D1334354

The New Oxford Dictionary of English

The New Oxford Dictionary of English

EDITED BY
Judy Pearsall

CHIEF EDITOR, CURRENT ENGLISH DICTIONARIES
Patrick Hanks

OXFORD

UNIVERSITY PRESS

Great Clarendon Street, Oxford OX2 6DP

Oxford University Press is a department of the University of Oxford.
It furthers the University's objective of excellence in research, scholarship,
and education by publishing worldwide in

Oxford New York

Athens Auckland Bangkok Bogotá Buenos Aires Cape Town
Chennai Dar es Salaam Delhi Florence Hong Kong Istanbul Karachi
Kolkata Kuala Lumpur Madrid Melbourne Mexico City Mumbai Nairobi
Paris São Paulo Shanghai Singapore Taipei Tokyo Toronto Warsaw

with associated companies in Berlin Ibadan

Oxford is a registered trade mark of Oxford University Press
in the UK and in certain other countries

Published in the United States
by Oxford University Press Inc., New York

© Oxford University Press 1998, 2001

Database right Oxford University Press (maker)

First published 1998
Thumb index edition first published 1999
Reissued with corrections and printed thumb tabs 2001

All rights reserved. No part of this publication may be reproduced,
stored in a retrieval system, or transmitted, in any form or by any means,
without the prior permission in writing of Oxford University Press,
or as expressly permitted by law, or under terms agreed with the appropriate
reprographics rights organization. Enquiries concerning reproduction
outside the scope of the above should be sent to the Rights Department,
Oxford University Press, at the address above

You must not circulate this book in any other binding or cover
and you must impose this same condition on any acquirer

British Library Cataloguing in Publication Data

Data available

Library of Congress Cataloging in Publication Data

Data available
ISBN 0-19-860441-6
ISBN 0-19-860469-6 (Dictionary with CD-Rom)

10 9 8 7 6 5 4 3 2

Designed by Andrew Boag, Typographic problem solving, London
Typeset in Swift and Arial
by Selwood Systems, Midsomer Norton, Bath
Printed in Italy by
La Tipografica Varese

Contents

Editorial staff

Editor
Judy Pearsall

Chief Science Editor
Bill Trumble

Associate Editors
Georgia Hole
Helen Liebeck
Jeremy Marshall
Catherine Soanes
Angus Stevenson
Maurice Waite

Project Coordinator
Lesley Blake

Editors, Word Histories
Senior Editor: Glynnis Chantrell
Consultant Editor: Edmund Weiner

Senior Editor, Animals and Plants
David Shirt

Pronunciations Editor
Susan Wilkin

Senior & Senior Assistant Editors
Catherine Bailey
Katrina Campbell
Martin Coleman
Lucinda Coventry
Chris Cowley
Julia Elliott
Sara Hawker
Martin Nixon

Assistant Editors
Louise Jones
Michael Lacewing
Alyson McGaw
Rachel Unsworth
Sandy Vaughan

Editorial Assistants
Britt Coulthurst
Christopher Eley
Kirsten Hayman
Richard Jones
Kakoli Thompson

Specialist Subject Consultants

Aeronautics
Ron Wingrove

American Football, Baseball, Basketball
Frank Abate

American Indian Terms
Frank Abate

Ancient Near East
Jeremy Black

Architecture & Building
Harold Morgan

Australian Rules Football
Bruce Moore
Hilary Kent

Ballet
Katherine Barber

Chess
Gerard O'Reilly

Computing
Alan Gay

Costume & Textiles
Caroline Imlah

Finance & Commerce
Philip Nixon

Ice Hockey
Eric Sinkins

Islam
Kenneth Cragg

Languages & Peoples
Patrick Hanks

Law
Folla Christie

Linguistics & Grammar
Patrick Hanks

Mathematics
Mark Dunn

Military Terms
Charles Kirke

Nautical Terms
Moke Wall

Philosophy
Simon Blackburn

Statistics
Ken Church

**Chief Editor,
Current English Dictionaries**
Patrick Hanks

World English Consultants

US English
Frank Abate
Elizabeth Jewell
Paul Betz
Hannah Borgeson
Claude Conyers
Mary Jacobi
Katherine Kane
Karen Murphy
Laura Phipps
Daniel Radosh
Ellen Satrom
Liz Sonneborn
Michael Stern
Christine Stevens
Emile Thomas
Anita Vanca

Australian English
Bruce Moore
Hilary Kent

Canadian English
Katherine Barber
Alex Bisset

Caribbean English
Lise Winer

Indian English
Indira Chowdhury Sengupta
Sukanta Chaudhuri

New Zealand English
Tony Deverson

Scottish English
Christopher Bailey
Wylie Horn
Fiona McPherson
Michael Proffitt

South African English
Penny Silva

Preface

The *New Oxford Dictionary of English* is a completely new dictionary, written on new principles. It builds on the excellence of the lexicographical traditions of scholarship and analysis of evidence as set down by the *Oxford English Dictionary* over a century ago, but it is also very much a new departure. The *New Oxford Dictionary of English* is a dictionary of current English and it is informed by currently available evidence and current thinking about language and cognition. It is an inventory of the words and meanings of present-day English, both those in actual use and those found in the literature of the past. The compilers have gone to the heart of the traditional practices of dictionary making and reappraised the principles on which lexicography is based. In particular, the focus has been on a different approach to an understanding of 'meaning' and how this relates to the structure, organization, and selection of material for the dictionary.

Linguists, cognitive scientists, and others have been developing new techniques for analysing usage and meaning, and the *New Oxford Dictionary of English* has taken full advantage of these developments. Foremost among them is an emphasis on identifying what is 'central and typical', as distinct from the time-honoured search for 'necessary conditions' of meaning (i.e. a statement of the conditions that would enable someone to pick out all and only the cases of the term being defined). Past attempts to cover the meaning of all possible uses of a word have tended to lead to a blurred, unfocused result, in which the core of the meaning is obscured by many minor uses. In the *New Oxford Dictionary of English*, meanings are linked to central norms of usage as observed in the language. The result is fewer meanings, with sharper, crisper definitions.

The style of definition adopted for the *New Oxford Dictionary of English* aims in part to account for the dynamism, imaginativeness, and flexibility of ordinary usage. The *New Oxford Dictionary of English* records and explains all normal meanings and uses of all well-attested words, but also illustrates transferred, figurative, and derivative meanings, in so far as these are conventional within the language.

The layout and organization of each entry in the dictionary reflect this new approach to meaning. Each entry has at least one core meaning, to which a number of subsenses, logically connected to it, may be attached. The text design is open and accessible, making it easy to find the core meanings and so to navigate the entry as a whole.

At the heart of the dictionary lies the **evidence**. This evidence forms the basis for everything which we, as lexicographers, are able to say about the language and the words within it. In particular, the large body of texts collected together on line as the British National Corpus gives, with its 100 million words, a selection of real, modern, and everyday language, equivalent to an ordinary person's reading over ten years or more. Using computational tools to analyse the data in the British National Corpus and other corpora, the editors have been able to look at the behaviour of each word in detail in its natural contexts, and so to build up a picture for every word in the dictionary.

Corpus analysis has been complemented by analysis of other types of evidence: the *New Oxford Dictionary of English* makes extensive use of the citation database of the Oxford Reading Programme, a collection of citations (currently standing at over 40 million words and growing at a rate of about 4.5 million words a year) taken from a variety of sources from all the English-speaking countries of the world. In addition, a specially commissioned reading programme has targeted previously neglected specialist fields as diverse as computing, complementary medicine, antique collecting, and winter sports. Other research includes a detailed and comprehensive survey of plants and animals throughout the world, resulting in the inclusion of hundreds of entries not in any other one-volume dictionary.

The general approach to defining in the *New Oxford Dictionary of English* has particular application for specialist vocabulary. Here, in the context of dealing with highly technical information which may be unfamiliar to the non-specialist reader, the focus on clarity of expression is of great importance. Avoidance of over-technical terminology and an emphasis on explaining and describing as well as defining are balanced by the need to maintain a high level of technical information and accuracy. In many cases, additional technical information is presented separately in an easily recognizable alternative format.

The *New Oxford Dictionary of English* views the language from the perspective that English is a world language. A network of consultants throughout the English-speaking world has enabled us to ensure excellent coverage of world English, from Canada and the US to the Caribbean, India, South Africa, Australia, and New Zealand. We have been indebted to the opportunities provided for communication by the Internet; lively discussions by e-mail across the oceans have formed an everyday part of the dictionary-making process.

Many people have been involved in the preparation of this dictionary, and thanks are due to them all. Those not listed on the separate credits page who deserve special mention include: Valerie Grundy, for her contribution as managing editor during the early stages of the project; Nigel Clifford, for research in special subjects; Fred McDonald, for work on word histories; Sue Atkins, Bob Allen, and Rosamund Moon, for their contributions during the early development of the project; Judith Scott, for assistance with foreign pronunciations; and David Munro, for assistance in updating place-name entries.

Introduction

The *New Oxford Dictionary of English* has been compiled according to principles which are quite different from those of traditional dictionaries. New types of evidence are now available in sufficient quantity to allow lexicographers to construct a picture of the language that is more accurate than has been possible before. The approach to structuring and organizing within individual dictionary entries has been rethought, as has the approach to the selection and presentation of information in every aspect of the dictionary: definitions, choice of examples, grammar, word histories, and every other category. New approaches have been adopted in response to a reappraisal of the workings of language in general and its relationship to the presentation of information in a dictionary in particular. The aim of this introduction is to give the reader background information for using this dictionary and, in particular, to explain some of the thinking behind these new approaches.

Structure: Core Sense and Subsense

The first part of speech is the primary one for that word: thus, for **bag** and **balloon** the senses of the noun are given before those for the verb, while for **babble** and **bake** the senses of the verb are given before those of the noun.

cocoon

CORE SENSE

a silky case spun by the larvae of many insects for protection as pupae.

subsense	subsense	subsense
a similar structure made by other animals.	a covering that prevents the corrosion of metal equipment.	something that envelops or surrounds, especially in a protective or comforting way: *a cocoon of bedclothes* | figurative *a warm cocoon of love.*

Within each part of speech the first definition given is the **core sense**. The general principle on which the senses in the *New Oxford Dictionary of English* are organized is that each word has at least one core meaning, to which a number of subsenses may be attached. If there is more than one core sense (see below), this is introduced by a bold sense number. Core meanings represent typical, central uses of the word in question in modern standard English, as established by research on and analysis of the British National Corpus and other corpora and citation databases. The core meaning is the one that represents the most literal sense that the word has in ordinary modern usage. This is not necessarily the same as the oldest meaning, because word meanings change over time. Nor is it necessarily the most frequent meaning, because figurative senses are sometimes the most frequent. It is the meaning accepted by native speakers as the one that is most established as literal and central.

The core sense also acts as a gateway to other, related subsenses. These subsenses are grouped under the core sense, each one being introduced by a solid square symbol.

cocoon

CORE SENSE	a silky case spun by the larvae of many insects for protection as pupae.
subsense	■a similar structure made by other animals. ■ a covering that prevents the corrosion of metal equipment. ■ something that envelops or surrounds, especially in a protective or comforting way: *a cocoon of bedclothes* | figurative *a warm cocoon of love.*

There is a logical relationship between each subsense and the core sense under which it appears. The organization of senses according to this logical relationship is designed to help the user, not only in being able to navigate the entry more easily and find relevant senses more readily, but also in building up an understanding of how senses in the language relate to one another and how the language is constructed on this model. The main types of relationship of core sense to subsense are as follows:

(a) figurative extension of the core sense, e.g.

backbone

CORE SENSE	the series of vertebrae in a person or animal, extending from the skull to the pelvis; the spine.
subsense	■ figurative the chief support of a system or organization; the mainstay: *these firms are the backbone of our industrial sector.*
subsense	■ [mass noun] figurative strength of character: *he has enough backbone to see us through this difficulty.*

bankrupt

CORE SENSE	(of a person or organization) declared in law unable to pay their debts.
subsense	■ figurative completely lacking in a particular good quality or value: *their cause is morally bankrupt.*

(b) specialized case of the core sense, e.g.

ball

CORE SENSE	a single throw, kick, or other movement of the ball in the course of a game, in particular:
subsense	■ Cricket a delivery of the ball by the bowler to the batsman.
subsense	■ Baseball a pitch delivered outside the strike zone which the batter does not attempt to hit.

demand

CORE SENSE	an insistent and peremptory request, made as of right.
subsense	■ [mass noun] Economics the desire of purchasers, consumers, clients, employers, etc. for a particular commodity, service, or other item: *a recent slump in demand.*

(c) other extension or shift in meaning, retaining one or more elements of the core sense, e.g.

bamboo

CORE SENSE	[mass noun] a giant woody grass which grows chiefly in the tropics, where it is widely cultivated.
subsense	■ the hollow jointed stem of this plant, used as a cane or to make furniture and implements.

management

CORE SENSE	[mass noun] the process of dealing with or controlling things or people.
subsense	■ [treated as sing. or pl.] the people in charge of running a company or organization, regarded collectively: *management were extremely cooperative.*

mandarin

CORE SENSE	an official in any of the nine top grades of the former imperial Chinese civil service.
subsense	■ a powerful official or senior bureaucrat, especially one perceived as reactionary and secretive: *a civil service mandarin.*

Many entries have just one core sense. However some entries are more complex and have different strands of meaning, each constituting a core sense. In this case, each core sense is introduced by a bold sense number, and each potentially has its own block of subsenses relating to it.

belt

CORE SENSE	**1** a strip of leather or other material worn round the waist or across the chest, especially in order to support or hold in clothes or to carry weapons.
subsenses	■ short for **SEAT BELT**. ■ a belt worn as a sign of rank or achievement: *he was awarded the victor's belt.* ■ a belt of a specified colour, marking the attainment of a particular level in judo, karate, or similar sports: [as modifier] *brown-belt level.* ■ a person who has reached such a level: *Shaun became a brown belt in judo.* ■ **(the belt)** the punishment of being struck with a belt.
CORE SENSE	**2** a strip of material used in various technical applications, in particular:
subsenses	■ a continuous band of material used in machinery for transferring motion from one wheel to another. ■ a conveyor belt. ■ a flexible strip carrying machine-gun cartridges.
CORE SENSE	**3** a strip or encircling band of something having a specified nature or composition that is different from its surroundings: *the asteroid belt	a belt of trees.*
CORE SENSE	**4** informal a heavy blow: *she ran in to administer a good belt with her stick.*

Specialist Vocabulary

One of the most important uses of a dictionary is to provide explanations of terms in specialized fields which are unfamiliar to a general reader. Yet in many traditional dictionaries the definitions have been written by specialists as if for other specialists, and as a result the definitions are often opaque and difficult for the general reader to understand.

One of the primary aims of the *New Oxford Dictionary of English* has been to break down the barriers to understanding specialist vocabulary. The challenge has been, on the one hand, to give information which is comprehensible, relevant, and readable, suitable for the general reader, while on the other hand maintaining the high level of technical information and accuracy suitable for the more specialist reader.

This has been achieved in some cases, notably entries for plants and animals and chemical substances, by separating out technical information from the rest of the definition:

balloonfish

DEFINITION	a tropical porcupine fish which lives in shallow water and can inflate itself when threatened.
technical information	● *Diodon holocanthus*, family Diodontidae.

benzopyrene

DEFINITION	[mass noun] Chemistry a compound which is the major carcinogen present in cigarette smoke, and also occurs in coal tar.
technical information	● A polycyclic aromatic hydrocarbon; chem. formula: $C_{20}H_{12}$.

In other cases, it is achieved by giving additional explanatory information within the definition itself:

curling

DEFINITION additional information	[mass noun] a game played on ice, especially in Scotland and Canada, in which large round flat stones are slid across the surface towards a mark. Members of a team use brooms to sweep the surface of the ice in the path of the stone to control its speed and direction.

alchemy

DEFINITION additional information	[mass noun] the medieval forerunner of chemistry, based on the supposed transformation of matter. It was concerned particularly with attempts to convert base metals into gold or find a universal elixir.
subsense	■ figurative a process by which paradoxical results are achieved or incompatible elements combined with no obvious rational explanation: *his conducting managed by some alchemy to give a sense of fire and ice.*

As elsewhere, the purpose is to give information which is relevant and interesting, aiming not just to define the word but also to describe and explain its context in the real world. Additional information of this type, where it is substantial, is given in the form of separate boxed features:

earth

CORE SENSE	(also **Earth**) the planet on which we live; the world: *the diversity of life on earth.*
additional boxed information	The earth is the third planet from the sun in the solar system, orbiting between Venus and Mars at an average distance of 149.6 million km from the sun, and has one natural satellite, the moon. It has an equatorial diameter of 12,756 km, an average density 5.5 times that of water, and is believed to have formed about 4,600 million years ago. The earth, which is three-quarters covered by oceans and has a dense atmosphere of nitrogen and oxygen, is the only planet known to support life.

Eocene

CORE SENSE	Geology of, relating to, or denoting the second epoch of the Tertiary period, between the Palaeocene and Oligocene epochs.
subsense	■ [as noun **the Eocene**] the Eocene epoch or the system of rocks deposited during it.
additional boxed information	The Eocene epoch lasted from 56.5 to 35.4 million years ago. It was a time of rising temperatures, and there was an abundance of mammals, including the first horses, bats, and whales.

An especially important feature of the *New Oxford Dictionary of English* is the coverage of animals and plants. In-depth research and a thorough review have been carried out for animals and plants throughout the world and, as a result, a large number of entries have been included which have never before been included in general dictionaries. The style and presentation of these entries follow the general principles for specialist vocabulary in the *New Oxford Dictionary of English*: the entries not only give the technical information, but also describe, in everyday English, the appearance and other characteristics (of behaviour, medicinal or culinary use, mythological significance, reason for the name, etc.) and the typical habitat and distribution:

mesosaur

CORE SENSE	an extinct small aquatic reptile of the early Permian period, with an elongated body, flattened tail, and a long narrow snout with numerous needle-like teeth.
technical information	● Genus *Mesosaurus*, order Mesosauria, subclass Anapsida.

kowari

CORE SENSE	a small carnivorous marsupial with a pointed snout, large eyes, and a black bushy tip to the tail, found in central Australia.
technical information	● *Dasycercus byrnei*, family Dasyuridae.

hiba

CORE SENSE	a Japanese conifer with evergreen scale-like leaves which form flattened sprays of foliage, widely planted as an ornamental and yielding durable timber.
technical information	● *Thujopsis dolabrata*, family Cupressaceae.

Encyclopedic Material

Some British dictionaries do not include entries for the names of people and places and other proper names. The argument for this is based on a distinction between 'words' and 'facts', by which dictionaries are about 'words' while encyclopedias and other reference works are about 'facts'. The distinction is an interesting theoretical one but in practice there is a considerable overlap: names such as *Shakespeare* and *England* are as much part of the language as words such as *drama* or *language*, and belong in a large dictionary.

The *New Oxford Dictionary of English* includes all those terms forming part of the enduring common knowledge of English speakers, regardless of whether they are classified as 'words' or 'names'. The information given is the kind of information that people are likely to need from a dictionary, however that information may be traditionally classified. Both the style of definitions in the *New Oxford Dictionary of English* and the inclusion of additional material in separate blocks reflect this approach.

The *New Oxford Dictionary of English* includes more than 4,500 place-name entries, 4,000 biographical entries, and just under 3,000 other proper names. The entries are designed to provide not just the basic facts (such as birth and death dates, full name, and nationality), but also a brief context giving information about, for example, a person's life and why he or she is important.

For a few really important encyclopedic entries—for example, countries—a fuller treatment is given and additional information is given in a separate boxed note.

Grammar

In recent years grammar has begun to enjoy greater prominence than in previous decades. It is once again being taught explicitly in state schools throughout Britain and elsewhere. In addition there is a recognition that different meanings of a word are closely associated with different lexical and syntactic patterns. The *New Oxford Dictionary of English* records and exemplifies the most important of these patterns at the relevant senses of each word, thus giving guidance on language use as well as word meaning.

For example, with the word **bomb**, it is possible to distinguish the main senses of the verb simply on the basis of the grammar: whether the verb takes a direct object, no direct object, or no direct object plus an obligatory adverbial:

CORE SENSE	attack *(a place or object)* with a bomb or bombs: *they bombed *the city* at dawn.*
grammar	[with obj.]

(the asterisks match the direct object in the example with the bracketed item in the definition)

CORE SENSE	informal (of a film, play, or other event) fail badly: *it just became another big-budget film that bombed.*
grammar	[no obj.]
CORE SENSE	Brit. informal move or go very quickly: *we were bombing *down the motorway* at breakneck speed.*
grammar	[no obj., with adverbial of direction]

(asterisks show adverbial in example)

This has particular relevance for a dictionary such as the *New Oxford Dictionary of English*, where the aim is to present information in such a way that it helps to explain the structure of the language itself, not just the meanings of individual senses. For this reason, special attention has been paid to the grammar of each word, and grammatical structures are given explicitly.

Where possible, the syntactic behaviour of a word is presented directly: for example, if a verb is normally found in a particular sense followed by a certain preposition, this is indicated before the definition, in bold:

build

... (**build on**) use as a basis for further progress or development: *Britain should build on the talents of its workforce.*

In other cases, collocations which are typical of the word in use, though not obligatory, are shown highlighted within the example sentence:

ball game

... a situation of a particular type, especially one that is completely different from the previous one: *making the film was a **whole new ball game** for her.*

end

... (**end up**) eventually reach or come to a specified place, state, or course of action: *I **ended up in** Eritrea | you could **end up with** a higher income.*

Great efforts have been made to use a minimum of specialist terminology. Nevertheless, a small number of terms are essential in explaining the grammar of a word. The less familiar terms are explained below. All terms are, of course, defined and explained under their own entries in the dictionary.

Terms relating to nouns

[**mass noun**]: used to mark those nouns (and senses of nouns) which are not ordinarily used in the plural and are not used in the singular with the indefinite article 'a' (it is normal to talk about 'bacon', for example, but not 'a bacon' or 'three bacons'), e.g.

bacon

[mass noun] cured meat from the back or sides of a pig.

badminton

[mass noun] a game with rackets in which a shuttlecock is played back and forth across a net.

banking

[mass noun] the business conducted or services offered by a bank.

Occasionally, a mass noun may be used in the plural, with the sense 'different types of X' or 'portions of X', as in *the panel tasted a range of bacons.* Such uses are recorded in the *New Oxford Dictionary of English* only when they are particularly important.

[**count noun**]: used to mark those nouns (and senses of nouns) which can take a plural and can be used with 'a', where this is in contrast with an already stated mass noun. By default, in this dictionary all nouns are to be regarded as count nouns unless stated otherwise.

ballet

CORE SENSE   [mass noun] an artistic dance form performed to music, using precise and highly formalized set steps and gestures.

subsense   ■[count noun] a creative work of this form or the music written for it.

brokerage

CORE SENSE   [mass noun] the business or service of acting as a broker.

subsense   ■[count noun] a company that buys or sells goods or assets for clients.

[as modifier]: used to mark a noun which can be placed before another noun in order to modify its meaning, e.g.

boom

[often as modifier] a movable arm over a television or film set, carrying a microphone or camera: *a boom mike.*

bedside

the space beside a bed (used especially with reference to an invalid's bed): *he was summoned to the bedside of a dying man* | [as modifier] *a bedside lamp.*

[treated as sing.]: used to mark a noun which is plural in form but is used with a singular verb, e.g. **mumps** in *mumps is one of the major childhood diseases* or **genetics** in *genetics has played a major role in this work.*

[treated as sing. or pl.]: used to mark a noun which can be used with either a singular or a plural verb without any change in meaning or in the form of the headword (often called *collective nouns*, because they typically denote groups of people considered collectively), e.g. *the government are committed to this policy* or *the government is trying to gag its critics.*

[in sing.]: used to mark a noun which is used as a count noun but is never or rarely found in the plural, e.g. **ear** in *an ear for rhythm and melody.*

Terms relating to verbs

[with obj.]: used to mark a verb which takes a direct object, i.e. is transitive (the type of direct object often being shown in brackets in the definition), e.g.

belabour

[with obj.] argue or elaborate (a subject) in excessive detail: *there is no need to belabour the point.*

[no obj.]: used to mark a verb which takes no direct object, i.e. is intransitive, e.g.

bristle

[no obj.] (of hair or fur) stand upright away from the skin, typically as a sign of anger or fear.

[with adverbial]: used to mark a verb which takes an obligatory adverbial, typically a prepositional phrase, without which the sentence in which the verb occurs would sound unnatural or odd, e.g.

barge

[no obj., with adverbial of direction] move forcefully or roughly: *we can't just barge into a private garden.*

Terms relating to adjectives

[attrib.]: used to mark an adjective which is normally used attributively, i.e. comes before the noun which it modifies, e.g. **certain** in *a certain man* (not *the man is certain*, which has a very different meaning). Note that attributive use is standard for many adjectives, especially in specialist fields: the [attrib.] label is used only to mark those cases in which predicative use would be highly unusual.

[predic.]: used to mark an adjective which is normally used predicatively, i.e. comes after the verb, e.g. **ajar** in *the door was ajar* (not *the ajar door*).

[postpositive]: used to mark an adjective which is used postpositively, i.e. typically comes immediately after the noun which it modifies (such uses are unusual in English and generally arise because the adjective has been adopted from a language where postpositive use is standard), e.g. **galore** in *there were prizes galore.*

Terms relating to adverbs

[sentence adverb]: used to mark an adverb which stands outside a sentence or clause, providing commentary on it as a whole or showing the speaker's or writer's attitude to what is being said, rather than the manner in which something was done. Sentence adverbs most frequently express the speaker's or writer's point of view, although they may also be used to set a context by stating a field of reference, e.g.

certainly

[sentence adverb] used to convey the speaker's belief that what is said is true: *the prestigious address certainly adds to the firm's appeal.*

[as submodifier]: used to mark an adverb which is used to modify an adjective or another adverb, e.g.

comparatively

[as submodifier] to a moderate degree as compared to something else; relatively: *inflation was comparatively low.*

Evidence and Illustrative Examples

The information presented in the dictionary about individual words is based on close analysis of how words behave in real, natural language. Behind every dictionary entry are examples of the word in use—often hundreds and thousands of them—which have been analysed to give information about typical usage, about distribution (whether typically British or typically US, for example), about register (whether informal or derogatory, for example), about currency (whether archaic or dated, for example), and about subject field (whether used only in Medicine or Finance, for example).

1. Corpus

Extensive use has been made of the British National Corpus. This is a carefully balanced selection of 100 million words of written and spoken English text (equivalent to one person's reading over ten or twenty years) in machine-readable form, available for computational analysis. This resource means that, for the first time, lexicographers are in a position to see how words normally behave. By using concordancing techniques, each word can be viewed almost instantaneously in the immediate contexts in which it is used. (See Figure 1.)

Concordances show at a glance that some combinations of words (called 'collocations') occur together much more often than others. For example, in the concordance on page xiii, 'end in', 'end the', and 'end up' all occur quite often. But are any of these combinations important enough to be given special treatment in the dictionary?

Recent research has focused on identifying combinations that are not merely frequent but also statistically significant. In the British

```
EngRel  ts , no future history of the English Reformation will  end  in 1559 . Elizabeth 's reign is now seen to be of
BrFesA  2> <p_7> The first date of her world tour , which will   end  in a gala evening at The Cathedral of St Margaret
LastEn  alking of your death ? You told me once that you would    end  in a tomb , alive , you thought it would be in Bry
DgArts  till in power . Some 53 per cent of American marriages    end  in divorce , usually to the detriment of the women
GcHome  wanted to build a third . The feeder roads for it now     end  in empty air . " That was really the only project
Thirty  HIL : </spkr> <p_120> I think it 's a cop-out . It 'll    end  in tears . </sp> <sp> <spkr> HARRY : </spkr> <p_12
LaWldA  ance or Germany . .PP He forecast : " This Treaty will    end  in tears it is better that it ends in tears now th
Viking  sibility that she might be here , that her quest could    end  in the next hour or so and she would be spared the
krw101  y 11 to 33 in order to make it more broad-based and to    end  intra-party squabbles . .PP On Jan/NP. 7 , Murli M
UnPass  Jenny nodded . " Their final clash was always going to    end  in tragedy . I didn't want you to be caught in the
WheelS  my knife and pill-bottles in the tent in case I should    end  my life during my night 's sleep . <p_42> The firs
WAAFWr  lmost together . <p_158> It was a disenchanting way to    end  my service . I went into a small room and handed m
TourLf  ey . Fast and frequent trains run daily from Easter to    end  of September , weekends March and October . </DL>
bbcBas  instance , BBCBASIC ( Z80 ) does not have a " clear to    end  of screen " command . Some computers will perform
HansrC  jective No. 2 of " Community Support Frameworks " will    end  on 31 December 1991 . Discussions are currently pr
krw204  5 ; and the two rounds of presidential elections would    end  on Aug. 23 . No official reason was given for the
Factry  ing going on down there , and I was sure it would only    end  one way , but I couldn't move . I was stuck there
krw009  epartment announced on Sept/NP. 18 that it proposed to    end  or reduce operations at 151 military sites in 10 E
elSalv  1978 , the offices of the CUTS were bombed . We had to    end  our open activities and work secretly . Many women
EconoE  ar preparing for the strike , convinced that it had to    end  overmanning and weaken the unions '/$ grip on prod
SbWldA  ove that beautiful countryside when we are at our wits    end  over what to do with deep-mined coal . " <p_4> He
krw111  to US goods . .PP Chinese leaders called on the USA to    end  sanctions and to withdraw the threat of punitive t
GfCity  me , then you will have to reapply . However , it will    end  sooner if someone else claims income support or fa
IhTitl  s as the party of sound money . .PP Mr Baker failed to    end  speculation about opposition from Sir Alan Walters
krw209  nd the Soviet Union from concluding a formal treaty to    end  the Pacific War . The collapse of the Soviet Union
FedEur  made more public and the crucial Fifth Directive would    end  the abuse of special voting rights and outlaw exis
CntNeP  at an old woman ! " .PP Peter Scudamore will doubtless    end  the comparisons there ... He may be a former jocke
krw003  a programme of " national reconciliation " designed to    end  the conflict with the anti-government mujaheddin g
HairFA  ur photographer will be there to record the event . To    end  the day we will all have dinner before going to th
LcLeis  , is against Venables and wants him to go , if only to    end  the disastrous deadlock which is keeping the club
CntNeE  ron 's stepfather appealed for a concerted campaign to    end  the spate of car thefts that so often ended in tra
krw106  asked their followers at evening prayers in Algiers to    end  the strike . <ct> New government </ct> .PP On June
Charit  cough , tetanus or diphtheria . With your help we can    end  this needless tragedy . .PP And if you are a paren
ClimbF  tre of outdoor clothing ( don't laugh ) , then I could    end  this review here . But thankfully , function still
envd41  tained from dead whales . Some , however , continue to    end  up as whale meat in restaurants . Times 10 , 27 No
BORain  to wrench free . " If we don't move Seawitch she could    end  up as wreckage on the rocks _ that 's what you sai
SaWldA  Kilbride , increasing employment opportunities , could    end  up being moved away again should they be privatise
NewScV  er ) with the theory of island biogeography , we still    end  up concluding " that there are <regsic=insufficent
HoCard  326> " Yet paradoxically that is just the way we could    end  up drifting if that majority support for a pragmat
GlWldA  ally engineered wrinkle-free tomato ) the plants could    end  up growing in a sewage farm somewhere , and this w
ZES1E2  y believe in and nobody fights back so everybody would    end  up having to agree . <p_3> However a war like the
CntNe0  . .PP It was the first inkling she had that she could    end  up homeless . .PP Anne signed an agreement last Fe
citySP  the streetwise dealers require quicker money , and may    end  up in a bucket shop on the Continent . <p_9> Most
SMusic  king up a socio-cultural whole . ; Such theories always    end  up in some kind of <page=10> reductionism _ " upwa
20Ways  ! <DT> 2 <DD> <LI> <p_100> Fear that information will    end  up in the hands of competitors . Experience has sh
TwstTa  g sure you got a first-class education just to let you    end  up like me , putting wheels on cars for the rest o
TaArti  .PP Don't try to do too much in one day or you will    end  up making impulse buys that you will regret , and
GuitaA  an everyday instrument , or whether it is destined to    end  up mute behind glass in a collection somewhere . B
LadyKi  e annoying Kate and if he wasn't careful he just might    end  up on the receiving end of her tongue . She placed
NaComm  e Consumers '/$ Association has warned . Drivers could    end  up paying a " monopoly premium " to the big car fi
LdsUtD  per game and championships is a bit premature , we 'll    end  up sounding like scumites who always think they 'l
Formul  vers . Certainly I thought at the time that Hunt would    end  up sponsored by Marlboro and driving a McLaren . <
MaFeat  . But if the guy tries to lay a finger on me , he 'll    end  up staring at the moon ! " <ct> SMILER : Van Damme
SuitKi  oodily down your chin , but who cares ? You also often    end  up stuck in the loo with a tummy upset but honestl
Wychwo  ast , I ought to have tried , but I didn't think we 'd    end  up with a blizzard like this . I can't remember wh
deBono  ty and that house had a poor kitchen . The buyer might    end  up with a much more expensive house which had a be
Advert  e . Am going to a dance " . They might _ conceivably _    end  up with a picture of Doris Day singing Ten cents a
HansrA  requirement for a new air defence frigate we shall not    end  up with another fiasco of expensive and fruitless
EconoH  ing internal competition free rein . But the world may    end  up with both projects , a waste of resources that
DogTod  re a diagnosis is made , the more likely the dog is to    end  up with long-term arthritis , another disease wher
TaSpor  with intent to harm his opponent ? .PP " It will just    end  up with long , protracted cases dragging the name
```

Figure 1: Extract from a concordance from the British National Corpus, showing the word 'end'.

National Corpus, the two words 'end the' occur frequently together but they do not form a statistically significant unit, since the word 'the' is the commonest in the language. The combinations **end up** and **end in**, on the other hand, are shown to be more significant and tell the lexicographer something about the way the verb **end** behaves in normal use. Of course, a dictionary for general use cannot go into detailed statistical analysis of word combinations, but it can present examples that are typical of normal usage. In the *New Oxford Dictionary of English* particularly significant or important patterns are highlighted, in bold or in bold italics, e.g.

end

[no obj.] (**end in**) have as its final part, point, or result: *one in three marriages is now likely to end in divorce.*

[no obj.] (**end up**) eventually reach or come to a specified place, state, or course of action: *I ended up in Eritrea | you could end up with a higher income.*

For further details, see the section on *Grammar*.

2. Citations

While the British National Corpus has formed the backbone of the evidence used in compiling the *New Oxford Dictionary of English*, other corpora have also been used. These include, for example, a corpus of US English and a historical corpus. The *New Oxford Dictionary of English* has also made use of the citation database created by the Oxford Reading Programme, an ongoing research project in which readers select citations from a huge variety of specialist and non-specialist sources in all varieties of English. This database currently stands at around 40 million words and is growing at a rate of 4.5 million words a year.

3. Specialist reading

A general corpus does not, by definition, contain large quantities of specialized terminology. For this reason, a directed reading programme was set up specially for the *New Oxford Dictionary of English*, enabling additional research and collection of citations in a number of neglected fields, for example antique collecting, food and cooking, boats and sailing, photography, video and audio, martial arts, and complementary medicine.

4. Examples

The *New Oxford Dictionary of English* contains many more examples of words in use than any other comparable dictionary. Generally, they are there to show typical uses of the word or sense. All examples are authentic, in that they represent actual usage. In the past, dictionaries have used made-up examples, partly because not enough authentic text was available and partly through an assumption that made-up examples were somehow better in that they could be tailored to the precise needs of the dictionary entry. Such a view finds little favour today, and it is now generally recognized that the 'naturalness' provided by authentic examples is of the utmost importance in giving an accurate picture of language in use.

Word Histories

The etymologies in standard dictionaries explain the language from which a word was brought into English, the period at which it is first recorded in English, and the development of modern word forms. While the *New Oxford Dictionary of English* does this, it also goes further. It explains sense development as well as morphological (or form) development. Information is presented clearly and with a minimum of technical terminology, and the perspective taken is that of the general reader who would like to know about word origins but who is not a philological specialist. In this context, the history of how and why a particular meaning developed from an apparently quite different older meaning is likely to be at least as interesting as, for example, what the original form was in Latin or Greek.

For example, the word history for the word **oaf** shows how the present meaning developed from the meaning 'elf', while the entry for **conker** shows how the word may be related both to 'conch' and 'conquer' (explaining how the original game of conkers was played with snail shells rather than the nut of the horse chestnut):

oaf

DEFINITION   a stupid, uncultured, or clumsy man.

ORIGIN   – ORIGIN early 17th cent.: variant of obsolete *auf*, from Old Norse *álfr* 'elf '. The original meaning was 'elf's child, changeling', later 'idiot child' and 'halfwit', generalized in the current sense.

conker

DEFINITION   Brit. the hard shiny dark brown nut of a horse chestnut tree.

■ **(conkers)** [treated as sing.] a children's game in which each has a conker on the end of a string and takes turns in trying to break another's with it.

ORIGIN   – ORIGIN mid 19th cent. (a dialect word denoting a snail shell, with which the game, or a similar form of it, was originally played): perhaps from **CONCH**, but associated with (and frequently spelled) **CONQUER** in the 19th and early 20th cents: an alternative name was *conquerors*.

Additional special features of the *New Oxford Dictionary of English* include 'internal etymologies' and 'folk etymologies'. Internal etymologies are given within entries to explain the origin of particular senses, phrases, or idioms. For example, how did the figurative use of **red herring** come about? Why do we call something a **flash in the pan**?

red herring

DEFINITION   **1** a dried smoked herring, which is turned red by the smoke.
2 something, especially a clue, which is or is intended to be misleading or distracting: *the book is fast-paced, exciting, and full of red herrings.*

ORIGIN   [ORIGIN: so named from the practice of using the scent of red herring in training hounds.]

flash

DEFINITION   **flash in the pan** a thing or person whose sudden but brief success is not repeated or repeatable: *our start to the season was just a flash in the pan.*

ORIGIN   [ORIGIN: with allusion to priming of a firearm, the flash arising from an explosion of gunpowder within the lock.]

The *New Oxford Dictionary of English* presents the information in a straightforward, user-friendly fashion immediately following the relevant definition.

In a similar vein, folk etymologies—those explanations which are unfounded but nevertheless well known to many people—have traditionally simply been ignored in dictionaries. The *New Oxford Dictionary of English* gives an account of widely held but often erroneous folk etymologies for the benefit of the general reader, explaining competing theories and assessing their relative merits where applicable.

posh

ORIGIN   – ORIGIN early 20th cent.: perhaps from slang *posh*, denoting a dandy. There is no evidence to support the folk etymology that *posh* is formed from the initials of *port out starboard home* (referring to the practice of using the more comfortable accommodation, out of the heat of the sun, on ships between England and India).

cherub

ORIGIN   – ORIGIN Old English *cherubin*, ultimately (via Latin and Greek) from Hebrew *kĕrūḇ*, plural *kĕrūḇīm*. A rabbinic folk etymology, which explains the Hebrew singular form as representing Aramaic *kĕ-rabyā* 'like a child', led to the representation of the cherub as a child.

Researching word histories is similar in some respects to archaeology: the evidence is often partial or not there at all, and etymologists must make informed decisions using the evidence available, however inadequate it may be. From time to time new evidence becomes available, and the known history of a word may need to be reconsidered. In this, the *New Oxford Dictionary of English* has been able to draw on the extensive expertise and ongoing research of the *Oxford English Dictionary*.

Usage Notes

Interest in questions of good usage is widespread among English speakers everywhere, and many issues are hotly debated. In the *New Oxford Dictionary of English*, traditional issues have been reappraised, and guidance is given on various points, old and new. The aim is to help people to use the language more accurately, more clearly, and more elegantly, and to give information and offer reassurance in the face of some of the more baffling assertions about 'correctness' that are sometimes made.

This reappraisal has involved looking carefully at evidence of actual usage (in the British National Corpus, the citations collected by the Oxford Reading Programme, and other sources) in order to find out where mistakes are actually being made, and where confusion and ambiguity actually arise. The issues on which journalists and others tend to comment have been reassessed and a judgement made about whether their comments are justified.

From the 15th century onwards, traditionalists have been objecting to particular senses of certain English words and phrases, for example 'aggravate', 'due to', and 'hopefully'. Certain grammatical structures, too, have been singled out for adverse comment, notably the split infinitive and the use of a preposition at the end of a clause. Some of these objections are founded on very dubious arguments, for example the notion that English grammatical structures should precisely parallel those of Latin or that meaning change of any kind is inherently suspect.

preposition

USAGE NOTE

> **USAGE** There is a traditional view, first set forth by the 17th-century poet and dramatist John Dryden, that it is incorrect to put a preposition at the end of a sentence, as in *where do you come **from**?* or *she's not a writer I've ever come **across**.* The rule was formulated on the basis that, since in Latin a preposition cannot come after the word it governs or is linked with, the same should be true of English. The problem is that English is not like Latin in this respect, and in many cases (particularly in questions and with phrasal verbs) the attempt to move the preposition produces awkward, unnatural-sounding results. Winston Churchill famously objected to the rule, saying *'This is the sort of English **up with** which I will not **put**.'* In standard English the placing of a preposition at the end of a sentence is widely accepted, provided the use sounds natural and the meaning is clear.

due

USAGE NOTE

> **USAGE** **Due to** in the sense 'because of', as in *he had to retire **due to** an injury,* has been condemned as incorrect on the grounds that **due** is an adjective and should not be used as a preposition. However, the prepositional use, first recorded at the end of the 19th century, is now common in all types of literature and is regarded as part of standard English.

aggravate

USAGE NOTE

> **USAGE** **Aggravate** in the sense 'annoy or exasperate' dates back to the 17th century and has been so used by respected writers ever since. This use is still regarded as incorrect by some traditionalists on the grounds that it is too radical a departure from the etymological meaning of 'make heavy'. It is, however, comparable to meaning changes in hundreds of other words which have long been accepted without comment.

The usage notes in the *New Oxford Dictionary of English* take the view that English is English, not Latin, and that English is, like all languages, subject to change. Good usage is usage that gets the writer's message across, not usage that conforms to some arbitrary rules that fly in the face of historical fact or current evidence. The editors of the *New Oxford Dictionary of English* are well aware that the prescriptions of pundits in the past have had remarkably little practical effect on the way the language is actually used. A good dictionary reports the language as it is, not as the editors (or anyone else) would wish it to be, and the usage notes must give guidance that accords with observed facts about present-day usage.

This is not to imply that the issues are straightforward or that there are simple solutions, however. Much of the debate about use of language is highly political and controversy is, occasionally, inevitable. Changing social attitudes have stigmatized long-established uses such as the word 'man' to denote the human race in general, for example, and have highlighted the absence of a gender-neutral singular pronoun meaning both 'he' and 'she' (for which purpose 'they' is increasingly being used). Similarly, words such as 'race' and 'native' are now associated with particular problems of sensitivity in use. The usage notes in the *New Oxford Dictionary of English* offer information and practical advice on such issues.

man

USAGE NOTE

> **USAGE** Traditionally the word **man** has been used to refer not only to adult males but also to human beings in general, regardless of sex. There is a historical explanation for this: in Old English the principal sense of **man** was 'a human being', and the words **wer** and **wif** were used to refer specifically to 'a male person' and 'a female person' respectively. Subsequently, **man** replaced **wer** as the normal term for 'a male person', but at the same time the older sense 'a human being' remained in use.
> In the second half of the twentieth century the generic use of **man** to refer to 'human beings in general' (as in *reptiles were here long before **man** appeared on the earth*) became problematic; the use is now often regarded as sexist or at best old-fashioned. In some contexts, alternative terms such as **the human race** or

humankind may be used. Fixed phrases and sayings such as *time and tide wait for no **man*** can be easily rephrased, e.g. *time and tide wait for **nobody.*** However, in other cases, particularly in compound forms, alternatives have not yet become established: there are no standard accepted alternatives for **manpower** or the verb **man**, for example.

native

USAGE NOTE

> **USAGE** In contexts such as *a **native** of Boston* the use of the noun **native** is quite acceptable. But when used as a noun without qualification, as in *this dance is a favourite with the **natives,*** it is more problematic. In modern use it is used humorously to refer to the local inhabitants of a particular place *(New York in the summer was too hot even for the **natives**).* In other contexts it has an old-fashioned feel and, because of being closely associated with a colonial European outlook on non-white peoples living in remote places, it may cause offence.

Standard English

Unless otherwise stated, the words and senses recorded in this dictionary are all part of standard English; that is, they are in normal use in both speech and writing everywhere in the world, at many different levels of formality, ranging from official documents to casual conversation. Some words, however, are appropriate only in particular contexts, and these are labelled accordingly. The technical term for a particular level of use in language is **register**.

The *New Oxford Dictionary of English* uses the following register labels:

formal: normally used only in writing, in contexts such as official documents.

informal: normally used only in contexts such as conversations or letters between friends.

dated: no longer used by the majority of English speakers, but still encountered occasionally, especially among the older generation.

archaic: very old-fashioned language, not in ordinary use at all today, but sometimes used to give a deliberately old-fashioned effect or found in works of the past that are still widely read.

historical: still used today, but only to refer to some practice or artefact that is no longer part of the modern world, e.g.

baldric

> historical a belt for a sword or other piece of equipment, worn over one shoulder and reaching down to the opposite hip.

almoner

> historical an official distributor of alms.

literary: found only or mainly in literature written in an 'elevated' style.

poetic: found only or mainly in poetry.

technical: normally used only in technical and specialist language, though not necessarily restricted to any specific subject field.

rare: not in normal use.

humorous: used with the intention of sounding funny or playful.

dialect: not used in the standard language, but still widely used in certain local regions of the English-speaking world. A distinction is made between traditional dialect, which is generally to do with rural society and agricultural practices which have mostly died out, and contemporary dialect, where speakers may not even be aware that the term is in fact a regionalism. The *New Oxford Dictionary of English* aims to include the main contemporary dialect terms, but does not set out to record traditional dialect.

offensive: language that is likely to cause offence, particularly racial offence, whether the speaker intends it or not.

derogatory: language intended to convey a low opinion or cause personal offence.

vulgar slang: informal language that may cause offence, often because it refers to the bodily functions of sexual activity or excretion, which are still widely regarded as taboo.

World English

English is spoken as a first language by more than 300 million people throughout the world, and used as a second language by many millions more. It is the language of international communication in trade, diplomacy, sport, science, technology, and countless other fields.

The main regional standards are British, US and Canadian, Australian and New Zealand, South African, Indian, and West Indian. Within each of these regional varieties, a number of highly differentiated local dialects may be found. For example, within British English, Scottish and Irish English have a long history and a number of distinctive features, which have in turn influenced particular North American and other varieties.

The scope of a dictionary such as the *New Oxford Dictionary of English*, given the breadth of material it aims to cover, must be limited in the main to the vocabulary of the standard language throughout the world rather than local dialectal variation. Nevertheless, the *New Oxford Dictionary of English* includes thousands of regionalisms encountered in standard contexts in the different English-speaking areas of the world, e.g.

> **bakkie**
>
> S. African a light truck or pickup truck.

> **larrikin**
>
> Austral. a boisterous, often badly behaved young man.
> ■ a person with apparent disregard for convention; a maverick: [as modifier] *the larrikin trade union leader.*

> **ale**
>
> [mass noun] chiefly Brit. any beer other than lager, stout, or porter: *a draught of ale* | [count noun] *traditional cask-conditioned ales.*
> ■ N. Amer. beer brewed by top fermentation.

The underlying approach has been to get away from the traditional, parochial notion that 'correct' English is spoken only in England and more particularly only in Oxford or London. A network of consultants in all parts of the English-speaking world has assisted in this by giving information and answering queries—by e-mail, on a regular, often daily basis—on all aspects of the language in a particular region. Often, the aim has been to find out whether a particular word, sense, or expression, well known and standard in British English, is used anywhere else. The picture that emerges is one of complex interactions among an overlapping set of regional standards.

The vast majority of words and senses in the *New Oxford Dictionary of English* are common to all the major regional standard varieties of English, but where important local differences exist, the *New Oxford Dictionary of English* records them. There are over 14,000 geographical labels on words and senses in this dictionary, but this contrasts with more than ten times that number which are not labelled at all.

The complexity of the overall picture has necessarily been simplified, principally for reasons of space and clarity of presentation. For example, a label such as 'chiefly Brit.' implies but does not state that a term is not standard in American English, though it may nevertheless be found in some local varieties in the US. In addition, the label 'US' implies that the use is typically US (and probably originated in the US) and is not standard in British English, but it might be found in other varieties such as Australian or South African English. The label 'Brit.', on the other hand, implies that the use is found typically in standard British English but is not found in standard American English, though it may be found elsewhere.

Spelling

It is often said that English spelling is both irregular and illogical, and it is certainly true that it is only indirectly related to contemporary pronunciation. English spelling reflects not modern pronunciation but the pronunciation of the 14th century, as used by Chaucer. This traditional spelling was reinforced in the 16th and 17th centuries, in particular through the influence of the works of Shakespeare and the Authorized Version of the Bible. However, in the two centuries between Chaucer and Shakespeare English pronunciation had undergone huge changes, but spelling had failed to follow.

In the 18th century, standard spelling became almost completely fixed. The dictionaries written in this period, particularly Samuel Johnson's *Dictionary of the English Language* (1755), helped establish this national standard, which, with only minor change and variation, is the standard accepted in English today. The complex history of the English language, together with the absence of any ruling body imposing 'spelling reform', has ensured that many idiosyncrasies and anomalies in standard spelling have not only arisen but have also been preserved.

The *New Oxford Dictionary of English* gives advice and information on spelling, particularly those cases which are irregular or which otherwise cause difficulty for native speakers. The main categories are summarized below.

Variant spellings

The main form of each word given in the *New Oxford Dictionary of English* is always the standard British spelling. If there is a standard variant, e.g. a standard US spelling variant, this is indicated at the top of the entry and is cross-referred if its alphabetical position is more than three entries distant from the main entry.

> **oesophagus** (US **esophagus**)
> **esophagus** US spelling of **OESOPHAGUS**.

> **filo** (also **phyllo**)
> **phyllo** variant spelling of **FILO**.

Other variants, such as archaic, old-fashioned, or informal spellings, are cross-referred to the main entry, but are not themselves listed at the parent entry.

> **Esquimau** archaic spelling of **ESKIMO**.

Hyphenation

Although standard spelling in English is fixed, the use of hyphenation is not. In standard English a few general rules are followed, and these are outlined below.

Hyphenation of noun compounds: There is no hard-and-fast rule to determine whether, for example, **airstream**, **air stream**, or **air-stream** is correct. All forms are found in use: all are recorded in the British National Corpus and other standard texts. However, there is a broad tendency to avoid hyphenation for noun compounds in modern English (except when used to show grammatical function: see below). Thus there is, for example, a preference for **airstream** rather than **air-stream** and for **air raid** rather than **air-raid**. Although this is a tendency in both British and US English there is an additional preference in US English for the form to be one word and in British English for the form to be two words, e.g. **air fare** tends to be the commonest form in British English, while **airfare** tends to be the commonest form in US English. To save space and avoid confusion, only one of the three potential forms of each noun compound (the standard British one) is used as the headword form in the *New Oxford Dictionary of English*. This does not, however, imply that other forms are incorrect or not used.

Grammatical function: Hyphens are also used to perform certain grammatical functions. When a noun compound made up of two separate words (e.g. **credit card**) is placed before another noun and used to modify it, the general rule is that the noun compound becomes hyphenated, e.g. *I used my credit card* but *credit-card debt*. This sort of regular alternation is seen in example sentences in the *New Oxford Dictionary of English* but is not otherwise explicitly mentioned in the dictionary entries.

A similar alternation is found in compound adjectives such as **well intentioned**. When used predicatively (i.e. after the verb), such adjectives are unhyphenated, but when used attributively (i.e. before the noun), they are hyphenated: *his remarks were well intentioned* but *a well-intentioned remark*.

A general rule governing verb compounds means that, where a noun compound is two words (e.g. **beta test**), any verb derived from it is normally hyphenated (**to beta-test**: *the system was beta-tested*). Similarly, verbal nouns and adjectives are more often hyphenated than ordinary noun or adjective compounds (e.g. **glass-making**, **nation-building**).

Inflection

Compared with other European languages, English has comparatively few inflections, and those that exist are remarkably regular. We add an *-s* to most nouns to make a plural; we add *-ed* to most verbs to make a past tense or a past participle, and *-ing* to make a present participle.

Occasionally, a difficulty arises: for example, a single consonant after a short stressed vowel is doubled before adding *-ed* or *-ing* (**hum, hums, humming, hummed**). In addition, words borrowed from other languages generally bring their foreign inflections with them, causing problems for English speakers who are not proficient in those languages.

In all such cases, guidance is given in the *New Oxford Dictionary of English*. The main areas covered are outlined below.

Verbs

The following forms are regarded as regular and are therefore not shown in the dictionary:
- third person singular present forms adding *-s* to the stem (or *-es* to stems ending in *-s*, *-x*, *-z*, *-sh*, or soft *-ch*), e.g. **find** → **finds** or **change** → **changes**
- past tenses and past participles dropping a final silent *e* and adding *-ed* to the stem, e.g. **change** → **changed** or **dance** → **danced**
- present participles dropping a final silent *e* and adding *-ing* to the stem, e.g. **change** → **changing** or **dance** → **dancing**

Other forms are given in the dictionary, notably for:
- verbs which inflect by doubling a consonant, e.g. **bat** → **batted, batting**
- verbs ending in *-y* which inflect by changing *-y* to *-i*, e.g. **try** → **tries, tried**
- verbs in which past tense and past participle do not follow the regular *-ed* pattern, e.g. **feel** → past and past participle **felt**; **awake** → past **awoke**; past participle **awoken**
- present participles which add *-ing* but retain a final *e* (in order to make clear that the pronunciation of *g* remains soft), e.g. **singe** → **singeing**

Nouns

Plurals formed by adding *-s* (or *-es* when they end in *-s*, *-x*, *-z*, *-sh*, or soft *-ch*) are regarded as regular and are not shown.

Other plural forms are given in the dictionary, notably for:
- nouns ending in *-i* or *-o*, e.g. **agouti** → **agoutis**; **albino** → **albinos**
- nouns ending in *-a*, *-um*, or *-us* which are or appear to be Latinate forms, e.g. **alumna** → **alumnae**; **spectrum** → **spectra**; **alveolus** → **alveoli**
- nouns ending in *-y*, e.g. **fly** → **flies**
- nouns with more than one plural form, e.g. **storey** → **storeys** or **stories**
- nouns with plurals showing a change in the stem, e.g. **foot** → **feet**
- nouns with plurals unchanged from the singular form, e.g. **sheep** → **sheep**

Adjectives

The following forms for comparative and superlative are regarded as regular and are not shown in the dictionary:
- words of one syllable adding *-er* and *-est*, e.g. **great** → **greater, greatest**
- words of one syllable ending in silent *e*, which drop the *-e* and add *-er* and *-est*, e.g. **brave** → **braver, bravest**
- words which form the comparative and superlative by adding 'more' and 'most'

Other forms are given in the dictionary, notably for:
- adjectives which form the comparative and superlative by doubling a final consonant, e.g. **hot** → **hotter, hottest**
- two-syllable adjectives which form the comparative and superlative with *-er* and *-est* (typically adjectives ending in *-y* and their negative forms), e.g. **happy** → **happier, happiest**; **unhappy** → **unhappier, unhappiest**

Pronunciations

Generally speaking, native speakers of English do not need information about the pronunciation for ordinary, everyday words such as **bake, baby, beach, bewilder, boastful,** or **budget**. For this reason, no pronunciations are given for such words (or their compounds and derivatives) in the *New Oxford Dictionary of English*. Words such as **baba ganoush, baccalaureate, beatific, bijouterie, bucolic,** and **buddleia**, on the other hand, are less familiar and may give problems. Similarly, difficulties are often encountered in pronouncing names of people and places, especially foreign ones, such as **Chechnya, Kieslowski,** and **Althusser**.

In the *New Oxford Dictionary of English*, the principle followed is that pronunciations are given where they are likely to cause problems for the native speaker of English, in particular for foreign words, foreign names, scientific and other specialist terms, rare words, words with unusual stress patterns, and words where there are alternative pronunciations or where there is a dispute about the standard pronunciation.

The *New Oxford Dictionary of English* uses the International Phonetic Alphabet (IPA) to represent the standard accent of English as spoken in the south of England (sometimes called Received Pronunciation or RP). The transcriptions reflect pronunciation as it actually is in modern English, unlike some longer-established systems, which reflect the standard pronunciation of broadcasters and public schools in the 1930s. It is recognized that, although the English of southern England is the pronunciation given, many variations are heard in standard speech in other parts of the English-speaking world.

The symbols used for English words, with their values, are given below.

Consonants: *b*, *d*, *f*, *h*, *k*, *l*, *m*, *n*, *p*, *r*, *s*, *t*, *v*, *w*, and *z* have their usual English values. Other symbols are used as follows:

g	**g**et	x	lo**ch**	ð	**th**is	j	**y**es
tʃ	**ch**ip	ŋ	ri**ng**	ʃ	**sh**e	
dʒ	**j**ar	θ	**th**in	ʒ	deci**s**ion	

Vowels

SHORT VOWELS	LONG VOWELS (ː indicates length)	DIPHTHONGS	TRIPHTHONGS
a **c**at	ɑː **a**rm	ʌɪ **m**y	ʌɪə **f**ire
ɛ **b**ed	ɛː **h**air	aʊ **h**ow	aʊə **s**our
ə **a**go	əː **h**er	eɪ **d**ay	
ɪ **s**it	iː **s**ee	əʊ **n**o	
i **cos**y	ɔː **s**aw	ɪə **n**ear	
ɒ **h**ot	uː **t**oo	ɔɪ **b**oy	
ʌ **r**un		ʊə **p**oor	
ʊ **p**ut			

(ə) before /l/, /m/, or /n/ indicates that the syllable may be realized with a syllabic **l**, **m**, or **n**, rather than with a vowel and a consonant, e.g. /ˈbʌt(ə)n/ rather than /ˈbʌtən/.

(r) indicates an **r** that is sometimes sounded when a vowel follows, as in dra**w**er, cha-ch**a**ing.

Foreign pronunciations

Foreign words and phrases, whether naturalized or not, are always given an anglicized pronunciation. The anglicized pronunciation represents the normal pronunciation used by native speakers of standard English (who may not be speakers of other languages) when using the word in an English context. A foreign pronunciation is also given for words taken from other languages (principally French, Dutch, German, Italian, Russian, and Spanish) where this is appreciably different from the anglicized form and where the other language is familiar to a reasonable number of English speakers.

Where the native form of a foreign place name is given in addition to the anglicized form, only the foreign pronunciation of this form is given, e.g.

> **Wisła** /ˈviswa/
> Polish name for **VISTULA**.

Foreign-language transcriptions are based on current national standards. Regional variations have not been given, except in the case of Spanish transcriptions, where both Castilian and American Spanish variants are given (if distinct). Transcriptions are broad, and many symbols, identical to those used for transcribing English, have similar values to those of RP. In a few cases, where there is no English equivalent to a foreign sound, a symbol has been added to the inventory. The additional symbols used to represent foreign pronunciations are given on the right.

Consonants

ç	(German)	Ehrli**ch**, gemütli**ch**
ɲ	(French)	Monsei**gn**eur, Auver**gn**e, Daubi**gny**
	(Italian)	Emilia-Roma**gn**a
	(Portuguese)	Mi**nh**o
	(Spanish)	Espa**ñ**a, Bu**ñ**uel
β	(Spanish)	Bil**b**ao
ɣ	(Spanish)	Bur**g**os
ʎ	(Italian)	Ca**gl**iari
z	(Hungarian)	Ma**gy**arország
ʀ	French 'r'	Anve**r**s, A**r**les
r	all other values of 'r' in other featured languages	(German) B**r**aunschweig (Italian) Albe**r**ti (Russian) G**r**odno (Spanish) Algeci**r**as, za**r**zuela

Vowels

SHORT VOWELS			LONG VOWELS (ː indicates length)		
ɐ	(German)	Abitu**r**	aː	(Dutch)	Den H**aa**g
ɑ	(Dutch)	Nederl**a**nd		(German)	**Aa**chen
e	(French)	abb**é**	eː	(German)	W**eh**rmacht
	(Italian)	Croc**e**		(Dutch)	N**e**derland
	(Spanish)	Albac**e**te		(Irish)	G**ae**ltacht
o	(French)	**au**berge	oː	(German)	verb**o**ten
	(Italian)	Pali**o**		(Hungarian)	Brass**ó**
	(Spanish)	C**o**rtes			
ɔ	(French)	B**o**nnard			
	(German)	durchk**o**mponiert			
	(Greek)	Dhíl**o**s			
	(Hungarian)	Brass**ó**			
	(Italian)	B**o**rgia			
œ	(French)	Past**eu**r			
ø	(French)	Jussi**eu**	øː	(German)	Gasth**ö**fe
u	(French)	Anj**ou**			
	(Italian)	D**u**ccio			
	(Spanish)	As**u**nción			
y	(French)	cr**u**	yː	(German)	gem**ü**tlich
ʏ	(German)	M**ü**nchen			
j	(Irish)	Dáil			
	(Russian)	Arkhan**ge**lsk			
ˈ	(French)	**H**orta			

NASALIZED VOWELS (~ indicates nasality)			DIPHTHONGS		
ã		p**in**cette	} used for anglicized French pronunciations		
ɒ̃		cord**on** bleu		aɪ (German)	Gl**ei**chschaltung
ɑ̃	(French)	D**an**ton, Lac Lem**an**			
ɛ̃	(French)	Ami**ens**, Rod**in**			
œ̃	(French)	Verd**un**			
ɔ̃	(French)	arr**on**dissement			

Note on trademarks and proprietary status

This dictionary includes some words which have, or are asserted to have, proprietary status as trademarks or otherwise. Their inclusion does not imply that they have acquired for legal purposes a non-proprietary or general significance, nor any other judgement concerning their legal status. In cases where the editorial staff have some evidence that a word has proprietary status this is indicated in the entry for that word by the label trademark, but no judgement concerning the legal status of such words is made or implied thereby.

How to use this dictionary

Each new part of speech (introduced by ▶)

Part of speech

Core sense

ear[1] ▶ **noun** the organ of hearing and balance in humans and other vertebrates, especially the external part of this.

Subsenses (introduced by ■)

■ an organ sensitive to sound in other animals. ■ [in sing.] an ability to recognize, appreciate, and reproduce sounds, especially music or language: *an ear for rhythm and melody.* ■ used to refer to a person's willingness to listen and pay attention to something: *she offers a sympathetic ear to worried pet owners.*

Encyclopedic information (in separate block)

The ear of a mammal is composed of three parts. The outer or external ear consists of a fleshy external flap and a tube leading to the eardrum or tympanum. The middle ear is an air-filled cavity connected to the throat, containing three small linked bones that transmit vibrations from the eardrum to the inner ear. The inner ear is a complex fluid-filled labyrinth including the spiral cochlea (where vibrations are converted to nerve impulses) and the three semicircular canals (forming the organ of balance). The ears of other vertebrates are broadly similar.

Phrase

Example (showing typical use)

– PHRASES **be all ears** informal be listening eagerly and attentively. **bring something (down) about one's ears** bring something, especially misfortune, on oneself: *she brought her world crashing about her ears.* **one's ears are burning** one is subconsciously aware of being talked about or criticized. **grin** (or **smile**) **from ear to ear** smile broadly. **have something coming out of one's ears** informal have a substantial or excessive amount of something: *that man's got money coming out of his ears.* **have someone's ear** have access to and influence with someone: *he claimed to have the prime minister's ear.* **have** (or **keep**) **an ear to the ground** be well informed about events and trends. **in** (**at**) **one ear and out** (**at**) **the other** heard but disregarded or quickly forgotten: *whatever he tells me seems to go in one ear and out the other.* **listen with half an ear** not give one's full attention. **be out on one's ear** informal be dismissed or ejected ignominiously. **up to one's ears in** informal very busy with or deeply involved in: *I'm up to my ears in work here.*

Label (showing level of formality)

– DERIVATIVES **eared** adjective [in combination] *long-eared*, **earless** adjective.

– ORIGIN Old English *ēare*, of Germanic origin; related to Dutch *oor* and German *Ohr*, from an Indo-European root shared by Latin *auris* and Greek *ous*.

Homonym number (indicates different word with the same spelling)

ear[2] ▶ **noun** the seed-bearing head or spike of a cereal plant.
■ N. Amer. a head of maize.

– ORIGIN Old English *ēar*, of Germanic origin; related to Dutch *aar* and German *Ähre*.

Pronunciation (for selected words)

Earhart /ˈɛːhɑːt/, Amelia (1898–1937), American aviator. In 1932 she became the first woman to fly across the Atlantic solo. Her aircraft disappeared over the Pacific Ocean during a subsequent round-the-world flight.

Encyclopedic entry (biography)

Common collocation
(highlighted within the example)

earn ▶ **verb** [with obj.] (of a person) obtain (money) in return for labour or services: *he now **earns his living** as a lorry driver* | [with two objs] *earn yourself a few dollars*.
■ [with two objs] (of an activity or action) cause (someone) to obtain (money): *this latest win earned them $50,000 in prize money.* ■ (of capital invested) gain (money) as interest or profit. ■ gain or incur deservedly in return for one's behaviour or achievements: *through the years she has earned affection and esteem.*
– PHRASES **earn one's corn** Brit. informal put in a lot of effort to show that one deserves one's wages. **earn one's keep** work in return for food and accommodation. ■ be worth the time, money, or effort spent on one.
– ORIGIN Old English *earnian*, of West Germanic origin, from a base shared by Old English *esne* 'labourer'.

Label (showing regional distribution)

earwig ▶ **noun** a small elongated insect with a pair of terminal appendages that resemble pincers. The females typically care for their eggs and young until they are well grown.
● Order Dermaptera: several families.
▶ **verb** (**earwigged**, **earwigging**) [no obj.] informal eavesdrop on a conversation: *he looked behind him to see if anyone was earwigging.*
■ [with obj.] archaic influence (someone) by secret means.
– ORIGIN Old English *ēarwicga*, from *ēare* 'ear' + *wicga* 'earwig' (probably related to *wiggle*). The insect is so named because it was once thought to crawl into the human ear.

Label (showing level of formality)

Label (showing currency)

ebullient /ɪˈbʌljənt, -ˈbʊl- / ▶ **adjective 1** cheerful and full of energy: *she sounded ebullient and happy.*
2 archaic or poetic/literary (of liquid or matter) boiling or agitated as if boiling: *misted and ebullient seas.*
– DERIVATIVES **ebullience** noun, **ebulliently** adverb.
– ORIGIN late 16th cent. (in the sense 'boiling'): from Latin *ebullient-* 'boiling up', from the verb *ebullire*, from *e-* (variant of *ex-*) 'out' + *bullire* 'to boil'.

Word origin (showing morphological and sense development)

ecdysis /ˈɛkdɪsɪs, ɛkˈdʌɪsɪs/ ▶ **noun** [mass noun] Zoology the process of shedding the old skin (in reptiles) or casting off the outer cuticle (in insects and other arthropods).
– DERIVATIVES **ecdysial** /ɛkˈdɪzɪəl/ adjective.
– ORIGIN mid 19th cent.: from Greek *ekdusis*, from *ekduein* 'put off', from *ek-* 'out, off' + *duein* 'put'.

Subject label

echidna /ɪˈkɪdnə/ ▶ **noun** a spiny insectivorous egg-laying mammal with a long snout and claws, native to Australia and New Guinea. Also called **SPINY ANTEATER.**
● Family Tachyglossidae, order Monotremata: two genera and species, in particular *Tachyglossus aculeatus*.
– ORIGIN mid 19th cent.: modern Latin, from Greek *ekhidna* 'viper', also the name of a mythical creature which gave birth to the many-headed Hydra; compare with *ekhinos* 'sea-urchin, hedgehog'.

Alternative name

Technical information
(chiefly for animals and plants)

Ecuador /ˈɛkwədɔː, Spanish ekwaˈðor/ an equatorial republic in South America, on the Pacific coast; pop. 11,460,100 (est. 1995); languages, Spanish (official), Quechua; capital, Quito.

Ranges and plateaux of the Andes separate the coastal plain from the tropical forests of the Amazon basin. Formerly part of the Inca empire, Ecuador was conquered by the Spanish in 1534 and remained part of Spain's American empire until, after the first uprising against Spanish rule in 1809, independence was gained in 1822.

– DERIVATIVES **Ecuadorean** adjective & noun.

Encyclopedic entry (place name)

Additional information (in separate block)

Verb inflections

Typical form (in bold)

edit ▶ verb (**edited, editing**) [with obj.] (often **be edited**) prepare (written material) for publication by correcting, condensing, or otherwise modifying it: *Volume I was edited by J. Johnson.*
■ choose material for (a film or radio or television programme) and arrange it to form a coherent whole: [as adj. **edited**] *edited highlights of the match.* ■ be editor of (a newspaper or magazine). ■ (**edit something out**) remove unnecessary or inappropriate words, sounds, or scenes from a text, film, or radio or television programme.
▶ noun a change or correction made as a result of editing.
– ORIGIN late 18th cent. (as a verb): partly a back-formation from **EDITOR**, reinforced by French *éditer* 'to edit' (from *édition* 'edition').

Typical pattern (in bold)

Plural form

Derivatives (in alphabetical order)

elf ▶ noun (pl. **elves**) a supernatural creature of folk tales, typically represented as a small, delicate, elusive figure in human form with pointed ears, magical powers, and a capricious nature.
– DERIVATIVES **elfish** adjective, **elven** adjective (poetic/literary), **elvish** adjective.
– ORIGIN Old English, of Germanic origin; related to German *Alp* 'nightmare'.

Grammatical information (in square brackets)

enlarge ▶ verb make or become bigger or more extensive: [with obj.] *recently my son enlarged our garden pond* | [no obj.] *lymph nodes enlarge and become hard* | [as adj. **enlarged**] *an enlarged spleen.*
■ [with obj.] (often **be enlarged**) develop a bigger print of (a photograph).
– ORIGIN Middle English (formerly also as *inlarge*): from Old French *enlarger*, from *en-* (expressing a change of state) + *large* 'large'.
▶ **enlarge on/upon** speak or write about (something) in greater detail: *I would like to enlarge on this theme.*

Phrasal verbs (introduced by ▶)

Cross reference entry

eon ▶ noun variant spelling of **AEON**.

Variant spelling

epicentre (US **epicenter**) ▶ noun the point on the earth's surface vertically above the focus of an earthquake.
■ figurative the central point of something, typically a difficult or unpleasant situation: *the patient was at the epicentre of concern.*
– DERIVATIVES **epicentral** adjective.
– ORIGIN late 19th cent.: from Greek *epikentros* 'situated on a centre', from *epi* 'upon' + *kentron* 'centre'.

Aa

A¹ (also **a**) ▶ **noun** (pl. **As** or **A's**) **1** the first letter of the alphabet.
■ denoting the first in a set of items, categories, sizes, etc. ■ denoting the first of two or more hypothetical people or things: *suppose A had killed B.* ■ the highest class of academic mark. ■ (in the UK) denoting the most important category of road, other than a motorway: *the A34 | busy A-roads.* ■ denoting the highest-earning socio-economic category for marketing purposes, including top management and senior professional personnel. ■ (a) Chess denoting the first file from the left, as viewed from White's side of the board. ■ (usu. **a**) the first constant to appear in an algebraic expression. ■ Geology denoting the uppermost soil horizon, especially the topsoil. ■ the human blood type (in the ABO system) containing the A antigen and lacking the B. ■ (with numeral) denoting a series of international standard paper sizes each twice the area of the next, as *A0, A1, A2, A3, A4,* etc., A4 being 210 × 297 mm.
2 a shape like that of a capital A: [in combination] *an A-shape.* See also **A-FRAME**, **A-LINE**.
3 Music the sixth note of the diatonic scale of C major. The A above middle C is usually used as the basis for tuning and in modern music has a standard frequency of 440 Hz.
■ a key based on a scale with A as its keynote.
– PHRASES **from A to B** from one's starting point to one's destination: *most road atlases will get you from A to B.* **from A to Z** over the entire range; completely.

A² ▶ **abbreviation for** ■ ace (used in describing play in bridge and other card games): *you cash ♥AK.* ■ against (heading the column in a table of sports results which shows the goals or points scored against each club). ■ ampere(s). ■ (**Å**) ångstrom(s). ■ answer: *Q: What is a hung parliament? A: One in which no single party has an overall majority.* ■ (in names of sports clubs) Athletic: *Dunfermline A.* ■ Austria (international vehicle registration).

a¹ (**an** before a vowel sound) [called the indefinite article] ▶ **determiner 1** used when mentioning someone or something for the first time in a text or conversation: *a man came out of the room | it has been an honour to have you | we need people with a knowledge of languages.* Compare with **THE**.
■ used with units of measurement to mean one such unit: *a hundred | a quarter of an hour.* ■ [with negative] one single; any: *I simply haven't a thing to wear.* ■ used when mentioning the name of someone not known to the speaker: *a Mr Smith telephoned.* ■ someone like (the name specified): *you're no better than a Hitler.*
2 used to indicate membership of a class of people or things: *he is a lawyer | this car is a BMW.*
3 in, to, or for each; per (used when expressing rates or ratios): *typing 60 words a minute | a move to raise petrol prices by 3p a litre.*
– ORIGIN Middle English: weak form of Old English *ān* 'one'.

> **USAGE** On the question of using **a** or **an** before words beginning with h, see usage at **AN**.

a² ▶ **abbreviation for** ■ (in travel timetables) arrives: *Penzance a 0915.* ■ [in combination] (in units of measurement) atto- (10⁻¹⁸). ■ Brit. (with reference to sporting fixtures) away: *March 15 Sheffield United (a).* ■ (used before a date) before: *a1200.* [ORIGIN: from Latin *ante*.]

▶ **symbol for** (*a*) Physics acceleration.

a-¹ (often **an-** before a vowel) ▶ **prefix** not; without: *atheistic | acephalous.*
– ORIGIN from Greek.

a-² ▶ **prefix** to; towards: *aside | ashore.*
■ in the process of (an activity) *a-hunting.* ■ in a specified state: *aflutter.* ■ on: *afoot.* ■ in: *nowadays.*
– ORIGIN Old English, unstressed form of **ON**.

a-³ ▶ **prefix** variant spelling of **AD-** assimilated before *sc, sp,* and *st* (as in *ascend, aspire* and *astringent*).

a-⁴ ▶ **prefix 1** of: *anew.* [ORIGIN: unstressed form of **OF**.]
2 utterly: *abash.* [ORIGIN: from Anglo-Norman French *a-* (Old French *e-, es-*), from Latin *ex*.]

-a¹ ▶ **suffix** forming: **1** ancient or Latinized modern names of animals and plants: *primula.*
2 names of oxides: *baryta.*
3 geographical names: *Africa.*
4 ancient or Latinized modern feminine forenames: *Lydia.*
5 nouns from Italian, Portuguese and Spanish: *duenna | stanza.*
– ORIGIN representing a Greek, Latin, or Romance feminine singular.

-a² ▶ **suffix** forming plural nouns: **1** from Greek or Latin neuter plurals corresponding to a singular in *-um* or *-on* (such as *addenda, phenomena*).
2 in names (often from modern Latin) of zoological groups: *Protista | Insectivora.*

-a³ ▶ **suffix** informal **1** of: *coupla.*
2 have: *mighta.*
3 to: *oughta.*
– ORIGIN representing a casual pronunciation.

@ ▶ **symbol for** 'at', used: **1** to indicate cost or rate per unit: *30 items @ £29.99 each.*
2 in Internet addresses between the user's name and the domain name: *jsmith@oup.co.uk.*

A1 ▶ **adjective** informal very good or well; excellent: *guitar, A1 condition.*
▶ **noun** a first-class vessel in Lloyd's Register of Shipping.

A3 ▶ **noun** [mass noun] a standard European size of paper, 420 × 297 mm: [as modifier] *A3 posters.*
■ paper of this size: *a prospectus printed on A3.*

A4 ▶ **noun** [mass noun] a standard European size of paper, 297 × 210 mm: [as modifier] *an A4 page.*
■ paper of this size: *several sheets of A4.*

A5 ▶ **noun** [mass noun] a standard European size of paper, 210 × 148 mm: [as modifier] *a little A5 booklet.*
■ paper of this size: *printed on A5.*

AA ▶ **abbreviation for** ■ Alcoholics Anonymous. ■ anti-aircraft. ■ (in the UK) Automobile Association.

aa /ˈɑːɑː/ ▶ **noun** [mass noun] Geology basaltic lava forming very rough, jagged masses with a light frothy texture. Often contrasted with **PAHOEHOE**.
– ORIGIN mid 19th cent.: from Hawaiian *'a-'a.*

AAA ▶ **abbreviation for** ■ (in the UK) Amateur Athletic Association. ■ American Automobile Association. ■ Australian Automobile Association.

AAAS ▶ **abbreviation for** American Association for the Advancement of Science.

Aachen /ˈɑːx(ə)n, ˈɑːk(ə)n, German ˈaːxn/ an industrial city and spa in western Germany, in North Rhine-Westphalia; pop. 244,440 (1991). French name **AIX-LA-CHAPELLE**.

AAD ▶ **abbreviation for** analogue analogue digital, indicating that a musical recording was made and mastered in analogue form before being stored digitally.

Aalborg /ˈɔːlbɔːg/ (also **Ålborg**) an industrial city and port in north Jutland, Denmark; pop. 155,000 (1991).

Aalto /ˈɑːltəʊ/, (Hugo) Alvar (Henrik) (1898–1976), Finnish architect and designer. He often used materials such as brick, copper, and timber in his building designs to blend with the landscape. As a designer he is known as the inventor of bent plywood furniture.

AAM ▶ **abbreviation for** air-to-air missile.

A & E ▶ **abbreviation for** accident and emergency.

A & M ▶ **abbreviation for** Hymns Ancient and Modern.

A & R ▶ **abbreviation for** artist(s) and repertoire (or recording), used to denote employees of a record company who select and sign new artists.

aapa /ˈɑːpə/ ▶ **noun** Indian an elder sister.
– ORIGIN from Urdu *āpa.*

aardvark /ˈɑːdvɑːk/ ▶ **noun** a nocturnal badger-sized burrowing mammal of Africa, with long ears, a tubular snout, and a long extensible tongue, feeding on ants and termites. Also called **ANTBEAR**.
● *Orycteropus afer,* the only member of the family Orycteropidae and order Tubulidentata.
– ORIGIN late 18th cent.: from South African Dutch, from *aarde* 'earth' + *vark* 'pig'.

aardwolf /ˈɑːdwʊlf/ ▶ **noun** (pl. **aardwolves**) a nocturnal black-striped African mammal of the hyena family, feeding mainly on termites.
● *Proteles cristatus,* family Hyaenidae.
– ORIGIN mid 19th cent.: from South African Dutch, from *aarde* 'earth' + *wolf* 'wolf'.

aargh /ɑː/ ▶ **exclamation** used as an expression of anguish, horror, rage, or other strong emotion.
– ORIGIN late 18th cent.: imitative, lengthened form of **AH**, to express a prolonged cry.

Aarhus /ˈɔːhuːs/ (also **Århus**) a city on the coast of east Jutland, Denmark; pop. 261,440 (1990).

Aaron /ˈɛːrən/ (in the Bible) brother of Moses and traditional founder of the Jewish priesthood.

Aaron's beard ▶ **noun** a name given to the rose of Sharon and other plants.
– ORIGIN early 19th cent.: alluding to **AARON**, whose beard 'went down to the skirts of his garments' (Ps. 133:2), because of the hairy stamens or long runners which some of these plants put out.

Aaron's rod ▶ **noun** the common or great mullein.
– ORIGIN mid 18th cent.: alluding to **AARON**, whose staff was said to have flowered (Num. 17:8).

AARP ▶ **abbreviation for** American Association of Retired Persons.

A'asia ▶ **abbreviation for** Australasia.

AAU ▶ **abbreviation for** (in the US) Amateur Athletic Union.

AAUP ▶ **abbreviation for** American Association of University Professors.

AB¹ ▶ **noun** a human blood type (in the ABO system) containing both the A and B antigens. In blood transfusion, a person with blood of this group is a potential universal recipient.

AB² ▶ abbreviation for ■ able seaman. ■ Alberta (in official postal use). ■ US Bachelor of Arts. [ORIGIN: from Latin *Artium Baccalaureus*.]

Ab¹ (also **Av**) ▶ noun (in the Jewish calendar) the eleventh month of the civil and fifth of the religious year, usually coinciding with parts of July and August.
– ORIGIN from Hebrew *'āḇ*.

Ab² Biology ▶ abbreviation for antibody.

ab- (also **abs-**) ▶ prefix away; from: *abaxial* | *abdicate*.
– ORIGIN from Latin.

ABA ▶ abbreviation for ■ (in the UK) Amateur Boxing Association. ■ (in the US) American Bar Association. ■ (in the US) American Booksellers' Association.

abaca /'abəkə/ ▶ noun a large herbaceous Asian plant of the banana family, yielding Manila hemp.
● *Musa textilis*, family Musaceae.
■ [mass noun] Manila hemp.
– ORIGIN mid 18th cent.: via Spanish from Tagalog *abaká*.

aback ▶ adverb **1** archaic towards or situated to the rear.
2 Sailing with the sail pressed backwards against the mast by a headwind.
– PHRASES **take someone aback** shock or surprise someone: *he was taken aback by her directness*.
– ORIGIN Old English *on bæc* (see **A-²**, **BACK**). For long written as two words, the term came to be treated as a single word in nautical use.

abacus /'abəkəs/ ▶ noun (pl. **abacuses**) **1** an oblong frame with rows of wires or grooves along which beads are slid, used for calculating.
2 Architecture the flat slab on top of a capital, supporting the architrave.
– ORIGIN late Middle English (denoting a board strewn with sand on which to draw figures): from Latin, from Greek *abax, abak-* 'slab, drawing board', of Semitic origin; probably related to Hebrew *'āḇāq* 'dust'.

Abadan /ˌabə'dɑːn/ a major port and oil-refining centre on an island of the same name on the Shatt al-Arab waterway in western Iran; pop. 308,000 (1986).

Abaddon /ə'bad(ə)n/ a name for the Devil (Rev. 9:11) or for hell.
– ORIGIN late Middle English: via Greek from Hebrew *'ăḇaddōn* 'destruction'. Its use for 'hell' arose in the late 17th cent.

abaft /ə'bɑːft/ Nautical ▶ adverb in or behind the stern of a ship.
▶ preposition nearer the stern than; behind.
– ORIGIN Middle English (in the sense 'backwards'): from **A-²** (expressing motion) + archaic *baft* 'in the rear'.

abaht /ə'bɑːt/ ▶ adverb & preposition non-standard spelling of **ABOUT**, used in representing southern English (especially cockney) speech.

Abakan /ˌabə'kɑːn/ an industrial city in south central Russia, capital of the republic of Khakassia; pop. 157,600 (1993). Former name (until 1931) **UST-ABAKANSKOE**.

abalone /ˌabə'ləʊni/ ▶ noun an edible mollusc of warm seas, with a shallow ear-shaped shell lined with mother-of-pearl and pierced with a line of respiratory holes. Also called **ORMER**, **EAR SHELL**.
● Genus *Haliotis*, family Haliotidae, class Gastropoda.
– ORIGIN mid 19th cent. (originally North American): from American Spanish *abulones*, plural of *abulón*, from *aulón*, the name in an American Indian language of Monterey Bay, California.

abandon ▶ verb [with obj.] **1** give up completely (a course of action, practice, or way of thinking): *he had clearly abandoned all pretence of trying to succeed*.
■ discontinue (a scheduled event) before completion: *fans invaded the pitch and the match was abandoned*.
2 cease to support or look after (someone); desert: *her natural mother had abandoned her at an early age*.
■ leave (a place, typically a building) empty or uninhabited, without intending to return: *derelict houses were abandoned*. ■ leave (something, typically a vehicle) for good: *he abandoned his vehicle and tried to flee on foot*. ■ (**abandon someone/thing to**) condemn someone or something (to a specified fate) by ceasing to take an interest in or look after them: *it was an attempt to persuade businesses not to abandon the area to inner-city deprivation*.
3 (**abandon oneself to**) allow oneself to indulge in

(a desire or impulse): *abandoning herself to moony fantasies*.
▶ noun [mass noun] complete lack of inhibition or restraint: *she sings and sways with total abandon*.
– PHRASES **abandon ship** leave a ship because it is sinking.
– DERIVATIVES **abandonment** noun.
– ORIGIN late Middle English: from Old French *abandoner*, from *a-* (from Latin *ad* 'to, at') + *bandon* 'control' (related to **BAN¹**). The original sense was 'bring under control', later 'give in to the control of, surrender to' (sense 3).

abandoned ▶ adjective **1** (of a person) having been deserted or cast off: *a home for orphan and abandoned boys*.
2 (of a building or vehicle) remaining empty or unused; having been left for good: *an abandoned jeep stood in the street*.
3 unrestrained; uninhibited: *a wild, abandoned dance*.

abase /ə'beɪs/ ▶ verb [with obj.] behave in a way so as to belittle or degrade (someone): *I watched my colleagues abasing themselves before the board of trustees*.
– DERIVATIVES **abasement** noun.
– ORIGIN late Middle English: from Old French *abaissier*, from *a-* (from Latin *ad* 'to, at') + *baissier* 'to lower', based on late Latin *bassus* 'short of stature'. The spelling has been influenced by **BASE²**.

abash ▶ verb [with obj.] [usu. as adj. **abashed**] cause to feel embarrassed, disconcerted, or ashamed: *Harriet looked slightly abashed*.
– DERIVATIVES **abashment** noun.
– ORIGIN Middle English: from Anglo-Norman French *abaiss-*; compare with Old French *esbaiss-*, lengthened stem of *esbair*, from *es-* 'utterly' + *bair* 'astound'.

abate /ə'beɪt/ ▶ verb [no obj.] (of something perceived as hostile, threatening, or negative) become less intense or widespread: *the storm suddenly abated*.
■ [with obj.] cause to become less intense: *nothing abated his crusading zeal*. ■ [with obj.] Law lessen, reduce, or remove (a nuisance).
– ORIGIN Middle English (in the legal sense 'put a stop to (a nuisance)'): from Old French *abatre* 'to fell', from *a-* (from Latin *ad* 'to, at') + *batre* 'to beat' (from Latin *battere, battuere* 'to beat').

abatement ▶ noun [mass noun] (often in legal use) the ending, reduction, or lessening of something: *noise abatement* | [count noun] *an abatement in the purchase price*.
– ORIGIN Middle English: from Anglo-Norman French, from Old French *abatre* 'fell, put an end to' (see **ABATE**).

abatis /'abətɪs/ (also **abattis**) ▶ noun (pl. same, **abatises**, or **abattises**) historical a defence made of felled trees placed lengthwise over each other with the boughs pointing outwards.
– ORIGIN mid 18th cent.: from French, literally 'felled (trees)', from Old French *abatre* 'to fell' (see **ABATE**).

abattoir /'abətwɑː/ ▶ noun a slaughterhouse.
– ORIGIN early 19th cent.: from French, from *abattre* 'to fell'.

abaxial /ab'aksɪəl/ ▶ adjective Botany facing away from the stem of a plant (in particular denoting the lower surface of a leaf). The opposite of **ADAXIAL**.

abaya /ə'beɪjə/ ▶ noun a full-length, sleeveless outer garment worn by Arabs.
– ORIGIN mid 19th cent.: from Arabic *'abāya*.

Abba /'abə/ ▶ noun (in the New Testament) God as father.
■ (in the Syrian Orthodox and Coptic Churches) a title given to bishops and patriarchs. ■ (**abba**) Indian father (often as a familiar form of address). [ORIGIN: from Hindi *abbā*, from Arabic *ab*.]
– ORIGIN via Greek from Aramaic *'abbā* 'father'.

abbacy /'abəsi/ ▶ noun (pl. **-ies**) the office or period of office of an abbot or abbess.
– ORIGIN late Middle English: from ecclesiastical Latin *abbacia*, from *abbas, abbat-* (see **ABBOT**).

Abbas /'abas/, Ferhat (1899–1989), Algerian nationalist leader. President of the provisional government of the Algerian republic from 1958, he was appointed first President of independent Algeria in 1962 but fell from favour the following year.

Abbasid /ə'basɪd, 'abəsɪd/ ▶ adjective of or relating to a dynasty of caliphs who ruled in Baghdad from 750 to 1258.

▶ noun a member of this dynasty.
– ORIGIN named after *Abbas* (566–652), the prophet Muhammad's uncle and founder of the dynasty.

abbatial /ə'beɪʃ(ə)l/ ▶ adjective of or relating to an abbey, abbot, or abbess.
– ORIGIN late 17th cent.: from medieval Latin *abbatialis*, from *abbas, abbat-* (see **ABBOT**).

Abbe /'abə, 'abi/, Ernst (1840–1905), German physicist, inventor of the apochromatic lens.

abbé /'abeɪ, French abe/ ▶ noun (in France) an abbot or other cleric.
– ORIGIN mid 16th cent.: French, from ecclesiastical Latin *abbas, abbat-* (see **ABBOT**).

abbess /'abɛs/ ▶ noun a woman who is the head of an abbey of nuns.
– ORIGIN Middle English: from Old French *abbesse* 'female abbot', from ecclesiastical Latin *abbatissa*, from *abbas, abbat-* (see **ABBOT**).

Abbevillian /ab'vɪlɪən/ ▶ adjective Archaeology, dated of, relating to, or denoting the first Palaeolithic culture in Europe, now usually referred to as the Lower Acheulian.
■ [as noun **the Abbevillian**] the Abbevillian culture or period.
– ORIGIN 1930s: from French *Abbevillien* 'from *Abbeville*', a town in northern France where tools from this culture were discovered.

abbey ▶ noun (pl. **-eys**) the building or buildings occupied by a community of monks or nuns.
■ a church or house that was formerly an abbey.
– ORIGIN Middle English: from Old French *abbeie*, from medieval Latin *abbatia* 'abbacy', from *abbas, abbat-* (see **ABBOT**).

abbot ▶ noun a man who is the head of an abbey of monks.
– DERIVATIVES **abbotship** noun.
– ORIGIN Old English *abbod*, from ecclesiastical Latin *abbas, abbat-*, from Greek *abbas* 'father', from Aramaic *'abbā* (see **ABBA**).

abbreviate /ə'briːvɪeɪt/ ▶ verb [with obj.] (usu. be **abbreviated**) shorten (a word, phrase, or text): *the business of artists and repertoire, commonly abbreviated to A & R* | [as adj. **abbreviated**] *this book is an abbreviated version of the earlier work*.
– ORIGIN late Middle English: from late Latin *abbreviat-* 'shortened', from the verb *abbreviare*, from Latin *brevis* 'short'.

abbreviation ▶ noun a shortened form of a word or phrase.
■ [mass noun] the process or result of abbreviating something.

ABC¹ ▶ noun the alphabet.
■ the rudiments of a subject: *the business had been learning the ABC of its trade*. ■ an alphabetical guide: *an ABC of British Railways locomotives*.
– PHRASES **(as) easy (or simple) as ABC** extremely easy or straightforward.

ABC² ▶ abbreviation for ■ American Broadcasting Company. ■ Australian Broadcasting Corporation.

ABC Islands an acronym for the islands of Aruba, Bonaire, and Curaçao.

ABD N. Amer. ▶ abbreviation for all but dissertation, used to denote a student who has completed all other parts of a doctorate.

abdabs (also **habdabs**) Brit. informal ▶ plural noun nervous anxiety or irritation.
– PHRASES **give someone the screaming abdabs** induce an attack of extreme anxiety or irritation in someone.
– ORIGIN 1940s: of unknown origin.

abdicate /'abdɪkeɪt/ ▶ verb [no obj.] (of a monarch) renounce one's throne: *in 1918 Kaiser Wilhelm abdicated as German emperor* | [with obj.] *Ferdinand abdicated the throne in favour of the emperor's brother*.
■ [with obj.] fail to fulfil or undertake (a responsibility or duty): *the government was accused of abdicating its responsibility* | [no obj.] *the secretary of state should not abdicate from leadership on educational issues*.
– DERIVATIVES **abdication** noun, **abdicator** noun.
– ORIGIN mid 16th cent.: from Latin *abdicat-* 'renounced', from the verb *abdicare*, from *ab-* 'away, from' + *dicare* 'declare'.

abdomen /'abdəmən, ab'dəʊmən/ ▶ noun the part of the body of a vertebrate containing the digestive and reproductive organs; the belly. In humans and other mammals it is contained between the diaphragm and the pelvis.
■ Zoology the hinder part of the body of an arthropod,

especially the segments of an insect's body behind the thorax.

– DERIVATIVES **abdominal** /ab'dɒmɪn(ə)l/ adjective.

– ORIGIN mid 16th cent.: from Latin.

abducens nerve /ab'dju:s(ə)nz/ ▶ **noun** Anatomy each of the sixth pair of cranial nerves, supplying the muscles concerned with the lateral movement of the eyeballs.

– ORIGIN early 19th cent.: *abducens* (modern Latin, 'leading away'), from the Latin verb *abducere*.

abduct ▶ **verb** [with obj.] **1** take (someone) away illegally by force or deception; kidnap: *the millionaire who disappeared may have been abducted.*
2 Physiology (of a muscle) move (a limb or part) away from the midline of the body or from another part. The opposite of **ADDUCT**[1].

– ORIGIN early 17th cent.: from Latin *abduct-* 'led away', from the verb *abducere*, from *ab-* 'away, from' + *ducere* 'to lead'.

abductee ▶ **noun** a person who has been abducted.

abduction ▶ **noun** [mass noun] **1** the action of forcibly taking someone away against their will: *they organized the abduction of Mr Cordes on his way to the airport* | [count noun] *abductions by armed men in plain clothes.*
■ (in legal use) the illegal removal of a child from its parents or guardians.
2 Physiology the movement of a limb or other part away from the midline of the body, or from another part. The opposite of ***adduction*** (see **ADDUCT**[1]).

abductor ▶ **noun** **1** a person who abducts another person.
2 (also **abductor muscle**) Anatomy a muscle whose contraction moves a limb or part away from the midline of the body, or from another part. Compare with **ADDUCTOR**.
■ any of a number of specific muscles in the hand, forearm, or foot: [followed by Latin genitive] *abductor pollicis.*

– ORIGIN early 17th cent. (as a term in anatomy): modern Latin (see **ABDUCT**).

Abduh /'abdu:/, Muhammad (1849–1905), Egyptian Islamic scholar, jurist, and liberal reformer.

Abdul Hamid II /ˌabdʊl 'hamɪd/ (1842–1918), the last sultan of Turkey 1876–1909. An autocratic ruler, he was deposed after the revolt of the Young Turks.

Abdullah ibn Hussein /abˌdʊlə ˌɪb(ə)n hʊ'seɪn/ (1882–1951), king of Jordan 1946–51. He served as emir of Transjordan from 1921, becoming king of Jordan on its independence.

Abdul Rahman /ˌabdʊl 'rɑ:mən/, Tunku (1903–90), Malayan statesman, first Prime Minister of independent Malaya 1957–63 and of Malaysia 1963–70.

abeam ▶ **adverb** on a line at right angles to a ship's or an aircraft's length.
■ (**abeam of**) opposite the middle of (a ship or aircraft): *she was lying almost abeam of us.*

– ORIGIN mid 19th cent.: from **A-**[2] (expressing general direction) + **BEAM**.

abecedarian /ˌeɪbi:si:'dɛ:rɪən/ ▶ **adjective** arranged alphabetically: *in abecedarian sequence.*

– ORIGIN mid 17th cent.: from late Latin *abecedarius* 'alphabetical' (from the names of the letters *a, b, c, d*) + **-AN**.

abed ▶ **adverb** archaic in bed.

– ORIGIN Middle English: from **A-**[2] 'in, on' + **BED**.

Abel[1] /'eɪb(ə)l/ (in the Bible) the second son of Adam and Eve, murdered by his brother Cain.

Abel[2] /'ɑ:b(ə)l/, Niels Henrik (1802–29), Norwegian mathematician. He proved that equations of the fifth degree cannot be solved by conventional algebraic methods, and made advances in the fields of power series and elliptic functions.

Abelard /'abəlɑ:(d)/, Peter (1079–1142), French scholar, theologian, and philosopher. He is famous for his tragic love affair with his pupil Héloïse (see **HÉLOÏSE**).

abele /ə'bi:l, 'eɪb(ə)l/ ▶ **noun** the white poplar.

– ORIGIN Middle English: via Old French from medieval Latin *albellus*, diminutive of *albus* 'white'. The term was reintroduced in the late 16th cent. from Dutch *abeel* (from Old French *abel*), when specimens were imported from the Netherlands.

abelia /ə'bi:lɪə/ ▶ **noun** an East Asian shrub of the honeysuckle family, typically having small tubular pink or white flowers.
• Genus *Abelia*, family Caprifoliaceae.

– ORIGIN modern Latin; named after Clarke *Abel* (1780–1826), English botanist.

abelian /ə'bi:lɪən/ ▶ **adjective** Mathematics (of a group) having members related by a commutative operation (i.e. $a*b = b*a$).

– ORIGIN mid 19th cent.: from N. H. *Abel* (see **ABEL**[2]) + **-IAN**.

Abenaki /ˌabə'naki/ ▶ **noun** & **adjective** variant spelling of **ABNAKI**.

Abeokuta /ˌabɪəʊ'ku:tə/ a city in SW Nigeria, capital of the state of Ogun; pop. 386,800 (est. 1992).

Aberdeen[1] a city and seaport in NE Scotland; pop. 201,100 (1991). It is a centre of the offshore North Sea oil industry.

Aberdeen[2], George Hamilton Gordon, 4th Earl of (1784–1860), British Conservative statesman, Prime Minister 1852–5.

Aberdeen Angus ▶ **noun** an animal of a Scottish breed of hornless black beef cattle.

– ORIGIN mid 19th cent.: from **ABERDEENSHIRE** and **ANGUS**[1], where the breed originated.

Aberdeenshire an administrative region and former county of NE Scotland. Between 1975 and 1996 it was part of Grampian region.

Aberdonian /ˌabə'dəʊnɪən/ ▶ **adjective** of Aberdeen.
▶ **noun** a native or citizen of Aberdeen.

– ORIGIN mid 17th cent.: from medieval Latin *Aberdonia* 'Aberdeen' + **-AN**.

Aberfan /ˌabə'van/ a village in South Wales where, in 1966, a slag heap collapsed, overwhelming houses and a school and killing 28 adults and 116 children.

aberrant /ə'bɛr(ə)nt/ ▶ **adjective** departing from an accepted standard.
■ chiefly Biology diverging from the normal type: *aberrant chromosomes.*

– DERIVATIVES **aberrance** noun, **aberrancy** noun, **aberrantly** adverb.

– ORIGIN mid 16th cent.: from Latin *aberrant-* 'wandering away', from the verb *aberrare*, from *ab-* 'away, from' + *errare* 'to stray'.

aberration /ˌabə'reɪʃ(ə)n/ ▶ **noun** a departure from what is normal, usual, or expected, typically one that is unwelcome: *they described the outbreak of violence in the area as an aberration.*
■ a person whose beliefs or behaviour are unusual or unacceptable: *evil men are an aberration.* ■ a departure from someone's usual moral character or mental ability, typically for the worse: *I see these activities as some kind of mental aberration.* ■ Biology a characteristic that deviates from the normal type: *colour aberrations.* ■ Optics the failure of rays to converge at one focus because of a defect in a lens or mirror. ■ Astronomy the apparent displacement of a celestial object from its true position, caused by the relative motion of the observer and the object.

– DERIVATIVES **aberrational** adjective.

– ORIGIN late 16th cent.: from Latin *aberratio(n-)*, from *aberrare* 'to stray' (see **ABERRANT**).

Abertawe /ˌaber'tawe/ Welsh name for **SWANSEA**.

abet /ə'bɛt/ ▶ **verb** (**abetted**, **abetting**) [with obj.] encourage or assist (someone) to do something wrong, in particular to commit a crime or other offence: *he was not guilty of murder, but guilty of* ***aiding and abetting*** *others.*
■ encourage or assist someone to commit (a crime): *we are* ***aiding and abetting*** *this illegal traffic.*

– DERIVATIVES **abetment** noun, **abetter** (also **abettor**) noun.

– ORIGIN late Middle English (in the sense 'urge to do something good or bad'): from Old French *abeter*, from *a-* (from Latin *ad* 'to, at') + *beter* 'hound, urge on'.

abeyance /ə'beɪəns/ ▶ **noun** [mass noun] a state of temporary disuse or suspension: *matters were* ***held in abeyance*** *pending further enquiries.*
■ Law the position of being without, or waiting for, an owner or claimant.

– DERIVATIVES **abeyant** adjective.

– ORIGIN late 16th cent. (in the legal sense): from Old French *abeance* 'aspiration to a title', from *abeer* 'aspire after', from *a-* 'towards' + *beer* 'to gape'.

ABH ▶ **abbreviation for** actual bodily harm.

abhor /əb'hɔ:/ ▶ **verb** (**abhorred**, **abhorring**) [with obj.] regard with disgust and hatred: *we abhor the principles outlined in this motion.*

– DERIVATIVES **abhorrer** noun.

– ORIGIN late Middle English: from Latin *abhorrere*, from *ab-* 'away from' + *horrere* 'to shudder'.

abhorrence /əb'hɒr(ə)ns/ ▶ **noun** [mass noun] a feeling of revulsion; disgusted loathing: *the thought of marrying him filled her with abhorrence* | *society's* ***abhorrence of*** *crime.*

abhorrent ▶ **adjective** inspiring disgust and loathing; repugnant: *racial discrimination was* ***abhorrent to*** *us all.*

– ORIGIN late 16th cent.: from Latin *abhorrent-* 'shuddering away from in horror', from the verb *abhorrere* (see **ABHOR**).

abide ▶ **verb** **1** [no obj.] (**abide by**) accept or act in accordance with (a rule, decision, or recommendation): *I said I would abide by their decision.*
2 [with obj.] (**can/could not abide**) informal be unable to tolerate (someone or something): *if there is one thing I cannot abide it is a lack of discipline.*
3 [no obj.] (of a feeling or a memory) continue without fading or being lost.
■ archaic live; dwell.

– DERIVATIVES **abidance** noun (archaic).

– ORIGIN Old English *ābīdan* 'wait', from *ā-* 'onwards' + *bīdan* (see **BIDE**).

abiding ▶ **adjective** (of a feeling or a memory) lasting a long time; enduring: *he had an abiding respect for her.*

– DERIVATIVES **abidingly** adverb.

Abidjan /ˌabɪ'dʒɑ:n/ the chief port of the Ivory Coast, the capital 1935–83; pop. 1,850,000 (est. 1982).

abigail ▶ **noun** archaic a lady's maid.

– ORIGIN mid 17th cent.: from the name of a character in *The Scornful Lady* by Beaumont and Fletcher, possibly in allusion to 1 Sam. 25: 23–24: 'And when Abigail saw David, she ... fell at his feet, and said, "... hear the words of thine handmaid".'.

ability ▶ **noun** (pl. **-ies**) **1** [in sing., with infinitive] the capacity to do something: *the manager had lost his ability to motivate the players* | *the tax bears no relationship to people's ability to pay.*
2 [mass noun] talent that enables someone to achieve a great deal: *a man of exceptional ability.*
■ (in the context of education) a level of mental power: *a student of below average ability* | [count noun] *pupils of all abilities.* ■ [count noun] a particular talent or skill: *much depends on the person's abilities and aptitudes.*

– ORIGIN late Middle English: from Old French *ablete*, from Latin *habilitas*, from *habilis* 'able'.

-ability ▶ **suffix** forming nouns of quality corresponding to adjectives ending in *-able* (such as *suitability* corresponding to *suitable*).

– ORIGIN from French *-abilité* or Latin *-abilitas*.

ab initio /ˌab ɪ'nɪʃɪəʊ/ ▶ **adverb** & **adjective** from the beginning (used chiefly in formal or legal contexts): [as adv.] *the agreement should be declared void ab initio.*

– ORIGIN Latin.

abiogenesis /ˌeɪbʌɪə(ʊ)'dʒɛnɪsɪs/ ▶ **noun** technical term for **SPONTANEOUS GENERATION**.

– DERIVATIVES **abiogenic** adjective.

– ORIGIN late 19th cent.: from **A-**[1] 'not' + Greek *bios* 'life' + **GENESIS**.

abiotic /ˌeɪbʌɪ'ɒtɪk/ ▶ **adjective** physical rather than biological; not derived from living organisms.
■ devoid of life; sterile.

Abitur /ˌabɪ'tʊə, German ˌabi'tu:ɐ/ (also **abitur**) ▶ **noun** (in Germany) a set of examinations taken in the final year of secondary school, success in which formerly ensured a university place.

– ORIGIN from German, abbreviation of *Abiturientenexamen* 'leavers' examination'.

abject /'abdʒɛkt/ ▶ **adjective** **1** (of a situation or condition) extremely bad, unpleasant, and degrading: *many people are living in abject poverty.*
■ (of an unhappy state of mind) experienced to the maximum degree: *his letter plunged her into abject misery.* ■ (of a failure) absolute and humiliating.
2 (of a person or their behaviour) completely without pride or dignity; self-abasing: *an abject apology.*

– DERIVATIVES **abjection** noun, **abjectly** adverb, **abjectness** noun.

– ORIGIN late Middle English (in the sense 'rejected'): from Latin *abjectus*, past participle of *abicere* 'reject', from *ab-* 'away' + *jacere* 'to throw'.

abjure /əb'dʒʊə/ ▶ **verb** [with obj.] formal solemnly renounce (a belief, cause, or claim): *MPs were urged to abjure their Jacobite allegiance.*

– PHRASES **abjure the realm** historical swear an oath to leave a country or realm forever.
– DERIVATIVES **abjuration** noun.
– ORIGIN late Middle English: from Latin *abjurare*, from *ab-* 'away' + *jurare* 'swear'.

Abkhaz /abˈkɑːz/ ▶ **noun** (pl. same) **1** a member of a people living mainly in Abkhazia.
2 [mass noun] the North Caucasian language of this people.
▶ **adjective** of or relating to Abkhazia, its people, or their language.

Abkhazia /abˈkɑːzɪə/ an autonomous territory in NW Georgia, west of the Caucasus mountains on the Black Sea; pop. 537,500 (1990); capital, Sokhumi. In 1992 Abkhazia unilaterally declared itself independent, sparking armed conflict with Georgia, and the following year drove Georgian forces from its territory.
– DERIVATIVES **Abkhazian** /abˈkɑːzɪən, abˈkeɪzjən/ adjective & noun.

ablation /əˈbleɪʃ(ə)n/ ▶ **noun** [mass noun] **1** the surgical removal of body tissue.
2 the removal of snow and ice by melting or evaporation, typically from a glacier or iceberg.
■ the erosion of rock, typically by wind action. ■ the loss of surface material from a spacecraft or meteorite through evaporation or melting caused by friction with the atmosphere.
– DERIVATIVES **ablate** verb.
– ORIGIN late Middle English (in the general sense 'taking away, removal'): from late Latin *ablatio(n-)*, from Latin *ablat-* 'taken away', from *ab-* 'away' + *lat-* 'carried' (from the verb *ferre*).

ablative /ˈablətɪv/ ▶ **adjective** **1** Grammar denoting a case (especially in Latin) of nouns and pronouns and words in grammatical agreement with them indicating an agent, instrument, or source, expressed by 'by', 'with', or 'from' in English.
2 (of surgical treatment) involving ablation.
3 of, relating to, or subject to ablation through melting or evaporation: *the spacecraft's ablative heat shield.*
▶ **noun** Grammar a word in the ablative case.
■ (**the ablative**) the ablative case.
– ORIGIN late Middle English: from Old French *ablative* (feminine of *ablatif*), Latin *ablativus*, from *ablat-* 'taken away' (see **ABLATION**).

ablative absolute ▶ **noun** a construction in Latin consisting of a noun and participle or adjective in the ablative case and which functions as a sentence adverb, for example *mirabile dictu* 'wonderful to relate'.

ablaut /ˈablaʊt/ ▶ **noun** [mass noun] alternation in the vowels of related word forms, especially in Germanic strong verbs (e.g. in *sing, sang, sung*).
– ORIGIN mid 19th cent.: from German, from *ab* 'off' + *Laut* 'sound'.

ablaze ▶ **adjective** [predic.] burning fiercely: *his clothes were ablaze* | [as complement] *farm buildings were set ablaze.*
■ very brightly coloured or lighted: *New England is **ablaze with** colour in autumn.* ■ made bright by a strong emotion: *his eyes were **ablaze with** anger.*

able ▶ **adjective** (**abler**, **ablest**) **1** [with infinitive] having the power, skill, means, or opportunity to do something: *he was able to read Greek at the age of eight* | *they would never be able to afford such a big house.*
2 having considerable skill, proficiency, or intelligence: *the dancers were technically very able.*
– ORIGIN late Middle English (also in the sense 'easy to use, suitable'): from Old French *hable*, from Latin *habilis* 'handy', from *habere* 'to hold'.

-able ▶ **suffix** forming adjectives meaning: **1** able to be: *calculable.*
2 due to be: *payable.*
3 subject to: *taxable.*
4 relevant to or in accordance with: *fashionable.*
5 having the quality to: *suitable* | *comfortable.*
– ORIGIN from French *-able* or Latin *-abilis*; originally found in words only from these forms but later used to form adjectives directly from English verbs ending in *-ate*, e.g. *educable* from *educate*; subsequently used to form adjectives from verbs of all types (influenced by the unrelated word **ABLE**), e.g. *bearable, saleable.*

able-bodied ▶ **adjective** fit and healthy; not physically disabled: *he was the only able-bodied man on the farm.*

abled ▶ **adjective** having a full range of physical or mental abilities; not disabled. See also **DIFFERENTLY ABLED**.
– ORIGIN 1980s: back-formation from **DISABLED**.

ableism /ˈeɪblɪz(ə)m/ (also **ablism**) ▶ **noun** [mass noun] discrimination in favour of able-bodied people.
– DERIVATIVES **ableist** adjective.

able seaman ▶ **noun** a rank of sailor in the Royal Navy above ordinary seaman and below leading seaman.

abloom ▶ **adjective** [predic.] covered in flowers.

ablution /əˈbluːʃ(ə)n/ ▶ **noun** (usu. **ablutions**) an act of washing oneself (often used for humorously formal effect): *the women performed their ablutions.*
■ a ceremonial act of washing parts of the body or sacred containers. ■ (**the ablutions**) Brit. (in army slang) a building or room containing washing places and toilets.
– DERIVATIVES **ablutionary** adjective.
– ORIGIN late Middle English: from Latin *ablutio(n-)*, from *abluere*, from *ab-* 'away' + *luere* 'wash'. The original use was as a term in chemistry and alchemy meaning 'purification by using liquids', hence 'purification of the body by washing' (mid 16th cent.).

ably ▶ **adverb** skilfully; competently: *Steven has summed up our concerns very ably.*

-ably ▶ **suffix** forming adverbs corresponding to adjectives ending in *-able* (such as *suitably* corresponding to *suitable*).

ABM ▶ **abbreviation for** anti-ballistic-missile.

Abnaki /abˈnaki/ (also **Abenaki** /abəˈnaki/) ▶ **noun** (pl. same or **Abnakis**) **1** a member of an American Indian people of Maine and southern Quebec.
2 [mass noun] either or both of the two extinct Algonquian languages (**Eastern Abnaki** and **Western Abnaki**) of this people.
▶ **adjective** of or relating to this people or their language.
– ORIGIN from French *Abénaqui*, from Montagnais *ouabanākionek* 'people of the eastern land'.

abnegate /ˈabnɪgeɪt/ ▶ **verb** [with obj.] rare renounce or reject (something desired or valuable): *he attempts to abnegate personal responsibility.*
– DERIVATIVES **abnegator** noun.
– ORIGIN early 17th cent.: from Latin *abnegat-* 'renounced', from the verb *abnegare*, from *ab-* 'away, off' + *negare* 'deny'.

abnegation ▶ **noun** [mass noun] the action of renouncing or rejecting something: *abnegation of political law-making power.*
■ self-denial.
– ORIGIN Middle English: from Latin *abnegatio(n-)*, from the verb *abnegare* (see **ABNEGATE**).

Abney level /ˈabni/ ▶ **noun** Surveying a kind of clinometer consisting of a sighting tube, spirit level, and graduated scale.
– ORIGIN late 19th cent.: named after Sir William *Abney* (1844–1920), English scientist.

abnormal ▶ **adjective** deviating from what is normal or usual, typically in a way that is undesirable or worrying: *the illness is recognizable from the patient's abnormal behaviour.*
– DERIVATIVES **abnormally** adverb.
– ORIGIN mid 19th cent.: alteration (by association with Latin *abnormis* 'monstrous') of 16th-cent. *anormal*, from French, variant of *anomal*, via Latin from Greek *anōmalos* (see **ANOMALOUS**).

abnormality ▶ **noun** (pl. **-ies**) an abnormal feature, characteristic, or occurrence, typically in a medical context: *a chromosome abnormality.*
■ [mass noun] the quality or state of being abnormal.

Abo /ˈabəʊ/ (also **abo**) Austral. informal, offensive ▶ **noun** (pl. **Abos**) an Aborigine.
▶ **adjective** Aboriginal.
– ORIGIN early 20th cent.: abbreviation.

Åbo /ˈɔːbuː/ Swedish name for **TURKU**.

aboard ▶ **adverb** & **preposition** on or into (a ship, aircraft, train, or other vehicle): [as adv.] *welcome aboard, sir* | *the plane crashed, killing all 158 people aboard* | [as prep.] *climbing aboard the yacht.*
■ on or on to (a horse): [as adv.] *with Richard Migliore aboard, he won the cup at a gallop.* ■ figurative into an organization or team as a new member: [as adv.] *coming aboard as IBM's new chairman.* ■ Baseball on base: [as adv.] *putting their first batter aboard.*
– PHRASES **all aboard!** a call warning passengers to get on a ship, train, or bus that is about to depart.
– ORIGIN late Middle English: from **A-**[2] (expressing motion) + **BOARD**, reinforced by Old French *à bord*.

abode[1] ▶ **noun** formal or poetic/literary a place of residence; a house or home: *both defendants were said to be of **no fixed abode*** | *my humble abode.*
■ [mass noun] residence: *their right of abode in Britain.* ■ archaic a stay; a sojourn.
– ORIGIN Middle English (in the sense 'act of waiting'): verbal noun from **ABIDE**.

abode[2] ▶ **verb** archaic past of **ABIDE**.

abolish ▶ **verb** [with obj.] formally put an end to (a system, practice, or institution): *the tax was abolished in 1977.*
– DERIVATIVES **abolishable** adjective, **abolisher** noun, **abolishment** noun.
– ORIGIN late Middle English: from Old French *aboliss-*, lengthened stem of *abolir*, from Latin *abolere* 'destroy'.

abolition ▶ **noun** [mass noun] the action of abolishing a system, practice, or institution: *the abolition of the death penalty.*
– ORIGIN early 16th cent.: from Latin *abolitio(n-)*, from *abolere* 'destroy'.

abolitionist ▶ **noun** a person who favours the abolition of a practice or institution, especially capital punishment or (formerly) slavery.
– DERIVATIVES **abolitionism** noun.

abomasum /ˌabəʊˈmeɪsəm/ ▶ **noun** (pl. **abomasa** /-sə/) Zoology the fourth stomach of a ruminant, which receives food from the omasum and passes it to the small intestine.
– ORIGIN late 17th cent.: modern Latin, from *ab-* 'away, from' + *omasum* (see **OMASUM**).

A-bomb ▶ **noun** short for **ATOM BOMB**.

Abomey /əˈbəʊmeɪ, ˌabə(ʊ)ˈmeɪ/ a town in southern Benin, capital of the former kingdom of Dahomey; pop. 65,725 (1992).

abominable ▶ **adjective** causing moral revulsion: *the uprising was suppressed with abominable cruelty.*
■ informal terrible: *what an abominable mess!*
– DERIVATIVES **abominably** adverb.
– ORIGIN Middle English: via Old French from Latin *abominabilis*, from *abominari* (see **ABOMINATE**). The term was once widely believed to be from **AB-** 'away from' + Latin *homine* (from *homo* 'human being'), thus 'inhuman, beastly', and frequently spelled *abhominable* until the 17th cent.

Abominable Snowman ▶ **noun** (pl. **-men**) another term for **YETI**.

abominate /əˈbɒmɪneɪt/ ▶ **verb** [with obj.] formal detest; loathe: *they abominated the very idea of monarchy.*
– DERIVATIVES **abominator** noun.
– ORIGIN mid 17th cent.: from Latin *abominat-* 'deprecated', from the verb *abominari*, from *ab-* 'away, from' + *omen, omin-* 'omen'.

abomination ▶ **noun** a thing that causes disgust or hatred: *the Pharisees regarded Gentiles as an abomination to God* | *concrete abominations masquerading as hotels.*
■ [in sing.] a feeling of hatred: *a Calvinist abomination of indulgence.*
– ORIGIN Middle English: from Latin *abominatio(n-)*, from the verb *abominari* (see **ABOMINATE**).

aboral /abˈɔːr(ə)l/ ▶ **adjective** Zoology relating to or denoting the side or end that is furthest from the mouth, especially in animals that lack clear upper and lower sides such as echinoderms.
■ moving or leading away from the mouth.
– DERIVATIVES **aborally** adverb.

aboriginal ▶ **adjective** (of peoples, animals, and plants) inhabiting or existing in a land from the earliest times or from before the arrival of colonists; indigenous.
■ (**Aboriginal**) of or relating to the Australian Aboriginals or their languages.
▶ **noun** **1** an aboriginal inhabitant of a place.
■ (**Aboriginal**) a person belonging to one of the indigenous peoples of Australia.
2 (**Aboriginal**) [mass noun] any of the numerous Australian Aboriginal languages.
– ORIGIN mid 17th cent.: from Latin *aborigines* 'original inhabitants' (see **ABORIGINE**) + **-AL**.

USAGE Both **Aboriginals** and **Aborigines** are standard plural forms when referring to Australian Aboriginal peoples.

Aboriginality ▶ **noun** [mass noun] the distinctive culture of aboriginal peoples, especially those in Australia: *their music reflects their Aboriginality.*

aborigine /abəˈrɪdʒɪniː/ ▶ **noun** a person, animal, or plant that has been in a country or region from earliest times.
■(**Aborigine**) an aboriginal inhabitant of Australia.
– ORIGIN mid 19th cent.: back-formation from the 16th-cent. plural *aborigines* 'original inhabitants' (in classical times referring to those of Italy and Greece), from the Latin phrase *ab origine* 'from the beginning'.

USAGE See usage at **ABORIGINAL**.

aborning /əˈbɔːnɪŋ/ ▶ **adverb** chiefly N. Amer. while being born or produced: *the idea died aborning.*
– ORIGIN 1930s: from *a-* 'in the process of' + *borning*, verbal noun from *born* (North American dialect usage) 'to be born'.

abort ▶ **verb** [with obj.] **1** carry out or undergo the abortion of (a fetus).
■[no obj.] (of a pregnant woman or female animal) have a miscarriage, with loss of the fetus. ■ [no obj.] Biology (of an embryonic organ or organism) remain undeveloped; fail to mature.
2 bring to a premature end because of a problem or fault: *the flight crew aborted the take-off.*
▶ **noun** informal or technical an act of aborting a flight, space mission, or other enterprise: *an abort because of bad weather.*
■an aborted enterprise or undertaking: *I've wasted almost a year on an abort.*
– ORIGIN mid 16th cent.: from Latin *aboriri* 'miscarry', from *ab-* 'away, from' + *oriri* 'be born'.

abortifacient /əˌbɔːtɪˈfeɪʃ(ə)nt/ Medicine ▶ **adjective** (chiefly of a drug) causing abortion.
▶ **noun** an abortifacient drug.

abortion ▶ **noun 1** [mass noun] the deliberate termination of a human pregnancy, most often performed during the first 28 weeks: *concerns such as abortion and euthanasia* | [count noun] *illegal abortions.*
■the expulsion of a fetus from the womb by natural causes before it is able to survive independently. ■ Biology the arrest of the development of an organ, typically a seed or fruit.
2 an object or undertaking regarded as unpleasant or badly made or carried out.
– ORIGIN mid 16th cent.: from Latin *abortio(n-)*, from *aboriri* 'miscarry' (see **ABORT**).

abortionist ▶ **noun** a person who carries out abortions (often applied to someone not working in a hospital, or used to convey disapproval of abortion).

abortion mill ▶ **noun** informal, chiefly N. Amer. used pejoratively by opponents of abortion to refer to an abortion clinic.

abortion pill ▶ **noun** informal a drug which can induce abortion, especially mifepristone.

abortive ▶ **adjective 1** failing to produce the intended result: *she made two abortive attempts at suicide.*
2 Biology, dated (of an organ or organism) rudimentary; arrested in development: *abortive medusae.*
■Medicine (of a virus infection) failing to produce symptoms.
3 rare causing or resulting in abortion.
– DERIVATIVES **abortively** adverb.
– ORIGIN Middle English (as a noun denoting a stillborn child or animal): via Old French from Latin *abortivus*, from *aboriri* 'miscarry' (see **ABORT**).

abortus fever /əˈbɔːtəs/ ▶ **noun** [mass noun] the commonest form of undulant fever in humans.
• This disease is caused by the bacterium *Brucella abortus*, which is also the chief cause of brucellosis in cattle.
– ORIGIN 1920s: from Latin *abortus* 'miscarriage'.

ABO system ▶ **noun** a system of four basic types (A, AB, B, and O) into which human blood may be classified, based on the presence or absence of certain inherited antigens.

Aboukir Bay, Battle of /ˌabuːˈkɪə/ (also **Abukir Bay**) a naval battle in 1798 off Aboukir Bay at the mouth of the Nile, in which the British under Nelson defeated the French fleet. Also called **BATTLE OF THE NILE**.

aboulia ▶ **noun** variant spelling of **ABULIA**.

abound ▶ **verb** [no obj.] exist in large numbers or amounts: *rumours of a further scandal abound.*
■(**abound in/with**) have in large numbers or amounts: *this area abounds with caravan sites.*
– ORIGIN Middle English (in the sense 'overflow, be abundant'): from Old French *abunder*, from Latin *abundare* 'overflow', from *ab-* 'from' + *undare* 'surge' (from *unda* 'a wave').

about ▶ **preposition 1** on the subject of; concerning: *I was thinking about you* | *I asked him about his beliefs.*
■so as to affect: *there's nothing we can do about it.* ■ (**be about**) be involved or to do with; have the intention of: *it's **all about** having fun.*
2 used to indicate movement within a particular area: *she looked about the room.*
3 used to express location in a particular place: *rugs strewn about the hall* | *he produced a knife from somewhere about his person.*
■used to describe a quality apparent in a person: *there was a look about her that said everything.*
▶ **adverb 1** used to indicate movement within an area: *men were floundering about* | *finding my way about.*
2 used to express location in a particular place: *there was a lot of flu about* | *a thief about in the hotel.*
3 (used with a number or quantity) approximately: *reduced by about 5 per cent* | *he's about 35.*
– PHRASES **about to do something** intending to do something or close to doing something very soon: *the ceremony was about to begin.* **be not about to do something** be unwilling to do something: *he is not about to step down after so long.* **be on about** see **ON**. **how about** see **HOW**[1]. **just about** see **JUST**. **know what one is about** informal be aware of the implications of one's actions or of a situation, and of how best to deal with them. **what about** see **WHAT**.
– ORIGIN Old English *onbūtan*, from *on* 'in, on' + *būtan* 'outside of' (see **BUT**[2]).

about-face ▶ **noun** & **verb** chiefly N. Amer. another term for **ABOUT-TURN**.

about-turn Brit. ▶ **noun** (chiefly in military contexts) a turn made so as to face the opposite direction: *he did an about-turn and marched out of the tent.*
■informal a complete change of opinion or policy: *the government made an about-turn over the bill.*
▶ **verb** [no obj.] turn so as to face the opposite direction.
▶ **exclamation** (**about turn!**) (in military contexts) a command to make an about-turn.
– ORIGIN late 19th cent. (originally as a military command): shortening of *right about turn*.

above ▶ **preposition 1** in extended space over and not touching: *a display of fireworks above the town* | *a cable runs above the duct.*
■extending upwards over: *her arms above her head.* ■ higher than and to one side of; overlooking: *in the hills above the capital* | *on the wall above the altar.*
2 at a higher level or layer than: *from his 'des res' above the corner shop* | *bruises above both eyes.*
■higher in grade or rank than: *at a level above the common people.* ■ considered of higher status or worth than; too good for: *she **married above her*** | *above reproach.* ■ in preference to: *the firm cynically chose profit above car safety.* ■ at a higher volume or pitch than: *above a whisper* | *the doorbell went unheard above the din.*
3 higher than (a specified amount, rate, or norm): *above average* | *above freezing* | *above sea level* | *the unemployment rate will soar above its present level.*
▶ **adverb** at a higher level or layer: *place a quantity of mud in a jar with water above.*
■higher in grade or rank: *an officer of the rank of superintendent or above.* ■ higher than a specified amount, rate, or norm: *boats of 31 ft or above.* ■ (in printed text) mentioned earlier or further up on the same page: *the two cases described above* | *see above left* | [as adj.] *at the above address* | [as noun] *since writing the **above**, I have reconsidered.*
– PHRASES **above all** (**else**) more so than anything else: *he was concerned above all to speak the truth.* **above oneself** conceited; arrogant. **from above** from overhead: *branches rained from above.* ■ from a position of higher rank or authority: *mass culture is imposed from above.* **not be above** be capable of stooping to (an unworthy act): *he was not above practical jokes.* **over and above** see **OVER**.
– ORIGIN Old English *abufan* (as an adverb), from *a-* 'on' + *bufan* (from *bi* 'by' + *ufan* 'above').

above board ▶ **adjective** & **adverb** legitimate, honest, and open: [as adj.] *certain transactions were not totally above board* | [as adv.] *the accountants acted completely above board.*

ab ovo /ab ˈəʊvəʊ/ ▶ **adverb** from the very beginning.
– ORIGIN Latin, literally 'from the egg'.

Abp ▶ **abbreviation for** Archbishop.

abracadabra ▶ **exclamation** a word said by conjurors when performing a magic trick.
▶ **noun** [mass noun] informal the implausibly easy performance of difficult feats: *the creation of profits was a marvellous bit of abracadabra.*
■language used to give the impression of arcane knowledge or power: *I get so fed up with all the mumbo-jumbo and abracadabra.*
– ORIGIN late 17th cent. (as a mystical word engraved and used as a charm to ward off illness): from Latin, first recorded in a 2nd-cent. poem by Q. Serenus Sammonicus, from a Greek base.

abrade /əˈbreɪd/ ▶ **verb** [with obj.] scrape or wear away by friction or erosion: *a landscape slowly abraded by a fine, stinging dust.*
– DERIVATIVES **abrader** noun.
– ORIGIN late 17th cent.: from Latin *abradere*, from *ab-* 'away, from' + *radere* 'to scrape'.

Abraham /ˈeɪbrəham/ (in the Bible) the Hebrew patriarch from whom all Jews trace their descent (Gen. 11:27–25:10). In Gen. 22 he is ordered by God to sacrifice his son Isaac as a test of faith, a command later revoked.

Abraham, Plains of see **PLAINS OF ABRAHAM**.

Abrahams /ˈeɪbrəhamz/, Harold (Maurice) (1899–1978), English athlete. In 1924 he became the first Englishman to win the 100 metres in the Olympic Games. His story was the subject of the film *Chariots of Fire* (1981).

abrasion /əˈbreɪʒ(ə)n/ ▶ **noun** [mass noun] the process of scraping or wearing away: *the metal is resistant to abrasion.*
■[count noun] an area damaged by scraping or wearing away: *there were cuts and abrasions to the lips and jaw.*
– ORIGIN mid 17th cent.: from Latin *abrasio(n-)*, from the verb *abradere* (see **ABRADE**).

abrasive /əˈbreɪsɪv/ ▶ **adjective** (of a substance or material) capable of polishing or cleaning a hard surface by rubbing or grinding.
■tending to rub or graze the skin: *the trees were abrasive to the touch.* ■ figurative (of sounds or music) rough to the ear; harsh: *fast abrasive rhythms.* ■ figurative (of a person or their manner) showing little concern for the feelings of others; harsh: *her abrasive and arrogant personal style won her few friends.*
▶ **noun** a substance used for grinding, polishing, or cleaning a hard surface.
– ORIGIN mid 19th cent. (as a noun): from Latin *abras-* 'abraded', from the verb *abradere* (see **ABRADE**), + **-IVE**.

abrazo /əˈbrɑːzəʊ, əˈbrasəʊ/ ▶ **noun** (pl. **-os**) US an embrace.
– ORIGIN Spanish.

abreact /ˌabrɪˈakt/ ▶ **verb** [with obj.] Psychoanalysis release (an emotion) by abreaction.
■cause (someone) to undergo abreaction.
– ORIGIN early 20th cent.: back-formation from **ABREACTION**.

abreaction ▶ **noun** [mass noun] Psychoanalysis the expression and consequent release of a previously repressed emotion, achieved through reliving the experience that caused it (typically through hypnosis or suggestion).
– DERIVATIVES **abreactive** adjective.
– ORIGIN early 20th cent.: from **AB-** 'away from' + **REACTION**, translating German *Abreagierung*.

abreast ▶ **adverb 1** side by side and facing the same way: *the path was wide enough for two people to walk abreast* | *they were riding three abreast.*
2 alongside or level with something: *the cart came **abreast of** the Americans in their rickshaw* | *the car braked as it drew abreast.*
■figurative up to date with the latest news, ideas, or information: ***keeping abreast of** developments.*
– ORIGIN late Middle English: from **A-**[2] 'in' + **BREAST**.

abridge ▶ **verb** [with obj.] (usu. **be abridged**) **1** shorten (a book, film, speech, or other text) without losing the sense: *the cassettes have been abridged from the original stories* | [as adj. **abridged**] *an abridged text of his speech.*
2 Law curtail (a right or privilege).
– DERIVATIVES **abridgeable** adjective, **abridger** noun.
– ORIGIN Middle English (in the sense 'deprive of'): from Old French *abregier*, from late Latin *abbreviare* 'cut short' (see **ABBREVIATE**).

abridgement (also **abridgment**) ▶ **noun 1** a shortened version of a larger work: *an abridgement of Shakespeare's Henry VI.*
2 Law a curtailment of rights.
– ORIGIN late Middle English: from Old French *abregement*, from the verb *abreg(i)er* (see **ABRIDGE**).

abroad ▶ **adverb 1** in or to a foreign country or

countries: *we usually* **go abroad** *for a week in May | competition from companies* **at home and abroad**.
■dated or humorous out of doors: *few people ventured abroad from their warm houses.*
2 in different directions; over a wide area: *millions of seeds are annually scattered abroad.*
■(of a feeling or rumour) widely current: *there is a new buccaneering spirit abroad.* ■freely moving about: *hospital inmates abroad on the streets of the town.*
3 archaic wide of the mark; in error.
▶**noun** [mass noun] foreign countries considered collectively: *servicemen returning from abroad.*
– ORIGIN Middle English: from **A-**[2] 'on' + **BROAD**.

abrogate /ˈabrəgeɪt/ ▶**verb** [with obj.] formal repeal or do away with (a law, right, or formal agreement): *a proposal to abrogate temporarily the right to strike.*
– DERIVATIVES **abrogation** noun, **abrogator** noun.
– ORIGIN early 16th cent.: from Latin *abrogat-* 'repealed', from the verb *abrogare*, from *ab-* 'away, from' + *rogare* 'propose a law'.

USAGE The verbs **abrogate** and **arrogate** are quite different in meaning. While **abrogate** means 'repeal (a law)', **arrogate** means 'take or claim (something for oneself) without justification', often in the structure **arrogate something to oneself**, as in *the emergency committee* ***arrogated to itself*** *whatever powers it chose.*

abrupt ▶**adjective 1** sudden and unexpected: *I was surprised by the abrupt change of subject | the match came to an abrupt end on the 13th hole.*
2 brief to the point of rudeness; curt: *you were rather abrupt with that young man.*
■(of a style of speech or writing) not flowing smoothly; disjointed.
3 steep; precipitous: *the abrupt double peak.*
– DERIVATIVES **abruptly** adverb, **abruptness** noun.
– ORIGIN late 16th cent.: from Latin *abruptus* 'broken off, steep', past participle of *abrumpere*, from *ab-* 'away, from' + *rumpere* 'break'.

abruption ▶**noun** [mass noun] technical the sudden breaking away of a portion from a mass.
■(also **placental abruption**) Medicine separation of the placenta from the wall of the womb during pregnancy, especially when it occurs prematurely.
– ORIGIN early 17th cent.: from Latin *abruptio(n-)*, from *abrumpere* 'break off' (see **ABRUPT**).

Abruzzi /aˈbrʊtsi/ a mountainous region of east central Italy; capital, Aquila.
– DERIVATIVES **Abruzzian** noun & adjective.

ABS ▶**abbreviation for** ■acrylonitrile-butadiene-styrene, a hard composite plastic used to make car bodies and cases for computers and other appliances. ■anti-lock braking system (for motor vehicles).

abs- ▶**prefix** variant spelling of **AB-** before *c*, *q*, and *t* (as in *abscond*, *abstain*).

abscess ▶**noun** a swollen area within body tissue, containing an accumulation of pus.
– DERIVATIVES **abscessed** adjective.
– ORIGIN mid 16th cent.: from Latin *abscessus* 'a going away', from the verb *abscedere*, from *ab-* 'away from' + *cedere* 'go', referring to the elimination of infected matter via the pus.

abscisic acid /abˈsɪsɪk/ ▶**noun** [mass noun] Biochemistry a plant hormone which promotes leaf detachment, induces seed and bud dormancy, and inhibits germination.
– ORIGIN 1960s: *abscisic* from *abscisin* (the earlier name for the hormone), from **ABSCISSION**.

abscissa /abˈsɪsə/ ▶**noun** (pl. **abscissae** /-siː/ or **abscissas**) Mathematics (in a system of coordinates) the distance from a point to the vertical or *y*-axis, measured parallel to the horizontal or *x*-axis; the *x*-coordinate. Compare with **ORDINATE**.
– ORIGIN early 17th cent. (denoting the part of a line between a point on it and the point of intersection with an ordinate): from modern Latin *abscissa (linea)* 'cut-off (line)', feminine past participle of *abscindere* (see **ABSCISSION**).

abscission /əbˈsɪʃ(ə)n/ ▶**noun** [mass noun] Botany the natural detachment of parts of a plant, typically dead leaves and ripe fruit.
– DERIVATIVES **abscise** /əbˈsʌɪz/ verb.
– ORIGIN early 17th cent.: from Latin *abscissio(n-)*, from *abscindere*, from *ab-* 'off' + *scindere* 'to cut'.

abscond /əbˈskɒnd, ab-/ ▶**verb** [no obj.] leave hurriedly and secretly, typically to avoid detection of or arrest for an unlawful action such as theft: *the barman absconded with a week's takings.*
■(of a person on bail) fail to surrender oneself for custody at the appointed time. ■(of a person kept in detention or under supervision) escape: *176 detainees absconded.* ■(of a colony of honeybees, especially Africanized ones) entirely abandon a hive or nest.
– DERIVATIVES **absconder** noun.
– ORIGIN mid 16th cent. (in the sense 'hide, conceal (oneself)'): from Latin *abscondere* 'hide', from *ab-* 'away, from' + *condere* 'stow'.

abseil /ˈabseɪl, -zʌɪl/ ▶**verb** [no obj., with adverbial of direction] descend a rock face or other near-vertical surface by using a doubled rope coiled round the body and fixed at a higher point: [as noun **abseiling**] *facilities for abseiling and rock climbing.*
▶**noun** a descent made by abseiling.
– DERIVATIVES **abseiler** noun.
– ORIGIN 1930s: from German *abseilen*, from *ab* 'down' + *Seil* 'rope'.

absence ▶**noun** [mass noun] the state of being away from a place or person: *the letter had arrived during his absence | I supervised the rehearsal* **in the absence of** *the director.*
■[count noun] an occasion or period of being away from a place or person: *repeated absences from school.* ■(**absence of**) the non-existence or lack of: *she found his total absence of facial expression disconcerting.*
– PHRASES **absence makes the heart grow fonder** proverb you feel more affection for those you love when parted from them. **absence of mind** failure to concentrate on or remember what one is doing.
– ORIGIN late Middle English: from Old French, from Latin *absentia*, from *absens*, *absent-* (see **ABSENT**).

absent ▶**adjective** /ˈabs(ə)nt/ **1** not present in a place or at an occasion: *most pupils were* **absent from** *school at least once | absent colleagues.*
■(of a part or feature of the body) not forming part of a creature in which it might be expected: *wings are absent in several species of crane flies.*
2 (of an expression or manner) showing that someone is not paying attention to what is being said or done: *she looked up with an absent smile.*
▶**verb** /abˈsɛnt/ (**absent oneself**) stay or go away: *various people absented themselves because of his presence | halfway through the meal, he* **absented himself from** *the table.*
▶**preposition** formal, N. Amer. without: *absent a willingness to negotiate, you can't have collective bargaining.*
– DERIVATIVES **absently** adverb (only in sense 2).
– ORIGIN Middle English: via Old French from Latin *absens*, *absent-* 'being absent', present participle of *abesse*, from *ab-* 'from, away' + *esse* 'to be'.

absentee ▶**noun** a person who is expected or required to be present at a place or event but is not.

absentee ballot ▶**noun** N. Amer. a ballot completed and usually sent by post before an election by a voter who is unable to vote in their place of registration.

absenteeism ▶**noun** [mass noun] the practice of regularly staying away from work or school without good reason.

absentee landlord ▶**noun** a landlord who does not live at and rarely visits the property they let.

absent-minded ▶**adjective** (of a person or their behaviour or manner) having or showing a forgetful or inattentive disposition: *an absent-minded smile.*
– DERIVATIVES **absent-mindedly** adverb, **absent-mindedness** noun.

absinth /ˈabsɪnθ/ ▶**noun 1** the shrub wormwood.
■[mass noun] an essence made from this.
2 (usu. **absinthe**) [mass noun] a potent green aniseed-flavoured liqueur which turns milky when water is added. It was originally an alcoholic drink made with wormwood, now banned because of its toxicity.
– ORIGIN late Middle English: from French *absinthe*, via Latin from Greek *apsinthion* 'wormwood'.

absit omen /ˌabsɪt ˈəʊmɛn/ ▶**exclamation** used to express the hope that a reference to something undesirable should not foreshadow its arrival or occurrence.
– ORIGIN Latin, literally 'may this (evil) omen be absent'.

absolute /ˈabsəluːt/ ▶**adjective 1** not qualified or diminished in any way; total: *absolute secrecy | absolute silence | the attention he gave you was absolute.*
■used for general emphasis when expressing an opinion: *the policy is absolute folly.* ■(of powers or rights) not subject to any limitation; unconditional: *no one dare challenge her absolute authority | the right to life is absolute.* ■(of a ruler) having unrestricted power: *Dom Miguel proclaimed himself absolute monarch.* ■Law (of a decree) final: *the decree of nullity was made absolute.* See also **DECREE ABSOLUTE**. ■Law see **ABSOLUTE TITLE**.
2 viewed or existing independently and not in relation to other things; not relative or comparative: *absolute moral standards.*
■Grammar (of a construction) syntactically independent of the rest of the sentence, as in *dinner being over, we left the table.* ■Grammar (of a transitive verb) used without an expressed object (e.g. *guns kill*). ■Grammar (of an adjective) used without an expressed noun (e.g. *the brave*).
▶**noun** Philosophy a value or principle which is regarded as universally valid or which may be viewed without relation to other things: *good and evil are presented as absolutes.*
■(**the absolute**) Philosophy that which exists without being dependent on anything else. ■(**the Absolute**) ultimate reality; God.
– DERIVATIVES **absoluteness** noun.
– ORIGIN late Middle English: from Latin *absolutus* 'freed, unrestricted', past participle of *absolvere* (see **ABSOLVE**).

absolute advantage ▶**noun** Economics the ability of an individual or group to carry out a particular economic activity more efficiently than another individual or group.

absolute alcohol ▶**noun** [mass noun] ethanol containing less than one per cent of water by weight.

absolutely ▶**adverb 1** with no qualification, restriction, or limitation; totally: *she trusted him absolutely |* [as submodifier] *you're absolutely right.*
■used to emphasize the truth or appropriateness of a very strong or exaggerated statement: *he absolutely adores that car |* [as submodifier] *Dad was absolutely furious.* ■[with negative] none whatsoever: *she had absolutely no idea what he was talking about.* ■used to emphasize a statement or opinion: *it's absolutely pouring down | it's absolutely ages since I went to a party.* ■[as exclamation] informal used to express and emphasize one's assent or agreement: *'Did they give you a free hand when you joined the band?' 'Absolutely!'*
2 not viewed in relation to other things or factors: *white-collar crime increased both absolutely and in comparison with other categories.*
■Grammar (of a verb) without a stated object.

absolute magnitude ▶**noun** Astronomy the magnitude (brightness) of a celestial object as it would be seen at a standard distance of 10 parsecs. Compare with **APPARENT MAGNITUDE**.

absolute majority ▶**noun** a majority over all rivals combined; more than half.

absolute music ▶**noun** [mass noun] instrumental music composed purely as music, and not intended to represent or illustrate something else. Compare with **PROGRAMME MUSIC**.

absolute pitch ▶**noun** [mass noun] Music another term for **PERFECT PITCH**.
■pitch according to a fixed standard defined by the frequency of the sound vibration.

absolute privilege ▶**noun** see **PRIVILEGE**.

absolute temperature ▶**noun** a temperature measured from absolute zero in kelvins. (Symbol: **T**)

absolute title ▶**noun** [mass noun] Law the guarantee of title to the ownership of a property or lease.

absolute unit ▶**noun** a unit of measurement which is defined in terms of the fundamental units of a system (mass, length, and time), and is not based on arbitrary definitions.

absolute value ▶**noun 1** Mathematics the magnitude of a real number without regard to its sign. Also called **MODULUS**.
• The absolute value of a complex number $a + ib$ is the positive square root of $a^2 + b^2$.
2 technical the actual magnitude of a numerical value or measurement, irrespective of its relation to other values.

absolute zero ▶**noun** the lowest temperature that is theoretically possible, at which the motion of particles which constitutes heat would be minimal. It is zero on the Kelvin scale, equivalent to −273.15°C.

absolution ▶**noun** [mass noun] formal release from guilt, obligation, or punishment.
■an ecclesiastical declaration of forgiveness of sins: *the priest had the right to administer absolution.*

– ORIGIN Middle English: via Old French from Latin *absolutio(n-)*, from the verb *absolvere* (see **ABSOLVE**).

absolutism ▶ **noun** [mass noun] the acceptance of or belief in absolute principles in political, philosophical, ethical, or theological matters.
– DERIVATIVES **absolutist** noun & adjective.

absolutize (also **-ise**) ▶ **verb** [with obj.] chiefly Philosophy & Theology make or treat as absolute.
– DERIVATIVES **absolutization** noun.

absolve /əbˈzɒlv/ ▶ **verb** [with obj.] declare (someone) free from blame, guilt, or responsibility: *the pardon **absolved** them **of** any crimes.*
■ (in church use) give absolution for (a sin).
– ORIGIN late Middle English: from Latin *absolvere* 'set free, acquit', from *ab-* 'from' + *solvere* 'loosen'.

absonant /ˈabs(ə)nənt/ ▶ **adjective** archaic discordant or unreasonable.
– ORIGIN mid 16th cent.: from Latin *ab-* 'away, from' + *sonant-* 'sounding' (from the verb *sonare*), on the pattern of words such as *dissonant*.

absorb /əbˈzɔːb, -ˈsɔːb/ ▶ **verb** [with obj.] **1** take in or soak up (energy or a liquid or other substance) by chemical or physical action, especially in a gradual way: *buildings can be designed to absorb and retain heat | steroids are **absorbed into** the bloodstream.*
■ take in and assimilate (information, ideas, or experience): *she absorbed the information in silence.* ■ take control of (a smaller or less powerful entity), making it a part of oneself by assimilation: *the family firm was **absorbed into** a larger group.* ■ use or take up (time or resources): *arms spending absorbs roughly two per cent of the national income.* ■ take up and reduce the effect or intensity of (sound or an impact): *deep-pile carpets absorbed all sound of the outside world.*
2 engross the attention of (someone): *the work absorbed him and continued to make him happy.*
– DERIVATIVES **absorber** noun.
– ORIGIN late Middle English: from Latin *absorbere*, from *ab-* 'from' + *sorbere* 'suck in'.

absorbable ▶ **adjective** able to be absorbed, especially into the body.
– DERIVATIVES **absorbability** noun.

absorbance ▶ **noun** Physics a measure of the capacity of a substance to absorb light of a specified wavelength. It is equal to the logarithm of the reciprocal of the transmittance.

absorbed ▶ **adjective** intensely engaged; engrossed: *she sat in an armchair, **absorbed in** a book.*
– DERIVATIVES **absorbedly** adverb.

absorbed dose ▶ **noun** Physics the quantity of ionizing radiation absorbed by a body, measured (usually in grays) as the energy absorbed per unit mass.

absorbent ▶ **adjective** (of a material) able to soak up liquid easily: *drain on absorbent kitchen paper.*
▶ **noun** a substance or item that soaks up liquid easily.
– DERIVATIVES **absorbency** noun.
– ORIGIN early 18th cent.: from Latin *absorbent-* 'swallowing up', from the verb *absorbere* (see **ABSORB**).

absorbent cotton ▶ **noun** North American term for **COTTON WOOL**.

absorbing ▶ **adjective** intensely interesting; engrossing: *an absorbing account of their marriage.*
– DERIVATIVES **absorbingly** adverb.

absorptiometer /əbˌzɔːpʃɪˈɒmɪtə, -ˌsɔːp-/ ▶ **noun** Physics an instrument for measuring the absorption of light or other radiation.
– DERIVATIVES **absorptiometric** adjective, **absorptiometry** noun.

absorption /əbˈzɔːpʃ(ə)n, -ˈsɔːp-/ ▶ **noun** [mass noun] **1** the process or action by which one thing absorbs or is absorbed by another: *East Germany's **absorption into** West Germany | shock absorption.*
2 the fact or state of being engrossed in something: *her **absorption in** the problems of the Third World.*
– DERIVATIVES **absorptive** adjective.
– ORIGIN late 16th cent. (in the sense 'the swallowing up of something'): from Latin *absorptio(n-)*, from *absorbere* 'swallow up' (see **ABSORB**).

absorption costing ▶ **noun** [mass noun] a method of calculating the cost of a product or enterprise by taking into account indirect expenses (overheads) as well as direct costs.

absorption nebula ▶ **noun** Astronomy another term for **DARK NEBULA**.

absorption spectrum ▶ **noun** Physics a spectrum of electromagnetic radiation transmitted through a substance, showing dark lines or bands due to absorption at specific wavelengths. Compare with **EMISSION SPECTRUM**.

absquatulate /əbˈskwɒtjʊleɪt/ ▶ **verb** [no obj., with adverbial] humorous, chiefly N. Amer. leave abruptly: *some overthrown dictator who had absquatulated to the USA.*
– DERIVATIVES **absquatulation** noun.
– ORIGIN mid 19th cent.: blend (simulating a Latin form) of **ABSCOND**, *squattle* 'depart', and **PERAMBULATE**.

abstain ▶ **verb** [no obj.] **1** restrain oneself from doing or enjoying something: ***abstaining from** chocolate.*
■ refrain from drinking alcohol: *most pregnant women abstain or drink very little.*
2 formally decline to vote either for or against a proposal or motion: *forty-one voted with the Opposition, and some sixty more abstained.*
– DERIVATIVES **abstainer** noun.
– ORIGIN late Middle English: from Old French *abstenir*, from Latin *abstinere*, from *ab-* 'from' + *tenere* 'hold'.

abstemious /əbˈstiːmɪəs/ ▶ **adjective** not self-indulgent, especially when eating and drinking: *'We only had a bottle.' 'Very abstemious of you.'*
– DERIVATIVES **abstemiously** adverb, **abstemiousness** noun.
– ORIGIN early 17th cent.: from Latin *abstemius*, (from *ab-* 'from' + a word related to *temetum* 'alcoholic liquor') + **-OUS**.

abstention /əbˈstɛnʃ(ə)n/ ▶ **noun** **1** an instance of declining to vote for or against a proposal or motion: *a resolution passed by 126 votes to none, with six abstentions.*
2 [mass noun] the fact or practice of restraining oneself from indulging in something; abstinence: *alcohol consumption versus abstention.*
– DERIVATIVES **abstentionism** noun.
– ORIGIN early 16th cent. (denoting the action of keeping back or restraining): from late Latin *abstentio(n-)*, from the verb *abstinere* (see **ABSTAIN**).

abstinence /ˈabstɪnəns/ ▶ **noun** [mass noun] the fact or practice of restraining oneself from indulging in something, typically alcohol: *I started drinking again after six years of abstinence.*
– ORIGIN Middle English: from Old French, from Latin *abstinentia*, from the verb *abstinere* (see **ABSTAIN**).

abstinent ▶ **adjective** (of a person) refraining from an activity or from the use or enjoyment of something, typically alcohol: *the patients are best advised to be totally abstinent from alcohol.*
– DERIVATIVES **abstinently** adverb.
– ORIGIN late Middle English: via Old French from Latin *abstinent-* 'abstaining', from the verb *abstinere* (see **ABSTAIN**).

abstract ▶ **adjective** /ˈabstrakt/ existing in thought or as an idea but not having a physical or concrete existence: *abstract concepts such as love or beauty.*
■ dealing with ideas rather than events: *the novel was too abstract and esoteric to sustain much attention.* ■ not based on a particular instance; theoretical: *we have been discussing the problem in a very abstract manner.* ■ (of a word, especially a noun) denoting an idea, quality, or state rather than a concrete object: *abstract words like truth or equality.* ■ of or relating to abstract art: *abstract pictures.*
▶ **verb** /əbˈstrakt/ [with obj.] **1** consider (something) theoretically or separately from something else: *to **abstract** science and religion **from** their historical context can lead to anachronism.*
■ [no obj.] form a general idea in this way: *he cannot form a general notion by **abstracting from** particulars.*
2 extract or remove (something): *applications to **abstract** more water **from** streams.*
■ used euphemistically to indicate that someone has stolen something: *his pockets contained all he had been able to **abstract from** the flat.* ■ (**abstract oneself**) withdraw: *as our relationship deepened you seemed to abstract yourself.*
3 make a written summary of (an article or book): *staff who index and abstract material for an online database.*
▶ **noun** /ˈabstrakt/ **1** a summary or statement of the contents of a book, article, or formal speech: *an abstract of her speech.*
2 an abstract work of art: *a big unframed abstract.*
3 (**the abstract**) that which is abstract; the theoretical consideration of something: *the abstract must be made concrete by examples.*
– PHRASES **in the abstract** in a general way; without reference to specific instances: *there's a fine line between promoting US business interests in the abstract and promoting specific companies.*
– DERIVATIVES **abstractly** adverb, **abstractor** noun.
– ORIGIN Middle English: from Latin *abstractus*, literally 'drawn away', past participle of *abstrahere*, from *ab-* 'from' + *trahere* 'draw off'.

abstract art ▶ **noun** [mass noun] art that does not attempt to represent external, recognizable reality but seeks to achieve its effect using shapes, forms, colours, and textures.

abstracted ▶ **adjective** showing a lack of concentration on what is happening around one: *she seemed abstracted and unaware of her surroundings | an abstracted smile.*
– DERIVATIVES **abstractedly** adverb.

abstract expressionism ▶ **noun** [mass noun] a development of abstract art which originated in New York in the 1940s and 1950s and aimed at subjective emotional expression with particular emphasis on the spontaneous creative act (e.g. action painting). Leading figures were Jackson Pollock and Willem de Kooning.
– DERIVATIVES **abstract expressionist** noun & adjective.

abstraction ▶ **noun** [mass noun] **1** the quality of dealing with ideas rather than events: *topics will vary in degrees of abstraction.*
■ [count noun] something which exists only as an idea: *the question can no longer be treated as an academic abstraction.*
2 freedom from representational qualities in art: *geometric abstraction has been a mainstay in her work.*
■ [count noun] an abstract work of art.
3 a state of preoccupation: *she sensed his momentary abstraction.*
4 the process of considering something independently of its associations, attributes, or concrete accompaniments: *Christians tend to interpret Christ's words **in abstraction from** any historical context.*
5 the process of removing something, especially water from a river or other source.
– ORIGIN late Middle English: from Latin *abstractio(n-)*, from the verb *abstrahere* 'draw away' (see **ABSTRACT**).

abstractionism ▶ **noun** [mass noun] the principles and practice of abstract art.
■ the presentation of ideas in abstract terms.
– DERIVATIVES **abstractionist** noun & adjective.

abstract of title ▶ **noun** Law (in unregistered conveyancing) a summary giving details of the title deeds and documents that prove an owner's right to dispose of land, together with any encumbrances that relate to the property.

abstruse /əbˈstruːs/ ▶ **adjective** difficult to understand; obscure: *an abstruse philosophical inquiry.*
– DERIVATIVES **abstrusely** adverb, **abstruseness** noun.
– ORIGIN late 16th cent.: from Latin *abstrusus* 'put away, hidden', from *abstrudere* 'conceal', from *ab-* 'from' + *trudere* 'to push'.

absurd ▶ **adjective** (of an idea or suggestion) wildly unreasonable, illogical, or inappropriate: *it would be absurd to blame contemporary Germans for Nazi crimes | So you think I'm a spy? How absurd!*
■ (of a person or their behaviour) foolish; unreasonable: *she was being absurd—and imagining things.* ■ (of an object or situation) arousing amusement or derision; ridiculous: *gym tunics and knee socks looked absurd on such a tall girl.*
▶ **noun** (**the absurd**) a state of affairs that is or seems wildly unreasonable, illogical, or inappropriate: *the incidents that followed bordered on the absurd.*
– DERIVATIVES **absurdly** adverb.
– ORIGIN mid 16th cent.: from Latin *absurdus* 'out of tune', hence 'irrational'; related to *surdus* 'deaf, dull'.

absurdism ▶ **noun** [mass noun] the belief that human beings exist in a purposeless, chaotic universe.
– DERIVATIVES **absurdist** adjective & noun.

absurdity ▶ **noun** (pl. **-ies**) [mass noun] the quality or state of being ridiculous or wildly unreasonable: *Duncan laughed at the absurdity of the situation |* [count noun] *the absurdities of haute cuisine.*
– ORIGIN late Middle English (in the sense 'dissonance'): from Latin *absurditas*, from *absurdus* (see **ABSURD**).

a

ABTA ▶ **abbreviation for** (in the UK) Association of British Travel Agents.

abubble ▶ **adjective** [predic.] full of excitement and enthusiasm: *he was* ***abubble with*** *the news.*
– ORIGIN 1930s: from **A-**[2] 'in the process of' + **BUBBLE**.

Abu Dhabi /ˌabuː ˈdɑːbi/ the largest of the seven member states of the United Arab Emirates, lying between Oman and the Gulf coast; pop. 928,360 (1995). The former sheikhdom joined the federation of the United Arab Emirates in 1971.
■ the capital of this state; pop. 242,975 (est. 1980). It is also the federal capital of the United Arab Emirates.

Abuja /əˈbuːdʒə/ a newly built city in central Nigeria, replacing Lagos as the national capital in 1991; pop. 378,670 (1991).

Abukir Bay, Battle of see **ABOUKIR BAY, BATTLE OF**.

abulia /əˈbuːlɪə/ (also **aboulia**) ▶ **noun** [mass noun] Psychiatry an absence of will power or an inability to act decisively, being a symptom of schizophrenia or other mental illness.
– DERIVATIVES **abulic** adjective.
– ORIGIN mid 19th cent.: coined from **A-**[1] 'without' + Greek *boulē* 'the will'.

Abu Musa /ˌabuː ˈmuːsə/ a small island in the Persian Gulf. Formerly held by the emirate of Sharjah, it has been occupied by Iran since 1971.

Abuna /əˈbuːnə/ ▶ **noun** a title given to the Patriarch of the Ethiopian Orthodox Church.
– ORIGIN Amharic, from Arabic *'abūnā* 'our father'.

abundance /əˈbʌnd(ə)ns/ ▶ **noun** a very large quantity of something: *the tropical island boasts* ***an abundance of*** *wildlife.*
■ [mass noun] the state or condition of having a copious quantity of something; plentifulness: *vines and figs grew* ***in abundance*** | *she was blessed with talent and charm* ***in abundance.*** ■ [mass noun] plentifulness of the good things of life; prosperity: *the growth of industry promised wealth and abundance.* ■ the quantity or amount of something, e.g. a chemical element or an animal or plant species, present in a particular area, volume, or sample: *estimates of the abundance of harp seals* | *the* ***relative abundances*** *of carbon and nitrogen.* ■ (in solo whist) a bid by which a player undertakes to make nine or more tricks.
– ORIGIN Middle English: from Latin *abundantia*, from *abundant-* 'overflowing', from the verb *abundare* (see **ABOUND**).

abundant ▶ **adjective** existing or available in large quantities; plentiful: *there was abundant evidence to support the theory.*
■ [predic.] (**abundant in**) having plenty of: *the riverbanks were abundant in beautiful wild plants.*
– ORIGIN late Middle English: from Latin *abundant-* 'abounding', from the verb *abundare* (see **ABOUND**).

abundantly ▶ **adverb** in large quantities; plentifully: *the plant grows abundantly in the wild.*
■ [as submodifier] extremely: *my boss* ***made it abundantly clear*** *that if I didn't like it, I should look for another job.*

abura /əˈbjʊərə/ ▶ **noun** a West African tree which yields soft pale timber, and leaves that are used in herbal medicine.
● *Mitragyna stipulosa*, family Rubiaceae.
– ORIGIN early 20th cent.: from Yoruba.

abuse ▶ **verb** /əˈbjuːz/ [with obj.] **1** use (something) to bad effect or for a bad purpose; misuse: *the judge abused his power by imposing the fines.*
■ make excessive and habitual use of (alcohol or drugs, especially illegal ones).
2 treat (a person or an animal) with cruelty or violence, especially regularly or repeatedly: *riders who abuse their horses should be prosecuted.*
■ assault (someone, especially a woman or child) sexually: *he was a depraved man who had abused his two young daughters* | [as adj. **abused**] *abused children.* ■ use or treat in such a way as to cause damage or harm: *he had been abusing his body for years.*
3 speak in an insulting and offensive way to or about (someone): *the referee was abused by players from both teams.*
▶ **noun** /əˈbjuːs/ [mass noun] **1** the improper use of something: *alcohol abuse* | [count noun] ***an abuse of*** *public funds.*
■ unjust or corrupt practice: *protection against fraud and abuse* | [count noun] *human rights abuses.*
2 cruel and violent treatment of a person or animal: *a black eye and other signs of physical abuse.*
■ violent treatment involving sexual assault, especially on a regular basis: *young people who have suffered sexual abuse.*
3 insulting and offensive language: *waving his fists and* ***hurling abuse at*** *the driver.*
– ORIGIN late Middle English: via Old French from Latin *abus-* 'misused', from the verb *abuti*, from *ab-* 'away' (i.e. 'wrongly') + *uti* 'to use'.

abuser ▶ **noun** [usu. with modifier] someone who regularly or habitually abuses someone or something, in particular:
■ someone who makes excessive use of alcohol or illegal drugs: *intravenous drug abusers.* ■ someone who sexually assaults another person, especially a woman or child: *an alleged child abuser.*

Abu Simbel /ˌabuː ˈsɪmb(ə)l/ the site of two huge rock-cut temples in southern Egypt, built during the reign of Ramses II in the 13th century BC and commemorating him and his first wife Nefertari. Following the building of the High Dam at Aswan, the monument was rebuilt higher up the hillside.

abusive ▶ **adjective** **1** extremely offensive and insulting: *the goalkeeper was sent off for using abusive language* | *he became quite abusive and swore at her.*
2 engaging in or characterized by habitual violence and cruelty: *abusive parents* | *an abusive relationship.*
3 involving injustice or illegality: *the abusive and predatory practices of businesses.*
– DERIVATIVES **abusively** adverb, **abusiveness** noun.

abustle ▶ **adjective** [predic.] bustling; busy: *the pier was* ***abustle with*** *voyagers and well-wishers.*
– ORIGIN 1930s: from **A-**[2] 'in the process of' + **BUSTLE**.

abut /əˈbʌt/ ▶ **verb** (**abutted**, **abutting**) [with obj.] (of an area of land or a building) be next to or have a common boundary with: *gardens abutting Great Prescott Street* | [no obj.] *a park* ***abutting on*** *an area of waste land.*
■ touch or lean upon: *masonry may crumble where a roof abuts it.*
– ORIGIN late Middle English: the sense 'have a common boundary' from Anglo-Latin *abuttare*, from *a-* (from Latin *ad* 'to, at') + Old French *but* 'end'; the sense 'lean upon' (late 16th cent.) from Old French *abouter*, from *a-* (from Latin *ad* 'to, at') + *bouter* 'strike, butt', of Germanic origin.

abutilon /əˈbjuːtɪlɒn/ ▶ **noun** a herbaceous plant or shrub of warm climates, typically bearing showy yellow, red, or mauve flowers and sometimes used for fibre.
● Genus *Abutilon*, family Malvaceae.
– ORIGIN modern Latin, from Arabic *ūbūṭīlūn* 'Indian mallow'.

abutment ▶ **noun** a structure built to support the lateral pressure of an arch or span, e.g. at the ends of a bridge.
■ [mass noun] the process of supporting something with such a structure. ■ a point at which something abuts against something else.

abutter ▶ **noun** chiefly US the owner of an adjoining property.

abuzz ▶ **adjective** [predic.] filled with a continuous humming sound: *the room was* ***abuzz with*** *mosquitoes* | figurative *the city was* ***abuzz with*** *rumours.*

ABV ▶ **abbreviation for** alcohol by volume.

abysm /əˈbɪz(ə)m/ ▶ **noun** poetic/literary an abyss: *the abysm from which nightmares crawl.*
– ORIGIN Middle English: from Old French *abisme*, medieval Latin *abysmus*, alteration of late Latin *abyssus* 'bottomless pit', the ending being assimilated to the Greek ending *-ismos*.

abysmal ▶ **adjective** **1** informal extremely bad; appalling: *the quality of her work is abysmal.*
2 poetic/literary very deep.
– DERIVATIVES **abysmally** adverb [as submodifier] *a boy who is abysmally lazy.*
– ORIGIN mid 17th cent. (used literally as in sense 2): from **ABYSM**. Sense 1 dates from the early 19th cent.

abyss /əˈbɪs/ ▶ **noun** a deep or seemingly bottomless chasm: *a rope led down into the dark abyss.*
■ figurative a wide or profound difference between people; a gulf: *the* ***abyss between*** *the two nations.* ■ figurative the regions of hell conceived of as a bottomless pit: *Satan's dark abyss.* ■ (**the abyss**) figurative a catastrophic situation seen as likely to occur: *teetering on the* ***edge of the abyss*** *of a total political wipeout.*
– ORIGIN late Middle English (in the sense 'infernal pit'): via late Latin from Greek *abussos* 'bottomless', from *a-* 'without' + *bussos* 'depth'.

abyssal ▶ **adjective** chiefly technical relating to or denoting the depths or bed of the ocean, especially between about 3000 and 6000 metres down.
■ Geology another term for **PLUTONIC** (in sense 1).
– ORIGIN mid 17th cent.: from late Latin *abyssalis* 'belonging to an abyss' (see **ABYSS**).

Abyssinia /ˌabɪˈsɪnɪə/ former name for **ETHIOPIA**.

Abyssinian ▶ **adjective** historical of or relating to Abyssinia or its people.
▶ **noun** **1** historical a native of Abyssinia.
2 (also **Abyssinian cat**) a cat of a breed having long ears and short brown hair flecked with grey.

AC ▶ **abbreviation for** ■ (**ac.**) N. Amer. acre: *a 22-ac. site.* ■ (also **ac**) air conditioning: *a sedan with power steering and AC.* ■ Aircraftman. ■ (also **ac**) alternating current. ■ appellation contrôlée: *AC Sauvignon and Chardonnay.* ■ athletic club. ■ before Christ. [ORIGIN: from Latin *ante Christum*.] ■ Companion of the Order of Australia.

Ac ▶ **symbol for** the chemical element actinium.

a/c ▶ **abbreviation for** ■ account. [ORIGIN: from the obsolete phrase *account current*, denoting a continuous account detailing sums paid and received.] ■ (also **A/C**) air conditioning.

ac- ▶ **prefix** variant spelling of **AD-** assimilated before *c*, *k*, and *q* (as in *accept*, *acquit*, and *acquiesce*).

-ac ▶ **suffix** forming adjectives which are often also (or only) used as nouns, such as *maniac*. Compare with **-ACAL**.
– ORIGIN via Latin *-acus* or French *-aque* from Greek *-akos*.

acacia /əˈkeɪʃə, -sɪə/ (also **acacia tree**) ▶ **noun** a tree or shrub of warm climates which bears spikes or clusters of yellow or white flowers and is typically thorny. Also called **WATTLE**[1], especially in Australia.
● Genus *Acacia*, family Leguminosae: numerous species, including *A. senegal*, which yields gum arabic.
– ORIGIN late Middle English: via Latin from Greek *akakia*.

academe /ˈakədiːm/ ▶ **noun** [mass noun] the academic environment or community; academia: *bridging the gap between industry and academe* | ***the groves of academe.***
– ORIGIN late 16th cent. (in the sense 'academy'): from Latin *academia*, reinforced by Greek *Akadēmos* (see **ACADEMY**).

academia /ˌakəˈdiːmɪə/ ▶ **noun** [mass noun] the environment or community concerned with the pursuit of research, education, and scholarship: *he spent his working life in academia.*
– ORIGIN 1950s: from Latin (see **ACADEMY**).

academic ▶ **adjective** **1** of or relating to education and scholarship: *academic achievement* | *he had no academic qualifications.*
■ of or relating to an educational or scholarly institution or environment: *students resplendent in academic dress.* ■ (of an institution or a course of study) placing a greater emphasis on reading and study than on technical or practical work: *a very academic school aiming to get pupils into Oxford or Cambridge.* ■ (of a person) interested in or excelling at scholarly pursuits and activities: *Ben is not an academic child but he tries hard.* ■ (of an art form) conventional, especially in an idealized or excessively formal way: *academic painting.*
2 not of practical relevance; of only theoretical interest: *the debate has been largely academic.*
▶ **noun** a teacher or scholar in a university or institute of higher education.
– DERIVATIVES **academically** adverb.
– ORIGIN mid 16th cent.: from French *académique* or medieval Latin *academicus*, from *academia* (see **ACADEMY**).

academical ▶ **adjective** of or relating to a college or university: *the academical year.*
▶ **noun** (**academicals**) Brit. dated formal university attire.

academician /əˌkadəˈmɪʃ(ə)n/ ▶ **noun** **1** a member of an academy, especially the Royal Academy of Arts, the Académie française, or the Russian Academy of Sciences.
2 N. Amer. an academic; an intellectual.
– ORIGIN mid 18th cent.: from French *académicien*, from medieval Latin *academicus* (see **ACADEMIC**).

academicism /ˌakəˈdɛmɪsɪz(ə)m/ (also **academism**) ▶ **noun** [mass noun] adherence to formal or conventional rules and traditions in art or literature.

academic year ▶ **noun** the period of the year

during which students attend school or university, usually reckoned from the beginning of the autumn term to the end of the summer term.

Académie française /ə,kadəmi: frɒ̃'seɪz, French akademi frɑ̃sɛz/ a French literary academy responsible for the standard form of the French language and for compiling and revising a definitive dictionary of the French language.

academy ▶ noun (pl. **-ies**) **1** a place of study or training in a special field: *a police academy.*
■ dated a place of study. ■ US & Scottish a secondary school, in the US typically a private one. ■ (**the Academy**) the teaching school founded by Plato.
2 a society or institution of distinguished scholars and artists or scientists that aims to promote and maintain standards in its particular field: *the Royal Academy of Arts.*
– ORIGIN late Middle English (denoting the garden where Plato taught): from French *académie* or Latin *academia*, from Greek *akadēmeia*, from *Akadēmos*, the hero after whom Plato's garden was named.

Academy award ▶ noun any of a series of awards of the Academy of Motion Picture Arts and Sciences (Hollywood, US) given annually since 1928 for achievement in the film industry in various categories; an Oscar.

Acadia /ə'keɪdɪə/ a former French colony established in 1604 in the territory now forming Nova Scotia in Canada. It was contested by France and Britain until it was eventually ceded to Britain in 1763; French-speaking Acadians were deported to other parts of North America, especially Louisiana.
– ORIGIN from *Acadie*, the French name for Nova Scotia.

Acadian chiefly historical ▶ **adjective** of or relating to Acadia or its people.
▶ noun a native or inhabitant of Acadia.
■ chiefly Canadian a French-speaking descendant of the early French settlers in Acadia. ■ US a descendant of the Acadians deported to Louisiana in the 18th century; a Cajun.

acajou /'akəʒu:/ ▶ noun another term for **CASHEW**.
– ORIGIN late 16th cent.: from French, via Portuguese from Tupi *acajú*.

-acal ▶ suffix forming adjectives such as *maniacal*, often making a distinction from nouns ending in *-ac* (as in *maniacal* compared with *maniac*).

acalculia /,eɪkal'kju:lɪə/ ▶ noun [mass noun] Medicine loss of the ability to perform simple calculations, typically resulting from disease or injury of the parietal lobe of the brain.
– ORIGIN early 20th cent.: from **A-**[1] 'not' + Latin *calculare* 'calculate' + **-IA**[1].

acanthamoeba /ə,kanθə'mi:bə/ ▶ noun (pl. **acanthamoebae** /-'mi:bi:/) an amoeba of a genus which includes a number that can cause opportunistic infections in humans. They have pseudopodia with thin tapering projections.
● Genus *Acanthamoeba*, phylum Rhizopoda.

acantho- /ə'kanθəʊ/ (also **acanth-** before a vowel) ▶ **combining form** having thorn-like characteristics.
– ORIGIN from Greek *akantha* 'thorn'.

Acanthocephala /ə,kanθə(ʊ)'sɛfələ, -'kɛf-/ Zoology a small phylum of parasitic invertebrates that comprises the thorny-headed worms.
– DERIVATIVES **acanthocephalan** adjective & noun, **acanthocephalid** adjective & noun.
– ORIGIN modern Latin (plural), from **ACANTHO-** 'thornlike' + Greek *kephalē* 'head'.

acanthodian /ə,kan'θəʊdɪən/ ▶ noun a small spiny-finned fossil fish of a group found chiefly in the Devonian period.
● Class (or subclass) Acanthodii.
– ORIGIN mid 19th cent.: from modern Latin *Acanthodii* (from **ACANTHO-**) + **-AN**.

acanthus /ə'kanθəs/ ▶ noun a herbaceous plant or shrub with bold flower spikes and spiny decorative leaves, found in warm regions of the Old World.
● Genus *Acanthus*, family Acanthaceae: many species, including bear's breeches.
■ Architecture a conventionalized representation of an acanthus leaf, used especially as a decoration for Corinthian column capitals.
– ORIGIN via Latin from Greek *akanthos*, from *akantha* 'thorn', from *akē* 'sharp point'; the architectural term dates from the mid 18th cent.

a cappella /,a kə'pɛlə, ,ɑ:/ ▶ **adjective** & **adverb** (with reference to choral music) sung without instrumental accompaniment: [as adj.] *an a cappella Mass* | [as adv.] *the consorts usually perform a cappella.*
– ORIGIN Italian, literally 'in chapel style'.

Acapulco /akə'pʊlkəʊ/ a port and resort in southern Mexico, on the Pacific coast; pop. 592,290 (1990). Full name **ACAPULCO DE JUÁREZ** /deɪ 'hwɑ:rɛz, Spanish ðe 'xwares, -reθ/.

acara /ə'kɑ:rə/ ▶ noun a small deep-bodied freshwater fish native to Central and South America. Acaras have elongated dorsal and anal fins which in some kinds form long streamers.
● Genera *Aequidens* and *Cichlisoma*, family Cichlidae: several species, including the **blue acara** (*A. latifrons*).
– ORIGIN from Portuguese *acaré*, from Tupi.

Acari /ə'kɑ:ri/ (also **Acarina** /,akə'rʌɪnə/) Zoology a large order (or subclass) of small arachnids which comprises the mites and ticks. They are distinguished by an apparent lack of body divisions.
– DERIVATIVES **acarid** /'akərɪd/ noun & adjective, **acarine** /'akərʌɪn/ noun & adjective.
– ORIGIN modern Latin (plural), from *acarus*, from Greek *akari* 'mite'.

acaricide /'akərɪsʌɪd/ ▶ noun a substance poisonous to mites or ticks.
– ORIGIN late 19th cent.: from Greek *akari* 'mite, tick' + **-CIDE**.

acaroid /'akərɔɪd/ (also **acaroid resin**, **accaroid**) ▶ noun [mass noun] a resin obtained in Australia from some kinds of grass tree, used in making varnish.
– ORIGIN mid 19th cent.: of unknown origin.

acarology /,akə'rɒlədʒi/ ▶ noun [mass noun] the study of mites and ticks.
– DERIVATIVES **acarologist** noun.
– ORIGIN early 20th cent.: from Greek *akari* 'mite, tick' + **-LOGY**.

ACAS /'eɪkas/ ▶ **abbreviation for** (in the UK) Advisory, Conciliation, and Arbitration Service.

acatalectic /ə,katə'lɛktɪk/ Prosody ▶ **adjective** (of a line of verse) having the full number of syllables.
▶ noun a line of verse of such a type.

acausal ▶ **adjective** not governed or operating by the laws of cause and effect.

acca /'akə/ ▶ noun & **adjective** Austral. informal short for **ACADEMIC**.

accaroid ▶ noun variant spelling of **ACAROID**.

accede /ək'si:d/ ▶ verb [no obj.] formal **1** assent or agree to a demand, request, or treaty: *the authorities did not accede to the strikers' demands.*
2 assume an office or position: *Elizabeth I acceded to the throne in 1558.*
■ become a member of a community or organization: *Albania acceded to the IMF in 1990.*
– ORIGIN late Middle English (in the general sense 'come forward, approach'): from Latin *accedere*, from *ad-* 'to' + *cedere* 'give way, yield'.

accelerando /ək,sɛlə'randəʊ, ə,tʃɛl-/ Music ▶ **adverb** & **adjective** (especially as a direction) with a gradual increase of speed.
▶ noun (pl. **accelerandos** or **accelerandi** /-di/) a passage performed with such an acceleration.
– ORIGIN Italian.

accelerant ▶ noun a substance used to aid the spread of fire.
▶ **adjective** technical accelerating or causing acceleration: *accelerant factors for carcinoma.*

accelerate /ək'sɛləreɪt/ ▶ verb [no obj.] (of a vehicle or other physical object) begin to move more quickly: *the car accelerated towards her.*
■ increase in amount or extent: *inflation started to accelerate* | [as adj. **accelerating**] *accelerating industrial activity.* ■ Physics undergo a change in velocity. ■ [with obj.] cause to go faster: *the key question is whether stress accelerates ageing.*
– DERIVATIVES **accelerative** adjective.
– ORIGIN early 16th cent. (in the sense 'hasten the occurrence of'): from Latin *accelerat-* 'hastened', from the verb *accelerare*, from *ad-* 'towards' + *celer* 'swift'.

accelerated learning ▶ noun [mass noun] **1** an intensive method of study which enables material to be learnt in a relatively short time.
2 a programme of learning which allows academically able children to progress through school more rapidly than others.

acceleration ▶ noun [mass noun] increase in the rate or speed of something: *the acceleration of the industrialization process* | [in sing.] *an acceleration in the divorce rate.*
■ Physics the rate of change of velocity per unit of time. ■ a vehicle's capacity to gain speed within a short time: *the three-litre model has spectacular acceleration.*

accelerator ▶ noun something which brings about acceleration, in particular:
■ a device, typically a foot pedal, which controls the speed of a vehicle's engine. ■ Physics an apparatus for accelerating charged particles to high velocities. ■ a substance that speeds up a chemical process, typically the vulcanization of rubber or the curing of a plastic. ■ Computing short for **ACCELERATOR BOARD**.

accelerator board (also **accelerator card**) ▶ noun an accessory circuit board which can be plugged into a small computer to increase the speed of its processor or input/output operations.

accelerometer /ək,sɛlə'rɒmɪtə/ ▶ noun an instrument for measuring the acceleration of a moving or vibrating body.
– ORIGIN early 20th cent.: from **ACCELERATE** + **-METER**.

accent ▶ noun /'aks(ə)nt, -sɛnt/ **1** a distinctive mode of pronunciation of a language, especially one associated with a particular country, area, or social class: *a strong American accent.*
■ the mode of pronunciation used by native speakers of a language: *she never mastered the French accent.*
2 a distinct emphasis given to a syllable or word in speech by stress or pitch.
■ a mark on a letter or word to indicate pitch, stress, or vowel quality. ■ Music an emphasis on a particular note or chord.
3 [in sing.] a special or particular emphasis: *the accent is on participation.*
■ a feature which gives a distinctive visual emphasis to something: *blue woodwork and accents of red.*
▶ verb /ak'sɛnt/ [with obj.] emphasize (a particular feature): *fabrics which accent the background colours in the room.*
■ Music play (a note or beat) with emphasis.
– DERIVATIVES **accentual** adjective.
– ORIGIN late Middle English (in the sense 'intonation'): from Latin *accentus* 'tone, signal, or intensity' (from *ad-* 'to' + *cantus* 'song'), translating Greek *prosōidia* 'a song sung to music, intonation'.

accented ▶ **adjective** **1** spoken with or characterized by a particular accent: *he spoke in slightly accented English.*
2 (of a word or syllable) stressed.

accentor /ək'sɛntə/ ▶ noun a small Eurasian songbird with generally drab-coloured plumage.
● Family Prunellidae and genus *Prunella*: several species, including the dunnock and the **alpine accentor** (*P. collaris*).
– ORIGIN early 19th cent.: from late Latin, from *ad-* 'to' + *cantor* 'singer'.

accentuate /ək'sɛntʃʊeɪt, -tjʊ-/ ▶ verb [with obj.] make more noticeable or prominent: *his jacket unfortunately accentuated his paunch.*
– ORIGIN mid 18th cent.: from medieval Latin *accentuat-* 'accented', from the verb *accentuare*, from *accentus* 'tone' (see **ACCENT**).

accentuation ▶ noun [mass noun] the action of emphasizing something: *the accentuation of the Treasury's currency policy.*
■ the prominence of a thing relative to a norm: *a condition with accentuation of female characteristics.* ■ the pattern of relative prominence of syllables in a phrase or utterance.

accept ▶ verb [with obj.] **1** consent to receive (a thing offered): *he accepted a pen as a present.*
■ agree to undertake (an offered position or responsibility). ■ give an affirmative answer to (an offer or proposal); say yes to: *he would accept their offer and see what happened* | [no obj.] *Tim offered Brian a lift home and he accepted.* ■ dated say yes to a proposal of marriage from (a man): *Reginald was a good match and she ought to accept him.* ■ receive as adequate, valid, or suitable: *the college accepted her as a student* | *credit cards are widely accepted.* ■ regard favourably or with approval; welcome: *the Irish literati never accepted him as one of them.* ■ agree to meet (a draft or bill of exchange) by signing it. ■ (of a thing) be designed to allow (something) to be inserted or applied: *vending machines that accepted 100-yen coins for cans of beer.*
2 believe or come to recognize (a proposition) as valid or correct: *this tentative explanation came to be accepted by the men* | [with clause] *it is accepted that ageing is a continuous process* | [as adj. **accepted**] *he wasn't handsome in the accepted sense.*
■ be prepared to subscribe to (a belief or philosophy): *accept the tenets of the Episcopalian faith.* ■ take upon

a

oneself (a responsibility or liability); acknowledge: *Jenkins is willing to accept his responsibility* | [with clause] *he accepts that he made a mistake.* ■ tolerate or submit to (something unpleasant or undesired): *they accepted the need to cut overheads.*
– DERIVATIVES **accepter** noun.
– ORIGIN late Middle English: from Latin *acceptare*, frequentative of *accipere* 'take something to oneself', from *ad-* 'to' + *capere* 'take'.

acceptable ▶ **adjective 1** able to be agreed on; suitable: *the electoral arrangements must be **acceptable to** the people.*
■ adequate; satisfactory: *an acceptable substitute for champagne.* ■ pleasing; welcome: *some coffee would be most acceptable.* ■ Linguistics (of a sentence, phrase, or other linguistic unit) judged by a native speaker to conform to the rules of grammar of a particular language.
2 able to be tolerated or allowed: *pollution in the city had reached four times the acceptable level.*
– PHRASES **the acceptable face of** the tolerable or attractive manifestation or aspect of (something typically considered suspect or immoral).
– DERIVATIVES **acceptability** noun, **acceptableness** noun, **acceptably** adverb.
– ORIGIN late Middle English: from Old French, from late Latin *acceptabilis*, from *acceptare* (see **ACCEPT**).

acceptance ▶ **noun** [mass noun] **1** the action of consenting to receive or undertake something offered: *charges involving the acceptance of bribes* | [as modifier] *an acceptance speech.*
■ agreement to meet a draft or bill of exchange, effected by signing it. ■ [count noun] a draft or bill so accepted.
2 the action or process of being received as adequate or suitable, typically to be admitted into a group: *you must wait for acceptance into the village.*
3 agreement with or belief in an idea, opinion, or explanation: *acceptance of the teaching of the Church.*
■ willingness to tolerate a difficult or unpleasant situation: *a mood of resigned acceptance.*
– ORIGIN mid 16th cent.: from Old French, from *accepter* (see **ACCEPT**).

acceptant ▶ **adjective** [predic.] (**acceptant of**) rare willingly accepting (something).
– ORIGIN late 16th cent.: from French, 'accepting', present participle of *accepter.*

acceptation /ˌaksɛpˈteɪʃ(ə)n/ ▶ **noun** a particular sense or the generally recognized meaning (**common acceptation**) of a word or phrase.
– ORIGIN late Middle English (originally in the sense 'favourable reception, approval'): from late Latin *acceptatio(n-)*, from the verb *acceptare* (see **ACCEPT**). The current sense dates from the early 17th cent.

acceptor ▶ **noun** a person or thing that accepts something, in particular:
■ a person or bank that accepts a draft or bill of exchange. ■ Chemistry an atom or molecule which is able to bind to or accept an electron or other species. ■ Physics such an atom forming a positive hole in a semiconductor.

access ▶ **noun 1** [mass noun] the means or opportunity to approach or enter a place: *the staircase gives **access to** the top floor* | *wheelchair access* | [count noun] *the building has a side access.*
■ the right or opportunity to use or benefit from something: *do you **have access to** a computer?* | *awards to help people **gain access to** training.* ■ the right or opportunity to approach or see someone: *we were denied access to our grandson.* ■ the action or process of obtaining or retrieving information stored in a computer's memory: *this prevents unauthorized access or inadvertent deletion of the file.* ■ [as modifier] denoting broadcasting produced by minority and specialist interest groups, rather than by professionals: *access television.*
2 [in sing.] an attack or outburst of an emotion: *I was suddenly overcome with **an access of** rage.*
▶ **verb** [with obj.] (usu. **be accessed**) **1** Computing obtain, examine, or retrieve (data or a file).
2 approach or enter (a place): *single rooms have private facilities accessed via the balcony.*
– ORIGIN Middle English (in the sense 'sudden attack of illness'): from Latin *accessus*, from the verb *accedere* 'to approach' (see **ACCEDE**). Sense 1 is first recorded in the early 17th cent.

accessary ▶ **noun** variant spelling of **ACCESSORY**.

access charge (also **access fee**) ▶ **noun** a charge made for the use of computer or local telephone-network facilities.

access course ▶ **noun** an educational course enabling those without traditional qualifications to become eligible for higher education.

accessible ▶ **adjective 1** (of a place) able to be reached or entered: *the building has been made **accessible to** disabled people.*
■ able to be easily obtained or used: *making learning opportunities more **accessible to** adults.* ■ easily understood or appreciated: *his Latin grammar is lucid and accessible.*
2 (of a person, especially one in a position of authority or importance) friendly and easy to talk to; approachable: *he is more accessible than most tycoons.*
– DERIVATIVES **accessibility** noun, **accessibly** adverb.
– ORIGIN late Middle English: from late Latin *accessibilis*, from Latin *access-* 'approached', from the verb *accedere* (see **ACCEDE**).

accession ▶ **noun 1** [mass noun] the attainment or acquisition of a position of rank or power, typically that of monarch or president: *the Queen's **accession to** the throne.*
■ the action or process of formally joining or being accepted by an association, institution, or group: *the **accession** of Spain and Portugal **to** the EC.* ■ the formal acceptance of a treaty or agreement: ***accession to** the Treaty of Rome was effected in 1971.*
2 a new item added to an existing collection of books, paintings, or artefacts.
■ an amount added to an existing quantity of something: *substantial accessions of gold.*
▶ **verb** [with obj.] (usu. **be accessioned**) record the addition of (a new item) to a library, museum, or other collection.
– ORIGIN late 16th cent. (in the general sense 'something added'): from Latin *accessio(n-)*, from the verb *accedere* 'approach, come to' (see **ACCEDE**).

accessorize (also **-ise**) ▶ **verb** [with obj.] provide or complement (a garment) with or as a fashion accessory: *sequined catsuits were accessorized with cork-heeled shoes.*

accessory (also **accessary**) ▶ **noun** (pl. **-ies**) **1** a thing which can be added to something else in order to make it more useful, versatile, or attractive: *a range of bathroom accessories.*
■ a small article or item of clothing carried or worn to complement a garment or outfit: *she wore the suit with perfectly matching accessories—hat, bag, shoes.*
2 Law someone who give assistance to the perpetrator of a crime without taking part in it: *she was charged as an **accessory to** murder.*
▶ **adjective** chiefly technical contributing to or aiding an activity or process in a minor way; subsidiary or supplementary: *functionally the maxillae are a pair of accessory jaws.*
– PHRASES **accessory before** (or **after**) **the fact** Law, dated a person who incites or assists someone to commit an arrestable offence (or knowingly aids someone who has committed such an offence).
– DERIVATIVES **accessorial** adjective (chiefly Law).
– ORIGIN late Middle English: from medieval Latin *accessorius* 'additional thing', from Latin *access-* 'increased', from the verb *accedere* (see **ACCEDE**).

accessory cell ▶ **noun** Physiology any of various cells of the immune system that interact with T lymphocytes in the initiation of the immune response.

accessory mineral ▶ **noun** Geology a constituent mineral present in small quantity and not taken into account in identifying a rock.

accessory nerve ▶ **noun** Anatomy each of the eleventh pair of cranial nerves, supplying certain muscles in the neck and shoulder.

access time ▶ **noun** Computing the time taken to retrieve data from storage.

acciaccatura /əˌtʃakəˈtjʊərə/ ▶ **noun** (pl. **acciaccaturas** or **acciaccature**) Music a grace note performed as quickly as possible before an essential note of a melody.
– ORIGIN Italian, from *acciaccare* 'to crush'.

accidence /ˈaksɪd(ə)ns/ ▶ **noun** [mass noun] dated the part of grammar that deals with the inflections of words.
– ORIGIN early 16th cent.: from late Latin *accidentia* (translation of Greek *parepomena* 'things happening alongside'), neuter plural of the present participle of *accidere* 'happen' (see **ACCIDENT**).

accident ▶ **noun 1** an unfortunate incident that happens unexpectedly and unintentionally, typically resulting in damage or injury: *he had an accident at the factory* | [mass noun] *if you are unable to work owing to accident or sickness.*
■ a crash involving road or other vehicles, typically one that causes serious damage or injury: *four people were killed in a road accident.* ■ informal used euphemistically to refer to an incidence of incontinence, typically by a child or an animal.
2 an event that happens by chance or that is without apparent or deliberate cause: *the pregnancy was an accident* | ***it is no accident that** Manchester has produced more than its fair share of professional comics.*
■ [mass noun] the working of fortune; chance: *I opened it **by accident*** | *members belong to the House of Lords through hereditary right or **accident of birth**.*
3 Philosophy (in Aristotelian thought) a property of a thing which is not essential to its nature.
– PHRASES **accident and emergency** Brit. denoting a hospital department concerned with the provision of immediate treatment to people who are seriously injured in an accident or who are suddenly taken seriously ill. **an accident waiting to happen** informal a potentially disastrous situation, typically caused by negligent or faulty procedures. ■ a person certain to cause trouble. **accidents will happen in the best regulated families** proverb however careful you try to be, it is inevitable that some unfortunate or unforeseen events will occur: *problems like these should not occur, but accidents will happen.* **without accident** safely: *he was able to stop the train without accident.*
– ORIGIN late Middle English (in the general sense 'an event'): via Old French from Latin *accident-* 'happening', from the verb *accidere*, from *ad-* 'towards, to' + *cadere* 'to fall'.

accidental ▶ **adjective 1** happening by chance, unintentionally, or unexpectedly: *a verdict of accidental death* | *the damage might have been accidental.*
2 incidental; subsidiary: *the location is accidental and contributes nothing to the poem.*
3 Philosophy (in Aristotelian thought) relating to or denoting properties which are not essential to a thing's nature.
▶ **noun 1** Music a sign indicating a momentary departure from the key signature by raising or lowering a note.
2 Ornithology another term for **VAGRANT**.
– DERIVATIVES **accidentally** adverb.
– ORIGIN late Middle English (in senses 2 and 3 of the adjective): from late Latin *accidentalis*, from Latin *accident-* 'happening' (see **ACCIDENT**).

accident-prone ▶ **adjective** tending to be involved in a greater than average number of accidents.

accidie /ˈaksɪdi/ ▶ **noun** [mass noun] spiritual or mental sloth; apathy.
– ORIGIN Middle English: via Old French from medieval Latin *accidia*, alteration of **ACEDIA**. Obsolete after the 16th cent., the term was revived in the late 19th cent.

accipiter /akˈsɪpɪtə/ ▶ **noun** Ornithology a hawk of a group distinguished by short, broad wings and relatively long legs, adapted for fast flight in wooded country.
● *Accipiter* and related genera, family Accipitridae: numerous species, including the goshawk.
– ORIGIN from Latin, 'hawk, bird of prey'.

accipitrine /akˈsɪpɪtrʌɪn/ ▶ **adjective** Ornithology of or relating to birds of a family that includes most diurnal birds of prey other than falcons, New World vultures, and the osprey.
● Family Accipitridae; treated as a subfamily (Accipitrinae) in this sense when the osprey is included in this family.
– ORIGIN mid 19th cent.: from French, from Latin *accipiter* 'bird of prey'.

acclaim ▶ **verb** [with obj.] (usu. **be acclaimed**) praise enthusiastically and publicly: *the conference was **acclaimed as** a considerable success* | [with obj. and complement] *he was acclaimed a great painter.*
▶ **noun** [mass noun] enthusiastic and public praise: *she has won acclaim for her commitment to democracy.*
– ORIGIN early 17th cent. (in the sense 'express approval'): from Latin *acclamare*, from *ad-* 'to' + *clamare* 'to shout'. The change in the ending was due to association with **CLAIM**. Current senses date from the 17th cent.

acclamation ▶ **noun** [mass noun] loud and enthusiastic approval, typically to welcome or honour someone or something: *the tackle brought the supporters to their feet in acclamation.*
– PHRASES **by acclamation 1** (of election,

agreement, etc.) by overwhelming vocal approval and without ballot. **2** Canadian (of election) by virtue of being the sole candidate.
– ORIGIN mid 16th cent.: from Latin *acclamatio(n-)*, from *acclamare* 'shout at', later 'shout in approval' (see **ACCLAIM**).

acclimate /ˈaklɪmeɪt, əˈklʌɪmət/ ▶ **verb** [no obj.] chiefly N. Amer. acclimatize: *we had to give the soldiers time to acclimate.*
■ Biology respond physiologically or behaviourally to a change in a single environmental factor: *trees may* ***acclimate to*** *high CO_2 levels by reducing the number of stomata.* Compare with **ACCLIMATIZE**. ■ [with obj.] Botany & Horticulture harden off (a plant).
– DERIVATIVES **acclimation** noun.
– ORIGIN late 18th cent.: from French *acclimater*, from *a-* (from Latin *ad* 'to, at') + *climat* 'climate'.

acclimatize (also **-ise**) ▶ **verb** [no obj.] become accustomed to a new climate or to new conditions: *it's unknown whether people will* ***acclimatize to*** *increasingly warm weather | they like to* ***acclimatize themselves*** *properly before doing anything.*
■ Biology respond physiologically or behaviourally to changes in a complex of environmental factors. Compare with **ACCLIMATE**. ■ [with obj.] Botany & Horticulture harden off (a plant).
– DERIVATIVES **acclimatization** noun.
– ORIGIN mid 19th cent.: from French *acclimater* 'acclimatize' + **-IZE**.

acclivity /əˈklɪvɪti/ ▶ **noun** (pl. **-ies**) an upward slope.
– DERIVATIVES **acclivitous** adjective.
– ORIGIN early 17th cent.: from Latin *acclivitas*, from *acclivis*, from *ad-* 'towards' + *clivus* 'a slope'.

accolade /ˈakəleɪd, ˌakəˈleɪd/ ▶ **noun 1** an award or privilege granted as a special honour or as an acknowledgement of merit: *the ultimate official accolade of a visit by the Queen.*
■ an expression of praise or admiration.
2 a touch on a person's shoulders with a sword at the bestowing of a knighthood.
– ORIGIN early 17th cent.: from French, from Provençal *acolada*, literally 'embrace around the neck (when bestowing knighthood)', from Latin *ad-* 'at, to' + *collum* 'neck'.

accommodate ▶ **verb** [with obj.] **1** (of physical space, especially a building) provide lodging or sufficient space for: *the cottages accommodate up to six people.*
2 fit in with the wishes or needs of: *any language must accommodate new concepts.*
■ [no obj.] (**accommodate to**) adapt to: *making users accommodate to the realities of today's marketplace.*
– DERIVATIVES **accommodative** adjective.
– ORIGIN mid 16th cent.: from Latin *accommodat-* 'made fitting', from the verb *accommodare*, from *ad-* 'to' + *commodus* 'fitting'.

accommodating ▶ **adjective** fitting in with someone's wishes or demands in a helpful way.
– DERIVATIVES **accommodatingly** adverb.

accommodation ▶ **noun 1** [mass noun] a room, group of rooms, or building in which someone may live or stay: *they were living in temporary accommodation.*
■ (**accommodations**) chiefly N. Amer. lodgings, sometimes also including board: *the company offers a number of guest house accommodations in Oberammergau.* ■ the available space for occupants in a building, vehicle, or vessel: *there was lifeboat accommodation for 1,178 people.* ■ the providing of a room or lodgings: *the building is used exclusively for the accommodation of guests.*
2 a convenient arrangement; a settlement or compromise: *the prime minister was seeking an accommodation with Labour.*
■ [mass noun] the process of adapting or adjusting to someone or something: *accommodation to a separate political entity was not possible.* ■ [mass noun] the automatic adjustment of the focus of the eye by flattening or thickening of the lens.
– ORIGIN early 17th cent.: from Latin *accommodatio(n-)*, from *accommodare* 'fit one thing to another' (see **ACCOMMODATE**).

accommodation address ▶ **noun** Brit. an address for correspondence used by a person who wishes to conceal or does not have a permanent address.

accommodationist ▶ **noun** US a person who seeks compromise with an opposing point of view, typically a political one.

accommodation ladder ▶ **noun** a ladder or flight of steps up the side of a ship allowing access from a small boat or a quayside.

accommodation platform ▶ **noun** an offshore platform serving as accommodation for workers in offshore oil or gas production.

accompaniment ▶ **noun 1** a musical part which supports or partners a solo instrument, voice, or group: *she sang to a guitar accompaniment* | [mass noun] *sonatas for piano with violin accompaniment.*
■ a piece of music played as a complement or background to an activity: *lush string accompaniments to romantic scenes in films.*
2 something that supplements or complements something else, especially food: *these biscuits are a lovely accompaniment to tea.*
– PHRASES **to the accompaniment of** with accompanying or background music or sound from: *we filed out to the accompaniment of the organ.* ■ with another event happening at the same time as.
– ORIGIN early 18th cent.: from French *accompagnement*, from *accompagner* 'accompany'.

accompanist ▶ **noun** a person who provides a musical accompaniment to another musician or to a singer.

accompany ▶ **verb** (**-ies**, **-ied**) [with obj.] **1** go somewhere with (someone) as a companion or escort: *the two sisters were to accompany us to London.*
2 (usu. **be accompanied**) be present or occur at the same time as (something else): *the illness is often accompanied by nausea.*
■ provide (something) as a complement or addition to something else: *home-cooked ham accompanied by brown bread.*
3 play a musical accompaniment for.
– ORIGIN late Middle English: from Old French *accompagner*, from *a-* (from Latin *ad* 'to, at') + *compagne*, from Old French *compaignon* 'companion'. The spelling change was due to association with **COMPANY**.

accomplice /əˈkʌmplɪs, əˈkɒm-/ ▶ **noun** a person who helps another commit a crime.
– ORIGIN mid 16th cent.: alteration (probably by association with **ACCOMPANY**) of Middle English *complice* 'an associate', via Old French from late Latin *complex, complic-* 'allied', from *com-* 'together' + the root of *plicare* 'to fold'.

accomplish ▶ **verb** [with obj.] achieve or complete successfully: *the planes accomplished their mission.*
– ORIGIN late Middle English: from Old French *acompliss-*, lengthened stem of *acomplir*, based on Latin *ad-* 'to' + *complere* 'to complete'.

accomplished ▶ **adjective** highly trained or skilled in a particular activity: *an accomplished pianist.*
■ well educated and having good social skills.

accomplishment ▶ **noun** something that has been achieved successfully: *the reduction of inflation was a remarkable accomplishment.*
■ [mass noun] the successful achievement of a task: *the accomplishment of planned objectives.* ■ an activity that a person can do well, typically as a result of study or practice: *typing was another of her accomplishments.* ■ [mass noun] skill or ability in an activity: *a poet of considerable accomplishment.*

accord ▶ **verb 1** [with obj.] give or grant someone (power, status, or recognition): *the powers* ***accorded to*** *the head of state* | [with two objs] *the national assembly accorded the General more power.*
2 [no obj.] (**accord with**) (of a concept or fact) be harmonious or consistent with.
▶ **noun** an official agreement or treaty.
■ [mass noun] agreement or harmony: *the government and the rebels are* ***in accord*** *on one point.*
– PHRASES **in accord with** according to. **of one's own accord** voluntarily or without outside intervention: *he would not seek treatment of his own accord.* **with one accord** in a united way.
– ORIGIN Old English, from Old French *acorder* 'reconcile, be of one mind', from Latin *ad-* 'to' + *cor, cord-* 'heart'; influenced by **CONCORD**.

accordance ▶ **noun** (in phrase **in accordance with**) in a manner conforming with: *the ballot was held in accordance with trade union rules.*
– ORIGIN Middle English: from Old French *acordance*, from *acorder* 'bring to an agreement' (see **ACCORD**).

accordant ▶ **adjective** archaic agreeing or compatible: *I found the music* ***accordant with*** *the words of the service.*
– ORIGIN Middle English: from Old French *acordant*, from *acorder* 'bring to an agreement' (see **ACCORD**).

according ▶ **adverb 1** (**according to**) as stated by or in: *the outlook for investors is not bright, according to financial experts.*
■ in a manner corresponding or conforming to: *cook the rice according to the instructions.* ■ in proportion or relation to: *salary will be fixed according to experience.*
2 (**according as**) depending on whether.

accordingly ▶ **adverb 1** in a way that is appropriate to the particular circumstances: *we have to discover what his plans are and act accordingly.*
2 [sentence adverb] consequently; therefore: *there was no breach of the rules; accordingly, there will be no disciplinary inquiry.*

accordion /əˈkɔːdɪən/ ▶ **noun** a musical instrument played by stretching and squeezing with the hands to work a central bellows that blows air over metal reeds, the melody and chords being sounded by buttons or keys. Compare with **CONCERTINA**.
■ [as modifier] folding like the bellows of an accordion: *an accordion pleat.*
– DERIVATIVES **accordionist** noun.
– ORIGIN mid 19th cent.: from German *Akkordion*, from Italian *accordare* 'to tune'.

accost ▶ **verb** [with obj.] approach and address (someone) boldly or aggressively: *reporters accosted him in the street | a man tried to accost the girl on the way to school.*
– ORIGIN late 16th cent. (originally in the sense 'lie or go alongside'): from French *accoster*, from Italian *accostare*, from Latin *ad-* 'to' + *costa* 'rib, side'.

accouchement /əˈkuːʃmɒ̃/ ▶ **noun** [mass noun] archaic the action of giving birth to a baby.
– ORIGIN late 18th cent.: French, from *accoucher* 'act as midwife', from *a-* (from Latin *ad* 'to, at') + *coucher* 'put to bed' (see **COUCH**[1]).

accoucheur /ˌakuːˈʃəː/ ▶ **noun** a male midwife.
– ORIGIN mid 18th cent.: French, from *accoucher* (see **ACCOUCHEMENT**).

account ▶ **noun 1** a report or description of an event or experience: *a detailed account of what has been achieved.*
■ an interpretation or rendering of a piece of music: *a lively account of Offenbach's score.*
2 a record or statement of financial expenditure and receipts relating to a particular period or purpose: *the barman was doing his accounts | he submitted a quarterly account.*
■ (**Accounts**) the department of a company that deals with such records. ■ chiefly Brit. a bill taking the form of such a record: *there's no money to pay the tradesmen's accounts this month.*
3 an arrangement by which a body holds funds on behalf of a client or supplies goods or services to them on credit: *a bank account | charge it to my account | I began buying things* ***on account.***
■ a client having such an arrangement with a supplier: *selling bibles to established accounts in the North.* ■ a contract to do work periodically for a client: *another agency were awarded the account.* ■ Stock Exchange, Brit. a fixed period on a stock exchange, at the end of which payment must be made for stock that has been bought.
4 [mass noun] importance: *money was* ***of no account*** *to her.*
▶ **verb 1** [with obj. and complement] consider or regard in a specified way: *her visit could not be accounted a success | he* ***accounted himself*** *the unluckiest man alive.*
2 [no obj.] archaic give or receive an account for money received: *after 1292 he* ***accounted to*** *the Westminster exchequer.*
– PHRASES **by** (or **from**) **all accounts** according to what one has heard or read: *by all accounts he is a pretty nice guy.* **call** (or **bring**) **someone to account** require someone to explain a mistake or poor performance. **give a good** (or **bad**) **account of oneself** make a favourable (or unfavourable) impression through one's performance. **keep an account of** keep a record of. **leave something out of account** fail or decline to consider a factor. **money of account** denominations of money used in reckoning but not current as coins. **on someone's account** for a specified person's benefit: *don't bother on my account.* **on account of** because of. **on no account** under no circumstances: *on no account let anyone know we're interested.* **on one's own account** with one's own money or assets, rather than for an employer or client: *he began trading on his own account.* **settle** (or **square**) **accounts with** pay money owed to

(someone). ■ have revenge on. **take something into account** (or **take account of**) consider a specified thing along with other factors before reaching a decision or taking action. **there's no accounting for tastes** (or **taste**) proverb it's impossible to explain why different people like different things, especially those things which the speaker considers unappealing. **turn something to (good) account** turn something to one's advantage.
– ORIGIN Middle English (in the sense 'counting', 'to count'): from Old French *acont* (noun), *aconter* (verb), based on *conter* 'to count'.

▶**account for 1** give a satisfactory record of (something, typically money, that one is responsible for). ■ provide or serve as a satisfactory explanation or reason for: *he was brought before the Board to account for his behaviour.* ■ (usually **be accounted for**) know the fate or whereabouts of (someone or something), especially after an accident: *everyone was accounted for after the floods.* ■ succeed in killing, destroying, or defeating: *a mishit drive accounted for Jones, who had scored 32.* **2** supply or make up (a specified amount or proportion): *social security accounts for about a third of total public spending.*

accountable ▶ **adjective 1** (of a person, organization, or institution) required or expected to justify actions or decisions; responsible: *ministers are **accountable to** Parliament | parents cannot be **held accountable for** their children's actions.*
2 explicable; understandable: *the delayed introduction of characters' names is accountable, if we consider that names have a low priority.*
– DERIVATIVES **accountability** noun, **accountably** adverb.

accountancy ▶ **noun** [mass noun] the profession or duties of an accountant.

accountant ▶ **noun** a person whose job is to keep or inspect financial accounts.
– ORIGIN Middle English: from Law French, present participle of Old French *aconter* (see **ACCOUNT**). The original use was as an adjective meaning 'liable to give an account', hence denoting a person who must do so.

account executive ▶ **noun** a business executive who manages the interests of a particular client, typically in advertising.

accounting ▶ **noun** [mass noun] the action or process of keeping financial accounts.

accounts payable ▶ **plural noun** money owed by a company to its creditors.

accounts receivable ▶ **plural noun** money owed to a company by its debtors.

accoutre /əˈkuːtə/ (US **accouter**) ▶ **verb** (**accoutred**, **accoutring**; US **accoutered**, **accoutering**) [with obj.] (usu. **be accoutred**) clothe or equip, typically in something noticeable or impressive.
– ORIGIN mid 16th cent.: from French *accoutrer*, from Old French *acoustrer*, from *a-* (from Latin *ad* 'to, at') + *cousture* 'sewing'.

accoutrement /əˈkuːtəm(ə)nt, -trə-/ (US **accouterment**) ▶ **noun** (usu. **accoutrements**) additional items of dress or equipment, or other items carried or worn by a person or used for a particular activity: *the accoutrements of religious ritual.*
■ a soldier's outfit other than weapons and garments.
– ORIGIN mid 16th cent.: from French, from *accoutrer* 'clothe, equip' (see **ACCOUTRE**).

Accra /əˈkrɑː/ the capital of Ghana, a port on the Gulf of Guinea; pop. 867,460 (1984) (pop. of Greater Accra 1,431,100).

accra /ˈakrə, əˈkrɑː/ (also **akara**) ▶ **noun** (in West Africa and the Caribbean) a fritter made with black-eyed peas or a similar pulse, or, especially in Trinidad, mashed fish.
– ORIGIN from Yoruba *àkàrà* 'bean cake'.

accredit ▶ **verb** (**accredited**, **accrediting**) [with obj.] (usu. **be accredited**) **1** give credit to (someone) for something: *he was **accredited with** being one of the world's fastest sprinters.*
■ (**accredit something to**) attribute an action, saying, or quality to: *the discovery of distillation is usually accredited to the Arabs.*
2 (of an official body) give authority or sanction to (someone or something) when recognized standards have been met: *institutions that do not meet the standards will not be accredited for teacher training.*
3 give official authorization for (someone, typically a diplomat or journalist) to be in a particular place or to hold a particular post: *Arab ambassadors **accredited to** Baghdad.*
– DERIVATIVES **accreditation** noun.
– ORIGIN early 17th cent. (in sense 2): from French *accréditer*, from *a-* (from Latin *ad* 'to, at') + *crédit* 'credit'.

accredited ▶ **adjective** (of a person, organization, or course of study) officially recognized or authorized: *an accredited practitioner.*

accrete /əˈkriːt/ ▶ **verb** [no obj.] grow by accumulation or coalescence: *ice that had accreted grotesquely into stalactites.*
■ [with obj.] form (a composite whole or a collection of things) by gradual accumulation: *the collection of art he had accreted was to be sold.* ■ Astronomy (of matter) come together or cause to come together under the influence of gravitation: [no obj.] *the gas will cool and then **accrete to** the galaxy's core.* ■ Astronomy (of a body) be formed from such matter.
– ORIGIN late 18th cent.: from Latin *accret-* 'grown', from the verb *accrescere*, from *ad-* 'to' + *crescere* 'grow'.

accretion ▶ **noun** [mass noun] the process of growth or increase, typically by the gradual accumulation of additional layers or matter: *the accretion of sediments in coastal mangroves* | figurative *the growing accretion of central government authority.*
■ [count noun] a thing formed or added by such growth or increase: *the city has a historic core surrounded by recent accretions.* ■ Astronomy the coming together and cohesion of matter under the influence of gravitation to form larger bodies.
– DERIVATIVES **accretive** adjective.
– ORIGIN early 17th cent.: from Latin *accretio(n-)*, from *accrescere* 'become larger' (see **ACCRETE**).

accretionary prism (also **accretionary wedge**) ▶ **noun** Geology a mass of sedimentary material scraped off a region of oceanic crust during subduction and piled up at the edge of a continental crustal plate.

accretion disc ▶ **noun** Astronomy a rotating disc of matter formed by accretion around a massive body (such as a black hole) under the influence of gravitation.

accrue /əˈkruː/ ▶ **verb** (**accrues**, **accrued**, **accruing**) [no obj.] (of a benefit or sum of money) be received by someone in regular or increasing amounts over time: *financial benefits will **accrue from** restructuring* | [as adj. **accrued**] *the accrued interest.*
■ [with obj.] accumulate or receive (such payments or benefits): *they accrue entitlements to holiday pay.* ■ [with obj.] make provision for (a charge) at the end of a financial period for work that has been done but not yet invoiced.
– DERIVATIVES **accrual** noun.
– ORIGIN late Middle English: from Old French *acreue*, past participle of *acreistre* 'increase', from Latin *accrescere* 'become larger' (see **ACCRETE**).

acculturate /əˈkʌltʃəreɪt/ ▶ **verb** assimilate or cause to assimilate a different culture, typically the dominant one: [no obj.] *those who have **acculturated to** the United States* | [with obj.] *the next weeks were spent acculturating the field staff.*
– DERIVATIVES **acculturation** noun, **acculturative** adjective.
– ORIGIN mid 20th cent.: from **AC-** + **CULTURE** + **-ATE**[3]. The noun *acculturation* dates from the late 19th cent.

accumulate /əˈkjuːmjʊleɪt/ ▶ **verb** [with obj.] gather together or acquire an increasing number or quantity of: *investigators have yet to accumulate enough evidence.*
■ gradually gather or acquire (a resulting whole): *her goal was to accumulate a huge fortune.* ■ [no obj.] gather; build up: *the toxin accumulated in their bodies.*
– ORIGIN late 15th cent.: from Latin *accumulat-* 'heaped up', from the verb *accumulare*, from *ad-* 'to' + *cumulus* 'a heap'.

accumulation ▶ **noun** [mass noun] the acquisition or gradual gathering of something: *the accumulation of wealth.*
■ [count noun] a mass or quantity of something that has gradually gathered or been acquired: *the accumulation of paperwork on her desk.* ■ the growth of a sum of money by the regular addition of interest.

accumulative /əˈkjuːmjʊlətɪv/ ▶ **adjective** gathering or growing by gradual increases: *the accumulative effects of pollution.*

accumulator ▶ **noun** a person or thing that accumulates: *an accumulator of capital.*
■ Brit. a large rechargeable electric cell. ■ Brit. a bet placed on a series of races (or other events), the winnings and stake from each being placed on the next: *an eight-horse accumulator.* ■ Computing a register used to contain the results of an arithmetical or logical operation.

accuracy ▶ **noun** (pl. **-ies**) [mass noun] the quality or state of being correct or precise: *we have confidence in the accuracy of the statistics.*
■ technical the degree to which the result of a measurement, calculation, or specification conforms to the correct value or a standard: *the accuracy of radiocarbon dating* | [count noun] *accuracies of 50–70 per cent.* Compare with **PRECISION**.

accurate /ˈakjʊrət/ ▶ **adjective 1** (especially of information, measurements, or predictions) correct in all details; exact: *accurate information about the illness is essential.*
■ (of an instrument or method) capable of giving such information: *an accurate thermometer.* ■ (of a piece of work) done with meticulous care and free from errors. ■ faithfully or fairly representing the truth about someone or something: *the portrait is an accurate likeness of Mozart.*
2 (of a weapon or the person using it) capable of reaching the intended target.
■ (of a shot or throw, or the person making it) successful in reaching a target.
– DERIVATIVES **accurately** adverb.
– ORIGIN late 16th cent.: from Latin *accuratus* 'done with care', past participle of *accurare*, from *ad-* 'towards' + *cura* 'care'.

accursed /əˈkəːsɪd, əˈkəːst/ ▶ **adjective 1** poetic/literary under a curse: *the Angel of Death walks this accursed house.*
2 [attrib.] informal, dated used to express strong dislike of or anger at someone or something: *this accursed country!*
– ORIGIN Middle English: past participle of obsolete *accurse*, from *a-* (expressing intensity) + **CURSE**.

accurst ▶ **adjective** archaic spelling of **ACCURSED**.

accusal ▶ **noun** another term for **ACCUSATION**.

accusation ▶ **noun** a charge or claim that someone has done something illegal or wrong: *accusations of bribery.*
■ [mass noun] the action or process of making such a charge or claim: *there was accusation in Brian's voice.*
– ORIGIN late Middle English: from Old French, from Latin *accusatio(n-)*, from *accusare* 'call to account' (see **ACCUSE**).

accusative /əˈkjuːzətɪv/ Grammar ▶ **adjective** (in Latin, Greek, German, and some other languages) denoting a case of nouns, pronouns, and adjectives which expresses the object of an action or the goal of motion.
▶ **noun** a word in the accusative case.
■ (**the accusative**) the accusative case.
– ORIGIN late Middle English: from Latin (*casus*) *accusativus*, literally 'relating to an accusation or (legal) case', translating Greek (*ptōsis*) *aitiatikē* '(the case) showing cause'.

accusatorial /əˌkjuːzəˈtɔːrɪəl/ ▶ **adjective** Law (of a trial or legal procedure) involving accusation by a prosecutor and a verdict reached by an impartial judge or jury. Compare with **ADVERSARIAL**, **INQUISITORIAL**.

accusatory /əˈkjuːzət(ə)ri/ ▶ **adjective** indicating or suggesting that one believes a person has done something wrong: *he pointed an accusatory finger in her direction.*

accuse ▶ **verb** [with obj.] (often **be accused**) charge (someone) with an offence or crime: *he was **accused of** murdering his wife's lover.*
■ claim that (someone) has done something wrong: *he was **accused of** favouritism.*
– DERIVATIVES **accuser** noun.
– ORIGIN Middle English: from Old French *acuser*, from Latin *accusare* 'call to account', from *ad-* 'towards' + *causa* 'reason, motive, lawsuit'.

accused ▶ **noun** (**the accused**) [treated as sing. or pl.] a person or group of people who are charged with or on trial for a crime.

accusing ▶ **adjective** (of an expression, gesture, or tone of voice) indicating a belief in someone's guilt or culpability: *she stared at him with accusing eyes.*
– DERIVATIVES **accusingly** adverb.

accustom ▶ **verb** [with obj.] make (someone or something) accept something as normal or usual: *I* *accustomed my eyes to the lenses* | [with obj. and infinitive] *sixth-form education is supposed to accustom pupils to think for themselves.*

■(**be accustomed to**) be used to: *I am not accustomed to having my word questioned.*

– ORIGIN late Middle English: from Old French *acostumer*, from *a-* (from Latin *ad* 'to, at') + *costume* 'custom'.

accustomed ▶ **adjective** [attrib.] customary; usual: *his accustomed route.*

AC/DC ▶ **adjective** alternating current/direct current.

■informal bisexual.

ace ▶ **noun 1** a playing card with a single spot on it, ranked as the highest card in its suit in most card games: *the ace of diamonds* | figurative *life had started dealing him aces again.*

2 [often with modifier] informal a person who excels at a particular sport or other activity: *a motorcycle ace.*

■a pilot who has shot down many enemy aircraft.

3 (in tennis and similar games) a service that an opponent is unable to return and thus wins a point.

■Golf, informal a hole in one.

▶ **adjective** informal very good: *an ace swimmer* | [as an exclamation] *Ace! You've done it!*

▶ **verb** [with obj.] informal (in tennis and similar games) serve an ace against (an opponent).

■Golf score an ace on (a hole) or with (a shot). ■ N. Amer. get an A or its equivalent in (a test or exam): *I aced my grammar test.* ■(**ace someone out**) N. Amer. outdo someone in a competitive situation: *it wasn't our intention to ace Phil out of a job.*

– PHRASES **ace up one's sleeve** (or N. Amer. **in the hole**) a plan or piece of information kept secret until it becomes necessary to use it. **hold all the aces** have all the advantages. **play one's ace** use one's best resource: *deciding to play her ace, Emily showed the letter to Vic.* **within an ace of** very close to: *they came within an ace of death.*

– ORIGIN Middle English (denoting the 'one' on dice): via Old French from Latin *as* 'unity, a unit'.

-acea ▶ **suffix** Zoology forming the names of zoological groups: *Crustacea.* Compare with **-ACEAN**.

– ORIGIN from Latin, 'of the nature of', neuter plural adjectival ending.

-aceae ▶ **suffix** Botany forming the names of families of plants: *Liliaceae.*

– ORIGIN from Latin, 'of the nature of', feminine plural adjectival ending.

-acean ▶ **suffix** Zoology forming the singular of group names ending in *-acea* (such as *crustacean* from *Crustacea*).

– ORIGIN from Latin *-aceus* 'of the nature of' + **-AN**.

acedia /əˈsiːdɪə/ ▶ **noun** another term for **ACCIDIE**.

– ORIGIN early 17th cent.: via late Latin from Greek *akēdia* 'listlessness', from *a-* 'without' + *kēdos* 'care'.

acellular ▶ **adjective** Biology not consisting of, divided into, or containing cells.

■(especially of protozoa) consisting of one cell only.

acentric ▶ **adjective** without a centre; not centralized.

■Genetics (of a chromosome) having no centromere.

-aceous ▶ **suffix 1** Botany forming adjectives from family names ending in *-aceae* (such as *ericaceous* from *Ericaceae*).

2 chiefly Biology & Geology forming adjectives describing similarity, especially in shape, texture, or colour: *arenaceous* | *foliaceous* | *olivaceous.*

– ORIGIN from Latin *-aceus* 'of the nature of' + **-OUS**.

acephalous /eɪˈsɛf(ə)ləs, -ˈkɛf-/ ▶ **adjective 1** no longer having a head: *an acephalous skeleton.*

■Zoology not having a head. ■ having no leader or chief: *an acephalous society.*

2 Prosody (of a hexameter beginning with a short syllable) lacking a syllable or syllables in the first foot.

– ORIGIN mid 18th cent.: via medieval Latin from Greek *akephalos* 'headless' (from *a-* 'without' + *kephalē* 'head') + **-OUS**.

acer /ˈeɪsə/ ▶ **noun** a Eurasian or North American deciduous tree or shrub which typically has five-lobed leaves and is widely grown for its ornamental foliage and bright autumn colours.

● Genus *Acer*, family Aceraceae: numerous species, including the maples and the European sycamore.

– ORIGIN from Latin, 'maple'.

acerb /əˈsəːb/ ▶ **adjective** chiefly US another term for **ACERBIC**.

– ORIGIN early 17th cent.: from Latin *acerbus* 'sour-tasting'.

acerbic ▶ **adjective 1** (especially of a comment or style of speaking) sharp and forthright: *his acerbic wit.*

2 archaic or technical tasting sour or bitter.

– DERIVATIVES **acerbically** adverb, **acerbity** noun.

– ORIGIN mid 19th cent.: from Latin *acerbus* 'sour-tasting' + **-IC**.

acesulfame /ˌasɪˈsʌlfeɪm/ ▶ **noun** [mass noun] a white crystalline compound used as a low-calorie artificial sweetener, typically in the form of a potassium salt (**acesulfame-K**).

● A sulphur-containing heterocyclic compound; chem. formula: $C_4H_5NO_4S$.

– ORIGIN 1980s: of unknown origin.

acet- ▶ **combining form** variant spelling of **ACETO-** shortened before a vowel (as in *acetaldehyde*).

acetabulum /ˌasɪˈtabjʊləm/ ▶ **noun** (pl. **acetabula** /-lə/) Anatomy the socket of the hip bone, into which the head of the femur fits.

■Zoology any cup-shaped structure, especially a sucker.

– ORIGIN late Middle English (denoting a vinegar cup, hence a cup-shaped cavity): from Latin, from *acetum* 'vinegar' + *-abulum*, denoting a container.

acetal /ˈasɪtal/ ▶ **noun** Chemistry an organic compound formed by the condensation of two alcohol molecules with an aldehyde molecule.

● Acetals have the general formula $R^1CH(OR^2)_2$, where R^1 and R^2 are alkyl groups.

– ORIGIN mid 19th cent.: from **ACETIC ACID** + *al* from **ALCOHOL**.

acetaldehyde /ˌasɪtˈaldɪhʌɪd/ ▶ **noun** [mass noun] Chemistry a colourless volatile liquid aldehyde obtained by oxidizing ethanol.

● Alternative name: **ethanal**; chem. formula: CH_3CHO.

acetamide /əˈsiːtəmʌɪd, əˈsɛt-/ ▶ **noun** [mass noun] Chemistry the amide of acetic acid. It is a crystalline solid with a characteristic musty odour.

● Alternative name: **ethanamide**; chem. formula: CH_3CONH_2.

– ORIGIN mid 19th cent.: from **ACETYL** + **AMIDE**.

acetaminophen /əˌsiːtəˈmɪnəfɛn, əˌsɛtə-, ˌasɪtə-/ ▶ **noun** North American term for **PARACETAMOL**.

– ORIGIN 1960s: from *para-acetylaminophenol*.

acetanilide /ˌasɪtˈanɪlʌɪd/ ▶ **noun** [mass noun] Chemistry a crystalline solid prepared by acetylation of aniline, used in dye manufacture.

● Chem. formula: $C_6H_5NHCOCH_3$.

– ORIGIN mid 19th cent.: from *acet(yl)* + *anil(ine)* + **-IDE**.

acetate /ˈasɪteɪt/ ▶ **noun 1** Chemistry a salt or ester of acetic acid, containing the anion CH_3COO^- or the group $—OOCCH_3$.

2 [mass noun] cellulose acetate, especially as used to make textile fibres or plastic: [as modifier] *acetate silk.*

■[count noun] a transparency made of cellulose acetate film. ■ [count noun] a direct-cut recording disc coated with cellulose acetate.

acetic acid /əˈsiːtɪk, əˈsɛt-/ ▶ **noun** [mass noun] Chemistry the acid that gives vinegar its characteristic taste. The pure acid is a colourless viscous liquid or glassy solid.

● Alternative name: **ethanoic acid**; chem. formula: CH_3COOH.

– ORIGIN late 18th cent.: *acetic* from French *acétique*, from Latin *acetum* 'vinegar'.

acetic anhydride ▶ **noun** [mass noun] Chemistry the anhydride of acetic acid. It is a colourless pungent liquid, used in making synthetic fibres.

● Chem. formula: $(CH_3CO)_2O$.

aceto- (also **acet-** before a vowel) ▶ **combining form** Chemistry representing **ACETIC ACID** or **ACETYL**.

acetobacter /əˌsiːtə(ʊ)ˈbaktə, ˌasɪtəʊ-/ ▶ **noun** [mass noun] bacteria that oxidize organic compounds to acetic acid, as in vinegar formation.

● Genus *Acetobacter*, Gram-negative oval or rod-shaped bacteria.

– ORIGIN modern Latin (genus name), from **ACETO-** + **BACTERIUM**.

acetogenic /əˌsiːtə(ʊ)ˈdʒɛnɪk, ˌasɪtəʊ-/ ▶ **adjective** (of bacteria) forming acetate or acetic acid as a product of metabolism.

acetonaemia /ˌasɪtə(ʊ)ˈniːmɪə/ ▶ **noun** another term for **KETOSIS**.

acetone /ˈasɪtəʊn/ ▶ **noun** [mass noun] Chemistry a colourless volatile liquid ketone made by oxidizing isopropanol, used as an organic solvent and synthetic reagent.

● Alternative name: **propanone**; chem. formula: CH_3COCH_3.

– ORIGIN mid 19th cent.: from **ACETIC ACID** + **-ONE**.

acetonitrile /əˌsiːtə(ʊ)ˈnʌɪtrʌɪl, ˌasɪtəʊ-/ ▶ **noun** [mass noun] Chemistry a toxic odoriferous liquid, used as a solvent in high-performance liquid chromatography.

● Alternative name: **methyl cyanide**; chem. formula: $CH_3C{\equiv}N$.

acetous /əˈsiːtəs/ ▶ **adjective** producing or resembling vinegar: *acetous fermentation.*

– ORIGIN late Middle English (rare before the late 18th cent.): from late Latin *acetosus* 'sour', from Latin *acetum* 'vinegar'.

acetyl /ˈasɪtʌɪl, -tɪl/ ▶ **noun** [as modifier] Chemistry of or denoting the acyl radical $—C(O)CH_3$, derived from acetic acid: *acetyl chloride* | *an acetyl group.*

acetylate /əˈsɛtɪleɪt/ ▶ **verb** [with obj.] Chemistry introduce an acetyl group into (a molecule or compound): [as adj. **acetylated**] *the acetylated forms of chloramphenicol.*

– DERIVATIVES **acetylation** noun.

acetylcholine /ˌasɪtʌɪlˈkəʊliːn, -tɪl-/ ▶ **noun** [mass noun] Biochemistry a compound which occurs throughout the nervous system, in which it functions as a neurotransmitter.

acetylcholinesterase /ˌasɪtʌɪlˌkəʊlɪnˈɛstəreɪz, -tɪl-/ ▶ **noun** [mass noun] Biochemistry an enzyme that causes rapid hydrolysis of acetylcholine. Its action serves to stop excitation of a nerve after transmission of an impulse.

acetyl coenzyme A ▶ **noun** [mass noun] Biochemistry the acetyl ester of coenzyme A, involved as an acetylating agent in many biochemical processes.

acetylene /əˈsɛtɪliːn/ ▶ **noun** Chemistry a colourless pungent-smelling hydrocarbon gas, which burns with a bright flame, used in welding and formerly in lighting.

● Alternative name: **ethyne**; chem. formula: C_2H_2.

– ORIGIN mid 19th cent.: from **ACETIC ACID** + **-YL** + **-ENE**.

acetylide /əˈsɛtɪlʌɪd/ ▶ **noun** Chemistry a salt-like compound formed from acetylene and a metal, containing the anion $(C{\equiv}C)^{2-}$ or $HC{\equiv}C^-$. Acetylides are typically unstable or explosive.

acetylsalicylic acid /ˌasɪtʌɪlˌsalɪˈsɪlɪk, -tɪl-/ ▶ **noun** systematic chemical name for **ASPIRIN**.

ach /ɑːx/ ▶ **exclamation** dialect (chiefly Scottish) form of **AH**: *ach well, win some lose some.*

– ORIGIN late 15th cent.: Scottish Gaelic, Dutch, and German.

achaar ▶ **noun** variant spelling of **ACHAR**.

Achaea /əˈkiːə/ a region of ancient Greece on the north coast of the Peloponnese.

Achaean ▶ **adjective** of or relating to Achaea in ancient Greece.

■poetic/literary (especially in Homeric contexts) Greek.

▶ **noun** an inhabitant of Achaea.

■poetic/literary (especially in Homeric contexts) a Greek.

The Achaeans were among the earliest Greek-speaking inhabitants of Greece, being established there well before the 12th century BC. Some scholars identify them with the Mycenaeans of the 14th–13th centuries BC. The Greek protagonists in the Trojan War are regularly called Achaeans in the *Iliad*, though this may have referred only to the leaders.

Achaemenid /əˈkiːmənɪd/ (also **Achaemenian** /ˌakɪˈmiːnɪən/) ▶ **adjective** of or relating to the dynasty ruling in Persia from Cyrus I to Darius III (553–330 BC).

▶ **noun** a member of this dynasty.

– ORIGIN from Greek *Akhaimenēs* 'Achaemenes' (the reputed ancestor of the dynasty) + **-ID**³.

achalasia /ˌakəˈleɪzɪə/ ▶ **noun** [mass noun] Medicine a condition in which the muscles of the lower part of the oesophagus fail to relax, preventing food from passing into the stomach.

– ORIGIN early 20th cent.: from **A-**¹ 'without, not' + Greek *khalasis* 'loosening' (from *khalan* 'relax') + **-IA**¹.

achar /əˈtʃɑː/ (also **achaar**) ▶ **noun** [mass noun] (in Indian cookery) a type of pickle in which the food is preserved in spiced oil: *mango achar.*

– ORIGIN from Hindi *acār*, from Persian.

acharnement /əˈʃɑːnmɒ̃/ ▶ **noun** [mass noun] archaic bloodthirsty fury or ferocity.

– ORIGIN French, from *acharner* 'give (to dogs, falcons, etc.) a taste of flesh', from *charn*, archaic variant of *chair*, from Latin *caro, carn-* 'flesh'.

Achates /əˈkeɪtiːz/ Greek & Roman Mythology a companion of Aeneas. His loyalty to his friend was

a

so exemplary as to become proverbial, hence the term *fidus Achates* ('faithful Achates').

achcha /əˈtʃɑː/ ▶ **exclamation** Indian **1** okay; all right. **2** is that so? (used in responses to indicate the speaker's surprise, joy, or doubt).
– ORIGIN from Hindi *acchā*.

ache ▶ **noun** a continuous or prolonged dull pain in a part of one's body: *the ache in her head worsened* | [mass noun] *he had stomach ache.*
■ [in sing.] figurative an emotion experienced with painful or bitter-sweet intensity: *an ache in her heart.*
▶ **verb** [no obj.] **1** (of a person or bodily part) suffer from a continuous dull pain: *I'm aching all over* | *my legs ached from the previous day's exercise* | [as adj. **aching**] *aching feet.*
■ figurative feel intense sadness or compassion: *she sat still and silent, her heart aching* | *she looked so tired that my heart **ached for** her.*
2 feel an intense desire for: *she **ached for** his touch* | [with infinitive] *he was aching to get his hands on the ball.*
– PHRASES **aches and pains** minor pains and discomforts, especially in the muscles.
– DERIVATIVES **achingly** adverb [as submodifier] *a sound which was achingly familiar to me.*
– ORIGIN Old English *æce* (noun), *acan* (verb). In Middle and early modern English the noun was spelled *atche* and rhymed with 'batch' and the verb was spelled and pronounced as it is today. The noun began to be pronounced like the verb around 1700. The modern spelling is largely due to Dr Johnson, who mistakenly assumed its derivation to be from Greek *akhos* 'pain'.

Achebe /əˈtʃeɪbi/, Chinua (b.1930), Nigerian novelist, poet, short-story writer, and essayist; born *Albert Chinualumgu*. Notable works: *Things Fall Apart* (1958).

achene /əˈkiːn/ ▶ **noun** Botany a small, dry one-seeded fruit that does not open to release the seed.
– ORIGIN mid 19th cent.: from modern Latin *achaenium*, derived irregularly from *a-* 'not' + Greek *khainein* 'to gape'.

Achernar /ˈeɪkənɑː/ Astronomy the ninth brightest star in the sky and the brightest in the constellation Eridanus, visible only in the southern hemisphere.
– ORIGIN from Arabic, 'end of the river (i.e. Eridanus)'.

Acheron /ˈakərɒn/ Greek Mythology one of the rivers of Hades.
■ poetic/literary hell.
– ORIGIN Latin, from Greek *Akherōn*.

Acheson /ˈeɪtʃɪs(ə)n/, Dean (Gooderham) (1893–1971), American statesman, Secretary of State 1949–53.

Acheulian /əˈʃuːlɪən/ (also **Acheulean**) ▶ **adjective** Archaeology of, relating to, or denoting the main Lower Palaeolithic culture in Europe (preceding the Mousterian) and a similar culture in Africa. It is represented by hand-axe industries, which are dated as a whole to about 1,500,000–150,000 years ago. See also **ABBEVILLIAN**.
■ [as noun **the Acheulian**] the Acheulian culture or period.
– ORIGIN early 20th cent.: from French *Acheuléen*, from *St-Acheul* near Amiens in northern France, where objects from this culture were found.

achieve ▶ **verb** [with obj.] reach, attain, or successfully bring about (a desired objective, level, or result) by effort, skill, or courage: *he achieved his ambition to become a press baron* | *the communist system achieved a basic economic modernization.*
– DERIVATIVES **achievable** adjective.
– ORIGIN Middle English (in the sense 'complete successfully'): from Old French *achever* 'come or bring to a head', from *a chief* 'to a head'.

achievement ▶ **noun 1** a thing done successfully, typically by effort, courage, or skill: *to reach this stage is a great achievement.*
2 [mass noun] the process or fact of achieving something: *the achievement of professional recognition* | *a sense of achievement.*
■ a child's or student's progress in a course of learning, typically as measured by standardized tests or objectives: *assessing ability in terms of academic achievement* | [as modifier] *an achievement test.*
3 Heraldry a representation of a coat of arms with all the adjuncts to which a bearer of arms is entitled.

achiever ▶ **noun** a person who achieves a high or specified level of success.

achillea /ˌakɪˈliːə, əˈkɪlɪə/ ▶ **noun** a Eurasian and North African plant of a genus that includes the yarrow, typically having heads of small white or yellow flowers and fern-like leaves.
• Genus *Achillea*, family Compositae: numerous species.
– ORIGIN via Latin from Greek *Akhilleios*, denoting a plant supposed to have been used medicinally by Achilles.

Achilles /əˈkɪliːz/ Greek Mythology a hero of the Trojan War, son of Peleus and Thetis. During his infancy his mother plunged him in the Styx, thus making his body invulnerable except for the heel by which she held him. During the Trojan War Achilles killed Hector but was later wounded in the heel by an arrow shot by Paris and died.

Achilles' heel ▶ **noun** a weakness or vulnerable point.
– ORIGIN early 19th cent.: alluding to the vulnerability of **ACHILLES**.

Achilles tendon ▶ **noun** the tendon connecting calf muscles to the heel.

achimenes /əˈkɪmɪniːz/ ▶ **noun** (pl. same) a Central American plant with tubular or trumpet-shaped flowers.
• Genus *Achimenes*, family Gesneriaceae.
– ORIGIN modern Latin, either from Greek *akhaimenis*, denoting a different plant (euphorbia), or from *a-* 'not' + *kheimanein* 'expose to the cold'.

Achinese /ˈatʃɪniːz/ ▶ **noun** (pl. same) **1** a member of a people living in northern Sumatra.
2 [mass noun] the Indonesian language of this people.
▶ **adjective** of or relating to this people or their language.
– ORIGIN from *Acheh*, *Atjeh*, a territory in northern Sumatra + *-n-* + **-ESE**.

achiote /ˌatʃɪˈɒti/ ▶ **noun** North American term for **ANNATTO**.
– ORIGIN mid 17th cent.: from Spanish, from Nahuatl *achiotl*.

achiral /eɪˈkʌɪr(ə)l/ ▶ **adjective** Chemistry (chiefly of a molecule) symmetric in such a way that it can be superimposed on its mirror image; not chiral.

achkan /ˈatʃk(ə)n/ ▶ **noun** a knee-length coat buttoned in front, worn by men from the Indian subcontinent.
– ORIGIN from Hindi *ackan*.

achlorhydria /ˌeɪkləːˈhʌɪdrɪə, ˌakləː-/ ▶ **noun** [mass noun] Medicine absence of hydrochloric acid in the gastric secretions.
– ORIGIN late 19th cent.: from **A-**[1] 'without' + **CHLOR-** + **HYDRO-** + **-IA**[1].

Acholi /əˈtʃəʊli/ ▶ **noun** (pl. same) **1** a member of a farming and pastoral people of northern Uganda and southern Sudan.
2 [mass noun] the Nilotic language of this people.
▶ **adjective** of or relating to this people or their language.
– ORIGIN the name in Acholi.

achondrite /əˈkɒndrʌɪt/ ▶ **noun** a stony meteorite containing no small mineral granules (chondrules).
– DERIVATIVES **achondritic** adjective.
– ORIGIN early 20th cent.: from **A-**[1] 'without' + **CHONDRITE**.

achondroplasia /əˌkɒndrə(ʊ)ˈpleɪzɪə, eɪ-/ ▶ **noun** [mass noun] a hereditary condition in which the growth of long bones by ossification of cartilage is retarded, resulting in very short limbs and sometimes a face which is small in relation to the (normal sized) skull.
– DERIVATIVES **achondroplasic** adjective, **achondroplastic** adjective.
– ORIGIN late 19th cent.: from **A-**[1] 'without' + Greek *khondros* 'cartilage' + *plasis* 'moulding' + **-IA**[1].

achromat /ˈakrə(ʊ)mat/ ▶ **noun** a lens that transmits light without separating it into constituent colours.

achromatic /ˌakrə(ʊ)ˈmatɪk/ ▶ **adjective 1** relating to, employing, or denoting lenses that transmit light without separating it into constituent colours.
2 poetic/literary without colour: *the achromatic gloom.*
– DERIVATIVES **achromaticity** noun, **achromatism** noun.
– ORIGIN late 18th cent.: via French from Greek *a-* 'without' + *khrōmatikos* (from *khrōma* 'colour').

achy ▶ **adjective** (**-ier**, **-est**) suffering from continuous dull pain: *she felt tired and achy.*

acicular /əˈsɪkjʊlə/ ▶ **adjective** technical (chiefly of crystals) needle-shaped.
– ORIGIN early 18th cent.: from late Latin *acicula* 'small needle' (diminutive of *acus*) + **-AR**[1].

acid ▶ **noun** a substance with particular chemical properties including turning litmus red, neutralizing alkalis, and dissolving some metals; typically, a corrosive or sour-tasting liquid of this kind. Often contrasted with **ALKALI** or **BASE**.
■ [mass noun] figurative bitter or cutting remarks or tone of voice: *she was unable to quell the acid in her voice.* ■ [mass noun] informal the drug LSD. ■ Chemistry a molecule or other species which can donate a proton or accept an electron pair in reactions.

> Acids are compounds which release hydrogen ions (H^+) when dissolved in water. Any solution with a pH of less than 7 is acidic, strong acids such as sulphuric or hydrochloric acid having a pH as low as 1 or 2. Most organic acids (**carboxylic** or **fatty acids**) contain the carboxyl group —COOH.

▶ **adjective 1** containing acid or having the properties of an acid; having a pH of less than 7: *poor, acid soils.* Often contrasted with **ALKALINE** or **BASIC**.
■ Geology (of rock, especially lava) containing a relatively high proportion of silica. ■ Metallurgy relating to or denoting steel-making processes involving silica-rich refractories and slags.
2 sharp-tasting or sour: *acid fruit.*
■ (of a person's remarks or tone) bitter or cutting: *she was stung into acid defiance.* ■ (of a colour) strikingly intense or bright: *an acid green.*
– PHRASES **put the acid on** Austral./NZ informal seek to extract a loan or favour from (someone). [ORIGIN: *acid* from **ACID TEST**, referring to possible resistance (because gold resists nitric acid).]
– DERIVATIVES **acidy** adjective.
– ORIGIN early 17th cent. (in the sense 'sour-tasting'): from Latin *acidus*, from *acere* 'be sour'.

acid drop ▶ **noun** Brit. a kind of boiled sweet with a sharp taste.

acid-fast ▶ **adjective** Microbiology denoting bacteria that cannot be decolorized by an acid after staining, which is characteristic of the mycobacteria that cause tuberculosis and leprosy.

acid house ▶ **noun** [mass noun] a kind of popular synthesized dance music with a fast repetitive beat, popular in the 1980s and associated with the taking of drugs such as Ecstasy.

acidic ▶ **adjective 1** having the properties of an acid, or containing acid; having a pH below 7. Often contrasted with **ALKALINE** or **BASIC**.
■ Geology (of rock, especially lava) relatively rich in silica. ■ Metallurgy relating to or denoting steel-making processes involving silica-rich refractories and slags.
2 sharp-tasting or sour: *acidic wine.*
■ (of a person's remarks or tone) bitter or cutting: *the occasional acidic comment.* ■ (of a colour) strikingly intense or bright: *an acidic yellow.*

acidify /əˈsɪdɪfʌɪ/ ▶ **verb** (**-ies**, **-ied**) make or become acid: [with obj.] *pollutants can acidify surface water.*
– DERIVATIVES **acidification** noun.

acidimetry /ˌasɪˈdɪmɪtri/ ▶ **noun** [mass noun] measurement of the strengths of acids.

acidity ▶ **noun** [mass noun] **1** the level of acid in substances such as water, soil, or wine.
■ such a level in the gastric juices, typically when excessive and causing discomfort.
2 bitterness or sharpness in a person's remarks or tone: *the cutting acidity in his voice.*

acid jazz ▶ **noun** [mass noun] a kind of popular dance music incorporating elements of jazz, funk, soul, and hip hop.
– ORIGIN apparently coined from **ACID HOUSE** and popularized by the *Acid Jazz* record label founded in 1988.

acidly ▶ **adverb** with bitterness or sarcasm: *'Is it up to you to make that decision?' she asked acidly.*

acidophil /əˈsɪdə(ʊ)fɪl/ ▶ **noun** Physiology an acidophilic white blood cell.

acidophilic /ˌasɪdə(ʊ)ˈfɪlɪk, əˌsɪd-/ ▶ **adjective** Biology **1** (of a cell or its contents) readily stained with acid dyes.
2 (of a micro-organism or plant) growing best in acidic conditions.

acidophilus /ˌasɪˈdɒfɪləs/ ▶ **noun** [mass noun] a bacterium that is used to make yogurt and to supplement the intestinal flora.
• *Lactobacillus acidophilus*; a Gram-positive rod-shaped bacterium.
– ORIGIN 1920s: modern Latin, literally 'acid-loving'.

b but | d dog | f few | g get | h he | j yes | k cat | l leg | m man | n no | p pen | r red | s sit | t top | v voice | w we | z zoo | ʃ she | ʒ decision | θ thin | ð this | ŋ ring | x loch | tʃ chip | dʒ jar

acidosis /ˌasɪˈdəʊsɪs/ ▶ **noun** [mass noun] Medicine an excessively acid condition of the body fluids or tissues.
– DERIVATIVES **acidotic** adjective.

acid rain ▶ **noun** [mass noun] rainfall made sufficiently acidic by atmospheric pollution that it causes environmental harm, chiefly to forests and lakes. The main cause is the industrial burning of coal and other fossil fuels, the waste gases from which contain sulphur and nitrogen oxides which combine with atmospheric water to form acids.

acid rock ▶ **noun** [mass noun] a style of rock music popular chiefly in the late 1960s, associated with or inspired by hallucinogenic drugs.

acid salt ▶ **noun** Chemistry a salt formed by incomplete replacement of the hydrogen of an acid, e.g. potassium hydrogen sulphate ($KHSO_4$).

acid test ▶ **noun** [in sing.] a conclusive test of the success or value of something: *gritstone is the acid test of a climber's ability.*
– ORIGIN figuratively, from the original use denoting a test for gold using nitric acid.

acidulate /əˈsɪdjʊleɪt/ ▶ **verb** [with obj.] [usu. as adj. **acidulated**] make slightly acidic: *acidulated water.*
– DERIVATIVES **acidulation** noun.
– ORIGIN mid 18th cent.: from Latin *acidulus* (from *acidus* 'sour') + **-ATE**[3].

acidulous /əˈsɪdjʊləs/ ▶ **adjective** sharp-tasting; sour.
■(of a person's remarks or tone) bitter; cutting.
– ORIGIN mid 18th cent.: from Latin *acidulus* (from *acidus* 'sour') + **-OUS**.

acinus /ˈasɪnəs/ ▶ **noun** (pl. **acini** /-nʌɪ/) Anatomy **1** a small sac-like cavity in a gland, surrounded by secretory cells.
2 a region of the lung supplied with air from one of the terminal bronchioles.
– ORIGIN mid 18th cent.: Latin, literally 'a kernel'.

-acious ▶ **suffix** (forming adjectives) inclined to; having as a capacity: *audacious* | *capacious.*
– ORIGIN from Latin *-ax, -ac-* (especially forming adjectives from verbal stems) + **-OUS**.

-acity ▶ **suffix** forming nouns of quality or state corresponding to adjectives ending in *-acious* (such as *audacity* corresponding to *audacious*).
– ORIGIN from French *-acité* or Latin *-acitas.*

ack-ack ▶ **noun** Military, informal an anti-aircraft gun or regiment.
■[mass noun] anti-aircraft gunfire.
– ORIGIN signallers' name for the letters *AA*; *ack* for *A* was replaced in military use by *able* in 1942.

ackee /ˈaki/ (also **akee**) ▶ **noun** a tropical West African tree which is cultivated for its fruit and has been introduced into the Caribbean and elsewhere.
● *Blighia sapida*, family Sapindaceae.
■[mass noun] the fruit of this tree, which is widely eaten as a vegetable but is poisonous until fully ripe.
– ORIGIN late 18th cent.: from Kru *ākee.*

ack emma ▶ **adverb** Brit., dated informal term for **A.M.**
– ORIGIN First World War: signallers' name for these letters.

acknowledge ▶ **verb 1** [reporting verb] accept or admit the existence or truth of: [with obj.] *the plight of the refugees was acknowledged by the authorities* | [with clause] *the government* ***acknowledged that*** *the tax was unfair* | [with direct speech] *'That's true,' she acknowledged.*
2 [with obj.] (of a body of opinion) recognize the fact or importance or quality of: *the art world has begun to acknowledge his genius* | [with obj. and infinitive] *he's generally acknowledged to be the game's finest coach.*
■express or display gratitude for or appreciation of: *he received a letter acknowledging his services.* ■ accept the validity or legitimacy of: *Henry acknowledged Richard as his heir.*
3 [with obj.] show that one has noticed or recognized (someone) by making a gesture or greeting: *she refused to acknowledge my presence.*
■confirm (receipt of something).
– DERIVATIVES **acknowledgeable** adjective.
– ORIGIN late 15th cent.: from the obsolete Middle English verb *knowledge*, influenced by obsolete *acknow* 'acknowledge, confess'.

acknowledgement (also **acknowledgment**) ▶ **noun** [mass noun] **1** acceptance of the truth or existence of something: *there was no acknowledgement of the family's trauma.*
2 the action of expressing or displaying gratitude or appreciation for something: *he received an award* ***in acknowledgement of*** *his work.*
■the action of showing that one has noticed someone or something: *he touched his hat* ***in acknowledgement.***
■ [count noun] a letter confirming receipt of something: *I received an acknowledgement of my application.*
3 (usu. **acknowledgements**) an author's or publisher's statement of indebtedness to others, typically one printed at the beginning of a book.

ACL ▶ **abbreviation for** anterior cruciate ligament.

aclinic line /əˈklɪnɪk/ ▶ **noun** another term for **MAGNETIC EQUATOR**.
– ORIGIN mid 19th cent.: *aclinic* from Greek *aklinēs*, from *a-* 'not' + *klinein* 'to bend'.

ACLU ▶ **abbreviation for** American Civil Liberties Union.

acme /ˈakmi/ ▶ **noun** [in sing.] the point at which someone or something is best, perfect, or most successful: *physics is the acme of scientific knowledge.*
– ORIGIN late 16th cent.: from Greek *akmē* 'highest point'. Until the 18th cent. it was often consciously used as a Greek word and often written in Greek letters.

Acmeist /ˈakmiːɪst/ ▶ **adjective** denoting or relating to an early 20th century movement in Russian poetry which rejected the values of symbolism in favour of formal technique and clarity of exposition. Notable members were Anna Akhmatova and Osip Mandelstam.
▶ **noun** a member of this movement.
– DERIVATIVES **Acmeism** noun.

acne ▶ **noun** [mass noun] a skin condition characterized by red pimples on the skin, especially on the face, due to inflamed or infected sebaceous glands and prevalent chiefly among adolescents.
– DERIVATIVES **acned** adjective.
– ORIGIN mid 19th cent.: via modern Latin from Greek *aknas*, a misreading of *akmas*, accusative plural of *akmē* 'highest point, peak, or facial eruption'; compare with **ACME**.

acne rosacea ▶ **noun** see **ROSACEA**.

Acol /ˈeɪkɒl/ ▶ **noun** Bridge a commonly used British system of bidding designed to enable partners with weaker hands to find suitable contracts.
– ORIGIN 1930s: from *Acol* Road, Hampstead in London, the address of a house in which the system was devised.

acolyte /ˈakəlʌɪt/ ▶ **noun** an assistant or follower.
■a person assisting a priest in a religious service or procession.
– ORIGIN Middle English: from Old French *acolyt* or ecclesiastical Latin *acolytus*, from Greek *akolouthos* 'follower'.

Aconcagua /ˌakɒnˈkɑːgwə/ an extinct volcano in the Andes, on the border between Chile and Argentina, rising to 6,960 m (22,834 ft). It is the highest mountain in the western hemisphere.

aconite /ˈakənʌɪt/ ▶ **noun 1** a poisonous plant of the buttercup family, bearing hooded pink or purple flowers and found in temperate regions of the northern hemisphere.
● Genus *Aconitum*, family Ranunculaceae: many species, including monkshood and wolfsbane.
■[mass noun] an extract of such a plant, used as a poison or in pharmacy.
2 (also **winter aconite**) a small herbaceous Eurasian plant, widely cultivated for its yellow flowers in early spring.
● Genus *Eranthis*, family Ranunculaceae: several species, in particular *E. hyemalis*.
– ORIGIN mid 16th cent.: via French and Latin from Greek *akoniton*.

aconitine /əˈkɒnɪtiːn/ ▶ **noun** [mass noun] Chemistry a poisonous alkaloid obtained from monkshood and related plants.

acorn ▶ **noun** the fruit of the oak, a smooth oval nut in a rough cup-like base.
– ORIGIN Old English *æcern*, of Germanic origin; related to Dutch *aker*, also to **ACRE**, later associated with **OAK** and **CORN**[1].

acorn barnacle ▶ **noun** a stalkless barnacle that attaches itself, often in large numbers, to a variety of surfaces including rocks, ships, and marine animals.
● Genus *Balanus*, family Balanidae.

acorn squash ▶ **noun** a winter squash of a variety with ridged dark green to orange rind and yellow flesh.

acorn worm ▶ **noun** a burrowing worm-like marine animal of shallow waters. Its body consists of a proboscis, a collar, and a long trunk with gill slits, and contains a structure resembling a notochord.
● Class Enteropneusta, phylum Hemichordata.

acouchi /əˈkuːtʃi/ ▶ **noun** (pl. **acouchis**) a large forest rodent resembling an agouti, found in the Amazon basin.
● Genus *Myoprocta*, family Dasyproctidae: two species.
– ORIGIN late 18th cent.: from French, from Tupi.

acoustic /əˈkuːstɪk/ ▶ **adjective 1** relating to sound or the sense of hearing: *dogs have a much greater acoustic range than humans.*
■(of building materials) used for soundproofing or modifying sound: *acoustic tiles.* ■(of a device or system) utilizing sound energy in its operation. ■(of an explosive mine or other weapon) able to be set off by sound waves.
2 (of popular music or musical instruments) not having electrical amplification: *an acoustic guitar.*
▶ **noun 1** (usu. **acoustics**) the properties or qualities of a room or building that determine how sound is transmitted in it: *the Symphony Hall has perfect acoustics.*
■(**acoustic**) the acoustic properties or ambience of a sound recording or of a recording studio.
2 (**acoustics**) [treated as sing.] the branch of physics concerned with the properties of sound.
3 a musical instrument without electrical amplification, typically a guitar.
– DERIVATIVES **acoustical** adjective, **acoustically** adverb.
– ORIGIN mid 17th cent.: from Greek *akoustikos*, from *akouein* 'hear'.

acoustic coupler ▶ **noun** Electronics a modem which converts digital signals into audible signals and vice versa so that they can be transmitted and received over telephone lines. This typically takes the form of a sound-absorbent cradle, incorporating a microphone and loudspeaker, into which a telephone handset is placed.

acoustician /ˌakuːˈstɪʃ(ə)n/ ▶ **noun** an expert in the branch of physics concerned with the properties of sound.

acoustic impedance ▶ **noun** Physics the ratio of the pressure over an imaginary surface in a sound wave to the rate of particle flow across the surface.

acquaint ▶ **verb** [with obj.] (**acquaint someone with**) make someone aware of or familiar with: *new staff should be acquainted with fire exit routes* | *you need to acquaint yourself with the house style.*
■(**be acquainted**) be an acquaintance: *I am not* ***acquainted with*** *any young lady of that name* | *I'll leave you two to* ***get acquainted.***
– ORIGIN Middle English: from Old French *acointier* 'make known', from late Latin *accognitare*, from Latin *accognoscere*, from *ad-* 'to' + *cognoscere* 'come to know'.

acquaintance ▶ **noun 1** [mass noun] a person's knowledge or experience of something: *the pupils had little* ***acquaintance with*** *the language.*
■one's slight knowledge of or friendship with someone: *I renewed my* ***acquaintance with*** *Herbert.*
2 a person one knows slightly, but who is not a close friend: *a wide circle of friends and acquaintances.*
■[mass noun] such people considered collectively: *his extensive acquaintance included Oscar Wilde and Yeats.*
– PHRASES **make the acquaintance of** (or **make someone's acquaintance**) meet someone for the first time and come to know them slightly.
– DERIVATIVES **acquaintanceship** noun.
– ORIGIN Middle English (in the sense 'mutual knowledge, being acquainted'): from Old French *acointance*, from *acointier* 'make known' (see **ACQUAINT**).

acquaintance rape ▶ **noun** [mass noun] chiefly N. Amer. rape by a person who is known to the victim.

acquiesce /ˌakwɪˈɛs/ ▶ **verb** [no obj.] accept something reluctantly but without protest: *Sara* ***acquiesced in*** *his decision.*
– DERIVATIVES **acquiescence** noun.
– ORIGIN early 17th cent.: from Latin *acquiescere*, from *ad-* 'to, at' + *quiescere* 'to rest'.

acquiescent ▶ **adjective** (of a person) ready to accept something without protest, or to do what someone else wants.
– ORIGIN early 17th cent.: from Latin *acquiescent-* 'remaining at rest', from the verb *acquiescere* (see **ACQUIESCE**).

acquire ▶ **verb** [with obj.] buy or obtain (an asset or object) for oneself.
■learn or develop (a skill, habit, or quality): *you must*

a

acquire the rudiments of Greek | *I've acquired a taste for whisky.* ■ achieve (a particular reputation) as a result of one's behaviour or activities.

– PHRASES **acquired taste** a thing that one has come to like only through experience: *pumpkin pie is an acquired taste.* ■ a liking of this kind.

– DERIVATIVES **acquirable** adjective, **acquiree** noun (Finance), **acquirer** noun.

– ORIGIN late Middle English *acquere*, from Old French *aquerre*, based on Latin *acquirere* 'get in addition', from *ad-* 'to' + *quaerere* 'seek'. The English spelling was modified (*c.*1600) by association with the Latin word.

acquired character (also **acquired characteristic**) ▶ **noun** Biology a modification or change in an organ or tissue during the lifetime of an organism due to use, disuse, or environmental effects, and not inherited. See also **LAMARCK**.

acquired immune deficiency syndrome ▶ **noun** see **AIDS**.

acquirement ▶ **noun** [mass noun] the action of acquiring something: *the acquirement of self control.* ■ [count noun] something acquired, typically a skill.

acquisition /ˌakwɪˈzɪʃ(ə)n/ ▶ **noun** **1** an asset or object bought or obtained, typically by a library or museum.
■ an act of purchase of one company by another.
■ [mass noun] buying or obtaining assets or objects: *western culture places a high value on material acquisition.*
2 [mass noun] the learning or developing of a skill, habit, or quality: *the acquisition of management skills.*

– ORIGIN late Middle English (in the sense 'act of acquiring something'): from Latin *acquisitio(n-)*, from the verb *acquirere* (see **ACQUIRE**).

acquisition accounting ▶ **noun** [mass noun] a procedure in accounting in which the value of the assets of a company is changed from book to fair market level after a takeover.

acquisitive ▶ **adjective** excessively interested in acquiring money or material things.

– DERIVATIVES **acquisitively** adverb, **acquisitiveness** noun.

– ORIGIN mid 19th cent.: from French *acquisitif, -ive*, from late Latin *acquisitivus*, from Latin *acquisit-* 'acquired', from the verb *acquirere* (see **ACQUIRE**).

acquit ▶ **verb** (**acquitted**, **acquitting**) **1** [with obj.] (usu. **be acquitted**) free (someone) from a criminal charge by a verdict of not guilty: *she was acquitted on all counts* | *the jury* **acquitted** *Bream* **of** *murder.*
2 (**acquit oneself**) conduct oneself or perform in a specified way: *the goalkeeper acquitted himself well.*
■ (**acquit oneself of**) archaic discharge (a duty or responsibility).

– ORIGIN Middle English (originally in the sense 'pay a debt, discharge a liability'): from Old French *acquiter*, from medieval Latin *acquitare* 'pay a debt', from *ad-* 'to' + *quitare* 'set free'.

acquittal ▶ **noun** a judgement or verdict that a person is not guilty of the crime with which they have been charged.

acquittance ▶ **noun** Law, dated a written receipt attesting the settlement of a fine or debt.

– ORIGIN Middle English: from Old French, from *aquiter* 'discharge (a debt)' (see **ACQUIT**).

acrasia ▶ **noun** variant spelling of **AKRASIA**.

Acre **1** /ˈeɪkə/ an industrial seaport of Israel; pop. 39,100 (1982). Also called **Akko**.
2 /ˈɑːkrə/ a state of western Brazil, on the border with Peru; capital, Rio Branco.

acre /ˈeɪkə/ ▶ **noun** a unit of land area equal to 4,840 square yards (0.405 hectare).
■ (**acres of**) informal a large extent or amount of something: *acres of space.*

– DERIVATIVES **acred** adjective [in combination] *a many-acred park.*

– ORIGIN Old English *æcer* (denoting the amount of land a yoke of oxen could plough in a day), of Germanic origin; related to Dutch *akker* and German *Acker* 'field', from an Indo-European root shared by Sanskrit *ajra* 'field', Latin *ager*, and Greek *agros*.

acreage /ˈeɪk(ə)rɪdʒ/ ▶ **noun** [mass noun] an area of land, typically when used for agricultural purposes, but not necessarily measured in acres: *a 35% increase in net acreage* | [count noun] *a modest acreage in Drake's Prairie.*

acre-foot ▶ **noun** (pl. **acre-feet**) a unit of volume equal to the volume of a sheet of water one acre (0.405 hectare) in area and one foot (30.48 cm) in depth; 43,560 cubic feet (1233.5 cubic metres).

acrid /ˈakrɪd/ ▶ **adjective** having an unpleasantly bitter or pungent taste or smell: *acrid fumes.*
■ angry and bitter: *an acrid farewell.*

– DERIVATIVES **acridity** noun, **acridly** adverb.

– ORIGIN early 18th cent.: formed irregularly from Latin *acer, acri-* 'sharp, pungent' + **-ID**[1], probably influenced by *acid*.

acridine /ˈakrɪdiːn/ ▶ **noun** [mass noun] Chemistry a colourless solid compound obtained from coal tar, used in the manufacture of dyes and drugs.
● Chem. formula: $C_{13}H_9N$.

– ORIGIN late 19th cent.: coined in German from **ACRID** + **-INE**[4].

acriflavine /ˌakrɪˈfleɪvɪn, -iːn/ ▶ **noun** [mass noun] a bright orange-red dye derived from acridine, used as an antiseptic.

– ORIGIN early 20th cent.: formed irregularly from **ACRIDINE** + Latin *flavus* 'yellow' + **-INE**[4].

Acrilan /ˈakrɪlan/ ▶ **noun** [mass noun] trademark a synthetic acrylic textile fibre.

– ORIGIN 1950s: from **ACRYLIC** + Latin *lana* 'wool'.

acrimonious /ˌakrɪˈməʊnɪəs/ ▶ **adjective** (typically of speech or a debate) angry and bitter: *an acrimonious dispute about wages.*

– DERIVATIVES **acrimoniously** adverb.

– ORIGIN early 17th cent. (in the sense 'bitter, pungent'): from **ACRIMONY** + **-OUS**.

acrimony /ˈakrɪməni/ ▶ **noun** [mass noun] bitterness or ill feeling: *the AGM dissolved into acrimony.*

– ORIGIN mid 16th cent. (in the sense 'bitter taste or smell'): from French *acrimonie* or Latin *acrimonia*, from *acer, acri-* 'pungent, acrid'.

acrobat ▶ **noun** an entertainer who performs spectacular gymnastic feats.

– ORIGIN early 19th cent.: from French *acrobate*, from Greek *akrobatēs*, from *akrobatos* 'walking on tiptoe', from *akron* 'tip' + *bainein* 'to walk'.

acrobatic ▶ **adjective** performing, involving, or adept at spectacular gymnastic feats.

– DERIVATIVES **acrobatically** adverb.

acrobatics ▶ **plural noun** [usu. treated as sing.] spectacular gymnastic feats.

acrocyanosis /ˌakrə(ʊ)sʌɪəˈnəʊsɪs/ ▶ **noun** [mass noun] Medicine bluish or purple colouring of the hands and feet caused by slow circulation.

– ORIGIN late 19th cent.: from Greek *akron* 'tip' + **CYANOSIS**.

acrolect /ˈakrə(ʊ)lɛkt/ ▶ **noun** Linguistics the most prestigious dialect or variety of a particular language. Contrasted with **BASILECT**.

– DERIVATIVES **acrolectal** adjective.

– ORIGIN 1960s: from Greek *akron* 'summit' + *-lect* as in *dialect*.

acromegaly /ˌakrə(ʊ)ˈmɛɡəli/ ▶ **noun** [mass noun] Medicine abnormal growth of the hands, feet, and face, caused by overproduction of growth hormone by the pituitary gland.

– DERIVATIVES **acromegalic** /-mɪˈɡalɪk/ adjective.

– ORIGIN late 19th cent.: coined in French from Greek *akron* 'tip, extremity' + *megas, megal-* 'great'.

acronym /ˈakrənɪm/ ▶ **noun** a word formed from the initial letters of other words (e.g. *laser, Aids*).

– ORIGIN 1940s: from Greek *akron* 'end, tip' + *onuma* 'name', on the pattern of *homonym*.

acropetal /əˈkrɒpɪt(ə)l/ ▶ **adjective** Botany (of growth or development) upwards from the base or point of attachment. The opposite of **BASIPETAL**.
■ (of the movement of dissolved substances) outwards towards the shoot and root apices.

– DERIVATIVES **acropetally** adverb.

– ORIGIN late 19th cent.: from Greek *akron* 'tip' + Latin *petere* 'seek' + **-AL**.

acrophobia /ˌakrəˈfəʊbɪə/ ▶ **noun** [mass noun] extreme or irrational fear of heights.

– DERIVATIVES **acrophobic** adjective.

– ORIGIN late 19th cent.: from Greek *akron* 'summit' + **-PHOBIA**.

acropolis /əˈkrɒpəlɪs/ ▶ **noun** a citadel or fortified part of an ancient Greek city, typically one built on a hill.
■ (**the Acropolis**) the ancient citadel at Athens, containing the Parthenon and other notable buildings, mostly dating from the 5th century BC.

– ORIGIN Greek, from *akron* 'summit' + *polis* 'city'.

across ▶ **preposition** & **adverb** from one side to the other of (something):
■ expressing movement over a place or region: [as prep.] *I ran across the street* | *travelling across Europe* | [as adv.] *he had swum across.* ■ expressing position or orientation: [as prep.] *they lived across the street from one another* | *the bridge across the river* | [as adv.] *he looked across at me* | *halfway across, Jenny jumped.* ■ [as adv.] used with an expression of measurement: *mounds some 30 metres across.* ■ [as adv.] a crossword answer which reads horizontally: *19 across.*

– PHRASES **across the board** applying to all: *the cutbacks might be across the board.* ■ US (in horse racing) denoting a bet in which equal amounts are staked on the same horse to win, place, or show in a race. **across from** opposite: *she sat across from me.* **be** (or **get**) **across something** Austral. be or become fully cognizant of the details or complexity of an issue or situation.

– ORIGIN Middle English (as an adverb meaning 'in the form of a cross'): from Old French *a croix, en croix* 'in or on a cross', later regarded as being from **A-**[2] + **CROSS**.

acrostic /əˈkrɒstɪk/ ▶ **noun** a poem, word puzzle, or other composition in which certain letters in each line form a word or words.

– ORIGIN late 16th cent.: from French *acrostiche*, from Greek *akrostikhis*, from *akron* 'end' + *stikhos* 'row, line of verse'. The change in the ending was due to association with **-IC**.

Acrux /ˈeɪkrʌks/ Astronomy the star Alpha Crucis, which is the brightest star in the southern constellation Crux and the twelfth brightest in the sky.

– ORIGIN from *A* for alpha + **CRUX**.

acrylamide /əˈkrɪləmʌɪd/ ▶ **noun** [mass noun] Chemistry a colourless crystalline solid which readily forms water-soluble polymers.
● The amide of acrylic acid; chem. formula: $CH_2{=}CHCONH_2$.

– ORIGIN late 19th cent.: from **ACRYLIC** + **AMIDE**.

acrylic ▶ **adjective** (of synthetic resins and textile fibres) made from polymers of acrylic acid or acrylates: *a red acrylic jumper.*
■ of, relating to, or denoting paints based on acrylic resin as a medium: *acrylic colours* | *an acrylic painting.*
▶ **noun** **1** [mass noun] an acrylic textile fibre: *a sweater in four-ply acrylic.*
2 (often **acrylics**) an acrylic paint.

– ORIGIN mid 19th cent.: from the liquid aldehyde *acrolein* (from Latin *acer, acri-* 'pungent' + *ol(eum)* 'oil' + **-IN**[1]) + **-YL** + **-IC**.

acrylic acid ▶ **noun** [mass noun] Chemistry a pungent liquid organic acid which can be polymerized to make synthetic resins.
● Alternative name: **propenoic acid**; chem. formula: $CH_2CH{=}COOH$.

– DERIVATIVES **acrylate** noun.

acrylonitrile /ˌakrɪlə(ʊ)ˈnʌɪtrʌɪl/ ▶ **noun** [mass noun] Chemistry a pungent, toxic liquid, used in making artificial fibres and other polymers.
● The nitrile of acrylic acid; chem. formula: $CH_2{=}CHCN$.

ACT ▶ **abbreviation for** ■ advance corporation tax. ■ Australian Capital Territory.

act ▶ **verb** [no obj.] **1** take action; do something: *they urged Washington to act* | [with infinitive] *governments must act to reduce pollution.*
■ (**act on**) take action according to or in the light of: *I shall certainly act on his suggestion.* ■ (**act for**) take action in order to bring about: *one's ability to act for community change.* ■ (**act for/on behalf of**) represent (someone) on a contractual, legal, or paid basis: *he chose a solicitor to act for him.* ■ (**act from/out of**) be motivated by: *you acted from greed.*
2 [with adverbial] behave in the way specified: *they challenged a man who was seen acting suspiciously* | *he acts as if he owned the place.*
■ (**act as/like**) behave in the manner of: *try to act like civilized adults.*
3 (**act as**) fulfil the function or serve the purpose of: *they need volunteers to act as foster-parents.*
■ have the effect of: *a five-year sentence will act as a deterrent.*
4 take effect; have a particular effect: *bacteria* **act on** *proteins and sugar.*
5 perform a fictional role in a play, film, or television: *she acted in her first professional role at the age of six.*
■ [with obj.] perform (a part or role): *he acted the role of the dragon* | *doctors do not always* **act out** *the role of doctor.* ■ [with complement] behave so as to appear to be; pretend to be: *I acted dumb at first.* ■ [with obj.] (**act something out**) perform a narrative as if it were a play: *encouraging pupils to act out the stories.* ■ [with obj.] (**act something out**) Psychoanalysis express repressed

emotion or impulses in overt behaviour as a defensive substitute for conscious recall, typical of some behavioural disorders.

▶**noun 1** a thing done; a deed: *a criminal act | the act of writing down one's thoughts | an act of heroism.*
▪(**Acts** or **Acts of the Apostles**) a New Testament book immediately following the Gospels and relating the history of the early Church.
2 [in sing.] a pretence: *she was putting on an act and laughing a lot.*
▪[with adj. or noun modifier] a particular type of behaviour or routine: *he did his Sir Galahad act.*
3 Law a written ordinance of Parliament, Congress, etc.: *the 1989 Children's Act.*
▪a document attesting a legal transaction. ▪(often **acts**) dated the recorded decisions or proceedings of a committee or an academic body.
4 a main division of a play, ballet, or opera.
▪a set performance: *her one-woman poetry act.* ▪a performing group: *an act called the Apple Blossom Sisters.*

– PHRASES **act of God** an instance of uncontrollable natural forces in operation (often used in insurance claims). **act of grace** a privilege or concession that cannot be claimed as a right. **catch someone in the act** (usu. **be caught in the act**) surprise someone in the process of doing something wrong: *the thieves were caught in the act.* **clean up one's act** behave in a more acceptable manner. **get one's act together** informal galvanize oneself into organizing one's life or affairs effectively. **get** (or **be**) **in on the act** informal become or be involved in a particular activity, in order to gain profit or advantage. **a hard** (or **tough**) **act to follow** an achievement or performance which sets a standard regarded as being hard for others to measure up to. **in the act of** in the process of: *they photographed him in the act of reading other people's mail.*

– DERIVATIVES **actability** noun, **actable** adjective.

– ORIGIN late Middle English: from Latin *actus* 'event, thing done', *act-* 'done', from the verb *agere*, reinforced by the French noun *acte*.

▶**act up 1** (of a thing) fail to function properly: *the plane's engine was acting up.* ▪(of a person) misbehave. **2** (of a person) take over or be promoted to a more senior position, typically on a temporary basis.

Actaeon /akˈtiːən, ˈaktɪən/ Greek Mythology a hunter who, because he accidentally saw Artemis bathing, was changed by her into a stag and killed by his own hounds.

actant /ˈaktənt/ ▶**noun 1** Grammar a noun or noun phrase involved in the action expressed by a verb.
2 (in literary theory) a person, creature, or object playing any of a set of active roles in a narrative.

ACTH Biochemistry ▶**abbreviation for** adrenocorticotrophic hormone.

actin /ˈaktɪn/ ▶**noun** [mass noun] Biochemistry a protein which forms (together with myosin) the contractile filaments of muscle cells, and is also involved in motion in other types of cell.
– ORIGIN 1940: from Greek *aktis, aktin-* 'ray' + **-IN**[1].

acting ▶**noun** [mass noun] the art or occupation of performing fictional roles in plays, films, or television.
▶**adjective** [attrib.] temporarily doing the duties of another person: *an acting director.*

acting pilot officer ▶**noun** a rank in the RAF above warrant officer and below pilot officer.

actinian /akˈtɪnɪən/ ▶**noun** Zoology a sea anemone.
– ORIGIN mid 18th cent.: from the modern Latin genus name *Actinia* (from Greek *aktis, aktin-* 'ray') + **-AN**.

actinic /akˈtɪnɪk/ ▶**adjective** technical (of light or lighting) able to cause photochemical reactions, as in photography, through having a significant short wavelength or ultraviolet component.
▪relating to or caused by such light.
– DERIVATIVES **actinism** noun.
– ORIGIN mid 19th cent.: from Greek *aktis, aktin-* 'ray' + **-IC**.

actinide /ˈaktɪnʌɪd/ ▶**noun** Chemistry any of the series of fifteen metallic elements from actinium (atomic number 89) to lawrencium (atomic number 103) in the periodic table. They are all radioactive, the heavier members being extremely unstable and not of natural occurrence.
– ORIGIN 1940s: from **ACTINIUM** + **-IDE**, on the pattern of *lanthanide*.

actinium /akˈtɪnɪəm/ ▶**noun** [mass noun] the chemical element of atomic number 89, a radioactive metallic element of the actinide series. It is rare in nature, occurring as an impurity in uranium ores. (Symbol: **Ac**)
– ORIGIN early 20th cent.: from Greek *aktis, aktin-* 'ray' + **-IUM**.

actinolite /akˈtɪnəlʌɪt/ ▶**noun** [mass noun] a green mineral of the amphibole group containing calcium, magnesium, and iron and occurring chiefly in metamorphic rocks and as a form of asbestos.
– ORIGIN late 18th cent.: from Greek *aktis, aktin-* 'ray' + *lithos* 'stone' (because of the ray-like crystals).

actinometer /ˌaktɪˈnɒmɪtə/ ▶**noun** Physics an instrument for measuring the intensity of radiation, typically ultraviolet radiation.
– ORIGIN mid 19th cent.: from Greek *aktis, aktin-* 'ray' + **-METER**.

actinomorphic /ˌaktɪnə(ʊ)ˈmɔːfɪk/ ▶**adjective** Biology characterized by radial symmetry, such as a starfish or the flower of a daisy. Compare with **ZYGOMORPHIC**.
– DERIVATIVES **actinomorphy** noun.
– ORIGIN late 19th cent.: from Greek *aktis, aktin-* 'ray' + *morphē* 'form' + **-IC**.

actinomycete /ˌaktɪnə(ʊ)ˈmʌɪsiːt/ ▶**noun** a bacterium of an order of typically non-motile filamentous forms. They include the economically important streptomycetes, and were formerly regarded as fungi.
• Order Actinomycetales; Gram-positive.
– ORIGIN 1920s (originally only in the plural): modern Latin, from Greek *aktis, aktin-* 'ray' + *mukētes*, plural of *mukēs* 'fungus'.

action ▶**noun 1** [mass noun] the fact or process of doing something, typically to achieve an aim: *demanding tougher action against terrorism | if there is a breach of regulations, we will* ***take action.***
▪the way in which something such as a chemical has an effect or influence: *the seeds require the catalytic action of water to release heat.* ▪short for **INDUSTRIAL ACTION**: *the rank and file want to call the action off.* ▪armed conflict: *servicemen listed as* ***missing in action*** *during the war.* ▪[count noun] a military engagement: *a rearguard action.* ▪the events represented in a story or play: *the action is set in a country house.* ▪informal exciting or notable activity: *the weekend sporting action begins on Saturday | people in media want to be* ***where the action is.*** ▪[as exclamation] used by a film director as a command to begin: *lights, camera, action.*
2 a thing done; an act: *I would not be responsible for my actions if I saw him.*
▪a legal process; a lawsuit: *a civil action for damages.* ▪a gesture or movement.
3 [usu. with modifier] a manner or style of doing something, typically the way in which a mechanism works or a person moves: *a high paddle action in canoeing.*
▪the mechanism that makes a machine or instrument work: *a piano with an escapement action.*
▶**verb** [with obj.] (usu. **be actioned**) take action on; deal with: *your request will be actioned.*
– PHRASES **actions speak louder than words** proverb what someone actually does means more than what they say they will do. **go into action** start work or activity. **in action** engaged in a certain activity; in operation: *watching him in action, normal workers are left in awe.* **man** (or **woman**) **of action** a person whose life is characterized by physical activity or deeds rather than by words or intellectual matters. **out of action** temporarily unable to engage in a certain activity; not working: *a heart attack put him out of action.* **put into action** put into effect; carry out.
– ORIGIN late Middle English: via Old French from Latin *actio(n-)*, from *agere* 'do, act'.

actionable ▶**adjective** Law giving sufficient reason to take legal action: *their remarks were bordering on actionable.*

action at a distance ▶**noun** [mass noun] Physics, chiefly historical the exertion of force by one body on another separated from the first by empty space.

action committee (also **action group**) ▶**noun** a body formed to campaign politically, especially on a particular issue.

Action Directe /ˌaksjɔ̃ dɪˈrɛkt, French aksjɔ̃ dirɛkt/ a group of extreme left-wing French terrorists.
– ORIGIN 1980s: French, literally 'direct action'.

actioner ▶**noun** informal a film predominantly consisting of exciting action and adventure.

action figure ▶**noun** a doll representing a person or fictional character known for vigorous action, such as a soldier or superhero.

action for declarator ▶**noun** see **DECLARATOR**.

action-packed ▶**adjective** informal full of activity or excitement: *an action-packed programme of events.*

action painting ▶**noun** [mass noun] a technique and style of abstract painting in which paint is randomly splashed, thrown, or poured on to the canvas. It was made famous by Jackson Pollock, and formed part of the more general movement of abstract expressionism.

action point ▶**noun** a specific proposal for action to be taken, typically one arising from a discussion or meeting.

action potential ▶**noun** Physiology the change in electrical potential associated with the passage of an impulse along the membrane of a muscle cell or nerve cell.

action replay ▶**noun** Brit. a playback of part of a television broadcast, typically one in slow motion of an incident in a sporting event.
▪informal an exact repetition of an action or event.

action research ▶**noun** [mass noun] studies carried out in the course of an activity or occupation, typically in the field of education, to improve the methods and approach of those involved.

action stations ▶**plural noun** chiefly Brit. the positions taken up by military personnel in preparation for action (often as a command or signal to prepare for action).

Actium, Battle of /ˈaktɪəm/ a naval battle which took place in 31 BC off the promontory of Actium in western Greece, in the course of which Octavian defeated Mark Antony.

activate ▶**verb** [with obj.] make (something) active or operative: *fumes from cooking are enough to activate the alarm.*
▪convert (a substance, molecule, etc.) into a reactive form: [as adj. **activated**] *activated chlorine.*
– DERIVATIVES **activation** noun, **activator** noun.

activated carbon (also **activated charcoal**) ▶**noun** [mass noun] charcoal that has been heated or otherwise treated to increase its adsorptive power.

activated sludge ▶**noun** [mass noun] aerated sewage containing aerobic micro-organisms which help to break it down.

activation analysis ▶**noun** [mass noun] Chemistry a technique of analysis in which atoms of a particular element in a sample are made radioactive, typically by irradiation with neutrons, and their concentration is then determined radiologically.

activation energy ▶**noun** Chemistry the minimum quantity of energy which the reacting species must possess in order to undergo a specified reaction.

active ▶**adjective 1** (of a person) engaging or ready to engage in physically energetic pursuits: *I needed to change my lifestyle and become more active.*
▪moving or tending to move about vigorously or frequently: *active fish need a larger tank.* ▪characterized by energetic activity: *they enjoyed an active social life | an active outdoors holiday.* ▪(of a person's mind or imagination) alert and lively.
2 doing things for an organization, cause, or campaign, rather than simply giving it one's support: *she was an active member of the society | he had never been very* ***active in*** *the affairs of the Institute.*
▪(of a person) participating or engaged in a particular sphere or activity: *sexually active teenagers.* ▪[predic.] (of a person or animal) pursuing their usual occupation or activity, typically at a particular place or time: *tigers are active mainly at night.*
3 working; operative: *the old watermill was active until 1960.*
▪(of a bank account) in continuous use. ▪(of an electric circuit) capable of modifying its state or characteristics automatically in response to input or feedback. ▪(of a volcano) that is erupting or has erupted in historical times. ▪(of a disease) in which the symptoms are manifest; not in remission or latent: *active colitis.* ▪having a chemical or biological effect on something: *active ingredients.*
4 Grammar denoting a voice of verbs in which the subject is typically the person or thing performing the action and which can take a direct object (e.g. *she loved him* as opposed to *he was loved*). The opposite of **PASSIVE**.
▶**noun** Grammar an active form of a verb.

■(**the active**) the active voice.
– DERIVATIVES **actively** adverb.

active birth ▶ noun [mass noun] childbirth during which the mother is encouraged to be as active as possible, mainly by moving around freely and assuming any position which feels comfortable.

active carbon (also **active charcoal**) ▶ noun another term for ACTIVATED CARBON.

active citizen ▶ noun a person who actively takes responsibility and initiative in areas of public concern such as crime prevention and the local community.
– DERIVATIVES **active citizenship** noun.

active duty ▶ noun [mass noun] the playing of a direct role in the operational work of the police or armed forces as opposed to doing administrative work.

active immunity ▶ noun [mass noun] Physiology the immunity which results from the production of antibodies by the immune system in response to the presence of an antigen. Compare with PASSIVE IMMUNITY.

active layer ▶ noun Geography the seasonally thawed surface layer above permafrost.

active list ▶ noun a list of the officers in an armed service who are liable to be called on for duty.

active matrix ▶ noun Electronics a display system in which each pixel is individually controlled.

active service ▶ noun [mass noun] direct participation in military operations as a member of the armed forces.

active site ▶ noun Biochemistry a region on an enzyme that binds to a protein or other substance during a reaction.

active transport ▶ noun [mass noun] Biology the movement of ions or molecules across a cell membrane into a region of higher concentration, assisted by enzymes and requiring energy.

activism ▶ noun [mass noun] the policy or action of using vigorous campaigning to bring about political or social change.
– DERIVATIVES **activist** noun & adjective.

activity ▶ noun (pl. **-ies**) **1** [mass noun] the condition in which things are happening or being done: *there has been a sustained level of activity in the economy.*
■busy or vigorous action or movement: *the room was a hive of activity.*
2 (usu. **activities**) a thing that a person or group does or has done: *the firm's marketing activities.*
■a recreational pursuit or pastime: *a range of sporting activities.* ■(**activities**) actions taken by a group in order to achieve their aims: *the police were investigating communist activities.*
3 the degree to which something displays its characteristic property or behaviour: *abnormal liver enzyme activities.*
■Chemistry a thermodynamic quantity representing the effective concentration of a particular component in a solution or other system, equal to its concentration multiplied by an **activity coefficient**.
– ORIGIN late Middle English: from French *activité* or late Latin *activitas*, from Latin *act-* 'done', from the verb *agere*.

act of contrition ▶ noun (in the Roman Catholic Church) a penitential prayer.

Act of Settlement, Act of Uniformity, etc. see SETTLEMENT, ACT OF; UNIFORMITY, ACT OF, etc.

actomyosin /ˌaktə(ʊ)ˈmʌɪəsɪn/ ▶ noun [mass noun] Biochemistry a complex of actin and myosin of which the contractile protein filaments of muscle tissue are composed.
– ORIGIN 1940s: from ACTIN + MYOSIN.

actor ▶ noun a person whose profession is acting on the stage, in films, or on television.
■a person who behaves in a way that is not genuine: *in war one must be a good actor.* ■a participant in an action or process: *employers are key actors within industrial relations.*
– ORIGIN late Middle English (originally denoting an agent or administrator): from Latin, 'doer, actor', from *agere* 'do, act'. The theatre sense dates from the 16th cent.

actor-manager ▶ noun a person who is both manager and actor in a theatre company.

Actors' Studio an acting workshop in New York City, founded in 1947 by Elia Kazan and others, and a leading centre of method acting.

actress ▶ noun a female actor.

actressy ▶ adjective characteristic of an actress in being self-consciously theatrical or emotionally volatile: *her actressy manner.*

actual /ˈaktʃʊəl, -tjʊəl/ ▶ adjective **1** existing in fact, typically as contrasted with what was intended, expected, or believed: *the estimate was much less than the actual cost* | *those were his actual words.*
■used to emphasize the important aspect of something: *the book could be condensed into half the space, but what of the actual content?*
2 existing now; current: *using actual income to measure expected income.*
– PHRASES **in actual fact** used to emphasize a comment, typically one that modifies or contradicts a previous statement: *people talk as if he was a monster—in actual fact he was a very kind guy.*
your actual —— informal the real, genuine, or important thing specified: *is this a drop of your actual feminine intuition?*
– ORIGIN Middle English: from Old French *actuel* 'active, practical', from late Latin *actualis*, from *actus* (see ACT).

actual bodily harm (abbrev.: **ABH**) ▶ noun [mass noun] Law minor injury, such as bruising, inflicted on a person by the deliberate action of another, considered less serious than grievous bodily harm.

actuality ▶ noun (pl. **-ies**) [mass noun] actual existence, typically as contrasted with what was intended, expected, or believed: *the building looked as impressive in actuality as it did in magazines.*
■(**actualities**) existing conditions or facts: *the grim actualities of prison life.*
– ORIGIN late Middle English (in the sense 'activity'): from Old French *actualite* or medieval Latin *actualitas*, from *actualis* 'active, practical', from *actus* (see ACT).

actualize (also **-ise**) ▶ verb [with obj.] make a reality of: *he had actualized his dream and achieved the world record.*
– DERIVATIVES **actualization** noun.

actually ▶ adverb **1** as the truth or facts of a situation: *we must pay attention to what young people are actually doing* | *the time actually worked on a job.*
2 [sentence adverb] used to emphasize that something someone has said or done is surprising: *he actually expected me to be pleased about it!*
■used when expressing an opinion, typically one that is not expected: *'Actually,' she said icily, 'I don't care who you go out with.'* ■used when expressing a contradictory opinion or correcting someone: *'Tom's happy anyway.' 'He isn't, actually, not any more.'* ■used to introduce a new topic or to add information to a previous statement: *he had a thick Cockney accent—he sounded like my grandad actually.*

actuary /ˈaktʃʊəri, -tjʊ-/ ▶ noun (pl. **-ies**) a person who compiles and analyses statistics and uses them to calculate insurance risks and premiums.
– DERIVATIVES **actuarial** adjective, **actuarially** (also **actuarily**) adverb.
– ORIGIN mid 16th cent. (originally denoting a clerk or registrar of a court): from Latin *actuarius* 'bookkeeper', from *actus* (see ACT). The current sense dates from the mid 19th cent.

actuate /ˈaktʃʊeɪt, -tjʊ-/ ▶ verb **1** [with obj.] cause (a machine or device) to operate: *the pendulum actuates an electrical switch.*
2 (usu. **be actuated**) cause (someone) to act in a particular way; motivate: *the defendants were actuated by malice.*
– DERIVATIVES **actuation** noun, **actuator** noun.
– ORIGIN late 16th cent.: from medieval Latin *actuat-* 'carried out, caused to operate', from the verb *actuare*, from Latin *actus* (see ACT). The original sense was 'carry out in practice', later 'stir into activity, enliven'; sense 1 dates from the mid 17th cent.

actus reus /ˌaktəs ˈreɪəs/ ▶ noun [mass noun] Law action or conduct which is a constituent element of a crime, as opposed to the mental state of the accused. Compare with MENS REA.
– ORIGIN Latin, literally 'guilty act'.

acuity /əˈkjuːɪti/ ▶ noun [mass noun] sharpness or keenness of thought, vision, or hearing: *intellectual acuity* | *visual acuity.*
– ORIGIN late Middle English: from Old French *acuite* or medieval Latin *acuitas*, from Latin *acuere* 'sharpen' (see ACUTE).

aculeate /əˈkjuːlɪət/ ▶ adjective **1** Entomology (of an insect) having a sting.
2 Botany sharply pointed; prickly.
▶ noun Entomology a stinging insect of a group that includes the bees, wasps, and ants.
●Section Aculeata, suborder Apocrita, order Hymenoptera.
– ORIGIN mid 17th cent.: from Latin *aculeatus*, from *aculeus* 'a sting', diminutive of *acus* 'needle'.

acumen /ˈakjʊmən, əˈkjuːmən/ ▶ noun [mass noun] the ability to make good judgements and take quick decisions, typically in a particular domain: *business acumen.*
– ORIGIN late 16th cent.: from Latin, 'sharpness, point', from *acuere* 'sharpen' (see ACUTE).

acuminate /əˈkjuːmɪnət/ ▶ adjective Biology (of a plant or animal structure, e.g. a leaf) tapering to a point.
– ORIGIN late 16th cent.: from late Latin *acuminatus* 'pointed', from *acuminare* 'sharpen to a point', from *acuere* 'sharpen' (see ACUTE).

acupressure /ˈakjʊˌprɛʃə/ ▶ noun [mass noun] a form of alternative therapy in which manual pressure is used to stimulate supposed energy points on the body.
– ORIGIN 1950s: blend of ACUPUNCTURE and PRESSURE.

acupuncture /ˈakjʊˌpʌŋ(k)tʃə/ ▶ noun [mass noun] a system of complementary medicine in which fine needles are inserted in the skin at specific points along what are considered to be lines of energy (meridians), used in the treatment of various physical and mental conditions.
– DERIVATIVES **acupuncturist** noun.
– ORIGIN late 17th cent.: from Latin *acu* 'with a needle' + PUNCTURE.

acushla /əˈkʊʃlə/ ▶ noun Irish, dated an affectionate form of address.
– ORIGIN mid 19th cent.: from Irish *a chuisle* (moi chroi) 'O pulse (of my heart)!'

acutance /əˈkjuːt(ə)ns/ ▶ noun [mass noun] the sharpness of a photographic or printed image.
– ORIGIN 1950s: from ACUTE + -ANCE.

acute ▶ adjective **1** (of a bad, difficult, or unwelcome situation or phenomenon) present or experienced to a severe or intense degree: *an acute housing shortage* | *the problem is acute and getting worse.*
■(of a disease or its symptoms) of short duration but typically severe: *acute appendicitis.* Often contrasted with CHRONIC. ■ denoting or designed for patients with such conditions: *an acute ward* | *acute patients.*
2 having or showing a perceptive understanding or insight; shrewd: *an acute awareness of changing fashions.*
■(of a physical sense or faculty) highly developed; keen: *an acute sense of smell.*
3 (of an angle) less than 90°.
■having a sharp end; pointed.
4 (of a sound) high; shrill.
▶ noun short for ACUTE ACCENT.
– DERIVATIVES **acutely** adverb, **acuteness** noun.
– ORIGIN late Middle English (describing a disease or its symptoms): from Latin *acutus*, past participle of *acuere* 'sharpen', from *acus* 'needle'.

acute abdomen ▶ noun Medicine a condition of severe abdominal pain, usually requiring emergency surgery, caused by acute disease of or injury to the internal organs.

acute accent ▶ noun a mark (´) placed over certain letters in some languages to indicate a feature such as altered sound quality (e.g. in *fiancée*).

acute rheumatism ▶ noun another term for RHEUMATIC FEVER.

ACW ▶ abbreviation for aircraftwoman.

-acy ▶ suffix forming nouns of state or quality: *celibacy* | *lunacy.*
– ORIGIN variant of -CY, from Latin *-atia* (medieval Latin *-acia*), or from Greek *-ateia.*

acyclic /eɪˈsʌɪklɪk, -ˈsɪk-/ ▶ adjective not displaying or forming part of a cycle.
■(of a woman) not having a menstrual cycle. ■ Chemistry (of a compound or molecule) containing no rings of atoms.

acyclovir /eɪˈsʌɪklə(ʊ)ˌvʌɪə/ ▶ noun [mass noun] Medicine an antiviral drug used chiefly in the treatment of herpes and Aids. Also called ZOVIRAX (trademark).
– ORIGIN 1970s: from *acycl(ic)* + *vir(al DNA).*

acyl /ˈeɪsʌɪl, ˈasɪl/ ▶ noun [as modifier] Chemistry of or

a

denoting a radical of general formula —C(O)R, where R is an alkyl group, derived from a carboxylic acid: *acyl groups.*
– ORIGIN late 19th cent.: coined in German, from Latin *acidus* (see **ACID**) + **-YL**.

acylate /ˈeɪsʌleɪt, ˈasɪl-/ ▶ **verb** [with obj.] Chemistry introduce an acyl group into (a molecule or compound): [as adj. **acylated**] *an acylated glycine derivative.*
– DERIVATIVES **acylation** noun.

AD ▶ **abbreviation for** Anno Domini (used to indicate that a date comes the specified number of years after the traditional date of Christ's birth).

USAGE AD is normally written in small capitals and should be placed before the numerals, as in AD *375* (not *375* AD). The reason for this is that AD is an abbreviation of *anno domini*, which means 'in the year of our Lord'. However, when the date is spelled out, it is normal to write *the third century* AD (**not** AD *the third century*). Compare with **BC**.

A/D Electronics ▶ **abbreviation for** analogue to digital.

ad ▶ **noun** informal **1** an advertisement.
2 Tennis advantage.
– ORIGIN mid 19th cent.: abbreviation.

ad- ▶ **prefix** denoting motion or direction to: *advance* | *adduce.*
■ reduction or change into: *adapt* | *adulterate.* ■ addition, increase, or intensification: *adjunct.*
– ORIGIN from Latin *ad* 'to'; in the 16th cent. the use of *ad-* and its variants was extended to replace *a-* from a different origin such as Latin *ab-* (e.g. *advance,* from French *avancer* based on late Latin *abante* 'in front').

USAGE **Ad-** is also found assimilated in the following forms: **a-** before **sc, sp, st**; **ac-** before **c, k, q**; **af-** before **f**; **ag-** before **g**; **al-** before **l**; **an-** before **n**; **ap-** before **p**; **ar-** before **r**; **as-** before **s**; **at-** before **t**.

-ad[1] /ad, əd/ ▶ **suffix** forming nouns: **1** in collective numerals: *myriad* | *triad.*
2 in names of females in classical mythology, such as *dryad* and *naiad.*
3 in names of poems and similar compositions: *Iliad* | *jeremiad.*
4 forming names of members of some taxonomic groupings: *bromeliad.*
– ORIGIN from the Greek ending *-as, -ad-.*

-ad[2] /əd/ ▶ **suffix** forming nouns such as *ballad, salad.* Compare with **-ADE**[1].
– ORIGIN from French *-ade.*

Ada /ˈeɪdə/ ▶ **noun** [mass noun] a high-level computer programming language used chiefly in real-time computerized control systems, e.g. for aircraft navigation.
– ORIGIN 1980s: named after *Ada* Lovelace (see **LOVELACE**[1]).

adage /ˈadɪdʒ/ ▶ **noun** a proverb or short statement expressing a general truth.
– ORIGIN mid 16th cent.: from French, from Latin *adagium* 'saying', based on an early form of *aio* 'I say'.

adagio /əˈdɑː(d)ʒɪəʊ/ Music ▶ **adverb** & **adjective** (especially as a direction) in slow time.
▶ **noun** (pl. **-os**) a movement, passage, or composition marked to be performed adagio.
– ORIGIN Italian, from *ad agio* 'at ease'.

Adam[1] (in the biblical and Koranic traditions) the name of the first man. According to the Book of Genesis, Adam was created by God as the progenitor of the human race and lived with Eve in the garden of Eden.
– PHRASES **not know someone from Adam** not know or be completely unable to recognize the person in question.
– ORIGIN from Hebrew *'ādām* 'man', later taken to be a name.

Adam[2], Robert (1728–92), Scottish architect. He was influenced by neoclassical theory and, assisted by his brother **James** (1730–94), he initiated a lighter, more decorative style than the Palladianism favoured by the British architecture of the previous half-century.

adamant ▶ **adjective** refusing to be persuaded or to change one's mind: *he is* **adamant that** *he is not going to resign.*
▶ **noun** [mass noun] archaic a legendary rock or mineral to which many, often contradictory, properties were attributed, formerly associated with diamond or lodestone.
– DERIVATIVES **adamance** noun, **adamancy** noun, **adamantly** adverb.
– ORIGIN Old English (as a noun), from Old French *adamaunt-,* via Latin from Greek *adamas, adamant-,* 'untameable, invincible' (later used to denote the hardest metal or stone, hence diamond), from *a-* 'not' + *daman* 'to tame'. The phrase *to be adamant* dates from the 1930s, although adjectival use had been implied in such collocations as 'an adamant heart' since the 16th cent.

adamantine /ˌadəˈmantʌɪn/ ▶ **adjective** poetic/literary unbreakable: *adamantine chains* | figurative *her adamantine will.*

Adams[1], Ansel (Easton) (1902–84), American photographer, noted for his black-and-white photographs of American landscapes.

Adams[2], John (1735–1826), American Federalist statesman, 2nd President of the US 1797–1801; father of John Quincy Adams. He helped draft the Declaration of Independence (1776).

Adams[3], John Couch (1819–92), English astronomer. In 1843 he calculated the position of a supposed planet beyond Uranus; similar calculations performed by Le Verrier resulted in the discovery of Neptune three years later.

Adams[4], John Quincy (1767–1848), American statesman, 6th President of the US 1825–9; eldest son of John Adams.

Adam's ale ▶ **noun** [mass noun] dated, humorous water.

Adam's apple ▶ **noun** the projection at the front of the neck formed by the thyroid cartilage of the larynx, often prominent in men.
– ORIGIN mid 18th cent.: so named from the notion that a piece of the forbidden fruit became lodged in Adam's throat.

Adam's Bridge a line of shoals lying between NW Sri Lanka and the SE coast of Tamil Nadu in India, separating the Palk Strait from the Gulf of Mannar.

Adam's needle ▶ **noun** another term for **YUCCA**.

Adam's Peak a mountain in south central Sri Lanka, rising to 2,243 m (7,360 ft). A rock near the top bears a depression resembling a footprint, which is the focus of religious pilgrimages.

Adana /ˈadənə/ a town in southern Turkey, capital of a province of the same name; pop. 916,150 (1990).

adapt ▶ **verb** [with obj.] make (something) suitable for a new use or purpose; modify: *hospitals have had to be* **adapted for** *modern medical practice* | [with obj. and infinitive] *the policies can be adapted to suit individual needs and requirements.*
■ [no obj.] become adjusted to new conditions: *a large organization can be slow to* **adapt** *to change.* ■ alter (a text) to make it suitable for filming, broadcasting, or the stage: *the film was* **adapted from** *a Turgenev short story.*
– DERIVATIVES **adaptive** adjective.
– ORIGIN late Middle English: from French *adapter,* from Latin *adaptare,* from *ad-* 'to' + *aptare* (from *aptus* 'fit').

adaptable ▶ **adjective** able to adjust to new conditions: *rats are highly* **adaptable to** *change.*
■ able to be modified for a new use or purpose.
– DERIVATIVES **adaptability** noun, **adaptably** adverb.

adaptation ▶ **noun** [mass noun] the action or process of adapting or being adapted: *the adaptation of teaching strategy to meet students' needs* | [count noun] *adaptations to the school curriculum.*
■ [count noun] a film, television drama, or stage play that has been adapted from a written work: *a three-part adaptation of* Hard Times. ■ [count noun] Biology a change by which an organism or species becomes better suited to its environment. ■ the process of making such changes: *biochemical adaptation in parasites.*
– ORIGIN early 17th cent.: from French, from late Latin *adaptatio(n-),* from Latin *adaptare* (see **ADAPT**).

adaptationism ▶ **noun** [mass noun] Biology the axiom or assumption that each feature of an organism is the result of evolutionary adaptation for a particular function.
– DERIVATIVES **adaptationist** noun & adjective.

adaption ▶ **noun** another term for **ADAPTATION**.

adaptive expectations hypothesis ▶ **noun** Economics the hypothesis that expectations of future values of a variable can be based primarily on its values in the recent past. Compare with **RATIONAL EXPECTATIONS HYPOTHESIS**.

adaptive radiation ▶ **noun** [mass noun] Biology the diversification of a group of organisms into forms filling different ecological niches.

adaptogen /əˈdaptədʒ(ə)n/ ▶ **noun** (in herbal medicine) a natural substance considered to help the body adapt to stress and to exert a normalizing effect upon bodily processes. The best-known example is ginseng.
– DERIVATIVES **adaptogenic** adjective.
– ORIGIN 1960s: from Russian (see **ADAPT**, **-GEN**).

adaptor (also **adapter**) ▶ **noun** **1** a device for connecting pieces of equipment that cannot be connected directly.
■ Brit. a device for connecting several electric plugs to one socket.
2 a person who adapts a text to make it suitable for filming, broadcasting, or the stage.

Adar /aˈdɑː/ ▶ **noun** (in the Jewish calendar) the sixth month of the civil and twelfth of the religious year, usually coinciding with parts of February and March. It is known in leap years as **Second Adar**.
■ an intercalary month preceding this in leap years, also called **First Adar**.
– ORIGIN from Hebrew *'ăḏār.*

ADAS /ˈeɪdas/ ▶ **abbreviation for** Agricultural Development and Advisory Service, set up in Britain in 1971.

adaxial /adˈaksɪəl/ ▶ **adjective** Botany facing toward the stem of a plant (in particular denoting the upper surface of a leaf). The opposite of **ABAXIAL**.

ADC ▶ **abbreviation for** ■ aide-de-camp. ■ analogue to digital converter.

ADD ▶ **abbreviation for** ■ analogue digital digital, indicating that a music recording was made in analogue format before being mastered and stored digitally. ■ attention deficit disorder.

add ▶ **verb** [with obj.] **1** join (something) to something else so as to increase the size, number, or amount: *a new wing was* **added to** *the building* | *some box offices now* **add on** *a convenience charge* | [as adj. **added**] *one vitamin tablet daily will give added protection.*
■ [no obj.] (**add up**) increase in amount, number, or degree: *watch those air miles add up!* ■ put or mix (an ingredient) together with another as one of the stages in the preparation of a dish: **add** *the flour* **to** *the eggs, stirring continuously.* ■ put (something) in or on something else so as to improve or alter its quality or nature: *chlorine is* **added to** *the water to kill bacteria* | [as adj. **added**] *the fruit juice contains no added sugar.* ■ contribute (an enhancing quality) to something: *the suite will* **add** *a touch of class* **to** *your bedroom.*
2 put together (two or more numbers or amounts) to calculate their total value: *they* **added** *all the figures* **up** | **add** *the two numbers* **together.**
■ [no obj.] (**add up to**) amount to: *this adds up to a total of 400 calories* | figurative *these isolated incidents don't add up to a true picture of the situation.* ■ [no obj.] [usu. with negative] (**add up**) informal seem reasonable or consistent; make sense: *many things in her story didn't add up.*
3 [reporting verb] say as a further remark: [with direct speech] *'I hope we haven't been too much trouble,' she added politely* | [with obj.] *we would like to add our congratulations.*
– ORIGIN late Middle English: from Latin *addere,* from *ad-* 'to' + the base of *dare* 'put'.

adda /ˈədˌdɑː/ ▶ **noun** Indian **1** an illicit drinking place.
2 [mass noun] informal conversation among a group of people.
– ORIGIN from Hindi *aḍḍā,* originally in the sense 'perch for tame birds'.

Addams, Jane (1860–1935), American social reformer, feminist, and pacifist. In 1889 she founded Hull House, a centre for the care and education of the poor of Chicago. Nobel Peace Prize (1931).

addax /ˈadaks/ ▶ **noun** a large antelope with a mainly greyish and white coat, native to the deserts of North Africa.
• *Addax nasomaculatus,* family Bovidae.
– ORIGIN late 17th cent.: from Latin, from an African word recorded by Pliny.

addendum /əˈdɛndəm/ ▶ **noun** (pl. **addenda** /-də/) **1** an item of additional material added at the end of a book or other publication.
2 Engineering the radial distance from the pitch circle of a cogwheel or wormwheel to the crests of the teeth or ridges. Compare with **DEDENDUM**.
– ORIGIN late 17th cent.: Latin, 'that which is to be added', gerundive of *addere* (see **ADD**).

a

adder[1] ▶ **noun** a small venomous Eurasian snake which has a dark zigzag pattern on its back and bears live young. It is the only poisonous snake in Britain. Also called **VIPER**.
• *Vipera berus*, family Viperidae.
■used in names of similar or related snakes, e.g. **death adder**, **puff adder**.
– ORIGIN Old English *nædre* 'serpent, adder', of Germanic origin; related to Dutch *adder* and German *Natter*. The initial *n* was lost in Middle English by wrong division of *a naddre*; compare with **APRON**, **AUGER**, and **UMPIRE**.

adder[2] ▶ **noun** Electronics a unit which adds together two input variables. A **full adder** can add a bit carried from another addition as well as the two inputs, whereas a **half adder** can only add the inputs together.

adder's tongue (also US **adder-tongue**) ▶ **noun**
1 a widely distributed fern of open country, with a single pointed oval frond and a straight unbranched spore-bearing stem.
• Genus *Ophioglossum*, family Ophioglossaceae, in particular *O. vulgatum*.
2 North American term for **DOG'S-TOOTH VIOLET**.

addict ▶ **noun** a person who is addicted to a particular substance, typically an illegal drug.
■[with modifier] informal an enthusiastic devotee of a specified thing or activity: *a self-confessed chocolate addict.*
– ORIGIN early 20th cent.: from the obsolete verb *addict*, which was a back-formation from **ADDICTED**.

addicted ▶ **adjective** physically and mentally dependent on a particular substance, and unable to stop taking it without incurring adverse effects: *she became* ***addicted to*** *alcohol and diet pills.*
■enthusiastically devoted to a particular thing or activity: *he's* ***addicted to*** *computers.*
– ORIGIN mid 16th cent.: from the obsolete adjective *addict* 'bound or devoted (to someone)', from Latin *addict-* 'assigned', from the verb *addicere*, from *ad-* 'to' + *dicere* 'say'.

addiction ▶ **noun** [mass noun] the fact or condition of being addicted to a particular substance, thing, or activity: *he committed the offence to finance his drug addiction.*
– ORIGIN late 16th cent. (denoting a person's inclination or proclivity): from Latin *addictio(n-)*, from *addicere* 'assign' (see **ADDICTED**).

addictive ▶ **adjective** (of a substance or activity) causing or likely to cause someone to become addicted to it: *a highly addictive drug.*
■of, relating to, or susceptible to the fact of being or becoming addicted to something: *addictive behaviour.*

add-in ▶ **noun** a printed circuit board capable of being fitted internally to a computer or accommodated in an externally accessible slot.

Addington, Henry, 1st Viscount Sidmouth (1757–1844), British Tory statesman, Prime Minister 1801–4 and Home Secretary (1812–21).

Addis Ababa /ˌadɪs ˈabəbə/ (also **Adis Abeba**) the capital of Ethiopia, situated at an altitude of about 2,440 m (8,000 ft); pop. 2,316,400 (est. 1994).

Addison, Joseph (1672–1719), English essayist, poet, dramatist, and Whig politician, noted for his simple, unornamented prose style. In 1711 he founded the *Spectator* with Sir Richard Steele.

Addisonian /ˌadɪˈsəʊnɪən/ ▶ **adjective** **1** of, relating to, or characteristic of the works or style of Joseph Addison.
2 Medicine of, relating to, or characterized by Addison's disease.

Addisonian anaemia ▶ **noun** another term for **PERNICIOUS ANAEMIA**.

Addison's disease ▶ **noun** [mass noun] a disease characterized by progressive anaemia, low blood pressure, great weakness, and bronze discoloration of the skin. It is caused by inadequate secretion of hormones by the adrenal cortex.
– ORIGIN mid 19th cent.: named after Thomas *Addison* (1793–1860), the English physician who described the disease.

addition ▶ **noun** [mass noun] **1** the action or process of adding something to something else: *the hotel has been extended* ***with the addition of*** *more rooms.*
■[count noun] a person or thing added or joined, typically in order to improve something: *you will find the coat a useful* ***addition to*** *your wardrobe.*
2 the process or skill of calculating the total of two or more numbers or amounts: *she began with simple arithmetic, addition and then subtraction.*
■Mathematics the process of combining matrices, vectors, or other quantities under specific rules to obtain their sum or resultant.
– PHRASES **in addition** as an extra person, thing, or circumstance: *members of the board were paid a small allowance* ***in addition to*** *their normal salary.*
– ORIGIN late Middle English: from Latin *additio(n-)*, from the verb *addere* (see **ADD**).

additional ▶ **adjective** added, extra, or supplementary to what is already present or available: *we require additional information.*

additionally ▶ **adverb** as an extra factor or circumstance: *brokers finance themselves additionally by short-term borrowing.*
■[sentence adverb] used to introduce a new fact or argument: *additionally, many countries levy taxes that do not apply in Britain.*

additional member system ▶ **noun** a type of proportional representation in which each elector votes separately for a party and for a representative.

addition reaction ▶ **noun** Chemistry a reaction in which one molecule combines with another to form a larger molecule with no other products.

additive ▶ **noun** a substance added to something in small quantities, typically so as to improve or preserve it: *many foods contain chemical additives.*
▶ **adjective** characterized by, relating to, or produced by addition: *an additive process.*
■technical of or relating to the reproduction of colours by the superimposition of primary colours.
– ORIGIN late 17th cent. (as an adjective): from late Latin *additivus*, from Latin *addit-* 'added', from the verb *addere* (see **ADD**). The noun dates from the 1940s.

addle ▶ **verb** [with obj.] chiefly humorous make (someone) unable to think clearly; confuse: *being in love must have addled your brain.*
▶ **adjective** **1** [in combination] chiefly N. Amer. lacking in common sense; muddled: *the film is addle-brained.*
2 archaic (of an egg) rotten.
– ORIGIN Middle English (in sense 2): from Old English *adela* 'liquid filth', of Germanic origin; related to Dutch *aal* and German *Adel* 'mire, puddle'.

addled ▶ **adjective** **1** (of an egg) rotten.
2 unable to think clearly; confused: [in combination] *drug-addled visions.*
– ORIGIN mid 17th cent.: from the adjective **ADDLE**.

Addled Parliament the Parliament of James I of England (James VI of Scotland), so known because it refused to accede to the king's requests and was dissolved without having passed any legislation.

add-on ▶ **noun** something that has been or can be added to an existing object or arrangement: [as modifier] *cars with add-on extras.*
■an accessory device designed to increase the capability of a computer or hi-fi system.

addorsed /əˈdɔːst/ ▶ **adjective** chiefly Heraldry placed back to back.
– ORIGIN late 16th cent.: from Latin *ad* 'to' + *dorsum* 'back' + **-ED**[2].

addra gazelle /ˈadrə/ ▶ **noun** another term for **DAMA GAZELLE**.
– ORIGIN *addra* probably a local African word.

address ▶ **noun** **1** the particulars of the place where someone lives or an organization is situated: *they exchanged addresses and agreed to keep in touch.*
■the place itself: *our officers called at the address.* ■Computing a string of characters which identifies a destination for e-mail messages. ■Computing a binary number which identifies a particular location in a data storage system or computer memory.
2 a formal speech delivered to an audience: *an address to the European Parliament.*
■[mass noun] archaic a person's manner of speaking to someone else: *his address was abrupt and unceremonious.* ■(**addresses**) archaic courteous or amorous approaches to someone: *he persecuted her with his addresses.*
3 [mass noun] dated skill, dexterity, or readiness: *he rescued me with the most consummate address.*
▶ **verb** [with obj.] **1** write the name and address of the intended recipient on (an envelope, letter, or parcel): *I* ***addressed*** *my letter* ***to*** *him personally* | [as adj. **addressed**] *please enclose a stamped addressed envelope.*
2 speak to (a person or an assembly), typically in a formal way: *she addressed the open-air meeting* | *they* ***addressed themselves to*** *my father.*
■(**address someone as**) name someone in the specified way when talking to them: *she addressed my father as 'Mr Stevens'.* ■(**address something to**) say or write remarks or a protest to: *address your complaints to the Trading Standards Board.*
3 think about and begin to deal with (an issue or problem): *a fundamental problem has still to be addressed.*
4 Golf take up one's stance and prepare to hit (the ball).
– PHRASES **form of address** a name or title used in speaking or writing to a person of a specified rank or function.
– DERIVATIVES **addresser** noun.
– ORIGIN Middle English (as a verb in the senses 'set upright' and 'guide, direct', hence 'write directions for delivery on' and 'direct spoken words to'): from Old French, based on Latin *ad-* 'towards' + *directus* (see **DIRECT**). The noun is of mid 16th-cent. origin in the sense 'act of approaching or speaking to someone'.

addressable ▶ **adjective** Computing relating to or denoting a memory unit in which all locations can be separately accessed by a particular program.

addressee /ˌadrɛˈsiː/ ▶ **noun** the person to whom something, typically a letter, is addressed.

adduce /əˈdjuːs/ ▶ **verb** [with obj.] cite as evidence: *a number of factors are adduced to explain the situation.*
– DERIVATIVES **adducible** adjective.
– ORIGIN late Middle English: from Latin *adducere*, from *ad-* 'towards' + *ducere* 'to lead'.

adduct[1] /əˈdʌkt/ ▶ **verb** [with obj.] (of a muscle) move (a limb or other part of the body) towards the midline of the body or towards another part. The opposite of **ABDUCT**.
– DERIVATIVES **adduction** noun.
– ORIGIN mid 19th cent.: back-formation from late Middle English *adduction*, from late Latin *adductio(n-)* 'bringing forward', from the verb *adducere* 'bring in' (see **ADDUCE**).

adduct[2] /ˈadʌkt/ ▶ **noun** Chemistry the product of an addition reaction between two compounds.
– ORIGIN 1940s: from German *Addukt* (blend of *Addition* and *Produkt*).

adductor /əˈdʌktə/ (also **adductor muscle**) ▶ **noun** Anatomy a muscle whose contraction moves a limb or other part of the body towards the midline of the body or towards another part. Compare with **ABDUCTOR**.
■any of a number of specific muscles in the hand, foot, or thigh: [followed by Latin genitive] *adductor hallucis.*
– ORIGIN early 17th cent.: modern Latin, from Latin *adduct-* 'brought in', from the verb *adducere* (see **ADDUCE**).

-ade[1] ▶ **suffix** forming nouns: **1** denoting an action that is completed: *barricade* | *blockade.*
2 denoting the body concerned in an action or process: *brigade* | *cavalcade.*
3 denoting the product or result of an action or process: *arcade* | *marmalade.*
– ORIGIN from French, via Portuguese, Provençal, and Spanish *-ada* or via Italian *-ata*, from Latin *-atus* (past participial suffix of verbs ending in *-are*).

-ade[2] ▶ **suffix** forming nouns such as *decade.*
– ORIGIN variant of **-AD**[1], from French *-ade*, from Greek *-as*, *-ad-*.

-ade[3] ▶ **suffix** forming nouns: **1** equivalent in sense to nouns ending in **-ADE**[1]: *brocade.*
2 denoting a person: *renegade.*
– ORIGIN from Spanish or Portuguese *-ado*, masculine form of *-ada* (see **-ADE**[1]).

Adelaide /ˈadəleɪd/ a city in Australia, the capital and chief port of the state of South Australia; pop. 1,049,870 (1990).

Adélie Land /aˈdeɪli/ (also **Adélie Coast**) a section of the Antarctic continent south of the 60th parallel, between Wilkes Land and King George V Land.

Aden /ˈeɪd(ə)n/ a port in Yemen at the mouth of the Red Sea; pop. 400,800 (est. 1993). Aden was formerly under British rule, first as part of British India (from 1839), then from 1935 as a Crown Colony. It was capital of the former South Yemen from 1967 until 1990.

Aden, Gulf of a part of the eastern Arabian Sea lying between the south coast of Yemen and the Horn of Africa.

Adenauer /'ædɪnaʊə, German 'a:dənaʊɐ/, Konrad (1876–1967), German statesman, first Chancellor of the Federal Republic of Germany 1949–63.

adenine /'ædɪniːn/ ▶ noun [mass noun] Biochemistry a compound which is one of the four constituent bases of nucleic acids. A purine derivative, it is paired with thymine in double-stranded DNA.
● Alternative name: **6-aminopurine**; chem. formula: $C_5H_5N_5$.
– ORIGIN late 19th cent.: coined in German from Greek *adēn* 'gland' + **-INE**⁴.

adeno- ▶ combining form relating to a gland or glands: *adenocarcinoma*.
– ORIGIN from Greek *adēn* 'gland'.

adenocarcinoma /ˌædɪnəʊˌkɑːsɪ'nəʊmə/ ▶ noun (pl. **adenocarcinomas** or **adenocarcinomata** /-mətə/) Medicine a malignant tumour formed from glandular structures in epithelial tissue.

adenoids /'ædɪnɔɪdz/ ▶ plural noun a mass of enlarged lymphatic tissue between the back of the nose and the throat, often hindering speaking and breathing in young children.
– DERIVATIVES **adenoidal** adjective.
– ORIGIN late 19th cent.: *adenoid* from Greek *adēn* 'gland' + **-OID**.

adenoma /ˌædɪ'nəʊmə/ ▶ noun (pl. **adenomas** or **adenomata** /-mətə/) Medicine a benign tumour formed from glandular structures in epithelial tissue.
– ORIGIN late 19th cent.: modern Latin, from Greek *adēn* 'gland'.

adenosine /ə'dɛnə(ʊ)siːn/ ▶ noun [mass noun] Biochemistry a compound consisting of adenine combined with ribose, present in all living tissue in combined form as nucleotides.
– ORIGIN early 20th cent.: blend of **ADENINE** and **RIBOSE**.

adenosine deaminase /diː'amɪneɪz/ ▶ noun [mass noun] Biochemistry an enzyme which catalyses the deamination of adenosine to inosine.

adenosine monophosphate (abbrev.: **AMP**) ▶ noun another term for **ADENYLIC ACID**.

adenosine triphosphate (abbrev.: **ATP**) ▶ noun [mass noun] Biochemistry a compound consisting of an adenosine molecule bonded to three phosphate groups, present in all living tissue. The breakage of one phosphate linkage (to form **adenosine diphosphate**, **ADP**) provides energy for physiological processes such as muscular contraction.

adenovirus /'ædɪnəʊˌvʌɪrəs/ ▶ noun Medicine any of a group of DNA viruses first discovered in adenoid tissue, most of which cause respiratory diseases.

adenylate cyclase /ə,dɛnɪleɪt 'sʌɪkleɪz, 'sɪk-/ ▶ noun [mass noun] Biochemistry an enzyme that catalyses the formation of cyclic adenylic acid from adenosine triphosphate.

adenylic acid /ˌædɪ'nɪlɪk/ ▶ noun [mass noun] Biochemistry a compound consisting of an adenosine molecule bonded to one acidic phosphate group, present in most DNA and RNA. It typically exists in a cyclic form with the phosphate bonded to the nucleoside at two points.
– DERIVATIVES **adenylate** noun.
– ORIGIN late 19th cent.: *adenylic* from **ADENINE** + **-YL** + **-IC**.

adept ▶ adjective /'ædɛpt, ə'dɛpt/ very skilled or proficient at something: *she is* **adept at** *cutting through red tape* | *an adept negotiator*.
▶ noun /'ædɛpt/ a person who is skilled or proficient at something: *adepts at kung fu and karate*.
– DERIVATIVES **adeptly** adverb, **adeptness** noun.
– ORIGIN mid 17th cent.: from Latin *adeptus* 'achieved', past participle of *adipisci* 'obtain, attain'.

adequate ▶ adjective satisfactory or acceptable in quality or quantity: *this office is perfectly* **adequate for** *my needs* | *adequate resources and funding*.
– DERIVATIVES **adequacy** noun, **adequately** adverb.
– ORIGIN early 17th cent.: from Latin *adaequatus* 'made equal to', past participle of the verb *adaequare*, from *ad-* 'to' + *aequus* 'equal'.

à deux /ɑː 'dəː, French a døˈ/ ▶ adverb for or involving two people: *dinner à deux*.
– ORIGIN French.

ADF ▶ abbreviation for automatic direction-finder, a device used by pilots to aid navigation.

ad fin. /ad 'fɪn/ ▶ adverb at or near the end of a piece of writing.
– ORIGIN from Latin *ad finem* 'at the end'.

ADH Biochemistry ▶ abbreviation for antidiuretic hormone.

ADHD ▶ abbreviation for attention deficit hyperactivity disorder.

adhere /əd'hɪə/ ▶ verb [no obj.] (**adhere to**) stick fast to (a surface or substance): *paint won't adhere well to a greasy surface*.
■ believe in and follow the practices of: *the people adhere to the Muslim religion*. ■ represent truthfully and in detail: *the account adhered firmly to fact*.
– ORIGIN late 15th cent.: from Latin *adhaerere*, from *ad-* 'to' + *haerere* 'to stick'.

adherent ▶ noun someone who supports a particular party, person, or set of ideas: *he was a strong adherent of monetarism*.
▶ adjective sticking fast to an object or surface: *any adherent sand grains are easily removed*.
– DERIVATIVES **adherence** noun.
– ORIGIN late Middle English: from Old French *adherent*, from Latin *adhaerent-* 'sticking to', from the verb *adhaerere* (see **ADHERE**).

adhesion /əd'hiːʒ(ə)n/ ▶ noun [mass noun] **1** the action or process of adhering to a surface or object: *the adhesion of the gum strip to the paper*.
■ the frictional grip of wheels, shoes, etc. on a road, track, or other surface: *the front tyres were struggling for adhesion*. ■ Physics the sticking together of particles of different substances. ■ allegiance or faithfulness to a particular person, party, or set of ideas: *he was harshly criticized for his* **adhesion to** *Say's law*.
2 Medicine an abnormal union of surfaces due to inflammation or injury: *endoscopic surgery for pelvic adhesions*.
– ORIGIN late 15th cent.: from French *adhésion*, from Latin *adhaesio(n-)*, from the verb *adhaerere* (see **ADHERE**).

adhesive /əd'hiːsɪv, -zɪv/ ▶ adjective able to stick fast to a surface or object; sticky: *an adhesive label*.
▶ noun a substance used for sticking objects or materials together; glue.
– DERIVATIVES **adhesively** adverb, **adhesiveness** noun.
– ORIGIN late 17th cent. (in the sense 'tending to adhere or cling to'): from French *adhésif, -ive*, from the verb *adhérer*, from Latin *adhaerere* 'stick to' (see **ADHERE**).

adhibit /əd'hɪbɪt/ ▶ verb (**adhibited**, **adhibiting**) [with obj.] formal apply or affix (something) to something else: *signed by a partner who would either adhibit the firm's signature or his own*.
– DERIVATIVES **adhibition** noun.
– ORIGIN early 16th cent. (in the sense 'take in, include'): from Latin *adhibit-* 'brought in', from the verb *adhibere*, from *ad-* 'to' + *habere* 'hold, have'.

ad hoc /ad 'hɒk/ ▶ adjective & adverb formed, arranged, or done for a particular purpose only: [as adj.] *an ad hoc committee* | *the discussions were on an ad hoc basis* | [as adv.] *the group was constituted ad hoc*.
– ORIGIN Latin, literally 'to this'.

adhocracy /ad'hɒkrəsi/ ▶ noun [mass noun] the replacement of over-rigid bureaucracy with more flexible and informal forms of organization and management.
– ORIGIN 1970s: blend of **AD HOC** and **-CRACY**.

ad hominem /ad 'hɒmɪnɛm/ ▶ adverb & adjective **1** relating to or associated with a particular person: [as adv.] *the office was created ad hominem for Fenton*.
2 (of an argument or reaction) directed against a person rather than the position they are maintaining: [as adj.] *an ad hominem response*.
– ORIGIN Latin, literally 'to the person'.

adiabatic /ˌeɪdʌɪə'batɪk, ˌadɪə-/ Physics ▶ adjective relating to or denoting a process or condition in which heat does not enter or leave the system concerned.
■ impassable to heat.
▶ noun a curve or formula representing adiabatic phenomena.
– DERIVATIVES **adiabatically** adverb.
– ORIGIN late 19th cent.: from Greek *adiabatos* 'impassable', from *a-* 'not' + *dia* 'through' + *batos* 'passable' (from *bainein* 'go'), + **-IC**.

adiabatic lapse rate ▶ noun Meteorology the rate at which atmospheric temperature decreases with increasing altitude in conditions of thermal equilibrium.

adieu /ə'djuː/ chiefly poetic/literary ▶ exclamation goodbye.
▶ noun (pl. **adieus** or **adieux** /ə'djuːz/) a goodbye: *he whispered a fond adieu* | *they bade us all adieu*.

– ORIGIN late Middle English: from Old French, from *a* 'to' + *Dieu* 'God'; compare with **ADIOS**.

Adi Granth /ˌɑːdɪ 'ɡrʌnt/ the principal sacred scripture of Sikhism. Originally compiled under the direction of Arjan Dev (1563–1606), the fifth Sikh guru, it contains hymns and religious poetry as well as the teachings of the first five gurus. Also called **GRANTH**, **GRANTH SAHIB** ('Revered Book').
– ORIGIN from Sanskrit *ādigrantha*, literally 'first book', based on *grantha* 'literary composition', from *granth* 'to tie'.

ad infinitum /ˌad ɪnfɪ'nʌɪtəm/ ▶ adverb again and again in the same way; forever: *registration is for seven years and may be renewed ad infinitum*.
– ORIGIN Latin, literally 'to infinity'.

ad interim /ad 'ɪntərɪm/ ▶ adverb for an intervening or temporary period of time.
▶ adjective temporary.
– ORIGIN Latin, from *ad* 'to' and *interim* 'meanwhile', used as a noun.

adios /ˌadɪ'ɒs/ ▶ exclamation & noun Spanish term for **GOODBYE**.
– ORIGIN Spanish *adiós*, from *a* 'to' + *Dios* 'God'; compare with **ADIEU**.

adipic acid /ə'dɪpɪk/ ▶ noun [mass noun] Chemistry a crystalline fatty acid obtained from natural fats and used especially in the manufacture of nylon.
● Alternative name: **hexanedioic acid**; chem. formula: $HOOC(CH_2)_4COOH$.
– DERIVATIVES **adipate** noun.
– ORIGIN mid 19th cent.: from Latin *adeps, adip-* 'fat' (because the acid was first prepared by oxidizing fats) + **-IC**.

adipocere /ˌadɪpə(ʊ)'sɪə/ ▶ noun [mass noun] a greyish waxy substance formed by the decomposition of soft tissue in dead bodies subjected to moisture.
– ORIGIN early 19th cent.: from French *adipocire*, from Latin *adeps, adip-* 'fat' + French *cire* 'wax' (from Latin *cera*).

adipocyte /'adɪpə(ʊ)sʌɪt/ ▶ noun Biology a cell specialized for the storage of fat, found in connective tissue.
– ORIGIN 1930s: from **ADIPOSE** + **-CYTE**.

adipose /'adɪpəʊs, -z/ ▶ adjective technical (especially of body tissue) used for the storage of fat.
– DERIVATIVES **adiposity** noun.
– ORIGIN mid 18th cent.: from modern Latin *adiposus*, from *adeps, adip-* 'fat'.

adipose fin ▶ noun Zoology a small, rayless, fleshy, dorsal fin present in certain fishes, notably in the salmon family.

Adirondack Mountains /ˌadɪ'rɒndak/ (also **the Adirondacks**) a range of mountains in New York State, source of the Hudson and Mohawk Rivers.

Adis Abeba variant spelling of **ADDIS ABABA**.

adit /'adɪt/ ▶ noun a horizontal passage leading into a mine for the purposes of access or drainage.
– ORIGIN early 17th cent.: from Latin *aditus* 'approach, entrance', from *adit-* 'approached', from the verb *adire*, from *ad-* 'towards' + *ire* 'go'.

Adivasi /ˌɑːdɪ'vɑːsi/ ▶ noun (pl. same or **Adivasis**) a member of any of the aboriginal tribal peoples living in India before the arrival of the Aryans in the second millennium BC.
■ a descendant of any of these peoples.
– ORIGIN from modern Sanskrit *ādivāsī*, from *ādi* 'the beginning' + *vāsin* 'inhabitant'.

Adj. ▶ abbreviation for adjutant.

adjacent /ə'dʒeɪs(ə)nt/ ▶ adjective **1** next to or adjoining something else: *adjacent rooms* | *the area adjacent to the station*.
2 Geometry (of a pair of angles) formed on the same side of a straight line when intersected by another line.
– DERIVATIVES **adjacency** noun.
– ORIGIN late Middle English: from Latin *adjacent-* 'lying near to', from *adjacere*, from *ad-* 'to' + *jacere* 'lie down'.

adjective ▶ noun Grammar a word naming an attribute of a noun, such as *sweet*, *red*, or *technical*.
– DERIVATIVES **adjectival** adjective, **adjectivally** adverb.
– ORIGIN late Middle English: from Old French *adjectif, -ive*, from Latin *adject-* 'added', from the verb *adicere*, from *ad-* 'towards' + *jacere* 'throw'. The term was originally used in the phrase *noun adjective*, translating Latin *nomen adjectivum*, a

translation of Greek *onoma epitheton* 'attributive name'.

adjigo /ˈadʒɪɡəʊ/ (also **adjiko** /ˈadʒɪkəʊ/) ▶ **noun** a yam with edible tubers, native to near-coastal areas of SW Australia.
• *Dioscorea hastifolia*, family Dioscoreaceae.
– ORIGIN mid 19th cent.: probably from Nhanta (an Aboriginal language) *ajuga* 'vegetable food'.

adjoin ▶ **verb** [with obj.] be next to and joined with (a building, room, or piece of land): *the dining room adjoins a conservatory* | [as adj. **adjoining**] *the adjoining room.*
■ archaic or technical add or join something to.
– ORIGIN Middle English: from Old French *ajoindre*, from Latin *adjungere*, from *ad-* 'to' + *jungere* 'to join'.

adjoint Mathematics ▶ **adjective** relating to or denoting a function or quantity related to a given function or quantity by a particular process of transposition.
■ denoting a matrix that is the transpose of the complex conjugates or the cofactors of a given square matrix.
▶ **noun** an adjoint matrix, function, or quantity.
– ORIGIN late 19th cent.: from French, literally 'joined to', from *adjoindre* (see **ADJOIN**).

adjourn /əˈdʒəːn/ ▶ **verb** [with obj.] (usu. **be adjourned**) break off (a meeting, legal case, or game) with the intention of resuming it later: *the meeting was adjourned until December 4* | [no obj.] *let's adjourn and reconvene at 2 o'clock.*
■ [no obj., with adverbial] (of people who are together) go somewhere else, typically for refreshment: *they* ***adjourned to*** *a local pub.* ■ put off or postpone (a resolution or sentence): *sentence was adjourned for a social inquiry report.*
– DERIVATIVES **adjournment** noun.
– ORIGIN Middle English (in the sense 'summon someone to appear on a particular day'): from Old French *ajorner*, from the phrase *a jorn (nome)* 'to an (appointed) day'.

adjournment debate ▶ **noun** a debate in the UK House of Commons on the motion that the House be adjourned, used as an opportunity for raising various matters.

Adjt ▶ **abbreviation for** adjutant.

adjudge ▶ **verb** [with obj. and complement] (usu. **be adjudged**) consider or declare to be true or the case: *she was adjudged guilty.*
■ (**adjudge something to**) (in legal use) award something judicially to (someone): *the court adjudged legal damages to her.* ■ [with obj. and infinitive] (in legal use) condemn (someone) to pay a penalty: *the defaulter was adjudged to pay the whole amount.*
– DERIVATIVES **adjudgement** (also **adjudgment**) noun.
– ORIGIN late Middle English: from Old French *ajuger*, from Latin *adjudicare*, from *ad-* 'to' + *judicare*, from *judex, judic-* 'a judge'.

adjudicate /əˈdʒuːdɪkeɪt/ ▶ **verb** [no obj.] make a formal judgement or decision about a problem or disputed matter: *the Committee* ***adjudicates on*** *all betting disputes* | [with obj.] *the case was adjudicated in the High Court.*
■ act as a judge in a competition: *we asked him to adjudicate at the local flower show.* ■ [with obj. and complement] pronounce or declare judicially: *he was adjudicated bankrupt.*
– DERIVATIVES **adjudication** noun, **adjudicative** adjective, **adjudicator** noun.
– ORIGIN early 18th cent. (in the sense 'award judicially'): from Latin *adjudicat-* 'awarded judicially', from the verb *adjudicare* (see **ADJUDGE**). The noun *adjudication* (as a Scots legal term) dates from the early 17th cent.

adjunct /ˈadʒʌŋ(k)t/ ▶ **noun 1** a thing added to something else as a supplementary rather than an essential part: *computer technology is an* ***adjunct to*** *learning.*
■ a person who is another's assistant or subordinate.
2 Grammar a word or phrase, typically an adverbial, that constitutes an optional element or is considered of secondary importance in a sentence, for example *on the table* in *we left some flowers on the table.*
■ (in some systemic grammar) an obligatory or optional adverbial functioning as a constituent of clause structure.
▶ **adjective** [attrib.] connected or added to something, typically in an auxiliary way: *other alternative or adjunct therapies include immunotherapy.*
■ N. Amer. (of an academic post) attached to the staff of a university in a temporary or assistant capacity: *an adjunct professor of entomology.*
– DERIVATIVES **adjunctive** adjective.
– ORIGIN early 16th cent. (as an adjective meaning 'joined on, subordinate'): from Latin *adjunctus*, past participle of *adjungere* (see **ADJOIN**).

adjunction ▶ **noun** [mass noun] **1** Mathematics the joining of two sets which without overlapping jointly constitute a larger set, or the relation between two such sets.
2 Logic the asserting in a single formula of two previously asserted formulae.
– ORIGIN late 16th cent.: from Latin *adjunctio(n)-*, from the verb *adjungere* (see **ADJOIN**).

adjure /əˈdʒʊə/ ▶ **verb** [with obj. and infinitive] formal urge or request (someone) solemnly or earnestly to do something: *I adjure you to tell me the truth.*
– DERIVATIVES **adjuration** noun, **adjuratory** /-rət(ə)ri/ adjective.
– ORIGIN late Middle English (in the sense 'put a person on oath'): from Latin *adjurare*, from *ad-* 'to' + *jurare* 'swear' (from *jus, jur-* 'oath').

adjust ▶ **verb 1** [with obj.] alter or move (something) slightly in order to achieve the desired fit, appearance, or result: *he smoothed his hair and adjusted his tie* | *the interest rate should be* ***adjusted for*** *inflation.*
■ [no obj.] permit small alterations or movements so as to allow a desired fit, appearance, or result to be achieved: *a harness that* ***adjusts to*** *the correct fit.* ■ [no obj.] adapt or become used to a new situation: *she must be allowed to grieve and to adjust in her own way* | *his eyes had* ***adjusted to*** *semidarkness.*
2 [with obj.] assess (loss or damages) when settling an insurance claim.
– DERIVATIVES **adjustability** noun, **adjustable** adjective, **adjuster** noun, **adjustment** noun.
– ORIGIN early 17th cent. (in the senses 'harmonize discrepancies' and 'assess (loss or damages)'): from obsolete French *adjuster*, from Old French *ajoster* 'to approximate', based on Latin *ad-* 'to' + *juxta* 'near'.

adjutant /ˈadʒʊt(ə)nt/ ▶ **noun 1** a military officer who acts as an administrative assistant to a senior officer.
■ a person's assistant or deputy.
2 (also **adjutant stork** or **adjutant bird**) a large black-and-white stork with a massive bill and a bare head and neck, found in India and SE Asia.
• Genus *Leptoptilos*, family Ciconiidae: two species.
– DERIVATIVES **adjutancy** noun.
– ORIGIN early 17th cent. (in the sense 'assistant, helper'): from Latin *adjutant-* 'being of service to', from *adjutare*, frequentative of *adjuvare* 'assist' (see **ADJUVANT**).

Adjutant General ▶ **noun** (pl. **Adjutants General**) (in the British army) a high-ranking administrative officer.
■ (in the US army) the chief administrative officer.

adjuvant /ˈadʒʊv(ə)nt/ ▶ **adjective** Medicine (of therapy) applied after initial treatment for cancer, especially to suppress secondary tumour formation.
▶ **noun** Medicine a substance which enhances the body's immune response to an antigen.
– ORIGIN late 16th cent.: from Latin *adjuvant-* 'helping towards', from the verb *adjuvare*, from *ad-* 'towards' + *juvare* to 'help'.

adland ▶ **noun** [mass noun] informal the business world of advertising and advertisers.

Adler /ˈadlə, German ˈaːdlɐ/, Alfred (1870–1937), Austrian psychologist and psychiatrist. Adler disagreed with Freud's idea that mental illness was caused by sexual conflicts in infancy, arguing that society and culture were significant factors. He introduced the concept of the inferiority complex.
– DERIVATIVES **Adlerian** /adˈlɪərɪən/ adjective & noun.

ad-lib ▶ **verb** (**ad-libbed**, **ad-libbing**) [no obj.] speak or perform in public without previously preparing one's words: *Charles had to ad-lib because he'd forgotten his script* | [with obj.] *she ad-libbed half the speech.*
▶ **noun** something spoken or performed in such a way.
▶ **adverb** & **adjective 1** spoken or performed without previous preparation: [as adj.] *an ad-lib commentary* | [as adv.] *I spoke ad lib.*
■ Music (especially as a direction) to be performed with free rhythm and expression.
2 as much and as often as desired: [as adv.] *the price includes meals and drinks ad lib* | [as adj.] *the pigs are fed on an ad-lib basis.*
– ORIGIN early 19th cent. (as an adverb): abbreviation of **AD LIBITUM**.

ad libitum /ad ˈlɪbɪtəm/ ▶ **adverb** & **adjective** more formal term for **AD LIB**.
– ORIGIN Latin, literally 'according to pleasure'.

ad litem /ad ˈlʌɪtɛm/ ▶ **adjective** Law (especially of a guardian) appointed to act in a lawsuit on behalf of a child or other person who is not considered capable of representing themselves.
– ORIGIN Latin, literally 'for the lawsuit'.

Adm. ▶ **abbreviation for** Admiral.

adman ▶ **noun** (pl. **-men**) informal a person who works in advertising.

admass ▶ **noun** [in sing.] dated, chiefly Brit. the section of the community regarded as readily influenced by advertising and the mass media.

admeasurement ▶ **noun** [mass noun] archaic the action of ascertaining and apportioning just shares in something.
– ORIGIN early 16th cent.: from Old French *amesurement*, from the verb *amesurer*, from medieval Latin *admensurare*, based on Latin *metiri* 'to measure'.

admi /ˈɑːdmi/ ▶ **noun** Indian informal a man.
– ORIGIN from Hindi and Urdu *ādmī*.

admin ▶ **noun** [mass noun] informal, chiefly Brit. the administration of a business, organization, etc.: *day-to-day admin* | [as modifier] *admin staff.*
– ORIGIN 1940s: abbreviation.

adminicle /ədˈmɪnɪk(ə)l/ ▶ **noun** rare something that helps or supports something else.
■ Scots Law a document giving evidence as to the existence or contents of another, missing document.
– DERIVATIVES **adminicular** /admɪˈnɪkjʊlə/ adjective.
– ORIGIN mid 16th cent.: from Latin *adminiculum* 'prop, support'.

administer ▶ **verb** [with obj.] **1** manage and be responsible for the running of (a business, organization, etc.): *each school was administered separately.*
■ be responsible for the implementation or use of (law or resources): *a Health and Safety agency would administer new regulations.*
2 dispense or apply (a remedy or drug): *paramedic crews are capable of administering drugs.*
■ deal out or inflict (punishment): *retribution was administered to those found guilty.* ■ (of a priest) perform the rites of (a sacrament, typically the Eucharist). ■ archaic or Law direct the taking of (an oath).
– DERIVATIVES **administrable** adjective.
– ORIGIN late Middle English: via Old French from Latin *administrare*, from *ad-* 'to' + *ministrare* (see **MINISTRATION**).

administrate ▶ **verb** less common term for **ADMINISTER** (in sense 1): *the cost of administrating VAT.*
– ORIGIN mid 16th cent.: from Latin *administrat-* 'managed', from the verb *administrare* (see **ADMINISTER**).

administration ▶ **noun 1** [mass noun] the process or activity of running a business, organization, etc.: *the day-to-day administration of the company* | *a career in arts administration* | [as modifier] *administration costs.*
■ (**the administration**) the people responsible for this, regarded collectively: *the university administration took their demands seriously.* ■ the management of public affairs; government: *the inhabitants of the island voted to remain under French administration.* ■ Law the management and disposal of the property of a deceased person, debtor, or other individual, or of an insolvent company, by a legally appointed administrator: *the company* ***went into administration.***
2 the government in power: *successive Conservative administrations enjoyed a comfortable majority.*
■ chiefly N. Amer. the term of office of a political leader or government: *the early years of the Reagan Administration.* ■ (in the US) a government agency: *the US Food and Drug Administration.*
3 [mass noun] the action of dispensing, giving, or applying something: *the oral administration of the antibiotic* | *the administration of justice.*
– ORIGIN Middle English: from Latin *administratio(n-)*, from the verb *administrare* (see **ADMINISTER**).

administrative ▶ **adjective** of or relating to the running of a business, organization, etc.: *administrative problems* | *administrative staff.*
– DERIVATIVES **administratively** adverb.
– ORIGIN mid 18th cent.: from Latin *administrativus*,

a

from *administrat-* 'managed', from the verb *administrare* (see **ADMINISTRATE**).

administrator ▶ **noun** **1** a person responsible for running a business or organization.
■ Law a person legally appointed to manage and dispose of the estate of a deceased person, debtor, or other individual, or of an insolvent company.
2 a person who dispenses or administers something, especially justice or a religious sacrament: *administrators of justice*.

administratrix /ədˌmɪnɪˈstreɪtrɪks/ ▶ **noun** (pl. **administratrixes**, **administratrices** /-trɪsiːz/) Law a female administrator of an estate.

admirable ▶ **adjective** arousing or deserving respect and approval: *he has one admirable quality—he is totally honest | their temperance is admirable.*
– DERIVATIVES **admirably** adverb.
– ORIGIN late Middle English: via Old French from Latin *admirabilis* 'to be wondered at', from *admirari* (see **ADMIRE**).

admiral ▶ **noun** **1** a commander of a fleet or naval squadron.
■ (**Admiral**) a naval officer of the second most senior rank, above vice admiral and below Admiral of the Fleet or Fleet Admiral. ■ the commander-in-chief of a country's navy. ■ short for **VICE ADMIRAL** or **REAR ADMIRAL**.
2 [with modifier] a butterfly which has dark wings with bold red or white markings.
• Several species in the subfamily Nymphalinae, family Nymphalidae. See **RED ADMIRAL**, **WHITE ADMIRAL**.
– DERIVATIVES **admiralship** noun.
– ORIGIN Middle English (denoting an emir or Saracen commander): from Old French *amiral*, *admirail*, via medieval Latin from Arabic *'amīr* 'commander' (from *'amara* 'to command'). The ending *-al* was from Arabic *-al-* 'of the', used in titles (e.g. *'amīr-al-'umarā* 'ruler of rulers'), later assimilated to the familiar Latinate suffix **-AL**.

Admiral of the Fleet ▶ **noun** the highest rank of admiral in the Royal Navy.

Admiral's Cup a yacht-racing competition held every two years since 1957 between international teams of three yachts.

Admiralty ▶ **noun** (pl. **-ies**) **1** (in the UK) the government department that administered the Royal Navy, now incorporated in the Ministry of Defence and current only in titles.
2 (**admiralty**) [mass noun] Law the jurisdiction of courts of law over cases concerning ships or the sea and other navigable waters.
– ORIGIN late Middle English: from Old French *admiralte*, from *admirail* 'emir, leader' (see **ADMIRAL**).

Admiralty Board ▶ **noun** Brit. historical a committee of the Ministry of Defence superintending the Royal Navy.

Admiralty Islands a group of about forty islands in the western Pacific, part of Papua New Guinea.

admiration ▶ **noun** [mass noun] respect and warm approval: *I have the greatest* ***admiration for*** *all those involved in the project.*
■ (**the admiration of**) the object of such feelings: *her house was the admiration of everyone.* ■ pleasurable contemplation: *they were lost in admiration of the scenery.*
– ORIGIN late Middle English (in the sense 'marvelling, wonder'): from Latin *admiratio(n-)*, from the verb *admirari* (see **ADMIRE**).

admire ▶ **verb** [with obj.] regard (an object, quality, or person) with respect or warm approval: *I admire your courage* | [as adj. **admiring**] *she couldn't help but notice his admiring glance.*
■ look at with pleasure: *we were just admiring your garden.*
– DERIVATIVES **admiringly** adverb.
– ORIGIN late 16th cent.: from Latin *admirari*, from *ad-* 'at' + *mirari* 'wonder'.

admirer ▶ **noun** someone who has a particular regard for someone or something: *he was a great admirer of Henry James.*
■ a man who is attracted to a particular woman: *she's got a secret admirer.*

admissible ▶ **adjective** **1** acceptable or valid, especially as evidence in a court of law: *the case is admissible | legally admissible evidence.*
2 having the right to be admitted to a place: *foreigners were admissible only as temporary workers.*
– DERIVATIVES **admissibility** noun.
– ORIGIN early 17th cent.: from medieval Latin *admissibilis*, from Latin *admittere* (see **ADMIT**).

admission ▶ **noun** **1** a statement acknowledging the truth of something: *an admission of guilt | a tacit* ***admission that*** *things had gone wrong | a man who,* ***by his own admission****, fell in love easily.*
2 [mass noun] the process or fact of entering or being allowed to enter a place, organization, or institution: *I had some difficulty securing admission to the embassy | the country's admission to the UN* | [count noun] *her condition required frequent hospital admissions.*
■ the money charged for allowing someone to enter a public place: *admission is £1 for adults and 50p for children.* ■ (**admissions**) the number of people entering a place: *cinema admissions have been rising recently.* ■ a person admitted to hospital for treatment: *all admissions over 75 are seen by the geriatricians.*
– ORIGIN late Middle English: from Latin *admissio(n-)*, from the verb *admittere* (see **ADMIT**).

admit ▶ **verb** (**admitted**, **admitting**) **1** [reporting verb] confess to be true or to be the case, typically with reluctance: [with clause] *the Home Office finally admitted that several prisoners had been injured* | ***I have to admit*** *I was relieved when he went* | [with direct speech] *'I am feeling pretty tired,' Jane admitted* | [with obj.] *she admitted her terror of physical contact.*
■ [with obj.] confess to (a crime or fault, or one's responsibility for it): *he was sentenced to prison after admitting 47 charges of burglary* | [no obj.] *the paramilitaries* ***admitted to*** *the illegal possession of arms.* ■ [with obj.] acknowledge (a failure or fault): *after searching for an hour, she finally had to* ***admit defeat*** | [no obj.] *he readily* ***admits to*** *being something of a tearaway.*
2 [with obj.] allow (someone) to enter a place: *old-age pensioners are* ***admitted*** *free* ***to*** *the museum.*
■ (of a ticket) give (someone) the right to enter a place: *the voucher* ***admits*** *up to four people* ***to*** *the theme park.* ■ carry out the procedures necessary for (someone) to be received into hospital for treatment: *she was* ***admitted to*** *hospital suffering from a chest infection.* ■ allow (a person, country, or organization) to join an organization or group: *Canada was* ***admitted to*** *the League of Nations.* ■ allow (someone) to share in a privilege: *he was* ***admitted to*** *the freedom of the city in 1583.* ■ accept as valid: *the courts can refuse to admit police evidence which has been illegally obtained.*
3 [no obj.] (**admit of**) allow the possibility of: *the need to inform him was too urgent to admit of further delay.*
– ORIGIN late Middle English: from Latin *admittere*, from *ad-* 'to' + *mittere* 'send'.

admittance ▶ **noun** [mass noun] **1** the process or fact of entering or being allowed to enter a place or institution: *people were unable to* ***gain admittance*** *to the hall.*
2 Physics a measure of electrical conduction, numerically equal to the reciprocal of the impedance.

admittedly ▶ **adverb** [sentence adverb] used to introduce a concession or recognition that something is true or the case: *admittedly, the salary was not wonderful but the duties were light | this is admittedly an extreme case.*

admix ▶ **verb** [with obj.] chiefly technical mix (something) with something else.
– ORIGIN late Middle English: back-formation from the obsolete adjective 'admixt', from Latin *admixtus* 'mixed together', past participle of *admiscere*, from *ad-* 'to' + *miscere* 'to mix'.

admixture ▶ **noun** a mixture: *he felt that his work was an admixture of aggression and creativity.*
■ something mixed with something else, typically as a minor ingredient: *green with an admixture of black.* ■ [mass noun] the action of adding such an ingredient.
– ORIGIN early 17th cent. (in the sense 'act of admixing'): from **AD-** (expressing addition) + **MIXTURE**.

admonish ▶ **verb** [with obj.] warn or reprimand someone firmly: *she admonished me for appearing at breakfast unshaven* | [with obj. and direct speech] *'You mustn't say that, Shiona,' Ruth admonished her.*
■ [with obj. and infinitive] advise or urge (someone) earnestly: *she admonished him to drink no more than one glass of wine.* ■ archaic warn (someone) of something to be avoided: *he* ***admonished*** *the people* ***against*** *the evil of such practices.*
– DERIVATIVES **admonishment** noun.
– ORIGIN Middle English *amonest* 'urge, exhort', from Old French *amonester*, based on Latin *admonere* 'urge by warning'. Later, the final *-t* of *amonest* was taken to indicate the past tense, and the present tense changed on the pattern of verbs such as *abolish*; the prefix became *ad-* in the 16th cent. by association with the Latin form.

admonitory /ədˈmɒnɪt(ə)ri/ ▶ **adjective** giving or conveying a warning or reprimand: *the sergeant lifted an admonitory finger.*
– DERIVATIVES **admonition** noun, **admonitor** noun.
– ORIGIN late 16th cent.: from medieval Latin *admonitorius*, from *admonit-* 'urged', from Latin *admonere* (see **ADMONISH**).

ADN ▶ **abbreviation for** Yemen (international vehicle registration).
– ORIGIN from **ADEN**.

adnate /ˈadneɪt/ ▶ **adjective** Botany joined by having grown together.
– ORIGIN mid 17th cent.: from Latin *adnatus*, variant of *agnatus* (see **AGNATE**), by association with **AD-**.

ad nauseam /ad ˈnɔːzɪam, -sɪam/ ▶ **adverb** used to refer to the fact that something has been done or repeated so often that it has become annoying or tiresome: *the inherent risks of nuclear power have been debated ad nauseam.*
– ORIGIN Latin, literally 'to sickness'.

adnexa /adˈnɛksə/ ▶ **plural noun** Anatomy the parts adjoining an organ.
– DERIVATIVES **adnexal** adjective.
– ORIGIN late 19th cent.: Latin, neuter plural of *adnexus* 'joined', from *adnectere* 'fasten to'.

adnominal /ədˈnɒmɪn(ə)l/ ▶ **adjective** Grammar attached to or modifying a noun.
– ORIGIN mid 19th cent.: from Latin *adnomen* 'added name' + **-AL**.

Adnyamathanha /ˈadnjəˌmʌdənə/ ▶ **noun** [mass noun] an Aboriginal language of South Australia.

ado ▶ **noun** [mass noun] trouble or difficulty: *she had* ***much ado*** *to keep up with him.*
■ fuss, especially about something that is unimportant: *this is* ***much ado*** *about almost nothing.*
– PHRASES **what's ado** archaic what's the matter? **without further** (or **more**) **ado** without any fuss or delay; immediately.
– ORIGIN late Middle English (originally in the sense 'action, business'): from northern Middle English *at do* 'to do', from Old Norse *at* (used to mark an infinitive) and **DO**[1].

-ado /ˈeɪdəʊ, ˈɑː-/ ▶ **suffix** forming nouns such as *bravado*, *desperado*. Compare with **-ADE**[3].
– ORIGIN from Spanish and Portuguese *-ado*, or refashioning of Italian *-ata*, Spanish *-ada*, based on Latin *-atus* (past participial suffix of verbs ending in *-are*).

adobe /əˈdəʊbi, əˈdəʊb/ ▶ **noun** [mass noun] a kind of clay used as a building material, typically in the form of sun-dried bricks: [as modifier] *adobe houses.*
■ [count noun] a brick of such a type. ■ [count noun] US a building constructed from such material.
– ORIGIN mid 18th cent.: from Spanish, from *adobar* 'to plaster', from Arabic *aṭ-ṭūb*, from *al* 'the' + *ṭūb* 'bricks'.

adolescence ▶ **noun** [mass noun] the period following the onset of puberty during which a young person develops from a child into an adult.
– ORIGIN late Middle English: from French, from Latin *adolescentia*, from *adolescere* 'grow to maturity' (see **ADOLESCENT**).

adolescent ▶ **adjective** (of a young person) in the process of developing from a child into an adult.
■ relating to or characteristic of this process: *his adolescent years | adolescent problems.*
▶ **noun** an adolescent boy or girl.
– ORIGIN late Middle English (as a noun): via French from Latin *adolescent-* 'coming to maturity', from *adolescere*, from *ad-* 'to' + *alescere* 'grow, grow up', from *alere* 'nourish'. The adjective dates from the late 18th cent.

Adonai /ˌadɒˈnʌɪ, -ˈneɪʌɪ/ ▶ **noun** a Hebrew name for God.
– ORIGIN from Hebrew *'ăḏōnāy*; see also **JEHOVAH**.

Adonis /əˈdəʊnɪs/ Greek Mythology a beautiful youth loved by both Aphrodite and Persephone. He was killed by a boar, but Zeus decreed that he should spend the winter of each year in the underworld with Persephone and the summer months with Aphrodite.
■ [as noun **an Adonis**] an extremely handsome young man.

Adonis blue ▶ **noun** a small Eurasian butterfly, the male of which has vivid sky-blue wings.
• *Lysandra bellargus*, family Lycaenidae.

a

adopt ▶ verb [with obj.] legally take (another's child) and bring it up as one's own: *there are many people eager to adopt a baby.*
■ take up or start to use or follow (something, especially an idea, method, or course of action): *this approach has been adopted by many big banks.* ■ choose and move to (a country or city) as one's permanent place of residence. ■ take on or assume (an attitude or position): *he adopted a patronizing tone | adopt a slightly knees-bent position.* ■ Brit. choose (someone) as a candidate for office: *she was recently adopted as Labour candidate for the constituency.* ■ formally approve or accept (a report or suggestion): *the committee voted 5–1 to adopt the proposal.* ■ choose (a textbook) as standard or required for a course of study. ■ Brit. (of a local authority) accept responsibility for the maintenance of (a road).
– DERIVATIVES **adoptable** adjective, **adoptee** noun, **adopter** noun.
– ORIGIN late 15th cent.: via French from Latin *adoptare*, from *ad-* 'to' + *optare* 'choose'.

adoption ▶ noun [mass noun] the action or fact of adopting or being adopted: *she gave up her children for adoption | the widespread adoption of agricultural technology |* [as modifier] *an adoption agency.*
– ORIGIN Middle English: from Latin *adoptio(n-)*, from *ad-* 'to' + *optio(n-)* 'choosing' (see **OPTION**).

Adoptionist ▶ noun Christian Theology, chiefly historical a person holding the view that Christ is the son of God by adoption only.

adoptive ▶ adjective as a result of the adoption of another's child: *adoptive parents.*
■ denoting a country or city to which a person has moved and in which they have chosen to make their permanent place of residence.
– DERIVATIVES **adoptively** adverb.
– ORIGIN late Middle English: via Old French from Latin *adoptivus*, from *adoptare* 'select for oneself' (see **ADOPT**).

adorable ▶ adjective inspiring great affection; delightful; charming: *she looked just adorable | I have four adorable Siamese cats.*
– DERIVATIVES **adorability** noun, **adorableness** noun, **adorably** adverb.
– ORIGIN early 17th cent. (in the sense 'worthy of divine worship'): from French, from Latin *adorabilis*, from the verb *adorare* (see **ADORE**).

adoral /ad'ɔːr(ə)l/ ▶ adjective Zoology relating to or denoting the side or end where the mouth is situated, especially in animals that lack clear upper and lower sides such as echinoderms: *the adoral shields.*
– DERIVATIVES **adorally** adverb.
– ORIGIN late 19th cent.: from **AD-** 'at' + **ORAL**.

adore ▶ verb [with obj.] love and respect (someone) deeply: *he adored his mother.*
■ worship; venerate: *he adored the Sacred Host.* ■ informal like (something or someone) very much: *she adores Mexican cuisine |* [as adj. **adoring**] *blowing a farewell kiss to an adoring crowd.*
– DERIVATIVES **adoration** noun, **adorer** noun, **adoringly** adverb.
– ORIGIN late Middle English: via Old French from Latin *adorare* 'to worship', from *ad-* 'to' + *orare* 'speak, pray'.

adorn ▶ verb [with obj.] make more beautiful or attractive: *pictures and prints adorned his walls.*
– DERIVATIVES **adorner** noun, **adornment** noun.
– ORIGIN late Middle English: via Old French from Latin *adornare*, from *ad-* 'to' + *ornare* 'deck, add lustre'.

Adorno /ə'dɔːnəʊ, German a'dɔrno/, Theodor Wiesengrund (1903–69), German philosopher, sociologist, and musicologist; born *Theodor Wiesengrund*. A member of the Frankfurt School, Adorno argued that philosophical authoritarianism is inevitably oppressive and that all theories should be rejected.

ADP ▶ abbreviation for ■ Biochemistry adenosine diphosphate. ■ automatic data processing.

ad personam /ˌad pəː'səʊnam/ ▶ adverb formal (of an appointment) assigned personally or on an individual basis.
– ORIGIN Latin.

adpressed ▶ adjective Botany lying closely against the adjacent part, or against the ground.
– ORIGIN early 19th cent.: from Latin *adpress-* 'pressed near', from *adprimere*, from *ad* 'to, at' + *premere* 'to press', + **-ED**[2].

ADR ▶ abbreviation for ■ alternative dispute resolution. ■ (in the US) American depositary receipt.

Adrar des Iforas /aˌdrɑː deɪz ɪ'fɔːrɑː/ a massif region in the central Sahara, on the border between Mali and Algeria.

ad rem /ad 'rɛm/ ▶ adverb & adjective formal relevant to what is being done or discussed at the time.
– ORIGIN late 16th cent.: Latin, literally 'to the matter'.

adrenal /ə'driːn(ə)l/ ▶ adjective of, relating to, or denoting a pair of ductless glands situated above the kidneys. Each consists of a core region (**adrenal medulla**) secreting adrenalin and noradrenaline, and an outer region (**adrenal cortex**) secreting corticosteroids.
▶ noun (usu. **adrenals**) an adrenal gland.
– ORIGIN late 19th cent.: from **AD-** + **RENAL**.

adrenalin /ə'drɛn(ə)lɪn/ (also **adrenaline**, US **Adrenalin** (trademark)) ▶ noun [mass noun] a hormone secreted by the adrenal glands, especially in conditions of stress, increasing rates of blood circulation, breathing, and carbohydrate metabolism and preparing muscles for exertion: *performing live really gets your adrenalin going.* Also called **EPINEPHRINE**.
– ORIGIN early 20th cent.: from **ADRENAL** + **-IN**[1].

adrenergic /ˌadrɪ'nəːdʒɪk/ ▶ adjective Physiology relating to or denoting nerve cells in which adrenalin, noradrenaline, or a similar substance acts as a neurotransmitter. Contrasted with **CHOLINERGIC**.
– ORIGIN 1930s: from **ADRENALIN** + Greek *ergon* 'work' + **-IC**.

adrenocorticotrophic hormone /əˌdriːnə(ʊ)ˌkɔːtɪkə(ʊ)'trəʊfɪk, -'trɒfɪk/ (also **adrenocorticotropic hormone** /-'trəʊpɪk, -'trɒpɪk/) (abbrev.: **ACTH**) ▶ noun [mass noun] Biochemistry a hormone secreted by the pituitary gland and stimulating the adrenal cortex.
– ORIGIN 1930s: from *adreno-* and *cortico-* (combining forms of **ADRENAL** and **CORTEX**) + **-TROPHIC** or **-TROPIC**.

adrenocorticotrophin /əˌdriːnə(ʊ)ˌkɔːtɪkə(ʊ)'trəʊfɪn, -'trɒfɪn/ (also **adrenocorticotropin** /-pɪn/) ▶ noun another term for **ADRENOCORTICOTROPHIC HORMONE**.

adret /'adreɪ/ ▶ noun Geography a mountain slope which faces the sun. Compare with **UBAC**.
– ORIGIN from French, from dialect variants of *à* 'to' and *droit* 'straight'.

Adrian IV (*c*.1100–59), pope 1154–9; born *Nicholas Breakspear*. He is the only Englishman to have held this office.

Adriatic /ˌeɪdrɪ'atɪk/ ▶ adjective of or relating to the region comprising the Adriatic Sea and its coasts and islands.
▶ noun (**the Adriatic**) the Adriatic Sea or its coasts and islands.

Adriatic, Marriage of the see **MARRIAGE OF THE ADRIATIC**.

Adriatic Sea an arm of the Mediterranean Sea between the Balkans and the Italian peninsula.

adrift ▶ adjective & adverb (of a boat or its passengers) floating without being either moored or steered: [as adv.] *a cargo ship **went adrift** |* [as predic. adj.] *the seamen are adrift in lifeboats.*
■ [as adv.] Brit. informal no longer fixed in position: *one of my fillings has **come adrift**.* ■ figurative (of a person) without purpose or guidance; lost and confused: [as predic. adj.] *he was adrift in a strange country |* [as adv.] *they were **cast adrift** in a sea of events.* ■ Brit. informal not working or reasoning properly: [as adv.] *the author **comes adrift** in tackling ethical issues |* [as predic. adj.] *his instincts were not entirely adrift.* ■ [as predic. adj.] Brit. informal failing to reach a target, typically a winning score in a sporting contest: *the team are three points **adrift of** the leaders.*
– ORIGIN late 16th cent.: from **A-**[2] 'on, in' + **DRIFT**.

adroit /ə'drɔɪt/ ▶ adjective clever or skilful in using the hands or mind: *he was **adroit at** tax avoidance.*
– DERIVATIVES **adroitly** adverb, **adroitness** noun.
– ORIGIN mid 17th cent.: from French, from *à droit* 'according to right, properly'.

adscititious /ˌadsɪ'tɪʃəs/ ▶ adjective rare forming an addition or supplement; not integral or intrinsic.
– ORIGIN early 17th cent.: from Latin *adscit-* 'admitted, adopted', from *adsciscere*, + **-ITIOUS**[1], on the pattern of *adventitious*.

adsorb /əd'zɔːb, -'sɔːb/ ▶ verb [with obj.] (of a solid) hold (molecules of a gas or liquid or solute) as a thin film on the outside surface or on internal surfaces within the material: *charcoal will not adsorb nitrates | the dye is **adsorbed on to** the fibre.*
– DERIVATIVES **adsorbable** adjective, **adsorption** noun, **adsorptive** adjective.
– ORIGIN late 19th cent.: blend of **AD-** (expressing adherence) + **ABSORB**.

adsorbate ▶ noun a substance adsorbed.

adsorbent ▶ noun a substance which adsorbs another.
▶ adjective able to adsorb substances.

adstratum /'adstrɑːtəm, ad'strɑːtəm/ ▶ noun (pl. **adstrata**) Linguistics a language or group of elements within it that is responsible for changes in a neighbouring language.
– DERIVATIVES **adstrate** adjective.
– ORIGIN 1930s: modern Latin, from Latin *ad* 'to' + *stratum* 'something laid down'.

ADT ▶ abbreviation for Atlantic Daylight Time (see **ATLANTIC TIME**).

aduki /ə'duːki/ ▶ noun variant spelling of **ADZUKI**.

adulate /'adjʊleɪt/ ▶ verb [with obj.] praise (someone) excessively or obsequiously.
– DERIVATIVES **adulator** noun, **adulatory** adjective.
– ORIGIN mid 18th cent.: from Latin *adulat-* 'fawned on', from the verb *adulari*.

adulation ▶ noun [mass noun] obsequious flattery; excessive admiration or praise: *he found it difficult to cope with the adulation of the fans.*
– ORIGIN late Middle English: from Latin *adulatio(n)-*, from *adulari* 'fawn on'.

Adullamite /ə'dʌləmʌɪt/ ▶ noun a member of a dissident political group (originally applied to a group of British MPs who seceded from the Liberal party in 1866).
– ORIGIN adopted in allusion to the cave of Adullam, where those discontented with the rule of Saul came to join David (1 Sam. 22:1–2).

adult /'adʌlt, ə'dʌlt/ ▶ noun a person who is fully grown or developed: *children should be accompanied by an adult.*
■ a fully developed animal. ■ Law a person who has reached the age of majority.
▶ adjective (of a person or animal) fully grown or developed: *the adult inhabitants of Britain.*
■ of or for adult people: *adult education | the responsibilities of adult life.* ■ emotionally and mentally mature: *an effort to be adult and civilized.* ■ suitable only for adults (used euphemistically to refer to a sexually explicit film, book, or magazine).
– DERIVATIVES **adulthood** noun, **adultly** adverb.
– ORIGIN mid 16th cent.: from Latin *adultus*, past participle of *adolescere* 'grow to maturity' (see **ADOLESCENT**).

adulterant ▶ noun a substance used to adulterate another.
▶ adjective used in adulterating something.
– ORIGIN mid 18th cent.: from Latin *adulterant-* 'corrupting', from the verb *adulterare* (see **ADULTERATE**).

adulterate ▶ verb /ə'dʌltəreɪt/ [with obj.] render (something) poorer in quality by adding another substance, typically an inferior one: *the food provided by industry is often adulterated.*
▶ adjective /ə'dʌlt(ə)rət/ archaic not pure or genuine: *adulterate remedies.*
– DERIVATIVES **adulteration** noun, **adulterator** noun.
– ORIGIN early 16th cent. (as an adjective): from Latin *adulterat-* 'corrupted', from the verb *adulterare*.

adulterer ▶ noun a person who commits adultery.
– ORIGIN early 16th cent.: from the obsolete verb *adulter* 'commit adultery', from Latin *adulterare* 'debauch, corrupt', replacing an earlier Middle English noun *avouterer*, from Old French *avoutrer* 'commit adultery'.

adulteress ▶ noun a female adulterer.

adulterine /ə'dʌlt(ə)rʌɪn/ ▶ adjective (of a child) born as the result of an adulterous relationship.
■ archaic or historical illegal, unlicensed, or spurious: *an adulterine castle.*
– ORIGIN mid 18th cent. (in the sense 'due to adulteration'): from Latin *adulterinus*, from *adulterare* 'debauch, corrupt'.

adulterous ▶ adjective of or involving adultery: *an adulterous affair.*
– DERIVATIVES **adulterously** adverb.
– ORIGIN mid 16th cent.: from the obsolete noun *adulter* 'adulterer' (see **ADULTERY**) + **-OUS**.

adultery ▶ **noun** [mass noun] voluntary sexual intercourse between a married person and a person who is not their spouse: *she was* ***committing adultery*** *with a much younger man.*
– ORIGIN late 15th cent.: from the obsolete noun *adulter*, from Latin *adulter* 'adulterer', replacing an earlier form *avoutrie*, from Old French *avouterie*.

adumbrate /'adʌmbreɪt/ ▶ **verb** [with obj.] formal report or represent in outline: *Hobhouse had already adumbrated the idea of a welfare state.*
■ indicate faintly: *the walls were only adumbrated by the meagre light.* ■ foreshadow or prefigure (a future event): *tenors solemnly adumbrate the fate of the convicted sinner.* ■ overshadow: *her happy reminiscences were adumbrated by consciousness of something else.*
– DERIVATIVES **adumbration** noun, **adumbrative** adjective.
– ORIGIN late 16th cent.: from Latin *adumbrat-* 'shaded', from the verb *adumbrare*, from *ad-* 'to' (as an intensifier) + *umbrare* 'cast a shadow' (from *umbra* 'shade').

adust /ə'dʌst/ ▶ **adjective** archaic **1** scorched; burnt.
2 gloomy; melancholic.
– ORIGIN late Middle English: from French *aduste* or Latin *adustus* 'burnt', from *adurere*, from *ad* 'to' (as an intensifier) + *urere* 'to burn'.

Advaita /ʌd'vʌɪtʌ/ ▶ **noun** [mass noun] Hinduism a Vedantic doctrine that identifies the individual self (atman) with the ground of reality (brahman). It is associated especially with the Indian philosopher Shankara (*c.*788–820).
– ORIGIN Sanskrit, literally 'non-duality'.

ad valorem /ˌad və'lɔːrɛm/ ▶ **adverb** & **adjective** (of the levying of tax or customs duties) in proportion to the estimated value of the goods or transaction concerned.
– ORIGIN Latin, 'according to the value'.

advance ▶ **verb 1** [no obj.] move forwards, typically in a purposeful way: *the troops* ***advanced on*** *the capital | she stood up and advanced towards him.*
■ make progress: *our knowledge is advancing all the time.* ■ [with obj.] cause (an event) to occur at an earlier date than planned: *I advanced the schedule by several weeks.* ■ [with obj.] promote or help the progress of (a person, cause, or plan): *it was a chance to advance his own interests.* ■ put forward (a theory or suggestion): *the hypothesis I wish to advance in this article.* ■ (especially of shares) increase in price.
2 [with two objs] lend (money) to (someone): *the building society advanced them a loan.*
■ pay (money) to (someone) before it is due: *he advanced me a month's salary.*
▶ **noun 1** a forward movement: *the rebels' advance on Madrid was well under way |* figurative *the advance of civilization.*
■ a development or improvement: *genuine* ***advances in*** *engineering techniques |* [mass noun] *decades of great scientific advance.* ■ an increase or rise in amount, value, or price: *any advance on £40?*
2 an amount of money paid before it is due or for work only partly completed: *the author was paid a £250,000 advance | I asked for an* ***advance on*** *next month's salary.*
■ a loan: *an advance from the bank.*
3 (usu. **advances**) an approach made to someone, typically with the aim of initiating a sexual or amorous relationship or encounter: *her tutor* ***made advances to*** *her.*
▶ **adjective** [attrib.] done, sent, or supplied beforehand: *advance notice | advance payment.*
– PHRASES **in advance** ahead in time: *you need to book weeks in advance.* **in advance of** ahead of in time or space; before.
– DERIVATIVES **advancer** noun.
– ORIGIN Middle English: from Old French *avance* (noun), *avancer* (verb), from late Latin *abante* 'in front', from *ab* 'from' + *ante* 'before'. The initial *a-* was erroneously assimilated to **AD-** in the 16th cent.

Advance Australia ▶ **noun** a catchphrase used as a patriotic slogan or motto in Australia.

Advance Australia Fair the national anthem of Australia, composed *c.*1878 by P. D. McCormick (*c.*1834–1916), a Scot, under the pen-name 'Amicus'. It officially replaced 'God Save the Queen' in 1984.

advanced ▶ **adjective** far on or ahead in development or progress: *negotiations are at an advanced stage | the cancer is hopelessly advanced | people of advanced years.*
■ new and not yet generally accepted: *his advanced views made him unpopular.*

advanced gas-cooled reactor (abbrev.: **AGR**) ▶ **noun** a nuclear reactor in which the coolant is carbon dioxide, with uranium oxide fuel clad in steel and using graphite as a moderator.

advance directive ▶ **noun** a living will which gives durable power of attorney to a surrogate decision-maker, remaining in effect during the incompetency of the person making it.

advanced level ▶ **noun** [mass noun] (in the UK except Scotland) the higher of the two main levels of the GCE examination. Compare with **ORDINARY LEVEL**.

advanced subsidiary level ▶ **noun** [mass noun] (in the UK except Scotland) a GCE examination at a level between GCSE and advanced level.

advance guard (also **advanced guard**) ▶ **noun** a body of soldiers preceding and making preparations for the main body of an army.

advance man ▶ **noun** chiefly N. Amer. a person who visits a location before the arrival of an important visitor to make the appropriate arrangements.

advancement ▶ **noun** [mass noun] the process of promoting a cause or plan: *their lives were devoted to the advancement of science.*
■ the promotion of a person in rank or status: *opportunities for career advancement.* ■ [count noun] a development or improvement: *technological advancements.*
– ORIGIN Middle English: from Old French *avancement*, from *avancer* 'to advance'.

advantage ▶ **noun** a condition or circumstance that puts one in a favourable or superior position: *companies with a computerized database are* ***at an advantage*** *| she had an* ***advantage over*** *her mother's generation.*
■ [mass noun] the opportunity to gain something; benefit or profit: *you could learn something* ***to your advantage*** *| he saw some advantage in the proposal.* ■ a favourable or desirable circumstance or feature; a benefit: *the village's proximity to the town is an advantage.* ■ Tennis a player's score in a game when they have won the first point after deuce (and will win the game if they win the next point).
▶ **verb** [with obj.] put in a favourable or more favourable position.
– PHRASES **have the advantage of** dated be in a stronger position than. **take advantage of 1** exploit or make unfair use of for one's own benefit: *people tend to take advantage of a placid nature.* ■ dated (of a man) seduce (a woman). **2** make good use of the opportunities offered by (something): *take full advantage of the facilities available.* **to advantage** in a way which displays or makes good use of the best aspects of something: *her shoes showed off her legs to advantage | plan your space* ***to its best advantage.*** **turn something to advantage** (or **to one's advantage**) handle or respond to something in such a way as to benefit from it.
– DERIVATIVES **advantageous** /adv(ə)n'teɪdʒəs/ adjective, **advantageously** adverb.
– ORIGIN Middle English: from Old French *avantage*, from *avant* 'in front', from late Latin *abante* (see **ADVANCE**).

advantaged ▶ **adjective** having a comparatively favourable position, typically in terms of economic or social circumstances: *children from less advantaged homes.*

advection /əd'vɛkʃ(ə)n/ ▶ **noun** [mass noun] the transfer of heat or matter by the flow of a fluid, especially horizontally in the atmosphere or the sea.
– DERIVATIVES **advect** verb, **advective** adjective.
– ORIGIN early 20th cent.: from Latin *advectio(n-)*, from *advehere* 'bring', from *ad-* 'to' + *vehere* 'carry'.

advent /'adv(ə)nt, -vɛnt/ ▶ **noun** [in sing.] the arrival of a notable person, thing, or event: *the advent of television.*
■ (**Advent**) the first season of the church year, leading up to Christmas and including the four preceding Sundays. ■ (**Advent**) Christian Theology the coming or second coming of Christ.
– ORIGIN Old English, from Latin *adventus* 'arrival', from *advenire*, from *ad-* 'to' + *venire* 'come'.

Advent calendar ▶ **noun** a calendar made of card containing small numbered flaps, one of which is opened on each day of Advent to reveal a picture appropriate to the season.

Adventist ▶ **noun** a member of any of various Christian sects emphasizing belief in the imminent second coming of Christ. See also **SEVENTH-DAY ADVENTIST**.
– DERIVATIVES **Adventism** noun.

adventitia /ˌadvɛn'tɪʃə/ ▶ **noun** [mass noun] the outermost layer of the wall of a blood vessel.
– DERIVATIVES **adventitial** adjective.
– ORIGIN late 19th cent.: shortening of modern Latin *tunica adventitia* 'additional sheath'.

adventitious /ˌadv(ə)n'tɪʃəs/ ▶ **adjective** happening or carried on according to chance rather than design or inherent nature: *adventitious similarities.*
■ coming from outside; not native: *the adventitious population.* ■ Biology formed accidentally or in an unusual anatomical position: *adventitious lobes may appear between the primaries.* ■ Botany (of a root) growing directly from the stem or other upper part of a plant.
– DERIVATIVES **adventitiously** adverb.
– ORIGIN early 17th cent.: from Latin *adventicius* 'coming to us from abroad' (from *advenire* 'arrive') + **-OUS** (see also **-ITIOUS**[2]).

Advent Sunday ▶ **noun** the first Sunday in Advent, falling on or near 30 November.

adventure ▶ **noun** an unusual and exciting, often hazardous, experience or activity: *her recent adventures in Italy.*
■ [mass noun] excitement arising from or associated with danger or the taking of risks: *she travelled the world in search of adventure | a sense of adventure.* ■ archaic a commercial speculation.
▶ **verb** [no obj.] dated engage in hazardous and exciting activity, especially the exploration of unknown territory: *they had* ***adventured into*** *the forest.*
■ [with obj.] dated put (something, typically money or one's life) at risk: *he adventured £300 in the purchase of land.*
– DERIVATIVES **adventuresome** adjective.
– ORIGIN Middle English: from Old French *aventure* (noun), *aventurer* (verb), based on Latin *adventurus* 'about to happen', from *advenire* 'arrive'.

adventure game ▶ **noun** a type of computer game in which the participant plays a fantasy role in an episodic adventure story.

adventure playground ▶ **noun** Brit. a playground containing various different objects or structures, such as ropes, slides, and tunnels, for children to play on or in.

adventurer ▶ **noun** a person who enjoys or seeks adventure.
■ a person willing to take risks or use dishonest methods for personal gain: *a political adventurer.* ■ archaic a financial speculator. ■ archaic a mercenary soldier.
– ORIGIN late 15th cent. (denoting a gambler): from French *aventurier*, from *aventurer* 'venture upon' (see **ADVENTURE**).

adventuress ▶ **noun** a woman who enjoys or seeks adventure.
■ a woman who seeks social or financial advancement by dishonest or unscrupulous methods.

adventurism ▶ **noun** [mass noun] the willingness to take risks in business or politics (especially in the context of foreign policy); actions, tactics, or attitudes regarded as reckless or potentially hazardous.
– DERIVATIVES **adventurist** noun & adjective.

adventurous ▶ **adjective** willing to take risks or to try out new methods, ideas, or experiences: *let's be adventurous | an adventurous traveller.*
■ involving new ideas or methods: *they wanted more adventurous meals.* ■ full of excitement: *my life couldn't be more adventurous.*
– DERIVATIVES **adventurously** adverb, **adventurousness** noun.
– ORIGIN Middle English: from Old French *aventureus*, from *aventure* (see **ADVENTURE**).

adverb ▶ **noun** Grammar a word or phrase that typically modifies the meaning of an adjective, verb, or other adverb, typically expressing manner, place, time, or degree (e.g. *gently, here, now, very*). Some adverbs, for example **sentence adverbs**, can also be used to modify whole sentences.
– ORIGIN late Middle English: from Latin *adverbium*, from *ad-* 'to' (expressing addition) + *verbum* 'word, verb'.

adverbial Grammar ▶ **noun** a word or phrase (typically a prepositional phrase) functioning as a major clause constituent and typically expressing place (*in the garden*), time (*in May*), or manner (*in a strange way*).

a

▶ **adjective** relating to or functioning as an adverb or adverbial.
– DERIVATIVES **adverbially** adverb.

adversarial /ˌadvəˈsɛːrɪəl/ ▶ **adjective** involving or characterized by conflict or opposition: *the industry and the government have had an adversarial relationship.*
■ Law (of a trial or legal procedure) in which the parties in a dispute have the responsibility for finding and presenting evidence: *an adversarial system of justice.* Compare with **ACCUSATORIAL**, **INQUISITORIAL**.
– DERIVATIVES **adversarially** adverb.

adversary /ˈadvəs(ə)ri/ ▶ **noun** (pl. **-ies**) one's opponent in a contest, conflict, or dispute: *Davis beat his old adversary in the quarter-finals.*
■ (**the Adversary**) the Devil.
▶ **adjective** /ˈadvəs(ə)ri, adˈvəːsəri/ another term for **ADVERSARIAL**: *the confrontations of adversary politics.*
– ORIGIN Middle English: from Old French *adversarie*, from Latin *adversarius* 'opposed, opponent', from *adversus* (see **ADVERSE**).

adversative /ədˈvəːsətɪv/ ▶ **adjective** Grammar (of a word or phrase) expressing opposition or antithesis.
– ORIGIN late Middle English: from French *adversatif*, *-ive* or late Latin *adversativus*, from Latin *adversari* 'oppose', from *adversus* (see **ADVERSE**).

adverse /ˈadvəːs/ ▶ **adjective** preventing success or development; harmful; unfavourable: *taxes are having an adverse effect on production* | *adverse weather conditions.*
– DERIVATIVES **adversely** adverb.
– ORIGIN late Middle English: from Old French *advers*, from Latin *adversus* 'against, opposite', past participle of *advertere*, from *ad-* 'to' + *vertere* 'to turn'. Compare with **AVERSE**.

USAGE The two words **adverse** and **averse** are related in origin but they do not have the same meaning. **Adverse** means 'unfavourable or harmful' and is normally used of conditions and effects rather than people, as in ***adverse** weather conditions.* **Averse**, on the other hand, is used of people, nearly always with **to**, and means 'having a strong dislike or opposition to something', as in *I am not **averse to** helping out.* A common error is to use **adverse** instead of **averse**, as in *he is not **adverse to** making a profit.* Around 15 per cent of citations in the British National Corpus where the meaning is **averse** use the incorrect form **adverse**.

adversity ▶ **noun** (pl. **-ies**) [mass noun] difficulties; misfortune: *resilience in the face of adversity* | [count noun] *she overcame many adversities.*
– ORIGIN Middle English: from Old French *adversite*, from Latin *adversitas*, from *advertere* 'turn towards'.

advert[1] /ˈadvəːt/ ▶ **noun** Brit. informal an advertisement.
– ORIGIN mid 19th cent.: abbreviation.

advert[2] /ədˈvəːt/ ▶ **verb** [no obj.] (**advert to**) formal refer to in speaking or writing.
– ORIGIN late Middle English: from Old French *avertir*, from Latin *advertere* 'turn towards' (see **ADVERSE**). The original sense was 'turn one's attention to', later 'bring to someone's attention'.

advertise ▶ **verb** [with obj.] describe or draw attention to (a product, service, or event) in a public medium in order to promote sales or attendance: *a billboard advertising beer* | *many rugs are **advertised as** machine washable* | [no obj.] *we had a chance to advertise on television.*
■ seek to fill (a vacancy) by putting a notice in a newspaper or other medium: *for every job we advertise we get a hundred applicants* | [no obj.] *he **advertised for** dancers in the trade papers.* ■ make (a quality or fact) known: *Meryl coughed briefly to advertise her presence.* ■ archaic notify (someone) of something: *some prisoners **advertised** the French **of** this terrible danger.*
– DERIVATIVES **advertiser** noun.
– ORIGIN late Middle English: from Old French *advertiss-*, lengthened stem of *advertir*, from Latin *advertere* 'turn towards' (see **ADVERT**[2]).

advertisement ▶ **noun** a notice or announcement in a public medium promoting a product, service, or event or publicizing a job vacancy: ***advertisements for** alcoholic drinks.*
■ (**advertisement for**) informal a person or thing regarded as a means of recommending something: *unhappy clients are not a good advertisement for the firm.* ■ archaic a notice to readers in a book.
– ORIGIN late Middle English (denoting a statement calling attention to something): from Old French *advertissement*, from the verb *advertir* (see **ADVERTISE**).

advertising ▶ **noun** [mass noun] the activity or profession of producing advertisements for commercial products or services: *cinema audiences are receptive to advertising* | [as modifier] *an advertising agency.*

Advertising Standards Authority (abbrev.: **ASA**) (in the UK) an independent regulatory body set up in 1962 to monitor standards within advertising and to ensure that advertisements comply with the requirement that they be legal, decent, honest, and truthful.

advertorial /ˌadvəːˈtɔːrɪəl/ ▶ **noun** a newspaper or magazine advertisement giving information about a product in the style of an editorial or objective journalistic article.
– ORIGIN 1960s (originally US): blend of **ADVERTISEMENT** and **EDITORIAL**.

advice ▶ **noun** [mass noun] guidance or recommendations concerning prudent future action, typically given by someone regarded as knowledgeable or authoritative: *she visited the island **on** her doctor's **advice*** | *even successful businessmen **asked** his **advice**.*
■ [count noun] a formal notice of a financial transaction: *remittance advices.* ■ (also **advices**) archaic information; news: *the want of fresh advices from Europe.*
– PHRASES **take advice** obtain information and guidance, typically from an expert: *he should take advice from his accountant.* **take someone's advice** act according to recommendations given by someone: *he took my advice and put his house up for sale.*
– ORIGIN Middle English: from Old French *avis*, based on Latin *ad* 'to' + *visum*, past participle of *videre* 'to see'. The original sense was 'way of looking at something, judgement', hence later 'an opinion given'.

advisable ▶ **adjective** [often with infinitive] (of a course of action) to be recommended; sensible: *it is advisable to carry one of the major credit cards* | *early booking is advisable.*
– DERIVATIVES **advisability** noun, **advisably** adverb.

advise ▶ **verb** [reporting verb] offer suggestions about the best course of action to someone: [with obj. and infinitive] *I advised him to go home* | [with obj.] *he advised caution* | [no obj.] *we **advise against** sending cash by post* | [with direct speech] *'Go to Paris,' he advised.*
■ [with obj.] recommend (something): *sleeping pills are not advised.* ■ [with obj.] inform (someone) about a fact or situation, typically in a formal or official way: *you will **be advised of** the requirements* | [with obj. and clause] *the lawyer advised the court that his client wished to give evidence.*
– ORIGIN Middle English: from Old French *aviser*, based on Latin *ad-* 'to' + *visere*, frequentative of *videre* 'to see'. The original senses included 'look at' and 'consider', hence 'consult with others'.

advised ▶ **adjective** behaving as someone, especially the speaker, would recommend; sensible; wise: *you **would be advised to** check on increases to your pension.*

advisedly ▶ **adverb** deliberately and after consideration (used especially of what might appear a mistake or oversight): *I've used the term 'old' advisedly.*

advisement ▶ **noun** [mass noun] archaic or N. Amer. careful consideration.
■ advice or counsel.
– PHRASES **take something under advisement** N. Amer. reserve judgement while considering something.
– ORIGIN Middle English: from Old French *avisement*, from *aviser* 'look at' (see **ADVISE**).

adviser (also **advisor**) ▶ **noun** a person who gives advice, typically someone who is expert in a particular field: *the military **adviser to** the President.*

USAGE The spelling **advisor** is much less common than **adviser** (in the British National Corpus only around 10 per cent of citations are for the **-or** spelling) and is more common in North America than in Britain (in the Oxford Reading Programme, 7 out of every 8 citations for **advisor** are from North American sources). The **-or** spelling is a more recent development and is still regarded by some people as incorrect.

advisory ▶ **adjective** having or consisting in the power to make recommendations but not to take action enforcing them: *an independent advisory committee* | *the Commission acts in an advisory capacity.*
■ recommended but not compulsory: *the EC has put forward an advisory maximum figure.*
▶ **noun** (pl. **-ies**) N. Amer. an official announcement, typically a warning about bad weather conditions.

advocaat /ˈadvəkɑː/ ▶ **noun** [mass noun] a liqueur made with eggs, sugar, and brandy.
– ORIGIN 1930s: from Dutch, literally 'advocate' (being originally considered a lawyer's drink).

advocacy /ˈadvəkəsi/ ▶ **noun** [mass noun] public support for or recommendation of a particular cause or policy: *their **advocacy of** family values.*
■ the profession or work of a legal advocate.
– ORIGIN late Middle English: via Old French from medieval Latin *advocatia*, from *advocare* 'summon, call to one's aid' (see **ADVOCATE**).

advocate ▶ **noun** /ˈadvəkət/ a person who publicly supports or recommends a particular cause or policy: *he was an untiring **advocate of** economic reform.*
■ a person who puts a case on someone else's behalf: *care managers can become advocates for their clients.* ■ a professional pleader in a court of justice. ■ Scottish term for **BARRISTER**. ■ (in South Africa) a lawyer who pleads the cause of a client in the Supreme and Appeal Courts.
▶ **verb** /ˈadvəkeɪt/ [with obj.] publicly recommend or support: *voters supported candidates who advocated an Assembly.*
– DERIVATIVES **advocateship** noun, **advocation** noun.
– ORIGIN Middle English: from Old French *avocat*, from Latin *advocatus*, past participle (used as a noun) of *advocare* 'call (to one's aid)', from *ad-* 'to' + *vocare* 'to call'.

advocate-depute ▶ **noun** (in Scotland) any of a number of officers who assist the Lord Advocate in prosecutions.

advocate-general ▶ **noun** any of a number of officers assisting the judges in the European Court of Justice.

advowson /ədˈvaʊz(ə)n/ ▶ **noun** Brit. (in ecclesiastical law) the right to recommend a member of the Anglican clergy for a vacant benefice, or to make such an appointment.
– ORIGIN Middle English (in the sense 'patronage of a religious house or benefice', with the obligation to defend it and speak for it): from Old French *avoeson*, from Latin *advocatio(n-)*, from *advocare* 'summon' (see **ADVOCATE**).

advt ▶ **abbreviation for** advertisement.

Adygea /ˈɑːdɪgeɪə, ˌɑːdɪˈgjeɪə/ an autonomous republic in the NW Caucasus in SW Russia, with a largely Muslim population; pop. 432,000 (1989); capital, Maikop. Full name **ADYGEI AUTONOMOUS REPUBLIC** /ˈɑːdɪgeɪ, ˌɑːdɪˈgjeɪ/.

Adyghe /ˈadɪgeɪ, ˌɑːdɪˈgjeɪ/ (also **Adygei**) ▶ **noun** (pl. same) **1** a member of a mainly Sunni Muslim people of the NW Caucasus, especially Adygea. Also called **CIRCASSIAN**.
2 [mass noun] the North Caucasian language of this people, with about 100,000 speakers in the Caucasus and 100,000 elsewhere.
▶ **adjective** of or relating to this people or their language.

adytum /ˈadɪtəm/ ▶ **noun** (pl. **adyta** /-tə/) the innermost sanctuary of an ancient Greek temple.
– ORIGIN Latin, from Greek *aduton*, neuter singular of *adutos* 'impenetrable', from *a-* 'not' + *duein* 'enter'.

adze /adz/ (US **adz**) ▶ **noun** a tool similar to an axe, with an arched blade at right angles to the handle, used for cutting or shaping large pieces of wood.
– ORIGIN Old English *adesa*, of unknown origin.

adzuki /ədˈzuːki/ (also **adzuki bean**) (also **aduki**) ▶ **noun** (pl. **adzukis**) **1** a small, round dark-red edible bean.
2 the bushy Asian plant which produces this bean.
• *Vigna angularis*, family Leguminosae.
– ORIGIN early 18th cent.: from Japanese *azuki*.

AE ▶ **abbreviation for** auto-exposure.

Æ (also **æ**) ▶ **noun** a letter used in Old English to represent a vowel intermediate between a and e (see **ASH**[2]).

-ae /iː, ʌɪ/ ▶ **suffix** forming plural nouns: **1** used in names of animal and plant families and other groups: *Felidae* | *Gymnospermae.*
2 used instead of *-as* in the plural of many non-naturalized or unfamiliar nouns ending in *-a* derived from Latin or Greek: *striae* | *larvae.*
– ORIGIN Latin plural suffix, or representing the Greek plural ending *-ai.*

AEA ▶ abbreviation for (in the UK) Atomic Energy Authority.

AEC historical ▶ abbreviation for (in the US) Atomic Energy Commission.

aedile /'iːdʌɪl/ ▶ noun Roman History either of two (later four) Roman magistrates responsible for public buildings and originally also for the public games and the supply of corn to the city.
– DERIVATIVES **aedileship** noun.
– ORIGIN mid 16th cent.: from Latin *aedilis* 'concerned with buildings', from *aedes* 'building'.

AEEU ▶ abbreviation for (in the UK) Amalgamated Engineering and Electrical Union.

Aegean /iːˈdʒiːən, ɪ-/ ▶ adjective of or relating to the region comprising the Aegean Sea and its coasts and islands.
▶ noun (**the Aegean**) the Aegean Sea or its region.
– ORIGIN early 17th cent.: via Latin from Greek *Aigaios* + **-EAN**.

Aegean Islands a group of islands in the Aegean Sea, forming a region of Greece. The principal islands of the group are Chios, Samos, Lesbos, the Cyclades, and the Dodecanese.

Aegean Sea a part of the Mediterranean Sea lying between Greece and Turkey, bounded to the south by Crete and Rhodes and linked to the Black Sea by the Dardanelles, the Sea of Marmara, and the Bosporus.

aegis /'iːdʒɪs/ ▶ noun [in sing.] the protection, backing, or support of a particular organization or person: *the negotiations were conducted **under the aegis of the** UN.*
■ (in classical art and mythology) an attribute of Zeus and Athena (or their Roman counterparts Jupiter and Minerva) usually represented as a goatskin shield.
– ORIGIN early 17th cent. (denoting armour or a shield, especially that of a god): via Latin from Greek *aigis* 'shield of Zeus'.

Aegisthus /ɪˈɡɪsθəs/ Greek Mythology the son of Thyestes and lover of Agamemnon's wife Clytemnestra.

aegrotat /ʌɪˈɡrəʊtat, 'iː-, iːˈɡrəʊ-/ ▶ noun Brit. a certificate stating that a university student is too ill to attend an examination.
■ an examination pass awarded to a student having such a certificate.
– ORIGIN late 18th cent.: Latin, literally 'he is sick'.

Aelfric /'alfrɪk/ (c.955–c.1020), Anglo-Saxon monk, writer, and grammarian; known as **Grammaticus**. Notable works: *Lives of the Saints* (993–6).

-aemia (also **-haemia**, US **-emia** or **-hemia**) ▶ combining form in nouns denoting that a substance is present in the blood, especially in excess: *septicaemia* | *leukaemia*.
– ORIGIN modern Latin, from Greek *-aimia*, from *haima* 'blood'.

Aeneas /ɪˈniːəs/ Greek & Roman Mythology a Trojan leader, son of Anchises and Aphrodite, and legendary ancestor of the Romans. When Troy fell to the Greeks he escaped and after wandering for many years eventually reached Italy. The story of his voyage is recounted in Virgil's *Aeneid*.

Aeneid /ɪˈniːɪd, 'iːnɪɪd/ a Latin epic poem in twelve books by Virgil which relates the travels and experiences of Aeneas after the fall of Troy.

aeolian /iːˈəʊlɪən/ (US **eolian**) ▶ adjective chiefly Geology relating to or arising from the action of the wind.
– ORIGIN early 17th cent.: from the name **AEOLUS** + **-IAN**.

aeolian harp ▶ noun a stringed instrument that produces musical sounds when a current of air passes through it.

Aeolian Islands ancient name for **LIPARI ISLANDS**.

Aeolian mode /iːˈəʊlɪən/ ▶ noun Music the mode represented by the natural diatonic scale A–A (containing a minor 3rd, 6th, and 7th).
– ORIGIN late 18th cent.: from Latin *Aeolius*, 'from *Aeolis*' (an ancient coastal district of Asia Minor) + **-AN**.

Aeolus /'iːələs/ Greek Mythology the god of the winds.
– ORIGIN from Greek *Aiolos*, from *aiolos* 'swift, changeable'.

aeon /'iːən/ (US or technical also **eon**) ▶ noun (often **aeons**) an indefinite and very long period of time, especially a period exaggerated for humorous or rhetorical effect: *the shows were made aeons ago.*
■ Astronomy & Geology a unit of time equal to a thousand million years. ■ Geology a major division of geological time, subdivided into eras: *the Precambrian aeon.* ■ Philosophy (in Neoplatonism, Platonism, and Gnosticism) a power existing from eternity; an emanation or phase of the supreme deity.
– ORIGIN mid 17th cent.: via ecclesiastical Latin from Greek *aiōn* 'age'.

aepyornis /ˌiːpɪˈɔːnɪs/ ▶ noun another term for **ELEPHANT BIRD**.
– ORIGIN mid 19th cent.: modern Latin, from Greek *aipus* 'high' + *ornis* 'bird'.

aerate /'ɛːreɪt/ ▶ verb [with obj.] introduce air into (a material): *aerate the lawn using a garden fork.*
– DERIVATIVES **aeration** noun, **aerator** noun.
– ORIGIN late 18th cent.: from Latin *aer* 'air' + **-ATE**³, influenced by French *aérer*.

aerated ▶ adjective 1 (of a liquid) made effervescent by being charged with carbon dioxide or some other gas: *aerated spring water.*
2 Brit. informal agitated, angry, or over-excited: *don't get so aerated!*

aerenchyma /ɛːˈrɛŋkɪmə/ ▶ noun [mass noun] Botany a soft plant tissue containing air spaces, found especially in many aquatic plants.
– DERIVATIVES **aerenchymatous** adjective.
– ORIGIN late 19th cent.: from Greek *aēr* 'air' + *enkhuma* 'infusion'.

aerial /'ɛːrɪəl/ ▶ noun 1 a rod, wire, or other structure by which signals are transmitted or received as part of a radio or television transmission or receiving system.
2 (**aerials**) a type of freestyle skiing in which the skier jumps from a ramp and carries out manoeuvres in the air.
▶ adjective [attrib.] existing, happening, or operating in the air: *an aerial battle* | *an intrepid aerial adventurer.*
■ coming or carried out from the air, especially using aircraft: *aerial bombardment of civilian targets* | *aerial photography.* ■ (of a part of a plant) growing above ground. ■ (of a bird) spending much of its time in flight. ■ of or in the atmosphere; atmospheric. ■ figurative insubstantial and hard to grasp or define.
– DERIVATIVES **aeriality** noun, **aerially** adverb.
– ORIGIN late 16th cent. (in the sense 'thin as air, imaginary'): via Latin *aerius* from Greek *aerios* (from *aēr* 'air') + **-AL**.

aerialist ▶ noun a person who performs acrobatics high above the ground on a tightrope or trapezes.

aerial perspective ▶ noun [mass noun] Art the technique of representing more distant objects as fainter and more blue.

aerie ▶ noun US spelling of **EYRIE**.

aero ▶ adjective [attrib.] informal 1 aeronautical: *an aero club.*
2 aerodynamic: *we softened the lines for a more aero look.*
– ORIGIN early 20th cent. (in sense 1): abbreviation.

aero- /'ɛːrəʊ/ ▶ combining form 1 of or relating to air: *aerobe* | *aerobics.*
2 of or relating to aircraft: *aerotowing* | *aerodrome.*
– ORIGIN from Greek *aēr* 'air'.

aerobatics ▶ plural noun [usu. treated as sing.] loops, rolls, and other feats of spectacular flying performed in one or more aircraft to entertain an audience on the ground.
– DERIVATIVES **aerobatic** adjective.
– ORIGIN First World War: from **AERO-** + a shortened form of **ACROBATICS**.

aerobe /'ɛːrəʊb/ ▶ noun a micro-organism which grows in the presence of air or requires oxygen for growth.
– ORIGIN late 19th cent.: coined in French from Greek *aēr* + *bios* 'life'.

aerobic /ɛːˈrəʊbɪk/ ▶ adjective Biology relating to, involving, or requiring free oxygen: *simple aerobic bacteria.*
■ relating to or denoting exercise which improves or is intended to improve the efficiency of the body's cardiovascular system in absorbing and transporting oxygen.
– DERIVATIVES **aerobically** adverb.
– ORIGIN late 19th cent.: from **AERO-** + Greek *bios* 'life' + **-IC**.

aerobics ▶ plural noun [often treated as sing.] vigorous exercises designed to increase cardiovascular efficiency.

aerobiology ▶ noun [mass noun] the study of airborne micro-organisms, pollen, spores, and seeds, especially as agents of infection.

aerobrake ▶ verb [no obj.] technical cause a spacecraft to slow down by flying through a planet's rarefied atmosphere to produce aerodynamic drag.
▶ noun a mechanism for aerobraking.

aerodrome ▶ noun Brit. a small airport or airfield.

aerodynamic ▶ adjective of or relating to aerodynamics: *aerodynamic forces.*
■ of or having a shape which reduces the drag from air moving past: *the plane has a more aerodynamic shape.*
– DERIVATIVES **aerodynamically** adverb.

aerodynamics ▶ plural noun [treated as sing.] the study of the properties of moving air and especially of the interaction between the air and solid bodies moving through it.
■ [treated as pl.] the properties of a solid object regarding the manner in which air flows around it. ■ [treated as pl.] these properties in so far as they result in maximum efficiency of motion.
– DERIVATIVES **aerodynamicist** noun.

aeroelasticity ▶ noun [mass noun] the science of the interaction between aerodynamic forces and non-rigid structures.
– DERIVATIVES **aeroelastic** adjective.

aerofoil ▶ noun Brit. a structure with curved surfaces designed to give the most favourable ratio of lift to drag in flight, used as the basic form of the wings, fins, and tailplanes of most aircraft.

aerogel ▶ noun a solid material of extremely low density, produced by removing the liquid component from a conventional gel.

aerogramme (US **aerogram**) ▶ noun another term for **AIR LETTER**.

aerolite ▶ noun a meteorite made of stone.

aerology ▶ noun [mass noun] dated the study of the atmosphere, especially away from ground level.
– DERIVATIVES **aerological** adjective.

aeromagnetic ▶ adjective relating to or denoting the measurement of the earth's magnetic field using airborne instruments.

aeromedical ▶ adjective of or relating to the use of aircraft for medical purposes such as transporting patients to hospital.

aeromodelling ▶ noun [mass noun] the hobby of building and flying model aircrafts.
– DERIVATIVES **aeromodeller** noun.

aeronaut ▶ noun dated a traveller in a hot-air balloon, airship, or other flying craft.
– ORIGIN late 18th cent.: from French *aéronaute*, from Greek *aēr* 'air' + *nautēs* 'sailor'.

aeronautics ▶ plural noun [treated as sing.] the study or practice of travel through the air.
– DERIVATIVES **aeronautic** adjective, **aeronautical** adjective.
– ORIGIN early 19th cent.: from modern Latin *aeronautica* 'matters relating to aeronautics', from Greek (see **AERONAUT**).

aeronomy /ɛːˈrɒnəmi/ ▶ noun [mass noun] the study of the upper atmosphere, especially those regions where the ionization is important.

aerophagy /ɛːˈrɒfədʒi/ ▶ noun [mass noun] Medicine the swallowing of air, whether deliberately to stimulate belching, accidentally, or as an involuntary habit.

aerophone ▶ noun Music, technical a wind instrument.

aeroplane ▶ noun chiefly Brit. a powered flying vehicle with fixed wings and a weight greater than that of the air it displaces.
– ORIGIN late 19th cent.: from French *aéroplane*, from *aéro-* 'air' + Greek *-planos* 'wandering'.

aeroshell ▶ noun a casing which protects a spacecraft during re-entry.

aerosol ▶ noun a substance enclosed under pressure and able to be released as a fine spray, typically by means of a propellant gas.
■ a container holding such a substance. ■ Chemistry a colloidal suspension of particles dispersed in air or gas.
– ORIGIN 1920s: from **AERO-** + **SOL**².

aerosolize (also **-ise**) ▶ verb [with obj.] technical convert into a fine spray or colloidal suspension in air: [as adj. **aerosolized**] *the drug is being tested in an aerosolized form.*

aerospace ▶ noun [mass noun] the branch of technology and industry concerned with both aviation and space flight.

a

aerostat /ˈɛːrəstat/ ▶**noun** an airship or hot-air balloon.
– ORIGIN late 18th cent.: from French *aérostat*, from Greek *aēr* 'air' + *statos* 'standing'.

aerotowing ▶**noun** [mass noun] the towing of a glider by a powered aircraft to a height suitable for launching.

Aeschines /ˈiːskɪniːz/ (*c*.390–*c*.314 BC), Athenian orator and statesman. He opposed Demosthenes' efforts to unite the Greek city states against Macedon, with which he attempted to make peace.

Aeschylus /ˈiːskɪləs/ (*c*.525–*c*.456 BC), Greek dramatist. Aeschylus is best known for his trilogy the *Oresteia* (458 BC, consisting of the tragedies *Agamemnon*, *Choephoroe*, and *Eumenides*), which tells the story of Agamemnon's murder at the hands of his wife Clytemnestra and the vengeance of their son Orestes.

Aesculapian /ˌiːskjʊˈleɪpɪən/ ▶**adjective** archaic of or relating to medicine or physicians.
– ORIGIN late 16th cent.: from Latin *Aesculapius*, the name of the Roman god of medicine, + **-IAN**.

Aesculapian snake ▶**noun** a long, slender olive-brown to greyish snake found in Europe and SW Asia. In ancient times it was protected owing to its mythical link with the god of healing, Aesculapius.
• *Elaphe longissima*, family Colubridae.

Æsir /ˈiːsə/ Scandinavian Mythology the Norse gods and goddesses collectively, including Odin, Thor, and Balder.

Aesop /ˈiːsɒp/ (6th century BC), Greek storyteller. The moral animal fables associated with him were probably collected from many sources, and initially communicated orally. Aesop is said to have lived as a slave on the island of Samos.

aesthete /ˈiːsθiːt, ˈɛs-/ (US also **esthete**) ▶**noun** a person who is appreciative of or sensitive to art and beauty.
– ORIGIN late 19th cent.: from Greek *aisthētēs* 'a person who perceives', or from **AESTHETIC**, on the pattern of the pair *athlete, athletic*.

aesthetic /iːsˈθɛtɪk, ɛs-/ (US also **esthetic**) ▶**adjective** concerned with beauty or the appreciation of beauty: *the pictures give great aesthetic pleasure.*
■giving or designed to give pleasure through beauty; of pleasing appearance.
▶**noun** [in sing.] a set of principles underlying and guiding the work of a particular artist or artistic movement: *the Cubist aesthetic.*
– DERIVATIVES **aesthetically** adverb *an aesthetically pleasing colour combination.*
– ORIGIN late 18th cent. (in the sense 'relating to perception by the senses'): from Greek *aisthētikos*, from *aisthēta* 'perceptible things', from *aisthesthai* 'perceive'. The sense 'concerned with beauty' was coined in German in the mid 18th cent. and adopted into English in the early 19th cent., but its use was controversial until much later in the century.

aesthetician (US also **esthetician**) ▶**noun** **1** a person who is knowledgeable about the nature and appreciation of beauty, especially in art.
2 N. Amer. a beautician.

aestheticism (US also **estheticism**) ▶**noun** [mass noun] the approach to art exemplified by (but not restricted to) the Aesthetic Movement.

aestheticize (US also **estheticize**) ▶**verb** [with obj.] rare represent as being beautiful or artistically pleasing.

Aesthetic Movement a literary and artistic movement which flourished in England in the 1880s, devoted to 'art for art's sake' and rejecting the notion that art should have a social or moral purpose. Its chief exponents included Oscar Wilde, Max Beerbohm, Aubrey Beardsley, and others associated with the journal the *Yellow Book*.

aesthetics (US also **esthetics**) ▶**plural noun** [usu. treated as sing.] a set of principles concerned with the nature and appreciation of beauty, especially in art.
■the branch of philosophy which deals with questions of beauty and artistic taste.

aestival /ˈiːstɪv(ə)l, iːˈstʌɪv(ə)l, ˈɛst-, ɛˈstʌɪv(ə)l/ (US also **estival**) ▶**adjective** technical belonging to or appearing in summer.
– ORIGIN late Middle English: from Latin *aestivalis*, from *aestivus*, from *aestus* 'heat'.

aestivate /ˈiːstɪveɪt, ˈɛst-/ (US **estivate**) ▶**verb** [no obj.] Zoology (of an animal, especially an insect, fish, or amphibian) spend a hot or dry period in a prolonged state of torpor or dormancy.
– ORIGIN early 17th cent. (in the sense 'pass the summer'): from Latin *aestivat-*, from *aestivare* 'spend the summer', from *aestus* 'heat'.

aestivation /ˌiːstɪˈveɪʃ(ə)n, ˌɛst-/ (US **estivation**) ▶**noun** [mass noun] **1** Zoology prolonged torpor or dormancy of an animal during a hot or dry period.
2 Botany the arrangement of petals and sepals in a flower bud before it opens. Compare with **VERNATION**.

aet. (also **aetat.**) ▶**abbreviation for** aetatis.

a.e.t. ▶**abbreviation for** after extra time (in a soccer match).

aetatis /ʌɪˈtɑːtɪs, iː-/ ▶**adjective** of or at the age of.
– ORIGIN Latin.

aether ▶**noun** variant spelling of **ETHER** (in senses 2 and 3).

aetiology /ˌiːtɪˈɒlədʒi/ (US **etiology**) ▶**noun** [mass noun] **1** Medicine the cause, set of causes, or manner of causation of a disease or condition.
■the causation of diseases and disorders as a subject of investigation.
2 the investigation or attribution of the cause or reason for something, often expressed in terms of historical or mythical explanation.
– DERIVATIVES **aetiologic** adjective, **aetiological** adjective, **aetiologically** adverb.
– ORIGIN mid 16th cent.: via medieval Latin from Greek *aitiologia*, from *aitia* 'a cause' + *-logia* (see **-LOGY**).

AEU historical ▶**abbreviation for** (in the UK) Amalgamated Engineering Union.

AF ▶**abbreviation for** ■ audio frequency. ■ autofocus.

af- ▶**prefix** variant spelling of **AD-** assimilated before *f* (as in *affiliate, affirm*).

Afar /ˈɑːfɑː/ ▶**noun** (pl. same or **Afars**) **1** a member of a people living in Djibouti and NE Ethiopia. Also called **DANAKIL**.
2 [mass noun] the Cushitic language of this people, with about 700,000 speakers.
▶**adjective** of or relating to this people or their language.
– ORIGIN from Afar *qafar*.

afar ▶**adverb** chiefly poetic/literary at or to a distance: *our hero travelled afar* | *for months he had loved her* ***from afar.***
– ORIGIN Middle English *of feor* 'from far'.

afara /əˈfɑːrə/ ▶**noun** a tall West African hardwood tree with a characteristic pagodalike shape. Also called **LIMBA**.
• *Terminalia superba*, family Combretaceae.
– ORIGIN 1920s: from Yoruba.

Afars and Issas, French Territory of the /ˈɑːfɑːz, ˈiːsɑːz/ former name (1946–77) for the Republic of **DJIBOUTI**.

AFC ▶**abbreviation for** ■ (in the UK) Air Force Cross, awarded for bravery while flying but not in active service against an enemy. ■ (in the UK) Association Football Club: *Leeds United AFC.* ■ automatic frequency control, a system in radios and television which keeps them tuned on to an incoming signal.

AFDC ▶**abbreviation for** (in the US) Aid to Families with Dependent Children, a welfare benefit paid by the federal government.

afeared ▶**adjective** archaic or dialect afraid.
– ORIGIN Old English, from *āfǣran* 'frighten', from *ā-* (expressing intensity) + *fǣran* (see **FEAR**); used commonly by Shakespeare, but rarely after 1700 in written form.

afebrile ▶**adjective** Medicine not feverish.
– ORIGIN late 19th cent.: from **A-**[1] 'not' + **FEBRILE**.

affable ▶**adjective** friendly, good-natured, or easy to talk to: *an affable and agreeable companion.*
– DERIVATIVES **affability** noun, **affably** adverb.
– ORIGIN late Middle English: via Old French from Latin *affabilis*, from the verb *affari*, from *ad-* 'to' + *fari* 'speak'.

affair ▶**noun** **1** an event or sequence of events of a specified kind or that has previously been referred to: *the board admitted responsibility for the affair* | *I wanted the funeral to be a family affair.*
■a matter that is a particular person's concern or responsibility: *what you do in your spare time is your affair.* ■ **(affairs)** matters of public interest and importance: *commissions were created to advise on foreign affairs.* ■ **(affairs)** business and financial dealings: *his time was spent in winding up his affairs.* ■ [with adj.] informal an object of a particular type: *her dress was a black low-cut affair.*
2 a love affair: *his wife is having an affair.*
– ORIGIN Middle English: from Old French *afaire*, from *à faire* 'to do'; compare with **ADO**.

affaire /aˈfɛː, French afɛʀ/ (also **affaire de** or **du cœur** /də ˈkəː, djuː, French də , dy kœʀ/) ▶**noun** a love affair.
– ORIGIN early 19th cent.: French, literally 'affair (of the heart)'.

affairé /aˈfɛːreɪ, French afeʀe/ ▶**adjective** busy; involved.
– ORIGIN French, from *affaire*, from *à* 'to' + *faire* 'do'.

affect[1] /əˈfɛkt/ ▶**verb** [with obj.] have an effect on; make a difference to: *the dampness began to affect my health* | [with clause] *your attitude will* ***affect how*** *successful you are.*
■touch the feelings of (someone); move emotionally: [as adj. **affecting**] *a highly affecting account of her experiences in prison.* ■ (of an illness) attack or infect.
– DERIVATIVES **affectingly** adverb.
– ORIGIN late Middle English (in the sense 'attack as a disease'): from French *affecter* or Latin *affect-* 'influenced, affected', from the verb *afficere* (see **AFFECT**[2]).

> **USAGE** Affect and effect are quite different in meaning, though frequently confused. **Affect** is primarily a verb meaning 'make a difference to', as in *their gender need not* ***affect*** *their career.* **Effect** on the other hand is commonly used both as a noun and a verb, meaning 'a result' as a noun (*move the cursor until you get the* ***effect*** *you want*) or 'bring about (a result)' as a verb (*growth in the economy can only be* ***effected*** *by stringent economic controls*). In the British National Corpus, nearly 10 per cent of uses of **effect** are in fact incorrect uses where **affect** should be used.

affect[2] /əˈfɛkt/ ▶**verb** [with obj.] pretend to have or feel (something): *as usual I affected a supreme unconcern* | [with infinitive] *a book that affects to loathe the modern world.*
■use, wear, or assume (something) pretentiously or so as to make an impression on others: *an Anglophile who had affected a British accent.*
– ORIGIN late Middle English: from French *affecter* or Latin *affectare* 'aim at', frequentative of *afficere* 'work on, influence', from *ad-* 'at, to' + *facere* 'do'. The original sense was 'like, love', hence '(like to) use, assume, etc.'.

affect[3] /ˈafɛkt/ ▶**noun** [mass noun] Psychology emotion or desire, especially as influencing behaviour or action.
– DERIVATIVES **affectless** adjective, **affectlessness** noun.
– ORIGIN late 19th cent.: coined in German from Latin *affectus* 'disposition', from *afficere* 'to influence' (see **AFFECT**[2]).

affectation ▶**noun** [mass noun] behaviour, speech, or writing that is artificial and designed to impress: *the affectation of a man who measures every word for effect* | [count noun] *she called the room her boudoir, which he thought an affectation.*
■[count noun] a studied display of real or pretended feeling: *an affectation of calm.*
– ORIGIN mid 16th cent.: from Latin *affectatio(n-)*, from the verb *affectare* (see **AFFECT**[2]).

affected ▶**adjective** **1** influenced or touched by an external factor: *affected areas.*
2 artificial, pretentious, and designed to impress: *the gesture appeared both affected and stagy.*
3 [predic.] archaic disposed or inclined in a specified way: *you might become differently affected towards him.*
– DERIVATIVES **affectedly** adverb.

affection ▶**noun** [mass noun] **1** a gentle feeling of fondness or liking: *she felt* ***affection for*** *the wise old lady* | [count noun] *he won a place in her affections.*
2 archaic the action or process of affecting or being affected.
■[count noun] a condition of disease: *an affection of the skin.* ■ [count noun] a mental state; an emotion.
– DERIVATIVES **affectional** adjective.
– ORIGIN Middle English: via Old French from Latin *affectio(n-)*, from *afficere* 'to influence' (see **AFFECT**[2]).

affectionate ▶**adjective** readily feeling or showing fondness or tenderness: *his affectionate nature.*
■expressing fondness: *an affectionate kiss.*
– DERIVATIVES **affectionately** adverb.
– ORIGIN late 15th cent. (in the sense 'disposed, inclined towards'): from French *affectionné* 'beloved'

or medieval Latin *affectionatus* 'devoted', from *affectio(n-)*, from *afficere* 'to influence' (see **AFFECT**[2]).

affective ▶ **adjective** chiefly Psychology relating to moods, feelings, and attitudes: *affective disorders.*
– DERIVATIVES **affectively** adverb, **affectivity** noun.
– ORIGIN late Middle English: via French from late Latin *affectivus*, from *afficere* (see **AFFECT**[2]).

affenpinscher /ˈafən,pɪnʃə/ ▶ **noun** a dog of a small breed resembling the griffon.
– ORIGIN early 20th cent.: from German, from *Affe* 'monkey' + *Pinscher* 'terrier'.

afferent /ˈaf(ə)r(ə)nt/ ▶ **adjective** Physiology conducting or conducted inwards or towards something (for nerves, the central nervous system; for blood vessels, the organ supplied). The opposite of **EFFERENT**.
▶ **noun** an afferent nerve fibre or vessel.
– ORIGIN mid 19th cent.: from Latin *afferent-* 'bringing towards', from the verb *afferre*, from *ad-* 'to' + *ferre* 'bring'.

affiance /əˈfʌɪəns/ ▶ **verb** (**be affianced**) poetic/literary be engaged to marry: *Edward was* **affianced to** *Lady Eleanor Butler.*
– ORIGIN late 15th cent.: from Old French *afiancer*, from *afier* 'promise, entrust', from medieval Latin *affidare* 'declare on oath', from *ad-* 'towards' + *fides* 'trust'.

affiant /əˈfʌɪənt/ ▶ **noun** US Law a person who makes an affidavit.
– ORIGIN early 19th cent.: from French, present participle of *afier*, from medieval Latin *affidare* 'declare on oath' (see **AFFIANCE**).

affidavit /,afɪˈdeɪvɪt/ ▶ **noun** Law a written statement confirmed by oath or affirmation, for use as evidence in court.
– ORIGIN mid 16th cent.: from medieval Latin, literally 'he has stated on oath', from *affidare*.

affiliate ▶ **verb** /əˈfɪlieɪt/ [with obj.] (usu. **be affiliated to/with**) officially attach or connect (a subsidiary group or a person) to an organization: *a non-political union, not affiliated to any party.*
■ (of an organization) admit as a member: *the main party agreed to affiliate four Conservative associations.* ■ [no obj.] officially join or become attached to an organization: *almost all students* **affiliate to** *the Students' Union.*
▶ **noun** /əˈfɪlɪət/ a person or organization officially attached to a larger body.
– DERIVATIVES **affiliative** adjective.
– ORIGIN mid 18th cent.: from medieval Latin *affiliat-* 'adopted as a son', from the verb *affiliare*, from *ad-* 'towards' + *filius* 'son'.

affiliation ▶ **noun** [mass noun] the state or process of affiliating or being affiliated: *the group has no* **affiliation to** *any preservation society* | [count noun] *his political affiliations.*
– ORIGIN late 18th cent.: from French, from medieval Latin *affiliatio(n-)*, from the verb *affiliare* (see **AFFILIATE**).

affiliation order ▶ **noun** UK Law, historical a legal order that the man judged to be the father of an illegitimate child must help to support it.

affinal /əˈfʌɪn(ə)l/ ▶ **adjective** Anthropology concerning or having a family relationship by marriage.
– ORIGIN mid 19th cent.: from Latin *affinis* 'related' (see **AFFINITY**) + **-AL**.

affine /əˈfʌɪn/ ▶ **adjective** Mathematics allowing for or preserving parallel relationships.
▶ **noun** Anthropology a relative by marriage.
– ORIGIN early 16th cent. (as a noun): from Old French *afin* or Latin *affinis* 'related' (see **AFFINITY**). The mathematical sense dates from the early 20th cent.

affined ▶ **adjective** archaic related or connected.
– ORIGIN late 16th cent.: from Latin *affinis* 'related' (see **AFFINITY**) + **-ED**[1].

affinity ▶ **noun** (pl. **-ies**) a spontaneous or natural liking or sympathy for someone or something: *he had a special affinity with horses.*
■ a similarity of characteristics suggesting a relationship, especially a resemblance in structure between animals, plants, or languages. ■ [mass noun] relationship, especially by marriage as opposed to blood ties. ■ chiefly Biochemistry the degree to which a substance tends to combine with another.
– ORIGIN Middle English (in the sense 'relationship by marriage'): via Old French from Latin *affinitas*, from *affinis* 'related' (literally 'bordering on'), from *ad-* 'to' + *finis* 'border'.

affinity card ▶ **noun** a cheque card or credit card for which the bank donates a portion of the money spent using the card to a specific charity or other organization.

affinity group ▶ **noun** chiefly US a group of people linked by a common interest or purpose.

affirm ▶ **verb** [reporting verb] state as a fact; assert strongly and publicly: [with obj.] *he affirmed the country's commitment to peace* | [with clause] *they affirmed that policies were to be judged by their contribution to social justice* | [with direct speech] *'Pessimism,' she affirmed, 'is the most rational view.'*
■ [with obj.] declare one's support for; uphold; defend: *the referendum affirmed the republic's right to secede.* ■ [with obj.] Law accept or confirm the validity of (a judgement or agreement); ratify. ■ [no obj.] Law make a formal declaration rather than taking an oath.
– DERIVATIVES **affirmatory** adjective, **affirmer** noun.
– ORIGIN Middle English (in the sense 'make firm'): via Old French from Latin *affirmare*, from *ad-* 'to' + *firmus* 'strong'.

affirmation ▶ **noun** [mass noun] the action or process of affirming something: *he nodded in affirmation* | [count noun] *an affirmation of basic human values.*
■ [count noun] Law a formal declaration by a person who declines to take an oath for reasons of conscience.
– ORIGIN late Middle English: from Latin *affirmatio(n-)*, from the verb *affirmare* (see **AFFIRM**).

affirmative ▶ **adjective** agreeing with or consenting to a statement or request: *an affirmative answer.*
■ Grammar & Logic stating that a fact is so; making an assertion: *affirmative sentences.* Contrasted with **NEGATIVE** and **INTERROGATIVE**. ■ (of a vote) expressing approval or agreement. ■ offering support, help, or encouragement: *the family is usually a source of encouragement from which affirmative influences come.* ■ relating to or denoting proposed legislation which must receive a parliamentary vote in its favour before it can come into force.
▶ **noun** a statement of agreement with or consent to an assertion or request: *he accepted her reply as an affirmative.*
■ Grammar a word used in making assertions or to express consent. ■ Logic a statement asserting that something is true of the subject of a proposition. ■ (**the affirmative**) a position of agreement or confirmation: *his answer veered towards the affirmative.*
▶ **exclamation** chiefly N. Amer. expressing agreement with or consent to a statement or request; yes.
– PHRASES **in the affirmative** so as to accept or agree to a statement or request: *he answered the question in the affirmative.*
– DERIVATIVES **affirmatively** adverb.
– ORIGIN late Middle English (in the sense 'assertive, positive'): via Old French from late Latin *affirmativus*, from *affirmare* 'assert' (see **AFFIRM**).

affirmative action ▶ **noun** [mass noun] chiefly N. Amer. action favouring those who tend to suffer from discrimination, especially in relation to employment or education; positive discrimination.

affix ▶ **verb** /əˈfɪks/ [with obj.] stick, attach, or fasten (something) to something else: *he licked the stamp and* **affixed** *it* **to** *the envelope.*
■ [no obj.] be able to be fixed: *the strings* **affix to** *the back of the bridge.*
▶ **noun** /ˈafɪks/ Grammar an addition to the base form or stem of a word in order to modify its meaning or create a new word. Compare with **PREFIX**, **SUFFIX**, **INFIX**.
– DERIVATIVES **affixation** noun.
– ORIGIN late Middle English: from Old French *affixer* or medieval Latin *affixare*, frequentative of Latin *affigere*, from *ad-* 'to' + *figere* 'to fix'.

afflatus /əˈfleɪtəs/ ▶ **noun** formal a divine creative impulse or inspiration.
– ORIGIN mid 17th cent.: from Latin, from the verb *afflare*, from *ad-* 'to' + *flare* 'to blow'.

afflict ▶ **verb** [with obj.] (of a problem or illness) cause pain or suffering to; affect; trouble: *his younger child was afflicted with a skin disease* | *serious ills afflict the industry* | [as plural noun **the afflicted**] *he comforted the afflicted.*
■ Astrology (of a celestial body) be in a stressful aspect with (another celestial body or a point on the ecliptic): *Jupiter is afflicted by Mars in opposition.*
– DERIVATIVES **afflictive** adjective (archaic).
– ORIGIN late Middle English (in the sense 'deject, humiliate'): from Latin *afflictare* 'knock about, harass', or from *afflict-* 'knocked down, weakened': both from the verb *affligere*, from *ad-* 'to' + *fligere* 'to strike, dash'.

affliction ▶ **noun** something that causes pain or suffering: *a crippling affliction of the nervous system.*
■ [mass noun] pain; suffering: *poor people in great affliction.* ■ Astrology an instance of one celestial body afflicting another.
– ORIGIN Middle English (originally in the sense 'infliction of pain or humiliation', specifically 'religious self-mortification'): via Old French from Latin *afflictio(n-)*, from the verb *affligere* (see **AFFLICT**).

affluent ▶ **adjective 1** (especially of a group or area) having a great deal of money; wealthy: *the affluent societies of the western world* | [as plural noun **the affluent**] *only the affluent could afford to travel abroad.*
2 archaic (of water) flowing freely or in great quantity.
▶ **noun** archaic a tributary stream.
– DERIVATIVES **affluence** noun, **affluently** adverb.
– ORIGIN late Middle English (in sense 2): via Old French from Latin *affluent-* 'flowing towards, flowing freely', from the verb *affluere*, from *ad-* 'to' + *fluere* 'to flow'.

afflux /ˈaflʌks/ ▶ **noun** archaic a flow of something, especially water or air.
– ORIGIN early 17th cent.: from medieval Latin *affluxus*, from *affluere* 'flow freely' (see **AFFLUENT**).

afforce ▶ **verb** [with obj.] rare reinforce (a body of people) with new members: *research teams were sometimes afforced by temporary staff.*
– ORIGIN Middle English (in the sense 'to force'): from Old French *aforcier*, from *a-* (from Latin *ad* 'to, at') + *force* (from Latin *fortis* 'strong').

afford ▶ **verb** [with obj.] **1** (**can/could afford**) have enough money to pay for: *the best that I could afford was a first-floor room* | [with infinitive] *we could never have afforded to heat the place.*
■ have (a certain amount of something, especially money or time) available or to spare: *it was taking up more time than he could afford.* ■ [with infinitive] be able to do something without risk of adverse consequences: *only aristocrats could afford to stoop to such practices.*
2 provide or supply (an opportunity or facility): *the rooftop terrace affords beautiful views* | [with two objs] *they were afforded the luxury of bed and breakfast.*
– ORIGIN late Old English *geforthian*, from *ge-* (prefix implying completeness) + *forthian* 'to further', from **FORTH**. The original sense was 'promote, perform, accomplish', later 'manage, be in a position to do'.

affordable ▶ **adjective** inexpensive; reasonably priced: *affordable homes.*
– DERIVATIVES **affordability** noun.

afforest /əˈfɒrɪst/ ▶ **verb** [with obj.] convert (land) into forest, especially for commercial exploitation.
■ Brit. historical bring (woodland) under the jurisdiction of forest law for the purpose of hunting.
– DERIVATIVES **afforestation** noun.
– ORIGIN early 16th cent.: from medieval Latin *afforestare*, from *ad-* 'to' (expressing change) + *foresta* 'forest'.

affranchise ▶ **verb** [with obj.] archaic release from servitude.
– ORIGIN late 15th cent.: from Old French *afranchiss-*, lengthened stem of *afranchir*, from *a-* (from Latin *ad* 'to, at') + *franc* 'free'.

affray ▶ **noun** Law, dated an instance of group fighting in a public place that disturbs the peace: *Lowe was charged with causing an affray* | [mass noun] *a person guilty of affray.*
– ORIGIN Middle English (in the general sense 'disturbance, fray'): from Anglo-Norman French *afrayer* 'disturb, startle', based on an element of Germanic origin related to Old English *frithu* 'peace, safety' (compare with German *Friede* 'peace').

affricate /ˈafrɪkət/ ▶ **noun** Phonetics a phoneme which combines a plosive with an immediately following fricative or spirant sharing the same place of articulation, e.g. *ch* as in *chair* and *j* as in *jar.*
– ORIGIN late 19th cent.: from Latin *affricatus*, past participle of *affricare*, from *ad-* 'to' + *fricare* 'to rub'.

affright archaic ▶ **verb** [with obj.] frighten (someone): *ghosts could never affright her.*
▶ **noun** [mass noun] fright: *the deer gazed at us in affright.*
– ORIGIN late Middle English: in early use from *āfyrhted* 'frightened' in Old English; later by vague form association with **FRIGHT**.

affront ▶ **noun** an action or remark that causes

a

outrage or offence: *he took his son's desertion as a personal affront* | *the sackings were* ***an affront to*** *justice.*
▶ **verb** [with obj.] (usu. **be affronted**) offend the modesty or values of: *she was affronted by his familiarity.*
– ORIGIN Middle English (as a verb): from Old French *afronter* 'to slap in the face, insult', based on Latin *ad frontem* 'to the face'.

affronté /əˈfrʌnti/ (also **affronty**) ▶ **adjective** [predic. or postpositive] Heraldry (especially of an animal's head) facing the observer.
– ORIGIN mid 16th cent. (as *affronty*): French, past participle of *affronter* 'to face'.

AFG ▶ **abbreviation for** Afghanistan (international vehicle registration).

Afghan /ˈafgan/ ▶ **noun 1** a native or national of Afghanistan, or a person of Afghan descent.
2 another term for **PASHTO**.
3 (**afghan**) a woollen blanket or shawl, typically one knitted or crocheted in strips or squares.
4 short for **AFGHAN COAT** or **AFGHAN HOUND**.
▶ **adjective** of or relating to Afghanistan, its people, or their language.
– ORIGIN from Pashto *afghānī*.

Afghan coat ▶ **noun** Brit. a kind of sheepskin coat with the skin outside, typically having a shaggy border.

Afghan hound ▶ **noun** a tall hunting dog of a breed with long silky hair.

afghani /afˈgɑːni/ ▶ **noun** (pl. **afghanis**) the basic monetary unit of Afghanistan, equal to 100 puls.
– ORIGIN from Pashto *afghānī*.

Afghanistan /afˈganɪstɑːn, -stan/ a mountainous landlocked republic in central Asia; pop. 16,600,000 (est. 1991); official languages, Pashto and Dari (the local form of Persian); capital, Kabul.

Part of the Indian Mogul empire, Afghanistan became independent in the mid 18th century, and in the 19th and early 20th centuries was a focal point for conflicting Russian and British interests on the North-West Frontier. Afghanistan was invaded by the Soviet Union in 1979; Soviet forces withdrew in 1988–9 and in 1996 the fundamentalist Taliban took Kabul and set up an Islamic state. This was overthrown in 2001 by US-led forces in conjunction with Afghan groups following the attacks on the World Trade Center and the Pentagon by Islamic terrorists.

aficionado /əˌfɪsjəˈnɑːdəʊ, -ˌfɪʃjə-/ ▶ **noun** (pl. **-os**) a person who is very knowledgeable and enthusiastic about an activity, subject, or pastime.
– ORIGIN mid 19th cent. (denoting a devotee of bullfighting): from Spanish, 'amateur', past participle of *aficionar* 'become fond of' used as a noun, based on Latin *affectio(n-)* '(favourable) disposition towards' (see **AFFECTION**).

afield ▶ **adverb 1** to or at a distance: *competitors from* ***as far afield*** *as Aberdeen.*
2 in the field (usually in reference to hunting): *the satisfaction of a day afield.*
– ORIGIN Middle English (in sense 2): from **A-**[2] 'on, in' + **FIELD**.

afire ▶ **adverb** & **adjective** chiefly poetic/literary on fire; burning: [as predic. adj.] *the whole mill was afire.*

AFL ▶ **abbreviation for** Australian Football League.

aflame ▶ **adverb** & **adjective** in flames; burning: [as adv.] *pour brandy over the steaks and then set aflame.*

aflatoxin /ˌafləˈtɒksɪn/ ▶ **noun** Chemistry any of a class of toxic compounds produced by certain moulds found in food, which can cause liver damage and cancer.
• These are produced by fungi of the *Aspergillus flavus* group, subdivision Deuteromycotina.
– ORIGIN 1960s: from elements of the modern Latin taxonomic name (see above) + **TOXIN**.

AFL-CIO ▶ **abbreviation for** American Federation of Labor and Congress of Industrial Organizations.

afloat ▶ **adjective** & **adverb** floating in water; not sinking: [as adv.] *they trod water to keep afloat* | [as predic. adj.] *the canoes were still afloat.*
■ on board a ship or boat: [as adv.] *flotilla sailing is a sociable way to explore while living afloat.* ■ figurative out of debt or difficulty: [as adv.] *professional management will be needed to keep firms afloat.* ■ in general circulation; current.
– ORIGIN Old English *on flote* (see **A-**[2], **FLOAT**), influenced in Middle English by Old Norse *á flot(i)* and Old French *en flot*.

AFM ▶ **abbreviation for** (in the UK) Air Force Medal, awarded for bravery.

afoot ▶ **adverb** & **adjective 1** in preparation or progress; happening or beginning to happen: [as predic. adj.] *plans are afoot for a festival.*
2 chiefly N. Amer. on foot: [as adv.] *they were forced to go afoot.*

afore ▶ **preposition** archaic or dialect before.
– ORIGIN Old English *onforan* (see **A-**[2], **FORE**).

afore- ▶ **prefix** before; previously.

aforementioned ▶ **adjective** denoting a thing or person previously mentioned: *songs from the aforementioned album.*

aforesaid ▶ **adjective** another term for **AFOREMENTIONED**.

aforethought ▶ **adjective** see **MALICE AFORETHOUGHT**.

a fortiori /ˌeɪ fɔːtɪˈɔːrʌɪ, ˌɑː, -riː/ ▶ **adverb** & **adjective** used to express a conclusion for which there is stronger evidence than for a previously accepted one: [as adv.] *they reject all absolute ideas of justice, and a fortiori the natural-law position.*
– ORIGIN early 17th cent.: Latin, from *a fortiori argumento* 'from stronger argument'.

afoul ▶ **adverb** N. Amer. into conflict or difficulty with.

afraid ▶ **adjective** [predic.] feeling fear or anxiety; frightened: *I'm* ***afraid of*** *dogs.*
■ worried that something undesirable will occur or be done: *she was* ***afraid that*** *he would be angry.* ■ [with infinitive] unwilling or reluctant to do something for fear of the consequences: *I'm often afraid to go out on the streets.* ■ (**afraid for**) anxious about the well-being or safety of: *William was suddenly afraid for her.*
– PHRASES **I'm afraid** [with clause] used to express polite or formal apology or regret: *I'm afraid I don't understand.*
– ORIGIN Middle English: past participle of the obsolete verb *affray*, from Anglo-Norman French *afrayer* (see **AFFRAY**).

A-frame ▶ **noun** a frame shaped like a capital letter A.
■ N. Amer. a house built around such a timber frame.

afreet /ˈafriːt/ (also **afrit**) ▶ **noun** (in Arabian and Muslim mythology) a powerful jinn or demon.
– ORIGIN late 18th cent.: from Arabic *ʿifrīt*.

afresh ▶ **adverb** in a new or different way: *she left the job to start afresh.*

Africa the second largest continent, a southward projection of the Old World land mass divided roughly in two by the equator and surrounded by sea except where the Isthmus of Suez joins it to Asia.

African ▶ **noun** a person from Africa, especially a black person.
■ a person of black African descent.
▶ **adjective** of or relating to Africa or people of African descent.
– ORIGIN from Latin *Africanus*, from *Africa (terra)* '(land) of the *Afri*', an ancient people of North Africa.

Africana /ˌafrɪˈkɑːnə/ ▶ **plural noun** books, artefacts, and other collectors' items connected with Africa, especially southern Africa.

African American chiefly US ▶ **noun** an American of African origin.
▶ **adjective** of or relating to Americans of African origin.

USAGE **African American** is the currently accepted term in the US for Americans of African origin, having first become prominent in the late 1980s.

African buffalo ▶ **noun** a buffalo with large horns, native to Africa south of the Sahara.
• *Syncerus caffer*, family Bovidae; sometimes considered to be two species, the **Cape buffalo** and the **forest** (or **dwarf**) **buffalo**.

African daisy ▶ **noun** a plant of the daisy family, sometimes cultivated for its bright flowers.
• *Dimorphotheca* and other genera, family Compositae.

Africander /ˌafrɪˈkandə/ ▶ **noun** variant spelling of **AFRIKANDER**.

African elephant ▶ **noun** the elephant native to Africa, which is larger than the Indian elephant and has larger ears and a two-lipped trunk.
• *Loxodonta africana*, family Elephantidae.

African grey parrot ▶ **noun** another term for **GREY PARROT**.

African horse sickness ▶ **noun** a notifiable viral disease of horses, which is usually fatal. It is transmitted by biting insects and occurs chiefly in Africa, the Middle East, and the Mediterranean.

Africanism ▶ **noun 1** a feature of language or culture regarded as characteristically African.
2 [mass noun] the belief that black Africans and their culture should predominate in Africa.
– DERIVATIVES **Africanist** noun & adjective.

Africanize (also **-ise**) ▶ **verb** [with obj.] **1** make African in character: [as adj. **Africanized**] *an Africanized form of Cajun music.*
■ (in Africa) restructure (an organization) by replacing white employees with black Africans.
2 [usu. as adj. **Africanized**] hybridize (honeybees of European stock) with bees of African stock, producing an aggressive strain.
– DERIVATIVES **Africanization** noun.

African lynx ▶ **noun** another term for **CARACAL**.

African National Congress (abbrev.: **ANC**) a South African political party and black nationalist organization. Having been banned by the South African government 1960–90, the ANC was victorious in the country's first democratic elections in 1994 and its leader Nelson Mandela became the country's President.

African violet ▶ **noun** a small East African plant with heart-shaped velvety leaves and violet, pink, or white flowers.
• Genus *Saintpaulia*, family Gesneriaceae: several species, in particular *S. ionantha*, a popular house plant.

Afrikaans /ˌafrɪˈkɑːns/ ▶ **noun** [mass noun] a language of southern Africa, derived from the form of Dutch brought to the Cape by Protestant settlers in the 17th century. It is an official language of South Africa, spoken by around 6 million people.
▶ **adjective** relating to the Afrikaner people, their way of life, or their language.
– ORIGIN the name in Afrikaans, from Dutch, literally 'African'.

Afrika Korps /ˈafrɪkə ˌkɔː/ a German army force sent to North Africa in 1941 under General Rommel.

Afrikander /ˌafrɪˈkɑːndə/ (also **Africander**) ▶ **noun** an animal of a South African breed of sheep or longhorn cattle.
– ORIGIN early 19th cent. (an early form of **AFRIKANER**, having the same senses): via Afrikaans from South African Dutch.

Afrikaner /ˌafrɪˈkɑːnə/ ▶ **noun 1** an Afrikaans-speaking white person in South Africa, especially one descended from the Dutch and Huguenot settlers of the 17th century.
2 S. African a gladiolus native to southern Africa.
• *Gladiolus* and related genera, family Iridaceae.
– DERIVATIVES **Afrikanerdom** noun.
– ORIGIN Afrikaans, from South African Dutch *Africander*, from Dutch *Afrikaan* 'an African' + the personal suffix *-der*, on the pattern of *Hollander* 'Dutchman'.

afrit ▶ **noun** variant spelling of **AFREET**.

Afro ▶ **noun** a hairstyle consisting of a mass of very tight curls that stick out all round the head, like the natural hair of some black people.
– ORIGIN 1930s: independent usage of **AFRO-**, or an abbreviation of **AFRICAN**.

Afro- ▶ **combining form** African; African and ...: *Afro-Asiatic* | *Afro-Belizean.*
■ relating to Africa: *Afrocentric.*
– ORIGIN from Latin *Afer, Afr-* 'African'.

Afro-American chiefly US ▶ **adjective** & **noun** another term for **AFRICAN AMERICAN**.

USAGE The term **Afro-American**, first recorded in the 19th century and popular in the 1960s and 1970s, has now largely given way to **African American** as the current accepted term in the US for Americans of African origin. In Britain, **black** is the standard term.

Afro-Asiatic ▶ **adjective** relating to or denoting a family of languages spoken in the Middle East and North Africa. They can be divided into five groups: Semitic, Omotic, Berber, Cushitic, and Chadic. Ancient Egyptian was also a member of this family. Also called **HAMITO-SEMITIC**.

Afro-Caribbean ▶ **noun** a person of African descent living in or coming from the Caribbean.
▶ **adjective** of or relating to Afro-Caribbeans.

Afrocentric ▶ **adjective** regarding African or black culture as pre-eminent.
– DERIVATIVES **Afrocentrism** noun, **Afrocentrist** noun.

afrormosia /ˌafrɔːˈməʊzɪə/ ▶ **noun 1** [mass noun] the

valuable timber of a tropical tree, resembling teak and used for furniture.
2 the tree that yields this timber, occurring mainly in West Africa.
• Genus *Pericopsis* (formerly *Afrormosia*), family Leguminosae: several species, especially *P. elata* and *P. laxiflora*.
– ORIGIN 1920s: modern Latin, from **AFRO-** + the related genus name *Ormosia*, formed irregularly from Greek *hormos* 'necklace' (because necklaces were strung from the seeds).

Afrotropical ▶ **adjective** another term for **ETHIOPIAN** (sense 2).

aft /ɑːft/ ▶ **adverb** & **adjective** at, near, or towards the stern of a ship or tail of an aircraft: [as adv.] *Travis made his way aft* | [as adj.] *the aft cargo compartment.*
– ORIGIN early 17th cent.: probably from obsolete *baft* (see **ABAFT**), influenced by Low German and Dutch *achter* 'abaft, after'.

after ▶ **preposition 1** during the period of time following (an event): *shortly after Christmas* | *there's only one thing to do after an experience like that.*
■ with a period of time rather than an event: *after a while he returned.* ■ in phrases indicating something happening continuously or repeatedly: ***day after day*** *we kept studying.* ■ N. Amer. past (used in specifying a time): *I strolled in about ten minutes after two.* ■ during the time following the departure of (someone): *she cooks for him and cleans up after him.*
2 behind: *she went out, shutting the door after her.*
■ (with reference to looking or speaking) in the direction of someone who is moving further away: *she stared after him.*
3 in pursuit or quest of: *chasing after something you can't have* | *most of them are after money.*
4 next to and following in order or importance: *in their order of priorities health* ***comes after*** *housing* | *x comes after y in the series.*
5 in allusion to (someone or something with the same or a related name): *they named her Pauline, after Barbara's mother.*
■ in imitation of: *a drawing after Millet's* The Reapers.
▶ **conjunction** & **adverb** during the period of time following (an event): [as conjunction] *bathtime ended in a flood after the taps were left running* | [as adv.] *Duke Frederick died soon after.*
▶ **adjective** [attrib.] **1** archaic later: *he was sorry in after years.*
2 nearer the stern of a ship: *the after cabin.*
– PHRASES **after all** in spite of any indications or expectations to the contrary: *I rang and told her I couldn't come after all* | *you are my counsellor, after all.* **after hours** after normal working or opening hours, typically those of licensed premises. **after you** a polite formula used to suggest that someone goes in front of or takes a turn before oneself: *after you, Mr Pritchard.* **be after doing something** Irish be on the point of doing something or have just done it: *the pigs were after breaking loose.*
– ORIGIN Old English *æfter*, of Germanic origin; related to Dutch *achter*.

afterbirth ▶ **noun** [mass noun] the placenta and fetal membranes discharged from the womb after the birth of offspring.

afterburner ▶ **noun** an auxiliary burner in which extra fuel is burned in the exhaust of a jet engine, to increase thrust.

aftercare ▶ **noun** [mass noun] subsequent care or maintenance, in particular:
■ care of a patient after a stay in hospital or of a person on release from prison. ■ support or advice offered to a customer following the purchase of a product or service.

afterdamp ▶ **noun** [mass noun] choking gas left after an explosion of firedamp in a mine, rich in carbon monoxide.

afterdeck ▶ **noun** an open deck toward the stern of a ship.

after-effect ▶ **noun** an effect that follows after the primary action of something: *he was suffering the after-effects of the drug.*

afterglow ▶ **noun** [in sing.] light or radiance remaining in the sky after the sun has set.
■ good feelings remaining after a pleasurable or successful experience: *basking in the afterglow of victory.*

after-image ▶ **noun** an impression of a vivid sensation (especially a visual image) retained after the stimulus has ceased.

afterlife ▶ **noun** [in sing.] **1** (in some religions) life after death: *most Christians believe in an afterlife.*
2 later life: *they spent much of their afterlife trying to forget the fire.*

aftermarket ▶ **noun** chiefly US the market for spare parts, accessories, and components, especially for motor vehicles.
■ Stock Exchange the market for shares and bonds after their original issue.

aftermath ▶ **noun 1** the consequences or after-effects of an event, especially when unpleasant: *food prices soared* ***in the aftermath of*** *the drought.*
2 Farming new grass growing after mowing or harvest.
– ORIGIN late 15th cent. (in sense 2): from **AFTER** (as an adjective) + dialect *math* 'mowing', of Germanic origin; related to German *Mahd*.

aftermost ▶ **adjective** [attrib.] nearest the stern of a ship or tail of an aircraft.
– ORIGIN late 18th cent.: from **AFTER** (as an adjective) + **-MOST**.

afternoon ▶ **noun** the time from noon or lunchtime to evening: *I telephoned* ***this afternoon*** | *I'll be back at three in the afternoon* | *she worked on Tuesday afternoons* | [as modifier] *the afternoon sunshine.*
■ this time on a particular day, characterized by a specified type of activity or particular weather conditions: *it was an afternoon of drama and tension.*
▶ **adverb** (**afternoons**) informal in the afternoon; every afternoon.
▶ **exclamation** informal short for **GOOD AFTERNOON**.

afterpains ▶ **plural noun** pains after childbirth caused by contraction of the womb.

afters ▶ **plural noun** Brit. informal the sweet course following the main course of a meal; pudding.

aftershave ▶ **noun** [mass noun] an astringent scented lotion for applying to the skin after shaving.

aftershock ▶ **noun** a smaller earthquake following the main shock of a large earthquake.

aftersun ▶ **adjective** denoting a product intended for application to the skin after exposure to the sun: *aftersun lotion.*
▶ **noun** [mass noun] a product of this type.

aftertaste ▶ **noun** a taste, typically an unpleasant one, remaining in the mouth after eating or drinking something.

afterthought ▶ **noun** an item or thing that is thought of or added later: *as an afterthought she said 'Thank you'.*

aftertouch ▶ **noun** [mass noun] a facility on an electronic music keyboard by which an effect is produced by depressing a key after striking it.

afterwards (US also **afterward** /-wəd/) ▶ **adverb** at a later or future time; subsequently: *the offender was arrested shortly afterwards.*
– ORIGIN Old English *æftewearde*, from *æftan* 'aft' + **-WARDS**, influenced by **AFTER**.

afterword ▶ **noun** a concluding section in a book, typically by a person other than the author.

afterworld ▶ **noun** a world entered after death.

AG ▶ **abbreviation for** ■ Adjutant General. ■ Aktiengesellschaft, used in the names of German joint-stock companies. ■ Attorney General.

Ag[1] ▶ **symbol for** the chemical element silver.
– ORIGIN from Latin *argentum*.

Ag[2] Biochemistry ▶ **abbreviation for** antigen.

ag[1] /ag/ N. Amer. informal ▶ **adjective** short for **AGRICULTURAL**.
▶ **noun** short for **AGRICULTURE**.

ag[2] /ax, ʌx/ ▶ **exclamation** S. African used to express a range of emotions from irritation or grief to pleasure: *ag man, there's nothing anyone can do.*
– ORIGIN Afrikaans, from Dutch *ach* (see **ACH**).

ag- ▶ **prefix** variant spelling of **AD-** assimilated before g (as in *aggravate*, *aggression*).

Aga /ˈɑːgə/ ▶ **noun** Brit. trademark a type of heavy heat-retaining cooking stove or range and intended for continuous heating.
– ORIGIN 1930s: from the Swedish name (*Svenskaa*) *A*(*ktiebolaget*) *Ga*(*sackumulator*) 'Swedish Gas Accumulator Company', the original manufacturer.

aga /ˈɑːgə/ ▶ **noun** chiefly historical (in Muslim countries, especially under the Ottoman Empire) a military commander or official.
– ORIGIN mid 16th cent.: from Turkish *ağa* 'master, lord', from Mongolian *aqa*.

Agadir /ˌagəˈdɪə/ a seaport and resort on the Atlantic coast of Morocco; pop. 137,000 (1993).

again /əˈgɛn, əˈgeɪn/ ▶ **adverb** another time; once more: *it was great to meet old friends again* | *they were disappointed* ***yet again.***
■ returning to a previous position or condition: *he rose, tidied the bed, and sat down again.* ■ in addition to what has already been mentioned: *the wages were low but they made half as much again in tips.* ■ [sentence adverb] used to introduce a further point for consideration, supporting or contrasting with what has just been said: *I never saw any signs, but* ***then again,*** *maybe I wasn't looking.* ■ used to ask someone to repeat something: *what was your name again?*
– PHRASES **again and again** repeatedly.
– ORIGIN Old English *ongēan*, *ongægn*, etc., of Germanic origin; related to German *entgegen* 'opposite'.

against /əˈgɛnst, əˈgeɪnst/ ▶ **preposition 1** in opposition to: *the fight against crime* | *arguing against the ordination of women* | *you've turned her against me* | *he decided against immediate publication* | *swimming against the tide.*
■ with reference to legal action: *allegations against police officers* | *the first victim gave evidence against him* | *the council said it would appeal against the decision.* ■ with reference to a sporting contest: *the championship match against Somerset.* ■ (in betting) in anticipation of the failure of: *the odds were 5–1 against England.*
2 in anticipation of and preparation for (a problem or difficulty): *insurance against sickness and unemployment* | *he gritted his teeth against the pain* | *makeshift barricades against tank attacks.*
■ in resistance to; as protection from: *he turned up his collar against the wind.* ■ in relation to (an amount of money owed, due, or lent) so as to reduce, cancel, or secure it: *money was advanced against the value of the property.*
3 in conceptual contrast to: *the benefits must be weighed against the costs* | *the instilling of habits* ***as against*** *the development of understanding.*
■ in visual contrast to: *he was silhouetted against the light of the stair window.*
4 in or into physical contact with (something), typically so as to be supported by or collide with it: *she stood with her back against the door* | *she sank back against the pillows* | *frustration made him bang his head against the wall.*
– PHRASES **have something against someone** dislike or bear a grudge against someone: *I have nothing against you personally.*
– ORIGIN Middle English: from **AGAIN** + *-s* (adverbial genitive) + *-t* probably by association with superlatives (as in *amongst*).

Aga Khan /ˌɑːgə ˈkɑːn/ ▶ **noun** the title of the spiritual leader of the Nizari sect of Ismaili Muslims. The first Aga Khan was given his title in 1818 by the shah of Persia. The present (fourth) Aga Khan (**Karim Al-Hussain Shah**, b.1937) inherited the title in 1957.

agal /aˈgɑːl/ ▶ **noun** a headband worn by Bedouin Arab men to keep the keffiyeh in place.
– ORIGIN mid 19th cent.: representing a Bedouin pronunciation of Arabic *ʿiḳāl* 'bond, hobble'.

agama /əˈgɑːmə/ ▶ **noun** an Old World lizard with a large head and a long tail, typically showing a marked difference in colour and form between the sexes.
• Genus *Agama*, family Agamidae: many species.
■ any lizard of the agama family.
– ORIGIN late 18th cent.: perhaps from Carib.

Agamemnon /ˌagəˈmɛmnɒn/ Greek Mythology king of Mycenae and brother of Menelaus, commander-in-chief of the Greek expedition against Troy. On his return home from Troy he was murdered by his wife Clytemnestra and her lover Aegisthus; his murder was avenged by his son Orestes and daughter Electra.

agamic /əˈgamɪk/ ▶ **adjective** Biology asexual; reproducing asexually: *winged agamic females.*
– ORIGIN mid 19th cent.: from Greek *agamos* 'unmarried' + **-IC**.

agamid /əˈgamɪd/ ▶ **noun** Zoology a lizard of the agama family (Agamidae).
– ORIGIN late 19th cent.: from modern Latin *Agamidae* (plural), from **AGAMA**.

agammaglobulinaemia /eɪˌgaməˌglɒbjʊlɪˈniːmɪə/ (also **agammaglobulinemia**) ▶ **noun** [mass noun] Medicine lack of gamma globulin in the blood plasma, causing immune deficiency.

agamospermy /ˈagəmə(ʊ)ˌspəːmi/ ▶ **noun** [mass noun] Botany asexual reproduction in which seeds are produced from unfertilized ovules.
– DERIVATIVES **agamospermous** adjective.

a

– ORIGIN 1930s: from Greek *agamos* 'unmarried' + *sperma* 'seed'.

agapanthus /ˌagəˈpanθəs/ ▶ **noun** a South African plant of the lily family, with funnel-shaped bluish flowers which grow in rounded clusters.
• Genus *Agapanthus*, family Liliaceae (or Alliaceae).
– ORIGIN modern Latin, from Greek *agapē* 'love' + *anthos* 'flower'.

agape[1] /əˈgeɪp/ ▶ **adjective** [predic.] (of a person's mouth) wide open, especially with surprise or wonder.
– ORIGIN mid 17th cent.: from **A-**[2] 'on' + **GAPE**.

agape[2] /ˈagəpi/ ▶ **noun** [mass noun] Christian Theology Christian love, especially as distinct from erotic love or simple affection.
■ [count noun] a communal meal in token of Christian fellowship, as held by early Christians in commemoration of the Last Supper.
– ORIGIN early 17th cent.: from Greek *agapē* 'brotherly love'.

agar /ˈeɪgɑː/ (also **agar-agar** /eɪgɑːrˈeɪgɑː/) ▶ **noun** [mass noun] a gelatinous substance obtained from various kinds of red seaweed and used in biological culture media and as a thickener in foods.
– ORIGIN early 19th cent.: from Malay.

agarbatti /ˈʌgəːˌbʌtiː/ ▶ **noun** (pl. same or **agarbattis**) Indian term for **JOSS STICK**.
– ORIGIN from Hindi *agarbattī*.

agaric /ˈag(ə)rɪk, əˈgɑːrɪk/ ▶ **noun** a fungus with a fruiting body that resembles a mushroom, having a convex or flattened cap with gills on the underside.
• Order Agaricales, class Hymenomycetes, in particular the mushroom family Agaricaceae.
– ORIGIN late Middle English (originally denoting various bracket fungi with medicinal or other uses): from Latin *agaricum*, from Greek *agarikon* 'tree fungus'.

agarose /ˈagərəʊz, -s/ ▶ **noun** [mass noun] Biochemistry a substance which is the main constituent of agar and is used especially in gels for electrophoresis. It is a polysaccharide mainly containing galactose residues.

Agartala /ˈʌgətəˌlɑː/ a city in the far north-east of India, capital of the state of Tripura, situated near the border with Bangladesh; pop. 157,640 (1991).

Agassi /ˈagəsi/, André (b.1970), American tennis player. Ranked third in the world by the age of 18, he won the Wimbledon men's singles title in 1992 and a gold medal in the 1996 Olympics.

Agassiz /ˈagəsi/, Jean Louis Rodolphe (1807–73), Swiss-born American zoologist, geologist, and palaeontologist. In 1837 Agassiz was the first to propose that much of Europe had once been in the grip of an ice age.

agate /ˈagət/ ▶ **noun** [mass noun] an ornamental stone consisting of a hard variety of chalcedony, typically banded in appearance.
■ [count noun] a coloured toy marble resembling a banded gemstone.
– ORIGIN late 15th cent.: from French, via Latin from Greek *akhatēs*.

agave /əˈgeɪvi/ ▶ **noun** a succulent plant with rosettes of narrow spiny leaves and tall flower spikes, native to the southern US and tropical America.
• Genus *Agave*, family Agavaceae: numerous species, including the century plant.
– ORIGIN Latin, from Greek *Agauē*, the name of one of the daughters of Cadmus in Greek mythology, from *agauos* 'illustrious'.

AGC Electronics ▶ **abbreviation for** automatic gain control.

age ▶ **noun 1** the length of time that a person has lived or a thing has existed: *he died from a heart attack at the age of 51 | his wife is the same age as Una | he must be nearly 40 years* **of age** *| young people between the ages of 11 and 18.*
■ a particular stage in someone's life: *children of primary school age.* ■ [mass noun] the latter part of life or existence; old age: *with age this gland can become sluggish.*
2 a distinct period of history: *an age of technological growth | a child of the television age.*
■ Geology a division of time that is a subdivision of an epoch, corresponding to a stage in chronostratigraphy. ■ archaic a lifetime taken as a measure of time; a generation: *Nestor is said to have lived three ages when he was ninety years old.* ■ **(ages/an age)** informal a very long time: *I haven't seen her for ages.*
▶ **verb (ageing** or **aging)** [no obj.] grow old or older, especially visibly and obviously so: *you haven't aged a lot | the tiredness we feel as we age.*
■ [with obj.] cause to grow, feel, or appear older: *he even tried ageing the painting with a spoonful of coffee.* ■ (especially with reference to an alcoholic drink) mature or allow to mature: [no obj.] *the wine ages in open vats or casks.* ■ [with obj.] determine how old (something) is: *we didn't have a clue how to age these animals.*
– PHRASES **act** (or **be**) **one's age** [usu. in imperative] behave in a manner appropriate to someone of one's age and not to someone much younger. **come of age** (of a person) reach adult status (in UK law at 18, formerly 21). ■ (of a movement or activity) become fully established: *space travel will then finally come of age.* **of an age 1** old enough to be able or expected to do something: *the sons are of an age to marry.* **2** (of two or more people or things) of a similar age: *the children all seemed of an age.* **through the ages** throughout history.
– ORIGIN Middle English: from Old French, based on Latin *aetas, aetat-*, from *aevum* 'age, era'.

-age ▶ **suffix** forming nouns: **1** denoting an action: *leverage | voyage.*
■ the product of an action: *spillage | wreckage.* ■ a function; a sphere of action: *homage | peerage.*
2 denoting an aggregate or number of: *mileage | percentage.*
■ fees payable for; the cost of using: *postage | tonnage.*
3 denoting a place or abode: *vicarage | village.*
– ORIGIN from Old French, based on Latin *-aticum*, neuter form of the adjectival ending *-aticus*.

aged ▶ **adjective 1** /eɪdʒd/ [predic. or postpositive] having lived for a specified length of time; of a specified age: *young people aged 14 to 18 | he died aged 60.*
■ (of a horse or farm animal) over a certain defined age of maturity, typically 6 to 12 years for horses, 3 or 4 years for cattle.
2 /ˈeɪdʒɪd/ having lived or existed for a long time; old: *aged men with white hair |* [as plural noun **the aged**] *Methodist homes for the aged.*
3 /eɪdʒd/ that has been subjected to ageing: *replica guitar with aged finish.*

age gap ▶ **noun** a difference in age between people, especially as a potential source of misunderstanding.

age group ▶ **noun** a number of people or things classed together as being of similar age.

age hardening ▶ **noun** [mass noun] spontaneous hardening of a metal which occurs if it is quenched and then stored at ambient temperature or treated with mild heat.
– DERIVATIVES **age-hardened** adjective.

ageing (also **aging**) ▶ **noun** [mass noun] the process of growing old: *the external signs of ageing |* [as modifier] *the ageing process.*
■ the process of change in the properties of a material occurring over a period, either spontaneously or through deliberate action.
▶ **adjective** (of a person) growing old; elderly: *looking after ageing relatives | an ageing population.*
■ (of a thing) reaching the end of useful life: *the world's ageing fleet of oil tankers.*

ageism (also **agism**) ▶ **noun** [mass noun] prejudice or discrimination on the grounds of a person's age.
– DERIVATIVES **ageist** (also **agist**) adjective & noun.

ageless ▶ **adjective** never growing or appearing to grow old: *the town retains an ageless charm.*
– DERIVATIVES **agelessness** noun.

age-long ▶ **adjective** [attrib.] having existed for a very long time: *the will to change age-long habits.*

agency ▶ **noun 1** [often with adj. or noun modifier] a business or organization established to provide a particular service, typically one that involves organizing transactions between two other parties: *an advertising agency | aid agencies.*
■ a department or body providing a specific service for a government or other organization: *the Environmental Protection Agency.*
2 [mass noun] action or intervention, especially such as to produce a particular effect: *canals carved by the agency of running water.*
■ [count noun] a thing or person that acts to produce a particular result: *the movies could be an agency moulding the values of the public.*
– ORIGIN mid 17th cent.: from medieval Latin *agentia*, from *agent-* 'doing' (see **AGENT**).

agenda /əˈdʒɛndə/ ▶ **noun** a list of items of business to be considered and discussed at a meeting: *the question of nuclear weapons had been removed from the agenda.*
■ a list or programme of things to be done or problems to be addressed: *he vowed to put jobs at the top of his agenda | the government had its own agenda.*
– PHRASES **on the agenda** scheduled for discussion at a meeting: *the rights of minorities would be high on the agenda at the conference.* ■ likely or needing to be dealt with or done: *his release was not on the agenda.* **set the agenda** draw up a list of items to be discussed at a meeting. ■ influence or determine a programme of action: *he has set the agenda for future work in this field.*
– ORIGIN early 17th cent. (in the sense 'things to be done'): from Latin, neuter plural of *agendum*, gerundive of *agere* 'do'.

USAGE Although **agenda** is the plural of **agendum** in Latin, in standard modern English it is normally used as a singular noun with a standard plural form (**agendas**). See also **usage** at **DATA** and **MEDIA**[1].

agent ▶ **noun 1** a person who acts on behalf of another, in particular:
■ a person who manages business, financial, or contractual matters for an actor, performer, or writer. ■ a person or company that provides a particular service, typically one that involves organizing transactions between two other parties: *a travel agent | shipping agents | a letting agent.* ■ a person who obtains information for a government or other official body, typically in secret: *a trained intelligence agent | KGB agents | an FBI agent.*
2 a person or thing that takes an active role or produces a specified effect: *agents of environmental change | bleaching agents.*
■ Grammar the doer of an action, typically expressed as the subject of an active verb or in a *by* phrase with a passive verb.
– DERIVATIVES **agentive** adjective (Grammar).
– ORIGIN late Middle English (in the sense 'someone or something that produces an effect'): from Latin *agent-* 'doing', from *agere*.

agent-general ▶ **noun** (pl. **agents general**) the representative of an Australian state or Canadian province in London or another major foreign city.

agent noun ▶ **noun** a noun denoting someone or something that performs the action of a verb, usually ending in *-er* or *-or*, e.g. *worker, accelerator.*

Agent Orange ▶ **noun** [mass noun] a defoliant chemical used by the US in the Vietnam War.

agent provocateur /ˌaʒɒ̃ prəˌvɒkəˈtəː, French aʒɑ̃ pʀɔvɔkatœʀ/ ▶ **noun** (pl. **agents provocateurs** pronunc. same) a person who induces others to break the law so that they can be convicted.
– ORIGIN late 19th cent.: French, literally 'provocative agent'.

age of consent ▶ **noun** the age at which a person's consent to sexual intercourse is valid in law.

age of discretion ▶ **noun** the age at which someone is considered able to manage their own affairs or take responsibility for their actions.

age-old ▶ **adjective** having existed for a very long time: *the age-old quest for knowledge.*

Aggadah ▶ **noun** variant spelling of **HAGGADAH**.

agglomerate ▶ **verb** /əˈglɒməreɪt/ collect or form into a mass or group: [with obj.] *companies agglomerate multiple sites such as chains of shops |* [no obj.] *these small particles soon agglomerate together.*
▶ **noun** /əˈglɒmərət/ a mass or collection of things: *a multimedia agglomerate.*
■ [mass noun] Geology a volcanic rock consisting of large fragments bonded together.
▶ **adjective** /əˈglɒmərət/ collected or formed into a mass.
– DERIVATIVES **agglomeration** noun, **agglomerative** adjective.
– ORIGIN late 17th cent.: from Latin *agglomerat-* 'added to', from the verb *agglomerare*, from *ad-* 'to' + *glomerare* (from *glomus* 'ball').

agglutinate /əˈgluːtɪneɪt/ ▶ **verb** firmly stick or be stuck together to form a mass: [as adj. **agglutinated**] *rhinoceros horns are agglutinated masses of hair.*
■ Biology (with reference to bacteria or red blood cells) clump together: [with obj.] *these strains agglutinate human red cells |* [no obj.] *cell fragments agglutinate and form intricate meshes.* ■ [with obj.] Linguistics (of a language) combine (word elements) to express compound ideas.
– DERIVATIVES **agglutination** noun.
– ORIGIN mid 16th cent.: from Latin *agglutinat-*

'caused to adhere', from the verb *agglutinare*, from *ad-* 'to' + *glutinare* (from *gluten* 'glue').

agglutinative /əˈgluːtɪnətɪv/ ▶ **adjective** Linguistics denoting a language that typically expresses concepts in complex words consisting of many elements, rather than by inflection or by using isolated elements. Examples include Hungarian, Turkish, Korean, and Swahili. Contrasted with **ANALYTIC** and **SYNTHETIC**.

agglutinin /əˈgluːtɪnɪn/ ▶ **noun** Biology an antibody, lectin, or other substance that causes agglutination.
– ORIGIN late 19th cent.: from **AGGLUTINATE** + **-IN**[1].

aggradation /ˌagrəˈdeɪʃ(ə)n/ ▶ **noun** [mass noun] Geology the deposition of material by a river, stream, or current.
– ORIGIN late 19th cent.: from **AG-** (expressing increase) + (*de*)*gradation*.

aggrandize /əˈgrandʌɪz/ (also **-ise**) ▶ **verb** [with obj.] increase the power, status, or wealth of: *an action intended to aggrandize the Frankish dynasty.*
▪enhance the reputation of (someone) beyond what is justified by the facts: *he hoped to aggrandize himself by dying a hero's death.*
– DERIVATIVES **aggrandizement** noun, **aggrandizer** noun.
– ORIGIN mid 17th cent. (in the general sense 'increase, magnify'): from French *agrandiss-*, lengthened stem of *agrandir*, probably from Italian *aggrandire*, from Latin *grandis* 'large'. The ending was changed by association with verbs ending in **-IZE**.

aggravate ▶ **verb** [with obj.] **1** make (a problem, injury, or offence) worse or more serious: *military action would only aggravate the situation.*
2 informal annoy or exasperate (someone), especially persistently: [as adj. **aggravating**] *she found him thoroughly aggravating and unprofessional.*
– DERIVATIVES **aggravatingly** adverb, **aggravation** noun.
– ORIGIN mid 16th cent.: from Latin *aggravat-* 'made heavy', from the verb *aggravare*, from *ad-* (expressing increase) + *gravis* 'heavy'.

USAGE Aggravate in the sense 'annoy or exasperate' dates back to the 17th century and has been so used by respected writers ever since. This use is still regarded as incorrect by some traditionalists on the grounds that it is too radical a departure from the etymological meaning of 'make heavy'. It is, however, comparable to meaning changes in hundreds of other words which have long been accepted without comment.

aggravated ▶ **adjective** [attrib.] (of an offence) made more serious by attendant circumstances: *aggravated burglary.*
▪(of a penalty) made more severe in recognition of the seriousness of an offence: *aggravated damages.*

aggregate ▶ **noun** /ˈagrɪgət/ **1** a whole formed by combining several (often disparate) elements: *the council was an aggregate of three regional assemblies.*
▪the total score of a player or team in a fixture comprising more than one game or round: [mass noun] *the result put the sides level* **on aggregate**.
2 a material or structure formed from a mass of fragments or particles loosely compacted together.
▪[mass noun] pieces of broken or crushed stone or gravel used to make concrete, or more generally in building and construction work.
▶**adjective** /ˈagrɪgət/ [attrib.] formed or calculated by the combination of many separate units or items; total: *the aggregate amount of grants made.*
▪Botany (of a group of species) comprising several very similar species formerly regarded as a single species. ▪Economics denoting the total supply or demand for goods and services in an economy at a particular time: *aggregate demand | aggregate supply.*
▶**verb** /ˈagrɪgeɪt/ form or group into a class or cluster: [with obj.] *socio-occupational groups aggregate men sharing similar kinds of occupation.*
– PHRASES **in (the) aggregate** in total; as a whole.
– DERIVATIVES **aggregation** noun, **aggregative** /ˈagrɪgətɪv/ adjective.
– ORIGIN late Middle English: from Latin *aggregat-* 'herded together', from the verb *aggregare*, from *ad-* 'towards' + *grex*, *greg-* 'a flock'.

aggregate fruit ▶ **noun** Botany a fruit formed from several carpels derived from the same flower, e.g. a raspberry.

aggression ▶ **noun** [mass noun] hostile or violent behaviour or attitudes towards another; readiness to attack or confront: *his chin was jutting with aggression | territorial aggression between individuals of the same species.*
▪the action of attacking without provocation, especially in beginning a quarrel or war: *the dictator resorted to armed aggression | he called for an end to foreign aggression against his country.* ▪forceful and sometimes overly assertive pursuit of one's aims and interests.
– ORIGIN early 17th cent. (in the sense 'an attack'): from Latin *aggressio(n-)*, from *aggredi* 'to attack', from *ad-* 'towards' + *gradi* 'proceed, walk'.

aggressive ▶ **adjective** ready or likely to attack or confront; characterized by or resulting from aggression: *he's very uncooperative and aggressive | aggressive behaviour.*
▪pursuing one's aims and interests forcefully, sometimes unduly so: *an aggressive businessman.*
– DERIVATIVES **aggressively** adverb, **aggressiveness** noun.
– ORIGIN early 19th cent.: from Latin *aggress-* 'attacked' (from the verb *aggredi*) + **-IVE**; compare with French *agressif*, *-ive*.

aggressor ▶ **noun** a person or country that attacks another first.
– ORIGIN mid 17th cent.: from late Latin, from *aggredi* 'to attack' (see **AGGRESSION**).

aggrieved ▶ **adjective** feeling resentment at having been unfairly treated: *they were aggrieved at the outcome | she did not see herself as the aggrieved party.*
– DERIVATIVES **aggrievedly** adverb.
– ORIGIN Middle English (in the sense 'distressed'): past participle of *aggrieve*, from Old French *agrever* 'make heavier', based on Latin *aggravare* (see **AGGRAVATE**).

aggro ▶ **noun** [mass noun] Brit. informal aggressive, violent behaviour.
▪problems and difficulties.
– ORIGIN 1960s: abbreviation of *aggravation* (see **AGGRAVATE**), or of **AGGRESSION**.

aghast /əˈgɑːst/ ▶ **adjective** filled with horror or shock: *when the news came out they were aghast.*
– ORIGIN late Middle English: past participle of the obsolete verb *agast*, *gast* 'frighten', from Old English *gǣsten*. The spelling with *gh* (originally Scots) became general by about 1700, probably influenced by **GHOST**; compare with **GHASTLY**.

Aghios Nikolaos /ˌagɪɒs ˌnɪkəˈlʌɪɒs/ a fishing port and holiday resort on the north coast of Crete, east of Heraklion; pop. 8,100 (1981). Greek name **ÁYIOS NIKÓLAOS**.

agile ▶ **adjective** able to move quickly and easily: *Ruth was as agile as a monkey |* figurative *his vague manner concealed an agile mind.*
– DERIVATIVES **agilely** adverb, **agility** noun.
– ORIGIN late Middle English: via French from Latin *agilis*, from *agere* 'do'.

agile gibbon ▶ **noun** a gibbon with colour varying from light buff to black, found in SE Asia.
• *Hylobates agilis*, family Hylobatidae.

agin /əˈgɪn/ ▶ **preposition** dialect form of **AGAINST**.
– ORIGIN early 19th cent.: variant of the obsolete preposition *again*, with the same meaning.

Agincourt, Battle of /ˈadʒɪnˌkɔː, -ˌkɔːt, French aʒɛ̃kuʀ/ a battle in northern France in 1415 during the Hundred Years War, in which the English under Henry V defeated a large French army. The victory, achieved largely by use of the longbow, allowed Henry to occupy Normandy.

aging ▶ **adjective** & **noun** variant spelling of **AGEING**.

agism ▶ **noun** variant spelling of **AGEISM**.

agist[1] /əˈdʒɪst/ ▶ **verb** [with obj.] take in and feed (livestock) for payment.
– DERIVATIVES **agister** noun, **agistment** noun.
– ORIGIN late Middle English (in the sense 'use or allow the use of land for pasture'): from Old French *agister*, from *a-* (from Latin *ad* 'to, at') + *gister*, from *giste* 'lodging'.

agist[2] /ˈeɪdʒɪst/ ▶ **adjective** & **noun** variant spelling of *ageist* (see **AGEISM**).

agitate ▶ **verb** [with obj.] **1** make (someone) troubled or nervous: *the thought of questioning Toby agitated him extremely |* [as adj. **agitated**] *she was red and agitated with the effort of arguing.*
▪[no obj.] campaign to arouse public concern about an issue in the hope of prompting action: *they agitated for a reversal of the decision.*
2 stir or disturb (something, especially a liquid) briskly: *agitate the water to disperse the oil.*
– DERIVATIVES **agitatedly** adverb.
– ORIGIN late Middle English (in the sense 'drive away'): from Latin *agitat-* 'agitated, driven', from *agitare*, frequentative of *agere* 'do, drive'.

agitation ▶ **noun** [mass noun] **1** a state of anxiety or nervous excitement: *she was wringing her hands in agitation.*
▪the action of arousing public concern about an issue and pressing for action on it: *widespread agitation for social reform.*
2 the action of briskly stirring or disturbing something, especially a liquid.
– ORIGIN mid 16th cent. (in the sense 'action, being active'): from Latin *agitatio(n-)*, from the verb *agitare* (see **AGITATE**).

agitato /ˌadʒɪˈtɑːtəʊ/ ▶ **adverb** & **adjective** Music (especially as a direction) agitated in manner: *allegro agitato.*
– ORIGIN Italian, literally 'agitated'.

agitator ▶ **noun** **1** a person who urges others to protest or rebel: *a communist agitator.*
2 an apparatus for stirring liquid, as in a washing machine or a photographic developing tank.
– ORIGIN mid 17th cent. (denoting a delegate of private soldiers in the Parliamentary army during the English Civil War): from Latin, from *agitare* (see **AGITATE**). Sense 1 dates from the mid 18th cent.

agitprop /ˈadʒɪtprɒp, ˈag-/ ▶ **noun** [mass noun] political (originally communist) propaganda, especially in art or literature: [as modifier] *agitprop painters.*
– ORIGIN 1930s: Russian, blend of *agitatsiya* 'agitation' and *propaganda* 'propaganda'.

agleam ▶ **adjective** [predic.] gleaming: *his eyes were agleam with the intensity of his fervour.*

aglet /ˈaglət/ ▶ **noun** a metal or plastic tube fixed tightly round each end of a shoelace.
– ORIGIN late Middle English: from French *aiguillette* 'small needle', diminutive of *aiguille* (see **AIGUILLE**).

agley /əˈgleɪ, əˈgliː/ ▶ **adverb** Scottish askew; awry.
– ORIGIN late 18th cent.: from **A-**[2] 'on' + Scots *gley* 'squint', of unknown origin.

aglow ▶ **adjective** [predic.] glowing.

AGM ▶ **abbreviation for** annual general meeting.

agma /ˈagmə/ ▶ **noun** the speech sound of 'ng' as in *thing*, a velar nasal consonant.
▪the symbol /ŋ/, used to represent this sound in the International Phonetic Alphabet.
– ORIGIN 1950s: from late Greek, from Greek, literally 'fragment'.

agnail /ˈagneɪl/ ▶ **noun** another term for **HANGNAIL**.

agnate /ˈagneɪt/ chiefly Law ▶ **noun** a person descended from the same male ancestor as another specified or implied person, especially through the male line.
▶**adjective** descended in this way. Compare with **COGNATE** (in sense 2).
▪of the same clan or nation.
– DERIVATIVES **agnatic** /-ˈnatɪk/ adjective, **agnation** noun.
– ORIGIN late 15th cent. (as a noun): from Latin *agnatus*, from *ad-* 'to' + *gnatus*, *natus* 'born'.

Agnatha /agˈneɪθə/ Zoology a group of primitive jawless vertebrates which includes the lampreys, hagfishes, and many fossil fishlike forms. Compare with **CYCLOSTOME**.
• Superclass Agnatha: the living forms are in the classes Myxini (hagfishes) and Cephalaspidomorphi (lampreys).
– DERIVATIVES **agnathan** noun & adjective.
– ORIGIN from modern Latin *Agnatha*, from **A-**[1] 'without' + Greek *gnathos* 'jaw'.

Agnes, St[1] (died *c.*304), Roman martyr, said to have been a Christian virgin who refused to marry. She is the patron saint of virgins and her emblem is a lamb (Latin *agnus*). Feast day, 21 January.

Agnes, St[2] (*c.*1211–82), patron saint of Bohemia. She was canonized in 1989. Feast day, 2 March.

Agnesi /anˈjeɪzi/, Maria Gaetana (1718–99), Italian mathematician and philosopher, regarded as the first female mathematician of the Western world.

Agni /ˈagni/ the Vedic god of fire, the priest of the gods and the god of the priests.

agnolotti /ˌanjəˈlɒti/ ▶ **plural noun** pasta squares stuffed with a variety of fillings, like small ravioli.
– ORIGIN Italian.

agnosia /agˈnəʊsɪə/ ▶ **noun** [mass noun] Medicine inability to interpret sensations and hence to recognize things, typically as a result of brain damage.

a

– ORIGIN early 20th cent.: coined in German from Greek *agnōsia* 'ignorance'.

agnostic /ag'nɒstɪk/ ▶ **noun** a person who believes that nothing is known or can be known of the existence or nature of God.
▶ **adjective** of or relating to agnostics or agnosticism.
– DERIVATIVES **agnosticism** noun.
– ORIGIN mid 19th cent.: from **A-**[1] 'not' + **GNOSTIC**.

Agnus Dei /ˌagnʊs 'deɪiː, ˌanjʊs, 'diːʌɪ/ ▶ **noun 1** a figure of a lamb bearing a cross or flag, as an emblem of Christ.
2 Christian Church an invocation beginning with the words 'Lamb of God' forming a set part of the Mass. ■a musical setting of this.
– ORIGIN late Middle English: from Latin, literally 'Lamb of God'.

ago ▶ **adverb** before the present; earlier (used with a measurement of time): *he went five minutes ago* | *as long ago as 1942* | *not long ago.*
– ORIGIN Middle English *ago, agone*, past participle of the obsolete verb *ago* 'pass', used to express passage of time.

USAGE When **ago** is followed by a clause, the clause should be introduced by **that** rather than **since**, e.g. *it was sixty years ago* ***that*** *I left this place* (not *it was sixty years ago* ***since*** *I left this place*). The use of **since** is not correct in standard English.

agog ▶ **adjective** [predic.] very eager or curious to hear or see something: *I'm* ***all agog*** | *he came from the kitchen, agog to hear everything.*
– ORIGIN mid 16th cent.: from Old French *en gogues*, from *en* 'in' + the plural of *gogue* 'fun'.

agogic /ə'gɒdʒɪk/ Music ▶ **adjective** relating to or denoting accentuation within musical phrases by slight lengthening of notes.
▶ **noun** (**agogics**) [usu. treated as sing.] the use of agogic accents.
– ORIGIN late 19th cent.: coined in German from Greek *agōgos* 'leading', from *agein* 'to lead', + **-IC**.

agogo /ə'gəʊgəʊ/ ▶ **noun** a small bell made of two joined metal cones, used as a percussion instrument in African and Latin music.
– ORIGIN from Yoruba.

a gogo /ə 'gəʊgəʊ/ ▶ **adjective** [postpositive] informal in abundance; galore: *Gershwin a gogo—all the hits.*
– ORIGIN 1960s: from French *à gogo*, from Old French *gogue* 'fun'.

agonic line /ə'gɒnɪk/ ▶ **noun** an imaginary line round the earth passing through both the north pole and the north magnetic pole, at any point on which a compass needle points to true north.
– ORIGIN mid 19th cent.: from Greek *agōnios, agōnos* (from *a-* 'without' + *gonia* 'angle') + **-IC**.

agonist /'agənɪst/ ▶ **noun 1** Biochemistry a substance which initiates a physiological response when combined with a receptor. Compare with **ANTAGONIST**.
2 Anatomy a muscle whose contraction moves a part of the body directly. Compare with **ANTAGONIST**.
3 another term for **PROTAGONIST**.
– DERIVATIVES **agonism** noun.
– ORIGIN early 20th cent.: from Greek *agōnistēs* 'contestant' (a sense reflected in English in the early 17th cent.), from *agōn* 'contest'.

agonistic ▶ **adjective** polemical; combative. ■Zoology (of animal behaviour) associated with conflict. ■ Biochemistry of, relating to, or acting as an agonist.
– DERIVATIVES **agonistically** adverb.
– ORIGIN mid 17th cent.: via late Latin from Greek *agōnistikos*, from *agōnistēs* 'contestant', from *agōn* 'contest'.

agonize (also **-ise**) ▶ **verb** [no obj.] undergo great mental anguish through worrying about something: *I didn't agonize over the problem.* ■[with obj.] cause mental anguish to (someone).
– ORIGIN late 16th cent.: from French *agoniser* or late Latin *agonizare*, from Greek *agōnizesthai* 'contend', from *agōn* 'contest'.

agonized (also **-ised**) ▶ **adjective** manifesting, suffering, or characterized by great physical or mental pain: *she gave an agonized cry* | *months of agonized discussion.*

agonizing (also **-ising**) ▶ **adjective** causing great physical or mental pain: *an agonizing death* | *there is an agonizing choice to make.*
– DERIVATIVES **agonizingly** adverb [as submodifier] *agonizingly slow steps.*

agony ▶ **noun** (pl. **-ies**) [mass noun] extreme physical or mental suffering: *he crashed to the ground in agony.* ■[with adj. or noun modifier] the final stages of a difficult or painful death: *his last agony* | *the death agony.*
– ORIGIN late Middle English (originally denoting 'mental' anguish alone): via Old French and late Latin from Greek *agōnia*, from *agōn* 'contest'. The sense of 'physical' suffering dates from the early 17th cent.

agony aunt ▶ **noun** Brit. informal a woman who answers letters in an agony column.

agony column ▶ **noun** Brit. informal a column in a newspaper or magazine offering advice on personal problems to readers who write in. ■dated a personal column.

agony uncle ▶ **noun** Brit. informal a man who answers letters in an agony column.

agora[1] /'agɒrə/ ▶ **noun** (pl. **agorae** /-riː/or **agoras**) (in ancient Greece) a public open space used for assemblies and markets.
– ORIGIN from Greek.

agora[2] /ˌagə'rɑː/ ▶ **noun** (pl. **agorot** or **agoroth** /ˌagə'rəʊt, -rəʊθ/) a monetary unit of Israel, equal to one hundredth of a shekel.
– ORIGIN from Hebrew *'ăgōrāh* 'small coin'.

agoraphobia /ˌag(ə)rə'fəʊbɪə/ ▶ **noun** [mass noun] extreme or irrational fear of open or public places, leading to panic attacks and reclusive behaviour.
– DERIVATIVES **agoraphobe** noun, **agoraphobic** adjective & noun.
– ORIGIN late 19th cent.: from Greek *agora* 'place of assembly, marketplace' + **-PHOBIA**.

Agostini /ˌagə'stiːni/, Giacomo (b.1944), Italian racing motorcyclist. Between 1966 and 1975 he won a record fifteen world titles, and won the Isle of Man TT ten times.

agouti /ə'guːti/ ▶ **noun** (pl. same or **agoutis**) a large long-legged burrowing rodent related to the guinea pig, native to Central and South America.
● Genera *Agouti* and *Dasyprocta*, family Dasyproctidae: several species.
■[mass noun] fur in which each hair has alternate dark and light bands, producing a grizzled appearance. ■ a rodent, especially a mouse, having fur of this type.
– ORIGIN mid 16th cent.: via French or from Spanish *aguti*, from Tupi *akutí*.

AGR ▶ **abbreviation for** advanced gas-cooled (nuclear) reactor.

Agra /'ɑːgrə/ a city on the River Jumna in Uttar Pradesh state, northern India; pop. 899,000 (1991). Founded in 1566, Agra was the capital of the Mogul empire until 1658. It is the site of the Taj Mahal.

agrammatism /ə'gramətɪz(ə)m/ ▶ **noun** [mass noun] Medicine a tendency to form sentences without the correct inflectional structure as a result of brain damage, as in Broca's aphasia.

agranulocytosis /əˌgranjʊlə(ʊ)sʌɪ'təʊsɪs/ ▶ **noun** [mass noun] Medicine a deficiency of granulocytes in the blood, causing increased vulnerability to infection.

agraphia /ə'grafɪə, eɪ-/ ▶ **noun** [mass noun] Medicine inability to write, as a language disorder resulting from brain damage.
– ORIGIN mid 19th cent.: from **A-**[1] 'without' + Greek *-graphia* 'writing'.

agrarian /ə'grɛːrɪən/ ▶ **adjective** of or relating to cultivated land or the cultivation of land. ■relating to landed property.
▶ **noun** a person who advocates a redistribution of landed property.
– ORIGIN early 17th cent. (originally designating a Roman law for the division of conquered lands): from Latin *agrarius*, from *ager, agr-* 'field'.

Agrarian Revolution the transformation of British agriculture during the 18th century, characterized by the enclosure of common land and the introduction of technological innovations such as the seed drill and the rotation of crops.

agree ▶ **verb** (**agrees, agreed, agreeing**) [no obj.] **1** have the same opinion about something; concur: *I completely* ***agree with*** *your recent editorial* | *we both agreed on issues such as tougher penalties for criminals* | [with clause] *everybody agrees that jobs will go* | [with direct speech] *'Yes, dreadful, isn't it,' she agreed.* ■(**agree with**) approve of (something) with regard to its moral correctness: *I'm not sure I agree with abortion.*
2 (**agree to** or **to do something**) consent to do something which has been suggested by another person: *she had agreed to go and see a movie with him* ■[with obj.] chiefly Brit. reach agreement about (something), typically after a period of negotiation: *if they had agreed a price the deal would have gone through* | [no obj.] *the commission* ***agreed on*** *a proposal to limit imports.* ■ [with obj.] chiefly Brit. (of a government or organization) consent to or authorize (a plan or proposal): *the cabinet has agreed a plan on the country's territorial waters.*
3 (**agree with**) be consistent with: *your body language does not agree with what you are saying.* ■Grammar have the same number, gender, case, or person as: *the verb agrees with the final noun.* ■ [usu. with negative] be healthy or appropriate for (someone): *she's eaten something which did not agree with her.*
– PHRASES **agree to differ** see **DIFFER**.
– ORIGIN late Middle English: from Old French *agreer*, based on Latin *ad-* 'to' + *gratus* 'pleasing'.

agreeable ▶ **adjective 1** quite enjoyable and pleasurable; pleasant: *a cheerful and agreeable companion.*
2 [predic.] willing to agree to something: *they were agreeable to its publication.* ■(of a course of action) acceptable: *a compromise which might be agreeable to both coal owners and unions.*
– DERIVATIVES **agreeableness** noun, **agreeably** adverb [as submodifier] *an agreeably warm day.*
– ORIGIN late Middle English: from Old French *agreable*, from *agreer* 'make agreeable to' (see **AGREE**).

agreed ▶ **adjective** [attrib.] discussed or negotiated and then accepted by all parties: *the agreed date* | *the agreed term of the loan.* ■(of two or more parties) holding the same view or opinion on something: *all the republics are agreed on the necessity of a common defence policy* | [with clause] *we are agreed that what is needed is a catchy title.*

agreement ▶ **noun** [mass noun] harmony or accordance in opinion or feeling; a position or result of agreeing: *the governments failed to* ***reach agreement*** | *the two officers nodded* ***in agreement*** | *there is wide* ***agreement that*** *investment is necessary.* ■[count noun] a negotiated and typically legally binding arrangement between parties as to a course of action: *a trade agreement* | *a verbal agreement to sell.* ■the absence of incompatibility between two things; consistency: *agreement between experimental observations and theory.* ■ Grammar the condition of having the same number, gender, case, and/or person as another word.
– ORIGIN late Middle English: from Old French, from *agreer* 'make agreeable to' (see **AGREE**).

agrestal /ə'grɛst(ə)l/ ▶ **adjective** Botany growing wild in cultivated fields.
– ORIGIN mid 19th cent.: from Latin *agrestis* 'relating to the country' (see **AGRESTIC**) + **-AL**.

agrestic /ə'grɛstɪk/ ▶ **adjective** chiefly poetic/literary of or relating to the country; rural; rustic.
– ORIGIN early 17th cent.: from Latin *agrestis*, from *ager, agr-* 'field' + **-IC** .

agribusiness ▶ **noun** [mass noun] **1** agriculture conducted on strictly commercial principles. ■[count noun] an organization engaged in this.
2 the group of industries dealing with agricultural produce and services required in farming.
– DERIVATIVES **agribusinessman** noun (pl. **-men**).
– ORIGIN 1950s (originally US): blend of **AGRICULTURE** and **BUSINESS**.

Agricola /ə'grɪkələ/, Gnaeus Julius (AD 40–93), Roman general and governor of Britain 78–84. As governor he completed the subjugation of Wales and defeated the Scottish Highland tribes.

agricultural ▶ **adjective** of or relating to agriculture: *agricultural land* | *an agricultural worker.* ■Brit. informal (in a sporting context) denoting a clumsy shot or player: *Keith took an agricultural swing at the ball.*
– DERIVATIVES **agriculturalist** noun, **agriculturally** adverb.

agriculture ▶ **noun** [mass noun] the science or practice of farming, including cultivation of the soil for the growing of crops and the rearing of animals to provide food, wool, and other products.
– DERIVATIVES **agriculturist** noun.
– ORIGIN late Middle English: from Latin *agricultura*, from *ager, agr-* 'field' + *cultura* 'growing, cultivation'.

agrimony /'agrɪməni/ ▶ **noun** (pl. **-ies**) a plant of the rose family which bears slender flower spikes and hooked fruits, found in north temperate regions.

• Genus *Agrimonia*, family Rosaceae: several species, in particular the Eurasian *A. eupatoria*, with small yellow flowers.
– ORIGIN late Middle English: directly or (in early use) via Old French from Latin *agrimonia*, alteration of *argemonia*, from Greek *argemōnē* 'poppy'.

agrion /ˈagrɪɒn/ ▶ **noun** a large damselfly that has a body with a metallic sheen. Also called DEMOISELLE.
• Genus *Agrion* (or *Calopteryx*), family Calopterygidae: numerous species, including the common European *A. virgo*.
– ORIGIN Greek, neuter of *agrios* 'wild'.

Agrippa /əˈgrɪpə/, Marcus Vipsanius (63–12 BC), Roman general. Augustus' adviser and son-in-law, he played an important part in the naval victories over Mark Antony.

agriproduct ▶ **noun** a product of agribusiness.

agriscience ▶ **noun** [mass noun] the application of science to agriculture.
– DERIVATIVES **agriscientist** noun.

agro- /ˈagrəʊ/ ▶ **combining form** agricultural: *agro-industry* | *agrobiology*.
■ agriculture and ...: *agroforestry*.
– ORIGIN from Greek *agros* 'field'.

agrobiology ▶ **noun** [mass noun] the branch of biology that deals with soil science and plant nutrition and its application to crop production.
– DERIVATIVES **agrobiological** adjective, **agrobiologist** noun.

agrochemical ▶ **noun** a chemical used in agriculture, such as a pesticide or a fertilizer.

agroecosystem ▶ **noun** an ecosystem on agricultural land.

agroforestry ▶ **noun** [mass noun] agriculture incorporating the cultivation of trees.

agro-industry ▶ **noun** [mass noun] industry connected with agriculture.
■ agriculture developed along industrial lines.
– DERIVATIVES **agro-industrial** adjective.

agrology ▶ **noun** [mass noun] Canadian the application of science to agriculture.
– DERIVATIVES **agrologist** noun.

agronomy /əˈgrɒnəmi/ ▶ **noun** [mass noun] the science of soil management and crop production.
– DERIVATIVES **agronomic** adjective, **agronomical** adjective, **agronomically** adverb, **agronomist** noun.
– ORIGIN early 19th cent.: from French *agronomie*, from *agronome* 'agriculturist', from Greek *agros* 'field' + *-nomos* 'arranging' (from *nemoein* 'arrange').

Agro Pontino /ˌagro ponˈtino/ Italian name for PONTINE MARSHES.

agrostology /ˌagrəˈstɒlədʒi/ ▶ **noun** [mass noun] the branch of botany concerned with grasses.
– ORIGIN mid 19th cent.: from Greek *agrōstis* (denoting a kind of grass) + -LOGY.

aground ▶ **adjective** & **adverb** (with reference to a ship) on or on to the bottom in shallow water: [as adv.] *the ships must slow to avoid **running aground*** | [as predic. adj.] *a cargo ship aground in the Pentland Firth.*
– ORIGIN Middle English (in the sense 'on the ground'): from A-[2] 'on' + GROUND[1].

aguardiente /əˌgwɑːdɪˈɛnteɪ, Spanish aɣwarˈðjente/ ▶ **noun** [mass noun] (in Spanish-speaking countries) a distilled liquor resembling brandy, especially as made in South America from sugar cane.
– ORIGIN from Spanish, from *agua* 'water' + *ardiente* 'fiery'.

Aguascalientes /ˌagwəskaˈljɛnteɪz/ a state of central Mexico.
■ its capital, a health resort noted for its hot springs; pop. 506,380 (1990).
– ORIGIN Spanish, literally 'hot waters'.

ague /ˈeɪgjuː/ ▶ **noun** [mass noun] archaic malaria or some other illness involving fever and shivering.
■ [count noun] a fever or shivering fit.
– DERIVATIVES **agued** adjective, **aguish** adjective.
– ORIGIN Middle English: via Old French from medieval Latin *acuta (febris)* 'acute (fever)'.

Agulhas, Cape /əˈgʌləs/ the most southerly point of the continent of Africa, in the province of Western Cape, South Africa.

Agulhas Current an ocean current flowing southward along the east coast of Africa.

AH ▶ **abbreviation** in the year of the Hegira (used in the Muslim calendar for reckoning years from Muhammad's departure from Mecca in AD 622); of the Muslim era: *a Koran dated 556 AH.*
– ORIGIN from Latin *anno Hegirae*.

ah ▶ **exclamation** used to express a range of emotions including surprise, pleasure, sympathy, and realization: *ah, there you are!* | *ah, this is the life.*
– ORIGIN Middle English: from Old French.

AHA ▶ **abbreviation for** alpha-hydroxy acid.

aha ▶ **exclamation** used to express satisfaction, triumph, or surprise.
– ORIGIN Middle English: from AH + HA[1].

Ahaggar Mountains /ɑːˈhɑːgə/ another name for HOGGAR MOUNTAINS.

ahead ▶ **adverb** further forward in space; in the line of one's forward motion: *he had to give his attention to the road ahead* | *he was striding ahead towards the stream.*
■ further forward in time; in advance; in the near future: *he contemplated the day ahead* | *we have to plan ahead.* ■ onward so as to make progress. ■ in the lead: *the Bucks were ahead by four* | *he was slightly ahead on points.* ■ higher in number, amount, or value than previously: *profits were slightly ahead.*
– PHRASES **ahead of** in front of or before: *she walked ahead of him along the corridor* ■ in store for; awaiting: *we have a long drive ahead of us.* ■ earlier than planned or expected: *elimination of trade barriers came five years ahead of schedule.* **ahead of one's** (or **its**) **time** innovative and radical by the standards of the time; more characteristic of a later age.
– ORIGIN mid 16th cent. (originally in nautical use): from A-[2] 'in, at' + HEAD.

ahem ▶ **exclamation** used to represent the noise made when clearing the throat, typically to attract attention or express disapproval or embarrassment.
– ORIGIN mid 18th cent.: lengthened form of HEM[2].

Ahern /əˈhəːn/, Bertie (b.1951), Irish Fianna Fáil statesman, Taoiseach (Prime Minister) since 1997.

ahimsa /əˈhɪmsɑː/ ▶ **noun** [mass noun] (in the Hindu, Buddhist, and Jainist tradition) respect for all living things and avoidance of violence towards others.
– ORIGIN Sanskrit, from *a* 'non-, without' + *hiṃsā* 'violence'.

ahistorical ▶ **adjective** lacking historical perspective or context.

Ahmadabad /ˈɑːmədəbad/ (also **Ahmedabad**) an industrial city in the state of Gujarat in western India; pop. 2,873,000 (1991).

aholehole /əˌhəʊlɪˈhəʊli/ ▶ **noun** a small silvery fish occurring only in the shallow waters around the Hawaiian islands, where it is a food fish.
• *Kuhlia sandvicensis*, family Kuhliidae.
– ORIGIN from Hawaiian.

-aholic (also **-oholic**) ▶ **suffix** denoting a person addicted to something: *shopaholic* | *workaholic.*
– ORIGIN on the pattern of *(alc)oholic*.

ahoy ▶ **exclamation** Nautical or humorous a call used in hailing: *ahoy there!* | *ship ahoy!*
– PHRASES **land ahoy!** an exclamation announcing the sighting of land from a ship.
– ORIGIN mid 18th cent.: from AH + HOY[1].

Ahriman /ˈɑːrɪmən/ the evil spirit in the doctrine of Zoroastrianism, the opponent of Ahura Mazda.

Ahura Mazda /əˌhʊərə ˈmazdə/ the creator god of Zoroastrianism, the force for good and the opponent of Ahriman. Also called ORMAZD.
– ORIGIN Avestan, literally 'wise deity'.

Ahvaz /ɑːˈvɑːz/ (also **Ahwaz** /ɑːˈwɑːz/) a town in western Iran; pop. 725,000 (1991).

Ahvenanmaa /ˈɑːvənənmɑː/ Finnish name for ÅLAND ISLANDS.

AI ▶ **abbreviation for** ■ Amnesty International. ■ artificial insemination. ■ artificial intelligence.

ai /ˈɑːi/ ▶ **noun** (pl. **ais**) the three-toed sloth.
– ORIGIN early 17th cent.: from Tupi, imitative of its cry.

AID ▶ **abbreviation for** artificial insemination by donor.

aid ▶ **noun** [mass noun] help, typically of a practical nature: *he saw the pilot slumped in his cockpit and **went to his aid*** | *within six weeks he was walking **with the aid of** a frame.*
■ financial or material help given to a country or area in need: *700,000 tons of food aid* | [as modifier] *an aid agency.* ■ [count noun] a person or thing that is a source of help or assistance: *exercise is an important **aid to** recovery after heart attacks* | *a teaching aid.* ■ [count noun] historical a grant of subsidy or tax to a king.
▶ **verb** [with obj.] help, assist, or support (someone or something) in the achievement of something: *women were aided in childbirth by midwives* | [no obj.] *research was conducted to aid in making decisions.*
■ promote or encourage (something): *diet and exercise aid healthy skin.*
– PHRASES **aid and abet** see ABET. **in aid of** chiefly Brit. in support of; for the purpose of raising money for: *a charity show in aid of Leukaemia Research.* **what's (all) this in aid of?** Brit. informal what is the purpose of this?
– ORIGIN late Middle English: from Old French *aide* (noun), *aidier* (verb), based on Latin *adjuvare*, from *ad-* 'towards' + *juvare* 'to help'.

aida /ˈeɪdə/ (also **aida cloth** or **aida fabric**) ▶ **noun** [mass noun] a material consisting of a mesh of small holes, used in cross stitch embroidery.

Aidan, St /ˈeɪd(ə)n/ (d. AD 651), Irish missionary. While a monk in the monastery at Iona he set out to Christianize Northumbria, founding a church and monastery at Lindisfarne in 635 and becoming its first bishop.

aid climbing ▶ **noun** [mass noun] rock climbing using the assistance of objects such as pegs placed in the rock. Compare with FREE CLIMBING.
– DERIVATIVES **aid climb** noun, **aid-climb** verb.

aide /eɪd/ ▶ **noun** an assistant to an important person, especially a political leader.
■ short for AIDE-DE-CAMP.

aide-de-camp /ˌeɪddəˈkɒ̃/ ▶ **noun** (pl. **aides-de-camp** pronunc. same) a military officer acting as a confidential assistant to a senior officer.
– ORIGIN late 17th cent.: from French, 'camp adjutant'.

aide-memoire /ˌeɪd mɛmˈwɑː, French ɛd mɛmwaʀ/ ▶ **noun** (pl. **aides-memoires** or **aides-memoire** pronunc. same) an aid to the memory, especially a book or document.
■ an informal diplomatic message.
– ORIGIN mid 19th cent.: from French *aide-mémoire*, from *aider* 'to help' and *mémoire* 'memory'.

Aids (also **AIDS**) ▶ **noun** [mass noun] acquired immune deficiency syndrome, a disease in which there is a severe loss of the body's cellular immunity, greatly lowering the resistance to infection and malignancy.

> The cause is a virus (called the human immunodeficiency virus or HIV) transmitted in blood and in sexual fluids, and though the incubation period may be long the fully developed disease is invariably fatal. Aids was first identified in the early 1980s and now affects millions of people. In the developed world the disease first spread among homosexuals, intravenous drug users, and recipients of infected blood transfusions, before reaching the wider population. This has tended to overshadow a greater epidemic in parts of Africa, where transmission is mainly through heterosexual contact.

– ORIGIN 1980s: acronym.

Aids-related complex ▶ **noun** [mass noun] the symptoms of a person who is affected with HIV but does not necessarily develop the disease.

aigrette /ˈeɪgrɛt, eɪˈgrɛt/ ▶ **noun** a headdress consisting of a white egret's feather or other decoration such as a spray of gems.
– ORIGIN mid 18th cent.: from French, 'egret'.

aiguille /ˈeɪgwiːl/ ▶ **noun** a sharp pinnacle of rock in a mountain range.
– ORIGIN mid 18th cent.: from French, literally 'needle', from medieval Latin *acucula* 'little needle', diminutive of Latin *acus*.

aiguillette /ˌeɪgwɪˈlɛt/ ▶ **noun** an ornament on some military and naval uniforms, consisting of braided loops hanging from the shoulder and on dress uniforms ending in points that resemble pencils.
– ORIGIN mid 16th cent.: from French, literally 'small needle', diminutive of *aiguille*.

AIH ▶ **abbreviation for** artificial insemination by husband.

aikido /ʌɪˈkiːdəʊ/ ▶ **noun** [mass noun] a Japanese form of self-defence and martial art that uses locks, holds, throws, and the opponent's own movements.
– ORIGIN 1950s.: from Japanese *aikidō*, literally 'way of adapting the spirit', from *ai* 'together, unify' + *ki* 'spirit' + *dō* 'way'.

ail ▶ **verb** [with obj.] archaic trouble or afflict (someone) in mind or body: *exercise is good for whatever ails one.*
– ORIGIN Old English *eglian*, *eglan*, from *egle* 'troublesome', of Germanic origin; related to Gothic *agls* 'disgraceful'.

ailanthus /eɪˈlanθəs/ ▶ **noun** a tall large-leaved deciduous tree which is widely grown as an ornamental or shade tree. Native to Asia and

Australasia, it has been naturalized in North America and Europe.
• Genus *Ailanthus*, family Simaroubaceae: several species, in particular the tree of heaven.
– ORIGIN modern Latin, from French *ailante*, from Amboinese *ailanto*, literally 'tree of heaven' (the ending being influenced by names ending with *-anthus*, from Greek *anthos* 'flower').

aileron /ˈeɪlərɒn/ ▶ **noun** a hinged surface in the trailing edge of an aeroplane wing, used to control the roll of an aircraft about its longitudinal axis.
– ORIGIN early 20th cent.: from French, literally 'small wing', diminutive of *aile*, from Latin *ala* 'wing'.

ailing ▶ **adjective** in poor health: *I went to see my ailing mother* | figurative *the ailing economy.*

ailment ▶ **noun** an illness, typically a minor one.

ailurophobia /ˌʌɪljʊrəˈfəʊbɪə/ ▶ **noun** [mass noun] extreme or irrational fear of cats.
– DERIVATIVES **ailurophobe** noun.
– ORIGIN early 20th cent.: from Greek *ailuros* 'cat' + **-PHOBIA**.

AIM ▶ **abbreviation for** (in the UK) Alternative Investment Market.

aim ▶ **verb 1** [with obj.] point or direct (a weapon or camera) at a target: *aim the camcorder* ***at*** *some suitable object* | [no obj.] ***aim for*** *the middle of the target.*
■ direct (a missile or blow) at someone or something: *she had* ***aimed*** *the bottle* ***at*** *Gary's head.* ■ (**aim something at**) direct information or an action towards (a particular group): *the TV campaign is aimed at the 16–24 age group.*
2 [no obj.] have the intention of achieving: *the programme will* ***aim at*** *deepening understanding* | [with infinitive] *we aim to give you the best possible service.*
▶ **noun 1** a purpose or intention; a desired outcome: *our primary aim is to achieve financial discipline.*
2 [in sing.] the directing of a weapon or missile at a target: *his aim was perfect.*
– PHRASES **aim high** be ambitious. **take aim** point a weapon or camera at a target.
– ORIGIN Middle English: from Old French *amer*, variant of *esmer* (from Latin *aestimare* 'assess, estimate'), reinforced by *aemer, aesmer* (from late Latin *adaestimare*, intensified form of *aestimare*).

aimless ▶ **adjective** without purpose or direction: *an aimless, ungratifying life.*
– DERIVATIVES **aimlessly** adverb, **aimlessness** noun.

ainhum /ˈeɪnhəm/ ▶ **noun** [mass noun] Medicine a condition in which a band of fibrous tissue grows around the base of a toe, eventually resulting in loss of the digit. It occurs mainly in the tropics and is associated with going barefoot.
– ORIGIN late 19th cent.: from Portuguese, based on Yoruba *eyun* 'saw'.

ain't informal ▶ **contraction of** ■ am not; are not; is not: *if it ain't broke, don't fix it.* [ORIGIN: originally representing London dialect.] ■ has not; have not: *they ain't got nothing to say.* [ORIGIN: from dialect *hain't*.]

USAGE The use of **ain't** was widespread in the 18th century, typically as a contraction for **am not**. It is still perfectly normal in many dialects and informal speech in both Britain and North America. Today, however, it does not form part of standard English and should never be used in formal or written contexts. See also **usage** at **AREN'T**.

Aintab /ˈʌntɑːb/ former name (until 1921) for **GAZIANTEP**.

Aintree /ˈeɪntriː/ a suburb of Liverpool, site of a racecourse over which the Grand National is run.

Ainu /ˈeɪnuː/ ▶ **noun** (pl. same or **Ainus**) **1** a member of an aboriginal people of northern Japan, physically distinct (with light skin colour and round eyes) from the majority population.
2 [mass noun] the language of this people, perhaps related to Altaic. It is no longer in everyday use.
▶ **adjective** of or relating to this people or their language.
– ORIGIN the name in Ainu, literally 'man, person'.

aïoli /ʌɪˈəʊli/ (also **aioli**) ▶ **noun** [mass noun] mayonnaise seasoned with garlic.
– ORIGIN French, from Provençal *ai* 'garlic' + *oli* 'oil'.

air ▶ **noun 1** [mass noun] the invisible gaseous substance surrounding the earth, a mixture mainly of oxygen and nitrogen:
■ this substance regarded as necessary for breathing: *the air was stale* | *the doctor told me to get some fresh air.* ■ the free or unconfined space above the surface of the earth: *he celebrated by tossing his hat high in the air.* ■ [as modifier] used to indicate that something involves the use of aircraft: *air travel.* ■ the earth's atmosphere as a medium for transmitting radio waves: *radio stations have successfully sold products* ***over the air.*** ■ one of the four elements in ancient and medieval philosophy and in astrology (considered essential to the nature of the signs of Gemini, Aquarius, and Libra): [as modifier] *an air sign.* ■ [count noun] a breeze or light wind. See also **LIGHT AIR**. ■ [count noun] a jump off the ground on a snowboard. [ORIGIN: Middle English: from Old French *air*, from Latin *aer*, from Greek *aēr*, denoting the gas.]
2 (**air of**) an impression of a quality or manner given by someone or something: *she answered with a faint air of boredom.*
■ (**airs**) an annoyingly affected and condescending manner: *he began to* ***put on airs*** *and think he could boss us around.* [ORIGIN: late 16th cent.: from French *air*, probably from Old French *aire* 'site, disposition', from Latin *ager, agr-* 'field' (influenced by sense 1).]
3 Music a tune or short melodious composition, typically a song. [ORIGIN: late 16th cent.: from Italian *aria* (see **ARIA**).]
▶ **verb 1** [with obj.] (often **be aired**) express (an opinion or grievance) publicly: *a meeting in which long-standing grievances were aired.*
■ broadcast (a programme) on radio or television: *the programmes were aired on India's state TV network.* ■ archaic parade or show (something) ostentatiously.
2 [with obj.] expose (a room) to the open air in order to ventilate it: *the window sashes were lifted regularly to air the room.*
■ Brit. warm (washed laundry) to remove dampness, typically in a heated cupboard. ■ [no obj.] (of laundry) be warmed in this way. ■ (**air oneself**) archaic go out in the fresh air.
– PHRASES **airs and graces** derogatory an affectation of superiority. **by air** in an aircraft: *all goods must come in by air.* **in the air** noticeable all around; becoming prevalent: *I smell violence in the air.* **on** (or **off**) **the air** being (or not being) broadcast on radio or television. **take the air** go out of doors. **up in the air** (of a plan or issue) still to be settled; unresolved: *the fate of the power station is up in the air.* **walk** (or **tread**) **on air** feel elated.

air bag ▶ **noun** a safety device fitted inside a road vehicle, consisting of a cushion designed to inflate rapidly in the event of a collision and positioned so as to protect passengers from being flung against the vehicle's structure.

airband ▶ **noun** a range of frequencies allocated for radio communications involving aircraft.

airbase ▶ **noun** a base for the operation of military aircraft.

air bearing ▶ **noun** a bearing in which moving surfaces are kept apart by a layer of air provided by jets.

air bed ▶ **noun** Brit. an inflatable mattress.

air bladder ▶ **noun** an air-filled bladder or sac found in certain animals and plants.
■ another term for **SWIM BLADDER**.

airboat ▶ **noun** a shallow-draught boat powered by an aircraft engine, for use in swamps.

airborne ▶ **adjective** transported by air: *airborne pollutants.*
■ (of an aircraft) in the air after taking off.

air brake ▶ **noun** a brake worked by air pressure.
■ a movable flap or other device on an aircraft to reduce its speed.

airbrick ▶ **noun** Brit. a brick perforated with small holes for ventilation.

air bridge ▶ **noun** Brit. a portable bridge put against an aircraft door to allow passengers to embark or disembark.

airbrush ▶ **noun** an artist's device for spraying paint by means of compressed air.
▶ **verb** [with obj.] paint with an airbrush: *a cab airbrushed with a mural of a sunset.*
■ alter or conceal (a photograph or a detail in one) using an airbrush: *a picture of a man with wings airbrushed on to his shoulders.* ■ [usu. as adj. **airbrushed**] figurative represent or describe (someone or something) as better or more beautiful than they in fact are: *an airbrushed vision of the decade.*

airburst ▶ **noun** an explosion in the air, especially of a nuclear bomb or large meteorite.
▶ **verb** [no obj.] explode in the air.

air chief marshal ▶ **noun** a high rank of officer in the RAF, above air marshal and below Marshal of the RAF.

air cleaner ▶ **noun** another term for **AIR FILTER**.

air commodore ▶ **noun** a rank of officer in the RAF, above group captain and below air vice-marshal.

air con ▶ **noun** short for **AIR CONDITIONING**.

air conditioning ▶ **noun** [mass noun] a system for controlling the humidity, ventilation, and temperature in a building or vehicle, typically to maintain a cool atmosphere in warm conditions.
– DERIVATIVES **air-conditioned** adjective, **air conditioner** noun.

air corridor ▶ **noun** a route to which aircraft are restricted, especially over a foreign country.

air cover ▶ **noun** [mass noun] protection by aircraft for land-based or naval operations in war situations.

aircraft ▶ **noun** (pl. same) an aeroplane, helicopter, or other machine capable of flight.

aircraft carrier ▶ **noun** a large warship equipped to serve as a base for aircraft which can take off and land from its deck.

aircraftman ▶ **noun** (pl. **-men**) the lowest male rank in the RAF, below leading aircraftman.

aircraftwoman ▶ **noun** (pl. **-women**) the lowest female rank in the RAF, below leading aircraftwoman.

aircrew ▶ **noun** (pl. **aircrews**) [treated as sing. or pl.] the crew manning an aircraft.
■ (pl. same) a member of such a crew.

air cushion ▶ **noun 1** an inflatable cushion.
2 the layer of air supporting a hovercraft or similar vehicle.

air dam ▶ **noun** a streamlining device below the front bumper of a vehicle; a front spoiler.

airdrop ▶ **noun** an act of dropping supplies, troops, or equipment by parachute from an aircraft.
▶ **verb** (**-dropped, -dropping**) [with obj.] drop (such things) by parachute.

air-dry ▶ **verb** make or become dry through contact with unheated air.
▶ **adjective** not giving off any moisture on exposure to air.

Airedale /ˈɛːdeɪl/ ▶ **noun** a large terrier of a rough-coated black-and-tan breed.
– ORIGIN late 19th cent.: from *Airedale*, a district in Yorkshire, where the dog was bred.

airer ▶ **noun** Brit. a frame or stand for airing or drying clothes.

airfield ▶ **noun** an area of land set aside for the take-off, landing, and maintenance of aircraft.

air filter ▶ **noun** a device for filtering particles from the air passing through it, especially one protecting the air inlet of an internal-combustion engine.

airflow ▶ **noun** the flow of air, especially that encountered by a moving aircraft or vehicle.

airfoil ▶ **noun** North American term for **AEROFOIL**.

air force ▶ **noun** a branch of the armed forces concerned with fighting or defence in the air.

Air Force One the official aircraft of the President of the United States.

airframe ▶ **noun** the body of an aircraft as distinct from its engine.

airframer ▶ **noun** informal an aircraft designer or builder.

airfreight ▶ **noun** [mass noun] the carriage of goods by aircraft.
■ goods in transit, or to be carried, by aircraft.
▶ **verb** [with obj.] carry or send (goods) by aircraft.
▶ **adverb** by airfreight: *the exhibit was flown airfreight.*

air-freshener ▶ **noun** a substance or device for making the air in a room smell fresh or clean.

airglow ▶ **noun** [mass noun] a glow in the night sky caused by radiation from the upper atmosphere.

air guitar ▶ **noun** informal used to describe the actions of someone playing an imaginary guitar: *we like our audiences to sing along and play air guitar.*

air gun ▶ **noun 1** a gun which fires pellets using compressed air.
2 (also **hot-air gun**) a tool used to strip paint by means of a stream of very hot air.

airhead[1] ▶ **noun** Military a base close to the area of active operations where supplies and troops can be received and evacuated by air.

– ORIGIN Second World War: on the pattern of *bridgehead*.

airhead² ▶ noun informal a silly or foolish person.

air hostess ▶ noun Brit. a stewardess in a passenger aircraft.

airing ▶ noun [in sing.] **1** an exposure to warm or fresh air, for the purpose of ventilating or removing dampness from something: *somebody had given the place a thorough airing* | [as modifier] *he got a towel from the airing cupboard*.
■ a walk or outing to take air or exercise: *taking the baby out for an airing*.
2 a public expression of an opinion or subject: *these are ideas I feel might be worth an airing*.
■ a transmission of a television or radio programme.

air-kiss ▶ verb [with obj.] purse the lips as if kissing (someone), without making contact: *the media crowd who lunch, gossip, and air-kiss one another*.
▶ noun (**air kiss**) a simulated kiss, without physical contact.

air lane ▶ noun a path or course regularly used by aircraft.

air layering ▶ noun [mass noun] Horticulture a form of layering in which the branch is potted or wrapped in a moist growing medium to promote root growth.

airless ▶ adjective stuffy; not ventilated: *a dusty, airless basement*.
■ without wind or breeze; still: *a hot, airless night*.
– DERIVATIVES **airlessness** noun.

air letter ▶ noun a sheet of light paper folded and sealed to form a letter for sending by airmail.

airlift ▶ noun an act of transporting supplies by aircraft, typically in a blockade or other emergency: *a massive airlift of food, blankets, and medical supplies*.
▶ verb [with obj.] transport (troops or supplies) by aircraft, typically when transportation by land is difficult: *helicopters were employed to airlift the troops out of danger*.

airline ▶ noun **1** an organization providing a regular public service of air transport on one or more routes.
■ (usu. **air line**) a route which forms part of a system regularly used by aircraft.
2 (usu. **air line**) a pipe supplying air.

airliner ▶ noun a large passenger aircraft.

airlock ▶ noun **1** a stoppage of the flow in a pump or pipe, caused by an air bubble.
2 a compartment with controlled pressure and parallel sets of doors, to permit movement between areas at different pressures.

airmail ▶ noun [mass noun] a system of transporting mail by aircraft, typically overseas.
■ [count noun] a letter carried by aircraft.
▶ verb [with obj.] send (mail) by aircraft: *a sheaf of letters to airmail*.

airman ▶ noun (pl. **-men**) a male pilot or member of the crew of an aircraft, especially in an air force.
■ a male member of the RAF below commissioned rank. ■ a male member of the US air force of the lowest rank, below staff sergeant. ■ a male member of the US navy whose general duties are concerned with aircraft.

airmanship ▶ noun [mass noun] skill in flying an aircraft.

air marshal ▶ noun a high rank of officer in the RAF, above air vice-marshal and below air chief marshal.

air mass ▶ noun Meteorology a body of air with horizontally uniform levels of temperature, humidity, and pressure.

air mattress ▶ noun North American term for **AIR BED**.

air mile ▶ noun a nautical mile used as a measure of distance flown by aircraft.
■ (**Air Miles**) trademark points (equivalent to miles of free air travel) accumulated by buyers of airline tickets and other products and redeemable against the cost of air travel with a particular airline.

airmiss ▶ noun Brit. an instance of two or more aircraft in flight on different routes being less than a prescribed distance apart.

airmobile /ɛːˈməʊbʌɪl/ ▶ adjective (of troops) moved about by air.

air officer ▶ noun any rank of officer in the RAF above that of group captain.

air pistol ▶ noun a pistol which fires pellets using compressed air.

airplane ▶ noun North American term for **AEROPLANE**.

air plant ▶ noun a tropical American plant that grows on trees as an epiphyte, with long narrow leaves that absorb water and nutrients from the atmosphere.
● Genus *Tillandsia*, family Bromeliaceae: several species, including Spanish moss.

airplay ▶ noun [mass noun] broadcasting time devoted to a particular record, performer, or musical genre.

air pocket ▶ noun a cavity containing air.
■ a region of low pressure causing an aircraft to lose height suddenly.

airport ▶ noun a complex of runways and buildings for the take-off, landing, and maintenance of civil aircraft, with facilities for passengers.
■ [as modifier] relating to or denoting light popular fiction such as is offered for sale to travellers in airports: *another airport thriller*.

air power ▶ noun [mass noun] the ability to defend or attack by means of aircraft.

air pump ▶ noun a device for pumping air into or out of an enclosed space.

air quality ▶ noun the degree to which the ambient air is pollution-free, assessed by measuring a number of indicators of pollution.

air raid ▶ noun an attack in which bombs are dropped from aircraft on to a ground target.

air rank ▶ noun [mass noun] the rank attained by air officers.

air rifle ▶ noun a rifle which fires pellets using compressed air.

air sac ▶ noun a lung compartment containing air; an alveolus.
■ an extension of a bird's lung cavity into a bone or other part of the body.

airscrew ▶ noun Brit. an aircraft propeller.

air-sea rescue ▶ noun a rescue from the sea using aircraft.

air shaft ▶ noun a straight, typically vertical passage admitting air into a mine, tunnel, or building.

airship ▶ noun a power-driven aircraft that is kept buoyant by a body of gas (usually helium, formerly hydrogen) which is lighter than air.

air shot ▶ noun informal a missed attempt to hit or kick a ball.

air show ▶ noun a show at which aircraft perform aerial displays.

airsick ▶ adjective affected with nausea due to travel in an aircraft.
– DERIVATIVES **airsickness** noun.

airside ▶ noun the side of an airport terminal from which aircraft can be observed; the area beyond passport and customs control.
▶ adverb on or to this side of an airport terminal: *a new executive lounge has opened airside*.

airspace ▶ noun [mass noun] room available in the atmosphere immediately above the earth: *temples and mosques fight for airspace with skyscrapers*.
■ the air available to aircraft to fly in, especially the part subject to the jurisdiction of a particular country. ■ Law the right of a private landowner to the space above his land and any structures on it, which he can use for ordinary purposes such as the erection of signposts or fences. ■ space left to be occupied by air for purposes of insulation.

airspeed ▶ noun [mass noun] the speed of an aircraft relative to the air through which it is moving. Compare with **GROUND SPEED**.

air station ▶ noun an airfield operated by a navy or marine corps.

airstream ▶ noun a current of air.

air strike ▶ noun an attack made by aircraft.

airstrip ▶ noun a strip of ground set aside for the take-off and landing of aircraft.

air support ▶ noun [mass noun] assistance given to ground or naval forces in an operation by their own or allied aircraft.

airtight ▶ adjective not allowing air to escape or pass through.
■ having no weaknesses; unassailable: *she had an airtight alibi*.

airtime ▶ noun [mass noun] time during which a broadcast is being transmitted.

air-to-air ▶ adjective directed or operating from one aircraft to another in flight.

air-to-ground ▶ adjective directed or operating from an aircraft in flight to the land surface.

air-to-surface ▶ adjective directed or operating from an aircraft in flight to the surface of the sea or other body of water.

air traffic control ▶ noun [mass noun] the ground-based personnel and equipment concerned with controlling and monitoring air traffic within a particular area.
– DERIVATIVES **air traffic controller** noun.

air vice-marshal ▶ noun a high rank of officer in the RAF, above air commodore and below air marshal.

airwaves ▶ plural noun the radio frequencies used for broadcasting: *football pervades the airwaves*.

airway ▶ noun **1** the passage by which air reaches a person's lungs.
■ a tube for supplying air to a person's lungs in an emergency. ■ a ventilating passage in a mine.
2 a recognized route followed by aircraft.
■ (**Airways**) in names of airlines: *British Airways*.

airwoman ▶ noun (pl. **-women**) a woman pilot or member of the crew of an aircraft, especially in an air force.
■ a female member of the RAF below commissioned rank. ■ a female member of the US air force of the lowest rank, below staff sergeant. ■ a female member of the US navy whose general duties are concerned with aircraft.

airworthy ▶ adjective (of an aircraft) safe to fly.
– DERIVATIVES **airworthiness** noun.

Airy, Sir George Biddell (1801–92), English astronomer and geophysicist, who proposed the concept of isostasy and gave an improved estimate of the earth's density.

airy ▶ adjective (**airier**, **airiest**) **1** (of a room or building) spacious, well lit, and well ventilated.
■ delicate, as though filled with or made of air: *airy clouds*. ■ figurative giving an impression of light gracefulness and elegance: *her airy presence filled the house*.
2 giving an impression of being unconcerned or not serious, typically about something taken seriously by others: *her airy unconcern for economy*.
– DERIVATIVES **airily** adverb, **airiness** noun.

airy-fairy ▶ adjective informal, chiefly Brit. impractical and foolishly idealistic: *love might seem an airy-fairy, romantic concept*.

aisle /ʌɪl/ ▶ noun a passage between rows of seats in a building such as a church or theatre, an aircraft, or train: *the musical had the audience dancing in the aisles*.
■ a passage between cabinets and shelves of goods in a supermarket or other building. ■ Architecture (in a church) a lower part parallel to and at the side of a nave, choir, or transept, from which it is divided by pillars.
– PHRASES **lead someone up the aisle** get married to someone.
– DERIVATIVES **aisled** adjective.
– ORIGIN late Middle English *ele*, *ile*, from Old French *ele*, from Latin *ala* 'wing'. The spelling change in the 17th cent. was due to confusion with *isle* and influenced by French *aile* 'wing'.

ait /eɪt/ (also **eyot**) ▶ noun [in place names] Brit. a small island in a river: *Raven's Ait*.
– ORIGIN Old English *īggath*, *īgeth*, based on *īeg* 'island' + a diminutive suffix.

aitch ▶ noun the letter H.
– PHRASES **drop one's aitches** fail to pronounce the letter *h* at the beginning of words, a characteristic feature of certain dialects.
– ORIGIN mid 16th cent.: from Old French *ache*.

aitchbone ▶ noun the buttock or rump bone of cattle.
■ a cut of beef lying over this.
– ORIGIN late 15th cent., from dialect *nache* 'rump', from Old French, based on Latin *natis* 'buttock(s)', + **BONE**. The initial *n* in *a nache bone* was lost by wrong division; compare with **ADDER¹**.

Aitken /ˈeɪtkɪn/, William Maxwell, see **BEAVERBROOK**.

Aix-en-Provence /ˌɛksɑ̃prɒˈvɒ̃s/, French

εksăpʀovǎs/ a city in Provence in southern France; pop. 126,850 (1990).

Aix-la-Chapelle /ɛkslaʃapɛl/ French name for **AACHEN**.

Aizawl /ʌɪdʒəl/ a city in the far north-east of India, capital of the state of Mizoram; pop. 154,000 (1991).

Ajaccio /əˈdʒaksɪəʊ, French aʒaksjo/ a port on the west coast of Corsica; pop. 59,320 (1990). It is the capital of the southern department of Corse-du-Sud.

Ajanta Caves /əˈdʒʌntə/ a series of caves in the state of Maharashtra, south central India, containing Buddhist frescoes and sculptures dating from the 1st century BC to the 7th century AD.

ajar¹ ▶ adverb & adjective (of a door or other opening) slightly open: [as adv.] *the home help had left the window ajar that morning* | [as predic. adj.] *the door to the sitting room was ajar.*
– ORIGIN late 17th cent.: from **A-²** 'on' + obsolete *char* (Old English *cerr*) 'a turn, return'.

ajar² ▶ adverb archaic out of harmony.
– ORIGIN mid 19th cent.: from **A-²** 'in, at' + **JAR**².

Ajax /ˈeɪdʒaks/ Greek Mythology **1** a Greek hero of the Trojan war, son of Telamon, king of Salamis. He was proverbial for his size and strength.
2 a Greek hero, son of Oileus, king of Locris.

Ajman /adʒˈmaːn/ one of the seven member states of the United Arab Emirates; pop. 118,800 (1995).

Ajmer /adʒˈmɪə/ a city in NW India, in Rajasthan; pop. 402,000 (1991).

ajuga /əˈdʒuːgə/ ▶ noun a plant of a genus that includes bugle.
● Genus *Ajuga*, family Labiatae.
– ORIGIN modern Latin, from medieval Latin *ajuga*.

AK ▶ abbreviation for Alaska (in official postal use).

aka ▶ abbreviation for also known as: *John Merrick, aka the Elephant Man.*

Akali /əˈkɑːli/ ▶ noun (pl. **Akalis**) a member of a militant Sikh political group.
– ORIGIN from Punjabi *akālī*, literally 'follower of the Immortal One'.

Akan /ˈaːk(ə)n/ ▶ noun (pl. same) **1** a member of a people inhabiting southern Ghana and adjacent parts of Ivory Coast.
2 [mass noun] the language of this people, belonging to the Kwa group and having over 4 million speakers. Its main dialects are Ashanti and Fante. Also called **TWI**.
▶ adjective of or relating to this people or their language.
– ORIGIN the name in Akan.

akara /əˈkarə/ ▶ noun variant spelling of **ACCRA**.

akasha /ɑːˈkɑːʃə/ ▶ noun chiefly Indian Religion a supposed universal etheric field in which a record of past events is imprinted.
– DERIVATIVES **akashic** adjective.
– ORIGIN from Sanskrit *ākāśa.*

Akbar /ˈakbə/, Jalaludin Muhammad (1542–1605), Mogul emperor of India 1556–1605; known as **Akbar the Great**. Akbar expanded the Mogul empire to incorporate northern India and established an efficient but enlightened administration.

akebia /əˈkiːbɪə/ ▶ noun an East Asian climbing shrub with purplish flowers and deeply divided leaves.
● Genus *Akebia*, family Lardizabalaceae.
– ORIGIN 1837: modern Latin, coined by J. Decaisne, French botanist, from Japanese *akebi.*

akee ▶ noun variant spelling of **ACKEE**.

Akela /ɑːˈkeɪlə/ ▶ noun informal the adult leader of a group of Cub Scouts, officially termed Cub Scout Leader.
– ORIGIN 1920s: from the name of the leader of a wolf pack in Kipling's *Jungle Books* (1894–5).

Akhenaten /ˌakəˈnɑːt(ə)n/ (also **Akhenaton** or **Ikhnaton**) (14th century BC), Egyptian pharaoh of the 18th dynasty, reigned 1379–1362 BC; came to the throne as *Amenhotep IV*. The husband of Nefertiti, he introduced the monotheistic solar cult of Aten and moved the capital from Thebes to the newly built city of Akhetaten. He was succeeded by his son-in-law Tutankhamen, who abandoned the new religion.

Akhetaten /ˌakəˈtɑːt(ə)n/ an ancient Egyptian capital built by Akhenaten in *c.*1375 BC when he established the new worship of the sun disc Aten,

but abandoned after his death. See also **AMARNA, TELL EL-**.

Akhmatova /akˈmɑːtəvə/, Anna (1889–1966), Russian poet; pseudonym of *Anna Andreevna Gorenko*. Akhmatova was a member of the Acmeist group of poets.

Akihito /akɪˈhiːtəʊ/ (b.1933), son of Emperor Hirohito, emperor of Japan since 1989; full name *Tsugu Akihito.*

akimbo /əˈkɪmbəʊ/ ▶ adverb with hands on the hips and elbows turned outwards: *she stood with arms akimbo, frowning at the small boy.*
■ (of other limbs) flung out widely or haphazardly.
– ORIGIN late Middle English: from *in kenebowe* in Middle English, probably from Old Norse.

akin ▶ adjective [predic.] of similar character: *something akin to gratitude overwhelmed her* | *genius and madness are akin.*
■ related by blood.
– ORIGIN late 16th cent.: contracted form of *of kin*.

akinesia /ˌeɪkɪˈniːsɪə, a-/ ▶ noun [mass noun] Medicine loss or impairment of the power of voluntary movement.
– DERIVATIVES **akinetic** adjective.
– ORIGIN mid 19th cent.: from Greek *akinēsia* 'quiescence', from *a-* 'without' + *kinēsis* 'motion'.

Akita /əˈkiːtə/ ▶ noun a spitz (dog) of a Japanese breed.
– ORIGIN early 20th cent.: from *Akita*, the name of a district in northern Japan.

Akkad /ˈakad, aˈkad/ the capital city which gave its name to an ancient kingdom traditionally founded by Sargon in north central Mesopotamia. Its site is lost.

Akkadian /əˈkeɪdɪən, -ˈkad-/ ▶ adjective of or relating to Akkad in ancient Babylonia or its people or their language.
▶ noun **1** an inhabitant of Akkad.
2 [mass noun] the extinct language of Akkad, written in cuneiform, with two dialects, Assyrian and Babylonian, widely used from about 3500 BC. It is the oldest Semitic language for which records exist.

Akko /ˈakəʊ/ another name for **ACRE** 1.

Ak-Mechet /ˌakməˈtʃɛt/ former name for **SIMFEROPOL**.

Akmola /akˈmɒlə/ former name for **ASTANA**.

akrasia /əˈkreɪzɪə, əˈkrasɪə/ (also **acrasia**) ▶ noun [mass noun] chiefly Philosophy the state of mind in which someone acts against their better judgement through weakness of will.
– DERIVATIVES **akratic** (also **acratic**) adjective.
– ORIGIN early 19th cent.: from Greek, from *a-* 'without' + *kratos* 'power, strength'. The term is used especially with reference to Aristotle's *Nicomachean Ethics.*

Akron /ˈakrən/ a city in NE Ohio; pop. 223,000 (1990).

Aksai Chin /ˌaksʌɪ ˈtʃɪn/ a region of the Himalayas occupied by China since 1950, but claimed by India as part of Kashmir.

Aksum /ˈaːksəm/ (also **Axum**) a town in the province of Tigray in northern Ethiopia. It was a religious centre and the capital of a powerful kingdom between the 1st and 6th centuries AD.
– DERIVATIVES **Aksumite** adjective & noun.

akvavit /ˈakvəvɪt/ ▶ noun variant spelling of **AQUAVIT**.

AL ▶ abbreviation for ■ Alabama (in official postal use). ■ Albania (international vehicle registration). ■ American League (in baseball).

Al ▶ symbol for the chemical element aluminium.

al- ▶ prefix variant spelling of **AD-** assimilated before *-l* (as in *alleviate, allocate*).

-al ▶ suffix **1** (forming adjectives) relating to; of the kind of:
■ from Latin words: *annual* | *infernal*. ■ from Greek words: *historical* | *comical*. ■ from English nouns: *tidal.*
2 forming nouns chiefly denoting verbal action: *arrival* | *transmittal.*
– ORIGIN sense 1 from French *-el* or Latin *-alis*; sense 2 from French *-aille* or from Latin *-alis* functioning as a noun ending.

Ala. ▶ abbreviation for Alabama.

à la /ˈaː laː; a laː/ ▶ preposition (of a dish) cooked or prepared in a specified style or manner: *fish cooked à la meunière.*

■ informal in the style or manner of: *afternoon talk shows à la Oprah.*
– ORIGIN French, from **À LA MODE**.

Alabama /ˌaləˈbamə/ a state in the south-eastern US, on the Gulf of Mexico; pop. 4,040,600 (1990); capital, Montgomery. It became the 22nd state in 1819.
– DERIVATIVES **Alabaman** adjective & noun.

alabaster /ˈaləbɑːstə, -bastə, ˌaləˈbaːstə, -ˈbastə/ ▶ noun [mass noun] a translucent form of gypsum, typically white, often carved into ornaments.
▶ adjective made of alabaster.
■ poetic/literary like alabaster in whiteness and smoothness: *her alabaster cheeks flushed with warmth.*
– ORIGIN late Middle English: via Old French from Latin *alabaster, alabastrum*, from Greek *alabastos, alabastros.*

à la carte /aː laː ˈkaːt, a la, French a la kaʀt/ ▶ adjective (of a menu or restaurant) listing or serving food that can be ordered as separate items, rather than part of a set meal.
■ (of food) available on such a menu.
▶ adverb as separately priced items from a menu, not as part of a set meal: *good food served à la carte.*
– ORIGIN early 19th cent.: French, literally 'according to the (menu) card'.

alack (also **alack-a-day**) ▶ exclamation archaic an expression of regret or dismay.
– ORIGIN late Middle English: probably from **AH** + **LACK**.

alacrity /əˈlakrɪti/ ▶ noun [mass noun] brisk and cheerful readiness: *she accepted the invitation with alacrity.*
– ORIGIN late Middle English: from Latin *alacritas*, from *alacer* 'brisk'.

Aladdin /əˈladɪn/ the hero of a story in the *Arabian Nights*, who finds an old lamp which, when rubbed, summons a genie who obeys the will of the owner.
– ORIGIN from Arabic 'Alā' al-dīn.

Aladdin's cave ▶ noun a place filled with a great number and variety of strange or precious items: *the market is an Aladdin's cave of goodies.*
– ORIGIN from **ALADDIN**.

Aladdin's lamp ▶ noun a talisman enabling its holder to gratify any wish.
– ORIGIN from **ALADDIN**.

Alagoas /ˌaləˈgəʊəs/ a state in eastern Brazil, on the Atlantic coast; capital, Maceió.

Alain-Fournier /ˌalɛ̃ˈfʊənɪeɪ, French alɛ̃fuʀnje/ (1886–1914), French novelist; pseudonym of *Henri-Alban Fournier*. A literary columnist, he completed only one novel, *Le Grand Meaulnes* (1913), before his death in the First World War.

alameda /ˌaləˈmeɪdə/ ▶ noun (in Spain and Spanish-speaking areas) a public walkway or promenade, shaded with trees.
– ORIGIN late 18th cent.: Spanish.

Alamein see **EL ALAMEIN, BATTLE OF**.

Alamo /ˈaləməʊ/ (the Alamo) a mission in San Antonio, Texas, site of a siege in 1836 by Mexican forces, in which all 180 defenders were killed.

à la mode /aː laː ˈməʊd, a la/ ▶ adverb & adjective **1** in fashion; up to date.
2 (of beef) braised in wine, typically with vegetables.
3 N. Amer. served with ice cream.
– ORIGIN late 16th cent.: French, literally 'in the fashion'.

Åland Islands /ˈɔːlənd/ a group of islands in the Gulf of Bothnia, forming an autonomous region of Finland; capital, Mariehamn (known in Finnish as Maarianhamina). Finnish name **AHVENANMAA**.

alanine /ˈaləniːn/ ▶ noun [mass noun] Biochemistry an amino acid which is a constituent of most proteins.
● Alternative name: **2-aminopropanoic acid**; chem. formula: $CH_3CH(NH_2)COOH$. **β-alanine**, is an isomer of this, is 3-aminopropanoic acid, $(NH_2)CH_2CH_2COOH$.
– ORIGIN mid 19th cent.: coined in German as *Alanin*, from **ALDEHYDE** + *-an* (for ease of pronunciation) + **-INE**⁴.

alannah /əˈlanə/ (also **alanna**) ▶ noun Irish my child (used as an affectionate form of address).
– ORIGIN mid 19th cent.: from Irish *a leanbh* 'O child'.

Al-Anon /ˌaləˈnɒn/ a mutual support organization for the families and friends of alcoholics, especially those of members of Alcoholics Anonymous.

alap /əˈlaːp/ ▶ noun (in Indian music) the improvised

liquid obtained when acetaldehyde dimerizes in dilute alkali or acid.
● Alternative name: **3-hydroxybutanal**; chem. formula: $CH_3CH(OH)CH_2CHO$.
– ORIGIN late 19th cent.: from al(dehyde) + -OL.

aldosterone /alˈdɒstərəʊn/ ▶ noun [mass noun] Biochemistry a corticosteroid hormone which stimulates absorption of sodium by the kidneys and so regulates water and salt balance.
– ORIGIN 1950s: blend of ALDEHYDE and STEROID, + -ONE.

aldosteronism /ˌaldə(ʊ)ˈstɛrənɪz(ə)m/ ▶ noun [mass noun] Medicine a condition in which there is excessive secretion of aldosterone. This disturbs the balance of sodium, potassium, and water in the blood and so leads to high blood pressure.

Aldrin /ˈɔːldrɪn/, Buzz (b.1930), American astronaut; full name *Edwin Eugene Aldrin*. In 1969 he took part in the first moon landing, the Apollo 11 mission, becoming the second person to set foot on the moon, after Neil Armstrong.

aldrin /ˈɔːldrɪn/ ▶ noun [mass noun] a toxic synthetic insecticide, now generally banned.
● A chlorinated polycyclic hydrocarbon; chem. formula: $C_{12}H_8Cl_6$.
– ORIGIN 1940s: from the name of K. *Alder* (see DIELS–ALDER REACTION) + -IN[1].

Aldus Manutius /ˌɔːldəs məˈnjuːʃɪəs/ (1450–1515), Italian scholar, printer, and publisher; Latinized name of *Teobaldo Manucci*; also known as **Aldo Manuzio**. He printed fine first editions of many Greek and Latin classics.

ale ▶ noun [mass noun] chiefly Brit. any beer other than lager, stout, or porter: *a draught of ale* | [count noun] *traditional cask-conditioned ales*.
■ N. Amer. beer brewed by top fermentation. ■ historical a drink made like beer but without the addition of hops.
– ORIGIN Old English *alu*, *ealu*, of Germanic origin; related to Old Norse *ǫl*. Formerly the word referred especially to unhopped or the paler varieties of beer.

aleatoric /ˌeɪlɪəˈtɒrɪk, ˌal-/ ▶ adjective another term for ALEATORY.
– ORIGIN 1960s: from Latin *aleatorius*, from *aleator* 'dice player', from *alea* 'die', + -IC.

aleatory /ˈeɪlɪət(ə)ri, ˈal-/ ▶ adjective depending on the throw of a die or on chance; random.
■ relating to or denoting music or other forms of art involving elements of random choice (sometimes using statistical or computer techniques) during their composition, production, or performance.
– ORIGIN late 17th cent.: from Latin *aleatorius* (see ALEATORIC).

alec /ˈalɪk/ (also **aleck** or **alick**) ▶ noun Austral. informal a stupid person: *what sort of alec do you take me for?*
– ORIGIN late 20th cent.: shortening of SMART ALEC.

alecost /ˈeɪlkɒst/ ▶ noun another term for COSTMARY.
– ORIGIN late 16th cent.: from ALE + cost.

Alecto /əˈlɛktəʊ/ (also **Allecto**) Greek Mythology one of the Furies.

alee /əˈliː/ ▶ adjective & adverb Nautical on the side of a ship that is sheltered from the wind.
■ (of the helm) moved round to leeward in order to tack a vessel or to bring its bows up into the wind.
– ORIGIN late Middle English: from A-[2] 'on' + LEE.

alehouse ▶ noun chiefly dated an inn or public house.

Alekhine /ˈalɪkiːn, ˈaljəkɪn/, Alexander (1892–1946), Russian-born French chess player, world champion 1927–35 and from 1937 until his death.

Aleksandropol /ˌalɪkˈsɑːndrəpɒl/ (also **Alexandropol**) former name (1840–1924) for GYUMRI.

Aleksandrovsk /ˌalɪkˈsɑːndrəfsk/ former name (until 1921) for ZAPORIZHZHYA.

alembic /əˈlɛmbɪk/ ▶ noun a distilling apparatus, now obsolete, consisting of a gourd-shaped container and a cap with a long beak for conveying the products to a receiver.
– ORIGIN Middle English: via Old French from medieval Latin *alembicus*, from Arabic *al-'anbīk*, from *al-* 'the' + *'anbīk* 'still' (from Greek *ambix*, *ambik-* 'cup, cap of a still').

Alentejo /ˌalənˈteɪʒuː/ a region and former province of east central Portugal.

aleph /ˈɑːlɛf/ ▶ noun the first letter of the Hebrew alphabet.
– ORIGIN Middle English: from Hebrew *'ālep*, literally 'ox' (the character in Phoenician and ancient Hebrew possibly being derived from a hieroglyph of an ox's head).

Aleppo /əˈlɛpəʊ/ a city in northern Syria; pop. 1,494,000 (1993). Arabic name HALAB.

Aleppo gall ▶ noun a hard nut-like gall that forms on the valonia oak (formerly known as the Aleppo oak) in response to the developing larva of a gall wasp. It is used as a source of gallic acid and tannin.
● The wasp is *Cynips tinctoria*, family Cynipidae.

alerce /əˈlɔːsi/ ▶ noun a cypress tree that is valued for its timber.
● Several species in the family Cupressaceae, in particular *Tetraclinis articulata* of southern Spain and north Africa, from which the resin sandarac is obtained.
– ORIGIN mid 19th cent.: from Spanish, 'larch'.

alert ▶ adjective quick to notice any unusual and potentially dangerous or difficult circumstances; vigilant: *an alert police officer discovered a lorry full of explosive* | *schools need to be constantly alert to this problem*.
■ able to think clearly; intellectually active: *she remained active and alert until well into her eighties*.
▶ noun [mass noun] the state of being watchful for possible danger: *security forces were placed on alert*.
■ [count noun] an announcement or signal warning of danger: *a bomb alert* | *an alert sounded and all the fighters took off*. ■ [count noun] a period of vigilance in response to such a warning: *traffic was halted during the alert*.
▶ verb [with obj.] warn (someone) of a danger, threat, or problem, typically with the intention of having it avoided or dealt with: *he alerted people to the dangers of smoking* | *police were alerted after three men drove away without paying*.
– PHRASES **on the alert** vigilant and prepared: *security forces are on the alert for an upsurge in violence*.
– DERIVATIVES **alertly** adverb, **alertness** noun.
– ORIGIN late 16th cent. (originally in military use): from French *alerte*, from Italian *all' erta* 'to the watchtower'.

-ales /ˈeɪliːz/ ▶ suffix Botany forming the names of orders of plants: *Rosales*.
– ORIGIN from the plural of the Latin adjectival suffix *-alis* (see -AL).

alethic /əˈliːθɪk/ ▶ adjective Philosophy denoting modalities of truth, such as necessity, contingency, or impossibility.
– ORIGIN 1950s: from Greek *alētheia* 'truth' + -IC.

Aletschhorn /ˈɑːlɛtʃˌhɔːn/ a mountain in Switzerland, in the Bernese Alps, rising to 4,195 m (13,763 ft). Its glaciers are among the largest in Europe.

aleurone /əˈljʊərəʊn/ ▶ noun [mass noun] Botany protein stored as granules in the cells of plant seeds.
– ORIGIN mid 19th cent.: from Greek *aleuron* 'flour'.

Aleut /əˈljuːt, ˈaljuːt/ ▶ noun **1** a member of a people inhabiting the Aleutian Islands, other islands in the Bering Sea, and parts of western Alaska.
2 [mass noun] the language of this people, related to Eskimo. It is now almost extinct.
▶ adjective of or relating to this people or their language.
– ORIGIN of unknown origin.

Aleutian Islands /əˈl(j)uːʃ(ə)n/ (also **the Aleutians**) a chain of volcanic islands in US possession, extending south-west from the Alaska Peninsula.

A level ▶ noun Brit. short for ADVANCED LEVEL.
■ an exam or pass at this level.

alevin /ˈaləvɪn/ ▶ noun a newly spawned salmon or trout still carrying the yolk.
– ORIGIN mid 19th cent.: from French, based on Latin *allevare* 'raise up'.

alewife ▶ noun (pl. **alewives**) a NW Atlantic fish of the herring family, swimming up rivers to spawn.
● *Alosa pseudoharengus*, family Clupeidae.
– ORIGIN mid 17th cent.: possibly from earlier *alewife* 'woman who keeps an ale house', with reference to the fish's large belly.

Alexander[1] (356–323 BC), king of Macedon 336–323, son of Philip II; known as **Alexander the Great**. He conquered Persia, Egypt, Syria, Mesopotamia, Bactria, and the Punjab; in Egypt he founded the city of Alexandria.

Alexander[2] the name of three kings of Scotland:

■ Alexander I (c.1077–1124), son of Malcolm III, reigned 1107–24.
■ Alexander II (1198–1249), son of William I of Scotland, reigned 1214–49.
■ Alexander III (1241–86), son of Alexander II, reigned 1249–86.

Alexander[3] the name of three tsars of Russia:
■ Alexander I (1777–1825), reigned 1801–25.
■ Alexander II (1818–81), son of Nicholas I, reigned 1855–81; known as **Alexander the Liberator**. His reforms included limited emancipation of the serfs.
■ Alexander III (1845–94), son of Alexander II, reigned 1881–94.

Alexander[4], Harold (Rupert Leofric George), 1st Earl Alexander of Tunis (1891–1969), British Field Marshal and Conservative statesman, holding commands during the Second World War.

Alexander Archipelago a group of about 1,100 islands off the coast of SE Alaska.

Alexander Nevsky /ˈnjɛfski/ (also **Nevski**) (c.1220–63), prince of Novgorod 1236–63. He defeated the Swedes on the banks of the River Neva in 1240. Feast day, 30 August or 23 November.

alexanders ▶ plural noun [treated as sing.] a European plant of the parsley family with yellowish flowers, formerly used in salads.
● *Smyrnium olusatrum*, family Umbelliferae.
■ N. Amer. any of a number of other plants of the parsley family.
– ORIGIN Old English *alexandre*, from medieval Latin *alexandrum*.

Alexander technique ▶ noun a system designed to promote well-being by retraining one's awareness and habits of posture to ensure minimum effort and strain.
– ORIGIN 1930s: named after Frederick Matthias *Alexander* (1869–1955), the Australian-born actor and elocutionist who developed it.

Alexandretta /ˌalɪgzɑːnˈdrɛtə/ former name for ISKENDERUN.

Alexandria /ˌalɪgˈzɑːndrɪə/ the chief port of Egypt; pop. 3,170,000 (est. 1990). Alexandria was a major centre of Hellenistic culture.

Alexandrian ▶ adjective of or relating to Alexandria in Egypt.
■ belonging to or akin to the schools of literature and philosophy of ancient Alexandria. ■ (of a writer) derivative or imitative rather than creative; fond of recondite learning.

alexandrine /ˌalɪgˈzɑːndrɪn, -ʌɪn/ Prosody ▶ adjective (of a line of verse) having six iambic feet.
▶ noun (usu. **alexandrines**) an alexandrine line.
– ORIGIN late 16th cent.: from French *alexandrin*, from *Alexandre* (see ALEXANDER[1]), the subject of an Old French poem in this metre.

alexandrite /ˌalɪgˈzɑːndrʌɪt/ ▶ noun [mass noun] a gem variety of chrysoberyl which appears green in daylight and red in artificial light.
– ORIGIN mid 19th cent.: from the name of Tsar *Alexander* II of Russia (see ALEXANDER[3]) + -ITE[1].

Alexandropol variant spelling of ALEKSANDROPOL.

alexia /əˈlɛksɪə, eɪ-/ ▶ noun [mass noun] Medicine inability to recognize or read written words or letters, typically as a result of brain damage. Compare with DYSLEXIA.
– ORIGIN late 19th cent.: from A-[1] 'without' + Greek *lexis* 'speech', from *legein* 'speak', which was confused with Latin *legere* 'read'.

Alf ▶ noun Austral. informal an uneducated and unthinkingly conservative Australian man.
– ORIGIN 1960s: abbreviation of the given name *Alfred*.

alfalfa /alˈfalfə/ ▶ noun a leguminous plant with clover-like leaves and bluish flowers, native to SW Asia and widely grown for fodder. Also called LUCERNE.
● *Medicago sativa*, family Leguminosae.
– ORIGIN mid 19th cent.: from Spanish, from Arabic *al-fasfaṣa*, a green fodder.

Al Fatah see FATAH, AL.

alfisol /ˈalfɪsɒl/ ▶ noun Soil Science a soil of an order comprising leached basic or slightly acid soils with a clay-enriched B horizon.
– ORIGIN 1960s: from the arbitrary element *Alfi-* + -SOL.

Alfonso XIII /alˈfɒnsəʊ/ (1886–1941), king of Spain

1886–1931, forced into exile after elections indicating a preference for a republic.

Alfred (849–99), king of Wessex 871–99; known as **Alfred the Great**. Alfred's military resistance saved SW England from Viking occupation. A great reformer, he is credited with the foundation of the English navy and with a revival of learning.

Alfredo /al'freɪdəʊ/ ▶**noun** [mass noun] a sauce for pasta incorporating butter, cream, garlic, and Parmesan cheese.
– ORIGIN named after *Alfredo* di Lelio, the Italian chef and restaurateur who invented the sauce.

alfresco /al'frɛskəʊ/ ▶**adverb** & **adjective** in the open air: [as adj.] *we had an alfresco supper.*
– ORIGIN mid 18th cent.: from Italian *al fresco* 'in the fresh (air)'.

Al Fujayrah another name for **FUJAIRAH**.

Alfvén /'alvɛn/, Hannes Olof Gösta (1908–95), Swedish theoretical physicist. His work was important for controlled thermonuclear fusion. Nobel Prize for Physics (1970).

Alfvén wave ▶**noun** Physics a transverse magnetohydrodynamic wave travelling in the direction of the magnetic field in a magnetized plasma. The velocity of such waves (the **Alfvén velocity** or **speed**) is characteristic for a plasma of given properties.

alga /'algə/ ▶**noun** (pl. **algae** /'aldʒiː, 'algiː/) a simple, non-flowering, and typically aquatic plant of a large assemblage that includes the seaweeds and many single-celled forms. Algae contain chlorophyll but lack true stems, roots, leaves, and vascular tissue.
• Divisions Chlorophyta (**green algae**), Heterokontophyta (**brown algae**), and Rhodophyta (**red algae**); some (or all) are frequently placed in the kingdom Protista.
– DERIVATIVES **algal** adjective.
– ORIGIN mid 16th cent.: from Latin, 'seaweed'.

algal bloom ▶**noun** a rapid growth of microscopic algae or cyanobacteria in water, often resulting in a coloured scum on the surface.

Algarve /al'gɑːv/ (**the Algarve**) the southernmost province of Portugal, on the Atlantic coast; capital, Faro.

algebra /'aldʒɪbrə/ ▶**noun** [mass noun] the part of mathematics in which letters and other general symbols are used to represent numbers and quantities in formulae and equations.
■ a system of this based on given axioms.
– DERIVATIVES **algebraist** /aldʒɪ'breɪɪst/ noun.
– ORIGIN late Middle English: from Italian, Spanish, and medieval Latin, from Arabic *al-jabr* 'the reunion of broken parts', 'bone-setting', from *jabara* 'reunite, restore'. The original sense, 'the surgical treatment of fractures', probably came via Spanish, in which it survives; the mathematical sense comes from the title of a book, *'ilm al-jabr wa'l-mukābala* 'the science of restoring what is missing and equating like with like', by the mathematician al-Kwārizmī (see **ALGORITHM**).

algebraic ▶**adjective** relating to or involving algebra.
■ (of a mathematical expression or equation) in which a finite number of symbols are combined using only the operations of addition, subtraction, multiplication, division, and exponentiation with constant rational exponents. Compare with **TRANSCENDENTAL**.
– DERIVATIVES **algebraical** adjective, **algebraically** adverb.

Algeciras /ˌaldʒɪ'sɪərəs, Spanish alxe'θiras, -'siras/ a ferry port and resort in southern Spain; pop. 101,365 (1991).

Algeria /al'dʒɪərɪə/ a republic on the Mediterranean coast of North Africa; pop. 25,800,000 (est. 1991); official language, Arabic; capital, Algiers.

> Algeria was colonized by France in the mid 19th century and was for a time closely integrated with metropolitan France, but following civil war in the 1950s the country achieved independence in 1962. A brief period of multiparty democracy was ended by a military takeover in 1992 after the fundamentalist Islamic Salvation Front had won the first round of the national elections; violent civil strife ensued.

– DERIVATIVES **Algerian** adjective & noun.

-algia ▶**combining form** denoting pain in a specified part of the body: *neuralgia* | *myalgia*.
– DERIVATIVES **-algic** combining form in corresponding adjectives.
– ORIGIN from Greek *algos* 'pain'.

algicide /'aldʒɪsʌɪd, 'algɪ-/ ▶**noun** a substance which is poisonous to algae.

Algiers /al'dʒɪəz/ the capital of Algeria and one of the leading Mediterranean ports of North Africa; pop. 2,168,000 (1995).

alginic acid /al'dʒɪnɪk/ ▶**noun** [mass noun] Chemistry an insoluble gelatinous carbohydrate found (chiefly as salts) in many brown seaweeds. The sodium salt is used as a thickener in foods and many other materials.
– DERIVATIVES **alginate** noun.
– ORIGIN late 19th cent.: *alginic* from **ALGA** + **-IN**[1] + **-IC**.

Algol[1] /'algɒl/ Astronomy a variable star in the constellation Perseus, regarded as the prototype of eclipsing binary stars.
– ORIGIN from Arabic *al ġūl* 'the ghoul'.

Algol[2] /'algɒl/ ▶**noun** [mass noun] one of the early, high-level computer programming languages which was devised to carry out scientific calculations.
– ORIGIN 1950s: from *algo(rithmic)* + the initial letter of **LANGUAGE**.

algolagnia /ˌalgə(ʊ)'lagnɪə/ ▶**noun** [mass noun] Psychiatry desire for sexual gratification through inflicting pain on oneself or others; sadomasochism.
– ORIGIN early 20th cent.: coined in German from Greek *algos* 'pain' + *lagneia* 'lust'.

algology /əl'gɒlədʒi/ ▶**noun** [mass noun] the study of algae.
– DERIVATIVES **algological** adjective, **algologist** noun.

Algonquian /al'gɒŋkwɪən, -kɪ-/ (also **Algonkian** /-kɪən/) ▶**adjective** denoting, belonging to, or relating to a large family of North American Indian languages formerly spoken across a vast area from the Atlantic seaboard to the Great Lakes and the Great Plains, and including Ojibwa, Cree, Blackfoot, Cheyenne, and Delaware. Many words in English have been adopted from these languages, e.g. *moccasin*, *moose*, and *toboggan*.
▶**noun 1** [mass noun] this family of languages.
2 a speaker of any of these languages.
– ORIGIN from **ALGONQUIN** + **-IAN**.

Algonquin /al'gɒŋkwɪn/ (also **Algonkin**) ▶**noun 1** a member of an American Indian people living in Canada along the Ottawa River and its tributaries and westward to the north of Lake Superior.
2 [mass noun] the Algonquian language of this people, with about 3,000 speakers.
▶**adjective** of or relating to this people or their language.
– ORIGIN French, contraction of obsolete *Algoumequin*, from a Micmac word meaning 'at the place of spearing fish and eels'.

> **USAGE** The terms **Algonquin** and **Algonquian** do not mean the same thing. **Algonquian** refers to a large family of languages, of which **Algonquin** is a specific member. **Algonquin** is also the term used for the American Indian people speaking the Algonquin language.

algorithm /'algərɪð(ə)m/ ▶**noun** a process or set of rules to be followed in calculations or other problem-solving operations, especially by a computer: *a basic algorithm for division.*
– DERIVATIVES **algorithmic** adjective, **algorithmically** adverb.
– ORIGIN late 17th cent. (denoting the Arabic or decimal notation of numbers): variant (influenced by Greek *arithmos* 'number') of Middle English *algorism*, via Old French from medieval Latin *algorismus*. The Arabic source, *al-Kwārizmī* 'the man of Kwārizm' (now Khiva), was the cognomen of the 9th-cent. mathematician Abū Ja'far Muhammad ibn Mūsa, author of widely translated works on algebra and arithmetic.

Algren /'ɔːlgrən/, Nelson (Abraham) (1909–81), American novelist. He drew on his childhood experiences in the slums of Chicago for his novels of social realism, for example *The Man with the Golden Arm* (1949) and *Walk on the Wild Side* (1956).

alguacil /ˌalgwa'θiːl, Spanish ˌalɣwa'θil, -'sil/ ▶**noun** (pl. **alguaciles** /ˌalgwa'θiːlɪz, Spanish ˌalɣwa'θiles, -'siles/) a mounted constable (one of two) acting as an official at a bullfight.
– ORIGIN Spanish, from Arabic *al-wazīr* 'the helper, aide, or vizier'.

alhaji /al'hadʒi/ ▶**noun** (pl. **alhajis**) (fem. **alhaja**) (in West Africa) a Muslim who has been to Mecca as a pilgrim (often used as a title).
– ORIGIN Hausa, from Persian and Turkish, from *al* 'the' + *hājī* 'pilgrim'.

Alhambra /al'hambrə/ a fortified Moorish palace, the last stronghold of the Muslim kings of Granada, built between 1248 and 1354 near Granada in Spain.

Al-Hudayda /ˌalhuː'deɪdə/ Arabic name for **HODEIDA**.

Ali[1], Muhammad, see **MUHAMMAD ALI**[1].

Ali[2], Muhammad, see **MUHAMMAD ALI**[2].

alias /'eɪlɪəs/ ▶**adverb** used to indicate that a named person is also known or more familiar under another specified name: *Eric Blair, alias George Orwell.*
■ informal indicating another term or synonym.
▶**noun** a false or assumed identity: *a spy operating under the alias Barsad.*
■ Computing an alternative name or label that refers to a file, command, address, or other item, and can be used to locate or access it. ■ Physics & Telecommunications each of a set of signal frequencies which, when sampled at a given uniform rate, would give the same set of sampled values, and thus might be incorrectly substituted for one another when reconstructing the original signal.
▶**verb** [with obj.] (usu. **be aliased**) Physics & Telecommunications misidentify (a signal frequency), introducing distortion or error.
– ORIGIN late Middle English: from Latin, 'at another time, otherwise'.

aliasing ▶**noun** [mass noun] **1** Physics & Telecommunications the misidentification of a signal frequency, introducing distortion or error.
2 Computing the use of aliases to designate files, commands, addresses, or other items.

Ali Baba /ˌalɪ 'bɑːbə/ the hero of a story supposed to be from the *Arabian Nights*, who discovered the magic formula ('Open Sesame!') which opened a cave where forty thieves kept their treasure.

alibi /'alɪbʌɪ/ ▶**noun** (pl. **alibis**) a claim or piece of evidence that one was elsewhere when an act, typically a criminal one, is alleged to have taken place: *she has an alibi for the whole of yesterday evening* | [mass noun] *a defence of alibi.*
■ informal an excuse or pretext: *a catch-all alibi for failure and inadequacy.*
▶**verb** (**alibis**, **alibied**, **alibiing**) [with obj.] informal offer an excuse or defence for (someone), especially by providing an account of their whereabouts at the time of an alleged act: *her friend agreed to alibi her.*
– ORIGIN late 17th cent. (as an adverb in the sense 'elsewhere'): from Latin, 'elsewhere'. The noun use dates from the late 18th cent.

> **USAGE** The word **alibi**, which in Latin means 'elsewhere', has been used since the 18th century to mean 'an assertion by a person that he or she was elsewhere'. In the 20th century a new sense arose (originally in the US) with the meaning 'an excuse'. This use is an example of a fairly common and natural extension of the core meaning, and, though widely accepted in standard English, it is still regarded as incorrect by some traditionalists.

Alicante /ˌalɪ'kanti, -teɪ/ a seaport on the Mediterranean coast of SE Spain, the capital of a province of the same name; pop. 270,950 (1991).

Alice band ▶**noun** a flexible band worn to hold back the hair.
– ORIGIN *Alice*, from the name of the heroine of two books by Lewis Carroll.

Alice Springs a railway terminus and supply centre serving the outback of Northern Territory, Australia; pop. 20,450 (1991).

alick ▶**noun** variant spelling of **ALEC**.

alicyclic /ˌalɪ'sʌɪklɪk, -'sɪk-/ Chemistry ▶**adjective** relating to or denoting organic compounds which combine cyclic structure with aliphatic properties, e.g. cyclohexane and other saturated cyclic hydrocarbons. Compare with **AROMATIC**.
▶**noun** (usu. **alicyclics**) an alicyclic compound.
– ORIGIN late 19th cent.: blend of **ALIPHATIC** and **CYCLIC**.

alidade /'alɪdeɪd/ ▶**noun** a sighting device or pointer for determining directions or measuring angles, used in surveying and (formerly) astronomy.
– ORIGIN late Middle English: directly or (in modern use) via French and Spanish from Arabic *al-'iḍāda* 'the revolving radius', probably based on *'aḍud* 'upper arm'.

alien ▶ **adjective** belonging to a foreign country or nation.
■ unfamiliar and disturbing or distasteful: *principles that are **alien to** them.* ■ relating to or denoting beings supposedly from other worlds; extraterrestrial: *an alien spacecraft.* ■ (of a plant or animal species) introduced from another country and later naturalized.
▶ **noun** a foreigner, especially one who is not a naturalized citizen of the country where he or she is living: *an enemy alien.*
■ a hypothetical or fictional being from another world. ■ a plant or animal species originally introduced from another country and later naturalized.
– DERIVATIVES **alienness** noun.
– ORIGIN Middle English: via Old French from Latin *alienus* 'belonging to another', from *alius* 'other'.

alienable ▶ **adjective** Law able to be transferred to new ownership.
– DERIVATIVES **alienability** noun.

alienage ▶ **noun** [mass noun] the state or condition of being an alien.

alienate ▶ **verb** [with obj.] **1** cause (someone) to feel isolated or estranged: *an urban environment which would alienate its inhabitants* | [as adj. **alienated**] *an alienated angst-ridden twenty-two-year-old.*
■ cause (someone) to become unsympathetic or hostile: *the association does not wish to alienate its members.*
2 Law transfer ownership of (property rights) to another person or group.
– PHRASES **alienate someone's affections** US Law induce someone to transfer their affection from a person (such as a spouse) with legal rights or claims on them.
– DERIVATIVES **alienator** noun.
– ORIGIN early 16th cent.: from Latin *alienat-* 'estranged', from the verb *alienare*, from *alienus* 'of another' (see **ALIEN**).

alienation ▶ **noun** [mass noun] **1** the state or experience of being isolated from a group or an activity to which one should belong or in which one should be involved: *unemployment may generate a sense of political alienation.*
■ loss or lack of sympathy; estrangement: *public **alienation from** bureaucracy.* ■ (in Marxist theory) a condition of workers in a capitalist economy, resulting from a lack of identity with the products of their labour and a sense of being controlled or exploited. ■ Psychiatry a state of depersonalization or loss of identity in which the self seems unreal, thought to be caused by difficulties in relating to society and the resulting prolonged inhibition of emotion. ■ a type of faulty recognition where familiar situations or people appear unfamiliar. Compare with **DÉJÀ VU**. ■ (also **alienation effect**) Theatre an effect, sought by some dramatists, whereby the audience remains objective and does not identify with the actors.
2 Law the transfer of the ownership of property rights.
– ORIGIN late Middle English: from Latin *alienatio(n-)*, from the verb *alienare* 'estrange', from *alienus* (see **ALIEN**). The term *alienation effect* (1940s) is a translation of German *Verfremdungseffekt*.

alienee ▶ **noun** Law old-fashioned term for **GRANTEE**.

alienist ▶ **noun** former term for **PSYCHIATRIST**.
■ chiefly US a psychiatrist who assesses the competence of a defendant in a law court.
– ORIGIN mid 19th cent.: from French *aliéniste*, based on Latin *alienus* 'of another' (see **ALIEN**).

alienor /ˌeɪlɪəˈnɔː/ ▶ **noun** Law old-fashioned term for **GRANTOR**.

aliform /ˈeɪlɪfɔːm/ ▶ **adjective** wing-shaped.
– ORIGIN early 18th cent.: from modern Latin *aliformis*, from Latin *ala* 'wing' + *-formis* (see **-FORM**).

Aligarh /ˌɑːlɪˈgɑː/ a city in northern India, in Uttar Pradesh; pop. 480,000 (1991). The city comprises the ancient fort of Aligarh and the former city of Koil.

Alighieri /ˌalɪˈgjɛːri/, Dante, see **DANTE**.

alight[1] ▶ **verb** [no obj., with adverbial of place] formal, chiefly Brit. descend from a train, bus, or other form of transport: *visitors should alight at the Fort Road stop.*
■ (of a bird) descend from the air and settle.
– ORIGIN Old English *ālīhtan*, from *ā-* (as an intensifier) + *līhtan* 'descend' (see **LIGHT**[3]).
▶ **alight on** find by chance; notice: *her eyes alighted on the item in question.*

alight[2] ▶ **adverb** & **adjective** on fire; burning: [as adj.] *the house was well alight when the firemen arrived* | [as adv.] *flammable liquid was **set alight**.*
■ shining brightly: [as adj.] *a single lamp was alight* | figurative *the boy's face was **alight with** excitement.*
– PHRASES **set the world** (or **the place**) **alight** informal achieve something which causes great excitement and makes one famous.
– ORIGIN late Middle English: probably from the phrase *on a light* (= lighted) *fire*.

align ▶ **verb 1** [with obj.] place or arrange (things) in a straight line: *gently brush the surface to align the fibres.*
■ put (things) into correct or appropriate relative positions: *the fan blades are carefully aligned* | figurative *aligning domestic prices with prices in world markets.* ■ [no obj.] lie in a straight line, or in correct relative positions: *the pattern of the border at the joint should align perfectly.*
2 (**align oneself with**) give support to (a person, organization, or cause): *newspapers usually align themselves with certain political parties.*
■ [no obj.] come together in agreement or alliance: *all of them must now align against the foe* | [as adj. **aligned**] *forces aligned with Russia.*
– ORIGIN late 17th cent.: from French *aligner*, from *à ligne* 'into line'.

alignment ▶ **noun 1** [mass noun] arrangement in a straight line, or in correct or appropriate relative positions: *the tiles had slipped out of alignment.*
■ [count noun] the route or course of a railway or road: *four railways, all on different alignments.* ■ [count noun] Archaeology a linear arrangement of stones.
2 a position of agreement or alliance: *a firm famous for its liberal alignment.*
– ORIGIN late 18th cent.: from French *alignement*, from *aligner* (see **ALIGN**).

alike ▶ **adjective** [predic.] (of two or more subjects) similar to each other: *the brothers were very much alike* | *the houses all looked alike.*
▶ **adverb** in the same or a similar way: *the girls dressed alike in black trousers and jackets.*
■ used to show that something applies equally to a number of specified subjects: *he talked in a friendly manner to staff and patients alike.*
– ORIGIN Old English *gelīc*, of Germanic origin; related to Dutch *gelijk* and German *gleich*, reinforced in Middle English by Old Norse *álíkr* (adjective) and *álíka* (adverb).

aliment /ˈalɪm(ə)nt/ ▶ **noun** [mass noun] **1** archaic food; nourishment.
2 Scots Law maintenance; alimony.
– ORIGIN late 15th cent.: from Latin *alimentum*, from *alere* 'nourish'.

alimentary ▶ **adjective** of or relating to nourishment or sustenance.
– ORIGIN late 16th cent.: from Latin *alimentarius*, from *alimentum* 'nourishment' (see **ALIMENT**).

alimentary canal ▶ **noun** the whole passage along which food passes through the body from mouth to anus during digestion.

alimentation ▶ **noun** [mass noun] formal the provision of nourishment or other necessities of life.
– ORIGIN late 16th cent. (in the sense 'maintenance, support'): from medieval Latin *alimentatio(n-)*, from late Latin *alimentare* 'to feed', from *alimentum* 'nourishment' (see **ALIMENT**).

alimony /ˈalɪməni/ ▶ **noun** [mass noun] chiefly US a husband's (or wife's) provision for a spouse after separation or divorce; maintenance.
– ORIGIN early 17th cent. (in the sense 'nourishment, means of subsistence'): from Latin *alimonia* 'nutriment', from *alere* 'nourish'.

A-line ▶ **adjective** (of a garment) slightly flared from a narrow waist or shoulders: *A-line skirts.*

aliphatic /ˌalɪˈfatɪk/ Chemistry ▶ **adjective** relating to or denoting organic compounds in which carbon atoms form open chains (as in the alkanes), not aromatic rings.
▶ **noun** (usu. **aliphatics**) an aliphatic compound.
– ORIGIN late 19th cent. (originally used of the fatty acids): from Greek *aleiphar*, *aleiphat-* 'fat' + **-IC**.

aliquot /ˈalɪkwɒt/ ▶ **noun** a portion of a larger whole, especially a sample taken for chemical analysis or other treatment.
■ (also **aliquot part** or **portion**) Mathematics a quantity which can be divided into another an integral number of times.
▶ **verb** [with obj.] (usu. **be aliquoted**) divide (a whole) into aliquots; take aliquots from (a whole).
– ORIGIN late 16th cent.: from French *aliquote*, from Latin *aliquot* 'some, so many', from *alius* 'one of two' + *quot* 'how many'.

alisphenoid /ˌalɪˈsfiːnɔɪd/ (also **alisphenoid bone**) ▶ **noun** Anatomy & Zoology a wing-like cartilaginous bone within the mammalian skull forming part of the socket of the eye.
– ORIGIN mid 19th cent.: from Latin *ala* 'wing' + **SPHENOID**.

aliterate /eɪˈlɪt(ə)rət/ ▶ **adjective** unwilling to read, although able to do so.
▶ **noun** an aliterate person.
– DERIVATIVES **aliteracy** noun.

alive ▶ **adjective** [predic.] **1** (of a person, animal, or plant) living, not dead: *hopes of finding anyone still alive were fading* | *he was kept alive by a feeding tube.*
■ (of a feeling or quality) continuing in existence: *keeping hope alive.* ■ continuing to be supported or in use: *militarism was kept alive by pure superstition.*
2 (of a person or animal) alert and active; animated: *Ken **comes alive** when he hears his music played.*
■ figurative having interest and meaning: *we hope we will make history **come alive** for the children.*
3 (**alive to**) aware of and interested in; responsive to: *always alive to new ideas.*
4 (**alive with**) swarming or teeming with: *in spring those cliffs are alive with auks and gulls.*
– PHRASES **alive and kicking** informal prevalent and very active: *bigotry is still alive and kicking.* **alive and well** still existing or active (often used to deny rumours or beliefs that something has disappeared or declined): *the sports car industry is alive and well.*
– DERIVATIVES **aliveness** noun.
– ORIGIN Old English *on līfe*, literally 'in life'.

aliyah /ˈalɪjə/ ▶ **noun** (pl. **aliyoth** /ˈalɪjəʊt/) Judaism **1** [mass noun] immigration to Israel: *students **making aliyah**.*
2 the honour of being called upon to read from the Torah: *I was called up for an aliyah.*
– ORIGIN from Hebrew *ʻălīyyāh* 'ascent'.

alizarin /əˈlɪz(ə)rɪn/ ▶ **noun** [mass noun] Chemistry a red pigment present in madder root, used in dyeing.
• Alternative name: **1,2-dihydroxyanthraquinone**; chem. formula: $C_{14}H_8O_4$.
■ [as modifier] denoting dyes derived from or similar to this pigment: *alizarin crimson.*
– ORIGIN mid 19th cent.: from French *alizarine*, from *alizari* 'madder', from Arabic *al-ʻiṣāra* 'pressed juice', from *ʻaṣara* 'to press fruit'.

Al Jizah /al ˈdʒiːzə/ Arabic name for **GIZA**.

alkahest /ˈalkəhɛst/ (also **alcahest**) ▶ **noun** historical the hypothetical universal solvent sought by alchemists.
– ORIGIN mid 17th cent.: sham Arabic, probably invented by Paracelsus.

alkali /ˈalkəlʌɪ/ ▶ **noun** (pl. **alkalis**) a compound with particular chemical properties including turning litmus blue and neutralizing or effervescing with acids; typically, a caustic or corrosive substance of this kind such as lime or soda. Often contrasted with **ACID**; compare with **BASE**.
■ [as modifier] chiefly N. Amer. alkaline.

Alkalis release hydroxide ions (OH^-) when dissolved in water. Any solution with a pH of more than 7 is alkaline.

– ORIGIN late Middle English (denoting a saline substance derived from the ashes of various plants, including glasswort): from medieval Latin, from Arabic *al-ḳalī* 'calcined ashes (of the glasswort etc.)', from *ḳalā* 'fry, roast'.

alkalic /alˈkalɪk/ ▶ **adjective** Geology (of a rock or mineral) richer in sodium and/or potassium than is usual for its type.

alkali feldspar ▶ **noun** Geology any of the group of feldspars rich in sodium and/or potassium.

alkali metal ▶ **noun** Chemistry any of the elements lithium, sodium, potassium, rubidium, caesium, and francium, occupying Group IA (1) of the periodic table. They are very reactive, electropositive, monovalent metals forming strongly alkaline hydroxides.

alkaline ▶ **adjective** having the properties of an alkali, or containing alkali; having a pH greater than 7. Often contrasted with **ACID** or **ACIDIC**; compare with **BASIC**.
– DERIVATIVES **alkalinity** noun.

alkaline earth (also **alkaline earth metal**) ▶ **noun** any of the elements beryllium, magnesium, calcium, strontium, barium, and radium, occupying Group IIA (2) of the periodic table. They

a

are reactive, electropositive, divalent metals, and form basic oxides which react with water to form comparatively insoluble hydroxides.

alkalize (also **-ise**) ▶ **verb** [with obj.] [usu. as adj. **alkalized** or **alkalizing**] treat with alkali.

– DERIVATIVES **alkalization** noun, **alkalizer** noun.

alkaloid /ˈalkəlɔɪd/ ▶ **noun** Chemistry any of a class of nitrogenous organic compounds of plant origin which have pronounced physiological actions on humans. They include many drugs (morphine, quinine) and poisons (atropine, strychnine).

– ORIGIN early 19th cent.: coined in German from **ALKALI**.

alkalosis /ˌalkəˈləʊsɪs/ ▶ **noun** [mass noun] Medicine an excessively alkaline condition of the body fluids or tissues, which may cause weakness or cramp.

alkane /ˈalkeɪn/ ▶ **noun** Chemistry any of the series of saturated hydrocarbons including methane, ethane, propane, and higher members.

• Alkanes have the general formula: C_nH_{2n+2}.

– ORIGIN late 19th cent.: from **ALKYL** + **-ANE**[2].

alkanet /ˈalkənɛt/ ▶ **noun** a Eurasian plant of the borage family, typically having a hairy stem and blue flowers.

• *Anchusa* and other genera, family Boraginaceae: several species, including the European *A. officinalis*, **dyer's alkanet** (*Alkanna tinctoria*) of the Mediterranean region, and **green alkanet** (*Pentaglottis sempervirens*), grown as an ornamental.

– ORIGIN Middle English: from colloquial Arabic *al-ḥannat* (classical Arabic *al-ḥinnā'*) 'the henna shrub'.

alkene /ˈalkiːn/ ▶ **noun** Chemistry any of the series of unsaturated hydrocarbons containing a double bond, including ethylene and propene.

• Alkenes have the general formula: C_nH_{2n}.

– ORIGIN late 19th cent.: from **ALKYL** + **-ENE**.

alky (also **alkie**) ▶ **noun** (pl. **-ies**) informal an alcoholic.

alkyd /ˈalkɪd/ ▶ **noun** Chemistry any of a group of synthetic polyester resins derived from various alcohols and acids.

– ORIGIN 1920s: blend of **ALKYL** and **ACID**.

alkyl /ˈalkʌɪl, -kɪl/ ▶ **noun** [as modifier] Chemistry of or denoting a hydrocarbon radical derived from an alkane by removal of a hydrogen atom.

– ORIGIN late 19th cent.: German, from *Alkohol* 'alcohol' + **-YL**.

alkylate /ˈalkɪleɪt/ ▶ **verb** [with obj.] [usu. as adj. **alkylating** or **alkylated**] Chemistry introduce an alkyl radical into (a compound): *alkylating agents*.

– DERIVATIVES **alkylation** noun.

alkyne /ˈalkʌɪn/ ▶ **noun** Chemistry any of the series of unsaturated hydrocarbons containing a triple bond, including acetylene.

• Alkynes have the general formula: C_nH_{2n-2}.

– ORIGIN early 20th cent.: from **ALKYL** + **-YNE**.

all ▶ **predeterminer, determiner, & pronoun** used to refer to the whole quantity or extent of a particular group or thing: [as predeterminer] *all the people I met* | *she left all her money to him* | [as determiner] *10% of all cars sold* | *he slept all day* | [as pronoun] *four bedrooms, all with balconies* | *carry* ***all of*** *the blame* | *the men are all bearded.*

■ [determiner] any whatever: *assured beyond all doubt* | *he denied all knowledge.* ■ [determiner] used to emphasize the greatest possible amount of a quality: *they were* ***in all*** *probability completely unaware* | ***with all*** *due respect* | *hand it over* ***with all*** *speed.* ■ [pronoun] [with clause] the only thing (used for emphasis): *all I want is to be left alone.* ■ [pronoun] (used to refer to surroundings or a situation in general) everything: *all was well* | *all is not lost yet* | *it was all very strange.*

▶ **adverb 1** used for emphasis:

■ completely: *dressed all in black* | *she's been all round the world* | *all by himself.* ■ Brit. informal used to emphasize a temporary quality: *my ankle's gone all wobbly* | *he was* ***all of a*** *dither.*

2 (in games) used after a number to indicate an equal score: *after extra time it was still two all.*

– PHRASES **all along** all the time; from the beginning: *she'd known all along.* **all and sundry** everyone. **all but 1** very nearly: *the subject was all but forgotten.* **2** all except: *we have support from all but one of the networks.* **all comers** chiefly informal anyone who chooses to take part in an activity, typically a competition: *the champion took on all comers* | (**all-comers**) [as modifier] *she set a new all-comers record.* **all for** informal strongly in favour of: *I was all for tolerance.* **all get-out** see *as —— as all get-out* at **GET-OUT**. **all in** informal exhausted: *he was all in by half-time.* See also **ALL-IN**. **all in all** all things considered; on the whole: *all in all it's been a good year.* **all kinds** (or **sorts**) **of** many different kinds of: *he gets into all kinds of trouble.* **all manner of** see **MANNER**. **all of** as much as (often used ironically of an amount or quantity considered small by the speaker): *the show lasted all of six weeks.* **all of a sudden** see **SUDDEN**. **all one to someone** making no difference to someone: *simple cases or hard cases, it's all one to me.* **all out** using all one's strength or resources: *going all out to win* | [as adj.] *an all-out effort.* **all over 1** completely finished: *it's all over between us.* **2** informal everywhere: *there were bodies all over.* ■ with reference to all parts of the body: *I was shaking all over.* **3** informal typical of the person mentioned: *that's our management all over!* **4** informal effusively attentive to (someone): *James was all over her.* **all over the place** (or N. Amer. also **map**, Brit. also **shop**) informal everywhere: *we've been all over the place looking for you.* ■ in a state of disorder: *my hair was all over the place.* **all round** (US also **all around**) **1** in all respects: *it was a bad day all round* | [as modifier] *a man of all-round ability.* **2** for or by each person: *drinks all round* | *good acting all round.* **all sorts of** see ***all kinds of*** above. **all's well that ends well** proverb if the outcome of a situation is happy, this compensates for any previous difficulty or unpleasantness. **all that ——** see **THAT**. **all the same** see **SAME**. **all the ——** see **THE** (sense 6). **all there** [usu. with negative] informal in full possession of one's mental faculties: *he's not quite all there.* **all the time** see **TIME**. **all together** all in one place or in a group; all at once. Compare with **ALTOGETHER**. **all told** in total: *they tried a dozen times all told.* **all very well** informal used to express criticism or rejection of a favourable or consoling remark: *your proposal is all very well in theory, but in practice it will not pay.* **all the way** informal without limit or reservation: *I'm with you all the way.* **—— and all** used to emphasize something additional that is being referred to: *she threw her coffee over him, mug and all.* ■ informal as well: *get one for me and all.* **at all** [with negative or in questions] (used for emphasis) in any way; to any extent: *I don't like him at all* | *did he suffer at all?* ■ Irish added at the end of an utterance for emphasis: *what is the matter with you at all?* **for all ——** in spite of ——: *for all its clarity and style, the book is not easy reading.* **give** (or **put**) **one's all** use one's whole strength or resources: *I was giving it my all in the last 50 yards.* **in all** in total number; altogether: *there were about 5,000 people in all.* **it is all up with** see **UP**. **of all** see **OF**. **on all fours** see **ALL FOURS**. **one and all** see **ONE**.

– ORIGIN Old English *all, eall*, of Germanic origin; related to Dutch *al* and German *all*.

alla breve /ˌalə ˈbreɪvi, ˈbrɛveɪ/ ▶ **noun** Music a time signature indicating 2 or 4 minim beats in a bar.

– ORIGIN Italian, literally 'according to the breve'.

alla cappella /kəˈpɛlə/ ▶ **adjective & adverb** another term for **A CAPPELLA**.

Allah /ˈalə, əlˈlɑː/ the name of God among Muslims (and Arab Christians).

– ORIGIN from Arabic *'allāh*, contraction of *al-'ilāh* 'the god'.

Allahabad /ˈaləhəˌbad/ a city in the state of Uttar Pradesh, north central India; pop. 806,000 (1991). Situated at the confluence of the sacred Jumna and Ganges Rivers, it is a place of Hindu pilgrimage.

allamanda /ˌaləˈmandə/ (also **allamander**) ▶ **noun** any of a number of tropical shrubs or climbers which bear showy flowers, typically of yellow or purple.

• Species in several families, particularly in the genus *Allamanda* (family Apocynaceae), including the ornamental South American **yellow allamanda** (*A. cathartica*).

– ORIGIN modern Latin, named after Jean-Nicholas-Sébastien *Allamand* (1713–87), Swiss naturalist.

all-American ▶ **adjective 1** possessing qualities characteristic of American ideals, such as honesty, industriousness, and health: *his all-American wholesomeness.*

2 having members or contents drawn only from America or the US: *an all-American anthology.*

■ involving or representing the whole of America or the US: *an all-American final.* ■ (also **all-America**) US (of a sports player) honoured as one of the best amateur competitors in the US.

▶ **noun** (also **all-America**) US a sports player honoured as one of the best amateurs in the US.

allanite /ˈalənʌɪt/ ▶ **noun** [mass noun] a brownish-black mineral of the epidote group, consisting of a silicate of rare earth metals, aluminium, and iron.

– ORIGIN early 19th cent.: named after Thomas *Allan* (1777–1833), Scottish mineralogist, + **-ITE**[1].

allantoin /əˈlantəʊɪn/ ▶ **noun** [mass noun] Biochemistry a crystalline compound formed in the nitrogen metabolism of many mammals (excluding primates).

• A cyclic compound related to hydantoin; chem. formula: $C_4H_6N_4O_3$.

– ORIGIN mid 19th cent.: from **ALLANTOIS** (because it was discovered in the allantoic fluid of cows) + **-IN**[1].

allantois /əˈlantəʊɪs/ ▶ **noun** (pl. **allantoides** /-ɪdiːz/) the fetal membrane lying below the chorion in many vertebrates, formed as an outgrowth of the embryo's gut. In birds and reptiles it grows to surround the embryo; in eutherian mammals it forms part of the placenta.

– DERIVATIVES **allantoic** adjective, **allantoid** adjective.

– ORIGIN mid 17th cent.: modern Latin, based on Greek *allantoeidēs* 'sausage-shaped'.

allargando /ˌalɑːˈgandəʊ/ Music ▶ **adverb & adjective** (especially as a direction) getting slower and broader.

▶ **noun** (pl. **allargandi** /-di/ or **allargandos**) a passage performed in such a way.

– ORIGIN Italian, 'broadening'.

all-around ▶ **adjective** US term for **ALL-ROUND**.

allay /əˈleɪ/ ▶ **verb** [with obj.] diminish or put at rest (fear, suspicion, or worry): *the report attempted to educate the public and allay fears.*

■ relieve or alleviate (pain or hunger): *some stale figs partly allayed our hunger.*

– ORIGIN Old English *ālecgan* 'lay down or aside'.

All Blacks the New Zealand international rugby union team, so called because of their black strip.

all-clear ▶ **noun** a signal that danger or difficulty is over: *she was given* ***the all-clear*** *to travel home.*

all-day ▶ **adjective** [attrib.] lasting or available throughout the day: *we went on an all-day excursion to Blackpool.*

Allecto variant spelling of **ALECTO**.

allée /ˈaleɪ/ ▶ **noun** an alley in a formal garden or park, bordered by trees or bushes.

– ORIGIN mid 18th cent.: French.

allegation ▶ **noun** a claim or assertion that someone has done something illegal or wrong, typically one made without proof: *he made allegations of corruption against the administration* | ***allegations that*** *the army was operating a shoot-to-kill policy* | [mass noun] *years of rumour and allegation.*

– ORIGIN late Middle English: from Latin *allegatio(n-)*, from *allegare* 'allege'.

allege /əˈlɛdʒ/ ▶ **verb** [reporting verb] claim or assert that someone has done something illegal or wrong, typically without proof that this is the case: [with clause] *he* ***alleged that*** *he had been assaulted* | [with obj. and infinitive] *the offences are alleged to have been committed outside the woman's home* | *he is alleged to have assaulted five men.*

– ORIGIN Middle English (in the sense 'declare on oath'): from Old French *esligier*, based on Latin *lis, lit-* 'lawsuit'; confused in sense with Latin *allegare* 'allege'.

alleged ▶ **adjective** [attrib.] (of an incident or a person) said, without proof, to have taken place or to have a specified illegal or undesirable quality: *the alleged conspirators.*

– DERIVATIVES **allegedly** adverb [sentence adverb] *he was allegedly a leading participant in the coup attempt.*

Allegheny Mountains /ˌaləˈgeɪni/ (also **the Alleghenies**) a mountain range of the Appalachian system in the eastern US.

allegiance ▶ **noun** [mass noun] loyalty or commitment of a subordinate to a superior or of an individual to a group or cause: *those wishing to receive citizenship must* ***swear allegiance to*** *the republic* | [count noun] *a complex pattern of cross-party allegiances.*

– ORIGIN late Middle English: from Anglo-Norman French, variant of Old French *ligeance*, from *lige, liege* (see **LIEGE**), perhaps by association with Anglo-Latin *alligantia* 'alliance'.

allegorical ▶ **adjective** constituting or containing allegory: *an allegorical painting.*

– DERIVATIVES **allegoric** adjective, **allegorically** adverb.

allegorize (also **-ise**) ▶ **verb** [with obj.] interpret or represent symbolically: *the picture is interpreted as allegorizing an alienated society.*

– DERIVATIVES **allegorization** noun.

allegory ▶ noun (pl. **-ies**) a story, poem, or picture which can be interpreted to reveal a hidden meaning, typically a moral or political one: *Pilgrim's Progress is an allegory of the spiritual journey.* ■[mass noun] the genre to which such works belong: *he had given up realism for allegory.* ■ a symbol.
– DERIVATIVES **allegorist** noun.
– ORIGIN late Middle English: from Old French *allegorie*, via Latin from Greek *allēgoria*, from *allos* 'other' + *-agoria* 'speaking'.

allegretto /ˌalɪˈɡrɛtəʊ/ Music ▶ adverb & adjective (especially as a direction) at a fairly brisk speed.
▶ noun (often **Allegretto**) (pl. **-os**) a movement or passage marked to be performed allegretto.
– ORIGIN Italian, diminutive of **ALLEGRO**.

Allegri /aˈlɛɡri, -ˈleɪ-/, Gregorio (1582–1652), Italian priest and composer, noted especially for his *Miserere*, written for performance in the Sistine Chapel.

allegro /əˈlɛɡrəʊ, -ˈleɪɡ-/ Music ▶ adverb & adjective (especially as a direction) at a brisk speed.
▶ noun (often **Allegro**) (pl. **-os**) a movement, passage, or composition marked to be performed allegro.
– ORIGIN Italian, literally 'lively, gay'.

allele /ˈaliːl/ ▶ noun Genetics one of two or more alternative forms of a gene that arise by mutation and are found at the same place on a chromosome. Also called **ALLELOMORPH**.
– DERIVATIVES **allelic** adjective.
– ORIGIN 1930s: from German *Allel*, abbreviation of **ALLELOMORPH**.

allelochemical /əˌliːləʊˈkɛmɪk(ə)l/ ▶ noun a chemical produced by a living organism, exerting a detrimental physiological effect on the individuals of another species when released into the environment.
– ORIGIN 1970s: from Greek *allēl-* 'one another' + **CHEMICAL**.

allelomorph /əˈliːləʊmɔːf/ ▶ noun another term for **ALLELE**.
– DERIVATIVES **allelomorphic** adjective.
– ORIGIN early 20th cent.: from Greek *allēl-* 'one another' + *morphē* 'form'.

allelopathy /ˌaliːˈlɒpəθi/ ▶ noun [mass noun] Ecology the chemical inhibition of one plant (or other organism) by another, due to the release into the environment of substances acting as germination or growth inhibitors.
– DERIVATIVES **allelopathic** /əˌliːlə(ʊ)ˈpaθɪk/ adjective.
– ORIGIN 1950s: from Greek *allēl-* 'one another' + **-PATHY**.

alleluia /ˌalɪˈluːjə/ ▶ exclamation & noun variant spelling of **HALLELUJAH**.

allemande /ˈalmɑːnd/ ▶ noun any of a number of German dances, in particular an elaborate court dance popular in the 16th century.
■ the music for such a dance, especially as a movement of a suite. ■ a figure in country dancing in which adjacent dancers link arms or join hands and make a full or partial turn.
– ORIGIN late 17th cent.: from French, 'German (dance)'.

all-embracing ▶ adjective including or covering everything or everyone; comprehensive: *the goal is not one, all-embracing religion.*

Allen[1], Ethan (1738–89), American soldier. He fought the British in the War of Independence and led the irregular force the Green Mountain Boys in their campaign to gain independence for the state of Vermont.

Allen[2], Woody (b.1935), American film director, writer, and actor; born *Allen Stewart Konigsberg*. Allen stars in most of his own films, many of which have won Oscars and which humorously explore themes of neurosis and sexual inadequacy. Notable works: *Play it Again, Sam* (1972), *Annie Hall* (1977).

Allenby /ˈalənbi/, Edmund Henry Hynman, 1st Viscount (1861–1936), British soldier. Commander of the Egyptian Expeditionary Force against the Turks, he captured Jerusalem in 1917 and defeated the Turkish forces at Megiddo in 1918.

Allende /aˈjɛndeɪ/, Salvador (1908–73), Chilean statesman, President 1970–3. The first avowed Marxist to win a presidency in a free election, Allende was overthrown and killed in a military coup led by General Pinochet.

Allen key ▶ noun trademark a spanner designed to fit into and turn an Allen screw.

– ORIGIN 1960s: from the name of the manufacturer, the *Allen* Manufacturing Company, of Hartford, Connecticut.

Allen screw ▶ noun trademark a screw with a hexagonal socket in the head.
– ORIGIN 1930s: from the name of the manufacturer (see **ALLEN KEY**).

Allenstein /ˈalən.ʃtaɪn/ German name for OLSZTYN.

allergen /ˈalədʒ(ə)n/ ▶ noun a substance that causes an allergic reaction.
– DERIVATIVES **allergenic** adjective, **allergenicity** noun.
– ORIGIN early 20th cent.: blend of **ALLERGY** and **-GEN**.

allergic /əˈlɜːdʒɪk/ ▶ adjective of, caused by, or relating to an allergy: *an allergic reaction to penicillin.*
■ having an allergy to a substance: *one and a half per cent of the population is allergic to bee venom.* ■ [predic.] (**allergic to**) informal having a strong dislike for: *it's just that I'm allergic to the hype.*

allergist ▶ noun a medical practitioner specializing in the diagnosis and treatment of allergies.

allergy /ˈalədʒi/ ▶ noun (pl. **-ies**) a damaging immune response by the body to a substance, especially a particular food, pollen, fur, or dust, to which it has become hypersensitive.
■ informal an antipathy: *their allergy to free enterprise.*
– ORIGIN early 20th cent.: from German *Allergie*, from Greek *allos* 'other', on the pattern of *Energie* 'energy'.

Allerød /ˈalərəːd/ ▶ noun (**the Allerød**) Geology the second climatic stage of the late-glacial period in northern Europe, between the two Dryas stages (about 12,000 to 10,800 years ago). It was an interlude of warmer weather marked by the spread of birch.
– ORIGIN 1920s: place name near Copenhagen in Denmark.

alleviate /əˈliːvɪeɪt/ ▶ verb [with obj.] make (suffering, deficiency, or a problem) less severe: *he couldn't prevent her pain, only alleviate it | measures to alleviate unemployment.*
– DERIVATIVES **alleviation** noun, **alleviative** adjective, **alleviator** noun.
– ORIGIN late Middle English: from late Latin *alleviat-* 'lightened', from the verb *alleviare*, from Latin *allevare*, from *ad-* 'to' + *levare* 'raise', influenced by *levis* 'light'.

alley[1] ▶ noun (pl. **-eys**) a narrow passageway between or behind buildings.
■ a path lined with trees, bushes, or stones. Compare with **ALLÉE**. ■ [with modifier] a long, narrow area in which games such as skittles and bowling are played. ■ Tennis, N. Amer. either of the two side strips between the service court and the sidelines which count as part of the court in a doubles match. ■ Baseball the area between the outfielders in left-centre or right-centrefield.
– PHRASES **up one's alley** see **up one's street** at **STREET**.
– ORIGIN late Middle English: from Old French *alee* 'walking or passage', from *aler* 'go', from Latin *ambulare* 'to walk'.

alley[2] ▶ noun (pl. **-eys**) variant spelling of **ALLY**[2].

alley cat ▶ noun a cat that lives wild in a town.

alley-oop ▶ exclamation used to encourage or draw attention to the performance of some physical, especially acrobatic, feat.
▶ noun (also **alley-oop pass**) Basketball a high pass caught by a leaping teammate who tries to dunk the ball before landing.
– ORIGIN early 20th cent.: perhaps from French *allez!* 'go on!' (expressing encouragement) + a supposedly French pronunciation of **UP**.

alleyway ▶ noun another term for **ALLEY**[1].

All Fools' Day ▶ noun another term for **APRIL FOOL'S DAY**.

all fours ▶ noun a card game, now rarely played, in which points are scored for being dealt the highest or lowest trump, capturing the jack of trumps, and taking the highest value of cards in tricks.
– PHRASES **on** (or **on to**) **all fours** on (or on to) hands and knees or (of an animal) on all four legs rather than just the hind ones: *Frankie scuttled away on all fours.*

All Hallows ▶ noun another term for **ALL SAINTS' DAY**.

allheal ▶ noun any of a number of plants used in herbal medicine and traditionally considered to be effective in treating a variety of conditions, in particular common valerian.

alliaceous /ˌalɪˈeɪʃəs/ ▶ adjective Botany of, relating to, or denoting plants of a group that comprises the onions and other alliums.
– ORIGIN late 18th cent.: from Latin *allium* 'garlic' + **-ACEOUS**; compare with the modern Latin taxonomic family name *Alliaceae*.

alliance ▶ noun a union or association formed for mutual benefit, especially between countries or organizations: *a defensive alliance between Australia and New Zealand | divisions within the alliance.*
■ a relationship based on an affinity in interests, nature, or qualities: *an alliance between medicine and morality.* ■ [mass noun] a state of being joined or associated: *his party is in alliance with the Greens.* ■ (**Alliance**) used in names of political parties formed by the combination or association of separate parties. ■ Ecology a group of closely related plant associations.
– ORIGIN Middle English: from Old French *aliance*, from *alier* 'to ally' (see **ALLY**[1]).

allicin /ˈalɪsɪn/ ▶ noun [mass noun] Chemistry a pungent oily liquid with antibacterial properties, present in garlic.
● Chem. formula: $(C_3H_5S)_2O$.
– ORIGIN 1940s: from Latin *allium* 'garlic' + **-IN**[1].

allied /ˈalaɪd, əˈlaɪd/ ▶ adjective joined by or relating to members of an alliance: *allied territories | the allied fleet.*
■ (usu. **Allied**) of or relating to Britain and her allies in the First and Second World Wars and after: *the liberation of Paris by Allied troops.* ■ [predic.] (**allied to/with**) in combination or working together with: *skilled craftsmanship allied to advanced technology.* ■ connected; related: *members of the medical and allied professions.*

Allier /ˈalɪeɪ, French alje/ a river of central France which rises in the Cévennes and flows 410 km (258 miles) north-west to meet the Loire.

alligator ▶ noun **1** a large semiaquatic reptile similar to a crocodile but with a broader and shorter head, native to the Americas and China.
● Genus *Alligator*, family Alligatoridae, order Crocodylia: the **American alligator** (*A. mississippiensis*) and the **Chinese alligator** (*A. sinensis*).
■ [mass noun] the skin of the alligator or material resembling it.
– ORIGIN late 16th cent.: from Spanish *el lagarto* 'the lizard', probably based on Latin *lacerta*.

alligator clip ▶ noun chiefly N. Amer. another term for **CROCODILE CLIP**.

alligator fish ▶ noun a small, slender bottom-dwelling fish of the NW Atlantic, with an armour of bony plates and two curved spines on the snout.
● *Aspidophoroides monopterygius*, family Agonidae.

alligator lizard ▶ noun a heavily built slow-moving lizard native to North America and Mexico.
● Genus *Gerrhonotus*, family Anguidae: several species, in particular *G. coeruleus*.

alligator pear ▶ noun North American term for **AVOCADO**.

alligator snapper (also **alligator snapping turtle**) ▶ noun a large snapping turtle occurring in fresh water around the Gulf of Mexico.
● *Macroclemys temminckii*, family Chelydridae.

all-important ▶ adjective vitally important; crucial: *the town's all-important tourist industry.*

all-in ▶ adjective [attrib.] Brit. (especially of a price) inclusive of everything.

all-inclusive ▶ adjective including everything or everyone.

all-in-one ▶ adjective [attrib.] combining two or more items or functions in a single unit: *an all-in-one shampoo/conditioner.*
▶ noun a thing combining two or more items or functions, especially a garment that takes the place of two or more other garments.

all-in wrestling ▶ noun [mass noun] chiefly Brit. wrestling with few or no restrictions.

allis shad /ˈalɪs/ ▶ noun a European shad (fish) with a deep blue back and silvery sides. Also called **KING OF THE HERRINGS**.
● *Alosa alosa*, family Clupeidae.
– ORIGIN late 16th cent.: *allis* from Old French *alose*, from late Latin *alausa*.

alliterate /əˈlɪtəreɪt/ ▶ verb [no obj.] (of a phrase or

line of verse) contain words which begin with the same sound or letter: *his first and last names alliterated.*
■use words beginning with the same sound or letter.
– ORIGIN late 18th cent.: back-formation from ALLITERATION.

alliteration ▶ **noun** [mass noun] the occurrence of the same letter or sound at the beginning of adjacent or closely connected words.
– ORIGIN early 17th cent.: from medieval Latin *alliteratio(n-)*, from Latin *ad-* (expressing addition) + *littera* 'letter'.

alliterative /əˈlɪt(ə)rətɪv/ ▶ **adjective** relating to or marked by alliteration.
– DERIVATIVES **alliteratively** adverb.

allium /ˈalɪəm/ ▶ **noun** (pl. **alliums**) a bulbous plant of a genus that includes the onion and its relatives (e.g. garlic, leek, and chives).
● Genus *Allium*, family Liliaceae (or Alliaceae).
– ORIGIN Latin, 'garlic'.

all-night ▶ **adjective** [attrib.] lasting, open, or operating throughout the night: *an all-night party.*

allo- /ˈaləʊ/ ▶ **combining form** other; different: *allopatric* | *allotrope.*
– ORIGIN from Greek *allos* 'other'.

allocate ▶ **verb** [with obj.] distribute (resources or duties) for a particular purpose: *the authorities **allocated** 50,000 places **to** refugees* | [with two objs] *students are allocated accommodation on a yearly basis.*
– DERIVATIVES **allocable** adjective, **allocator** noun.
– ORIGIN mid 17th cent.: from medieval Latin *allocat-* 'allotted', from the verb *allocare*, from *ad-* 'to' + *locare* (see LOCATE).

allocation ▶ **noun** [mass noun] the action or process of allocating or sharing out something: *more efficient allocation of resources* | *ticket allocation.*
■[count noun] an amount or portion of a resource assigned to a particular recipient.
– DERIVATIVES **allocative** adjective (chiefly Economics).
– ORIGIN late Middle English: from medieval Latin *allocatio(n-)*, from the verb *allocare* (see ALLOCATE).

allochthonous /əˈlɒkθənəs/ ▶ **adjective** Geology denoting a deposit or formation that originated at a distance from its present position. Often contrasted with AUTOCHTHONOUS.
– ORIGIN early 20th cent.: from ALLO- 'other' + Greek *khthōn* 'earth' + -OUS.

allocution /ˌaləˈkjuːʃ(ə)n/ ▶ **noun** a formal speech giving advice or a warning.
– ORIGIN early 17th cent.: from Latin *allocutio(n-)*, from *alloqui* 'speak to', from *ad-* 'to' + *loqui* 'speak'.

allod /ˈalɒd/ (also **allodium** /əˈləʊdɪəm/) ▶ **noun** historical an estate held in absolute ownership, without acknowledgement to a superior.
– ORIGIN early 17th cent. (as *allodium*): from medieval Latin *al(l)odium*, used frequently in the Domesday Book, from a Germanic cognate of ALL + *ōd* 'estate'.

allodial /əˈləʊdɪəl/ ▶ **adjective** chiefly historical (with reference to land) held in absolute ownership.
– ORIGIN mid 17th cent.: from medieval Latin *al(l)odialis*, from *al(l)odium* (see ALLOD).

allogamy /əˈlɒɡəmi/ ▶ **noun** [mass noun] Botany the fertilization of a flower by pollen from another flower, especially one on a different plant. Compare with AUTOGAMY.
– DERIVATIVES **allogamous** adjective.
– ORIGIN late 19th cent.: from ALLO- 'other, different' + Greek *-gamia* (from *gamos* 'marriage').

allogeneic /ˌalə(ʊ)dʒɪˈniːɪk, -dʒɪˈneɪɪk/ ▶ **adjective** Immunology denoting, relating to, or involving tissues or cells which are genetically dissimilar and hence immunologically incompatible, although from individuals of the same species. Compare with XENOGENEIC.
– ORIGIN 1960s: from ALLO- 'different' + Greek *genea* 'race, stock' + -IC.

allogenic /ˌaləˈdʒɛnɪk/ ▶ **adjective** **1** Geology (of a mineral or sediment) transported to its present position from elsewhere. Often contrasted with AUTHIGENIC.
2 Ecology (of a successional change) caused by non-living factors in the environment.

allograft /ˈaləɡrɑːft/ ▶ **noun** a tissue graft from a donor of the same species as the recipient but not genetically identical. Compare with HOMOGRAFT.

allograph /ˈaləɡrɑːf/ ▶ **noun** Linguistics each of two or more alternative forms of a letter of an alphabet or other grapheme, for example the capital, lower case, italic, and various handwritten forms of a letter.
■Phonetics each of two or more letters or letter-combinations representing a single phoneme in different words. Allographs of the phoneme /f/ include the (f) of 'fake' and the (ph) of 'phase'.
– ORIGIN 1950s: from ALLO- 'other, different' + GRAPHEME.

allometry /əˈlɒmɪtri/ ▶ **noun** [mass noun] Biology the growth of body parts at different rates, resulting in a change of body proportions.
■the study of such growth.
– DERIVATIVES **allometric** adjective.

allomorph /ˈaləmɔːf/ ▶ **noun** Linguistics any of two or more actual representations of a morpheme, such as the plural endings /s/ (as in *bats*), /z/ (as in *bugs*), and /ɪz/ (as in *buses*).
– DERIVATIVES **allomorphic** adjective.
– ORIGIN 1940s: from ALLO- 'other, different' + MORPHEME.

allopath /ˈaləpaθ/ ▶ **noun** a person who practises allopathy.

allopathy /əˈlɒpəθi/ ▶ **noun** [mass noun] the treatment of disease by conventional means, i.e. with drugs having effects opposite to the symptoms. Often contrasted with HOMEOPATHY.
– DERIVATIVES **allopathic** adjective, **allopathist** noun.

allopatric /ˌaləˈpatrɪk/ ▶ **adjective** Biology (of animals or plants, especially of related species or populations) occurring in separate non-overlapping geographical areas. Compare with SYMPATRIC.
■(of speciation) taking place as a result of such separation.
– DERIVATIVES **allopatry** noun.
– ORIGIN 1940s: from ALLO- 'other' + Greek *patra* 'fatherland' + -IC.

allophone /ˈaləfəʊn/ ▶ **noun** Phonetics any of the various phonetic realizations of a phoneme in a language, which do not contribute to distinctions of meaning. For example, in English an aspirated *p* (as in *pin*) and unaspirated *p* (as in *spin*) are allophones of /p/, whereas in ancient Greek the distinction was phonemic.
– DERIVATIVES **allophonic** adjective.
– ORIGIN 1930s: from ALLO- 'other, different' + PHONEME.

allopurinol /ˌalə(ʊ)ˈpjʊərɪnɒl/ ▶ **noun** [mass noun] Medicine a synthetic drug which inhibits uric acid formation in the body and is used to treat gout and related conditions.
– ORIGIN 1960s: from ALLO- 'other' + PURINE + -OL.

All Ordinaries index (on the Australian stock exchanges) an index based on the weighted average of selected ordinary share prices.

all-ords short for ALL ORDINARIES INDEX.

all-or-none ▶ **adjective** another way of saying ALL-OR-NOTHING.
■Physiology (of a response) having a strength independent of the strength of the stimulus that caused it.

all-or-nothing ▶ **adjective** having no middle position or compromise available: *an all-or-nothing decision.*

allosaurus /ˌaləˈsɔːrəs/ ▶ **noun** a large bipedal carnivorous dinosaur of the late Jurassic period.
● Genus *Allosaurus*, suborder Theropoda, order Saurischia.
– ORIGIN modern Latin, from Greek *allos* 'other' + *sauros* 'lizard'.

allosteric /ˌaləˈstɛrɪk, -ˈstɪərɪk/ ▶ **adjective** Biochemistry relating to or denoting the alteration of the activity of an enzyme by means of a conformational change induced by a different molecule.
– DERIVATIVES **allosterically** adverb.

allot ▶ **verb** (**allotted**, **allotting**) [with obj.] give or apportion (something) to someone: *equal time was allotted to each* | [with two objs] *I was allotted a little room in the servant's block.*
– ORIGIN late 15th cent.: from Old French *aloter*, from *a-* (from Latin *ad* 'to') + *loter* 'divide into lots'.

allotment ▶ **noun** **1** Brit. a small piece of land, typically belonging to a local authority, that is rented by an individual for growing vegetables or other plants.
■US, chiefly historical a piece of land made over by the government to an American Indian.
2 [mass noun] the action of allotting something.
■[count noun] an amount of something allocated to a particular person.

allotrope /ˈalətrəʊp/ ▶ **noun** Chemistry each of two or more different physical forms in which an element can exist. Graphite, charcoal, and diamond are all allotropes of carbon.
– ORIGIN late 19th cent.: back-formation from ALLOTROPY.

allotropy /əˈlɒtrəpi/ ▶ **noun** [mass noun] Chemistry the existence of two or more different physical forms of a chemical element.
– DERIVATIVES **allotropic** adjective.
– ORIGIN mid 19th cent.: from Greek *allotropos* 'of another form', from *allo-* 'other' + *tropos* 'manner' (from *trepein* 'to turn').

allottee ▶ **noun** a person to whom something is allotted, especially land or shares.

all-over ▶ **adjective** [attrib.] covering the whole of something, especially uniformly: *a carpet with an all-over pattern.*

allow ▶ **verb** [with obj.] **1** admit (an event or activity) as legal or acceptable: *a plan to allow Sunday shopping* | *political advertising on television is not allowed.*
■[with obj. and infinitive] give (someone) permission to do something: *the dissident was allowed to leave the country.* ■[with two objs] permit (someone) to have (something): *she was allowed a higher profile.* ■[with obj. and adverbial of direction] permit (someone) to enter a place or go in a particular direction: *the river was patrolled and few people were allowed across.* ■[with obj. and infinitive] fail to prevent (something) from happening: *I could not believe that we would allow the opportunity to slip away.*
2 give the necessary time or opportunity for: *they agreed to a ceasefire to allow talks with the government* | [with obj. and infinitive] *he stopped for a moment to allow his eyes to adjust* | [no obj.] dated *my household duties were too many to **allow of** a visit to the hospital.*
■[no obj.] (**allow for**) make provision or provide scope for (something): *the house was demolished to allow for road widening.* ■take something into consideration when making plans or calculations: *income rose by 11 per cent allowing for inflation.* ■[with obj.] provide or set aside (an amount of something) for a particular purpose: *allow an hour or so for driving.*
3 [reporting verb] admit the truth of; concede: [with clause] *he allowed that the penalty appeared too harsh for the crime* | [with direct speech] *'Could happen,' she allowed indifferently.*
■[with clause] N. Amer. informal or dialect assert; be of the opinion: *Lincoln allowed that he himself could never support the man.*
– DERIVATIVES **allowable** adjective, **allowably** adverb.
– ORIGIN Middle English (originally in the senses 'commend, sanction' and 'assign as a right'): from Old French *alouer*, from Latin *allaudare* 'to praise', reinforced by medieval Latin *allocare* 'to place' (see ALLOCATE).

allowance ▶ **noun** the amount of something that is permitted, especially within a set of regulations or for a specified purpose: *your baggage allowance.*
■a sum of money paid regularly to a person, typically to meet specified needs or expenses. ■chiefly N. Amer. a small amount of money given regularly to a child by its parents. ■an amount of money that can be earned or received free of tax: *a personal allowance.* ■Horse Racing a deduction in the weight that a horse is required to carry in a race. ■[mass noun] archaic tolerance; sufferance: *the allowance of slavery in the South.*
▶ **verb** [with obj.] archaic give (someone) a sum of money regularly as an allowance:
– PHRASES **make allowance(s) for** **1** take into consideration when planning or making calculations. **2** regard or treat leniently on account of mitigating circumstances.
– ORIGIN late Middle English: from Old French *alouance*, from *alouer* (see ALLOW).

allowedly ▶ **adverb** [sentence adverb] as is generally admitted to be true.

alloxan /aˈlɒks(ə)n/ ▶ **noun** [mass noun] Chemistry an acidic compound obtained by the oxidation of uric acid and isolated as an efflorescent crystalline hydrate.
● Chem. formula: $C_4H_2N_2O_4$.
– ORIGIN mid 19th cent.: from *all(antoin)* + *ox(alic)* + -AN.

alloy ▶ **noun** /ˈalɔɪ/ a metal made by combining two or more metallic elements, especially to give greater strength or resistance to corrosion: *an alloy of nickel, bronze, and zinc* | [mass noun] *flat pieces of alloy* | [as modifier] *alloy wheels.*
■an inferior metal mixed with a precious one.

▶**verb** /əˈlɔɪ/ [with obj.] mix (metals) to make an alloy: *alloying tin with copper to make bronze.*
■figurative debase (something) by adding something inferior: *a salutary fear alloyed their admiration.*
– ORIGIN late 16th cent.: from Old French *aloi* (noun) and French *aloyer* (verb), both from Old French *aloier, aleier* 'combine', from Latin *alligare* 'bind'. In early use the term denoted the comparative purity of gold or silver; the sense 'mixture of metals' arose in the mid 17th cent.

all-party ▶ **adjective** [attrib.] Brit. involving all political parties: *the measure received all-party support.*

all-pervading (also **all-pervasive**) ▶ **adjective** occurring or having an effect through or into every part of something: *the all-pervading excitement.*

all-points bulletin (abbrev.: **APB**) ▶ **noun** (in the US) a radio message sent to every officer in a police force giving details of a suspected criminal or stolen vehicle.

all-powerful ▶ **adjective** having complete power: *an all-powerful dictator.*

all-purpose ▶ **adjective** having many uses, especially all that might be expected from something of its type: *an all-purpose kitchen knife.*

all right ▶ **adjective** [predic.] satisfactory; acceptable: *the tea was all right.*
■(of a person) in a satisfactory mental or physical state: *do you feel all right to walk home?* ■ permissible; allowable: *it's all right for you to go now.*
▶**adverb 1** in a satisfactory manner or to a satisfactory extent; fairly well: *we get on all right.*
2 used to emphasize how certain one is about something: *'Are you sure it's him?' 'It's him all right.'*
▶**exclamation** expressing or asking for assent, agreement, or acceptance: *all right, I'll tell you.*

all-roader ▶ **noun** another term for **ALL-TERRAIN VEHICLE**.

all-round ▶ **adjective** [attrib.] having a great many abilities or uses; versatile: *an all-round artist.*
■in many or all respects: *his all-round excellence.* ■ on or from every side or in every direction: *the car's large glass area provides excellent all-round vision.*

all-rounder ▶ **noun** Brit. a versatile person or thing, especially a cricketer who can both bat and bowl well.

All Saints' Day ▶ **noun** a Christian festival in honour of all the saints in heaven, held (in the Western Church) on 1 November.

all-seater ▶ **adjective** Brit. (of a sports stadium) having a seat for every spectator and no standing places.

allseed ▶ **noun** any of a number of plants producing a large number of seeds for their size.
• Species in several families, in particular the small *Radiola linoides* (family Linaceae) of Europe.

All Souls' Day ▶ **noun** a Catholic festival with prayers for the souls of the dead in Purgatory, held on 2 November.

allspice ▶ **noun 1** [mass noun] the dried aromatic fruit of a Caribbean tree, used whole or ground as a culinary spice and in the production of certain liqueurs such as Benedictine.
2 a tree of the myrtle family from which this spice is obtained. Also called **PIMENTO** or **JAMAICA PEPPER**.
• *Pimenta dioica*, family Myrtaceae.
3 an aromatic North American tree or shrub.
• Genus *Calycanthus*, family Calycanthaceae: **Carolina allspice** (*C. floridus*) and **Californian allspice** (*C. occidentalis*).

all-star ▶ **adjective** [attrib.] composed wholly of outstanding performers or players: *an all-star cast.*
▶**noun** N. Amer. a member of such a group or team.

Allston /ˈɔːlst(ə)n/, Washington (1779–1843), American landscape painter, the first major artist of the American romantic movement.

all-terrain vehicle (abbrev.: **ATV**) ▶ **noun** a small open motor vehicle with one seat and three or more wheels fitted with large tyres, designed for use on rough ground.

all-ticket ▶ **adjective** denoting or relating to an event, especially a sports match, for which spectators must buy tickets in advance.

all-time ▶ **adjective** [attrib.] unsurpassed: *her all-time favourite | interest rates hit an all-time high.*

allude ▶ **verb** [no obj.] (**allude to**) suggest or call attention to indirectly; hint at: *she had a way of alluding to Jean but never saying her name.*
■mention without discussing at length: *we will allude briefly to the main points.* ■ (of an artist or a work of art) recall (an earlier work or style) in such a way as to suggest a relationship with it: *the photographs allude to Italian Baroque painting.*
– ORIGIN late 15th cent. (in the sense 'hint at, suggest'): from Latin *alludere*, from *ad-* 'towards' + *ludere* 'to play'.

all-up weight ▶ **noun** chiefly Brit. the total weight of an aircraft with passengers, cargo, and fuel, or of a vehicle or mechanical part.

allure ▶ **noun** [mass noun] the quality of being powerfully and mysteriously attractive or fascinating: *people for whom gold holds no allure.*
▶**verb** [with obj.] powerfully attract or charm; tempt: [as adj. **alluring**] *the town offers alluring shops and restaurants.*
– DERIVATIVES **allurement** noun, **alluringly** adverb.
– ORIGIN late Middle English (in the sense 'tempt, entice'): from Old French *aleurier* 'attract', from *a-* (from Latin *ad* 'to') + *luere* 'a lure' (originally a falconry term).

allus /ˈɔːləz, ˈaləz/ ▶ **adverb** non-standard spelling of **ALWAYS**.
– ORIGIN mid 19th cent.: representing a regional pronunciation.

allusion ▶ **noun** an expression designed to call something to mind without mentioning it explicitly; an indirect or passing reference: *an **allusion to** Shakespeare | a classical allusion.*
■[mass noun] the practice of making such references, especially as an artistic device.
– ORIGIN mid 16th cent. (denoting a pun, metaphor, or parable): from French, or from late Latin *allusio(n-)*, from the verb *alludere* (see **ALLUDE**).

allusive ▶ **adjective** working by, containing, or employing suggestion rather than explicit mention: *allusive references to the body | a highly allusive poet.*
– DERIVATIVES **allusively** adverb, **allusiveness** noun.

alluvial /əˈl(j)uːvɪəl/ ▶ **adjective** of, relating to, or derived from alluvium: *rich alluvial soils.*

alluvion /əˈl(j)uːvɪən/ ▶ **noun** [mass noun] the action of the sea or a river in adding to the area of land by deposition (used in legal contexts). Compare with **AVULSION**.
– ORIGIN mid 16th cent. (originally denoting a flood, especially one carrying suspended material which is then deposited): from French, from Latin *alluvio(n-)*, from *ad-* 'towards' + *luere* 'to wash'.

alluvium /əˈl(j)uːvɪəm/ ▶ **noun** [mass noun] a deposit of clay, silt, and sand left by flowing flood water in a river valley or delta, typically producing fertile soil.
– ORIGIN mid 17th cent.: Latin, neuter of *alluvius* 'washed against', from *ad-* 'towards' + *luere* 'to wash'.

all-weather ▶ **adjective** in or suitable for all types of weather: *an all-weather soccer pitch.*
▶**noun** an artificial surface used for an activity such as horse racing.

all-wheel drive ▶ **noun** North American term for **FOUR-WHEEL DRIVE**.

ally[1] /ˈalʌɪ/ ▶ **noun** (pl. **-ies**) a state formally cooperating with another for a military or other purpose, typically by treaty.
■a person or organization that cooperates with or helps another in a particular activity: *he was forced to dismiss his closest political ally.* ■ (**the Allies**) a group of nations taking military action together, in particular the countries that fought with Britain in the First and Second World Wars.
▶**verb** /also əˈlʌɪ/ (**-ies, -ied**) [with obj.] (**ally something to/with**) combine or unite a resource or commodity with (another) for mutual benefit: *he allied his racing experience with his father's business acumen.*
■(**ally oneself with**) side with or support (someone or something): *he allied himself with the forces of change.*
– ORIGIN Middle English (as a verb): from Old French *alier*, from Latin *alligare* 'bind together', from *ad-* 'to' + *ligare* 'to bind'; the noun is partly via Old French *alie* 'allied'. Compare with **ALLOY**.

ally[2] /ˈali/ (also **alley**) ▶ **noun** (pl. **-ies**) a toy marble made of marble, alabaster, or glass.
– ORIGIN early 18th cent.: perhaps a diminutive of **ALABASTER**.

-ally ▶ **suffix** forming adverbs from adjectives ending in *-al* (such as *radically* from *radical*). Compare with **-AL, -LY**[2], **-ICALLY**.

allyl /ˈalʌɪl, -lɪl/ ▶ **noun** [as modifier] Chemistry of or denoting the unsaturated hydrocarbon radical $-CH{=}CHCH_2$: *allyl alcohol.*
– DERIVATIVES **allylic** adjective.
– ORIGIN mid 19th cent.: from Latin *allium* 'garlic' + **-YL**.

Alma-Ata /ˌalmə əˈtɑː/ variant spelling of **ALMATY**.

Al Madinah /ˌal maˈdiːnə/ Arabic name for **MEDINA**.

Almagest /ˈalmədʒɛst/ ▶ **noun** (**the Almagest**) an Arabic version of Ptolemy's astronomical treatise.
■(also **almagest**) (in the Middle Ages) any celebrated textbook on astrology and alchemy.
– ORIGIN late Middle English: from Old French *almageste*, based on Arabic, from *al* 'the' + Greek *megistē* 'greatest (composition)'.

alma mater /ˌalmə ˈmɑːtə, ˈmeɪt-/ ▶ **noun** (**one's Alma Mater**) the university, school, or college that one once attended.
– ORIGIN mid 17th cent. (in the general sense 'someone or something providing nourishment'): Latin, literally 'bounteous mother'.

almanac /ˈɔːlmənak, ˈɒl-/ (also, especially in titles, **almanack**) ▶ **noun** an annual calendar containing important dates and statistical information such as astronomical data and tide tables.
■a handbook, typically published annually, containing information of general interest or on a sport or pastime.
– ORIGIN late Middle English: via medieval Latin from Greek *almenikhiaka*, of unknown origin.

Almanach de Gotha /ˌɔːlmənak də ˈgəʊtə, ˌɒl-/ an annual publication giving information about European royalty, nobility, and diplomats, published in Gotha 1763–1944 and revived in 1968.

almandine /ˈalmәndiːn, -dʌɪn/ ▶ **noun** [mass noun] a kind of garnet with a violet tint.
– ORIGIN late Middle English: from obsolete French, alteration of *alabandine*, from medieval Latin *alabandina (gemma)*, 'jewel from *Alabanda*', an ancient city in Asia Minor where these stones were cut.

Alma-Tadema /ˌalməˈtadəmə/, Sir Lawrence (1836–1912), Dutch-born British painter known for lush genre scenes set in the ancient world.

Almaty /ˈalmɑːti/ (also **Alma-Ata**) the former capital of the central Asian republic of Kazakhstan (replaced in 1997 by Astana); pop. 1,515,300 (1991). Former name (until 1921) **VERNY**.

Almería /ˌalməˈrɪə/ a town in a province of the same name in Andalusia, Spain; pop. 157,760 (1991).

almighty ▶ **adjective** having complete power; omnipotent: *God almighty.*
■informal very great; enormous: *the silence was broken by an almighty roar.*
▶**noun** (**the Almighty**) a name or title for God.
– ORIGIN Old English *ælmihtig* (see **ALL, MIGHTY**).

almirah /alˈmʌɪrə/ ▶ **noun** Indian a free-standing cupboard or wardrobe.
– ORIGIN from Hindi *almārī*, via Portuguese from Latin *armarium* 'closet, chest'.

Almirante Brown /ˌalmɪˈranti/ a city in eastern Argentina, forming part of the conurbation of Buenos Aires; pop. 449,100 (1991).

Almodóvar /ˌalməˈdəʊvɑː/, Spanish almoˈðoβar/, Pedro (b.1951), Spanish film director. His films, such as *Women on the Verge of a Nervous Breakdown* (1988), are outlandishly inventive and deal outrageously with sexual matters.

Almohad /ˈalməhad/ (also **Almohade** /-heɪd/) ▶ **noun** (pl. **Almohads**) a member of a Berber Muslim movement and dynasty that conquered the Spanish and North African empire of the Almoravids in the 12th century.

almond ▶ **noun 1** the oval nut-like seed (kernel) of the almond tree, growing in a woody shell and used as food.
2 (also **almond tree**) the tree that produces this seed, related to the peach and plum. Native to western Asia, it is widely cultivated in warm climates.
• *Prunus dulcis*, family Rosaceae.
– ORIGIN Middle English: from Old French *alemande*, from medieval Latin *amandula*, from Greek *amugdalē*.

almond eyes ▶ **plural noun** eyes that are narrow and oval with pointed ends.

almond oil ▶ **noun** [mass noun] oil expressed from bitter almonds, used for cosmetic preparations, flavouring, and medicinal purposes.

almond paste ▶ **noun** another term for **MARZIPAN**.

almoner /ˈɑːmənə, ˈalm-/ ▶ **noun** historical an official distributor of alms.
– ORIGIN Middle English: from Old French *aumonier*, based on medieval Latin *eleemosynarius*, from *eleemosyna* 'alms' (see **ALMS**).

almonry /ˈɑːmənri, ˈalm-/ ▶ **noun** (pl. **-ies**) a building or place where alms were formerly distributed.
– ORIGIN late Middle English: from Old French *au(l)mosnerie*, from medieval Latin *eleemosynarius* (see **ALMONER**).

Almoravid /alˈmɔːrəvɪd/ (also **Almoravide** /-vʌɪd/) ▶ **noun** (pl. **Almoravids**) a member of a federation of Muslim Berber peoples that established an empire in Morocco, Algeria, and Spain in the 11th century. They were in turn driven out by the Almohads, losing their capital Marrakesh in 1147.

almost ▶ **adverb** not quite; very nearly: *he almost knocked Georgina over | Rachel laughed, almost apologetically | the place was almost empty | it will eat almost anything | the storm was almost upon them.*
– ORIGIN Old English *æl mæst* 'for the most part' (see **ALL**, **MOST**).

alms /ɑːmz/ ▶ **plural noun** (in historical contexts) money or food given to poor people.
– ORIGIN Old English *ælmysse, ælmesse*, from Christian Latin *eleemosyna*, from Greek *eleēmosunē* 'compassion', from *eleēmōn* 'compassionate', from *eleos* 'mercy'.

almshouse ▶ **noun** a house built originally by a charitable person or organization for poor people to live in.

almucantar /ˌalməˈkantə/ ▶ **noun** Astronomy a circle on the celestial sphere parallel to the horizon; a parallel of altitude.
■ a telescope mounted on a float resting on mercury, used to determine stellar altitude and azimuth.
– ORIGIN Middle English: from medieval Latin *almucantarath* or obsolete French *almucantara*, from Arabic *almuḳanṭarāt* 'lines of celestial latitude', based on *al* 'the' + *ḳanṭara* 'arch'.

aloe /ˈaləʊ/ ▶ **noun** **1** a succulent plant with a rosette of thick tapering leaves and bell-shaped or tubular flowers on long stems. Native to the Old World tropics, several kinds are cultivated commercially or as ornamentals.
• Genus *Aloe*, family Liliaceae (or Aloaceae).
■ (**aloes** or **bitter aloes**) [mass noun] a strong laxative obtained from the bitter juice of various kinds of aloe. ■ (also **American aloe**) another term for **CENTURY PLANT**.
2 (also **aloes wood**) [mass noun] the fragrant heartwood of a tropical Asian tree.
• The tree belongs to the genus *Aquilaria*, family Thymelaeaceae, in particular *A. agallocha*.
■ the resin obtained from this wood, used in perfume, incense, and medicine.
– ORIGIN Old English *alewe, alwe* (denoting the fragrant resin or heartwood of certain oriental trees), via Latin from Greek *aloē*; reinforced in late Middle English by Old French *aloes* 'aloe', hence frequently used in the plural.

aloe vera /ˈvɪərə/ ▶ **noun** **1** [mass noun] a gelatinous substance obtained from a kind of aloe, used especially in cosmetics as an emollient.
2 the plant that yields this substance, grown chiefly in the Caribbean area and the southern US.
• *Aloe vera*, family Liliaceae (or Aloaceae).
– ORIGIN early 20th cent.: modern Latin, literally 'true aloe', probably in contrast to the American agave, which closely resembles aloe vera: both plants were formerly classified together in the lily family.

aloft ▶ **adjective** & **adverb** up in or into the air; overhead: [as predic. adj.] *the congregation sways, hands aloft* | [as adv.] *she held her glass aloft.*
■ up the mast or into the rigging of a ship.
– ORIGIN Middle English: from Old Norse *á lopt, á lopti*, from *á* 'in, on, to' + *lopt* 'air'.

alogical ▶ **adjective** opposed to or lacking in logic.

aloha /əˈləʊhə/ ▶ **exclamation** & **noun** Hawaiian word used when greeting or parting from someone.

aloha shirt ▶ **noun** a loose, brightly patterned Hawaiian shirt.

Aloha State informal name for **HAWAII**.

alone ▶ **adjective** & **adverb** **1** having no one else present; on one's own: [as predic. adj.] *she was alone that evening* | [as adv.] *he lives alone.*
■ without others' help or participation; single-handed: [as adv.] *team members are more effective than individuals working alone.* ■ [as adj.] isolated and lonely: *she was terribly alone and exposed.* ■ having no companions in a particular position or course of action: [as predic. adj.] *they were not alone in dissenting from the advice.*
2 [as adv.] indicating that something is confined to the specified subject or recipient: *he is answerable to Parliament alone | it was a smile for him alone.*
■ used to emphasize that only one factor out of several is being considered and that the whole is greater or more extreme: *there were fifteen churches in the town centre alone.*
– PHRASES **go it alone** informal act by oneself without assistance. **leave** (or **let**) **someone/thing alone** **1** abandon or desert someone or something. **2** stop disturbing or interfering with someone or something. **let alone** see **LET**[1].
– DERIVATIVES **aloneness** noun.
– ORIGIN Middle English: from **ALL** + **ONE**.

along ▶ **preposition** & **adverb** **1** moving in a constant direction on (a path or any more or less horizontal surface): [as prep.] *soon we were driving along a narrow road | he saw Gray run along the top of the wall* | [as adv.] *she sailed along | we continued to plod along.*
■ used metaphorically to refer to the passage of time or the making of progress: [as prep.] *they can be helped along the road to modernity | you'll pick up some valuable tips along the way* | [as adv.] *they asked how the construction was coming along.*
2 [prep.] extending in a more or less horizontal line on: *cars were parked along the grass verge | the path along the cliff | hotels are springing up all along the coast.*
3 [adverb] in or into company with others: *he had brought along a friend of his.*
– PHRASES **along about** N. Amer. informal or dialect round about (a specified time or date): *we could head out along about six.* **along of** archaic or dialect **1** on account of: *the trouble I've had along of that lady's crankiness.* **2** with: *you'll have to make a break for it along of me.* **along with** in company with or at the same time as: *I was chosen, along with twelve other artists.* **be** (or **come**) **along** arrive: *she'll be along soon.*
– ORIGIN Old English *andlang*, of West Germanic origin; related to **LONG**[1].

alongshore ▶ **adverb** along or by the shore: *currents flowing alongshore.*

alongside ▶ **preposition** (N. Amer. also **alongside of**) close to the side of; next to: *she was sitting alongside him | the road passes alongside the viaduct* | [as adv.] *the boat came alongside.*
■ together and in cooperation with: *a care assistant was working alongside him.* ■ at the same time as or in coexistence with: *they aim to encourage coverage of disabled sport alongside able-bodied achievement.*

aloo /ˈɑːluː, ˈaluː/ (also **alu**) ▶ **noun** Indian potato: *aloo jeera.*
– ORIGIN from Hindi, Urdu, and Sanskrit *ālū*.

aloof ▶ **adjective** not friendly or forthcoming; cool and distant: *they were courteous but faintly aloof | an aloof and somewhat austere figure.*
■ conspicuously uninvolved and uninterested, typically through distaste: *he stayed **aloof from** the bickering.*
– DERIVATIVES **aloofly** adverb, **aloofness** noun.
– ORIGIN mid 16th cent.: from **A-**[2] (expressing direction) + **LUFF**. The term was originally an adverb in nautical use, meaning 'away and to windward!', i.e. with the ship's head kept close to the wind away from a lee shore etc. towards which it might drift. From this arose the sense 'at a distance'.

alopecia /ˌaləˈpiːʃə/ ▶ **noun** [mass noun] Medicine the partial or complete absence of hair from areas of the body where it normally grows; baldness.
– ORIGIN late Middle English: via Latin from Greek *alōpekia*, literally 'fox mange', from *alōpēx* 'fox'.

Alor Setar /ˌɑːlɔː səˈtɑː/ the capital of the state of Kedah in Malaysia, near the west coast of the central Malay Peninsula; pop. 71,682 (1980).

aloud ▶ **adverb** **1** audibly; not silently or in a whisper: *he read the letter aloud.*
2 archaic loudly: *he wept aloud.*
– ORIGIN Middle English: from **A-**[2] (expressing manner) + **LOUD**.

alow /əˈləʊ/ ▶ **adverb** archaic or dialect below; downwards.
■ Nautical, archaic on or near the deck of a ship.
– ORIGIN late Middle English (in nautical use since the early 16th cent.): from **A-**[2] 'on' + **LOW**[1].

ALP ▶ **abbreviation for** Australian Labor Party.

alp ▶ **noun** a high mountain, especially a snow-capped one.
■ (in Switzerland) an area of green pasture on a mountainside.
– ORIGIN late Middle English: singular of **ALPS**.

alpaca /alˈpakə/ ▶ **noun** (pl. same or **alpacas**) a long-haired domesticated South American mammal related to the llama, valued for its wool.
• *Lama pacos*, family Camelidae, probably descended from the wild guanaco.
■ [mass noun] the wool of the alpaca. ■ [mass noun] fabric made from this wool, with or without other fibres: [as modifier] *an alpaca jersey.*
– ORIGIN late 18th cent.: from Spanish, from Aymara *allpaca*.

alpargata /ˌalpɑːˈgɑːtə/ ▶ **noun** a light canvas shoe with a plaited fibre sole; an espadrille.
– ORIGIN early 19th cent.: from Spanish.

alpenglow /ˈalpəngləʊ/ ▶ **noun** [mass noun] the rosy light of the setting or rising sun seen on high mountains.
– ORIGIN late 19th cent.: a partial translation of German *Alpenglühen*, literally 'Alp glow'.

alpenhorn /ˈalpənhɔːn/ (also **alphorn**) ▶ **noun** a very long valveless wooden wind instrument played like a horn and used for signalling in the Alps.
– ORIGIN late 19th cent.: from German, literally 'Alp horn'.

alpenstock /ˈalpənstɒk/ ▶ **noun** a longish iron-tipped stick used by hillwalkers and formerly by mountaineers.
– ORIGIN early 19th cent.: from German, literally 'Alp stick'.

alpha /ˈalfə/ ▶ **noun** **1** the first letter of the Greek alphabet (**Α, α**), transliterated as 'a'.
■ [as modifier] denoting the first of a series of items or categories, e.g. forms of a chemical compound: *alpha interferon | the α and β chains of haemoglobin.* ■ Brit. a first-class mark given for an examination paper or piece of school or college work: *he had been awarded alpha double plus.* ■ short for **ALPHA TEST**. ■ (**Alpha**) [followed by Latin genitive] Astronomy the first (typically the brightest) star in a constellation: *Alpha Orionis.* ■ [as modifier] relating to alpha decay or alpha particles: *an alpha emitter.*
2 a code word representing the letter A, used in radio communication.
▶ **symbol for** ■ (**α**) a plane angle. ■ (**α**) angular acceleration. ■ (**α**) Astronomy right ascension.
– PHRASES **alpha and omega** the beginning and the end (especially used by Christians as a title for Jesus). ■ the essence or most important features.
– ORIGIN via Latin from Greek.

alphabet ▶ **noun** a set of letters or symbols in a fixed order used to represent the basic set of speech sounds of a language, especially the set of letters from A to Z.
■ the basic elements in a system which combine to form complex entities: *DNA's 4-letter alphabet.*

> The origin of the alphabet goes back to the Phoenician system of the 2nd millennium BC, from which the modern Hebrew and Arabic systems are ultimately derived. The Greek alphabet, which emerged in 1000–900 BC, developed two branches, Cyrillic (which became the script of Russian) and Etruscan (from which derives the Roman alphabet used in the West).

– ORIGIN early 16th cent.: from late Latin *alphabetum*, from Greek *alpha, bēta*, the first two letters of the Greek alphabet.

alphabetical ▶ **adjective** of or relating to an alphabet: *alphabetical characters.*
■ in the order of the letters of the alphabet: *an alphabetical index | in alphabetical order.*
– DERIVATIVES **alphabetic** adjective, **alphabetically** adverb.

alphabetize /ˈalfəbətʌɪz/ (also **-ise**) ▶ **verb** [with obj.] arrange in alphabetical order: *the listings are arranged by state and alphabetized by city.*
– DERIVATIVES **alphabetization** noun.

alphabet soup ▶ **noun** [mass noun] informal incomprehensible or confusing language, typically containing many abbreviations or symbols.
– ORIGIN early 20th cent.: alluding to a kind of clear soup containing pasta in the shapes of letters.

alpha blocker ▶ **noun** Medicine any of a class of drugs which prevent the stimulation of the adrenergic receptors responsible for increased blood pressure.

Alpha Centauri /ˌalfə sɛnˈtɔːrʌɪ/ Astronomy the third brightest star in the sky, in the constellation

b **but** | d **dog** | f **few** | g **get** | h **he** | j **yes** | k **cat** | l **leg** | m **man** | n **no** | p **pen** | r **red** | s **sit** | t **top** | v **voice** | w **we** | z **zoo** | ʃ **she** | ʒ **decision** | θ **thin** | ð **this** | ŋ **ring** | x **loch** | tʃ **chip** | dʒ **jar**

Centaurus, visible only to observers in the southern hemisphere. It is the nearest bright star to the solar system (distance 4.34 light years), and is a visual binary. Also called **RIGIL KENTAURUS**.

alphafetoprotein /ˌalfəˌfiːtəʊˈprəʊtiːn/ ▶ **noun** [mass noun] Medicine a protein produced by a fetus which is present in amniotic fluid and the bloodstream of the mother. Levels of the protein can be measured to detect certain congenital defects such as spina bifida and Down's syndrome.

alpha-hydroxy acid ▶ **noun** Chemistry an organic acid containing a hydroxyl group bonded to the carbon atom adjacent to the carboxylic acid group. A number of such compounds are used in skincare preparations for their exfoliating properties.

alphanumeric ▶ **adjective** consisting of or using both letters and numerals: *alphanumeric data* | *an alphanumeric keyboard*.
▶ **noun** a character that is either a letter or a number.
– DERIVATIVES **alphanumerical** adjective.
– ORIGIN 1950s: blend of **ALPHABET** and **NUMERIC**.

alpha particle ▶ **noun** Physics a helium nucleus emitted by some radioactive substances, originally regarded as a ray.

alpha radiation ▶ **noun** [mass noun] ionizing radiation consisting of alpha particles, emitted by some substances undergoing radioactive decay.

alpha rhythm ▶ **noun** [mass noun] Physiology the normal electrical activity of the brain when conscious and relaxed, consisting of oscillations (**alpha waves**) with a frequency of 8 to 13 hertz.

alpha test ▶ **noun** a trial of machinery, software, or other products carried out by a developer before a product is made available for beta testing.
▶ **verb** (**alpha-test**) [with obj.] subject (a product) to a test of this kind.

alphonso /alˈfɒnsəʊ/ ▶ **noun** (pl. **-os**) a type of mango from western India.
– ORIGIN from Portuguese *Alfonso*.

alphorn /ˈalphɔːn/ ▶ **noun** another term for **ALPENHORN**.

alpine ▶ **adjective** of or relating to high mountains: *alpine and subalpine habitats*.
■ (in the names of plants and animals) growing or found on high mountains: *the alpine chough*. ■ (**Alpine**) of or relating to the Alps: *Alpine guides*. ■ (also **Alpine**) relating to or denoting skiing downhill: *an alpine ski team*. Often contrasted with **NORDIC**.
▶ **noun 1** a plant native to mountain districts, often suitable for growing in rock gardens.
2 a North American butterfly which has brownish-black wings with orange-red markings.
• Genus *Erebia*, subfamily Satyrinae, family Nymphalidae.
– ORIGIN late Middle English: from Latin *Alpinus*, from *Alpes* 'Alps' (see **ALP**).

alpine house ▶ **noun** an unheated greenhouse used to grow alpine plants.

alpine salamander ▶ **noun** a mainly or entirely black salamander with a flat head and large protruding eyes, native to the Alps and other mountainous regions of southern Europe.
• *Salamandra atra*, family Salamandridae.

alpinist ▶ **noun** chiefly dated a climber of high mountains, especially in the Alps.
– ORIGIN late 19th cent.: from French *alpiniste*, from Latin *Alpinus* (see **ALPINE**).

alprazolam /alˈpreɪzə(ʊ)lam/ ▶ **noun** [mass noun] Medicine a drug of the benzodiazepine group, used in the treatment of anxiety.
– ORIGIN 1970s: from *al-* of unknown origin + *p(henyl)* + *(t)r(i)azol(e)* + *(-azep)am*.

Alps a mountain system in Europe extending in a curve from the coast of SE France through NW Italy, Switzerland, Liechtenstein, and southern Germany into Austria. The highest peak of the Alps, Mont Blanc, rises to a height of 4,807 m (15,771 ft).
– ORIGIN late Middle English: via French from Latin *Alpes*, from Greek *Alpeis*, of unknown origin.

Al Qahira /al ˈkɑːhiːrɑː/ (also **El Qahira**) Arabic name for **CAIRO**.

already ▶ **adverb 1** before or by now or the time in question: *Anna has suffered a great deal already*.
■ as surprisingly soon or early as this: *at 31, he already suffers from arthritis* | *already it was past four o' clock*.
2 N. Amer. informal used as an intensive after a word or phrase to express impatience: *enough already with these crazy kids and their wacky dances!*
– ORIGIN Middle English: from **ALL** (as an adverb) + **READY**; sense 2 is influenced by Yiddish use.

alright ▶ **adjective**, **adverb**, & **exclamation** variant spelling of **ALL RIGHT**.

> **USAGE** The merging of **all** and **right** to form the one-word spelling **alright** is not recorded until the end of the 19th century (unlike other similar merged spellings such as **altogether** and **already**, which date from much earlier). There is no logical reason for insisting on **all right** as two words, when other single-word forms such as **altogether** have long been accepted. Nevertheless it is still considered by many people to be unacceptable in formal writing. In the British National Corpus around 5 per cent of citations for the two forms are for the one-word form **alright**.

Alsace /alˈsas, French alzas/ a region of NE France, on the borders with Germany and Switzerland. Alsace was annexed by Prussia, along with part of Lorraine (forming **Alsace-Lorraine**), after the Franco-Prussian War of 1870–1, and restored to France after the First World War.

Alsatian ▶ **noun 1** Brit. a large dog of a breed typically used as guard dogs or for police work. Also called **GERMAN SHEPHERD**.
2 a native or inhabitant of Alsace.
▶ **adjective** of or relating to Alsace or its inhabitants.
– ORIGIN from medieval Latin *Alsatia* 'Alsace' + **-AN**.

alsike /ˈalsɪk/ (also **alsike clover**) ▶ **noun** a tall clover which is widely grown for fodder, native to Europe and naturalized in North America.
• *Trifolium hybridum*, family Leguminosae.
– ORIGIN mid 19th cent.: named after *Alsike* in Sweden; Linnaeus mentions the plant growing there.

also ▶ **adverb** in addition; too: *a brilliant linguist, he was also interested in botany* | *dyslexia, also known as word-blindness* | [sentence adverb] *also, a car's very expensive to run*.
– ORIGIN Old English *alswā* 'quite so, in that manner, similarly' (see **ALL**, **SO**[1]).

also-ran ▶ **noun** a loser in a race or contest, especially by a large margin.
■ an undistinguished or unsuccessful person or thing.

alstroemeria /ˌalstrəˈmɪərɪə/ ▶ **noun** a South American plant with showy lily-like flowers, widely cultivated as an ornamental.
• Genus *Alstroemeria*, family Liliaceae: several species, in particular the Peruvian lily.
– ORIGIN late 18th cent.: modern Latin, named after Klas von *Alstroemer* (1736–96), Swedish naturalist.

Alt ▶ **noun** short for **ALT KEY**.

Alta ▶ **abbreviation for** Alberta.

Altai /ˈaltʌɪ/ (also **Altay**) a krai (administrative territory) of Russia in SW Siberia, on the border with Kazakhstan; capital, Barnaul.

Altaic /alˈteɪɪk/ ▶ **adjective 1** of or relating to the Altai Mountains.
2 denoting or belonging to a phylum or superfamily of languages which includes the Turkic, Mongolian, Tungusic, and Manchu languages. They are characterized by agglutination and vowel harmony.
▶ **noun** [mass noun] the Altaic family of languages.

Altai Mountains a mountain system of central Asia extending about 1,600 km (1,000 miles) eastwards from Kazakhstan into western Mongolia and northern China.

Altair /ˈaltɛː/ Astronomy the brightest star in the constellation Aquila.
– ORIGIN Arabic, literally 'flying eagle'.

Altamira /ˌaltəˈmɪərə/ the site of a cave with Palaeolithic rock paintings, south of Santander in northern Spain, discovered in 1879.

altar /ˈɔːltə, ˈɒl-/ ▶ **noun** the table in a Christian church at which the bread and wine are consecrated in communion services.
■ a table or flat-topped block used as the focus for a religious ritual, especially for making sacrifices or offerings to a deity.
– PHRASES **lead someone to the altar** marry a woman. **sacrifice someone/thing on/at the altar of** cause someone or something to suffer in the interests of: *no businessman is going to sacrifice his company on the altar of such altruism*.
– ORIGIN Old English *altar*, *alter*, based on late Latin *altar*, *altarium*, from Latin *altus* 'high'.

altar boy ▶ **noun** a boy who acts as a priest's assistant during a service, especially in the Roman Catholic Church.

altarpiece ▶ **noun** a painting or other work of art designed to be set above and behind an altar.

Altay variant spelling of **ALTAI**.

altazimuth /alˈtazɪməθ/ ▶ **noun 1** (also **altazimuth mount** or **mounting**) Astronomy a telescope mounting that moves in azimuth (about a vertical axis) and in altitude (about a horizontal axis). Compare with **EQUATORIAL MOUNT**.
■ (also **altazimuth telescope**) a telescope on such a mounting.
2 a surveying instrument for measuring vertical and horizontal angles, resembling a theodolite but larger and more precise.
– ORIGIN mid 19th cent.: blend of **ALTITUDE** and **AZIMUTH**.

Altdorfer /ˈaltdɔːfə, German ˈaltdɔrfɐ/, Albrecht (*c.*1485–1538), German painter and engraver. He was one of the first modern European landscape painters and was principal artist of the Danube School.

alter /ˈɔːltə, ˈɒl-/ ▶ **verb** change or cause to change in character or composition, typically in a comparatively small but significant way: [with obj.] *Eliot was persuaded to alter the passage* | *nothing alters the fact that children are our responsibility* | [no obj.] *our outward appearance alters as we get older* | [as adj. **altered**] *an altered state*.
■ [with obj.] make structural changes to (a building): *plans to alter the dining hall*. ■ [with obj.] N. Amer. & Austral. castrate or spay (a domestic animal).
– DERIVATIVES **alterable** adjective.
– ORIGIN late Middle English: from Old French *alterer*, from late Latin *alterare*, from Latin *alter* 'other'.

alteration ▶ **noun** [mass noun] the action or process of altering or being altered: *careful alteration of old buildings* | [count noun] *alterations had to be made*.
– ORIGIN late Middle English: from Old French, or from late Latin *alteratio(n-)*, from the verb *alterare* (see **ALTER**).

altercate /ˈɔːltəkeɪt, ˈɒl-/ ▶ **verb** [no obj.] archaic dispute or argue noisily and publicly.
– ORIGIN mid 16th cent.: from Latin *altercat-* 'wrangled', from *altercari*.

altercation ▶ **noun** a noisy argument or disagreement, especially in public: *I had an altercation with the ticket collector*.
– ORIGIN late Middle English: from Latin *altercatio(n-)*, from the verb *altercari* (see **ALTERCATE**).

alter ego /ˌaltər ˈɛɡəʊ, ˌɒlt-, ˈiːɡ-/ ▶ **noun** a person's secondary or alternative personality.
■ an intimate and trusted friend.
– ORIGIN mid 16th cent.: Latin, 'other self'.

alterity /alˈtɛrɪti, ɒl-/ ▶ **noun** [mass noun] formal the state of being other or different; otherness.
– ORIGIN mid 17th cent.: from late Latin *alteritas*, from *alter* 'other'.

alternant /ɔːlˈtəːnənt, ɒl-/ ▶ **noun** an alternative form of a word or other linguistic unit; a variant.
▶ **adjective** changing from one to the other; alternating.
– ORIGIN mid 17th cent.: from Latin *alternant-* 'doing things by turns', from the verb *alternare* (see **ALTERNATE**).

alternate ▶ **verb** /ˈɔːltəneɪt, ˈɒl-/ [no obj.] occur in turn repeatedly: *bouts of depression* ***alternate with*** *periods of elation* | [as adj. **alternating**] *a season of alternating hot days and cool nights*.
■ [with obj.] do or perform in turn repeatedly: *some adults who wish to* ***alternate*** *work* ***with*** *education*. ■ (of a thing) change repeatedly between two contrasting conditions: *the government* ***alternated between*** *the Labour and Conservative parties*.
▶ **adjective** /ɔːlˈtəːnət, ɒl-/ [attrib.] **1** every other; every second: *she was asked to attend on alternate days*.
■ (of two things) each following and succeeded by the other in a regular pattern: *alternate bouts of intense labour and of idleness*. ■ (of a sequence) consisting of alternate items. ■ Botany (of leaves or shoots) placed alternately on the two sides of the stem.
2 chiefly N. Amer. another term for **ALTERNATIVE**: *a novel set in an alternate universe*.
▶ **noun** /ɔːlˈtəːnət, ɒl-/ N. Amer. a person who acts as a deputy or substitute.
– DERIVATIVES **alternately** adverb, **alternation** noun.
– ORIGIN early 16th cent.: from Latin *alternat-* 'done by turns', from *alternare*, from *alternus* 'every other', from *alter* 'other'.

a

alternate angles ▶**plural noun** Mathematics two angles, formed when a line crosses two other lines, that lie on opposite sides of the transversal line and on opposite relative sides of the other lines. If the two lines crossed are parallel, the alternate angles are equal.

alternating current (abbrev.: **AC** or **ac**) ▶**noun** an electric current that reverses its direction many times a second at regular intervals, typically used in power supplies. Compare with **DIRECT CURRENT**.

alternation of generations ▶**noun** [mass noun] Biology a pattern of reproduction occurring in the life cycles of many lower plants and some invertebrates, involving a regular alternation between two distinct forms. The generations are alternately sexual and asexual (as in ferns) or dioecious and parthenogenetic (as in some jellyfishes).

alternative ▶**adjective** [attrib.] (of one or more things) available as another possibility: *the various alternative methods for resolving disputes* | *the alternative definition of democracy as popular power.*
■(of two things) mutually exclusive: *the facts fit two alternative scenarios.* ■ of or relating to behaviour that is considered unconventional and is typically seen as a challenge to traditional norms: *an alternative lifestyle.*
▶**noun** one of two or more available possibilities: *audio cassettes are an interesting* ***alternative to*** *reading* | *she had no alternative but to break the law.*
– ORIGIN mid 16th cent. (in the sense 'alternating, alternate'): from French *alternatif, -ive* or medieval Latin *alternativus*, from Latin *alternare* 'interchange' (see **ALTERNATE**).

USAGE 1 The adjective **alternate** is sometimes used in place of **alternative**, especially in American English. Strictly speaking, the two words are quite distinct: **alternative** means 'available as another possibility or choice', as in *some European countries follow an* ***alternative*** *approach*, while **alternate** means 'every other or every second', as in *they meet on* ***alternate*** *Sundays*, or '(of two things) each following and succeeded by the other in a regular pattern', as in ***alternate*** *layers of potato and sauce.* The use of **alternate** to mean **alternative**, as in *we will need to find* ***alternate*** *sources of fuel*, is common in North America, and many dictionaries now record the two simply as variants of one another. The Oxford Reading Programme records a quarter of all uses in this sense using the spelling **alternate**. It is, however, still regarded as incorrect by many people in Britain.
2 Some traditionalists maintain, from an etymological standpoint, that you can only have a maximum of two alternatives (from the Latin *alter* 'other (of two)') and that uses where there are more than two alternatives are erroneous. Such uses are, however, normal in modern standard English.

alternative comedy ▶**noun** [mass noun] a style of comedy rejecting established (especially racist or sexist) stereotypes and sometimes having a political component.

alternative dispute resolution (abbrev.: **ADR**) ▶**noun** [mass noun] chiefly N. Amer. the use of methods such as mediation or arbitration to resolve a dispute without resort to litigation.

alternative energy ▶**noun** [mass noun] energy fuelled in ways that do not use up the earth's natural resources or otherwise harm the environment, especially by avoiding the use of fossil fuels or nuclear power.

alternative fuel ▶**noun** a fuel other than petrol or diesel for powering motor vehicles, such as natural gas, methanol, or electricity.

alternatively ▶**adverb** [sentence adverb] as another option or possibility: *alternatively, you may telephone us direct if you wish.*

alternative medicine ▶**noun** [mass noun] any of a range of medical therapies that are not regarded as orthodox by the medical profession, such as herbalism, naturopathy, and crystal healing. See also **COMPLEMENTARY MEDICINE**.

Alternative Service Book (abbrev.: **ASB**) ▶**noun** a book containing the public liturgy of the Church of England published in 1980 for use as the alternative to the Book of Common Prayer.

alternator ▶**noun** a dynamo that generates an alternating current.

Althing /'ɔːlθɪŋ, 'ɒl-/ the bicameral legislative assembly of Iceland.
– ORIGIN Icelandic, from Old Norse.

althorn /'althɔːn/ ▶**noun** a musical instrument of the saxhorn family, especially the alto or tenor saxhorn in E flat.
– ORIGIN mid 19th cent.: from German, from *alt* 'high' (from Latin *altus*) + *Horn* 'horn'.

although ▶**conjunction** in spite of the fact that; even though: *although the sun was shining it wasn't that warm* | *although small, the room has a spacious feel.*
■however; but: *he says he has the team strip, although I've never seen him wear it.*
– ORIGIN Middle English: from **ALL** (as an adverb) + **THOUGH**.

USAGE The form **although** can be replaced by **though**, the only difference being that **although** tends to be more formal than **though**. Some uses of **though** are not interchangeable with **although** however: e.g. adverbial uses (*it was nice of him to phone,* ***though***) and uses in phrases with 'as' or 'even' (*she doesn't look* ***as though*** *she's listening*).

Althusser /'altʊsɛː, French altysɛʀ/, Louis (1918–90), French philosopher. In giving a reinterpretation of traditional Marxism in the light of structuralist theories his work had a significant influence on literary and cultural theory.

altimeter /'altɪmiːtə/ ▶**noun** an instrument for determining altitude attained, especially a barometric or radar device fitted in an aircraft.
– ORIGIN early 20th cent.: from Latin *altus* 'high' + **-METER**.

altimetry /al'tɪmɪtri/ ▶**noun** [mass noun] the measurement of height or altitude.
– DERIVATIVES **altimetric** adjective, **altimetrically** adverb.
– ORIGIN late Middle English: from medieval Latin *altimetria*.

altiplano /ˌaltɪ'plɑːnəʊ/ ▶**noun** (pl. **-os**) the high tableland of central South America.
– ORIGIN early 20th cent.: from Spanish.

altissimo /al'tɪsɪməʊ/ ▶**adjective** Music very high in pitch: *the extreme altissimo range of his horn.*
– ORIGIN Italian, superlative of *alto* 'high'.

altitude ▶**noun** [mass noun] the height of an object or point in relation to sea level or ground level: *flight data including airspeed and altitude* | [count noun] *flying at altitudes over 15,000 feet.*
■great height: *the mechanism can freeze at altitude.* ■ Astronomy the apparent height of a celestial object above the horizon, measured in angular distance. ■ Geometry the length of the perpendicular line from a vertex to the opposite side of a figure.
– DERIVATIVES **altitudinal** adjective.
– ORIGIN late Middle English: from Latin *altitudo*, from *altus* 'high'.

altitude sickness ▶**noun** [mass noun] illness caused by ascent to high altitude, characterized chiefly by hyperventilation, nausea, and exhaustion resulting from shortage of oxygen.

Alt key (also **ALT key**) ▶**noun** Computing a key on a keyboard which, when pressed simultaneously with another key, gives the latter an alternative function.
– ORIGIN late 20th cent.: abbreviation of *alt(ernative) key*.

Altman /'ɔːltm(ə)n, 'ɒlt-/, Robert (b.1925), American film director. He made his name with *MASH* (1970), a black comedy about an army surgical hospital at the front in the Korean war.

alto /'altəʊ/ ▶**noun** (pl. **-os**) Music a voice, instrument, or part below the highest range and above tenor, in particular:
■(especially in church music) the highest adult male singing voice (sometimes distinguished from the counter-tenor voice as using falsetto). ■ the lowest female singing voice; contralto. ■ a person with such a voice. ■ a part written for such a voice. ■ [as modifier] denoting the member of a family of instruments pitched second or third highest: *alto flute.* ■ an alto instrument, especially an alto saxophone.
– ORIGIN late 16th cent.: from Italian *alto (canto)* 'high (song)'.

alto clef ▶**noun** a clef placing middle C on the middle line of the stave, used chiefly for viola music.

altocumulus ▶**noun** (pl. **-cumuli**) [mass noun] cloud forming a layer of rounded masses with a level base, occurring at medium altitude (typically 2 to 7 km, 6,500 to 23,000 ft).
– ORIGIN late 19th cent.: from modern Latin *alto-* (from Latin *altus* 'high') + **CUMULUS**.

altogether ▶**adverb** completely; totally: *I stopped seeing her altogether* | [as submodifier] *I'm not altogether sure that I'd trust him.*
■including everything or everyone; in total: *he had married several times and had forty-six children altogether.* ■ [sentence adverb] taking everything into consideration; on the whole: *altogether it was a great evening.*
– PHRASES **in the altogether** informal without any clothes on; naked: *she's agreed to pose in the altogether.*
– ORIGIN Old English (see **ALL, TOGETHER**).

USAGE Note that **altogether** and **all together** do not mean the same thing. **Altogether** means 'in total', as in *there are six bedrooms* ***altogether***, whereas **all together** means 'all in one place' or 'all at once', as in *it was good to have a group of friends* ***all together***; *they came in* ***all together***.

alto-relievo /ˌaltəʊrɪ'liːvəʊ/ (also **alto-rilievo** /-rɪ'ljeɪvəʊ/) ▶**noun** (pl. **-os**) [mass noun] another term for ***high relief*** at **RELIEF** (in sense 4).
■[count noun] a sculpture or carving in high relief.
– ORIGIN mid 17th cent.: from Italian *alto-rilievo*.

altostratus ▶**noun** [mass noun] cloud forming a continuous uniform layer which resembles stratus but occurs at medium altitude (typically 2 to 7 km, 6,500 to 23,000 ft).
– ORIGIN late 19th cent.: from modern Latin *alto-* (from Latin *altus* 'high') + **STRATUS**.

altricial /al'trɪʃ(ə)l/ Zoology ▶**adjective** (of a young bird or other animal) hatched or born in an undeveloped state and requiring care and feeding by the parents. Also called **NIDICOLOUS**. Often contrasted with **PRECOCIAL**.
■(of a particular species) having such young.
▶**noun** an altricial bird.
– ORIGIN late 19th cent.: from Latin *altrix, altric-*, feminine of *altor* 'nourisher', from *alere* 'nourish'.

altruism /'altruːɪz(ə)m/ ▶**noun** [mass noun] the belief in or practice of disinterested and selfless concern for the well-being of others: *some may choose to work with vulnerable elderly people out of altruism.*
■Zoology behaviour of an animal that benefits another at its own expense.
– DERIVATIVES **altruist** noun, **altruistic** adjective, **altruistically** adverb.
– ORIGIN mid 19th cent.: from French *altruisme*, from Italian *altrui* 'somebody else', from Latin *alteri huic* 'to this other'.

ALU Computing ▶**abbreviation for** arithmetic logic unit.

alu /'ɑːluː/ ▶**noun** (pl. **alus**) variant spelling of **ALOO**.

aludel /'aljʊdɛl/ ▶**noun** a pear-shaped earthenware or glass pot, open at both ends to enable a series to be fitted one above another, formerly used in sublimation and other chemical processes.
– ORIGIN late Middle English: from Old French *alutel*, via Spanish from Arabic *al-'uṯāl* 'the sublimation vessel'.

alula /'aljʊlə/ ▶**noun** (pl. **alulae** /'aljʊliː/) technical term for **BASTARD WING**.
– ORIGIN late 18th cent.: modern Latin, literally 'small wing', diminutive of *ala*.

alum /'aləm/ (also **potash alum**) ▶**noun** [mass noun] Chemistry a colourless astringent compound which is a hydrated double sulphate of aluminium and potassium, used in solution in dyeing and tanning.
• Chem. formula: $AlK(SO_4)_2.12H_2O$.
■[count noun] any of a number of analogous crystalline double sulphates of a monovalent metal (or group) and a trivalent metal.
– ORIGIN late Middle English: via Old French from Latin *alumen, alumin-* related to *aluta* 'tawed leather'.

alumina /ə'luːmɪnə/ ▶**noun** [mass noun] a white solid that is a major constituent of many rocks, especially clays, and is found crystallized as corundum, sapphire, and other minerals.
• Alternative name: **aluminium oxide**; chem. formula: Al_2O_3.
– ORIGIN late 18th cent.: from Latin *alumen* (see **ALUM**), on the pattern of words such as *magnesia*.

aluminium (US **aluminum**) ▶**noun** [mass noun] the chemical element of atomic number 13, a light silvery-grey metal. (Symbol: **Al**)

Aluminium is the most abundant metal in the earth's crust and is obtained mainly from bauxite. Its resistance to corrosion, lightness, and strength (especially in alloys) have led to widespread use in domestic utensils, engineering parts, and aircraft construction.

– ORIGIN early 19th cent.: from **ALUMINA** + **-IUM**.

aluminium bronze ▶ noun [mass noun] an alloy of copper and aluminium.

aluminize /ə'lu:mɪnʌɪz/ (also **-ise**) ▶ verb [with obj.] [usu. as adj. **aluminized**] coat with aluminium.

aluminosilicate /ə,lu:mɪnə(ʊ)'sɪlɪkeɪt/ ▶ noun Chemistry a silicate in which aluminium replaces some of the silicon, especially a rock-forming mineral such as a feldspar or a clay mineral.
– ORIGIN early 20th cent.: from *alumino-* (combining form of **ALUMINIUM**) + **SILICATE**.

aluminous /ə'lu:mɪnəs/ ▶ adjective (chiefly of minerals and rocks) containing alumina or aluminium.
– ORIGIN late Middle English: from Latin *aluminosus*, from *alumen*, *alumin-* (see **ALUM**).

aluminum /ə'lu:mɪnəm/ ▶ noun US spelling of **ALUMINIUM**.

alumna /ə'lʌmnə/ ▶ noun (pl. **alumnae** /-ni:/) a female former pupil or student of a particular school, college, or university.
– ORIGIN late 19th cent.: from Latin, feminine of *alumnus* (see **ALUMNUS**).

alumnus /ə'lʌmnəs/ ▶ noun (pl. **alumni** /-nɪ/) a male former pupil or student of a particular school, college, or university: *a Harvard alumnus*.
– ORIGIN mid 17th cent.: from Latin, 'nursling, pupil', from *alere* 'nourish'.

> USAGE In the singular, **alumnus** nearly always means a male, but the plural **alumni** can be used to refer to pupils or students of either sex. See also **ALUMNA**.

alum root ▶ noun chiefly N. Amer. another term for **HEUCHERA**.

Al Uqsur /al 'ʊksʊə/ variant spelling of **EL UQSUR**.

Alvarez /al'vɑ:rɛz/, Luis Walter (1911–88), American physicist. In 1980 Alvarez and his son identified iridium in sediment from the Cretaceous–Tertiary boundary and proposed that this resulted from a catastrophic meteorite impact.

alveolar /al'vɪələ, ,alvɪ'əʊlə/ ▶ adjective of or relating to an alveolus, in particular:
■ Anatomy relating to or denoting the bony ridge that contains the sockets of the upper teeth. ■ Phonetics (of a consonant) pronounced with the tip of the tongue on or near this ridge (e.g. *n*, *s*, *d*, *t*). ■ Anatomy of or relating to an alveolus or the alveoli of the lung.
▶ noun Phonetics an alveolar consonant.

alveolitis /,alvɪə(ʊ)'lʌɪtɪs/ ▶ noun [mass noun] Medicine inflammation of the air sacs of the lungs.

alveolus /al'vɪələs, ,alvɪ'əʊləs/ ▶ noun (pl. **alveoli** /-lʌɪ, -li:/) chiefly Anatomy a small cavity, pit, or hollow, in particular:
■ any of the many tiny air sacs of the lungs which allow for rapid gaseous exchange. ■ the bony socket for the root of a tooth. ■ an acinus in a gland.
– DERIVATIVES **alveolate** /al'vɪələt/ adjective.
– ORIGIN late 17th cent.: from Latin, 'small cavity', diminutive of *alveus*.

alway ▶ adverb archaic form of **ALWAYS**.

always ▶ adverb **1** at all times; on all occasions: *the sun always rises in the east.*
■ throughout a long period of the past: *Isabel had always been in rude health.* ■ for all future time; forever: *she will always be missed.* ■ repeatedly and annoyingly: *she is always making derogatory remarks.*
2 as a last resort; failing all else: *if the marriage doesn't work out, we can always get divorced*
– ORIGIN Middle English: genitive case of *all way*, the inflection probably giving the sense 'at every time' as opposed to 'at one uninterrupted time': the difference between the two is no longer distinct.

alyssum /'alɪs(ə)m, ə'lɪs(ə)m/ ▶ noun (pl. **alyssums**) a herbaceous Eurasian plant which typically bears small white or yellow flowers. Some kinds are widely cultivated in gardens.
● Genera *Alyssum* and *Lobularia*, family Cruciferae: many species, including **sweet alyssum** (*L. maritima*), with fragrant white flowers.
– ORIGIN mid 16th cent. (used loosely to denote various medicinal herbs): modern Latin, from Latin *alysson*, from Greek *alusson*, from *a-* 'without' + *lussa* 'rabies' (referring to early herbalist use).

Alzheimer's disease /'altshʌɪməz/ ▶ noun [mass noun] progressive mental deterioration that can occur in middle or old age, due to generalized degeneration of the brain. It is the commonest cause of premature senility.
– ORIGIN early 20th cent.: named after Alois

Alzheimer (1864–1915), the German neurologist who first identified it.

AM ▶ abbreviation for ■ amplitude modulation. ■ **(A.M.)** Hymns Ancient and Modern. ■ US Master of Arts. [ORIGIN: Latin *artium magister*.] ■ Member of the Order of Australia.

Am ▶ symbol for the chemical element americium.

am first person singular present of **BE**.

a.m. ▶ abbreviation before noon (used after times of day between midnight and noon not expressed using the twenty-four-hour clock): *at 7.45 a.m.*
– ORIGIN from Latin *ante meridiem*.

amacrine cell /'aməkrʌɪn, -krɪn/ ▶ noun Anatomy a small nerve cell within the retina which has dendrites but no axon.
– ORIGIN early 20th cent.: from **A-**¹ 'not' + Greek *makros* 'large' + *is*, *in-* 'sinew or strip'.

amadavat /'amədəvat/ ▶ noun variant spelling of **AVADAVAT**.

amadou /'amədu:/ ▶ noun [mass noun] historical a spongy substance made by drying certain bracket fungi and formerly used as an absorbent in medicine, as tinder, and for drying fishing flies.
– ORIGIN late 18th cent.: from French, from Latin *amator* 'lover' (because it easily ignites).

amah /'ɑːmə/ ▶ noun a nursemaid or maid in the Far East or India.
– ORIGIN from Portuguese *ama* 'nurse'.

Amal /ə'mɑːl/ a Lebanese Shiite Muslim organization founded in 1975 and having political and paramilitary wings.
– ORIGIN from Arabic *amal* 'hope'.

Amalfi /ə'malfi/ a port and resort on the west coast of Italy, on the Gulf of Salerno; pop. 5,900 (1990).

amalgam /ə'malgəm/ ▶ noun a mixture or blend: *a curious amalgam of the traditional and the modern.*
■ Chemistry an alloy of mercury with another metal, especially one used for dental fillings.
– ORIGIN late 15th cent.: from French *amalgame* or medieval Latin *amalgama*, from Greek *malagma* 'an emollient'.

amalgamate /ə'malgəmeɪt/ ▶ verb combine or unite to form one organization or structure: [with obj.] *he amalgamated his company with another* | [no obj.] *numerous small British railway companies amalgamated.*
■ [with obj.] Chemistry alloy (a metal) with mercury: [as adj. **amalgamated**] *amalgamated zinc.*
– ORIGIN early 17th cent.: from medieval Latin *amalgamat-* 'formed into a soft mass', from the verb *amalgamare*, from *amalgama* (see **AMALGAM**).

amalgamation ▶ noun [mass noun] the action, process, or result of combining or uniting: *the threat of amalgamation with another college* | [count noun] *an amalgamation of two separate companies.*
■ Chemistry the action or process of alloying a metal with mercury.
– ORIGIN early 17th cent.: from medieval Latin *amalgamare* (see **AMALGAMATE**).

Amalthea /ə'malθɪə/ Astronomy a satellite of Jupiter, the third closest to the planet, being reddish in colour and heavily cratered (262 km long and 146 km across).
– ORIGIN from the name of a goat in Greek Mythology, which suckled the infant Zeus.

amanuensis /ə,manjʊ'ɛnsɪs/ ▶ noun (pl. **amanuenses** /-si:z/) a literary or artistic assistant, in particular one who takes dictation or copies manuscripts.
– ORIGIN early 17th cent.: Latin, from (*servus*) *a manu* '(slave) at hand(writing), secretary' + *-ensis* 'belonging to'.

Amapá /,amə'pa:/ a state of northern Brazil, on the Atlantic coast, lying between the Amazon delta and the border with French Guiana; capital, Macapá. It is a region of dense rainforest.

amaranth /'aməranθ/ ▶ noun a plant of a chiefly tropical family that includes love-lies-bleeding.
● Family Amaranthaceae: several genera, especially *Amaranthus*.
– ORIGIN mid 16th cent.: from French *amarante* or modern Latin *amaranthus*, alteration (on the pattern of plant names ending in *-anthus*, from Greek *anthos* 'flower') of Latin *amarantus*, from Greek *amarantos* 'not fading'.

amaretti /,amə'rɛti/ ▶ plural noun Italian almond-flavoured biscuits.

– ORIGIN Italian, based on *amaro* 'bitter'; compare with **AMARETTO**.

amaretto /,amə'rɛtəʊ/ ▶ noun [mass noun] a brown almond-flavoured liqueur produced in Italy.
– ORIGIN Italian, diminutive of *amaro* 'bitter' (with reference to bitter almonds).

Amarna, Tell el- /ə'mɑːnə, ,tɛl ɛl/ the site of the ruins of the ancient Egyptian capital Akhetaten, on the east bank of the Nile.

amaryllis /,amə'rɪlɪs/ ▶ noun a bulbous plant with showy trumpet-shaped flowers and strap-shaped leaves.
● Two plants of the family Liliaceae (or Amaryllidaceae): the South African *Amaryllis belladonna* (also called **BELLADONNA LILY**), and (popularly) a tropical South American plant of the genus *Hippeastrum*, grown as a house plant.
– ORIGIN modern Latin, from Latin *Amaryllis* (from Greek *Amarullis*), a name for a country girl in pastoral poetry.

amass ▶ verb [with obj.] gather together or accumulate (a large amount or number of valuable material or things) over a period of time: *he amassed a fortune estimated at close to a million pounds.*
■ [no obj.] archaic (of people) gather together in a crowd or group: *the soldiers were amassing from all parts of Spain.*
– DERIVATIVES **amasser** noun.
– ORIGIN late 15th cent.: from French *amasser* or medieval Latin *amassare*, based on Latin *massa* 'lump' (see **MASS**).

Amaterasu /ə,mɑːtə'rɑːsu:/ the principal deity of the Japanese Shinto religion, the sun goddess and ancestor of Jimmu, founder of the imperial dynasty.

amateur /'amətə, -tʃə, -tjʊə, ,amə'tə:/ ▶ noun a person who engages in a pursuit, especially a sport, on an unpaid basis.
■ a person considered contemptibly inept at a particular activity: *that bunch of stumbling amateurs.*
▶ adjective engaging or engaged in without payment; non-professional: *an amateur archaeologist* | *amateur athletics.*
■ inept; unskilful: *it's all so amateur!*
– DERIVATIVES **amateurism** noun.
– ORIGIN late 18th cent.: from French, from Italian *amatore*, from Latin *amator* 'lover', from *amare* 'to love'.

amateurish ▶ adjective unskilful; inept: *her amateurish interviewing technique* | *the music was amateurish.*
– DERIVATIVES **amateurishly** adverb, **amateurishness** noun.

Amati /ə'mɑːti/ a family of Italian violin-makers from Cremona. In the 16th and 17th centuries three generations of the Amatis developed the basic proportions of the violin, viola, and cello.

amatol /'amətɒl/ ▶ noun [mass noun] a high explosive consisting of a mixture of TNT and ammonium nitrate.
– ORIGIN early 20th cent.: formed irregularly from *am*(monium) + *tol*(uene).

amatory /'amət(ə)ri/ ▶ adjective relating to or induced by sexual love or desire: *his amatory exploits.*
– ORIGIN late 16th cent.: from Latin *amatorius*, from *amator* (see **AMATEUR**).

amaurosis /,amɔː'rəʊsɪs/ ▶ noun [mass noun] Medicine partial or total blindness without visible change in the eye, typically due to disease of the optic nerve, spinal cord, or brain.
– DERIVATIVES **amaurotic** adjective.
– ORIGIN mid 17th cent.: from Greek *amaurōsis*, from *amauroun* 'darken', from *amauros* 'dim'.

amaze ▶ verb [with obj.] (often **be amazed**) surprise (someone) greatly; fill with astonishment: *he was amazed at how modern everything was* | [with obj. and clause] *she was amazed that Paul should notice her* | [as adj. **amazed**] *she shook her head in amazed disbelief.*
– ORIGIN Old English *āmasian*, of unknown origin.

amazement ▶ noun [mass noun] a feeling of great surprise or wonder: *she shook her head in amazement* | *to her amazement, Bill was keen.*

amazing ▶ adjective causing great surprise or wonder; astonishing: *an amazing number of people registered* | *it is amazing how short memories are.*
■ informal startlingly impressive: *she makes the most amazing cakes.*
– DERIVATIVES **amazingly** adverb [sentence adverb] *amazingly, Alan escaped with a few cuts and bruises* | [as submodifier] *an amazingly good idea*, **amazingness** noun.

Amazon[1] /ˈaməz(ə)n/ a river in South America, flowing over 6,683 km (4,150 miles) through Peru, Colombia, and Brazil into the Atlantic Ocean. It drains two fifths of the continent and in terms of water flow it is the largest river in the world.
– DERIVATIVES **Amazonian** adjective.
– ORIGIN the river bore various names after its discovery in 1500 and was finally called *Amazon* after a legendary race of female warriors believed to live on its banks.

Amazon[2] /ˈaməz(ə)n/ ▶ noun **1** a member of a legendary race of female warriors believed by the ancient Greeks to exist in Scythia or elsewhere on the edge of the known world.
■ a very tall and strong or athletic woman.
2 (**amazon**) a parrot, typically green and with a broad rounded tail, found in Central and South America.
● Genus *Amazona*, family Psittacidae: numerous species.
– DERIVATIVES **Amazonian** /aməˈzəʊnɪən/ adjective.
– ORIGIN late Middle English: via Latin from Greek *Amazōn*, explained by the Greeks as 'breastless' (as if from *a-* 'without' + *mazos* 'breast'), referring to the fable that the Amazons cut off the right breast so as not to interfere with the use of a bow, but probably a folk etymology of an unknown foreign word.

amazon ant ▶ noun a small reddish ant which captures the pupae of other ant colonies to raise as slaves.
● Genus *Polyergus*, family Formicidae.

Amazonas /aməˈzəʊnəs/ a state of NW Brazil; capital, Manaus. It is traversed by the Amazon and its numerous tributaries.

Amazon dolphin ▶ noun another term for **BOUTU**.

Amazonia /aməˈzəʊnɪə/ the area around the River Amazon in South America, principally in Brazil, but also extending into Peru, Colombia, and Bolivia. The region comprises approximately one third of the world's remaining tropical rainforest.
■ a national park protecting 10,000 sq. km (3,850 sq. miles) of tropical rainforest in the state of Pará, northern Brazil.

ambassador ▶ noun an accredited diplomat sent by a state as its permanent representative in a foreign country: *the French ambassador to Portugal*.
■ a person who acts as a representative or promoter of a specified activity: *he is a good ambassador for the industry*.
– DERIVATIVES **ambassadorial** adjective, **ambassadorship** noun.
– ORIGIN late Middle English: from French *ambassadeur*, from Italian *ambasciator*, based on Latin *ambactus* 'servant'.

ambassador-at-large ▶ noun N. Amer. an ambassador with special duties not appointed to a particular country.

ambassador extraordinary ▶ noun a diplomat sent by one state or monarch on a diplomatic mission to another. An **ambassador extraordinary and plenipotentiary** is one of the highest rank permanently representing a state or monarch at a foreign government or court.

ambassador plenipotentiary ▶ noun an ambassador with full powers to sign treaties or otherwise act for the state or monarch.

ambassadress ▶ noun a female ambassador.
■ archaic an ambassador's wife.

ambatch /ˈambatʃ/ ▶ noun a tropical African tree of the pea family, with light spongy timber that is used chiefly for rafts and floats.
● *Aeschynomene elaphroxylon*, family Leguminosae.
– ORIGIN mid 19th cent.: of Ethiopic origin.

Ambato /amˈbɑːtəʊ/ a market town in the Andes of central Ecuador; pop. 229,190 (1990).

amber ▶ noun [mass noun] hard translucent fossilized resin originating from extinct coniferous trees of the Tertiary period, typically yellowish in colour. It is found chiefly along the southern shores of the Baltic Sea and has been used in jewellery since antiquity.
■ a honey-yellow colour typical of this substance. ■ a yellow light used as a cautionary signal between green for 'go' and red for 'stop': *the lights were at amber*.
▶ adjective made of amber: *amber beads*.
■ having the yellow colour of amber: *her amber eyes*.
– ORIGIN late Middle English (also in the sense 'ambergris'): from Old French *ambre*, from Arabic *'anbar* 'ambergris', later 'amber'.

ambergris /ˈambəɡrɪs, -iːs/ ▶ noun [mass noun] a waxlike substance that originates as a secretion in the intestines of the sperm whale, found floating in tropical seas and used in perfume manufacture.
– ORIGIN late Middle English: from Old French *ambre gris* 'grey amber', as distinct from *amber jaune* 'yellow amber' (the resin).

amberjack ▶ noun a large marine game fish which occurs in inshore tropical and subtropical waters of the Atlantic and South Pacific.
● Genus *Seriola*, family Carangidae: several species.
– ORIGIN late 19th cent.: from **AMBER** (because of its yellowish tail) + **JACK**[1].

amber liquid (also **amber fluid**) ▶ noun [mass noun] informal, chiefly Austral. beer.

ambidextrous /ˌambɪˈdɛkstrəs/ ▶ adjective (of a person) able to use the right and left hands equally well: *few of us are naturally ambidextrous*.
■ (of an implement) designed to be used by left-handed and right-handed people with equal ease.
– DERIVATIVES **ambidexterity** noun, **ambidextrously** adverb, **ambidextrousness** noun.
– ORIGIN mid 17th cent.: from late Latin *ambidexter* (from Latin *ambi-* 'on both sides' + *dexter* 'right-handed') + **-OUS**.

ambience /ˈambɪəns/ (also **ambiance**) ▶ noun [usu. in sing.] the character and atmosphere of a place: *the relaxed ambience of the cocktail lounge is popular with guests*.
■ background noise added to a musical recording to give the impression that it was recorded live.
– ORIGIN late 19th cent.: from **AMBIENT** + **-ENCE**, or from French *ambiance*, from *ambiant* 'surrounding'.

ambient /ˈambɪənt/ ▶ adjective [attrib.] of or relating to the immediate environs of something: *the liquid is stored at below ambient temperature*.
■ of or relating to ambient music.
▶ noun (also **ambient music**) [mass noun] a style of instrumental music with electronic textures and no persistent beat, used to create or enhance a mood or atmosphere.
– ORIGIN late 16th cent.: from French *ambiant* or Latin *ambient-* 'going round', from *ambire*.

ambiguity ▶ noun (pl. **-ies**) [mass noun] uncertainty or inexactness of meaning in language: *we can detect no ambiguity in this section of the Act* | [count noun] *ambiguities in such questions are potentially very dangerous*.
■ a lack of decisiveness or commitment resulting from a failure to make a choice between alternatives: *the film is fraught with moral ambiguity*.
– ORIGIN late Middle English: from Old French *ambiguite* or Latin *ambiguitas*, from *ambiguus* 'doubtful' (see **AMBIGUOUS**).

ambiguous /amˈbɪɡjʊəs/ ▶ adjective (of language) open to more than one interpretation; having a double meaning: *the question is rather ambiguous* | *ambiguous phrases*.
■ unclear or inexact because a choice between alternatives has not been made: *this whole society is morally ambiguous* | *the election result was ambiguous*.
– DERIVATIVES **ambiguously** adverb, **ambiguousness** noun.
– ORIGIN early 16th cent. (in the sense 'indistinct, obscure'): from Latin *ambiguus* 'doubtful' (from *ambigere* 'waver, go around', from *ambi-* 'both ways' + *agere* 'to drive') + **-OUS**.

ambisexual /ˌambɪˈsɛksjʊəl, -ʃʊəl/ ▶ adjective bisexual or androgynous.
▶ noun an ambisexual person.
– DERIVATIVES **ambisexually** adverb.
– ORIGIN 1930s: from Latin *ambi-* 'on both sides' + **SEXUAL**.

ambisonic ▶ adjective denoting or relating to a high-fidelity audio system that reproduces the directional and acoustic properties of recorded sound using two or more channels.
▶ noun (**ambisonics**) [treated as sing.] ambisonic reproduction or systems.
– ORIGIN 1970s: from Latin *ambi-* 'on both sides' + **SONIC**.

ambit /ˈambɪt/ ▶ noun [in sing.] the scope, extent, or bounds of something: *incitement to religious hatred is outside the ambit of the British law*.
– ORIGIN late Middle English (in the sense 'precincts, environs'): from Latin *ambitus* 'circuit', from *ambire* 'go round'.

ambition ▶ noun a strong desire to do or achieve something, typically requiring determination and hard work: *her ambition was to become a model* | *he achieved his ambition of making a fortune*.
■ [mass noun] desire and determination to achieve success: *life offered few opportunities for young people with ambition*.
– ORIGIN Middle English: via Old French from Latin *ambitio(n-)*, from *ambire* 'go around (canvassing for votes)'.

ambitious ▶ adjective having or showing a strong desire and determination to succeed: *his mother was hard-working and ambitious for her four children*.
■ (of a plan or piece of work) intended to satisfy high aspirations and therefore difficult to achieve: *the scope of the book is very ambitious* | *an ambitious enterprise*.
– DERIVATIVES **ambitiously** adverb, **ambitiousness** noun.
– ORIGIN late Middle English: from Old French *ambitieux* or Latin *ambitiosus*, from *ambitio* (see **AMBITION**).

ambivalent /amˈbɪv(ə)l(ə)nt/ ▶ adjective having mixed feelings or contradictory ideas about something or someone: *some loved her, some hated her, few were ambivalent about her* | *an ambivalent attitude to terrorism*.
– DERIVATIVES **ambivalence** noun, **ambivalently** adverb.
– ORIGIN early 20th cent.: from *ambivalence* (from German *Ambivalenz*), on the pattern of *equivalent*.

ambivert /ˈambɪvəːt/ ▶ noun Psychology a person who has a balance of extrovert and introvert features in their personality.
– DERIVATIVES **ambiversion** noun.
– ORIGIN 1920s: from Latin *ambi-* 'on both sides', on the pattern of *extrovert* and *introvert*.

amble ▶ verb [no obj., with adverbial of direction] walk or move at a slow, relaxed pace: *they ambled along the riverbank* | *he ambled into the foyer*.
▶ noun a walk at a slow, relaxed pace, especially for pleasure: *a peaceful riverside amble*.
– DERIVATIVES **ambler** noun.
– ORIGIN Middle English (originally denoting a horse's gait): from Old French *ambler*, from Latin *ambulare* 'to walk'.

amblyopia /ˌamblɪˈəʊpɪə/ ▶ noun [mass noun] Medicine impaired or dim vision without obvious defect or change in the eye.
– DERIVATIVES **amblyopic** adjective.
– ORIGIN early 18th cent.: from Greek *ambluōpia* 'dim-sightedness', from *ambluōpos* (adjective), from *amblus* 'dull' + *ōps, ōp-* 'eye'.

ambo /ˈambəʊ/ ▶ noun (pl. **ambos** or **ambones** /-ˈbəʊniːz/) (in an early Christian church) an oblong pulpit with steps at each end.
– ORIGIN mid 17th cent.: via medieval Latin from Greek *ambōn* 'rim' (in medieval Greek 'pulpit').

Ambon /amˈbɒn/ (also **Amboina** /-ˈbɔɪnə/) a mountainous island in eastern Indonesia, one of the Molucca Islands.
■ a port on this island, the capital of the Molucca Islands; pop. 79,636 (1980).
– DERIVATIVES **Ambonese** (also **Amboinese**) noun & adjective.

amboyna /amˈbɔɪnə/ (also **amboyna wood**) ▶ noun [mass noun] the decorative timber of a rapidly growing SE Asian tree, typically used for cabinetmaking.
● The tree is *Pterocarpus indicus*, family Leguminosae.
– ORIGIN mid 19th cent.: named after *Amboina* Island (see **AMBON**).

Ambrose, St /ˈambrəʊz/ (c.339–97), Doctor of the Church, bishop of Milan. A champion of orthodoxy, he also encouraged developments in church music. Feast day, 7 December.
– DERIVATIVES **Ambrosian** adjective.

ambrosia ▶ noun [mass noun] Greek & Roman Mythology the food of the gods.
■ something very pleasing to taste or smell: *the tea was ambrosia after the slop I'd been suffering*. ■ a fungal product used as food by pinhole borers and ambrosia beetles. ■ another term for **BEE BREAD**.
– DERIVATIVES **ambrosial** adjective.
– ORIGIN mid 16th cent.: via Latin from Greek, 'elixir of life', from *ambrotos* 'immortal'.

ambrosia beetle ▶ noun a small dark wood-boring beetle whose adults and larvae both feed on ambrosia produced by fungus in the wood.

• Genus *Platypus* (family Platypodidae), and *Xyleborus* and other genera (family Scolytidae).

ambry /ˈambri/ ▶ **noun** variant spelling of **AUMBRY**.

ambulacrum /ˌambjʊˈleɪkrəm, -ˈlakrəm/ ▶ **noun** (pl. **ambulacra** /-ˈleɪkrə, -ˈlakrə/) Zoology (in an echinoderm) each of the radially arranged bands, together with their underlying structures, through which the double rows of tube feet protrude.
– DERIVATIVES **ambulacral** adjective.
– ORIGIN early 19th cent.: Latin, 'avenue', from *ambulare* 'to walk'.

ambulance ▶ **noun** a vehicle specially equipped for taking sick or injured people to and from hospital, especially in emergencies: [as modifier] *the ambulance service.*
▶ **verb** [with obj. and adverbial of direction] convey (someone) somewhere in an ambulance: *he was ambulanced to accident and emergency.*
– ORIGIN early 19th cent.: French, from *hôpital ambulant* 'mobile (horse-drawn) field hospital', from Latin *ambulant-* 'walking' (see **AMBULANT**).

ambulance-chaser ▶ **noun** derogatory, chiefly N. Amer. a lawyer who specializes in bringing cases seeking damages for personal injury.
– ORIGIN late 19th cent.: from the reputation gained by certain lawyers for attending accidents and encouraging victims to sue.

ambulant /ˈambjʊl(ə)nt/ ▶ **adjective** Medicine (of a patient) able to walk about; not confined to bed.
■ (of treatment) not confining a patient to bed.
– ORIGIN early 17th cent.: from Latin *ambulant-* 'walking', from *ambulare*.

ambulate /ˈambjʊleɪt/ ▶ **verb** [no obj.] formal or technical walk; move about: *people who make use of crutches to ambulate.*
– DERIVATIVES **ambulation** noun.
– ORIGIN early 17th cent.: from Latin *ambulat-* 'walked', from the verb *ambulare*.

ambulatory /ˈambjʊlət(ə)ri/ ▶ **adjective** relating to or adapted for walking.
■ another term for **AMBULANT**. ■ movable; mobile: *an ambulatory ophthalmic service.*
▶ **noun** (pl. **-ies**) a place for walking, especially an aisle or cloister in a church or monastery.
– ORIGIN mid 16th cent. (as a noun): from Latin *ambulatorius*, from *ambulare* 'to walk'.

ambuscade /ˌambəˈskeɪd/ ▶ **noun** dated an ambush.
▶ **verb** [with obj.] archaic attack from an ambush.
■ [no obj.] archaic lie in ambush.
– ORIGIN late 16th cent.: from French *embuscade*, from Italian *imboscata*, Spanish *emboscada*, or Portuguese *embuscada*, based on a late Latin word meaning 'to place in a wood'; related to **BUSH**[1].

ambush ▶ **noun** a surprise attack by people lying in wait in a concealed position: *seven members of a patrol were killed in an ambush* | [mass noun] *there might be terrorists waiting* ***in ambush.***
▶ **verb** [with obj.] (often **be ambushed**) make a surprise attack on (someone) from a concealed position: *they were ambushed and taken prisoner by the enemy* | figurative *Tory representatives were ambushed by camera crews.*
– ORIGIN Middle English (in the sense 'place troops in hiding in order to surprise an enemy'): from Old French *embusche* (noun), *embuschier* (verb), based on a late Latin word meaning 'to place in a wood'; related to **BUSH**[1].

ameba ▶ **noun** (pl. **amebae** or **amebas**) US spelling of **AMOEBA**.
– DERIVATIVES **amebic** adjective, **ameboid** adjective.

amebiasis ▶ **noun** US spelling of **AMOEBIASIS**.

amelanchier /ˌaməˈlaŋkɪə/ ▶ **noun** a shrub of a genus that includes juneberry and snowy mespilus, typically bearing white flowers.
• Genus *Amelanchier*, family Rosaceae.
– ORIGIN from French dialect *amelancier* 'medlar'.

ameliorate /əˈmiːlɪəreɪt/ ▶ **verb** [with obj.] make (something bad or unsatisfactory) better: *the reform did much to ameliorate living standards.*
– DERIVATIVES **amelioration** noun, **ameliorative** adjective, **ameliorator** noun.
– ORIGIN mid 18th cent.: alteration of **MELIORATE**, influenced by French *améliorer*, from *meilleur* 'better'.

amen /ɑːˈmɛn, eɪ-/ ▶ **exclamation** uttered at the end of a prayer or hymn, meaning 'so be it'.
■ used to express agreement or assent: *amen to that!*
▶ **noun** an utterance of 'amen'.
– ORIGIN Old English, from ecclesiastical Latin, from Greek *amēn*, from Hebrew *'āmēn* 'truth, certainty', used adverbially as expression of agreement, and adopted in the Septuagint as a solemn expression of belief or affirmation.

amenable /əˈmiːnəb(ə)l/ ▶ **adjective** open and responsive to suggestion; easily persuaded or controlled: *parents who have had easy babies and amenable children.*
■ [predic.] (**amenable to**) (of a thing) capable of being acted upon in a particular way; susceptible: *the patients had cardiac failure not amenable to medical treatment.*
– DERIVATIVES **amenability** noun, **amenably** adverb.
– ORIGIN late 16th cent. (in the sense 'liable to answer (to a law or tribunal)'): an Anglo-Norman French legal term, from Old French *amener* 'bring to' from *a-* (from Latin *ad*) 'to' + *mener* 'bring' (from late Latin *minare* 'drive (animals)', from Latin *minari* 'threaten').

amend ▶ **verb** [with obj.] make minor changes in (a text or piece of legislation or other ruling) in order to make it fairer or more accurate, or to reflect changing circumstances: *the rule was amended to apply only to non-members.*
■ improve the texture or fertility of (soil): *amend your soil with peat moss or compost.* ■ archaic put right: *a few things had gone wrong, but these had been amended.*
– DERIVATIVES **amendable** adjective, **amender** noun.
– ORIGIN Middle English: from Old French *amender*, based on Latin *emendare* (see **EMEND**).

amende honorable /əˌmɒ̃d ɒnɔːˈrɑːbl(ə), French amɑ̃d ɔnɔʀabl/ ▶ **noun** (pl. **amendes honorables** pronunc. same) poetic/literary a public or open apology, typically with some form of reparation.
– ORIGIN French, literally 'honourable reparation'.

amendment ▶ **noun** a minor change or addition designed to improve something: *an* ***amendment to*** *existing bail laws.*
■ [mass noun] the formal proposing of changes to a bill being considered by Parliament: *it is rare for a bill's main proposals to be overturned by amendment* | [count noun] *a lobby from industry tried to force an amendment.* ■ (**Amendment**) an article added to the US Constitution: *the First Amendment.* ■ something which is added to soil in order to improve its texture or fertility.
– ORIGIN Middle English (in the sense 'improvement, correction'): from Old French *amendement*, from *amender* (see **AMEND**).

amends ▶ **plural noun** [treated as sing.] reparation or compensation: *try to* ***make amends for*** *the rude way you spoke to Lucy.*
– PHRASES **an offer of amends** Law an offer to publish a correction and an apology for an act of libel.
– ORIGIN Middle English: from Old French *amendes* 'penalties, fine', plural of *amende* 'reparation', from *amender* (see **AMEND**).

Amenhotep /ˌɑːmɛnˈhəʊtɛp/ the name of four Egyptian pharaohs of the 18th dynasty; Greek name *Amenophis*.
■ Amenhotep I (16th century BC), son of Ahmose I (founder of the 18th dynasty), reigned 1546–1526.
■ Amenhotep II (15th century BC), son of Hatshepsut and Tuthmosis III, reigned 1450–1425.
■ Amenhotep III (15th–14th centuries BC), son of Tuthmosis IV, reigned 1417–1379. He embarked on an extensive building programme centred on his capital, Thebes, including the colossi of Memnon and the Luxor temple.
■ Amenhotep IV see **AKHENATEN**.

amenity /əˈmiːnɪti, -ˈmɛn-/ ▶ **noun** (pl. **-ies**) (usu. **amenities**) a desirable or useful feature or facility of a building or place: *the property is situated in a convenient location, close to all local amenities.*
■ [mass noun] the pleasantness or attractiveness of a place: *developments which would clash with amenity.*
– ORIGIN late Middle English: from Old French *amenite* or Latin *amoenitas*, from *amoenus* 'pleasant'.

amenity bed ▶ **noun** Brit. a bed in a private room in a National Health Service hospital available for a payment to a patient receiving free treatment.

amenorrhoea /əˌmɛnəˈriːə/ (US **amenorrhea**) ▶ **noun** [mass noun] an abnormal absence of menstruation.
– ORIGIN early 19th cent.: from **A-**[1] 'without' + **MENORRHOEA**.

ament /ˈeɪmənt, əˈmɛnt/ ▶ **noun** Botany a catkin.
– ORIGIN mid 18th cent.: from Latin *amentum* 'thong'.

amentia /eɪˈmɛnʃə, ə-/ ▶ **noun** [mass noun] Medicine, dated severe congenital mental handicap.
– ORIGIN late Middle English: from Latin, literally 'madness', from *amens, ament-* 'mad', from *a-* 'without' + *mens* 'the mind'.

Amerasian /ˌaməˈreɪʃ(ə)n, -ʒ(ə)n/ ▶ **adjective** having one American and one Asian parent.
▶ **noun** a person with one American and one Asian parent.
– ORIGIN 1960s: blend of **AMERICAN** and **ASIAN**.

amercement /əˈməːsmənt/ ▶ **noun** English Law, historical a fine.
– DERIVATIVES **amerce** verb.
– ORIGIN late Middle English: from Anglo-Norman French *amerciment*, based on *estre amercie* 'be at the mercy of another' (with respect to the amount of a fine), from *a merci* 'at (the) mercy'.

America (also **the Americas**) a land mass of the western hemisphere consisting of the continents of North and South America joined by the Isthmus of Panama.
■ used as a name for the United States.

> America was originally inhabited by American Indians and Inuit peoples. The NE coastline of North America was visited by Norse seamen in the early 11th century, but for the modern world America was first reached by Christopher Columbus, who arrived in the Caribbean in 1492 and the South American mainland in 1498.

– ORIGIN the name *America* dates from the early 16th cent. and is believed to derive from the Latin form (*Americus*) of the name of Amerigo Vespucci, who sailed along the west coast of South America in 1501.

American ▶ **adjective** of, relating to, or characteristic of the United States or its inhabitants: *the election of a new American president.*
■ relating to or denoting the continents of America: *the American continent south of the tropic of Cancer.*
▶ **noun 1** a native or citizen of the United States.
■ a native or inhabitant of any of the countries of North, South, or Central America.
2 [mass noun] the English language as it is used in the United States; American English.
– DERIVATIVES **Americanness** noun.
– ORIGIN from modern Latin *Americanus*, from **AMERICA**.

Americana /əˌmɛrɪˈkɑːnə/ ▶ **plural noun** things associated with America, especially the United States.

American aloe ▶ **noun** another term for **CENTURY PLANT**.

American blackbird ▶ **noun** see **BLACKBIRD** (sense 2).

American chameleon ▶ **noun** see **CHAMELEON**.

American Civil War the war between the northern US states (usually known as the Union) and the Confederate states of the South, 1861–5.

> The war was fought over the issues of slavery and states' rights. The pro-slavery Southern states seceded from the Federal Union following the election of Abraham Lincoln on an anti-slavery platform, but were defeated by the North after failing to gain foreign recognition.

American depositary receipt (also **American depositary share**) ▶ **noun** (in the US) a negotiable certificate of title to a number of shares in a non-US company which are deposited in an overseas bank.

American dream ▶ **noun** the traditional social ideals of the United States, such as equality, democracy, and material prosperity.

American English ▶ **noun** [mass noun] the English language as spoken and written in the US.

> As well as differences from British English in spelling, pronunciation, and grammar, there are specifically American uses of words and meanings, principally: adoptions from languages with which the early settlers came in contact (*moccasin, prairie*), changes in meaning (*corn, vest*), survivals of 17th- and 18th-century English (*gotten*), and different words for the same referent (*elevator* for *lift*).

American Federation of Labor a federation of North American trade unions, merged in 1955 with the Congress of Industrial Organizations to form the American Federation of Labor and Congress of Industrial Organizations (AFL-CIO).

American football ▶ **noun** [mass noun] a kind of football played with an oval ball on a field marked out as a gridiron. Points are scored mainly through touchdowns and goals. Each side has eleven players on the field at any time. In the US called simply **FOOTBALL**.

a

American Independence, War of the war of 1775–83 in which the American colonists won independence from British rule. Called in the US and Canada the **AMERICAN REVOLUTION**.

The war was triggered by resentment of the economic policies of Britain, particularly the right of Parliament to tax the colonies, and by the exclusion of the colonists from participation in political decisions affecting their interests. Following disturbances such as the Boston Tea Party of 1773, fighting broke out in 1775; a year later the Declaration of Independence was signed. The Americans gained the support of France and Spain, and French sea power eventually played a crucial role in the decisive surrender of a British army at Yorktown in 1781.

American Indian ▶ **noun** a member of any of the groups of indigenous peoples of North, Central, and South America, especially those of North America.
▶ **adjective** of or relating to any of these groups.

USAGE The term **American Indian** has been steadily replaced in the US, especially in official contexts, by the more recent term **Native American** (first recorded in the 1950s and becoming prominent in the 1970s). The latter is preferred by some as being a more accurate and respectful description (the word **Indian** recalling Columbus' assumption that, on reaching America, he had reached the east coast of India), as well as avoiding the stereotype of cowboys and Indians in the stories of the Wild West. **American Indian** is still widespread in general use even in the US, however, perhaps at least partly owing to the fact that it is not normally regarded as offensive by American Indians themselves, and it is the term used in this dictionary. Nevertheless, since the category **American Indian** is very broad, it is preferable, where possible, to name the specific people, as **Apache**, **Comanche**, or **Sioux**. See also **usage** at **NATIVE AMERICAN** and comments at **AMERINDIAN**.

Americanism ▶ **noun** a word or phrase peculiar to or originating in the United States.
■ [mass noun] the qualities regarded as definitive of America and Americans: *the vigilantes felt he did not conform to their definition of Americanism.*

Americanize (also **-ise**) ▶ **verb** [with obj.] make American in character or nationality: *trying to Americanize the immigrant children* | [as adj. **Americanized**] *an Americanized accent.*
– DERIVATIVES **Americanization** /-ˈzeɪʃ(ə)n/ noun.

American Legion (in the US) an association of ex-servicemen formed in 1919.

American organ ▶ **noun** a type of reed organ resembling the harmonium but in which air is sucked (not blown) through reeds.

American plan ▶ **noun** North American term for **FULL BOARD**. Often contrasted with **EUROPEAN PLAN**.

American Revolution US and Canadian term for **WAR OF AMERICAN INDEPENDENCE**.

American Saddle Horse ▶ **noun** a light, strong horse of a breed developed in America to be comfortable to ride over long distances.

American Samoa an unincorporated overseas territory of the US comprising a group of islands in the southern Pacific Ocean, to the east of Samoa and south of the Kiribati group; pop. 46,770 (1990); capital, Fagatogo. In 1899 the US acquired rights to the islands by agreement with Germany and Britain, and in April 1900 the two main islands were ceded to the US by their chiefs. Further islands were handed over in succeeding years.

American Sign Language ▶ **noun** [mass noun] a form of sign language developed in the US for the use of the deaf, consisting of over 4,000 signs.

American Standard Version (abbrev.: **ASV**) ▶ **noun** an English translation of the Bible published in the US in 1901, based on the Revised Version of 1881–95 with additional work by American scholars.

American wormseed ▶ **noun** see **WORMSEED**.

Americas (**the Americas**) another name for **AMERICA**.

America's Cup an international yachting race held every three to four years.

americium /ˌaməˈrɪsjəm/ ▶ **noun** [mass noun] the chemical element of atomic number 95, a radioactive metal of the actinide series. Americium does not occur naturally and was first made by bombarding plutonium with neutrons. (Symbol: **Am**)
– ORIGIN 1940s: from **AMERICA** (where it was first made) + **-IUM**.

Amerindian /ˌaməˈrɪndɪən/ (also **Amerind** /ˈamərɪnd/) ▶ **adjective** & **noun** another term for **AMERICAN INDIAN**, used chiefly in anthropological and linguistic contexts.
– ORIGIN late 19th cent.: blend of **AMERICAN** and **INDIAN**.

Ameslan /ˈamɪslan/ ▶ **noun** another term for **AMERICAN SIGN LANGUAGE**.
– ORIGIN 1970s: acronym.

Ames test /eɪmz/ ▶ **noun** Medicine a test to determine the mutagenic activity of chemicals by observing whether they cause mutations in sample bacteria.
– ORIGIN 1970s: named after Bruce N. *Ames* (born 1928), the American biochemist who devised it.

amethyst /ˈaməθɪst/ ▶ **noun** [mass noun] a precious stone consisting of a violet or purple variety of quartz.
■ a violet or purple colour: [as modifier] *an amethyst dress.*
– DERIVATIVES **amethystine** /-ˈθɪstiːn/ adjective.
– ORIGIN Middle English: via Old French from Latin *amethystus*, from Greek *amethustos* 'not drunken' (because the stone was believed to prevent intoxication).

amethyst deceiver ▶ **noun** an edible woodland mushroom with a lilac cap and stem, found in both Eurasia and North America.
• *Laccaria amethystea*, family Tricholomataceae, class Hymenomycetes.

Amex ▶ **abbreviation for** ■ trademark American Express. ■ American Stock Exchange.

Amhara /amˈhɑːrə/ ▶ **noun** (pl. same or **Amharas**) a member of a Semitic people of central Ethiopia.

Amharic /amˈharɪk/ ▶ **noun** [mass noun] the official language of Ethiopia, a Semitic language descended from Ge'ez and spoken by about 9 million people.
▶ **adjective** of or relating to this language.
– ORIGIN mid 18th cent.: from **AMHARA** + **-IC**.

amiable ▶ **adjective** having or displaying a friendly and pleasant manner: *the amiable young man greeted me enthusiastically.*
– DERIVATIVES **amiability** noun, **amiableness** noun, **amiably** adverb.
– ORIGIN late Middle English (originally in the senses 'kind', and 'lovely, lovable'): via Old French from late Latin *amicabilis* 'amicable'. The current sense, influenced by modern French *aimable* 'trying to please', dates from the mid 18th cent.

amianthus /ˌamɪˈanθəs/ ▶ **noun** [mass noun] a variety of asbestos with fine silky fibres which can be woven.
– ORIGIN early 17th cent.: from Latin *amiantus*, from Greek *amiantos* 'undefiled' (i.e. purified of stains by fire, it being incombustible), from *a-* 'not' + *miainein* 'defile'. The spelling was changed from the Latin on the pattern of plant names ending in *-anthus*, from Greek *anthos* 'flower'.

amicable /ˈamɪkəb(ə)l/ ▶ **adjective** (of relations between people) having a spirit of friendliness; without serious disagreement or rancour: *there will be an amicable settlement of the dispute* | *the meeting was relatively amicable.*
– DERIVATIVES **amicability** noun, **amicableness** noun, **amicably** adverb.
– ORIGIN late Middle English (in the sense 'pleasant, benign', applied to things): from late Latin *amicabilis*, from Latin *amicus* 'friend'.

amicable numbers ▶ **plural noun** Mathematics a pair of numbers, each of which is the sum of the factors of the other (e.g. 220 and 284).

amice[1] /ˈamɪs/ ▶ **noun** a white linen cloth worn on the neck and shoulders, under the alb, by a priest celebrating the Eucharist.
– ORIGIN late Middle English: from medieval Latin *amicia*, *amisia*, of unknown origin.

amice[2] /ˈamɪs/ ▶ **noun** a cap, hood, or cape worn by members of certain religious orders.
– ORIGIN late Middle English: from Old French *aumusse*, from medieval Latin *almucia*, of unknown origin.

amicus /aˈmʌɪkəs/ (in full **amicus curiae** /ˈkjʊərɪiː/) ▶ **noun** (pl. **amici** /-siː/, **amici curiae**) an impartial adviser to a court of law in a particular case.
– ORIGIN early 17th cent.: modern Latin, literally 'friend', (in full) 'friend of the court'.

amid ▶ **preposition** surrounded by; in the middle of: *our dream home, set amid magnificent rolling countryside.*
■ in an atmosphere or against a background of: *talks broke down amid accusations of a hostile takeover bid.*
– ORIGIN Middle English *amidde(s)* (see **A**[2], **MID**).

Amidah /əˈmiːdə/ ▶ **noun** Judaism a prayer, part of the Jewish liturgy, consisting of a varying number of blessings recited while the worshippers stand.
– ORIGIN late 19th cent.: Hebrew, literally 'standing'.

amide /ˈeɪmʌɪd, ˈamʌɪd/ ▶ **noun** Chemistry an organic compound containing the group $—C(O)NH_2$, related to ammonia by replacing a hydrogen atom by an acyl group.
■ a compound derived from ammonia by replacement of a hydrogen atom by a metal, containing the anion NH_2^-.
– ORIGIN mid 19th cent.: from **AMMONIA** + **-IDE**.

amidships (US also **amidship**) ▶ **adverb** & **adjective** in the middle of a ship, either longitudinally or laterally: [as adv.] *the destroyer rammed her amidships* | [as adj.] *an amidships engine room.*
– ORIGIN late 17th cent.: from **A-**[2] (expressing position or direction) + **MIDSHIP**, influenced by **AMID**.

amidst ▶ **preposition** poetic/literary variant of **AMID**.

Amiens /ˈamɪənz, French amjɛ̃/ a town in northern France; pop. 136,230 (1990).

amigo /əˈmiːɡəʊ/ ▶ **noun** (pl. **-os**) informal, chiefly N. Amer. used to address or refer to a friend, chiefly in Spanish-speaking areas.
– ORIGIN mid 19th cent.: Spanish.

Amin /aˈmiːn/, Idi (b.1925), Ugandan soldier and head of state 1971–9; full name *Idi Amin Dada*. Amin overthrew President Obote in a coup, and was deposed after a period of rule characterized by the murder of political opponents and the expulsion of non-Africans.

Amindivi Islands /ˌamɪnˈdiːvi/ the northernmost group of islands in the Indian territory of Lakshadweep in the Indian Ocean.

amine /ˈeɪmiːn/ ▶ **noun** Chemistry an organic compound derived from ammonia by replacement of one or more hydrogen atoms by organic radicals. Amines are distinguished as **primary** (RNH_2), **secondary** (R_2NH), and **tertiary amines** (R_3N), where R is an organic group.
– ORIGIN mid 19th cent.: from **AMMONIA** + **-INE**[4].

amino /əˈmiːnəʊ, əˈmʌɪnəʊ/ ▶ **noun** [as modifier] Chemistry the group $—NH_2$, present in amino acids, amides, and many amines.
– ORIGIN late 19th cent.: from **AMINE**.

amino acid ▶ **noun** Biochemistry a simple organic compound containing both a carboxyl ($—COOH$) and an amino ($—NH_2$) group.

Amino acids occur naturally in plant and animal tissues and form the basic constituents of proteins. There are about twenty common amino acids, of which the simplest is glycine (H_2NCH_2COOH).

amir /əˈmɪə/ ▶ **noun** variant spelling of **EMIR**.
– ORIGIN late 16th cent.: from Persian and Urdu, from Arabic *'amīr* 'commander', from *'amara* 'to command'; compare with **EMIR**.

Amirante Islands /ˈamɪrant, ˌamɪˈranti/ a group of coral islands in the Indian Ocean, forming part of the Seychelles.

Amis[1] /ˈeɪmɪs/, Sir Kingsley (1922–95), English novelist. He achieved popular success with his first novel *Lucky Jim* (1954); his later novels include *The Old Devils* (Booker Prize, 1986) and *The Folks that Live on the Hill* (1990).

Amis[2] /ˈeɪmɪs/, Martin (Louis) (b.1949), English novelist, son of Kingsley Amis. Notable works: *The Rachel Papers* (1973), *Money* (1984), and *Time's Arrow* (1991).

Amish /ˈamɪʃ, ˈɑː-, ˈeɪ-/ ▶ **plural noun** the members of a strict Mennonite sect which established major settlements in Pennsylvania, Ohio, and elsewhere in North America from 1720 onwards.
▶ **adjective** of or relating to this sect.
– ORIGIN mid 19th cent.: apparently from German *amisch*, from the name Jakob *Amman* (c.1645–c.1730), a Swiss preacher.

amiss ▶ **adjective** [predic.] not quite right, inappropriate or out of place: *there was something amiss about his calculations.*
▶ **adverb** dated wrongly or inappropriately: *the prime minister may have constructed his cabinet a little amiss.*
– PHRASES **take something amiss** be offended by

something that is said, especially through misinterpreting the intentions behind it. **something would not go** (or **come**) **amiss** the specified thing would be welcome and useful: *you look as if a good meal wouldn't come amiss.*
– ORIGIN Middle English: probably from Old Norse *á mis* 'so as to miss', from *á* 'on' + *mis* (related to **MISS**[1]).

amitotic /ˌeɪmaɪˈtɒtɪk, ˌamaɪ-/ ▶ **adjective** Biology relating to or denoting the division of a cell nucleus without mitosis.
– DERIVATIVES **amitosis** noun, **amitotically** adverb.

amitriptyline /ˌamɪˈtrɪptɪliːn/ ▶ **noun** [mass noun] Medicine an antidepressant drug of the tricyclic group, with a mild tranquillizing action.
– ORIGIN 1960s: from *ami(ne)* + **TRI-** + *(he)ptyl* + **-INE**[4].

amity /ˈamɪti/ ▶ **noun** [mass noun] a friendly relationship.
– ORIGIN late Middle English: from Old French *amitie*, based on Latin *amicus* 'friend'.

amma /ˈʌmɑː/ ▶ **noun** Indian informal one's mother (often used as a familiar form of address).
– ORIGIN probably derived from a child's word, perhaps influenced by **AMAH**.

Amman /əˈmɑːn/ the capital of Jordan; pop. 965,000 (est. 1991).

ammeter /ˈamɪtə/ ▶ **noun** an instrument for measuring electric current in amperes.
– ORIGIN late 19th cent.: from **AMPERE** + **-METER**.

ammo /ˈaməʊ/ ▶ **noun** informal term for **AMMUNITION**.

Ammon Greek and Roman form of **AMUN**.

ammonia /əˈməʊnɪə/ ▶ **noun** [mass noun] a colourless gas with a characteristic pungent smell, which dissolves in water to give a strongly alkaline solution.
● Chem. formula: NH_3.
■ a solution of this gas, used as a cleaning fluid.
– ORIGIN late 18th cent.: modern Latin, from *sal ammoniacus* (see **SAL AMMONIAC**).

ammoniacal /ˌamə(ʊ)ˈnʌɪək(ə)l/ ▶ **adjective** of or containing ammonia.
– ORIGIN mid 18th cent.: from Middle English *ammoniac*, via Old French from Latin *ammoniacus*. This represented the Greek word *ammōniakos* 'of Ammon', used as a name for the salt and gum obtained near the temple of *Jupiter Ammon* at Siwa in Egypt. Compare with **SAL AMMONIAC**.

ammoniated ▶ **adjective** combined or treated with ammonia.

ammonite /ˈamənʌɪt/ ▶ **noun** an ammonoid fossil, especially one of a later type found chiefly in the Jurassic and Cretaceous periods, typically with intricately frilled suture lines. Compare with **CERATITE** and **GONIATITE**.
● Typified by ammonoids of the order Ammonitida.
– ORIGIN mid 18th cent.: from modern Latin *ammonites*, from medieval Latin *cornu Ammonis* 'horn of Ammon', from the fossil's resemblance to the ram's horn associated with Jupiter Ammon (see **AMMONIACAL**).

ammonium /əˈməʊnɪəm/ ▶ **noun** [as modifier] Chemistry the cation NH_4^+, present in solutions of ammonia and in salts derived from ammonia.
– ORIGIN early 19th cent.: from **AMMONIA** + **-IUM**.

ammonium carbonate ▶ **noun** [mass noun] Chemistry a white crystalline solid which slowly decomposes giving off ammonia and is an ingredient of sal volatile.
● Chem. formula: $(NH_4)_2CO_3$. Commercial forms often contain other, related, salts.

ammonium chloride ▶ **noun** [mass noun] Chemistry a white crystalline salt used chiefly in dry cells, as a mordant, and as soldering flux. Also called **SAL AMMONIAC**.
● Chem. formula: NH_4Cl.

ammonium nitrate ▶ **noun** [mass noun] Chemistry a white crystalline solid used as a fertilizer and as a component of some explosives.
● Chem. formula: NH_4NO_3.

ammonoid /ˈamənɔɪd/ Palaeontology ▶ **noun** an extinct cephalopod mollusc with a flat-coiled spiral shell, found commonly as a fossil in marine deposits from the Devonian to the Cretaceous periods.
● Subclass Ammonoidea, class Cephalopoda: numerous families. See **AMMONITE**, **CERATITE**, and **GONIATITE**.
▶ **adjective** of or relating to the ammonoids.

– ORIGIN mid 19th cent.: from modern Latin *Ammonoidea*, based on **AMMON** (see **AMMONITE**).

ammunition ▶ **noun** [mass noun] a supply or quantity of bullets and shells.
■ figurative considerations that can be used to support one's case in debate: *these figures provide ammunition to the argument for more resources.*
– ORIGIN late 16th cent.: from obsolete French *amunition*, alteration (by wrong division) of *la munition* 'the munition' (see **MUNITION**).

amnesia /amˈniːzɪə/ ▶ **noun** [mass noun] a partial or total loss of memory.
– DERIVATIVES **amnesiac** noun & adjective, **amnesic** adjective & noun.
– ORIGIN late 18th cent.: from Greek *amnēsia* 'forgetfulness'.

amnesty ▶ **noun** (pl. **-ies**) an official pardon for people who have been convicted of political offences: *an amnesty for political prisoners* | [mass noun] *the new law granted amnesty to those who illegally left the country.*
■ an undertaking by the authorities to take no action against specified offences or offenders during a fixed period: *a month-long weapons amnesty.*
▶ **verb** (**-ies**, **-ied**) [with obj.] grant an official pardon to: *the guerrillas would be amnestied and allowed to return to civilian life.*
– ORIGIN late 16th cent.: via Latin from Greek *amnēstia* 'forgetfulness'.

Amnesty International an independent international organization in support of human rights, especially for prisoners of conscience. The organization was awarded the Nobel Peace Prize in 1977.

amnio /ˈamnɪəʊ/ ▶ **noun** (pl. **-os**) informal term for **AMNIOCENTESIS**.

amniocentesis /ˌamnɪəʊsɛnˈtiːsɪs/ ▶ **noun** (pl. **amniocenteses** /-siːz/) a process in which amniotic fluid is sampled using a hollow needle inserted into the uterus, to screen for abnormalities in the developing fetus.
– ORIGIN 1950s: from **AMNION** + Greek *kentēsis* 'pricking' (from *kentein* 'to prick').

amnion /ˈamnɪən/ ▶ **noun** (pl. **amnions** or **amnia**) the innermost membrane that encloses the embryo of a mammal, bird, or reptile.
– ORIGIN mid 17th cent.: from Greek, 'caul', diminutive of *amnos* 'lamb'.

amniote /ˈamnɪəʊt/ ▶ **noun** Zoology an animal whose embryo develops in an amnion and chorion and has an allantois; a mammal, bird, or reptile.
– ORIGIN late 19th cent.: from modern Latin *Amniota*, back-formation from **AMNIOTIC**.

amniotic ▶ **adjective** of or relating to the amnion.
– ORIGIN early 19th cent.: formed irregularly from obsolete *amnios* 'amnion' + **-OTIC**, perhaps via French *amniotique*.

amniotic fluid ▶ **noun** [mass noun] the fluid surrounding a fetus within the amnion.

amn't /ˈam(ə)nt/ chiefly Scottish & Irish ▶ **contraction of** am not.

amoeba /əˈmiːbə/ (US also **ameba**) ▶ **noun** (pl. **amoebas** or **amoebae** /-biː/) a single-celled animal which catches food and moves about by extending finger-like projections of protoplasm. Amoebas are either free-living in damp environments or parasitic.
● Many families and genera in the phylum Rhizopoda, kingdom Protista, including the aquatic *Amoeba proteus*.
– DERIVATIVES **amoebic** adjective, **amoeboid** adjective.
– ORIGIN mid 19th cent.: modern Latin, from Greek *amoibē* 'change, alternation'.

amoebiasis /ˌamiːˈbʌɪəsɪs/ (US also **amebiasis**) ▶ **noun** [mass noun] Medicine infection with amoebas, especially as causing dysentery.
– ORIGIN early 20th cent.: from **AMOEBA** + **-ASIS**.

amok /əˈmɒk/ (also **amuck**) ▶ **adverb** (in phrase **run amok**) behave uncontrollably and disruptively: *with stone-throwing anarchists running amok* | figurative *her feelings seemed to be running amok.*
– ORIGIN mid 17th cent.: via Portuguese *amouco*, from Malay *amok* 'rushing in a frenzy'. Early use was as a noun denoting a Malay in a homicidal frenzy; the adverb use dates from the late 17th cent.

Amon variant spelling of **AMUN**.

among (chiefly Brit. also **amongst**) ▶ **preposition**
1 situated more or less centrally in relation to

(several other things): *wild narcissi hidden among the roots of the trees* | *you're among friends.*
2 being a member or members of (a larger set): *a British woman was among the 54 victims of the disaster* | *snakes are among the animals most feared by man.*
3 occurring in or shared or practised by (some members of a community): *a drop in tooth decay among children* | *this pronunciation is not popular among the general public.*
■ involving most or all members of a group reciprocally: *members of the government bickered among themselves.*
4 indicating a division, choice, or differentiation involving three or more participants: *the old king called the three princesses to divide his kingdom among them* | *choosing a privatization scheme from among five models.*
– ORIGIN Old English *ongemang* (from *on* 'in' + *gemang* 'assemblage, mingling'). The *-st* of *amongst* represents *-s* (adverbial genitive) + *-t* probably by association with superlatives (as in *against*).

amontillado /əˌmɒntɪˈlɑːdəʊ, -ˈljɑː-/ ▶ **noun** (pl. **-os**) [mass noun] a medium dry sherry.
– ORIGIN Spanish, from *Montilla*, the name of a town in southern Spain where the original wine was produced.

amoral /eɪˈmɒr(ə)l/ ▶ **adjective** lacking a moral sense; unconcerned with the rightness or wrongness of something: *an amoral attitude to sex.*
– DERIVATIVES **amoralism** noun, **amoralist** noun, **amorality** noun.

USAGE Amoral is distinct in meaning from **immoral**: while **immoral** means 'not conforming to accepted standards of morality', **amoral** implies 'not concerned with morality'. The difference is illustrated in the following two examples: *the client pays for the amoral expertise of the lawyer; the council judged the film to be immoral and obscene.*

amoretto /ˌaməˈrɛtəʊ/ ▶ **noun** (pl. **amoretti** /-ti/) a representation of Cupid in a work of art.
– ORIGIN (denoting a lover or a love song): Italian, diminutive of *amore* 'love', from Latin *amor*.

amorist /ˈamərɪst/ ▶ **noun** a person who is in love or who writes about love.
– ORIGIN late 16th cent.: from Latin *amor* or French *amour* 'love' + **-IST**.

Amorite /ˈamərʌɪt/ ▶ **noun** a member of a semi-nomadic people living in Mesopotamia, Palestine, and Syria in the 3rd millennium BC, founders of Mari on the Euphrates and the first dynasty of Babylon.
▶ **adjective** of or relating to this people.
– ORIGIN from Hebrew *'ĕmōrī* + **-ITE**[1].

amoroso[1] /ˌaməˈrəʊzəʊ, -səʊ/ ▶ **adverb** & **adjective** Music (especially as a direction) in a loving or tender manner.
– ORIGIN Italian, from medieval Latin *amorosus* (see **AMOROUS**).

amoroso[2] /ˌaməˈrəʊzəʊ, -səʊ/ ▶ **noun** [mass noun] a dark, sweet sherry.
– ORIGIN from Spanish, literally 'amorous', from medieval Latin *amorosus* (see **AMOROUS**).

amorous ▶ **adjective** showing, feeling, or relating to sexual desire: *she rejected his amorous advances.*
– DERIVATIVES **amorously** adverb, **amorousness** noun.
– ORIGIN Middle English: via Old French from medieval Latin *amorosus*, from Latin *amor* 'love'.

amorphous /əˈmɔːfəs/ ▶ **adjective** without a clearly defined shape or form: *an amorphous, characterless conurbation.*
■ (of a group of people or an organization) lacking a clear structure or focus: *an amorphous and leaderless legislature.* ■ Mineralogy & Chemistry (of a solid) not crystalline, or not apparently crystalline.
– DERIVATIVES **amorphously** adverb, **amorphousness** noun.
– ORIGIN mid 18th cent.: from modern Latin *amorphus*, from Greek *amorphos* 'shapeless' (from *a-* 'without' + *morphē* 'form') + **-OUS**.

amortize /əˈmɔːtʌɪz/ (also **-ise**) ▶ **verb** [with obj.] write off the initial cost of (an asset) by instalments over a period or by charging to a number of different cost centres.
■ reduce or extinguish (a debt) by money regularly put aside. ■ historical transfer (land) to a corporation in mortmain.
– DERIVATIVES **amortization** noun.
– ORIGIN late Middle English (in the senses 'deaden'

and 'transfer (land) to a corporation in mortmain'): from Old French *amortiss-*, lengthened stem of *amortir*, based on Latin *ad* 'to, at' + *mors, mort-* 'death'.

Amos /ˈeɪmɒs/ a Hebrew minor prophet (*c.*760 BC), a shepherd of Tekoa, near Jerusalem.
▪ a book of the Bible containing his prophecies.

amosite /ˈeɪməsʌɪt/ ▶ **noun** [mass noun] an iron-rich amphibole asbestos, mined in South Africa.
– ORIGIN early 20th cent.: from the initial letters of Asbestos Mines of South Africa + **-ITE**[1].

amount ▶ **noun** a quantity of something, especially the total of a thing or things in number, size, value, or extent: *sport gives an enormous* **amount** *of pleasure to many people* | *the substance is harmless if taken in small amounts.*
▪ a sum of money: *they have spent a colossal amount rebuilding the stadium.*
▶ **verb** [no obj.] (**amount to**) come to be (the total) when added together: *losses amounted to over 10 million pounds.*
▪ be the equivalent of: *their actions amounted to a conspiracy.*
– PHRASES **any amount of** a great deal or number of: *the second half produced any amount of action.* **no amount of** not even the greatest possible amount of: *no amount of talk is going to change anything.*
– ORIGIN Middle English (as a verb): from Old French *amunter*, from *amont* 'upward', literally 'uphill', from Latin *ad montem*. The noun use dates from the early 18th cent.

amour /əˈmʊə/ ▶ **noun** a love affair or lover, especially one that is secret: *he is enraged at this revelation of his past amours.*
– ORIGIN Middle English (originally in the sense 'love, affection'): via Old French from Latin *amor* 'love'. The current sense dates from the late 16th cent.

amour courtois /əˌmʊə kɔːˈtwɑ, French amuʀ kuʀtwa/ ▶ **noun** another term for **COURTLY LOVE**.
– ORIGIN French.

amour fou /əˌmʊə ˈfuː, French amuʀ fu/ ▶ **noun** [mass noun] uncontrollable or obsessive passion.
– ORIGIN 1970s: French, 'insane love'.

amour propre /aˌmʊə ˈprɒpr(ə), French amuʀ pʀɔpʀ/ ▶ **noun** [mass noun] a sense of one's own worth; self-respect: *Pablo's amour propre must have been tested by his short stature.*
– ORIGIN French.

Amoy /əˈmɔɪ/ another name for **XIAMEN**.

AMP Biochemistry ▶ **abbreviation for** adenosine monophosphate.

amp[1] ▶ **noun** short for **AMPERE**.

amp[2] ▶ **noun** informal short for **AMPLIFIER**.

ampelopsis /ˌampɪˈlɒpsɪs/ ▶ **noun** (pl. same) a bushy climbing plant of the vine family.
● Genus *Ampelopsis*, family Vitaceae: two species, especially the North American *A. cordata*.
– ORIGIN modern Latin, from Greek *ampelos* 'vine' + *opsis* 'appearance'.

amperage /ˈamp(ə)rɪdʒ/ ▶ **noun** the strength of an electric current in amperes.

Ampère /ˈampɛː, French ɑ̃pɛʀ/, André-Marie (1775–1836), French physicist, mathematician, and philosopher, who analysed the relationship between magnetic force and electric current.

ampere /ˈampɛː/ (abbrev.: **A**) ▶ **noun** a unit of electric current equal to a flow of one coulomb per second.
● The SI base unit of electric current, 1 ampere is precisely defined as that constant current which, if maintained in two straight parallel conductors of infinite length, of negligible circular cross section, and placed 1 metre apart in a vacuum, would produce between these conductors a force of 2×10^{-7} newton per metre.
– ORIGIN late 19th cent.: named after A-M **AMPÈRE**.

ampersand /ˈampəsand/ ▶ **noun** the sign & (standing for *and*, as in *Smith & Co.*, or the Latin *et*, as in *&c.*).
– ORIGIN mid 19th cent.: alteration of *and per se and* '& by itself is *and*', chanted as an aid to learning the sign.

amphetamine /amˈfɛtəmiːn, -ɪn/ ▶ **noun** [mass noun] a synthetic, addictive, mood-altering drug, used illegally as a stimulant.
▪ [count noun] a tablet of this drug.

Alternative name: 1-phenyl-2-aminopropane (or one of its salts, especially **amphetamine sulphate**); chem. formula: $C_6H_5CH_2CH(CH_3)NH_2$.

– ORIGIN 1930s: abbreviation of its chemical name, *a(lpha-)m(ethyl) phe(ne)t(hyl)amine.*

amphi- /ˈamfi/ ▶ **combining form 1** both: *amphibian*.
▪ of both kinds: *amphipod*. ▪ on both sides: *amphiprostyle*.
2 around: *amphitheatre*.
– ORIGIN from Greek.

amphibian ▶ **noun** Zoology a cold-blooded vertebrate animal of a class that comprises the frogs, toads, newts, salamanders, and caecilians. They are distinguished by having an aquatic gill-breathing larval stage followed (typically) by a terrestrial lung-breathing adult stage.
● Class Amphibia: orders Urodela (newts and salamanders), Anura (frogs and toads), and Gymnophiona (caecilians).
▪ a seaplane, tank, or other vehicle that can operate on land and on water.
▶ **adjective** Zoology of or relating to this class of animals: *amphibian eggs.*
– ORIGIN mid 17th cent. (in the sense 'having two modes of existence or of doubtful nature'): from modern Latin *amphibium* 'an amphibian', from Greek *amphibion* (noun use of *amphibios* 'living both in water and on land', from *amphi* 'both' + *bios* 'life').

amphibious /amˈfɪbɪəs/ ▶ **adjective** relating to, living in, or suited for both land and water: *an amphibious vehicle.*
▪ (of a military operation) involving forces landed from the sea: *an amphibious assault.* ▪ (of forces) trained for such operations.
– DERIVATIVES **amphibiously** adverb.
– ORIGIN mid 17th cent.: from modern Latin *amphibium*, from Greek *amphibion* (see **AMPHIBIAN**) + **-OUS**.

amphibole /ˈamfɪbəʊl/ ▶ **noun** any of a class of rock-forming silicate or aluminosilicate minerals typically occurring as fibrous or columnar crystals.
– ORIGIN early 19th cent.: from French, from Latin *amphibolus* 'ambiguous' (because of the varied structure of these minerals), from Greek *amphibolos*, from *amphi-* 'both, on both sides' + *ballein* 'to throw'.

amphibolite /amˈfɪbəlʌɪt/ ▶ **noun** [mass noun] Geology a granular metamorphic rock consisting mainly of hornblende and plagioclase.
– ORIGIN early 19th cent.: from **AMPHIBOLE** + **-ITE**[1].

amphibology /ˌamfɪˈbɒlədʒi/ ▶ **noun** (pl. **-ies**) a phrase or sentence that is grammatically ambiguous, such as *She sees more of her children than her husband.*
– ORIGIN late Middle English: from Old French *amphibologie*, from late Latin *amphibologia*, from Latin *amphibolia*, from Greek *amphibolos* 'ambiguous' (see **AMPHIBOLE**).

amphiboly /amˈfɪbəli/ ▶ **noun** (pl. **-ies**) another term for **AMPHIBOLOGY**.

amphibrach /ˈamfɪbrak/ ▶ **noun** Prosody a metrical foot consisting of a stressed syllable between two unstressed syllables or (in Greek and Latin) a long syllable between two short syllables.
– ORIGIN late 16th cent. (originally in the Latin forms *amphibrachus, amphibrachys*): via Latin from Greek *amphibrakhus* 'short at both ends'.

amphimixis /ˌamfɪˈmɪksɪs/ ▶ **noun** [mass noun] Botany sexual reproduction involving the fusion of two different gametes to form a zygote. Often contrasted with **APOMIXIS**.
– DERIVATIVES **amphimictic** adjective.
– ORIGIN late 19th cent.: from **AMPHI-** + Greek *mixis* 'mingling'.

amphioxus /ˌamfɪˈɒksəs/ ▶ **noun** a small lancelet which is caught for food in parts of Asia.
● Genus *Branchiostoma* (formerly *Amphioxus*), family Branchiostomidae.
– ORIGIN mid 19th cent.: modern Latin, from **AMPHI-** + Greek *oxus* 'sharp'.

amphipathic /ˌamfɪˈpaθɪk/ ▶ **adjective** Biochemistry (of a molecule, especially a protein) having both hydrophilic and hydrophobic parts.
– ORIGIN 1930s: from **AMPHI-** + Greek *pathikos* (from *pathos* 'experience').

amphiphilic /ˌamfɪˈfɪlɪk/ ▶ **adjective** Biochemistry another term for **AMPHIPATHIC**.

Amphipoda /ˌamfɪˈpəʊdə/ Zoology an order of chiefly marine crustaceans with a laterally compressed body and a large number of leg-like appendages.
– DERIVATIVES **amphipod** /ˈamfɪpɒd/ noun.
– ORIGIN modern Latin (plural), from **AMPHI-** 'of both kinds' (because some legs are specialized for swimming and some for feeding) + Greek *pous, pod-* 'foot'.

amphiprostyle /amˈfɪprəstʌɪl/ ▶ **adjective** (of a classical building) having a portico at each end but not at the sides.
– ORIGIN early 18th cent.: via Latin from Greek *amphiprostulos*, from *amphi-* 'both, on both sides' + *prostulos* 'having pillars in front' (see **PROSTYLE**).

amphisbaena /ˌamfɪsˈbiːnə/ ▶ **noun** poetic/literary a mythical serpent with a head at each end.
– ORIGIN late Middle English: via Latin from Greek *amphisbaina*, from *amphis* 'both ways' + *bainein* 'go'.

Amphisbaenia /ˌamfɪsˈbiːnɪə/ Zoology a group of reptiles which comprises the worm lizards.
● Suborder Amphisbaenia, order Squamata.
– DERIVATIVES **amphisbaenian** noun & adjective.
– ORIGIN modern Latin, from Greek *amphisbaina*, from *amphis* 'both' + *bainein* 'go, walk'.

amphitheatre (US **amphitheater**) ▶ **noun** (especially in Greek and Roman architecture) a round building, typically unroofed, with a central space for the presentation of dramatic or sporting events surrounded by tiers of seats for spectators.
▪ a semicircular seating gallery in a theatre.
– ORIGIN late Middle English: via Latin from Greek *amphitheatron*, from *amphi* 'on both sides' + *theatron* (see **THEATRE**).

Amphitrite /ˌamfɪˈtrʌɪti/ Greek Mythology a sea goddess, wife of Poseidon and mother of Triton.

amphiuma /ˌamfɪˈjuːmə/ ▶ **noun** a fully aquatic eel-like amphibian with very small limbs, occurring in stagnant water and swamps in the south-eastern US.
● Family Amphiumidae and genus *Amphiuma*: three species.
– ORIGIN modern Latin, probably formed irregularly from **AMPHI-** 'both' + Greek *pneuma* 'breath'.

amphora /ˈamf(ə)rə/ ▶ **noun** (pl. **amphorae** /-riː/ or **amphoras**) a tall ancient Greek or Roman jar or jug with two handles and a narrow neck.
– ORIGIN Latin, from Greek *amphoreus*, or from French *amphore*.

amphoteric /ˌamfəˈtɛrɪk/ ▶ **adjective** Chemistry (of a compound, especially a metal oxide or hydroxide) able to react both as a base and as an acid.
– ORIGIN mid 19th cent.: from Greek *amphoteros*, comparative of *amphō* 'both', + **-IC**.

ampicillin /ˌampɪˈsɪlɪn/ ▶ **noun** [mass noun] Medicine a semi-synthetic form of penicillin used chiefly to treat infections of the urinary and respiratory tracts.
– ORIGIN 1960s: blend of **AMINO** and a contraction of **PENICILLIN**.

ample ▶ **adjective** (**ampler, amplest**) enough or more than enough; plentiful: *there is ample time for discussion* | *an ample supply of consumer goods.*
▪ large and accommodating: *he leaned back in his ample chair.* ▪ used euphemistically to convey that someone is stout: *she stood with her hands on her ample hips.*
– DERIVATIVES **ampleness** noun, **amply** adverb.
– ORIGIN late Middle English: via French from Latin *amplus* 'large, capacious, abundant'.

amplexus /amˈplɛksəs/ ▶ **noun** [mass noun] Zoology the mating position of frogs and toads, in which the male clasps the female about the back.
– ORIGIN 1930s: from Latin, 'an embrace'.

amplifier ▶ **noun** an electronic device for increasing the amplitude of electrical signals, used chiefly in sound reproduction.
▪ a device of this kind combined with a loudspeaker, used to amplify electric guitars and other musical instruments.

amplify ▶ **verb** (**-ies, -ied**) [with obj.] (often **be amplified**) increase the volume of (sound), especially using an amplifier: *the accompanying chords have been amplified in our arrangement.*
▪ increase the amplitude of (an electrical signal or other oscillation). ▪ cause to become more marked or intense: *urban policy initiatives amplified social polarization.* ▪ Genetics make multiple copies of (a gene or DNA sequence). ▪ enlarge upon or add detail to (a story or statement): *the notes amplify information contained in the statement.*
– DERIVATIVES **amplification** noun.
– ORIGIN late Middle English (in the general sense 'increase, augment'): from Old French *amplifier*, from Latin *amplificare*, from *amplus* 'large, abundant'.

amplitude ▶ **noun** [mass noun] **1** Physics the maximum

extent of a vibration or oscillation, measured from the position of equilibrium.
■the maximum difference of an alternating electric current or potential from the average value.
2 Astronomy the angular distance of a celestial object from the true east or west point of the horizon at rising or setting.
3 breadth, range, or magnitude: *the amplitude of the crime of manslaughter lies beneath murder.*
4 Mathematics the angle between the real axis of an Argand diagram and a vector representing a complex number.
– ORIGIN mid 16th cent. (in the senses 'physical extent' and 'grandeur'): from Latin *amplitudo*, from *amplus* 'large, abundant'.

amplitude modulation (abbrev.: **AM**) ▶ **noun** [mass noun] the modulation of a wave by varying its amplitude, used chiefly as a means of radio broadcasting, in which an audio signal is combined with a carrier wave. Often contrasted with **FREQUENCY MODULATION**.

ampoule /ˈampuːl/ (US also **ampul** or **ampule** /ˈampjuːl/) ▶ **noun** a small sealed glass capsule containing a liquid, especially a measured quantity ready for injecting: *an ampoule of adrenalin.*
– ORIGIN early 20th cent.: from French, from Latin *ampulla* (see **AMPULLA**).

ampster /ˈampstə/ (also **amster** /ˈamstə/) ▶ **noun** Austral. informal the accomplice of a sideshow operator who acts as a purchaser in an attempt to persuade others to do the same.
– ORIGIN 1940s: of unknown origin.

ampulla /amˈpʊlə/ ▶ **noun** (pl. **ampullae** /-liː/) a roughly spherical Roman flask with two handles.
■a flask for sacred uses such as holding the oil for anointing the sovereign at a coronation. ■ Anatomy & Zoology a cavity, or the dilated end of a vessel, shaped like a Roman ampulla.
– ORIGIN late Middle English: from Latin, diminutive of *ampora*, variant of *amphora* (see **AMPHORA**).

amputate /ˈampjʊteɪt/ ▶ **verb** [with obj.] cut off (a limb) by surgical operation: *surgeons had to amputate her left hand.*
– DERIVATIVES **amputation** noun, **amputator** noun.
– ORIGIN mid 16th cent.: from Latin *amputat-* 'lopped off', from *amputare*, from *am-* (for *amb-* 'about') + *putare* 'to prune'.

amputee ▶ **noun** a person who has had a limb amputated.

AMRAAM ▶ **abbreviation for** advanced medium range air-to-air missile.

amrit /ˈʌmrɪt/ (also **amrita** /ˈʌmriːtə/) ▶ **noun** [mass noun] a syrup considered divine by Sikhs and taken by them at baptism and in religious observances.
– ORIGIN from Sanskrit *amṛta* 'immortal'.

Amritsar /ʌmˈrɪtsə/ a city in the state of Punjab in NW India; pop. 709,000 (1991). It became the centre of the Sikh faith and the site of its holiest temple, the Golden Temple. It was the scene of a riot in 1919, in which 400 people were killed by British troops.

amster ▶ **noun** variant spelling of **AMPSTER**.

Amsterdam /ˌamstəˈdam/ the capital and largest city of the Netherlands; pop. 702,440 (1991). It is built on some ninety islands separated by canals. Although Amsterdam is the capital, the country's seat of government and administrative centre is at The Hague.

AMT ▶ **abbreviation for** (in the US) alternative minimum tax, introduced to prevent companies and individuals using deductions and credits to pay no tax.

amtrac /ˈamtrak/ (also **amtrak**) ▶ **noun** US an amphibious tracked vehicle used for landing assault troops on a shore.
– ORIGIN Second World War: blend of **AMPHIBIOUS** and **TRACTOR**.

Amtrak /ˈamtrak/ trademark a federal passenger railway service in the US, operated by the National Railroad Passenger Corporation.

amu ▶ **abbreviation for** atomic mass unit.

amuck /əˈmʌk/ ▶ **adverb** variant spelling of **AMOK**.

Amu Darya /ˌɑːmuː ˈdɑːrɪə/ a river of central Asia, rising in the Pamirs and flowing 2,400 km (1,500 miles) into the Aral Sea. In classical times it was known as the Oxus.

amulet /ˈamjʊlɪt/ ▶ **noun** an ornament or small piece of jewellery thought to give protection against evil, danger, or disease.
– ORIGIN late 16th cent.: from Latin *amuletum*, of unknown origin.

Amun /ˈɑːmən/ (also **Amon**) Egyptian Mythology a supreme god of the ancient Egyptians, identified with the sun god Ra, and in Greek and Roman times with Zeus and Jupiter (under the name **Ammon**).

Amundsen /ˈɑːmʊnds(ə)n/, Roald (1872–1928), Norwegian explorer. Amundsen was the first to navigate the North-West Passage (1903–6), during which expedition he located the site of the magnetic north pole. In 1911 he became the first to reach the South Pole.

Amur /əˈmʊə/ a river of NE Asia, forming for the greater part of its length the boundary between Russia and China. Its length is about 4,350 km (2,737 miles). Chinese name **HEILONG**.

amuse ▶ **verb** [with obj.] **1** cause (someone) to find something funny: [as adj. **amused**] *people looked on with amused curiosity.*
2 provide interesting and enjoyable occupation for (someone); entertain: *they* ***amused themselves*** *digging through an old encyclopedia* | [as adj. **amused**] *elegant shops that will keep any browser amused for hours.*
– DERIVATIVES **amusedly** adverb (only in sense 1).
– ORIGIN late 15th cent. (in the sense 'delude, deceive'): from Old French *amuser* 'entertain, deceive', from *a-* (expressing causal effect) + *muser* 'stare stupidly'. Current senses date from the mid 17th cent.

amuse-gueule /əˌmjuːzˈɡəːl, French amyzɡœl/ ▶ **noun** (pl. **amuse-gueules** or same) a small savoury item of food served as an appetizer before a meal.
– ORIGIN French, literally 'amuse mouth'.

amusement ▶ **noun** [mass noun] the state or experience of finding something funny: *we looked with amusement at our horoscopes.*
■the provision or enjoyment of entertainment: *an evening's amusement.* ■ [count noun] something that causes laughter or provides entertainment: *his daughter was an amusement to him.* ■ [count noun] Brit. a mechanical device such as a roundabout to provide entertainment, typically at a fairground or a seaside resort.
– ORIGIN early 17th cent. (in the sense 'musing, diversion of the attention'): from French, from the verb *amuser* (see **AMUSE**).

amusement arcade ▶ **noun** Brit. an indoor area containing coin-operated game machines.

amusement park ▶ **noun** a large outdoor area with fairground rides, shows, refreshments, and other entertainments.

amusing ▶ **adjective** causing laughter and providing entertainment: *such a likable, amusing man!*
– DERIVATIVES **amusingly** adverb.

amygdala /əˈmɪɡdələ/ ▶ **noun** (pl. **amygdalae** /əˈmɪɡdəliː/) Anatomy a roughly almond-shaped mass of grey matter deep inside each cerebral hemisphere, associated with the sense of smell.
– ORIGIN Late Middle English: via Latin from Greek *amugdalē* 'almond'.

amygdale /əˈmɪɡdeɪl/ ▶ **noun** Geology a vesicle in an igneous rock, containing secondary minerals.
– ORIGIN late 19th cent.: from French, from Latin *amygdala* (see **AMYGDALA**).

amygdalin /əˈmɪɡd(ə)lɪn/ ▶ **noun** [mass noun] Chemistry a bitter crystalline compound found in bitter almonds and the stones of peaches, apricots, and other fruit.
– ORIGIN mid 19th cent.: from Latin *amygdala* 'almond' + **-IN**[1].

amygdaloid /əˈmɪɡdəlɔɪd/ ▶ **adjective** technical shaped like an almond.
▶ **noun** (also **amygdaloid nucleus**) Anatomy another term for **AMYGDALA**.
– ORIGIN mid 18th cent.: from Latin *amygdala* 'almond' + **-OID**.

amygdaloidal ▶ **adjective** Geology relating to or containing amygdales.

amyl /ˈeɪmʌɪl, ˈamɪl/ ▶ **noun** [as modifier] Chemistry of or denoting the straight-chain pentyl radical —C_5H_{11}.
■[mass noun] informal short for **AMYL NITRITE**.
– ORIGIN mid 19th cent.: from Latin *amylum* 'starch' + **-YL**.

amylase /ˈamɪleɪz/ ▶ **noun** [mass noun] Biochemistry an enzyme, found chiefly in saliva and pancreatic fluid, that converts starch and glycogen into simple sugars.

amyl nitrate ▶ **noun** [mass noun] Chemistry a colourless synthetic liquid used as an additive in diesel fuel to improve its ignition properties.
• Chem. formula: $C_5H_{11}NO_3$.

USAGE Amyl nitrate and **amyl nitrite** are distinct substances, but **amyl nitrate** is often mistakenly used to refer to the street drug (inhaled and used as a stimulant and vasodilator), which is correctly called **amyl nitrite**.

amyl nitrite ▶ **noun** [mass noun] a yellowish volatile synthetic liquid used medicinally as a vasodilator. It is rapidly absorbed by the body on inhalation, and is sometimes used for its stimulatory effects.
• Chem. formula: $C_5H_{11}NO_2$.

amyloid /ˈamɪlɔɪd/ ▶ **noun** [mass noun] Medicine a starch-like protein which is deposited in the liver, kidneys, spleen, or other tissues in certain diseases.
■another term for **AMYLOIDOSIS**.

amyloidosis /ˌamɪlɔɪˈdəʊsɪs/ ▶ **noun** [mass noun] Medicine deposition of amyloid in the body.

amylopectin /ˌamɪləʊˈpɛktɪn/ ▶ **noun** [mass noun] Biochemistry the non-crystallizable form of starch, consisting of branched polysaccharide chains.

amylose /ˈamɪləʊs/ ▶ **noun** [mass noun] Biochemistry the crystallizable form of starch, consisting of long unbranched polysaccharide chains.

amyotrophic lateral sclerosis ▶ **noun** another term for **LOU GEHRIG'S DISEASE**.

amyotrophy /ˌamɪˈɒtrəfi/ ▶ **noun** [mass noun] Medicine muscular atrophy.
– DERIVATIVES **amyotrophic** adjective.
– ORIGIN late 19th cent.: from **A-**[1] 'not' + Greek *mus*, *muo-* 'muscle' + Greek *trophē* 'nourishment'.

Amytal /ˈamɪt(ə)l/ ▶ **noun** [mass noun] trademark a barbiturate drug used as a sedative and a hypnotic.
• Alternative name: 5-ethyl-5-isopropylbarbituric acid, or its sodium salt (**sodium amytal**); chem. formula: $C_{11}H_{18}N_2O_3$.
– ORIGIN 1920s: from **AMYL** + *-t-* (for ease of pronunciation) + **-AL**.

an ▶ **determiner** the form of the indefinite article (see **A**[1]) used before words beginning with a vowel sound.

USAGE There is still some divergence of opinion over the form of the indefinite article to use preceding certain words beginning with **h-** when the first syllable is unstressed: '**a** historical document' or '**an** historical document'; '**a** hotel' or '**an** hotel'. The form depends on whether the initial **h** is sounded or not: **an** was common in the 18th and 19th centuries, because the initial **h** was commonly not pronounced for these words. In standard modern English the norm is for the **h** to be pronounced in words like **hotel** and **historical**, and therefore the indefinite article **a** is used; however, the older form, with the silent **h** and the indefinite article **an**, is still encountered, especially among older speakers.

an-[1] ▶ **prefix** variant spelling of **A-**[1] before a vowel (as in *anaemia*).

an-[2] ▶ **prefix** variant spelling of **AD-** assimilated before *n* (as in *annihilate, annotate*).

an-[3] ▶ **prefix** variant spelling of **ANA-** shortened before a vowel (as in *aneurysm*).

-an ▶ **suffix 1** forming adjectives and nouns, especially from:
■names of places: *Cuban.* ■ names of systems: *Anglican.* ■ names of zoological classes or orders: *crustacean.* ■ names of founders: *Lutheran.*
2 /an/ Chemistry forming names of organic compounds, chiefly polysaccharides: *dextran.*
– ORIGIN from Latin *-anus, -ana, -anum.*

ana- (usu. **an-** before a vowel) ▶ **prefix 1** up: *anabatic.*
2 back: *anamnesis.*
3 again: *anabiosis.*
– ORIGIN from Greek *ana* 'up'.

-ana ▶ **suffix** (forming plural nouns) denoting things associated with a person, place, or field of interest: *Americana* | *Victoriana.*
– ORIGIN from Latin, neuter plural of *-anus*, adjectival ending.

Anabaptism /ˌanəˈbaptɪz(ə)m/ ▶ **noun** [mass noun] the doctrine that baptism should only be administered to believing adults, held by a radical Protestant sect which emerged during the 1520s and 1530s.
– DERIVATIVES **Anabaptist** noun & adjective.
– ORIGIN mid 16th cent.: via ecclesiastical Latin from Greek *anabaptismos*, from *ana-* 'over again' + *baptismos* 'baptism'.

a **cat** | ɑː **arm** | ɛ **bed** | ɛː **hair** | ə **ago** | əː **her** | ɪ **sit** | i **cosy** | iː **see** | ɒ **hot** | ɔː **saw** | ʌ **run** | ʊ **put** | uː **too** | ʌɪ **my** | aʊ **how** | eɪ **day** | əʊ **no** | ɪə **near** | ɔɪ **boy** | ʊə **poor** | ʌɪə **fire** | aʊə **sour**

anabatic /ˌanəˈbatɪk/ ▶ **adjective** Meteorology (of a wind) caused by local upward motion of warm air.
– ORIGIN early 20th cent.: from Greek *anabatikos*, from *anabatēs* 'a person who ascends', from *anabainein* 'walk up'.

anabiosis /ˌanəbʌɪˈəʊsɪs/ ▶ **noun** [mass noun] Zoology a temporary state of suspended animation or greatly reduced metabolism.
– DERIVATIVES **anabiotic** /-ˈɒtɪk/ adjective.
– ORIGIN late 19th cent.: from Greek *anabiōsis*, from *anabioein* 'return to life'.

anabolic /ˌanəˈbɒlɪk/ ▶ **adjective** Biochemistry relating to or promoting anabolism.

anabolic steroid ▶ **noun** a synthetic steroid hormone which resembles testosterone in promoting the growth of muscle. Such hormones are used medicinally to treat some forms of weight loss and (illegally) by some athletes, sports players, and others to enhance physical performance.

anabolism /əˈnabəlɪz(ə)m/ ▶ **noun** [mass noun] Biochemistry the synthesis of complex molecules in living organisms from simpler ones together with the storage of energy; constructive metabolism.
– ORIGIN late 19th cent.: from Greek *anabolē* 'ascent', from *ana-* 'up' + *ballein* 'to throw'.

anabranch /ˈanəbrɑːn(t)ʃ/ ▶ **noun** chiefly Austral. a stream that leaves a river and re-enters it lower down.
– ORIGIN mid 19th cent.: from *ana(stomosing)* (present participle of **ANASTOMOSE**) + **BRANCH**.

anachronic /ˌanəˈkrɒnɪk/ ▶ **adjective** relating to or involving anachronism: *an anachronic atmosphere in which time seems to have stood still.*
– ORIGIN early 19th cent.: from **ANACHRONISM**, on the pattern of pairs such as *synchronism, synchronic*.

anachronism /əˈnakrəˌnɪz(ə)m/ ▶ **noun** a thing belonging or appropriate to a period other than that in which it exists, especially a thing that is conspicuously old-fashioned: *their shop persisted almost as an anachronism into the 1980s.*
■ [mass noun] the action of attributing a custom, event, or object to a period to which it does not belong: *it is anachronism to suppose that the official morality of the age was mere window dressing.*
– DERIVATIVES **anachronistic** adjective, **anachronistically** adverb.
– ORIGIN mid 17th cent.: from Greek *anakhronismos*, from *ana-* 'backwards' + *khronos* 'time'.

anaclitic /ˌanəˈklɪtɪk/ ▶ **adjective** Psychoanalysis relating to or characterized by a strong emotional dependence on another or others: *anaclitic depression.*
– ORIGIN 1920s: from Greek *anaklitos* 'for reclining', from *anaklinein* 'recline'.

anacoluthon /ˌanəkəˈluːθɒn, -θ(ə)n/ ▶ **noun** (pl. **anacolutha** /-θə/) a sentence or construction in which the expected grammatical sequence is absent, for example *while in the garden, the door banged shut.*
– DERIVATIVES **anacoluthic** adjective.
– ORIGIN early 18th cent.: via late Latin from Greek *anakolouthon*, from *an-* 'not' + *akolouthos* 'following'.

anaconda /ˌanəˈkɒndə/ ▶ **noun** a semiaquatic snake of the boa family which may grow to a great size, native to tropical South America.
• Genus *Eunectes*, family Boidae: several species, in particular the **green anaconda** (*E. murinus*).
– ORIGIN mid 18th cent. (originally denoting a kind of Sri Lankan snake): unexplained alteration of Latin *anacandaia* 'python', from Sinhalese *henakaňdayā* 'whip snake', from *hena* 'lightning' + *kaňda* 'stem'.

Anacreon /əˈnakrɪən/ (*c.*570–478 BC), Greek lyric poet, best known for his celebrations of love and wine.
– DERIVATIVES **anacreontic** adjective & noun.

anacrusis /ˌanəˈkruːsɪs/ ▶ **noun** (pl. **anacruses** /-siːz/)
1 Prosody one or more unstressed syllables at the beginning of a verse.
2 Music one or more unstressed notes before the first bar line of a piece or passage.
– ORIGIN mid 19th cent.: modern Latin, from Greek *anakrousis* 'prelude', from *ana-* 'up' + *krousis*, from *krouein* 'to strike'.

anadromous /əˈnadrəməs/ ▶ **adjective** Zoology (of a fish, such as the salmon) migrating up rivers from the sea to spawn. The opposite of **CATADROMOUS**.
– ORIGIN mid 18th cent.: from Greek *anadromos* (from *ana-* 'up' + *dromos* 'running') + **-OUS**.

anaemia /əˈniːmɪə/ (US **anemia**) ▶ **noun** [mass noun] a condition in which there is a deficiency of red blood cells or of haemoglobin in the blood, resulting in pallor and weariness.
– ORIGIN early 19th cent.: via modern Latin from Greek *anaimia*, from *an-* 'without' + *haima* 'blood'.

anaemic (US **anemic**) ▶ **adjective** suffering from anaemia.
■ figurative lacking in colour, spirit, or vitality.

anaerobe /ˈanərəʊb, əˈnɛːrəʊb/ ▶ **noun** Biology a micro-organism that is able to, or can only, live in the absence of oxygen.
– ORIGIN late 19th cent.: from **AN-**[1] + **AEROBE**.

anaerobic ▶ **adjective** Biology relating to, involving, or requiring an absence of free oxygen: *anaerobic bacteria.*
■ relating to or denoting exercise which does not improve or is not intended to improve the efficiency of the body's cardiovascular system in absorbing and transporting oxygen.
– DERIVATIVES **anaerobically** adverb.

anaesthesia /ˌanɪsˈθiːzɪə/ (US **anesthesia**) ▶ **noun** [mass noun] insensitivity to pain, especially as artificially induced by the administration of gases or the injection of drugs before surgical operations.
■ the induction of this state. ■ the branch of medicine concerned with the induction of this state.
– ORIGIN early 18th cent.: modern Latin, from Greek *anaisthēsia*, from *an-* 'without' + *aisthēsis* 'sensation'.

anaesthesiology /ˌanɪsˌθiːzɪˈɒlədʒi/ (US **anesthesiology**) ▶ **noun** [mass noun] the branch of medicine concerned with anaesthesia and anaesthetics.
– DERIVATIVES **anaesthesiologist** noun.

anaesthetic /ˌanɪsˈθɛtɪk/ (US **anesthetic**) ▶ **noun**
1 a substance that induces insensitivity to pain.
2 (**anaesthetics**) [treated as sing.] the study or practice of anaesthesia.
▶ **adjective** inducing or relating to insensitivity to pain.
– ORIGIN mid 19th cent.: from Greek *anaisthētos* 'insensible', related to *anaisthēsia* (see **ANAESTHESIA**), + **-IC**.

anaesthetist /əˈniːsθətɪst/ (US **anesthetist**) ▶ **noun** a medical specialist who administers anaesthetics.

anaesthetize /əˈniːsθətʌɪz/ (also **-ise**, US **anesthetize**) ▶ **verb** [with obj.] administer an anaesthetic to: *I was called to Casualty to anaesthetize a patient.*
■ figurative deprive of feeling or awareness: *the feeling of numb unreality persisted and anaesthetized me.*
– DERIVATIVES **anaesthetization** noun.

anagen /ˈanədʒ(ə)n/ ▶ **noun** [mass noun] Physiology the growing phase of a hair follicle. Often contrasted with **TELOGEN**.
– ORIGIN 1920s: from **ANA-** + **-GEN**.

anagenesis /ˌanəˈdʒɛnɪsɪs/ ▶ **noun** [mass noun] Biology species formation without branching of the evolutionary line of descent.
– DERIVATIVES **anagenetic** adjective.

anaglyph /ˈanəglɪf/ ▶ **noun 1** Photography a stereoscopic photograph with the two images superimposed and printed in different colours, usually red and green, producing a stereo effect when the photograph is viewed with a filter of a colour corresponding to that of one of the images over each eye.
2 an object, such as a cameo, embossed or carved in low relief.
– DERIVATIVES **anaglyphic** adjective.
– ORIGIN late 16th cent. (in sense 2): from Greek *anagluphē*, from *ana-* 'up' + *gluphē* (from *gluphein* 'carve'). Sense 1 dates from the late 19th cent.

Anaglypta /ˌanəˈglɪptə/ ▶ **noun** [mass noun] trademark a type of thick embossed wallpaper, designed to be painted over.
– ORIGIN late 19th cent.: from Latin *anaglypta* 'work in low relief'; compare with **ANAGLYPH**.

anagram /ˈanəgram/ ▶ **noun** a word, phrase, or name formed by rearranging the letters of another, such as *spar*, formed from *rasp*.
▶ **verb** (**anagrammed**, **anagramming**) another term for **ANAGRAMMATIZE**.
– DERIVATIVES **anagrammatic** adjective, **anagrammatical** adjective.
– ORIGIN late 16th cent.: from French *anagramme* or modern Latin *anagramma*, from Greek *ana-* 'back, anew' + *gramma* 'letter'.

anagrammatize /ˌanəˈgramətʌɪz/ (also **-ise**) ▶ **verb** [with obj.] make an anagram of (a word, phrase, or name).
– DERIVATIVES **anagrammatization** noun.

Anaheim /ˈanəhʌɪm/ a city in California, on the SE side of the Los Angeles conurbation; pop. 266,400 (1990). It is the site of the amusement park Disneyland.

anal /ˈeɪn(ə)l/ ▶ **adjective** involving, relating to, or situated near the anus.
■ Psychoanalysis (in Freudian theory) relating to or denoting a stage of infantile psychosexual development in which defecation is the major source of sensuous pleasure and the anus forms the centre of self-awareness. ■ informal anal-retentive: *he's anal about things like that.*
– DERIVATIVES **anally** adverb.
– ORIGIN mid 18th cent.: from modern Latin *analis*, from Latin *anus* (see **ANUS**).

analects /ˈanəlɛkts/ (also **analecta** /ˌanəˈlɛktə/) ▶ **plural noun** a collection of short literary or philosophical extracts.
– ORIGIN late Middle English: via Latin from Greek *analekta* 'things gathered up', from *analegein* 'pick up', from *ana-* 'up' + *legein* 'gather'.

analeptic /ˌanəˈlɛptɪk/ Medicine ▶ **adjective** (chiefly of a drug) tending to restore a person's health or strength; restorative.
▶ **noun** a restorative drug.
■ a drug that stimulates the central nervous system.
– ORIGIN late 16th cent.: via late Latin from Greek *analēptikos* 'restorative'.

anal fin ▶ **noun** Zoology an unpaired fin located on the underside of a fish posterior to the anus.

analgesia /ˌan(ə)lˈdʒiːzɪə/ ▶ **noun** [mass noun] Medicine the inability to feel pain.
■ medication that acts to relieve pain.
– ORIGIN early 18th cent.: from Greek *analgēsia* 'painlessness', from *an-* 'not' + *algeein* 'feel pain'.

analgesic /ˌan(ə)lˈdʒiːzɪk, -sɪk/ Medicine ▶ **adjective** (chiefly of a drug) acting to relieve pain.
▶ **noun** an analgesic drug.

analogize /əˈnalədʒʌɪz/ (also **-ise**) ▶ **verb** [with obj.] make a comparison of (something) with something else to assist understanding: *he could **analogize** birth **to** the coming into being of a poem.*

analogous /əˈnaləgəs/ ▶ **adjective** comparable in certain respects, typically in a way which makes clearer the nature of the things compared: *they saw the relationship between a ruler and his subjects as **analogous to** that of father and children.*
■ Biology (of organs) performing a similar function but having a different evolutionary origin, such as the wings of insects and birds. Often contrasted with **HOMOLOGOUS**.
– DERIVATIVES **analogously** adverb.
– ORIGIN mid 17th cent.: via Latin from Greek *analogos* 'proportionate' + **-OUS**.

analogue /ˈanəlɒg/ (US also **analog**) ▶ **noun** a person or thing seen as comparable to another: *an interior analogue of the exterior world.*
■ Chemistry a compound with a molecular structure closely similar to that of another.
▶ **adjective** (also **analog**) relating to or using signals or information represented by a continuously variable physical quantity such as spatial position, voltage, etc. Often contrasted with **DIGITAL** (sense 1).
■ (of a clock or watch) showing the time by means of hands or a pointer rather than displayed digits.
– ORIGIN early 19th cent.: from French, from Greek *analogon*, neuter of *analogos* 'proportionate'.

analogue to digital converter ▶ **noun** a device for converting analogue signals to digital form.

analogy /əˈnalədʒi/ ▶ **noun** (pl. **-ies**) a comparison between one thing and another, typically for the purpose of explanation or clarification: *an **analogy between** the workings of nature and those of human societies* | [mass noun] *he interprets logical functions **by analogy with** machines.*
■ a correspondence or partial similarity. ■ a thing which is or is represented as being comparable to something else in significant respects: *works of art were seen as an analogy for works of nature.* ■ [mass noun] Logic a process of arguing from similarity in known respects to similarity in other respects. ■ [mass noun] Linguistics a process by which new words and inflections are created on the basis of regularities in the form of existing ones. ■ [mass noun] Biology the resemblance of function between organs that have a different evolutionary origin.

– DERIVATIVES **analogical** adjective, **analogically** adverb.
– ORIGIN late Middle English (in the sense 'appropriateness, correspondence'): from French *analogie*, Latin *analogia* 'proportion', from Greek, from *analogos* 'proportionate'.

analphabetic ▶ **adjective 1** representing sounds by composite signs rather than by single letters or symbols.
2 completely illiterate.

anal-retentive Psychoanalysis ▶ **adjective** (of a person) excessively orderly and fussy (supposedly owing to conflict over toilet-training in infancy).
▶ **noun** a person who is excessively orderly and fussy.
– DERIVATIVES **anal retention** noun, **anal retentiveness** noun.

anal-sadistic ▶ **adjective** Psychoanalysis displaying abnormal aggressive and destructive tendencies supposedly caused by fixation at the anal stage of development.
– DERIVATIVES **anal-sadism** noun.

analysand /əˈnalɪsand/ ▶ **noun** a person undergoing psychoanalysis.

analyse (US **analyze**) ▶ **verb** [with obj.] examine methodically and in detail the constitution or structure of (something, especially information), typically for purposes of explanation and interpretation: *we need to analyse our results more clearly.*
■ discover or reveal (something) through such examination: *I intend to analyse the sexism in such texts* | [with clause] *he tried to analyse exactly what was going on.* ■ psychoanalyse (someone). ■ identify and measure the chemical constituents of (a substance or specimen). ■ Grammar resolve (a sentence) into its grammatical elements; parse.
– DERIVATIVES **analysable** adjective, **analyser** noun.
– ORIGIN late 16th cent.: influenced by French *analyser*, from medieval Latin *analysis* (see **ANALYSIS**).

analysis /əˈnalɪsɪs/ ▶ **noun** (pl. **analyses** /-siːz/) [mass noun] detailed examination of the elements or structure of something, typically as a basis for discussion or interpretation: *statistical analysis* | [count noun] *an analysis of popular culture.*
■ the process of separating something into its constituent elements. Often contrasted with **SYNTHESIS**. ■ the identification and measurement of the chemical constituents of a substance or specimen. ■ short for **PSYCHOANALYSIS**. ■ Mathematics the part of mathematics concerned with the theory of functions and the use of limits, continuity, and the operations of calculus. ■ [count noun] Cricket a statement of a bowler's performance, especially in an innings, giving the numbers of wickets taken and runs conceded.
– PHRASES **in the final** (or **last** or **ultimate**) **analysis** when everything has been considered (used to suggest that a statement expresses the basic truth about a complex situation): *in the final analysis it is a question of political history.*
– ORIGIN late 16th cent.: via medieval Latin from Greek *analusis*, from *analuein* 'unloose', from *ana-* 'up' + *luein* 'loosen'.

analyst ▶ **noun** a person who conducts analysis, in particular:
■ an investment expert, typically one in a specified field: *the stockbrokers' brewing analyst.* ■ short for **PSYCHOANALYST**. ■ a chemist who analyses substances.
– ORIGIN mid 17th cent.: from French *analyste*, from the verb *analyser* (see **ANALYSE**).

analytic ▶ **adjective** another term for **ANALYTICAL**.
■ Logic true by virtue of the meaning of the words or concepts used to express it, so that its denial would be a self-contradiction. Compare with **SYNTHETIC**. ■ Linguistics (of a language) tending not to alter the form of its words but to use word order to express grammatical structure. Chinese and English are examples of analytic languages. Contrasted with **SYNTHETIC** and **AGGLUTINATIVE**.
– ORIGIN early 17th cent.: via Latin from Greek *analutikos*, from *analuein* 'unloose'. The term was adopted in the late 16th cent. as a noun denoting the branch of logic dealing with analysis, with specific reference to Aristotle's treatises on logic, the Analytics (Greek *analutika*).

analytical ▶ **adjective** relating to or using analysis or logical reasoning.
– DERIVATIVES **analytically** adverb.

analytical geometry ▶ **noun** [mass noun] geometry using coordinates.

analytical philosophy (also **analytic philosophy**) ▶ **noun** [mass noun] a method of approaching philosophical problems through analysis of the terms in which they are expressed, associated with Anglo-American philosophy of the early 20th century.

analytical psychology ▶ **noun** [mass noun] the psychoanalytical system of psychology developed and practised by Carl Gustav Jung.

analyze ▶ **verb** US spelling of **ANALYSE**.

anamnesis /ˌanəmˈniːsɪs/ ▶ **noun** (pl. **anamneses** /-siːz/) [mass noun] recollection, in particular:
■ the remembering of things from a supposed previous existence (often used with reference to Platonic philosophy). ■ [count noun] Medicine a patient's account of their medical history. ■ Christian Church the part of the Eucharist in which the Passion, Resurrection, and Ascension of Christ are recalled.
– ORIGIN late 16th cent.: from Greek *anamnēsis* 'remembrance'.

anamnestic /ˌanəmˈnɛstɪk/ ▶ **adjective** Medicine denoting an enhanced reaction of the body's immune system to an antigen which is related to one previously encountered.

anamorphic /ˌanəˈmɔːfɪk/ ▶ **adjective** denoting an anamorphosis: *an anamorphic picture.*
■ relating to anamorphosis: *an anamorphic lens.*

anamorphosis /ˌanəˈmɔːfəsɪs/ ▶ **noun** a distorted projection or drawing which appears normal when viewed from a particular point or with a suitable mirror or lens.
■ [mass noun] the process by which such images are produced.
– ORIGIN early 18th cent.: from Greek *anamorphōsis* 'transformation', from *ana-* 'back, again' + *morphosis* 'a shaping' (from *morphoun* 'to shape', from *morphē* 'shape, form').

ananda /ɑːˈnʌndə/ ▶ **noun** [mass noun] (in Hinduism, Buddhism, and Jainism) extreme happiness, one of the highest states of being.
– ORIGIN from Sanskrit *ānanda* 'blessedness, bliss'.

Anangu /ˈɑːnɑːŋuː/ ▶ **noun** (pl. same) Austral. an Aboriginal, especially one from central Australia.

Ananias /ˌanəˈnʌɪəs/ two figures in the New Testament, the husband of Sapphira, struck dead because he lied (Acts 5), and the Jewish high priest before whom St Paul was brought (Acts 23).

anapaest /ˈanəpiːst, -pɛst/ (US **anapest**) ▶ **noun** Prosody a metrical foot consisting of two short or unstressed syllables followed by one long or stressed syllable.
– DERIVATIVES **anapaestic** /-ˈpiːstɪk, -ˈpɛstɪk/ adjective.
– ORIGIN late 16th cent.: via Latin from Greek *anapaistos* 'reversed', from *ana-* 'back' + *paiein* 'strike' (because it is the reverse of a dactyl).

anaphase /ˈanəfeɪz/ ▶ **noun** [mass noun] Genetics the third stage of cell division, between metaphase and telophase, during which the chromosomes move away from one another to opposite poles of the spindle.

anaphor /ˈanəfə, -fɔː/ ▶ **noun** Grammar a word or phrase that refers back to an earlier word or phrase (e.g. in *my cousin said she was coming*, *she* is used as an anaphor for *my cousin*).
■ (in Chomskyan linguistics) a word or expression that has the same reference as another word in the same sentence; a reflexive pronoun or a reciprocal, e.g. *each other.*
– ORIGIN 1970s: back-formation from **ANAPHORA**.

anaphora /əˈnaf(ə)rə/ ▶ **noun** [mass noun] **1** Grammar the use of a word referring back to a word used earlier in a text or conversation, to avoid repetition, for example the pronouns *he, she, it,* and *they* and the verb *do* in *I like it and so do they.* Compare with **CATAPHORA**.
■ (in Chomskyan linguistics) co-reference within a sentence.
2 Rhetoric the repetition of a word or phrase at the beginning of successive clauses.
3 Christian Church the part of the Eucharist which contains the consecration, anamnesis, and communion.
– DERIVATIVES **anaphoric** /ˌanəˈfɒrɪk/ adjective.
– ORIGIN late 16th cent.: senses 1 and 2 via Latin from Greek, 'repetition', from *ana-* 'back' + *pherein* 'to bear'; sense 3 from late Greek.

anaphrodisiac /əˌnafrəˈdɪzɪak/ Medicine ▶ **adjective** (chiefly of a drug) tending to reduce sexual desire.
▶ **noun** an anaphrodisiac drug.

anaphylaxis /ˌanəfɪˈlaksɪs/ ▶ **noun** [mass noun] Medicine an extreme allergic reaction to an antigen (e.g. a bee sting) to which the body has become hypersensitive following an earlier exposure.
– DERIVATIVES **anaphylactic** adjective.
– ORIGIN early 20th cent.: modern Latin, from Greek *ana-* 'again' + *phulaxis* 'guarding'.

anapsid /əˈnapsɪd/ ▶ **noun** Zoology a reptile of a group characterized by a lack of temporal openings in the skull, including the turtles and their relatives.
• Sometimes placed in a subclass Anapsida, though this taxon is now often not recognized.
– ORIGIN 1930s: from modern Latin *Anapsida*, from Greek *an-* 'without' + *apsis, apsid-* 'arch'.

anaptyxis /ˌanəpˈtɪksɪs/ ▶ **noun** [mass noun] Phonetics the insertion of a vowel between two consonants to aid pronunciation, as in *he went thataway.*
– DERIVATIVES **anaptyctic** adjective.
– ORIGIN late 19th cent.: modern Latin, from Greek *anaptuxis* 'unfolding', from *ana-* 'back, again' + *ptuxis* 'folding'.

anarch /ˈanɑːk/ poetic/literary ▶ **noun** an anarchist.
▶ **adjective** anarchic.
– ORIGIN mid 17th cent.: from Greek *anarkhos* 'without a chief' (see **ANARCHY**).

anarchic ▶ **adjective** with no controlling rules or principles to give order: *an anarchic and bitter civil war.*
■ (of comedy or a person's sense of humour) uncontrolled by convention: *his anarchic wit.*
– DERIVATIVES **anarchical** adjective, **anarchically** adverb.

anarchism ▶ **noun** [mass noun] belief in the abolition of all government and the organization of society on a voluntary, cooperative basis without recourse to force or compulsion.
■ a political force or movement based on such a belief: *socialism and anarchism emerged to offer organized protest against the injustices of Spanish society.*
– ORIGIN mid 17th cent.: from Greek *anarkhos* 'without a chief' (see **ANARCHY**) + **-ISM**; later influenced by French *anarchisme*.

anarchist ▶ **noun** a person who believes in or tries to bring about anarchy.
▶ **adjective** relating to or supporting anarchy or anarchists: *an anarchist newspaper.*
– DERIVATIVES **anarchistic** adjective.
– ORIGIN mid 17th cent.: from Greek *anarkhos* 'without a chief' (see **ANARCHY**) + **-IST**; later influenced by French *anarchiste*.

anarchy ▶ **noun** [mass noun] a state of disorder due to absence or non-recognition of authority or other controlling systems: *he must ensure public order in a country threatened with anarchy.*
■ absence of government and absolute freedom of the individual, regarded as a political ideal.
– ORIGIN mid 16th cent.: via medieval Latin from Greek *anarkhia*, from *anarkhos*, from *an-* 'without' + *arkhos* 'chief, ruler'.

Anasazi /ˌanəˈsɑːzi/ ▶ **noun** (pl. same or **Anasazis**) a member of an ancient American Indian people of the south-western US, who flourished between *c.*200 BC and AD 1500. The earliest phase of their culture is known as the Basket Maker period; the present day Pueblo culture developed from a later stage.
– ORIGIN from Navajo, 'ancient one' or 'enemy ancestor'.

anastigmat /əˈnastɪgmat/ ▶ **noun** an anastigmatic lens system.

anastigmatic /ˌanəstɪgˈmatɪk/ ▶ **adjective** (of a lens system) constructed so that the astigmatism of each element is cancelled out.
– ORIGIN late 19th cent.: from **AN-**[1] 'not' + *astigmatic* (see **ASTIGMATISM**).

anastomose /əˈnastəməʊz/ ▶ **verb** [no obj.] Medicine be linked by anastomosis: *adjacent veins may anastomose.*
■ [with obj.] (usu. **be anastomosed**) link by anastomosis: *the graft is anastomosed to the vein of the recipient.*
– ORIGIN late 17th cent.: coined in French from Greek *anastomōsis* (see **ANASTOMOSIS**).

anastomosis /əˌnastəˈməʊsɪs/ ▶ **noun** (pl. **anastomoses** /-siːz/) technical a cross-connection between adjacent channels, tubes, fibres, or other parts of a network.
■ Medicine a connection made surgically between adjacent blood vessels, parts of the intestine, or

other channels of the body. ■ an operation in which such a connection is constructed.
– DERIVATIVES **anastomotic** adjective & noun.
– ORIGIN late 16th cent.: modern Latin, from Greek *anastomōsis*, from *anastomoun* 'provide with a mouth'.

anastrophe /əˈnastrəfi/ ▶ **noun** [mass noun] Rhetoric the inversion of the usual order of words or clauses.
– ORIGIN mid 16th cent.: from Greek *anastrophē* 'turning back', from *ana-* 'back' + *strephein* 'to turn'.

anathema /əˈnaθəmə/ ▶ **noun** **1** [mass noun] something or someone that one vehemently dislikes: *racial hatred was* ***anathema to*** *her.*
2 a formal curse by a pope or a council of the Church, excommunicating a person or denouncing a doctrine.
■ poetic/literary a strong curse: *the sergeant clutched the ruined communicator, muttering anathemas.*
– ORIGIN early 16th cent.: from ecclesiastical Latin, 'excommunicated person, excommunication', from Greek *anathema* 'thing dedicated', (later) 'thing devoted to evil, accursed thing', from *anatithenai* 'to set up'.

anathematize /əˈnaθəmətʌɪz/ (also **-ise**) ▶ **verb** [with obj.] curse; condemn: *he anathematized them as 'bloody scroungers'.*
– ORIGIN mid 16th cent.: from French *anathématiser*, from Latin *anathematizare*, from Greek *anathematizein*, from *anathema* (see **ANATHEMA**).

Anatolia /ˌanəˈtəʊlɪə/ the western peninsula of Asia, bounded by the Black Sea, the Aegean, and the Mediterranean, that forms the greater part of Turkey.

Anatolian ▶ **adjective** of or relating to Anatolia, its inhabitants, or their ancient languages.
▶ **noun** **1** a native or inhabitant of Anatolia.
2 [mass noun] an extinct group of ancient languages constituting a branch of the Indo-European language family and including Hittite, Luwian, Lydian, and Lycian.

anatomical ▶ **adjective** of or relating to bodily structure: *anatomical abnormalities.*
■ of or relating to the study of anatomy: *anatomical lectures.*
– DERIVATIVES **anatomically** adverb.
– ORIGIN late 16th cent.: from late Latin *anatomicus*, from *anatomia* (see **ANATOMY**), + **-AL**.

anatomist ▶ **noun** an expert in anatomy.
– ORIGIN mid 16th cent.: from French *anatomiste*, from a medieval Latin derivative of *anatomizare* (see **ANATOMIZE**).

anatomize (also **-ise**) ▶ **verb** [with obj.] dissect (a body).
■ examine and analyse in detail: *successful comedy is notoriously difficult to anatomize.*
– ORIGIN late Middle English: from medieval Latin *anatomizare*, from *anatomia* (see **ANATOMY**).

anatomy ▶ **noun** (pl. **-ies**) [mass noun] the branch of science concerned with the bodily structure of humans, animals, and other living organisms, especially as revealed by dissection and the separation of parts: *he studied physiology and anatomy.*
■ [count noun] the bodily structure of an organism: *descriptions of the cat's anatomy and behaviour.* ■ [count noun] informal, humorous a person's body. ■ [count noun] figurative a study of the structure or internal workings of something: *to undertake a comprehensive anatomy of primary school management.*
– ORIGIN late Middle English: from Old French *anatomie* or late Latin *anatomia*, from Greek, from *ana-* 'up' + *tomia* 'cutting' (from *temnein* 'to cut').

anatto ▶ **noun** variant spelling of **ANNATTO**.

Anaxagoras /ˌanakˈsagərəs/ (*c.*500–*c.*428 BC), Greek philosopher, teaching in Athens. He believed that all matter was infinitely divisible and motionless until animated by mind (*nous*).

Anaximander /aˌnaksɪˈmandə/ (*c.*610–*c.*545 BC), Greek scientist, who lived at Miletus. He believed the earth to be cylindrical and poised in space, and is reputed to have taught that life began in water and that humans originated from fish.

Anaximenes /ˌanakˈsɪmɪniːz/ (*c.*546 BC), Greek philosopher and scientist, who lived at Miletus. Anaximenes believed the earth to be flat and shallow, a view of astronomy that was a retrograde step from that of Anaximander.

ANC ▶ **abbreviation for** African National Congress.

-ance ▶ **suffix** forming nouns: **1** denoting a quality or state or an instance of one: *allegiance | extravagance | perseverance.*
2 denoting an action: *appearance | utterance.*
– ORIGIN from French *-ance*, from Latin *-antia*, *-entia* (from present participial stems *-ant-*, *-ent-*).

ancestor ▶ **noun** a person, typically one more remote than a grandparent, from whom one is descended: *he could trace his ancestors back to James the First.*
■ an early type of animal or plant from which others have evolved. ■ an early version of a machine, artefact, system, etc., which later became more developed.
– ORIGIN Middle English: from Old French *ancestre*, from Latin *antecessor*, from *antecedere*, from *ante* 'before' + *cedere* 'go'.

ancestral ▶ **adjective** of, belonging to, inherited from, or denoting an ancestor or ancestors: *the family's ancestral home | the only records of the ancestral forms are their fossils.*
– ORIGIN late Middle English: from Old French *ancestrel*, from *ancestre* (see **ANCESTOR**).

ancestress ▶ **noun** a female ancestor.

ancestry ▶ **noun** (pl. **-ies**) [usu. in sing.] one's family or ethnic descent: *his dark eyes came from his Jewish ancestry.*
■ the evolutionary or genetic line of descent of an animal or plant: *the ancestry of the rose is extremely complicated.* ■ figurative the origin or background of something: *the book traces the ancestry of women's poetry.*
– ORIGIN Middle English: alteration of Old French *ancesserie*, from *ancestre* (see **ANCESTOR**).

Anchises /anˈkʌɪsiːz/ Greek & Roman Mythology the father of the Trojan hero Aeneas.

ancho /ˈantʃəʊ/ (also **ancho chilli**) ▶ **noun** a large aromatic variety of chilli, used (usually dried) in dishes of Mexican origin or style.
– ORIGIN from Mexican Spanish (*chile*) *ancho*, 'wide (chilli)'.

anchor ▶ **noun** **1** a heavy object attached to a cable or chain and used to moor a ship to the sea bottom, typically one having a metal shank with a ring at one end for the cable and a pair of curved and/or barbed flukes at the other.
■ (**anchors**) Brit. informal the brakes of a car: *this idiot in front slammed on his anchors at a crossing.* ■ figurative a person or thing which provides stability or confidence in an otherwise uncertain situation: *the European Community is the economic anchor of the New Europe.* ■ [usu. as modifier] a large and prestigious department store prominently sited in a new shopping centre with the object of attracting trade and business: *an anchor tenant.*
2 an anchorman or anchorwoman, especially in broadcasting or athletics: *he signed off after nineteen years as CBS news anchor.*
▶ **verb** [with obj.] **1** moor (a ship) to the sea bottom with an anchor so as to cause it to remain in the same place: *the ship was anchored in the lee of the island* | [no obj., with adverbial of place] *we anchored in the harbour.*
■ secure firmly in position: *with cords and pitons they* ***anchored*** *him* ***to*** *the rock | the tail is used as a hook with which the fish* ***anchors itself to*** *coral.* ■ provide with a firm basis or foundation: *it is important that policy be anchored to some acceptable theoretical basis.*
2 present and coordinate (a television or radio programme): *she anchored a television documentary series in the early 1980s.*
– PHRASES **at anchor** (of a ship) moored by means of an anchor. **drop anchor** (of a ship) let down the anchor and moor. **weigh** (or **raise**) **anchor** (of a ship) take up the anchor when ready to start sailing.
– ORIGIN Old English *ancor*, *ancra*, via Latin from Greek *ankura*; reinforced in Middle English by Old French *ancre*. The current form is from *anchora*, an erroneous Latin spelling. The verb (from Old French *ancrer*) dates from Middle English.

Anchorage the largest city in Alaska, a seaport on an inlet of the Pacific Ocean; pop. 226,340 (1990).

anchorage ▶ **noun** **1** an area off the coast which is suitable for a ship to anchor.
■ [mass noun] the action of securing something to a base or the state of being secured: *the plant needs firm anchorage* | figurative *the mother provides emotional anchorage.*
2 historical an anchorite's dwelling place.

anchor escapement ▶ **noun** a form of escapement in clocks and watches in which the teeth of the crown- or balance-wheel act on the pallets by recoil.

anchoress ▶ **noun** historical a female anchorite.

anchorite /ˈaŋkərʌɪt/ ▶ **noun** historical a religious recluse.
– DERIVATIVES **anchoritic** adjective.
– ORIGIN late Middle English: from medieval Latin *anchorita*, (ecclesiastical Latin *anchoreta*), from ecclesiastical Greek *anakhōrētēs*, from *anakhōrein* 'retire', from *ana-* 'back' + *khōra*, *khōr-* 'a place'.

anchorman ▶ **noun** (pl. **-men**) a man who presents and coordinates a live television or radio programme involving other contributors.
■ a man who plays the most crucial part or is the most dependable contributor: *the anchorman of the Hampshire batting.* ■ the member of a relay team who runs the last leg.

anchorwoman ▶ **noun** (pl. **-women**) a female presenter of a television or radio programme.

anchoveta /ˌantʃə(ʊ)ˈvɛtə/ ▶ **noun** an anchovy found off the Pacific coasts of South America, of great commercial importance to Peru.
● *Engraulis ringens*, family Engraulidae.
– ORIGIN 1940s: from Spanish, diminutive of *anchova* (see **ANCHOVY**).

anchovy /ˈantʃəvi, anˈtʃəʊvi/ ▶ **noun** (pl. **-ies**) a small shoaling fish of commercial importance as a food fish and as bait. It is strongly flavoured and is usually preserved in salt and oil.
● Genus *Engraulis*, family Engraulidae: several species, including *E. encrasicolus* of European waters.
– ORIGIN late 16th cent.: from Spanish and Portuguese *anchova*, of unknown origin.

anchusa /əŋˈkjuːzə, anˈtʃuːzə/ ▶ **noun** an Old World plant of the borage family, which is widely cultivated for its bright, typically blue, flowers.
● Genus *Anchusa*, family Boraginaceae.
– ORIGIN via Latin from Greek *ankhousa*.

ancien régime /ˌɒsɪã reɪˈʒiːm, French ɑ̃sjɛ̃ ʀeʒim/ ▶ **noun** (pl. **anciens régimes** pronunc. same) a political or social system that has been displaced, typically by one that is more modern.
■ (**Ancien Régime**) the political and social system in France before the Revolution of 1789.
– ORIGIN French, literally 'old rule'.

ancient[1] ▶ **adjective** belonging to the very distant past and no longer in existence: *the ancient civilizations of the Mediterranean.*
■ having been in existence for a very long time: *an ancient gateway | ancient forests.* ■ chiefly humorous showing or feeling signs of age or wear: *an ancient pair of jeans | you make me feel ancient.*
▶ **noun** archaic or humorous an old man: *a solitary ancient in a tweed jacket.*
– PHRASES **the Ancient of Days** a biblical title for God. **the ancients** the people of ancient times, especially the Greeks and Romans of classical antiquity. ■ the classical Greek and Roman authors.
– DERIVATIVES **ancientness** noun.
– ORIGIN late Middle English: from Old French *ancien*, based on Latin *ante* 'before'.

ancient[2] ▶ **noun** archaic a standard, flag, or ensign.
– ORIGIN mid 16th cent.: alteration of **ENSIGN** by association with *ancien*, an early form of **ANCIENT**[1].

ancient demesne ▶ **noun** [mass noun] land recorded in Domesday Book as belonging to the Crown.

ancient history ▶ **noun** [mass noun] the history of the ancient civilizations of the Mediterranean area and the Near East up to the fall of the Western Roman Empire in AD 476.
■ informal something that is already long familiar and no longer new, interesting, or relevant: *the New Wave is ancient history now.*
– DERIVATIVES **ancient historian** noun.

ancient lights ▶ **plural noun** [treated as sing.] English Law the right of access to light of a property, established by custom and used to prevent the construction of buildings on adjacent property which would obstruct such access.
– ORIGIN mid 18th cent.: from *lights* meaning 'light from the sky'. In England the sign 'Ancient Lights' was often placed on a house, adjacent to a site where a high building might be erected.

anciently ▶ **adverb** long ago: *the area was anciently called Dalriada.*

ancient monument ▶ **noun** Brit. an old building,

or the site of one, that is preserved by an official agency.

ancient world ▶ **noun** the region around the Mediterranean and the Near East before the fall of the Western Roman Empire in AD 476.

ancillary /anˈsɪləri/ ▶ **adjective** providing necessary support to the primary activities or operation of an organization, institution, industry, or system: *ancillary staff such as radiotherapists.*
■additional; subsidiary: *paragraph 19 was merely* **ancillary** *to paragraph 16.*
▶ **noun** (pl. **-ies**) a person whose work provides necessary support to the primary activities of an organization, institution, or industry: *the employment of specialist teachers and ancillaries.*
■something which functions in a supplementary or supporting role: *undergraduate courses of three main subjects with related ancillaries.*
– ORIGIN mid 17th cent.: from Latin *ancillaris*, from *ancilla* 'maidservant'.

ancon /ˈaŋkɒn, -k(ə)n/ ▶ **noun** (pl. **ancones** /aŋˈkəʊniːz/) Architecture **1** a console, typically consisting of two volutes, that supports or appears to support a cornice.
2 each of a pair of projections on either side of a block of stone or other material, used for lifting it.
– ORIGIN early 18th cent. (denoting the corner or quoin of a wall or rafter): via Latin from Greek *ankōn* 'bend, elbow'.

Ancona[1] /aŋˈkəʊnə/ a port on the Adriatic coast of central Italy, capital of Marche region; pop. 103,270 (1990).

Ancona[2] /ənˈkəʊnə/ ▶ **noun** a chicken of a breed with black-and-white mottled plumage.

-ancy ▶ **suffix** (forming nouns) denoting a quality or state: *buoyancy* | *expectancy.* Compare with **-ANCE**.
– ORIGIN from Latin *-antia* (see also **-ENCY**).

ancylostomiasis /ˌaŋkɪlə(ʊ)stə(ʊ)ˈmʌɪəsɪs, ˌansɪ-/ (also **ankylostomiasis**) ▶ **noun** [mass noun] Medicine hookworm infection of the small intestine, often leading to anaemia.
● The worm is typically *Ancylostoma duodenale*, class Phasmida.
– ORIGIN late 19th cent.: from modern Latin *Ancylostoma* (from Greek *ankulos* 'crooked' + *stoma* 'mouth') + **-IASIS**.

Ancyra /anˈsʌɪrə/ ancient Roman name for **ANKARA**.

AND ▶ **abbreviation for** Andorra (international vehicle registration).

and ▶ **conjunction 1** used to connect words of the same part of speech, clauses, or sentences, that are to be taken jointly: *bread and butter* | *red and black tiles* | *they can read and write* | *a hundred and fifty.*
■used to connect two clauses when the second refers to something that happens after the first: *he turned round and walked out.* ■ used to connect two clauses, the second of which refers to something that results from the first: *do that once more and I'll skin you alive.* ■ connecting two identical comparatives, to emphasize a progressive change: *getting better and better.* ■ connecting two identical words, implying great duration or great extent: *I cried and cried.* ■ used to connect two identical words to indicate that things of the same name or class have different qualities: *all human conduct is determined or caused—but there are causes and causes.* ■ used to connect two numbers to indicate that they are being added together: *six and four makes ten.* ■ archaic used to connect two numbers, implying succession: *a line of men marching two and two.*
2 used to introduce an additional comment or interjection: *if it came to a choice—and this was the worst thing—she would turn her back on her parents.*
■used to introduce a question in connection with what someone else has just said: *'I found the letter in her bag.' 'And did you steam it open?'* ■ (especially in broadcasting) used to introduce a statement about a new topic: *and now to the dessert.*
3 informal used after some verbs and before another verb to indicate intention, instead of 'to': *I would* **try and** *do what he said.* See **usage** below.
▶ **noun** (**AND**) Electronics a Boolean operator which gives the value one if and only if all the operands are one, and otherwise has a value of zero.
■(also **AND gate**) a circuit which produces an output signal only when signals are received simultaneously through all input connections.
– PHRASES **and/or** either or both of two stated possibilities: *audio and/or video components.*
– ORIGIN Old English *and, ond*, of Germanic origin; related to Dutch *en* and German *und*.

USAGE 1 It is still widely taught and believed that conjunctions such as **and** (and also **but** and **because**) should not be used to start a sentence, the argument being that a sentence starting with **and** expresses an incomplete thought and is therefore incorrect. Writers down the centuries from Shakespeare to David Lodge and the *New York Times Book Review* have readily ignored this advice, however, using **and** to start a sentence, typically for rhetorical effect, as in the following example: *What are the government's chances of winning in court? **And** what are the consequences?*
2 A small number of verbs, notably **try**, **come**, and **go** can be followed by **and** with another verb, as in sentences like *we're going to **try and** explain it to them* or *why don't you **come and** see the film?* The structures in these verbs correspond to the use of the infinitive **to**, as in *we're going to **try to** explain it to them* or *why don't you **come to** see the film?* Since these structures are grammatically odd—for example, the use is normally only idiomatic with the infinitive of the verb and not with other forms (i.e. it is not possible to say ***I tried and** explained it to them*)—they are regarded as wrong by some traditionalists. However, these uses are extremely common in just about every context and can certainly be regarded as part of standard English.
3 For information about whether it is more correct to say *both **the boys** and **the girls*** or *both **the boys** and **girls***, see **usage** at **BOTH**.
4 Where a list of items are separated by **and**, the following verb needs to be in the plural: see **usage** at **OR**.

-and ▶ **suffix** (forming nouns) denoting a person or thing to be treated in a specified way: *analysand.*
– ORIGIN from Latin gerundive ending *-andus*.

Andalusia /ˌandəˈluːsɪə/ the southernmost region of Spain, bordering on the Atlantic and the Mediterranean; capital, Seville. The region was under Moorish rule from 711 to 1492. Spanish name **ANDALUCÍA** /andaluˈθia, -ˈsia/.

Andalusian /ˌandəˈluːzɪən, -sɪən/ ▶ **adjective** of or relating to Andalusia or its people or their dialect.
▶ **noun 1** a native or inhabitant of Andalusia.
2 [mass noun] the dialect of Spanish spoken in Andalusia.
3 a light horse of a strong breed from Andalusia.

andalusite /ˌandəˈluːsʌɪt/ ▶ **noun** [mass noun] a grey, green, brown, or pink aluminosilicate mineral occurring mainly in metamorphic rocks as elongated rhombic prisms, sometimes of gem quality.
– ORIGIN early 19th cent.: from the name of the Spanish region of **ANDALUSIA** + **-ITE**[1].

Andaman and Nicobar Islands /ˈandəmən, ˈnɪkəbɑː/ two groups of islands in the Bay of Bengal, constituting a Union Territory in India; pop. 279,110 (1991); capital, Port Blair.

andante /anˈdanteɪ/ Music ▶ **adverb** & **adjective** (especially as a direction) in a moderately slow tempo.
▶ **noun** a movement, passage, or composition marked to be performed andante.
– ORIGIN Italian, literally 'going', present participle of *andare*.

andantino /ˌandanˈtiːnəʊ/ Music ▶ **adverb** & **adjective** (especially as a direction) lighter than andante, and usually quicker.
▶ **noun** (pl. **-os**) a movement or passage marked to be performed andantino.
– ORIGIN Italian, diminutive of **ANDANTE**.

Andean /anˈdiːən, ˈandɪən/ ▶ **adjective** of or relating to the Andes.
▶ **noun** a native or inhabitant of the Andes.

Andean condor ▶ **noun** see **CONDOR**.

Andersen, Hans Christian (1805–75), Danish author. He is famous for his fairy tales, published from 1835, such as 'The Snow Queen', 'The Ugly Duckling', and 'The Little Match Girl'.

Anderson[1], Carl David (1905–91), American physicist. In 1932 he discovered the positron—the first antiparticle known. Nobel Prize for Physics (1936, shared).

Anderson[2], Elizabeth Garrett (1836–1917), English physician. She established a dispensary for women and children in London (renamed the Elizabeth Garrett Anderson Hospital) and was the first woman elected to the BMA (1873).

Anderson[3], Lindsay (Gordon) (1923–94), English film director, best known for *This Sporting Life* (1963), *If ...* (1968), and *O Lucky Man* (1973).

Anderson[4], Marian (1902–93), American operatic contralto. In 1955 she became the first black singer to perform at the New York Metropolitan Opera.

Anderson shelter ▶ **noun** historical a small prefabricated air-raid shelter of a type built in the UK during the Second World War.
– ORIGIN 1930s: named after Sir John *Anderson*, the Home Secretary in 1939–40 when the shelter was adopted.

Andes /ˈandiːz/ a major mountain system running the length of the Pacific coast of South America. Its highest peak is Aconcagua, which rises to a height of 6,960 m (22,834 ft).

andesite /ˈandɪzʌɪt, -sʌɪt/ ▶ **noun** [mass noun] Geology a dark, fine-grained, brown or greyish intermediate volcanic rock which is a common constituent of lavas in some areas.
– DERIVATIVES **andesitic** adjective.
– ORIGIN mid 19th cent.: named after the **ANDES** mountains, where it is found + **-ITE**[1].

Andhra Pradesh /ˌɑːndrə prəˈdɛʃ/ a state in SE India, on the Bay of Bengal; capital, Hyderabad.

andiron /ˈandʌɪən/ ▶ **noun** a metal support, typically one of a pair, for wood burning in a fireplace.
– ORIGIN Middle English: from Old French *andier*, of unknown origin. The ending was altered by association with **IRON**.

andisol /ˈandɪsɒl/ ▶ **noun** Soil Science a black or dark brown soil formed from volcanic material, with an A horizon rich in organic material.

Andorra /anˈdɔːrə/ a small autonomous principality in the southern Pyrenees, between France and Spain; pop. 61,600 (est. 1993); official languages, Catalan and French; capital, Andorra la Vella. Its independence dates from the late 8th century, when Charlemagne is said to have granted the Andorrans self-government for their help in defeating the Moors.
– DERIVATIVES **Andorran** adjective & noun.

andouille /ɒ̃ˈduːj/ ▶ **noun** [mass noun] chiefly N. Amer. a type of pork sausage, served typically as an hors d'oeuvre.
– ORIGIN French.

andradite /ˈandrədʌɪt/ ▶ **noun** [mass noun] a mineral of the garnet group, containing calcium and iron. It occurs as yellow, green, brown, or black crystals, sometimes of gem quality.
– ORIGIN mid 19th cent.: named after J. B. de *Andrada* e Silva (c.1763–1838), Brazilian geologist, + **-ITE**[1].

Andre /ˈɑːndreɪ/, Carl (b.1935), American minimalist sculptor. His most famous works consist of ready-made units such as bricks, stacked according to a mathematical system and without adhesives or joints.

Andretti /anˈdrɛti/, Mario (Gabriele) (b.1940), Italian-born American motor-racing driver. He won the Formula One world championship in 1978, and also won the Indycar championship four times.

Andrew, Prince, Andrew Albert Christian Edward, Duke of York (b.1960), second son of Elizabeth II. He married Sarah Ferguson in 1986 but the couple divorced in 1993; they have two children, Princess Beatrice (b.1988) and Princess Eugenie (b.1990).

Andrew, St, an Apostle, the brother of St Peter. The X-shaped cross became associated with his name during the Middle Ages because he is said to have died by crucifixion on such a cross. St Andrew is the patron saint of Scotland and Russia. Feast day, 30 November.

Andrews[1], Dame Julie (b.1935), English actress and singer; born *Julia Elizabeth Wells*. She is best known for the films *Mary Poppins* (1964), for which she won an Oscar, and *The Sound of Music* (1965).

Andrews[2], Thomas (1813–85), Irish physical chemist. He discovered the critical temperature of carbon dioxide, and showed that ozone is an allotrope of oxygen.

androcentric /ˌandrə(ʊ)ˈsɛntrɪk/ ▶ **adjective** focused or centred on men: *in the radical feminist view science is sexist and androcentric.*
– ORIGIN early 20th cent.: from Greek *anēr, andr-* 'man' + **-CENTRIC**.

Androcles /ˈandrəkliːz/ a runaway slave in a story by Aulus Gellius (2nd century AD) who extracted a

a

thorn from the paw of a lion, which later recognized him and refrained from attacking him when he faced it in the arena.

androcracy /an'drɒkrəsi/ ▶ **noun** (pl. **-ies**) a social system ruled or dominated by men.
– DERIVATIVES **androcratic** adjective.

androecium /an'driːsɪəm/ ▶ **noun** (pl. **androecia** /-sɪə/) Botany the stamens of a flower collectively.
– ORIGIN mid 19th cent.: modern Latin, from Greek *anēr, andr-*, 'man' + *oikion* 'house'.

androgen /'andrədʒ(ə)n/ ▶ **noun** Biochemistry a male sex hormone, such as testosterone.
– DERIVATIVES **androgenic** adjective.
– ORIGIN 1930s: from Greek *anēr, andr-* 'man' + **-GEN**.

androgenize /an'drɒdʒənʌɪz/ (also **-ise**) ▶ **verb** [with obj.] [usu. as adj. **androgenized**] treat with or expose to male hormones, typically with the result that male sexual characteristics are produced.
– DERIVATIVES **androgenization** noun.

androgyne /'andrədʒʌɪn/ ▶ **noun** an androgynous individual.
■ a hermaphrodite.
– ORIGIN mid 16th cent. (as a noun): via Latin from Greek *androgunos*, from *anēr, andr-* 'man' + *gunē* 'woman'.

androgynous /an'drɒdʒɪnəs/ ▶ **adjective** partly male and partly female in appearance; of indeterminate sex.
■ hermaphrodite.
– DERIVATIVES **androgyny** noun.
– ORIGIN early 17th cent.: from Latin *androgynus* (see **ANDROGYNE**) + **-OUS**.

android /'andrɔɪd/ ▶ **noun** (in science fiction) a robot with a human appearance.
– ORIGIN early 18th cent. (in the modern Latin form): from modern Latin *androides*, from Greek *anēr, andr-* 'man' + **-OID**.

Andromache /an'drɒməki/ Greek Mythology the wife of Hector. She became the slave of Neoptolemus (son of Achilles) after the fall of Troy.

Andromeda /an'drɒmɪdə/ **1** Greek Mythology an Ethiopian princess whose mother Cassiopeia boasted that she herself (or, in some stories, her daughter) was more beautiful than the nereids. In revenge Poseidon sent a sea monster to ravage the country; to placate him Andromeda was fastened to a rock and exposed to the monster, from which she was rescued by Perseus.
2 Astronomy a large northern constellation between Perseus and Pegasus, with few bright stars. It is chiefly notable for the **Andromeda Galaxy** (or **Great Nebula of Andromeda**), a conspicuous spiral galaxy probably twice as massive as our own and located 2 million light years away.
■ [as genitive **Andromedae** /an'drɒmɪdiː, -dʌɪ/] used with preceding letter or numeral to designate a star in this constellation: *the star Gamma Andromedae.*

andromeda /an'drɒmɪdə/ ▶ **noun** a bog rosemary, especially (**marsh andromeda**) the common bog rosemary.

Andropov[1] /an'drɒpɒf/ former name (1984–9) for **RYBINSK**.

Andropov[2] /an'drɒpɒf/, Yuri (Vladimirovich) (1914–84), Soviet statesman, General Secretary of the Communist Party of the USSR 1982–4 and President 1983–4. As President he initiated the reform process carried through by Mikhail Gorbachev, his chosen successor.

androsterone /ˌandrə(ʊ)'stɪərəʊn, an'drɒstərəʊn/ ▶ **noun** [mass noun] Biochemistry a relatively inactive male sex hormone produced by metabolism of testosterone.
– ORIGIN 1930s: from Greek *anēr, andr-* 'man' + **STEROL** + **-ONE**.

-androus ▶ **combining form** Botany having male organs or stamens of a specified number: *polyandrous.*
– ORIGIN from modern Latin *-andrus* (from Greek *-andros*, from *anēr, andr-* 'man') + **-OUS**.

-ane[1] ▶ **suffix** variant spelling of **-AN**, usually with a distinction of sense (such as *humane* compared with *human*) but sometimes with no corresponding form in *-an* (such as *mundane*).

-ane[2] ▶ **suffix** Chemistry forming names of saturated hydrocarbons: *methane | propane.*
– ORIGIN on the pattern of words such as *-ene, -ine.*

anecdotage /'anɪkdəʊtɪdʒ/ ▶ **noun** [mass noun] **1** anecdotes collectively: *a number of reports cannot be dismissed as anecdotage.* [ORIGIN: early 19th cent.: from **ANECDOTE** + **-AGE**.]
2 humorous old age, especially in someone who is inclined to be garrulous. [ORIGIN: late 18th cent.: from a blend of **ANECDOTE** and **DOTAGE**.]

anecdotal ▶ **adjective** (of an account) not necessarily true or reliable, because based on personal accounts rather than facts or research: *while there was much anecdotal evidence there was little hard fact.*
■ characterized by or fond of telling anecdotes: *her book is anecdotal and chatty.* ■ (of a painting) depicting small narrative incidents: *nineteenth century French anecdotal paintings.*
– DERIVATIVES **anecdotalist** noun, **anecdotally** adverb.

anecdote /'anɪkdəʊt/ ▶ **noun** a short amusing or interesting story about a real incident or person: *he told anecdotes about his job* | [mass noun] *he had a rich store of anecdote.*
■ an account regarded as unreliable or hearsay: [mass noun] *his wife's death has long been the subject of rumour and anecdote.* ■ [mass noun] the depiction of a minor narrative incident in a painting.
– ORIGIN late 17th cent.: from French, or via modern Latin from Greek *anekdota* 'things unpublished', from *an-* 'not' + *ekdotos*, from *ekdidōnai* 'publish'.

anechoic /ˌanɪ'kəʊɪk/ ▶ **adjective** technical free from echo: *an anechoic chamber.*
■ (of a coating or material) tending to deaden sound.

anele /ə'niːl/ ▶ **verb** [with obj.] archaic anoint (someone), especially as part of the Christian rite of giving extreme unction to the dying.
– ORIGIN Middle English: from *an-* 'on' + archaic *elien* 'to oil' (from Old English *ele*, from Latin *oleum* 'oil').

anemia ▶ **noun** US spelling of **ANAEMIA**.

anemic ▶ **adjective** US spelling of **ANAEMIC**.

anemograph /ə'nɛməgrɑːf/ ▶ **noun** an anemometer which records the speed, duration, and sometimes also the direction of the wind.
– ORIGIN mid 19th cent.: from Greek *anemos* 'wind' + **-GRAPH**.

anemometer /ˌanɪ'mɒmɪtə/ ▶ **noun** an instrument for measuring the speed of the wind, or of any current of gas.
– DERIVATIVES **anemometric** adjective, **anemometry** noun.
– ORIGIN early 18th cent.: from Greek *anemos* 'wind' + **-METER**.

anemone /ə'nɛməni/ ▶ **noun 1** a plant of the buttercup family which typically has brightly coloured flowers and deeply divided leaves.
• Genus *Anemone*, family Ranunculaceae: numerous species, including the common Eurasian **wood anemone** (*A. nemorosa*).
2 short for **SEA ANEMONE**.
– ORIGIN mid 16th cent.: from Latin, said to be from Greek *anemōnē* 'windflower', literally 'daughter of the wind', from *anemos* 'wind', thought to be so named because the flowers open only when the wind blows.

anemone fish ▶ **noun** another term for **CLOWNFISH**.

anemophilous /ˌanɪ'mɒfɪləs/ ▶ **adjective** Botany (of a plant) wind-pollinated.
– DERIVATIVES **anemophily** noun.
– ORIGIN late 19th cent.: from Greek *anemos* 'wind' + *-philous* (see **-PHILIA**).

anencephalic /ˌanɛnsɪ'falɪk, -kɛ'falɪk/ Medicine ▶ **adjective** having part or all of the cerebral hemispheres and the rear of the skull congenitally absent.
▶ **noun** an anencephalic fetus or infant.
– DERIVATIVES **anencephaly** noun.
– ORIGIN mid 19th cent.: from Greek *anenkephalos* 'without brain' + **-IC**.

anent /ə'nɛnt/ ▶ **preposition** chiefly archaic or Scottish concerning; about: *I'll say a few words anent the letter.*
– ORIGIN Old English *on efen* 'in line with, in company with' .

-aneous ▶ **suffix** forming adjectives from Latin words: *cutaneous | spontaneous.*
– ORIGIN from the Latin suffix *-aneus* + **-OUS**.

anergia /a'nɔːdʒɪə/ ▶ **noun** [mass noun] Psychiatry abnormal lack of energy.
– ORIGIN late 19th cent.: modern Latin, from Greek *an-* 'without' + *ergon* 'work'.

anergy /'anədʒi/ ▶ **noun** [mass noun] Medicine absence of the normal immune response to a particular antigen or allergen.
– ORIGIN early 20th cent.: from German *Anergie*, from Greek *an-* 'not', on the pattern of *Allergie* 'allergy'.

aneroid /'anərɔɪd/ ▶ **adjective** relating to or denoting a barometer that measures air pressure by the action of the air in deforming the elastic lid of an evacuated box.
▶ **noun** a barometer of this type.
– ORIGIN mid 19th cent.: coined in French from Greek *a-* 'without' + *nēros* 'water'.

anesthesia etc. ▶ **noun** US spelling of **ANAESTHESIA** etc.

aneurysm /'anjʊrɪz(ə)m/ (also **aneurism**) ▶ **noun** Medicine an excessive localized swelling of the wall of an artery.
– DERIVATIVES **aneurysmal** adjective.
– ORIGIN late Middle English: from Greek *aneurusma* 'dilatation', from *aneurunein* 'widen out'.

anew ▶ **adverb** chiefly poetic/literary in a new or different and typically more positive way: *her career had **begun anew**, with a lucrative Japanese modelling contract.*
■ once more; again: *tears filled her eyes anew.*

anfractuous /ən'fraktjʊəs/ ▶ **adjective** rare sinuous or circuitous.
– DERIVATIVES **anfractuosity** noun.
– ORIGIN late 16th cent.: from late Latin *anfractuosus*, from Latin *anfractus* 'a bending'.

angel ▶ **noun 1** a spiritual being believed to act as an attendant, agent, or messenger of God, conventionally represented in human form with wings and a long robe: *God sent an angel to talk to Gideon | the Angel of Death |* figurative *Ella, ever the **angel of mercy**, organized the girls into baking biscuits.*
■ an attendant spirit, especially a benevolent one: *there was an angel watching over me.* See also **GUARDIAN ANGEL**. ■ informal a financial backer of an enterprise, typically in the theatre. ■ (in traditional Christian angelology) a being of the lowest order of the ninefold celestial hierarchy. ■ (**Angel**) short for **HELL'S ANGEL**. ■ informal an unexplained radar echo.
2 a person of exemplary conduct or virtue: *women were then seen as angels or whores | I know I'm **no angel**.*
■ used in similes or comparisons to refer to a person's outstanding beauty, qualities, or abilities: *you sang **like an angel**.* ■ used in approval when a person has been or is expected to be kind or willing to oblige: ***be an angel** and let us come in.* ■ used as a term of endearment: *I miss you too, angel.*
3 a former English coin minted between the reigns of Edward IV and Charles I and bearing the figure of the archangel Michael killing a dragon.
4 (**angels**) aviation slang an aircraft's altitude (often used with a numeral indicating thousands of feet): *we rendezvous at angels nine.*
– PHRASES **the angel in the house** chiefly ironic a woman who is completely devoted to her husband and family. [ORIGIN: phrase from a poem by Coventry Patmore.] **on the side of the angels** on the side of what is right: *we're not in the business of polluting the environment, we're on the side of the angels.*
– ORIGIN Old English *engel*, ultimately via ecclesiastical Latin from Greek *angelos* 'messenger'; superseded in Middle English by forms from Old French *angele*.

angel cake (N. Amer. also **angel food cake**) ▶ **noun** a very light, pale sponge cake made of flour, egg whites, and no fat, typically baked in a ring shape and covered with soft icing.

angel dust ▶ **noun** [mass noun] informal **1** the hallucinogenic drug phencyclidine hydrochloride.
2 another term for **CLENBUTEROL**.

Angeleno /ˌandʒə'liːnəʊ/ (also **Los Angeleno**, **Angelino**) ▶ **noun** (pl. **-os**) a native or inhabitant of Los Angeles: [as modifier] *Angeleno sports fans.*
– ORIGIN late 19th cent.: from American Spanish.

Angel Falls a waterfall in the Guiana Highlands of SE Venezuela. It is the highest waterfall in the world, with an uninterrupted descent of 978 m (3,210 ft). The falls were discovered in 1935 by the American aviator and prospector **James Angel** (*c.*1899–1956).

angelfish ▶ **noun** (pl. same or **-fishes**) any of a number of laterally compressed deep-bodied fishes with extended dorsal and anal fins, typically brightly coloured or boldly striped:
• a freshwater fish native to the Amazon basin (genus *Pterophyllum*, family Cichlidae), in particular *P. scalare*.
• a marine or reef-dwelling fish (several genera in the

a

family Chaetodontidae). • another term for **BATFISH** (in sense 2).

angel hair (also **angel's hair**) ▶ **noun** [mass noun] a type of pasta consisting of very fine long strands.

angelic ▶ **adjective** of or relating to angels: *the angelic hosts.*
▪(of a person) exceptionally beautiful, innocent, or kind: *she looks remarkably young and angelic.*
– DERIVATIVES **angelical** adjective, **angelically** adverb.
– ORIGIN late Middle English: from French *angélique*, via late Latin from Greek *angelikos*, from *angelos* (see **ANGEL**).

angelica /an'dʒɛlɪkə/ ▶ **noun** a tall aromatic plant of the parsley family, with large leaves and yellowish-green flowers. Native to both Eurasia and North America, it is used in cooking and herbal medicine.
• Genus *Angelica*, family Umbelliferae: many species, especially the cultivated *A. archangelica*.
▪[mass noun] the candied stalk of this plant, used in confectionery and cake decoration.
– ORIGIN early 16th cent.: from medieval Latin (*herba*) *angelica* 'angelic (herb)', so named because it was believed to be efficacious against poisoning and disease.

angelica tree ▶ **noun** a tree of the ginseng family, with large leaves and black berries.
• Genus *Aralia*, family Araliaceae, including the devil's walking stick of North America and several Asian species.

Angelic Doctor the nickname of St Thomas Aquinas.

Angelico /an'dʒɛlɪkəʊ/, Fra (*c.*1400–55), Italian painter and Dominican friar; born *Guido di Pietro*; monastic name *Fra Giovanni da Fiesole*. Notable works: the frescoes in the convent of San Marco, Florence (*c.*1438–47).

Angelino ▶ **noun** variant spelling of **ANGELENO**.

Angelman's syndrome (also **Angelman syndrome**) ▶ **noun** [mass noun] a rare congenital disorder characterized by mental retardation and a tendency to jerky movement, caused by the absence of certain genes normally present on the copy of chromosome 15 inherited from the mother.
– ORIGIN 1970s: named after Harold *Angelman*, the British doctor who described the condition.

angelology ▶ **noun** [mass noun] theological doctrine concerning angels.

Angelou /'andʒəluː/, Maya (b.1928), American novelist and poet, acclaimed for the first volume of her autobiography, *I Know Why the Caged Bird Sings* (1970), which recounts her harrowing experiences as a black child in the American South.

angel shark ▶ **noun** a large, active bottom-dwelling cartilaginous fish with broad wing-like pectoral fins.
• Family Squatinidae and genus *Squatina*: several species, in particular *S. squatina* (also called **MONKFISH**).

angels on horseback ▶ **plural noun** Brit. an appetizer consisting of oysters individually wrapped in bacon and served on toast.

angel's trumpet ▶ **noun** a South American shrub or small tree with large pendulous trumpet-shaped flowers, cultivated as an ornamental and in some regions consumed for its narcotic properties.
• Genus *Brugmansia*, family Solanaceae; often placed in the genus *Datura*.

angelus /'andʒ(ə)ləs/ (also **Angelus**) ▶ **noun** [in sing.] a Roman Catholic devotion commemorating the Incarnation of Jesus and including the Hail Mary, said at morning, noon, and sunset.
▪a ringing of church bells announcing this.
– ORIGIN mid 17th cent.: from the Latin phrase *Angelus domini* 'the angel of the Lord', the opening words of the devotion.

angel wings ▶ **plural noun** [treated as sing.] a large white edible piddock (mollusc) which occurs in the Caribbean and on the east coast of North America.
• *Barnea costata*, family Pholadidae.

anger ▶ **noun** [mass noun] a strong feeling of annoyance, displeasure, or hostility: *the colonel's anger at his daughter's disobedience.*
▶ **verb** [with obj.] (often **be angered**) fill (someone) with such a feeling; provoke anger in: *she was angered by his terse answer* | [with obj. and infinitive] *I was angered to receive a further letter from them* | [with obj. and clause] *he was angered that he had not been told.*
– ORIGIN Middle English: from Old Norse *angr* 'grief', *angra* 'vex'. The original use was in the Old Norse senses; current senses date from late Middle English.

Angers /'ɑ̃ʒeɪ, French ɑ̃ʒe/ a town in western France, capital of the former province of Anjou; pop. 146,160 (1990).

Angevin /'andʒəvɪn/ ▶ **noun** a native, inhabitant, or ruler of Anjou.
▪any of the Plantagenet kings of England, especially those who were also counts of Anjou (Henry II, Richard I, and John).
▶ **adjective** of or relating to Anjou.
▪of, relating to, or denoting the Plantagenets.
– ORIGIN from French, from medieval Latin *Andegavinus*, from *Andegavum* 'Angers' (see **ANGERS**).

angina /an'dʒʌɪnə/ ▶ **noun** [mass noun] **1** (also **angina pectoris** /'pɛkt(ə)rɪs/) a condition marked by severe pain in the chest, often also spreading to the shoulders, arms, and neck, owing to an inadequate blood supply to the heart. [ORIGIN: Latin *pectoris* 'of the chest'.]
2 [with modifier] any of a number of disorders in which there is an intense localized pain: *Ludwig's angina.*
– ORIGIN mid 16th cent. (in the Latin sense): from Latin, 'quinsy', from Greek *ankhonē* 'strangling'.

angio- /'andʒɪəʊ/ ▶ **combining form** relating to blood vessels: *angiography.*
▪relating to seed vessels: *angiosperm.*
– ORIGIN from Greek *angeion* 'vessel'.

angiogenesis ▶ **noun** [mass noun] Medicine the development of new blood vessels.

angiogram /'andʒɪə(ʊ)gram/ ▶ **noun** an X-ray photograph of blood or lymph vessels, made by angiography.

angiography /ˌandʒɪ'ɒgrəfi/ ▶ **noun** [mass noun] radiography of blood or lymph vessels, carried out after introduction of a radiopaque substance.
– DERIVATIVES **angiographic** adjective, **angiographically** adverb.

angioma /ˌandʒɪ'əʊmə/ ▶ **noun** (pl. **angiomas** or **angiomata** /-mətə/) Medicine an abnormal growth produced by the dilatation or new formation of blood vessels.
– ORIGIN late 19th cent.: from Greek *angeion* 'vessel' + **-OMA**.

angioneurotic ▶ **adjective** Medicine (of oedema) marked by swelling and itching of areas of skin, usually allergic in origin.

angioplasty /'andʒɪə(ʊ)ˌplasti/ ▶ **noun** (pl. **-ies**) [mass noun] surgical repair or unblocking of a blood vessel, especially a coronary artery.

angiosperm ▶ **noun** Botany a plant of a large group that comprises those that have flowers and produce seeds enclosed within a carpel, including herbaceous plants, shrubs, grasses, and most trees. Compare with **GYMNOSPERM**.
• Subdivision Angiospermae, division Spermatophyta.
– DERIVATIVES **angiospermous** /-'spəːməs/ adjective.

angiotensin /ˌandʒɪə(ʊ)'tɛnsɪn/ ▶ **noun** [mass noun] Biochemistry a protein whose presence in the blood promotes aldosterone secretion and tends to raise blood pressure.
– ORIGIN 1950s: from **ANGIO-** + (*hyper*)*tens*(*ion*) + **-IN**[1].

Angkor /'aŋkɔː/ the capital of the ancient kingdom of Khmer in NW Cambodia, noted for its temples, especially the Angkor Wat (mid 12th century); the site was rediscovered in 1860.

Angle ▶ **noun** a member of a Germanic people, originally inhabitants of what is now Schleswig-Holstein, who came to England in the 5th century AD. The Angles founded kingdoms in Mercia, Northumbria, and East Anglia and gave their name to England and the English.
– ORIGIN from Latin *Anglus*, (plural) *Angli* 'the people of *Angul*', a district of Schleswig (now in northern Germany), so named because of its shape; of Germanic origin, related to Old English *angul* (see **ANGLE**[2]). Compare with **ENGLISH**.

angle[1] ▶ **noun** **1** the space (usually measured in degrees) between two intersecting lines or surfaces at or close to the point where they meet.
▪a corner, especially an external projection or an internal recess of a part of a building or other structure: *a skylight in the angle of the roof.* ▪ a measure of the inclination of one line or surface with respect to another, equal to the amount that one would have to be turned in order to have the same inclination as the other: *sloping at an angle of 33° to the horizontal.* ▪ a position from which something is viewed or along which it travels or acts, typically as measured by its inclination from an implicit horizontal or vertical baseline: *from this angle Maggie could not see Naomi's face.*
2 a particular way of approaching or considering an issue or problem: *discussing the problems from every conceivable angle* | *he always had a fresh* ***angle on*** *life.*
3 [often with modifier] Astrology each of the four cardinal points of a chart, from which the first, fourth, seventh, and tenth houses extend anticlockwise respectively.
4 [mass noun] angle iron or a similar constructional material made of another metal.
▶ **verb** [with obj. and adverbial of direction] direct or incline at an angle: *Anna angled her camera towards the tree* | *he angled his chair so that he could watch her.*
▪[no obj., with adverbial of direction] move or be inclined at an angle: *still the rain angles down.* ▪ [with obj.] present (information) to reflect a particular view or have a particular focus: *angle your answer so that it is relevant to the job for which you are applying.*
– PHRASES **at an angle** in a direction or at an inclination markedly different from parallel, vertical, or horizontal with respect to an implicit baseline: *she wore her beret at an angle* | *an armchair was drawn up* ***at an angle to*** *his desk.* **from all angles** from every direction or point of view: *they come shooting at us from all angles.*
– ORIGIN late Middle English: from Old French, from Latin *angulus* 'corner'.

angle[2] ▶ **verb** [no obj.] fish with a rod and line: *there are no big fish left to* ***angle for.***
▪seek something desired by indirectly prompting someone to offer it: *Ralph had begun to* ***angle for*** *an invitation* | [with infinitive] *her husband was angling to get into the cabinet.*
▶ **noun** archaic a fish-hook.
– ORIGIN Old English *angul* (noun); the verb dates from late Middle English.

angle bead ▶ **noun** a strip of metal or wood fixed to an external corner before it is plastered to reinforce and protect it.

angle bracket ▶ **noun** **1** either of a pair of marks in the form < >, used to enclose words or figures so as to separate them from their context.
2 another term for **BRACKET** (in sense 3).

angled ▶ **adjective** **1** placed or inclined at an angle to something else: *he sent an angled shot into the net.*
▪(of information) presented so as to reflect a particular view or to have a particular focus.
2 [in combination] (of an object or shape) having an angle or angles of a specified type or number: *a right-angled bend* | *an obtuse-angled triangle.*

angle grinder ▶ **noun** a device with a rotating abrasive disc, used to grind, polish, or cut metal and other materials.

angle iron ▶ **noun** [mass noun] a constructional material consisting of pieces of iron or steel with an L-shaped cross section, able to be bolted together.
▪[count noun] a piece of metal of this kind.

angle of attack ▶ **noun** Aeronautics the angle between the line of the chord of an aerofoil and the relative airflow.

angle of incidence ▶ **noun** Physics the angle which an incident line or ray makes with a perpendicular to the surface at the point of incidence.

angle of reflection ▶ **noun** Physics the angle made by a reflected ray with a perpendicular to the reflecting surface.

angle of refraction ▶ **noun** Physics the angle made by a refracted ray with a perpendicular to the refracting surface.

angle of repose ▶ **noun** the steepest angle at which a sloping surface formed of loose material is stable.

anglepoise ▶ **noun** trademark a type of desk lamp with a jointed arm and counterbalancing springs that hold it in any position to which it is adjusted: [as modifier] *an anglepoise lamp.*

angler ▶ **noun** a person who fishes with a rod and line.
▪short for **ANGLERFISH**.

anglerfish ▶ **noun** (pl. same or **-fishes**) a fish that lures prey with a fleshy lobe on filament arising from the snout, typically with a very large head and wide mouth, and a small body and tail.
• Order Lophiiformes: several families. Some rest motionless on the seabed, in particular those of the family Lophiidae

(which includes *Lophius piscatorius* of European coasts); many others are deep-sea fish.

Anglesey /ˈaŋg(ə)lsi/ an island and county (since 1996) of NW Wales, separated from the mainland by the Menai Strait; pop. 70,000 (1996). Welsh name **YNYS MÔN**.

angle shades ▶ plural noun [treated as sing.] a European moth with wings patterned in muted green, red, and pink.
● *Phlogophora meticulosa*, family Noctuidae.

angle wings ▶ plural noun [treated as sing.] a North American butterfly that is related to and resembles the comma.
● Genus *Polygonia*, subfamily Nymphalinae, family Nymphalidae: several species.

Anglian /ˈaŋglɪən/ ▶ adjective **1** of or relating to the ancient Angles.
2 Geology of, relating to, or denoting a Pleistocene glaciation in Britain, identified with the Elsterian of northern Europe (and perhaps the Mindel of the Alps).
■ [as noun **the Anglian**] the Anglian glaciation or the system of deposits laid down during it.
– ORIGIN from Latin *Angli* (see **ANGLE**) + **-IAN**.

Anglican ▶ adjective of, relating to, or denoting the Church of England or any Church in communion with it.
▶ noun a member of any of these Churches.
– DERIVATIVES **Anglicanism** noun.
– ORIGIN early 17th cent.: from medieval Latin *Anglicanus* (its adoption suggested by *Anglicana ecclesia* 'the English church' in the Magna Carta), from *Anglicus*, from *Angli* (see **ANGLE**).

Anglican chant ▶ noun [mass noun] a method of singing unmetrical psalms and canticles to short harmonized melodies, the first note being extended to accommodate as many syllables as necessary.

Anglican communion the group of Christian Churches derived from or related to the Church of England, including the Episcopal Church in the US and other national, provincial, and independent Churches. The body's senior bishop is the Archbishop of Canterbury.

anglice /ˈaŋglɪsi/ ▶ adverb formal in English.
– ORIGIN from medieval Latin, from Latin *Anglus* (see **ANGLE**).

Anglicism ▶ noun a word or phrase that is peculiar to British English: *this new autobiography is studded with Anglicisms like lorries, plimsolls, and doing a bunk.*
■ [mass noun] the quality of being typically English or of favouring English things.
– ORIGIN mid 17th cent.: from Latin *Anglicus*, from *Angli* (see **ANGLE**) + **-ISM**.

anglicize (also **-ise**) ▶ verb [with obj.] make English in form or character: *he anglicized his name to Goodman* | [as adj. **anglicized**] *an anglicized form of a Navajo word.*
– DERIVATIVES **anglicization** noun.

angling ▶ noun [mass noun] the sport or pastime of fishing with a rod and line.

Anglo ▶ noun (pl. **Anglos**) **1** a white English-speaking person of British (sometimes including also northern European) origin (typically used outside Britain and Ireland, chiefly in North America and Australia).
■ chiefly US such a person as distinct from a Hispanic American: [as modifier] *Anglo neighbourhoods.* ■ Canadian such a person as distinct from one of French descent. ■ Indian, often offensive an Anglo-Indian.
2 Brit. informal a person selected for a Scottish, Irish, or Welsh national sports team who plays for an English club.
– ORIGIN early 19th cent.: independent usage of **ANGLO-**.

Anglo- ▶ combining form English: *anglophone.*
■ of English origin: *Anglo-Saxon.* ■ English and …: *Anglo-Latin.* ■ British and …: *Anglo-Indian.*
– ORIGIN modern Latin, from Latin *Anglus* 'English'.

Anglo-Boer War ▶ noun S. African the second Boer War. See **BOER WARS**.

Anglo-Catholic ▶ adjective of or relating to Anglo-Catholicism.
▶ noun a member of an Anglo-Catholic Church.

Anglo-Catholicism ▶ noun [mass noun] a tradition within the Anglican Church which is close to Catholicism in its doctrine and worship and is broadly identified with High Church Anglicanism.

As a movement, Anglo-Catholicism grew out of the Oxford Movement of the 1830s and 1840s.

Anglo-Celt ▶ noun a person of British or Irish descent (typically used outside Britain and Ireland).
– DERIVATIVES **Anglo-Celtic** adjective.

Anglocentric ▶ adjective centred on or considered in terms of England or Britain: *an Anglocentric, white view of Australian history.*

Anglo-Indian ▶ adjective of, relating to, or involving both Britain and India: *Anglo-Indian business cooperation.*
■ (of a person) of mixed British and Indian parentage. ■ chiefly historical (of a person) of British descent or birth but living or having lived long in India. ■ (of a word) adopted into English from an Indian language.
▶ noun an Anglo-Indian person.

Anglo-Irish ▶ adjective of or relating to both Britain and Ireland (or specifically the Republic of Ireland).
■ (of a person) of English descent but born or resident in Ireland. ■ of mixed English and Irish parentage.
▶ noun [mass noun] the English language as used in Ireland.
■ [as plural noun **the Anglo-Irish**] people of English descent but born or resident in Ireland.

Anglo-Irish Agreement an agreement made between Britain and the Republic of Ireland in 1985, admitting the Republic to discussions on Northern Irish affairs and providing for greater cooperation between the security forces in border areas.

Anglo-Irish Treaty an agreement signed in 1921 by representatives of the British government and the provisional Irish Republican government, by which Ireland was partitioned and the Irish Free State created.

Anglo-Latin ▶ adjective of, in, or relating to Latin as used in medieval England.
▶ noun [mass noun] this form of Latin.

Anglomania ▶ noun [mass noun] excessive admiration of English customs.
– DERIVATIVES **Anglomaniac** noun.

Anglo-Norman French (also **Anglo-Norman**) ▶ noun [mass noun] the variety of Norman French used in England after the Norman Conquest. It remained the language of the English nobility for several centuries and has had a strong influence on legal phraseology in English.
▶ adjective of or relating to this language.

Anglo-Nubian ▶ noun a goat of a coloured breed with a short glossy coat and lop ears, kept for its rich milk.

Anglophile ▶ noun a person who is fond of or greatly admires England or Britain.
– DERIVATIVES **Anglophilia** noun.

Anglophobe ▶ noun a person who greatly hates or fears England or Britain.
– DERIVATIVES **Anglophobia** noun.

anglophone ▶ adjective English-speaking: *the population is largely anglophone.*
▶ noun an English-speaking person.
– ORIGIN early 20th cent. (as a noun; rare before the 1960s): from **ANGLO-** + **-PHONE**, on the pattern of *francophone.*

Anglo-Saxon ▶ adjective relating to or denoting the Germanic inhabitants of England from their arrival in the 5th century up to the Norman Conquest.
■ of English descent. ■ of, in, or relating to the Old English language. ■ informal (of an English word or expression) plain, in particular vulgar: *using a lot of good old Anglo-Saxon expletives.*
▶ noun **1** a Germanic inhabitant of England between the 5th century and the Norman Conquest.
■ a person of English descent. ■ chiefly N. Amer. any white, English-speaking person.
2 [mass noun] the Old English language.
■ informal plain English, in particular vulgar slang.
– ORIGIN from modern Latin *Anglo-Saxones* (plural), medieval Latin *Angli Saxones.*

Angola /aŋˈgəʊlə/ a republic on the west coast of southern Africa; pop. 10,301,000 (est. 1991); languages, Portuguese (official), Bantu languages; capital, Luanda.

Angola was a Portuguese possession from the end of the 16th century until it achieved independence in 1975. Independence was followed by years of civil war, chiefly between the ruling Marxist MPLA and the UNITA movement.

– DERIVATIVES **Angolan** adjective & noun.

Angora /aŋˈgɔːrə/ former name (until 1930) for **ANKARA**.

angora /aŋˈgɔːrə/ ▶ noun [often as modifier] a cat, goat, or rabbit of a long-haired breed: *angora rabbits.*
■ [mass noun] a fabric made from the hair of the angora goat or rabbit: [as modifier] *an angora cardigan.*
– ORIGIN early 19th cent. (denoting a long-haired breed): from the place name **ANGORA**.

angora wool ▶ noun [mass noun] a mixture of sheep's wool and angora rabbit hair.

Angostura /ˌaŋgəˈstjʊərə/ former name (until 1846) for **CIUDAD BOLÍVAR**.

angostura /ˌaŋgəˈstjʊərə/ (also **angostura bark**) ▶ noun [mass noun] an aromatic bitter bark from certain South American trees, used as a flavouring, and formerly as a tonic and to reduce fever.
● The trees are *Angostura febrifuga* and *Galipea officinalis*, family Rutaceae.
■ short for **ANGOSTURA BITTERS**.
– ORIGIN late 18th cent.: from the place name **ANGOSTURA**.

Angostura bitters ▶ plural noun trademark a kind of tonic first made in Angostura.

angrez /ʌŋˈreɪz/ Indian informal ▶ noun (pl. **angrezi** /ʌŋˈreɪzi/ or **angrezlog** /ʌŋˈreɪzləʊg/) an English person: *the angrezi are your people.*
▶ adjective (also **angrezi**) English.
– ORIGIN Hindi, 'Englishman'.

angry ▶ adjective (**angrier**, **angriest**) having a strong feeling of or showing annoyance, displeasure, or hostility: full of anger: *why are you angry with me?* | *I'm angry that she didn't call me.*
■ figurative (of the sea or sky) stormy, turbulent, or threatening: *the wild, angry sea.* ■ (of a wound or sore) red and inflamed.
– DERIVATIVES **angrily** adverb.

angry white male ▶ noun chiefly US a right-wing or anti-liberal white man, especially a working-class one.

angry young man ▶ noun a young man dissatisfied with and outspoken against existing social and political structures.
■ (**Angry Young Men**) a number of British playwrights and novelists of the early 1950s whose work was marked by irreverence towards the Establishment and disgust at the survival of class distinctions and privilege. Notable members of the group were John Osborne and Kingsley Amis.

angst /aŋst/ ▶ noun [mass noun] a feeling of deep anxiety or dread, typically an unfocused one about the human condition or the state of the world in general: *angst-ridden sixth-formers.*
■ informal a feeling of persistent worry about something trivial: *my hair causes me angst.*
– DERIVATIVES **angsty** adjective.
– ORIGIN 1920s: from German, 'fear'.

Ångström /ˈɒŋstrəm/, Anders Jonas (1814–1874), Swedish physicist. He proposed a relationship between the emission and absorption spectra of chemical elements, and measured optical wavelengths in the unit later named in his honour.

angstrom /ˈaŋstrəm/ (also **ångström** /ˈɒŋstrəm/ **angstrom unit**) (abbrev.: **Å**) ▶ noun a unit of length equal to one hundred-millionth of a centimetre, 10^{-10} metre, used mainly to express wavelengths and interatomic distances.
– ORIGIN late 19th cent.: named after A. J. **ÅNGSTRÖM**.

Anguilla /aŋˈgwɪlə/ the most northerly of the Leeward Islands in the Caribbean; pop. 8,960 (est. 1992); languages, English (official), English Creole; capital, The Valley. Formerly a British colony, and briefly united with St Kitts and Nevis (1967), the island is now a self-governing dependency of the UK.
– DERIVATIVES **Anguillan** adjective & noun.

anguilliform /aŋˈgwɪlɪfɔːm/ ▶ adjective rare shaped like or resembling an eel.
■ Zoology of or relating to a large order of fishes (Anguilliformes) that comprises the eels.
– ORIGIN late 17th cent.: from Latin *anguilla* 'eel' + **-IFORM**.

anguish ▶ noun [mass noun] severe mental or physical pain or suffering: *she shut her eyes in anguish* | *Philip gave a cry of anguish.*
– ORIGIN Middle English: via Old French from Latin *angustia* 'tightness', (plural) 'straits, distress', from *angustus* 'narrow'.

anguished ▶ **adjective** experiencing or expressing severe mental or physical pain or suffering: *he gave an anguished cry.*
– ORIGIN early 17th cent.: past participle of the rare verb *anguish*, from Old French *anguissier*, from ecclesiastical Latin *angustiare* 'to distress', from Latin *angustia* (see **ANGUISH**).

angular /ˈaŋɡjʊlə/ ▶ **adjective** **1** (of an object, outline, or shape) having angles or sharp corners: *angular chairs | Adam's angular black handwriting*
■ (of a person or part of their body) lean and having a prominent bone structure: *her angular face.* ■ placed or directed at an angle: *Pittman launched an angular shot across the face of the goal.*
2 Physics denoting physical properties or quantities measured with reference to or by means of an angle, especially those associated with rotation: *angular acceleration.*
3 Astrology located in, relating to, or denoting any of the houses that begin at the four cardinal points of a chart.
– DERIVATIVES **angularity** noun, **angularly** adverb.
– ORIGIN late Middle English (as an astrological term): from Latin *angularis*, from *angulus* (see **ANGLE**[1]).

angular diameter ▶ **noun** Astronomy the apparent diameter of a planet or other celestial object measured by the angle which it subtends at the point of observation.

angular frequency ▶ **noun** Physics the frequency of a steadily recurring phenomenon expressed in radians per second. A frequency in hertz can be converted to an angular frequency by multiplying it by 2π. (Symbol: **ω**)

angular momentum ▶ **noun** Physics the quantity of rotation of a body, which is the product of its moment of inertia and its angular velocity.

angular velocity ▶ **noun** Physics the rate of change of angular position of a rotating body.

angulate ▶ **verb** [with obj.] (often **be angulated**) technical hold, bend, or distort (a part of the body, especially of an animal) so as to form an angle or angles: [as adj. **angulated**] *the hindquarters are more strongly angulated than the forequarters.*
■ Skiing incline (the upper body) sideways and outwards during a turn: [no obj.] *angulate slightly with the knees.*
– DERIVATIVES **angulation** noun.
– ORIGIN late 15th cent. (as *angulated*, used chiefly as a botanical or zoological term): from Latin *angulatus*, past participle of *angulare*, from *angulus* 'angle'. The ski term dates from the 1970s.

Angus[1] /ˈaŋɡəs/ an administrative region of NE Scotland; administrative centre, Forfar. It was known from the 16th century until 1928 as Forfarshire, and between 1975 and 1996 was part of Tayside region.

Angus[2] /ˈaŋɡəs/ ▶ **noun** short for **ABERDEEN ANGUS**.

angwantibo /əŋˈɡwɒntɪbəʊ/ ▶ **noun** (pl. **-os**) a small rare nocturnal primate of west central Africa, related to the potto.
● *Arctocebus calabarensis*, family Lorisidae.
– ORIGIN mid 19th cent.: from Efik.

anharmonic ▶ **adjective** Physics relating to or denoting motion that is not simple harmonic.
– DERIVATIVES **anharmonicity** noun.

anhedonia /ˌanhiːˈdəʊnɪə/ ▶ **noun** [mass noun] Psychiatry inability to feel pleasure in normally pleasurable activities.
– DERIVATIVES **anhedonic** adjective.
– ORIGIN late 19th cent.: from French *anhédonie*, from Greek *an-* 'without' + *hēdonē* 'pleasure'.

anhedral /anˈhiːdr(ə)l, -ˈhɛd-/ ▶ **adjective** Crystallography (of a crystal) having no plane faces.
▶ **noun** [mass noun] Aeronautics downward inclination of an aircraft's wing, or the angle of this. Compare with **DIHEDRAL**.
– ORIGIN late 19th cent. (as an adjective): from **AN-**[1] 'not' + *-hedral* (see **-HEDRON**).

anhinga /anˈhɪŋɡə/ ▶ **noun** chiefly N. Amer. another term for **DARTER** (in sense 1).
– ORIGIN mid 18th cent.: from Portuguese, from Tupi *áyinga*.

Anhui /anˈhweɪ/ (also **Anhwei**) a province in eastern China; capital, Hefei.

anhydride /anˈhʌɪdrʌɪd/ ▶ **noun** Chemistry the compound obtained by removing the elements of water from a particular acid.
■ [usu. with modifier] an organic compound containing the group —C(O)OC(O)—, derived from a carboxylic acid.
– ORIGIN mid 19th cent.: from Greek *anudros* (see **ANHYDROUS**) + **-IDE**.

anhydrite /anˈhʌɪdrʌɪt/ ▶ **noun** [mass noun] a white mineral consisting of anhydrous calcium sulphate. It typically occurs in evaporite deposits.
– ORIGIN early 19th cent.: from Greek *anudros* (see **ANHYDROUS**) + **-ITE**[1].

anhydrous /anˈhʌɪdrəs/ ▶ **adjective** Chemistry (of a substance, especially a crystalline compound) containing no water.
– ORIGIN early 19th cent.: from Greek *anudros* (from *an-* 'without' + *hudōr* 'water') + **-OUS**.

ani /ˈɑːni/ ▶ **noun** (pl. **anis**) a glossy black long-tailed bird of the cuckoo family, with a large deep bill, found in Central and South America.
● Genus *Crotophaga*, family Cuculidae: three species.
– ORIGIN early 19th cent.: from Spanish *ani*, Portuguese *anum*, from Tupi *anú*.

aniline /ˈanɪliːn, -lɪn/ ▶ **noun** [mass noun] Chemistry a colourless oily liquid present in coal tar. It is used in the manufacture of dyes, drugs, and plastics, and was the basis of the earliest synthetic dyes.
● Chem. formula: $C_6H_5NH_2$.
– ORIGIN mid 19th cent.: from *anil* 'indigo' (from which it was originally obtained), via French and Portuguese from Arabic *an-nīl* (from Sanskrit *nīlī*, from *nīla* 'dark blue').

aniline dye ▶ **noun** chiefly historical a synthetic dye, especially one made from aniline.

anilingus /ˌeɪnɪˈlɪŋɡəs/ ▶ **noun** [mass noun] sexual stimulation of the anus by the tongue or mouth.
– ORIGIN 1960s: from Latin *anus* 'anus' on the pattern of *cunnilingus*.

anima /ˈanɪmə/ ▶ **noun** [mass noun] Psychoanalysis Jung's term for the feminine part of a man's personality. Often contrasted with **ANIMUS** (sense 3).
■ [count noun] the part of the psyche which is directed inwards, in touch with the subconscious. Often contrasted with **PERSONA**.
– ORIGIN 1920s: from Latin, 'mind, soul'.

animadversion /ˌanɪmədˈvəːʃ(ə)n/ ▶ **noun** [mass noun] formal criticism or censure: *her animadversion against science.*
■ [count noun] a comment or remark, especially a critical one: *animadversions that the poet receives quite humbly.*
– ORIGIN mid 16th cent.: from French, or from Latin *animadversio(n-)*, from the verb *animadvertere* (see **ANIMADVERT**).

animadvert /ˌanɪmədˈvəːt/ ▶ **verb** [no obj.] (**animadvert on/upon/against**) formal pass criticism or censure on; speak out against: *we shall be obliged to animadvert most severely upon you in our report.*
– ORIGIN late Middle English (in the sense 'pay attention to'): from Latin *animadvertere*, from *animus* 'mind' + *advertere* (from *ad-* 'towards' + *vertere* 'to turn').

animal ▶ **noun** a living organism which feeds on organic matter, typically having specialized sense organs and nervous system and able to respond rapidly to stimuli: *animals such as spiders | wild animals adapt badly to a caged life | humans are the only animals who weep.*
■ any such living organism other than a human being: *are humans superior to animals, or just different?* ■ a mammal, as opposed to a bird, reptile, fish, or insect: *the snowfall seemed to have chased all birds, animals, and men indoors.* ■ a person whose behaviour is regarded as devoid of human attributes or civilizing influences, especially someone who is very cruel, violent, or repulsive: *those men have to be animals—what they did to that boy was savage.* ■ [with adj. or noun modifier] a particular type of person or thing: *a regular party animal | I am a political animal.*

> Animals are generally distinguished from plants by being unable to synthesize organic molecules from inorganic ones, so that they have to feed on plants or on other animals. They are typically able to move about, though this ability is sometimes restricted to a particular stage in the life cycle. The great majority of animals are invertebrates, of which there are some thirty phyla; the vertebrates constitute but a single subphylum. See also **HIGHER ANIMALS**, **LOWER ANIMALS**.

▶ **adjective** [attrib.] of, relating to, or characteristic of animals: *the evolution of animal life | animal welfare.*
■ of animals as distinct from plants: *tissues of animal and vegetable protein.* ■ characteristic of the physical and instinctive needs of animals; of the flesh rather than the spirit or intellect: *a crude surrender to animal lust.*
– ORIGIN Middle English: the noun from Latin *animal*, based on Latin *animalis* 'having breath' from *anima* 'breath'; the adjective via Old French from Latin *animalis*.

animalcule /ˌanɪˈmalkjuːl/ ▶ **noun** archaic a microscopic animal.
– DERIVATIVES **animalcular** adjective.
– ORIGIN late 16th cent.: from modern Latin *animalculum*, from *animal* 'an animal' + **-CULE**.

animalism ▶ **noun** [mass noun] behaviour that is characteristic of or appropriate to animals, particularly in being physical and instinctive.
■ religious worship of or concerning animals.
– DERIVATIVES **animalistic** adjective.

animalist ▶ **noun** an animal liberationist.

animality ▶ **noun** [mass noun] animal nature or character: *a pre-human condition of animality.*
■ physical, instinctive behaviour or qualities: *what attracted me to her was her animality.*
– ORIGIN early 17th cent.: from French *animalité*, from *animal* (adjective), from Latin *animalis* 'animate, living' (see **ANIMAL**).

animalize (also **-ise**) ▶ **verb** [with obj.] make into or like an animal.
– DERIVATIVES **animalization** noun.

animal liberation ▶ **noun** [mass noun] the freeing of animals from exploitation and cruel treatment by humans.
– DERIVATIVES **animal liberationist** noun.

animal magnetism ▶ **noun** [mass noun] **1** a quality of sexual attractiveness: *he had an animal magnetism that women found irresistible.*
2 historical a supposed emanation to which the action of mesmerism was ascribed.

animal rights ▶ **plural noun** the rights of animals to live free from human exploitation and abuse: [as modifier] *animal rights activists.*

animal spirits ▶ **plural noun** natural exuberance.

animate ▶ **verb** /ˈanɪmeɪt/ [with obj.] **1** chiefly figurative bring to life: *the desert is like a line drawing waiting to be animated with colour.*
■ give inspiration, encouragement, or renewed vigour to: *she has animated the government with a sense of political direction.*
2 (usu. **be animated**) give (a film or character) the appearance of movement using animation techniques.
▶ **adjective** /ˈanɪmət/ alive or having life (often as a contrast with **INANIMATE**): *gods in a wide variety of forms, both animate and inanimate.*
■ lively and active: *party photos of animate socialites.*
– ORIGIN late Middle English: from Latin *animat-* 'instilled with life', from the verb *animare*, from *anima* 'life, soul'.

animated ▶ **adjective** **1** full of life or excitement; lively: *an animated conversation.*
2 (of a film) made using animation techniques: *an animated version of the classic fairy tale.*
■ moving or appearing to move as if alive: *push-button commentaries and animated life-size figures.*
– DERIVATIVES **animatedly** adverb.

animated stick ▶ **noun** a stick insect of the eastern Australian coast, which is one of the world's longest insects at up to 25 cm.
● *Acrophylla titan*, family Phasmatidae, order Phasmida.

animateur /ˌanɪməˈtəː/ ▶ **noun** a person who enlivens or encourages something, especially a promoter of artistic projects.
– ORIGIN 1950s: French, from medieval Latin *animator*.

animatic /ˌanɪˈmatɪk/ ▶ **noun** a preliminary version of a film, produced by shooting successive sections of a storyboard and adding a soundtrack.
– ORIGIN 1970s: from *animat(ed)* + **-IC**, or a blend of **ANIMATED** and **SCHEMATIC**.

animation ▶ **noun** [mass noun] **1** the state of being full of life or vigour; liveliness: *they started talking with animation.*
■ chiefly archaic the state of being alive.
2 the technique of filming successive drawings or positions of puppets or models to create an illusion of movement when the film is shown as a sequence.
■ (also **computer animation**) the manipulation of electronic images by means of a computer in order to create moving images.
– ORIGIN mid 16th cent. (in the sense 'encouragement'): from Latin *animatio(n-)*, from *animare* 'instil with life' (see **ANIMATE**). Sense 1 dates from the early 19th cent.

animato /anɪˈmɑːtəʊ/ Music ▶ adverb & adjective (especially as a direction) in an animated manner.
▶ noun (pl. **animatos** or **animati** /ˌanɪˈmɑːtiː/) a passage marked to be performed animato.
– ORIGIN Italian.

animator ▶ noun a person who animates something, in particular:
■ a person who prepares animated films. ■ a person who provides entertainment and organizes activities such as sports at a holiday centre or tourist attraction. [ORIGIN: from French *animateur*, used in this sense.]

animatronics /ˌanɪməˈtrɒnɪks/ ▶ plural noun [treated as sing.] the technique of making and operating lifelike robots, typically for use in film or other entertainment.
– DERIVATIVES **animatronic** adjective.
– ORIGIN 1970s: blend of **ANIMATED** and **ELECTRONICS**.

anime /ˈanɪmeɪ, ˈanɪmə/ ▶ noun [mass noun] Japanese film and television animation, typically having a science-fiction theme and sometimes including violent or explicitly sexual material. Compare with **MANGA**.
– ORIGIN 1980s: Japanese.

animism /ˈanɪmɪz(ə)m/ ▶ noun [mass noun] **1** the attribution of a living soul to plants, inanimate objects, and natural phenomena.
2 the belief in a supernatural power that organizes and animates the material universe.
– DERIVATIVES **animist** noun, **animistic** adjective.
– ORIGIN mid 19th cent.: from Latin *anima* 'life, soul' + -**ISM**.

animosity /ˌanɪˈmɒsɪti/ ▶ noun (pl. -**ies**) [mass noun] strong hostility: *he no longer felt any* **animosity** *towards her.*
– ORIGIN late Middle English (originally in the sense 'spirit, courage'): from Old French *animosite* or late Latin *animositas*, from *animosus* 'spirited', from Latin *animus* 'spirit, mind'. The current sense dates from the early 17th cent.

animus /ˈanɪməs/ ▶ noun [mass noun] **1** hostility or ill feeling: *the author's animus towards her.*
2 motivation to do something: *the reformist animus came from within the Party.*
3 Psychoanalysis Jung's term for the masculine part of a woman's personality. Often contrasted with **ANIMA**.
– ORIGIN early 19th cent.: from Latin, 'spirit, mind'.

anion /ˈanʌɪən/ ▶ noun Chemistry a negatively charged ion, i.e. one that would be attracted to the anode in electrolysis. The opposite of **CATION**.
– DERIVATIVES **anionic** adjective.
– ORIGIN mid 19th cent.: from **ANODE** or **ANA-**, + **ION**.

anise /ˈanɪs/ ▶ noun **1** a Mediterranean plant of the parsley family, cultivated for its aromatic seeds which are used in cooking and herbal medicine.
● *Pimpinella anisum*, family Umbelliferae. See also **ANISEED**.
2 an Asian or American tree or shrub which bears fruit with an aniseed-like odour.
● Genus *Illicium*, family Illiciaceae: many species, especially star anise (*I. verum*), used in Chinese cooking.
– ORIGIN Middle English: via Old French from Latin *anisum*, from Greek *anison* 'anise, dill'.

anise cap ▶ noun a pale greenish mushroom which has a funnel-shaped cap and smells strongly of aniseed, found in both Eurasia and North America.
● *Clitocybe odora*, family Tricholomataceae, class Hymenomycetes.

aniseed ▶ noun [mass noun] the seed of the anise, used in cooking and herbal medicine.
– ORIGIN late Middle English: from **ANISE** + **SEED**.

anisette /ˌanɪˈzɛt/ ▶ noun [mass noun] a liqueur flavoured with aniseed.
– ORIGIN mid 19th cent.: from French, diminutive of *anis* (see **ANISE**).

anisogamy /ˌanʌɪˈsɒɡəmi/ ▶ noun [mass noun] Biology sexual reproduction by the fusion of dissimilar gametes. Compare with **ISOGAMY**.
– DERIVATIVES **anisogamous** adjective.
– ORIGIN late 19th cent.: from Greek *anisos* 'unequal' + -*gamy* (from *gamos* 'marriage').

Anisoptera /ˌanʌɪˈzɒptərə/ Entomology a group of insects which comprises the dragonflies. Compare with **ZYGOPTERA**.
● Suborder Anisoptera, order Odonata.
– DERIVATIVES **anisopteran** noun & adjective.

– ORIGIN modern Latin (plural), from Greek *anisos* 'unequal' + *pteron* 'wing'.

anisotropic /ˌanʌɪsə'trɒpɪk/ ▶ adjective Physics (of an object or substance) having a physical property which has a different value when measured in different directions. An example is wood, which is stronger along the grain than across it. Often contrasted with **ISOTROPIC**.
■ (of a property or phenomenon) varying in magnitude according to the direction of measurement.
– DERIVATIVES **anisotropically** adverb, **anisotropy** /-'sɒtrəpi/ noun.
– ORIGIN late 19th cent.: from Greek *anisos* 'unequal' + *tropos* 'turn' + -**IC**.

Anjou /ˈãʒuː, French ãʒu/ a former province of western France, on the Loire. It was an English possession from 1154 until 1204.

Ankara /ˈaŋkərə/ the capital of Turkey since 1923; pop. 2,559,470 (1990). Prominent in Roman times as Ancyra, it later declined in importance until chosen by Kemal Atatürk in 1923 as his seat of government. Former name (until 1930) **ANGORA**.

ankh /aŋk/ ▶ noun an object or design resembling a cross but having a loop instead of the top arm, used in ancient Egypt as a symbol of life.
– ORIGIN late 19th cent.: from Egyptian, literally 'life, soul'.

ankle ▶ noun the joint connecting the foot with the leg.
■ the narrow part of the leg between this and the calf: *her slim ankles* | *I stood up to my ankles in* snow | *the men are ankle-deep in mud* | [as modifier] *ankle socks*.
▶ verb [no obj.] **1** [with adverbial of direction] informal, chiefly US walk: *we can ankle off to a new locale*.
■ [with obj.] leave: *he ankled the series to do a movie*.
2 [usu. as noun **ankling**] flex the ankles while cycling in order to increase pedalling efficiency.
– ORIGIN Old English *ancleow*, of Germanic origin; superseded in Middle English by forms from Old Norse; related to Dutch *enkel* and German *Enkel*, from an Indo-European root shared by **ANGLE**[1].

ankle-biter ▶ noun humorous, chiefly N. Amer. & Austral./NZ a child.

ankle bone ▶ noun the chief bone of the ankle joint; the talus.

anklet ▶ noun **1** an ornament worn round an ankle.
2 chiefly N. Amer. a sock that reaches just above the ankle.
– ORIGIN early 19th cent.: from **ANKLE** + -**LET**, on the pattern of *bracelet*.

ankus /ˈaŋkəs/ ▶ noun Indian a goad for elephants.
– ORIGIN via Hindi from Sanskrit *aṅkuśa*.

ankylosaur /ˈaŋkɪlɔːsɔː/ ▶ noun a heavily built quadrupedal herbivorous dinosaur of the Cretaceous period, armoured with bony plates.
● Infraorder Ankylosauria, order Ornithischia: several genera, in particular *Ankylosaurus*.
– ORIGIN early 20th cent.: from modern Latin *Ankylosaurus*, from Greek *ankulos* (see **ANKYLOSIS**) + *sauros* 'lizard'.

ankylose /ˈaŋkɪləʊz/ ▶ verb (be/become **ankylosed**) Medicine (of bones or a joint) be or become stiffened or united by ankylosis.
– ORIGIN late 18th cent.: back-formation from **ANKYLOSIS**, on the pattern of words such as *anastomose*.

ankylosing spondylitis ▶ noun [mass noun] Medicine a form of spinal arthritis, chiefly affecting young males, that eventually causes ankylosis of vertebral and sacro-iliac joints.

ankylosis /ˌaŋkɪˈləʊsɪs/ ▶ noun [mass noun] Medicine abnormal stiffening and immobility of a joint due to fusion of the bones.
– DERIVATIVES **ankylotic** adjective.
– ORIGIN early 18th cent.: from Greek *ankulōsis*, from *ankuloun* 'to crook', from *ankulos* 'crooked'.

ankylostomiasis /ˌaŋkɪlə(ʊ)stə(ʊ)ˈmʌɪəsɪs/ ▶ noun variant spelling of **ANCYLOSTOMIASIS**.

anlage /ˈanlaːɡə/ ▶ noun (pl. **anlagen** /-ɡ(ə)n/) Biology the rudimentary basis of a particular organ or other part, especially in an embryo.
– ORIGIN late 19th cent.: from German, 'foundation, basis'.

anna /ˈanə/ ▶ noun a former monetary unit of India and Pakistan, equal to one sixteenth of a rupee.
– ORIGIN from Hindi *ānā*.

Annaba /ˈanəbə/ a port of NE Algeria; pop. 348,000

(est. 1989). The modern town is adjacent to the site of Hippo Regius, a prominent city in Roman Africa and the home and bishopric of St Augustine of Hippo from 396 to 430. Former name **BÔNE**.

An Najaf /an/ another name for **NAJAF**.

annal /ˈan(ə)l/ ▶ noun a record of the events of one year: *the annal for 1032.*
■ a record of one item in a chronicle.
– ORIGIN late 17th cent.: back-formation from **ANNALS**.

annalist ▶ noun a person who writes annals.
– DERIVATIVES **annalistic** adjective, **annalistically** adverb.

annals ▶ plural noun a record of events year by year: *eighth-century Northumbrian annals.*
■ historical records: *the annals of the police courts* | figurative *the deed will live forever in the annals of infamy.* ■ (**Annals**) used in titles of learned journals: *Annals of Neurobiology.*
– ORIGIN mid 16th cent.: from Latin *annales (libri)* 'yearly (books)', from *annus* 'year'.

Annan /ˈanan, ˈan(ə)n/, Kofi (Atta) (b.1938), Ghanaian diplomat, Secretary General of the United Nations since 1997.

Annapolis /əˈnapəlɪs/ the state capital of Maryland, on Chesapeake Bay; pop. 33,190 (1990). It is the home of the US Naval Academy.

Annapurna /ˌanəˈpʊənə/ a ridge of the Himalayas, in north central Nepal. Its highest peak rises to 8,078 m (26,503 ft).

Anna's hummingbird ▶ noun a North American hummingbird which lives chiefly in California. The male has an iridescent rose-red head and throat.
● *Calypte anna*, family Trochilidae.
– ORIGIN mid 19th cent.: named after *Anna*, the wife of Prince François Massena (*c.*1795–1863), Duc de Ravoli, who obtained the original specimen.

annates /ˈaneɪts/ ▶ plural noun chiefly historical a year's revenue of a Roman Catholic see or benefice, paid to the Pope by a bishop or other cleric on his appointment.
– ORIGIN early 16th cent.: from French, from medieval Latin *annata* 'year's proceeds', from *annus* 'year'.

annatto /əˈnatəʊ/ (also **anatto**) ▶ noun (pl. -**os**) **1** [mass noun] an orange-red dye obtained from the seed coat of a tropical fruit, used for colouring foods.
2 the tropical American tree from which this fruit is obtained.
● *Bixa orellana*, family Bixaceae.
– ORIGIN early 17th cent.: from Carib.

Anne (1665–1714), queen of England and Scotland (known as Great Britain from 1707) and Ireland 1702–14. The last of the Stuart monarchs, daughter of the Catholic James II (but herself a Protestant), she succeeded her brother-in-law William III to the throne. None of her children survived into adulthood, and by the Act of Settlement (1701) the throne passed to the House of Hanover on her death.

Anne, Princess, Anne Elizabeth Alice Louise, the Princess Royal (b.1950), daughter of Elizabeth II. She is a skilled horsewoman (riding for Great Britain in the 1976 Olympics) and is president of Save the Children Fund. Her two children are Peter (b.1977) and Zara Philips (b.1981), by her former husband Captain Mark Philips.

Anne, St, traditionally the mother of the Virgin Mary, first mentioned by name in the apocryphal gospel of James (2nd century). She is the patron saint of Brittany and the province of Quebec in Canada. Feast day, 26 July.

anneal /əˈniːl/ ▶ verb [with obj.] heat (metal or glass) and allow it to cool slowly, in order to remove internal stresses and toughen it.
■ Biochemistry recombine (DNA) in the double-stranded form. ■ [no obj.] Biochemistry (of DNA) undergo this process.
– DERIVATIVES **annealer** noun.
– ORIGIN Old English *onǣlan*, from *on* + *ǣlan* 'burn, bake' from *āl* 'fire, burning'. The original sense was 'set on fire', hence (in late Middle English) 'subject to fire, alter by heating'.

Anne Boleyn see **BOLEYN**.

Annelida /əˈnɛlɪdə/ Zoology a large phylum that comprises the segmented worms, which include earthworms, lugworms, ragworms, and leeches.

– DERIVATIVES **annelid** /ˈan(ə)lɪd/ noun & adjective, **annelidan** noun & adjective.
– ORIGIN modern Latin (plural), from French (*animaux*) *annelés* 'ringed (animals)', from Old French *anel* 'a ring', from Latin *anellus*, diminutive of *anulus* 'a ring'.

Anne of Cleves /kliːvz/ (1515–57), fourth wife of Henry VIII. Arranged for political purposes, the marriage was dissolved after only six months; Henry, initially deceived by a flattering portrait of Anne by Holbein, took an instant dislike to her.

annex ▶ **verb** /əˈnɛks/ [with obj.] (often **be annexed**) append or add as an extra or subordinate part, especially to a document: *the first ten amendments were* ***annexed to*** *the Constitution in 1791.*
■ add (territory) to one's own territory by appropriation: *Zululand was* ***annexed to*** *Natal in 1897.* ■ informal take for oneself; appropriate: *it was bad enough that Richard should have annexed his girlfriend.* ■ archaic add or attach as a condition or consequence.
▶ **noun** /ˈanɛks/ (chiefly Brit. also **annexe**) (pl. **annexes**) **1** a building joined to or associated with a main building, providing additional space or accommodation.
2 an addition to a document: *an annex to the report.*
– DERIVATIVES **annexation** noun, **annexationist** noun & adjective.
– ORIGIN late Middle English: from Old French *annexer*, from Latin *annectere* 'connect', from *ad-* 'to' + *nectere* 'tie, fasten'.

Annigoni /ˌanɪˈɡəʊni/, Pietro (1910–88), Italian painter. He is famous for his portraits of Queen Elizabeth II (1955, 1970) and President Kennedy (1961).

annihilate /əˈnʌɪleɪt/ ▶ **verb** [with obj.] destroy utterly; obliterate: *a simple bomb of this type could annihilate them all* | *a crusade to annihilate evil.*
■ defeat utterly: *the stronger force annihilated its opponent virtually without loss.* ■ Physics convert (a subatomic particle) into radiant energy.
– DERIVATIVES **annihilator** noun.
– ORIGIN late Middle English (originally as an adjective meaning 'destroyed, annulled'): from late Latin *annihilatus* 'reduced to nothing', from the verb *annihilare*, from *ad-* 'to' + *nihil* 'nothing'. The sense 'destroy utterly' dates from the mid 16th cent.

annihilation ▶ **noun** [mass noun] complete destruction or obliteration: *the threat of global annihilation.*
■ total defeat: *a show of independence is its only hope of avoiding annihilation in next year's elections.* ■ Physics the conversion of matter into energy, especially the mutual conversion of a particle and an antiparticle into electromagnetic radiation.
– ORIGIN mid 16th cent.: from late Latin *annihilatio(n-)*, from the verb *annihilare* (see **ANNIHILATE**).

anniversary ▶ **noun** (pl. **-ies**) the date on which an event took place in a previous year: *the 50th anniversary of the Battle of Britain.*
■ the date on which a country or other institution was founded in a previous year: *the 75th anniversary of the RAF.* ■ the date on which a couple were married in a previous year: *he even forgot our tenth anniversary!*
– ORIGIN Middle English: from Latin *anniversarius* 'returning yearly', from *annus* 'year' + *versus* 'turning'.

Annobón /ˈanəbɒn/ an island of Equatorial Guinea, in the Gulf of Guinea. Former name (1973–9) **PAGALU**.

Anno Domini /ˌanəʊ ˈdɒmɪnʌɪ/ ▶ **adverb** full form of **AD**.
▶ **noun** [mass noun] informal advancing age: *since retirement Anno Domini has restricted my activities.*
– ORIGIN Latin, 'in the year of the Lord'.

annotate /ˈanəteɪt/ ▶ **verb** [with obj.] add notes to (a text or diagram) giving explanation or comment: [as adj. **annotated**] *an annotated bibliography.*
– DERIVATIVES **annotatable** adjective, **annotative** adjective, **annotator** noun.
– ORIGIN late 16th cent.: from Latin *annotat-* 'marked', from the verb *annotare*, from *ad-* 'to' + *nota* 'a mark'.

annotation ▶ **noun** a note by way of explanation or comment added to a text or diagram: *marginal annotations.*
■ [mass noun] the action of annotating a text or diagram: *annotation of prescribed texts.*
– ORIGIN late Middle English: from French, or from Latin *annotatio(n-)*, from the verb *annotare* (see **ANNOTATE**).

announce ▶ **verb** [reporting verb] make a public and typically formal declaration about a fact, occurrence, or intention: [with clause] *the President's office announced that the state of siege would be lifted* | [with obj.] *he announced his retirement from international football* | [with direct speech] *'I have a confession to make,' she announced.*
■ give information about (transport) in a station or airport via a public address system: *they were announcing her train.* ■ make known the arrival or imminence of (a guest or a meal) at a formal social occasion: *dinner was announced.*
– ORIGIN late 15th cent.: from French *annoncer*, from Latin *annuntiare*, from *ad-* 'to' + *nuntiare* 'declare, announce' (from *nuntius* 'messenger').

announcement ▶ **noun** a public and typically formal statement about a fact, occurrence, or intention: *the minister was about to* ***make an announcement*** | *a policy announcement.*
■ [mass noun] the action of making such a statement: *the announcement of the decision of the European Parliament.* ■ a notice appearing in a newspaper or public place and announcing something such as a birth, death, or marriage: *an announcement is appearing in the* Morning Post *tomorrow.* ■ a statement of information given over a public address system.

announcer ▶ **noun** a person who announces something, in particular someone who introduces or gives information about programmes on radio or television.

annoy ▶ **verb** [with obj.] (often **be annoyed**) irritate (someone); make (someone) a little angry: *he was* ***annoyed at*** *being woken up so early* | *your damned cheerfulness has always annoyed me.*
■ archaic harm or attack repeatedly: *a gallant Saxon, who annoyed this Coast.*
– DERIVATIVES **annoyer** noun.
– ORIGIN Middle English (in the sense 'be hateful to'): from Old French *anoier* (verb), *anoi* (noun), based on Latin *in odio* in the phrase *mihi in odio est* 'it is hateful to me'.

annoyance ▶ **noun** [mass noun] the feeling or state of being annoyed; irritation: *there was* ***annoyance at*** *government interference* | *he turned his charm on Tara,* ***much to*** *Hegarty's* ***annoyance.***
■ [count noun] a thing that annoys someone; a nuisance: *the Council found him an annoyance.*
– ORIGIN late Middle English: from Old French *anoiance*, from *anoier* (see **ANNOY**).

annoying ▶ **adjective** causing irritation or annoyance: *annoying habits* | *unsolicited calls are annoying.*
– DERIVATIVES **annoyingly** adverb [as submodifier] *the car is annoyingly noisy.*

annual ▶ **adjective** occurring once every year: *the sponsored walk became an annual event* | *an annual report.*
■ calculated over or covering a period of a year: *an annual rate of increase* | *his basic annual income.* ■ (of a plant) living only for a year or less, perpetuating itself by seed. Compare with **BIENNIAL**, **PERENNIAL**.
▶ **noun** a book or magazine that is published once a year under the same title but with different contents.
■ an annual plant.
– DERIVATIVES **annually** adverb.
– ORIGIN late Middle English: from Old French *annuel*, from late Latin *annualis*, based on Latin *annus* 'year'.

annual general meeting (abbrev.: **AGM**) ▶ **noun** Brit. a yearly meeting of the members or shareholders of a club, company, or other organization, especially for holding elections and reporting on the year's events.

annualized ▶ **adjective** (of a rate of interest, inflation, or return on an investment) recalculated as an annual rate.

annual ring ▶ **noun** a ring in the cross section of the stem or root of a temperate woody plant, produced by one year's growth.

annuitant /əˈnjuːɪt(ə)nt/ ▶ **noun** formal a person who receives an annuity.
– ORIGIN early 18th cent.: from **ANNUITY**, on the pattern of *accountant*.

annuity ▶ **noun** (pl. **-ies**) a fixed sum of money paid to someone each year, typically for the rest of their life: *he left her an annuity of £1,000 in his will.*
■ a form of insurance or investment entitling the investor to a series of annual sums: [as modifier] *an annuity scheme.*
– ORIGIN late Middle English: from French *annuité*, from medieval Latin *annuitas*, from Latin *annuus* 'yearly', from *annus* 'year'.

annul /əˈnʌl/ ▶ **verb** (**annulled**, **annulling**) [with obj.] (usu. **be annulled**) declare invalid (an official agreement, decision, or result): *the elections were annulled by the general amid renewed protests.*
■ declare (a marriage) to have had no legal existence: *her first marriage was finally annulled by His Holiness.*
– DERIVATIVES **annulment** noun.
– ORIGIN late Middle English: from Old French *anuller*, from late Latin *annullare*, from *ad-* 'to' + *nullum* 'nothing'.

annular /ˈanjʊlə/ ▶ **adjective** technical ring-shaped.
– DERIVATIVES **annularly** adverb.
– ORIGIN late 16th cent.: from French *annulaire* or Latin *annularis*, from *anulus*, *annulus* 'a ring'.

annular eclipse ▶ **noun** an eclipse of the sun in which the edge of the sun remains visible as a bright ring around the moon.

annulate /ˈanjʊlət/ ▶ **adjective** chiefly Zoology having rings; marked with or formed of rings: *an annulate worm.*
– DERIVATIVES **annulated** adjective, **annulation** noun.
– ORIGIN early 19th cent.: from Latin *annulatus*, from *anulus*, *annulus* 'a ring'.

annulet /ˈanjʊlɪt/ ▶ **noun** **1** Architecture a small fillet or band encircling a column.
2 Heraldry a charge in the form of a small ring.
– ORIGIN late Middle English (in the general sense 'small ring'): from Old French *anelet*, from Latin *anulus*, *annulus* 'ring' + **-ET**[1]. The spelling change in the 16th cent. was due to association with the Latin.

annulus /ˈanjʊləs/ ▶ **noun** (pl. **annuli** /-lʌɪ, -liː/) technical a ring-shaped object, structure, or region.
■ Mathematics a plane figure consisting of the area between a pair of concentric circles.
– ORIGIN mid 16th cent.: from Latin *anulus*, *annulus*.

annunciate /əˈnʌnsɪeɪt/ ▶ **verb** [with obj.] archaic announce (something).
■ (of a bell or other device) give a warning of (a malfunction or dangerous condition).
– ORIGIN late Middle English (originally as a past participle): from medieval Latin *annunciat-*, variant spelling of Latin *annuntiat-* 'announced', from the verb *annuntiare*.

annunciation ▶ **noun** (usu. **the Annunciation**) the announcement of the Incarnation by the angel Gabriel to Mary (Luke 1:26–38).
■ a church festival commemorating this, held on 25 March (Lady Day). ■ a painting or sculpture depicting this. ■ [mass noun] formal or archaic the announcement of something: *the annunciation of a set of rules applying to the relationships between states.*
– ORIGIN Middle English: from Old French *annonciation*, from late Latin *annuntiatio(n-)*, from the verb *annuntiare* (see **ANNUNCIATE**).

annunciator ▶ **noun** a bell, light, or other device that provides information on the state or condition of something by indicating which of several electric circuits has been activated.

annus horribilis /ˌanəs hɒˈriːbɪlɪs/ ▶ **noun** a year of disaster or misfortune.
– ORIGIN modern Latin, suggested by **ANNUS MIRABILIS**.

annus mirabilis /mɪˈrɑːbɪlɪs/ ▶ **noun** a remarkable or auspicious year.
– ORIGIN modern Latin, 'wonderful year'.

anoa /əˈnəʊə/ ▶ **noun** (pl. same or **anoas**) a small deer-like water buffalo, native to Sulawesi.
● Genus *Bubalus*, family Bovidae: two species.
– ORIGIN mid 19th cent.: a local word.

anode /ˈanəʊd/ ▶ **noun** the positively charged electrode by which the electrons leave an electrical device. The opposite of **CATHODE**.
■ the negatively charged electrode of an electrical device, such as a primary cell, that supplies current.
– DERIVATIVES **anodal** adjective, **anodic** adjective.
– ORIGIN mid 19th cent.: from Greek *anodos* 'way up', from *ana* 'up' + *hodos* 'way'.

anodize /ˈanədʌɪz/ (also **-ise**) ▶ **verb** [with obj.] [usu. as adj. **anodized**] coat (a metal, especially aluminium) with a protective oxide layer by an electrolytic process in which the metal forms the anode.
– DERIVATIVES **anodizer** noun.

anodyne /ˈanədʌɪn/ ▶ **adjective** not likely to cause

offence or disagreement and somewhat dull: *anodyne music*.
▶ **noun** a painkilling drug or medicine.
■figurative something which alleviates a person's mental distress: *an anodyne to the misery she had put him through*.
– ORIGIN mid 16th cent.: via Latin from Greek *anōdunos* 'painless', from *an-* 'without' + *odunē* 'pain'.

anogenital /ˌeɪnəʊˈdʒɛnɪt(ə)l/ ▶ **adjective** Medicine & Anatomy of or relating to the anus and genitals.
– ORIGIN early 20th cent.: from Latin *ano-* (combining form of **ANUS**) + **GENITAL**.

anoint ▶ **verb** [with obj.] smear or rub with oil, typically as part of a religious ceremony: *bodies were anointed after death for burial*.
■(**anoint something with**) smear or rub something with (any other substance): *Cuna Indians anoint the tips of their arrows with poison*. ■ceremonially confer divine or holy office upon (a priest or monarch) by smearing or rubbing with oil: [with obj. and infinitive] *the Lord has anointed me to preach to the poor* | [with obj. and complement] *Samuel anointed him king*. ■figurative nominate or choose (someone) as successor to or leading candidate for a position: *he was anointed as the organizational candidate of the party* | [as adj. **anointed**] *his officially anointed heir*.
– PHRASES **Anointing of the Sick** (in the Roman Catholic Church) the sacramental anointing of the ill or infirm with blessed oil; unction. **God's** (or **the Lord's**) **anointed** a monarch ruling by divine right.
– DERIVATIVES **anointer** noun.
– ORIGIN Middle English: from Old French *enoint* 'anointed', past participle of *enoindre*, from Latin *inungere*, from *in-* 'upon' + *ungere* 'anoint, smear with oil'.

anole /əˈnəʊli/ ▶ **noun** a small, mainly arboreal American lizard with a throat fan that (in the male) is typically brightly coloured. Anoles have some ability to change colour. Also called **CHAMELEON** in North America.
●Genus *Anolis*, family Iguanidae: numerous species, in particular the **green anole** (*A. carolinensis*), which is popular as a pet in North America.
– ORIGIN early 18th cent.: from Carib.

anomalistic month ▶ **noun** Astronomy a month measured between successive perigees of the moon (approximately 27½ days).

anomalistic year ▶ **noun** Astronomy a year measured between successive perihelia of the earth (approximately 365¼ days).

anomalous /əˈnɒm(ə)ləs/ ▶ **adjective** deviating from what is standard, normal, or expected: *an anomalous situation* | *sentences which are grammatically anomalous*.
– DERIVATIVES **anomalously** adverb, **anomalousness** noun.
– ORIGIN mid 17th cent.: via late Latin from Greek *anōmalos* (from *an-* 'not' + *homalos* 'even') + **-OUS**.

anomaly /əˈnɒm(ə)li/ ▶ **noun** (pl. **-ies**) **1** something that deviates from what is standard, normal, or expected: *there are a number of anomalies in the present system* | [with clause] *the apparent anomaly that those who produced the wealth were the poorest* | [mass noun] *the position abounds in anomaly*.
2 Astronomy the angular distance of a planet or satellite from its last perihelion or perigee.
– ORIGIN late 16th cent.: via Latin from Greek *anōmalia*, from *anōmalos* (see **ANOMALOUS**).

anomia /əˈnəʊmɪə/ ▶ **noun** [mass noun] Medicine a form of aphasia in which the patient is unable to recall the names of everyday objects.
– DERIVATIVES **anomic** adjective.
– ORIGIN early 20th cent.: formed irregularly from **A-**[1] 'without, not' + Latin *nomen* 'name' + **-IA**[1].

anomie /ˈanəmi/ (also **anomy**) ▶ **noun** [mass noun] lack of the usual social or ethical standards in an individual or group: *the theory that high-rise architecture leads to anomie in the residents*.
– DERIVATIVES **anomic** /əˈnɒmɪk/ adjective.
– ORIGIN 1930s: from French, from Greek *anomia*, from *anomos* 'lawless'.

anon ▶ **adverb** archaic or informal soon; shortly: *I'll see you anon*.
– ORIGIN Old English *on ān* 'into one', *on āne* 'in one'. The original sense was 'in or into one state, course, etc.', which developed into the temporal sense 'at once'.

anon. ▶ **abbreviation for** anonymous.

anonym ▶ **noun 1** an anonymous person or publication.
2 a pseudonym.
– ORIGIN early 19th cent.: from French *anonyme*, from Greek *anōnumos* (see **ANONYMOUS**).

anonymize (also **-ise**) ▶ **verb** [with obj.] [usu. as adj. **anonymized**] Medicine remove identifying particulars from (test results) for statistical or other purposes: *anonymized testing of routine blood samples*.
– ORIGIN 1970s: from **ANONYMOUS** + **-IZE**.

anonymous ▶ **adjective** (of a person) not identified by name; of unknown name: *the donor's wish to remain anonymous* | *an anonymous phone call*.
■having no outstanding, individual, or unusual features; unremarkable or impersonal: *his impeccable, slightly anonymous Chelsea flat*.
– DERIVATIVES **anonymity** /anəˈnɪmɪti/ noun, **anonymously** adverb.
– ORIGIN late 16th cent.: via late Latin from Greek *anōnumos* 'nameless' (from *an-* 'without' + *onoma* 'name') + **-OUS**.

anonymous FTP ▶ **noun** [mass noun] Computing an implementation of the FTP server that allows anyone who can use FTP to log on to the server, using a general username and without a password check.

anopheles /əˈnɒfɪliːz/ (also **anopheles mosquito**) ▶ **noun** a mosquito of a genus which is particularly common in warmer countries and includes the mosquitoes that transmit the malarial parasite to humans. Compare with **CULEX**.
●Genus *Anopheles*, subfamily Anophelinae, family Culicidae.
– DERIVATIVES **anopheline** /əˈnɒfɪlʌɪn, -liːn/ adjective & noun.
– ORIGIN late 19th cent.: modern Latin, from Greek *anōphelēs* 'unprofitable, useless'.

Anoplura /ˌanə(ʊ)ˈplʊərə/ Entomology an order of insects that comprises the sucking lice. Also called **SIPHUNCULATA**. See also **PHTHIRAPTERA**.
– DERIVATIVES **anopluran** noun & adjective.
– ORIGIN modern Latin (plural), from *anoplos* 'unarmed' + *oura* 'tail'.

anorak ▶ **noun** a waterproof jacket, typically with a hood, of a kind originally used in polar regions.
■Brit. informal, derogatory a socially inept and studious or obsessive person with unfashionable and largely solitary interests.
– ORIGIN 1920s: from Greenland Eskimo *anoraq*. The British English informal sense dates from the 1980s and derives from the anoraks worn by trainspotters, regarded as typifying this kind of person.

anorectal /ˌeɪnəʊˈrɛkt(ə)l/ ▶ **adjective** Medicine & Anatomy of or relating to the anus and rectum.
– ORIGIN late 19th cent.: from French *ano-rectal*, from Latin *ano-* (combining form of **ANUS**) + *rectal* (see **RECTAL**).

anorexia /ˌanəˈrɛksɪə/ ▶ **noun** [mass noun] lack or loss of appetite for food (as a medical condition), in particular:
■(also **anorexia nervosa**) an emotional disorder characterized by an obsessive desire to lose weight by refusing to eat, and a distorted perception of one's own body.
– ORIGIN late 16th cent.: via late Latin from Greek, from *an-* 'without' + *orexis* 'appetite'.

anorexic (also **anorectic**) ▶ **adjective** relating to, characterized by, or suffering from anorexia.
■informal extremely thin.
▶ **noun 1** a person suffering from anorexia.
2 (**anorectic**) a medicine which produces a loss of appetite.

anorgasmia /ˌanɔːˈgazmɪə/ ▶ **noun** [mass noun] Medicine persistent inability to achieve orgasm despite responding to sexual stimulation.
– DERIVATIVES **anorgasmic** adjective.
– ORIGIN 1970s: from **AN-**[1] + **ORGASM** + **-IA**[1].

anorthite /əˈnɔːθʌɪt/ ▶ **noun** [mass noun] a calcium-rich mineral of the feldspar group, typically white, occurring in many basic igneous rocks.
– ORIGIN mid 19th cent.: from **AN-**[1] + Greek *orthos* 'straight' + **-ITE**[1].

anorthosite /əˈnɔːθəsʌɪt/ ▶ **noun** [mass noun] Geology a granular igneous rock composed largely of labradorite or another plagioclase.
– ORIGIN mid 19th cent.: from French *anorthose* 'plagioclase' + **-ITE**[1].

anosmia /aˈnɒzmɪə/ ▶ **noun** [mass noun] Medicine the loss of the sense of smell, either total or partial. It

may be caused by head injury, infection, or blockage of the nose.
– DERIVATIVES **anosmic** adjective.
– ORIGIN early 19th cent.: from **AN-**[2] + Greek *osmē* 'smell'.

A. N. Other ▶ **pronoun** Brit. used when listing sports teams to refer to a player who is not named or whose selection has not been confirmed.

another ▶ **determiner** & **pronoun 1** used to refer to an additional person or thing of the same type as one already mentioned or known about; one more; a further: [as determiner] *have another drink* | *I didn't say another word* | [as pronoun] *she was to become another of his stars*.
■[as determiner] used with a proper name to indicate someone or something's similarity to the person or event specified: *this will not be another Vietnam*.
2 used to refer to a different person or thing from one already mentioned or known about: [as determiner] *his wife left him for another man* | [as pronoun] *moving from one place to another*.
■[as determiner] used to refer to someone sharing an attribute in common with the person already mentioned: *his kiss with another man caused a tabloid rumpus*.
– ORIGIN Middle English: as *an other* until the 16th cent.

another place ▶ **noun** Brit. the other House of Parliament (used in the Commons to refer to the Lords, and vice versa).

anothery (also **anotherie**) ▶ **noun** Austral. informal another one: *I'll have anothery*.

Anouilh /ˈɒnwiː, French anɥij/, Jean (1910–87), French dramatist. He wrote many plays but is best known for his reworking of the Greek myth of Antigone in *Antigone* (1944).

ANOVA /aˈnəʊvə/ ▶ **noun** [mass noun] analysis of variance, a statistical method in which the variation in a set of observations is divided into distinct components.
– ORIGIN 1960s: acronym.

anovulant /aˈnɒvjʊl(ə)nt/ Medicine ▶ **adjective** (chiefly of a drug) preventing ovulation.
▶ **noun** an anovulant drug.
– ORIGIN 1960s: from **AN-**[1] + *ovul*(ation) + **-ANT**.

anovulatory /ˌanɒvjʊˈleɪt(ə)ri/ ▶ **adjective** Medicine (of a menstrual cycle) in which ovulation does not occur.

anoxia /aˈnɒksɪə/ ▶ **noun** [mass noun] technical an absence of oxygen.
■Medicine an absence or deficiency of oxygen reaching the tissues; severe hypoxia.
– DERIVATIVES **anoxic** adjective.
– ORIGIN 1930s: from **AN-**[1] + *ox*(*ygen*) + **-IA**[1].

ANS ▶ **abbreviation for** autonomic nervous system.

ansatz /ˈansats/ ▶ **noun** Mathematics an assumption about the form of an unknown function which is made in order to facilitate solution of an equation or other problem.
– ORIGIN 1940s: from German *Ansatz* 'approach, attempt'.

Anschluss /ˈanʃlʊs/ the annexation of Austria by Germany in 1938. Hitler had forced the resignation of the Austrian Chancellor by demanding that he admit Nazis into his cabinet. The new Chancellor, a pro-Nazi, invited German troops to enter the country on the pretext of restoring law and order.
– ORIGIN German, from *anschliessen* 'to join'.

Anselm, St /ˈansɛlm/ (c.1033–1109), Italian-born philosopher and theologian, Archbishop of Canterbury 1093–1109. He worked to free the Church from secular control and believed that the best way to defend the faith was by intellectual reasoning. His writings include *Cur Deus Homo?* a mystical study on the Atonement. Feast day, 21 April.

anserine /ˈansərʌɪn/ ▶ **adjective** of or like a goose.
– ORIGIN mid 19th cent.: from Latin *anserinus*, from *anser* 'goose'.

Anshan /anˈʃan/ a city in Liaoning, China; pop. 1,370,000 (1990). Anshan is situated close to major iron-ore deposits and China's largest iron and steel complex is nearby.

ANSI ▶ **abbreviation for** American National Standards Institute.

answer ▶ **noun** a thing that is said, written, or done to deal with or as a reaction to a question,

statement, or situation: *he knocked and entered without waiting for an answer.*
■ a thing written or said in reaction to a question in a test or quiz: *write your answers on a postcard.* ■ the correct solution to such a question: *the answer is 280°.* ■ a solution to a problem or dilemma: *the **answer to** poverty and unemployment is a properly funded range of services.* ■ [in sing.] (**answer to**) a thing or person regarded as being of equivalent status or fulfilling the same role as something or someone from another place: *the press called her Britain's answer to Marilyn Monroe.*
▶ **verb 1** [reporting verb] say or write something to deal with or as a reaction to someone or something: [with direct speech] *'Of course I can,' she answered* | [with clause] *she answered that she would take nothing but the ring* | [with obj.] *she tried to answer his questions truthfully* | [no obj.] *Steve was about to answer, but Hazel spoke first.*
■ [with obj.] provide the required responses to (a test or quiz): *answer the questions below for a chance to win a holiday.* ■ [no obj.] (**answer back**) respond impudently or disrespectfully to someone, especially when being criticized or told to do something: *I'd usually talk him round, but never answer back* | [with obj.] *Mary resisted the temptation to answer her mother back.* ■ [with obj.] act in reaction to (a sound such as a telephone ringing or a knock or ring on a door): *Digby answered the door* | [no obj.] *she rang Edward's house, hoping the housekeeper would answer.* ■ [with obj.] defend oneself against (a charge, accusation, or criticism): *he said he would return to Spain to answer all charges.* ■ [no obj.] (**answer for**) be responsible or to blame for: *if you persist in clinging to me in that way I will not answer for the consequences* | *the dust mite **has a lot to answer for**, especially if you are asthmatic.* ■ [no obj.] (**answer to**) be responsible or report to (someone): *I answer to the Assistant Commissioner of Specialist Operations.* ■ [no obj.] (**answer to**) be required to explain or justify oneself to (someone): *you will have the police to answer to.*
2 [with obj.] be suitable for fulfilling (a need); satisfy: *entrepreneurship is necessary to answer the needs of national and international markets.*
– PHRASES **answer the description of** correspond to a description, especially one of a suspect issued by the police. **answer to (the name of)** often humorous be called: *an attractive woman answering to the name of Suzanne.* **have** (or **know**) **all the answers** informal be confident in one's knowledge of something, typically without justification. **in answer to** as a response to or as a result of: *I hurried along the passage in answer to the doorbell's ring.*
– ORIGIN Old English *andswaru* (noun), *andswarian* (verb), of Germanic origin; from a base shared by **SWEAR**.

answerable ▶ **adjective 1** [predic.] (**answerable to**) required to explain or justify one's actions to; responsible or having to report to: *I'm not answerable to you for my every movement* | *the Attorney General is answerable only to Parliament for his decisions.*
■ (**answerable for**) responsible for: *an employer is answerable for the negligence of his employees.*
2 (of a question) able to be answered: *straightforward and answerable questions.*

answering machine ▶ **noun** a tape recorder or digital device which supplies a recorded answer to a telephone call and can record a message from the caller.

answering service ▶ **noun** a business that receives and answers telephone calls for its clients.

answerphone ▶ **noun** Brit. a telephone answering machine.

ant ▶ **noun** a small insect typically having a sting and living in a complex social colony with one or more breeding queens. It is wingless except for fertile adults, which form large mating swarms, and is proverbial for its industry.
● Family Formicidae, order Hymenoptera: several subfamilies.
– PHRASES **have ants in one's pants** informal be fidgety or restless.
– ORIGIN Old English *ǣmete* of West Germanic origin; related to German *Ameise*. Compare with **EMMET**.

ant- ▶ **prefix** variant spelling of **ANTI-** shortened before a vowel or *h* (as in *Antarctic*).

-ant ▶ **suffix 1** (forming adjectives) denoting attribution of an action or state: *arrogant* | *pendant.* **2** (forming nouns) denoting an agent: *deodorant* | *propellant.*
– ORIGIN from French or Latin present participial verb stems (see also **-ENT**).

Antabuse /ˈantəbjuːs/ ▶ **noun** trademark for **DISULFIRAM**.
– ORIGIN 1940s: from **ANTI-** + **ABUSE**.

antacid /anˈtasɪd/ ▶ **adjective** (chiefly of a medicine) preventing or correcting acidity, especially in the stomach.
▶ **noun** an antacid medicine.

Antaeus /anˈtiːəs/ Greek Mythology a giant, the son of Poseidon and Earth, who compelled all comers to wrestle with him, overcoming and killing them all until he was defeated by Hercules.

antagonism /anˈtag(ə)nɪz(ə)m/ ▶ **noun** [mass noun] active hostility or opposition: *the **antagonism between** them* | *his **antagonism towards** the local people* | [count noun] *petty antagonisms and jealousies.*
– ORIGIN early 19th cent.: from French *antagonisme*, from Greek *antagōnizesthai* 'struggle against' (see **ANTAGONIST**).

antagonist ▶ **noun** a person who actively opposes or is hostile to someone or something; an adversary: *the woman was forcing her antagonist's face into the mud.*
■ Biochemistry a substance which interferes with or inhibits the physiological action of another. Compare with **AGONIST**. ■ Anatomy a muscle whose action counteracts that of another specified muscle. Compare with **AGONIST**.
– ORIGIN late 16th cent.: from French *antagoniste* or late Latin *antagonista*, from Greek *antagōnistēs*, from *antagōnizesthai* 'struggle against' (see **ANTAGONIZE**).

antagonistic ▶ **adjective** showing or feeling active opposition or hostility towards someone or something: *he was **antagonistic to** the government's reforms* | *an antagonistic group of bystanders.*
■ Biochemistry & Physiology of or relating to an antagonist or its action.
– DERIVATIVES **antagonistically** adverb.

antagonize (also **-ise**) ▶ **verb** [with obj.] cause (someone) to become hostile: *the aim was to antagonize visiting supporters.*
■ Biochemistry (of a substance) act as an antagonist of (a substance or its action).
– ORIGIN mid 18th cent. (in the sense 'struggle against'): from Greek *antagōnizesthai*, from *ant-* 'against' + *agōnizesthai* 'struggle' (from *agōn* 'contest').

Antakya /ʌnˈtʌkjʌ/ Turkish name for **ANTIOCH**.

Antalya /anˈtaljə/ a port in southern Turkey; pop. 378,200 (1990).

Antananarivo /ˌantəˌnanəˈriːvəʊ/ the capital of Madagascar, situated in the central plateau; pop. 802,390 (1990). Former name (until 1975) **TANANARIVE**.

Antarctic ▶ **adjective** of or relating to the south polar region or Antarctica.
■ Botany of, relating to, or denoting a phytogeographical kingdom comprising New Zealand, southern parts of Chile and Argentina, and islands in the South Atlantic and southern Indian Ocean.
▶ **noun** (**the Antarctic**) the Antarctic region.
– ORIGIN late Middle English: from Old French *antartique* or Latin *antarcticus*, from Greek *antarktikos* 'opposite to the north', from *ant-* 'against' + *arktikos* (see **ARCTIC**).

Antarctica a continent round the South Pole, situated mainly within the Antarctic Circle and almost entirely covered by ice sheets.

Antarctic Circle the parallel of latitude 66° 33′ south of the equator. It marks the southernmost point at which the sun is visible on the southern winter solstice and the northernmost point at which the midnight sun can be seen on the southern summer solstice.

Antarctic Convergence the zone of the Antarctic Ocean where the cold, nutrient-laden Antarctic surface water sinks beneath the warmer waters to the north.

Antarctic Ocean the sea surrounding Antarctica, consisting of parts of the South Atlantic, the South Pacific, and the southern Indian Ocean. Also called **SOUTHERN OCEAN**.

Antarctic Peninsula a mountainous peninsula of Antarctica between the Bellingshausen Sea and the Weddell Sea, extending northwards towards Cape Horn and the Falkland Islands.

Antares /anˈtɑːriːz/ Astronomy the brightest star in the constellation Scorpius. It is a binary star of which the main component is a red supergiant.
– ORIGIN Greek, literally 'simulating Mars (in colour)'.

antbear ▶ **noun** another term for **AARDVARK**.

antbird ▶ **noun** an insectivorous, long-legged, short-tailed bird which typically has dark grey plumage in the male and brown in the female. Antbirds are found mainly in the tropical forests of South America.
● Family Formicariidae: several genera, in particular *Myrmeciza*, *Cercomacra*, and *Drymophila*.

ante /ˈanti/ ▶ **noun** a stake put up by a player in poker or brag before receiving cards.
▶ **verb** (**antes**, **anted**, **anteing**) [with obj.] (**ante something up**) put up an amount as an ante in poker or brag and similar games.
■ N. Amer. informal pay an amount of money in advance: *he anted up $925,000 of his own money.* ■ [no obj.] (**ante up**) N. Amer. informal put up one's money; pay up: *the owners have to ante up if they want to attract the best talent.*
– PHRASES **up** (or **raise**) **the ante** increase what is at stake or under discussion, especially in a conflict or dispute: *he decided to up the ante in the trade war.*
– ORIGIN early 19th cent.: from Latin, literally 'before'.

ante- /ˈanti/ ▶ **prefix** before; preceding: *antechapel* | *antecedent.*
– ORIGIN from Latin *ante* 'before'.

anteater ▶ **noun** a mammal that feeds on ants and termites, with a long snout and sticky tongue.
● Most anteaters are edentates of the Central and South American family Myrmecophagidae, which includes the **giant anteater** and the tamanduas. The echidna, numbat, and pangolin are alternatively known as **spiny**, **banded**, and **scaly anteater** respectively.

antebellum /ˌantɪˈbɛləm/ ▶ **adjective** [attrib.] occurring or existing before a particular war, especially the US Civil War: *the conventions of the antebellum South.*
– ORIGIN mid 19th cent.: from Latin, from *ante* 'before' and *bellum* 'war'.

antecedent /ˌantɪˈsiːd(ə)nt/ ▶ **noun** a thing or event that existed before or logically precedes another: *some antecedents to the African novel might exist in Africa's oral traditions.*
■ (**antecedents**) a person's ancestors or family and social background: *her early life and antecedents have been traced.* ■ Grammar an earlier word, phrase, or clause to which another word (especially a following relative pronoun) refers back. ■ Logic the statement contained in the 'if' clause of a conditional proposition.
▶ **adjective** preceding in time or order; previous or preexisting: *the antecedent events that prompt you to break a diet.*
■ denoting or counting as a grammatical antecedent.
– DERIVATIVES **antecedence** noun, **antecedently** adverb.
– ORIGIN late Middle English: from Old French or from Latin *antecedent-* 'going before', from *antecedere*, from *ante* 'before' + *cedere* 'go'.

antechamber ▶ **noun** a small room leading to a main one.
– ORIGIN mid 17th cent. (as *antichamber*): from French *antichambre*, from Italian *anticamera*, from *anti-* 'preceding' + *camera* (see **CHAMBER**).

antechapel ▶ **noun** a distinct part of a college chapel between the entrance and the nave or choir.

antechinus /ˌantɪˈkʌɪnəs/ ▶ **noun** a marsupial mouse of shrew-like habits and appearance, found in Australia, New Guinea, and Tasmania.
● Genera *Antechinus* and *Parantechinus*, family Dasyuridae: several species.
– ORIGIN modern Latin, from Greek *anti-* 'simulating' + *ekhinos* 'sea urchin, hedgehog' (from its bristly fur).

antedate ▶ **verb** [with obj.] precede in time; come before (something) in date: *a civilization that antedated the Roman Empire.*
■ indicate that (a document or event) should be assigned to an earlier date: *there are no references to him that would antedate his birth.*

antediluvian /ˌantɪdɪˈluːvɪən/ ▶ **adjective** of or belonging to the time before the biblical Flood: *gigantic bones of antediluvian animals.*
■ chiefly humorous ridiculously old-fashioned: *they maintain antediluvian sex-role stereotypes.*
– ORIGIN mid 17th cent.: from **ANTE-** + Latin *diluvium* 'deluge' + **-AN**.

antelope ▶ **noun** (pl. same or **antelopes**) a swift-running deer-like ruminant with smooth hair and upward-pointing horns, native to Africa and Asia, and including the gazelles, impala, gnus, and elands.
● Many genera and species, in the family Bovidae.

■N. Amer. another term for **PRONGHORN**.
– ORIGIN late Middle English (originally the name of a fierce mythical creature with long serrated horns, said to live on the banks of the Euphrates): via Old French and medieval Latin from late Greek *antholops*, of unknown origin and meaning.

ante-mortem ▶ adjective & adverb before death: [as adj.] *the ante-mortem instructions of the dead leader* | [as adv.] *abnormalities of the sinus are difficult to demonstrate ante-mortem.*
– ORIGIN Latin 'before death'.

antenatal ▶ adjective before birth; during or relating to pregnancy: *antenatal care.*
▶ noun informal a medical examination during pregnancy.
– DERIVATIVES **antenatally** adverb.

antenna ▶ noun (pl. **antennae** /-niː/) **1** Zoology either of a pair of long, thin sensory appendages on the heads of insects, crustaceans, and some other arthropods.
■(**antennae**) figurative the faculty of instinctively detecting and interpreting subtle signs: *he has the political antennae of a party whip.*
2 (pl. also **antennas**) chiefly N. Amer. or technical another term for **AERIAL**: *a TV antenna.*
– DERIVATIVES **antennal** adjective, **antennary** adjective.
– ORIGIN mid 17th cent.: from Latin, alteration of *antemna* 'yard' (of a ship), used in the plural to translate Greek *keraioi* 'horns (of insects)', used by Aristotle.

antennule /anˈtɛnjuːl/ ▶ noun Zoology a small antenna, especially either of the first pair of antennae in a crustacean.
– ORIGIN mid 19th cent.: diminutive of **ANTENNA**.

antenuptial ▶ adjective chiefly Brit. another term for **PRENUPTIAL**.
– ORIGIN early 19th cent.: from late Latin *antenuptialis* (see **ANTE-, NUPTIAL**).

antepartum /antɪˈpɑːtəm/ ▶ adjective Medicine occurring not long before childbirth.
– ORIGIN late 19th cent.: from Latin, 'before birth'.

antepenultimate ▶ adjective last but two in a series; third last: *the antepenultimate item on the agenda.*

ante-post ▶ adjective [attrib.] Brit. (of a bet on a horse race) placed at odds fixed at the time, and before the runners are known, on a horse thought likely to be entered.
– ORIGIN early 20th cent.: from **ANTE-** + **POST**[1].

anterior ▶ adjective **1** technical, chiefly Anatomy & Biology nearer the front, especially situated in the front of the body, or nearer to the head or forepart: *the veins anterior to the heart.* The opposite of **POSTERIOR**.
■Botany (of a part of a flower or leaf) situated further away from the main stem. ■ Phonetics pronounced with an obstruction located in front of the palato-alveolar region of the mouth, e.g. *b, p, d, t.*
2 formal coming before in time; earlier: *an incident anterior to her troubles.*
– DERIVATIVES **anteriority** noun, **anteriorly** adverb.
– ORIGIN mid 16th cent.: from French *antérieur* or Latin *anterior*, comparative of *ante* 'before'.

antero- /ˈantərəʊ/ ▶ combining form chiefly Anatomy representing **ANTERIOR**: *anteroposterior.*

anterograde ▶ adjective directed forwards in time.
■of or denoting a form of amnesia which involves inability to remember information encountered after its onset.
– ORIGIN late 19th cent.: from **ANTERIOR**, on the pattern of *retrograde.*

anterolateral ▶ adjective chiefly Anatomy both anterior and lateral.

ante-room ▶ noun an antechamber, typically serving as a waiting room.
■Military a large room in an officers' mess, typically adjacent to the dining room.

anteroposterior ▶ adjective chiefly Anatomy relating to or directed towards both front and back.

anteverted /ˈantɪvɜːtɪd/ ▶ adjective Anatomy & Medicine (of an organ of the body, especially the womb) inclined forward.
– ORIGIN mid 19th cent.: from Latin *antevertere*, from *ante* 'before' + *vertere* 'to turn' + **-ED**[2].

ant heap ▶ noun another term for **ANTHILL**.

anthelion /antˈhiːlɪən, anˈθiːl-/ ▶ noun (pl. **anthelia** /-lɪə/) a luminous halo round a shadow projected by the sun on to a cloud or fog bank.

■a parhelion seen opposite the sun in the sky.
– ORIGIN late 17th cent.: from Greek *anthēlion*, neuter of *anthēlios* 'opposite to the sun', from *anth-* (variant of *anti-* 'against') + *hēlios* 'sun'.

anthelmintic /ˌanθ(ə)lˈmɪntɪk/ Medicine ▶ adjective (chiefly of medicines) used to destroy parasitic worms.
▶ noun a medicine of this kind.
– ORIGIN late 17th cent. (as an adjective): from *anth-* (variant of *anti* 'against') + Greek *helmins, helminth-* 'worm' + **-IC**.

anthem ▶ noun **1** a rousing or uplifting song identified with a particular group, body, or cause: *the song became the anthem for hippie activists.*
■(also **national anthem**) a solemn patriotic song officially adopted by a country as an expression of national identity.
2 a musical setting of a religious text to be sung by a choir during a church service, especially in Anglican or Protestant Churches.
– ORIGIN Old English *antefn, antifne* (denoting a composition sung antiphonally), from late Latin *antiphona* (see **ANTIPHON**). The spelling with *th*, which began in the 16th cent., was on the pattern of similar words such as *Antony, Anthony.*

anthemic /anˈθiːmɪk/ ▶ adjective (of a song) like an anthem in being rousing or uplifting.

anthemion /anˈθiːmɪən/ ▶ noun (pl. **anthemia** /-mɪə/) an ornamental design of alternating motifs resembling clusters of narrow leaves or honeysuckle petals.
– ORIGIN mid 19th cent.: from Greek, literally 'flower'.

Anthemius /anˈθiːmɪəs/ (6th century AD), Greek mathematician, engineer, and artist; known as **Anthemius of Tralles**.

anther ▶ noun Botany the part of a stamen that contains the pollen.
– ORIGIN early 18th cent.: from French *anthère* or modern Latin *anthera*, from Greek *anthēra* 'flowery', from *anthos* 'flower'.

antheridium /ˌanθəˈrɪdɪəm/ ▶ noun (pl. **antheridia** /-dɪə/) Botany the male sex organ of algae, mosses, ferns, fungi, and other non-flowering plants.
– DERIVATIVES **antheridial** adjective.
– ORIGIN mid 19th cent.: modern Latin, from *anthera* (see **ANTHER**) + *-idium* (from the Greek diminutive suffix *-idion*).

antherozoid /ˌanθ(ə)rə(ʊ)ˈzɔɪd/ ▶ noun Botany another term for **SPERMATOZOID**.
– ORIGIN mid 19th cent.: from **ANTHER** + **ZOOID**.

anthesis /anˈθiːsɪs/ ▶ noun [mass noun] Botany the flowering period of a plant, from the opening of the flower bud.
– ORIGIN mid 19th cent.: from Greek *anthēsis* 'flowering', from *anthein* 'to blossom'.

anthill ▶ noun a nest in the form of a mound built by ants or termites.

antho- /ˈanθəʊ/ ▶ combining form of or relating to flowers: *anthophilous.*
– ORIGIN from Greek *anthos* 'flower'.

anthocyanin /ˌanθə(ʊ)ˈsʌɪənɪn/ ▶ noun [mass noun] Chemistry a blue, violet, or red flavonoid pigment found in plants.
– ORIGIN mid 19th cent.: from German *Anthocyan*, from Greek *anthos* 'flower' + *kuanos* 'blue' + **-IN**[1].

anthologize (also **-ise**) ▶ verb [with obj.] [usu. as adj. **anthologized**] include (an author or work) in an anthology: *the most anthologized of today's poets.*

anthology ▶ noun (pl. **-ies**) a published collection of poems or other pieces of writing.
■a similar collection of songs or musical compositions issued in one album.
– DERIVATIVES **anthologist** noun.
– ORIGIN mid 17th cent.: via French or medieval Latin from Greek *anthologia*, from *anthos* 'flower' + *-logia* 'collection' (from *legein* 'gather'). In Greek, the word originally denoted a collection of the 'flowers' of verse, i.e. small choice poems or epigrams, by various authors.

Anthony, St /ˈantəni, ˈanθəni/ (also **Antony**) (c.251–356), Egyptian hermit, the founder of monasticism. Feast day, 17 January.

Anthony of Padua, St (also **Antony**) (1195–1231), Portuguese Franciscan friar. His devotion to the poor is commemorated by alms known as St Anthony's bread; he is invoked to find lost articles. Feast day, 13 June.

anthophilous /anˈθɒfɪləs/ ▶ adjective Zoology (of insects or other animals) frequenting flowers.

Anthozoa /ˌanθəˈzəʊə/ Zoology a large class of sedentary marine coelenterates that includes the sea anemones and corals. They are either solitary or colonial, and have a central mouth surrounded by tentacles.
– DERIVATIVES **anthozoan** noun & adjective.
– ORIGIN modern Latin (plural), from Greek *anthos* 'flower' + *zōia* 'animals'.

anthracene /ˈanθrəsiːn/ ▶ noun [mass noun] Chemistry a colourless crystalline aromatic hydrocarbon obtained by the distillation of crude oils and used in chemical manufacture.
● A tricyclic compound; chem. formula: $C_{14}H_{10}$.
– ORIGIN mid 19th cent.: from Greek *anthrax, anthrak-* 'coal' + **-ENE**.

anthracite /ˈanθrəsʌɪt/ ▶ noun [mass noun] coal of a hard variety that contains relatively pure carbon and burns with little flame and smoke.
■a dark grey colour.
– DERIVATIVES **anthracitic** adjective.
– ORIGIN late 16th cent. (denoting a gem described by Pliny and said to resemble coals, supposedly hydrophane): from Greek *anthrakitēs*, from *anthrax, anthrak-* 'coal'.

anthracnose /anˈθraknəʊs/ ▶ noun [mass noun] a mainly fungal disease of plants, causing dark lesions.
● This is usually caused by fungi of the subdivision Deuteromycotina.
– ORIGIN late 19th cent.: coined in French from Greek *anthrax, anthrak-* 'coal' + *nosos* 'disease'.

anthranilic acid /ˌanθrəˈnɪlɪk/ ▶ noun [mass noun] Chemistry a colourless or yellow crystalline compound first obtained by alkaline hydrolysis of indigo.
● Alternative name: *ortho-***aminobenzoic acid**; chem. formula: $NH_2C_6H_4COOH$.
– DERIVATIVES **anthranilate** noun.
– ORIGIN mid 19th cent.: *anthranilic* from Greek *anthrax* 'coal' + *anil* (being any imine derived from aniline) + **-IC**.

anthraquinone /ˌanθrəˈkwɪnəʊn/ ▶ noun [mass noun] Chemistry a yellow crystalline compound obtained by oxidation of anthracene. It is the basis of many natural and synthetic dyes.
● Chem. formula: $C_{14}H_8O_2$.
– ORIGIN late 19th cent.: from *anthra(cene)* + **QUINONE**.

anthrax /ˈanθraks/ ▶ noun [mass noun] a serious bacterial disease of sheep and cattle, typically affecting the skin and lungs. It can be transmitted to humans, causing severe skin ulceration (see **MALIGNANT PUSTULE**) or a form of pneumonia (**wool-sorters' disease**).
– ORIGIN late Middle English: Latin, 'carbuncle' (the earliest sense in English), from Greek *anthrax, anthrak-* 'coal, carbuncle', with reference to the skin ulceration in humans.

anthropic principle /anˈθrɒpɪk/ ▶ noun the cosmological principle that theories of the universe are constrained by the necessity to allow human existence.
– ORIGIN 1970s: *anthropic* from Greek *anthrōpikos*, from *anthrōpos* 'human being'.

anthropo- /ˈanθrəpəʊ/ ▶ combining form human; of a human being: *anthropometry.*
■relating to humankind: *anthropology.*
– ORIGIN from Greek *anthrōpos* 'human being'.

anthropocentric ▶ adjective regarding humankind as the central or most important element of existence, especially as opposed to God or animals.
– DERIVATIVES **anthropocentrically** adverb, **anthropocentrism** noun.

anthropogenic /ˌanθrəpə(ʊ)ˈdʒɛnɪk/ ▶ adjective (chiefly of environmental pollution and pollutants) originating in human activity: *anthropogenic emissions of sulphur dioxide.*
– DERIVATIVES **anthropogenically** adverb.

anthropoid ▶ adjective resembling a human being in form: *an anthropoid coffin.*
■Zoology of or relating to the group of higher primates, which includes monkeys, apes, and humans. ■ Zoology (of an ape) belonging to the family of great apes. ■ informal, derogatory (of a person) ape-like in appearance or behaviour.
▶ noun Zoology a higher primate, especially an ape or apeman.

● Suborder Anthropoidea, order Primates.
■ informal, derogatory a person that resembles an ape in appearance or behaviour.
– ORIGIN mid 19th cent.: from Greek *anthrōpoeidēs*, from *anthrōpos* 'human being' + **-OID**.

anthropology /ˌanθrəˈpɒlədʒi/ ▶ noun [mass noun] the study of humankind, in particular:
■ (also **cultural** or **social anthropology**) the comparative study of human societies and cultures and their development. ■ (also **physical anthropology**) the science of human zoology, evolution, and ecology.
– DERIVATIVES **anthropological** adjective, **anthropologist** noun.

anthropometrics ▶ plural noun [treated as sing.] anthropometry, especially as it relates to the design of furniture and machinery.

anthropometry /ˌanθrəˈpɒmɪtri/ ▶ noun [mass noun] the scientific study of the measurements and proportions of the human body.
– DERIVATIVES **anthropometric** adjective.

anthropomorphic /ˌanθrəpəˈmɔːfɪk/ ▶ adjective relating to or characterized by anthropomorphism.
■ having human characteristics: *anthropomorphic bears and monkeys*.
– DERIVATIVES **anthropomorphically** adverb.
– ORIGIN early 19th cent.: from Greek *anthrōpomorphos* (see **ANTHROPOMORPHOUS**) + **-IC**.

anthropomorphism /ˌanθrəpəˈmɔːfɪz(ə)m/ ▶ noun [mass noun] the attribution of human characteristics or behaviour to a god, animal, or object.
– DERIVATIVES **anthropomorphize** (also **-ise**) verb.

anthropomorphous ▶ adjective (of a god, animal, or object) human in form or nature.
– ORIGIN mid 18th cent.: from Greek *anthrōpomorphos* (from *anthrōpos* 'human being' + *morphē* 'form') + **-OUS**.

anthropopathy /ˌanθrəˈpɒpəθi/ ▶ noun [mass noun] the attribution of human emotions to a god.

anthropophagi /ˌanθrəˈpɒfəɡʌɪ/ ▶ plural noun cannibals, especially in legends or fables.
– ORIGIN mid 16th cent.: from Latin, plural of *anthropophagus*, from Greek *anthrōpophagos* 'maneating', from *anthrōpos* 'human being' + *-phagos* (see **-PHAGOUS**).

anthropophagy /ˌanθrəˈpɒfədʒi/ ▶ noun the eating of human flesh by human beings.
– DERIVATIVES **anthropophagous** /-ɡəs/ adjective.
– ORIGIN mid 17th cent.: from Greek *anthrōpophagia*, from *anthrōpophagos* (see **ANTHROPOPHAGI**).

anthroposophy /ˌanθrəˈpɒsəfi/ ▶ noun [mass noun] a formal educational, therapeutic, and creative system established by Rudolf Steiner, seeking to use mainly natural means to optimize physical and mental health and well-being.
– DERIVATIVES **anthroposophical** adjective.
– ORIGIN early 20th cent.: from **ANTHROPO-** + Greek *sophia* 'wisdom'.

anthurium /anˈθ(j)ʊərɪəm/ ▶ noun (pl. **anthuriums**) a tropical American plant which is widely grown for its ornamental foliage or brightly coloured flowering spathes.
● Genus *Anthurium*, family Araceae.
– ORIGIN modern Latin, from Greek *anthos* 'flower' + *oura* 'tail'.

anti ▶ preposition opposed to; against: *I'm anti the abuse of drink and the hassle that it causes*.
▶ adjective [predic.] informal opposed: *the local councils are anti*.
▶ noun (pl. **antis**) informal a person opposed to a particular policy, activity, or idea: *the threat to field sports from the antis is a serious one*.
– ORIGIN late 18th cent. (as a noun): independent usage of **ANTI-**.

anti- (also **ant-**) ▶ prefix **1** opposed to; against: *anti-aircraft*.
■ preventing: *antibacterial*. ■ relieving: *antipruritic*. ■ the opposite of: *anticlimax*. ■ acting as a rival: *antipope*. ■ unlike the conventional form: *anti-hero*.
2 Physics the antiparticle of a specified particle: *antiproton*.
– ORIGIN from Greek *anti* 'against'.

anti-abortion ▶ adjective [attrib.] opposing or legislating against medically induced abortion.
– DERIVATIVES **anti-abortionist** noun & adjective.

anti-aircraft ▶ adjective (especially of a gun or missile) used to attack enemy aircraft.

anti-apartheid ▶ adjective [attrib.] opposed to a policy or system of apartheid.

antibacterial ▶ adjective active against bacteria.

Antibes /ɒ̃ˈtiːb, French ɑ̃tib/ a fishing port and resort in SE France; pop. 70,690 (1990).

antibiosis /ˌantɪbʌɪˈəʊsɪs/ ▶ noun [mass noun] Biology an antagonistic association between two organisms (especially micro-organisms), in which one is adversely affected. Compare with **SYMBIOSIS**.
– ORIGIN late 19th cent.: from **ANTI-** + a shortened form of **SYMBIOSIS**.

antibiotic ▶ noun a medicine (such as penicillin or its derivatives) that inhibits the growth of or destroys micro-organisms.
▶ adjective relating to, involving, or denoting antibiotics.
– ORIGIN mid 19th cent. (in the sense 'doubting the possibility of life in a particular environment'): from **ANTI-** + Greek *biōtikos* 'fit for life' (from *bios* 'life').

antibody ▶ noun (pl. **-ies**) a blood protein produced in response to and counteracting a specific antigen. Antibodies combine chemically with substances which the body recognizes as alien, such as bacteria, viruses, and foreign substances in the blood.
– ORIGIN early 20th cent.: from **ANTI-** + **BODY**, translating German *Antikörper*, from *anti-* 'against' + *Körper* 'body'.

antic ▶ adjective poetic/literary grotesque or bizarre.
– ORIGIN early 16th cent.: from Italian *antico* 'antique', used to mean 'grotesque'.

anticathode ▶ noun Physics the target (or anode) of an X-ray tube which is struck by electrons from the cathode and from which X-rays are emitted.

anti-choice ▶ adjective opposed to granting choice, especially the right to choose abortion.

anticholinergic /ˌantɪkəʊlɪˈnəːdʒɪk/ Medicine ▶ adjective (chiefly of a drug) inhibiting the physiological action of acetylcholine, especially as a neurotransmitter.
▶ noun an anticholinergic drug.

Antichrist ▶ noun (**the Antichrist**) a postulated personal opponent of Christ expected by the early Church to appear before the end of the world.
■ a person or force seen as opposing Christ or the Christian Church.
– ORIGIN Old English, via Old French or ecclesiastical Latin from Greek *antikhristos*, from *anti* 'against' + *Khristos* (see **CHRIST**).

anti-christian ▶ adjective opposed to Christianity or Christian values.
■ of or relating to the Antichrist.

anticipate ▶ verb [with obj.] **1** regard as probable; expect or predict: *she anticipated scorn on her return to the theatre* | [with clause] *it was anticipated that the rains would slow the military campaign*.
■ guess or be aware of (what will happen) and take action in order to be prepared: *they failed to anticipate a full scale invasion*. ■ look forward to: *Stephen was eagerly anticipating the break from the routine of business*.
2 act as a forerunner or precursor of: *he anticipated Bates's theories on mimicry and protective coloration*.
■ come or take place before (an event or process expected or scheduled for a later time).
– DERIVATIVES **anticipative** adjective, **anticipator** noun.
– ORIGIN mid 16th cent. (in the senses 'to take something into consideration', 'mention something before the proper time'): from Latin *anticipat-* 'acted in advance', from *anticipare*, based on *ante-* 'before' + *capere* 'take'.

anticipation ▶ noun [mass noun] the action of anticipating something; expectation or prediction: *her eyes sparkled with anticipation*.
■ Music the introduction in a composition of part of a chord which is about to follow in full.
– PHRASES **in anticipation** with the probability or expectation of something happening.
– ORIGIN late Middle English: from Latin *anticipatio(n-)*, from the verb *anticipare* (see **ANTICIPATE**).

anticipatory /anˈtɪsɪpəˌt(ə)ri/ ▶ adjective happening, performed, or felt in anticipation of something: *an anticipatory flash of excitement*.
■ Law (of a breach of contract) taking the form of an announcement or indication that a contract will not be honoured. ■ Grammar denoting the use of 'it' as a dummy subject or object, anticipating the true subject or object, which comes later in the sentence (as in *it is easy to please John*).

anticlerical chiefly historical ▶ adjective opposed to the power or influence of the clergy, especially in politics.
▶ noun a person holding such views.
– DERIVATIVES **anticlericalism** noun.

anticlimax ▶ noun a disappointing end to an exciting or impressive series of events: *the rest of the journey was an anticlimax by comparison* | [mass noun] *a sense of anticlimax and incipient boredom*.
– DERIVATIVES **anticlimactic** adjective, **anticlimactically** adverb.

anticline /ˈantɪklʌɪn/ ▶ noun Geology a ridge or fold of stratified rock in which the strata slope downwards from the crest. Compare with **SYNCLINE**.
– DERIVATIVES **anticlinal** adjective.
– ORIGIN mid 19th cent.: from **ANTI-** + Greek *klinein* 'lean', on the pattern of *incline*.

anticlockwise ▶ adverb & adjective Brit. in the opposite direction to the way in which the hands of a clock move round: [as adv.] *stopcocks are opened by turning them anticlockwise* | [as adj.] *an anticlockwise direction*.

anticoagulant ▶ adjective having the effect of retarding or inhibiting the coagulation of the blood.
▶ noun an anticoagulant substance.

anticodon /ˌantɪˈkəʊdɒn/ ▶ noun Biochemistry a sequence of three nucleotides forming a unit of genetic code in a transfer RNA molecule, corresponding to a complementary codon in messenger RNA.

anti-communist ▶ adjective opposed to communism: *anti-communist demonstrators*.
▶ noun a person who is opposed to communism.

anti-constitutional ▶ adjective violating a political constitution: *anti-constitutional activity*.

anticonvulsant ▶ adjective (chiefly of a drug) used to prevent or reduce the severity of epileptic fits or other convulsions.
▶ noun an anticonvulsant drug.

Anti-Corn-Law League a pressure group formed in Britain in 1838 to campaign for the repeal of the Corn Laws, under the leadership of Richard Cobden and John Bright.

antics ▶ plural noun foolish, outrageous, or amusing behaviour: *the antics of our political parties*.
– ORIGIN early 16th cent.: from **ANTIC**.

anticyclone ▶ noun a weather system with high barometric pressure at its centre, around which air slowly circulates in a clockwise (northern hemisphere) or anticlockwise (southern hemisphere) direction. Anticyclones are associated with calm, fine weather.
– DERIVATIVES **anticyclonic** adjective.

antidepressant ▶ adjective (chiefly of a drug) used to alleviate depression.
▶ noun an antidepressant drug.

antidiarrhoeal ▶ adjective (of a drug) used to alleviate diarrhoea.
▶ noun an antidiarrhoeal drug.

antidiuretic hormone (abbrev.: **ADH**) ▶ noun another term for **VASOPRESSIN**.

antidote ▶ noun a medicine taken or given to counteract a particular poison.
■ something that counteracts or neutralizes an unpleasant feeling or situation: *laughter is a good antidote to stress*.
– DERIVATIVES **antidotal** adjective.
– ORIGIN late Middle English: via Latin, from Greek *antidoton*, neuter of *antidotos* 'given against', from *anti-* 'against' + *didonai* 'give'.

antidromic /ˌantɪˈdrəʊmɪk/ ▶ adjective Physiology (of an impulse) travelling in the opposite direction to that normal in a nerve fibre. The opposite of **ORTHODROMIC**.
– ORIGIN early 20th cent.: from **ANTI-** + Greek *dromos* 'running' + **-IC**.

anti-emetic ▶ adjective (chiefly of a drug) preventing vomiting.
▶ noun an anti-emetic drug.

anti-establishment ▶ adjective against the establishment or established authority.

antifeedant ▶ noun a naturally occurring substance in certain plants which adversely affects insects or other animals which eat them.
– ORIGIN 1960s: from **ANTI-** + **FEED** + **-ANT**.

antiferromagnetic ▶ adjective Physics denoting or

exhibiting a form of magnetism characterized by an antiparallel alignment of adjacent electron spins in a crystal lattice. Compare with **FERRIMAGNETIC**.

antifouling ▶ noun [mass noun] treatment of a boat's hull with a paint or similar substance designed to prevent fouling.
■ a substance of this kind.

antifreeze ▶ noun [mass noun] a liquid, typically one based on ethylene glycol, which can be added to water to lower the freezing point, chiefly used in the radiator of a motor vehicle.

anti-g ▶ adjective short for **ANTIGRAVITY**.
– ORIGIN 1940s: from **ANTI-** + g, the symbol for acceleration due to gravity.

antigen ▶ noun a toxin or other foreign substance which induces an immune response in the body, especially the production of antibodies.
– DERIVATIVES **antigenic** adjective.
– ORIGIN early 20th cent.: via German from French antigène (see **ANTI-**, **-GEN**).

antigenic determinant ▶ noun Biochemistry another term for **EPITOPE**.

Antigone /anˈtɪɡəni/ Greek Mythology daughter of Oedipus and Jocasta, the subject of a tragedy by Sophocles. She was sentenced to death for defying her uncle Creon, king of Thebes, but she took her own life before the sentence could be carried out, and Creon's son Haemon, who was engaged to her, killed himself over her body.

antigorite /anˈtɪɡərʌɪt/ ▶ noun [mass noun] a mineral of the serpentine group, occurring typically as thin green plates.

anti-government ▶ adjective against a government or the administration in office.

antigravity ▶ noun [mass noun] Physics a hypothetical force opposing gravity.
▶ adjective [attrib.] (chiefly of clothing for a pilot or astronaut) designed to counteract the effects of high acceleration.

Antigua /anˈtiːɡwə/ (also **Antigua Guatemala**) a town in the central highlands of Guatemala; pop. 26,630 (1988).

Antigua and Barbuda /bɑːˈbuːdə/ a country consisting of three islands (Antigua, Barbuda, and Redonda) in the Leeward Islands in the Eastern Caribbean; pop. 59,355 (1991); languages, English (official), Creole; capital, St John's (on Antigua). Discovered in 1493 by Columbus and settled by the English in 1632, Antigua became a British colony with Barbuda as its dependency; the islands gained independence within the Commonwealth in 1981.
– DERIVATIVES **Antiguan** adjective & noun.

anti-hero ▶ noun a central character in a story, film, or drama who lacks conventional heroic attributes.

anti-heroine ▶ noun a female anti-hero.

antihistamine ▶ noun [usu. as modifier] a drug or other compound that inhibits the physiological effects of histamine, used especially in the treatment of allergies: an antihistamine injection.

anti-infective ▶ adjective (of a drug) used to prevent infection.
▶ noun an anti-infective drug.

anti-inflammatory ▶ adjective (chiefly of a drug) used to reduce inflammation.
▶ noun (pl. **-ies**) an anti-inflammatory drug.

anti-knock ▶ noun [mass noun] a substance (such as tetraethyl lead) added to petrol to inhibit pre-ignition.

Anti-Lebanon Mountains a range of mountains running north to south along the border between Lebanon and Syria, east of the Lebanon range.

anti-life ▶ adjective opposed to or restricting the full development of natural life.

Antilles /anˈtɪliːz/ a group of islands, forming the greater part of the West Indies. The **Greater Antilles**, extending roughly east to west, comprise Cuba, Jamaica, Hispaniola (Haiti and the Dominican Republic), and Puerto Rico; the **Lesser Antilles**, to the south-east, include the Virgin Islands, Leeward Islands, Windward Islands, and various small islands to the north of Venezuela. See also **NETHERLANDS ANTILLES**.

anti-lock ▶ adjective [attrib.] (of brakes) designed so as to prevent the wheels locking and the vehicle skidding if applied suddenly.

antilog ▶ noun short for **ANTILOGARITHM**.

antilogarithm ▶ noun the number of which a given number is the logarithm.

antilogy /anˈtɪlədʒi/ ▶ noun (pl. **-ies**) archaic a contradiction in terms or ideas.
– ORIGIN early 17th cent.: from French antilogie, from Greek antilogia, from anti- 'against' + -logia (see **-LOGY**).

antimacassar /ˌantɪməˈkasə/ ▶ noun a piece of cloth put over the back of a chair to protect it from grease and dirt or as an ornament.
– ORIGIN mid 19th cent.: from **ANTI-** + **MACASSAR**.

anti-magnetic ▶ adjective (especially of watches) resistant to magnetization.

antimatter ▶ noun [mass noun] Physics matter consisting of elementary particles which are the antiparticles of those making up normal matter.

antimetabolite ▶ noun Physiology a substance that interferes with the normal metabolic processes within cells, typically by combining with enzymes.

anti-monarchist ▶ noun an opponent of monarchy.

antimony /ˈantɪməni/ ▶ noun [mass noun] the chemical element of atomic number 51, a brittle silvery-white semimetal. (Symbol: **Sb**)

Antimony was known from ancient times; the naturally occurring black sulphide was used as the cosmetic kohl. The element is used in alloys, usually with lead, such as pewter, type metal, and Britannia metal.

– DERIVATIVES **antimonial** adjective, **antimonic** adjective, **antimonious** adjective.
– ORIGIN late Middle English (denoting stibnite, the most common ore of the metal): from medieval Latin antimonium, of unknown origin. The current sense dates from the early 19th cent.

anti-national ▶ adjective opposed to national interests or nationalism: the Communists were seen as an anti-national party.

anting ▶ noun [mass noun] Ornithology behaviour seen in some birds, in which the bird either picks up ants and rubs them on the feathers or stands with the wings spread and allows the ants to crawl over it. It is probable that the ants' secretions help to keep the feathers in good condition.

antinode ▶ noun Physics the position of maximum displacement in a standing wave system.

anti-noise ▶ noun [mass noun] sound generated for the purpose of reducing noise by interference.

antinomian /ˌantɪˈnəʊmɪən/ ▶ adjective of or relating to the view that Christians are released by grace from the obligation of observing the moral law.
▶ noun a person holding such a view.
– DERIVATIVES **antinomianism** noun.
– ORIGIN mid 17th cent.: from medieval Latin Antinomi, the name of a 16th-cent. sect in Germany alleged to hold this view, from Greek anti- 'opposite, against' + nomos 'law'.

antinomy /anˈtɪnəmi/ ▶ noun (pl. **-ies**) a contradiction between two beliefs or conclusions that are in themselves reasonable; a paradox.
– ORIGIN late 16th cent. (in the sense 'a conflict between two laws'): from Latin antinomia, from Greek, from anti 'against' + nomos 'law'.

anti-nuclear ▶ adjective opposed to the development of nuclear weapons or nuclear power.

Antioch /ˈantɪɒk/ **1** a city in southern Turkey, near the Syrian border; pop. 123,871 (1990). Antioch was the ancient capital of Syria under the Seleucid kings, who founded it c.300 BC. Turkish name **ANTAKYA**.
2 a city in ancient Phrygia.

Antiochus /anˈtʌɪəkəs/ the name of eight Seleucid kings, notably:
■ **Antiochus III** (c.242–187 BC), reigned 223–187 BC; known as **Antiochus the Great**. He restored and expanded the Seleucid empire.
■ **Antiochus IV** (c.215–163 BC), son of Antiochus III, reigned 175–163 BC; known as **Antiochus Epiphanes**. His firm control of Judaea and his attempt to Hellenize the Jews resulted in the revival of Jewish nationalism and the Maccabean revolt.

antioxidant ▶ noun a substance that inhibits oxidation, especially one used to counteract the deterioration of stored food products.
■ a substance such as vitamin C or E that removes

potentially damaging oxidizing agents in a living organism.

antiparallel ▶ adjective Physics parallel but moving or oriented in opposite directions.

antiparticle ▶ noun Physics a subatomic particle having the same mass as a given particle but opposite electric or magnetic properties. Every kind of subatomic particle has a corresponding antiparticle, e.g. the positron has the same mass as the electron but an equal and opposite charge.

antipasto /ˌantɪˈpastəʊ/ ▶ noun (pl. **antipasti** /-tiː/) (in Italian cookery) an hors d'oeuvre.
– ORIGIN Italian, from anti- 'before' + pasto (from Latin pastus 'food').

antipathetic ▶ adjective showing or feeling a strong aversion: it is human nature to be antipathetic to change.
– ORIGIN mid 19th cent.: from **ANTIPATHY**, on the pattern of pathetic.

antipathy /anˈtɪpəθi/ ▶ noun (pl. **-ies**) [mass noun] a deep-seated feeling of aversion: his fundamental antipathy to capitalism.
– ORIGIN late 16th cent. (in the sense 'opposition of feeling, nature, or disposition'): from French antipathie, or via Latin from Greek antipatheia, from antipathēs 'opposed in feeling', from anti 'against' + pathos 'feeling'.

anti-personnel ▶ adjective [attrib.] (of weapons, especially bombs) designed to kill or injure people rather than to damage buildings or equipment.

antiperspirant ▶ noun [mass noun] a substance that is applied to the skin, especially under the arms, to prevent or reduce perspiration.

antiphon /ˈantɪf(ə)n/ ▶ noun (in traditional Western Christian liturgy) a short sentence sung or recited before or after a psalm or canticle.
■ a musical setting of such a sentence or sentences.
– ORIGIN late Middle English: via ecclesiastical Latin from Greek antiphōna 'harmonies', neuter plural of antiphōnos 'responsive', from anti 'in return' + phōnē 'sound'.

antiphonal ▶ adjective (of music, especially church music, or a section of a church liturgy) sung, recited, or played alternately by two groups.
▶ noun another term for **ANTIPHONARY**.
– DERIVATIVES **antiphonally** adverb.

antiphonary /anˈtɪf(ə)nəri/ ▶ noun (pl. **-ies**) (in the Western Christian Church) a book of plainsong for the Divine Office.
– ORIGIN early 17th cent.: from ecclesiastical Latin antiphonarium, from antiphona (see **ANTIPHON**).

antiphony ▶ noun [mass noun] antiphonal singing, playing, or chanting.

antipodal /anˈtɪpəd(ə)l/ ▶ adjective relating to or situated on the opposite side of the earth.
■ [predic.] (**antipodal to**) diametrically opposed to.
■ Botany relating to or denoting cells formed at the chalazal end of the embryo sac.

antipode /ˈantɪpəʊd/ ▶ noun the direct opposite of something : the pole and its antipode.
– ORIGIN early 17th cent.: back-formation from **ANTIPODES**.

Antipodean /ˌantɪpəˈdiːən/ ▶ adjective of or relating to Australia or New Zealand (used by inhabitants of the northern hemisphere): Antipodean wines.
▶ noun a person from Australia or New Zealand (used by inhabitants of the northern hemisphere).
– ORIGIN mid 17th cent.: formed irregularly from **ANTIPODES** + **-AN**.

antipodes /anˈtɪpədiːz/ ▶ plural noun (**the Antipodes**) Australia and New Zealand (used by inhabitants of the northern hemisphere).
■ the direct opposite of something: we are the very antipodes of trade unions.
– ORIGIN late Middle English: via French or late Latin from Greek antipodes 'having the feet opposite', from anti 'against, opposite' + pous, pod- 'foot'. The term originally denoted the inhabitants of opposite sides of the earth.

antipope ▶ noun a person established as pope in opposition to one held by others to be canonically chosen.
– ORIGIN late Middle English antipape, via French from medieval Latin antipapa (on the pattern of Antichrist). The change in the ending in the 17th cent. was due to association with **POPE**[1].

antiproton ▶ noun Physics the negatively charged antiparticle of a proton.

antipruritic /ˌantɪprʊ'rɪtɪk/ ▶ adjective (chiefly of a drug) used to relieve itching.
▶ noun an antipruritic drug.
– ORIGIN late 19th cent.: from **ANTI-** + *pruritic* (see **PRURITUS**).

antipsychotic ▶ adjective (chiefly of a drug) used to treat psychotic disorders.
▶ noun an antipsychotic drug.

antipyretic ▶ adjective (chiefly of a drug) used to prevent or reduce fever.
▶ noun an antipyretic drug.

antiquarian /ˌantɪ'kwɛːrɪən/ ▶ adjective relating to or dealing in antiques or rare books.
■ relating to the study of antiquities.
▶ noun a person who studies or collects antiques or antiquities.
– DERIVATIVES **antiquarianism** noun.
– ORIGIN early 17th cent.: from Latin *antiquarius* (see **ANTIQUARY**).

antiquark ▶ noun Physics the antiparticle of a quark.

antiquary /'antɪkwəri/ ▶ noun (pl. **-ies**) another term for **ANTIQUARIAN**.
– ORIGIN mid 16th cent.: from Latin *antiquarius*, from *antiquus* (see **ANTIQUE**).

antiquated ▶ adjective old-fashioned or outdated: *this antiquated central heating system.*
– ORIGIN late 16th cent. (in the sense 'old, of long standing'): from ecclesiastical Latin *antiquare* 'make old', from *antiquus* (see **ANTIQUE**).

antique ▶ noun a collectable object such as a piece of furniture or work of art that has a high value because of its considerable age.
▶ adjective 1 (of a collectable object) having a high value because of considerable age: *an antique clock.*
■ (of a method of finishing a wooden surface) intended to resemble the appearance of high quality old furniture: *bookshelves with an antique finish.*
2 belonging to ancient times: *statues of antique gods.*
■ old-fashioned or outdated: *trade unions defending antique work practices.* ■ often humorous showing signs of great age or wear: *the kitchen had an antique cooker.*
▶ verb (**antiques, antiqued, antiquing**) [with obj.] [usu. as adj. **antiqued**] make (something) resemble an antique by artificial means: *an antiqued door.*
– ORIGIN late 15th cent. (as an adjective): from Latin *antiquus, anticus* 'former, ancient', from *ante* 'before'.

antiquity ▶ noun (pl. **-ies**) [mass noun] 1 the ancient past, especially the period of classical and other human civilizations before the Middle Ages: *the great civilizations of antiquity* | *cameos dating from classical antiquity.*
■ [count noun] (usu. **antiquities**) an object, building, or work of art from the ancient past: *a collection of Islamic antiquities.*
2 great age: *a church of great antiquity.*
– ORIGIN Middle English: from Old French *antiquite*, from Latin *antiquitas*, from *antiquus* 'old, former' (see **ANTIQUE**).

anti-racism ▶ noun [mass noun] the policy or practice of opposing racism and promoting racial tolerance.
– DERIVATIVES **anti-racist** noun & adjective.

anti-roll bar ▶ noun a rubber-mounted bar fitted in the suspension of a vehicle to increase its stability, especially when cornering.

antirrhinum /ˌantɪ'rʌɪnəm/ ▶ noun (pl. **antirrhinums**) a plant of a genus that includes the snapdragon.
● Genus *Antirrhinum*, family Scrophulariaceae.
– ORIGIN from Latin, from Greek *antirrhinon*, from *anti-* 'counterfeiting' + *rhis, rhin-* 'nose', from the resemblance of the flower to an animal's snout.

antiscorbutic Medicine ▶ adjective (chiefly of a drug) having the effect of preventing or curing scurvy.
▶ noun an antiscorbutic food or drug.

anti-self ▶ noun an adopted persona that is the opposite of one's conscious normal self.
▶ adjective Physiology (of antibodies) directed against the body's own tissues.

anti-Semitism ▶ noun [mass noun] hostility to or prejudice against Jews.
– DERIVATIVES **anti-Semite** noun, **anti-Semitic** adjective.

antisense ▶ adjective Genetics having a sequence of nucleotides complementary to (and hence capable of binding to) a coding (or sense) sequence, which may be either that of the strand of a DNA double helix which undergoes transcription, or that of a messenger RNA molecule.

antisepsis ▶ noun [mass noun] the practice of using antiseptics to eliminate the micro-organisms that cause disease. Compare with **ASEPSIS**.

antiseptic ▶ adjective of, relating to, or denoting substances that prevent the growth of disease-causing micro-organisms.
■ (of medical techniques) based on the use of such substances. ■ figurative scrupulously clean or pure, especially so as to be bland or characterless: *their squeaky-clean home epitomizes this antiseptic respectability.*
▶ noun an antiseptic compound or preparation.
– DERIVATIVES **antiseptically** adverb.

antiserum ▶ noun (pl. **antisera**) a blood serum containing antibodies against specific antigens, injected to treat or protect against specific diseases.

antisocial ▶ adjective 1 contrary to the laws and customs of society; causing annoyance and disapproval in others: *children's antisocial behaviour.*
■ Psychiatry sociopathic.
2 not sociable or wanting the company of others.

USAGE On the difference in use between **antisocial**, **unsocial**, and **unsociable**, see usage at **UNSOCIABLE**.

antispasmodic ▶ adjective (chiefly of a drug) used to relieve spasm of involuntary muscle.
▶ noun an antispasmodic drug.

anti-static ▶ adjective preventing the build-up of static electricity or reducing its effects.

antistrophe /an'tɪstrəfi/ ▶ noun the second section of an ancient Greek choral ode or of one division of it. Compare with **STROPHE**.
– ORIGIN mid 16th cent. (as a term in rhetoric denoting the repetition of words in reverse order): via late Latin from Greek *antistrophē*, from *antistrephein* 'turn against', from *anti* 'against' + *strephein* 'to turn'.

antisymmetric ▶ adjective Mathematics & Physics unaltered in magnitude but changed in sign by exchange of two variables or by a particular symmetry operation.

anti-tank ▶ adjective [attrib.] for use against enemy tanks.

anti-tetanus ▶ adjective preventing or effective against tetanus: *an anti-tetanus injection.*

antithesis /an'tɪθəsɪs/ ▶ noun (pl. **antitheses** /-siːz/) a person or thing that is the direct opposite of someone or something else: *love is the antithesis of selfishness.*
■ a contrast or opposition between two things: *the antithesis between occult and rational mentalities.* ■ [mass noun] a rhetorical or literary device in which an opposition or contrast of ideas is expressed by parallelism of words which are the opposites of, or strongly contrasted with, each other. ■ [mass noun] (in Hegelian philosophy) the negation of the thesis as the second stage in the process of dialectical reasoning. Compare with **SYNTHESIS**.
– ORIGIN late Middle English (originally denoting the substitution of one grammatical case for another): from late Latin, from Greek *antitithenai* 'set against', from *anti* 'against' + *tithenai* 'to place'. The earliest current sense, denoting a rhetorical or literary device, dates from the early 16th cent.

antithetical /ˌantɪ'θɛtɪk(ə)l/ ▶ adjective 1 directly opposed or contrasted; mutually incompatible: *people whose religious beliefs are antithetical to mine.*
2 connected with, containing, or using the rhetorical device of antithesis.
– DERIVATIVES **antithetic** adjective, **antithetically** adverb.
– ORIGIN late 16th cent. (in sense 2): from Greek *antithetikos*, from *antithetos* 'placed in opposition', from *antitithenai* 'set against'.

antitoxin ▶ noun Physiology an antibody that counteracts a toxin.
– DERIVATIVES **antitoxic** adjective.

antitrades (also **antitrade winds**) ▶ plural noun steady winds that blow in the opposite direction to and overlie the trade winds.

antitrust ▶ adjective [attrib.] (of legislation, chiefly in the US) preventing or controlling trusts or other monopolies, and so promoting fair competition in business.

antitype ▶ noun a person or thing that represents the opposite of someone or something else: *the antitype of Christian moralization.*
– DERIVATIVES **antitypical** adjective.
– ORIGIN early 17th cent.: from late Latin *antitypus*, from Greek *antitupos* 'corresponding as an impression to the die', from *anti* 'against, opposite' + *tupos* 'type, a stamp'.

antivenin /ˌantɪ'vɛnɪn/ ▶ noun an antiserum containing antibodies against specific poisons, especially those in the venom of snakes, spiders, and scorpions.
– DERIVATIVES **antivenom** noun.
– ORIGIN late 19th cent.: from **ANTI-** + *ven(om)* + **-IN**[1].

antiviral ▶ adjective Medicine (chiefly of a drug or treatment) effective against viruses.

antivirus ▶ adjective [attrib.] Computing (of software) designed to detect and destroy computer viruses.

antivivisection ▶ adjective [attrib.] opposed to the use of live animals for scientific research.
– DERIVATIVES **antivivisectionism** noun, **antivivisectionist** noun & adjective.

antler ▶ noun one of the branched horns on the head of an adult deer (typically a male one), which are made of bone and are grown and cast annually.
■ one of the branches on such a horn.
– DERIVATIVES **antlered** adjective.
– ORIGIN late Middle English (originally denoting the lowest (forward-directed) branch of the antler): from Anglo-Norman French, variant of Old French *antoillier*, of unknown origin. The current sense dates from the early 19th cent.

Antlia /'antlɪə/ ▶ noun Astronomy a small and faint southern constellation (the Air Pump), between Hydra and Vela.
■ [as genitive **Antliae** /'antlɪʌɪ, -liːʃ/] used with preceding letter or numeral to designate a star in this constellation: *the star Alpha Antliae.*
– ORIGIN Latin, from Greek.

ant lion ▶ noun an insect that resembles a dragonfly, with predatory larvae that construct conical pits into which insect prey, especially ants, fall.
● Family Myrmeleontidae, order Neuroptera.

Antofagasta /ˌantəfə'gastə/ a port in northern Chile, capital of a region of the same name; pop. 226,750 (1992).

Antonine /'antənʌɪn/ ▶ adjective of or relating to the Roman emperors Antoninus Pius and Marcus Aurelius or their rules (AD 137–80).
▶ plural noun (**the Antonines**) the Antonine emperors.

Antonine Wall a defensive barrier about 59 km (37 miles) long, built (c.140 AD) across the narrowest part of southern Scotland between the Firth of Forth and the Firth of Clyde. It was intended to mark the frontier of the Roman province of Britain.

Antoninus Pius /ˌantə'nʌɪnəs 'pʌɪəs/ (86–161), Roman emperor 138–61. The adopted son and successor of Hadrian, he had a generally peaceful and harmonious reign.

Antonioni /anˌtəʊnɪ'əʊni/, Michelangelo (b.1912), Italian film director. Notable films: *L'avventura* (1960), *Blow-Up* (1966), and *Zabriskie Point* (1970).

antonomasia /ˌantənə'meɪzɪə, anˌtɒnə-/ ▶ noun [mass noun] Linguistics the substitution of an epithet or title for a proper name (e.g. *the Maid of Orleans* for Joan of Arc).
■ the use of a proper name to express a general idea (e.g. *a Scrooge* for a miser).
– ORIGIN mid 16th cent.: via Latin from Greek, from *antonomazein* 'name instead', from *anti-* 'against, instead' + *onoma* 'a name'.

Anton Piller order ▶ noun English Law a court order which requires the defendant in proceedings to permit the plaintiff or his or her legal representatives to enter the defendant's premises in order to obtain evidence essential to the plaintiff's case.
– ORIGIN 1970s: named after *Anton Piller*, German manufacturers of electric motors, who were involved in legal proceedings (1975) in which such an order was granted.

Antony /'antəni/, Mark (c.83–30 BC), Roman general and triumvir; Latin name *Marcus Antonius*. A supporter of Julius Caesar, in 43 he was appointed one of the triumvirate after Caesar's murder. Following the battle of Philippi he took charge of the Eastern Empire, where he established his association with Cleopatra. Quarrels with Octavian led finally to his defeat at the battle of Actium and to his suicide.

Antony, St see **ANTHONY, ST**.

antonym /ˈantənɪm/ ▶ **noun** a word opposite in meaning to another (e.g. *bad* and *good*).
– DERIVATIVES **antonymous** adjective.
– ORIGIN mid 19th cent.: from French *antonyme*, from *ant-* (from Greek *anti-* 'against') + Greek *onuma* 'a name'.

Antony of Padua, St see **ANTHONY OF PADUA, ST**.

antrectomy /anˈtrɛktəmi/ ▶ **noun** [mass noun] surgical removal of the walls of an antrum, especially the antrum of the stomach.

Antrim one of the Six Counties of Northern Ireland, formerly an administrative area.
■ a town in this county, on the NE shore of Lough Neagh; pop. 22,340 (1981).

Antron /ˈantrɒn/ ▶ **noun** [mass noun] trademark a type of strong, light nylon fibre used chiefly in making carpets and upholstery.
– ORIGIN 1960s: an invented name.

antrum /ˈantrəm/ ▶ **noun** (pl. **antra** /-trə/) Anatomy a natural chamber or cavity in a bone or other anatomical structure.
■ the part of the stomach just inside the pylorus.
– DERIVATIVES **antral** adjective.
– ORIGIN early 19th cent.: from Latin, from Greek *antron* 'cave'.

ants' eggs ▶ **plural noun** the pupae of ants, especially when used as food for pet fish.

antsy /ˈantsi/ ▶ **adjective** (**-ier**, **-iest**) N. Amer. informal agitated, impatient, or restless: *Dick* **got antsy** *the day he put to sea.*
– ORIGIN mid 19th cent.: probably from the phrase *have ants in one's pants* (see **ANT**).

ant-thrush ▶ **noun** any of a number of thrush-sized ant-eating birds:
• a large antbird (three genera in the family Formicariidae). • an African thrush (genus *Neocossyphus*, family Turdidae: four species). • another term for **PITTA**[2].

Antung /anˈtʊŋ/ former name for **DANDONG**.

Antwerp /ˈantwəːp/ a port in northern Belgium, on the Scheldt; pop. 467,520 (1991). By the 16th century it had become a leading European commercial and financial centre. French name **ANVERS**, Flemish name **ANTWERPEN** /ˈɑntwɛrpə(n)/.
■ a province of Belgium of which Antwerp is the capital.

Anubis /əˈnjuːbɪs/ Egyptian Mythology the god of mummification, protector of tombs, typically represented as having a dog's head.

Anura /əˈnjʊərə/ Zoology an order of tailless amphibians that comprises the frogs and toads. Also called **SALIENTIA** or **BATRACHIA**.
■ [as plural noun **anura**] amphibians of this order; frogs and toads.
– DERIVATIVES **anuran** noun & adjective.
– ORIGIN modern Latin (plural), from **AN-**[1] 'without' + Greek *oura* 'tail'.

Anuradhapura /ənʊˈrɑːdəˌpʊərə/ a city in north central Sri Lanka, capital of a district of the same name; pop. 36,000 (1981). The ancient capital of Sri Lanka, it is a centre of Buddhist pilgrimage.

anuria /əˈnjʊərɪə/ ▶ **noun** [mass noun] Medicine failure of the kidneys to produce urine.
– DERIVATIVES **anuric** adjective.
– ORIGIN mid 19th cent.: from **AN-**[1] + **-URIA**.

anus /ˈeɪnəs/ ▶ **noun** Anatomy & Zoology the opening at the end of the alimentary canal through which solid waste matter leaves the body.
– ORIGIN late Middle English: from Latin, originally 'a ring'.

Anvers /ɑ̃vɛʀ/ French name of **ANTWERP**.

anvil ▶ **noun** a heavy iron block with a flat top, concave sides, and typically a pointed end, on which metal can be hammered and shaped.
■ the horizontally extended upper part of a cumulonimbus cloud: [as modifier] *anvil clouds.* ■ Anatomy another term for **INCUS**.
– ORIGIN Old English *anfilte*, from the Germanic base of **ON** + a verbal stem meaning 'beat'.

anxiety ▶ **noun** (pl. **-ies**) [mass noun] a feeling of worry, nervousness, or unease, typically about an imminent event or something with an uncertain outcome: *he felt a surge of anxiety* | [count noun] *anxieties about the moral decline of today's youth.*
■ [with infinitive] desire to do something, accompanied by apprehension: *the housekeeper's eager anxiety to please.* ■ Psychiatry a nervous disorder marked by excessive uneasiness and apprehension, typically with compulsive behaviour or panic attacks.
– ORIGIN early 16th cent.: from French *anxiété* or Latin *anxietas*, from *anxius* (see **ANXIOUS**).

anxiolytic /ˌaŋzɪəˈlɪtɪk/ Medicine ▶ **adjective** (chiefly of a drug) used to reduce anxiety.
▶ **noun** an anxiolytic drug.
– ORIGIN 1960s: from **ANXIETY** + **-LYTIC**.

anxious ▶ **adjective 1** experiencing worry, nervousness, or unease, typically about an imminent event or something with an uncertain outcome: *she was extremely anxious about her exams.*
■ [attrib.] (of a period of time or situation) causing or characterized by worry or nervousness: *there were some anxious moments.*
2 [usu. with infinitive] wanting something very much, typically with a feeling of unease: *the company was anxious to avoid any trouble* | [with clause] *my parents were anxious that I get an education.*
– DERIVATIVES **anxiously** adverb, **anxiousness** noun.
– ORIGIN early 17th cent.: from Latin *anxius* (from *angere* 'to choke') + **-OUS**.

any ▶ **determiner** & **pronoun 1** [usu. with negative or in questions] used to refer to one or some of a thing or number of things, no matter how much or how many: [as determiner] *I don't have any choice* | *do you have any tips to pass on?* | [as pronoun] *you don't know* **any of** *my friends* | *if there is any left throw it away.*
■ anyone: *it ceased payments to any but the aged.*
2 whichever of a specified class might be chosen: [as determiner] *these constellations are visible at any hour of the night* | [as pronoun] *the illness may be due to* **any of** *several causes.*
▶ **adverb** [usu. with negative or in questions] [as submodifier] at all; in some degree (used for emphasis): *he wasn't any good at basketball* | *no one would be* **any the wiser**.
■ US informal used alone, not qualifying another word: *I didn't hurt you any.*
– PHRASES **any amount of** see **AMOUNT**. **any more** (also **anymore**) [usu. with negative or in questions] to any further extent; any longer: *she refused to listen any more.* **any old** see **OLD**. **any time** (also **anytime**) at whatever time: *she can come any time.* **any time** (or **day** or **minute** etc.) **now** informal very soon: *we'll get them back any day now.* **be not having any** (**of it**) informal be unwilling to cooperate: *I tried to make polite conversation, but he wasn't having any.* **hardly any** see **HARDLY**. **not just any** —— a particular or special thing of its type rather than any ordinary one of that type: *he had an acting job at last, and not just any part, but the lead in a new film.*
– ORIGIN Old English *ǣnig* (see **ONE**, **-Y**[1]), of Germanic origin; related to Dutch *eenig* and German *einig*.

USAGE When used as a pronoun **any** can be used with either a singular or a plural verb, depending on the context: *we needed more sugar but there* ***wasn't any*** *left* (**singular verb**) or ***are any*** *of the new videos available?* (**plural verb**).

anybody ▶ **pronoun** anyone: *there wasn't anybody around.*
– PHRASES **anybody's guess** see **GUESS**.

anyhow ▶ **adverb 1** another term for **ANYWAY**.
2 in a careless or haphazard way: *two suitcases flung anyhow.*

anymore ▶ **adverb** chiefly N. Amer. variant of *any more* at **ANY**.

anyone ▶ **pronoun 1** [usu. with negative or in questions] any person or people: *there wasn't anyone there* | *does anyone remember him?* | *I was afraid to tell anyone.*
■ [without negative] used for emphasis: *anyone could do it.*
2 a person of importance or authority: *they are read by* **anyone who's anyone**.
– PHRASES **be anyone's** informal (of a person) be open to sexual advances from anyone: *three shandies and he's anyone's.* **anyone's game** an evenly balanced contest: *it was still anyone's game at half-time.* **anyone's guess** see **GUESS**.

USAGE The two-word form **any one** is not the same as the one-word form **anyone** and the two forms cannot be used interchangeably. **Any one** means 'any single (person or thing)', as in: *not more than twelve new members are admitted in* ***any one*** *year.*

anyplace ▶ **adverb** N. Amer. informal term for **ANYWHERE**: *Miami is hotter than anyplace else.*

any road ▶ **adverb** chiefly N. English informal term for **ANYWAY**: *it won't make no difference now any road.*

anything ▶ **pronoun** [usu. with negative or in questions] used to refer to a thing, no matter what: *nobody was saying anything* | *have you found anything?* | *he inquired whether there was anything he could do.*
■ [without negative] used for emphasis: *I was ready for anything.* ■ used to indicate a range: *he trains anything from seven to eight hours a day.*
– PHRASES **anything but** not at all (used for emphasis): *he is anything but racist.* **anything like** —— [with negative] at all like —— (used for emphasis): *it doesn't taste anything like wine.* (**as**) —— **as anything** informal extremely ——: *she said it out loud, clear as anything.* **if anything** see **IF**. **like anything** see **LIKE**[1]. **or anything** [usu. with negative or in questions] informal added as a general reference to other things similar to the thing mentioned: *no strings attached, you don't have to join up or anything.*

anytime ▶ **adverb** chiefly N. Amer. variant of **ANY TIME** at **ANY**.

anyway ▶ **adverb 1** used to confirm or support a point or idea just mentioned: *I told you, it's all right, and anyway, it was my fault* | *it's too late now anyway.*
■ used in questions to emphasize the speaker's wish to obtain the truth: *'What are you doing here, anyway?'*
2 used in conversations to change the subject or to resume a subject after interruption: *How she lives with him is beyond me. Anyway I really like her.*
■ used to indicate that the speaker wants to end the conversation: *'Anyway, Dot, I must dash.'* ■ used to indicate that the speaker is passing over less significant aspects of an account in order to focus on the most important points: *'Poor John always enjoyed a drink. Anyway, he died last year.'*
3 used to indicate that something happened or will happen in spite of something else: *nobody invited Miss Honey to sit down but she sat down anyway.*

anyways ▶ **adverb** N. Amer. informal or dialect form of **ANYWAY**: *you wouldn't understand all them long words anyways.*

anywhere ▶ **adverb** [usu. with negative or in questions] in or to any place: *he couldn't be found anywhere.*
■ [without negative] used for emphasis: *I could go anywhere in the world.* ■ used to indicate a range: *he could get* **anywhere from** *three to seven years* | *she could have been* **anywhere between** *twenty-five and forty.*
▶ **pronoun** any place: *he doesn't have anywhere to live.*
– PHRASES **anywhere near** [with negative or in questions] at all near (used for emphasis): *I wouldn't dream of letting a surgeon anywhere near my eyes.* ■ remotely close to in extent, level, or scope: *imitations rarely look anywhere as good as the real thing.*

anywheres ▶ **adverb** & **pronoun** chiefly N. Amer. informal or dialect form of **ANYWHERE**: [as adv.] *I'll see if I can see your clothes anywheres.*

anywise ▶ **adverb** archaic in any manner or way.
– ORIGIN Old English *on ǣnige wīsan* 'in any wise'.

Anzac ▶ **noun** a soldier in the Australian and New Zealand Army Corps (1914–18).
■ dated a person, especially a member of the armed services, from Australia or New Zealand.
– ORIGIN acronym.

Anzac Day ▶ **noun** (in Australia and New Zealand) the day on which the Anzac landing at Gallipoli in 1915 is annually commemorated, 25 April.

Anzus /ˈanzəs/ an alliance between Australia, New Zealand, and the US, established in 1951 and designed to protect those countries in the Pacific area from armed attack. Also called **PACIFIC SECURITY TREATY**.

AO ▶ **abbreviation for** Officer of the Order of Australia.

AOB Brit. ▶ **abbreviation for** (at the end of an agenda for a meeting) any other business.

AOC ▶ **abbreviation for** ***appellation d'origine contrôlée*** (see **APPELLATION CONTRÔLÉE**).

ao dai /ˈaʊ ˌdʌɪ/ ▶ **noun** (pl. **ao dais**) a Vietnamese woman's long-sleeved tunic with ankle-length panels at front and back, worn over trousers.
– ORIGIN 1960s: Vietnamese.

A-OK (also **A-okay**) N. Amer. informal ▶ **adjective** in good order or condition; all right: *everything will be A-OK.*
▶ **adverb** in a good manner or way; all right: *we hit it off A-OK.*
– ORIGIN 1960s (originally an astronauts' term): from all systems *OK*.

AOR ▶ **noun** [mass noun] a style of popular music in which a hard rock background is combined with softer or more melodic elements.

– ORIGIN 1970s (originally US): from *album-oriented rock* or *adult-oriented rock*.

Aorangi /aʊˈraŋi/ Maori name for Mount Cook (see **COOK, MOUNT**).

aorist /ˈeɪərɪst, ˈɛ:r-/ Grammar ▶ **noun** a past tense of a verb (especially in Greek), which does not contain any reference to duration or completion of the action.
▶ **adjective** relating to or denoting this tense.
– DERIVATIVES **aoristic** adjective.
– ORIGIN late 16th cent.: from Greek *aoristos* 'indefinite', from *a-* 'not' + *horizein* 'define, limit'.

aorta /eɪˈɔ:tə/ ▶ **noun** the main artery of the body, supplying oxygenated blood to the circulatory system. In humans it passes over the heart from the left ventricle and runs down in front of the backbone.
– DERIVATIVES **aortic** adjective.
– ORIGIN mid 16th cent.: from Greek *aortē* (used in the plural by Hippocrates for the branches of the windpipe, and by Aristotle for the great artery), from *aeirein* 'raise'.

Aosta /ɑ:ˈɒstə/ a city in NW Italy, capital of Valle d'Aosta region; pop. 36,095 (1990).

Aotearoa /aʊˌteɪəˈrəʊə/ Maori name for **NEW ZEALAND**.
– ORIGIN Maori, literally 'land of the long white cloud'.

aoudad /ˈɑ:ʊdad/ ▶ **noun** another term for **BARBARY SHEEP**.
– ORIGIN early 19th cent.: from French, from Berber *udād*.

à outrance /ɑ: ˈu:trɒs, French a utʀɑ̃s/ ▶ **adverb** poetic/literary to the death or the very end: *a duel à outrance*.
– ORIGIN French, literally 'to the utmost'.

Aozou Strip /aʊˈzu:/ (also **Aouzou Strip**) a narrow corridor of disputed desert land in northern Chad, stretching the full length of the border between Chad and Libya.

AP ▶ **abbreviation for** Associated Press.

ap-[1] ▶ **prefix** variant spelling of **AD-** assimilated before *p* (as in *apposite, apprehend*).

ap-[2] ▶ **prefix** variant spelling of **APO-** shortened before a vowel or *h* (as in *aphelion*).

apace ▶ **adverb** poetic/literary swiftly; quickly: *work continues apace*.
– ORIGIN late Middle English: from Old French *a pas* 'at (a considerable) pace'.

Apache /əˈpatʃi/ ▶ **noun** (pl. same or **Apaches**) **1** a member of an American Indian people living chiefly in New Mexico and Arizona. The Apache put up fierce resistance to the European settlers and were, under the leadership of Geronimo, the last American Indian people to be conquered.
2 [mass noun] any of the Athabaskan languages of this people, which have about 14,000 speakers altogether, though some are virtually extinct.
▶ **adjective** of or relating to the Apache or their language.
– ORIGIN from Mexican Spanish, probably from Zuñi *Apachu*, literally 'enemy'.

apache /əˈpaʃ, French apaʃ/ ▶ **noun** (pl. **apaches** pronunc. same) a violent street ruffian, originally in Paris.
– ORIGIN early 20th cent.: French, from **APACHE**, by association with the reputed ferocity of the American Indian people.

apanage ▶ **noun** variant spelling of **APPANAGE**.

apart ▶ **adverb** **1** (of two or more people or things) separated by a distance; at a specified distance from each other in time or space: *two stone gateposts some thirty feet apart | studies from* **as far apart as** *America and Iceland |* figurative *the two sides remained far apart on the issue of cruise missiles*.
■ no longer living together or close emotionally: *alcoholism had driven us apart*.
2 to or on one side; at a distance from the main body: *Isabel stepped away from Joanna and stood apart*.
■ used after a noun to indicate that someone or something has distinctive qualities which mark them out from other people or things: *wrestlers were a breed apart*. ■ used after a noun to indicate that someone or something has been dealt with sufficiently or is being excluded from what follows: *Alaska apart, much of America's energy business concentrates on producing gas*.
3 so as to be shattered; into pieces: *he leapt out of the car just before it was blown apart*.
– PHRASES **apart from 1** except for: *the whole world seemed to be sleeping, apart from Barbara*. **2** in addition to; as well as: *quite apart from all the work, he had such financial problems*.
– DERIVATIVES **apartness** noun.
– ORIGIN late Middle English: from Old French, from Latin *a parte* 'at the side'.

apartheid /əˈpɑ:theɪt, əˈpɑ:tʌɪd/ ▶ **noun** [mass noun] historical (in South Africa) a policy or system of segregation or discrimination on grounds of race.
■ segregation in other contexts: *sexual apartheid*.

Adopted by the successful Afrikaner National Party as a slogan in the 1948 election, apartheid extended and institutionalized existing racial segregation. Despite rioting and terrorism at home and isolation abroad from the 1960s onwards, the white regime maintained the apartheid system with only minor relaxation until February 1991.

– ORIGIN 1940s: from Afrikaans, literally 'separateness', from Dutch *apart* 'separate' + *-heid* (equivalent of **-HOOD**).

aparthotel (also **apartotel**) ▶ **noun** a type of hotel providing self-catering apartments as well as ordinary hotel facilities.
– ORIGIN 1960s: from Spanish *Apartotel*, the name of a company specializing in this type of accommodation, from a blend of *apartamento* 'apartment' and *hotel*.

apartment ▶ **noun** chiefly N. Amer. a suite of rooms forming one residence, typically in a building containing a number of these; a flat.
■ a block containing such flats; an apartment building. ■ (**apartments**) a suite of rooms in a very large or grand house set aside for the private use of a monarch or noble: *the Imperial apartments*.
– ORIGIN mid 17th cent. (denoting a suite of rooms for the use of a particular person or group): from French *appartement*, from Italian *appartamento*, from *appartare* 'to separate', from *a parte* 'apart'.

apartment building (also **apartment block** or chiefly US **apartment house**) ▶ **noun** a block of apartments.

apartment hotel ▶ **noun** N. Amer. a hotel with furnished suites of rooms including kitchen facilities, available for long-term or short-term rental.

apathetic ▶ **adjective** showing or feeling no interest, enthusiasm, or concern: *an apathetic electorate*.
– DERIVATIVES **apathetically** adverb.
– ORIGIN mid 18th cent.: from **APATHY**, on the pattern of *pathetic*.

apathy /ˈapəθi/ ▶ **noun** [mass noun] lack of interest, enthusiasm, or concern: *widespread apathy among students*.
– ORIGIN early 17th cent.: from French *apathie*, via Latin from Greek *apatheia*, from *apathēs* 'without feeling', from *a-* 'without' + *pathos* 'suffering'.

apatite /ˈapətʌɪt/ ▶ **noun** [mass noun] a widely occurring pale green to purple mineral, consisting of calcium phosphate with some fluorine, chlorine, and other elements. It is used in the manufacture of fertilizers.
– ORIGIN early 19th cent.: coined in German from Greek *apatē* 'deceit' (from the mineral's diverse forms and colours).

apatosaurus /əˌpatəˈsɔ:rəs/ ▶ **noun** a huge herbivorous dinosaur of the late Jurassic period, with a long neck and tail. Formerly called **BRONTOSAURUS**.
● Genus *Apatosaurus* (formerly *Brontosaurus*), infraorder Sauropoda, order Saurischia.
– ORIGIN modern Latin, from Greek *apatē* 'deceit' + *sauros* 'lizard'.

APB US ▶ **abbreviation for** all-points bulletin.

APC ▶ **abbreviation for** armoured personnel carrier.

ape ▶ **noun** a large primate that lacks a tail, including the gorilla, chimpanzees, orang-utan, and gibbons. See also **GREAT APE, GIBBON**.
● Families Pongidae and Hylobatidae.
■ used in names of macaque monkeys with short tails, e.g. **Barbary ape**. ■ (in general use) any monkey. ■ an unintelligent or clumsy person. ■ archaic an inferior imitator or mimic: *cunning is but the ape of wisdom*.
▶ **verb** [with obj.] imitate the behaviour or manner of (someone or something), especially in an absurd or unthinking way: *new architecture can respect the old without aping its style*.
– PHRASES **go ape** (or vulgar slang, chiefly N. Amer. **apeshit**) informal go wild or out of one's mind: *your kids will go ape over these frozen pops!*
– DERIVATIVES **ape-like** adjective.
– ORIGIN Old English *apa*, of Germanic origin; related to Dutch *aap* and German *Affe*.

APEC ▶ **abbreviation for** Asia Pacific Economic Cooperation, a regional economic forum established in 1989, including the US, Japan, China, Australia, Indonesia, Hong Kong, and Thailand.

Apeldoorn /ˈap(ə)ldɔ:n/ a town in the east central Netherlands; pop. 148,200 (1991). It is the site of the summer residence of the Dutch royal family.

Apelles /əˈpɛli:z/ (4th century BC), Greek painter. He is now known only from written sources, but was highly acclaimed throughout the ancient world.

apeman ▶ **noun** (pl. **-men**) an extinct ape-like primate believed to be related or ancestral to present-day humans.

Apennines /ˈapɪnʌɪnz/ a mountain range running 1,400 km (880 miles) down the length of Italy, from the north-west to the southern tip of the peninsula.

aperçu /ˌapɛ:ˈsju:/ ▶ **noun** (pl. **aperçus**) a comment or brief reference which makes an illuminating or entertaining point.
– ORIGIN early 19th cent.: from French, past participle of *apercevoir* 'perceive'.

aperient /əˈpɪərɪənt/ Medicine ▶ **adjective** (chiefly of a drug) used to relieve constipation.
▶ **noun** an aperient drug.
– ORIGIN early 17th cent.: from Latin *aperient-* 'opening', from *aperire*.

aperiodic ▶ **adjective** technical not periodic; irregular.
■ Physics denoting a potentially oscillating or vibrating system (such as an instrument with a pointer) that is damped to prevent oscillation or vibration.
– DERIVATIVES **aperiodicity** noun.

aperitif /əˈpɛrɪti:f, əˌpɛrɪˈti:f/ ▶ **noun** an alcoholic drink taken before a meal to stimulate the appetite.
– ORIGIN late 19th cent.: from French *apéritif*, from medieval Latin *aperitivus*, based on Latin *aperire* 'to open'.

aperture /ˈapətʃə, -tj(ʊ)ə/ ▶ **noun** chiefly technical an opening, hole, or gap: *the bell ropes passed through apertures in the ceiling*.
■ a space through which light passes in an optical or photographic instrument, especially the variable opening by which light enters a camera.
– ORIGIN late Middle English: from Latin *apertura*, from *apert-* 'opened', from *aperire* 'to open'.

aperture priority ▶ **noun** [mass noun] Photography a system used in some automatic cameras in which the aperture is selected by the user and the appropriate shutter speed is controlled automatically. Compare with **SHUTTER PRIORITY**.

apery /ˈeɪpəri/ ▶ **noun** [mass noun] archaic the action of imitating the behaviour or manner of someone, especially in an absurd or unthinking way.

apetalous /eɪˈpɛt(ə)ləs, ə-/ ▶ **adjective** Botany (of a flower) having no petals.
– ORIGIN early 18th cent.: from modern Latin *apetalus*, from Greek *apetalos* 'leafless' (from *a-* 'without' + *petalon* 'leaf') + **-OUS**.

APEX ▶ **abbreviation for** (in the UK) Association of Professional, Executive, Clerical, and Computer Staff.

Apex /ˈeɪpɛks/ ▶ **noun** [mass noun] a system of reduced fares for scheduled airline flights and railway journeys which must be booked and paid for before a certain period in advance of departure.
– ORIGIN 1970s: from Advance Purchase Excursion.

apex /ˈeɪpɛks/ ▶ **noun** (pl. **apexes** or **apices** /ˈeɪpɪsi:z/) the top or highest part of something, especially one forming a point: *the apex of the roof |* figurative *the apex of his career was when he hoisted aloft the World Cup*.
■ Geometry the highest point in a plane or solid figure, relative to a base line or plane. ■ Botany the growing point of a shoot. ■ the highest level of a hierarchy, organization, or other power structure regarded as a triangle or pyramid: *the central bank is at the apex of the financial system*. ■ Motor Racing the point in turning a corner when the vehicle is closest to the edge of the track.
▶ **verb 1** [no obj.] reach a high point or climax: *melodic lines build up to the chorus and it apexes at the solo*.

a cat | ɑ: arm | ɛ bed | ɛ: hair | ə ago | ə: her | ɪ sit | i cosy | i: see | ɒ hot | ɔ: saw | ʌ run | ʊ put | u: too | ʌɪ my | aʊ how | eɪ day | əʊ no | ɪə near | ɔɪ boy | ʊə poor | ʌɪə fire | aʊə sour

2 [with obj.] Motor Racing turn (a corner) very close to the edge of the track.
– ORIGIN early 17th cent.: from Latin, 'peak, tip'.

Apgar score /'apgə/ ▶ noun Medicine a measure of the physical condition of a newborn infant. It is obtained by adding points (2, 1, or 0) for heart rate, respiratory effort, muscle tone, response to stimulation, and skin coloration; a score of ten represents the best possible condition.
– ORIGIN 1960s: named after Virginia *Apgar* (1909–74), the American anaesthesiologist who devised this method of assessment in 1953.

aphasia /ə'feɪzɪə/ ▶ noun [mass noun] Medicine inability (or impaired ability) to understand or produce speech, as a result of brain damage. Compare with **APHONIA**.
– DERIVATIVES **aphasic** adjective & noun.
– ORIGIN mid 19th cent.: from Greek, from *aphatos* 'speechless', from *a-* 'not' + *phanai* 'speak'.

aphelion /ap'hi:lɪən/ ▶ noun (pl. **aphelia** /-lɪə/) Astronomy the point in the orbit of a planet, asteroid, or comet at which it is furthest from the sun: *Mars is at aphelion*. The opposite of **PERIHELION**.
– ORIGIN mid 17th cent.: alteration of modern Latin *aphelium* (by substitution of the Greek inflection *-on*), from Greek *aph' hēlion* 'from the sun'.

apheresis /ə'fɪərɪsɪs/ ▶ noun [mass noun] **1** Linguistics omission of the initial sound of a word, as when *he is* is pronounced *he's*.
2 Medicine a technique by which a particular substance or component is removed from the blood, the main volume being returned to the body.
– ORIGIN mid 16th cent.: via late Latin from Greek *aphairesis*, from *aphairein* 'take away', from *apo* 'from' + *hairein* 'take'.

aphesis /'afɪsɪs/ ▶ noun [mass noun] Linguistics the gradual loss of an unstressed vowel at the beginning of a word (e.g. of *e* from *esquire* to form *squire*).
– DERIVATIVES **aphetic** /ə'fɛtɪk/ adjective, **aphetically** adverb.
– ORIGIN late 19th cent.: from Greek, literally 'letting go', from *apo* 'from' + *hienai* 'let go, send'.

aphicide /'eɪfɪsʌɪd/ ▶ noun an insecticide used against aphids.

aphid /'eɪfɪd/ ▶ noun a small bug which feeds by sucking sap from plants; a blackfly or greenfly. Aphids reproduce rapidly, sometimes producing live young without mating, and large numbers can cause extensive damage to plants.
● Superfamily Aphidoidea, suborder Homoptera.
– ORIGIN late 19th cent.: back-formation from *aphides*, plural of **APHIS**.

aphis /'eɪfɪs/ ▶ noun (pl. **aphides** /-diːz/) an aphid, especially one of the genus *Aphis* (which includes the common greenfly and blackfly).
– ORIGIN late 18th cent.: modern Latin, from Greek, perhaps a misreading of *koris* 'bug' (interpreting the characters κορ 'kor' as αφ 'aph').

aphonia /eɪ'fəʊnɪə, ə-/ (also **aphony** /'af(ə)ni/) ▶ noun [mass noun] Medicine inability to speak through disease of or damage to the larynx or mouth. Compare with **APHASIA**.
– ORIGIN late 17th cent.: modern Latin, from Greek *aphōnia*, from *aphōnos* 'voiceless', from *a-* 'without' + *phōnē* 'voice'.

aphorism /'afərɪz(ə)m/ ▶ noun a pithy observation which contains a general truth.
■ a concise statement of a scientific principle, typically by a classical author.
– DERIVATIVES **aphorist** noun, **aphoristic** adjective, **aphoristically** adverb, **aphorize** (also **-ise**) verb.
– ORIGIN early 16th cent.: from French *aphorisme* or late Latin *aphorismus*, from Greek *aphorismos* 'definition', from *aphorizein* 'define'.

aphrodisiac /ˌafrə'dɪzɪak/ ▶ noun a food, drink, or drug that stimulates sexual desire.
■ figurative an abstract quality regarded as having such an effect: *power is an aphrodisiac*.
– ORIGIN early 18th cent.: from Greek *aphrodisiakos*, from *aphrodisios*, from *Aphroditē* (see **APHRODITE**).

Aphrodisias /ˌafrə'dɪsɪas/ an ancient city of western Asia Minor, site of a temple dedicated to Aphrodite. Now in ruins, it is situated 80 km (50 miles) west of Aydin, in modern Turkey.

Aphrodite /ˌafrə'dʌɪti/ Greek Mythology the goddess of beauty, fertility, and sexual love. She is variously described as the daughter of Zeus and Dione, or as being born from the sea. Roman equivalent **VENUS**.
– ORIGIN Greek, literally 'foam-born', from *aphros* 'foam'.

aphtha /'afθə/ ▶ noun (pl. **aphthae** /'afθiː/) Medicine a small ulcer occurring in groups in the mouth or on the tongue.
■ [mass noun] a condition in which such ulcers occur.
– DERIVATIVES **aphthous** adjective.
– ORIGIN mid 17th cent.: via Latin from Greek, connected with *haptein* 'set on fire'.

API Computing ▶ abbreviation for application programming interface.

Apia /'apɪə/ the capital of Samoa; pop. 32,000 (1992).

apian /'eɪpɪən/ ▶ adjective of or relating to bees: *purple flowers are the most attractive to the apian mind*.
– ORIGIN early 19th cent.: from Latin *apianus*, from *apis* 'bee'.

apiary /'eɪpɪəri/ ▶ noun (pl. **-ies**) a place where bees are kept; a collection of beehives.
– DERIVATIVES **apiarian** adjective, **apiarist** noun.
– ORIGIN mid 17th cent.: from Latin *apiarium*, from *apis* 'bee'.

apical /'eɪpɪk(ə)l, 'ap-/ ▶ adjective technical of, relating to, or denoting an apex.
■ Phonetics (of a consonant) formed with the tip of the tongue at or near the front teeth or the alveolar ridge, for example *th* or trilled *r*.
– ORIGIN early 19th cent.: from Latin *apex, apic-* (see **APEX**) + **-AL**.

apices plural form of **APEX**.

Apicomplexa /ˌeɪpɪkɒm'plɛksə/ another term for **SPOROZOA**.

apiculture /'eɪpɪˌkʌltʃə/ ▶ noun technical term for **BEE-KEEPING**.
– DERIVATIVES **apicultural** adjective, **apiculturist** noun.
– ORIGIN mid 19th cent.: from Latin *apis* 'bee' + **CULTURE**, on the pattern of words such as *agriculture*.

apiece ▶ adverb to, for, or by each one of a group (used after a noun or an amount): *we sold 385 prints at £10 apiece*.
– ORIGIN late Middle English: from **A**[1] + **PIECE**.

Apis /'ɑːpɪs, 'ap-/ Egyptian Mythology a god depicted as a bull, symbolizing fertility and strength in war.

apish /'eɪpɪʃ/ ▶ adjective of or resembling an ape in appearance: *Australopithecus had an apish cranium*.
■ resembling or likened to an ape in being foolish or silly.
– DERIVATIVES **apishly** adverb, **apishness** noun.

aplanat /'aplənat/ ▶ noun Physics a reflecting or refracting surface which is free from spherical aberration.
– DERIVATIVES **aplanatic** adjective.
– ORIGIN late 19th cent.: coined in German from Greek *aplanētos*, from *a-* 'not' + *planan* 'wander'.

aplasia /ə'pleɪzɪə/ ▶ noun [mass noun] Medicine the failure of an organ or tissue to develop or to function normally.
– DERIVATIVES **aplastic** adjective.
– ORIGIN late 19th cent.: from **A-**[1] 'without' + Greek *plasis* 'formation'.

aplastic anaemia ▶ noun [mass noun] Medicine deficiency of all types of blood cell caused by failure of bone marrow development.

aplenty ▶ adjective [postpositive] in abundance: *there is passion aplenty in the events described*.

aplomb /ə'plɒm/ ▶ noun [mass noun] self-confidence or assurance, especially when in a demanding situation: *Diana passed the test with aplomb*.
– ORIGIN late 18th cent. (in the sense 'perpendicularity, steadiness'): from French, from *à plomb* 'according to a plummet'.

apnoea /ap'niːə/ (US **apnea**) ▶ noun [mass noun] Medicine temporary cessation of breathing, especially during sleep: *thousands suffer from sleep apnoea*.
– ORIGIN early 18th cent.: modern Latin, from Greek *apnoia*, from *apnous* 'breathless'.

apo- /'apəʊ/ ▶ prefix **1** away from: *apocrine*.
■ separate: *apocarpous*.
2 Astronomy denoting the furthest point in the orbit of a body in relation to the primary: *apolune*. Compare with **PERI-**.
– ORIGIN from Greek *apo* 'from, away, quite, un-'.

Apoc. ▶ abbreviation for ■ Apocalypse. ■ Apocrypha.

apocalypse /ə'pɒkəlɪps/ ▶ noun (often **the Apocalypse**) the complete final destruction of the world, especially as described in the biblical book of Revelation.
■ an event involving destruction or damage on an awesome or catastrophic scale: *a stock market apocalypse*. ■ **(the Apocalypse)** (especially in the Vulgate Bible) the book of Revelation.
– ORIGIN Old English, via Old French and ecclesiastical Latin from Greek *apokalupsis*, from *apokaluptein* 'uncover, reveal', from *apo-* 'un-' + *kaluptein* 'to cover'.

apocalyptic ▶ adjective describing or prophesying the complete destruction of the world: *the apocalyptic visions of ecologists*.
■ resembling the end of the world; momentous or catastrophic: *the struggle between the two countries is assuming apocalyptic proportions*. ■ of or resembling the biblical Apocalypse: *apocalyptic imagery*.
– DERIVATIVES **apocalyptically** adverb.
– ORIGIN early 17th cent. (as a noun denoting the writer of the Apocalypse, St. John): from Greek *apokaluptikos*, from *apokaluptein* 'uncover' (see **APOCALYPSE**).

apocarpous /ˌapə'kɑːpəs/ ▶ adjective Botany (of a flower, fruit, or ovary) having distinct carpels that are not joined together. Often contrasted with **SYNCARPOUS**.
– ORIGIN mid 19th cent.: from **APO-** + Greek *karpos* 'fruit' + **-OUS**.

apochromat /'apəkrəmat/ ▶ noun Physics a lens or lens system that reduces spherical and chromatic aberration.
– DERIVATIVES **apochromatic** adjective.
– ORIGIN early 20th cent.: from **APO-** + **CHROMATIC**.

apocope /ə'pɒkəpi/ ▶ noun [mass noun] Linguistics omission of the final sound of a word, as when *cup of tea* is pronounced as *cuppa tea*.
– ORIGIN mid 16th cent.: from late Latin, from Greek *apokoptein* 'cut off', from *apo-* 'from' + *koptein* 'to cut'.

Apocr. ▶ abbreviation for Apocrypha.

apocrine /'apəkrʌɪn, -krɪn/ ▶ adjective Physiology relating to or denoting multicellular glands which release some of their cytoplasm in their secretions, especially the sweat glands associated with hair follicles in the armpits and pubic regions. Compare with **ECCRINE**.
– ORIGIN early 20th cent.: from **APO-** + Greek *krinein* 'to separate'.

Apocrypha /ə'pɒkrɪfə/ ▶ plural noun [treated as sing. or pl.] biblical or related writings not forming part of the accepted canon of Scripture.
■ **(apocrypha)** writings or reports not considered genuine.
– ORIGIN late Middle English: from ecclesiastical Latin *apocrypha (scripta)* 'hidden (writings)', from Greek *apokruphos*, from *apokruptein* 'hide away'.

apocryphal ▶ adjective (of a story or statement) of doubtful authenticity, although widely circulated as being true: *an apocryphal story about a former president*.
■ of or belonging to the Apocrypha: *the apocryphal Gospel of Thomas*.

apodictic /ˌapə'dɪktɪk/ (also **apodeictic** /-'dʌɪktɪk/) ▶ adjective formal clearly established or beyond dispute.
– ORIGIN mid 17th cent.: via Latin from Greek *apodeiktikos*, from *apodeiknunai* 'show off, demonstrate'.

apodosis /ə'pɒdəsɪs/ ▶ noun (pl. **apodoses** /-siːz/) Grammar the main clause of a conditional sentence (e.g. *I would agree* in *if you asked me I would agree*). Often contrasted with **PROTASIS**.
– ORIGIN early 17th cent.: via Latin from Greek, from *apodidonai* 'give back'.

apodous /'apədəs/ ▶ adjective Zoology without feet or having only rudimentary feet.
– ORIGIN early 19th cent.: from Greek *apous, apod-* 'footless' (from *a-* 'without' + *pous, pod-* 'foot') + **-OUS**.

apogee /'apədʒiː/ ▶ noun Astronomy the point in the orbit of the moon or a satellite at which it is furthest from the earth. The opposite of **PERIGEE**.
■ figurative the highest point in the development of something; the climax or culmination of something: *the idea for that poster was the apogee of my career*.
– ORIGIN late 16th cent.: from French *apogée* or modern Latin *apogaeum*, from Greek *apogaion (diastēma)*, '(distance) away from earth', from *apo* 'from' + *gaia, gē* 'earth'.

apolar ▶ **adjective** chiefly Biochemistry having no electrical polarity.

apolitical ▶ **adjective** not interested or involved in politics: *he took an apolitical stance.*

Apollinaire /əˌpɒlɪˈnɛː, French apɔlinɛʀ/, Guillaume (1880–1918), French poet; pseudonym of *Wilhelm Apollinaris de Kostrowitzki*. He coined the term *surrealist* and was acknowledged by the surrealist poets as their precursor. Notable works: *Les Alcools* (1913) and *Calligrammes* (1918).

Apollinaris /əˌpɒlɪˈnɛːrɪs/ (*c*.310–*c*.390), bishop of Laodicea in Asia Minor. He upheld the heretical doctrine that Christ had a human body and soul but no human spirit, this being replaced by the divine Logos.
– DERIVATIVES **Apollinarian** adjective & noun.

Apollo 1 Greek Mythology a god, son of Zeus and Leto and brother of Artemis. He is associated with music, poetic inspiration, archery, prophecy, medicine, pastoral life, and the sun.
2 the American space programme for landing astronauts on the moon. *Apollo 8* was the first mission to orbit the moon (1968), *Apollo 11* was the first to land astronauts (1969), and five further landings took place up to 1972.

apollo ▶ **noun** (pl. **-os**) a large butterfly which has creamy-white wings marked with black and red spots, found chiefly on the mountains of mainland Europe.
• *Parnassius apollo*, family Papilionidae.
– ORIGIN mid 19th cent.: from **APOLLO**.

Apollonian /ˌapəˈləʊnɪən/ ▶ **adjective 1** Greek Mythology of or relating to the god Apollo.
2 of or relating to the rational, ordered, and self-disciplined aspects of human nature. Compare with **DIONYSIAC**.

Apollonius[1] /ˌapəˈləʊnɪəs/ (*c*.260–190 BC), Greek mathematician; known as **Apollonius of Perga**. He examined and redefined conic sections and was the first to use the terms *ellipse*, *parabola*, and *hyperbola* for these classes of curve.

Apollonius[2] /ˌapəˈləʊnɪəs/ (3rd century BC), Greek poet and grammarian; known as **Apollonius of Rhodes**. He is known for his *Argonautica*, an epic poem in Homeric style dealing with the expedition of the Argonauts.

Apollyon /əˈpɒljən/ a name for the Devil (Rev. 9:11).
– ORIGIN from late Latin (Vulgate), from Greek *Apolluōn* (translating **ABADDON**), from *apollunai*, from *apo-* 'quite' + *ollunai* 'destroy'.

apologetic ▶ **adjective** regretfully acknowledging or excusing an offence or failure: *she was very apologetic about the whole incident.*
■ expressing such regret: *she gave an apologetic smile.* ■ of the nature of a formal defence or justification of something such as a theory or religious doctrine: *the apologetic proposition that production for profit is the same thing as production for need.*
– DERIVATIVES **apologetically** adverb.
– ORIGIN late Middle English (as a noun denoting a formal justification): from French *apologétique* or late Latin *apologeticus*, from Greek *apologētikos*, from *apologeisthai* 'speak in one's own defence', from *apologia* (see **APOLOGY**). The current sense dates from the mid 19th cent.

apologetics ▶ **plural noun** [treated as sing. or pl.] reasoned arguments or writings in justification of something, typically a theory or religious doctrine: *apologetics for the slave trade are quite out of order.*
– ORIGIN mid 18th cent.: from **APOLOGETIC**.

apologia /ˌapəˈləʊdʒɪə/ ▶ **noun** a formal written defence of one's opinions or conduct: *an apologia for book-banning.*
– ORIGIN late 18th cent.: from Latin (see **APOLOGY**).

apologist ▶ **noun** a person who offers an argument in defence of something controversial: *an enthusiastic **apologist for** fascism in the 1920s.*
– ORIGIN mid 17th cent.: from French *apologiste*, from Greek *apologizesthai* 'give an account' (see **APOLOGIZE**).

apologize (also **-ise**) ▶ **verb** [no obj.] express regret for something that one has done wrong: *I must **apologize for** disturbing you like this | we **apologize** to him for our error.*
– ORIGIN late 16th cent. (in the sense 'make a defensive argument'): from Greek *apologizesthai* 'give an account', from *apologos* (see **APOLOGUE**). In English the verb has always been used as if it were a direct derivative of *apology*.

apologue /ˈapəlɒg/ ▶ **noun** a moral fable, especially one with animals as characters.
– ORIGIN mid 16th cent.: from French, via Latin from Greek *apologos* 'story'.

apology ▶ **noun** (pl. **-ies**) **1** a regretful acknowledgement of an offence or failure: *we owe you an apology | my apologies for the delay.*
■ a formal public statement of regret, such as one issued by a newspaper, government, or other organization: *the Prime Minister demanded an apology from the ambassador.* ■ (**apologies**) used to express formally one's regret at being unable to attend a meeting or social function: ***apologies for absence*** *were received from Miss Brown.*
2 (**an apology for**) a very poor or inadequate example of: *we were shown into an apology for a bedroom.*
– PHRASES **with apologies to** used before the name of an author or artist to indicate that something is a parody or adaptation of their work.
– ORIGIN mid 16th cent. (denoting a formal defence against an accusation): from French *apologie*, or via late Latin from Greek *apologia* 'a speech in one's own defence', from *apo* 'away'+ *-logia* (see **-LOGY**).

apolune /ˈapə(ʊ)luːn/ ▶ **noun** [mass noun] the point at which a spacecraft in lunar orbit is furthest from the moon. The opposite of **PERILUNE**.
– ORIGIN 1960s: from **APO-** + Latin *luna* 'moon', on the pattern of *apogee*.

apomict /ˈapəmɪkt/ ▶ **noun** Botany a plant which reproduces by apomixis.

apomixis /ˌapəˈmɪksɪs/ ▶ **noun** [mass noun] Botany asexual reproduction in plants, in particular agamospermy. Often contrasted with **AMPHIMIXIS**.
– DERIVATIVES **apomictic** adjective.
– ORIGIN early 20th cent.: from **APO-** + Greek *mixis* 'mingling'.

apomorphine /ˌapəˈmɔːfiːn/ ▶ **noun** [mass noun] Medicine a white crystalline compound used as an emetic and in the treatment of Parkinsonism.
• A morphine derivative; chem. formula: $C_{17}H_{17}NO_2$.

aponeurosis /ˌapənjʊˈrəʊsɪs/ ▶ **noun** (pl. **aponeuroses** /-siːz/) Anatomy a sheet of pearly white fibrous tissue which takes the place of a tendon in sheet-like muscles having a wide area of attachment.
– DERIVATIVES **aponeurotic** adjective.
– ORIGIN late 17th cent.: modern Latin, from Greek *aponeurōsis*, from *apo* 'off, away' + *neuron* 'sinew' + **-OSIS**.

apophatic /ˌapəˈfatɪk/ ▶ **adjective** Theology (of knowledge of God) obtained through negation. The opposite of **CATAPHATIC**.
– ORIGIN mid 19th cent.: from Greek *apophatikos* 'negative', from *apophasis* 'denial', from *apo-* 'other than' + *phanai* 'speak'.

apophthegm /ˈapəθɛm/ (US **apothegm**) ▶ **noun** a concise saying or maxim; an aphorism.
– DERIVATIVES **apophthegmatic** /-θɛgˈmatɪk/ adjective.
– ORIGIN mid 16th cent.: from French *apophthegme* or modern Latin *apothegma*, from Greek, from *apophthengesthai* 'speak out'.

apophyllite /əˈpɒfɪlʌɪt/ ▶ **noun** [mass noun] a mineral occurring typically as white glassy prisms, usually as a secondary mineral in volcanic rocks. It is a hydrated silicate and fluoride of calcium and potassium.
– ORIGIN early 19th cent.: from **APO-** + Greek *phullon* 'leaf' + **-ITE**[1].

apophysis /əˈpɒfɪsɪs/ ▶ **noun** (pl. **apophyses**) Zoology & Anatomy a natural protuberance from a bone, or inside the shell or exoskeleton of a sea urchin or insect, for the attachment of muscles.
■ Botany a swelling at the base of the sporangium in some mosses. ■ Geology a small offshoot extending from an igneous intrusion into the surrounding rock.
– DERIVATIVES **apophyseal** adjective.
– ORIGIN late 16th cent.: modern Latin, from Greek *apophusis* 'offshoot', from *apo-* 'from, away' + *phusis* 'growth'.

apoplectic /ˌapəˈplɛktɪk/ ▶ **adjective** informal overcome with anger; extremely indignant: *Mark was **apoplectic with** rage at the decision.*
■ dated relating to or denoting apoplexy (stroke): *an apoplectic attack.*
– DERIVATIVES **apoplectically** adverb.
– ORIGIN early 17th cent.: from French *apoplectique* or late Latin *apoplecticus*, from Greek *apoplēktikos*, from *apoplēssein* 'disable by a stroke'.

apoplexy /ˈapəplɛksi/ ▶ **noun** (pl. **-ies**) [mass noun] dated unconsciousness or incapacity resulting from a cerebral haemorrhage or stroke.
■ informal incapacity or speechlessness caused by extreme anger: *of all transport policies, road pricing seems most likely to cause apoplexy.*
– ORIGIN late Middle English: from Old French *apoplexie*, from late Latin *apoplexia*, from Greek *apoplēxia*, from *apoplēssein* 'disable by a stroke'.

apoprotein /ˌapəˈprəʊtiːn/ ▶ **noun** Biochemistry a protein which together with a prosthetic group forms a particular biochemical molecule such as a hormone or enzyme.

apoptosis /ˌapə(p)ˈtəʊsɪs/ ▶ **noun** [mass noun] Physiology the death of cells which occurs as a normal and controlled part of an organism's growth or development. Also called **PROGRAMMED CELL DEATH**.
– DERIVATIVES **apoptotic** /-ˈtɒtɪk/ adjective.
– ORIGIN 1970s: from Greek *apoptōsis* 'falling off', from *apo* 'from' + *ptōsis* 'falling, a fall'.

aporia /əˈpɔːrɪə, əˈpɒrɪə/ ▶ **noun** an irresolvable internal contradiction or logical disjunction in a text, argument, or theory.
■ [mass noun] Rhetoric the expression of doubt.
– ORIGIN mid 16th cent.: via late Latin from Greek, from *aporos* 'impassable', from *a-* 'without' + *poros* 'passage'.

aposematic /ˌapə(ʊ)sɪˈmatɪk/ ▶ **adjective** Zoology (of coloration or markings) serving to warn or repel predators.
■ (of an animal) having such coloration or markings.
– DERIVATIVES **aposematism** noun.
– ORIGIN late 19th cent.: from **APO-** 'away from' + Greek *sēma* 'sign' + **-ATIC**.

aposiopesis /ˌapə(ʊ)ˌsʌɪəˈpiːsɪs/ ▶ **noun** (pl. **aposiopeses** /-siːz/) [mass noun] Rhetoric the device of suddenly breaking off in speech.
– DERIVATIVES **aposiopetic** adjective.
– ORIGIN late 16th cent.: via Latin from Greek *aposiōpēsis*, from *aposiōpan* 'be silent'.

apostasy /əˈpɒstəsi/ ▶ **noun** [mass noun] the abandonment or renunciation of a religious or political belief or principle.
– ORIGIN Middle English: from ecclesiastical Latin *apostasia*, from a late Greek alteration of Greek *apostasis* 'defection'.

apostate /ˈapəsteɪt/ ▶ **noun** a person who renounces a religious or political belief or principle.
▶ **adjective** abandoning a religious or political belief or principle: *an apostate Roman Catholic.*
– DERIVATIVES **apostatical** adjective.
– ORIGIN Middle English: from ecclesiastical Latin *apostata*, from Greek *apostatēs* 'apostate, runaway slave'.

apostatize /əˈpɒstətʌɪz/ (also **-ise**) ▶ **verb** [no obj.] renounce a religious or political belief or principle.
– ORIGIN mid 16th cent.: from medieval Latin *apostatizare*, from *apostata* (see **APOSTATE**).

a posteriori /eɪ, ɑː, pɒˌstɛrɪˈɔːrʌɪ, pɒˌstɪə-/ ▶ **adjective** relating to or denoting reasoning or knowledge which proceeds from observations or experiences to the deduction of probable causes.
■ (in general use) of the nature of an afterthought or subsequent rationalization.
▶ **adverb** in a way based on reasoning from known facts or past events rather than by making assumptions or predictions.
■ [sentence adverb] informal with hindsight; as an afterthought.
– ORIGIN early 17th cent.: Latin, 'from what comes after'.

apostle ▶ **noun** (**Apostle**) each of the twelve chief disciples of Jesus Christ.
■ any important early Christian teacher, especially St Paul. ■ the first successful Christian missionary in a country or to a people. ■ a vigorous and pioneering advocate or supporter of a particular policy, idea, or cause: *he was the apostle of revolution against unjust government.*

The twelve Apostles were Peter, Andrew, James, John, Philip, Bartholomew, Thomas, Matthew, James (the Less), Judas (or Thaddaeus), Simon, and Judas Iscariot. After the suicide of Judas Iscariot his place was taken by Matthias.

– DERIVATIVES **apostleship** noun.
– ORIGIN Old English *apostol*, via ecclesiastical Latin from Greek *apostolos* 'messenger', from *apostellein* 'send forth'.

a

apostlebird ▶ **noun** a gregarious Australian bird of the mud-nester family, with grey, brown, and black plumage and a robust black bill.
• *Struthidea cinerea*, family Corcoracidae (or Grallinidae).
▪Austral. any of a number of other gregarious birds, especially babblers.
– ORIGIN early 20th cent.: named from the supposed habit of these birds of going about in flocks of twelve.

Apostles' Creed a statement of Christian belief used in the Western Church, dating from the 4th century and traditionally ascribed to the twelve Apostles.

Apostle spoon (also **Apostle teaspoon**) ▶ **noun** a teaspoon with the figure of an Apostle or saint on the handle.

apostolate /əˈpɒstəleɪt/ ▶ **noun** (chiefly in Roman Catholic contexts) the position or authority of an apostle or a religious leader.
▪a group of apostles or religious leaders. ▪ a form of religious or evangelistic activity or works.
– ORIGIN late Middle English: from ecclesiastical Latin *apostolatus*, from *apostulus* (see **APOSTLE**).

apostolic /ˌapəˈstɒlɪk/ ▶ **adjective** Christian Church of or relating to the Apostles: *apostolic writings.*
▪of or relating to the Pope, especially when he is regarded as the successor to St Peter: *an apostolic nuncio.*
– ORIGIN Middle English: from French *apostolique* or ecclesiastical Latin *apostolicus*, from Greek *apostolikos*, from *apostolos* (see **APOSTLE**).

Apostolic Fathers ▶ **plural noun** the Christian leaders immediately succeeding the Apostles.

apostolic succession ▶ **noun** (in Christian thought) the uninterrupted transmission of spiritual authority from the Apostles through successive popes and bishops, taught by the Roman Catholic Church but denied by most Protestants.

apostrophe[1] /əˈpɒstrəfi/ ▶ **noun** a punctuation mark (') used to indicate either possession (e.g. *Harry's book; boys' coats*) or the omission of letters or numbers (e.g. *can't; he's; 1 Jan. '99*).
– ORIGIN mid 16th cent. (denoting the omission of one or more letters): via late Latin, from Greek *apostrophos* 'accent of elision', from *apostrephein* 'turn away', from *apo* 'from' + *strephein* 'to turn'.

apostrophe[2] /əˈpɒstrəfi/ ▶ **noun** Rhetoric an exclamatory passage in a speech or poem addressed to a person (typically one who is dead or absent) or thing (typically one that is personified).
– ORIGIN mid 16th cent.: via Latin from Greek *apostrophē* 'turning away', from *apostrephein* 'turn away' (see **APOSTROPHE**[1]).

apostrophize /əˈpɒstrəfʌɪz/ (also **-ise**) ▶ **verb** [with obj.] **1** Rhetoric address an exclamatory passage in a speech or poem to (someone or something).
2 punctuate (a word) with an apostrophe.

apothecaries' measure (also **apothecaries' weight**) ▶ **noun** [mass noun] historical systems of units formerly used in pharmacy for liquid volume (or weight). They were based respectively on the fluid ounce (= 8 drachms or 480 minims) and the ounce troy (= 8 drachms or 24 scruples or 480 grains).

apothecary /əˈpɒθɪk(ə)ri/ ▶ **noun** (pl. **-ies**) archaic a person who prepared and sold medicines and drugs.
– ORIGIN late Middle English: via Old French from late Latin *apothecarius*, from Latin *apotheca*, from Greek *apothēkē* 'storehouse'.

apothegm ▶ **noun** US spelling of **APOPHTHEGM**.

apothem /ˈapəθɛm/ ▶ **noun** Geometry a line from the centre of a regular polygon at right angles to any of its sides.
– ORIGIN late 19th cent.: from Greek *apotithenai* 'put aside, deposit', from *apo* 'away' + *tithenai* 'to place'.

apotheosis /əˌpɒθɪˈəʊsɪs/ ▶ **noun** (pl. **apotheoses** /-siːz/) [usu. in sing.] the highest point in the development of something; a culmination or climax: *his appearance as Hamlet was the apotheosis of his career.*
▪the elevation of someone to divine status.
– ORIGIN late 16th cent.: via ecclesiastical Latin from Greek *apotheōsis*, from *apotheoun* 'make a god of', from *apo* 'from' + *theos* 'god'.

apotheosize /əˈpɒθɪəsʌɪz/ (also **-ise**) ▶ **verb** [with obj.] elevate to, or as if to, the rank of a god; idolize.

apotropaic /ˌapətrəˈpeɪɪk/ ▶ **adjective** supposedly having the power to avert evil influences or bad luck: *apotropaic statues.*
– DERIVATIVES **apotropaically** adverb.
– ORIGIN late 19th cent.: from Greek *apotropaios* 'averting evil', from *apotrepein* 'turn away or from' + **-IC**.

app ▶ **noun** Computing short for **APPLICATION** (in sense 5).

appal (US **appall**) ▶ **verb** (**appalled**, **appalling**) [with obj.] (usu. **be appalled**) greatly dismay or horrify: *bankers are* ***appalled at*** *the economic incompetence of some ministers* | [as adj. **appalled**] *Alison looked at me, appalled.*
– ORIGIN Middle English: from Old French *apalir* 'grow pale', from *a-* (from Latin *ad* 'to, at') + *palir* 'to pale'. The original sense was 'grow pale', later 'make pale', hence 'horrify' (late Middle English).

Appalachian Mountains /ˌapəˈleɪ(t)ʃ(ə)n/ (also **the Appalachians**) a mountain system of eastern North America, stretching from Quebec and Maine in the North to Georgia and Alabama in the South. Its highest peak is Mount Mitchell in North Carolina, which rises to 2,037 m (6,684 ft).

Appalachian Trail a 3,200-km (about 2,000-mile) footpath through the Appalachian Mountains from Mount Katahdin in Maine to Springer Mountain in Georgia.

appalling ▶ **adjective** horrifying; shocking: *the cat suffered appalling injuries during the attack.*
▪informal shockingly bad; awful: *his conduct was appalling.*
– DERIVATIVES **appallingly** adverb.

Appaloosa /ˌapəˈluːsə/ ▶ **noun** a horse of a North American breed having dark spots on a light background.
– ORIGIN 1920s: from *Opelousas* in Louisiana, or *Palouse*, a river in Idaho.

appanage /ˈap(ə)nɪdʒ/ (also **apanage**) ▶ **noun** historical a provision made for the maintenance of the younger children of kings and princes, consisting of a gift of land, an official position, or money.
▪archaic a benefit or right belonging to someone; a perquisite: *the appanages of her rank.*
– ORIGIN early 17th cent.: from French, based on medieval Latin *appanare* 'provide with the means of subsistence', from *ad-* 'to' + *panis* 'bread'.

apparat /ˌapəˈrɑːt/ ▶ **noun** chiefly historical the administrative system of a communist party, especially in a communist country.
– ORIGIN Russian, from German, literally 'apparatus'.

apparatchik /ˌapəˈratʃɪk/ ▶ **noun** (pl. **apparatchiks** or **apparatchiki** /-kiː/) derogatory or humorous an official in a large organization, especially a political one: *Tory apparatchiks.*
▪chiefly historical a member of a Communist Party apparat.
– ORIGIN 1940s: from Russian, from *apparat* (see **APPARAT**).

apparatus /ˌapəˈreɪtəs/ ▶ **noun** (pl. **apparatuses**) **1** [mass noun] the equipment needed for a particular activity or purpose: *laboratory apparatus.*
▪the organs used to perform a particular bodily function: *the specialized male and female sexual apparatus.*
2 a complex structure within an organization or system: *the apparatus of government.*
3 (also **critical apparatus**) a collection of notes, variant readings, and other matter accompanying a printed text. Also called **APPARATUS CRITICUS**.
– ORIGIN early 17th cent.: from Latin, from *apparare* 'make ready for', from *ad-* 'towards' + *parare* 'make ready'.

apparatus criticus /ˈkrɪtɪkəs/ ▶ **noun** (pl. **apparatus critici** /ˈkrɪtɪsʌɪ/) another term for **APPARATUS** (in sense 3).

apparel ▶ **noun** [mass noun] formal clothing.
▪(**apparels**) embroidered ornamentation on ecclesiastical vestments.
▶**verb** (**apparelled**, **apparelling**; US **appareled**, **appareling**) [with obj.] archaic clothe (someone): *all the vestments in which they used to apparel their Deities.*
– ORIGIN Middle English (as a verb in the sense 'make ready or fit'; as a noun 'furnishings, equipment'): from Old French *apareillier*, based on Latin *ad-* 'to' (expressing change) + *par* 'equal'.

apparent ▶ **adjective** clearly visible or understood; obvious: *for no apparent reason she laughed* | [with clause] *it became apparent that he was talented.*
▪seeming real or true, but not necessarily so: *his apparent lack of concern.* ▪ Astronomy as seen from the earth: *the apparent motion of the planets.*
– ORIGIN late Middle English: from Old French *aparant*, from Latin *apparent-* 'appearing', from the verb *apparere* (see **APPEAR**).

apparent horizon ▶ **noun** see **HORIZON** (sense 1).

apparently ▶ **adverb** [sentence adverb] as far as one knows or can see: *the child nodded, apparently content with the promise.*
▪used by speakers or writers to avoid committing themselves to the truth of what they are saying: *ministers met but apparently failed to make progress.*

apparent magnitude ▶ **noun** Astronomy the magnitude of a celestial object as it is actually measured from the earth. Compare with **ABSOLUTE MAGNITUDE**.

apparent time ▶ **noun** another term for **MEAN SOLAR TIME**.

apparent wind ▶ **noun** the wind as it is experienced on board a moving sailing vessel, as a result of the combined effects of the true wind and the boat's speed.

apparition ▶ **noun** a ghost or ghostlike image of a person.
▪[mass noun] the appearance of something remarkable or unexpected, especially an image of this type: *the transient apparition of a spectre.*
– DERIVATIVES **apparitional** adjective.
– ORIGIN late Middle English (in the sense 'the action of appearing'): from Latin *apparitio(n-)* 'attendance', from the verb *apparere* (see **APPEAR**).

appeal ▶ **verb** [no obj.] **1** make a serious, urgent, or heartfelt request: *police are* ***appealing for*** *information about the incident* | *she* ***appealed to*** *Germany for political asylum.*
▪(**appeal to**) address oneself to (a principle or quality in someone) in anticipation of a favourable response: *I appealed to his sense of justice.*
2 Law apply to a higher court for a reversal of the decision of a lower court: *he said he would* ***appeal against*** *the conviction* | [with obj.] N. Amer. *they have 48 hours to appeal the decision.*
▪Cricket (of the bowler or fielders) call on the umpire to declare a batsman out, traditionally with a shout of 'How's that?'
3 be attractive or interesting: *the range of topics will* ***appeal to*** *youngsters.*
▶**noun 1** a serious, urgent, or heartfelt request: *his mother made an appeal for the return of the ring.*
▪an attempt to obtain financial support: *a public appeal to raise £120,000.* ▪ [mass noun] entreaty: *a look of appeal on his face.* ▪ an address to a principle or quality in anticipation of a favourable response: *the debate was to be an appeal to homophobia.*
2 Law an application to a higher court for a decision to be reversed: *he has 28 days in which to* ***lodge an appeal*** | [mass noun] *the right of appeal.*
▪Cricket a shout of 'How's that?' or a similar call by a bowler or fielder to an umpire to declare a batsman out.
3 [mass noun] the quality of being attractive or interesting: *the popular appeal of football.*
– DERIVATIVES **appealer** noun.
– ORIGIN Middle English (in legal contexts): from Old French *apel* (noun), *apeler* (verb), from Latin *appellare* 'to address', based on *ad-* 'to' + *pellere* 'to drive'.

appealable ▶ **adjective** Law (of a case or ruling) able to be referred to a higher court for review.

appeal court ▶ **noun** a court that hears appeals, especially (**the Appeal Court**) the Court of Appeal.

appealing ▶ **adjective 1** attractive or interesting: *village life is somehow more appealing.*
2 (of an expression or tone of voice) showing that one wants help or sympathy: *an appealing look.*
– DERIVATIVES **appealingly** adverb.

appear ▶ **verb** [no obj.] **1** come into sight; become visible or noticeable, especially without visible agent or apparent cause: *smoke appeared on the horizon.*
▪come into existence or use: *the major life forms appeared on earth.* ▪ (of a book) be published: *the paperback edition didn't appear for another two years.* ▪ feature or be shown: *the symbol* ***appears in*** *many paintings of the period.* ▪ perform publicly in a film, play, etc.: *he* ***appeared on*** *Broadway.* ▪ (of an accused person, a witness, or a lawyer) make an official appearance in a court or tribunal: *he* ***appeared on*** *six*

charges of theft. ■ informal arrive at a place: *by ten o'clock Bill still hadn't appeared.*
2 seem; give the impression of being: [with infinitive] *she appeared not to know what was happening* | [with clause] ***it appears** unlikely that interest rates will fall.*
– ORIGIN Middle English: from Old French *apareir*, from Latin *apparere*, from *ad-* 'towards' + *parere* 'come into view'.

appearance ▶ **noun 1** [mass noun] the way that someone or something looks: *residents improve the appearance of their village* | *they are similar **in appearance**.*
■ [count noun] an impression given by someone or something, although this may be misleading: *she read it with every appearance of interest.*
2 an act of performing or participating in a public event: *he is well known for his television appearances.*
3 [usu. in sing.] an act of becoming visible or noticeable; an arrival: *the sudden appearance of her daughter startled her.*
■ a process of coming into existence or use: *the appearance of the railway.*
– PHRASES **keep up appearances** maintain an impression of wealth or well-being, especially to hide the true situation. **make** (or **put in**) **an appearance** attend an event briefly, especially as a matter of courtesy. **to** (or **by**) **all appearances** as far as can be seen: *to all appearances, it had been a normal day.*
– ORIGIN late Middle English: from Old French *aparance, aparence*, from late Latin *apparentia*, from Latin *apparere* (see **APPEAR**).

appearance money ▶ **noun** [mass noun] money paid to secure the appearance of a celebrity, especially a sports player, at a particular event.

appease ▶ **verb** [with obj.] **1** pacify or placate (someone) by acceding to their demands: *amendments have been added to appease local pressure groups.*
2 assuage or satisfy (a demand or a feeling): *we give to charity because it appeases our guilt.*
– DERIVATIVES **appeasement** noun, **appeaser** noun.
– ORIGIN Middle English: from Old French *apaisier*, from *a-* (from Latin *ad* 'to, at') + *pais* 'peace'.

Appel /ˈɑːp(ə)l/, Karel (b.1921), Dutch painter, sculptor, and graphic artist. An exponent of abstract expressionism, he is best known for his brightly coloured swirling images.

appellant /əˈpɛl(ə)nt/ ▶ **noun** Law a person who applies to a higher court for a reversal of the decision of a lower court.
– ORIGIN late Middle English: from French *apelant*, literally 'appealing', from the verb *apeler* (see **APPEAL**).

appellate /əˈpɛlət/ ▶ **adjective** [attrib.] Law (especially of a court) concerned with or dealing with applications for decisions to be reversed.
– ORIGIN late Middle English (originally in the sense 'appealed against, accused'): from Latin *appellatus* 'appealed against', from the verb *appellare* (see **APPEAL**). The current sense dates from the mid 18th cent.

appellation¹ /ˌapəˈleɪʃ(ə)n/ ▶ **noun** formal a name or title.
■ [mass noun] the action of giving a name to someone or something.
– ORIGIN late Middle English: via Old French from Latin *appellatio(n-)*, from the verb *appellare* (see **APPEAL**).

appellation² /ˌapəˈlasjɔ̃, French apɛlasjɔ̃/ ▶ **noun** an appellation contrôlée.
■ a wine bearing such a guarantee. ■ the district in which such wine is produced.
– ORIGIN late 20th cent.: abbreviation of *appellation (d'origine) contrôlée*.

appellation contrôlée /apəˌlasjɔ̃ kənˈtrəʊleɪ, French apɛlasjɔ̃ kɔ̃tʀole/ (also **appellation d'origine** /ˌdɒrɪˈʒiːn, French dɔʀiʒin/ **contrôlée**) ▶ **noun** a description awarded to French wine guaranteeing that it was produced in the region specified, using vines and production methods which satisfy the regulating body.
– ORIGIN French, literally 'controlled appellation'.

appellative /əˈpɛlətɪv/ ▶ **adjective** formal relating to or denoting the giving of a name.
▶ **noun** a common noun, such as 'doctor', 'mother', or 'sir', used as a vocative.
– ORIGIN late Middle English: from late Latin *appellativus*, from *appellat-* 'addressed', from the verb *appellare* (see **APPEAL**).

appellee /ˌapəˈliː, ˌapɛˈliː/ ▶ **noun** Law, chiefly US the defendant in a case taken to a higher court.
– ORIGIN mid 16th cent.: from French *appelé*, past participle of *appeler* 'call', from Latin *appellare* 'to address' (see **APPEAL**).

append ▶ **verb** [with obj.] add (something) to the end of a written document: *the results of the survey are **appended to** this chapter.*
– ORIGIN late Middle English: from Latin *appendere* 'hang on', from *ad-* 'to' + *pendere* 'hang'.

appendage ▶ **noun** a thing that is added or attached to something larger or more important (often used with negative or pejorative connotations): *they treat Scotland as a mere appendage of England.*
■ Biology a projecting part of an invertebrate or other living organism, with a distinct appearance or function: *many species have specialized clutching appendages.*

appendant formal or archaic ▶ **adjective** attached or added, especially in a subordinate capacity.
▶ **noun** a subordinate person or thing.
– ORIGIN late Middle English (in legal contexts): from Old French *apendant*, from *apendre* 'depend on, belong to', from Latin *appendere* (see **APPEND**).

appendectomy /ˌap(ə)nˈdɛktəmi/ (Brit. also **appendicectomy** /əˌpɛndɪˈsɛktəmi/) ▶ **noun** (pl. **-ies**) a surgical operation to remove the appendix.

appendicitis ▶ **noun** [mass noun] a serious medical condition in which the appendix becomes inflamed and painful.

appendicular /ˌap(ə)nˈdɪkjʊlə/ ▶ **adjective** technical relating to or denoting an appendage or appendages.
■ Anatomy of or relating to a limb or limbs.
– ORIGIN mid 17th cent.: from Latin *appendicula* 'small appendage', diminutive of *appendix*, + **-AR**¹.

appendix ▶ **noun** (pl. **appendices** or **appendixes**)
1 Anatomy a tube-shaped sac attached to and opening into the lower end of the large intestine in humans and some other mammals. In humans the appendix is small and has no known function, but in rabbits, hares, and some other herbivores it is involved in the digestion of cellulose. Also called **VERMIFORM APPENDIX**.
2 a section or table of subsidiary matter at the end of a book or document.
– ORIGIN mid 16th cent. (in sense 2): from Latin, from *appendere* 'hang upon' (see **APPEND**). Sense 1 dates from the early 17th cent.

apperception ▶ **noun** [mass noun] Psychology, dated the mental process by which a person makes sense of an idea by assimilating it to the body of ideas he or she already possesses.
– DERIVATIVES **apperceptive** adjective.
– ORIGIN mid 18th cent.: from French *aperception* or modern Latin *apperceptio(n-)*, from Latin *ad-* 'to' + *percipere* 'perceive'.

appertain /ˌapəˈteɪn/ ▶ **verb** [no obj.] **1** (**appertain to**) relate to; concern: *the answers generally appertain to improvements in standard of service.*
2 be appropriate or applicable: *the institutional arrangements which appertain under the system.*
– ORIGIN late Middle English: from Old French *apertenir*, from late Latin *appertinere*, from *ad-* 'to' + Latin *pertinere* 'to pertain'.

appestat /ˈapɪstat/ ▶ **noun** Physiology the region of the hypothalamus of the brain which is believed to control a person's appetite for food.
– ORIGIN 1950s: from **APPETITE**, probably on the pattern of *thermostat*.

appetency /ˈapɪt(ə)nsi/ ▶ **noun** (pl. **-ies**) archaic a longing or desire.
■ a natural tendency or affinity.
– ORIGIN early 17th cent.: from Latin *appetentia*, from *appetere* 'seek after' (see **APPETITE**).

appetite ▶ **noun** [usu. in sing.] a natural desire to satisfy a bodily need, especially for food: *he has a healthy appetite* | [mass noun] *they suffered from loss of appetite.*
■ a strong desire or liking for something: *her appetite for life.*
– ORIGIN Middle English: from Old French *apetit* (modern *appétit*), from Latin *appetitus* 'desire for', from *appetere* 'seek after', from *ad-* 'to' + *petere* 'seek'.

appetitive /əˈpɛtɪtɪv/ ▶ **adjective** characterized by a natural desire to satisfy bodily needs: *the appetitive behaviour of animals.*
– ORIGIN mid 16th cent.: from French *appétitif* or medieval Latin *appetitivus*, from *appetire* 'seek after' (see **APPETITE**).

appetizer (also **-iser**) ▶ **noun** a small dish of food or a drink taken before a meal or the main course of a meal to stimulate one's appetite.

appetizing (also **-ising**) ▶ **adjective** stimulating one's appetite: *the appetizing aroma of sizzling bacon.*
– DERIVATIVES **appetizingly** adverb.
– ORIGIN mid 17th cent.: from French *appétissant*, irregular formation from *appétit* (see **APPETITE**).

Appian Way /ˈapɪən/ the principal road southward from Rome in classical times, named after the censor Appius Claudius Caecus, who in 312 BC built the section to Capua; it was later extended to Brindisi. Latin name **VIA APPIA**.

applaud ▶ **verb** [no obj.] show approval or praise by clapping: *the crowd whistled and applauded* | [with obj.] *his speech was loudly applauded.*
■ [with obj.] show strong approval of (a person or action); praise: *Jill applauded the decision.*
– ORIGIN late 15th cent.: from Latin *applaudere*, from *ad-* 'to' + *plaudere* 'to clap', reinforced by French *applaudir*.

applause ▶ **noun** [mass noun] approval or praise expressed by clapping: *they gave him **a round of applause**.*
– ORIGIN late Middle English: from medieval Latin *applausus*, from the verb *applaudere* (see **APPLAUD**).

applause line ▶ **noun** US a statement in a political speech calculated to win a favourable response from an audience: *an urgent plea for health-care reform is still a reliable applause line.*

apple ▶ **noun 1** the round fruit of a tree of the rose family, which typically has thin green or red skin and crisp flesh. Many varieties have been developed as dessert or cooking fruit or for making cider.
■ used in names of unrelated fruits or other plant growths that resemble apples in some way, e.g. **custard apple**, **oak apple**.
2 (also **apple tree**) the tree bearing such fruit, with hard pale timber that is used in carpentry and to smoke food.
• Genus *Malus*, family Rosaceae: numerous hybrids and cultivars.
– PHRASES **the apple never falls far from the tree** proverb salient family characteristics are usually inherited. **the apple of one's eye** a person of whom one is extremely fond and proud. [ORIGIN: originally denoting the pupil of the eye, considered to be a globular solid body, extended as a symbol of something cherished.] **apples and oranges** N. Amer. (of two people or things) irreconcilably or fundamentally different. **apples and pears** Brit. rhyming slang stairs: *he hasn't made it up those apples and pears in ten years.* **a rotten** (or **bad**) **apple** informal a bad or corrupt person in a group, especially one whose behaviour is likely to have a detrimental influence on their associates. [ORIGIN: with reference to the effect that a rotten apple has on fruit with which it is in contact.] **she's apples** Austral. informal used to indicate that everything is in good order and there is nothing to worry about: *'Is the fire safe?' 'Yeah, she's apples.'* [ORIGIN: from *apples and spice* or *apples and rice*, rhyming slang for 'nice'.] **upset the apple cart** spoil a plan or disturb the status quo.
– ORIGIN Old English *æppel*, of Germanic origin; related to Dutch *appel* and German *Apfel*.

apple butter ▶ **noun** [mass noun] N. Amer. a paste of spiced stewed apple used as a spread or condiment, typically made with cider.

apple-cheeked ▶ **adjective** (of a person) having round rosy cheeks.

apple cider ▶ **noun** see **CIDER**.

apple green ▶ **noun** [mass noun] a bright green.

Apple Isle (also **Apple Island**) Austral. informal name for **TASMANIA**.
– ORIGIN so named because it is a region popularly associated with apple-growing.

applejack ▶ **noun** [mass noun] N. Amer. an alcoholic drink distilled from fermented cider.
– ORIGIN early 19th cent.: from **APPLE** + **JACK**¹.

apple-knocker ▶ **noun** US informal a person who picks or sells apples.
■ derogatory an ignorant or unsophisticated person.

apple pie ▶ **noun** [mass noun] N. Amer. used to represent a cherished ideal of homeliness: *to say I'm fed up* *with the Olympics is like being against **motherhood and apple pie**.*

– PHRASES **as American as apple pie** N. Amer. typically American in character.

apple-pie bed ▶ noun a bed which, as a practical joke, has been made with one of the sheets folded back on itself so that a person's legs cannot be stretched out.

apple-pie order ▶ noun [mass noun] perfect order or neatness: *everything was **in apple-pie order**.*

apple-polisher ▶ noun N. Amer. informal a toady.

– DERIVATIVES **apple-polishing** noun.

applet /ˈaplɪt/ ▶ noun Computing a very small application, especially a utility program performing one or a few simple functions.

– ORIGIN 1990s: blend of **APPLICATION** and **-LET**.

Appleton, Sir Edward Victor (1892–1965), English physicist. He discovered a region of ionized gases (the Appleton layer) in the atmosphere above the Heaviside or E layer, and won the Nobel Prize for Physics in 1947.

appley ▶ adjective (especially of white wine) smelling or tasting of apples.

appliance ▶ noun **1** a device or piece of equipment designed to perform a specific task, especially a domestic one: *electrical and gas appliances.*
■a fire engine.
2 [mass noun] Brit. the action or process of bringing something into operation: *the appliance of science could increase crop yields.*

applianced ▶ adjective US (of a kitchen) having or fitted with appliances.

applicable ▶ adjective relevant or appropriate: *the same considerations are equally **applicable to** accident claims.*

– DERIVATIVES **applicability** noun, **applicably** adverb.

– ORIGIN mid 16th cent. (in the sense 'compliant'): from Old French, or from medieval Latin *applicabilis*, from the verb *applicare* (see **APPLY**).

applicant ▶ noun a person who makes a formal application for something, especially a job.

– ORIGIN early 19th cent.: from **APPLICATION** + **-ANT**.

application ▶ noun **1** a formal request to an authority for something: *an **application for** leave* | [mass noun] *licences are available **on application*** | [as modifier] *an application form.*
2 [mass noun] the action of putting something into operation: *the application of general rules to particular cases* | [count noun] *massage has far-reaching medical applications.*
■practical use or relevance: *this principle has no application to the present case.*
3 [mass noun] the action of putting something on a surface: *paints suitable for application on fabric* | [count noun] *a fresh application of make-up.*
■a medicinal substance put on the skin.
4 [mass noun] sustained effort; hard work: *the job takes a great deal of patience and application.*
5 Computing a program or piece of software designed and written to fulfil a particular purpose of the user: *a database application.*

– DERIVATIVES **applicational** adjective.

– ORIGIN Middle English: via Old French from Latin *applicatio(n-)*, from the verb *applicare* (see **APPLY**).

application program ▶ noun another term for **APPLICATION** (in sense 5).

application programming interface ▶ noun Computing a system of tools and resources in an operating system, enabling developers to create software applications.

applicative /ˈaplɪkeɪtɪv, -kətɪv/ ▶ adjective relating to or involving the application of a subject or idea; practical or applied: *applicative algebra.*

– ORIGIN mid 17th cent.: from Latin *applicat-* 'set close or in contact, fastened to', from the verb *applicare* (see **APPLY**).

applicator ▶ noun a device used for inserting something or for applying a substance to a surface.

– ORIGIN mid 17th cent.: from Latin *applicat-* 'fastened to' (from the verb *applicare*) + **-OR**[1].

applied ▶ adjective [attrib.] (of a subject or type of study) put to practical use as opposed to being theoretical: *applied chemistry.* Compare with **PURE**.

applied linguistics ▶ plural noun [treated as sing.] the branch of linguistics concerned with practical applications of language studies, for example language teaching, translation, and speech therapy.

applied mathematics ▶ plural noun see **MATHEMATICS**.

appliqué /əˈpliːkeɪ/ ▶ noun [mass noun] ornamental needlework in which pieces of fabric are sewn or stuck on to a fabric ground to form pictures or patterns.
▶verb (**appliqués**, **appliquéd**, **appliquéing**) [with obj.] (usu. **be appliquéd**) decorate (a garment or piece of fabric) in such a way: *the coat is **appliquéd with** exotic-looking cloth* | [as adj. **appliquéd**] *19th-century appliquéd silks.*
■sew or stick (pieces of fabric) on to fabric to form pictures or patterns: *the floral motifs are appliquéd to christening robes.*

– ORIGIN mid 18th cent.: from French, past participle of *appliquer* 'apply', from Latin *applicare* (see **APPLY**).

apply ▶ verb (**-ies**, **-ied**) **1** [no obj.] make a formal application or request: *you need to **apply to** the local authority for a grant* | [with infinitive] *a number of people have applied to vote by proxy.*
■put oneself forward formally as a candidate for a job: *she had **applied for** a number of positions.*
2 [no obj.] be applicable or relevant: *prices do not **apply to** public holiday periods* | *normal rules apply.*
3 [with obj.] put or spread (something) on a surface: *the sealer can be **applied to** new wood.*
■administer: *smooth over with a cloth, applying even pressure.* ■bring or put into operation or use: *the oil industry has failed to apply appropriate standards of care.*
4 (**apply oneself**) give one's full attention to a task; work hard.

– DERIVATIVES **applier** noun.

– ORIGIN late Middle English: from Old French *aplier*, from Latin *applicare* 'fold, fasten to', from *ad-* 'to' + *plicare* 'to fold'.

appoggiatura /əˌpɒdʒəˈtjʊərə/ ▶ noun (pl. **appoggiaturas** or **appoggiature**) Music a grace note which delays the next note of the melody, taking half or more of its written time value.

– ORIGIN Italian, from *appoggiare* 'lean upon, rest'.

appoint ▶ verb [with obj.] **1** assign a job or role to (someone): *she has been **appointed to** the board* | *they **appointed** her **as** personnel manager.*
2 determine or decide on (a time or a place): *they appointed a day in May for the meeting.*
■archaic decree: *such laws are appointed by God.*
3 Law decide the disposal of (property of which one is not the owner) under powers granted by the owner: *trustees appoint the capital to the beneficiaries.*

– DERIVATIVES **appointee** noun, **appointer** noun.

– ORIGIN late Middle English: from Old French *apointer*, from *a point* 'to a point'.

appointed ▶ adjective **1** (of a time or place) decided on beforehand; designated: *she arrived at the appointed time.*
2 (of a building or room) equipped or furnished in a specified way or to a specified standard: *a luxuriously appointed lounge.*

appointive ▶ adjective N. Amer. (of a job) relating to or filled by appointment rather than election.

appointment ▶ noun **1** an arrangement to meet someone at a particular time and place: *she **made an appointment** with my receptionist.*
2 an act of assigning a job or position to someone: *his appointment as President.*
■a job or position: *she took up an appointment as head of communications.* ■a person appointed to a job or position.
3 (**appointments**) furniture or fittings: *the room was spartan in its appointments.*

– PHRASES **by appointment** having previously made an arrangement to do something: *visits are by appointment only.* **by appointment to the Queen** (in the UK) used by manufacturers to indicate that their products are sold to the queen and are therefore of guaranteed quality. **power of appointment 1** power to select the holder of a particular job or position. **2** Law power to decide the disposal of property, in exercise of a right conferred by the owner.

– ORIGIN Middle English: from Old French *apointement*, from *apointer* (see **APPOINT**).

apport /əˈpɔːt/ ▶ noun a material object produced supposedly by occult means, especially at a seance.

– ORIGIN late 19th cent.: from French *apport* 'something brought', from *apporter* 'bring to'.

apportion ▶ verb [with obj.] divide up and share out: *voting power will be apportioned according to contribution.*
■assign: *they did not **apportion** blame or liability **to** any one individual.*

– DERIVATIVES **apportionable** adjective.

– ORIGIN late 16th cent.: from Old French *apportionner* or medieval Latin *apportionare*, from *ad-* 'to' + *portionare* 'divide into portions'.

apportionment ▶ noun [mass noun] the action or result of apportioning something: *an exercise in apportionment of blame.*
■the determination of the proportional number of members each US state sends to the House of Representatives, based on population figures.

appose /əˈpəʊz/ ▶ verb [with obj.] technical place (something) side by side with or close to something else: *the specimen was **apposed to** X-ray film.*

– ORIGIN late 16th cent.: from Latin *apponere*, on the pattern of words such as *compose*, *expose*.

apposite /ˈapəzɪt/ ▶ adjective apt in the circumstances or in relation to something: *an apposite quotation* | *the observations are **apposite to** the discussion.*

– DERIVATIVES **appositely** adverb, **appositeness** noun.

– ORIGIN late 16th cent.: from Latin *appositus*, past participle of *apponere* 'apply', from *ad-* 'towards' + *ponere* 'put'.

apposition ▶ noun [mass noun] **1** chiefly technical the positioning of things or condition of being side by side or close together.
2 Grammar a relationship between two or more words or phrases in which the two units are grammatically parallel and have the same referent (e.g. *my friend Sue*; *the first US president, George Washington*).

– DERIVATIVES **appositional** adjective & noun.

– ORIGIN late Middle English: from late Latin *appositio(n-)*, from *apponere* 'to apply' (see **APPOSITE**).

appositive ▶ adjective & noun Grammar another term for ***appositional*** (see **APPOSITION**).

– ORIGIN late 17th cent.: from late Latin *appositivus* 'subsidiary'.

appraisal ▶ noun an act of assessing something or someone: *she carried out a thorough appraisal* | [mass noun] *the report has been subject to appraisal.*
■a formal assessment, typically in an interview, of the performance of an employee over a particular period.

appraisal drilling ▶ noun [mass noun] drilling undertaken to establish the quality, quantity, and other characteristics of oil or gas in a newly discovered field.

appraise ▶ verb [with obj.] assess the value or quality of: *there is a need to appraise existing techniques.*
■assess the performance of (an employee) formally. ■(of an official valuer) set a price on; value: *they appraised the painting at £200,000.*

– DERIVATIVES **appraisable** adjective, **appraisee** noun, **appraisement** noun, **appraiser** noun, **appraisingly** adverb, **appraisive** adjective.

– ORIGIN late Middle English (in the sense 'set a price on'): alteration of **APPRIZE**, by association with **PRAISE**. The current sense dates from the mid 19th cent.

USAGE The verb **appraise** is frequently confused with **apprise**. **Appraise** means 'assess (someone or something)', as in *a need to **appraise** existing techniques*, while **apprise** means 'inform (someone)' and is often used in the structure **apprise someone of something**, as in *psychiatrists were **apprised of** his condition.* In the British National Corpus, 50 per cent of citations for the meaning 'inform' incorrectly use **appraise** rather than **apprise**, as in *once **appraised of** the real facts, there was only one person who showed any opposition.*

appreciable ▶ adjective large or important enough to be noticed: *pupils may have to travel appreciable distances.*

– DERIVATIVES **appreciably** adverb.

– ORIGIN early 19th cent.: from French *appréciable*, from *apprécier* (see **APPRECIATE**).

appreciate /əˈpriːʃɪeɪt, -sɪ-/ ▶ verb [with obj.] **1** recognize the full worth of: *she feels that he does not appreciate her.*
■be grateful for (something): *I'd appreciate any information you could give me.*
2 understand (a situation) fully; recognize the full implications of: *they failed to appreciate the pressure he was under* | [with clause] *I appreciate that you cannot be held totally responsible.*

3 [no obj.] rise in value or price: *they expected the house to appreciate in value.*
– DERIVATIVES **appreciative** /-ʃ(ɪ)ətɪv/ adjective, **appreciatively** adverb, **appreciativeness** noun, **appreciator** noun, **appreciatory** /-ʃ(ɪ)ət(ə)ri/ adjective.
– ORIGIN mid 16th cent.: from late Latin *appretiat-* 'set at a price, appraised', from the verb *appretiare*, from *ad-* 'to' + *pretium* 'price'.

appreciation ▶ noun **1** [mass noun] recognition and enjoyment of the good qualities of someone or something: *I smiled in appreciation* | [count noun] *he had a fine appreciation of drawing.*
■ gratitude for something: *they would be the first to show their appreciation.* ■ [count noun] a piece of writing in which the qualities of a person or their work are discussed and assessed.
2 a full understanding of a situation: *they have an appreciation of the needs of users* | [mass noun] *the bank's lack of appreciation of their problems.*
3 [mass noun] increase in monetary value: *the appreciation of the franc against the pound.*
– ORIGIN early 17th cent.: from French *appréciation*, from late Latin *appretiatio(n-),* from the verb *appretiare* 'set at a price, appraise' (see **APPRECIATE**).

apprehend ▶ verb [with obj.] **1** arrest (someone) for a crime: *a warrant was issued but he has not been apprehended.*
2 understand or perceive: *we enter a field of vision we could not otherwise apprehend.*
■ archaic anticipate (something) with uneasiness or fear.
– ORIGIN late Middle English (originally in the sense 'grasp, get hold of (physically or mentally)'): from French *appréhender* or Latin *apprehendere,* from *ad-* 'towards' + *prehendere* 'lay hold of'.

apprehensible ▶ adjective archaic or poetic/literary capable of being understood or perceived: *a bat whirred, apprehensible only from the displacement of air.*
– ORIGIN early 17th cent.: from late Latin *apprehensibilis,* from Latin *apprehendere* (see **APPREHEND**).

apprehension ▶ noun [mass noun] **1** anxiety or fear that something bad or unpleasant will happen: *he felt sick with apprehension* | [count noun] *she had some apprehensions about the filming.*
2 understanding; grasp: *his first apprehension of such large issues.*
3 the action of arresting someone: *they acted with intent to prevent lawful apprehension.*
– ORIGIN late Middle English (in the sense 'learning, acquisition of knowledge'): from late Latin *apprehensio(n-),* from *apprehendere* 'seize, grasp' (see **APPREHEND**).

apprehensive ▶ adjective **1** anxious or fearful that something bad or unpleasant will happen: *he felt apprehensive about going home.*
2 archaic or poetic/literary of or relating to perception or understanding.
– DERIVATIVES **apprehensively** adverb, **apprehensiveness** noun.
– ORIGIN late Middle English (in sense 2): from French *appréhensif* or medieval Latin *apprehensivus,* from Latin *apprehendere* 'seize, grasp' (see **APPREHEND**).

apprentice ▶ noun a person who is learning a trade from a skilled employer, having agreed to work for a fixed period at low wages: [as modifier] *an apprentice electrician.*
▶ verb [with obj.] (usu. **be apprenticed**) employ (someone) as an apprentice: *Edward was apprenticed to a printer.*
■ [no obj.] N. Amer. serve as an apprentice: *she apprenticed with midwives in San Francisco.*
– DERIVATIVES **apprenticeship** noun.
– ORIGIN Middle English: from Old French *aprentis* (from *apprendre* 'learn', from Latin *apprehendere* 'apprehend'), on the pattern of words ending in *-tis, -tif,* from Latin *-tivus* (see **-IVE**).

appress /əˈprɛs/ ▶ verb [with obj.] (usu. **be appressed**) technical press (something) close to something else: *the two cords can be closely appressed to one another.*
– ORIGIN early 17th cent.: from Latin *appress-* 'pressed close', from the verb *apprimere,* from *ad-* 'to' + *premere* 'to press'.

apprise /əˈprʌɪz/ ▶ verb [with obj.] inform or tell (someone): *I thought it right to apprise Chris of what had happened.*
– ORIGIN late 17th cent.: from French *appris, apprise,* past participle of *apprendre* 'learn, teach', from Latin *apprehendere* (see **APPREHEND**).

USAGE The verb **apprise** is frequently confused with **appraise**. See usage at **APPRAISE**.

apprize /əˈprʌɪz/ (also **-ise**) ▶ verb [with obj.] archaic put a price upon; appraise: *the sheriff was to apprize the value of the lands.*
■ value highly; esteem: *how highly your Highness apprizeth peace.*
– ORIGIN late Middle English: from Old French *aprisier,* from *a-* (from Latin *ad* 'to, at') + *prisier* 'to price, prize', from *pris* (see **PRICE**). The change in the ending in the 17th cent. was due to association with **PRIZE**[1].

appro ▶ noun (in phrase **on appro**) Brit. informal on approval.

approach ▶ verb [with obj.] **1** come near or nearer to (someone or something) in distance: *the train approached the main line* | [no obj.] *she hadn't heard him approach* | [as adj. **approaching**] *an approaching car.*
■ come near or nearer to (a future time or event): *he was approaching retirement.* ■ [no obj.] (of a future time) come nearer: *the time is approaching when you will be destroyed.* ■ come close to (a number, level, or standard) in quality or quantity: *the population will approach 12 million by the end of the decade.* ■ archaic bring nearer: *all those changes shall serve to approach him the faster to the blest mansion.*
2 speak to (someone) for the first time about something, typically with a proposal or request: *the department had been approached about funding.*
3 start to deal with (something) in a certain way: *one must approach the matter with caution.*
▶ noun **1** a way of dealing with something: *we need a whole new approach to the job.*
2 an act of speaking to someone for the first time about something, typically a proposal or request: *the landowner made an approach to the developer.*
■ (**approaches**) dated behaviour intended to propose personal or sexual relations with someone: *feminine resistance to his approaches.*
3 [in sing.] the action of coming near or nearer to someone or something in distance or time: *the approach of winter.*
■ (**approach to**) an approximation to something: *the past is impossible to recall with any approach to accuracy.* ■ the part of an aircraft's flight in which it descends gradually towards an airfield or runway for landing. ■ (usu. **approaches**) a road, sea passage, or other way leading to a place: *the northern approaches to London.*
– ORIGIN Middle English: from Old French *aprochier, aprocher,* from ecclesiastical Latin *appropiare* 'draw near', from *ad-* 'to' + *propius* (comparative of *prope* 'near').

approachable ▶ adjective **1** friendly and easy to talk to: *managers should be approachable.*
2 (of a place) able to be reached from a particular direction or by a particular means: *the site is approachable from the roundabout.*
– DERIVATIVES **approachability** noun.

approach road ▶ noun Brit. a road leading up to a particular place or feature.

approach shot ▶ noun Golf a stroke which sends the ball from the fairway on to or nearer the green.

approbate /ˈaprəbeɪt/ ▶ verb [with obj.] US rare approve formally; sanction: *a letter approbating the affair.*
– ORIGIN late Middle English: from Latin *approbat-* 'approved', from the verb *approbare,* from *ad-* 'to' + *probare* 'try, test' (from *probus* 'good').

approbation ▶ noun [mass noun] formal approval or praise: *a term of approbation.*
– DERIVATIVES **approbative** adjective, **approbatory** adjective.
– ORIGIN late Middle English: via Old French from Latin *approbatio(n-),* from the verb *approbare* (see **APPROBATE**).

appropriate ▶ adjective /əˈprəʊprɪət/ suitable or proper in the circumstances: *a measure appropriate to a wartime economy.*
■ archaic assigned to a particular person; special; individual: *the end of her deliberation was to show general gaiety, without appropriate favour.*
▶ verb /əˈprəʊprɪeɪt/ [with obj.] **1** take (something) for one's own use, typically without the owner's permission: *the accused had appropriated the property.*
2 devote (money or assets) to a special purpose: *there can be problems in appropriating funds for legal expenses.*
– DERIVATIVES **appropriately** adverb [sentence adverb] *appropriately, the first recital will be given at the festival,* **appropriateness** noun, **appropriator** noun.

– ORIGIN late Middle English: from late Latin *appropriatus,* past participle of *appropriare* 'make one's own', from *ad-* 'to' + *proprius* 'own, proper'.

appropriation ▶ noun **1** [mass noun] the action of taking something for one's own use, typically without the owner's permission: *the appropriation of parish funds.*
■ often derogatory the artistic practice or technique of reworking images from well-known paintings, photographs, or other works in one's own work.
2 a sum of money or total of assets devoted to a special purpose.
– ORIGIN late Middle English: from late Latin *appropriatio(n-),* from *appropriare* 'make one's own' (see **APPROPRIATE**).

appropriationist ▶ noun often derogatory an artist whose work contains reworkings of well-known images by other artists: [as modifier] *appropriationist art.*

approval ▶ noun [mass noun] the action of officially agreeing to something or accepting something as satisfactory: *the road schemes have been given approval* | [count noun] *they have delayed the launch to await project approvals.*
■ the belief that someone or something is good or acceptable: *step-parents need to win a child's approval.*
– PHRASES **on approval** (of goods) supplied on condition that they may be returned if not satisfactory. **seal** (or **stamp**) **of approval** an official statement or indication that something is accepted or regarded favourably.

approve ▶ verb [with obj.] **1** officially agree to or accept as satisfactory: *the budget was approved by parliament* | [as adj. **approved**] *places on approved courses.*
■ [no obj.] believe that someone or something is good or acceptable: *I don't approve of romance.*
2 archaic prove; show: *he approved himself ripe for military command.*
– DERIVATIVES **approvingly** adverb.
– ORIGIN Middle English: from Old French *aprover,* from Latin *approbare* (see **APPROBATE**). The original sense was 'prove, demonstrate', later 'corroborate, confirm', hence 'pronounce to be satisfactory' (late Middle English).

approved school ▶ noun Brit. historical a residential institution for young offenders.

approx. ▶ abbreviation for approximate(ly).

approximant ▶ noun **1** Mathematics a function, series, or other expression which is an approximation to the solution of a problem.
2 Phonetics a consonant produced by bringing one articulator (the tongue or lips) close to another without actually touching it, as in English r and w.

approximate ▶ adjective /əˈprɒksɪmət/ close to the actual, but not completely accurate or exact: *the calculations are very approximate.*
▶ verb /əˈprɒksɪmeɪt/ [no obj.] come close or be similar to something in quality, nature, or quantity: *a leasing agreement approximating to ownership* | [with obj.] *reality can be approximated by computational techniques.*
■ [with obj.] estimate or calculate (a quantity) fairly accurately: *I had to approximate the weight of my horse.*
– DERIVATIVES **approximately** adverb, **approximation** noun.
– ORIGIN late Middle English (in the adjectival sense 'close, similar'): from late Latin *approximatus,* past participle of *approximare,* from *ad-* 'to' + *proximus* 'very near'. The verb (originally meaning 'bring close') arose in the mid 17th cent.; the current adjectival sense dates from the early 19th cent.

approximative ▶ adjective (of a method, description, etc.) giving only an approximation to something: *a crudely approximative outline.*

appurtenance /əˈpəːt(ɪ)nəns/ ▶ noun (usu. **appurtenances**) an accessory or other item associated with a particular activity or style of living: *the appurtenances of consumer culture.*
– ORIGIN Middle English: from Old French *apertenance,* based on late Latin *appertinere* 'belong to' (see **APPERTAIN**).

appurtenant ▶ adjective belonging; pertinent: *properties appurtenant to the main building.*
– ORIGIN late Middle English: from Old French *apartenant* 'appertaining', from the verb *apartenir* (see **APPERTAIN**).

APR ▶ abbreviation for annual or annualized percentage rate (used typically of interest on loans or credit).

Apr. ▶ abbreviation for April.

apraxia /əˈpraksɪə/ ▶ noun [mass noun] Medicine inability to perform particular purposive actions, as a result of brain damage.
– DERIVATIVES **apraxic** adjective.
– ORIGIN late 19th cent.: from German *Apraxie*, from Greek *apraxia* 'inaction'.

après- /ˈapreɪ/ ▶ prefix informal, humorous coming after in time, typically specifying a period following an activity: *après-shopping*.
– ORIGIN French, 'after', used in combinations on the pattern of *après-ski*.

après-ski ▶ noun [mass noun] the social activities and entertainment following a day's skiing.
– DERIVATIVES **après-skiing** noun.
– ORIGIN 1950s: from French, literally 'after skiing'.

apricot /ˈeɪprɪkɒt, ˈaprɪ-/ ▶ noun 1 a juicy, soft fruit, resembling a small peach, of an orange-yellow colour.
■ [mass noun] an orange-yellow colour like the skin of a ripe apricot: *Rose had her shops decorated in apricot* | [as modifier] *an apricot cotton dress.*
2 (also **apricot tree**) the tree bearing this fruit.
● *Prunus armeniaca*, family Rosaceae.
– ORIGIN mid 16th cent.: from Portuguese *albricoque* or Spanish *albaricoque*, from Spanish Arabic *al* 'the' + *barkūk* (via late Greek from Latin *praecoquum*, variant of *praecox* 'early-ripe'); influenced by Latin *apricus* 'ripe' and French *abricot*.

April ▶ noun the fourth month of the year, in the northern hemisphere usually considered the second month of spring: *the prison was to close in April* | *the show opens next April.*
– ORIGIN Old English, from Latin *Aprilis*.

April Fool ▶ noun a person who is the victim of a trick or hoax on April Fool's Day.
■ a trick or hoax on April Fool's Day.

April Fool's Day (also **April Fools' Day**) ▶ noun 1 April, in many Western countries traditionally an occasion for playing tricks. This custom has been observed for hundreds of years, but its origin is unknown. Also called **ALL FOOLS' DAY**.

a priori /ˌeɪ prʌɪˈɔːrʌɪ, ˌɑː prɪˈɔːri/ ▶ adjective relating to or denoting reasoning or knowledge which proceeds from theoretical deduction rather than from observation or experience: *a priori assumptions about human nature.*
▶ adverb in a way based on theoretical deduction rather than empirical observation: *sexuality may be a factor but it cannot be assumed a priori.*
– DERIVATIVES **apriorism** /eɪˈprʌɪɒrɪz(ə)m/ noun.
– ORIGIN late 16th cent.: Latin, 'from what is before'.

apron ▶ noun 1 a protective garment worn over the front of one's clothes, either from chest or waist level, and tied at the back.
■ a similar garment worn as part of official dress, as by a bishop or Freemason. ■ a sheet of lead worn to shield the body during an X-ray examination.
2 a small area adjacent to another larger area or structure: *a tiny apron of garden.*
■ a hard-surfaced area on an airfield used for manoeuvring or parking aircraft. ■ (also **apron stage**) a projecting strip of stage for playing scenes in front of the curtain. ■ US an area of tarmac where the drive of a house meets the road. ● Geology an extensive outspread deposit of sediment, typically at the foot of a glacier or mountain.
3 an object resembling an apron in shape or function, in particular:
■ a covering protecting an area or structure, for example from water erosion. ■ [often as modifier] an endless conveyor made of overlapping plates: *apron feeders bring coarse ore to a grinding mill.*
– PHRASES (**tied to**) **someone's apron strings** (too much under) the influence and control of someone: *we have all met sturdy adults who are tied to mother's apron strings.*
– ORIGIN Middle English *naperon*, from Old French, diminutive of *nape*, *nappe* 'tablecloth', from Latin *mappa* 'napkin'. The *n* was lost by wrong division of *a napron*; compare with **ADDER**[1].

aproned ▶ adjective wearing an apron: *aproned waiters in white caps.*

apropos /ˌaprəˈpəʊ, ˈaprəpəʊ/ ▶ preposition with reference to; concerning: *she remarked apropos of the initiative, 'It's not going to stop the abuse'.*
▶ adverb [sentence adverb] (**apropos of nothing**) used to state a speaker's belief that someone's comments or acts are unrelated to any previous discussion or situation: *Isabel kept smiling apropos of nothing.*

▶ adjective [predic.] very appropriate to a particular situation: *the song feels apropos to a midnight jaunt.*
– ORIGIN mid 17th cent.: from French *à propos* '(with regard) to (this) purpose'.

apsara /ˈʌpsəraː/ (also **apsaras** /ˈʌpsərɑːs/) ▶ noun (pl. **apsaras** or **apsarases**) Hindu Mythology a celestial nymph, typically the wife of a heavenly musician.
– ORIGIN from Hindi *apsarā*, from Sanskrit *apsarās*.

apse /aps/ ▶ noun 1 a large semicircular or polygonal recess in a church, arched or with a domed roof and typically at the church's eastern end.
2 another term for **APSIS**.
– DERIVATIVES **apsidal** /ˈapsɪd(ə)l/ adjective.
– ORIGIN early 19th cent. (in sense 2): from Latin *apsis* (see **APSIS**).

apsis /ˈapsɪs/ ▶ noun (pl. **apsides** /-diːz/) either of two points on the orbit of a planet or satellite that are nearest to or furthest from the body round which it moves.
– DERIVATIVES **apsidal** adjective.
– ORIGIN early 17th cent. (denoting the orbit of a planet): via Latin from Greek *apsis*, *hapsis* 'arch, vault', perhaps from *haptein* 'fasten, join'.

apt ▶ adjective 1 appropriate or suitable in the circumstances: *an apt description of her nature.*
2 [predic., with infinitive] having a tendency to do something: *he is apt to be swayed by irrational considerations.*
3 quick to learn: *she proved an apt pupil.*
– DERIVATIVES **aptly** adverb, **aptness** noun.
– ORIGIN late Middle English (in the sense 'suited, appropriate'): from Latin *aptus* 'fitted', past participle of *apere* 'fasten'.

apterous /ˈapt(ə)rəs/ ▶ adjective Entomology (of an insect) having no wings.
– ORIGIN late 18th cent.: from Greek *apteros* (from *a*- 'without' + *pteron* 'wing') + **-OUS**.

Apterygota /apˈtɛrɪˌɡəʊtə/ Entomology a group of insects which includes the bristletails and springtails, having a primitive body form without wings and no distinct larval stage. Compare with **PTERYGOTA**.
● Subclass Apterygota, class Insecta (or Hexapoda): several orders, some of which are sometimes excluded from the Insecta.
– DERIVATIVES **apterygote** noun.
– ORIGIN modern Latin *Apterygota*, from Greek *a*- 'not' + *pterugōtos* 'winged'.

aptitude ▶ noun a natural ability to do something: *he had a remarkable aptitude for learning words* | [mass noun] *the staff show aptitude for managerial responsibility.*
■ a natural tendency: *his natural aptitude for failure.*
– ORIGIN late Middle English: via Old French from late Latin *aptitudo*, from *aptus* (see **APT**).

aptitude test ▶ noun a test designed to determine a person's ability in a particular skill or field of knowledge.

APU ▶ abbreviation for auxiliary power unit, a device used on aircraft to provide power while on the ground and to start the main engines.

Apuleius /ˌapjʊˈliːəs/ (born *c.*123 AD), Roman writer, born in Africa. His writings are characterized by an exuberant and bizarre use of language. Notable works: *Metamorphoses* (*The Golden Ass*).

Apulia /əˈpjuːlɪə/ a region of SE Italy, extending into the 'heel' of the peninsula; capital, Bari. Italian name **PUGLIA**.
– DERIVATIVES **Apulian** noun & adjective.

Apus /ˈeɪpəs/ Astronomy a faint southern constellation (the Bird of Paradise), close to the south celestial pole.
■ [as genitive **Apodis** /eɪˈpəʊdɪs/] used with preceding letter or numeral to designate a star in this constellation: *the star Beta Apodis.*
– ORIGIN Latin, denoting a kind of bird, from Greek *apous.*

Aqaba /ˈakəbə/ Jordan's only port, at the head of the Gulf of Aqaba; pop. 40,000 (est. 1983).

Aqaba, Gulf of a part of the Red Sea extending northwards between the Sinai and Arabian peninsulas.

aqua /ˈakwə/ ▶ noun [mass noun] a light bluish-green colour; aquamarine.
– ORIGIN 1930s: abbreviation of **AQUAMARINE**.

aqua- /ˈakwə/ ▶ combining form relating to water: *aquaculture.*

■ relating to water sports or aquatic entertainment: *aquacade.*
– ORIGIN from Latin *aqua* 'water'.

aqua aura ▶ noun [mass noun] quartz or other mineral to which a thin film of gold has been applied, giving it a blue iridescent colour.

aquacade /ˈakwəˌkeɪd/ ▶ noun US a spectacle involving swimming and diving, usually with musical accompaniment.

aquaculture ▶ noun [mass noun] Botany the rearing of aquatic animals or the cultivation of aquatic plants for food.
– ORIGIN mid 19th cent.: from Latin *aqua* 'water' + **CULTURE**, on the pattern of words such as *agriculture.*

aqua fortis /ˈfɔːtɪs/ ▶ noun archaic term for **NITRIC ACID**.
– ORIGIN late 15th cent.: from Latin, literally 'strong water'.

aqualung ▶ noun a portable breathing apparatus for divers, consisting of cylinders of compressed air strapped on the diver's back, feeding air automatically through a mask or mouthpiece.
– ORIGIN 1950s (originally a proprietary name in the US): from Latin *aqua* 'water' + **LUNG**.

aquamanile /ˌakwəmə'nʌɪli, -'niːli/ ▶ noun a water container or ewer, typically in the form of a mammal or bird, used in medieval times.
– ORIGIN late 19th cent.: from late Latin, from Latin *aquaemanalis*, literally 'ewer of water'.

aquamarine ▶ noun [mass noun] a precious stone consisting of a light bluish-green variety of beryl.
■ a light bluish-green colour: *the aquamarine of the Atlantic Ocean* | [as modifier] *the aquamarine water.*
– ORIGIN early 18th cent.: from Latin *aqua marina* 'seawater'.

aquanaut ▶ noun a person who swims under water using an aqualung.
– ORIGIN late 19th cent.: from Latin *aqua* 'water' + Greek *nautēs* 'sailor'.

aquaplane ▶ noun a board for riding on water, pulled by a speedboat.
▶ verb [no obj.] [often as noun **aquaplaning**] ride standing on an aquaplane.
■ (of a vehicle) slide uncontrollably on a wet surface: *the plane is believed to have aquaplaned on the runway.*
– ORIGIN early 20th cent. (originally US): from Latin *aqua* 'water' + **PLANE**[1].

aqua regia /ˈriːdʒə/ ▶ noun [mass noun] Chemistry a mixture of concentrated nitric and hydrochloric acids. It is a highly corrosive liquid able to attack gold and other resistant substances.
– ORIGIN early 17th cent.: Latin, literally 'royal water'.

aquarelle /ˌakwə'rɛl/ ▶ noun [mass noun] the technique of painting with thin, transparent watercolours (as distinct from gouache).
■ [count noun] a painting of this kind.
– ORIGIN mid 19th cent.: from French, from Italian *acquarella* 'watercolour', diminutive of *acqua*, from Latin *aqua* 'water'.

Aquarian /əˈkwɛːrɪən/ Astrology ▶ noun a person born under the sign of Aquarius.
▶ adjective of or relating to the sign of Aquarius.
■ of or relating to the Age of Aquarius.

aquarist /ˈakwərɪst/ ▶ noun a person who keeps an aquarium.

aquarium ▶ noun (pl. **aquaria** /-rɪə/ or **aquariums**) a transparent tank of water in which live fish and other water creatures and plants are kept.
■ a building containing such tanks, especially one that is open to the public.
– ORIGIN mid 19th cent.: from Latin, neuter of *aquarius* 'of water', on the pattern of *vivarium.*

Aquarius /əˈkwɛːrɪəs/ **1** Astronomy a large constellation (the Water Carrier or Water Bearer), said to represent a man pouring water from a jar. It contains no bright stars but has several planetary nebulae.
■ [as genitive **Aquarii** /əˈkwɛːrɪʌɪ/] used with preceding letter or numeral to designate a star in this constellation: *the star Alpha Aquarii.*
2 Astrology the eleventh sign of the zodiac, which the sun enters about 21 January.
■ (an Aquarius) a person born when the sun is in this sign.
– PHRASES **Age of Aquarius** an astrological age which is about to begin, marked by the precession

of the vernal equinox into Aquarius, believed by some to herald worldwide peace and harmony.
– ORIGIN Latin *aquarius* 'of water', used as a noun to mean 'water carrier'.

aquarobics /ˌakwəˈrəʊbɪks/ ▶ **plural noun** [often treated as sing.] aerobic exercises performed in water.
– ORIGIN 1980s: blend of **AQUA-** and **AEROBICS**.

aquatic /əˈkwatɪk, -ˈkwɒt-/ ▶ **adjective** of or relating to water.
■(of a plant or animal) growing or living in or near water: *the bay could support aquatic life.* ■ (of a sport) played in or on water. ■ (of a shop or dealer) specializing in products for ponds or aquaria.
▶**noun 1** an aquatic plant or animal, especially one suitable for a pond or aquarium.
2 (**aquatics**) sports played in or on water.
– ORIGIN late 15th cent. (in the sense 'watery, rainy'): from Old French *aquatique* or Latin *aquaticus*, from *aqua* 'water'.

aquatint ▶ **noun** a print resembling a watercolour, made by etching a copper plate with nitric acid, using resin and varnish to produce areas of tonal shading.
■[mass noun] the technique or process of producing such prints.
▶**verb** [with obj.] produce (a print) in this way.
– ORIGIN late 18th cent.: from French *aquatinte*, from Italian *acqua tinta* 'coloured water'.

aquavit /ˌakwəˈviːt/ (also **akvavit**) ▶ **noun** [mass noun] an alcoholic spirit made from potatoes or other starchy plants.
– ORIGIN late 19th cent.: from Norwegian, Swedish, and Danish *akvavit* (see **AQUA VITAE**).

aqua vitae /ˈvʌɪtiː, ˈviːtʌɪ/ ▶ **noun** [mass noun] strong alcoholic spirit, especially brandy.
– ORIGIN late Middle English: from Latin, literally 'water of life'; compare with **AQUAVIT**, **EAU DE VIE**, **USQUEBAUGH**, and **WHISKY**.

aqueduct /ˈakwɪdʌkt/ ▶ **noun** a bridge or viaduct carrying a waterway over a valley or other gap.
■an artificial channel for conveying water. ■ Anatomy a small canal containing fluid.
– ORIGIN mid 16th cent.: from obsolete French (now *aqueduc*), from Latin *aquae ductus* 'conduit', from *aqua* 'water' + *ducere* 'to lead'.

aqueduct of Sylvius /ˈsɪlvɪəs/ ▶ **noun** Anatomy a fluid-filled canal which runs through the midbrain connecting the third and fourth ventricles. Also called **CEREBRAL AQUEDUCT**.

aqueous /ˈeɪkwɪəs/ ▶ **adjective** of or containing water, especially as a solvent or medium: *an aqueous solution of potassium permanganate.*
■like water; watery: *an eerie, aqueous light.*
– ORIGIN mid 17th cent.: from medieval Latin *aqueus*, from Latin *aqua* 'water'.

aqueous humour ▶ **noun** [mass noun] the clear fluid filling the space in the front of the eyeball between the lens and the cornea. Compare with **VITREOUS HUMOUR**.

aquifer /ˈakwɪfə/ ▶ **noun** a body of permeable rock which can contain or transmit groundwater.
– ORIGIN early 20th cent.: from Latin *aqui-* (from *aqua* 'water') + *-fer* 'bearing'.

Aquila[1] /ˈakwɪlə, əˈkwɪlə/ Astronomy a small northern constellation (the Eagle), said to represent the eagle that carried Ganymede to Olympus. It contains the bright star Altair, and some rich star fields of the Milky Way.
■[as genitive **Aquilae** /ˈakwɪliː, əˈkwɪliː, -lʌɪ/] used with preceding letter or numeral to designate a star in this constellation: *the star Beta Aquilae.*
– ORIGIN Latin.

Aquila[2] /ˈakwɪlə/ a city in east central Italy, capital of Abruzzi region; pop. 67,820 (1990). Italian name **L'AQUILA**.

aquilegia /ˌakwɪˈliːdʒə/ ▶ **noun** a plant of the buttercup family, which bears showy flowers with backward-pointing spurs. Native to temperate regions of the northern hemisphere, it is widely grown in gardens.
● Genus *Aquilegia*, family Ranunculaceae. See also **COLUMBINE**.
– ORIGIN from medieval Latin, probably from Latin *aquilegus* 'water-collecting'.

aquiline /ˈakwɪlʌɪn/ ▶ **adjective** like an eagle.
■(of a person's nose) hooked or curved like an eagle's beak.
– ORIGIN mid 17th cent.: from Latin *aquilinus*, from *aquila* 'eagle'.

Aquinas, St Thomas /əˈkwʌɪnəs/ (1225–74), Italian philosopher, theologian, and Dominican friar; known as *the Angelic Doctor*.

He is regarded as the greatest figure of scholasticism; one of his most important achievements was the introduction of the work of Aristotle to Christian western Europe. His works include commentaries on Aristotle as well as the *Summa Contra Gentiles*, intended as a manual for missionaries, and *Summa Theologiae*, the greatest achievement of medieval systematic theology. He also devised the official Roman Catholic tenets. Feast day, 28 January.

Aquitaine[1] /ˌakwɪˈteɪn, French akitɛn/ a region and former province of SW France, on the Bay of Biscay, centred on Bordeaux. It became an English possession by the marriage of Eleanor of Aquitaine to Henry II, and remained so until 1453.

Aquitaine[2], Eleanor of, see **ELEANOR OF AQUITAINE**.

aquiver /əˈkwɪvə/ ▶ **adjective** [predic.] quivering; trembling: *her face was aquiver with pleasure.*

AR ▶ **abbreviation for** ■ US Arkansas (in official postal use). ■ Autonomous Republic.

Ar ▶ **symbol for** the chemical element argon.

ar- ▶ **prefix** variant spelling of **AD-** assimilated before *r* (as in *arrive, arrogate*).

-ar[1] ▶ **suffix 1** (forming adjectives) of the kind specified; relating to: *lunar* | *molecular.*
2 forming nouns such as *scholar.*
– ORIGIN from Old French *-aire, -ier*, or from Latin *-aris*.

-ar[2] ▶ **suffix** forming nouns such as *pillar.*
– ORIGIN via Old French from Latin *-are* (neuter of *-aris*).

-ar[3] ▶ **suffix** forming nouns such as *bursar, exemplar, vicar.*
– ORIGIN from Old French *-aire, -ier*, or from Latin *-arius, -arium*.

-ar[4] ▶ **suffix** alteration of **-ER**[1], **-OR**[1] (as in *liar, pedlar*).

ARA ▶ **abbreviation for** Associate of the Royal Academy.

Ara /ˈɑːrə/ Astronomy a small and faint southern constellation (the Altar), in the Milky Way near Scorpius.
■[as genitive **Arae** /ˈɑːrʌɪ, ˈɑːriː/] used with preceding letter or numeral to designate a star in this constellation: *the star Delta Arae.*
– ORIGIN Latin.

Arab /ˈarəb, ˈeɪrab/ ▶ **noun 1** a member of a Semitic people, originally from the Arabian peninsula and neighbouring territories, inhabiting much of the Middle East and North Africa.
2 a horse of a breed originating in Arabia, with a distinctive dished face and high-set tail.
▶**adjective** of or relating to Arabian people: *Arab countries.*
– ORIGIN via Latin and Greek from Arabic *ʿarab*.

arabesque /ˌarəˈbɛsk/ ▶ **noun 1** an ornamental design consisting of intertwined flowing lines, originally found in ancient and especially in Islamic decoration: [as modifier] *arabesque scrolls.*
■Music a passage or composition with fanciful ornamentation of the melody.
2 Ballet a posture in which one leg is lifted from the floor and extended backwards at right angles.
■a position of the arms in which both are extended palms downwards, one to the front and the other behind or to the side.
– ORIGIN mid 17th cent.: from French, from Italian *arabesco* 'in the Arabic style', from *arabo* 'Arab'.

Arabia /əˈreɪbɪə/ (also **Arabian peninsula**) a peninsula of SW Asia, largely desert, lying between the Red Sea and the Persian Gulf and bounded on the north by Jordan and Iraq. The original homeland of the Arabs and the historic centre of Islam, it comprises the states of Saudi Arabia, Yemen, Oman, Bahrain, Kuwait, Qatar, and the United Arab Emirates.

Arabian ▶ **adjective** of or relating to Arabia or its inhabitants.
▶**noun** historical a native or inhabitant of Arabia.
■an Arab horse.

Arabian camel ▶ **noun** the domesticated one-humped camel, probably native to the deserts of North Africa and SW Asia. See also **DROMEDARY**.
● *Camelus dromedarius*, family Camelidae.

Arabian Desert the desert in eastern Egypt, between the Nile and the Red Sea. Also called the **EASTERN DESERT**.

Arabian Gulf another name for **PERSIAN GULF**.

Arabian Nights a collection of stories and romances written in Arabic. The king of Samarkand has killed all his wives after one night's marriage until he marries Scheherazade, who saves her life by entertaining him with stories. The stories include the tales of Aladdin and Sinbad the Sailor. Also called **ARABIAN NIGHTS' ENTERTAINMENTS** or **THOUSAND AND ONE NIGHTS**.

Arabian peninsula another name for **ARABIA**.

Arabian Sea the north-western part of the Indian Ocean, between Arabia and India.

Arabic ▶ **noun** [mass noun] the Semitic language of the Arabs, spoken by some 150 million people throughout the Middle East and North Africa.
▶**adjective** of or relating to the literature or language of Arab people.

Arabic is written from right to left in a cursive script of twenty-eight consonants, the vowels being indicated by additional signs. The classical or literary language is based largely on that of the Koran; colloquial Arabic has many dialects. The script has been adapted for various languages, including Persian, Urdu, Malay, and (formerly) Turkish.

– ORIGIN Middle English: via Latin from Greek *arabikos*, from *Araps, Arab-* 'Arab'.

arabica /əˈrabɪkə/ ▶ **noun 1** [mass noun] coffee or coffee beans from the most widely grown kind of coffee plant.
2 the bush that produces these beans, native to the Old World tropics.
● *Coffea arabica*, family Rubiaceae. See also **ROBUSTA**.
– ORIGIN 1920s: from Latin, feminine of *arabicus* (see **ARABIC**).

Arabic numeral ▶ **noun** any of the numerals 0, 1, 2, 3, 4, 5, 6, 7, 8, and 9. Arabic numerals reached western Europe (replacing Roman numerals) through Arabia by about AD 1200 but probably originated in India.

arabinose /ˈarəbɪnəʊz, -s/ ▶ **noun** [mass noun] Chemistry a sugar of the pentose class which is a constituent of many plant gums.
– ORIGIN late 19th cent.: from **ARABICA** + **-IN**[1] + **-OSE**[2].

arabis /ˈarəbɪs/ ▶ **noun** a low-growing herbaceous plant which typically bears white or pink flowers, frequently grown in rock gardens. Also called **ROCK CRESS** or **WALL CRESS**.
● Genus *Arabis*, family Cruciferae.
– ORIGIN via medieval Latin from Greek, feminine of *Araps, Arab-* (see **ARAB**).

Arabism ▶ **noun 1** [mass noun] Arab culture or identity.
■support for Arab nationalism or political interests.
2 an Arabic linguistic usage, word, or phrase.
– DERIVATIVES **Arabist** noun & adjective.

Arabize (also **-ise**) ▶ **verb** [with obj.] [usu. as adj. **Arabized**] give (someone or something) an Arab or Arabic character: *an Arabized script.*
– DERIVATIVES **Arabization** noun.

arable ▶ **adjective** (of land) used or suitable for growing crops.
■(of crops) able to be grown on such land. ■ concerned with growing such crops: *arable farming.*
▶**noun** [mass noun] land or crops of this type.
– ORIGIN late Middle English: from Old French, or from Latin *arabilis*, from *arare* 'to plough'.

Arab League another name for **LEAGUE OF ARAB STATES**.

Araby /ˈarəbi/ archaic term for **ARABIA**.
– ORIGIN late Middle English: from Old French *Arabie*, from Latin *Arabia*, from Greek.

Aracajú /ˌarəkəˈʒuː/ a port in eastern Brazil, on the Atlantic coast, capital of the state of Sergipe; pop. 404,828 (1990).

aracari /ˌarəˈsɑːri, ˌarəˈkɑːri/ (also **araçari** /-ˈsɑːri/) ▶ **noun** (pl. **aracaris**) a small toucan with a serrated bill, and typically with a green back and wings, yellow underside, and red rump.
● Genus *Pteroglossus*, family Ramphastidae: several species.
– ORIGIN early 19th cent.: via Portuguese from Tupi *arasa'ri*.

arachidonic acid /əˌrakɪˈdɒnɪk/ ▶ **noun** [mass noun] Biochemistry a polyunsaturated fatty acid present in animal fats. It is important in metabolism, especially in the synthesis of prostaglandins and leukotrienes, and is an essential constituent of the diet.
● Alternative name: **eicosa-5,8,11,14-enoic acid**; chem. formula: $C_{19}H_{31}COOH$.

– ORIGIN early 20th cent.: *arachidonic* formed irregularly from *arachidic* (a saturated fatty acid) + **-ONE** + **-IC**.

arachis oil /ˈarəkɪs/ ▶ noun another term for **PEANUT OIL**.
– ORIGIN mid 19th cent.: modern Latin *arachis*, from Greek *arak(h)os*, *-kis*, a leguminous plant.

Arachne /əˈrakni/ Greek Mythology a woman of Colophon in Lydia, a skilful weaver who challenged Athene to a contest. Athene destroyed Arachne's work and Arachne tried to hang herself, but Athene changed her into a spider.
– ORIGIN from Greek *arakhnē* 'spider'.

Arachnida /əˈraknɪdə/ Zoology a class of chelicerate arthropods that includes spiders, scorpions, mites, and ticks. They have become adapted for a terrestrial life and possess book lungs and tracheae, and many have silk or poison glands.
– DERIVATIVES **arachnid** noun & adjective.
– ORIGIN modern Latin (plural), from Greek *arakhnē* 'spider'.

arachnoid /əˈraknɔɪd/ ▶ adjective like a spider or arachnid.
▶ noun (also **arachnoid membrane**) Anatomy a fine, delicate membrane, the middle one of the three membranes or meninges that surround the brain and spinal cord, situated between the dura mater and the pia mater.
– ORIGIN mid 18th cent.: from modern Latin *arachnoides*, from Greek *arakhnoeidēs* 'like a cobweb', from *arakhnē* 'spider'.

arachnophobia /əˌraknəˈfəʊbɪə/ ▶ noun [mass noun] extreme or irrational fear of spiders.
– DERIVATIVES **arachnophobe** noun, **arachnophobic** adjective.
– ORIGIN 1920s: modern Latin, from Greek *arakhnē* 'spider' + **-PHOBIA**.

Arafat /ˈarəfat/, Yasser (b.1929), Palestinian statesman, chairman of the Palestine Liberation Organization from 1968 and Palestinian President since 1996. He became leader of the new Palestine National Authority in 1994, following the signing of a PLO–Israeli peace accord for which he shared the 1994 Nobel Peace Prize with Yitzhak Rabin and Shimon Peres.

Arafura Sea /ˌarəˈfʊərə/ a sea lying between northern Australia, the islands of east Indonesia, and New Guinea.

Aragon[1] /ˈarəg(ə)n/ an autonomous region of NE Spain, bounded on the north by the Pyrenees and on the east by Catalonia and Valencia; capital, Saragossa. Formerly an independent kingdom, it was united with Catalonia in 1137 and with Castile in 1479.

Aragon[2], Catherine of, see **CATHERINE OF ARAGON**.

aragonite /ˈarəg(ə)nʌɪt/ ▶ noun [mass noun] a mineral consisting of calcium carbonate and typically occurring as colourless prisms in deposits from hot springs.
– ORIGIN early 19th cent.: from the place name **ARAGON**[1] + **-ITE**[1].

arak /əˈrak/ ▶ noun variant spelling of **ARRACK**.

aralia /əˈreɪlɪə/ ▶ noun a plant of a very diverse group of trees and shrubs native to America and Asia. Several kinds are cultivated for their foliage and profusion of tiny flowers, and some are used in herbal medicine.
● Genus *Aralia*, family Araliaceae: several species, including the Japanese angelica tree (*A. elata*).
– ORIGIN modern Latin, of unknown origin.

Aral Sea /ˈarəl/ an inland sea in central Asia, on the border between Kazakhstan and Uzbekistan. Its area was reduced to two thirds of its original size between 1960 and 1990, after water was diverted for irrigation, with serious consequences for the environment of the area.

Aramaean /ˌarəˈmiːən/ (also **Aramean**) ▶ noun a member of an ancient Aramaic-speaking people inhabiting Aram (modern Syria) and most of Mesopotamia in the 11th–8th centuries BC.
▶ adjective of or relating to Aram or the Aramaeans.
– ORIGIN from Latin *Aramaeus* (from Greek *Aramaios*: see **ARAMAIC**) + **-AN**.

Aramaic /ˌarəˈmeɪɪk/ ▶ noun [mass noun] a branch of the Semitic family of languages, especially the language of Syria used as a lingua franca in the Near East from the 6th century BC. It replaced Hebrew locally as the language of the Jews, and

though displaced by Arabic in the 7th century AD, it still has about 200,000 speakers in scattered communities.
▶ adjective of or relating to this language.
– ORIGIN mid 19th cent.: from Greek *Aramaios* 'of Aram' (the biblical name of Syria) + **-IC**.

arame /ˈarəmi/ ▶ noun [mass noun] an edible Pacific seaweed with broad brown leaves which is used in Japanese cookery.
● *Ecklonia bicyclis*, class Phaeophyceae.

Aran /ˈar(ə)n/ ▶ adjective [attrib.] denoting a type of knitwear or garment with traditional patterns, typically involving raised cable stitch and large diamond designs.
– ORIGIN 1960s: from the **ARAN ISLANDS**.

Aranda /əˈrʌntə, aˈruːndə/ (also **Arunta** or **Arrernte**) ▶ noun (pl. same or **Arandas**) **1** a member of an Aboriginal people of central Australia.
2 [mass noun] the language of this people, now with fewer than 2,000 speakers.
▶ adjective of or relating to this people or their language.
– ORIGIN Aboriginal.

araneid /əˈreɪnɪd/ ▶ noun Zoology an invertebrate of an order that comprises the spiders.
● Order Araneae, in particular the family Araneidae.
– ORIGIN late 19th cent.: from modern Latin *Araneida* (former order name), from *aranea* 'spider'.

Aran Islands a group of three islands, Inishmore, Inishmaan, and Inisheer, off the west coast of the Republic of Ireland.

Aranyaka /ˌarəˈnjakə/ ▶ noun each of a set of Hindu sacred treatises based on the Brahmanas, composed in Sanskrit c.700 BC. Intended only for initiates, the Aranyakas contain mystical and philosophical material and explications of esoteric rites.

Arapaho /əˈrapəhəʊ/ ▶ noun (pl. same or **-os**) **1** a member of a North American Indian people living chiefly on the Great Plains, especially in Wyoming.
2 [mass noun] the Algonquian language of this people, now almost extinct.
▶ adjective of or relating to this people or their language.
– ORIGIN from Crow *alappahó*, literally 'many tattoo marks'.

arapaima /ˌarəˈpʌɪmə/ ▶ noun a very large edible freshwater fish native to tropical South America.
● *Arapaima gigas*, family Osteoglossidae.
– ORIGIN late 19th cent.: from Tupi.

Ararat, Mount /ˈarərat/ a pair of volcanic peaks in eastern Turkey, near the borders with Armenia and Iran. The higher peak, which rises to 5,165 m (16,946 ft), is the traditional site of the resting place of Noah's ark after the Flood (Gen. 8:4).

arational ▶ adjective not based on or governed by logical reasoning.

Araucanian /ˌarɔːˈkeɪnɪən/ ▶ noun **1** a member of a group of American Indian peoples of Chile and adjacent parts of Argentina, of which the only group which has a surviving cultural identity is the Mapuche.
2 [mass noun] the language of this people, constituting a distinct language family sometimes linked to Penutian.
▶ adjective relating to or denoting this people or their language. See also **MAPUCHE**.
– ORIGIN from Spanish *Araucania*, a region in Chile, + **-AN**.

araucaria /ˌarɔːˈkɛːrɪə/ ▶ noun an evergreen conifer of a genus that includes the monkey puzzle, having stiff sharp leaves.
● Genus *Araucaria*, family Araucariaceae.
– ORIGIN modern Latin, from Spanish *Arauco*, the name of a province of Araucania, Chile.

Arawak /ˈarəwak/ ▶ noun (pl. same or **Arawaks**) **1** a member of a group of native peoples of the Greater Antilles and northern and western South America. They were forced out of the Antilles by the more warlike Caribs shortly before Spanish expansion in the Caribbean.
2 [mass noun] any of the languages of these peoples.
▶ adjective of or relating to this people or their languages.

Arawakan /ˌarəˈwak(ə)n/ ▶ adjective denoting or belonging to a widely scattered family of South American Indian languages, most of which are now extinct or nearly so.
▶ noun [mass noun] this family of languages.

arb /ɑːb/ ▶ noun informal short for **ARBITRAGEUR**.

arbalest /ˈɑːbəlɛst/ (also **arblast**) ▶ noun historical a crossbow with a special mechanism for drawing back and releasing the string.
– ORIGIN Old English *arblast*, from Old French *arbaleste*, from late Latin *arcubalista*, from Latin *arcus* 'bow' + *ballista* (see **BALLISTA**).

arbiter /ˈɑːbɪtə/ ▶ noun a person who settles a dispute or has ultimate authority in a matter: *the military acted as arbiter of conflicts between political groups.*
■ a person whose views or actions have great influence over trends in social behaviour: *an arbiter of taste.*
– ORIGIN late Middle English: from Latin, 'judge, supreme ruler'.

arbiter elegantiarum /ˌɛlɪgantɪˈɑːrəm/ (also **arbiter elegantiae** /ˌɛlɪˈgantɪʌɪ/) ▶ noun a judge of artistic taste and etiquette.
– ORIGIN Latin, 'judge of elegance', used by Tacitus to describe **PETRONIUS**, arbiter of taste at Nero's court.

arbitrage /ˈɑːbɪtrɪdʒ, ˌɑːbɪˈtrɑːʒ/ ▶ noun [mass noun] the simultaneous buying and selling of securities, currency, or commodities in different markets or in derivative forms in order to take advantage of differing prices for the same asset.
▶ verb [no obj.] buy and sell assets in such a way.
– ORIGIN late Middle English (originally denoting the exercise of individual judgement): from French, from *arbitrer* 'give judgement', from Latin *arbitrari* (see **ARBITRATE**). The current sense dates from the late 19th cent.

arbitrageur /ˌɑːbɪtrɑːˈʒəː/ (also **arbitrager** /ˈɑːbɪtrɪdʒə/) ▶ noun a person who engages in arbitrage.
– ORIGIN late 19th cent.: from French, from *arbitrer* 'give judgement', from Latin *arbitrari* (see **ARBITRATE**).

arbitral /ˈɑːbɪtr(ə)l/ ▶ adjective of, relating to, or resulting from the use of an arbitrator to settle a dispute.
– ORIGIN late 15th cent.: from late Latin *arbitralis*, from *arbiter* 'judge, supreme ruler'.

arbitrament /ɑːˈbɪtrəm(ə)nt/ ▶ noun [mass noun] the settling of a dispute by an arbitrator.
■ [count noun] an authoritative decision made by an arbitrator.
– ORIGIN late Middle English: from Old French *arbitrement*, from medieval Latin *arbitramentum*, from *arbitrari* (see **ARBITRATE**).

arbitrary /ˈɑːbɪt(rə)ri/ ▶ adjective based on random choice or personal whim, rather than any reason or system: *his mealtimes were entirely arbitrary.*
■ (of power or a ruling body) unrestrained and autocratic in the use of authority: *a country under arbitrary government.* ■ Mathematics (of a constant or other quantity) of unspecified value.
– DERIVATIVES **arbitrarily** adverb, **arbitrariness** noun.
– ORIGIN late Middle English (in the sense 'dependent on one's will or pleasure, discretionary'): from Latin *arbitrarius*, from *arbiter* 'judge, supreme ruler', perhaps influenced by French *arbitraire*.

arbitrate /ˈɑːbɪtreɪt/ ▶ verb [no obj.] (of an independent person or body) reach an authoritative judgement or settlement: *the board has the power to arbitrate in disputes* | [with obj.] *the insurance ombudsman arbitrates insurance matters.*
– ORIGIN mid 16th cent.: from Latin *arbitrat-* 'judged', from *arbitrari*, from *arbiter* 'judge, supreme ruler'.

arbitration ▶ noun [mass noun] the use of an arbitrator to settle a dispute.
– PHRASES **go to arbitration** use an arbitrator to settle a dispute.

arbitrator ▶ noun an independent person or body officially appointed to settle a dispute.

arblast /ˈɑːblɑːst/ ▶ noun variant spelling of **ARBALEST**.

arbor[1] /ˈɑːbə/ ▶ noun an axle or spindle on which something revolves.
■ a device holding a tool in a lathe.
– ORIGIN mid 17th cent.: from French *arbre* 'tree, axis'. The spelling change was due to association with Latin *arbor* 'tree'.

arbor[2] ▶ noun US spelling of **ARBOUR**.

Arbor Day ▶ noun a day dedicated annually to public tree planting in the US, Australia, and other

countries. It is usually observed in late April or early May.
– ORIGIN from Latin *arbor* 'tree'.

arboreal /ɑːˈbɔːrɪəl/ ▶ **adjective** (chiefly of animals) living in trees: *arboreal rodents.*
■of or relating to trees.
– DERIVATIVES **arboreality** noun.
– ORIGIN mid 17th cent.: from Latin *arboreus*, from *arbor* 'tree', + **-AL**.

arborescent /ˌɑːbəˈrɛs(ə)nt/ ▶ **adjective** chiefly Botany tree-like in growth or appearance.
– DERIVATIVES **arborescence** noun.
– ORIGIN late 17th cent.: from Latin *arborescent-* 'growing into a tree', from *arborescere*, from *arbor* 'tree'.

arboretum /ˌɑːbəˈriːtəm/ ▶ **noun** (pl. **arboretums** or **arboreta** /-tə/) a botanical garden devoted to trees.
– ORIGIN early 19th cent.: from Latin, 'a place with trees', from *arbor* 'tree'.

arboriculture /ˈɑːb(ə)rɪˌkʌltʃə, ɑːˈbɔː-/ ▶ **noun** [mass noun] the cultivation of trees and shrubs.
– DERIVATIVES **arboricultural** adjective, **arboriculturist** noun.
– ORIGIN early 19th cent.: from Latin *arbor* 'tree' + **CULTURE**, on the pattern of words such as *agriculture*.

Arborio /ɑːˈbɔːrɪəʊ/ ▶ **noun** [mass noun] a variety of round-grained rice produced in Italy and used in making risotto.
– ORIGIN Italian.

arborization /ˌɑːb(ə)rʌɪˈzeɪʃ(ə)n/ (also **-isation**) ▶ **noun** Anatomy a fine branching structure at the end of a nerve fibre.

arbor vitae /ˌɑːbə ˈvʌɪtiː, ˈviːtʌɪ/ ▶ **noun** another term for **THUJA**.
– ORIGIN mid 16th cent.: from Latin, literally 'tree of life', probably with reference to its medicinal use.

arbour /ˈɑːbə/ (US **arbor**) ▶ **noun** a shady garden alcove with the sides and roof formed by trees or climbing plants trained over a wooden framework.
– DERIVATIVES **arboured** adjective.
– ORIGIN Middle English (also denoting a lawn or flower bed): from Old French *erbier*, from *erbe* 'grass, herb', from Latin *herba*. The phonetic change to *ar-* (common in words having *er-* before a consonant) was assisted by association with Latin *arbor* 'tree'.

arbovirus /ˈɑːbə(ʊ)ˌvʌɪrəs/ ▶ **noun** Medicine any of a group of viruses which are transmitted by mosquitoes, ticks, or other arthropods. They include the virus of yellow fever.
– ORIGIN 1950s: from *ar(thropod)-bo(rne)* + **VIRUS**.

Arbus /ˈɑːbəs/, Diane (1923–71), American photographer. She is best known for her disturbing images of people on the streets of US cities.

Arbuthnot /ɑːˈbʌθnət/, John (1667–1735), Scottish physician and writer. His satirical *History of John Bull* (1712) was the origin of John Bull as the personification of the typical Englishman.

arbutus /ɑːˈbjuːtəs, ˈɑːbjʊtəs/ ▶ **noun** an evergreen tree or shrub of a genus that includes the strawberry tree. See also **TRAILING ARBUTUS**.
● Genus *Arbutus*, family Ericaceae.
– ORIGIN from Latin.

ARC ▶ **abbreviation for** ■historical (in the UK) Agricultural Research Council. ■Medicine Aids-related complex.

arc /ɑːk/ ▶ **noun 1** a part of a curve, especially a part of the circumference of a circle.
■a shape resembling this or something with such a shape: *the huge arc of the sky.* ■a curving trajectory: *he swung his torch in a wide arc.* ■[as modifier] Mathematics indicating the inverse of a trigonometrical function. [ORIGIN: from the former method of defining trigonometrical functions by arcs.]
2 a luminous electrical discharge between two electrodes or other points.
▶**verb** (**arced** /ɑːkt/, **arcing** /ˈɑːkɪŋ/) [no obj.] **1** [with adverbial of direction] move with a curving trajectory: *the ball arced across the room.*
2 [usu. as noun **arcing**] form an electric arc: *check that switches operate properly with no sign of arcing.*
– PHRASES **minute of arc** see **MINUTE**[1] (sense 2). **second of arc** see **SECOND**[2] (sense 2).
– ORIGIN late Middle English (denoting the path of a celestial object, especially the sun, from horizon to horizon): via Old French from Latin *arcus* 'bow, curve'.

arcade ▶ **noun 1** a covered passage with arches along one or both sides.
■chiefly Brit. a covered walk with shops along one or both sides. ■Architecture a series of arches supporting a wall, or set along it.
2 short for **AMUSEMENT ARCADE**.
– DERIVATIVES **arcaded** adjective, **arcading** noun.
– ORIGIN late 17th cent.: from French, from Provençal *arcada* or Italian *arcata*, based on Latin *arcus* 'bow'.

Arcadia /ɑːˈkeɪdɪə/ a mountainous district in the Peloponnese of southern Greece. In poetic fantasy it represents a pastoral paradise and in Greek mythology it is the home of Pan.

Arcadian ▶ **noun** a native of Arcadia.
■poetic/literary an idealized country dweller.
▶**adjective** of or relating to Arcadia.
■poetic/literary of or relating to an ideal rustic paradise.
– ORIGIN late 16th cent.: from Latin *Arcadius*, from Greek *Arkadia* (see **ARCADIA**).

Arcady /ˈɑːkədi/ ▶ **noun** poetic/literary an ideal rustic paradise.
– ORIGIN late 16th cent.: from Greek *Arkadia* (see **ARCADIA**).

arcana /ɑːˈkeɪnə/ ▶ **plural noun** [treated as sing. or pl.] (sing. **arcanum**) secrets or mysteries: *all sorts of arcana about medicines and treatments.*
■either of the two groups of cards in a tarot pack: the twenty-two trumps (the **major arcana**) and the fifty-six suit cards (the **minor arcana**).
– ORIGIN mid 16th cent.: from Latin, neuter plural of *arcanus* (see **ARCANE**).

arcane /ɑːˈkeɪn/ ▶ **adjective** understood by few; mysterious or secret: *arcane procedures for electing people.*
– DERIVATIVES **arcanely** adverb.
– ORIGIN mid 16th cent.: from Latin *arcanus*, from *arcere* 'to shut up', from *arca* 'chest'.

arc cosine (abbrev.: **arcos**) ▶ **noun** a mathematical function that is the inverse of the cosine function.

Arc de Triomphe /ˌɑːk də ˈtriːɒmf, French ark də tʀijɔ̃f/ a ceremonial arch standing at the top of the Champs Élysées in Paris, commissioned by Napoleon to commemorate his victories in 1805–6. Inspired by the Arch of Constantine in Rome, it was completed in 1836.

arc eye ▶ **noun** [mass noun] Medicine a painful eye condition caused by damage to the cornea from ultraviolet radiation during arc welding.

arch[1] ▶ **noun** a curved symmetrical structure spanning an opening and typically supporting the weight of a bridge, roof, or wall above it.
■a structure of this type forming a passage or an ornamental monument: *a triumphal arch.* ■a shape resembling such a structure or a thing with such a shape: *the delicate arch of his eyebrows.* ■the inner side of the foot.
▶**verb 1** [no obj., with adverbial of place] have the curved shape of such a structure: *a beautiful bridge that arched over a canal.*
■form or cause to form the curved shape of such a structure: [no obj.] *her eyebrows arched in surprise* | [with obj.] *she arched her back.*
2 [with obj.] [usu. as adj. **arched**] provide (a bridge, building, or part of a building) with an arch: *high arched windows.*
■archaic or poetic/literary span (something) by or as if by an arch: *the vine arched his evening seat.*
– ORIGIN Middle English: from Old French *arche*, based on Latin *arcus* 'bow'.

arch[2] ▶ **adjective** deliberately or affectedly playful and teasing: *a somewhat arch tone of voice.*
– DERIVATIVES **archly** adverb, **archness** noun.
– ORIGIN mid 17th cent.: from **ARCH-**, by association with the sense 'rogue' in combinations such as *arch-scoundrel*.

arch- ▶ **combining form** chief; principal: *archbishop* | *archdiocese.*
■pre-eminent of its kind; out-and-out: *arch-enemy.*
– ORIGIN via Latin from Greek *arkhi-*, from *arkhos* 'chief'.

archaea /ɑːˈkiːə/ ▶ **plural noun** Biology micro-organisms which are similar to bacteria in size and simplicity of structure but radically different in molecular organization. They are now believed to constitute an ancient group which is intermediate between the bacteria and eukaryotes. Also called **ARCHAEBACTERIA**.
– DERIVATIVES **archaean** adjective & noun.
– ORIGIN modern Latin (plural), from Greek *arkhaios* 'primitive'.

Archaean /ɑːˈkiːən/ (US **Archean**) ▶ **adjective** Geology of, relating to, or denoting the aeon that constitutes the earlier (or middle) part of the Precambrian, in which there was no life on the earth. It precedes the Proterozoic aeon and (in some schemes) is preceded by the Priscoan aeon. Also called **AZOIC**.
■[as noun **the Archaean**] the Archaean aeon or the system of rocks deposited during it.

The Archaean extended from the origin of the earth (see **PRECAMBRIAN**) to about 2,500 million years ago. In schemes which include the Priscoan aeon, the Archaean began about 4,000 million years ago.

– ORIGIN late 19th cent.: from Greek *arkhaios* 'ancient' + **-AN**.

archaebacteria /ˌɑːkɪbakˈtɪərɪə/ ▶ **plural noun** (sing. **archaebacterium**) another term for **ARCHAEA**.
– DERIVATIVES **archaebacterial** adjective.

archaeo- /ˈɑːkɪəʊ/ ▶ **combining form** relating to archaeology or prehistoric times: *archaeoastronomy.*
– ORIGIN from Greek *arkhaios* 'ancient'.

archaeoastronomy ▶ **noun** [mass noun] the investigation of the astronomical knowledge of prehistoric cultures. Also called **ASTRO-ARCHAEOLOGY**.

archaeology (US also **archeology**) ▶ **noun** [mass noun] the study of human history and prehistory through the excavation of sites and the analysis of artefacts and other physical remains.
– DERIVATIVES **archaeologic** adjective, **archaeological** adjective, **archaeologically** adverb, **archaeologist** noun, **archaeologize** (also **-ise**) verb.
– ORIGIN early 17th cent. (in the sense 'ancient history'): from modern Latin *archaeologia*, from Greek *arkhaiologia* 'ancient history', from *arkhaios* 'ancient' (see **ARCHAEO-**). The current sense dates from the mid 19th cent.

archaeomagnetism ▶ **noun** [mass noun] magnetism possessed by components of clay and rocks which have in the past been heated above a certain temperature. The orientation and intensity of this remanent magnetism was fixed by the earth's magnetic field when the material cooled, and can be used to study the earth's magnetism and as a method of geological and archaeological dating.
– DERIVATIVES **archaeomagnetic** adjective.

archaeometry /ˌɑːkɪˈɒmɪtri/ ▶ **noun** [mass noun] the application of scientific techniques to the dating of archaeological remains.
– DERIVATIVES **archaeometric** adjective.

archaeopteryx /ˌɑːkɪˈɒptərɪks/ ▶ **noun** the oldest known fossil bird, of the late Jurassic period. It had feathers, wings, and hollow bones like a bird, but teeth, a bony tail, and legs like a small coelurosaur dinosaur.
● *Archaeopteryx lithographica*, subclass Archaeornithes.
– ORIGIN from **ARCHAEO-** 'ancient' + Greek *pterux* 'wing'.

archaic /ɑːˈkeɪɪk/ ▶ **adjective** very old or old-fashioned: *prisons are run on archaic methods.*
■(of a word or a style of language) no longer in everyday use but sometimes used to impart an old-fashioned flavour. ■of an early period of art or culture, especially the 7th–6th centuries BC in Greece: *the archaic temple at Corinth.*
– DERIVATIVES **archaically** adverb.
– ORIGIN mid 19th cent.: from French *archaïque*, from Greek *arkhaikos*, from *arkhaios*, from *arkhē* 'beginning'.

archaism /ˈɑːkeɪɪz(ə)m/ ▶ **noun** a thing that is very old or old-fashioned.
■an archaic word or style of language or art. ■[mass noun] the use or conscious imitation of very old or old-fashioned styles or features in language or art.
– DERIVATIVES **archaistic** adjective.
– ORIGIN mid 17th cent.: from modern Latin *archaismus*, from Greek *arkhaismos*, from *arkhaizein* 'imitate archaic styles', from *arkhaios* 'ancient', from *arkhē* 'beginning'.

archaizing (also **archaising**) ▶ **adjective** consciously imitating a word or a style of language or art that is very old or old-fashioned.

Archangel /ˈɑːkeɪndʒ(ə)l/ a port of NW Russia, on the White Sea; pop. 419,000 (1990). It is named after the monastery of the Archangel Michael situated there. Russian name **ARKHANGELSK**.

archangel /ˈɑːkeɪndʒ(ə)l, ɑːkˈeɪn-/ ▶ **noun 1** an angel of greater than ordinary rank.
■(in traditional Christian angelology) a being of the

a

eighth highest order of the ninefold celestial hierarchy.
2 (also **yellow archangel**) a yellow-flowered Eurasian dead-nettle found in woodland.
● *Lamiastrum galeobdolon* (or *Galeobdolon luteum*), family Labiatae.
− DERIVATIVES **archangelic** adjective.
− ORIGIN Middle English, from Anglo-Norman French *archangele*, via ecclesiastical Latin from ecclesiastical Greek *arkhangelos*, from *arkhi-* 'chief' + *angelos* 'messenger, angel'.

archbishop ▶ noun the chief bishop responsible for a large district.
− ORIGIN Old English, from **ARCH-** 'chief' + *biscop* (see **BISHOP**), replacing earlier *heah-biscop* 'high-bishop'.

archbishopric ▶ noun the office of an archbishop.
■ an archdiocese.
− ORIGIN Old English *arcebiscoprice* (see **ARCH-**, **BISHOPRIC**).

archboard ▶ noun a block of shaped wood at the aft end of the counter at the stern of a ship.

archdeacon ▶ noun a senior Christian cleric (in the early church a deacon, in the modern Anglican Church a priest) to whom a bishop delegates certain responsibilities.
− ORIGIN Old English *arce-, ercediacon*, from ecclesiastical Latin *archidiaconus*, from ecclesiastical Greek *arkhidiakonos*, from *arkhi-* 'chief' + *diakonos* (see **DEACON**).

archdeaconry ▶ noun (pl. **-ies**) the office of an archdeacon.
■ the district for which an archdeacon is responsible.

archdiocese ▶ noun the district for which an archbishop is responsible.
− DERIVATIVES **archdiocesan** adjective.

archduchess ▶ noun historical the wife or widow of an archduke.
■ a daughter of the Emperor of Austria.

archduke ▶ noun historical a son of the Emperor of Austria.
− DERIVATIVES **archducal** adjective, **archduchy** noun.
− ORIGIN early 16th cent.: from Old French *archeduc*, from Merovingian Latin *archiducus, archiduc-*, from *archi-* 'chief' + *dux, duc-* (see **DUKE**).

Archean ▶ adjective US spelling of **ARCHAEAN**.

archegonium /ˌɑːkɪˈɡəʊnɪəm/ ▶ noun (pl. **archegonia** /-ɪə/) Botany the female sex organ in mosses, liverworts, ferns, and most conifers.
− ORIGIN mid 19th cent.: modern Latin, from Greek *arkhegonos*, from *arkhe-* 'chief' + *gonos* 'race'.

arch-enemy ▶ noun a person who is extremely opposed or hostile to someone or something: *the twins were arch-enemies*.
■ (**the Arch-enemy**) the Devil.

archenteron /ɑːˈkɛntərɒn/ ▶ noun Embryology the rudimentary alimentary cavity of an embryo at the gastrula stage.
− ORIGIN late 19th cent.: from Greek *arkhē* 'beginning' + *enteron* 'intestine'.

archeology ▶ noun US spelling of **ARCHAEOLOGY**.

Archer, Jeffrey (Howard), Baron Archer of Weston-super-Mare (b.1940), British writer and Conservative politician. He resigned as an MP after being declared bankrupt, and embarked on a career as a best-selling novelist; he was deputy chairman of the Conservative Party 1985–6, but resigned after a libel case.

archer ▶ noun a person who shoots with a bow and arrows, especially at a target as a sport.
■ (**the Archer**) the zodiacal sign or constellation Sagittarius.
− ORIGIN Middle English: from Old French *archier*, based on Latin *arcus* 'bow'.

archerfish ▶ noun (pl. same or **-fishes**) a freshwater fish that knocks insect prey off overhanging vegetation by shooting water at it from its mouth. It is native to Asia, Australia, and the Philippines.
● Genus *Toxotes*, family Toxotidae: several species, in particular *T. jaculator*.

archery ▶ noun [mass noun] shooting with a bow and arrows, especially at a target as a sport.
− ORIGIN late Middle English: from Old French *archerie*, from *archier* (see **ARCHER**).

arches ▶ plural noun [treated as sing.] used in names of moths with curving arch-like patterns on the wings, such as **dark arches**.
● Several genera in the families Noctuidae and Notodontidae.

archetypal /ˌɑːkɪˈtʌɪp(ə)l/ ▶ adjective very typical of a certain kind of person or thing: *the archetypal country doctor*.
■ recurrent as a symbol or motif in literature, art, or mythology: *an archetypal journey representing the quest for identity*. ■ of or relating to or denoting an original which has been imitated: *the archetypal believer, Abraham*. ■ relating to Jungian archetypes.

archetype /ˈɑːkɪtʌɪp/ ▶ noun a very typical example of a certain person or thing: *the book is a perfect archetype of the genre*.
■ an original which has been imitated: *Marx gave us the archetype of the capitalist*. ■ a recurrent symbol or motif in literature, art, or mythology: *mythological archetypes of good and evil*. ■ Psychoanalysis (in Jungian theory) a primitive mental image inherited from the earliest human ancestors, and supposed to be present in the collective unconscious.
− DERIVATIVES **archetypical** adjective.
− ORIGIN mid 16th cent.: via Latin from Greek *arkhetupon* 'something moulded first as a model', from *arkhe-* 'primitive' + *tupos* 'a model'.

archidiaconal /ˌɑːkɪdʌɪˈak(ə)n(ə)l/ ▶ adjective of or relating to an archdeacon.
− ORIGIN late Middle English: from medieval Latin *archidiaconalis*, from *archi-* 'chief' + *diaconalis* (see **DIACONAL**).

archiepiscopal /ˌɑːkɪɪˈpɪskəp(ə)l/ ▶ adjective of or relating to an archbishop.
− DERIVATIVES **archiepiscopacy** noun (pl. **-ies**), **archiepiscopate** noun.
− ORIGIN early 17th cent.: via ecclesiastical Latin from Greek *arkhiepiskopos* 'archbishop' (from *arkhi-* 'chief' + *episkopos* 'bishop') + **-AL**.

archil /ˈɑːtʃɪl/ ▶ noun archaic spelling of **ORCHIL**.

Archilochus /ɑːˈkɪləkəs/ (8th or 7th century BC), Greek poet. Acclaimed in his day as equal in stature to Homer and Pindar, he wrote satirical verse and fables and is credited with the invention of iambic metre.

archimandrite /ˌɑːkɪˈmandrʌɪt/ ▶ noun the superior of a large monastery or group of monasteries in the Orthodox Church.
■ an honorary title given to a monastic priest.
− ORIGIN mid 17th cent.: via ecclesiastical Latin, from ecclesiastical Greek *arkhimandritēs*, from *arkhi-* 'chief' + *mandra* 'monastery'.

Archimedean screw /ˌɑːkɪˈmiːdɪən/ ▶ noun a device invented by Archimedes for raising water by means of a helix rotating within a tube.

Archimedes /ˌɑːkɪˈmiːdiːz/ (*c.*287–212 BC), Greek mathematician and inventor, of Syracuse. He is famous for his discovery of Archimedes' principle (legend has it that he made this discovery while taking a bath, and ran through the streets shouting 'Eureka!'); among his mathematical discoveries are the ratio of the radius of a circle to its circumference, and formulas for the surface area and volume of a sphere and of a cylinder.
− DERIVATIVES **Archimedean** adjective.

Archimedes' principle Physics a law stating that a body totally or partially immersed in a fluid is subject to an upward force equal in magnitude to the weight of fluid it displaces.

archipelago /ˌɑːkɪˈpɛləɡəʊ/ ▶ noun (pl. **-os** or **-oes**) a group of islands.
■ a sea or stretch of water having many islands.
− ORIGIN early 16th cent.: from Italian *arcipelago*, from Greek *arkhi-* 'chief' + *pelagos* 'sea'. The word was originally used as a proper name (*the Archipelago* 'the Aegean Sea'): the general sense arose because the Aegean Sea is remarkable for its large numbers of islands.

Archipenko /ˌɑːkɪˈpjɛŋkəʊ/, Alexander (Porfirevich) (1887–1964), Russian-born American sculptor. He adapted cubist techniques to sculpture.

Archipiélago de Colón /arkiˈpjelavo ðe koˈlon/ official Spanish name for **GALAPAGOS ISLANDS**.

architect ▶ noun a person who designs buildings and in many cases also supervises their construction.
■ a person who is responsible for inventing or realizing a particular idea or project: *the architects of the reform programme*.
▶ verb [with obj.] (usu. **be architected**) Computing design and make (a program or system).
− ORIGIN mid 16th cent.: from French *architecte*, from Italian *architetto*, via Latin from Greek *arkhitektōn*, from *arkhi-* 'chief' + *tektōn* 'builder'.

architectonic /ˌɑːkɪtɛkˈtɒnɪk/ ▶ adjective of or relating to architecture or architects.
■ (of an artistic composition or physical appearance) having a clearly defined structure, especially one that is artistically pleasing: *the painting's architectonic harmony*.
▶ noun (**architectonics**) [usu. treated as sing.] the scientific study of architecture.
■ musical, literary, or artistic structure.
− DERIVATIVES **architectonically** adverb.
− ORIGIN mid 17th cent.: via Latin from Greek *arkhitektonikos*, from *arkhitektōn* (see **ARCHITECT**).

architecture ▶ noun [mass noun] **1** the art or practice of designing and constructing buildings.
■ the style in which a building is designed or constructed, especially with regard to a specific period, place, or culture: *Georgian architecture*.
2 the complex or carefully designed structure of something: *the chemical architecture of the human brain*.
■ [count noun] the conceptual structure and logical organization of a computer or computer-based system.
− DERIVATIVES **architectural** adjective, **architecturally** adverb.
− ORIGIN mid 16th cent.: from Latin *architectura*, from *architectus* (see **ARCHITECT**).

architrave /ˈɑːkɪtreɪv/ ▶ noun **1** (in classical architecture) a main beam resting across the tops of columns.
2 the moulded frame around a doorway or window.
■ a moulding round the exterior of an arch.
− ORIGIN mid 16th cent.: from French, from Italian, from *archi-* 'chief' + *-trave* from Latin *trabs, trab-* 'a beam'.

archive /ˈɑːkʌɪv/ ▶ noun (usu. **archives**) a collection of historical documents or records providing information about a place, institution, or group of people: *source materials in local archives* | [as modifier] *a section of archive film*.
■ the place where such documents or records are kept: *they were allowed to study in the archives*.
▶ verb [with obj.] place or store (something) in such a collection or place.
■ Computing transfer (data) to a less frequently used storage medium such as magnetic tape, typically external to the computer system and having a greater storage capacity.
− DERIVATIVES **archival** adjective.
− ORIGIN early 17th cent. (in the sense 'place where records are kept'): from French *archives* (plural), from Latin *archiva, archia*, from Greek *arkheia* 'public records', from *arkhē* 'government'. The verb dates from the late 19th cent.

archivist /ˈɑːkɪvɪst/ ▶ noun a person who maintains and is in charge of archives.

archivolt /ˈɑːkɪvəʊlt/ ▶ noun a band of mouldings round the lower curve of an arch.
■ the lower curve itself from impost to impost of the columns.
− ORIGIN mid 17th cent.: from French *archivolte* or Italian *archivolto*, based on Latin *arcus* 'bow, arch' + *volvere* 'to roll'.

archlute ▶ noun a bass lute with an extended neck which supports unstopped bass strings.
− ORIGIN mid 17th cent.: from French *archiluth*, from *archi-* 'chief' + *luth* 'lute'.

archon /ˈɑːkən/ ▶ noun each of the nine chief magistrates in ancient Athens.
− DERIVATIVES **archonship** noun.
− ORIGIN late 16th cent.: from Greek *arkhōn* 'ruler', noun use of the present participle of *arkhein* 'to rule'.

archosaur /ˈɑːkəsɔː/ ▶ noun Zoology & Palaeontology a reptile of a large group that includes the dinosaurs and pterosaurs, represented today only by the crocodilians.
● Subdivision Archosauria, subclass Diapsida.
− ORIGIN 1930s: from modern Latin *Archosauria*, from Greek *arkhos* 'chief' or *arkhōn* 'ruler' + **-SAUR**.

archpriest ▶ noun a chief priest.
■ a person whose opinions are widely regarded as authoritative in a particular field.

archway ▶ noun a curved structure forming a passage or entrance.

arc lamp (also **arc light**) ▶ noun a light source using an electric arc.

arc minute ▶ noun see **MINUTE**¹ (sense 2).

arco /ˈɑːkəʊ/ ▶ adverb & adjective Music (especially as a direction) played on a violin or other stringed instrument using the bow. Often contrasted with **PIZZICATO**.

arcology /ɑːˈkɒlədʒi/ ▶ noun (pl. **-ies**) an ideal integrated city contained within a massive vertical structure, allowing maximum conservation of the surrounding environment.
– ORIGIN 1969: blend of **ARCHITECTURE** and **ECOLOGY**.

arcos ▶ abbreviation for arc cosine.

arc second (also **second of arc**) ▶ noun see **SECOND**[2].

arc sine (abbrev.: **arcsin**) ▶ noun a mathematical function that is the inverse of the sine function.

arc tangent (abbrev.: **arctan**) ▶ noun a mathematical function that is the inverse of the tangent function.

Arctic ▶ adjective **1** of or relating to the regions around the North Pole: *an Arctic explorer.*
■ (of animals or plants) living or growing in such regions. ■ designed for use in such regions: *Arctic clothing.*
2 (**arctic**) informal (of weather conditions) very cold.
▶ noun **1** (**the Arctic**) the regions around the North Pole.
2 N. Amer. a thick waterproof overshoe extending to the ankle or above.
3 (**arctic**) a drab-coloured hairy butterfly of the arctic and subarctic regions of the New World.
● Genus *Oenis*, subfamily Satyrinae, family Nymphalidae.
– ORIGIN late Middle English: via Old French from Latin *arcticus, articus*, from Greek *arktikos*, from *arktos* 'bear, Ursa Major, pole star'.

Arctic charr ▶ noun see **CHARR**.

Arctic Circle the parallel of latitude 66° 33′ north of the equator. It marks the northernmost point at which the sun is visible on the northern winter solstice and the southernmost point at which the midnight sun can be seen on the northern summer solstice.

Arctic fox ▶ noun a small fox with a thick coat that turns white in winter, found on the tundra of North America and Eurasia.
● *Alopex lagopus*, family Canidae.

Arctic hare ▶ noun a hare whose coat turns white in winter, found in the arctic areas of North America.
● *Lepus arcticus*, family Leporidae; sometimes treated as the same species as the mountain hare of Eurasia.
■ another term for **MOUNTAIN HARE**.

Arctic Ocean the sea that surrounds the North Pole, lying within the Arctic Circle. Much of the sea is covered with pack ice throughout the year.

Arctic tern ▶ noun a red-billed tern which breeds in the Arctic and adjacent areas, migrating to antarctic regions to overwinter.
● *Sterna paradisaea*, family Sternidae.

Arctogaea /ˌɑːktəˈdʒiːə/ (US **Arctogea**) Zoology a major zoogeographical area comprising the Palaearctic, Nearctic, Ethiopian, and Oriental regions.
– DERIVATIVES **Arctogaean** adjective.
– ORIGIN modern Latin, from Greek *arktos* 'northern' + *gaia* 'earth'.

Arcturus /ɑːkˈtjʊərəs/ Astronomy the fourth brightest star in the sky, and the brightest in the constellation Boötes. It is an orange giant.
– ORIGIN from Greek *arktos* 'bear' + *ouros* 'guardian' (because of its position in line with the tail of Ursa Major).

arcuate /ˈɑːkjʊət/ ▶ adjective technical shaped like a bow; curved: *the arcuate sweep of the chain of islands.*
– ORIGIN late Middle English: from Latin *arcuatus*, past participle of *arcuare* 'to curve', from *arcus* 'bow, curve'.

arcus senilis /ˌɑːkəs sɪˈnʌɪlɪs/ ▶ noun Medicine a narrow opaque band encircling the cornea, common in old age.
– ORIGIN Latin, literally 'senile bow'.

arc welding ▶ noun [mass noun] a technique in which metals are welded using the heat generated by an electric arc.

-ard ▶ suffix forming nouns such as *bollard, wizard*.
■ forming nouns having a depreciatory sense: *drunkard | dullard.*
– ORIGIN from Old French, from German *-hard* 'hard, hardy'.

Arden /ˈɑːd(ə)n/, Elizabeth (c.1880–1966), Canadian-born American businesswoman; born *Florence Nightingale Graham*. She built up an international chain of beauty salons and an extensive range of cosmetics.

Ardennes /ɑːˈdɛn/ a forested upland region extending over parts of SE Belgium, NE France, and Luxembourg. It was the scene of fierce fighting in both world wars.

ardent /ˈɑːd(ə)nt/ ▶ adjective very enthusiastic or passionate: *an ardent supporter of the conservative cause.*
■ archaic or poetic/literary burning; glowing: *the ardent flames.*
– DERIVATIVES **ardency** noun, **ardently** adverb.
– ORIGIN Middle English: from Old French *ardant* from Latin *ardens, ardent-*, from *ardere* 'to burn'.

Ardnamurchan /ˌɑːdnəˈmɔːk(ə)n/ a peninsula on the coast of Highland region in western Scotland.

ardour /ˈɑːdə/ (US **ardor**) ▶ noun [mass noun] great enthusiasm or passion: *the rebuff did little to dampen his ardour.*
– ORIGIN late Middle English: via Old French from Latin *ardor*, from *ardere* 'to burn'.

arduous /ˈɑːdjʊəs/ ▶ adjective involving or requiring strenuous effort; difficult and tiring: *an arduous journey.*
– DERIVATIVES **arduously** adverb, **arduousness** noun.
– ORIGIN early 16th cent.: from Latin *arduus* 'steep, difficult' + **-OUS**.

are[1] second person singular present and first, second, third person plural present of **BE**.

are[2] /ɑː/ ▶ noun historical a metric unit of measurement, equal to 100 square metres.
– ORIGIN late 18th cent.: from French, from Latin *area* (see **AREA**).

area ▶ noun **1** a region or part of a town, a country, or the world: *rural areas of Britain | people living in the area are at risk.*
■ [with modifier] a space allocated for a specific use: *the dining area.* ■ a part of an object or surface: *areas of the body.* ■ a subject or range of activity or interest: *the key areas of science.* ■ (**the area**) Soccer short for **PENALTY AREA**. ■ [usu. as modifier] a sunken enclosure giving access to the basement of a building: *the area steps.*
2 the extent or measurement of a surface or piece of land: *the area of a triangle | [mass noun] the room is twelve square feet in area.*
– DERIVATIVES **areal** adjective.
– ORIGIN mid 16th cent. (in the sense 'space allocated for a specific purpose'): from Latin, literally 'vacant piece of level ground'.

area code ▶ noun North American term for **DIALLING CODE**.

areaway ▶ noun N. Amer. a sunken enclosure giving access to the basement of a building.
■ a passageway between buildings.

areca /ˈarɪkə, əˈriːkə/ (also **areca palm**) ▶ noun a tropical Asian palm.
● Genus *Areca*, family Palmae: several species, in particular *A. catechu.*
– ORIGIN via Portuguese from Malayalam *áḍekka.*

areca nut ▶ noun the astringent seed of an areca palm (*Areca catechu*), which is often chewed with betel leaves. Also called **BETEL NUT**.

areg plural form of **ERG**[2].

arena ▶ noun a level area surrounded by seating, in which sports, entertainments, and other public events are held.
■ a place or scene of activity, debate, or conflict: *he has re-entered the political arena.*
– ORIGIN early 17th cent.: from Latin *harena, arena* 'sand, sand-strewn place of combat'.

arenaceous /ˌarɪˈneɪʃəs/ ▶ adjective Geology consisting of sand or sand-like particles.
■ Biology (of animals or plants) living or growing in sand.
– ORIGIN mid 17th cent.: from Latin *arenaceus*, from *arena, harena* 'sand'.

arenavirus /əˈriːnəˌvʌɪrəs/ ▶ noun Medicine any of a group of RNA viruses (including that causing Lassa fever) which appear under an electron microscope to contain sand-like granules.
– ORIGIN 1970s: from Latin *arenosus* 'sandy' (from *arena* 'sand') + **VIRUS**.

Arendt /ˈɑːrənt/, Hannah (1906–75), German-born American philosopher and political theorist. A pupil of Heidegger, she established her reputation as a political thinker with one of the first works to

propose that Nazism and Stalinism had common roots. Notable works: *The Origins of Totalitarianism* (1951), *Eichmann in Jerusalem* (1963).

aren't ▶ contraction of ■ are not: *they aren't here.* ■ am not (only used in questions): *I'm right, aren't I? | why aren't I being given a pay rise?*

> **USAGE** The contraction **aren't** is used to mean 'am not' in questions, as in *I'm right, aren't I?* This is now standard, although it was first used as a hypercorrect form, following stigmatization of the earlier form **ain't**, a contraction of **amn't**. Outside questions, **aren't** used to mean 'am not' is incorrect (e.g. *I aren't going* is clearly wrong). The more logical form **amn't** is now non-standard and restricted to Scottish, Irish, and dialect use.

areola /əˈriːələ/ ▶ noun (pl. **areolae** /-liː/) Anatomy a small circular area, in particular the ring of pigmented skin surrounding a nipple.
■ Biology any of the small spaces between lines or cracks on a leaf or an insect's wing. ■ Medicine a reddened patch around a spot or papule.
– DERIVATIVES **areolar** adjective, **areolate** adjective.
– ORIGIN mid 17th cent. (in the sense 'small space or interstice'): from Latin, literally 'small open space', diminutive of *area* (see **AREA**).

areole /ˈɛːrɪəʊl/ ▶ noun Biology an areola, especially a small area bearing spines or hairs on a cactus.
– ORIGIN mid 19th cent.: from French *aréole*, from Latin (see **AREOLA**).

Areopagus /ˌarɪˈɒpəgəs/ (in ancient Athens) a hill on which was sited the highest governmental council and later a judicial court.
– ORIGIN from Greek *Areios pagos* 'hill of Ares'; the name for the site came to denote the court itself.

Arequipa /ˌarɛˈkiːpə/ a city in the Andes of southern Peru; pop. 619,150 (1993).

Ares /ˈɛːriːz/ Greek Mythology the Greek war god, son of Zeus and Hera. Roman equivalent **MARS**.

arête /əˈrɛt, əˈreɪt/ ▶ noun a sharp mountain ridge.
– ORIGIN early 19th cent.: from French, from Latin *arista* 'ear of corn, fishbone, spine'.

arf (usu. **arf arf**) ▶ exclamation used to imitate or represent laughter or a dog's bark.

'arf ▶ noun, predeterminer, pronoun, adjective, & adverb non-standard spelling of **HALF**, used to represent southern English (especially Cockney) speech.

argali /ˈɑːɡ(ə)li/ ▶ noun (pl. same) the largest wild sheep, which has massive horns and is found in mountainous areas of Asia.
● *Ovis ammon*, family Bovidae.
– ORIGIN late 18th cent.: from Mongolian.

Argand diagram /ˈɑːɡand/ ▶ noun Mathematics a diagram on which complex numbers are represented geometrically using Cartesian axes, the horizontal coordinate representing the real part of the number and the vertical coordinate the complex part.
– ORIGIN early 20th cent.: named after J. R. Argand (1768–1822), French mathematician.

Argand lamp ▶ noun historical an oil or gas lamp fitted with a cylindrical burner which allowed air to pass both inner and outer surfaces of the flame.
– ORIGIN late 18th cent.: named after Aimé *Argand* (1755–1803), French physicist.

argent /ˈɑːdʒ(ə)nt/ ▶ adjective poetic/literary & Heraldry silver; silvery white: *the argent moon.*
▶ noun [mass noun] Heraldry silver as a heraldic tincture.
– ORIGIN late Middle English (denoting silver coins): via Old French from Latin *argentum* 'silver'.

argentiferous /ˌɑːdʒ(ə)nˈtɪf(ə)rəs/ ▶ adjective (of rocks or minerals) containing silver.
– ORIGIN late 18th cent.: from Latin *argentum* 'silver' + **-FEROUS**.

Argentina /ˌɑːdʒ(ə)nˈtiːnə/ a republic occupying much of the southern part of South America; pop. 32,646,000 (1991); official language, Spanish; capital, Buenos Aires. Also called **THE ARGENTINE** /ˈɑːdʒənˌtʌɪn, -ˌtiːn/.

> Colonized by the Spanish in the 16th century, Argentina declared its independence in 1816. It emerged as a democratic republic in the mid 19th century, but has periodically fallen under military rule. In 1982 the Argentinian claim to the Falkland Islands led to an unsuccessful war with Britain.

– DERIVATIVES **Argentine** adjective & noun, **Argentinian** adjective & noun.

argentine /ˈɑːdʒ(ə)ntʌɪn/ ▶ adjective archaic of or resembling silver.

▶**noun** a small marine fish with a silvery sheen.
• Family Argentinidae: two genera and several species, in particular *Argentina silus* of the North Atlantic.
– ORIGIN late Middle English: from Old French *argentin, argentine*, from *argent* 'silver', from Latin *argentum*.

Argentine ant ▶**noun** a small South American ant that has become established in parts of Europe.
• *Iridomyrmex humilis*, family Formicidae.

argh ▶**exclamation** variant spelling of **AARGH**.

argillaceous /ˌɑːdʒɪˈleɪʃəs/ ▶**adjective** Geology (of rocks or sediment) consisting of or containing clay.
– ORIGIN late 17th cent.: from Latin *argillaceus* (from *argilla* 'clay') + **-OUS**.

argillite /ˈɑːdʒɪlʌɪt/ ▶**noun** [mass noun] Geology a sedimentary rock that does not split easily, formed from consolidated clay.
– ORIGIN late 18th cent.: from Latin *argilla* 'clay' + **-ITE**[1].

arginine /ˈɑːdʒɪniːn/ ▶**noun** [mass noun] Biochemistry a basic amino acid which is a constituent of most proteins. It is an essential nutrient in the diet of vertebrates.
• Chem. formula: $HN{=}C(NH_2)NH(CH_2)_3CH(NH_2)COOH$.
– ORIGIN late 19th cent.: from German *Arginin*, perhaps from Greek *arginoeis* 'bright-shining, white'.

Argive /ˈɑːgʌɪv, -dʒʌɪv/ ▶**adjective** of or relating to the ancient city of Argos.
■(especially in Homer) Greek.
▶**noun** a citizen of Argos.
■(especially in Homer) a Greek person.
– ORIGIN from Latin *Argivus*, from Greek *Argeios* 'relating to Argos'.

argle-bargle ▶**noun** [mass noun] **1** copious but meaningless talk or writing; waffle: *bureaucratic argle-bargle*.
2 another term for **ARGY-BARGY**.
– ORIGIN early 19th cent.: reduplication of dialect *argle*, a late 16th-cent. alteration of **ARGUE**.

Argo /ˈɑːgəʊ/ (in full **Argo Navis**) Astronomy, historical a large southern constellation (the ship *Argo*), which is now divided into the constellations Carina, Puppis, and Vela.
– ORIGIN Latin.

argol /ˈɑːg(ə)l/ ▶**noun** [mass noun] tartar obtained from wine fermentation.
– ORIGIN Middle English: from Anglo-Norman French *argoile*, of unknown origin.

argon /ˈɑːgɒn/ ▶**noun** [mass noun] the chemical element of atomic number 18, an inert gaseous element of the noble gas group. Argon is the commonest noble gas, making up nearly one per cent of the earth's atmosphere. (Symbol: **Ar**)
– ORIGIN late 19th cent.: from Greek, neuter of *argos* 'idle', from *a-* 'without' + *ergon* 'work'.

argonaut /ˈɑːg(ə)nɔːt/ ▶**noun** a small floating octopus, the female of which has webbed sail-like arms and secretes a thin coiled papery shell in which the eggs are laid. Also called **PAPER NAUTILUS**.
• Genus *Argonauta*, order Octopoda.

Argonauts /ˈɑːgənɔːts/ Greek Mythology a group of heroes who accompanied Jason on board the ship *Argo* in the quest for the Golden Fleece.
– ORIGIN *argonaut* from Greek *argonautēs* 'sailor in the ship *Argo*'.

Argos /ˈɑːgɒs/ a city in the NE Peloponnese of Greece; pop. 20,702 (1981). One of the oldest cities of ancient Greece, it dominated the Peloponnese and the western Aegean in the 7th century BC.

argosy /ˈɑːgəsi/ ▶**noun** (pl. **-ies**) poetic/literary a large merchant ship, originally one from Ragusa (now Dubrovnik) or Venice.
– ORIGIN late 16th cent.: apparently from Italian *Ragusea (nave)* '(vessel) of *Ragusa*'.

argot /ˈɑːgəʊ/ ▶**noun** [mass noun] the jargon or slang of a particular group or class: *teenage argot*.
– ORIGIN mid 19th cent. (originally denoting the jargon or slang of criminals): from French, of unknown origin.

arguable ▶**adjective** able to be argued or asserted: [with clause] *it was arguable that the bank had no authority to honour the cheques* | *an arguable case for judicial review*.
■open to disagreement; not obviously correct: *a highly arguable assumption*.

arguably ▶**adverb** [sentence adverb] it may be argued (used to qualify the statement of an opinion or belief): *she is arguably the greatest woman tennis player of all time*.

argue ▶**verb** (**argues, argued, arguing**) **1** [reporting verb] give reasons or cite evidence in support of an idea, action, or theory, typically with the aim of persuading others to share one's view: [with clause] *sociologists* ***argue that*** *inequalities in industrial societies are being reduced* | [with direct speech] *'It stands to reason,' she argued*.
■[with obj.] (**argue someone into/out of**) persuade someone to do or not to do (something) by giving reasons: *I tried to argue him out of it*.
2 [no obj.] exchange or express diverging or opposite views, typically in a heated or angry way: *don't* ***argue with*** *me* | figurative *I wasn't going to* ***argue with*** *a gun* | [with obj.] *she was too tired to* ***argue the point***.
– PHRASES **argue the toss** informal, chiefly Brit. dispute a decision or choice already made.
– DERIVATIVES **arguer** noun.
– ORIGIN Middle English: from Old French *arguer*, from Latin *argutari* 'prattle', frequentative of *arguere* 'make clear, prove, accuse'.

argufy /ˈɑːgjʊfʌɪ/ ▶**verb** (**-ies, -ied**) [no obj.] humorous or dialect argue or quarrel, typically about something trivial: *It won't do to argufy, I tell you*.
– ORIGIN late 17th cent.: fanciful formation from **ARGUE**; compare with *speechify*.

argument ▶**noun** **1** an exchange of diverging or opposite views, typically a heated or angry one: *I've had an* ***argument with*** *my father* | *heated arguments over public spending* | [mass noun] *there was some argument about the decision*.
2 a reason or set of reasons given with the aim of persuading others that an action or idea is right or wrong: *there is a strong argument for submitting a formal appeal* | [with clause] *he rejected the* ***argument that*** *keeping the facility would be costly*.
3 Mathematics & Logic an independent variable associated with a function or proposition and determining its value. For example, in the expression $y = F(x_1, x_2)$, the arguments of the function F are x_1 and x_2, and the value is y.
■another term for **AMPLITUDE** (in sense 4). ■ Linguistics any of the noun phrases in a clause that are related directly to the verb, typically the subject, direct object, and indirect object.
4 archaic a summary of the subject matter of a book.
– PHRASES **for the sake of argument** as a basis for discussion or reasoning.
– ORIGIN Middle English (in the sense 'process of reasoning'): via Old French from Latin *argumentum*, from *arguere* 'make clear, prove, accuse'.

argumentation ▶**noun** [mass noun] the action or process of reasoning systematically in support of an idea, action, or theory: *lines of argumentation used to support his thesis*.
– ORIGIN late Middle English: via Old French from Latin *argumentatio(n-)*, from *argumentat-* 'conducted as an argument', from *argumentari*.

argumentative ▶**adjective** **1** given to expressing divergent or opposite views: *an argumentative child*.
2 using or characterized by systematic reasoning: *the highest standards of argumentative rigour*.
– DERIVATIVES **argumentatively** adverb, **argumentativeness** noun.
– ORIGIN late Middle English: from Old French *argumentatif, -ive* or late Latin *argumentativus*, from *argumentari* 'conduct an argument'.

argument from design ▶**noun** Christian Theology the argument that God's existence is demonstrable from the evidence of design in the universe.

argus /ˈɑːgəs/ ▶**noun** **1** (also **argus pheasant**) a large long-tailed pheasant with generally brown plumage, found in SE Asia and Indonesia.
• Two species in the family Phasianidae: the male **great argus** (*Argusianus argus*) has lengthened secondary wing feathers bearing eyespots, spread during display; the **crested argus** (*Rheinartia ocellata*) has the longest tail feathers of any bird.
2 a small brown or bluish Eurasian butterfly which typically has eye-like markings near the wing margins.
• *Aricia* and other genera, family Lycaenidae.
3 (also **argus fish**) a silvery deep-bodied fish with round spots, widely distributed throughout the tropical Indo-Pacific region in both fresh and salt water.
• *Scatophagus argus*, family Scatophagidae.
– ORIGIN late Middle English: from Latin, from Greek *Argos*, the name of a mythical watchman with a hundred eyes.

Argus-eyed ▶**adjective** poetic/literary vigilant.

argute /ɑːˈgjuːt/ ▶**adjective** rare shrewd.
– ORIGIN late 16th cent.: from Latin *argutus* 'made clear, proved, accused', from *arguere*.

argy-bargy /ˌɑːdʒɪˈbɑːdʒi, ˌɑːgɪˈbɑːgi/ ▶**noun** (pl. **-ies**) [mass noun] informal, chiefly Brit. noisy quarrelling or wrangling: *a bit of argy-bargy between actor and director* | [count noun] *an argy-bargy over the price*.
– ORIGIN late 19th cent. (originally Scots): rhyming jingle based on **ARGUE**.

argyle /ɑːˈgʌɪl/ ▶**noun** [usu. as modifier] a pattern composed of diamonds of various colours on a plain background, used in knitted garments such as sweaters and socks.
– ORIGIN 1940s: from *Argyll*, a family name and a former county of Scotland. The pattern is based on the tartan of the *Argyll* branch of the Campbell clan.

Argyll and Bute /ɑːˈgʌɪl, bjuːt/ an administrative region in the west of Scotland, created in 1996; administrative centre, Lochgilphead.

Argyllshire a former county on the west coast of Scotland. It was divided between Strathclyde and Highland regions in 1975 and in 1996 became part of Argyll and Bute.

argyrophilic /ˌɑːdʒɪrə(ʊ)ˈfɪlɪk/ ▶**adjective** Biology (of cells or their contents) readily stained black by silver salts.
– DERIVATIVES **argyrophil** adjective, **argyrophilia** noun.
– ORIGIN 1930s: from Greek *arguro-* (from *arguros* 'silver') + *-philic* (see **-PHILIA**).

arhat /ˈɑːhat/ ▶**noun** (in Buddhism and Jainism) a saint of one of the highest ranks.
– ORIGIN from Sanskrit, literally 'meritorious'.

Århus variant spelling of **AARHUS**.

arhythmic ▶**adjective** variant spelling of **ARRHYTHMIC**.

aria /ˈɑːrɪə/ ▶**noun** Music a long accompanied song for a solo voice, typically one in an opera or oratorio.
– ORIGIN early 18th cent.: from Italian, from Latin *aer* 'air'.

Ariadne /ˌarɪˈadni/ Greek Mythology the daughter of King Minos of Crete and Pasiphaë. She helped Theseus to escape from the Minotaur's labyrinth by giving him a ball of thread, which he unravelled as he went in and used to trace his way out again after killing the Minotaur.

Arian /ˈɛːrɪən/ ▶**noun** **1** an adherent of the doctrine of Arianism.
2 (also **Arien**) a person born under the sign of Aries.
▶**adjective** **1** of or concerning Arianism.
2 (also **Arien**) of or relating to a person born under the sign of Aries.

-arian ▶**suffix** (forming adjectives and corresponding nouns) having a concern or belief in a specified thing: *humanitarian* | *vegetarian*.
– ORIGIN from the Latin suffix *-arius*.

Arianism ▶**noun** [mass noun] Christian Theology the main heresy denying the divinity of Christ, originating with the Alexandrian priest Arius (*c.*250–*c.*336). Arianism maintained that the son of God was created by the Father and was therefore neither coeternal nor consubstantial with the Father.

arid /ˈarɪd/ ▶**adjective** (of land or a climate) having little or no rain; too dry or barren to support vegetation: *hot and arid conditions*.
■figurative lacking in interest, excitement, or meaning: *his arid years in suburbia*.
– DERIVATIVES **aridity** noun, **aridly** adverb, **aridness** noun.
– ORIGIN mid 17th cent.: from French *aride* or Latin *aridus*, from *arere* 'be dry or parched'.

aridisol /əˈrɪdɪsɒl/ ▶**noun** Soil Science a soil of an order comprising typically saline or alkaline soils with very little organic matter, characteristic of arid regions.

Ariel /ˈɛːrɪəl/ **1** Astronomy a satellite of Uranus discovered in 1851, the twelfth closest to the planet and the fourth largest (diameter 1,160 km).
2 a series of six American and British satellites devoted to studies of the ionosphere and X-ray astronomy (1962–79).
– ORIGIN the name of a fairy in Shakespeare's *The Tempest*.

ariel /ˈɛːrɪəl/ ▶ **noun** a gazelle found in the Middle East and North Africa.
• Genus *Gazella*, family Bovidae: possibly the mountain gazelle (*G. gazella*) or the dorcas gazelle (*G. dorcas*).
– ORIGIN mid 19th cent.: from Arabic *ʿaryal*.

Arien ▶ **noun** & **adjective** variant spelling of **ARIAN** (in sense 2).

Aries /ˈɛːriːz/ **1** Astronomy a small constellation (the Ram), said to represent the ram whose Golden Fleece was sought by Jason and the Argonauts.
■ [as genitive **Arietis** /ˌarɪˈɛtɪs/] used with preceding letter or numeral to designate a star in this constellation: *the star Beta Arietis*.
2 Astrology the first sign of the zodiac, which the sun enters at the vernal equinox (about 20 March).
■ (**an Aries**) (pl. same) a person born when the sun is in this sign.
– PHRASES **First Point of Aries** Astronomy the point on the celestial sphere where the path of the sun crosses the celestial equator from south to north in March, marking the zero point of right ascension. Owing to precession of the equinoxes it has moved from Aries into Pisces, and is now approaching Aquarius. Also called **VERNAL EQUINOX**.
– ORIGIN Latin.

aright ▶ **adverb** dialect correctly; properly: *I wondered if I'd heard aright*.
– ORIGIN Old English *on riht, ariht* (see **A-**[2] 'in', **RIGHT**).

aril /ˈarɪl/ ▶ **noun** Botany an extra seed covering, typically coloured and hairy or fleshy, e.g. the red fleshy cup around a yew seed.
– DERIVATIVES **arillate** adjective.
– ORIGIN mid 18th cent.: from modern Latin *arillus*, of unknown origin; perhaps related to medieval Latin *arilli* 'dried grape stones'.

arioso /ˌarɪˈəʊzəʊ, -səʊ/ Music ▶ **noun** [mass noun] (especially in opera and oratorio) a style of vocal performance more melodic than recitative but less formal than an aria.
■ [count noun] (pl. **-os**) a passage in this style.
▶ **adjective** & **adverb** in such a style or manner.
– ORIGIN Italian, from **ARIA**.

Ariosto /ˌarɪˈɒstəʊ/, Ludovico (1474–1533), Italian poet noted for his romantic epic *Orlando Furioso* (final version 1532).

-arious ▶ **suffix** forming adjectives such as *gregarious, vicarious*.
– ORIGIN from the Latin suffix *-arius* + **-OUS**.

arise ▶ **verb** (past **arose**; past participle **arisen**) [no obj.]
1 (of a problem, opportunity, or situation) emerge; become apparent: *new difficulties had arisen*.
■ come into being; originate: *the practice arose in the nineteenth century*. ■ (**arise from/out of**) occur as a result of: *motorists are liable for damages arising out of accidents*.
2 formal or poetic/literary get or stand up: *he arose at 9.30*.
– ORIGIN Old English *ārīsan*, from *ā-* 'away' (as an intensifier) + the verb **RISE**.

arisings ▶ **plural noun** materials forming the secondary or waste products of industrial operations.

Aristarchus[1] /ˌarɪˈstɑːkəs/ (3rd century BC), Greek astronomer; known as **Aristarchus of Samos**. Founder of an important school of Hellenic astronomy, he was aware of the rotation of the earth around the sun and so was able to account for the seasons.

Aristarchus[2] /ˌarɪˈstɑːkəs/ (*c*.217–145 BC), Greek scholar; known as **Aristarchus of Samothrace**. The librarian at Alexandria, he is noted for his editions of the writings of Homer and other Greek authors.

Aristides /ˌarɪˈstʌɪdiːz/ (5th century BC), Athenian statesman and general; known as **Aristides the Just**. He commanded the Athenian army at the battle of Plataea.

Aristippus /aˈrɪstɪpəs, ˌarɪˈstɪpəs/ (late 5th century BC), Greek philosopher; known as **Aristippus the Elder**. He was a pupil of Socrates and is generally considered the founder of the Cyrenaic school.

aristo /əˈrɪstəʊ/ ▶ **noun** informal term for **ARISTOCRAT**.

aristocracy ▶ **noun** (pl. **-ies**) (usu. **the aristocracy**) [treated as sing. or pl.] the highest class in certain societies, typically comprising people of noble birth holding hereditary titles and offices: *members of the aristocracy*.
■ [mass noun] a form of government in which power is held by the nobility. ■ a state governed in this way.
– ORIGIN late 15th cent.: from Old French *aristocratie*, from Greek *aristokratia*, from *aristos* 'best' + *-kratia* 'power'. The term originally denoted the government of a state by its best citizens, later by the rich and well born, hence the sense 'nobility', regardless of the form of government (mid 17th cent.).

aristocrat /ˈarɪstəkrat, əˈrɪst-/ ▶ **noun** a member of the aristocracy.
– ORIGIN late 18th cent.: from French *aristocrate* (a word of the French Revolution), from *aristocratie* (see **ARISTOCRACY**).

aristocratic ▶ **adjective** of, belonging to, or typical of the aristocracy: *an aristocratic family*.
– DERIVATIVES **aristocratically** adverb.
– ORIGIN early 17th cent.: from French *aristocratique*, from Greek *aristokratikos*, from *aristokratia* (see **ARISTOCRACY**).

Aristophanes /ˌarɪˈstɒfəniːz/ (*c*.450–*c*.385 BC), Greek comic dramatist. His surviving plays are characterized by exuberant language and the satirization of leading contemporary figures. Notable works: *Lysistrata*, the *Birds*, the *Frogs*.

Aristotelian /ˌarɪstəˈtiːlɪən/ ▶ **adjective** of or relating to Aristotle or his philosophy.
▶ **noun** a student of Aristotle or an adherent of his philosophy.

Aristotelian logic ▶ **noun** [mass noun] the traditional system of logic expounded by Aristotle and developed in the Middle Ages, concerned chiefly with deductive reasoning as expressed in syllogisms. Compare with **SYMBOLIC LOGIC**.

Aristotle /ˈarɪstɒt(ə)l/ (384–322 BC), Greek philosopher and scientist.

A pupil of Plato and tutor to Alexander the Great, he founded a school (the Lyceum) outside Athens. He is one of the most influential thinkers in the history of Western thought and his work was central to Arabic and medieval philosophy. His surviving works cover a vast range of subjects, including logic, ethics, metaphysics, politics, natural science, and physics

aristotle /ˈarɪstɒt(ə)l/ ▶ **noun** Austral. rhyming slang a bottle.

Aristotle's lantern ▶ **noun** Zoology a conical structure of calcareous plates and muscles supporting the rasping teeth of a sea urchin.

Arita /əˈriːtə/ ▶ **noun** [mass noun] a type of Japanese porcelain characterized by asymmetric decoration.
– ORIGIN late 19th cent.: named after *Arita*, a town in Japan, where it is made.

arithmetic ▶ **noun** /əˈrɪθmətɪk/ [mass noun] the branch of mathematics dealing with the properties and manipulation of numbers: *the laws of arithmetic*.
■ the use of numbers in counting and calculation: *arithmetic had never been her strong point*. ■ figurative those aspects of a particular situation that can be expressed in numerical terms: *the parliamentary arithmetic facing the government*.
▶ **adjective** /ˌarɪθˈmɛtɪk/ [attrib.] of or relating to arithmetic: *arithmetic calculations*.
– DERIVATIVES **arithmetical** adjective, **arithmetically** adverb, **arithmetician** noun.
– ORIGIN Middle English: from Old French *arismetique*, based on Latin *arithmetica*, from Greek *arithmētikē* (*tekhnē*) '(art) of counting', from *arithmos* 'number'.

arithmetic logic unit ▶ **noun** a unit in a computer which carries out arithmetic and logical operations.

arithmetic mean ▶ **noun** the average of a set of numerical values, as calculated by adding them together and dividing by the number of terms in the set.

arithmetic progression (also **arithmetic series**) ▶ **noun** a sequence of numbers in which each differs from the preceding one by a constant quantity (e.g. 1, 2, 3, 4, etc.; 9, 7, 5, 3, etc.).
■ [mass noun] the relation between numbers in such a sequence: *the numbers are in arithmetic progression*.

arithmetic unit ▶ **noun** another term for **ARITHMETIC LOGIC UNIT**.

arithmetize /əˈrɪθmətʌɪz/ ▶ **verb** [with obj.] express arithmetically; reduce to arithmetical form.

-arium /ˈɛːrɪəm/ ▶ **suffix** forming nouns usually denoting a place: *planetarium* | *vivarium*.
– ORIGIN from Latin, neuter of *-arius*, adjectival ending.

Ariz. ▶ **abbreviation for** Arizona.

Arizona a state of the south-western US, on the border with Mexico; pop. 3,665,230 (1990); capital, Phoenix. It became the 48th state of the US in 1912.
– DERIVATIVES **Arizonan** noun & adjective.

Arjuna /ˈɑːdʒʊnə/ Hinduism a Kshatriya prince in the Mahabharata, one of the two main characters in the Bhagavadgita.

Ark. ▶ **abbreviation for** Arkansas.

ark ▶ **noun 1** (**the ark**) (in the Bible) the ship built by Noah to save his family and two of every kind of animal from the Flood; Noah's ark.
■ [usu. in names] a ship or boat: *the Ark Royal*. ■ informal used to refer to something perceived as extremely old-fashioned: *this kind of variety entertainment **went out with the ark***.
2 short for **ARK OF THE COVENANT**.
■ (also **Holy Ark**) a chest or cupboard housing the Torah scrolls in a synagogue.
3 (also **ark shell**) a small, widely distributed bivalve mollusc which typically attaches itself to rocks with byssus threads.
• Order Arcoidea: *Arca* and other genera.
– ORIGIN Old English *ærc*, from Latin *arca* 'chest'.

Arkansas /ˈɑːkənsɔː/ a state of the south central US; pop. 2,350,725 (1990); capital, Little Rock. It became the 25th state of the US in 1836.
– DERIVATIVES **Arkansan** noun & adjective.

Arkhangelsk /arˈxangʲilʲsk/ Russian name for **ARCHANGEL**.

Ark of the Covenant (also **Ark of the Testimony**) the wooden chest which contained the tablets of the laws of the ancient Israelites. Carried by the Israelites on their wanderings in the wilderness, it was later placed by Solomon in the Temple at Jerusalem.

arkose /ˈɑːkəʊs, -z/ ▶ **noun** [mass noun] Geology a coarse-grained sandstone which is at least 25 per cent feldspar.
– DERIVATIVES **arkosic** adjective.
– ORIGIN mid 19th cent.: from French, probably from Greek *arkhaios* 'ancient'.

Arkwright, Sir Richard (1732–92), English inventor and industrialist. In 1767 he patented a water-powered spinning machine capable of producing yarn strong enough to be used as warp.

Arles /ɑːl, French arl/ a city in SE France; pop. 52,590 (1990). It was the capital of the medieval kingdom of Arles, formed in the 10th century by the union of Provence and Burgundy.

Arlington /ˈɑːlɪŋtən/ **1** a county in northern Virginia, forming a suburb of Washington. It is the site of the Pentagon.
2 an industrial city in northern Texas, between Dallas and Fort Worth; pop. 261,720 (1990).

Arlon /ɑːˈlɔ̃, French arlɔ̃/ a town in SE Belgium, capital of the province of Luxembourg; pop. 23,420 (1991).

arm[1] ▶ **noun 1** each of the two upper limbs of the human body from the shoulder to the hand: *she held the baby in her arms*.
■ each of the forelimbs of an animal. ■ a flexible limb of an invertebrate animal, e.g. an octopus. ■ a sleeve of a garment. ■ an ability to bowl, pitch, or throw a ball skilfully: *he has a good arm*. ■ used to refer to the holding of a person's arm in support or companionship: *as they walked he offered her his arm* | *he arrived with a pretty girl on his arm*. ■ used to refer to something perceived as powerful or protective: *they have extended the arm of friendship to developing countries*.
2 a thing resembling an arm in form or function, in particular:
■ a side part of a chair or other seat on which a sitter can rest their arm. ■ a narrow strip of water or land projecting from a larger body. ■ a large branch of a tree. ■ figurative a long, narrow shape or object: *a long arm of sunshine*.
3 a branch or division of a company or organization: *the political arm of the separatist group*.
■ one of the types of troops of which an army is composed, such as infantry or artillery. [ORIGIN: also understood as a figurative use of **ARM**[2].]
4 Mathematics each of the lines enclosing an angle.
– PHRASES **arm in arm** (of two or more people) with arms linked. **as long as one's** (or **someone's**) **arm** informal very long: *I have a list of vices as long as your arm*. **at arm's length** away from the body, with one's arm fully extended: *I held the telephone at arm's length*. **beyond arm's reach** see ***within arm's reach*** below. **cost an arm and a leg** informal be extremely expensive. **give one's right arm** informal used to

convey how much one would like to have or do something: *I'd give my right arm to go with them.* **in arms** (of a baby) too young to walk: *a babe in arms.* **into the arms of** into the possession or control of: *the violin passed into the arms of a wealthy dilettante.* **keep someone/thing at arm's length** avoid intimacy or close contact with someone or something. **the long** (or **strong**) **arm of** the far-reaching power, authority, or influence of: *the long arm of the law caught up with him.* **put the arm on** N. Amer. informal attempt to force or coerce (someone) to do something: *she started putting the arm on them for donations.* **under one's arm** between one's arm and one's body: *Meryl tucked the papers under her arm.* **with open arms** with great affection or enthusiasm: *schools have welcomed such arrangements with open arms.* **within** (or **beyond**) **arm's reach** near (or not near) enough to reach by extending one's arm.
– DERIVATIVES **armful** noun (pl. **-fuls**), **armless** adjective.
– ORIGIN Old English *arm*, *earm*, of Germanic origin; related to Dutch *arm* and German *Arm*.

arm² ▶ verb [with obj.] supply or provide with weapons: *both sides armed themselves with grenades and machine guns.*
■ supply or provide with equipment, tools, or other items in preparation or readiness for something: *she armed them with brushes and mops.* ■ activate the fuse of (a bomb, missile or other explosive device) so that it is ready to explode.
– ORIGIN Middle English: from Old French *armer* (verb), from Latin *armare*, from *arma* 'armour, arms'.

armada /ɑːˈmɑːdə/ ▶ noun a fleet of warships.
■ (**the** (**Spanish**) **Armada**) a Spanish naval invasion force sent against England in 1588 by Philip II of Spain. It was defeated by the English fleet and almost completely destroyed by storms off the Hebrides.
– ORIGIN mid 16th cent.: from Spanish, from *armata*, feminine past participle of Latin *armare* 'to arm'.

armadillo /ˌɑːməˈdɪləʊ/ ▶ noun (pl. **-os**) a nocturnal insectivorous mammal that has large claws for digging and a body covered in bony plates. Armadillos are native to Central and South America and one kind is spreading into the southern US.
● Family Dasypodidae, order Xenarthra (or Edentata): several genera.
– ORIGIN late 16th cent.: from Spanish, diminutive of *armado* 'armed man', from Latin *armatus*, past participle of *armare* 'to arm'.

Armageddon /ˌɑːməˈɡɛd(ə)n/ ▶ noun (in the New Testament) the last battle between good and evil before the Day of Judgement.
■ the place where this will be fought. ■ a dramatic and catastrophic conflict, especially one seen as likely to destroy the world or the human race: *nuclear Armageddon.*
– ORIGIN Greek, from Hebrew *har měgiddōn* 'hill of Megiddo' (Rev. 16:16.)

Armagh /ɑːˈmɑː/ one of the Six Counties of Northern Ireland, formerly an administrative area.
■ the chief town of this county; pop. 12,700 (1981).

Armagnac /ˈɑːmənjak/ ▶ noun [mass noun] a type of brandy traditionally made in Aquitaine in SW France.
– ORIGIN from the former name of a district in Aquitaine.

Armalite /ˈɑːməlʌɪt/ ▶ noun trademark a type of light automatic rifle.

armament /ˈɑːməm(ə)nt/ ▶ noun [mass noun] (also **armaments**) military weapons and equipment: *national armaments could be kept to a minimum.*
■ the process of equipping military forces for war. ■ archaic a military force equipped for war.
– ORIGIN late 17th cent. (in the sense 'force equipped for war'): from Latin *armamentum*, from *armare* 'to arm' (see **ARM²**).

armamentarium /ˌɑːməmən'tɛːrɪəm/ ▶ noun (pl. **armamentaria** /-rɪə/) the medicines, equipment, and techniques available to a medical practitioner.
■ a collection of resources available for a certain purpose: *the technological armamentarium.*
– ORIGIN late 19th cent.: from Latin, 'arsenal, armoury'.

Armani /ɑːˈmɑːni, Italian arˈmɑːni/, Giorgio (b.1935), Italian fashion designer.

armature /ˈɑːmətʃə, -tj(ʊ)ə/ ▶ noun 1 the rotating coil or coils of a dynamo or electric motor.

■ any moving part of an electrical machine in which a voltage is induced by a magnetic field. ■ a piece of iron or other object acting as a keeper for a magnet.
2 an open framework on which a sculpture is moulded with clay or similar material.
3 Biology the protective covering of an animal or plant.
■ [mass noun] archaic armour.
– ORIGIN late Middle English: from French, from Latin *armatura* 'armour', from *armare* 'to arm' (see **ARM²**). The original sense was 'armour', hence 'protective covering' (sense 3, early 18th cent.), later 'keeper of a magnet' (source of sense 1 (mid 19th cent.).

armband ▶ noun a band worn around a person's upper arm to hold up a shirtsleeve or as a form of identification.
■ an inflatable plastic band worn around a person's upper arm as a swimming aid.

armchair ▶ noun a large, comfortable chair with side supports for a person's arms.
▶ adjective [attrib.] lacking or not involving practical or direct experience of a particular subject or activity: *an armchair traveller.*

Armco /ˈɑːmkəʊ/ ▶ noun [mass noun] trademark a very pure soft iron, used in particular for roadside crash barriers.
– ORIGIN early 20th cent.: acronym from *American Rolling Mill Company*.

armed ▶ adjective 1 equipped with or carrying a firearm or firearms: *the security forces are armed with automatic rifles* | *heavily armed troops.*
■ involving the use of firearms: *armed robbery.* ■ figurative supplied with equipment, tools, or other items in preparation or readiness for something: *he is armed with a list of questions.*
2 Heraldry having claws, a beak, etc. of a specified tincture.
– PHRASES **armed to the teeth** see **TOOTH**.

armed camp ▶ noun a town, territory, or group of people fully armed for war.

armed forces (also **armed services**) ▶ plural noun a country's army, navy, and air force.

Armenia /ɑːˈmiːnɪə/ a landlocked country in the Caucasus of SE Europe; pop. 3,360,000 (est. 1991); official language, Armenian; capital, Yerevan.

> The Armenian homeland fell under Turkish rule from the 16th century, and with the decline of the Ottomans was divided between Turkey, Iran, and Russia. In 1915 the Turks forcibly deported 1,750,000 Armenians to the deserts of Syria and Mesopotamia; more than 600,000 were killed or died on forced marches. Russian Armenia was absorbed into the Soviet Union in 1922, gaining independence as a member of the Commonwealth of Independent States in 1991.

Armenian /ɑːˈmiːnɪən/ ▶ adjective of or relating to Armenia, its language, or the Christian Church established there.
▶ noun 1 a native of Armenia or a person of Armenian descent.
2 [mass noun] the Indo-European language of Armenia, spoken by around 4 million people and written in a distinctive alphabet of thirty-eight letters.

Armenian Church (also **Armenian Apostolic Orthodox Church**) an independent Christian Church established in Armenia since *c.*300 and influenced by Roman and Byzantine as well as Syrian traditions. A small Armenian Catholic Church also exists (see **UNIATE**).

armhole ▶ noun each of two openings in a garment through which the wearer puts their arms.

armiger /ˈɑːmɪdʒə/ ▶ noun a person entitled to heraldic arms.
– DERIVATIVES **armigerous** adjective.
– ORIGIN mid 16th cent.: Latin, literally 'bearing arms', from *arma* 'arms' + *gerere* 'to bear'.

armillaria /ˌɑːmɪˈlɛːrɪə/ ▶ noun a fungus of a genus that includes the honey fungus, found chiefly in woodland. Its mycelia can grow for a considerable distance, enabling individuals of parasitic species to invade more than one tree.
● Genus *Armillaria*, family Tricholomataceae, class Hymenomycetes: many species, including *A. bulbosa*, a single individual of which may span several hectares.
– ORIGIN modern Latin: from Latin *armilla* 'bracelet' (because of the bracelet-like frill on the fruiting bodies).

armillary sphere ▶ noun a model of the celestial globe constructed from rings and hoops

representing the equator, the tropics, and other celestial circles, and able to revolve on its axis.
– ORIGIN mid 17th cent.: from modern Latin *armillaris* 'relating to an *armilla*', an astronomical instrument consisting of a hoop fixed in the plane of the equator (sometimes crossed by one in the plane of the meridian), used by the ancient astronomers to show the recurrence of equinoxes and solstices; from Latin *armilla* 'bracelet'.

Arminian /ɑːˈmɪnɪən/ ▶ adjective relating to the doctrines of Jacobus Arminius (Latinized name of Jakob Hermandszoon, 1560–1609), a Dutch Protestant theologian who rejected the Calvinist doctrine of predestination. His teachings had a considerable influence on Methodism.
▶ noun an adherent of these doctrines.
– DERIVATIVES **Arminianism** noun.

armistice /ˈɑːmɪstɪs/ ▶ noun an agreement made by opposing sides in a war to stop fighting for a certain time; a truce.
– ORIGIN early 18th cent.: from French, or from modern Latin *armistitium*, from *arma* 'arms' (see **ARM²**) + *-stitium* 'stoppage'.

Armistice Day ▶ noun the anniversary of the armistice of 11 November 1918, now replaced by Remembrance Sunday in the UK and Veterans Day in the US.

armlet ▶ noun a band or bracelet worn round the upper part of a person's arm.

armlock ▶ noun a method of restraining someone by holding their arm tightly behind their back.

armoire /ɑːˈmwɑː/ ▶ noun a cupboard or wardrobe, typically one that is ornate or antique.
– ORIGIN late 16th cent.: from French, from Old French *armarie* (see **AUMBRY**).

armor ▶ noun US spelling of **ARMOUR**.

armored ▶ adjective US spelling of **ARMOURED**.

armorer ▶ noun US spelling of **ARMOURER**.

armorial /ɑːˈmɔːrɪəl/ ▶ adjective of or relating to heraldry or heraldic devices: *armorial bearings.*
– ORIGIN late Middle English: from Old French *armoierie* (see **ARMOURY**).

Armorica /ɑːˈmɒrɪkə/ an ancient region of NW France between the Seine and the Loire.

Armorican ▶ adjective of or relating to Armorica.
■ Geology another term for **HERCYNIAN**.

armory¹ /ˈɑːməri/ ▶ noun [mass noun] heraldry.
– ORIGIN late Middle English: from Old French *armoierie* (see **ARMOURY**).

armory² noun US spelling of **ARMOURY**.

armour (US **armor**) ▶ noun [mass noun] the metal coverings formerly worn by soldiers or warriors to protect the body in battle: *knights in armour* | *a suit of armour.*
■ (also **armour plate**) the tough metal layer covering a military vehicle or ship to defend it from attack. ■ military vehicles collectively: *the contingent includes infantry, armour, and logistic units.* ■ the protective layer or shell of some animals and plants. ■ a person's emotional, social, or other defences: *his armour of self-confidence.*
▶ verb [with obj.] provide (someone) with emotional, social, or other defences: *the knowledge armoured him against her.*
– DERIVATIVES **armour-plated** adjective.
– ORIGIN Middle English: from Old French *armure*, from Latin *armatura*, from *armare* 'to arm' (see **ARM²**).

armoured (US **armored**) ▶ adjective (of a military vehicle or ship) covered with armour: *armoured vehicles.*
■ (of troops) equipped with such vehicles: *the 3rd Armoured Division.* ■ (of some animals and plants) having a protective layer or shell: *armoured fish.* ■ historical (of a soldier) wearing armour.

armoured personnel carrier ▶ noun an armoured military vehicle used to transport troops.

armourer (US **armorer**) ▶ noun 1 a maker, supplier, or repairer of weapons or armour.
2 an official in charge of the arms of a warship or regiment.
– ORIGIN Middle English: from Old French *armurier*, from *armure* (see **ARMOUR**).

armoury (US **armory**) ▶ noun (pl. **-ies**) 1 a place where arms are kept.
■ a supply of arms: *Britain's nuclear armoury expanded.* ■ US a place where arms are manufactured. ■ [in sing.]

figurative an array of resources available for a particular purpose: *his armoury of comic routines.*
2 N. Amer. a place where militia units drill and train.
– ORIGIN Middle English (in the sense 'armour'): from Old French *armoirie, armoierie*, from *armoier* 'to blazon', from *arme* 'weapon' (see **ARMS**). The change in the second syllable in the 17th cent. was due to association with **ARMOUR**.

armpit ▶ **noun** a hollow under the arm at the shoulder. Also called **AXILLA**.
▪ informal, chiefly N. Amer. a place regarded as extremely unpleasant: *they call the region the armpit of America.*
– PHRASES **up to one's armpits** chiefly US deeply involved in a particular unpleasant situation or enterprise: *the country is **up to its armpits** in drug trafficking.*

armrest ▶ **noun** a padded or upholstered arm of a chair or other seat on which a sitter can comfortably rest their arm.

arms ▶ **plural noun 1** weapons; armaments: *arms and ammunition* | [as modifier] *arms exports.*
2 distinctive emblems or devices, originally borne on shields in battle and now forming the heraldic insignia of families, corporations, or countries. See also **COAT OF ARMS**.
– PHRASES **a call to arms** a call to defend or make ready for confrontation. **in arms** armed; prepared to fight. **lay down (one's) arms** cease fighting. **take up arms** begin fighting. **under arms** equipped and ready for war or battle. **up in arms (about/over)** protesting vigorously about something: *teachers are up in arms about new school tests.*
– ORIGIN Middle English: from Old French *armes*, from Latin *arma*.

arms control ▶ **noun** [mass noun] international disarmament or arms limitation, especially by mutual consent.

arm's-length ▶ **adjective** [attrib.] avoiding intimacy or close contact: *they maintained an arm's-length relationship.*

arms race ▶ **noun** (usu. **the arms race**) a competition between nations for superiority in the development and accumulation of weapons.

Armstrong[1], Edwin Howard (1890–1954), American electrical engineer, inventor of the superheterodyne radio receiver and the frequency modulation (FM) system.

Armstrong[2], (Daniel) Louis (1900–71), American jazz musician; known as **Satchmo**. A major influence on Dixieland jazz, he was a trumpet and cornet player as well as a bandleader and a distinctive singer.

Armstrong[3], Neil (Alden) (b.1930), American astronaut. He commanded the Apollo 11 mission, during which he became the first man to set foot on the moon (20 July 1969).

arm-twisting ▶ **noun** [mass noun] informal persuasion by the use of physical force or moral pressure: *a day of arm-twisting by government whips.*
– DERIVATIVES **arm-twist** verb.

arm-waving ▶ **noun** [mass noun] the action of waving one's arms in order to attract attention.
▪ elaborate but unconvincing theoretical explanations of something.

arm-wrestling ▶ **noun** [mass noun] a trial of strength in which two people sit opposite each other with one elbow resting on a table, clasp each other's hands, and try to force each other's arm down on to the table.
– DERIVATIVES **arm-wrestle** verb.

army ▶ **noun** (pl. **-ies**) [treated as sing. or pl.] an organized military force equipped for fighting on land: *the two armies were in position* | [as modifier] *army officers.*
▪ (**the army**) the part of a particular country's military force trained to fight on land: *he joined the army at 16.* ▪ (**an army of/armies of**) a large number of people or things, typically formed or organized for a particular purpose: *an army of photographers.*
– PHRASES **an army marches on its stomach** see **STOMACH**. **you and whose army?** informal used as an expression of disbelief in someone's ability to carry out a threat: *'One word to him and I'll have you.' 'You and whose army?'*
– ORIGIN late Middle English: from Old French *armee*, from *armata*, feminine past participle of Latin *armare* 'to arm'.

army ant ▶ **noun** a blind nomadic tropical ant that forages in large columns, preying chiefly on insects and spiders. Also called **DRIVER ANT**.
● Subfamily Dorylinae, family Formicidae.

army disposal ▶ **noun** Australian term for **ARMY SURPLUS**.

army issue ▶ **noun** [mass noun] [usu. as modifier] equipment or clothing supplied by the army.

Army List ▶ **noun** (in the UK) an official list of commissioned officers.

army-navy ▶ **adjective** US denoting the type of shop which specializes in military surplus equipment, or the goods sold there.

army surplus ▶ **noun** [mass noun] goods and equipment which are surplus to the army's requirements: [as modifier] *an army surplus store.*

army worm ▶ **noun** any of a number of insect larvae which occur in destructive swarms, in particular:
● the caterpillars of some moths, which feed on cereals and other crops and move *en masse* when the food is exhausted (*Spodoptera* and other genera, family Noctuidae). ● the small maggots of certain fungus gnats, which move in large numbers within secreted slime (genus *Sciara*, family Mycetophilidae).

Arne /ɑːn/, Thomas (1710–78), English composer noted for 'Rule, Britannia' (whose words are attributed to James Thomson) and for his settings of Shakespearean songs.

Arnel /ˈɑːnɛl/ ▶ **noun** [mass noun] trademark a synthetic fibre or fabric made from cellulose triacetate.

Arnhem /ˈɑːnəm/ a town in the eastern Netherlands, situated on the River Rhine, capital of the province of Gelderland; pop. 131,700 (1991). During the Second World War, in September 1944, Allied airborne troops made a landing nearby but were overwhelmed by German forces.

Arnhem Land a peninsula in Northern Territory, Australia whose chief town is Nhulunbuy. In 1976 Arnhem Land was declared an Aboriginal reservation.

arnica /ˈɑːnɪkə/ ▶ **noun** a plant of the daisy family which bears yellow, daisy-like flowers, found in cooler regions of the northern hemisphere.
● Genus *Arnica*, family Compositae: many species, especially mountain tobacco (*A. montana*) of central Europe.
▪ [mass noun] a preparation of this plant used medicinally, especially for the treatment of bruises.
– ORIGIN mid 18th cent.: modern Latin, of unknown origin.

Arno /ˈɑːnəʊ/ a river which rises in the Apennines of northern Italy and flows westwards 240 km (150 miles) through Florence and Pisa to the Ligurian Sea.

Arnold[1], Sir Malcolm (Henry) (b.1921), English composer and trumpeter, noted especially for his orchestral works and film scores.

Arnold[2], Matthew (1822–88), English poet, essayist, and social critic. In works such as *Culture and Anarchy* (1869) he criticized the Victorian age in terms of its materialism, philistinism, and complacency. Notable poems: 'The Scholar Gipsy' (1853), 'Dover Beach' (1867).

aroha /ˈɑːrɒhə/ ▶ **noun** [mass noun] NZ love; affection.
▪ sympathy.
– ORIGIN Maori.

aroid /ˈɛːrɔɪd/ (also **aroid lily**) ▶ **noun** Botany a plant of the arum family (Araceae).
– ORIGIN late 19th cent.: from **ARUM** + **-OID**.

arolla /əˈrɒlə/ (also **arolla pine**) ▶ **noun** a tall pine tree of the Alps and Carpathian Mountains, frequently planted in dense clumps as an avalanche break.
● *Pinus cembra*, family Pinaceae. Alternative name: **Swiss stone pine**.
– ORIGIN late 19th cent.: from Swiss French *arol(l)e*.

aroma ▶ **noun** a distinctive, typically pleasant smell: *the tantalizing aroma of fresh coffee.*
▪ *figurative* a subtle, pervasive quality or atmosphere of a particular type: *the aroma of officialdom.*
– ORIGIN Middle English (usually in the plural denoting fragrant plants or spices): via Latin from Greek *arōma* 'spice'.

aromatherapy ▶ **noun** [mass noun] the use of aromatic plant extracts and essential oils for healing and cosmetic purposes.
– DERIVATIVES **aromatherapeutic** adjective, **aromatherapist** noun.

aromatic ▶ **adjective 1** having a pleasant and distinctive smell: *a massage with aromatic oils.*
2 Chemistry (of an organic compound) containing a planar unsaturated ring of atoms which is stabilized by an interaction of the bonds forming the ring. Such compounds are typified by benzene and its derivatives. Compare with **ALICYCLIC**.
▶ **noun 1** a substance or plant emitting a pleasant and distinctive smell.
2 (usu. **aromatics**) Chemistry an aromatic compound.
– DERIVATIVES **aromatically** adverb, **aromaticity** noun (Chemistry).
– ORIGIN late Middle English: via Old French from late Latin *aromaticus*, from Greek *arōmatikos*, from *arōma* (see **AROMA**).

aromatize (also **-ise**) ▶ **verb** [with obj.] **1** Chemistry convert (a compound) into an aromatic structure.
2 cause to have a pleasant and distinctive smell: *vinegar aromatized with plant juices and honey.*
– DERIVATIVES **aromatization** noun.
– ORIGIN late Middle English: from Old French *aromatiser*, from late Latin *aromatizare*, from Greek *arōmatizein* 'to spice'.

arose past of **ARISE**.

around ▶ **adverb 1** located or situated on every side: *the mountains towering all around.*
2 so as to face in the opposite direction: *Guy seized her by the shoulders and turned her around.*
3 in or to many places throughout a locality: *word got around that he was on the verge of retirement.*
4 aimlessly or unsystematically; here and there: *one of them was glancing nervously around.*
5 present, living, in the vicinity, or in active use: *there was no one around* | *maize has been around for a long time.*
6 (used with a number or quantity) approximately: *software costs would be around £1,500* | *I returned to my hotel around 3 a.m.*
▶ **preposition 1** on every side of: *the palazzo is built around a courtyard* | *the hills around the city.*
▪ (of something abstract) having (the thing mentioned) as a focal point: *our entire culture is built around those loyalties.*
2 in or to many places throughout (a community or locality): *cycling around the village* | *a number of large depots around the country.*
3 round:
▪ so as to encircle or embrace (someone or something): *he put his arm around her* | *warming her hands around a cup of coffee.* ▪ following an approximately circular route: *he walked around the airfield* | *it can drill around corners.*
– PHRASES **have been around** informal have a lot of varied experience and understanding of the world.
– ORIGIN Middle English: from **A-**[2] 'in, on' + **ROUND**.

USAGE On the difference in use between **round** and **around**, see **usage** at **ROUND**.

arouse ▶ **verb** [with obj.] **1** evoke or awaken (a feeling, emotion, or response): *something about the man aroused the guard's suspicions* | *the letter **aroused in** him a sense of urgency.*
▪ excite or provoke (someone) to anger or strong emotions: *an ability to influence the audience and to arouse the masses.* ▪ excite (someone) sexually: *his touch, which had so aroused her moments before, unnerved her now* | [as adj. **aroused**] *she told him how aroused she was.*
2 awaken (someone) from sleep: *she had been aroused from deep slumber.*
– DERIVATIVES **arousable** adjective, **arousal** noun.
– ORIGIN late 16th cent.: from **ROUSE**, on the pattern of the pair of *rise, arise*.

ARP Brit. historical ▶ **abbreviation for** air-raid precautions.

Arp /ɑːp, French aʀp/, Jean (1887–1966), French painter, sculptor, and poet; also known as **Hans Arp**. He was a co-founder of the Dada movement and is noted for his three-dimensional abstract curvilinear sculptures in marble and bronze.

arpeggiate /ɑːˈpɛdʒɪeɪt/ ▶ **verb** [with obj.] Music play (a chord) as a series of ascending or descending notes.
– DERIVATIVES **arpeggiation** noun, **arpeggiator** noun.

arpeggio /ɑːˈpɛdʒɪəʊ/ ▶ **noun** (pl. **-os**) Music the notes of a chord played in rapid succession, either ascending or descending.
– ORIGIN Italian, from *arpeggiare* 'play the harp', from *arpa* 'harp'.

arpeggione /ɑːˌpɛdʒɪˈəʊneɪ, -ni/ ▶ **noun** an early 19th-century stringed instrument resembling a guitar in shape and having six strings and frets, but played with a bow like a cello.

a

– ORIGIN late 19th cent.: from German, from **ARPEGGIO**.

arquebus /ˈɑːkwɪbəs/ ▶ noun variant spelling of **HARQUEBUS**.

arr. ▶ abbreviation for ■ (of a piece of music) arranged by: *Variations on a theme of Corelli (arr. Wild).* ■ (with reference to the arrival time of a bus, train, or aircraft) arrives.

arrack /ˈarək, əˈrak/ (also **arak**) ▶ noun [mass noun] an alcoholic spirit made in Eastern countries from the sap of the coco palm or from rice.
– ORIGIN early 17th cent.: from Arabic *ʿaraḳ* 'sweat', from the phrase *ʿarak al-tamr*, denoting an alcoholic spirit made from dates.

arrah /ˈarə/ ▶ exclamation Irish expressing excitement or strong emotion (used at the beginning of an utterance): *'Arrah, don't be talking nonsense,' Elmer exclaimed.*
– ORIGIN late 17th cent.: from Irish *ara, arú*.

arraign /əˈreɪn/ ▶ verb (often **be arraigned**) call or bring (someone) before a court to answer a criminal charge; indict: *her sister was* ***arraigned on*** *attempted murder charges.*
■ find fault with; censure: *social workers were relieved it was not they who were arraigned in the tabloids.*
– DERIVATIVES **arraignment** noun.
– ORIGIN late Middle English: from Old French *araisnier*, based on Latin *ad-* 'to' + *ratio(n-)* 'reason, account'.

Arran an island in the Firth of Clyde, in the west of Scotland.

arrange ▶ verb [with obj.] **1** put (things) in a neat, attractive, or required order: *she had just finished arranging the flowers | the columns are* ***arranged in*** *12 rows.*
2 organize or make plans for (a future event): *they hoped to arrange a meeting | we've* ***arranged*** *the funeral* ***for*** *Saturday |* [no obj.] *my aunt* ***arranged for*** *the furniture to be stored.*
■ [no obj.] reach agreement about an action or event in advance: *I* ***arranged with*** *my boss to have the time off |* [with infinitive] *they arranged to meet at eleven o'clock.* ■ ensure that (something) is done or provided by organizing it in advance: *accommodation can be arranged if required.*
3 Music adapt (a composition) for performance with instruments or voices other than those originally specified: *songs* ***arranged for*** *viola and piano.*
4 archaic settle (a dispute or claim): *the quarrel, partly by the interference of the Crown Prince, was arranged.*
– DERIVATIVES **arrangeable** adjective, **arranger** noun.
– ORIGIN late Middle English: from Old French *arangier*, from *a-* (from Latin *ad* 'to, at') + *rangier* 'put in order' (see **RANGE**).

arranged marriage ▶ noun a marriage planned and agreed by the families or guardians of the couple concerned, who have little or no say in the matter themselves.

arrangement ▶ noun **1** [mass noun] the action, process, or result of arranging or being arranged: *the arrangement of the furniture in the room.*
■ [count noun] a thing that has been arranged in a neat or attractive way: *flower arrangements | an intricate arrangement of gravel paths.*
2 (usu. **arrangements**) plans or preparations for a future event: *all the* ***arrangements for*** *the wedding were made.*
■ an agreement with someone to do something: *the travel agents have an* ***arrangement with*** *the hotel |* [mass noun] ***by special arrangement****, students can take a course in other degree programmes.*
3 Music a composition arranged for performance with instruments or voices differing from those originally specified: *Mozart's symphonies in* ***arrangements for*** *cello and piano.*
4 archaic a settlement of a dispute or claim.

arrant /ˈar(ə)nt/ ▶ adjective [attrib.] dated complete, utter: *what arrant nonsense!*
– DERIVATIVES **arrantly** adverb.
– ORIGIN Middle English: variant of **ERRANT**, originally in phrases such as *arrant thief* ('outlawed, roving thief').

Arras /ˈarəs, French aʀas/ a town in NE France; pop. 42,700 (1990). In medieval times it was a centre for the manufacture of tapestries.

arras /ˈarəs/ ▶ noun a wall hanging made of a rich tapestry fabric, typically used to conceal an alcove.
– ORIGIN late Middle English (originally denoting the fabric itself): named after the French town of **ARRAS**.

array /əˈreɪ/ ▶ noun **1** an impressive display or range of a particular type of thing: *there is a vast array of literature on the topic | a bewildering array of choices.*
2 an ordered arrangement, in particular:
■ an arrangement of troops. ■ Mathematics an arrangement of quantities or symbols in rows and columns; a matrix. ■ Computing an ordered set of related elements. ■ Law a list of jurors impanelled.
3 [mass noun] poetic/literary elaborate or beautiful clothing: *he was clothed in fine array.*
▶ verb **1** [with obj. and adverbial of place] (usu. **be arrayed**) display or arrange (things) in a particular way: *the forces arrayed against him.*
2 [with obj.] (usu. **be arrayed in**) dress (someone) in the clothes specified: *they were arrayed in Hungarian national dress.*
3 [with obj.] Law impanel (a jury).
– ORIGIN Middle English (in the senses 'preparedness' and 'place in readiness'): from Old French *arei* (noun), *areer* (verb), based on Latin *ad-* 'towards' + a Germanic base meaning 'prepare'.

arré /ˈəreɪ/ ▶ exclamation Indian used to express annoyance, surprise or interest, or to attract someone's attention.
– ORIGIN via Hindi from Sanskrit *are*, an interjection for calling to a person of inferior rank.

arrears ▶ plural noun money that is owed and should have been paid earlier: *he was suing the lessee for the arrears of rent.*
– PHRASES **in arrears** (also chiefly Law **in arrear**) **1** behind with paying money that is owed: *two out of three tenants are in arrears.* ■ (of payments made or due for wages, rent, etc.) at the end of each period in which work is done or a tenancy is occupied: *you will be paid monthly in arrears.* **2** (of a competitor in a sports race or match) having a lower score or weaker performance than other competitors: *she finished ten metres in arrears.*
– DERIVATIVES **arrearage** noun.
– ORIGIN Middle English (first used in the phrase *in arrear*): from *arrear* (adverb) 'behind, overdue', from Old French *arere*, from medieval Latin *adretro*, from *ad-* 'towards' + *retro* 'backwards'.

Arrernte /əˈrʌntə, aˈruːndə/ ▶ noun variant form of **ARANDA**.

arrest ▶ verb [with obj.] **1** seize (someone) by legal authority and take them into custody: *the police* ***arrested*** *him* ***for*** *possession of marijuana | two youths aged 16 were arrested.*
■ seize and detain (a ship) by legal authority.
2 stop or check (progress or a process): *the spread of the disease can be arrested.*
3 attract the attention of (someone): *the church's stillness arrested her.*
▶ noun **1** [mass noun] the action of seizing someone and taking them into custody: *I have a warrant for your arrest | they* ***placed*** *her* ***under arrest*** *|* [count noun] *at least 69 arrests were made.*
2 a stoppage or sudden cessation of motion: [with modifier] *a cardiac arrest.*
– PHRASES **arrest of judgement** Law the suspension of proceedings in a criminal trial between the verdict and the sentence on the grounds of a material irregularity in the course of the trial.
– ORIGIN late Middle English: from Old French *arester*, based on Latin *ad-* 'at, to' + *restare* 'remain, stop'.

arrestable offence ▶ noun Law an offence for which the offender may be arrested without a warrant; a felony.

arrestee ▶ noun chiefly N. Amer. a person who has been or is being legally arrested.

arrester (also **arrestor**) ▶ noun [usu. with modifier] a device which prevents or stops a specified thing: *a spark arrester | a lightning arrester.*
■ a device on an aircraft carrier that slows down aircraft after landing by means of a hook and cable.

arresting ▶ adjective striking; eye-catching: *at 6 ft 6 in he was an arresting figure.*
– DERIVATIVES **arrestingly** adverb.

arrestment ▶ noun Scots Law an attachment of property for the satisfaction of a debt.

Arretine /ˈarətʌɪn/ ▶ adjective denoting Samian ware (Roman pottery), especially that made at Arretium (modern Arezzo) in central Italy.
– ORIGIN late 18th cent.: from the name of the city + **-INE**[1].

Arrhenius /əˈreɪnɪəs, əˈriːn-/, Svante August (1859–1927), Swedish chemist, noted for his work on electrolytes. Nobel Prize for Chemistry (1903).

arrhythmia /əˈrɪðmɪə/ ▶ noun [mass noun] Medicine a condition in which the heart beats with an irregular or abnormal rhythm.
– ORIGIN late 19th cent.: from Greek *arruthmia* 'lack of rhythm', from *a-* 'without' + *rhuthmos* (see **RHYTHM**).

arrhythmic (also **arhythmic**) ▶ adjective not rhythmic; without rhythm or regularity: *the arrhythmic phrasing of the music.*
■ Medicine of, relating to, or suffering from cardiac arrhythmia.
– DERIVATIVES **arrhythmical** adjective, **arrhythmically** adverb.

arrière-pensée /ˌarɪɛːˈpɒ̃seɪ, French aʀjɛʀ pɑ̃se/ ▶ noun a concealed thought or intention; an ulterior motive.
– ORIGIN French, literally 'behind thought'.

arris /ˈarɪs/ ▶ noun Architecture a sharp edge formed by the meeting of two flat or curved surfaces.
– ORIGIN late 17th cent.: alteration of early modern French *areste* 'sharp ridge', earlier form of **ARÊTE**.

arris rail ▶ noun a fence rail with a triangular cross section.

arrival ▶ noun **1** [mass noun] the action or process of arriving: *Ruth's arrival in New York | he was dead* ***on arrival*** *at hospital.*
■ [count noun] a person who has arrived somewhere: *hotel staff greeted the late arrivals.* ■ the emergence or appearance of a new development, phenomenon, or product: *the arrival of democracy.* ■ [count noun] such a new development, phenomenon, or product: *sociology is a relatively new arrival on the academic scene.*
– ORIGIN late Middle English: from Anglo-Norman French *arrivaille*, from Old French *arriver* (see **ARRIVE**).

arrive ▶ verb [no obj.] reach a place at the end of a journey or a stage in a journey: *we* ***arrived at*** *his house and knocked at the door | the team* ***arrived in*** *New Delhi on July 30 | they had recently* ***arrived from*** *Turkey.*
■ (of a thing) be brought or delivered: *the invitation arrived a few days later.* ■ (**arrive at**) reach (a conclusion or decision): *they arrived at the same conclusion.* ■ (of an event or a particular moment) happen or come: *we will be in touch with them when the time arrives.* ■ (of a new development or product) come into existence or use: *microcomputers arrived at the start of the 1970s.* ■ (of a baby) be born: *he will feel jealous when a new baby arrives.* ■ informal achieve success or recognition.
– ORIGIN Middle English (in the sense 'reach the shore after a voyage'): from Old French *ariver*, based on Latin *ad-* 'to' + *ripa* 'shore'.

arriviste /ˌariːˈviːst/ ▶ noun an ambitious or ruthlessly self-seeking person.
– DERIVATIVES **arrivisme** /ˌariːˈviːzm(ə)/ noun.
– ORIGIN early 20th cent.: from French, from *arriver* (see **ARRIVE**).

arrogant ▶ adjective having or revealing an exaggerated sense of one's own importance or abilities: *he's arrogant and opinionated | a typically arrogant assumption.*
– DERIVATIVES **arrogance** noun, **arrogantly** adverb.
– ORIGIN late Middle English: via Old French from Latin *arrogant-* 'claiming for oneself', from the verb *arrogare* (see **ARROGATE**).

arrogate /ˈarəgeɪt/ ▶ verb [with obj.] take or claim (something) for oneself without justification: *they* ***arrogate to themselves*** *the ability to divine the nation's true interests.*
– DERIVATIVES **arrogation** noun.
– ORIGIN mid 16th cent.: from Latin *arrogat-* 'claimed for oneself', from the verb *arrogare*, from *ad-* 'to' + *rogare* 'ask'.

USAGE On the difference between **arrogate** and **abrogate**, see usage at **ABROGATE**.

arrondissement /aˈrɒndiːsmɒ̃, ˌarɒnˈdiːsmɒ̃, French aʀɔ̃dismɑ̃/ ▶ noun a subdivision of a French department, for local government administration purposes.
■ an administrative district of certain large French cities, in particular Paris.
– ORIGIN French, from *arrondir* 'make round'.

Arrow, Kenneth Joseph (b.1921), American economist, noted chiefly for his work on general economic equilibrium and social choice. Nobel Prize for Economics (1972).

arrow ▶ **noun** a weapon consisting of a thin, straight stick with a sharp point, designed to be shot from a bow.
■a mark or sign resembling such a weapon, used to show direction or position: *we followed a series of arrows.*
▶**verb** [no obj., with adverbial of direction] move or appear to move swiftly and directly, like an arrow shot from a bow: *lights* ***arrowed down*** *into the airport.*
– PHRASES **arrow of time** (or **time's arrow**) the direction of travel from past to future in time considered as a physical dimension.
– DERIVATIVES **arrowy** adjective.
– ORIGIN Old English *arewe, arwe*, from Old Norse.

arrowed ▶ **adjective** having marks or signs resembling an arrow: *the jackets were striped and arrowed.*

arrowgrass ▶ **noun** [mass noun] a grass-like marsh plant with a slender spike of tiny flowers.
• Genus *Triglochin*, family Juncaginaceae.

arrowhead ▶ **noun 1** the pointed end of an arrow.
■a decorative device resembling this. ■Geometry a quadrilateral in which one internal angle is more than 180°.
2 a Eurasian water plant with arrow-shaped leaves above the water surface.
• Genus *Sagittaria*, family Alismataceae: several species, in particular the common European *S. sagittaria*.

arrow rest ▶ **noun** Archery a small shelf fixed to a bow on which to support an arrow when shooting.

arrowroot ▶ **noun** a herbaceous Caribbean plant from which a starch is prepared.
• *Maranta arundinacea*, family Marantaceae.
■[mass noun] the fine-grained starch obtained from this plant, used in cookery and medicine.
– ORIGIN late 17th cent.: alteration of Arawak *aru-aru* (literally 'meal of meals') by association with **ARROW** and **ROOT**[1], the tubers being used to absorb poison from arrow wounds.

arrow slit ▶ **noun** (especially in a medieval fortified building) a narrow vertical slit in a wall for shooting or looking through or to admit light and air.

arrow-straight ▶ **adjective** & **adverb** completely straight: [as adj.] *the roads are empty and arrow-straight* | [as adv.] *an index leads you arrow-straight to documents of interest.*
■[as adv.] in a direct or undeviating manner; unswervingly: *an index at the back leads the reader arrow-straight to documents of interest.*

arrow worm ▶ **noun** a slender transparent worm-like animal with fins, having spines on the head for grasping prey. It is common in marine plankton. Also called ***chaetognath***.
• Phylum Chaetognatha.

arroyo /əˈrɔɪəʊ/ ▶ **noun** (pl. **-os**) a steep-sided gully cut by running water in an arid or semi-arid region, found chiefly in the south-western US.
– ORIGIN mid 19th cent.: from Spanish.

arroz /aˈrɒs, Spanish aˈroθ, aˈros/ ▶ **noun** Spanish word for **RICE**, used in the names of various dishes.

arse Brit. vulgar slang ▶ **noun** a person's buttocks or anus.
■a stupid, irritating, or contemptible person.
▶**verb 1** [no obj.] (**arse about/around**) behave in a stupid way; waste time.
2 (**can't/couldn't be arsed**) not want to do something because one has no interest in or enthusiasm for it.
– PHRASES **arse about face** contrary to what is usual, expected, or logical. **arse over tit** so as to fall over in a sudden or dramatic way. **get off one's arse** stop being lazy. **my arse** used to convey that one does not believe something that has just been said. **not know one's arse from one's elbow** be totally ignorant or incompetent. **a pain in the arse** see **PAIN**. **talk out of one's arse** talk rubbish. **up your arse** used to express contempt for someone or something.
– ORIGIN Old English *ærs*, of Germanic origin; related to Dutch *aars* and German *Arsch*.

arse bandit ▶ **noun** Brit. vulgar slang a male homosexual.

arsehole ▶ **noun** vulgar slang the anus.
■a stupid, irritating, or contemptible person.

arse-kissing ▶ **noun** another term for **ARSE-LICKING**.
– DERIVATIVES **arse-kisser** noun.

arse-licking ▶ **noun** [mass noun] vulgar slang the action or practice of behaving obsequiously in order to gain favour.
– DERIVATIVES **arse-licker** noun.

arsenal ▶ **noun** a collection of weapons and military equipment stored by a country, person, or group: *Britain's nuclear arsenal.*
■a place where weapons and military equipment are stored or made. ■[in sing.] figurative an array of resources available for a certain purpose: *we have an arsenal of computers at our disposal.*
– ORIGIN early 16th cent. (denoting a dock for the construction and repair of ships): from French, or from obsolete Italian *arzanale*, based on Arabic *dār-aṣ-ṣinā'a*, from *dār* 'house' + *al-* '(of) the' + *ṣinā'a* 'art, industry'.

arsenic ▶ **noun** /ˈɑːs(ə)nɪk/ [mass noun] the chemical element of atomic number 33, a brittle steel-grey semimetal. (Symbol: **As**)

Arsenic compounds (and their poisonous properties) have been known since ancient times, and the metallic form was isolated in the Middle Ages. Arsenic occurs naturally in orpiment, realgar, and other minerals, and rarely as the free element. Arsenic is used in semiconductors and some specialized alloys; its toxic compounds are widely used as herbicides and pesticides.

▶**adjective** /ɑːˈsɛnɪk/ of or relating to arsenic.
■Chemistry of arsenic with a valency of five; of arsenic(V). Compare with **ARSENIOUS**.
– ORIGIN late Middle English (denoting yellow orpiment, arsenic sulphide): via Old French from Latin *arsenicum*, from Greek *arsenikon* 'yellow orpiment', identified with *arsenikos* 'male', but in fact from Arabic *al-zarnīḵ* 'the orpiment', based on Persian *zar* 'gold'.

arsenic acid ▶ **noun** [mass noun] Chemistry a weakly acidic crystalline solid with oxidizing properties, formed when arsenic reacts with nitric acid.
• Chem. formula: H_3AsO_4.
– DERIVATIVES **arsenate** noun.

arsenical /ɑːˈsɛnɪk(ə)l/ ▶ **adjective** of or containing arsenic.
▶**noun** (usu. **arsenicals**) an arsenical drug or other compound.

arsenide ▶ **noun** Chemistry a binary compound of arsenic with a metallic element.

arsenious /ɑːˈsiːnɪəs/ ▶ **adjective** Chemistry of arsenic with a valency of three; of arsenic(III). Compare with **ARSENIC**.

arsenopyrite /ˌɑːs(ə)nəʊˈpʌɪrʌɪt/ ▶ **noun** [mass noun] a silvery-grey mineral consisting of an arsenide and sulphide of iron and cobalt.

arsey (also **arsie**) ▶ **adjective** Austral. informal very lucky.
– ORIGIN 1950s: alteration of slang *tin arse* 'lucky person', from *tin* 'money', figuratively 'luck'.

arsine /ˈɑːsiːn/ ▶ **noun** [mass noun] Chemistry a poisonous gas smelling slightly of garlic, made by the reaction of some arsenides with acids.
• Alternative name: **arsenic trihydride**; chem. formula: AsH_3.
– ORIGIN late 19th cent.: from **ARSENIC**, on the pattern of *amine*.

arsis /ˈɑːsɪs/ ▶ **noun** (pl. **arses** /-siːz/) Prosody a stressed syllable or part of a metrical foot in Greek or Latin verse. Often contrasted with **THESIS** (in sense 3).
– ORIGIN late Middle English: via late Latin from Greek, literally 'lifting', from *airein* 'raise'.

arson ▶ **noun** [mass noun] the criminal act of deliberately setting fire to property: *police are treating the fire as arson* | [as modifier] *an arson attack.*
– DERIVATIVES **arsonist** noun.
– ORIGIN late 17th cent.: an Anglo-Norman French legal term, from medieval Latin *arsio(n-)*, from Latin *ardere* 'to burn'.

arsphenamine /ɑːsˈfɛnəmiːn, -ɪn/ ▶ **noun** [mass noun] Medicine a synthetic organic arsenic compound formerly used to treat syphilis and other diseases. See also **EHRLICH**.
– ORIGIN early 20th cent.: blend of **ARSENIC**, **PHENYL**, and **AMINE**.

arsy-versy ▶ **adjective** & **adverb** informal in a confused, disordered, or perversely contrary state or manner: [as adj.] *the whole place was arsy-versy* | *they got things all arsy-versy.*
– ORIGIN mid 16th cent.: from **ARSE** + Latin *versus* 'turned', the addition of **-Y**[1] to both elements forming a jingle.

art[1] ▶ **noun 1** [mass noun] the expression or application of human creative skill and imagination, typically in a visual form such as painting or sculpture, producing works to be appreciated primarily for their beauty or emotional power: *the art of the Renaissance* | *great art is concerned with moral imperfections* | *she studied art in Paris.*
■works produced by such skill and imagination: *his collection of modern art* | *an exhibition of Tibetan art* | [as modifier] *an art critic.* ■creative activity resulting in the production of paintings, drawings, or sculpture: *she's good at art.*
2 (**the arts**) the various branches of creative activity, such as painting, music, literature, and dance: *the visual arts* | [in sing.] *the art of photography.*
3 (**arts**) subjects of study primarily concerned with the processes and products of human creativity and social life, such as languages, literature, and history (as contrasted with scientific or technical subjects): *the belief that the arts and sciences were incompatible* | *the Faculty of Arts.*
4 a skill at doing a specified thing, typically one acquired through practice: *the art of conversation.*
– PHRASES **art for art's sake** used to convey the idea that the chief or only aim of a work of art is the self-expression of the individual artist who creates it. **art is long, life is short** proverb there is so much knowledge to acquire that a lifetime is not sufficient. **art of war** the strategy, tactics, and techniques of combat.
– ORIGIN Middle English: via Old French from Latin *ars, art-*.

art[2] archaic or dialect second person singular present of **BE**.

art. ▶ **abbreviation for** article.

Artaud /ɑːˈtəʊ, French aʀto/, Antonin (1896–1948), French actor, director, and poet. He developed the concept of the non-verbal Theatre of Cruelty, which concentrated on the use of sound, mime, and lighting, expounding his theory in a series of essays *Le Théâtre et son double* (1938).

Artaxerxes /ˌɑːtəˈzəːksiːz/ the name of three kings of ancient Persia:
■Artaxerxes I son of Xerxes I, reigned 464–424 BC.
■Artaxerxes II son of Darius II, reigned 404–358 BC.
■Artaxerxes III son of Artaxerxes II, reigned 358–338 BC.

art deco /ˈdɛkəʊ/ ▶ **noun** [mass noun] the predominant decorative art style of the 1920s and 1930s, characterized by precise and boldly delineated geometric shapes and strong colours and used most notably in household objects and in architecture.
– ORIGIN 1960s: shortened from French *art décoratif* 'decorative art', from the 1925 *Exposition des Arts décoratifs* in Paris.

artefact /ˈɑːtɪfakt/ (US **artifact**) ▶ **noun 1** an object made by a human being, typically one of cultural or historical interest: *gold and silver artefacts.*
■Archaeology such an object as distinguished from a similar object naturally produced.
2 something observed in a scientific investigation or experiment that is not naturally present but occurs as a result of the preparative or investigative procedure.
– DERIVATIVES **artefactual** adjective.
– ORIGIN early 19th cent.: from Latin *arte* 'by or using art' + *factum* 'something made' (neuter past participle of *facere* 'make').

artel /ɑːˈtɛl/ ▶ **noun** (pl. **artels, arteli**) historical (in pre-revolutionary Russia) a cooperative association of craftsmen living and working together.
– ORIGIN from Russian *artel'*.

Artemis /ˈɑːtɪmɪs/ Greek Mythology a goddess, daughter of Zeus and sister of Apollo. She was a huntress and is typically depicted with a bow and arrows. Roman equivalent **DIANA**.

artemisia /ˌɑːtɪˈmɪzɪə/ ▶ **noun** an aromatic or bitter-tasting plant of a genus that includes wormwood, mugwort, and sagebrush. Several kinds are used in herbal medicine and many are cultivated for their feathery grey foliage.
• Genus *Artemisia*, family Compositae.
– ORIGIN Middle English: via Latin from Greek, 'wormwood', named after the goddess **ARTEMIS**, to whom it was sacred.

artemisinin /ˌɑːtɪˈmiːsɪnɪn/ ▶ **noun** [mass noun] a terpene-based antimalarial substance used in Chinese medicine.
• The drug is obtained from *Artemisia annua*, family Compositae.
– ORIGIN 1970s: blend of **ARTEMISIA** and **QUININE**.

Arte Povera /ˌɑːteɪ ˈpɒvərə/ ▶ **noun** [mass noun] an

artistic movement that originated in Italy in the 1960s, combining aspects of conceptual, minimalist, and performance art, and making use of worthless or common materials such as earth or newspaper, in the hope of subverting the commercialization of art.
– ORIGIN 1960s: Italian, literally 'impoverished art', from *arte* 'art' + *povera* (feminine of *povero* 'needy').

arterial /ɑːˈtɪərɪəl/ ▶ **adjective** of or relating to an artery or arteries.
■ denoting an important route in a system of roads, railway lines, or rivers: *one of the main arterial routes from York.*
– ORIGIN late Middle English: from medieval Latin *arterialis*, from Latin *arteria* (see **ARTERY**).

arterialize (also **-ise**) ▶ **verb** [with obj.] [usu. as adj. **arterialized**] convert venous into arterial (blood) by oxygenation, especially in the lungs.
– DERIVATIVES **arterialization** noun.

arterio- ▶ **combining form** of or relating to the arteries: *arteriosclerosis.*
– ORIGIN from Greek *artēria* (see **ARTERY**).

arteriography /ɑːˌtɪərɪˈɒɡrəfi/ ▶ **noun** [mass noun] Medicine radiography of an artery, carried out after injection of a radiopaque substance.

arteriole /ɑːˈtɪərɪəʊl/ ▶ **noun** Anatomy a small branch of an artery leading into capillaries.
– DERIVATIVES **arteriolar** adjective.
– ORIGIN mid 19th cent.: from French *artériole*, diminutive of *artère* (see **ARTERY**).

arteriosclerosis /ɑːˌtɪərɪəʊsklɪəˈrəʊsɪs, -sklə-/ ▶ **noun** [mass noun] Medicine the thickening and hardening of the walls of the arteries, occurring typically in old age.
– DERIVATIVES **arteriosclerotic** adjective.

arteriovenous /ɑːˌtɪərɪəʊˈviːnəs/ ▶ **adjective** Anatomy of, relating to, or affecting an artery and a vein.

arteritis ▶ **noun** [mass noun] Medicine inflammation of the walls of an artery.

artery ▶ **noun** (pl. **-ies**) any of the muscular-walled tubes forming part of the circulation system by which blood (mainly that which has been oxygenated) is conveyed from the heart to all parts of the body. Compare with **VEIN** (in sense 1).
■ an important route in a system of roads, rivers, or railway lines: *George Street, main artery of Edinburgh's Golden Mile.*
– ORIGIN late Middle English: from Latin *arteria*, from Greek *artēria*, probably from *airein* 'raise'.

artesian /ɑːˈtiːzɪən, -ʒ(ə)n/ ▶ **adjective** relating to or denoting a well bored perpendicularly into water-bearing strata lying at an angle, so that natural pressure produces a constant supply of water with little or no pumping.
– ORIGIN mid 19th cent.: from French *artésien* 'from Artois' (see **ARTOIS**), where such wells were first made.

Artex /ˈɑːtɛks/ ▶ **noun** [mass noun] trademark a kind of plaster applied to walls and ceilings to give a textured finish, typically in decorative patterns.
– ORIGIN 1950s: blend of **ART**[1] and **TEXTURE**.

art form ▶ **noun** a conventionally established form of artistic composition, such as the novel, sonata, or sonnet.
■ any activity regarded as a medium of imaginative or creative self-expression: *he elevates stage managing to an art form.*

artful ▶ **adjective** **1** (of a person or action) clever or skilful, especially in a crafty or cunning way: *her artful wiles.*
2 showing creative skill or taste: *an artful photograph of a striking woman.*
– DERIVATIVES **artfully** adverb, **artfulness** noun.

art history ▶ **noun** [mass noun] the academic study of the history and development of painting, sculpture, and the other visual arts.
– DERIVATIVES **art historian** noun, **art historical** adjective.

art house ▶ **noun** a cinema which specializes in showing films that are artistic or experimental rather than merely entertaining.

arthralgia /ɑːˈθraldʒə/ ▶ **noun** [mass noun] Medicine pain in a joint.
– ORIGIN mid 19th cent.: from Greek *arthron* 'joint' + **-ALGIA**.

arthritis /ɑːˈθrʌɪtɪs/ ▶ **noun** [mass noun] a disease causing painful inflammation and stiffness of the joints.
– DERIVATIVES **arthritic** adjective & noun.
– ORIGIN mid 16th cent.: via Latin from Greek, from *arthron* 'joint'. *Arthritic* was already used in late Middle English.

arthro- ▶ **combining form** of a joint; relating to joints: *arthroscope.*
– ORIGIN from Greek *arthron* 'joint'.

arthrodesis /ɑːˈθrɒdɪsɪs/ ▶ **noun** [mass noun] surgical immobilization of a joint by fusion of the bones.
– ORIGIN early 20th cent.: from **ARTHRO-** + Greek *desis* 'binding together'.

Arthropoda /ˌɑːθrəˈpəʊdə/ Zoology a large phylum of invertebrate animals that includes insects, spiders, crustaceans, and their relatives. They have a segmented body, an external skeleton, and jointed limbs, and are sometimes placed in different phyla.
– DERIVATIVES **arthropod** /ˈɑːθrəpɒd/ noun.
– ORIGIN modern Latin (plural), from Greek *arthron* 'joint' + *pous, pod-* 'foot'.

arthroscope /ˈɑːθrəskəʊp/ ▶ **noun** Medicine an instrument through which the interior of a joint may be inspected or operated on.
– DERIVATIVES **arthroscopic** adjective, **arthroscopy** noun.

Arthur[1] a legendary king of Britain, historically perhaps a 5th- or 6th-century Romano-British chieftain or general. Stories of his life, the exploits of his knights, and the Round Table of the court at Camelot were developed by Malory, Chrétien de Troyes, and other medieval writers and became the subject of many legends.
– DERIVATIVES **Arthurian** /ɑːˈθjʊərɪən/ adjective.

Arthur[2], Chester Alan (1830–86), American Republican statesman, 21st President of the US 1881–5.

artic /ˈɑːtɪk/ ▶ **noun** Brit. informal an articulated lorry.
– ORIGIN 1950s: abbreviation.

artichoke /ˈɑːtɪtʃəʊk/ ▶ **noun** **1** (also **globe artichoke**) a European plant cultivated for its large thistle-like flower heads.
• *Cynara scolymus*, family Compositae.
■ the unopened flower head of this, of which the heart and the fleshy bases of the bracts are edible.
2 see **JERUSALEM ARTICHOKE**.
– ORIGIN mid 16th cent.: from northern Italian *articiocco*, from Spanish *alcarchofa*, from Arabic *al-karšūfa*.

artichoke gall ▶ **noun** a hard egg-shaped gall which forms inside an artichoke bud in response to the developing larva of a gall wasp.
• The wasp is *Andricus fecundator*, family Cynipidae.

article ▶ **noun** **1** a particular item or object, typically one of a specified type: *small household articles | articles of clothing.*
2 a piece of writing included with others in a newspaper, magazine, or other publication: *an article about middle-aged executives.*
3 a separate clause or paragraph of a legal document or agreement, typically one outlining a single rule or regulation.
■ (**articles**) a period of training with a firm as a solicitor, architect, surveyor, or accountant, according to the terms of a legal contract: *he is already **in articles** | it may be worth **taking articles** in a specialized firm.* ■ (**articles**) the terms on which crew members take service on a ship.
4 Grammar the definite or indefinite article. See also **DETERMINER** (sense 2).
▶ **verb** [with obj.] (usu. **be articled**) bind (a trainee solicitor, architect, surveyor, or accountant) to undergo a period of training with a firm in order to become qualified: *he was **articled to** a firm of solicitors in York.*
– PHRASES **an article of faith** a firmly held belief. **article of virtu** see **VIRTU**. **the finished article** something that is complete and ready for use. **the genuine article** a person or thing considered to be an authentic and excellent example of their kind.
– ORIGIN Middle English (denoting a separate clause of the Apostles' Creed): from Old French, from Latin *articulus* 'small connecting part', diminutive of *artus* 'joint'.

articled clerk ▶ **noun** Brit. a trainee solicitor.

articular /ɑːˈtɪkjʊlə/ ▶ **adjective** of or relating to a joint or the joints: *articular cartilage.*
– ORIGIN late Middle English: from Latin *articularis*, from *articulus* 'small connecting part' (see **ARTICLE**).

articulate ▶ **adjective** /ɑːˈtɪkjʊlət/ **1** (of a person or their words) having or showing the ability to speak fluently and coherently: *she was not very articulate.*
2 technical having joints or jointed segments.
■ Zoology denoting a brachiopod which has projections and sockets that form a hinge joining the two halves of the shell.
▶ **verb** /ɑːˈtɪkjʊleɪt/ **1** [with obj.] express (an idea or feeling) fluently and coherently: *they were unable to articulate their emotions.*
■ pronounce (something) clearly and distinctly: *he articulated each word with precision | [no obj.] people who do not articulate well are more difficult to lip-read.*
2 [no obj.] form a joint: *the mandible is a solid piece **articulating with** the head.*
■ (**be articulated**) be connected by joints: *the wing is articulated to the thorax.*
– DERIVATIVES **articulable** adjective, **articulacy** noun, **articulately** adverb, **articulateness** noun.
– ORIGIN mid 16th cent.: from Latin *articulatus*, past participle of *articulare* 'divide into joints, utter distinctly', from *articulus* 'small connecting part' (see **ARTICLE**).

articulated ▶ **adjective** **1** having two or more sections connected by a flexible joint: *an articulated lorry | the trilobite's thorax has a variable number of articulated segments.*
2 (of an idea or feeling) expressed; put into words: *the lack of a clearly articulated policy.*

articulation ▶ **noun** [mass noun] **1** the action of putting into words an idea or feeling of a specified type: *it would involve the articulation of a theory of the just war.*
■ the formation of clear and distinct sounds in speech: *the articulation of vowels and consonants.* ■ Music clarity in the production of successive notes. ■ Phonetics the formation of a speech sound by constriction of the air flow in the vocal organs at a particular place (e.g. the tongue, teeth, or palate) and in a particular way (as a plosive, affricate, etc.).
2 the state of being jointed: *the area of articulation of the lower jaw.*
■ [count noun] [with modifier] a specified joint: *the leg articulation.* ■ [count noun] figurative a connection or link between structures or systems: *an increased articulation between the formal and informal sectors.*
– ORIGIN late Middle English (in the senses 'joint', 'joining'): from Latin *articulatio(n-)*, from the verb *articulare* (see **ARTICULATE**).

articulator ▶ **noun** any of the vocal organs above the larynx, including the tongue, lips, teeth, and hard palate.

articulatory /ɑːˈtɪkjʊlət(ə)ri, ɑːˌtɪkjʊˈleɪt(ə)ri/ ▶ **adjective** [attrib.] of or relating to the formation of speech sounds.

artifact ▶ **noun** US spelling of **ARTEFACT**.

artifice /ˈɑːtɪfɪs/ ▶ **noun** [mass noun] clever or cunning devices or expedients, especially as used to trick or deceive others: *an industry dominated by artifice | [count noun] the style is not free from the artifices of the period.*
– ORIGIN late Middle English (in the sense 'workmanship'): from Old French, from Latin *artificium*, based on *ars, art-* 'art' + *facere* 'make'.

artificer /ɑːˈtɪfɪsə/ ▶ **noun** a skilled mechanic in the armed forces.
■ archaic a skilled craftsman or inventor.
– ORIGIN late Middle English: from Anglo-Norman French, probably an alteration of Old French *artificien*, from *artifice* (see **ARTIFICE**).

artificial ▶ **adjective** **1** made or produced by human beings rather than occurring naturally, especially as a copy of something natural: *her skin glowed in the artificial light | an artificial limb | artificial flowers.*
■ (of a situation or concept) not existing naturally; contrived or false: *the artificial division of people into age groups.* ■ Bridge (of a bid) conventional as opposed to natural.
2 (of a person or their behaviour or manner) insincere or affected: *she gave an artificial smile.*
– DERIVATIVES **artificiality** noun, **artificially** adverb.
– ORIGIN late Middle English: from Old French *artificiel* or Latin *artificialis*, from *artificium* 'handicraft' (see **ARTIFICE**).

artificial horizon ▶ **noun** a gyroscopic instrument or a fluid surface, typically one of mercury, used to provide the pilot of an aircraft with a horizontal reference plane for navigational measurement when the natural horizon is obscured.

artificial insemination (abbrev.: **AI**) ▶ **noun** [mass noun] the injection of semen into the vagina or uterus other than by sexual intercourse.

artificial intelligence (abbrev.: **AI**) ▶ **noun** [mass noun] the theory and development of computer systems able to perform tasks normally requiring human intelligence, such as visual perception, speech recognition, decision-making, and translation between languages.

artificial kidney ▶ **noun** a machine or other mechanical device which performs the functions of the human kidney.

artificial life ▶ **noun** [mass noun] the production or action of computer programs or computerized systems which simulate the behaviour, population dynamics, or other characteristics of living organisms.

artificial respiration ▶ **noun** [mass noun] the restoration or initiation of someone's breathing by manual, mechanical, or mouth-to-mouth methods.

artificial satellite ▶ **noun** another term for **SATELLITE** (in sense 1).

artificial silk ▶ **noun** old-fashioned term for **VISCOSE**.

artillery /ɑːˈtɪləri/ ▶ **noun** (pl. **-ies**) [mass noun] large-calibre guns used in warfare on land: *tanks and heavy artillery*.
▪a military detachment or branch of the armed forces that uses such guns.
– DERIVATIVES **artillerist** noun.
– ORIGIN late Middle English: from Old French *artillerie*, from *artiller*, alteration of *atillier* 'equip, arm', probably a variant of *atirier*, from *a-* (from Latin *ad* 'to, at') + *tire* 'rank, order'.

artilleryman ▶ **noun** (pl. **-men**) a member of a regiment of artillery.

Artiodactyla /ˌɑːtɪə(ʊ)ˈdaktɪlə/ Zoology an order of mammals that comprises the even-toed ungulates. Compare with **PERISSODACTYLA**.
– DERIVATIVES **artiodactyl** noun & adjective.
– ORIGIN modern Latin (plural), from Greek *artios* 'even' + *daktulos* 'finger, toe'.

artisan /ˌɑːtɪˈzan, ˈɑːtɪzan/ ▶ **noun** a worker in a skilled trade, especially one that involves making things by hand.
– DERIVATIVES **artisanal** adjective.
– ORIGIN mid 16th cent.: from French, from Italian *artigiano*, based on Latin *artitus*, past participle of *artire* 'instruct in the arts', from *ars, art-* 'art'.

artist ▶ **noun** a person who produces paintings or drawings as a profession or hobby.
▪a person who practises any of the various creative arts, such as a sculptor, novelist, poet, or film-maker. ▪ a person skilled at a particular task or occupation: *a surgeon who is an artist with the scalpel*. ▪ a performer such as a singer, actor, or dancer. ▪ informal [with modifier] a habitual practitioner of a specified reprehensible activity: *a con artist | rip-off artists*.
– ORIGIN early 16th cent. (denoting a master of the liberal arts): from French *artiste*, from Italian *artista*, from *arte* 'art', from Latin *ars, art-*.

artiste /ɑːˈtiːst/ ▶ **noun** a professional entertainer, especially a singer or dancer: *cabaret artistes*.
– ORIGIN early 19th cent.: from French (see **ARTIST**).

artistic ▶ **adjective** having or revealing natural creative skill: *my lack of artistic ability*.
▪of, relating to, or characteristic of art or artists: *a denial of artistic freedom | her artistic temperament*. ▪ aesthetically pleasing: *computer programs which produce artistic designs*.
– DERIVATIVES **artistically** adverb.

artistic director ▶ **noun** the person with overall responsibility for the selection and interpretation of the works performed by a theatre, ballet, or opera company.

artistry ▶ **noun** [mass noun] creative skill or ability: *the artistry of the pianist*.

artist's fungus ▶ **noun** a bracket fungus which has the shape of an artist's palette, with a reddish-brown upper surface, found in both Eurasia and North America.
• *Ganoderma applanatum*, family Ganodermataceae, class Hymenomycetes.

artless ▶ **adjective** without guile or deception: *an artless, naive girl | artless sincerity*.
▪without effort or pretentiousness; natural and simple: *an artless literary masterpiece*. ▪ without skill or finesse: *her awkward, artless prose*.
– DERIVATIVES **artlessly** adverb.

art nouveau /ˌɑː(t) nuːˈvəʊ/ ▶ **noun** [mass noun] a style of decorative art, architecture, and design prominent in western Europe and the USA from about 1890 until the First World War and characterized by intricate linear designs and flowing curves based on natural forms.
– ORIGIN early 20th cent.: from French, literally 'new art'.

Artois /ɑːˈtwʌ, French artwa/ a region and former province of NW France.

art paper ▶ **noun** [mass noun] Brit. high-quality paper coated with china clay or a similar substance to give it a smooth surface.

arts and crafts ▶ **plural noun** decorative design and handicraft.

Arts and Crafts Movement an English decorative arts movement of the second half of the 19th century which sought to revive the ideal of craftsmanship in an age of increasing mechanization and mass production. William Morris was its most prominent member.

art therapy ▶ **noun** [mass noun] a form of psychotherapy involving the encouragement of free self-expression through painting, drawing, or modelling, used as a remedial or diagnostic activity.

artwork ▶ **noun** [mass noun] illustrations, photographs, or other non-textual material prepared for inclusion in a publication.
▪paintings, drawings, or other artistic works: *a collection of artwork from tribal cultures* | [count noun] *each artwork is reproduced in colour on a full page*.

arty (chiefly N. Amer. also **artsy**) ▶ **adjective** (**artier**, **artiest**) informal making a strong, affected, or pretentious display of being artistic or interested in the arts: *television people and arty types | a very arty film*.
– DERIVATIVES **artiness** noun.

arty-crafty informal, chiefly Brit. ▶ **adjective** interested or involved in making decorative, artistic objects, especially ones perceived as quaint or homespun: *he mixed with the arty-crafty set*.

arty-farty (also **artsy-fartsy**) ▶ **adjective** informal, derogatory associated with or showing an interest in the arts: *you'll have to forget that arty-farty nonsense here*.

Aruba /əˈruːbə/ an island in the Caribbean Sea, close to the Venezuelan coast; pop. 60,000 (est. 1991); capital, Oranjestad. Formerly part of the Netherlands Antilles, it separated from that group in 1986 to become a self-governing territory of the Netherlands.

arugula /əˈruːgjʊlə/ (also **rucola**, **rugola**) ▶ **noun** [mass noun] N. Amer. the rocket plant, used in cookery.
– ORIGIN 1970s: from Italian dialect, ultimately a diminutive of Latin *eruca* 'down-stemmed plant'.

arum /ˈɛːrəm/ ▶ **noun** a European plant which has arrow-shaped leaves and a broad leafy spathe enclosing a club-shaped spadix. Pollination is by small flies which are temporarily trapped by the plant.
• Genus *Arum*, family Araceae (the **arum family**): several species, in particular the common **wild arum** or cuckoo pint. The arum family contains a number of popular house plants, such as the Swiss cheese plant, philodendrons, and arum lilies.
– ORIGIN late Middle English: from Latin, from Greek *aron*.

arum lily ▶ **noun** chiefly Brit. a tall lily-like African plant which bears a large showy spathe. Also called ***calla lily***, especially in North America.
• Genus *Zantedeschia*, family Araceae: several species, in particular *Z. aethiopica*, which, in Britain, is often associated with funerals.

Arunachal Pradesh /ɑːrəˌnɑːtʃəl prəˈdɛʃ/ a mountainous state in the far north-east of India, lying on the borders of Tibet to the north and Burma (Myanmar) to the east; capital, Itanagar. It became a state of India in 1986.

Arunta /əˈrʌntə, aˈruːndə/ ▶ **noun** variant spelling of **ARANDA**.

arvo /ˈɑːvəʊ/ ▶ **noun** (pl. **-os**) Austral./NZ informal afternoon: *four in the arvo*.
– ORIGIN 1930s: abbreviation of **AFTERNOON** (with voicing of the *f*) + **-O**.

-ary[1] ▶ **suffix 1** forming adjectives such as *budgetary, primary*.
2 forming nouns such as *dictionary, granary*.
– ORIGIN from French *-aire* or Latin *-arius* 'connected with'.

-ary[2] ▶ **suffix** forming adjectives such as *capillary, military*.
– ORIGIN from French *-aire* or Latin *-aris* 'relating to'.

Aryabhata I /ˌarɪəˈbɑːtə/, (476–*c*.550), Indian astronomer and mathematician. His surviving work, the *Aryabhatiya* (499), has sections dealing with mathematics, the measurement of time, planetary models, the sphere, and eclipses.

Aryan /ˈɛːrɪən/ ▶ **adjective** relating to or denoting a people speaking an Indo-European language who invaded northern India in the 2nd millennium BC, displacing the Dravidian and other aboriginal peoples.
▪old-fashioned term for **PROTO-INDO-EUROPEAN** or for **INDO-IRANIAN**. ▪ (in Nazi ideology) relating to or denoting people of Caucasian race not of Jewish descent.

The idea that there was an 'Aryan' race corresponding to the parent Indo-European language was proposed by certain 19th-century writers, and was taken up by Hitler and other proponents of racist ideology, but it has been generally rejected by scholars.

▶ **noun** a member of the ancient Aryan people.
▪[mass noun] the language of this people. ▪ (in Nazi ideology) a person of Caucasian race not of Jewish descent.
– ORIGIN from Sanskrit *ārya* 'noble' + **-AN**.

aryl /ˈarʌɪl, -rɪl/ ▶ **noun** [as modifier] Chemistry of or denoting a radical derived from an aromatic hydrocarbon by removal of a hydrogen atom: *aryl groups*.
– ORIGIN early 20th cent.: from **AROMATIC** + **-YL**.

arytenoid /ˌarɪˈtiːnɔɪd/ Anatomy ▶ **adjective** [attrib.] of, relating to, or denoting a pair of cartilages at the back of the larynx, used in the production of different kinds of voice quality (for example creaky voice).
▶ **noun** either of these cartilages.
– ORIGIN early 18th cent.: from modern Latin *arytaenoides*, from Greek *arutainoeidēs*, from *arutaina* 'funnel'.

AS ▶ **abbreviation for** Anglo-Saxon.

As ▶ **symbol for** the chemical element arsenic.

as[1] /az, əz/ ▶ **adverb** used in comparisons to refer to the extent or degree of something: *hailstones **as** big **as** tennis balls | it tasted like grape juice but not as sweet*.
▪used to emphasize an amount: ***as** many **as** twenty-two rare species may be at risk*.
▶ **conjunction 1** used to indicate that something happens during the time when something else is taking place: *Frank watched him as he ambled through the crowd | as she grew older, she kept more to herself*.
2 used to indicate by comparison the way that something happens or is done: *dress as you would if you were having guests | they can do as they wish | she kissed him goodbye, **as usual***.
▪used to add or interject a comment relating to the statement of a fact: *as you can see, I didn't go after all*.
3 because; since: *I must stop now as I have to go out*.
4 even though: *sweet as he is, he doesn't pay his bills | try as he might, he failed to pull it off*.
▶ **preposition 1** used to refer to the function or character that someone or something has: *it came as a shock | as prime minister, he is a target for terrorism*.
2 during the time of being (the thing specified): *he had often been ill as a child*.
– PHRASES **as and when** at the time when (used to refer to an uncertain future event): *they deal with an issue as and when it rears its head*. **as for** with regard to: *as for you, you'd better be quick*. **as from** (or **of**) chiefly Brit. used to indicate the time or date from which something starts: *as from 1 January, a free market will be created | I'm on the dole as from now*. **as if** (or **though**) as would be the case if: *she behaved as if he wasn't there*. **as if!** informal I very much doubt it: *You know how pools winners always say it won't change their lives? Yeah, as if*. **as (it) is** in the existing circumstances: *I've got enough on my plate as it is*. **as it were** in a way (used to be less precise): *areas which have been, as it were, pushed aside*. **as long as** see **LONG**[1]. **as much** see **MUCH**. **as of** see *as from* above. **as per** see **PER**. **as such** see **SUCH**. **as though** see *as if* above. **as to** with respect to; concerning: *decisions as to which patients receive treatment*. **as well** see **WELL**[1]. **as yet** [usu. with negative] until now or a particular time in the past: *the damage is as yet undetermined*. **as you do** Brit. used as an ironic comment on a previous statement: *She only acts part-time now: she prefers helping out with her hubby's real estate business. As you do.*

– ORIGIN Middle English: reduced form of Old English *alswā* 'similarly' (see **ALSO**).

USAGE For a discussion of whether it is correct to say *he's not as shy as I* rather than *he's not as shy as me* or *I live in the same street as she* rather than *I live in the same street as her* see usage at **PERSONAL PRONOUN**.

as² /as/ ▶ **noun** an ancient Roman copper coin.
– ORIGIN Latin, 'a unit'.

as- ▶ **prefix** variant spelling of **AD-** assimilated before *s* (as in *assemble, assess*).

ASA ▶ **abbreviation for** ■ Advertising Standards Authority. ■ Amateur Swimming Association. ■ American Standards Association (especially in film-speed specification): *colour film from 50 to 400 ASA*).

asafoetida /ˌasəˈfiːtɪdə, -ˈfɛt-/ (US **asafetida**) ▶ **noun** **1** [mass noun] a fetid resinous gum obtained from the roots of a herbaceous plant, used in herbal medicine and Indian cooking.
2 a Eurasian plant of the parsley family, from which this gum is obtained.
● *Ferula assa-foetida*, family Umbelliferae.
– ORIGIN late Middle English: from medieval Latin, from *asa* (from Persian *azā* 'mastic') + *foetida* (see **FETID**).

asana /ˈɑːsənə/ ▶ **noun** a posture adopted in performing hatha yoga.
– ORIGIN from Sanskrit *āsana*.

Asansol /ˌasənˈsəʊl/ an industrial city in NE India, in West Bengal, north-west of Calcutta; pop. 262,000 (1991).

Asante variant spelling of **ASHANTI**[1], **ASHANTI**[2].

asap ▶ **abbreviation for** as soon as possible.

asarabacca /ˈasərəˌbakə/ ▶ **noun** a low-growing European evergreen plant of the birthwort family, formerly used in medicine and as an ingredient in snuff.
● *Asarum europaeum*, family Aristolochiaceae.
– ORIGIN early 16th cent.: from Latin *asarum* (from Greek *asaron*), probably compounded with a shortened form of another name for the plant in Greek.

ASB ▶ **abbreviation for** Alternative Service Book.

asbestos /azˈbɛstɒs, as-, -təs/ ▶ **noun** [mass noun] a highly heat-resistant fibrous silicate mineral that can be woven into fabrics, and is used in brake linings and other fire-resistant and insulating materials.
■ fabric containing such a mineral.

The asbestos minerals include chrysotile (**white asbestos**) and several kinds of amphibole, notably amosite (**brown asbestos**) and crocidolite (**blue asbestos**). The danger to health caused by breathing in highly carcinogenic asbestos particles has led to more stringent control of its use.

– ORIGIN early 17th cent., via Latin from Greek *asbestos* 'unquenchable' (applied by Dioscurides to quicklime), from *a-* 'not' + *sbestos* (from *sbennumi* 'quench').

asbestosis /ˌazbɛˈstəʊsɪs, ˌas-/ ▶ **noun** [mass noun] a lung disease resulting from the inhalation of asbestos particles, marked by severe fibrosis and a high risk of mesothelioma (cancer of the pleura).

Ascalon /ˈaskələn/ ancient Greek name for **ASHQELON**.

ascariasis /ˌaskəˈrʌɪəsɪs/ ▶ **noun** [mass noun] Medicine infection of the intestine with ascarids.

ascarid /ˈaskərɪd/ (also **ascaris** /-rɪs/) ▶ **noun** Zoology a parasitic nematode worm of a family (Ascaridae) whose members typically live in the intestines of vertebrates.
– ORIGIN late 17th cent.: from modern Latin *Ascaridae* (plural), from Greek *askarides*, plural of *askaris* 'intestinal worm'.

ascend ▶ **verb** **1** [with obj.] go up or climb: *she ascended the stairs* | [no obj.] *we had ascended 3,000 ft.*
■ climb to the summit of (a mountain or hill): *the first traveller to ascend the mountain.* ■ (of a fish or boat) move upstream along (a river).
2 [no obj.] rise or move up through the air: *the lift ascended from his sight.*
■ (of a road or flight of steps) slope or lead up: *the road ascends to the loch.* ■ move up the social or professional scale: *he took exams to* ***ascend through*** *the ranks.* ■ (**ascend to**) rise to (an important position or a higher level): *some executives ascend to top-level positions.* ■ (**ascend to/into heaven**) (of a spiritual being or soul) go to heaven: *the Prophet ascended to heaven* | [as adj. **ascended**] *the risen and ascended Christ.* ■ (of a voice or sound) rise in pitch: *Carolyn's voice had ascended into high-pitched giggles.*
– PHRASES **ascend the throne** become king or queen.
– ORIGIN late Middle English: from Latin *ascendere*, from *ad-* 'to' + *scandere* 'to climb'.

ascendancy (also **ascendency**) ▶ **noun** [mass noun] occupation of a position of dominant power or influence: *the ascendancy of good over evil* | [count noun] *they have a moral ascendancy over the rich.*
■ short for **PROTESTANT ASCENDANCY**.

ascendant (also **ascendent**) ▶ **adjective** **1** rising in power or influence: *ascendant moderate factions in the party.*
2 Astrology (of a planet, zodiacal degree, or sign) on or close to the intersection of the ecliptic with the eastern horizon.
▶ **noun** Astrology the point on the ecliptic at which it intersects the eastern horizon at a particular time, typically that of a person's birth.
■ the point on a birth chart representing this.
– PHRASES **in the ascendant** rising in power or influence: *the reformers are in the ascendant.*
– ORIGIN late Middle English: via Old French from Latin *ascendent-* 'climbing up', from the verb *ascendere* (see **ASCEND**).

ascender ▶ **noun** a person or thing that ascends, in particular:
■ a part of a letter that extends above the level of the top of an *x* (as in *b* and *f*). ■ a letter having such a part. ■ Climbing a device which can be clipped to a rope to act as a foothold or handhold, or to keep something in position.

ascending ▶ **adjective** [attrib.] **1** increasing in size or importance: *incomes ranked* ***in ascending order*** *of size.*
2 sloping or leading upwards: *a gently ascending forest track* | *blood pressure in the ascending aorta.*

ascending colon ▶ **noun** Anatomy the first main part of the large intestine, which passes upwards from the caecum on the right side of the abdomen.

ascension ▶ **noun** [in sing.] the action of rising to an important position or a higher level: *his* ***ascension to*** *the ranks of pop star.*
■ (**Ascension**) the ascent of Christ into heaven on the fortieth day after the Resurrection.
– DERIVATIVES **ascensional** adjective.
– ORIGIN Middle English (referring to the ascent of Christ): via Old French from Latin *ascensio(n-)*, from the verb *ascendere* (see **ASCEND**).

Ascension Day ▶ **noun** the Thursday forty days after Easter, on which Christ's Ascension is celebrated in the Christian Church.

Ascension Island a small island in the South Atlantic, incorporated with St Helena, with which it is a dependency of the UK; pop. 1,007 (1988).

Ascensiontide ▶ **noun** the period of ten days from Ascension Day to Whitsun Eve.

ascent ▶ **noun** **1** a climb or walk to the summit of a mountain or hill: *the first ascent of the Matterhorn* | [mass noun] *the routes of ascent can be retraced.*
■ an upward slope or path that one may walk or climb: *the ascent grew steeper.*
2 [in sing.] an instance of rising or moving up through the air: *the first balloon ascent was in 1783.*
■ [in sing.] a rise to an important position or a higher level: *his* ***ascent to*** *power.*
– ORIGIN late 16th cent.: from **ASCEND**, on the pattern of the pair of *descend, descent*.

ascertain /ˌasəˈteɪn/ ▶ **verb** [with obj.] find (something) out for certain; make sure of: *an attempt to ascertain the cause of the accident* | [with clause] *management should* ***ascertain whether*** *adequate funding can be provided.*
– DERIVATIVES **ascertainable** adjective, **ascertainment** noun.
– ORIGIN late Middle English (in the sense 'assure, convince'): from Old French *acertener*, based on Latin *certus* 'settled, sure'.

ascesis /əˈsiːsɪs/ ▶ **noun** [mass noun] the practice of severe self-discipline, typically for religious reasons.
– ORIGIN late 19th cent.: from Greek *askēsis* 'training', from *askein* 'to exercise'.

ascetic /əˈsɛtɪk/ ▶ **adjective** characterized by or suggesting the practice of severe self-discipline and abstention from all forms of indulgence, typically for religious reasons: *an ascetic life of prayer, fasting, and manual labour* | *an ascetic face.*
▶ **noun** a person who practises such self-discipline and abstention.
– DERIVATIVES **ascetically** adverb, **asceticism** noun.
– ORIGIN mid 17th cent.: from medieval Latin *asceticus* or Greek *askētikos*, from *askētēs* 'monk', from *askein* 'to exercise'.

Ascham /ˈaskəm/, Roger (*c.*1515–68), English humanist scholar and writer, noted for his treatise on archery, *Toxophilus* (1545), and *The Scholemaster* (1570), a practical and influential tract on education.

aschelminth /ˈaʃhɛlmɪnθ, ˈask-/ ▶ **noun** (pl. **aschelminths** or **aschelminthes**) Zoology an invertebrate animal belonging to a group of phyla that are distinguished by the lack of a well-developed coelom and blood vessels. Most are minute worm-like animals, including the nematodes, rotifers, and water bears.
● Phylum Nematoda and about seven minor phyla, formerly placed in a phylum Aschelminthes.
– ORIGIN from modern Latin *Aschelminthes* (former phylum name), from Greek *askos* 'sac' + *helminth* 'worm' (from the former belief that animals of this group had a fluid-filled internal sac).

asci plural form of **ASCUS**.

ascidian /əˈsɪdɪən/ ▶ **noun** Zoology a sea squirt.
– ORIGIN mid 19th cent.: from modern Latin plural *Ascidia* (genus name), from Greek *askidion*, diminutive of *askos* 'wineskin'.

ASCII /ˈaski/ Computing ▶ **abbreviation for** American Standard Code for Information Interchange, a set of digital codes representing letters, numerals, and other symbols, widely used as a standard format in the transfer of text between computers.

ascites /əˈsʌɪtiːz/ ▶ **noun** [mass noun] Medicine the accumulation of fluid in the peritoneal cavity, causing abdominal swelling.
– DERIVATIVES **ascitic** adjective.
– ORIGIN late Middle English: via late Latin from Greek *askitēs*, from *askos* 'wineskin'.

Asclepius /əˈskliːpɪəs/ Greek Mythology a hero and god of healing, son of Apollo.

ascomycete /ˌaskəˈmʌɪsiːt/ ▶ **noun** (pl. **ascomycetes** /-ˈmʌɪsiːts, -mʌɪˈsiːtiːz/) Botany a fungus whose spores develop within asci. They include most moulds, mildews, and yeasts, the fungal component of most lichens, and a few large forms such as morels and truffles. Compare with **BASIDIOMYCETE**.
● Subdivision Ascomycotina (formerly class Ascomycetes): several classes.
– ORIGIN mid 19th cent.: from modern Latin *Ascomycetes* (former class name), from Greek *askos* 'sac' + *mukētes* 'fungi'.

ascon /ˈaskɒn/ ▶ **noun** Zoology a sponge of a grade of structure of the simplest type, in the form of a tube or bag lined with choanocytes. Compare with **LEUCON** and **SYCON**.
– DERIVATIVES **asconoid** adjective.
– ORIGIN late 19th cent.: modern Latin (genus name), from Greek *askos* 'bag'.

ascorbic acid /əˈskɔːbɪk/ ▶ **noun** [mass noun] a vitamin found particularly in citrus fruits and green vegetables. It is essential in maintaining healthy connective tissue, and is also thought to act as an antioxidant. Severe deficiency causes scurvy. Also called **VITAMIN C**.
● A lactone; chem. formula: $C_6H_8O_6$.
– DERIVATIVES **ascorbate** noun.
– ORIGIN 1930s: from **A-**[1] 'without' + medieval Latin *scorbutus* 'scurvy' + **-IC**.

Ascot a town in southern England, south-west of Windsor. Its racecourse is the site of an annual race meeting.

ascot (also **ascot tie**) ▶ **noun** a man's broad silk necktie.
– ORIGIN early 20th cent.: from the place name **ASCOT**, by association with formal dress at race meetings held there.

ascribe ▶ **verb** [with obj.] (**ascribe something to**) attribute something to (a cause): *he ascribed Jane's short temper to her upset stomach.*
■ (usu. **be ascribed to**) attribute (a text, quotation, or work of art) to a particular person or period: *a quotation ascribed to Thomas Cooper.* ■ (usu. **be ascribed to**) regard (a quality) as belonging to: *toughmindedness is a quality commonly ascribed to top bosses.*
– DERIVATIVES **ascribable** adjective.

– ORIGIN Middle English: from Latin *ascribere*, from *ad-* 'to' + *scribere* 'write'.

ascription ▶ noun the attribution of something to a cause: *an ascription of effect to cause.*
■ the attribution of a text, quotation, or work of art to a particular person or period: *her ascription of the text to Boccaccio* | [mass noun] *questions of authorial ascription.* ■ [mass noun] the action of regarding a quality as belonging to someone or something: *the ascription of special personal qualities to political leaders.* ■ a preacher's words ascribing praise to God at the end of a sermon.
– ORIGIN late 16th cent.: from Latin *ascriptio(n-)*, from the verb *ascribere* (see **ASCRIBE**).

ascus /ˈaskəs/ ▶ noun (pl. **asci** /ˈaskaɪ, -iː/) Botany a sac, typically cylindrical in shape, in which the spores of ascomycete fungi develop.
– ORIGIN mid 19th cent.: modern Latin, from Greek *askos* 'bag'.

asdic /ˈazdɪk/ ▶ noun [mass noun] chiefly Brit. an early form of sonar used to detect submarines.
– ORIGIN Second World War: acronym from *Allied Submarine Detection Investigation Committee*.

-ase ▶ suffix Biochemistry forming names of enzymes: *amylase.*
– ORIGIN from (di*ast*)*ase*.

ASEAN /ˈasɪən/ ▶ abbreviation for Association of South-East Asian Nations.

aseismic /eɪˈsʌɪzmɪk/ ▶ adjective Geology not characterized by earthquake activity.

asepsis /eɪˈsɛpsɪs/ ▶ noun [mass noun] the absence of bacteria, viruses, and other micro-organisms.
■ the exclusion of bacteria and other micro-organisms, typically during surgery. Compare with **ANTISEPSIS**.

aseptic ▶ adjective free from contamination caused by harmful bacteria, viruses, or other micro-organisms.
■ (of surgical practice) aiming at the complete exclusion of harmful micro-organisms. ■ (of a wound, instrument, or dressing) surgically sterile or sterilized.

asexual ▶ adjective without sex or sexuality, in particular:
■ Biology (of reproduction) not involving the fusion of gametes. ■ Biology without sex or sexual organs: *asexual parasites.* ■ without sexual feelings or associations: *she wore a grey frock, discreet and asexual.*
– DERIVATIVES **asexuality** noun, **asexually** adverb.

Asgard /ˈazɡɑːd/ Scandinavian Mythology a region in the centre of the universe, inhabited by the gods.

ASH ▶ abbreviation for (in the UK) Action on Smoking and Health.

ash[1] ▶ noun 1 [mass noun] the powdery residue left after the burning of a substance: *cigarette ash* | [count noun] *I turned over the ashes.*
■ [count noun] (**ashes**) the remains of the human body after cremation or burning. ■ the mineral component of an organic substance, as assessed from the residue left after burning: *coal contains higher levels of ash than premium fuels.*
2 (**the Ashes**) a trophy for the winner of a series of test matches in a cricket season between England and Australia. [ORIGIN: from a mock obituary notice published in the *Sporting Times* (2 September 1882), with reference to the symbolical remains of English cricket being taken to Australia after a sensational victory by the Australians at the Oval.]
▶ verb [with obj.] (usu. **be ashed**) burn to ash, typically for chemical analysis.
■ cover or sprinkle with ash.
– PHRASES (**turn to**) **ashes in one's mouth** (become) something that is bitterly disappointing or worthless. **rise** (or **emerge**) **from the ashes** be renewed after destruction. [ORIGIN: compare with *rise like a phoenix from the ashes* (see **PHOENIX**).]
– ORIGIN Old English *æsce, aexe*, of Germanic origin; related to Dutch *as* and German *Asche*.

ash[2] ▶ noun 1 (also **ash tree**) a tree with compound leaves, winged fruits, and hard pale timber. It is widely distributed throughout north temperate regions.
● Genus *Fraxinus*, family Oleaceae: many species, especially the **common** (or **European**) ash (*F. excelsior*).
■ used in names of unrelated trees with similar leaves, e.g. **mountain ash**.
2 an Old English runic letter, ⊦. [ORIGIN: so named from the word of which it was the first letter.]
■ the symbol æ or Æ, used in the Roman alphabet in place of the runic letter and as a phonetic symbol. See also **Æ**.

– ORIGIN Old English *æsc*, of Germanic origin; related to Dutch *es* and German *Esche*.

ashamed ▶ adjective [predic.] embarrassed or guilty because of something one has done or characteristics one has: *you should be ashamed of yourself* | [with clause] *she felt ashamed that she had hit him.*
■ [with infinitive] reluctant to do something through fear of embarrassment or humiliation: *I'm ashamed to say I followed him home* | *I am not ashamed to be seen with them.* ■ embarrassed or humiliated to be associated with a person: *his clothes and manners made us ashamed of him.*
– DERIVATIVES **ashamedly** adverb.
– ORIGIN Old English *āscamod*, past participle of *āscamian* 'feel shame', from *ā-* (as an intensifier) + the verb **SHAME**.

Ashanti[1] /əˈʃanti/ (also **Asante**) a region of central Ghana. It was annexed by Britain in 1902, becoming part of the former British colony of the Gold Coast.

Ashanti[2] /əˈʃanti/ (also **Asante**) ▶ noun (pl. same) 1 a member of a people of south central Ghana.
2 [mass noun] the dialect of Akan spoken by this people.
▶ adjective relating to or denoting this people or their language.
– ORIGIN the name in Akan.

ash blonde (also **ash blond**) ▶ adjective (of a person or their hair) very pale blonde.
▶ noun [mass noun] a very pale blonde colour.
■ [count noun] a person with hair of such a colour.

ashcan ▶ noun US a dustbin.

Ashcan School a group of American realist painters active from *c*.1908 until the First World War, who painted scenes from the slums of New York. The school grew out of the group called 'the Eight'.

Ashcroft, Dame Peggy (1907–91), English actress; born *Edith Margaret Emily Ashcroft*. She made her name on the stage with a number of Shakespearean roles, and won an Oscar for best supporting actress in the film *A Passage to India* (1984).

Ashdod /ˈaʃdɒd/ a seaport on the Mediterranean coast of Israel, situated to the south of Tel Aviv; pop. 103,600 (est. 1993).

Ashdown, Sir Paddy (b.1941), British Liberal Democrat politician, born in India; full name *Jeremy John Durham Ashdown*. He became the first leader of the Liberal Democrats (originally the Social and Liberal Democrats) in 1988, resigning in 1999.

Ashe, Arthur (Robert) (1943–93), American tennis player. He won the US Open championship in 1968 and Wimbledon in 1975, and was the first black male player to achieve world rankings.

ashen[1] ▶ adjective of the pale grey colour of ash: *the ashen morning sky.*
■ (of a person's face) very pale with shock, fear, or illness. ■ of or resembling ashes: *the volcano's ashen breath.*

ashen[2] ▶ adjective archaic or poetic/literary made of timber from the ash tree.

ashen-faced ▶ adjective very pale with shock, fear, or illness.

Asher /ˈaʃə/ (in the Bible) a Hebrew patriarch, son of Jacob and Zilpah (Gen. 30:12, 13).
■ the tribe of Israel traditionally descended from him.

ashet /ˈaʃɪt/ ▶ noun Scottish & N. English a large plate or dish.
– ORIGIN mid 16th cent.: from French *assiette*.

Ashgabat /ˈaʃɡəbat/ (also **Ashkhabad**) the capital of the central Asian republic of Turkmenistan; pop. 407,200 (1990). Former name (1919–27) **POLTORATSK**.

ashine ▶ adjective [predic.] poetic/literary shining: *eyes ashine in the darkness.*

Ashkelon variant spelling of **ASHQELON**.

Ashkenazi /ˌaʃkəˈnɑːzi/ ▶ noun (pl. **Ashkenazim** /-zɪm/) a Jew of central or eastern European descent. More than 80 per cent of Jews today are Ashkenazim; they preserve Palestinian rather than Babylonian Jewish traditions and some still use Yiddish. Compare with **SEPHARDI**.
– DERIVATIVES **Ashkenazic** adjective.
– ORIGIN from modern Hebrew, from *Ashkenaz*, grandson of Japheth, one of the sons of Noah (Gen. 10:3).

Ashkenazy /ˌaʃkəˈnɑːzi/, Vladimir (Davidovich)

(b.1937), Russian-born pianist. A child prodigy, he left the Soviet Union in 1963, finally settling in Iceland in 1973.

ash key ▶ noun Brit. the winged fruit of an ash tree, growing in clusters resembling bunches of keys.

Ashkhabad /ˌaʃkəˈbad/ variant spelling of **ASHGABAT**.

ashlar /ˈaʃlə/ ▶ noun [mass noun] masonry made of large square-cut stones, typically used as a facing on walls of brick or stone rubble.
■ [count noun] a stone used in such masonry.
– ORIGIN Middle English: from Old French *aisselier* from Latin *axilla*, diminutive of *axis* 'plank'.

ashlaring ▶ noun [mass noun] 1 ashlar masonry.
2 upright boarding fixed from the joists to the rafters of an attic to cut off the acute angle between the roof and the floor.

Ashley, Laura (1925–85), Welsh fashion and textile designer, known for her use of floral patterns and romantic Victorian and Edwardian styles.

Ashmole, Elias (1617–92), English antiquary. His collection of rarities, presented to Oxford University in 1677, formed the nucleus of the Ashmolean Museum.

Ashmolean Museum /aʃˈməʊlɪən/ a museum of art and antiquities in Oxford. It opened in 1683 and was the first public institution of its kind in England.

Ashmore and Cartier Islands /ˈaʃmɔː, ˈkɑːtɪeɪ/ an external territory of Australia in the Indian Ocean, comprising the uninhabited Ashmore Reef and Cartier Islands.

Ashoka /əˈʃəʊkə/ variant spelling of **ASOKA**.

ashore ▶ adverb to or on the shore or land from the direction of the sea: *the seals come ashore to breed.*
■ on land as opposed to at sea: *we spent the day ashore.*

ash pan ▶ noun a tray fitted beneath a grate in which ashes can be collected and removed.

ashplant ▶ noun a sapling from an ash tree, typically used as a walking stick.

Ashqelon /ˈaʃkələn/ (also **Ashkelon**) an ancient Mediterranean city, situated to the south of modern Tel Aviv, in Israel. Greek name **ASCALON**.

ashram /ˈaʃrəm/ ▶ noun (in the Indian subcontinent) a hermitage, monastic community, or other place of religious retreat.
■ a place of religious retreat or community life modelled on the Indian ashram.
– ORIGIN from Sanskrit *āśrama* 'hermitage'.

ashrama /ˈaʃrəmə/ ▶ noun Hinduism any of the four stages of an ideal life, ascending from the status of pupil to the total renunciation of the world.
– ORIGIN from Sanskrit *āśrama*.

Ash Shariqah /ˌaʃ ʃɑːˈriːkə/ Arabic name for **SHARJAH**.

Ashton, Sir Frederick (William Mallandaine) (1904–88), British ballet dancer, choreographer, and director. As a choreographer he created successful new works as well as popular adaptations of classical ballets.

ashtray ▶ noun a small receptacle for tobacco ash and cigarette ends.

Ashur /ˈaʃʊə/ variant spelling of **ASSUR**.

Ashurbanipal /ˌaʃʊəˈbanɪpal, -ˈbanɪpɑːl/, king of Assyria *c*.668–627 BC, grandson of Sennacherib. A patron of the arts, he established a library of more than 20,000 clay tablets at Nineveh.

Ash Wednesday ▶ noun the first day of Lent in the Western Christian Church, marked by services of penitence.
– ORIGIN from the custom of marking the foreheads of penitents with ashes on that day.

ashy ▶ adjective 1 of a pale greyish colour; ashen: *the ashy shadows of the mountains.*
2 covered with, consisting of, or resembling ashes: *an ashy sediment.*

ASI ▶ abbreviation for airspeed indicator.

Asia /ˈeɪʃə, -ʒə/ the largest of the world's continents, constituting nearly one third of the land mass, lying entirely north of the equator except for some SE Asian islands. It is connected to Africa by the Isthmus of Suez, and borders Europe (part of the same land mass) along the Ural Mountains and across the Caspian Sea.

Asia Minor the western peninsula of Asia, which now constitutes the bulk of modern Turkey.

Asian /ˈeɪʃ(ə)n, -ʒ(ə)n/ ▶ **adjective** of or relating to Asia or its people, customs, or languages.
▶ **noun** a native of Asia or a person of Asian descent.
– ORIGIN late Middle English: from Latin *Asianus*, from Greek *Asianos*, from *Asia* (see **ASIA**).

USAGE In Britain **Asian** is used to refer to people who come from (or whose parents came from) the Indian subcontinent, while in North America it is used to refer to people from the Far East.

Asian American ▶ **noun** an American who is of Asian (chiefly Far Eastern) descent.
▶ **adjective** of or relating to such people.

Asian Development Bank a bank with forty-seven member countries (thirty-two are from the Asia-Pacific region) located in Manila. Its aim is to promote the economic and social progress of its developing member countries.

Asian elephant ▶ **noun** another term for **INDIAN ELEPHANT**.

Asian pear ▶ **noun** another term for **NASHI**.

Asia-Pacific (also **Asia-Pacific region**) ▶ **noun** a business region consisting of the whole of Asia as well as the countries of the Pacific Rim.

Asiatic /ˌeɪʃɪˈatɪk, ˌeɪzɪ-/ ▶ **adjective** relating to or deriving from Asia: *Asiatic coastal regions*.
▶ **noun** offensive an Asian person.
– ORIGIN via Latin *Asiaticus* from Greek *Asiatikos*, from *Asia* (see **ASIA**).

USAGE The standard and accepted term when referring to individual people is **Asian** rather than **Asiatic**, which can be offensive. However, **Asiatic** is standard in scientific and technical use, for example in biological and anthropological classifications. See **usage** at **ASIAN**.

ASIC Electronics ▶ **abbreviation for** application specific integrated circuit.

A-side ▶ **noun** the side of a pop single regarded as the main one.

aside ▶ **adverb** to one side; out of the way: *he pushed his plate aside | they stood aside to let a car pass | she must put aside all her antagonistic feelings*.
■ in reserve; for future use: *she set aside some money for rent*. ■ used to indicate that one is dismissing something from consideration or that one is shifting from one topic or tone of discussion to another: *joking aside, I've certainly had my fill*.
▶ **noun 1** a remark or passage in a play spoken by an actor that is intended to be heard by the audience but is supposed to be unheard by the other characters in the play.
■ a remark not intended to be heard by everyone present: *'Does that make him a murderer?' whispered Alice in an aside to Fred*.
2 a remark that is not directly related to the main topic of discussion: *the recipe book has little asides about the importance of home and family*.
– PHRASES **aside from** apart from. **set something aside 1** remove land from agricultural production for fallow or other use. **2** annul a legal decision or process. **take** (or **draw**) **someone aside** move someone away from a group of people in order to talk to them privately.
– ORIGIN Middle English (originally *on side*): see **A**², **SIDE**.

Asimov /ˈazɪmɒf/, Isaac (1920–92), Russian-born American writer and scientist, particularly known for his works of science fiction and books on science for non-scientists. Notable science-fiction works: *I, Robot* (1950) and *Foundation* (trilogy, 1951–3).

asinine /ˈasɪnʌɪn/ ▶ **adjective** extremely stupid or foolish: *Lydia ignored his asinine remark*.
– DERIVATIVES **asininity** noun.
– ORIGIN late 15th cent.: from Latin *asininus*, from *asinus* 'ass'.

Asir Mountains /əˈsɪə/ a range of mountains in SW Saudi Arabia, running parallel to the Red Sea.

-asis (often **-iasis**) ▶ **suffix** forming the names of diseases: *onchocerciasis | psoriasis*.
– ORIGIN via Latin from Greek.

asity /ˈasɪti/ ▶ **noun** (pl. **-ies**) a stocky perching bird related to the pittas, found only in Madagascar.
● Family Philepittidae: two genera, in particular *Philepitta* (two species). See also **FALSE SUNBIRD**.
– ORIGIN probably a local word.

ask ▶ **verb 1** [reporting verb] say something in order to obtain an answer or some information: [with obj. and clause] *I **asked** her **what** she meant* | [with obj.] *people are always asking questions* | [with direct speech] *'How much further?' I asked* | [no obj.] *the old man **asked about** her job*.
■ [no obj.] (**ask around**) talk to different people in order to find out something: *there are fine meals to be had if you ask around*. ■ [no obj.] (**ask after** or Scottish **for**) enquire about the health or well-being of: *if I see him I'll tell him you were asking after him*.
2 [with obj.] request (someone) to do or give something: *Mary **asked** her father **for** money* | [with obj. and infinitive] *I asked him to call the manager* | [no obj.] *don't be afraid to **ask for** advice*.
■ [with clause] request permission to do something: *she **asked if** she could move in* | [with infinitive] *he asked to see the officer involved*. ■ request (permission) of someone. ■ [no obj.] (**ask for**) request to speak to: *when I arrived I asked for Katrina*. ■ request (a specified amount) as a price for selling something: *he was **asking** £250 **for** the guitar*. ■ expect or demand (something) of someone: *it's asking a lot, but could you look through Billy's things?*
3 [with obj.] invite someone to (one's home or a function): *it's about time we **asked** Pam **to** dinner | she **asked** him **round for** a drink*.
■ (**ask someone along**) invite someone to join one on an outing, typically with a group of others: *do you want to ask him along?* ■ (**ask someone out**) invite someone out socially, especially on a date.
▶ **noun** [in sing.] chiefly N. Amer. the price at which an item, especially a financial security, is offered for sale: [as modifier] *ask prices for bonds*.
– PHRASES **ask me another** informal used to indicate that one does not know the answer to a question: *'What do they quarrel about?' queried Ruth. 'Ask me another.'* **be asking for trouble** (or **it**) informal behave in a way that is likely to result in difficulty for oneself. **a big ask** Austral./NZ informal a difficult demand to fulfil. **don't ask me!** informal used to indicate that one does not know the answer to a question and that one is surprised or irritated to be questioned. **for the asking** used to indicate that someone can easily have something if they want it: *the job was his for the asking*. **I ask you!** informal an exclamation of shock or disapproval intended to elicit agreement from one's listener: *ringing me up on Christmas Day, I ask you!* **if you ask me** informal used to emphasize that a statement is one's personal opinion: *if you ask me, it's just an excuse for laziness*.
– DERIVATIVES **asker** noun.
– ORIGIN Old English *āscian, āhsian, āxian*, of West Germanic origin.

askance /əˈskans, əˈskɑːns/ (also **askant** /-ˈskant, -ˈskɑːnt/) ▶ **adverb** with an attitude or look of suspicion or disapproval: *the reformers **looked askance** at the mystical tradition | a waiter **looked askance at** his jeans*.
– ORIGIN late 15th cent.: of unknown origin.

askari /əˈskɑːri/ ▶ **noun** (pl. same or **askaris**) (in East Africa) a soldier or police officer.
– ORIGIN late 19th cent.: from Arabic *ʿaskarī* 'soldier'.

askew /əˈskjuː/ ▶ **adverb** & **adjective** not in a straight or level position: [as adv.] *the door was hanging askew on one twisted hinge* | [as predic. adj.] *her hat was slightly askew*.
■ figurative wrong; awry: [as adv.] *the plan went sadly askew* | [as predic. adj.] *the judging was a bit askew*.
– ORIGIN mid 16th cent.: from **A-**² 'on' + **SKEW**.

Askey /ˈaski/, Arthur (Bowden) (1900–82), English comedian and actor.

asking price ▶ **noun** the price at which something is offered for sale.

ASL ▶ **abbreviation for** American Sign Language.

aslant ▶ **adverb** at an angle or in a sloping direction: *some of the paintings hung aslant*.
▶ **preposition** across at an angle or in a sloping direction: *rays of light fell aslant a door*.

asleep ▶ **adjective** & **adverb** in or into a state of sleep: [as adj.] *she had been asleep for over three hours* | [as adv.] *a man lay asleep*.
■ not attentive or alert; inactive: [as adj.] *the competition was not asleep*. ■ (of a limb) having no feeling; numb: [as adj.] *his legs were asleep*. ■ poetic/literary used euphemistically to indicate that someone is dead.
– PHRASES **asleep at the switch** N. Amer. informal not attentive or alert; inactive: *our industry is asleep at the switch*.

ASLEF /ˈazlɛf/ ▶ **abbreviation for** (in the UK) Associated Society of Locomotive Engineers and Firemen.

AS level ▶ **noun** (in the UK except Scotland) an examination or pass at advanced subsidiary level.

aslope ▶ **adjective** & **adverb** archaic or poetic/literary in a sloping position: [as adj.] *the steps are aslope and broken* | [as adv.] *against the mast he leans aslope*.
– ORIGIN late Middle English: origin uncertain; this form appears earlier than **SLOPE**.

ASM ▶ **abbreviation for** ■ air-to-surface missile. ■ assistant stage manager.

Asmara /asˈmɑːrə/ (also **Asmera** /-ˈmɛːrə/) the capital of Eritrea; pop. 358,000 (est. 1990).

asocial ▶ **adjective** avoiding social interaction; inconsiderate of or hostile to others: *a tendency to asocial behaviour*.

Asoka /əˈsəʊkə/ (also **Ashoka**) (died *c.*232 BC), emperor of India *c.*269–232 BC. He converted to Buddhism and established it as the state religion.

Asoka Chakra /ˈtʃʌkrə/ the wheel on the Indian flag, designed after a wheel on a column set up by the Emperor Asoka.

Asoka pillar a pillar with four lions on the capital, built by the Emperor Asoka at Sarnath in Uttar Pradesh to mark the spot where the Buddha publicly preached his doctrine, and adopted as a symbol by the government of India.

asp /asp/ ▶ **noun 1** (also **asp viper**) a small southern European viper with an upturned snout.
● *Vipera aspis*, family Viperidae.
■ another term for **EGYPTIAN COBRA**.
2 a large predatory Eurasian freshwater fish of the carp family.
● *Aspius aspius*, family Cyprinidae.
– ORIGIN Middle English: from Latin *aspis*, from Greek.

asparagine /əˈsparədʒiːn/ ▶ **noun** [mass noun] Biochemistry a hydrophilic amino acid which is a constituent of most proteins.
● An amide of aspartic acid; chem. formula: $CONH_2CH_2CH(NH_2)COOH$.
– ORIGIN early 19th cent.: from **ASPARAGUS** (which contains it) + **-INE**⁴.

asparagus /əˈsparəgəs/ ▶ **noun** a tall plant of the lily family with fine feathery foliage, cultivated for its edible shoots.
● *Asparagus officinalis*, family Liliaceae.
■ [mass noun] the tender young shoots of this plant, eaten as a vegetable and considered a delicacy.
– ORIGIN mid 16th cent.: via Latin from Greek *asparagos*.

asparagus beetle ▶ **noun** a small boldly marked leaf beetle whose adults and larvae both feed on the leaves of asparagus.
● *Crioceris asparagi*, family Chrysomelidae.

asparagus fern ▶ **noun** a decorative indoor or greenhouse plant with feathery foliage, which is related to the edible asparagus.
● Genus *Asparagus*, family Liliaceae: several species, in particular *A. plumosus*.

asparagus pea ▶ **noun** a pea plant which has edible cylindrical pods with four longitudinal wavy flanges.
● *Tetragonolobus* (or *Lotus*) *purpurea*, family Leguminosae.

aspartame /əˈspɑːteɪm/ ▶ **noun** [mass noun] a very sweet substance used as an artificial sweetener, chiefly in low-calorie products. It is a derivative of aspartic acid and phenylalanine.

aspartic acid /əˈspɑːtɪk/ ▶ **noun** [mass noun] Biochemistry an acidic amino acid which is a constituent of most proteins, and also occurs in sugar cane. It is important in the metabolism of nitrogen in animals, and also acts as a neurotransmitter.
● Chem. formula: $COOHCH_2CH(NH_2)COOH$.
– DERIVATIVES **aspartate** noun.
– ORIGIN mid 19th cent.: *aspartic* from French *aspartique*, formed arbitrarily from Latin *asparagus* (see **ASPARAGUS**).

aspect ▶ **noun 1** a particular part or feature of something: *personal effectiveness in all aspects of life | the financial aspect can be overstressed*.
■ a particular way in which something may be considered: *from every aspect theirs was a changing world*. ■ [in sing., with modifier] a particular appearance or quality: *the air of desertion lent the place a sinister aspect* | [mass noun] *a man of decidedly foreign aspect*.
2 [usu. in sing.] the positioning of a building or thing in a particular direction: *a greenhouse with a southern aspect*.
■ the side of a building facing a particular direction: *the front aspect of the hotel was unremarkable*. ■ Astrology any of a number of particular angular relationships

between one celestial body or point on the ecliptic and another: *the sun in Aries formed an adverse aspect with Uranus in Capricorn.*
3 [mass noun] Grammar a grammatical category or form which expresses the way in which time is denoted by the verb: *the semantics of tense and aspect* | [count noun] *four verbal aspects.*

There are three aspects in English, the progressive or continuous aspect (expressing duration, typically using the auxiliary verb *be* with a form in *-ing*, as in *I was reading a book*), the perfect or perfective (expressing completed action, typically using the auxiliary verb *have* with a past participle, as in *I have read the book*), and unmarked aspect (as in *he reads books*).

▶**verb** [with obj.] (often **be aspected**) Astrology (of a planet) form an aspect with (another celestial body): *the sun is superbly aspected by your ruler Mars on the 19th.*
– DERIVATIVES **aspectual** adjective.
– ORIGIN late Middle English (denoting the action or a way of looking at something): from Latin *aspectus*, from *aspicere* 'look at', from *ad-* 'to, at' + *specere* 'to look'.

aspect ratio ▶**noun** the ratio of two dimensions of something as considered from a particular direction, in particular:
▪the ratio of the width to the height of the image on a television screen. ▪ Aeronautics the ratio of the span to the mean chord of an aerofoil.

Aspen a ski resort in south central Colorado; pop. 6,850 (1990).

aspen ▶**noun** a poplar tree with small rounded long-stalked leaves that tremble in the breeze.
• Genus *Populus*, family Salicaceae: several species, in particular the European *P. tremula* and the North American **quaking aspen** (*P. tremuloides*).
– ORIGIN late Middle English: from dialect *asp* (in the same sense) + **-EN**^{2}, forming an adjective later used as a noun (late 16th cent.).

Asperger's syndrome /ˈaspəːdʒə(r)z/ ▶**noun** [mass noun] Psychiatry a rare and relatively mild autistic disorder characterized by awkwardness in social interaction, pedantry in speech, and preoccupation with very narrow interests.
– ORIGIN named after Hans *Asperger* (1906–80), the Austrian psychiatrist who described the condition in 1944.

asperges /əˈspəːdʒiːz/ ▶**noun** [mass noun] Christian Church the rite of sprinkling holy water at the beginning of the Mass, still used occasionally in Catholic churches.
▪[count noun] another term for **ASPERGILLUM**.
– ORIGIN late 16th cent.: the first word of the Latin text of Psalms 50(51):9 (literally 'thou shalt purge'), recited before mass during the sprinkling of holy water.

aspergillosis /ˌaspədʒɪˈləʊsɪs/ ▶**noun** [mass noun] a condition in which certain fungi infect the tissues. It most commonly affects the lungs, owing to inhalation of spores from mouldy hay, and is then informally called **farmer's lung**.
• The fungi are blackish moulds of the genus *Aspergillus*, subdivision Deuteromycotina.
– ORIGIN late 19th cent.: from modern Latin *Aspergillus*, from **ASPERGILLUM**, + **-OSIS**.

aspergillum /ˌaspəˈdʒɪləm/ ▶**noun** (pl. **aspergilla** or **aspergillums**) an implement for sprinkling holy water.
– ORIGIN mid 17th cent.: from Latin.

asperity /əˈspɛrɪti/ ▶**noun** (pl. **-ies**) [mass noun] harshness of tone or manner: *he pointed this out with some asperity* | [count noun] *a faint asperity in his tone.*
▪[count noun] (**asperities**) harsh qualities or conditions: *the asperities of a harsh and divided society.* ▪ [count noun] (usu. **asperities**) a rough edge on a surface: *the asperities of the metal surfaces.*
– ORIGIN Middle English (in the sense 'hardship, rigour'): from Old French *asperite*, or Latin *asperitas*, from *asper* 'rough'.

aspermia /eɪˈspəːmɪə/ ▶**noun** [mass noun] Medicine failure to produce semen, or absence of sperms from the semen.

asperse /əˈspəːs/ ▶**verb** [with obj.] rare attack or criticize the reputation or integrity of: *he aspersed the place and its inhabitants.*
– ORIGIN late 15th cent. (in the sense 'spatter with liquid'): from Latin *aspers-* 'sprinkled', from the verb *aspergere*, from *ad-* 'to' + *spargere* 'sprinkle'.

aspersion /əˈspəːʃ(ə)n/ ▶**noun** (usu. **aspersions**) an attack on the reputation or integrity of someone or something: *I don't think anyone is* ***casting aspersions*** *on you.*
– ORIGIN late Middle English (denoting the sprinkling of water, especially at baptism): from Latin *aspersio(n-)*, from *aspergere* (see **ASPERSE**).

asphalt /ˈasfalt, -əlt/ ▶**noun** [mass noun] a mixture of dark bituminous pitch with sand or gravel, used for surfacing roads, flooring, roofing, etc.
▪the pitch used in this mixture, sometimes found in natural deposits but usually made by the distillation of crude oil.
▶**verb** [with obj.] surface with asphalt.
– DERIVATIVES **asphaltic** adjective.
– ORIGIN late Middle English: from French *asphalte*, based on late Latin *asphalton*, *asphaltum*, from Greek *asphalton*.

aspherical ▶**adjective** (especially of an optical lens) not spherical.
– DERIVATIVES **aspheric** adjective.

asphodel /ˈasfədɛl/ ▶**noun 1** a Eurasian plant of the lily family, typically having long slender leaves and flowers borne on a spike.
• Genera *Asphodelus* and *Asphodeline*, family Liliaceae. See also **BOG ASPHODEL**.
2 poetic/literary an everlasting flower said to grow in the Elysian fields.
– ORIGIN late Middle English: via Latin from Greek *asphodelos*; compare with **DAFFODIL**.

asphyxia /əsˈfɪksɪə/ ▶**noun** [mass noun] a condition arising when the body is deprived of oxygen, causing unconsciousness or death; suffocation.
– DERIVATIVES **asphyxial** adjective, **asphyxiant** adjective & noun.
– ORIGIN early 18th cent. (in the sense 'stopping of the pulse'): modern Latin, from Greek *asphuxia*, from *a-* 'without' + *sphuxis* 'pulse'.

asphyxiate ▶**verb** [with obj.] (usu. **be asphyxiated**) kill (someone) by depriving them of air: *they were asphyxiated by the carbon monoxide fumes* | [as adj. **asphyxiating**] figurative *the asphyxiating boredom of the good-taste gardener.*
▪[no obj.] die in this way: *they slowly asphyxiated.*
– DERIVATIVES **asphyxiation** noun, **asphyxiator** noun.

aspic ▶**noun** [mass noun] a savoury jelly made with meat stock, used as a garnish, or to contain pieces of food such as meat, seafood, or eggs, set in a mould.
– ORIGIN late 18th cent.: from French, literally 'asp', from the colours of the jelly as compared with those of the snake.

aspidistra /ˌaspɪˈdɪstrə/ ▶**noun** a bulbous plant of the lily family with broad tapering leaves, native to East Asia and widely grown as a house plant.
• Genus *Aspidistra*, family Liliaceae.
– ORIGIN early 19th cent.: modern Latin, from Greek *aspis, aspid-* 'shield' (because of the shape of the stigma), on the pattern of *Tupistra*, a related genus.

aspirant /əˈspʌɪər(ə)nt, ˈasp(ɪ)r-/ ▶**adjective** [attrib.] (of a person) having ambitions to achieve something, typically to follow a particular career: *an aspirant politician.*
▶**noun** a person who has ambitions to achieve something: ***an aspirant to*** *the throne.*
– ORIGIN mid 18th cent. (as a noun): from Latin *aspirant-* 'aspiring', from the verb *aspirare* (see **ASPIRE**).

aspirate ▶**verb** /ˈaspəreɪt/ [with obj.] **1** Phonetics pronounce (a sound) with an exhalation of breath: [as adj. **aspirated**] *the aspirated allophone of p occurs in 'pie'.*
▪[no obj.] pronounce the sound of *h* at the beginning of a word.
2 (usu. **be aspirated**) Medicine draw (fluid) by suction from a vessel or cavity.
▪draw fluid in such a way from (a vessel or cavity). ▪ breathe (something) in; inhale: *some drowning victims don't aspirate any water.*
3 [usu. as adj. **aspirated**] provide (an internal-combustion engine) with air: *the superchargers produce twice the power of standard aspirated engines.* See also **NORMALLY ASPIRATED**.
▶**noun** /ˈasp(ə)rət/ **1** Phonetics an aspirated consonant.
▪a sound of *h*.
2 [mass noun] Medicine matter that has been drawn from the body by aspiration: *gastric aspirate* | [count noun] *oesophageal aspirates.*
▶**adjective** /ˈasp(ə)rət/ Phonetics (of a sound) pronounced with an exhalation of breath; aspirated.
– ORIGIN mid 16th cent. (as an adjective): from Latin *aspiratus* 'breathed', past participle of *aspirare* (see **ASPIRE**).

aspiration ▶**noun 1** (usu. **aspirations**) a hope or ambition of achieving something: *the needs and aspirations of the people* | [mass noun] | *the yawning gulf between aspiration and reality.*
2 [mass noun] the action of pronouncing a sound with an exhalation of breath.
3 [mass noun] Medicine the action of drawing fluid by suction from a vessel or cavity.
– DERIVATIVES **aspirational** adjective (only in sense 1).
– ORIGIN late Middle English (in sense 2): from Latin *aspiratio(n-)*, from the verb *aspirare* (see **ASPIRE**).

aspirator ▶**noun** Medicine an instrument or apparatus for aspirating fluid from a vessel or cavity.

aspire ▶**verb** [no obj.] direct one's hopes or ambitions towards achieving something: *we never thought that we might* ***aspire to*** *those heights* | [with infinitive] *other people will aspire to be like you* | [as adj. **aspiring**] *an aspiring artist.*
▪poetic/literary rise high; tower.
– ORIGIN late Middle English: from French *aspirer* or Latin *aspirare*, from *ad-* 'to' + *spirare* 'breathe'.

aspirin ▶**noun** (pl. same or **aspirins**) [mass noun] a synthetic compound used medicinally to relieve mild or chronic pain and to reduce fever and inflammation.
• Alternative name: **acetylsalicylic acid**; chem. formula: $C_6H_4(OCOCH_3)COOH$.
▪[count noun] a tablet containing this.
– ORIGIN late 19th cent.: from German, from *acetylierte Spirsäure* 'acetylated salicylic acid' (the element *Spir-* being from the plant genus name *Spiraea*).

asportation ▶**noun** [mass noun] English Law, rare the detachment, movement, or carrying away of property, formerly an essential component of the crime of larceny.
– ORIGIN late 15th cent.: from Latin *asportatio(n-)*, from *asportare* 'carry away'.

asprawl ▶**adverb** & **adjective** sprawling: [as adv.] *he slipped on the greasy tiles and fell asprawl* | [as predic. adj.] *she lay, legs and arms asprawl.*

asp viper ▶**noun** see **ASP** (sense 1).

asquint ▶**adverb** & **adjective** with a glance to one side or from the corner of the eyes: [as adv.] *a woman* ***looked asquint at*** *me* | [as predic. adj.] *his bright eyes asquint with emotion.*
– ORIGIN Middle English: perhaps from **A-**^{2} 'on' + a Low German or Dutch word related to modern Dutch *schuinte* 'slant'.

Asquith /ˈaskwɪθ/, Herbert Henry, 1st Earl of Oxford and Asquith (1852–1928), British Liberal statesman, Prime Minister 1908–16.

ass^{1} /as/ ▶**noun 1** a hoofed mammal of the horse family, which is typically smaller than a horse and has longer ears and a braying call.
• Genus *Equus*, family Equidae: *E. africanus* of Africa, which is the ancestor of the domestic ass or donkey, and *E. hemionus* of Asia.
▪(in general use) a donkey.
2 informal a foolish or stupid person: *that ass of a young man.*
– ORIGIN Old English *assa*, from a Celtic word related to Welsh *asyn*, Breton *azen*, based on Latin *asinus*.
▶**make an ass of oneself** informal behave in a way that makes one look foolish or stupid.

ass^{2} /ɑːs, as/ ▶**noun** US vulgar slang a person's buttocks or anus.
▪[mass noun] women regarded as a source of sexual gratification. ▪ oneself (used in phrases for emphasis): *get your ass in here fast* | *the bureaucrat who wants everything in writing so as to cover his ass.*
– PHRASES **bust one's ass** try very hard to do something. **chew** (**someone's**) **ass** reprimand severely. **drag** (or **tear** or **haul**) **ass** hurry or move fast: *he better drag ass to get here.* **get your ass in** (or **into**) **gear** hurry: *if you get your ass in gear, you can make it out of here tonight.* **kick** (**some**) **ass** (or **kick someone's ass**) see **KICK**^{1}. **kiss ass** see **KISS**. **not give a rat's ass** not care at all about something. **a pain in the ass** see **PAIN**. **a piece of ass** see **PIECE**. **put** (or **have**) **someone's ass in a sling** get someone in trouble. **whip** (or **bust**) **someone's ass** use physical force to beat someone in a fight. **you bet your ass** you can be very sure: [with clause] *you can bet your ass I'll go for it every time.*

a

– DERIVATIVES **assed** adjective [in combination] *fat-assed guys.*

Assad /ˈasad/, Hafiz al- (1928–2000), Syrian Baath statesman, President 1971–2000.

assagai ▶ noun & verb variant spelling of **ASSEGAI**.

assai /aˈsʌɪ/ ▶ adverb [usu. postpositive as submodifier] Music (in directions) very: *allegro assai.*
– ORIGIN Italian, 'very much'.

assail /əˈseɪl/ ▶ verb [with obj.] make a concerted or violent attack on: *the Scots army assailed Edward's army from the rear.*
■ (usu. **be assailed**) (of an unpleasant feeling or physical sensation) come upon (someone) suddenly and strongly: *she was assailed by doubts and regrets.* ■ criticize (someone) strongly.
– DERIVATIVES **assailable** adjective.
– ORIGIN Middle English: from Old French *asaill-*, stressed stem of *asalir*, from medieval Latin *assalire*, from Latin *assilire*, from *ad-* 'to' + *salire* 'to leap'; compare with **ASSAULT**.

assailant ▶ noun a person who physically attacks another.

Assam /aˈsam/ a state in NE India; capital, Dispur. Most of the state lies in the valley of the Brahmaputra River; it is noted for the production of tea.

Assamese /ˌasəˈmiːz/ ▶ noun (pl. same) **1** a native or inhabitant of Assam.
2 [mass noun] the Indic language which is the official language of Assam. It is related to Bengali and is spoken by around 20 million people, roughly half in Assam and half in Bangladesh.
▶ adjective of or relating to Assam, its people, or their language.

assart /əˈsɑːt/ Brit. historical ▶ noun a piece of land converted from forest to arable use.
■ [mass noun] the action of so converting land.
▶ verb [with obj.] convert (forest or shrubland) to arable use.
– ORIGIN late Middle English (as a noun): from Old French *essarter*, from medieval Latin *ex(s)artare*, based on *ex* 'out' + *sar(r)ire* 'to weed'. The verb dates from the early 16th cent.

assassin /əˈsasɪn/ ▶ noun a murderer of an important person in a surprise attack for political or religious reasons.
■ (**Assassin**) historical a member of the Nizari branch of Ismaili Muslims at the time of the Crusades, when the newly established sect ruled part of northern Persia (1094–1256). They were renowned as militant fanatics, and were popularly reputed to use hashish before going on murder missions.
– ORIGIN mid 16th cent.: from French, or from medieval Latin *assassinus*, from Arabic *ḥašīšī* 'hashish-eater'.

assassinate ▶ verb [with obj.] (often **be assassinated**) murder (an important person) in a surprise attack for political or religious reasons.
– DERIVATIVES **assassination** noun.
– ORIGIN early 17th cent.: from medieval Latin *assassinat-* 'killed', from the verb *assassinare*, from *assassinus* (see **ASSASSIN**).

assassin bug ▶ noun a long-legged predatory or bloodsucking bug which occurs chiefly in the tropics and feeds mainly on other arthropods. Some of those that bite man can transmit micro-organisms such as that causing Chagas' disease.
● Family Reduviidae, suborder Heteroptera: numerous species, including the common European **heath assassin bug** (*Coranus subapterus*).

assault ▶ verb [with obj.] make a physical attack on: *he pleaded guilty to assaulting a police officer | she was sexually assaulted as a child.*
■ figurative attack or bombard (someone or the senses) with something undesirable or unpleasant: *thunder assaulted the ears.* ■ carry out a military attack or raid on (an enemy position).
▶ noun **1** a physical attack: *his imprisonment for an* ***assault on*** *the film director | a sexual assault.*
■ Law an act that threatens physical harm to a person, whether or not actual harm is done: *he admitted an assault and two thefts |* [mass noun] *he appeared in court charged with assault.* ■ a military attack or raid on an enemy position: *troops began an* ***assault on*** *the city |* [as modifier] *an assault boat.* ■ a strong verbal attack: *the* ***assault on*** *the party's tax policies.*
2 a concerted attempt to do something demanding: *a winter* ***assault on*** *Mt. Everest.*
– DERIVATIVES **assaulter** noun.
– ORIGIN Middle English: from Old French *asaut* (noun), *assauter* (verb), based on Latin *ad-* 'to' + *saltare*, frequentative of *salire* 'to leap'. Compare with **ASSAIL**.

assault and battery ▶ noun [mass noun] Law the action of threatening a person together with the action of making physical contact with them.

assault course ▶ noun Brit. a course through which the participants must run, negotiating obstacles to be climbed, crawled under, crossed on suspended ropes, etc., as used for training soldiers.

assaultive ▶ adjective tending or likely to commit an assault: *they found that assaultive men had abusive parents.*
■ extremely aggressive or forcefully assertive: *his loud, assaultive playing style can leave you cowering.*

assay /əˈseɪ, ˈaseɪ/ ▶ noun [mass noun] the testing of a metal or ore to determine its ingredients and quality: *submission of plate for assay.*
■ [count noun] a procedure for measuring the biochemical or immunological activity of a sample: *each assay was performed in duplicate |* [mass noun] *the results of sequential assay of serum were analysed | immunofluorescence assay.*
▶ verb [with obj.] **1** determine the content or quality of (a metal or ore).
■ determine the biochemical or immunological activity of (a sample): *cell contents were* ***assayed for*** *enzyme activity.* ■ examine (something) in order to assess its nature: *stepping inside, I quickly assayed the clientele.*
2 archaic attempt: *I assayed a little joke of mine on him.*
– DERIVATIVES **assayer** noun.
– ORIGIN Middle English (in the general sense 'testing, or a test of, the merit of someone or something'): from Old French *assai* (noun), *assaier* (verb), variant of *essai* 'trial', *essayer* 'to try' (see **ESSAY**).

assay office ▶ noun an establishment for the assaying of ores and metals.
■ Brit. an institution authorized to award hallmarks to articles made from precious metals. There are currently four in Britain, at London, Birmingham, Sheffield, and Edinburgh.

assegai /ˈasəgʌɪ/ (also **assagai**) ▶ noun (pl. **assegais**) **1** a slender, iron-tipped, hardwood spear used chiefly by southern African peoples.
2 (also **assegai wood**) a South African tree of the dogwood family, which yields hard timber.
● *Curtisia dentata*, family Cornaceae.
▶ verb (**assegaied**, **assegaing**) [with obj.] (often **be assegaied**) wound or kill with an assegai.
– ORIGIN early 17th cent.: from obsolete French *azagaie* or Portuguese *azagaia*, from Arabic *az-zaḡāyah*, from *az, al* 'the' + Berber *zaḡāyah* 'spear'.

assemblage ▶ noun a collection or gathering of things or people: *a loose assemblage of diverse groups.*
■ a machine or object made of pieces fitted together: *some vast assemblage of gears and cogs.* ■ a work of art made by grouping together found or unrelated objects. ■ [mass noun] the action of gathering or fitting things together.

assemble ▶ verb **1** [no obj.] (of people) gather together in one place for a common purpose: *a crowd had assembled outside the gates.*
■ [with obj.] cause (people or things) to gather together for a common purpose: *he assembled the surviving members of the group for a tour.* ■ [usu. as noun **assembling**] Entomology (of male moths) gather for mating in response to a pheromone released by a female.
2 [with obj.] fit together the separate component parts of (a machine or other object): *a factory that assembled parts for trucks.*
■ Computing translate (a program) from a symbolic language into machine code.
– ORIGIN Middle English: from Old French *asembler*, based on Latin *ad-* 'to' + *simul* 'together'.

assemblé /ˌasɒ̃ˈbleɪ/ ▶ noun (pl. pronounced same) Ballet a leap in which the feet are brought together before landing.

assembler ▶ noun **1** a person who assembles a machine or its parts.
2 Computing a program for converting instructions written in low-level symbolic code into machine code.
■ another term for **ASSEMBLY LANGUAGE**.

assembly ▶ noun (pl. **-ies**) **1** a group of people gathered together in one place for a common purpose: *an assembly of dockers and labourers.*
■ a group of such a type elected to make laws or decisions for a particular country or region.
2 [mass noun] the action of gathering together as a group for a common purpose: *a decree guaranteeing freedom of assembly.*
■ the regular gathering of the teachers and pupils of a school at the start or end of the day: *he was told off for talking in assembly.* ■ (usu. **the assembly**) chiefly historical a signal for troops to assemble, given by drum or bugle.
3 [mass noun] [often as modifier] the action of fitting together the component parts of a machine or other object: *a car assembly plant.*
■ [count noun] a unit consisting of components that have been fitted together: *the tail assembly of the aircraft.* ■ [usu. as modifier] Computing the conversion of instructions in low-level code to machine code by an assembler.
– ORIGIN Middle English: from Old French *asemblee*, feminine past participle of *asembler* (see **ASSEMBLE**).

assembly language ▶ noun Computing a low-level symbolic code converted by an assembler.

assembly line ▶ noun a series of workers and machines in a factory by which a succession of identical items is progressively assembled.

assembly room ▶ noun **1** (usu. **assembly rooms**) chiefly Brit. a public room or hall in which meetings or social functions are held.
2 another term for **ASSEMBLY SHOP**.

assembly shop ▶ noun a place where a machine or its components are assembled.

assent /əˈsɛnt/ ▶ noun [mass noun] the expression of approval or agreement: *a loud murmur of assent | he* ***nodded assent.***
■ official agreement or sanction: *the act was given the Royal Assent.*
▶ verb [no obj.] express approval or agreement, typically officially: *the Prime Minister assented to the change |* [with direct speech] *'Guest house, then,' Frank assented cheerfully.*
– ORIGIN Middle English: from Old French *as(s)enter* (verb), *as(s)ente* (noun), based on Latin *assentire*, from *ad-* 'towards' + *sentire* 'feel, think'.

assenter (also **assentor**) ▶ noun a person who assents to something, in particular:
■ (usu. **assentor**) Brit. any of the people, typically eight in number, other than the proposer and seconder who are required to sign the nomination papers for a candidate in parliamentary and some local government elections.

assentient /əˈsɛnʃ(ə)nt, -ʃɪənt/ archaic ▶ adjective assenting.
▶ noun a person who assents to something.
– ORIGIN mid 19th cent.: from Latin *assentient-* 'assenting', from the verb *assentire* (see **ASSENT**).

assert ▶ verb [reporting verb] state a fact or belief confidently and forcefully: [with clause] *the company asserts that the cuts will not affect development |* [with obj.] *he asserted his innocence |* [with direct speech] *'I don't know why she came,' he asserted.*
■ [with obj.] cause others to recognize (one's authority or a right) by confident and forceful behaviour: *the good librarian is able to assert authority when required.* ■ (**assert oneself**) behave or speak in a confident and forceful manner: *it was time to assert himself.*
– DERIVATIVES **asserter** (also **-or**) noun.
– ORIGIN early 17th cent.: from Latin *asserere* 'claim, affirm', from *ad-* 'to' + *serere* 'to join'.

assertion ▶ noun a confident and forceful statement of fact or belief: [with clause] *his assertion that his father had deserted the family.*
■ [mass noun] the action of stating something or exercising authority confidently and forcefully: *the assertion of his legal rights.*

assertive ▶ adjective having or showing a confident and forceful personality: *the job may call for assertive behaviour.*
– DERIVATIVES **assertively** adverb, **assertiveness** noun.

asses plural form of **AS**[2], **ASS**[1], **ASS**[2].

asses' bridge ▶ noun English term for **PONS ASINORUM**.

assess ▶ verb [with obj.] evaluate or estimate the nature, ability, or quality of: *the committee must assess the relative importance of the issues |* [with clause] *it is difficult to assess whether this is a new trend.*
■ (usu. **be assessed**) calculate or estimate the price or value of: *the damage was assessed at £5 billion.* ■ (usu. **be assessed**) set the value of a tax, fine, etc., for (a person or property) at a specified level: *all empty properties will be* ***assessed at*** *50 per cent.*
– DERIVATIVES **assessable** adjective.

– ORIGIN late Middle English: from Old French *assesser*, based on Latin *assidere* 'sit by' (in medieval Latin 'levy tax'), from *ad-* 'to, at' + *sedere* 'sit'. Compare with **ASSIZE**.

assessment ▶ **noun** [mass noun] the action of assessing someone or something: *the assessment of educational needs* | [count noun] *he made a rapid assessment of the situation* | *assessments of market value.*

assessor ▶ **noun** a person who assesses someone or something, in particular:
■ a person who judges the quality of performance, typically in an exam or coursework. ■ a person who calculates or estimates an amount to be paid or what something is worth, chiefly for tax or insurance purposes. ■ a person who is knowledgeable in a particular field and is called upon for advice, typically by a judge or committee of inquiry.
– ORIGIN late Middle English: from Old French *assessour*, from Latin *assessor* 'assistant judge' (in medieval Latin 'assessor of taxes'), from Latin *assidere* (see **ASSESS**).

asset ▶ **noun** a useful or valuable thing, person, or quality: *quick reflexes were his chief assets* | *the school is an asset to the community.*
■ (usu. **assets**) property owned by a person or company, regarded as having value and available to meet debts, commitments, or legacies: *growth in net assets* | [as modifier] *an asset scale.*
– ORIGIN mid 16th cent. (in the plural in the sense 'sufficient estate to allow discharge of a will'): from an Anglo-Norman French legal term, from Old French *asez* enough, based on Latin *ad* 'to' + *satis* 'enough'.

asset-backed ▶ **adjective** denoting securities having as collateral the return on a series of mortgages, credit agreements, or other forms of lending.

asset-stripping ▶ **noun** [mass noun] the practice of taking over a company in financial difficulties and selling each of its assets separately at a profit without regard for the company's future.
– DERIVATIVES **asset-stripper** noun.

asseveration /əˌsɛvəˈreɪʃ(ə)n/ ▶ **noun** [mass noun] the solemn or emphatic declaration or statement of something: *I fear that you offer only unsupported asseveration* | [count noun] *the dogmatic outlook marks many of his asseverations.*
– DERIVATIVES **asseverate** verb.
– ORIGIN mid 16th cent.: from Latin *asseveratio(n-)*, from the verb *asseverare*, from *ad-* 'to' + *severus* 'serious'.

asshole ▶ **noun** vulgar slang US spelling of **ARSEHOLE**.

assibilate /əˈsɪbɪleɪt/ ▶ **verb** [with obj.] Phonetics pronounce (a sound) as a sibilant or affricate ending in a sibilant (e.g. sound *t* as *ts*).
– DERIVATIVES **assibilation** noun.
– ORIGIN mid 19th cent.: from Latin *assibilat-* 'hissed at', from the verb *assibilare*, from *ad-* 'to' + *sibilare* 'to hiss'.

assiduity /ˌasɪˈdjuːɪti/ ▶ **noun** (pl. **-ies**) [mass noun] constant or close attention to what one is doing: *the assiduity with which he could wear down his opponents.*
■ [count noun] (**assiduities**) archaic or poetic/literary constant attentions to someone.
– ORIGIN late Middle English: from Latin *assiduitas*, from *assiduus* 'occupied with' (see **ASSIDUOUS**).

assiduous /əˈsɪdjʊəs/ ▶ **adjective** showing great care and perseverance: *she was* **assiduous in** *pointing out every feature.*
– DERIVATIVES **assiduously** adverb, **assiduousness** noun.
– ORIGIN mid 16th cent.: from Latin *assiduus*, from *assidere* 'be engaged in doing' (see **ASSESS**), + **-OUS**.

assign ▶ **verb** [with obj.] **1** allocate (a job or duty): *Congress had* **assigned** *the task* **to** *the agency* | [with two objs] *his leader assigned him this mission.*
■ (often **be assigned**) appoint (someone) to a particular job, task, or organization: *she has been* **assigned to** *a new job* | [with obj. and infinitive] *he was assigned to prosecute the case.*
2 designate or set (something) aside for a specific purpose: *managers happily* **assign** *large sums of money* **to** *travel budgets.*
■ (**assign something to**) attribute something as belonging to: *it is difficult to decide whether to assign the victory to Godwin.*
3 transfer (legal rights or liabilities): *they will ask you to assign your rights against the airline.*
▶ **noun** Law another term for **ASSIGNEE** (in sense 1).
– DERIVATIVES **assignable** adjective, **assigner** noun, **assignor** noun (only in sense 3 of the verb).
– ORIGIN Middle English: from Old French *asigner, assiner*, from Latin *assignare*, from *ad-* 'to' + *signare* 'to sign'.

assignation ▶ **noun 1** an appointment to meet someone in secret, typically one made by lovers: *his* **assignation with** *an older woman.*
2 [mass noun] the allocation or attribution of someone or something as belonging to something.
– ORIGIN late Middle English (in the senses 'command, appointment to office, or allotment of revenue'): via Old French from Latin *assignatio(n-)*, from the verb *assignare* (see **ASSIGN**).

assignee ▶ **noun** chiefly Law **1** a person to whom a right or liability is legally transferred.
2 a person appointed to act for another.
– ORIGIN Middle English: from Old French *assigne*, past participle of *assigner* 'allot' (see **ASSIGN**).

assignment ▶ **noun 1** a task or piece of work allocated to someone as part of a job or course of study: *a homework assignment.*
■ [mass noun] the allocation of a job or task to someone or the fact of being allocated a job or task: *the effective assignment of tasks* | *I was* **on assignment** *for a German magazine.*
2 [mass noun] the allocation or attribution of someone or something as belonging: *the* **assignment** *of individuals* **to** *particular social positions.*
3 an act of making a legal transfer of a right or liability: *an assignment of leasehold property.*
■ a document effecting such a transfer.
– ORIGIN late Middle English: from Old French *assignement*, from medieval Latin *assignamentum*, from Latin *assignare* 'allot' (see **ASSIGN**).

assimilate ▶ **verb** [with obj.] **1** take in and understand fully (information, ideas, or culture): *Marie tried to assimilate the week's events.*
■ (usu. **be assimilated**) absorb and integrate (people, ideas, or culture) into a wider society or culture: *pop trends are* **assimilated into** *the mainstream with alarming speed.* ■ [no obj.] become absorbed and integrated in this way: *the older generation had more trouble assimilating.* ■ absorb or integrate and use for one's own benefit: *the music business assimilated whatever aspects of punk it could turn into profit.* ■ (usu. **be assimilated**) (of the body or any biological system) absorb and digest (food or nutrients).
2 regard as similar; liken: *philosophers had* **assimilated** *thought* **to** *perception.*
■ [no obj.] become similar: *the churches* **assimilated to** *a certain cultural norm.* ■ Phonetics make (a sound) more like another in the same or next word.
– DERIVATIVES **assimilable** adjective, **assimilation** noun, **assimilative** adjective, **assimilator** noun, **assimilatory** adjective.
– ORIGIN late Middle English: from Latin *assimilat-* 'absorbed, incorporated', from the verb *assimilare*, from *ad-* 'to' + *similis* 'like'.

assimilationist ▶ **noun** a person who advocates or participates in racial or cultural integration.

Assisi[1] /əˈsiːsi/ a town in the region of Umbria in central Italy; pop. 24,790 (1990). It is famous as the birthplace of St Francis, whose tomb is located there.

Assisi[2] see **CLARE OF ASSISI, ST.**

Assisi[3] see **FRANCIS OF ASSISI, ST.**

assist ▶ **verb** [with obj.] help (someone), typically by doing a share of the work: *a senior academic would assist him in his work* | [with obj. and infinitive] *he assisted her to find employment* | [no obj.] *their presence would* **assist in** *keeping the peace.*
■ help by providing money or information: *they were assisting police with their inquiries* | [no obj.] *funds to* **assist with** *capital investment.* ■ [no obj.] be present as a helper: *two midwives who* **assisted at** *a water birth.*
▶ **noun** chiefly N. Amer. an act of help, typically by providing money: *the budget must have an assist from tax policies.*
■ (chiefly in ice hockey, basketball, or baseball) the act of touching the ball in a play in which a teammate scores or an opposing batter is put out: *Elliot had 10 points and five assists.* ■ [in combination] a mechanical device that provides help: *the implant is a ventricular-assist device.*
– DERIVATIVES **assister** noun.
– ORIGIN late Middle English: from Old French *assister*, from Latin *assistere* 'take one's stand by', from *ad-* 'to, at' + *sistere* 'take one's stand'.

assistance ▶ **noun** [mass noun] the provision of money, resources, or information to help someone: *schemes offering financial* **assistance to** *employers* | *she will be glad to give advice and assistance*
■ the action of helping someone with a job or task: *the work was completed* **with the assistance of** *carpenters.*
– PHRASES **be of assistance** be of practical use or help: *the guide will* **be of assistance to** *development groups.* **come to someone's assistance** act to help someone.
– ORIGIN late Middle English: from Old French, or from medieval Latin *assistentia*, from Latin *assistere* (see **ASSIST**).

assistant ▶ **noun** a person who ranks below a senior person: *the managing director and his assistant* | [as modifier] *an assistant manager.*
■ [with adj. or noun modifier] a person who helps in particular work: *a care assistant.*
– ORIGIN late Middle English: from Old French, or from medieval Latin *assistent-* 'taking one's stand beside', from the verb *assistere* (see **ASSIST**).

assistant professor ▶ **noun** N. Amer. a university teacher ranking immediately below an associate professor.

assistantship ▶ **noun** N. Amer. a paid academic appointment made to a graduate student that involves part-time teaching or research.

assisted area ▶ **noun** (in the UK) a region receiving government grants or loans for industrial development.

assisted place ▶ **noun** (in the UK) a place in an independent school for a pupil whose fees are wholly or partially subsidized by the state.

assisted suicide ▶ **noun** [mass noun] the suicide of a patient suffering from an incurable disease, effected by the taking of lethal drugs provided by a doctor for this purpose.

assize /əˈsʌɪz/ ▶ **noun** (usu. **assizes**) historical a court which formerly sat at intervals in each county of England and Wales to administer the civil and criminal law. In 1972 the civil jurisdiction of assizes was transferred to the High Court, and the criminal jurisdiction to the Crown Court.
– ORIGIN Middle English: from Old French *assise*, feminine past participle of *asseeir* 'sit, settle, assess', from Latin *assidere* (see **ASSESS**).

ass-kissing ▶ **noun** [mass noun] N. Amer. vulgar slang obsequious behaviour in order to gain favour.
– DERIVATIVES **ass-kisser** noun.

ass-licking ▶ **noun** vulgar slang US spelling of **ARSE-LICKING**.

Assoc. ▶ **abbreviation for** (as part of a title) Association.

associate ▶ **verb** /əˈsəʊʃɪeɪt, -sɪeɪt/ [with obj.] connect (someone or something) with something else in one's mind: *I* **associated** *wealth* **with** *freedom.*
■ (usu. **be associated**) connect (something) with something else because they occur together or one produces the other: *the environmental problems* **associated with** *nuclear waste.* ■ (**associate oneself with**) allow oneself to be connected with or seen to be supportive of: *I cannot associate myself with some of the language used.* ■ (**be associated with**) be involved with. ■ [no obj.] meet or have dealings with someone regarded with disapproval: *she began* **associating with** *socialists.*
▶ **noun** /əˈsəʊʃɪət, -sɪət/ **1** a partner or companion in business or at work: *a close associate of the Minister.*
2 a person with limited or subordinate membership of an organization.
3 chiefly Psychology a concept connected with another.
▶ **adjective** /əˈsəʊʃɪət, -sɪət/ [attrib.] joined or connected with an organization or business: *an associate company.*
■ denoting shared function or membership but with a lesser status: *the associate director of the academy.*
– DERIVATIVES **associability** noun, **associable** adjective, **associateship** noun, **associator** noun.
– ORIGIN late Middle English (as a verb in the sense 'join with in a common purpose'; as an adjective in the sense 'allied'): from Latin *associat-* 'joined', from the verb *associare*, from *ad-* 'to' + *socius* 'sharing, allied'.

associated ▶ **adjective** (of a person or thing) connected with something else: *two associated events.*
■ (of a company) connected or amalgamated with another company or companies. ■ Chemistry (of liquids) in which the molecules are held together by hydrogen bonding or other weak interaction.

Associated Press (abbrev.: **AP**) an international news agency based in New York City.

associate professor ▶ **noun** N. Amer. an academic ranking immediately below full professor.

association ▶ **noun 1** (often in names) a group of people organized for a joint purpose: *the National Association of Probation Officers.*
■Ecology a stable plant community including a characteristic group of dominant plant species.
2 a connection or cooperative link between people or organizations: *he developed a close **association with** the university* | [mass noun] *the programme was promoted **in association with** the Department of Music.*
■[mass noun] the action or state of becoming a member of an organization with subordinate status: [as modifier] *an association agreement between Bulgaria and the EC.* ■Chemistry the linking of molecules through hydrogen bonding or other interaction short of full bond formation.
3 (usu. **associations**) a mental connection between ideas or things: *the word bureaucracy has unpleasant associations.*
■[mass noun] the action of making such a connection: *the association of alchemy with 'hieroglyphics' and 'cabala.'* ■[mass noun] the fact of occurring with something else; co-occurrence: *cases of cancer found **in association with** colitis.*
– DERIVATIVES **associational** adjective.
– ORIGIN mid 16th cent. (in the sense 'uniting in a common purpose'): from medieval Latin *associatio(n-)*, from Latin *associare* 'to unite, ally' (see **ASSOCIATE**).

association area ▶ **noun** Anatomy a region of the cortex of the brain which connects sensory and motor areas, and which is thought to be concerned with higher mental activities.

Association Football ▶ **noun** [mass noun] more formal term for **SOCCER**.

associationism ▶ **noun** [mass noun] a theory in philosophy or psychology which regards the simple association or co-occurrence of ideas or sensations as the primary basis of meaning, thought, or learning.
– DERIVATIVES **associationist** noun & adjective.

Association of South-East Asian Nations (abbrev.: **ASEAN**) a regional organization intended to promote economic cooperation and now comprising the countries of Indonesia, Malaysia, the Philippines, Singapore, Thailand, Vietnam, and Brunei.

associative ▶ **adjective 1** of or involving the action of associating ideas or things.
■[attrib.] Computing of or denoting computer storage in which items are identified by content rather than by address.
2 Mathematics involving the condition that a group of quantities connected by operators gives the same result whatever their grouping, i.e. in whichever order the operations are performed, as long as the order of the quantities remains the same, e.g. $(a \times b) \times c = a \times (b \times c)$.

assonance /ˈas(ə)nəns/ ▶ **noun** [mass noun] the resemblance of sound between syllables in nearby words, arising particularly from the rhyming of two or more stressed vowels, but not consonants (e.g. *sonnet, porridge*), but also from the use of identical consonants with different vowels (e.g. *killed, cold, culled*).
– DERIVATIVES **assonant** adjective, **assonate** /-neɪt/ verb.
– ORIGIN early 18th cent.: from French, from Latin *assonare* 'respond to', from *ad-* 'to' + *sonare* (from *sonus* 'sound').

assort ▶ **verb 1** [no obj.] Genetics (of genes or characteristics) become distributed among cells or progeny.
2 [with obj.] archaic place in a group; classify: *he would **assort** it **with** the fabulous dogs as a monstrous invention.*
– ORIGIN late 15th cent.: from Old French *assorter*, from *a-* (from Latin *ad* 'to, at') + *sorte* 'sort, kind'.

assortative ▶ **adjective** denoting or involving the preferential mating of animals or marriage between people with similar characteristics.

assorted ▶ **adjective** [attrib.] of various sorts put together; miscellaneous: *bowls in assorted colours.*

assortment ▶ **noun** a miscellaneous collection of things or people: *the room was filled with **an assortment of** clothes.*

ASSR historical ▶ **abbreviation for** Autonomous Soviet Socialist Republic.

Asst ▶ **abbreviation for** Assistant.

assuage /əˈsweɪdʒ/ ▶ **verb** [with obj.] make (an unpleasant feeling) less intense: *the letter assuaged the fears of most members.*
■satisfy (an appetite or desire): *an opportunity occurred to assuage her desire for knowledge.*
– DERIVATIVES **assuagement** noun.
– ORIGIN Middle English: from Old French *assouagier, asouagier*, based on Latin *ad-* 'to' (expressing change) + *suavis* 'sweet'.

As Sulaymaniyah /as/ full name of **SULAYMANIYAH**.

assume ▶ **verb** [with obj.] **1** suppose to be the case, without proof: *topics which assume detailed knowledge of local events* | [with clause] *it is reasonable to assume that such changes have significant social effects* | [with obj. and infinitive] *they were assumed to be foreign.*
2 take or begin to have (power or responsibility): *he assumed full responsibility for all organizational work.*
■seize (power or control).
3 begin to have (a quality, appearance, or extent): *militant activity had assumed epidemic proportions.*
■adopt falsely: *Oliver assumed an expression of penitence* | [as adj. **assumed**] *a man living under an assumed name.*
– DERIVATIVES **assumable** adjective, **assumedly** adverb.
– ORIGIN late Middle English: from Latin *assumere*, from *ad-* 'towards' + *sumere* 'take'.

assuming ▶ **conjunction** used for the purpose of argument to indicate a premise on which a statement can be based: ***assuming that** the treaty is ratified, what is its relevance?*
▶ **adjective** archaic arrogant or presumptuous.

assumption ▶ **noun 1** a thing that is accepted as true or as certain to happen, without proof: *they made certain assumptions about the market* | [with clause] *we're working on the assumption that the time of death was after midnight.*
2 [mass noun] the action of taking or beginning to take power or responsibility.
3 (**Assumption**) the reception of the Virgin Mary bodily into heaven. This was formally declared a doctrine of the Roman Catholic Church in 1950. See also **DORMITION**.
■the feast in honour of this, celebrated on 15 August.
4 [mass noun] archaic arrogance or presumption.
– ORIGIN Middle English (in sense 3): from Old French *asompsion* or Latin *assumptio(n-)*, from the verb *assumere* (see **ASSUME**).

assumptive ▶ **adjective 1** rare of the nature of an assumption.
2 archaic arrogant or presumptuous.
– ORIGIN mid 16th cent.: from Latin *assumptivus*, from the verb *assumere* (see **ASSUME**).

Assur /ˈaʃʊə/ (also **Asur** or **Ashur**) an ancient city state of Mesopotamia, situated on the River Tigris to the south of modern Mosul. It was the traditional capital of the Assyrian empires.

assurance ▶ **noun 1** a positive declaration intended to give confidence; a promise: [with clause] *he **gave an assurance that** work would not recommence until Wednesday.*
2 [mass noun] confidence or certainty in one's own abilities: *she drove with assurance.*
■certainty about something: *assurance of faith depends on our trust in God.*
3 [mass noun] chiefly Brit. insurance, specifically life insurance.
– ORIGIN late Middle English (in sense 2): from Old French, from *assurer* 'assure'.

USAGE In the context of life insurance, a technical distinction is made between **assurance** and **insurance**. **Assurance** is used of policies under whose terms a payment is guaranteed, either after a fixed term or on the death of the insured person; **insurance** is the general term, and is used in particular of policies under whose terms a payment would be made only in certain circumstances (e.g. accident or death within a limited period).

assure ▶ **verb 1** [reporting verb] tell someone something positively or confidently to dispel any doubts they may have: [with obj. and clause] *Tony assured me that there was a supermarket in the village* | [with obj. and direct speech] *'I quite understand,' Mrs Lewis assured her* | [with obj.] *they **assured** him **of** their full confidence.*
■make (someone) sure of something: *you would be assured of a welcome* | *she assured herself that he was asleep.*
2 [with obj.] (often **be assured**) make (something) certain to happen: *victory was now assured* | [with clause] *their influence assured that the report would be tough.*
■chiefly Brit. cover (a life) by assurance. ■secure the future payment of (an amount) with insurance.
– DERIVATIVES **assurer** noun.
– ORIGIN late Middle English: from Old French *assurer*, based on Latin *ad-* 'to' (expressing change) + *securus* (see **SECURE**).

assured ▶ **adjective 1** confident: *'Certainly not' was her assured reply.*
2 [attrib.] protected against discontinuance or change: *an assured tenancy.*
– DERIVATIVES **assuredly** adverb [sentence adverb] *if they lose their hold, they will assuredly drown.*

Assyria /əˈsɪrɪə/ an ancient country in what is now northern Iraq. From the early part of the 2nd millennium BC Assyria was the centre of a succession of empires; it was at its peak in the 8th and late 7th centuries BC, when its rule stretched from the Persian Gulf to Egypt. It fell in 612 BC to a coalition of Medes and Babylonians.

Assyrian ▶ **noun 1** an inhabitant of ancient Assyria.
2 [mass noun] the language of ancient Assyria, a dialect of Akkadian.
3 [mass noun] a dialect of Aramaic still spoken by a group of people of mainly Christian faith living in the mountains of Syria, northern Iraq, and surrounding regions.
▶ **adjective 1** of or relating to ancient Assyria or its language.
2 relating to or denoting modern Assyrian.

Assyriology /əˌsɪrɪˈɒlədʒi/ ▶ **noun** [mass noun] the study of the language, history, and antiquities of ancient Assyria.
– DERIVATIVES **Assyriological** adjective, **Assyriologist** noun.

AST ▶ **abbreviation for** Atlantic Standard Time (see **ATLANTIC TIME**).

astable /əˈsteɪb(ə)l, eɪ-/ ▶ **adjective** chiefly Electronics of or relating to a system or electric circuit which oscillates spontaneously between unstable states.

Astaire /əˈstɛː/, Fred (1899–1987), American dancer, singer, and actor; born *Frederick Austerlitz*. He is famous for starring in a number of film musicals, including *Top Hat* (1935), in a successful partnership with Ginger Rogers.

Astana /əˈstɑːnə/ a city in Kazakhstan, the capital since 1997; pop. (1990) 281,400. Former name **AKMOLA**.

Astarte /əˈstɑːti/ Near Eastern Mythology a Phoenician goddess of fertility and sexual love who corresponds to the Babylonian and Assyrian goddess Ishtar and who became identified with the Egyptian Isis, the Greek Aphrodite, and others.

astatic /əˈstatɪk/ ▶ **adjective** not keeping a steady position or direction, in particular:
■Physics (of a system or instrument) consisting of or employing a combination of magnets suspended in a uniform magnetic field on a single wire or thread in such a way that no torque is present (e.g. to minimize the effect of the earth's magnetic field).
– ORIGIN early 19th cent.: from Greek *astatos* 'unstable' + **-IC**.

astatine /ˈastətiːn/ ▶ **noun** [mass noun] the chemical element of atomic number 85, a radioactive member of the halogen group. Astatine was first produced by bombarding bismuth with alpha particles, and it occurs in traces in nature as a decay product. (Symbol: **At**)
– ORIGIN 1940s: from Greek *astatos* 'unstable' + **-INE**[4].

aster /ˈastə/ ▶ **noun** a plant of a large genus that includes the Michaelmas daisy, typically having purple or pink rayed flowers.
• Genus *Aster*, family Compositae: numerous species. See also **CHINA ASTER**.
– ORIGIN early 17th cent. (in the Greek sense): via Latin from Greek *astēr* 'star'.

-aster ▶ **suffix** forming nouns: **1** denoting poor quality: *criticaster* | *poetaster.*
2 Botany denoting incomplete resemblance: *oleaster.*
– ORIGIN from Latin.

asterisk ▶ **noun** a symbol (*) used to mark printed or written text, typically as a reference to an annotation or to stand for omitted matter.
▶ **verb** [with obj.] [usu. as adj. **asterisked**] mark (printed or written text) with an asterisk: *asterisked entries.*
– ORIGIN late Middle English: via late Latin from Greek *asteriskos* 'small star', diminutive of *astēr*.

asterism /ˈastərɪz(ə)m/ ▶ noun 1 Astronomy a prominent pattern or group of stars, typically having a popular name but smaller than a constellation.
2 a group of three asterisks (⁂) drawing attention to following text.
– ORIGIN late 16th cent.: from Greek *asterismos*, from *astēr* 'star'.

astern ▶ adverb behind or towards the rear of a ship or aircraft: *the engine rooms lay astern* | *the lifeboat was carried astern by the tide.*
■ (of a ship's engine) backwards: *run the engine hard astern.*
– ORIGIN late Middle English: from A-² (expressing position or direction) + **STERN**².

asteroid /ˈastərɔɪd/ ▶ noun a small rocky body orbiting the sun. Large numbers of these, ranging enormously in size, are found between the orbits of Mars and Jupiter, though some have more eccentric orbits.
– DERIVATIVES **asteroidal** adjective.
– ORIGIN early 19th cent.: from Greek *asteroeidēs* 'starlike', from *astēr* 'star'.

Asteroidea /ˌastəˈrɔɪdɪə/ Zoology a class of echinoderms that comprises the starfishes.
– DERIVATIVES **asteroid** noun & adjective.
– ORIGIN modern Latin (plural), from Greek *asteroeidēs* 'starlike', from *astēr* 'star'.

asthenia /əsˈθiːnɪə/ ▶ noun [mass noun] Medicine abnormal physical weakness or lack of energy.
– DERIVATIVES **asthenic** adjective.
– ORIGIN late 18th cent.: modern Latin, from Greek *astheneia*, from *asthenēs* 'weak'.

asthenosphere /əsˈθɛnəsfɪə/ ▶ noun Geology the upper layer of the earth's mantle, below the lithosphere, in which there is relatively low resistance to plastic flow and convection is thought to occur.
– DERIVATIVES **asthenospheric** adjective.
– ORIGIN early 20th cent.: from Greek *asthenēs* 'weak' + **SPHERE**.

asthma /ˈasmə/ ▶ noun [mass noun] a respiratory condition marked by attacks of spasm in the bronchi of the lungs, causing difficulty in breathing. It is usually connected to allergic reaction or other forms of hypersensitivity.
– ORIGIN late Middle English: from medieval Latin *asma*, from Greek *asthma*, from *azein* 'breathe hard'.

asthmatic ▶ adjective relating to or suffering from asthma.
▶ noun a person who suffers from asthma.
– DERIVATIVES **asthmatically** adverb.
– ORIGIN early 16th cent.: via Latin from Greek *asthmatikos*, from *asthma* (see **ASTHMA**).

Asti /ˈasti/ ▶ noun [mass noun] 1 a white wine from the province of Asti and neighbouring parts of Piedmont.
2 a light sparkling wine from this region.

astigmatism /əˈstɪgmətɪz(ə)m/ ▶ noun [mass noun] a defect in the eye or in a lens caused by a deviation from spherical curvature, which results in distorted images, as light rays are prevented from meeting at a common focus.
– DERIVATIVES **astigmatic** /ˌastɪgˈmatɪk/ adjective.
– ORIGIN mid 19th cent.: from A-¹ 'without' + Greek *stigma* 'point' + -ISM.

astilbe /əˈstɪlbi/ ▶ noun an Old World plant of the saxifrage family, with plumes of tiny white, pink, or red flowers.
● Genus *Astilbe*, family Saxifragaceae.
– ORIGIN modern Latin, from Greek *a-* 'not' + *stilbē*, feminine of *stilbos* 'glittering' (because the individual flowers are small and inconspicuous).

astir ▶ adjective [predic.] in a state of excited movement: *the streets are all astir.*
■ awake and out of bed: *he woke before anyone else was astir.*
– ORIGIN late 18th cent.: from A-² 'on' + the noun **STIR**¹.

Asti Spumante /sp(j)uːˈmanteɪ, -ti/ ▶ noun another term for **ASTI** (in sense 2).

Aston, Francis William (1877–1945), English physicist. He invented the mass spectrograph (with J. J. Thomson) and eventually discovered many of the 287 naturally occurring isotopes of non-radioactive elements. Nobel Prize for Chemistry (1922).

astonish ▶ verb [with obj.] surprise or impress (someone) greatly: *you never fail to astonish me* | [with obj. and clause] *it astonished her that Mrs Browning could seem so anxious* | [as adj. **astonishing**] *an astonishing achievement.*
– DERIVATIVES **astonishingly** adverb [as submodifier] *an astonishingly successful programme.*
– ORIGIN early 16th cent. (as *astonished*, in the sense 'stunned, bewildered, dismayed'): from obsolete *astone* 'stun, stupefy', from Old French *estoner*, based on Latin *ex-* 'out' + *tonare* 'to thunder'.

astonishment ▶ noun [mass noun] great surprise: *she looked at him in astonishment.*

Astor /ˈastə/, Nancy Witcher Langhorne, Viscountess (1879–1964), American-born British Conservative politician. She became the first woman to sit in the House of Commons when she succeeded her husband as MP for Plymouth in 1919.

astound ▶ verb [with obj.] shock or greatly surprise: *her bluntness astounded him.*
– ORIGIN Middle English (as an adjective in the sense 'stunned'): from *astoned*, past participle of obsolete *astone* (see **ASTONISH**).

astounding ▶ adjective surprisingly impressive or notable: *the summit offers astounding views.*
– DERIVATIVES **astoundingly** adverb [as submodifier] *an astoundingly good performance.*

astraddle ▶ preposition with the legs stretched widely on each side of: *policemen sitting astraddle motorcycles.*
▶ adjective & adverb with the legs stretched widely on each side: [as predic. adj.] *with her legs astraddle* | [as adv.] *the guys got me astraddle of the wheel.*

Astraea /aˈstriːə/ Astronomy asteroid 5, discovered in 1845 (diameter 125 km).
– ORIGIN from the name of a Roman goddess associated with justice.

astragal /ˈastrag(ə)l/ ▶ noun a convex moulding or wooden strip across a surface or separating panels, typically semicircular in cross section.
■ Architecture a small semicircular moulding round the top or bottom of a column. ■ a glazing bar, typically one used in cabinetmaking.
– ORIGIN mid 17th cent.: from **ASTRAGALUS**, partly via French *astragale*.

astragalus /əˈstrag(ə)ləs/ ▶ noun (pl. **astragali** /-lʌɪ/) 1 chiefly Zoology another term for **TALUS**¹ (ankle bone).
■ (astragali) historical small bones used as dice.
2 a plant of a genus that includes milk vetch.
● Genus *Astragalus*, family Leguminosae.
– ORIGIN mid 16th cent.: via Latin from Greek *astragalos* 'ankle bone, moulding', also the name of a plant.

Astrakhan /ˌastrəˈkɑːn/ a city in southern Russia, on the delta of the River Volga; pop. 507,700 (1993).

astrakhan /ˌastrəˈkan/ ▶ noun [mass noun] the dark curly fleece of young karakul lambs from central Asia: [as modifier] *an astrakhan collar.*
■ a fabric imitating this.
– ORIGIN mid 18th cent.: named after the city of **ASTRAKHAN** in Russia, from which the fleeces were exported.

astral /ˈastr(ə)l/ ▶ adjective [attrib.] of, relating to, or resembling the stars: *astral navigation.*
■ of or relating to a supposed non-physical realm of existence to which various psychic and paranormal phenomena are ascribed, and in which the physical human body is said to have a counterpart.
– ORIGIN early 17th cent.: from late Latin *astralis*, from *astrum* 'star'.

astrantia /əˈstrantɪə/ ▶ noun a plant of the parsley family with small compact starlike heads of tiny flowers surrounded by prominent bracts, native to Europe and western Asia.
● Genus *Astrantia*, family Umbelliferae: several species, in particular *A. major*, which is often grown in gardens.
– ORIGIN modern Latin, perhaps from Greek *astēr* 'star'.

astray ▶ adverb 1 away from the correct path or direction: *we went astray but a man redirected us.*
2 into error or morally questionable behaviour: *he was led astray by boozy colleagues.*
– PHRASES **go astray** (of an object) become lost or mislaid: *the money had gone astray.*
– ORIGIN Middle English (in the sense 'distant from the correct path'): from an Anglo-Norman French variant of Old French *estraie*, past participle of *estraier*, based on Latin *extra* 'out of bounds' + *vagari* 'wander'.

astride ▶ preposition & adverb with a leg on each side of: [as prep.] *he was sitting astride the bike* | *a figure astride a horse* | [as adv.] *he sat on the chair astride.*
■ [as prep.] extending across: *the port stands astride an international route* | *this picturesque village astride the River Coln.* ■ [as adv.] (of a person's legs) apart: *he stood, legs astride.*

astringent /əˈstrɪn(d)ʒ(ə)nt/ ▶ adjective 1 causing the contraction of body tissues, typically of the cells of the skin: *an astringent skin lotion.*
2 sharp or severe in manner or style: *her astringent words had their effect.*
■ (of taste or smell) sharp or bitter.
▶ noun a substance that causes the contraction of body tissues, typically used to protect the skin and to reduce bleeding from minor abrasions.
– DERIVATIVES **astringency** noun, **astringently** adverb.
– ORIGIN mid 16th cent.: from French, from Latin *astringent-* 'pulling tight', from the verb *astringere*, from *ad-* 'towards' + *stringere* 'bind, pull tight'.

astro- /ˈastrəʊ/ ▶ combining form relating to the stars or celestial objects: *astrodome* | *astrophotography.*
■ relating to outer space: *astrochemistry.*
– ORIGIN from Greek *astron* 'star'.

astro-archaeology ▶ noun another term for ARCHAEOASTRONOMY.

astrobleme /ˈastrəʊbliːm/ ▶ noun Geology an eroded remnant of a large crater made by the impact of a meteorite or comet.
– ORIGIN mid 20th cent.: from Greek *astron* 'star' + *blēma* 'wound'.

astrochemistry ▶ noun [mass noun] the study of molecules and ions occurring in stars and interstellar space.
– DERIVATIVES **astrochemical** adjective, **astrochemist** noun.

astrocompass ▶ noun an instrument designed to indicate direction with respect to the stars.

astrocyte /ˈastrə(ʊ)sʌɪt/ ▶ noun Anatomy a star-shaped glial cell of the central nervous system.
– DERIVATIVES **astrocytic** adjective.

astrodome ▶ noun 1 chiefly US an enclosed stadium with a domed roof.
2 a domed window in an aircraft for astronomical observations.

astrogation /ˌastrə(ʊ)ˈgeɪʃ(ə)n/ ▶ noun [mass noun] (in science fiction) navigation in outer space.
– DERIVATIVES **astrogator** noun.
– ORIGIN 1930s: blend of **ASTRO-** and **NAVIGATION**.

astroid /ˈastrɔɪd/ ▶ noun Mathematics a hypocycloid with four cusps (like a square with concave sides).

astrolabe /ˈastrəleɪb/ ▶ noun chiefly historical an instrument used to make astronomical measurements, typically of the altitudes of celestial bodies, and in navigation for calculating latitude, before the development of the sextant. In its basic form it consists of a disc with the edge marked in degrees and a pivoted pointer.
– ORIGIN late Middle English: from Old French *astrelabe*, from medieval Latin *astrolabium*, from Greek *astrolabon*, neuter of *astrolabos* 'star-taking'.

astrology ▶ noun [mass noun] the study of the movements and relative positions of celestial bodies interpreted as having an influence on human affairs and the natural world.

Ancient observers of the heavens developed elaborate systems of explanation based on the movements of the sun, moon, and planets through the constellations of the zodiac, for predicting events and for casting horoscopes. By 1700 astrology had lost intellectual credibility in the West, but continued to have popular appeal. Modern astrology is based on that of the Greeks, but other systems are extant, e.g. that of China.

– DERIVATIVES **astrologer** noun, **astrological** adjective, **astrologist** noun.
– ORIGIN late Middle English: from Old French *astrologie*, from Latin *astrologia*, from Greek, from *astron* 'star'.

astrometric binary ▶ noun Astronomy a binary star system in which one companion is invisible, but is known to be present from its effect on measurements relating to the other.

astrometry ▶ noun [mass noun] the measurement of the positions, motions, and magnitudes of stars.
– DERIVATIVES **astrometric** adjective.

astronaut ▶ noun a person who is trained to travel in a spacecraft.
– DERIVATIVES **astronautical** adjective.

a

– ORIGIN 1920s: from **ASTRO-**, on the pattern of *aeronaut* and *aquanaut*.

astronautics ▶ **plural noun** [treated as sing.] the science and technology of space travel and exploration.

astronomer ▶ **noun** an expert in or student of astronomy.

astronomical ▶ **adjective** **1** of or relating to astronomy.
2 informal (of an amount) extremely large: *he wanted an astronomical fee.*
– DERIVATIVES **astronomic** adjective (only in sense 2), **astronomically** adverb.
– ORIGIN mid 16th cent.: via Latin from Greek *astronomikos*, from *astronomia* (see **ASTRONOMY**).

astronomical unit (abbrev.: **AU**) ▶ **noun** Astronomy a unit of measurement equal to 149.6 million kilometres, the mean distance from the centre of the earth to the centre of the sun.

astronomical year ▶ **noun** see **YEAR** (sense 1).

astronomy ▶ **noun** [mass noun] the branch of science which deals with celestial objects, space, and the physical universe as a whole.

In ancient times, observation of the sun, moon, stars, and planets formed the basis of timekeeping and navigation. Astronomy was greatly furthered by the invention of the telescope, but modern observations are made in all parts of the spectrum, including X-ray and radio frequencies, using terrestrial and orbiting instruments and space probes.

– ORIGIN Middle English (also denoting astrology): from Old French *astronomie*, from Latin *astronomia*, from Greek, from *astronomos* (adjective) 'star-arranging'.

astrophotography ▶ **noun** [mass noun] the use of photography in astronomy; the photographing of celestial objects and phenomena.
– DERIVATIVES **astrophotographer** noun, **astrophotographic** adjective.

astrophysics ▶ **plural noun** [treated as sing.] the branch of astronomy concerned with the physical nature of stars and other celestial bodies, and the application of the laws and theories of physics to the interpretation of astronomical observations.
– DERIVATIVES **astrophysical** adjective, **astrophysicist** noun.

AstroTurf ▶ **noun** [mass noun] trademark an artificial grass surface, used for sports fields.
– ORIGIN 1960s: from sense 1 of **ASTRODOME** (where it was first used) + **TURF**.

Asturias /a'stʊərɪəs/ an autonomous region and former principality of NW Spain; capital, Oviedo.

astute ▶ **adjective** having or showing an ability to accurately assess situations or people and turn this to one's advantage: *an astute businessman.*
– DERIVATIVES **astutely** adverb, **astuteness** noun.
– ORIGIN early 17th cent.: from obsolete French *astut* or Latin *astutus*, from *astus* 'craft'.

astylar /ə'stʌɪlə/ ▶ **adjective** Architecture (of a classical building) lacking columns or pilasters.
– ORIGIN mid 19th cent.: from **A-**[1] 'without' + Greek *stulos* 'column' + **-AR**[1].

Asunción /əˌsʊnsɪ'ɒn, Spanish asun'sjon, -'θjon/ the capital and chief port of Paraguay; pop. 637,740 (1992).

asunder ▶ **adverb** archaic or poetic/literary apart: *those whom God hath joined together let no man put asunder.*
– ORIGIN Old English *on sundran* 'in or into a separate place'; compare with **SUNDER**.

Asur /'aʃʊə/ variant spelling of **ASSUR**.

asura /'ʌsʊrə/ ▶ **noun** a member of a class of divine beings in the Vedic period, which in Indian mythology tend to be evil and in Zoroastrianism are benevolent. Compare with **DEVA**.

ASV ▶ **abbreviation for** American Standard Version (of the Bible).

Aswan /as'wɑːn/ a city on the Nile in southern Egypt, 16 km (10 miles) north of Lake Nasser; pop. 195,700 (est. 1986). Two dams across the Nile have been built nearby. The controlled release of water from Lake Nasser behind the High Dam produces the greater part of Egypt's electricity.

aswarm ▶ **adjective** [predic.] crowded or full: *the streets were aswarm with vendors.*

aswim ▶ **adjective** [predic.] swimming: *sardines aswim in oil.*

aswirl ▶ **adjective** & **adverb** swirling; covered or surrounded with something swirling: [as predic. adj.] *flowers aswirl with bees* | [as adv.] *she shook her head, sending the streamers aswirl.*

asylum ▶ **noun** **1** [mass noun] (also **political asylum**) the protection granted by a state to someone who has left their native country as a political refugee: *people seeking asylum in Britain.*
■shelter or protection from danger: *asylum for those too ill to care for themselves.*
2 dated an institution offering shelter and support to the mentally ill: *he'd been committed to an asylum.*
– ORIGIN late Middle English (in the sense 'place of refuge', especially for criminals): via Latin from Greek *asulon* 'refuge', from *asulos* 'inviolable', from *a-* 'without' + *sulon* 'right of seizure'. Current senses date from the 18th cent.

asymmetrical ▶ **adjective** having parts which fail to correspond to one another in shape, size, or arrangement; lacking symmetry: *the church has an asymmetrical plan with an aisle only on one side.*
■having parts or aspects which are not equal or equivalent; unequal in some respect: *the asymmetrical relationship between a landlord and a tenant.*
– DERIVATIVES **asymmetric** adjective, **asymmetrically** adverb.

asymmetric bars ▶ **plural noun** a pair of bars of different heights used in women's gymnastics.

asymmetry /ə'sɪmɪtri, eɪ-/ ▶ **noun** (pl. **-ies**) [mass noun] lack of equality or equivalence between parts or aspects of something; lack of symmetry.
– ORIGIN mid 17th cent.: from Greek *asummetria*, from *a-* 'without' + *summetria* (see **SYMMETRY**).

asymptomatic ▶ **adjective** Medicine (of a condition or a person) producing or showing no symptoms.

asymptote /'asɪm(p)təʊt/ ▶ **noun** a straight line that continually approaches a given curve but does not meet it at any finite distance.
– DERIVATIVES **asymptotic** /ˌasɪm(p)'tɒtɪk/ adjective, **asymptotically** adverb.
– ORIGIN mid 17th cent.: from modern Latin *asymptota (linea)* '(line) not meeting', from Greek *asumptōtos* 'not falling together', from *a-* 'not' + *sun* 'together' + *ptōtos* 'apt to fall' (from *piptein* 'to fall').

asynchronous ▶ **adjective** **1** Computing & Telecommunications (of equipment or methods of working) making use of pulses to control the timing of operations that are sent when the previous operation is completed, rather than at regular intervals.
2 not going at the same rate and exactly together with something else, in particular:
■(of a machine or motor) not working in time with the alternations of current. ■ Astronomy (of a satellite) revolving round the parent planet at a different rate from that at which the planet rotates. ■ Astronomy (of an orbit) such that a satellite in it is asynchronous.
3 (of two or more objects or events) not existing or happening at the same time.
– DERIVATIVES **asynchronously** adverb.

asyndeton /ə'sɪndɪt(ə)n/ ▶ **noun** (pl. **asyndeta** /-tə/) [mass noun] the omission or absence of a conjunction between parts of a sentence, as in *I came, I saw, I conquered.*
– DERIVATIVES **asyndetic** /asɪn'dɛtɪk/ adjective.
– ORIGIN mid 16th cent.: modern Latin, from Greek *asundeton*, neuter of *asundetos* 'unconnected', from *a-* 'not' + *sundetos* 'bound together'.

At ▶ **symbol for** the chemical element astatine.

at[1] ▶ **preposition** **1** expressing location or arrival in a particular place or position: *they live at Conway House* | *she was constantly at the telex machine* | *they stopped at a small trattoria.*
2 expressing the time when an event takes place: *the children go to bed at nine o'clock* | *his death came at a time when the movement was split* | *he was defeated at the election of December 1910.*
■(followed by a noun without a determiner) denoting a particular period of time: *the sea is cooler at night* | *the force landed at dawn.* ■(followed by a noun without a determiner) denoting the time spent by someone attending an educational institution, a workplace, or their home: *it was at university that he first began to perform* | *we all need to get involved in fighting crime whether it's at work, at home, or at school.*
3 denoting a particular point or segment on a scale: *prices start at £18,500* | *driving at 50 mph* | *learners of English at advanced levels.*
■referring to someone's age: *at fourteen he began to work as a postman.*
4 expressing a particular state or condition: *with a ready smile to put Mrs Jones at ease* | *placed them at a serious disadvantage* | *the coroner accepted that the machines were at fault.*
■expressing a relationship between an individual and a skill: *boxing was the only sport I was any good at* | *he is poor at giving instructions.*
5 expressing the object of a look, gesture, thought, action, or plan: *I looked at my watch* | *Leslie pointed at him* | *I was amazed at how well the hair kept its shape* | *policies aimed at reducing taxation.*
■expressing the target of a shot from a weapon: *they tore down the main street, firing at anyone in sight.* ■ expressing an incomplete or attempted action, typically involving repeated movements: *she clutched at the thin gown* | *Shelley grabbed at his arm.*
6 expressing the means by which something is done: *holding a prison officer at knifepoint* | figurative *her pride had taken a beating at his hands.*
– PHRASES **at all** see **ALL**. **at first** see **FIRST**. **at it** engaged in some activity, typically a reprehensible one: *the guy who faked the Hitler diaries is at it again.* **at last** see **LAST**[1]. **at least** see **LEAST**. **at most** see **MOST**. **at once** see **ONCE**. **at that** in addition; furthermore: *it was not fog but smoke, and very thick at that.* **not at all** see **NOT**. **where it's at** informal the fashionable place, possession, or activity: *New York is where it's at, stylewise.*
– ORIGIN Old English *æt*, of Germanic origin; related to Old Frisian *et* and Old Norse *at*, from an Indo-European root shared by Latin *ad* 'to'.

at[2] /ɑːt, at/ ▶ **noun** a monetary unit of Laos, equal to one hundredth of a kip.
– ORIGIN Thai.

at- ▶ **prefix** variant spelling of **AD-** assimilated before *t* (as in *attend, attenuate*).

Atabrine /'atɪbriːn/ ▶ **noun** variant spelling of **ATEBRIN**.

Atacama Desert /ˌatə'kɑːmə/ an arid region of western Chile, extending roughly 965 km (600 miles) southwards from the Peruvian border.

atactic /ə'taktɪk/ ▶ **adjective** Chemistry (of a polymer or polymer structure) in which the repeating units have no regular stereochemical configuration.
– ORIGIN mid 19th cent.: from Greek *ataktos*, from *a-* 'not' + *taktos* 'arranged' + **-IC**.

Atalanta /ˌatə'lantə/ Greek Mythology a huntress who would marry only someone who could beat her in a foot race. She was beaten when a suitor threw down three golden apples which she stopped to pick up.

ataman /'atəman/ ▶ **noun** (pl. **atamans**) a Cossack leader.
– ORIGIN mid 19th cent.: from Russian.

atap ▶ **noun** variant spelling of **ATTAP**.

ataraxy /'atəraksi/ (also **ataraxia** /ˌatə'raksɪə/) ▶ **noun** [mass noun] a state of serene calmness.
– DERIVATIVES **ataractic** adjective, **ataraxic** adjective.
– ORIGIN early 17th cent.: from French *ataraxie*, from Greek *ataraxia* 'impassiveness', from *a-* 'not' + *tarassein* 'disturb'.

Atatürk /'atətəːk/, Kemal (1881–1938), Turkish general and statesman, President 1923–38; also called **Kemal Pasha**. He was elected the first President of the Turkish republic, taking the name of Atatürk ('father of the Turks') in 1934. He abolished the caliphate and introduced other policies designed to make Turkey a modern secular state.

atavistic /ˌatə'vɪstɪk/ ▶ **adjective** relating to or characterized by reversion to something ancient or ancestral: *atavistic fears and instincts.*
– DERIVATIVES **atavism** noun, **atavistically** adverb.
– ORIGIN late 19th cent.: based on Latin *atavus* 'forefather' + the adjectival suffix *-istic*.

ataxia /ə'taksɪə/ (also **ataxy** /-si/) ▶ **noun** [mass noun] Medicine the loss of full control of bodily movements.
– DERIVATIVES **ataxic** adjective.
– ORIGIN late 19th cent.: modern Latin, from Greek, from *a-* 'without' + *taxis* 'order'. The original sense was 'irregularity, disorder', later (in medical use) denoting irregularity of function or symptoms.

ATB ▶ **abbreviation for** all-terrain bike.

at bat Baseball ▶ **noun** a player's turn at batting, as officially recorded: *he had three singles in four at bat.*
▶ **adverb** batting.

ATC ▶ **abbreviation for** ■ air traffic control or air traffic controller. ■ (in Britain) Air Training Corps.

ATE ▶ **abbreviation for** automated test equipment.

a

ate past of **EAT**.

-ate[1] ▶ **suffix** forming nouns: **1** denoting status or office: *doctorate* | *episcopate*.
■ denoting a state or function: *curate* | *mandate*.
2 denoting a group: *electorate*.
3 Chemistry denoting a salt or ester, especially of an acid with a corresponding name ending in *-ic*: *chlorate* | *nitrate*.
4 denoting a product of a chemical process: *condensate* | *filtrate*.
– ORIGIN from Old French *-at* or Latin *-atus*, *-ata*, *-atum*.

-ate[2] ▶ **suffix 1** forming adjectives and nouns such as *associate*, *duplicate*, *separate*.
2 forming adjectives from Latin: *caudate*.
– ORIGIN from Latin *-atus*, *-ata*, *-atum*.

-ate[3] ▶ **suffix** forming verbs such as *fascinate*, *hyphenate*.
– ORIGIN from **-ATE**[2]; originally forms were based on existing past participial adjectives ending in *-atus*, but were later extended to any Latin verb ending in *-are* and to French verbs ending in *-er*.

A-team ▶ **noun** a group of elite soldiers or the top advisers or workers in an organization.
– ORIGIN 1970s: from sports terminology in which an organization's A-team is its best team.

Atebrin /ˈatɪbrɪn/ (US **Atabrine**) ▶ **noun** trademark for **QUINACRINE**.
– ORIGIN 1930s: of unknown origin.

atelectasis /ˌatɪˈlɛktəsɪs/ ▶ **noun** [mass noun] Medicine partial collapse or incomplete inflation of the lung.
– ORIGIN mid 19th cent.: from Greek *atelēs* 'imperfect' + *ektasis* 'extension'.

atelier /əˈtɛlɪeɪ/ ▶ **noun** a workshop or studio, especially one used by an artist or designer.
– ORIGIN late 17th cent.: from French, from Old French *astelle* 'splinter of wood', from Latin *astula*.

a tempo /ɑː ˈtɛmpəʊ/ ▶ **adverb** & **adjective** Music (especially as a direction) in the previous tempo.
– ORIGIN Italian, literally 'in time'.

atemporal /eɪˈtɛmp(ə)r(ə)l/ ▶ **adjective** existing or considered without relation to time.
– DERIVATIVES **atemporality** noun.

Aten /ˈɑːt(ə)n/ (also **Aton**) Egyptian Mythology the sun or solar disc, the deity of a strong monotheistic cult, particularly during the reign of Akhenaten.

atenolol /əˈtɛnəlɒl/ ▶ **noun** [mass noun] Medicine a beta blocker used mainly to treat angina and high blood pressure.
– ORIGIN 1970s: perhaps from *a(ngina)* + *ten(sion)* + *(propran)olol*, a related compound.

ATF ▶ **abbreviation for** (in the US) (Federal Bureau of) Alcohol, Tobacco, and Firearms.

Athabaskan /ˌaθəˈbask(ə)n/ (also **Athapaskan**) ▶ **adjective** denoting, belonging to, or relating to a family of North American Indian languages, including a southern group of which the most important are Navajo and Apache, and a northern group in Alaska and the Canadian North-West, many of which are now rare or extinct.
▶ **noun 1** [mass noun] this family of languages, sometimes classified in the Na-Dene phylum.
2 a speaker of any of these languages.
– ORIGIN from *Athabasca*, the name of a lake in western Canada, from Cree *Athap-askaw* 'grass and reeds here and there', + **-AN**.

Athanasian Creed /ˌaθəˈneɪʃ(ə)n/ a summary of Christian doctrine formerly attributed to St Athanasius, but probably dating from the 5th century.

Athanasius, St /ˌaθəˈneɪʃəs/ (*c.*296–373), Greek theologian and upholder of Christian orthodoxy against Arianism. Feast day, 2 May.

athanor /ˈaθənɔː/ ▶ **noun** historical a type of furnace used by alchemists, able to maintain a steady heat for long periods.
– ORIGIN late 15th cent.: from Arabic *at-tannūr*, from *al-* 'the' + *tannūr* 'baker's oven'.

Atharva Veda /əˌtɑːvə ˈveɪdə, ˈviːdə/ Hinduism a collection of hymns and ritual utterances in early Sanskrit, added at a later stage to the existing Veda material.
– ORIGIN from Sanskrit *Atharvan* (the name of Brahma's eldest son, said to be the author of the collection) + *veda* '(sacred) knowledge'.

atheism /ˈeɪθɪɪz(ə)m/ ▶ **noun** [mass noun] the theory or belief that God does not exist.
– DERIVATIVES **atheist** noun, **atheistic** adjective, **atheistical** adjective.
– ORIGIN late 16th cent.: from French *athéisme*, from Greek *atheos*, from *a-* 'without' + *theos* 'god'.

atheling /ˈaθ(ə)lɪŋ/ ▶ **noun** historical a prince or lord in Anglo-Saxon England.
– ORIGIN Old English *ætheling*, of West Germanic origin, from a base meaning 'race, family'.

Athelstan /ˈaθəlstən/ (895–939), king of England 925–39. Athelstan came to the thrones of Wessex and Mercia in 924 before effectively becoming the first king of all England.

athematic /ˌaθɪˈmatɪk, eɪ-/ ▶ **adjective 1** Music (of a composition) not based on the use of themes.
2 Grammar (of a verb form) having a suffix attached to the stem without a connecting (thematic) vowel.

Athenaeum /ˌaθɪˈniːəm/ (US also **Atheneum**) ▶ **noun** used in the names of libraries or institutions for literary or scientific study: *the Boston Athenaeum*.
■ used in the titles of periodicals concerned with literature, science, and art. ■ (**the Athenaeum**) a London club founded in 1824, originally for men of distinction in literature, art, and learning.
– ORIGIN mid 18th cent.: via Latin from Greek *Athēnaion*, denoting the temple of Athene.

Athene /əˈθiːni/ (also **Athena**) Greek Mythology the patron goddess of Athens, typically allegorized into a personification of wisdom. Also called **PALLAS**. Roman equivalent **MINERVA**.

Athenian empire see **DELIAN LEAGUE**.

Athens /ˈaθɪnz/ the capital of Greece; pop. 3,096,775 (1991). Greek name **ATHÍNAI**.

> A flourishing city state of ancient Greece, Athens was an important cultural centre in the 5th century BC. It came under Roman rule in 146 BC and fell to the Goths in AD 267. After its capture by the Turks in 1456 Athens declined to the status of a village, until chosen as the capital of a newly independent Greece in 1834.

– DERIVATIVES **Athenian** adjective & noun.

atherogenic /ˌaθərə(ʊ)ˈdʒɛnɪk/ ▶ **adjective** Physiology tending to promote the formation of fatty plaques in the arteries.
– DERIVATIVES **atherogenesis** noun.
– ORIGIN 1950s: from **ATHEROMA** + **-GENIC**.

atheroma /ˌaθəˈrəʊmə/ ▶ **noun** [mass noun] Medicine degeneration of the walls of the arteries caused by accumulated fatty deposits and scar tissue, and leading to restriction of the circulation and a risk of thrombosis. See also **ATHEROSCLEROSIS**.
■ the fatty material which forms plaques in the arteries.
– DERIVATIVES **atheromatous** adjective.
– ORIGIN late 16th cent.: via Latin from Greek *athērōma*, from *athērē*, *atharē* 'groats'.

atherosclerosis /ˌaθərəʊsklɪəˈrəʊsɪs, -sklə-/ ▶ **noun** [mass noun] Medicine a disease of the arteries characterized by the deposition of plaques of fatty material on their inner walls. See also **ATHEROMA**.
– DERIVATIVES **atherosclerotic** adjective.
– ORIGIN early 20th cent.: coined in German from Greek *athērē* 'groats' + *sklērōsis* 'hardening' (see **SCLEROSIS**).

Atherton Tableland /ˈaθət(ə)n/ a plateau in the Great Dividing Range in NE Queensland, Australia.

athetize /ˈaθɪtʌɪz/ ▶ **verb** [with obj.] rare reject (a passage in a text) as spurious.
– DERIVATIVES **athetesis** noun.
– ORIGIN late 19th cent.: from Greek *athetos* 'without position' + **-IZE**, rendering the Greek verb *athetein*.

athetosis /ˌaθɪˈtəʊsɪs/ ▶ **noun** [mass noun] Medicine a condition in which abnormal muscle contraction causes involuntary writhing movements. It affects some people with cerebral palsy, impairing speech and use of the hands.
– DERIVATIVES **athetoid** adjective, **athetotic** adjective.
– ORIGIN late 19th cent.: from Greek *athetos* 'without position' + **-OSIS**.

Athínai /aˈθine/ Greek name for **ATHENS**.

athirst ▶ **adjective** [predic.] archaic thirsty.
■ very eager to get something: *she was athirst for news*.
– ORIGIN Old English *ofthyrst*, shortened from *ofthyrsted*, past participle of *ofthyrstan* 'be thirsty'.

athlete ▶ **noun** a person who is proficient in sports and other forms of physical exercise.
■ chiefly Brit. a person who takes part in competitive track and field events (athletics).
– ORIGIN late Middle English: from Latin *athleta*, from Greek *athlētēs*, from *athlein* 'compete for a prize', from *athlon* 'prize'.

athlete's foot ▶ **noun** [mass noun] a fungal infection affecting mainly the skin between the toes. It is a form of ringworm.

athletic ▶ **adjective 1** physically strong, fit, and active: *big, muscular, athletic boys*.
2 [attrib.] of or relating to athletes or athletics: *athletic events* | *an athletic club*.
– DERIVATIVES **athletically** adverb, **athleticism** noun.
– ORIGIN mid 17th cent.: from French *athlétique* or Latin *athleticus*, from Greek *athlētikos*, from *athlētēs* (see **ATHLETE**).

athletics ▶ **plural noun** [usu. treated as sing.] chiefly Brit. the sport of competing in track and field events, including running races and various competitions in jumping and throwing.
■ N. Amer. physical sports and games of any kind.

at-home ▶ **noun** a party in a person's home.
■ dated a period when a person has announced that they will receive visitors in their home.

Athos, Mount /ˈaθɒs, ˈeɪθ-/ a narrow, mountainous peninsula in NE Greece, projecting into the Aegean Sea. It is inhabited by monks of the Orthodox Church, who forbid women and even female animals to set foot on the peninsula.
– DERIVATIVES **Athonite** /ˈaθəˌnʌɪt/ adjective & noun.

athwart /əˈθwɔːt/ ▶ **preposition 1** from side to side of; across: *a counter was placed athwart the entrance*.
2 in opposition to; counter to: *these statistics run sharply **athwart** conventional presumptions*.
▶ **adverb 1** across from side to side; transversely: *one table running athwart was all the room would hold*.
2 so as to be perverse or contradictory: *our words ran **athwart** and we ended up at cross purposes*.
– ORIGIN late Middle English: from **A-**[2] 'on' + **THWART**.

-atic ▶ **suffix** forming adjectives and nouns such as *aquatic*, *idiomatic*.
– ORIGIN from French *-atique* or Latin *-aticus*, sometimes based on Greek *-atikos*.

-ation ▶ **suffix** (forming nouns) denoting an action or an instance of it: *exploration* | *hesitation*.
■ denoting a result or product of action: *plantation*.
– ORIGIN from French *-ation* or Latin *-ation-*.

Ativan /ˈatɪvan/ ▶ **noun** trademark for **LORAZEPAM**.

-ative ▶ **suffix** (forming adjectives) denoting a characteristic or propensity: *pejorative* | *talkative*.
– ORIGIN from French *-atif*, *-ative* or Latin *-ativus* (from past participial stems ending in *-at*).

Atkinson, Sir Harry (Albert) (1831–92), British-born New Zealand statesman, Prime Minister 1876–7, 1883–4, and 1887–91.

Atlanta the state capital of Georgia in the US; pop. 394,000 (1990).
– DERIVATIVES **Atlantan** noun & adjective.

atlantes plural form of **ATLAS** (in sense 3).

Atlantic ▶ **adjective** [attrib.] **1** of or adjoining the Atlantic Ocean: *the Atlantic coast of Europe*.
2 Geology of, relating to, or denoting the third climatic stage of the postglacial period in northern Europe, between the Boreal and Sub-Boreal stages (about 7,500 to 5,000 years ago). The stage was the warmest since the last glaciation, and was marked by a moist oceanic climate.
▶ **noun** (**the Atlantic**) **1** short for **ATLANTIC OCEAN**.
2 Geology the Atlantic climatic stage.
– ORIGIN late Middle English: via Latin from Greek *Atlantikos*, from *Atlas*, *Atlant-* (see **ATLAS**). The term originally referred to Mount Atlas in Libya, hence to the sea near the west African coast, later extended to the whole ocean.

Atlantic, Battle of the a succession of sea operations during the Second World War in which Axis naval and air forces attempted to destroy ships carrying supplies from North America to the UK.

Atlantic Charter a declaration of eight common principles in international relations drawn up by Churchill and Roosevelt in August 1941, which provided the ideological basis for the United Nations organization.

Atlanticism /atˈlantɪˌsɪz(ə)m/ ▶ **noun** [mass noun] belief in or support for a close relationship between western Europe and the US, or particularly for Nato.
– DERIVATIVES **Atlanticist** noun & adjective.

Atlantic Ocean the ocean lying between Europe and Africa to the east and North and South

America to the west. It is divided by the equator into the North Atlantic and the South Atlantic oceans.

Atlantic Provinces the Canadian provinces of Newfoundland, Labrador, and the Maritime Provinces.

Atlantic seal ▶ noun another term for GREY SEAL.

Atlantic time the standard time in a zone including the easternmost parts of mainland Canada, Puerto Rico, and the Virgin Islands, specifically:
● (**Atlantic Standard Time** abbrev.: **AST**) standard time based on the mean solar time at longitude 60° W, four hours behind GMT. ● (**Atlantic Daylight Time** abbrev.: **ADT**) Atlantic time during daylight saving, five hours behind GMT.

Atlantis a legendary island, beautiful and prosperous, which was overwhelmed by the sea.
– DERIVATIVES **Atlantean** adjective.

Atlas Greek Mythology one of the Titans, who was punished for his part in their revolt against Zeus by being made to support the heavens. He became identified with the Atlas Mountains.
– DERIVATIVES **Atlantean** adjective.

atlas ▶ noun **1** a book of maps or charts: *I looked in the atlas to see where Naples was* | *a road atlas.*
■ a book of illustrations or diagrams in any subject.
2 (also **atlas vertebra**) Anatomy the topmost vertebra of the backbone, articulating with the occipital bone of the skull.
3 (pl. **atlantes** /atˈlantiːz/) Architecture a stone carving of a male figure, used as a column to support the entablature of a Greek or Greek-style building.
– ORIGIN late 16th cent. (originally denoting a person who supported a great burden): via Latin from Greek *Atlas* (see ATLAS).

atlas moth ▶ noun a very large boldly marked silk moth which occurs in both the Old and New World tropics.
● Genus *Attacus*, family Saturniidae: several species, in particular *A. atlas* of Asia, which is the largest moth in the world.

Atlas Mountains a range of mountains in North Africa extending from Morocco to Tunisia in a series of chains.

ATM ▶ abbreviation for ■ Telecommunications asynchronous transfer mode. ■ automated teller machine.

atman /ˈɑːtmən/ ▶ noun [mass noun] Hinduism the spiritual life principle of the universe, especially when regarded as immanent in the real self of the individual.
■ [count noun] a person's soul.
– ORIGIN from Sanskrit *ātman*, literally 'essence, breath'.

atmosphere ▶ noun [usu. in sing.] **1** the envelope of gases surrounding the earth or another planet: *part of the sun's energy is absorbed by the earth's atmosphere.*
■ the air in any particular place: *the atmosphere was unbreathable with cigar smoke.* ■ (abbrev.: **atm**) Physics a unit of pressure equal to mean atmospheric pressure at sea level, 101,325 pascals.
2 the pervading tone or mood of a place, situation, or creative work: *the hotel has won commendations for its friendly, welcoming atmosphere* | *this crisis further compounded the prevailing atmosphere of gloom.*
■ [mass noun] a pleasurable and interesting or exciting mood: *a superb restaurant, full of atmosphere.*
– ORIGIN mid 17th cent.: from modern Latin *atmosphaera*, from Greek *atmos* 'vapour' + *sphaira* 'ball, globe'.

atmospheric ▶ adjective **1** of or relating to the atmosphere of the earth or (occasionally) another planet: *atmospheric conditions such as fog, snow, rain.*
2 creating a distinctive mood, typically of romance, mystery, or nostalgia: *atmospheric lighting.*
– DERIVATIVES **atmospherical** adjective (archaic), **atmospherically** adverb.

atmospheric perspective ▶ noun another term for AERIAL PERSPECTIVE.

atmospheric pressure ▶ noun [mass noun] the pressure exerted by the weight of the atmosphere, which at sea level has a mean value of 101,325 pascals (roughly 14.6959 pounds per square inch).

atmospherics ▶ plural noun **1** electrical disturbances in the atmosphere due to lightning and other phenomena, especially as they interfere with telecommunications.
2 effects intended to create a particular atmosphere or mood, especially in music: *a smoky jazz sound with spooky atmospherics.*

ATOL /ˈatɒl/ ▶ abbreviation for (in the UK) Air Travel Organizer's Licence.

atoll /ˈatɒl, əˈtɒl/ ▶ noun a ring-shaped reef, island, or chain of islands formed of coral.
– ORIGIN early 17th cent.: from Maldivian *atolu.*

atom ▶ noun the smallest particle of a chemical element that can exist.
■ (usu. **the atom**) such particles as a source of nuclear energy: *the power of the atom.* ■ [usu. with negative] an extremely small amount of a thing or quality: *I shall not have one atom of strength left.* ■ [usu. as modifier] Canadian a level of amateur sport, typically involving children aged between nine and eleven: *eight atom hockey teams.*

> Atoms consist of a tiny, dense, positively charged nucleus made of neutrons and protons, surrounded by a cloud of negatively charged electrons, roughly 10^{-8} cm in diameter. Each chemical element consists of atoms with a characteristic number of protons. Atoms are held together in molecules by the sharing of electrons.

– ORIGIN late 15th cent.: from Old French *atome*, via Latin from Greek *atomos* 'indivisible', based on *a-* 'not' + *temnein* 'to cut'.

atom bomb ▶ noun a bomb which derives its destructive power from the rapid release of nuclear energy by fission of heavy atomic nuclei, causing damage through heat, blast, and radioactivity.

> Such a bomb contains a critical mass of a material such as uranium-235 or plutonium-239, which when detonated by a conventional explosive charge is capable of maintaining a nuclear chain reaction, releasing large amounts of energy almost instantaneously.

atomic ▶ adjective of or relating to an atom or atoms: *the atomic nucleus.*
■ Chemistry (of a substance) consisting of uncombined atoms rather than molecules: *atomic hydrogen.* ■ of or forming a single irreducible unit or component in a larger system: *a society made up of atomic individuals pursuing private interests.* ■ relating to, denoting, or using the energy released in nuclear fission or fusion: *the atomic age required a new way of political thinking* | *atomic weapons.*
– DERIVATIVES **atomically** adverb.
– ORIGIN late 17th cent.: from modern Latin *atomicus*, from *atomus* 'indivisible' (see ATOM).

atomic clock ▶ noun an extremely accurate type of clock which is regulated by the vibrations of an atomic or molecular system such as caesium or ammonia.

atomicity ▶ noun **1** Chemistry the number of atoms in the molecules of an element.
2 [mass noun] the state or fact of being composed of indivisible units.

atomic mass ▶ noun the mass of an atom of a chemical element expressed in atomic mass units. It is approximately equivalent to the number of protons and neutrons in the atom (the mass number) or to the average number allowing for the relative abundances of different isotopes.

atomic mass unit (abbrev.: **amu**) ▶ noun a unit of mass used to express atomic and molecular weights, equal to one twelfth of the mass of an atom of carbon-12.

atomic number ▶ noun Chemistry the number of protons in the nucleus of an atom, which is characteristic of a chemical element and determines its place in the periodic table. (Symbol: **Z**)

atomic physics ▶ plural noun [treated as sing.] the branch of physics concerned with the structure of the atom and the characteristics of subatomic particles.

atomic pile ▶ noun old-fashioned term for NUCLEAR REACTOR.

atomic power ▶ noun another term for NUCLEAR POWER.

atomic spectrum ▶ noun the spectrum of frequencies of electromagnetic radiation emitted or absorbed during transitions of electrons between energy levels within an atom. Each element has a characteristic spectrum by which it can be recognized.

atomic theory ▶ noun [mass noun] the theory that all matter is made up of tiny indivisible particles (atoms). According to the modern version, the atoms of each element are effectively identical, but differ from those of other elements, and unite to form compounds in fixed proportions.
■ [count noun] a theory in any field which proposes the

existence of distinct, separable, independent components: *an atomic theory of heredity.*

atomic volume ▶ noun Chemistry the volume occupied by one gram-atom of an element under standard conditions.

atomic weight ▶ noun Chemistry another term for RELATIVE ATOMIC MASS.

atomism ▶ noun [mass noun] chiefly Philosophy a theoretical approach that regards something as interpretable through analysis into distinct, separable, and independent elementary components. The opposite of HOLISM.
– DERIVATIVES **atomist** noun, **atomistic** adjective.

atomize (also **-ise**) ▶ verb [with obj.] convert (a substance) into very fine particles or droplets.
■ reduce (something) to atoms or other small distinct units: *by disrupting our ties with our neighbours, crime atomizes society.*
– DERIVATIVES **atomization** noun.

atomizer (also **-iser**) ▶ noun a device for emitting water, perfume, or other liquids as a fine spray.

atom smasher ▶ noun informal term for PARTICLE ACCELERATOR.

atomy /ˈatəmi/ ▶ noun (pl. **-ies**) archaic a skeleton or emaciated body.
– ORIGIN late 16th cent.: from ANATOMY, taken as *an atomy.*

Aton variant spelling of ATEN.

atonal /eɪˈtəʊn(ə)l, ə-/ ▶ adjective Music not written in any key or mode.
– DERIVATIVES **atonalism** noun, **atonalist** noun, **atonality** noun.

atone ▶ verb [no obj.] make amends or reparation: *a human sacrifice to atone for the sin.*
– ORIGIN Middle English (originally in the sense 'make or become united or reconciled', rare before the 16th cent.): from *at one* in early use; later by back-formation from ATONEMENT.

atonement ▶ noun [mass noun] reparation for a wrong or injury: *he submitted his resignation as an act of atonement.*
■ Religion reparation or expiation for sin: *the High Priest offered the sacrifice as atonement for all the sins of Israel.*
■ (**the Atonement**) Christian Theology the reconciliation of God and mankind through Jesus Christ.
– ORIGIN early 16th cent. (denoting unity or reconciliation, especially between God and man): from *at one* + -MENT, influenced by medieval Latin *adunamentum* 'unity', and earlier *onement* from an obsolete verb *one* 'to unite'.

atonic /əˈtɒnɪk/ ▶ adjective **1** Linguistics (of a syllable) without accent or stress.
2 Physiology lacking muscular tone.
– DERIVATIVES **atony** /ˈatəni/ noun.

atop poetic/literary, chiefly US ▶ preposition on the top of: *the weathervane is perched atop the Great Tower.*
▶ adverb on the top: *the air-raid siren atop of the County Courthouse.*

atopic /ˈatəpi/ ▶ adjective denoting a form of allergy in which a hypersensitivity reaction such as eczema or asthma may occur in a part of the body not in contact with the allergen.
– DERIVATIVES **atopy** noun.
– ORIGIN early 20th cent.: from Greek *atopia* 'unusualness', from *atopos* 'unusual', from *a-* 'without' + *topos* 'place'.

-ator ▶ suffix forming agent nouns such as *agitator.*
■ used in names of implements, machines, etc.: *escalator.*
– ORIGIN from Latin, or sometimes representing French *-ateur.*

-atory ▶ suffix (forming adjectives) relating to or involving an action: *explanatory* | *predatory.*
– ORIGIN from Latin *-atorius.*

A to Z ▶ noun an alphabetically arranged handbook; a complete guide to a subject: *an A to Z of tools.*
■ a guidebook listing city streets.

ATP ▶ abbreviation for ■ Biochemistry adenosine triphosphate. ■ Brit. automatic train protection, a system for automatically stopping a train if its driver does not observe signal warnings or speed restrictions.

atrabilious /ˌatrəˈbɪliəs/ ▶ adjective poetic/literary melancholy or ill-tempered.
– DERIVATIVES **atrabiliousness** noun.
– ORIGIN mid 17th cent. (in the sense 'affected by black bile', one of the four supposed cardinal humours of the body, believed to cause

melancholy): from Latin *atra bilis* 'black bile', translation of Greek *melankholia* 'melancholy', + **-IOUS**.

atraumatic ▶ adjective (of a medical or surgical procedure) causing minimal tissue injury.

atrazine /ˈatrəziːn/ ▶ noun [mass noun] a synthetic compound derived from triazine, used as an agricultural herbicide.
– ORIGIN 1960s: blend of **AMINO** and **TRIAZINE**.

atremble ▶ adjective [predic.] poetic/literary trembling.

atresia /əˈtriːʃə, -zɪə/ ▶ noun [mass noun] **1** Medicine absence or abnormal narrowing of an opening or passage in the body.
2 Physiology the degeneration of those ovarian follicles which do not ovulate during the menstrual cycle.
– ORIGIN early 19th cent.: from **A-**[1] 'without' + Greek *trēsis* 'perforation' + **-IA**[1].

Atreus /ˈeɪtrɪəs/ Greek Mythology the son of Pelops and father of Agamemnon and Menelaus. He quarrelled with his brother Thyestes and invited him to a banquet at which he served up the flesh of Thyestes' own children.

atrioventricular /ˌeɪtrɪə(ʊ)vɛnˈtrɪkjʊlə/ ▶ adjective Anatomy & Physiology relating to the atrial and ventricular chambers of the heart, or the connection or coordination between them.

atrium /ˈeɪtrɪəm/ ▶ noun (pl. **atria** /ˈeɪtrɪə/ or **atriums**) **1** Architecture an open-roofed entrance hall or central court in an ancient Roman house.
■ a central hall or court in a modern building, typically rising through several stories and having a glazed roof. ■ the forecourt of a large church built on the basilican plan.
2 Anatomy each of the two upper cavities of the heart from which blood is passed to the ventricles. The right atrium receives deoxygenated blood from the veins of the body, the left atrium oxygenated blood from the pulmonary vein. Also called **AURICLE**.
– DERIVATIVES **atrial** adjective.
– ORIGIN late 16th cent.: from Latin.

atrocious ▶ adjective horrifyingly wicked: *atrocious cruelties*.
■ of a very poor quality; extremely bad or unpleasant: *he attempted an atrocious imitation of my English accent | atrocious weather.*
– DERIVATIVES **atrociously** adverb, **atrociousness** noun.
– ORIGIN mid 17th cent.: from Latin *atrox, atroc-* 'cruel' + **-IOUS**.

atrocity ▶ noun (pl. **-ies**) an extremely wicked or cruel act, typically one involving physical violence or injury: *a textbook which detailed war atrocities* | [mass noun] *scenes of hardship and atrocity.*
■ humorous a highly unpleasant or distasteful object: *atrocities in cheap red nylon.*
– ORIGIN mid 16th cent. (in the sense 'cruelty'): from French *atrocité* or Latin *atrocitas*, from *atrox, atroc-* 'cruel'.

atrophy /ˈatrəfi/ ▶ verb (**-ies**, **-ied**) [no obj.] (of body tissue or an organ) waste away, especially as a result of the degeneration of cells, or become vestigial during evolution: *the calf muscles will atrophy* | [as adj. **atrophied**] *in some beetles, the hindwings are atrophied.*
■ figurative gradually decline in effectiveness or vigour due to underuse or neglect: *the imagination can atrophy from lack of use.*
▶ noun [mass noun] the condition or process of atrophying: *gastric atrophy.*
– DERIVATIVES **atrophic** adjective.
– ORIGIN late 16th cent.: from French *atrophier* (verb), *atrophie* (noun), from late Latin *atrophia*, from Greek, 'lack of food', from *a-* 'without' + *trophē* 'food'.

atropine /ˈatrəpiːn, -ɪn/ ▶ noun [mass noun] Chemistry a poisonous compound found in deadly nightshade and related plants. It is used in medicine as a muscle relaxant, e.g. in dilating the pupil of the eye.
• An alkaloid; chem. formula: $C_{17}N_{23}NO_3$.
– ORIGIN mid 19th cent.: modern Latin *Atropa belladonna* 'deadly nightshade', from **ATROPOS** + **-INE**[4].

Atropos /ˈatrəpɒs/ Greek Mythology one of the three Fates.
– ORIGIN Greek, literally 'inflexible'.

at sign ▶ noun the symbol @.

attaboy ▶ exclamation an informal expression of encouragement or admiration to a man or boy.
– ORIGIN early 20th cent.: probably representing a casual pronunciation of *that's the boy*.

attacca /əˈtakə/ ▶ imperative verb a musical instruction used to indicate that the next section should follow without a pause.
– ORIGIN Italian, literally 'attack'.

attach ▶ verb [with obj.] fasten; join: *he ensured the trailer was securely* ***attached to*** *the minibus.*
■ fasten (a related document) to another: *I attach a copy of the memo for your information.* ■ include (a condition) as part of an agreement: *the Commission can attach appropriate conditions to the operation of the agreement.* ■ ascribe (value or importance) to something: *he doesn't* ***attach*** *too much importance* ***to*** *fixed ideas.* ■ [no obj.] (**attach to**) (of importance or value) be ascribed to: *a good deal of prominence attaches to the central union federations.* ■ (**attach oneself to**) join (someone or something) without being invited: *they were all too ready to attach themselves to you for the whole day.* ■ (usu. **be attached**) appoint (someone) for special or temporary duties: *I was* ***attached to*** *another working group.* ■ Law, archaic seize (a person or property) by legal authority: *the Earl Marshal attached Gloucester for high treason.*
– DERIVATIVES **attachable** adjective.
– ORIGIN Middle English (in the sense 'seize by legal authority'): from Old French *atachier* or *estachier* 'fasten, fix', based on an element of Germanic origin related to **STAKE**[1]; compare with **ATTACK**.

attaché /əˈtaʃeɪ/ ▶ noun **1** a person on the staff of an ambassador, typically one having a specialized area of responsibility: *naval and air attachés.*
2 N. Amer. short for **ATTACHÉ CASE**.
– ORIGIN early 19th cent.: from French, literally 'attached', past participle of *attacher*.

attaché case ▶ noun a small, flat, rigid, rectangular case used for carrying documents.

attached ▶ adjective **1** joined or fastened to something: *please complete the attached form.*
■ (of a building or room) adjacent to and typically connected with another building or room: *a ground floor bedroom with a toilet attached.*
2 full of affection or fondness: *during the journey Mark became increasingly* ***attached to*** *Tara.*
3 [predic.] (**attached to**) (of a person) appointed to (an organization or group) for special or temporary duties: *he was attached to Military Intelligence.*
■ (of an organization or body) affiliated to (another larger organization or body): *a science policy agency attached to the Council of Ministers.*

attachment ▶ noun **1** an extra part or extension that is or may be attached to something to perform a particular function: *the processor comes complete with a blender attachment.*
2 [mass noun] the condition of being attached to something or someone, in particular:
■ affection, fondness, or sympathy for someone or something: *she felt a sentimental* ***attachment to*** *the place creep over her.* ■ [count noun] an affectionate relationship between two people: *he formed an attachment with a young widow.* ■ Brit. temporary secondment to an organization: *the students are placed* ***on attachment*** *to schools for one day a week.*
3 [mass noun] the action of attaching something: *the case has a loop for attachment to your waist belt.*
■ legal seizure of property.
– PHRASES **attachment of earnings** English Law payment of debts by direct deduction from the debtor's earnings, under a court order.
– ORIGIN late Middle English (in the sense 'arrest for contempt of court'): from Old French *attachement*, from *atachier* 'fasten, fix' (see **ATTACH**).

attack ▶ verb [with obj.] take aggressive action against (a place or enemy forces) with weapons or armed force, typically in a battle or war: *in February the Germans attacked Verdun* | [no obj.] *the terrorists did not attack again until March.*
■ (of a person or animal) act against (someone or something) aggressively in an attempt to injure or kill: *a doctor was attacked by two youths.* ■ (of a disease, chemical, or insect) act harmfully on: *HIV is thought to attack certain cells in the brain.* ■ criticize or oppose fiercely and publicly: *he attacked the government's defence policy.* ■ begin to deal with (a problem or task) in a determined and vigorous way: *a plan of action to attack unemployment.* ■ [no obj.] make an aggressive or forceful attempt to score a goal or point or gain or exploit an advantage in a game against an opposing team or player: *Crystal Palace attacked swiftly down the left* | [as adj. **attacking**] *Leeds showed some good attacking play.* ■ [with obj.] Chess move into or be in a position to capture (an opponent's piece or pawn).
▶ noun **1** an aggressive and violent act against a person or place: *he was killed in an* ***attack on*** *a checkpoint | three classrooms were gutted in the arson attack.*
■ [mass noun] destructive action by a disease, chemical, or insect: *the tissue is open to attack by fungus.* ■ a sudden short bout of an illness or stress: *an attack of nausea | an asthma attack.* ■ an instance of fierce public criticism or opposition: *he launched a stinging* ***attack on*** *the Prime Minister.* ■ a determined attempt to tackle a problem or task: *an* ***attack on*** *inflation.* ■ [mass noun] Music the manner of beginning to play or sing a passage. ■ [mass noun] forceful and decisive style in performing music or another art: *the sheer attack of Hendrix's playing.* ■ an aggressive attempt to score a goal, win points, or gain or exploit an advantage in a game. ■ the players in a team who are in the position of trying to score a goal or win points: *Baxter was recalled to the attack.* ■ Chess a threat to capture an opponent's piece or pawn.
– PHRASES **under attack** subject to aggressive, violent, or harmful action: *the north-western suburbs came under attack in the latest fighting.*
– ORIGIN early 17th cent.: from French *attaque* (noun), *attaquer* (verb), from Italian *attacco* 'an attack', *attaccare* 'join battle', based on an element of Germanic origin (see **ATTACH**).

attacker ▶ noun a person or animal that attacks someone or something.
■ (in football and other games) a player whose task is to attack the other side's goal in the attempt to score; a forward.

attagirl ▶ exclamation an informal expression of encouragement or admiration to a woman or girl.
– ORIGIN 1920s: on the pattern of *attaboy*.

attain ▶ verb [with obj.] succeed in achieving (something that one desires and has worked for): *clarify your objectives and ways of attaining them | he attained the rank of Brigadier | human beings can attain happiness.*
■ reach (a specified age, size, or amount): *dolphins can attain speeds in water which man cannot yet emulate.*
– DERIVATIVES **attainability** noun, **attainable** adjective, **attainableness** noun.
– ORIGIN Middle English (in the senses 'bring to justice' and 'reach (a state)'): from Old French *ateindre*, from Latin *attingere*, from *ad-* 'at, to' + *tangere* 'to touch'.

attainder /əˈteɪndə/ ▶ noun historical the forfeiture of land and civil rights suffered as a consequence of a sentence of death for treason or felony.
– PHRASES **act** (or **bill**) **of attainder** an item of legislation inflicting attainder without judicial process.
– ORIGIN late Middle English: from Anglo-Norman French, variant (used as a noun) of Old French *ateindre* in the sense 'convict, bring to justice' (see **ATTAIN**).

attainment ▶ noun [mass noun] the action or fact of achieving a goal towards which one has worked: *the attainment of corporate aims.*
■ [count noun] (often **attainments**) a thing achieved, especially a skill or educational achievement.

attaint ▶ verb [with obj.] **1** (usu. **be attainted**) historical subject to attainder.
2 archaic affect or infect with disease or corruption.
– ORIGIN Middle English (in the sense 'touch, reach, attain'): from obsolete *attaint* (adjective), from Old French *ataint, ateint*, past participle of *ateindre* 'bring to justice' (see **ATTAIN**); influenced in meaning by **TAINT**.

Attalid /ˈatəlɪd/ ▶ noun a member of a Hellenistic dynasty named after Attalus I (reigned 241–197 BC), which flourished in the 3rd and 2nd centuries BC.
▶ adjective of or relating to this dynasty.

attap /ˈatəp/ (also **atap**) ▶ noun [mass noun] thatch made in SE Asia from palm fronds.
– ORIGIN early 19th cent.: from Malay *atap* 'roof, thatch'.

attar /ˈatə/ (also **otto**) ▶ noun a fragrant essential oil, typically made from rose petals.
– ORIGIN late 17th cent.: via Persian from Arabic *ʿitr* 'perfume, essence'.

attempt ▶ verb [with obj.] make an effort to achieve or complete (something, typically a difficult task or action): *she attempted a comeback in 1989* | [with infinitive] *troops shot civilians who attempted to flee.*
■ try to climb to the top of (a mountain): *the expedition was the first to attempt Panch Chuli V.* ■ archaic try to take (a life): *he would not have attempted the life of a friend.*
▶ noun an act of trying to achieve something, typically

a

one that is unsuccessful or not certain to succeed: [with infinitive] *an attempt to halt the bombings* | *any* ***attempt at*** *talking politics ended in a fit of the giggles* | *an abortive coup attempt.*
■an effort to surpass a record or conquer a mountain. ■ a bid to kill someone: *Karakozov made an* ***attempt on*** *the Tsar's life.* ■ a thing produced as a result of trying to make or achieve something: *she picked her first* ***attempt at*** *a letter out of the wastebasket.*
– DERIVATIVES **attemptable** adjective.
– ORIGIN late Middle English: from Old French *attempter*, from Latin *attemptare*, from *ad-* 'to' + *temptare* 'to tempt'.

Attenborough[1] /ˈat(ə)nb(ə)rə/, Sir David (Frederick) (b.1926), English naturalist and broadcaster, brother of Richard Attenborough. He is known for films of animals in their natural habitats, including *Life on Earth* (1979), *The Living Planet* (1983), and *The Trials of Life* (1990).

Attenborough[2] /ˈat(ə)nb(ə)rə/, Richard (Samuel), Baron Attenborough of Richmond-upon-Thames (b.1923), English film actor, producer, and director; brother of David Attenborough. Notable films directed: *Oh! What a Lovely War* (1969), *Gandhi* (1982), and *Shadowlands* (1993).

attend ▶**verb 1** [with obj.] be present at (an event, meeting, or function): *the whole sales force attended the conference* | *he left hospital to attend his wife's funeral.*
■go regularly to (a school, church, or clinic): *all children are required to attend school.*
2 [no obj.] (**attend to**) deal with: *he muttered that he had business to attend to.*
■give practical help and care to; look after: *the severely wounded had two medics to attend to their wounds* | [with obj.] *each of the beds in the intensive-care unit is attended by a nurse.* ■ pay attention to: *Alice hadn't attended to a word of his sermon.*
3 [with obj.] (usu. **be attended**) occur with or as a result of: *people feared that the switch to a peacetime economy would be attended by a severe slump.*
■escort or accompany (a member of royalty or other important person) so as to assist them; wait on: *Her Royal Highness was attended by Mrs Jane Stevens.*
– DERIVATIVES **attender** noun.
– ORIGIN Middle English (in the sense 'apply one's mind, one's energies to'): from Old French *atendre*, from Latin *attendere*, from *ad-* 'to' + *tendere* 'stretch'.

attendance ▶**noun** [mass noun] the action or state of going regularly to or being present at a place or event: *my* ***attendance at*** *church was very patchy.*
■[count noun] the number of people present at a particular event, function, or meeting: *falling attendances for first-class matches.*
– PHRASES **in attendance** present at a function or a place. ■ accompanying a member of royalty or other important person as an assistant or servant.
– ORIGIN late Middle English: from Old French, from *atendre* 'give one's attention to' (see **ATTEND**).

attendance allowance ▶**noun** [mass noun] **1** (in the UK) a state benefit paid to disabled people who need constant care at home.
2 (in the UK) money paid to local councillors for their time spent on council business.

attendance centre ▶**noun** (in the UK) a place to which young offenders are ordered by a court to report regularly for a set period, as a minor penalty.

attendant ▶**noun 1** a person employed to provide a service to the public in a particular place: *a cloakroom attendant* | *a garage attendant.*
■an assistant to an important person; a servant or courtier.
2 a person who is present at an event, meeting, or function: *he had become a regular attendant at chapel.*
▶**adjective** occurring with or as a result of; accompanying: *the sea and its attendant attractions* | *he warns against the dangers* ***attendant on*** *solitary life.*
■(of a person or animal) accompanying another as a companion or assistant: *a child in a pram with attendant nursemaid.*
– ORIGIN late Middle English (as an adjective): from Old French, from *atendre* 'give one's attention to' (see **ATTEND**).

attendee ▶**noun** a person who attends a conference or other gathering.

attention ▶**noun** [mass noun] **1** notice taken of someone or something; the regarding of someone or something as interesting or important: *he* ***drew attention to*** *three spelling mistakes* | *you've never* ***paid*** *that much* ***attention*** *to her opinions.*
■the mental faculty of considering or taking notice of someone or something: *he* ***turned his attention to*** *the educational system.*
2 the action of dealing with or taking special care of someone or something: *her business needed her attention* | *he was found guilty of failing to give a patient adequate medical attention.*
■[count noun] (**attentions**) a person's interest in someone, especially when unwelcome or regarded as excessive: *his primary aim was to avoid the attentions of the newspapers.* ■ [count noun] (**attentions**) a person's actions intended to express sexual or romantic interest in someone, sometimes when unwelcome: *she felt flattered by his attentions.*
3 Military a position assumed by a soldier, standing very straight with the feet together and the arms straight down the sides of the body: *Saunders* ***stood*** *stolidly* ***to attention*** | *we paraded outside for the Sergeant-Major, shivering* ***at attention.***
■[as exclamation] an order to assume such a position.
– DERIVATIVES **attentional** adjective.
– ORIGIN late Middle English: from Latin *attentio(n-)*, from the verb *attendere* (see **ATTEND**).

attention deficit disorder (N. Amer. also **attention deficit hyperactivity disorder**) (abbrev.: **ADD** or **ADHD**) ▶**noun** any of a range of behavioural disorders occurring primarily in children, including such symptoms as poor concentration, hyperactivity, and learning difficulties.

attention span ▶**noun** the length of time for which a person is able to concentrate mentally on a particular activity.

attentive ▶**adjective** paying close attention to something: *never before had she had such an attentive audience* | *ministers should be more* ***attentive to*** *the interests of taxpayers.*
■assiduously attending to the comfort or wishes of others; very polite or courteous: *the hotel has a pleasant atmosphere and attentive service.*
– DERIVATIVES **attentively** adverb, **attentiveness** noun.
– ORIGIN late Middle English: from Old French *attentif, -ive*, from *atendre* 'give one's attention to' (see **ATTEND**).

attenuate ▶**verb** /əˈtɛnjʊeɪt/ [with obj.] (often **be attenuated**) reduce the force, effect, or value of: *her intolerance was attenuated by an unexpected liberalism.*
■reduce the amplitude of (a signal, electric current, or other oscillation). ■ [no obj.] (of a signal, electric current, or other oscillation) be reduced in amplitude. ■ [usu. as adj. **attenuated**] reduce the virulence of (a pathogenic organism or vaccine): *attenuated strains of rabies virus.* ■ reduce in thickness; make thin.
▶**adjective** /əˈtɛnjʊət/ rare reduced in force, effect, or physical thickness.
– DERIVATIVES **attenuation** noun.
– ORIGIN mid 16th cent.: from Latin *attenuat-* 'made slender', from the verb *attenuare*, from *ad-* 'to' + *tenuare* 'make thin' (from *tenuis* 'thin').

attenuated ▶**adjective** unnaturally thin: *she was a drooping, attenuated figure.*
■weakened in force or effect: *Roman influence became attenuated.*

attenuator ▶**noun** a device consisting of an arrangement of resistors which reduces the strength of a radio or audio signal.

attest /əˈtɛst/ ▶**verb 1** [with obj.] provide or serve as clear evidence of: *his status is attested by his becoming an alderman* | [no obj.] *his numerous drawings of babies* ***attest to*** *his fascination with them.*
■[no obj.] declare that something exists or is the case: *I can* ***attest to*** *his tremendous energy* | [with clause] *the deceased's solicitor attested that he had been about to institute divorce proceedings.* ■ witness or certify formally.
2 [no obj.] historical, chiefly Brit. declare oneself as ready for military service.
■[with obj.] recruit (someone) by putting them on oath to serve if called upon.
– DERIVATIVES **attestable** adjective, **attestation** noun, **attestor** noun.
– ORIGIN early 16th cent.: from French *attester*, from Latin *attestari*, from *ad-* 'to' + *testari* 'to witness' (from *testis* 'a witness').

Attic /ˈatɪk/ ▶**adjective** of or relating to Athens or Attica, or the dialect of Greek spoken there, in ancient times.
▶**noun** [mass noun] the dialect of Greek used by the ancient Athenians. It was the chief literary form of classical Greek.
– ORIGIN late 16th cent.: via Latin from Greek *Attikos*.

attic ▶**noun** a space or room inside or partly inside the roof of a building.
– ORIGIN late 17th cent. (as an architectural term designating a small order (column and entablature) above a taller one): from French *attique*, from Latin *Atticus* 'relating to Athens or Attica'.

Attica /ˈatɪkə/ a triangular promontory of eastern Greece. With the islands in the Saronic Gulf it forms a department of Greece, of which Athens is the capital.

Atticism /ˈatɪsɪz(ə)m/ (also **atticism**) ▶**noun** a word or form characteristic of Attic Greek, regarded as having particular literary elegance.
– ORIGIN late 16th cent.: from Greek *Attikismos*, from *Attikos* (see **ATTIC**).

Attila /əˈtɪlə/ (406–53), king of the Huns 434–53. He ravaged vast areas between the Rhine and the Caspian Sea before being defeated by the joint forces of the Roman army and the Visigoths at Châlons in 451.

Attila Line the boundary separating Greek and Turkish-occupied Cyprus, named after the Attila Plan, a secret Turkish plan of 1964 to partition the country. Also called **SAHIN LINE**.

attire ▶**noun** [mass noun] clothes, especially fine or formal ones: *the usually sober attire of British security service personnel.*
▶**verb** (**be attired**) be dressed in clothes of a specified kind: *Lady Agatha was* ***attired in*** *an elaborate evening gown* | [as adj., with submodifier] (**attired**) *the outrageously attired hippy freaks.*
– ORIGIN Middle English: from Old French *atirier, atirer* 'equip', from *a tire* 'in order', of unknown origin.

Attis /ˈatɪs/ Anatolian Mythology the youthful consort of Cybele. His death and resurrection were associated with the spring festival.

attitude ▶**noun** a settled way of thinking or feeling about someone or something, typically one that is reflected in a person's behaviour: *he was questioned on his* ***attitude to*** *South Africa* | *being competitive is an* ***attitude of mind*** | [mass noun] *differences in attitude were apparent between ethnic groups.*
■a position of the body proper to or implying an action or mental state: *the boy was standing in an* ***attitude of*** *despair, his chin sunk on his chest.* ■ [mass noun] informal, chiefly N. Amer. truculent or uncooperative behaviour: *I asked the waiter for a clean fork and all I got was attitude.* ■ [mass noun] informal, chiefly N. Amer. individuality and self-confidence as manifested by behaviour or appearance: *she snapped her fingers* ***with attitude.*** ■ the orientation of an aircraft or spacecraft, relative to the direction of travel. ■ Ballet a position in which one leg is lifted behind with the knee bent at right angles and turned out, and the corresponding arm is raised above the head, the other extended to the side.
– DERIVATIVES **attitudinal** adjective.
– ORIGIN late 17th cent. (denoting the placing or posture of a figure in art): from French, from Italian *attitudine* 'fitness, posture', from late Latin *aptitudo*, from *aptus* 'fit'.

attitudinize /ˌatɪˈtjuːdɪnʌɪz/ (also **-ise**) ▶**verb** [no obj.] adopt or express a particular attitude or attitudes, typically just for effect.
– DERIVATIVES **attitudinizer** noun.
– ORIGIN late 16th cent.: from Italian *attitudine* (see **ATTITUDE**) + **-IZE**.

Attlee /ˈatli/, Clement Richard, 1st Earl Attlee (1883–1967), British Labour statesman, Prime Minister 1945–51. His term saw the creation of the modern welfare state and the nationalization of major industries.

attn ▶**abbreviation for** (on an envelope or at the top of a letter or fax) attention (i.e. for the attention of): *attn: Harold Carter.*

atto- /ˈatəʊ/ ▶**combining form** (used in units of measurement) denoting a factor of 10^{-18}: *attowatt.*
– ORIGIN from Danish or Norwegian *atten* 'eighteen'.

attorn /əˈtəːn/ ▶**verb** [no obj.] Law formally make or acknowledge a transfer of something.
■[with obj.] archaic transfer (something) to someone else.
– PHRASES **attorn tenant** Law formally make or acknowledge a transfer of tenancy.
– ORIGIN Middle English (in the senses 'turn, change, transform'): from Old French *atorner* 'appoint, assign', from *a-* (from Latin *ad* 'to, at') +

torner 'to turn'. The spelling with *o*, rather than *u* or *ou*, is due to the late Anglo-Norman French form *attorner*, adopted in legal use.

attorney /əˈtəːni/ ▶ **noun** (pl. **-eys**) a person, typically a lawyer, appointed to act for another in business or legal matters. Compare with **BARRISTER, SOLICITOR**.
■ chiefly US a qualified lawyer. ■ South African term for **SOLICITOR**.
– DERIVATIVES **attorneyship** noun.
– ORIGIN Middle English: from Old French *atorne*, past participle of *atorner* 'assign', from *a* 'towards' + *torner* 'turn'.

Attorney-General ▶ **noun** (pl. **Attorneys General**) the principal legal officer who represents the Crown or a state in legal proceedings and gives legal advice to the government.

attract ▶ **verb** [with obj.] cause to come to a place or participate in a venture by offering something of interest or advantage: *a campaign to attract more visitors to Shetland | he hoped this strategy would attract foreign investment by multinationals.*
■ evoke (a specified reaction): *I did not want to attract attention | his criticism of the government attracted widespread support.* ■ cause (someone) to have a liking for or interest in something: *I was* **attracted to** *the idea of working for a ballet company.* ■ cause (someone) to have a sexual or romantic interest in someone: *it was her beauty that attracted him.* ■ exert a force on (an object) which is directed towards the source of the force: *the negatively charged ions attract particles of dust.*
– DERIVATIVES **attractable** adjective, **attractor** noun.
– ORIGIN late Middle English: from Latin *attract-* 'drawn near', from the verb *attrahere*, from *ad-* 'to' + *trahere* 'draw'.

attractant ▶ **noun** a substance which attracts something (especially animals): *a sex attractant given off by female moths to attract a mate.*
▶ **adjective** attracting.

attraction ▶ **noun** [mass noun] the action or power of evoking interest, pleasure, or liking for someone or something: *she has very romantic ideas about sexual attraction | the timeless attraction of a good tune.*
■ [count noun] a quality or feature that evokes interest, liking, or desire: *this reform has many* **attractions for** *those on the left.* ■ [count noun] a thing or place which draws visitors by providing something of interest or pleasure: *the church is the town's main tourist attraction.*
■ Physics a force under the influence of which objects tend to move towards each other: *gravitational attraction.* ■ Grammar the influence exerted by one word on another which causes it to change to an incorrect form, e.g. *the wages of sin is* (for *are*) *death*.
– ORIGIN late Middle English (denoting the action of a poultice in drawing matter from the tissues): from Latin *attractio(n-)*, from the verb *attrahere* (see **ATTRACT**).

attractive ▶ **adjective** (of a thing) pleasing or appealing to the senses: *an attractive village | foliage can be as attractive as flowers.*
■ (of a person) appealing to look at; sexually alluring: *a stunningly attractive, charismatic man.* ■ (of a thing) having beneficial qualities or features which induce someone to take up what is being offered: *the site is close to other prestige schemes which should make it* **attractive to** *developers.* ■ of or relating to attraction between physical objects.
– DERIVATIVES **attractively** adverb, **attractiveness** noun.
– ORIGIN late Middle English (in the sense 'absorbent'): from French *attractif, -ive*, from late Latin *attractivus*, from the verb *attrahere* (see **ATTRACT**).

attribute ▶ **verb** /əˈtrɪbjuːt/ [with obj.] (**attribute something to**) regard something as being caused by: *he attributed the firm's success to the efforts of the managing director | the bombing was attributed to the IRA.*
■ ascribe a work or remark to (a particular author, artist, or speaker): *the building was attributed to Inigo Jones.* ■ regard a quality or feature as characteristic of or possessed by: *ancient peoples attributed magic properties to certain stones.*
▶ **noun** /ˈatrɪbjuːt/ a quality or feature regarded as a characteristic or inherent part of someone or something: *flexibility and mobility are the key attributes of Britain's army.*
■ a material object recognized as symbolic of a person, especially a conventional object used in art to identify a saint or mythical figure. ■ Grammar an attributive adjective or noun. ■ Statistics a real property which a statistical analysis is attempting to describe.
– DERIVATIVES **attributable** /əˈtrɪbjʊtəb(ə)l/ adjective, **attribution** noun.
– ORIGIN late 15th cent.: the noun from Old French *attribut*; the verb from Latin *attribut-* 'allotted': both from the verb *attribuere*, from *ad-* 'to' + *tribuere* 'assign'.

attribution theory ▶ **noun** [mass noun] Psychology a theory which supposes that people attempt to understand the behaviour of others by attributing feelings, beliefs, and intentions to them.

attributive /əˈtrɪbjʊtɪv/ ▶ **adjective** Grammar (of an adjective or other modifier) preceding the word that it modifies and expressing an attribute, as *old* in *the old dog* (but not in *the dog is old*) and *expiry* in *expiry date*. Contrasted with **PREDICATIVE**.
– DERIVATIVES **attributively** adverb.
– ORIGIN mid 18th cent. (as a noun in the sense 'a word expressing an attribute'): from French *attributif, -ive*, from *attribut* 'an attribute', from Latin *attribuere* 'add to' (see **ATTRIBUTE**).

attrit /əˈtrɪt/ ▶ **verb** (**attritted**, **attritting**) [with obj.] US informal wear down (an opponent or enemy) by sustained action: *his defense was designed to attrit us.*
– ORIGIN 1950s: back-formation from **ATTRITION**.

attrition /əˈtrɪʃ(ə)n/ ▶ **noun** [mass noun] **1** the action or process of gradually reducing the strength or effectiveness of someone or something through sustained attack or pressure: *the council is trying to wear down the opposition by attrition | the squadron suffered severe attrition of its bombers.*
■ chiefly N. Amer. & Austral./NZ the gradual reduction of a workforce by employees leaving and not being replaced rather than by redundancy. ■ wearing away by friction; abrasion: *the skull shows attrition of the edges of the teeth.*
2 (in scholastic theology) sorrow for sin falling short of contrition.
– DERIVATIVES **attritional** adjective.
– ORIGIN late Middle English (in sense 2): from late Latin *attritio(n-)*, from *atterere* 'to rub'.

attune ▶ **verb** [with obj.] (usu. **be attuned**) make receptive or aware: *a society more* **attuned to** *consumerism than ideology |* [as adj. **attuned**] *the Department is very attuned politically.*
■ accustom or acclimatize: *students are not* **attuned to** *making decisions.* ■ [no obj.] become receptive to or aware of: *a conscious attempt to* **attune to** *the wider audience.* ■ make harmonious.
– ORIGIN late 16th cent.: from **AT-** + **TUNE**.

Atty ▶ **abbreviation for** Attorney.

ATV ▶ **abbreviation for** ■ all-terrain vehicle. ■ historical (in the UK) Associated Television, an independent television company founded in 1956 and replaced in 1981 by Central Television.

Atwood, Margaret (Eleanor) (b.1939), Canadian novelist, poet, critic, and short-story writer. Notable novels: *The Edible Woman* (1969), *Cat's Eye* (1989), *The Blind Assassin* (Booker Prize, 2000).

atypical ▶ **adjective** not representative of a type, group, or class: *a sample of people who are rather atypical of the target audience | there were somewhat atypical results in May and November.*
– DERIVATIVES **atypically** adverb.

AU ▶ **abbreviation for** ■ ångström unit(s). ■ (also **a.u.**) astronomical unit(s).

Au ▶ **symbol for** the chemical element gold.
– ORIGIN from Latin *aurum*.

aubade /əʊˈbɑːd/ ▶ **noun** a poem or piece of music appropriate to the dawn or early morning.
– ORIGIN late 17th cent.: from French, from Spanish *albada*, from *alba* 'dawn'.

auberge /əʊˈbɛːʒ, French obɛʀʒ/ ▶ **noun** an inn in French-speaking countries.
– ORIGIN French, from Provençal *alberga* 'lodging'.

aubergine /ˈəʊbəʒiːn/ ▶ **noun** chiefly Brit. **1** the purple egg-shaped fruit of a tropical Old World plant, eaten as a vegetable. Also called **EGGPLANT**.
■ [mass noun] a dark purple colour like the skin of this fruit.
2 the large plant of the nightshade family which bears this fruit.
● *Solanum melongena*, family Solanaceae.
– ORIGIN late 18th cent.: from French, from Catalan *albergínia*, from Arabic *al-bāḏinjān* (based on Persian *bādingān*, from Sanskrit *vātiṃgaṇa*).

aubretia /ɔːˈbriːʃə/ (also **aubrietia**) ▶ **noun** a dwarf evergreen Eurasian trailing plant with dense masses of foliage and purple, pink, or white flowers, widely cultivated in rock gardens.
● *Aubrieta deltoidea*, family Cruciferae.
– ORIGIN early 19th cent.: modern Latin, named after Claude *Aubriet* (1668–1743), French botanist.

USAGE In popular use the forms **aubretia** and **aubrietia** have become more frequent than the strictly correct form **aubrieta**.

Aubrey /ˈɔːbri/, John (1626–97), English antiquarian and author. He is chiefly remembered for *Brief Lives*, a collection of biographies of eminent people.

auburn /ˈɔːbən, ˈɔːbəːn/ ▶ **adjective** (chiefly of a person's hair) of a reddish-brown colour.
▶ **noun** [mass noun] a reddish-brown colour.
– ORIGIN late Middle English: from Old French *auborne, alborne*, from Latin *alburnus* 'whitish', from *albus* 'white'. The original sense was 'yellowish white', but the word became associated with *brown* because in the 16th and 17th centuries it was often written *abrune* or *abroun*.

Aubusson /ˈəʊbjʊsɒn, -sɔ̃/ ▶ **noun** a fine tapestry or carpet made at Aubusson, a town in central France, especially one from the late 18th century.

AUC ▶ **abbreviation** used to indicate a date reckoned from 753 BC, the year of the foundation of Rome: *765 AUC*.
– ORIGIN from Latin *ab urbe condita* 'from the foundation of the city', also *anno urbis conditae* 'in the year of the foundation of the city'.

Auckland /ˈɔːklənd/ the largest city and chief seaport of New Zealand, on North Island; pop. 309,400 (1990). It was the site of the first Parliament of New Zealand in 1854, remaining the capital until 1865.

au courant /ˌəʊ kʊˈrɒ̃/ ▶ **adjective** aware of what is going on; well informed: *they were* **au courant with** *the literary scene.*
■ fashionable: *light, low-fat, au courant recipes.*
– ORIGIN mid 18th cent.: from French, literally 'in the (regular) course'.

auction /ˈɔːkʃ(ə)n/ ▶ **noun** a public sale in which goods or property are sold to the highest bidder: *the books are expected to fetch a six-figure sum at tomorrow's auction |* [as modifier] *an auction sale.*
■ [mass noun] the action or process of selling something in this way: *the Ferrari sold* **at auction** *for £10 million.*
■ Bridge the part of the play in which players bid to decide the contract in which the hand shall be played.
▶ **verb** [with obj.] (often **be auctioned**) sell or offer for sale at an auction: *his collection of vintage cars is to be* **auctioned off** *tomorrow.*
– PHRASES **on the auction block** see ***on the block*** at **BLOCK**.
– ORIGIN late 16th cent.: from Latin *auctio(n-)* 'increase, auction', from the verb *augere* 'to increase'.

auction bridge ▶ **noun** [mass noun] an obsolete form of the card game bridge, in which all tricks won counted towards the game whether bid or not.

auctioneer ▶ **noun** a person who conducts auctions by accepting bids and declaring goods sold.
– DERIVATIVES **auctioneering** noun.

auction house ▶ **noun** a company that runs auctions.

auction room (also **auction rooms**) ▶ **noun** a building in which auctions are held.

aucuba /ˈɔːkjʊbə/ ▶ **noun** a hardy East Asian evergreen shrub of the dogwood family, resembling a laurel.
● Genus *Aucuba*, family Cornaceae: several species, in particular the Japanese laurel (*A. japonica*).
– ORIGIN modern Latin, from Japanese *aokiba*.

audacious /ɔːˈdeɪʃəs/ ▶ **adjective** **1** showing a willingness to take surprisingly bold risks: *a series of audacious takeovers.*
2 showing an impudent lack of respect: *he made an audacious remark.*
– DERIVATIVES **audaciously** adverb, **audaciousness** noun.
– ORIGIN mid 16th cent.: from Latin *audax, audac-* 'bold' (from *audere* 'dare') + **-IOUS**.

audacity /ɔːˈdasɪti/ ▶ **noun** [mass noun] **1** the willingness to take bold risks: *he whistled at the sheer audacity of the plan.*
2 rude or disrespectful behaviour; impudence: *she*

had the **audacity to** suggest I'd been carrying on with him.
– ORIGIN late Middle English: from medieval Latin *audacitas*, from *audax*, *audac-* 'bold' (see **AUDACIOUS**).

Auden /ˈɔːd(ə)n/, W. H. (1907–73), British-born poet, resident in America from 1939; full name *Wystan Hugh Auden*. *Look, Stranger!* (1936) and *Spain* (1937, on the Civil War) secured his position as a leading left-wing poet. He was awarded the Pulitzer Prize for *The Age of Anxiety* (1947).

Audh /ˈʌwəd/ variant spelling of **OUDH**.

audial /ˈɔːdɪəl/ ▶ adjective relating to or perceived through the sense of hearing.
– ORIGIN late 20th cent.: formed irregularly from Latin *audire* 'hear' (compare with **AUDILE**), on the pattern of *visual*.

audible ▶ adjective able to be heard: *ultrasound is audible to dogs.*
▶ noun American Football a change of playing tactics called by the quarterback at the line of scrimmage.
– DERIVATIVES **audibility** noun, **audibly** adverb.
– ORIGIN late 15th cent.: from late Latin *audibilis*, from *audire* 'hear'.

audience ▶ noun **1** the assembled spectators or listeners at a public event, such as a play, film, concert, or meeting: *the orchestra were given an enthusiastic ovation from the audience.*
■ the people who watch or listen to a television or radio programme: *the programme attracted an audience of almost twenty million.* ■ the readership of a book, magazine, or newspaper: *the newspaper has a sophisticated audience.* ■ the people giving or likely to give attention to something: *there is an audience for films with sociological relevance.*
2 a formal interview with a person in authority: *he demanded an audience with the Pope.*
3 [mass noun] archaic formal hearing.
– ORIGIN late Middle English: from Old French, from Latin *audientia*, from *audire* 'hear'.

audile /ˈɔːdʌɪl/ ▶ adjective another term for **AUDITORY**.
– ORIGIN late 19th cent.: formed irregularly from Latin *audire* 'hear', on the pattern of *tactile*.

audio ▶ noun [mass noun] [usu. as modifier] sound, especially when recorded, transmitted, or reproduced: *audio equipment* | *the machine can retrieve and play audio from a CD-ROM.*
– ORIGIN 1930s: independent usage of **AUDIO-**.

audio- ▶ combining form relating to hearing or sound: *audiometer* | *audio-visual.*
– ORIGIN from Latin *audire* 'hear'.

Audio-Animatronics ▶ plural noun trademark for **ANIMATRONICS**.
– DERIVATIVES **Audio-Animatronic** adjective.

audiobook ▶ noun an audio cassette recording of a reading of a book, typically a novel.

audio cassette ▶ noun a cassette of audio tape.

audio frequency ▶ noun a frequency of oscillation capable of being perceived by the human ear, generally between 20 and 20,000 Hz.

audiogram ▶ noun a graphic record produced by audiometry.

audiology /ˌɔːdɪˈɒlədʒi/ ▶ noun [mass noun] the branch of science and medicine concerned with the sense of hearing.
– DERIVATIVES **audiological** adjective, **audiologist** noun.

audiometry /ˌɔːdɪˈɒmɪtri/ ▶ noun [mass noun] measurement of the range and sensitivity of a person's sense of hearing.
– DERIVATIVES **audiometer** noun, **audiometric** adjective.

audiophile ▶ noun informal a hi-fi enthusiast.

audio tape ▶ noun [mass noun] magnetic tape on which sound can be recorded.
■ [count noun] a length of this, typically in the form of a cassette.
▶ verb (**audiotape**) [with obj.] record (sound) on tape: *each interview was audiotaped and transcribed.*

audio typist ▶ noun a typist who transcribes letters or other documents from recorded dictation.

audio-visual ▶ adjective using both sight and sound, typically in the form of slides or video and recorded speech or music: *learners can be encouraged to use audio-visual aids.*

audit ▶ noun an official inspection of an organization's accounts, typically by an independent body.
■ a systematic review or assessment of something: *a complete audit of flora and fauna at the site.*
▶ verb (**audited**, **auditing**) [with obj.] **1** conduct an official financial inspection of (a company or its accounts): *unlimited companies must also have their accounts audited.*
■ conduct a systematic review of: *a method of auditing obstetric and neonatal care.*
2 N. Amer. attend (a class) informally, without working for credit.
– ORIGIN late Middle English: from Latin *auditus* 'hearing', from *audire* 'hear', in medieval Latin *auditus (compoti)* 'audit (of an account)', an audit originally being presented orally.

Audit Commission (in the UK) an independent body that monitors public spending, especially that by local government, on behalf of the government.

audition /ɔːˈdɪʃ(ə)n/ ▶ noun **1** an interview for a particular role or job as a singer, actor, dancer, or musician, consisting of a practical demonstration of the candidate's suitability and skill.
2 [mass noun] archaic the power of hearing or listening.
▶ verb [no obj.] perform an audition: *he was auditioning for the lead role in the play.*
■ [with obj.] assess the suitability of (someone) for a role by means of an audition: *she was auditioning people for her new series.*
– ORIGIN late 16th cent. (in the sense 'power of hearing or listening'): from Latin *auditio(n-)*, from *audire* 'hear'. Sense 1 of the noun dates from the late 19th cent.

auditive ▶ adjective another term for **AUDITORY**.

auditor ▶ noun **1** a person who conducts an audit.
2 a listener: *so low was Deems's voice that his auditors had to give it close attention.*
■ N. Amer. a person who attends a class informally without working for credit.
– DERIVATIVES **auditorial** adjective.
– ORIGIN Middle English: from Old French *auditeur*, from Latin *auditor*, from *audire* 'to hear'.

auditorium ▶ noun (pl. **auditoriums** or **auditoria**) **1** the part of a theatre, concert hall, or other public building in which the audience sits.
2 chiefly N. Amer. a large building or hall used for public gatherings, typically concerts or sports events.
■ a large room, especially a school hall.
– ORIGIN early 17th cent. (originally in the general sense 'a place for hearing'): from Latin, neuter of *auditorius* 'relating to hearing' (see **AUDITORY**).

auditory ▶ adjective of or relating to the sense of hearing: *the auditory nerves* | *teaching methods use both visual and auditory stimulation.*
– ORIGIN late 16th cent.: from Latin *auditorius*, from *audire* 'hear'.

Audubon /ˈɔːdəb(ə)n/, John James (1785–1851), American naturalist and artist. Notable works: *The Birds of America* (1827–38).

Auer /ˈaʊə, German ˈaʊɐ/, Carl, Baron von Welsbach (1858–1929), Austrian chemist, who separated the supposed rare earth element didymium into neodymium and praseodymium.

Auerbach /ˈɔːbak, German ˈaʊɐbax/, Frank (b.1931), German-born British painter.

AUEW ▶ abbreviation for (in the UK) Amalgamated Union of Engineering Workers.

au fait /əʊ ˈfeɪ, French o fɛ(t)/ ▶ adjective [predic.] (**au fait with**) having a good or detailed knowledge of: *you should be au fait with the company and its products.*
– ORIGIN mid 18th cent.: from French, literally 'to the fact, to the point'.

au fond /əʊ ˈfɔ̃, French o fɔ̃/ ▶ adverb in essence.
– ORIGIN French.

Aug. ▶ abbreviation for August.

Augean /ɔːˈdʒiːən/ ▶ adjective of or relating to Augeas: *the Augean stables.*
■ (of a task or problem) requiring so much effort to complete or solve as to seem impossible: *there are Augean amounts of debris to clear.*

Augeas /ɔːˈdʒiːəs/ Greek Mythology a legendary king whose vast stables had never been cleaned. Hercules cleaned them in a day by diverting the River Alpheus to flow through them.

auger /ˈɔːgə/ ▶ noun **1** a tool resembling a large corkscrew, for boring holes in wood.
■ a similar larger tool for boring holes in the ground.
2 (also **auger shell**) a marine mollusc of warm seas

which has a slender tapering spiral shell that is typically large and brightly coloured.
● *Terebra* and other genera, family Terebridae, class Gastropoda.
– ORIGIN Old English *nafogār*, from *nafu* (see **NAVE**[2]) + *gār* 'piercer'. The *n* was lost by wrong division of *a nauger*; compare with **ADDER**[1] and **APRON**.

> USAGE See usage at **AUGUR**.

Auger effect /ˈəʊʒeɪ/ ▶ noun [mass noun] Physics an effect whereby an atom which has been ionized by removal of an electron from an inner shell loses energy by emitting an electron from an outer shell.
– ORIGIN 1930s: named after Pierre V. *Auger* (born 1899), French physicist.

aught[1] /ɔːt/ (also **ought**) ▶ pronoun archaic anything at all: *know you aught of this fellow, young sir?*
– ORIGIN Old English *āwiht* (see **AYE**[2], **WIGHT**).

aught[2] ▶ noun variant spelling of **OUGHT**[2].

augite /ˈɔːdʒʌɪt/ ▶ noun [mass noun] a dark green or black aluminosilicate mineral of the pyroxene group. It occurs in many igneous rocks, including basalt, gabbro, and dolerite.
– ORIGIN early 19th cent.: from Latin *augites*, denoting a precious stone (probably turquoise), from Greek *augitēs*, from *augē* 'lustre'.

augment ▶ verb /ɔːɡˈmɛnt/ [with obj.] make (something) greater by adding to it; increase: *her secretarial work helped to augment her husband's income.*
▶ noun /ˈɔːɡm(ə)nt/ Linguistics a vowel prefixed to past tenses of verbs in Greek and certain other Indo-European languages.
– DERIVATIVES **augmenter** noun.
– ORIGIN late Middle English: from Old French *augmenter* (verb), *augment* (noun), or late Latin *augmentare*, from Latin *augere* 'to increase'.

augmentation ▶ noun [mass noun] the action or process of making or becoming greater in size or amount.
■ Music the lengthening of the time values of notes in a melodic part. ■ [count noun] Heraldry an addition to a coat of arms granted as a mark of special honour.
– ORIGIN late Middle English: from late Latin *augmentatio(n-)*, from the verb *augmentare* (see **AUGMENT**).

augmentative ▶ adjective Linguistics (of an affix or derived word) reinforcing the idea of the original word, especially by meaning 'a large one of its kind', as with the Italian suffix *-one* in *borrone* 'ravine', compared with *borro* 'ditch'.
– ORIGIN late Middle English (in the sense 'having a tendency to increase'): from Old French *augmentatif*, *-ive* or medieval Latin *augmentativus*, from the verb *augmentare* (see **AUGMENT**).

augmented ▶ adjective **1** having been made greater in size or value: *augmented pensions for those retiring at 65.*
2 Music denoting or containing an interval which is one semitone greater than the corresponding major or perfect interval: *augmented fourths.*

augmented transition network ▶ noun Linguistics a grammar that represents a sentence as a series of states and possible continuations, augmented with rules for such matters as word agreement.

Augrabies Falls /əˈɡrɑːbiːz/ a series of waterfalls on the Orange River in the province of Northern Cape, South Africa.

au gratin /əʊ ˈɡratã, French o ɡʀatɛ̃/ ▶ adjective [postpositive] sprinkled with breadcrumbs or grated cheese and browned: *lentil and mushroom au gratin.*
– ORIGIN French, literally 'by grating', from the verb *gratter* 'to grate'.

Augsburg /ˈaʊɡzbəːɡ, German ˈaʊksbʊrk/ a city in southern Germany, in Bavaria; pop. 259,880 (1991).

Augsburg Confession a statement of the Lutheran position, drawn up mainly by Melanchthon and approved by Luther before being presented to the Emperor Charles V at Augsburg on 25 June 1530.

augur /ˈɔːɡə/ ▶ verb [no obj.] (**augur well/badly/ill**) (of an event or circumstance) portend a good or bad outcome: *the end of the cold war seemed to augur well.*
■ [with obj.] portend or bode (a specified outcome): *they feared that these happenings augured a neo-Nazi revival.* ■ [with obj.] archaic foresee or predict.
▶ noun historical (in ancient Rome) a religious official who observed natural signs, especially the

a

behaviour of birds, interpreting these as an indication of divine approval or disapproval of a proposed action.
– DERIVATIVES **augural** /ˈɔːgjʊ(ə)r(ə)l/ adjective (archaic).
– ORIGIN late Middle English (as a noun): from Latin, 'diviner'.

USAGE The spellings **augur** (a verb meaning 'portend a good or bad outcome', as in *this augurs well*) and **auger** (a type of tool used for boring) are sometimes confused, but the two words are quite different in both their present meaning and their origins.

augury /ˈɔːgjʊri/ ▶ noun (pl. **-ies**) a sign of what will happen in the future; an omen: *they heard the sound as an augury of death.*
■ [mass noun] the interpretation of omens.
– ORIGIN late Middle English (in the sense 'divination'): from Old French *augurie* or Latin *augurium* 'interpretation of omens', from *augur* (see **AUGUR**).

August ▶ noun the eighth month of the year, in the northern hemisphere usually considered the last month of summer: *the sultry haze of late August | the wettest August in six years.*
– ORIGIN Old English, from Latin *augustus* 'consecrated, venerable'; named after **AUGUSTUS** Caesar, the first Roman emperor.

august /ɔːˈgʌst/ ▶ adjective respected and impressive: *she was in august company.*
– DERIVATIVES **augustly** adverb, **augustness** noun.
– ORIGIN mid 17th cent.: from French *auguste* or Latin *augustus* 'consecrated, venerable'.

Augusta /ɔːˈgʌstə/ **1** a resort in eastern Georgia in the US; pop. 44,640 (1990).
2 the state capital of Maine; pop. 21,320 (1990).

Augustan /ɔːˈgʌst(ə)n/ ▶ adjective connected with or occurring during the reign of the Roman emperor Augustus.
■ relating to or denoting Latin literature of the reign of Augustus, including the works of Virgil, Horace, Ovid, and Livy. ■ relating to or denoting 17th- and 18th-century English literature of a style considered refined and classical, including the works of Pope, Addison, and Swift.
▶ noun a writer of the (Latin or English) Augustan age.
– ORIGIN from Latin *Augustanus* 'relating to Augustus' (see **AUGUSTUS**).

Augustine /ɔːˈgʌstɪn/ ▶ noun an Augustinian friar.
– ORIGIN late Middle English: from Old French *augustin*, from Latin *Augustinus* 'Augustine' (see **AUGUSTINIAN**).

Augustine, St[1] /ɔːˈgʌstɪn/ (died *c.*604), Italian churchman; known as **St Augustine of Canterbury**. Sent from Rome by Pope Gregory the Great to refound the Church in England in 597, he founded a monastery at Canterbury and became its first archbishop. Feast day, 26 May.

Augustine, St[2] /ɔːˈgʌstɪn/ (354–430), Doctor of the Church; known as **St Augustine of Hippo**. He became bishop of Hippo in North Africa in 396. His writings, such as *Confessions* and the *City of God*, dominated subsequent Western theology. Feast day, 28 August.

Augustinian /ˌɔːgəˈstɪnɪən/ ▶ adjective **1** of or relating to St Augustine of Hippo or his doctrines.
2 of or relating to a religious order observing a rule derived from St Augustine's writings.
▶ noun **1** a member of an Augustinian order.
2 an adherent of the doctrines of St Augustine.

Augustus /ɔːˈgʌstəs/ (63 BC–AD 14), the first Roman emperor; born *Gaius Octavius*; also called (until 27 BC) **Octavian**. He was adopted by the will of his great-uncle Julius Caesar and gained supreme power by his defeat of Antony in 31 BC. In 27 BC he was given the title Augustus ('venerable') and became in effect the first Roman emperor.

auk /ɔːk/ ▶ noun a short-winged diving seabird found in northern oceans, typically with a black head and back and white underparts.
• Family Alcidae (the **auk family**), which comprises the guillemots, razorbills, puffins, and their relatives.
– ORIGIN late 17th cent.: from Old Norse *álka* 'razorbill'.

auklet /ˈɔːklɪt/ ▶ noun a small stubby auk found in the North Pacific, typically with grey underparts.
• *Aethia* and three other genera, family Alcidae: several species.

auld /ɔːld, ɑːld/ ▶ adjective Scottish form of **OLD**.
– ORIGIN Old English *ald*, Anglian form of **OLD**.

auld lang syne /ˌɔːld laŋ ˈsʌɪn/ ▶ noun [mass noun] times long past.
– PHRASES **for auld lang syne** for old times' sake.
– ORIGIN late 18th cent.: Scots (see **AULD**, **LANG SYNE**). The phrase was popularized as the title and refrain of a song by Robert Burns (1788).

aumbry /ˈɔːmbri/ (also **ambry**) ▶ noun (pl. **-ies**) a small recess or cupboard in the wall of a church.
■ historical a small cupboard.
– ORIGIN Middle English: from Old French *armarie*, from Latin *armarium* 'closet, chest', from *arma* 'utensils'.

au naturel /ˌəʊ natjʊˈrɛl, French o natyʀɛl/ ▶ adjective & adverb with no elaborate treatment, dressing, or preparation: [as adv.] *I wear my hair au naturel these days* | [as adj.] *the cheese is delicious whether au naturel or seasoned.*
– ORIGIN French, literally 'in the natural (state)'.

Aung San /ˌaʊŋ ˈsan/ (1914–47), Burmese nationalist leader. As leader of the Council of Ministers he negotiated a promise of self-government from the British shortly before his assassination.

Aung San Suu Kyi /aʊŋ ˌsan suː ˈtʃiː/ (b.1945), Burmese political leader, daughter of Aung San and leader of the National League for Democracy (NLD) since 1988. She was kept under house arrest from 1989 to 1995, and the military government refused to recognize her party's victory in the 1990 elections. Nobel Peace Prize (1991).

aunt ▶ noun the sister of one's father or mother or the wife of one's uncle.
■ informal an unrelated adult female friend, especially of a child.
– PHRASES **my sainted aunt!** informal, chiefly Brit. an exclamation expressing surprise or disbelief.
– ORIGIN Middle English: from Old French *ante*, from Latin *amita*.

auntie (also **aunty**) ▶ noun (pl. **-ies**) informal term for **AUNT**.
■ **(Auntie)** Brit. the BBC.

Aunt Sally ▶ noun (pl. **-ies**) [mass noun] a game played in some parts of Britain in which players throw sticks or balls at a wooden dummy.
■ [count noun] a dummy used in this game. ■ [count noun] figurative a person or thing subjected to much criticism, especially one set up as an easy target for it.

au pair /əʊ ˈpɛː/ ▶ noun a young foreign person, typically a woman, who helps with housework or childcare in exchange for food, a room, and some pocket money.
– ORIGIN late 19th cent.: from French, literally 'on equal terms'. The phrase was originally adjectival, describing an arrangement between two parties paid for by the exchange of mutual services; the noun usage dates from the 1960s.

aura /ˈɔːrə/ ▶ noun (pl. **aurae** /-riː/ or **auras**) [usu. in sing.] the distinctive atmosphere or quality that seems to surround and be generated by a person, thing, or place: *the ceremony retains an aura of mystery.*
■ a supposed emanation surrounding the body of a living creature, allegedly visible to some, which is viewed by many spiritualists, mystics, and practitioners of alternative medicine as an essential part of the individual. ■ any invisible emanation, especially an odour. ■ Medicine a warning sensation experienced before an attack of epilepsy or migraine.
– ORIGIN late Middle English (originally denoting a gentle breeze): via Latin from Greek, 'breeze, breath'. Current senses date from the 18th cent.

aural /ˈɔːr(ə)l/ ▶ adjective of or relating to the ear or the sense of hearing: *aural anatomy | information held in written, aural, or visual form.*
– DERIVATIVES **aurally** adverb.
– ORIGIN mid 19th cent.: from Latin *auris* 'ear' + **-AL**.

USAGE The words **aural** and **oral** have the same pronunciation in standard English, which is sometimes a source of confusion. However, although a distinctive pronunciation for **aural** has been proposed (/ˈaʊr(ə)l/, the first syllable rhyming with *cow*), it has not yet become standard.

Aurangzeb /ˈɔːrəŋzɛb, ˈaʊərəŋ-/ (1618–1707), Mogul emperor of Hindustan 1658–1707, who increased the Mogul empire to its greatest extent.

aurar plural form of **EYRIR**.

aureate /ˈɔːrɪət/ ▶ adjective denoting, made of, or having the colour of gold.
■ (of language) highly ornamented or elaborate.
– ORIGIN late Middle English: from late Latin *aureatus*, from Latin *aureus* 'golden', from *aurum* 'gold'.

Aurelian /ɔːˈriːlɪən/ (*c.*215–75), Roman emperor 270–5; Latin name *Lucius Domitius Aurelianus*. Originally a common soldier, he rose through the ranks and was elected emperor by the army.

Aurelius /ɔːˈriːlɪəs/, Marcus (121–80), Roman emperor 161–80; full name *Caesar Marcus Aurelius Antoninus Augustus*. He was occupied for much of his reign with wars against invading Germanic tribes. His *Meditations*, a collection of aphorisms and reflections, are evidence of his philosophical nature.

aureole /ˈɔːrɪəʊl/ (also **aureola** /ɔːˈrɪələ/) ▶ noun a circle of light or brightness surrounding something, especially as depicted in art around the head or body of a person represented as holy.
■ another term for **CORONA**[1] (in sense 1, of the sun or moon). ■ another term for **AREOLA**. ■ Geology the zone of metamorphosed rock surrounding an igneous intrusion.
– ORIGIN Middle English: from Old French *aureole*, from Latin *aureola (corona)* 'golden (crown)', feminine of *aureolus* (diminutive of *aureus*, from *aurum* 'gold').

aureus /ˈɔːrɪəs/ ▶ noun (pl. **aurei**) a Roman coin of the late republic and empire, worth 25 silver denarii.
– ORIGIN Latin, noun use of *aureus* 'golden', from *aurum* 'gold'.

au revoir /ˌəʊ rəˈvwɑː, French o ʀəvwaʀ/ ▶ exclamation goodbye until we meet again.
– ORIGIN late 17th cent.: from French, literally 'to the seeing again'.

Auric /ˈɔːrɪk, French ɔʀik/, Georges (1899–1983), French composer. Auric was one of the anti-romantic group Les Six. He is probably best known for film music such as the scores for *The Lavender Hill Mob* (1951) and *Moulin Rouge* (1952).

auric[1] /ˈɔːrɪk/ ▶ adjective of or relating to the aura supposedly surrounding a living creature.

auric[2] /ˈɔːrɪk/ ▶ adjective Chemistry of gold with a valency of three; of gold(III).
– ORIGIN early 19th cent.: from Latin *aurum* 'gold' + **-IC**.

auricle /ˈɔːrɪk(ə)l/ ▶ noun Anatomy & Biology a structure resembling an ear or ear lobe.
■ another term for **ATRIUM** (of the heart). ■ a small muscular flap on the surface of each atrium. ■ the external part or pinna of the ear.
– ORIGIN late Middle English: from Latin *auricula* 'external part of the ear', diminutive of *auris* 'ear'.

auricula /ɔːˈrɪkjʊlə/ ▶ noun an Alpine primula from which a wide range of flowering cultivars have been developed. It has leaves that supposedly resemble bears' ears. Also called **BEAR'S EAR**.
• *Primula auricula*, family Primulaceae.
– ORIGIN mid 17th cent.: from Latin, diminutive of *auris* 'ear'.

auricular /ɔːˈrɪkjʊlə/ ▶ adjective **1** of or relating to the ear or hearing.
2 of, relating to, or shaped like an auricle.
– ORIGIN late Middle English: from late Latin *auricularis*, from *auricula*, diminutive of *auris* 'ear'.

auriculate /ɔːˈrɪkjʊlət/ ▶ adjective chiefly Botany & Zoology having one or more structures shaped like an ear or ear lobe.
– ORIGIN early 18th cent.: from Latin *auricula* 'external part of the ear' (diminutive of *auris* 'ear') + **-ATE**[2].

auriferous /ɔːˈrɪf(ə)rəs/ ▶ adjective (of rocks or minerals) containing gold.
– ORIGIN mid 17th cent.: from Latin *aurifer* 'gold-bearing' (from *aurum* 'gold') + **-OUS**.

Auriga /ɔːˈrʌɪgə/ Astronomy a large northern constellation (the Charioteer), said to represent a man holding a whip.
■ [as genitive **Aurigae** /ɔːˈrʌɪgiː, -gʌɪ/] used with preceding letter or numeral to designate a star in this constellation: *the star Theta Aurigae.*
– ORIGIN Latin.

Aurignacian /ˌɔːrɪˈnjeɪʃ(ə)n, ˌɔːrɪgˈneɪ-/ ▶ adjective Archaeology of, relating to, or denoting the early stages of the Upper Palaeolithic culture in Europe and the Near East. It is dated in most places to about 34,000–29,000 years ago, and is associated with Cro-Magnon Man.

■[as noun **the Aurignacian**] the Aurignacian culture or period.

– ORIGIN early 20th cent.: from French *Aurignacien*, from *Aurignac* in SW France, where objects from this culture were found.

auriscope /ˈɔːrɪskəʊp/ (also **auroscope** /ˈɔːrəskəʊp/) ▶ **noun** another term for **OTOSCOPE**.

– ORIGIN mid 19th cent.: from Latin *auris* 'ear' + **-SCOPE**.

aurochs /ˈɔːrɒks, ˈaʊ-/ ▶ **noun** (pl. same) a large wild Eurasian ox that was the ancestor of domestic cattle. It was probably exterminated in Britain in the Bronze Age, and the last one was killed in Poland in 1627. Also called **URUS**.

● *Bos primigenius*, family Bovidae.

– ORIGIN late 18th cent.: from German, early variant of *Auerochs*, from Old High German *ūrohso*, from *ūr* (form also found in Old English, of unknown origin) + *ohso* 'ox'.

Aurora /ɔːˈrɔːrə/ Roman Mythology goddess of the dawn. Greek equivalent **Eos**.

aurora /ɔːˈrɔːrə/ ▶ **noun** (pl. **auroras** or **aurorae** /-riː/)

1 a natural electrical phenomenon characterized by the appearance of streamers of reddish or greenish light in the sky, especially near the northern or southern magnetic pole. The effect is caused by the interaction of charged particles from the sun with atoms in the upper atmosphere. In northern and southern regions it is respectively called **aurora borealis** or **northern lights** and **aurora australis** or **southern lights**. [ORIGIN: *borealis* from Latin, 'northern', based on Greek *Boreas*, the god of the north wind; *australis* from Latin, 'southern', from *Auster* 'the south, the south wind'.]

2 [in sing.] poetic/literary the dawn.

– DERIVATIVES **auroral** adjective.

– ORIGIN late Middle English (originally in sense 2): from Latin, 'dawn, goddess of the dawn'. Sense 1 dates from the early 18th cent.

AUS ▶ **abbreviation for** Australia (international vehicle registration).

Auschwitz /ˈaʊʃvɪts/ a Nazi concentration camp in the Second World War, near the town of Oświęcim (Auschwitz) in Poland.

auscultation /ˌɔːsk(ə)lˈteɪʃ(ə)n/ ▶ **noun** [mass noun] the action of listening to sounds from the heart, lungs, or other organs, typically with a stethoscope, as a part of medical diagnosis.

– DERIVATIVES **auscultate** verb, **auscultatory** /ɔːˈskʌltət(ə)ri/ adjective.

– ORIGIN mid 17th cent.: from Latin *auscultatio(n-)*, from *auscultare* 'listen to'.

Auslese /ˈaʊsleɪzə/ ▶ **noun** [mass noun] a white wine of German origin or style made from selected bunches of grapes picked later than the general harvest.

– ORIGIN from German, from *aus* 'out' + *Lese* 'picking, vintage'.

auspice /ˈɔːspɪs/ ▶ **noun** archaic a divine or prophetic token.

– PHRASES **under the auspices of** with the help, support, or protection of: *the delegation's visit was arranged under UN auspices.*

– ORIGIN mid 16th cent. (originally denoting the observation of bird-flight in divination): from French, or from Latin *auspicium*, from *auspex* 'observer of birds', from *avis* 'bird' + *specere* 'to look'.

auspicious /ɔːˈspɪʃəs/ ▶ **adjective** conducive to success; favourable: *it was not the most auspicious moment to hold an election.*

■giving or being a sign of future success: *they said it was an auspicious moon—it was rising.* ■ archaic characterized by success; prosperous: *he was respectful to his auspicious customers.*

– DERIVATIVES **auspiciously** adverb, **auspiciousness** noun.

– ORIGIN late 16th cent.: from **AUSPICE** + **-OUS**.

Aussie /ˈɒzi, ˈɒsi/ (also **Ozzie**) ▶ **noun** (pl. **-ies**) & **adjective** informal term for **AUSTRALIA** or **AUSTRALIAN**.

Austen /ˈɒstɪn, ˈɔː-/, Jane (1775–1817), English novelist. Her major novels are *Sense and Sensibility* (1811), *Pride and Prejudice* (1813), *Mansfield Park* (1814), *Emma* (1815), *Northanger Abbey* (1818), and *Persuasion* (1818). They are notable for skilful characterization, dry wit, and penetrating social observation.

austenite /ˈɒstɪnʌɪt, ˈɔː-/ ▶ **noun** [mass noun] Metallurgy a solid solution of carbon in a non-magnetic form of iron stable at high temperatures. It is a constituent of some forms of steel.

– DERIVATIVES **austenitic** adjective.

– ORIGIN early 20th cent.: from the name of Sir William Roberts-*Austen* (1843–1902), English metallurgist, + **-ITE**[1].

austere /ɒˈstɪə, ɔː-/ ▶ **adjective** (**austerer**, **austerest**) severe or strict in manner, attitude, or appearance: *he was an austere man, with a rigidly puritanical outlook | an austere expression.*

■(of living conditions or a way of life) having no comforts or luxuries; harsh or ascetic: *conditions in the prison could hardly be more austere.* ■ having an extremely plain and simple style or appearance; unadorned: *the cathedral is impressive in its austere simplicity.* ■ (of an economic policy or measure) designed to reduce a budget deficit, especially by cutting public expenditure.

– DERIVATIVES **austerely** adverb.

– ORIGIN Middle English: via Old French from Latin *austerus*, from Greek *austēros* 'severe'.

austerity ▶ **noun** (pl. **-ies**) [mass noun] sternness or severity of manner or attitude: *he was noted for his austerity and his authoritarianism.*

■extreme plainness and simplicity of style or appearance: *the room was decorated with a restraint bordering on austerity.* ■ (**austerities**) conditions characterized by severity, sternness, or asceticism: *his uncle's austerities had undermined his health* | [mass noun] *the simple life of prayer and personal austerity.* ■ difficult economic conditions created by government measures to reduce a budget deficit, especially by reducing public expenditure: *a period of austerity* | [as modifier] *austerity measures.*

– ORIGIN late Middle English: from French *austérité*, from Latin *austeritas*, from *austerus* 'severe' (see **AUSTERE**).

Austerlitz, Battle of /ˈaʊstəlɪts, ˈɔːstə-/ a battle in 1805 near the town of Austerlitz (now in the Czech Republic), in which Napoleon defeated the Austrians and Russians.

Austin[1] /ˈɒstɪn, ˈɔː-/ the state capital of Texas; pop. 465,620 (1990). First settled in 1835, it was named in 1839 after Stephen F. Austin, son of Moses Austin, leader of the first Texas colony.

Austin[2] /ˈɒstɪn, ˈɔː-/, Herbert, 1st Baron Austin of Longbridge (1866–1941), British motor manufacturer. Among the cars produced by his factory the Austin Seven ('Baby Austin') was particularly popular. His company merged with Morris Motors in 1952 to form the British Motor Corporation.

Austin[3] /ˈɒstɪn, ˈɔː-/, John (1790–1859), English jurist. His work is significant for its strict delimitation of the sphere of law and its distinction from that of morality.

Austin[4] /ˈɒstɪn, ˈɔː-/, J. L. (1911–60), English philosopher; full name *John Langshaw Austin*. A careful exponent of linguistic philosophy, he pioneered the theory of speech acts, pointing out that utterances can be used to perform actions as well as to convey information. Notable works: *Sense and Sensibilia* and *How to Do Things with Words* (both 1962).

Austin Friars ▶ **plural noun** another name for Augustinian Friars.

austral /ˈɒstr(ə)l, ˈɔː-/ ▶ **adjective** of or relating to the south, in particular:

■technical of the southern hemisphere: *the austral spring.* ■ (**Austral**) of Australia or Australasia.

– ORIGIN late 15th cent.: from Latin *australis*, from *Auster* 'the south, the south wind'.

Australasia /ˌɒstrəˈleɪʒə, -ʃə/ the region consisting of Australia, New Zealand, New Guinea, and the neighbouring islands of the Pacific.

– DERIVATIVES **Australasian** adjective & noun.

Australia an island country and continent of the southern hemisphere, in the SW Pacific, a member state of the Commonwealth; pop. 17,500,000 (est. 1991); official language, English; capital, Canberra.

> Inhabited by Aboriginal peoples since prehistoric times, Australia was explored by the Dutch from 1606; British colonization began in 1788, as did the transportation of convicts (discontinued in 1868). Australia was declared a Commonwealth in 1901, when the six colonies (New South Wales, Victoria, Queensland, South Australia, Western Australia, and the offshore island of Tasmania) federated as sovereign states; Northern Territory achieved similar status in 1978.

Australia Day ▶ **noun** a national public holiday in Australia, commemorating the founding on 26 January 1788 of the colony of New South Wales.

Australian ▶ **noun** a native or national of Australia, or a person of Australian descent.

▶ **adjective** of or relating to Australia.

■Zoology of, relating to, or denoting a zoogeographical region comprising Australasia together with Indonesia east of Wallace's line, in which monotremes and marsupials dominate the fauna. Compare with **NOTOGAEA**. ■ Botany of, relating to, or denoting a phytogeographical kingdom comprising only Australia and Tasmania.

– DERIVATIVES **Australianism** noun.

– ORIGIN from French *australien*, from Latin *australis* in the phrase *Terra Australis* 'the southern land', the name of the supposed southern continent.

Australian Antarctic Territory an area of Antarctica administered by Australia, lying between longitudes 142° east and 136° east.

Australian Capital Territory a federal territory in New South Wales, Australia, consisting of two enclaves ceded by New South Wales, one in 1911 to contain Canberra, the other in 1915 containing Jervis Bay; the latter became the Jervis Bay territory in 1988.

Australian crawl ▶ **noun** chiefly Austral. another term for **CRAWL** (sense 2).

Australian flatworm ▶ **noun** an orange or yellow terrestrial flatworm up to 8 cm in length, accidentally introduced from Australia to Britain where it is destroying earthworm populations.

● *Coenoplana alba*, order Tricladida, class Turbellaria.

Australian Labor Party (abbrev.: **ALP**) Australia's oldest political party, founded in 1891. The party is moderate left-of-centre; it has provided three recent Australian Prime Ministers, Gough Whitlam, Bob Hawke, and Paul Keating.

Australian Rules (also **Australian Rules football**) ▶ **noun** [mass noun] a form of football played on an oval ground with an oval ball by teams of eighteen players.

> The game dates from 1858. Players may run with the ball if they touch it to the ground every fifteen metres, and may pass it in any direction by punching. There are both inner and outer goalposts: a behind (between the outer posts) scores one point and a goal (between the inner posts) scores six.

Australian salmon ▶ **noun** see **SALMON** (sense 2).

Australian salute ▶ **noun** Austral. humorous a wave of the hand to brush flies off the face.

Australian terrier ▶ **noun** a wire-haired terrier of a breed originating in Australia.

Austral Islands another name for **TUBUAI ISLANDS**.

Australite /ˈɒstrəlʌɪt, ˈɔː-/ ▶ **noun** Geology a tektite from the strewn field in Australia.

Australoid /ˈɒstrəlɔɪd, ˈɔː-/ ▶ **adjective** of or relating to the broad division of humankind represented by Australian Aboriginal peoples.

▶ **noun** a person belonging to this division of humankind.

> **USAGE** The term **Australoid** belongs to a set of terms introduced by 19th-century anthropologists attempting to categorize human races. Such terms are associated with outdated notions of racial types, and so are now potentially offensive and best avoided. See **usage** at **MONGOLOID**.

Australopithecus /ˌɒstrələʊˈpɪθɪkəs, ˌɔː-/ ▶ **noun** a fossil bipedal primate with both ape-like and human characteristics, found in Pliocene and Lower Pleistocene deposits (*c.*4 million to 1 million years old) in Africa.

● Genus *Australopithecus*, family Hominidae: several species, including the lightly built *A. africanus*, which is thought to be the immediate ancestor of the human genus *Homo*.

– DERIVATIVES **australopithecine** /-ɪsiːn/ noun & adjective.

– ORIGIN modern Latin, from Latin *australis* 'southern' (see **AUSTRAL**) + Greek *pithēkos* 'ape'.

Australorp /ˈɒstrəlɔːp, ˈɔː-/ ▶ **noun** a black Orpington chicken of an Australian breed.

– ORIGIN early 20th cent.: blend of **AUSTRALIAN** and **ORPINGTON**.

Austria a republic in central Europe; pop. 7,700,000 (est. 1991); official language, German; capital, Vienna. German name **ÖSTERREICH**.

Austria was dominated from the early Middle Ages by the Habsburg family, and became the centre of a massive central European empire which lasted until 1918. The country was incorporated within the Nazi Reich in 1938 and after the Second World War was occupied by the Allies, regaining its sovereignty in 1955. A referendum in 1994 approved Austria's entry into the European Union.

– DERIVATIVES **Austrian** adjective & noun.

Austria–Hungary (also **Austro-Hungarian empire**) the dual monarchy established in 1867 by the Austrian emperor Franz Josef, according to which Austria and Hungary became autonomous states under a common sovereign.

Austrian blind ▶ **noun** a blind made from ruched fabric, which extends about a third of the way down a window.

Austrian Succession, War of the a group of several related conflicts (1740–8), involving most of the states of Europe, that were triggered by the death of the Emperor Charles VI and the accession of his daughter Maria Theresa in 1740 to the Austrian throne. See also **PRAGMATIC SANCTION**.

Austro-[1] /ˈɒstrəʊ, ˈɔː-/ ▶ **combining form** Austrian; Austrian and ...: *Austro-Hungarian.*

Austro-[2] /ˈɒstrəʊ, ˈɔː-/ ▶ **combining form** Australian; Australian and ...: *Austro-Malayan.*
▪southern: *Austro-Asiatic.*
– ORIGIN from Latin *australis* 'southern'.

Austro-Asiatic ▶ **adjective** of, relating to, or denoting a phylum or superfamily of languages spoken in SE Asia, consisting of the Mon-Khmer family, the Munda family, and one or two other isolated languages.
▶ **noun** [mass noun] this phylum of languages.
– ORIGIN from **AUSTRO-**[2] 'southern' + **ASIATIC**.

Austronesian /ˌɒstrə(ʊ)ˈniːzɪən, -ʒ(ə)n, ˌɔː-/ ▶ **adjective** of, relating to, or denoting a family of languages spoken in an area extending from Madagascar in the west to the Pacific islands in the east. Also called **MALAYO-POLYNESIAN**.
▶ **noun** [mass noun] this family of languages.

Austronesian languages are spoken by about 140 million people, of whom all but 1 million speak a language of the Indonesian group, which includes Indonesian, Javanese, Tagalog, and Malagasy. The other groups are Micronesian, Melanesian, and Polynesian, scattered across the islands of the South Pacific.

– ORIGIN from German *austronesisch*, based on Latin *australis* 'southern' (see **AUSTRAL**) + Greek *nēsos* 'island'.

AUT ▶ **abbreviation for** (in the UK) Association of University Teachers.

aut- ▶ **prefix** variant spelling of **AUTO-** shortened before a vowel (as in *autoxidation*).

autarch /ˈɔːtɑːk/ ▶ **noun** a ruler who has absolute power.
– ORIGIN early 19th cent.: from Greek *autarkhos*, from *autos* 'self' + *arkhos* 'leader'.

autarchy /ˈɔːtɑːki/ ▶ **noun** (pl. **-ies**) **1** another term for **AUTOCRACY**.
2 variant spelling of **AUTARKY**.
– DERIVATIVES **autarchic** adjective.

autarky (also **autarchy**) ▶ **noun** [mass noun] economic independence or self-sufficiency.
▪[count noun] a country, state, or society which is economically independent.
– DERIVATIVES **autarkic** adjective.
– ORIGIN early 17th cent.: from Greek *autarkeia*, from *autarkēs* 'self-sufficiency', from *autos* 'self' + *arkein* 'suffice'.

autecology /ˌɔːtɪˈkɒlədʒi/ (also **autoecology**) ▶ **noun** [mass noun] Biology the ecological study of a particular species. Contrasted with **SYNECOLOGY**.
– DERIVATIVES **autecological** adjective.

auteur /əʊˈtəː, ɔː-/ ▶ **noun** a film director who influences their films so much that they rank as their author.
– DERIVATIVES **auteurism** noun, **auteurist** adjective.
– ORIGIN 1960s: from French, literally 'author'.

authentic ▶ **adjective** **1** of undisputed origin; genuine: *the letter is now accepted as an authentic document | authentic 14th-century furniture.*
▪made or done in the traditional or original way, or in a way that faithfully resembles an original: *the restaurant serves authentic Italian meals | every detail of the film was totally authentic.* ▪ based on facts; accurate or reliable: *an authentic depiction of the situation.* ▪ (in existentialist philosophy) relating to or denoting an emotionally appropriate, significant, purposive, and responsible mode of human life.
2 Music (of a church mode) containing notes between the principal note or final and the note an octave higher. Compare with **PLAGAL**.
– DERIVATIVES **authentically** adverb [as submodifier] *the food is authentically Cajun*, **authenticity** /ɔːθɛnˈtɪsɪti/ noun.
– ORIGIN late Middle English: via Old French from late Latin *authenticus*, from Greek *authentikos* 'principal, genuine'.

authenticate ▶ **verb** [with obj.] prove or show (something, especially a claim or an artistic work) to be true or genuine: *they were invited to authenticate artefacts from the Italian Renaissance.*
▪validate: *the nationalist statements authenticated their leadership among the local community.* ▪ [no obj.] Computing (of a user or process) have one's identity verified.
– DERIVATIVES **authentication** /-ˈkeɪʃ(ə)n/ noun, **authenticator** noun.
– ORIGIN early 17th cent.: from medieval Latin *authenticat-* 'established as valid', from the verb *authenticare*, from late Latin *authenticus* 'genuine' (see **AUTHENTIC**).

authigenic /ˌɔːθɪˈdʒɛnɪk/ ▶ **adjective** Geology (of minerals and other materials) formed in their present position. Often contrasted with **ALLOGENIC**.
– ORIGIN late 19th cent.: from Greek *authigenēs* 'born on the spot' + **-IC**.

author ▶ **noun** a writer of a book, article, or report: *he is the author of several books on the subject.*
▪someone who writes books as a profession. ▪ the writings of such a person: *I had to read authors I disliked.* ▪ figurative an originator or creator of something, especially a plan or idea: *the authors of the peace plan.*
▶ **verb** [with obj.] be the author of (a book or piece of writing): *she has authored several articles on wildlife.*
▪figurative be the originator of: *the concept has been authored largely by insurance companies.*
– DERIVATIVES **authorial** /ɔːˈθɔːrɪəl/ adjective.
– ORIGIN Middle English (in the sense 'a person who invents or causes something'): from Old French *autor*, from Latin *auctor*, from *augere* 'increase, originate, promote'. The spelling with *th* arose in the 15th cent., and perhaps became established under the influence of *authentic*.

USAGE In the sense 'be the author of' the verb **author** is objected to by some traditionalists. It is well established, though, especially in North America (in the Oxford Reading Programme, US and Canadian usage accounts for around 85 per cent of the total number of uses collected), and has been around since the end of the 16th century.

authoress ▶ **noun** a female author.

authoring ▶ **noun** [mass noun] Computing the creation of programs and databases for computer applications such as computer-assisted learning or multimedia products: [as modifier] *an authoring system.*

authoritarian /ɔːˌθɒrɪˈtɛːrɪən/ ▶ **adjective** favouring or enforcing strict obedience to authority, especially that of the state, at the expense of personal freedom: *the transition from an authoritarian to a democratic regime.*
▪showing a lack of concern for the wishes or opinions of others; dictatorial: *he had an authoritarian and at times belligerent manner.*
▶ **noun** an authoritarian person.
– DERIVATIVES **authoritarianism** noun.

authoritative /ɔːˈθɒrɪtətɪv, -ˌteɪtɪv/ ▶ **adjective** **1** able to be trusted as being accurate or true; reliable: *clear, authoritative information and advice | an authoritative source.*
▪(of a text) considered to be the best of its kind and unlikely to be improved upon: *this is likely to become the authoritative study of the subject.*
2 commanding and self-confident; likely to be respected and obeyed: *she had an authoritative air | his voice was calm and authoritative.*
▪proceeding from an official source and requiring compliance or obedience: *authoritative directives.*
– DERIVATIVES **authoritatively** adverb, **authoritativeness** noun.

authority ▶ **noun** (pl. **-ies**) **1** [mass noun] the power or right to give orders, make decisions, and enforce obedience: *he had absolute **authority over** his subordinates | positions of authority | a rebellion against those **in authority**.*
▪the right to act in a specified way, delegated from one person or organization to another: [often with infinitive] *military forces have the legal authority to arrest drug traffickers.* ▪ official permission; sanction: *the money was spent without parliamentary authority.*
2 (often **authorities**) a person or organization having power or control in a particular, especially political or administrative, sphere: *the health authorities | the Civil Aviation Authority |* [mass noun] *she wasn't used to dealing with authority.*
3 [mass noun] the power to influence others, especially because of one's commanding manner or one's recognized knowledge about something: *he has the natural authority of one who is used to being obeyed | he spoke **with authority** on the subject.*
▪the confidence resulting from personal expertise: *he hit the ball with authority.* ▪ [count noun] a person with extensive or specialized knowledge about a subject; an expert: *he was **an authority on** the stock market.* ▪ [count noun] a book or other source able to supply reliable information or evidence, typically to settle a dispute.
– PHRASES **have something on good authority** have ascertained something from a reliable source.
– ORIGIN Middle English: from Old French *autorite*, from Latin *auctoritas*, from *auctor* 'originator, promoter' (see **AUTHOR**).

authorization (also **-isation**) ▶ **noun** [mass noun] the action or fact of authorizing or being authorized: *the raising of revenue and the authorization of spending |* [count noun] *power stations will have to obtain authorizations to continue their operations.*
▪[count noun] a document giving permission or authority.

authorize (also **-ise**) ▶ **verb** [with obj.] give official permission for or approval to (an undertaking or agent): *the government authorized further aircraft production |* [as adj. **authorized**] *an authorized dealer |* [with obj. and infinitive] *the troops were authorized to use force.*
– ORIGIN late Middle English: from Old French *autoriser*, from medieval Latin *auctorizare*, from *auctor* 'originator, promoter' (see **AUTHOR**).

Authorized Version ▶ **noun** chiefly Brit. an English translation of the Bible made in 1611 at the order of James I and still widely used, though never formally 'authorized'. Also called **KING JAMES BIBLE**.

authorship ▶ **noun** [mass noun] the fact or position of someone's having written a book or other work: *an investigation into the authorship of the Gospels | joint authorship.*
▪the occupation of writing: *he took to authorship.*

autism /ˈɔːtɪz(ə)m/ ▶ **noun** [mass noun] Psychiatry a mental condition, present from early childhood, characterized by great difficulty in communicating and forming relationships with other people and in using language and abstract concepts.
▪a mental condition in which fantasy dominates over reality, as a symptom of schizophrenia and other disorders.
– DERIVATIVES **autistic** adjective & noun.
– ORIGIN early 20th cent.: from Greek *autos* 'self' + **-ISM**.

auto[1] ▶ **noun** (pl. **-os**) [usu. as modifier] informal, chiefly N. Amer. a motor car: *the auto industry.*
– ORIGIN late 19th cent.: abbreviation of **AUTOMOBILE**.

auto[2] ▶ **adjective** & **noun** short for **AUTOMATIC**.

auto- (usu. **aut-** before a vowel) ▶ **combining form** self: *auto-analysis.*
▪one's own: *autograph.* ▪ by oneself or spontaneous: *autoxidation.* ▪ by itself or automatic: *autofocusing.*
– ORIGIN from Greek *autos* 'self'.

autoantibody ▶ **noun** (pl. **-ies**) Physiology an antibody produced by an organism in response to a constituent of its own tissues.

Autobahn /ˈɔːtə(ʊ)bɑːn, German ˈaʊtobaːn/ ▶ **noun** a German, Austrian, or Swiss motorway.
– ORIGIN 1930s: from German, from *Auto* 'motor car' + *Bahn* 'path, road'.

autobiographical ▶ **adjective** (of a written work) dealing with the writer's own life: *an autobiographical account | the book is partly autobiographical.*
– DERIVATIVES **autobiographic** adjective.

autobiography ▶ **noun** (pl. **-ies**) an account of a person's life written by that person: *he gives a vivid description of his childhood in his autobiography.*
▪[mass noun] such writing as a literary genre.
– DERIVATIVES **autobiographer** noun.

auto bra ▶ noun see **BRA**.

autocar ▶ noun archaic a motor vehicle.

autocatalysis ▶ noun [mass noun] Chemistry catalysis of a reaction by one of its products.
– DERIVATIVES **autocatalyst** noun, **autocatalytic** adjective.

autocephalous /ˌɔːtə(ʊ)ˈsɛf(ə)ləs, -ˈkɛf-/ ▶ adjective (of an Eastern Christian Church) appointing its own head, not subject to the authority of an external patriarch or archbishop.
– ORIGIN mid 19th cent.: from Greek *autokephalos* (from *autos* 'self' + *kephalē* 'head') + **-OUS**.

autochanger (also **autochange**) ▶ noun a mechanism for the automatic substitution of one gramophone record or compact disc for another during use.

autochrome ▶ noun [mass noun] [usu. as modifier] an early form of colour photography using plates coated with dyed starch grains, patented by the Lumière brothers in 1904: *the autochrome process.*
■ [count noun] a colour photograph made by this process.

autochthon /ɔːˈtɒkθ(ə)n, -θɒn/ ▶ noun (pl. **autochthons** or **autochthones** /-θəniːz/) an original or indigenous inhabitant of a place; an aborigine.
– ORIGIN late 16th cent.: from Greek, literally 'sprung from the earth', from *autos* 'self' + *khthōn* 'earth, soil'.

autochthonous /ɔːˈtɒkθənəs/ ▶ adjective (of an inhabitant of a place) indigenous rather than descended from migrants or colonists.
■ Geology (of a deposit or formation) formed in its present position. Often contrasted with **ALLOCHTHONOUS**.

autoclave /ˈɔːtə(ʊ)kleɪv/ ▶ noun a strong heated container used for chemical reactions and other processes using high pressures and temperatures, e.g. steam sterilization.
▶ verb [with obj.] heat (something) in an autoclave.
– ORIGIN late 19th cent.: from French, from *auto-* 'self' + Latin *clavus* 'nail' or *clavis* 'key' (so named because it is self-fastening).

autocorrelation ▶ noun [mass noun] Mathematics & Statistics correlation between the elements of a series and others from the same series separated from them by a given interval.
■ [count noun] a calculation of such correlation.

autocracy /ɔːˈtɒkrəsi/ ▶ noun (pl. **-ies**) [mass noun] a system of government by one person with absolute power.
■ [count noun] a regime based on such a principle of government. ■ [count noun] a country, state, or society governed in such a way. ■ domineering rule or control: *a boss who shifts between autocracy and consultation.*
– ORIGIN mid 17th cent. (in the sense 'autonomy'): from Greek *autokrateia*, from *autokratēs* (see **AUTOCRAT**).

autocrat ▶ noun a ruler who has absolute power.
■ someone who insists on complete obedience from others; an imperious or domineering person.
– ORIGIN early 19th cent.: from French *autocrate*, from Greek *autokratēs*, from *autos* 'self' + *kratos* 'power'.

autocratic ▶ adjective of or relating to a ruler who has absolute power: *the constitutional reforms threatened his autocratic power.*
■ taking no account of other people's wishes or opinions; domineering: *a man with a reputation for an autocratic management style.*
– DERIVATIVES **autocratically** adverb.

autocross ▶ noun [mass noun] Brit. a form of motor racing in which cars are driven singly or in heats over a course including rough terrain or unmade roads. Compare with **RALLYCROSS**.
■ N. Amer. a form of competition in which cars are driven around an obstacle course, typically marked out by cones on an empty car park.
– ORIGIN 1960s: blend of **AUTOMOBILE** and **CROSS-COUNTRY**.

autocue ▶ noun trademark, chiefly Brit. a device which projects an enlarged image of a script on to a clear glass screen in front of someone speaking on television or in public, so enabling the speaker to read their speech while appearing to be looking at the viewers or audience.

auto-da-fé /ˌɔːtəʊdɑːˈfeɪ/ ▶ noun (pl. **autos-da-fé** /ˌɔːtəʊz-/) the burning of a heretic by the Spanish Inquisition.

■ a sentence of such a kind.
– ORIGIN early 18th cent.: from Portuguese, literally 'act of the faith'.

autodidact /ˈɔːtəʊdɪdakt/ ▶ noun a self-taught person.
– DERIVATIVES **autodidactic** adjective.
– ORIGIN mid 18th cent.: from Greek *autodidaktos* 'self-taught', from *autos* 'self' + *didaskein* 'teach'.

autoecology /ˌɔːtiːˈkɒlədʒi/ ▶ noun variant spelling of **AUTECOLOGY**.

auto-erotic ▶ adjective of or relating to sexual excitement generated by stimulating or fantasizing about one's own body.
– DERIVATIVES **auto-eroticism** noun.

auto-exposure ▶ noun a device which sets the exposure automatically on a camera or other device.
■ [mass noun] the facility to set exposure automatically.

autofocus ▶ noun a device focusing a camera or other device automatically.
■ [mass noun] automatic focusing.
– DERIVATIVES **autofocusing** noun.

autogamy /ɔːˈtɒɡəmi/ ▶ noun [mass noun] Biology self-fertilization, especially the self pollination of a flower. Compare with **ALLOGAMY**.
– DERIVATIVES **autogamous** adjective.
– ORIGIN late 19th cent.: from **AUTO-** 'self' + Greek *-gamia* (from *gamos* 'marriage').

autogenic /ˌɔːtə(ʊ)ˈdʒɛnɪk/ ▶ adjective technical self-generated: *autogenic succession.*

autogenic training ▶ noun [mass noun] a form of relaxation therapy involving auto-suggestion.

autogenous /ɔːˈtɒdʒɪnəs/ ▶ adjective arising from within or from a thing itself.
■ (of welding) done either without a filler or with a filler of the same metal as the pieces being welded.

autogiro (also **autogyro**) ▶ noun (pl. **-os**) a form of aircraft with freely rotating horizontal vanes and a propeller. It differs from a helicopter in that the vanes are not powered but rotate in the slipstream, propulsion being by a conventional mounted engine.
– ORIGIN 1920s: from Spanish, from *auto-* 'self' + *giro* 'gyration'.

autograft ▶ noun a graft of tissue from one point to another of the same individual's body.

autograph ▶ noun **1** a signature, especially that of a celebrity written as a memento for an admirer: *fans surged around the car asking for autographs.* **2** a manuscript or musical score in an author's or musician's own handwriting.
■ [mass noun] a person's handwriting.
▶ verb [with obj.] (of a celebrity) write one's signature on (something); sign: *the whole team autographed a shirt for him* | [as adj. **autographed**] *an autographed photo.*
▶ adjective written in the author's own handwriting: *an autograph manuscript.*
■ (of a painting or sculpture) done by the artist himself, not by a copier.
– DERIVATIVES **autographic** adjective.
– ORIGIN early 17th cent.: from French *autographe* or late Latin *autographum*, from Greek *autographon*, neuter of *autographos* 'written with one's own hand', from *autos* 'self' + *graphos* 'written'.

autoharp ▶ noun a kind of zither fitted with a series of sprung and padded bars which allow the playing of chords by damping selected strings.

autohypnosis ▶ noun [mass noun] induction of a hypnotic state in oneself; self-hypnosis.
– DERIVATIVES **autohypnotic** adjective.

autoimmune ▶ adjective Medicine of or relating to disease caused by antibodies or lymphocytes produced against substances naturally present in the body: *the infection triggers an autoimmune response.*
– DERIVATIVES **autoimmunity** noun.

autointoxication ▶ noun [mass noun] Medicine poisoning by a toxin formed within the body itself.

autologous /ɔːˈtɒləɡəs/ ▶ adjective (of cells or tissues) obtained from the same individual.

autolysis /ɔːˈtɒlɪsɪs/ ▶ noun [mass noun] Biology the destruction of cells or tissues by their own enzymes, especially those released by lysosomes.
– DERIVATIVES **autolytic** adjective.

automat ▶ noun US historical a cafeteria in which food and drink were obtained from slot machines.
– ORIGIN late 17th cent. (denoting an automaton): from German, from French *automate*, from Latin

automaton (see **AUTOMATON**). The current sense dates from the early 20th cent.

automate ▶ verb [with obj.] convert (a process or facility) to be operated by largely automatic equipment: *industry is investing in automating production* | [as adj. **automated**] *a fully automated process.*
– ORIGIN 1950s: back-formation from **AUTOMATION**.

automated teller machine ▶ noun a machine that automatically provides cash and performs other banking services on insertion of a special card by the account holder.

automatic ▶ adjective **1** (of a device or process) working by itself with little or no direct human control: *an automatic kettle that switches itself off when it boils* | *calibration is fully automatic.*
■ (of a firearm) self-loading and able to fire continuously until the ammunition is exhausted or the pressure on the trigger is released: *automatic weapons.* ■ (of a motor vehicle or its transmission) using gears that change by themselves according to speed and acceleration: *a four-speed automatic gearbox.*
2 done or occurring spontaneously, without conscious thought or attention: *automatic physical functions such as breathing* | *'Nice to meet you,' he said, with automatic politeness.*
■ occurring as a matter of course and without debate: *he is the automatic choice for the senior team.* ■ (especially of a legal sanction) given or imposed as a necessary and inevitable result of a fixed rule or particular set of circumstances: *he received an automatic one-match suspension.*
▶ noun an automatic machine or device, in particular:
■ a gun that continues firing until the ammunition is exhausted or the pressure on the trigger is released. ■ a vehicle with automatic transmission.
– DERIVATIVES **automatically** adverb, **automaticity** noun.
– ORIGIN mid 18th cent.: from Greek *automatos* 'acting of itself' (see **AUTOMATON**) + **-IC**.

automatic gain control ▶ noun [mass noun] Electronics a feature of certain amplifier circuits which gives a constant output over a wide range of input levels.

automatic pilot ▶ noun a device for keeping an aircraft on a set course without the intervention of the pilot.

automatic translation ▶ noun another term for **MACHINE TRANSLATION**.

automatic writing ▶ noun [mass noun] writing said to be produced by a spiritual, occult, or subconscious agency rather than by the conscious intention of the writer.

automation ▶ noun [mass noun] the use or introduction of automatic equipment in a manufacturing or other process or facility.
– ORIGIN 1940s (originally US): irregular formation from **AUTOMATIC** + **-ATION**.

automatism /ɔːˈtɒmətɪz(ə)m/ ▶ noun [mass noun] Psychiatry the performance of actions without conscious thought or intention, typically without awareness, or with detached awareness as if observing.
■ Art the avoidance of conscious intention in producing works of art, especially by using mechanical techniques or subconscious associations. ■ [count noun] an action performed unconsciously or involuntarily.
– ORIGIN mid 19th cent.: from French *automatisme*, from *automate* 'automaton', from Greek *automatos* 'acting of itself' (see **AUTOMATON**).

automatize /ɔːˈtɒmətʌɪz/ (also **-ise**) ▶ verb [with obj.] [usu. as adj. **automatized**] make automatic or habitual: *the need to refresh automatized forms of literature.*
– DERIVATIVES **automatization** noun.

automaton /ɔːˈtɒmət(ə)n/ ▶ noun (pl. **automata** /-tə/ or **automatons**) a moving mechanical device made in imitation of a human being.
■ a machine which performs a function according to a predetermined set of coded instructions, especially one capable of a range of programmed responses to different circumstances. ■ used in similes and comparisons to refer to a person who seems to act in a mechanical or unemotional way.
– ORIGIN early 17th cent.: via Latin from Greek, neuter of *automatos* 'acting of itself', from *autos* 'self'.

automize ▶ verb **1** another term for **AUTOMATE**. **2** another term for **AUTOMATIZE**.

automobile ▶ noun chiefly N. Amer. a motor car.
– ORIGIN late 19th cent.: from French, from *auto-* 'self' + *mobile* 'mobile'.

automotive /ˌɔːtəˈməʊtɪv/ ▶ adjective [attrib.] of, relating to, or concerned with motor vehicles.

autonomic /ˌɔːtəˈnɒmɪk/ ▶ adjective [attrib.] chiefly Physiology involuntary or unconscious; relating to the autonomic nervous system.
– ORIGIN mid 19th cent. (in the sense 'self-governing'): from **AUTONOMY** + **-IC**.

autonomic nervous system ▶ noun the part of the nervous system responsible for control of the bodily functions not consciously directed, such as breathing, the heartbeat, and digestive processes.

autonomous ▶ adjective (of a country or region) having self-government, at least to a significant degree: *the federation included sixteen autonomous republics.*
■ acting independently or having the freedom to do so: *school governors are legally autonomous.* ■ (in Kantian moral philosophy) acting in accordance with one's moral duty rather than one's desires. Compare with **HETERONOMOUS**.
– DERIVATIVES **autonomously** adverb.
– ORIGIN early 19th cent.: from Greek *autonomos* 'having its own laws' + **-OUS**.

autonomy /ɔːˈtɒnəmi/ ▶ noun (pl. **-ies**) [mass noun] (of a country or region) the right or condition of self-government, especially in a particular sphere: *Tatarstan demanded greater autonomy within the Russian Federation.*
■ [count noun] a self-governing country or region. ■ freedom from external control or influence; independence. ■ (in Kantian moral philosophy) the capacity of an agent to act in accordance with objective morality rather than under the influence of desires.
– DERIVATIVES **autonomist** noun & adjective.
– ORIGIN early 17th cent.: from Greek *autonomia*, from *autonomos* 'having its own laws', from *autos* 'self' + *nomos* 'law'.

autopilot ▶ noun short for **AUTOMATIC PILOT**.

autopista /ˌɔːtə(ʊ)ˈpiːstə, Spanish autoˈpista/ ▶ noun a motorway in a Spanish-speaking country.
– ORIGIN 1950s: from Spanish, from *auto* 'automobile' + *pista* 'track'.

autopsy /ˈɔːtɒpsi, ɔːˈtɒpsi/ ▶ noun (pl. **-ies**) a post-mortem examination to discover the cause of death or the extent of disease.
▶ verb (**-ies, -ied**) [with obj.] perform an autopsy on (a body or organ): [as adj. **autopsied**] *an autopsied brain.*
– ORIGIN mid 17th cent. (in the sense 'personal observation'): from French *autopsie* or modern Latin *autopsia*, from Greek, from *autoptēs* 'eyewitness', from *autos* 'self' + *optos* 'seen'.

autoradiogram /ˌɔːtəʊˈreɪdɪə(ʊ)gram/ ▶ noun another term for **AUTORADIOGRAPH**.

autoradiograph ▶ noun a photograph of an object produced by radiation from radioactive material in the object.
▶ verb [with obj.] make an autoradiograph of.
– DERIVATIVES **autoradiographic** adjective, **autoradiography** noun.

autorickshaw ▶ noun (in the Indian subcontinent) a motorized, three-wheeled rickshaw for public hire.

autorotation ▶ noun [mass noun] rotation of an object caused by the flow of moving air or water around the shape of the object (e.g. a winged seed).
■ such rotation in the rotor blades of a helicopter that is descending without engine power.
– DERIVATIVES **autorotate** verb.

autoroute ▶ noun a French motorway.
– ORIGIN 1960s: from French, from *auto(mobile)* 'car' + *route* 'route'.

autosave Computing ▶ noun [in sing.] a software facility which automatically saves a user's word-processed or other work at regular intervals.
▶ verb [with obj.] save (work) automatically using such a facility.

autoshaping ▶ noun [mass noun] Psychology conditioning in which the conditioned response has not been reinforced by reward or punishment, but is a modified instinctive response to certain stimuli.

autosome /ˈɔːtəsəʊm/ ▶ noun Biology any chromosome that is not a sex chromosome.
– DERIVATIVES **autosomal** adjective.

autostrada /ˈɔːtə(ʊ)ˌstrɑːdə, Italian autoˈstrada/ ▶ noun (pl. **autostradas** or **autostrade** /-deɪ, Italian -de/) an Italian motorway.
– ORIGIN 1920s: from Italian, from *auto* 'automobile' + *strada* 'road'.

auto-suggestion ▶ noun [mass noun] the hypnotic or subconscious adoption of an idea which one has originated oneself.

autotelic /ˌɔːtə(ʊ)ˈtɛlɪk/ ▶ adjective formal (of an activity or a creative work) having an end or purpose in itself.
– ORIGIN early 20th cent.: from **AUTO-** 'self' + Greek *telos* 'end' + **-IC**.

autotomy /ɔːˈtɒtəmi/ ▶ noun [mass noun] Zoology the casting off of a part of the body (e.g. the tail of a lizard) by an animal under threat.

autotoxin ▶ noun a substance produced by an organism which is toxic to itself.
– DERIVATIVES **autotoxic** adjective.

autotransformer ▶ noun an electrical transformer which has a single winding of which part is common to both primary and secondary circuits.

autotransplantation ▶ noun [mass noun] transplantation of tissue from one site to another in the same individual.
– DERIVATIVES **autotransplant** noun, **autotransplanted** adjective.

autotroph /ˈɔːtə(ʊ)trəʊf, -trɒf/ ▶ noun Biology an organism that is able to form nutritional organic substances from simple inorganic substances such as carbon dioxide. Compare with **HETEROTROPH**.
– DERIVATIVES **autotrophic** adjective, **autotrophy** noun.

autowinder ▶ noun a device which automatically winds on the film in a camera after a picture has been taken.
– DERIVATIVES **autowind** noun & verb.

autoxidation /ˌɔːtɒksɪˈdeɪʃ(ə)n/ ▶ noun [mass noun] Chemistry spontaneous oxidation of a substance at ambient temperatures in the presence of oxygen.
– DERIVATIVES **autoxidize** (also **-ise**) verb.

autumn ▶ noun chiefly Brit. the season after summer and before winter, when crops and fruits are gathered and leaves fall, in the northern hemisphere from September to November and in the southern hemisphere from March to May: *the countryside is ablaze with colour in autumn* | [as modifier] *autumn leaves* | figurative *he was in the autumn of his life.*
■ Astronomy the period from the autumn equinox to the winter solstice.
– ORIGIN late Middle English: from Old French *autompne*, or later directly from Latin *autumnus*.

autumnal ▶ adjective of, characteristic of, or occurring in autumn: *rich autumnal colours.*
– ORIGIN late 16th cent.: from Latin *autumnalis*, from *autumnus* 'autumn'.

autumn crocus ▶ noun a crocus-like Eurasian plant of the lily family, cultivated for its autumn-blooming flowers.
• Genus *Colchicum*, family Liliaceae: several species, in particular meadow saffron.

autumn equinox (also **autumnal equinox**) ▶ noun the equinox in autumn, on about 22 September in the northern hemisphere and 20 March in the southern hemisphere.
■ Astronomy the equinox in September.

autunite /ˈɔːtʌnʌɪt/ ▶ noun [mass noun] a yellow mineral occurring as square crystals which fluoresce in ultraviolet light. It is a hydrated phosphate of calcium and uranium.
– ORIGIN mid 19th cent.: from *Autun*, the name of a town in eastern France, + **-ITE**[1].

Auvergne /əʊˈvɛːn, French ovɛʀɲ/ a region of south central France and a province of the Roman Empire. The region is mountainous and contains the extinct volcanic cones known as the Puys.
– ORIGIN from Latin *Arverni*, the name of a Celtic tribe who lived there in Roman times.

auxiliary /ɔːgˈzɪlɪəri, ɒg-/ ▶ adjective providing supplementary or additional help and support: *an auxiliary nurse* | *auxiliary airport staff* | *the ship has an auxiliary power source.*
■ (of troops) engaged in the service of a nation at war but not part of the regular army, and typically of foreign origin. ■ (of a sailing vessel) equipped with a supplementary engine: *an auxiliary schooner.*
▶ noun (pl. **-ies**) an auxiliary person or thing: *a nursing auxiliary* | *there are two main fuel tanks and two auxiliaries.*
■ N. Amer. a group of volunteers giving supplementary support to an organization or institution: *members of the Volunteer Fire Department's women's auxiliary.* ■ Grammar an auxiliary verb. ■ a naval vessel with a supporting role, not armed for combat.
– ORIGIN late Middle English: from Latin *auxiliarius*, from *auxilium* 'help'.

auxiliary verb ▶ noun Grammar a verb used in forming the tenses, moods, and voices of other verbs. The primary auxiliary verbs in English are *be*, *do*, and *have*; the modal auxiliaries are *can, could, may, might, must, shall, should, will*, and *would*.

auxin /ˈɔːksɪn/ ▶ noun [mass noun] a plant hormone which causes the elongation of cells in shoots and is involved in regulating plant growth. See also **INDOLEACETIC ACID**.
– ORIGIN 1930s: coined in German from Greek *auxein* 'to increase' + **-IN**[1].

auxotroph /ˈɔːksətrəʊf, -trɒf/ ▶ noun Biology a mutant organism (especially a bacterium or fungus) that requires a particular additional nutrient which the normal strain does not.
– DERIVATIVES **auxotrophic** adjective.
– ORIGIN 1950s: from Latin *auxilium* 'help' + Greek *trophos* 'feeder'.

AV ▶ abbreviation for ■ audio-visual (teaching aids). ■ Authorized Version.

Av ▶ noun variant spelling of **AB**[1].

avadavat /ˈavədəvat/ (also **amadavat**) ▶ noun a small South Asian waxbill that is widely kept as a cage bird. The male has red or green plumage and a red bill. Also called **MUNIA**.
• Genus *Amandava*, family Estrildidae: the **red avadavat** (*A. amandava*) and the **green avadavat** (*A. formosa*).
– ORIGIN late 17th cent.: named after the city of **AHMADABAD** in India, where the birds were sold.

avail ▶ verb **1** (**avail oneself of**) use or take advantage of (an opportunity or available resource): *my daughter did not avail herself of my advice.*
2 help or benefit: [with obj.] *no amount of struggle availed Charles* | [no obj., with infinitive] *the dark and narrow hiding place did not avail to save the fugitives.*
– PHRASES **avail someone nothing** archaic (of an action) be of no help at all to someone. **of little** (or **no**) **avail** not very (or not at all) effective or successful. **to little** (or **no**) **avail** with little (or no) success or benefit: *he tried to get his work recognized, but to little avail.*
– ORIGIN Middle English: from obsolete *vail* 'be of use or value' (apparently on the pattern of pairs such as *amount, mount*), from Old French *valoir*, from Latin *valere* 'be strong, be of value'.

available ▶ adjective able to be used or obtained; at someone's disposal: *refreshments will be available all afternoon* | *community health services* ***available to*** *Londoners.*
■ [predic.] (of a person) not otherwise occupied; free to do something: *the nurse is only available at certain times* | *the minister was not available for comment.* ■ informal not currently involved in a sexual or romantic relationship: *there's no available women here.*
– DERIVATIVES **availability** noun, **availableness** noun.
– ORIGIN late Middle English (in the senses 'effectual, serviceable' and 'legally valid'): from **AVAIL** + **-ABLE**. The sense 'at someone's disposal' dates from the early 19th cent.

avalanche /ˈavəlɑːnʃ/ ▶ noun a mass of snow, ice, and rocks falling rapidly down a mountainside.
■ a large mass of any material moving rapidly downhill: *an avalanche of mud.* ■ figurative a sudden arrival or occurrence of something in overwhelming quantities: *we have had an avalanche of applications for the post.* ■ Physics a cumulative process in which a fast-moving ion or electron generates further ions and electrons by collision.
▶ verb [no obj.] (of a mass of snow, ice, and rocks) descend rapidly down a mountainside.
■ [with obj.] (usu. **be avalanched**) engulf or carry off by such a mass of material. *the climbers were avalanched down the south face of the mountain.* ■ [no obj.] Physics undergo a rapid increase in conductivity due to an avalanche process.
– ORIGIN late 18th cent.: from French, alteration of the Alpine dialect word *lavanche* (of unknown origin), influenced by *avaler* 'descend'; compare with Italian *valanga*.

Avalon /ˈavəlɒn/ (in Arthurian legend) the place to which Arthur was conveyed after death.

avant-garde /ˌavɒ̃ˈgɑːd/ ▶ noun (usu. **the avant-garde**) new and unusual or experimental ideas,

especially in the arts, or the people introducing them: *works by artists of the Russian avant-garde.*
▶ **adjective** favouring or introducing such new ideas: *a controversial avant-garde composer.*
– DERIVATIVES **avant-gardism** noun, **avant-gardist** noun.
– ORIGIN late Middle English (denoting the vanguard of an army): from French, literally 'vanguard'. Current senses date from the early 20th cent.

Avar /əˈvɑː/ ▶ **noun 1** a member of a nomadic equestrian people from central Asia who built up a large kingdom in SE Europe from the 6th century but were conquered by Charlemagne (791–9).
2 a pastoral people of Dagestan in Russia, of uncertain relationship to the ancient Avars.
3 [mass noun] the North Caucasian language of the modern Avars.
▶ **adjective** of or relating to the Avars or their language.
– ORIGIN the name in Avar.

avarice ▶ **noun** [mass noun] extreme greed for wealth or material gain.
– ORIGIN Middle English: from Old French, from Latin *avaritia*, from *avarus* 'greedy'.

avaricious ▶ **adjective** having or showing an extreme greed for wealth or material gain: *an avaricious, manipulative woman.*
– DERIVATIVES **avariciously** adverb, **avariciousness** noun.
– ORIGIN late Middle English: from Old French *avaricieux*, based on Latin *avarus* 'greedy'.

avascular /əˈvaskjʊlə, eɪ-/ ▶ **adjective** Medicine characterized by or associated with a lack of blood vessels.

avast /əˈvɑːst/ ▶ **exclamation** Nautical stop; cease: *a sailor is expected to keep hauling until the mate hollers, 'Avast!'*
– ORIGIN early 17th cent.: from Dutch *hou'vast, houd vast* 'hold fast!'

avatar /ˈavətɑː/ ▶ **noun** chiefly Hinduism a manifestation of a deity or released soul in bodily form on earth; an incarnate divine teacher.
■ an incarnation, embodiment, or manifestation of a person or idea: *he set himself up as a new avatar of Arab radicalism.* ■ Computing a movable icon representing a person in cyberspace or virtual reality graphics.
– ORIGIN from Sanskrit *avatāra* 'descent', from *ava* 'down' + *tar-* 'to cross'.

avaunt /əˈvɔːnt/ ▶ **exclamation** archaic go away: *avaunt, you worm-faced fellows of the night!*
– ORIGIN late Middle English: from an Anglo-Norman French variant of Old French *avant*, from Latin *ab* 'from' + *ante* 'before'.

Ave. ▶ **abbreviation for** Avenue.

ave /ˈɑːveɪ/ ▶ **exclamation** poetic/literary used to express good wishes on meeting or parting.
▶ **noun 1** (**Ave**) short for **AVE MARIA**.
2 poetic/literary a shout of welcome or farewell.
– ORIGIN Middle English: from Latin, 'fare well!', singular imperative of *avere*.

Avebury /ˈeɪvb(ə)ri/ a village in Wiltshire, site of one of Britain's major henge monuments of the late Neolithic period. The monument consists of a bank and ditch containing the largest known stone circle, with two smaller circles within it.

Ave Maria /ˌɑːveɪ məˈriːə/ ▶ **noun** a prayer to the Virgin Mary used in Catholic worship. The first line is adapted from Luke 1:28. Also called **HAIL MARY**.
– ORIGIN the opening words in Latin, literally 'hail, Mary!'.

avenge ▶ **verb** [with obj.] inflict harm in return for (an injury or wrong done to oneself or another): *his determination to avenge the murder of his brother | they are keen to avenge a 3–0 early-season defeat.*
■ inflict such harm on behalf of (oneself or someone else previously wronged or harmed): *we must avenge our dead | they* ***avenged*** *themselves* ***on*** *the interlopers | the warrior swore he would be* ***avenged on*** *their prince.*
– DERIVATIVES **avenger** noun.
– ORIGIN late Middle English: from Old French *avengier*, from *a-* (from Latin *ad* 'to') + *vengier*, from Latin *vindicare* 'vindicate'.

avens /ˈeɪv(ə)nz/ ▶ **noun** a plant of the rose family, typically having serrated, divided leaves and seeds bearing small hooks.
• Genus *Geum*, family Rosaceae: several species, including the widespread **water avens** (*G. rivale*), with drooping pinkish flowers, and **wood avens** or herb bennet.
– ORIGIN Middle English: from Old French *avence* (medieval Latin *avencia*), of unknown origin.

aventurine /əˈvɛntʃərɪn/ ▶ **noun** [mass noun] brownish glass containing sparkling particles of copper or gold: [as modifier] *aventurine glass.*
■ a translucent mineral containing small reflective particles, especially quartz containing mica or iron compounds, or feldspar containing haematite.
– ORIGIN early 18th cent.: from French, from Italian *avventurino*, from *avventura* 'chance' (because of its accidental discovery).

avenue ▶ **noun 1** a broad road in a town or city, typically having trees at regular intervals along its sides: *tree-lined avenues surround the hotel |* [in names] *Shaftesbury Avenue.*
■ [in names] N. Amer. a thoroughfare running at right angles to the streets in a city laid out on a grid pattern: *7th Avenue.* ■ a tree-lined road or path, especially one that leads to a country house or similar building: *an avenue of limes.*
2 a way of approaching a problem or making progress towards something: *three possible avenues of research suggested themselves.*
– ORIGIN early 17th cent. (in sense 2): from French, feminine past participle of *avenir* 'arrive, approach', from Latin *advenire*, from *ad-* 'towards' + *venire* 'come'.

aver /əˈvəː/ ▶ **verb** (**averred**, **averring**) [reporting verb] formal state or assert to be the case: [with clause] *he averred that he was innocent of the allegations |* [with direct speech] *'I don't have to do anything—it's his problem,' Rory averred.*
■ [with obj.] Law allege as a fact in support of a plea.
– ORIGIN late Middle English (in the sense 'declare or confirm to be true'): from Old French *averer*, based on Latin *ad* 'to' (implying 'cause to be') + *verus* 'true'.

average ▶ **noun 1** the result obtained by adding several amounts together and then dividing this total by the number of amounts; the mean: *the proportion of over-60s is above the EU average of 19 per cent.*
■ an amount, standard, level, or rate regarded as usual or ordinary: *underground water reserves are* ***below average*** *| they take about thirty minutes* ***on average****.*
2 [mass noun] the apportionment of financial liability resulting from loss of or damage to a ship or its cargo.
■ reduction in the amount payable under an insurance policy, e.g. in respect of partial loss.
▶ **adjective** constituting the result obtained by adding together several amounts and then dividing this total by the number of amounts: *the average temperature in May was 4°C below normal.*
■ of the usual or ordinary standard, level, or quantity: *a woman of average height.* ■ having qualities that are seen as typical of a particular person or thing: *the average lad likes a good night out.* ■ mediocre; not very good: *a very average director making very average movies.*
▶ **verb** [with obj.] amount to or achieve as an average rate or amount over a period of time: *annual inflation averaged 2.4 per cent.*
■ calculate or estimate the average of (figures or measurements): *the women earned only £35 weekly when their seasonal earnings were* ***averaged out****.* ■ [no obj.] (**average out**) result in an even distribution; even out: *it is reasonable to hope that the results will average out.* ■ [no obj.] (**average out at/to**) result in an average figure of: *the cost should average out at about £6 per page.*
– DERIVATIVES **averagely** adverb, **averageness** noun.
– ORIGIN late 15th cent.: from French *avarie* 'damage to ship or cargo', earlier 'customs duty', from Italian *avaria*, from Arabic *ʿawār* 'damage to goods'; the suffix *-age* is on the pattern of *damage*. Originally denoting a duty payable by the owner of goods to be shipped, the term later denoted the financial liability from goods lost or damaged at sea, and specifically the equitable apportionment of this between the owners of the vessel and of the cargo (late 16th cent.); this gave rise to the general sense of calculating the mean (mid 18th cent.).

avermectin /ˌeɪvəˈmɛktɪn/ ▶ **noun** any of a group of compounds with strong anthelmintic properties, isolated from a strain of bacteria. Chemically, they are macrocyclic lactones with a disaccharide ring attached.
– ORIGIN 1970s: from modern Latin (*Streptomyces*) *averm(itilis)*, the name of the source actinomycete, + *ect-* (of unknown origin) + **-IN**[1].

averment /əˈvəːm(ə)nt/ ▶ **noun** formal an affirmation or allegation.
■ Law a formal statement by a party in a case of a fact or circumstance which the party offers to prove or substantiate.
– ORIGIN late Middle English: from Old French *averrement, averement*, from *averer* 'declare true' (see **AVER**).

Avernus /əˈvəːnəs/ a lake near Naples in Italy, which fills the crater of an extinct volcano. It was described by Virgil and other Latin writers as the entrance to the underworld.

Averroës /əˈvɛrəʊiːz/ (*c.*1126–98), Spanish-born Islamic philosopher, judge, and physician; Arabic name *ibn-Rushd*. His highly influential commentaries on Aristotle sought to reconcile Aristotle with Plato and the Greek philosophical tradition with the Arabic.

averse ▶ **adjective** [predic.] [usu. with negative] having a strong dislike of or opposition to something: *as a former CIA director, he is* ***not averse to*** *secrecy |* [in combination] *the bank's approach has been risk-averse.*
– ORIGIN late 16th cent.: from Latin *aversus* 'turned away from', past participle of *avertere* (see **AVERT**).

> **USAGE** 1 On the confusion of **averse** and **adverse**, see **usage** at **ADVERSE**.
> 2 Traditionally, and according to Dr Johnson, **averse** ***from*** is preferred to **averse *to***. The latter is condemned on etymological grounds (the Latin root translates as 'turn ***from***'). However, **averse to** is entirely consistent with ordinary usage in modern English (on the analogy of ***hostile to***, ***disinclined to***, etc.) and is part of normal standard English.

aversion ▶ **noun** a strong dislike or disinclination: *he had a deep-seated* ***aversion to*** *most forms of exercise.*
■ someone or something that arouses such feelings.
– DERIVATIVES **aversive** adjective.
– ORIGIN late 16th cent. (originally denoting the action of turning away or averting one's eyes): from Latin *aversio(n-)*, from *avertere* 'turn away from' (see **AVERT**).

aversion therapy ▶ **noun** [mass noun] a type of behaviour therapy designed to make patients give up an undesirable habit by causing them to associate it with an unpleasant effect.

avert ▶ **verb** [with obj.] **1** turn away (one's eyes or thoughts).
2 prevent or ward off (an undesirable occurrence): *talks failed to avert a rail strike.*
– DERIVATIVES **avertable** adjective.
– ORIGIN late Middle English (in the sense 'divert or deter someone from a place or a course of action'): from Latin *avertere*, from *ab-* 'from' + *vertere* 'to turn'; reinforced by Old French *avertir*.

Aves /ˈeɪviːz, ˈɑːveɪz/ Zoology a class of vertebrates which comprises the birds.
– ORIGIN Latin, plural of *avis* 'bird'.

Avesta /əˈvɛstə/ ▶ **noun** the sacred writings of Zoroastrianism, compiled in the 4th century.
– ORIGIN Persian.

Avestan /əˈvɛst(ə)n/ ▶ **adjective** of or relating to the Avesta or to the ancient Iranian language in which it is written, closely related to Vedic Sanskrit.
▶ **noun** [mass noun] the Avestan language.

avgas /ˈavgas/ ▶ **noun** [mass noun] aircraft fuel.
– ORIGIN 1940s: from *av(iation)* + **GAS**.

avian /ˈeɪvɪən/ ▶ **adjective** of or relating to birds: *avian tuberculosis.*
▶ **noun** a bird.
– ORIGIN late 19th cent.: from Latin *avis* 'bird' + **-AN**.

aviary /ˈeɪvɪəri/ ▶ **noun** (pl. **-ies**) a large cage, building, or enclosure for keeping birds in.
– ORIGIN late 16th cent.: from Latin *aviarium*, from *avis* 'bird'.

aviate /ˈeɪvɪeɪt/ ▶ **verb** pilot or fly in an aircraft: [with obj.] *an aircraft that can be aviated without effort |* [no obj.] *there are fewer opportunities to aviate in winter.*
– ORIGIN late 19th cent.: back-formation from **AVIATION**.

aviation ▶ **noun** [mass noun] the flying or operating of aircraft: [as modifier] *the aviation industry.*
– ORIGIN mid 19th cent.: from French, formed irregularly from Latin *avis* 'bird'.

aviator ▶ **noun** dated a pilot.

aviatrix /ˌeɪvɪˈeɪtrɪks/ ▶ **noun** (pl. **aviatrices** /-trɪsiːz/) dated a female pilot.

Avicenna /ˌavɪˈsɛnə/ (980–1037), Persian-born Islamic philosopher and physician; Arabic name *ibn-Sina*. His philosophical system, drawing on Aristotle but in many ways closer to Neoplatonism, was the major influence on the development of scholasticism. His *Canon of Medicine* was a standard medieval medical text.

avicularium /əˌvɪkjʊˈlɛːrɪəm/ ▶ **noun** (pl. **avicularia** /-rɪə/) Zoology (in some bryozoans) any of a number of modified zooids that take the form of a pair of snapping jaws resembling a bird's head, serving to prevent other organisms from settling on the colony. Compare with **VIBRACULUM**.
– ORIGIN mid 19th cent.: modern Latin, from *avicula*, diminutive of *avis* 'bird'.

aviculture /ˈeɪvɪˌkʌltʃə/ ▶ **noun** [mass noun] the breeding and rearing of birds.
– DERIVATIVES **avicultural** adjective, **aviculturalist** noun, **aviculturist** noun.
– ORIGIN late 19th cent.: from Latin *avis* 'bird' + **CULTURE**.

avid /ˈavɪd/ ▶ **adjective** having or showing a keen interest in or enthusiasm for something: *an avid reader of science fiction | she took an avid interest in the project.*
■ [predic.] (**avid for**) having an eager desire for: *she was avid for information about the murder inquiry.*
– DERIVATIVES **avidly** adverb.
– ORIGIN mid 18th cent.: from French *avide* or Latin *avidus*, from *avere* 'crave'.

avidin /ˈavɪdɪn/ ▶ **noun** [mass noun] Biochemistry a protein found in raw egg white, which combines with biotin and hinders its absorption.
– ORIGIN 1940s: from **AVID** + **-IN**[1].

avidity ▶ **noun** [mass noun] keen interest or enthusiasm.
■ Biochemistry the overall strength of binding between an antibody and an antigen.
– ORIGIN late Middle English: from French *avidité* or Latin *aviditas*, from *avidus* 'eager, greedy'.

avifauna /ˈeɪvɪfɔːnə/ ▶ **noun** [mass noun] Zoology the birds of a particular region, habitat, or geological period.
– DERIVATIVES **avifaunal** adjective.
– ORIGIN late 19th cent.: from Latin *avis* 'bird' + **FAUNA**.

Avignon /ˈavɪnjɒ̃, French avɪɲɔ̃/ a city on the Rhône in SE France; pop. 89,440 (1990). From 1309 until 1377 it was the residence of the popes during their exile from Rome, and was papal property until the French Revolution.

Ávila, Teresa of see **TERESA OF ÁVILA, ST.**

avionics /ˌeɪvɪˈɒnɪks/ ▶ **plural noun** [usu. treated as sing.] electronics as applied to aviation.
■ [usu. treated as pl.] electronic equipment fitted in an aircraft.
– ORIGIN 1940s: blend of **AVIATION** and **ELECTRONICS**.

avirulent /eɪˈvɪrjʊl(ə)nt, a-/ ▶ **adjective** (of a micro-organism) not virulent.

avitaminosis /eɪˌvɪtəmɪˈnəʊsɪs, -ˌvʌɪt-/ ▶ **noun** (pl. **avitaminoses** /-siːz/) Medicine a condition resulting from a deficiency of a particular vitamin.

avizandum /ˌavɪˈzandəm/ ▶ **noun** [mass noun] Scots Law time taken for further consideration of a judgement.
– ORIGIN early 17th cent.: from medieval Latin, literally 'something to be considered', gerund of *avizare* 'consider, advise', from *ad-* 'to' + *visere*, frequentative of *videre* 'to see'.

avo /ˈɑːvəʊ/ ▶ **noun** (pl. **-os**) a monetary unit of Macao, equal to one hundredth of a pataca.
– ORIGIN Portuguese.

avocado /ˌavəˈkɑːdəʊ/ ▶ **noun** (pl. **-os**) **1** (also **avocado pear**) a pear-shaped fruit with a rough leathery skin, smooth oily edible flesh, and a large stone. Also called **ALLIGATOR PEAR**.
■ [mass noun] a light green colour like that of the flesh of avocados.
2 the tropical evergreen tree which bears this fruit, native to Central America and widely cultivated elsewhere.
• *Persea americana*, family Lauraceae.
– ORIGIN mid 17th cent.: from Spanish, alteration (influenced by *avocado* 'advocate') of *aguacate*, from Nahuatl *ahuacatl*.

avocation /ˌavəˈkeɪʃ(ə)n/ ▶ **noun** a hobby or minor occupation.
– DERIVATIVES **avocational** adjective.
– ORIGIN mid 17th cent.: from Latin *avocatio(n-)*, from *avocare* 'call away', from *ab-* 'from' + *vocare* 'to call'.

avocet /ˈavəsɛt/ ▶ **noun** a long-legged wading bird with a slender upturned bill and strikingly patterned plumage.
• Genus *Recurvirostra*, family Recurvirostridae: four species, in particular the widespread **pied avocet** (*R. avosetta*), which has black-and-white plumage.
– ORIGIN late 17th cent.: from French *avocette*, from Italian *avosetta*.

Avogadro /ˌavəˈgɑːdrəʊ/, Amedeo (1776–1856), Italian chemist and physicist. His law, formulated in 1811, was used to derive both molecular weights and a system of atomic weights.

Avogadro's constant (also **Avogadro's number**) Chemistry the number of atoms or molecules in one mole of a substance, equal to 6.023×10^{23}.

Avogadro's law (also **Avogadro's hypothesis**) Chemistry a law stating that equal volumes of gases at the same temperature and pressure contain equal numbers of molecules.

avoid ▶ **verb** [with obj.] **1** keep away from or stop oneself from doing (something): *avoid excessive exposure to the sun | Gerard avoided meeting his eye | a place that Robyn normally* **avoided like the plague.**
■ contrive not to meet (someone): *boys queued up to take Gloria out, but avoided Deirdre.* ■ prevent from happening: *book early to avoid disappointment.*
2 Law repudiate, nullify, or render void (a decree or contract).
– DERIVATIVES **avoidable** adjective, **avoidably** adverb, **avoidance** noun, **avoider** noun.
– ORIGIN late Middle English: from Old French *evuider* 'clear out, get rid of', from *vuide* 'empty' (see **VOID**).

avoidance relationship ▶ **noun** a familial relationship that is forbidden according to rules operating in some traditional societies. In Australian Aboriginal society, for example, mothers-in-law and sons-in-law may not meet face to face or speak directly with one another.

avoirdupois /ˌavwɑːdjʊˈpwɑː, ˌavədəˈpɔɪz/ ▶ **noun** a system of weights based on a pound of 16 ounces or 7,000 grains, widely used in English-speaking countries: [as modifier] *avoirdupois weights* | [postpositive] *a pound avoirdupois.* Compare with **TROY**.
■ humorous weight; heaviness: *she was putting on the avoirdupois like nobody's business.*
– ORIGIN Middle English (denoting merchandise sold by weight): from Old French *aveir de peis* 'goods of weight', from *aveir* 'to have' (infinitive used as a noun, from Latin *habere*) + *peis* 'weight' (see **POISE**[1]).

Avon 1 a river of central England which rises near the Leicestershire–Northamptonshire border and flows 154 km (96 miles) south-west through Stratford to the River Severn.
2 a river of SW England which rises near the Gloucestershire–Wiltshire border and flows 121 km (75 miles) through Bath and Bristol to the River Severn.
3 a former county of SW England, formed in 1974 from parts of north Somerset and Gloucestershire and replaced in 1996 by unitary councils of NW Somerset, Bristol, South Gloucestershire, and Bath and NE Somerset.

avouch ▶ **verb** [with obj.] archaic affirm or assert.
– DERIVATIVES **avouchment** noun.
– ORIGIN late 15th cent.: from Old French *avochier*, from Latin *advocare* 'summon in defence', from *ad-* 'to' + *vocare* 'to call'.

avow ▶ **verb** [reporting verb] assert or confess openly: [with clause] *he avowed that he had voted Labour in every election* | [with obj.] *he avowed his change of faith* | [as adj. **avowed**] *an avowed Marxist.*
– DERIVATIVES **avowal** noun, **avowedly** adverb.
– ORIGIN Middle English (in the senses 'acknowledge, approve' and 'vouch for'): from Old French *avouer* 'acknowledge', from Latin *advocare* 'summon in defence' (see **AVOUCH**).

avulsion /əˈvʌlʃ(ə)n/ ▶ **noun** [mass noun] chiefly Medicine the action of pulling or tearing away.
■ Law the sudden separation of land from one property and its attachment to another, especially by flooding or a change in the course of a river. Compare with **ALLUVION**.
– DERIVATIVES **avulse** verb.
– ORIGIN early 17th cent.: from Latin *avulsio(n-)*, from the verb *avellere*, from *ab-* 'from' + *vallere* 'pluck'.

avuncular /əˈvʌŋkjʊlə/ ▶ **adjective 1** kind and friendly towards a younger or less experienced person: *an avuncular manner.*
2 Anthropology of or relating to the relationship between men and their siblings' children.
– ORIGIN mid 19th cent.: from Latin *avunculus* 'maternal uncle', diminutive of *avus* 'grandfather'.

avunculate /əˈvʌŋkjʊlət/ ▶ **noun** (**the avunculate**) Anthropology the special relationship in some societies between a man and his sister's son.
– ORIGIN early 20th cent.: from Latin *avunculus* 'maternal uncle' + **-ATE**[2].

aw ▶ **exclamation** chiefly N. Amer. & Scottish used to express mild protest, entreaty, commiseration, or disapproval: *aw, come on, Andy.*
– ORIGIN natural exclamation: first recorded in American English in the mid 19th cent.

AWACS /ˈeɪwaks/ ▶ **abbreviation for** airborne warning and control system, denoting a long-range airborne military radar system.

Awadh /ˈʌwəd/ variant spelling of **OUDH**.

await ▶ **verb** [with obj.] (of a person) wait for (an event): *we await the proposals with impatience | remand prisoners awaiting trial* | [as adj., with submodifier] (**awaited**) *an eagerly awaited debut.*
■ (of an event or circumstance) be in store for (someone): *many dangers await them.*
– ORIGIN Middle English: from Anglo-Norman French *awaitier*, from *a-* (from Latin *ad* 'to, at') + *waitier* 'to wait'.

awake ▶ **verb** (past **awoke**; past participle **awoken**) [no obj.] stop sleeping; wake from sleep: *she awoke to find the streets covered in snow.*
■ [with obj.] cause (someone) to wake from sleep: *my screams awoke my parents.* ■ regain consciousness: *I awoke none the worse for the operation.* ■ (**awake to**) figurative become aware of; come to a realization of: *the authorities finally awoke to the extent of the problem.* ■ make or become active again: [with obj.] *there were echoes and scents which awoke some memory in me.*
▶ **adjective** [predic.] not asleep: *the noise might keep you awake at night.*
■ (**awake to**) aware of: *too few are awake to the dangers.*
– ORIGIN Old English *āwæcnan, āwacian*, both used in the sense 'come out of sleep' (see **A-**[2], **WAKE**[1]).

awaken ▶ **verb** [with obj.] rouse from sleep; cause to stop sleeping: *Anna was awakened by the telephone.*
■ [no obj.] stop sleeping: *he sighed but did not awaken.* ■ rouse (a feeling): *different images can awaken new emotions within us.* ■ (**awaken someone to**) make someone aware of (something) for the first time: *the film helped to awaken many to the horrors of apartheid.*
– ORIGIN Old English *onwæcnan*, from *on* 'on' + **WAKEN**.

awakening ▶ **noun** [in sing.] **1** an act or moment of becoming suddenly aware of something: *the war came as a* **rude awakening** *to the hardships of life.*
■ formal an act of waking from sleep. ■ the beginning or rousing of something: *her sexual awakening | the awakening of democracy in eastern Europe.*
▶ **adjective** [attrib.] coming into existence or awareness: *his awakening desire | an awakening conscience.*

award ▶ **verb** [with two objs] give or order the giving of (something) as an official payment, compensation, or prize to (someone): *he was awarded the Military Cross | a 3.5 per cent pay rise was awarded to staff.*
■ grant or assign (a contract or commission) to (a person or organization).
▶ **noun** a prize or other mark of recognition given in honour of an achievement: *the company's annual award for high-quality service* | [as modifier] *an award ceremony.*
■ an amount of money paid to someone as an official payment, compensation, or grant: *a 1.5 per cent pay award.* ■ [mass noun] the action of giving a payment, compensation, or prize: *the award of an honorary doctorate* | [count noun] *an award of damages.*
– DERIVATIVES **awardee** noun, **awarder** noun.
– ORIGIN late Middle English (in the sense 'issue a judicial decision', also denoting the decision itself): from Anglo-Norman French *awarder*, variant of Old French *esguarder* 'consider, ordain', from *es-* (from Latin *ex* 'thoroughly') + *guarder* 'watch (over)', based on a word of Germanic origin related to **WARD**; compare with **GUARD**.

aware ▶ **adjective** [predic.] having knowledge or perception of a situation or fact: *most people are* **aware of** *the dangers of sunbathing | he was suddenly* **aware of** *the numbing cold* | [with clause] *he was aware that a problem existed |* **as far as I'm aware**, *no one has complained.*
■ [with adv.] concerned and well informed about a particular situation or development: *everyone needs to become more* **environmentally aware.**

a

– DERIVATIVES **awareness** noun.
– ORIGIN Old English *gewær*, of West Germanic origin; related to German *gewahr*, also to **WARE**[3].

awash ▶ **adjective** [predic.] covered or flooded with water, especially seawater or rain: *the boat rolled violently, her decks awash* | figurative *the city was* ***awash with*** *journalists.*
■ level with the surface of water, especially the sea, so that it just washes over: *a rock awash outside the reef entrance.*

away ▶ **adverb** **1** to or at a distance from a particular place, person, or thing: *she landed badly, and crawled away* | *they walked* ***away from*** *the vicarage in silence* | *stay indoors,* ***away from*** *the trouble* | *Bernice pushed him away* | *we'll only be away for four nights* | *there's a river* ***not far away.***
■ at a specified distance: *when he was ten or twelve feet away he stopped* | *a loud explosion* ***a short distance away*** | *we have had patients* ***from as far away as*** *Wales.* ■ at a specified future distance in time: *the wedding is only weeks away.* ■ towards a lower level; downwards: *in front of them the land fell away to the river.* ■ conceptually to one side, so as no longer to be the focus of attention: *the Museum has shifted its emphasis* ***away from*** *research towards exhibitions.* ■ (with reference to sports fixtures) at the opponents' ground.
2 into an appropriate place for storage or safe keeping: *he put away the pistol* | *Philip locked away all the takings every night.*
■ towards or into non-existence: *the sound of hoof-beats died away* | *Marie felt her distress ebbing away.*
3 constantly, persistently, or continuously: *there was Morrissey crooning away* | *have your camera at the ready and click away when you spot something.*
▶ **adjective** (of a sporting contest) played at the opponents' ground: *tomorrow night's away game at Leicester.*
▶ **noun** an away match or win.
– PHRASES **away with** said as an exhortation to overcome or be rid of something; let us be rid of: *away with poverty!* ■ (**away with you**) Scottish expressing scepticism.
– ORIGIN Old English *onweg, aweg* 'on one's way' (see **A-**[2], **WAY**).

AWB an extreme right-wing white political party in South Africa violently opposed to majority rule.
– ORIGIN abbreviation from *Afrikaner Weerstandsbeweging* 'Afrikaner Resistance Movement'.

awe ▶ **noun** [mass noun] a feeling of reverential respect mixed with fear or wonder: *they gazed in awe at the small mountain of diamonds* | *the sight filled me with awe* | *his staff members* ***are in awe of*** *him.*
■ archaic capacity to inspire awe: *is it any wonder that Christmas Eve has lost its awe?*
▶ **verb** [with obj.] (usu. **be awed**) inspire with awe: *they were both awed by the vastness of the forest* | [as adj. **awed**] *he spoke in a hushed, awed whisper.*
– ORIGIN Old English *ege* 'terror, dread, awe', replaced in Middle English by forms related to Old Norse *agi*.

aweary ▶ **adjective** poetic form of **WEARY**: *I am well* ***aweary of*** *it now.*
– ORIGIN mid 16th cent.: from *a-* (imitating **A-**[2]) + **WEARY**.

aweigh ▶ **adjective** [predic.] Nautical (of an anchor) raised just clear of the seabed.
– ORIGIN early 17th cent.: from **A-**[2] 'on'+ **WEIGH**[1].

awe-inspiring ▶ **adjective** arousing awe through being impressive or formidable: *Michelangelo's awe-inspiring masterpiece.*

awesome ▶ **adjective** extremely impressive or daunting; inspiring great admiration, apprehension, or fear: *the awesome power of the atomic bomb.*
■ informal extremely good; excellent: *the band is truly awesome!*
– DERIVATIVES **awesomely** adverb, **awesomeness** noun.
– ORIGIN late 16th cent. (in the sense 'filled with awe'): from **AWE** + **-SOME**[1].

awestruck (also **awestricken**) ▶ **adjective** filled with or revealing awe: *people were awestruck by the pictures sent back to earth.*

awful ▶ **adjective** **1** very bad or unpleasant: *the place smelled awful* | *I look awful in a swimsuit* | *an awful speech.*
■ extremely shocking; horrific: *awful, bloody images.* ■ [attrib.] used to emphasize the extent of something, especially something unpleasant or negative: *I've made an awful fool of myself.* ■ (of a person) very unwell or troubled: *I felt awful for being so angry with him* | *you look awful—you should go and lie down.*
2 archaic inspiring reverential wonder or fear.
▶ **adverb** [as submodifier] informal, chiefly N. Amer. awfully; very: *we're an awful long way from the motorway.*
– PHRASES **an awful lot** a very large amount; a great deal: *we've had an awful lot of letters* | *you've still got an awful lot to learn.*
– DERIVATIVES **awfulness** noun.
– ORIGIN Old English (see **AWE**, **-FUL**).

awfully ▶ **adverb** **1** [as submodifier] (used especially in spoken English) very: *I'm awfully sorry to bother you so late* | *an awfully nice man.*
■ very much: *thanks awfully for the tea, Mr Oakley.*
2 very badly or unpleasantly: *we played awfully.*

awhile ▶ **adverb** for a short time: *stand here awhile.*
– ORIGIN Old English *āne hwīle* '(for) a while'.

awhirl ▶ **adjective** [predic.] in a whirl; whirling: *her mind was* ***awhirl with*** *images.*

awkward ▶ **adjective** **1** causing difficulty; hard to do or deal with: *one of the most awkward jobs is painting a ceiling* | *some awkward questions* | *the wheelbarrow can be awkward to manoeuvre.*
■ chiefly Brit. deliberately unreasonable or uncooperative: *you're being damned awkward!*
2 causing or feeling uneasy embarrassment or inconvenience: *he had put her in a very awkward position* | *she felt awkward alone with him.*
3 not smooth or graceful; ungainly: *Luther's awkward movements impeded his progress.*
■ uncomfortable or abnormal: *make sure the baby isn't sleeping in an awkward position.*
– DERIVATIVES **awkwardly** adverb, **awkwardness** noun.
– ORIGIN late Middle English (in the sense 'the wrong way round, upside down)': from dialect *awk* 'backwards, perverse, clumsy' (from Old Norse *afugr* 'turned the wrong way') + **-WARD**.

awl /ɔːl/ ▶ **noun** a small pointed tool used for piercing holes, especially in leather.
– ORIGIN Old English *æl*, of Germanic origin; related to German *Ahle*.

awn /ɔːn/ ▶ **noun** Botany a stiff bristle, especially one of those growing from the ear or flower of barley, rye, and many grasses.
– DERIVATIVES **awned** adjective.
– ORIGIN Old English, from Old Norse *ǫgn*; related to Swedish *agn*, Danish *avn*.

awning ▶ **noun** a sheet of canvas or other material stretched on a frame and used to keep the sun or rain off a shop window, doorway, or ship's deck.
– ORIGIN early 17th cent. (originally in nautical use): of unknown origin.

awoke past of **AWAKE**.

awoken past participle of **AWAKE**.

AWOL /ˈeɪwɒl/ ▶ **adjective** [usu. predic.] Military absent from where one should be but without intent to desert: *the men have* ***gone AWOL*** | humorous *now the parrot has* ***gone AWOL.***
– ORIGIN 1920s: acronym from *absent without (official) leave.*

awry /əˈrʌɪ/ ▶ **adverb** & **adjective** away from the appropriate, planned, or expected course; amiss: [as adv.] *many youthful romances* ***go awry*** | [as predic. adj.] *I got the impression that something was awry.*
■ out of the normal or correct position; askew: [as predic. adj.] *he was hatless, his silver hair awry.*
– ORIGIN late Middle English: from **A-**[2] 'on' + **WRY**.

AWS Brit. ▶ **abbreviation for** automatic warning system, a system of providing train drivers with audible indications regarding signals and where necessary applying brakes automatically.

aw-shucks ▶ **adjective** [attrib.] N. Amer. informal (of a personal quality or manner) self-deprecating and shy: *he's filled with aw-shucks niceness.*
– ORIGIN late 20th cent.: from **AW** + *shucks* (see **SHUCK**).

axe (US also **ax**) ▶ **noun** **1** a tool used for chopping wood and cutting down trees, typically of iron with a steel edge and wooden handle.
■ (**the axe**) a measure intended to reduce costs drastically, especially one involving redundancies: *thirty staff are* ***facing the axe*** *at the Royal Infirmary.*
2 informal a musical instrument used in popular music or jazz, especially a guitar or (originally) a saxophone.
▶ **verb** [with obj.] **1** end, cancel, or dismiss suddenly and ruthlessly: *the company is axing 125 jobs* | *2,500 staff were axed as part of a rationalization programme.*
■ reduce (costs or services) drastically: *the Chancellor warned the cabinet to axe public spending.*
2 cut or strike with an axe, especially violently or destructively: *the mahogany panelling had been axed.*
– PHRASES **have an axe to grind** have a private reason for doing or being involved in something.
– ORIGIN Old English *æx*, of Germanic origin; related to Dutch *aaks* and German *Axt*.

axe kick ▶ **noun** a type of kick used in tae kwon do and other martial arts, in which the opponent's head is struck with the heel of the foot.

axel /ˈaks(ə)l/ ▶ **noun** a jump in skating from the forward outside edge of one skate to the backward outside edge of the other, with one (or more) and a half turns in the air.
– ORIGIN 1930s: named after *Axel* R. Paulsen (1885–1938), Norwegian skater.

axeman (US also **axman**) ▶ **noun** (pl. **-men**) **1** a man who works, fights, or commits violent attacks with an axe: *a mad axeman.*
■ informal a man who cuts costs drastically or ruthlessly.
2 informal a male rock or jazz guitarist.

axenic /eɪˈzɛnɪk/ ▶ **adjective** chiefly Botany of, relating to, or denoting a culture that is free from living organisms other than the species required.
– DERIVATIVES **axenically** adverb.
– ORIGIN 1940s: from *a-* 'not' + *xenikos* 'alien, strange' + **-IC**.

axes plural form of **AXIS**[1].

axial /ˈaksɪəl/ ▶ **adjective** of, forming, or relating to an axis: *the main axial road.*
■ around an axis: *the axial rotation rate of the Earth.*
– DERIVATIVES **axially** adverb.

axil /ˈaksɪl/ ▶ **noun** Botany the upper angle between a leaf stalk or branch and the stem or trunk from which it is growing.
– ORIGIN late 18th cent.: from Latin *axilla* 'armpit' (see **AXILLA**).

axilla /akˈsɪlə/ ▶ **noun** (pl. **axillae** /-liː/) Anatomy a person's armpit.
■ Botany an axil.
– ORIGIN early 17th cent.: from Latin, diminutive of *ala* 'wing'.

axillary /akˈsɪləri/ ▶ **adjective** Anatomy of or relating to the armpit: *enlargement of the axillary lymph nodes.*
■ Botany in or growing from an axil: *axillary buds.* Often contrasted with **TERMINAL**.

axiom /ˈaksɪəm/ ▶ **noun** a statement or proposition which is regarded as being established, accepted, or self-evidently true: *the* ***axiom that*** *sport builds character.*
■ chiefly Mathematics a statement or proposition on which an abstractly defined structure is based.
– ORIGIN late 15th cent.: from French *axiome* or Latin *axioma*, from Greek *axiōma* 'what is thought fitting', from *axios* 'worthy'.

axiomatic /ˌaksɪəˈmatɪk/ ▶ **adjective** self-evident or unquestionable: *it is* ***axiomatic that*** *dividends have to be financed.*
■ [attrib.] chiefly Mathematics relating to or containing axioms.
– DERIVATIVES **axiomatically** adverb.
– ORIGIN late 18th cent.: from Greek *axiōmatikos*, from *axiōma* 'what is thought fitting' (see **AXIOM**).

axiomatize /ˌaksɪˈɒmətʌɪz/ (also **-ise**) ▶ **verb** [with obj.] express (a theory) as a set of axioms: *the attempts that are made to axiomatize linguistics.*

axion /ˈaksɪɒn/ ▶ **noun** Physics a hypothetical subatomic particle postulated to account for the rarity of processes which break charge–parity symmetry. It is very light, electrically neutral, and pseudoscalar.
– ORIGIN 1970s: from **AXIAL** + **-ON**.

axis[1] /ˈaksɪs/ ▶ **noun** (pl. **axes** /-siːz/) **1** an imaginary line about which a body rotates: *the Earth revolves on its axis once every 24 hours.*
■ Geometry an imaginary straight line passing through the centre of a symmetrical solid, and about which a plane figure can be conceived as rotating to generate the solid. ■ an imaginary line which divides something into equal or roughly equal halves, especially in the direction of its greatest length.
2 Mathematics a fixed reference line for the measurement of coordinates.
3 a straight central part in a structure to which other parts are connected.
■ Botany the central column of an inflorescence or other growth. ■ Zoology the skull and backbone of a vertebrate animal.

4 Anatomy the second cervical vertebra, below the atlas at the top of the backbone.
5 an agreement or alliance between two or more countries that forms a centre for an eventual larger grouping of nations: *the Anglo-American axis.*
■ **(the Axis)** the alliance of Germany and Italy formed before and during the Second World War, later extended to include Japan and other countries: [as modifier] *the Axis Powers.*
– ORIGIN late Middle English: from Latin, 'axle, pivot'.

axis² /'aksɪs/ (also **axis deer**) ▶ noun (pl. same) another term for CHITAL.
– ORIGIN early 17th cent.: from Latin, the name of an Indian animal mentioned by Pliny.

axisymmetric /ˌaksɪsɪ'mɛtrɪk/ ▶ adjective Geometry symmetrical about an axis.

axle /'aks(ə)l/ ▶ noun a rod or spindle (either fixed or rotating) passing through the centre of a wheel or group of wheels.
– ORIGIN Middle English (originally *axle-tree*): from Old Norse *ǫxultré.*

axle box ▶ noun (on a railway vehicle) a metal enclosure within which the end of an axle revolves.

axman ▶ noun US spelling of AXEMAN.

Axminster /'aksmɪnstə/ (also **Axminster carpet**) ▶ noun a kind of machine-woven patterned carpet with a cut pile.
– ORIGIN early 19th cent.: named after the town of *Axminster* in southern England, noted since the 18th cent. for the production of carpets.

axolemma /'aksə(ʊ)lɛmə/ ▶ noun [mass noun] Biology the plasma membrane of an axon.
– ORIGIN late 19th cent.: from Greek *axōn* 'axis' + *lemma* 'husk'.

axolotl /'aksəlɒt(ə)l/ ▶ noun a Mexican salamander which in natural conditions retains its aquatic newt-like larval form throughout life but is able to breed.
● *Ambystoma mexicanum,* family Ambystomatidae.
– ORIGIN late 18th cent.: from Nahuatl, from *atl* 'water' + *xolotl* 'servant'.

axon /'aksɒn/ ▶ noun the long thread-like part of a nerve cell along which impulses are conducted from the cell body to other cells. Compare with DENDRITE.
– DERIVATIVES **axonal** adjective.
– ORIGIN mid 19th cent. (denoting the body axis): from Greek *axōn* 'axis'.

axoneme /'aksə(ʊ)ni:m/ ▶ noun Biology the central strand of a cilium or flagellum. It is composed of an array of microtubules, typically in nine pairs around two single central ones.
– DERIVATIVES **axonemal** adjective.
– ORIGIN early 20th cent.: from Greek *axōn* 'axis' + *nēma* 'thread'.

axonometric /ˌaks(ə)nə(ʊ)'mɛtrɪk/ ▶ adjective using or denoting an orthographic projection of an object, such as a building, on a plane inclined to each of the three principal axes of the object; three-dimensional but without perspective.

axoplasm /'aksə(ʊ)plaz(ə)m/ ▶ noun [mass noun] Biology the cytoplasm of a nerve axon.
– DERIVATIVES **axoplasmic** adjective.

Axum variant spelling of AKSUM.

ay ▶ exclamation & noun variant spelling of AYE¹.

Ayacucho /ˌʌɪə'ku:tʃəʊ/ a city in the Andes of south central Peru; pop. 101,600 (est. 1990).

ayah /'ʌɪə/ ▶ noun a nursemaid or nanny employed by Europeans in India or another former British territory.
– ORIGIN Anglo-Indian, from Portuguese *aia* 'nurse', feminine of *aio* 'tutor'.

ayahuasca /ˌʌɪə'waskə/ ▶ noun a tropical vine of the Amazon region, noted for its hallucinogenic properties.
● Genus *Banisteriopsis,* family Malpighiaceae: several species, in particular *B. caapi.*
■ [mass noun] a hallucinogenic drink prepared from the bark of this.
– ORIGIN 1940s: from South American Spanish, from Quechua *ayawáskha,* from *aya* 'corpse' + *waskha* 'rope'.

ayatollah /ˌʌɪə'tɒlə/ ▶ noun a high-ranking religious leader among Shiite Muslims, chiefly in Iran.
– ORIGIN 1950s: from Persian, from Arabic *'āyatu-llāh,* literally 'token of God'.

Ayatollah Khomeini see KHOMEINI.

Ayckbourn /'eɪkbɔ:n/, Sir Alan (b.1939), English dramatist, known chiefly for comedies dealing with suburban and middle-class life. Notable plays: *Relatively Speaking* (1967), *Absurd Person Singular* (1973).

aye¹ /ʌɪ/ (also **ay**) ▶ exclamation archaic or dialect said to express assent; yes: *aye, you're right there.*
■ **(aye aye)** Nautical a response accepting an order: *aye aye, captain.* ■ (in voting) I assent: *all in favour say aye.*
▶ noun an affirmative answer, especially in voting.
– PHRASES **the ayes have it** the affirmative votes are in the majority.
– ORIGIN late 16th cent.: probably from *I*, first person personal pronoun, expressing assent.

aye² /eɪ, ʌɪ/ ▶ adverb archaic or Scottish always or still.
– PHRASES **for aye** forever.
– ORIGIN Middle English: from Old Norse *ei, ey*; related to Latin *aevum* 'age' and Greek *aie(i)* 'ever', *aiōn* 'aeon'.

aye-aye /'ʌɪʌɪ/ ▶ noun a rare nocturnal Madagascan primate related to the lemurs. It has rodent-like incisor teeth and an elongated twig-like finger on each hand with which it prises insects from bark.
● *Daubentonia madagascariensis,* the only member of the family Daubentoniidae.
– ORIGIN late 18th cent.: from French, from Malagasy *aiay.*

Ayer /ɛ:/, Sir A. J. (1910–89), English philosopher; full name *Alfred Jules Ayer*. Involved with the Vienna Circle in 1932, he was an important proponent of logical positivism. Notable work: *Language, Truth, and Logic* (1936).

Ayers Rock /ɛ:z/ a red rock mass in Northern Territory, Australia, south-west of Alice Springs. The largest monolith in the world, it is 348 m (1,143 ft) high and about 9 km (6 miles) in circumference. Aboriginal name ULURU.
– ORIGIN named after Sir Henry *Ayers*, Premier of South Australia in 1872–3.

Ayesha /ɑ:'(j)i:ʃə/ the youngest wife of Muhammad.

Áyios Nikólaos /ˌajios ni'kɔlaɔs/ Greek name for AGHIOS NIKOLAOS.

Aylesbury¹ /'eɪlzb(ə)ri/ a town in south central England, the county town of Buckinghamshire; pop. 50,000 (1985).

Aylesbury² /'eɪlzb(ə)ri/ ▶ noun (pl. **Aylesburys**) a domestic duck of a breed with white plumage.

Aymara /'ʌɪmərɑ:/ ▶ noun (pl. same or **Aymaras**) **1** a member of an American Indian people inhabiting the high plateau region of Bolivia and Peru near Lake Titicaca.
2 [mass noun] the language of this people, with over 2 million speakers. It may be related to Quechua.
▶ adjective of or relating to this people or their language.
– ORIGIN Bolivian Spanish.

Ayrshire¹ /'ɛ:ʃɪə, -ʃə/ a former county of SW Scotland, on the Firth of Clyde, now divided into the administrative regions of **North Ayrshire**, **East Ayrshire**, and **South Ayrshire**.

Ayrshire² /'ɛ:ʃə/ ▶ noun an animal of a mainly white breed of dairy cattle.

Ayub Khan /ˌʌɪjʊb 'kɑ:n/, Muhammad (1907–74), Pakistani soldier and statesman, President 1958–69.

Ayurveda /ˌɑ:jʊə'veɪdə, -'vi:də/ ▶ noun [mass noun] the traditional Hindu system of medicine, which is based on the idea of balance in bodily systems and uses diet, herbal treatment, and yogic breathing.
– DERIVATIVES **Ayurvedic** adjective.
– ORIGIN from Sanskrit *āyus* 'life' + *veda* '(sacred) knowledge'.

AZ ▶ abbreviation for Arizona (in official postal use).

Azad Kashmir /ˌɑ:zad kaʃ'mɪə/ an autonomous state in NE Pakistan, formerly part of Kashmir; administrative centre, Muzzafarabad. It was established in 1949 after Kashmir was split as a result of the partition of India.
– ORIGIN from Urdu, literally 'Free Kashmir'.

azalea /ə'zeɪlɪə/ ▶ noun a deciduous flowering shrub with clusters of brightly coloured, sometimes fragrant, flowers. Azaleas are typically smaller than other rhododendrons and there are numerous cultivars.
● Genus *Rhododendron,* family Ericaceae.
– ORIGIN mid 18th cent.: modern Latin, from Greek, feminine of *azaleos* 'dry', because the shrub flourishes in dry soil.

azan /ə'zɑ:n/ ▶ noun the Muslim call to ritual prayer made by a muezzin from the minaret of a mosque (or now often played from a recording).
– ORIGIN mid 19th cent.: from Arabic *'aḏān* 'announcement'.

Azande /ə'zandi/ ▶ noun & adjective see ZANDE.

Azania /ə'zeɪnɪə/ an alternative name for South Africa, proposed in the time of apartheid by some supporters of majority rule for the country.
– DERIVATIVES **Azanian** noun & adjective.
– ORIGIN Greek (taken from classical geography), probably based on Arabic *Zanj,* denoting a black African.

azarole /'azərəʊl/ ▶ noun **1** an edible Mediterranean fruit which resembles a tiny apple and is chiefly used for making preserves.
2 the small hawthorn-like tree bearing this fruit.
● *Crataegus azarolus,* family Rosaceae.
– ORIGIN mid 17th cent.: from French *azerole,* from Spanish *azarolla.*

azeotrope /'eɪzɪətrəʊp, ə'zi:ə-/ ▶ noun Chemistry a mixture of two liquids which has a constant boiling point and composition throughout distillation.
– DERIVATIVES **azeotropic** /-'trəʊpɪk, -'trɒpɪk/ adjective.
– ORIGIN early 20th cent.: from A-¹ 'without' + Greek *zein* 'to boil' + *tropos* 'turning'.

Azerbaijan /ˌazəbʌɪ'dʒɑ:n/ a country in the Caucasus of SE Europe, on the western shore of the Caspian Sea; pop. 7,219,000 (est. 1991); languages, Azerbaijani (official), Russian; capital, Baku.

> Historically, the name Azerbaijan referred to a larger region which formed part of Persia. The northern part of this was ceded to Russia in the early 19th century, the southern part remaining a region of NW Iran. Russian Azerbaijan was absorbed into the Soviet Union in 1922, gaining independence on the break-up of the USSR in 1991.

Azerbaijani ▶ adjective of or relating to Azerbaijan or its people or their language.
▶ noun (pl. **Azerbaijanis**) **1** a native or national of Azerbaijan or a person of Azerbaijani descent.
2 [mass noun] the Turkic language spoken by over 14 million people in Azerbaijan and adjacent regions.

Azeri /ə'zɛ:ri/ ▶ noun (pl. **Azeris**) **1** a member of a Turkic people forming the majority population of Azerbaijan, and also living in Armenia and northern Iran.
2 [mass noun] the Azerbaijani language.
▶ adjective of, relating to, or denoting this people or their language.
– ORIGIN from Turkish *azeri.*

azide /'eɪzʌɪd/ ▶ noun Chemistry a compound containing the anion N_3^- or the group —N_3.
– ORIGIN early 20th cent.: from AZO- + -IDE.

azidothymidine /ˌeɪzɪdəʊ'θʌɪmɪdi:n, eɪˌzʌɪdəʊ-/ ▶ noun trademark for the drug ZIDOVUDINE.

Azikiwe /ˌɑ:zɪ'ki:weɪ/, (Benjamin) Nnamdi (1904–96), Nigerian statesman, the first Governor General of an independent Nigeria 1960–3 and its first President 1963–6.

Azilian /ə'zɪlɪən/ ▶ adjective Archaeology of, relating to, or denoting an early Mesolithic culture in Europe, succeeding the Magdalenian and dated to about 11,500–9,500 years ago. It is characterized by flat bone harpoons, painted pebbles, and microliths.
■ [as noun **the Azilian**] the Azilian culture or period.
– ORIGIN late 19th cent.: named after *Mas d'Azil* in the French Pyrenees, where objects from this culture were found.

azimuth /'azɪməθ/ ▶ noun the direction of a celestial object from the observer, expressed as the angular distance from the north or south point of the horizon to the point at which a vertical circle passing through the object intersects the horizon.
■ the horizontal angle or direction of a compass bearing.
– DERIVATIVES **azimuthal** /-'mju:θ(ə)l/ adjective.
– ORIGIN late Middle English (denoting the arc of a celestial circle from the zenith to the horizon): from Old French *azimut,* from Arabic *as-samt,* from *al* 'the' + *samt* 'way, direction'.

azimuthal projection /ˌazɪ'mju:θ(ə)l/ ▶ noun a map projection in which a region of the earth is projected on to a plane tangential to the surface, usually at a pole or the equator.

azine /'eɪzi:n/ ▶ noun Chemistry a cyclic organic compound having a ring including one or (usually) more nitrogen atoms.
– ORIGIN late 19th cent.: from AZO- + -INE⁴.

azo- /'eɪzəʊ/ ▶ prefix Chemistry containing two adjacent nitrogen atoms between carbon atoms: *azobenzene.*
– ORIGIN from obsolete *azote* 'nitrogen', from French, from Greek *a-* 'without' + *zōē* 'life'.

azobenzene /ˌeɪzəʊ'bɛnziːn/ ▶ noun [mass noun] Chemistry a synthetic crystalline organic compound used chiefly in dye manufacture.
● Chem. formula: $(C_6H_5)N=N(C_6H_5)$.

azo dye ▶ noun Chemistry any of a large class of synthetic dyes whose molecules contain two adjacent nitrogen atoms between carbon atoms.

azoic /eɪ'zəʊɪk/ ▶ adjective having no trace of life or organic remains.
■ (Azoic) Geology another term for ARCHAEAN.
– ORIGIN mid 19th cent.: from Greek *azōos* 'without life' + -IC.

azonal /eɪ'zəʊn(ə)l/ ▶ adjective (especially of soils) having no zonal organization or structure.

azoospermia /ˌeɪzəʊə'spɜːmɪə, ə'zəʊ-/ ▶ noun [mass noun] Medicine absence of motile (and hence viable) sperm in the semen.
– DERIVATIVES **azoospermic** adjective.

Azores /ə'zɔːz/ a group of volcanic islands in the Atlantic Ocean, west of Portugal, in Portuguese possession but partially autonomous; pop. 241,590 (1991); capital, Ponta Delgada.

azoturia /ˌazə(ʊ)'tjʊərɪə/ ▶ noun [mass noun] Medicine abnormal excess of nitrogen compounds in the urine.
■ Veterinary Medicine a condition that can affect horses exercised after a period of stabling, causing painful stiffness in the hindquarters and back, and dark urine containing products of muscle cell destruction. Also called **TYING UP**.
– ORIGIN mid 19th cent.: from obsolete *azote* 'nitrogen' + -URIA.

Azov, Sea of /'azɒf/ an inland sea of southern Russia and Ukraine, separated from the Black Sea by the Crimea and linked to it by a narrow strait.

Azrael /'azreɪl/ Jewish & Islamic Mythology the angel who severs the soul from the body at death.

AZT trademark ▶ abbreviation for azidothymidine.

Aztec /'aztɛk/ ▶ noun 1 a member of the American Indian people dominant in Mexico before the Spanish conquest of the 16th century.
2 [mass noun] the extinct language of this people, a Uto-Aztecan language from which modern Nahuatl is descended.
▶ adjective of, relating to, or denoting this people or their language.
– ORIGIN from French *Aztèque* or Spanish *Azteca*, from Nahuatl *aztecatl* 'person of Aztlan', their legendary place of origin.

azulejo /ˌazjʊ'leɪhəʊ/ ▶ noun (pl. **azulejos**) a kind of glazed coloured tile traditionally used in Spanish and Portuguese buildings.
– ORIGIN from Spanish, from *azul* 'blue'.

azure /'aʒə, -ʒj(ʊ)ə, 'eɪ-/ ▶ adjective 1 bright blue in colour like a cloudless sky.
■ Heraldry blue: [postpositive] *a saltire azure.*
▶ noun 1 [mass noun] a bright blue colour.
■ poetic/literary the clear sky.
2 a small butterfly which is typically blue or purplish, with colour differences between the sexes.
● *Celastrina* and other genera, family Lycaenidae.
– ORIGIN Middle English (denoting a blue dye): from Old French *asur, azur,* from medieval Latin *azzurum, azolum,* from Arabic *al* 'the' + *lāzaward* (from Persian *lāžward* 'lapis lazuli').

azurite /'aʒʊrʌɪt, -ʒj(ʊ)ə-/ ▶ noun [mass noun] a blue mineral consisting of basic copper carbonate. It occurs as blue prisms or crystal masses, typically with malachite.
– ORIGIN early 19th cent.: from AZURE + -ITE[1].

azygos vein /'azɪgəs/ ▶ noun Anatomy a large vein on the right side at the back of the thorax, draining into the superior vena cava.
– ORIGIN mid 17th cent.: *azygos* from Greek *azugos,* from *a-* 'without' + *zugon* 'yoke', the vein not being one of a pair.

azygous /'azɪgəs/ ▶ adjective Anatomy & Biology (of an organic structure) single; not existing in pairs.
– ORIGIN mid 19th cent.: from Greek *azugos* 'unyoked' (compare with AZYGOS VEIN) + -OUS.

Az Zarqa /az/ variant form of ZARQA.

Bb

B¹ (also **b**) ▶ noun (pl. **Bs** or **B's**) **1** the second letter of the alphabet.
■ denoting the second of two or more hypothetical people or things. ■ the second highest class of academic mark. ■ (in the UK) denoting a secondary road: *the B4248 | B-roads*. ■ denoting the second-highest-earning socio-economic category for marketing purposes, including intermediate management and professional personnel. ■ (**b**) Chess denoting the second file from the left, as viewed from White's side of the board. ■ (usu. **b**) the second fixed constant to appear in an algebraic equation. ■ Geology denoting a soil horizon of intermediate depth, typically the subsoil. ■ the human blood type (in the ABO system) containing the B antigen and lacking the A. ■ (with numeral) denoting a series of international standard paper sizes each twice the area of the next, as *B0, B1, B2, B3, B4*, etc., *B4* being 250 × 353 mm.
2 (usu. **B**) Music the seventh note of the diatonic scale of C major. (In the German system this note is called H, with B denoting B flat.)
■ a key based on a scale with B as its keynote.
– PHRASES **plan B** an alternative strategy.

B² ▶ abbreviation for ■ Belgium (international vehicle registration). ■ bishop (used in recording moves in chess): *Be5*. ■ black (used in describing grades of pencil lead): *2B pencils*. ■ bomber (in designations of US aircraft types): *a B52*.
▶ symbol for ■ the chemical element boron. ■ Physics magnetic flux density.

b ▶ abbreviation for ■ Physics barn(s). ■ (**b.**) born (used to indicate a date of birth): *George Lloyd (b. 1913)*. ■ Cricket (on scorecards) bowled by: *AC Hudson b Prasad 146*. ■ Cricket (on scorecards) bye(s): *extras (b 6, lb 24, nb 9) 39*.

BA ▶ abbreviation for ■ Bachelor of Arts: *David Brown, BA*. ■ British Airways. ■ British Association (for the Advancement of Science). ■ Buenos Aires.

Ba ▶ symbol for the chemical element barium.

ba /bɑː/ ▶ noun in ancient Egypt, the supposed soul of a person or god, which survived after death but had to be sustained with offerings of food. It was typically represented as a human-headed bird. See also **KA**.

baa ▶ verb (**baas, baaed, baaing**) [no obj.] (of a sheep or lamb) bleat.
▶ noun the cry of a sheep or lamb.
– ORIGIN early 16th cent.: imitative.

Baade /ˈbɑːdə/ (Wilhelm Heinrich) Walter (1893–1960), German-born American astronomer. He proved that the Andromeda galaxy was much further away than had been thought, which implied that the universe was much older and more extensive than had been supposed.

Baader-Meinhof Group /ˌbɑːdəˈmʌɪnhɒf/ another name for **RED ARMY FACTION**.

Baal /bɑːl/ (also **Bel**) a male fertility god whose cult was widespread in ancient Phoenician and Canaanite lands.
– ORIGIN from Hebrew *baʿal* 'lord'.

baa-lamb ▶ noun a child's name for a lamb.

Baalbek /ˈbɑːlbɛk/ a town in eastern Lebanon, site of the ancient city of Heliopolis.

baap /bɑːp/ ▶ noun Indian a father.

baas /bɑːs/ ▶ noun S. African, offensive a boss or master, especially a white man in charge of coloureds or blacks: [as title] *Baas O'Brien*.
– ORIGIN Dutch, 'master'; compare with **BOSS**[1].

baasie /ˈbɑːsi/ ▶ noun S. African, offensive a form of address to a young white male.
– ORIGIN Afrikaans (from earlier Dutch *baasje*), literally 'little master'.

Baath Party /bɑːθ/ (also **Ba'ath**) a pan-Arab socialist party founded in Syria in 1943. Different factions of the Baath Party hold power in Syria and Iraq.
– DERIVATIVES **Baathism** noun, **Baathist** adjective & noun.
– ORIGIN *Baath*, from Arabic *baʿṯ* 'resurrection, renaissance'.

baba[1] /ˈbɑːbɑː/ (also **rum baba**) ▶ noun a small rich sponge cake, typically soaked in rum-flavoured syrup.
– ORIGIN via French from Polish, literally 'married peasant woman'.

baba[2] /ˈbɑːbɑː/ ▶ noun Indian informal **1** father (often as a proper name or as a familiar form of address).
■ a respectful form of address for an older man. ■ (often **Baba**) a holy man (often as a proper name or form of address).
2 a child, especially a male one (often in names or as an affectionate form of address).
– ORIGIN from Hindi *bābā*.

baba ganoush /ˌbɑːbə ɡaˈnuːʃ/ (also **baba ghanouj** /ɡaˈnuːʒ/) ▶ noun [mass noun] a thick sauce or spread made from puréed aubergines and sesame seeds, olive oil, lemon, and garlic, typical of eastern Mediterranean cuisine.
– ORIGIN from Egyptian Arabic, from Arabic *bābā*, literally 'father' + *ghannūj*, perhaps a personal name.

babalaas /ˈbabəlɑːs, -lɑːs/ ▶ noun [mass noun] S. African the unpleasant after-effects of drinking an excess of alcohol.
– ORIGIN Afrikaans, from Zulu *ibhabhalazi*.

babassu /ˌbabəˈsuː/ (also **babaçú**) ▶ noun a Brazilian palm that yields an edible oil which is sometimes used in cosmetics.
● Genus *Orbignya*, family Palmae.
– ORIGIN 1920s: from Brazilian Portuguese *babaçú*, from Tupi *ybá* 'fruit' + *guasu* 'large'.

Babbage /ˈbabɪdʒ/, Charles (1791–1871), English mathematician, inventor, and pioneer of machine computing. He designed a mechanical computer with Ada Lovelace but was unable to complete it in his lifetime.

Babbitt[1] /ˈbabɪt/, Milton (Byron) (b.1916), American composer and mathematician. His compositions developed from the twelve-note system of Schoenberg and Webern.

Babbitt[2] /ˈbabɪt/ ▶ noun dated, chiefly US a materialistic, complacent, and conformist businessman.
– DERIVATIVES **Babbittry** noun.
– ORIGIN 1922: from the name George *Babbitt*, the protagonist of the novel *Babbitt* by Sinclair Lewis.

babbitt metal ▶ noun [mass noun] a soft alloy of tin, antimony, copper, and usually lead, used to line bearings.
– ORIGIN late 19th cent.: named after Isaac *Babbitt* (1799–1862), the American inventor of the lining.

babble ▶ verb [no obj.] talk rapidly and continuously in a foolish, excited, or incomprehensible way: *they babbled on about their holiday*.
■ [reporting verb] utter something rapidly and incoherently: [with direct speech] *'Thank goodness you're all right,' she babbled* | [with obj.] *he began to babble an apology*. ■ reveal something secret or confidential by talking impulsively or carelessly: *he babbled to another convict while he was in jail* | [with obj.] *my father babbled out the truth*. ■ [usu. as adj.] **babbling** (of a stream) make the continuous murmuring sound of water flowing over stones: *a gently babbling brook*.
▶ noun [in sing.] the sound of a person or a group of people babbling: *a babble of protest*.
■ foolish, excited, or confused talk: *her soft voice stopped his babble*. ■ [usu. in combination or with modifier] pretentious jargon from a specified field: *New Age babble*. ■ the continuous murmuring sound of water flowing over stones in a stream: *the babble of a brook*. ■ [mass noun] background disturbance caused by interference from conversations on other telephone lines.
– DERIVATIVES **babblement** noun.
– ORIGIN Middle English: from Middle Low German *babbelen*, or an independent English formation, as a frequentative based on the repeated syllable *ba*, typical of a child's early speech.

babbler ▶ noun **1** a thrush-like Old World songbird with a long tail, short rounded wings, and typically a loud chattering or musical voice. See also **RAIL-BABBLER**.
● Family Timaliidae (the **babbler family**): numerous genera.
2 a person who babbles.

babby ▶ noun (pl. **-ies**) dialect form of **BABY**.

babe ▶ noun **1** chiefly poetic/literary a baby: *a babe in arms, less than twelve months old*.
■ figurative an innocent or helpless person.
2 informal an affectionate form of address, typically for someone with whom one has a romantic relationship.
■ a sexually attractive young woman or girl.
– ORIGIN late Middle English: probably imitative of an infant's first attempts at speech. Compare with **BABY**.

babel /ˈbeɪb(ə)l/ ▶ noun [in sing.] a confused noise, typically that made by a number of voices: *the babel of voices on the road*.
■ a scene of noisy confusion.
– ORIGIN early 16th cent.: from *Babel* (see **TOWER OF BABEL**), where, according to the biblical story, God confused the languages of the builders.

Babel, Tower of see **TOWER OF BABEL**.

babesiosis /bəˌbiːzɪˈəʊsɪs/ (also **babesiasis** /ˌbabɪˈzʌɪəsɪs/) ▶ noun [mass noun] a disease of cattle and other livestock, transmitted by the bite of ticks. It affects the red blood cells and causes the passing of red or blackish urine. Also called **PIROPLASMOSIS**, **REDWATER**, or **MURRAIN**.
● The disease is caused by protozoans of the genus *Babesia*, phylum Sporozoa.
– ORIGIN early 20th cent.: from modern Latin *Babesia*, from the name Victor *Babès* (1854–1926), Romanian bacteriologist.

Babi /ˈbɑːbi/ ▶ noun an adherent of Babism.

babiche /bəˈbiːʃ/ ▶ noun [mass noun] raw hide, typically formed into strips, as used by North American Indians for making fastenings, animal snares, and other items.

– ORIGIN early 19th cent.: from Canadian French, from Micmac *a:papi:č*.

babirusa /ˌbɑːbɪˈruːsə/ ▶ **noun** a forest-dwelling wild pig with several upturned horn-like tusks, native to Malaysia.

● *Babyrousa babyrussa*, family Suidae.

– ORIGIN late 17th cent.: from Malay, from *babi* 'hog' + *rusa* 'deer'.

Babism /ˈbɑːbɪz(ə)m/ ▶ **noun** [mass noun] a religion founded in 1844 by the Persian Mirza Ali Muhammad of Shiraz (1819–50) (popularly known as 'the Bab'), who taught that a new prophet would follow Muhammad. See also **BAHA'I**.

– ORIGIN mid 19th cent.: via Persian from Arabic *bāb* 'intermediary', literally 'gate' (taken as a name by the founder) + **-ISM**.

baboon ▶ **noun** a large Old World ground-dwelling monkey with a long doglike snout, large teeth, and naked callosities on the buttocks. Baboons are social animals and live in troops.

● Genera *Papio* and *Mandrillus*, family Cercopithecidae: several species, including the drill and mandrill.

■an ugly or uncouth person.

– ORIGIN Middle English (denoting a grotesque figure used in architecture): from Old French *babuin* or medieval Latin *babewynus*, perhaps from Old French *baboue* 'muzzle, grimace'.

baboon spider ▶ **noun** a large hairy burrowing spider found in Africa.

● *Ceratogyrus, Harpactira*, and other genera, family Theraphosidae, suborder Mygalomorphae.

babouche /bəˈbuːʃ/ ▶ **noun** a heelless slipper, typically in oriental style.

– ORIGIN late 17th cent.: from French, from Arabic *bābūj*, Persian *pāpūš*, literally 'foot covering'.

Babruisk /bəˈbruːɪsk/ (also **Babruysk**) a river port in central Belarus, on the Byarezina River south-east of Minsk; pop. 222,900 (1990). Russian name **BOBRUISK** or **BOBRUYSK**.

babu /ˈbɑːbuː/ ▶ **noun** (pl. **babus**) Indian a respectful title or form of address for a man, especially an educated one: *I could see Kana-babu's shop.*

■an office worker; a clerk.

– ORIGIN from Hindi *bābū*, literally 'father'.

babul /bəˈbuːl/ ▶ **noun** (in the Indian subcontinent) a tropical acacia introduced from Africa, used as a source of fuel, gum arabic, and (formerly) tannin.

● *Acacia nilotica*, family Leguminosae.

– ORIGIN early 19th cent.: from Hindi *babūl*.

Babur /ˈbɑːbʊə/ (1483–1530), first Mogul emperor of India *c.*1525–30, descendant of Tamerlane; born *Zahir ad-Din Muhammad*. He invaded India *c.*1525 and conquered the territory from the Oxus to Patna.

babushka /bəˈbʊʃkə, ˈbabʊʃˌkə/ ▶ **noun** (in Russia) an old woman or grandmother.

■N. Amer. a headscarf tied under the chin, typical of those traditionally worn by Russian women.

– ORIGIN Russian, 'grandmother'.

Babuyan Islands /ˌbɑːbʊˈjɑːn/ a group of twenty-four volcanic islands lying to the north of the island of Luzon in the northern Philippines.

baby ▶ **noun** (pl. **-ies**) **1** a very young child, especially one that is newly or recently born: *his wife's just had a baby* | [as modifier] *a baby girl.*

■a young or newly born animal. ■the youngest member of a family or group: *Clara was the baby of the family.* ■a timid or childish person: *'Don't be such a baby!' she said witheringly.* ■figurative (**one's baby**) one's particular responsibility, achievement, or concern.

2 informal a young woman or a person with whom one is having a romantic relationship (often as a form of address): *my baby left me for another guy.*

■a thing regarded with affection or familiarity: *this baby can reach speeds of 120 mph.*

▶ **adjective** [attrib.] comparatively small or immature of its kind: *a baby version of the Oxford movement.*

■(of vegetables) picked before reaching their usual size: *baby carrots.*

▶ **verb** (**-ies**, **-ied**) [with obj.] treat (someone) as a baby; pamper or be overprotective towards.

– PHRASES **throw the baby out** (or **away**) **with the bathwater** discard something valuable along with other things that are inessential or undesirable.

– DERIVATIVES **babyhood** noun.

– ORIGIN late Middle English: probably imitative of an infant's first attempts at speech.

baby blue ▶ **noun** [mass noun] a pale shade of blue.

■(**baby blues**) informal blue eyes. ■(**baby blues**) informal term for **POST-NATAL DEPRESSION**.

baby boom ▶ **noun** informal a temporary marked increase in the birth rate, especially the one following the Second World War.

– DERIVATIVES **baby boomer** noun.

baby bouncer ▶ **noun** Brit. a harness suspended by elastic or a spring, into which a baby is put, with its feet within reach of the floor, to exercise its legs.

baby buggy ▶ **noun** trademark, chiefly Brit. a pushchair, typically a light one with a soft seat that allows the chair to be collapsed inwards.

baby bust ▶ **noun** informal, chiefly N. Amer. a temporary marked decrease in the birth rate.

– DERIVATIVES **baby buster** noun.

baby carriage ▶ **noun** N. Amer. a pram.

baby doll ▶ **noun** a doll designed to look like a baby.

■a girl or woman with pretty, ingenuous, childlike looks.

▶ **adjective** [attrib.] denoting a style of women's clothing resembling that traditionally worn by a doll or young child, especially short, high-waisted, short-sleeved dresses.

baby-faced ▶ **adjective** having a youthful or innocent face: *baby-faced tough guys.*

baby grand ▶ **noun** the smallest size of grand piano, about 1.5 metres long.

Babygro ▶ **noun** (pl. **-os**) trademark an all-in-one stretch garment for babies.

– ORIGIN 1950s (originally US): from **BABY** + **GROW**.

babyish ▶ **adjective** derogatory (of appearance or behaviour) similar to or characteristic of a baby: *he pursed his mouth into a babyish pout.*

■(of clothes or toys) suitable for a baby: *a babyish frock.*

– DERIVATIVES **babyishly** adverb, **babyishness** noun.

Babylon[1] /ˈbabɪlən/ an ancient city in Mesopotamia, the capital of Babylonia in the 2nd millennium BC. The city (of which only ruins now remain) lay on the Euphrates and was noted by Classical writers for its luxury, its fortifications, and its legendary Hanging Gardens.

– ORIGIN Greek *Babulōn* (from Hebrew *bāḇel*), also the name of the mystical city of the Apocalypse. Compare with **BABEL**.

Babylon[2] /ˈbabɪlɒn/ ▶ **noun** [mass noun] black English (chiefly among Rastafarians) a contemptuous or dismissive term for aspects of white culture seen as degenerate or oppressive, especially the police.

– ORIGIN 1940s: by association with **BABYLON**[1].

Babylonia /ˌbabɪˈləʊnɪə/ an ancient region of Mesopotamia, formed when the kingdoms of Akkad in the north and Sumer in the south combined in the first half of the 2nd millennium BC.

Babylonian /ˌbabɪˈləʊnɪən/ ▶ **noun 1** an inhabitant of Babylon or Babylonia.

2 [mass noun] the dialect of Akkadian spoken in ancient Babylon.

▶ **adjective** of or relating to Babylon or Babylonia.

Babylonian Captivity the captivity of the Israelites in Babylon, lasting from their deportation by Nebuchadnezzar in 586 BC until their release by Cyrus the Great in 539 BC.

baby oil ▶ **noun** [mass noun] a mineral oil used to soften the skin.

baby's breath ▶ **noun** a herbaceous plant of delicate appearance which bears tiny scented pink or white flowers.

● *Gypsophila paniculata*, family Caryophyllaceae.

babysit ▶ **verb** (**-sitting**; past and past participle **-sat**) [no obj.] look after a child or children while the parents are out: *I babysit for my neighbour sometimes* | [with obj.] *she was babysitting Sophie* | [as noun **babysitting**] *part-time jobs such as babysitting.*

– DERIVATIVES **babysitter** noun.

baby-snatcher ▶ **noun** informal **1** a person who abducts a very young child.

2 Brit. another term for **CRADLE-SNATCHER**.

baby stay ▶ **noun** Sailing an additional forestay sometimes used on offshore racing yachts.

baby talk ▶ **noun** [mass noun] childish talk used by or to young children.

baby tooth ▶ **noun** another term for **MILK TOOTH**.

baby walker ▶ **noun** a wheeled frame in which a baby is suspended in a harness and can move itself about a room with its feet.

bacalao /ˌbakəˈlaʊ/ ▶ **noun** [mass noun] codfish, typically dried or salted, as used in Spanish and Latin American cookery.

– ORIGIN Spanish.

Bacall /bəˈkɔːl/, Lauren (b.1924), American actress. She co-starred with her husband, Humphrey Bogart, in a number of successful thrillers, including *The Big Sleep* (1946) and *Key Largo* (1948).

baccalaureate /ˌbakəˈlɔːrɪət/ ▶ **noun 1** an examination intended to qualify successful candidates for higher education. See also **INTERNATIONAL BACCALAUREATE**.

2 a university bachelor's degree.

– ORIGIN mid 17th cent. (in sense 2): from French *baccalauréat* or medieval Latin *baccalaureatus*, from *baccalaureus* 'bachelor'. The earlier form *baccalarius* was altered by wordplay to conform with *bacca lauri* 'laurel berry', because of the laurels awarded to scholars. Sense 1 dates from 1970.

baccarat /ˈbakərɑː/ ▶ **noun** [mass noun] a gambling card game in which players hold two- or three-card hands, the winning hand being that giving the highest remainder when its face value is divided by ten.

– ORIGIN mid 19th cent.: from French *baccara*, of unknown origin.

Bacchae /ˈbakiː/ the priestesses or female devotees of the Greek god Bacchus.

bacchanal /ˈbakən(ə)l, -nal/ chiefly poetic/literary ▶ **noun**

1 an occasion of wild and drunken revelry.

2 a priest, worshipper, or follower of Bacchus.

▶ **adjective** another term for **BACCHANALIAN**.

– ORIGIN mid 16th cent.: from Latin *bacchanalis*, from the name of the god **BACCHUS**.

Bacchanalia /ˌbakəˈneɪlɪə/ ▶ **plural noun** [also treated as sing.] the Roman festival of Bacchus.

■(**bacchanalia**) drunken revelry.

– ORIGIN late 16th cent.: from Latin *bacchanalia*, neuter plural of the adjective *bacchanalis* (see **BACCHANAL**).

bacchanalian /ˌbakəˈneɪlɪən/ ▶ **adjective** characterized by or given to drunken revelry: *a bacchanalian orgy.*

bacchant /ˈbakənt/ ▶ **noun** (pl. **bacchants** or **bacchantes** /bəˈkantiːz/; fem. **bacchante** /bəˈkant, bəˈkanti/) a priest, priestess, or follower of Bacchus.

– ORIGIN late 16th cent.: from French *bacchante*, from Latin *bacchari* 'celebrate the feast of Bacchus'.

Bacchus /ˈbakəs/ Greek Mythology another name for **DIONYSUS**.

– DERIVATIVES **Bacchic** adjective.

– ORIGIN Latin, from Greek *Bakkhos*.

baccy ▶ **noun** Brit. informal term for **TOBACCO**.

Bach /bɑːx/, Johann Sebastian (1685–1750), German composer.

An exceptional and prolific baroque composer, he produced works ranging from violin concertos, suites, and the six *Brandenburg Concertos* (1720–1) to clavier works and sacred cantatas. Large-scale choral works include *The Passion according to St John* (1723), *The Passion according to St Matthew* (1729), and the *Mass in B minor* (1733–8). He had twenty children: **Carl Philipp Emanuel Bach** (1714–88) wrote church music, keyboard sonatas, and a celebrated treatise on clavier playing, and **Johann Christian Bach** (1735–82) became music master to the British royal family and composed thirteen operas.

Bacharach /ˈbakərak/, Burt (b.1929), American writer of popular songs. His songs, many of which were written with lyricist Hal David (b.1921), include 'Walk On By' (1961), 'Alfie' (1966), and 'Raindrops Keep Falling on my Head' (1969).

bachcha /ˈbʌtʃəː/ ▶ **noun** Indian informal a young person.

– ORIGIN from Hindi *baccā* 'child'.

bachelor ▶ **noun 1** a man who is not and has never been married: *one of the country's most* ***eligible bachelors***.

■Zoology a male bird or mammal without a mate, especially one prevented from breeding by a dominant male. ■Canadian a bachelor apartment.

2 a person who holds a first degree from a university or other academic institution (only in titles or set expressions): *a Bachelor of Arts.*

3 historical a young knight serving under another's banner. See also **KNIGHT BACHELOR**. [ORIGIN: said to be from French *bas chevalier*, literally 'low knight' (i.e. knight of a low order).]

– DERIVATIVES **bachelorhood** noun.

– ORIGIN Middle English: from Old French *bacheler*; of uncertain origin.

bachelor apartment ▶ **noun** N. Amer. an apartment occupied by a bachelor.

■Canadian an apartment consisting of a single large room serving as bedroom and living room, with a separate bathroom.

bachelorette ▶ **noun** **1** N. Amer. a young unmarried woman.
2 Canadian a very small bachelor apartment.

bachelorette party ▶ **noun** N. Amer. a party given for a woman who is about to get married, typically one attended by women only.

bachelor girl ▶ **noun** an independent, unmarried young woman.

bachelor party ▶ **noun** N. Amer. a party given for a man who is about to get married, typically attended by men only.

bachelor's buttons ▶ **plural noun** [treated as sing. or pl.] any of a number of ornamental plants which bear small, button-like, double flowers, in particular:
• a white flower of the daisy family (*Achillea ptarmica*, family Compositae). • a yellow buttercup (*Ranunculus acris*, family Ranunculaceae).

Bach flower remedies /batʃ/ (also **Bach remedies**) ▶ **plural noun** preparations of the flowers of various plants used in a system of complementary medicine intended to relieve ill health by influencing underlying emotional states.
– ORIGIN 1970s: named after Edward *Bach* (1886–1936), British physician.

bacilliform /bəˈsɪlɪfɔːm/ ▶ **adjective** chiefly Biology rod-shaped.

bacillus /bəˈsɪləs/ ▶ **noun** (pl. **bacilli** /-lʌɪ, -liː/) a disease-causing bacterium.
■a rod-shaped bacterium.
– DERIVATIVES **bacillary** adjective.
– ORIGIN late 19th cent.: from late Latin, diminutive of Latin *baculus* 'stick'.

USAGE All bacteria belonging to the genus *Bacillus* are called **bacilli**. However, there are some bacteria, also called **bacilli**, which do not belong to the genus *Bacillus*.

back ▶ **noun** **1** the rear surface of the human body from the shoulders to the hips: *he lay on his back* | *Forbes slapped me on the back* | [as modifier] *back pain.*
■the corresponding upper surface of an animal's body. ■ the spine of a person or animal. ■ the main structure of a ship's hull or an aircraft's fuselage. ■ the part of a chair against which the sitter's back rests. ■ the part of a garment that covers a person's back. ■ a person's torso or body regarded in terms of wearing clothes: *all he owned were the clothes on his back.* ■ a person's back regarded as carrying a load or bearing an imposition: *the Press are* ***on my back.***
2 the side or part of something that is away from the spectator or from the direction in which it moves or faces; the rear: *at the back of the hotel is a secluded garden* | *the backs of four high buildings.*
■[in sing.] the position directly behind someone or something: *she unbuttoned her dress from the back.* ■ the side or part of an object opposed to the one that is normally seen or used; the less active, visible, or important part of something: *write on the back of a postcard.*
3 a player in a team game who plays in a defensive position behind the forwards.
4 (**the Backs**) the grounds of Cambridge colleges which back on to the River Cam.
▶ **adverb** **1** towards the rear; in the opposite direction from the one that one is facing or travelling: *she moved back a pace* | *she walked away without looking back.*
■expressing movement of the body into a reclining position: *he leaned back in his chair* | *sit back and relax.* ■ at a distance away: *keep back from the roadside* | *I thought you were miles back.* ■ (**back of**) N. Amer. behind: *he knew that other people were back of him.* ■ N. Amer. losing by a specified margin: *the team was five points back.*
2 used to express a return to an earlier or normal position or condition: *she put the book back on the shelf* | *drive to Montreal and back* | *I went back to sleep* | *he was given his job back* | *things were back to normal.*
■fashionable again: *sideburns are back.*
3 in or into the past: *he made his fortune back in 1955.*
■at a place previously left or mentioned: *the folks back home are counting on him.*
4 in return: *they wrote back to me.*
▶ **verb** **1** [with obj.] give financial, material, or moral support to: *he had a newspaper empire backing him* | *go up there and tell them—I'll* ***back you up.***
■bet money on (a person or animal) winning a race or contest: *he backed the horse at 33–1.* ■ be in favour of: *the Borough Council backs the scheme.* ■ supplement in order to reinforce or strengthen: *US troops were* ***backed up*** *by forces from European countries.*
2 [with obj.] (often **be backed**) cover the back of (an article) in order to support, protect, or decorate it: *a mirror backed with tortoiseshell.*
■(especially in popular music) provide musical accompaniment to (a singer or musician): *on his new album he is backed by an American group.* ■ put a song or piece of music on the less important side of (a recording): *the new single is backed with a track from the LP.*
3 [no obj., with adverbial of direction] walk or drive backwards: *she tried to back away* | figurative *the government* ***backed away from*** *the plan* | [with obj.] *he backed the Mercedes into the yard.*
■[no obj.] (of the wind) change direction anticlockwise around the points of the compass: *the wind had backed to the north-west.* The opposite of **VEER**[1]. ■ [with obj.] Sailing put (a sail) aback in order to slow the vessel down or assist in turning through the wind.
4 [no obj.] (**back on/ on to**) (of a building or other structure) have its back or rear facing or adjacent to: *his garage wall backs on to the neighbouring property.*
■[with obj.] (usu. **be backed**) lie behind or at the back of: *the promenade is backed by lots of cafes.*
▶ **adjective** [attrib.] **1** of or at the back of something: *the back garden* | *the back pocket of his jeans.*
■situated in a remote or subsidiary position: *back roads.*
2 (especially of wages or something published or released) from or relating to the past: *the band's back catalogue* | *she was owed back pay.*
3 directed towards the rear or in a reversed course: *a back header.*
4 Phonetics (of a sound) articulated at the back of the mouth.
– PHRASES **at someone's back** in pursuit or support of someone. **back and forth** to and fro. **someone's back is turned** someone's attention is elsewhere: *he kissed her quickly, when the landlady's back was turned.* **the back of beyond** a very remote or inaccessible place. **the back of one's mind** used to express that something is in one's mind but is not consciously thought of or remembered: *she had a little nagging worry at the back of her mind.* **back to front** Brit. with the back at the front and the front at the back: *the exhausts had been fitted back to front* | *a back-to-front baseball cap.* **back water** reverse the action of the oars, causing a boat to slow down or stop. **back the wrong horse** make a wrong or inappropriate choice. **behind someone's back** without a person's knowledge and in an unfair or dishonourable way: *Carla made fun of him behind his back.* **get** (or **put**) **someone's back up** make someone annoyed or angry. **in back** N. Amer. at the back of something, especially a building: *dad demolished an old shed* ***in back of*** *his barn.* **know something like the back of one's hand** be entirely familiar with a place or route. **on one's back** in bed recovering from an injury or illness. **put one's back into** approach (a task) with vigour. **turn one's back on** ignore (someone) by turning away from them. ■ reject or abandon (a person or thing that one was previously involved with). **with one's back to** (or **up against**) **the wall** in a desperate situation; hard-pressed.
– ORIGIN Old English *bæc*, of Germanic origin; related to Middle Dutch and Old Norse *bak*. The adverb use dates from late Middle English and is a shortening of **ABACK**.
▶ **back down** withdraw a claim or assertion in the face of opposition: *the contenders* ***backed down from*** *their original pledge.*
back off draw back from action or confrontation: *they* ***backed off from*** *fundamental reform of the system.* ■ another way of saying ***back down.***
back out withdraw from a commitment: *if he* ***backs out of*** *the deal they'll sue him.*
back up 1 (of vehicles) form into a queue due to congestion: *the traffic began to back up.* **2** (of running water) accumulate behind an obstruction.
back something up 1 Computing make a spare copy of data or a disk. **2** (usu. **be backed up**) cause vehicles to form into a queue due to congestion: *the traffic was backed up a couple of miles in each direction.*

backache ▶ **noun** [mass noun] prolonged pain in one's back: *a cure for backache.*

backacter ▶ **noun** another term for **BACKHOE**.

back alley ▶ **noun** a narrow passage behind or between buildings.
▶ **adjective** [attrib.] secret and illegal: *a back-alley abortion.*

back-arc ▶ **adjective** [attrib.] Geology relating to or denoting the area behind an island arc.

backbar ▶ **noun** chiefly US a structure behind a bar counter, with shelves for holding bottles, other supplies, and equipment.

backbeat ▶ **noun** Music a strong accent on one of the normally unaccented beats of the bar, used especially in jazz and popular music.

back bench ▶ **noun** (in the UK) any of the benches behind the front benches on either side of the House of Commons, occupied by members of parliament who do not hold office in the government or opposition: [as modifier] *back-bench MPs.*
■(**the back benches**) these members of parliament.
– DERIVATIVES **back-bencher** noun.

backbiting ▶ **noun** [mass noun] malicious talk about someone who is not present.
– DERIVATIVES **backbiter** noun.

backblocks ▶ **plural noun** (**the backblocks**) Austral./NZ land in the remote and sparsely inhabited interior: [as modifier] *backblocks roads.*

backboard ▶ **noun** a board placed at or forming the back of something, such as a collage or piece of electronic equipment.
■a board used to support or straighten a person's back, especially after an accident. ■ Basketball an upright board behind the basket, off which the ball may rebound.

back boiler ▶ **noun** Brit. a boiler supplying hot water or heating that is built in behind a fireplace or is an integral part of a gas fire.

backbone ▶ **noun** the series of vertebrae in a person or animal, extending from the skull to the pelvis; the spine.
■figurative the chief support of a system or organization; the mainstay: *these firms are the backbone of our industrial sector.* ■ [mass noun] figurative strength of character: *he has enough backbone to see us through this difficulty.* ■ US the spine of a book. ■ Biochemistry the main chain of a polymeric molecule.

back-breaking ▶ **adjective** (especially of manual labour) physically demanding: *a day's back-breaking work.*
■(of an inefficient tool) tending to make a task difficult: *put away those old back-breaking hand tools.*

back bulb ▶ **noun** (in orchids) a leafless enlargement of the stem behind a bulb with leaves or flowers.

back-burner ▶ **verb** [with obj.] (usu. **be back-burnered**) US postpone consideration of or action on: *a planned test of the new ale has been back-burnered.*
– PHRASES **on the back burner** see **BURNER**.

backcast ▶ **noun** a backward swing of a fishing line preparatory to casting.
▶ **verb** (past and past participle **backcast**) [no obj.] make such a backward swing.

backchannel ▶ **noun** a secondary or covert route for the passage of information: *we have used him as a diplomatic backchannel* | [as modifier] *backchannel reports.*
■Psychology a sound or gesture made to give continuity to a conversation by a person who is listening to another.

backchat ▶ **noun** [mass noun] Brit. informal rude or cheeky remarks made in reply to someone in authority.

backcloth ▶ **noun** Brit. another term for **BACKDROP**.

backcomb ▶ **verb** [with obj.] chiefly Brit. comb (the hair) from the ends of the strands towards the scalp to make it look thicker.

backcountry ▶ **noun** (**the backcountry**) chiefly N. Amer. sparsely inhabited rural areas.

backcourt ▶ **noun** **1** (especially in Glasgow) a courtyard behind a house or tenement.
2 (in tennis, basketball, and other games) the part of each side of the court nearest the back wall or back boundary line.
■the defensive players in a basketball team.

backcrawl ▶ **noun** another term for **BACKSTROKE**.

backcross Genetics ▶ **verb** [with obj.] cross (a hybrid) with one of its parents or an organism with the same genetic characteristics as one of the parents: [as adj. **backcrossed**] *after five generations the backcrossed dogs were indistinguishable from pure-bred Dalmatians.*
▶ **noun** an instance of backcrossing.
■the product of such a cross.

backdate ▶ **verb** [with obj.] (usu. **be backdated**) Brit. make (something, especially a pay increase)

retrospectively valid: *the company have agreed a 5 per cent increase, backdated to January 1.*
■put an earlier date to (a document or agreement) than the actual one: *they backdated the sale documents to evade a court order.*

back door ▶ noun the door or entrance at the back of a building.
▶ adjective [attrib.] achieved by using indirect or dishonest means: *a back-door tax increase.*
– PHRASES **by** (or **through**) **the back door** using indirect or dishonest means to achieve an objective.

backdown ▶ noun an act of backing down.

backdraught (US **backdraft**) ▶ noun **1** a current of air or water that flows backwards down a chimney, pipe, etc.
2 a phenomenon in which a fire that has consumed all available oxygen suddenly explodes when more oxygen is made available, typically because a door or window has been opened.
– DERIVATIVES **backdraughting** noun.

backdrop ▶ noun a painted cloth hung at the back of a theatre stage as part of the scenery.
■figurative the setting or background for a scene, event, or situation: *the conference took place* ***against a backdrop of*** *increasing diplomatic activity.*

back end ▶ noun the one end of something which is furthest from the front or the working end: *the back end of the car swung round.*
■informal the rump or buttocks. ■ the latter part of a period of time, process, etc.: *the book takes us up to the back end of last year.*
▶ adjective [attrib.] **1** relating to the end or outcome of a project, process, or investment: *many annuities have back-end surrender charges.*
2 Computing denoting a subordinate processor or program, not directly accessed by the user, which performs a specialized function on behalf of a main processor or software system.

backer ▶ noun a person, institution, or country that supports someone or something, especially financially: *a struggle to find a new financial backer.*
■a person that bets on a horse.

back-fanged ▶ adjective Zoology (of a snake such as a boomslang) having the rear one or two pairs of teeth modified as fangs, with grooves to conduct the venom. Compare with **FRONT-FANGED**.

back fat ▶ noun [mass noun] fat on the back of a meat-producing animal.

backfield ▶ noun [mass noun] American Football the area of play behind the line of scrimmage.
■the players (quarterback and running backs) positioned in this area.

backfill ▶ verb [with obj.] refill (an excavated hole) with the material dug out of it.
▶ noun [mass noun] material used for backfilling.

backfire ▶ verb /bakˈfʌɪə/ [no obj.] **1** (of a vehicle or its engine) undergo a mistimed explosion in the cylinder or exhaust.
2 (of a plan or action) rebound adversely on the originator; have the opposite effect to what was intended: *over-zealous publicity* ***backfired on*** *her.*
▶ noun /ˈbakfʌɪə/ a mistimed explosion in the cylinder or exhaust of a vehicle or engine.

backfist ▶ noun (in martial arts) a punch made with the back of the fist.

backflip ▶ noun a backward somersault done in the air with the arms and legs stretched out straight.

back focus ▶ noun Photography the distance between the back of a lens and the image of an object at infinity.

back-formation ▶ noun a word that is formed from an already existing word which looks as though it is a derivative, typically by removal of a suffix (e.g. *laze* from *lazy* and *edit* from *editor*).
■[mass noun] the process by which such words are formed.

backgammon ▶ noun [mass noun] a board game in which two players move their pieces around twenty-four triangular points according to the throw of dice, the winner being the first to remove all their pieces from the board. It is among the most ancient of all games, having been played in its present form by the Romans.
■[count noun] the most complete form of win in this game.
– ORIGIN mid 17th cent.: from **BACK** + **GAMMON**².

background ▶ noun **1** [in sing.] the area or scenery behind the main object of contemplation, especially when perceived as a framework for it: *the house stands against a background of sheltering trees.*
■the part of a picture or design that serves as a setting to the main figures or objects, or appears furthest from the viewer: *the background shows a landscape of domes and minarets | the word is written in white on a red background.* ■ a position or function which is not prominent or conspicuous: *after that evening, she remained* ***in the background.***
2 the general scene, surroundings, or circumstances: *the events occurred against a background of continuing civil war.*
■a person's education, experience, and social circumstances: *she has a background in nursing | a mix of students from many different backgrounds.* ■ the circumstances, facts, or events that influence, cause, or explain something: *the political and economic background* | [as modifier] *background information.*
3 a persistent level of some phenomenon or process, against which particular events or measurements are distinguished, in particular:
■Physics low-intensity radiation from radioisotopes present in the natural environment. ■ unwanted signals, such as noise in the reception or recording of sound.
4 Computing used to describe tasks or processes running on a computer that do not need input from the user: *programs can be left running in the background* | [as modifier] *background processing.*

backgrounder ▶ noun N. Amer. an official briefing or handout giving background information.

background music ▶ noun [mass noun] music intended as an unobtrusive accompaniment to some activity, such as dining in a restaurant, or to provide atmosphere in a film.

backhand ▶ noun (in tennis and other racket sports) a stroke played with the back of the hand facing in the direction of the stroke, typically with the arm across the body: *he drove a backhand into the net* | [as modifier] *a backhand volley.*
■a blow or stroke of any kind made in this way, or in a direction opposite to the usual.
▶ verb [with obj.] strike with a backhanded blow or stroke: *in a flash, he backhanded Ace across the jaw.*

backhanded ▶ adjective **1** made with the back of the hand facing in the direction of movement: *a backhanded pass.*
■figurative indirect; ambiguous: *coming from me, teasing is a* ***backhanded compliment.***
▶ adverb with the back of the hand or with the hand turned backwards: *Ellwood hit him backhanded.*

backhander ▶ noun **1** a blow made with the back of the hand: *shut up, or I'll give you a backhander.*
■a backhand stroke or shot in a game.
2 Brit. informal a secret payment, typically one made illegally; a bribe: *a fortune had been paid in backhanders to local officials and politicians.*

back-heel ▶ verb [with obj.] kick (something) backwards with the heel: *Johnson back-heeled the ball.*

backhoe (Brit. also **backhoe loader**) ▶ noun a mechanical excavator which draws towards itself a bucket attached to a hinged boom.

backing ▶ noun [mass noun] **1** help or support: *the foreign secretary won the backing of opposition parties | they had financial backing from local firms.*
■a layer of material that forms, protects, or strengthens the back of something: [count noun] *the fabric has a special backing for durability.* ■ (especially in popular music) the music or singing that accompanies the main singer or soloist: *the trio provided backing* | [as modifier] *a backing group.*
2 Phonetics the movement of the place of formation of a sound towards the back of the mouth.

backing store ▶ noun Computing a device for secondary storage of data, such as a drum or disk, that typically has greater capacity than the primary store but is slower to access.

backing track ▶ noun a recorded musical accompaniment, especially one for a soloist to play or sing along with.

back issue ▶ noun a past issue of a journal or magazine.

backland ▶ noun [mass noun] **1** (also **backlands**) another term for **BACKCOUNTRY**.
2 land behind or beyond an area which is built on or otherwise developed.

backlash ▶ noun **1** [in sing.] a strong and adverse reaction by a large number of people, especially to a social or political development: *a public* ***backlash against*** *racism.*
2 [mass noun] recoil arising between parts of a mechanism.
■degree of play between parts of a mechanism.

backless ▶ adjective (of a woman's garment) cut low at the back: *a backless lycra dress.*

backlight ▶ noun [mass noun] illumination from behind.
▶ verb (past **-lit**; past participle **-lit** or **lighted**) [with obj.] illuminate from behind: [as adj. **backlit**] *a backlit LCD screen.*
– DERIVATIVES **backlighting** noun.

backline ▶ noun a line marking the back of something, especially the area of play in a game.
■Rugby the players lined out across the field behind a scrum or line-out. ■ the amplifiers used by a popular music group for guitars and other instruments, typically placed across the back of the stage.

backlist ▶ noun a publisher's list of books published before the current season and still in print.

backload ▶ noun a load transported on the return journey of a delivery truck.
▶ verb **1** [no obj.] transport a load on a return journey.
2 [with obj.] (usu. **be backloaded**) place more charges at the later stages of (a financial agreement) that at the earlier stages: [as adj. **backloaded**] *backloaded rentals.*

backlog ▶ noun an accumulation of uncompleted work or matters needing to be dealt with: *the company took on extra staff to clear the backlog of work.*

backlot ▶ noun an outdoor area in a film studio where large exterior sets are made and some outside scenes are filmed.

backmarker ▶ noun Brit. a competitor who is among the last in a race.

backmost ▶ adjective furthest back: *the backmost tooth.*
– ORIGIN late 18th cent.: from **BACK**, on the pattern of *foremost* and *hindmost*.

back number ▶ noun an issue of a periodical earlier than the current one.
■informal a person or thing seen as outdated or past their prime.

backpack ▶ noun a rucksack.
■a load or piece of equipment carried on a person's back.
▶ verb [no obj.] [usu. as noun **backpacking**] travel or hike carrying one's belongings in a rucksack: *a week's backpacking in the Pyrenees.*
– DERIVATIVES **backpacker** noun.

back pass ▶ noun Soccer a deliberate pass to one's own goalkeeper (who is not allowed to pick up the ball if the pass was kicked).

back passage ▶ noun Brit. used euphemistically to refer to a person's rectum.

back-pedal ▶ verb [no obj.] move the pedals of a bicycle backwards in order to brake.
■move hastily backwards: *Cook forced the goalkeeper to back-pedal and push a shot over the bar.* ■ reverse one's previous action or opinion: *Boyd quickly back-pedalled when asked to explain her suggestion.*

backplane ▶ noun a board to which the main circuit boards of a computer may be connected, and which provides connections between them.

backplate ▶ noun a plate placed at or forming the back of something.

back-projection ▶ noun [mass noun] the projection of a picture on to the back of a translucent screen for viewing or for use as a background in filming.
■[count noun] an image projected in this way.

backrest ▶ noun a support for a person's back when they are seated.

back room ▶ noun a place where secret, administrative, or supporting work is done: *this would lead to weak government, and deals in back rooms* | [as modifier] *the back-room staff.*

back row ▶ noun [treated as sing. or pl.] Rugby the forwards who are in the second row in a scrum.
– DERIVATIVES **back-rower** noun.

backscatter ▶ noun [mass noun] Physics deflection of radiation or particles through an angle of 180°.
■radiation or particles that have been deflected in this way. ■ Photography light from a flash gun or other light source that is deflected directly into a lens.
▶ verb [with obj.] Physics deflect (radiation or particles) through an angle of 180°: [as adj. **backscattered**] *backscattered sound reaches the sonar receiver.*

backscratcher ▶ noun an implement consisting

of a small hand attached to a long handle for scratching one's own back.

backscratching ▸ noun [mass noun] the reciprocal provision of help or support, typically in an underhand or illicit manner.

back seat ▸ noun a seat at the back of a vehicle.
– PHRASES **take a back seat** take or be given a less important position or role: *in future he would take a back seat in politics.*

back-seat driver ▸ noun a passenger in a car who gives the driver unwanted advice.
▪ a person who is eager to advise without responsibility.
– DERIVATIVES **back-seat driving** noun.

backsheesh ▸ noun variant spelling of BAKSHEESH.

backshift ▸ noun [mass noun] Grammar the changing of a present tense in direct speech to a past tense in reported speech (or a past tense to pluperfect).

backside ▸ noun 1 informal a person's buttocks or anus.
2 chiefly N. Amer. the reverse or rearward side of a thing: *the backside of the hill.*

backsight ▸ noun 1 the sight of a rifle or other weapon that is nearer the eye of the person aiming.
2 Surveying a sight or reading taken backwards or towards the point of starting.

back slang ▸ noun [mass noun] slang in which words are spoken as though they were spelled backwards (e.g. *redraw* for *warder*).

backslapping ▸ noun [mass noun] the action of slapping a person's back in congratulation or encouragement.
▪ the action of congratulating someone, typically as a mere gesture or in return for favours: *the awards are about industry politics and backslapping.*
▸ adjective vigorously hearty: *those cheerful, backslapping journalists.*
– DERIVATIVES **backslapper** noun.

backslash ▸ noun a backward-sloping diagonal line (\), used in computer commands.

backslide ▸ verb (past **-slid**; past participle **-slid** or **-slidden**) [no obj.] relapse into bad ways or error: *there are many things that can cause slimmers to backslide* | [as noun **backsliding**] *there would be no backsliding from the government's sound policies.*
– DERIVATIVES **backslider** noun.

backspace ▸ noun 1 a key on a typewriter or computer keyboard used to cause the carriage or cursor to move backwards.
2 [mass noun] a device on a video recorder or camcorder which produces a slight backward run between shots to eliminate disturbance caused by the interruption of the scanning process.
▸ verb [no obj.] move a typewriter carriage or computer cursor back one or more spaces.

backspin ▸ noun [mass noun] a backward spin given to a moving ball, causing it to stop more quickly or rebound at a steeper angle on hitting a surface.

back-stabbing ▸ noun [mass noun] the action or practice of criticizing someone in a treacherous manner while feigning friendship: *the media world of back-stabbing, scheming, and downright malice.*
▸ adjective (of a person) behaving in such a way.
– DERIVATIVES **back-stabber** noun.

backstage ▸ adverb in or to the area behind the stage in a theatre, especially the wings or dressing rooms: *I went backstage after the show.*
▪ figurative in secret: *we planned our strategies backstage.*
▸ adjective of, relating to, or situated in the area behind the stage in a theatre: *a backstage tour of the opera house.*
▪ figurative secret: *backstage deals.*

backstairs ▸ plural noun stairs at the back or side of a building.
▸ adjective [attrib.] underhand; clandestine: *I won't make backstairs deals with politicians.*

backstamp ▸ noun a mark stamped on the back of a plate or a letter.

backstay ▸ noun a stay on a sailing ship leading downwards and aft from the top or upper part of a mast.

backstitch ▸ noun [mass noun] a method of sewing with overlapping stitches.
▸ verb [with obj.] sew using backstitch: *you can simply backstitch the edges* | [no obj.] *this method avoids having to backstitch through open loops.*

backstop ▸ noun a person or thing placed at the rear of something as a barrier or support.
▪ Baseball a high fence or similar structure behind the home plate area. ▪ Baseball a catcher. ▪ figurative an emergency precaution or last resort: *the human operator has to act as the ultimate backstop when things go badly wrong.*
▸ verb [with obj.] Baseball act as backstop for: *the man who backstopped the Edmonton Oilers* | figurative *reinsurers might become reluctant to continue backstopping American insurers.*

back straight ▸ noun Brit. the part of a racecourse that is farthest from the grandstand and parallel to the home straight.

backstreet ▸ noun a minor street away from the main roads: *we took a short cut through the backstreets of Kings Cross* | [as modifier] *a backstreet garage.*
▪ [as modifier] denoting someone or something acting, operating, or occurring secretly and typically illegally: *backstreet abortions.*

backstretch ▸ noun N. Amer. another term for BACK STRAIGHT.
▪ the area adjacent to a race course where the horses are stabled and stable employees have temporary living accommodation.

backstroke ▸ noun 1 [in sing.] a swimming stroke performed on the back with the arms lifted alternately out of the water in a backward circular motion and the legs extended and kicking.
2 Bell-ringing a pull of the tail end of the rope from its highest position so as to swing the bell through a full circle. Compare with HANDSTROKE.
– DERIVATIVES **backstroker** noun (only in sense 1).

backswimmer ▸ noun a predatory aquatic bug that swims on its back using its long back legs as oars. It is able to capture large prey such as tadpoles and fish. See also WATER BOATMAN.
● Family Notonectidae, suborder Heteroptera: *Notonecta* and other genera.

backswing ▸ noun a backward swing, especially of an arm or of a golf club when about to hit a ball.

backsword ▸ noun a sword with only one cutting edge.

back talk ▸ noun informal North American term for BACKCHAT.

back-to-back ▸ adjective 1 chiefly Brit. (of houses) built in a continuous terrace divided along its length by a party wall or a narrow alley, to produce two terraces of houses.
2 consecutive: *his back-to-back victories in the Hungarian and Belgian grands prix.*
▸ noun a house in a back-to-back terrace.
▸ adverb (**back to back**) 1 (of two people) facing in opposite directions with their backs touching.
2 consecutively; in succession: *the games were played back to back.*

back-to-nature ▸ adjective [attrib.] advocating or relating to reversion to a simpler way of life: *a back-to-nature lifestyle.*

backtrack ▸ verb 1 [no obj.] retrace one's steps: *Marilyn backtracked and went down into the basement* | figurative *to backtrack a little, the case is a complex one.*
▪ reverse one's previous position or opinion: *the unions have had to backtrack on their demands.*
2 [with obj.] chiefly US pursue, trace, or monitor: *he was able to backtrack the buck to a ridge nearby.*

back-up ▸ noun 1 [mass noun] help or support: *no police back-up could be expected.*
▪ someone or something that can be called upon if necessary; a reserve: *I've got a security force as back-up* | [as modifier] *a back-up generator.*
2 [mass noun] Computing the procedure for making extra copies of data in case the original is lost or damaged.
▪ [count noun] a copy made in such a way.
3 N. Amer. a queue of vehicles, especially in congested traffic.

back-up light ▸ noun North American term for REVERSING LIGHT.

backveld /ˈbakfɛlt/ ▸ noun (usu. **the backveld**) S. African remote country districts, especially when considered to be unsophisticated or conservative.
– DERIVATIVES **backvelder** noun.
– ORIGIN partial translation of Afrikaans *agterveld*, literally 'back countryside'.

backward ▸ adjective 1 directed behind or to the rear: *she left the room without a backward glance* | *a gradual backward movement.*

▪ reverting to an inferior state; retrograde: *the decision was a backward step.*
2 (of a person) having learning difficulties.
▪ having made less progress than is normal or expected: *the Russian Empire was economically backward.*
3 [predic.] [with negative] (**backward in**) lacking the confidence to do (something): *he was not backward in displaying his talents.*
4 Cricket (of a fielding position) behind an imaginary line passing through the stumps at the batsman's end at right angles to the wicket.
▸ adverb another word for BACKWARDS.
– DERIVATIVES **backwardly** adverb, **backwardness** noun.
– ORIGIN Middle English: from earlier *abackward*, from ABACK.

USAGE In most adverbial uses **backward** and **backwards** are interchangeable: *the car rolled slowly backward* and *the car rolled slowly backwards* are both equally acceptable. In North American English **backward** tends to be preferred to **backwards**, while in British English it is the other way round. As an adjective, on the other hand, the standard form is **backward** rather than **backwards**: uses such as *a backwards glance* (as opposed to *a backward glance*) are unusual (though not incorrect).

backwardation ▸ noun [mass noun] Stock Exchange, Brit. a situation in which the spot or cash price of a commodity is higher than the forward price. Often contrasted with CONTANGO.
▪ a situation in which the offer price for stock is lower than the bid. ▪ historical a percentage paid by a person selling stock for the right of delaying its delivery.

backward-looking ▸ adjective opposing progress and innovation; reactionary.

backwards (also **backward**) ▸ adverb 1 (of a movement) away from one's front; in the direction of one's back: *Penny glanced backwards* | *he took a step backwards.*
▪ in reverse of the usual direction or order: *count backwards from twenty to ten.*
2 (of an object's motion) back towards the starting point: *the tape rolled backwards.*
▪ towards or into the past: *the film looks backwards towards the stage melodramas from which it springs.* ▪ towards or into a worse state: *a step backwards for the economy.*
– PHRASES **backwards and forwards** in both directions alternately; to and fro: *he paced backwards and forwards nervously.* **bend** (or **fall** or **lean**) **over backwards** informal make every effort to achieve something, especially to be fair or helpful: *we have bent over backwards to ensure a fair trial for the defendants.* **know something backwards** be entirely familiar with something.

backwards compatible (also **backward compatible**) ▸ adjective (of computer hardware or software) able to be used with an older piece of hardware or software without special adaptation or modification.
– DERIVATIVES **backwards compatibility** noun.

backwash ▸ noun [mass noun] the motion of receding waves.
▪ a backward current created by an object moving through water or air. ▪ figurative repercussions: *the backwash of the Cuban missile crisis.*
▸ verb [with obj.] clean (a filter) by reversing the flow of fluid through it.

backwater ▸ noun a part of a river not reached by the current, where the water is stagnant.
▪ an isolated or peaceful place. ▪ a place or condition in which no development or progress is taking place: *the country remained an economic backwater.*

backwind Sailing ▸ verb [with obj.] (of a sail or vessel) deflect a flow of air into the back of (another sail or vessel).
▸ noun a flow of air deflected into the back of a sail.

backwoods ▸ plural noun [often as modifier] chiefly N. Amer. remote uncleared forest land: *backwoods homesteads.*
▪ a remote or sparsely inhabited region, especially one considered backward or conservative.

backwoodsman ▸ noun (pl. **-men**) chiefly N. Amer. an inhabitant of backwoods, especially one regarded as uncouth or backward.
▪ Brit. informal a peer who very rarely attends the House of Lords.

backyard ▸ noun Brit. a yard at the back of a house or other building.

■N. Amer. a back garden. ■ informal the area close to where one lives, or the territory close to a particular country, regarded with proprietorial concern: *anything was preferable to a nuclear dump **in their own backyard**.* ■ one's area of interest or operation.

baclava ▶ noun variant spelling of **BAKLAVA**.

Bacolod /bɑːˈkəʊlɒd/ a city on the NW coast of the island of Negros in the central Philippines; pop. 364,180 (1990). It is the chief city of the island and a major port.

Bacon[1], Francis, Baron Verulam and Viscount St Albans (1561–1626), English statesman and philosopher. As a scientist he advocated the inductive method; his views were instrumental in the founding of the Royal Society in 1660. Notable works: *The Advancement of Learning* (1605) and *Novum Organum* (1620).

Bacon[2], Francis (1909–92), Irish painter. His work chiefly depicts human figures in grotesquely distorted postures, set in confined interior spaces.

Bacon[3], Roger (*c.*1214–94), English philosopher, scientist, and Franciscan friar. Most notable for his work in the field of optics, he emphasized the need for an empirical approach to scientific study.

bacon ▶ noun [mass noun] cured meat from the back or sides of a pig.
– PHRASES **bring home the bacon** informal **1** supply material provision or support: *I have to go to work because it brings home the bacon.* **2** achieve success.
– ORIGIN Middle English: from Old French, from a Germanic word meaning 'ham, flitch'; related to **BACK**.

bacon-and-eggs ▶ noun Austral. another term for **EGGS AND BACON**.

bacon beetle ▶ noun another term for **LARDER BEETLE**.

baconer ▶ noun a pig fit for being made into bacon and ham, typically heavier than both a porker and a cutter.

Baconian /beɪˈkəʊnɪən/ ▶ adjective of or relating to Sir Francis Bacon or his inductive method of reasoning and philosophy.
■relating to or denoting the theory that Bacon wrote the plays attributed to Shakespeare.
▶ noun an adherent of Bacon's philosophical system.
■a supporter of the theory that Bacon wrote the plays attributed to Shakespeare.

bacteraemia /ˌbaktəˈriːmɪə/ (US **bacteremia**) ▶ noun [mass noun] Medicine the presence of bacteria in the blood.
– DERIVATIVES **bacteraemic** adjective.
– ORIGIN late 19th cent.: from **BACTERIUM** + **-AEMIA**.

bacteria plural form of **BACTERIUM**.

bactericide /bakˈtɪərɪsʌɪd/ ▶ noun a substance which kills bacteria.
– DERIVATIVES **bactericidal** adjective.

bacterio- /bakˈtɪərɪəʊ/ ▶ combining form representing **BACTERIUM**.

bacteriocin /bakˈtɪərɪə(ʊ)sɪn/ ▶ noun Biology a protein produced by bacteria of one strain and active against those of a closely related strain.
– ORIGIN 1950s: from French *bactériocine*, from Greek *baktērion* 'small cane' + a shortened form of **COLICIN**.

bacteriological ▶ adjective of or relating to bacteriology or bacteria.
■relating to or denoting germ warfare.
– DERIVATIVES **bacteriologic** adjective, **bacteriologically** adverb.

bacteriology ▶ noun [mass noun] the study of bacteria.
– DERIVATIVES **bacteriologist** noun.

bacteriolysis /bakˌtɪərɪˈɒlɪsɪs/ ▶ noun [mass noun] Biology the rupture of bacterial cells, especially by an antibody.
– DERIVATIVES **bacteriolytic** adjective.

bacteriophage /bakˈtɪərɪə(ʊ)feɪdʒ, -fɑːʒ/ ▶ noun Biology a virus which parasitizes a bacterium by infecting it and reproducing inside it. Bacteriophages are much used in genetic research.
– ORIGIN 1920s: from **BACTERIUM** + Greek *phagein* 'eat'.

bacteriostat /bakˈtɪərɪə(ʊ)stat/ ▶ noun a substance that prevents the multiplying of bacteria without destroying them.
– DERIVATIVES **bacteriostasis** noun, **bacteriostatic** adjective, **bacteriostatically** adverb.
– ORIGIN early 20th cent.: from **BACTERIUM** + Greek *statos* 'standing'.

bacterium /bakˈtɪərɪəm/ ▶ noun (pl. **bacteria** /-rɪə/) a member of a large group of unicellular microorganisms which have cell walls but lack organelles and an organized nucleus, including some which can cause disease.

Bacteria are widely distributed in soil, water, and air, and on or in the tissues of plants and animals. Formerly included in the plant kingdom, they are now classified separately (as prokaryotes). They play a vital role in global ecology, as the chemical changes they bring about include those of organic decay and nitrogen fixation. Much modern biochemical knowledge has been gained from the study of bacteria, as they grow easily and reproduce rapidly in laboratory cultures.

– DERIVATIVES **bacterial** adjective.
– ORIGIN mid 19th cent.: modern Latin, from Greek *baktērion*, diminutive of *baktēria* 'staff, cane' (because the first ones to be discovered were rod-shaped). Compare with **BACILLUS**.

USAGE **Bacteria** is the plural form (derived from Latin) of **bacterium**. Like any other plural it should be used with the plural form of the verb: *the **bacteria** causing salmonella **are** killed by thorough cooking*, **not** *the **bacteria** causing salmonella **is** killed by thorough cooking.* However, the unfamiliarity of the form means that **bacteria** is sometimes mistakenly treated as a singular form, as in the example above.

bacteriuria /bakˌtɪərɪˈjʊərɪə/ ▶ noun [mass noun] Medicine the presence of bacteria in the urine.

Bactria /ˈbaktrɪə/ an ancient country in central Asia, corresponding to the northern part of modern Afghanistan. It was the seat of a powerful Indo-Greek kingdom in the 3rd and 2nd centuries BC.
– DERIVATIVES **Bactrian** adjective & noun.

Bactrian camel ▶ noun the two-humped camel, which has been domesticated but is still found wild in central Asia.
● *Camelus ferus* (including the domesticated *C. bactrianus*), family Camelidae.

baculovirus /ˈbakjʊlə(ʊ),vʌɪrəs/ ▶ noun Biology a member of a family of DNA viruses infecting only invertebrate animals. Some have a very specific insect host, and may be used in biological pest control.
– ORIGIN 1980s: from Latin *baculum* 'rod, stick' + **VIRUS**.

baculum /ˈbakjʊləm/ ▶ noun (pl. **bacula** /-lə/) another term for **OS PENIS**.
– ORIGIN 1930s: modern Latin.

bad ▶ adjective (**worse**, **worst**) **1** of poor quality: *a bad diet | a bad film.*
■not functioning to a required or expected standard: *bad eyesight.* ■ not able to do something specified well: *I'm so **bad at** names | a bad listener.* ■ [attrib.] not appropriate to a particular purpose: *morning was a bad time to ask Andy about anything.*
2 not such as to be hoped for or desired; unpleasant or unwelcome: *bad news | bad weather | bad luck.*
■unfavourable: *a bad reputation.* ■ (of something causing pain, danger, or other unwelcome consequences) severe or intense: *bad headaches | a bad crash | a bad mistake.* ■ [predic.] (**bad for**) having a harmful effect on: *soap was bad for his face.*
3 (of food) decayed; putrid: *everything in the fridge would go bad.*
■(of the atmosphere) polluted; unhealthy: *bad air.*
4 (of a part of the body) injured, diseased, or causing pain: *a bad back.*
■[as complement] (of a person) unwell: *I feel bad.*
5 [as complement] regretful, guilty, or ashamed about something: *working mothers who feel bad about leaving their child.*
6 lacking or failing to conform to moral virtue: *the bad guys | bad behaviour.*
■(of language) using words generally considered offensive.
7 worthless; not valid: *he ran up 87 bad cheques.*
8 (**badder**, **baddest**) informal, chiefly US good; excellent: *they want the baddest, best-looking Corvette there is.*
▶ adverb N. Amer. informal badly: *he beat her up real bad.*
– PHRASES **a bad penny always turns up** see **PENNY**. **a bad workman always blames his tools** see **WORKMAN**. **come to a bad end** see **END**. **from bad to worse** into an even worse state. **in a bad way** ill or in trouble. **not** (or **not so**) **bad** informal fairly good: *she discovered he wasn't so bad after all.* **to the bad** **1** to ruin: *I hate to see you going to the bad.* **2** in deficit: *he was £80 to the bad.* **too bad** informal used to indicate that something is regrettable but now beyond retrieval: *too bad, but that's the way it is.*
– DERIVATIVES **baddish** adjective, **badness** noun.
– ORIGIN Middle English: perhaps from Old English *bǣddel* 'hermaphrodite, womanish man'.

BADA ▶ abbreviation for British Antique Dealers' Association.

badam /bʌˈdɑːm/ ▶ noun Indian term for **ALMOND**.
– ORIGIN from Hindi *badām*.

badass informal, chiefly N. Amer. ▶ noun a tough, aggressive, or uncooperative person.
▶ adjective **1** tough; aggressive: *a badass demeanour.* **2** formidable; excellent: *this was one badass camera.*
– ORIGIN 1950s: from the adjective **BAD** + **ASS**[2].

bad blood ▶ noun [mass noun] ill feeling: *there has always been bad blood between these families.*

bad break ▶ noun informal a piece of bad luck.
■a mistake or blunder.

bad breath ▶ noun [mass noun] unpleasant-smelling breath; halitosis.

bad debt ▶ noun a debt that cannot be recovered.

baddeleyite /ˈbad(ə)lɪʌɪt/ ▶ noun [mass noun] a mineral consisting largely of zirconium dioxide, ranging from colourless to yellow, brown, or black.
– ORIGIN late 19th cent.: named after Joseph *Baddeley*, English traveller, + **-ITE**[1].

badderlocks /ˈbadəlɒks/ (also **dabberlocks**) ▶ plural noun chiefly Scottish an edible seaweed with a long greenish frond and prominent midrib, occurring in northern Europe.
● *Alaria esculenta*, class Phaeophyceae.
– ORIGIN late 18th cent.: perhaps from *Balderlocks*, based on the name of the god **BALDER**.

baddy (also **baddie**) ▶ noun (pl. **-ies**) informal a villain or criminal in a book, film, etc.

bade /beɪd, bad/ past of **BID**[2].

Baden /ˈbɑːd(ə)n/ a spa town in Austria, south of Vienna; pop. 24,000 (1991). It was a royal summer retreat and fashionable resort in the 19th century.

Baden-Baden /ˌbɑːd(ə)nˈbɑːd(ə)n/ a spa town in the Black Forest; pop. 48,700 (est. 1984). It was a fashionable resort in the 19th century.

Baden-Powell /ˌbeɪd(ə)nˈpəʊəl/, Robert (Stephenson Smyth), 1st Baron Baden-Powell of Gilwell (1857–1941), English soldier and founder of the Boy Scout movement. He became a national hero after his successful defence of Mafeking (1899–1900) in the Boer War.

Baden-Württemberg /ˌbɑːd(ə)nˈvəːtəmˌbəːg, German ˌbaːdnˈvʏrtəmˌbɛrk/ a state of western Germany; capital, Stuttgart.

Bader /ˈbɑːdə/, Sir Douglas (Robert Steuart) (1910–82), British airman. Despite having lost both legs in a flying accident in 1931, he saw action as a fighter pilot during the Battle of Britain (1940–1). After the war he was noted for his work on behalf of disabled people.

bad faith ▶ noun [mass noun] intent to deceive: *the slave owners had acted **in bad faith**.*
■(in existentialist philosophy) refusal to confront facts or choices.

bad form ▶ noun [mass noun] an offence against current social conventions: *it was considered bad form to talk about money.*

badge ▶ noun a small piece of metal, plastic, or cloth bearing a design or words, typically worn to show a person's name, rank, membership of an organization, or support for a particular cause.
■a distinguishing object or emblem: *the car's front badge is much loved by thieves.* ■ figurative a feature or sign which reveals a particular condition or quality: *philanthropy was regarded as a badge of social esteem.*
▶ verb [with obj.] mark with a badge or other distinguishing emblem: [with obj. and complement] *vendors can badge their products 'OSF certified'.*
– ORIGIN late Middle English: of unknown origin.

badge engineering ▶ noun [mass noun] the practice of marketing a motor vehicle under two or more brand names or badges.

badger ▶ noun a heavily built omnivorous nocturnal mammal of the weasel family, typically having a grey and black coat. Badgers live in extensive burrow systems called setts.
● Several genera and species in the family Mustelidae, in particular the Eurasian *Meles meles*, which has a white head with two black stripes, and the North American *Taxidea taxus*, with a white stripe on the head.
▶ verb [with obj.] repeatedly and annoyingly ask

(someone) to do something or give one something: *journalists badgered him about the deals | Tom had finally* ***badgered*** *her* ***into*** *going.*
– ORIGIN early 16th cent.: perhaps from **BADGE**, with reference to its distinctive head markings. The verb sense (late 18th cent.) originates from the formerly popular sport of badger-baiting.

badger-baiting ▶ **noun** [mass noun] a sport in which dogs draw a badger from its sett and kill it, illegal in the UK since 1830.

Badger State informal name for **WISCONSIN**[1].

bad hair day ▶ **noun** informal, chiefly US a day on which everything seems to go wrong, characterized as a day on which one's hair is particularly unmanageable.

badinage /ˈbadɪnɑːʒ/ ▶ **noun** [mass noun] humorous or witty conversation: *he developed a nice line in badinage with the Labour leader.*
– ORIGIN mid 17th cent.: from French, from *badiner* 'to joke', from *badin* 'fool', based on Provençal *badar* 'gape'.

badlands ▶ **plural noun** extensive tracts of heavily eroded, uncultivable land with little vegetation.
■ (**Badlands**) a barren plateau region of the western US, mainly in North and South Dakota and Nebraska.
– ORIGIN mid 19th cent. (originally US): translation of French *mauvaises terres*.

badly ▶ **adverb** (**worse**, **worst**) **1** in an unsatisfactory, inadequate, or unsuccessful way: *England have played badly this year | the war was going badly.*
■ in a critical or unfavourable way: *try not to think badly of me.* ■ in an unacceptable or unpleasant way: *she realized she was behaving rather badly.*
2 to a great or serious degree (used of a harmful or unpleasant event or action): *the building was badly damaged by fire.*
■ very much or intensely (used of lack or desire): *I wanted a baby so badly.*
3 used to convey that someone feels guilty about something: *I felt badly about my unfriendliness of the previous evening.*
– PHRASES **badly off** in an unfavourable situation. ■ having little money.

badmash /bʌdˈmɑːʃ/ ▶ **noun** Indian a hooligan.
– ORIGIN from Urdu, from Persian *bad* 'evil' + Arabic *ma'āš* 'means of livelihood'.

badminton ▶ **noun** [mass noun] a game with rackets in which a shuttlecock is played back and forth across a net.
– ORIGIN named after *Badminton* in SW England, country seat of the Duke of Beaufort.

bad-mouth ▶ **verb** [with obj.] informal criticize (someone) behind their back: *no one wants to hire an individual who bad-mouths a prior employer.*

bad news ▶ **noun** [mass noun] informal an unpleasant or undesirable person or thing: *dry weather is always bad news for gardeners.*

Badon Hill, Battle of /ˈbeɪd(ə)n/ an ancient British battle (the location of which is uncertain), in AD 516, in which the forces of King Arthur successfully defended themselves against the Saxons. Another source implies that the battle was fought *c.*500 but does not connect it with King Arthur.

bad-tempered ▶ **adjective** easily annoyed or made angry: *in a heatwave many people become increasingly bad-tempered.*
■ characterized by anger or ungraciousness: *a bad-tempered match.*
– DERIVATIVES **bad-temperedly** adverb.

BAe ▶ **abbreviation for** British Aerospace.

Baedeker /ˈbeɪdɪkə, German ˈbɛːdəkɐ/, Karl (1801–59), German publisher. He is remembered chiefly for the series of guidebooks to which he gave his name and which are still published today.

Baer /bɛː, German bɛːɐ/, Karl Ernest von (1792–1876), German biologist. He discovered that ova were particles within the ovarian follicles and he formulated the principle that in the developing embryo general characteristics appear before special ones. His studies were used by Darwin in the theory of evolution.

Baeyer /ˈbʌɪə, German ˈbaɪɐ/, Adolph Johann Friedrich Wilhelm von (1835–1917), German organic chemist. He prepared the first barbiturates and investigated dyes, synthesizing indigo and determining its structural formula. Nobel Prize for Chemistry (1905).

Baez /ˈbʌɪɛz/, Joan (b.1941), American folk singer. She is best known for her performances at civil rights demonstrations in the early 1960s.

Baffin, William (*c.*1584–1622), English navigator and explorer, the pilot of several expeditions in search of the North-West Passage 1612–16.

Baffin Bay an extension of the North Atlantic between Baffin Island and Greenland, linked to the Arctic Ocean by three passages. It is largely ice-bound in winter.

Baffin Island a large island in the Canadian Arctic, situated at the mouth of Hudson Bay. It is separated from Greenland by Baffin Bay.

baffle ▶ **verb** [with obj.] **1** totally bewilder or perplex: *an unexplained occurrence that baffled everyone* | [as adj. **baffling**] *the baffling murder of her sister.*
2 restrain or regulate (a fluid, a sound, etc.): *to baffle the noise further, I pad the gunwales.*
▶ **noun** a device used to restrain the flow of a fluid, gas, or loose material or to prevent the spreading of sound or light in a particular direction.
– DERIVATIVES **bafflement** noun (only in sense 1 of the verb), **bafflingly** adverb (only in sense 1 of the verb).
– ORIGIN late 16th cent. (in the sense 'cheat, deceive'): perhaps related to French *bafouer* 'ridicule' or obsolete French *beffer* 'mock, deceive'.

bafflegab /ˈbaf(ə)lgab/ ▶ **noun** [mass noun] informal, chiefly N. Amer. incomprehensible or pretentious verbiage, especially bureaucratic jargon.

baffler ▶ **noun** another term for **BAFFLE**.

BAFTA /ˈbaftə/ ▶ **abbreviation for** British Academy of Film and Television Arts.
■ [as noun] an award made by this institution.

bafta /ˈbɑːftə/ (also **baft**) ▶ **noun** [mass noun] coarse fabric, typically of cotton.
– ORIGIN late 16th cent.: from Urdu, from Persian *bāft* 'textile', *bāfta* 'woven'.

bag ▶ **noun 1** a container of flexible material with an opening at the top, used for carrying things: *brown paper bags.*
■ the amount held by such a container: *a* ***bag of*** *sugar.* ■ a woman's handbag. ■ a piece of luggage: *she began to unpack her bags.* ■ (**bags of**) informal, chiefly Brit. plenty of: *I had bags of energy.* ■ Baseball a square, typically padded, marking each of the first, second, and third bases.
2 the amount of game shot by a hunter.
3 (usu. **bags**) a loose fold of skin under a person's eye: *the bags under his eyes gave him a sad appearance.*
4 informal a woman, especially an older one, perceived as unpleasant, bad-tempered, or unattractive: *an interfering* ***old bag.***
5 (**bags**) Brit. dated loose-fitting trousers.
6 (**one's bag**) informal one's particular interest or taste: *if religion and politics are your bag you'll find something to interest you here.*
7 (in southern Africa) a unit of measurement, used especially of grain, equal to 70 kg (formerly 200 lb).
▶ **verb** (**bagged**, **bagging**) [with obj.] **1** put (something) in a bag: *customers bagged their own groceries | we* ***bagged up*** *the apples.*
2 succeed in killing or catching (an animal): *Mike bagged nineteen cod.*
■ figurative succeed in securing (something): *we've bagged three awards for excellence | get there early to bag a seat in the front row.*
3 [no obj.] (of clothes, especially trousers) hang loosely or become out of shape: *these trousers never bag at the knee.*
4 [often as noun **bagging**] Austral./NZ informal criticize; disparage: *it's a pretty suspect outfit, deserving of the consistent bagging it gets from customers.* [ORIGIN: 1960s: extended use of colloquial *bag* 'sack, dismiss'.]
– PHRASES **bag and baggage** with all one's belongings: *he threw her out bag and baggage.* **a bag of bones** informal an emaciated person or animal. **a bag** (or **bundle**) **of nerves** informal a person who is extremely timid or tense. **a bag** (or **whole bag**) **of tricks** informal a set of ingenious plans, techniques, or resources. **bags** (or **bags I**) Brit. informal a child's expression used to make a claim to something: *bags I his jacket.* **in the bag** informal **1** (of something desirable) as good as secured: *the election is in the bag.* **2** US drunk.
– DERIVATIVES **bagful** noun (pl. **-fuls**), **bagger** noun.
– ORIGIN Middle English: perhaps from Old Norse *baggi*.

Baganda /bəˈgandə/ ▶ **plural noun** (sing. **Muganda**) an African people of the kingdom of Buganda, now forming part of Uganda. Their language is Luganda.
▶ **adjective** of or relating to the Baganda.
– ORIGIN a local name; compare with Kiswahili *Waganda*.

bagasse /bəˈgas/ ▶ **noun** [mass noun] the dry pulpy residue left after the extraction of juice from sugar cane.
– ORIGIN early 19th cent.: from French, from Spanish *bagazo* 'pulp'.

bagatelle /ˌbagəˈtɛl/ ▶ **noun 1** [mass noun] a game in which small balls are hit and then allowed to roll down a sloping board on which there are holes, each numbered with the score achieved if a ball goes into it, with pins acting as obstructions.
2 a thing regarded as too unimportant or easy to be worth much consideration: *dealing with these boats was* ***a mere bagatelle*** *for the world's oldest yacht club.*
3 a short, light piece of music, especially one for the piano.
– ORIGIN mid 17th cent. (in sense 2): from French, from Italian *bagatella*, perhaps from *baga* 'baggage' or from a diminutive of Latin *baca* 'berry'. Sense 1 dates from the early 19th cent.

Bagehot /ˈbadʒət/, Walter (1826–77), English economist and journalist. He became editor of the *Economist* in 1860, a post which he held until his death. Notable works: *The English Constitution* (1867), *Lombard Street* (1873).

bagel /ˈbeɪg(ə)l/ ▶ **noun** a dense bread roll in the shape of a ring, characteristic of Jewish baking.
– ORIGIN early 20th cent. (as *beigel*): from Yiddish *beygel*.

baggage ▶ **noun 1** [mass noun] personal belongings packed in suitcases for travelling; luggage.
■ the portable equipment of an army. ■ [usu. with adj.] figurative past experiences or long-held ideas and opinions perceived as burdensome encumbrances: *the emotional baggage I'm hauling around.*
2 dated a cheeky or disagreeable girl or woman.
– ORIGIN late Middle English: from Old French *bagage* (from *baguer* 'tie up'), or *bagues* 'bundles'; perhaps related to **BAG**.

baggage reclaim ▶ **noun** [in sing.] the area in an airport where arriving passengers collect luggage that has been transported in the hold of the aircraft.

Baggie ▶ **noun** (pl. **-ies**) N. Amer. trademark a plastic bag typically used for storing food.

baggy ▶ **adjective** (**baggier**, **baggiest**) (of clothing) loose and hanging in folds: *baggy trousers.*
■ (of eyes) with folds of puffy skin below them: *his eyes were baggy with the fatigue of overwork.*
▶ **noun** informal **1** (**baggies**) loose, wide-legged trousers or shorts.
2 [mass noun] a style of popular music combining indie rock and dance music, popular in the early 1990s.
– DERIVATIVES **baggily** adverb, **bagginess** noun.

baggywrinkle ▶ **noun** [mass noun] rope yarns wound around parts of a ship's rigging to prevent chafe.

bagh /bɑːg/ ▶ **noun** [usu. in place names] Indian a large garden or orchard: *Roshanara Bagh.*
– ORIGIN via Hindi from Persian *bāg*.

Baghdad /bagˈdad/ the capital of Iraq, on the River Tigris; pop. 4,648,600 (est. 1985). A thriving city under the Abbasid caliphs in the 8th and 9th centuries, it was taken by the Ottoman sultan Suleiman in 1534 and remained under Ottoman rule until the First World War. In 1920 it became the capital of the newly created state of Iraq.

bag lady ▶ **noun** informal a homeless woman who carries her possessions around in shopping bags.

bagman ▶ **noun** (pl. **-men**) **1** Brit. informal, dated a travelling salesman.
2 Austral. a tramp. [ORIGIN: mid 19th cent.: probably facetiously from sense 1.]
3 Canadian a political fund-raiser.
4 US & Austral./NZ informal an agent who collects or distributes the proceeds of illicit activities.

bagnio /ˈbɑːnjəʊ, ˈbanjəʊ/ ▶ **noun** (pl. **-os**) **1** archaic a brothel.
2 historical (in the Far East) a prison.
– ORIGIN late 16th cent. (in sense 2): from Italian *bagno*, from Latin *balneum* 'bath'.

Bagot /ˈbagət/ ▶ noun a goat of a horned white breed with a black head, neck, and shoulders.

bagpipe ▶ noun (usu. **bagpipes**) a musical instrument with reed pipes that are sounded by the pressure of wind emitted from a bag squeezed by the player's arm. Bagpipes are associated especially with Scotland, but are also used in folk music in Ireland, Northumberland, and France, and in varying forms across Europe and western Asia.
– DERIVATIVES **bagpiper** noun.

ba gua /baː ˈgwaː/ (also **pa kua**) ▶ noun a Chinese religious motif incorporating the eight trigrams of the *I Ching*, typically arranged octagonally around a symbol denoting the balance of yin and yang, or around a mirror.
■ this motif regarded in feng shui as a pattern determining the significance and auspicious qualities of spatial relationships. ■ a Chinese martial art in which movements are focused on a circle and the defence of eight points around it.
– ORIGIN from Chinese *bā* 'eight' + *guà* 'divinatory symbols'.

baguette /baˈgɛt/ ▶ noun **1** a long, narrow French loaf.
2 [often as modifier] a gem, especially a diamond, cut in a long rectangular shape: *a baguette diamond.*
3 Architecture a small moulding, semicircular in section.
– ORIGIN early 18th cent. (in sense 3): from French, from Italian *bacchetto*, diminutive of *bacchio*, from Latin *baculum* 'staff'. Senses 1 and 2 date from the 20th cent.

bagwash ▶ noun a laundry at which clothes are washed but not pressed.
■ a bundle of clothes for rough washing of this kind.

bagworm ▶ noun a drab moth, the caterpillar and flightless female of which live in a portable protective case constructed out of plant debris.
● Family Psychidae: many genera.

bah ▶ exclamation an expression of contempt or disagreement: *You think it was an accident? Bah!*
– ORIGIN early 19th cent.: probably from French.

bahada /bəˈhɑːdə/ ▶ noun variant spelling of **BAJADA**.

bahadur /ˌbaːhəˈduːə/ ▶ noun Indian a brave man.
■ an honorific title, originally given to officers in British India: *Bahadur Shah.*
– ORIGIN from Urdu and Persian *bahādur*, from Mongolian.

Baha'i /baːˈhaːi/ (also **Bahai**) ▶ noun (pl. **Baha'is**) [mass noun] a monotheistic religion founded in the 19th century as a development of Babism, emphasizing the essential oneness of humankind and of all religions and seeking world peace. The Baha'i faith was founded by the Persian Baha'ullah (1817–92) and his son Abdul Baha (1844–1921).
■ [count noun] an adherent of the Baha'i faith.
– DERIVATIVES **Baha'ism** /baːˈhaːɪz(ə)m/ noun.
– ORIGIN Persian, from Arabic *bahā'* 'splendour'.

Bahamas a country consisting of an archipelago off the SE coast of Florida, part of the West Indies; pop. 255,050 (1990); languages, English (official), Creole; capital, Nassau.

It was there that Columbus made his first landfall in the New World (12 October 1492). The islands were a British colony from the 18th century until they gained independence within the Commonwealth in 1973.

– DERIVATIVES **Bahamian** /bəˈheɪmɪən/ adjective & noun.

Bahasa Indonesia /bəˈhaːsə/ ▶ noun [mass noun] the official language of Indonesia. See **INDONESIAN**.
– ORIGIN from Malay *bahasa* 'language'.

Bahasa Malaysia ▶ noun [mass noun] the official language of Malaysia. See **MALAY**.

Bahawalpur /bəˈhaːwəlˌpʊə/ a city of central Pakistan, in Punjab province; pop. 250,000 (1991). It was formerly the capital of a princely state established by the nawabs of Bahawalpur.

Bahia /bəˈiːə/ **1** a state of eastern Brazil, on the Atlantic coast; capital, Salvador.
2 former name for **SALVADOR**.

Bahía Blanca /baːˌiːə ˈblaŋkə/ a port in Argentina serving the southern part of the country; pop. 271,500 (1991).

Bahrain /baːˈreɪn/ a sheikhdom consisting of a group of islands in the Persian Gulf; pop. 518,000 (est. 1991); official language, Arabic; capital, Manama.

Ruled by the Portuguese in the 16th century and the Persians in the 17th century, the islands became a British protectorate in 1861 and gained independence in 1971. Bahrain's economy is dependent on the refining and export of oil.

– DERIVATIVES **Bahraini** adjective & noun.

baht /baːt/ ▶ noun (pl. same) the basic monetary unit of Thailand, equal to 100 satangs.
– ORIGIN from Thai *bāt*.

Bahutu plural form of **HUTU**.

bai /baɪ/ ▶ noun (pl. **bais**) Indian **1** [often as name] a polite form of address for a woman.
2 a maid.
– ORIGIN Marathi, 'lady'.

Baikal, Lake /baɪˈkaːl/ (also **Baykal**) a large lake in southern Siberia, the largest freshwater lake in Europe and Asia and, with a depth of 1,743 m (5,714 ft), the deepest lake in the world.

Baikonur /ˌbaɪkəˈnʊə/ (also **Baykonur**) a mining town in central Kazakhstan. The world's first satellite (1957) and the first manned space flight (1961) were launched from the former Soviet space centre nearby.

bail[1] ▶ noun [mass noun] the temporary release of an accused person awaiting trial, sometimes on condition that a sum of money is lodged to guarantee their appearance in court: *he has been released on bail.*
■ money paid by or for such a person as security.
▶ verb [with obj.] (usu. **be bailed**) release or secure the release of (a prisoner) on payment of bail: *his son called home to get bailed out of jail.*
– PHRASES **go bail** (or **stand bail**) act as surety for an accused person. **jump bail** informal fail to appear for trial after being released on bail. **post bail** pay a sum of money as bail.
– DERIVATIVES **bailable** adjective.
– ORIGIN Middle English: from Old French, literally 'custody, jurisdiction', from *bailler* 'take charge of', from Latin *bajulare* 'bear a burden'.

bail[2] ▶ noun **1** (usu. **bails**) Cricket either of the two crosspieces bridging the stumps, which the bowler and fielders try to dislodge with the ball to get the batsman out.
2 a bar which holds something in place, in particular:
■ a bar on a typewriter or computer printer which holds the paper steady. ■ Climbing a bar on a crampon which fits into a groove in the sole of a boot. ■ a bar separating horses in an open stable. ■ Austral./NZ a movable framework for securing the head of a cow during milking.
▶ verb Austral./NZ [with obj.] **1** secure (a cow) during milking.
2 confront (someone) with the intention of robbing them: *they bailed up Mr Dyason and demanded his money.*
■ detain (someone) in conversation, especially against their will.
– ORIGIN Middle English (denoting the outer wall of a castle): from Old French *baile* 'palisade, enclosure', *baillier* 'enclose', perhaps from Latin *baculum* 'rod, stick'.

bail[3] (Brit. also **bale**) ▶ verb [with obj.] scoop water out of (a ship or boat): *the first priority is to bail out the boat with buckets.*
■ scoop (water) out of a ship or boat.
– DERIVATIVES **bailer** noun.
– ORIGIN early 17th cent.: from obsolete *bail* 'bucket', from French *baille*, based on Latin *bajulus* 'carrier'.
▶ **bail out** make an emergency parachute descent from an aircraft. ■ figurative become free of an obligation or commitment; discontinue an activity: *she felt ready to bail out of the corporate rat race.*
bail someone/thing out release someone or something from a difficulty; rescue: *the state will not bail out loss-making enterprises.*

Baile Átha Cliath /ˌblʲaː ˈklʲɪə/ Irish name for **DUBLIN**.

bailee /beɪˈliː/ ▶ noun Law a person or party to whom goods are delivered for a purpose, such as custody or repair, without transfer of ownership.

Bailey[1] a shipping forecast area in the NE Atlantic north of Rockall and south-west of the Faeroes.

Bailey[2], David (b.1938), English photographer. He was a prominent figure of 1960s pop culture.

bailey ▶ noun (pl. **-eys**) the outer wall of a castle.

■ a court enclosed by this. See also **MOTTE-AND-BAILEY**.
– ORIGIN Middle English: probably from Old French *baile* 'palisade, enclosure' (see **BAIL**[2]).

Bailey bridge ▶ noun a temporary bridge of lattice steel designed for rapid assembly from prefabricated standard parts, used especially in military operations.
– ORIGIN Second World War: named after Sir D. Bailey (1901–85), the English engineer who designed it.

bailie /ˈbeɪli/ ▶ noun (pl. **-ies**) chiefly historical a municipal officer and magistrate in Scotland.
– ORIGIN Middle English (originally used interchangeably with **BAILIFF**): from Old French *bailli*.

bailiff /ˈbeɪlɪf/ ▶ noun a person who performs certain actions under legal authority, in particular:
■ chiefly Brit. a sheriff's officer who executes writs and processes and carries out distraints and arrests. ■ Brit. the agent or steward of a landlord. ■ N. Amer. an official in a court of law who keeps order, looks after prisoners, etc. ■ Brit. historical the sovereign's representative in a district, especially the chief officer of a hundred. ■ the first civil officer in the Channel Islands.
– ORIGIN Middle English: from Old French *baillif*, inflected form of *bailli* (see **BAILIE**), based on Latin *bajulus* 'carrier, manager'.

bailiwick /ˈbeɪlɪwɪk/ ▶ noun Law the district or jurisdiction of a bailie or bailiff.
■ (one's bailiwick) informal one's sphere of operations or particular area of interest.
– ORIGIN late Middle English: from **BAILIE** + **WICK**[2].

bailment ▶ noun Law an act of delivering goods to a bailee for a particular purpose, without transfer of ownership.

bailor /ˈbeɪlɔː/ ▶ noun Law a person or party that entrusts goods to a bailee.

bailout ▶ noun informal an act of giving financial assistance to a failing business or economy to save it from collapse.

Baily's beads Astronomy a string of bright points seen at the edge of the darkened moon at the beginning or end of totality in an eclipse of the sun, caused by the unevenness of the lunar topography.
– ORIGIN mid 19th cent.: named after Francis Baily (1774–1844), English astronomer.

bain-marie /ˌbanməˈriː/ ▶ noun (pl. **bains-marie** or **bain-maries** pronunc. same) a pan or tin of hot water in which a cooking container is placed for slow cooking.
■ Brit. a double boiler.
– ORIGIN early 18th cent.: French, translation of medieval Latin *balneum Mariae* 'bath of Maria', translating Greek *kaminos Marias* 'furnace of Maria', said to be a Jewish alchemist.

Bairam /baɪˈraːm/ ▶ noun either of two annual Muslim festivals. See **GREATER BAIRAM**, **LESSER BAIRAM**.
– ORIGIN from Turkish *bairam* (earlier form of *bayram*), from Persian *bazrām*.

Baird /bɛːd/, John Logie (1888–1946), Scottish pioneer of television. He made the first transatlantic transmission and demonstration of colour television in 1928 using a mechanical system which was soon superseded by an electronic system.

bairn /bɛːn/ ▶ noun chiefly Scottish & N. English a child.
– ORIGIN Old English *bearn*, of Germanic origin; related to the verb **BEAR**[1].

Baisakhi /baɪˈsaːkhi/ ▶ noun a Sikh festival held annually to commemorate the founding of the khalsa by Gobind Singh in 1699.
– ORIGIN from Sanskrit *Vaiśākha*, denoting a month of the Hindu lunar year corresponding to April–May, regarded in some areas as the start of the new year.

bait ▶ noun **1** [mass noun] food placed on a hook or in a net, trap, or fishing area to entice fish or other animals as prey.
■ something intended to entice someone to do something: *she used the prospect of freedom as bait to trap him into talking.*
2 variant spelling of **BATE**[1].
▶ verb [with obj.] **1** deliberately annoy or taunt (someone): *the other boys revelled in baiting him about his love of literature.*

■torment (a trapped or restrained animal), especially by allowing dogs to attack it.
2 put bait on (a hook) or in (a trap, net, or fishing area) to entice fish or animals as prey: *I used a hook baited with fat* | [no obj.] *I baited up with a fresh squid.*
3 [no obj.] archaic stop on a journey to take food or a rest: *we shall bait at Inver inn.*
■[with obj.] give food to (horses) on a journey.
– PHRASES **fish or cut bait** N. Amer. informal stop vacillating and decide to act on or disengage from something. **rise to the bait** react to a provocation or temptation exactly as intended.
– ORIGIN Middle English: from Old Norse *beit* 'pasture, food', *beita* 'to hunt or chase'.

bait-and-switch ▶ **noun** the action (generally illegal) of advertising goods which are an apparent bargain, with the intention of substituting inferior or more expensive goods.

baitcasting ▶ **noun** [mass noun] fishing by throwing a bait or lure into the water on the end of a line using a rod and reel.
– DERIVATIVES **baitcaster** noun.

baiza /ˈbʌɪzɑː/ ▶ **noun** (pl. same or **baizas**) a monetary unit of Oman, equal to one thousandth of a rial.

baize /beɪz/ ▶ **noun** [mass noun] a coarse felt-like woollen material that is typically green, used for covering billiard and card tables and for aprons.
– ORIGIN late 16th cent.: from French *baies*, feminine plural of *bai* 'chestnut-coloured' (see **BAY**[4]), treated as a singular noun. The name is presumably from the original colour of the cloth, although several colours are recorded.

baize door (also **green baize door**) ▶ **noun** used to refer to a door which divides different areas of a stately home or office according to status.

Baja California /ˈbɑːhɑː/ a mountainous peninsula in NW Mexico, which extends southwards from the border with California and separates the Gulf of California from the Pacific Ocean. It consists of two states of Mexico: **Baja California** (capital, Mexicali) and **Baja California Sur** (capital, La Paz). Also called **LOWER CALIFORNIA**.

bajada /bəˈhɑːdə/ (also **bahada**) ▶ **noun** a broad slope of alluvial material at the foot of an escarpment.
– ORIGIN mid 19th cent.: from Spanish, 'descent, slope'.

Bajan /ˈbeɪdʒ(ə)n/ ▶ **adjective** & **noun** informal term for *Barbadian* (see **BARBADOS**).

bajra /ˈbɑːdʒrɑː/ ▶ **noun** [mass noun] (in the Indian subcontinent) pearl millet or similar grain.
– ORIGIN from Hindi *bājrā*, *bājrī*.

bake ▶ **verb** [with obj.] **1** cook (food) by dry heat without direct exposure to a flame, typically in an oven or on a hot surface: *they bake their own bread and cakes* | [as adj. **baked**] *baked apples.*
■[no obj.] (of food) be cooked in such a way: *the bread was baking on hot stones.*
2 (of the sun or other agency) subject (something) to dry heat, especially so as to harden it.
■[no obj.] informal (of a person or place) be or become extremely hot in prolonged sun or hot weather: *the city was baking in a heat wave.*
▶ **noun** [with modifier] a dish consisting of a number of ingredients mixed together and cooked in an oven: *a vegetable bake.*
■[with modifier] N. Amer. a social gathering at which food of a specified kind is eaten: *lobster bakes.*
– PHRASES **bake blind** see **BLIND**.
– ORIGIN Old English *bacan*, of Germanic origin; related to Dutch *bakken* and German *backen*.

bakeapple ▶ **noun** Canadian the fruit of the cloudberry.

baked Alaska ▶ **noun** [mass noun] sponge cake and ice cream in a meringue covering, cooked in a hot oven for a very short time.

baked beans ▶ **plural noun** baked haricot beans, typically cooked in tomato sauce and tinned.

baked potato ▶ **noun** a potato baked in its skin.

bakehouse ▶ **noun** dated a building or area in which bread is made.

Bakelite /ˈbeɪk(ə)lʌɪt/ ▶ **noun** [mass noun] trademark an early form of brittle plastic, typically dark brown, made from formaldehyde and phenol, used chiefly for electrical equipment.
– ORIGIN early 20th cent.: named after Leo H. *Baekeland* (1863–1944), the Belgian-born American chemist who invented it, + **-ITE**[1].

Baker[1], Dame Janet (Abbott) (b.1933), English operatic mezzo-soprano.

Baker[2], Josephine (1906–75), American dancer. She was a star of the Folies-Bergère in the 1930s, famed for her exotic dancing and risqué clothing.

baker ▶ **noun** a person whose trade is making and selling bread and cakes.
■[often with modifier] an oven for a particular purpose: *a waffle baker.*
– ORIGIN Old English *bæcere*, from *bacan* (see **BAKE**).

baker's dozen ▶ **noun** a group of thirteen: *a baker's dozen of love songs.*
– ORIGIN late 16th cent.: from the former bakers' custom of adding an extra loaf to a dozen sold, this representing the retailer's profit.

bakery ▶ **noun** (pl. **-ies**) a place where bread and cakes are made or sold.
■[mass noun] baked goods such as bread and cakes.

bakeshop ▶ **noun** North American term for **BAKERY**.

bakeware ▶ **noun** [mass noun] tins, trays, and other items used during baking.

Bakewell, Robert (1725–95), English pioneer in scientific methods of livestock breeding and husbandry. He produced pedigree herds of sheep and cattle and increased the meat production from his animals through selective breeding.

Bakewell tart ▶ **noun** Brit. a baked open pie consisting of a pastry case lined with jam and filled with almond sponge cake.
– ORIGIN named after the town of *Bakewell* in Derbyshire.

baking powder ▶ **noun** [mass noun] a mixture of sodium bicarbonate and cream of tartar, used instead of yeast in baking.

baking soda ▶ **noun** [mass noun] sodium bicarbonate used in cooking, for cleaning, or in toothpaste.

Bakker, Robert T. (b.1945), American palaeontologist. He proposed the controversial idea that dinosaurs were both active and warm-blooded.

bakkie /ˈbaki, ˈbʌki/ ▶ **noun** (pl. **-ies**) S. African a light truck or pickup truck.
– ORIGIN Afrikaans, from *bak*, denoting the load-bearing part of a truck, + the diminutive suffix *-ie*.

baklava /ˈbɑːkləvə, ˈbak-/ (also **baclava**) ▶ **noun** [mass noun] a dessert originating in the Middle East made of filo pastry filled with chopped nuts and soaked in honey.
– ORIGIN Turkish.

baksheesh /bakˈʃiːʃ/ (also **backsheesh**) ▶ **noun** [mass noun] (in parts of the Middle East, Far East, and the Indian subcontinent) a small sum of money given as alms, a tip, or a bribe.
– ORIGIN based on Persian *bakšīš*, from *bakšīdan* 'give'.

Bakst /bakst/, Léon (1866–1924), Russian painter and designer; born *Lev Samuilovich Rozenberg*. He was a member of the Diaghilev circle and the Ballets Russes, for which he designed exotic, richly coloured sets and costumes.

Baku /baˈkuː/ the capital of Azerbaijan, on the Caspian Sea; pop. 1,780,000 (1990). It is an industrial port and a centre of the oil industry.

Bakunin /baˈkuːnɪn/, Mikhail (Aleksandrovich) (1814–76), Russian anarchist. He took part in the revolutions of 1848, and participated in the First International until his expulsion in 1872.

balaclava /ˌbaləˈklɑːvə/ (also **balaclava helmet**) ▶ **noun** a close-fitting garment covering the whole head and neck except for parts of the face, typically made of wool.
– ORIGIN late 19th cent. (worn originally by soldiers on active service in the Crimean War): named after the village of *Balaclava* in the Crimea (see **BALACLAVA, BATTLE OF**).

Balaclava, Battle of /ˌbaləˈklɑːvə/ a battle of the Crimean War, fought between Russia and an alliance of British, French, and Turkish forces in and around the port of Balaclava (now Balaklava) in the southern Crimea in 1854. The battle ended inconclusively; it is chiefly remembered as the scene of the Charge of the Light Brigade.

balafon /ˈbaləfɒn/ ▶ **noun** a large xylophone with hollow gourds as resonators, used in West African music.
– ORIGIN late 18th cent.: via French from Manding *bala* 'xylophone' + *fo* 'to play'.

balalaika /ˌbaləˈlʌɪkə/ ▶ **noun** a Russian musical instrument like a guitar with a triangular body and typically three strings.
– ORIGIN late 18th cent.: from Russian, of Tartar origin.

balance ▶ **noun** **1** [mass noun] an even distribution of weight enabling someone or something to remain upright and steady: *slipping in the mud but* ***keeping their balance*** | *she* ***lost*** *her* ***balance*** *and fell.*
■mental or emotional stability: *the way to some kind of peace and personal balance.* ■ Sailing the ability of a boat to stay on course without adjustment of the rudder.
2 [mass noun] a condition in which different elements are equal or in the correct proportions: *the obligations of political balance in broadcasting* | [in sing.] *try to keep a* ***balance between*** *work and relaxation.*
■Art harmony of design and proportion. ■ the relative volume of various sources of sound: *the balance of the voices is good.*
3 an apparatus for weighing, especially one with a central pivot, beam, and two scales.
■(**the Balance**) the zodiacal sign or constellation Libra.
4 a counteracting weight or force.
■(also **balance wheel**) the regulating device in a clock or watch.
5 [mass noun] a predominating weight or amount: ***the balance of*** *opinion was that work was more important than leisure.*
6 a figure representing the difference between credits and debits in an account; the amount of money held in an account: *he accumulated a healthy balance with the savings bank.*
■[usu. in sing.] the difference between an amount due and an amount paid: *the holiday balance must be paid by 8 weeks before departure.* ■ [in sing.] an amount left over.
▶ **verb** [with obj.] **1** keep or put (something) in a steady position so that it does not fall: *a mug that she balanced on her knee.*
■[no obj.] remain in a steady position without falling: *Richard balanced on the ball of one foot.*
2 offset or compare the value of (one thing) with another: *the cost of obtaining such information needs to be* ***balanced against*** *its benefits.*
■counteract, equal, or neutralize the weight or importance of: *he balanced his radical remarks with more familiar declarations.* ■ establish equal or appropriate proportions of elements in: *balancing work and family life.*
3 compare debits and credits in (an account) so as to ensure that they are equal: *the law requires the council to* ***balance its books*** *each year.*
■[no obj.] (of an account) have credits and debits equal.
– PHRASES **balance of payments** the difference in total value between payments into and out of a country over a period. **balance of power 1** a situation in which states of the world have roughly equal power. **2** the power held by a small group when larger groups are of equal strength. **balance of trade** the difference in value between a country's imports and exports. **in the balance** uncertain; at a critical stage: *his survival* ***hung in the balance*** *for days.* **on balance** when all factors are taken into consideration: *on balance, he was pleased with how things had gone.* **strike a balance** choose a moderate course or compromise. **throw** (or **catch**) **someone off balance** cause someone to become unsteady and in danger of falling. ■ figurative confuse or bewilder someone.
– DERIVATIVES **balancer** noun.
– ORIGIN Middle English (in sense 3 of the noun): from Old French *balance* (noun), *balancer* (verb), based on late Latin *(libra) bilanx* '(balance) having two scale-pans', from *bi-* 'twice, having two' + *lanx* 'scale-pan'.

balanced ▶ **adjective** keeping or showing a balance; in good proportions: *she assembled a balanced team.*
■taking everything into account; fairly judged or presented: *accurate and balanced information.* ■ (especially of food) having different elements in the correct proportions: *a healthy, balanced diet.* ■ (of a person or state of mind) having no emotion too strong or too weak; stable: *a balanced personality.* ■ (of an electric circuit or signal) being symmetrical with respect to a reference point, usually ground.

balance sheet ▶ **noun** a statement of the assets, liabilities, and capital of a business or other organization at a particular point in time, detailing the balance of income and expenditure over the preceding period.

balance tab ▶ **noun** a tab on a control surface of

an aircraft which reduces the amount of force needed to move the control surface by moving in the opposite direction.

balance wheel ▶ noun the regulating device in a watch or clock.

Balanchine /ˈbalənʃiːn, -tʃiːn/, George (1904–83), Russian-born American ballet dancer and choreographer; born *Georgi Melitonovich Balanchivadze*. He was chief choreographer of Diaghilev's Ballets Russes during the 1920s, and in 1934 he co-founded the company which later became the New York City Ballet.

balancing act ▶ noun an action or activity that requires a delicate balance between different situations or requirements.

balander /bəˈlandə/ (also **balanda**) ▶ noun derogatory (in Australian Aboriginal English) a white man.
– ORIGIN mid 19th cent.: from Makasarese *balanda*, from Malay *belanda* (alteration of **HOLLANDER** in the sense 'Dutchman').

balanitis /ˌbaləˈnʌɪtɪs/ ▶ noun [mass noun] Medicine inflammation of the glans penis.
– ORIGIN mid 19th cent.: from Greek *balanos* 'glans penis' (literally 'acorn') + **-ITIS**.

balas ruby /ˈbaləs/ ▶ noun a ruby of a delicate rose-red variety.
– ORIGIN late Middle English: from Old French *balais*, from Arabic *balakš*, from Persian *Badakšān*, a district of Afghanistan, where it is found.

balata /ˈbalətə, bəˈlɑːtə/ ▶ noun a tropical American tree which bears edible fruit and produces latex.
• Several species in the family Sapotaceae, in particular *Manilkara bidentata*.
■ [mass noun] the dried sap of this tree used as a substitute for rubber.
– ORIGIN early 17th cent.: from Carib *balatá*.

Balaton, Lake /ˌbɒləˈtɒn/ a large shallow lake in west central Hungary, situated in a resort and wine-producing region to the south of the Bakony mountains.

Balboa /balˈbəʊə/, Vasco Núñez de (1475–1519), Spanish explorer. In 1513 he reached the western coast of the isthmus of Darien (Panama), thereby becoming the first European to see the Pacific Ocean.

balboa /balˈbəʊə/ ▶ noun the basic monetary unit of Panama, equal to 100 centésimos.
– ORIGIN named after Vasco Núñez de **BALBOA**.

balbriggan /balˈbrɪg(ə)n/ ▶ noun [mass noun] a knitted cotton fabric, used for stockings and underwear.
– ORIGIN late 19th cent.: named after the town of *Balbriggan* in Ireland, where it was originally made.

Balcon /ˈbɔːlk(ə)n/, Sir Michael (1896–1977), English film producer associated chiefly with Ealing Studios. He produced such famous comedies as *Kind Hearts and Coronets* and *Whisky Galore* (both 1949).

balcony ▶ noun (pl. **-ies**) **1** a platform enclosed by a wall or balustrade on the outside of a building, with access from an upper-floor window or door.
2 (**the balcony**) the highest tier of seats in a theatre, above the dress or upper circle.
■ the upstairs seats in a cinema. ■ N. Amer. the dress circle in a theatre.
– DERIVATIVES **balconied** adjective.
– ORIGIN early 17th cent.: from Italian *balcone*.

bald ▶ adjective **1** having a scalp wholly or partly lacking hair: *a little man with a bald head* | *he was starting to* **go bald**.
■ (of an animal) not covered by the usual fur, hair, or feathers: *hedgehogs are born bald.* ■ (of a plant or an area of land) not covered by the usual leaves, bark, or vegetation. ■ (of a tyre) having the tread worn away.
2 without any extra detail or explanation; plain or blunt: *the bald statement in the preceding paragraph requires amplification.*
– PHRASES (**as**) **bald as a coot** completely bald.
– DERIVATIVES **balding** noun & adjective (only in sense 1), **baldish** adjective, **baldly** adverb (only in sense 2), **baldness** noun.
– ORIGIN Middle English: probably from a base meaning 'white patch', whence the archaic sense 'marked or streaked with white'. Compare with Welsh *ceffyl bal*, denoting a horse with a white mark on its face.

baldachin /ˈbaldəkɪn, ˈbɔːld-/ (also **baldaquin** /ˈbɔːldəkɪn/ or **baldacchino** /ˌbaldəˈkiːnəʊ/) ▶ noun a ceremonial canopy of stone, metal, or fabric over an altar, throne, or doorway.
– ORIGIN late 16th cent. (denoting a rich brocade of silk and gold thread): from Italian *baldacchino*, from *Baldacco* 'Baghdad', place of origin of the original brocade.

bald crow ▶ noun the rockfowl (in allusion to its bare head).

bald cypress ▶ noun another term for **SWAMP CYPRESS**.

bald eagle ▶ noun a white-headed North American eagle that includes fish among its prey. It is the national bird of the US but is now common only in Alaska.
• *Haliaeetus leucocephalus*, family Accipitridae.

Balder /ˈbɔːldə/ Scandinavian Mythology a son of Odin and god of the summer sun. He was invulnerable to all things except mistletoe, with which the god Loki, by a trick, induced the blind god Hödur to kill him.

balderdash /ˈbɔːldədaʃ/ ▶ noun [mass noun] senseless talk or writing; nonsense.
– ORIGIN late 16th cent. (denoting a frothy liquid; later, an unappetizing mixture of drinks): of unknown origin.

baldie ▶ noun & adjective variant spelling of **BALDY**.

baldmoney /ˈbɔːldmʌni/ ▶ noun (pl. **-eys**) another term for **SPIGNEL**.
– ORIGIN late Middle English (denoting the gentian; now only Scots): origin unknown.

baldpate ▶ noun the American wigeon (in allusion to its white-crowned head).

baldric /ˈbɔːldrɪk/ ▶ noun historical a belt for a sword or other piece of equipment, worn over one shoulder and reaching down to the opposite hip.
– ORIGIN Middle English *baudry*, from Old French *baudre*, of unknown ultimate origin.

Baldwin[1] /ˈbɔːldwɪn/, James (Arthur) (1924–87), American novelist and black civil rights activist. Notable works: *Go Tell it on the Mountain* (1953), *Giovanni's Room* (1956).

Baldwin[2] /ˈbɔːldwɪn/, Stanley, 1st Earl Baldwin of Bewdley (1867–1947), British Conservative statesman, Prime Minister 1923–4, 1924–9, and 1935–7. Despite the German occupation of the Rhineland and the outbreak of the Spanish Civil War (both 1936), Baldwin opposed demands for rearmament, believing that the public would not support it.

baldy (also **baldie**) ▶ noun (pl. **-ies**) informal, derogatory a bald-headed person.
▶ adjective chiefly Scottish & Irish bald.

Bâle /bal/ French name for **BASLE**.

bale[1] ▶ noun a large wrapped or bound bundle of paper, hay, or cotton.
■ the quantity in a bale as a measure, specifically (in the US) 500 lb of cotton.
▶ verb [with obj.] make up into bales: *the straw is left on the field to be baled later.*
– ORIGIN Middle English: probably from Middle Dutch, from Old French; ultimately of Germanic origin and related to **BALL**[1].

bale[2] ▶ noun [mass noun] archaic evil considered as a destructive force.
■ evil suffered; physical or mental torment.
– ORIGIN Old English *balu*, *bealu*, of Germanic origin.

bale[3] ▶ noun & verb Brit. variant spelling of **BAIL**[3].

Balearic Islands /ˌbalɪˈarɪk, bəˈlɪərɪk/ (also **the Balearics**) a group of Mediterranean islands off the east coast of Spain, forming an autonomous region of that country, with four large islands (Majorca, Minorca, Ibiza, Formentera) and seven smaller ones; capital, Palma (on Majorca).

baleen /bəˈliːn/ ▶ noun [mass noun] whalebone.
– ORIGIN Middle English (also denoting a whale): from Old French *baleine*, from Latin *balaena* 'whale'.

baleen whale ▶ noun a whale that has plates of whalebone in the mouth for straining plankton from the water. Baleen whales include the rorqual, humpback, right whale, and grey whale. Also called **WHALEBONE WHALE**.
• Suborder Mysticeti, order Cetacea: three families and ten species.

balefire ▶ noun US a large open-air fire.
– ORIGIN Old English (recorded in poetry), from obsolete *bale* 'great fire' + **FIRE**.

baleful ▶ adjective threatening harm; menacing: *Bill shot a baleful glance in her direction.*
■ having a harmful or destructive effect: *drug money has had a baleful impact on the country.*
– DERIVATIVES **balefully** adverb, **balefulness** noun.
– ORIGIN Old English *bealufull* (see **BALE**[2], **-FUL**).

Balenciaga /baˌlɛnsɪˈɑːgə, Spanish balenˈθjaɣa, -ˈsjaɣa/, Cristóbal (1895–1972), Spanish couturier. In the 1950s he contributed to the move away from the tight-waisted New Look originated by Christian Dior to a looser, semi-fitted style.

baler ▶ noun a machine for making up material such as paper, hay, or cotton into bales.

Balfour /ˈbalfə/, Arthur James, 1st Earl of Balfour (1848–1930), British Conservative statesman, Prime Minister 1902–5. In 1917, in his capacity as Foreign Secretary, Balfour issued the declaration in favour of a Jewish national home in Palestine that came to be known as the Balfour Declaration.

Bali /ˈbɑːli/ a mountainous island of Indonesia, to the east of Java; chief city, Denpasar; pop. 2,856,000 (1993).

balibuntal /ˌbalɪˈbʌnt(ə)l/ ▶ noun [mass noun] a fine close-woven straw, used for making hats.
– ORIGIN early 20th cent.: from *Baliuag* in the Philippines, where it originated, + **BUNTAL**.

Balinese /ˌbɑːlɪˈniːz/ ▶ adjective of or relating to Bali or its people or language.
▶ noun (pl. same) **1** a native of Bali.
2 [mass noun] the Indonesian language of Bali, with around 4 million speakers.
– ORIGIN from **BALI**, on the pattern of Dutch *Balinees*.

balk ▶ verb & noun chiefly US variant spelling of **BAULK**.

Balkanize /ˈbɔːlkənʌɪz, ˈbɒl-/ (also **-ise**) ▶ verb [with obj.] divide (a region or body) into smaller mutually hostile states or groups.
– DERIVATIVES **Balkanization** /-ˈzeɪʃ(ə)n/ noun.
– ORIGIN 1920s: from *Balkan* Peninsula (where this was done in the late 19th and early 20th cent.) + **-IZE**.

Balkans /ˈbɔːlkənz/ **1** (also **Balkan Mountains**) a range of mountains stretching eastwards across Bulgaria from the Serbian frontier to the Black Sea. The highest peak is Botev Peak (2,375 m; 7,793 ft).
2 the countries occupying the part of SE Europe lying south of the Danube and Sava Rivers, forming a peninsula bounded by the Adriatic and Ionian Seas in the west, the Aegean and Black Seas in the east, and the Mediterranean in the south.
– DERIVATIVES **Balkan** adjective.

Balkan Wars two wars of 1912–13 that were fought over the last European territories of the Ottoman Empire.

> In 1912 Bulgaria, Serbia, Greece, and Montenegro forced Turkey to give up Albania and Macedonia, leaving the area around Constantinople (Istanbul) as the only Ottoman territory in Europe. The following year Bulgaria disputed with Serbia, Greece, and Romania for possession of Macedonia, which was partitioned between Greece and Serbia.

Balkhash, Lake variant spelling of **BALQASH, LAKE**.

Balkis /ˈbɔːlkɪs, ˈbɒl-/ the name of the queen of Sheba in Arabic literature.

balky /ˈbɔːlki, ˈbɔːki/ (Brit. also **baulky**) ▶ adjective (**balkier**, **balkiest**) chiefly US awkward; uncooperative.

Ball[1], John (d.1381), English rebel. Ball was a priest who preached an egalitarian social message. He was excommunicated and imprisoned for heresy, and following the Peasants' Revolt was hanged as a traitor.

Ball[2], Lucille (1911–89), American comedienne, known in particular for the popular television series *I Love Lucy* (1951–5).

ball[1] ▶ noun **1** a solid or hollow sphere or ovoid, especially one that is kicked, thrown, or hit in a game: *a cricket ball.*
■ an object or mass of material having a similar shape: *a* **ball of** *wool* | *he crushed the card into a ball.* ■ historical a solid spherical non-explosive projectile for a cannon. ■ [mass noun] N. Amer. a game played with a ball, especially baseball: *young men would graduate from college and enter pro ball.*
2 a single throw, kick, or other movement of the ball in the course of a game, in particular:
■ Cricket a delivery of the ball by the bowler to the batsman. ■ Baseball a pitch delivered outside the strike zone which the batter does not attempt to hit. ■ Soccer a pass of the ball in a specified direction or manner: *Whelan sent a long ball to Goddard.*
▶ verb [with obj.] **1** squeeze or form (something) into a

rounded shape: *Robert **balled up** his napkin and threw it on to his plate.*
■clench or screw up (one's fist) tightly: *she balled her fist so that the nails dug into her palms.* ■[no obj.] form a round shape: *the fishing nets eventually **ball up** and sink.* ■wrap the root ball of (a tree or shrub) in hessian to protect it during transportation.
2 N. Amer. vulgar slang have sexual intercourse with.
3 [no obj.] Brit. (of a flower) fail to open properly, decaying in the half-open bud.
– PHRASES **the ball is in your court** it is up to you to make the next move. **a ball of fire** a person who is full of energy and enthusiasm. **the ball of the foot** the rounded protuberant part of the foot at the base of the big toe. **the ball of the thumb** the rounded protuberant part of the hand at the base of the thumb. **have a lot** (or **not much**) **on the ball** US have a lot of (or not much) ability. **keep the ball rolling** maintain the momentum of an activity. **keep one's eye on** (or **take one's eye off**) **the ball** keep (or fail to keep) one's attention focused on the matter in hand. **on the ball** alert to new ideas, methods, and trends. **play ball** play a ball game such as baseball or cricket. ■informal work willingly with others; cooperate: *if his solicitors won't play ball, there's nothing we can do.* **start** (or **get** or **set**) **the ball rolling** set an activity in motion; make a start. **the whole ball of wax** N. Amer. informal everything.
– ORIGIN Middle English: from Old Norse *bǫllr*, of Germanic origin.

ball[2] ▶ **noun** a formal social gathering for dancing.
– PHRASES **have a ball** informal enjoy oneself greatly.
– ORIGIN early 17th cent.: from French *bal* 'a dance', from late Latin *ballare* 'to dance'; related to Greek *ballizein* 'to dance' (also *ballein* 'to throw').

ballad ▶ **noun** a poem or song narrating a story in short stanzas. Traditional ballads are typically of unknown authorship, having been passed on orally from one generation to the next as part of the folk culture.
■a slow sentimental or romantic song.
– ORIGIN late 15th cent. (denoting a light, simple song): from Old French *balade*, from Provençal *balada* 'dance, song to dance to', from *balar* 'to dance', from late Latin *ballare* (see **BALL**[2]). The sense 'narrative poem' dates from the mid 18th cent.

ballade /baˈlɑːd/ ▶ **noun** **1** a poem consisting of one or more triplets of stanzas with a repeated refrain and an envoy.
2 a piece of music in romantic style with dramatic elements, typically for piano.
– ORIGIN late Middle English: earlier spelling and pronunciation of **BALLAD**.

balladeer /ˌbaləˈdɪə/ ▶ **noun** a singer or composer of ballads.

ballad metre ▶ **noun** another term for **COMMON METRE**.

ballad opera ▶ **noun** a theatrical entertainment popular in early 18th-century England, taking the form of a satirical play interspersed with traditional or operatic songs. The best-known example is John Gay's *The Beggar's Opera* (1728).

balladry ▶ **noun** [mass noun] ballads collectively.
■the art of writing or performing ballads.

ball and chain ▶ **noun** a heavy metal ball secured by a chain to the leg of a prisoner to prevent escape.
■used in similes and metaphors to convey the idea that someone or something is a crippling encumbrance: *the ball and chain of debt.*

ball-and-socket joint ▶ **noun** a natural or manufactured joint or coupling, such as the hip joint, in which a partially spherical end lies in a socket, allowing multidirectional movement and rotation.

Ballantyne /ˈbalәntʌɪn/, R. M. (1825–94), Scottish author; full name *Robert Michael Ballantyne*. He wrote acclaimed stories for boys, such as *The Coral Island* (1857).

ballan wrasse /ˈbalәn/ ▶ **noun** a large European wrasse of rocky shores and reefs, popular as an angling fish.
• *Labrus bergylta*, family Labridae.
– ORIGIN mid 18th cent.: *ballan* from Irish *ballán*, from *ball* 'spot'.

Ballarat /ˈbalәrat/ a mining and sheep-farming centre in Victoria, Australia; pop. 64,980 (1991). It is the site of the discovery in 1851 of the largest gold reserves in Australia.

Ballard, J. G. (b.1930), British novelist and short-story writer; full name *James Graham Ballard*. He is known for dystopian science fiction such as his first novel, *The Drowned World* (1962), and *Crash* (1973).

ballast /ˈbalәst/ ▶ **noun** [mass noun] **1** heavy material, such as gravel, sand, iron, or lead, placed in the bilge of a ship to ensure its stability.
■a similar substance carried in an airship or on a hot-air balloon to stabilize it and jettisoned when greater altitude is required. ■figurative something that gives stability or substance: *the film is an entertaining comedy with some serious ideas thrown in for ballast.*
2 gravel or coarse stone used to form the bed of a railway track or the substratum of a road.
■a mixture of coarse and fine aggregate for making concrete.
3 [count noun] a passive component used in an electric circuit to moderate changes in current.
▶ **verb** [with obj.] (usu. **be ballasted**) **1** give stability to (a ship) by putting a heavy substance in its bilge.
2 form (the bed of a railway line or the substratum of a road) with gravel or coarse stone.
– PHRASES **in ballast** (of a ship) laden only with ballast.
– ORIGIN mid 16th cent.: probably of Low German or Scandinavian origin.

ball bearing ▶ **noun** a bearing which allows one part (such as a wheel) to rotate around an axle and consists of a set of freely rotating metal balls loosely held in a ring.
■a ball used in such a bearing.

ballboy ▶ **noun** a boy who retrieves balls that go out of play during a game such as tennis or baseball.

ball-breaker (also **ball-buster**) ▶ **noun** informal a sexually demanding woman who destroys men's self-confidence.
– DERIVATIVES **ball-breaking** adjective.

ball-carrier ▶ **noun** American Football a player in possession of the ball and attempting to advance it.

ball clay ▶ **noun** [mass noun] a fine-textured clay used in the manufacture of ceramics.

ballcock ▶ **noun** a valve which is linked by a hinged arm to a ball floating on top of a liquid and opens or closes a tap automatically according to the height of the ball, especially in the cistern of a flushing toilet.

ballerina ▶ **noun** a female ballet dancer.
– ORIGIN late 18th cent.: from Italian, feminine of *ballerino* 'dancing master', from *ballare* 'to dance', from late Latin.

Ballesteros /ˌbaləˈstɛːrɒs, Spanish bajesˈteros/, Sevvy (b.1957), Spanish golfer; full name *Severiano Ballesteros*. In 1979 he became the youngest player in the 20th century to win the British Open; the following year he was the youngest-ever winner of the US Masters.

ballet ▶ **noun** [mass noun] an artistic dance form performed to music, using precise and highly formalized set steps and gestures. Classical ballet, which originated in Renaissance Italy and established its present form during the 19th century, is characterized by light, graceful, fluid movements and the use of pointe shoes with reinforced toes.
■[count noun] a creative work of this form or the music written for it. ■[treated as sing. or pl.] a group of dancers who regularly perform such works: *the Bolshoi Ballet.* ■[in sing.] figurative an elaborate or complicated interaction between people: *that delicate and cautious ballet known as the planning process.*
– ORIGIN mid 17th cent.: from French, from Italian *balletto*, diminutive of *ballo* 'a dance', from late Latin *ballare* 'to dance' (see **BALL**[2]).

balletic /bәˈlɛtɪk/ ▶ **adjective** of, relating to, or characteristic of ballet: *a graceful, balletic movement.*
– DERIVATIVES **balletically** adverb.

ballet master ▶ **noun** a person employed by a ballet company to teach and rehearse dancers.

balletomane /ˈbalɪtәʊˌmeɪn/ ▶ **noun** a ballet enthusiast.
– DERIVATIVES **balletomania** noun.

Ballets Russes /ˌbaleɪ ˈruːs, French bale ʀys/ a ballet company formed in Paris in 1909 by Sergei Diaghilev.

The company commissioned music from the composers Stravinsky, Satie, and Rimsky-Korsakov, while Picasso and Jean Cocteau designed sets. The company's choreographers and dancers included Michel Fokine, Anna Pavlova, Vaslav Nijinsky, and George Balanchine. It was responsible for reviving ballet as an art form in western Europe.

ball float ▶ **noun** the spherical float attached to a hinged arm in the ballcock of a water cistern.

ball game ▶ **noun** **1** a game played with a ball.
■N. Amer. a baseball match.
2 [in sing.] informal a situation of a particular type, especially one that is completely different from a previous one: *making the film was **a whole new ball game** for her.*

ballgirl ▶ **noun** a girl who retrieves balls that go out of play during a game such as tennis or baseball.

ballhawk ▶ **noun** N. Amer. informal a player who is good at getting possession of or catching the ball in a game.
– DERIVATIVES **ballhawking** noun.

ballista /bәˈlɪstә/ ▶ **noun** (pl. **ballistae** /-stiː/ or **ballistas**) a catapult used in ancient warfare for hurling large stones.
■a large crossbow for firing a spear.
– ORIGIN early 16th cent.: from Latin, based on Greek *ballein* 'to throw'.

ballistic /bәˈlɪstɪk/ ▶ **adjective** **1** of or relating to projectiles or their flight.
2 moving under the force of gravity only.
– PHRASES **go ballistic** informal fly into a rage.
– DERIVATIVES **ballistically** adverb.
– ORIGIN late 18th cent.: from **BALLISTA** + **-IC**.

ballistic missile ▶ **noun** a missile with a high, arching trajectory, which is initially powered and guided but falls under gravity on to its target.

Ballistic Missile Defense Organization name given to **STRATEGIC DEFENSE INITIATIVE** after 1993.

ballistics ▶ **plural noun** [treated as sing.] the science of projectiles and firearms.
■the study of the effects of being fired on a bullet, cartridge, or gun.

ball lightning ▶ **noun** [mass noun] a rare and little known kind of lightning having the form of a moving globe of light several centimetres across which persists for periods of up to a minute.

ballock ▶ **verb** variant spelling of **BOLLOCK**.

ballocking ▶ **noun** variant spelling of **BOLLOCKING**.

ballocks ▶ **noun** variant spelling of **BOLLOCKS**.

ballon /ˈbalɒ̃/ ▶ **noun** **1** [mass noun] (in dancing) the ability to appear effortlessly suspended while performing movements during a jump.
2 variant spelling of **BALLOON** (in sense 3).
– ORIGIN French, from Italian *ballone*, from *balla* 'ball'.

balloon ▶ **noun** **1** a brightly coloured rubber sac which is inflated with air and then sealed at the neck, and used as a child's toy or a decoration.
■a round or pear-shaped outline in which the words or thoughts of characters in a comic strip or cartoon are written.
2 a large bag filled with hot air or gas to make it rise in the air, typically one carrying a basket for passengers: *a hot-air balloon.*
3 (also **balloon glass**) a large rounded drinking glass, used for brandy and other drinks.
4 Scottish informal a stupid person.
▶ **verb** [no obj.] **1** swell out or cause to swell out in a spherical shape: *the trousers **ballooned out** below his waist.*
■(of an amount of money spent, earned, or owed) increase rapidly: *the company's debt has ballooned in the last five years* | [as adj. **ballooning**] *ballooning government spending.* ■(of a person) increase rapidly and dramatically in weight: *I ate out of boredom and I just **ballooned up**.*
2 Brit. (of a ball) be kicked or struck so that it floats high in the air: *the ball ballooned into the air.*
■[with obj.] hit or kick (a ball) in such a way: *he ballooned the penalty over the bar.*
3 travel by hot-air balloon: *he is famous for ballooning across oceans.*
– PHRASES **when** (or **before**) **the balloon goes up** informal when (or before) the action or trouble starts. [ORIGIN: probably with allusion to the release of a balloon to mark the start of an event.]
– ORIGIN late 16th cent. (originally denoting a game played with a large inflated leather ball): from French *ballon* or Italian *ballone* 'large ball'.

balloon angioplasty ▶ noun [mass noun] Medicine surgical widening of a blocked or narrowed blood vessel, especially a coronary artery, by means of a balloon catheter.

balloon catheter ▶ noun Medicine a type of catheter incorporating a small balloon which may be introduced into a canal, duct, or blood vessel and then inflated in order to clear an obstruction or dilate a narrowed region.

balloonfish ▶ noun (pl. same or **-fishes**) a tropical porcupine fish which lives in shallow water and can inflate itself when threatened.
● *Diodon holocanthus*, family Diodontidae.

ballooning ▶ noun [mass noun] the sport or pastime of flying in a balloon.
– DERIVATIVES **balloonist** noun.

balloon payment ▶ noun a repayment of the outstanding principal sum made at the end of a loan period, interest only having been paid hitherto.

balloon tyre ▶ noun a large tyre containing air at low pressure for travel on soft or uneven surfaces.
– DERIVATIVES **balloon-tyred** adjective.

balloon vine ▶ noun a tropical American vine with inflated balloon-like pods.
● *Cardiospermum halicacabum*, family Sapiondaceae.

balloon whisk ▶ noun a hand whisk made of loops of metal wire.

ballot ▶ noun a procedure by which people vote secretly on a particular issue: *a strike ballot* | [mass noun] *the commissioners were elected by ballot.*
■ (**the ballot**) the total number of votes cast in such a process: *he won 54 per cent of the ballot.* ■ the piece of paper used to record someone's vote. ■ a lottery held to decide the allocation of tickets, shares, or other things among a number of applicants.
▶ verb (**balloted**, **balloting**) [with obj.] (of an organization) elicit a secret vote from (members) on a particular issue: *the union is preparing to ballot its members on further industrial action.*
■ [no obj.] cast one's vote on a particular issue: [with infinitive] *ambulance crews balloted unanimously to reject the deal.* ■ decide the allocation of (something) to applicants by drawing lots.
– ORIGIN mid 16th cent. (originally denoting a small coloured ball placed in a container to register a vote): from Italian *ballotta*, diminutive of *balla* (see **BALL**[1]).

ballot box ▶ noun a sealed box into which voters put completed ballot papers.
■ (**the ballot box**) democratic principles and methods: *the proper remedy was the ballot box and not the court.*

ballpark chiefly N. Amer. ▶ noun a baseball ground.
■ informal a particular area or range: *we can make a pretty good guess that this figure's in the ballpark.*
▶ adjective [attrib.] informal (of a price or cost) approximate; rough: *the ballpark figure is $400–500.*

ballpoint (also **ballpoint pen**) ▶ noun a pen with a tiny ball as its writing point, especially one using stiffer ink than a rollerball.

ballroom ▶ noun a large room for formal dancing.

ballroom dancing ▶ noun [mass noun] formal social dancing in couples, popular as a recreation and also as a competitive activity. The ballroom dance repertoire includes dances developed from old European folk dances such as the waltz and minuet, Latin American dances such as the tango, rumba, and cha-cha, and dances of 20th-century origin such as the foxtrot and quickstep.

balls vulgar slang ▶ plural noun testicles.
■ [treated as sing.] Brit. nonsense; rubbish (often said to express strong disagreement). ■ [mass noun] courage or nerve.
▶ verb [with obj.] (**balls something up**) bungle something.

balls-aching ▶ adjective vulgar slang causing annoyance, revulsion, or boredom.
– DERIVATIVES **balls-ache** noun, **balls-achingly** adverb.

balls-up ▶ noun Brit. vulgar slang a bungled or badly carried out task or action; a mess.

ballsy ▶ adjective (**ballsier**, **ballsiest**) informal bold; courageous: *she was a cool, ballsy woman.*
– DERIVATIVES **ballsiness** noun.
– ORIGIN 1950s: from **BALLS** + **-Y**[1].

ball-tampering ▶ noun [mass noun] Cricket illegal alteration of the surface or seam of a ball on the field, to affect its motion when bowled.

ball-tearer ▶ noun Austral. informal something outstanding of its kind.

ball valve ▶ noun a one-way valve that is opened and closed by pressure on a ball which fits into a cup-shaped opening.
■ Brit. another term for **BALLCOCK**.

bally /ˈbali/ ▶ adjective & adverb Brit. old-fashioned euphemism for **BLOODY**[2].

ballyhoo informal ▶ noun [mass noun] extravagant publicity or fuss: *after all the ballyhoo, the film was a flop.*
▶ verb (**ballyhoos**, **ballyhooed**) [with obj.] chiefly N. Amer. praise or publicize extravagantly.
– ORIGIN late 19th cent.: American coinage of unknown origin.

Ballymena /ˌbaliˈmiːnə/ a town in Northern Ireland, to the north of Lough Neagh, capital of a district of the same name; pop. 18,150 (1981).

ballyrag ▶ verb variant spelling of **BULLYRAG**.

balm /bɑːm/ ▶ noun 1 a fragrant ointment or preparation used to heal or soothe the skin.
■ figurative something that has a comforting, soothing, or restorative effect: *the murmur of the water can provide balm for troubled spirits.*
2 a tree which yields a fragrant resinous substance, especially one used in medicine.
● Species in several families, in particular those of the genus *Commiphora* (family Burseraceae).
■ [mass noun] resinous substance from such a tree.
3 (also **lemon** or **sweet balm**) [mass noun] a bushy herb of the mint family, with leaves smelling and tasting of lemon.
● *Melissa officinalis*, family Labiatae.
■ used in names of other aromatic herbs of the mint family, e.g. **bee balm**.
– ORIGIN Middle English (in the sense 'preparation for embalming, fragrant resinous substance'): from Old French *basme*, from Latin *balsamum* (see **BALSAM**).

bal masqué /ˌbal maˈskeɪ, French bal maske/ ▶ noun (pl. **bals masqués** pronunc. same) a masked ball.
– ORIGIN French.

Balmer series /ˈbɑːmə/ Physics a series of lines in the visible and ultraviolet spectrum of atomic hydrogen, between 656 and 365 nanometres.

balm of Gilead /ˈɡɪliəd/ ▶ noun 1 [mass noun] a fragrant medicinal resin obtained from certain trees.
2 a tree that yields such a resin, in particular:
● an Arabian tree traditionally of importance in medicine and perfumery (*Commiphora gileadensis*, family Burseraceae).
● either of two poplars with sticky aromatic buds (*Populus* × *gileadensis* (or *candicans*)) and the balsam poplar, family Salicaceae. ● the balsam fir.
– ORIGIN early 16th cent.: *balm* from a translation in Coverdale's Bible (Gen. 37:25), rendered 'resin' in the Vulgate; *Gilead* from the assumption that this resin is the substance mentioned in the Bible as coming from Gilead.

balmoral /balˈmɒr(ə)l/ ▶ noun 1 a round brimless hat with a cockade or ribbons attached, worn by certain Scottish regiments.
2 a heavy laced leather walking boot.
– ORIGIN mid 19th cent. (in sense 2): named after **BALMORAL CASTLE** in Scotland.

Balmoral Castle a holiday residence of the British royal family, on the River Dee in Scotland.

bal musette /ˌbal mjuːˈzɛt, French bal myzɛt/ ▶ noun (pl. **bals musettes** pronunc. same) (in France) a dance hall with an accordion band.
– ORIGIN French, originally denoting dancing outdoors to bagpipe accompaniment.

balmy /ˈbɑːmi/ ▶ adjective (**balmier**, **balmiest**) 1 characterized by pleasantly warm weather: *the balmy days of late summer.*
2 chiefly US variant spelling of **BARMY**.
– DERIVATIVES **balmily** adverb, **balminess** noun.

balneology /ˌbalnɪˈɒlədʒi/ ▶ noun [mass noun] the study of therapeutic bathing and medicinal springs.
■ another term for **BALNEOTHERAPY**.
– DERIVATIVES **balneological** adjective, **balneologist** noun.
– ORIGIN mid 19th cent.: from Latin *balneum* 'bath' and **-LOGY**.

balneotherapy /ˌbalnɪə(ʊ)ˈθɛrəpi/ ▶ noun [mass noun] the treatment of disease by bathing in mineral springs.

– ORIGIN late 19th cent.: from Latin *balneum* 'bath' + **THERAPY**.

baloney /bəˈləʊni/ (also **boloney**) ▶ noun informal
1 [mass noun] foolish or deceptive talk; nonsense. [ORIGIN: said to be a corruption of **BOLOGNA**, from **BOLOGNA SAUSAGE**: the connection remains conjectural.]
2 North American term for **BOLOGNA**.

BALPA /ˈbalpə/ ▶ abbreviation for British Air Line Pilots Association.

Balqash, Lake /balˈkaʃ/ (also **Balkhash**) a shallow salt lake in Kazakhstan.

balsa /ˈbɒlsə/ ▶ noun [mass noun] 1 (also **balsa wood**) very lightweight timber used chiefly for making models and rafts.
2 the fast-growing tropical American tree from which this timber is obtained.
● *Ochroma lagopus* (or *pyramidale*), family Bombacaceae.
– ORIGIN early 17th cent. (denoting a kind of South American raft or fishing boat): from Spanish, 'raft'.

balsam /ˈbɔːlsəm, ˈbɒl-/ ▶ noun 1 [mass noun] an aromatic resinous substance, such as balm, exuded by various trees and shrubs and used as a base for certain fragrances and medical preparations.
■ [count noun] an aromatic ointment or other resinous medicinal or cosmetic preparation. ■ [count noun] a tree or shrub which yields balsam.
2 a herbaceous plant cultivated for its helmeted flowers, which are typically pink or purple.
● Genus *Impatiens*, family Balsaminaceae: several species, including **garden balsam** (*I. balsamina*) and **Himalayan balsam** (*I. glandulifera*), which is naturalized in Europe and North America.
– DERIVATIVES **balsamic** /-ˈsamɪk/ adjective.
– ORIGIN Old English, via Latin from Greek *balsamon*.

balsam fir ▶ noun a North American fir tree which yields Canada balsam.
● *Abies balsamea*, family Pinaceae.

balsamic vinegar ▶ noun [mass noun] dark, sweet Italian vinegar that has been matured in wooden barrels.

balsam poplar ▶ noun a North American poplar tree which yields balsam.
● *Populus balsamifera*, family Salicaceae.

balsa wood ▶ noun see **BALSA** (sense 1).

bals masqués plural form of **BAL MASQUÉ**.

bals musettes plural form of **BAL MUSETTE**.

Balt /bɔːlt, bɒlt/ ▶ noun 1 a speaker of a Baltic language; a Lithuanian or Latvian.
2 a native or inhabitant of one of the Baltic States of Lithuania, Latvia, and Estonia.
■ historical a German-speaking inhabitant of any of these states.
▶ adjective of or relating to the Balts.
– ORIGIN late 19th cent.: from late Latin *Balthae* 'dwellers near the Baltic Sea'.

Balthasar /ˈbalθəzɑː/ the name of one of the three Magi.

Balthazar /balˈθazə/ ▶ noun a very large wine bottle, equivalent in capacity to sixteen regular bottles.
– ORIGIN 1930s: from *Balthazar*, the name of the king of Babylon, who 'made a great feast … and drank wine before a thousand' (Dan. 5:1).

Balti /ˈbalti/ ▶ noun 1 a native or inhabitant of Baltistan.
2 [mass noun] the Tibetan language of this people, with around 400,000 speakers.
▶ adjective of or relating to the Baltis or their language.
– ORIGIN the name in Ladakhi dialect.

balti /ˈbɒlti, ˈbalti/ ▶ noun (pl. **baltis**) [mass noun] a type of Pakistani cuisine in which the food is cooked in a small two-handled pan known as a karahi.
■ [count noun] a meal prepared in this way.
– ORIGIN from Urdu *bāltī*, literally 'pail'.

Baltic /ˈbɔːltɪk, ˈbɒl-/ ▶ adjective 1 of or relating to the Baltic Sea or the region surrounding it.
2 denoting, belonging to, or relating to a branch of the Indo-European family of languages consisting of Lithuanian, Latvian, and Old Prussian.
▶ noun 1 (**the Baltic**) the Baltic Sea or the Baltic States.
2 [mass noun] the Baltic languages collectively.
– ORIGIN late 16th cent.: from medieval Latin *Balticus*, from late Latin *Balthae* 'dwellers near the Baltic Sea'.

Baltic Exchange an association of companies,

based in London, whose members are engaged in numerous international trading activities, especially the chartering of vessels to carry cargo.

– ORIGIN from the name *Virginia and Baltic*, one of many coffee houses where shipowners and merchants met in London in the 18th cent., the coffee house being so named by association with areas of much of the trade.

Baltic Sea an almost landlocked sea of northern Europe, between Sweden, Finland, Russia, Poland, Germany, and Denmark. It is linked with the North Sea by the Kattegat strait and the Øresund channel.

Baltic States 1 the independent republics of Estonia, Latvia, and Lithuania.
2 the ten members of the Council of Baltic States established in 1992: Denmark, Estonia, Finland, Germany, Latvia, Lithuania, Norway, Poland, Russia, and Sweden.

Baltimore /ˈbɔːltɪmɔː, ˈbɒl-/ a seaport in north Maryland; pop. 736,000 (1990).
– ORIGIN named after George Calvert, the first Baron *Baltimore* (*c*.1580–1632), who in 1632 obtained a grant of land for the colony later to become Maryland.

Baltistan /ˌbɔːltɪˈstɑːn, ˌbɒl-, -ˈstan/ a region of the Karakoram range of the Himalayas, to the south of K2. Also called **LITTLE TIBET**.

Baluchi /bəˈluːtʃi/ ▶ noun **1** a native or inhabitant of Baluchistan.
2 [mass noun] the language of the Iranian group spoken by over 5 million people in and around Baluchistan.
▶ adjective of or relating to this people or their language.
– ORIGIN from Persian *Balūč(ī)*.

Baluchistan /bəˌluːtʃɪˈstɑːn, -ˈstan/ **1** a mountainous region of western Asia, which includes part of SE Iran, SW Afghanistan, and western Pakistan.
2 a province of western Pakistan; capital, Quetta.

balun /ˈbalʌn/ ▶ noun a type of electrical transformer used to connect an unbalanced circuit to a balanced one.
– ORIGIN from *bal(ance to) un(balance transformer)*.

Balunda plural form of **LUNDA**.

baluster /ˈbaləstə/ ▶ noun a short pillar or column, typically decorative in design, forming part of a series supporting a rail or coping.
■ [as modifier] (of a furniture leg or other decorative item) having the form of a baluster.
– ORIGIN early 17th cent.: from French *balustre*, from Italian *balaustro*, from *balaust(r)a* 'wild pomegranate flower' (via Latin from Greek *balaustion*), so named because part of the pillar resembles the curving calyx tube of the flower.

balustrade /ˌbaləˈstreɪd/ ▶ noun a railing supported by balusters, especially one forming an ornamental parapet to a balcony, bridge, or terrace.
– DERIVATIVES **balustraded** adjective.
– ORIGIN mid 17th cent.: from French, from *balustre* (see **BALUSTER**).

Balzac /ˈbalzak/, Honoré de (1799–1850), French novelist. He is chiefly remembered for his series of ninety-one interconnected novels and stories known collectively as *La Comédie humaine*, which includes *Eugénie Grandet* (1833) and *Le Père Goriot* (1835).
– DERIVATIVES **Balzacian** /balˈzakɪən/ adjective.

bam ▶ exclamation used to imitate the sound of a hard blow or to convey something happening abruptly: *he'll have to make a dash for it, and when he does, bam, he's dead.*
– ORIGIN 1920s: imitative.

bama /ˈbamə/ (also **pama**) ▶ noun Austral. an Aboriginal person, especially one from northern Queensland.

Bamako /ˈbaməkəʊ/ the capital of Mali, in the south of the country, on the River Niger; pop. 646,000 (est. 1990).

Bambara /bamˈbɑːrə/ ▶ noun (pl. same or **Bambaras**) **1** a member of a West African people living chiefly in Mali.
2 [mass noun] the language of this people, belonging to the Mande group. It has about 1.5 million speakers.
▶ adjective of or relating to this people or their language.

bambino /bamˈbiːnəʊ/ ▶ noun (pl. **bambini** /-ni/) a baby or young child.
■ an image of the infant Jesus.
– ORIGIN early 18th cent.: Italian, diminutive of *bambo* 'silly'.

bamboo ▶ noun [mass noun] a giant woody grass which grows chiefly in the tropics, where it is widely cultivated.
● *Bambusa* and other genera, family Gramineae.
■ the hollow jointed stem of this plant, used as a cane or to make furniture and implements.
– ORIGIN late 16th cent.: from Dutch *bamboes*, based on Malay *mambu*.

bamboo rat ▶ noun a large nocturnal burrowing rat that feeds chiefly on the roots of bamboo and other plants, found in the forests of SE Asia.
● Genus *Rhyzomys*, family Muridae: several species.

bamboo shoot ▶ noun a young shoot of bamboo, eaten as a vegetable.

bamboozle /bamˈbuːz(ə)l/ ▶ verb [with obj.] informal cheat or fool: *he bamboozled Canada's largest banks in a massive counterfeit scam.*
– DERIVATIVES **bamboozler** noun.
– ORIGIN early 18th cent.: of unknown origin.

Bamian /ˌbɑːmiˈɑːn/ a city in central Afghanistan; pop. 8,000 (1984). Nearby are the remains of two colossal statues of Buddha and the ruins of the city of Ghulghuleh, which was destroyed by Genghis Khan *c*.1221.

ban[1] /ban/ ▶ verb (**banned**, **banning**) [with obj.] (often **be banned**) officially or legally prohibit: *he was banned from driving for a year | a proposal to ban all trade in ivory.*
■ officially exclude (someone) from a place: *her son was banned for life from the Centre.*
▶ noun an official or legal prohibition: *a proposed ban on cigarette advertising | a three-year driving ban.*
■ an official exclusion of a person from an organization, country, or activity: *a ban on homosexuals in the armed forces.* ■ historical a sentence of outlawry. ■ archaic a curse.
– ORIGIN Old English *bannan* 'summon by a public proclamation', of Germanic origin, reinforced by Old Norse *banna* 'curse, prohibit'; the noun is partly from Old French *ban* 'proclamation, summons, banishment'.

ban[2] /bɑːn/ ▶ noun (pl. **bani** /ˈbɑːni/) a monetary unit of Romania, equal to one hundredth of a leu.
– ORIGIN Romanian.

Banaba /bəˈnabə/ an island in the western Pacific, just south of the equator to the west of the Gilbert Islands. Formerly within the Gilbert and Ellice Islands, the island has been part of Kiribati since 1979. Also called **OCEAN ISLAND**.

banal /bəˈnɑːl, -ˈnal/ ▶ adjective so lacking in originality as to be obvious and boring: *songs with banal, repeated words.*
– DERIVATIVES **banality** noun (pl. **-ies**), **banally** adverb.
– ORIGIN mid 18th cent. (originally relating to feudal service in the sense 'compulsory', hence 'common to all'): from French, from *ban* 'a proclamation or call to arms'; ultimately of Germanic origin and related to **BAN**[1].

banana ▶ noun **1** a long curved fruit which grows in clusters and has soft pulpy flesh and yellow skin when ripe.
2 (also **banana plant** or **banana tree**) the tropical and subtropical palm-like plant which bears this fruit, having very large leaves but lacking a woody trunk.
● Genus *Musa*, family Musaceae: several species, in particular *M. sapientum*.
– PHRASES **go** (or **be**) **bananas** informal become (or be) mad or extremely silly: *everyone's beginning to think I'm bananas.* ■ become extremely angry or excited: *she went bananas when I said I was going to leave the job.* **top** (or **second**) **banana** informal, chiefly N. Amer. the most (or second most) important person in an organization or activity.
– ORIGIN late 16th cent.: via Portuguese or Spanish from Mande.

banana belt ▶ noun N. Amer. informal a region with a comparatively warm climate.

Banana bender ▶ noun Austral. informal a person from Queensland.

Bananaland ▶ noun Austral. informal Queensland.
– DERIVATIVES **Bananalander** noun.

banana plug ▶ noun Electronics, informal a single-pole

connector with a curved strip of metal forming a spring along its tip.

bananaquit /bəˈnɑːnəkwɪt/ ▶ noun a small songbird with a curved bill, typically with a white stripe over the eye, a sooty grey back, and yellow underparts. It is common in the Caribbean and Central and South America.
● *Coereba flaveola*, the only member of the family Coerebidae; sometimes placed in the family Parulidae.
– ORIGIN see **QUIT**[2].

banana republic ▶ noun derogatory a small state dependent on foreign capital, typically as a result of the domination of the economy by a single trade, and hence politically unstable.

banana skin ▶ noun the skin of a banana, especially when peeled off and discarded.
■ informal used to refer to a cause of difficulty or embarrassment: *the insurance market has an unhappy knack of slipping on banana skins.*

banana split ▶ noun a sweet dish made with bananas cut down the middle and filled with ice cream, sauce, and nuts.

banausic /bəˈnɔːsɪk/ ▶ adjective formal not operating on a refined or elevated level; mundane.
■ relating to technical work.
– ORIGIN mid 19th cent.: from Greek *banausikos* 'of or for artisans'.

Banbury cake ▶ noun Brit. a flat pastry with a spicy currant filling.
– ORIGIN late 16th cent.: named after the town of *Banbury* in central England, where it was originally made.

bancassurance /ˈbaŋkəˌʃɔːrəns/ (also **bank-assurance**) ▶ noun [mass noun] Brit. the selling of life assurance and other insurance products and services by banking institutions.
– DERIVATIVES **bancassurer** noun.

banco /ˈbaŋkəʊ/ ▶ exclamation used in baccarat, chemin de fer, and similar games to express a player's willingness to meet the banker's whole stake single-handed.
– ORIGIN late 18th cent.: via French from Italian.

band[1] ▶ noun **1** a flat, thin strip or loop of material, typically one used to fasten things together, to reinforce something, or as decoration.
■ Ornithology, N. Amer. a ring of metal placed round a bird's leg to identify it. ■ a plain ring for the finger, especially a gold wedding ring. ■ (**bands**) a collar with two hanging strips, worn by certain lawyers, clerics, and academics as part of their formal dress. ■ a belt or strap transmitting motion between two wheels or pulleys.
2 a stripe, line, or elongated area of a different colour, texture, or composition from its surroundings: *a long, narrow band of cloud.*
■ a narrow stratum of rock or coal.
3 a range of values or a specified category within a series (used especially in financial contexts): *your home was placed in one of eight valuation bands.*
■ a range of frequencies or wavelengths in a spectrum: *channels in the UHF band.* ■ any of several groups into which school pupils of the same age are divided on the basis of broadly similar ability: *the top band of pupils.*
4 archaic a thing that restrains, binds, or unites: *must I fall, and die in bands?*
▶ verb [with obj.] (usu. **be banded**) **1** surround (an object) with something in the form of a strip or ring, typically for reinforcement or decoration: *doors are banded with iron to make them stronger.*
■ Ornithology, N. Amer. put a band on (a bird) for identification.
2 mark (something) with a stripe or stripes of a different colour: *the bird's bill is banded across the middle with black | [as adj. **banded**] banded agate.*
3 allocate to a range or category (used especially in financial contexts): *single adults in a property banded above D will pay more.*
■ group (school pupils) into classes or sets for teaching purposes.
– ORIGIN late Old English (in sense 4), from Old Norse, reinforced in late Middle English by Old French *bande*, of Germanic origin; related to **BIND**.

band[2] ▶ noun **1** a group of people who have a common interest or purpose or who are characterized by a common feature: *a band of eminent British researchers.*
■ Anthropology a subgroup of a tribe.
2 a group of musicians who play together, in particular:

■a small group of musicians and vocalists who play pop, jazz, or rock music. ■ a group of musicians who play brass, wind, or percussion instruments. ■ informal an orchestra.
3 N. Amer. a herd or flock: *moving **bands of** caribou.*
▶**verb** [no obj.] (of people or organizations) form a group for a mutual purpose, especially to campaign for a common cause: *local people **banded together** to fight the company.*
– ORIGIN late Middle English: from Old French *bande*, of Germanic origin; related to **BANNER**.

Banda /ˈbandə/, Hastings Kamuzu (1906–97), Malawian statesman, Prime Minister 1964–94 and the first President of the Republic of Malawi 1966–94. Banda was defeated in Malawi's first multiparty elections in 1994; the following year he was acquitted on charges of murdering four political opponents.

bandage ▶**noun** a strip of woven material used to bind up a wound or to protect an injured part of the body: *her leg was swathed in bandages* | [mass noun] *a strip of bandage.*
▶**verb** [with obj.] bind (a wound or a part of the body) with a protective strip of material: *bandage the foot so that the ankle is supported* | *the doctors **bandaged up** his wounds.*
– ORIGIN late 16th cent.: from French, from *bande* (see **BAND**[1]).

bandaging ▶**noun** [mass noun] the action of binding a strip or strips of woven material round a wound or injured part of the body.
■the material used for this.

Band-Aid (also **band-aid**) ▶**noun** trademark a piece of sticking plaster of a type having a gauze pad.
■[often as modifier] figurative a makeshift or temporary solution: *a band-aid solution to a much deeper problem.*

bandanna /banˈdanə/ ▶**noun** a large coloured handkerchief or neckerchief, typically of silk or cotton and with white spots.
– ORIGIN mid 18th cent.: probably via Portuguese from Hindi.

Bandaranaike /ˌbandərəˈnʌɪkə/, Sirimavo Ratwatte Dias (1916–2000), Sinhalese stateswoman, Prime Minister of Sri Lanka 1960–5, 1970–7, and 1994–2000. The world's first woman Prime Minister, she succeeded her husband, S. W. R. D. Bandaranaike, after his assassination.

Bandar Lampung /ˌbandə ˈlampʊŋ/ a city at the southern tip of Sumatra, in Indonesia; pop. 284,275 (1980). It was created in the 1980s as a result of the amalgamation of the city of Tanjungkarang and the nearby port of Telukbetung.

Bandar Seri Begawan /ˌbandə ˌsɛrɪ bəˈɡɑːwən/ the capital of Brunei; pop. 46,000 (1991).

Banda Sea /ˈbandə/ a sea in eastern Indonesia, between the central and south Molucca Islands.

B. & B. ▶**abbreviation for** bed and breakfast.

bandbox ▶**noun** a cardboard box, typically circular, for carrying hats.
■dated used in comparisons to convey the freshness and neatness of someone's appearance: *I'd go out looking fresh **out of a bandbox**.*
– ORIGIN mid 17th cent.: from **BAND**[1] + **BOX**[1], the box being used originally for neckbands.

bandeau /ˈbandəʊ/ ▶**noun** (pl. **bandeaux** /-dəʊz/) a narrow band worn round the head to hold the hair in position.
– ORIGIN early 18th cent.: from French, from Old French *bandel*, diminutive of *bande* (see **BAND**[1]).

banded anteater ▶**noun** another term for **NUMBAT**.

banded snail ▶**noun** a snail with a yellow or reddish shell typically marked with dark spiral bands, common in hedgerows and grassland.
• Genus *Cepaea*, family Helicinidae.

bander ▶**noun** North American term for **RINGER**[2] (in sense 3).

banderilla /ˌbandəˈriːjə, -rɪljə/ ▶**noun** a decorated dart thrust into a bull's neck or shoulders during a bullfight.
– ORIGIN Spanish, diminutive of *bandera* 'banner'.

banderillero /ˌbandərɪlˈjɛːrəʊ, -riːˈjɛːrəʊ/ ▶**noun** (pl. **-os**) a bullfighter who uses banderillas.
– ORIGIN Spanish.

banderole /ˈbandərəʊl/ (also **banderol**) ▶**noun** a narrow flag-like object, in particular:
■a long, narrow flag with a cleft end, flown at a masthead. ■ an ornamental streamer on a knight's lance. ■ a ribbon-like stone scroll bearing an inscription. ■ a rectangular banner carried at the funerals of public figures and placed over the tomb.
– ORIGIN mid 16th cent.: from French, from Italian *banderuola*, diminutive of *bandiera* 'banner'.

bandersnatch /ˈbandəsnatʃ/ ▶**noun** a fierce mythical creature immune to bribery and capable of moving very fast.
– ORIGIN 1871: coined by Lewis Carroll in *Through the Looking Glass*; probably a portmanteau word.

bandfish ▶**noun** (pl. same or **-fishes**) **1** an elongated marine fish with dorsal and often anal fins that extend the length of the body.
• Family Cepolidae: several genera and species, including the burrowing European **red bandfish** (*Cepola rubescens*).
2 a large edible freshwater fish that has a long trunk-like snout and lacks dorsal, pelvic, and tail fins, native to tropical South America.
• *Rhamphichthys rostratus*, family Rhamphichthyidae.

bandh /bʌnd/ ▶**noun** Indian a general strike.
– ORIGIN via Hindi from Sanskrit *bandh* 'to stop'.

bandicoot /ˈbandɪkuːt/ ▶**noun** a mainly insectivorous marsupial native to Australia and New Guinea.
• Family Peramelidae: several genera and species, some of which are endangered or extinct.
■chiefly Indian a bandicoot rat.
– ORIGIN late 18th cent.: from Telugu *pandikokku*, literally 'pig-rat'.

bandicoot rat ▶**noun** an Asian rat that is a destructive pest in many places.
• Genera *Bandicota* and *Nesokia*, family Muridae: four species, in particular the large *B. indica*.

banding ▶**noun** [mass noun] **1** the presence or formation of visible stripes of contrasting colour: *the yellow and black banding of bees and wasps.*
■Biochemistry the pattern of regions on a chromosome made visible by staining.
2 the division of something into a series of ranges or categories (used especially in financial contexts): *the earnings-related banding of contributions.*
■the practice of dividing school pupils into broad categories according to ability, for teaching purposes.
3 N. Amer. the marking of individual birds or other animals with bands or rings.

bandit ▶**noun** (pl. **bandits** or **banditti** /banˈdiːti/) a robber or outlaw belonging to a gang or small group and typically operating in an isolated or lawless area.
■military slang an enemy aircraft.
– DERIVATIVES **banditry** noun.
– ORIGIN late 16th cent.: from Italian *bandito*, literally 'banned', past participle of *bandire*.

bandito /banˈdiːtəʊ/ (also **bandido**) ▶**noun** (pl. **-os**) N. Amer. a Mexican bandit, especially as represented in films and popular culture.

Bandjarmasin variant spelling of **BANJARMASIN**.

bandleader ▶**noun** a player at the head of a musical band.

bandmaster ▶**noun** the conductor of a musical band, especially a brass or military one.

Band of Hope a British organization promoting total abstinence from alcohol.

bandog ▶**noun** a fighting dog bred for its strength and ferocity by crossing aggressive breeds.
– ORIGIN Middle English (originally denoting a dog kept on a chain or 'band'): from **BAND**[1] + **DOG**.

bandolier /ˌbandəˈlɪə/ (also **bandoleer**) ▶**noun** a shoulder belt with loops or pockets for cartridges.
– ORIGIN late 16th cent.: from French *bandoulière*; perhaps from Spanish *bandolera* (from *banda* 'sash'), or from Catalan *bandolera* (from *bandoler* 'bandit').

bandoneon /banˈdəʊnɪən/ ▶**noun** a type of square concertina, especially popular in Argentina.
– ORIGIN via Spanish from German *Bandonion*, named after Heinrich *Band*, the 19th-cent. German musician who invented it, + *-on-* (as in *Harmonika* 'harmonica') + *-ion* (as in *Akkordion* 'accordion').

bandora /banˈdɔːrə/ (also **bandore** /banˈdɔː/) ▶**noun** a kind of bass lute with a scallop-shaped body and metal strings, typical of English consorts of the late 16th and 17th centuries.
– ORIGIN mid 16th cent.: origin uncertain; compare with Dutch *bandoor*, Spanish *bandurria*, also with **BANJO**: probably based on Greek *pandoura* 'three-stringed lute'.

bandpass ▶**adjective** (of a filter) transmitting only a set range of frequencies: *a 1–40 Hz bandpass filter.*
▶**noun** the range of frequencies which are transmitted through such a filter.

bandsaw ▶**noun** a saw consisting of an endless moving steel belt with a serrated edge.

bandshell ▶**noun** chiefly N. Amer. a bandstand in the form of a large concave shell with special acoustic properties.

bandsman ▶**noun** (pl. **-men**) a player in a musical band, especially a military or brass one.

bandstand ▶**noun** a covered outdoor platform for a band to play on, typically in a park.

Bandung /ˈbandʊŋ/ a city in Indonesia; pop. 2,056,900 (1990). Founded by the Dutch in 1810, it was the capital of the former Dutch East Indies.

bandura /banˈduːrə/ ▶**noun** a Ukrainian stringed instrument resembling a large asymmetrical lute with many strings, held vertically and plucked like a zither.
– ORIGIN Ukrainian; compare with **BANDORA**.

bandwagon ▶**noun** **1** (especially formerly) a wagon used for carrying a band in a parade or procession.
2 [usu. in sing.] a particular activity or cause that has suddenly become fashionable or popular: *the Green bandwagon provided a fillip for many companies tackling environmental problems.*
– PHRASES **jump** (or **climb**) **on the bandwagon** join others in doing or supporting something fashionable or likely to be successful.

bandwidth ▶**noun** Electronics a range of frequencies within a given band, in particular:
■the range of frequencies used for transmitting a signal. ■ the range of frequencies over which a system or a device can operate effectively. ■ the transmission capacity of a computer network or other telecommunication system.

bandy[1] ▶**adjective** (**bandier**, **bandiest**) (of a person's legs) curved outwards so that the knees are wide apart.
■(often **bandy-legged**) having legs that are curved in such a way.
– ORIGIN late 17th cent.: perhaps from obsolete *bandy* 'curved stick used in hockey'.

bandy[2] ▶**verb** (**-ies**, **-ied**) [with obj.] (usu. **be bandied about/around**) pass on or discuss (an idea or rumour) in a casual or uninformed way: *£40,000 is the figure that has been bandied about.*
– PHRASES **bandy words** argue pointlessly or rudely: *I'm not going to **bandy words with** you.*
– ORIGIN late 16th cent. (in the sense 'pass (a ball) to and fro'): perhaps from French *bander* 'take sides at tennis', from *bande* 'band, crowd' (see **BAND**[2]).

bandy-bandy ▶**noun** (pl. **bandy-bandys**) a small mildly venomous nocturnal snake marked with distinctive black-and-white bands, native to Australia.
• *Vermicella annulata*, family Elapidae.
– ORIGIN 1920s: from Kattah (an Aboriginal language) *bandi bandi*.

bane ▶**noun** [usu. in sing.] a cause of great distress or annoyance: *the telephone was **the bane of my life**.*
■archaic something, typically poison, which causes death.
– DERIVATIVES **baneful** adjective (archaic).
– ORIGIN Old English *bana* 'thing causing death, poison', of Germanic origin.

baneberry ▶**noun** (pl. **-ies**) a plant of the buttercup family, which bears fluffy spikes of creamy-white flowers followed by shiny berries, found in north temperate regions.
• Genus *Actaea*, family Ranunculaceae, especially the common Eurasian *A. spicata* (also called **HERB CHRISTOPHER**), with black berries.
■the bitter berry of this plant, which can be dangerously poisonous.
– ORIGIN mid 18th cent.: from **BANE** in the sense 'poison' + **BERRY**.

Banffshire /ˈbamfʃɪə, -ʃə/ a former county of NE Scotland which became a part of Grampian region in 1975.

bang[1] ▶**noun** **1** a sudden loud, sharp noise: *the door slammed with a bang.*
■a sharp blow causing such a noise: *I went to answer a bang on the front door.* ■ a sudden painful blow: *a nasty bang on the head.*
2 (**bangs**) chiefly N. Amer. a fringe of hair cut straight across the forehead. [ORIGIN: from a use of the adverb *bang* to mean 'abruptly'.]
3 vulgar slang an act of sexual intercourse.

4 Computing, chiefly US the character '!'
▶**verb** [with obj.] **1** strike or put down (something) forcefully and noisily, typically in anger or in order to attract attention: *he began to bang the table with his fist* | *Sarah* ***banged*** *the phone* ***down*** | [no obj.] *someone was* ***banging on*** *the door.*
■[with obj. and adverbial] cause to come into contact with something suddenly and sharply, typically by accident: *I banged my head on the low beams* | [no obj.] *she banged into some shelves in the darkness.* ■ [no obj.] make a sudden loud noise, typically repeatedly: *the shutter was banging in the wind.* ■ (with reference to something such as a door) open or close violently and noisily: [with obj. and complement] *he* ***banged*** *the kitchen door* ***shut*** *behind him* | [no obj., with complement] *the door* ***banged open*** *and a man staggered out.* ■ [no obj., with adverbial of direction] (of a person) move around or do something noisily, especially as an indication of anger or irritation: *she was banging around the kitchen.* ■ [with obj. and adverbial of direction] (of a sports player) hit (a ball or a shot) forcefully and successfully: *he banged home four penalties in the opening twenty minutes.* ■ vulgar slang (of a man) have sexual intercourse with (a woman).
2 chiefly N. Amer. cut (hair) in a fringe.
▶**adverb** informal, chiefly Brit. exactly: *the train arrived bang on time.*
■completely: *bring your wardrobe bang up to date.*
▶**exclamation 1** used to express or imitate the sound of a sudden loud noise: *party poppers* ***went bang.***
2 used to convey the suddenness of an action or process: *the minute something becomes obsolete, bang, it's gone.*
– PHRASES **bang for one's** (or **the**) **buck** informal, chiefly US value for money; performance for cost. **bang goes ——** used to express the sudden or complete destruction of a plan or ambition: *my first thought when I heard the news was 'Bang goes my knighthood!'* **bang on** Brit. informal exactly right: *the programme is bang on about the fashion world.* **bang** (or **knock**) **people's heads together** see **HEAD**. **get a bang out of** informal, chiefly N. Amer. derive excitement or pleasure from: *some people get a bang out of reading that stuff.* **go** (**off**) **with a bang** go successfully. **with a bang 1** abruptly: *the remark brought me down to earth with a bang.* **2** impressively or spectacularly: *the day starts with a bang—the steep climb to the mountain top.*
– ORIGIN mid 16th cent.: imitative, perhaps of Scandinavian origin; compare with Old Norse *bang* 'hammering'.
▶**bang away at** informal do something in a persistent or dogged way: *he was banging away at his novel.*
bang on about informal talk tediously and at length about (something): *the government banged on about competition, efficiency, and the free market.*
bang something out informal **1** play music or a tune noisily, enthusiastically, and unskilfully. **2** produce something hurriedly or in great quantities: *they weren't banging out ads in my day the way they are now.*
bang someone/thing up Brit. informal imprison someone: *they've been banged up for something they didn't do.* ■ N. Amer. informal damage or injure someone or something: *he banged up his knee.*

bang[2] /baŋ/ ▶**noun** variant spelling of **BHANG**.

Bangalore /ˌbaŋgəˈlɔː/ a city in south central India, capital of the state of Karnataka; pop. 2,651,000 (1991).

Bangalore torpedo ▶**noun** a tube containing explosive used by infantry for blowing up wire entanglements or other barriers.

banger ▶**noun** chiefly Brit. **1** informal a sausage.
2 informal a car in poor condition, especially a noisy one: *they've only got an old banger.*
3 a loud explosive firework.

banging ▶**adjective** [attrib.] **1** making a sudden loud, sharp noise: *the banging carriages of electric typewriters.*
2 (also **bangin'**) Brit. informal (of dance music) having a loud relentless beat.
■excellent: *a bangin' night out.*

Bangkok /baŋˈkɒk/ the capital and chief port of Thailand, on the Chao Phraya waterway, 40 km (25 miles) upstream from its outlet into the Gulf of Thailand; pop. 5,876,000 (est. 1990).

Bangla /ˈbʌŋlə:/ ▶**noun** [mass noun] the Bengali language.
– ORIGIN from Bengali *bāṅglā*.

Bangladesh /ˌbaŋgləˈdɛʃ/ a country of the Indian subcontinent, in the Ganges delta; pop. 107,992,140 (est. 1991); official language, Bengali; capital, Dhaka.

Formerly part of British India, the region became (as East Pakistan) one of the two geographical units of Pakistan. After civil war the independent republic of Bangladesh was proclaimed in 1971; it became a Commonwealth state in 1972.

– DERIVATIVES **Bangladeshi** adjective & noun.

bangle ▶**noun** a rigid ornamental band worn round the arm or occasionally the ankle.
– ORIGIN late 18th cent.: from Hindi *baṅglī* 'glass bracelet'.

bangtail ▶**noun** a horse's tail that has been cut straight across just below the level of the hocks.
■US informal a racehorse.

bangtail muster ▶**noun** Austral. a count of cattle on a station, involving cutting across the tufts at the tail ends as each is counted.
– ORIGIN late 19th cent.: *bang* in the sense 'cut (the tail of an animal) straight across'; compare with verb sense 2 of **BANG**[1].

Bangui /ˈbaŋgiː/ the capital of the Central African Republic; pop. 596,800 (est. 1988).

bang-up ▶**adjective** N. Amer. informal excellent: *for a novice, he has done a bang-up job.*

bani plural form of **BAN**[2].

bania /ˈbʌnɪə/ ▶**noun** (in India) a trader or merchant.
– ORIGIN from Hindi *baniyā*, from Sanskrit *vāṇija*.

banian ▶**noun** variant spelling of **BANYAN**.

banish ▶**verb** [with obj.] (often **be banished**) send (someone) away from a country or place as an official punishment: *a number of people were banished to Siberia for political crimes.*
■get rid of, abolish, or forbid (something unwanted): *all thoughts of romance were* ***banished from*** *her head.*
– DERIVATIVES **banishment** noun.
– ORIGIN late Middle English: from Old French *baniss-*, lengthened stem of *banir*; ultimately of Germanic origin and related to **BAN**[1].

banister /ˈbanɪstə/ (also **bannister**) ▶**noun** (also **banisters**) the structure formed by the uprights and handrail at the side of a staircase.
■a single upright at the side of the staircase: *I stuck my head between the banisters.*
– ORIGIN mid 17th cent.: from earlier *barrister*, alteration of **BALUSTER**.

Banjarmasin /ˌbandʒəˈmɑːsɪn/ (also **Bandjarmasin**) a deep-water port and capital of the province of Kalimantan in Indonesia, on the island of Borneo; pop. 480,700 (1990).

banjax /ˈbandʒaks/ ▶**verb** [with obj.] informal ruin; incapacitate: *he said the scheme was banjaxing the tourist industry.*
– ORIGIN 1930s: originally Anglo-Irish, of unknown origin.

banjo ▶**noun** (pl. **-os** or **-oes**) a stringed instrument of the guitar family, with an open-backed soundbox of vellum (or plastic) stretched over a round hoop, typically of wood. It is used especially in jazz and American folk music.
■an object resembling this in shape: [as modifier] *a banjo clock.* ■ Austral./NZ a shovel.
– DERIVATIVES **banjoist** noun.
– ORIGIN mid 18th cent.: originally a black American alteration of *bandore* (see **BANDORA**).

Banjul /banˈdʒuːl/ the capital of Gambia; pop. 44,540 (1983). Former name (until 1973) **BATHURST**.

bank[1] ▶**noun 1** the land alongside or sloping down to a river or lake: *willows lined the riverbank.*
2 a long, high slope, mass, or mound of a particular substance: *a grassy bank* | *a bank of snow.*
■an elevation in the seabed or a river bed; a mudbank or sandbank. ■ a transverse slope given to a road, railway, or sports track to enable vehicles or runners to maintain speed round a curve. ■ [mass noun] the sideways tilt of an aircraft when turning in flight: *flying with small amounts of bank* | [count noun] *the aeroplane flew through banks of up to 30 degrees.*
3 a set or series of similar things, especially electrical or electronic devices, grouped together in rows: *the DJ had big banks of lights and speakers on either side of his console.*
■a tier of oars.
4 the cushion of a pool table.
▶**verb** [with obj.] **1** heap (a substance) into a mass or mound: *the rain* ***banked*** *the soil* ***up*** *behind the gate* | *snow was banked in humps at the roadside.*
■[no obj.] rise or form into a mass or mound: *purple clouds* ***banked up*** *over the hills.* ■ heap a mass or mound of a substance against (something): *people were banking their houses with earth.* ■ heap up (a fire) with tightly packed fuel so that it burns slowly: *she* ***banked up*** *the fire.* ■ edge or surround with a ridge or row of something: *steps banked with pots of chrysanthemums.*
2 (with reference to an aircraft or vehicle) tilt or cause to tilt sideways in making a turn: [no obj.] *the plane banked as if to return to the airport* | [with obj.] *I banked the aircraft steeply and turned.*
■build (a road, railway, or sports track) higher at the outer edge of a bend to facilitate fast cornering.
3 [often as noun **banking**] Brit. (of a locomotive) provide additional power for (a train) in ascending an incline.
4 (of an angler) succeed in bringing (a fish) to the side of a river or lake: *it was the biggest rainbow trout that had ever been banked.*
5 N. Amer. (in pool) play (a ball) so that it rebounds off a surface such as a backboard or cushion.
– ORIGIN Middle English: from Old Norse *bakki*, of Germanic origin; related to **BENCH**. The senses 'set of similar things in sloping rows' and 'tier of oars' are from French *banc*, of the same ultimate origin.

bank[2] ▶**noun** a financial establishment that uses money deposited by customers for investment, pays it out when required, makes loans at interest, and exchanges currency: [as modifier] *a bank account.*
■a stock of something available for use when required: *a blood bank* | figurative *Britain has a bank of highly exportable skills.* ■ a site or receptacle where something may be deposited for recycling: *a paper bank.* ■ (**the bank**) the store of money or tokens held by the banker in some gambling or board games. ■ the person holding this store; the banker.
▶**verb** [with obj.] deposit (money or valuables) in a bank: *I banked the cheque.*
■[no obj.] have an account at a particular bank: *the family has* ***banked with*** *Coutts for generations.* ■ informal (especially of a competitor in a game or race) win or earn (a sum of money): *he banked £100,000 for a hole-in-one.* ■ store (something, especially blood, tissue, or sperm) for future use.
– PHRASES **break the bank** (in gambling) win more money than is held by the bank. ■ [usu. with negative] informal cost more than one can afford: *we're offering five-night breaks at a price that won't break the bank.*
– ORIGIN late 15th cent. (originally denoting a money dealer's table): from French *banque* or Italian *banca*, from medieval Latin *banca*, *bancus*, of Germanic origin; related to **BANK**[1] and **BENCH**.
▶**bank on** rely on confidently: *the prime minister cannot bank on their support.*

bankable ▶**adjective** (especially in the entertainment industry) certain to bring profit and success: *he needed some bankable names to star in the film.*
■reliable: *a bankable assurance.*
– DERIVATIVES **bankability** /-əˈbɪlɪti/ noun.

bankassurance ▶**noun** variant spelling of **BANCASSURANCE**.

bank balance ▶**noun** the amount of money held in a bank account at a given moment.

bank barn ▶**noun** chiefly N. Amer. a barn built on a slope.

bank bill ▶**noun 1** Brit. a bill of exchange drawn by one bank on another.
2 chiefly US another term for **BANKNOTE**.

bank book ▶**noun** another term for **PASSBOOK**.

bank card ▶**noun** another term for **CHEQUE CARD**.

bank draft ▶**noun** a cheque drawn by a bank on its own funds.

banker[1] ▶**noun 1** a person who manages or owns a bank or group of banks.
■the person running the table, controlling play, or acting as dealer in some gambling or board games.
2 Brit. a supposedly certain bet: *the horse should be a banker for him in the Members' race.*
■a result forecast identically (while other forecasts differ) in several football-pool entries on one coupon.
– ORIGIN mid 16th cent.: from French *banquier*, from *banque* (see **BANK**[2]).

banker[2] ▶**noun 1** a boat employed in cod fishing off Newfoundland.
■a Newfoundland fisherman.
2 Austral. informal a river flooded to the top of its banks.
3 an additional locomotive used to assist a train in ascending an incline.

banker's card ▶**noun** Brit. another term for **CHEQUE CARD**.

banker's draft ▶ noun another term for **BANK DRAFT**.

banker's hours ▶ plural noun N. Amer. short working hours (in reference to the typical opening hours of a bank).

banker's order ▶ noun Brit. a standing order to a bank to make specified payments from one's account to a particular recipient.

banket /'baŋ'kɛt/ ▶ noun [mass noun] S. African compact gold-bearing conglomerate.
– ORIGIN Dutch, literally 'almond sweets', with reference to the smooth quartz pebbles on the outcrop, said to resemble such sweets.

Bank for International Settlements (abbrev.: **BIS**) a bank founded in 1930 to promote the cooperation of central banks and to provide facilities for international financial operations. It is located at Basle in Switzerland.

Bankhead, Tallulah (1903–68), American actress noted for her uninhibited public persona. Her most successful film appearance was in Alfred Hitchcock's *Lifeboat* (1944).

bank holiday ▶ noun Brit. a day on which banks are officially closed, kept as a public holiday.

banking[1] ▶ noun [mass noun] the business conducted or services offered by a bank: *with this account, you are entitled to free banking*.

banking[2] ▶ noun an embankment or artificial bank.

bank machine ▶ noun another term for **CASH DISPENSER**.

bank manager ▶ noun a person in charge of a local branch of a bank.

banknote ▶ noun a piece of paper money, constituting a central bank's promissory note to pay a stated sum to the bearer on demand.

Bank of England the central bank of England and Wales, which issues legal tender, manages the national debt, administers exchange rate policy, and since 1997 sets interest rates. Founded in 1694, it was nationalized in 1946.

bank rate ▶ noun another term for **BASE RATE** or **DISCOUNT RATE**.

bankroll chiefly N. Amer. ▶ noun a roll of banknotes.
■ figurative financial resources.
▶ verb [with obj.] informal support (a person, organization, or project) financially: *the project is bankrolled by wealthy expatriates*.

bankrupt ▶ adjective (of a person or organization) declared in law unable to pay their debts: *he committed suicide after going bankrupt*.
■ figurative completely lacking in a particular good quality or value: *their cause is morally bankrupt*.
▶ noun a person judged by a court to be insolvent, whose property is taken and disposed of for the benefit of their creditors.
▶ verb [with obj.] reduce (a person or organization) to bankruptcy: *the strike nearly bankrupted the union*.
– ORIGIN mid 16th cent.: from Italian *banca rotta* 'broken bench', from *banca* (see **BANK**[2]) and *rompere* 'to break'. The change in the ending was due to association with Latin *rupt-* 'broken'.

bankruptcy ▶ noun (pl. **-ies**) [mass noun] the state of being bankrupt: *many companies were facing bankruptcy* | [count noun] *bankruptcies are up on a year ago*.
■ figurative the state of being completely lacking in a specified good quality or value: *the moral bankruptcy of terrorism*.

bankruptcy order ▶ noun English Law an order of the court declaring a person bankrupt and placing their affairs under the control of a receiver or trustee. Compare with **RECEIVING ORDER**.

Banks[1], Gordon (b.1937), English footballer. An outstanding goalkeeper, he played in the 1966 and 1970 World Cups. In 1972 a serious eye injury sustained in a car crash effectively ended his playing career.

Banks[2], Sir Joseph (1743–1820), English botanist. He accompanied Captain James Cook on his first voyage to the Pacific, and helped to establish the Royal Botanic Gardens at Kew.

banksia /'baŋksɪə/ ▶ noun an evergreen Australian shrub which typically has narrow leathery leaves and spikes of bottlebrush-like flowers.
● Genus *Banksia*, family Proteaceae.
– ORIGIN modern Latin, named after Sir Joseph Banks (see **BANKS**[2]).

banksia rose ▶ noun a small-flowered climbing rose native to China.
● *Rosa banksiae*, family Rosaceae.

bank statement ▶ noun a printed record of the balance in a bank account and the amounts that have been paid into it and withdrawn from it, issued periodically to the holder of the account.

bank swallow ▶ noun N. Amer. see **SAND MARTIN**.

bank vole ▶ noun a common reddish-brown Eurasian vole that lives in woodland and scrub.
● *Clethrionomys glareolus*, family Muridae.

banner ▶ noun a long strip of cloth bearing a slogan or design, carried in a demonstration or procession or hung in a public place.
■ a flag on a pole used as the standard of a king, knight, or army. ■ used in reference to support for or adherence to a belief or principle: *the government is flying the free trade banner*.
▶ adjective [attrib.] N. Amer. excellent; outstanding: *I predict that 1998 will be a banner year*.
– PHRASES **under the banner of** claiming to support a specified set or set of ideas: *campaigns fought under the banner of multiculturalism*. ■ as part of a specified group or organization: *the party is running under the banner of the Left-Wing Alliance*.
– DERIVATIVES **bannered** adjective.
– ORIGIN Middle English: from Old French *baniere*, ultimately of Germanic origin and related to **BAND**[2].

banneret /'banərɪt/ ▶ noun historical **1** a knight who commanded his own troops in battle under his own banner.
2 a knighthood given on the battlefield for courage.
– ORIGIN Middle English: from Old French *baneret*, literally 'bannered', from *baniere* 'banner'.

banner headline ▶ noun a large newspaper headline, especially one across the top of the front page.

Bannister, Sir Roger (Gilbert) (b.1929), British middle-distance runner and neurologist. In May 1954 he became the first man to run a mile in under 4 minutes, with a time of 3 minutes 59.4 seconds.

bannister ▶ noun variant spelling of **BANISTER**.

bannock /'banək/ ▶ noun a round, flat loaf, typically unleavened, associated with Scotland and northern England.
– ORIGIN Old English *bannuc*, of Celtic origin; related to Welsh *ban*, Breton *bannac'h*, *banne*, and Cornish *banna* 'a drop'.

Bannockburn, Battle of /'banəkbə:n/ a battle which took place near Stirling in central Scotland in 1314, in which the English army of Edward II, advancing to break the siege of Stirling Castle, was defeated by the Scots under Robert the Bruce.

banns ▶ plural noun a notice read out on three successive Sundays in a parish church, announcing an intended marriage and giving the opportunity for objections.
– PHRASES **forbid the banns** archaic raise an objection to an intended marriage, especially in church following the reading of the banns.
– ORIGIN Middle English: plural of **BAN**[1].

banoffi pie /bə'nɒfi/ (also **banoffee pie**) ▶ noun a pie or tart made with toffee, bananas, and cream.
– ORIGIN *banoffi* from a blend of **BANANA** and **TOFFEE**.

banquet /'baŋkwɪt/ ▶ noun an elaborate and formal evening meal for many people, typically followed by speeches: *a state banquet at Buckingham Palace*.
■ an elaborate, extensive, and delicious meal; a feast: *a four-course Asian banquet*.
▶ verb (**banqueted, banqueting**) [with obj.] entertain with a banquet: *there are halls for banqueting up to 3,000 people* | [as noun modifier] (**banqueting**) *a banqueting hall*.
– DERIVATIVES **banqueter** noun.
– ORIGIN late 15th cent.: from French, diminutive of *banc* 'bench' (see **BANK**[2]).

banquette /baŋ'kɛt/ ▶ noun **1** an upholstered bench along a wall, especially in a restaurant or bar.
2 a raised step behind a rampart.
– ORIGIN early 17th cent. (in sense 2): from French, from Italian *banchetta*, diminutive of *banca* 'bench' (see **BANK**[2]). Sense 1 dates from the mid 19th cent.

bansela ▶ noun variant spelling of **BONSELA**.

banshee /ban'ʃiː, 'banʃiː/ ▶ noun (in Irish legend) a

female spirit whose wailing warns of a death in a house: *the little girl dropped her ice cream and began to howl like a banshee* | [as modifier] *a horrible banshee wail*.
– ORIGIN late 17th cent.: from Irish *bean sídhe*, from Old Irish *ben síde* 'woman of the fairies'.

bantam ▶ noun a chicken of a small breed, the cock of which is noted for its aggression.
■ [usu. as modifier] Canadian a level of amateur sport typically involving children aged between 13 and 15: *bantam hockey*. ■ short for **BANTAMWEIGHT**.
– ORIGIN mid 18th cent.: apparently named after the province of *Bantam* in Java, although the fowl is not native there.

bantamweight ▶ noun [mass noun] a weight in boxing and other sports intermediate between flyweight and featherweight. In the amateur boxing scale it ranges from 51 to 54 kg.
■ [count noun] a boxer or other competitor of this weight.

banteng /'bantɛŋ/ ▶ noun a SE Asian forest ox that resembles the domestic cow. It has been domesticated in Bali.
● *Bos javanicus*, family Bovidae.
– ORIGIN early 19th cent.: from Malay.

banter ▶ noun [mass noun] the playful and friendly exchange of teasing remarks: *there was much singing and good-natured banter*.
▶ verb [no obj.] talk or exchange remarks in a good-humoured teasing way: *the men bantered with the waitresses* | [as adj.] **bantering** *a bantering tone*.
– DERIVATIVES **banterer** noun.
– ORIGIN late 17th cent.: of unknown origin.

Banting, Sir Frederick Grant (1891–1941), Canadian physiologist and surgeon. With the assistance of C. H. Best, Banting discovered insulin in 1921–2, using it to treat the previously incurable and fatal disease diabetes. Nobel Prize for Physiology or Medicine (1923, shared with J. J. R. Macleod).

Bantu /ban'tuː, 'bantuː/ ▶ noun (pl. same or **Bantus**)
1 a member of an extensive group of indigenous peoples of central and southern Africa.
2 [mass noun] the group of Niger–Congo languages spoken by these peoples, including Swahili, Xhosa, and Zulu.
▶ adjective of or relating to these peoples or their languages.
– ORIGIN plural (in certain Bantu languages) of *-ntu* 'person'.

> **USAGE** The word **Bantu** became a strongly offensive term under the old apartheid regime in South Africa, especially when used to refer to a single individual. In standard current use in South Africa the term **black** or **African** is used as a collective or non-specific term for African peoples. The term **Bantu** has, however, continued to be accepted as a neutral 'scientific' term outside South Africa used to refer to the group of languages and their speakers collectively.

Bantu education ▶ noun historical, derogatory (in South Africa under apartheid) the official system of education for black South Africans.

Bantustan /ˌbantu:'staːn, -'stan/ ▶ noun S. African historical, derogatory a partially self-governing area set aside for a particular indigenous African people; a homeland.
– ORIGIN from **BANTU** + -*stan*, on the pattern of words such as *Hindustan*.

banyan /'banɪən, -njən/ (also **banian**) ▶ noun **1** (also **banyan tree**) an Indian fig tree, the branches of which produce aerial roots which later become accessory trunks. A mature tree may cover several hectares in this manner.
● *Ficus benghalensis*, family Moraceae.
2 a loose flannel jacket, shirt, or gown worn in India.
– ORIGIN late 16th cent.: from Portuguese, from Gujarati *vāniyo* 'man of the trading caste', from Sanskrit. Originally denoting a Hindu merchant, the term was applied, by Europeans in the mid 17th cent., to a particular tree under which such traders had built a pagoda.

banzai /ban'zʌɪ/ ▶ exclamation **1** a Japanese battle cry.
2 a form of greeting used to the Japanese emperor.
▶ adjective (especially of Japanese troops) attacking fiercely and recklessly: *a banzai charge*.
– ORIGIN Japanese, literally 'ten thousand years (of life to you)'.

baobab /'beɪə(ʊ)bab/ ▶ noun a short tree with a very thick trunk and large edible fruit, living to a great age.

• Genus *Adansonia*, family Bombacaceae: several species, in particular the African *A. digitata* and the Australian *A. gregorii*.
– ORIGIN mid 17th cent.: probably from an African language; first recorded in Latin (1592), in a treatise on the plants of Egypt by Prosper Alpinus, Italian botanist.

BAOR ▶ **abbreviation for** British Army of the Rhine.

Baotou /baʊˈtəʊ/ an industrial city in Inner Mongolia, northern China, on the Yellow River; pop. 1,180,000 (1990).

bap ▶ **noun** Brit. a large, round, flattish bread roll, typically with a spongy texture and floury top.
– ORIGIN late 16th cent.: of unknown origin.

baptism ▶ **noun** [mass noun] (in the Christian Church) the religious rite of sprinkling water on to a person's forehead or of immersing them in water, symbolizing purification or regeneration and admission to the Christian Church. In many denominations, baptism is performed on young children and is accompanied by name-giving.
■ [count noun] a ceremony or occasion at which this takes place. ■ figurative a person's initiation into a particular activity or role, typically one perceived as difficult: *this event constituted his baptism as a politician.*
– PHRASES **baptism of fire** a difficult or painful new undertaking or experience. [ORIGIN: from the original sense of 'a soldier's first battle'.]
– DERIVATIVES **baptismal** adjective.
– ORIGIN Middle English: from Old French *baptesme*, via ecclesiastical Latin from ecclesiastical Greek *baptismos* 'ceremonial washing', from *baptizein* 'immerse, baptize'.

baptismal name ▶ **noun** a personal name given at baptism.

baptist ▶ **noun 1** (**Baptist**) a member of a Protestant Christian denomination advocating baptism only of adult believers by total immersion. Baptists form one of the largest Protestant bodies and are found throughout the world and especially in the US.
2 a person who baptizes someone.
– ORIGIN Middle English (in sense 2): from Old French *baptiste*, via ecclesiastical Latin from ecclesiastical Greek *baptistēs*, from *baptizein* 'immerse, baptize'.

baptistery (also **baptistry**) ▶ **noun** (pl. **-ies**) the part of a church used for baptism.
■ historical a building next to a church, used for baptism. ■ (in a Baptist chapel) a sunken receptacle used for baptism by total immersion.
– ORIGIN Middle English: from Old French *baptistere*, via ecclesiastical Latin from ecclesiastical Greek *baptistērion*, from *baptizein* 'immerse, baptize'.

baptize (also **-ise**) ▶ **verb** [with obj. and often with complement] administer baptism to (someone); christen: *he was baptized Joshua.*
■ admit (someone) into a specified Church by baptism: *Mark had been baptized a Catholic.* ■ give a name or nickname to: *he baptized the science of narrative 'narratology'.*
– ORIGIN Middle English: via Old French from ecclesiastical Latin *baptizare*, from Greek *baptizein* 'immerse, baptize'.

Bar. ▶ **abbreviation for** Baruch (Apocrypha) (in biblical references).

bar[1] ▶ **noun 1** a long rod or rigid piece of wood, metal, or similar material, typically used as an obstruction, fastening, or weapon.
■ an amount of food or another substance formed into a regular narrow block: *a bar of chocolate.* ■ a band of colour or light, especially on a flat surface: *bars of sunlight shafting through the broken windows.* ■ Brit. the heating element of an electric fire. ■ (**the bar**) the crossbar of a goal. ■ Brit. a metal strip below the clasp of a medal, awarded as an additional distinction. ■ a sandbank or shoal at the mouth of a harbour or an estuary. ■ Brit. a rail marking the end of each chamber in the Houses of Parliament. ■ Heraldry a charge in the form of a narrow horizontal stripe across the shield.
2 a counter in a public house, restaurant, or cafe across which alcoholic drinks or refreshments are served.
■ a room in a public house, restaurant, or hotel in which alcohol is served. ■ an establishment where alcohol is served. ■ [with modifier] a small shop or stall serving refreshments or providing a specified service: *a sandwich bar.* ■ a specialized department in a large store.
3 a barrier or restriction to an action or advance: *political differences are not necessarily **a bar to** a good relationship.*
4 Music any of the short sections or measures, typically of equal time value, into which a piece of music is divided, shown on a score by vertical lines across the stave.
■ chiefly N. Amer. short for **BAR LINE**.
5 (**the bar**) a partition in a court room, now usually notional, at which an accused person stands: *the prisoner **at the bar**.*
■ a similar partition in a legislative assembly. ■ a plea arresting an action or claim in a law case. ■ a particular court of law.
6 (**the Bar**) the profession of barrister.
■ Brit. barristers collectively. ■ N. Amer. lawyers collectively.
▶ **verb** (**barred**, **barring**) [with obj.] **1** fasten (something, especially a door or window) with a bar or bars: *she bolts and bars the door.*
■ (usu. **be barred**) prevent or forbid the entrance, movement, or progress of: *all reporters were barred | boulders barred her passage.* ■ prohibit (someone) from doing something: *journalists had been **barred from** covering the elections.* ■ forbid (an activity) to someone: *the job she loved had been **barred to** her.* ■ exclude (something) from consideration: *nothing is barred in the crime novel.* ■ Law prevent or delay (an action) by objection.
2 (usu. **be barred**) mark (something) with bars or stripes: *his face was barred with light.*
▶ **preposition** chiefly Brit. except for; apart from: *everyone, bar a few ascetics, thinks it desirable.*
■ Horse Racing, Brit. except the horses indicated (used when stating the odds).
– PHRASES **bar none** with no exceptions: *the greatest living American poet bar none.* **be called** (or **go**) **to the Bar** Brit. be admitted as a barrister. **be called within the Bar** Brit. be appointed a Queen's Counsel. **behind bars** in prison.
– DERIVATIVES **barred** adjective *barred windows* | [in combination] *a five-barred gate.*
– ORIGIN Middle English: from Old French *barre* (noun), *barrer* (verb), of unknown origin.

bar[2] ▶ **noun** a unit of pressure equivalent to a hundred thousand newtons per square metre or approximately one atmosphere.
– ORIGIN early 20th cent.: from Greek *baros* 'weight'.

bara brith /ˌbarə ˈbrɪθ/ ▶ **noun** [mass noun] a traditional Welsh tea bread, typically made with raisins, currants, and candied peel.

Barak /baˈrak/, Ehud (b.1942), Israeli Labour Statesman, Prime Minister 1999–2001.

barasingha /ˌbarəˈsɪŋgə/ ▶ **noun** (pl. same) another term for **SWAMP DEER**.
– ORIGIN mid 19th cent.: from Hindi *bārahsiṅghā*, literally 'twelve-tined'.

barathea /ˌbarəˈθɪə/ ▶ **noun** [mass noun] a fine woollen cloth, sometimes mixed with silk or cotton, used chiefly for coats and suits.
– ORIGIN mid 19th cent.: of unknown origin.

baraza /bəˈrɑːzə/ ▶ **noun** (in East Africa) a public meeting place.
– ORIGIN Kiswahili.

barb[1] ▶ **noun 1** a sharp projection near the end of an arrow, fish-hook, or similar object, which is angled away from the main point so as to make extraction difficult.
■ a cluster of spikes on barbed wire. ■ figurative a deliberately hurtful remark: *his barb hurt more than she cared to admit.* ■ a beard-like filament at the mouth of some fish, such as barbel and catfish. ■ one of the fine hair-like filaments growing from the shaft of a feather, forming the vane.
2 a freshwater fish that typically has barbels around the mouth, popular in aquaria.
• *Barbus* and other genera, family Cyprinidae: numerous species, including the **tiger barb** (*B. pentazona*) and the **rosy barb** (*B. conchonius*).
– DERIVATIVES **barbless** adjective.
– ORIGIN Middle English (denoting a piece of linen worn over or under the chin by nuns): from Old French *barbe*, from Latin *barba* 'beard'.

barb[2] ▶ **noun** a small horse of a hardy breed originally from North Africa.
– ORIGIN mid 17th cent.: from French *barbe*, from Italian *barbero* 'of Barbary'.

Barbados /bɑːˈbeɪdɒs/ the most easterly of the Caribbean islands, one of the Windward Islands group; pop. 260,490 (1990); official language, English; capital, Bridgetown. Barbados became a British colony in the 1630s and remained British until 1966, when it gained independence as a Commonwealth state.
– DERIVATIVES **Barbadian** adjective & noun.

barbarian ▶ **noun** (in ancient times) a member of a community or tribe not belonging to one of the great civilizations (Greek, Roman, Christian).
■ an uncultured or brutish person.
▶ **adjective** of or relating to ancient barbarians: *barbarian invasions.*
■ uncultured; brutish.
– ORIGIN Middle English (as an adjective used depreciatively to denote a person with different speech and customs): from Old French *barbarien*, from *barbare*, or from Latin *barbarus* (see **BARBAROUS**).

barbaric ▶ **adjective 1** savagely cruel: *he had carried out barbaric acts in the name of war.*
2 primitive; unsophisticated: *the barbaric splendour he found in civilizations since destroyed.*
■ uncivilized and uncultured.
– DERIVATIVES **barbarically** adverb.
– ORIGIN late Middle English (as a noun in the sense 'a barbarian'): from Old French *barbarique*, or via Latin from Greek *barbarikos*, from *barbaros* 'foreign' (especially with reference to speech).

barbarism ▶ **noun** [mass noun] **1** absence of culture and civilization: *the collapse of civilization and the return to barbarism.*
■ [count noun] a word or expression which is badly formed according to traditional philological rules, e.g. a word formed from elements of different languages, such as *breathalyser* (English and Greek) or *television* (Greek and Latin).
2 extreme cruelty or brutality: *she called the execution an act of barbarism.*
– ORIGIN late Middle English: from Old French *barbarisme*, via Latin from Greek *barbarismos*, from *barbarizein* 'speak like a foreigner', from *barbaros* 'foreign'.

barbarity ▶ **noun** (pl. **-ies**) [mass noun] **1** extreme cruelty or brutality: *the barbarity displayed by the terrorists* | [count noun] *the Nazi barbarities of the last war.*
2 absence of culture and civilization: *beyond the Empire lay barbarity.*

barbarize (also **-ise**) ▶ **verb** [with obj.] [usu. as adj. **barbarizing**] cause to become savage or uncultured: *the barbarizing effect of four decades of rock 'n' roll.*
– DERIVATIVES **barbarization** noun.
– ORIGIN late Middle English (in the sense 'speak using barbarisms'): from late Latin *barbarizare*, from Greek *barbarizein* 'speak like a foreigner'.

Barbarossa[1] /ˌbɑːbəˈrɒsə/ see **FREDERICK I**.

Barbarossa[2] /ˌbɑːbəˈrɒsə/, (*c.*1483–1546), Barbary pirate; born *Khair ad-Din*. He was notorious for his successes against Christian vessels in the eastern Mediterranean.

barbarous ▶ **adjective 1** exceedingly brutal: *many early child-rearing practices were barbarous by modern standards.*
2 primitive; uncivilized: *a remote and barbarous country.*
■ (especially of language) coarse and unrefined.
– DERIVATIVES **barbarously** adverb, **barbarousness** noun.
– ORIGIN late Middle English (in sense 2): via Latin from Greek *barbaros* 'foreign' + **-OUS**.

Barbary /ˈbɑːbəri/ (also **Barbary States**) a former name for the Saracen countries of North and NW Africa, together with Moorish Spain. Compare with **MAGHRIB**.
– ORIGIN based on Arabic *barbar* (see **BERBER**).

Barbary ape ▶ **noun** a tailless macaque monkey that is native to NW Africa and also found on the Rock of Gibraltar.
• *Macaca sylvana*, family Cercopithecidae.

Barbary Coast a former name for the Mediterranean coast of North Africa from Morocco to Egypt.

Barbary sheep ▶ **noun** a short-coated sheep with a long neck ruff, found in the high deserts of northern Africa. Also called **AOUDAD**.
• *Ammotragus lervia*, family Bovidae.

Barbary States another name for **BARBARY**.

barbastelle /ˌbɑːbəˈstɛl, ˈbɑːbəstɛl/ ▶ **noun** an Old World bat with broad ears that meet over the head.
• Genus *Barbastella*, family Vespertilionidae: two species, in

b

particular the rare *B. barbastellus* of western Europe and North Africa.
– ORIGIN late 18th cent.: from French, from Italian *barbastello*.

barbecue ▶ noun a meal or gathering at which meat, fish, or other food is cooked out of doors on a rack over an open fire or on a special appliance. ■a metal appliance used for the preparation of food at a barbecue, or a brick fireplace containing such an appliance. ■ [mass noun] N. Amer. food cooked in such a way.
▶verb (**barbecues, barbecued, barbecuing**) [with obj.] cook (meat, fish, or other food) on a barbecue.
– ORIGIN mid 17th cent.: from Spanish *barbacoa*, perhaps from Arawak *barbacoa* 'wooden frame on posts'. The original sense was 'wooden framework for sleeping on, or for storing meat or fish to be dried'.

barbecue sauce ▶ noun a highly seasoned sauce containing vinegar, spices, and usually chillies.

barbed ▶ adjective having a barb or barbs: *barbed arrows.*
■figurative (of a remark or joke) deliberately hurtful: *a fair degree of barbed wit.*

barbed wire ▶ noun [mass noun] wire with clusters of short, sharp spikes set at short intervals along it, used to make fences or in warfare as an obstruction.

barbel /'bɑːb(ə)l/ ▶ noun **1** a fleshy filament growing from the mouth or snout of a fish.
2 a large European freshwater fish of the carp family, which has such filaments hanging from the mouth.
● *Barbus barbus,* family Cyprinidae.
3 [with modifier] an African marine or freshwater fish with barbels round the mouth.
● Species in several families, including *Tachysurus feliceps* (family Aniidae), of southern African coasts and estuaries, whose toxin-coated spines can inflict a dangerous wound.
– ORIGIN late Middle English (in sense 2): via Old French from late Latin *barbellus,* diminutive of *barbus* 'barbel', from *barba* 'beard'.

barbell /'bɑːbɛl/ ▶ noun a long metal bar to which discs of varying weights are attached at each end, used for weightlifting.
– ORIGIN late 19th cent.: from **BAR**[1] + **BELL**[1].

Barber, Samuel (1910–81), American composer. He developed a style based on romanticism allied to classical forms; his music includes operas and orchestral and chamber music.

barber ▶ noun a person who cuts men's hair and shaves or trims beards as an occupation.
▶verb [with obj.] cut or trim (a man's hair).
– ORIGIN Middle English: via Anglo-Norman French from Old French *barbe* (see **BARB**[1]).

barberry ▶ noun (pl. **-ies**) a spiny shrub which typically has yellow flowers and red berries, frequently grown for ornamental hedging.
● Genus *Berberis,* family Berberidaceae: many species, including the **European** (or **common**) **barberry** (*B. vulgaris*).
– ORIGIN late Middle English: from Old French *berberis* (see **BERBERIS**). The change in the ending was due to association with **BERRY**.

barbershop ▶ noun chiefly N. Amer. a shop where a barber works.
■[mass noun] [often as modifier] a popular style of close harmony singing, typically for four male voices. [ORIGIN: from the custom in the 16th and 17th cents of passing time in a barber's shop by harmonizing to a lute or guitar provided to entertain customers waiting their turn.]

barber's itch (also **barber's rash**) ▶ noun [mass noun] ringworm of the face or neck communicated by unsterilized shaving apparatus.

barber's pole ▶ noun a pole painted with spiralling red and white stripes and hung outside barbers' shops as a business sign.

barbet /'bɑːbɪt/ ▶ noun a large-headed, brightly coloured fruit-eating bird that has a stout bill with tufts of bristles at the base. Barbets are found on all continents, especially in the tropics.
● Family Capitonidae: numerous genera and species.
– ORIGIN late 16th cent. (denoting a poodle until the early 19th cent.): from French, from *barbe* 'beard' (see **BARB**[1]). The current sense dates from the early 19th cent.

barbette /bɑː'bɛt/ ▶ noun a fixed armoured housing at the base of a gun turret on a warship or armoured vehicle.

■historical a platform on which a gun is placed to fire over a parapet.
– ORIGIN late 18th cent.: from French, diminutive of *barbe* 'beard' (see **BARB**[1]).

barbican /'bɑːbɪk(ə)n/ ▶ noun the outer defence of a city or castle, especially a double tower above a gate or drawbridge.
– ORIGIN Middle English: from Old French *barbacane*; probably based on Arabic.

barbie ▶ noun (pl. **-ies**) informal, chiefly Austral. a barbecue.
– ORIGIN 1970s: abbreviation.

Barbie doll ▶ noun trademark a doll representing a conventionally attractive young woman.
■informal, chiefly N. Amer. a woman who is attractive in a glossily artificial way, typically one considered to be stupid and characterless.
– ORIGIN 1950s: *Barbie,* diminutive of the given name *Barbara.*

bar billiards ▶ noun Brit. a form of billiards played on a small table, typically in a public bar, in which balls are struck into holes guarded by pegs.

Barbirolli /,bɑːbɪ'rɒli/, Sir John (Giovanni Battista) (1899–1970), English conductor, of Franco-Italian descent, conductor of the Hallé Orchestra from 1943.

barbital /'bɑːbɪt(ə)l/ ▶ noun North American term for **BARBITONE**.
– ORIGIN early 20th cent.: from **BARBITURIC ACID**, on the pattern of *veronal* (an alternative name).

barbitone /'bɑːbɪtəʊn/ ▶ noun [mass noun] a long-acting sedative and sleep-inducing drug of the barbiturate type.
● Alternative name: **diethylbarbituric acid**; chem. formula: $C_6H_{12}O_3N_2$.
– ORIGIN early 20th cent.: from **BARBITURIC ACID** + **-ONE**.

barbiturate /bɑː'bɪtjʊrət, -reɪt/ ▶ noun any of a class of sedative and sleep-inducing drugs derived from barbituric acid.
■Chemistry a salt or ester of barbituric acid.

barbituric acid /,bɑːbɪ'tjʊərɪk, -'tʃʊərɪk/ ▶ noun [mass noun] Chemistry a synthetic organic acid from which the barbiturates are derived.
● A cyclic derivative of urea and malonic acid; chem. formula: $C_4H_4O_3N_2$.
– ORIGIN mid 19th cent.: from French *barbiturique,* from German *Barbitursäure,* from the given name *Barbara* + *Säure* 'acid'.

Barbizon School a mid 19th-century school of French landscape painters who reacted against classical conventions and based their art on direct study of nature. Led by Théodore Rousseau, the group included Charles Daubigny and Jean-François Millet.
– ORIGIN named after *Barbizon,* a small village in the forest of Fontainebleau, near Paris, where Rousseau and others worked.

barbola /bɑː'bəʊlə/ (also **barbola work**) ▶ noun [mass noun] the craft of making small models of fruit or flowers from a plastic paste.
■articles such as mirrors decorated with these models.
– ORIGIN 1920s: an arbitrary formation from **BARBOTINE**.

barbotine /'bɑːbətɪn/ ▶ noun [mass noun] slip (liquid clay) used to decorate pottery.
■pottery decorated with this.
– ORIGIN mid 19th cent.: from French.

Barbour[1] /'bɑːbə/, John (c.1320–95), Scottish poet and prelate. The poem ascribed to him with certainty is *The Bruce,* a verse chronicle relating the deeds of Robert the Bruce.

Barbour[2] /'bɑːbə/ (also **Barbour jacket**) ▶ noun trademark a type of green waxed outdoor jacket.
– ORIGIN named after John *Barbour* (died 1918), a draper in NE England who sold waterproof clothing.

Barbuda see **ANTIGUA AND BARBUDA**.
– DERIVATIVES **Barbudan** adjective & noun.

barbule /'bɑːbjuːl/ ▶ noun a minute filament projecting from the barb of a feather.
– ORIGIN mid 19th cent.: from Latin *barbula,* diminutive of *barba* 'beard'.

barbwire ▶ noun N. Amer. barbed wire.

barcarole /'bɑːkərəʊl, ,bɑːkə'rəʊl/ (also **barcarolle** /-rɒl, -'rɒl/) ▶ noun a song traditionally sung by Venetian gondoliers.
■a musical composition in the style of such a song.

– ORIGIN late 18th cent.: from French *barcarolle,* from Venetian Italian *barcarola* 'boatman's song', from *barca* 'boat'.

Barcelona /,bɑːsə'ləʊnə, Spanish barθe'lona, barse-/ a city on the coast of NE Spain, capital of Catalonia; pop. 1,653,175 (1991).

barchan /'bɑːk(ə)n/ ▶ noun a crescent-shaped shifting sand dune, as found in the deserts of Turkestan.
– ORIGIN late 19th cent.: from Turkic *barkhan.*

bar chart (also **bar graph**) ▶ noun a diagram in which the numerical values of variables are represented by the height or length of lines or rectangles of equal width.

Bar-Cochba /bɑː'kɒkbə/ Jewish rebel leader; known as **Simeon** in Jewish sources. He led the rebellion against the Romans in AD 132, and was accepted by some of his Jewish contemporaries as the Messiah.

bar code ▶ noun a machine-readable code in the form of numbers and a pattern of parallel lines of varying widths, printed on and identifying a commodity and used especially for stock control.

Barcoo /bɑː'kuː/ ▶ adjective Austral. of or relating to the remote inland area of Australia: *Barcoo sickness.*
– ORIGIN late 19th cent.: from the name of a river (and the surrounding country) in western Queensland.

Barcoo rot ▶ noun [mass noun] Austral. scurvy.

bard[1] ▶ noun archaic or poetic/literary a poet, traditionally one reciting epics and associated with a particular oral tradition.
■(**the Bard** or **the Bard of Avon**) Shakespeare. ■ (**Bard**) the winner of a prize for Welsh verse at an Eisteddfod.
– DERIVATIVES **bardic** adjective.
– ORIGIN Middle English: from Scottish Gaelic *bàrd,* Irish *bard,* Welsh *bardd,* of Celtic origin. In Scotland in the 16th cent. it was a derogatory term for an itinerant musician, but was later romanticized by Sir Walter Scott.

bard[2] ▶ noun a rasher of fat bacon placed on meat or game before roasting.
▶verb [with obj.] cover (meat or game) with rashers of fat bacon.
– ORIGIN early 18th cent.: from French *barde,* a transferred sense of *barde* 'armour for the breast and flanks of a warhorse', based on Arabic *barda'a* 'saddlecloth, padded saddle'.

bardie /'bɑːdi/ (also **bardee** or **bardy**) ▶ noun (pl. **-ies**) Austral. the edible larva or pupa of certain insects, in particular:
● a longhorn beetle that bores within stems (*Bardistus cibarius,* family Cerambycidae). ● a moth that develops underground on roots (family Hepialidae, especially *Trictena argentata*).
– ORIGIN mid 19th cent.: from Nyungar (and other Aboriginal languages) *bardi.*

bardolatry /bɑː'dɒlətri/ ▶ noun [mass noun] humorous excessive admiration of Shakespeare.
– DERIVATIVES **bardolater** (or **bardolator**) noun.

Bardolino /,bɑːdə'liːnəʊ/ ▶ noun [mass noun] a red wine from the Veneto region of Italy.
– ORIGIN Italian.

Bardot /bɑː'dəʊ, French bardo/, Brigitte (b.1934), French actress; born *Camille Javal.* The film *And God Created Woman* (1956) established her reputation as an international sex symbol.

bardy ▶ noun (pl. **-ies**) variant spelling of **BARDIE**.

bare ▶ adjective **1** (of a person or part of the body) not clothed or covered: *he was bare from the waist up | she padded in bare feet towards the door.*
■without the appropriate, usual, or natural covering: *leaf fall had left the trees bare | bare floorboards.* ■ without the appropriate or usual contents: *a bare cell with just a mattress.*
2 without addition; basic and simple: *he outlined the bare essentials of the story.*
■[attrib.] only just sufficient: *a bare majority.* ■ [attrib.] surprisingly small in number or amount: *all you need to get started with this program is a bare 10K bytes of memory.*
▶verb [with obj.] uncover (a part of the body or other thing) and expose it to view: *he bared his chest to show his scar.*
– PHRASES **bare all** take off all of one's clothes and display oneself to others. **the bare bones** the basic facts about something, without any detail: *the bare bones of the plot.* **bare of** without: *the interior was bare of plaster.* **bare one's soul** reveal one's innermost

secrets and feelings to someone. **bare one's teeth** show one's teeth, typically when angry. **with one's bare hands** without using tools or weapons.
– DERIVATIVES **bareness** noun.
– ORIGIN Old English *bær* (noun), *barian* (verb), of Germanic origin; related to Dutch *baar*.

bareback ▶ **adjective** & **adverb** on an unsaddled horse or donkey: [as adj.] *a bareback circus rider* | [as adv.] *riding bareback*.

bareboat ▶ **adjective** [attrib.] relating to or denoting a boat or ship hired without a crew: *bareboat charters*.

Barebones Parliament the nickname of Cromwell's Parliament of 1653, from one of its members, Praise-God Barbon, an Anabaptist leather seller of Fleet Street. It replaced the Rump Parliament, but was itself dissolved within a few months.

barefaced ▶ **adjective** **1** shameless and undisguised: *a barefaced lie*.
2 having an uncovered face and therefore exposed or vulnerable to something: *his years of working barefaced, breathing down dust*.
– DERIVATIVES **barefacedly** adverb, **barefacedness** noun.

barefoot (also **barefooted**) ▶ **adjective** & **adverb** wearing nothing on the feet: [as adv.] *I won't walk barefoot*.

barefoot doctor ▶ **noun** a paramedical worker with basic medical training working in a rural district in China.

barège /bəˈreɪʒ/ (also **barege**) ▶ **noun** [mass noun] a light, silky dress fabric resembling gauze, typically made from wool.
– ORIGIN French, named after the village of *Barèges* in SW France, where it was originally made.

barehanded ▶ **adjective** & **adverb** with nothing in or covering one's hands.
■ carrying no weapons.

bareheaded ▶ **adjective** & **adverb** without a covering for one's head.

Bareilly /bəˈreɪli/ an industrial city in northern India, in Uttar Pradesh; pop. 583,000 (1991).

bare-knuckle (also **bare-knuckled** or **bare-knuckles**) ▶ **adjective** [attrib.] (of a boxer or boxing match) without gloves.
■ informal with no scruples or reservations: *an apostle of bare-knuckled capitalism*.

barely ▶ **adverb** **1** only just; almost not: *she nodded, barely able to speak* | [as submodifier] *a barely perceptible pause*.
■ only a very short time before: *they had barely sat down before forty policemen swarmed in*.
2 in a simple and sparse way: *their barely furnished house*.
3 archaic openly; explicitly.

Barenboim /ˈbarənbɔɪm/, Daniel (b.1942), Israeli pianist and conductor, musical director of the Orchestre de Paris 1975–88 and of the Chicago Symphony Orchestra since 1991. In 1967 he married the cellist Jacqueline du Pré.

Barents /ˈbarənts/, Willem (d.1597), Dutch explorer. The leader of several expeditions in search of the North-East Passage to Asia, Barents discovered Spitsbergen and reached Novaya Zemlya, off the coast of which he died.

Barents Sea a part of the Arctic Ocean to the north of Norway and Russia, bounded to the west by Svalbard, to the north by Franz Josef Land, and to the east by Novaya Zemlya.

barf informal, chiefly N. Amer. ▶ **verb** [no obj.] vomit.
▶ **noun** an attack of vomiting.
■ [mass noun] vomited food.
– ORIGIN 1960s (originally US): of unknown origin.

barfi /ˈbʌrfiː/ ▶ **noun** variant spelling of **BURFI**.

barfly /ˈbɑːflʌɪ/ ▶ **noun** (pl. **-flies**) informal a person who spends much of their time drinking in bars.

barfly jumping ▶ **noun** [mass noun] the sport of jumping at and sticking to a Velcro-covered wall while wearing a Velcro suit.

bargain ▶ **noun** an agreement between two or more people or groups as to what each will do for the other: *bargains between political parties supporting the government*.
■ Brit. an agreement to buy or sell shares on the stock market. ■ a thing bought or offered for sale much more cheaply than is usual or expected: *the second-hand table was a real bargain* | [as modifier] *get this guide at the bargain price of 80p*.
▶ **verb** [no obj.] negotiate the terms and conditions of a transaction: *he* ***bargained with*** *the local council to rent the stadium*.
■ [with obj.] (**bargain something away**) part with something after negotiation but get little or nothing in return: *his determination not to bargain away any of the province's economic powers*. ■ (**bargain for/on**) be prepared for; expect: *I got more information than I'd bargained for* | *he didn't bargain on this storm*.
– PHRASES **drive a hard bargain** be uncompromising in making a deal. **into** (N. Amer. **in**) **the bargain** in addition to what has been already mentioned or was expected: *I am now tired and extremely hungry—with a headache into the bargain*. **keep one's side of the bargain** carry out the promises one has made as part of an agreement.
– DERIVATIVES **bargainer** noun.
– ORIGIN Middle English: from Old French *bargaine* (noun), *bargaignier* (verb); probably of Germanic origin and related to German *borgen* 'borrow'.

bargain basement ▶ **noun** a store or part of a store where goods are sold cheaply, typically because they are old or imperfect: [as modifier] *bargain-basement prices*.

bargaining counter (also **bargaining chip**) ▶ **noun** a potential concession or other factor which can be used to advantage in negotiations.

barge ▶ **noun** a long flat-bottomed boat for carrying freight on canals and rivers, either under its own power or towed by another.
■ a long ornamental boat used for pleasure or ceremony. ■ a boat used by the chief officers of a warship.
▶ **verb** **1** [no obj., with adverbial of direction] move forcefully or roughly: *we can't just* ***barge into*** *a private garden*.
■ (**barge in**) intrude or interrupt rudely or awkwardly: *sorry to* ***barge in on*** *your cosy evening*. ■ [with obj.] (chiefly in a sporting context) run into and collide with, typically intentionally: *you can use this method to barge an opponent*.
2 [with obj.] convey (freight) by barge.
– ORIGIN Middle English (denoting a small seagoing vessel): from Old French, perhaps based on Greek *baris* 'Egyptian boat'.

bargeboard ▶ **noun** a board, typically an ornamental one, fixed to the gable end of a roof to hide the ends of the roof timbers.
– ORIGIN mid 19th cent.: from mid 16th-cent. *barge-* (used in architectural terms relating to the gable of a building), perhaps from medieval Latin *bargus* 'gallows'.

bargee /bɑːˈdʒiː/ ▶ **noun** chiefly Brit. a person in charge of or working on a barge.

Bargello /bɑːˈdʒɛləʊ/ ▶ **noun** [mass noun] a kind of embroidery worked on canvas in stitch patterns suggestive of flames.
– ORIGIN 1940s: named after *Bargello* Palace, in Florence, Italy.

bargepole ▶ **noun** a long pole used to propel a barge and fend off obstacles.
– PHRASES **would not touch someone/thing with a bargepole** informal used to express a refusal to have anything to do with someone or something.

bar girl ▶ **noun** N. Amer. an attractive woman employed to encourage customers to buy drinks at a bar.

bar graph ▶ **noun** another term for **BAR CHART**.

Bari /ˈbɑːri/ an industrial seaport on the Adriatic coast of SE Italy, capital of Apulia region; pop. 353,030 (1990).

barilla /bəˈrɪlə/ ▶ **noun** [mass noun] an impure alkali formerly made from the ashes of burnt plants, especially saltworts.
– ORIGIN early 17th cent.: from Spanish *barrilla*, diminutive of *barra* 'bar'.

Barisal /ˈbʌrɪsʌl/ a river port in southern Bangladesh, on the Ganges delta; pop. 180,010 (1991).

barite /ˈbarʌɪt, ˈbɛː-/ ▶ **noun** variant spelling of **BARYTE**.

baritone ▶ **noun** **1** an adult male singing voice between tenor and bass.
■ a singer with such a voice. ■ a part written for such a voice.
2 an instrument that is second lowest in pitch in its family.
■ a brass instrument similar to a euphonium, sounding in B flat and used in brass bands.
▶ **adjective** second lowest in musical pitch.
– ORIGIN early 17th cent.: from Italian *baritono*, from Greek *barutonos*, from *barus* 'heavy' + *tonos* (see **TONE**).

barium /ˈbɛːrɪəm/ ▶ **noun** [mass noun] the chemical element of atomic number 56, a soft white reactive metal of the alkaline earth group. (Symbol: **Ba**)
■ a mixture of barium sulphate and water, opaque to X-rays, which is swallowed to permit radiological examination of the stomach or intestines: [as modifier] *a barium meal*.

Barium compounds are used in water purification, the glass industry, and pigments, and as an ingredient of signal flares and fireworks, to which they give a bright yellowish-green colour. Barium oxide is a component of high-temperature superconductors.

– ORIGIN early 19th cent.: from **BARYTA** + **-IUM**.

bark[1] ▶ **noun** the sharp explosive cry of a dog, fox, or seal.
■ a sound resembling this cry, typically one made by someone laughing or coughing: *a short bark of laughter*.
▶ **verb** **1** [no obj.] (of a dog, fox, or seal) give a bark.
■ (of a person) make a sound, such as a cough or a laugh, resembling a bark: *she barked with laughter*.
2 [with obj.] utter (a command or question) abruptly or aggressively: *he began* ***barking out*** *his orders* | [with direct speech] *'Nobody is allowed up here,' he barked*.
■ [no obj.] US call out in order to sell or advertise something: *doormen bark at passers-by, promising hot girls and cold beer*.
– PHRASES **someone's bark is worse than their bite** someone is not as ferocious as they appear or sound. **be barking up the wrong tree** informal pursue a mistaken or misguided line of thought or course of action.
– ORIGIN Old English *beorc* (noun), *beorcan* (verb), of Germanic origin; possibly related to **BREAK**[1].

bark[2] ▶ **noun** [mass noun] the tough protective outer sheath of the trunk, branches, and twigs of a tree or woody shrub.
■ this material used for tanning leather, making dyestuffs, or as a mulch in gardening.
▶ **verb** [with obj.] **1** strip the bark from (a tree or piece of wood).
■ scrape the skin off (one's shin) by accidentally hitting it against something hard.
2 technical tan or dye (leather or other materials) using the tannins found in bark.
– DERIVATIVES **barked** adjective [in combination] *the red-barked dogwood*.
– ORIGIN Middle English: from Old Norse *bǫrkr*; perhaps related to **BIRCH**.

bark[3] ▶ **noun** archaic or poetic/literary a ship or boat.
– ORIGIN late Middle English: variant of **BARQUE**.

bark beetle ▶ **noun** a small wood-boring beetle that tunnels under the bark of trees, which may die if heavily infested.
• Family Scolytidae: many genera and species, including the **elm bark beetle** (*Scolytus scolytus*), which is responsible for the spread of the fungus which causes Dutch elm disease.

barkcloth ▶ **noun** [mass noun] cloth made from the inner bark of the paper mulberry or similar tree.

barkeeper (US also **barkeep**) ▶ **noun** chiefly N. Amer. a person who owns or serves drinks in a bar.

barkentine ▶ **noun** US spelling of **BARQUENTINE**.

barker ▶ **noun** informal a tout at an auction, sideshow, etc., who calls out to passers-by to attract custom.
– ORIGIN late Middle English: from **BARK**[1] + **-ER**[1]. The original sense was 'a person or animal that barks; noisy protestor', hence the current sense (late 17th cent.).

barking ▶ **adjective** [predic.] Brit. informal completely mad or demented: *we are all a bit barking* | [as submodifier] *has she gone completely* ***barking mad?***

barking deer ▶ **noun** another term for **MUNTJAC**.

barking gecko (also **barking lizard**) ▶ **noun** any of a number of geckos with a bark-like call, in particular:
• a South African lizard with a characteristic clicking call (genus *Ptenopus*, family Pygopodidae). • a southern Australian lizard (genus *Nephrurus*, family Gekkonidae, including *N. milii*).

Barkly Tableland a plateau region lying to the north-east of Tennant Creek in Northern Territory, Australia.

barley ▶ **noun** [mass noun] a hardy cereal which has coarse bristles extending from the ears. It is widely cultivated, chiefly for use in brewing and stockfeed.
• Genus *Hordeum*, family Gramineae.
■ the grain of this plant. See also **PEARL BARLEY**.
– ORIGIN Old English *bærlic* (adjective), from *bære*, *bere* 'barley' + *-lic* (see **-LY**[1]).

barleycorn ▶ noun a grain of barley.
■ a former unit of measurement (about a third of an inch) based on the length of a grain of barley.

barleymow ▶ noun Brit. archaic a stack of barley.

barley sugar ▶ noun [mass noun] an amber-coloured sweet made of boiled sugar, traditionally shaped as a twisted stick.
▶ adjective [attrib.] shaped like twisted barley-sugar sticks.

barley water ▶ noun [mass noun] a drink made from water and a boiled barley mixture, usually flavoured with orange or lemon.

barley wine ▶ noun [mass noun] a strong English ale.

bar line ▶ noun Music a vertical line used in a musical score to mark a division between bars.

barm ▶ noun [mass noun] the froth on fermenting malt liquor.
■ archaic or dialect yeast or leaven.
– ORIGIN Old English beorma, of West Germanic origin.

barmaid ▶ noun 1 Brit. a woman serving behind the bar of a public house or hotel.
2 N. Amer. a waitress who serves drinks in a bar.

barman ▶ noun (pl. -men) chiefly Brit. a man serving behind the bar of a public house or hotel.

barmbrack (also **barnbrack**) ▶ noun [mass noun] a kind of soft, spicy bread containing dried fruit, originating in Ireland.
– ORIGIN from Irish bairín breac 'speckled cake'.

barm cake ▶ noun N. English a soft, flattish bread roll.

Barmecide /'bɑːmɪsaɪd/ ▶ adjective rare illusory or imaginary and therefore disappointing.
– ORIGIN early 18th cent. (as a noun): from Arabic Barmakī, the name of a prince in the Arabian Nights' Entertainments, who gave a beggar a feast consisting of ornate but empty dishes.

bar mitzvah /bɑː 'mɪtzvə/ ▶ noun the religious initiation ceremony of a Jewish boy who has reached the age of 13 and is regarded as ready to observe religious precepts and eligible to take part in public worship.
■ the boy undergoing this ceremony.
▶ verb [with obj.] (usu. be bar mitzvahed) administer the bar mitzvah ceremony to (a boy).
– ORIGIN from Hebrew bar miṣwāh, literally 'son of the commandment'.

barmy ▶ adjective (barmier, barmiest) informal, chiefly Brit. extremely foolish: this is a barmy decision.
– DERIVATIVES barmily adverb, barminess noun.
– ORIGIN late 15th cent. (in the sense 'frothy'): from BARM + -Y[1].

barn[1] ▶ noun a large farm building used for storing grain, hay, or straw or for housing livestock.
■ N. Amer. a large shed used for storing road or railway vehicles. ■ a large and uninviting building: a great barn of a pub.
– ORIGIN Old English bern, berern, from bere 'barley' + ern, ærn 'house'.

barn[2] (abbrev.: b) ▶ noun Physics a unit of area, 10^{-28} square metres, used especially in particle physics.
– ORIGIN 1940s: apparently from the phrase as big as a barn door.

Barnabas, St /'bɑːnəbəs/ (died c.61), a Cypriot Levite and Apostle. He accompanied St Paul on the first missionary journey to Cyprus and Asia Minor. The traditional founder of the Cypriot Church, he is said to have been martyred in Cyprus. Feast day, 11 June.

barnacle /'bɑːnək(ə)l/ ▶ noun a marine crustacean with an external shell, which attaches itself permanently to a variety of surfaces. Barnacles feed by filtering particles from the water using their modified feathery legs.
● Class Cirripedia. See ACORN BARNACLE, GOOSE BARNACLE.
■ used in similes to describe a tenacious person or thing: buses careered along with men hanging from their doors like barnacles.
– DERIVATIVES barnacled adjective.
– ORIGIN late 16th cent.: from medieval Latin bernaca, of unknown origin. In Middle English the term denoted the barnacle goose, whose breeding grounds were long unknown and which was believed to hatch from the shell of the crustacean to which it gave its name.

barnacle goose ▶ noun a goose with a white face and black neck, breeding in the arctic tundra of Greenland, Spitsbergen, and Novaya Zemlya.

● Branta leucopsis, family Anatidae.
– ORIGIN mid 18th cent.: see BARNACLE.

Barnard /'bɑːnɑːd/, Christiaan Neethling (b.1922), South African surgeon. He pioneered human heart transplantation, performing the first operation of this kind in December 1967.

Barnardo /bə'nɑːdəʊ/, Thomas John (1845–1905), Irish-born doctor and philanthropist. He founded the East End Mission for destitute children in 1867, the first of many such homes. Now known as Dr Barnardo's Homes, they cater chiefly for those with physical and mental disabilities.

Barnard's star Astronomy a red dwarf in the constellation Ophiuchus. It has a large proper motion and is one of the closest stars to the sun.
– ORIGIN named after Edward E. Barnard (1857–1923), the American astronomer who discovered it in 1916.

Barnaul /ˌbɑːnɑ'uːl/ the capital of Altai territory on the River Ob; pop. 603,000 (1990).

barnbrack ▶ noun variant spelling of BARMBRACK.

barn burner ▶ noun N. Amer. informal a very exciting or dramatic event, especially a sports contest.

barn dance ▶ noun 1 an informal social gathering for country dancing.
2 a dance for a number of couples moving round a circle, typically involving changes of partner.

barn door ▶ noun the large door of a barn.
■ used to refer to a large and easy target: on the shooting range he could not hit a barn door. ■ a hinged metal flap fitted to a spotlight to control the direction and intensity of its beam.

barnet /'bɑːnɪt/ ▶ noun Brit. informal a person's hair.
– ORIGIN mid 19th cent.: from rhyming slang barnet fair, the name of a famous horse fair held at Barnet, Herts.

barney ▶ noun (pl. -eys) Brit. informal a quarrel, especially a noisy one.
– ORIGIN mid 19th cent.: of unknown origin.

barn owl ▶ noun an owl with a heart-shaped face, black eyes, and relatively long, slender legs. It typically nests in farm buildings or in holes in trees. Also called SCREECH OWL.
● Genus Tyto, family Tytonidae: three species, especially T. alba, which is found throughout the world and (in western Europe) has a white face and underparts.

Barnsley a town in northern England, a unitary council formerly in Yorkshire; pop. 217,300 (1991).

barnstorm ▶ verb [no obj.] chiefly N. Amer. tour rural districts giving theatrical performances, originally often in barns.
■ [with obj.] make a rapid tour of (an area), typically as part of a political campaign. ■ travel around giving exhibitions of flying and performing aeronautical stunts.
– DERIVATIVES barnstormer noun.

barnstorming ▶ adjective (of a performance or a person giving a performance) flamboyantly energetic and successful: his barnstorming oratory has been sorely missed.

barn swallow ▶ noun see SWALLOW[2].

Barnum /'bɑːnəm/, P. T. (1810–91), American showman; full name Phineas Taylor Barnum. He billed his circus, opened in 1871, as 'The Greatest Show on Earth'; ten years later he founded the Barnum and Bailey circus with his former rival Anthony Bailey (1847–1906).

Barnum effect ▶ noun [mass noun] Psychology the tendency to accept as true types of information such as character assessments or horoscopes, even when the information is so vague as to be worthless.
– ORIGIN named after P. T. BARNUM; the word Barnum was in use from the mid 19th cent. as a noun in the sense 'nonsense, humbug'.

barnyard ▶ noun the area of open ground around a barn; a farmyard.

baro- /'bærəʊ/ ▶ combining form relating to pressure: barotrauma | barotitis.
– ORIGIN from Greek baros 'weight'.

Baroda /bə'rəʊdə/ a former princely state of western India, now part of Gujarat.
■ former name (until 1976) for VADODARA.

barograph ▶ noun a barometer that records its readings on a moving chart.
– ORIGIN mid 19th cent.: from Greek baros 'weight' + -GRAPH.

Barolo /bə'rəʊləʊ, Italian ba'rɔlo/ ▶ noun [mass noun] a

full-bodied red wine from the area around Barolo in NW Italy.

barometer ▶ noun an instrument measuring atmospheric pressure, used especially in forecasting the weather and determining altitude.
■ something which reflects changes in circumstances or opinions: furniture is a barometer of changing tastes.
– DERIVATIVES barometric adjective, barometrical adjective, barometry noun.
– ORIGIN mid 17th cent.: from Greek baros 'weight' + -METER.

baron ▶ noun a member of the lowest order of the British nobility. Baron is not used as a form of address, barons usually being referred to as 'Lord'.
■ a similar member of a foreign nobility. ■ historical a person who held lands or property from the sovereign or a powerful overlord. ■ [with modifier] an important or powerful person in a specified business or industry: a press baron.
– ORIGIN Middle English: from Old French, from medieval Latin baro, baron- 'man, warrior', probably of Germanic origin.

baronage ▶ noun 1 [treated as sing. or pl.] barons or nobles collectively.
2 an annotated list of barons or peers.
– ORIGIN Middle English: from Old French barnage (from baron), or from medieval Latin baronagium, from baro (see BARON).

baroness ▶ noun the wife or widow of a baron. Baroness is not used as a form of address, baronesses usually being referred to as 'Lady'.
■ a woman holding the rank of baron either as a life peerage or as a hereditary rank.
– ORIGIN late Middle English: from Old French baronesse (see BARON).

baronet /'bær(ə)nɪt/ ▶ noun a member of the lowest hereditary titled British order, with the status of a commoner but able to use the prefix 'Sir'.
– ORIGIN late Middle English: from Anglo-Latin baronettus, from Latin baro, baron- 'man, warrior'. The term originally denoted a gentleman, not a nobleman, summoned by the king to attend parliament; the current order was instituted in the early 17th cent.

baronetage ▶ noun 1 [treated as sing. or pl.] baronets collectively.
2 an annotated list of baronets.

baronetcy ▶ noun (pl. -ies) the rank of a baronet.

baronial ▶ adjective 1 of or relating to a baron or barons.
2 in the turreted style characteristic of Scottish country houses.

baron of beef ▶ noun Brit. a joint of beef consisting of two sirloins joined at the backbone.

barony ▶ noun (pl. -ies) 1 the rank and estates of a baron.
2 historical (in Ireland) a division of a county.
3 historical (in Scotland) a large manor or estate.

baroque /bə'rɒk, -'rəʊk/ ▶ adjective relating to or denoting a style of European architecture, music, and art of the 17th and 18th centuries that followed mannerism and is characterized by ornate detail. In architecture the period is exemplified by the palace of Versailles and by the work of Wren in England. Major composers include Vivaldi, Bach, and Handel; Caravaggio and Rubens are important baroque artists.
■ highly ornate and extravagant in style.
▶ noun [mass noun] the baroque style.
■ the baroque period.
– ORIGIN mid 18th cent.: from French (originally designating a pearl of irregular shape), from Portuguese barroco, Spanish barrueco, or Italian barocco; of unknown ultimate origin.

baroreceptor ▶ noun Zoology a receptor sensitive to changes in pressure.

barotitis /ˌbærə(ʊ)'taɪtɪs/ ▶ noun [mass noun] Medicine discomfort and inflammation in the ear caused by the changes of pressure occurring during air travel.

barotrauma ▶ noun [mass noun] Medicine injury caused by a change in air pressure, affecting typically the ear or the lung.

barouche /bə'ruːʃ/ ▶ noun historical a four-wheeled horse-drawn carriage with a collapsible hood over the rear half, a seat in front for the driver, and seats facing each other for the passengers.
– ORIGIN early 19th cent.: from German dialect Barutsche, from Italian baroccio, based on Latin

birotus 'two-wheeled', from *bi-* 'having two' + *rota* 'wheel'.

barque /bɑːk/ ▶ noun a sailing ship, typically with three masts, in which the foremast and mainmast are square-rigged and the mizzenmast is rigged fore and aft.
■ poetic/literary a boat.
– ORIGIN Middle English: from Old French, probably from Provençal *barca*, from late Latin *barca* 'ship's boat'.

barquentine /ˈbɑːk(ə)ntiːn/ (US **barkentine**) ▶ noun a sailing ship similar to a barque but with only the foremast square-rigged and the remaining masts rigged fore and aft.
– ORIGIN late 17th cent.: from **BARQUE**, on the pattern of *brigantine*.

Barquisimeto /ˌbɑːkɪsɪˈmeɪtəʊ/ a city in NW Venezuela; pop. 602,620 (1991).

Barra /ˈbarə/ a small island towards the southern end of the Outer Hebrides, to the south of South Uist, from which it is separated by the Sound of Barra.

barrack[1] ▶ verb [with obj.] (often **be barracked**) provide (soldiers) with accommodation in a building or set of buildings.
– ORIGIN early 18th cent.: from **BARRACKS**.

barrack[2] ▶ verb [with obj.] Brit. & Austral./NZ jeer loudly at (someone performing or speaking in public) in order to express disapproval or to distract them: *opponents barracked him when he addressed the opening parliamentary session* | [as noun **barracking**] *the disgraceful barracking which came from the mob.*
■ [no obj.] (**barrack for**) Austral./NZ give support and encouragement to: *I take it you'll be barracking for Labour tonight?*
– ORIGIN late 19th cent.: probably from Northern Irish dialect.

barrack-room lawyer ▶ noun Brit. a person who likes to give authoritative-sounding opinions on subjects in which they are not qualified, especially legal matters.

barracks ▶ plural noun [often treated as sing.] a large building or group of buildings used to house soldiers: *the troops were ordered back to barracks.*
■ (**barrack**) a large, ugly building: *that great barrack of a house.*
– ORIGIN late 17th cent.: *barrack* from French *baraque*, from Italian *baracca* or Spanish *barraca* 'soldier's tent', of unknown origin.

barrack square ▶ noun Brit. a drill ground near a barracks.

barracoon /ˌbarəˈkuːn/ ▶ noun historical an enclosure in which black slaves were confined for a limited period.
– ORIGIN mid 19th cent.: from Spanish *barracón*, from *barraca* 'soldier's tent' (see **BARRACKS**).

barracouta /ˌbarəˈkuːtə/ ▶ noun (pl. same or **barracoutas**) **1** a long, slender fish of southern oceans, highly valued as food. Also called **SNOEK** in South Africa.
● *Thyrsites atun*, family Gempylidae.
2 NZ a long loaf of bread.
– ORIGIN mid 19th cent.: alteration of **BARRACUDA**. Sense 2 dates from the late 20th cent.

barracuda /ˌbarəˈkuːdə/ ▶ noun (pl. same or **barracudas**) a large predatory tropical marine fish with a slender body and large jaws and teeth.
● Family Sphyraenidae and genus *Sphyraena*: several species, in particular *S. barracuda*.
– ORIGIN late 17th cent.: of unknown origin.

barracudina /ˌbarəkuːˈdiːnə/ ▶ noun a slender-bodied predatory fish with a long head, found in open oceans.
● Family Paralepididae: numerous species, including *Paralepis atlantica*.
– ORIGIN from American Spanish, diminutive of *barracuda* (see **BARRACUDA**), which it resembles.

barrage /ˈbarɑːʒ/ ▶ noun **1** a concentrated artillery bombardment over a wide area.
■ figurative an overwhelming number of questions, criticisms, or complaints delivered simultaneously or in rapid succession: *a barrage of questions.*
2 Brit. an artificial barrier, typically across a river, to prevent flooding, aid irrigation or navigation, or to generate electricity by tidal power.
▶ verb [with obj.] (usu. **be barraged**) bombard (someone) with questions, criticisms, or complaints: *his doctor was barraged with unsolicited advice.*

– ORIGIN mid 19th cent. (in sense 2): from French, from *barrer* 'to bar', of unknown origin.

barrage balloon ▶ noun a large balloon anchored to the ground by cables and typically with netting suspended from it, serving as an obstacle to low-flying enemy aircraft.

barramundi /ˌbarəˈmʌndi/ ▶ noun (pl. same or **barramundis**) any of a number of large, chiefly freshwater fishes of Australia and SE Asia:
● a fish that migrates between the sea and rivers and is valued as a food fish (*Lates calcarifer*, family Centropomidae). ● a mouthbrooder (genus *Scleropages*, family Osteoglossidae), in particular *S. leichardti*.
– ORIGIN late 19th cent.: probably from an Aboriginal language of Queensland.

barranca /bəˈraŋkə/ (also **barranco**) ▶ noun (pl. **barrancas** or **barrancos**) chiefly US a narrow, winding river gorge.
– ORIGIN late 17th cent.: from Spanish.

Barranquilla /ˌbarəŋˈkiːjə/ the chief port of Colombia; pop. 1,018,700 (1992). Founded in 1629, the city lies at the mouth of the Magdalena River, near the Caribbean Sea.

barratry /ˈbarətri/ ▶ noun [mass noun] **1** archaic fraud or gross negligence of a ship's master or crew at the expense of its owners or users.
2 Law vexatious litigation or incitement to it. This offence was abolished in Britain in 1967 but is still current in other jurisdictions.
3 historical trade in the sale of Church or state appointments.
– DERIVATIVES **barrator** noun (only in sense 2), **barratrous** adjective.
– ORIGIN late Middle English (in sense 3): from Old French *baraterie*, from *barater* 'deceive', based on Greek *prattein* 'do, perform, manage' (sometimes dishonestly); perhaps influenced by Old Norse *barátta* 'contest'.

Barrault /baˈrəʊ, French baʁo/, Jean-Louis (1910–94), French actor and director. He directed a number of films, including *Les Enfants du Paradis* (1945).

Barr body ▶ noun Physiology a small, densely staining structure in the cell nuclei of females, consisting of a condensed, inactive X chromosome. It is regarded as diagnostic of genetic femaleness.

barre /bɑː/ ▶ noun **1** a horizontal bar at waist level on which ballet dancers rest a hand for support during certain exercises.
2 [as modifier] denoting a chord played using the barré method.
– ORIGIN French.

barré /ˈbareɪ/ ▶ noun Music a method of playing a chord on the guitar or a similar instrument in which one finger is laid across all the strings at a particular fret.
– ORIGIN late 19th cent.: French, literally 'barred', past participle of *barrer*.

barrel /ˈbar(ə)l/ ▶ noun **1** a cylindrical container bulging out in the middle, traditionally made of wooden staves with metal hoops round them.
■ such a container together with its contents: *a barrel of beer.* ■ a measure of capacity used for oil and beer. It is usually equal to 36 imperial gallons for beer and 35 imperial gallons or 42 US gallons (roughly 159 litres) for oil.
2 a cylindrical tube forming part of an object such as a gun or a pen.
3 the belly and loins of a four-legged animal such as a horse.
▶ verb (**barrelled**, **barrelling**; N. Amer. **barreled**, **barreling**) **1** [no obj., with adverbial of direction] informal, chiefly N. Amer. drive or move in a way that is so fast as to almost be out of control: *they shot him and then barreled away in the truck.*
2 [with obj.] put into a barrel or barrels.
– PHRASES **a barrel of laughs** [with negative] informal a source of amusement or pleasure: *life is not exactly a barrel of laughs at the moment.* **over a barrel** informal in a helpless position; at someone's mercy: *I like doing business with a man who knows he's over a barrel.* **with both barrels** informal, chiefly US with unrestrained force or emotion.
– ORIGIN Middle English: from Old French *baril*, from medieval Latin *barriclus* 'small cask'.

barrel-chested ▶ adjective having a large rounded chest.

barrel distortion ▶ noun [mass noun] a type of defect in optical or electronic images in which vertical or horizontal straight lines appear as convex curves.

barrelfish ▶ noun (pl. same or **-fishes**) a fish which lives in the deep waters of the Atlantic when adult, and on the surface, typically among flotsam, when young.
● *Schedophilus medusophagus* and *Hyperoglyphe perciforma*, family Centrolophidae.

barrelhead ▶ noun the flat top of a barrel.
– PHRASES **on the barrelhead** North American term for *on the nail* (see **NAIL**).

barrelhouse ▶ noun **1** N. Amer. a cheap or disreputable bar.
2 [mass noun] [usu. as modifier] an unrestrained and unsophisticated style of jazz music.
– ORIGIN late 19th cent.: so named because of the rows of barrels along the walls of such a bar.

barrel organ ▶ noun a small pipe organ played by turning a handle, which rotates a cylinder studded with pegs that open the valves to produce a preset tune, formerly much used by street musicians.

barrel roll ▶ noun an aerobatic manoeuvre in which an aircraft follows a single turn of a spiral while rolling once about its longitudinal axis.

barrel vault ▶ noun Architecture a vault forming a half cylinder.
– DERIVATIVES **barrel-vaulted** adjective.

barren ▶ adjective **1** (of land) too poor to produce much or any vegetation.
■ (of a tree or plant) not producing fruit or seed. ■ archaic (of a woman) infertile. ■ (of a female animal) not pregnant or unable to become so. ■ figurative showing no results or achievements; unproductive.
2 (of a place or building) bleak and lifeless.
■ empty of meaning or value. ■ [predic.] (**barren of**) devoid of: *the room was barren of furniture.*
▶ noun (usu. **barrens**) chiefly N. Amer. a barren tract or tracts of land: *the Newfoundland barrens.*
– DERIVATIVES **barrenly** adverb, **barrenness** noun.
– ORIGIN Middle English: from Old French *barhaine*, of unknown origin.

barrenwort ▶ noun an Old World plant with cup-shaped spurred flowers, cultivated for its colourful foliage. It was formerly thought to cause infertility.
● Genus *Epimedium*, family Berberidaceae.

Barrett, Elizabeth, see **BROWNING**[1].

barrette /baˈrɛt/ ▶ noun a hairslide.
– ORIGIN early 20th cent.: from French, diminutive of *barre* 'bar'.

barricade /ˌbarɪˈkeɪd/ ▶ noun an improvised barrier erected across a street or other thoroughfare to prevent or delay the movement of opposing forces.
▶ verb [with obj.] block or defend with such a barrier: *they barricaded the building and occupied it all night.*
■ shut (oneself or someone) into a place by blocking all the entrances: *detainees who barricaded themselves into their dormitory.*
– ORIGIN late 16th cent.: from French, from *barrique* 'cask', from Spanish *barrica*; related to **BARREL** (barrels being often used to build barricades).

Barrie, Sir J. M. (1860–1937), Scottish dramatist and novelist; full name *James Matthew Barrie*. Barrie's most famous play is *Peter Pan* (1904), a fantasy for children about a boy who would not grow up.

barrier ▶ noun a fence or other obstacle that prevents movement or access.
■ Brit. a gate at a car park or railway station that controls access by being raised or lowered. ■ figurative a circumstance or obstacle that keeps people or things apart or prevents communication or progress: *a language barrier* | *the cultural barriers to economic growth* | *an attempt to break the 100-mile-an-hour barrier.*
– ORIGIN late Middle English (denoting a palisade or fortification defending an entrance): from Old French *barriere*, of unknown origin; related to **BARRE**.

barrier cream ▶ noun Brit. a cream used to protect the skin from damage or infection.

barrier method ▶ noun a method of contraception using a device or preparation which prevents live sperm from reaching an ovum.

barrier reef ▶ noun a coral reef close and running parallel to the shore but separated from it by a channel of deep water.

barring ▶ preposition except for; if not for: *barring accidents, we should win.*
– ORIGIN late 15th cent.: from the verb **BAR**[1] + **-ING**[2].

barrio /'bariəʊ/ ▶ noun (pl. **-os**) a district of a town in Spain and Spanish-speaking countries.
■(in the US) the Spanish-speaking quarter of a town or city.
– ORIGIN Spanish, perhaps from Arabic.

barrister (also **barrister-at-law**) ▶ noun chiefly Brit. a person called to the bar and entitled to practise as an advocate, particularly in the higher courts. Compare with **ATTORNEY**, **SOLICITOR**.
– ORIGIN late Middle English: from the noun **BAR**[1], perhaps on the pattern of *minister*.

barroom ▶ noun chiefly N. Amer. a room where alcoholic drinks are served over a counter.

barrow[1] ▶ noun Brit. a two-wheeled handcart used especially by street vendors.
■a wheelbarrow.
– DERIVATIVES **barrowload** noun.
– ORIGIN Old English *bearwe* 'stretcher, bier', of Germanic origin; related to **BEAR**[1].

barrow[2] ▶ noun Archaeology an ancient burial mound.
– ORIGIN Old English *beorg*, of Germanic origin; related to Dutch *berg*, German *Berg* 'hill, mountain'.

barrow boy ▶ noun Brit. a boy or man who sells wares from a barrow in the street.

Barry, Sir Charles (1795–1860), English architect, designer of the Houses of Parliament.

barry /'ba:ri/ ▶ adjective Heraldry divided into typically four, six, or eight equal horizontal bars of alternating tinctures.
– ORIGIN late 15th cent.: from French *barré* 'barred, striped', past participle of *barrer*.

Barrymore an American family of film and stage actors, notably **Lionel** (1878–1954), his sister **Ethel** (1879–1959), and their brother **John** (1882–1942).

Barsac /'ba:sak, French baʀsak/ ▶ noun [mass noun] a sweet white wine from the district of Barsac, a department of the Gironde in France.

bar sinister ▶ noun popular and erroneous term for **BEND SINISTER**.

bar stool ▶ noun a tall stool for customers at a bar to sit on.

Bart[1], Lionel (1930–99), English composer and lyricist. His musicals include *Oliver!* (1960).

Bart[2] ▶ abbreviation for Baronet.

bar tack ▶ noun a stitch made to strengthen a potential weak spot in a garment or other sewn item.
– DERIVATIVES **bar-tacked** adjective, **bar tacking** noun.

bartender ▶ noun a person serving drinks at a bar.

barter ▶ verb [with obj.] exchange (goods or services) for other goods or services without using money: *he often bartered a meal for drawings* | [no obj.] *the company is prepared to barter for Russian oil*.
▶ noun [mass noun] the action or system of bartering.
■the goods or services used for such an exchange: *I took a supply of coffee and cigarettes to use as barter*.
– DERIVATIVES **barterer** noun.
– ORIGIN late Middle English: probably from Old French *barater* 'deceive' (see **BARRATRY**).

Barth[1] /ba:θ/, John (Simmons) (b.1930), American novelist and short-story writer noted for complex experimental novels such as *The Sot-Weed Factor* (1960).

Barth[2] /ba:t, ba:θ/, Karl (1886–1968), Swiss Protestant theologian. His seminal work *Epistle to the Romans* (1919) established a neo-orthodox or theocentric approach to contemporary religious thought which remains influential on Protestant theology.
– DERIVATIVES **Barthian** /'ba:tɪən/ adjective.

Barthes /ba:t, French baʀt/, Roland (1915–80), French writer and critic. Barthes was a leading exponent of structuralism and semiology in literary criticism, while later works were influential in the development of deconstruction and post-structuralism.

Bartholdi /ba:'tɒldi, -'θɒldi, French baʀtɔldi/, (Frédéric) Auguste (1834–1904), French sculptor, known especially for the *Statue of Liberty*, which was presented to the US in 1886.

bartholinitis /ˌba:təlɪ'naɪtɪs/ ▶ noun [mass noun] Medicine inflammation of Bartholin's gland, typically accompanied by cysts or abscesses.

Bartholin's gland /'ba:təlɪnz/ ▶ noun Anatomy either of a pair of glands lying near the entrance of the vagina, which secrete a fluid that lubricates the vulva.
– ORIGIN early 18th cent.: named by Caspar *Bartholin* (1655–1738), Danish anatomist, as a tribute to his father.

Bartholomew, St /ba:'θɒlə,mju:/ an Apostle. He is said to have been flayed alive in Armenia, and is hence regarded as the patron saint of tanners. Feast day, 24 August.

Bartlett /'ba:tlɪt/ (also **Bartlett pear**) ▶ noun a dessert pear of a juicy early ripening variety.

Bartók /'ba:tɒk/, Béla (1881–1945), Hungarian composer. His work owes much to Hungarian folk music and includes six string quartets, three piano concertos, and the *Concerto for Orchestra* (1943).

Bartolommeo /ˌba:tɒlə'meɪəʊ, Italian ˌbartolom-'mɛɔ/, Fra (c.1472–1517), Italian painter; born *Baccio della Porta*. He was a Dominican friar and worked chiefly in Florence.

Barton, Sir Edmund (1849–1920), Australian statesman and jurist, first Prime Minister of Australia 1901–3.

bar tracery ▶ noun [mass noun] Architecture tracery with strips of stone across an aperture.

bartsia /'ba:tsɪə/ ▶ noun a herbaceous plant of the figwort family, some kinds being partly parasitic on the roots of other plants, especially grasses.
● *Bartsia* and related genera, family Scrophulariaceae: several species, in particular the common purple-flowered **red bartsia** (*Odontites verna*).
– ORIGIN modern Latin, named after Johann *Bartsch* (1709–38), Prussian botanist.

Baruch /'ba:rʊk/ a book of the Apocrypha, attributed in the text to Baruch, the scribe of Jeremiah (Jer. 36).

barwing ▶ noun an Asian bird of the babbler family, with barred feathers on the wings and tail.
● Genus *Actinodura*, family Timaliidae: several species.

barycentric /ˌbarɪ'sɛntrɪk/ ▶ adjective of or relating to the centre of gravity.
– DERIVATIVES **barycentre** noun.
– ORIGIN late 19th cent.: from Greek *barus* 'heavy' + **-CENTRIC**.

baryon /'barɪɒn/ ▶ noun Physics a subatomic particle, such as a nucleon or hyperon, that has a mass equal to or greater than that of a proton.
– DERIVATIVES **baryonic** adjective.
– ORIGIN 1950s: from Greek *barus* 'heavy' + **-ON**.

Baryshnikov /bə'rɪʃnɪˌkɒf/, Mikhail (Nikolaevich) (b.1948), American ballet dancer, born in Latvia of Russian parents. In 1974 he defected to the West while touring with the Kirov Ballet.

baryta /bə'raɪtə/ ▶ noun [mass noun] Chemistry barium hydroxide.
● Chem. formula: Ba(OH)$_2$.
– ORIGIN early 19th cent.: from **BARYTE**, on the pattern of words such as *soda*.

baryte /'barʌɪt, 'bɛ:-/ (also **barytes** /bə'rʌɪti:z/, **barite**) ▶ noun a mineral consisting of barium sulphate, typically occurring as colourless prismatic crystals or thin white flakes.
– ORIGIN mid 19th cent.: from **BARIUM** + variant endings based on Greek *-ites*.

baryton /'barɪtɒn/ ▶ noun an obsolete stringed instrument similar to a bass viol, with additional sympathetic strings, used mainly in 18th-century Germany and Austria.
– ORIGIN variant of **BARITONE**.

bas /bʌs/ ▶ exclamation Indian stop; enough: *Bas! Stop pestering me!*
– ORIGIN from Hindi, from Persian.

basal /'beɪs(ə)l/ ▶ adjective chiefly technical forming or belonging to a bottom layer or base.

basal cell carcinoma ▶ noun technical term for **RODENT ULCER**.

basal ganglia ▶ plural noun Anatomy a group of structures linked to the thalamus in the base of the brain and involved in coordination of movement.

basal metabolic rate ▶ noun the rate at which the body uses energy while at rest to maintain vital functions such as breathing and keeping warm.
– DERIVATIVES **basal metabolism** noun.

basalt /'basɔ:lt, -(ə)lt/ ▶ noun [mass noun] a dark fine-grained volcanic rock that sometimes displays a columnar structure. It is typically composed largely of plagioclase with pyroxene and olivine.
■a kind of black stoneware developed by Josiah Wedgwood.
– DERIVATIVES **basaltic** /bə'sɔ:ltɪk/ adjective.
– ORIGIN early 17th cent. (in the Latin form): from Latin *basaltes* (variant of *basanites*), from Greek *basanitēs*, from *basanos* 'touchstone'.

basanite /'basənʌɪt/ ▶ noun [mass noun] a dark grey or black basaltic rock consisting of plagioclase, augite, olivine, and a feldspathoid.
– ORIGIN late 18th cent.: from Latin *basanites* (see **BASALT**) + **-ITE**[1].

bascinet ▶ noun variant spelling of **BASINET**.

bascule /'baskju:l/ (also **bascule bridge**) ▶ noun a type of bridge with a section which can be raised and lowered using counterweights.
■a movable section of road forming part of such a bridge.
– ORIGIN late 19th cent.: earlier denoting a lever apparatus of which one end is raised while the other is lowered, from French (earlier *bacule*), 'see-saw', from *battre* 'to bump' + *cul* 'buttocks'.

base[1] ▶ noun **1** the lowest part or edge of something, especially the part on which it rests or is supported: *she sat down at the base of a tree*.
■Architecture the part of a column between the shaft and pedestal or pavement. ■ Botany & Zoology the end at which a part or organ is attached to the trunk or main part. ■ Geometry a line or surface on which a figure is regarded as standing: *the base of the triangle*. ■ Surveying a known line used as a geometrical base for trigonometry. ■ Heraldry the lowest part of a shield. ■ Heraldry the lower third of the field.
2 a conceptual structure or entity on which something draws or depends: *the town's economic base collapsed*.
■something used as a foundation or starting point for further work: *she uses existing data as the base for the study*. ■ [with modifier] a group of people regarded as supporting an organization, for example by buying its products: *a client base*.
3 the main place where a person works or stays: *she makes the studio her base*.
■chiefly Military a place used as a centre of operations by the armed forces or others; a headquarters: *he headed back to base*. ■ a place from which a particular activity can be carried out: *a base for shipping operations*.
4 a main or important element or ingredient to which other things are added: *soaps with a vegetable oil base*.
■[mass noun] a substance used as a foundation for make-up. ■ [mass noun] a substance into which a pigment is mixed to form paint, such as water, oil, or powdered aluminium hydroxide.
5 Chemistry a substance capable of reacting with an acid to form a salt and water, or (more broadly) of accepting or neutralizing hydrogen ions. Compare with **ALKALI**.
■Biochemistry a purine or pyrimidine group in a nucleotide or nucleic acid.
6 Electronics the middle part of a bipolar transistor, separating the emitter from the collector.
7 Linguistics the root or stem of a word or a derivative.
■the uninflected form of a verb.
8 Mathematics a number used as the basis of a numeration scale.
■a number in terms of which other numbers are expressed as logarithms.
9 Baseball one of the four stations that must be reached in turn to score a run.
▶ verb [with obj.] **1** (often **be based**) use something specified as the foundation or starting-point for (something): *the film is based on a novel by Pat Conroy* | *entitlement will be based on income*.
2 (usu. **be based**) situate at a specified place as the centre of operations: *the Science Policy Review Unit is based at the University of Sussex* | [as adj., in combination **-based**] *a London-based band*.
– PHRASES **get to first base** [usu. with negative] informal, chiefly N. Amer. achieve the first step towards one's objective. **off base** informal, chiefly N. Amer. mistaken. **touch base (with)** informal, chiefly N. Amer. briefly make or renew contact (with).
– ORIGIN Middle English: from Old French, from Latin *basis* 'base, pedestal', from Greek.

base[2] ▶ adjective (of a person or their actions or feelings) without moral principles; ignoble: *the electorate's baser instincts of greed and selfishness*.
■archaic denoting or befitting a person of low social class. ■ (of coins or other articles) not made of precious metal.

- DERIVATIVES **basely** adverb, **baseness** noun.
- ORIGIN late Middle English: from Old French *bas*, from medieval Latin *bassus* 'short' (found in classical Latin as a cognomen). Early senses included 'low, short' and 'of inferior quality'; from the latter arose a sense 'low in the social scale', and hence (mid 16th cent.) 'reprehensibly cowardly, selfish, or mean'.

baseball ▶ noun [mass noun] a ball game played between two teams of nine on a diamond-shaped circuit of four bases. It is played chiefly as a warm-weather sport in the US and Canada. ■ [count noun] the hard ball used in this game.

baseball cap ▶ noun a cotton cap of a kind originally worn by baseball players, with a large peak and an adjustable strap at the back.

baseboard ▶ noun North American term for **SKIRTING**.

baseborn ▶ adjective archaic of low birth or origin. ■ illegitimate.

base camp ▶ noun a camp from which mountaineering expeditions set out or from which a particular activity can be carried out.

base dressing ▶ noun [mass noun] the application of manure or fertilizer to the earth, which is then ploughed or dug in. Compare with **TOP DRESSING**. ■ manure or fertilizer applied in this way.

basehead ▶ noun US informal a habitual user of freebase or crack.
- ORIGIN 1980s: from a shortened form of **FREEBASE** + **-HEAD**[2].

base hit ▶ noun Baseball a fair ball hit such that the batter can advance safely to a base without an error by the team in the field.

base hospital ▶ noun a military hospital situated at some distance from the area of active operations during a war. ■ Austral./NZ a hospital serving a large rural area.

base jump (also **BASE jump**) ▶ noun a parachute jump from a fixed point, typically a high building or promontory, rather than an aircraft. ▶ verb [no obj.] [often as noun **base jumping**] perform such a jump.
- DERIVATIVES **base jumper** noun.
- ORIGIN 1980s: *base* from building, *a*ntenna-tower, *s*pan, *e*arth (denoting the types of structure used).

Basel /ˈbɑːzl/ German name for **BASLE**.

baseless ▶ adjective 1 without foundation in fact: *baseless allegations.*
2 Architecture (of a column) not having a base between the shaft and pedestal.
- DERIVATIVES **baselessly** adverb, **baselessness** noun.

baseline ▶ noun 1 a minimum or starting point used for comparisons.
2 (in tennis, volleyball, and other games) the line marking each end of a court. ■ Baseball the line between bases which a runner must stay close to when running.

baseload ▶ noun the permanent minimum load that a power supply system is required to deliver.

baseman ▶ noun (pl. **-men**) Baseball a fielder designated to cover either first, second, or third base.

basement ▶ noun the floor of a building which is partly or entirely below ground level. ■ Geology the oldest formation of rocks underlying a particular area.
- ORIGIN mid 18th cent.: probably from archaic Dutch *basement* 'foundation', perhaps from Italian *basamento* 'column base'.

basement membrane ▶ noun Anatomy a thin, delicate membrane of protein fibres and mucopolysaccharides separating an epithelium from underlying tissue.

base metal ▶ noun a common metal that is not considered precious, such as copper, tin, or zinc.

basenji /bəˈsɛndʒi/ ▶ noun (pl. **basenjis**) a smallish hunting dog of a central African breed, which growls and yelps but does not bark.
- ORIGIN 1930s: a local word.

base pair ▶ noun Biochemistry a pair of complementary bases in a double-stranded nucleic acid molecule, consisting of a purine in one strand linked by hydrogen bonds to a pyrimidine in the other. Cytosine always pairs with guanine, and adenine with thymine (in DNA) or uracil (in RNA).

- DERIVATIVES **base pairing** noun.

baseplate ▶ noun a sheet of metal forming the bottom of an object.

base rate ▶ noun (in the UK) the interest rate set by the Bank of England for lending to other banks, used as the benchmark for interest rates generally.

bases plural form of **BASE**[1] and **BASIS**.

base unit ▶ noun a fundamental unit that is defined arbitrarily and not by combinations of other units. The base units of the SI system are the metre, kilogram, second, ampere, kelvin, mole, and candela.

bash ▶ verb [with obj.] informal strike hard and violently: *she bashed him with the book | his head's been bashed about a bit | [no obj.] people bashed on the doors.*
■ (**bash something in**) damage or break something by striking it violently: *the car's rear window had been bashed in.* ■ [no obj.] (**bash into**) collide with: *the other vehicle bashed into the back of them.* ■ figurative criticize severely: *bashing the trade unions.*
▶ noun informal 1 a heavy blow: *a bash on the head.*
2 [usu. with modifier] informal a party or social event: *a birthday bash.*
3 [in sing.] Brit. informal an attempt: *she will have a bash at anything.*
- ORIGIN mid 17th cent. (as a verb): imitative, perhaps a blend of **BANG**[1] and **SMASH**, **DASH**, etc. Sense 2 is a 20th-cent. usage.
▶ **bash on** continue despite difficulties.
bash something out produce something rapidly without preparation or attention to detail.

basha /ˈbɑːʃə/ ▶ noun an improvised shelter for one or a few soldiers.
- ORIGIN 1920s (originally denoting a bamboo hut with a thatched roof): Assamese.

bashful ▶ adjective reluctant to draw attention to oneself; shy.
- DERIVATIVES **bashfully** adverb, **bashfulness** noun.
- ORIGIN late 15th cent.: from obsolete *bash* 'make or become abashed' (from **ABASH**) + **-FUL**.

bashing ▶ noun [mass noun] [usu. in combination] informal violent physical assault: *nine incidents of gay-bashing were reported to the police.*
■ figurative severe criticism: *press-bashing.*

Bashkir /baʃˈkɪə/ ▶ noun 1 a member of a Muslim people living in the southern Urals.
2 [mass noun] the Turkic language of this people, with about 1 million speakers.
▶ adjective of or relating to this people or their language.
- ORIGIN via Russian from Turkic *Başkurt.*

Bashkiria /baʃˈkɪərɪə/ an autonomous republic in central Russia, west of the Urals; pop. 3,964,000 (1990); capital, Ufa. Also called **BASHKIR AUTONOMOUS REPUBLIC**, **BASHKORTOSTAN** /baʃˌkɔːtəˈstɑːn, -ˈstan/.

bashment /ˈbaʃmənt/ ▶ noun W. Indian a large popular party or dance.

basho /ˈbaʃəʊ/ ▶ noun (pl. same or **-os**) a sumo wrestling tournament.
- ORIGIN Japanese, from *ba* 'place, occasion' + *shō* 'place, locality'.

BASIC ▶ noun [mass noun] a simple high-level computer programming language that uses familiar English words, designed for beginners and formerly utilized on microcomputers.
- ORIGIN 1960s: acronym from *Beginners' All-purpose Symbolic Instruction Code.*

basic ▶ adjective 1 forming an essential foundation or starting point; fundamental: *certain basic rules must be obeyed | the laying down of arms is basic to the agreement.*
■ offering or consisting in the minimum required without elaboration or luxury: *the food was good, if a bit basic.* ■ common to or required by everyone; primary and ineradicable or inalienable: *basic human rights.*
2 Chemistry having the properties of a base, or containing a base; having a pH above 7. Often contrasted with **ACID** or **ACIDIC**; compare with **ALKALINE**.
■ Geology (of rock, especially lava) relatively poor in silica. ■ Metallurgy relating to or denoting steel-making processes involving lime-rich refractories and slags.
▶ noun (**basics**) informal the essential facts or principles of a subject or skill: *I learnt the basics of programming on a course | teachers are going back to basics to encourage pupils to learn English.*

■ essential food and other supplies: *people are facing a shortage of basics like flour.*
- ORIGIN mid 19th cent.: from **BASE**[1] + **-IC**.

basically ▶ adverb [often as submodifier] in the most essential respects; fundamentally: *we started from a basically simple idea.*
■ [sentence adverb] used to indicate that a statement summarizes the most important aspects, or gives a roughly accurate account, of a more complex situation: *I basically played the same thing every night.*

Basic English ▶ noun [mass noun] a simplified form of English limited to 850 selected words, intended for international communication.

basicity /beɪˈsɪsɪti/ ▶ noun [mass noun] Chemistry the number of hydrogen atoms replaceable by a base in a particular acid.

basic oxygen process ▶ noun a steel-making process in which a jet of oxygen is delivered by a lance on to a molten mixture of pig iron and scrap steel in a retort lined with a basic refractory. Excess carbon is burnt away, producing enough heat to keep the iron molten, and the oxidized impurities are removed as gases or slag.

basic pay ▶ noun [mass noun] a standard rate of pay before additional payments such as allowances and bonuses.

basic slag ▶ noun [mass noun] slag formed as a by-product of basic steel-making processes. It is generally rich in lime and sometimes also in phosphates, and can be used as fertilizer.

basic wage ▶ noun a minimum wage earned before additional payments such as overtime.
■ [in sing.] Austral./NZ the minimum living wage, as determined by industrial tribunal.

basidiomycete /bəˌsɪdɪəˈmʌɪsiːt/ ▶ noun (pl. **basidiomycetes** /-ˈmʌɪsiːts, -mʌɪˈsiːtiːz/) Botany a fungus whose spores develop in basidia. They include the majority of familiar mushrooms and toadstools. Compare with **ASCOMYCETE**.
● Subdivision Basidiomycotina (formerly class Basidiomycetes): several classes.
- ORIGIN late 19th cent.: Anglicized singular of modern Latin *Basidiomycetes*, from *basidium* (see **BASIDIUM**) + Greek *mukētes* 'fungi'.

basidium /bəˈsɪdɪəm/ ▶ noun (pl. **basidia** /-dɪə/) a microscopic club-shaped spore-bearing structure produced by certain fungi.
- ORIGIN mid 19th cent.: modern Latin, from Greek *basidion*, diminutive of *basis* (see **BASIS**).

Basie /ˈbeɪsi/, Count (1904–84), American jazz pianist, organist, and bandleader; born *William Basie.* In 1935 he formed a big band, known as the Count Basie Orchestra, which became one of the most successful bands of the swing era.

basil /ˈbaz(ə)l, -zɪl/ ▶ noun [mass noun] 1 an aromatic plant of the mint family, native to tropical Asia. The leaves are used as a culinary herb, especially in Mediterranean dishes.
● Genus *Ocimum*, family Labiatae: several species, in particular the annual **sweet basil** (O. basilicum).
2 (also **wild basil**) a similar European plant which grows in hedges and scrub.
● *Clinopodium vulgare*, family Labiatae.
- ORIGIN late Middle English: from Old French *basile*, via medieval Latin from Greek *basilikon*, neuter of *basilikos* 'royal' (see **BASILICA**).

Basil, St (c.330–79), Doctor of the Church, bishop of Caesarea; known as **St Basil the Great**. Brother of St Gregory of Nyssa, he staunchly opposed Arianism and put forward a monastic rule which is still the basis of monasticism in the Eastern Church. Feast day, 14 June.

basilar /ˈbasɪlə/ ▶ adjective of or situated at the base of something, especially of the skull, or of the organ of Corti in the ear.
- ORIGIN mid 16th cent.: from modern Latin *basilaris*, formed irregularly from Latin *basis* (see **BASIS**).

Basildon /ˈbazɪldən/ a town in SE Essex; pop. 157,500 (1991). It was developed as a new town from 1949.

basilect /ˈbasɪlɛkt, ˈbeɪsɪ-/ ▶ noun Linguistics a less prestigious dialect or variety of a particular language. Often contrasted with **ACROLECT**.
- DERIVATIVES **basilectal** /ˈlɛkt(ə)l/ adjective.

Basilian /bəˈzɪlɪən/ ▶ adjective of or relating to St Basil the Great, or the order of monks and nuns following his monastic rule.
▶ noun a Basilian monk or nun.

b

basilica /bə'sɪlɪkə, -'zɪl-/ ▶ noun a large oblong hall or building with double colonnades and a semicircular apse, used in ancient Rome as a law court or for public assemblies. ■ a similar building used as a Christian church. ■ the name given to certain churches granted special privileges by the Pope.
– DERIVATIVES **basilican** adjective.
– ORIGIN mid 16th cent.: from Latin, literally 'royal palace', from Greek *basilikē*, feminine of *basilikos* 'royal', from *basileus* 'king'.

Basilicata /bə,sɪlɪ'kɑːtə/ a region of southern Italy, lying between the 'heel' of Apulia and the 'toe' of Calabria; capital, Potenza.

basilisk /'bazɪlɪsk/ ▶ noun 1 a mythical reptile with a lethal gaze or breath, hatched by a serpent from a cock's egg.
■ Heraldry another term for COCKATRICE.
2 a long, slender, and mainly bright green lizard found in Central America, the male of which has a crest running from the head to the tail. It can swim well, and is able to run on its hind legs across the surface of water.
● *Basiliscus plumifrons*, family Iguanidae.
– ORIGIN late Middle English: via Latin from Greek *basiliskos* 'little king, serpent', from *basileus* 'king'.

basin ▶ noun 1 a bowl for washing, typically attached to a wall and having taps connected to a water supply; a washbasin.
2 a wide, round open container, typically one used for preparing food or for holding liquid.
3 a circular or oval valley or natural depression on the earth's surface, especially one containing water: *the Indian Ocean basin.*
■ the tract of country drained by a river and its tributaries, or which drains into a lake or sea: *the Amazon basin.* ■ an enclosed area of water where boats can be moored. ■ Geology a circumscribed rock formation where the strata dip towards the centre.
– DERIVATIVES **basinful** noun (pl. -**fuls**).
– ORIGIN Middle English: from Old French *bacin*, from medieval Latin *bacinus*, from *bacca* 'water container', perhaps of Gaulish origin.

basinet /'basɪnɪt/ (also **bascinet**) ▶ noun historical a light, close-fitting steel helmet, typically having a visor.
– ORIGIN Middle English: from Old French *bacinet* 'little basin'.

basipetal /beɪ'sɪpɪt(ə)l/ ▶ adjective Botany (of growth or development) downwards towards the base or point of attachment. The opposite of ACROPETAL.
■ (of the movement of dissolved substances) inwards from the shoot and root apices.
– DERIVATIVES **basipetally** adverb.
– ORIGIN mid 19th cent.: from BASIS + Latin *petere* 'seek' + -AL.

basis ▶ noun (pl. **bases** /-siːz/) the underlying support or foundation for an idea, argument, or process: *trust is the only basis for a good working relationship.*
■ [with adj.] the system or principles according to which an activity or process is carried on: *she needed coaching on a regular basis.* ■ the justification for or reasoning behind something: *on the basis of these statistics important decisions are made.*
– ORIGIN late 16th cent. (denoting a base or pedestal): via Latin from Greek, 'stepping'. Compare with BASE[1].

basis point ▶ noun Finance one hundredth of one per cent (used chiefly in expressing differences of interest rates).

bask ▶ verb [no obj.] lie exposed to warmth and light, typically from the sun, for relaxation and pleasure.
■ (**bask in**) figurative revel in and make the most of (something pleasing): *he went on basking in the glory of his first book.*
– ORIGIN late Middle English (originally in the sense 'bathe'): perhaps related to Old Norse *batha* 'bathe'.

Baskerville /'baskəvɪl/ ▶ noun [mass noun] a typeface much used in books.
– ORIGIN early 19th cent.: named after John *Baskerville* (1706–75), English printer, designer of the typeface.

basket ▶ noun 1 a container used to hold or carry things, typically made from interwoven strips of cane or wire.
■ Finance a group or range of currencies or investments: *a basket of ten currencies.*
2 Basketball a net fixed on a hoop used as the goal.
■ a goal scored.

3 Brit. informal euphemism for BASTARD (in sense 2).
– DERIVATIVES **basketful** noun.
– ORIGIN Middle English: from Old French *basket*, of unknown ultimate origin.

basketball ▶ noun [mass noun] a game played between two teams of five players in which goals are scored by throwing a ball through a netted hoop fixed at each end of the court.
■ [count noun] the inflated ball used in this game.

basket case ▶ noun informal a person or thing regarded as useless or unable to cope.
– ORIGIN early 20th cent.: originally US slang denoting a soldier who had lost all four limbs, thus unable to move independently.

basket hilt ▶ noun a sword hilt with a guard resembling basketwork.
– DERIVATIVES **basket-hilted** adjective.

Basket Maker ▶ noun a member of a culture of the south-western US, forming the early stages of the Anasazi culture, from the 1st century BC until *c.*700 AD. The name comes from the basketry and other woven fragments found in early cave sites.

basketry ▶ noun [mass noun] the craft of basket-making.
■ baskets collectively.

basket shell ▶ noun a small burrowing bivalve mollusc, the left valve of which fits into the larger right valve.
● Genus *Corbula*, family Corbulidae.

basket weave ▶ noun [mass noun] a style of weave or a pattern resembling basketwork.

basketwork ▶ noun [mass noun] material woven in the style of a basket.
■ the craft of making such material.

basking shark ▶ noun a large shark which feeds exclusively on plankton and typically swims slowly close to the surface, found chiefly in the open ocean.
● *Cetorhinus maximus*, the only member of the family Cetorhinidae.

Basle /bɑːl/ a commercial and industrial city on the Rhine in NW Switzerland; pop. 171,000 (1991). French name **BÂLE**, German name **BASEL**.

basmati /bas'mɑːti, -z-/ (also **basmati rice**) ▶ noun [mass noun] a kind of long-grain Indian rice with a delicate fragrance.
– ORIGIN from Hindi *bāsmatī*, literally 'fragrant'.

basophil /'beɪsə(ʊ)fɪl/ ▶ noun Physiology a basophilic white blood cell.

basophilic /,beɪsə(ʊ)'fɪlɪk/ ▶ adjective Physiology (of a cell or its contents) readily stained with basic dyes.

Basotho /bæ'suːtuː/ ▶ plural noun (sing. **Mosotho**) the South Sotho people collectively, living chiefly in Lesotho.
– ORIGIN the name in Sesotho.

Basque /bask, bɑːsk/ ▶ noun 1 a member of a people living in the Basque Country of France and Spain. Culturally one of the most distinct groups in Europe, the Basques were largely independent until the 19th century; the Basque separatist movement ETA carried on an armed struggle against the Spanish government until September 1998, when it declared a ceasefire.
2 [mass noun] the language of this people, which is not known to be related to any other language. It has about 1 million speakers.
▶ adjective of or relating to the Basques or their language.
– ORIGIN from French, from Latin *Vasco*; compare with GASCON.

basque /bask, bɑːsk/ ▶ noun a close-fitting bodice extending from the shoulders to the waist and typically with a short continuation below waist level.
– ORIGIN mid 19th cent.: from **BASQUE**, referring to Basque dress.

Basque Country a region of the western Pyrenees in both France and Spain, the homeland of the Basque people. French name **PAYS BASQUE**.

Basque Provinces an autonomous region of northern Spain, on the Bay of Biscay; capital, Vitoria.

Basra /'bazrə/ an oil port of Iraq, on the Shatt al-Arab waterway; pop. 616,700 (est. 1985).

bas-relief /'basrɪ,liːf, 'bɑː(s)-/ ▶ noun [mass noun] another term for *low relief* (see RELIEF sense 4).

■ [count noun] a sculpture, carving, or moulding in low relief.
– ORIGIN early 17th cent. (as *basse relieve*): from Italian *basso-rilievo* 'low relief', later altered to the French form.

bass[1] /beɪs/ ▶ noun a voice, instrument, or sound of the lowest range, in particular:
■ the lowest adult male singing voice. ■ a singer with such a voice. ■ a part written for such a voice. ■ [as modifier] denoting the member of a family of instruments that is the lowest in pitch: *a bass clarinet.* ■ informal a bass guitar or double bass. ■ [mass noun] the low-frequency output of a radio or audio system, corresponding to the bass in music.
– ORIGIN late Middle English: alteration of BASE[2], influenced by BASSO.

bass[2] /bas/ ▶ noun (pl. same or **basses**) 1 the common European freshwater perch.
2 any of a number of fish similar to or related to this, in particular:
● a mainly marine fish found in temperate waters (family Percichthyidae or Moronidae, including *Dicentrarchus labrax* of European waters and genus *Morone* of North America). ● an American freshwater fish of the sunfish family, popular with anglers (genera *Ambloplites* and *Micropterus*, family Centrarchidae). ● a sea bass.
– ORIGIN late Middle English: alteration of dialect *barse*, of Germanic origin; related to Dutch *baars* and German *Barsch*.

bass[3] /bas/ ▶ noun another term for BAST.
– ORIGIN late 17th cent.: alteration.

bass clef ▶ noun Music a clef placing F below middle C on the second-highest line of the stave.

bass drum ▶ noun a large drum of indefinite low pitch.

Bassein /bæ'seɪn/ a port on the Irrawaddy delta in SW Burma (Myanmar); pop. 144,100 (1983).

Basse-Normandie /bas'nɔːməndi, French basnɔrmɑ̃di/ a region of NW France, on the coast of the English Channel, including the Cherbourg peninsula and the city of Caen.

basset (also **basset hound**) ▶ noun a sturdy hunting dog of a breed with a long body, short legs, and long, drooping ears.
– ORIGIN early 17th cent.: from French, diminutive of *bas* 'low', from medieval Latin *bassus* 'short'.

Basseterre /bas'tɛː/ the capital of St Kitts and Nevis in the Leeward Islands, on the island of St Kitts; pop. 12,600 (est. 1994).

Basse-Terre /bas'tɛː/ the main island of Guadeloupe in the Caribbean.

basset horn ▶ noun an alto clarinet in F, typically with a bent mouthpiece and upturned bell.
– ORIGIN mid 19th cent.: from German, translation of French *cor de bassette*, from Italian *corno di bassetto*, from *corno* 'horn' + *di* 'of' + *bassetto* (diminutive of *basso* 'low', from Latin *bassus* 'short').

bassinet /,basɪ'nɛt/ ▶ noun a child's wicker cradle.
– ORIGIN mid 19th cent.: from French, diminutive of *bassin* 'basin'; compare with BASINET.

bassist /'beɪsɪst/ ▶ noun a person who plays a double bass or bass guitar.

basslet /'baslɪt/ ▶ noun a small, brightly coloured fish related to the sea basses.
● Genera *Gramma* and *Lipogramma*, family Grammidae: several species.

basso /'basəʊ/ ▶ noun (pl. **bassos** or **bassi** /-siː/) a bass voice or vocal part.
– ORIGIN early 18th cent.: Italian, 'low', from Latin *bassus* 'short, low'.

basso continuo ▶ noun see CONTINUO.

bassoon ▶ noun a bass woodwind instrument of the oboe family, with a doubled-back tube over four feet long, played with a double reed.
– DERIVATIVES **bassoonist** noun.
– ORIGIN early 18th cent.: from French *basson*, from Italian *bassone*, from *basso* 'low', from Latin *bassus* 'short, low'.

basso profundo /prə'fʌndəʊ/ ▶ noun (pl. **bassos profundos** or **bassi profundi** /-di/) a bass singer with an exceptionally low range.
– ORIGIN mid 19th cent.: Italian, from *basso* 'low' + *profondo* 'deep'.

basso-relievo /,basəʊrɪ'liːvəʊ/ ▶ noun (pl. -**os**) another term for *low relief* (see RELIEF sense 4).
– ORIGIN mid 17th cent.: from Italian *basso-rilievo*.

Bass Strait /bas/ a channel separating Tasmania from the mainland of Australia.

bass viol ▶ **noun** a bass instrument of the viol family; a viola da gamba.
■N. Amer. a double bass.

basswood /ˈbaswʊd/ ▶ **noun** a North American lime tree with large leaves, commonly planted as a street tree in the US.
• *Tilia americana*, family Tiliaceae.
– ORIGIN late 17th cent.: from **BASS**[3] + **WOOD**.

bast /bast/ ▶ **noun** (also **bast fibre**) [mass noun] fibrous material from a plant, in particular the inner bark of a tree such as the lime, used as fibre in matting, cord, etc.
■Botany the phloem or vascular tissue of a plant.
– ORIGIN Old English *bæst*; related to Dutch *bast*, German *Bast*; of unknown origin.

bastard /ˈbɑːstəd, ˈbast-/ ▶ **noun 1** archaic or derogatory a person born of parents not married to each other.
2 informal an unpleasant or despicable person.
■[with adj.] a person of a specified kind: *he was a lucky bastard.* ■ a difficult or awkward thing, undertaking, or situation: *it's been a **bastard of a** week.*
▶ **adjective** [attrib.] **1** archaic or derogatory born of parents not married to each other; illegitimate.
2 (of a thing) no longer in its pure or original form; debased: *a bastard Darwinism.*
■(of a handwriting script or typeface) showing a mixture of different styles.
– DERIVATIVES **bastardy** noun (only in sense 1 of the noun).
– ORIGIN Middle English: via Old French from medieval Latin *bastardus*, probably from *bastum* 'packsaddle'; compare with Old French *fils de bast*, literally 'packsaddle son' (i.e. the son of a mule driver who uses a packsaddle for a pillow and is gone by morning).

USAGE In the past the word **bastard** was the standard term in both legal and non-legal use for 'an illegitimate child'. Today, however, it has little importance as a legal term and is retained today in this older sense only as a term of abuse.

bastardize (also **-ise**) ▶ **verb** [with obj.] **1** [often as adj. **bastardized**] corrupt or debase (something such as a language or art form), typically by adding new elements: *a strange, bastardized form of French.*
2 archaic declare (someone) illegitimate.
– DERIVATIVES **bastardization** noun.

bastard-trench ▶ **verb** [with obj.] Horticulture dig (ground) by digging over the lower soil with the topsoil temporarily removed.

bastard wing ▶ **noun** a group of small quill feathers on the first digit of a bird's wing.

baste[1] ▶ **verb** [with obj.] pour fat or juices over (meat) during cooking in order to keep it moist.
– ORIGIN late 15th cent.: of unknown origin.

baste[2] ▶ **verb** [with obj.] Needlework tack with long, loose stitches in preparation for sewing.
– ORIGIN late Middle English: from Old French *bastir* 'sew lightly', ultimately of Germanic origin and related to **BAST**.

baste[3] ▶ **verb** [with obj.] informal, dated beat (someone) soundly; thrash.
– ORIGIN mid 16th cent.: perhaps a figurative use of **BASTE**[1].

Bastet /ˈbastɛt/ Egyptian Mythology a goddess usually shown as a woman with the head of a cat, wearing one gold earring. See also **SEKHMET**.

bast fibre ▶ **noun** see **BAST**.

Bastia /ˈbastjə/ the chief port of Corsica; pop. 38,730 (1990).

bastide /baˈstiːd/ ▶ **noun** (in southern France) a country house.
■historical a fortified village or town in France.
– ORIGIN early 16th cent.: via Old French from Provençal *bastida*.

Bastille /baˈstiːl/ a fortress in Paris built in the 14th century and used in the 17th–18th centuries as a state prison. Its storming by the mob on 14 July 1789 marked the start of the French Revolution.
– ORIGIN via Old French from Provençal *bastida*, from *bastir* 'build'.

bastinado /ˌbastɪˈneɪdəʊ, -ˈnɑːdəʊ/ chiefly historical ▶ **noun** [mass noun] a form of punishment or torture that involves caning the soles of someone's feet.
▶ **verb** (**-oes**, **-oed**) [with obj.] (usu. **be bastinadoed**) punish or torture (someone) in such a way.
– ORIGIN late 16th cent. (denoting a blow with a stick): from Spanish *bastonada*, from *bastón* 'stick, cudgel', from late Latin *bastum* 'stick'.

bastion /ˈbastɪən/ ▶ **noun** a projecting part of a fortification built at an angle to the line of a wall, so as to allow defensive fire in several directions.
■a natural rock formation resembling such a fortification. ■ figurative an institution, place, or person strongly maintaining particular principles, attitudes, or activities: *cricket's last bastion of discrimination.*
– ORIGIN mid 16th cent.: from French, from Italian *bastione*, from *bastire* 'build'.

bastnaesite /ˈbastneɪˌsʌɪt/ ▶ **noun** [mass noun] a yellow to brown mineral consisting of a fluoride and carbonate of cerium and other rare earth metals.
– ORIGIN late 19th cent.: from *Bastnäs*, the name of a district in Västmanland, Sweden, + **-ITE**[1].

basuco /bəˈsuːkəʊ/ ▶ **noun** [mass noun] impure or low-grade cocaine, especially when mixed with coca paste and tobacco and cannabis.
– ORIGIN 1980s: from Colombian Spanish; perhaps related to Spanish *bazucar* 'shake violently'.

Basutoland /bəˈsuːtəʊland/ former name (until 1966) for **LESOTHO**.

bat[1] ▶ **noun** an implement with a handle and a solid surface, typically of wood, used for hitting the ball in games such as cricket, baseball, and table tennis.
■a turn at playing with a bat. ■ a person batting, especially in cricket; a batsman. ■ each of a pair of objects resembling table tennis bats, used by a person on the ground to guide a taxiing aircraft. ■ a slab on which pottery is formed, dried, or fired.
▶ **verb** (**batted**, **batting**) **1** [no obj.] (of a team or a player in sports such as cricket and baseball) take the role of hitting rather than throwing the ball.
2 [with obj. and adverbial of direction] hit at (someone or something) with the flat of one's hand: *he batted the flies away.*
– PHRASES **off one's own bat** Brit. at one's own instigation; spontaneously. **right off the bat** N. Amer. at the very beginning; straight away.
– ORIGIN late Old English *batt* 'club, stick, staff', perhaps partly from Old French *batte*, from *battre* 'to strike'.
▶**bat around** (or **about**) informal, chiefly N. Amer. travel widely, frequently, or casually.
bat something around (or **about**) informal, chiefly N. Amer. discuss an idea or proposal casually or idly.
bat for (or **go to bat for**) informal, chiefly N. Amer. defend the interests of; support: *she turned out to have the law batting for her.*

bat[2] ▶ **noun 1** a mainly nocturnal mammal capable of sustained flight, with membranous wings that extend between the fingers and limbs.
• Order Chiroptera: many families and numerous species. The large tropical fruit bats (suborder Megachiroptera) generally have good eyesight and feed mainly on fruit; the numerous smaller bats (suborder Microchiroptera) are mouse-like in appearance, mainly insectivorous, and use ultrasonic echolocation.
2 (usu. **old bat**) informal a woman regarded as unattractive or unpleasant. [ORIGIN: from *bat*, a slang term for 'prostitute', or from **BATTLEAXE**.]
– PHRASES **have bats in the** (or **one's**) **belfry** informal be eccentric or mad. **like a bat out of hell** informal very fast and wildly.
– ORIGIN late 16th cent.: alteration, perhaps by association with medieval Latin *batta*, *blacta*, of Middle English *bakke*, of Scandinavian origin.

bat[3] ▶ **verb** (**batted**, **batting**) [with obj.] flutter (one's eyelashes), typically in a flirtatious manner: *she batted her long dark eyelashes at him.*
– PHRASES **not bat** (or **without batting**) **an eyelid** (or **eye**) informal show (or showing) no surprise or concern: *she paid the bill without batting an eyelid.*
– ORIGIN late 19th cent. (originally US): from dialect and US *bat* 'to wink, blink', variant of obsolete *bate* 'to flutter'.

Bata /ˈbɑːtə/ a seaport in Equatorial Guinea; pop. 17,000 (est. 1986).

Batak /ˈbatək/ ▶ **noun** (pl. same or **Bataks**) **1** a member of a people of the northern part of Sumatra.
2 [mass noun] the Indonesian language of this people, with about 6 million speakers.
▶**adjective** of or relating to the Batak or their language.
– ORIGIN the name in Batak.

Batan Islands /bəˈtɑːn/ the most northerly islands of the Philippines.

batata /bəˈtɑːtə/ ▶ **noun** [mass noun] (in the southern Caribbean) sweet potato.
– ORIGIN via Spanish from Taino.

Batavia /bəˈteɪvɪə/ former name (until 1949) for **DJAKARTA**.

Batavian historical or archaic ▶ **adjective** of or relating to the ancient Germanic people who inhabited the island of Betuwe between the Rhine and the Waal (now part of the Netherlands).
■of or relating to the people of the Netherlands. ■ of or relating to Djakarta in Indonesia (formerly the Dutch East Indies).
▶**noun** a Batavian person.
– ORIGIN from Latin *Batavia* (from *Batavi* 'the people of Betuwe') + **-AN**.

Batavian lettuce ▶ **noun** another term for *Batavian endive* (see **ENDIVE**).

batch ▶ **noun** a quantity or consignment of goods produced at one time.
■informal a number of things or people regarded as a group or set: *a **batch of** loyalists and sceptics.* ■ Computing a group of records processed as a single unit, usually without input from a user.
▶**verb** [with obj.] arrange (things) in sets or groups.
– ORIGIN late 15th cent. (in the senses 'process of baking', 'quantity produced at one baking'): based on an Old English word related to *bacan* (see **BAKE**). Current senses date from the early 18th cent.

batch file ▶ **noun** a computer file containing a list of instructions to be carried out in turn.

batch processing ▶ **noun** [mass noun] the performing of an industrial process on material in batches of a limited quantity or number.
■Computing the processing of previously collected jobs in a single batch.

Batdambang variant spelling of **BATTAMBANG**.

bate[1] (also **bait**) ▶ **noun** [in sing.] Brit. informal, dated an angry mood.
– ORIGIN mid 19th cent.: from the verb **BAIT** 'torment', expressing the notion 'state of a baited person'.

bate[2] ▶ **verb** [no obj.] Falconry (of a hawk) beat the wings in agitation and flutter off the perch.
– ORIGIN late Middle English: from Old French *batre* 'to beat' (see also **BATTER**[1]).

bat-eared fox ▶ **noun** a small fox found in southern and East Africa, with very large ears that are used to locate insect prey.
• *Otocyon megalotis*, family Canidae.

bateau /ˈbatəʊ/ ▶ **noun** (pl. **bateaux** /-əʊz/) a light flat-bottomed riverboat used in Canada.
– ORIGIN early 18th cent.: French, 'boat'.

bateau mouche /ˌbatəʊ ˈmuːʃ, French bato muʃ/ ▶ **noun** (pl. **bateaux mouches** pronunc. same) a pleasure boat that takes sightseers on the Seine in Paris.
– ORIGIN French, literally 'fly boat', because of the boat's mobility.

bated ▶ **adjective** (in phrase **with bated breath**) in great suspense; very anxiously or excitedly: *he waited for a reply to his offer with bated breath.*
– ORIGIN late 16th cent.: from the past participle of obsolete *bate* 'restrain', from **ABATE**.

USAGE The spelling **baited breath** instead of **bated breath** is a common mistake. 14 per cent of citations for this idiom in the British National Corpus are for the incorrect spelling.

bateleur /ˈbat(ə)ləː/ (also **bateleur eagle**) ▶ **noun** a short-tailed African eagle with mainly black plumage and a bare red face.
• *Terathopius ecaudatus*, family Accipitridae.
– ORIGIN mid 19th cent.: from French, literally 'acrobat, juggler' (with reference to the side-to-side tilting motion of the bird in flight).

Bateman, H. M. (1887–1970), Australian-born British cartoonist; full name *Henry Mayo Bateman*. He is known for the series of cartoons entitled 'The Man Who …', which illustrated social gaffes based on snobbery.

Bates, H. E. (1905–74), English novelist and short-story writer; full name *Herbert Ernest Bates*. Notable novels: *The Darling Buds of May* (1958).

Batesian mimicry /ˈbeɪtsɪən/ ▶ **noun** [mass noun] Zoology mimicry in which an edible animal is protected by its resemblance to one avoided by predators. Compare with **MÜLLERIAN MIMICRY**.
– ORIGIN late 19th cent.: named after Henry W. Bates (1825–92), the English naturalist who first described it.

Bates method ▶ **noun** [mass noun] a technique

b

1840) and Ferdinand (1760–1826) *Bauer*, Austrian botanical draughtsmen.

Bauhaus /ˈbaʊhaʊs/ a school of applied arts established by Walter Gropius in Weimar in 1919 and noted for its refined functionalist approach to architecture and industrial design.
– ORIGIN German, 'house of architecture', from *Bau* 'building' + *Haus* 'house'.

baulk /bɔːlk, bɔːk/ (chiefly US also **balk**) ▶ verb [no obj.] hesitate or be unwilling to accept an idea or undertaking: *he baulked at such a drastic solution.*
■ [with obj.] thwart or hinder (a plan or person): *he raised every objection he could to baulk this plan.* ■ [with obj.] (**baulk someone of**) prevent a person or animal from having (something): *a tiger baulked of its prey.* ■ [with obj.] archaic miss or refuse (a chance or invitation). ■ (with reference to a horse) refuse or cause to refuse to go on.
▶ noun **1** a roughly squared timber beam.
2 the area on a billiard table between the baulk line and the bottom cushion, within which in some circumstances a ball is protected from a direct stroke.
3 Baseball an illegal action made by a pitcher that may deceive a base-runner.
4 a ridge left unploughed between furrows.
– ORIGIN late Old English *balc*, from Old Norse *bálkr* 'partition'. The original use was 'unploughed ridge', later 'land left unploughed by mistake', hence 'blunder, omission', giving rise to the verb use 'miss (a chance)'. A late Middle English sense 'obstacle' gave rise to the verb senses 'hesitate' and 'hinder'.

baulk line ▶ noun a transverse line marked on a billiard table, extending the diameter of the D to the sides of the table.

baulky ▶ adjective British spelling of **BALKY**.

bauxite /ˈbɔːksʌɪt/ ▶ noun [mass noun] an amorphous clayey rock that is the chief commercial ore of aluminium. It consists largely of hydrated alumina with variable proportions of iron oxides.
– DERIVATIVES **bauxitic** adjective.
– ORIGIN mid 19th cent.: from French, from *Les Baux* (the name of a village near Arles in SE France, near which it was first found) + **-ITE**[1].

bavardage /ˌbavaˈdɑːʒ, French bavaʀdaʒ/ ▶ noun [mass noun] idle gossip.
– ORIGIN French, from *bavarder* 'to chatter', from *bavard* 'talkative', from *bave* 'drivel'.

Bavaria /bəˈvɛːrɪə/ a state of southern Germany, formerly an independent kingdom; capital, Munich. German name **BAYERN**.

Bavarian ▶ adjective of or relating to Bavaria, its people, or their language.
▶ noun **1** a native or inhabitant of Bavaria.
2 [mass noun] the dialect of German used in Bavaria.

bavarois /ˌbavəˈwɑː/ (also **bavaroise** /ˌbavəˈwɑːz/) ▶ noun a dessert containing gelatin and whipped cream, served cold.
– ORIGIN French, literally 'Bavarian.'

bawbee /ˈbɔːbiː/ ▶ noun Scottish a coin of low value.
■ a former silver coin worth three (later six) Scottish pennies.
– ORIGIN mid 16th cent.: from the name of the laird of Sille*bawby*, mint-master under James V.

bawd /bɔːd/ ▶ noun archaic a woman in charge of a brothel.
– ORIGIN late Middle English: shortened from obsolete *bawdstrot*, from Old French *baudestroyt* 'procuress', from *baude* 'shameless'.

bawdry ▶ noun [mass noun] obscenity in speech or writing.

bawdy ▶ adjective (**bawdier**, **bawdiest**) dealing with sexual matters in a comical way; humorously indecent.
▶ noun [mass noun] humorously indecent talk or writing.
– DERIVATIVES **bawdily** adverb, **bawdiness** noun.

bawdy house ▶ noun archaic a brothel.

bawl ▶ verb **1** [reporting verb] shout or call out noisily and unrestrainedly: [with direct speech] *'Move!' bawled the drill corporal* | [with obj.] *lustily bawling out the hymns.*
2 [no obj.] weep or cry noisily: [as adj. **bawling**] *bawling babies.*
▶ noun a loud, unrestrained shout.
– ORIGIN late Middle English (in the sense '(of an animal) howl, bark'): imitative; possibly related to medieval Latin *baulare* 'to bark' or Icelandic *baula* 'to low'.

▶**bawl someone out** informal reprimand someone angrily: *tales of how she bawled out employees.*

bawley /ˈbɔːli/ ▶ noun (pl. **-eys**) a fishing smack of a kind formerly used on the coasts of Essex and Kent.
– ORIGIN late 19th cent.: of unknown origin.

bawn /bɔːn/ ▶ noun **1** Irish & Canadian an area of grassy land near a house; a meadow.
2 Canadian a flat expanse of rocks on a beach, on which fish are spread to dry.
– ORIGIN from Irish.

Bax, Sir Arnold (Edward Trevor) (1883–1953), English composer, noted for tone poems such as *Tintagel* (1917).

bay[1] ▶ noun a broad inlet of the sea where the land curves inwards: [in place names] *Sandy Bay* | *the Bay of Biscay.*
■ an indentation or recess in a range of hills or mountains.
– ORIGIN late Middle English: from Old French *baie*, from Old Spanish *bahia*, of unknown origin.

bay[2] (also **bay tree**, **bay laurel**, or **sweet bay**) ▶ noun an evergreen Mediterranean shrub with deep green leaves and purple berries. Its aromatic leaves are used in cookery and were formerly used to make triumphal crowns for victors.
● *Laurus nobilis*, family Lauraceae.
– ORIGIN late Middle English (denoting the laurel berry): from Old French *baie*, from Latin *baca* 'berry'.

bay[3] ▶ noun a recessed or enclosed area, in particular:
■ a space created by a window-line projecting outwards from a wall. ■ a section of wall between two buttresses or columns, especially in the nave of a church. ■ [with modifier] a compartment with a specified function in a motor vehicle, aircraft, or ship: *an engine bay.* ■ an area specially allocated or marked off: *a loading bay.* ■ (also **bay platform**) Brit. a short terminal platform at a railway station also having through lines.
– ORIGIN late Middle English: from Old French *baie*, from *baer* 'to gape', from medieval Latin *batare*, of unknown origin.

bay[4] ▶ adjective (of a horse) brown with black points.
▶ noun a bay horse.
– ORIGIN Middle English: from Old French *bai*, from Latin *badius*.

bay[5] ▶ verb [no obj.] (of a dog, especially a large one) bark or howl loudly.
■ (of a group of people) shout loudly, typically to demand something: *the crowd bayed for an encore.* ■ [with obj.] archaic bay at: *a pack of wolves baying the moon.*
▶ noun [mass noun] the sound of baying, especially that of hounds in close pursuit of their quarry.
– PHRASES **at bay** forced to face or confront one's attackers or pursuers; cornered. **bay for blood** demand punishment or retribution. **bring someone/thing to bay** trap or corner a person or animal being hunted or chased. **hold** (or **keep**) **someone/thing at bay** prevent someone or something from approaching or having an effect.
– ORIGIN Middle English (as a noun): from Old French (*a*)*bai* (noun), (*a*)*baiier* (verb) 'to bark', of imitative origin.

baya /ˈbʌɪə/ (also **baya weaver**) ▶ noun a weaver bird that typically has a brown back, yellow cap, and black face, common throughout the Indian subcontinent and in SE Asia.
● *Ploceus philippinus*, family Ploceidae.
– ORIGIN from Hindi.

bayadère /ˌbʌɪəˈdɛː/ ▶ noun a Hindu dancing girl, especially one at a southern Indian temple.
– ORIGIN from French, from Portuguese *bailadeira*, from *bailar* 'to dance' (related to medieval Latin *ballare* 'to dance').

Bayard /ˈbeɪɑːd, French bajaʀ/, Pierre du Terrail, Chevalier de (1473–1524), French soldier. He became known as the knight 'sans peur et sans reproche' (fearless and above reproach).

bayberry ▶ noun (pl. **-ies**) a North American shrub with aromatic leathery leaves and waxy berries. Also called **WAX MYRTLE**.
● Genus *Myrica*, family Myricaceae: several species, in particular *M. cerifera*.
– ORIGIN late 17th cent.: from **BAY**[2] + **BERRY**.

Bayern /ˈbaɪɛn/ German name for **BAVARIA**.

Bayes' theorem Statistics a theorem describing how the conditional probability of each of a set of possible causes for a given observed outcome can be computed from knowledge of the probability of each cause and the conditional probability of the outcome of each cause.
– DERIVATIVES **Bayesian** adjective.
– ORIGIN mid 19th cent.: named after Thomas *Bayes* (1702–61), English mathematician.

Bayeux Tapestry /bʌɪˈjə/ an embroidered cloth, about 70 metres (230 feet) long, illustrating events leading up to the Norman Conquest and made between 1066 and 1077 for the bishop of Bayeux in Normandy.

Baykal, Lake variant spelling of **BAIKAL, LAKE**.

Baykonur variant spelling of **BAIKONUR**.

bay laurel ▶ noun another term for **BAY**[2].

bay leaf ▶ noun the aromatic dried leaf of the bay tree, used in cooking.

Baylis, Lilian Mary (1874–1937), English theatre manager, noted for her management of the Old Vic and for her initiative in reopening the old Sadler's Wells Theatre in 1931.

Bay of Bengal, Bay of Fundy, etc. see **BENGAL, BAY OF; FUNDY, BAY OF;** etc.

bayonet ▶ noun **1** a sword-like stabbing blade which may be fixed to the muzzle of a rifle for use in hand-to-hand fighting.
2 [as modifier] denoting a fitting for a light bulb, camera lens, or other appliance which is engaged by being pushed into a socket and then twisted to lock it in place.
▶ verb (**bayoneted**, **bayoneting**) [with obj.] stab (someone) with a bayonet.
– ORIGIN late 17th cent. (denoting a kind of short dagger): from French *baïonnette*, from *Bayonne*, the name of a town in SW France, where they were first made.

bayou /ˈbʌɪuː/ ▶ noun (pl. **bayous**) (in the southern US) a marshy outlet of a lake or river.
– ORIGIN mid 18th cent.: from Louisiana French, from Choctaw *bayuk*.

bay platform ▶ noun see **BAY**[3].

Bayreuth /bʌɪˈrɔɪt/ a town in Bavaria where Wagner is buried and where festivals of his operas are held regularly.

bay rum ▶ noun [mass noun] a perfume, chiefly for the hair, distilled originally from rum and bayberry leaves.

Bay State informal name for **MASSACHUSETTS**.

bay tree ▶ noun another term for **BAY**[2].

bay window ▶ noun a window built to project outwards from an outside wall.

baza /ˈbɑːzə/ ▶ noun an Asian and Australasian hawk related to and resembling the cuckoo hawks of Africa.
● Genus *Aviceda*, family Accipitridae: three species, including the **crested baza** or crested hawk (*A. subcristata*).
– ORIGIN modern Latin, via Hindi from Arabic *bāz*, denoting a goshawk.

bazaar /bəˈzɑː/ ▶ noun a market in a Middle-Eastern country.
■ a fund-raising sale of goods, typically for charity. ■ dated a large shop selling miscellaneous goods.
– ORIGIN late 16th cent.: from Italian *bazarro*, from Turkish, from Persian *bāzār* 'market'.

bazoo /bəˈzuː/ ▶ noun US informal a person's mouth.
– ORIGIN late 19th cent.: of unknown origin; compare with Dutch *bazuin* 'trombone, trumpet'.

bazooka ▶ noun **1** a short-range tubular rocket launcher used against tanks.
2 a kazoo shaped like a trumpet.
– ORIGIN 1930s (in sense 2; originally US): apparently from US slang **BAZOO** in the original sense 'kazoo'.

bazoom ▶ noun (usu. **bazooms**) informal, chiefly N. Amer. a woman's breast.
– ORIGIN 1950s: probably an alteration of **BOSOM**.

BB ▶ symbol for ■ Brit. double-black (used in describing grades of pencil lead). ■ N. Amer. a standard size of lead pellet used in air rifles.

BBC ▶ abbreviation for British Broadcasting Corporation.

BBC English ▶ noun [mass noun] a form of standard spoken English associated with BBC announcers.

bbl. ▶ abbreviation for barrels (especially of oil).

b-boy ▶ noun informal, chiefly US a young man involved with hip-hop culture.

– ORIGIN 1980s: *b*-probably from the noun **BEAT** or from **BREAK-DANCING**.

BBQ informal ▶ **abbreviation for** a barbecue.

BBS Computing ▶ **abbreviation for** bulletin board system.

BC ▶ **abbreviation for** ■ before Christ (used to indicate that a date is before the Christian era). ■ British Columbia (in official postal use).

USAGE BC is normally written in small capitals and placed **after** the numerals, as in *72* BC (**not** BC *72*). Compare with **AD**.

bcc (also **b.c.c.**) ▶ **abbreviation for** blind carbon copy (used as an indication that a duplicate has been or should be sent to another person without the knowledge of the main recipient). Compare with **CC**.

BCD ▶ **abbreviation for** binary coded decimal.

BCE ▶ **abbreviation for** before the Common Era (used of dates before the Christian era, especially by non-Christians).

B-cell ▶ **noun** Physiology another term for **B-LYMPHOCYTE**.

BCF ▶ **abbreviation for** ■ bromochlorodifluoromethane, a substance formerly used in fire extinguishers. ■ British Cycling Federation.

BCG ▶ **abbreviation for** Bacillus Calmette-Guérin, an anti-tuberculosis vaccine.

BD ▶ **abbreviation for** ■ Bachelor of Divinity. ■ Bangladesh (international vehicle registration).

Bde ▶ **abbreviation for** Brigade.

bdellium /ˈdɛlɪəm/ ▶ **noun** [mass noun] a fragrant resin produced by a number of trees related to myrrh, used in perfumes.

– ORIGIN late Middle English: via Latin from Greek *bdellion*, of Semitic origin.

Bdr Brit. ▶ **abbreviation for** Bombardier.

BDS ▶ **abbreviation for** Bachelor of Dental Surgery.

BE ▶ **abbreviation for** ■ Bachelor of Education. ■ Bachelor of Engineering. ■ bill of exchange.

Be ▶ **symbol for** the chemical element beryllium.

be ▶ **verb** (sing. present **am**; **are**; **is**; pl. present **are**; 1st and 3rd sing. past **was**; 2nd sing. past and pl. past **were**; present subjunctive **be**; past subjunctive **were**; present participle **being**; past participle **been**) **1** (usu. **there is/are**) exist: *there are no easy answers | there once was a man | there must be something wrong | I think, therefore I am.*
■ be present: *there were no curtains around the showers | are there any castles in this area?*
2 [with adverbial] occur; take place: *the exhibition will be in November | the opening event is on October 16 | that was before the war.*
■ occupy a position in space: *Salvation Street was on his left | she was not at the window.* ■ stay in the same place or condition: *he's a tough customer—**let him be**.* ■ attend: *I'm at school doing A levels.* ■ come; go; visit: *he's from Missouri | I have just been to Thailand | the doctor's been twice today.*
3 [as copular verb] having the state, quality, identity, nature, role, etc., specified: *Amy was 91 | the floor was uneven | I want to be a teacher | father was not well | it will be Christmas soon | 'Be careful,' Mr Carter said.*
■ cost: *the tickets were £25.* ■ amount to: *one and one is two.* ■ represent: *let A be a square matrix of order n.* ■ signify: *we were everything to each other.* ■ consist of; constitute: *the monastery was several three-storey buildings.*
▶ **auxiliary verb 1** used with a present participle to form continuous tenses: *they are coming | he had been reading | she will be waiting.*
2 used with a past participle to form the passive voice: *it was done | it is said | his book will be published.*
3 [with infinitive] used to indicate something that is due or destined to happen: *construction is to begin next summer | his mum was never to see him win.*
■ used to express obligation or necessity: *you are to follow these orders | they said I was to remain on board.* ■ used to express possibility: *these snakes are **to be** found in North America | she was nowhere **to be** seen.* ■ used to hypothesize about something that might happen: ***if I were** to lose | **if I was to** tell you, you'd think I was mad | were she to cure me, what could I offer her?*
4 archaic used with the past participle of intransitive verbs to form perfect tenses: *I am returned.*

– PHRASES **as/that was** as someone or something was previously called: *former Sex Pistol John Lydon (Rotten, as was).* **the be-all and end-all** informal a feature of an activity or a way of life that is of greater importance than any other. **be oneself** act naturally, according to one's character and instincts. **been** (or **been and gone**) **and ——** informal used to express surprise or annoyance at someone's actions: *they've been and carted Mum off to hospital.* **been there, done that** see **THERE**. **be that as it may** see **MAY**[1]. **be there for someone** be available to support or comfort someone while they are experiencing difficulties or adversities. **not be oneself** not feel in one's usual physical or mental state. **-to-be** [in combination] of the future: *my bride-to-be.*

– ORIGIN Old English *bēon*, an irregular and defective verb, whose full conjugation derives from several originally distinct verbs. The forms *am* and *is* are from an Indo-European root shared by Latin *sum* and *est*. The forms *was* and *were* are from an Indo-European root meaning 'remain'. The forms *be* and *been* are from an Indo-European root shared by Latin *fui* 'I was', *fio* 'I become' and Greek *phuein* 'bring forth, cause to grow'. The origin of *are* is uncertain.

▶ **be about** see **ABOUT** (sense 1 of the preposition).
be at be doing or trying to do: *what are you at there?*
be away leave or set out at once: *I'm away to my work.*
be off [often in imperative] go away; leave: ***be off with** you!*

USAGE For a discussion of whether it is correct to say *that must **be he** at the door* and *it **is I*** rather than *that must **be him** at the door* and *it **is me***, see **usage** at **PERSONAL PRONOUN**.

be- ▶ **prefix** forming verbs. **1** all over; all round: *bespatter.*
■ thoroughly; excessively: *bewilder.*
2 (added to intransitive verbs) expressing transitive action: *bemoan.*
3 (added to adjectives and nouns) expressing transitive action: *befool | befriend.*
4 (added to nouns) affect with: *befog.*
■ (added to adjectives) cause to be: *befoul.*
5 (forming adjectives ending in *-ed*) having; covered with: *bejewelled.*

– ORIGIN Old English, weak form of *bī* 'by'.

beach ▶ **noun** a pebbly or sandy shore, especially by the sea between high- and low-water marks.
▶ **verb** [with obj.] run or haul up (a boat or ship) on to a beach: *at the water's edge a rowing boat was beached |* [no obj.] *crews would not beach for fear of damaging their crafts.*
■ [often as adj. **beached**] cause (a whale or similar animal) to become stranded out of the water. ■ [no obj.] (of a whale or similar animal) become stranded out of the water. ■ (of an angler) land (a fish) on a beach. ■ figurative leave (someone) at a loss: *competitive procurement seems to have beached several firms.*

– ORIGIN mid 16th cent. (denoting shingle on the seashore): perhaps related to Old English *bæce*, *bece* 'brook' (an element that survives in place names such as Wisbech and Sandbach), assuming an intermediate sense 'pebbly river valley'.

beach ball ▶ **noun** a large inflatable ball used for playing games on the beach.

beach buggy ▶ **noun** a low wide-wheeled motor vehicle for recreational driving on sand.

beach bum ▶ **noun** informal a person who spends time idly on or around a beach.

beachcomber ▶ **noun 1** a vagrant who makes a living by searching beaches for articles of value and selling them.
2 a long wave rolling in from the sea.

beachfront ▶ **noun** chiefly N. Amer. another term for **SEAFRONT**.

beachhead ▶ **noun** a defended position on a beach taken from the enemy by landing forces, from which an attack can be launched.

– ORIGIN Second World War (originally US): formed on the pattern of *bridgehead*.

Beach-la-mar /ˌbiːtʃlәˈmɑː/ ▶ **noun** variant spelling of **BISLAMA**.

beach plum ▶ **noun** a maritime shrub related to the plum, found on the east coast of North America.
● *Prunus maritima*, family Rosaceae.
■ the edible fruit of this tree.

beachside ▶ **adjective** [attrib.] next to the beach.

beach volleyball ▶ **noun** [mass noun] a form of volleyball played on sand by teams of two players.

beachwear ▶ **noun** [mass noun] clothing suitable for wearing on the beach, though not necessarily for swimming in.

beacon ▶ **noun** a fire or light set up in a high or prominent position as a warning, signal, or celebration.
■ [often in place names] Brit. a hill suitable for such a fire or light: *Ivinghoe Beacon.* ■ a light or other visible object serving as a signal, warning, or guide, especially at sea or on an airfield. ■ a radio transmitter whose signal helps to fix the position of a ship, aircraft, or spacecraft.

– ORIGIN Old English *bēacn* 'sign, portent, ensign', of West Germanic origin; related to **BECKON**.

beaconfish ▶ **noun** (pl. same or **-fishes**) a popular aquarium characin from tropical South America, with a red and gold spot near the base of the tail fin and another near the eye.
● *Hemigrammus ocellifer*, family Characidae.

bead ▶ **noun 1** a small piece of glass, stone, or similar material, typically rounded and perforated for threading with others to make a necklace or rosary or for sewing on to fabric.
2 something resembling a bead or a string of beads, in particular:
■ a drop of a liquid on a surface: ***beads of** sweat.* ■ a small knob forming the foresight of a gun. ■ the reinforced inner edge of a pneumatic tyre that grips the rim of the wheel. ■ an ornamental plaster moulding resembling a string of beads or having a semicircular cross section. ■ a narrow moulding of any cross section.
▶ **verb** [with obj.] **1** [often as adj. **beaded**] decorate or cover with beads: *a beaded evening bag.*
■ string (beads) together.
2 (often **be beaded**) cover (a surface) with drops of moisture: *his face was **beaded with** perspiration.*

– PHRASES **draw** (or **get**) **a bead on** chiefly N. Amer. take aim at with a gun. **tell one's beads** use the beads of a rosary in counting prayers.

– ORIGIN Old English *gebed* 'prayer', of Germanic origin; related to Dutch *bede* and German *Gebet*, also to **BID**[2]. Current senses derive from the use of a rosary, each bead representing a prayer.

beaded lizard ▶ **noun** a lizard with a stout body, short limbs, a large blunt head, and bead-like scales, occurring from the south-western US to Guatemala. Beaded lizards are the only venomous lizards.
● Family Helodermatidae and genus *Heloderma*: the **Mexican beaded lizard** (*H. horridum*) and the Gila monster.

beading ▶ **noun** [mass noun] **1** decoration or ornamental moulding resembling a string of beads or having a semicircular cross section.
2 the bead of a tyre.

beadle ▶ **noun** Brit. a ceremonial officer of a church, college, or similar institution.
■ Scottish a church officer attending on the minister. ■ historical a minor parish officer dealing with petty offenders.

– ORIGIN Old English *bydel* 'a person who makes a proclamation', gradually superseded in Middle English by forms from Old French *bedel*, ultimately of Germanic origin; related to German *Büttel*, also to **BID**[1]. Compare with **BEDEL**.

beadlet anemone ▶ **noun** a common European coastal sea anemone which is typically rust-red with several rings of tentacles around the mouth.
● *Actinia equina*, order Actiniaria.

beadsman ▶ **noun** (pl. **-men**) historical a pensioner provided for by a benefactor in return for prayers, especially one living in an almshouse.

beadwork ▶ **noun** [mass noun] decorative work made of beads.

beady ▶ **adjective** (of a person's eyes) small, round, and gleaming.
■ (of a look) bright and penetrating.

– DERIVATIVES **beadily** adverb, **beadiness** noun.

beady-eyed ▶ **adjective** having small, glinting eyes.
■ informal keenly observant.

beagle ▶ **noun** a small hound of a breed with a short coat, used for hunting hares.
▶ **verb** [no obj.] [usu. as noun **beagling**] hunt with beagles.

– DERIVATIVES **beagler** noun.

– ORIGIN late 15th cent.: perhaps from Old French *beegueule* 'open-mouthed', from *beer* 'open wide' + *gueule* 'throat'.

Beagle Channel a channel through the islands of Tierra del Fuego at the southern tip of South America.

– ORIGIN named after HMS *Beagle*, the ship of Charles Darwin's voyage of 1831–6.

beak¹ ▶ noun a bird's horny projecting jaws; a bill.
■ the similar horny projecting jaw of other animals, for example a turtle or squid. ■ informal a person's nose: *she can't wait to stick her beak in.* ■ a projection at the prow of an ancient warship, typically shaped to resemble the head of a bird or other animal, used to pierce the hulls of enemy ships.
– DERIVATIVES **beaked** adjective [in combination] *a yellow-beaked alpine chough*, **beak-like** adjective.
– ORIGIN Middle English: from Old French *bec*, from Latin *beccus*, of Celtic origin.

beak² ▶ noun Brit. informal a magistrate or a schoolmaster.
– ORIGIN late 18th cent.: probably from criminals' slang.

beaked whale ▶ noun a medium-sized whale with elongated jaws that form a beak, typically showing marked differences in size and body form between the sexes.
● Family Ziphiidae: four genera and several species, including the bottlenose whales.

beaker ▶ noun Brit. a tall drinking container, typically tumbler-shaped and made of plastic.
■ a lipped cylindrical glass container for laboratory use. ■ archaic or poetic/literary a large drinking container with a wide mouth. ■ Archaeology a waisted pot characteristic of graves of the Beaker folk.
– ORIGIN Middle English (in the sense 'large drinking container'): from Old Norse *bikarr*, perhaps based on Greek *bikos* 'drinking bowl'.

Beaker folk ▶ plural noun Archaeology a late Neolithic and early Bronze Age European people (*c.*2700–1700 BC), named after distinctive waisted pots (**Beaker ware**) that were associated with their burials and appear to have been used for alcoholic drinks. It is now thought that the Beaker folk were not a separate race, but that the use of such pots spread as a result of migration, trade, and fashion.

beaky ▶ adjective informal (of a person's nose) resembling a bird's beak; hooked.
■ (of a person) having such a nose.

Beale, Dorothea (1831–1906), English educationist. She was principal of Cheltenham Ladies' College 1858–1906 and a campaigner for women's suffrage and higher education.

beam ▶ noun 1 a long, sturdy piece of squared timber or metal spanning an opening or part of a building, typically to support the roof or floor above.
■ a narrow, raised horizontal piece of squared timber on which a gymnast balances while performing exercises. ■ a horizontal piece of squared timber or metal supporting the deck and joining the sides of a ship. ■ Nautical the direction of an object visible from the port or starboard side of a ship when it is perpendicular to the centre line of the vessel: *there was land in sight* **on the port beam**. ■ a ship's breadth at its widest point: *a cutter with a beam of 16 feet.* ■ [in sing.] informal the width of a person's hips: *notice how broad in the beam she's getting?* ■ the main stem of a stag's antler. ■ the crossbar of a balance. ■ an oscillating shaft which transmits the vertical piston movement of a beam engine to the crank or pump. ■ the shank of an anchor. ■ historical the main timber of a horse-drawn plough.
2 a ray or shaft of light: *a beam of light flashed in front of her* | *the torch beam dimmed perceptibly.*
■ a directional flow of particles or radiation: *beams of electrons.* ■ a series of radio or radar signals emitted as a navigational guide for ships or aircraft.
3 [in sing.] a radiant or good-natured look or smile: *a beam of satisfaction.*
▶ verb 1 [with obj. and adverbial of direction] transmit (a radio signal or broadcast) in a specified direction: *beaming a distress signal into space* | [no obj.] *the TV company begins beaming into homes in the new year.*
■ [with obj.] (**beam someone up/down**) (in science fiction) transport someone instantaneously to another place, especially to or from a spaceship. [ORIGIN: phrase from the American television series *Star Trek*.]
2 [no obj., with adverbial of direction] (of a light or light source) shine brightly: *the sun's rays beamed down.*
3 [no obj.] smile radiantly: *she beamed with pleasure* | [as adj. **beaming**] *a beaming smile.*
■ [with obj.] express (an emotion) with a radiant smile: *the instructress beamed her approval.*
– PHRASES **a beam in one's eye** a fault that is greater in oneself than in the person one is finding fault with. [ORIGIN: with biblical allusion to Matt. 7:3.] **off**, or **way off**, **beam** informal on the wrong track; mistaken. **on the beam** informal on the right

track. **on her** (or **its**) **beam-ends** (of a ship) heeled over on its side; almost capsized. **on one's beam-ends** near the end of one's resources; desperate. **put the low beams on** N. Amer. dip the headlights of one's car.
– ORIGIN Old English *bēam* 'tree, beam', of West Germanic origin; related to Dutch *boom* and German *Baum.*

beam compass (also **beam compasses**) ▶ noun a drawing compass consisting of a horizontal rod or beam connected by sliding sockets to two vertical legs, used for drawing large circles.

beam engine ▶ noun a stationary steam engine with a large oscillating beam that transmits the vertical movement of the pistons to a crank or pump.

beamer ▶ noun Cricket a ball bowled directly at a batsman's head or upper body without bouncing (regarded as unsporting).

Beamon /ˈbiːmən/, Bob (b.1946), American long jumper; full name *Robert Beamon.* At the 1968 Olympic Games he set a world record that stood until 1991.

beam sea ▶ noun Nautical a sea which is rolling against a ship's side approximately at right angles.

beam splitter ▶ noun a device for dividing a beam of light or other electromagnetic radiation into two or more separate beams.

beamy ▶ adjective (of a ship) broad-beamed.

bean ▶ noun 1 an edible seed, typically kidney-shaped, growing in long pods on certain leguminous plants.
■ the hard seed of coffee, cocoa, and certain other plants.
2 a leguminous plant that bears such seeds in pods.
● *Phaseolus* and other genera, family Leguminosae: numerous species, including the **runner bean** (*P. coccineus*), **French bean** (*P vulgaris*), and **broad bean** (*Vicia faba*).
3 (N. Amer. also **beans**) [with negative] informal a very small amount or nothing at all of something (used emphatically): *there is not a single bean of substance in the report* | *I didn't know beans about being a step-parent.*
■ used in reference to money: *he didn't have a bean.* [ORIGIN: from early 19th-cent. slang denoting a sovereign or guinea.]
4 informal, dated a person's head, especially when regarded as a source of common sense.
▶ verb [with obj.] informal, chiefly N. Amer. hit (someone) on the head: *she picked up a rock and beaned him on the forehead.*
– PHRASES **full of beans** informal lively; in high spirits. **a hill** (or **row**) **of beans** [with negative] anything of any importance or value: *three little people don't amount to a hill of beans in this crazy world.* **know how many beans make five** Brit. informal be intelligent; have one's wits about one. **old bean** Brit. informal, dated a friendly form of address, typically to a man.
– ORIGIN Old English *bēan*, of Germanic origin; related to Dutch *boon* and German *Bohne.*

beanbag ▶ noun 1 a small bag filled with dried beans and used in children's games.
2 a large cushion, typically filled with polystyrene beads, used as a seat.

bean counter ▶ noun informal a person, typically an accountant or bureaucrat, perceived as placing excessive emphasis on controlling expenditure and budgets.

bean curd ▶ noun another term for TOFU.

beanery ▶ noun (pl. **-ies**) N. Amer. informal a cheap restaurant.

beanfeast ▶ noun Brit. informal a celebratory party with plentiful food and drink.
– ORIGIN early 19th cent.: from BEAN + FEAST. The term originally denoted an annual dinner given to employees by their employers, where beans and bacon were regarded as an indispensable dish.

bean goose ▶ noun a grey goose with orange-yellow bill and legs, breeding in the arctic tundra of Lapland and Siberia and overwintering in parts of Europe and Asia.
● *Anser fabalis*, family Anatidae.

beanie ▶ noun (pl. **-ies**) a small close-fitting hat worn on the back of the head.
– ORIGIN 1940s (originally US): perhaps from BEAN (in the sense 'head') + -IE.

beano ▶ noun (pl. **-os**) Brit. informal a party.
– ORIGIN late 19th cent.: abbreviation of BEANFEAST.

beanpole ▶ noun a stick for supporting bean plants.
■ informal a tall, thin person.

bean sprouts ▶ plural noun the sprouting seeds of certain beans, especially mung beans, used chiefly in oriental cookery.

beanstalk ▶ noun the stem of a bean plant, proverbially fast-growing and tall.

bear¹ ▶ verb (past **bore**; past participle **borne**) [with obj.]
1 (of a person) carry: *he was bearing a tray of brimming glasses* | *the warriors bore lances tipped with iron.*
■ (of a vehicle or boat) convey (passengers or cargo): *steamboats bear the traveller out of Kerrerra Sound.* ■ have or display as a visible mark or feature: *many of the papers bore his flamboyant signature.* ■ be called by (a name or title): *he bore the surname Tiller.* ■ [with adverbial] (**bear oneself**) carry or conduct oneself in a specified manner: *she bore herself with dignity.*
2 support: *walls which cannot bear a stone vault.*
■ take responsibility for: *no one likes to bear the responsibility for such decisions* | *the expert's fee shall be borne by the tenant.* ■ be able to accept or stand up to: *it is doubtful whether either of these distinctions would bear scrutiny.*
3 endure (an ordeal or difficulty): *she bore the pain stoically.*
■ [with modal and negative] manage to tolerate (a situation or experience): *she could hardly bear his sarcasm* | [with infinitive] *I cannot bear to see you hurt* ■ (**cannot bear someone/thing**) strongly dislike: *I can't bear caviar.*
4 give birth to (a child): *she bore sixteen daughters* | [with two objs] *his wife had borne him a son.*
■ (of a tree or plant) produce (fruit or flowers).
5 [no obj., with adverbial of direction] turn and proceed in a specified direction: *bear left and follow the old drove road.*
– PHRASES **bear arms 1** carry firearms. **2** wear or display a coat of arms. **bear the brunt of** see BRUNT. **bear the burden of** suffer the consequences of. **bear fruit** figurative yield positive results. **bear someone a grudge** nurture a feeling of resentment against someone. **bear a hand** archaic help in a task or enterprise. **bear in mind** remember and take into account: [with clause] *you need to bear in mind that the figures vary from place to place.* **bear someone malice** (or **ill will**) [with negative] wish someone harm. **bear a relation** (or **relationship**) **to** [with negative] be logically consistent with: *the map didn't seem to bear any relation to the roads.* **bear a resemblance** (or **similarity**) **to** resemble. **bear the stamp of** strongly resemble in a way that suggests influence: *their tactics bear the stamp of Soviet military training.* **bear witness** (or **testimony**) **to** testify to: *little is left to bear witness to the past greatness of the city.* ■ state or show one's belief in: *people bearing witness to Jesus.* **be borne in upon** come to be realized by: *the folly of her action was borne in on her.* **bring pressure to bear on** attempt to coerce. **bring to bear 1** muster and use to effect: *she had reservations about how much influence she could bring to bear.* **2** aim (a weapon): *bringing his rifle to bear on a distant target.* **does not bear thinking about** is too terrible to contemplate. **grin and bear it** see GRIN.
– ORIGIN Old English *beran*, of Germanic origin; from an Indo-European root shared by Sanskrit *bharati*, Greek *pherein*, and Latin *ferre.*

USAGE Until the 18th century **borne** and **born** were simply variant forms of the past participle of **bear**, used interchangeably with no distinction in meaning. By around 1775, however, the present distinction in use had become established. At that time **borne** became the standard past participle used in all the senses listed in this dictionary entry, e.g. *she has* **borne** *you another son*, *the findings have been* **borne** *out*, and so on. **Born** became restricted to just one very common use, which remains the case today: in the passive, without *by*, as the standard, neutral way to refer to birth: *she was* **born** *in 1965*, *he was* **born** *lucky*, or *I was* **born** *and bred in Gloucester.*

▶ **bear away** another way of saying *bear off.*
bear down (of a woman in labour) exert downwards pressure in order to push the baby out.
bear down on move directly towards someone or something in a purposeful or intimidating manner. ■ take strict measures to deal with: *a commitment to bear down on inflation.*
bear off Sailing change course away from the wind.
bear on be relevant to (something): *two kinds of theories which bear on literary studies.* ■ [with adverbial] be a burden on (someone): *the extension of VAT to*

domestic fuel will **bear hard on** *the low paid.*

bear something out support or confirm something: *this assumption is not borne out by any evidence.*

bear up remain cheerful in the face of adversity: *she's bearing up remarkably well.*

bear with be patient or tolerant with.

bear[2] ▶ **noun 1** a large, heavy mammal which walks on the soles of its feet, with thick fur and a very short tail. Bears are related to the dog family but have an omnivorous diet.

• Family Ursidae: several genera and species.

■ a teddy bear. ■ informal a rough, ill-mannered, or uncouth person. ■ a large, heavy, cumbersome man. ■ (**the Bear**) informal a nickname for Russia.

2 Stock Exchange a person who sells shares hoping to buy them back later at a lower price. Often contrasted with **BULL**[1]. [ORIGIN: said to be from a proverb warning against 'selling the bear's skin before one has caught the bear'.]

3 (pl. same or **bears**) informal, chiefly US a police officer.

– PHRASES **like a bear with a sore head** Brit. informal (of a person) very irritable. **loaded for bear** N. Amer. informal fully prepared for any eventuality, especially a confrontation or challenge.

– ORIGIN Old English *bera*, of West Germanic origin; related to Dutch *beer* and German *Bär*.

bearable ▶ **adjective** able to be endured.

– DERIVATIVES **bearability** noun, **bearably** adverb.

bear-baiting ▶ **noun** [mass noun] historical a form of entertainment which involved setting dogs to attack a captive bear.

bearberry ▶ **noun** (pl. **-ies**) a creeping dwarf shrub of the heather family, with pinkish flowers and bright red berries.

• Genus *Arctostaphylos*, family Ericaceae: several species, in particular *A. uva-ursi* of circumpolar regions.

bearcat ▶ **noun** a bear-like climbing mammal, especially the red panda.

beard ▶ **noun 1** a growth of hair on the chin and lower cheeks of a man's face.

■ a tuft of hair on the chin of certain mammals, for example a lion or goat. ■ an animal's growth or marking that is likened to a beard, for example the gills of an oyster, or the beak bristles of certain birds. ■ a tuft of hairs or bristles on certain plants, especially the awn of a grass.

2 N. Amer. informal a woman who accompanies a homosexual man as an escort to a social occasion, in order to help conceal his homosexuality.

▶ **verb** [with obj.] boldly confront or challenge (someone formidable).

– PHRASES **beard the lion in his den** (or **lair**) confront or challenge someone on their own ground.

– DERIVATIVES **bearded** adjective [often in combination] *a grey-bearded man*, **beardless** adjective.

– ORIGIN Old English, of West Germanic origin; related to Dutch *baard* and German *Bart*.

bearded collie ▶ **noun** a dog of a shaggy breed of collie with long hair on the face.

bearded dragon (also **bearded lizard**) ▶ **noun** a semi-arboreal Australian lizard with spiny scales and a large throat pouch bearing sharp spines.

• Genus *Pogona* (or *Amphibolurus*), family Agamidae; now split into several species, in particular *P. barbata*.

bearded tit ▶ **noun** a small long-tailed Eurasian songbird of the parrotbill family, the male of which has dark markings resembling a moustache, frequenting reed beds. Also called **REEDLING**.

• *Panurus biarmicus*, family Panuridae (or Paradoxornithidae); formerly placed in the tit family.

bearded vulture ▶ **noun** another term for **LAMMERGEIER**.

beardfish ▶ **noun** (pl. same or **-fishes**) a small bottom-dwelling marine fish of deep water, with a long pair of fleshy barbels beneath the chin.

• Family Polymixiidae and genus *Polymixia*: several species, in particular *P. lowei*.

beardie ▶ **noun** (pl. **-ies**) Brit. informal **1** a bearded man, especially one regarded as lacking in style.

2 a bearded collie.

Beardmore Glacier a glacier in Antarctica, flowing from the Queen Maud Mountains to the Ross Ice Shelf, at the southern edge of the Ross Sea.

Beardsley, Aubrey (Vincent) (1872–98), English artist and illustrator, associated with art nouveau and the Aesthetic movement. He is known for original and controversial illustrations, such as those for Oscar Wilde's *Salome* (1894).

bearer ▶ **noun 1** a person or thing that carries or holds something: [in combination] *a flag-bearer* | figurative *I'm sorry to be the bearer of bad tidings.*

■ a carrier of equipment on an expedition. ■ Indian a domestic servant or other menial worker. ■ Indian a waiter. ■ a person who carries the coffin at a funeral.

2 a person who presents a cheque or other order to pay money: *promissory notes payable to the bearer.*

■ [as modifier] payable to the possessor: *bearer bonds.*

bear garden (also **bear pit**) ▶ **noun** a scene of uproar and confusion.

– ORIGIN late 16th cent.: *bear* from **BEAR**[2]. The original sense was 'a place set apart for bear-baiting'; bear gardens were often used for other rough sports, hence the figurative meaning.

beargrass ▶ **noun** a North American plant with long, coarse, grass-like leaves, in particular:

• a wild yucca (genus *Yucca*, family Agavaceae). • a cultivated ornamental plant, the leaves of which were formerly used by American Indians to make watertight baskets (*Xerophyllum tenax*, family Liliaceae).

bear hug ▶ **noun** a rough, tight embrace.

bearing ▶ **noun 1** [in sing.] a person's way of standing or moving: *a man of precise military bearing.*

■ the way a person behaves or conducts themselves: *she has the bearing of a First Lady.*

2 [mass noun] relation; relevance: *the case has no direct* **bearing on** *the issues being considered.*

3 [mass noun] the ability to tolerate something bad or to be tolerated: *school was bad enough, but now it's past bearing.*

4 (often **bearings**) a part of a machine that allows one part to rotate or move in contact with another part with as little friction as possible.

5 the direction or position of something, or the direction of movement, relative to a fixed point. It is usually measured in degrees, typically with magnetic north as zero.

■ (**one's bearings**) awareness of one's position relative to one's surroundings: *he flashed the torch around, trying to get his bearings.*

6 Heraldry a device or charge: *armorial bearings.*

bearing rein ▶ **noun** a fixed rein which causes the horse to raise its head and arch its neck.

bearish ▶ **adjective 1** resembling or likened to a bear, typically in being rough, surly, or clumsy.

2 Stock Exchange characterized by falling share prices.

■ (of a dealer) inclined to sell because of an anticipated fall in prices.

– DERIVATIVES **bearishly** adverb, **bearishness** noun.

bear market ▶ **noun** Stock Exchange a market in which share prices are falling, encouraging selling.

Béarnaise sauce /ˌbeɪəˈneɪz/ ▶ **noun** [mass noun] a rich sauce thickened with egg yolks and flavoured with tarragon.

– ORIGIN *Béarnaise*, feminine of French *béarnais* 'of *Béarn*', a region of SW France.

bear pit ▶ **noun** another term for **BEAR GARDEN**.

bear's breech ▶ **noun** a Mediterranean plant with large deep-cut leaves and tall spikes of purple-veined white flowers.

• *Acanthus mollis*, family Acanthaceae.

bear's ear ▶ **noun** another term for **AURICULA**.

bear's foot ▶ **noun** a hellebore, which has leaves that are said to resemble a bear's foot.

bearskin ▶ **noun** the pelt of a bear, especially when used as a rug or wrap.

■ a tall cap of black fur worn ceremonially by certain troops, such as the Guards in the British army.

Beas /beɪˈɑːs, biːˈɑːs/ a river of northern India which rises in the Himalayas and flows through Himachal Pradesh to join the Sutlej River in Punjab. It is one of the five rivers that gave Punjab its name.

beast ▶ **noun** an animal, especially a large or dangerous four-footed one: *a wild beast.*

■ (usu. **beasts**) a domestic animal, especially a bovine farm animal. ■ an inhumanly cruel, violent, or depraved person: *he is a filthy drunken beast.* ■ informal an objectionable or unpleasant person or thing: *a scheming, manipulative little beast.* ■ (**the beast**) a person's brutish or untamed characteristics: **the beast in you** *is rearing its ugly head.* ■ [with adj.] informal a thing possessing a specified quality: *that much-maligned beast, the rave record.*

– ORIGIN Middle English: from Old French *beste*, based on Latin *bestia*.

beastie ▶ **noun** (pl. **-ies**) Scottish or humorous a small animal or insect.

■ [with adj.] informal a vehicle or device of a specified kind: *these little beasties only have three wheels.*

beastly ▶ **adjective** (**beastlier**, **beastliest**) **1** Brit. informal very unpleasant: *this beastly war.*

■ unkind; malicious: *don't be beastly to him.*

2 archaic cruel and unrestrained: *beastly immorality.*

▶ **adverb** [as submodifier] Brit. informal, dated to an extreme and unpleasant degree: *a beastly dull wedding party.*

– DERIVATIVES **beastliness** noun.

beast of burden ▶ **noun** an animal, such as a mule or donkey, that is used for carrying loads.

beast of prey ▶ **noun** an animal, especially a mammal, that kills and eats other animals.

beat ▶ **verb** (past **beat**; past participle **beaten**) [with obj.]

1 strike (a person or an animal) repeatedly and violently so as to hurt or injure them, typically with an implement such as a club or whip: *she beat me with a stick for the slightest misdemeanour.*

■ strike (an object) repeatedly so as to make a noise: *he beat the table with his hand.* ■ [no obj.] (of an instrument) make a rhythmical sound through being struck: *drums were beating in the distance.* ■ strike (a carpet, blanket, etc.) repeatedly in order to remove dust. ■ remove (dust) from something by striking it repeatedly. ■ flatten or shape (metal) by striking it repeatedly with a hammer: *pure gold can be* **beaten out** *to form very thin sheets.* ■ (**beat something against/on**) strike something against (something): *she beat her fists against the wood.* ■ [no obj.] (**beat on/against**) strike repeatedly on: *Sidney beat on the door with the flat of his hand.* ■ [no obj.] (**beat at**) make striking movements towards: *Emmie seized the hearthrug and began to beat at the flames.* ■ move across (an area of land) repeatedly striking at the ground cover in order to raise game birds for shooting.

2 defeat (someone) in a game or other competitive situation: *she beat him easily at chess* | *Juventus were beaten 2–1.*

■ informal baffle: **it beats me how** *you manage to work in this heat.* ■ overcome (a problem or disease): *the battle to beat car crime* | *he beat heroin addiction in 1992.* ■ do or be better than (a record or score): *he beat his own world record.* ■ informal be better than: **you can't beat** *the taste of fresh raspberries.*

3 succeed in getting somewhere ahead of (someone): *the defender beat him to the ball.*

■ take action to avoid (difficult or inconvenient effects of an event or circumstance): *they set off early to beat the traffic.*

4 [no obj.] (of the heart) pulsate: *her heart beat faster with panic.*

5 (of a bird) move (the wings) up and down.

■ (of a bird or its wings) make rhythmic movements through (the air). ■ [no obj.] (of a bird) fly making rhythmic wing movements: *an owl beat low over the salt marsh.*

6 stir (cooking ingredients) vigorously to make a smooth or frothy mixture.

7 (**beat it**) informal leave: [in imperative] *now beat it, will you!*

8 [no obj., with adverbial of direction] Sailing sail into the wind, following a zigzag course with repeated tacking: *we beat southwards all that first day.*

▶ **noun 1** a main accent or rhythmic unit in music or poetry: *the glissando begins on the second beat.*

■ a strong rhythm in popular music: *the music changed to a funky disco beat.* ■ [in sing.] a regular, rhythmic sound or movement: *the beat of the wipers became almost hypnotic.* ■ the sound made when something, especially a musical instrument, is struck: *he heard a regular drum beat.* ■ a pulsation of the heart. ■ a periodic variation of sound or amplitude due to the combination of two sounds, electrical signals, or other vibrations having similar but not identical frequencies. ■ the movement of a bird's wings.

2 an area allocated to a police officer and patrolled on foot: *his beat was in North London* | *public clamour for more policemen* **on the beat**.

■ a spell of duty allocated to a police officer: *his beat ended at 6 a.m.* ■ an area regularly frequented by someone, especially a prostitute. ■ figurative a person's area of interest: *his beat is construction, property, and hotels.* ■ an area regularly occupied by a shoal of freshwater fish. ■ a stretch of water fished by an angler.

3 a brief pause or moment of hesitation, typically one lasting a specified length: *she waited for a beat of three seconds.* [ORIGIN: referring to such a pause as a stage direction.]

4 informal short for **BEATNIK**.

▶ **adjective 1** [predic.] informal completely exhausted: *I'm dead beat.*

2 [attrib.] of or relating to the beat generation or its philosophy: *beat poet Allen Ginsberg.*

– PHRASES **beat about the bush** discuss a matter without coming to the point. **beat someone at their own game** see **GAME**[1]. **beat the bounds** historical mark parish boundaries by walking round them and striking certain points with rods. **beat someone's brains out** see **BRAIN**. **beat one's breast** see **BREAST**. **beat the bushes** N. Amer. informal search thoroughly: *I was out beating the bushes for investors to split the risk.* **beat the clock** perform a task quickly or within a fixed time limit. **beat the drum for** see **DRUM**[1]. **beat the hell out of** informal **1** beat (someone) very severely. **2** surpass or defeat easily. **beat the living daylights out of** see **DAYLIGHT** (sense 2). **beat the pants off** informal prove to be vastly superior to. **beat a path to someone's door** (of a large number of people) hasten to make contact with someone regarded as interesting or inspiring. **beat a (hasty) retreat** withdraw, typically in order to avoid something unpleasant. **beat the shit out of** vulgar slang beat (someone) very severely. **beat the system** succeed in finding a means of getting round rules, regulations, or other means of control. **beat time** indicate or follow a musical tempo with a baton or other means. **beat someone to it** succeed in doing something or getting somewhere before someone else, to their annoyance. **if you can't beat them, join them** humorous if you are unable to outdo rivals in some endeavour, you might as well cooperate with them and thereby possibly gain an advantage. **miss a beat** see **MISS**[1]. **to beat all ——s** infinitely better than all the things of the specified type: *a PC screen saver to beat all screen savers.* **to beat the band** informal, chiefly N. Amer. in such a way as to surpass all competition: *they were talking to beat the band.*

– DERIVATIVES **beatable** adjective.

– ORIGIN Old English *bēatan*, of Germanic origin.

▶**beat someone back** (usu. **be beaten back**) force (someone attempting to do something) to retreat: *I tried to get in but was beaten back by the flames.*

beat down (of the sun) radiate intense heat and brightness. ■ (of rain) fall hard and continuously.

beat something down quell defence or resistance. ■ fight to suppress a feeling or emotion.

beat someone down force someone to reduce the price of something.

beat off vulgar slang (of a man) masturbate.

beat someone/thing off succeed in resisting an attacker or an attack. ■ win against a challenge or rival.

beat something out 1 produce a loud, rhythmic sound by striking something: *he beat out a rhythm on the drums.* **2** extinguish flames by striking at them with a suitable object.

beat someone up assault and severely injure someone by hitting, kicking, or punching them repeatedly.

beat up on someone North American way of saying ***beat someone up***.

beatbox ▶ **noun** informal a drum machine.
■ a radio or radio cassette player used to play loud music, especially rap.

beaten past participle of **BEAT**. ▶ **adjective 1** having been defeated: *last year's beaten finalist.*
■ exhausted and dejected: *he sat feeling old and beaten.*
2 having been beaten or struck: *he trudged home like a beaten cur.*
■ (of food) stirred vigorously to a uniform consistency: *beaten egg.* ■ (of metal) shaped by hammering, typically so as to give the surface a dimpled texture. ■ (of precious metal) hammered to form thin foil for ornamental use.
3 (of a path) well trodden; much used.

– PHRASES **off the beaten track** (or **path**) in or into an isolated place. ■ unusual.

beater ▶ **noun 1** a person who hits someone or something, in particular:
■ a person employed to flush out or drive game birds for shooting by striking at the ground cover. ■ a person who beats metal in manufacturing. ■ [in combination] a person who habitually hits someone: *a wife-beater.*
2 [often with modifier] an implement or machine used for beating something, in particular:
■ (in cookery) a device for whisking or blending ingredients. ■ an implement used to dislodge dirt from rugs and carpets by hitting them.
3 [in combination] informal a means of defeating or preventing something: *a recession-beater.*
4 N. Amer. informal an old or dilapidated vehicle.

beat frequency ▶ **noun** Physics the number of beats per second, equal to the difference in the frequencies of two interacting tones or oscillations.

beat generation ▶ **noun** a movement of young people in the 1950s and early 1960s who rejected conventional society, valuing free self-expression and favouring modern jazz. Among writers associated with the movement were Jack Kerouac and Allen Ginsberg.

beatific /biːəˈtɪfɪk/ ▶ **adjective** feeling or expressing blissful happiness: *a beatific smile.*
■ Christian Theology imparting holy bliss.

– DERIVATIVES **beatifically** adverb.

– ORIGIN mid 17th cent.: from French *béatifique* or Latin *beatificus*, from *beatus* 'blessed'.

beatification /bɪˌatɪfɪˈkeɪʃ(ə)n/ ▶ **noun** [mass noun] (in the Roman Catholic Church) declaration by the Pope that a dead person is in a state of bliss, constituting a first step towards canonization and permitting public veneration.

– ORIGIN early 16th cent. (in the sense 'action of making blessed'): from Old French, or from ecclesiastical Latin *beatificatio(n-)*, from *beatificare* 'make blessed', from Latin *beatus* 'blessed'.

beatify /bɪˈatɪfʌɪ/ ▶ **verb** (**-ies**, **-ied**) [with obj.] (in the Roman Catholic Church) announce the beatification of.
■ make (someone) blissfully happy.

– ORIGIN mid 16th cent. (in the sense 'make blessed or supremely happy'): from Old French *beatifier* or ecclesiastical Latin *beatificare*, from Latin *beatus* 'blessed'.

beating ▶ **noun 1** a punishment or assault in which the victim is hit repeatedly: *if he got dirt on his clothes he'd get a beating* | [mass noun] *torture methods included beating.*
2 [mass noun] pulsation or throbbing, typically of the heart.
3 a defeat in a competitive situation.

– PHRASES **take a beating** informal suffer damage or hurt. **take some** (or **a lot of**) **beating** informal be difficult to surpass.

beatitude /bɪˈatɪtjuːd/ ▶ **noun** [mass noun] supreme blessedness.
■ (**the Beatitudes**) [count noun] the blessings listed by Jesus in the Sermon on the Mount (Matt. 5:3–11). ■ (**His/Your Beatitude**) a title given to patriarchs in the Orthodox Church.

– ORIGIN late Middle English: from Old French *beatitude* or Latin *beatitudo*, from *beatus* 'blessed'.

Beatles a pop and rock group from Liverpool consisting of George Harrison, John Lennon, Paul McCartney, and Ringo Starr. Remembered for the quality and stylistic diversity of their songs (mostly written by Lennon and McCartney), they achieved success with their first single 'Love Me Do' (1962) and went on to produce albums such as *Sergeant Pepper's Lonely Hearts Club Band* (1967).

beatnik ▶ **noun** a young person in the 1950s and early 1960s belonging to a subculture associated with the beat generation.

– ORIGIN 1950s: from **BEAT** + *-nik* on the pattern of *sputnik*, perhaps influenced by US use of Yiddish *-nik*, denoting someone or something who acts in a particular way.

Beaton, Sir Cecil (Walter Hardy) (1904–80), English photographer famous for his fashion features and portraits of celebrities, particularly the British royal family. He later diversified into costume and set design, winning two Oscars for the film *My Fair Lady* (1964).

Beatty[1] /ˈbiːti/, David, 1st Earl Beatty of the North Sea and of Brooksby (1871–1936), British admiral. During the First World War he played a major role in the Battle of Jutland and was Commander-in-Chief of the Grand Fleet from 1916.

Beatty[2] /ˈbeɪti, ˈbiːti/, Warren (b.1937), American actor, film director, and screenwriter; born *Henry Warren Beaty*. He starred in and produced *Bonnie and Clyde* (1967), and was producer, co-writer, star, and Oscar-winning director of *Reds* (1981).

beat-up ▶ **adjective** informal worn out by overuse; in a state of disrepair.

beau /bəʊ/ ▶ **noun** (pl. **beaux** or **beaus** /bəʊz, bəʊ/) dated **1** a boyfriend or male admirer.
2 a rich, fashionable young man; a dandy.

– ORIGIN late 17th cent. (in sense 2): from French, literally 'handsome', from Latin *bellus*.

Beaubourg Centre /ˈbəʊbɔːɡ, French boburʀ/ another name for **POMPIDOU CENTRE**.

Beau Brummell see **BRUMMELL**.

Beaufort scale /ˈbəʊfət/ a scale of wind speed based on a visual estimation of the wind's effects, ranging from force 0 (less than 1 knot or 1 kph, 'calm') to force 12 (64 knots or 118 kph and above, 'hurricane').

– ORIGIN mid 19th cent.: named after Sir Francis *Beaufort* (1774–1857), the English admiral and naval hydrographer who devised it.

Beaufort Sea a part of the Arctic Ocean lying to the north of Alaska and Canada.

– ORIGIN named after the English admiral Sir Francis *Beaufort* (see **BEAUFORT SCALE**).

beau geste /bəʊ ˈʒɛst, French bo ʒɛst/ ▶ **noun** (pl. **beaux gestes** pronunc. same) a noble and generous act.

– ORIGIN French, literally 'splendid gesture'.

beau idéal /ˌbəʊ iːdeɪˈal, French bo ideal/ ▶ **noun** a person or thing representing the highest possible standard of excellence in a particular respect.

– ORIGIN French, literally 'ideal beauty'.

Beaujolais /ˈbəʊʒəleɪ, French boʒolɛ/ ▶ **noun** [mass noun] a light red or (less commonly) white burgundy wine produced in the Beaujolais district of SE France.

Beaujolais Nouveau /ˌbəʊʒəleɪ nuːˈvəʊ, French boʒolɛ nuvo/ ▶ **noun** [mass noun] a Beaujolais wine sold in the first year of a vintage.

– ORIGIN from **BEAUJOLAIS** + French *nouveau* 'new'.

Beaumarchais /ˈbəʊmɑːˌʃeɪ, French bomaʀʃɛ/, Pierre Augustin Caron de (1732–99), French dramatist. He is chiefly remembered for his comedies *The Barber of Seville* (1775) and *The Marriage of Figaro* (1784), which inspired operas by Rossini and Mozart.

beau monde /bəʊ ˈmɒnd, French bo mɔ̃d/ ▶ **noun** (**the beau monde**) fashionable society.

– ORIGIN French, literally 'fine world'.

Beaumont /ˈbəʊmɒnt/, Francis (1584–1616), English dramatist. He collaborated with John Fletcher on *Philaster* (1609), *The Maid's Tragedy* (1610–11), and many other plays. *The Knight of the Burning Pestle* (*c.*1607) is attributed to Beaumont alone.

Beau Nash see **NASH**[4].

Beaune /bəʊn/ ▶ **noun** [mass noun] a red burgundy wine from the region around Beaune in eastern France.

beau sabreur /ˌbəʊ saˈbrəː, French bo sabʀœʀ/ ▶ **noun** (pl. **beaux sabreurs** pronunc. same) a dashing adventurer.

– ORIGIN French, 'handsome swordsman', originally a sobriquet of Joachim Murat (1767–1815), French cavalry officer and brother-in-law of Napoleon.

beaut /bjuːt/ informal, chiefly Austral./NZ ▶ **noun** a particularly fine example of something: *the idea was a beaut.*
■ a beautiful person.
▶ **adjective** very good or beautiful: *a beaut view.*

– ORIGIN mid 19th cent.: abbreviation of **BEAUTY** or **BEAUTIFUL**.

beauteous ▶ **adjective** poetic/literary beautiful.

– ORIGIN late Middle English: from **BEAUTY**, on the pattern of *bounteous* and *plenteous*.

beautician ▶ **noun** a person whose job is to give people beauty treatment.

beautiful ▶ **adjective** very pleasing aesthetically; delightful to the senses: *beautiful poetry* | *a beautiful young woman.*
■ of a very high standard; excellent: *the house had been left in beautiful order* | *she spoke in beautiful English.*

– PHRASES **the beautiful people 1** fashionable, glamorous, and privileged people. **2** (in the 1960s) hippies. **the body beautiful** an ideal of physical beauty.

– DERIVATIVES **beautifully** adverb [as submodifier] *the rules are beautifully simple.*

beautify ▶ **verb** (**-ies**, **-ied**) [with obj.] improve the appearance of.

– DERIVATIVES **beautification** noun, **beautifier** noun.

beauty ▶ **noun** (pl. **-ies**) **1** [mass noun] a combination of qualities, such as shape, colour, or form, that pleases the aesthetic senses, especially the sight: *I was struck by her beauty* | *an area of outstanding natural beauty.*
■ a combination of qualities that pleases the intellect or moral sense. ■ [as modifier] denoting something

intended to make someone more attractive: *beauty treatment.*

2 a beautiful or pleasing thing or person, in particular:

■a beautiful woman: *a blonde beauty.* ■an excellent specimen or example of something: *the fish was a beauty, around 14 pounds.* ■(**the beauties of**) the pleasing or attractive features of (something): *the beauties of the English countryside.* ■[in sing.] the best feature or advantage of something: ***the beauty of** keeping cats is that they don't tie you down.*

3 used in names of moths with muted brown or grey wing patterns that provide camouflage in trees and shrubs, e.g. **pine beauty**.

● Several species in the families Geometridae and Noctuidae.

– PHRASES **beauty is in the eye of the beholder** proverb that which one person finds beautiful or admirable may not appeal to another. **beauty is only skin-deep** proverb a pleasing appearance is not a guide to character.

– ORIGIN Middle English: from Old French *beaute*, based on Latin *bellus* 'beautiful, fine'.

beauty contest ▶ **noun** a competition for a prize given to the woman judged the most beautiful.

■informal a contest between rival institutions which depends heavily on presentation.

beauty pageant ▶ **noun** see **PAGEANT**.

beauty parlour (also **beauty salon**) ▶ **noun** an establishment in which hairdressing, make-up, and similar cosmetic treatments are carried out professionally.

beauty queen ▶ **noun** a woman judged most beautiful in a beauty contest.

beauty sleep ▶ **noun** [mass noun] humorous sleep considered to be sufficient to keep one looking young and beautiful.

beauty spot ▶ **noun 1** a place known for its beautiful scenery.

2 a small natural or artificial mark such as a mole on a woman's face, considered to enhance another feature.

Beauvoir, Simone de, see **DE BEAUVOIR**.

beaux plural form of **BEAU**.

beaux arts /bəʊz ˈɑː, French boz aʀ/ ▶ **plural noun 1** fine arts.

2 (usu. **Beaux Arts**) [as modifier] relating to the classical decorative style maintained by the École des Beaux-Arts in Paris, especially in the 19th century.

– ORIGIN from French *beaux-arts*.

beaux yeux /bəʊz ˈjəː, French boz jœ/ ▶ **plural noun** poetic/literary beautiful eyes.

■admiring glances; favourable regard.

– ORIGIN French.

beaver[1] ▶ **noun** (pl. same or **beavers**) **1** a large semiaquatic broad-tailed rodent that is native to North America and northern Eurasia. It is noted for its habit of gnawing through tree trunks to fell the trees in order to make dams.

● Family Castoridae and genus *Castor*: the North American *C. canadensis* and the Eurasian *C. fiber*, which was exterminated in Britain in about the 12th century.

■[mass noun] the soft light brown fur of the beaver. ■(also **beaver hat**) chiefly historical a hat made of felted beaver fur. ■(also **beaver cloth**) [mass noun] a heavy woollen cloth resembling felted beaver fur. ■figurative a very hard-working person.

2 (**Beaver**) a boy aged about 6 or 7 who is an affiliated member of the Scout Association.

▶**verb** [no obj.] informal work hard: *Bridget **beavered away** to keep things running smoothly.*

– ORIGIN Old English *beofor, befor*, of Germanic origin; related to Dutch *bever* and German *Biber*, from an Indo-European root meaning 'brown'.

beaver[2] ▶ **noun** the lower part of the face guard of a helmet in a suit of armour. The term is also used to refer to the upper part or visor, or to a single movable guard.

– ORIGIN late 15th cent.: from Old French *baviere* 'bib', from *baver* 'slaver'.

beaver[3] ▶ **noun 1** vulgar slang, chiefly N. Amer. a woman's genitals or pubic area.

■a woman regarded in sexual terms.

2 Brit. informal, dated a bearded man.

– ORIGIN early 20th cent.: of unknown origin.

beaverboard ▶ **noun** [mass noun] chiefly N. Amer. a kind of fibreboard used in building.

– ORIGIN early 20th cent.: from **BEAVER**[1] + **BOARD**.

Beaverbrook, Max Aitken, 1st Baron (1879–1964), Canadian-born British Conservative politician and newspaper proprietor; full name *William Maxwell Aitken*. He bought the *Daily Express* in 1916 and expanded it to a world record circulation. Beaverbrook was also Minister of Aircraft Production in Churchill's cabinet (1940).

beaver lamb ▶ **noun** [mass noun] lambskin made to look like beaver fur.

Beaver State informal name for **OREGON**.

bebop /ˈbiːbɒp/ ▶ **noun** [mass noun] a type of jazz originating in the 1940s and characterized by complex harmony and rhythms. It is associated particularly with Charlie Parker, Thelonious Monk, and Dizzy Gillespie.

– DERIVATIVES **bebopper** noun.

– ORIGIN 1940s (originally US): imitative of the typical rhythm of this music.

becalm ▶ **verb** [with obj.] (usu. **be becalmed**) leave (a sailing ship) unable to move through lack of wind.

became past participle of **BECOME**.

becard /ˈbɛkəd, bəˈkɑːd/ ▶ **noun** a small bird of the tyrant flycatcher family, with a large head, strong bill, and plumage varying from mainly black to brightly coloured. Becards are found mainly in Central and South America.

● Genus *Pachyramphus*, family Tyrannidae: several species, including the **rose-throated becard** (*P. aglaiae*), which reaches the southern US.

– ORIGIN mid 19th cent.: from French *bécarde*, from *bec* 'beak'.

because ▶ **conjunction** for the reason that; since: *we did it because we felt it our duty* | ***just because** I'm inexperienced doesn't mean that I lack perception.*

– PHRASES **because of** on account of; by reason of: *they moved here because of the baby.*

– ORIGIN Middle English: from the phrase *by cause*, influenced by Old French *par cause de* 'by reason of'.

USAGE **1** When **because** follows a negative construction the meaning can be ambiguous. In the sentence *he did not go **because** he was ill*, for example, it is not clear whether it means either 'the reason he did not go was that he was ill' or 'being ill wasn't the reason for him going; there was another reason'. Some usage guides recommend using a comma when the first interpretation is intended (*he did not go, because he was ill*) and no comma where the second interpretation is intended, but it is probably wiser to avoid using **because** after a negative altogether.
2 As with other conjunctions such as **but** and **and**, it is still widely held that it is incorrect to begin a sentence with **because**. It has, however, long been used in this way in both written and spoken English (typically for rhetorical effect), and is quite acceptable.
3 On the construction **the reason … is because**, see usage at **REASON**.

béchamel /ˈbeɪʃəmɛl/ (also **béchamel sauce**) ▶ **noun** [mass noun] a rich white sauce made with milk infused with herbs and other flavourings.

– ORIGIN named after the Marquis Louis de *Béchamel* (died 1703), steward to Louis XIV of France, who is said to have invented a similar sauce.

bêche-de-mer /ˌbɛʃdəˈmɛː/ ▶ **noun** (pl. same or **bêches-de-mer** pronunc. same) **1** [mass noun] a large sea cucumber which is eaten as a delicacy in China and Japan. Also called **TREPANG**.

2 (**Bêche-de-mer**) another term for **BISLAMA**.

– ORIGIN late 18th cent.: pseudo-French, alteration of Portuguese *bicho do mar*, literally 'sea-worm'.

Bechstein /ˈbɛkstʌɪn, ˈbɛx-/ ▶ **noun** a piano made by the German piano-builder Friedrich Wilhelm Carl Bechstein (1826–1900) or by the firm which he founded in 1856.

Bechuanaland /ˌbɛtʃʊˈɑːnəland/ former name (until 1966) for **BOTSWANA**.

beck[1] ▶ **noun** N. English a stream.

– ORIGIN Middle English: from Old Norse *bekkr*, of Germanic origin; related to Dutch *beek* and German *Bach*. Used as the common term for a brook in northern areas, *beck* often refers, in literature, to a brook with a stony bed or following a rugged course, typical of such areas.

beck[2] ▶ **noun** poetic/literary a gesture requesting attention, such as a nod or wave.

– PHRASES **at someone's beck and call** always having to be ready to obey someone's orders immediately.

– ORIGIN Middle English: from archaic *beck*, abbreviated form of **BECKON**.

Beckenbauer /ˈbɛk(ə)nˌbaʊə, German ˈbɛknˌbaʊɐ/, Franz (b.1945), German footballer. A defender, he captained Germany when they won the World Cup in 1974. He was manager of the national team that won the World Cup again in 1990.

Becker /ˈbɛkə, German ˈbɛkɐ/, Boris (b.1967), German tennis player. In 1985 he became the youngest man and first unseeded player to win the men's singles championship at Wimbledon. He won at Wimbledon again in 1986 and 1989.

becket /ˈbɛkɪt/ ▶ **noun** a loop of rope or similar device for securing loose items on a ship.

– ORIGIN early 18th cent.: of unknown origin.

Becket, St Thomas à /ˈbɛkɪt/ (*c.*1118–70), English prelate and statesman, Archbishop of Canterbury 1162–70. He came into open opposition to Henry II, who uttered words in anger which led four knights to assassinate Becket in his cathedral. Henry was obliged to do public penance at Becket's tomb, which became a major centre of pilgrimage until its destruction under Henry VIII (1538). Feast day, 29 December.

Beckett /ˈbɛkɪt/, Samuel (Barclay) (1906–89), Irish dramatist, novelist, and poet. He is best known for his plays, especially *Waiting for Godot* (1952), a seminal work in the Theatre of the Absurd. Nobel Prize for Literature (1969).

Beckford, William (1759–1844), English writer and collector. As an author he is remembered for the oriental romance *Vathek* (1786, originally written in French).

Beckmann[1] /ˈbɛkmən, German ˈbɛkman/, Ernst Otto (1853–1923), German chemist. He devised a method of determining a compound's molecular weight by measuring the rise in boiling point of a solvent containing the compound.

Beckmann[2] /ˈbɛkmən, German ˈbɛkman/, Max (1884–1950), German painter and graphic artist. Beckmann's paintings reflect his first-hand experience of human evil during the First World War.

beckon ▶ **verb** [no obj.] make a gesture with the hand, arm, or head to encourage or instruct someone to come nearer or follow: *Miranda **beckoned to** Adam.*

■[with obj. and adverbial of direction] attract the attention of and summon (someone) in this way: *he beckoned Cameron over* | [with obj. and infinitive] *he beckoned Duncan to follow.* ■figurative seem to be appealing or inviting: *the going is tough and soft options beckon.*

– ORIGIN Old English *bīecnan, bēcnan*, of West Germanic origin; related to **BEACON**.

becloud ▶ **verb** [with obj.] cause to become obscure or muddled: *confusion beclouds the issue.*

■(usu. **be beclouded**) cover or surround with clouds.

become ▶ **verb** (past **became**; past participle **become**) **1** [no obj., with complement] begin to be: *they became angry when asked about it* | *it is becoming clear that we are in a totally new situation.*

■grow to be; turn into: *the child will become an adult.* ■(of a person) qualify or be accepted as; acquire the status specified: *she wanted to become a doctor.* ■(**become of**) (in questions) happen to: *what would become of her now?*

2 [with obj.] (of clothing) look well on or suit (someone): *mourning regalia became her.*

■be appropriate or suitable to (someone): *minor celebrity status did not become Potter.*

– ORIGIN Old English *becuman* 'come to a place, come (to be or do something)' (see **BE-**, **COME**), of Germanic origin; related to Dutch *bekomen* and German *bekommen* 'get, receive'.

becoming ▶ **adjective** (of clothing) looking well on someone: *what a becoming dress!*

■decorous: *a becoming modesty.*

– DERIVATIVES **becomingly** adverb, **becomingness** noun.

Becquerel /ˈbɛkərɛl, French bɛkʀɛl/, Antoine-Henri (1852–1908), French physicist. With Marie and Pierre Curie he discovered the natural radioactivity in uranium salts. Nobel Prize for Physics (1903, shared with the Curies).

becquerel /ˈbɛkərɛl/ (abbrev.: **Bq**) ▶ **noun** Physics the SI unit of radioactivity, corresponding to one disintegration per second.

– ORIGIN late 19th cent.: named after A-H. **BECQUEREL**.

BEd ▶ **abbreviation for** Bachelor of Education.

bed ▶ **noun 1** a piece of furniture for sleep or rest,

typically a framework with a mattress and coverings: *a large double bed* | *she was in bed by nine* | *I'm ready for bed.*
■ a bed and associated facilities comprising a place for a patient in a hospital: *in 1987 nearly 4,000 beds were closed.* ■ a bedroom: [in combination] *a three-bed detached house.* ■ a place or article used by a person or animal for sleep or rest: *a bed of straw.* ■ informal used with reference to a bed as the typical place for sexual activity: *she'd gone to bed with Tony willingly.*
2 an area of ground, typically in a garden, where flowers and plants are grown: *a bed of tulips.*
3 a flat base or foundation on which something rests or is supported, in particular:
■ the foundation of a road or railway. ■ chiefly N. Amer. the open part of a truck, wagon, or cart, where goods are carried. ■ the flat surface beneath the baize of a billiard table.
4 a layer of something, in particular:
■ a layer of food on which other foods are served: *the salad is served on a bed of raw spinach.* ■ a stratum or layer of rock: *a bed of clay.*
5 the bottom of the sea or a lake or river.
■ [with modifier] a place on the seabed where shellfish, especially oysters or mussels, breed or are bred: *the Conwy mussel beds.*
▶ verb (**bedded, bedding**) [with obj.] **1** (usu. **be bedded**) provide with sleeping accommodation: *the children were bedded in the attic.*
■ [no obj.] settle down to sleep or rest for the night, typically in an improvised place: *he usually bedded down on newspapers in the church porch.* ■ (**bed someone/thing down**) settle a person or animal down to sleep or rest for the night. ■ informal have sexual intercourse with: *he should bed a woman of his own age and leave this girl alone.*
2 transfer (a plant) from a pot or seed tray to a garden plot: *I bedded out these house plants.*
3 (usu. **be bedded in/on**) fix firmly; embed: *the posts should be firmly bedded in concrete.*
■ lay or arrange (something, especially stone) in a layer. ■ [no obj.] (**bed in**) settle down and become established: *a period of calm will allow the changes to bed in.*
– PHRASES **bed of nails** a board with nails pointing out of it, as lain on by fakirs and ascetics. ■ figurative a problematic or uncomfortable situation. **a bed of roses** [often with negative] used in reference to a situation or activity that is comfortable or easy: *farming is no bed of roses.* **be brought to bed** archaic (of a woman) give birth to a child: *she was brought to bed of a daughter.* **get out of bed on the wrong side** start the day in a bad mood, which continues all day long. **in bed with** informal having sexual intercourse with. ■ figurative in undesirably close association with. **keep one's bed** archaic stay in bed because of illness. **one has made one's bed and must lie in** (or **on**) **it** one must accept the consequences of one's own actions. **put someone to bed** take or prepare someone, typically a child, for rest in bed. **put something to bed** informal make a newspaper or book ready for press. **take to one's bed** stay in bed because of illness.
– ORIGIN Old English *bed, bedd* (noun), *beddian* (verb), of Germanic origin; related to Dutch *bed* and German *Bett.*

bedabble /bɪˈdab(ə)l/ ▶ verb [with obj.] (usu. **be bedabbled**) archaic stain or splash with dirty liquid or blood.

bedad /bɪˈdad/ ▶ exclamation Irish used to express surprise or for emphasis.
– ORIGIN early 18th cent.: alteration of *by God*; compare with BEGAD and GAD[2].

bed and board ▶ noun lodging and food, typically forming part of someone's wages or included in some other agreement.

bed and breakfast ▶ noun sleeping accommodation for a night and a meal in the morning, provided in guest houses and small hotels.
■ a guest house.
▶ verb (**bed-and-breakfast**) [with obj.] Stock Exchange, Brit. sell (shares) and buy them back by agreement the next day.

bedaub ▶ verb [with obj.] (usu. **be bedaubed**) poetic/literary smear or daub with a sticky substance.

bedazzle ▶ verb [with obj.] (often **be bedazzled**) greatly impress (someone) with brilliance or skill: *bedazzled by him, they offered him a post in Paris.*
■ cleverly outwit.
– DERIVATIVES **bedazzlement** noun.

bedbug ▶ noun a bloodsucking bug which is a parasite of birds and mammals.
● Family Cimicidae, suborder Heteroptera: *Cimex* and other genera, and many species, in particular *C. lectularius*, which comes out to feed on humans at night.

bedchamber ▶ noun archaic a bedroom.
■ used in the title of some of the British sovereign's attendants: *groom of the bedchamber.*

bedclothes ▶ plural noun coverings for a bed, such as sheets and blankets.

beddable /ˈbɛdəb(ə)l/ ▶ adjective informal sexually attractive or available.

bedded ▶ adjective **1** [in combination] (of a place) having a specified number or type of beds: *a double-bedded room* | *a 34-bedded acute medical ward.*
2 Geology (of rock) deposited in layers or strata, especially in a specified way: *thinly bedded carbonate mudstones.*

bedder ▶ noun **1** a plant suitable for use as a bedding plant.
2 Brit. a servant employed to clean and tidy rooms in Cambridge colleges.
3 [in combination] informal a house or flat with a specified number of bedrooms: *a studio or one-bedder.*

bedding ▶ noun [mass noun] **1** bedclothes.
■ straw or similar material for animals to sleep on.
2 a base or bottom layer: [as modifier] *a bedding course of sand.*
3 a display of bedding plants.
4 Geology the stratification or layering of rocks: [as modifier] *bedding planes.*

bedding plant ▶ noun a plant set into a garden bed or container when it is about to bloom, typically an annual used for display and discarded at the end of the season.

beddy-byes ▶ noun a child's word for bed: *beddy-byes for both of us—I'm worn out.*
– ORIGIN early 20th cent.: from BED + -Y[2] and BYE-BYES.

Bede, St /biːd/ (c.673–735), English monk, theologian, and historian; known as **the Venerable Bede**. Bede wrote *The Ecclesiastical History of the English People* (completed in 731), a primary source for early English history. Feast day, 27 May.

bedeck ▶ verb [with obj.] (often **be bedecked**) decorate: *he led us into a room bedecked with tinsel.*

bedeguar /ˈbɛdɪɡɑː/ (also **bedeguar gall**) ▶ noun a reddish moss-like growth on rose bushes, forming in response to the developing larvae of a gall wasp. Also called ROBIN'S PINCUSHION.
● The wasp is *Diplolepis rosae*, family Cynipidae.
– ORIGIN late Middle English: from French *bédégar*, from Persian *bād-āwar*, literally 'wind-brought'.

bedel /ˈbiːd(ə)l, bɪˈdɛl/ (also **bedell**) ▶ noun Brit. (in some British universities) an official with largely ceremonial duties.
– ORIGIN late Middle English: archaic spelling of BEADLE.

bedevil ▶ verb (**bedevilled, bedevilling**; US **bedeviled, bedeviling**) [with obj.] (of something bad) cause great and continual trouble to: *the problems that have recently bedevilled the club.*
■ (of a person) torment or harass: *he bedevilled them with petty practical jokes.*
– DERIVATIVES **bedevilment** noun.

bedew /bɪˈdjuː/ ▶ verb [with obj.] poetic/literary cover or sprinkle with drops of water or other liquid.

bedfellow ▶ noun a person who shares a bed with another.
■ figurative a person or thing allied or closely connected with another: *big business and politics were inseparable bedfellows.*

Bedford a town in south central England, on the River Ouse, the county town of Bedfordshire; pop. 89,200 (est.1983).

Bedford cord ▶ noun [mass noun] a tough woven fabric with prominent ridges, similar to corduroy.
– ORIGIN late 19th cent.: named after the town of BEDFORD.

Bedfordshire a county of south central England; county town, Bedford.

bedhead ▶ noun Brit. an upright board or panel fixed at the head of a bed.

bed-hop ▶ verb [no obj.] informal engage in successive casual sexual affairs.
– DERIVATIVES **bed-hopper** noun.

bedight /bɪˈdʌɪt/ ▶ adjective archaic adorned: *a Christmas pudding bedight with holly.*

– ORIGIN late Middle English: past participle of archaic *bedight* 'equip, array' (see BE-, DIGHT).

bedim ▶ verb (**bedimmed, bedimming**) [with obj.] poetic/literary cause to become dim.

bedizen /bɪˈdʌɪz(ə)n, -ˈdɪz-/ ▶ verb [with obj.] (usu. **be bedizened**) poetic/literary dress up or decorate gaudily: *a uniform bedizened with resplendent medals.*
– ORIGIN mid 17th cent.: from BE- (as an intensifier) + obsolete *dizen* 'deck out', probably of Dutch origin.

bedjacket ▶ noun a jacket worn for extra warmth when sitting up in bed.

bed joint ▶ noun a horizontal layer of mortar underneath a layer of masonry.

bedlam /ˈbɛdləm/ ▶ noun **1** [mass noun] a scene of uproar and confusion: *there was bedlam in the courtroom.*
2 archaic an asylum.
– ORIGIN late Middle English: early form of BETHLEHEM, referring to the hospital of St Mary of Bethlehem in London, used as an asylum for the insane.

bedlinen ▶ noun [mass noun] sheets, pillowcases, and duvet covers.

Bedlington terrier /ˈbɛdlɪŋt(ə)n/ ▶ noun a terrier of a breed with a narrow head, long legs, and curly grey hair.
– ORIGIN mid 19th cent.: named after the village of *Bedlington* in northern England, where the breed originated.

bedload ▶ noun [mass noun] Geology the sediment transported by a river in the form of particles too heavy to be in suspension.

bedmaker ▶ noun Brit. a person employed to clean and tidy students' rooms in a college, especially at Cambridge.

Bedouin /ˈbɛdʊɪn/ (also **Beduin**) ▶ noun (pl. same) a nomadic Arab of the desert.
▶ adjective of or relating to the Bedouin.
– ORIGIN from Old French *beduin*, based on Arabic *badawī*, (plural) *badawīn* 'dwellers in the desert', from *badw* 'desert'.

bedpan ▶ noun a receptacle used by a bedridden patient for urine and faeces.

bedplate ▶ noun a metal plate forming the base of a machine.

bedpost ▶ noun any of the four upright supports of a bedstead.
– PHRASES **between you and me and the bedpost** (or **the gatepost** or **the wall**) informal in strict confidence.

bedraggled ▶ adjective dishevelled: *we got there, tired and bedraggled.*
– ORIGIN early 18th cent.: from BE- 'thoroughly' + DRAGGLE + -ED[2].

bed rest ▶ noun [mass noun] confinement of an invalid to bed as part of treatment.

bedridden ▶ adjective confined to bed by sickness or old age.
– ORIGIN Middle English: formed irregularly from archaic *bedrid* 'bedridden person', from the base of the verb RIDE.

bedrock ▶ noun [mass noun] solid rock underlying loose deposits such as soil or alluvium.
■ figurative the fundamental principles on which something is based: *honesty is the bedrock of a good relationship.*

bedroll ▶ noun chiefly N. Amer. a sleeping bag or other bedding rolled into a bundle.

bedroom ▶ noun a room for sleeping in.
■ [as modifier] relating to sexual relations: *bedroom secrets.* ■ [as modifier] N. Amer. denoting a small town or suburb whose residents travel to work in a nearby city.

Beds. ▶ abbreviation for Bedfordshire.

bedside ▶ noun the space beside a bed (used especially with reference to an invalid's bed): *he was summoned to the bedside of a dying man* | [as modifier] *a bedside lamp.*
– PHRASES **bedside manner** a doctor's approach or attitude to a patient.

bedsit (also **bedsitter** or **bed-sitting room**) ▶ noun Brit. informal a one-roomed unit of accommodation typically consisting of combined bedroom and sitting room with cooking facilities.

bedskirt ▶ noun N. Amer. a valance for a bed.

bedsock ▶ noun chiefly Brit. one of a pair of thick socks worn for extra warmth in bed.

bedsore ▶ noun a sore developed by an invalid because of pressure caused by lying in bed in one position. Also called DECUBITUS ULCER.

bedspread ▶ noun a decorative cloth used to cover a bed when it is not in use.

bedstead ▶ noun the framework of a bed on which the mattress and bedclothes are placed.

bedstraw ▶ noun a herbaceous plant with small, lightly perfumed, white or yellow flowers and whorls of slender leaves, formerly used for stuffing mattresses.
● Genus *Galium*, family Rubiaceae: several species.

bedtime ▶ noun [in sing.] the usual time when someone goes to bed: *it was well past her bedtime* | [as modifier] *a bedtime story*.

Bedu /'bɛduː/ ▶ noun & adjective another term for BEDOUIN.
– ORIGIN from Arabic *badw*.

Beduin ▶ noun & adjective variant spelling of BEDOUIN.

bed-warmer ▶ noun a device for warming a bed, typically a metal pan filled with warm coals.

bed-wetting ▶ noun [mass noun] involuntary urination during the night.
– DERIVATIVES **bed-wetter** noun.

bee ▶ noun 1 (also **honeybee** or **hive bee**) a stinging winged insect which collects nectar and pollen, produces wax and honey, and lives in large communities. It was domesticated for its honey around the end of the Neolithic period, and is typically kept in hives.
● Four species in the genus *Apis*, family Apidae, in particular the widespread *A. mellifera*.
2 an insect of a large group to which the honeybee belongs, including many solitary as well as social kinds.
● Superfamily Apoidea, order Hymenoptera: several families, often now placed in the single family Apidae.
3 [with modifier] a meeting for communal work or amusement: *a sewing bee*.
– PHRASES **the bee's knees** informal an outstandingly good person or thing. [ORIGIN: first used to denote something small and insignificant, transferred to the opposite sense in US slang.] **have a bee in one's bonnet** informal be preoccupied or obsessed with something.
– ORIGIN Old English *bēo*, of Germanic origin; related to Dutch *bij* and German dialect *Beie*.

Beeb Brit. informal name for the BBC.

bee balm ▶ noun see BERGAMOT[1] (sense 3).

bee beetle ▶ noun a hairy yellowish chafer with broad black stripes, which flies by day and is typically seen on flowers.
● Genus *Trichius*, family Scarabaeidae: several species, in particular *T. fasciatus*.

bee bread ▶ noun [mass noun] honey or pollen used as food by bees.

beech ▶ noun (also **beech tree**) a large tree with smooth grey bark, glossy leaves, and hard, pale, fine-grained timber.
● Genera *Fagus* (of the northern temperate zone) and *Notofagus* (the **southern beeches**, of Australasia and South America), family Fagaceae: many species, in particular the common **European beech** (*F. sylvaticus*).
– ORIGIN Old English *bēce*, of Germanic origin; related to Latin *fagus* 'beech', Greek *phagos* 'edible oak'.

Beecham, Sir Thomas (1879–1961), English conductor and impresario, founder of the London Philharmonic (1932) and the Royal Philharmonic (1947). He did much to stimulate interest in new or neglected composers such as Sibelius, Delius, and Richard Strauss.

Beecher, Henry Ward (1813–87), American congregationalist clergyman, orator, and writer. He became famous as an orator attacking political corruption and slavery.

beech fern ▶ noun a fern with triangular, deeply lobed fronds, found in moist woodland habitats and streamsides in both Eurasia and North America.
● Genus *Phegopteris*, family Thelypteridaceae.

Beeching, Richard, Baron (1913–85), English businessman and engineer. As Chairman of the British Railways Board (1963–5) he was responsible for the closure of a substantial proportion of the British rail network.

beech marten ▶ noun another term for STONE MARTEN.

beechmast ▶ noun [mass noun] the angular brown nuts of the beech tree, pairs of which are enclosed in a prickly case.
– ORIGIN late 16th cent.: from BEECH + MAST[2].

bee dance ▶ noun another term for WAGGLE DANCE.

beedi ▶ noun (pl. **beedis**) variant spelling of BIDI.

bee-eater ▶ noun a brightly coloured insectivorous bird with a large head and a long downcurved bill, and typically with long central tail feathers.
● Family Meropidae: three genera, in particular *Merops*, and including the **European bee-eater** (*M. apiaster*).

beef ▶ noun 1 [mass noun] the flesh of a cow, bull, or ox, used as food.
■ [count noun] (pl. **beeves** /biːvz/ or US also **beefs**) Farming a cow, bull, or ox fattened for its meat. ■ informal flesh or muscle, especially when well developed: *he needs a little more beef on his bones*. ■ informal strength or power: *he's been brought in to give the team more beef*. ■ informal the substance of a matter: *it's more a sketch than a policy—where's the beef?*
2 (pl. **beefs**) informal a complaint or grievance: *the beef about the warehouse was that it was too big*.
▶ verb [no obj.] informal complain: *he was beefing about how the recession was killing the business*.
– ORIGIN Middle English: from Old French *boef*, from Latin *bos, bov-* 'ox'.
▶ **beef something up** informal give more substance or strength to something: *cost-cutting measures are planned to beef up performance*.

beefalo ▶ noun (pl. same or **-oes**) a hybrid animal of a cross between cattle and buffalo.
– ORIGIN 1970s: blend of BEEF and BUFFALO.

beefburger ▶ noun a flat round cake of minced beef, fried or grilled and typically eaten in a bun.

beefcake ▶ noun [mass noun] informal attractive men with well-developed muscles.

beefeater ▶ noun a Yeoman Warder or Yeoman of the Guard in the Tower of London.
– ORIGIN early 17th cent. (originally a derogatory term for a well-fed servant): the current sense dates from the late 17th cent.

bee fly ▶ noun a squat, hairy bee-like fly that hovers to feed from flowers using its long tongue. Its larvae typically parasitize other insects, especially bees and wasps.
● Family Bombyliidae: many genera.

beef road ▶ noun Austral. a road built in a remote area for transporting beef cattle to market.

beefsteak ▶ noun a thick slice of lean beef, typically from the rump and eaten grilled or fried.

beefsteak fungus ▶ noun a reddish-brown bracket fungus which resembles raw beef and is sometimes considered edible, found in both Eurasia and North America.
● *Fistulina hepatica*, family Fistulinaceae, class Hymenomycetes.

beef tea ▶ noun [mass noun] Brit. a drink made from stewed extract of beef, used as nourishment for invalids.

beef tomato (chiefly N. Amer. also **beefsteak tomato**) ▶ noun a tomato of an exceptionally large and firm variety.

beef Wellington ▶ noun [mass noun] a dish consisting of beef coated in pâté and wrapped in puff pastry.

beefwood ▶ noun a tropical hardwood tree with close-grained red timber.
● Species in several families, in particular *Casuarina equisetifolia* (family Casuarinaceae), native to Australia and SE Asia.

beefy ▶ adjective (**beefier**, **beefiest**) 1 informal muscular or robust: *he shrugged his beefy shoulders*.
■ large and impressively powerful.
2 tasting like beef.
– DERIVATIVES **beefily** adverb, **beefiness** noun.

bee hawkmoth ▶ noun a small day-flying hawkmoth with partly transparent wings, resembling a bumblebee and hovering at flowers to feed.
● Genus *Hemaris*, family Sphingidae: several species.

beehive ▶ noun 1 a structure in which bees are kept, typically in the form of a dome or box.
■ [usu. as modifier] something having the domed shape of a traditional wicker beehive: *a beehive hut*. ■ a busy crowded place: *the church became a beehive of activity*. ■ (**the Beehive**) the dome-shaped parliament building in Wellington, New Zealand. ■ (**the Beehive**) another term for PRAESEPE.
2 a woman's domed and lacquered hairstyle popular in the 1960s.
– DERIVATIVES **beehived** adjective (only in sense 2).

Beehive State informal name for UTAH.

bee-keeping ▶ noun [mass noun] the occupation of owning and breeding bees for their honey.
– DERIVATIVES **bee-keeper** noun.

beeline ▶ noun a straight line between two places.
– PHRASES **make a beeline for** hurry directly to.
– ORIGIN early 19th cent.: with reference to the straight line supposedly taken instinctively by a bee when returning to the hive.

bee louse ▶ noun a minute fly which is a parasite of honeybees, the larvae feeding on wax and stored pollen.
● *Braula coeca*, family Braulidae.

Beelzebub /bɪˈɛlzɪbʌb/ a name for the Devil.
– ORIGIN from late Latin *Beëlzebub*, translating Hebrew *ba'al zĕbūb* 'lord of flies', the name of a Philistine god (2 Kings 1:2), and Greek *Beelzeboul* 'the Devil' (Matt. 12:24).

been past participle of BE.

been-to ▶ noun (in Africa and Asia) a person who has been to Britain, especially for education.

bee orchid ▶ noun a European orchid with a flower that resembles a bee.
● *Ophrys apifera* and related species, family Orchidaceae.

beep ▶ noun a short, high-pitched sound emitted by electronic equipment or a vehicle horn.
▶ verb [no obj.] (of a horn or electronic device) produce such a sound.
■ [with obj.] chiefly N. Amer. summon (someone) by means of a pager.
– ORIGIN 1920s: imitative.

beeper ▶ noun a device that emits short, high-pitched sounds as a signal.

beer ▶ noun [mass noun] an alcoholic drink made from yeast-fermented malt flavoured with hops: *a pint of beer* | [count noun] *he ordered a beer*. Compare with ALE.
■ N. Amer. such a drink brewed by bottom fermentation. ■ used in names of certain other fermented drinks, e.g. **ginger beer**.
– PHRASES **beer and skittles** [often with negative] Brit. amusement or enjoyment: *life isn't all beer and skittles*.
– ORIGIN Old English *bēor*, of West Germanic origin, based on monastic Latin *biber* 'a drink', from Latin *bibere* 'to drink'; related to Dutch *bier* and German *Bier*.

beer belly (also informal **beer gut**) ▶ noun a man's fat stomach, caused by excessive consumption of beer.
– DERIVATIVES **beer-bellied** adjective.

Beerbohm /'brəbəʊm/, Max (1872–1956), English caricaturist, essayist, and critic; full name *Sir Henry Maximilian Beerbohm*. A central figure of the Aesthetic Movement, he is remembered chiefly for his novel, *Zuleika Dobson* (1911).

beer cellar ▶ noun 1 an underground room for storing beer.
2 a basement bar where beer is served.

beer drink ▶ noun S. African (in African society) a traditional gathering for the drinking of beer.

Beerenauslese /'bɛːrənˌaʊsleːzə/ ▶ noun [mass noun] a white wine of German origin or style made from selected individual grapes picked later than the general harvest.
– ORIGIN German, from *Beeren* 'berries' + *aus* 'out' + *lese* 'picking'.

beer engine ▶ noun Brit. a machine that draws up beer from a barrel in a cellar.

beer garden ▶ noun a garden, typically one attached to a public house, where beer is served.

beer gut ▶ noun informal term for BEER BELLY.

beer hall ▶ noun a large room or building where beer is served.
■ (in black townships in South Africa) a state-run establishment selling beer.

beerhouse ▶ noun Brit. historical a public house licensed to sell beer but not spirits.

beer mat ▶ noun a small cardboard table mat for resting glasses on in a bar or public house.

beer money ▶ noun [mass noun] informal a small amount of money allowed or earned.
– ORIGIN early 19th cent.: so named because the allowance of money was made instead of beer.

beer parlour ▶ **noun** Canadian a room in a hotel or tavern where beer is served.

Beersheba /ˌbɪəˈʃiːbə/ a town in southern Israel on the northern edge of the Negev desert; pop. 138,100 (est. 1993).

beer-up ▶ **noun** informal a drinking bout or party.

beery ▶ **adjective** informal **1** relating to or influenced by the drinking of beer in large amounts: *many beery pledges were made.*
2 smelling or tasting of beer: *stale beery breath.*
– DERIVATIVES **beerily** adverb, **beeriness** noun.

beestings ▶ **plural noun** [treated as sing.] the first milk produced by a cow or goat after giving birth.
– ORIGIN Old English *bȳsting*, of West Germanic origin; related to Dutch *biest* and German *Biest(milch)*.

bee-stung ▶ **adjective** [attrib.] informal (of a woman's lips) full, red, and pouting.

beeswax ▶ **noun** [mass noun] **1** the wax secreted by bees to make honeycombs and used to make wood polishes and candles.
2 N. Amer. informal a person's concern or business: *that's none of your beeswax.*
▶ **verb** [with obj.] [often as adj. **beeswaxed**] polish (furniture) with beeswax.

beeswing /ˈbiːzwɪŋ/ ▶ **noun** [mass noun] a filmy second crust on old port.

beet ▶ **noun** a herbaceous plant widely cultivated as a source of food for humans and livestock, and for processing into sugar. Some varieties are grown for their leaves and some for their swollen nutritious root.
• *Beta vulgaris*, family Chenopodiaceae: several subspecies.
– ORIGIN Old English *bēte*, of West Germanic origin, from Latin *beta*, perhaps of Celtic origin; related to Dutch *beet* and German *Bete*.

Beethoven /ˈbeɪtˌ(h)əʊv(ə)n/, Ludwig van (1770–1827), German composer.

> Despite increasing deafness Beethoven was responsible for a prodigious output: nine symphonies, thirty-two piano sonatas, sixteen string quartets, the opera *Fidelio* (1814), and the Mass in D (the *Missa Solemnis*, 1823). In his Ninth Symphony (1824) he broke with precedent in the finale by introducing voices to sing Schiller's *Ode to Joy*. He is often seen as bridging the classical and romantic movements.

– DERIVATIVES **Beethovenian** /ˌbeɪt(h)əʊˈviːnɪən/ adjective.

beetle[1] ▶ **noun** **1** an insect of a large order distinguished by having forewings that are typically modified into hard wing cases (elytra), which cover and protect the hindwings and abdomen.
• Order Coleoptera: see **COLEOPTERA**.
2 [mass noun] Brit. a dice game in which a picture of a beetle is drawn or assembled.
▶ **verb** [no obj., with adverbial of direction] informal make one's way hurriedly or with short, quick steps: *the tourist beetled off.*
– ORIGIN Old English *bitula, bitela* 'biter', from the base of *bītan* 'to bite'.

beetle[2] ▶ **noun** **1** a very heavy mallet, typically with a wooden head, used for ramming, crushing, driving wedges, etc.
2 a machine used for heightening the lustre of cloth by pressure from rollers.
▶ **verb** [with obj.] ram, crush, or drive with a beetle.
■ finish (cloth) with a beetle.
– ORIGIN Old English *bētel*, of Germanic origin; related to **BEAT**.

beetle[3] ▶ **verb** [no obj.] [usu. as adj. **beetling**] (of a person's eyebrows) project or overhang: *piercing eyes glittered beneath a great beetling brow.*
▶ **adjective** [attrib.] (of a person's eyebrows) shaggy and projecting.
– DERIVATIVES **beetle-browed** adjective.
– ORIGIN mid 16th cent. (as an adjective): back-formation from *beetle-browed*. The verb was apparently used as a nonce-word by Shakespeare and was later adopted by other writers.

beetle-crusher ▶ **noun** Brit. humorous a large boot, shoe, or foot.

beetle mite ▶ **noun** a small heavily armoured mite which inhabits leaf litter and soil.
• Order Oribatida.

Beeton, Mrs Isabella Mary (1836–65), English author on cookery, famous for her best-selling *Book of Cookery and Household Management* (1861).

beetroot ▶ **noun** chiefly Brit. **1** the edible root of a kind of beet which is typically dark red and spherical and eaten as a vegetable.
2 the variety of beet which produces this root.
• *Beta vulgaris* subsp. *vulgaris*, family Chenopodiaceae.

beeves plural form of **BEEF** (in sense 1 of the noun).

beezer ▶ **adjective** [attrib.] Brit. informal excellent: *a beezer time was had by all.*
– ORIGIN 1950s: from the earlier noun *beezer*, denoting something large or impressive, of unknown origin.

BEF ▶ **abbreviation for** British Expeditionary Force.

befall ▶ **verb** (past **befell**; past participle **befallen**) [with obj.] poetic/literary (especially of something bad) happen to (someone): *a tragedy befell his daughter* | [no obj.] *she was to blame for anything that befell.*
– ORIGIN Old English *befeallan* 'to fall' (early use being chiefly figurative); related to German *befallen*.

befit ▶ **verb** (**befitted**, **befitting**) [with obj.] be appropriate for; suit: *as befits a Quaker, he was a humane man* | [as adj. **befitting**] *he made a befitting reply.*
– DERIVATIVES **befittingly** adverb.

befog ▶ **verb** (**befogged**, **befogging**) [with obj.] cause to become confused: *her brain was befogged with lack of sleep.*

befool ▶ **verb** [with obj.] archaic make a fool of.

before ▶ **preposition**, **conjunction**, & **adverb** **1** during the period of time preceding (a particular event, date, or time): [as prep.] *she had to rest before dinner* | *the day before yesterday* | [as conjunction] *they lived rough for four days before they were arrested* | *it* **wasn't long before** *I had my first bite* | [as adv.] *his playing days had ended six years before* | *it's never happened to me before.*
2 in front of: [as prep.] *Matilda stood before her, panting* | *the patterns swam before her eyes* | [as adv.] archaic *trotting through the city with guards running before and behind.*
■ [prep.] in front of and required to answer to (a court of law, tribunal, or other authority): *he could be taken before a magistrate for punishment.*
3 in preference to; with a higher priority than: [as prep.] *rangers are taught to put their horses' comfort before their own* | *a woman who placed duty before all else* | [as conjunction] *they would die before they would cooperate with each other.*
– ORIGIN Old English *beforan* (see **BY**, **FORE**), of Germanic origin; related to German *bevor*.

beforehand ▶ **adverb** before an action or event; in advance: *rooms must be booked beforehand.*
– PHRASES **be beforehand with** archaic anticipate or forestall.
– ORIGIN Middle English (originally as two words): from **BEFORE** + **HAND**; probably influenced by Old French *avant main*.

befoul ▶ **verb** [with obj.] make dirty; pollute: *the dangers of letting industry befoul the environment.*

befriend ▶ **verb** [with obj.] act as or become a friend to (someone), especially when they are in need of help or support.

befuddle ▶ **verb** [with obj.] [usu. as adj. **befuddled**] cause to become unable to think clearly: *his befuddled mind.*
– DERIVATIVES **befuddlement** noun.

befur ▶ **verb** (**befurred**, **befurring**) [with obj.] [often as adj. **befurred**] dress in or cover with furs.

beg ▶ **verb** (**begged**, **begging**) **1** [reporting verb] ask someone earnestly or humbly for something: [with obj.] *a leper* **begged** *Jesus* **for** *help* | [with obj. and infinitive] *she begged me to say nothing to her father* | [no obj.] *I must* **beg of** *you not to act impulsively.*
■ [with obj.] ask for (something) earnestly or humbly: *he begged their forgiveness* | [with direct speech] *'Don't leave me,' she begged.* ■ [with obj.] ask formally for (permission to do something): *I will now* **beg leave** *to make some observations* | [no obj., with infinitive] *I beg to second the motion.*
2 [no obj.] ask for something, typically food or money, as charity or a gift: *they had to* **beg for** *food.*
■ [with obj.] acquire (something) from someone in this way: *a piece of bread which I begged from a farmer.* ■ live by acquiring food or money in this way. ■ (of a dog) sit up with the front paws raised expectantly in the hope of a reward.
– PHRASES **beg one's bread** archaic live by begging. **beg the question** **1** (of a fact or action) raise a question or point that has not been dealt with; invite an obvious question. **2** assume the truth of an argument or proposition to be proved, without arguing it. **beg to differ** see **DIFFER**. **go begging** (of an article) be available for use because unwanted by others. ■ (of an opportunity) fail to be taken.
– ORIGIN Middle English: probably from Old English *bedecian*, of Germanic origin; related to **BID**[2].

> **USAGE** The original meaning of the phrase **beg the question** belongs to the field of logic and is a translation of Latin *petitio principii*, literally meaning 'laying claim to a principle', i.e. assuming something that ought to be proved first, as in the following sentence: *by devoting such a large part of the budget for the fight against drug addiction to education, we are* **begging the question** *of its significance in the battle against drugs.* To some traditionalists this is still the only correct meaning. However, over the last 100 years or so another, more general use has arisen: 'invite an obvious question', as in *some definitions of mental illness* **beg the question** *of what constitutes normal behaviour.* This is by far the commonest use today and is widely accepted in modern standard English.

▶ **beg off** withdraw from a promise or undertaking.

begad /bɪˈɡad/ ▶ **exclamation** archaic used to express surprise or for emphasis.
– ORIGIN late 16th cent.: altered form; compare with **BEDAD** and **GAD**[2].

began past of **BEGIN**.

begat archaic past of **BEGET**.

begem ▶ **verb** (**begemmed**, **begemming**) [with obj.] [usu. as adj. **begemmed**] set or stud with gems.

beget ▶ **verb** (**begetting**; past **begot**; past participle **begotten**) [with obj.] poetic/literary **1** (typically of a man, also of a man and a woman) bring (a child) into existence by the process of reproduction: *they hoped that the King might beget an heir by his new queen.*
2 cause; bring about: *killings beget more killings.*
– DERIVATIVES **begetter** noun.
– ORIGIN Old English *begietan* 'get, obtain by effort' (see **BE-**, **GET**).

beggar ▶ **noun** **1** a person, typically a homeless one, who lives by asking for money or food.
2 [with adj.] informal a person of a specified type, especially one to be envied or pitied: *poor little beggars.*
▶ **verb** [with obj.] reduce (someone) to poverty: *why should I beggar myself for you?*
– PHRASES **beggar belief** (or **description**) be too extraordinary to be believed or described. **beggars can't be choosers** proverb people with no other options must be content with what is offered. **set a beggar on horseback and he'll ride to the Devil** proverb someone unaccustomed to power or luxury will abuse or be corrupted by it.
– ORIGIN Middle English: from **BEG** + **-AR**[3].

beggarly ▶ **adjective** poverty-stricken.
■ pitifully or deplorably bad: *the beggarly physical condition to which I had been reduced.* ■ meagre and ungenerous: *the stipend in 1522 was a beggarly £26.*
– DERIVATIVES **beggarliness** noun.

beggar-my-neighbour ▶ **noun** [mass noun] a card game for two players in which the object is to acquire one's opponent's cards. Players alternately turn cards up and if an honour is revealed, the other player must find an honour within a specified number of turns or else forfeit the cards already played.
▶ **adjective** [attrib.] (especially of national policy) self-aggrandizing at the expense of competitors.

beggar's purse ▶ **noun** N. Amer. an appetizer consisting of a crêpe stuffed with a savoury filling, typically caviar and crème fraiche.

beggarticks ▶ **plural noun** [often treated as sing.] another term for **BUR-MARIGOLD**.
– ORIGIN mid 19th cent. (also as *beggar's ticks*): apparently from the resemblance of the seed pods to ticks.

beggary ▶ **noun** [mass noun] a state of extreme poverty.

begging bowl ▶ **noun** a bowl held out by a beggar for food or alms.
■ figurative an earnest appeal for financial help.

begging letter ▶ **noun** a letter asking for a gift or a charitable donation.

Begin /ˈbeɪɡɪn, ˈbeɡɪn/, Menachem (1913–92), Israeli statesman, Prime Minister 1977–83. His hard line on Arab–Israeli relations softened in a series of meetings with President Sadat of Egypt, which led to a peace treaty between the countries. Nobel Peace Prize (1978, shared with Sadat).

begin ▶ **verb** (**beginning**; past **began**; past participle **begun**) **1** [with obj.] perform or undergo the first part of (an action or activity): *Peter had just begun a life sentence for murder* | *Nadia began work on a new project* | [with infinitive or present participle] *it was beginning to snow* | [no obj.] *she* **began by** *rewriting the syllabus.*
■ [no obj.] come into being or have its starting point at a certain time or place: *a new era had begun* | *the tale* **begins with** *a sickly youth, Robin* | *the cycleway* **begins at** *Livingston village.* ■ [no obj.] (of a person) hold a specified position or role before holding any other: *he* **began as** *a drummer.* ■ [no obj.] (of a thing) originate: *Watts Lake* **began as** *a marine inlet.* ■ [no obj.] (**begin with**) have as a first element: *words beginning with a vowel.* ■ [no obj.] (**begin on/upon**) set to work at: *Picasso began on a great canvas.* ■ [with direct speech] start speaking by saying: *'Mr Smith,' he began.* ■ [no obj.] (**begin at**) (of an article) cost at least (a specified amount): *rooms begin at $139.*
2 [no obj., with infinitive] [with negative] informal not have any chance or likelihood of doing a specified thing: *circuitry that Karen could not begin to comprehend.*
– PHRASES **to begin with** at first. ■ used to introduce the first of several points: *such a fate is unlikely to befall him: to begin with, his is a genuine talent.*
– ORIGIN Old English *beginnan*, of Germanic origin; related to Dutch and German *beginnen*.

beginner ▶ **noun** a person just starting to learn a skill or take part in an activity.
– PHRASES **beginner's luck** good luck supposedly experienced by a beginner at a particular activity.

beginning ▶ **noun** [usu. in sing.] the point in time or space at which something begins: *he left at the beginning of February* | *they had reached the beginning of the wood.*
■ the process of coming or bringing something into being: *the ending of one relationship and the beginning of another.* ■ the first part or earliest stage of something: *on the paper was the beginning of a letter* | *she had the beginnings of a headache.* ■ (usu. **beginnings**) the background or origins of a person or organization: *he had risen from humble beginnings to great wealth.*
– PHRASES **the beginning of the end** the point or event to which ending or failure can be traced.

begob /bɪˈɡɒb/ ▶ **exclamation** Irish expressing amazement or emphasis.
– ORIGIN late 19th cent.: alteration of *by God!*; compare with **BEGAD**.

begone ▶ **exclamation** poetic/literary go away (as an expression of annoyance): *begone from my sight!*

begonia /bɪˈɡəʊnɪə/ ▶ **noun** a herbaceous plant of warm climates, the flowers of which have brightly coloured sepals but no petals. Numerous cultivars are grown for their flowers or striking foliage.
• Genus *Begonia*, family Begoniaceae.
– ORIGIN modern Latin, named after Michel Bégon (1638–1710), the French amateur botanist who discovered the plant on the island of Santo Domingo and introduced it to Europe.

begorra /bɪˈɡɒrə/ ▶ **exclamation** an exclamation of surprise traditionally attributed to the Irish.
– ORIGIN mid 19th cent.: alteration of *by God*.

begot past of **BEGET**.

begotten past participle of **BEGET**.

beg-pardon ▶ **noun** Austral./NZ informal an apology.

begrime ▶ **verb** [with obj.] [often as adj. **begrimed**] blacken with ingrained dirt.

begrudge ▶ **verb 1** [with two objs] envy (someone) the possession or enjoyment of (something): *she begrudged Martin his affluence.*
2 [with obj.] give reluctantly or resentfully: *nobody begrudges a single penny spent on health* | [as adj. **begrudging**] *begrudging admiration from a rival.*
– DERIVATIVES **begrudgingly** adverb.

beguile ▶ **verb** [with obj.] **1** charm or enchant (someone), typically in an underhand or deceptive way: *he beguiled the voters with his good looks* | [as adj. **beguiling**] *a beguiling smile.*
■ trick (someone) into doing something: *they were* **beguiled into** *signing a peace treaty.*
2 help (time) pass pleasantly: *to beguile some of the time they went to the cinema.*
– DERIVATIVES **beguilement** noun, **beguiler** noun, **beguilingly** adverb.
– ORIGIN Middle English (in the sense 'deceive, deprive of by fraud'): from **BE-** 'thoroughly' + obsolete *guile* 'to deceive' (see **GUILE**).

beguine /beɪˈɡiːn/ ▶ **noun** a popular dance of Caribbean origin, similar to the foxtrot.
– ORIGIN 1930s: from West Indian French, from French *béguin* 'infatuation'.

begum /ˈbeɪɡəm/ ▶ **noun** Indian a Muslim woman of high rank.
■ (**Begum**) the title of a married Muslim woman, equivalent to Mrs.
– ORIGIN from Urdu *begam*, from eastern Turkish *bigim* 'princess', feminine of *big* 'prince'.

begun past participle of **BEGIN**.

behalf ▶ **noun** (in phrase **on** (US also **in**) **behalf of** or **on someone's behalf**) **1** in the interests of a person, group, or principle: *he campaigned on behalf of the wrongly convicted four.*
2 as a representative of: *he had to attend the funeral on Mama's behalf.*
– ORIGIN Middle English: from a mixture of the earlier phrases *on his halve* and *bihalve him*, both meaning 'on his side' (see **BY**, **HALF**).

Behan /ˈbiːən/, Brendan (Francis) (1923–64), Irish dramatist and poet who supported Irish nationalism and was convicted for terrorism. Notable works: *Borstal Boy* (novel, 1958), *The Quare Fellow* (play, 1956).

behave ▶ **verb** [no obj.] **1** [with adverbial] act or conduct oneself in a specified way, especially towards others: *he always behaved like a gentleman* | *you should* **behave** *affectionately* **towards** *the patient.*
■ (of a machine or natural phenomenon) work or function in a specified way: *each car behaves differently.*
2 [often in imperative] conduct oneself in accordance with the accepted norms of a society or group: *'Just behave, Tom,' he said* | *they were expected to* **behave themselves**.
– ORIGIN late Middle English: from **BE-** 'thoroughly' + **HAVE** in the sense 'have or bear (oneself) in a particular way' (corresponding to modern German *sich behaben*).

behaved ▶ **adjective** [in combination or with submodifier] conducting oneself in a specified way: *a well-behaved child* | *some of the boys had been badly behaved.*

behaviour (US **behavior**) ▶ **noun** [mass noun] the way in which one acts or conducts oneself, especially towards others: *good behaviour* | *his insulting* **behaviour towards** *me.*
■ the way in which an animal or person behaves in response to a particular situation or stimulus: *the feeding behaviour of predators.* ■ the way in which a machine or natural phenomenon works or functions: *the erratic behaviour of the old car.*
– PHRASES **be on one's best behaviour** behave well when being observed.
– ORIGIN late Middle English: from **BEHAVE**, on the pattern of *demeanour*, and influenced by obsolete *haviour* from **HAVE**.

behavioural (US **behavioral**) ▶ **adjective** involving, relating to, or emphasizing behaviour: *closely related species have similar behavioural patterns* | *a behavioural approach to children's language.*

behaviouralism (US **behavioralism**) ▶ **noun** [mass noun] the methods and principles of the scientific study of animal (and human) behaviour.
■ advocacy of or adherence to a behavioural approach to social phenomena.
– DERIVATIVES **behaviouralist** noun & adjective.

behavioural science ▶ **noun** [mass noun] the scientific study of human and animal behaviour.

behaviourism (US **behaviorism**) ▶ **noun** [mass noun] Psychology the theory that human and animal behaviour can be explained in terms of conditioning, without appeal to thoughts or feelings, and that psychological disorders are best treated by altering behaviour patterns.
■ such treatment in practice.
– DERIVATIVES **behaviourist** noun & adjective, **behaviouristic** adjective.

behaviour therapy ▶ **noun** [mass noun] the treatment of neurotic symptoms by training the patient's reactions to stimuli.

behead ▶ **verb** cut off the head of (someone), especially as a form of execution.
– ORIGIN Old English *behēafdian*; from **BE-** 'off' (expressing removal) + *hēafod* (see **HEAD**).

beheld past and past participle of **BEHOLD**.

behemoth /bɪˈhiːmɒθ, ˈbiːhɪˌməʊθ/ ▶ **noun** a huge or monstrous creature.
■ something enormous, especially a big and powerful organization.
– ORIGIN late Middle English: from Hebrew *bĕhēmōṯ*, intensive plural of *bĕhēmāh* 'beast'.

behest /bɪˈhɛst/ ▶ **noun** poetic/literary a person's orders or command: *they had assembled* **at his behest**.
– ORIGIN Old English *behǣs* 'a vow', from a Germanic base meaning 'bid'; related to **HIGHT**.

behind ▶ **preposition 1** at or to the far side of (something), typically so as to be hidden by it:
■ expressing location: *the recording machinery was kept behind screens* | *she was sitting behind a luggage trolley.* ■ figurative hidden from the observer: *the agony behind his decision to retire.* ■ expressing movement: *she stopped and drew me behind a screen* | *Jannie instinctively hid her cigarette behind her back.* ■ at the back of (someone), after they have passed through a door: *she ran out of the room, slamming the door behind her.*
2 in a queue or procession, following or further back than (another member of the queue or procession): *stuck behind a slow-moving tractor.*
3 in support of or giving guidance to (someone else): *whatever you decide to do, I'll be behind you* | *the power behind the throne.*
■ guiding, controlling, or responsible for (an event or plan): *the chances were that he was behind the death of the girl* | *the reasoning behind their decisions* | *the meticulous organization behind the coup.*
4 after the departure or death of (the person referred to): *he left behind him a manuscript which was subsequently published.*
5 less advanced than (someone else) in achievement or development: *the government admitted it is ten years behind the West in PC technology.*
6 having a lower score than (another competitor): *Woosnam moved to ten under par, five shots behind Fred Couples.*
▶ **adverb 1** at or to the far side of something: *Campbell grabbed him from behind.*
2 in a particular place after leaving or after others have moved on: *Marie had left a load of mags behind* | *don't leave me behind.*
3 further back than other members of a moving group: *Bigwig led the way, with Buckthorn a short distance behind.*
4 (in a contest or match) having a score lower than that of the opposing team: *England were still 382 runs behind.*
5 late in accomplishing a task: *I'm getting* **behind with** *my work.*
■ in arrears: *she was* **behind with** *her rent.*
▶ **noun 1** informal the backside: *sitting on her behind.*
2 Australian Rules a kick that sends the ball over a behind line, or a touch that sends it between the inner posts, scoring one point.
– ORIGIN Old English *behindan*, *bihindan*, from *bi* 'by' + *hindan* 'from behind'.

behindhand ▶ **adjective** [predic.] late or slow in doing something, especially paying a debt: *I do not want to be* **behindhand with** *my shipmates* | *the Yoruba have not been* **behindhand in** *economic activity.*
■ archaic unaware of recent events: *you are miserably behindhand—Mr Cole gave me a hint of it six weeks ago.*
– ORIGIN mid 16th cent.: from **BEHIND** + **HAND**, on the pattern of *beforehand*.

behind line ▶ **noun** Australian Rules the line between an inner and outer goalpost.

Behn /beɪn, bɛn/, Aphra (1640–89), English novelist and dramatist, regarded as the first professional woman writer in England. Notable works: *The Rover* (comic play, 1678) and *Oroonoko, or the History of the Royal Slave* (novel, 1688).

behold ▶ **verb** (past and past participle **beheld**) [with obj.] [often in imperative] archaic or poetic/literary see or observe (someone or something, especially of remarkable or impressive nature): *behold your lord and prince!* | *the botanical gardens were a wonder* **to behold**.
– DERIVATIVES **beholder** noun.
– ORIGIN Old English *bihaldan*, from *bi-* 'thoroughly' + *haldan* 'to hold'. Parallel Germanic words have the sense 'maintain, retain'; the notion of 'looking' is found only in English.

beholden ▶ **adjective** [predic.] owing thanks or having a duty to someone in return for help or a service: *I don't like to be* **beholden to** *anybody.*
– ORIGIN late Middle English: archaic past participle of **BEHOLD**, in the otherwise unrecorded sense 'bound'.

behoof /bɪˈhuːf/ ▶ **noun** [mass noun] archaic benefit or advantage: *to make laws* **for the behoof of** *the colony.*
– ORIGIN Old English *behōf*, of West Germanic origin;

related to Dutch *behoef* and German *Behuf*, also to **HEAVE**.

behove /bɪˈhəʊv/ (US **behoove** /-ˈhuːv/) ▶ **verb** [with obj.] (**it behoves someone to do something**) formal it is a duty or responsibility for someone to do something; it is incumbent on: *it behoves the House to assure itself that there is no conceivable alternative.*
■[with negative] it is appropriate or suitable; it befits: ***it ill behoves** Opposition Members constantly to decry the sale of arms to friendly countries.*
– ORIGIN Old English *behōfian*, from *behōf* (see **BEHOOF**).

Behrens /ˈbɛːr(ə)nz/, Peter (1868–1940), German architect and designer. He trained Walter Gropius and Le Corbusier.

Behring /ˈbɛːrɪŋ/, Emil Adolf von (1854–1917), German bacteriologist and one of the founders of immunology. Nobel Prize for Physiology/Medicine (1901).

Beiderbecke /ˈbʌɪdəbɛk/, Bix (1903–31), American jazz musician and composer; born *Leon Bismarck Beiderbecke*. A self-taught cornettist and pianist, he was one of a handful of white musicians who profoundly influenced the development of jazz.

beige ▶ **adjective** of a pale sandy fawn colour: *the beige tiles of the kitchen floor.*
▶ **noun** [mass noun] a pale sandy fawn: *tones of beige and green* | [count noun] *matching fawns and beiges.*
– ORIGIN mid 19th cent. (denoting a usually undyed and unbleached woollen fabric of this colour): from French, of unknown ultimate origin.

beignet /ˈbɛnjeɪ/ ▶ **noun** chiefly N. Amer. **1** a fritter.
2 a square of fried dough eaten hot sprinkled with icing sugar.
– ORIGIN French, from archaic *buyne* 'hump, bump'.

Beijing /beɪˈ(d)ʒɪŋ/ (also **Peking**) the capital of China, in the north-east of the country; pop. 6,920,000 (1990). Beijing became the country's capital in 1421, at the start of the Ming period, and survived as the capital of the Republic of China after the revolution of 1912.

being ▶ **noun** **1** [mass noun] existence: *the railway brought many towns **into being** | the single market **came into being** in 1993 | Communist factions remained **in being**.*
■living; being alive: *a unified way of being.*
2 [in sing.] the nature or essence of a person: *sometimes one aspect of our being has been developed at the expense of the others.*
3 a real or imaginary living creature or entity, especially an intelligent one: *alien beings | a rational being.*

Beira /ˈbʌɪrə/ a port on the coast of Mozambique, capital of Sofala province; pop. 299,300 (1990).

beira /ˈbeɪrə/ (also **beira antelope**) ▶ **noun** a rare, slender antelope found in Somalia and Ethiopia.
● *Dorcatragus megalotis*, family Bovidae.
– ORIGIN a local name.

Beirut /beɪˈruːt/ the capital and chief port of Lebanon; pop. 1,500,000 (est. 1988). The city was badly damaged during the Lebanese civil war of 1975–89.

beisa /ˈbeɪzə/ (also **beisa oryx**) ▶ **noun** a gemsbok of a race that is native to the Horn of Africa.
● *Oryx gazella beisa*, family Bovidae.
– ORIGIN mid 19th cent.: from Amharic.

Beja /ˈbɛdʒə/ ▶ **noun** (pl. same) **1** a member of a nomadic people living between the Nile and the Red Sea.
2 [mass noun] the Cushitic language of this people, with about 1 million speakers.
▶ **adjective** of or relating to this people or their language.

bejabers /bɪˈdʒeɪbəz/ (also **bejabbers** /-ˈdʒabəz/) ▶ **exclamation** another way of saying **BEJESUS**.
– ORIGIN early 19th cent.: alteration of *by Jesus*.

Béjart /beɪˈʒɑː, French beʒaʀ/, Maurice (b.1927), French choreographer; born *Maurice Jean Berger*. He is chiefly identified with The Ballet of the 20th Century, the company which he founded in Brussels in 1959. His choreography is noted for its fusion of classic and modern dance.

bejesus /bɪˈdʒiːzəs/ (also **bejeezus**) ▶ **noun** informal an exclamation traditionally attributed to the Irish, used to express surprise or for emphasis.
– PHRASES **beat the bejesus out of** hit (someone) very hard or for a long time. **scare the bejesus out of** frighten (someone) very much.

bejewelled (US **bejeweled**) ▶ **adjective** adorned with jewels.

Bekaa /bɪˈkɑː/ (also **El Beqa'a**) a fertile valley in central Lebanon between the Lebanon and Anti-Lebanon Mountains.

Bel /bɛl/ another name for **BAAL**.

bel ▶ **noun** a unit used in the comparison of power levels in electrical communication or of intensities of sound, corresponding to an intensity ratio of 10 to 1. See also **DECIBEL**.
– ORIGIN 1920s: from the name of A. G. *Bell* (see **BELL**[1]).

belabour (US **belabor**) ▶ **verb** [with obj.] **1** attack or assault (someone) physically or verbally: *Bernard was belabouring Jed with his fists.*
2 argue or elaborate (a subject) in excessive detail: *there is no need to belabour the point.*
– ORIGIN late Middle English: from **BE-** (expressing transitivity) + the verb **LABOUR**.

Bel and the Dragon a book of the Apocrypha containing additional stories of Daniel, concerned mainly with his refusal to worship Bel and his slaying of a dragon.

Belarus /ˌbɛləˈruːs/ a country in eastern Europe; pop. 10,328,000 (est. 1991); official language, Belorussian; capital, Minsk. Formerly called **BELORUSSIA**, **WHITE RUSSIA**.

> Successively part of the grand duchy of Lithuania, Poland, and the Russian empire, the country became a republic of the USSR in 1921. Belarus gained independence as a member of the Commonwealth of Independent States in 1991 but in 1996 signed a treaty with Russia that established a Community of Sovereign Republics.

– DERIVATIVES **Belarusian** noun & adjective.

belated ▶ **adjective** coming or happening later than should have been the case: *a belated apology.*
– DERIVATIVES **belatedly** adverb, **belatedness** noun.
– ORIGIN early 17th cent. (in the sense 'overtaken by darkness'): past participle of obsolete *belate* 'delay' (see **BE-**, **LATE**).

Belau /bəˈlaʊ/ variant spelling of **PALAU**.

belay /ˈbiːleɪ, bɪˈleɪ/ ▶ **verb** [with obj.] **1** fix (a running rope) round a cleat, pin, rock, or other object, to secure it.
■secure (a rock climber) in this way: *he belayed his partner across the ice* | [no obj.] *it is possible to belay here.*
2 [usu. in imperative] Nautical slang stop; desist from: *'Belay that, mister. Man your post.'*
▶ **noun** **1** an act of belaying.
2 a spike of rock or other hard material used for belaying.
– DERIVATIVES **belayer** noun.
– ORIGIN mid 16th cent. (originally in nautical use): from **BE-** + **LAY**[1], on the pattern of Dutch *beleggen*.

belaying pin ▶ **noun** a fixed pin, typically of metal or wood, used on board ship and in rock climbing to secure a rope which is fastened around it.

bel canto /bɛl ˈkantəʊ/ ▶ **noun** [mass noun] a lyrical style of operatic singing using a full, rich, broad tone and smooth phrasing.
– ORIGIN late 19th cent.: Italian, literally 'fine song'.

belch ▶ **verb** **1** [no obj.] emit wind noisily from the stomach through the mouth.
2 [with obj.] (often **belch out/forth/into**) (especially of a chimney) send (smoke or flames) out or up: *a factory chimney belches out smoke.*
■[no obj.] (**belch from**) (of smoke or flames) pour out from (a chimney or other opening): *flames belch from the wreckage.*
▶ **noun** an act of belching.
– ORIGIN Old English *belcettan*, probably imitative.

beldam /ˈbɛldəm/ (also **beldame**) ▶ **noun** archaic an old woman.
■a malicious and ugly woman, especially an old one; a witch.
– ORIGIN late Middle English (originally in the sense 'grandmother'): from Old French *bel* 'beautiful' + **DAM**[3].

beleaguer ▶ **verb** [with obj.] [usu. as adj. **beleaguered**] lay siege to: *he is leading a relief force to the aid of the beleaguered city.*
■put in a very difficult situation: *the board is supporting the beleaguered director amid calls for his resignation.*
– ORIGIN late 16th cent.: from Dutch *belegeren* 'camp round', from *be-* '(all) about' + *leger* 'a camp'.

Belém /bɛˈlɛm/ a city and port of northern Brazil, at the mouth of the Amazon, capital of the state of Pará; pop. 1,244,690 (1992). It is the country's chief commercial centre.

belemnite /ˈbɛləmnʌɪt/ ▶ **noun** an extinct cephalopod mollusc with a bullet-shaped internal shell that is typically found as a fossil in marine deposits of the Jurassic and Cretaceous periods.
● Order Belemnoidea, class Cephalopoda: many genera.
– ORIGIN early 17th cent.: from modern Latin *belemnites*, based on Greek *belemnon* 'dart'.

bel esprit /ˌbɛl ɛˈspriː, French bɛl ɛspʀi/ ▶ **noun** (pl. **beaux esprits** /ˌbəʊz ɛˈspriː, French boz ɛspʀi/) archaic a witty person.
– ORIGIN French, literally 'fine mind'.

Belfast /bɛlˈfɑːst/ the capital and chief port of Northern Ireland; pop. 280,970 (1991). The city suffered damage and population decline from the early 1970s as a result of sectarian violence by the IRA and Loyalist paramilitary groups.

belfry ▶ **noun** (pl. **-ies**) a bell tower or steeple housing bells, especially one that is part of a church.
■a space for hanging bells in a church tower.
– PHRASES **bats in the** (or **one's**) **belfry** see **BAT**[2].
– ORIGIN Middle English *berfrey*, from Old French *berfrei*, later *belfrei*, of West Germanic origin. The change in the first syllable was due to association with **BELL**[1].

Belgae /ˈbɛldʒiː, ˈbɛlgʌɪ/ ▶ **plural noun** an ancient Celtic people inhabiting Gaul north of the Seine and Marne Rivers.
– ORIGIN from Latin.

Belgaum /ˈbɛlgaʊm/ an industrial city in western India, in the state of Karnataka; pop. 326,000 (1991).

Belgian ▶ **adjective** of or relating to Belgium.
▶ **noun** a native or national of Belgium or a person of Belgian descent.

Belgian Blue ▶ **noun** a heavily muscled animal of a breed of cattle kept for its meat.

Belgian Congo former name (1908–60) for **ZAIRE** (Democratic Republic of Congo).

Belgian endive ▶ **noun** another term for **ENDIVE** (in sense 2).

Belgian hare ▶ **noun** a rabbit of a dark red long-eared domestic breed.

Belgian sheepdog ▶ **noun** a dog of a medium-sized breed, similar in appearance to an Alsatian.

Belgian waffle ▶ **noun** N. Amer. a waffle with large, deep indentations.

Belgic /ˈbɛldʒɪk/ ▶ **adjective** of or relating to the Belgae.

Belgium a low-lying country in western Europe on the south shore of the North Sea and English Channel; pop. 9,978,700 (1991); official languages, Flemish and French; capital, Brussels. French name **BELGIQUE** /bɛlʒik/, Flemish name **BELGIË** /ˈbɛlxiːə/.

> Belgium became independent from the Netherlands after a nationalist revolt in 1830. Occupied and devastated during both world wars, Belgium formed the Benelux Customs Union with the Netherlands and Luxembourg in 1948 and became a founder member of the EEC. Flemish is spoken mainly in the north of the country, and French and Walloon in the south.

– ORIGIN Latin, from **BELGAE**.

Belgorod /ˈbɛlgərɒd/ an industrial city in southern Russia, on the Donets River close to the border with Ukraine; pop. 306,000 (1990).

Belgrade /bɛlˈgreɪd/ the capital of Serbia, on the River Danube; pop. 1,168,450 (1991). Serbian name **BEOGRAD**.

Belial /ˈbiːlɪəl/ a name for the Devil.
– ORIGIN from Hebrew *bĕlîyyaʻal* 'worthlessness'.

belie ▶ **verb** (**belying**) [with obj.] **1** (of an appearance) fail to give a true notion or impression of (something): *his lively, alert manner belied his years.*
2 fail to fulfil or justify (a claim or expectation): *the quality of the music seems to belie the criticism.*
– ORIGIN Old English *belēogan* 'deceive by lying', from **BE-** 'about' + *lēogan* 'to lie'. Current senses date from the 17th cent.

belief ▶ **noun** **1** an acceptance that a statement is true or that something exists: *his **belief in** God* | [with clause] *a belief that climate can be modified beneficially.*
■something one accepts as true or real; a firmly held opinion or conviction: *we're prepared to fight for our beliefs* | [mass noun] *contrary to popular belief existing safety regulations were adequate.* ■a religious conviction: *Christian beliefs.*
2 (**belief in**) trust, faith, or confidence in (someone

or something): *a belief in democratic politics* | [mass noun] *I've still got belief in myself.*

– PHRASES **be of the belief that** hold the opinion that; think. **beyond belief** astonishingly great, good, or bad; incredible: *riches beyond belief* | *the driving we have witnessed was beyond belief.* **in the belief that** thinking or believing that: *he took the property in the belief that he had consent.* **to the best of my belief** in my genuine opinion; as far as I know.

– ORIGIN Middle English: alteration of Old English *gelēafa*; compare with **BELIEVE**.

believable ▶ **adjective** (of an account or the person relating it) able to be believed; credible.

■(of a fictional character or situation) convincing or realistic.

– DERIVATIVES **believability** noun, **believably** adverb.

believe ▶ **verb** [with obj.] **1** accept (something) as true; feel sure of the truth of: *the superintendent believed Lancaster's story* | [with clause] *Christians believe that Jesus rose from the dead.*

■accept the statement of (someone) as true: *he didn't believe her or didn't want to know.* ■ [no obj.] have faith, especially religious faith: *there are those on the fringes of the Church who do not really believe.* ■ (**believe something of someone**) feel sure that someone is capable of a particular action: *I wouldn't have believed it of Lavinia—what an extraordinary woman!*

2 [with clause] hold (something) as an opinion; think or suppose: *I believe we've already met* | *things were not as bad as the experts believed* | (**believe some-one/thing to be**) *four men were believed to be trapped in the burning building.*

– PHRASES **believe it or not** used to concede that a proposition or statement is surprising: *believe it or not, the speaker was none other than Horace.* **believe me** (or **believe you me**) used to emphasize the truth of a statement or assertion: *believe me, it is well worth the effort.* **be unable to** (or **be hardly able to**) **believe** be amazed by (something): *Clarke could hardly believe his luck as he put the ball into the empty net.* **be unable to** (or **be hardly able to**) **believe one's eyes** (or **ears**) be amazed by what one sees or hears. **don't you believe it!** used to express disbelief in the truth of a statement: *he says he is left of centre, but don't you believe it.* **would you believe (it)?** used to express surprise at something one is relating: *they're still arguing, would you believe it?*

– ORIGIN late Old English *belyfan, belēfan*, alteration of *gelēfan*, of Germanic origin; related to Dutch *geloven* and German *glauben*, also to **LIEF**.

▶ **believe in 1** have faith in the truth or existence of: *those who believe in God.* **2** be of the opinion that (something) is right, proper, or desirable: *I don't believe in censorship of the arts.* **3** have confidence in (a person or a course of action): *he had finally begun to believe in her.*

believer ▶ **noun 1** a person who believes in the truth or existence of something: [with clause] *a firm* ***believer that*** *party politics has no place in local government* | *a* ***believer in*** *ghosts.*

■a person who believes that a specified thing is effective, proper, or desirable: *I'm a great* ***believer in*** *community policing.*

2 an adherent of a particular religion; someone with religious faith.

Belisha beacon /bəˈliːʃə/ ▶ **noun** (in the UK) an orange ball containing a flashing light, mounted on a striped post on the pavement at each end of a zebra crossing.

– ORIGIN 1930s: named after Leslie Hore-*Belisha* (1893–1957), British politician, Minister of Transport when the beacons were introduced.

belittle ▶ **verb** [with obj.] dismiss (someone or something) as unimportant: *this is not to belittle his role.*

– DERIVATIVES **belittlement** noun, **belittler** noun, **belittlingly** adverb.

Belitung /bɪˈliːtʊŋ/ (also **Billiton**) an Indonesian island in the Java Sea, between Borneo and Sumatra.

Belize /bɛˈliːz/ a country on the Caribbean coast of Central America; pop. 190,800 (1991); languages, English (official), Creole, Spanish; capital, Belmopan. Former name (until 1973) **BRITISH HONDURAS**.

Proclaimed as a British Crown Colony in 1862, Belize became an independent Commonwealth state in 1981. Guatemala, which bounds it on the west and south, has always claimed the territory on the basis of old Spanish treaties, although in 1992 it agreed to recognize the existence of Belize.

– DERIVATIVES **Belizean** (also **Belizian**) adjective & noun.

– ORIGIN named after a river with a Mayan name meaning 'muddy water'.

Belize City the principal seaport and former capital (until 1970) of Belize; pop. 46,000 (1991).

Bell[1], Alexander Graham (1847–1922), Scottish-born American scientist, the inventor of the telephone and the gramophone.

Bell[2], Currer, Ellis, and Acton, the pseudonyms used by Charlotte, Emily, and Anne Brontë.

Bell[3], Gertrude (Margaret Lowthian) (1868–1926), English archaeologist, traveller, and supporter of Arab independence.

Bell[4], Vanessa (1879–1961), English painter and designer; born *Vanessa Stephen.* Together with her sister Virginia Woolf she was a prominent member of the Bloomsbury Group.

bell[1] ▶ **noun 1** a hollow object, typically made of metal and having the shape of a deep inverted cup widening at the lip, that sounds a clear musical note when struck, especially by means of a clapper inside.

■a device that includes or sounds like a bell, used to give a signal or warning: *a bicycle bell.* ■ (**the bell**) (in boxing and other sports) a bell rung to mark the start or end of a round: *they were dragged off each other at the final bell.*

2 a bell-shaped object or part of an object, in particular:

■the end of a trumpet. ■ the corolla of a bell-shaped flower.

3 (**bells**) a musical instrument consisting of a set of cylindrical metal tubes of different lengths, suspended in a frame and played by being struck with a hammer. Also called **TUBULAR BELLS**.

4 Nautical (preceded by a numeral) the time as indicated every half-hour of a watch by the striking of the ship's bell one to eight times: *at five bells in the forenoon of June 11.*

▶ **verb 1** [with obj.] provide with a bell or bells; attach a bell or bells to: [as adj. **belled**] *animals in gaudy belled harnesses.*

2 [no obj.] make a ringing sound likened to that of a bell: *your ears are still belling when the cars come around again.*

■[with obj.] Brit. informal telephone (someone).

3 [no obj.] spread or flare outwards like the lip of a bell: *her shirt* ***belled out*** *behind.*

– PHRASES **bell the cat** take the danger of a shared enterprise upon oneself. [ORIGIN: an allusion to a fable in which the mice (or rats) suggest hanging a bell around the cat's neck to have warning of its approach.] **bells and whistles** informal attractive additional features or trimmings. [ORIGIN: an allusion to the various bells and whistles of old fairground organs.] **be saved by the bell** (in boxing and other sports) be saved from being counted out by the ringing of the bell at the end of a round. ■ escape from a difficult situation narrowly or by an unexpected intervention. **(as) clear** (or **sound**) **as a bell** perfectly clear or sound. **give someone a bell** Brit. informal telephone someone. **ring a bell** informal revive a distant recollection; sound familiar: *the name rings a bell.* **with bells on** N. Amer. informal enthusiastically: *everybody's waiting for you with bells on.*

– ORIGIN Old English *belle*, of Germanic origin; related to Dutch *bel*, and perhaps to **BELL**[2].

bell[2] ▶ **noun** the cry of a stag or buck at rutting time.

▶ **verb** [no obj.] (of a stag or buck) make this cry.

– ORIGIN Old English *bellan* 'to bellow', of Germanic origin; related to German *bellen* 'to bark, bray', and perhaps also to **BELL**[1].

belladonna /ˌbɛləˈdɒnə/ ▶ **noun** deadly nightshade.

■[mass noun] a drug prepared from the leaves and root of this plant, containing atropine.

– ORIGIN mid 18th cent.: from modern Latin, from Italian *bella donna* 'fair lady', perhaps from the use of its juice to add brilliance to the eyes by dilating the pupils.

belladonna lily ▶ **noun** the South African amaryllis.

bellbird ▶ **noun 1** a tropical American bird of the cotinga family, with loud explosive calls. There are wattles on the head of the male.

● Genus *Procnias*, family Cotingidae: four species.

2 any of a number of Australasian songbirds with ringing bell-like calls:

● (**New Zealand bellbird**) a New Zealand honeyeater (*Anthornis melanura*, family Meliphagidae). ● (**crested bellbird**) an Australian whistler (*Oreoica gutturalis*, family Pachycephalidae). ● the bell miner. See **MINER** (sense 2).

bell-bottoms ▶ **plural noun** trousers with a marked flare below the knee: [as modifier] (**bell-bottom**) *bell-bottom trousers.*

– DERIVATIVES **bell-bottomed** adjective.

bellboy ▶ **noun** chiefly N. Amer. an attendant in a hotel who performs services such as carrying guests' luggage.

bell-buoy ▶ **noun** a buoy equipped with a bell rung by the motion of the sea, warning shipping of shoal waters.

bell captain ▶ **noun** N. Amer. the supervisor of a group of bellboys.

bell crank (also **bell-crank lever**) ▶ **noun** a lever with two arms which have a common fulcrum at their junction.

bell curve ▶ **noun** Mathematics a graph of a normal (Gaussian) distribution, with a large rounded peak tapering away at each end.

belle /bɛl/ ▶ **noun** a beautiful girl or woman, especially the most beautiful at a particular event or in a particular group: *the belle of the ball.*

– ORIGIN early 17th cent.: from French, feminine of *beau*, from Latin *bella*, feminine of *bellus* 'beautiful'.

belle époque /ˌbɛl eɪˈpɒk, French bɛl epɔk/ ▶ **noun** the period of settled and comfortable life preceding the First World War: [as modifier] *a romantic, belle-époque replica of a Paris bistro.*

– ORIGIN French, 'fine period'.

belle laide /bɛl ˈlɛd/ ▶ **noun** (pl. **belles laides** pronunc. same) another way of saying **JOLIE LAIDE**.

– ORIGIN French, from *belle* 'beautiful' and *laide* 'ugly', feminine adjectives.

Bellerophon /bɪˈlɛrəf(ə)n/ Greek Mythology a hero who slew the monster Chimera with the help of the winged horse Pegasus.

belles-lettres /bɛlˈlɛtr(ə), French bɛllɛtʀ/ ▶ **plural noun** [also treated as sing.] essays, particularly on literary and artistic criticism, written and read primarily for their aesthetic effect.

– DERIVATIVES **belletrism** /bɛlˈlɛtrɪz(ə)m/ noun, **belletrist** noun, **belletristic** adjective.

– ORIGIN mid 17th cent.: from French, literally 'fine letters'.

bellflower ▶ **noun** a plant with bell-shaped flowers that are typically blue, purple, or white, many kinds being cultivated as ornamentals.

● Genus *Campanula*, family Campanulaceae (the **bellflower family**): many species, including the Eurasian **clustered bellflower** (*C. glomerata*) and the harebell.

bell glass ▶ **noun** a bell-shaped glass cover used, especially formerly, as a cloche.

bell heather ▶ **noun** a common European heather with relatively large purplish-red flowers.

● *Erica cinerea*, family Ericaceae.

bellhop ▶ **noun** N. Amer. another term for **BELLBOY**.

bellicose /ˈbɛlɪkəʊs/ ▶ **adjective** demonstrating aggression and willingness to fight: *a mood of bellicose jingoism.*

– DERIVATIVES **bellicosity** /-ˈkɒsɪti/ noun.

– ORIGIN late Middle English: from Latin *bellicosus*, from *bellicus* 'warlike', from *bellum* 'war'.

belligerence /bəˈlɪdʒ(ə)r(ə)ns/ (also **belligerency**) ▶ **noun** [mass noun] aggressive or warlike behaviour.

belligerent ▶ **adjective** hostile and aggressive: *the mood at the meeting was belligerent.*

■engaged in a war or conflict, as recognized by international law.

▶ **noun** a nation or person engaged in war or conflict, as recognized by international law.

– DERIVATIVES **belligerently** adverb.

– ORIGIN late 16th cent.: from Latin *belligerant-* 'waging war', from the verb *belligerare*, from *bellum* 'war'.

Bellingshausen Sea /ˈbɛlɪŋzˌhaʊz(ə)n/ a part of the SE Pacific off the coast of Antarctica, bounded to the east and south by the Antarctic Peninsula and Ellsworth Land.

– ORIGIN named after the Russian explorer Fabian Gottlieb von *Bellingshausen* (1778–1852), who in 1819–21 became the first to circumnavigate Antarctica.

Bellini[1] /bɛˈliːni/, a family of Italian painters in Venice, **Jacopo** (*c.*1400–70) and his sons **Gentile** (*c.*1429–1507) and **Giovanni** (*c.*1430–1516).

Bellini² /bɛ'li:ni/, Vincenzo (1801–35), Italian composer. Notable operas: *La Sonnambula* (1831), *Norma* (1831), and *I Puritani* (1835).

bell jar ▶ noun a bell-shaped glass cover used in a laboratory, typically for enclosing samples.
■ figurative an environment in which someone is protected or cut off from the outside world. [ORIGIN: with allusion to Sylvia Plath's novel, *The Bell Jar* (1963).]

bell magpie ▶ noun see **CURRAWONG** and **MAGPIE** (sense 2).

bellman ▶ noun (pl. **-men**) historical a town crier.

bell metal ▶ noun [mass noun] an alloy of copper and tin for making bells, with a higher tin content than in bronze.

Belloc /'bɛlɒk/ (Joseph) Hilaire (Pierre René) (1870–1953), French-born British writer, historian, and poet remembered chiefly for *Cautionary Tales* (1907).

Bellow, Saul (b.1915), Canadian-born American novelist, of Russian-Jewish descent. Notable works: *The Adventures of Augie March* (1953) and *Herzog* (1964). Nobel Prize for Literature (1976).

bellow ▶ verb [no obj.] (of a person or animal) emit a deep loud roar, typically in pain or anger: *he bellowed in agony.*
■ [reporting verb] shout something with a deep loud roar: [with obj.] *he* **bellowed out** *the order* | [with direct speech] *'Not sausage and mash again!' he bellowed* | [with infinitive] *her parents were* **bellowing at** *her to stop.* ■ [with obj.] sing (a song) loudly and tunelessly: *a dozen large men were bellowing 'Jerusalem'.*
▶ noun a deep roaring shout or sound: *a bellow of rage* | *he delivers his lines in a bellow.*
– ORIGIN Middle English: perhaps from late Old English *bylgan*.

bellows ▶ plural noun [also treated as sing.] **1** a device with an air bag that emits a stream of air when squeezed:
■ (also **a pair of bellows**) a kind with two handles used for blowing air at a fire. ■ a kind used in a harmonium or small organ.
2 an object or device with concertinaed sides to allow it to expand and contract, such as a tube joining a lens to a camera body.
– ORIGIN Middle English: probably from Old English *belga*, plural of *belig* (see **BELLY**), used as a shortened form of earlier *blæstbelig* 'blowing-bag'.

bell pepper ▶ noun North American term for **SWEET PEPPER**.

bell pull ▶ noun a cord or handle which rings a bell when pulled, typically used to summon someone from another room.

bell push ▶ noun Brit. a button that operates an electric bell when pushed.

bell-ringing ▶ noun [mass noun] the activity or pastime of ringing church bells or handbells.
– DERIVATIVES **bell-ringer** noun.

bell sheep ▶ noun Austral./NZ a sheep caught by a shearer just before the bell rings to signal the end of a shift, which he is allowed to shear.

Bell's palsy ▶ noun [mass noun] paralysis of the facial nerve causing muscular weakness in one side of the face.
– ORIGIN mid 19th cent.: named after Sir Charles Bell (1774–1842), the Scottish anatomist who first described it.

bell tent ▶ noun a cone-shaped tent supported by a central pole.

bellwether ▶ noun the leading sheep of a flock, with a bell on its neck.
■ an indicator or predictor of something: *Basildon is now the bellwether of Britain's voting behaviour.*

belly ▶ noun (pl. **-ies**) the human trunk below the ribs, containing the stomach and bowels.
■ the front of this part of the body: *he fell flat on his belly.* ■ the stomach, especially as representing the body's need for food: *they'll fight all the better on empty bellies.* ■ the underside of a bird or other animal. ■ (also **belly pork**) [mass noun] a cut of pork from the underside between the legs. ■ a pig's belly as food, especially as a traded commodity. ■ the rounded underside of a ship or aircraft. ■ the top surface of an instrument of the violin family, over which the strings are placed.
▶ verb (**-ies**, **-ied**) **1** [no obj.] swell; bulge: *as she leaned forward her pullover* **bellied out**.
■ [with obj.] cause to swell or bulge: *the wind* **bellied** *the sail out.*
2 [no obj.] (**belly up to**) N. Amer. informal move or sit close to (a bar or table): *regulars who first bellied up to the bar years before.*
– PHRASES **go belly up** informal go bankrupt.
– DERIVATIVES **bellied** adjective [in combination] *fat-bellied men.*
– ORIGIN Old English *belig* 'bag', of Germanic origin, from a base meaning 'swell, be inflated'.

bellyache informal ▶ noun a stomach pain.
▶ verb [no obj.] complain noisily or persistently: *Heads of Department* **bellyaching about** *lack of resources.*
– DERIVATIVES **bellyacher** noun.

bellyband ▶ noun a band placed round a horse's belly to harness it to the shafts of a cart.

belly button ▶ noun informal a person's navel.

belly dance ▶ noun a dance originating in the Middle East, typically performed by a woman and involving undulating movements of the belly and rapid gyration of the hips.
– DERIVATIVES **belly dancer** noun, **belly dancing** noun.

bellyflop informal ▶ noun a dive into water, landing flat on one's front.
▶ verb (**-flopped**, **-flopping**) [no obj.] perform such a dive.
■ (of an aircraft) perform an emergency landing without lowering the undercarriage.

bellyful ▶ noun (pl. **-fuls**) a quantity of food sufficient to fill one's stomach; a sustaining meal.
– PHRASES **have a** (or **one's**) **bellyful** informal become intolerant of someone or something after lengthy or repeated contact: *he had had his bellyful of hospitals.*

belly landing ▶ noun a crash-landing of an aircraft on the underside of the fuselage, without lowering the undercarriage.

belly laugh ▶ noun a loud unrestrained laugh.

belly pork ▶ noun see **BELLY**.

Belmopan /ˌbɛlməʊ'pan/ the capital of Belize; pop. 3,850 (1991).

Belo Horizonte /ˌbɛl ɒrɪ'zɒnteɪ, -ti/ a city in eastern Brazil, capital of the state of Minas Gerais; pop. 2,020,160 (1991).

belong ▶ verb [no obj.] **1** [with adverbial of place] (of a thing) be rightly placed in a specified position: *learning to place the blame where it belongs* | *such statements do not belong in a modern student textbook.*
■ be rightly classified in or assigned to a specified category: *bony fish: the vast majority of living fish belong here* | *the Howard letter does* **belong to** *the year 1469.*
2 [usu. with adverbial of place] (of a person) fit in a specified place or environment: *she is a stranger, and doesn't belong here* | *you and me, we belong together* | [as noun **belonging**] *we feel a real* **sense of belonging**.
■ have the right personal or social qualities to be a member of a particular group: *young people are generally very anxious to belong.* ■ (**belong to**) be a member or part of (a particular group, organization, or class): *they belong to garden and bridge clubs.*
3 (**belong to**) be the property of: *the vehicle did not belong to him.*
■ be the rightful possession of; be due to: *most of the credit belongs to Paul.* ■ (of a contest or period of time) be dominated by: *the race belonged completely to Fogarty.*
– DERIVATIVES **belongingness** noun.
– ORIGIN Middle English (in the sense 'be appropriately assigned to'): from **BE-** (as an intensifier) + the archaic verb *long* 'belong', based on Old English *gelang* 'at hand, together with'.

belongings ▶ plural noun a person's movable possessions.

Belorussia /ˌbɛlə(ʊ)'rʌʃə/ (also **Byelorussia**) former name for **BELARUS**.
– ORIGIN from Russian *Belorossiya*, from *belyĭ* 'white' + *Rossiya* 'Russia'.

Belorussian (also **Byelorussian**) ▶ adjective of or relating to Belarus, its people, or its language.
▶ noun **1** a native of Belarus, or a person of Belorussian descent.
2 [mass noun] the Eastern Slavic language of Belarus, with about 9 million speakers.

Belostok /bʲila'stok/ Russian name for **BIAŁYSTOK**.

beloved ▶ adjective dearly loved.
■ [predic.] (**beloved by/of**) very popular with or much used by (a specified set of people): *the mountain hut is beloved of families on a day's outing.*
▶ noun a much loved person: *he watched his beloved.*
– ORIGIN late Middle English: past participle of obsolete *belove* 'be pleasing', later 'love'.

below ▶ preposition **1** extending underneath: *the tunnel below the crags* | *cables running below the floorboards* | *hanging space below a top storage shelf.*
2 at a lower level or layer than: *just below the pocket was a stain* | *blistered skin below his collar.*
■ lower in grade or rank than: *below us in the League* | *they rated its financial soundness below its competitor's.*
3 lower than (a specified amount, rate, or norm): *below average* | *below freezing* | *a dive to below 60 feet* | *below 50 mph* | *if your account falls below $5000.*
▶ adverb at a lower level or layer: *he jumped from the window into the moat below.*
■ (in printed text) mentioned later or further down on the same page: *our nutritionist is pictured below right.* ■ Nautical below deck: *I'll* **go below** *and fix us a drink.*
– PHRASES **below** (**the**) **ground** beneath the surface of the ground. **below stairs** Brit. dated in the basement of a house as occupied by servants.
– ORIGIN late Middle English (as an adverb): from **BE-** 'by' + the adjective **LOW¹**. Not common until the 16th cent., the word developed a prepositional use and was frequent in Shakespeare.

below decks (also **below deck**) ▶ adjective & adverb in or into the space below the main deck of a ship.
▶ plural noun (**belowdecks**) the space below the main deck of a ship.

Bel Paese /ˌbɛl pɑː'eɪzeɪ, -zi/ ▶ noun [mass noun] trademark a rich, white, mild, creamy cheese of a kind originally made in Italy.
– ORIGIN Italian, literally 'fair country'.

Belsen /'bɛls(ə)n/ a Nazi concentration camp in the Second World War, near the village of Belsen in NW Germany.

Belshazzar /bɛl'ʃazə/ (6th century BC), viceroy and son of the last king of Babylon. The Bible (Daniel 5) tells how his death in the sack of the city was foretold by a mysterious hand which wrote on the palace wall at a banquet.

belt ▶ noun **1** a strip of leather or other material worn round the waist or across the chest, especially in order to support or hold in clothes or to carry weapons.
■ short for **SEAT BELT**. ■ a belt worn as a sign of rank or achievement: *he was awarded the victor's belt.* ■ a belt of a specified colour, marking the attainment of a particular level in judo, karate, or similar sports: [as modifier] *brown-belt level.* ■ a person who has reached such a level: *Shaun became a brown belt in judo.* ■ (**the belt**) the punishment of being struck with a belt.
2 a strip of material used in various technical applications, in particular:
■ a continuous band of material used in machinery for transferring motion from one wheel to another. ■ a conveyor belt. ■ a flexible strip carrying machine-gun cartridges.
3 a strip or encircling band of something having a specified nature or composition that is different from its surroundings: *the asteroid belt* | *a belt of trees.*
4 informal a heavy blow: *she ran in to administer a good belt with her stick.*
▶ verb [with obj.] **1** [with obj. and adverbial] fasten with a belt: *she paused only to belt a towelling robe about her waist* | *she belted her raincoat firmly.*
■ [no obj., with adverbial] be fastened with a belt: *the jacket belts at the waist.* ■ attach or secure with a belt: *he was securely belted into the passenger seat.*
2 beat or strike (someone), especially with a belt as a punishment: *I was belted and sent to my room.*
■ hit (something) hard: *he belted the ball downfield.*
3 [no obj., with adverbial of direction] informal rush or dash in a specified direction: *he belted out of the side door.*
■ (of rain) fall hard: *the rain* **belted down** *on the tin roof.*
– PHRASES **below the belt** unfair or unfairly; disregarding the rules: *she said one of them had to work; Eddie thought that was below the belt.* [ORIGIN: from the notion of an unfair and illegal blow in boxing.] **belt and braces** Brit. (of a policy or action) using two means to the same end. [ORIGIN: from the literal *belt* and *braces* for holding up a pair of loose trousers.] **tighten one's belt** cut one's expenditure; live more frugally. **under one's belt 1** safely or satisfactorily achieved, experienced, or acquired: *he now has almost a year as minister under his belt.* **2** (of food or drink) consumed: *Gus already had a large brandy under his belt.*
– DERIVATIVES **belted** adjective (usu. in sense 1 of the noun).
– ORIGIN Old English, of Germanic origin, from Latin *balteus* 'girdle'.
▶ **belt something out** sing or play a song loudly and

forcefully.

belt up informal **1** [usu. in imperative] be quiet. **2** put on a seat belt.

Beltane /ˈbɛlteɪn/ ▶ noun an ancient Celtic festival celebrated on May Day.
– ORIGIN late Middle English: from Scottish Gaelic *bealltainn*.

belt drive ▶ noun a mechanism in which power is transmitted by the movement of a continuous flexible belt.

belted galloway ▶ noun an animal belonging to a variety of the galloway breed of cattle. See **GALLOWAY**.

belted sandfish ▶ noun see **SANDFISH** (sense 2).

belter ▶ noun informal **1** an exceptional or outstanding example of something: *Magilton made the goal with a belter of a pass.*
2 a loud, forceful singer or song.

belting ▶ noun **1** [mass noun] belts collectively, or material for belts.
2 a beating, especially with a belt as a punishment.
▶ adjective informal outstanding: *they've come up with some belting songs.*

beltman ▶ noun (pl. **-men**) Austral. the member of a surf life-saving team who swims out, wearing a belt with a line attached for safety, to give assistance to bathers or surfers in difficulties.

belt sander ▶ noun a sander that uses a moving abrasive belt to smooth surfaces.

beltway ▶ noun US a ring road.
■ (**Beltway**) [often as modifier] Washington DC, especially as representing the perceived insularity of the US government: *conventional Beltway wisdom.* [ORIGIN: transferred use by association with the ring road encircling Washington.]

beluga /bəˈluːɡə/ ▶ noun (pl. same or **belugas**) **1** a small white toothed whale related to the narwhal, living in herds mainly in Arctic coastal waters. Also called **WHITE WHALE**.
● *Delphinapterus leucas*, family Monodontidae.
2 a very large sturgeon occurring in the inland seas and associated rivers of central Eurasia.
● *Huso huso*, family Acipenseridae.
■ (also **beluga caviar**) [mass noun] caviar obtained from this fish.
– ORIGIN late 16th cent. (in sense 2): from Russian *belukha* (sense 1), *beluga* (sense 2), both from *belyǐ* 'white'.

belvedere /ˈbɛlvɪdɪə/ ▶ noun a summer house or open-sided gallery, typically at rooftop level, commanding a fine view.
– ORIGIN late 16th cent.: from Italian, literally 'fair sight', from *bel* 'beautiful' + *vedere* 'to see'.

belying present participle of **BELIE**.

BEM historical ▶ abbreviation for British Empire Medal, an award for public service (discontinued in 1993).

bema /ˈbiːmə/ ▶ noun (pl. **bemas** or **bemata**) the altar part or sanctuary in ancient and Orthodox churches.
■ historical the platform from which orators spoke in ancient Athens.
– ORIGIN late 17th cent.: from Greek *bēma* 'step, raised place'.

Bemba /ˈbɛmbə/ ▶ noun (pl. same) **1** a member of an African people of Zambia.
2 [mass noun] the Bantu language of this people, with nearly 2 million speakers.
▶ adjective of or relating to this people or their language.
– ORIGIN of Bemba origin.

bemire /bɪˈmaɪə/ ▶ verb [with obj.] archaic cover or stain with mud.
– ORIGIN mid 16th cent.: from BE- (expressing transitivity) + MIRE.

bemoan ▶ verb [with obj.] express discontent or sorrow over (something): *it was no use bemoaning her lot.*
– ORIGIN Old English *bemǣnan* 'complain, lament'. The change in the second syllable (16th cent.) was due to association with **MOAN**, to which it is related.

bemuse ▶ verb [with obj.] [usu. as adj. **bemused**] puzzle, confuse, or bewilder: *her bemused expression | he was bemused by what was happening.*
– DERIVATIVES **bemusedly** adverb, **bemusement** noun.

– ORIGIN mid 18th cent.: from BE- (as an intensifier) + MUSE[2].

ben[1] ▶ noun Scottish a high mountain or mountain peak (especially in place names): *Ben Nevis.*
– ORIGIN late 18th cent.: from Scottish Gaelic and Irish *beann*.

ben[2] ▶ noun Scottish the inner room in a two-roomed cottage. See also **BUT**[2].
– ORIGIN late 18th cent.: dialect variant of Middle English *binne* 'within' (adverb), from Old English *binnan* (related to Dutch and German *binnen*).

Benares /bɪˈnɑːrɪz/ former name for **VARANASI**.

Benbecula /bɛnˈbɛkjʊlə/ a small island in the Outer Hebrides, situated between North and South Uist and linked to them by causeways.

Ben Bella /bɛn ˈbɛlə/, (Muhammad) Ahmed (b.1916), Algerian statesman, Prime Minister 1962–3 and President 1963–5. The first President of an independent Algeria, he was overthrown in a military coup.

bench ▶ noun **1** a long seat for several people, typically made of wood or stone.
2 a long, sturdy work table in a workshop or laboratory.
3 (**the bench**) the office of judge or magistrate.
■ a judge's seat in a law court. ■ judges or magistrates collectively: *he's the Chairman of our local Bench.*
4 Brit. a long seat in Parliament for politicians of a specified party or position: *the Conservative benches.*
■ the politicians occupying such a seat: *the pledge that was given by the Opposition benches yesterday.*
5 (**the bench**) a seat at the side of a sports field for coaches, substitutes, and players not taking part in a game.
6 a flat ledge in masonry or on sloping ground.
▶ verb [with obj.] **1** exhibit (a dog) at a show: *Affenpinschers and Afghans were benched side by side.* [ORIGIN: from the practice of exhibiting dogs on benches.]
2 N. Amer. withdraw (a sports player) from play: *the coach benched quarterback Randall Cunningham in favour of Jim McMahon.*
3 short for **BENCH-PRESS**.
– PHRASES **on the bench 1** appointed as or in the capacity of a judge or magistrate: *he retired after twenty-five years on the bench.* **2** acting as one of the possible substitutes in a sports match.
– ORIGIN Old English *benc*, of Germanic origin; related to Dutch *bank* and German *Bank*, also to **BANK**[1].

bencher ▶ noun Law (in the UK) a senior member of any of the Inns of Court.

benchmark ▶ noun **1** a standard or point of reference against which things may be compared or assessed: [as modifier] *a benchmark case.*
■ a problem designed to evaluate the performance of a computer system.
2 a surveyor's mark cut in a wall, pillar, or building and used as a reference point in measuring altitudes.
▶ verb [with obj.] evaluate or check (something) by comparison with a standard: *we are benchmarking our performance against external criteria* | [no obj.] *we continue to benchmark against the competition.*
■ [no obj., with adverbial] give particular results during a benchmark test: *the device should benchmark at between 100 and 150 MHz.*

benchmark test ▶ noun a test using a benchmark to evaluate a computer system's performance.

bench press ▶ noun a bodybuilding and weightlifting exercise in which a lifter lies on a bench with feet on the floor and raises a weight with both arms.
▶ verb (**bench-press**) [with obj.] raise (a weight) in a bench press.

bench run ▶ noun & verb another term for **BENCH TEST**.

bench seat ▶ noun a seat across the whole width of a car.

bench table ▶ noun a low stone seat on the inside of a wall or round the base of a pillar in a church, cloister, or other religious building.

bench test chiefly Computing ▶ noun a test carried out on a machine, a component, or software before it is released for use, to ensure that it works properly.
▶ verb (**bench-test**) [with obj.] run a bench test on.
■ [no obj., with adverbial] give particular results during a

bench test: *it bench-tests two times faster than the previous version.*

benchwarmer ▶ noun N. Amer. informal a sports player who does not get selected to play; a substitute.

benchwork ▶ noun [mass noun] work carried out at a bench in a laboratory or workshop.

bend[1] ▶ verb (past and past participle **bent**) **1** [with obj.] shape or force (something straight) into a curve or angle: *the wire has to be bent back tightly.*
■ [no obj.] (of something straight) be shaped or forced into a curve or angle: *poppies bending in the wind.*
■ figurative force or be forced to submit: [with obj.] *they want to bend me to their will* | [no obj.] *a refusal to bend to mob rule.* ■ [no obj., usu. with adverbial of direction] (of a road, river, or path) deviate from a straight line in a specified direction; have a sharply curved course: *the road bent left and then right* | *the river slowly bends around Dittisham.*
2 [no obj.] (of a person) incline the body downwards from the vertical: *she bent down and yanked out the flex* | *I bent over my plate* | *he bent and kissed Dot on her forehead.*
■ [with obj.] move (a jointed part of the body) to an angled position: *extend your left leg and bend your right* | *Ianthe bent her head over her work.*
3 [with obj.] interpret or modify (a rule) to suit someone: *we cannot bend the rules, even for Darren.*
4 [with obj.] direct or devote (one's attention or energies) to a task: *Eric bent all his efforts to persuading them to donate some blankets* | [no obj.] *she bent once more to the task of diverting the wedding guests.*
5 [with obj.] Nautical attach (a sail or cable) by means of a knot: *sailors were bending sails to the spars.*
▶ noun **1** a curve, especially a sharp one, in a road, river, path, or racing circuit.
2 a curved or angled part or form of something: *making a bend in the wire.*
3 a kind of knot used to join two ropes together, or to tie a rope to another object, e.g. a carrick bend.
4 (**the bends**) decompression sickness, especially in divers.
– PHRASES **bend someone's ear** informal talk to someone, especially with great eagerness or in order to ask a favour. **bend one's elbow** N. Amer. drink alcohol. **bend one's (or the) knee** figurative submit: *a country no longer willing to bend its knee to foreign powers.* **bend over backwards** see **BACKWARDS**. **on bended knee (or knees)** kneeling, especially when pleading or showing great respect. **round (or US around) the bend** informal mad: *I'd round the bend looking after kids all day* | *it used to drive my wife round the bend.*
– DERIVATIVES **bendable** adjective.
– ORIGIN Old English *bendan* 'put in bonds, tension a bow by means of a string', of Germanic origin; related to **BAND**[1].

bend[2] ▶ noun Heraldry an ordinary in the form of a broad diagonal stripe from top left (dexter chief) to bottom right (sinister base) of a shield or part of one.
– ORIGIN late Middle English: from Anglo-Norman French *bande*, Old French *bende* 'flat strip'.

bender informal ▶ noun **1** [usu. with modifier or in combination] an object or person that bends something else: *a fender bender.*
2 a wild drinking spree.
3 offensive a homosexual.
4 Brit. a shelter made by covering a framework of bent branches with canvas or tarpaulin.
– ORIGIN late 15th cent. (denoting instruments such as pliers, for bending things): from **BEND**[1] + **-ER**[1].

Bendigo /ˈbɛndɪɡəʊ/ a former gold-mining town in the state of Victoria, Australia; pop. 57,430 (1991).
– ORIGIN named after a local boxer who had adopted the nickname of William Thompson (1811–80), a well-known English prizefighter.

bendlet ▶ noun Heraldry a bend of half the normal width, usually borne in groups of two or three.
– ORIGIN late 16th cent.: probably from the earlier heraldic term *bendel* 'little bend' (Old French diminutive of *bende* 'band') + **-ET**[1].

bend sinister ▶ noun Heraldry a broad diagonal stripe from top right to bottom left of a shield (a supposed sign of bastardy).

bendy ▶ adjective (**bendier**, **bendiest**) informal **1** capable of bending; soft and flexible.
2 (especially of a road) having many bends.
– DERIVATIVES **bendiness** noun.

b

berceuse /bɛːˈsəːz/ ▶ **noun** (pl. **berceuses** pronunc. same) a lullaby.
– ORIGIN French, from *bercer* 'to rock'.

Berchtesgaden /ˈbɛːxtəsˌgɑːd(ə)n, German ˈbɛrçtəsˌgaːdn/ a town in southern Germany, in the Bavarian Alps close to the border with Austria; pop. 8,186 (1983). Hitler had a fortified retreat there.

bereave ▶ **verb** (**be bereaved**) be deprived of a close relation or friend through their death: *the year after they had been bereaved* | [as adj. **bereaved**] *bereaved families* | [as plural noun **the bereaved**] *those who counsel the bereaved.*
– DERIVATIVES **bereavement** noun.
– ORIGIN Old English *berēafian* (see **BE-**, **REAVE**). The original sense was 'deprive of' in general.

bereft ▶ **adjective** deprived of or lacking something, especially a non-material asset: *her room was stark and bereft of colour.*
■ (of a person) lonely and abandoned, especially through someone's death or departure: *his death in 1990 left her bereft.*
– ORIGIN late 16th cent.: archaic past participle of **BEREAVE**.

Berenice /ˌbɛrɪˈnʌɪsi/ (3rd century BC), Egyptian queen, wife of Ptolemy III.

beret /ˈbɛreɪ, -ri/ ▶ **noun** a round flattish cap of felt or cloth.
– ORIGIN early 19th cent.: from French *béret* 'Basque cap', from Old Provençal *berret*, based on late Latin *birrus* 'hooded cape'. Compare with **BIRETTA**.

Berg /bɛːg/, Alban (Maria Johannes) (1885–1935), Austrian composer, a leading exponent of twelve-note composition. Notable works: the operas *Wozzeck* (1914–21) and *Lulu* (1928–35) and his violin concerto (1935).

berg[1] /bəːg/ ▶ **noun** short for **ICEBERG**.

berg[2] /bəːg/ ▶ **noun** S. African a mountain or hill.
■ (**the Berg**) the Drakensberg mountain range.
– ORIGIN Dutch.

bergamot[1] /ˈbəːgəmɒt/ ▶ **noun** **1** [mass noun] an oily substance extracted from the rind of a dwarf variety of Seville orange, used in cosmetics and as flavouring in Earl Grey tea.
2 (also **bergamot orange**) the tree which bears this fruit.
● *Citrus aurantium* subsp. *bergamia*, family Rutaceae.
3 an aromatic North American herb of the mint family.
● Genus *Monarda*, family Labiatae: several species, in particular **sweet bergamot** (*M. didyma*) (also called **BEE BALM**, **OSWEGO TEA**), grown for its bright flowers and used in American Indian medicine.
– ORIGIN late 17th cent. (in sense 2): named after the city and province of *Bergamo* in northern Italy.

bergamot[2] /ˈbəːgəmɒt/ ▶ **noun** a dessert pear of a rich and sweet variety.
– ORIGIN early 17th cent.: from French *bergamotte*, from Italian *bergamotta*, from Turkish *begarmudu* 'prince's pear', from *beg* 'prince' + *armud* 'pear' + the possessive suffix *-u*.

Bergen 1 /ˈbɛːg(ə)n/ a seaport in SW Norway; pop. 213,344 (1991). It is a centre of the fishing and North Sea oil industries.
2 /ˈbɛrxə(n)/ Flemish name for **MONS**.

bergen /ˈbəːg(ə)n/ ▶ **noun** Brit. a type of rucksack supported by a frame, used by the military.
– ORIGIN early 20th cent.: of unknown origin.

bergenia /bəˈgiːnɪə/ ▶ **noun** an evergreen Asian plant with large, thick leaves and typically pink, red, or purple flowers.
● Genus *Bergenia*, family Saxifragaceae.
– ORIGIN modern Latin, named after Karl A. von *Bergen* (1704–60), German botanist and physician.

Berger /ˈbəːgə, German ˈbɛrgɐ/, Hans (1873–1941), German psychiatrist who detected electric currents in the cerebral cortex and developed encephalography.

Bergerac[1] /ˈbɛːʒərak/ a wine-producing region in the Dordogne valley in SW France.
■ a town on the Dordogne River; pop. 27,890 (1990).

Bergerac[2] see **CYRANO DE BERGERAC**.

bergère /bɛːˈʒɛː/ ▶ **noun** a long-seated upholstered armchair fashionable in the 18th century.

Bergie /ˈbəːgi/ ▶ **noun** (pl. **-ies**) S. African informal a vagabond.
– ORIGIN from Dutch *berg* 'mountain' + the informal suffix **-IE**.

Bergius /ˈbəːgɪəs, German ˈbɛrgɪʊs/, Friedrich Karl Rudolf (1884–1949), German industrial chemist. Nobel Prize for Chemistry (1931).

Bergman[1] /ˈbəːgmən/, (Ernst) Ingmar (b.1918), Swedish film and theatre director. He used haunting imagery and symbolism often derived from Jungian dream analysis. Notable films: *Smiles of a Summer Night* (1955), *The Seventh Seal* (1956), and *Hour of the Wolf* (1968).

Bergman[2] /ˈbəːgmən/, Ingrid (1915–82), Swedish actress. Notable films: *Casablanca* (1942), *Anastasia* (1956), and *Murder on the Orient Express* (1974).

bergschrund /ˈbəːgʃrʊnd/ ▶ **noun** a crevasse at the junction of a glacier or snowfield with a steep upper slope.
– ORIGIN mid 19th cent.: from German, from *Berg* 'mountain' + *Schrund* 'crevice'.

Bergson /ˈbəːgs(ə)n, French bɛrksɔn/, Henri (Louis) (1859–1941), French philosopher. Dividing the world into life (or consciousness) and matter, he rejected Darwinian evolution and argued that life possesses an inherent creative impulse (*elan vital*) which creates new forms as life seeks to impose itself on matter. Nobel Prize for Literature (1927).
– DERIVATIVES **Bergsonian** adjective.

berg wind ▶ **noun** S. African a hot dry northerly wind blowing from the interior to coastal districts.

Beria /ˈbɛrɪə/, Lavrenti (Pavlovich) (1899–1953), Soviet politician and head of the secret police 1938–53. He was involved in the elimination or deportation of Stalin's opponents, but after Stalin's death he was arrested and executed.

beribboned ▶ **adjective** decorated with many ribbons.

beriberi /ˌbɛrɪˈbɛri/ ▶ **noun** [mass noun] a disease causing inflammation of the nerves and heart failure, ascribed to a deficiency of vitamin B_1.
– ORIGIN early 18th cent.: from Sinhalese, from *beri* 'weakness'.

Bering /ˈbɛːrɪŋ/, Vitus (Jonassen) (1681–1741), Danish navigator and explorer. He led several Russian expeditions aimed at discovering whether Asia and North America were connected by land.

Beringia /bɛˈrɪndʒɪə/ the area comprising the Bering Strait and adjacent parts of Siberia and Alaska (used especially in connection with the migration of animals across the former Bering land bridge).
– DERIVATIVES **Beringian** adjective.

Bering Sea an arm of the North Pacific lying between NE Siberia and Alaska, bounded to the south by the Aleutian Islands. It is linked to the Arctic Ocean by the Bering Strait. Both the sea and the strait are named after Vitus Bering.

Bering Strait a narrow sea passage which separates the eastern tip of Siberia from Alaska and links the Arctic Ocean with the Bering Sea, about 85 km (53 miles) wide at its narrowest point. During the Ice Age, as a result of a drop in sea levels, the **Bering land bridge** formed between the two continents, allowing the migration of animals and dispersal of plants in both directions.

Berio /ˈbɛrɪəʊ/, Luciano (b.1925), Italian composer, an experimentalist who has adopted serial, aleatory, and electronic techniques. Notable works: *Circles* (1960), *Sequenza* series (1958–75), and *Un Re in Ascolto* (opera, 1984).

berk /bəːk/ (also **burk** or **burke**) ▶ **noun** Brit. informal a stupid person.
– ORIGIN 1930s: abbreviation of *Berkeley* or *Berkshire Hunt*, rhyming slang for 'cunt'.

Berkeley[1] /ˈbəːkli/ a city in western California, on San Francisco Bay, site of a campus of the University of California; pop. 102,724 (1990).

Berkeley[2] /ˈbəːkli/, Busby (1895–1976), American choreographer and film director; born *William Berkeley Enos*. He is remembered for his spectacular and dazzling sequences in which huge casts of rhythmically moving dancers formed kaleidoscopic patterns on the screen. Notable films: the *Gold Diggers* series (1922–37) and *Babes in Arms* (1939).

Berkeley[3] /ˈbɑːkli/, George (1685–1753), Irish philosopher and bishop. He argued that material objects exist solely by being perceived, so there are only minds and mental events. Since God perceives everything all the time, objects have a continuous existence in the mind of God. Notable works: *A Treatise Concerning the Principles of Human Knowledge* (1710).

Berkeley[4] /ˈbɑːkli/, Sir Lennox (Randall Francis) (1903–89), English composer of four operas, four symphonies, music for ballet and film, and sacred choral music.

berkelium /bəːˈkiːlɪəm, ˈbəːklɪəm/ ▶ **noun** [mass noun] the chemical element of atomic number 97, a radioactive metal of the actinide series. Berkelium does not occur naturally and was first made by bombarding americium with helium ions. (Symbol: **Bk**)
– ORIGIN 1949: from **BERKELEY**[1] (where it was first made) + **-IUM**.

Berkoff /ˈbəːkɒf/, Steven (b.1937), English dramatist, director, and actor. Much of his work is politically radical in content and shocking and aggressive in style.

Berks. ▶ **abbreviation for** Berkshire.

Berkshire[1] /ˈbɑːkʃɪə, -ʃə/ a county of southern England, west of London, divided in 1998 into six unitary authorities.

Berkshire[2] /ˈbɑːkʃə/ ▶ **noun** a pig of a black breed, now rarely kept commercially.

Berlin[1] /bəːˈlɪn/ the capital of Germany; pop. 3,102,500 (est. 1990).

> At the end of the Second World War the city was occupied by the Allies and divided into two parts: **West Berlin**, comprising the American, British, and French sectors, later a state of the Federal Republic of Germany despite forming an enclave within the German Democratic Republic; and **East Berlin**, the sector of the city occupied by the USSR and later capital of the German Democratic Republic. Between 1961 and 1989 the Berlin Wall separated the two parts, which were reunited in 1990; occupation formally ended in 1994.

Berlin[2] /bəːˈlɪn/, Irving (1888–1989), Russian-born American songwriter; born *Israel Baline*. Notable works: the songs 'God Bless America' (1939) and 'White Christmas' (1942) and the film score for *Annie get Your Gun* (1946).

Berlin[3] /bəːˈlɪn/, Sir Isaiah (1909–97), Latvian-born British philosopher who concerned himself with the history of ideas. Notable works: *Karl Marx* (1939), *Four Essays on Liberty* (1959), and *Vico and Herder* (1976).

Berlin airlift an operation by British and American aircraft to airlift food and supplies to Berlin in 1948–9, while Russian forces blockaded the city to isolate it from the West and terminate the joint Allied military government of the city. After the blockade was lifted the city was formally divided into East and West Berlin.

Berliner ▶ **noun** **1** a native or citizen of Berlin.
2 a doughnut with jam filling and vanilla icing.
– ORIGIN German.

Berlin Wall a fortified and heavily guarded wall built in 1961 by the communist authorities on the boundary between East and West Berlin, chiefly to curb the flow of East Germans to the West. It was opened in November 1989 after the collapse of the communist regime in East Germany and subsequently dismantled.

Berlin work ▶ **noun** [mass noun] worsted embroidery on canvas.

Berlioz /ˈbɛːlɪəʊz, French bɛrljɔz/, Hector (1803–69), French composer; full name *Louis-Hector Berlioz*. Notable works: *Les Troyens* (opera, 1856–9), *Symphonie fantastique* (1830), and *La Damnation de Faust* (cantata, 1846).

berm /bəːm/ ▶ **noun** a flat strip of land, raised bank, or terrace bordering a river or canal.
■ a path or grass strip beside a road. ■ an artificial ridge or embankment, such as one built as a defence against tanks. ■ a narrow space, especially one between a ditch and the base of a parapet.
– ORIGIN early 18th cent. (denoting a narrow space): from French *berme*, from Dutch *berm*.

Bermuda /bəˈmjuːdə/ (also **the Bermudas**) a country consisting of about 150 small islands off the coast of North Carolina; pop. 58,000 (est. 1991); official language, English; capital, Hamilton. It is a British dependency with full internal self-government.
– DERIVATIVES **Bermudan** adjective & noun, **Bermudian** adjective & noun.
– ORIGIN named after a Spanish sailor, Juan *Bermúdez*, who sighted the islands early in the 16th cent.

Bermuda grass ▶ **noun** [mass noun] a creeping grass common in warmer parts of the world, used for lawns and pasture.

• *Cynodon dactylon*, family Gramineae.

Bermuda rig ▶ **noun** a fore-and-aft yachting rig with a tall tapering mainsail.

Bermuda shorts (also **Bermudas**) ▶ **plural noun** casual knee-length shorts.

Bermuda Triangle an area of the western Atlantic Ocean where a large number of ships and aircraft are said to have mysteriously disappeared.

Bern variant spelling of **BERNE**.

Bernadette, St /ˌbəːnəˈdɛt/ (1844–79), French peasant girl; born *Marie Bernarde Soubirous*. Her visions of the Virgin Mary in Lourdes in 1858 led to the town's establishment as a centre of pilgrimage. Bernadette later became a nun and she was canonized in 1933. Feast day, 18 February.

Bernadotte[1] /ˌbəːnəˈdɒt/, Folke, Count (1895–1948), Swedish statesman. As vice-president of the Swedish Red Cross he arranged the exchange of prisoners of war and in 1945 conveyed a German offer of capitulation to the Allies.

Bernadotte[2] /ˌbəːnəˈdɒt, French bɛʀnadɔt/, Jean Baptiste Jules (1763–1844), French soldier, king of Sweden (as Charles XIV) 1818–44. One of Napoleon's marshals, he was adopted by Charles XIII of Sweden in 1810 and later became king, thus founding Sweden's present royal house.

Bernard /bɛːˈnɑː, French bɛʀnaʀ/, Claude (1813–78), French physiologist. Bernard showed the role of the pancreas in digestion, the method of regulation of body temperature, and the function of nerves supplying the internal organs.

Bernard, St /ˈbəːnəd/ (*c.*996–*c.*1081), French monk who founded two hospices for travellers in the Alps. The St Bernard passes, where the hospices were situated, and St Bernard dogs are named after him. Feast day, 28 May.

Bernard of Clairvaux, St /klɛːˈvəʊ, French klɛʀvo/ (1090–1153), French theologian and abbot. He was the first abbot of Clairvaux and his monastery became one of the chief centres of the Cistercian order. Feast day, 20 August.

Berne /bəːn, bɛːn, French bɛʀn, German bɛrn/ (also **Bern**) the capital of Switzerland since 1848; pop. 134,620 (1990).
■ a canton of Switzerland.
– DERIVATIVES **Bernese** adjective & noun.

Berne Convention an international copyright agreement of 1886, later revised. The US has never been party to it.

Bernhardt /ˈbəːnhɑːt, French bɛʀnaʀ/, Sarah (1844–1923), French actress; born *Henriette Rosine Bernard*. She was best known for her portrayal of Marguerite in *La Dame aux Camélias* and Cordelia in *King Lear*.

Bernini /bɛːˈniːni, Italian berˈnini/, Gian Lorenzo (1598–1680), Italian baroque sculptor, painter, and architect. His work includes the great canopy over the altar and the colonnade round the piazza at St Peter's, Rome.

Bernoulli /bəːˈnuːi/ the name of a Swiss family that produced many eminent mathematicians and scientists:
■ **Jakob** (1654–1705); also known as *Jacques* or *James Bernoulli*. He made discoveries in calculus and contributed to geometry and the theory of probabilities.
■ **Johann** (1667–1748), the brother of Jakob, who contributed to differential and integral calculus; also known as *Jean* or *John Bernoulli*.
■ **Daniel** (1700–82), son of Johann. His greatest contributions were to hydrodynamics and mathematical physics.

Bernstein /ˈbəːnstiːn, -stʌɪn/, Leonard (1918–90), American composer, conductor, and pianist. Notable works: *Candide* (operetta, 1954–6), *West Side Story* (musical, 1957), *Chichester Psalms* (1965), and film music for *On the Waterfront* (1954).

Berra /ˈbɛrə/, Yogi (b.1925), American baseball player; born *Lawrence Peter Berra*. He was especially famous as a catcher with the New York Yankees.

Berry[1] a former province of central France; chief town, Bourges.

Berry[2], Chuck (b.1931), American rock-and-roll singer, guitarist, and songwriter; born *Charles Edward Berry*. Notable songs: 'Johnny B Goode' (1958).

berry ▶ **noun** (pl. **-ies**) a small roundish juicy fruit without a stone: *juniper berries.*
■ Botany any fruit that has its seeds enclosed in a fleshy pulp, for example a banana or tomato. ■ any of various kernels or seeds, such as the coffee bean. ■ a fish egg or roe of a lobster or similar creature.
– DERIVATIVES **berried** adjective [often in combination] *red-berried elder trees.*
– ORIGIN Old English *berie*, of Germanic origin; related to Dutch *bes* and German *Beere*.

berrying ▶ **noun** [mass noun] the activity of gathering berries.

berserk /bəˈsəːk, -z-/ ▶ **adjective** out of control with anger or excitement; wild or frenzied: *a man went* **berserk** *with an arsenal of guns.*
– ORIGIN early 19th cent. (originally as a noun denoting a wild Norse warrior who fought with frenzy): from Old Norse *berserkr* (noun), probably from *birn-*, *bjorn* (see **BEAR**[2]) + *serkr* 'coat', but also possibly from *berr* 'bare' (i.e. without armour).

berserker ▶ **noun** an ancient Norse warrior who fought with a wild frenzy.

berth ▶ **noun 1** a ship's allotted place at a wharf or dock.
2 a fixed bed or bunk on a ship, train, or other means of transport.
3 informal (often in a sporting context) a situation or position in an organization or event: *he looked at home in an unfamiliar right-back berth.*
▶ **verb** [with obj.] **1** moor (a ship) in its allotted place.
■ [no obj.] (of a ship) dock.
2 (of a passenger ship) provide a sleeping place for (someone).
– PHRASES **give someone/thing a wide berth** steer a ship well clear of something while passing it. ■ stay away from someone or something.
– ORIGIN early 17th cent. (in the sense 'adequate sea room'): probably from a nautical use of **BEAR**[1] + **-TH**[2].

bertha ▶ **noun** chiefly historical a deep collar, typically made of lace, attached to the top of a dress that has a low neckline.
– ORIGIN mid 19th cent.: from the given name *Bertha*.

berthing ▶ **noun 1** the action of mooring a ship.
2 [mass noun] accommodation for ships in berths: *there were more than 12 miles of berthing.*

Bertillon /ˈbɛːtiːjɔ̃, French bɛʀtijɔ̃/, Alphonse (1853–1914), French criminologist. He devised a system of body measurements for the identification of criminals, which was widely used until superseded by fingerprinting at the beginning of the 20th century.

Bertolucci /ˌbɛːtəˈluːtʃi, Italian bertoˈluttʃi/, Bernardo (b.1940), Italian film director. Notable works: *The Spider's Stratagem* (1970), *Last Tango in Paris* (1972), and *The Last Emperor* (1988).

Berwickshire /ˈbɛrɪkʃɪə, -ʃə/ a former county of SE Scotland, on the border with England. It became a part of Borders region (now Scottish Borders) in 1975.

Berwick-upon-Tweed /ˌbɛrɪkəpɒnˈtwiːd/ a town at the mouth of the River Tweed in NE England, close to the Scottish border; pop. 13,000 (1981). Having been held alternately by England and Scotland, it was ceded by Scotland to England in 1482.

beryl /ˈbɛrɪl/ ▶ **noun** [mass noun] a transparent pale green, blue, or yellow mineral consisting of a silicate of beryllium and aluminium, sometimes used as a gemstone.
– ORIGIN Middle English: from Old French *beril*, via Latin from Greek *bērullos*.

berylliosis /bəˌrɪlɪˈəʊsɪs/ ▶ **noun** [mass noun] Medicine poisoning by beryllium or beryllium compounds, especially by inhalation causing fibrosis of the lungs.

beryllium /bəˈrɪlɪəm/ ▶ **noun** [mass noun] the chemical element of atomic number 4, a hard grey metal. (Symbol: **Be**)

> Beryllium is the lightest of the alkaline earth metals, and its chief source is the mineral beryl. It is used in the manufacture of light corrosion-resistant alloys and in windows in X-ray equipment.

Berzelius /bəːˈziːlɪəs/, Jöns Jakob (1779–1848), Swedish analytical chemist. He determined the atomic weights of many elements and discovered cerium, selenium, and thorium.

Bes /bɛs/ Egyptian Mythology a grotesque god depicted as having short legs, an obese body, and an almost bestial face, who dispelled evil spirits.

Besançon /ˈbɛz(ə)nsɒn, French bəzɑ̃sɔ̃/ the capital of Franche-Comté in NE France; pop. 119,200 (1990).

Besant /ˈbɛz(ə)nt, bɪˈzant/, Annie (1847–1933), English theosophist, writer, and politician, president of the Theosophical Society. She settled in Madras, where she worked for Indian self-government.

beseech ▶ **verb** (past and past participle **besought** or **beseeched**) [reporting verb] poetic/literary ask someone urgently and fervently to do or give something: [with obj. and infinitive] *they beseeched him to stay* | [with obj. and direct speech] *'You have got to believe me,' Violet beseeched him* | [with obj.] *they earnestly beseeched his forgiveness.*
– DERIVATIVES **beseechingly** adverb.
– ORIGIN Middle English: from **BE-** (as an intensifier) + Old English *sēcan* (see **SEEK**).

beset ▶ **verb** (**besetting**; past and past participle **beset**) [with obj.] **1** (of a problem or difficulty) trouble or threaten persistently: *the social problems that beset the UK* | *she was* **beset with** *self-doubt.*
■ surround and harass: *I was beset by clouds of flies.* ■ hem in: *the ship was beset by ice and finally sank.*
2 archaic (**be beset with**) be covered or studded with: *springy grass all beset with tiny jewel-like flowers.*
– PHRASES **besetting sin** a fault to which a person or institution is especially prone.
– ORIGIN Old English *besettan*, from **BE-** 'about' + *settan* (see **SET**[1]).

beside ▶ **preposition 1** at the side of; next to: *he sat beside me in the front seat* | *on the table beside the bed.*
■ compared with: *beside Paula she always felt clumsy.*
2 in addition to; apart from: *he commissioned work from other artists beside Minton.*
– PHRASES **beside oneself** overcome with worry, grief, or anger; distraught: *she was* **beside herself** *with anguish.* **beside the point** see **POINT**.
– ORIGIN Old English *be sīdan* (adverb) 'by the side' (see **BY, SIDE**).

> **USAGE** It is sometimes said that **beside** should not be used to mean 'apart from' and that **besides** should be used instead (*he commissioned work from other artists* **besides** *Minton* rather than *he commissioned work from other artists* **beside** *Minton*). Although there is little logical basis for such a view, and in standard English both **beside** and **besides** are used for this sense, it is worth being aware of the potential ambiguity in the use of **beside**: ***beside*** *the cold meat, there are platters of trout and salmon* means either 'the cold meat is next to the trout and salmon' or 'apart from the cold meat, there are also trout and salmon'.

besides ▶ **preposition** in addition to; apart from: *I have no other family besides my parents* | *besides being a player, he was my friend.*
▶ **adverb** in addition; as well: *I'm capable of doing the work, and a lot more besides.*
■ [sentence adverb] used to introduce an additional idea or explanation: *I had no time to warn you. Besides, I wasn't sure.*

besiege ▶ **verb** [with obj.] surround (a place) with armed forces in order to capture it or force its surrender; lay siege to: *the king marched north to besiege Berwick* | [as adj. **besieged**] *the besieged city.*
■ crowd round oppressively; surround and harass: *she spent the whole day besieged by newsmen.* ■ (**be besieged**) be inundated by large numbers of requests or complaints: *the television station was* **besieged with** *calls.*
– DERIVATIVES **besieger** noun.
– ORIGIN Middle English: alteration (by change of prefix) of *assiege*, from Old French *asegier*.

besmear ▶ **verb** [with obj.] poetic/literary smear or cover with a greasy or sticky substance.
– ORIGIN Old English *bismierwan* (see **BE-, SMEAR**).

besmirch /bɪˈsməːtʃ/ ▶ **verb** [with obj.] damage (someone's reputation): *he had besmirched the good name of his family.*
■ poetic/literary make (something) dirty or discoloured: *the ground was* **besmirched with** *blood.*

besom /ˈbiːz(ə)m, ˈbɪz-/ ▶ **noun 1** a broom made of twigs tied round a stick.
2 derogatory, chiefly Scottish & N. English a woman or girl.
– ORIGIN Old English *besema*, of West Germanic origin; related to Dutch *bezem* and German *Besen*.

besotted /bɪˈsɒtɪd/ ▶ **adjective 1** strongly infatuated: *he became* **besotted with** *a local barmaid.*
2 archaic intoxicated; drunk.
– ORIGIN late 16th cent.: past participle of *besot* 'make foolishly affectionate', from **BE-** 'cause to be' + **SOT**.

besought past and past participle of **BESEECH**.

bespangle ▶ **verb** [with obj.] poetic/literary cover or adorn with something that glitters or sparkles.

bespatter ▶ **verb** [with obj.] splash small drops of a liquid substance all over (an object or surface): *his elegant shoes and trousers were **bespattered with** mud.*

bespeak ▶ **verb** (past **bespoke**; past participle **bespoken**) [with obj.] **1** suggest the presence of; be evidence of: *the attractive tree-lined road bespoke money.*
2 order or reserve (something) in advance: *obtaining the affidavits that it has been necessary to bespeak.*
3 archaic speak to.
– ORIGIN Old English *bisprecan* 'speak up, speak out' (see **BE-**, **SPEAK**), later 'discuss, decide on', hence 'arrange, order' (sense 2, late 16th cent.).

bespectacled ▶ **adjective** (of a person) wearing glasses.

bespoke ▶ **adjective** Brit. (of goods, especially clothing) made to order: *a bespoke suit.*
■(of a trader) making such goods: *bespoke tailors.* ■(of a computer program) written or adapted for a specific user or purpose.

bespoken past participle of **BESPEAK**.

besprinkle ▶ **verb** [with obj.] poetic/literary sprinkle all over with small drops or amounts of a substance.

Bessarabia /ˌbɛsəˈreɪbɪə/ a region in eastern Europe between the Dniester and Prut Rivers, from 1918 to 1940 part of Romania. The major part of the region now falls in Moldova, the remainder in Ukraine.
– DERIVATIVES **Bessarabian** adjective & noun.

Bessel /ˈbɛs(ə)l/, Friedrich Wilhelm (1784–1846), German astronomer and mathematician. He determined the positions of some 75,000 stars, obtained accurate measurements of stellar distances, and following a study of the orbit of Uranus, predicted the existence of an eighth planet.

Bessemer /ˈbɛsəmə/, Sir Henry (1813–98), English engineer and inventor. By 1860 he had developed the Bessemer process, the first successful method of making steel in quantity at low cost.

Bessemer process ▶ **noun** a steel-making process, now largely superseded, in which carbon, silicon, and other impurities are removed from molten pig iron by oxidation in a blast of air in a special tilting retort (a **Bessemer converter**).

Best[1], Charles Herbert (1899–1978), American-born Canadian physiologist who assisted F. G. Banting in research leading to the discovery of insulin in 1922.

Best[2], George (b.1946), Northern Irish footballer. A winger for Manchester United, he was named European Footballer of the Year in 1968.

best ▶ **adjective** of the most excellent or desirable type or quality: *the best midfielder in the country | how to obtain the best results from your machine | her best black suit.*
■most enjoyable: *some of the best times of my life.* ■most appropriate, advantageous, or well advised: *do whatever you think best | it's best if we both go.*
▶ **adverb** to the highest degree; most (used with verbs suggesting a desirable action or state or a successful outcome): *the one we liked best | you knew him best | well-drained soil suits it best.*
■to the highest standard: *the best-dressed man in Britain | the things we do best.* ■most suitably, appropriately, or usefully: *this is best done at home | jokes are best avoided in essays.*
▶ **noun** (usu. **the best**) that which is the most excellent, outstanding, or desirable: *buy the best you can afford | Sarah always had **to be the best at** everything | a theory embodying the best of both socialism and capitalism.*
■the most meritorious aspect of a thing or person: *he **brought out the best in** people.* ■**(one's best)** the highest standard or level that someone or something can reach: *beyond the date shown the product will be **past its best** | this is jazz **at its best** | try to **look your best**.* ■**(one's best)** one's smartest or most formal clothes: *she dressed in her best.* ■(in sport) a record performance, especially a personal one: *a lifetime best of 12.0 seconds | **a personal best**.* ■chiefly N. Amer. written at the end of a letter to wish a person well: *See you soon, best, Michael.*
▶ **verb** [with obj.] informal outwit or get the better of (someone): *she refused to allow herself to be bested.*
– PHRASES **all the best** said or written to wish a person well on ending a letter or parting. **as best one can** (or **may**) as effectively as possible under the circumstances: *I went about my job as best I could.* **at best** taking the most optimistic or favourable view: *what signs there are of recovery are patchy at best.* **at the best of times** even in the most favourable circumstances: *his memory is poor at the best of times.* **be best friends** be mutually closest friends: *he's **best friends with** Eddie.* **be for** (or **all for**) **the best** be desirable in the end, although not at first seeming so. **best end** Brit. the rib end of a neck of lamb or other meat. **one's best friend** one's closest or favourite friend. **the best-laid plans of mice and men gang aft agley** proverb even the most careful planning doesn't necessarily ensure success: *in the tradition of all best-laid plans, subsequent events overturned the scheme.* [ORIGIN: see **GANG**[2].] **the best of friends** very close friends. **the best of three** (or **five** etc.) victory achieved by winning the majority of a specified odd number of games. **the best part of** most of: *it took them the best part of 10 years.* **best wishes** an expression of hope for someone's future happiness or welfare, often written at the end of a letter: *best wishes, Celia.* **one's best years** the most vigorous and productive period of one's life; one's prime. **do** (or **try**) **one's best** do all one can: *Ruth **did her best to** reassure her.* **get the best of** overcome (someone): *his drinking got the best of him and he was fired.* **give someone/thing best** Brit. admit the superiority of someone or something. **had best do something** find it most sensible or well advised to do the thing mentioned: *I'd best be going.* **make the best of** derive what limited advantage one can from (something unsatisfactory or unwelcome): *you'll just have to make the best of the situation.* ■use (resources) as well as possible: *he tried to make the best of his talents.* **make the best of a bad job** Brit. do something as well as one can under difficult circumstances. **six of the best** Brit., chiefly historical or humorous a caning as a punishment, traditionally with six strokes of the cane. **to the best of one's ability** (or **knowledge**) as far as one can do (or know): *the text is free of factual errors, to the best of my knowledge.* **with the best of them** as well or as much as anyone: *he'll be out there dancing with the best of them.*
– ORIGIN Old English *betest* (adjective), *betost*, *betst* (adverb), of Germanic origin; related to Dutch and German *best*, also to **BETTER**[1].

best ball ▶ **noun** Golf the better score at a hole of two or more players competing as a team: [as modifier] *a best-ball match.*

best bower ▶ **noun** see **BOWER**[2].

best boy ▶ **noun** the assistant to the chief electrician of a film crew.

bestial /ˈbɛstɪəl/ ▶ **adjective** of or like an animal or animals: *Darwin's revelations about our bestial beginnings.*
■savagely cruel and depraved: *bestial and barbaric acts.*
– DERIVATIVES **bestialize** (also **-ise**) verb, **bestially** adverb.
– ORIGIN late Middle English: via Old French from late Latin *bestialis*, from Latin *bestia* 'beast'.

bestiality ▶ **noun** [mass noun] **1** savagely cruel or depraved behaviour.
2 sexual intercourse between a person and an animal.
– ORIGIN late Middle English: from Old French *bestialite*, from *bestial* (see **BESTIAL**).

bestiary /ˈbɛstɪəri/ ▶ **noun** (pl. **-ies**) a descriptive or anecdotal treatise on various kinds of animal, especially a medieval work with a moralizing tone.
– ORIGIN mid 19th cent.: from medieval Latin *bestiarium*, from Latin *bestia* 'beast'.

bestir ▶ **verb** (**bestirred**, **bestirring**) (**bestir oneself**) make a physical or mental effort; exert or rouse oneself: *they rarely bestir themselves except in the most pressing of circumstances.*

best man ▶ **noun** a male friend or relative chosen by a bridegroom to assist him at his wedding.

bestow ▶ **verb** [with obj.] confer or present (an honour, right, or gift): *the office was **bestowed on** him by the monarch of this realm.*
■[with adverbial of place] archaic put (something) in a specified place: *stooping to bestow the presents into eager hands.*
– DERIVATIVES **bestowal** noun.
– ORIGIN Middle English (in the sense 'use for, devote to'): from **BE-** (as an intensifier) + Old English *stōw* 'place'.

bestrew ▶ **verb** (past participle **bestrewed** or **bestrewn**) [with obj.] poetic/literary cover or partly cover (a surface) with scattered objects: *the court was all **bestrewn with** herbs.*
■(of objects) lie scattered over (a surface): *to sweep away the sand and rubbish which bestrewed the floor.*
– ORIGIN Old English *bestrēowian* (see **BE-**, **STREW**).

bestride ▶ **verb** (past **bestrode**; past participle **bestridden**) [with obj.] stand astride over; span or straddle: *he bestrode me, defending my prone body |* figurative *creatures that bestride the dividing line between amphibians and reptiles.*
■sit astride on: *he bestrode his horse with the easy grace of a born horseman.* ■figurative dominate: *he bestrides Alberta politics today.*
– ORIGIN Old English *bestrīdan* (see **BE-**, **STRIDE**).

best-seller ▶ **noun** a book or other product that sells in very large numbers.

best-selling ▶ **adjective** [attrib.] (of a book or other product) having very large sales; very popular.

bet ▶ **verb** (**betting**; past and past participle **bet** or **betted**) **1** [no obj.] risk something, typically a sum of money, against someone else's on the basis of the outcome of a future event, such as the result of a race or game: ***betting on** horses | I wouldn't **bet against** him winning |* [with clause] *I would be prepared to bet that what he really wanted was to settle down |* [with obj.] *most people would **bet** their life savings **on** the prospect |* [with obj. and clause] *he bet a hundred pounds that he could complete 200 miles.*
■[with obj. and clause] risk a sum of money against (someone) on the outcome or happening of a future event: [with two objs] *I bet you £15 you won't chat her up.*
2 [with clause] informal used to express certainty: ***I bet** this place is really spooky late at night | he'll be surprised to see me, **I'll bet**.*
▶ **noun** an act of risking a sum of money in this way: *every Saturday she had **a bet on** the horses | **for a bet** he once rode 200 miles in nine hours.*
■a sum of money staked in this way: *the bookies are taking bets on his possible successor.* ■[with adj.] informal a candidate or course of action to choose, offering likelihood of success to a specified degree: *Town looked **a good bet** for victory | **your best bet** is to call the official liquidators.* ■**(one's bet)** informal an opinion, typically one formed quickly or spontaneously: *my bet is that Liverpool won't win anything.*
– PHRASES **all bets are off** informal the outcome of a situation is unpredictable. **don't** (or **I wouldn't**) **bet on it** informal used to express doubt about an assertion or situation: *he may be a suitable companion—but don't bet on it.* **want to bet?** informal used to express vigorous disagreement with a confident assertion: *'You can't be with me every moment.' 'Want to bet?'* **you bet** informal you may be sure; certainly: *'Would you like this piece of pie?' 'You bet!'*
– ORIGIN late 16th cent.: perhaps a shortening of the obsolete noun *abet* 'abetment'.

beta /ˈbiːtə/ ▶ **noun** the second letter of the Greek alphabet (**Β**, **β**), transliterated as 'b'.
■[as modifier] denoting the second of a series of items, categories, forms of a chemical compound, etc.: *beta carotene | β blocker.* ■Brit. a second-class mark given for an essay, examination paper, or other piece of work. ■informal short for **BETA TEST**. ■**(Beta)** [followed by Latin genitive] Astronomy the second (typically second-brightest) star in a constellation: *Beta Virginis.* ■[as modifier] relating to beta decay or beta particles: *beta emitters.* ■(also **beta coefficient**) a measure of the movement in price of a security relative to the stock market as a whole, used to indicate possible risk.
– ORIGIN via Latin from Greek.

beta blocker ▶ **noun** any of a class of drugs which prevent the stimulation of the adrenergic receptors responsible for increased cardiac action, used to control heart rhythm, treat angina, and reduce high blood pressure.

Betacam /ˈbiːtəkam/ ▶ **noun** [mass noun] trademark a high-quality format for video cameras and recorders.
■[count noun] a camera using this format.

beta-carotene ▶ **noun** see **CAROTENE**.

beta decay ▶ **noun** [mass noun] radioactive decay in which an electron is emitted.

betaine /ˈbiːtəiːn/ ▶ **noun** [mass noun] Chemistry a crystalline compound with basic properties found in many plant juices.
• Chem. formula: $(CH_3)_3N^+—CH_2CO_2^-$.
■[count noun] any zwitterionic compound of the type represented by this.
– ORIGIN mid 19th cent.: formed irregularly from

Latin *beta* 'beet' (because originally isolated from sugar beet) + **-INE**[4].

betake ▶ **verb** (past **betook**; past participle **betaken**) [with obj.] (**betake oneself to**) poetic/literary go to: *I shall betake myself to my lodgings.*

Betamax /ˈbiːtəmaks/ ▶ **noun** [mass noun] trademark a format for video recorders, now largely obsolete.
– ORIGIN 1970s: from Japanese *beta* 'all over' + *-max* from **MAXIMUM**.

beta particle (also **beta ray**) ▶ **noun** Physics a fast-moving electron emitted by radioactive decay of substances (originally regarded as rays).

beta rhythm ▶ **noun** [mass noun] Physiology the normal electrical activity of the brain when conscious and alert, consisting of oscillations (**beta waves**) with a frequency of 18 to 25 hertz.

beta test ▶ **noun** a trial of machinery, software, or other products, in the final stages of its development, carried out by a party unconnected with its development.
▶ **verb** (**beta-test**) [with obj.] subject (a product) to such a test.

betatron /ˈbiːtətrɒn/ ▶ **noun** Physics an apparatus for accelerating electrons in a circular path by magnetic induction.
– ORIGIN 1940s: from **BETA** + **-TRON**.

betcha ▶ **verb** a non-standard contraction of 'bet you', used in representing informal speech.

betel /ˈbiːt(ə)l/ ▶ **noun** [mass noun] **1** the leaf of an Asian evergreen climbing plant, used in the East as a mild stimulant. Parings of areca nut, lime, and cinnamon are wrapped in the leaf, which is then chewed, causing the saliva to go red and, with prolonged use, the teeth to go black. Also called **PAAN**.
2 the plant, related to pepper, from which these leaves are taken.
• *Piper betle*, family Piperaceae.
– ORIGIN mid 16th cent.: via Portuguese from Malayalam *verrila*.

Betelgeuse /ˈbiːt(ə)lˌdʒəːz/ (also **Betelgeux**) Astronomy the tenth brightest star in the sky, in the constellation Orion. It is a red supergiant, and variations in its brightness are associated with pulsations in its outer envelope.
– ORIGIN French, alteration of Arabic *yad al-jauzā* 'hand of the giant' (the giant being Orion).

betel nut ▶ **noun** another term for **ARECA NUT**.
– ORIGIN Portuguese *betel*.

bête noire /beɪt ˈnwɑː, bɛt, French bɛt nwaʀ/ ▶ **noun** (pl. **bêtes noires** pronunc. same) (**one's bête noire**) a person or thing that one particularly dislikes.
– ORIGIN French, literally 'black beast'.

Beth Din /beɪt ˈdiːn/ ▶ **noun** a Jewish court of law composed of three rabbinic judges, responsible for matters of Jewish religious law and the settlement of civil disputes between Jews.
– ORIGIN from Hebrew *bēṯ dīn*, literally 'house of judgement'.

bethink ▶ **verb** (past and past participle **bethought**) (**bethink oneself**) formal or archaic come to think: *he **bethought himself of** the verse from the Book of Proverbs.*
– ORIGIN Old English *bithencan* (see **BE-**, **THINK**).

Bethlehem /ˈbɛθlɪhɛm/ a small town 8 km (5 miles) south of Jerusalem, in the West Bank; pop. 14,000 (est. 1980). It was the native city of King David and is the reputed birthplace of Jesus.

betide ▶ **verb** [no obj.] poetic/literary happen: *I waited with beating heart, not knowing what would betide.*
▪ [with obj.] happen to (someone): *she was trembling with fear lest worse might betide her.*
– PHRASES **woe betide** see **WOE**.
– ORIGIN Middle English: from **BE-** (as an intensifier) + obsolete *tide* 'befall', from Old English *tīdan* 'happen', from *tīd* (see **TIDE**).

betimes ▶ **adverb** poetic/literary before the usual or expected time; early: *next morning I was up betimes.*
– ORIGIN Middle English: from obsolete *betime* (see **BY**, **TIME**).

bêtise /beɪˈtiːz, bɛˈtiːz, French betiz/ ▶ **noun** a foolish or ill-timed remark or action.
– ORIGIN French, 'stupidity', from *bête* 'foolish'.

Betjeman /ˈbɛtʃəmən/, Sir John (1906–84), English poet, noted for his self-deprecating, witty, and gently satirical poems. He was appointed Poet Laureate in 1972.

betoken ▶ **verb** [with obj.] poetic/literary be a sign of: *she wondered if his cold, level gaze betokened indifference or anger.*
▪ be a warning or indication of (a future event): *the falling comet betokened the true end of Merlin's powers.*
– ORIGIN Old English *betācnian*, from **BE-** (as an intensifier) + *tācnian* 'signify', of Germanic origin; related to **TOKEN**.

betony /ˈbɛtəni/ ▶ **noun** (pl. **-ies**) a Eurasian plant of the mint family, which bears spikes of showy purple flowers.
• *Stachys officinalis*, family Labiatae.
▪ used in names of plants that resemble the betony, e.g. **water betony**.
– ORIGIN Middle English: from Old French *betoine*, based on Latin *betonica*, perhaps from the name of an Iberian tribe.

betook past of **BETAKE**.

betray ▶ **verb** [with obj.] be disloyal to: *the men who have betrayed British people's trust.*
▪ be disloyal to (one's country, organization, or ideology) by acting in the interests of an enemy: *he could betray his country for the sake of communism.* ▪ treacherously inform an enemy of the existence or location of (a person or organization): *this group was betrayed by an informer.* ▪ treacherously reveal (secrets or information): *many of those employed by diplomats betrayed secrets and sold ciphers.* ▪ figurative reveal the presence of; be evidence of: *she drew a deep breath that betrayed her indignation.*
– DERIVATIVES **betrayal** noun, **betrayer** noun.
– ORIGIN Middle English: from **BE-** 'thoroughly' + obsolete *tray* 'betray', from Old French *trair*, based on Latin *tradere* 'hand over'.

betroth /bɪˈtrəʊð, -θ/ ▶ **verb** [with obj.] (usu. **be betrothed**) dated formally engage (someone) to be married: *in no time I shall be **betrothed to** Isabel* | [as noun **betrothed**] *how long have you known your betrothed?*
– DERIVATIVES **betrothal** noun.
– ORIGIN Middle English *betreuthe*: from **BE-** (expressing transitivity) + **TRUTH**. The change in the second syllable was due to association with **TROTH**.

better[1] ▶ **adjective** **1** more desirable, satisfactory, or effective: *hoping for better weather* | *the new facilities were far better* | *I'm **better at** doing sums than Alice.* [ORIGIN: comparative of the adjective **GOOD**.]
▪ more appropriate, advantageous, or well advised: *there couldn't be a better time to take up this job* | *it might be better to borrow the money.*
2 [predic. or as complement] partly or fully recovered from illness or injury: *his leg was getting better* | *Henry will be completely better after some rest.* [ORIGIN: comparative of the adjective **WELL**[1].]
▪ fitter and healthier; less unwell: *we'll feel a lot better after a decent night's sleep.*
▶ **adverb** more excellently or effectively: *Jonathon could do better if he tried* | *sound travels better in water than in air* | *instruments are generally better made these days.*
▪ to a greater degree; more (used in connection with success or with desirable actions or conditions): *I liked it better when we lived in the country* | *you may find alternatives that suit you better* | *well-fed people are better able to fight off infection.* ▪ more suitably, appropriately, or usefully: *the money could be better spent on more urgent cases.*
▶ **noun** **1** [mass noun] the better one; that which is better: *the Natural History Museum book is by far the better of the two* | *you've a right to expect better than that* | *a change **for the better**.*
2 (**one's betters**) chiefly dated or humorous one's superiors in social class or ability: *educating the young to respect their **elders and betters**.*
▶ **verb** [with obj.] improve on or surpass (an existing or previous level or achievement): *his account can hardly be bettered* | *bettering his previous time by ten minutes.*
▪ make (something) better; improve: *his ideas for bettering the lot of the millhands.* ▪ (**better oneself**) achieve a higher social position or status: *the residents are mostly Londoners who have bettered themselves.* ▪ overcome or defeat (someone): *she had almost bettered him at archery.*
– PHRASES **the —— the better** used to emphasize the importance or desirability of the quality or thing specified: *the sooner we're off the better.* **better the devil you know than the devil you don't know** proverb it's wiser to deal with an undesirable but familiar person or situation than to risk a change that might lead to a situation with worse difficulties or a person whose faults you have yet to discover. **better off** in a more desirable or advantageous position, especially in financial terms: *the proposals would make her about £40 a year better off.* **the better part of** almost all of; most of: *it is the better part of a mile.* **better safe than sorry** proverb it's wiser to be cautious and careful than to be hasty or rash and so do something you may later regret. **better than** N. Amer. more than: *he'd lived there for better than twenty years.* **the better to ——** so as to —— better: *he leaned closer the better to hear her.* **for better or** (**for**) **worse** whether the outcome is good or bad. **get the better of** (of a person) gain an advantage over or defeat (someone) by superior strength or ability: *no one has ever got the better of her yet.* ▪ (of a feeling or urge) be too strong to conceal or resist: *curiosity got the better of her.* **go one better** narrowly surpass a previous effort or achievement: *I want to go one better this time and score.* ▪ narrowly outdo (another person). **had better do something** would find it wiser to do something; ought to do something: *you had better be careful.* **have the better of** be more successful in (a contest): *Attlee had the better of these exchanges.* **no** (or **little**) **better than** just (or almost) the same as (something bad); merely: *viceroys who were often no better than bandits.* **no better than one should** (or **ought to**) **be** perceived as sexually promiscuous or of doubtful moral character.
– ORIGIN Old English *betera* (adjective), of Germanic origin; related to Dutch *beter* and German *besser*, also to **BEST**.

USAGE In the verb phrase **had better do something** the word **had** acts like an auxiliary verb and in informal spoken contexts it is often dropped, as in *you **better** not come tonight.* In writing, the **had** may be contracted to **'d** but it should not be dropped altogether.

better[2] ▶ **noun** variant spelling of **BETTOR**.

better half ▶ **noun** informal a person's wife, husband, or partner.

betterment ▶ **noun** [mass noun] the improvement of something: *they believed that what they were doing was vital for the betterment of society.*
▪ the enhanced value of real property arising from local improvements: [as modifier] *a betterment charge.*

Betterton, Thomas (1635–1710), English actor. A leading actor of the Restoration period, he also adapted the plays of John Webster, Molière, and Beaumont and Fletcher for his own productions.

Betti /ˈbɛti/, Ugo (1892–1953), Italian dramatist, poet, and short-story writer. Notable plays: *Corruption in the Palace of Justice* (1949), *Crime on Goat Island* (1950).

betting ▶ **noun** [mass noun] the action of gambling money on the outcome of a race, game, or other unpredictable event.
▪ the odds offered by bookmakers for such events: *Atlantic Way headed the betting at 2–1.*
– PHRASES **the betting is** informal it is likely: *the betting is that the company will slash the dividend.* **in** (or **out of**) **the betting** likely (or unlikely) to be among the winners of a horse race and given appropriate odds. **what's the betting?** Brit. informal used to express a belief that something is likely: *what's the betting he's up to no good?*

betting shop (also **betting office**) ▶ **noun** Brit. an establishment licensed to handle bets on races and other events.

bettong /ˈbɛtɒŋ/ ▶ **noun** a short-nosed rat-kangaroo found in Australia.
• Family Potoroidae: two genera, in particular *Bettongia*, and several species. See also **BOODIE**, **WOYLIE**.
– ORIGIN early 19th cent.: from Dharuk.

bettor (also **better**) ▶ **noun** chiefly US a person who bets, especially on a regular basis.

between ▶ **preposition** **1** at, into, or across the space separating (two objects or regions):
▪ expressing location: *they stopped on the A64 between York and Leeds* | *a rope bridge strung between two cliff ledges* | *the border between Mexico and the United States.* ▪ expressing movement to a point: *the dog crawled between us and lay down at our feet.* ▪ expressing movement from one side or point to the other and back again: *those who travel by train between London and Paris.*
2 in the period separating (two points in time): *they snack between meals* | *the long, cold nights between autumn and spring.*
3 in the interval separating (two points on a scale): *a man aged between 18 and 30* | *between 25 and 40 per cent off children's clothes.*
4 indicating a connection or relationship involving two or more parties: *links between science and*

industry | negotiations between Russia, Ukraine, and Romania.
■with reference to a collision or conflict: *a collision in mid-air between two light aircraft above Geneva | the wars between Russia and Poland.* ■with reference to a contrast or failure to correspond: *the difference between income and expenditure.* ■with reference to a choice or differentiation involving two or more things being considered together: *if you have to choose between two or three different options.*
5 by combining the resources or actions of (two or more people or other entities): *we have created something between us | China and India between them account for a third of the global population.*
■shared by (two or more people or things): *they had drunk between them a bottle of Chianti.*
▶**adverb 1** in or along the space separating two objects or regions: *layers of paper with tar* ***in between*** *| from Leipzig to Dresden, with the gentle Elbe flowing between.*
2 in the period separating two points in time: *sets of exercises with no rest* ***in between.***
– PHRASES **between ourselves** (or **you and me**) in confidence: *just between you and me, I don't think it was going to happen.* (**in**) **between times** (or **whiles**) in the intervals between other actions.
– ORIGIN Old English *betwēonum*, from *be* 'by' + a Germanic word related to **TWO**.

USAGE In standard English it is correct to say **between you and me** but incorrect to say **between you and I**. Why is this? A preposition such as **between** takes the object case and is correctly followed by object pronouns such as **me**, **him**, **her**, and **us** rather than subject pronouns such as **I**, **he**, **she**, and **we**. Thus it is correct to say **between us** or **between him and her** and it is clearly incorrect to say **between we** or **between he and she**. The mistake **between you and I** arises from a confusion between what follows a preposition and what ordinarily comes at the beginning of a sentence in the subject case. Many people know that it is not correct to say ***John and me*** *went to the shops* and that the correct sentence is ***John and I*** *went to the shops*. Thus, people concerned about correcting mistakes in one context have assumed that 'and me' should in all cases be replaced by 'and I'. In trying to avoid one kind of error, another one has been created.

betwixt ▶**preposition** & **adverb** archaic term for **BETWEEN**.
– PHRASES **betwixt and between** informal neither one thing nor the other.
– ORIGIN Old English *betwēox*, from *be* 'by' + a Germanic word related to **TWO**.

beurré /ˈbjʊəri/ ▶**noun** a class of pear of a mellow variety.
– ORIGIN early 18th cent.: French, literally 'buttered, buttery'.

beurre blanc /bəː ˈblɒ̃, French bœʀ blɑ̃/ ▶**noun** [mass noun] a creamy sauce made with butter, onions, and vinegar or lemon juice, usually served with seafood dishes.
– ORIGIN French, literally 'white butter'.

beurre manié /bəː ˈmanjeɪ, French bœʀ manje/ ▶**noun** [mass noun] a mixture of flour and butter used for thickening sauces or soups.
– ORIGIN French, literally 'worked butter'.

beurre noir /bəː ˈnwɑː, French bœʀ nwaʀ/ ▶**noun** French term for **BLACK BUTTER**.

Beuthen /ˈbɔytn/ German name for **BYTOM**.

Beuys /bɔɪs/, Joseph (1921–86), German artist. One of the most influential figures of the avant-garde movement in Europe in the 1970s and 1980s, his work consisted of 'assemblages' of various articles of rubbish. In 1979 he co-founded the German Green Party.

BeV ▶**abbreviation** another term for **GEV**.
– ORIGIN 1940s: from *billion* (10^9) electronvolts.

Bevan /ˈbɛv(ə)n/, Nye (1897–1960), British Labour politician; full name *Aneurin Bevan*. MP for Ebbw Vale 1929–60, his most notable contribution was the creation of the National Health Service (1948) during his time as Minister of Health 1945–51.

bevatron /ˈbɛvətrɒn/ ▶**noun** a synchrotron used to accelerate protons to energies in the billion electronvolt range.
– ORIGIN 1940s: from **BEV** + **-TRON**.

bevel /ˈbɛv(ə)l/ ▶**noun** a slope from the horizontal or vertical in carpentry and stonework; a sloping surface or edge.
■(also **bevel square**) a tool for marking angles in carpentry and stonework.
▶**verb** (**bevelled**, **bevelling**; US **beveled**, **beveling**) [with obj.] [often as adj. **bevelled**] reduce (a square edge on an object) to a sloping edge: *a bevelled mirror.*
– ORIGIN late 16th cent. (as an adjective in the sense 'oblique'): from an Old French diminutive of *baif* 'open-mouthed', from *baer* 'to gape' (see **BAY**[3]).

bevel gear ▶**noun** a gear working another gear at an angle to it by means of bevel wheels.

bevel wheel ▶**noun** a toothed wheel whose working face is oblique to the axis.

beverage /ˈbɛv(ə)rɪdʒ/ ▶**noun** (chiefly in commercial use) a drink other than water.
– ORIGIN Middle English: from Old French *bevrage*, based on Latin *bibere* 'to drink'.

Beveridge /ˈbɛvərɪdʒ/, William Henry, 1st Baron (1879–1963), British economist and social reformer, born in India. He was chairman of the committee which prepared the Beveridge Report, which formed the basis of much of the social legislation on which the welfare state in the UK is founded.

Beverly Hills a largely residential city in California, on the NW side of the Los Angeles conurbation; pop. 31,970 (1990). It is famous as the home of many film stars.

Bevin /ˈbɛvɪn/, Ernest (1881–1951), British Labour statesman and trade unionist. He was one of the founders of the Transport and General Workers' Union and a leading organizer of the General Strike (1926).

Bevin boy ▶**noun** (during the Second World War), a young man of age for National Service selected by lot to work as a miner.
– ORIGIN named after Ernest **BEVIN**.

bevvied /ˈbɛvɪd/ ▶**adjective** Brit. informal having consumed a lot of alcohol; drunk.

bevvy /ˈbɛvi/ ▶**noun** (pl. **-ies**) Brit. informal an alcoholic drink.
– ORIGIN late 19th cent.: abbreviation of **BEVERAGE**.

bevy /ˈbɛvi/ ▶**noun** (pl. **-ies**) a large group of people or things of a particular kind: *he was surrounded by* ***a bevy of*** *beautiful girls.*
– ORIGIN late Middle English: of unknown origin.

bewail ▶**verb** [with obj.] express great regret, disappointment, or bitterness over (something) by complaining about it to others: *men will bewail the loss of earlier freedoms.*
– DERIVATIVES **bewailer** noun.

beware ▶**verb** [no obj.] [in imperative or infinitive] be cautious and alert to risks or dangers: *shoppers were warned to* ***beware of*** *cut-price fakes | Beware! Dangerous submerged rocks ahead |* [with obj.] *we should beware the incompetence of legislators.*
– ORIGIN Middle English: from the phrase *be ware* (see **BE-**, **WARE**[3]).

bewdy ▶**noun** non-standard Australian spelling of **BEAUTY**.

bewhiskered ▶**adjective** having hair or whiskers growing on the face.

Bewick /ˈbjuːɪk/, Thomas (1753–1828), English artist and wood engraver, noted especially for the animal studies in such books as *A History of British Birds* (1797, 1804).

Bewick's swan ▶**noun** a bird of the Eurasian race of the tundra swan, breeding in Arctic regions of Russia and overwintering in northern Europe and central Asia.
• *Cygnus columbianus bewickii*, family Anatidae.

bewigged ▶**adjective** (of a person) wearing a wig.

bewilder ▶**verb** [with obj.] [often as adj. **bewildered**] cause (someone) to become perplexed and confused: *she seemed frightened and bewildered | his reaction had bewildered her |* [as adj. **bewildering**] *there is a bewildering array of holidays to choose from.*
– DERIVATIVES **bewilderedly** adverb, **bewilderingly** adverb, **bewilderment** noun.
– ORIGIN late 17th cent.: from **BE-** 'thoroughly' + obsolete *wilder* 'lead or go astray', of unknown origin.

bewitch ▶**verb** [with obj.] (often **be bewitched**) gain control over (someone) by casting a spell on them: *his relatives were convinced that he was bewitched.*
■enchant and delight (someone): *they both were bewitched by the golden luminosity of Italy |* [as adj. **bewitching**] *she was certainly a bewitching woman.*
– DERIVATIVES **bewitchingly** adverb, **bewitchment** noun.
– ORIGIN Middle English: from **BE-** 'thoroughly' + **WITCH**.

bey /beɪ/ ▶**noun** (pl. **-eys**) historical the governor of a district or province in the Ottoman Empire.
■formerly used in Turkey and Egypt as a courtesy title.
– ORIGIN Turkish, modern form of *beg* 'prince, governor'.

beyond ▶**preposition** & **adverb 1** at or to the further side of: [as prep.] *he pointed to a spot beyond the concealing trees | passengers travelling to destinations beyond London |* [as adv.] *from south of Dortmund as far as Essen* ***and beyond*** *| a view of Hobart with Mount Wellington beyond.*
■[prep.] outside the physical limits or range of: *the hook which held the chandelier was beyond her reach.* ■ figurative more extensive or extreme than; further-reaching than: [as prep.] *what these children go through is* ***far beyond*** *what most adults endure in a lifetime | the authority of the inspectors goes beyond ordinary police powers |* [as adv.] *pushing the laws to their limits* ***and beyond.***
2 happening or continuing after (a specified time, stage, or event): [as prep.] *training beyond the age of 14 |* [as adv.] *music going on into the night* ***and beyond.***
3 having progressed or achieved more than (a specified stage or level): [as prep.] *we need to get beyond square one | his failure to rise beyond the rank of Undersecretary.*
■above or greater than (a specified amount): [as prep.] *raising its stake beyond 15% |* [as adv.] *he could count up to a hundred thousand million now,* ***and beyond.***
4 [prep.] to or in a degree or condition where a specified action is impossible: *the landscape has changed beyond recognition | their integrity remains beyond question.*
■too much for (someone) to achieve or understand: *I did something that I thought was beyond me | the questions were well beyond the average adult.*
5 [prep.] [with negative] apart from; except: *beyond telling us that she was well educated, he has nothing to say about her | there was little vegetation beyond scrub and brush-growth.*
▶**noun** (**the beyond**) the unknown after death: *messages from the beyond.*
– PHRASES **the back of beyond** see **BACK**.
– ORIGIN Old English *begeondan*, from *be* 'by' + *geondan* of Germanic origin (related to **YON** and **YONDER**).

bezant /ˈbɛz(ə)nt/ ▶**noun 1** historical a gold or silver coin originally minted at Byzantium.
2 Heraldry a roundel or (i.e. a solid gold circle).
– ORIGIN Middle English: from Old French *besant*, from Latin *Byzantius* 'Byzantine'. Sense 2 dates from the late 15th cent.

bezel /ˈbɛz(ə)l/ ▶**noun** a grooved ring holding the cover of a watch face or other instrument in position.
■a groove holding the crystal of a watch or the stone of a gem in its setting.
– ORIGIN late 16th cent.: from Old French, of unknown origin.

bezique /bɪˈziːk/ ▶**noun** [mass noun] a trick-taking card game for two, played with a double pack of 64 cards, including the seven to ace only in each suit.
■the holding of the queen of spades and the jack of diamonds in this game.
– ORIGIN mid 19th cent.: from French *bésigue*, perhaps from Persian *bāzīgar* 'juggler' or *bāzī* 'game'.

bezoar /ˈbiːzɔː, ˈbɛzəʊɑː/ ▶**noun 1** a small stony concretion which may form in the stomachs of certain animals, especially ruminants, and which was once used as an antidote for various ailments.
2 a wild goat with flat scimitar-shaped horns, found from Greece to Pakistan. It is the ancestor of the domestic goat and is the best-known source of the above stony concretions.
• *Capra aegagrus*, family Bovidae.
– ORIGIN late 15th cent. (in the general sense 'stone or concretion'): from French *bezoard*, based on Arabic *bāzahr*, *bādizahr*, from Persian *pādzahr* 'antidote'.

b.f. ▶**abbreviation for** ■ Brit. informal bloody fool. ■ (in bookkeeping) brought forward.

BFI ▶**abbreviation for** British Film Institute.

B-film ▶**noun** another term for **B-MOVIE**.

BFPO ▶**abbreviation for** British Forces Post Office (or British Field Post Office, when in a combat zone).

BG ▶**abbreviation for** Bulgaria (international vehicle registration).

BH ▶ abbreviation for Belize (international vehicle registration).
– ORIGIN from *British Honduras*.

Bh ▶ symbol for the chemical element bohrium.

Bhagavadgita /ˌbʌɡəvədˈɡiːtə/ Hinduism a poem composed between the 2nd century BC and the 2nd century AD and incorporated into the Mahabharata. Presented as a dialogue between the Kshatriya prince Arjuna and his divine charioteer Krishna, it stresses the importance of doing one's duty and of faith in God. Also called **GITA**.

Bhagwan /bʌɡˈwɑːn/ ▶ noun Indian God.
■ a guru or revered person (often used as a proper name or form of address).
– ORIGIN from Hindi *bhagwān*, from Sanskrit *bhagavān*, from the root *bhaj* 'adore'.

bhai /bʌɪ/ ▶ noun Indian a brother.
■ a friendly form of address for a man.
– ORIGIN from Hindi *bhāī*, based on Sanskrit *bhrātr* 'brother'.

bhajan /ˈbʌdʒ(ə)n/ ▶ noun Hinduism a devotional song.
– ORIGIN from Sanskrit *bhajana*.

bhaji /ˈbɑːdʒi/ (also **bhajia**) ▶ noun (pl. **bhajis**, **bhajia**) (in Indian cuisine) a small flat cake or ball of vegetables, fried in batter.
■ an Indian dish of fried vegetables.
– ORIGIN from Hindi *bhājī* 'fried vegetables'.

bhakti /ˈbʌkti/ ▶ noun [mass noun] Hinduism devotional worship directed to one supreme deity, usually Vishnu (especially in his incarnations as Rama and Krishna) or Shiva, by whose grace salvation may be attained by all regardless of sex, caste, or class. It is followed by the majority of Hindus today.
– ORIGIN Sanskrit.

bhang /baŋ/ (also **bang**) ▶ noun [mass noun] the leaves and flower-tops of cannabis, used as a narcotic.
– ORIGIN from Hindi *bhāng*.

bhangra /ˈbɑːŋɡrə/ ▶ noun [mass noun] a type of popular music combining Punjabi folk traditions with Western pop music.
– ORIGIN 1960s (denoting a traditional folk dance): from Punjabi *bhāngrā*.

bharal /ˈbʌr(ə)l/ ▶ noun a Himalayan wild sheep with a bluish coat and backward-curving horns. Also called **BLUE SHEEP**.
● *Pseudois nayaur*, family Bovidae.
– ORIGIN mid 19th cent.: from Hindi.

Bharat /ˈbʌrət/ Hindi name for **INDIA**.

Bharatanatyam /ˌbʌrətəˈnɑːtjʌm/ ▶ noun [mass noun] a classical dance form of southern India.
– ORIGIN from Sanskrit *bharatanātya*, literally 'the dance of Bharata', from *Bharata*, reputed to be the author of the *Nātyaśāstra*, a manual of dramatic art.

bhavan /ˈbɑːvʌn/ ▶ noun [often in place names] Indian a building used for a special purpose, such as meetings or concerts.
– ORIGIN Hindi.

Bhavnagar /bʌvˈnʌɡə/ an industrial port in NW India, in Gujarat, on the Gulf of Cambay; pop. 401,000 (1991). It was the capital of a former Rajput princely state of the same name.

BHC ▶ noun another term for **LINDANE**.
– ORIGIN from *benzene hexachloride*.

bhelpuri /ˈbeɪlˌpuːri/ ▶ noun [mass noun] an Indian dish of puffed rice, onions, spices, and hot chutney.
– ORIGIN from Hindi *bhel* 'mixture' + *pūrī* 'deep-fried bread'.

Bhil /biːl/ (also **Bheel**) ▶ noun a member of an indigenous people of central India.
▶ adjective of or relating to this people.
– ORIGIN from Hindi *Bhīl*, from Sanskrit *Bhilla*.

Bhili /ˈbiːli/ ▶ noun [mass noun] the Indic language of the Bhils.

bhindi /ˈbɪndi/ ▶ noun Indian term for **OKRA**.
– ORIGIN from Hindi *bhindī*.

Bhojpuri /ˌbəʊdʒˈpʊəri/ ▶ noun [mass noun] one of the Bihari group of languages, spoken by some 20 million people in western Bihar and eastern Uttar Pradesh.

Bhopal /bəʊˈpɑːl/ a city in central India, the capital of the state of Madhya Pradesh; pop. 1,604,000 (1991). In December 1984 leakage of poisonous gas from an American-owned pesticide factory in the city caused the death of about 2,500 people.

b.h.p. ▶ abbreviation for brake horsepower.

Bhubaneswar /ˌbʊbəˈneɪʃwə/ a city in eastern India, capital of the state of Orissa; pop. 412,000 (1991).

Bhutan /buːˈtɑːn/ a small independent kingdom on the south-eastern slopes of the Himalayas, a protectorate of the Republic of India; pop. 600,000 (est. 1994); languages, Dzongkha (official), Nepali; capital, Thimphu.
– DERIVATIVES **Bhutanese** /ˌbuːtəˈniːz/ adjective & noun.

Bhutto[1] /ˈbuːtəʊ/, Benazir (b.1953), Pakistani stateswoman, Prime Minister 1988–90 and 1993–96, daughter of Zulfikar Ali Bhutto. She was the first woman Prime Minister of a Muslim country. In 1999, while she was abroad, she was sentenced to imprisonment for corruption.

Bhutto[2] /ˈbuːtəʊ/, Zulfikar Ali (1928–79), Pakistani statesman, President 1971–3 and Prime Minister 1973–7. He was ousted by a military coup and executed for conspiring to murder a political rival.

Bi ▶ symbol for the chemical element bismuth.

bi /bʌɪ/ informal ▶ adjective for bisexual.

bi- /bʌɪ/ ▶ combining form two; having two: *bicoloured | biathlon*. See also **BIN-**.
■ occurring twice in every one or once in every two: *bicentennial*. ■ lasting for two: *biennial*. ■ doubly; in two ways: *biconcave*. ■ Chemistry (in names of compounds) containing two atoms or groups of a specified kind: *bicarbonate*. ■ Botany & Zoology (of division and subdivision) twice over: *bipinnate*.
– ORIGIN from Latin, 'doubly, having two'; related to Greek *di-* 'two'.

Biafra /bɪˈafrə/ a state proclaimed in 1967, when part of eastern Nigeria, inhabited chiefly by the Ibo people, sought independence from the rest of the country. In the ensuing civil war the new state's troops were overwhelmed by numerically superior forces, and by 1970 it had ceased to exist.
– DERIVATIVES **Biafran** adjective & noun.

bialy /bɪˈɑːli/ ▶ noun (pl. **bialys**) US a flat bread roll topped with chopped onions.
– ORIGIN Yiddish, from **BIAŁYSTOK**, where such bread was originally made.

Białystok /biːˈalɪstɒk/ an industrial city in NE Poland, close to the border with Belarus; pop. 270,568 (1990). Russian name **BELOSTOK**.

bi-amping ▶ noun [mass noun] informal the use of two amplifiers for high- and low-frequency ranges in an audio circuit.

biannual ▶ adjective occurring twice a year: *the biannual meeting of the planning committee*. Compare with **BIENNIAL**.
– DERIVATIVES **biannually** adverb.

Biarritz /ˌbɪəˈrɪts/, French bjarits/ a seaside resort in SW France, on the Bay of Biscay; pop. 28,890 (1990).

bias ▶ noun 1 [mass noun] prejudice in favour of or against one thing, person, or group compared with another, especially in a way considered to be unfair: *there was evidence of bias against black applicants | the bias towards younger people in recruitment | [in sing.] a systematic bias in favour of the powerful*.
■ [in sing.] a concentration on or interest in one particular area or subject: *his work showed a discernible bias towards philosophy*. ■ a systematic distortion of a statistical result due to a factor not allowed for in its derivation.
2 an edge cut obliquely across the grain of a fabric.
3 Bowls the irregular shape given to a bowl.
■ the oblique course that such a shape causes a bowl to run.
4 Electronics a steady voltage, magnetic field, or other factor applied to an electronic system or device to cause it to operate over a pre-determined range.
▶ verb (**biased**, **biasing** or **biassed**, **biassing**) **1** [with obj.] (usu. **be biased**) cause to feel or show prejudice for or against someone or something: *readers said their paper was biased towards the Conservatives | editors were biased against authors from provincial universities | [as adj.] **biased** a biased view of the world*.
2 Electronics give a bias to.
– PHRASES **cut on the bias** (of a fabric or garment) cut obliquely across the grain.
– ORIGIN mid 16th cent. (in the sense 'oblique line'; also as an adjective meaning 'oblique'): from French *biais*, from Provençal, perhaps based on Greek *epikarsios* 'oblique'.

bias binding ▶ noun [mass noun] a narrow strip of fabric cut obliquely and used to bind edges or for decoration.

bias-cut ▶ adjective (of a garment or fabric) cut obliquely or diagonally across the grain.

bias-ply ▶ adjective North American term for **CROSS-PLY**.

biathlon ▶ noun a Nordic skiing event in which competitors combine cross-country skiing and rifle shooting.
– DERIVATIVES **biathlete** noun.
– ORIGIN 1950s: from **BI-** 'two' + Greek *athlon* 'contest', on the pattern of *pentathlon*.

biaxial ▶ adjective having or relating to two axes.
■ (of crystals) having two optic axes, as in the orthorhombic, monoclinic, and triclinic systems.

bib[1] ▶ noun **1** a piece of cloth or plastic fastened round a child's neck to keep its clothes clean while eating.
■ a loose-fitting sleeveless garment worn for identification, especially by competitors and officials at sporting events. ■ the part above the waist of the front of an apron or pair of dungarees. ■ a patch of colour on the throat of a bird or other animal.
2 a common European inshore fish of the cod family. Also called **POUT**[2] or **POUTING**.
● *Trisopterus luscus*, family Gadidae.
– PHRASES **one's best bib and tucker** informal one's smartest clothes. **stick** (or **poke**) **one's bib in** Austral./NZ informal interfere.
– ORIGIN late 16th cent.: probably from **BIB**[2].

bib[2] ▶ verb (**bibbed**, **bibbing**) [with obj.] archaic drink (something alcoholic).
– ORIGIN late Middle English: probably from Latin *bibere* 'to drink'.

bibber ▶ noun [in combination] a person who regularly drinks a specified drink: *a wine-bibber*.

bibb lettuce ▶ noun N. Amer. a butterhead lettuce of a variety that has crisp dark green leaves.
– ORIGIN late 19th cent.: named after Jack *Bibb* (1789–1884), the American horticulturalist who developed it.

bib cock ▶ noun a tap with a bent nozzle fixed at the end of a pipe.
– ORIGIN late 18th cent.: perhaps from **BIB**[1] and **COCK**[1].

bibelot /ˈbɪbələʊ/ ▶ noun a small, decorative ornament or trinket.
– ORIGIN late 19th cent.: from French, fanciful formation based on *bel* 'beautiful'.

bibi /ˈbiːbiː/ ▶ noun (pl. **bibis**) Indian a man's non-European girlfriend.
– ORIGIN from Urdu *bībī*, from Persian.

Bible ▶ noun (**the Bible**) the Christian scriptures, consisting of the Old and New Testaments.
■ (**the Bible**) the Jewish scriptures, consisting of the Torah or Law, the Prophets, and the Hagiographa or Writings. ■ (also **bible**) a copy of the Christian or Jewish scriptures. ■ a particular edition or translation of the Bible: *the New English Bible*. ■ (**bible**) informal a book regarded as authoritative: *for many teachers Lehninger has been a biochemical bible*. ■ the scriptures of any religion.
– ORIGIN Middle English: via Old French from ecclesiastical Latin *biblia*, from Greek (*ta*) *biblia* '(the) books', from *biblion* 'book', originally a diminutive of *biblos* 'papyrus, scroll', of Semitic origin.

Bible-bashing (also **Bible-thumping** or **Bible-punching**) ▶ adjective [attrib.] informal denoting a person who expounds or follows the teachings of the Bible in an aggressively evangelical way.
– DERIVATIVES **Bible-basher** (also **Bible-thumper**, **Bible-puncher**) noun.

Bible Belt ▶ noun (**the Bible Belt**) those areas of the southern and middle western United States and western Canada where Protestant fundamentalism is widely practised.

biblical (also **Biblical**) ▶ adjective of, relating to, or contained in the Bible: *the biblical account of creation | biblical times*.
■ resembling the language or style of the Bible: *there is a biblical cadence in the last words he utters*. ■ very great; on a large scale: *they see themselves as victims of almost biblical proportions*.
– DERIVATIVES **biblically** adverb.

biblio- /ˈbɪblɪəʊ/ ▶ combining form relating to a book or books: *bibliomania | bibliophile*.
– ORIGIN from Greek *biblion* 'book'.

bibliography /ˌbɪblɪˈɒɡrəfi/ ▶ noun (pl. **-ies**) a list of the books referred to in a scholarly work, typically printed as an appendix.

▪a list of the books of a specific author or publisher, or on a specific subject. ▪[mass noun] the history or systematic description of books, their authorship, printing, publication, editions, etc. ▪any book containing such information.
– DERIVATIVES **bibliographer** noun, **bibliographic** /-əˈgrafɪk/ adjective, **bibliographical** /-əˈgrafɪk(ə)l/ adjective, **bibliographically** /-əˈgrafɪk(ə)li/ adverb.
– ORIGIN early 19th cent.: from French *bibliographie* or modern Latin *bibliographia*, from Greek *biblion* 'book' + *-graphia* 'writing'.

bibliomancy /ˈbɪblɪə(ʊ)mansi/ ▶ **noun** [mass noun] the practice of foretelling the future by interpreting a randomly chosen passage from a book, especially the Bible.

bibliomania ▶ **noun** [mass noun] passionate enthusiasm for collecting and possessing books.
– DERIVATIVES **bibliomaniac** noun & adjective.

bibliometrics ▶ **plural noun** [treated as sing.] statistical analysis of books, articles, or other publications.
– DERIVATIVES **bibliometric** adjective.

bibliophile ▶ **noun** a person who collects or has a great love of books.
– DERIVATIVES **bibliophilic** adjective, **bibliophily** /-ˈɒfɪli/ noun.
– ORIGIN early 19th cent.: from French, from Greek *biblion* 'book' + *philos* 'loving'.

bibliopole /ˈbɪblɪə(ʊ)pəʊl/ ▶ **noun** archaic a person who buys and sells books, especially rare ones.
– ORIGIN late 18th cent.: via Latin from Greek *bibliopōlēs*, from *biblion* 'book' + *pōlēs* 'seller'.

Bibliothèque nationale /ˌbɪblɪəʊˌtɛk ˌnasjəˈnɑːl, French bibljotɛk nasjɔnal/ the national library of France, in Paris, which receives a copy of every book and periodical etc. published in France.

bib tap ▶ **noun** another term for **BIB COCK**.

bibulous /ˈbɪbjʊləs/ ▶ **adjective** formal excessively fond of drinking alcohol.
– DERIVATIVES **bibulously** adverb, **bibulousness** noun.
– ORIGIN late 17th cent. (in the sense 'absorbent'): from Latin *bibulus* 'freely or readily drinking' (from *bibere* 'to drink') + **-OUS**.

bicameral /bʌɪˈkam(ə)r(ə)l/ ▶ **adjective** (of a legislative body) having two chambers.
– DERIVATIVES **bicameralism** noun.
– ORIGIN mid 19th cent.: from **BI-** 'two' + Latin *camera* 'chamber' + **-AL**.

bicarb ▶ **noun** [mass noun] informal sodium bicarbonate.

bicarbonate /bʌɪˈkɑːbəneɪt, -nət/ ▶ **noun** Chemistry a salt containing the anion HCO_3^-.
▪(also **bicarbonate of soda**) [mass noun] sodium bicarbonate.

bice /bʌɪs/ ▶ **noun** [mass noun] dated a medium blue or blue-green pigment made from basic copper carbonate.
– ORIGIN Middle English (originally in the sense 'dark or brownish grey'): from Old French *bis* 'dark grey', of unknown ultimate origin.

bicentenary /ˌbʌɪsɛnˈtiːnəri, -ˈtɛn-/ ▶ **noun** (pl. **-ies**) the two-hundredth anniversary of a significant event.
▶ **adjective** of or relating to such an anniversary: *the huge bicentenary celebrations.*

bicentennial ▶ **noun** & **adjective** another term for **BICENTENARY**.

bicephalous /bʌɪˈsɛf(ə)ləs, -ˈkɛf-/ ▶ **adjective** having two heads.
– ORIGIN early 19th cent.: from **BI-** 'two' + Greek *kephalē* 'head' + **-OUS**.

biceps /ˈbʌɪsɛps/ ▶ **noun** (pl. same) any of several muscles having two points of attachment at one end, in particular:
▪(also **biceps brachii** /ˈbreɪkɪʌɪ/) a large muscle in the upper arm which turns the hand to face palm uppermost and flexes the arm and forearm: *he clenched his fist and exhibited his bulging biceps.* ▪(also **biceps femoris** /fɪˈmɔːrɪs/ or **leg biceps**) Anatomy a muscle in the back of the thigh which helps to flex the leg.
– ORIGIN mid 17th cent.: from Latin, literally 'two-headed', from *bi-* 'two' + *-ceps* (from *caput* 'head').

bichir /ˈbɪʃɪə/ ▶ **noun** an elongated African freshwater fish with an armour of hard shiny scales and a series of separate fins along its back.
• Genus *Polypterus*, family *Polypteridae*: several species, including *P. senegalus*.
– ORIGIN 1960s: via French from dialect Arabic *abu shīr*.

bicker ▶ **verb** [no obj.] **1** argue about petty and trivial matters: *whenever the phone rings, they* **bicker over** *who must answer it.*
2 poetic/literary (of water) flow or fall with a gentle repetitive noise; patter.
▪(of a flame or light) flash, gleam, or flicker.
– DERIVATIVES **bickerer** noun.
– ORIGIN Middle English: of unknown origin.

bicky (also **bikky**) ▶ **noun** (pl. **-ies**) informal a biscuit.
– PHRASES **big bickies** Austral. informal a large sum of money: *just showing up is worth big bickies.*
– ORIGIN 1930s: diminutive of **BISCUIT**.

Bicol ▶ **noun** & **adjective** variant spelling of **BIKOL**.

bicolour ▶ **adjective** having two colours: *a male bicolour damselfish.*
▶ **noun** a bicolour flower or breed.
– DERIVATIVES **bicoloured** adjective & noun.

biconcave ▶ **adjective** concave on both sides.

biconvex ▶ **adjective** convex on both sides.

bicultural ▶ **adjective** having or combining the cultural attitudes and customs of two nations, peoples, or ethnic groups.
– DERIVATIVES **biculturalism** noun.

bicuspid ▶ **adjective** having two cusps or points.
▶ **noun** a tooth with two cusps, especially a human premolar tooth.
– ORIGIN mid 19th cent.: from **BI-** 'two' + Latin *cuspis, cuspid-* 'sharp point'.

bicuspid valve ▶ **noun** Anatomy another term for **MITRAL VALVE**.

bicycle ▶ **noun** a vehicle composed of two wheels held in a frame one behind the other, propelled by pedals and steered with handlebars attached to the front wheel.
▶ **verb** [no obj., with adverbial of direction] ride a bicycle in a particular direction: *they had spent the holidays bicycling around the beautiful Devonshire countryside.*
– DERIVATIVES **bicyclist** noun.
– ORIGIN mid 19th cent.: from **BI-** 'two' + Greek *kuklos* 'wheel'.

bicycle chain ▶ **noun** a chain that transmits the driving power from the pedals of a bicycle to its rear wheel.

bicycle clip ▶ **noun** either of a pair of metal clips worn by a cyclist round their ankles to prevent their trouser legs from becoming entangled with the bicycle chain.

bicycle pump ▶ **noun** a portable pump for inflating bicycle tyres.

bicycle rickshaw ▶ **noun** another term for **CYCLE RICKSHAW**.

bicyclic /bʌɪˈsʌɪklɪk, -ˈsɪk-/ ▶ **adjective** Chemistry having two rings of atoms in its molecule.

bid[1] ▶ **verb** (**bidding**; past and past participle **bid**) [with obj.] offer (a certain price) for something, especially at an auction: *a consortium of dealers bid a world record price for a snuff box | what am I bid?* | [no obj.] *guests will* **bid for** *pieces of fine jewellery.*
▪[no obj.] (**bid for**) (of a contractor) offer to do (work) for a stated price; tender for: *nineteen companies have indicated their intention to bid for the contract.* ▪[no obj.] (**bid for**) make an effort or attempt to achieve: *the two forwards are bidding for places in the England side.* ▪Bridge make a statement during the auction undertaking to make (a certain number of tricks with a stated suit as trumps) if the bid is successful and one becomes the declarer: *North bids four hearts* | [no obj.] *with this hand, South should not bid.*
▶ **noun** an offer of a price, especially at an auction: *at the fur tables, several buyers make bids for the pelts.*
▪an offer to buy the shares of a company in order to gain control of it: *a takeover bid.* ▪an offer to do work or supply goods at a stated price; a tender. ▪an attempt or effort to achieve something: *Edward helped him* **make a bid for** *the Scottish throne* | [with infinitive] *an investigation would be carried out* **in a bid** *to establish what had happened.* ▪Bridge an undertaking by a player in the auction to make a stated number of tricks with a stated suit as trumps.
– DERIVATIVES **bidder** noun.
– ORIGIN Old English *bēodan* 'to offer, command', of Germanic origin; related to Dutch *bieden* and German *bieten*.

bid[2] ▶ **verb** (**bidding**; past **bid** or **bade**; past participle **bid**) [with obj.] **1** utter (a greeting or farewell) to: *a chance to bid farewell to their president and welcome the new man.*
2 archaic or poetic/literary command or order (someone) to do something: *I did as he bade me.*
▪invite (someone) to do something: *he bade his companions enter.*
– PHRASES **bid fair to** archaic or poetic/literary seem likely to: *the girl bade fair to be pretty.*
– ORIGIN Old English *biddan* 'ask', of Germanic origin; related to German *bitten*.

bidarka /bʌɪˈdɑːkə/ ▶ **noun** a canoe covered with animal skins, used by the Inuit of Alaska and adjacent regions.
– ORIGIN early 19th cent.: from Russian *baĭdarka*, diminutive of *baĭdara* 'an umiak'.

biddable ▶ **adjective 1** meekly ready to accept and follow instructions.
2 Bridge strong enough to justify a bid.
– DERIVATIVES **biddability** /-ˈbɪlɪti/ noun.

bidden archaic or poetic/literary past participle of **BID**[2].

bidding ▶ **noun** [mass noun] **1** the offering of particular prices for something, especially at an auction.
▪the offers made in such a situation: *from a cautious opener of £30, the bidding soared to a top of £48.* ▪(in bridge and whist) the action of stating before play how many tricks one intends to make.
2 the ordering or requesting of someone to do something: *women came running* **at his bidding** | [in sing.] *I never needed a second bidding.*
– PHRASES **do someone's bidding** do what someone orders or requests, especially in a way considered overly slavish.

bidding paddle ▶ **noun** a paddle-shaped baton, typically marked with an identifying number, used to signal bids at auctions.

bidding prayer ▶ **noun** (in church use) a prayer in the form of an invitation by a minister or leader to the congregation to pray about something.

biddy ▶ **noun** (pl. **-ies**) informal a woman, especially an elderly one, regarded as annoying or interfering: *the* **old biddies** *were muttering in his direction.*
– ORIGIN early 17th cent. (originally denoting a chicken): of unknown origin; probably influenced by the use of *biddy* denoting an Irish maidservant, from *Biddy*, pet form of the given name *Bridget*.

bide ▶ **verb** [no obj., with adverbial of place] archaic or dialect remain or stay somewhere: *how long must I bide here to wait for the answer?*
– PHRASES **bide one's time** wait quietly for a good opportunity to do something: *she patiently bided her time before making an escape bid.*
– ORIGIN Old English *bīdan*, of Germanic origin.

bidet ▶ **noun** a low oval basin used for washing one's genital and anal area.
– ORIGIN mid 17th cent. (in the sense 'horse'): from French, literally 'pony', from *bider* 'to trot', of unknown origin.

bidi /ˈbiːdiː/ (also **beedi** or **biri**) ▶ **noun** (pl. **bidis**) (in the Indian subcontinent) a type of cheap cigarette made of unprocessed tobacco wrapped in leaves.
– ORIGIN from Hindi *bīḍī* 'betel plug, cigar', from Sanskrit *vīṭikā*.

bidirectional ▶ **adjective** functioning in two directions.

bidonville /ˈbɪd(ə)nvɪl/ ▶ **noun** a shanty town built of oil drums or other metal containers, especially on the outskirts of a North African city.
– ORIGIN 1950s: from French, from *bidon* 'container for liquids' + *ville* 'town'.

bid price ▶ **noun** the price at which a market-maker or dealer is prepared to buy securities or other assets. Compare with **OFFER PRICE**.

bidri /ˈbɪdri/ ▶ **noun** [mass noun] an alloy of copper, lead, tin, and zinc, used as a ground for inlaying with gold and silver.
– ORIGIN late 18th cent.: from Urdu *bidrī*, from *Bidar*, the name of a town in India.

Biedermeier /ˈbiːdəˌmʌɪə/ ▶ **adjective** denoting or relating to a style of furniture and interior decoration current in Germany in the period 1815–48, characterized by restraint, conventionality, and utilitarianism.
– ORIGIN from the name of Gottlieb *Biedermaier*, a fictitious German provincial schoolmaster and poet created by L. Eichrodt (1854).

Bielefeld /ˈbiːləˌfɛlt/ an industrial city in North Rhine-Westphalia in western Germany; pop. 322,130 (1991).

biennale /ˌbiːɛˈnɑːleɪ, -li/ ▶ **noun** a large art

exhibition or music festival,especially one held biennially.

– ORIGIN 1930s (used originally as the name of an international art exhibition held in Venice): from Italian, literally 'biennial'.

biennial /bʌɪˈɛnɪəl/ ▶ **adjective 1** taking place every other year: *summit meetings are normally biennial.* Compare with **BIANNUAL**.
2 (of a plant) taking two years to grow from seed to fruition and die. Compare with **ANNUAL**, **PERENNIAL**.
▶ **noun 1** a biennial plant.
2 an event celebrated or taking place every two years.
– DERIVATIVES **biennially** adverb.
– ORIGIN early 17th cent.: from Latin *biennis* (from *bi-* 'twice' + *annus* 'year') + **-AL**.

biennium /bʌɪˈɛnɪəm/ ▶ **noun** (pl. **biennia** /-nɪə/ or **bienniums**) (usu. **the biennium**) a specified period of two years: *the budget for the next biennium.*
– ORIGIN early 20th cent.: from Latin, from *bi-* 'twice' + *annus* 'year'.

bien pensant /ˌbjã pɒ̃sɒ̃, French bjɛ̃ pɑ̃sɑ̃/ ▶ **adjective** right-thinking; orthodox.
▶ **noun** (**bien-pensant**) a right-thinking or orthodox person.
– ORIGIN French, from *bien* 'well' + *pensant*, present participle of *penser* 'think'.

bier /bɪə/ ▶ **noun** a movable frame on which a coffin or a corpse is placed before burial or cremation or on which they are carried to the grave.
– ORIGIN Old English *bēr*, of Germanic origin; related to German *Bahre*, also to **BEAR**[1].

Bierce /bɪəs/, Ambrose (Gwinnett) (1842–*c.*1914), American writer, best known for his sardonic short stories and *The Devil's Dictionary* (1911). In 1913 he travelled to Mexico and mysteriously disappeared.

biface /ˈbʌɪfeɪs/ ▶ **noun** Archaeology a type of prehistoric stone implement flaked on both faces.

bifacial ▶ **adjective** having two faces, in particular:
■ Botany (of a leaf) having upper and lower surfaces that are structurally different. ■ Archaeology (of a flint or other artefact) worked on both faces.

biff informal ▶ **verb** [with obj.] strike (someone) roughly or sharply, typically with the fist: *he biffed me on the nose.*
▶ **noun** a sharp blow with the fist.
– ORIGIN mid 19th cent. (originally US): symbolic of a short sharp movement.

bifid /ˈbʌɪfɪd/ ▶ **adjective** Botany & Zoology (of a part of a plant or animal) divided by a deep cleft or notch into two parts: *a bifid leaf* | *the gut is bifid.*
– ORIGIN mid 17th cent.: from Latin *bifidus*, from *bi-* 'doubly' + *fidus* (from *findere* 'to split').

bifilar /bʌɪˈfʌɪlə/ ▶ **adjective** consisting of or involving two threads or wires.
– ORIGIN mid 19th cent.: from **BI-** 'two' + *filum* 'thread' + **-AR**[1].

bifocal ▶ **adjective** (especially of a pair of glasses) having lenses with two parts with different focal lengths, one for distant vision and one for near vision.
▶ **noun** (**bifocals**) a pair of glasses having two such parts.

bifold ▶ **adjective** double or twofold.

BIFU ▶ **abbreviation for** (in the UK) Banking, Insurance, and Finance Union.

bifurcate ▶ **verb** /ˈbʌɪfəkeɪt/ divide into two branches or forks: [no obj.] *just below Cairo the river bifurcates* | [with obj.] *the trail was bifurcated by a mountain stream.*
▶ **adjective** /bʌɪˈfəːkət/ forked; branched: *a bifurcate tree.*
– ORIGIN early 17th cent.: from medieval Latin *bifurcat-* 'divided into two forks', from the verb *bifurcare*, from Latin *bifurcus* 'two-forked', from *bi-* 'having two' + *furca* 'a fork'.

bifurcation ▶ **noun** [mass noun] the division of something into two branches or parts.
■ [count noun] the point at which something divides into two branches. ■ [count noun] either of two branches into which something divides.

big ▶ **adjective** (**bigger**, **biggest**) **1** of considerable size or extent: *big hazel eyes* | *big buildings* | *big cuts in staff.*
■ [attrib.] larger than other items of the same kind: *my big toe.* ■ grown-up: *I'm a big girl now.* ■ [attrib.] elder: *my big sister.* ■ [predic.] (**big with**) archaic advanced in pregnancy with: *my wife was big with child* | figurative *a word big with fate.* ■ informal on an ambitiously large scale: *a small company with big plans.* ■ [attrib.] informal doing a specified action very often or on a very large scale: *a big eater* | *a big gambler.* ■ informal showing great enthusiasm: *a big tennis fan.* ■ informal exciting great interest or popularity: *African bands which are big in Britain.*
2 of considerable importance or seriousness: *it's a big decision* | *his biggest problem is money* | *he made a big mistake.*
■ informal holding an important position or playing an influential role: *as a senior in college, he was a big man on campus.*
3 [predic.] informal, often ironic generous: *'I'm inclined to take pity on you.' 'That's big of you!'*
▶ **verb** [with obj.] (**big something up**) black slang praise or recommend something highly: *the record's been on the streets a while now, but it's certainly still worth bigging up.*
▶ **noun** (**the bigs**) N. Amer. informal the major league in a professional sport.
– PHRASES **big idea** chiefly ironic a clever or important intention or scheme: *okay, what's the big idea?* **the big lie** a gross distortion or misrepresentation of the facts, especially when used as a propaganda device by a politician or official body. **big money** (chiefly N. Amer. also **big bucks**) informal large amounts of money, especially as pay or profit. **big screen** informal the cinema: [as modifier] *her big-screen debut.* **big shot** (also **big noise**) informal an important or influential person. **the big stick** informal the use or threat of force or power: *the authorities used quiet persuasion instead of the big stick.* **the Big Three, Four,** etc. informal the three, four, etc., most important or powerful figures in a particular field: *increased competition between the Big Three cider-makers.* **come** (or **go**) **over big** informal have a great effect; be a success: *the story went over big with the children.* **give someone the big E** Brit. informal reject someone, typically in an insensitive or dismissive way. [ORIGIN: *E* from *elbow*.] **in a big way** informal to a great extent or high degree: *he contributed to the film in a big way* | *they go for it in a big way.* **make it big** informal become very successful or famous. **talk big** informal talk confidently or boastfully. **think big** informal be ambitious. **too big for one's boots** (or dated **breeches**) informal conceited.
– DERIVATIVES **biggish** adjective, **bigness** noun.
– ORIGIN Middle English (in the sense 'strong, mighty'): of unknown origin.

bigamy ▶ **noun** [mass noun] the offence of marrying someone while already married to another person.
– DERIVATIVES **bigamist** noun, **bigamous** adjective.
– ORIGIN Middle English: from Old French *bigamie*, from *bigame* 'bigamous', from late Latin *bigamus*, from *bi-* 'twice' + Greek *-gamos* 'married'.

Big Apple informal name for New York City.

big band ▶ **noun** a large group of musicians playing jazz or dance music: [as modifier] *the big-band sound.*

big bang ▶ **noun 1** Astronomy the explosion of dense matter which according to current cosmological theories marked the origin of the universe.

In the beginning a fireball of radiation at extremely high temperature and density, but occupying a tiny volume, is believed to have formed. This expanded and cooled, extremely fast at first, but more slowly as subatomic particles condensed into matter which later accumulated to form galaxies and stars. The galaxies are currently still retreating from one another. What was left of the original radiation continued to cool and has been detected as a uniform background of weak microwave radiation.

2 (**Big Bang**) (in the UK) the introduction in 1986 of major changes in trading in the Stock Exchange, principally involving widening of membership, relaxation of rules for brokers, and computerization.

Big Ben the great clock tower of the Houses of Parliament in London and its bell.

Big Board US informal name for the New York Stock Exchange.

Big Brother ▶ **noun** informal a person or organization exercising total control over people's lives.
– ORIGIN 1950s: from the name of the head of state in Orwell's *Nineteen Eighty-four* (1949).

big bud ▶ **noun** [mass noun] a disease of blackcurrant bushes in which the buds become swollen due to the presence of gall mites.
• The mite is *Cecidophyopsis ribis*, family Eriophyidae.

big bug ▶ **noun** informal another term for **BIGWIG**.

big business ▶ **noun** [mass noun] large-scale or important financial or commercial activity: *the children's toy market is big business now.*

big cat ▶ **noun** any of the large members of the cat family, including the lion, tiger, leopard, jaguar, snow leopard, clouded leopard, cheetah, and puma.
• *Panthera* and other genera, family Felidae.

big cheese ▶ **noun** informal an important person: *he was a really big cheese in the business world.*
– ORIGIN 1920s: *cheese*, probably via Urdu from Persian *čīz* 'thing': the phrase *the cheese* was used earlier to mean 'first-rate' (i.e. *the* thing).

Big Chief (also **Big Daddy**) ▶ **noun** informal a person in authority; the head of an organization or enterprise.

big dipper ▶ **noun 1** Brit. a roller coaster.
2 (**the Big Dipper**) North American term for **PLOUGH** (in sense 2).

big end ▶ **noun** (in a piston engine) the larger end of the connecting rod, encircling the crankpin.

bigeneric /ˌbʌɪdʒɪˈnɛrɪk/ ▶ **adjective** Botany relating to or denoting a hybrid between two genera.

bigeye ▶ **noun 1** (also **bigeye tuna**) a large migratory tuna which is found in warm seas and is very important to the fishing industry.
• *Thunnus obesus*, family Scombridae.
2 a reddish fish with large eyes which lives in moderately deep waters of the tropical Atlantic and the western Indian Ocean. Also called **CATALUFA**.
• *Priacanthus arenatus*, family Priacanthidae.

big five ▶ **noun** (**the big five**) a name given by hunters to the five largest and most dangerous African mammals: rhinoceros, elephant, buffalo, lion, and leopard.

Bigfoot ▶ **noun** (pl. **Bigfeet**) a large, hairy ape-like creature resembling a yeti, supposedly found in NW America. See also **SASQUATCH**.
– ORIGIN so named because of the size of its footprints.

big game ▶ **noun** [mass noun] large animals hunted for sport.

biggie ▶ **noun** (pl. **-ies**) informal a big, important, or successful person or thing: *composers including most of the biggies like Brahms, Wagner, Mendelssohn.*

big government ▶ **noun** [mass noun] chiefly N. Amer. government perceived as excessively interventionist and intruding into all aspects of the lives of its citizens.

big gun ▶ **noun** informal a powerful or influential person.

bigha /ˈbiːɡə/ ▶ **noun** (in the Indian subcontinent) a measure of land area varying locally from ⅓ to 1 acre (⅛ to ⅖ hectare).
– ORIGIN from Hindi *bīghā*.

big hair ▶ **noun** [mass noun] informal a bouffant hairstyle, especially one that has been teased, permed, or sprayed to create volume.

big-head ▶ **noun** informal a conceited or arrogant person.
– DERIVATIVES **big-headed** adjective, **big-headedness** noun.

big-hearted ▶ **adjective** (of a person or action) kind and generous.

bighorn (also **bighorn sheep**) ▶ **noun** (pl. same or **-horns**) a stocky brown wild sheep with large horns, found in North America and NE Asia.
• Genus *Ovis*, family Bovidae: two species, in particular the American *O. canadensis* (also called **MOUNTAIN SHEEP**), found chiefly in the Rocky Mountains.

big house ▶ **noun** (usu. **the big house**) the largest house in a village or area, typically inhabited by a family of high social standing.
■ informal a prison: *he's doing a stint in the big house.*

bight /bʌɪt/ ▶ **noun** a curve or recess in a coastline, river, or other geographical feature.
■ a loop of rope.
– ORIGIN Old English *byht* 'a bend or angle', of Germanic origin; related to **BOW**[2].

big league ▶ **noun** a group of teams in a professional sport, especially baseball, competing for a championship at the highest level.
■ (**the big league**) informal a very successful or important group: *the film brought him into the movie world's big league.*
– DERIVATIVES **big leaguer** noun.

big mouth ▶ **noun** informal an indiscreet or boastful person.
– DERIVATIVES **big-mouthed** adjective.

big name ▶ noun informal a person who is famous in a particular sphere: *he's a big name in athletics.*

big noise ▶ noun another term for *big shot* (see BIG).

bigot /ˈbɪɡət/ ▶ noun a person who is bigoted.
– ORIGIN late 16th cent. (denoting a superstitious religious hypocrite): from French, of unknown origin.

bigoted ▶ adjective obstinately convinced of the superiority or correctness of one's own opinions and prejudiced against those who hold different opinions: *a bigoted group of reactionaries.*
  ■ expressing or characterized by prejudice and intolerance: *a thoughtless and bigoted article.*
– DERIVATIVES **bigotedly** adverb.

bigotry ▶ noun [mass noun] intolerance towards those who hold different opinions from oneself: *the report reveals racism and right-wing bigotry.*
– ORIGIN late 17th cent.: from BIGOT, reinforced by French *bigoterie.*

big science ▶ noun [mass noun] informal scientific research that is expensive and involves large teams of scientists.

big smoke ▶ noun (**the big smoke**) Brit. informal London.
  ■ chiefly Austral. any large town.

big-ticket ▶ adjective [attrib.] N. Amer. informal constituting a major expense: *big-ticket items such as cars, houses, and expensive vacations.*

big time informal ▶ noun (**the big time**) the highest or most successful level in a career, especially in entertainment: *a bit-part actor who finally made the big time in Hollywood.*
▶ adverb on a large scale; to a great extent: *this time they've messed up big time.*
– DERIVATIVES **big-timer** noun.

big top ▶ noun the main tent in a circus.

big tree ▶ noun North American term for *giant redwood* (see REDWOOD).

biguanide /baɪˈɡwɑːnaɪd/ ▶ noun [mass noun] Chemistry a crystalline compound with basic properties, made by condensation of two guanidine molecules.
  ● Chem. formula: $NH:C(NH)(NH_2)_2.$

big wheel ▶ noun 1 a Ferris wheel.
2 North American term for BIGWIG.

bigwig ▶ noun informal an important person, especially in a particular sphere: *government bigwigs.*
– ORIGIN early 18th cent.: so named from the large wigs formerly worn by distinguished men.

Bihar /bɪˈhɑː/ a state in NE India; capital, Patna.

Bihari /bɪˈhɑːri/ ▶ noun (pl. **-ies**) 1 a native or inhabitant of Bihar.
2 [mass noun] a group of three closely related Indic languages spoken principally in Bihar. The three languages are Bhojpuri, Maithili, and Magahi.
▶ adjective of or relating to Bihar, its peoples, or their languages.
– ORIGIN from Hindi *Bihārī.*

bijection /baɪˈdʒɛkʃ(ə)n/ ▶ noun Mathematics a mapping that is both one-to-one (an injection) and onto (a surjection), i.e. a function which relates each member of a set *S* (the domain) to a separate and distinct member of another set *T* (the range), where each member in *T* also has a corresponding member in *S*.
– DERIVATIVES **bijective** adjective.

bijou /ˈbiːʒuː/ ▶ adjective (especially of a house or flat) small and elegant.
▶ noun (pl. **bijoux** pronounced same) archaic a jewel or trinket.
– ORIGIN French, from Breton *bizou* 'finger-ring', from *biz* 'finger'.

bijouterie /biˈʒuːt(ə)ri, French bijutri/ ▶ noun [mass noun] jewellery or trinkets.
– ORIGIN French, from BIJOU.

bike informal ▶ noun a bicycle or motorcycle: *I'm going by bike* | [as modifier] *a bike ride.*
▶ verb [no obj.] ride a bicycle or motorcycle: *we hope to encourage people to bike to work.*
– PHRASES **get off one's bike** Austral./NZ informal become annoyed. **on your bike!** Brit. informal go away (used as an expression of annoyance).
– ORIGIN late 19th cent.: abbreviation.

biker ▶ noun informal a motorcyclist, especially one who is a member of a gang.
  ■ a cyclist.

bikeway ▶ noun chiefly N. Amer. a path or lane for the use of bicycles.

bikie ▶ noun (pl. **-ies**) Austral. informal a member of a gang of motorcyclists.

Bikini an atoll in the Marshall Islands, in the western Pacific, used by the US between 1946 and 1958 as a site for testing nuclear weapons.

bikini ▶ noun (pl. **bikinis**) a two-piece swimsuit for women.
– ORIGIN 1940s: named after BIKINI, where an atom bomb was exploded in 1946 (because of the supposed 'explosive' effect created by the garment).

bikini briefs ▶ plural noun scanty briefs worn by women as underwear.

bikini line ▶ noun the area of skin around the edge of the bottom half of a bikini (used especially with reference to the cosmetic removal of the pubic hair in this area).

bikky ▶ noun (pl. **-ies**) variant spelling of BICKY.

Biko /ˈbiːkəʊ/, Steve (1946–77), South African radical leader; full name *Stephen Biko.* He was banned from political activity in 1973; after his death in police custody he became a symbol of heroic resistance to apartheid.

Bikol /bɪˈkɒl/ (also **Bicol**) ▶ noun (pl. same or **Bikols**)
1 a member of an indigenous people of SE Luzon in the Philippines.
2 [mass noun] the Austronesian language of this people, with over 3 million speakers.
▶ adjective of or relating to this people or their language.

bilabial ▶ adjective Phonetics (of a speech sound) formed by closure or near closure of the lips, e.g. *p, b, m, w.*
▶ noun a consonant sound made in such a way.

bilateral ▶ adjective having or relating to two sides; affecting both sides: *bilateral hearing.*
  ■ involving two parties, especially countries: *the recently concluded bilateral agreements with Japan.*
– DERIVATIVES **bilaterally** adverb.

bilateral symmetry ▶ noun [mass noun] the property of being divisible into symmetrical halves on either side of a unique plane.

bilayer ▶ noun Biochemistry a film two molecules thick (formed e.g. by lipids), in which each molecule is arranged with its hydrophobic end directed inwards towards the opposite side of the film and its hydrophilic end directed outwards.

Bilbao /bɪlˈbaʊ, -ˈbeɪaʊ, Spanish bilˈβao/ a seaport and industrial city in northern Spain; pop. 372,200 (1991).

bilberry ▶ noun (pl. **-ies**) a hardy dwarf shrub with red drooping flowers and dark blue edible berries, growing on heathland and mountains in northern Eurasia.
  ● Genus *Vaccinium,* family Ericaceae: several species, in particular *V. myrtillus.*
  ■ the small blue edible berry of this plant.
– ORIGIN late 16th cent.: probably of Scandinavian origin; compare with Danish *bøllebær.*

bilbo ▶ noun (pl. **-os** or **-oes**) a sword used in former times, noted for the temper and elasticity of its blade.
– ORIGIN mid 16th cent.: from *Bilboa,* an earlier English form of the name BILBAO, noted for the manufacture of fine blades.

bilboes ▶ plural noun an iron bar with sliding shackles, formerly used for confining a prisoner's ankles.
– ORIGIN mid 16th cent.: of unknown origin.

bilby /ˈbɪlbi/ ▶ noun (pl. **-ies**) another term for RABBIT-EARED BANDICOOT.
– ORIGIN late 19th cent.: probably from an Aboriginal language.

Bildungsroman /ˈbɪldʊŋzrəʊˌmɑːn/ ▶ noun a novel dealing with one person's formative years or spiritual education.
– ORIGIN German, from *Bildung* 'education' + *Roman* 'a novel'.

bile ▶ noun [mass noun] a bitter greenish-brown alkaline fluid which aids digestion and is secreted by the liver and stored in the gall bladder.
  ■ figurative anger; irritability.
– ORIGIN mid 16th cent.: from French, from Latin *bilis.*

bile duct ▶ noun the duct which conveys bile from the liver and the gall bladder to the duodenum.

bi-level ▶ adjective having or functioning on two levels; arranged on two planes: *the unit's bi-level design keeps water in the sink.*
  ■ N. Amer. denoting a style of two-storey house in which the lower storey is partially sunk below ground level, and the main entrance is between the two storeys. ■ denoting a railway carriage with seats on two levels.
▶ noun N. Amer. a bi-level house: *a three-bedroom bi-level.*

bilge ▶ noun the area on the outer surface of a ship's hull where the bottom curves to meet the vertical sides.
  ■ (**bilges**) the lowest internal portion of the hull. ■ (also **bilge water**) [mass noun] dirty water that collects inside the bilges. ■ [mass noun] figurative, informal nonsense; rubbish: *romantic bilge dreamed up by journalists.*
▶ verb [with obj.] archaic break a hole in the bilge of (a ship).
– ORIGIN late 15th cent.: probably a variant of BULGE.

bilge keel ▶ noun each of a pair of plates or timbers fastened under the sides of the hull of a ship to provide lateral resistance to the water, prevent rolling, and support its weight in dry dock.

bilharzia /bɪlˈhɑːtsɪə/ ▶ noun [mass noun] a chronic disease, endemic in parts of Africa and South America, caused by infestation with blood flukes (schistosomes). Also called BILHARZIASIS or SCHISTOSOMIASIS.
  ■ a blood fluke (schistosome).
– ORIGIN mid 19th cent.: modern Latin, former name of the genus *Schistosoma,* named after T. Bilharz (1825–62), the German physician who discovered the parasite.

bilharziasis /ˌbɪlhɑːˈtsaɪəsɪs/ ▶ noun Medicine another term for BILHARZIA (the disease).

biliary /ˈbɪlɪəri/ ▶ adjective Medicine of or relating to bile or the bile duct.
– ORIGIN mid 18th cent.: from French *biliaire,* from *bile* 'bile'.

bilinear ▶ adjective Mathematics 1 rare of, relating to, or contained by two straight lines.
2 of, relating to, or denoting a function of two variables that is linear and homogeneous in both independently.

bilingual ▶ adjective speaking two languages fluently: *a bilingual secretary.*
  ■ (of a text or an activity) written or conducted in two languages: *bilingual dictionaries* | *bilingual education.* ■ (of a country, city, or other community) using two languages, especially officially: *the town is virtually bilingual in Dutch and German.*
▶ noun a person fluent in two languages.
– DERIVATIVES **bilingualism** noun.
– ORIGIN mid 19th cent.: from Latin *bilinguis,* from *bi-* 'having two' + *lingua* 'tongue' + **-AL**.

bilious ▶ adjective affected by or associated with nausea or vomiting: *having eaten something which disagreed with me, I was a little bilious* | *a bilious attack.*
  ■ (of a colour) lurid or sickly: *a bilious olive hue.* ■ figurative spiteful; bad-tempered: *outbursts of bilious misogyny.* ■ Physiology of or relating to bile.
– DERIVATIVES **biliously** adverb, **biliousness** noun.
– ORIGIN mid 16th cent. (in the sense 'biliary'): from Latin *biliosus,* from *bilis* 'bile'.

bilirubin /ˌbɪlɪˈruːbɪn/ ▶ noun [mass noun] Biochemistry an orange-yellow pigment formed in the liver by the breakdown of haemoglobin and excreted in bile.
– ORIGIN late 19th cent.: coined in German from Latin *bilis* 'bile' + *ruber* 'red' + **-IN**[1].

biliverdin /ˌbɪlɪˈvɜːdɪn/ ▶ noun [mass noun] Biochemistry a green pigment excreted in bile. It is an oxidized derivative of bilirubin.

bilk informal ▶ verb [with obj.] 1 obtain or withhold money from (someone) by deceit or without justification; cheat or defraud: *government waste has bilked the taxpayer of billions of dollars.*
  ■ obtain (money) fraudulently: *some businesses bilk thousands of dollars from unsuspecting elderly consumers.*
2 archaic evade; elude.
– DERIVATIVES **bilker** noun.
– ORIGIN mid 17th cent. (originally used in cribbage meaning 'spoil one's opponent's score'): perhaps a variant of BAULK.

Bill ▶ noun (**the Bill** or **the Old Bill**) [treated as sing. or pl.] Brit. informal the police.
– ORIGIN 1960s: pet form of the given name *William.*

bill[1] ▶ noun 1 an amount of money owed for goods supplied or services rendered, set out in a printed or written statement of charges: *the bill for their meal came to £17.* **2** a draft of a proposed law presented to parliament for discussion: *a debate over the civil rights bill.* **3** a programme of entertainment, especially at a theatre or cinema: *she was top of the bill at America's leading vaudeville house.* **4** N. Amer. a banknote: *a ten-dollar bill.* **5** a poster or handbill.

▶ **verb** [with obj.] **1** (usu. **be billed**) list (a person or event) in a programme: *they were billed to appear but did not show up.*

■ (**bill someone/thing as**) describe someone or something in a particular way, especially in order to advertise them or emphasize their importance: *he was billed as 'the new Sean Connery'.* **2** send a note of charges to (someone): *we shall be billing them for the damage caused* | [with two objs] *he had been billed £3,000 for his licence.*

■ charge (a sum of money): *we billed £400,000.*

– PHRASES **fit** (or **fill**) **the bill** be suitable for a particular purpose.

– DERIVATIVES **billable** adjective.

– ORIGIN Middle English (denoting a written list or catalogue): from Anglo-Norman French *bille*, probably based on medieval Latin *bulla* 'seal, sealed document' (see also **BULL**[2]).

bill[2] ▶ **noun 1** the beak of a bird, especially when it is slender, flattened, or weak, or belongs to a web-footed bird or a bird of the pigeon family.

■ the muzzle of a platypus. ■ the point of an anchor fluke. **2** [in place names] a narrow promontory: *Portland Bill.*

▶ **verb** [no obj.] (of birds, especially doves) stroke bill with bill during courtship.

– PHRASES **bill and coo** informal behave or talk in a very loving or sentimental way.

– DERIVATIVES **billed** adjective [usu. in combination] *the red-billed weaver bird.*

– ORIGIN Old English *bile*, of unknown origin.

bill[3] ▶ **noun** a medieval weapon like a halberd with a hook instead of a blade.

– ORIGIN Old English *bil*, of West Germanic origin; related to German *Bille* 'axe'.

billabong ▶ **noun** Austral. a branch of a river forming a backwater or stagnant pool, made by water flowing from the main stream during a flood.

– ORIGIN mid 19th cent.: from Wiradhuri *bilabang* (originally as the name of the Bell River, NSW), from *billa* 'water' + *bang* 'channel that is dry except after rain'.

billboard ▶ **noun** a large outdoor board for displaying advertisements; a hoarding.

billet[1] ▶ **noun** a place, especially a civilian's house, where soldiers are lodged temporarily.

■ informal a place to stop or stay: *the young people's stay at each of their billets was short.*

▶ **verb** (**billeted, billeting**) [with obj. and adverbial of place] (often **be billeted**) lodge (soldiers) in a particular place, especially a civilian's house: *he didn't belong to the regiment billeted at the Hall.*

– ORIGIN late Middle English (originally denoting a short written document): from Anglo-Norman French *billette*, diminutive of *bille* (see **BILL**[1]). The verb is recorded in the late 16th cent., and the noun sense 'a written order requiring a householder to lodge the bearer, usually a soldier', from the mid 17th cent.; hence the current meaning.

billet[2] ▶ **noun** a thick piece of wood.

■ a small bar of metal for further processing. ■ Architecture each of a series of short cylindrical pieces inserted at intervals in Norman decorative mouldings. ■ Heraldry a rectangle placed vertically as a charge.

– ORIGIN late Middle English: from Old French *billette* and *billot*, diminutives of *bille* 'tree trunk', from medieval Latin *billa, billus* 'branch, trunk', probably of Celtic origin.

billet-doux /ˌbɪlɪˈduː/ ▶ **noun** (pl. **billets-doux** /-ˈduːz/) dated or humorous a love letter.

– ORIGIN late 17th cent.: French, literally 'sweet note'.

billfish ▶ **noun** (pl. same or **-fishes**) a large, fast-swimming fish of open seas, with a streamlined body and a long pointed spear-like snout. It occurs on the surface in warmer waters and is a popular sporting fish.

● Family Istiophoridae: three genera and several species, including the marlins, sailfish, and spearfishes.

billfold ▶ **noun** N. Amer. a wallet.

billhook ▶ **noun** a tool having a sickle-shaped blade with a sharp inner edge, used for pruning or lopping branches or other vegetation.

billiards /ˈbɪljədz/ ▶ **plural noun** [usu. treated as sing.] a game for two people, played on a billiard table, in which three balls are struck with cues into pockets round the edge of the table: [as modifier] (**billiard**) *billiard ball.*

– ORIGIN late 16th cent.: from French *billard*, denoting both the game and the cue, diminutive of *bille* (see **BILLET**[2]).

billiard table ▶ **noun** a smooth rectangular cloth-covered table used for billiards, snooker, and some forms of pool, with six pockets at the corners and sides into which the balls can be struck.

billing ▶ **noun** [mass noun] **1** the action or fact of publicizing or being publicized in a particular way: *they can justify their billing as Premier League favourites.*

■ prominence in publicity, especially as an indication of importance: *he shared top billing with his wife.* **2** the process of making out or sending invoices: *faster, more accurate order fulfilment and billing.*

■ the total amount of business conducted in a given time, especially that of an advertising agency: [count noun] *the account was worth about $2 million a year in billings.*

Billingsgate a London fish market dating from the 16th century. In 1982 the market moved to the Isle of Dogs in the East End.

Billings method ▶ **noun** a system for finding the time of ovulation by examining cervical mucus. It can be used as a form of birth control by avoiding sexual intercourse at that time.

– ORIGIN 1960s: named after Drs John and Evelyn Billings, who devised the method.

billion ▶ **cardinal number** (pl. **billions** or (with numeral or quantifying word) same) the number equivalent to the product of a thousand and a million; 1,000,000,000 or 10^9: *a world population of nearly 5 billion* | *half a billion dollars.*

■ (**billions**) informal a very large number or amount of something: *our immune systems are killing billions of germs right now.* ■ a billion pounds or dollars: *the problem persists despite the billions spent on it.* ■ dated, chiefly Brit. a million million (1,000,000,000,000 or 10^{12}).

– DERIVATIVES **billionth** ordinal number.

– ORIGIN late 17th cent.: from French, from *million*, by substitution of the prefix *bi-* 'two' for the initial letters.

billionaire ▶ **noun** a person possessing assets worth at least a billion pounds or dollars.

– ORIGIN mid 19th cent.: from **BILLION**, on the pattern of *millionaire.*

Billiton /bɪˈliːtɒn/ variant spelling of **BELITUNG**.

bill of costs ▶ **noun** Brit. a solicitor's account of charges and expenses incurred while carrying out a client's business.

bill of exchange ▶ **noun** a written order to a person requiring them to make a specified payment to the signatory or to a named payee; a promissory note.

bill of fare ▶ **noun** dated a menu.

■ a programme for a theatrical event.

bill of goods ▶ **noun** N. Amer. a consignment of merchandise.

– PHRASES **sell someone a bill of goods** deceive someone, especially by persuading them to accept something untrue or undesirable.

bill of health ▶ **noun** a certificate relating to the incidence of infectious disease on a ship or in the port from which it has sailed.

– PHRASES **a clean bill of health** a declaration or confirmation that someone is healthy or that something is in good condition.

bill of indictment ▶ **noun** historical or N. Amer. a written accusation as presented to a grand jury.

bill of lading ▶ **noun** a detailed list of a ship's cargo in the form of a receipt given by the master of the ship to the person consigning the goods.

bill of quantities ▶ **noun** a detailed statement of work, prices, dimensions, and other details, for the erection of a building by contract.

Bill of Rights ▶ **noun** Law a statement of the rights of a class of people, in particular:

■ the English constitutional settlement of 1689, confirming the deposition of James II and the accession of William and Mary, guaranteeing the

Protestant succession, and laying down the principles of parliamentary supremacy. ■ the first ten amendments to the Constitution of the US, ratified in 1791.

bill of sale ▶ **noun** a certificate of transfer of personal property, used especially where something is transferred as security for a debt.

billon /ˈbɪlən/ ▶ **noun** [mass noun] an alloy formerly used for coinage, containing gold or silver with a predominating amount of copper or other base metal.

– ORIGIN early 18th cent.: from French, literally 'bronze or copper money', in Old French 'ingot', from *bille* (see **BILLET**[2]).

billow ▶ **noun** a large undulating mass of something, typically cloud, smoke, or steam.

■ archaic a large sea wave.

▶ **verb** [no obj., with adverbial of direction] (of fabric) fill with air and swell outwards: *her dress billowed out around her.*

■ (of smoke, cloud, or steam) move or flow outward with an undulating motion: *smoke was billowing from the chimney-mouth* | [as adj.] (**billowing**) *a billowing cloud.*

– DERIVATIVES **billowy** adjective.

– ORIGIN mid 16th cent.: from Old Norse *bylgja.*

billposter (also **billsticker**) ▶ **noun** a person who pastes up advertisements on hoardings.

– DERIVATIVES **billposting** noun.

billy[1] (also **billycan**) ▶ **noun** (pl. **-ies**) a tin or enamel cooking pot with a lid and a wire handle, for use when camping.

– ORIGIN mid 19th cent.: perhaps from Aboriginal *billa* 'water'.

billy[2] ▶ **noun** (pl. **-ies**) **1** short for **BILLY GOAT**.

2 (also **billy club**) N. Amer. a truncheon.

– ORIGIN mid 19th cent.: from *Billy*, pet form of the given name *William.*

billy-bread ▶ **noun** [mass noun] NZ bread cooked over an open fire.

billycart ▶ **noun** Austral. a small handcart.

■ a go-kart.

– ORIGIN 1920s: *billy* perhaps from **BILLY GOAT**; formerly such carts were sometimes pulled by a goat.

billycock ▶ **noun** historical a kind of bowler hat.

– ORIGIN mid 19th cent.: said to be from the name of William Coke, nephew of Thomas William Coke, Earl of Leicester (1752–1842).

billy goat ▶ **noun** a male goat.

billy-o ▶ **noun** (in phrase **like billy-o**) Brit. informal very much, hard, or strongly: *I had to run like billy-o.*

– ORIGIN late 19th cent.: of unknown origin.

Billy the Kid see **BONNEY**.

bilobed (also **bilobate**) ▶ **adjective** having or consisting of two lobes.

bilocation ▶ **noun** [mass noun] the supposed phenomenon of being in two places simultaneously.

biltong /ˈbɪltɒŋ, ˈbəl-/ ▶ **noun** [mass noun] chiefly S. African lean meat which is salted and dried in strips.

– ORIGIN Afrikaans, from Dutch *bil* 'buttock' + *tong* 'tongue'.

BIM ▶ **abbreviation** for British Institute of Management.

Bim /bɪm/ ▶ **noun** informal a native or inhabitant of Barbados.

– ORIGIN mid 19th cent.: of unknown origin.

bim ▶ **noun** US informal short for **BIMBO**.

bimanual ▶ **adjective** performed with both hands.

– DERIVATIVES **bimanually** adverb.

bimbo ▶ **noun** (pl. **-os**) informal, derogatory an attractive but unintelligent or frivolous young woman.

– DERIVATIVES **bimbette** noun.

– ORIGIN early 20th cent. (originally in the sense 'fellow, chap'): from Italian, literally 'little child'.

bi-media ▶ **adjective** involving or working in two of the mass communication media, especially radio and television: *a bi-media journalist.*

bimetallic ▶ **adjective** made or consisting of two metals.

■ historical of or relating to bimetallism.

– ORIGIN late 19th cent.: from French *bimétallique*, from *bi-* 'two' + *métallique* 'metallic'.

bimetallic strip ▶ **noun** a temperature sensitive electrical contact used in some thermostats, consisting of two bands of different metals joined

b

lengthwise. When heated, the metals expand at different rates, causing the strip to bend.

bimetallism /bʌɪˈmɛt(ə)lɪz(ə)m/ ▶ **noun** [mass noun] historical a system of allowing the unrestricted currency of two metals (e.g. gold and silver) as legal tender at a fixed ratio to each other.
– DERIVATIVES **bimetallist** noun.

bimillenary /ˌbʌɪmɪˈlɛnəri, -ˈliːn-, bʌɪˈmɪlənəri/ ▶ **adjective** [attrib.] of or relating to a period of two thousand years or a two-thousandth anniversary.
▶ **noun** (pl. **-ies**) a period of two thousand years or a two-thousandth anniversary.

bimodal ▶ **adjective** having or involving two modes, in particular (of a statistical distribution) having two maxima.

bimolecular ▶ **adjective** Chemistry consisting of or involving two molecules.

bimonthly ▶ **adjective** occurring or produced twice a month or every two months: *a bimonthly newsletter.*
▶ **adverb** twice a month or every two months.
▶ **noun** (pl. **-ies**) a periodical produced twice a month or every two months.

USAGE The meaning of **bimonthly** (and other similar words such as **biweekly** and **biyearly**) is ambiguous, as the above definition shows. The only way to avoid this ambiguity is to use alternative expressions like *every two months* and *twice a month*. In the publishing world, the meaning of **bimonthly** is more fixed and is invariably used to mean 'every two months'.

bin Brit. ▶ **noun** a receptacle in which to deposit rubbish.
■ [with modifier] a similar receptacle for storing a specified substance: *a compost bin.* ■ a partitioned stand for storing bottles of wine. ■ Statistics each of a series of ranges of numerical value into which data are sorted in statistical analysis. ■ informal, offensive a mental home or hospital.
▶ **verb** (**binned**, **binning**) [with obj.] throw (something) away by putting it in a bin: *he binned those awful golf shoes.*
■ informal discard or reject (something): *the whole idea had to be binned.* ■ store (something, especially wine) in a bin. ■ Statistics group together (data) in bins.
– ORIGIN Old English *bin(n)*, *binne*, of Celtic origin; related to Welsh *ben* 'cart'. The original meaning was 'receptacle' in a general sense; also specifically 'a receptacle for provender in a stable' and 'container for grain, bread, or other foodstuffs'. The sense 'receptacle for rubbish' dates from the mid 19th cent.

bin- ▶ **prefix** variant form of **BI-** before a vowel (as in *binaural*).

binary /ˈbʌɪnəri/ ▶ **adjective 1** relating to, using, or expressed in a system of numerical notation that has 2 rather than 10 as a base.
■ in binary format: *it is stored as a binary file.*
2 relating to, composed of, or involving two things: *binary chemical weapons.*
▶ **noun** (pl. **-ies**) **1** [mass noun] the binary system: binary notation: *the device is counting in binary.*
2 something having two parts.
■ a binary star.
– ORIGIN late Middle English (in the sense 'duality, a pair'): from late Latin *binarius*, from *bini* 'two together'.

binary code ▶ **noun** [mass noun] Electronics a coding system using the binary digits 0 and 1 to represent a letter, digit, or other character in a computer or other electronic device.

binary coded decimal (abbrev.: **BCD**) ▶ **noun** [mass noun] Electronics a system for coding a number in which each digit of a decimal number is represented individually by its binary equivalent.
■ [count noun] a number represented in this way.

binary digit ▶ **noun** one of two digits (0 or 1) in a binary system of notation.

binary star ▶ **noun** Astronomy a system of two stars in which one star revolves round the other or both revolve round a common centre.

binary system ▶ **noun 1** a system in which information can be expressed by combinations of the digits 0 and 1.
2 a system consisting of two parts: *the binary system of state and public schools.*
■ Astronomy a star system containing two stars orbiting around each other.

binary tree ▶ **noun** Computing a data structure in which a record is linked to two successor records, usually referred to as the left branch when greater and the right when less than the previous record.

binational ▶ **adjective** concerning or consisting of two nations.

binaural /bɪˈnɔːr(ə)l, bʌɪ-/ ▶ **adjective** of, relating to, or used with both ears: *human hearing is binaural.*
■ of or relating to sound recorded using two microphones and usually transmitted separately to the two ears of the listener.

bin bag ▶ **noun** Brit. a large, strong plastic bag used as a container for household rubbish.

bind ▶ **verb** (past and past participle **bound**) [with obj.] **1** tie or fasten (something) tightly together: *floating bundles of logs* ***bound together*** *with ropes | they bound her hands and feet.*
■ restrain (someone) by tying their hands and feet: *the raider then bound and gagged Mr Glenn.* ■ wrap (something) tightly: *her hair was* ***bound up*** *in a towel.* ■ bandage (a wound): *Shelley cleaned the wound and* ***bound*** *it* ***up*** *with a clean dressing.* ■ (**be bound with**) (of an object) be encircled by something, typically metal bands, so as to have greater strength: *an ancient oak chest bound with brass braces.* ■ Linguistics (of a rule or set of grammatical conditions) determine the relationship between (coreferential noun phrases).
2 cause (people) to feel that they belong together or form a cohesive group: *the comradeship that had* ***bound*** *such a disparate bunch of lads* ***together.***
■ (**bind someone to**) cause someone to feel strongly attached to (a person or place): *touches like that had bound men to him for life.* ■ cohere or cause to cohere in a single mass: [with obj.] *the trees bind soil and act as a windbreak* | [no obj.] *clay is made up chiefly of tiny soil particles which* ***bind together*** *tightly.* ■ cause (ingredients) to cohere by adding another ingredient: *mix the flour with the coconut and enough egg white to bind them.* ■ cause (painting pigments) to form a smooth medium by mixing them with oil. ■ hold by chemical bonding. ■ [no obj.] (**bind to**) combine with (a substance) through chemical bonding.
3 formal impose a legal or contractual obligation on: *a party who signs a document will normally be bound by its terms.*
■ indenture (someone) as an apprentice: *he was* ***bound apprentice*** *at the age of sixteen.* ■ (**bind oneself**) formal make a contractual or enforceable undertaking: *the government cannot bind itself as to the form of subsequent legislation.* ■ secure (a contract), typically with a sum of money. ■ (**be bound by**) be hampered or constrained by: *Sarah did not want to be bound by a rigid timetable.*
4 fix together and enclose (the pages of a book) in a cover: *a small, fat volume, bound in red morocco.*
5 trim (the edge of a piece of material) with a decorative strip: *a frill with the edges* ***bound in*** *a contrasting colour.*
6 Logic (of a quantifier) be applied to (a given variable) so that the variable falls within its scope. For example, in an expression of the form 'For every *x*, if *x* is a dog, *x* is an animal', the universal quantifier is binding the variable *x*.
7 (of a food or medicine) make (someone) constipated.
▶ **noun 1** informal an annoyance: *I know being disturbed on Christmas Day is a bind.*
■ a problematical situation: *he is in a political bind over the abortion issue.*
2 formal a statutory constraint: *the moral bind of the law.*
3 Music another term for **TIE**.
4 another term for **BINE**.
– PHRASES **bind someone hand and foot** see **HAND**.
– ORIGIN Old English *bindan*, of Germanic origin; related to Dutch and German *binden*, from an Indo-European root shared by Sanskrit *bandh*.
▶ **bind off** N. Amer. cast off in knitting.
bind someone over (usu. **be bound over**) (of a court of law) require someone to fulfil an obligation, typically by paying a sum of money as surety: *he was bound over to keep the peace by magistrates.*

binder ▶ **noun** a thing or person that binds something, in particular:
■ a cover for holding magazines or loose sheets of paper together. ■ a substance that acts cohesively. ■ a reaping machine that binds grain into sheaves. ■ a bookbinder.

binder twine ▶ **noun** [mass noun] (in farming) strong cord made from plastic or natural fibre, used in a baling machine to tie hay and straw bales.

bindery ▶ **noun** (pl. **-ies**) a workshop or factory in which books are bound.

bindi /ˈbɪndiː/ ▶ **noun** (pl. **bindis**) a decorative mark worn in the middle of the forehead by Indian women, especially Hindus.
– ORIGIN from Hindi *bindī*.

bindi-eye /ˈbɪndɪʌɪ/ ▶ **noun** a small perennial Australian plant of the daisy family, which has a bur-like fruit.
• *Calotis cuneifolia*, family Compositae.
– ORIGIN early 20th cent.: perhaps from an Aboriginal language.

binding ▶ **noun 1** a strong covering holding the pages of a book together.
■ [mass noun] fabric such as braid used for binding the edges of a piece of material.
2 (also **ski binding**) Skiing a mechanical device fixed to a ski to grip a ski boot, especially either of a pair used for downhill skiing which hold the toe and heel of the boot and release it automatically in a fall.
3 [mass noun] the action of fastening or holding together, or of being linked by chemical bonds: *the binding of antibodies to cell surfaces.*
4 (in Chomskyan linguistics) the relationship between a referentially dependent noun (such as a reflexive) and the independent noun phrase which determines its reference.
▶ **adjective** (of an agreement or promise) involving an obligation that cannot be broken: *business agreements are intended to be legally binding.*

binding energy ▶ **noun** [mass noun] Physics the energy that holds a nucleus together. This is equal to the mass defect of the nucleus.

binding post ▶ **noun** Electronics a connector consisting of a threaded screw to which bare wires are attached and held in place by a nut.

bindlestiff /ˈbɪnd(ə)lstɪf/ ▶ **noun** US informal a tramp.
– ORIGIN early 20th cent.: probably from an alteration of **BUNDLE** + **STIFF** (in the sense 'useless person').

bindweed /ˈbʌɪndwiːd/ ▶ **noun** [mass noun] a twining plant with trumpet-shaped flowers, several kinds of which are invasive weeds.
• Genera *Convolvulus* and *Calystegia*, family Convolvulaceae: several species, in particular the **hedge** (or **larger**) **bindweed** (*Calystegia sepium*).
■ used in names of similar twining plants, e.g. **black bindweed**.

bine /bʌɪn/ ▶ **noun** a long, flexible stem of a climbing plant, especially the hop.
– ORIGIN early 19th cent.: originally a dialect form of **BIND**.

bin-end ▶ **noun** Brit. one of the last bottles from a bin of wine, usually sold at a reduced price.

Binet /ˈbiːneɪ/, Alfred (1857–1911), French psychologist. He devised a mental age scale which described performance in relation to the average performance of students of the same physical age, and with the psychiatrist **Théodore Simon** (1873–1961) was responsible for a pioneering system of intelligence tests.

bing[1] ▶ **noun** chiefly Scottish a heap, especially of metallic ore or of waste from a mine.
– ORIGIN early 16th cent.: from Old Norse *bingr* 'heap'.

bing[2] ▶ **exclamation** indicating a sudden action or event: *Bing! They've hit you with something.*
– ORIGIN late 19th cent.: (originally dialect in the sense 'sudden bang'): imitative.

binge informal ▶ **noun** a short period devoted to indulging in an activity, especially drinking alcohol, to excess: *he* ***went on a binge*** *and was in no shape to drive | a spending binge |* [as modifier] *binge eating.*
▶ **verb** (**bingeing** or US also **binging**) [no obj.] indulge in an activity, especially eating, to excess: *some dieters say they cannot help* ***bingeing on*** *chocolate.*
– DERIVATIVES **binger** noun.
– ORIGIN early 19th cent.: of unknown origin.

bingee ▶ **noun** variant spelling of **BINGY**.

binghi /ˈbɪŋʌɪ/ ▶ **noun** (pl. **binghis**) Austral. informal, chiefly derogatory an Aboriginal.
– ORIGIN from Awabakal (an Aboriginal language), literally 'elder brother'.

bingle /ˈbɪŋg(ə)l/ ▶ **noun** Austral. informal a collision.
– ORIGIN 1940s: diminutive of dialect *bing* 'thump, blow' (compare **BING**[2]).

bingo ▶ noun a game in which players mark off numbers on cards as the numbers are drawn randomly by a caller, the winner being the first person to mark off all their numbers.
▶ exclamation **1** a call by someone who wins a game of bingo.
2 used to express satisfaction or surprise at a sudden positive event or outcome: *bingo, she leapfrogged into a sales trainee position.*
– ORIGIN 1920s (as an interjection): of unknown origin.

bingy /ˈbɪn(d)ʒi/ (also **bingee**) ▶ noun Austral. informal the stomach.
– ORIGIN from Dharuk *bindi.*

bin liner ▶ noun Brit. a plastic bag used for lining a rubbish bin.

binman ▶ noun (pl. **-men**) Brit. informal a dustman.

binnacle /ˈbɪnək(ə)l/ ▶ noun a built-in housing for a ship's compass.
– ORIGIN late 15th cent. (as *bittacle*): from Spanish *bitácula, bitácora* or Portuguese *bitacola,* from Latin *habitaculum* 'dwelling place', from *habitare* 'inhabit'. The change to *binnacle* occurred in the mid 18th cent.

binocs ▶ plural noun informal short for BINOCULARS.

binocular /bɪˈnɒkjʊlə/ ▶ adjective adapted for or using both eyes: *a binocular microscope.*
– ORIGIN early 18th cent. (in the sense 'having two eyes'): from Latin *bini* 'two together' + *oculus* 'eye', on the pattern of *ocular.*

binoculars (also **a pair of binoculars**) ▶ plural noun an optical instrument with a lens for each eye, used for viewing distant objects.
– ORIGIN late 19th cent.: plural of BINOCULAR.

binocular vision ▶ noun [mass noun] vision using two eyes with overlapping fields of view, allowing good perception of depth.

binomial /bʌɪˈnəʊmɪəl/ ▶ noun **1** Mathematics an algebraic expression of the sum or the difference of two terms.
2 a two-part name, especially the Latin name of a species of living organism (consisting of the genus followed by the specific epithet).
3 Grammar a noun phrase with two heads joined by a conjunction, in which the order is relatively fixed (as in *knife and fork*).
▶ adjective **1** Mathematics consisting of two terms.
■ of or relating to a binomial or to the binomial theorem.
2 having or using two names (used especially of the Latin name of a species of living organism).
– ORIGIN mid 16th cent.: from French *binôme* or modern Latin *binomium* (from *bi-* 'having two' + Greek *nomos* 'part, portion') + -AL.

binomial distribution ▶ noun Statistics a frequency distribution of the possible number of successful outcomes in a given number of trials in each of which there is the same probability of success.

binomial nomenclature ▶ noun [mass noun] Biology the system of nomenclature in which two terms are used to denote a species of living organism, the first one indicating the genus and the second the species.

binomial theorem ▶ noun a formula for finding any power of a binomial without multiplying at length.

binominal ▶ adjective another term for BINOMIAL (in sense 2).
– ORIGIN late 19th cent.: from Latin *binominis,* from *bi-* 'having two' + *nomen, nomin-* 'name' + -AL.

bins ▶ plural noun informal short for BINOCULARS.

bint ▶ noun Brit. informal a girl or woman.
– ORIGIN mid 19th cent.: from Arabic, literally 'daughter, girl'.

binturong /ˈbɪntjʊrɒŋ/ ▶ noun a tree-dwelling Asian civet with a coarse blackish coat and a muscular prehensile tail.
● *Arctictis binturong,* family Viverridae.
– ORIGIN early 19th cent.: from Malay.

binucleate /bʌɪˈnjuːklɪət/ ▶ adjective Biology (of a cell) having two nuclei.

bio informal ▶ noun (pl. **-os**) **1** [mass noun] biology.
2 chiefly N. Amer. a biography.
▶ adjective biological.
– ORIGIN mid 20th cent.: abbreviation.

bio- /ˈbʌɪəʊ/ ▶ combining form of or relating to life: *biosynthesis.*
■ biological; relating to biology: *biohazard.* ■ of living beings: *biogenesis.*
– ORIGIN from Greek *bios* '(course of) human life'. The sense is extended in modern scientific usage to mean 'organic life'.

bioaccumulate ▶ verb [no obj.] (of a substance) become concentrated inside the bodies of living things.
– DERIVATIVES **bioaccumulation** noun.

bioactive ▶ adjective (of a substance) having a biological effect.
– DERIVATIVES **bioactivity** noun.

bioassay /ˌbʌɪəʊəˈseɪ/ ▶ noun [mass noun] measurement of the concentration or potency of a substance by its effect on living cells or tissues.

bioavailability ▶ noun [mass noun] Physiology the proportion of a drug or other substance which enters the circulation when introduced into the body and so is able to have an active effect.
– DERIVATIVES **bioavailable** adjective.

biocenosis ▶ noun US spelling of BIOCOENOSIS.

biocentrism ▶ noun [mass noun] the view or belief that the rights and needs of humans are not more important than those of other living things.
– DERIVATIVES **biocentric** adjective, **biocentrist** noun.

biochemistry ▶ noun [mass noun] the branch of science concerned with the chemical and physico-chemical processes which occur within living organisms.
■ processes of this kind: *abnormal brain biochemistry.*
– DERIVATIVES **biochemical** adjective, **biochemically** adverb, **biochemist** noun.

biochip ▶ noun a microchip designed or intended to function in a biological environment, especially inside a living organism.
■ a logical device analogous to the silicon chip, whose components are formed from biological molecules or structures.

biocide ▶ noun **1** a poisonous substance, especially a pesticide.
2 [mass noun] the destruction of life: *our whims have brought us to the brink of biocide.*
– DERIVATIVES **biocidal** adjective.

biocircuit ▶ noun an integrated circuit incorporating biological molecules or structures.

bioclast /ˈbʌɪə(ʊ)klast/ ▶ noun Geology a fragment of a shell or fossil forming part of a sedimentary rock.
– DERIVATIVES **bioclastic** adjective.

bioclimatic ▶ adjective Ecology of or relating to the interrelation of climate and the activities and distribution of living organisms.

biocoenosis /ˌbʌɪə(ʊ)sɪˈnəʊsɪs/ (US **biocenosis**) ▶ noun (pl. **-noses** /-siːz/) Ecology an association of different organisms forming a closely integrated community.
– ORIGIN late 19th cent.: modern Latin, from BIO- 'life' + Greek *koinōsis* 'sharing' (from *koinos* 'common').

biocompatible ▶ adjective (especially of material used in surgical implants) not harmful or toxic to living tissue.
– DERIVATIVES **biocompatibility** noun.

biocomputer ▶ noun a computer based on circuits and components formed from biological molecules or structures which would be smaller and faster than an equivalent computer built from semiconductor components.
■ a human being, or the human mind, regarded as a computer.

biocomputing ▶ noun [mass noun] the design and construction of computers using biochemical components.
■ an approach to programming that seeks to emulate or model biological processes. ■ computing in a biological context or environment.

biocontrol ▶ noun short for BIOLOGICAL CONTROL.

biodata ▶ plural noun [treated as sing. or pl.] biographical details.
■ [treated as sing.] Indian a curriculum vitae.

biodegradable ▶ adjective (of a substance or object) capable of being decomposed by bacteria or other living organisms and thereby avoiding pollution.
– DERIVATIVES **biodegradability** noun.

biodegrade ▶ verb [no obj.] (of a substance or object) be decomposed by bacteria or other living organisms.
– DERIVATIVES **biodegradation** noun.

bio-diesel ▶ noun [mass noun] a biofuel intended as a substitute for diesel.

biodiversity ▶ noun [mass noun] the variety of plant and animal life in the world or in a particular habitat. A high level of biodiversity is usually considered to be important and desirable.

biodynamics ▶ plural noun [treated as sing.] **1** the study of physical motion or dynamics in living systems.
2 a method of organic farming involving the observation of lunar phases and planetary cycles and the use of incantations and ritual substances.
– DERIVATIVES **biodynamic** adjective.

bioelectric ▶ adjective of or relating to electricity or electrical phenomena produced within living organisms.
– DERIVATIVES **bioelectrical** adjective.

bioenergetics ▶ plural noun [treated as sing.] **1** the study of the transformation of energy in living organisms.
2 a system of alternative psychotherapy based on the belief that emotional healing can be aided through resolution of bodily tension.
– DERIVATIVES **bioenergetic** adjective.

bioengineering ▶ noun [mass noun] **1** another term for GENETIC ENGINEERING.
2 the use of artificial tissues, organs, or organ components to replace damaged or absent parts of the body.
3 the use in engineering or industry of organisms or biological processes.
– DERIVATIVES **bioengineer** noun & verb.

bioethics ▶ plural noun [treated as sing.] the ethics of medical and biological research.
– DERIVATIVES **bioethical** adjective, **bioethicist** noun.

biofeedback ▶ noun [mass noun] the use of electronic monitoring of a normally automatic bodily function in order to train someone to acquire voluntary control of that function.

bioflavonoid ▶ noun any of a group of compounds occurring mainly in citrus fruits and blackcurrants, sometimes regarded as vitamins.

biofouling ▶ noun [mass noun] the fouling of underwater pipes and other surfaces by organisms such as barnacles and algae.

biofuel ▶ noun a fuel derived immediately from living matter.

biog ▶ noun informal a biography.
– ORIGIN 1940s: abbreviation.

biogas ▶ noun [mass noun] gaseous fuel, especially methane, produced by the fermentation of organic matter.

biogenesis /ˌbʌɪə(ʊ)ˈdʒɛnɪsɪs/ ▶ noun [mass noun] the synthesis of substances by living organisms.
■ historical the hypothesis that living matter arises only from other living matter.
– DERIVATIVES **biogenetic** adjective.

biogenic /ˌbʌɪə(ʊ)ˈdʒɛnɪk/ ▶ adjective produced or brought about by living organisms: *biogenic sediments.*

biogeochemical ▶ adjective relating to or denoting the cycle in which chemical elements and simple substances are transferred between living systems and the environment.
– DERIVATIVES **biogeochemist** noun, **biogeochemistry** noun.

biogeography ▶ noun [mass noun] the branch of biology that deals with the geographical distribution of plants and animals.
– DERIVATIVES **biogeographer** noun, **biogeographic** adjective, **biogeographical** adjective, **biogeographically** adverb.

biography ▶ noun (pl. **-ies**) an account of someone's life written by someone else.
■ [mass noun] writing of such a type as a branch of literature. ■ the course of a person's life: *although their individual biographies are different, both are motivated by a similar ambition.*
– DERIVATIVES **biographer** noun, **biographic** adjective, **biographical** adjective, **biographically** adverb.
– ORIGIN late 17th cent.: from French *biographie* or modern Latin *biographia,* from medieval Greek, from *bios* 'life' + *-graphia* 'writing'.

biohazard ▶ noun a risk to human health or the

environment arising from biological work, especially with micro-organisms.

Bioko /bɪˈəʊkəʊ/ an island of Equatorial Guinea, in the eastern part of the Gulf of Guinea. Its chief town is Malabo, the capital of Equatorial Guinea. Former names **FERNANDO PÓO** (until 1973) and **MACIAS NGUEMA** (1973–9).

biolistics ▶ plural noun [treated as sing.] a technique in genetic engineering in which tiny metal pellets coated with DNA are propelled into living cells at high velocities.
– DERIVATIVES **biolistic** adjective.
– ORIGIN late 20th cent.: apparently from **BIO-** and **BALLISTICS**.

biological ▶ adjective of or relating to biology or living organisms.
■another term for **NATURAL** (in sense 3). ■ (of a detergent or other cleaning product) containing enzymes to assist the process of cleaning. ■ relating to, involving, or denoting the use of toxins of biological origin or micro-organisms as weapons of war.
– DERIVATIVES **biologically** adverb.

biological clock ▶ noun an innate mechanism that controls the physiological activities of an organism which change on a daily, seasonal, yearly, or other regular cycle.

biological control ▶ noun [mass noun] the control of a pest by the introduction of a natural enemy or predator.

biologism /baɪˈɒlədʒɪz(ə)m/ ▶ noun [mass noun] the interpretation of human life from a strictly biological point of view.
– DERIVATIVES **biologistic** adjective.

biology ▶ noun [mass noun] the study of living organisms, divided into many specialized fields that cover their morphology, physiology, anatomy, behaviour, origin, and distribution.
■the plants and animals of a particular area: *the biology of the Chesapeake Bay.* ■ the physiology, behaviour, and other qualities of a particular organism or class of organisms: *human biology.*
– DERIVATIVES **biologist** noun.
– ORIGIN early 19th cent.: coined in German, via French from Greek *bios* 'life' + **-LOGY**.

bioluminescence ▶ noun [mass noun] the biochemical emission of light by living organisms such as glow-worms and deep-sea fishes.
■the light emitted in such a way.
– DERIVATIVES **bioluminescent** adjective.

biomagnetism ▶ noun [mass noun] the interaction of living organisms with magnetic fields.

biomass ▶ noun [mass noun] the total quantity or weight of organisms in a given area or volume.
■organic matter used as a fuel, especially in a power station for the generation of electricity.

biomathematics ▶ plural noun [treated as sing.] the science of the application of mathematics to biology.

biome /ˈbaɪəʊm/ ▶ noun Ecology a large naturally occurring community of flora and fauna occupying a major habitat, e.g. forest or tundra.
– ORIGIN early 20th cent.: from **BIO-** 'life' + **-OME**.

biomechanics ▶ plural noun [treated as sing.] the study of the mechanical laws relating to the movement or structure of living organisms.

biomedical ▶ adjective of or relating to both biology and medicine.
– DERIVATIVES **biomedicine** noun.

biometry /baɪˈɒmɪtri/ (also **biometrics** /baɪəʊˈmɛtrɪks/) ▶ noun [mass noun] the application of statistical analysis to biological data.
– DERIVATIVES **biometric** adjective, **biometrical** adjective, **biometrician** noun.

biomimetic ▶ adjective Biochemistry relating to or denoting synthetic methods which mimic biochemical processes.

biomorph ▶ noun a decorative form or object based on or resembling a living organism.
■a graphical representation of an organism generated on a computer, used to model evolution.
– DERIVATIVES **biomorphic** adjective.

bionic ▶ adjective having artificial body parts, especially electro-mechanical ones.
■informal having ordinary human powers increased by or as if by the aid of such devices (real or fictional): *working out in gymnasiums to become bionic men.* ■ of or relating to bionics.

bionically adverb.
– ORIGIN 1960s: from **BIO-** 'human', on the pattern of *electronic.*

bionics ▶ plural noun [treated as sing.] the study of mechanical systems that function like living organisms or parts of living organisms.

bionomics /ˌbaɪə(ʊ)ˈnɒmɪks/ ▶ plural noun [treated as sing.] the study of the mode of life of organisms in their natural habitat and their adaptations to their surroundings; ecology.
– DERIVATIVES **bionomic** adjective.
– ORIGIN late 19th cent.: from **BIO-** 'life', on the pattern of *economics.*

biophilia ▶ noun [mass noun] (according to a theory of the biologist E.O. Wilson) an innate and genetically determined affinity of human beings with the natural world.
– ORIGIN 1980s: from **BIO-** + **PHILIA**.

biophysics ▶ plural noun [treated as sing.] the science of the application of the laws of physics to biological phenomena.
– DERIVATIVES **biophysical** adjective, **biophysicist** noun.

biopic ▶ noun informal a biographical film.

biopolymer ▶ noun a polymeric substance occurring in living organisms, e.g. a protein, cellulose, or DNA.

bioprospecting ▶ noun [mass noun] the search for plant and animal species from which medicinal drugs and other commercially valuable compounds can be obtained.
– DERIVATIVES **bioprospector** noun.
– ORIGIN 1990s: from *bio(diversity) prospecting.*

biopsy /ˈbaɪɒpsi/ ▶ noun (pl. **-ies**) an examination of tissue removed from a living body to discover the presence, cause, or extent of a disease.
– ORIGIN late 19th cent.: coined in French from Greek *bios* 'life' + *opsis* 'sight', on the pattern of *necropsy.*

biopsychology ▶ noun [mass noun] the branch of psychology concerned with its biological and physiological aspects.
– DERIVATIVES **biopsychological** adjective.

bioreactor ▶ noun an apparatus in which a biological reaction or process is carried out, especially on an industrial scale.

bioregion ▶ noun a region defined by characteristics of the natural environment rather than by man-made divisions.
– DERIVATIVES **bioregional** adjective.

bioregionalism ▶ noun [mass noun] advocacy of the belief that human activity should be largely restricted to within the boundaries of distinct ecological and geographical regions.
– DERIVATIVES **bioregionalist** noun.

bioremediation /ˌbaɪə(ʊ)rɪˌmiːdɪˈeɪʃ(ə)n/ ▶ noun [mass noun] the use of either naturally occurring or deliberately introduced micro-organisms to consume and break down environmental pollutants, in order to clean up a polluted site.

biorhythm ▶ noun a recurring cycle in the physiology or functioning of an organism, such as the daily cycle of sleeping and waking.
■a cyclic pattern of physical, emotional, or mental activity said to occur in the life of a person.
– DERIVATIVES **biorhythmic** adjective.

BIOS /ˈbaɪɒs/ ▶ noun Computing a set of computer instructions in firmware which control input and output operations.
– ORIGIN acronym from *Basic Input-Output System.*

bioscience ▶ noun any of the life sciences.
– DERIVATIVES **bioscientist** noun.

bioscope ▶ noun S. African dated a cinema or film.

biosensor ▶ noun a device which uses a living organism or biological molecules, especially enzymes or antibodies, to detect the presence of chemicals.

biosocial ▶ adjective of or relating to the interaction of biological and social factors.

biosolids ▶ plural noun organic matter recycled from sewage, especially for use in agriculture.

biosphere ▶ noun the regions of the surface and atmosphere of the earth or another planet occupied by living organisms.
– DERIVATIVES **biospheric** adjective.
– ORIGIN late 19th cent.: coined in German from Greek *bios* 'life' + *sphaira* (see **SPHERE**).

biostatistics ▶ plural noun [treated as sing.] the branch of statistics that deals with data relating to living organisms.
– DERIVATIVES **biostatistical** adjective, **biostatistician** noun.

biostratigraphy /ˌbaɪə(ʊ)strəˈtɪɡrəfi/ ▶ noun [mass noun] the branch of stratigraphy concerned with fossils and their use in dating rock formations.
– DERIVATIVES **biostratigrapher** noun, **biostratigraphic** adjective, **biostratigraphical** adjective, **biostratigraphically** adverb.

biosynthesis ▶ noun [mass noun] the production of complex molecules within living organisms or cells.
– DERIVATIVES **biosynthetic** adjective.

biosystematics ▶ plural noun [treated as sing.] taxonomy based on the study of the genetic evolution of plant and animal populations.
– DERIVATIVES **biosystematist** noun.

biota /baɪˈəʊtə/ ▶ noun [mass noun] Ecology the animal and plant life of a particular region, habitat, or geological period: *the biota of the river.*
– ORIGIN early 20th cent.: modern Latin, from Greek *biotē* 'life'.

biotech ▶ noun short for **BIOTECHNOLOGY**.

biotechnology ▶ noun [mass noun] the exploitation of biological processes for industrial and other purposes, especially the genetic manipulation of micro-organisms for the production of antibiotics, hormones, etc.
– DERIVATIVES **biotechnological** adjective, **biotechnologist** noun.

biotecture /ˈbaɪəʊˌtɛktʃə/ ▶ noun [mass noun] the use of living plants as an integral part of the design of buildings.
– ORIGIN 1980s: from **BIO-** 'of living organisms' + a shortened form of **ARCHITECTURE**.

biotic /baɪˈɒtɪk/ ▶ adjective of, relating to, or resulting from living things, especially in their ecological relations.
– ORIGIN mid 19th cent.: from French *biotique*, or via late Latin from Greek *biōtikos*, from *bios* 'life'.

biotin /ˈbaɪətɪn/ ▶ noun [mass noun] Biochemistry a vitamin of the B complex, found in egg yolk, liver, and yeast. It is involved in the synthesis of fatty acids and glucose. Also called **VITAMIN H**, especially in North America.
– ORIGIN 1930s: coined in German from Greek *bios* 'life' + **-IN**[1].

biotite /ˈbaɪətʌɪt/ ▶ noun [mass noun] a black, dark brown, or greenish black micaceous mineral, occurring as a constituent of many igneous and metamorphic rocks.
– ORIGIN mid 19th cent.: named after J.-B. *Biot* (1774–1862), French mineralogist.

biotope /ˈbaɪətəʊp/ ▶ noun Ecology the region of a habitat associated with a particular ecological community.
– ORIGIN 1920s: from German *Biotop*, based on Greek *topos* 'place'.

bioturbation /ˌbaɪəʊtəːˈbeɪʃ(ə)n/ ▶ noun [mass noun] Geology the disturbance of sedimentary deposits by living organisms.
– DERIVATIVES **bioturbated** adjective.

biotype ▶ noun a group of organisms having an identical genetic constitution.

bipartisan /ˌbaɪpɑːtɪˈzan/ ▶ adjective of or involving the agreement or cooperation of two political parties that usually oppose each other's policies: *the reforms received considerable bipartisan approval.*
– DERIVATIVES **bipartisanship** noun.

bipartite /baɪˈpɑːtʌɪt/ ▶ adjective involving or made by two separate parties: *the bipartite system of grammar and secondary modern schools.*
■technical consisting of two parts: *a bipartite uterus.*
– ORIGIN late Middle English (in the sense 'divided into two parts'): from Latin *bipartitus*, past participle of *bipartire*, from *bi-* 'two' + *partire* 'to part'.

bipedal /baɪˈpiːd(ə)l/ ▶ adjective Zoology (of an animal) using only two legs for walking.
– DERIVATIVES **biped** /ˈbaɪpɛd/ noun & adjective, **bipedalism** noun, **bipedality** /ˌbaɪpiːˈdalɪti/ noun.
– ORIGIN early 17th cent.: from Latin *bipes, biped-* (from *bi-* 'having two' + *pes, ped-* 'foot') + **-AL**.

biphasic /baɪˈfeɪzɪk/ ▶ adjective having two phases.

biphenyl /baɪˈfiːnʌɪl, baɪˈfɛnɪl/ ▶ noun Chemistry an

organic compound containing two phenyl groups bonded together, e.g. the PCBs.

bipinnate /bʌɪˈpɪneɪt/ ▶ **adjective** Botany (of a pinnate leaf) having leaflets that are further subdivided in a pinnate arrangement.

biplane ▶ **noun** an early type of aircraft with two pairs of wings, one above the other.

bipod /ˈbʌɪpɒd/ ▶ **noun** a two-legged stand or support.

bipolar ▶ **adjective** having or relating to two poles or extremities: *a sharply bipolar division of affluent and underclass.*
■(of psychiatric illness) characterized by both manic and depressive episodes, or manic ones only. ■ (of a plant or animal species) of or occurring in both polar regions. ■ (of a nerve cell) having two axons, one either side of the cell body. ■ Electronics (of a transistor or other device) using both positive and negative charge carriers.
– DERIVATIVES **bipolarity** noun.

biracial ▶ **adjective** concerning or containing members of two racial groups.

biramous /bʌɪˈreɪməs/ ▶ **adjective** Zoology (especially of crustacean limbs and antennae) dividing to form two branches.
– ORIGIN late 19th cent.: from **BI-** 'two' + **RAMUS** + **-OUS**.

birch ▶ **noun 1** (also **birch tree**) a slender hardy tree which has thin peeling bark and bears catkins. Birch trees grow chiefly in northern temperate regions and yield hard, pale, fine-grained timber.
● Genus *Betula*, family Betulaceae: many species, including the **silver birch** (*B. pendula*) of Europe.
2 (**the birch**) chiefly historical a formal punishment in which a person is flogged with a bundle of birch twigs: *there were calls to bring back the birch.*
▶ **verb** [with obj.] chiefly historical beat (someone) with a bundle of birch twigs as a formal punishment.
– DERIVATIVES **birchen** adjective (archaic).
– ORIGIN Old English *bierce, birce*, of Germanic origin; related to German *Birke*.

birchbark ▶ **noun** [mass noun] the impervious bark of the North American paper birch, which was formerly used, especially by American Indians, to make canoes, cups, and wigwam covers.

Bircher /ˈbəːtʃə/ ▶ **noun** a member or supporter of the John Birch Society, an extreme right-wing and anti-communist American organization founded in 1958.
– ORIGIN from the name of John Birch, a USAF officer and 'first casualty of the cold war', killed by Chinese communists in 1945.

bird ▶ **noun 1** a warm-blooded egg-laying vertebrate animal distinguished by the possession of feathers, wings, a beak, and typically by being able to fly.
● Class Aves; birds probably evolved in the Jurassic period from small dinosaurs that may already have been warm-blooded.
■an animal of this type that is hunted for sport or used for food: *carve the bird and arrange on a warmed serving plate.* ■ a clay pigeon. ■ informal, chiefly N. Amer. an aircraft, spacecraft, or satellite.
2 [usu. with adj.] informal a person of a specified kind or character: *she's a sharp old bird.*
■Brit. informal a young woman or girlfriend.
– PHRASES **the bird has flown** the person one is looking for has escaped or left. **a bird in the hand is worth two in the bush** proverb it's better to be content with what you have than to risk losing everything by seeking to get more. **the birds and the bees** informal basic facts about sex and reproduction as told to a child. **birds of a feather flock together** proverb people of the same sort or with the same tastes and interests will be found together: *these health professionals sure were birds of a feather.* **do (one's) bird** Brit. informal serve a prison sentence. [ORIGIN: *bird* from rhyming slang *birdlime* 'time'.] **flip someone the bird** (or **flip the bird**) US stick one's middle finger up at someone as a sign of contempt or anger. (**strictly**) **for the birds** informal not worthy of consideration: *mothering's for the birds.* **get the bird** Brit. informal be booed or jeered at. **give someone the bird** Brit. informal boo or jeer at someone. ■ N. Amer. another way of saying *flip someone the bird.* **have a bird** N. Amer. informal be very shocked or agitated. **a little bird told me** humorous used to indicate that the speaker knows something but prefers to keep the identity of the informant a secret: *a little bird told me it was your birthday.*
– DERIVATIVES **bird-like** adjective.
– ORIGIN Old English *brid* 'chick, fledgling', of unknown origin.

bird banding ▶ **noun** North American term for **BIRD RINGING**.
– DERIVATIVES **bird bander** noun.

bird bath ▶ **noun** a small basin placed in a garden and filled with water for birds to bathe in.

birdbrain ▶ **noun** informal an annoyingly stupid and shallow person.
– DERIVATIVES **birdbrained** adjective.

birdcage ▶ **noun** a cage for pet birds, typically made of wire or cane.
■an object resembling such a cage.

bird call ▶ **noun** a note uttered by a bird for the purpose of contact or alarm.
■an instrument imitating such a sound, used especially by hunters.

bird cherry ▶ **noun** a small wild cherry tree or shrub, with bitter black fruit that is eaten by birds.
● *Prunus padus*, family Rosaceae.

bird dog N. Amer. ▶ **noun** a gun dog trained to retrieve birds.
■informal a person whose job involves searching, especially a talent scout for a sports team.
▶ **verb** (**bird-dog**) [with obj.] informal search out or pursue with dogged determination.

bird-eating spider (also **bird spider**) ▶ **noun** another term for **TARANTULA** (in sense 1).

birder ▶ **noun** chiefly N. Amer. a birdwatcher.

bird fancier's lung ▶ **noun** [mass noun] a respiratory disease caused by inhaling dust consisting of feathers, droppings, and other organic matter from birds.

bird house ▶ **noun** North American term for **NEST BOX**.

birdie ▶ **noun** (pl. **-ies**) **1** informal a little bird.
2 Golf a score of one stroke under par at a hole.
▶ **verb** (**birdying**) [with obj.] Golf play (a hole) with a score of one stroke under par.
– ORIGIN late 18th cent.: diminutive of **BIRD**; the golf term from US slang *bird*, denoting any first-rate thing.

birding ▶ **noun** [mass noun] chiefly N. Amer. the observation of birds in their natural habitats as a hobby.

birdlime ▶ **noun** [mass noun] a sticky substance spread on to twigs to trap small birds.

bird observatory ▶ **noun** a place or building where research on birds, especially ringing, is carried out.

bird of paradise ▶ **noun 1** (pl. **birds of paradise**) a tropical Australasian bird, the male of which is noted for the beauty and brilliance of its plumage and its spectacular courtship display. Most kinds are found in New Guinea, where their feathers are used in ornamental dress. [ORIGIN: early 17th cent.: so named because when the skins were first brought back to Spain (16th cent.) their beauty suggested they were from paradise.]
● Family Paradisaeidae: numerous genera.
2 (also **bird of paradise flower**) a southern African plant related to the banana, which bears a showy irregular flower with a long projecting tongue. [ORIGIN: late 19th cent.: named from the protrusion of flowers from a green spathe, resembling a bird of paradise in flight.]
● Genus *Strelitzia*, family Strelitziaceae: several species, in particular *S. regina*, with orange and dark blue flowers.

bird of passage ▶ **noun** dated a migratory bird.
■a person who passes through or visits a place without staying for long.

bird of prey ▶ **noun** a bird that feeds on animal flesh, distinguished by a hooked bill and sharp talons; a raptor.
● Orders Falconiformes (the diurnal birds of prey) and Strigiformes (the owls).

bird pepper ▶ **noun** a tropical American capsicum pepper which is thought to be the ancestor of both sweet and chilli peppers.
● *Capsicum annuum* var. *glabriusculum* (or *C. frutescens* var. *typicum*), family Solanaceae.
■the small, red, very hot fruit of this plant. ■ a variety of small hot pepper grown in Asia or Africa.

bird ringing ▶ **noun** [mass noun] the practice of catching birds, marking them with an identifying band around the leg, and then releasing them.

birdseed ▶ **noun** [mass noun] a blend of seed for feeding pet birds.

Birdseye, Clarence (1886–1956), American businessman and inventor. He developed a process of rapid freezing of foods in small packages suitable for retail, creating a revolution in eating habits.

bird's-eye ▶ **noun 1** [usu. as modifier] any of a number of plants with small flowers that have contrasting petals and centres, in particular:
● (also **bird's-eye primrose**) a primrose with yellow-centred purple flowers (*Primula farinosa*, family Primulaceae). ● (also **bird's-eye speedwell**) North American term for **GERMANDER SPEEDWELL**.
2 (also **bird's-eye chilli** or **bird's-eye pepper**) a small very hot chilli pepper.
3 a small geometric pattern woven with a dot in the centre, typically used in suiting and lining fabrics.

bird's-eye maple ▶ **noun** [mass noun] the timber of an American maple which contains eye-like markings, used in decorative woodwork.

bird's-eye view ▶ **noun** a general view from above.

bird's-foot ▶ **noun** (pl. **bird's-foots**) a European plant of the pea family, which bears pods shaped like the foot of a bird.
● *Ornithopus perpusillus*, family Leguminosae.

bird's-foot trefoil ▶ **noun** a small plant of the pea family which has three-lobed leaves, yellow flowers streaked with red, and triple pods that resemble the feet of a bird. Also called **EGGS AND BACON** or **TOM THUMB**.
● *Lotus corniculatus*, family Leguminosae.

birdshot ▶ **noun** [mass noun] the smallest size of shot for sporting rifles or other guns.

bird's-nest ▶ **noun 1** a brownish or yellowish flowering plant of the wintergreen family, with scale-like leaves. Bird's-nests are saprophytes that lack chlorophyll.
● Two species in the family Monotropaceae (or Pyrolaceae): the **yellow bird's-nest** (*Monotropa hypopitys*) of north temperate regions, and the **giant bird's-nest** (*Pterospora andromeda*) of North America.
2 (also **bird's-nest fungus**) a Eurasian and North American fungus with a small bowl-shaped fruiting body that opens to reveal egg-shaped organs containing the spores.
● Family Nidulariaceae, class Gasteromycetes, including the **common bird's-nest** (*Crucibulum laeve*).

bird's-nesting ▶ **noun** [mass noun] the action or practice of hunting for birds' nests in order to take the eggs.

bird's-nest orchid ▶ **noun** a European woodland orchid which lacks chlorophyll, the whole plant being yellowish-brown. Its nest-like mass of thick roots absorbs nutrients from a soil-dwelling fungus.
● *Neottia nidus-avis*, family Orchidaceae.

bird's nest soup ▶ **noun** [mass noun] a soup made in Chinese cookery from the dried gelatinous coating of the nests of swifts and other birds.

birdsong ▶ **noun** [mass noun] the musical vocalizations of a bird or birds, typically uttered by a male songbird in characteristic bursts or phrases for territorial purposes.

bird-strike ▶ **noun** a collision between a bird and an aircraft.

bird table ▶ **noun** Brit. a small platform or table in a garden on which food for birds is placed.

birdwatcher ▶ **noun** a person who observes birds in their natural surroundings as a hobby.

birdwatching ▶ **noun** [mass noun] the practice of observing birds in their natural environment as a hobby.

birdwing (also **bird-winged butterfly**) ▶ **noun** a very large boldly marked butterfly occurring in the tropical parts of Australasia.
● Genus *Ornithoptera*, family Papilionidae: several species, including **Queen Alexandra's birdwing** (*O. alexandrae*), which is the world's largest butterfly.

birefringent /ˌbʌɪrɪˈfrɪn(d)ʒ(ə)nt/ ▶ **adjective** Physics having two different refractive indices.
– DERIVATIVES **birefringence** noun.

bireme /ˈbʌɪriːm/ ▶ **noun** an ancient warship with two files of oarsmen on each side.
– ORIGIN late 16th cent.: from Latin *biremis*, from *bi-* 'having two' + *remus* 'oar'.

biretta /bɪˈrɛtə/ ▶ **noun** a square cap with three flat projections on top, worn by Roman Catholic clergymen.

b

– ORIGIN late 16th cent.: from Italian *berretta* or Spanish *birreta*, based on late Latin *birrus* 'hooded cape'. Compare with **BERET**.

Birgitta, St /ˌbɪəˈɡɪtə/ variant spelling of **BRIDGET, ST**².

biri ▶ noun (pl. **biris**) variant spelling of **BIDI**.

biriani /ˌbɪrɪˈɑːni/ (also **biriyani** or **biryani**) ▶ noun [mass noun] an Indian dish made with highly seasoned rice and meat, fish, or vegetables.
– ORIGIN Urdu, from Persian *biryānī*, from *biriyān* 'fried, grilled'.

Birkenhead /ˈbəːkənhɛd/ a town in NW England on the Wirral Peninsula, across the River Mersey from Liverpool; pop. 116,000 (1991).

birl /bəːl/ Scottish ▶ verb spin or whirl: [with obj.] *laying his hand on her shoulder and birling her about* | [no obj.] *his head must have been birling.*
▶ noun a spin or whirl.
– ORIGIN early 18th cent.: imitative.

birlinn /ˈbəːlɪn, ˈbɪə-/ ▶ noun a large rowing boat or barge of a kind formerly used in the Western Islands of Scotland.
– ORIGIN late 16th cent.: Scottish Gaelic.

Birman /ˈbəːmən/ ▶ noun a cat of a long-haired breed, typically with a cream body, dark head, tail, and legs, and white paws.
– ORIGIN variant of **BURMAN**.

Birmingham 1 an industrial city in west central England; pop. 934,900 (1991). **2** an industrial city in north central Alabama; pop. 265,968 (1990).

biro /ˈbaɪrəʊ/ ▶ noun (pl. **-os**) Brit. trademark a kind of ballpoint pen.
– ORIGIN 1940s: named after László József *Biró* (1899–1985), Hungarian inventor of the ballpoint.

birr /bəː/ ▶ noun the basic monetary unit of Ethiopia, equal to 100 cents.
– ORIGIN from Amharic.

birth ▶ noun [mass noun] the emergence of a baby or other young from the body of its mother; the start of life as a physically separate being: *he was blind from birth* | [count noun] *despite a difficult birth he's fit and healthy.*
 ■ [count noun] a baby born: *the overall rate of incidence of Down's syndrome is one in every 800 live births.* ■ the beginning or coming into existence of something: *the birth of Socialist Realism.* ■ origin, descent, or ancestry: *the mother is English by birth* | *he is of noble birth.* ■ high or noble descent: *she was proud of her beauty and her birth.*
▶ verb [with obj.] chiefly N. Amer. give birth to (a baby or other young): *she had carried him and birthed him* | [no obj.] *in spring the cows birthed.*
– PHRASES **give birth** bear a child or young: *her mother had died giving birth* | *she gave birth to a son.*
– ORIGIN Middle English: from Old Norse *byrth*; related to **BEAR**¹.

birth certificate ▶ noun an official document issued to record a person's birth and identify them by name, place, date of birth, and parentage.

birth control ▶ noun [mass noun] the practice of preventing unwanted pregnancies, especially by use of contraception.

birthday ▶ noun the annual anniversary of the day on which a person was born, typically treated as an occasion for celebration and present-giving: *his twenty-ninth birthday* | *I'm going to get a doll's house for my birthday* | [as modifier] *a birthday cake.*
 ■ the day of one's birth: *he shares a birthday with Rod Stewart.* ■ the anniversary of something starting or being founded: *staff celebrated the twenty-fifth birthday of the paper.*
– PHRASES **in one's birthday suit** humorous naked.

birthday book ▶ noun a book in diary form for recording birthdays.

Birthday Honours ▶ plural noun (in Britain) the titles and decorations awarded on a sovereign's official birthday: [as modifier] *the Birthday Honours list.*

birthing ▶ noun [mass noun] the action or process of giving birth.

birthing pool ▶ noun a large bath in which a woman may give birth.

birthmark ▶ noun an unusual, typically permanent, brown or red mark on someone's body which is there from birth.

birth mother ▶ noun a woman who has given birth to a child, as opposed to an adoptive mother.

---

birth parent ▶ noun a biological as opposed to an adoptive parent.

birthplace ▶ noun the place where a person was born.
 ■ the place where something started or originated: *Florence was the birthplace of the Renaissance.*

birth rate ▶ noun the number of live births per thousand of population per year.

birthright ▶ noun a particular right of possession or privilege a person has from birth, especially as an eldest son.
 ■ a natural or moral right, possessed by everyone: *she saw a liberal education as the birthright of every child.*

birth sign ▶ noun Astrology the zodiacal sign through which the sun is passing when a person is born.

birthstone ▶ noun a gemstone popularly associated with the month or astrological sign of a person's birth.

birthweight ▶ noun [mass noun] the weight of a baby at birth.

birthwort ▶ noun a climbing or herbaceous plant which typically has heart-shaped leaves and deep-throated, pipe-shaped, flowers. It was formerly used as an aid to childbirth and to induce abortion.
 ● Genus *Aristolochia*, family Aristolochiaceae.

Birtwistle /ˈbəːtˌwɪs(ə)l/, Sir Harrison (Paul) (b.1934), English composer and clarinettist. His early work was influenced by Stravinsky; later compositions are more experimental.

biryani ▶ noun variant spelling of **BIRIANI**.

BIS ▶ abbreviation for Bank for International Settlements.

bis /bɪs/ ▶ adverb Music (as a direction) again.
– ORIGIN via French and Italian from Latin, literally 'twice'.

bis- /bɪs/ ▶ combining form Chemistry used to form the names of compounds containing two groups identically substituted or coordinated: *bis*(2-aminoethyl) *ether.*

Biscay, Bay of /ˈbɪskeɪ/ a part of the North Atlantic between the north coast of Spain and the west coast of France, noted for its strong currents and storms. The shipping forecast area **Biscay** extends approximately as far west as the longitude of Gijón in Spain.

biscotti /bɪˈskɒti/ ▶ plural noun small rectangular biscuits containing nuts, made originally in Italy.
– ORIGIN Italian.

biscuit ▶ noun **1** Brit. a small baked unleavened cake, typically crisp, flat, and sweet: *a chocolate biscuit* | [mass noun] *a piece of biscuit.*
 ■ N. Amer. a small, soft round cake like a scone. ■ Carpentry a small flat piece of wood used to join two larger pieces of wood together, fitting into slots in each. **2** [mass noun] porcelain or other pottery which has been fired but not glazed: [as modifier] *biscuit ware.* **3** [mass noun] a light brown colour.
– DERIVATIVES **biscuity** adjective.
– ORIGIN Middle English: from Old French *bescuit*, based on Latin *bis* 'twice' + *coctus*, past participle of *coquere* 'to cook' (so named because originally biscuits were cooked in a twofold process: first baked and then dried out in a slow oven so that they would keep).

biscuit barrel ▶ noun Brit. a small barrel-shaped container for biscuits.

biscuit beetle ▶ noun a small beetle related to the furniture beetle, with larvae that feed on dried foodstuffs and stored products such as biscuits, pasta, and seeds. Also called **DRUGSTORE BEETLE**.
 ● *Stegobium paniceum*, family Anobiidae.

biscuit firing (also **biscuit fire**) ▶ noun [in sing.] the first firing of pottery, which permanently hardens the clay.

biscuit jointer ▶ noun a tool used to cut slots into pieces of wood so that they can be joined using a biscuit (see **BISCUIT** sense 1).

bisect ▶ verb [with obj.] divide into two parts: *a landscape of ploughland bisected by long straight roads.*
 ■ Geometry divide (a line, angle, or shape) into two exactly equal parts.
– DERIVATIVES **bisection** noun, **bisector** noun.
– ORIGIN mid 17th cent.: from **BI-** 'two' + Latin *sect-* (from *secare* 'to cut').

biserial ▶ adjective Botany & Zoology arranged in or consisting of two series or rows.

---

bisexual ▶ adjective sexually attracted to both men and women.
 ■ Biology having characteristics of both sexes.
▶ noun a person who is sexually attracted to both men and women.
– DERIVATIVES **bisexuality** noun.

bish¹ ▶ noun Brit. informal, dated a mistake or blunder.
– ORIGIN 1930s: of unknown origin.

bish² ▶ verb [with obj.] NZ informal throw (something): *they'd just sort of bished them into the cupboard.*
– ORIGIN 1940s: imitative.

Bishkek /bɪʃˈkɛk/ the capital of Kyrgyzstan; pop. 625,000 (1990). Former names **PISHPEK** (until 1926), **FRUNZE** (1926–91).

Bisho /ˈbiːʃəʊ/ a town in southern South Africa, the capital of the province of Eastern Cape, situated near the coast to the north-east of Port Elizabeth; pop. (with East London) 270,130 (1991).

Bishop, Elizabeth (1911–79), American poet awarded the Pulitzer Prize for her first two collections, *North and South* (1946) and *A Cold Spring* (1955).

bishop ▶ noun **1** a senior member of the Christian clergy, usually in charge of a diocese and empowered to confer holy orders. **2** (also **bishop bird**) an African weaver bird, the male of which has red, orange, yellow, or black plumage.
 ● Genus *Euplectes*, family Ploceidae: several species, including the **red bishop** (*E. orix*), which has scarlet plumage with a black face and underparts.
 3 a chess piece, typically with its top shaped like a mitre, that can move in any direction along a diagonal on which it stands. Each player starts the game with two bishops, one moving on white squares and the other on black. **4** [mass noun] mulled and spiced wine.
– ORIGIN Old English *biscop*, *bisceop*, based on Greek *episkopos* 'overseer', from *epi* 'above' + *-skopos* '-looking'.

bishopric /ˈbɪʃəprɪk/ ▶ noun the office or rank of a bishop.
 ■ a district under a bishop's control; a diocese.
– ORIGIN Old English *bisceoprīce*, from *bisceop* (see **BISHOP**) + *rīce* 'realm'.

bishop suffragan ▶ noun see **SUFFRAGAN**.

Bislama /ˈbɪʃləˌmɑː/ (also **Beach-la-mar** or **Bêche-de-mer**) ▶ noun [mass noun] an English-based pidgin language used as a lingua franca in Fiji and the Solomon Islands and as an official language in Vanuatu.
– ORIGIN alteration of Portuguese *bicho do mar* 'sea cucumber' (traded as a commodity, the word later being applied to the language of trade).

Bismarck¹ /ˈbɪzmɑːk/ the state capital of North Dakota; pop. 49,256 (1990). A terminus of the Northern Pacific Railway, it took the name of the German Chancellor in order to attract German capital for railroad-building.

Bismarck² /ˈbɪzmɑːk, German ˈbɪsmark/, Otto Eduard Leopold von, Prince of Bismarck, Duke of Lauenburg (1815–98), Prussian minister and German statesman, Chancellor of the German Empire 1871–90; known as the **Iron Chancellor**. He was the driving force behind the unification of Germany, orchestrating wars with Denmark (1864), Austria (1866), and France (1870–1) in order to achieve this end.
– DERIVATIVES **Bismarckian** adjective.

Bismarck Sea an arm of the Pacific Ocean north-east of New Guinea and north of New Britain.

bismillah /bɪsˈmɪlə/ ▶ exclamation in the name of God (an invocation used by Muslims at the beginning of an undertaking).
– ORIGIN from Arabic *bi-smi-llāh(i)*, the first word of the Koran.

bismuth /ˈbɪzməθ/ ▶ noun [mass noun] the chemical element of atomic number 83, a brittle reddish-tinged grey metal. (Symbol: **Bi**)
 ■ a compound of this element used medicinally.
– ORIGIN mid 17th cent.: from modern Latin *bisemutum*, Latinization of German *Wismut*, of unknown origin.

bison /ˈbaɪs(ə)n/ ▶ noun (pl. same) a humpbacked shaggy-haired wild ox native to North America and Europe.
 ● Genus *Bison*, family Bovidae: *B. bison* of North American prairies (also called **BUFFALO**), and *B. bonasus* of European

---

forests (also called **WISENT**), now found only in Poland. These are sometimes regarded as a single species.
– ORIGIN late Middle English: from Latin, ultimately of Germanic origin and related to **WISENT**.

bisphenol A /ˈbɪsfiːnɒl/ ▶ **noun** [mass noun] Chemistry a synthetic organic compound used in the manufacture of epoxy resins and other polymers.
• A two-ringed phenol; chem. formula: $C(CH_3)_2(C_6H_4OH)_2$.

bisque[1] /bɪsk, biːsk/ ▶ **noun** [mass noun] a rich shellfish soup, typically made from lobster.
– ORIGIN French, 'crayfish soup'.

bisque[2] /bɪsk/ ▶ **noun** an extra turn or stroke allowed to a weaker player in croquet.
– ORIGIN mid 17th cent. (originally a term in real tennis): from French, of unknown ultimate origin.

bisque[3] /bɪsk/ ▶ **noun** another term for **BISCUIT** (in sense 2).

Bissagos Islands /bɪˈsɑːgəs/ a group of islands off the coast of Guinea-Bissau, West Africa.

Bissau /bɪˈsaʊ/ the capital of Guinea-Bissau; pop. 125,000 (est. 1994).

bistable ▶ **noun** an electronic circuit which has two stable states.
▶ **adjective** (of a system) having two stable states.

Bisto /ˈbɪstəʊ/ ▶ **noun** [mass noun] trademark a powder used to thicken, flavour, and brown gravy.

bistort /ˈbɪstɔːt/ ▶ **noun** a Eurasian herbaceous plant with a spike of flesh-coloured flowers and a twisted root.
• Genus *Polygonum*, family Polygonaceae: several species, in particular *P. bistorta*.
– ORIGIN early 16th cent.: from French *bistorte* or medieval Latin *bistorta*, from *bis* 'twice' + *torta* (feminine past participle of *torquere* 'to twist').

bistoury /ˈbɪstʊri/ ▶ **noun** (pl. **-ies**) a surgical knife with a long, narrow, straight or curved blade.
– ORIGIN mid 18th cent.: from French *bistouri*, originally *bistorie* 'dagger', of unknown origin.

bistre /ˈbɪstə/ (US also **bister**) ▶ **noun** [mass noun] a brownish-yellow pigment made from the soot of burnt wood.
■ the colour of this pigment.
– ORIGIN early 18th cent.: from French, of unknown origin.

bistro /ˈbiːstrəʊ, ˈbɪs-/ ▶ **noun** (pl. **-os**) a small, inexpensive restaurant.
– ORIGIN 1920s: French; perhaps related to *bistouille*, a northern colloquial term meaning 'bad alcohol', perhaps from Russian *bystro* 'rapidly'.

bisulphate (US **bisulfate**) ▶ **noun** Chemistry a salt of the anion HSO_4^-.

bit[1] ▶ **noun 1** a small piece, part, or quantity of something: *give the duck **a bit of** bread* | *he read **bits of** his work to me* | *I like this bit because it is funny.*
■ **(a bit)** a fair amount: *there's a bit to talk about there.* ■ **(a bit)** a short time or distance: *I fell asleep for a bit.* ■ [with adj.] informal a set of actions or ideas associated with a specific group or activity: *Miranda could go off and do her theatrical bit.* ■ informal a girl or young woman: *he went and married some young bit half his age.*
2 N. Amer. informal a unit of 12½ cents (used only in even multiples).
– PHRASES **a bit** somewhat; to some extent: *he came back looking a bit annoyed.* **bit by bit** gradually: *the school was built bit by bit over the years.* **a bit of a ——** used to suggest that something is not severe or extreme, or is the case only to a limited extent: *I have had a bit of an accident* | *he's a bit of a womanizer.* ■ used to denote a young person of slight build: *you're just a bit of a girl yourself.* **a bit of all right** Brit. informal a pleasing person or thing, especially a woman regarded sexually: *that blonde's a bit of all right.* **bit of fluff** (or **skirt** or **stuff**) Brit. informal a woman regarded in sexual terms. **bit of rough** see **ROUGH**. **bit on the side** informal **1** a person with whom one is unfaithful to one's partner. **2** money earned outside one's normal job: *I'd like to make a bit on the side.* **bits and pieces** (or **bobs**) an assortment of small items. **do one's bit** informal make a useful contribution to an effort or cause: *she was keen to do her bit to help others.* **every bit as** see **EVERY**. **not a bit** not at all: *I'm not a bit tired.* **not a bit of it** Brit. not at all: *Am I being unduly cynical? Not a bit of it.* **to bits 1** into pieces: *he smashed it to bits with a hammer.* **2** informal very much; to a great degree: *we've got two great kids whom I love to bits.*
– ORIGIN Old English *bita* 'bite, mouthful', of Germanic origin; related to German *Bissen*, also to **BITE**.

bit[2] past of **BITE**.

bit[3] ▶ **noun 1** a mouthpiece, typically made of metal, which is attached to a bridle and used to control a horse.
2 a tool or piece for boring or drilling: *a drill bit.*
■ the cutting or gripping part of a plane, pincers, or other tool. ■ the part of a key that engages with the lock lever. ■ the copper head of a soldering iron.
▶ **verb** [with obj.] put a bit into the mouth of (a horse).
■ figurative restrain: *my own hysteria was bitted by upbringing and respect.*
– PHRASES **above the bit** (of a horse) carrying its head too high so that it evades correct contact with the bit. **behind the bit** (of a horse) carrying its head with the chin tucked in so that it evades contact with the bit. **get** (or **take** or **have**) **the bit between** (or N. Amer. **in**) **one's teeth** begin to tackle a problem or task in a determined or independent way. **off the bit** (or **bridle**) (of a horse) ridden on a loose rein to allow it to gallop freely, especially at the end of a race. **on the bit** (or **bridle**) (of a horse) ridden with a light but firm contact on the mouth, and accepting the bit in a calm and relaxed manner.
– DERIVATIVES **bitted** adjective [in combination] *a double-bitted axe.*
– ORIGIN Old English *bite* 'biting, a bite', of Germanic origin; related to Dutch *beet* and German *Biss*, also to **BITE**.

bit[4] ▶ **noun** Computing a unit of information expressed as either a 0 or 1 in binary notation.
– ORIGIN 1940s: blend of **BINARY** and **DIGIT**.

bitch ▶ **noun 1** a female dog, wolf, fox, or otter.
2 informal a woman whom one dislikes or considers to be malicious or unpleasant.
■ black English a woman (used in a non-derogatory sense). ■ **(a bitch)** informal a thing or situation that is unpleasant or difficult to deal with: *life's a bitch* | *the stove is a bitch to fix.*
▶ **verb** [no obj.] informal make malicious or spitefully critical comments: *everybody was **bitching about** their colleagues.*
– ORIGIN Old English *bicce*, of Germanic origin.

bitchery ▶ **noun** [mass noun] informal malicious or spiteful behaviour.

bitching (also **bitchen**) ▶ **adjective** informal, chiefly US excellent: *a bitching new album.*
▶ **adverb** [as submodifier] extremely: *it's bitchin' hot, ain't it?*

bitchy ▶ **adjective** (**bitchier**, **bitchiest**) informal (of a person or their comments) malicious or spitefully critical: *bitchy remarks.*
– DERIVATIVES **bitchily** adverb, **bitchiness** noun.

bite ▶ **verb** (past **bit**; past participle **bitten**) [no obj.] **1** (of a person or animal) use the teeth to cut into something in order to eat it: *Rosa **bit into** a cream cake* | [with obj.] *he bit a mouthful from the sandwich* | *the woman's arm was **bitten off** by an alligator.*
■ [with obj.] (of an animal or a person) use the teeth in order to inflict injury on: *she had bitten, scratched, and kicked her assailant* | [no obj.] *it is not unusual for a dog to **bite at** its owner's hand.* ■ [with obj.] (of a snake, insect, or spider) wound with a sting, pincers, or fangs: *while on holiday she was bitten by an adder.* ■ (of an acid) corrode a surface: *chemicals have **bitten** deep **into** the stone.* ■ (of a fish) take the bait or lure on the end of a fishing line into the mouth. ■ figurative (of a person) be persuaded to accept a deal or offer: *a hundred or so retailers should bite.* ■ [with obj.] informal annoy or worry: *what's biting you today?*
2 (of a tool, tyre, boot, etc.) grip or take hold on a surface: *once on the slab, my boots failed to bite.*
■ (of an object) press into a part of the body, causing pain: *the handcuffs **bit into** his wrists.* ■ figurative cause emotional pain: *Cheryl's betrayal had bitten deep.* ■ (of a policy or situation) take effect, with unpleasant consequences: *the cuts in art education were starting to bite.*
▶ **noun 1** an act of biting into something in order to eat it: *Stephen ate a hot dog in three big bites.*
■ a piece cut off by biting: *Robyn took a large bite out of her sandwich.* ■ informal a quick snack: *I plan to stop off in the village and have **a bite to eat**.* ■ a small morsel of prepared food, intended to constitute one mouthful: *bacon bites with cheese.* ■ figurative a short piece of information: *snack-sized bites of information.* See also **SOUND BITE**. ■ a wound inflicted by an animal's or a person's teeth: *Percy's dog had given her a nasty bite.* ■ a wound inflicted by an insect or snake: *my legs were covered in mosquito bites.* ■ an instance of bait being taken by a fish: *by four o'clock he still hadn't had a single bite.* ■ Dentistry the bringing together of the teeth in occlusion. ■ Dentistry the imprint of this in a plastic material.
2 a sharp or pungent flavour: *a fresh, lemony bite.*
■ [mass noun] incisiveness or cogency of style: *the tale has added bite if its characters appear to be real.* ■ a feeling of cold in the air or wind: *by early October there's a bite in the air.*
– PHRASES **someone's bark is worse than their bite** said of someone whose fierce and intimidating manner does not reflect their nature. **be bitten by the —— bug** develop a passionate interest in a specified activity: *Joe was badly bitten by the showbiz bug at the age of four.* **bite the big one** N. Amer. informal die. **bite the bullet** decide to do something difficult or unpleasant that one has been putting off or hesitating over. [ORIGIN: from the old custom of giving wounded soldiers a bullet to bite on when undergoing surgery without anaesthetic.] **bite the dust** informal be killed. ■ figurative fail; come to an end: *she hoped the new course would not bite the dust for lack of funding.* **bite the hand that feeds one** deliberately hurt or offend a benefactor. **bite someone's head off** see **HEAD**. **bite one's lip** dig one's front teeth into one's lip in embarrassment, grief, or annoyance, or to prevent oneself from saying something. **bite one's nails** chew at one's nails as a nervous habit. **bite off more than one can chew** take on a commitment one cannot fulfil. **the biter bitten** (or **bit**) used to indicate that someone is being treated in the same way as they have treated others, typically badly. **bite one's tongue** make a desperate effort to avoid saying something: *I had to bite my tongue and accept his explanation.* **one could have bitten one's tongue off** used to convey that one profoundly and immediately regrets having said something. **once bitten, twice shy** proverb an unpleasant experience induces caution. **put the bite on** N. Amer. & Austral. informal borrow or extort money from. [ORIGIN: 1930s (originally US): *bite*, from the slang sense 'deception'.] **take a bite out of** informal reduce by a significant amount: *commissions that can take a bite out of your retirement funds.*
– DERIVATIVES **biter** noun.
– ORIGIN Old English *bītan*, of Germanic origin; related to Dutch *bijten* and German *beissen*.
▶ **bite something back** refrain with difficulty from saying something, making a sound, or expressing an emotion: *Melissa bit back a scathing comment.*
bite something off cut short an utterance.

biternate /bʌɪˈtəːneɪt/ ▶ **adjective** Botany (especially of a ternate leaf) having leaflets or other parts that are further subdivided in a ternate arrangement.

bite-sized (also **bite-size**) ▶ **adjective** (of a piece of food) small enough to be eaten in one mouthful: *cut the potatoes into bite-sized pieces.*
■ informal very small or short: *a series of bite-sized essays.*

Bithynia /bɪˈθɪnɪə/ the ancient name for the region of NW Asia Minor west of ancient Paphlagonia, bordering the Black Sea and the Sea of Marmara.

biting ▶ **adjective** (of insects and certain other animals) able to wound the skin with a sting or fangs.
■ (of wind or cold) so cold as to be painful: *he leant forward to protect himself against the biting wind.* ■ (of wit or criticism) harsh or cruel: *his biting satire on corruption and power.*
– DERIVATIVES **bitingly** adverb.

biting midge ▶ **noun** a minute fly which typically occurs in large swarms. The female has piercing mouthparts and feeds on the blood of a variety of animals, including humans.
• Family Ceratopogonidae: numerous genera and species, including the common European *Culicoides obsoletus*.

bitmap Computing ▶ **noun** a representation in which each item corresponds to one or more bits of information, especially the information used to control the display of a computer screen.
▶ **verb** (**-mapped**, **-mapping**) [with obj.] represent (an item) as a bitmap.

bitonal /bʌɪˈtəʊn(ə)l/ ▶ **adjective** (of music) having parts in two different keys sounding together.
– DERIVATIVES **bitonality** noun.

bit part ▶ **noun** a small acting role in a play or a film.

bit rate ▶ **noun** Electronics the number of bits per second that can be transmitted along a digital network.

Bitrex /ˈbɪtrɛks/ ▶ **noun** [mass noun] trademark a bitter-tasting synthetic organic compound added to cleaning fluids or other products to make them unpalatable.

b

– ORIGIN 1960s: an invented name.

bitstream /ˈbɪtstriːm/ ▶ noun Electronics a stream of data in binary form.
■ **(Bitstream)** trademark a system of digital-to-analogue signal conversion used in some audio CD players, in which the signal from the CD is digitally processed to give a signal at a higher frequency before being converted to an analogue signal.

bitten past participle of **BITE**.

bitter ▶ adjective 1 having a sharp, pungent taste or smell; not sweet: *raw berries have an intensely bitter flavour.*
■ (of chocolate) dark and unsweetened.
2 feeling or showing anger, hurt, or resentment because of bad experiences or a sense of unjust treatment: *I don't feel jealous or bitter* | *she wept bitter tears of self-reproach.*
3 painful or unpleasant to accept or contemplate: *today's decision has come as a bitter blow* | *she knew from bitter experience how treacherous such feelings could be.*
■ (of a conflict, argument, or opponent) full of anger and acrimony: *a bitter five-year legal battle.* ■ (of wind or weather) intensely cold: *a bitter wind blowing from the east.*
▶ noun **1** [mass noun] Brit. beer that is strongly flavoured with hops and has a bitter taste.
2 (**bitters**) [treated as sing.] liquor that is flavoured with the sharp pungent taste of plant extracts and is used as an additive in cocktails or as a medicinal substance to promote appetite or digestion.
– PHRASES **to the bitter end** used to indicate that one will continue doing something until it is finished, no matter what: *the workers would fight to the bitter end.* [ORIGIN: perhaps associated with a nautical word *bitter* denoting the last part of a cable inboard of the **BITTS**, perhaps influenced by the biblical phrase 'her end is bitter as wormwood' (Prov. 5:4).]
– DERIVATIVES **bitterly** adverb, **bitterness** noun.
– ORIGIN Old English *biter*, of Germanic origin; related to Dutch and German *bitter*, and probably to **BITE**.

bitter aloes ▶ noun see **ALOE**.

bitter apple ▶ noun another term for **COLOCYNTH**.

bittercress ▶ noun a plant with small white flowers, which grows widely as a temperate weed, especially in damp soils.
● Genus *Cardamine*, family Cruciferae: several species.

bitter-ender (also **bitter-einder**) ▶ noun chiefly S. African a person who holds out until the end, no matter what.
■ (in southern African history) a Boer who refused to surrender towards the end of the Second Boer War.
– ORIGIN the form *bitter-ender* probably entered South African English at approximately the same time that *bitter-einder* entered South African Dutch.

bitter greens ▶ plural noun N. Amer. mixed green leaves of a variety of salad vegetables with a bitter taste, such as endives, chicory, or spinach.

bitter lemon ▶ noun [mass noun] Brit. a carbonated semi-sweet soft drink flavoured with lemons.

bitterling ▶ noun a small brightly coloured freshwater fish of central Europe. The eggs are deposited inside a mussel, in which they are fertilized and the young eventually hatch.
● *Rhodeus amarus*, family Cyprinidae.
– ORIGIN late 19th cent.: from German *Bitterling*, from *bitter* 'bitter'(translating Latin *amarus*) + **-LING**.

bittern¹ /ˈbɪtən/ ▶ noun a large marshbird of the heron family, which is typically smaller than a heron, with brown streaked plumage. The larger kinds are noted for the deep booming call of the male in the breeding season.
● Genera *Botaurus* and *Ixobrychus*, family Ardeidae: several species, especially the **Eurasian bittern** (*B. stellaris*) and the **American bittern** (*B. lentiginosus*).
– ORIGIN late Middle English: from Old French *butor*, based on Latin *butio* 'bittern' + *taurus* 'bull' (because of its call). The *-n* was added in the 16th cent., perhaps by association with *hern*, obsolete variant of **HERON**.

bittern² /ˈbɪt(ə)n/ (also **bitterns**) ▶ noun [mass noun] a concentrated solution of various salts remaining after the crystallization of salt from seawater.
– ORIGIN late 17th cent.: probably from the adjective **BITTER**.

bitter orange ▶ noun another term for **SEVILLE ORANGE**.

bitter pit ▶ noun [mass noun] a disease of apples caused by calcium deficiency, characterized by sunken brown spots.

bitter-sweet ▶ adjective (of food, drink, flavour, or smell) sweet with a bitter aftertaste.
■ arousing pleasure tinged with sadness or pain: *the room, with all its bitter-sweet memories.*
▶ noun (usu. **bittersweet**) **1** another term for *woody nightshade* (see **NIGHTSHADE**).
2 a vine-like American climbing plant which bears clusters of bright orange pods.
● Genus *Celastrus*, family Celastraceae: several species, in particular *C. scandens*.
3 (also **bittersweet shell**) a widely distributed bivalve mollusc which has a pale rounded shell that is typically marked with wavy lines.
● Genus *Glycymeris*, family Glycymeridae.

bitts ▶ plural noun a pair of posts on the deck of a ship for fastening mooring lines or cables.
– ORIGIN Middle English: probably of Low German origin.

bitty informal ▶ adjective (**bittier**, **bittiest**) **1** chiefly Brit. made up of small parts that seem unrelated: *the text is rather bitty.*
2 [usu. in combination] N. Amer. tiny: *a little-bitty girl.*
– DERIVATIVES **bittily** adverb, **bittiness** noun.

Bitumastic /ˌbɪtjʊˈmastɪk/ ▶ noun [mass noun] trademark an asphaltic composition used as a protective coating.
– ORIGIN late 19th cent.: blend of **BITUMEN** and **MASTIC**.

bitumen /ˈbɪtjʊmən/ ▶ noun [mass noun] a black viscous mixture of hydrocarbons obtained naturally or as a residue from petroleum distillation. It is used for road surfacing and roofing.
■ Austral. informal a tarred road surface: *a kilometre and a half of bitumen.*
– ORIGIN late Middle English (denoting naturally occurring asphalt used as mortar): from Latin.

bituminize /bɪˈtjuːmɪnʌɪz/ (also **-ise**) ▶ verb [with obj.] convert into, impregnate with, or cover with bitumen.
– DERIVATIVES **bituminization** noun.

bituminous /bɪˈtjuːmɪnəs/ ▶ adjective of, containing, or of the nature of bitumen.
– ORIGIN mid 16th cent.: from French *bitumineux*, from Latin *bituminosus*.

bituminous coal ▶ noun [mass noun] black coal having a relatively high volatile content and burning with a characteristically bright smoky flame.

bitwise ▶ adjective Computing denoting an operator in a programming language which manipulates the individual bits in a byte or word.

bitzer /ˈbɪtsə/ ▶ noun Austral. informal a contraption made from previously unrelated parts.
■ a mongrel dog.
– ORIGIN 1920s: abbreviation of the phrase *bits and pieces*.

bivalence /bʌɪˈveɪl(ə)ns/ ▶ noun [mass noun] Logic the existence of only two states or truth values (e.g. true and false).

bivalent ▶ adjective **1** /ˈbɪv(ə)l(ə)nt/ Biology (of homologous chromosomes) associated in pairs.
2 /bʌɪˈveɪl(ə)nt/ Chemistry another term for **DIVALENT**.
▶ noun /ˈbɪv(ə)l(ə)nt/ Biology a pair of homologous chromosomes.
– ORIGIN mid 19th cent.: from **BI-** 'two' + Latin *valent-* 'being strong' (from the verb *valere*).

bivalve ▶ noun an aquatic mollusc which has a compressed body enclosed within two hinged shells, such as oysters, mussels, and scallops. Also called **PELECYPOD** or **LAMELLIBRANCH**.
● Class Bivalvia, phylum Mollusca.
▶ adjective (also **bivalved**) (of a mollusc or other aquatic invertebrate) having a hinged double shell.
■ Botany having two valves.

bivariate /bʌɪˈvɛːrɪət/ ▶ adjective Statistics involving or depending on two variates.

bivouac /ˈbɪvʊak, ˈbɪvwak/ ▶ noun a temporary camp without tents or cover, used especially by soldiers or mountaineers.
▶ verb [no obj., with adverbial of place] (**bivouacked**, **bivouacking**) stay in such a camp: *the party bivouacked for the night.*
– ORIGIN early 18th cent. (denoting a night watch by the whole army): from French, probably from Swiss German *Bîwacht* 'additional guard at night',

apparently denoting a citizens' patrol supporting the ordinary town watch.

bivvy informal ▶ noun (pl. **-ies**) a small tent or temporary shelter: [as modifier] *a bivvy bag.*
▶ verb (**-ies**, **-ied**) [no obj.] use such a tent or shelter.
– ORIGIN early 20th cent.: abbreviation of **BIVOUAC**.

biweekly ▶ adjective & adverb appearing or taking place every two weeks or twice a week: [as adj.] *a biweekly bulletin* | [as adv.] *she followed her doctor's instructions to undergo health checks biweekly.*
▶ noun (pl. **-ies**) a periodical that appears every two weeks or twice a week.

> **USAGE** See usage at **BIMONTHLY**.

bi-wiring ▶ noun [mass noun] the use of two wires between an amplifier and a loudspeaker to operate the low- and high-frequency speaker circuits separately.

biyearly ▶ adjective & adverb appearing or taking place every two years or twice a year.

> **USAGE** See usage at **BIMONTHLY**.

biz ▶ noun [usu. with modifier] informal a business, especially one connected with entertainment: *the music biz.*
– ORIGIN mid 19th cent. (originally US): abbreviation.

bizarre /bɪˈzɑː/ ▶ adjective very strange or unusual, especially so as to cause interest or amusement: *his behaviour became more and more bizarre.*
– DERIVATIVES **bizarreness** noun.
– ORIGIN mid 17th cent.: from French, from Italian *bizzarro* 'angry', of unknown origin.

bizarrely ▶ adverb in a very strange or unusual manner: *bizarrely attired musicians.*
■ [sentence adverb] used to express the opinion that something is very strange or unusual: *bizarrely enough, she began to take them seriously.*

bizarrerie /bɪˈzɑːrəri/ ▶ noun (pl. **-ies**) a thing considered extremely strange and unusual, especially in an amusing way: *the bizarreries of small talk.*
– ORIGIN mid 18th cent.: from French, from **BIZARRE**.

Bizerta /bɪˈzɜːtə/ (also **Bizerte**) a seaport on the northern coast of Tunisia; pop. 94,500 (1984).

Bizet /ˈbiːzeɪ/, Georges (1838–75), French composer; born *Alexandre César Léopold Bizet*. He is best known for the opera *Carmen* (1875).

bizzy ▶ noun (pl. **-ies**) variant spelling of **BUSY**.

Bjerknes /ˈbjɜːknəs/, Vilhelm Frimann Koren (1862–1951), Norwegian geophysicist and meteorologist. He developed a theory of physical hydrodynamics for atmospheric and oceanic circulation, and mathematical models for weather prediction.

Bk ▶ symbol for the chemical element berkelium.

bk ▶ abbreviation for book.

BL ▶ abbreviation for ■ (in Scotland and Ireland) Bachelor of Law. ■ bill of lading. ■ historical British Leyland. ■ British Library.

bl ▶ abbreviation for barrel.

blab informal ▶ verb (**blabbed**, **blabbing**) [no obj.] reveal secrets by indiscreet talk: *she blabbed to the press* | [with obj.] *there's no need to blab the whole story.*
■ talk foolishly or mindlessly: *they blab on about responsibility.*
▶ noun a person who blabs.
– ORIGIN Middle English (as a noun): probably of Germanic origin; ultimately imitative.

blabber informal ▶ verb [no obj.] talk foolishly, indiscreetly, or excessively: *she blabbered on and on.*
▶ noun a person who talks in such a way.
■ [mass noun] talk of such a kind: *the obsequious blabber of her servants.*

blabbermouth ▶ noun informal a person who talks excessively or indiscreetly.

Black, Joseph (1728–99), Scottish chemist. He was important in developing accurate techniques for following chemical reactions by weighing reactants and products, and formulated the concepts of latent heat and thermal capacity.

black ▶ adjective **1** of the very darkest colour due to the absence of or complete absorption of light; the opposite of white: *black smoke* | *her hair was black.*
■ (of the sky or night) completely dark due to non-visibility of the sun, moon, or stars, normally because of dense cloud cover: *the sky was moonless and*

black. ▪ deeply stained with dirt: *the walls were black with age and dirt.* ▪ (of a plant or animal) dark in colour as distinguished from a lighter variety: *Japanese black pine.* ▪ (of coffee or tea) served without milk. ▪ of or denoting the suits spades and clubs in a pack of cards. ▪ (of a ski run) of the highest level of difficulty, as indicated by black markers positioned along it.

2 (also **Black**) of any human group having dark-coloured skin, especially of African or Australian Aboriginal ancestry.

▪ of or relating to black people: *black culture.*

3 figurative (of a situation or period of time) characterized by tragic or disastrous events; causing despair or pessimism: *five thousand men were killed on the blackest day of the war | the future looks black.*

▪ (of a person's state of mind) full of gloom or misery; very depressed: *Jean had disappeared and Mary was in a black mood.* ▪ (of humour) presenting tragic or harrowing situations in comic terms: *'Good place to bury the bodies,' she joked with black humour.* ▪ full of anger or hatred: *Rory shot her a black look.* ▪ archaic very evil or wicked: *my soul is steeped in the blackest sin.*

4 Brit. dated (of goods or work) not to be handled or undertaken by trade union members, especially so as to express support for an industrial dispute elsewhere: *the union declared the ship black.*

▶**noun 1** [mass noun] black colour or pigment: *a tray decorated in black and green.*

▪ black clothes or material, typically worn as a sign of mourning: *only one or two of the mourners were in black.* ▪ darkness, especially of night or an overcast sky: *the only thing visible in the black was the light of the torch.*

2 a black thing, in particular:

▪ the black ball in snooker. ▪ (**Black**) the player of the black pieces in chess or draughts. ▪ Brit. informal blackcurrant cordial: *a rum and black.*

3 (also **Black**) a member of a dark-skinned people, especially one of African or Australian Aboriginal ancestry.

▶**verb** [with obj.] **1** make black, especially by the application of black polish: *the steps of the house were neatly blacked.*

▪ make (one's face, hands, and other visible parts of one's body) black with polish or make-up, so as not to be seen at night or to play the role of a black person in a play or film: *white extras **blacking up** their faces to play Ethiopians.* ▪ [no obj.] (of a television screen) show no pictures and go blank.

2 Brit. dated refuse to handle (goods), undertake (work), or have dealings with (a person or business) as a way of taking industrial action: *the printers blacked firms trying to employ women.*

– PHRASES **black someone's eye** hit someone in the eye so as to cause bruising. **in the black** (of a person or organization) not owing any money; solvent. **in someone's black books** informal in disfavour with someone. **look on the black side** informal view a situation from a pessimistic angle. **not as black as one is painted** informal not as bad as one is said to be.

– DERIVATIVES **blackish** adjective, **blackly** adverb, **blackness** noun.

– ORIGIN Old English *blæc*, of Germanic origin.

> **USAGE** Evidence for the use of **black** to refer to African peoples (and their descendants) dates back at least to the late 14th century. Although the word has been in continuous use ever since, other terms have enjoyed prominence too: in the US **coloured** was the term adopted in preference by emancipated slaves following the American Civil War, and **coloured** was itself superseded in the US in the early 20th century by **Negro** as the term preferred by prominent black American campaigners such as Booker T. Washington. In Britain on the other hand, **coloured** was the most widely used and accepted term in the 1950s and early 1960s. With the civil rights and Black Power movements of the 1960s, **black** was adopted by Americans of African origin to signify a sense of racial pride, and it remains the most widely used and generally accepted term in Britain today. See also **AFRICAN AMERICAN** and **AFRO-AMERICAN**.

▶**black out** (of a person) undergo a sudden and temporary loss of consciousness.

black something out 1 (usu. **be blacked out**) extinguish all lights or completely cover windows, especially for protection against an air attack or in order to provide darkness in which to show a film. ▪ subject a place to an electricity failure: *Chicago was blacked out yesterday after a freak flood.* **2** obscure something completely so that it cannot be read or seen: *the number plate had been blacked out with masking tape.* ▪ (of a television company) decide not to broadcast a disputed or controversial programme.

black Africa the area of Africa, generally south of the Sahara, where black people predominate.

blackamoor /ˈblakəmɔː, -mʊə/ ▶**noun** archaic a black African or a very dark-skinned person.

– ORIGIN early 16th cent.: from **BLACK** + **MOOR**.

black and blue ▶**adjective** (of a person) covered in livid bruises.

black and tan ▶**noun 1** a terrier of a breed with a black back and tan markings on face, flanks, and legs.

2 [mass noun] Brit. a drink composed of stout and bitter.

Black and Tans an armed force recruited by the British government to fight Sinn Fein in Ireland in 1921. Their harsh methods caused an outcry in Britain and America.

– ORIGIN so named because of the mixture of military khaki and black constabulary colours of their uniform.

black and white ▶**adjective 1** (of a photograph, film, television programme, or illustration) in black, white, shades of grey, and no other colour: *old black-and-white movies.*

▪ (of a television) displaying images in black, white, and shades of grey.

2 (of a situation or debate) involving clearly defined opposing principles or issues: *it was all grey areas; no black-and-white certainties.*

▶**noun** US informal a police car.

– PHRASES **in black and white 1** in writing or in print (regarded as more reliable, credible, or formal than speech): *she had abandoned all hope of getting her contract down in black and white.* **2** in terms of clearly defined opposing principles or issues: *children think in black and white, good and bad.*

black ant ▶**noun** a small ant which is black in colour and is typically found in and around houses.

● Several species in the family Formicidae, in particular *Lasius niger*, of both Eurasia and North America.

black art ▶**noun** (usu. **the black art**) another term for **BLACK MAGIC**.

▪ often humorous a technique or practice considered mysterious and sinister: *the black art of political news management.*

blackball ▶**verb** [with obj.] reject (a candidate applying to become a member of a private club), typically by means of a secret ballot.

– ORIGIN late 18th cent.: from the practice of registering an adverse vote by placing a black ball in a ballot box.

black bass ▶**noun** a North American freshwater fish of the sunfish family, which is a popular sporting and food fish.

● Genus *Micropterus*, family Centrarchidae: several species, in particular the **largemouth bass** (*M. salmoides*) and the **smallmouth bass** (*M. dolomieui*).

black bean ▶**noun 1** either of two cultivated varieties of bean plant having small black seeds:

● a variety of soy bean, used fermented in oriental cooking. ● a Mexican variety of the French bean.

▪ the dried seed of such a plant used as a vegetable.

2 either of two Australian plants of the pea family:

● a liana with blackish flowers (*Kennedia nigricans*, family Leguminosae). ● another term for **MORETON BAY CHESTNUT**.

black bear ▶**noun** a medium-sized forest-dwelling bear with blackish fur and a paler face, found in North America and east Asia.

● Two species, family Ursidae: the **American black bear** (*Ursus americanus*), with a wide range of coat colour, and the smaller **Asian black bear** (*Selenarctos thibetanus*).

black beetle ▶**noun** Brit. informal the common cockroach.

black belt ▶**noun** a black belt worn by an expert in judo, karate, and other martial arts.

▪ a person qualified to wear this.

blackberry ▶**noun** (pl. **-ies**) **1** an edible soft fruit consisting of a cluster of soft purple-black drupelets.

2 the prickly climbing shrub of the rose family which bears this fruit and which grows extensively in the wild. Also called **BRAMBLE**.

● *Rubus fruticosus*, family Rosaceae (sometimes treated as an aggregate of many species).

▶**verb** (**-ies, -ied**) [no obj.] [usu. as noun **blackberrying**] gather blackberries in the wild.

black bile ▶**noun** [mass noun] (in medieval science and medicine) one of the four bodily humours, believed to be associated with a melancholy temperament. Also called **MELANCHOLY**.

– ORIGIN late 18th cent.: translation of Greek *melankholia* (see **MELANCHOLY**). Compare with **ATRABILIOUS**.

black bindweed ▶**noun** [mass noun] a twining European weed related to the docks, with heart-shaped leaves and small white flowers.

● *Fallopia convolvulus*, family Polygonaceae.

blackbird ▶**noun 1** an Old World thrush with mainly black plumage.

● Genus *Turdus*, family Turdidae: four species, in particular *T. merula*, the male of which has all-black plumage and a yellow bill.

2 (also **American blackbird**) a New World songbird with a strong pointed bill. The male has black plumage that is iridescent or has patches of red or yellow.

● Family Icteridae (the **American blackbird family**): several genera and species, including the abundant **red-winged blackbird** (*Agelaius phoeniceus*).

3 historical a black or Polynesian captive on a slave ship.

blackboard ▶**noun** a large board with a smooth dark surface attached to a wall or supported on an easel and used by teachers in schools for writing on with chalk.

black body ▶**noun** Physics a hypothetical perfect absorber and radiator of energy, with no reflecting power.

black bottom ▶**noun** a popular American dance of the 1920s.

black box ▶**noun** a flight recorder in an aircraft.

▪ any complex piece of equipment, typically a unit in an electronic system, with contents which are mysterious to the user.

blackboy ▶**noun** an Australian tree or erect shrub with long stiff grass-like leaves. Flowering in some species is stimulated by fire. Also called **GRASS TREE**.

● Genus *Xanthorrhoea*, family Xanthorrhoeaceae: several species, including a tree (*X. preissii*) with a thick dark trunk and a palm-like crown of leaves, and a shrub (*X. australis*) with a short buried trunk and leaves on the surface of the ground.

black bread ▶**noun** [mass noun] a coarse dark-coloured type of rye bread.

black bryony ▶**noun** a climbing European hedgerow plant with broad glossy leaves, poisonous red berries, and black tubers.

● *Tamus communis*, the only European member of the yam family (Dioscoreaceae).

blackbuck ▶**noun** a small Indian gazelle, the horned male of which has a black back and white underbelly, the female being hornless. Also called **SASIN**.

● *Antilope cervicapra*, family Bovidae.

black bulgar ▶**noun** a cup-shaped stemless black fungus which grows on the fallen trunks and branches of broadleaved trees in Europe.

● *Bulgaria inquinans*, family Helotiaceae, subdivision Ascomycotina.

black bun ▶**noun** [mass noun] rich fruit cake in a pastry case, traditionally eaten in Scotland at New Year.

Blackburn an industrial town in NW England; pop. 132,800 (1991).

blackbutt ▶**noun** a tall straight-trunked Australian eucalyptus tree, typically with fire-charred fibrous bark on the lower trunk and with pale brown timber.

● *Eucalyptus pilularis*, family Myrtaceae.

– ORIGIN early 19th cent.: from **BLACK** + **BUTT**[3] in the sense 'tree trunk'.

black butter ▶**noun** [mass noun] a sauce made by heating butter until it is brown and usually adding vinegar.

blackcap ▶**noun 1** a mainly European warbler with a black cap in the male and a reddish-brown one in the female.

● *Sylvia atricapilla*, family Sylviidae.

2 N. Amer. the black-capped chickadee.

● *Parus atricapillus*, family Paridae.

Black Carib ▶**noun** [mass noun] a language derived from Island Carib with borrowings from Spanish, English, and French, spoken in isolated parts of Central America by descendants of people transported from the Lesser Antilles.

black caucus ▶**noun** US a political caucus

composed of black people interested in advancing the concerns of blacks.

blackcock ▶ noun (pl. same) the male of the black grouse.

black cohosh /kəˈhɒʃ/ ▶ noun see COHOSH.

black consciousness ▶ noun [mass noun] awareness of one's identity as a black person.
■ a political movement or ideology (particularly in the US and South Africa) seeking to unite black people in affirming their common identity.

Black Country a district of the Midlands with much heavy industry.

blackcurrant ▶ noun 1 a small round edible black berry which grows in loose hanging clusters.
2 the widely cultivated shrub which bears this fruit.
● *Ribes nigrum*, family Grossulariaceae.

Black Death the great epidemic of bubonic plague that killed a large proportion of the population of Europe in the mid 14th century. It originated in central Asia and China and spread rapidly through Europe, carried by the fleas of black rats, reaching England in 1348 and killing between one third and one half of the population in a matter of months.
– ORIGIN a modern term (compare with earlier *the (great) pestilence, great death, the plague*), said to have been introduced into English history by Mrs Markham (pseudonym of Mrs Penrose) in 1823, and into medical literature by a translation of German *der Schwarze Tod* (1833).

black diamond ▶ noun 1 informal a lump of coal.
2 a dark, opaque form of diamond. Also called CARBONADO.
3 [usu. as modifier] N. Amer. a difficult ski slope: *a steep, black-diamond run*.

black dog ▶ noun informal a metaphorical representation of melancholy or depression.
– ORIGIN early 19th cent.: figuratively from a cant name used during Queen Anne's reign for a base silver coin (usually a bad shilling).

black durgon /ˈdɑːɡ(ə)n/ ▶ noun a black triggerfish that occurs worldwide in tropical seas.
● *Melichthys niger*, family Balistidae.
– ORIGIN mid 20th cent.: *durgon* perhaps from English dialect *durgan* or *durgen* 'undersized person or animal'.

black economy ▶ noun the part of a country's economic activity which is unrecorded and untaxed by its government.

blacken ▶ verb become or make black or dark, especially as a result of burning, decay, or bruising: [no obj.] *he set light to the paper, watching the end blacken as it burned* | [with obj.] *stone blackened by the soot of ages* | [as adj. **blackened**] *she smiled at Mary, revealing blackened teeth*.
■ [with obj.] dye or colour (the face or hair) black for camouflage or cosmetic effect. ■ [no obj.] (of the sky) become dark as night or a storm approaches. ■ [with obj.] figurative damage or destroy (someone's reputation) by speaking badly of them: *she won't thank you for blackening her husband's name*.

black English ▶ noun [mass noun] any of various forms of English spoken by black people, especially as an urban dialect in the US.

Blackett /ˈblakɪt/, Patrick Maynard Stuart, Baron (1897–1974), English physicist. Blackett was a member of the Maud Committee which dealt with the development of the atom bomb. He also modified the cloud chamber for the study of cosmic rays. Nobel Prize for Physics (1948).

black eye ▶ noun an area of bruised skin around the eye resulting from a blow.

black-eyed bean (also **black-eye bean**, US **black-eyed pea**) ▶ noun a creamy-white edible bean which has a black mark at the point where it was attached to the pod.
● This bean is obtained from *Vigna sinensis*, family Leguminosae.

black-eyed Susan ▶ noun any of a number of plants having flowers with yellowish petals and a dark centre:
● a slender tropical climber popular as an indoor or greenhouse plant (*Thunbergia alata*, family Acanthaceae). ● a rudbeckia grown in gardens (*Rudbeckia hirta* and its hybrids, family Compositae).

blackface ▶ noun 1 a sheep of a breed with a black face.

2 [mass noun] the make-up used by a non-black performer playing a black role.

blackfellow ▶ noun Austral. offensive an Aboriginal.

black-figure ▶ noun [usu. as modifier] a type of ancient Greek pottery, originating in Corinth in the 7th century BC, in which figures are painted in black, details being added by incising through to the red clay background: *a black-figure amphora*. Compare with RED-FIGURE.

blackfish ▶ noun (pl. same or **-fishes**) 1 any of a number of dark-coloured fish:
● an open-ocean fish related to the perches (genera *Centrolophus* and *Schedophilus*, family Centrolophidae), in particular the large and widespread *C. niger*. ● (**Alaska blackfish**) a small fish occurring along the Arctic coasts of Alaska and Siberia, noted for its ability to withstand freezing (*Dallia pectoralis*, family Umbridae). ● (**river blackfish**) a large fish of Australian rivers (*Gadopsis marmoratus*, family Gadopsidae). ● another term for LUDERICK. ● another term for GALJOEN. ● a salmon just after spawning.
2 another term for PILOT WHALE.

black flag ▶ noun 1 historical a pirate's ensign, typically thought to feature a white skull and crossbones on a black background.
2 historical a black flag hoisted outside a prison to announce an execution.
3 Motor Racing a black flag used to signal to a driver that he must stop at the pits as a punishment for a misdemeanour.

blackfly ▶ noun (pl. same or **-flies**) 1 a black or dark green aphid which is a common pest of crops and gardens.
● Several species in the family Aphididae, in particular *Aphis fabae*.
2 (also **black fly**) a small black fly, the female of which sucks blood and can transmit a number of serious human and animal diseases. Large numbers sometimes build up and cause distress to livestock and humans.
● Family Simuliidae: *Simulium* and other genera.

Blackfoot ▶ noun (pl. same or **Blackfeet**) 1 a member of a confederacy of North American Indian peoples of the north-western plains. The Blackfoot confederacy was made up of three closely related tribes: the Blackfoot proper or Siksika, the Bloods, and the Peigan.
2 [mass noun] the Algonquian language of this people, with about 6,000 speakers.
▶ adjective of or relating to this people or their language.

Black Forest a hilly wooded region of SW Germany, lying to the east of the Rhine valley. German name SCHWARZWALD.

Black Forest gateau (N. Amer. **Black Forest cake**) ▶ noun a chocolate sponge having layers of morello cherries or cherry jam and whipped cream and topped with chocolate icing.

Black Friar ▶ noun a Dominican friar.
– ORIGIN early 16th cent.: so named because of the colour of the order's habit.

black frost ▶ noun [mass noun] frost which does not have a white surface.

black game ▶ noun [treated as pl.] black grouse regarded collectively.

black gold ▶ noun [mass noun] N. Amer. informal oil.

black grouse ▶ noun (pl. same) a large Eurasian grouse, the male of which has glossy blue-black plumage and a lyre-shaped tail. The males display in communal leks.
● *Tetrao tetrix*, family Tetraonidae (or Phasianidae); the male is called a **blackcock** and the female a **greyhen**.

blackguard /ˈblagɑːd, -gəd/ dated ▶ noun a man who behaves in a dishonourable or contemptible way.
▶ verb [with obj.] abuse or disparage (someone) scurrilously.
– DERIVATIVES **blackguardly** adjective.
– ORIGIN early 16th cent. (originally as two words): from BLACK + GUARD. The term originally denoted a body of attendants or servants, especially the menials who had charge of kitchen utensils, but the exact significance of the epithet 'black' is uncertain. The sense 'scoundrel, villain' dates from the mid 18th cent., and was formerly considered highly offensive.

black guillemot ▶ noun a seabird of the auk family with black summer plumage and large white wing patches, breeding on the coasts of the Arctic and North Atlantic.
● *Cepphus grylle*, family Alcidae.

Black Hamburg ▶ noun see HAMBURG[2].

blackhead ▶ noun 1 a plug of sebum in a hair follicle, darkened by oxidation.
2 [mass noun] an infectious disease of turkeys producing discoloration of the head, caused by a protozoon.

Black Hills a range of mountains in east Wyoming and west South Dakota. The highest point is Harney Peak (2,207 m, 7,242 ft); the range also includes the sculptured granite face of Mount Rushmore.

black hole ▶ noun Astronomy a region of space having a gravitational field so intense that no matter or radiation can escape.
■ informal a place where money or lost items are thought of as going, never to be seen again.

Black holes are probably formed when a massive star exhausts its nuclear fuel and collapses under its own gravity. If the star is massive enough no known force can counteract the increasing gravity, and it will collapse to a point of infinite density. Before this stage is reached, within a certain radius (the event horizon) light itself becomes trapped and the object becomes invisible.

Black Hole of Calcutta a dungeon 6 metres (20 feet) square in Fort William, Calcutta, where perhaps as many as 146 English prisoners were confined overnight following the capture of Calcutta by the nawab of Bengal in 1756. Only twenty-three of them were still alive the next morning.

black house ▶ noun a traditional single-storeyed Scottish house built of turf or unmortared stone, typically lacking a chimney and roofed with turf or thatch. Examples survive mainly in the Outer Hebrides.

black ice ▶ noun [mass noun] a transparent coating of ice, especially on a road surface.

black information ▶ noun [mass noun] information held by banks, credit agencies, or other financial institutions about people who are considered bad credit risks.

blacking ▶ noun [mass noun] black paste or polish, especially that used on shoes.

blackjack ▶ noun 1 [mass noun] chiefly N. Amer. a gambling card game in which players try to acquire cards with a face value totalling 21 and no more. See also PONTOON[1], VINGT-ET-UN.
2 a widely distributed weed related to the bur-marigold, with barbed black seeds. [ORIGIN: perhaps from sense 3, drawing a comparison between the shape of the seeds and a bludgeon.]
● *Bidens pilosa*, family Compositae.
3 N. Amer. a flexible lead-filled truncheon, used as a weapon.
4 historical a pirates' black ensign.
5 historical a tarred-leather container used for alcoholic liquor.

Black Jew ▶ noun another term for FALASHA.

black kite ▶ noun a bird of prey with dark plumage and a slightly forked tail, feeding mainly by scavenging and found throughout much of the Old World.
● *Milvus migrans*, family Accipitridae.

black knight ▶ noun Stock Exchange a person or company making an unwelcome takeover bid for another company.
– ORIGIN by association with WHITE KNIGHT.

blacklead ▶ noun another term for GRAPHITE.
▶ verb [with obj.] polish (metal, especially cast iron) with graphite.

blackleg ▶ noun 1 Brit. derogatory a person who continues working when fellow workers are on strike. [ORIGIN: the reason for the name remains unknown.]
2 [mass noun] an acute infectious bacterial disease of cattle and sheep, causing necrosis in one or more legs.
● The bacterium is *Clostridium chauvoei*.
3 [mass noun] any of a number of plant diseases in which part of the stem blackens and decays, in particular:
● a fungal disease of cabbages and related plants (caused by *Leptosphaeria, Pleospora*, and other genera). ● a bacterial disease of potatoes (caused by *Erwinia carotovora* subsp. *atroseptica*).
▶ verb (**-legged**, **-legging**) [no obj.] Brit. derogatory continue working when one's fellow workers are on strike.

black letter ▶ noun [mass noun] an early, ornate, bold style of type.

black light ▶ noun [mass noun] ultraviolet or infrared radiation, invisible to the eye.

blacklist ▶ noun a list of people or groups regarded as unacceptable or untrustworthy and often marked down for punishment or exclusion.
▶verb [with obj.] (often **be blacklisted**) put on such a list.

black lung ▶ noun [mass noun] chiefly US pneumoconiosis caused by inhalation of coal dust.

black magic ▶ noun [mass noun] magic involving the supposed invocation of evil spirits for evil purposes.

blackmail ▶ noun [mass noun] the action, treated as a criminal offence, of demanding money from someone in return for not revealing compromising information which one has about them.
■money demanded in this way: we do not pay blackmail. ■ the use of threats or the manipulation of someone's feelings to force them to do something: some people use emotional blackmail.
▶verb [with obj.] demand money from (someone) in return for not revealing compromising information about them.
■force (someone) to do something by using threats or manipulating their feelings: he had blackmailed her into sailing with him.
– DERIVATIVES **blackmailer** noun.
– ORIGIN mid 16th cent. (denoting protection money levied by Scottish chiefs): from **BLACK** + obsolete mail 'tribute, rent', from Old Norse mál 'speech, agreement'.

black mamba ▶ noun a highly venomous slender olive-brown to dark grey snake that moves with great speed and agility. Native to eastern and southern Africa, it is the largest poisonous snake on the continent.
● Dendroaspis polylepis, family Elapidae.

Black Maria ▶ noun **1** informal a police vehicle for transporting prisoners.
2 [mass noun] a card game in which players try to avoid winning tricks containing the queen of spades or any hearts.
■a name for the queen of spades in this game.
– ORIGIN mid 19th cent. (originally US): said to be named after a black woman, Maria Lee, who kept a boarding house in Boston and helped police in escorting drunk and disorderly customers to jail.

black mark ▶ noun informal a record or impression of a person's misdemeanour or discreditable action: a black mark went down against his name for turning down the job.

black market ▶ noun an illegal traffic or trade in officially controlled or scarce commodities.
– DERIVATIVES **black marketeer** noun.

black mass ▶ noun a travesty of the Roman Catholic Mass in worship of the Devil.

black metal ▶ noun [mass noun] a type of heavy metal music having lyrics which deal with the Devil and the supernatural.

Black Monday ▶ noun **1** Monday 19 October 1987, when massive falls in the value of stocks on Wall Street triggered similar falls in markets around the world.
2 archaic Easter Monday (probably so called because Mondays in general were held to be unlucky).

black money ▶ noun [mass noun] income illegally obtained or not declared for tax purposes.

Black Monk ▶ noun a Benedictine monk.
– ORIGIN Middle English: so named because of the colour of the order's habit.

Blackmore, R. D. (1825–1900), English novelist and poet; full name Richard Doddridge Blackmore. He is known for his romantic novel Lorna Doone (1869), set in 17th-century Exmoor.

black Muslim ▶ noun a member of the **NATION OF ISLAM**.

black nationalism ▶ noun [mass noun] the advocacy of the national civil rights of black people, especially in the US.

black nightshade ▶ noun see **NIGHTSHADE**.

blackout ▶ noun **1** a period when all lights must be turned out or covered to prevent them being seen by the enemy during an air raid.
■(usu. **blackouts**) dark curtains put up in windows to cover lights during an air raid. ■ a failure of electrical power supply: due to a power blackout their hotel was in total darkness. ■ a moment in the theatre when the lights on stage are suddenly dimmed. ■ a

suppression of information, especially one imposed on the media by government: there is a total information blackout on minority interests.
2 a temporary loss of consciousness.

Black Panther ▶ noun a member of a militant political organization set up in the US in 1966 to fight for black rights.

black panther ▶ noun a leopard that has black fur rather than the typical spotted coat.

black pepper ▶ noun [mass noun] the dried black berries of the pepper, which are harvested while still green and unripe. Black pepper is widely used as a spice and a condiment, and may be used whole (peppercorns) or ground. Compare with **WHITE PEPPER**.

blackpoll /ˈblakpəʊl/ (also **blackpoll warbler**) ▶ noun a North American warbler with a black cap, white cheeks, and white underparts streaked with black.
● Dendroica striata, family Parulidae.

Blackpool a seaside resort in NW England; pop. 144,500 (1991).

black powder ▶ noun [mass noun] gunpowder.

Black Power ▶ noun [mass noun] a movement in support of rights and political power for black people, especially prominent in the US in the 1960s and 1970s.

Black Prince (1330–76), eldest son of Edward III of England; name given to Edward, Prince of Wales and Duke of Cornwall. He was responsible for the English victory at Poitiers in 1356. He predeceased his father, but his son became king as Richard II.

black pudding ▶ noun Brit. a black sausage containing pork, dried pig's blood, and suet.

black rat ▶ noun a rat with dark fur, large ears, and a long tail. It is found throughout the world, being particularly common in the tropics, and is the chief host of the plague-transmitting flea. Also called **SHIP RAT**, **HOUSE RAT**, or **ROOF RAT**.
● Rattus rattus, family Muridae.

black rhinoceros ▶ noun a two-horned rhinoceros with a prehensile upper lip, found in Africa south of the Sahara.
● Diceros bicornis, family Rhinocerotidae.

Black Rod (in full **Gentleman Usher of the Black Rod**) ▶ noun (in the UK) the chief usher of the Lord Chamberlain's department of the royal household, who is also usher to the House of Lords.
– ORIGIN mid 17th cent.: so named because of the black wand carried as a symbol of office.

black rot ▶ noun [mass noun] [usu. with modifier] any of a number of fungal or bacterial diseases of plants, fruits, and vegetables, producing blackening, rotting, and shrivelling.

black salsify ▶ noun another term for **SCORZONERA**.

Black Sea a tideless almost landlocked sea bounded by Ukraine, Russia, Georgia, Turkey, Bulgaria, and Romania, connected to the Mediterranean through the Bosporus and the Sea of Marmara.

black sheep ▶ noun informal a member of a family or group who is regarded as a disgrace to it: the black sheep of the family.
– ORIGIN late 18th cent.: from the proverb there is a black sheep in every flock.

blackshirt ▶ noun a member of a Fascist organization, in particular:
■(in Italy) a member of a paramilitary group founded by Mussolini. ■ (in Nazi Germany) a member of the SS. ■ (in the UK) a supporter of Oswald Mosley's British Union of Fascists.
– ORIGIN 1920s: so named because of the colour of the Italian Fascist uniform.

blacksmith ▶ noun a person who makes and repairs things in iron by hand.
■a farrier.

black smoker ▶ noun Geology a geothermal vent on the seabed which ejects superheated water containing much suspended matter, typically black sulphide minerals.

black spot ▶ noun **1** Brit. a place or area marked by a particular trouble or concern: an unemployment black spot | an accident black spot.
2 [mass noun] a fungal or bacterial disease of plants, especially roses, producing black blotches on the leaves.

● Rose black spot is caused by the fungus Diplocarpon rosae, subdivision Ascomycotina.

black stinkwood ▶ noun see **STINKWOOD**.

Blackstone, Sir William (1723–80), English jurist. His major work was the Commentaries on the Laws of England (1765–9), an exposition of English law.

Black Stone the sacred reddish-black stone built into the outside wall of the Kaaba and ritually touched by Muslim pilgrims.

black stump ▶ noun Austral. informal a mythical marker of distance in the outback.
– PHRASES **beyond the black stump** in the remote outback.
– ORIGIN early 20th cent.: black in the sense 'fire-blackened'.

black swan ▶ noun a mainly black swan with white flight feathers which is common in Australia and Tasmania and has been introduced widely elsewhere.
● Cygnus atratus, family Anatidae.
■archaic or kind of person that is extremely rare: husbands without faults, if such black swans there be. [ORIGIN: proverbial, from Juvenal's Satires.]

black-tailed deer ▶ noun another term for **MULE DEER**.

black tea ▶ noun [mass noun] **1** tea served without milk.
2 tea of the most usual type, that is fully fermented before drying. Compare with **GREEN TEA**.

blackthorn ▶ noun a thorny Eurasian shrub which bears white flowers before the leaves appear, followed by astringent blue-black fruits (sloes). Also called **SLOE**.
● Prunus spinosa, family Rosaceae.
■a walking stick or cudgel made from a stem of this shrub.

blackthorn winter ▶ noun Brit. a spell of cold weather at the time in early spring when the blackthorn flowers.

black tie ▶ noun a black bow tie worn with a dinner jacket.
■[mass noun] formal evening dress: the audience wears black tie.
▶adjective (**black-tie**) (of an event) requiring formal evening dress: evening meals were black-tie affairs.

blacktop chiefly N. Amer. ▶ noun [mass noun] asphalt, tarmacadam, or other black material used for surfacing roads: [as modifier] blacktop roads.
■[count noun] a road or area surfaced with such material.
▶verb [with obj.] surface (a road or area) with such material: 41 km had been blacktopped to date.

black tracker ▶ noun Austral. an Aboriginal employed to help find people lost or hiding in the bush.

black velvet ▶ noun [mass noun] a drink consisting of a mixture of stout and champagne.

black vulture ▶ noun **1** a very large Old World vulture with blackish-brown plumage, now rare in Europe. Also called **CINEREOUS VULTURE**.
● Aegypius monachus, family Accipitridae.
2 a New World vulture with black plumage and a bare black head.
● Coragyps atratus, family Cathartidae.

blackwall tyre ▶ noun a tyre with black side walls.

Black Watch the Royal Highland Regiment.
– ORIGIN in the early 18th cent. the term Watch was given to certain companies of irregular troops in the Highlands; Black Watch referred to some of these companies raised c.1729–30, distinctive by their dark-coloured tartan.

black water ▶ noun [mass noun] technical waste water and sewage from toilets. Compare with **GREY WATER**.

blackwater fever ▶ noun [mass noun] a severe form of malaria in which blood cells are rapidly destroyed, resulting in dark urine.

black widow ▶ noun a highly venomous American spider which has a black body with red markings.
● Latrodectus mactans, family Theridiidae; subspecies also occur on other continents (see **KATIPO**, **REDBACK**, and **BUTTON SPIDER**).

blackwood ▶ noun a tropical hardwood tree of the pea family, which produces high-quality dark timber.
● Dalbergia and other genera, family Leguminosae: several species, in particular the **African blackwood** (D.

melanoxylon), and the Australian *Acacia melanoxylon*, which has become naturalized in SW Europe.

blackwork ▶ **noun** [mass noun] a type of embroidery done in black thread on white cloth, popular especially in Tudor times.

bladder ▶ **noun 1** a membranous sac in humans and other animals, in which urine is collected for excretion.
2 anything inflated and hollow, in particular an inflated fruit or vesicle in various plants.
– ORIGIN Old English *blædre*, of Germanic origin; related to Dutch *blaar* and German *Blatter*, also to **BLOW**[1].

bladder campion ▶ **noun** a white-flowered Eurasian campion with a swollen bladder-like calyx behind the deeply cut petals.
• *Silene vulgaris*, family Caryophyllaceae.

bladder fern ▶ **noun** a small, delicate fern with rounded spore cases, growing on rocks and walls in both Eurasia and North America.
• Genus *Cystopteris*, family Woodsiaceae: several species.

bladder nut ▶ **noun** a shrub or small tree of northern temperate regions, which bears white flowers and inflated seed capsules.
• Genus *Staphylea*, family Staphyleaceae: several species, in particular the central European *S. pinnata*.

bladder senna ▶ **noun** a Mediterranean shrub of the pea family, which bears yellow flowers followed by inflated reddish pods.
• *Colutea arborescens*, family Leguminosae.

bladder snail ▶ **noun** a freshwater snail which typically lives in slow-running water with abundant vegetation.
• Family Physidae: *Physa* and other genera.

bladder worm ▶ **noun** an immature form of a tapeworm, which lives in the flesh of the secondary host. Further development is suspended until it is eaten by the primary host.

bladderwort /ˈbladəwəːt/ ▶ **noun** an aquatic plant of north temperate regions, with small air-filled bladders which keep the plant afloat and trap tiny animals that provide additional nutrients.
• Genus *Utricularia*, family Lentibulariaceae.

bladderwrack ▶ **noun** [mass noun] a common brown shoreline seaweed which has tough strap-like fronds containing air bladders that give buoyancy.
• *Fucus vesiculosus*, class Phaeophyceae.

blade ▶ **noun 1** the flat cutting edge of a knife, saw, or other tool or weapon.
■ poetic/literary a sword. ■ Archaeology a long, narrow flake. ■ (**blades**) Austral./NZ hand shears.
2 the flat, wide section of an implement or device such as an oar or a propeller.
■ a thin, flat metal runner on an ice skate. ■ (also **blade bone**) a shoulder bone in a joint of meat, or the joint itself. ■ the flat part of the tongue behind the tip.
3 a long, narrow leaf of grass or another similar plant: ***a blade of** grass.*
■ Botany the broad thin part of a leaf apart from the stalk.
4 informal, dated a dashing or energetic young man.
– DERIVATIVES **bladed** adjective [in combination] *double-bladed paddles.*
– ORIGIN Old English *blæd* 'leaf of a plant' (also in sense 2), of Germanic origin; related to Dutch *blad* and German *Blatt*.

blaeberry /ˈbleɪb(ə)ri, -bɛri/ ▶ **noun** (pl. **-ies**) Scottish and northern English term for **BILBERRY**.
– ORIGIN Middle English: from Scots and northern English dialect *blae* 'blackish-blue' (from Old Norse *blár*, related to **BLUE**[1]) + **BERRY**.

blag Brit. informal ▶ **noun 1** a violent robbery or raid.
2 an act of using clever talk or lying to obtain something: *blags and scams on the allowance scheme.*
▶ **verb** (**blagged**, **blagging**) [with obj.] **1** steal (something) in a violent robbery or raid: *I could lie in wait and blag her fur coat.*
2 obtain (something) by clever talk or lying: *students who irritate by trying to blag tickets.*
– DERIVATIVES **blagger** noun.
– ORIGIN late 19th cent.: sense 1 of unknown origin; sense 2 perhaps from French *blaguer* 'tell lies'.

blague /blɑːg/ ▶ **noun** rare a joke or piece of nonsense.
– ORIGIN French.

blagueur /blaˈgəː, French blagœʀ/ ▶ **noun** rare a person who talks nonsense.
– ORIGIN French, from **BLAGUE**.

blah informal ▶ used to substitute for actual words in contexts where they are felt to be too tedious or lengthy to give in full: *he said nations great and small could come together to blah blah blah.*
▶ **noun 1** (also **blah-blah**) [mass noun] used to refer to something which is boring or without meaningful content: *talking all kinds of blah to him.*
2 (**the blahs**) N. Amer. depression: *a case of the blahs.*
– ORIGIN early 20th cent. (originally US): imitative.

blain /bleɪn/ ▶ **noun** rare an inflamed swelling or sore on the skin.
– ORIGIN Old English *blegen*, of West Germanic origin; related to Dutch *blein*.

Blair, Tony (b.1953), British Labour statesman, Prime Minister since 1997; full name *Anthony Charles Lynton Blair*. His landslide victory in the election of 1997 gave his party its biggest-ever majority and made him the youngest Prime Minister since Lord Liverpool in 1812.
– DERIVATIVES **Blairism** noun, **Blairite** noun & adjective.

Blake[1], Peter (b.1932), English painter, prominent in the pop art movement in the late 1950s and early 1960s. He is best known for the cover design for the Beatles album *Sergeant Pepper's Lonely Hearts Club Band* (1967).

Blake[2], William (1757–1827), English artist and poet. Blake's poems mark the beginning of romanticism and a rejection of the Age of Enlightenment. His watercolours and engravings, like his writings, were only fully appreciated after his death. Notable collections of poems: *Songs of Innocence* (1789) and *Songs of Experience* (1794).
– DERIVATIVES **Blakeian** adjective.

Blakey[1], Art (1919–90), American jazz drummer, a pioneer of the bebop movement known for his group the Jazz Messengers; full name *Arthur Blakey*.

Blakey[2] ▶ **noun** (pl. **-eys**) Brit. a protective metal plate fitted to the sole of a shoe or boot.
– ORIGIN late 19th cent.: named after the manufacturers, E. Blakey and Sons, of Leeds.

blame ▶ **verb** [with obj.] assign responsibility for a fault or wrong to (someone or something): *the inquiry **blamed** the train driver **for** the accident.*
■ (**blame something on**) assign the responsibility for something bad to (someone or something): *they blame youth crime on unemployment.*
▶ **noun** [mass noun] responsibility for a fault or wrong: *his players had to **take the blame** for the defeat | they are trying to **put the blame on** us.*
■ the action of assigning responsibility for a fault: *he singled out food additives for blame.*
– PHRASES **be to blame** be responsible for a fault or wrong: *he **was to blame for** their deaths.* **I don't** (or **can't**) **blame you** (or **her** etc.) used to indicate that one agrees that the action or attitude taken was reasonable: *he was becoming impatient and I couldn't blame him.* **have only oneself to blame** be solely responsible for something bad that has happened.
– DERIVATIVES **blameable** (US also **blamable**) adjective, **blameful** adjective.
– ORIGIN Middle English: from Old French *blamer*, *blasmer* (verb), from a popular Latin variant of ecclesiastical Latin *blasphemare* 'reproach, revile, blaspheme', from Greek *blasphēmein* (see **BLASPHEME**).

blameless ▶ **adjective** innocent of wrongdoing: *he led a blameless life.*
– DERIVATIVES **blamelessly** adverb, **blamelessness** noun.

blameworthy ▶ **adjective** responsible for wrongdoing and deserving of censure or blame.
– DERIVATIVES **blameworthiness** noun.

blanch /blɑːn(t)ʃ/ ▶ **verb 1** [with obj.] make white or pale by extracting colour; bleach: *the cold light blanched her face.*
■ [with obj.] whiten (a plant) by depriving it of light. ■ [no obj.] figurative (of a person) grow pale from shock, fear, or a similar emotion: *many **people blanch at** the suggestion | their faces blanched with fear.*
2 [with obj.] prepare (vegetables) for freezing or further cooking by immersing briefly in boiling water.
■ [often as adj. **blanched**] peel (almonds) by scalding them.
– ORIGIN Middle English: from Old French *blanchir*, from *blanc* 'white', ultimately of Germanic origin.

Blanchard /ˈblɑ̃ʃɑː, French blɑ̃ʃaʀ/, Jean Pierre François (1753–1809), French balloonist. He made the first crossing of the English Channel by air, flying by balloon, on 7 January 1785.

blancmange /bləˈmɒnʒ, -ˈmɑːnʒ/ ▶ **noun** a sweet opaque gelatinous dessert made with flavoured cornflour and milk.
– ORIGIN late Middle English *blancmanger*: from Old French *blanc mangier*, from *blanc* 'white' + *mangier* 'eat' (used as a noun to mean 'food'). The shortened form without *-er* arose in the 18th cent.

blanco /ˈblaŋkəʊ/ ▶ **noun** [mass noun] Brit. a white substance used for whitening belts and other items of military equipment.
▶ **verb** (**-oes**, **-oed**) [with obj.] whiten (equipment) with blanco.
– ORIGIN late 19th cent.: from French *blanc* 'white', ultimately of Germanic origin.

bland ▶ **adjective** lacking strong features or characteristics and therefore uninteresting: *rebelling against the bland uniformity.*
■ (of food or drink) unseasoned, mild-tasting, or insipid. ■ (of a person or their behaviour) showing no strong emotion; dull and unremarkable: *his expression was bland and unreadable.*
– DERIVATIVES **blandly** adverb, **blandness** noun.
– ORIGIN late Middle English (in the sense 'gentle in manner'): from Latin *blandus* 'soft, smooth'.

blandish /ˈblandɪʃ/ ▶ **verb** [with obj.] archaic coax (someone) with kind words or flattery.
– ORIGIN Middle English: from Old French *blandiss-*, lengthened stem of *blandir*, from Latin *blandiri*, from *blandus* 'soft, smooth'.

blandishment ▶ **noun** (often **blandishments**) a flattering or pleasing statement or action used to gently persuade someone to do something.

blank ▶ **adjective 1** (of a surface or background) unrelieved by decorative or other features; bare, empty, or plain: *a blank wall | the screen went blank.*
■ not written or printed on: *a blank sheet of paper.* ■ (of a document) with spaces left for a signature or details: *blank tax-return forms.* ■ (of a tape) with nothing recorded on it: *blank cassettes.*
2 showing incomprehension or no reaction: *we were met by blank looks.*
■ having temporarily no knowledge or understanding: *her mind went blank.* ■ lacking incident or result: *those blank moments aboard airplanes.*
3 [attrib.] complete; absolute (used emphatically with negative force): *he was met with a blank refusal to discuss the issue.*
4 used euphemistically in place of an adjective regarded as obscene, profane, or abusive: *show the miserable blank-blank Englishman how to fight this war.*
▶ **noun 1** a space left to be filled in a document: *leave blanks to type in the appropriate names.*
■ a document with blank spaces to be filled.
2 (also **blank cartridge**) a cartridge containing gunpowder but no bullet, used for training or as a signal.
3 an empty space or period of time, especially in terms of a lack of knowledge or understanding: *my mind was a total blank.*
4 an object which has no mark or design on it, in particular:
■ a roughly cut metal or wooden block intended for further shaping or finishing. ■ a domino with one or both halves blank. ■ a plain metal disc from which a coin is made by stamping a design on it.
5 a dash written instead of a word or letter, especially instead of an obscenity or profanity.
■ used euphemistically in place of a noun regarded as obscene, profane, or abusive.
▶ **verb** [with obj.] **1** cover up, obscure, or cause to appear blank or empty: *electronic countermeasures **blanked out** the radar signals.*
■ [no obj.] become blank or empty: *the picture **blanked out**.* ■ cut (a metal blank).
2 N. Amer. defeat (a sports team) without allowing them to score: *Baltimore blanked Toronto in a 7–0 victory.*
3 Brit. informal deliberately ignore (someone): *I just blanked them and walked out.*
– PHRASES **be firing blanks** humorous (of a man) be infertile. **draw a blank** elicit no successful response; fail: *the search drew a blank.*
– DERIVATIVES **blankly** adverb, **blankness** noun.
– ORIGIN Middle English (in the sense 'white, colourless'): from Old French *blanc* 'white', ultimately of Germanic origin.

blank cheque ▶ **noun** a cheque with the amount left for the payee to fill in.
■ [in sing.] figurative an unlimited freedom of action: *he was effectively granted a blank cheque to conduct a war without Congressional authorization.*

blanket ▶ **noun 1** a large piece of woollen or similar material used as a covering on a bed or elsewhere for warmth.
■figurative a thick mass or layer of a specified material that covers something completely: *a dense grey blanket of cloud.*
2 Printing a rubber surface used for transferring the image in ink from the plate to the paper in offset printing.
▶ **adjective** [attrib.] covering all cases or instances; total and inclusive: *a blanket ban on tobacco advertising.*
▶ **verb** (**blanketed**, **blanketing**) [with obj.] cover completely with a thick layer of something: *the countryside **was blanketed in** snow.*
■stifle or keep quiet (sound): *the double glazing blankets the noise a bit.* ■ Sailing take wind from the sails of (another craft) by passing to windward.
– PHRASES **born on the wrong side of the blanket** dated illegitimate.
– ORIGIN Middle English (denoting undyed woollen cloth): via Old Northern French from Old French *blanc* 'white', ultimately of Germanic origin.

blanket bath ▶ **noun** Brit. an all-over wash given to a person confined to bed.

blanket bog ▶ **noun** [mass noun] an extensive flat peat bog formed in cool regions of high rainfall or humidity.

blanket coat ▶ **noun** N. Amer. a coat made from a blanket or from blanket-like material.

blanket finish ▶ **noun** a very close finish in a race.

blanketing ▶ **noun 1** [mass noun] material used for making blankets.
2 the action of covering something with or as if with a blanket: *the blanketing of large areas with trees.*

blanket roll ▶ **noun** N. Amer. a soldier's blanket and kit made into a roll for use on active service.

blanket stitch ▶ **noun** [mass noun] a buttonhole stitch used on the edges of a blanket or other material too thick to be hemmed.

blanket weed ▶ **noun** [mass noun] a common green freshwater alga which forms long unbranched filaments, sometimes becoming a problem in over-enriched water and garden ponds.
• Genus *Spirogyra*, division Chlorophyta (or phylum Chlorophyta, kingdom Protista).

blankety (also **blankety-blank**) ▶ **adjective** & **noun** informal used euphemistically to replace a word considered coarse or vulgar: [as adj.] *it's time to ditch the blankety-blank tax code.*

blanking plate ▶ **noun** a plate that covers an opening in a device or a wall to protect it from moisture or dust.

blank verse ▶ **noun** [mass noun] verse without rhyme, especially that which uses iambic pentameters.

blanquette /blɒ̃ˈkɛt/ ▶ **noun** a dish consisting of white meat in a white sauce.
– ORIGIN French, based on *blanc* 'white'.

Blantyre /blanˈtʌɪə/ the chief commercial and industrial city of Malawi; pop. 331,600 (1987) (with Limbe, a town 8 km south-east of Blantyre).

blare ▶ **verb** [no obj.] sound loudly and harshly: *the ambulance arrived outside, siren blaring.*
■[with obj.] cause (something) to sound loudly and harshly: *the wireless was **blaring out** organ music.*
▶ **noun** [in sing.] a loud, harsh sound: *a blare of trumpets.*
– ORIGIN late Middle English (in the sense 'roar, bellow'): from Middle Dutch *blaren, bleren*, or Low German *blaren*, of imitative origin. Current senses date from the late 18th cent.

blarney ▶ **noun** [mass noun] talk which aims to charm, pleasantly flatter, or persuade (often considered especially typical of Irish people): *it took all my Irish blarney to keep us out of court.*
■amusing and harmless nonsense: *this story is perhaps just a bit of blarney.*
▶ **verb** (**-eys**, **-eyed**) [with obj.] influence or persuade (someone) using charm and pleasant flattery.
– ORIGIN late 18th cent.: named after *Blarney*, a castle near Cork in Ireland, where there is a stone said to give the gift of persuasive speech to anyone who kisses it.

blasé /ˈblɑːzeɪ/ ▶ **adjective** unimpressed with or indifferent to something because one has experienced or seen it so often before: *she was becoming quite blasé about the dangers.*
– ORIGIN early 19th cent.: French, past participle of *blaser* 'cloy', probably ultimately of Germanic origin.

blaspheme /blasˈfiːm/ ▶ **verb** [no obj.] speak irreverently about God or sacred things: *allegations that he had **blasphemed against** Islam.*
– DERIVATIVES **blasphemer** noun.
– ORIGIN Middle English: via Old French from ecclesiastical Latin *blasphemare* 'reproach, revile, blaspheme', from Greek *blasphēmein*, from *blasphēmos* 'evil-speaking'. Compare with **BLAME**.

blasphemous ▶ **adjective** sacrilegious against God or sacred things; profane: *blasphemous and heretical talk.*
– DERIVATIVES **blasphemously** adverb.
– ORIGIN late Middle English: via ecclesiastical Latin from Greek *blasphēmos* 'evil-speaking' + **-OUS**.

blasphemy ▶ **noun** (pl. **-ies**) [mass noun] the action or offence of speaking sacrilegiously about God or sacred things; profane talk: *he was detained on charges of blasphemy* | [count noun] *screaming incomprehensible blasphemies.*
– ORIGIN Middle English: from Old French, via ecclesiastical Latin from Greek *blasphēmia* 'slander, blasphemy'.

blast /blɑːst/ ▶ **noun 1** a destructive wave of highly compressed air spreading outwards from an explosion: *they were thrown backwards by the blast.*
■an explosion or explosive firing, especially of a bomb: *a bomb blast* | *a shotgun blast.* ■ figurative a forceful attack or assault: *United's four-goal blast.*
2 a strong gust of wind or air: *the icy blast hit them.*
■a strong current of air used in smelting.
3 a single loud note of a horn, whistle, or similar: *a blast of the ship's siren.*
4 informal a severe reprimand: *I braced myself for the inevitable blast.*
5 N. Amer. informal an enjoyable experience or lively party: *it could turn out to be a real blast.*
▶ **verb** [with obj.] **1** blow up or break apart (something solid) with explosives: *quantities of solid rock had to be **blasted away*** | *the explosion **blasted out** hundreds of windows.*
■produce (damage or a hole) by means of an explosion: *the force of the collision **blasted out** a tremendous crater.* ■ [with obj. and adverbial of direction] force or throw (something) in a specified direction by impact or explosion: *the car was blasted thirty feet into the sky.* ■ shoot with a gun: *Fowler was blasted with an air rifle.* ■ [no obj., with adverbial of direction] move very quickly and loudly in a specified direction: *four low-flying jets blasted down the glen.* ■ informal criticize fiercely: *the school was blasted by government inspectors.*
2 produce or cause to produce loud continuous music or other noise: [no obj.] *music blasted out at full volume* | [with obj.] *an impatient motorist blasted his horn.*
3 kick or strike (a ball) hard: *the striker blasted the free kick into the net.*
4 poetic/literary (of a wind or other natural force) wither, shrivel, or blight (a plant): *corn blasted before it be grown up.*
■strike with divine anger (used to express annoyance or dislike): *damn and blast this awful place!* ■ destroy or ruin: *your reputation is blasted already in the village.*
▶ **exclamation** Brit. informal expressing annoyance: *'Blast! The car won't start!'*
– PHRASES **a blast from the past** informal something powerfully nostalgic: *a request for a real old blast from the past.* **(at) full blast** at maximum power or intensity: *the heat is on full blast.*
– ORIGIN Old English *blǣst*, of Germanic origin; related to **BLAZE**[3].
▶ **blast off** (of a rocket or spacecraft) take off from a launching site.

-blast ▶ **combining form** Biology denoting an embryonic cell: *erythroblast.* Compare with **-CYTE**.
■denoting a germ layer of an embryo: *epiblast.*
– ORIGIN from Greek *blastos* 'germ, sprout'.

blast chiller ▶ **noun** a machine used in commercial kitchens to cool food rapidly by circulating very cold air over it.

blasted ▶ **adjective 1** [attrib.] informal used to express annoyance: *make your own blasted coffee!*
2 [attrib.] poetic/literary withered or blighted; laid waste: *a blasted heath* | *an area of blasted trees.*
3 [predic.] informal drunk: *I got really blasted.*

blaster ▶ **noun** a person or thing that blasts.
■(in science fiction) a weapon that emits a destructive blast. ■ Golf old-fashioned term for **SAND WEDGE**.

blast furnace ▶ **noun** a smelting furnace in the form of a tower into which a blast of hot compressed air can be introduced from below. Such furnaces are used chiefly to make iron from a mixture of iron ore, coke, and limestone.

blasting gelatin ▶ **noun** another term for **GELATIN**.

blasto- /ˈblastəʊ/ ▶ **combining form** relating to germination: *blastoderm.*
– ORIGIN from Greek *blastos* 'germ, sprout'.

blastocyst ▶ **noun** Embryology a mammalian blastula in which some differentiation of cells has occurred.

blastoderm ▶ **noun** Embryology a blastula having the form of a disc of cells on top of the yolk.

blast-off ▶ **noun** [mass noun] the launching of a rocket or spacecraft.

blastomere /ˈblastə(ʊ)mɪə/ ▶ **noun** Embryology a cell formed by cleavage of a fertilized ovum.

blastomycosis /ˌblastə(ʊ)mʌɪˈkəʊsɪs/ ▶ **noun** [mass noun] Medicine a disease caused by infection with parasitic fungi affecting the skin or the internal organs.
• The fungi belong to the genus *Blastomyces*, subdivision Deuteromycotina.

blastula /ˈblastjʊlə/ ▶ **noun** (pl. **blastulae** /-liː/ or US **blastulas**) Embryology an animal embryo at the early stage of development when it is a hollow ball of cells.
– ORIGIN late 19th cent.: modern Latin, from Greek *blastos* 'sprout'.

blat informal, chiefly N. Amer. ▶ **verb** (**blatted**, **blatting**) [no obj.] **1** make a bleating sound.
2 [no obj., with adverbial of direction] travel quickly, typically in a car: *blatting down the motorway.*
▶ **noun** a bleat or similar noise: *the blat of Jack's horn.*
– ORIGIN mid 19th cent.: imitative.

blatant /ˈbleɪt(ə)nt/ ▶ **adjective** (of bad behaviour) done openly and unashamedly: *blatant lies.*
■completely lacking in subtlety; very obvious: *forcing herself to resist his blatant charm.*
– DERIVATIVES **blatancy** noun, **blatantly** adverb.
– ORIGIN late 16th cent.: perhaps an alteration of Scots *blatand* 'bleating'. It was first used by Spenser as an epithet for a thousand-tongued monster produced by Cerberus and Chimaera, a symbol of calumny, which he called the *blatant beast*. It was subsequently used to mean 'clamorous, offensive to the ear', first of people (mid 17th cent.), later of things (late 18th cent.); the sense 'unashamedly conspicuous' arose in the late 19th cent.

blather /ˈblaðə/ (also **blether** or **blither**) ▶ **verb** [no obj.] talk long-windedly without making very much sense: *she began **blathering on** about spirituality and life after death* | [as noun **blathering**] *now stop your blathering and get back to work.*
▶ **noun** [mass noun] long-winded talk with no real substance.
– ORIGIN late Middle English (as a verb; originally Scots and northern English dialect): from Old Norse *blathra* 'talk nonsense', from *blathr* 'nonsense'.

blatherskite /ˈblaðəskʌɪt/ (also **bletherskate**) ▶ **noun** chiefly N. Amer. a person who talks at great length without making much sense.
■[mass noun] foolish talk; nonsense.
– ORIGIN mid 17th cent.: from **BLATHER** + *skite*, a Scots derogatory term adopted into American colloquial speech during the War of Independence from the Scottish song *Maggie Lauder*, by F. Semphill, which was popular with American troops.

blatter ▶ **verb** [no obj., with adverbial] informal move with a clatter: *the pickup blattered down the road.*
■strike repeatedly and noisily: *blattering away at an old typewriter.*
– ORIGIN early 18th cent.: originally Scots, of imitative origin.

Blaue Reiter /ˌblaʊə ˈrʌɪtə/ a group of German expressionist painters formed in 1911, based in Munich. The group included Wassily Kandinsky, Jean Arp, and Paul Klee.
– ORIGIN German, literally 'blue rider', the title of a painting by Kandinsky.

Blavatsky /bləˈvatski/, Helena (Petrovna) (1831–91), Russian spiritualist, born in Ukraine; born *Helena Petrovna Hahn*; known as **Madame Blavatsky**. In 1875 she co-founded the Theosophical Society in New York.

blaxploitation /ˌblaksplɔɪˈteɪʃ(ə)n/ ▶ **noun** [mass noun] chiefly US the exploitation of black people, especially with regard to stereotyped roles in films.

b

– ORIGIN 1970s: blend of *blacks* (see **BLACK**) and **EXPLOITATION**.

blaze[1] ▶ **noun 1** a very large or fiercely burning fire: *twenty fireman fought the blaze.*
■ a harsh bright light: *a lightning flash changed the gentle illumination of the office into a sudden white blaze.* ■ [in sing.] a very bright display of light or colour: *the gardens in summer are **a blaze of colour**.* ■ [in sing.] figurative a conspicuous display or outburst of something: *their relationship broke up in **a blaze of publicity**.*
2 (**blazes**) informal used in various expressions of anger, bewilderment, or surprise as a euphemism for 'hell': *'Go to blazes!' he shouted | what the blazes are you all talking about?* [ORIGIN: with reference to the flames associated with hell.]
▶ **verb** [no obj.] **1** burn fiercely or brightly: *the fire blazed merrily.*
■ shine brightly or powerfully: *the sun **blazed down** |* figurative *Barbara's eyes were **blazing with** anger.*
2 (of a gun or a person firing a gun) fire repeatedly or indiscriminately: *two terrorists burst into the house with guns blazing.*
3 informal achieve something in an impressive manner: *she blazed to a gold medal in the 200-metre sprint.*
■ [with obj.] hit (a ball) with impressive strength: *he blazed a drive into the rough.*
– PHRASES **like blazes** informal very fast or forcefully: *I ran like blazes homewards.* [ORIGIN: see sense 2 of the noun.] **with all guns blazing** informal with great determination and energy, especially without thought for the consequences.
– ORIGIN Old English *blæse* 'torch, bright fire', of Germanic origin; related ultimately to **BLAZE**[2].
▶ **blaze up** burst into flame: *he attacked the fire with poker and tongs until it blazed up.* ■ figurative suddenly become angry: *he blazed up without warning.*

blaze[2] ▶ **noun 1** a white spot or stripe on the face of a mammal or bird.
■ a broad white stripe running the length of a horse's face.
2 a mark made on a tree by cutting the bark so as to mark a route.
▶ **verb** (**blaze a trail**) mark out a path or route.
■ figurative set an example by being the first to do something; pioneer: *small firms would set the pace, blazing a trail for others to follow.*
– ORIGIN mid 17th cent.: ultimately of Germanic origin; related to German *Blässe* 'blaze' and *blass* 'pale', also to **BLAZE**[1], and probably to **BLEMISH**.

blaze[3] ▶ **verb** [with obj.] (of a newspaper) present or proclaim (news) in a prominent, typically sensational, manner.
– ORIGIN late Middle English (in the sense 'blow out on a trumpet'): from Middle Low German or Middle Dutch *blāzen* 'to blow'; related to **BLOW**[1].

blazer ▶ **noun** a coloured summer jacket worn by schoolchildren or sports players as part of a uniform.
■ a plain jacket, typically dark blue, not forming part of a suit but considered appropriate for formal wear.
– ORIGIN late 19th cent.: from **BLAZE**[1] + **-ER**[1]. The original general sense was 'a thing that blazes or shines' (mid 17th cent.), giving rise to the term for a brightly coloured sporting jacket.

blazing ▶ **adjective** very hot: *the delicious cool of marble corridors after the blazing heat outside.*
■ (of an argument) very heated: *she had a blazing row with Eddie and stormed out.*
– DERIVATIVES **blazingly** adverb.

blazing star ▶ **noun** any of a number of North American plants, some of which are cultivated for their flowers, in particular:
• a plant of the daisy family with tall spikes of purple or white flowers (genus *Liatris*, family Compositae). • a plant of the lily family bearing spikes of white flowers (*Chamaelirium luteum*, family Liliaceae). Also called **DEVIL'S BIT**, **UNICORN ROOT**.

blazon /ˈbleɪz(ə)n/ ▶ **verb** [with obj.] **1** [with adverbial of place] display prominently or vividly: *they saw their company name blazoned all over the media.*
■ report (news), especially in a sensational manner: *accounts of their ordeal were blazoned to the entire nation.*
2 Heraldry describe or depict (armorial bearings) in a correct heraldic manner.
■ inscribe or paint (an object) with arms or a name.
▶ **noun** Heraldry a correct description of armorial bearings.
■ archaic a coat of arms.
– ORIGIN Middle English (denoting a shield, later one bearing a heraldic device): from Old French *blason* 'shield', of unknown origin. The sense of the verb has been influenced by **BLAZE**[3].

blazonry ▶ **noun** [mass noun] Heraldry the art of describing or painting heraldic devices or armorial bearings.
■ [treated as pl.] devices or bearings of this type.

bleach ▶ **verb** [with obj.] cause (a material such as cloth, paper, or hair) to become white or much lighter by a chemical process or by exposure to sunlight: *a new formula to bleach and brighten clothing |* [as adj. **bleached**] *permed and bleached hair.*
■ figurative deprive of vitality or substance: *his contributions to the album are bleached of personality.*
▶ **noun** [mass noun] a chemical (typically a solution of sodium hypochlorite or hydrogen peroxide) used to make cloth, paper, hair, or other materials whiter and often also for sterilizing drains, sinks, etc.
– ORIGIN Old English *blǣcan* (verb), *blǣce* (noun), from *blǣc* 'pale', of Germanic origin; related to **BLEAK**[1].

bleacher ▶ **noun 1** a person who bleaches textiles or other material.
■ a container or chemical used in bleaching.
2 (usu. **bleachers**) chiefly N. Amer. a cheap bench seat at a sports ground, typically in an outdoor uncovered stand.
– DERIVATIVES **bleacherite** noun (only in sense 2).

bleaching powder ▶ **noun** [mass noun] a powder containing calcium hypochlorite, used chiefly to remove colour from materials.

bleak[1] ▶ **adjective** (of an area of land) lacking vegetation and exposed to the elements: *a bleak and barren moor.*
■ (of a building or room) charmless and inhospitable; dreary: *he looked round the bleak little room in despair.* ■ (of the weather) cold and miserable: *a bleak midwinter's day.* ■ (of a situation or future prospect) not hopeful or encouraging; unlikely to have a favourable outcome: *he paints a bleak picture of a company that has lost its way | the future looks bleak.* ■ (of a person or a person's expression) cold and forbidding: *his mouth was set and his eyes were bleak.*
– DERIVATIVES **bleakly** adverb, **bleakness** noun.
– ORIGIN Old English *blāc* 'shining, white', or in later use from synonymous Old Norse *bleikr*; ultimately of Germanic origin and related to **BLEACH**.

bleak[2] ▶ **noun** a small silvery shoaling fish of the carp family, found in Eurasian rivers.
• Genera *Alburnus* and *Chalcalburnus*, family Cyprinidae: several species, in particular *A. alburnus*.
– ORIGIN late 15th cent.: from Old Norse *bleikja*.

blear archaic ▶ **adjective** dim, dull, or filmy: *a medicine to lay to sore and blear eyes.*
▶ **verb** [with obj.] make dim; blur: *he bleared his eyes with books.*
– ORIGIN Middle English (as a verb): probably related to Middle High German *blerre* 'blurred vision' and Low German *blarroged* 'bleary-eyed'.

bleary ▶ **adjective** (**blearier**, **bleariest**) (of the eyes) looking or feeling dull and unfocused from sleep or tiredness: *Boris opened a bleary eye.*
– DERIVATIVES **blearily** adverb, **bleariness** noun.

bleary-eyed ▶ **adjective** (of a person) having bleary eyes.

bleat ▶ **verb** [no obj.] (of a sheep, goat, or calf) make a characteristic weak, wavering cry: *the lamb was bleating weakly |* [as noun **bleating**] *the silence was broken by the plaintive bleating of sheep.*
■ [reporting verb] speak or complain in a weak, querulous, or foolish way: *it's no good just **bleating on** about the rising tide of crime.*
▶ **noun** [in sing.] the weak, wavering cry made by a sheep, goat, or calf: *the distant bleat of sheep.*
■ a person's weak or plaintive cry: *his despairing bleat touched her heart.* ■ informal a complaint: *they're hoping that I'll bow to their idiotic arrangements without a bleat.*
– DERIVATIVES **bleater** noun.
– ORIGIN Old English *blǣtan*, of imitative origin.

bleb ▶ **noun** a small blister on the skin.
■ a small bubble in glass or in a fluid. ■ Biology a rounded outgrowth on the surface of a cell.
– ORIGIN early 17th cent.: variant of **BLOB**.

bleed ▶ **verb** (past and past participle **bled**) **1** [no obj.] lose blood from the body as a result of injury or illness: *the cut was bleeding steadily | some casualties were left to **bleed to death** |* [as noun **bleeding**] *the bleeding has stopped now.*
■ (of a liquid substance such as dye or colour) seep into an adjacent colour or area: *I worked loosely with the oils, allowing colours to bleed into one another.* ■ [no obj.] Printing (of an illustration or a design) be printed so that it runs off the page after trimming: *the picture bleeds on three sides.* ■ [with obj.] Printing print and trim (an illustration or a design) in such a way.
2 [with obj.] draw blood from (someone), especially as a former method of treatment in medicine.
■ [with obj.] informal drain (someone) of money or resources: *his policy of attempting to bleed British unions of funds.* ■ [with obj.] allow (fluid or gas) to escape from a closed system through a valve. ■ [with obj.] treat (a system) in this way: *air can be got rid of by bleeding the radiator at the air vent.*
▶ **noun** an instance of bleeding: *a lot of blood was lost from the placental bleed.*
■ Printing an instance of printing an illustration or piece of text so as to leave no margin after the page has been trimmed: *the picture has an unfortunate bleed.* ■ [mass noun] the escape of fluid or gas from a closed system through a valve: *the amount of air bleed from the compressor.* ■ [mass noun] the action or process of a dye or colour seeping into an adjacent colour or area: *colour bleed is apparent on brighter hues.*
– PHRASES **bleed someone dry** (or **white**) drain someone of all their money or resources. **my heart bleeds** (**for you**) used ironically to express the speaker's belief that the person referred to does not deserve the sympathetic response they are seeking: *'I flew out here feeling tired and overworked.' 'My heart bleeds for you!' she replied.*
– ORIGIN Old English *blēdan*, of Germanic origin; related to **BLOOD**.

bleeder ▶ **noun 1** [with adj.] Brit. informal a person regarded with contempt, disrespect, or pity: *lucky little bleeder!*
2 informal a person who bleeds easily, especially a haemophiliac.
3 Baseball a ground ball hit that barely passes between two infielders.

bleeding ▶ **adjective** [attrib.] Brit. informal used for emphasis, or to express annoyance: *the watch was a bleeding copy |* [as submodifier] *she looks so bleeding bored all day.*

bleeding heart ▶ **noun 1** informal, derogatory a person considered to be dangerously soft-hearted, typically someone considered too liberal or left-wing in their political beliefs: [as modifier] *a bleeding-heart liberal.*
2 any of a number of plants which have red, or partly red, heart-shaped flowers, in particular:
• a popular herbaceous garden plant related to Dutchman's breeches (genus *Dicentra*, family Fumariaceae, in particular *D. cucullaria*). • a tropical twining shrub with cream and red flowers, widely cultivated under glass (*Clerodendrum thomsoniae*, family Verbenaceae).
3 (also **bleeding heart dove**) a dove with an oval red patch on the breast, found on islands around the Philippines.
• Genus *Gallicolumba*, family Columbidae: several species.

bleep ▶ **noun** a short high-pitched sound made by an electronic device as a signal or to attract attention.
■ a sound of this type used in broadcasting as a substitute for a censored word or phrase. ■ another term for **BLEEPER**.
▶ **verb** [no obj.] (of an electronic device) make a short high-pitched sound or repeated sequence of sounds as a signal or to attract attention: *the screen flickered for a few moments and bleeped.*
■ [with obj.] summon (someone) with a bleeper: *I'll get Janine to bleep you if I need transport.* ■ [with obj.] substitute a bleep or bleeps for (a censored word or phrase): *I may have to bleep a few words in his testimony.*
– ORIGIN 1950s: imitative.

bleeper ▶ **noun** Brit. a small portable electronic device which emits a series of high-pitched sounds when someone wants to contact the wearer.

blemish ▶ **noun** a small mark or flaw which spoils the appearance of something: *the merest blemish on a Rolls Royce might render it unsaleable.*
■ figurative a moral defect or fault: *the offences were an uncharacteristic blemish on an otherwise clean record |* [mass noun] *local government is not without blemish.*
▶ **verb** [with obj.] [often as adj. **blemished**] spoil the appearance of (something) that is otherwise aesthetically perfect: *my main problem was a blemished skin |* figurative *his reign as world champion has been blemished by controversy.*
– ORIGIN late Middle English (as a verb): from Old French *ble(s)miss-*, lengthened stem of *ble(s)mir* 'make pale, injure'; probably of Germanic origin.

blench[1] /blɛn(t)ʃ/ ▶ **verb** [no obj.] make a sudden flinching movement out of fear or pain: *he blenched and struggled to regain his composure.*
– ORIGIN Old English *blencan* 'deceive', of Germanic origin; later influenced by **BLINK**.

blench[2] /blɛntʃ/ ▶ **verb** chiefly dialect variant spelling of **BLANCH**.

blend ▶ **verb** [with obj.] mix (a substance) with another substance so that they combine together as a mass: *blend the cornflour* ***with*** *a tablespoon of water* | [no obj.] *add the grated cheese and blend well.*
■ [often as adj. **blended**] mix (different types of the same substance, such as tea, coffee, spirits, etc.) together so as to make a product of the desired quality: *a blended whisky.* ■ put or combine (abstract things) together: *I blend basic information for the novice with some scientific gardening for the more experienced* | [as noun **blending**] *a blending of romanticism with a more detached modernism.* ■ merge (a colour) with another so that one is not clearly distinguishable from the other. ■ [no obj.] form a harmonious combination: *costumes, music, and lighting all* ***blend together*** *beautifully.* ■ (**blend in/into**) be an unobtrusive or harmonious part of a greater whole by being similar in appearance or behaviour: *she would have to employ a permanent bodyguard in the house, someone who would blend in.*
▶ **noun** a mixture of different things or people: *knitting yarns in mohair blends.*
■ a mixture of different types of the same substance, such as tea, coffee, spirits, etc. ■ a combination of different abstract things or qualities: *a blend of Marxist and anarchist ideas* | *Ontario offers a cultural blend you'll find nowhere else on earth.* ■ a word made up of the parts and combining the meanings of two others, for example *motel* from *motor* and *hotel*.
– ORIGIN Middle English: probably of Scandinavian origin and related to Old Norse *blanda* 'to mix'.

blende /blɛnd/ ▶ **noun** another term for **SPHALERITE**.
– ORIGIN late 17th cent.: from German, from *blenden* 'deceive' (so named because it often resembles galena, but is deceptive in that it yields no lead).

blended family ▶ **noun** chiefly N. Amer. a family consisting of a couple and their children from this and all previous relationships.

blender ▶ **noun** a person or thing that mixes things together, in particular an electric mixing machine used in food preparation for liquidizing, chopping, or puréeing.

Blenheim[1] /ˈblɛnɪm/ **1** a battle in 1704 in Bavaria, near the village of Blindheim, in which the English, under the Duke of Marlborough, defeated the French and the Bavarians.
2 (also **Blenheim Palace**) the Duke of Marlborough's seat at Woodstock near Oxford, a stately home designed by Vanbrugh (1705). The house and its estate were given to the first Duke of Marlborough in honour of his victory at Blenheim.

Blenheim[2] /ˈblɛnɪm/ ▶ **noun** a dog of a small red and white breed of spaniel.
– ORIGIN mid 19th cent.: from the name of *Blenheim* palace (see **BLENHEIM**[1]).

Blenheim Orange ▶ **noun** an English dessert apple of a golden or orange-red variety which ripens late in the season.
– ORIGIN so named because it was discovered growing by the boundary wall of the Blenheim estate (see **BLENHEIM**[1]) in the 18th cent.

blenny ▶ **noun** (pl. **-ies**) a small spiny-finned marine fish with scaleless skin and a blunt head, typically living in shallow inshore or intertidal waters.
• Family Blenniidae: several genera, in particular *Blennius*.
■ used in names of other small fishes that resemble or are related to the true blennies, e.g. **eel blenny**.
– ORIGIN mid 18th cent.: from Latin *blennius*, from Greek *blennos* 'mucus' (because of its mucous coating).

blent poetic/literary past and past participle of **BLEND**.

bleomycin /ˌbliːəʊˈmʌɪsɪn/ ▶ **noun** [mass noun] Medicine an antibiotic used to treat Hodgkin's disease and other cancers.
• The drug is obtained from the bacterium *Streptomyces verticillus*.
– ORIGIN 1960s: an arbitrary alteration of earlier *phleomycin*, the name of a related antibiotic.

blepharitis /ˌblɛfəˈrʌɪtɪs/ ▶ **noun** [mass noun] Medicine inflammation of the eyelid.
– ORIGIN mid 19th cent.: from Greek *blepharon* 'eyelid' + **-ITIS**.

blepharoplasty /ˈblɛf(ə)rə(ʊ)ˌplasti/ ▶ **noun** [mass noun] Medicine surgical repair or reconstruction of an eyelid.
– ORIGIN mid 19th cent.: from Greek *blepharon* 'eyelid' + **-PLASTY**.

blepharospasm /ˈblɛf(ə)rəʊˌspaz(ə)m/ ▶ **noun** [mass noun] involuntary tight closure of the eyelids.
– ORIGIN late 19th cent.: from Greek *blepharon* 'eyelid' + **SPASM**.

Blériot /ˈblɛrɪəʊ, French blerjo/, Louis (1872–1936), French aviation pioneer. On 25 July 1909 he became the first to fly the English Channel (Calais to Dover), in a monoplane of his own design.

blesbok /ˈblɛsbɒk/ ▶ **noun** an antelope with a mainly reddish-brown coat and white face, found in south-western South Africa. It belongs to the same species as the bontebok.
• *Damaliscus dorcas phillipsi*, family Bovidae.
– ORIGIN early 19th cent.: from Afrikaans, from Dutch *bles* 'blaze' (because of the white mark on its forehead) + *bok* 'buck'.

bless ▶ **verb** [with obj.] (of a priest) pronounce words in a religious rite, to confer or invoke divine favour upon; ask God to look favourably on: *he blessed the dying man and anointed him.*
■ consecrate (something) by a religious rite, action, or spoken formula. ■ (especially in Christian church services) call (God) holy; praise (God). ■ (**bless someone with**) (of God or some notional higher power) endow (someone) with a particular cherished thing or attribute: *we have been blessed with a beautiful baby boy.* ■ express or feel gratitude to; thank: *she silently blessed the premonition which had made her pack her best dress.* ■ (**bless oneself**) archaic make the sign of the cross. ■ used in expressions of surprise, endearment, gratitude, etc.: *bless my soul, Alan, what are you doing?* | *Nurse Jones, bless her, had made a pot of tea.*
– PHRASES **bless you!** said to a person who has just sneezed. [ORIGIN: from the phrase (*may*) *God bless you*.] **not have a penny to bless oneself with** dated be completely impoverished. [ORIGIN: alluding to the cross on an old silver penny or to the practice of crossing a person's palm with silver for luck.]
– ORIGIN Old English *blēdsian*, *blētsian*, based on *blōd* 'blood' (i.e. originally perhaps 'mark or consecrate with blood'). The meaning was influenced by its being used to translate Latin *benedicere* 'to praise, worship', and later by association with **BLISS**.

blessed /ˈblɛsɪd, blɛst/ ▶ **adjective 1** made holy; consecrated: *the Blessed Sacrament.*
■ a title preceding the name of a dead person considered to have led a holy life, especially a person formally beatified by the Roman Catholic Church: *the Convent of the Blessed Agnes.* ■ endowed with divine favour and protection: *blessed are the meek.* ■ bringing pleasure or relief as a welcome contrast to what one has previously experienced: *he half stumbled out of the room up to his bed and blessed, blessed sleep.*
2 informal used in mild expressions of annoyance or exasperation: *he'll want to go and see his blessed allotment.*
▶ **plural noun** (**the Blessed**) those who live with God in heaven.
– DERIVATIVES **blessedly** adverb.

blessedness /ˈblɛsɪdnɪs/ ▶ **noun** [mass noun] the state of being blessed with divine favour.

Blessed Sacrament ▶ **noun** see **SACRAMENT**.

Blessed Virgin Mary, a title given to Mary, the mother of Jesus (see **MARY**[1]).

blessing ▶ **noun** God's favour and protection: *may God continue to give us his blessing.*
■ a prayer asking for such favour and protection: *a priest gave a blessing as the ship was launched.* ■ grace said before or after a meal. ■ a beneficial thing for which one is grateful; something that brings well-being: *great intelligence can be a curse as well as a blessing* | *it's a blessing we're alive.* ■ a person's sanction or support: *he gave the plan his blessing even before it was announced.*
– PHRASES **a blessing in disguise** an apparent misfortune that eventually has good results.

blest ▶ **adjective** archaic or literary term for **BLESSED**.

blether /ˈblɛðə/ ▶ **noun** chiefly Scottish another term for **BLATHER**.

bletherskate /ˈblɛðəskeɪt/ ▶ **noun** variant spelling of **BLATHERSKITE**.

blew past of **BLOW**[1] and **BLOW**[3].

blewit /ˈbluːɪt/ (also **blewits**) ▶ **noun** an edible European mushroom with a pale buff or lilac cap and a lilac stem.
• Genus *Lepista*, family Tricholomataceae, class Hymenomycetes: several species, including **common blewit** (*L. saeva*) and **wood blewit** (*L. nuda*).
– ORIGIN early 19th cent.: probably from **BLUE**[1].

Bligh /blʌɪ/, William (1754–1817), British naval officer, captain of HMS *Bounty*. In 1789 part of his crew, led by the first mate Fletcher Christian, mutinied and Bligh was set adrift in an open boat, arriving safely at Timor, nearly 6,400 km (4,000 miles) away, a few weeks later.

blight ▶ **noun** [mass noun] a plant disease, typically one caused by fungi such as mildews, rusts, and smuts: *the vines suffered blight and disease* | *potato blight.*
■ informal anything that causes a plant disease or interferes with the healthy growth of a plant. ■ [in sing.] a thing that spoils or damages something: *her remorse could be* ***a blight on*** *that happiness.* ■ [mass noun] an ugly or neglected urban area: *the depressing urban blight that lies to the south of the city.*
▶ **verb** [with obj.] (usu. **be blighted**) infect (plants or a planted area) with blight: *a peach tree blighted by leaf curl.*
■ spoil, harm, or destroy: *the scandal blighted the careers of several leading politicians* | [as adj. **blighted**] *his father's blighted ambitions.* ■ [usu. as adj. **blighted**] subject (an urban area) to neglect: *plans to establish enterprise zones in blighted areas.*
– ORIGIN mid 16th cent. (denoting inflammation of the skin): of unknown origin.

blighter ▶ **noun** [with adj.] Brit. informal a person who is regarded with contempt, irritation, or pity: *you little blighter!*
– ORIGIN early 19th cent.: from **BLIGHT** + **-ER**[1].

Blighty ▶ **noun** Brit. an informal and often affectionate term for Britain or England, chiefly as used by soldiers of the First and Second World Wars.
■ military slang a wound suffered by a soldier in the First World War which was sufficiently serious to merit being shipped home to Britain: *he had copped a Blighty and was on his way home.*
– ORIGIN first used by soldiers in the Indian army; Anglo-Indian alteration of Urdu *bilāyatī*, *wilāyatī* 'foreign, European', from Arabic *wilāyat*, *wilāya* 'dominion, district'.

blimey (also **cor blimey**) ▶ **exclamation** Brit. informal used to express one's surprise, excitement, or alarm.
– ORIGIN late 19th cent.: altered form of (*God*) *blind* (*or blame*) *me!*

blimp ▶ **noun 1** (also **Colonel Blimp**) Brit. a pompous, reactionary type of person: *you'll still find Colonel Blimps at local party level.*
2 informal a small airship or barrage balloon.
■ N. Amer. an obese person: *I could work out four hours a day and still end up a blimp.*
3 a soundproof cover for a cine camera.
– DERIVATIVES **blimpish** adjective.
– ORIGIN First World War (in sense 2): of uncertain origin. Sense 1 derives from the character invented by cartoonist David Low, used in anti-German or anti-government drawings before and during the Second World War.

blin /blɪn/ singular form of **BLINI**.

blind ▶ **adjective 1** unable to see because of injury, disease, or a congenital condition: *a blind man with a stick* | *he was blind in one eye* | [as plural noun **the blind**] *guide dogs for the blind.*
■ (of an action, especially a test or experiment) done without being able to see or without being in possession of certain information: *a blind tasting of eight wines.* ■ Aeronautics (of flying) using instruments only: *blind landings during foggy conditions.*
2 [predic.] lacking perception or discernment: *she was ignorant, but not stupid or blind.*
■ (**blind to**) unwilling or unable to appreciate or notice (a fact or situation which is apparent to others): *she was blind to the realities of her position.* ■ (of an action or state of mind) not controlled by reason or judgement: *a blind acceptance of conventional opinions* | *they left in blind panic.* ■ not governed by purpose: *moving purposelessly in a world of blind chance.*
3 concealed or closed, in particular:
■ (of a corner or bend in a road) impossible to see round: *two trucks collided on a blind curve in the road.* ■ (of a door or window) walled up. ■ closed at one end: *a blind pipe.* ■ (of a plant) without buds, eyes, or terminal flowers.
4 [attrib.] [with negative] informal not the slightest (used in emphatic expressions): *this declaration is not a blind bit of good to the workers.*
▶ **verb** [with obj.] **1** cause (someone) to be unable to see, permanently or temporarily: *the injury temporarily blinded him* | *eyes blinded with tears.*
■ (of rain) make (a window) difficult or impossible to see through.

b

2 (usu. **be blinded**) deprive (someone) of understanding, judgement, or perception: *Malik was blinded by his faith | somehow Clare and I were blinded to the truth.*
■(**blind someone with**) confuse or overawe someone with something they do not understand: *they try to blind you with science.*
3 [no obj., with adverbial of direction] Brit. informal, dated move very fast and dangerously: *I could see the bombs blinding along above the roof tops.*
▶**noun 1** an obstruction to sight or light, in particular:
■a screen for a window, especially one on a roller or made of slats: *she pulled down the blinds.* ■Brit. an awning over a shop window.
2 [in sing.] something designed to conceal one's real intentions: *he phoned again from his own home: that was just a blind for his wife.*
■N. Amer. a hide, as for example used by hunters.
3 Brit. informal, dated a heavy drinking bout: *he's off on a blind again.*
▶**adverb** without being able to see clearly: *he was the first pilot in history to fly blind | wines were tasted blind.*
■without having all the relevant information; unprepared: *he was going into the interview blind.* ■(of a stake in poker or brag) put up by a player before the cards dealt are seen.
– PHRASES **bake something blind** bake a pastry or flan case without a filling. **(as) blind as a bat** informal having very bad eyesight. **blind drunk** informal extremely drunk. **there's none so blind as those who will not see** proverb there's no point trying to reason with someone who does not want to listen to reason. **turn a blind eye** pretend not to notice. [ORIGIN: said to be in allusion to Nelson, who lifted a telescope to his blind eye at the Battle of Copenhagen (1801), thus not seeing the signal to 'discontinue the action'.] **when the blind lead the blind, both shall fall into a ditch** proverb those people without knowledge or experience should not try to guide or advise others in a similar position: *I didn't know anything about fighting and neither did my students—it was the blind leading the blind.*
– DERIVATIVES **blindness** noun.
– ORIGIN Old English, of Germanic origin; related to Dutch and German *blind*.

blind alley ▶**noun** a cul-de-sac.
■figurative a course of action leading nowhere.

blind coal ▶**noun** [mass noun] chiefly Scottish anthracite.

blind date ▶**noun** a social engagement with a person one has not previously met, designed to have a romantic or sexual aim.

blinder ▶**noun 1** Brit. informal an excellent performance in a game or race: *Marinello played a blinder in his first game.*
2 (**blinders**) N. Amer. blinkers on a horse's bridle.

blindfold ▶**verb** [with obj.] (often **be blindfolded**) deprive (someone) of sight by tying a piece of cloth around their head so as to cover their eyes.
▶**noun** a piece of cloth tied around the head to cover someone's eyes.
▶**adjective** poetic/literary wearing a blindfold.
■(of a game of chess) conducted without sight of board and pieces.
▶**adverb** with a blindfold covering the eyes: *the reporter was driven blindfold to meet the gangster.*
■done with great ease and confidence, as if it could have been done wearing a blindfold: *missing putts that he would normally hole blindfold.*
– ORIGIN mid 16th cent.: alteration, by association with **FOLD**[1], of *blindfeld*, past participle of obsolete *blindfell* 'strike blind, blindfold', from Old English *geblindfellan* (see **BLIND**, **FELL**[2]).

Blind Freddie (also **Blind Freddy**) ▶**noun** Austral. informal an imaginary person supposed to have little or no perception.
– ORIGIN 1940s: said to be from the name of a Sydney hawker.

blind gut ▶**noun** the caecum.

blinding ▶**noun** [mass noun] the process of covering a newly made road with grit to fill cracks.
■the grit used in such a process. ■a thin bed of concrete laid down over an area before the main mass of concrete is put in place.
▶**adjective** (of light) very bright and likely to dazzle or temporarily blind someone: *a massive explosion with a blinding flash of light.*
■(of a thing) temporarily obstructing a person's vision: *blinding rain.* ■figurative suddenly and overwhelmingly obvious: *in a blinding flash, everything fell into place | I woke up with the blinding realization that it was time to go.* ■figurative (of pain or an emotion) very intense: *I've got a blinding headache.* ■informal (of an action) remarkably skilful and exciting: *he denied Norwich victory with two blinding saves.*
– DERIVATIVES **blindingly** adverb [as submodifier] *the reason was blindingly obvious.*

blindly ▶**adverb** as if blind; without seeing or noticing: *she ran, blindly, as for her life.*
■without reasoning or questioning: *the government has blindly followed US policy.*

blind man's buff (US also **blind man's bluff**) ▶**noun** a game in which a blindfold player tries to catch others while being pushed about by them.
– ORIGIN early 17th cent.: from *buff* 'a blow', from Old French *bufe* (see **BUFFET**[2]).

blind pig (also **blind tiger**) ▶**noun** N. Amer. informal an illegal bar.
– ORIGIN late 19th cent.: from **BLIND** (with reference to its anonymous blank facade) + **PIG** (used as a disparaging term).

blind side ▶**noun** [in sing.] a direction in which a person has a poor view, typically of approaching danger.
■Rugby the side of the scrum opposite that on which the main line of the opponents' backs is ranged.
▶**verb** (**blindside**) [with obj.] N. Amer. hit or attack (someone) on their blind side.
■(usu. **be blindsided**) cause (someone) to be unable to perceive the truth of a situation.

blindsight ▶**noun** [mass noun] Medicine the ability to respond to visual stimuli without consciously perceiving them. This condition can occur after certain types of brain damage.

blind snake ▶**noun** a small burrowing insectivorous snake which lacks a distinct head and has very small inefficient eyes. Also called **WORM SNAKE**.
• Infraorder Scolecophidia: three families, in particular Typhlopidae, and several genera.

blind spot ▶**noun 1** Anatomy the point of entry of the optic nerve on the retina, insensitive to light.
2 an area where a person's view is obstructed.
■an area in which a person lacks understanding or impartiality: *Ed had a blind spot where these ethical issues were concerned.*
3 Telecommunications a point within the normal range of a transmitter where there is unusually weak reception.

blind stamping (also **blind tooling**) ▶**noun** [mass noun] the impressing of text or a design on a book cover without the use of colour or gold leaf.

blind stitch ▶**noun** [mass noun] a sewing stitch producing stitches visible on one side only.
▶**verb** (**blind-stitch**) [with obj.] sew (something) using such a stitch.

blind tiger ▶**noun** another term for **BLIND PIG**.

blind trust ▶**noun** chiefly N. Amer. a trust independently administering the private business interests of a person in public office to prevent conflict of interest.

blindworm ▶**noun** another term for **SLOW-WORM**.

blini /ˈblɪni, ˈbliːniː/ (also **bliny** or **blinis**) ▶**plural noun** (sing. **blin**) pancakes made from buckwheat flour and served with sour cream.
– ORIGIN Russian (plural).

blink ▶**verb** [no obj.] **1** shut and open the eyes quickly: *she blinked, momentarily blinded |* [with obj.] *he blinked his eyes nervously.*
■[with obj. and adverbial of direction] clear (dust or tears) from the eyes by this action: *she blinked away her tears.* ■[with obj.] (**blink something back**) try to control or prevent tears by such an action. ■(**blink at**) look at (someone or something) with one's eyes opening and shutting, typically to register surprise or bewilderment. ■[usu. with negative] (**blink at**) figurative react to (something) with surprise or disapproval: *he doesn't blink at the unsavoury aspects of his subject.*
2 (of a light or light source) shine unsteadily or intermittently: *the car's right-hand indicator was blinking.*
▶**noun** [usu. in sing.] **1** an act of shutting and opening the eyes very quickly: *he was observing her every blink.*
■figurative a moment's hesitation: *Feargal would have given her all this without a blink.*
2 a momentary gleam of light.
– PHRASES **in the blink of an eye** (or **in a blink**) informal very quickly. **not blink an eye** show no reaction. **on the blink** informal (of a machine) not working properly; out of order: *the computer's on the blink.*
– ORIGIN Middle English: from *blenk*, Scots variant of **BLENCH**[1], reinforced by Middle Dutch *blinken* 'to shine'. Early senses included 'deceive', 'flinch' (compare with **BLENCH**), and also 'open the eyes after sleep': hence sense 1 (mid 16th cent.).

blinker ▶**noun 1** (**blinkers**) chiefly Brit. a pair of small leather screens attached to a horse's bridle to prevent it seeing sideways and behind and being startled.
■figurative something which prevents someone from gaining a full understanding of a situation: *we are having a fresh look at ourselves without blinkers.*
2 (usu. **blinkers**) a vehicle indicator or other device that gives out an intermittent light.
▶**verb** [with obj.] (often **be blinkered**) put blinkers on (a horse) to prevent it from looking to the side and being startled during a race.
■figurative cause (someone) to have a narrow or limited outlook on a situation.

blinkered ▶**adjective** (of a horse) wearing blinkers.
■figurative having or showing a narrow or limited outlook: *a blinkered attitude.*

blinking ▶**adjective** [attrib.] Brit. informal used to express annoyance: *computers can be a blinking nuisance to operators |* [as submodifier] *I'll sign off however I blinking well like.*

blinks (also **water blinks**) ▶**plural noun** [usu. treated as sing.] a small fleshy plant with tiny white flowers, which grows in damp and wet habitats in temperate regions. The leaves are sometimes eaten as salad.
• *Montia fontana*, family Portulacaceae.
– ORIGIN late 17th cent.: from **BLINK** in the sense 'momentary gleam of light' (referring to the small flowers).

blintze /blɪn(t)s/ ▶**noun** a thin rolled pancake filled with cheese or fruit and then fried or baked.
– ORIGIN from Yiddish *blintse*, from Russian *blinets* 'little pancake'; compare with **BLINI**.

bliny ▶**plural noun** variant spelling of **BLINI**.

blip ▶**noun 1** an unexpected, minor, and typically temporary deviation from a general trend: *the Chancellor dismissed rising inflation as a temporary blip.*
2 a very short high-pitched sound made by an electronic device.
■a small flashing point of light on a radar screen representing an object, often accompanied by such a sound.
▶**verb** (**blipped**, **blipping**) **1** [no obj.] (of an electronic device) make a very short high-pitched sound or succession of sounds.
2 [with obj.] open (the throttle of a motor vehicle) momentarily.
– ORIGIN late 19th cent. (denoting a sudden rap or tap): imitative; the noun sense 'unexpected deviation' dates from the 1970s.

Bliss, Sir Arthur (Edward Drummond) (1891–1975), English composer. He moved from the influence of Stravinsky, in works such as *A Colour Symphony* (1922), to a rich style closer to Elgar, as in his choral symphony *Morning Heroes* (1930).

bliss ▶**noun** [mass noun] perfect happiness; great joy: *she gave a sigh of bliss.*
■an experience or situation providing such happiness: *the steam room was bliss.* ■a state of spiritual blessedness, typically that reached after death.
– ORIGIN Old English *blīths*, *bliss*, of Germanic origin; related to **BLITHE**.
▶**bliss out** [often as adj. **blissed out**] informal reach a state of perfect happiness, especially so as to be oblivious of everything else: *blissed-out hippies.*

blissful ▶**adjective** extremely happy; full of joy: *a blissful couple holding a baby.*
■providing perfect happiness or great joy: *the blissful caress of cool cotton sheets.*
– PHRASES **blissful ignorance** complete unawareness of something important or unpleasant.
– DERIVATIVES **blissfully** adverb [as submodifier] *she was blissfully happy*, **blissfulness** noun.

blister ▶**noun 1** a small bubble on the skin filled with serum and caused by friction, burning, or other damage.
■a similar swelling, filled with air or fluid, on the surface of a plant, heated metal, painted wood, or other object. ■Medicine, chiefly historical a preparation applied to the skin to form a blister.

2 Brit. informal, dated an annoying person: *the child is a disgusting little blister.*
▶ **verb** [no obj.] form swellings filled with air or fluid on the surface of something: *the surface of the door began to blister* | [as adj. **blistered**] *he had blistered feet.*
■ [with obj.] cause blisters to form on the surface of: *a caustic liquid which blisters the skin.*
– ORIGIN Middle English: perhaps from Old French *blestre* 'swelling, pimple'.

blister beetle ▶ **noun** a beetle that secretes a substance that causes blisters when it is alarmed. The larvae are typically parasites of other insects.
● *Lytta* and other genera, family Meloidae: several species.

blister copper ▶ **noun** [mass noun] partly purified copper with a blistered surface formed during smelting.

blister gas ▶ **noun** [mass noun] poison gas which causes blisters on and intense irritation to the skin.

blistering ▶ **adjective** (of heat) intense: *the blistering heat of the desert.*
■ figurative (of criticism) expressed with great vehemence: *a blistering attack on the government's transport policy.* ■ (in sports journalism) extremely fast, forceful, or impressive: *Burke set a blistering pace.*

blister pack ▶ **noun** another term for BUBBLE PACK.

blithe ▶ **adjective** showing a casual and cheerful indifference considered to be callous or improper: *a blithe disregard for the rules of the road.*
■ poetic/literary happy or joyous: *a blithe seaside comedy.*
– DERIVATIVES **blithely** adverb, **blitheness** noun, **blithesome** /-s(ə)m/ adjective (poetic/literary).
– ORIGIN Old English *blīthe*, of Germanic origin; related to Dutch *blijde*, also to BLISS.

blither /ˈblɪðə/ ▶ **verb** & **noun** variant spelling of BLATHER.

blithering ▶ **adjective** [attrib.] informal complete; utter (used to express annoyance or contempt): *a blithering idiot.*
– ORIGIN late 19th cent.: from BLITHER + -ING².

BLitt ▶ **abbreviation** for Bachelor of Letters.
– ORIGIN from Latin *Baccalaureus Litterarum*.

blitz ▶ **noun** an intensive or sudden military attack.
■ (**the Blitz**) the German air raids on Britain in 1940–1. ■ informal a sudden, energetic, and concerted effort to deal with something: *the annual booze blitz by the Health Promotion Agency.* ■ another term for LIGHTNING CHESS.
▶ **verb** [with obj.] (often **be blitzed**) attack or seriously damage (a place or building) in a blitz: *news came that Rotterdam had been blitzed* | figurative *City blitzed United with a three-goal burst.*
– ORIGIN abbreviation of BLITZKRIEG.

blitzkrieg /ˈblɪtskriːɡ/ ▶ **noun** an intense military campaign intended to bring about a swift victory.
– ORIGIN Second World War: from German, literally 'lightning war'.

Blixen, Karen (Christentze), Baroness Blixen-Finecke (1885–1962), Danish novelist and short-story writer; born *Karen Dinesen*; also known by the pseudonym of **Isak Dinesen**. She is best known for *Seven Gothic Tales* (1934) and her autobiography *Out of Africa* (1937), which she wrote after living in Kenya from 1914 to 1931.

blizzard ▶ **noun** a severe snowstorm with high winds.
■ figurative a large or overwhelming number or amount of something, typically arriving suddenly: *a blizzard of forms.*
– ORIGIN early 19th cent. (originally US, denoting a violent blow): of unknown origin.

BL Lac object ▶ **noun** Astronomy a type of remote elliptical galaxy with a very compact starlike nucleus, remarkable for its considerable short-term variations in brightness and radio emissions.
– ORIGIN *BL Lac*, short for *BL Lacertae*, the designation of the first such object discovered (originally thought to be a variable star).

bloat¹ ▶ **verb** [with obj.] cause to swell with fluid or gas: *the fungus has bloated their abdomens.*
■ [no obj.] become swollen with fluid or gas: [as noun **bloating**] *she suffered from abdominal bloating.*
▶ **noun** [mass noun] a disease of livestock characterized by an accumulation of gas in the stomach.
– ORIGIN late 17th cent. (in the sense 'cause to swell'): from obsolete *bloat* 'swollen, soft', perhaps from Old Norse *blautr* 'soft, flabby'. The noun sense dates from the late 19th cent.

bloat² ▶ **verb** [with obj.] cure (a herring) by salting and smoking it lightly.
– ORIGIN late 16th cent.: related to the adjective *bloat* used in the compound *bloat herring* 'bloater' from the late 16th to mid 17th cent.; of obscure origin.

bloated ▶ **adjective** (of part of the body) swollen with fluid or gas: *he had a bloated, unshaven face.*
■ figurative excessive in size or amount: *the company trimmed its bloated labour force.* ■ figurative (of a person) excessively wealthy and pampered: *the bloated captains of industry.*

bloater ▶ **noun** a herring cured by salting and light smoking.

bloatware ▶ **noun** [mass noun] Computing, informal software whose usefulness is reduced because of the excessive memory it requires.

blob ▶ **noun** a drop of a thick liquid or viscous substance: *blobs of paint.*
■ a spot of colour: *the town is much more than a brown blob on the map.* ■ an indeterminate roundish mass or shape: *a big pink blob of a face was at the window.* ■ informal a score of 0 in a game.
▶ **verb** [with obj.] (often **be blobbed**) put small drops of thick liquid or spots of colour on: *her nose was blobbed with paint.*
– DERIVATIVES **blobby** adjective.
– ORIGIN late Middle English (denoting a bubble): perhaps symbolic of a drop of liquid; compare with BLOTCH, BLUBBER¹, and PLOP.

bloc ▶ **noun** a group of countries or political parties with common interests who have formed an alliance: *the Soviet bloc* | *a parliamentary bloc.*
– ORIGIN early 20th cent.: from French, literally 'block'.

Bloch /blɒx/, Ernest (1880–1959), Swiss-born American composer, of Jewish descent. His work reflects the influence of the late 19th-century romanticism of Liszt and Richard Strauss and Jewish musical forms. Notable works: the *Israel Symphony* (1912–16) and *Solomon* (1916).

block ▶ **noun** **1** a large solid piece of hard material, especially rock, stone, or wood, typically with flat surfaces on each side: *a block of marble.*
■ a sturdy flat-topped piece of wood used as a work surface, typically for chopping food. ■ a commercially packaged rectangular portion of solid food, typically butter, ice cream, or chocolate: *a family block of ice cream.* ■ (usu. **blocks**) a starting block: *Jackson jetted out of his blocks.* ■ Printing a piece of wood or metal engraved for printing on paper or fabric. ■ (also **cylinder block** or **engine block**) a large metal moulding containing the cylinders of an internal-combustion engine. ■ a head-shaped mould used for shaping hats or wigs.
2 chiefly Brit. a large single building subdivided into separate rooms, flats, or offices: *an apartment block.*
■ [with modifier] a building, especially part of a complex, used for a particular purpose: *a shower block.* ■ a group of buildings bounded by four streets: *she went for a run round the block.* ■ chiefly N. Amer. any urban or suburban area so bounded: *ours was the ugliest house on the block.* ■ chiefly N. Amer. the length of one side of such an area, especially as a measure of distance: *he lives a few blocks away from the museum.*
3 a large quantity or allocation of things regarded as a unit: *a block of shares* | *final examinations will be taken in a block at the end of the course* | [as modifier] *a block booking.*
■ chiefly Brit. a set of sheets of paper glued along one edge, used for drawing or writing on: *a sketching block.* ■ Computing a large piece of text processed as a unit.
4 an obstacle to the normal progress or functioning of something: *substantial demands for time off may constitute a block to career advancement* | *an emotional block.*
■ an act of blocking someone or something: *Marshall's shot drew a fine block from the goalkeeper.* ■ a chock for stopping the motion of a wheel. ■ (also **blockhole**) Cricket the spot on which a batsman rests the end of the bat while waiting to receive a ball.
5 a flat area of something, especially a solid area of colour: *cover the eyelid with a neutral block of colour.*
■ Austral./NZ an area of land, in particular a tract offered to an individual settler by a government. ■ Austral./NZ an urban or suburban building plot.
6 a pulley or system of pulleys mounted in a case.
▶ **verb** [with obj.] **1** make the movement or flow in (a passage, pipe, road, etc.) difficult or impossible: *block up the holes with sticky tape* | *the narrow roads were blocked by cars* | [as adj. **blocked**] *a blocked nose.*
■ put an obstacle in the way of (something proposed or

attempted): *he stood up, blocking her escape* | *the government tried to block an agreement on farm subsidies.*
■ restrict the use or conversion of (currency or any other asset). ■ American Football impede the progress of (a tackler) with one's body. ■ (in martial arts or soccer) stop (a blow or ball) from finding its mark: *Pears did well to block Soloman's shot.* ■ Cricket stop (a ball) with the bat defensively. ■ Bridge play in such a way that opponents are prevented from establishing (a long suit).
2 impress text or a design on (a book cover).
3 shape or reshape (a hat) using a wooden mould.
– PHRASES **the new kid on the block** informal a newcomer to a particular place or sphere of activity, especially one who has yet to prove themselves. **on the (auction) block** chiefly N. Amer. for sale at auction: *the original first manuscript for Ravel's Bolero goes on the block today.* **put** (or **lay**) **one's head** (or **neck**) **on the block** informal put one's standing or reputation at risk by proceeding with a particular course of action. [ORIGIN: with reference to an executioner's block.]
– ORIGIN Middle English (denoting a log or tree stump): from Old French *bloc* (noun), *bloquer* (verb), from Middle Dutch *blok*, of unknown ultimate origin.
▶ **block something in 1** paint something with solid areas of colour. ■ add something in a unit: *it's a good idea to block in regular periods of exercise.* ■ mark something out roughly. **2** park one's car in such a way as to prevent another car from moving away: *he blocked in Vera's Mini.*
block something out 1 stop something, typically light or noise, from reaching somewhere: *you're blocking out my sun.* ■ figurative exclude something unpleasant from one's thoughts or memory. **2** mark or sketch something out roughly.

blockade ▶ **noun** an act of sealing off a place to prevent goods or people from entering or leaving: *they voted to lift a blockade of major railway junctions.*
■ a person or thing that prevents access or progress: *trucks stuck in the lorry blockade.* ■ an obstruction of a physiological or mental function, especially of a biochemical receptor.
▶ **verb** [with obj.] seal off (a place) to prevent goods or people from entering or leaving.
– PHRASES **run a blockade** (of a ship) manage to enter or leave a blockaded port.
– DERIVATIVES **blockader** noun.
– ORIGIN late 17th cent.: from BLOCK + -ADE¹, probably influenced by *ambuscade*.

blockage ▶ **noun** an obstruction which makes movement or flow difficult or impossible: *a blockage in the pipes* | [mass noun] *the pumps are prone to blockage.*

block and tackle ▶ **noun** a lifting mechanism consisting of ropes, a pulley block, and a hook.

blockboard ▶ **noun** [mass noun] Brit. a building material consisting of a core of wooden strips between two layers of plywood.

blockbuster ▶ **noun** informal a thing of great power or size, in particular a film, book, or other product that is a great commercial success: [as modifier] *a blockbuster film.*
– ORIGIN 1940s (denoting a huge aerial bomb): from BLOCK + BUSTER.

blockbusting informal ▶ **adjective** very successful commercially: *his blockbusting novel.*
▶ **noun** [mass noun] N. Amer. the practice of persuading owners to sell property cheaply because of the fear of people of another race or class moving into the neighbourhood, and then profiting by reselling at a higher price.

block capitals ▶ **plural noun** plain capital letters.

block diagram ▶ **noun** a diagram showing in schematic form the general arrangement of parts or components of a complex system or process, such as an industrial apparatus or an electronic circuit.

blocker ▶ **noun** a person or thing that blocks something, in particular:
■ Cricket a habitually defensive batsman. ■ American Football a player whose task it is to block for the ball-carrier. ■ a substance which prevents or inhibits a given physiological function.

block grant ▶ **noun** a grant from central government which a local authority can allocate to a wide range of services.

blockhead ▶ **noun** informal a very stupid person.
– DERIVATIVES **blockheaded** adjective.

block heater ▶ **noun 1** Brit. a storage heater.

b

2 N. Amer. a device for heating the engine block of a vehicle.

blockhole ▶ **noun** see **BLOCK** (sense 4).

blockhouse ▶ **noun** a reinforced concrete shelter used as an observation point.
■ historical a one-storeyed timber building with loopholes, used as a fort. ■ US a house made of squared logs.

blocking ▶ **noun** [mass noun] **1** the action or process of obstructing movement, progress, or activity, in particular:
■ obstructing or impeding the actions of an opponent in a game, especially (in ball sports) one who does not have control of the ball. ■ Psychiatry the sudden halting of the flow of thought or speech, as a symptom of schizophrenia or other mental disorder. ■ failure to recall or consider an unpleasant memory or train of thought.
2 the grouping or treatment of things (e.g. items of data or shades of colour) in blocks.
■ the physical arrangement of actors on a stage or film set.

blockish ▶ **adjective** **1** big, bulky, or crude in form or appearance: *his blockish architecture is ugly if functional.*
2 unintelligent and stupid.

block letters ▶ **plural noun** another term for **BLOCK CAPITALS**.

block mountain ▶ **noun** Geology a mountain formed by natural faults in the earth's crust.

block plane ▶ **noun** a carpenter's plane with a blade set at an acute angle, used especially for planing across the end grain of wood.

block release ▶ **noun** [mass noun] Brit. a system of allowing employees the whole of a stated period off work for education.

blockship ▶ **noun** a ship which is moored or grounded in a channel in order to block it, for purposes of war or to provide shelter.

block system ▶ **noun** a system of railway signalling which divides the track into sections and allows no train to enter a section that is not completely clear.

block vote ▶ **noun** Brit. a vote proportional in power to the number of people a delegate represents, used particularly at a trade-union conference.

blocky ▶ **adjective** of the nature of or resembling a block or blocks: *blocky granite.*

Bloemfontein /ˈbluːmfɒnˌteɪn, ˈblʊm-/ the capital of Free State province and judicial capital of South Africa; pop. 300,150 (1991).

bloke ▶ **noun** Brit. informal a man: *he's a nice bloke.*
– ORIGIN mid 19th cent.: from Shelta.

blokeish (also **blokish**) ▶ **adjective** Brit. informal indulging in or relating to stereotypically male behaviour and interests.
– DERIVATIVES **blokeishness** noun.

blokey ▶ **adjective** another term for **BLOKEISH**.

blonde ▶ **adjective** (also **blond**) (chiefly of hair) fair or pale yellow: *her long blonde hair | I had my hair dyed blonde.*
■ (of a person) having hair of a fair or pale yellow colour: *a tall blonde woman.* ■ (of a person) having fair hair and a light complexion (especially when regarded as a racial characteristic).
▶ **noun** a woman with fair or yellow hair.
■ [mass noun] the colour of blonde hair.
– DERIVATIVES **blondish** adjective, **blondness** noun.
– ORIGIN late 17th cent. (earlier as *blond*): from French, feminine of *blond*.

> **USAGE** The alternative spellings **blonde** and **blond** correspond to the feminine and masculine forms in French, but in English the distinction is not always made, as English does not have such distinctions of grammatical gender. Thus, ***blond** woman* or ***blonde** woman*; ***blond** man* or ***blonde** man* are all used. The word is undoubtedly more commonly used of women, though, and in the noun the spelling is invariably **blonde**.

Blondin /ˈblɒndɪn, French blɔ̃dɛ̃/, Charles (1824–97), French acrobat; born *Jean-François Gravelet*. He is famous for walking across a tightrope suspended over Niagara Falls on several occasions.

Blood /blʌd/ ▶ **noun** (pl. same or **Bloods**) a member of a North American Indian people belonging to the Blackfoot Confederacy.

blood ▶ **noun** [mass noun] **1** the red liquid that circulates in the arteries and veins of humans and other vertebrate animals, carrying oxygen to and carbon dioxide from the tissues of the body: *drops of blood.*
■ an internal bodily fluid, not necessarily red, which performs a similar function in invertebrates. ■ figurative violence involving bloodshed: *a commando operation full of blood and danger.* ■ figurative a person's downfall or punishment, typically as retribution: *the press is baying for blood.*

> Blood consists of a mildly alkaline aqueous fluid (plasma) containing red cells (erythrocytes), white cells (leucocytes), and platelets; it is red when oxygenated and purple when deoxygenated. Red blood cells carry the protein haemoglobin, which gives blood its colour and can combine with oxygen, thus enabling the blood to carry oxygen from the lungs to the tissues. White blood cells protect the body against the invasion of foreign agents (e.g. bacteria). Platelets and other factors present in plasma are concerned in the clotting of blood, preventing haemorrhage. In medieval science and medicine, blood was regarded as one of the four bodily humours, believed to be associated with a confident and optimistic temperament.

2 figurative fiery or passionate temperament: *a ritual that fires up his blood.*
3 [with modifier] family background; descent or lineage: *she must have Irish blood in her.*
■ [count noun] [in combination] a person of specified descent: *a mixed-blood.* ■ [count noun] US informal a fellow black person.
4 [count noun] dated, chiefly Brit. a fashionable and dashing young man: *a group of young bloods.*
▶ **verb** [with obj.] initiate (someone) in a particular activity: *clubs are too slow in blooding young players.*
■ (in hunting) smear the face of (a novice) with the blood of the kill. ■ (in hunting) give (a hound) a first taste of blood.
– PHRASES **be like getting blood out of** (or **from**) **a stone** (N. Amer. also **turnip**) be extremely difficult (said in reference to obtaining something from someone): *getting a story out of her is like getting blood out of a stone!* **blood and guts** informal violence and bloodshed, especially in fiction. **blood and thunder** informal unrestrained and violent action or behaviour, especially in sport or fiction. **blood is thicker than water** proverb family relationships and loyalties are the strongest and most important ones. **one's blood is up** one is in a fighting mood. **blood, sweat, and tears** extremely hard work; unstinting effort. **blood will tell** proverb family characteristics cannot be concealed. **first blood** **1** the first shedding of blood, especially in a boxing match or formerly in duelling with swords. **2** the first point or advantage gained in a contest: *King drew first blood when he took the opening set.* **give blood** allow blood to be removed medically from one's body in order to be stored for use in transfusions. **have blood on one's hands** be responsible for someone's death. **in one's blood** ingrained in or fundamental to one's character: *racing is in his blood.* **make someone's blood boil** informal infuriate someone. **make someone's blood run cold** horrify someone. **new** (or **fresh**) **blood** new members admitted to a group, especially as an invigorating force. **of the blood** (**royal**) poetic/literary royal. **out for** (**someone's**) **blood** set on getting revenge. **taste blood** achieve an early success that stimulates further efforts: *the speculators have tasted blood and could force a devaluation of the franc.* **young blood** a younger member or members of a group, especially as an invigorating force.
– ORIGIN Old English *blōd*, of Germanic origin; related to German *Blut* and Dutch *bloed*.

blood bank ▶ **noun** a place where supplies of blood or plasma for transfusion are stored.

bloodbath ▶ **noun** an event or situation in which many people are killed in an extremely violent manner.

blood boosting ▶ **noun** another term for **BLOOD DOPING**.

blood-borne ▶ **adjective** (typically of a disease or pathogen) carried by the blood.

blood brother ▶ **noun** a man who has sworn to treat another man as a brother, typically by a ceremonial mingling of blood.

blood cell ▶ **noun** any of the kinds of cell normally found circulating in the blood.

blood count ▶ **noun** a determination of the number of corpuscles in a specific volume of blood.
■ the number found in such a procedure: *a low blood count.*

blood-curdling ▶ **adjective** causing or expressing terror or horror: *a blood-curdling scream.*

blood donor ▶ **noun** a person who gives blood for transfusion.

blood doping ▶ **noun** [mass noun] the injection of oxygenated blood into an athlete before an event in an (illegal) attempt to enhance athletic performance.

blooded ▶ **adjective** [usu. in combination] having blood or a temperament of a specified kind: *thin-blooded.*
■ chiefly N. Amer. (of horses or cattle) of good pedigree: *a blooded stallion.*

blood feud ▶ **noun** a lengthy conflict between families involving a cycle of retaliatory killings.

bloodfin ▶ **noun** a small South American freshwater fish that is silvery-yellow with bright red fins, popular in aquaria.
• *Aphyocharax rubripinnis*, family Characidae.

blood fluke ▶ **noun** another term for **SCHISTOSOME**.

blood group ▶ **noun** any of the various types of human blood whose antigen characteristics determine compatibility in transfusion. The best-known blood groups are those of the ABO system.

blood heat ▶ **noun** [mass noun] the normal body temperature of a healthy human being, about 37 °C or 98.4 °F.

blood horse ▶ **noun** dated a thoroughbred horse.

bloodhound ▶ **noun** a large hound of a breed with a very keen sense of smell, used in tracking.

blood knot ▶ **noun** a type of knot used by anglers to join two fishing lines.

bloodless ▶ **adjective** **1** (of a revolution or conflict) without violence or killing: *a bloodless coup.*
2 (of the skin or a part of the body) drained of colour: *his bloodless lips.*
■ (of a person) cold or ruthless. ■ lacking in vitality; feeble: *a bloodless chorus.*
– DERIVATIVES **bloodlessly** adverb, **bloodlessness** noun.

bloodletting ▶ **noun** [mass noun] chiefly historical the surgical removal of some of a patient's blood for therapeutic purposes.
■ the violent killing and wounding of people during a war or conflict: *gang members have halted their internecine bloodletting.* ■ bitter division and quarrelling within an organization.

bloodline ▶ **noun** an animal's set of ancestors or pedigree, especially as considered with regard to the desirable characteristics bred into it.
■ a set of ancestors or line of descent of a person, especially an important one.

bloodlust ▶ **noun** [mass noun] uncontrollable desire to kill or maim others.

blood meal ▶ **noun** [mass noun] dried blood used for feeding animals and as a fertilizer.

blood money ▶ **noun** [mass noun] money paid in compensation to the family of someone who has been killed.
■ money paid to a hired killer. ■ money paid for information about a killer or killing.

blood orange ▶ **noun** an orange of a variety with red or red-streaked flesh.

blood platelet ▶ **noun** see **PLATELET**.

blood poisoning ▶ **noun** [mass noun] the presence of micro-organisms or their toxins in the blood, causing a diseased state; septicaemia.

blood pressure ▶ **noun** [mass noun] the pressure of the blood in the circulatory system, often measured for diagnosis since it is closely related to the force and rate of the heartbeat and the diameter and elasticity of the arterial walls.

blood pudding (also **blood sausage**) ▶ **noun** [mass noun] black pudding.

blood-red ▶ **adjective** of the deep red colour of blood.
▶ **noun** [mass noun] a deep red.

blood relation (also **blood relative**) ▶ **noun** a person who is related to another by birth rather than by marriage.

bloodroot ▶ **noun** **1** a North American plant of the poppy family, which has white flowers and fleshy underground rhizomes which exude red sap when cut.
• *Sanguinaria canadensis*, family Papaveraceae.
2 a lily-like Australian plant with a red rhizome which is roasted and eaten by some Aboriginals.

● *Haemodorum coccineum*, family Haemodoraceae.

blood sausage ▶ noun another term for **BLOOD PUDDING**.

bloodshed ▶ noun [mass noun] the killing or wounding of people, typically on a large scale during a conflict.

bloodshot ▶ adjective (of the eyes) inflamed or tinged with blood, typically as a result of tiredness.

blood sport ▶ noun (usu. **blood sports**) a sport involving the hunting, wounding, or killing of animals.

bloodstain ▶ noun a mark or discoloration on fabric or a surface caused by blood.

bloodstained ▶ adjective marked or covered with blood.

bloodstock ▶ noun [treated as sing. or pl.] thoroughbred horses considered collectively.

bloodstone ▶ noun [mass noun] a type of green chalcedony spotted or streaked with red, used as a gemstone.

bloodstream ▶ noun [in sing.] the blood circulating through the body of a person or animal.

bloodsucker ▶ noun **1** an animal or insect that sucks blood, especially a leech or a mosquito.
2 a long-tailed arboreal Asian lizard which carries its head in a raised position. The head and shoulders of the male become bright red when it is excited.
● *Calotes versicolor*, family Agamidae.
3 informal a person who extorts money or otherwise lives off other people.
– DERIVATIVES **bloodsucking** adjective.

blood sugar ▶ noun [mass noun] the concentration of glucose in the blood.

blood test ▶ noun a scientific examination of a sample of blood, typically for the diagnosis of illness or for the detection and measurement of drugs or other substances.

bloodthirsty ▶ adjective (**bloodthirstier, bloodthirstiest**) having or showing a desire to kill and maim, typically on a large scale: *a bloodthirsty dictator.*
■ (of a story or film) containing or depicting much violence.
– DERIVATIVES **bloodthirstily** adverb, **bloodthirstiness** noun.

blood transfusion ▶ noun an injection of a volume of blood, previously taken from a healthy person, into a patient.

blood vessel ▶ noun a tubular structure carrying blood through the tissues and organs; a vein, artery, or capillary.

bloodwood ▶ noun any of a number of hardwood trees with deep red timber, in particular:
● an Australian gum tree (genus *Eucalyptus*, family Myrtaceae, in particular *E. gummifera*). ● a tree of the Old World tropics (genus *Pterocarpus*, family Leguminosae), including kiaat.

bloodworm ▶ noun **1** the bright red aquatic larva of a non-biting midge, the blood of which contains haemoglobin that allows it to live in poorly oxygenated water.
● Genus *Chironomus*, family Chironomidae.
2 another term for **TUBIFEX**.

bloody¹ ▶ adjective (**bloodier, bloodiest**) **1** covered, smeared, or running with blood: *a bloody body.*
■ composed of or resembling blood: *a bloody discharge.*
2 involving or characterized by bloodshed or cruelty: *a bloody coup* | *the bloody tyrannies of Europe.*
▶ verb (**-ies, -ied**) [with obj.] (often **be bloodied**) cover or stain with blood.
– PHRASES **bloody** (or **bloodied**) **but unbowed** proud of what one has achieved despite having suffered great difficulties or losses.
– DERIVATIVES **bloodily** adverb, **bloodiness** noun.
– ORIGIN Old English *blōdig* (see **BLOOD, -Y¹**).

bloody² ▶ adjective informal, chiefly Brit. **1** [attrib.] used to express anger, annoyance, or shock, or simply for emphasis: *you took your bloody time* | [as exclamation] *bloody Hell!—what was that?* | [as submodifier] *it's bloody cold outside.*
2 dated unpleasant or perverse: *don't be too bloody to poor Nigel.*
– ORIGIN mid 17th cent.: from **BLOODY¹**. The use of *bloody* to add emphasis to an expression is of uncertain origin, but is thought to have a connection with the 'bloods' (aristocratic rowdies) of the late 17th and early 18th centuries; hence the phrase *bloody drunk* (= as drunk as a blood) meant

'very drunk indeed'. After the mid 18th cent. until quite recently *bloody* used as a swear word was regarded as unprintable, probably from the mistaken belief that it implied a blasphemous reference to the blood of Christ, or that the word was an alteration of 'by Our Lady'; hence a widespread caution in using the term even in phrases such as *bloody battle* merely referring to bloodshed.

Bloody Assizes the trials of the supporters of the Duke of Monmouth after their defeat at the Battle of Sedgemoor, held in SW England in 1685. The government's representative, Judge Jeffreys, sentenced several hundred rebels to death and about 1,000 others to transportation to America as plantation slaves.

bloody hand ▶ noun Heraldry another term for **RED HAND**.

Bloody Mary¹ the nickname of Mary I of England (see **MARY²**).

Bloody Mary² ▶ noun (pl. **Bloody Marys**) a drink consisting of vodka and tomato juice.

bloody-minded ▶ adjective Brit. informal deliberately uncooperative.
– DERIVATIVES **bloody-mindedly** adverb, **bloody-mindedness** noun.

bloody-nosed beetle ▶ noun a large black leaf beetle which exudes a red liquid from its mouth and leg joints when disturbed.
● Genus *Timarcha*, family Chrysomelidae, in particular the common *T. tenebricosa.*

Bloody Sunday 1 (in Northern Ireland) 30 January 1972, when British troops shot dead thirteen marchers in Londonderry who were protesting against the government's policy of internment.
2 (in Britain) 13 November 1887, when police violently broke up a socialist demonstration in Trafalgar Square, London against the British government's Irish policy.
3 (in Russia) 9 January 1905 (22 January in the New Style calendar), when troops attacked and killed hundreds of unarmed workers who had gathered in St Petersburg to present a petition to the tsar.

blooey /ˈbluːi/ (also **blooie**) US informal ▶ adverb & adjective awry; amiss: [as adv.] *the ignition switch went blooey* | [as adj.] *a blooey television.*
▶ exclamation used to convey that something has happened in an abrupt way: *Blooey! He shot himself dead.*
– ORIGIN 1920s: of unknown origin.

bloom¹ ▶ noun **1** a flower, especially one cultivated for its beauty: *an exotic bloom.*
■ [mass noun] the state or period of flowering: *the apple trees were in bloom.* ■ [mass noun] the state or period of greatest beauty, freshness, or vigour: *a young girl, still in the bloom of youth.* ■ [in sing.] a youthful or healthy glow in a person's complexion: *her face had lost its usual bloom.* ■ [mass noun] a full bright sound, especially in a musical recording: *the remastering has lost some of the bloom of the strings.*
2 a delicate powdery surface deposit on certain fresh fruits, leaves, or stems.
■ [mass noun] a greyish-white appearance on chocolate caused by cocoa butter rising to the surface. ■ short for **ALGAL BLOOM**.
▶ verb **1** [no obj.] produce flowers; be in flower: *a chalk pit where cowslips bloomed.*
■ come into or be in full beauty or health; flourish: *the children had bloomed in the soft Devonshire air.* ■ (of fire, colour, or light) become radiant and glowing: *colour bloomed in her cheeks.*
2 [with obj.] technical coat (a lens) with a special surface layer so as to reduce reflection from its surface.
– PHRASES **the bloom is off the rose** N. Amer. the thing in question is no longer new, fresh, or exciting.
– ORIGIN Middle English: from Old Norse *blóm* 'flower, blossom', *blómi* 'prosperity', *blómar* 'flowers'.

bloom² ▶ noun a mass of iron, steel, or other metal hammered or rolled into a thick bar for further working.
■ historical an unworked mass of puddled iron.
▶ verb [with obj.] [usu. as noun **blooming**] make (metal) into such a mass.
– ORIGIN Old English *blōma*, of unknown origin.

bloomer¹ ▶ noun Brit. informal, dated a serious or stupid mistake.
– ORIGIN late 19th cent.: equivalent to *blooming error.*

bloomer² ▶ noun Brit. a large loaf with diagonal slashes on a rounded top.
– ORIGIN 1930s: of unknown origin.

bloomer³ ▶ noun [usu. in combination] a plant that produces flowers at a specified time: *fragrant night-bloomers such as nicotiana.*
■ [with adj.] a person who matures or flourishes at a specified time: *he was a late bloomer.*

bloomers ▶ plural noun women's loose-fitting knee-length knickers, considered old-fashioned.
■ historical women's and girls' loose-fitting trousers, gathered at the knee or, originally, the ankle.
– ORIGIN mid 19th cent.: named after Mrs Amelia J. *Bloomer* (1818–94), an American social reformer who advocated a similar garment.

bloomery ▶ noun (pl. **-ies**) historical a forge or mill producing blooms of wrought iron.

Bloomfield, Leonard (1887–1949), American linguist, one of the founders of American structural linguistics. His primary aim was to establish linguistics as an autonomous and scientific discipline. Notable works: *Language* (1933).
– DERIVATIVES **Bloomfieldian** adjective.

blooming ▶ adjective [attrib.] Brit. informal used to express annoyance or for emphasis: *of all the blooming cheek!* | [as submodifier] *a blooming good read.*

Bloomsbury an area of central London noted for its large squares and gardens and for its associations with the Bloomsbury Group. The British Museum is located there.
■ [as modifier] associated with or similar to the Bloomsbury Group.

Bloomsbury Group a group of writers, artists, and philosophers living in or associated with Bloomsbury in the early 20th century. Members of the group, which included Virginia Woolf, Lytton Strachey, Vanessa Bell, Duncan Grant, and Roger Fry, were known for their unconventional lifestyles and attitudes and were a powerful force in the growth of modernism.

bloop informal, chiefly N. Amer. ▶ verb **1** [no obj.] (of an electronic device) emit a short low-pitched noise: *a fruit machine blooping in the corner.*
2 [no obj.] make a mistake: *the company admitted it had blooped.*
■ [with obj.] Baseball make (a hit) from a poorly hit fly ball landing just beyond the reach of the infielders.
▶ noun **1** a short low-pitched noise emitted by an electronic device.
2 a mistake: *a typical beginner's bloop.*
■ Baseball another term for **BLOOPER** (in sense 2).
– DERIVATIVES **bloopy** adjective.
– ORIGIN 1920s: imitative.

blooper ▶ noun informal, chiefly N. Amer. **1** an embarrassing error: [as modifier] *blooper shows consisting of out-takes from films.*
2 Baseball a poorly hit fly ball landing just beyond the reach of the infielders.
– ORIGIN 1926 (originally US, denoting a radio which caused others to *bloop*, i.e. emit a loud howling noise): from imitative **BLOOP** + **-ER¹**.

blossom ▶ noun a flower or a mass of flowers, especially on a tree or bush: *tiny white blossoms* | [mass noun] *the slopes were ablaze with almond blossom.*
■ [mass noun] the state or period of flowering: *fruit trees in blossom.* ■ informal a person who is considered lovely or full of promise (often as a form of address): *Linda, my blossom, you needn't say anything.*
▶ verb [no obj.] (of a tree or bush) produce flowers or masses of flowers: *a garden in which roses blossom* | [as adj. **blossoming**] *blossoming magnolia.*
■ mature or develop in a promising or healthy way: *their friendship blossomed into romance* | [as noun **blossoming**] *the blossoming of experimental theatre.* ■ seem to grow or open like a flower: *the smile blossomed on his lips.*
– DERIVATIVES **blossomy** adjective.
– ORIGIN Old English *blōstm, blōstma* (noun), *blōstmian* (verb), of Germanic origin; related to Dutch *bloesem*, also to **BLOOM¹**.

blot ▶ noun a dark mark or stain, typically one made by ink, paint, or dirt: *an ink blot.*
■ a shameful act or quality that tarnishes an otherwise good character or reputation: *the only blot on an otherwise clean campaign.* ■ a thing that mars the beauty or perfection of something: *wind power turbines are a blot on the landscape.* ■ Biochemistry a procedure in which proteins or nucleic acids separated on a gel are transferred directly to an immobilizing medium for identification.

▶ **verb** (**blotted**, **blotting**) [with obj.] **1** dry (a wet surface or substance) using an absorbent material: *Henry blotted the page.*
■ Biochemistry transfer by means of a blot.
2 mark or stain (something): [as adj. **blotted**] *the writing was messy and blotted.*
■ tarnish the good character or reputation of: *the turmoil blotted his memory of the school.*
3 (**blot something out**) cover writing or pictures with ink or paint so that they cannot be seen.
■ obscure a view: *a dust shield blotting out the sun.* ■ obliterate or disregard something painful in one's memory or existence: *the concentration necessary to her job blotted out all the feelings.*
– PHRASES **blot one's copybook** Brit. tarnish one's good reputation.
– ORIGIN late Middle English: probably of Scandinavian origin and related to Old Norse *blettr.*

blotch ▶ **noun** a large irregular patch or unsightly mark on a surface, typically the skin: *red blotches on her face.*
▶ **verb** (usu. **be blotched**) cover with blotches.
– DERIVATIVES **blotchy** adjective.
– ORIGIN early 17th cent. (as a verb): partly an alteration of obsolete *plotch* in the same sense (of unknown origin), influenced by **BLOT**; partly a blend of **BLOT** and **BOTCH**.

blotter ▶ **noun** **1** a sheet or pad of blotting paper inserted into a frame and kept on a desk.
2 N. Amer. a temporary recording book, especially a police charge sheet.

blotting paper ▶ **noun** [mass noun] absorbent paper used for soaking up excess ink when writing.

blotto ▶ **adjective** [predic.] informal extremely drunk: *we got blotto.*
– ORIGIN early 20th cent.: from **BLOT** + **-O**.

blouse ▶ **noun** a woman's loose upper garment resembling a shirt, typically with a collar, buttons, and sleeves.
■ a loose linen or cotton garment of a type worn by peasants and manual workers, typically belted at the waist. ■ a type of jacket worn as part of military uniform.
▶ **verb** [with obj. and adverbial] make (a garment) hang in loose folds: *I bloused my trousers over my boots* | [no obj.] *my dress bloused out above my waist.*
– PHRASES **big** (or **great**) **girl's blouse** Brit. informal a weak, cowardly, or over-sensitive man.
– ORIGIN early 19th cent. (denoting a belted loose garment worn by peasants): from French, of unknown origin.

blouson /ˈbluːzɒn/ ▶ **noun** a short loose-fitting jacket, typically bloused and finishing at the waist.
– ORIGIN early 20th cent.: from French, diminutive of **BLOUSE**.

Blow, John (*c.*1649–1708), English composer and organist. The organist of Westminster Abbey 1668–79 and 1695–1708, he wrote much church music and taught Henry Purcell. His masque *Venus and Adonis* (*c.*1682) was a forerunner of English opera.

blow[1] ▶ **verb** (past **blew**; past participle **blown**) **1** [no obj.] (of wind) move creating an air current: *a cold wind began to blow.*
■ [with obj. and adverbial of direction] (of wind) cause to move; propel: *a gust of wind blew a cloud of smoke into his face* | *the spire was blown down during a gale.* ■ [no obj., with adverbial of direction] be carried, driven, or moved by the wind or an air current: *it was so windy that the tent nearly blew away* | *cotton curtains blowing in the breeze.* ■ informal leave: *I'd better blow.*
2 [no obj.] (of a person) expel air through pursed lips: *Willie took a deep breath, and blew* | *he **blew on** his tea to cool it.*
■ [with obj.] use one's breath to propel: *he blew cigar smoke in her face.* ■ breathe hard; pant: *Uncle Albert was soon puffing and blowing.* ■ [with obj.] cause to breathe hard; exhaust of breath: [as adj. **blown**] *an exhausted, blown horse.* ■ [with obj.] (of a person) force air through the mouth into (an instrument) in order to make a sound: *the umpire blew his whistle.* ■ (of such an instrument) make a noise through being blown into in such a way: *police whistles blew.* ■ [with obj.] sound (the horn of a vehicle). ■ informal play jazz or rock music in an unrestrained style. ■ [with obj.] force air through a tube into (molten glass) in order to create an artefact. ■ [with obj.] remove the contents of (an egg) by forcing air through it. ■ [with obj.] (of flies) lay eggs in or on (something). ■ (of a whale) eject air and vapour through the blowhole.
3 [with obj. and adverbial of direction] (of an explosion or explosive device) displace violently or send flying: *the blast had blown the windows out of the van.*
■ [no obj.] (of a vehicle tyre) burst suddenly while the vehicle is in motion. ■ burst or cause to burst due to pressure or overheating: [no obj.] *the engines sounded as if their exhausts had blown* | [with obj.] *frost will have blown a compression joint.* ■ (of an electric circuit) burn out or cause to burn out through overloading: [no obj.] *the fuse in the plug had blown* | [with obj.] *the floodlights blew a fuse.*
4 [with obj.] informal spend recklessly: *they blew £100,000 in just eighteen months.*
5 informal completely bungle (an opportunity): *the wider issues were to show that politicians had **blown it**.*
■ (usu. **be blown**) expose (a stratagem): *a man whose cover was blown.*
6 (past participle **blowed**) [with obj.] [usu. as imperative] Brit. informal damn: *'Well, **blow me**', he said, 'I never knew that'* | [with clause] ***I'm blowed if*** *I want to see him again.*
7 [with obj.] vulgar slang perform fellatio on (a sexual partner).
▶ **noun** **1** [in sing.] a strong wind: *we're in for a bit of a blow.*
■ an act of getting some fresh air: *I'll go down to the sea and get a blow before supper.*
2 an act of blowing on an instrument: *a number of blows on the whistle.*
■ [in sing.] an act of blowing one's nose: *give your nose a good blow.* ■ [in sing.] informal a spell of playing jazz or rock music. ■ (in steel-making) an act of sending an air or oxygen blast through molten metal in a converter.
3 [mass noun] informal cannabis.
– PHRASES **be blown off course** (of a project) be disrupted by some circumstance. **be blown out of the water** (of a person, idea, or project) be shown to lack all credibility. **blow away the cobwebs** refresh oneself when feeling weary, especially by having some fresh air. **blow someone's brains out** informal kill someone with a shot in the head with a firearm. **blow cold on** regard unfavourably. **blow the doors off** N. Amer. informal be considerably better or more successful than: *a package that blows the doors off anything on the market.* **blow a fuse** (or **gasket**) informal lose one's temper. **blow the gaff** see **GAFF**[2]. **blow hot and cold** vacillate. **blow someone a kiss** kiss the tips of one's fingers then blow across them towards someone as a gesture of affection. **blow someone's mind** informal impress or otherwise affect someone very strongly: *the sound of a twelve-string guitar just blew my mind.* **blow one's nose** clear one's nose of mucus by blowing through it into a handkerchief. **blow off steam** see ***let off steam*** at **STEAM**. **blow someone's socks off** see **SOCK**. **blow one's top** (or chiefly N. Amer. **lid** or **stack**) informal lose one's temper. **blow one's trumpet** see **TRUMPET**. **blow up in one's face** (of an action, project, or situation) go drastically wrong with damaging effects to oneself. **blow the whistle on** see **WHISTLE**. **blow with the wind** be incapable of maintaining a consistent course of action.
– ORIGIN Old English *blāwan*, of Germanic origin; related to German *blähen* 'blow up, swell', from an Indo-European root shared by Latin *flare* 'blow'.
▶ **blow someone away** informal **1** kill someone using a firearm. **2** (**be blown away**) be extremely impressed: *I'm blown away by his new poem.*
blow in informal (of a person) arrive casually and unannounced.
blow off 1 lose one's temper and shout. **2** informal break wind noisily.
blow someone off N. Amer. informal fail to keep an appointment with someone. ■ end a romantic or sexual relationship with someone.
blow something off N. Amer. informal ignore or make light of something. ■ fail to attend something: *Ivy blew off class.*
blow out 1 be extinguished by an air current: *the candles blew out.* **2** (of a tyre) puncture while the vehicle is in motion. **3** (of an oil or gas well) emit gas suddenly and forcefully. **4** (**blow itself out**) (of a storm) finally lose its force.
blow someone out N. Amer. informal defeat someone convincingly.
blow something out 1 use one's breath to extinguish a flame: *he blew out the candle.* **2** puff out one's cheeks. **3** N. Amer. informal render a part of the body useless.
blow over (of trouble) fade away without serious consequences.
blow up 1 explode. ■ (of a person) lose one's temper: *Mum had **blown up at** Dad with more than her usual vehemence.* **2** (of a wind or storm) begin to develop. ■ (of a scandal or dispute) emerge or become public. **3** inflate: *my stomach had started to blow up.*
blow someone up informal, dated reprimand someone severely: *she got blown up by her boss for being late.*
blow something up 1 cause something to explode. **2** inflate something: *a small pump for blowing up balloons.* ■ figurative inflate the importance of something: *it was a domestic tiff which had been blown up out of all proportion.* ■ enlarge a photograph or text.

blow[2] ▶ **noun** a powerful stroke with a hand, weapon, or hard object: *he received a blow to the skull.*
■ a sudden shock or disappointment: *the news came as a crushing blow to the cast.*
– PHRASES **at one blow** by a single stroke; in one operation: *the letter had destroyed his certainty at one blow.* **come to blows** start fighting after a disagreement. **soften** (or **cushion**) **the blow** make it easier to cope with a difficult change or upsetting news: *monetary compensation was offered to soften the blow.* **strike a blow for** (or **against**) act in support of (or opposition to): *a chance to strike a blow for freedom.*
– ORIGIN late Middle English: of unknown origin.

blow[3] archaic or poetic/literary ▶ **verb** (past **blew**; past participle **blown**) [no obj.] produce flowers or be in flower: *I know a bank where the wild thyme blows.*
▶ **noun** [mass noun] the state or period of flowering: *stocks in fragrant blow.*
– ORIGIN Old English *blōwan*, of Germanic origin; related to Dutch *bloeien* and German *blühen*, also to **BLOOM**[1] and **BLOSSOM**.

blowback ▶ **noun** a process in which gases expand or travel in a direction opposite to the usual one, especially through escape of pressure or delayed combustion.

blow-by-blow ▶ **adjective** [attrib.] (of a description of an event) giving all the details in the order in which they occurred: *a blow-by-blow account of how England lost to Portugal.*

blowdown ▶ **noun** **1** N. Amer. a tree that has been blown down by the wind.
■ [mass noun] such trees collectively: *work to remove blowdown.* ■ [mass noun] the blowing down of a tree or trees.
2 [mass noun] the removal of solids or liquids from a container or pipe using pressure.

blow-dry ▶ **verb** [with obj.] arrange (the hair) into a particular style while drying it with a hand-held dryer.
▶ **noun** [in sing.] an act of arranging the hair in such a way.
– DERIVATIVES **blow-dryer** noun.

blower ▶ **noun** **1** a person or thing that blows, especially a mechanical device for creating a current of air used to dry or heat something.
2 informal, chiefly Brit. a telephone.

blowfish ▶ **noun** (pl. same or **-fishes**) any of a number of fishes that are able to inflate their bodies when alarmed, such as a globefish.

blowfly ▶ **noun** (pl. **-flies**) a large and typically metallic fly which lays its eggs on meat and carcasses.
• Family Calliphoridae: numerous species, including the bluebottle.

blowgun ▶ **noun** another term for **BLOWPIPE**.

blowhard N. Amer. informal ▶ **noun** a person who blusters and boasts in an unpleasant way.
▶ **adjective** acting or appearing in such a way.

blowhole ▶ **noun** a hole for blowing or breathing through, in particular:
■ the nostril of a whale or dolphin on the top of its head. ■ a hole in ice for breathing or fishing through. ■ a vent for air or smoke in a tunnel or other structure.

blowie ▶ **noun** (pl. **-ies**) Austral./NZ informal a blowfly.

blow-in ▶ **noun** Austral. informal a newcomer or recent arrival.

blow job ▶ **noun** vulgar slang an act of fellatio.

blowlamp ▶ **noun** British term for **BLOWTORCH**.

blown[1] past participle of **BLOW**[1]. ▶ **adjective** informal (of a vehicle or its engine) provided with a turbocharger.

blown[2] past participle of **BLOW**[3].

blow-off ▶ **noun** [mass noun] the action of emitting a gas, typically to reduce pressure to a safe level.

blowout ▶ **noun** **1** a sudden rupture or malfunction

of a part or apparatus due to pressure, in particular:
■an occasion when a tyre on a vehicle bursts or an electric fuse melts. ■ an uprush of oil or gas from a well. ■ N. Amer. informal an outburst of anger or an argument.
2 informal a large or lavish meal or social gathering.
3 N. Amer. informal an easy victory over someone in a sporting contest or an election.
4 a hollow eroded by the wind.

blowpipe ▶ **noun** a primitive weapon consisting of a long tube through which an arrow or dart is propelled by force of the breath.
■a long tube by means of which molten glass is blown into the required shape. ■ a tube used to intensify the heat of a flame by blowing air or other gas through it at high pressure.

blowsy /ˈblaʊzi/ (also **blowzy**) ▶ **adjective** (of a woman) coarse, untidy, and red-faced.
– DERIVATIVES **blowsily** adverb, **blowsiness** noun.
– ORIGIN early 17th cent.: from obsolete *blowze* 'beggar's female companion', of unknown origin.

blowtorch ▶ **noun** a portable device producing a hot flame which can be directed on to a surface, typically to burn off paint.

blow-up ▶ **noun 1** an enlargement of a photograph.
2 informal an outburst of anger.
▶ **adjective** [attrib.] inflatable: *a blow-up pillow.*

blowy ▶ **adjective** (**blowier**, **blowiest**) having or affected by strong winds; windy or windswept: *a blowy day.*

BLT ▶ **noun** informal, chiefly N. Amer. a sandwich filled with bacon, lettuce, and tomato.

blub ▶ **verb** (**blubbed**, **blubbing**) [no obj.] informal sob noisily and uncontrollably.
– ORIGIN early 19th cent.: abbreviation of **BLUBBER**[2].

blubber[1] ▶ **noun** [mass noun] the fat of sea mammals, especially whales and seals.
■informal, derogatory excessive human fat.
▶ **adjective** [attrib.] archaic (of a person's lips) swollen or protruding. [ORIGIN: alteration of obsolete *blabber* 'swollen'.]
– DERIVATIVES **blubbery** adjective.
– ORIGIN late Middle English (denoting the foaming of the sea, also a bubble on water): perhaps symbolic; compare with **BLOB** and **BLOTCH**.

blubber[2] ▶ **verb** [no obj.] informal sob noisily and uncontrollably: *he was blubbering like a child* | [with direct speech] *'I don't like him,' blubbered Jonathan.*
– DERIVATIVES **blubberer** noun.
– ORIGIN late Middle English: probably symbolic; compare with **BLOB** and **BLUBBER**[1].

bluchers /ˈbluːkəz/ ▶ **plural noun** historical strong leather half-boots or high shoes.
– ORIGIN mid 19th cent.: named after G. L. von *Blücher* (1742–1819), Prussian general.

bludge Austral./NZ informal ▶ **verb** [no obj.] shirk responsibility and live off the efforts of others: *they were sick of* ***bludging on*** *the public.*
■[with obj.] cadge or scrounge: *the girls bludged smokes.*
▶ **noun** an easy job or assignment.
– ORIGIN late 19th cent.: back-formation from **BLUDGER**.

bludgeon /ˈblʌdʒ(ə)n/ ▶ **noun** a thick stick with a heavy end, used as a weapon.
▶ **verb** [with obj.] beat (someone) repeatedly with a bludgeon or other heavy object.
■force or bully (someone) to do something: *she was determined not to be* ***bludgeoned into*** *submission.* ■ (**bludgeon one's way**) make one's way by brute force.
– ORIGIN mid 18th cent.: of unknown origin.

bludger ▶ **noun** Austral./NZ informal a scrounger.
■an idler or loafer.
– ORIGIN mid 19th cent. (originally British slang denoting a pimp, specifically one who robbed his prostitute's clients): abbreviation of *bludgeoner*, from **BLUDGEON**.

blue[1] ▶ **adjective** (**bluer**, **bluest**) **1** of a colour intermediate between green and violet, as of the sky or sea on a sunny day: *the clear blue sky* | *blue jeans* | *deep blue eyes.*
■(of a person's skin) having or turning such a colour, especially as a result of cold or breathing difficulties: *Ashley went blue and I panicked.* ■ (of a bird or other animal) having blue markings: *a blue jay.* ■ (of a cat, fox, or rabbit) having fur of a smoky grey colour: *the blue fox.* ■ (of a ski run) of the second lowest level of difficulty, as indicated by coloured markers positioned along it. ■ Physics denoting one of three colours of quark.
2 informal (of a person or mood) melancholy, sad, or depressed: *he's feeling blue.*
3 informal (of a film, joke, or story) with sexual or pornographic content: *a blue movie.*
4 Brit. informal politically conservative: *the successful blue candidate.*
▶ **noun 1** [mass noun] blue colour or pigment: *she was dressed* ***in blue*** | *the dark blue of his eyes* | [count noun] *armchairs in pastel blues and greens.*
■blue clothes or material: *Susan wore blue.*
2 a blue thing, in particular:
■a blue ball, piece, etc. in a game or sport. ■ the blue ball in snooker. ■ (**the blue**) poetic/literary the sky or sea, or the unknown: *far out upon the blue were many sails.* ■ another term for **BLUING**.
3 [usu. with modifier] a small butterfly, the male of which is predominantly blue while the female is typically brown.
• Numerous genera in the family Lycaenidae.
4 (also **Blue**) [usu. with modifier] Brit. a person who has represented Cambridge University (a **Cambridge blue**) or Oxford University (an **Oxford blue**) in a particular sport: *a flyweight boxing blue.*
■a distinction awarded to such a person: *a centre forward who won a rugby blue.*
5 Austral./NZ informal an argument or fight. [ORIGIN: 1940s: perhaps by association with phrases such as *make the air blue*, alluding to swearing with annoyance.]
6 Austral./NZ informal a mistake.
7 Austral./NZ informal a nickname for a red-headed person. [ORIGIN: 1930s: of unknown origin.]
▶ **verb** (**blues**, **blued**, **bluing** or **blueing**) **1** make or become blue: [with obj.] *the light dims, bluing the retina* | [no obj.] *the day would haze, the air bluing with afternoon.*
■[with obj.] heat (metal) so as to give it a greyish-blue finish: [as adj. **blued**] *nickel-plated or blued hooks.*
2 [with obj.] chiefly historical wash (white clothes) with bluing.
– PHRASES **do something until** (or **till**) **one is blue in the face** informal put all one's efforts into doing something to no avail: *she could talk to him until she was blue in the face, but he was just not hearing.* **once in a blue moon** informal very rarely. [ORIGIN: because a 'blue moon' is a phenomenon that never occurs.] **out of the blue** (or **out of a clear blue sky**) informal without warning; unexpectedly: *she phoned me out of the blue.* [ORIGIN: with reference to a 'blue' (i.e. clear) sky, from which nothing unusual is expected.] **scream** (or **yell**) **blue murder** see **MURDER**. **talk a blue streak** N. Amer. informal speak continuously and at great length.
– DERIVATIVES **blueness** noun.
– ORIGIN Middle English: from Old French *bleu*, ultimately of Germanic origin and related to Old English *blǣwen* 'blue' and Old Norse *blár* 'dark blue' (see also **BLAEBERRY**).

blue[2] ▶ **verb** (**blues**, **blued**, **bluing** or **blueing**) Brit. informal, dated squander or recklessly spend (money).
– ORIGIN mid 19th cent.: perhaps a variant of **BLOW**[1].

blue baby ▶ **noun** a baby with a blue complexion from lack of oxygen in the blood due to a congenital defect of the heart or major blood vessels.

blueback ▶ **noun** chiefly N. Amer. a bird or fish, especially a trout or a sockeye salmon, having a bluish back.

Bluebeard a character in a tale by Charles Perrault, who killed several wives in turn for disobeying his order to avoid a locked room, which contained the bodies of his previous wives. Local tradition in Brittany identifies him with Gilles de Rais (*c.*1400–40), a perpetrator of atrocities, although he had only one wife (who left him).
■[as noun **a Bluebeard**] a man who murders his wives.

blue beat ▶ **noun** another term for **SKA**.

bluebell ▶ **noun 1** a European woodland plant of the lily family, which produces clusters of blue bell-shaped flowers in spring. Also called **WILD HYACINTH**.
• *Hyacinthoides* (or *Endymion*) *nonscripta*, family Liliaceae.
2 any of a number of other plants with blue bell-shaped flowers, in particular:
• Scottish term for **HAREBELL**. • a North American plant of the borage family (genus *Mertensia*, family Boraginaceae). • an Australian and South African plant of the bellflower family (genus *Wahlenbergia*, family Campanulaceae).

blueberry ▶ **noun** (pl. **-ies**) **1** a small sweet blue-black edible berry which grows in clusters on North American shrubs related to the bilberry.
2 one of the dwarf shrubs that produces this berry, some kinds being cultivated for their fruit or as ornamentals.
• Genus *Vaccinium*, family Ericaceae: several species.

bluebill ▶ **noun 1** a large African waxbill with a stout metallic blue bill and red and black plumage.
• Genus *Spermophaga*, Estrildidae: three species.
2 any of a number of ducks with blue bills:
• N. Amer. the scaup duck. • Austral. the blue-billed duck (*Oxyura australis*, family Anatidae), a stiff-tailed duck with chestnut plumage.

bluebird ▶ **noun** an American songbird of the thrush family, the male of which has a blue head, back, and wings.
• Genus *Sialia*, family Turdidae: three species, including the **eastern bluebird** (*S. sialis*).

blue-black ▶ **adjective** black with a tinge of blue.

blue blood ▶ **noun** [mass noun] noble birth.
■[count noun] a person of noble birth.
– DERIVATIVES **blue-blooded** adjective.

blue bonnet ▶ **noun** a pale grey-brown Australian parrot with a deep blue face and variously coloured wings, tail, and belly.
• *Psephotus* (or *Northiella*) *haematogaster*, family Psittacidae.

blue book ▶ **noun 1** (in the UK) a report bound in a blue cover and issued by Parliament or the Privy Council.
2 (in the US) an official book listing government officials.

bluebottle ▶ **noun 1** a common blowfly with a metallic-blue body, the female of which often comes into houses searching for a suitable food source on which to lay her eggs.
• *Calliphora vomitoria*, family Calliphoridae.
2 Austral. & S. African the Portuguese man-of-war. [ORIGIN: so named because of the organism's blue balloon-like float.]
3 Brit. the wild cornflower.
4 Brit. informal, dated a police officer.

blue box ▶ **noun 1** chiefly US an electronic device used to access long-distance telephone lines illegally.
2 chiefly Canadian a blue plastic box for the collection of recyclable household materials.

blue buck ▶ **noun** S. African another term for ***blue duiker*** (see **DUIKER**).
– ORIGIN early 19th cent.: translating South African Dutch *blauwbok.*

blue channel ▶ **noun** (at a customs area in an airport or port) the passage which should be taken by arriving passengers who have only travelled within the European Community.

blue cheese ▶ **noun** [mass noun] cheese containing veins of blue mould, such as Stilton and Danish Blue.

blue-chip ▶ **adjective** [attrib.] denoting companies or their shares considered to be a reliable investment, though less secure than gilt-edged stock.
■of the highest quality: *blue-chip art.*
– ORIGIN early 20th cent. (originally US): from the *blue chip* used in gambling games, which usually has a high value.

blue chipper ▶ **noun** N. Amer. informal a highly valued person, especially a sports player.

blue coat ▶ **noun** a person who wears a blue coat, in particular:
■historical a soldier in a blue uniform. ■ (**Blue Coat**) Brit. a student at a charity school with a blue uniform.

blue cohosh ▶ **noun** see **COHOSH**.

blue-collar ▶ **adjective** chiefly N. Amer. of or relating to manual work or workers, particularly in industry: *a blue-collar neighbourhood.*

blue corn ▶ **noun** [mass noun] N. Amer. a variety of maize with bluish grains.

blue crab ▶ **noun** a large edible swimming crab of the Atlantic coast of North America.
• *Callinectes sapidus*, family Portunidae.

blue crane ▶ **noun** a large South African crane with blue-grey plumage, the national bird of South Africa. Also called **STANLEY CRANE**.
• *Anthropoides paradisea*, family Gruidae.

blue ensign ▶ **noun** a blue flag with the Union Jack in the top corner next to the flagstaff, flown chiefly by British naval auxiliary vessels.

blue-eyed boy ▶ **noun** Brit. informal, chiefly derogatory a

b

person highly regarded by someone and treated with special favour.

blue-eyed grass ▶ noun a North American plant of the iris family, cultivated for its blue flowers.
● Genus *Sisyrinchium*, family Iridaceae: several species, including *S. bermudiana*, which also occurs in Ireland.

blue-eyed Mary ▶ noun a low-growing southern European plant of the borage family, which bears bright blue flowers and spreads by means of runners.
● *Omphalodes verna*, family Boraginaceae.

Blue-faced Leicester ▶ noun see LEICESTER³ (sense 3).

Bluefields a port on the Mosquito Coast of Nicaragua, situated on an inlet of the Caribbean Sea; pop. 18,000 (1985).

bluefin (also **bluefin tuna**) ▶ noun the commonest large tuna, which occurs worldwide in warm seas. It is probably the largest bony fish, and is very important as a food and game fish. Also called TUNNY.
● *Thunnus thynnus*, family Scombridae.

bluefish ▶ noun (pl. same or **-fishes**) a predatory blue-coloured marine fish, which inhabits tropical and temperate waters and is popular as a game fish.
● *Pomatomus saltatrix*, the only member of the family Pomatomidae.

blue flag ▶ noun **1** a European award for beaches based on cleanliness and safety.
2 Motor Racing a blue flag used to indicate to a driver that there is another driver trying to lap him.

blue flyer ▶ noun Austral. a female red kangaroo.
– ORIGIN mid 19th cent.: *blue*, by association with the informal nickname for red-headed people (see sense 7 of BLUE¹).

blue funk ▶ noun see FUNK¹.

bluegill /'bluːɡɪl/ ▶ noun an edible North American freshwater fish of the sunfish family, with a deep body and bluish cheeks and gill covers.
● *Lepomis macrochirus*, family Centrarchidae.

blue gopher snake ▶ noun see GOPHER SNAKE.

bluegrass ▶ noun [mass noun] **1** (also **Kentucky bluegrass**) a bluish-green grass which was introduced into North America from northern Europe. It is widely grown for fodder, especially in Kentucky and Virginia.
● Genus *Poa*, family Gramineae: several species, in particular the common Eurasian meadow grass.
2 a kind of country music influenced by jazz and blues and characterized by virtuosic playing of banjos and guitars and high-pitched, close-harmony vocals.

Bluegrass State informal name for KENTUCKY.

blue-green algae ▶ plural noun another term for cyanobacteria (see CYANOBACTERIA).

blue groper ▶ noun see GROPER¹ (sense 2).

blue ground ▶ noun another term for KIMBERLITE.

bluegum ▶ noun a Eucalyptus tree with blue-green aromatic leaves and smooth bark.
● Genus *Eucalyptus*, family Myrtaceae: several species, in particular *E. regnans*.

blue hare ▶ noun another term for MOUNTAIN HARE.

bluehead ▶ noun a small wrasse of the tropical East Atlantic, the large males of which have a blue head and green body with vertical stripes, and the females and smaller males are predominantly yellowish.
● *Thalassoma bifasciatum*, family Labridae.

blue heeler ▶ noun Austral./NZ a cattle dog with a dark speckled body.
– ORIGIN early 20th cent.: *blue* from the characteristic blue (or red) flecked coat of the breed.

blue helmet ▶ noun a member of a United Nations peacekeeping force.

blue ice ▶ noun [mass noun] ice of a vivid blue colour, formed when a large body of water freezes suddenly.

blueing ▶ noun variant spelling of BLUING.

blueish ▶ adjective variant spelling of BLUISH.

bluejacket ▶ noun informal a sailor in the navy.

blue jay ▶ noun a common North American jay with a blue crest, back, wings, and tail.
● *Cyanocitta cristata*, family Corvidae.
■ another term for ROLLER¹ (in sense 2).

blue jet ▶ noun a very faint short-lived cone of deep

blue light sometimes observed in the upper atmosphere above an intense thunderstorm.

Blue John ▶ noun [mass noun] a blue or purple banded variety of fluorite found in Derbyshire.

blue law ▶ noun N. Amer. a law prohibiting certain activities, such as shopping, on a Sunday.
■ (in colonial New England) a strict puritanical law, particularly one preventing entertainment or leisure activities on a Sunday.

blue lias ▶ noun see LIAS.

blue line ▶ noun Ice Hockey either of the two lines running across the ice between the centre line and the goal line.

blue metal ▶ noun [mass noun] Brit. broken blue stone used for road-making.

blue mould ▶ noun a bluish fungus which grows on food, some kinds of which are used to produce blue cheeses or antibiotics such as penicillin.
● *Penicillium* and other genera, subdivision Deuteromycotina.

Blue Mountains 1 a section of the Great Dividing Range in New South Wales, Australia.
2 a range of mountains in eastern Jamaica.
3 a range of mountains running from central Oregon to SE Washington State in the US.

Blue Nile one of the two principal headwaters of the Nile. Rising from Lake Tana in NW Ethiopia, it flows some 1,600 km (1,000 miles) southwards then north-westwards into Sudan, where it meets the White Nile at Khartoum.

bluenose ▶ noun informal, chiefly N. Amer. **1** (**Bluenose**) a person from Nova Scotia.
2 a priggish or puritanical person.
– DERIVATIVES **bluenosed** adjective (only in sense 2).

blue note ▶ noun Music a minor interval where a major would be expected, used especially in jazz.

blue-pencil ▶ verb [with obj.] censor or make cuts in (a manuscript, film, or other work).

Blue Peter ▶ noun a blue flag with a white square in the centre, raised by a ship about to leave port.

blue-plate ▶ adjective [attrib.] N. Amer. (of a restaurant meal) consisting of a full main course ordered as a single menu item.
– ORIGIN with reference to the original blue plates divided into compartments, on which fixed-price restaurant meals were served.

blue pointer ▶ noun another term for MAKO¹.

blueprint ▶ noun a design plan or other technical drawing.
■ figurative something which acts as a plan, model, or template: *the scheme was a blueprint for future development programmes*.
▶ verb [with obj.] N. Amer. draw up (a plan or model): [as adj. **blueprinted**] *a neatly blueprinted scheme*.
– ORIGIN late 19th cent.: from the original process in which prints were composed of white lines on a blue ground or of blue lines on a white ground.

blue riband ▶ noun **1** (also **blue ribbon**) a ribbon of blue silk worn as a badge of honour, in particular:
■ a badge given as first prize to the winner of a competition. ■ a competition or award of the greatest distinction in its own field. ■ (in the UK) a badge worn by members of the Order of the Garter.
2 (**Blue Riband** or **Ribbon**) a trophy for the ship making the fastest eastward sea crossing of the Atlantic Ocean on a regular commercial voyage.

blue-ribbon ▶ adjective [attrib.] N. Amer. of the highest quality; first-class: *blue-ribbon service*.
■ (of a jury or committee) carefully or specially selected.

Blue Ridge Mountains a range of the Appalachian Mountains in the eastern US, stretching from southern Pennsylvania to northern Georgia. Mount Mitchell is the highest peak, rising to a height of 2,037 m (6,684 ft).

blue rinse ▶ noun a preparation used as a rinse on grey or white hair so as to give it a temporary blue tint.
▶ adjective (also **blue-rinsed**) [attrib.] informal, derogatory of or relating to elderly and conservative women: *the blue-rinse brigade*.

blue roan ▶ adjective denoting an animal's coat consisting of black-and-white hairs evenly mixed, giving it a blue-grey hue.
▶ noun an animal with such a coat.

blue rock ▶ noun (in pigeon-fancying) a pigeon showing the coloration of the wild rock dove.

blues ▶ plural noun **1** (often **the blues**) [treated as sing. or

pl.] melancholic music of black American folk origin, typically in a twelve-bar sequence. It developed in the rural southern US towards the end of the 19th century, finding a wider audience in the 1940s, as blacks migrated to the cities. This urban blues gave rise to rhythm and blues and rock and roll.
■ [treated as sing.] a piece of such music: *a blues in C*.
2 (**the blues**) informal feelings of melancholy, sadness, or depression: *she's got the blues*.
– DERIVATIVES **bluesy** adjective (in sense 1).
– ORIGIN mid 19th cent. (in sense 2): elliptically from *blue devils* 'depression or delirium tremens'.

Blues and Royals ▶ plural noun Brit. a regiment of the Household Cavalry.
– ORIGIN formed from the amalgamation (1969) of the Royal Horse Guards (also known as the *Blues*) and the *Royal Dragoons*.

blueschist /'bluːʃɪst/ ▶ noun [mass noun] a metamorphic rock with a blue colour, formed under conditions of high pressure and low temperature.

blue-screen ▶ adjective [attrib.] denoting a special-effects technique used in films in which scenes shot against a blue background are superimposed on other scenes.

blue shark ▶ noun a long, slender shark with an indigo-blue back and white underparts, found typically in the open sea.
● *Prionace glauca*, family Carcharhinidae.

blue sheep ▶ noun another term for BHARAL.

blue shift ▶ noun [mass noun] Astronomy the displacement of the spectrum to shorter wavelengths in the light coming from distant celestial objects moving towards the observer. Compare with RED SHIFT.

blue-sky (also **blue-skies**) ▶ adjective [attrib.] informal not yet practicable or profitable: *blue-sky research*.

bluestocking ▶ noun often derogatory an intellectual or literary woman.
– ORIGIN late 17th cent.: originally used to describe a man wearing blue worsted (instead of formal black silk) stockings; extended to mean 'in informal dress'. Later the term denoted a person who attended the literary assemblies held (c.1750) by three London society ladies, where some of the men favoured less formal dress. The women who attended became known as *blue-stocking ladies* or *blue-stockingers*.

bluestone ▶ noun [mass noun] any of various bluish or grey building stones.
■ [count noun] any of the smaller stones made of dolerite found in the inner part of Stonehenge.

bluet /'bluːɪt/ ▶ noun a low-growing evergreen North American plant with milky-blue flowers.
● *Hedyotis* (or *Houstonia*) *caerulea*, family Rubiaceae.
– ORIGIN early 18th cent.: from French, diminutive of *bleu* 'blue'.

bluethroat ▶ noun a songbird resembling the robin, found in northern Eurasia and Alaska. The male has a blue throat with a red or white spot in the centre.
● *Luscinia svecica*, family Turdidae.

blue tit ▶ noun a small tit (songbird) with a blue cap, greenish-blue back, and yellow underparts, widespread in Eurasia and NW Africa.
● *Parus caeruleus*, family Paridae.

bluetongue ▶ noun [mass noun] an insect-borne viral disease of sheep (transmissible with less serious effects to cattle and goats), characterized by fever, lameness, and a blue, swollen mouth and tongue.

blue-tongued skink ▶ noun a heavily built Australian skink with a large head, short limbs, and a blue tongue which is displayed in defence.
● Genus *Tiliqua*, family Scincidae: several species, in particular *T. scincoides*, which is occasionally kept as a pet.

blue vinny /'vɪni/ (also **blue vinney**) ▶ noun [mass noun] a blue-mould skimmed-milk cheese from Dorset.

blue vitriol ▶ noun [mass noun] archaic crystalline copper sulphate.

blue water ▶ noun open sea: [as modifier] *blue-water navigation*.

blue whale ▶ noun a mottled bluish-grey rorqual which is the largest living animal and reaches lengths of up to 27 m (90 ft).
● *Balaenoptera musculus*, family Balaenopteridae.

bluey ▶ **adjective** [often in combination] almost or partly blue: *bluey-green foliage.*
▶ **noun** (pl. **-eys**) Austral./NZ informal **1** a bundle of possessions carried by a bushman. [ORIGIN: so named because the outer covering was generally a blue blanket.]
2 a nickname for a red-headed person. [ORIGIN: early 20th cent.: of unknown origin.]

bluff[1] ▶ **noun** an attempt to deceive someone into believing that one can or is going to do something: *the offer was denounced as a bluff* | [mass noun] *his game of bluff.*
▶ **verb** [no obj.] try to deceive someone as to one's abilities or intentions: *he's been bluffing all along.*
■ [with obj.] mislead (someone) in this way: *the object is to* ***bluff** your opponent **into** submission.* ■ (**bluff one's way**) contrive a difficult escape or other achievement by maintaining a pretence. ■ (**bluff it out**) survive a difficult situation by maintaining a pretence.
– PHRASES **call someone's bluff** challenge someone to carry out a stated intention, in the expectation of being able to expose it as a pretence. ■ (in poker or brag) make an opponent show their hand in order to reveal that its value is weaker than their heavy betting suggests.
– DERIVATIVES **bluffer** noun.
– ORIGIN late 17th cent. (originally in the sense 'blindfold, hoodwink'): from Dutch *bluffen* 'brag', or *bluf* 'bragging'. The current sense (originally US, mid 19th cent.) originally referred to bluffing in the game of poker.

bluff[2] ▶ **adjective** direct in speech or behaviour but in a good-natured way: *a big, bluff, hearty man.*
– DERIVATIVES **bluffly** adverb, **bluffness** noun.
– ORIGIN early 18th cent. (in the sense 'surly, abrupt in manner'): figurative use of **BLUFF**[3]. The current positive connotation dates from the early 19th cent.

bluff[3] ▶ **noun** **1** a steep cliff, bank, or promontory.
2 Canadian a grove or clump of trees.
▶ **adjective** (of a cliff or a ship's bows) having a vertical or steep broad front.
– ORIGIN early 17th cent. (as an adjective, originally in nautical use): of unknown origin. The Canadian sense dates from the mid 18th cent.

bluing (also **blueing**) ▶ **noun** [mass noun] **1** chiefly historical blue powder used to preserve the whiteness of laundry.
2 a greyish-blue finish on metal produced by heating.

bluish (also **blueish**) ▶ **adjective** having a blue tinge; slightly blue.

Blum /bluːm/, Léon (1872–1950), French statesman, Prime Minister 1936–7, 1938, 1946–7. As France's first socialist and Jewish Prime Minister, Blum introduced significant labour reforms.

Blumenbach /ˈbluːmənbaːx/, Johann Friedrich (1752–1840), German physiologist and anatomist. He is regarded as the founder of physical anthropology, though his approach has since been much modified. He classified modern humans into five broad categories (Caucasian, Mongoloid, Malayan, Ethiopian, and American) based mainly on cranial measurements.

Blunden, Edmund (Charles) (1896–1974), English poet and critic. His poetry reveals his love of the English countryside, while his prose work *Undertones of War* (1928) deals with his experiences in the First World War.

blunder ▶ **noun** a stupid or careless mistake.
▶ **verb** [no obj.] make such a mistake; act or speak clumsily: *he knew he'd blundered* | *I* ***blundered on** in my explanation* | [as adj. **blundering**] *one's first blundering attempts.*
■ [no obj., with adverbial of direction] move clumsily or as if unable to see: *we were blundering around in the darkness.*
– DERIVATIVES **blunderer** noun, **blunderingly** adverb.
– ORIGIN Middle English: probably of Scandinavian origin and related to **BLIND**.

blunderbuss ▶ **noun** historical a short large-bored gun firing balls or slugs.
■ figurative an action or way of doing something regarded as lacking in subtlety and precision: *economists resort too quickly to the blunderbuss of regulation.*
– ORIGIN mid 17th cent.: alteration (by association with **BLUNDER**) of Dutch *donderbus*, literally 'thunder gun'.

blunge /blʌn(d)ʒ/ ▶ **verb** [with obj.] mix (clay or other materials) with water in a revolving apparatus, for use in ceramics.
– DERIVATIVES **blunger** noun.
– ORIGIN early 19th cent.: blend of **BLEND** and **PLUNGE**.

Blunt, Anthony (Frederick) (1907–83), British art historian, Foreign Office official, and Soviet spy. He confessed in 1965 that he had been a Soviet agent since the 1930s and had facilitated the escape of Guy Burgess and Donald Maclean. When these facts were made public in 1979 he was stripped of his knighthood.

blunt ▶ **adjective** **1** (of a cutting implement) not or no longer having a sharp edge or point: *a blunt knife.*
■ having a flat or rounded end: *the blunt tip of the leaf.*
2 (of a person or remark) uncompromisingly forthright: *a blunt statement of fact.*
▶ **verb** make or become less sharp: [with obj.] *wood can blunt your axe* | [no obj.] *the edge may blunt very rapidly.*
■ [with obj.] figurative weaken or reduce the force of (something): *their determination had been blunted.*
– DERIVATIVES **bluntly** adverb, **bluntness** noun.
– ORIGIN Middle English (in the sense 'dull, insensitive'): perhaps of Scandinavian origin and related to Old Norse *blunda* 'shut the eyes'.

blunt instrument ▶ **noun** a heavy object without a sharp edge or point, used as a weapon.
■ figurative an imprecise or heavy-handed way of doing something: *as a promotional method direct mail is a blunt instrument.*

blur ▶ **verb** (**blurred**, **blurring**) make or become unclear or less distinct: [with obj.] *tears blurred her vision* | *his novels blur the boundaries between criticism and fiction* | [no obj.] *in front of him the page blurred.*
▶ **noun** a thing that cannot be seen or heard clearly: *the pale blur of her face* | *the words were a blur.*
■ something remembered or perceived indistinctly, typically because it happened very fast: *the day before was a blur.*
– DERIVATIVES **blurry** adjective (**blurrier**, **blurriest**).
– ORIGIN mid 16th cent. (in the sense 'smear that partially obscures something)': perhaps related to **BLEAR**.

blurb ▶ **noun** a short description of a book, film, or other product written for promotional purposes and appearing on the cover of a book or in an advertisement.
▶ **verb** [with obj.] informal, chiefly N. Amer. write or contribute such a passage for (a book, film, or other product).
– ORIGIN early 20th cent.: coined by Gelett Burgess (died 1951), American humorist.

blurt ▶ **verb** [with obj.] say (something) suddenly and without careful consideration: *she wouldn't* ***blurt out** words she did not mean* | [with direct speech] *'It wasn't my idea,' Gordon blurted.*
– ORIGIN late 16th cent.: probably imitative.

blush ▶ **verb** [no obj.] show shyness, embarrassment, or shame by becoming red in the face: *she blushed at the unexpected compliment* | [with complement] *Kate felt herself blushing scarlet.*
■ feel embarrassed or ashamed: [with infinitive] *he blushed to think of how he'd paraded himself.* ■ [often as adj. **blushing**] (especially of a flower) be or become pink or pale red: *the trees are loaded with blushing blossoms.*
▶ **noun** **1** a reddening of the face as a sign of shyness, embarrassment, or shame: *he had brought a faint blush to her cheeks.*
■ a pink or pale red tinge: *the roses were white with a lovely pink blush.*
2 [mass noun] [often as modifier] a wine with a slight pink tint made in the manner of white wine but from red grape varieties.
– PHRASES **at first blush** at the first glimpse or impression. **spare** (or **save**) **someone's blushes** refrain from causing someone embarrassment.
– ORIGIN Old English *blyscan*; related to modern Dutch *blozen*.

blusher ▶ **noun** **1** [mass noun] a cosmetic of a powder or cream consistency used to give a warm colour to the cheeks.
2 a toadstool with a buff cap bearing fluffy white spots and with white flesh that turns pink when bruised or cut, found in woodland in both Eurasia and North America.
• *Amanita rubescens*, family Amanitaceae, class Hymenomycetes.

bluster ▶ **verb** [no obj.] talk in a loud, aggressive, or indignant way with little effect: *you threaten and bluster, but won't carry it through* | [with direct speech] *'I don't care what he says,' I blustered* | [as adj. **blustering**] *a blustering bully.*
■ (of a storm, wind, or rain) blow or beat fiercely and noisily: *a winter gale* ***blustered against** the sides of the house* | [as adj. **blustering**] *the blustering wind.*
▶ **noun** [mass noun] loud, aggressive, or indignant talk with little effect: *their threats contained a measure of bluster.*
– DERIVATIVES **blusterer** noun.
– ORIGIN late Middle English: ultimately imitative.

blustery ▶ **adjective** (of weather or a period of time) characterized by strong winds: *a gusty, blustery day.*
■ (of a wind) blowing in strong gusts.

Blu-tack Brit. ▶ **noun** [mass noun] trademark a blue sticky material used to attach paper to walls.
▶ **verb** [with obj.] attach (something) using such material.

B-lymphocyte ▶ **noun** Physiology a lymphocyte not processed by the thymus gland, and responsible for producing antibodies. Also called **B-CELL**. Compare with **T-LYMPHOCYTE**.
– ORIGIN *B* for **BURSA**, referring to the organ in birds where it was first identified.

Blyton, Enid (1897–1968), English writer of children's fiction. Her best-known creation for young children is the character Noddy, who first appeared in 1949; her books for older children include the series of *Famous Five* and *Secret Seven* adventure stories.

BM ▶ **abbreviation for** ■ Bachelor of Medicine. ■ British Museum.

BMA ▶ **abbreviation for** British Medical Association.

B-movie ▶ **noun** a low-budget film of poor quality made for use as a supporting feature in a cinema programme: [as modifier] *a B-movie actress.*

BMR ▶ **abbreviation for** basal metabolic rate.

BMus ▶ **abbreviation for** Bachelor of Music.

BMX ▶ **noun** [as modifier] denoting or relating to bicycles of a robust design suitable for cross-country racing: *a BMX bike* | [count noun] *he'd seen Barry on his BMX.*
– ORIGIN 1970s: from the initial letters of *bicycle motocross*, with *X* standing for *cross*.

Bn ▶ **abbreviation for** ■ Baron. ■ Battalion.

bn ▶ **abbreviation for** billion.

B'nai B'rith /bəˌneɪ bəˈriːθ, ˈbrɪθ/ a Jewish organization founded in New York in 1843, which pursues educational, humanitarian, and cultural activities and attempts to safeguard the rights and interests of Jews around the world.
– ORIGIN Hebrew, literally 'sons of the covenant'.

BNP ▶ **abbreviation for** British National Party.

BO informal ▶ **abbreviation for** body odour.

bo[1] ▶ **exclamation** another term for **BOO**.
– ORIGIN late Middle English: imitative.

bo[2] ▶ **noun** US informal used as a friendly form of address.
– ORIGIN early 19th cent.: perhaps an abbreviated form of **BOY**.

boa /ˈbəʊə/ ▶ **noun** **1** a constrictor snake which bears live young and may reach great size, native to America, Africa, Asia, and some Pacific islands.
• Family Boidae, several genera and numerous species.
■ any snake which is a constrictor.
2 a long, thin stole of feathers or fur worn around a woman's neck, typically as part of evening dress.
– ORIGIN late Middle English: from Latin (mentioned in the writings of Pliny), of unknown ultimate origin.

boab /ˈbəʊab/ ▶ **noun** Austral. another term for **BAOBAB**.

boa constrictor ▶ **noun** a large snake, typically with bold markings, that kills by coiling around its prey and asphyxiating it, native to tropical America.
• *Boa constrictor*, family Boidae.

Boadicea /ˌbəʊdɪˈsiːə/ another name for **BOUDICCA**.

boak /ˈbəʊk/ ▶ **verb** variant spelling of **BOKE**.

boar ▶ **noun** (pl. same or **boars**) **1** (also **wild boar**) a tusked Eurasian wild pig from which domestic pigs are descended, exterminated in Britain in the 17th century.
• *Sus scrofa*, family Suidae.
■ [mass noun] the flesh of the wild boar as food.
2 an uncastrated domestic male pig.

■the full-grown male of certain other animals, especially a badger, guinea pig, or hedgehog.
– ORIGIN Old English *bār*, of West Germanic origin; related to Dutch *beer* and German *Bär*.

b

board ▶ **noun 1** a long, thin, flat piece of wood or other hard material, typically used for floors or other building purposes: *loose boards creaked as I walked on them* | [mass noun] *sections of board.*
■(**the boards**) informal the stage of a theatre. ■ (**the board**) Austral./NZ the part of the floor of a shearing shed where the shearers work. [ORIGIN: late 19th cent.: originally boards running alongside the pens.]
2 a thin, flat, rectangular piece of wood or other stiff material used for various purposes, in particular:
■a vertical surface on which to write or pin notices. ■ a horizontal surface on which to cut things, play games, or perform other activities. ■ a flat insulating sheet used as a mounting for an electronic circuit: *a graphics board.* ■ the piece of equipment on which a person stands in surfing, skateboarding, snowboarding, and certain other sports. ■ (**boards**) pieces of thick stiff card used for book covers. ■ (**boards**) the structure, typically of wood surmounted with panels of glass, surrounding an ice-hockey rink. ■ (**boards**) Basketball informal term for **BACKBOARD**.
3 [treated as sing. or pl.] a group of people constituted as the decision-making body of an organization: *he sits on the board of directors* | [in names] *the English Tourist Board* | [as modifier] *a board meeting.*
4 [mass noun] the provision of regular meals when one stays somewhere, in return for payment or services: *board and lodging.*
■[count noun] archaic a table set for a meal.
5 Sailing a distance covered by a vessel in a single tack.
▶ **verb 1** [with obj.] get on or into (a ship, aircraft, or other vehicle): *we boarded the plane for Oslo* | [no obj.] *they would not be able to board without a ticket.*
■(**be boarding**) (of an aircraft) be ready for passengers to get on: *Flight 172 to Istanbul is now boarding.*
2 [no obj.] live and receive regular meals in a house in return for payment or services: *the cousins boarded for a while with Ruby.*
■(of a pupil) live in school during term time in return for payment. ■ [with obj.] (usu. **be boarded**) provide (a person or animal) with regular meals and somewhere to live in return for payment: *dogs may have to be boarded at kennels.*
3 [with obj.] (**board something up/over**) cover or seal a window, shop, or other structure with pieces of wood: *the shop was still boarded up.*
4 [no obj.] ride on a snowboard.
– PHRASES **go by the board** (of something planned or previously upheld) be abandoned, rejected, or ignored: *my education just went by the board.* [ORIGIN: earlier in nautical use meaning 'fall overboard', used of a mast falling past the *board*, i.e. the side of the ship.] **on board** on or in a ship, aircraft, or other vehicle. ■ informal on to a team or group as a member: *the need to bring on board a young manager.* ■ informal (of a jockey) riding. **take something on board** informal fully consider or assimilate a new idea or situation. **tread** (or **walk**) **the boards** informal appear on stage as an actor.
– ORIGIN Old English *bord*, of Germanic origin; related to Dutch *boord* and German *Bort*; reinforced in Middle English by Old French *bort* 'edge, ship's side' and Old Norse *borth* 'board, table'.

boarded ▶ **adjective** (of a floor, roof, or other structure) built with pieces of wood.
■(of a window, shop, or other structure) covered or sealed with pieces of wood.

boarder ▶ **noun 1** a person who receives regular meals when staying somewhere, in return for payment or services.
■a pupil who lives in school during term time in return for payment.
2 a person who forces their way on to a ship in an attack.
3 a person who takes part in a sport using a board, such as surfing or snowboarding.

board foot ▶ **noun** (pl. **board feet**) a unit of volume for timber equal to 144 cu. inches.

board game ▶ **noun** a game that involves the movement of counters or other objects around a board.

boarding ▶ **noun** [mass noun] **1** long, flat, thin pieces of wood used to build or cover something.
2 the procedure according to which pupils live in school during term time in return for payment.
3 the action of getting on or into a ship, aircraft, or other vehicle.
4 Ice Hockey the illegal action of body-checking an opponent violently into the boards from behind.

boarding house ▶ **noun** a private house providing food and lodging for paying guests.

boarding kennel ▶ **noun** a place in which dogs are kept and looked after, especially while their owners are on holiday.

boarding pass (also **boarding card**) ▶ **noun** a pass for boarding an aircraft, given to passengers when checking in.

boarding school ▶ **noun** a school in which the pupils live during term time.

Board of Green Cloth ▶ **noun** full form of **GREEN CLOTH**.

Board of Trade ▶ **noun 1** North American term for **CHAMBER OF COMMERCE**.
■(in full **Chicago Board of Trade**) the Chicago futures exchange.
2 a now nominal British government department within the Department of Trade and Industry concerned with commerce and industry.

boardroom ▶ **noun** a room in which a board of directors of a company or other organization meets regularly.
■the directors of a company or organization considered collectively.

boardsailing ▶ **noun** another term for **WINDSURFING**.
– DERIVATIVES **boardsailor** noun.

board school ▶ **noun** historical an elementary school under the management of a School Board, established in Britain by the Education Act of 1870.

boardwalk ▶ **noun** a wooden walkway across sand or marshy ground.
■N. Amer. a promenade along a beach or waterfront, typically made of wood.

boarfish ▶ **noun** (pl. same or **-fishes**) any of a number of deep-bodied fishes with a protruding snout, a small mouth, small toothed scales, and a spiny dorsal fin:
● a temperate marine fish occurring around southern Africa, the North Pacific, and Australasia (*Pentaceros richardsoni* and others in the family Pentacerotidae). ● a marine fish of the NE Atlantic (family Caproidae, in particular *Capros aper*).

boart ▶ **noun** variant spelling of **BORT**.

Boas /ˈbəʊaz/, Franz (1858–1942), German-born American anthropologist. A pioneer of modern anthropology, he developed the linguistic and cultural components of ethnology. He did much to overturn the theory that Nordic peoples constitute an essentially superior race; his writings were burnt by the Nazis.

boast[1] ▶ **verb 1** [reporting verb] talk with excessive pride and self-satisfaction about one's achievements, possessions, or abilities: [with direct speech] *Ted used to boast 'I manage ten people'* | [with clause] *he boasted that he had taken part in the crime* | [no obj.] *she boasted about her many conquests.*
2 [with obj.] (of a person, place, or thing) possess (a feature that is a source of pride): *the hotel boasts high standards of comfort.*
▶ **noun** an act of talking with excessive pride and self-satisfaction: *I said I would score and it wasn't an idle boast.*
– DERIVATIVES **boaster** noun, **boastingly** adverb.
– ORIGIN Middle English (as a noun): of unknown origin.

boast[2] ▶ **noun** (in squash) a stroke in which the ball is made to hit one of the side walls before hitting the front wall.
– ORIGIN late 19th cent.: perhaps from French *bosse* denoting a rounded projection in the wall of a court for real tennis.

boastful ▶ **adjective** showing excessive pride and self-satisfaction in one's achievements, possessions, or abilities.
– DERIVATIVES **boastfully** adverb, **boastfulness** noun.

boat ▶ **noun 1** a small vessel for travelling over water, propelled by oars, sails, or an engine: *a fishing boat* | [as modifier] *a boat trip.*
■a vessel of any size, especially a large one carrying passengers.
2 a gravy boat or sauce boat.
▶ **verb** [no obj.] travel or go in a boat for pleasure: *they boated through fjords.*
■[with obj. and adverbial of direction] transport (someone or something) in a boat: *they boated the timber down the lake.* ■ [with obj.] (of an angler) draw (a hooked fish) into a boat.
– PHRASES **be in the same boat** informal be in the same unfortunate or difficult circumstances as others. **off the boat** informal, often offensive recently arrived from a foreign country, and by implication naive or an outsider: *What are you, fresh off the boat?* **push the boat out** Brit. informal be lavish in one's spending or celebrations. **rock the boat** informal say or do something to disturb an existing situation and upset other people.
– DERIVATIVES **boatful** noun (pl. **-fuls**).
– ORIGIN Old English *bāt*, of Germanic origin.

boatbill ▶ **noun 1** (also **boat-billed heron**) a small Central and South American heron with a broad flattened bill and a prominent black crest.
● *Cochlearius cochlearius*, family Ardeidae.
2 a flycatcher that has a very broad flattened bill with a hooked tip, found mainly in New Guinea. Also called **FLATBILL FLYCATCHER**.
● Genus *Machaerirhynchus*, family Monarchidae: two species, in particular the **yellow-breasted boatbill** (*M. flaviventer*).

boatbuilding ▶ **noun** [mass noun] the occupation or industry of building boats.
– DERIVATIVES **boatbuilder** noun.

boat deck ▶ **noun** the deck from which a ship's lifeboats are launched.

boatel /bəʊˈtɛl/ (also **botel**) ▶ **noun 1** a waterside hotel with facilities for mooring boats.
2 a ship moored at a wharf and used as a hotel.
– ORIGIN 1950s (originally US): blend of **BOAT** and **HOTEL**.

boater ▶ **noun 1** a flat-topped hardened straw hat with a brim. [ORIGIN: so named because originally worn while boating.]
2 a person who uses or travels in a boat for pleasure.

boathook ▶ **noun** a long pole with a hook and a spike at one end, used for fending off or pulling a boat.

boathouse ▶ **noun** a shed at the edge of a river or lake used for housing boats.

boatie ▶ **noun** (pl. **-ies**) informal, chiefly Austral./NZ a boating enthusiast.
■Brit. derogatory a university rower.

boating ▶ **noun** [mass noun] rowing or sailing in boats as a sport or form of recreation.

boatload ▶ **noun** an amount of cargo or number of passengers which will fill a ship or boat: *a* **boatload** *of coal.*
■informal a large number of people: *the company has signed a* **boatload of** *distributors for the new product.*

boatman ▶ **noun** (pl. **-men**) a person who hires out boats or provides transport by boat.

boat people ▶ **plural noun** refugees who have left a country by sea, in particular the Vietnamese people who fled in small boats to Hong Kong, Australia, and elsewhere after the conquest of South Vietnam by North Vietnam in 1975.

boat race ▶ **noun 1** a race between rowing crews.
■(**the Boat Race**) the annual boat race between Oxford and Cambridge. First rowed at Henley in 1829, it has been held over its present course, from Putney to Mortlake (6.8 km, 4.25 miles), since 1845.
2 Brit. rhyming slang a person's face.

boat shell ▶ **noun** North American term for **SLIPPER LIMPET**.

boatswain /ˈbəʊs(ə)n/ (also **bo'sun** or **bosun**) ▶ **noun** a ship's officer in charge of equipment and the crew.
– ORIGIN late Old English *bātswegen* (see **BOAT**, **SWAIN**).

boatswain's chair ▶ **noun** a seat suspended from ropes, used for work on the body or masts of a ship or the face of a building.

boat train ▶ **noun** a train scheduled to connect with the arrival or departure of a boat.

boatyard ▶ **noun** an enclosed area of land where boats are built or stored.

Boa Vista /ˌbəʊə ˈvɪstə/ a town in northern Brazil, capital of the state of Roraima; pop. 130,426 (1990).

Bob ▶ **noun** (in phrase **Bob's your uncle**) Brit. informal used to express the ease with which a task can be achieved: *fill in the form, and Bob's your uncle.*
– ORIGIN 1930s: pet form of the given name *Robert*.

bob[1] ▶ **verb** (**bobbed**, **bobbing**) [no obj., with adverbial of

direction] make a quick, short movement up and down: *I could see his ginger head bobbing about* | *the boat bobbed up and down.*
  ■[with obj.] cause (something) to make such a movement: *she bobbed her head.* ■ [no obj., with adverbial of direction] make a sudden move in a particular direction so as to appear or disappear: *a lady bobbed up from beneath the counter.* ■ [no obj.] move up and down briefly in a curtsy.
▶ noun a quick, short movement up and down: *she could only manage a slight bob of her head.*
  ■ a brief curtsy.
− PHRASES **bob and weave** make rapid bodily movements up and down and from side to side, for example as an evasive tactic by a boxer. **bob for apples** try to catch floating or hanging apples with one's mouth alone, as a game.
− ORIGIN late Middle English: of unknown origin.

bob² ▶ noun **1** a style in which the hair is cut short and evenly all round so that it hangs above the shoulders. **2** a weight on a pendulum, plumb line, or kite-tail. **3** a bobsleigh. **4** a short line at or towards the end of a stanza.
▶ verb (**bobbed**, **bobbing**) **1** [with obj.] [usu. as adj. **bobbed**] cut (someone's hair) in a bob. **2** [no obj.] ride on a bobsleigh.
− ORIGIN late Middle English (denoting a bunch or cluster): of unknown origin.

bob³ ▶ noun (pl. same) Brit. informal a shilling.
  ■ used with reference to a moderately large but unspecified amount of money: *those vases are worth a few bob.*
− ORIGIN late 18th cent.: of unknown origin.

bob⁴ ▶ noun a change of order in bell-ringing.
  ■ used in names of change-ringing methods: *plain bob* | *bob minor.*
− ORIGIN late 17th cent.: perhaps connected with **BOB¹** in the noun sense 'sudden movement up and down'.

bobber ▶ noun **1** a person who rides on a bobsleigh. **2** a float used in angling.

bobbin ▶ noun **1** a cylinder or cone holding thread, yarn, or wire, used especially in weaving and machine sewing.
  ■ a spool or reel. **2** a small bar attached to a string used for raising a door latch.
− ORIGIN mid 16th cent.: from French *bobine*, of unknown origin.

bobbinet /ˈbɒbɪnɛt/ ▶ noun [mass noun] machine-made cotton net (imitating lace made with bobbins on a pillow).
− ORIGIN mid 19th cent.: from **BOBBIN** + **NET¹**.

bobbin lace ▶ noun [mass noun] lace made by hand with thread wound on bobbins.

bobble¹ ▶ noun a small ball made of strands of wool used as a decoration on a hat or on furnishings.
− DERIVATIVES **bobbly** adjective.
− ORIGIN 1920s: diminutive of **BOB²**.

bobble² /ˈbɒb(ə)l/ informal ▶ verb **1** [no obj.] move with a feeble or irregular bouncing motion: *some of those goals have bobbled in off the post.* **2** [with obj.] N. Amer. mishandle (a ball): *Andy bobbled the ball, so his throw home was too late.*
▶ noun **1** a feeble or irregular bouncing motion. **2** N. Amer. a mishandling of a ball.
− ORIGIN early 19th cent.: frequentative of **BOB¹**.

bobby ▶ noun (pl. **-ies**) Brit. informal, dated a police officer.
− ORIGIN mid 19th cent.: pet form of *Robert*, given name of Sir Robert **PEEL**.

bobby calf ▶ noun (pl. **-ies**) an unweaned calf slaughtered for veal.
− ORIGIN 1920s: perhaps from **BOB²**, *bobby calf* being one of a number of collocations where *bobby* has the sense 'small, short'. Compare with the dialect term *staggering bob* for a very young calf or its meat, recorded from the late 18th cent., perhaps from the pet form of *Robert*, and describing a calf too young to walk steadily.

bobby-dazzler ▶ noun Brit. informal, dated a person or thing considered remarkable or excellent.
− ORIGIN mid 19th cent. (originally northern English dialect): related to **DAZZLE**; the origin of the first element is unknown.

bobby pin ▶ noun N. Amer. & Austral./NZ a kind of sprung hairpin or small clip.

▶ verb (**bobby-pin**) [with obj.] fix (hair) in place with such a pin or clip.
− ORIGIN 1930s: from **BOB²** (because bobby pins were originally used with bobbed hair) + **-Y²**.

bobby socks (also **bobby sox**) ▶ plural noun N. Amer. short socks reaching just above the ankle, as worn by teenage girls in the 1940s and 1950s.
− ORIGIN compare with **BOB²** in the sense 'cut short'.

bobby-soxer ▶ noun N. Amer. informal, dated an adolescent girl.

bobcat ▶ noun a small North American lynx with a barred and spotted coat and a short tail.
  ● *Felis rufus*, family Felidae.
− ORIGIN late 19th cent.: from **BOB²** (with reference to its short tail) + **CAT¹**.

bobol /ˈbʌbɔːl/ W. Indian ▶ noun a fraud committed with public funds.
▶ verb (**bobolled**, **bobolling**) [no obj.] commit such a fraud.
− ORIGIN of unknown origin.

bobolink /ˈbɒbəlɪŋk/ ▶ noun a North American songbird of the American blackbird family, with a finch-like bill. The male has black, buff, and white plumage.
  ● *Dolichonyx oryzivorus*, family Icteridae.
− ORIGIN late 18th cent. (originally *Bob o'Lincoln, Bob Lincoln*): imitative of its call.

bobotie /bəˈbuːti, -ˈbʊəti/ ▶ noun [mass noun] a South African dish of curried minced meat baked with a savoury custard topping.
− ORIGIN Afrikaans, probably of Malay or Javanese origin.

Bobruisk /bəˈbrujsk/ (also **Bobruysk**) Russian name for **BABRUISK**.

bobskate ▶ noun Canadian an adjustable skate for a child, consisting of two sections of double runners.

bobsled /ˈbɒbslɛd/ ▶ noun North American term for **BOBSLEIGH**.
− DERIVATIVES **bobsledding** noun.

bobsleigh ▶ noun Brit. a mechanically steered and braked sledge, typically for two or four people, used for racing down an ice-covered run.
− DERIVATIVES **bobsleighing** noun.
− ORIGIN mid 19th cent. (originally US, denoting a sleigh made of two short sleighs coupled together and used for hauling logs): from **BOB²** in the sense 'short' + **SLEIGH**.

bobstay ▶ noun a rope used to hold down the bowsprit of a ship and keep it steady.
− ORIGIN mid 18th cent.: probably from **BOB¹** + **STAY²**.

bobsy-die /ˌbɒbzɪˈdʌɪ/ ▶ noun [mass noun] dialect & NZ a great deal of fuss or trouble: *kicking up bobsy-die.*
− ORIGIN early 19th cent.: contraction of earlier *Bob's-a-dying.*

bobtail ▶ noun a docked tail of a horse or dog.
− ORIGIN mid 16th cent.: probably from **BOB²** + **TAIL¹**. It was originally recorded as a humorous term for a kind of broad-headed arrow, probably because it looked as though it had been cut short.

bobweight ▶ noun a component used as a counterweight to a moving part in a machine.

bobwhite (also **bobwhite quail**) ▶ noun a New World quail with mottled reddish-brown plumage, and typically a pale throat and eyestripe.
  ● Genus *Colinus*, family Phasianidae: two species, in particular the **northern bobwhite** (*C. virginianus*).
− ORIGIN early 19th cent.: imitative of its call.

bocage /bəˈkɑːʒ/ ▶ noun [mass noun] (in France) pastureland divided into small hedged fields interspersed with groves of trees.
  ■ the modelling of leaves, flowers, and plants in clay, especially for porcelain figurines.
− ORIGIN late 16th cent.: from French, from Old French *boscage* (see **BOSCAGE**).

Boccaccio /bɒˈkatʃɪəʊ/, Giovanni (1313–75), Italian writer, poet, and humanist. He is most famous for the *Decameron* (1348–58), a collection of a hundred tales told by ten young people who have moved to the country to escape the Black Death.

bocce /ˈbɒtʃeɪ, ˈbɒtʃi/ (also **boccia** /ˈbɒtʃə/) ▶ noun [mass noun] an Italian game similar to bowls but played on a shorter, narrower green.
− ORIGIN Italian, 'bowls', plural of *boccia* 'ball'.

Boccherini /ˌbɒkəˈriːni/, Luigi (1743–1805), Italian composer and cellist, known chiefly for his cello concertos and sonatas.

bocconcini /ˌbɒkɒnˈtʃiːni/ ▶ plural noun small balls of mozzarella cheese.
− ORIGIN Italian.

Boche /bɒʃ/ informal, dated ▶ noun a German, especially a soldier.
  ■ (the Boche) Germans, especially German soldiers, considered collectively.
▶ adjective German.
− ORIGIN French soldiers' slang, originally in the sense 'rascal', later used in the First World War meaning 'German'.

Bochum /ˈbɒʊxɒm, German ˈboːxʊm/ an industrial city in the Ruhr valley, North Rhine-Westphalia, Germany; pop. 398,580 (1991).

bock ▶ noun [mass noun] a strong, dark German beer.
− ORIGIN mid 19th cent.: via French from an abbreviation of German *Eimbockbier* 'beer from *Einbeck*', a town in Hanover.

BOD ▶ abbreviation for biochemical oxygen demand.

bod ▶ noun informal a body: *a line-up of stunning bods.*
  ■ chiefly Brit. a person: *some clever bod wrote a song about them.*
− ORIGIN late 18th cent. (originally Scots): abbreviation of **BODY**.

bodach /ˈbɒʊdaːx/ ▶ noun Scottish & Irish **1** a man, especially a peasant or an old man. **2** a ghost; a spectre.
− ORIGIN early 19th cent. (earlier as *buddough*): from Scottish Gaelic.

bodacious /bəʊˈdeɪʃəs/ ▶ adjective N. Amer. informal excellent, admirable, or attractive: *bodacious babes.*
  ■ US audacious in a way considered admirable.
− ORIGIN mid 19th cent.: perhaps a variant of SW dialect *boldacious*, blend of **BOLD** and **AUDACIOUS**.

bode ▶ verb [no obj.] (**bode well/ill**) be a portent of a particular outcome: *their argument did not bode well for the future* | [with obj.] *the 12 per cent interest rate bodes dark days ahead for retailers.*
− ORIGIN Old English *bodian* 'proclaim, foretell', from *boda* 'messenger', of Germanic origin; related to German *Bote*, also to **BID¹**.

bodega /bəˈdeɪɡə/ ▶ noun a cellar or shop selling wine and food, especially in a Spanish-speaking country or area.
− ORIGIN mid 19th cent.: from Spanish, via Latin from Greek *apothēkē* 'storehouse'. Compare with **BOUTIQUE**.

Bodensee /ˈboːdnˌzeː/ German name for Lake Constance (see **CONSTANCE, LAKE**).

Bode's law /ˈbəʊdz, ˈbəʊdəz/ Astronomy a formula by which the distances of the first seven planets from the sun are roughly derived in terms of powers of two.
− ORIGIN mid 19th cent.: named after Johann E. *Bode* (1747–1826), the German astronomer who drew attention to the law, which was discovered earlier by his countryman, Johann D. Titius (1729–96).

bodge ▶ verb [with obj.] Brit. informal make or repair (something) badly or clumsily: *the door was bodged together from old planks.*
− ORIGIN mid 16th cent.: alteration of **BOTCH**.

bodger informal ▶ noun Brit. a person who makes or repairs something badly or clumsily.
▶ adjective Austral. worthless or inferior.

bodgie ▶ noun (pl. **-ies**) Austral. informal **1** a youth, especially of the 1950s, analogous to the British Teddy boy. **2** something flawed or worthless.
− ORIGIN probably from **BODGER**; a term said to have arisen as a result of the post-war black market trade in American-made cloth in Sydney, Australia; when inferior cloth was passed off as American-made, it was called *bodgie*, extended to denote any young man who adopted an American accent and manner.

Bodhgaya /ˌbɒdɡəˈjɑː, ˌbəʊd-/ (also **Buddh Gaya**) a village in the state of Bihar, NE India, where the Buddha attained enlightenment.

bodhisattva /ˌbɒdɪˈsɑːtvə/ ▶ noun (in Mahayana Buddhism) a person who is able to reach nirvana but delays doing so through compassion for suffering beings.
− ORIGIN Sanskrit, 'a person whose essence is perfect knowledge', from *bodhi* 'perfect knowledge' (from *budh-* 'know perfectly') + *sattva* 'being, essence'.

bodhrán /ˈbaʊrɑːn, baʊˈrɑːn/ ▶ noun a shallow one-sided Irish drum typically played using a short stick with knobbed ends.

– ORIGIN Irish.

bodh tree ▶ noun variant spelling of **BO TREE**.

bodice ▶ noun the part of a woman's dress (excluding sleeves) which is above the waist.
■ a woman's undergarment for this part of the body, like a vest.
– ORIGIN mid 16th cent. (originally *bodies*): plural of **BODY**, retaining the original pronunciation. The term probably first denoted an undergarment, then known as a *pair of bodice*, although this sense is not recorded until the early 17th cent.

bodice-ripper ▶ noun informal, derogatory or humorous a sexually explicit romantic novel or film with a historical setting.
– DERIVATIVES **bodice-ripping** adjective.

bodiless ▶ adjective lacking a body: *a bodiless head.*
■ incorporeal or insubstantial: *a sinister, bodiless voice.*

bodily ▶ adjective [attrib.] of or concerning the body: *children learn to control their bodily functions.*
■ material or actual as opposed to spiritual or incorporeal: *God is not present in bodily form.*
▶ adverb by taking hold of a person's body, especially with force: *he hauled her bodily from the van.*
■ with one's whole body; with great force: *he launched himself bodily at the door.*

bodkin ▶ noun a thick, blunt needle with a large eye, used especially for drawing tape or cord through a hem.
■ historical a long pin used by women for fastening up the hair. ■ Printing a pointed tool used for removing pieces of metal type for correction.
– ORIGIN Middle English: perhaps of Celtic origin and related to Irish *bod*, Welsh *bidog*, Scottish Gaelic *biodag* 'dagger'.

Bodleian Library /ˈbɒdlɪən/ the library of Oxford University, one of six copyright libraries in the UK.

Bodley, Sir Thomas (1545–1613), English scholar and diplomat. He refounded and greatly enlarged the Oxford University library, which was renamed the Bodleian in 1604.
■ an informal name for the Bodleian Library.

Bodoni /bəˈdəʊni/, Giambattista (1740–1813), Italian printer. He designed a typeface characterized by extreme contrast between uprights and diagonals, which is named after him.

Bodrum /ˈbɒdrəm/ a resort town on the Aegean coast of western Turkey, site of the ancient city of Halicarnassus.

body ▶ noun (pl. **-ies**) **1** the physical structure, including the bones, flesh, and organs, of a person or an animal: *it's important to keep your body in good condition* | [as modifier] *body temperature.*
■ a corpse: *they found his body washed up on the beach.* ■ [mass noun] the physical and mortal aspect of a person as opposed to the soul or spirit: *we're together in body and spirit.* ■ informal a person's body regarded as an object of sexual desire: *he was just after her body.* ■ informal, dated a person, typically one of a specified type or character: *a motherly body.*
2 the trunk apart from the head and the limbs: *the blow almost severed his head from his body.*
■ (**the body of**) the main or central part of something, especially a building or text, as distinct from subordinate or additional parts: *information that changes regularly is kept apart from the main body of the text.* ■ the main section of a car or aircraft: *the body of the aircraft was filled with smoke.* ■ a large or substantial amount of something; a mass or collection of something: *a rich* **body** *of Canadian folklore* | *large* **bodies** *of seawater.* ■ a woman's close-fitting stretch garment for the upper body, fastening at the crotch. ■ (in pottery) a clay used for making the main part of ceramic ware, as distinct from a glaze.
3 a group of people with a common purpose or function acting as an organized unit: *a regulatory body* | *international bodies of experts.*
4 [often with adj.] technical a distinct piece of matter; a material object: *the path taken by the falling body.*
5 [mass noun] a full or substantial quality of flavour in wine.
■ fullness or thickness of a person's hair: *restructuring formulations help to add body.*
▶ verb (**-ies**, **-ied**) [with obj.] **1** (**body something forth**) give material form to something abstract: *he bodied forth the traditional Prussian remedy for all ills.*
2 build the bodywork of (a motor vehicle): *an era when cars were bodied over wooden frames.*
– PHRASES **body and soul** involving every aspect of a person: *the company owned them body and soul.* **in a body** all together; as a group: *they departed*

in a body. **keep body and soul together** stay alive, especially in difficult circumstances: *do you think a man can keep body and soul together by selling coconuts?* **over my dead body** informal used to emphasize that one completely opposes something and would do anything to prevent it from happening: *she moves into our home over my dead body.*
– DERIVATIVES **bodied** adjective [in combination] *a wide-bodied jet.*
– ORIGIN Old English *bodig*, of unknown origin.

body armour ▶ noun [mass noun] clothing worn by army and police personnel to protect against gunfire.

body art ▶ noun [mass noun] **1** items of jewellery or clothing worn on the body and regarded as art.
■ the practice of decorating the body by means of tattooing, piercing, plastic surgery, etc.
2 an artistic genre, originating in the 1970s, in which the actual body of the artist or model is integral to the work.

body bag ▶ noun a bag used for carrying a corpse from a battlefield or the scene of an accident or crime.

body blow ▶ noun a heavy punch to the body.
■ figurative a severe disappointment or crushing setback: *a tax on books would be a body blow for education.*

bodyboard ▶ noun a short, light type of surfboard ridden in a prone position.
– DERIVATIVES **bodyboarder** noun, **bodyboarding** noun.

body brush ▶ noun a soft brush for grooming a horse.

bodybuilder ▶ noun **1** a person who strengthens and enlarges the muscles of their body through strenuous exercise.
2 a person or company that builds the bodies of vehicles.
– DERIVATIVES **bodybuilding** noun.

body-centred ▶ adjective denoting a crystal structure in which there is an atom at each vertex and at the centre of the unit cell.

body-check ▶ noun (especially in ice hockey) an attempt to obstruct a player by bumping into them, typically with the shoulder or hip.
▶ verb [with obj.] obstruct (a player) in such a way.

body clock ▶ noun a person's or animal's biological clock.

body colour ▶ noun [mass noun] opaque pigment used in painting, especially gouache.

body corporate ▶ noun formal term for **CORPORATION**.

body double ▶ noun a stand-in for a film actor used during stunt or nude scenes.

body English ▶ noun [mass noun] N. Amer. **1** a follow-through bodily action after throwing or hitting a ball, intended as an attempt to control the ball's trajectory.
2 another term for **BODY LANGUAGE**.

bodyguard ▶ noun a person or group of people employed to escort and protect an important or famous person.

body language ▶ noun [mass noun] the conscious and unconscious movements and postures by which attitudes and feelings are communicated: *his intent was clearly expressed in his body language.*

bodyline ▶ noun [mass noun] Cricket, historical persistent short-pitched fast bowling on the leg side, threatening the batsman's body, especially as employed by England in the Ashes series in Australia in 1932–3.

body louse ▶ noun a louse which infests the human body and is especially prevalent where hygiene is poor. It is able to transmit several diseases through its bite, including typhus.
● *Pediculus humanus humanus*, family Pediculidae, order Anoplura. See also **HEAD LOUSE**.

body odour ▶ noun [mass noun] the unpleasant smell of a person's unwashed body.

body piercing ▶ noun [mass noun] the piercing of holes in parts of the body other than the ear lobes in order to insert rings or other decorative objects.

body politic ▶ noun (usu. **the body politic**) the people of a nation, state, or society considered collectively as an organized group of citizens.

body-popping ▶ noun [mass noun] a kind of street dancing characterized by jerky robotic movements of the joints.

body press ▶ noun Wrestling a move in which a wrestler uses their body weight to pin an opponent to the floor.

body scrub ▶ noun an exfoliating cosmetic preparation applied to the body to cleanse the skin.
■ a type of beauty treatment in which the skin is cleaned and exfoliated.

body search ▶ noun a search of a person's body and clothing for illicit weapons, drugs, or other articles, conducted typically by customs officials or the police.

bodyshell ▶ noun the metal frame of a motor or railway vehicle, to which the metal panels are attached.

body shop ▶ noun chiefly N. Amer. a garage where repairs to the bodywork of vehicles are carried out.

bodyside ▶ noun the side of the body of a vehicle.

body slam ▶ noun Wrestling a move (illegal in some codes) in which the opponent's body is lifted and then thrown hard on to the floor.

bodysnatcher ▶ noun historical a person who illicitly disinterred corpses for dissection, for which there was no legal provision until 1832.
– DERIVATIVES **bodysnatching** noun.

body stocking ▶ noun a woman's one-piece undergarment which covers the torso and legs.

bodysuit ▶ noun a close-fitting one-piece stretch garment for women, worn typically for sporting activities.

bodysurf ▶ verb [no obj.] [often as noun **bodysurfing**] float on the crest of incoming waves without using a board.

body swerve ▶ noun an abrupt swerving movement of the whole body, used as a tactic to avoid contact or collision.

body text ▶ noun (usu. **the body text**) the main part of a printed text, excluding items such as headings and footnotes.

body warmer ▶ noun a sleeveless quilted or padded jacket worn as an outdoor garment.

body wave ▶ noun a soft, light permanent wave designed to give the hair fullness.

bodywork ▶ noun [mass noun] **1** the metal outer shell of a vehicle.
2 therapies and techniques in complementary medicine which involve touching or manipulating the body.
– DERIVATIVES **bodyworker** noun (only in sense 2).

body wrap ▶ noun a type of beauty treatment intended to result in a reduction in body measurements, involving the application of skin-cleansing ingredients to the body, which is then wrapped in hot bandages.

Boeotia /biˈəʊʃə/ a department of central Greece, to the north of the Gulf of Corinth, and a region of ancient Greece of which the chief city was Thebes.
– DERIVATIVES **Boeotian** adjective & noun.

Boer /bɔː, ˈbəʊə, bʊə/ chiefly historical ▶ noun a member of the Dutch and Huguenot population which settled in southern Africa in the late 17th century.

The Boers were Calvinist in religion and fiercely self-sufficient. Conflict with the British administration of Cape Colony after 1806 led to the Great Trek of 1835–7 and the Boer Wars, after which the Boer republics of Transvaal and Orange Free State became part of the Republic of South Africa. The Boers' present-day descendants are the Afrikaners.

▶ adjective of or relating to the Boers.
– ORIGIN from Dutch *boer* 'farmer'.

boerbull /ˈbʊəbʊl/ ▶ noun S. African a large cross-breed dog bred from the mastiff and indigenous African dogs.
– ORIGIN 1960s: from Afrikaans *boerboel*, from *boer* (commonly applied to indigenous plants and animals) + *boel*, from Dutch *bul* (as in *bulhond* 'mastiff').

boeremusiek /ˈbʊərəmjuːzɪk/ ▶ noun [mass noun] S. African traditional Afrikaner music, often for dancing.
– ORIGIN Afrikaans, from *boere* 'Afrikaner' + *musiek* 'music'.

boerewors /ˈbuːrəvɔːs, ˈbʊ-/ ▶ noun [mass noun] S. African a type of traditional sausage, typically containing coarsely ground beef and pork seasoned with spices.
– ORIGIN Afrikaans, from *boere* 'Afrikaner or farmer's' + *wors* 'sausage'.

boer goat ▶**noun** a goat of a hardy breed, originally from South Africa.
– ORIGIN from Afrikaans *boer* 'farmer' + **GOAT**.

boerie /ˈbʊri/ ▶**noun** S. African informal another term for **BOEREWORS**.

Boer Wars two wars fought by Great Britain in southern Africa between 1880 and 1902.

> The first war (1880–1) began with the revolt of the Boer settlers in Transvaal against British rule and ended with the establishment of an independent Boer Republic under British suzerainty. The second (1899–1902) was caused by the Boer refusal to grant equal rights to recent British immigrants and by the imperialist ambitions of Cecil Rhodes. The British eventually won through superior numbers and the employment of concentration camps to control the countryside.

Boethius /bəʊˈiːθɪəs/, Anicius Manlius Severinus (*c.*480–524), Roman statesman and philosopher, best known for *The Consolation of Philosophy*, which he wrote while in prison on a charge of treason.

boeuf /bœf/ ▶**noun** [mass noun] French word for **BEEF**, used in the names of various beef dishes.

boeuf bourguignon /ˌbəːf ˈbɔːɡɪnjɒ̃/ ▶**noun** [mass noun] a dish consisting of beef stewed in red wine.
– ORIGIN French, literally 'Burgundy beef'.

boff[1] N. Amer. informal ▶**verb** [with obj.] **1** hit or strike (someone).
2 have sexual intercourse with (someone).
▶**noun 1** a blow or punch.
2 an act of sexual intercourse.
– ORIGIN 1920s: imitative. Sense 2 dates from the 1950s.

boff[2] ▶**noun** short for **BOFFIN**.

boffin ▶**noun** informal, chiefly Brit. a person engaged in scientific or technical research: *a computer boffin.*
■a person with knowledge or a skill considered to be complex, arcane, and difficult: *he had a reputation as a tax boffin, a learned lawyer.*
– DERIVATIVES **boffiny** adjective.
– ORIGIN Second World War: of unknown origin.

boffo N. Amer. informal ▶**adjective 1** (of a theatrical production or film, or a review of one) resoundingly successful or wholeheartedly commendatory: *a boffo box office certainty.*
2 (of a laugh) deep and unrestrained.
■boisterously funny.
▶**noun** (pl. **-os**) a success: *the finale is a genuine boffo.*
– ORIGIN 1940s: from US *boff* 'roaring success' + **-O**.

boffola /bɒˈfəʊlə/ N. Amer. informal ▶**noun** a joke or a line in a script meant to get a laugh.
▶**adjective** (of a laugh) hearty and unrestrained.
– ORIGIN 1940s: extension of slang *boff* 'hearty laugh'.

Bofors gun /ˈbəʊfəz/ ▶**noun** a type of light anti-aircraft gun.
– ORIGIN 1930s: named after *Bofors* in Sweden, where it was first manufactured.

bog ▶**noun 1** an area of wet muddy ground that is too soft to support a heavy body: *a peat bog* | figurative *a bog of legal complications* | [mass noun] *the island is a wilderness of bog and loch.*
■Ecology wetland with acid, peaty soil, typically dominated by peat moss. Compare with **FEN**[1].
2 (usu. **the bog**) Brit. informal a toilet.
▶**verb** (**bogged**, **bogging**) [with obj.] (usu. **be bogged down**) cause (a vehicle, person, or animal) to become stuck in mud or wet ground: *the family Rover became bogged down on the beach road* | figurative *you must not* **get bogged down in** *detail.*
– DERIVATIVES **bogginess** noun, **boggy** adjective.
– ORIGIN Middle English: from Irish or Scottish Gaelic *bogach*, from *bog* 'soft'.
▶**bog in** Austral./NZ start a task enthusiastically: *if he saw a trucker in difficulty, he would just bog in and give a hand.* [ORIGIN: early 20th cent.: *bog* probably in the sense 'sink, immerse (oneself)'.]
bog off Brit. informal go away: *I told him to bog off.*

bogan[1] /ˈbəʊɡ(ə)n/ ▶**noun** Austral. informal a foolish person.

bogan[2] /ˈbəʊɡ(ə)n/ ▶**noun** Canadian a side stream.
– ORIGIN Algonquian.

Bogarde /ˈbəʊɡɑːd/, Sir Dirk (1921–99), British actor and writer, of Dutch descent; born *Derek Niven van den Bogaerde*. He became famous in the 'Doctor' series of comedy films. Other notable films: *The Servant* (1963) and *Death in Venice* (1971).

Bogart /ˈbəʊɡɑːt/, Humphrey (DeForest) (1899–1957), American actor. His many films include *Casablanca* (1942), *The Big Sleep* (1946, in which he played opposite his fourth wife Lauren Bacall), and *The African Queen* (1951, for which he won an Oscar).

bog arum ▶**noun** a plant of the arum family, with heart-shaped leaves, a white spathe, and a green spadix. It grows in swamps and boggy ground in north temperate regions. Also called **CALLA** or **WATER CALLA**.
● *Calla palustris*, family Araceae.

bog asphodel ▶**noun** a yellow-flowered European marsh plant of the lily family.
● *Narthecium ossifragum*, family Liliaceae.

bogbean ▶**noun** a plant of bogs and shallow water which has creeping rhizomes, bean-like three-lobed leaves, and hairy white or pinkish flowers. Also called **BUCKBEAN**.
● *Menyanthes trifoliata*, family Menyanthaceae.

bog cotton ▶**noun** another term for **COTTON GRASS**.

bogey[1] Golf ▶**noun** (pl. **-eys**) a score of one stroke over par at a hole.
■old-fashioned term for **PAR**[1] in sense 1.
▶**verb** (**-eys**, **-eyed**) [with obj.] play (a hole) in one stroke over par.
– ORIGIN late 19th cent.: perhaps from *Bogey*, denoting the Devil (see **BOGEY**[2]), regarded as an imaginary player.

bogey[2] (also **bogy**) ▶**noun** (pl. **-eys**) **1** an evil or mischievous spirit.
■a person or thing that causes fear or alarm: *the bogey of recession.* ■US military slang an enemy aircraft. ■informal, dated a detective or policeman.
2 Brit. informal a piece of nasal mucus.
– ORIGIN mid 19th cent. (as a proper name applied to the Devil): of unknown origin; probably related to **BOGLE**.

bogeyman (also **bogyman**) ▶**noun** (pl. **-men**) (usu. **the bogeyman**) an imaginary evil spirit, used to frighten children.
■a person or thing that is widely regarded as an object of fear: *the violent criminal has replaced the communist as the bogeyman.*

bog garden ▶**noun** a piece of land laid out and irrigated to grow plants which prefer a damp habitat.

boggart /ˈbɒɡət/ ▶**noun** Scottish & N. English an evil or mischievous spirit.
– ORIGIN late 16th cent.: related to obsolete *bog* 'bugbear', **BOGGLE**, and **BOGLE**.

boggle ▶**verb** [no obj.] informal (of a person or their mind) be astonished or alarmed when trying to imagine something: **the mind boggles at** *the spectacle.*
■[with obj.] cause (a person or their mind) to be astonished in such a way: *the inflated salary of a star boggles the mind* | [as adj. **boggling**] *the total was a boggling 1.5 trillion miles.* ■(**boggle at**) (of a person) hesitate or be anxious at: *you never boggle at plain speaking.*
– ORIGIN late 16th cent.: probably of dialect origin and related to **BOGLE** and **BOGEY**[2].

bogie /ˈbəʊɡi/ ▶**noun** (pl. **-ies**) chiefly Brit. an undercarriage with four or six wheels pivoted beneath the end of a railway vehicle.
■Indian a railway carriage. ■chiefly N. English a low truck on four small wheels; a trolley.
– ORIGIN early 19th cent. (originally in northern English dialect use): of unknown origin.

bog iron (also **bog iron ore**) ▶**noun** [mass noun] an impure, porous form of limonite deposited in bogs.

bogland ▶**noun** [mass noun] marshy land.

bogle ▶**noun** a phantom or goblin.
■Scottish & N. English a scarecrow.
– ORIGIN early 16th cent.: of unknown origin; probably related to **BOGEY**[2].

bog moss ▶**noun** another term for **PEAT MOSS** (in sense 1).

bog myrtle ▶**noun** a deciduous shrub of boggy places, with short upright catkins and aromatic grey-green leaves with insecticidal properties. Also called **SWEET GALE**.
● *Myrica gale*, family Myricaceae.

bog oak ▶**noun** an ancient oak tree which has been preserved in peat, with hard black wood.

Bogomil /ˈbəʊɡəmɪl, ˈbɒɡ-/ ▶**noun** historical a member of a heretical medieval Balkan sect professing a modified form of Manichaeism.
– DERIVATIVES **Bogomilism** noun.
– ORIGIN mid 19th cent.: from medieval Greek *Bogomilos*, from *Bogomil*, literally 'beloved of God', the name of the person who first disseminated the heresy, from Old Church Slavonic.

bogong /ˈbəʊɡɒŋ/ (also **bogong moth**) ▶**noun** a large brown moth of southern Australia, formerly eaten by Aboriginals.
● *Agrotis infusa*, family Noctuidae.
– ORIGIN mid 19th cent.: from Ngayawung (an Aboriginal language).

Bogotá /ˌbɒɡəˈtɑː/ the capital of Colombia, situated in the eastern Andes at about 2,610 m (8,560 ft); pop. 4,921,200 (est. 1994). It was founded by the Spanish in 1538 on the site of a pre-Columbian centre of the Chibcha culture. Official name **SANTA FÉ DE BOGOTÁ**.

bog rosemary ▶**noun** a pink-flowered evergreen dwarf shrub, which grows in boggy soils in north temperate regions. Also called **ANDROMEDA**.
● Genus *Andromeda*, family Ericaceae: two species, in particular the common *A. polifolia*.

bog spavin ▶**noun** a soft swelling of the joint capsule of the hock of horses, which most commonly occurs in young, fast-growing horses.

bog-standard ▶**adjective** informal, derogatory ordinary or basic: *most are just bog-standard PCs or workstations.*

bogtrotter ▶**noun** informal, offensive an Irish person.

bogus /ˈbəʊɡəs/ ▶**adjective** not genuine or true (used in a disapproving manner when deception has been attempted): *a bogus insurance claim.*
– DERIVATIVES **bogusly** adverb, **bogusness** noun.
– ORIGIN late 18th cent. (originally US, denoting a machine for making counterfeit money): of unknown origin.

bogy ▶**noun** (pl. **-ies**) variant spelling of **BOGEY**[2].

bogyman ▶**noun** variant spelling of **BOGEYMAN**.

Bo Hai /bəʊ ˈhʌɪ/ (also **Po Hai**) a large inlet of the Yellow Sea, on the coast of eastern China. Also called **GULF OF CHIHLI**.

bohea /bəʊˈhiː/ ▶**noun** [mass noun] a black China tea that comes from the last crop of the season and is usually regarded as of low quality.
– ORIGIN early 18th cent.: named after the *Bu-yi* (*Wuyi*) hills in China, from where black tea first came to Britain.

Bohemia /bəʊˈhiːmɪə/ a region forming the western part of the Czech Republic. Formerly a Slavic kingdom, it became a province of the newly formed Czechoslovakia by the Treaty of Versailles in 1919.

Bohemian ▶**noun 1** a native or inhabitant of Bohemia.
2 (also **bohemian**) a person who has informal and unconventional social habits, especially an artist or writer. [ORIGIN: mid 19th cent.: from French *bohémien* 'gypsy' (because gypsies were thought to come from Bohemia, or because they perhaps entered the West through Bohemia).]
▶**adjective 1** of or relating to Bohemia or its people.
2 (also **bohemian**) having informal and unconventional social habits: *she revelled in the Bohemian life of Montparnasse.*
– DERIVATIVES **Bohemianism** noun (in sense 2).

boho /ˈbəʊhəʊ/ ▶**noun** (pl. **-os**) informal term for **BOHEMIAN** (in sense 2).
▶**adjective** informal term for **BOHEMIAN** (in sense 2).

Bohol /bəʊˈhɒl/ an island lying to the north of Mindanao in the central Philippines; chief town, Tagbilaran.

Bohr /bɔː/, Niels Hendrik David (1885–1962), Danish physicist and pioneer in quantum physics. Bohr's theory of the structure of the atom incorporated quantum theory for the first time, and is the basis for present-day quantum-mechanical models. Bohr helped to develop the atom bomb in Britain and then in the US. Nobel Prize for Physics (1922).

bohrium /ˈbɔːrɪəm/ ▶**noun** [mass noun] the chemical element of atomic number 107, a very unstable element made by high-energy atomic collisions. (Symbol: **Bh**)

bohunk /ˈbəʊhʌŋk/ ▶**noun** N. Amer. informal, derogatory an immigrant from central or SE Europe.
– ORIGIN early 20th cent.: apparently from **BOHEMIAN** + *-hunk*, alteration of **HUNGARIAN**.

boil[1] ▶**verb 1** [with obj.] heat (a liquid) to the temperature at which it bubbles and turns to vapour: *we tried to get people to boil their drinking water* | *I'll* **boil up** *the stock.*
■[no obj.] (of a liquid) be at or reach this temperature: *he waited for the water to boil* | *check that the water has not* **boiled away**. ■heat (a kettle, pan, or other

container) until the liquid in it reaches such a temperature: *she boiled the kettle and took down a couple of mugs.* ■ [no obj.] (of a container) be heated until the liquid in it reaches such a temperature: *the kettle boiled and he filled the teapot.*
2 [with obj.] subject (something) to the heat of boiling liquid, in particular:
■cook (food) by immersing in boiling water or stock: *boil the potatoes until well done* | [as adj. **boiled**] *two boiled eggs.* ■ [no obj.] (of food) be cooked in boiling water: *make the sauce while the lobsters are boiling.* ■ wash or sterilize (clothes) in water of a very high temperature. ■ historical execute (someone) by subjecting them to the heat of boiling liquid.
3 [no obj.] (of the sea or clouds) be turbulent and stormy: *a huge cliff with the black sea boiling below.*
■(of a person or strong emotion) be stirred up or inflamed: *he was boiling with rage.*
▶**noun** [in sing.] the temperature at which a liquid bubbles and turns to vapour: ***bring to the boil*** *and simmer for 30 minutes | she waited for the water to* ***come to the boil.***
■an act or process of heating a liquid to such a temperature: *the kettle's* ***on the boil.*** ■ figurative a state of vigorous activity or excitement: *he has* ***gone off the boil*** *since opening the campaign.* ■ Fishing a sudden rise of a fish at a fly.
– PHRASES **keep the pot boiling** maintain the momentum or interest value of something: *a home win over Sheffield kept the pot boiling.*
– ORIGIN Middle English: from Old French *boillir*, from Latin *bullire* 'to bubble', from *bulla* 'bubble'.
▶**boil down to** amount to or be in essence a matter of: *everything boiled down to cash in the end.*
boil something down reduce the volume of a liquid by boiling: *they boil down the syrup until it is very thick.*
boil over (of a liquid) flow over the sides of the container in boiling. ■ figurative (of a situation or strong emotion) become so excited or tense as to get out of control: *one woman's anger boiled over.*

boil[2] ▶**noun** an inflamed pus-filled swelling on the skin, caused typically by the infection of a hair follicle.
– ORIGIN Old English *b**ȳ**le, b**ȳ**l*, of West Germanic origin; related to Dutch *buil* and German *Beule*.

Boileau /'bwʌləʊ, French bwalo/, Nicholas (1636–1711), French critic and poet; full name *Nicholas Boileau-Despréaux*. Boileau is considered particularly important as one of the founders of French literary criticism. His didactic poem *Art poétique* (1674) defined principles of composition and criticism.

boiled shirt ▶**noun** dated a dress shirt with a starched front.

boiled sweet ▶**noun** Brit. a hard sweet made of boiled sugar.

boiler ▶**noun 1** a fuel-burning apparatus or container for heating water, in particular:
■a household device providing a hot-water supply or serving a central heating system. ■ a tank for generating steam under pressure in a steam engine. ■ dated a metal tub for washing or sterilizing clothes at a very high temperature.
2 Brit. informal a chicken suitable for cooking only by boiling.
3 Brit. informal an unattractive or unpleasant woman.

boilermaker ▶**noun 1** a worker employed in making metal boilers for use in generating steam.
2 N. Amer. a shot of whisky followed immediately by a glass of beer as a chaser.

boilerplate ▶**noun 1** [mass noun] rolled steel plates for making boilers.
■(**boilerplates**) Climbing smooth, overlapping, and undercut slabs of rock.
2 [mass noun] chiefly US writing that is clichéd or expresses a generally accepted opinion or belief: *he accepted Soviet boilerplate at face value.*
■standardized pieces of text for use as clauses in contracts or as part of a computer program.

boiler room ▶**noun** a room in a building (typically in the basement) or a compartment in a ship containing a boiler and related heating equipment.
■chiefly N. Amer. a room used for intensive telephone selling: [as modifier] *boiler-room stock salesmen.*

boiler suit ▶**noun** Brit. a one-piece suit worn as overalls for heavy manual work.

boilie /'bɔɪli/ ▶**noun** (pl. **-ies**) a type of flavoured fishing bait, spherical in shape with a hard outer layer, used chiefly to catch carp.

boiling ▶**adjective** at or near boiling point: *boiling water.*
■informal extremely hot: *Saturday is forecast to be boiling and sunny* | [as submodifier] *I felt boiling hot.*
▶**noun** [mass noun] the action of bringing a liquid to the temperature at which it bubbles and turns to vapour.
■the temperature at which such an event occurs: *reheat gently to just below boiling.*

boiling point ▶**noun** the temperature at which a liquid boils and turns to vapour.
■figurative the point at which anger or excitement breaks out into violent expression: *racial tension surged to boiling point.*

boiling-water reactor (abbrev.: **BWR**) ▶**noun** a nuclear reactor in which the fuel is uranium oxide clad in zircaloy and the coolant and moderator is water, which is boiled to produce steam for driving turbines.

boilover ▶**noun** Austral. informal a surprise result; the defeat of a favourite in a sporting event.

boing /bɔɪŋ/ ▶**exclamation** representing the noise of a compressed spring suddenly released or a reverberating sound.
▶**noun** such a noise.
▶**verb** [no obj.] make such a noise.
– ORIGIN 1950s: imitative.

Boise /'bɔɪsi/ the state capital of Idaho; pop. 125,738 (1990).

boisterous ▶**adjective** (of a person, event, or behaviour) noisy, energetic, and cheerful: *the children's boisterous behaviour.*
■(of wind, weather, or water) wild or stormy: *the boisterous wind was lulled.*
– DERIVATIVES **boisterously** adverb, **boisterousness** noun.
– ORIGIN late Middle English (in the sense 'rough, stiff'): variant of earlier *boistuous* 'rustic, coarse, boisterous', of unknown origin.

boîte /bwʌt/ ▶**noun** (pl. pronounced same) a small restaurant or nightclub.
– ORIGIN French, literally 'box'.

Bokassa /bə'kasə/, Jean Bédel (1921–96), African statesman and military leader, President 1972–6 of the Central African Republic, self-styled emperor 1976–9.

bok choy /bɒk 'tʃɔɪ/ ▶**noun** US spelling of **PAK CHOI**.

boke /bəʊk/ (also **boak**) ▶**verb** [no obj.] Scottish vomit.
▶**noun** a vomiting fit.
– ORIGIN Middle English *bolke*; related to **BELCH**.

Bokhara /bə'kɑːrə/ variant spelling of **BUKHORO**.

bokken /'bɒk(ə)n/ ▶**noun** a wooden sword used as a practice weapon in kendo.
– ORIGIN Japanese.

bokmakierie /ˌbɒkmə'kɪəri/ (also **bokmakierie shrike**) ▶**noun** (pl. **-ies**) a bush shrike with conspicuous yellow underparts and a black band across the breast, common in southern Africa.
● *Telophorus* (or *Malaconotus*) *zeylonus*, family Laniidae.
– ORIGIN mid 19th cent.: from Afrikaans, imitative of its call.

Bokmål /'buːkmɔːl/ ▶**noun** [mass noun] one of two standard forms of the Norwegian language, a modified form of Danish. See **NORWEGIAN**.
– ORIGIN from Norwegian *bok* 'book' + *mål* 'language'.

bolas /'bəʊləs/ ▶**noun** [treated as sing. or pl.] (especially in South America) a missile consisting of a number of balls connected by strong cord, which when thrown entangles the limbs of the quarry.
– ORIGIN early 19th cent.: from Spanish and Portuguese, plural of *bola* 'ball'.

bold ▶**adjective 1** (of a person, action, or idea) showing a willingness to take risks; confident and courageous: *a bold attempt to solve the crisis | no journalist was bold enough to take on the Prime Minister.*
■dated (of a person or manner) so confident as to suggest a lack of shame or modesty: *she tossed him a bold look.*
2 (of a colour, pattern, or design) having a strong or vivid appearance: *a coat with bold polka dots.*
■(of type) having thick strokes.
3 (of a cliff or coastline) steep or projecting.
▶**noun** [mass noun] a typeface with thick strokes: *Shadow cabinet members listed* ***in bold.***
– PHRASES **be** (or **make**) **so bold** (**as to do something**) formal dare to do something (often used when politely asking a question or making a suggestion): *what would he be calling for,* ***if I might make so bold*** *as to ask?* (**as**) **bold as brass** confident to the point of impudence: *she marched into the library as bold as brass.* **bold stroke** a daring action or initiative.
– DERIVATIVES **boldly** adverb, **boldness** noun.
– ORIGIN Old English *bald*, of Germanic origin; related to Dutch *boud* and to German *bald* 'soon'.

boldface ▶**noun** [mass noun] a typeface with thick strokes.
▶**adjective** printed or displayed in such a typeface.
– DERIVATIVES **boldfaced** adjective.

boldo /'bɒldəʊ/ ▶**noun** an evergreen Chilean tree from which are obtained an edible fruit, a dye, and a medicinal leaf infusion.
● *Peumus boldus*, family Monimiaceae.
■[mass noun] a medicinal preparation of the leaves of this tree, used as a tonic and digestive aid.
– ORIGIN early 18th cent.: via American Spanish from Araucanian *voldo*.

bole[1] ▶**noun** the trunk of a tree.
– ORIGIN Middle English: from Old Norse *bolr*; perhaps related to **BAULK**.

bole[2] ▶**noun** [mass noun] a fine, smooth, reddish clay containing iron oxide, used especially as a ground for oil painting and gilding.
– ORIGIN Middle English: from late Latin *bolus* 'rounded mass' (see **BOLUS**).

bolection /bə'lɛkʃ(ə)n/ ▶**noun** [usu. as modifier] Architecture a decorative moulding above or around a panel or other architectural feature.
– ORIGIN mid 17th cent.: of unknown origin.

bolero /bə'lɛːrəʊ/ ▶**noun** (pl. **-os**) **1** a Spanish dance in simple triple time.
■a piece of music for or in the time of this dance.
2 /also 'bɒlərəʊ/ a woman's short open jacket.
– ORIGIN late 18th cent.: from Spanish.

boletus /bə'liːtəs/ (also **bolete**) ▶**noun** (pl. **boletuses**) a toadstool with pores rather than gills on the underside of the cap, typically having a thick stem.
● Genus *Boletus*, family Boletaceae, class Hymenomycetes.
– ORIGIN from Latin, from Greek *bōlitēs*, perhaps from *bōlos* 'lump'.

Boleyn /bə'lɪn/, Anne (1507–36), second wife of Henry VIII and mother of Elizabeth I. Henry divorced Catherine of Aragon in order to marry Anne (1533), but she fell from favour when she failed to provide him with a male heir and was eventually executed because of alleged infidelities.

Bolger /'bɒldʒə/, James (Brendan) (b.1935), New Zealand National Party statesman, Prime Minister 1990–7.

bolide /'bəʊlʌɪd/ ▶**noun** a large meteor which explodes in the atmosphere.
– ORIGIN early 19th cent.: from French, from Latin *bolis, bolid-*, from Greek *bolis* 'missile'.

Bolingbroke /'bɒlɪŋbrʊk/, the surname of Henry IV of England (see **HENRY**[1]).

Bolívar /'bɒlɪvɑː, Spanish bo'liβar/, Simón (1783–1830), Venezuelan patriot and statesman; known as **the Liberator.** He succeeded in driving the Spanish from Venezuela, Colombia, Peru, and Ecuador. Upper Peru was named Bolivia in his honour.

bolivar /ˌbɒlɪ'vɑː, bɒ'liːvɑː, Spanish bo'liβar/ ▶**noun** the basic monetary unit of Venezuela, equal to 100 centimos.
– ORIGIN named after S. **BOLÍVAR**.

Bolivia /bə'lɪvɪə, Spanish bo'liβja/ a landlocked country in South America; pop. 6,420,800 (1992); languages, Spanish (official), Aymara, and Quechua; capital, La Paz; legal capital and seat of the judiciary, Sucre.

Bolivia's chief topographical feature is the altiplano, the high central plateau between the eastern and western chains of the Andes. Following Pizarro's defeat of the Incas the country became part of Spain's American empire. It was freed from Spanish rule in 1825, but has suffered continually from political instability.

– DERIVATIVES **Bolivian** adjective & noun.
– ORIGIN named after Simón *Bolívar*, the liberator of the country from Spanish rule.

boliviano /bəˌlɪvɪ'ɑːnəʊ, Spanish boli'βjano/ ▶**noun** (pl. **-os**) the basic monetary unit of Bolivia (1863–1962 and since 1987), equal to 100 centavos or cents.
– ORIGIN Spanish, literally 'Bolivian', from **BOLIVIA**.

Böll /bəːl, German bœl/, Heinrich (Theodor) (1917–85), German novelist and short-story writer. Notable works: *Billiards at Half Past Nine* (1959) and *The Lost Honour of Katharina Blum* (1974). Nobel Prize for Literature (1972).

boll /bəʊl/ ▶ **noun** the rounded seed capsule of plants such as cotton or flax.
– ORIGIN Middle English (originally denoting a bubble): from Middle Dutch *bolle* 'rounded object'; related to **BOWL**[1].

bollard /ˈbɒlɑːd, -ləd/ ▶ **noun 1** Brit. a short post used to prevent traffic from entering an area or using part of a road.
2 a short, thick post on the deck of a ship or a quayside, to which a ship's rope may be secured.
– ORIGIN Middle English (in sense 2): perhaps from Old Norse *bolr* (see **BOLE**[1]) + **-ARD**.

bollix (also **bollux**) vulgar slang ▶ **verb** [with obj.] (usu. **bollix something up**) bungle (a task).
▶ **plural noun** variant spelling of **BOLLOCKS**.

bollock /ˈbɒlək/ (also **ballock**) ▶ **verb** [with obj.] Brit. vulgar slang reprimand (someone) severely.

bollocking (also **ballocking**) ▶ **noun** Brit. vulgar slang a severe reprimand.

bollocks (also **ballocks**) Brit. vulgar slang ▶ **plural noun 1** the testicles.
2 [treated as sing.] nonsense; rubbish (used to express contempt or disagreement, or as an exclamation of annoyance).
– ORIGIN mid 18th cent.: plural of *bollock*, variant of earlier *ballock*, of Germanic origin; related to **BALL**[1].

bollocky ▶ **adjective** Austral. informal naked.

boll weevil ▶ **noun** a small weevil which feeds on the fibres of the cotton boll and is a major pest of the American cotton crop.
• *Anthonomus grandis*, family Curculionidae.

bollworm ▶ **noun** a moth caterpillar which attacks the cotton boll, in particular:
• (**pink bollworm**) a small moth which is a serious pest of the North American cotton crop (*Pectinophora gossypiella*, family Gelechiidae). • (also **cotton bollworm**) another term for **CORN EARWORM**.

Bollywood ▶ **noun** informal the Indian popular film industry, based in Bombay.
– ORIGIN 1970s: blend of **BOMBAY** and **HOLLYWOOD**.

bolo /ˈbəʊləʊ/ ▶ **noun** (pl. **-os**) a large single-edged knife used in the Philippines.
– ORIGIN Spanish.

Bologna /bəˈləʊnjə, -ˈlɒnjə, Italian boˈlɔɲɲa/ a city in northern Italy, capital of Emilia-Romagna region; pop. 411,800 (1990). Its university, which dates from the 11th century, is the oldest in Europe.

bologna /bəˈləʊnjə, bəˈlɒnjə/ (also **bologna sausage**) ▶ **noun** a large smoked sausage made of bacon, veal, pork suet, and other meats.

bolometer /bəˈlɒmɪtə/ ▶ **noun** a sensitive electrical instrument for measuring radiant energy.
– DERIVATIVES **bolometric** adjective.
– ORIGIN late 19th cent.: from Greek *bolē* 'ray of light' + **-METER**.

boloney ▶ **noun** variant spelling of **BALONEY**.

bolo tie ▶ **noun** N. Amer. a type of tie consisting of a cord worn around the neck with a large ornamental fastening at the throat.

Bolshevik /ˈbɒlʃɪvɪk/ ▶ **noun** historical a member of the majority faction of the Russian Social Democratic Party, which was renamed the Communist Party after seizing power in the October Revolution of 1917.
■ chiefly derogatory (in general use) a person with politically subversive or radical views; a revolutionary.
▶ **adjective** of, relating to, or characteristic of Bolsheviks or Bolshevism.
– DERIVATIVES **Bolshevism** noun, **Bolshevist** noun.
– ORIGIN Russian, from *bol'she* 'greater' (with reference to the greater faction).

bolshie (also **bolshy**) Brit. informal, derogatory ▶ **adjective** (of a person or attitude) deliberately combative or uncooperative: *policemen with bolshie attitudes.*
▶ **noun** (pl. **-ies**) (**Bolshie**) dated a Bolshevik or socialist.
– DERIVATIVES **bolshiness** noun.
– ORIGIN early 20th cent.: abbreviation of **BOLSHEVIK**.

Bolshoi Ballet /ˈbɒlʃɔɪ/ a Moscow ballet company. Since 1825 it has been established at the Bolshoi Theatre, where it staged the first production of Tchaikovsky's *Swan Lake* (1877).

bolster[1] /ˈbəʊlstə/ ▶ **noun** (also **bolster pillow**) a long, thick pillow that is placed under other pillows for support.
■ a part on a vehicle or tool providing structural support or reducing friction. ■ Building a short timber cap over a post designed to increase the bearing of the beams it supports.
▶ **verb** [with obj.] support or strengthen; prop up: *the fall in interest rates is starting to bolster confidence | he wished to* **bolster up** *his theories with hard data.*
■ provide (a seat) with padded support: [as adj. **bolstered**] *I snuggled down into the heavily bolstered seat.*
– DERIVATIVES **bolsterer** noun.
– ORIGIN Old English (in the sense 'long, thick pillow'), of Germanic origin; related to Dutch *bolster* and German *Polster*.

bolster[2] /ˈbəʊlstə/ ▶ **noun** a heavy chisel used for cutting bricks.
– ORIGIN early 20th cent.: of unknown origin.

Bolt, Robert (Oxton) (1924–95), English writer best known for the play *A Man for All Seasons* (1960) and the screenplays for *Lawrence of Arabia* (1962) and *Dr Zhivago* (1965).

bolt[1] ▶ **noun 1** a large metal pin, in particular:
■ a bar that slides into a socket to fasten a door or window. ■ a long pin with a head that screws into a nut and is used to fasten things together. ■ the sliding piece of the breech mechanism of a rifle. ■ Climbing a long pin that is driven into a rock face so that a rope can be attached to it.
2 a short, heavy arrow shot from a crossbow.
3 a flash of lightning that can be seen shooting across the sky in a jagged white line.
▶ **verb** [with obj.] fasten with a bolt, in particular:
■ fasten (a door or window) with a bar that slides into a socket: *all the doors were locked and bolted.* ■ [with obj. and adverbial of place] fasten (something) to something else with a long pin that screws into a nut.
– PHRASES **a bolt from** (or **out of**) **the blue** a sudden and unexpected event or piece of news: *the job came like a bolt from the blue.* [ORIGIN: with reference to the unlikelihood of a thunderbolt coming from a clear blue sky.] **bolt upright** with the back very straight: *she sat bolt upright in bed.* **have shot one's bolt** informal have done all that is in one's power.
– ORIGIN Old English, 'arrow', of unknown origin; related to Dutch *bout* and German *Bolzen* 'arrow, bolt for a door'.

bolt[2] ▶ **verb 1** [no obj.] (of a horse or other animal) run away suddenly out of control: *the horses shied and bolted.*
■ [no obj., with adverbial of direction] (of a person) move or run away suddenly in an attempt to escape: *they bolted down the stairs.* ■ [with obj.] (in hunting) cause (a rabbit or fox) to run out of its burrow or hole. ■ (of a plant) grow quickly upwards and stop flowering as seeds develop: *the lettuces have bolted.*
2 [with obj.] eat or swallow (food) quickly: *it is normal for puppies to* **bolt down** *their food.*
– PHRASES **make a bolt for** try to escape by moving suddenly towards (something): *Ellie made a bolt for the door.*
– ORIGIN Middle English: from **BOLT**[1], expressing the sense 'fly like an arrow'.

bolt[3] ▶ **noun 1** a roll of fabric, originally as a measure: *the room is stacked with* **bolts of** *cloth.*
2 a folded edge of a piece of paper that is trimmed off to allow it to be opened, as on a section of a book.
– ORIGIN Middle English: transferred use of **BOLT**[1].

bolt[4] (also **boult**) ▶ **verb** [with obj.] archaic pass (flour, powder, or other material) through a sieve.
– ORIGIN Middle English: from Old French *bulter*, of unknown ultimate origin. The change in the first syllable was due to association with **BOLT**[1].

bolt-action ▶ **adjective** (of a gun) having a breech which is opened by turning a bolt and sliding it back.

bolter ▶ **noun** a person or thing that bolts.
■ Austral. an outsider in a sporting event or other competition. ■ Austral. historical an escaped convict or absconder.

bolt-hole ▶ **noun** chiefly Brit. a hole or burrow by which a rabbit or other wild animal can escape.
■ figurative a place where a person can escape and hide: *he thought of Antwerp as a possible bolt-hole.*

bolting ▶ **noun** [mass noun] Climbing the action of driving long metal pins into a rock face so that ropes can be attached to them.

Bolton a town in NW England, near Manchester; pop. 253,300 (1991).

bolt-on ▶ **adjective** [attrib.] (of an extra part of a machine) able to be fastened on with a bolt or catch.
▶ **noun** an extra part that can be fastened on to a machine with a bolt or catch.

bolt rope ▶ **noun** a rope sewn round the edge of a vessel's sail to prevent tearing.

Boltzmann /ˈbɒltsman/, Ludwig (1844–1906), Austrian physicist, who made contributions to the kinetic theory of gases, statistical mechanics, and thermodynamics.

Boltzmann distribution another term for **MAXWELL–BOLTZMANN DISTRIBUTION**.

Boltzmann's constant Chemistry the ratio of the gas constant to Avogadro's constant, equal to 1.381 $\times 10^{-23}$ joule per kelvin.

bolus /ˈbəʊləs/ ▶ **noun** (pl. **boluses**) a small rounded mass of a substance, especially of chewed food at the moment of swallowing.
■ a type of large pill used in veterinary medicine. ■ Medicine a single dose of a drug or other medicinal preparation given all at once.
– ORIGIN mid 16th cent. (denoting a large pill or medicine): via late Latin from Greek *bōlos* 'clod'.

Bolzano /bɒlˈtsɑːnəʊ/ a city in NE Italy, capital of the Trentino-Alto Adige region; pop. 100,380 (1990).

boma /ˈbəʊmə/ ▶ **noun** (in eastern and southern Africa) an enclosure, especially for animals.
– ORIGIN Kiswahili.

bomb ▶ **noun 1** a container filled with explosive or incendiary material, designed to explode on impact or when detonated by a timing, proximity, or remote-control device.
■ [with modifier] an explosive device fitted into a specified object: *a 100 lb van bomb.* ■ (**the bomb**) nuclear weapons considered collectively as agents of mass destruction: *she joined the fight against the bomb.*
2 a thing resembling a bomb in impact or shape, in particular:
■ (also **volcanic bomb**) a lump of lava thrown out by a volcano. ■ informal a cannabis cigarette. ■ informal a film, play, or other event that fails badly: *that bomb of an old movie.* ■ (**a bomb**) Brit. informal a large sum of money: *it will cost a bomb in call charges.* ■ a long forward pass or hit in a ball game: *a two-run bomb.* ■ a pear-shaped weight used to anchor a fishing line to the bottom.
▶ **verb 1** [with obj.] attack (a place or object) with a bomb or bombs: *they bombed the city at dawn* | [as noun **bombing**] *a series of bombings.*
■ (**bomb someone out**) make someone homeless by destroying their home with bombs.
2 [no obj., with adverbial of direction] Brit. informal move or go very quickly: *we were bombing down the motorway at breakneck speed.*
3 [no obj.] informal (of a film, play, or other event) fail badly: *it just became another big-budget film that bombed.*
– PHRASES **go down a bomb** Brit. informal be very well received: *those gigs we did went down a bomb.* **go like a bomb** Brit. informal **1** be very successful: *the party went like a bomb.* **2** (of a vehicle or person) move very fast. **look like a bomb's hit it** informal (of a place) be extremely messy or untidy in appearance.
– ORIGIN late 17th cent.: from French *bombe*, from Italian *bomba*, probably from Latin *bombus* 'booming, humming', from Greek *bombos*, of imitative origin.

bombard /bɒmˈbɑːd/ ▶ **verb** [with obj.] attack (a place or person) continuously with bombs, shells, or other missiles: *the city was bombarded by federal forces | supporters bombarded police with bottles.*
■ subject (someone) to a continuous flow of questions, criticisms, or information: *they will be* **bombarded with** *complaints.* ■ Physics direct a stream of high-speed particles at (a substance).
▶ **noun** /ˈbɒmbɑːd/ historical a cannon of the earliest type, which fired a stone ball or large shot.
– DERIVATIVES **bombardment** noun.
– ORIGIN late Middle English (as a noun denoting an early form of cannon, also a shawm) from Old French *bombarde*, probably based on Latin *bombus* 'booming, humming' (see **BOMB**). The verb (late 16th cent.) is from French *bombarder*.

bombarde /ˈbɒmbɑːd/ ▶ **noun** Music a shawm of alto pitch, used in medieval bands and in Breton folk music.
■ a powerful bass reed organ stop.
– ORIGIN late Middle English: from Old French, denoting a shawm (see **BOMBARD**).

bombardier /ˌbɒmbəˈdɪə/ ▶ **noun 1** a rank of non-commissioned officer in certain artillery regiments, equivalent to corporal.

2 a member of a bomber crew in the US air force responsible for sighting and releasing bombs.
3 (**Bombardier**) Canadian trademark a type of snowmobile.
– ORIGIN mid 16th cent. (denoting a soldier in charge of a *bombard*, an early form of cannon): from French, from Old French *bombarde* 'cannon' (see **BOMBARD**).

bombardier beetle ▶ noun a ground beetle that discharges a puff of irritant vapour from its anus with an audible pop when alarmed.
● Several species in the family Carabidae, in particular the European *Brachinus crepitans*.

bombardon /'bɒmbɑːd(ə)n/ ▶ noun a bass tuba.
– ORIGIN mid 19th cent.: from Italian *bombardone*, from *bombardo* 'cannon'. Compare with **BOMBARDE**.

bombast /'bɒmbast/ ▶ noun [mass noun] high-sounding language with little meaning, used to impress people.
– DERIVATIVES **bombastic** adjective, **bombastically** adverb.
– ORIGIN mid 16th cent. (denoting raw cotton or cotton wool used as padding, later used figuratively): from Old French *bombace*, from medieval Latin *bombax*, *bombac-*, alteration of *bombyx* 'silkworm' (see **BOMBAZINE**).

Bombay a city and port on the west coast of India, capital of the state of Maharashtra; pop. 9,990,000 (1991). Official name (from 1995) **MUMBAI**.

Bombay duck ▶ noun [mass noun] the bummalo (fish), especially when dried and eaten as an accompaniment with curries.
– ORIGIN mid 19th cent.: alteration of **BUMMALO** by association with **BOMBAY** in India, from which bummalo were exported.

Bombay mix ▶ noun [mass noun] (especially in Britain) an Indian snack consisting of lentils, peanuts, sev, and spices.

bombazine /'bɒmbəziːn/ ▶ noun [mass noun] a twilled dress fabric of worsted and silk or cotton, especially a black kind formerly used for mourning clothes.
– ORIGIN mid 16th cent. (denoting raw cotton): from French *bombasin*, from medieval Latin *bombacinum*, from *bombycinum*, neuter of *bombycinus* 'silken', based on Greek *bombux* 'silkworm'.

bomb bay ▶ noun a compartment in the fuselage of an aircraft in which bombs are held and from which they may be dropped.

bomb calorimeter ▶ noun a thick-walled steel container used to determine the energy contained in a substance by measuring the heat generated during its combustion.

bomb disposal ▶ noun [mass noun] the defusing or removal and detonation of unexploded and delayed-action bombs.

bombe /bɒmb/ ▶ noun a frozen dome-shaped dessert.
■ a dome-shaped mould in which this dessert is made.
– ORIGIN French, literally 'bomb'.

bombé /'bɔ̃beɪ, French bɔ̃be/ ▶ adjective (of furniture) rounded.
– ORIGIN early 20th cent.: French, literally 'swollen out'.

bombed ▶ adjective **1** (of an area or building) subjected to bombing.
2 informal intoxicated by drink or drugs.

bombed-out ▶ adjective **1** [attrib.] (of a person) driven out of a place by bombing: *bombed-out families.*
■ (of a building or city) destroyed by bombing.
2 informal another term for **BOMBED** in sense 2.

bomber ▶ noun **1** an aircraft designed to carry and drop bombs.
2 a person who plants, detonates, or throws bombs in a public place, especially as a terrorist.
3 informal a large cigarette containing cannabis.
4 short for **BOMBER JACKET**.

bomber jacket ▶ noun a short jacket tightly gathered at the waist and cuffs by elasticated bands and typically having a zip front.

bombinate /'bɒmbɪneɪt/ ▶ verb [no obj.] poetic/literary buzz; hum.
– ORIGIN late 19th cent.: from medieval Latin *bombinat-* 'buzzed', from the verb *bombinare*, from Latin *bombus* 'humming' (see **BOMBARD**).

bombing run ▶ noun the part of the flight path of a bomber which brings it into position to release its weapons.

bomblet ▶ noun a small bomb.

bombora /bɒm'bɔːrə/ ▶ noun Austral. a wave which forms over a submerged offshore reef or rock, sometimes breaking heavily and producing a dangerous stretch of broken water.
– ORIGIN 1930s: from an Aboriginal word, perhaps Dharuk *bumbora*.

bombproof ▶ adjective strong enough to resist the effects of blast from a bomb.

bombshell ▶ noun **1** an overwhelming surprise or disappointment: *the news came as a bombshell.*
2 informal a very attractive woman: *a twenty-year-old blonde bombshell.*
3 dated an artillery shell.

bombsight ▶ noun a mechanical or electronic device used in an aircraft for aiming bombs.

bomb site ▶ noun an area in a town or city where the buildings have been destroyed by bombs.

bomb squad ▶ noun a division of a police force appointed to investigate the planting and detonation of terrorist bombs.

Bon /bɒn/ (also **O-Bon**) ▶ noun a Japanese Buddhist festival held annually in August to honour the dead. Also called **FESTIVAL OF THE DEAD** and **LANTERN FESTIVAL**.

Bon, Cape a peninsula of NE Tunisia, extending into the Mediterranean Sea.

bona fide /ˌbəʊnə 'fʌɪdi/ ▶ adjective genuine; real: *only bona fide members of the company are allowed to use the logo.*
▶ adverb chiefly Law without intention to deceive: *the court will assume that they have acted bona fide.*
– ORIGIN Latin, literally 'with good faith', ablative singular of **BONA FIDES**.

bona fides /ˌbəʊnə 'fʌɪdiːz/ ▶ noun [mass noun] a person's honesty and sincerity of intention: *he went to great lengths to establish his liberal bona fides.*
■ [treated as pl.] informal documentary evidence showing that a person is what they claim to be; credentials.
– ORIGIN Latin, literally 'good faith'.

Bonaire /bɒˈnɛː/ one of the two principal islands of the Netherlands Antilles (the other is Curaçao); chief town, Kralendijk; pop. 10,190 (1992).

bonanza /bəˈnanzə/ ▶ noun a situation or event which creates a sudden increase in wealth, good fortune, or profits: *a natural gas bonanza for Britain |* [as modifier] *a bonanza year for the computer industry.*
■ a large amount of something desirable: *the festive feature film bonanza.*
– ORIGIN early 19th cent. (originally US, especially with reference to success when mining): from Spanish, literally 'fair weather, prosperity', from Latin *bonus* 'good'.

Bonaparte /'bəʊnəpɑːt, French bɔnapaʁt/ (Italian **Buonaparte**) a Corsican family including the three French rulers named Napoleon.
– DERIVATIVES **Bonapartism** noun, **Bonapartist** noun & adjective.

bon appétit /ˌbɒn apeˈtiː, French bɔn apeti/ ▶ exclamation used as a salutation to a person about to eat.
– ORIGIN French, literally 'good appetite'.

bona vacantia /ˌbəʊnə vəˈkantɪə/ ▶ noun [mass noun] Law (in the UK) goods without an apparent owner, such as treasure trove or the estate of a person dying intestate and without heirs, to which the Crown may have right.
– ORIGIN Latin, 'ownerless goods'.

Bonaventura, St /ˌbɒnəvɛnˈtjʊərə/ (1221–74), Franciscan theologian; born *Giovanni di Fidanza*; known as the **Seraphic Doctor**. He wrote the official biography of St Francis and had a lasting influence as a spiritual writer. Feast day, 15 (formerly 14) July.

bonbon ▶ noun a piece of confectionery; a sweet.
– ORIGIN late 18th cent.: from French, reduplication of *bon* 'good', from Latin *bonus*.

bonbonnière /ˌbɒnbɒnˈjɛː/ ▶ noun a small ornamental box or lidded jar for confectionery.

bonce ▶ noun Brit. informal a person's head.
– ORIGIN mid 19th cent. (denoting a large marble): of unknown origin.

Bond[1], Edward (b.1934), English dramatist. Many of his plays are marked by scenes of violence and cruelty. Notable works: *Saved* (1965) and *Lear* (1971).

Bond[2], James, a British secret agent in the spy novels of Ian Fleming, known also by his code name 007.

bond[1] /bɒnd/ ▶ noun **1** (**bonds**) physical restraints used to hold someone prisoner, especially ropes or chains.
■ a thing used to tie something or to fasten or link things together: *she brushed back a curl which had strayed from its bonds.* ■ figurative a force or feeling that unites people: *a common emotion or interest: there was a bond of understanding between them.*
2 an agreement or promise with legal force, in particular:
■ Law a deed by which a person is committed to make payment to another. ■ South African term for **MORTGAGE**. ■ a certificate issued by a government or a public company promising to repay borrowed money at a fixed rate of interest at a specified time. ■ an insurance policy held by a company, which protects against losses resulting from circumstances such as bankruptcy or misconduct by employees.
3 (also **chemical bond**) a strong force of attraction holding atoms together in a molecule or crystal, resulting from the sharing or transfer of electrons.
4 [with modifier] Building any of the various patterns in which bricks are conventionally laid in order to ensure the strength of the resulting structure.
▶ verb **1** join or be joined securely to something else, especially by means of an adhesive substance, heat, or pressure: [with obj.] *press the material to bond the layers together |* [no obj.] *this material will bond well to stainless steel rods |* [as adj. **bonding**] *a bonding agent.*
■ [no obj.] figurative establish a relationship or link with someone based on shared feelings, interests, or experiences: *the failure to properly bond with their children | the team has bonded together well.*
2 join or be joined by a chemical bond.
3 [with obj.] [usu. as adj. **bonding**] lay (bricks) in an overlapping pattern so as to form a strong structure: *a bonding course.*
4 [usu. as noun **bonding**] place (dutiable goods) in bond.
– PHRASES **in bond** (of dutiable goods) stored in a bonded warehouse until the importer pays the duty owing.
– ORIGIN Middle English: variant of **BAND**[1].

bond[2] /bɒnt/ ▶ noun S. African an Afrikaner league or association.
– ORIGIN Afrikaans, 'league, fellowship'.

bondage ▶ noun [mass noun] **1** the state of being a slave: *the deliverance of the Israelites from Egypt's bondage |* figurative *young women lost to the bondage of early motherhood.*
2 sexual practice that involves the tying up or restraining of one partner.
– ORIGIN Middle English: from Anglo-Latin *bondagium*, from Middle English *bond* 'serf' (earlier 'peasant, householder', from Old Norse *bóndi* 'tiller of the soil', based on *búa* 'dwell'; influenced in sense by **BOND**[1].

bondager ▶ noun historical a person who performed services as a condition of feudal tenure.
■ (in southern Scotland and NE England) a female outworker supplied to a proprietor by a tenant.

bonded ▶ adjective **1** (of a thing or things) joined securely to another or each other, especially by an adhesive, heat process, or pressure.
■ figurative emotionally or psychologically linked: *a strongly bonded group of females.* ■ held by a chemical bond: *bonded atoms.*
2 (of a person or company) bound by a legal agreement, in particular:
■ (of a travel agent or tour operator) holding an insurance policy which protects travellers' holidays and money should the company go bankrupt. ■ (of a worker or workforce) obliged to work for a particular employer, typically in a condition close to slavery.
3 (of dutiable goods) placed in bond.

bonded warehouse ▶ noun a customs-controlled warehouse for the retention of imported goods until the duty owed is paid.

Bondi /'bɒndʌɪ/ a coastal resort in New South Wales, Australia, a suburb of Sydney. It is noted for its popular beach.

bondi /'bɒndʌɪ/ ▶ noun Austral. a heavy club with a knob on the end.
– PHRASES **give someone bondi** informal attack someone savagely.
– ORIGIN probably from Wiradhuri and Kamilaroi.

bondieuserie /bɒnˈdjəːz(ə)ri, French bɔ̃djøzʁi/ ▶ noun (pl. **-ies**) a church ornament or devotional object, especially one of little artistic merit.

■[mass noun] such objects collectively.
– ORIGIN 1940s: from French, from *bon* 'good' + *Dieu* 'God'.

bond paper ▶ **noun** [mass noun] high-quality writing paper.

bondsman ▶ **noun** (pl. **-men**) **1** a person who stands surety for a bond. [ORIGIN: early 18th cent.: from **BOND**[1] + **MAN**.]
2 archaic a slave. [ORIGIN: mid 18th cent.: variant of Middle English *bondman*, from obsolete *bond* 'serf' (see also **BONDAGE**).]

bondstone ▶ **noun** a stone or brick running through a wall to bind or strengthen it.

Bône /bəʊn/ former name for **ANNABA**.

bone ▶ **noun 1** any of the pieces of hard, whitish tissue making up the skeleton in humans and other vertebrates: *his injuries included many broken bones* | *a shoulder bone*.
■(**one's bones**) one's body: *he hauled his tired bones upright*. ■(**bones**) a corpse or skeleton: *the diggers turned up the bones of a fifteen-year-old girl*. ■(**bones**) figurative the basic or essential framework of something: *you need to put some flesh on the bones of your idea*. ■a bone of an animal with meat on it fed to a dog.

The substance of bones is formed by specialized cells (osteoblasts) which secrete around themselves a material containing calcium salts (which provide hardness and strength in compression) and collagen fibres (which provide tensile strength). Many bones have a central cavity containing marrow.

2 [mass noun] the calcified material of which bones consist: *an earring of bone*.
■a substance similar to this such as ivory, dentine, or whalebone. ■(often **bones**) a thing made or formerly made of such a substance, such as a strip of stiffening for a foundation garment or strapless dress. ■(usu. **bones**) (in southern Africa) one of a set of carved dice or bones used by traditional healers in divination.
▶**verb 1** [with obj.] remove the bones from (meat or fish) before cooking it.
2 [with obj.] US vulgar slang (of a man) have sexual intercourse with (someone).
3 [no obj.] (**bone up on**) informal study (a subject) intensively, typically in preparation for something: *she boned up on languages she had learned long ago and went back to New Guinea*.
– PHRASES **bone of contention** a subject or issue over which there is continuing disagreement: *the examination system has long been a serious bone of contention*. **close to** (or **near**) **the bone** (of a remark) penetrating and accurate to the point of causing hurt or discomfort. ■(of a joke or story) likely to cause offence because near the limit of decency. **cut** (or **pare**) **something to the bone** reduce something to the bare minimum: *costs will have to be cut to the bone*. **have a bone to pick with someone** informal have reason to disagree or be annoyed with someone. **in one's bones** felt, understood, believed, or known very deeply or instinctively: *something good was bound to happen; he could feel it in his bones*. **make no bones about** have no hesitation in stating or dealing with (something), however unpleasant, awkward, or distasteful it is: *he makes no bones about his feelings towards the militants*. **not have a —— bone in one's body** have not the slightest trace of the specified quality: *she hasn't got a sympathetic bone in her body*. **off the bone** (of meat or fish) having had the bone or bones removed before being cooked, served, or sold. **on the bone** (of meat or fish) having the bone or bones left in when cooked, served, or sold. **point the bone at** Austral. (of an Aboriginal) cast a spell on (someone) so as to cause their sickness or death. ■figurative betray (someone); let (someone) down. [ORIGIN: from an Australian Aboriginal ritual, in which a bone is pointed at a victim.] **throw the bones** S. African use divining bones to foretell the future or discover the source of a difficulty by studying the pattern they form when thrown on the ground. **to the bone 1** (of a wound) so deep as to expose a person's bone: *his thigh had been axed open to the bone* | figurative *his contempt cut her to the bone*. ■(especially of cold) affecting a person in a very penetrating way. **2** see *to one's bones* below. **to one's bones** (or **to the bone**) used to emphasize that a person has a specified quality or experience in an overwhelming or very fundamental way: *he's a cop to the bone*. **what's bred in the bone will come out in the flesh** (or **blood**) proverb a person's behaviour or characteristics are determined by their heredity. **work one's fingers to the bone** work very hard.
– ORIGIN Old English *bān*, of Germanic origin; related to Dutch *been* and German *Bein*.

bone ash ▶ **noun** [mass noun] the mineral residue of calcined bones.

bone china ▶ **noun** [mass noun] white porcelain containing bone ash, made in Britain since about 1800.

boned ▶ **adjective 1** (of meat or fish) having had the bones removed before being cooked, served, or sold.
2 [in combination] (of a person) having bones of the specified type: *she was fine-boned and boyishly slim*.
3 (of a garment) stiffened with strips of plastic or whalebone to give shape to the figure or the garment.

bone dry ▶ **adjective** completely or extremely dry.

bonefish ▶ **noun** (pl. same or **-fishes**) a silvery game fish of warm coastal waters. Also called **LADYFISH**.
• Family Albulidae and genus *Albula*: several species, in particular *A. vulpes*.

bonehead ▶ **noun** informal a stupid person.
– DERIVATIVES **boneheaded** adjective.

bone idle (also **bone lazy**) ▶ **adjective** extremely idle or lazy.
– ORIGIN early 19th cent.: expressing *idle through to the bone*.

boneless ▶ **adjective** (of meat or fish) having had the bones removed ready for cooking or serving.
■figurative lacking physical or mental strength: *the slack and boneless character of his writing*.
– DERIVATIVES **bonelessly** adverb.

bone marrow ▶ **noun** see **MARROW** (sense 3).

bonemeal ▶ **noun** [mass noun] crushed or ground bones used as a fertilizer.

boner ▶ **noun 1** informal a stupid mistake.
2 informal an erection of the penis.
3 NZ a low-grade farm animal, with meat only suitable for use in sausages, pies, or processed products.
– PHRASES **pull a boner** N. Amer. informal make a stupid mistake.
– ORIGIN early 20th cent. (originally US): from **BONE** or (in sense 1) from **BONEHEAD**, + **-ER**[1].

boneset ▶ **noun** a North American plant of the daisy family, which bears clusters of small white flowers and is used in herbal medicine.
• *Eupatorium perfoliatum*, family Compositae.
■Brit. the common comfrey, the ground-up root of which was formerly used as a 'plaster' to set broken bones.

bone-setter ▶ **noun** historical a person, usually not formally qualified, who set broken or dislocated bones.

boneshaker ▶ **noun** Brit. informal an old vehicle with poor suspension: *a bone-shaker of a van*.
■historical an early type of bicycle without rubber tyres.

bone spavin ▶ **noun** osteoarthritis of the hock in horses, which may cause swelling and lameness.

bone-tired (also **bone-weary**) ▶ **adjective** extremely tired.

boney ▶ **noun** (pl. **-eys**) variant spelling of **BONY**[2].

boneyard ▶ **noun** informal a cemetery.

bonfire ▶ **noun** a large open-air fire used for burning rubbish or as part of a celebration.
– ORIGIN late Middle English: from **BONE** + **FIRE**. The term originally denoted a large open-air fire on which bones were burnt (sometimes as part of a celebration), also one for burning heretics or proscribed literature. Dr Johnson accepted the mistaken idea that the word came from French *bon* 'good'.

Bonfire Night ▶ **noun** (in the UK) 5 November, on which fireworks are displayed and figures representing Guy Fawkes burnt in memory of the Gunpowder Plot.

bong[1] ▶ **noun** a low-pitched sound, as of a bell.
▶**verb** [no obj.] emit such a sound.
– ORIGIN 1920s (originally US): imitative.

bong[2] ▶ **noun** a water pipe used for smoking cannabis or other drugs.
– ORIGIN 1970s: from Thai *baung*, literally 'cylindrical wooden tube'.

bong[3] ▶ **noun** Climbing a large piton.
– ORIGIN 1960s: probably imitative.

bongo[1] /ˈbɒŋɡəʊ/ ▶ **noun** (pl. **-os** or **-oes**) each of a joined pair of small deep-bodied drums, typically held between the knees and played with the fingers.
– ORIGIN 1920s: from Latin American Spanish *bongó*.

bongo[2] /ˈbɒŋɡəʊ/ ▶ **noun** (pl. same or **-os**) a forest antelope that has a chestnut coat with narrow white vertical stripes, native to central Africa.
• *Tragelaphus euryceros*, family Bovidae.
– ORIGIN mid 19th cent.: from Kikongo.

Bonhoeffer /ˈbɒnhəːfə, German ˈbɔnhœfɐ/, Dietrich (1906–45), German Lutheran theologian and pastor. He was an active opponent of Nazism and was involved in the German resistance movement. Arrested in 1943, he was sent to Buchenwald concentration camp and later executed.

bonhomie /ˈbɒnəmiː, ˌbɒnəˈmiː/ ▶ **noun** [mass noun] cheerful friendliness; geniality: *he exuded good humour and bonhomie*.
– DERIVATIVES **bonhomous** adjective.
– ORIGIN late 18th cent.: from French, from *bonhomme* 'good fellow'.

boniato /ˌbɒnɪˈɑːtəʊ/ ▶ **noun** a variety of sweet potato with white flesh.
– ORIGIN Spanish.

Boniface, St /ˈbɒnɪfeɪs/ (680–754), Anglo-Saxon missionary; born *Wynfrith*; known as **the Apostle of Germany**. He was sent to Frisia and Germany to spread the Christian faith and was appointed Primate of Germany in 732; he was martyred in Frisia. Feast day, 5 June.

Bonington /ˈbɒnɪŋtən/, Chris (b.1934), English mountaineer; full name *Christian John Storey Bonington*. He made the first British ascent of the north face of the Eiger in 1962 and led expeditions to Mount Everest in 1975 and 1985 (when he reached the summit).

bonito /bəˈniːtəʊ/ ▶ **noun** (pl. **-os**) a smaller relative of the tunas, having dark oblique stripes on the back and important as a food and game fish.
• *Sarda* and related genera, family Scombridae: several species.
■another term for **SKIPJACK** (in sense 1).
– ORIGIN late 16th cent.: from Spanish.

bonk informal ▶ **verb 1** [with obj.] knock or hit (someone or something) so as to cause a reverberating sound: *he bonked his head on the plane's low bulkhead*.
2 [no obj.] Brit. have sexual intercourse.
3 [no obj.] (of a cyclist or runner) reach a point of exhaustion that makes it impossible to go further.
▶**noun 1** an act of knocking or hitting someone or something so as to cause a reverberating sound: *give it a bonk with a hammer*.
■a reverberating sound caused in such a way.
2 Brit. an act of sexual intercourse.
3 (**the bonk**) a level of exhaustion that makes a cyclist or runner unable to go further.
– ORIGIN 1930s: imitative.

bonkbuster ▶ **noun** Brit. informal a type of popular novel characterized by frequent explicit sexual encounters.
– ORIGIN 1980s: from **BONK**, on the pattern of *blockbuster*.

bonkers ▶ **adjective** [predic.] informal mad; crazy: *you're stark raving bonkers!*
– ORIGIN 1940s: of unknown origin.

bon mot /bɒn ˈməʊ/ ▶ **noun** (pl. **bons mots** pronunc. same or /-məʊz/) a witty remark.
– ORIGIN mid 18th cent.: French, literally 'good word'.

Bonn a city in the state of North Rhine-Westphalia in Germany; pop. 296,240 (1991). From 1949 until the reunification of Germany in 1990 Bonn was the capital of the Federal Republic of Germany.

Bonnard /ˈbɒnɑː, French bɔnaʀ/, Pierre (1867–1947), French painter and graphic artist, a member of the Nabi Group. Notable for their rich, glowing colours, his works continue and develop the Impressionist tradition; they mostly depict domestic interior scenes, nudes, and landscapes.

bonne /bɒn/ ▶ **noun** dated a nursemaid or housemaid, typically a French one.
– ORIGIN late 18th cent.: from French, feminine of *bon* 'good'.

bonne bouche /bɒn ˈbuːʃ, French bɔn buʃ/ ▶ **noun** (pl. **bonne bouches** or **bonnes bouches** pronunc. same) an appetizing item of food, especially something sweet eaten at the end of a meal.
– ORIGIN French, literally 'a good taste in the

mouth', from *bonne*, feminine of *bon* 'good', and *bouche* 'mouth'.

bonne femme /bɒn ˈfam/ ▶ **adjective** [postpositive] (of fish dishes, stews, and soups) cooked in a simple way: *sole bonne femme*.
– ORIGIN French, from the phrase *à la bonne femme* 'in the manner of a good housewife'.

bonnet ▶ **noun 1** a woman's or child's hat tied under the chin, typically with a brim framing the face.
■ a soft, round brimless hat like a beret, especially as worn by men and boys in Scotland. ■ Heraldry the velvet cap within a coronet. ■ (also **war bonnet**) the ceremonial feathered headdress of an American Indian.
2 a protective cover or cap, in particular:
■ Brit. a metal part covering the engine of a motor vehicle. ■ a cowl on a chimney.
3 Sailing, historical an additional canvas laced to the foot of a sail to catch more wind.
– DERIVATIVES **bonneted** adjective.
– ORIGIN late Middle English (denoting a soft brimless hat for men): from Old French *bonet*, from medieval Latin *abonnis* 'headgear'. Sense 1 dates from the late 15th cent.

bonnethead (also **bonnethead shark**) ▶ **noun** a small hammerhead shark with a relatively narrow rounded head, found in American waters. Also called **SHOVELHEAD**.
● *Sphyrna tiburo*, family Sphyrnidae.

bonnet macaque (also **bonnet monkey**) ▶ **noun** a South Indian macaque with a bonnet-like tuft of hair on the head.
● *Macaca radiata*, family Cercopithecidae.

bonnetmouth ▶ **noun** a small, slender shoaling fish with an extensible mouth and a long spiny dorsal fin, occurring in the tropical western Atlantic.
● *Inermia vittata*, family Emmelichthyidae.

Bonney, William H. (1859–81), American outlaw; born *Henry McCarty*; known as **Billy the Kid**. A notorious robber and murderer, he was captured by Sheriff Pat Garrett in 1880, and was shot by Garrett after he escaped.

Bonnie Prince Charlie see STUART[1].

bonny (also **bonnie**) chiefly Scottish & N. English ▶ **adjective** (**bonnier**, **bonniest**) attractive or beautiful: *a bonny lass*.
■ (of a baby) plump and healthy-looking. ■ sizeable; considerable (usually expressing approval): *it's worth a thousand pounds, a bonny sum*.
▶ **noun** (**my bonny**) poetic/literary used as a form of address for one's beloved or baby.
– DERIVATIVES **bonnily** adverb, **bonniness** noun.
– ORIGIN late 15th cent.: perhaps related to Old French *bon* 'good'.

bonny clabber ▶ **noun** another term for CLABBER.
– ORIGIN early 17th cent.: from Irish *bainne clabair*, denoting thick milk for churning.

bonobo /ˈbɒnəbəʊ/ ▶ **noun** (pl. **-os**) a chimpanzee with a black face and black hair, found in the rainforests of Zaire (Democratic Republic of Congo). It is believed to be the closest living relative of humans. Also called **PYGMY CHIMPANZEE**.
● *Pan paniscus*, family Pongidae.
– ORIGIN 1950s: a local word.

bonsai /ˈbɒnsʌɪ/ ▶ **noun** (pl. same) (also **bonsai tree**) an ornamental tree or shrub grown in a pot and artificially prevented from reaching its normal size.
■ [mass noun] the art of growing trees or shrubs in such a way.
– ORIGIN 1950s: from Japanese, from *bon* 'tray' + *sai* 'planting'.

bonsella /bɒnˈsɛlə/ (also **bonsela** or **bansela**) ▶ **noun** S. African a tip or bonus.
– ORIGIN from Zulu *bansela* 'express thanks for a gift', or from *umbansela* 'small gift'.

bonspiel /ˈbɒnspiːl/ ▶ **noun** a curling match.
– ORIGIN mid 16th cent. (originally Scots): probably of Low German origin.

bontebok /ˈbɒntəbɒk/ ▶ **noun** (pl. same or **bonteboks**) an antelope with a mainly reddish-brown coat and white face, found in eastern South Africa. It belongs to the same species as the blesbok.
● *Damaliscus dorcas dorcas*, family Bovidae.
– ORIGIN late 18th cent.: from Afrikaans, from Dutch *bont* 'pied' + *bok* 'buck'.

bonus ▶ **noun** a payment or gift added to what is usual or expected, in particular:
■ an amount of money added to a person's wages, especially as a reward for good performance: *big Christmas bonuses.* ■ Brit. an extra dividend or issue paid to the shareholders of a company. ■ Brit. a distribution of profits to holders of an insurance policy. ■ a welcome and often unexpected circumstance, action, or service that accompanies and enhances something that is itself good: *good weather is **an added bonus** but the real appeal is the landscape.*
– ORIGIN late 18th cent. (probably originally Stock Exchange slang): from Latin *bonus* (masculine) 'good', used in place of *bonum* (neuter) 'good, good thing'.

bonus issue ▶ **noun** Brit. an issue of additional shares to shareholders instead of a dividend, in proportion to the shares already held.

bon vivant /bɒ viːˈvɒ̃, French bɔ̃ vivɑ̃/ ▶ **noun** (pl. **bon vivants** or **bons vivants** pronunc. same) a person who devotes themselves to a sociable and luxurious lifestyle.
– ORIGIN late 17th cent.: from French, literally 'person living well', from *bon* 'good' and *vivre* 'to live'.

bon viveur /viːˈvɜː/ ▶ **noun** (pl. **bon viveurs** or **bons viveurs** pronunc. same) another term for BON VIVANT.
– ORIGIN mid 19th cent.: pseudo-French, from French *bon* 'good' and *viveur* 'a living person', on the pattern of *bon vivant*.

bon voyage /ˌbɒn vɔɪˈjɑːʒ, French bɔ̃ vwajaʒ/ ▶ **exclamation** used to express good wishes to someone about to set off on a journey.
– ORIGIN late 17th cent.: French, literally 'good journey'.

bonxie /ˈbɒŋksi/ ▶ **noun** (pl. **-ies**) Scottish the great skua.
– ORIGIN late 18th cent.: from Norwegian *bunksi*, from *bunke* 'dumpy body'.

bony[1] ▶ **adjective** (**bonier**, **boniest**) of or like bone: *the bony plates that protect turtles and tortoises.*
■ (of a person or part of the body) so thin that the bones can be seen: *he held up his bony fingers.* ■ (of a fish eaten as food) having many bones.
– DERIVATIVES **boniness** noun.

bony[2] (also **boney**) ▶ **noun** (pl. **-ies**) S. African informal a motorbike.
– ORIGIN 1970s: probably from BONESHAKER.

bony fish ▶ **noun** a fish of a large class distinguished by a skeleton of bone, and comprising the majority of modern fishes. Compare with CARTILAGINOUS FISH.
● Class Osteichthyes: two or three subclasses.

bony labyrinth ▶ **noun** see LABYRINTH.

bonze /bɒnz/ ▶ **noun** a Japanese or Chinese Buddhist religious teacher.
– ORIGIN late 16th cent.: probably from Japanese *bonzō*, *bonsō* 'priest'.

bonzer ▶ **adjective** Austral./NZ informal excellent; first-rate.
– ORIGIN early 20th cent.: perhaps an alteration of BONANZA.

boo ▶ **exclamation 1** said suddenly to surprise someone who is unaware of one's presence: *'Boo!' she cried, jumping up to frighten him.* [ORIGIN: probably an alteration of earlier *bo*, used in the same way since late Middle English.]
2 said to show disapproval or contempt: *'There's only one bar.' 'Boo!'*
▶ **noun** an utterance of 'boo' to show disapproval or contempt of a speaker or performer: *the audience greeted this comment with boos and hisses.*
▶ **verb** (**boos**, **booed**) say 'boo' to show disapproval or contempt of a speaker or performer: [no obj.] *they booed and hissed when he stepped on stage* | [with obj.] *the team were booed off the pitch.*
– PHRASES **wouldn't say boo to a goose** (or US **not say boo**) used to emphasize that someone is very shy or reticent.
– ORIGIN early 19th cent. (in sense 2): imitative of the lowing of oxen. The sound was considered to be derisive; compare with HISS and HOOT.

booay /ˈbuːʌɪ/ (also **booai** or **boohai**) ▶ **noun** (**the booay**) NZ remote rural districts.
– PHRASES **up the booay** completely wrong or astray.
– ORIGIN perhaps from the place name *Puhoi* in North Auckland, New Zealand.

boob[1] informal ▶ **noun 1** Brit. an embarrassing mistake.

2 N. Amer. a foolish or stupid person.
▶ **verb** [no obj.] Brit. make an embarrassing mistake.
– ORIGIN early 20th cent.: abbreviation of BOOBY[1].

boob[2] ▶ **noun** (usu. **boobs**) informal a woman's breast.
– ORIGIN 1950s (originally US): abbreviation of BOOBY[1], from dialect *bubby*, of uncertain origin; perhaps related to German dialect *Bübbi* 'teat'.

booboisie /ˌbuːbwɑːˈziː/ ▶ **noun** [mass noun] US informal stupid people as a class.
– ORIGIN 1920s: from BOOB[1], humorous formation on the pattern of *bourgeoisie*.

boo-boo ▶ **noun** informal a mistake.
– ORIGIN 1950s (originally US): reduplication of BOOB[1].

boobook /ˈbuːbʊk/ (also **boobook owl**) ▶ **noun** a small Australasian owl with spotted brown plumage and a dark patch round each eye. It has a characteristic double hoot, reminiscent of the call of the European cuckoo. Also called MOPOKE or MOREPORK.
● Genus *Ninox*, family Strigidae: two species, especially the common *N. novaeseelandiae*.
– ORIGIN early 19th cent.: imitative of its call.

boob tube informal ▶ **noun 1** Brit. a tight-fitting strapless top made of stretchy material and worn by women or girls.
2 (usu. **the boob tube**) N. Amer. television or a television set: *librarians are scrambling for ways to compete with the boob tube.*

booby[1] ▶ **noun** (pl. **-ies**) **1** a stupid or childish person.
2 a large tropical seabird of the gannet family, with brown, black, or white plumage and typically having brightly coloured feet.
● Genus *Sula*, family Sulidae: several species, including the common **red-footed booby** (*S. sula*).
– ORIGIN early 17th cent.: probably from Spanish *bobo* (in both senses), from Latin *balbus* 'stammering'.

booby[2] ▶ **noun** (pl. **-ies**) (usu. **boobies**) informal a woman's breast.
– ORIGIN 1930s: alteration of dialect *bubby* (see BOOB[2]).

booby-hatch ▶ **noun** N. Amer. informal, offensive a psychiatric hospital.

booby prize ▶ **noun** a prize given as a joke to the person who is last in a race or competition.

booby trap ▶ **noun** a thing designed to catch the unwary, in particular:
■ an apparently harmless object containing a concealed explosive device designed to kill or injure anyone who touches it: [as modifier] *a booby trap bomb.* ■ a trap intended as a practical joke, especially one involving an object placed on top of a door ajar ready to fall on the next person to pass through.
▶ **verb** (**booby-trap**) [with obj.] place such a thing in or on (an object or area): [as adj. **booby-trapped**] *a booby-trapped parcel.*

boodie /ˈbuːdi/ ▶ **noun** a burrowing rat-kangaroo found only on islands off Western Australia.
● *Bettongia lesueur*, family Potoroidae. Also called **burrowing bettong**.
– ORIGIN mid 19th cent.: from Nyungar *burdi*.

boodle ▶ **noun** [mass noun] informal money, especially that gained or spent illegally or improperly.
– ORIGIN early 17th cent. (denoting a pack or crowd): from Dutch *boedel*, *boel* 'possessions, disorderly mass'. Compare with CABOODLE.

boofhead ▶ **noun** Austral. informal a fool.
– ORIGIN 1940s: probably from *bufflehead* 'simpleton', based on obsolete *buffle* 'buffalo'.

boogaloo /ˌbuːgəˈluː/ US ▶ **noun** a modern dance to rock-and-roll music performed with swivelling and shuffling movements of the body, originally popular in the 1960s.
▶ **verb** (**boogaloos**, **boogalooed**) [no obj.] perform this dance.
– ORIGIN 1960s: perhaps an alteration of BOOGIE-WOOGIE.

boogie ▶ **noun** (also **boogie-woogie**) (pl. **-ies**) [mass noun] a style of blues played on the piano with a strong, fast beat.
■ [count noun] informal a dance to fast pop or rock music.
▶ **verb** (**boogieing**) [no obj.] informal dance to fast pop or rock music: *Pat went off to boogie to a steel band.*
■ [no obj., with adverbial of direction] N. Amer. move or leave somewhere fast: *I think we'd better boogie on out of here.*
– ORIGIN early 20th cent. (originally US in the sense 'party'): of unknown origin.

boogie board ▶noun a short light type of surfboard ridden in a prone position.
– DERIVATIVES **boogie-boarder** noun.

boohai ▶noun variant spelling of BOOAY.

boohoo ▶exclamation used to represent the sound of someone crying noisily.
▶verb (**boohoos**, **boohooed**) [no obj.] cry noisily.
– ORIGIN mid 19th cent.: imitative.

boojum /ˈbuːdʒəm/ ▶noun an imaginary dangerous animal.
– ORIGIN 1876: nonsense word coined by Lewis Carroll in *The Hunting of the Snark*.

book ▶noun 1 a written or printed work consisting of pages glued or sewn together along one side and bound in covers: *a book of selected poems* | *a book on cats.*
  ■ a literary composition that is published or intended for publication as such a work: *the book is set in the 1940s* | *I'm writing a book.* ■ (**one's books**) used to refer to studying: *he is so deep in his books he would forget to eat.* ■ a main division of a literary work or of the Bible: *the Book of Genesis.* ■ (also **book of words**) the libretto of a musical or opera, or the script of a play. ■ (**the book**) the telephone directory for the area in which someone lives: *is your name in the book?* ■ informal a magazine. ■ figurative an imaginary record or list (often used to emphasize the thoroughness or comprehensiveness of someone's actions or experience): *she felt every emotion in the book of love.*
  2 [with modifier] a bound set of blank sheets for writing or keeping records in: *an accounts book.*
  ■ (**books**) a set of records or accounts: *a bid to balance the books.* ■ a bookmaker's record of bets accepted and money paid out. ■ Soccer the notebook in which a referee writes the names of players who are cautioned for foul play.
  3 a set of tickets, stamps, matches, cheques, samples of cloth, etc., bound together: *a pattern book.*
  ■ (**the book**) the first six tricks taken by declarer in a hand of bridge, after which further tricks count towards fulfilling the contract.
▶verb [with obj.] **1** reserve (accommodation, a place, etc.); buy (a ticket) in advance: *I have booked a table at the Swan* | [no obj.] *book early to avoid disappointment.*
  ■ reserve accommodation for (someone): *his secretary had booked him into the Howard Hotel* | [with two objs] *book me a single room at my usual hotel.* ■ [no obj.] (**book in**) register one's arrival at a hotel. ■ engage (a performer or guest) for an occasion or event. ■ (**be booked up**) have all places reserved; be full.
  2 make an official note of the name and other personal details of (an offender): *the cop booked me and took me down to the station.*
  ■ Soccer (of a referee) note down the name of (a player) who is cautioned for foul play.
– PHRASES **bring someone to book** officially punish someone or cause them to account for their behaviour. **by the book** strictly according to the rules: *a cop who doesn't exactly play it by the book.* **close the books** make no further entries at the end of an accounting period; cease trading. **in someone's bad** (or **good**) **books** in disfavour (or favour) with someone. **in my book** in my opinion: *that counts as a lie in my book.* **make** (or **open**) **a book** (US **make book**) take bets and pay out winnings on the outcome of a race or other contest or event. **on the books** contained in a list of members, employees, or clients. **People of the Book** Jews and Christians as regarded by Muslims. **suit one's book** Brit. be convenient to one: *it didn't suit her book at all to be moved.* **take a leaf out of someone's book** imitate or emulate someone in a particular way. **throw the book at** informal charge or punish (someone) as severely as possible or permitted. **you can't judge a book by its cover** proverb outward appearances are not a reliable indication of the true character of someone or something.
– ORIGIN Old English *bōc* (originally also 'a document or charter'), *bōcian* 'to grant by charter', of Germanic origin; related to Dutch *boek* and German *Buch*, and probably to BEECH (on which runes were carved).

bookable ▶adjective **1** able to be reserved: *tickets are bookable in advance.*
  2 Soccer (of an offence) serious enough for the offending player to be cautioned by the referee.

bookbinder ▶noun a person who binds books as a profession.
– DERIVATIVES **bookbinding** noun.

bookcase ▶noun an open cabinet containing shelves on which to keep books.

book club ▶noun a society which sells its members selected books, typically at reduced prices.

bookend ▶noun a support placed at the end of a row of books to keep them upright, typically ornamental and forming one of a pair.
▶verb [with obj.] (usu. **be bookended**) informal occur or be positioned at the end or on either side of (something): *the narrative is bookended by a pair of incisive essays.*

booker ▶noun a person employed to engage performers for a theatre or similar.

Booker Prize a literary prize awarded annually for a novel published by a British or Commonwealth citizen during the previous year, financed by the multinational company Booker McConnell.

book hand ▶noun [mass noun] a formal style of handwriting as used by professional copiers of books before the invention of printing.

bookie ▶noun (pl. **-ies**) informal a bookmaker.

booking ▶noun an act of reserving accommodation, a place, etc. or of buying a ticket in advance: *the hotel does not handle group bookings* | [mass noun] *early booking is essential* | [as modifier] *a booking form.*
  ■ Soccer an instance of a player being cautioned by the referee for foul play.

booking clerk ▶noun Brit. an official selling tickets, especially at a railway station.

booking hall ▶noun Brit. a room or area at a railway station in which tickets are sold.

booking office ▶noun chiefly Brit. a place where tickets are sold, especially at a railway station or theatre.

bookish ▶adjective (of a person or way of life) devoted to reading and studying.
  ■ (of language or writing) literary in style or allusion.
– DERIVATIVES **bookishly** adverb, **bookishness** noun.

bookkeeping ▶noun [mass noun] the activity or occupation of keeping records of the financial affairs of a business.
– DERIVATIVES **bookkeeper** noun.

bookland ▶noun [mass noun] Brit. historical an area of common land granted by charter to a private owner before the Norman conquest.
– ORIGIN Old English, from *bóc* 'charter' + LAND. The term was applied eventually to all land that was not *folcland*, i.e. land subject to traditional communal obligations.

book learning ▶noun [mass noun] knowledge gained from books or study rather than personal experience.

booklet ▶noun a small, thin book with paper covers, typically giving information on a particular subject.

booklouse ▶noun (pl. **booklice**) a minute insect that typically has reduced or absent wings, frequently found in buildings where it may cause damage to books and paper. See also PSOCID.
  ● Liposcelidae and related families in the order Psocoptera: many species, in particular the common *Liposcelis bostrychophilus.*

book lung ▶noun Zoology (in a spider or other arachnid) each of a pair of respiratory organs composed of many fine leaves. They are situated in the abdomen and have openings on the underside.

bookmaker ▶noun a person whose job is to take bets, especially on horse races, calculate odds, and pay out winnings; the manager of a betting shop.
– DERIVATIVES **bookmaking** noun.

bookman ▶noun (pl. **-men**) archaic a literary man.

bookmark ▶noun a strip of leather, card, or other material, used to mark one's place in a book.
  ■ Computing a record of the address of a file, Internet page, or other data used to enable quick access by a user.

bookmobile ▶noun N. Amer. a mobile library.
– ORIGIN 1930s: from BOOK, on the pattern of *automobile.*

Book of Changes ▶noun English name for I CHING.

Book of Common Prayer ▶noun the official service book of the Church of England, compiled by Thomas Cranmer and others, first issued in 1549, and largely unchanged since the revision of 1662.

book of hours ▶noun a book of prayers appointed for particular canonical hours or times of day, used

by Roman Catholics for private devotions and popular especially in the Middle Ages, when they were often richly illuminated.

Book of Life ▶noun (in South Africa) a name given to the comprehensive personal identity document, introduced originally for whites only (in general use since 1986).

Book of Proverbs see PROVERBS.

Book of the Dead ▶noun **1** a collection of ancient Egyptian religious and magical texts, selections from which were often written on or placed in tombs.
  2 (in full **Tibetan Book of the Dead**) a Tibetan Buddhist text recited during funerary rites, describing the passage from death to rebirth.

book of words ▶noun see BOOK (sense 1).

bookplate ▶noun a decorative label stuck in the front of a book, bearing the name of the book's owner.

bookrest ▶noun Brit. an adjustable support for an open book on a table.

bookshelf ▶noun (pl. **-shelves**) a shelf on which books can be stored.

Books of the Maccabees ▶plural noun see MACCABEES.

bookstall ▶noun a stand where books and sometimes newspapers are sold, especially out of doors or at a station.

booksy ▶adjective Brit. informal having literary or bookish pretensions.

book token ▶noun Brit. a voucher which can be exchanged for books costing up to a specified amount.

book value ▶noun the value of a security or asset as entered in a firm's books. Often contrasted with MARKET VALUE.

bookwork ▶noun [mass noun] **1** the activity of keeping records of accounts.
  2 the studying of textbooks, as opposed to practical work.

bookworm ▶noun **1** informal a person who enjoys reading.
  2 (especially formerly) the larva of a wood-boring beetle which feeds on the paper and glue in books.

Boole, George (1815–64), English mathematician responsible for Boolean algebra. The study of mathematical or symbolic logic developed mainly from his ideas.

Boolean /ˈbuːlɪən/ ▶adjective denoting a system of algebraic notation used to represent logical propositions by means of the binary digits 0 (false) and 1 (true), especially in computing and electronics.
▶noun Computing a binary variable with these possible values.
– ORIGIN mid 19th cent.: from the name of G. BOOLE + -AN.

boom¹ ▶noun a loud, deep, resonant sound: *the deep boom of the bass drum.*
  ■ the characteristic resonant cry of the bittern.
▶verb [no obj.] make a loud, deep, resonant sound: *thunder boomed in the sky* | *her voice boomed out.*
  ■ [with direct speech] say in a loud, deep, resonant voice: *'Stop right there,' boomed the Headmaster.* ■ (of a bittern) utter its characteristic resonant cry.
– DERIVATIVES **boominess** noun, **boomy** adjective.
– ORIGIN late Middle English (as a verb): ultimately imitative; perhaps from Dutch *bommen* 'to hum, buzz'.

boom² ▶noun a period of great prosperity or rapid economic growth: *the London property boom* | [as modifier] *the boom years of the late 1980s.*
▶verb [no obj.] experience a period of great prosperity or rapid economic growth: *business is booming.*
– DERIVATIVES **boomlet** noun, **boomy** adjective.
– ORIGIN late 19th cent. (originally US): probably from BOOM¹.

boom³ ▶noun a long pole or rod, in particular:
  ■ a pivoted spar to which the foot of a vessel's sail is attached, allowing the angle of the sail to be changed. ■ [often as modifier] a movable arm over a television or film set, carrying a microphone or camera: *a boom mike.* ■ a floating beam used to contain oil spills or to form a barrier across the mouth of a harbour or river.
– ORIGIN mid 16th cent. (in the general sense 'beam, pole'): from Dutch, 'beam, tree, pole'; related to BEAM.

b

boom box ▶ noun informal a large portable radio and cassette player capable of powerful sound.

boomer ▶ noun informal **1** something large or notable of its kind, in particular:
■ Austral. a large male kangaroo. ■ a large wave.
2 chiefly N. Amer. short for **baby boomer** (see **BABY BOOM**).
– ORIGIN early 19th cent.: probably from the verb **BOOM**¹ + **-ER**¹.

boomerang ▶ noun a curved flat piece of wood that can be thrown so as to return to the thrower, traditionally used by Australian Aboriginals as a hunting weapon.
▶ verb [no obj.] (of a plan or action) recoil on the originator: *misleading consumers about quality will eventually boomerang on a car-maker.*
– ORIGIN early 19th cent.: from Dharuk.

booming ▶ adjective **1** having a period of great prosperity or rapid economic growth: *the booming economy of southern China.*
2 (of a sound or voice) loud, deep, and resonant: *his booming voice | a booming laugh.*
3 struck or projected with great force: *a booming kick from the touchline.*

boomslang ▶ noun a large, highly venomous southern African tree snake, the male of which is bright green and the female dull olive brown.
● *Dispholidus typus,* family Colubridae.
– ORIGIN late 18th cent.: from Afrikaans, from Dutch *boom* 'tree' + *slang* 'snake'.

boom vang ▶ noun see **VANG**.

boon ▶ noun **1** [usu. in sing.] a thing that is helpful or beneficial: *the route will be a boon to many travellers.*
2 archaic a favour or request.
– ORIGIN Middle English (originally in the sense 'request for a favour'): from Old Norse *bón.*

boon companion ▶ noun a close friend with whom one enjoys spending time.
– ORIGIN mid 16th cent.: *boon* from Old French *bon,* from Latin *bonus* 'good'. The early literal sense was 'good fellow', originally denoting a drinking companion.

boondocks /ˈbuːndɒks/ ▶ plural noun N. Amer. informal rough or isolated country: *this place is out in the boondocks, you'll never get here by bus.*
– ORIGIN 1940s: *boondock* from Tagalog *bundok* 'mountain'.

boondoggle /ˈbuːndɒɡ(ə)l/ N. Amer. informal ▶ noun an unnecessary, wasteful, or fraudulent project.
▶ verb [no obj.] waste money or time on such projects.
– ORIGIN 1930s: of unknown origin.

Boone, Daniel (c.1734–1820), American pioneer. Boone made trips west from Pennsylvania into the unexplored area of Kentucky, organizing settlements and successfully defending them against hostile American Indians.

boong /bʊŋ/ ▶ noun Austral. offensive an Aboriginal.
– ORIGIN 1920s: from an Aboriginal word meaning 'human being'.

boonies /ˈbuːnɪz/ ▶ plural noun short for **BOONDOCKS**.

boor /bʊə/ ▶ noun a rough and bad-mannered person.
– DERIVATIVES **boorish** adjective, **boorishly** adverb, **boorishness** noun.
– ORIGIN mid 16th cent. (in the sense 'peasant'): from Low German *būr* or Dutch *boer* 'farmer'.

boost ▶ verb [with obj.] help or encourage (something) to increase or improve: *a range of measures to boost tourism.*
■ amplify (an electrical signal).
▶ noun a source of help or encouragement leading to increase or improvement: *the cut in interest rates will give a further boost to the economy.*
■ an increase or improvement: *a boost in exports.*
– ORIGIN early 19th cent. (originally US, in the sense 'push from below'): of unknown origin.

booster ▶ noun **1** a thing or person that helps increase or promote something, in particular:
■ Medicine a dose of an immunizing agent increasing or renewing the effect of an earlier one. ■ the first stage of a rocket or spacecraft, used to give initial acceleration and then jettisoned. ■ a device for increasing electrical voltage or signal strength. ■ [in combination] a source of help or encouragement: *job fairs are a great morale booster.* ■ N. Amer. a keen promoter of a person, organization, or cause.
2 N. Amer. informal a shoplifter.

boosterism ▶ noun [mass noun] chiefly N. Amer. the keen promotion of a person, organization, or cause.

booster seat (also **booster cushion**) ▶ noun an extra seat or cushion placed on an existing seat for a small child to sit on.

boot¹ ▶ noun **1** a sturdy item of footwear covering the foot and ankle, and sometimes also the leg below the knee: *walking boots.*
■ a covering to protect the lower part of a horse's leg. ■ historical an instrument of torture encasing and crushing the foot. ■ US a wheel clamp.
2 informal a hard kick: *he got a boot in the stomach.*
3 Brit. a space at the back of a car for carrying luggage or other goods.
4 (also **boot-up**) [usu. as modifier] the process of starting a computer and putting it into a state of readiness for operation: *a boot disk.*
▶ verb [with obj.] **1** [with obj. and adverbial of direction] kick (something) hard in a specified direction: *he ended up booting the ball into the stand.*
■ (**boot someone off**) informal force someone to leave something, especially a vehicle, unceremoniously: *a guard booted two children off a train.* ■ (**boot someone out**) informal force someone to leave a place, institution, or job unceremoniously: *she had been booted out of school.*
2 start (a computer) and put it into a state of readiness for operation: *the menu will be ready as soon as you boot up your computer | [no obj.] the system won't boot from the original drive.* [ORIGIN: from sense 2 of **BOOTSTRAP**.]
3 US place a wheel clamp on (an illegally parked car).
– PHRASES **the boot** (or N. Amer. **shoe**) **is on the other foot** the situation, in particular the holding of advantage, has reversed. **die with one's boots on** die in battle or while actively occupied. **get the boot** informal be dismissed from one's job. **give someone the boot** informal dismiss someone from their job. **old boot** informal an old woman considered to be ugly and contemptible. **put the boot in** (or **into someone**) Brit. informal kick someone hard when they are on the ground. ■ figurative treat someone in a cruel way, especially when they are vulnerable. **with one's heart in one's boots** in a state of great depression or trepidation. **you** (**can**) **bet your boots** informal used to express absolute certainty about a situation or statement: *you can bet your boots that the patrol has raised the alarm.*
– DERIVATIVES **booted** adjective (in senses 1 and 3 of the noun).
– ORIGIN Middle English: from Old Norse *bóti* or its source, Old French *bote,* of unknown ultimate origin.

boot² ▶ noun (in phrase **to boot**) as well; in addition: *she was a woman of uninspiring appearance and a dreadful bore to boot.*
– ORIGIN Old English *bōt* 'advantage, remedy', of Germanic origin; related to Dutch *boete* and German *Busse* 'penance, fine', also to **BETTER**¹ and **BEST**.

bootable ▶ adjective (of a disk) containing the software required to boot a computer.

bootblack ▶ noun chiefly historical a person employed to polish boots and shoes.

bootboy ▶ noun **1** informal a rowdy or violent youth typically having close-cropped hair and wearing heavy boots.
2 chiefly historical a boy employed to clean boots and shoes.

boot camp ▶ noun chiefly N. Amer. a military training camp for new recruits, with very harsh discipline.
■ a prison for young offenders, run on military lines.

bootee /buːˈtiː/ (also **bootie**) ▶ noun **1** a soft shoe, typically woollen, worn by a baby.
2 a woman's short boot.
3 a protective shoe or lining for a shoe.

Boötes /bəʊˈəʊtiːz/ Astronomy a northern constellation (the Herdsman), said to represent a man holding the leash of two dogs (Canes Venatici) while driving a bear (Ursa Major). It contains the bright star Arcturus.
■ [as genitive **Boötis** /bəʊˈəʊtɪs/] used with preceding letter or numeral to designate a star in this constellation: *the star Gamma Boötis.*
– ORIGIN Greek.

Booth, William (1829–1912), English religious leader, founder and first general of the Salvation Army. A Methodist revivalist preacher, in 1865 he established a mission in the East End of London which later became the Salvation Army.

booth /buːð, buːθ/ ▶ noun **1** a small temporary tent or structure used for selling goods, providing information, or staging shows, especially at a market or fair.
2 an enclosed compartment that allows privacy, for example when telephoning, voting, or sitting in a restaurant.
– ORIGIN Middle English (in the general sense 'temporary dwelling or shelter'): from Old Norse *buth,* based on *búa* 'dwell'.

Boothia, Gulf of /ˈbuːθɪə/ a gulf in the Canadian Arctic, between the Boothia Peninsula and Baffin Island, in the Northwest Territories.
– ORIGIN named in honour of Sir Felix Booth (1775–1850), patron of the expedition to the Arctic (1829–33) led by Sir John Ross.

Boothia Peninsula a peninsula of northern Canada, in the Northwest Territories, situated between Victoria Island and Baffin Island.

bootie ▶ noun (pl. **-ies**) variant spelling of **BOOTEE**.

bootjack ▶ noun a device for holding a boot by the heel to ease withdrawal of one's foot.

bootlace ▶ noun a cord or leather strip for lacing boots.

bootlace fungus ▶ noun another term for **HONEY FUNGUS**.

bootlace tie ▶ noun Brit. a narrow necktie, popular in the 1950s.

bootleg ▶ adjective (of alcoholic drink or a recording) made, distributed, or sold illegally: *bootleg cassettes | bootleg whisky.*
▶ verb (**-legged**, **-legging**) [with obj.] make, distribute, or sell (alcoholic drink or a recording) illegally: [as noun **bootlegging**] *bootlegging is rife in America.*
▶ noun an illegal musical recording, especially one made at a concert.
– DERIVATIVES **bootlegger** noun.
– ORIGIN late 19th cent.: from the smugglers' practice of concealing bottles in their boots.

bootless ▶ adjective archaic (of a task or undertaking) ineffectual; useless: *remonstrating with him seems ever to have been a bootless task.*
– ORIGIN Old English *bōtlēas* 'not able to be compensated for by payment' (see **BOOT**², **-LESS**).

bootlicker ▶ noun informal an obsequious or servile person.
– DERIVATIVES **bootlicking** noun.

boots ▶ noun Brit. dated a person employed in a hotel to clean boots and shoes, carry luggage, and perform other menial tasks.
– ORIGIN late 18th cent.: plural of **BOOT**¹, used as a singular.

boot sale ▶ noun short for **CAR BOOT SALE**.

boot-scooting ▶ noun another term for **LINE DANCING**.

bootstrap ▶ noun **1** a loop at the back of a boot, used to pull it on.
■ [usu. as modifier] the technique of using existing resources as a base and modifying them to create something more complex and effective: *a bootstrap process.*
2 Computing a technique of loading a program into a computer by means of a few initial instructions which enable the introduction of the rest of the program from an input device.
▶ verb [with obj. and adverbial of direction] get (oneself or something) into or out of a particular situation using existing resources: *the company is bootstrapping itself out of a marred financial past.*
– PHRASES **pull** (or **drag**) **oneself up by one's** (**own**) **bootstraps** improve one's position by one's own efforts.

boot top ▶ noun the part of the hull of a ship just above the waterline, typically marked by a line of contrasting colour.

boot-up ▶ noun see **BOOT**¹ (sense 4).

booty¹ ▶ noun [mass noun] valuable stolen goods, especially those seized in war.
– ORIGIN late Middle English (originally denoting plunder acquired in common): from Middle Low German *būte,* *buite* 'exchange, distribution', of uncertain origin.

booty² ▶ noun (pl. **-ies**) N. Amer. informal a person's bottom.
– PHRASES **shake one's booty** dance energetically.

booze informal ▶**noun** [mass noun] alcoholic drink: *he was on the booze somewhere.*
▶**verb** [no obj.] drink alcohol, especially in large quantities: [as noun **boozing**] *Michael is trying to quit boozing.*
– ORIGIN Middle English *bouse*, from Middle Dutch *būsen* 'drink to excess'. The spelling *booze* dates from the 18th cent.

boozer ▶**noun** informal a person who drinks large quantities of alcohol.
■Brit. a pub or bar.

booze-up ▶**noun** informal a heavy drinking session.

boozy ▶**adjective** (**boozier**, **booziest**) informal characterized by drinking large quantities of alcohol: *a boozy lunch.*
– DERIVATIVES **boozily** adverb, **booziness** noun.

bop[1] informal ▶**noun 1** chiefly Brit. a dance to pop music.
■an organized social occasion with such dancing.
2 short for **BEBOP**.
▶**verb** (**bopped**, **bopping**) [no obj.] dance to pop music: *everyone was bopping until the small hours.*
■move or travel energetically: *entrepreneurial types bopping around Italy.*
– DERIVATIVES **bopper** noun.
– ORIGIN 1940s: shortening of **BEBOP**.

bop[2] informal ▶**verb** (**bopped**, **bopping**) [with obj.] hit or punch quickly: *Rex bopped him on the head.*
▶**noun** a quick blow or punch.
– ORIGIN 1930s (originally US): imitative.

bo-peep ▶**noun 1** [mass noun] a game of hiding and suddenly reappearing, played with a young child.
2 Austral./NZ informal a quick look.
– ORIGIN early 16th cent. (in sense 1): from *bo*, an exclamation intended to startle someone (compare with **BOO**) + the verb **PEEP**[1]. Sense 2 dates from the 1940s.

Bophuthatswana /ˌbə(ʊ)puːtətˈswɑːnə/ a former homeland established in South Africa for the Tswana people, now part of North-West Province and Mpumalanga.

bora[1] /ˈbɔːrə/ ▶**noun** a strong, cold, dry NE wind blowing in the upper Adriatic.
– ORIGIN mid 19th cent.: dialect variant of Italian *borea*, from Latin *boreas* 'north wind' (see **BOREAL**).

bora[2] /ˈbɔːrə/ ▶**noun** an Australian Aboriginal rite in which boys are initiated into manhood.
– ORIGIN mid 19th cent.: from Kamilaroi *buuru*.

Bora-Bora /ˌbɔːrəˈbɔːrə/ an island of the Society Islands group in French Polynesia.

boracic /bəˈrasɪk/ ▶**adjective** consisting of, containing, or denoting boric acid, especially as an antiseptic.
■Brit. informal having no money. [ORIGIN: from *boracic lint*, rhyming slang for 'skint'.]
– ORIGIN late 18th cent.: from medieval Latin *borax*, *borac-* (see **BORAX**[1]) + **-IC**.

borage /ˈbɒrɪdʒ/ ▶**noun** a European herbaceous plant with bright blue flowers and hairy leaves, which is attractive to bees.
● *Borago officinalis*, family Boraginaceae (the **borage family**). This family includes many plants that typically have blue or purple flowers, including forget-me-not, comfrey, bugloss, and alkanet.
– ORIGIN Middle English: from Old French *bourrache*, from medieval Latin *borrago*, perhaps from Arabic *'abū ḥurāš* 'father of roughness' (referring to the leaves).

boraginaceous /ˌbɒrɪdʒɪˈneɪʃəs/ ▶**adjective** Botany of, relating to, or denoting plants of the borage family (Boraginaceae).

borak /ˈbɔːrak/ (also **borax**) ▶**noun** [mass noun] Austral./NZ informal banter; ridicule.
– ORIGIN early 19th cent.: originally Australian pidgin (expressing negation), based on Aboriginal *burag* 'no, not'.

borane /ˈbɔːreɪn/ ▶**noun** Chemistry any of a series of unstable binary compounds of boron and hydrogen, analogous to the alkanes. The simplest example is diborane, B_2H_6.
– ORIGIN early 20th cent.: from **BORON** + **-ANE**[2].

Borås /bʊˈrɔːs/ an industrial city in SW Sweden; pop. 101,770 (1990).

borate /ˈbɔːreɪt/ ▶**noun** Chemistry a salt in which the anion contains both boron and oxygen, as in borax.

borax[1] /ˈbɔːraks/ ▶**noun** [mass noun] a white compound which occurs as a mineral in some alkaline salt deposits and is used in making glass and ceramics, as a metallurgical flux, and as an antiseptic.
● A hydrated sodium borate; chem. formula: $Na_2B_4O_7.10H_2O$.
– ORIGIN late Middle English: from medieval Latin, from Arabic *būraḳ*, from Pahlavi *būrak*.

borax[2] /ˈbɔːraks/ ▶**noun** variant spelling of **BORAK**.

Borazon /ˈbɔːrəzɒn/ ▶**noun** [mass noun] trademark an industrial abrasive consisting of boron nitride.
– ORIGIN 1950s: from **BORON**, with the insertion of **AZO-**.

borborygmus /ˌbɔːbəˈrɪgməs/ ▶**noun** (pl. **borborygmi** /-mʌɪ/) technical a rumbling or gurgling noise made by the movement of fluid and gas in the intestines.
– DERIVATIVES **borborygmic** adjective.
– ORIGIN early 18th cent.: modern Latin, from Greek *borborugmos*.

Bordeaux[1] /bɔːˈdəʊ, French bɔrdo/ a port of SW France on the River Garonne, capital of Aquitaine; pop. 213,270 (1990). It is a centre of the wine trade.

Bordeaux[2] /bɔːˈdəʊ/ ▶**noun** (pl. same /-ˈdəʊz/) [mass noun] a red, white, or rosé wine from the district of Bordeaux.

Bordeaux mixture ▶**noun** [mass noun] a fungicide for vines, fruit trees, and other plants composed of equal quantities of copper sulphate and calcium oxide in water.
– ORIGIN late 19th cent.: first used in the vineyards of the Bordeaux region.

bordelaise /ˌbɔːdəˈleɪz/ ▶**adjective** denoting or served with a sauce of red wine and onions: *bordelaise sauce* | [postpositive] *lobster bordelaise.*
– ORIGIN French, from (*à la*) *bordelaise* 'Bordeaux-style'.

bordello /bɔːˈdɛləʊ/ ▶**noun** (pl. **-os**) chiefly N. Amer. a brothel.
– ORIGIN late 16th cent. (gradually replacing Middle English *bordel*): from Italian, probably from Old French *bordel*, diminutive of *borde* 'small farm, cottage', ultimately of Germanic origin.

Border, Allan (Robert) (b.1955), Australian cricketer. A batsman and occasional spin bowler, he had made 156 test match appearances (93 as captain) and scored 11,174 runs (all three figures being world records) at the time of his retirement from international cricket in 1994.

border ▶**noun 1** a line separating two countries, administrative divisions, or other areas: *Iraq's northern border with Turkey* | [as modifier] *border controls.*
■a district near such a line: *a refugee camp on the border.* ■(**the Border**) the boundary and adjoining districts between Northern Ireland and the Republic of Ireland. ■(**the Border** or **the Borders**) the boundary and adjoining districts between Scotland and England. ■figurative an edge, boundary, or limit of something: *the unknown regions at the borders of physics and electronics.*
2 a band or strip, especially a decorative one, around the edge of something.
■a strip of ground along the edge of a lawn or path for planting flowers or shrubs.
▶**verb** [with obj.] form an edge along or beside (something): *a pool bordered by palm trees.*
■(of a country or area) be adjacent to (another country or area): *regions bordering Azerbaijan* | [no obj.] *the states bordering on the Black Sea.* ■[no obj.] (**border on**) figurative come close to or be developing into (a particular extreme condition): *Sam arrived in a state of excitement bordering on hysteria.* ■(usu. **be bordered with**) provide (something) with a decorative edge: *the walls were bordered with carved scrolls and cornices.*
– ORIGIN late Middle English: from Old French *bordeure*; ultimately of Germanic origin and related to **BOARD**.

Border collie ▶**noun** a common working sheepdog, typically with a black-and-white coat, of a medium-sized breed originating near the border between England and Scotland.

borderer ▶**noun** (chiefly in historical contexts) a person living near the border between two countries, especially that between Scotland and England.

borderland ▶**noun** (usu. **borderlands**) a district near the line separating two countries or areas.
■figurative an area of overlap between two things: *the murky borderland between history and myth.*

Border Leicester ▶**noun** see **LEICESTER**[3] (sense 2).

borderline ▶**noun** a boundary separating two countries or areas.
■figurative a division between two distinct or opposite things: *the borderline between ritual and custom.*
▶**adjective** only just acceptable in quality or as belonging to a category: *references may be requested in borderline cases.*

Border terrier ▶**noun** a small terrier of a breed with rough hair, originating in the Cheviot Hills.

Bordet /ˈbɔːdeɪ, French bɔrdɛ/, Jules (1870–1961), Belgian bacteriologist and immunologist. He discovered the complement system of blood serum, and developed a vaccine for whooping cough. Nobel Prize for Physiology or Medicine (1919).

bordure /ˈbɔːdjʊə/ ▶**noun** Heraldry a broad border used as a charge in a coat of arms, often as a mark of difference.
– ORIGIN late Middle English: variant of **BORDER**.

bore[1] ▶**verb 1** [with obj.] make (a hole) in something with a tool or by digging: *they bored holes in the sides* | [no obj.] *the drill can bore through rock.*
■[no obj.] (**bore into**) figurative (of a person's eyes) stare harshly at: *his eyes bored into hers.* ■[with obj.] hollow out (a gun barrel or other tube): *an 1100 cc road bike bored out to 1168 cc.*
2 [no obj.] (of an athlete or racehorse) push another competitor out of the way.
▶**noun 1** the hollow part inside a gun barrel or other tube.
■[often in combination] the diameter of this; the calibre: *a small-bore rifle.* ■[in combination] a gun of a specified bore: *he shot a guard in the leg with a twelve-bore.*
2 short for **BOREHOLE**.
– ORIGIN Old English *borian* (verb), of Germanic origin; related to German *bohren*.

bore[2] ▶**noun** a person whose talk or behaviour is dull and uninteresting: *he can be a crashing bore.*
■[in sing.] a tedious or annoying situation, activity, or thing: *it's such a bore cooking when one's alone.*
▶**verb** [with obj.] cause (someone) to feel weary and uninterested by dull talk or qualities: *she is too polite to bore us with anecdotes* | [with obj. and complement] *timid women quickly bore her silly.*
– PHRASES **bore someone to death** (or **to tears**) make someone feel extremely bored.
– ORIGIN mid 18th cent. (as a verb): of unknown origin.

bore[3] ▶**noun** a steep-fronted wave caused by the meeting of two tides or by the constriction of a tide rushing up a narrow estuary.
– ORIGIN early 17th cent.: perhaps from Old Norse *bára* 'wave'; the term was used in the general sense 'billow, wave' in Middle English.

bore[4] past of **BEAR**[1].

boreal /ˈbɔːrɪəl/ ▶**adjective** of the North or northern regions, in particular:
■Ecology of, relating to, or characteristic of the climatic zone south of the Arctic, especially the cold temperate region dominated by taiga and forests of birch, poplar, and conifers: *northern boreal forest.* ■(**Boreal**) Botany of, relating to, or denoting a phytogeographical kingdom comprising the arctic and temperate regions of Eurasia and North America. ■(**Boreal**) Geology relating to or denoting the second climatic stage of the postglacial period in northern Europe, between the Preboreal and Atlantic stages (about 9,000 to 7,500 years ago).
– ORIGIN late Middle English: from late Latin *borealis*, from Latin *Boreas*, denoting the god of the north wind, from Greek.

bored[1] ▶**adjective** feeling weary and impatient because one is unoccupied or lacks interest in one's current activity: *she* ***got bored with*** *staring out of the window* | *they hung around all day,* ***bored stiff*** | *bored teenagers.*

USAGE The normal constructions for **bored** are **bored by** or **bored with**. More recently, **bored of** has emerged (probably by analogy with other words, such as **tired of**), but this construction, though common in informal English, is not yet considered acceptable in standard English.

bored[2] ▶**adjective** [in combination] (of a gun) having a specified bore: *large-bored guns.*

boredom ▶**noun** [mass noun] the state of feeling bored: *I'll die of boredom if I live that long.*

boreen /bɔːˈriːn/ ▶**noun** Irish a narrow country road.
– ORIGIN mid 19th cent.: from Irish *bóithrín*, diminutive of *bóthar* 'road'.

borehole ▶**noun** a deep, narrow hole made in the ground, especially to locate water or oil.

borer ▶**noun 1** a worm, mollusc, insect, or insect larva which bores into wood, other plant material, or rock.

b

2 a tool for boring.

borescope ▶ noun an instrument used to inspect the inside of a structure through a small hole.

Borg, Björn (Rune) (b.1956), Swedish tennis player. He won five consecutive men's singles titles at Wimbledon (1976–80), beating the record of three consecutive wins held by Fred Perry.

Borges /ˈbɔːxɛs/, Jorge Luis (1899–1986), Argentinian poet, short-story writer, and essayist. The volume of short stories *A Universal History of Infamy* (1935, revised 1954) is regarded as a founding work of magic realism.

Borgia[1] /ˈbɔːʒə, Italian ˈbɔrdʒa/, Cesare (c.1476–1507), Italian statesman, cardinal, and general. The illegitimate son of Cardinal Rodrigo Borgia (later Pope Alexander VI) and brother of Lucrezia Borgia, he was captain general of the papal army from 1499, and became master of a large portion of central Italy.

Borgia[2] /ˈbɔːʒə, Italian ˈbɔrdʒa/, Lucrezia (1480–1519), Italian noblewoman, sister of Cesare Borgia. She married three times, according to the political alliances useful to her family; after her third marriage in 1501 she established herself as a patron of the arts.

boric /ˈbɔːrɪk/ ▶ adjective Chemistry of boron: *boric oxide.*

boric acid ▶ noun Chemistry a weakly acid crystalline compound derived from borax, used as a mild antiseptic and in the manufacture of heat-resistant glass and enamels. See also **BORACIC**.
• Chem. formula: $B(OH)_3$.

boring ▶ adjective not interesting; tedious: *I've got a boring job in an office.*
– DERIVATIVES **boringly** adverb [as submodifier] *my boringly respectable uncle*, **boringness** noun.

Boris Godunov /ˈbɒrɪs/ see **GODUNOV**.

bork ▶ verb [with obj.] US informal obstruct (someone, especially a candidate for public office) by systematically defaming or vilifying them.
– ORIGIN 1980s: from the name of Robert *Bork* (born 1927), an American judge whose nomination to the Supreme Court (1987) was rejected following unfavourable publicity for his allegedly extreme views.

borlotti bean /bɔːˈlɒti/ ▶ noun a type of kidney bean with a pink speckled skin that turns brown when cooked.
– ORIGIN Italian *borlotti*, plural of *borlotto* 'kidney bean'.

Bormann /ˈbɔːmən, German ˈbɔːɐman/, Martin (1900–c.1945), German Nazi politician. Considered to be Hitler's closest collaborator, he disappeared at the end of the Second World War; his skeleton, exhumed in Berlin, was identified in 1973.

Born /bɔːn, German bɔrn/, Max (1882–1970), German theoretical physicist, a founder of quantum mechanics. Nobel Prize for Physics (1954).

born ▶ adjective existing as a result of birth: *she was born in Aberdeen | babies* **born to** *women aged 25–9 | I was* **born with** *a sense of curiosity | a newly born baby |* [in combination] *a German-born philosopher.*
■ [attrib.] having a natural ability to do a particular job or task: *he's a born engineer.* ■ [predic., with infinitive] perfectly suited or trained to do a particular job or task: *men born to rule.* ■ (of an organization, movement, or idea) brought into existence: *her own business was born.* ■ [predic.] **(born of)** existing as a result of (a particular situation or feeling): *a power born of obsession.*
– PHRASES **born and bred** by birth and upbringing, especially when considered a typical product of a place: *he was a Cambridge man born and bred.* **born on the wrong side of the blanket** see **BLANKET**. **be born with a silver spoon in one's mouth** see **SILVER**. **in all one's born days** used to express surprise or shock at something one has not encountered before: *in all my born days I've never seen the like of it.* **not know one is born** used to convey that someone has an easy life without realizing how easy it is. **there's one** (or **a sucker**) **born every minute** informal there are many gullible people. **I (she, etc.) wasn't born yesterday** used to indicate that one is not foolish or gullible.
– ORIGIN Old English *boren*, past participle of *beran* 'to bear' (see **BEAR**[1]).

USAGE On the difference between **born** and **borne**, see **usage** at **BEAR**[1].

Borna disease ▶ noun [mass noun] an infectious neurological disease affecting horses and other mammal and bird species, caused by an RNA virus (**Borna disease virus**).
– ORIGIN mid 20th cent.: from *Borna*, the name of a town and district near Leipzig in Germany where an outbreak occurred.

born-again ▶ adjective relating to or denoting a person who has converted to a personal faith in Christ (with reference to John 3:3): *a born-again Christian.*
■ figurative having the extreme enthusiasm of the newly converted or reconverted: *born-again environmentalists.*
▶ noun chiefly N. Amer. a born-again Christian.

borne past participle of **BEAR**[1]. ▶ adjective [in combination] carried or transported by the thing specified: *water-borne bacteria.*

Borneo /ˈbɔːnɪəʊ/ a large island of the Malay Archipelago, comprising Kalimantan (a region of Indonesia), Sabah and Sarawak (states of Malaysia), and Brunei.
– DERIVATIVES **Bornean** adjective & noun.

Bornholm /ˈbɔːnhəʊm/ a Danish island in the Baltic Sea, south-east of Sweden.

Bornholm disease ▶ noun [mass noun] a viral infection with fever and pain in the muscles of the ribs.
– ORIGIN 1930s: named after the island of **BORNHOLM**, where it was first described.

bornite /ˈbɔːnʌɪt/ ▶ noun [mass noun] a brittle reddish-brown crystalline mineral with an iridescent purple tarnish, consisting of a sulphide of copper and iron.
– ORIGIN early 19th cent.: from the name of Ignatius von *Born* (1742–91), Austrian mineralogist, + **-ITE**[1].

boro- /ˈbɔːrəʊ/ ▶ combining form Chemistry representing **BORON**.

Borobudur /ˌbɒrəʊbʊˈdʊə/ a Buddhist monument in central Java, built c.800.

Borodin /ˈbɒrədɪn/, Aleksandr (Porfirevich) (1833–87), Russian composer. He is best known for the epic opera *Prince Igor* (completed after his death by Rimsky-Korsakov and Glazunov).

Borodino, Battle of /ˌbɒrəˈdiːnəʊ/ a battle in 1812 at Borodino, a village about 110 km (70 miles) west of Moscow, at which Napoleon's forces defeated the Russian army.

boron /ˈbɔːrɒn/ ▶ noun [mass noun] the chemical element of atomic number 5, a non-metallic solid. (Symbol: **B**)

Boron is usually prepared as an amorphous brown powder, but when very pure it forms hard, shiny, black crystals with semiconducting properties. The element has some specialized uses, such as in alloy steels and in nuclear control rods.

– DERIVATIVES **boride** noun.
– ORIGIN early 19th cent.: from **BORAX**[1], on the pattern of *carbon* (which it resembles in some respects).

boronia /bəˈrəʊnɪə/ ▶ noun a sweet-scented Australian shrub which is cultivated for its perfume and for the cut-flower trade.
• Genus *Boronia*, family Rutaceae.
– ORIGIN modern Latin, named after Francesco *Borone* (1769–94), Italian botanist.

borosilicate /ˌbɔːrəʊˈsɪlɪkeɪt/ ▶ noun [usu. as modifier] a low-melting glass made from a mixture of silica and boric oxide (B_2O_3).

borough /ˈbʌrə/ ▶ noun a town or district which is an administrative unit, in particular:
■ Brit. a town (as distinct from a city) with a corporation and privileges granted by a royal charter. ■ Brit. historical a town sending representatives to Parliament. ■ an administrative division of London. ■ a municipal corporation in certain US states. ■ each of five divisions of New York City. ■ (in Alaska) a district corresponding to a county elsewhere in the US.
– ORIGIN Old English *burg*, *burh* 'fortress, citadel', later 'fortified town', of Germanic origin; related to Dutch *burg* and German *Burg*. Compare with **BURGH**.

Borromini /ˌbɒrəˈmiːni/, Francesco (1599–1667), Italian architect, a leading figure of the Italian baroque.

Borrow, George (Henry) (1803–81), English writer. His travels with gypsies provided material for the picaresque narrative *Lavengro* (1851) and its sequel *The Romany Rye* (1857).

borrow ▶ verb [with obj.] take and use (something that belongs to someone else) with the intention of returning it: *he had* **borrowed** *a car* **from** *one of his colleagues.*
■ take and use (money) from a person or bank under an agreement to pay it back later, typically in instalments. ■ take and use (a book) from a library for a fixed period of time. ■ take (a word, idea, or method) from another language, person, or source and use it in one's own language or work: *the term is* **borrowed from** *Greek.* ■ Golf allow (a certain distance) when playing a shot to compensate for sideways motion of the ball due to a slope or other irregularity.
▶ noun Golf a slope or other irregularity on a golf course which must be compensated for when playing a shot.
– PHRASES **be (living) on borrowed time** used to convey that someone has continued to survive against expectations, with the implication that they will not do so for much longer. **borrow trouble** N. Amer. take needless action that may have detrimental effects.
– DERIVATIVES **borrower** noun.
– ORIGIN Old English *borgian* 'borrow against security', of Germanic origin; related to Dutch and German *borgen.*

USAGE Some people confuse the two words **lend** and **borrow**, which have reciprocal but different meanings: see **usage** at **LEND**.

borrowing ▶ noun [mass noun] the action of borrowing something: *the borrowing of clothes.*
■ the action of taking and using money from a bank under an agreement to pay it back later: *a curb on government borrowing |* [count noun] *the group had total borrowings of $570 million.* ■ [count noun] a word, idea, or method taken from another language, person, or source and used in one's own language or work: *the majority of designs were* **borrowings from** *the continent.*

borrow pit ▶ noun a pit resulting from the excavation of material for use in embankments.

Borsalino /ˌbɔːsəˈliːnəʊ/ ▶ noun (pl. **-os**) trademark a man's wide-brimmed felt hat.
– ORIGIN early 20th cent.: from the name of the manufacturer.

borscht /bɔːʃt/ (also **borsch** /bɔːʃ/) ▶ noun [mass noun] a Russian or Polish soup made with beetroot and usually served with sour cream.
– ORIGIN from Russian *borshch.*

Borscht Belt /bɔːʃt/ ▶ noun N. Amer. humorous a resort area in the Catskill Mountains frequented chiefly by Jewish people of eastern European origin: [as modifier] *Borscht Belt comedians.*

borstal /ˈbɔːst(ə)l/ ▶ noun [mass noun] Brit. historical a custodial institution for young offenders.
– ORIGIN early 20th cent.: named after the village of *Borstal* in southern England, where the first of these was established.

bort /bɔːt/ (also **boart**) ▶ noun [mass noun] small, granular, opaque diamonds, used as an abrasive in cutting tools.
– ORIGIN early 17th cent.: from Dutch *boort.*

borzoi /ˈbɔːzɔɪ/ ▶ noun (pl. **borzois**) a large Russian wolfhound of a breed with a narrow head and silky, typically white, coat.
– ORIGIN late 19th cent.: from Russian *borzoĭ* (adjective), *borzaya* (noun), from *borzyĭ* 'swift'.

boscage /ˈbɒskɪdʒ/ (also **boskage**) ▶ noun [mass noun] a mass of trees or shrubs.
– ORIGIN late Middle English: from Old French; ultimately of Germanic origin and related to **BUSH**[1]. Compare with **BOCAGE**.

Bosch /bɒʃ/, Hieronymus (c.1450–1516), Dutch painter. Bosch's highly detailed works are typically crowded with half-human, half-animal creatures and grotesque demons in settings symbolic of sin and folly. His individual style prefigures that of the surrealists.

Bose /bəʊs/, Satyendra Nath (1894–1974), Indian physicist. With Einstein he described fundamental particles which later came to be known as *bosons.*

bosh ▶ noun [mass noun] informal something regarded as absurd or untrue; nonsense: *that's a load of bosh.*
– ORIGIN mid 19th cent.: from Turkish *boş* 'empty, worthless'.

bosie /ˈbəʊzi/ (also **bosey**) ▶ noun Cricket Australian term for **GOOGLY**.
– ORIGIN early 20th cent.: from the name of Bernard J. T. *Bosanquet* (1877–1936), English all-round cricketer, + **-IE**.

boskage ▶ noun variant spelling of BOSCAGE.

bosky /ˈbɒski/ ▶ adjective poetic/literary covered by trees or bushes; wooded: *a slow-moving river meandering between bosky banks.*
– ORIGIN late 16th cent.: from Middle English *bosk*, variant of BUSH[1].

Bosnia /ˈbɒznɪə/ short for BOSNIA–HERZEGOVINA.
▪a region in the Balkans forming the larger, northern part of Bosnia–Herzegovina.
– DERIVATIVES **Bosnian** adjective & noun.

Bosnia–Herzegovina (also **Bosnia and Herzegovina**) a country in the Balkans, formerly a constituent republic of Yugoslavia; pop. 4,365,000 (est. 1991); capital, Sarajevo.

Bosnia and Herzegovina were conquered by the Turks in 1463. The province of Bosnia–Herzegovina was annexed by Austria in 1908, an event which contributed towards the outbreak of the First World War. In 1918 it became part of the Kingdom of Serbs, Croats, and Slovenes, which changed its name to Yugoslavia in 1929. In 1992 Bosnia–Herzegovina followed Slovenia and Croatia in declaring independence, but ethnic conflict among Muslims, Serbs, and Croats quickly reduced the republic to a state of civil war. An accord signed in December 1995 formally brought the conflict to an end.

bosom ▶ noun a woman's chest: *her ample bosom* | [mass noun] *the dress offered a fair display of bosom.*
▪(usu. **bosoms**) a woman's breast. ▪a part of a woman's dress covering the chest. ▪the space between a person's clothing and their chest used for carrying things: *he carried a letter* ***in his bosom.*** ▪(**the bosom of**) poetic/literary the loving care and protection of: *Bruno went home each night* ***to the bosom of*** *his family.* ▪used to refer to the chest as the seat of emotions: *quivering dread was settling in her bosom.*
▶adjective [attrib.] (of a friend) very close or intimate: *the two girls had become bosom friends.*
– DERIVATIVES **bosomed** adjective [in combination] *her small-bosomed physique.*
– ORIGIN Old English *bōsm*, of West Germanic origin; related to Dutch *boezem* and German *Busen*.

bosomy ▶ adjective (of a woman) having large breasts.

boson /ˈbəʊzɒn/ ▶ noun Physics a subatomic particle, such as a photon, which has zero or integral spin and follows the statistical description given by S. N. Bose and Einstein.
– ORIGIN 1940s: named after S. N. BOSE + -ON.

Bosporus /ˈbɒspərəs/ (also **Bosphorus** /ˈbɒsfə-/) a strait connecting the Black Sea with the Sea of Marmara, and separating Europe from the Anatolian peninsula of western Asia. Istanbul is located at its south end.

BOSS ▶ abbreviation for Bureau of State Security.

boss[1] informal ▶ noun a person who is in charge of a worker or organization: *her boss offered her promotion* | *union bosses.*
▪a person in control of a group or situation: *does he see you as a partner, or is he already* ***the boss?***
▶verb [with obj.] give (someone) orders in an annoyingly domineering manner: *you're always* ***bossing us about.***
▶adjective [attrib.] N. Amer. excellent; outstanding: *she's a real boss chick.*
– PHRASES **be one's own boss** be self-employed. **show someone who's boss** make it clear that it is oneself who is in charge.
– ORIGIN early 19th cent. (originally US): from Dutch *baas* 'master'.

boss[2] ▶ noun a round knob, stud, or other projecting part, in particular:
▪a stud on the centre of a shield. ▪Architecture a piece of ornamental carving covering the point where the ribs in a vault or ceiling cross. ▪Geology a large mass of igneous rock protruding through other strata. ▪the central part of a propeller.
– ORIGIN Middle English: from Old French *boce*, of unknown origin.

boss[3] ▶ noun US informal a cow.
– ORIGIN early 19th cent.: of unknown origin.

bossa nova /ˌbɒsə ˈnəʊvə/ ▶ noun a dance like the samba, originating in Brazil.
▪a piece of music for this dance or in its rhythm.
– ORIGIN 1960s: from Portuguese, from *bossa* 'tendency' and *nova* (feminine of *novo*) 'new'.

boss-cocky ▶ noun (pl. **-ies**) Austral. informal a farmer who employs labour.
▪a person in authority.

boss-eyed ▶ adjective Brit. informal cross-eyed or squinting.
– ORIGIN mid 19th cent.: compare with dialect *boss* 'miss, bungle', of unknown origin.

bossism ▶ noun [mass noun] US a situation whereby a political party is controlled by party managers.

boss-shot ▶ noun dialect or informal a bad shot or aim.
– ORIGIN late 19th cent.: from dialect *boss* 'miss, bungle', of unknown origin.

bossy[1] ▶ adjective (**bossier**, **bossiest**) informal fond of giving people orders; domineering.
– DERIVATIVES **bossily** adverb, **bossiness** noun.

bossy[2] ▶ noun (pl. **-ies**) N. Amer. informal a cow or calf.
– ORIGIN mid 19th cent. of unknown origin.

bossyboots ▶ noun Brit. informal a domineering person.

Boston[1] the state capital of Massachusetts; pop. 574,280 (1990). It was founded *c.*1630 and named after Boston in Lincolnshire.
– DERIVATIVES **Bostonian** noun & adjective.

Boston[2] ▶ noun [mass noun] **1** a card game resembling solo whist.
2 a variation of the waltz or of the two-step.

Boston baked beans ▶ plural noun an American dish of baked beans with salt pork and molasses.

Boston crab ▶ noun Wrestling a hold in which a wrestler sits astride a prone opponent and pulls upwards on the opponent's legs.

Boston ivy ▶ noun a Virginia creeper with three-lobed leaves, which is cultivated for its foliage.
• *Parthenocissus tricuspidata*, family Vitaceae.

Boston Tea Party a violent demonstration in 1773 by American colonists prior to the War of American Independence. Colonists boarded vessels in Boston harbour and threw the cargoes of tea into the water in protest at the imposition of a tax on tea by the British Parliament, in which the colonists had no representation.

Boston terrier ▶ noun a small smooth-coated terrier of a breed originating in Massachusetts from a crossing of the bulldog and terrier.

bosun /ˈbəʊs(ə)n/ (also **bo'sun**) ▶ noun variant spelling of BOATSWAIN.

Boswell, James (1740–95), Scottish author, companion and biographer of Samuel Johnson. He is known for *Journal of a Tour to the Hebrides* (1785) and *The Life of Samuel Johnson* (1791).
– DERIVATIVES **Boswellian** adjective.

Bosworth Field /ˈbɒzwəθ/ (also **Battle of Bosworth**) a battle of the Wars of the Roses fought in 1485 near Market Bosworth in Leicestershire. Henry Tudor defeated and killed the Yorkist king Richard III, enabling him to take the throne as Henry VII.

bot[1] ▶ noun the larva of the botfly, which is an internal parasite of horses. It lives typically in the stomach, finally passing out in the dung and pupating on the ground.
▪(**sheep bot**) the sheep nostril fly. See NOSTRIL FLY.
– ORIGIN early 16th cent.: probably of Low German origin.

bot[2] ▶ noun (chiefly in science fiction) a robot.
▪Computing an autonomous program on a network (especially the Internet) which can interact with computer systems or users, especially one designed to respond or behave like a player in an adventure game.
– ORIGIN 1980s: shortening of ROBOT.

bot. ▶ abbreviation for ▪(with reference to journal titles) botanic; botanical; botany. ▪bottle. ▪bought.

botanical ▶ adjective of or relating to botany: *botanical specimens* | *a botanical illustrator.*
▶noun (usu. **botanicals**) a substance obtained from a plant and used as an additive, especially in gin or cosmetics.
– DERIVATIVES **botanically** adverb.

botanic garden (also **botanical garden**) ▶ noun an establishment where plants are grown for scientific study and display to the public.

botanize (also **-ise**) ▶ verb [no obj.] [usu. as noun **botanizing**] study plants, especially in their natural habitat.
– ORIGIN mid 18th cent.: from modern Latin *botanizare*, from Greek *botanizein* 'gather plants', from *botanē* 'plant'.

Botany /ˈbɒt(ə)ni/ (also **Botany wool**) ▶ noun [mass noun] merino wool, especially from Australia.
– ORIGIN late 19th cent.: named after BOTANY BAY, from where the wool originally came.

botany /ˈbɒt(ə)ni/ ▶ noun [mass noun] the scientific study of the physiology, structure, genetics, ecology, distribution, classification, and economic importance of plants.
▪the plant life of a particular region, habitat, or geological period: *the botany of North America.*
– DERIVATIVES **botanic** adjective, **botanist** noun.
– ORIGIN late 17th cent.: from earlier *botanic* (from French *botanique*, based on Greek *botanikos*, from *botanē* 'plant') + -Y[3].

Botany Bay an inlet of the Tasman Sea in New South Wales, Australia, just south of Sydney. It was the site of Captain James Cook's landing in 1770 and of an early British penal settlement.
– ORIGIN named by Cook after the large variety of plants collected there by his companion, Sir Joseph Banks.

botch ▶ verb [with obj.] informal carry out (a task) badly or carelessly: *he was accused of botching the job* | [as adj. **botched**] *a botched attempt to kill them.*
▶noun (also **botch-up**) informal a bungled or badly carried out task or action: *I've probably* ***made a botch of things.***
– DERIVATIVES **botcher** noun.
– ORIGIN late Middle English (in the sense 'repair' but originally not implying clumsiness): of unknown origin.

botel ▶ noun variant spelling of BOATEL.

botfly /ˈbɒtflʌɪ/ ▶ noun (pl. **-flies**) a stout hairy-bodied fly whose larvae are internal parasites of mammals, in particular:
• a fly whose larvae (bots) develop within the guts of horses (*Gasterophilus* and other genera, family Gasterophilidae).
• chiefly N. Amer. a fly of the warble fly family (Oestridae).

both ▶ predeterminer, determiner, & pronoun used for emphasis to refer to two people or things, regarded and identified together: [as predeterminer] *both his parents indulged him* | *I urge you to read both these books* | [as determiner] *she held on with both hands* | *he was blind in both eyes* | [as pronoun] *a picture of* ***both of*** *us together* | *Jackie and I are both self-employed* | *he looked at them both.*
▶adverb used before the first of two alternatives to emphasize that the statement being made applies to each (the other alternative being introduced by 'and'): *it has won favour with both young and old* | *studies of zebra finches, both in the wild and in captivity.*
– PHRASES **have it both ways** benefit from two incompatible ways of thinking or behaving: *countries cannot have it both ways: the cost of a cleaner environment may sometimes be fewer jobs.*
– ORIGIN Middle English: from Old Norse *báthir*.

USAGE When **both** is used in constructions with **and**, the structures following 'both' and 'and' should be symmetrical in well-formed English. Thus, *studies of zebra finches, both* ***in the wild*** *and* ***in captivity*** is better than, for example, *studies of zebra finches, both* ***in the wild*** *and* ***captivity.*** In the second example, the symmetry of 'in the wild' and 'in captivity' has been lost. Other examples: *her article is detrimental both to* ***understanding*** *and* ***to peace*** (not *her article is detrimental to both* ***understanding*** *and* ***to peace***).

Botha[1] /ˈbəʊtə/, Louis (1862–1919), South African soldier and statesman, first Prime Minister of the Union of South Africa 1910–19.

Botha[2] /ˈbəʊtə/, P. W. (b.1916), South African statesman, Prime Minister 1978–84, State President 1984–9; full name *Pieter Willem Botha*. An authoritarian leader, he continued to enforce apartheid but in response to pressure introduced limited reforms; his resistance to more radical change ultimately led to his fall from power.

Botham /ˈbəʊθəm/, Ian (Terence) (b.1955), English all-round cricketer. In 1978 he became the first player to score 100 runs and take eight wickets in a single test match; in 1982 he also achieved the record of 3,000 runs and 250 wickets in test matches overall.

bother ▶ verb **1** [no obj., with negative] take the trouble to do something: *scientists rarely* ***bother with*** *such niceties* | [with infinitive] *the driver didn't bother to ask why.*
2 [with obj.] (of a circumstance or event) worry, disturb, or upset (someone): *secrecy is an issue which bothers journalists* | [with obj. and clause] *it* ***bothered*** *me that I hadn't done anything.*
▪[no obj.] [usu. with negative] feel concern about or interest in: *don't* ***bother about*** *me—I'll find my own way home* | *he wasn't to* ***bother himself with*** *day-to-day things* | [as adj. **bothered**] *I'm not particularly* ***bothered about*** *how I look.* ▪cause trouble or annoyance to (someone) by

interrupting or otherwise inconveniencing them: *I'm sorry to bother you at this time of night.*

▶ noun [mass noun] effort, trouble, or difficulty: *he saved me the bother of having to come up with a speech* | *it may seem like too much bother to cook just for yourself* | *it's no bother, it's on my way home.* ■ Brit. used to refer to serious trouble in an understated way: *I'm afraid there's been a bit of bother.* ■ (**a bother**) a person or thing that causes annoyance or difficulty: *I hope she hasn't been a bother.*

▶ exclamation chiefly Brit. used to express mild irritation or impatience: '*Bother!' she muttered.*

– PHRASES **can't be bothered** (**to do something**) be unwilling to make the effort needed to do something: *they couldn't be bothered to look it up.* **hot and bothered** in a state of anxiety or physical discomfort, especially as a result of being pressured.

– ORIGIN late 17th cent. (as a noun in the dialect sense 'noise, chatter'): of Anglo-Irish origin; probably related to Irish *bodhaire* 'noise', *bodhraim* 'deafen, annoy'. The verb (originally dialect) meant 'confuse with noise' in the early 18th cent.

botheration informal ▶ noun [mass noun] effort, worry, or difficulty; bother.

▶ exclamation dated used to express mild irritation or annoyance.

bothersome ▶ adjective annoying; troublesome: *most childhood stomach aches, though bothersome, aren't serious.*

Bothnia, Gulf of /ˈbɒθnɪə/ a northern arm of the Baltic Sea, between Sweden and Finland.

both ways ▶ adverb & adjective another term for **EACH-WAY**: [as adv.] *put me down for a fiver both ways.*

Bothwell /ˈbɒθwɛl/, James Hepburn, 4th Earl of (c.1536–78), Scottish nobleman and third husband of Mary, Queen of Scots. He was implicated in the murder of Mary's previous husband, Lord Darnley (1567), a crime for which he was tried but acquitted; he married Mary later the same year.

bothy /ˈbɒθi/ (also **bothie**) ▶ noun (pl. **-ies**) (in Scotland) a small hut or cottage, especially one for housing farm labourers or for use as a mountain refuge.

– ORIGIN late 18th cent.: obscurely related to Irish and Scottish Gaelic *both*, *bothan*, and perhaps to **BOOTH**.

boto ▶ noun variant spelling of **BOUTU**.

bo tree /bəʊ/ (also **bodh tree**) ▶ noun a fig tree native to India and SE Asia, regarded as sacred by Buddhists. Also called **PEEPUL** or **PIPAL**.
● *Ficus religiosa*, family Moraceae.

– ORIGIN mid 19th cent.: representing Sinhalese *bōgaha* 'tree of knowledge' (Buddha's enlightenment having occurred beneath such a tree), from *bō* (from Sanskrit *budh* 'understand thoroughly') + *gaha* 'tree'.

botryoidal /ˌbɒtrɪˈɔɪd(ə)l/ ▶ adjective (chiefly of minerals) having a shape reminiscent of a cluster of grapes.

– ORIGIN late 18th cent.: from Greek *botruoeidēs* (from *botrus* 'bunch of grapes') + **-AL**.

botrytis /bəˈtrʌɪtɪs/ ▶ noun [mass noun] a greyish powdery mould which causes a number of plant diseases and is deliberately cultivated (as noble rot) on the grapes used for certain wines.
● Genus *Botrytis*, subdivision Deuteromycotina (or Ascomycotina), in particular the grey mould *B. cinerea*.

– ORIGIN modern Latin, from Greek *botrus* 'cluster of grapes'.

Botswana /bɒˈtswɑːnə/ a landlocked country in southern Africa; pop. 1,300,000 (est. 1991); official languages, Setswana and English; capital, Gaborone.

> Inhabited by Sotho people and, in the Kalahari Desert, San (Bushmen), the area was made the British Protectorate of Bechuanaland in 1885. It became an independent republic within the Commonwealth in 1966, adopting the name Botswana.

– DERIVATIVES **Botswanan** adjective & noun.

bott ▶ abbreviation for bottle.

botte /bɒt/ ▶ noun Fencing an attack or thrust.
– ORIGIN French.

Botticelli /ˌbɒtɪˈtʃɛli/, Sandro (1445–1510), Italian painter; born *Alessandro di Mariano Filipepi*. He worked in Renaissance Florence under the patronage of the Medicis. Botticelli is best known for his mythological works such as *Primavera* (c.1478) and *The Birth of Venus* (c.1480).

bottle ▶ noun **1** a glass or plastic container, typically one with a narrow neck, used for storing drinks or other liquids. ■ the contents of such a container: *he managed to get through a bottle of wine.* ■ (**the bottle**) informal used in reference to the heavy drinking of alcohol: *more women are taking to the bottle* | *some turn to the bottle for comfort.* ■ Brit. a baby's feeding bottle. ■ short for **HOT-WATER BOTTLE**. ■ a large metal cylinder holding liquefied gas.

2 [mass noun] Brit. informal the courage or confidence needed to do something difficult or dangerous: *I lost my bottle completely and ran.*

▶ verb **1** [with obj.] (usu. **be bottled**) place (drinks or other liquid) in glass or plastic containers for storage. ■ Brit. place (fruit or vegetables) in glass jars with other ingredients in order to preserve them. ■ [usu. as adj. **bottled**] store (gas) in a container in liquefied form.
2 [no obj.] (**bottle out**) Brit. informal lose one's nerve and decide not to do something: *the Minister has bottled out of real reforms.*
3 [with obj.] informal throw a glass bottle at (someone): *he was bottled offstage at a club last Saturday.*

– PHRASES **bottle and glass** Brit. rhyming slang arse. **hit the bottle** informal start to drink alcohol heavily, especially as a form of spurious comfort. **in bottle** (of wine) having been aged for a specified number of years in its bottle: *the wine is ready for drinking after eight years in bottle.*

– ORIGIN late Middle English (denoting a leather bottle): from Old French *boteille*, from medieval Latin *butticula*, diminutive of late Latin *buttis* 'cask, wineskin' (see **BUTT**[4]).

▶ **bottle someone up** keep an enemy force trapped or contained: *the army was bottled up inside the citadel.*
bottle something up repress or conceal feelings over a period of time: *if she bottles it up, it will only be worse later* | [as adj. **bottled up**] *Lily's bottled-up fury.*

bottle age ▶ noun [mass noun] time spent by a wine maturing in its bottle.

bottle bank ▶ noun Brit. a place where used glass bottles may be deposited for recycling.

bottle blonde (also **bottle blond**) derogatory ▶ adjective (of a woman's hair) of a shade of blonde that looks as if it has been artificially lightened or bleached.
▶ noun a woman with such hair.

bottlebrush ▶ noun **1** a cylindrical brush for cleaning inside bottles.
2 an Australian shrub or small tree with spikes of scarlet or yellow flowers which resemble a bottlebrush in shape.
● Genus *Callistemon*, family Myrtaceae.
■ any of a number of plants bearing similar flowers.

bottle-feed ▶ verb [with obj.] feed (a baby) with milk from a feeding bottle.

bottle green ▶ noun [mass noun] dark green: [as modifier] *a bottle-green uniform.*

bottle jack ▶ noun NZ a large jack used for lifting heavy objects.

bottleneck ▶ noun **1** the neck or mouth of a bottle.
2 a point of congestion or blockage, in particular: ■ a narrow section of road or a junction that impedes traffic flow. ■ a situation that causes delay in a process or system.
3 a device shaped like the neck of a bottle that is worn on a guitarist's finger and used to produce sliding effects on the strings. ■ (also **bottleneck guitar**) [mass noun] the style of playing that uses such a device.

bottlenose dolphin (also **bottle-nosed dolphin**) ▶ noun a stout-bodied dolphin with a distinct short beak, found in tropical and temperate coastal waters.
● *Tursiops truncatus*, family Delphinidae.

bottlenose whale (also **bottle-nosed whale**) ▶ noun a beaked whale of variable colour, with a bulbous forehead.
● Genus *Hyperoodon*, family Ziphiidae: two species.

bottle party ▶ noun Brit. a party to which guests bring bottles of drink.

bottler ▶ noun **1** a person or company that bottles drinks.
2 Austral./NZ informal an admirable person or thing: *he's getting married to a real little bottler.*

bottlescrew ▶ noun British term for **TURNBUCKLE**.

bottle store (also **bottle shop**) ▶ noun chiefly Austral./NZ & S. African another term for **OFF-LICENCE**.

bottle tree ▶ noun either of two Australian trees with swollen water-containing trunks: ● the Australian baobab of the Kimberley region (*Adansonia gregorii*, family Bombacaceae). ● a relative of the flame tree occurring in Queensland (*Brachychiton rupestre*, family Sterculiaceae).

bottom ▶ noun (usu. **the bottom**) **1** the lowest point or part of something: *the bottom of the page* | *she paused at the bottom of the stairs.* ■ the ground under a sea, river, or lake: *the liner plunged to the bottom of the sea.* ■ the inside or outside of the lower surface of something: *place the fruit on the bottom of the dish.* ■ the seat of a chair. ■ the furthest part or point of something: *the shed at the bottom of the garden.* ■ the lowest position in a competition or ranking: *he started at the bottom and now has his own business.* ■ (also **bottoms**) the lower half of a specified garment in two pieces: *a pair of pyjama bottoms* | *a skimpy bikini bottom.* ■ the keel or hull of a ship. ■ archaic a ship, especially considered as a cargo carrier. ■ [mass noun] archaic stamina or strength of character, especially of a horse.
2 chiefly Brit. the part of the body on which a person sits; a person's buttocks: *Toby pinched her bottom.*
3 [mass noun] Physics one of six flavours of quark.
▶ adjective in the lowest position: *the books on the bottom shelf.* ■ (of a place) in the furthest position away in a downhill direction: *the bottom field.* ■ in the lowest or last position in a competition or ranking: *I was put in the bottom class* | *they came bottom with 17 points.*
▶ verb [no obj.] (of a ship) reach or touch the ground under the sea: *nuclear submarines cannot bottom.* ■ (of a performance or situation) reach the lowest point before stabilizing or improving: *encouraging signs suggested the recession was bottoming out.* ■ [with obj.] Austral./NZ excavate (a hole or mine) to the level of a mineral-bearing stratum. ■ Austral./NZ find gold or other minerals while mining: *he's bottomed on opal there.* ■ archaic find the extent or real nature of.

– PHRASES **at bottom** basically; fundamentally: *at bottom, science is exploration.* **be at the bottom of** be the basic cause or origin of (something): *he knew what was at the bottom of it—Jane wanted them to live together.* **the bottom falls** (or **drops**) **out** used to refer to the sudden collapse or failure of something: *the bottom fell out of the market for classic cars.* **bottoms up!** informal used to express friendly feelings towards one's companions before drinking. **from the bottom of one's heart** see **HEART**. **from the bottom up** starting at the lower end or beginning of a hierarchy or process and proceeding to the top: *we began to study history from the bottom up.* **get to the bottom of** find an explanation for (a mystery). **knock the bottom out of** cause (something) to collapse or fail suddenly: *a shortfall in supplies would knock the bottom out of the engineering industry.* **you** (**can**) **bet your bottom dollar** informal, chiefly N. Amer. used to state one's conviction that a particular thing is going to happen: *you can bet your bottom dollar it'll end in tears.*

– DERIVATIVES **bottomed** adjective [in combination] *a glass-bottomed boat* | *bare-bottomed toddlers*, **bottommost** adjective.

– ORIGIN Old English *botm*, of Germanic origin; related to Dutch *bodem* 'bottom, ground' and German *Boden* 'ground, earth'.

bottom dog ▶ noun another term for **UNDERDOG**.

bottom drawer ▶ noun Brit., chiefly historical household linen stored by a woman in preparation for her marriage.

bottom fermentation ▶ noun [mass noun] the process by which lager-type beers are fermented, proceeding for a relatively long period at low temperature with the yeast falling to the bottom.

bottom house ▶ noun W. Indian an open area under a house built off the ground on pillars, sometimes used as additional housing space.

bottomland ▶ noun [mass noun] N. Amer. low-lying land, typically by a river.

bottomless ▶ adjective without a bottom. ■ very deep: *the cold dark sea in whose bottomless depths monsters swam.* ■ figurative (of a supply of money or other resources) inexhaustible: *I don't have a bottomless pit of money.*

bottom line ▶ noun (usu. in sing.) informal the final total of an account, balance sheet, or other financial document: *the rise in turnover failed to add to the company's bottom line.* ■ the ultimate criterion: *the bottom line is, does it work?*

■ the underlying and most important factor: *the bottom line is I'm still married to Denny.*

bottomry ▶ noun [mass noun] dated a system of merchant insurance in which a ship is used as security against a loan to finance a voyage, the lender losing their money if the ship sinks.
– ORIGIN late 16th cent.: from **BOTTOM** (in the sense 'ship') + **-RY**, influenced by Dutch *bodemerij*.

bottom-up ▶ adjective proceeding from the bottom or beginning of a hierarchy or process upwards; non-hierarchical: *bottom-up decisions.*

botty ▶ noun (pl. **-ies**) Brit. a child's word for a person's bottom.

botulin /ˈbɒtjʊlɪn/ ▶ noun [mass noun] the bacterial toxin involved in botulism.

botulinum toxin /ˌbɒtjʊˈlʌɪnəm/ (also **botulinus toxin**) ▶ noun another term for **BOTULIN**.

botulism /ˈbɒtjʊlɪz(ə)m/ ▶ noun [mass noun] food poisoning caused by a bacterium growing on improperly sterilized tinned meats and other preserved foods.
• The bacterium is *Clostridium botulinum*.
– ORIGIN late 19th cent.: from German *Botulismus*, originally 'sausage poisoning', from Latin *botulus* 'sausage'.

boubou /ˈbuːbuː/ (also **boubou shrike**) ▶ noun an African bush shrike with the upper parts mainly blackish in colour. It is noted for the duet of bell-like calls produced by the male and female together. Compare with **BRUBRU**.
• Genus *Laniarius*, family Laniidae: several species, in particular the **tropical boubou** (*L. aethiopicus*) and the **southern boubou** (*L. ferrugineus*).

bouchée /ˈbuːʃeɪ/ ▶ noun a small pastry with a sweet or savoury filling.

Boucher /ˈbuːʃeɪ, French buʃe/, François (1703–70), French painter and decorative artist, one of the foremost artists of the rococo style in France. Notable paintings: *The Rising of the Sun* (1753) and *Summer Pastoral* (1749).

bouclé /ˈbuːkleɪ/ ▶ noun [mass noun] [often as modifier] yarn with a looped or curled ply, or fabric woven from this yarn: *a bouclé sweater.*
– ORIGIN late 19th cent.: French, literally 'buckled, curled'.

Boudicca /bəʊˈdɪkə, ˈbuːdɪkə/ (d. AD 62), a queen of the Britons, ruler of the Iceni tribe in eastern England; also known as **Boadicea**. Boudicca led her forces in revolt against the Romans and sacked Colchester, St Albans, and London before being defeated by the Roman governor Suetonius Paulinus.

boudin /ˈbuːdã/ ▶ noun **1** (pl. same) a French type of black pudding.
2 /also ˈbuːdɪn/ (**boudins**) Geology a series of elongated parallel sections formed by the fracturing of a sedimentary rock stratum during folding.
– ORIGIN French.

boudoir /ˈbuːdwɑː/ ▶ noun chiefly historical or humorous a woman's bedroom or small private room.
– ORIGIN late 18th cent.: French, literally 'sulking-place', from *bouder* 'pout, sulk'.

bouffant /ˈbuːfɒ̃/ ▶ adjective (of a person's hair) styled so as to stand out from the head in a rounded shape.
▶ noun a bouffant hairstyle.
– ORIGIN early 19th cent.: from French, literally 'swelling', present participle of *bouffer*.

Bougainville[1] /ˈbuːgənvɪl/ a volcanic island in the South Pacific, the largest of the Solomon Islands.
– ORIGIN named after Louis de *Bougainville* (see **BOUGAINVILLE**[2]), who visited it in 1768.

Bougainville[2] /ˈbuːgənvɪl, French bugɛ̃vil/, Louis Antoine de (1729–1811), French explorer. Bougainville led the first French circumnavigation of the globe 1766–9, visiting many of the islands of the South Pacific and compiling an invaluable scientific record of his findings.

bougainvillea /ˌbuːg(ə)nˈvɪlɪə/ (also **bougainvillaea**) ▶ noun an ornamental shrubby climbing plant that is widely cultivated in the tropics. The insignificant flowers are surrounded by large, brightly coloured papery bracts which persist on the plant for a long time.
• Genus *Bougainvillea*, family Nyctaginaceae.
– ORIGIN named after L. A. de *Bougainville* (see **BOUGAINVILLE**[2]).

bough /baʊ/ ▶ noun a main branch of a tree: *apple boughs laden with blossom.*
– ORIGIN Old English *bōg, bōh* 'bough or shoulder', of Germanic origin; related to Dutch *boeg* 'shoulders or ship's bow', German *Bug* 'ship's bow' and 'horse's hock or shoulder', also to **BOW**[3].

bought past and past participle of **BUY**.

boughten /ˈbɔːt(ə)n/ ▶ adjective dialect, chiefly N. Amer. bought rather than home-made: *her first store-boughten doll.*
– ORIGIN late 18th cent.: dialect variant of **BOUGHT**.

bougie /ˈbuːʒiː/ ▶ noun (pl. **-ies**) Medicine a thin, flexible surgical instrument for exploring or dilating a passage of the body.
– ORIGIN mid 18th cent.: from French, literally 'wax candle', from Arabic *Bijāya*, the name of an Algerian town which traded in wax.

bouillabaisse /ˈbuːjəˌbeɪs/ ▶ noun [mass noun] a rich, spicy stew or soup made with various kinds of fish, originally from Provence.
– ORIGIN French, from modern Provençal *bouiabaisso*.

bouilli /ˈbuːjiː/ ▶ noun [mass noun] stewed or boiled meat.
– ORIGIN French, 'boiled'.

bouillon /ˈbuːjɒ̃/ ▶ noun [mass noun] thin soup or stock made by stewing meat, fish, or vegetables in water.
– ORIGIN French, literally 'liquid in which something has boiled', from *bouillir* 'to boil'.

boulder ▶ noun a large rock, typically one that has been worn smooth by erosion.
– DERIVATIVES **bouldery** adjective.
– ORIGIN late Middle English: shortened from earlier *boulderstone*, of Scandinavian origin.

boulder clay ▶ noun [mass noun] clay containing many large stones and boulders, formed by deposition from melting glaciers and ice sheets.

bouldering ▶ noun [mass noun] Climbing climbing on large boulders, either for practice or as a sport in its own right.

boule[1] /buːl/ (also **boules** pronunc. same) ▶ noun [mass noun] a French form of bowls, played on rough ground with metal balls.
– ORIGIN early 20th cent. (originally denoting a form of roulette): French, literally 'bowl'.

boule[2] /ˈbuːliː/ ▶ noun a legislative body of ancient or modern Greece.
– ORIGIN from Greek *boulē* 'senate'.

boulevard /ˈbuːləvɑːd/ ▶ noun a wide street in a town or city, typically one lined with trees: [in names] *Sunset Boulevard.*
– ORIGIN mid 18th cent.: French, 'a rampart' (later 'a promenade on the site of one'), from German *Bollwerk* (see **BULWARK**).

boulevardier /ˌbuːləvɑːˈdjeɪ/ ▶ noun a wealthy, fashionable socialite.
– ORIGIN late 19th cent.: from French, originally in the sense 'person who frequents boulevards'.

Boulez /ˈbuːlɛz/, Pierre (b.1925), French composer and conductor. His works explore and develop serialism and aleatory music, making use of both traditional and electronic instruments.

boulle /buːl/ (also **buhl**) ▶ noun [mass noun] brass, tortoiseshell, or other material cut to make a pattern and used for inlaying furniture: [as modifier] *boulle cabinets.*
■ work inlaid with brass, tortoiseshell, or other material in such a way.
– ORIGIN early 19th cent.: from French *boule*, from the name of André Charles *Boulle* (1642–1732), French cabinetmaker. The variant *buhl* is apparently a modern Germanized spelling.

Boulogne /bʊˈlɔɪn, French bulɔɲ/ a ferry port and fishing town in northern France; pop. 44,240 (1990). Full name **BOULOGNE-SUR-MER** /-sjʊəˈmɛː, French -syrmɛr/.

Boult /bəʊlt/, Sir Adrian (Cedric) (1889–1983), English conductor. Noted especially for his championship of English composers, he was music director of the BBC 1930–49 and principal conductor of the London Philharmonic Orchestra 1950–7.

boult ▶ verb variant spelling of **BOLT**[4].

Boulting /ˈbəʊltɪŋ/, John (1913–85) and Roy (b.1913), English film producers and directors. Twin brothers, they shared responsibilities as producer and director. Notable films: *Brighton Rock* (1947) and *I'm All Right Jack* (1959).

Boulton /ˈbəʊlt(ə)n/, Matthew (1728–1809), English engineer and manufacturer. With his partner James Watt he pioneered the manufacture of steam engines, which they began to produce in 1774.

bounce ▶ verb [no obj., usu. with adverbial of direction] (of an object, especially a round one such as a ball) move quickly up, back, or away from a surface after hitting it: *the ball bounced away and he chased it* | [with obj.] *he was bouncing the ball against the wall.*
■ (of light, sound, or an electronic signal) come into contact with an object or surface and be reflected back: *short sound waves **bounce off** even small objects.* ■ (**bounce back**) figurative recover well after a setback or problem: *the savings rate has already started to bounce back and is sure to rise further.* ■ (of a springy object) move up and down while remaining essentially in the same position: *the gangplank bounced under his confident step.* ■ (of a person) jump repeatedly up and down, typically on something springy: *Emma was happily bouncing up and down on the mattress.* ■ [with obj.] cause (a child) to move lightly up and down on one's knee as a game. ■ [with adverbial of direction] move in a particular direction in an energetic, happy, or enthusiastic manner: *Linda bounced in through the open front door.* ■ [with adverbial of direction] (of a vehicle) move jerkily along a bumpy surface: *the car bounced down the narrow track.* ■ informal (of a cheque) be returned by a bank when there are insufficient funds in an account to meet it: *a further two cheques of £160 also bounced.* ■ [with obj.] (of a bank) return a cheque in such circumstances. ■ [with obj.] informal, chiefly N. Amer. dismiss (someone) from a job: *those who put in a dismal performance will be **bounced from** the tour.* ■ [with obj.] informal eject (a troublemaker) forcibly from a nightclub or similar establishment. ■ [with obj.] Brit. informal pressurize (someone) into doing something, typically by presenting them with a fait accompli: *the government should beware being **bounced into** any ill-considered foreign gamble.* ■ [with obj.] W. Indian come into sudden forceful contact with (someone or something); collide with: *people cross the road as slowly as possible, as if daring the cars to bounce them.*
▶ noun a rebound of a ball or other object: *the wicket was causing the occasional erratic bounce.*
■ an act of jumping or an instance of being moved up and down lightly or jerkily: *every bounce of the truck brought them into fresh contact.* ■ [mass noun] the ability of a surface to make a ball rebound in a specified way: *a pitch of low bounce.* ■ a sudden rise in the level of something: *economists agree that there could be a bounce in prices next year.* ■ [mass noun] exuberant self-confidence: *the bounce was now back in Jenny's step.* ■ [mass noun] health and body in a person's hair: *use conditioner to help hair regain its bounce.* ■ W. Indian a collision.
– PHRASES **be bouncing off the walls** N. Amer. informal be full of nervous excitement or agitation. **bounce an idea off someone** informal share an idea with another person in order to get feedback on it and refine it. **on the bounce** as something rebounds: *he caught the ball on the bounce.* ■ informal in quick succession: *it's nice to get four victories on the bounce.*
– ORIGIN Middle English *bunsen* 'beat, thump', perhaps imitative, or from Low German *bunsen* 'beat', Dutch *bons* 'a thump'.

bounce flash ▶ noun a device for giving reflected photographic flashlight.
■ [mass noun] flashlight reflected in this way.

bouncer ▶ noun **1** a person employed by a nightclub or similar establishment to prevent troublemakers and other unwanted people entering or to eject them from the premises.
2 Cricket a ball bowled fast and short so as to rise high after pitching.

bouncing ▶ adjective (of a ball) rebounding up and down.
■ informal (of a cheque) returned by a bank because there are insufficient funds in an account to meet it. ■ (of a baby) vigorous and healthy. ■ lively and confident: *by the next day she was her usual bouncing, energetic self.*

bouncing Bet ▶ noun another term for **SOAPWORT**.

bouncy ▶ adjective (**bouncier**, **bounciest**) bouncing or making something bounce well: *bouncy floorboards* | *a bouncy ball.*
■ (of a person) confident and lively: *she was still the girl he remembered, bouncy and full of life.* ■ (of music) having a pleasingly jaunty rhythm: *bouncy 1960s tunes.*
– DERIVATIVES **bouncily** adverb, **bounciness** noun.

bouncy castle ▶ noun a large inflatable structure, typically in the form of a stylized castle or other building, on which children can jump and play.

b

bound[1] ▶ **verb** [no obj., with adverbial of direction] walk or run with leaping strides: *Louis came* ***bounding down*** *the stairs | figurative shares* ***bounded ahead*** *in early dealing.*
■(of an object, typically a round one) rebound from a surface: *bullets* ***bounded off*** *the veranda.*
▶ **noun** a leaping movement upwards, typically towards or over something: *I went up the steps in two effortless bounds.*
– ORIGIN early 16th cent. (as a noun): from French *bond* (noun), *bondir* (verb) 'resound', later 'rebound', from late Latin *bombitare*, from Latin *bombus* 'humming'.

bound[2] ▶ **noun** (often **bounds**) a territorial limit; a boundary: *the ancient bounds of the forest.*
■a limitation or restriction on feeling or action: *it is not* ***beyond the bounds of possibility*** *that the issue could arise again | enthusiasm to join the union* ***knew no bounds.*** ■ technical a limiting value.
▶ **verb** [with obj.] (usu. **be bounded**) form the boundary of; enclose: *the ground was bounded by a main road on one side and a meadow on the other.*
■place within certain limits; restrict: *freedom of action is bounded by law.*
– PHRASES **in bounds** inside the part of a sports field or court in which play is conducted. **out of bounds** (of a place) outside the limits of where one is permitted to be: *his kitchen was* ***out of bounds to*** *me at mealtimes.* ■ outside the part of a sports field or court in which play is conducted. ■ figurative beyond what is acceptable: *Paul felt that this conversation was getting out of bounds.*
– ORIGIN Middle English (in the senses 'landmark' and 'borderland'): from Old French *bodne*, from medieval Latin *bodina*, earlier *butina*, of unknown ultimate origin.

bound[3] ▶ **adjective** going or ready to go towards somewhere: *an express train* ***bound for*** *Edinburgh* | [in combination] *the three moon-bound astronauts.*
■figurative destined or very likely to have a specified experience: *they were* ***bound for*** *disaster.*
– ORIGIN Middle English *boun* (in the sense 'ready, dressed'), from Old Norse *búinn*, past participle of *búa* 'get ready'; the final *-d* is euphonic, or influenced by **BOUND**[4].

bound[4] past and past participle of **BIND**. ▶ **adjective**
1 [in combination] restricted or confined to a specified place: *his job kept him city-bound.*
■prevented from going somewhere or from operating normally by the specified conditions: *blizzard-bound Boston.*
2 [with infinitive] certain to be or to do or have something: *there is bound to be a change of plan.*
■obliged by law, circumstances, or duty to do something: *I'm bound to do what I can to help Sam.*
3 [in combination] (of a book) having a specified binding: *fine leather-bound books.*
4 (of a grammatical element) occurring only in combination with another form.
■in Chomskyan linguistics, (of a reflexive, reciprocal, or other linguistic unit) dependent for its reference on another noun phrase in the same sentence.
– PHRASES **bound up in** focusing on to the exclusion of all else: *she was too bound up in her own misery to care that other people were hurt.* **bound up with** (or **in**) closely connected with or related to: *democracy is bound up with a measure of economic and social equality.* **I'll be bound** used to emphasize that one is sure of something: *she's hatching more little plots, I'll be bound!* **I'm bound to say** used to precede a statement which one feels it is one's duty to make, however unwelcome it may be to the hearer: *I'm bound to say that I have some doubts.*

boundary ▶ **noun** (pl. **-ies**) a line which marks the limits of an area; a dividing line: *a county boundary | the river marks the boundary between the two regions* | [as modifier] *a boundary wall.*
■(often **boundaries**) figurative a limit of something abstract, especially a subject or sphere of activity: *a community without class or political boundaries.* ■ Cricket a hit crossing the limits of the field, scoring four or six runs.
– ORIGIN early 17th cent.: variant of dialect *bounder*, from **BOUND**[2] + **-ER**[1], perhaps on the pattern of *limitary.*

boundary condition ▶ **noun** Mathematics a condition that is required to be satisfied at all or part of the boundary of a region in which a set of differential conditions is to be solved.

boundary layer ▶ **noun** a layer of more or less stationary fluid (such as water or air) immediately surrounding an immersed moving object.

boundary rider ▶ **noun** Austral./NZ a person employed to maintain the outer fences of a cattle or sheep station.

boundary umpire ▶ **noun** Australian Rules an umpire on the boundary line who signals when the ball is out and throws it back in to restart play.

boundary value ▶ **noun** Mathematics a value specified by a boundary condition.

bounden /ˈbaʊnd(ə)n/ archaic past participle of **BIND**.
– PHRASES **a** (or **one's**) **bounden duty** a responsibility regarded by oneself or others as obligatory: *his bounden duty to respond to the call for help.*

bounder ▶ **noun** informal, dated, chiefly Brit. a dishonourable man: *he is nothing but a fortune-seeking bounder.*

boundless ▶ **adjective** unlimited; immense: *enthusiasts who devote boundless energy to their hobby.*
– DERIVATIVES **boundlessly** adverb, **boundlessness** noun.

bounteous ▶ **adjective** archaic generously given or giving; bountiful: *the earth yields a bounteous harvest.*
– DERIVATIVES **bounteously** adverb, **bounteousness** noun.
– ORIGIN late Middle English: from Old French *bontif, -ive* 'benevolent' (from *bonte* 'bounty'), on the pattern of *plenteous.*

bountiful ▶ **adjective** large in quantity; abundant: *the ocean provided a bountiful supply of fresh food.*
■giving generously: *this bountiful God has thought of everything.*
– DERIVATIVES **bountifully** adverb.
– ORIGIN early 16th cent.: from **BOUNTY** + **-FUL**.

Bounty a ship of the British navy on which in 1789 part of the crew, led by Fletcher Christian, mutinied against their commander, William Bligh, and set him adrift in an open boat with eighteen companions.

bounty ▶ **noun** (pl. **-ies**) a monetary gift or reward in return for a service or action, in particular:
■a sum paid for killing or capturing a person or animal: *there was an increased* ***bounty on his head.*** ■ historical a sum paid by the state to encourage trade. ■ chiefly historical a sum paid by the state to army or navy recruits on enlistment. ■ poetic/literary something given or occurring in generous amounts: *the bounties of nature.* ■ [mass noun] chiefly poetic/literary generosity: *for millennia the people along the Nile have depended entirely on its bounty.*
– ORIGIN Middle English (denoting goodness or generosity): from Old French *bonte* 'goodness', from Latin *bonitas*, from *bonus* 'good'. The sense 'monetary reward' dates from the early 18th cent.

bounty hunter ▶ **noun** a person who pursues a criminal for whom a reward is offered.

bouquet /bʊˈkeɪ, bəʊˈkeɪ, ˈbʊkeɪ/ ▶ **noun** **1** an attractively arranged bunch of flowers, especially one presented as a gift or carried at a ceremony.
■figurative an expression of approval; a compliment: *we will happily publish the bouquets and brickbats.*
2 the characteristic scent of a wine or perfume: *the aperitif has a faint bouquet of almonds.*
– ORIGIN early 18th cent.: from French (earlier 'clump of trees'), from a dialect variant of Old French *bos* 'wood'. Sense 2 dates from the mid 19th cent.

bouquet garni /bʊˌkeɪ ˈɡɑːni, bəʊˈkeɪ, ˈbʊkeɪ/ ▶ **noun** (pl. **bouquets garnis**) a bunch of herbs, typically encased in a muslin bag, used for flavouring a stew or soup.
– ORIGIN French, literally 'garnished bouquet'.

Bourbaki /ˌbʊəˈbɑːki/, Nicolas, a pseudonym of a group of mathematicians, mainly French, attempting to give a complete account of the foundations of pure mathematics. Their first publication was in 1939.
– ORIGIN the group was named, humorously, after a defeated French general of the Franco-Prussian War (1870–1).

Bourbon[1] /ˈbʊəb(ə)n, ˈbɔːbɒn/ the surname of a branch of the royal family of France. The Bourbons ruled France from 1589, when Henry IV succeeded to the throne, until the monarchy was overthrown in 1848, and reached the peak of their power under Louis XIV in the late 17th century. Members of this family have also been kings of Spain (1700–1931 and since 1975).

Bourbon[2] /ˈbʊəb(ə)n/ ▶ **noun** **1** US a reactionary.
2 Brit. a chocolate-flavoured biscuit with a chocolate-cream filling.
3 (also **Bourbon rose**) a rose of a variety which flowers over a long period and has a rich scent. It arose as a natural hybrid on the island of Réunion (formerly Île de Bourbon) and was introduced into Europe in the early 19th century.
● *Rosa* × *borboniana*, a hybrid of *Rosa chinensis* and *R. damascena*, family Rosaceae.
– ORIGIN mid 19th cent. (in sense 1): from **BOURBON**[1]. Sense 2 dates from the 1930s.

bourbon /ˈbəːb(ə)n, ˈbʊə-/ ▶ **noun** [mass noun] a kind of American whisky distilled from maize and rye.
– ORIGIN mid 19th cent.: named after *Bourbon* County, Kentucky, where it was first made.

Bourbonnais /ˌbʊəbɒˈneɪ/ a former duchy and province of central France; chief town, Moulins. It forms part of the Auvergne and Centre regions.

bourdon /ˈbʊəd(ə)n/ ▶ **noun** Music a low-pitched stop in an organ or harmonium, typically a stopped diapason of 16-foot pitch.
– ORIGIN Middle English (in the sense 'drone of a bagpipe'): from Old French, 'drone', of imitative origin.

Bourdon gauge /ˈbʊədɒn/ ▶ **noun** a pressure gauge employing a coiled metallic tube which tends to straighten out when pressure is exerted within it.
– ORIGIN mid 19th cent.: named after Eugène *Bourdon* (1808–84), French hydraulic engineer.

bourgeois /ˈbʊəʒwɑː/ ▶ **adjective** of or characteristic of the middle class, typically with reference to its perceived materialistic values or conventional attitudes: *a rich, bored, bourgeois family | these views will shock the bourgeois critics.*
■(in Marxist contexts) upholding the interests of capitalism; not communist: *bourgeois society took for granted the sanctity of property.*
▶ **noun** (pl. same) a bourgeois person.
– ORIGIN mid 16th cent.: from French, from late Latin *burgus* 'castle' (in medieval Latin 'fortified town'), ultimately of Germanic origin and related to **BOROUGH**. Compare with **BURGESS**.

bourgeoise /ˈbʊəʒwɑːz/ ▶ **adjective** of or characteristic of female members of the bourgeoisie.
▶ **noun** a female member of the bourgeoisie.
– ORIGIN late 18th cent.: French, feminine of *bourgeois* 'citizen' (see **BOURGEOIS**).

bourgeoisie /ˌbʊəʒwɑːˈziː/ ▶ **noun** [treated as sing. or pl.] the middle class, typically with reference to its perceived materialistic values or conventional attitudes.
■(in Marxist contexts) the capitalist class who own most of society's wealth and means of production.
– ORIGIN early 18th cent.: French, from **BOURGEOIS**.

Bourgogne /burɡɔɲ/ French name for **BURGUNDY**.

Bourguiba /ˌbʊəˈɡiːbə/, Habib ibn Ali (1903–2000), Tunisian nationalist and statesman, the first President of independent Tunisia 1957–87.

Bourke-White /bəːk/, Margaret (1906–71), American photojournalist. During the Second World War she was the first female photographer to be attached to the US armed forces, at the end of the war accompanying the Allied forces when they entered the concentration camps.

bourn[1] /bɔːn, bʊən/ ▶ **noun** dialect a small stream, especially one that flows intermittently or seasonally.
– ORIGIN Middle English: southern English variant of **BURN**[2].

bourn[2] /bɔːn, bʊən/ (also **bourne**) ▶ **noun** poetic/literary a limit; a boundary.
■a goal; a destination.
– ORIGIN early 16th cent. (denoting a boundary of a field): from French *borne*, from Old French *bodne* (see **BOUND**[2]).

Bournemouth /ˈbɔːnməθ/ a resort on the south coast of England, a unitary council formerly in Dorset; pop. 154,400 (1991).

bourrée /ˈbʊəreɪ/ ▶ **noun** a lively French dance like a gavotte.
■Ballet a series of very fast little steps, with the feet close together, usually performed on the tips of the toes and giving the impression that the dancer is gliding over the floor.

▶ **verb** [no obj.] perform a bourrée.
– ORIGIN late 17th cent.: French, literally 'faggot of twigs' (the dance being performed around a fire made with such twigs).

bourse /bʊəs, French buʀs/ ▶ **noun** a stock market in a non-English-speaking country, especially France. Compare with **BURSE**.
■ (**Bourse**) the Paris stock exchange.
– ORIGIN mid 16th cent. (as *burse*, the usual form until the mid 19th cent.): from French, literally 'purse', via medieval Latin from Greek *bursa* 'leather'.

Boursin /ˈbʊəsã, French buʀsɛ̃/ ▶ **noun** [mass noun] trademark a kind of soft cheese from France.
– ORIGIN French.

boustrophedon /ˌbaʊstrəˈfiːd(ə)n, ˌbuː-/ ▶ **adjective & adverb** (of written words) from right to left and from left to right in alternate lines.
– ORIGIN early 17th cent.: from Greek, literally 'as an ox turns in ploughing', from *bous* 'ox' + *-strophos* 'turning'.

bout /baʊt/ ▶ **noun 1** a short period of intense activity of a specified kind: *occasional bouts of strenuous exercise | a drinking bout.*
■ an attack of illness or strong emotion of a specified kind: *a severe bout of flu.* ■ a wrestling or boxing match.
2 a curve in the side of a violin, guitar, or other musical instrument.
– ORIGIN mid 16th cent. (denoting a curve or circuit, hence later a 'turn' of activity): from dialect *bought* 'bend, loop'; probably of Low German origin.

boutade /buːˈtɑːd/ ▶ **noun** formal a sudden outburst or outbreak.
– ORIGIN early 17th cent.: French, from *bouter* 'to thrust'.

boutique /buːˈtiːk/ ▶ **noun** a small shop selling fashionable clothes or accessories.
– ORIGIN mid 18th cent.: from French, 'small shop', via Latin from Greek *apothēkē* 'storehouse'. Compare with **BODEGA**.

bouton /ˈbuːtɒn/ ▶ **noun** Anatomy an enlarged part of a nerve fibre or cell, especially an axon, where it forms a synapse with another nerve.
– ORIGIN mid 20th cent.: from French, literally 'button'.

boutonnière /ˌbuːtɒnˈjɛː/ ▶ **noun** a spray of flowers worn in a buttonhole.
– ORIGIN late 19th cent.: French, 'buttonhole', from *bouton* 'button'.

Boutros-Ghali /ˌbuːtrɒsˈɡɑːli/, Boutros (b.1922), Egyptian diplomat and politician, Secretary General of the United Nations 1992–97.

boutu /ˈbəʊtuː/ (also **boto**) ▶ **noun** a pink and grey river dolphin found in the Amazon and Orinoco River systems. Also called **AMAZON DOLPHIN**.
● *Inia geoffrensis*, family Platanistidae.

Bouvet Island /ˈbuːveɪ/ an uninhabited Norwegian island in the South Atlantic.
– ORIGIN named after the French navigator François Lozier-*Bouvet* (1705–86), who visited it in 1739.

bouvier /ˈbuːvɪeɪ/ ▶ **noun** a large, powerful dog of a rough-coated breed originating in Belgium.

bouzouki /bʊˈzuːki/ ▶ **noun** (pl. **bouzoukis**) a long-necked Greek form of mandolin.
– ORIGIN 1950s: from modern Greek *mpouzouki*, possibly related to Turkish *bozuk* 'spoilt' (with reference to roughly made instruments).

bovid /ˈbəʊvɪd/ ▶ **noun** Zoology a mammal of the cattle family (Bovidae).
– ORIGIN late 19th cent.: from modern Latin *Bovidae* (plural), from *bos, bov-* 'ox'.

bovine /ˈbəʊvʌɪn/ ▶ **adjective** of, relating to, or affecting cattle: *bovine tuberculosis | bovine tissue.*
■ (of a person or their manner or expression) sluggish or stupid: *a look of bovine contentment came into her face.*
▶ **noun** an animal of the cattle group, which also includes buffaloes and bisons.
– DERIVATIVES **bovinely** adverb.
– ORIGIN early 19th cent.: from late Latin *bovinus*, from Latin *bos, bov-* 'ox'.

bovine spongiform encephalopathy ▶ **noun** see **BSE**.

Bovril ▶ **noun** [mass noun] trademark a concentrated essence of beef diluted with hot water to make a drink.
– ORIGIN late 19th cent.: from Latin *bos, bov-* 'ox', the second element perhaps from *vril*, an imaginary form of energy described in E. Bulwer-Lytton's novel *The Coming Race* (1871).

bovver ▶ **noun** [usu. as modifier] Brit. informal hooliganism or violent disorder, especially as caused by gangs of skinheads: *a bovver boy.*
– ORIGIN 1960s: representing a cockney pronunciation of **BOTHER**.

bovver boots ▶ **noun** Brit. informal heavy laced boots extending to the mid-calf, typically worn by skinheads.

Bow /bəʊ/, Clara (1905–65), American actress. One of the most popular stars and sex symbols of the 1920s, she was known as the 'It Girl'.

bow¹ /bəʊ/ ▶ **noun 1** a knot tied with two loops and two loose ends, used especially for tying shoelaces and decorative ribbons: *a girl with long hair tied back in a bow.*
■ a decorative ribbon tied in such a knot.
2 a weapon for shooting arrows, typically made of a curved piece of wood joined at both ends by a taut string.
3 a long, partially curved rod with horsehair stretched along its length, used for playing the violin and other stringed instruments.
■ a single passage of such a rod over the strings.
4 a thing that is bent or curved in shape, in particular:
■ a curved stroke forming part of a letter (e.g. *b, p*). ■ a metal ring forming the handle of a key or pair of scissors. ■ N. Amer. a side piece or lens frame of a pair of glasses.
▶ **verb** [with obj.] play (a stringed instrument or music) using a bow.
– PHRASES **have** (or **add**) **another string to one's bow** Brit. have a further resource that one can make use of. **have many strings to one's bow** Brit. have a wide range of resources that one can make use of.
– ORIGIN Old English *boga* 'bend, bow, arch', of Germanic origin; related to Dutch *boog* and German *Bogen*, also to **BOW²**.

bow² /baʊ/ ▶ **verb** [no obj.] bend the head or upper part of the body as a sign of respect, greeting, or shame: *he turned and* **bowed to** *his father | they refused to* **bow down before** *the king* | [with obj.] *she knelt and bowed her head.*
■ [with obj.] express (thanks, agreement, or other sentiments) by bending one's head respectfully: *he looked at Hector before bowing grave thanks.* ■ [with obj.] cause (someone) to bend with age or under a heavy weight: *the creepers were* **bowed down with** *flowers.* ■ submit to pressure or someone's demands: *the government has* **bowed to** *pressure from farmers to increase compensation.* ■ [with obj. and adverbial of direction] usher (someone) in a specified direction while bowing respectfully: *a gorgeously dressed footman bowed her into the hallway.*
▶ **noun** an act of bending the head or upper body as a sign of respect or greeting: *the man gave a little bow.*
– PHRASES **bow and scrape** behave in an obsequious way to someone in authority. **make one's bow** make one's first formal appearance in a particular role: *the midfielder only made his England bow nine months ago.* **take a bow** (of an actor or entertainer) acknowledge applause after a performance by bowing.
– ORIGIN Old English *būgan* 'bend, stoop', of Germanic origin; related to German *biegen*, also to **BOW¹**.
▶ **bow out** withdraw or retire from an activity, role, or commitment: *many artists are forced to* **bow out of** *the profession at a relatively early age.*

bow³ /baʊ/ (also **bows**) ▶ **noun** the front end of a ship: *water sprayed high over her bows.*
– PHRASES **on the bow** Nautical within 45° of the point directly ahead. **a** (**warning**) **shot across the bows** a statement or gesture intended to frighten someone into changing their course of action: *supporters are firing a warning shot across the President's bows.*
– ORIGIN late Middle English: from Low German *boog*, Dutch *boeg*, 'shoulder or ship's bow'; related to **BOUGH**.

bow compass (also **bow compasses**) ▶ **noun** a compass with jointed legs.

bowdlerize /ˈbaʊdlərʌɪz/ (also **-ise**) ▶ **verb** [with obj.] remove material that is considered improper or offensive from (a text or account), especially with the result that the text becomes weaker or less effective: [as adj. **bowdlerized**] *a bowdlerized version of the story.*
– DERIVATIVES **bowdlerism** noun, **bowdlerization** noun.
– ORIGIN mid 19th cent.: from the name of Dr Thomas *Bowdler* (1754–1825), who published an expurgated edition of Shakespeare in 1818, + **-IZE**.

bowel /ˈbaʊəl/ ▶ **noun** (often **bowels**) the part of the alimentary canal below the stomach; the intestine.
■ (**the bowels of ——**) the deepest inner parts or areas of something: *the mineshaft descended deep into the bowels of the earth.*
– ORIGIN Middle English: from Old French *bouel*, from Latin *botellus*, diminutive of *botulus* 'sausage'.

bowel movement ▶ **noun** an act of defecation.
■ the faeces discharged in an act of defecation.

Bowen /ˈbəʊɪn/, Elizabeth (Dorothea Cole) (1899–1973), British novelist and short-story writer, born in Ireland. Notable novels: *The Death of the Heart* (1938) and *The Heat of the Day* (1949).

bower¹ /ˈbaʊə/ ▶ **noun** a pleasant shady place under trees or climbing plants in a garden or wood.
■ poetic/literary a summer house or country cottage. ■ poetic/literary a lady's private room or bedroom.
▶ **verb** [with obj.] poetic/literary shade or enclose (a place or person): [as adj. **bowered**] *the bowered pathways into the tangle of vines.*
– ORIGIN Old English *būr* 'dwelling, inner room', of Germanic origin; related to German *Bauer* 'birdcage'.

bower² /ˈbaʊə/ (also **bower anchor**) ▶ **noun** each of two anchors carried at a ship's bow, formerly distinguished as the **best bower** (starboard) or **small bower** (port).
– ORIGIN late 15th cent.: from **BOW³** + **-ER¹**.

bowerbird ▶ **noun** a strong-billed Australasian bird, noted for the male's habit of constructing an elaborate run or bower adorned with feathers, shells, and other objects to attract the female for courtship.
● Family Ptilonorhynchidae: several genera and species, especially the **satin bowerbird** (*Ptilonorhynchus violaceus*), which decorates the bower with blue-coloured articles.
■ Austral. informal a person who collects trivia or odds and ends.

Bowery /ˈbaʊəri/ a street and district in New York City associated with drunks and vagrants.
– ORIGIN mid 17th cent.: built on the site of governor Peter Stuyvesant's *bowery* 'farm', from Dutch *bouwerij*; the district became noted for its cheap lodging houses and saloons.

bowfin /ˈbəʊfɪn/ ▶ **noun** a predatory American freshwater fish with a large blunt head and a long dorsal fin. It is able to survive for long periods out of water.
● *Amia calva*, the only living member of the family Amiidae.
– ORIGIN late 19th cent.: from **BOW¹** + **FIN**.

bow-fronted ▶ **adjective** (of furniture) having a convexly curved front.
– DERIVATIVES **bow front** noun & adjective.

bowhead /ˈbəʊhɛd/ (also **bowhead whale**) ▶ **noun** an Arctic right whale with black skin, feeding by skimming the surface for plankton. Also called **GREENLAND RIGHT WHALE**.
● *Balaena mysticetus*, family Balaenidae.
– ORIGIN late 19th cent.: from **BOW¹** + **HEAD**.

bowhunting ▶ **noun** [mass noun] N. Amer. the practice of hunting animals with a bow rather than a gun.
– DERIVATIVES **bowhunter** noun.

Bowie¹ /ˈbəʊi/, David (b.1947), English rock singer, songwriter, and actor; born *David Robert Jones*. He is known for his theatrical performances and unconventional stage personae. Notable albums: *Ziggy Stardust* (1972) and *Heroes* (1977).

Bowie² /ˈbəʊi/, Jim (1799–1836), American frontiersman; full name *James Bowie*. He shared command of the garrison that resisted the Mexican attack on the Alamo, where he died.

bowie /ˈbəʊi/ (also **bowie knife**) ▶ **noun** (pl. **-ies**) a long knife with a blade double-edged at the point.
– ORIGIN mid 19th cent.: named after J. *Bowie* (see **BOWIE²**).

bowknot ▶ **noun** a double-looped ornamental knot in a ribbon, tie, or other fastening.

bowl¹ ▶ **noun 1** a round, deep dish or basin used for food or liquid: *a mixing bowl | a sugar bowl.*
■ the contents of such a container: *they ate huge* **bowls of** *steaming spaghetti.* ■ [usu. in names] a decorative round dish awarded as a prize in a competition: *the McGeorge Rose Bowl.* ■ a rounded, concave part of an

b

object: *a toilet bowl* | *the bowl of a spoon.* ■ Geography a natural basin.
2 [in names] chiefly US a stadium for sporting or musical events: *the Hollywood Bowl.*
■ an American football game played after the regular season between leading teams.
– DERIVATIVES **bowlful** noun (pl. **-fuls**).
– ORIGIN Old English *bolle, bolla*, of Germanic origin; related to Dutch *bol* 'round object', also to **BOLL**.

bowl² ▶ **noun 1** a wooden or hard rubber ball, slightly asymmetrical so that it runs on a curved course, used in the game of bowls.
■ a large ball with indents for gripping, used in tenpin bowling. ■ a wooden ball or disc used in playing skittles.
2 a spell or turn of bowling in cricket.
▶ **verb 1** [with obj. and adverbial of direction] roll (a ball, hoop, or other round object) along the ground: *she snatched her hat off and bowled it ahead of her.*
2 [with obj.] Cricket (of a bowler) propel (the ball), typically with a smooth overarm action while running, from one end of the pitch to the other for the batsman to attempt to hit: *Lillee bowled another bouncer* | [no obj.] *Sobers bowled to Willis.*
■ dismiss (a batsman) by knocking down the wicket with the ball which one has bowled: *Stewart* ***was bowled for*** *33.* ■ (**bowl a side out**) get (an entire team) out: *they* ***bowled*** *Lancashire* ***out for*** *143.*
3 [no obj., with adverbial of direction] move rapidly and smoothly in a specified direction: *they bowled along the country roads.*
– ORIGIN late Middle English (in the general sense 'ball'): from Old French *boule*, from Latin *bulla* 'bubble'.
▶ **bowl someone over** knock someone down. ■ (usu. **be bowled over**) informal completely overwhelm or astonish someone, for example by one's good qualities or looks: *when he met Angela he was just bowled over by her.*

bow legs ▶ **plural noun** legs that curve outwards at the knee; bandy legs.
– DERIVATIVES **bow-legged** adjective.

bowler¹ ▶ **noun 1** Cricket a member of the fielding side who bowls or is bowling.
2 a player at bowls, tenpin bowling, or skittles.

bowler² (also **bowler hat**) ▶ **noun** a man's hard felt hat with a round dome-shaped crown.
– ORIGIN mid 19th cent.: named after William *Bowler*, the English hatter who designed it in 1850.

Bowles /bəʊlz/, Paul (Frederick) (1910–99), American writer and composer. His novels, which include *The Sheltering Sky* (1949) and *The Spider's House* (1966), typically concern westerners in the Arab world.

bowline /ˈbəʊlɪn/ ▶ **noun 1** a rope attaching the weather side of a square sail to a ship's bow.
2 a simple knot for forming a non-slipping loop at the end of a rope.
– ORIGIN Middle English: from Middle Low German *bōlīne*, Middle Dutch *boechlijne*, from *boeg* 'ship's bow' + *lijne* 'line'.

bowling ▶ **noun** [mass noun] **1** the game of bowls as a sport or recreation.
■ the game of tenpin bowling. ■ the game of skittles.
2 Cricket the action of a bowler in sending down balls towards the batsman's wicket: *fast bowling.*
■ the strength or resources of the bowlers in a cricket team: *on paper their bowling looks thin.*

bowling alley ▶ **noun** a long narrow track along which balls are rolled in the games of skittles or tenpin bowling.
■ a building containing such tracks.

bowling average ▶ **noun** Cricket the number of runs conceded by a bowler per wicket taken.

bowling crease ▶ **noun** Cricket the line from behind which a bowler delivers the ball.

bowling green ▶ **noun** an area of closely mown grass on which the game of bowls is played.

bowling rink ▶ **noun** see **RINK**.

bowls /bəʊlz/ ▶ **plural noun** [treated as sing.] a game played with heavy wooden bowls, the object of which is to propel one's bowl so that it comes to rest as close as possible to a previously bowled small white ball (the jack) without touching it. Bowls is played chiefly out of doors (though indoor bowls is also popular) on a closely trimmed lawn called a green.
■ Brit. tenpin bowling or skittles.

bowman¹ /ˈbəʊmən/ ▶ **noun** (pl. **-men**) an archer.

bowman² /ˈbaʊmən/ ▶ **noun** (pl. **-men**) the rower who sits nearest the bow of a boat, especially a racing boat.

bowsaw /ˈbəʊsɔː/ ▶ **noun** a saw with a narrow blade stretched like a bowstring on a light frame.

bowser /ˈbaʊzə/ ▶ **noun** trademark a tanker used for fuelling aircraft and other vehicles or for supplying water.
■ Austral./NZ a petrol pump.
– ORIGIN 1920s: from the name of a company of oil storage engineers.

bowshot /ˈbəʊʃɒt/ ▶ **noun** [in sing.] the distance to which a bow can send an arrow: *the two armies camped almost* ***within bowshot*** *of each other.*

bowsie /ˈbaʊziː/ ▶ **noun** (pl. **-ies**) Irish a low-class or unruly person.
– ORIGIN of unknown origin.

bowsprit /ˈbəʊsprɪt/ ▶ **noun** a spar running out from a ship's bow, to which the forestays are fastened.
– ORIGIN Middle English: from Middle Low German *bōgsprēt*, Middle Dutch *boechspriet*, from *boech* 'bow' + *spriet* 'sprit'.

Bow Street Runner /bəʊ/ ▶ **noun** the popular name for a London policeman during the first half of the 19th century.
– ORIGIN named after *Bow Street* in London, site of the chief metropolitan magistrates' court.

bowstring /ˈbəʊstrɪŋ/ ▶ **noun** the string of an archer's bow, traditionally made of three strands of hemp.
▶ **verb** (past and past participle **-strung**) [with obj.] historical strangle with a bowstring (a former Turkish method of execution).

bow tie ▶ **noun** a necktie in the form of a bow or a knot with two loops.
■ a pattern used for patchwork quilts, resembling such a necktie: [as modifier] *a bow-tie quilt.*

bow wave ▶ **noun** a wave or system of waves set up at the bows of a moving ship.

bow window ▶ **noun** a curved bay window.

bow-wow ▶ **exclamation** /baʊˈwaʊ/ an imitation of a dog's bark.
▶ **noun** /ˈbaʊwaʊ/ informal a child's word for a dog.

bowyang /ˈbəʊjaŋ/ ▶ **noun** Austral./NZ a band or strap worn round the trouser leg below the knee.
– ORIGIN late 19th cent.: from British dialect *bow-yanks, bow-yankees* 'leather leggings', of unknown origin.

bowyer /ˈbəʊjə/ ▶ **noun** a person who makes or sells archers' bows.

box¹ ▶ **noun 1** a container with a flat base and sides, typically square or rectangular and having a lid: *a cigarette box* | *a hat box.*
■ the contents of such a container: *she ate a whole* ***box of*** *chocolates that night.* ■ (**the box**) informal, chiefly Brit. television or a television set: *light entertainment shows on the box* | *we sat around the box watching the match.* ■ informal a casing containing a computer. ■ informal a coffin: *I always thought I'd be in a box when I finally left here.* ■ historical a coachman's seat. ■ vulgar slang, chiefly N. Amer. a woman's vagina.
2 an area or space enclosed within straight lines, in particular:
■ an area on a page that is to be filled in or that contains separate printed matter: *tick the box on the coupon.* ■ an area on a computer screen for user input or displaying information. ■ a box junction. ■ (**the box**) Soccer the penalty area. ■ (**the box**) Baseball the area occupied by the batter.
3 a small structure or building for a specific purpose, in particular:
■ a separate section or enclosed area within a larger building, especially one reserved for a group of people in a theatre or sports ground or for witnesses or the jury in a law court: *the royal box.* ■ Brit. a small country house for use when shooting or fishing.
4 a protective casing for a piece of a mechanism.
■ informal short for **GEARBOX**. ■ Brit. a light shield for protecting a man's genitals in sport, especially in cricket.
5 a facility at a newspaper office for receiving replies to an advertisement: *write to me care of Box 112.*
■ a facility at a post office whereby letters are kept until called for by the addressee.
▶ **verb** [with obj.] **1** [often as adj. **boxed**] put in or provide with a box: *the books are sold as a boxed set* | *Muriel* ***boxed up*** *all Christopher's clothes.*
■ enclose (a piece of text) within printed lines: *boxed sections in magazines.* ■ (**box someone in**) restrict the ability of (someone) to move freely: *a van had double-parked alongside her car and totally boxed her in.*
2 (**box sheep up**) Austral./NZ mix up different flocks.
– PHRASES **be a box of birds** Austral./NZ informal be fine; be happy. **box of tricks** informal an ingenious gadget: *all those magical effects were produced by this little box of tricks here.* **out of the box** Austral./NZ informal unusually good: *the novel is nothing out of the box.* [ORIGIN: by association with the phrase *look fresh out of a bandbox* 'look very smart' (see **BANDBOX**).] **out of one's box** Brit. informal intoxicated with alcohol or drugs.
– DERIVATIVES **boxful** noun (pl. **-fuls**), **box-like** adjective.
– ORIGIN late Old English, probably from late Latin *buxis*, from Latin *pyxis* 'boxwood box', from Greek *puxos* (see **BOX³**).

box² ▶ **verb** [no obj.] fight an opponent using one's fists; compete in the sport of boxing: *he boxed for England* | [with obj.] *he had to box Benn for the title.*
▶ **noun** [in sing.] a slap with the hand on the side of a person's head given as a punishment or in anger: *she gave him* ***a box on the ear.***
– PHRASES **box clever** Brit. informal act so as to outwit someone: *she had to box clever, let Adam think she had accepted what he said.* **box someone's ears** slap someone on the side of the head as a punishment or in anger.
– ORIGIN late Middle English (in the general sense 'a blow'): of unknown origin.

box³ ▶ **noun 1** (also **box tree**) a slow-growing European evergreen shrub or small tree with small glossy dark green leaves. It is widely used in hedging and for topiary, and yields hard, heavy timber.
● *Buxus sempervirens*, family Buxaceae.
2 any of a number of trees which have similar timber or foliage, in particular:
● several Australian eucalyptus trees (genus *Eucalyptus*, family Myrtaceae). ● the tropical American **Venezuelan** (or **West Indian**) **box** (*Casearia praecox*, family Flacourtiaceae), the timber of which has now largely replaced that of the European box.
– ORIGIN Old English, via Latin from Greek *puxos*.

box⁴ ▶ **verb** (in phrase **box the compass**) chiefly Nautical
1 recite the compass points in correct order.
2 make a complete change of direction.
– ORIGIN mid 18th cent.: perhaps from Spanish *bojar* 'sail round', from Middle Low German *bōgen* 'bend', from the base of **BOW¹**.

Box and Cox Brit. ▶ **noun** [often as modifier] used to refer to an arrangement whereby people or things make use of the same accommodation or facilities at different times, according to a strict arrangement.
▶ **verb** [no obj.] share accommodation or facilities by a strictly timed arrangement.
– ORIGIN the title of a play (1847) by J. M. Morton, in which two characters, John Box and James Cox, unknowingly become tenants of the same room.

box-and-whisker plot ▶ **noun** another term for **BOX PLOT**.

box beam ▶ **noun** another term for **BOX GIRDER**.

boxboard ▶ **noun** [mass noun] a type of stiff cardboard used to make boxes.

box camera ▶ **noun** a simple box-shaped hand camera.

box canyon ▶ **noun** N. Amer. a narrow canyon with a flat bottom and vertical walls.

boxcar ▶ **noun** N. Amer. an enclosed railway freight wagon, typically with sliding doors on the sides.

box elder ▶ **noun** an American maple with leaves that resemble those of the elder and green or purplish twigs.
● *Acer negundo*, family Aceraceae.

Boxer ▶ **noun** a member of a fiercely nationalistic Chinese secret society which flourished in the 19th century. In 1899 the society led a Chinese uprising against Western domination which was eventually crushed by a combined European force, aided by Japan and the US.
– ORIGIN from **BOXER**, translating Chinese *yì hé quán*, literally 'righteous harmony fists'.

boxer ▶ **noun 1** a person who takes part in boxing, especially for sport.
2 a medium-sized dog of a breed with a smooth brown coat and pug-like face.

boxercise ▶ **noun** [mass noun] trademark a form of

exercise based on boxing training and using boxing equipment.
– ORIGIN 1980s: blend of **BOXER** and **EXERCISE**.

boxer shorts ▶ plural noun men's loose underpants similar in shape to the shorts worn by boxers.

boxfish ▶ noun (pl. same or **-fishes**) a tropical marine fish that has a shell of bony plates enclosing the body, from which spines project. Also called **TRUNKFISH**.
● Family Ostraciontidae: numerous species, including the widely distributed *Tetrosomus gibbosus*.

box girder ▶ noun a hollow girder square in cross section.

Boxgrove man ▶ noun a fossil hominid of the Middle Pleistocene period, whose fragmentary remains were found at Boxgrove near Chichester, SE England, in 1993 and 1995. Dated (controversially) to about 500,000 years ago, it is one of the earliest known humans in Europe.
● *Homo heidelbergensis* (or *H. erectus*), family Hominidae.

boxing ▶ noun the sport or practice of fighting with the fists, especially with padded gloves in a roped square ring according to prescribed rules (known as the Queensberry Rules after the Marquess of Queensberry, who codified them in 1885).

Boxing Day ▶ noun (in parts of the Commonwealth) a public holiday celebrated on the first day (strictly, the first weekday) after Christmas Day.
– ORIGIN mid 19th cent.: from the custom of giving tradespeople a Christmas box on this day.

boxing glove ▶ noun a heavily padded mitten worn in boxing.

boxing weight ▶ noun each of a series of fixed weight ranges at which boxers are matched.

box jelly ▶ noun a jellyfish with a box-shaped swimming bell, living in warm seas. See also **SEA WASP**.
● Class Cubozoa (formerly order Cubomedusae).

box junction ▶ noun Brit. a road area at a junction marked with a yellow grid, which a vehicle should enter only if its exit from it is clear.

box kite ▶ noun a tailless kite in the form of a long box open at each end.

box number ▶ noun a number identifying a private advertisement in a newspaper and functioning as an address for replies.

box office ▶ noun a place at a theatre, cinema, or other arts establishment where tickets are bought or reserved.
■ [in sing.] used to refer to the commercial success of a film, play, or actor in terms of the audience size or takings they command: [as modifier] *the movie was a huge box office hit*.

boxout ▶ noun a piece of text written to accompany a larger text and printed in a separate area of the page.

box pew ▶ noun an old-fashioned church pew enclosed by wooden partitions.

box pleat ▶ noun a pleat consisting of two parallel creases facing opposite directions and forming a raised band.

box plot (also **box-and-whisker plot**) ▶ noun Statistics a simple way of representing statistical data on a plot in which a rectangle is drawn to represent the second and third quartiles, usually with a vertical line inside to indicate the median value. The lower and upper quartiles are shown as horizontal lines either side of the rectangle.

boxroom ▶ noun Brit. a very small room used for storage or as a bedroom.

box score ▶ noun N. Amer. the tabulated results of a baseball game or other sporting event, with statistics given for each player's performance.

box seat ▶ noun **1** a seat in a box in a theatre or sports stadium.
2 historical a coachman's seat.
– PHRASES **in the box seat** Austral./NZ in an advantageous position.

box-shifter ▶ noun informal a retail company which aims to maximize sales with little regard for quality or customer care.

box spanner ▶ noun Brit. a cylindrical spanner with a hexagonal end fitting over the head of a nut.

box spring ▶ noun each of a set of vertical springs housed in a frame in a mattress or upholstered chair base.

boxthorn ▶ noun a thorny shrub of warm-temperate regions, which bears red berries. Some kinds are used for hedging.
● Genus *Lycium*, family Solanaceae: several species (see also **TEA TREE** sense 2).

box turtle ▶ noun a land-living turtle which has a lower shell with hinged lobes that can be drawn up tightly to enclose the animal. It is native to North America and Mexico and is commonly kept as a pet in the US.
● Genus *Terrapene*, family Emydidae: several species.

boxty /ˈbɒksti/ (also **boxty bread**) ▶ noun [mass noun] a type of bread made using grated raw potatoes and flour, originally made in Ireland.
– ORIGIN from Irish *bacstaí*.

boxy ▶ adjective (**boxier**, **boxiest**) squarish in shape: *a boxy jacket*.
■ (of a room or space) cramped. ■ (of recorded sound) restricted in tone.

boy ▶ noun **1** a male child or youth.
■ a person's son: *she put her little boy to bed.* ■ [with modifier] a male child or young man who does a specified job: *a delivery boy*.
2 [usu. with adj.] a man, especially a young or relatively young one: *the inspector was a local boy* | *I was the new boy at the office*.
■ (**boys**) informal men who mix socially or who belong to a particular group, team, or profession: *he wants to stay one of the boys* | *our boys have finished bombing.* ■ dated used as a friendly form of address from one man to another, often from an older man to a young man: *my dear boy, don't say another word!* ■ dated, offensive (often used as a form of address) a black male servant or worker. ■ used as a form of address to a male dog: *down boy, down!*
▶ exclamation informal used to express strong feelings, especially of excitement or admiration: *oh boy, that's wonderful!*
– PHRASES **boys in blue** informal policemen; the police. **boys will be boys** used to express the view that mischievous or childish behaviour is typical of boys or young men and should not cause surprise when it occurs. **the big boys** men or organizations considered to be the most powerful and successful.
– DERIVATIVES **boyhood** noun.
– ORIGIN Middle English (denoting a male servant): of unknown origin.

boyar /bɔːˈjɑː/ ▶ noun historical a member of the old aristocracy in Russia, next in rank to a prince.
– ORIGIN late 16th cent.: from Russian *boyarin* 'grandee'.

Boyce, William (1711–79), English composer and organist. His compositions include songs, overtures, and eight symphonies; one of his most famous songs is 'Hearts of Oak'. He is also noted for his *Cathedral Music* (1760–79).

Boycott, Geoffrey (b.1940), English cricketer. He was an opening batsman for England, and was captain of Yorkshire 1971–5.

boycott ▶ verb [with obj.] withdraw from commercial or social relations with (a country, organization, or person) as a punishment or protest.
■ refuse to buy or handle (goods) as a punishment or protest. ■ refuse to cooperate with or participate in (a policy or event).
▶ noun a punitive ban on relations with other bodies, cooperation with a policy, or the handling of goods.
– ORIGIN from the name of Captain Charles C. *Boycott* (1832–97), an Irish land agent so treated in 1880, in an attempt instigated by the Irish Land League to get rents reduced.

Boyd, Arthur (Merric Bloomfield) (1920–99), Australian painter, potter, etcher, and ceramic artist. He was famous for his large ceramic sculptures and for his pictures inspired by his travels among Aboriginals.

Boyer /ˈbɔɪeɪ/, Charles (1897–1977), French-born American actor. Before going to Hollywood in the 1930s he enjoyed a successful stage career in France. Notable films: *Mayerling* (1936), *Gaslight* (1944), and *Barefoot in the Park* (1968).

boyfriend ▶ noun a person's regular male companion with whom they have a romantic or sexual relationship.

boyish ▶ adjective of, like, or characteristic of a male child or young man: *his boyish charm* | *she looked boyish and defiant*.
– DERIVATIVES **boyishly** adverb, **boyishness** noun.

boyla /ˈbɔɪlə/ ▶ noun Austral. an Aboriginal witch doctor.
– ORIGIN from Nyungar *bolya*.

Boyle, Robert (1627–91), Irish-born scientist. Boyle advanced a corpuscular view of matter which was a precursor of the modern theory of chemical elements and a cornerstone of his mechanical philosophy which became very influential. He is best known for his experiments with the air pump, which led to the law named after him.

Boyle's law Chemistry a law stating that the pressure of a given mass of an ideal gas is inversely proportional to its volume at a constant temperature.

Boyne, Battle of the /bɔɪn/ a battle fought near the River Boyne in Ireland in 1690, in which the Protestant army of William of Orange, the newly crowned William III, defeated the Catholic army (including troops from both France and Ireland) led by the recently deposed James II. The battle is celebrated annually (on 12 July) in Northern Ireland as a victory for the Protestant cause.

boyo ▶ noun (pl. **-os**) Welsh & Irish informal a boy or man (used chiefly as a form of address).

boy racer ▶ noun informal a youth or young man fond of driving very fast and aggressively in high-powered cars.

Boys' Brigade the oldest of the national organizations for boys in Britain, founded in 1883 with the aim of promoting 'Christian manliness', discipline, and self-respect. Companies are now also found in the US and in Commonwealth countries; each is connected with a church.

Boy Scout ▶ noun old-fashioned term for **SCOUT**[1] (in sense 2).

boysenberry /ˈbɔɪz(ə)n,b(ə)ri, -,bɛri/ ▶ noun (pl. **-ies**)
1 a large red edible blackberry-like fruit.
2 the shrubby plant that bears this fruit, which is a hybrid of several kinds of bramble.
● *Rubus loganobaccus*, family Rosaceae.
– ORIGIN 1930s: named after Rudolph *Boysen* (died 1950), the American horticulturalist who developed it.

boy toy ▶ noun informal, derogatory a young woman considered sexually attractive to young men.
■ a young man considered sexually attractive to women.
– ORIGIN 1980s: inversion of **TOY BOY**.

boy wonder ▶ noun an exceptionally talented young man or boy.

Boz /bɒz/ the pseudonym used by Charles Dickens in his *Pickwick Papers* and contributions to the *Morning Chronicle*.

bozo /ˈbəʊzəʊ/ ▶ noun (pl. **-os**) informal, chiefly N. Amer. a stupid or insignificant person.
■ a man.
– ORIGIN 1920s: of unknown origin.

BP ▶ abbreviation for ■ before the present (era): *18,000 years BP*. ■ blood pressure. ■ British Petroleum, a large multinational oil company. ■ (indicating listing in the) British Pharmacopoeia.

Bp ▶ abbreviation for Bishop.

bp ▶ abbreviation for ■ Biochemistry base pair(s), as a unit of length in nucleic acid chains. ■ Finance basis point(s). ■ (**b.p.**) boiling point.

BPC ▶ abbreviation for British Pharmaceutical Codex.

BPH Medicine ▶ abbreviation for benign prostatic hyperplasia (or hypertrophy), an enlargement of the prostate gland common in elderly men.

BPhil ▶ abbreviation for Bachelor of Philosophy.

bpi Computing ▶ abbreviation for bits per inch, used to indicate the density of data that can be stored on magnetic tape or similar media.

B-picture ▶ noun another term for **B-MOVIE**.

BPR ▶ abbreviation for business process re-engineering.

bps Computing ▶ abbreviation for bits per second.

Bq ▶ abbreviation for becquerel.

BR ▶ abbreviation for ■ N. Amer. bedroom or bedrooms. ■ Brazil (international vehicle registration). ■ (in the UK) British Rail or (formerly) British Railways.

Br ▶ symbol for the chemical element bromine.

Br. ▶ abbreviation for ■ (with reference to journal titles) British. ■ (with reference to religious order) Brother.

bra ▶ noun an undergarment worn by women to support the breasts.
- ■ (also **auto bra**, **car bra**) N. Amer. a carbon-based cover that fits over the front bumper of a car, absorbing the microwaves used in police radar equipment to minimize the risk of detection for the speeding motorist.
- DERIVATIVES **braless** adjective.
- ORIGIN 1930s: abbreviation of **BRASSIERE**.

braai /'brʌɪ/ S. African ▶ noun (pl. **braais**) short for **BRAAIVLEIS**.
- ■ a structure on which a fire can be made for the outdoor grilling of meat.
- ▶ verb (**braaied**, **braaiing** or **braaing**) [with obj.] grill (meat) over an open fire.
- ORIGIN Afrikaans.

braaivleis /'brʌɪˌfleɪs/ ▶ noun S. African a picnic or barbecue where meat is grilled over an open fire.
- ■ [mass noun] meat cooked in this way.
- ORIGIN Afrikaans, 'grilled meat', from *braai* 'to grill' + *vleis* 'meat'.

braata /'brɑːtə/ (also **braatas**) ▶ noun W. Indian a small amount added to a purchase in a market to encourage the customer to return.
- ORIGIN probably from Spanish *barata* 'bargain'.

Brabant /brə'bant/ a former duchy in western Europe, lying between the Meuse and Scheldt Rivers. Its capital was Brussels. It is now divided into two provinces in two countries: North Brabant in the Netherlands, of which the capital is 's-Hertogenbosch; and Brabant in Belgium, of which the capital remains Brussels.

Brabham /'brabəm/, Sir Jack (b.1926), Australian motor-racing driver; full name *John Arthur Brabham*. He won the Formula One world championship three times (1959, 1960, 1966).

brace ▶ noun 1 a device that clamps things tightly together or that gives support, in particular:
- ■ (**braces**) Brit. a pair of straps that pass over the shoulders and fasten to the top of trousers at the front and back to hold them up. ■ a device fitted to a weak or injured part of the body, such as the neck or leg, to give support. ■ a wire device fitted in the mouth to straighten the teeth. ■ a strengthening piece of iron or timber used in building or carpentry. ■ (also **brace and bit**) a drilling tool with a crank handle and a socket to hold a bit. ■ a rope attached to the yard of a ship for trimming the sail.
2 (pl. same) a pair of something, typically of birds or mammals killed in hunting: *thirty brace of grouse.*
3 Printing either of the two marks { and }, used either to indicate that two or more items on one side have the same relationship as each other to the single item to which the other side points, or in pairs to show that words between them are connected.
- ■ Music a similar mark connecting staves to be performed at the same time.
▶ verb [with obj.] make (a structure) stronger or firmer with wood, iron, or other forms of support: *the posts were braced by lengths of timber.*
- ■ press (one's body or part of one's body) firmly against something in order to stay balanced: *she braced her feet against a projecting shelf* | [as adj. **braced**] *he stood with legs braced.* ■ prepare (someone or oneself) for something difficult or unpleasant: *both stations are bracing themselves for job losses.*
- ORIGIN Middle English (as a verb meaning 'clasp, fasten tightly'): from Old French *bracier* 'embrace', from *brace* 'two arms', from Latin *bracchia*, plural of *bracchium* 'arm', from Greek *brakhiōn*.
▶ **brace up** be strong or courageous.

bracelet ▶ noun an ornamental band, hoop, or chain worn on the wrist or arm.
- ■ (**bracelets**) informal handcuffs.
- ORIGIN late Middle English: from Old French, from *bras* 'arm', from Latin *bracchium*.

bracer¹ ▶ noun informal an alcoholic drink intended to prepare one for something difficult or unpleasant.

bracer² ▶ noun a sort of wristguard used in archery and other sports.
- ■ historical a portion of a suit of armour covering the arm.
- ORIGIN late Middle English: from Old French *braciere*, from *bras* 'arm' (see **BRACELET**).

brachial /'breɪkɪəl/ ▶ adjective Anatomy of or relating to the arm or an arm-like structure: *the brachial artery.*
- ■ like an arm. ■ Zoology denoting the upper valve of a brachiopod's shell.

- ORIGIN late Middle English: from Latin *brachialis*, from *brac(c)hium* 'arm'.

brachiate ▶ verb /'brakɪeɪt/ [no obj., usu. with adverbial of direction] (of certain apes) move by using the arms to swing from branch to branch.
▶ adjective /'brakɪət, 'breɪk-/ Biology branched, especially having widely spread paired branches on alternate sides.
- ■ having arms.
- DERIVATIVES **brachiation** noun, **brachiator** noun.
- ORIGIN mid 18th cent. (originally in the sense 'having paired branches'): from Latin *brachium* 'arm' + -**ATE**².

Brachiopoda /ˌbrakɪə'pəʊdə/ Zoology a phylum of marine invertebrates that comprises the lamp shells.
- DERIVATIVES **brachiopod** /'brakɪə(ʊ)pɒd/ noun.
- ORIGIN modern Latin (plural), from Greek *brakhiōn* 'arm' + *pous, pod-* 'foot'.

brachiosaurus /ˌbrakɪə(ʊ)'sɔːrəs/ ▶ noun a huge herbivorous dinosaur of the late Jurassic to mid Cretaceous periods, with forelegs much longer than the hind legs.
- ● Genus *Brachiosaurus*, infraorder Sauropoda, order Saurischia.
- ORIGIN modern Latin, from Greek *brakhiōn* 'arm' + *sauros* 'lizard'.

brachistochrone /brə'kɪstəkrəʊn/ ▶ noun a curve between two points along which a body can move under gravity in a shorter time than for any other curve.
- ORIGIN late 18th cent.: from Greek *brakhistos* 'shortest' + *khronos* 'time'.

brachy- /'braki/ ▶ combining form short: *brachycephalic.*
- ORIGIN from Greek *brakhus* 'short'.

brachycephalic /ˌbrakɪsɪ'falɪk, -kɛ'falɪk/ ▶ adjective having a relatively broad, short skull (typically with the breadth at least 80 per cent of the length). Often contrasted with **DOLICHO-CEPHALIC**.
- DERIVATIVES **brachycephaly** noun.

bracing ▶ adjective 1 fresh and invigorating: *the bracing sea air.*
2 [attrib.] (of a support) serving to brace a structure: *bracing struts.*
- DERIVATIVES **bracingly** adverb (in sense 1), **bracingness** noun (in sense 1).

brack ▶ noun Irish a cake or bun containing dried fruit.
- ORIGIN shortening of **BARMBRACK**.

bracken ▶ noun [mass noun] a tall fern with coarse lobed fronds, which occurs worldwide and can cover large areas.
- ● *Pteridium aquilinum*, family Dennstaedtiaceae.
- ■ informal any large coarse fern resembling this.
- ORIGIN Middle English: of Scandinavian origin; related to Danish *bregne*, Swedish *bräken*.

bracket ▶ noun 1 each of a pair of marks ( ) [ ] { } ⟨ ⟩ used to enclose words or figures so as to separate them from the context: *symbols are given in brackets.*
2 [with adj. or noun modifier] a category of people or things that are similar or fall between specified limits: *those in a high income bracket.*
3 a right-angled support attached to and projecting from a wall for holding a shelf, lamp, or other object.
- ■ a shelf fixed with such a support to a wall. ■ (**the bracket**) informal, dated a person's nose or jaw.
4 Military the distance between two artillery shots fired either side of the target to establish range.
▶ verb (**bracketed**, **bracketing**) [with obj.] 1 (usu. **be bracketed**) place (one or more people or things) in the same category or group: *he is sometimes bracketed with the 'new wave' of film directors.*
2 enclose (words or figures) in brackets: [as adj. **bracketed**] *the relevant data are included as bracketed points.*
- ■ Mathematics enclose (a complex expression) in brackets to denote that the whole of the expression rather than just a part of it has a particular relation, such as multiplication or division, to another expression.
- ■ figurative surround or enclose (someone or something) physically: *the lines of exhaustion bracketing his mouth.* ■ put (a belief or matter) aside temporarily: *he bracketed off the question of God himself.*
3 hold or attach (something) by means of a right-angled support: *pipes should be bracketed.*
4 Military establish the range of (a target) by firing

two preliminary shots, one short of the target and the other beyond it.
- ■ Photography establish (the correct exposure) by taking several pictures with slightly more or less exposure.
- ORIGIN late 16th cent.: from French *braguette* or Spanish *bragueta* 'codpiece, bracket, corbel', from Provençal *braga*, from Latin *braca*, (plural) *bracae* 'breeches'.

bracket fungus ▶ noun a fungus which forms shelf-like projections on the trunks of living or dead trees, sending hyphae into the wood and sometimes causing the death of the tree or decay of the timber.
- ● Several families in the order Aphyllophorales, class Hymenomycetes.

brackish ▶ adjective (of water) slightly salty, as present in river estuaries.
- ■ (of fish or other organisms) living in or requiring such water.
- DERIVATIVES **brackishness** noun.
- ORIGIN mid 16th cent.: from obsolete *brack* 'salty', from Middle Low German, Middle Dutch *brac*.

braconid /'brakənɪd/ ▶ noun Entomology a small parasitic wasp of a family (Braconidae) which is related to the ichneumons. Unlike the latter, braconids lay numerous eggs in a single host.
- ORIGIN late 19th cent.: from modern Latin *Braconidae* (plural), formed irregularly from Greek *brakhus* 'short'.

bract ▶ noun Botany a modified leaf or scale, typically small, with a flower or flower cluster in its axil. Bracts are sometimes larger and more brightly coloured than the true flower, as in poinsettia.
- DERIVATIVES **bracteate** /'braktɪət/ adjective.
- ORIGIN late 18th cent.: from Latin *bractea* 'thin plate of metal'.

bracteate /'braktɪət, -tɪeɪt/ ▶ noun Archaeology an ornament or plate of thinly beaten precious metal, typically a thin gold disc.
- ORIGIN early 19th cent.: from Latin *bracteatus*, from *bractea* (see **BRACT**).

brad ▶ noun a nail of rectangular cross section with a flat tip and a small, typically asymmetrical head.
- ORIGIN late Middle English: from Old Norse *broddr* 'spike'.

bradawl /'bradɔːl/ ▶ noun a tool for boring holes, resembling a small, sharpened screwdriver.
- ORIGIN early 19th cent.: from **BRAD** + **AWL**.

Bradbury¹, Sir Malcolm (Stanley) (1932–2000), English novelist, critic, and academic. As a novelist he was known for satires of university life such as *The History Man* (1975) and *Rates of Exchange* (1983).

Bradbury², Ray (b.1920), American writer of science fiction; full name *Raymond Douglas Bradbury*. Notable works: *The Martian Chronicles* (short story collection, 1950), *Fahrenheit 451* (novel, 1951).

Bradenham ham /'brad(ə)nəm/ ▶ noun [mass noun] trademark a dark sweet-cured ham.

Bradford an industrial city in northern England, a unitary council formerly in Yorkshire; pop. 449,100 (1990).

Bradley, James (1693–1762), English astronomer. Bradley was appointed Astronomer Royal in 1742. He discovered the aberration of light and also observed the oscillation of the earth's axis, which he termed nutation. His star catalogue was published posthumously.

Bradman, Don (1908–2001), Australian cricketer; full name *Sir Donald George Bradman*. Bradman holds the record for the highest Australian test score against England (334 in 1930). His test match batting average of 99.94 was well above that of any other cricketer of any era.

bradoon /brə'duːn/ ▶ noun variant spelling of **BRIDOON**.

Bradshaw ▶ noun a timetable of all passenger trains in Britain, issued 1839–1961.
- ORIGIN named after its first publisher, George Bradshaw (1801–53), printer and engraver.

bradycardia /ˌbradɪ'kɑːdɪə/ ▶ noun [mass noun] Medicine abnormally slow heart action.
- ORIGIN late 19th cent.: from Greek *bradus* 'slow' + *kardia* 'heart'.

bradykinin /ˌbradɪ'kʌɪnɪn/ ▶ noun [mass noun] Biochemistry a compound released in the blood in some circumstances which causes contraction of smooth muscle and dilation of blood vessels. It is a peptide with nine amino-acid residues.

– ORIGIN 1940s: from Greek *bradus* 'slow' + *kinēsis* 'motion' + **-IN**[1].

brae /breɪ/ ▶ noun Scottish a steep bank or hillside.
– ORIGIN Middle English: from Old Norse *brá* 'eyelash'. Compare with **BROW**[1], in which a similar sense development occurred.

Braeburn /'breɪbə:n/ ▶ noun a dessert apple of a variety with crisp flesh, first grown in New Zealand.
– ORIGIN 1950s: from *Braeburn Orchards*, where it was first grown commercially.

brag ▶ verb (**bragged**, **bragging**) [reporting verb] say something in a boastful manner: [with clause] *he bragged that he was sure of victory* | [no obj.] *they were bragging about how easy it had been.*
▶ noun 1 [mass noun] a gambling card game which is a simplified form of poker.
2 [in sing.] a boastful statement; an act of talking boastfully.
▶ adjective [attrib.] informal, chiefly US excellent; first-rate.
– DERIVATIVES **bragger** noun, **braggingly** adverb.
– ORIGIN Middle English (as an adjective in the sense 'boastful'): of unknown origin (French *braguer* is recorded only later).

Braga /'bra:gə/ a city in northern Portugal, capital of a mountainous district of the same name; pop. 90,535 (1991).

Braganza[1] /brə'ganzə/ a city in NE Portugal, capital of a mountainous district of the same name; pop. 16,550 (1991). It was the original seat of the Braganza dynasty. Portuguese name **BRAGANÇA** /brə'γãsə/.

Braganza[2] /brə'ganzə/ the dynasty that ruled Portugal from 1640 until the end of the monarchy in 1910 and Brazil (on its independence from Portugal) from 1822 until the formation of a republic in 1889.

Bragg, Sir William Henry (1862–1942), English physicist, a founder of solid-state physics. He collaborated with his son, **Sir (William) Lawrence Bragg** (1890–1971), in developing the technique of X-ray diffraction for determining the atomic structure of crystals; for this they shared the 1915 Nobel Prize for Physics.

braggadocio /ˌbragə'dəʊtʃɪəʊ/ ▶ noun [mass noun] boastful or arrogant behaviour.
– ORIGIN late 16th cent. (denoting a boaster): from *Braggadocchio*, the name of a braggart in Spenser's *Faerie Queene*, from **BRAG** or **BRAGGART** + the Italian suffix *-occio*, denoting something large of its kind.

braggart /'bragət, -a:t/ ▶ noun a person who boasts about their achievements or possessions.
– ORIGIN late 16th cent.: from French *bragard*, from *braguer* 'to brag'.

Brahe /'bra:hi, 'bra:ə/, Tycho (1546–1601), Danish astronomer. He built an observatory equipped with precision instruments, but despite demonstrating that comets follow sun-centred paths he adhered to a geocentric picture for the planets.

Brahma /'bra:mə/ 1 the creator god in Hinduism, who forms a triad with Vishnu and Shiva. Brahma was an important god of late Vedic religion, but has been little worshipped since the 5th century AD.
2 another term for **BRAHMAN** (in sense 2).
– ORIGIN from Sanskrit *brahman*.

brahma /'bra:mə/ ▶ noun short for **BRAHMAPUTRA**.

Brahman /'bra:mən/ ▶ noun (pl. **-mans**) 1 (also **Brahmin**) a member of the highest Hindu caste, that of the priesthood. [ORIGIN: from Sanskrit *brāhmaṇa*.]
2 [without article] the ultimate reality underlying all phenomena in the Hindu scriptures. [ORIGIN: from Sanskrit *brahman*.]
3 US spelling of **BRAHMIN** (in sense 3).
– DERIVATIVES **Brahmanic** /-'manɪk/ adjective, **Brahmanical** /-'manɪk(ə)l/ adjective.

Brahmana /'bra:mənə/ ▶ noun (in Hinduism) any of the lengthy commentaries on the Vedas, composed in Sanskrit c.900–700 BC and containing expository material relating to Vedic sacrificial ritual.

Brahmanism /'bra:mə,nɪz(ə)m/ (also **Brahminism**) ▶ noun [mass noun] the complex sacrificial religion that emerged in post-Vedic India (c.900 BC) under the influence of the dominant priesthood (Brahmans), an early stage in the development of Hinduism.

Brahmaputra /ˌbra:mə'pu:trə/ a river of southern Asia, rising in the Himalayas and flowing 2,900 km (1,800 miles) through Tibet, NE India, and Bangladesh, to join the Ganges at its delta on the Bay of Bengal.

brahmaputra /ˌbra:mə'pu:trə/ (also **brahma**) ▶ noun a chicken of a large Asian breed.
– ORIGIN mid 19th cent.: named after the **BRAHMAPUTRA**, where it originated.

Brahmin /'bra:mɪn/ ▶ noun 1 variant spelling of **BRAHMAN** (in sense 1).
2 US a socially or culturally superior person, especially one from New England.
3 (also **Brahminy bull** or US **Brahman**) an ox of a humped breed originally domesticated in India, which is tolerant of heat and drought and is now kept widely in tropical and warm-temperate countries. Also called **ZEBU**.
● *Bos indicus*, family Bovidae; now usually included under the name *B. taurus* with other domestic cattle.
– DERIVATIVES **Brahminical** adjective (only in senses 1 and 2).

Brahms /bra:mz/, Johannes (1833–97), German composer and pianist. He eschewed programme music and opera and concentrated on traditional forms. He wrote four symphonies, four concertos, chamber and piano music, choral works including the *German Requiem* (1857–68), and nearly 200 songs.
– DERIVATIVES **Brahmsian** adjective.

Brahms and Liszt ▶ adjective [predic.] Brit. informal drunk.
– ORIGIN 1970s: rhyming slang for 'pissed'.

Brahui /brə'hu:i/ ▶ noun (pl. same) 1 a member of a pastoral people of western Pakistan.
2 [mass noun] the language of this people, a Dravidian language isolated for several thousand years from other members of the family. It has nearly 2 million speakers.
▶ adjective of or relating to this people or their language.

braid ▶ noun 1 [mass noun] threads of silk, cotton, or other material woven into a decorative band for edging or trimming garments: *a coat trimmed with gold braid* | [count noun] *fancy braids.*
2 a length of hair made up of three or more interlaced strands: *her hair curled neatly in blonde braids.*
■ a length made up of three or more interlaced strands of any flexible material: *a flexible copper braid.*
▶ verb [with obj.] 1 interlace three or more strands of (hair or other flexible material) to form a length: *their long hair was tightly braided.*
2 (often as adj. **braided**) edge or trim (a garment) with braid: *braided red trousers.*
3 (usu. as adj. **braided**) (of a river or stream) flow into shallow interconnected channels divided by deposited earth or alluvium.
– ORIGIN Old English *bregdan* 'make a sudden movement', also 'interweave', of Germanic origin; related to Dutch *breien* (verb).

braiding ▶ noun [mass noun] decorative braid or braided work: *curtains heavy with gold braiding.*

brail Sailing ▶ noun (**brails**) small ropes that are led from the leech of a fore-and-aft sail to pulleys on the mast for temporarily furling it.
▶ verb [with obj.] (**brail a sail up**) furl (a sail) by hauling on such ropes.
– ORIGIN late Middle English: from Old French *braiel*, from medieval Latin *bracale* 'girdle', from *braca* 'breeches'.

Brăila /brə'i:lə/ an industrial city and port on the Danube, in eastern Romania; pop. 236,300 (1993).

Braille[1] /breɪl/, French bʀaj/, Louis (1809–52), French educationist. Blind from the age of 3, by the age of 15 he had developed his own system of raised-point reading and writing, which was officially adopted two years after his death.

Braille[2] /breɪl/ ▶ noun [mass noun] a form of written language for the blind, in which characters are represented by patterns of raised dots that are felt with the fingertips.
▶ verb [with obj.] print or transcribe in Braille.

Brain, Dennis (1921–57), English French-horn player. His mastery of the instrument's entire range inspired many composers, including Benjamin Britten and Paul Hindemith, to write works for him.

brain ▶ noun 1 an organ of soft nervous tissue contained in the skull of vertebrates, functioning as the coordinating centre of sensation and intellectual and nervous activity.
■ (**brains**) the substance of such an organ, typically that of an animal, used as food. ■ informal an electronic device with functions comparable to those of the human brain.

The human brain consists of three main parts. (i) The forebrain, greatly developed into the cerebrum, consists of two hemispheres joined by a bridge of nerve fibres, and is responsible for the exercise of thought and control of speech. (ii) The midbrain, the upper part of the tapering brainstem, contains cells concerned in eye movements. (iii) The hindbrain, the lower part of the brainstem, contains cells responsible for breathing and for regulating heart action, the flow of digestive juices, and other unconscious actions and processes. The cerebellum, which lies behind the brain stem, plays an important role in the execution of highly skilled movements.

2 intellectual capacity: *I didn't have enough brains for the sciences* | [mass noun] *success requires brain as well as brawn.*
■ (**the brains**) informal a clever person who supplies the ideas and plans for a group of people: *Tom was the brains of the outfit.* ■ a person's mind: *a tiny alarm bell began to ring in her brain.*
▶ verb [with obj.] informal hit (someone) hard on the head with an object: *she brained me with a rolling pin.*
– PHRASES **have (got) something on the brain** informal be obsessed with something: *John has cars on the brain.*
– ORIGIN Old English *brægen*, of West Germanic origin; related to Dutch *brein.*

brainbox ▶ noun Brit. informal a very clever person.

brain cell ▶ noun a cell in the tissue of the brain.
■ informal used to refer to someone's intellectual power: *it does help if the student has more than one brain cell.*

brainchild ▶ noun (pl. **-children**) informal an idea or invention which is considered to be a particular person's creation: *the statue is the brainchild of a local landscape artist.*

brain coral ▶ noun a compact coral with a convoluted surface resembling that of the brain.
● *Diploria* and other genera, order Scleractinia.

brain damage ▶ noun [mass noun] injury to the brain that impairs its functions, especially permanently.
– DERIVATIVES **brain-damaged** adjective.

brain-dead ▶ adjective having suffered brain death: *brain-dead patients.*
■ informal extremely stupid: *a brain-dead computer zombie.*

brain death ▶ noun [mass noun] irreversible brain damage causing the end of independent respiration, regarded as indicative of death.

brain drain ▶ noun [in sing.] informal the emigration of highly trained or qualified people from a particular country.

Braine, John (Gerard) (1922–86), English novelist, famous for his first novel, *Room at the Top* (1957), whose opportunistic hero was hailed as a representative example of an 'angry young man'.

brained ▶ adjective [in combination] (of vertebrates) having a brain of a certain size or kind: *large-brained mammals.*
■ derogatory (of a person) having an intellectual capacity of a certain quality or kind: *half-brained twits.*

brain fever ▶ noun [mass noun] dated inflammation of the brain.

brainfever bird ▶ noun the common hawk cuckoo of India and Sri Lanka, which has a monotonous and maddeningly persistent call.
● *Cuculus varius*, family Cuculidae.

brain fungus ▶ noun 1 (also **yellow brain fungus**) a soft yellow gelatinous fungus with a lobed and folded surface, living on dead wood in both Eurasia and North America.
● *Tremella mesenterica*, family Tremellaceae, class Hymenomycetes.
2 another term for **CAULIFLOWER FUNGUS**.

brainiac ▶ noun N. Amer. informal an exceptionally intelligent person.
– ORIGIN 1950s: from the name of a superintelligent alien character of the Superman comic strip, from a blend of **BRAIN** and **MANIAC**.

brainless ▶ adjective stupid; foolish: *a brainless bimbo.*
– DERIVATIVES **brainlessly** adverb, **brainlessness** noun.

brainpan ▶ noun informal, chiefly N. Amer. a person's skull.

brainpower ▸ noun [mass noun] mental ability; intelligence.

brainstem ▸ noun Anatomy the central trunk of the mammalian brain, consisting of the medulla oblongata, pons, and midbrain, and continuing downwards to form the spinal cord.

brainstorm ▸ noun **1** informal a moment in which one is suddenly unable to think clearly or act sensibly.
2 a spontaneous group discussion to produce ideas and ways of solving problems.
■ informal, chiefly N. Amer. a sudden clever idea.
▸ verb [no obj.] produce an idea or way of solving a problem by holding a spontaneous group discussion: [as noun modifier] (**brainstorming**) a brainstorming session.

brains trust ▸ noun Brit. a group of experts who give impromptu answers to questions on topics of general or current interest in front of an audience or on the radio.
■ another term for BRAIN TRUST.

brain-teaser (also **brain-twister**) ▸ noun informal a problem or puzzle, typically one designed to be solved for amusement.
– DERIVATIVES **brain-teasing** adjective.

brain trust ▸ noun N. Amer. a group of experts appointed to advise a government or politician.

brainwash ▸ verb [with obj.] pressurize (someone) into adopting radically different beliefs by using systematic and often forcible means: people are brainwashed into believing family life is the best | [as noun **brainwashing**] victims of brainwashing.

brainwave ▸ noun (usu. **brainwaves**) an electrical impulse in the brain.
■ [usu. in sing.] informal a sudden clever idea.

brainy ▸ adjective (**brainier**, **brainiest**) having or showing intelligence: a brainy discussion | she was brainy, except for maths.
– DERIVATIVES **brainily** adverb, **braininess** noun.

braise ▸ verb [with obj.] fry (food) lightly and then stew it slowly in a closed container: [as adj. **braised**] braised veal.
– ORIGIN mid 18th cent.: from French braiser, from braise 'live coals' (in which the container was formerly placed).

brak /brak/ S. African ▸ adjective (of water or soil) brackish or alkaline.
▸ noun [mass noun] brackishness or alkalinity of soil or water.
– ORIGIN Afrikaans, from Dutch.

brake¹ ▸ noun a device for slowing or stopping a moving vehicle, typically by applying pressure to the wheels: he slammed on his brakes | [as modifier] a brake pedal.
■ figurative a thing that slows or hinders a process: constrained resources will act as a brake on research. ■ another term for BRAKE VAN.
▸ verb [no obj.] make a moving vehicle slow down or stop by using a brake: she had to brake hard to avoid a milk float | [as adj. **braking**] an anti-lock braking system.
– ORIGIN late 18th cent.: of unknown origin.

brake² ▸ noun historical an open horse-drawn carriage with four wheels.
– ORIGIN mid 19th cent.: variant of BREAK².

brake³ ▸ noun a toothed instrument used for crushing flax and hemp.
■ (also **brake harrow**) a heavy machine formerly used in agriculture for breaking up large lumps of earth.
– ORIGIN late Middle English: possibly related to Middle Low German brake and Dutch braak, and perhaps also to BREAK¹.

brake⁴ ▸ noun archaic or poetic/literary a thicket. See also FERNBRAKE.
– ORIGIN Old English bracu (first recorded in the plural in fearnbraca 'thickets of fern'), related to Middle Low German brake 'branch, stump'.

brake⁵ (also **brake fern**) ▸ noun a coarse fern of warm and tropical countries, frequently having the fronds divided into long linear segments.
● Genus Pteris, family Pteridaceae.
■ archaic term for BRACKEN.
– ORIGIN Middle English: perhaps an abbreviation of BRACKEN (interpreted as plural).

brake⁶ archaic past of BREAK¹.

brake block ▸ noun a block of hard material pressed against the rim of a wheel to slow it down by friction, especially one of a pair made of hardened rubber used on a bicycle.

brake caliper ▸ noun see CALIPER (sense 1).

brake disc ▸ noun the disc attached to the wheel in a disc brake.

brake drum ▸ noun a broad, very short cylinder attached to a wheel, against which the brake shoes press in a drum brake.

brake fluid ▸ noun [mass noun] fluid used in a hydraulic brake system.

brake harrow ▸ noun see BRAKE³.

brake horsepower ▸ noun (pl. same) an imperial unit of power, equal to one horsepower but used only as a measure of the power available at the shaft of an engine.
■ the available power of an engine, assessed by measuring the force needed to brake it.

brake light ▸ noun a red light at the back of a vehicle that is automatically illuminated when the brakes are applied.

brake lining ▸ noun a layer of hard material attached to a brake shoe or brake pad to increase friction against the drum or disc.

brakeman ▸ noun (pl. **-men**) (Brit. also **brakesman**) chiefly N. Amer. **1** a railway worker responsible for a train's brakes or for other duties such as those of a guard.
2 a person in charge of brakes, especially in a bobsleigh.

brake pad ▸ noun a thin block, typically one of a pair, which presses on to the disc in a disc brake.

brake shoe ▸ noun a long curved block, typically one of a pair, which presses on to the drum in a drum brake.

brake van ▸ noun Brit. a railway carriage or wagon from which the train's brakes can be controlled by the guard.

Bramah /ˈbrɑːmə/, Joseph (1748–1814), English inventor. One of the most influential engineers of the Industrial Revolution, Bramah is best known for his hydraulic press, used for heavy forging.

Bramante /brəˈmanteɪ/, Donato (di Angelo) (1444–1514), Italian architect. As architect to Pope Julius II he drew up the first plan for the new St Peter's (begun in 1506), instigating the concept of a huge central dome.

bramble ▸ noun a prickly scrambling shrub of the rose family, especially a blackberry.
■ chiefly Brit. the fruit of the blackberry.
▸ verb [no obj.] [usu. as noun **brambling**] Brit. gather blackberries.
– DERIVATIVES **brambly** adjective.
– ORIGIN Old English bræmbel, bræmel, of Germanic origin; related to BROOM.

bramble shark ▸ noun a heavy-bodied, dull-coloured shark of the tropical Atlantic, with numerous thornlike spines on the back.
● Echinorhinus brucus, family Echinorhinidae.

brambling /ˈbramblɪŋ/ ▸ noun a northern Eurasian finch with a white rump, related to the chaffinch. The male has a black head and orange breast in summer.
● Fringilla montifringilla, family Fringillidae.
– ORIGIN mid 16th cent.: perhaps from or related to the obsolete German synonym Brämling, related to BRAMBLE.

Bramley (also **Bramley's seedling**) ▸ noun (pl. **-eys**) a green English cooking apple of a large variety with firm flesh.
– ORIGIN early 20th cent.: named after Matthew Bramley, the English butcher in whose garden it is said to have first grown c.1850.

bran ▸ noun [mass noun] pieces of grain husk separated from flour after milling.
– ORIGIN Middle English: from Old French, of unknown origin.

Branagh /ˈbranə/, Kenneth (Charles) (b.1960), English actor, producer, and director. With the Royal Shakespeare Company he attracted critical acclaim for roles such as Henry V. He has also directed and starred in films such as Hamlet (1996).

branch ▸ noun a part of a tree which grows out from the trunk or from a bough.
■ a lateral extension or subdivision extending from the main part of something, typically one extending from a river, road, or railway. ■ a division or office of a large business or organization, operating locally or having a particular function: he went to work at our Birmingham branch. ■ a conceptual subdivision of something, especially a family, group of languages, or a subject: a branch of mathematics called graph theory.
▸ verb [no obj.] (of a road or path) divide into one or more subdivisions: follow this track south until it branches into two.
■ (of a tree or plant) bear or send out branches: [as adj. **branched**] the common sea lavender can be identified by its branched stem. ■ (**branch off**) diverge from the main route or part: the road branched off at the market town. ■ (**branch out**) extend or expand one's activities or interests in a new direction: the company is branching out into Europe.
– DERIVATIVES **branchlet** noun, **branch-like** adjective, **branchy** adjective.
– ORIGIN Middle English: from Old French branche, from Late Latin branca 'paw'.

branchia /ˈbraŋkɪə/ ▸ noun (pl. **branchiae** /-kiː/) the gills of fish and some invertebrate animals.
– DERIVATIVES **branchial** adjective
– ORIGIN late 17th cent.: from Latin branchia, (plural) branchiae, from Greek brankhia (plural).

Branchiopoda /ˌbraŋkɪˈpəʊdə/ Zoology a class of small aquatic crustaceans that includes water fleas and fairy shrimps, which are distinguished by having gills upon the feet.
– DERIVATIVES **branchiopod** /ˈbraŋkɪ(ə)pɒd/ noun.
– ORIGIN modern Latin (plural), from Greek brankhia 'gills' + pous, pod- 'foot'.

branch line ▸ noun a secondary railway line running from a main line to a terminus.

branch water (also **branch**) ▸ noun [mass noun] US ordinary water, especially when added to alcoholic drinks.

Brancusi /braŋˈkuːzi/, Constantin (1876–1957), Romanian sculptor, who spent much of his working life in France. His sculpture represents an attempt to move away from a representational art and to capture the essence of forms by reducing them to their ultimate, almost abstract, simplicity.

brand ▸ noun **1** a type of product manufactured by a particular company under a particular name: a new brand of soap powder.
■ a brand name: the firm will market computer software under its own brand. ■ a particular type or kind of something: the Finnish brand of democratic socialism.
2 an identifying mark burned on livestock or (especially in former times) criminals or slaves with a branding iron.
■ archaic a branding iron. ■ figurative a habit, trait, or quality that causes someone public shame or disgrace: the brand of Paula's dipsomania.
3 a piece of burning or smouldering wood: he took two burning brands from the fire.
4 poetic/literary a sword.
▸ verb [with obj.] **1** mark (an animal or, in former times, a criminal or slave) with a branding iron.
■ mark indelibly: an ointment that branded her with unsightly violet-coloured splotches. ■ describe (someone or something) as having a nature or quality regarded as bad or shameful: the media was intent on branding us as communists | [with obj. and complement] she was branded a liar.
2 assign a brand name to: [as adj. **branded**] cut-price branded goods.
■ [as noun **branding**] the promotion of a particular product or company by means of advertising and distinctive design.
– DERIVATIVES **brander** noun.
– ORIGIN Old English brand 'burning' (also in sense 3), of Germanic origin; related to German Brand, also to BURN¹. The verb sense 'mark permanently with a hot iron' dates from late Middle English, giving rise to the noun sense 'a mark of ownership made by branding' (mid 17th cent.), whence sense 1 (early 19th cent.).

brandade /brɒˈdɑːd/ ▸ noun a Provençal dish consisting of salt cod mixed into a purée with olive oil and milk.
– ORIGIN French, from modern Provençal brandado, literally 'something that has been shaken'.

Brandenburg /ˈbrandənbəːɡ, German ˈbrandn̩ˌbʊrk/ a state of NE Germany; capital, Potsdam. The modern state corresponds to the western part of the former Prussian electorate, of which the eastern part was ceded to Poland after the Second World War.

Brandenburg Gate one of the city gates of Berlin (built 1788–91), the only one that survives. After the construction of the Berlin Wall in 1961 it stood in East Berlin, a conspicuous symbol of a divided city. It was reopened in December 1989.

brand extension ▶ noun an instance of using an established brand name or trademark on new products, so as to increase sales.

branding iron ▶ noun a metal implement which is heated and used to brand livestock (or especially in former times) criminals or slaves.

brandish ▶ verb [with obj.] wave or flourish (something, especially a weapon) as a threat or in anger or excitement.
– DERIVATIVES **brandisher** noun.
– ORIGIN Middle English: from Old French *brandiss-*, lengthened stem of *brandir*; ultimately of Germanic origin and related to **BRAND**.

brand leader ▶ noun the best-selling or most highly regarded product or brand of its type.

brandling ▶ noun a red earthworm with rings of a brighter colour, typically found in manure, and used as bait by anglers and in composting kitchen waste.
● *Eisenia fetida*, family Lumbricidae.
– ORIGIN mid 17th cent.: from **BRAND** + **-LING**.

brand loyalty ▶ noun [mass noun] the tendency of some consumers to continue buying the same brand of goods despite the availability of competing brands.

brand name ▶ noun a name given by the maker to a product or range of products, especially a trademark.

brand new ▶ adjective completely new.

Brando, Marlon (b.1924), American actor. An exponent of method acting, he first attracted critical acclaim in the stage production of *A Streetcar Named Desire* (1947); he starred in the film version four years later. Other notable films: *On the Waterfront* (1954, for which he won an Oscar) and *The Godfather* (1972).

Brands Hatch a motor-racing circuit near Farningham in Kent.

Brandt[1] /brant/, Bill (1904–83), German-born British photographer; full name *Hermann Wilhelm Brandt*. He is best known for his almost abstract treatment of the nude, as in *Perspectives of Nudes* (1961).

Brandt[2] /brant/, Willy (1913–92), German statesman, Chancellor of West Germany 1969–74; born *Karl Herbert Frahm*. He achieved international recognition for his policy of détente and the opening of relations with the countries of the Eastern bloc (Ostpolitik). Nobel Peace Prize (1971).

Brand X ▶ noun a name used for an unidentified brand contrasted unfavourably with a product of the same type which is being promoted.

brandy ▶ noun (pl. **-ies**) [mass noun] a strong alcoholic spirit distilled from wine or fermented fruit juice.
– ORIGIN mid 17th cent.: from earlier *brandwine*, *brandewine*, from Dutch *brandewijn*, from *branden* 'burn, distil' + *wijn* 'wine'.

brandy-bottle ▶ noun the common yellow water lily, the flowers of which produce an alcoholic smell which is attractive to beetles. See **WATER LILY**.

brandy butter ▶ noun [mass noun] Brit. a stiff mixture of brandy, butter, and sugar, served with hot desserts.

brandy snap ▶ noun a crisp, rolled, gingerbread wafer, typically filled with cream.

branks /braŋks/ ▶ plural noun historical an instrument of punishment for a scolding woman, consisting of an iron framework for the head and a sharp metal gag for restraining the tongue.
– ORIGIN mid 16th cent.: origin uncertain; compare with German *Pranger* 'a pillory or bit for a horse' and Dutch *prang* 'a fetter'; also with late Middle English *barnacle(s)*, denoting a powerful bit for restraining a horse.

branle /'bran(ə)l/ ▶ noun a 16th-century court dance of French origin.
– ORIGIN late 16th cent.: from French, from *branler* 'shake'.

brannigan /'braniɡ(ə)n/ (also **branigan**) ▶ noun N. Amer. informal a brawl or violent argument.
– ORIGIN late 19th cent.: of unknown origin; perhaps from the surname *Brannigan*.

Branson, Sir Richard (b.1950), English businessman. He made his name with the company Virgin Records, which he set up in 1969. He later influenced the opening up of air routes with Virgin Atlantic Airways, established in 1984.

brant ▶ noun North American term for **BRENT GOOSE**.

bran tub ▶ noun Brit. a lucky dip in which the hidden items are buried in bran.

Braque /brak, French bʀak/, Georges (1882–1963), French painter. His collages, which introduced commercial lettering and fragmented objects into pictures to contrast the real with the 'illusory' painted image, were the first stage in the development of synthetic cubism.

brash[1] ▶ adjective self-assertive in a rude, noisy, or overbearing way: *he was brash, cocky, and arrogant.*
■ (of a place or object) having an ostentatious or tasteless appearance: *the cafe was a brash new building.* ■ (of colour) too bright; loud: *the bright, brash scarlet of her hair.*
– DERIVATIVES **brashly** adverb, **brashness** noun.
– ORIGIN early 19th cent. (originally dialect); perhaps a form of **RASH**[1].

brash[2] ▶ noun [mass noun] a mass of fragments, in particular:
■ loose broken rock or ice. ■ clippings from hedges, shrubs, or other plants.
– ORIGIN late 18th cent.: of unknown origin.

Brasil /bra'ziw/ Portuguese name for **BRAZIL**[1].

Brasilia /brə'zɪlɪə/ the capital, since 1960, of Brazil; pop. 1,601,100 (1991). Designed by Lúcio Costa in 1956, the city was located in the centre of the country with the intention of drawing people away from the crowded coastal areas.

Brasov /bra'ʃov/ a city in Romania; pop. 352,640 (1989). It belonged to Hungary until after the First World War, and was ceded to Romania in 1920. Hungarian name **BRASSÓ**; German name **KRONSTADT**.

brass ▶ noun [mass noun] a yellow alloy of copper and zinc: [as modifier] *a brass plate on the door.*
■ [count noun] a decorative object made of such an alloy: *shining brasses stood on the mantelpiece.* ■ (also **horse brass**) [count noun] a round flat brass ornament for the harness of a draught horse. ■ [count noun] Brit. a memorial, typically a medieval one, consisting of a flat piece of inscribed brass, laid in the floor or set into the wall of a church. ■ [count noun] a brass block or die used for stamping a design on a book binding. ■ Brit. informal money: *they wanted to spend their newly acquired brass.* ■ Music brass wind instruments (including trumpet, horn, and trombone) forming a band or a section of an orchestra: *the brass and percussion were consistently too loud.* ■ (also **top brass**) informal people in authority or of high military rank. ■ informal in extended or metaphorical use referring to a person's hardness or effrontery: *I didn't think that his mother would have the brass neck to come round here.*
– PHRASES **brassed off** Brit. informal exasperated. **a brass farthing** [with negative] informal no money or assets at all: *she hasn't got two brass farthings to rub together.* **get down to brass tacks** informal start to consider the basic facts or practical details. **the brass ring** N. Amer. informal success, typically as regarded as a reward for ambition or hard work. [ORIGIN: with reference to the reward of a free ride given on a merry-go-round to the person hooking a brass ring suspended over the horses.] **where there's muck there's brass** see **MUCK**.
– ORIGIN Old English *bræs*, of unknown origin.

brassard /'brasɑːd/ ▶ noun a band worn on the sleeve, typically with a uniform.
■ historical a piece of armour for the upper arm.
– ORIGIN late 16th cent. (denoting a piece of armour for the upper arm): from French, from *bras* 'arm'.

brass band ▶ noun a group of musicians playing brass instruments and sometimes also percussion.

brasserie /'brasəri/ ▶ noun (pl. **-ies**) a restaurant in France or one in a French style, typically serving inexpensive food.
– ORIGIN mid 19th cent.: French, originally 'brewery', from *brasser* 'to brew'.

Brassey /'brasi/, Thomas (1805–70), English engineer and railway contractor. He built more than 10,000 km (6,500 miles) of railways in Europe, India, South America, and Australia.

brass hat ▶ noun Brit. informal a high-ranking officer in the armed forces.
– ORIGIN late 19th cent.: so named because of the gilt insignia on the caps of such officers.

brassica /'brasɪkə/ ▶ noun a plant of a genus that includes cabbage, swede, rape, and mustard.
● Genus *Brassica*, family Cruciferae.

– ORIGIN modern Latin, from Latin, literally 'cabbage'.

brassie /'brasi, 'brɑːsi/ (also **brassy**) ▶ noun (pl. **-ies**) Golf, informal a number two wood.
– ORIGIN late 19th cent.: so named because the wood was originally shod with brass.

brassiere /'brazɪə, -s-, 'braːzɪɛ/ ▶ noun full form of **BRA**.
– ORIGIN early 20th cent.: from French, literally 'bodice, child's vest'.

brass monkey ▶ noun informal used in phrases to refer to extremely cold weather: *it's brass monkey weather tonight* | *it was cold enough to freeze the balls off a brass monkey.*
– ORIGIN late 19th cent.: from a type of brass rack or 'monkey' in which cannonballs were stored and which contracted in very cold weather, ejecting the balls.

Brassó /'brɒʃoː/ Hungarian name for **BRASOV**.

brass rubbing ▶ noun [mass noun] the action of rubbing heelball or chalk over paper laid on an engraved brass to reproduce its design.
■ [count noun] an image created by doing this.

brassware ▶ noun [mass noun] utensils or other objects made of brass.

brassy[1] ▶ adjective (**brassier**, **brassiest**) resembling brass in colour; bright or harsh yellow.
■ sounding like a brass musical instrument; harsh and loud. ■ (of a person, typically a woman) tastelessly showy or loud in appearance or manner: *her brassy, audacious exterior.*
– DERIVATIVES **brassily** adverb, **brassiness** noun.

brassy[2] ▶ noun variant spelling of **BRASSIE**.

brat ▶ noun informal, derogatory or humorous a child, typically a badly behaved one.
– DERIVATIVES **brattish** adjective, **brattishness** noun, **bratty** adjective.
– ORIGIN mid 16th cent.: perhaps an abbreviation of synonymous Scots *bratchet*, from Old French *brachet* 'hound, bitch'; or perhaps from dialect *brat* 'rough garment, rag', based on Old Irish *bratt* 'cloak'.

Bratislava /ˌbratɪ'slɑːvə/ the capital of Slovakia, a port on the Danube; pop. 441,450 (1991). From 1526 to 1784 it was the capital of Hungary. German name **PRESSBURG**; Hungarian name **POZSONY**.

brat pack ▶ noun informal a rowdy and ostentatious group of young celebrities, typically film stars.
– DERIVATIVES **brat packer** noun.

brattice /'bratɪs/ ▶ noun a partition or shaft lining in a coal mine, typically made of wood or heavy cloth.
– DERIVATIVES **bratticed** adjective.
– ORIGIN Middle English (denoting a temporary wooden gallery for use in a siege): from Old French *bretesche*, from medieval Latin *britisca*, from Old English *brittisc* 'British'. The current sense dates from the mid 19th cent.

brattle dialect ▶ noun a sharp rattling sound: *a distant brattle of thunder.*
▶ verb [with obj.] rattle (something).
■ [no obj.] produce a rattling sound.
– ORIGIN early 16th cent.: probably imitative, from a blend of **BREAK** and **RATTLE**[1].

bratwurst /'bratvɜːst/ ▶ noun [mass noun] a type of fine German pork sausage that is generally fried or grilled.
– ORIGIN German, from *Brat* 'a spit' + *Wurst* 'sausage'.

Braun[1] /braʊn/, Eva (1910–45), German mistress of Adolf Hitler. Braun and Hitler are thought to have married during the fall of Berlin, shortly before committing suicide together in the air-raid shelter of his Berlin headquarters.

Braun[2] /braʊn/, Karl Ferdinand (1850–1918), German physicist. Braun invented the coupled system of radio transmission and the Braun tube (forerunner of the cathode ray tube), in which a beam of electrons could be deflected. Nobel Prize for Physics (1909).

Braun[3] /braʊn/, Wernher Magnus Maximilian von (1912–77), German-born American rocket engineer. Braun led development on the V-2 rockets used by Germany in the Second World War. After the war he moved to the US, where he pioneered the work which resulted in the US space programme.

Braunschweig /'braʊnʃvaɪk/ German name for **BRUNSWICK**.

b

bravado ▶ **noun** [mass noun] a bold manner or a show of boldness intended to impress or intimidate.
– ORIGIN late 16th cent.: from Spanish *bravada*, from *bravo* 'bold' (see **BRAVE**, **-ADO**).

brave ▶ **adjective** ready to face and endure danger or pain; showing courage: *she was very brave about the whole thing* | [as plural noun **the brave**] *it was a time to remember the brave.*
■ poetic/literary fine or splendid in appearance: *his medals made a brave show.*
▶ **noun** dated an American Indian warrior.
■ a young man who shows courage or a fighting spirit.
▶ **verb** [with obj.] endure or face (unpleasant conditions or behaviour) without showing fear: *he pulled on his coat ready to brave the elements* | *I'll **brave it out** and meet new people.*
– PHRASES **brave new world** used to refer, often ironically, to a new and hopeful period in history resulting from major changes in society: ***the brave new world of** the health care market.* **put a brave face on something** see **FACE**.
– DERIVATIVES **bravely** adverb, **braveness** noun.
– ORIGIN late 15th cent.: from French, from Italian *bravo* 'bold' or Spanish *bravo* 'courageous, untamed, savage', based on Latin *barbarus* (see **BARBAROUS**).

bravery ▶ **noun** [mass noun] courageous behaviour or character.
– ORIGIN mid 16th cent. (in the sense 'bravado'): from French *braverie* or Italian *braveria* 'boldness', based on Latin *barbarus* (see **BARBAROUS**).

bravo[1] /brɑːˈvəʊ, ˈbrɑːvəʊ/ ▶ **exclamation** used to express approval when a performer or other person has done something well: *people kept on clapping and shouting 'bravo!'*
▶ **noun** (pl. **-os**) **1** a cry of bravo: *bravos rang out.*
2 a code word representing the letter B, used in radio communication.
– ORIGIN mid 18th cent.: from French, from Italian, literally 'bold' (see **BRAVE**).

bravo[2] /ˈbrɑːvəʊ/ ▶ **noun** (pl. **-os** or **-oes**) a thug or hired assassin.
– ORIGIN late 16th cent.: from Italian, from *bravo* 'bold (one)' (see **BRAVE**).

bravura /brəˈv(j)ʊərə/ ▶ **noun** [mass noun] great technical skill and brilliance shown in a performance or activity: *the recital ended with a blazing display of bravura* | [as modifier] *a bravura performance.*
■ the display of great daring: *the show of bravura hid a guilty timidity.*
– ORIGIN mid 18th cent.: from Italian, from *bravo* 'bold'.

braw /brɔː/ ▶ **adjective** Scottish fine: *it was a braw day.*
– DERIVATIVES **brawly** adverb.
– ORIGIN late 16th cent.: variant of **BRAVE**.

brawl ▶ **noun** a rough or noisy fight or quarrel.
▶ **verb** [no obj.] fight or quarrel in a rough or noisy way.
■ poetic/literary (of a stream) flow noisily.
– DERIVATIVES **brawler** noun.
– ORIGIN late Middle English: perhaps ultimately imitative and related to **BRAY**[1].

brawn ▶ **noun** [mass noun] **1** physical strength in contrast to intelligence: *commando work required as much brain as brawn.*
2 Brit. meat from a pig's or calf's head that is cooked and pressed in a pot with jelly.
– ORIGIN Middle English: from Old French *braon* 'fleshy part of the leg', of Germanic origin; related to German *Braten* 'roast meat'.

brawny ▶ **adjective** (**brawnier**, **brawniest**) physically strong; muscular.
– DERIVATIVES **brawniness** noun.

Braxton Hicks contractions /ˌbrakstən ˈhɪks/ ▶ **plural noun** Medicine intermittent weak contractions of the uterus occurring during pregnancy.
– ORIGIN early 20th cent.: named after John *Braxton Hicks* (1823–97), English gynaecologist.

braxy /ˈbraksi/ ▶ **noun** [mass noun] a fatal bacterial infection of young sheep, occurring chiefly in upland areas in winter.
• The bacterium is *Clostridium septicum*.
– ORIGIN late 18th cent.: perhaps from obsolete *brack* 'break, flaw', from Germanic base of **BREAK**[1].

bray[1] ▶ **noun** [usu. in sing.] the loud, harsh cry of a donkey or mule.
■ a sound, voice, or laugh resembling such a cry.
▶ **verb** [no obj.] make a loud, harsh cry or sound: *he brayed with laughter.*
■ [with obj.] say (something) in a loud, harsh way: *hawkers brayed the merits of spiced sausages.*
– ORIGIN Middle English: from Old French *brait* 'a shriek', *braire* 'to cry' (the original senses in English), perhaps ultimately of Celtic origin.

bray[2] ▶ **verb** [with obj.] archaic pound or crush (something) to small pieces, typically with a pestle and mortar.
– ORIGIN late Middle English: from Old French *breier*, of Germanic origin; related to **BREAK**[1].

Bray, Vicar of the protagonist of an 18th-century song who kept his benefice from Charles II's reign to George I's by changing his beliefs to suit the times. The song is apparently based on an anecdote of an unidentified vicar of Bray, Berkshire, in Thomas Fuller's *Worthies of England* (1662).

braze ▶ **verb** [with obj.] [often as adj. **brazed**] form, fix, or join by soldering with an alloy of copper and zinc at high temperature.
▶ **noun** a brazed joint.
– ORIGIN late 17th cent.: from French *braser* 'solder', ultimately of Germanic origin.

brazen ▶ **adjective** **1** bold and without shame: *he went about his illegal business with a brazen assurance* | *a brazen hussy.*
2 chiefly poetic/literary made of brass.
■ harsh in sound: *the music's brazen chords.*
– DERIVATIVES **brazenly** adverb, **brazenness** /ˈbreɪz(ə)nnɪs/ noun.
– ORIGIN Old English *bræsen* 'made of brass', from *bræs* 'brass', of unknown ultimate origin.
▶ **brazen it** (or **something**) **out** endure an embarrassing or difficult situation by behaving with apparent confidence and lack of shame.

brazier[1] /ˈbreɪzɪə, -ʒə/ ▶ **noun** **1** a portable heater consisting of a pan or stand for holding lighted coals.
2 N. Amer. a barbecue.
– ORIGIN late 17th cent.: from French *brasier*, from *braise* 'hot coals'.

brazier[2] /ˈbreɪzjə, -ʒə/ ▶ **noun** a worker in brass.
– DERIVATIVES **braziery** noun.
– ORIGIN Middle English: probably from **BRASS** + **-IER**, on the pattern of *glass* and *glazier*.

Brazil[1] the largest country in South America; pop. 146,825,475 (1991); official language, Portuguese; capital, Brasilia. Portuguese name **BRASIL**.

> Brazil is the fifth largest country in the world. Previously inhabited largely by Tupi and Guarani peoples, Brazil was colonized by the Portuguese, who imported large numbers of slaves from West Africa to work on sugar plantations. The country was proclaimed an independent empire in 1822, becoming a republic after the overthrow of the monarchy in 1889.

– DERIVATIVES **Brazilian** adjective & noun.

Brazil[2] (also **brazil**) ▶ **noun** **1** (also **Brazil nut**) a large three-sided nut with an edible kernel, several of which develop inside a large woody capsule borne by a South American forest tree. Most are harvested from the wild.
• The tree is *Bertholletia excelsa*, family Lecythidaceae.
2 (also **Brazil wood**) [mass noun] hard red timber from which dye may be obtained.
• The timber is obtained from several tropical trees of the genus *Caesalpinia*, family Leguminosae.
– ORIGIN Middle English (in sense 2): from medieval Latin *brasilium*. The South American country *Brazil* (see **BRAZIL**[1]) takes its name from the wood.

Brazzaville /ˈbrazəvɪl/ the capital and a major port of the Republic of the Congo; pop. 2,936,000 (est. 1995). It was founded in 1880 by the French explorer Savorgnan de Brazza (1852–1905) and was capital of French Equatorial Africa from 1910 to 1958.

breach ▶ **noun** **1** an act of breaking or failing to observe a law, agreement, or code of conduct: *a breach of confidence* | [mass noun] *I sued for breach of contract.*
■ a break in relations: *a widening **breach between** government and Church.*
2 a gap in a wall, barrier, or defence, especially one made by an attacking army.
▶ **verb** [with obj.] **1** make a gap in and break through (a wall, barrier, or defence): *the river breached its bank.*
■ break or fail to observe (a law, agreement, or code of conduct).
2 [no obj.] (of a whale) rise and break through the surface of the water.
– PHRASES **breach of the peace** an act of violent or noisy behaviour that causes a public disturbance and is considered a criminal offence. **breach of promise** the action of breaking a sworn assurance to do something, formerly especially to marry someone. **step into the breach** replace someone who is suddenly unable to do a job or task.
– ORIGIN Middle English: from Old French *breche*, ultimately of Germanic origin; related to **BREAK**[1].

bread ▶ **noun** [mass noun] food made of flour, water, and yeast mixed together and baked: *a loaf of bread* | [as modifier] *a bread roll* | [count noun] *Italian breads.*
■ the bread or wafer used in the Eucharist: *altar bread.*
■ informal the money or food that one needs in order to live: *I hate doing this, but I need the bread* | *his day job puts bread on the table.*
– PHRASES **be the best** (or **greatest**) **thing since sliced bread** informal used to emphasize one's enthusiasm about a new idea, person, or thing. **bread and circuses** used to refer to a diet of entertainment or political policies on which the masses are fed to keep them happy and docile. [ORIGIN: translating Latin *panem et circenses* (Juvenal's *Satires*, x.80).] **bread and water** a frugal diet that is eaten in poverty, chosen in abstinence, or given as a punishment. **bread and wine** the consecrated elements used in the celebration of the Eucharist; the sacrament of the Eucharist. **the bread of life** something regarded as a source of spiritual nourishment. **break bread** celebrate the Eucharist. ■ dated share a meal with someone. **one cannot live by bread alone** people have spiritual as well as physical needs. [ORIGIN: with biblical allusion to Deut. 8:3, Matt. 4:4.] **cast one's bread upon the waters** do good without expecting gratitude or reward. [ORIGIN: with biblical allusion to Eccles. 11:1.] **one's daily bread** the money or food that one needs in order to live: *she earned her daily bread by working long hours.* **know which side one's bread is buttered** (**on**) informal know where one's advantage lies. **take the bread out of** (or **from**) **people's mouths** deprive people of their livings by competition or unfair working practices. **want one's bread buttered on both sides** informal want more than is practicable or than is reasonable to expect.
– ORIGIN Old English *brēad*, of Germanic origin; related to Dutch *brood* and German *Brot*.

bread and butter ▶ **noun** [mass noun] a person's livelihood or main source of income, typically as earned by routine work: *their bread and butter is reporting local events* | [as modifier] *bread-and-butter occupations.*
■ an everyday or ordinary person or thing: *the bread and butter of non-League soccer.*

bread-and-butter letter ▶ **noun** a letter expressing thanks for hospitality.

bread-and-butter pudding ▶ **noun** [mass noun] a dessert consisting of slices of bread and butter layered with dried fruit and sugar and baked with a mixture of milk and egg.

breadbasket ▶ **noun** **1** a part of a region that produces cereals for the rest of it.
2 informal a person's stomach, considered as the target for a blow.

bread bin ▶ **noun** Brit. a container for keeping bread in.

breadboard Electronics ▶ **noun** a board for making an experimental model of an electric circuit.
▶ **verb** [with obj.] make (an experimental circuit).

breadcrumb ▶ **noun** (usu. **breadcrumbs**) a small fragment of bread.
– DERIVATIVES **breadcrumbed** adjective.

breaded ▶ **adjective** (of food) coated with breadcrumbs and then fried: *breaded scampi.*

breadfruit ▶ **noun** **1** the large round starchy fruit of a tropical tree, which is used as a vegetable and sometimes to make a substitute for flour.
2 (also **breadfruit tree**) the large evergreen tree which bears this fruit, which is widely cultivated on the islands of the Pacific and the Caribbean.
• *Artocarpus altilis*, family Moraceae.
3 South African term for **BREAD TREE**.

bread-kind ▶ **noun** [mass noun] W. Indian food with a consistency resembling bread such as yams or sweet potatoes.

bread knife ▶ **noun** a long knife, typically with a serrated edge, for slicing bread.

breadline ▶ **noun** **1** (**the breadline**) Brit. the poorest condition in which it is acceptable to live: *they are not well off, but they are not **on the breadline**.*

2 N. Amer. a queue of people waiting to receive free food.

bread pudding ▶**noun** [mass noun] a rich, heavy cake or pudding made from pieces of bread soaked in milk and baked with eggs, sugar, dried fruit, and spices, eaten hot or cold.

bread sauce ▶**noun** [mass noun] white sauce thickened with breadcrumbs, typically eaten with roast chicken or turkey.

breadstick ▶**noun** a long, thin, crisp piece of baked dough.

breadth ▶**noun** [mass noun] the distance or measurement from side to side of something; width: *the boat measured 27 feet* ***in breadth*** | [in sing.] *the bank reaches a maximum breadth of about 100 km.*
■ wide range or extent: *she has the advantage of breadth of experience.* ■ the capacity to accept a wide range of ideas or beliefs: *the minister is not noted for his breadth of vision.* ■ [count noun] dated a piece of cloth of standard or full width. ■ overall unity of artistic effect: *these masterpieces showed a new breadth of handling.*
– ORIGIN early 16th cent.: from obsolete *brede* in the same sense (related to **BROAD**) + **-TH**[2], on the pattern of *length.*

breadthways (also **breadthwise**) ▶**adverb** in a direction parallel with a thing's width.

bread tree (also **bread palm**) ▶**noun** a cycad native to tropical and southern Africa, which yields an edible sago-like starch.
• Genus *Encephalartos*, family Zamiaceae.

breadwinner ▶**noun** a person who earns money to support their family, typically the sole one.
– DERIVATIVES **breadwinning** noun.

break[1] ▶**verb** (past **broke**; past participle **broken**) **1** separate or cause to separate into pieces as a result of a blow, shock, or strain: [no obj.] *the slate fell from my hand and broke in two on the hard floor* | [with obj.] *windows in the street were broken by the blast.*
■ [with obj.] (of a person or animal) sustain an injury involving the fracture of a bone or bones in (a part of the body): *she had broken her leg in two places.* ■ [no obj.] (of a part of the body or a bone) sustain a fracture: *what if his leg had broken?* ■ [with obj.] cause a cut or graze in (the skin): *the bite had scarcely broken the skin.* ■ make or become inoperative: [no obj.] *the machine has broken and they can't fix it until next week* | [with obj.] *he's broken the video.* ■ (of the amniotic fluid surrounding a fetus) be or cause to be discharged when the sac is ruptured in the first stages of labour: [no obj.] *she realized her waters had broken.* ■ [with obj.] open (a safe) forcibly. ■ [with obj.] use (a banknote) to pay for something and receive change out of the transaction: *she had to break a tenner.* ■ [no obj.] (of two boxers or wrestlers) come out of a clinch, especially at the referee's command. ■ [with obj.] unfurl (a flag or sail). ■ [with obj.] succeed in deciphering (a code). ■ [with obj.] disprove (an alibi).
2 [with obj.] interrupt (a continuity, sequence, or course): *the new government broke the pattern of growth* | *his concentration was broken by a sound.*
■ put an end to (a silence) by speaking or making contact. ■ make a pause in (a journey). ■ [no obj.] stop proceedings in order to have a pause or vacation: *at mid-morning they* ***broke for*** *coffee.* ■ lessen the impact of (a fall). ■ stop oneself being subject to (a habit): *try to break the habit of adding salt at the table.* ■ [no obj., with adverbial] (chiefly of an attacking player or team, or of a military force) make a rush or dash in a particular direction: *Mitchell won possession and broke quickly, allowing Hughes to score.* ■ surpass (a record): *the film broke box office records in the US.* ■ disconnect or interrupt (an electric circuit). ■ [no obj., with adverbial of direction] (of a bowled cricket ball) change direction on bouncing, due to spin. ■ [no obj., with adverbial of direction] Soccer (of the ball) rebound unpredictably: *the ball broke to Craig but his shot rebounded from the post.*
3 [with obj.] fail to observe (a law, regulation, or agreement): *the council says it will prosecute traders who break the law* | *a legally binding contract which can only be broken by mutual consent.*
■ fail to continue with (a self-imposed discipline): *diets started without preparation are broken all the time.*
4 [with obj.] crush the emotional strength, spirit, or resistance of: *the idea was to better the prisoners, not to break them.*
■ [no obj.] (of a person's emotional strength or control) give way: *her self-control finally broke.* ■ destroy the power of (a movement or organization). ■ destroy the effectiveness of (a strike), typically by moving in other people to replace the striking workers.
5 [no obj.] undergo a change or enter a new state, in particular:
■ (of the weather) change suddenly, especially after a fine spell: *the weather broke and thunder rumbled through a leaden sky.* ■ (of a storm) begin violently. ■ (of dawn or a day) begin as the sun rises: *dawn was just breaking.* ■ (of clouds) move apart and begin to disperse. ■ (of waves) curl over and dissolve into foam: *the Caribbean sea breaking gently on the shore.* ■ (of a person's voice) falter and change tone, due to emotion: *her voice broke as she relived the experience.* ■ (of a boy's voice) change in tone and register at puberty. ■ Phonetics (of a vowel) develop into a diphthong, under the influence of an adjacent sound. ■ (of prices on the stock exchange) fall sharply. ■ (of news or a scandal) suddenly become public: *since the news broke I've received thousands of wonderful letters.* ■ [with obj.] (**break something to someone**) make bad news known to someone. ■ make the first stroke at the beginning of a game of billiards, pool, or snooker.

▶**noun 1** an interruption of continuity or uniformity: *the magazine has been published without a break since 1950.*
■ an act of separating oneself from a pre-existing state of affairs: *a* ***break with*** *the past.* ■ a change in the weather. ■ [with modifier] a change of line, paragraph, or page: *dotted lines on the screen show page breaks.* ■ a change of tone in a person's voice due to emotion. ■ an interruption in an electric circuit. ■ Cricket a change in the direction of a bowled ball on bouncing. ■ a rush or dash in a particular direction, especially by an attacking player or team: *Norwich scored on a rare break with 11 minutes left.* ■ informal an opportunity or chance, especially one leading to professional success: *his big break came when a critic gave him a rave review.* ■ (also **break of serve** or **service break**) Tennis the winning of a game against an opponent's serve.
2 a pause in work: *I need a* ***break from*** *mental activity* | *they take long coffee breaks.*
■ Brit. an interval during the school day: *the bell went for break.* ■ a short holiday: *a weekend break in the Cotswolds.* ■ a period of time taken out of one's professional activity in order to do something else: *those returning to work after a career break.* ■ a short solo or instrumental passage in jazz or popular music.
3 a gap or opening: *the track bends left through a break in the hedge* | *he stopped to wait for a break in the traffic.*
4 an instance of breaking something; the point where something is broken: *he was stretchered off with a break to the leg.*
5 Snooker & Billiards a consecutive series of successful shots, scoring a specified number of points: *a break of 83 put him in front for the first time.*
■ a player's turn to make the opening shot of a game.
6 a bud or shoot sprouting from a stem.
– PHRASES **break one's back** put great effort into achieving something. **break the back of** accomplish the main or hardest part of (a task): *we've broken the back of the problem.* ■ overwhelm or defeat: *I thought we really had broken the back of inflation.* **break the bank** see **BANK**[2]. **break bread** see **BREAD**. **break camp** see **CAMP**. **break cover** (of game being hunted) emerge into the open. **break one's duck** see **DUCK**[3]. **break someone's heart** see **HEART**. **break the ice** see **ICE**. **break a leg!** theatrical slang good luck! **break the mould** see **MOULD**. **break of day** dawn. **break rank** see **RANK**[1]. **break (someone's) serve** (or **service**) win a game in a tennis match against an opponent's service. **break ship** Nautical fail to rejoin one's ship after absence on leave. **break step** see **STEP**. **break wind** release gas from the anus. **give someone a break** [usu. in imperative] informal stop putting pressure on someone about something. ■ (**give me a break**) used to express contemptuous disagreement or disbelief about what has been said: *He's seven times as quick and he's only 20 years old. Give me a break.* **make a break for** make a sudden dash in the direction of, especially in a bid to escape: *he made a break for the door.* **make a clean break** remove oneself completely and finally from a situation or relationship.
– ORIGIN Old English *brecan* (verb), of Germanic origin; related to Dutch *breken* and German *brechen*, from an Indo-European root shared by Latin *frangere* 'to break'.

▶**break away** (of a person) escape from someone's hold. ■ escape from the control of a person, group, or practice: *an attempt to* ***break away from*** *the elitism that has dominated the book trade.* ■ (of a competitor in a race) move into the lead. ■ (of a material or object) become detached from its base, typically through decay or under force.

break down 1 (of a machine or motor vehicle) suddenly cease to function: *his van broke down.* ■ (of a person) experience a sudden failure of function in the vehicle they are driving: *she broke down on the motorway.* ■ (of a relationship, agreement, or process) cease to continue; collapse: *pay negotiations with management broke down.* ■ lose control of one's emotions when in a state of distress: *the old woman broke down in tears.* ■ (of a person's health or emotional control) fail or collapse. **2** undergo chemical decomposition: *waste products which* ***break down into*** *low-level toxic materials.*

break something down 1 demolish a door or other barrier: *they had to get the police to break the door down* | figurative *class barriers can be broken down by educational reform.* **2** separate something into a number of parts: *each tutorial is broken down into more manageable units.* ■ analyse information: *bar graphs show how the information can be broken down.* ■ convert a substance into simpler compounds by chemical action: *almost every natural substance can be broken down by bacteria.*

break even reach a point in a business venture when the profits are equal to the costs.

break forth burst out suddenly; emerge.

break free another way of saying ***break away***.

break in 1 force entry to a building. **2** [with direct speech] interject: *'I don't want to interfere,' Mrs Hendry broke in.*

break someone in familiarize someone with a new job or situation: *there was no time to break in a new foreign minister.* ■ (**break a horse in**) accustom a horse to a saddle and bridle, and to being ridden.

break something in wear something, typically new shoes, until it becomes supple and comfortable.

break in on interrupt: *the doctor's voice* ***broke in on*** *her thoughts.*

break into 1 enter or open (a place, vehicle, or container) forcibly, especially for the purposes of theft: *two raiders broke into his home* | *a friend of mine had his car broken into.* ■ succeed in winning a share of (a market or a position in a profession): *foreign companies have largely failed to break into the domestic-equity business.* ■ interrupt (a conversation). **2** (of a person) suddenly or unexpectedly burst forth into (laughter or song). ■ (of a person's face or mouth) relax into (a smile). **3** change one's pace to (a faster one): *Greg broke into a sprint.*

break off become severed: *the fuselage had broken off just behind the pilot's seat.* ■ abruptly stop talking: *she broke off, stifling a sob.*

break something off remove something from a larger unit or whole: *Tucker broke off a piece of bread.* ■ abruptly end or discontinue something: *Britain threatened to break off diplomatic relations.*

break something open open something forcibly.

break out (of war, fighting, or similarly undesirable things) start suddenly: *forest fires have broken out across Indonesia.* ■ (of a physical discomfort) suddenly manifest itself: *prickles of sweat had broken out along her backbone.*

break out in (of a person or a part of their body) be suddenly affected by an unpleasant sensation or condition: *she had broken out in a rash.*

break out of escape from: *a prisoner broke out of his cell* | figurative *executives looking to break out of the corporate hierarchy.*

break something out informal open and start using something: *it was time to break out the champagne.*

break through make or force a way through (a barrier): *demonstrators attempted to break through the police lines* | *the sun might break through in a few spots.* ■ figurative (of a person) achieve success in a particular area: *so many talented players are struggling to break through.*

break up disintegrate; disperse: *the grey clouds had begun to break up.* ■ (of a gathering) disband; end. ■ Brit. end the school term: *we broke up for the summer.* ■ (of a couple in a relationship) part company. ■ start laughing uncontrollably: *the whole cast broke up.* ■ chiefly N. Amer. become emotionally upset.

break someone up chiefly N. Amer. cause someone to become extremely upset.

break something up cause something to separate into several pieces, parts, or sections: *break up the chocolate and place it in a bowl* | *he intends to break the company up into strategic business units.* ■ cut something up for scrap metal: *she was towed to Bo'Ness and broken up.* ■ disperse or put an end to a gathering: *police broke up a demonstration in the* *capital.* ■ bring a social event or meeting to an end by being the first person to leave: *Richard was sorry to break up the party.*

break with quarrel or cease relations with (someone): *he had broken with his family long before.* ■ act in a way that is not in accordance with (a custom or tradition).

break² ▶ noun **1** former term for **BREAKING CART**. **2** historical another term for **BRAKE²**.
– ORIGIN mid 19th cent.: perhaps from 16th-cent. *brake* 'cage', later 'framework', of unknown origin.

breakable ▶ adjective capable of breaking or being broken easily: *breakable ornaments | an encrypted password isn't easily breakable.*
▶ noun (**breakables**) things which are fragile and easily broken.

breakage ▶ noun [mass noun] the action of breaking something or the fact of being broken: *some breakage of bone has occurred |* [count noun] *there had been three breakages in the overhead wires.*
■ [count noun] a thing that has been broken: *they left minor breakages behind them.*

breakaway ▶ noun **1** a divergence or radical change from something established or long standing: *rock was a breakaway from pop.*
■ a secession of a number of people from an organization, especially following conflict or disagreement and resulting in the establishment of a new organization: [as modifier] *a breakaway group.* **2** a sudden attack or forward movement, especially in a race, soccer or hockey game, etc.
■ Austral./NZ a stampede of animals, typically at the sight or smell of water. ■ Rugby each of the two flank forwards on the outsides of the second row of a scrum formation.

breakbone fever ▶ noun another term for **DENGUE**.

break-bulk ▶ adjective [attrib.] denoting a system of transporting cargo as separate pieces rather than in containers.

break crop ▶ noun a crop grown between fields of cereals to ensure a varied planting pattern.

break-dancing ▶ noun [mass noun] an energetic and acrobatic style of street dancing, developed by US blacks.
– DERIVATIVES **break-dance** verb & noun, **break dancer** noun.

breakdown ▶ noun **1** a failure of a relationship or of communication: *differences in language can lead to a breakdown in communication |* [mass noun] *some of these women will have experienced marital breakdown.*
■ a collapse of a system of authority due to widespread transgression of the rules: *a breakdown in military discipline.* ■ a sudden collapse in someone's mental health. ■ a mechanical failure. ■ [in sing.] the chemical or physical decomposition of something: *the breakdown of ammonia to nitrites.* **2** an explanatory analysis, especially of statistics: *a detailed cost breakdown.*

breaker ▶ noun **1** a heavy sea wave that breaks into white foam on the shore. **2** a person or thing that breaks something: [in combination] *a rule-breaker | a seal-breaker.*
■ chiefly Brit. a person who breaks up disused machinery. ■ a person who breaks in horses. ■ short for **CIRCUIT-BREAKER**. **3** a person who interrupts the conversation of others on a Citizens' Band radio channel, indicating that they wish to transmit a message.
■ any CB radio user. **4** a break dancer.

break-even ▶ noun [mass noun] the point or state at which a person or company breaks even.

break-fall ▶ noun (in martial arts) a controlled fall in which most of the impact is absorbed by the arms or legs.

breakfast ▶ noun a meal eaten in the morning, the first of the day: *a breakfast of bacon and eggs |* [mass noun] *I don't eat breakfast.*
▶ verb [no obj.] eat this meal: *she breakfasted on fried bread and bacon.*
– PHRASES **have** (or **eat**) **someone for breakfast** informal deal with or defeat someone with contemptuous ease.
– DERIVATIVES **breakfaster** noun.
– ORIGIN late Middle English: from the verb **BREAK¹** + **FAST²**.

breakfast television ▶ noun [mass noun] television programmes broadcast early in the morning.

break feeding ▶ noun [mass noun] NZ a system of controlling the feeding of grazing animals by dividing their paddock with movable electric fences.

breakfront ▶ noun a piece of furniture having the line of its front broken by a curve or angle: [as modifier] *a breakfront bookcase.*

break-in ▶ noun an illegal forced entry into a building or car, typically to steal something.

breaking and entering ▶ noun [mass noun] (in North American, and formerly also British, legal use) the crime of entering a building by force so as to commit burglary.

breaking cart ▶ noun a two-wheeled, low, open carriage with a skeleton body, used for breaking in young horses.

breaking point ▶ noun [mass noun] the moment of greatest strain at which someone or something gives way: *the refugee crisis has reached breaking point | her nerves were stretched to breaking point.*

breakneck ▶ adjective [attrib.] dangerously or extremely fast: *he drove at breakneck speed.*

break-off ▶ noun an instance of breaking something off or of discontinuing something.

breakout ▶ noun **1** a forcible escape, typically from prison.
■ (in soccer and other sports) a sudden attack by a team that had been defending. **2** [in sing.] an outbreak: *a breakout of hostilities.* **3** [mass noun] the deformation or splintering of wood, stone, or other material being drilled or planed.
▶ adjective informal **1** suddenly and extremely popular or successful: *a breakout movie.* **2** chiefly US denoting or relating to groups which break away from a conference or other larger gathering for discussion.

break point ▶ noun **1** a place or time at which an interruption or change is made.
■ (usu. **breakpoint**) Computing a place in a computer program where the sequence of instructions is interrupted, especially by another program or operator intervention. **2** [in sing.] Tennis the state of a game when the player or side receiving service needs only one more point to win the game: *he hit a winner to reach break point.*
■ a point of this nature: *he saved three break points.* **3** another term for **BREAKING POINT**.

Breakspear, Nicholas, see **ADRIAN IV**.

breakthrough ▶ noun a sudden, dramatic, and important discovery or development, especially in science: *a major breakthrough in the fight against Aids.*
■ a significant and dramatic overcoming of a perceived obstacle, allowing the completion of a process: *the metalworkers' agreement was the key breakthrough on pay and conditions.*

breakthrough bleeding ▶ noun [mass noun] bleeding from the uterus occurring between menstrual periods, a side effect of some oral contraceptives.

break-up ▶ noun an end to a relationship, typically a marriage.
■ a division of a country or organization into smaller autonomous units: *the break-up of the Soviet Union.* ■ a physical disintegration of something: *large quantities of oil are released after the break-up of a tanker.*

breakwater ▶ noun a barrier built out into the sea to protect a coast or harbour from the force of waves.

breakwind ▶ noun Austral./NZ a windbreak.

Bream, Julian (Alexander) (b.1933), English guitarist and lute player. He formed the Julian Bream Consort for the performance of early consort music and revived and edited much early music. Britten, Walton, and others composed works for him.

bream¹ ▶ noun (pl. same) a greenish-bronze deep-bodied freshwater fish native to Europe.
● *Abramis brama*, family Cyprinidae.
■ used in names of other fishes resembling or related to this, e.g. **sea bream**, **Ray's bream**.
– ORIGIN late Middle English: from Old French *bresme*, of Germanic origin; related to German *Brachsen*, *Brassen*.

bream² ▶ verb [with obj.] Nautical, archaic clear (a ship or its bottom) of weeds, shells, or other accumulated matter by burning and scraping it.
– ORIGIN late 15th cent.: probably of Low German origin and related to **BROOM**.

breast ▶ noun either of the two soft, protruding organs on the upper front of a woman's body which secrete milk after pregnancy.
■ the corresponding less-developed part of a man's body. ■ a person's chest: *her heart was hammering in her breast.* ■ the corresponding part of a bird or mammal: [as modifier] *the breast feathers of the doves.* ■ a joint of meat or portion of poultry cut from such a part: *Lisa popped a breast of chicken into the microwave.* ■ the part of a garment that covers the chest: [as modifier] *a breast pocket.* ■ a person's chest regarded as the seat of the emotions: *wild feelings of frustration were rising up in his breast.*
▶ verb [with obj.] face and move forwards against or through (something): *I watched him breast the wave.*
■ reach the top of (a hill).
– PHRASES **beat one's breast** make an exaggerated show of sorrow, despair, or regret. **make a clean breast of something** see **CLEAN**.
– DERIVATIVES **breasted** adjective [in combination] *a bare-breasted woman | a crimson-breasted bird.*
– ORIGIN Old English *brēost*, of Germanic origin; related to Dutch *borst* and German *Brust*.

breastbone ▶ noun a thin flat bone running down the centre of the chest and connecting the ribs. Also called **STERNUM**.

breast collar ▶ noun a thick chest strap which forms part of a horse's harness, often used instead of an ordinary collar on horses pulling lightweight or show vehicles.

breast drill ▶ noun a drill on which pressure is brought to bear by the operator's chest.

breastfeed ▶ verb (past and past participle **-fed**) [with obj.] (of a woman) feed (a baby) with milk from the breast: *she breastfed her first child |* [no obj.] *sometimes it is not possible to breastfeed.*
■ [no obj.] (of a baby) feed from the breast.
▶ noun an instance of feeding a baby in such a way.

breast-high ▶ adjective & adverb submerged to or as high as the breast.

breasthook ▶ noun a large piece of shaped timber fitted in the bows of a ship, used to connect the sides to the stem.

breast implant ▶ noun Medicine a prosthesis consisting of a gel-like or fluid material in a flexible sac, implanted behind or in place of a female breast in reconstructive or cosmetic surgery.

breastpin ▶ noun archaic a small brooch or badge worn on the breast, typically to fasten a garment.

breastplate ▶ noun **1** a piece of armour covering the chest. **2** a set of straps attached to the front of a saddle, which pass across the horse's chest and prevent the saddle slipping backward.
■ the strap of a harness covering the chest of a horse.

breast pump ▶ noun a device for drawing milk from a woman's breasts by suction.

breast shell ▶ noun a shallow plastic receptacle that fits over the nipple of a lactating woman to catch any milk that flows.

breaststroke ▶ noun [in sing.] a style of swimming on one's front, in which the arms are pushed forwards and then swept back in a circular movement, while the legs are tucked in towards the body and then kicked out in a corresponding movement.

breastsummer ▶ noun Architecture a beam across a broad opening, sustaining a superstructure.
– ORIGIN early 17th cent.: from **BREAST** and **SUMMER²**.

breastwork ▶ noun a low temporary defence or parapet.

breath ▶ noun [mass noun] the air taken into or expelled from the lungs: *I was gasping for breath | his breath smelled of garlic.*
■ an inhalation or exhalation of air from the lungs: *she drew in a quick breath.* ■ [mass noun] archaic the power of breathing; life. ■ [in sing.] a slight movement of air: *the weather was balmy, not a breath of wind.* ■ [in sing.] a sign, hint, or suggestion: *he avoided the slightest breath of scandal.*
– PHRASES **before one can** (or **has time to**) **draw breath** before one can do anything, such is the speed of events. **a breath of fresh air** a small amount of or a brief time in the fresh air. ■ a refreshing change: *Mike, my present husband, was a breath of fresh air.* **the breath of life** a thing that someone needs or depends on: *politics has been the breath of life to her for 50 years.* **catch one's breath**

b

1 cease breathing momentarily in surprise or fear. 2 rest after exercise to restore normal breathing. **don't hold your breath** informal used to indicate that something is unlikely to happen: *Next thing you know I'll be knitting baby clothes. But don't hold your breath.* **draw breath** breathe in. **get one's breath** (**back**) begin to breathe normally again after exercise or exertion. **hold one's breath** cease breathing temporarily. ■ figurative be in a state of suspense or anticipation: *France held its breath while the Senate chose its new president.* **in the —— breath** used to refer to the place of a statement in a sequence of statements, typically one containing a contradiction or inconsistency: *she admitted it but said in the same breath that it was of no consequence.* **the** (or **one's**) **last breath** the last moment of one's life (often used hyperbolically); death: *she would fight to the last breath to preserve her good name.* **out of breath** gasping for air, typically after exercise. **take breath** pause to recover free and easy breathing. **take someone's breath away** astonish or inspire someone with awed respect or delight. **under** (or **below**) **one's breath** in a very quiet voice; almost inaudibly: *he swore violently under his breath.* **waste one's breath** talk or give advice without effect: *I've far better things to do than waste my breath arguing.*
– ORIGIN Old English *brǣth* 'smell, scent', of Germanic origin; related to **BROOD**.

breathable ▶ **adjective** (of the air) fit or pleasant to breathe.
■ (of clothes or material) admitting air to the skin and allowing sweat to evaporate.

breathalyse (US **breathalyze**) ▶ **verb** [with obj.] (of the police) use a breathalyser to test how much alcohol (a driver) has consumed.

breathalyser (US trademark **Breathalyzer**) ▶ **noun** a device used by police for measuring the amount of alcohol in a driver's breath.
– ORIGIN 1960s: blend of **BREATH** and **ANALYSE**, + **-ER**[1].

breathe ▶ **verb** [no obj.] take air into the lungs and then expel it, especially as a regular physiological process: *she was breathing deeply* | *breathe in through your nose* | *he breathed out heavily* | [with obj.] *we are polluting the air we breathe.*
■ be or seem to be alive because of this: *at least I'm still breathing.* ■ poetic/literary (of wind) blow softly. ■ [with direct speech] say something with quiet intensity: *'We're together at last', she breathed.* ■ (of an animal or plant) respire or exchange gases: *plants breathe through their roots.* ■ [with obj.] give an impression of (something): *the whole room breathed an air of hygienic efficiency.* ■ (of wine) be exposed to fresh air: *letting a wine breathe allows oxygen to enter.* ■ (of material or soil) admit or emit air or moisture: *let your lawn breathe by putting air into the soil.* ■ [with obj.] allow (a horse) to rest after exertion. ■ (**breathe upon**) archaic or poetic/literary tarnish or taint: *before the queen's fair name was breathed upon.*
– PHRASES **breathe** (**freely**) **again** relax after being frightened or tense about something: *she wouldn't breathe freely again until she was airborne.* **breathe down someone's neck** follow closely behind someone. ■ constantly check up on someone. **breathe one's last** die. **breathe** (**new**) **life into** fill with enthusiasm and energy; reinvigorate: *the Prime Minister would breathe new life into his party.* **not breathe a word** remain silent about something secret.
– ORIGIN Middle English (in the sense 'exhale, steam'): from **BREATH**.

breather ▶ **noun 1** [in sing.] informal a brief pause for rest: *regroup and take a breather.*
2 a vent or valve to release pressure or to allow air to move freely around something: *a cask breather* | [as modifier] *a breather pipe.*
3 [with adj. or noun modifier] a person or animal that breathes in a particular way, or breathes a particular substance: *a heavy breather.*

breathing ▶ **noun 1** [mass noun] the process of taking air into and expelling it from the lungs: *his breathing was shallow.*
2 a sign in Greek (ʻ or ʼ) indicating the presence of an aspirate (**rough breathing**) or the absence of an aspirate (**smooth breathing**) at the beginning of a word.

breathing space ▶ **noun** [in sing.] an opportunity to pause, relax, or decide what to do next.

breathless ▶ **adjective** gasping for breath, typically due to exertion: *the climb left me breathless.*
■ holding or as if holding the breath due to excitement or other strong feelings: *she was breathless with shock* | *there was a breathless silence.* ■ (of the air or weather) unstirred by a wind or breeze; stiflingly still: *the warm breathless air.*
– DERIVATIVES **breathlessly** adverb, **breathlessness** noun.

breathtaking ▶ **adjective** astonishing or awe-inspiring in quality, so as to take one's breath away: *the scene was one of breathtaking beauty.*
– DERIVATIVES **breathtakingly** adverb.

breath test ▶ **noun** a test in which a driver is made to blow into a breathalyser to check whether they have drunk more than the legally permitted amount.
▶ **verb** (**breath-test**) [with obj.] give (someone) such a test.

breathy ▶ **adjective** (**breathier**, **breathiest**) producing or causing an audible sound of breathing, typically as a result of physical exertion or strong feelings: *a breathy laugh.*
– DERIVATIVES **breathily** adverb, **breathiness** noun.

breccia /ˈbrɛtʃə, -tʃɪə/ ▶ **noun** [mass noun] Geology rock consisting of angular fragments of stones cemented by finer calcareous material.
– DERIVATIVES **brecciate** verb, **brecciation** noun.
– ORIGIN late 18th cent.: from Italian, literally 'gravel', ultimately of Germanic origin and related to **BREAK**[1].

Brecht /brɛxt, German brɛçt/, (Eugen) Bertolt (Friedrich) (1898–1956), German dramatist, producer, and poet. His interest in combining music and drama led to collaboration with Kurt Weill, for example in *The Threepenny Opera* (1928), an adaptation of John Gay's *The Beggar's Opera*. Brecht's later drama, written in exile after Hitler's rise to power, uses techniques of theatrical alienation and includes *Mother Courage* (1941) and *The Caucasian Chalk Circle* (1948).
– DERIVATIVES **Brechtian** adjective.

Breconshire /ˈbrɛkənˌʃɪə, ˈʃə/ (also **Brecknockshire** /ˈbrɛknɒk-/) a former county of south central Wales. It was divided between Powys and Gwent in 1974.

bred past and past participle of **BREED**. ▶ **adjective** [usu. in combination] (of a person or animal) reared in a specified environment or way: *the bareness of the scene intimidated the city-bred Elizabeth.*

Breda /ˈbreɪdə/ a manufacturing town in the SW Netherlands; pop. 124,800 (1991). It is noted for the Compromise of Breda of 1566, a protest against Spanish rule over the Netherlands; the 1660 manifesto of Charles II (who lived there in exile), stating his terms for accepting the throne of Britain; and the Treaty of Breda, which ended the Anglo-Dutch war of 1665–7.

bredie /ˈbriːdi, ˈbrɪədi/ ▶ **noun** a traditional southern African dish consisting of a stew of meat (typically mutton) and vegetables.
– ORIGIN Afrikaans, perhaps from Portuguese *bredo*, denoting several species of *Amaranthus*, sometimes cooked as a vegetable.

breech ▶ **noun 1** the part of a cannon behind the bore.
■ the back part of a rifle or gun barrel.
2 archaic a person's buttocks.
▶ **verb** [with obj.] archaic put (a boy) into breeches after being in petticoats since birth.
– ORIGIN Old English *brēc* (plural of *brōc*, of Germanic origin; related to Dutch *broek*), interpreted as a singular form. The original sense was 'garment covering the loins and thighs' (compare with **BREECHES**), hence 'the buttocks' (sense 2, mid 16th cent.), later 'the hind part' of anything.

breech birth (also **breech delivery**) ▶ **noun** a delivery of a baby which is so positioned in the womb that the buttocks or feet are delivered first.

breechblock ▶ **noun** a metal block which closes the aperture at the back part of a rifle or gun barrel.

breechclout ▶ **noun** North American term for **LOINCLOTH**.

breeches ▶ **plural noun** short trousers fastened just below the knee, now chiefly worn for riding or as part of ceremonial dress.
■ informal trousers.
– ORIGIN Middle English: plural of **BREECH**.

Breeches Bible ▶ **noun** the Geneva Bible of 1560, so named because the word *breeches* is used in Gen. 3:7 for the garments made by Adam and Eve.

breeches buoy ▶ **noun** a lifebuoy with canvas breeches attached which, when suspended from a rope, can be used to hold and transfer a passenger to safety from a ship.

breeching ▶ **noun 1** a strong leather strap passing round the hindquarters of a horse harnessed to a vehicle and enabling the horse to push backwards.
2 historical a thick rope used to secure the carriages of cannon on a ship and to absorb the force of the recoil.
3 the hair or wool on the hindquarters of an animal.

breech-loader ▶ **noun** a gun designed to have ammunition inserted at the breech rather than through the muzzle.
– DERIVATIVES **breech-loading** adjective.

breed ▶ **verb** (past and past participle **bred**) [with obj.] cause (an animal) to produce offspring, especially in a controlled and organized way: *bitches may not be **bred from** more than once a year.*
■ [no obj.] (of animals) mate and then produce offspring: *toads are said to return to the pond of their birth to breed.* ■ develop (a kind of animal or plant) for a particular purpose or quality: *these horses are **bred for** this sport.* ■ rear and train (someone) to behave in a particular way or have certain qualities: *Theodora had been beautifully bred.* ■ produce or lead to (something), typically over a period of time: *success had bred a certain arrogance.* ■ Physics create (fissile material) by nuclear reaction.
▶ **noun** a stock of animals or plants within a species having a distinctive appearance and typically having been developed by deliberate selection.
■ a sort or kind of person or thing: *a new breed of entrepreneurs was brought into being.*
– PHRASES **a breed apart** a sort or kind of person that is very different from the norm: *health-service staff are a breed apart with their dedication to duty.* **a dying breed** a sort or kind of person that is slowly disappearing: *the country's dying breed of elder statesmen.* **what's bred in the bone will come out in the flesh** (or **blood**) see **BONE**.
– ORIGIN Old English *brēdan* 'produce (offspring), bear (a child)', of Germanic origin; related to German *brüten*, also to **BROOD**.

breeder ▶ **noun** a person who breeds livestock, racehorses, other animals, or plants.
■ [with adj. or noun modifier] an animal that breeds at a particular time or in a particular way: *emperor penguins are winter breeders.* ■ informal, derogatory (among homosexuals) a heterosexual person.

breeder reactor ▶ **noun** a nuclear reactor which creates fissile material (typically plutonium-239 by irradiation of uranium-238) at a faster rate than it uses another fissile material (typically uranium-235) as fuel.

breeding ▶ **noun** [mass noun] the mating and production of offspring by animals: *the flooding of the rivers is a trigger for breeding to start.*
■ the activity or process of causing animals to mate and produce offspring: *the breeding of rats and mice for experiment.* ■ the good manners regarded as characteristic of the aristocracy and conferred by heredity: *a girl of good breeding.*

breeding ground ▶ **noun** an area where birds, fish, or other animals habitually breed.
■ [usu. in sing.] figurative a thing that favours the development or occurrence of something: *the situation is a breeding ground for political unrest.*

breeks ▶ **plural noun** chiefly Scottish & N. English another term for **BREECHES**.

breeze[1] ▶ **noun 1** a gentle wind.
■ [with modifier] a wind of force 2 to 6 on the Beaufort scale (4–27 knots or 7–50 kph).
2 informal a thing that is easy to do or accomplish: *travelling through London was a breeze.*
▶ **verb** [no obj., with adverbial of direction] informal come or go in a casual or light-hearted manner: *Roger breezed into her office.*
■ [no obj.] (**breeze through**) deal with something with apparently casual ease: *Milan had breezed through their first defence of the European Cup.*
– ORIGIN mid 16th cent.: probably from Old Spanish and Portuguese *briza* 'NE wind' (the original sense in English).

breeze[2] ▶ **noun** [mass noun] small cinders mixed with sand and cement to make breeze blocks.
– ORIGIN late 16th cent.: from French *braise*, (earlier) *brese* 'live coals'.

b

breeze block ▶ noun Brit. a lightweight building brick made from small cinders mixed with sand and cement.

breezeway ▶ noun N. Amer. a roofed outdoor passage, as between a house and a garage.

breezy ▶ adjective (**breezier**, **breeziest**) **1** pleasantly windy: *it was a bright, breezy day.* **2** appearing relaxed, informal, and cheerily brisk: *the text is written in a breezy matter-of-fact manner.*
– DERIVATIVES **breezily** adverb, **breeziness** noun.

Bregenz /ˈbreɪɡənts, German ˈbreːɡɛnts/ a city in western Austria, on the eastern shores of Lake Constance; pop. 27,240 (1991). It is the capital of the state of Vorarlberg.

brei /breɪ/ S. African ▶ noun an accent characterized by a rolled, sometimes uvular *r.*
▶ verb (**breis**, **breid**, **breiing**) [no obj.] speak with this accent.
– ORIGIN alteration of Afrikaans *bry*, from a Dutch variant of *brouwen* 'speak thickly'.

brekkie (also **brekky**) ▶ noun [mass noun] informal breakfast.

Brel /brɛl, French brɛl/, Jacques (1929–78), Belgian singer and composer. He gained a reputation in Paris as an original songwriter whose satirical wit was balanced by his idealism and hope.

Bremen /ˈbreɪmən/ a state of NE Germany. Divided into two parts, which centre on the city of Bremen and the port of Bremerhaven, it is surrounded by the state of Lower Saxony.
▪ its capital, an industrial city linked by the River Weser to the port of Bremerhaven and the North Sea; pop. 537,600 (1989).

bremsstrahlung /ˈbrɛmzˌʃtrɑːlʊŋ/ ▶ noun [mass noun] Physics electromagnetic radiation produced by the acceleration or especially the deceleration of a charged particle after passing through the electric and magnetic fields of a nucleus.
– ORIGIN 1940s: from German, from *bremsen* 'to brake' + *Strahlung* 'radiation'.

Bren (also **Bren gun**) ▶ noun a lightweight quick-firing machine gun used by the Allied forces in the Second World War.
– ORIGIN blend of *Brno* (a town in the Czech Republic where it was originally made) and *Enfield* in England (site of the Royal Small Arms Factory where it was later made).

Brendan, St (*c.*486–*c.*575), Irish abbot. The legend of the 'Navigation of St Brendan' (*c.*1050), describing his voyage with a band of monks to a promised land (possibly Orkney or the Hebrides), was widely popular in the Middle Ages. Feast day, 16 May.

Brenner Pass /ˈbrɛnə/ an Alpine pass at the border between Austria and Italy, on the route between Innsbruck and Bolzano, at an altitude of 1,371 m (4,450 ft).

brent goose ▶ noun a small goose with a mainly black head and neck, breeding in the arctic tundra of Eurasia and Canada. Called **BRANT** in North America.
• *Branta bernicla*, family Anatidae.
– ORIGIN late Middle English: of unknown origin.

Brescia /ˈbrɛʃə/ an industrial city in Lombardy, in northern Italy; pop. 196,770 (1990).

Breslau /ˈbrɛslaʊ/ German name for **WROCŁAW**.

Bresson /ˈbrɛsɒ̃, French brɛsɔ̃/, Robert (1907–99), French film director. His most notable films, most of which feature unknown actors, include *Diary of a Country Priest* (1951) and *The Trial of Joan of Arc* (1962).

Brest /brɛst, French brɛst/ **1** a port and naval base on the Atlantic coast of Brittany, in NW France; pop. 153,100 (1990).
2 a river port and industrial city in Belarus, situated close to the border with Poland; pop. 268,800 (1990). The peace treaty between Germany and Russia was signed there in March 1918. Former name (until 1921) **BREST-LITOVSK**. Polish name **BRZEŚĆ NAD BUGIEM**.

Bretagne /brəˈtaɲ/ French name for **BRITTANY**.

brethren archaic plural of **BROTHER**. ▶ plural noun fellow Christians or members of a male religious order. See also **BROTHER** (sense 2).
▪ used for humorous or rhetorical effect to refer to people belonging to a particular group: *our brethren in the popular national press.*

Breton¹ /ˈbrɛt(ə)n/ ▶ noun **1** a native of Brittany.
2 [mass noun] the Celtic language of Brittany, derived from Cornish. It has around 500,000 speakers.
▶ adjective of or relating to Brittany or its people or language.
– ORIGIN from Old French, 'Briton'.

Breton² /ˈbrɛt(ə)n, French brətɔ̃/, André (1896–1966), French poet, essayist, and critic. First involved with Dadaism, Breton later launched the surrealist movement, outlining the movement's philosophy in his manifesto of 1924. His creative writing is characterized by surrealist techniques such as 'automatic' writing.

Breughel variant spelling of **BRUEGEL**.

Breuil /ˈbrɔːi, French brœj/, Henri (Édouard Prosper) (1877–1961), French archaeologist. He is noted for his work on Palaeolithic cave paintings, in particular those at Altamira in Spain, which he was able to authenticate.

breve ▶ noun **1** Music a note, rarely used in modern music, having the time value of two semibreves, and represented as a semibreve with two short bars either side, or as a square.
2 a written or printed mark (˘) indicating a short or unstressed vowel.
3 historical an authoritative letter from a pope or monarch.
– ORIGIN Middle English: variant of **BRIEF**. In the musical sense, the term was originally used in a series where a *long* was of greater time value than a *breve.*

brevet /ˈbrɛvɪt/ ▶ noun [often as modifier] a former type of military commission conferred especially for outstanding service, by which an officer was promoted to a higher rank without the corresponding pay: *a brevet lieutenant.*
▶ verb (**breveted** or **brevetted**, **breveting** or **brevetting**) [with obj.] confer a brevet rank on.
– ORIGIN late Middle English (denoting an official letter, especially a papal indulgence): from Old French *brievet* 'little letter', diminutive of *bref.*

breviary /ˈbriːvɪəri/ ▶ noun (pl. **-ies**) a book containing the service for each day, to be recited by those in orders in the Roman Catholic Church.
– ORIGIN late Middle English (also denoting an abridged version of the psalms): from Latin *breviarium* 'summary, abridgement', from *breviare* 'abridge', from *brevis* 'short, brief'.

brevity /ˈbrɛvɪti/ ▶ noun [mass noun] concise and exact use of words in writing or speech.
▪ shortness of time: *the brevity of human life.*
– PHRASES **brevity is the soul of wit** proverb the essence of a witty statement lies in its concise wording and delivery. [ORIGIN: from Shakespeare's *Hamlet* (II. ii. 90).]
– ORIGIN late 15th cent.: from Old French *brievete*, from Latin *brevitas*, from *brevis* 'brief'.

brew ▶ verb [with obj.] **1** make (beer) by soaking, boiling, and fermentation.
2 make (tea or coffee) by mixing it with hot water: *I've just brewed some coffee* | [no obj.] *he did a crossword while the tea brewed.*
3 [no obj.] (of an unwelcome event or situation) begin to develop: *there was more trouble brewing as the miners went on strike* | *a storm was brewing.*
▶ noun **1** a kind of beer.
▪ informal a glass or can of beer.
2 a cup or mug of tea or coffee.
3 a mixture of events, people, or things which interact to form a more potent whole: *a dangerous brew of political turmoil and violent conflict.*
– DERIVATIVES **brewer** noun.
– ORIGIN Old English *brēowan* (verb), of Germanic origin; related to Dutch *brouwen* and German *brauen.*
▶ **brew up** Brit. make tea.

brewer's yeast ▶ noun [mass noun] a yeast which is used in the brewing of top-fermenting beer and is also eaten as a source of vitamin B.
• *Saccharomyces cerevisiae*, subdivision Ascomycotina.

brewery ▶ noun (pl. **-ies**) a place where beer is made commercially.
– ORIGIN mid 17th cent.: from **BREW**, probably on the pattern of Dutch *brouwerij.*

brewhouse ▶ noun a brewery.

brewmaster ▶ noun a person who supervises the brewing process in a brewery.

brewpub ▶ noun chiefly US an establishment, typically one including a restaurant, selling beer brewed on the premises.

Brewster, Sir David (1781–1868), Scottish physicist. He is best known for his work on the laws governing the polarization of light, and for his invention of the kaleidoscope.

brew-up ▶ noun Brit. informal a session of making tea.

Brezhnev /ˈbrɛʒnɛf/, Leonid (Ilich) (1906–82), Soviet statesman, General Secretary of the Communist Party of the USSR 1966–82 and President 1977–82. His period in power was marked by intensified persecution of dissidents at home and by attempted détente followed by renewed cold war in 1968; he was largely responsible for the invasion of Czechoslovakia (1968).

Briansk variant spelling of **BRYANSK**.

briar¹ (also **brier**) ▶ noun any of a number of prickly scrambling shrubs, especially a wild rose.
• Genus *Rosa*, family Rosaceae: several species, including the Eurasian **sweet briar** (*R. eglanteria*).
– DERIVATIVES **briary** adjective.
– ORIGIN Old English *brǣr*, *brēr*, of unknown origin.

briar² (also **brier**) ▶ noun **1** (also **briar pipe**) a tobacco pipe made from woody nodules borne at ground level by a large woody plant of the heather family.
2 the tree heath, which bears these nodules.
– ORIGIN mid 19th cent.: from French *bruyère* 'heath, heather', from medieval Latin *brucus.*

bribe ▶ verb [with obj.] persuade (someone) to act in one's favour, typically illegally or dishonestly, by a gift of money or other inducement: *they attempted to* **bribe** *opponents* **into** *losing* | [with obj. and infinitive] *they had bribed an official to sell them a certificate.*
▶ noun a sum of money or other inducement offered or given in this way.
– DERIVATIVES **bribable** adjective, **briber** noun.
– ORIGIN late Middle English: from Old French *briber*, *brimber* 'beg', of unknown origin. The original sense was 'rob, extort', hence (as a noun) 'theft, stolen goods', also 'money extorted or demanded for favours', later 'offer money as an inducement' (early 16th cent.).

bribery ▶ noun [mass noun] the giving or offering of a bribe: *his opponent had been guilty of bribery and corruption* | [as modifier] *a bribery scandal.*

bric-a-brac ▶ noun [mass noun] miscellaneous objects and ornaments of little value.
– ORIGIN mid 19th cent.: from French, from obsolete *à bric et à brac* 'at random'.

brick ▶ noun **1** a small rectangular block typically made of fired or sun-dried clay, used in building.
▪ [mass noun] bricks collectively as a building material: *this mill was built of brick* | [as modifier] *a large brick building.* ▪ a small, rectangular object: *a* **brick of** *ice cream.* ▪ Brit. a child's toy building block.
2 Brit. informal, dated a generous, helpful, and reliable person: *'You are really a brick, Vi,' Gloria said.*
▶ verb **1** [with obj. and usu. with adverbial] (often **be bricked**) block or enclose with a wall of bricks: *the doors have been* **bricked up**.
2 (**be bricking oneself**) Brit. vulgar slang be extremely worried or nervous.
– PHRASES **be built like a brick shithouse** see **SHITHOUSE**. **a brick short of a load** see **SHORT**. **bricks and mortar** buildings, typically housing: *untold acres are being buried under bricks and mortar.* ▪ a building, typically a house, considered in terms of its value as an investment. **come up against** (or **hit**) **a brick wall** face an insuperable problem or obstacle while trying to do something. **like a ton of bricks** informal with crushing weight, force, or authority: *the FA came down on him like a ton of bricks.* **you can't make bricks without straw** proverb nothing can be made or accomplished without proper or adequate material or information. [ORIGIN: with biblical allusion to Exod. V.; 'without straw' meant 'without having straw provided' (i.e. the Israelites were required to gather the straw for themselves). A misinterpretation has led to the current sense.]
– ORIGIN late Middle English: from Middle Low German, Middle Dutch *bricke*, *brike*; probably reinforced by Old French *brique*; of unknown ultimate origin.

brickbat ▶ noun a piece of brick, typically when used as a missile.
▪ a remark or comment which is highly critical and often insulting: *the plaudits were beginning to outnumber the brickbats.*

brick-built ▶ adjective (of a building or structure) made of bricks.

brickfield ▶ noun an area of ground where bricks are made.

brickfielder ▶ noun Austral. a hot, dry north wind, typically accompanied by dust.
– ORIGIN early 19th cent.: from the name of *Brickfield Hill*, the site (now part of central Sydney) of a former brickworks, associated with dust.

brickie ▶ noun (pl. **-ies**) Brit. informal a bricklayer.

bricklayer ▶ noun a person whose job is to build walls, houses, and other structures with bricks.
– DERIVATIVES **bricklaying** noun.

brick red ▶ noun [mass noun] a deep brownish red: [as modifier] *he had a brick-red face.*

brick veneer ▶ noun a covering of brick applied to a timber frame.
■[mass noun] timber frames covered in brick as a building material. ■ Austral. a house built with walls of such frames.

brickwork ▶ noun [mass noun] the bricks in a wall, house, or other structure, typically in terms of their type or layout: *the patterned brickwork of the gables.*
■the craft or occupation of building walls, houses, or other structures with bricks.

brickyard ▶ noun a place where bricks are made.

bricolage /ˌbrɪkəˈlɑːʒ/ ▶ noun (pl. same or **bricolages**) [mass noun] (in art or literature) construction or creation from a diverse range of available things.
■[count noun] something constructed or created in this way.
– ORIGIN French.

bricoleur /ˌbrɪkəˈləː/ ▶ noun a person who engages in bricolage.
– ORIGIN French, literally 'handyman'.

bridal ▶ adjective [attrib.] of or concerning a bride or a newly married couple: *her white bridal gown | the bridal party came out into the church porch.*
– ORIGIN late Middle English: from Old English *brȳd-ealu* 'wedding-feast', from *brȳd* 'bride' + *ealu* 'ale-drinking'. Since the late 16th cent., the word has been associated with adjectives ending in **-AL**.

bridal registry ▶ noun chiefly N. Amer. a service offered by a shop or other organization in which a bridal couple's gift preferences are recorded so as to be available to family and friends when shopping at the store.

bridal suite ▶ noun a suite of rooms in a hotel for the use of a newly married couple.

bride ▶ noun a woman on her wedding day or just before and after the event.
– ORIGIN Old English *brȳd*, of Germanic origin; related to Dutch *bruid* and German *Braut*.

Bride, St /ˈbriːdə, brʌɪd/ see **BRIDGET, ST**[1].

bridegroom ▶ noun a man on his wedding day or just before and after the event.
– ORIGIN Old English *brȳdguma*, from *brȳd* 'bride' + *guma* 'man'. The change in the second syllable was due to association with **GROOM**.

bride price ▶ noun a sum of money or quantity of goods given to a bride's family by that of the groom, especially in tribal societies.

bridesmaid ▶ noun a girl or woman, usually one of several, who accompanies a bride on her wedding day.
– ORIGIN late 18th cent.: alteration of earlier *bridemaid*.

bridewell ▶ noun archaic a prison or reform school for petty offenders.
– ORIGIN mid 16th cent.: named after *St Bride's Well* in the City of London, near which such a building stood.

Bridge, Frank (1879–1941), English composer, conductor, and violist. His compositions include chamber music, songs, and orchestral works, among them *The Sea* (1910–11) and *Oration* (for cello and orchestra, 1930).

bridge[1] ▶ noun **1** a structure carrying a road, path, railway, etc. across a river, ravine, road, railway, or other obstacle: *a bridge across the River Thames | a railway bridge.*
■something which makes a physical connection between two other things. ■ something which is intended to reconcile or form a connection between two seemingly incompatible things: *a committee which was formed to create a bridge between rival party groups.* ■ a partial denture supported by natural teeth on either side. See also **BRIDGEWORK**. ■ the support for the tip of a billiard cue formed by the hand. ■ a long stick with a frame at the end which is used to support a cue for a difficult shot. ■ Music an upright piece of wood on a stringed instrument over which the strings are stretched. ■ Music a bridge passage or middle eight. ■ short for **LAND BRIDGE**.
2 the elevated, enclosed platform on a ship from which the captain and officers direct operations.
3 the upper bony part of a person's nose: *he pushed his spectacles further up the bridge of his nose.*
■the central part of a pair of glasses, fitting over this: *these sunglasses have a special nose bridge for comfort.*
4 an electric circuit with two branches across which a detector or load is connected. These circuits are used to measure resistance or other property by equalizing the potential across the two ends of a detector, or to rectify an alternating voltage or current.
▶ verb [with obj.] be a bridge over (something): *a covered walkway bridged the gardens.*
■build a bridge over (something): *earlier attempts to bridge St George's Channel had failed.* ■ make (a difference between two groups) smaller or less significant: *new initiatives were needed to bridge the great abyss of class.*
– PHRASES **cross that bridge when one comes to it** deal with a problem when and if it arises.
– DERIVATIVES **bridgeable** adjective.
– ORIGIN Old English *brycg* (noun), of Germanic origin; related to Dutch *brug* and German *Brücke*.

bridge[2] ▶ noun [mass noun] a card game related to whist, played by two partnerships of two players who at the beginning of each hand bid for the right to name the trump suit, the highest bid also representing a contract to make a specified number of tricks with a specified suit as trumps.
– ORIGIN late 19th cent.: of unknown origin.

bridge-building ▶ noun [mass noun] the activity of building bridges.
■figurative the promotion of friendly relations between groups.
– DERIVATIVES **bridge-builder** noun.

bridgehead ▶ noun a strong position secured by an army inside enemy territory from which to advance or attack.

bridge loan ▶ noun North American term for **BRIDGING LOAN**.

bridge of boats ▶ noun a bridge formed by mooring boats side by side across a river.

Bridge of Sighs a 16th-century enclosed bridge in Venice between the Doges' Palace and the state prison, originally crossed by prisoners on their way to torture or execution.

bridge passage ▶ noun a transitional section in a musical composition leading to a new section or theme.

bridge roll ▶ noun Brit. a small, soft bread roll with a long, thin shape.

Bridges, Robert (Seymour) (1844–1930), English poet and literary critic. His long philosophical poem *The Testament of Beauty* (1929), written in the Victorian tradition, was instantly popular. He was Poet Laureate 1913–30.

Bridget, St[1] (also **Bride** or **Brigid**) (6th century), Irish abbess; also known as **St Bridget of Ireland**. She was venerated in Ireland as a virgin saint and noted in miracle stories for her compassion; her cult soon spread over most of western Europe. Feast day, 1 February.

Bridget, St[2] (also **Birgitta**) (*c.*1303–73), Swedish nun and visionary; also known as **St Bridget of Sweden**. She experienced her first vision of the Virgin Mary at the age of 7. Feast day, 23 July.

Bridgetown the capital of Barbados, a port on the south coast; pop. 6,720 (1990).

bridgework ▶ noun [mass noun] **1** dental bridges collectively.
■the construction or insertion of such bridges.
2 Building the component parts of a bridge.
■the construction of bridges.

bridging /ˈbrɪdʒɪŋ/ ▶ noun [mass noun] the action of constructing a bridge over something: *the bridging of a ditch.*
■Climbing a method of climbing a wide chimney by using the left hand and foot on one side wall and the right hand and foot on the other.

bridging loan ▶ noun chiefly Brit. a sum of money lent by a bank to cover an interval between two transactions, typically the buying of one house and the selling of another.

Bridgman, Percy Williams (1882–1961), American physicist. He worked with liquids and solids under very high pressures and his techniques were later used in making artificial minerals (including diamonds). Nobel Prize for Physics (1946).

bridie ▶ noun (pl. **-ies**) Scottish a meat pasty.
– ORIGIN origin uncertain; perhaps from obsolete *bride's pie*.

bridle ▶ noun the headgear used to control a horse, consisting of buckled straps to which a bit and reins are attached.
■a line, rope, or device that is used to restrain or control the action or movement of something. ■ Nautical a mooring cable.
▶ verb **1** [with obj.] put a bridle on (a horse).
■bring (something) under control; curb: *the fact that he was their servant bridled his tongue.*
2 [no obj.] show one's resentment or anger, especially by throwing up one's head and drawing in one's chin: *she* **bridled at** *his tone.*
– PHRASES **off the bridle** see **BIT**[3]. **on the bridle** see **BIT**[3].
– ORIGIN Old English *brīdel* (noun), *brīdlian* (verb), of Germanic origin; related to Dutch *breidel* (noun). Sense 2 of the verb use is from the action of a horse when reined in.

bridleway (also **bridle path**) ▶ noun Brit. a path or track along which horse riders have right of way.

bridoon /brɪˈduːn/ (also **bradoon**) ▶ noun a snaffle bit which is frequently used in conjunction with a curb bit in a double bridle.
– ORIGIN mid 18th cent.: from French *bridon*, from *bride* 'bridle', of Germanic origin.

Brie /briː/ ▶ noun [mass noun] a kind of soft, mild, creamy cheese with a firm, white skin.
– ORIGIN named after *Brie* in northern France, where it was originally made.

brief ▶ adjective of short duration: *the president made a brief working visit to Moscow.*
■concise in expression; using few words: *introductions were brief and polite | be brief and don't talk for longer than is necessary.* ■ (of a piece of clothing) not covering much of the body; scanty: *Alison sported a pair of extremely brief black shorts.*
▶ noun chiefly Brit. a set of instructions given to a person about a job or task: *his brief is to turn round the county's fortunes.*
■Law a summary of the facts and legal points in a case given to a barrister to argue in court. ■ a piece of work for a barrister. ■ informal a solicitor or barrister: *it was only his brief's eloquence that had saved him from prison.* ■ US a written summary of the facts and legal points supporting one side of a case, for presentation to a court. ■ a letter from the Pope to a person or community on a matter of discipline.
▶ verb [with obj.] instruct or inform (someone) thoroughly, especially in preparation for a task: *she briefed him on last week's decisions.*
■Brit. instruct (a barrister) by brief.
– PHRASES **hold a brief for** Brit. be retained as counsel for. **hold no brief for** not support or argue in favour of: *I hold no brief for dishonest policemen.* **in brief** in a few words; in short: *he is, in brief, the embodiment of evil | the news in brief.*
– DERIVATIVES **briefly** adverb [sentence adverb] *briefly, the plot is as follows …*, **briefness** noun.
– ORIGIN Middle English: from Old French *brief*, from Latin *brevis* 'short'. The noun is via late Latin *breve* 'note, dispatch', hence 'an official letter'.

briefcase ▶ noun a leather or plastic rectangular container with a handle for carrying books and documents.

briefing ▶ noun a meeting for giving information or instructions: *a media briefing in the House of Commons.*
■the information or instructions given: *this briefing explains the systems, products, and standards.* ■ [mass noun] the action of informing or instructing someone: *today's briefing of Nato allies.*

briefless ▶ adjective Law, Brit. (of a barrister) having no clients.

briefs ▶ plural noun short, close-fitting underpants or knickers.

brier[1] ▶ noun variant spelling of **BRIAR**[1].

brier[2] ▶ noun variant spelling of **BRIAR**[2].

Brig. ▶ abbreviation for Brigadier.

brig[1] ▶ noun a two-masted square-rigged ship,

typically having an additional lower fore-and-aft sail on the gaff and a boom to the mainmast.
▪informal a prison, especially on a warship.
– ORIGIN early 18th cent.: abbreviation of **BRIGANTINE** (the original sense).

brig[2] ▶ **noun** Scottish & N. English a bridge.
– ORIGIN from Old Norse *bryggja*.

brigade ▶ **noun** a subdivision of an army, typically consisting of a small number of infantry battalions and/or other units and typically forming part of a division: *he commanded a brigade of 3,000 men.*
▪an organization with a specific purpose, typically with a military or quasi-military structure: *a volunteer ambulance brigade.* ▪ [in sing.] [with adj. or noun modifier] informal, often derogatory a group of people with a characteristic in common: *the anti-smoking brigade.*
▶ **verb** [with obj.] rare form into a brigade.
▪associate with (someone or something): *they thought the speech too closely brigaded with illegal action.*
– ORIGIN mid 17th cent.: from French, from Italian *brigata* 'company', from *brigare* 'contend', from *briga* 'strife'.

brigade major ▶ **noun** Military the principal staff officer to the brigadier in command at the headquarters of a brigade.

brigadier ▶ **noun** a rank of officer in the British army, above colonel and below major general.
– ORIGIN late 17th cent.: from French (see **BRIGADE**, **-IER**).

brigadier general ▶ **noun** a rank of officer in the US army, air force, and marine corps, above colonel and below major general.

brigalow /'brɪgələʊ/ ▶ **noun** an Australian acacia tree.
• Genus *Acacia*, family Leguminosae: several species, in particular *A. harpophylla*, with silver leaves and dark furrowed bark.
– ORIGIN mid 19th cent.: from an Aboriginal word, perhaps Kamilaroi *burigal*.

brigand /'brɪg(ə)nd/ ▶ **noun** poetic/literary a member of a gang that ambushes and robs people in forests and mountains.
– DERIVATIVES **brigandage** noun, **brigandry** noun.
– ORIGIN late Middle English (also denoting an irregular foot soldier): from Old French, from Italian *brigante*, literally '(person) contending', from *brigare* 'contend' (see **BRIGADE**).

brigandine /'brɪg(ə)ndiːn/ ▶ **noun** historical a coat of mail, typically one made of iron rings or plates attached to canvas or other fabric.
– ORIGIN late Middle English: from Old French, from *brigand* (see **BRIGAND**).

brigantine /'brɪg(ə)ntiːn/ ▶ **noun** a two-masted sailing ship with a square-rigged foremast and a mainmast rigged fore and aft.
– ORIGIN early 16th cent. (denoting a small vessel used by pirates): from Old French, from Italian *brigantino*, from *brigante* (see **BRIGAND**).

Briggs, Henry (1561–1630), English mathematician. He was renowned for his work on logarithms, in which he introduced the decimal base, made the thousands of calculations necessary for the tables, and popularized their use. Briggs also devised the usual method used for long division.

Bright, John (1811–89), English Liberal politician and reformer. A noted orator, Bright was the leader, along with Richard Cobden, of the campaign to repeal the Corn Laws. He was also a vociferous opponent of the Crimean War (1854) and was closely identified with the 1867 Reform Act.

bright ▶ **adjective 1** giving out or reflecting a lot of light; shining: *the sun was dazzlingly bright | her bright, dark eyes | an aversion to bright light.*
▪full of light: *the rooms are bright and spacious.* ▪ (of a period of time) having sunny, cloudless weather: *the long, bright days of June.* ▪ having a vivid colour: *the bright flowers | a bright tie.* ▪ (of colour) vivid and bold: *the bright green leaves.*
2 (of sound) clear, vibrant, and typically high-pitched: *her voice is fresh and bright.*
3 (of a person, idea, or remark) intelligent and quick-witted: *she was amiable, but not very bright | a bright idea.*
4 giving an appearance of cheerful liveliness: *at breakfast she would be persistently bright and chirpy | she gave a bright smile.*
▪(of someone's future) likely to be successful and happy: *these young people have a bright future ahead of them.*
▶ **adverb** chiefly poetic/literary brightly: *a full moon shining bright.*
▶ **noun** (**brights**) **1** bold and vivid colours: *a choice of fashion colours from pastels through to brights.*
2 N. Amer. headlights switched to full beam: *he turned the brights on and we drove along the dirt road.*
– PHRASES **bright and early** very early in the morning. **(as) bright as a button** informal intelligently alert and lively. **the bright lights** the glamour and excitement of city life: *they hankered for the bright lights of the capital.* **look on the bright side** be optimistic or cheerful in spite of difficulties.
– DERIVATIVES **brightish** adjective, **brightly** adverb, **brightness** noun.
– ORIGIN Old English *beorht*, of Germanic origin.

brighten ▶ **verb** make or become more light: [no obj.] *most of the country should* ***brighten up*** *in the afternoon |* [with obj.] *the fire began to blaze fiercely, brightening the room.*
▪[with obj.] make (something) more attractively and cheerfully colourful: *daffodils* ***brighten up*** *many gardens and parks.* ▪ make or become happier and more cheerful: [no obj.] *Sarah* ***brightened up*** *considerably as she thought of Emily's words |* [with obj.] *she seems to brighten his life.*
– ORIGIN Old English *(ge)beorhtnian*.

bright-eyed ▶ **adjective** having shining eyes.
▪alert and lively: *bright-eyed young lawyers | a bright-eyed optimism.*
– PHRASES **bright-eyed and bushy-tailed** informal alert and lively; eager. [ORIGIN: from the conventional description of a squirrel.]

Brighton a resort on the south coast of England; pop. 133,400 (1991). It was patronized by the Prince of Wales (later George IV) from *c.*1780 to 1827, and is noted for its Regency architecture. It became a city (with Hove) in 2000.

Bright's disease ▶ **noun** [mass noun] a disease involving chronic inflammation of the kidneys.
– ORIGIN mid 19th cent.: named after Richard Bright, (1789–1858), the English physician who established its nature.

bright spark ▶ **noun** informal, often ironic a clever or witty person.

brightwork ▶ **noun** [mass noun] polished metalwork on ships or other vehicles.

bright young thing ▶ **noun** an enthusiastic, ambitious, and fashionable young person, a term originally applied in the 1920s to a member of a fashionable set noted for outrageous behaviour.

Brigid, St /'brɪdʒɪd/ see **BRIDGET, ST**[1].

brill[1] ▶ **noun** a European flatfish that resembles a turbot.
• *Scophthalmus rhombus*, family Scophthalmidae (or Bothidae).
– ORIGIN late 15th cent.: of unknown origin.

brill[2] ▶ **adjective** Brit. informal excellent; marvellous: *a brill new series |* [as exclamation] *'She says I can spend half-term with you.' 'Hey, brill!'*
– ORIGIN 1980s: abbreviation of **BRILLIANT**.

brilliance (also **brilliancy**) ▶ **noun** [mass noun] intense brightness of light: *the nights were dark, lit only by the brilliance of Aegean stars.*
▪vividness of colour. ▪ exceptional talent or intelligence: *he's played the stock market with great brilliance.*

brilliant ▶ **adjective 1** exceptionally clever or talented: *he was quite brilliant and was promoted almost at once | the germ of a brilliant idea hit her.*
▪outstanding; impressive: *his brilliant career at Harvard.* ▪ Brit. informal excellent; marvellous: *we had a brilliant time |* [as exclamation] *'Brilliant!' he declared excitedly.*
2 (of light) very bright and radiant: *brilliant sunshine illuminated the scene.*
▪(of a colour) brightly and intensely vivid.
▶ **noun** a diamond of brilliant cut.
– DERIVATIVES **brilliantly** adverb.
– ORIGIN late 17th cent.: from French *brillant* 'shining', present participle of *briller*, from Italian *brillare*, probably from Latin *beryllus* (see **BERYL**).

brilliant cut ▶ **noun** a circular cut for diamonds and other gemstones in the form of two many-faceted pyramids joined at their bases, the upper one truncated near its apex.

brilliantine ▶ **noun** [mass noun] **1** dated scented oil used on men's hair to make it look glossy.
2 US shiny dress fabric made from cotton and mohair or cotton and worsted.
– DERIVATIVES **brilliantined** adjective (only in sense 1).
– ORIGIN late 19th cent.: from French *brillantine*, from *brillant* 'shining' (see **BRILLIANT**).

brim ▶ **noun** the projecting edge around the bottom of a hat: *a soft hat with a turned-up brim.*
▪the upper edge or lip of a cup, bowl, or other container: *he filled her glass* ***to the brim***.
▶ **verb** (**brimmed**, **brimming**) [no obj.] [often as adj. **brimming**] be full to the point of overflowing: *a brimming cup.*
▪fill something so completely as almost to spill out of it: *large tears brimmed in her eyes.* ▪ figurative be full of a particular quality, feeling, etc.: *he is* ***brimming with*** *ideas.*
– DERIVATIVES **brimless** adjective, **brimmed** adjective [in combination] *a wide-brimmed hat.*
– ORIGIN Middle English (denoting the edge of the sea or other body of water): perhaps related to German *Bräme* 'trimming'.

brimful ▶ **adjective** [predic.] filled with something to the point of overflowing: *a jug brimful of custard.*

brimstone /'brɪmst(ə)n, -stəʊn/ ▶ **noun 1** [mass noun] archaic sulphur.
▪figurative fiery or passionate feeling.
2 a bright yellow butterfly or moth:
• (also **brimstone butterfly**) a European butterfly of the white family, the male of which is yellow and the female greenish-white (*Gonepteryx rhamni*, family Pieridae). • (also **brimstone moth**) a small yellow European moth (*Opisthograptis luteolata*, family Geometridae).
– ORIGIN late Old English *brynstān*, probably from *bryne* 'burning' + *stān* 'stone'.

brindle ▶ **noun** [mass noun] a brownish or tawny colour of animal fur, with streaks of other colour.
▪[count noun] an animal with such a coat.
▶ **adjective** (also **brindled**) (especially of domestic animals) brownish or tawny with streaks of other colour: *a brindle pup.*
– ORIGIN late 17th cent.: back-formation from *brindled*, alteration of Middle English *brinded* in the same sense, probably of Scandinavian origin.

Brindley /'brɪndli/, James (1716–72), pioneering English canal-builder. He designed some 600 km (375 miles) of waterway with a minimum of locks, cuttings, or tunnels, connecting most of the major rivers of England.

brine ▶ **noun** [mass noun] water saturated or strongly impregnated with salt.
▪seawater: *dolphins and whales can't help taking in the odd gulp of brine as they swallow a fish.* ▪ [count noun] technical a strong solution of a salt or salts.
▶ **verb** [with obj.] [often as adj. **brined**] soak in or saturate with salty water: *brined anchovies.*
– ORIGIN Old English *brīne*, of unknown origin.

brine shrimp ▶ **noun** a small fairy shrimp which lives in brine pools and salt lakes and is used as food for aquarium fish.
• *Artemia salina*, class Branchiopoda.

bring ▶ **verb** (past and past participle **brought**) [with obj. and usu. with adverbial of direction] come to a place with (someone or something): *she brought Luke home from hospital |* [with two objs] *Liz brought her a glass of water.*
▪cause (someone or something) to come to a place: *what brings you here? | a felony case brought before a jury |* figurative *his inner confidence has* ***brought*** *him* ***through*** *his ordeal.* ▪ cause (someone or something) to move in a particular direction or way: *he brought his hands out of his pockets | heavy rain* ***brought down*** *part of the ceiling.* ▪ cause (something): *the bad weather brought famine | her letter* ***brought forth*** *a torrent of criticism.* ▪ cause (someone or something) to be in or change to a particular state or condition: *I'll give you an aspirin to* ***bring down*** *your temperature | his approach* ***brought*** *him* ***into*** *conflict with government | the thought* ***brought him out in*** *a cold sweat.* ▪ (**bring someone in**) involve (someone) in a particular activity: *he has brought in a consultancy company.* ▪ initiate (legal action) against someone: *riot and conspiracy charges should be* ***brought against*** *them.* ▪ [usu. with negative] (**bring oneself to do something**) force oneself to do something unpleasant or distressing: *she could not bring herself to mention it.* ▪ cause someone to receive (an amount of money) as income or profit: *two important Chippendale lots brought £10,000 each |* [with two objs] *five more novels brought him £150,000.*
– PHRASES **bring home the bacon** see **BACON**. **bring something home to someone** see **HOME**. **bring the house down** make an audience respond with great enthusiasm, typically as shown by their laughter or applause. **bring something into play** cause something to begin operating or to have an effect; activate. **bring something to bear** exert influence

or pressure so as to cause a particular result: *he was released after pressure had been brought to bear by the aid agencies.* **bring someone to book** see **BOOK**. **bring something to light** see **LIGHT**[1]. **bring someone/thing to mind** cause one to remember or think of someone or something: *all that marble brought to mind a mausoleum.* **bring something to pass** chiefly poetic/literary cause something to happen.

– DERIVATIVES **bringer** noun.

– ORIGIN Old English *bringan*, of Germanic origin; related to Dutch *brengen* and German *bringen*.

▶**bring something about 1** cause something to happen: *she brought about a revolution in psychoanalysis.* **2** cause a ship to head in a different direction.

bring something back cause something to return: *the smell of the tiny church brought back every memory of my childhood.* ■ reintroduce something: *bringing back capital punishment would solve nothing.*

bring someone down cause someone to fall over, especially by tackling them during a football or rugby match. ■ cause someone to lose power: *the vote will not bring down the government.* ■ make someone unhappy.

bring someone/thing down cause an animal or person to fall over by shooting them. ■ cause an aircraft or bird to fall from the sky by shooting at it.

bring something forth archaic or poetic/literary give birth to: *why does Elsbeth not bring forth a child?*

bring something forward 1 move a meeting or event to an earlier date or time. **2** [often as adj. **brought forward**] (in bookkeeping) transfer a total sum from the bottom of one page to the top of the next. **3** propose a plan, subject, or idea for consideration.

bring something in 1 introduce something, especially a new law or product: *Congress brought in reforms to prevent abuse of presidential power.* **2** make or earn a particular amount of money: *their fund-raising efforts have brought in more than $1 million.* **3** (of a jury) give a decision in court: *the jury brought in a unanimous verdict.*

bring someone off 1 rescue someone from a ship in difficulties. **2** vulgar slang give someone or oneself an orgasm.

bring something off achieve something successfully: *a good omelette is very hard to bring off.*

bring someone on encourage someone who is learning something to develop or improve at a faster rate.

bring something on 1 cause something, typically something unpleasant, to occur or develop: *ulcers are not brought on by a rich diet.* ■ (**bring something on/upon**) be responsible for something, typically something unpleasant, that happens to (oneself or someone else): *he's brought it upon himself—he's not a victim.* **2** (of the weather) promote the growth of crops.

bring someone out 1 encourage someone to feel more confident: *she needs friends to* **bring** *her* **out of** *herself.* **2** Brit. cause someone to go on strike.

bring something out 1 produce and launch a new product or publication: *the band are bringing out a video.* **2** make something more evident; emphasize something: *the shawl brings out the colour of your eyes | playing for United will* **bring out the best in** *me.*

bring someone round (or US **around**) **1** restore someone to consciousness. **2** persuade someone to do something, especially to adopt one's own point of view: *she's not keen, but I think I can bring her round.*

bring someone to restore someone to consciousness.

bring something to cause a boat to stop, especially by turning into the wind.

bring up (chiefly of a ship) come to a stop.

bring someone up look after a child until it is an adult. ■ (**be brought up**) be taught as a child to adopt particular behaviour or attitudes: *he had been brought up to believe that marriage was forever.*

bring something up 1 vomit something. **2** raise a matter for discussion or consideration: *she tried repeatedly to bring up the subject of money.*

bring and buy (also **bring-and-buy sale**) ▶ **noun** Brit. a charity sale at which people bring items for sale and buy those brought by others.

brinjal /ˈbrɪndʒɔːl, -dʒɒl/ ▶ **noun** Indian & S. African an aubergine.

– ORIGIN based on Portuguese *berinjela*, from Arabic *al-bāḏinjān* (see **AUBERGINE**).

Brink, André (b.1935), South African novelist, short-story writer, and dramatist. He gained international recognition with his novel *Looking on Darkness* (1973), which became the first novel in Afrikaans to be banned by the South African government. Other notable novels: *A Dry White Season* (1979) and *A Chain of Voices* (1982).

brink ▶ **noun** an extreme edge of land before a steep or vertical slope: ***the brink of*** *the cliffs.*

■ a margin or bank of a body of water: *at* ***the brink of*** *the pond I hesitated.* ■ the verge of a particular state, event, or action, typically one that is unwelcome or disastrous: *the country was* ***on the brink of*** *a constitutional crisis.*

– ORIGIN Middle English: of Scandinavian origin.

brinkmanship /ˈbrɪŋkmənʃɪp/ (US also **brinksmanship**) ▶ **noun** [mass noun] the art or practice of pursuing a dangerous policy to the limits of safety before stopping, typically in politics.

brinny ▶ **noun** (pl. **-ies**) Austral. a stone, typically one thrown as a missile.

– ORIGIN 1940s: probably from an Aboriginal language.

briny /ˈbrʌɪni/ ▶ **adjective** (**-ier**, **-iest**) of salty water or the sea; salty: *the briny tang of the scallops.*

▶ **noun** (**the briny**) Brit. informal the sea.

brio /ˈbriːəʊ/ ▶ **noun** [mass noun] vigour or vivacity of style or performance: *she told her story with some brio.* See also **CON BRIO**.

– ORIGIN mid 18th cent.: from Italian.

brioche /briːˈɒʃ, ˈbriːɒʃ/ ▶ **noun** a light sweet yeast bread typically in the form of a small round roll.

– ORIGIN French, from Norman French *brier*, synonym of *broyer*, literally 'split up into very small pieces by pressure'.

briquette /brɪˈkɛt/ (also **briquet**) ▶ **noun** a block of compressed coal dust or peat used as fuel.

– ORIGIN late 19th cent.: from French, diminutive of *brique* 'brick'.

Brisbane[1] /ˈbrɪzbən/ the capital of Queensland, Australia; pop. 1,273,500 (1990). It was founded in 1824 as a penal colony.

– ORIGIN named after Sir Thomas *Brisbane* (see **BRISBANE**[2]).

Brisbane[2] /ˈbrɪzbən/, Sir Thomas Makdougall (1773–1860), Scottish soldier and astronomer. In 1790 he joined the army, becoming major general in 1813. He was governor of New South Wales (1821–5) and became an acclaimed astronomer.

brisé /ˈbriːzeɪ/ ▶ **noun** Ballet a jump in which the dancer sweeps one leg into the air to the side while jumping off the other, brings both legs together in the air and beats them before landing.

▶ **adjective** (of a fan) consisting entirely of pierced sticks of ivory, horn, or tortoiseshell.

– ORIGIN French, literally 'broken'.

brisk ▶ **adjective** active and energetic: *a good brisk walk | business appeared to be brisk.*

■ slightly brusque in manner or nature: *she adopted a brisk, businesslike tone.* ■ (of wind or the weather) cold but pleasantly invigorating.

▶ **verb** [with obj.] (**brisk something up**) quicken something: *Mary brisked up her pace.*

– DERIVATIVES **brisken** verb, **briskly** adverb, **briskness** noun.

– ORIGIN late 16th cent.: probably from French *brusque* (see **BRUSQUE**).

brisket ▶ **noun** [mass noun] meat cut from the breast of an animal, typically a cow.

– ORIGIN Middle English: perhaps from Old Norse *brjósk* 'cartilage, gristle'.

brisling /ˈbrɪslɪŋ, ˈbrɪz-/ ▶ **noun** (pl. same or **brislings**) a sprat, typically one seasoned and smoked in Norway and sold in a can.

– ORIGIN early 20th cent.: from Norwegian and Danish.

bristle /ˈbrɪs(ə)l/ ▶ **noun** (usu. **bristles**) a short stiff hair, typically one of those on an animal's skin or a man's face.

■ a stiff animal hair, or a man-made substitute, used to make a brush: *a toothbrush with nylon bristles* | [mass noun] *the heads are made with natural bristle.*

▶ **verb** [no obj.] (of hair or fur) stand upright away from the skin, typically as a sign of anger or fear: *the hair on the back of his neck bristled.*

■ (of an animal) react in such a way that its hair or fur stands on end: *the cat bristled in annoyance.* ■ (of a person) react angrily or defensively, typically by drawing oneself up: *she* ***bristled at*** *his rudeness | the staff are* ***bristling with*** *indignation.* ■ (**bristle with**) be covered with or abundant in: *the roof bristled with antennae.*

– ORIGIN Middle English: from Old English *byrst* (of Germanic origin, related to German *Borste*) + **-LE**[1].

bristlebird ▶ **noun** an Australian songbird with mainly brown plumage, a long cocked tail, a fringe of bristles around the bill, and secretive habits.

• Genus *Dasyornis*, family Acanthizidae (or Maluridae): two or three species, in particular the **rufous bristlebird** (*D. broadbenti*).

bristlecone pine ▶ **noun** a very long-lived shrubby pine of western North America. It has been used in dendrochronology to check and adjust radiocarbon dating.

• *Pinus longaeva*, family Pinaceae.

bristle fern ▶ **noun** a mainly tropical filmy fern with hair-like bristles protruding from the spore-containing bodies.

• Genus *Trichomanes*, family Hymenophyllaceae.

bristletail ▶ **noun** a small primitive wingless insect which has bristles at the end of the abdomen.

• Orders Thysanura (the **true bristletails**, with three bristles, including the silverfish) and Diplura (the **two-pronged bristletails**), subclass Apterygota.

bristle worm ▶ **noun** a marine annelid worm which has a segmented body with numerous bristles on the fleshy lobes of each segment. Also called ***polychaete***.

• Class Polychaeta: numerous species, including ragworms, lugworms, fan worms, and their relatives.

bristling ▶ **adjective** (especially of hair) close-set, stiff, and spiky: *a bristling beard.*

■ figurative aggressively brisk or tense: *he fills the screen with a restless, bristling energy.*

bristly ▶ **adjective** (of hair or foliage) having a stiff and prickly texture.

■ covered with short stiff hairs: *he rubbed his bristly chin.*

Bristol /ˈbrɪst(ə)l/ a city in SW England; pop. 370,300 (1991). Situated on the River Avon about 10 km (6 miles) from the Bristol Channel, it has been a leading port since the 12th century.

Bristol board ▶ **noun** [mass noun] a type of stiff, smooth cardboard used as a drawing surface or for cutting and shaping.

Bristol Channel a wide inlet of the Atlantic between South Wales and the south-western peninsula of England, narrowing into the estuary of the River Severn.

Bristol fashion ▶ **adjective** [predic.] Brit. informal, dated in good order; neat and clean: *it gave him pleasure to keep things* ***shipshape and Bristol fashion.***

– ORIGIN mid 19th cent.: originally in nautical use, referring to the commercial prosperity of Bristol, when its shipping was in good order.

bristols ▶ **plural noun** Brit. informal a woman's breasts.

– ORIGIN 1960s: from rhyming slang *Bristol Cities* 'titties'.

Brit informal ▶ **noun** a British person.

▶ **adjective** British.

– ORIGIN early 20th cent.: abbreviation.

Britain the island containing England, Wales, and Scotland, and including the small adjacent islands. The name is broadly synonymous with Great Britain, but the longer form is more usual for the political unit. See also **GREAT BRITAIN**, **UNITED KINGDOM**.

– ORIGIN Old English *Breoton*, from Latin *Brittones* 'Britons', superseded in Middle English by forms from Old French *Bretaigne* (from Latin *Brit(t)annia*). It became a largely historical term until revived in the mid 16th cent., as the possible union of England and Scotland became a subject of political concern.

Britain, Battle of a series of air battles fought over Britain (August–October 1940), in which the RAF successfully resisted raids by the numerically superior German air force. This led Hitler to abandon plans to invade Britain, although the Germans continued to bomb British cities by night for several months afterwards.

Britannia /brɪˈtanjə/ the personification of Britain, usually depicted as a helmeted woman with shield and trident. The figure had appeared on Roman coins and was revived with the name Britannia on the coinage of Charles II.

– ORIGIN the Latin name for **BRITAIN**.

Britannia metal ▶ **noun** [mass noun] a silvery alloy consisting of tin with about 5–15 per cent antimony and usually some copper, lead, or zinc.

Britannia silver ▶ **noun** [mass noun] hallmarked silver that is at least 95.8 per cent pure.

Britannic /brɪˈtanɪk/ ▸ adjective dated (chiefly in names or titles) of Britain or the British Empire: *he answered His Britannic Majesty's call to arms.*
– ORIGIN mid 17th cent.: from Latin *Britannicus*, from *Britannia* (see **BRITANNIA**).

Briticism /ˈbrɪtɪsɪz(ə)m/ (also **Britishism** /-ʃɪz(ə)m/) ▸ noun an idiom used in Britain but not in other English-speaking countries.
– ORIGIN mid 19th cent.: from **BRITISH**, on the pattern of words such as *Gallicism.*

British ▸ adjective **1** of or relating to Great Britain or the United Kingdom, or to its people or language.
2 of the British Commonwealth or (formerly) the British Empire.
▸ noun [as plural noun **the British**] the British people.
– DERIVATIVES **Britishness** noun.
– ORIGIN Old English *Brettisc* 'relating to the ancient Britons', from *Bret* 'Briton', from Latin *Britto*, or its Celtic equivalent.

British Academy an institution founded in 1901 for the promotion of historical, philosophical, and philological studies.

British Antarctic Territory that part of Antarctica claimed by Britain. Designated in 1962 from territory that was formerly part of the Falkland Islands Dependencies, it includes some 388,500 sq. km (150,058 sq. miles) of the continent of Antarctica as well as the South Orkney Islands and South Shetland Islands in the South Atlantic.

British Broadcasting Corporation (abbrev.: **BBC**) a public corporation for radio and television broadcasting in Britain.

> The BBC was established in 1927 by royal charter and held a monopoly until the introduction of the first commercial TV station in 1954. It is financed by the sale of television viewing licences rather than by revenue from advertising and has an obligation to remain impartial in its reporting.

British Columbia a province on the west coast of Canada; pop. 3,218,500 (1991); capital, Victoria. Formed in 1866 by the union of Vancouver Island (a former British colony) and the mainland area, then called New Caledonia, the province includes the Queen Charlotte Islands.

British Council an organization established in 1934 with the aims of promoting a wider knowledge of Britain and the English language abroad, and of developing closer cultural relations with other countries.

British disease ▸ noun [usu. in sing.] informal a problem or failing supposed to be characteristically British, especially (formerly) a proneness to industrial unrest.

British Empire a former empire consisting of Great Britain and its possessions, dominions, and dependencies.

> Colonization of North America and domination of India began in the 17th century. A series of small colonies, mostly in the West Indies, were gained during the late 17th–early 19th centuries, and Australia, New Zealand, various parts of the Far East, and large areas of Africa were added in the 19th century. Self-government was granted to Canada, Australia, New Zealand, and South Africa in the mid 19th century, and most of the remaining colonies have gained independence since the end of the Second World War.

British Empire, Order of the see ORDER OF THE BRITISH EMPIRE.

British English ▸ noun [mass noun] English as used in Great Britain, as distinct from that used elsewhere.

Britisher ▸ noun informal (in North America and old-fashioned British English) a native or inhabitant of Britain.

British Expeditionary Force (abbrev.: **BEF**) a British force made available by the army reform of 1908 for service overseas. Such forces were sent to France in 1914 and 1939.

British Guiana see GUYANA.

British Honduras former name (until 1973) for BELIZE.

British India that part of the Indian subcontinent administered by the British from 1765, when the East India Company acquired control over Bengal, until 1947, when India became independent and Pakistan was created. By 1850 British India was coterminous with India's boundaries in the west and north and by 1885 it included Burma in the east. The period of British rule was known as the Raj.

British Indian Ocean Territory a British dependency in the Indian Ocean, comprising the Chagos Archipelago and (until 1976) parts of the Seychelles. Ceded to Britain by France in 1814, the islands became a dependency in 1965. There are no permanent inhabitants, but British and US naval personnel occupy the island of Diego Garcia.

British Isles a group of islands lying off the coast of NW Europe, from which they are separated by the North Sea and the English Channel. They include Britain, Ireland, the Isle of Man, the Hebrides, the Orkney Islands, the Shetland Islands, the Scilly Isles, and the Channel Islands.

Britishism ▸ noun variant spelling of BRITICISM.

British Legion short for ROYAL BRITISH LEGION.

British Library the national library of Britain, containing the former library departments of the British Museum. The principal copyright library, it was established separately from the British Museum in 1972.

British Lion ▸ noun see LION.

British Museum a national museum of antiquities in London. Established with public funds in 1753, it includes among its holdings the Magna Carta, the Elgin Marbles, and the Rosetta Stone.

British National Party (abbrev.: **BNP**) an extreme right-wing political party in Britain supporting racial discrimination and strongly opposing immigration. The party arose in the 1980s as a breakaway group from the National Front.

British Sign Language ▸ noun [mass noun] a form of sign language developed in the UK for the use of the deaf, the fourth most widely used indigenous language in Britain.

British Somaliland /səˈmɑːlɪˌland/ a former British protectorate established on the Somali coast of East Africa in 1884. In 1960 it united with former Italian territory to form the independent republic of Somalia.

British Standard ▸ noun the specification of recommended procedure, quality of output, terminology, and other details, in a particular field, drawn up and published by the British Standards Institution.

British Summer Time (abbrev.: **BST**) time as advanced one hour ahead of Greenwich Mean Time for daylight saving in the UK between March and October.

British thermal unit ▸ noun the amount of heat needed to raise 1 lb of water at maximum density through one degree Fahrenheit, equivalent to 1.055 × 10³ joules.

British Union of Fascists an extreme right-wing British political party founded by Sir Oswald Mosley in 1932. It promoted strongly anti-Semitic views and its supporters were known as blackshirts. The party was effectively destroyed by the Public Order Act of 1936.

British Virgin Islands see VIRGIN ISLANDS.

British warm ▸ noun a short thick overcoat or duffel coat.

Briton ▸ noun **1** a citizen, native, or inhabitant of Great Britain.
■ a person of British descent.
2 one of the people of southern Britain before and during Roman times.
– ORIGIN from Old French *Breton*, from Latin *Britto*, *Britton-*, or its Celtic equivalent.

Britpop ▸ noun [mass noun] pop music by a loose affiliation of British groups of the mid 1990s, typically influenced by the Beatles and other British groups of the 1960s and perceived as a reaction against American grunge music.

Brittany /ˈbrɪtəni/ a region and former duchy of NW France, forming a peninsula between the Bay of Biscay and the English Channel. It was occupied in the 5th and 6th centuries by Britons fleeing the Saxons, and was incorporated into France in 1532. French name **BRETAGNE**.

Britten /ˈbrɪt(ə)n/, (Edward) Benjamin, Lord Britten of Aldeburgh (1913–76), English composer, pianist, and conductor. He founded the Aldeburgh festival with Peter Pears in 1948, and in 1976 became the first composer to be made a life peer. Notable

operas: *Peter Grimes* (1945), *A Midsummer Night's Dream* (1960), and *Death in Venice* (1973).

brittle ▸ adjective hard but liable to break or shatter easily: *her bones became fragile and brittle.*
■ (of a sound, especially a person's voice) unpleasantly hard and sharp and showing signs of instability or nervousness: *a brittle laugh.* ■ (of a person or behaviour) appearing decisive and aggressive but unstable or nervous within.
▸ noun [mass noun] a brittle sweet made from nuts and set melted sugar: *peanut brittle.*
– DERIVATIVES **brittlely** (or **brittly**) adverb, **brittleness** noun.
– ORIGIN late Middle English, ultimately of Germanic origin and related to Old English *brēotan* 'break up'.

brittle bone disease ▸ noun [mass noun] Medicine
1 another term for OSTEOGENESIS IMPERFECTA.
2 another term for OSTEOPOROSIS.

brittle fracture ▸ noun [mass noun] fracture of a metal or other material occurring without appreciable prior plastic deformation.

brittlestar ▸ noun a marine animal related to starfishes, with long thin flexible arms radiating from a small central disk.
● Class Ophiuroidea: *Ophiura* and other genera.

Brittonic /brɪˈtɒnɪk/ ▸ adjective & noun variant of BRYTHONIC.
– ORIGIN from Latin *Britto*, *Britton-* 'Briton' + -IC.

britzka /ˈbrɪtskə/ (also **britzska**) ▸ noun historical an open carriage with calash top and space for people to recline in.
– ORIGIN early 19th cent.: from Polish *bryczka.*

BRN ▸ abbreviation for Bahrain (international vehicle registration).

Brno /ˈbəː(r)nəʊ/ an industrial city in the Czech Republic; pop. 388,000 (1991). It is the capital of Moravia.

bro /brəʊ/ ▸ noun informal short for BROTHER: *his baby bro.*
■ [in sing.] chiefly US a friendly greeting or form of address: *'Yo bro!'* ■ (**Bro.**) Brother (used before a first name when referring in writing to a member of a religious order of men): *Bro. Felix.*

broach¹ ▸ verb [with obj.] **1** raise (a sensitive or difficult subject) for discussion: *he broached the subject he had been avoiding all evening.*
2 pierce (a cask) to draw liquor.
■ open and start using the contents of (a bottle or other container).
3 [no obj.] (of a fish or sea mammal) rise through the water and break the surface: *the salmon broach, then fall to slap the water.*
– ORIGIN Middle English: from Old French *brochier*, based on Latin *brocchus, broccus* 'projecting'. The earliest recorded sense was 'prick with spurs', generally 'pierce with something sharp', which gave rise (late Middle English) to sense 2. Sense 1, a figurative use of this, dates from the late 16th cent.

broach² Nautical ▸ verb [no obj.] (of a ship) veer and pitch forward, presenting a side to the wind and waves and losing steerage control: *we had broached badly, side on to the wind and sea.*
▸ noun a sudden and unwelcome veering of a ship having such consequences.
– ORIGIN early 18th cent.: of unknown origin.

broach spire ▸ noun an octagonal church spire rising from a square tower without a parapet.

broad ▸ adjective **1** having a distance larger than usual from side to side; wide: *a broad staircase.*
■ (after a measurement) giving the distance from side to side: *the valley is three miles long and half a mile broad.* ■ large in area: *a broad expanse of paddy fields.*
2 covering a large number and wide scope of subjects or areas: *the company has a broad range of experience.*
■ having or incorporating a wide range of meanings, applications, or kinds of things; loosely defined: *our range of programmes comprises three broad categories.* ■ including or coming from many people of many kinds: *the polls registered broad support for Labour.*
3 general; without detail: *a broad outline of the legal framework for pension schemes.*
■ (of a hint) clear and unambiguous; not subtle. ■ somewhat coarse and indecent: *what we regard as broad or even bawdy is a fact of nature to him.* ■ (of a phonetic transcription) showing only meaningful distinctions in sound and ignoring minor details.
4 (of a regional accent) very noticeable and strong: *the words had a distinct tang of broad Lancashire.*

▶**noun** N. Amer. informal a woman.
– PHRASES **broad in the beam** fat around the hips. **in broad daylight** during the day, when it is light, and surprising or unexpected for this reason: *the kidnap had taken place in broad daylight.*
– DERIVATIVES **broadness** noun.
– ORIGIN Old English *brād*, of Germanic origin; related to Dutch *breed* and German *breit*.

broadacre ▶**adjective** Austral. (of farming practices or equipment) used in or suitable for large-scale production.

broad arrow ▶**noun** a mark resembling a broad arrowhead, formerly used on British prison clothing and other government property.

broadband ▶**adjective** of or using signals over a wide range of frequencies in high-capacity telecommunications: *broadband networks.*
▶**noun** [mass noun] signals over such a range of frequencies: *our ability to uplink on broadband has been curtailed.*

broad bean ▶**noun 1** a large flat edible green bean which is usually eaten without the pod.
2 the plant which yields these beans, widely cultivated in gardens.
• *Vicia faba*, family Leguminosae.

broadbill ▶**noun 1** a small bird of the Old World tropics, with a stocky body, a large head, a flattened bill with a wide gape, and typically very colourful plumage.
• Family Eurylaimidae: several genera.
2 chiefly N. Amer. a bird with a broad bill, especially a duck such as the shoveler or the scaup.

broad-brush ▶**adjective** lacking in detail and finesse: *a broad-brush measure of inflation.*

broadcast ▶**verb** (past **broadcast**; past participle **broadcast** or **broadcasted**) [with obj.] **1** (often **be broadcast**) transmit (a programme or some information) by radio or television: *the announcement was broadcast live* | [as noun **broadcasting**] *the state monopoly on broadcasting.*
▪[no obj.] take part in a radio or television transmission: *they regularly **broadcast on** Radio 2.* ▪ tell (something) to many people; make widely known: *we don't want to broadcast our unhappiness to the world.*
2 scatter (seeds) by hand or machine rather than placing in drills or rows.
▶**noun** a radio or television programme or transmission.
▶**adjective** of or relating to such programmes: *a broadcast journalist.*
▶**adverb** by scattering: *green manures can be sown broadcast or in rows.*
– DERIVATIVES **broadcaster** noun.
– ORIGIN mid 18th cent. (in the sense 'sown by scattering'): from **BROAD** + the past participle of **CAST**[1].

Broad Church ▶**noun** a tradition or group within the Anglican Church favouring a liberal interpretation of doctrine.
▪a group, organization, or doctrine which allows for and caters to a wide range of opinions and people.

broadcloth ▶**noun** [mass noun] clothing fabric of fine twilled wool or worsted, or plain-woven cotton.
– ORIGIN late Middle English: originally denoting cloth made 72 inches wide, as opposed to 'strait' cloth, 36 inches wide. The term now implies quality rather than width.

broaden ▶**verb** [no obj.] become larger in distance from side to side; widen: *her smile broadened* | *the river slowed and **broadened out** slightly.*
▪expand to encompass more people, ideas, or things: *her interests broadened as she grew up* | [with obj.] *he has to broaden Labour's appeal to the whole community.*
– PHRASES **broaden one's horizons** expand one's range of interests, activities, and knowledge.

broad gauge ▶**noun** a railway gauge which is wider than the standard gauge of 4 ft 8½ in (1.435 m).

broad jump ▶**noun** North American term for **LONG JUMP**.

broadleaf ▶**adjective** another term for **BROADLEAVED**.
▶**noun** a tree or plant with wide flat leaves.

broadleaved ▶**adjective** [attrib.] (of a tree or plant) having relatively wide flat leaves rather than needles; non-coniferous.
▪(of a wood or woodland) consisting of trees with such leaves: *ancient broadleaved woodlands.*

broad left ▶**noun** a loose coalition of left-wing groups presenting a unified alternative to the right.

broadloom ▶**noun** [mass noun] carpet woven in wide widths: *wall-to-wall broadloom.*
– DERIVATIVES **broadloomed** adjective.

broadly ▶**adverb 1** [sentence adverb] in general and with the exception of minor details: *the climate is broadly similar in the two regions* | ***broadly speaking**, the risks are as follows.*
2 widely and openly: *he was grinning broadly.*

broad-minded ▶**adjective** tolerant or liberal in one's views and reactions; not easily offended: *a broad-minded approach to religion.*
– DERIVATIVES **broad-mindedly** adverb, **broad-mindedness** noun.

broad money ▶**noun** [mass noun] Economics money in any form including bank or other deposits as well as notes and coins.

Broadmoor /ˈbrɔːdmɔː, -mʊə/ a special hospital near Reading in southern England for the secure holding of patients regarded as both mentally ill and potentially dangerous. It was established in 1863.

broad pennant (also **broad pendant**) ▶**noun** a short swallow-tailed pennant distinguishing the commodore's ship in a squadron.

broad reach Sailing ▶**noun** a point of sailing in which the wind blows over a boat's quarter, between the beam and the stern: ***on a broad reach** they are magnificent craft.*
▶**verb** (**broad-reach**) [no obj.] sail with the wind in this position.

Broads (often **the Norfolk Broads**) a network of shallow freshwater lakes, traversed by slow-moving rivers, in Norfolk and Suffolk. They were formed by the gradual natural flooding of medieval peat diggings.

broadscale ▶**adjective** on a broad scale, extensive.

broadsheet ▶**noun** a large piece of paper printed on one side only with information.
▪(also **broadsheet newspaper**) a newspaper with a large format regarded as more serious and less sensationalist than tabloids.

broadside ▶**noun 1** historical a firing of all the guns from one side of a warship.
▪figurative a strongly worded critical attack: *he launched a **broadside against** both monetary and political union.* ▪ the set of guns which can fire on each side of a warship. ▪ the side of a ship above the water between the bow and quarter.
2 a sheet of paper printed on one side only, forming one large page: *a broadside of Lee's farewell address.*
▶**adverb** with the side turned in a particular direction: *the yacht was drifting **broadside to** the wind.*
▪on the side: *her car was hit broadside by another vehicle.*
▶**verb** [with obj.] N. Amer. collide with the side of (a vehicle): *I had to skid my bike sideways to avoid broadsiding her.*
– PHRASES **broadside on** sideways on: *the ship swung broadside on to the current of the river.*

broad-spectrum ▶**adjective** [attrib.] denoting antibiotics, pesticides, etc. effective against a large variety of organisms.

broadsword ▶**noun** a sword with a wide blade, used for cutting rather than thrusting.

broadtail ▶**noun** a karakul sheep.
▪[mass noun] the fleece or wool from a karakul lamb.

Broadway a street traversing the length of Manhattan, New York. It is famous for its theatres, and its name has become synonymous with show business.

broadway ▶**noun** [usu. in names] a large open or main road: *Fulham Broadway.*

Brobdingnagian /ˌbrɒbdɪŋˈnagɪən/ ▶**adjective** gigantic.
▶**noun** a giant.
– ORIGIN early 18th cent.: from *Brobdingnag*, the name given by Swift (in *Gulliver's Travels*) to a land where everything is of huge size, + **-IAN**.

brocade ▶**noun** [mass noun] a rich fabric, usually silk, woven with a raised pattern, typically with gold or silver thread: [as modifier] *a heavy brocade curtain.*
▶**verb** [with obj.] [usu. as adj. **brocaded**] weave (something) with this design: *a heavily brocaded blanket.*
– ORIGIN late 16th cent.: from Spanish and Portuguese *brocado* (influenced by French *brocart*), from Italian *broccato*, from *brocco* 'twisted thread'.

Broca's area /ˈbrəʊkəz/ ▶**noun** Anatomy a region of the brain concerned with the production of speech, located in the cortex of the dominant frontal lobe. Damage in this area causes **Broca's aphasia**, characterized by hesitant and fragmented speech with little grammatical structure.
– ORIGIN late 19th cent.: named after Paul *Broca* (1824–80), French surgeon.

broccoli /ˈbrɒkəli/ ▶**noun** [mass noun] a cabbage of a variety similar to the cauliflower, which bears heads of green or purplish flower buds. It is widely cultivated as a vegetable.
• There are several kinds of broccoli, in particular those in the 'Italica' group, including **sprouting broccoli**, which bears small loose clusters of heads on several shoots, and the bright green dense headed variety also called **CALABRESE**.
▪the flower stalk and head eaten as a vegetable.
– ORIGIN mid 17th cent.: from Italian, plural of *broccolo* 'cabbage sprout, head', diminutive of *brocco* 'shoot', based on Latin *brocchus, broccus* 'projecting'.

broch /brɒk, brɒx/ ▶**noun** a prehistoric circular stone tower in north Scotland and adjacent islands.
– ORIGIN late 15th cent.: alteration of **BURGH** (the original sense). The current sense dates from the mid 17th cent.

brochette /brɒˈʃɛt/ ▶**noun** a skewer or spit on which chunks of meat or fish are barbecued, grilled, or roasted: *beef and lamb **en brochette**.*
▪a dish of meat or fish chunks cooked in such a way.
– ORIGIN French, diminutive of *broche* 'skewer'.

brochure /ˈbrəʊʃə, brɒˈʃʊə/ ▶**noun** a small book or magazine containing pictures and information about a product or service.
– ORIGIN mid 18th cent.: from French, literally 'something stitched', from *brocher* 'to stitch' (see **BROACH**[1]).

brock ▶**noun** Brit. the badger.
– ORIGIN Old English *brocc, broc*, of Celtic origin; related to Welsh and Cornish *broch*, Irish and Scottish Gaelic *broc*, and Breton *broc'h*.

Brocken /ˈbrɒk(ə)n/ a mountain in the Harz Mountains of north central Germany, rising to 1,143 m (3,747 ft). It is noted for the phenomenon of the Brocken spectre and for witches' revels which reputedly took place there on Walpurgis night.

Brocken spectre ▶**noun** a magnified shadow of an observer, typically surrounded by rainbow-like bands, thrown on to a bank of cloud in high mountain areas when the sun is low.
– ORIGIN early 19th cent.: named after **BROCKEN**, the highest of the Harz Mountains, Germany, where the phenomenon was first reported.

brocket (also **brocket deer**) ▶**noun** a small deer with short straight antlers, found in Central and South America.
• Genus *Mazama*, family Cervidae: four species.
– ORIGIN late Middle English (denoting any red deer stag in its second year, with straight antlers): from Anglo-Norman French *broquet*, diminutive of *broque*, variant of *broche* (see **BROOCH**). The current sense dates from the mid 19th cent.

broderie anglaise /ˌbrəʊd(ə)rɪ ˈɒŋgleɪz/ ▶**noun** [mass noun] open embroidery, typically in floral patterns, on fine white cotton or linen.
– ORIGIN mid 19th cent.: French, literally 'English embroidery'.

Brodsky /ˈbrɒdski/, Joseph (1940–96), Russian-born American poet; born *Iosif Aleksandrovich Brodsky*. Writing both in Russian and in English, he was most famous for his collection *The End of a Beautiful Era* (1977). Nobel Prize for Literature (1987).

Broeder /ˈbruːdə/ ▶**noun** S. African a member of the Broederbond.
– ORIGIN Dutch, literally 'brother'.

Broederbond /ˈbruːdəbɒnd, -bɒnt/ a secret society in South Africa (founded in 1918) promoting the interests of and restricted in membership to male, Protestant Afrikaners.
– ORIGIN Afrikaans, from *broeder* 'brother' + *bond* 'league'.

brogan /ˈbrəʊg(ə)n/ ▶**noun** a coarse stout leather shoe reaching to the ankle.
– ORIGIN mid 19th cent.: from Irish *brógán*, Scottish Gaelic *brógan*, literally 'small brogue'.

brogue[1] ▶**noun** a strong outdoor shoe with ornamental perforated patterns in the leather.
▪historical a rough shoe of untanned leather, formerly worn in parts of Ireland and the Scottish Highlands.
– ORIGIN late 16th cent.: from Scottish Gaelic and

Irish *bróg*, from Old Norse *brók* (related to **BREECH**).

brogue² ▶ noun [usu. in sing.] a marked accent, especially Irish or Scottish, when speaking English.
– ORIGIN early 18th cent.: perhaps allusively from **BROGUE¹**, referring to the rough footwear of Irish peasants.

broil¹ ▶ verb [with obj.] chiefly N. Amer. cook (meat or fish) by exposure to direct heat.
■ [no obj.] become very hot, especially from the sun: *the countryside lay broiling in the sun.*
– ORIGIN late Middle English (also in the sense 'burn, char'): from Old French *bruler* 'to burn', of unknown origin.

broil² ▶ noun archaic a quarrel or a commotion.
– ORIGIN early 16th cent.: from obsolete *broil* 'to muddle'. Compare with **EMBROIL**.

broiler ▶ noun **1** (also **broiler chicken**) a young chicken suitable for roasting, grilling, or barbecuing.
2 N. Amer. a gridiron, grill, or special part of a stove for cooking meat or fish by exposure to direct heat.

broiler house ▶ noun a building for rearing broiler chickens in close confinement.

broke past (and archaic past participle) of **BREAK¹**.
▶ adjective [predic.] informal having completely run out of money: *he went broke owing two million pounds.*
– PHRASES **go for broke** informal risk everything in an all-out effort.

broken past participle of **BREAK¹**. ▶ adjective
1 having been fractured or damaged and no longer in one piece or in working order: *he had a broken arm.*
■ (of a person) having given up all hope; defeated and despairing: *he went to his grave a broken man.* ■ (of a relationship) ended, typically by betrayal or faithlessness: *a broken marriage.* ■ (of an agreement or promise) not observed by one of the parties involved.
2 having gaps or intervals which break a continuity: *a broken white line across the road.*
■ having an uneven and rough surface: *he pressed onwards over the broken ground.* ■ (of speech or a language) spoken falteringly and with many mistakes, as by a foreigner: *a young man talking in broken Italian.*
– DERIVATIVES **brokenly** adverb, **brokenness** /ˈbrəʊk(ə)nnɪs/ noun.

broken chord ▶ noun [usu. as modifier] Music a chord in which the notes are played successively: *the second entry is a straight broken-chord figure.*

broken colour ▶ noun [mass noun] a colour mixed or juxtaposed closely with another.

broken-down ▶ adjective worn out and dilapidated by age, use, or ill-treatment: *a broken-down council estate.*
■ (of a machine or vehicle) not functioning, due to mechanical failure. ■ (of a horse) with serious damage to the legs, in particular the tendons, caused by excessive strain.

broken field American Football ▶ noun the area beyond the line of scrimmage, where the defenders are relatively scattered.
▶ adjective (**broken-field**) relating to or occurring in this area of the field: *a broken-field run.*
■ informal (of a movement) done in the manner of a ball-carrier running in the broken field: *a broken-field chase.*

broken-hearted ▶ adjective overwhelmed by grief or disappointment.
– DERIVATIVES **broken-heartedness** noun.

Broken Hill 1 a town in New South Wales, Australia; pop. 23,260 (1991). It is a centre of lead, silver, and zinc mining.
2 former name (1904–65) for **KABWE**.

broken home ▶ noun a family in which the parents are divorced or separated.

broken reed ▶ noun see **REED**.

broken wind ▶ noun [mass noun] another term for **COPD** in horses.
– DERIVATIVES **broken-winded** adjective.

broker ▶ noun a person who buys and sells goods or assets for others. Compare with **BROKER-DEALER**.
▶ verb [with obj.] arrange or negotiate (a deal or plan): *fighting continued despite attempts to broker a ceasefire.*
– ORIGIN Middle English (denoting a retailer or pedlar): from Anglo-Norman French *brocour*, of unknown ultimate origin.

USAGE The term **broker** was officially replaced in the UK Stock Exchange by **broker-dealer** in 1986, broker-dealers being entitled to act both as agents and principals in share dealings.

brokerage ▶ noun [mass noun] the business or service of acting as a broker.
■ [mass noun] a fee or commission charged by a broker: *a revenue of £1,400 less a sales brokerage of £12.50.* ■ [count noun] a company that buys or sells goods or assets for clients.

broker-dealer ▶ noun (in the UK) a person combining the former functions of a broker and jobber on the Stock Exchange.

USAGE Now the official term on the UK Stock Exchange, replacing **broker** in 1986.

broking ▶ noun [mass noun] Brit. the business or service of buying and selling goods or assets for others: [as modifier] *a broking house.*

brolga /ˈbrɒlɡə/ ▶ noun a large grey Australian crane which has an elaborate courtship display that involves much leaping, wing-flapping, and trumpeting.
● *Grus rubicundus*, family Gruidae.
– ORIGIN late 19th cent.: from Kamilaroi *burralga* (also found in other Aboriginal languages).

brolly ▶ noun (pl. **-ies**) Brit. informal an umbrella.

brom- /ˈbrəʊm/ ▶ combining form variant spelling of **BROMO-**, shortened before a vowel (as in *bromide*).

Bromberg /ˈbrɒmbɛrk/ German name for **BYDGOSZCZ**.

brome /brəʊm/ ▶ noun [mass noun] an oat-like grass which is sometimes grown for fodder or ornamental purposes.
● Genus *Bromus*, family Gramineae.
– ORIGIN mid 18th cent.: from modern Latin *Bromus*, from Greek *bromos* 'oat'.

bromeliad /brəˈmiːlɪad/ ▶ noun a plant of tropical and subtropical America, typically having short stems with rosettes of stiff, spiny leaves. Some kinds are epiphytic and many are cultivated as pot plants.
● Family Bromeliaceae: *Bromelia* and other genera, and numerous species, including the pineapple and Spanish moss.
– ORIGIN mid 19th cent.: from modern Latin *Bromelia* (named by Linnaeus after Olaf *Bromel* (1639–1705), Swedish botanist) + **-AD¹**.

bromic acid ▶ noun [mass noun] Chemistry a strongly oxidizing acid known only in aqueous solutions.
● Chem. formula: $HBrO_3$.
– DERIVATIVES **bromate** noun.

bromide /ˈbrəʊmʌɪd/ ▶ noun **1** Chemistry a compound of bromine with another element or group, especially a salt containing the anion $Br^−$ or an organic compound with bromine bonded to an alkyl radical.
■ a reproduction or piece of typesetting on bromide paper.
2 dated a sedative preparation containing potassium bromide.
■ a trite and unoriginal idea or remark, especially one intended to soothe or placate: *feel-good bromides create the illusion of problem-solving.*
– DERIVATIVES **bromidic** adjective (in sense 2).

bromide paper ▶ noun [mass noun] photographic printing paper coated with silver bromide emulsion.

bromine /ˈbrəʊmiːn/ ▶ noun [mass noun] the chemical element of atomic number 35, a dark red fuming toxic liquid with a choking irritating smell. It is a member of the halogen group and occurs chiefly in the form of salts in seawater and brines. (Symbol: **Br**)
– ORIGIN early 19th cent.: from French *brome*, from Greek *brōmos* 'a stink', + **-INE⁴**.

bromism /ˈbrəʊmɪz(ə)m/ ▶ noun [mass noun] dated a condition of dullness and weakness due to excessive intake of bromide sedatives.

bromo- /ˈbrəʊməʊ/ (usu. **brom-** before a vowel) ▶ combining form Chemistry representing **BROMINE**.

bromocriptine /ˌbrəʊməʊˈkrɪptiːn/ ▶ noun [mass noun] Medicine a drug used in the treatment of Parkinsonism, galactorrhoea, and other conditions. It is a synthetic analogue of the ergot alkaloids and stimulates the dopaminergic receptors of the brain, inhibiting the release of prolactin.

Brompton cocktail /ˈbrɒmpt(ə)n/ ▶ noun a powerful painkiller and sedative consisting of vodka or other liquor laced with morphine and sometimes also cocaine.
– ORIGIN late 20th cent.: said to be from the name of *Brompton* Hospital, London, where the mixture was invented for cancer patients.

bronc /brɒŋk/ ▶ noun N. Amer. informal short for **BRONCO**.

bronchi plural form of **BRONCHUS**.

bronchial /ˈbrɒŋkɪəl/ ▶ adjective of or relating to the bronchi or bronchioles: *bronchial pneumonia.*

bronchial tree ▶ noun the branching system of bronchi and bronchioles, conducting air from the windpipe into the lungs.

bronchiectasis /ˌbrɒŋkɪˈɛktəsɪs/ ▶ noun [mass noun] Medicine abnormal widening of the bronchi or their branches, causing a risk of infection.
– ORIGIN late 19th cent.: from Greek *bronkhia* (denoting the branches of the main bronchi) + *ektasis* 'dilatation'.

bronchiole /ˈbrɒŋkɪəʊl/ ▶ noun Anatomy any of the minute branches into which a bronchus divides.
– DERIVATIVES **bronchiolar** adjective.
– ORIGIN mid 19th cent.: from modern Latin *bronchiolus*, *bronchiolum*, diminutives of late Latin *bronchia*, denoting the branches of the main bronchi.

bronchiolitis /ˌbrɒŋkɪəˈlʌɪtɪs/ ▶ noun [mass noun] Medicine inflammation of the bronchioles.

bronchitis /brɒŋˈkʌɪtɪs/ ▶ noun [mass noun] inflammation of the mucous membrane in the bronchial tubes. It typically causes bronchospasm and coughing.
– DERIVATIVES **bronchitic** adjective & noun.

broncho- /ˈbrɒŋkəʊ/ ▶ combining form of or relating to the bronchi: *bronchopneumonia.*
– ORIGIN from Greek *bronkho-*, from *bronkhos* 'windpipe'.

bronchocele /ˈbrɒŋkə(ʊ)siːl/ ▶ noun a goitre.
– ORIGIN mid 17th cent.: from Greek *bronkhokēlē*.

bronchodilator /ˌbrɒŋkə(ʊ)dʌɪˈleɪtə/ ▶ noun Medicine a drug that causes widening of the bronchi, for example any of those taken by inhalation for the alleviation of asthma.

bronchogenic /ˌbrɒŋkə(ʊ)ˈdʒɛnɪk/ ▶ adjective of bronchial origin.

bronchopneumonia /ˌbrɒŋkə(ʊ)njuːˈməʊnɪə/ ▶ noun [mass noun] inflammation of the lungs, arising in the bronchi or bronchioles.

bronchoscope ▶ noun a fibre optic cable that is passed into the windpipe in order to view the bronchi.
– DERIVATIVES **bronchoscopy** noun.

bronchospasm ▶ noun [mass noun] Medicine spasm of bronchial smooth muscle, producing narrowing of the bronchi.

bronchus /ˈbrɒŋkəs/ ▶ noun (pl. **bronchi** /-kʌɪ/) any of the major air passages of the lungs which diverge from the windpipe.
– ORIGIN mid 17th cent.: from late Latin, from Greek *bronkhos* 'windpipe'.

bronco ▶ noun (pl. **-os**) a wild or half-tamed horse of the western US.
– ORIGIN mid 19th cent.: from Spanish, literally 'rough, rude'.

broncobuster ▶ noun informal a cowboy who breaks in wild or half-tamed horses.

Bronowski /brəˈnɒfski/, Jacob (1908–74), Polish-born British scientist, writer, and broadcaster. He popularized science with such books as *The Common Sense of Science* (1951) and the 1970s television documentary series *The Ascent of Man.*

Brontë the name of three English novelists:
■ Charlotte (1816–55), author of *Jane Eyre* (1847), *Shirley* (1849), and *Villette* (1853).
■ Emily (1818–48), author of *Wuthering Heights* (1847); also a poet.
■ Anne (1820–49), author of *Agnes Grey* (1845) and *The Tenant of Wildfell Hall* (1847).

The three sisters (with their brother **Branwell**, 1817–48) grew up in the Yorkshire village of Haworth, and had limited experience of the outside world. Their works were published under the pseudonyms Currer, Ellis, and Acton Bell.

brontosaurus /ˌbrɒntəˈsɔːrəs/ (also **brontosaur** /ˈbrɒntəsɔː/) ▶ noun former term for **APATOSAURUS**.
– ORIGIN modern Latin (former genus name), from Greek *brontē* 'thunder' + *sauros* 'lizard'.

Bronx /brɒŋks/ (**the Bronx**) a borough in the north-east of New York City.

– ORIGIN named after Jonas *Bronck*, a Dutch settler who purchased land there in 1641.

Bronx cheer ▶ noun a sound of derision or contempt made by blowing through closed lips with the tongue between them.
– ORIGIN 1920s: named after the **BRONX** in New York.

bronze ▶ noun [mass noun] a yellowish-brown alloy of copper with up to one-third tin.
■ a yellowish-brown colour: *rich, gleaming shades of bronze.* ■ [count noun] a work of sculpture or other object made of bronze. ■ [count noun] short for **BRONZE MEDAL**.
▶ verb [with obj.] (usu. **be bronzed**) make (a person or part of the body) suntanned: *Alison was bronzed by outdoor life* | [as adj. **bronzed**] *bronzed and powerful arms.*
■ give a surface of bronze or something resembling bronze to: *the doors were bronzed with sculpted reliefs.*
– DERIVATIVES **bronzy** adjective.
– ORIGIN mid 17th cent. (as a verb): from French *bronze* (noun), *bronzer* (verb), from Italian *bronzo*, probably from Persian *birinj* 'brass'.

Bronze Age a prehistoric period that followed the Stone Age and preceded the Iron Age, when weapons and tools were made of bronze rather than stone. See also **COPPER AGE**.

> The Bronze Age began in the Near East and SE Europe in the late 4th and early 3rd millennium BC. It is associated with the first European civilizations, the beginnings of urban life in China, and the final stages of some Meso-American civilizations, but did not appear in Africa and Australasia at all.

bronze medal ▶ noun a medal made of or coloured bronze, customarily awarded for third place in a race or competition.

bronzewing (also **bronze-winged pigeon**) ▶ noun an Australian pigeon with a metallic bronze band on the wing.
● Genus *Phaps*, family Columbidae: three species, in particular the **common bronzewing** (*P. chalcoptera*) and the **flock bronzewing** or flock pigeon (*P. histrionica*).

Bronzino /brɒn'ziːnəʊ/, Agnolo (1503–72), Italian painter; born *Agnolo di Cosimo*. He spent most of his career in Florence as court painter to Cosimo de' Medici. Notable works: *Venus, Cupid, Folly, and Time* (c.1546).

broo /bruː/ ▶ noun informal, Scottish a social security office.
– PHRASES **on the broo** claiming unemployment benefit.
– ORIGIN 1930s: alteration of **BUREAU**.

brooch ▶ noun an ornament fastened to clothing with a hinged pin and catch.
– ORIGIN Middle English: variant of *broach*, a noun originally meaning 'skewer, bodkin', from Old French *broche* 'spit for roasting', based on Latin *brocchus, broccus* 'projecting'. Compare with **BROACH**[1].

brood ▶ noun **1** a family of young animals, typically birds, produced at one hatching or birth: *a brood of chicks.*
■ [mass noun] bee or wasp larvae. ■ informal all of the children in a family: *she was brought up by a loving stepfather as part of a brood of eight.* ■ a group of things or people having a similar character: *broods of sedentary clergymen.*
▶ verb **1** [no obj.] think deeply about something that makes one unhappy: *he brooded over his dead mother.*
2 [with obj.] (of a bird) sit on (eggs) to hatch them.
■ (of a fish, frog, or invertebrate) hold (developing eggs) within the body.
▶ adjective [attrib.] (of an animal) kept to be used for breeding: *a brood mare.*
– ORIGIN Old English *brōd*, of Germanic origin; related to Dutch *broed* and German *Brut*, also to **BREED**. Sense 1 of the verb was originally used with an object, i.e. 'to nurse (feelings) in the mind' (late 16th cent.), a figurative use of the notion of a hen nursing chicks under her wings.

brood comb ▶ noun Zoology the part of a comb used for the rearing of bee larvae.

brooder ▶ noun **1** a heated house for chicks or piglets.
2 a person who broods about something.

brooding ▶ adjective showing deep unhappiness of thought: *he stared with brooding eyes.*
■ appearing darkly menacing: *the brooding moorland.*
– DERIVATIVES **broodingly** adverb.

brood pouch ▶ noun a pouch in certain fish, frogs,

and invertebrates in which the eggs are protected before hatching.

broody ▶ adjective (**broodier**, **broodiest**) **1** (of a hen) wishing or inclined to incubate eggs.
■ informal (of a woman) having a strong desire to have a baby.
2 thoughtful and unhappy: *his broody concern for the future.*
– DERIVATIVES **broodily** adverb, **broodiness** noun.

Brook, Peter (Stephen Paul) (b.1925), English theatre director. As co-director of the Royal Shakespeare Company he earned critical acclaim with *King Lear* (1963) and *A Midsummer Night's Dream* (1970).

brook[1] ▶ noun a small stream.
– DERIVATIVES **brooklet** noun.
– ORIGIN Old English *brōc*, of unknown origin; related to Dutch *broek* and German *Bruch* 'marsh'.

brook[2] ▶ verb [with obj.] [with negative] formal tolerate or allow (something, typically dissent or opposition): *Jenny would brook no criticism of Matthew.*
– ORIGIN Old English *brūcan* 'use, possess', of Germanic origin; related to Dutch *bruiken* and German *brauchen*. The current sense dates from the mid 16th cent., a figurative use of an earlier sense 'digest, stomach'.

Brooke, Rupert (Chawner) (1887–1915), English poet. He is most famous for his wartime poetry *1914 and Other Poems* (1915). He died while on naval service in the Mediterranean.

Brooklands a motor-racing circuit near Weybridge in Surrey, England, opened in 1907. During the Second World War the course was converted for aircraft manufacture.

brooklime ▶ noun [mass noun] a Eurasian speedwell with smooth fleshy leaves and deep blue flowers on long stalks. It grows in wet areas, where the stems take root or float in the water.
● Veronica beccabunga, family Scrophulariaceae.
– ORIGIN Middle English *broklemok*, from **BROOK**[1] + *hleomoce*, the name of the plant in Old English.

Brooklyn a borough of New York City, at the south-western corner of Long Island. The Brooklyn Bridge (1869–83) links Long Island with lower Manhattan.

Brooklynese ▶ noun [mass noun] an uncultivated form of New York speech associated especially with the borough of Brooklyn.

Brookner /'brʊknə/, Anita (b.1928), English novelist and art historian. She won the Booker Prize for *Hotel du Lac* (1984).

Brooks[1], Cleanth (1906–94), American teacher and critic. A leading proponent of the New Criticism movement, he edited *The Southern Review* from 1935 to 1942 and taught at Yale University 1947–75. Notable works: *Modern Poetry and Tradition* (1939).

Brooks[2], Mel (b.1927), American film director and comic actor; born *Melvin Kaminsky*. His film debut *The Producers* (1967) was followed by the spoof western *Blazing Saddles* (1974).

brook trout ▶ noun N. Amer. the brook charr. See **CHARR**.

brookweed ▶ noun [mass noun] a small white-flowered European plant which grows in wet ground, typically near the sea.
● Samolus valerandi, family Primulaceae.

broom ▶ noun **1** a long-handled brush of bristles or twigs, used for sweeping. [ORIGIN: formerly made of twigs of broom.]
■ an implement for sweeping the ice in the game of curling.
2 a flowering shrub with long, thin green stems and small or few leaves, cultivated for its profusion of flowers.
● Cytisus, Genista, and related genera, family Leguminosae: many species and cultivars.
– PHRASES **a new broom sweeps clean** proverb people newly appointed to positions of responsibility tend to make far-reaching changes: *the company seems set to make a fresh start under a new broom.*
– ORIGIN Old English *brōm* (in sense 2), of Germanic origin; related to Dutch *braam*, also to **BRAMBLE**.

broomie ▶ noun (pl. **-ies**) Austral./NZ informal a person who sweeps the floor in a shearing shed.

broomrape ▶ noun a parasitic plant which bears tubular flowers on a leafless brown stem. It is attached by its tubers to the roots of the host plant.
● Genus *Orobanche*, family Orobanchaceae.

– ORIGIN late 16th cent.: from **BROOM** + Latin *rapum* 'tuber'.

broomstick ▶ noun a brush with twigs at one end and a long handle, on which, in children's literature, witches are said to fly.

Bros /brɒs/ ▶ plural noun brothers (in names of companies): *Moss Bros the tailors.*

brose /brəʊz/ ▶ noun chiefly Scottish a kind of porridge made with oatmeal or dried peas and boiling water or milk.
– ORIGIN mid 17th cent.: originally a Scots form of Middle English *brewis* 'broth', from Old French *brouez*; ultimately of Germanic origin and related to **BROTH**.

broth ▶ noun [mass noun] **1** soup consisting of meat or vegetable chunks cooked in stock and typically thickened with barley or other cereals.
■ meat or fish stock.
2 Microbiology a liquid medium containing proteins and other nutrients for the culture of bacteria: [as modifier] *broth cultures of intestinal tissue.*
■ a liquid mixture for the preservation of tissue: [count noun] *tissue samples were frozen in a cryoprotective broth.*
– PHRASES **a broth of a boy** informal, chiefly Irish used approvingly to refer to a very lively boy or young man.
– ORIGIN Old English, of Germanic origin; related to **BREW**.

brothel ▶ noun a house where men visit prostitutes.
– ORIGIN mid 16th cent. (originally *brothel-house*): from late Middle English *brothel* 'worthless man, prostitute', related to Old English *brēothan* 'degenerate, deteriorate'.

brothel creepers ▶ plural noun informal soft-soled suede shoes.

brother ▶ noun **1** a man or boy in relation to other sons and daughters of his parents.
■ a male associate or fellow member of an organization: *the time is coming, brothers, for us to act.* ■ informal, chiefly N. Amer. a black man (chiefly used as a term of address by other black people). ■ a thing which resembles or is connected to another thing: *the machine is almost identical to its larger brother.*
2 (pl. also **brethren**) Christian Church a (male) fellow Christian.
■ a member of a religious order of men: *a Benedictine brother.* ■ a member of a fundamentalist Protestant denomination: *the Plymouth Brethren.*
▶ exclamation used to express annoyance or surprise.
– PHRASES **brothers in arms** soldiers fighting together on the same side.
– DERIVATIVES **brotherliness** noun, **brotherly** adjective.
– ORIGIN Old English *brōthor*, of Germanic origin; related to Dutch *broeder* and German *Bruder*, from an Indo-European root shared by Latin *frater*.

brother-german ▶ noun (pl. **brothers-german**) archaic a brother sharing both parents, as opposed to a half-brother or stepbrother.

brotherhood ▶ noun **1** [mass noun] the relationship between brothers.
■ the feeling of kinship with and closeness to a group of people or all people: *a gesture of solidarity and brotherhood.*
2 an association, society, or community of people linked by a common interest, religion, or trade: *a religious brotherhood.*
■ N. Amer. a trade union.
– ORIGIN Middle English: probably from obsolete *brotherred* (based on Old English *-ræden* 'condition, state'; compare with **KINDRED**). The change of suffix was due to association with words ending in **-HOOD** and **-HEAD**[1].

brother-in-law ▶ noun (pl. **brothers-in-law**) the brother of one's wife or husband.
■ the husband of one's sister or sister-in-law.

brougham /'bruː(ə)m/ ▶ noun historical a horse-drawn carriage with a roof, four wheels, and an open driver's seat in front.
■ a motor car with an open driver's seat.
– ORIGIN mid 19th cent.: named after Lord Brougham (1778–1868), who designed the carriage.

brought past and past participle of **BRING**.

brouhaha /'bruːhɑːhɑː/ ▶ noun [usu. in sing.] a noisy and overexcited critical response, display of interest, or trail of publicity: *the brouhaha over those infamous commercials* | [mass noun] *all that election brouhaha.*

b

– ORIGIN late 19th cent.: from French, probably imitative.

Brouwer /ˈbraʊə/, Adriaen (c.1605–38), Flemish painter. His most typical works represent peasant scenes in taverns.

brow[1] ▶ noun **1** a person's forehead: *he wiped his brow.*
■ (usu. **brows**) an eyebrow: *his brows lifted in surprise.*
2 the summit of a hill or pass: *the cottages were built on the brow of a hill.*
– DERIVATIVES **browed** adjective [in combination] *furrow-browed.*
– ORIGIN Old English *brū* 'eyelash, eyebrow', of Germanic origin. Current senses arose in Middle English; compare with **BRAE**.

brow[2] ▶ noun a gangway from a ship to the shore.
■ a hinged part of a ferry or landing craft forming a landing platform or ramp.
– ORIGIN mid 19th cent.: probably from Norwegian *bru*, from Old Norse *brú* 'bridge'.

brow band ▶ noun the part of a bridle which passes across the horse's forehead.

browbeat ▶ verb (past **-beat**; past participle **-beaten**) [with obj.] intimidate (someone), typically into doing something, with stern or abusive words: *a witness is being browbeaten under cross-examination.*
– DERIVATIVES **browbeater** noun.

Brown[1], Sir Arthur Whitten (1886–1948), Scottish aviator. He made the first transatlantic flight in 1919 with Sir John William Alcock.

Brown[2], Ford Madox (1821–93), English painter. His early work was inspired by the Pre-Raphaelites, and in 1861 he became a founder member of William Morris's company, designing stained glass and furniture.

Brown[3], James (b.1928), American soul and funk singer and songwriter. In the 1960s he played a leading role in the development of funk with songs such as 'Papa's Got a Brand New Bag' (1965) and 'Sex Machine' (1970).

Brown[4], John (1800–59), American abolitionist. In 1859 he was executed after raiding a government arsenal at Harpers Ferry in Virginia, intending to arm black slaves and start a revolt. He became a hero of the abolitionists in the Civil War.

Brown[5], Lancelot (1716–83), English landscape gardener; known as **Capability Brown**. He evolved an English style of natural-looking landscape parks. Notable examples of his work are at Blenheim Palace, Chatsworth House in Derbyshire, and Kew Gardens.

brown ▶ adjective of a colour produced by mixing red, yellow, and black, as of dark wood or rich soil: *an old brown coat* | *she had warm brown eyes.*
■ dark-skinned or suntanned: *his face was brown from the sun.* ■ South African term for **COLOURED** (in sense 2). ■ (of bread) made from a dark, unsifted, or unbleached flour.
▶ noun **1** [mass noun] brown colour or pigment: *the brown of his eyes* | *a pair of boots **in brown*** | [count noun] *the print is rich with velvety browns.*
■ brown clothes or material: *a woman all in brown.*
2 a brown thing, in particular the brown ball in snooker.
3 [with modifier] a satyrid butterfly, which typically has brown wings with small eyespots.
● Subfamily Satyrinae, family Nymphalidae: many genera and species, including the **meadow brown** and **wall brown**.
4 South African term for **COLOURED** (in sense 1): *compulsory education for blacks and browns.*
▶ verb make or become brown, typically by cooking: [with obj.] *a skillet in which food has been browned* | [no obj.] *grill the pizza until the cheese has browned.*
– PHRASES **(as) brown as a berry** (of a person) very suntanned. **in a brown study** see **STUDY**.
– DERIVATIVES **brownish** adjective, **brownness** noun, **browny** adjective.
– ORIGIN Old English *brūn*, of Germanic origin; related to Dutch *bruin* and German *braun*.
▶ **brown someone off** [usu. as adj. **browned off**] make someone feel irritated or depressed: *they are getting browned off with the overtime.*

brown ale ▶ noun [mass noun] Brit. dark, mild beer sold in bottles.

brown algae ▶ plural noun a large group of algae that are typically olive brown or greenish in colour, including many seaweeds. They contain xanthophyll in addition to chlorophyll.

● Class Phaeophyceae, division Heterokontophyta (also phylum Heterokonta, kingdom Protista); formerly division Phaeophyta.

brown bag ▶ noun a bag made of opaque brown paper.
■ N. Amer. a bag of brown paper in which a lunch is packed and carried to work, school, or an informal function: [as modifier] *a brown bag lunch.*
▶ verb [with obj.] (**brown bag it**) N. Amer. take a packed lunch to work or school.
– DERIVATIVES **brown bagger** noun.

brown bear ▶ noun a large bear with a coat colour ranging from cream to black, occurring chiefly in forests in Eurasia and North America. It is widely persecuted, and was exterminated in Britain, probably before the 10th century. Compare with **GRIZZLY BEAR**.
● *Ursus arctos*, family Ursidae.

brown belt ▶ noun a belt of a brown colour marking a high level of proficiency in judo, karate, or other martial arts, below that of a black belt.
■ a person qualified to wear such a belt.

Brown Betty ▶ noun **1** chiefly N. Amer. a baked pudding made with apples or other fruit and breadcrumbs.
2 Brit. a large brown earthenware teapot.

brown coal ▶ noun another term for **LIGNITE**.

brown creeper ▶ noun see **CREEPER** (sense 2).

brown dwarf ▶ noun Astronomy a celestial object intermediate in size between a giant planet and a small star, believed to emit mainly infrared radiation.

Browne, Sir Thomas (1605–82), English author and physician. He achieved prominence with *Religio Medici* (1642), a collection of opinions on a vast number of subjects connected with religion.

brown earth ▶ noun [mass noun] Soil Science a type of soil having a brown humus-rich surface layer.

brown fat ▶ noun [mass noun] a dark-coloured adipose tissue with many blood vessels, involved in the rapid production of heat in hibernating animals and human babies.

brownfield ▶ adjective [attrib.] (of an urban site for potential building development) having had previous development on it. Compare with **GREENFIELD**.

brown goods ▶ plural noun television sets, audio equipment, and similar household appliances. Compare with **WHITE GOODS**.

brown hare ▶ noun a hare found commonly in much of Eurasia, though absent from Ireland.
● *Lepus europaeus* (or *capensis*), family Leporidae.

brown holland ▶ noun [mass noun] unbleached holland linen.

Brownian motion /ˈbraʊnɪən/ ▶ noun [mass noun] Physics the erratic random movement of microscopic particles in a fluid, as a result of continuous bombardment from molecules of the surrounding medium.
– ORIGIN late 19th cent.: named after Robert *Brown* (1773–1858), the Scottish botanist who first observed the motion.

Brownie ▶ noun (pl. **-ies**) **1** (**the Brownies**) the junior branch of the Guides Association, for girls aged between about 7 and 10. [ORIGIN: so named because of the colour of the uniform.]
■ (Brit. also **Brownie Guide**) a member of this organization. ■ (**Brownies**) a meeting of a branch of this organization: *I went to Brownies every week.*
2 (**brownie**) a small square of rich cake; typically chocolate cake, with nuts.
■ Austral./NZ a piece of sweet currant bread.
3 (**brownie**) a benevolent elf supposedly haunting houses and doing housework secretly. [ORIGIN: diminutive of **BROWN**; a 'wee brown man' often appears in Scottish ballads and fairy tales; compare with Old Norse *svartálfar*, the dark elves of the Edda.]
– PHRASES **brownie point** informal, humorous an imaginary award given to someone for a good deed or an attempt to please: *his policy will win brownie points with voters.*

Brownie Guider ▶ noun the adult leader of a group of Brownies. See also **BROWN OWL** (sense 2).

Browning[1], Elizabeth Barrett (1806–61), English poet; born *Elizabeth Barrett*. She established her reputation with *Poems* (1844). In 1846 she eloped with Robert Browning.

Browning[2], Robert (1812–89), English poet. In 1842

he established his name with *Dramatic Lyrics*, containing 'The Pied Piper of Hamelin' and 'My Last Duchess'.

Browning[3] ▶ noun (also **Browning machine gun**) a type of water-cooled automatic machine gun.
■ (also **Browning automatic**) a type of automatic pistol.
– ORIGIN early 20th cent.: named after John M. *Browning* (1855–1926), American designer of the weapons.

browning ▶ noun [mass noun] the process or result of making something brown, typically by cooking or burning.
■ Brit. darkened flour, typically with other additives, for colouring gravy.

brown-nose N. Amer. informal ▶ noun (also **brown-noser**) a person who acts in a grossly obsequious way.
▶ verb [with obj.] curry favour with (someone) by acting in such a way: *academics were brown-nosing the senior faculty* | [no obj.] *I dedicated a book to him—I was not brown-nosing.*

brown-out ▶ noun chiefly N. Amer. a partial blackout.

brown owl ▶ noun **1** another term for **TAWNY OWL**.
2 (**Brown Owl**) Brit. informal the adult leader of a group of Brownies, officially termed the Brownie Guider since 1968.

brown rat ▶ noun a rat found throughout the world, typically living in association with man and regarded as a pest. It is commonly kept as a laboratory animal and as a pet, and is also bred in the albino form. Also called **COMMON RAT**, **NORWAY RAT**.
● *Rattus norvegicus*, family Muridae.

brown rice ▶ noun [mass noun] unpolished rice with only the husk of the grain removed.

brown rot ▶ noun [mass noun] a fungal disease causing the rotting and browning of parts of plants, in particular:
● a disease producing discoloration and shrivelling of apples, pears, plums, and other fruit (caused by fungi of the genus *Sclerotinia*, subdivision Ascomycotina). ● a disease resulting in the softening and cracking of timber (caused by bracket fungi of the family Polyporaceae, class Hymenomycetes).

brown sauce ▶ noun **1** a savoury sauce made with fat and flour cooked to a brown colour.
2 a commercially prepared relish containing vinegar and spices.

Brownshirt ▶ noun historical a member of a Nazi militia founded by Hitler in Munich in 1921, with brown uniforms resembling those of Mussolini's Blackshirts. They aided Hitler's rise to power, but were eclipsed by the SS after the 'night of the long knives' in June 1934. Also called **STORM TROOPS** or **STURMABTEILUNG**.

brown silver-line ▶ noun see **SILVER-LINE**.

brown snake ▶ noun **1** a fast-moving venomous and aggressive Australian snake, with a variety of colour forms.
● *Pseudonaja* and other genera, family Elapidae: several species, in particular *P. textilis*.
2 a small secretive harmless North American snake that is typically brownish in colour.
● *Storeria dekayi*, family Colubridae.

brownstone ▶ noun [mass noun] N. Amer. a kind of reddish-brown sandstone used for building.
■ [count noun] a building faced with such sandstone.

brown sugar ▶ noun [mass noun] unrefined or partially refined sugar.

brown-tail (also **brown-tail moth**) ▶ noun a white European tussock moth with a tuft of brown hairs on the tip of the abdomen. The caterpillars have severely irritant hairs, overwinter in a communal web, and can be a pest of tree foliage.
● *Euproctis chrysorrhoea*, family Lymantriidae.

browntop (also **browntop bent**) ▶ noun another term for the grass *common bent* (see **BENT**[2]).

brown trout ▶ noun (pl. same) the common trout of Europe, especially one of a non-migratory race with dark spotted skin occurring in small rivers and pools.
● *Salmo trutta*, family Salmonidae, in particular *S. trutta fario*.

browse /braʊz/ ▶ verb [no obj.] **1** survey objects superficially and in a leisurely fashion, especially goods for sale: *he stopped to browse around a sporting store.*
■ scan through a book or magazine superficially to gain an impression of the contents: *she browsed*

through the newspaper. ■ [with obj.] Computing read or survey (data files), typically via a network.

2 (of an animal) feed on leaves, twigs, or other high-growing vegetation: *they reach upward to* ***browse on*** *bushes* | [with obj.] *the animals browse the high foliage of trees.*

▶ **noun 1** [in sing.] an act of casual looking or reading: *the brochure is well worth a browse.*

■ something to be casually looked through: *this book is a useful browse for a new worker in the field.*

2 [mass noun] vegetation, such as twigs and young shoots, eaten by animals.

– DERIVATIVES **browsable** adjective.

– ORIGIN late Middle English (in sense 2 of the verb): from Old French *broster*, from *brost* 'young shoot', probably of Germanic origin.

browser ▶ **noun** a person who looks casually through books or magazines or at things for sale.

■ an animal which feeds mainly on high-growing vegetation. ■ Computing a program with a graphical user interface for displaying HTML files, used to navigate the World Wide Web: *a Web browser.*

brrr ▶ **exclamation** used to express someone's reaction to feeling cold: *Brrr! It's a freezing cold day.*

BRU ▶ **abbreviation for** Brunei (international vehicle registration).

Brubeck /ˈbruːbɛk/, Dave (b.1920), American jazz pianist, composer, and bandleader; full name *David Warren Brubeck*. He formed the Dave Brubeck Quartet in 1951 and won international recognition with the album *Time Out*, which included 'Take Five' (1959).

brubru /ˈbruːbruː/ (also **brubru shrike**) ▶ **noun** a small tropical African shrike with striking black-and-white plumage and chestnut flanks. Compare with **BOUBOU**.

• *Nilaus afer*, family Laniidae.

Bruce[1], Robert the, see **ROBERT** I.

Bruce[2], James (1730–94), Scottish explorer. In 1770 he was the first European to discover the source of the Blue Nile, although his *Travels to Discover the Sources of the Nile* (1790), recounting his expedition, was dismissed by his contemporaries as fabrication.

Bruce[3], Lenny (1925–66), American comedian; born *Leonard Alfred Schneider*. He gained notoriety for flouting the bounds of respectability with his humour, and was imprisoned for obscenity in 1961. He died following an accidental drugs overdose.

Bruce anchor ▶ **noun** trademark a modern type of anchor made in one piece, with three flukes forming a scoop.

– ORIGIN from the name of the manufacturers.

brucellosis /ˌbruːsəˈləʊsɪs/ ▶ **noun** [mass noun] a bacterial disease typically affecting cattle and causing undulant fever in humans.

• This disease is caused by Gram-negative bacteria of the genus *Brucella*, in particular *B. abortus*.

– ORIGIN 1930s: from modern Latin *Brucella* + **-OSIS**: named after Sir David *Bruce* (1855–1931), the Scottish physician who identified the bacterium.

brucite /ˈbruːsʌɪt/ ▶ **noun** [mass noun] a white, grey, or greenish mineral typically occurring in the form of tabular crystals. It consists of hydrated magnesium hydroxide.

– ORIGIN early 19th cent.: named after Archibald *Bruce* (1777–1818), American mineralogist, + **-ITE**[1].

Bruckner /ˈbrʊknə/, Anton (1824–96), Austrian composer and organist. He wrote ten symphonies, four masses, and a *Te Deum* (1884).

Bruegel /ˈbrɔɪg(ə)l/ (also **Breughel** or **Brueghel**) the name of a family of Flemish artists:

■ Pieter (*c*.1525–69); known as **Pieter Bruegel the Elder**. He produced landscapes, religious allegories, and satires of peasant life. Notable works: *The Procession to Calvary* (1564).

■ **Pieter Bruegel the Younger** (1564–1638), son of Pieter Bruegel the Elder; known as **Hell Bruegel**. A very able copyist of his father's work, he is also noted for his paintings of devils.

■ **Jan** (1568–1623), son of Pieter Bruegel the Elder; known as **Velvet Bruegel**. He was a celebrated painter of flowers, landscapes, and mythological scenes.

Bruges /bruːʒ/ a city in NW Belgium, capital of the province of West Flanders; pop. 117,000 (1991). A centre of the Flemish textile trade until the 15th century, it is a well-preserved medieval city surrounded by canals. Flemish name **BRUGGE**.

Brugge /ˈbryxə/ Flemish name for **BRUGES**.

bruin /ˈbruːɪn/ ▶ **noun** a bear, especially in children's fables.

– ORIGIN late 15th cent.: from Dutch *bruin* (see **BROWN**); used as a name for the bear in the 13th-cent. fable *Reynard the Fox*.

bruise ▶ **noun** an injury appearing as an area of discoloured skin on the body, caused by a blow or impact rupturing underlying blood vessels.

■ a similar area of damage on a fruit, vegetable, or plant.

▶ **verb 1** [with obj.] [often as adj. **bruised**] inflict such an injury on (someone or something): *a bruised knee.*

■ hurt (someone's feelings): *she tried to bolster her bruised pride.* ■ [no obj.] be susceptible to bruising: *potatoes bruise easily, so treat them with care.* ■ crush or pound (something): *the mix contains bruised oats.*

– ORIGIN Old English *brȳsan* 'crush, injure or damage with a blow', reinforced in Middle English by Old French *bruisier* 'break'.

bruiser ▶ **noun** informal, derogatory a person who is tough and aggressive and enjoys a fight or argument.

■ a professional boxer.

bruising ▶ **adjective** causing a bruise or bruises: *his legs took the bruising blows.*

■ figurative (of an antagonistic or competitive situation) conducted in an aggressive way and likely to have a stressful or damaging effect on those involved: *a bruising cabinet battle over public spending.*

▶ **noun** [mass noun] bruises on the skin: *her arm showed signs of bruising.*

bruit /bruːt/ ▶ **verb** [with obj. and adverbial] spread (a report or rumour) widely: *I didn't want to have our relationship* ***bruited about*** *the office.*

▶ **noun 1** archaic a report or rumour.

2 Medicine a sound, especially an abnormal one, heard through a stethoscope; a murmur.

– ORIGIN late Middle English (as a noun): from Old French *bruit* 'noise', from *bruire* 'to roar'.

Brum /brʌm/ Brit. an informal name for Birmingham.

– ORIGIN mid 19th cent.: abbreviation of **BRUMMAGEM**.

Brumaire /bruːˈmɛː, French brymɛʀ/ ▶ **noun** the second month of the French Republican calendar (1793–1805), originally running from 22 October to 20 November.

– ORIGIN French, from *brume* 'mist'.

brumby /ˈbrʌmbi/ ▶ **noun** (pl. **-ies**) (in Australia) a wild or unbroken horse.

– ORIGIN late 19th cent.: of unknown origin.

brume /bruːm/ ▶ **noun** [mass noun] poetic/literary mist or fog: *the birds rise like brume.*

– ORIGIN early 18th cent.: from French, from Latin *bruma* 'winter'.

Brummagem /ˈbrʌmədʒ(ə)m/ ▶ **adjective** [attrib.]

1 informal of or relating to Birmingham or the dialect of English spoken there.

2 cheap, showy, or counterfeit: *a vile Brummagem substitute for the genuine article.*

– ORIGIN mid 17th cent.: dialect form of **BIRMINGHAM**, England; sense 2 is with reference to counterfeit coins and cheap plated goods once made there.

Brummell /ˈbrʌm(ə)l/, George Bryan (1778–1840), English dandy; known as **Beau Brummell**. He was the arbiter of British fashion for the first decade and a half of the 19th century, owing his social position to his friendship with the Prince Regent.

Brummie (also **Brummy**) ▶ **noun** (pl. **-ies**) Brit. informal a native of the British city of Birmingham.

▶ **adjective 1** Brit. informal of, from, or relating to Birmingham: *a Brummie accent.*

2 (**brummy**) Austral. counterfeit, showy, or cheaply made: *brummy jewels.* [ORIGIN: see **BRUMMAGEM**.]

– ORIGIN 1940s: from **BRUM**.

brumous /ˈbruːməs/ ▶ **adjective** poetic/literary foggy; wintry.

– ORIGIN mid 19th cent.: from French *brumeux*, from late Latin *brumosus* (from *bruma* 'winter').

brunch ▶ **noun** a late morning meal eaten instead of breakfast and lunch.

– ORIGIN late 19th cent.: blend of **BREAKFAST** and **LUNCH**.

Brundtland /ˈbrʊntland/, Gro Harlem (b.1939), Norwegian Labour stateswoman, Prime Minister 1981, 1986–89, and 1990–6. As Norway's first woman Prime Minister she chaired the World Commission on Environment and Development (known as the Brundtland Commission), which produced the report *Our Common Future* in 1987.

Brunei /bruːˈnʌɪ/ a small oil-rich sultanate on the NW coast of Borneo, pop. 264,000 (est. 1991); languages, Malay (official), English (official), Chinese; capital, Bandar Seri Begawan. Official name **BRUNEI DARUSSALAM**.

In the 16th century Brunei dominated Borneo and parts of the Philippines, but its power declined as that of the Portuguese and Dutch grew, and in 1888 it was placed under British protection. It became a fully independent Commonwealth state in 1984.

– DERIVATIVES **Bruneian** /bruːˈnʌɪən/ adjective & noun.

Brunel[1] /brʊˈnɛl/, Isambard Kingdom (1806–59), English engineer, son of Sir Marc Isambard Brunel. He was chief engineer of the Great Western Railway. His achievements include designing the Clifton suspension bridge (1829–30) and the first transatlantic steamship, the *Great Western* (1838).

Brunel[2] /brʊˈnɛl/, Sir Marc Isambard (1769–1849), French-born English engineer, father of Isambard Kingdom Brunel. He introduced mass-production machinery to Portsmouth dockyard and designed other machines for woodworking, boot-making, knitting, and printing. He also worked to construct the first tunnel under the Thames (1825–43).

Brunelleschi /ˌbruːnəˈlɛski/, Filippo (1377–1446), Italian architect; born *Filippo di Ser Brunellesco*. He is especially noted for the dome of Florence cathedral (1420–61), which he raised without the use of temporary supports. He is often credited with the Renaissance 'discovery' of perspective.

brunette /bruːˈnɛt, brʊ-/ (US also **brunet**) ▶ **noun** a woman or girl with dark brown hair: [as modifier] *her lustrous brunette tresses.*

– ORIGIN mid 16th cent.: from French, feminine of *brunet*, diminutive of *brun* 'brown'.

brung dialect past and past participle of **BRING**.

Brunhild /ˈbruːnhɪlt/ Germanic Mythology in the Nibelungenlied, the wife of Gunther, who instigated the murder of Siegfried. In the Norse versions she is a Valkyrie whom Sigurd (the counterpart of Siegfried) wins by penetrating the wall of fire behind which she lies in an enchanted sleep.

Bruno /ˈbruːnəʊ/, Giordano (1548–1600), Italian philosopher. He was a follower of Hermes Trismegistus and a supporter of the heliocentric Copernican view of the solar system. Bruno was tried by the Inquisition for heresy and burned at the stake.

Bruno, St /ˈbruːnəʊ/ (*c*.1032–1101), German-born French churchman. In 1084 he withdrew to the mountains of Chartreuse and founded the Carthusian order at La Grande Chartreuse. Feast day, 6 October.

Brunswick /ˈbrʌnzwɪk/ a former duchy and state of Germany, mostly incorporated into Lower Saxony. German name **BRAUNSCHWEIG**.

■ the capital of this former duchy, an industrial city in Lower Saxony, Germany; pop. 259,130 (1991).

Brunswick stew ▶ **noun** [mass noun] US a stew originally made with squirrel or rabbit, but now consisting of chicken and vegetables including onion and tomatoes.

brunt /brʌnt/ ▶ **noun** (**the brunt**) the worst part or chief impact of a specified action: *education will* ***bear the brunt*** *of the cuts.*

– ORIGIN late Middle English (denoting a blow or an attack, also the force or shock of something): of unknown origin.

bruschetta /brʊˈskɛtə/ ▶ **noun** [mass noun] toasted Italian bread drenched in olive oil and served typically with garlic or tomatoes.

– ORIGIN Italian.

brush[1] ▶ **noun 1** an implement with a handle, consisting of bristles, hair, or wire set into a block, used for cleaning or scrubbing, applying a liquid or powder to a surface, arranging the hair, or other purposes: *a shaving brush.*

■ an act of sweeping, applying, or arranging with such an implement or with one's hand: *he gave the seat a brush.* ■ (usu. **brushes**) a thin stick set with long wire bristles, used to make a soft hissing sound on drums or cymbals. ■ the bushy tail of a fox.

2 a slight and fleeting touch: *the lightest brush of his lips against her cheek.*

■ a brief and typically unpleasant or unwelcome

encounter with someone or something: *a brush with death.*
3 a piece of carbon or metal serving as an electrical contact with a moving part in a motor or alternator.
4 [mass noun] Austral./NZ informal girls or women, especially when regarded sexually: *'Beer first, brush later.'* [ORIGIN: 1940s: probably from *brush* in the sense 'animal's tail', by association with *tail* 'buttocks' (see **TAIL**[1]).]
▶**verb 1** [with obj. and adverbial] remove (dust or dirt) by sweeping or scrubbing: *we'll be able to* **brush** *the mud* **off** *easily* | *he* **brushed himself down**.
■[with obj.] use a brush or one's hand to remove dust or dirt from (something): *she* **brushed down** *her best coat.* ■ [with obj.] clean (one's teeth) by scrubbing with a brush. ■ [with obj.] arrange (one's hair) by running a brush through it. ■ [with obj.] apply a liquid to (a surface) with a brush: *brush the potatoes with oil.* ■ apply (a liquid or substance) to a surface: *a coat of French polish was* **brushed over** *the repair.*
2 [no obj.] touch lightly and gently: *stems of grass* **brush against** *her legs.*
■(**brush past**) touch fleetingly and in passing: *she brushed past him to leave the room.* ■ [with obj.] push (something) away with a quick movement of the hand: *she* **brushed** *a wisp of hair* **away** *from her face.* ■ [with obj.] (**brush something aside**) dismiss something curtly and confidently: *he brushed aside attacks on his policies.* ■ [with obj.] (**brush someone/thing off**) dismiss in an abrupt, contemptuous way: *the president brushed off a reporter's question about terrorism.*
– DERIVATIVES **brushless** adjective (chiefly technical) *a brushless motor*, **brush-like** adjective.
– ORIGIN Middle English: noun (except sense 4) from Old French *broisse*; verb partly from Old French *brosser* 'to sweep'.
▶**brush someone back** Baseball, informal (of a pitcher) force a batter to step back to avoid being hit by a ball pitched close to the body.
brush up on (or **brush something up**) improve one's previously good knowledge of or skill at a particular thing: *brush up on your telephone skills.*

brush[2] ▶**noun** [mass noun] chiefly N. Amer. & Austral./NZ undergrowth, small trees, and shrubs.
■land covered with such growth. ■N. Amer. cut brushwood. ■ Austral./NZ dense forest.
– ORIGIN Middle English: from Old French *broce*, perhaps based on Latin *bruscum*, denoting an excrescence on a maple.

brushback (also **brushback pitch**) ▶**noun** Baseball a pitch aimed close to the body so that the batter must step back to avoid it.

brush bar (also **brush guard**) ▶**noun** a metal grille fitted to a motor vehicle to protect it against impact damage.

brush discharge ▶**noun** a broad electrical discharge from a conductor occurring when the potential difference is high but not sufficient for a spark or arc.

brushed ▶**adjective** having been treated with a brush, in particular:
■(of fabric) having a soft raised nap: *brushed cotton.* ■ (of metal) finished with a non-reflective surface: *brushed aluminium.*

brush-off ▶**noun** [in sing.] informal a rejection or dismissal of someone by treating them as unimportant: *he's* **given** *her* **the brush-off**.

brushtail (also **brush-tailed possum**) ▶**noun** a nocturnal and mainly tree-dwelling Australasian marsupial, which has a pointed muzzle and a furred tail with a naked tip.
• Genus *Trichosurus*, family Phalangeridae: three species, in particular the **common brushtail** (*T. vulpecula*), frequently found in suburban areas.

brush-turkey ▶**noun** a large mound-building bird of the megapode family, resembling a turkey and found mainly in New Guinea. Also called **SCRUB-TURKEY**.
• Family Megapodiidae: several genera and species, including *Alectura lathami* of eastern Australia.

brush-up ▶**noun** (usu. **a brush-up**) Brit. an act of cleaning or smartening oneself or something up: *he must want* **a wash and brush-up** *after the long journey.*
■[usu. as modifier] an act of improving one's previously good knowledge or skill at a particular thing: *a two-day brush-up course.*

brush-weeder ▶**noun** an agricultural device that uses rotating brushes to remove weeds.

brush wolf ▶**noun** North American term for **COYOTE**.

brushwood ▶**noun** [mass noun] undergrowth, twigs, and small branches, typically used for firewood or kindling.

brushwork ▶**noun** [mass noun] the way in which painters use their brush, as evident in their paintings: *canvases characterized by lively, flowing brushwork.*

brushy ▶**adjective 1** covered in or consisting of brushwood: *a brushy hillside.*
2 Art relating to or displaying bold use of the brush in painting: *brushy outlining of form.*

brusque /brʊsk, bruːsk/ ▶**adjective** abrupt or offhand in speech or manner: *she could be brusque and impatient.*
– DERIVATIVES **brusquely** adverb, **brusqueness** noun, **brusquerie** /ˈbrʊsk(ə)riː, ˈbruː-/ noun (archaic).
– ORIGIN mid 17th cent.: from French, 'lively, fierce', from Italian *brusco* 'sour'.

Brussels[1] the capital of Belgium and of the Belgian province of Brabant; pop. 954,000 (1991). The headquarters of the European Commission is located there. French name **BRUXELLES**; Flemish name **BRUSSEL** /ˈbrys(ə)l/.

Brussels[2] ▶**plural noun** informal Brussels sprouts.

Brussels carpet ▶**noun** a carpet with a heavy woollen pile and a strong linen back.
– ORIGIN late 18th cent.: named after **BRUSSELS**[1].

Brussels griffon ▶**noun** see **GRIFFON** (sense 1).

Brussels lace ▶**noun** [mass noun] an elaborate kind of lace, typically with a raised design, made using a needle or lace pillow.

Brussels sprout (also **Brussel sprout**) ▶**noun** a vegetable consisting of the small compact bud of a variety of cabbage.
■the plant which yields this vegetable, bearing many such buds along a tall single stem.

brut /bruːt, French bʀy/ ▶**adjective** (of sparkling wine) unsweetened; very dry.
– ORIGIN French, literally 'raw, rough'.

brutal ▶**adjective** savagely violent: *a brutal murder.*
■punishingly unpleasant, hard, or uncomfortable: *the brutal morning light.* ■ without any attempt to disguise unpleasantness: *the brutal honesty of his observations.*
– DERIVATIVES **brutality** /-ˈtalɪti/ noun, **brutally** adverb.
– ORIGIN late 15th cent. (in the sense 'relating to the lower animals'): from Old French, or from medieval Latin *brutalis*, from *brutus* 'dull, stupid' (see **BRUTE**).

brutalism ▶**noun 1** [mass noun] cruelty and savageness.
2 a style of architecture or art characterized by a deliberate crudity or violence of imagery. The term was first applied to functionalist buildings of the 1950s and 1960s which made much use of steel and concrete in starkly massive blocks.
– DERIVATIVES **brutalist** noun & adjective.

brutalize (also **-ise**) ▶**verb** [with obj.] (often **be brutalized**) desensitize (someone) to the pain or suffering of others by exposing them to violent behaviour or situations: *he had been brutalized in prison and become cynical* | [as adj. **brutalizing**] *the brutalizing effects of warfare.*
■attack (someone) in a savage and violent way: *they brutalize and torture persons in their custody.*
– DERIVATIVES **brutalization** noun.

brute ▶**noun** a savagely violent person or animal: *he was a cold-blooded brute.*
■informal a cruel, unpleasant, or insensitive person: *what an unfeeling little brute you are.* ■ an animal as opposed to a human being. ■ something which is awkward, difficult, or unpleasant: *a great* **brute** *of a machine.*
▶**adjective** [attrib.] unreasoning and animal-like: *a brute struggle for social superiority.*
■merely physical: *we achieve little by brute force.* ■ harsh, fundamental, or inescapable: *the brute necessities of basic subsistence.*
– ORIGIN late Middle English (as an adjective): from Old French *brut(e)*, from Latin *brutus* 'dull, stupid'.

brutish ▶**adjective** resembling or characteristic of a brute: *he was coarse and brutish* | *brutish behaviour.*
– DERIVATIVES **brutishly** adverb, **brutishness** noun.

Bruton /ˈbruːt(ə)n/, John (Gerard) (b.1947), Irish Fine Gael statesman, Taoiseach (Prime Minister) 1994–7.

Brutus[1] legendary Trojan hero, great-grandson of Aeneas and supposed ancestor of the British people. In medieval legend he was said to have brought a group of Trojans to England and founded Troynovant or New Troy (London).

Brutus[2], Lucius Junius, legendary founder of the Roman Republic. Traditionally he led a popular uprising, after the rape of Lucretia, against the king (his uncle) and drove him from Rome. He and the father of Lucretia were elected as the first consuls of the Republic (509 BC).

Brutus[3], Marcus Junius (85–42 BC), Roman senator. With Cassius he led the conspirators who assassinated Julius Caesar in 44. They were defeated by Caesar's supporters, Antony and Octavian, at the battle of Philippi in 42, after which he committed suicide.

Bruxelles /bʀysɛl/ French name for **BRUSSELS**[1].

bruxism /ˈbrʌksɪz(ə)m/ ▶**noun** [mass noun] involuntary habitual grinding of the teeth, typically during sleep.
– ORIGIN 1930s: from Greek *brukhein* 'gnash the teeth' + **-ISM**.

Bryansk /brɪˈansk/ (also **Briansk**) an industrial city in European Russia, south-west of Moscow, on the Desna River; pop. 456,000 (1990).

Brylcreem /ˈbrɪlkriːm/ ▶**noun** [mass noun] trademark a cream used on men's hair to give it a smooth, shiny appearance.
– DERIVATIVES **Brylcreemed** adjective.

bryology /brʌɪˈɒlədʒi/ ▶**noun** [mass noun] the study of mosses and liverworts.
– DERIVATIVES **bryological** adjective, **bryologist** noun.
– ORIGIN mid 19th cent.: from Greek *bruon* 'moss' + **-LOGY**.

bryony /ˈbrʌɪəni/ (also **white bryony**) ▶**noun** (pl. **-ies**) a climbing Eurasian hedgerow plant with lobed hairy leaves, red berries, and spring-like tendrils. See also **BLACK BRYONY**.
• *Bryonia dioica*, the only British member of the gourd family (Cucurbitaceae).
– ORIGIN Old English, via Latin from Greek *bruōnia*.

Bryophyta /ˌbrʌɪə(ʊ)ˈfʌɪtə/ Botany a division of small flowerless green plants which comprises the mosses and liverworts. They lack true roots and reproduce by spores released from a stalked capsule.
• Division Bryophyta: classes Musci (mosses) and Hepaticae (liverworts).
– DERIVATIVES **bryophyte** noun.
– ORIGIN modern Latin (plural), from Greek *bruon* 'moss' + *phuta* 'plants'.

Bryozoa /ˌbrʌɪəˈzəʊə/ Zoology a phylum of sedentary aquatic invertebrates that comprises the moss animals. Also called **ECTOPROCTA**, **POLYZOA**.
– DERIVATIVES **bryozoan** noun & adjective.
– ORIGIN modern Latin (plural), from Greek *bruon* 'moss' + *zōia* 'animals'.

Brythonic /brɪˈθɒnɪk/ (also **Brittonic**) ▶**adjective** denoting, relating to, or belonging to the southern group of Celtic languages, consisting of Welsh, Cornish, and Breton. They were spoken in Britain before and during the Roman occupation, surviving as Welsh and Cornish after the Anglo-Saxon invasions, and being taken to Brittany by emigrants. Compare with **GOIDELIC**. Also called **P-CELTIC**.
▶**noun** [mass noun] these languages collectively.
– ORIGIN from Welsh *Brython* 'Britons' + **-IC**.

Brześć nad Bugiem /ˌbʒɛʃtʃ nad ˈbugjɛm/ Polish name for **BREST** (sense 2).

BS ▶**abbreviation for** ■ US Bachelor of Science. ■ Bachelor of Surgery. ■ Blessed Sacrament. ■ British Standard(s), usually preceding a reference number. ■ (in the UK) British Steel. ■ N. Amer. vulgar slang bullshit.

BSc ▶**abbreviation for** Bachelor of Science, a first degree in a science subject.

BSE ▶**abbreviation for** bovine spongiform encephalopathy, a disease of cattle which affects the central nervous system, causing agitation and staggering, and is usually fatal. It is believed to be caused by an agent such as a prion or a virino, and to be related to Creutzfeldt–Jakob disease in humans. Also (popularly) called **MAD COW DISEASE**.

BSI ▶**abbreviation for** British Standards Institution.

B-side ▶**noun** the side of a pop single regarded as the less important one.

BSL ▶**abbreviation for** British Sign Language.

BST ▶ abbreviation for ■ bovine somatotrophin, especially as an additive in cattle feed. ■ British Summer Time.

BT ▶ abbreviation for British Telecom.

Bt ▶ abbreviation for Baronet.

B-tree ▶ noun Computing an organizational structure for information storage and retrieval in the form of a tree in which all terminal nodes are the same distance from the base, and all non-terminal nodes have between n and $2n$ subtrees or pointers (where n is an integer).

Btu (also **BTU**) ▶ abbreviation for British thermal unit(s).

btw ▶ abbreviation for by the way.

Bual /ˈbuːal/ ▶ noun [mass noun] a variety of wine grape grown chiefly in Madeira.
■ a Madeira wine of a medium-sweet type made from such grapes.
– ORIGIN from Portuguese *boal*.

BUAV ▶ abbreviation for British Union for the Abolition of Vivisection.

bub ▶ noun N. Amer. informal an aggressive or rude way of addressing a boy or man: *hey, bub, I'm looking for someone.*
– ORIGIN mid 19th cent.: from earlier *bubby* (perhaps a child's form of **BROTHER**), or from German *Bube* 'boy'.

bubal /ˈbjuːb(ə)l/ ▶ noun a hartebeest, especially of an extinct race that was formerly found in North Africa.
● *Alcelaphus buselaphus buselaphus*, family Bovidae.
– ORIGIN late 18th cent.: from French *bubale*, via Latin from Greek *boubalos* 'wild ox, antelope'.

bubba /ˈbʌbə/ ▶ noun N. Amer. informal **1** used as an informal or affectionate form of address to a brother: *my sister has always called me bubba.*
2 derogatory an uneducated conservative white male of the southern US.
– ORIGIN late 20th cent.: alteration of **BROTHER**.

bubble ▶ noun **1** a thin sphere of liquid enclosing air or another gas.
■ an air- or gas-filled spherical cavity in a liquid or a solidified liquid such as glass or amber. ■ figurative used to refer to a state or feeling that is unstable and unlikely to last: *many companies enjoyed rapid expansion before the bubble burst* | *a bubble of confidence.*
2 (also **bubble shell**) a marine mollusc that typically has a thin scroll-like shell.
● Bullidae and other families, order Cephalaspidea, class Gastropoda.
3 a transparent domed cover or enclosure: *piglets born into a sterile bubble.*
▶ verb [no obj.] (of a liquid) contain bubbles of air or gas rising to the surface: *a pot of coffee bubbled away on the stove.*
■ [often as adj. **bubbling**] make a sound resembling this: *a bubbling fountain.* ■ (**bubble with/over with**) figurative (of a person) be exuberantly filled with an irrepressible positive feeling: *Ellen was bubbling with such enthusiasm.* ■ (**bubble up**) figurative (especially of a negative feeling) become more intense and approach the point of being vehemently expressed: *the fury bubbling up inside her.*
– PHRASES **burst someone's bubble** see **BURST**. **on the bubble** N. Amer. informal (of a sports player or team) occupying the last qualifying position on a team or for a tournament, and liable to be replaced by another. [ORIGIN: from *sit on the bubble*, with the implication that the bubble may burst.]
– ORIGIN Middle English: partly imitative, partly an alteration of **BURBLE**.

bubble and squeak ▶ noun [mass noun] Brit. cooked cabbage fried with cooked potatoes and often meat.
– ORIGIN late 18th cent.: from the sounds of the mixture cooking.

bubble bath ▶ noun [mass noun] liquid, crystals, or powder added to bathwater to make it foam and have a fragrant smell.
■ [count noun] a bath of water with such a substance added.

bubble canopy ▶ noun a transparent domed canopy on a fighter aircraft or bubble car.

bubble car ▶ noun a small car with a transparent domed canopy and typically three wheels.

bubble chamber ▶ noun Physics an apparatus designed to make the tracks of ionizing particles visible as a row of bubbles in a liquid.

bubblegum ▶ noun [mass noun] **1** chewing gum that can be blown into bubbles.

■ (also **bubblegum pink**) [mass noun] the bright pink colour that is typical of such gum.
2 [usu. as modifier] chiefly N. Amer. a thing considered to be insipid, simplistic, or adolescent in taste or style: *rockers hate bubblegum pop.*

bubblehead ▶ noun informal a foolish or empty-headed person.

bubblejet printer ▶ noun a form of ink-jet printer.

bubble lift ▶ noun informal a ski lift with suspended cabins.

bubble memory ▶ noun [mass noun] Computing a type of memory in which data is stored as a pattern of magnetized regions in a thin layer of magnetic material.

bubble pack ▶ noun a small package enclosing goods in transparent dome-shaped plastic on a flat cardboard backing.
■ another term for **BUBBLE WRAP**.

bubbler ▶ noun Austral. & US a drinking fountain.

bubble shell ▶ noun see **BUBBLE** (sense 2).

bubble wrap (US trademark **Bubble Wrap**) ▶ noun [mass noun] plastic packaging material in sheets containing numerous small air cushions designed to protect fragile goods.

bubbly ▶ adjective (**bubblier**, **bubbliest**) containing bubbles: *bake until the top is crisp and bubbly.*
■ figurative (of a person) full of cheerful high spirits: *a bright and bubbly personality.*
▶ noun [mass noun] informal champagne.

Buber /ˈbuːbə/, Martin (1878–1965), Israeli religious philosopher, born in Austria. In his existentialist work *I and Thou* (1923) he argues that religious experience involves reciprocal relationships with a personal subject, rather than knowledge of some 'thing'.

bubinga /bjuːˈbɪŋgə/ ▶ noun [mass noun] reddish-brown timber used chiefly for inlay work and as a veneer.
● The timber is obtained from several tropical African trees of the genus *Guibourtia*, family Leguminosae.

bubo /ˈbjuːbəʊ/ ▶ noun (pl. **-oes**) a swollen inflamed lymph node in the armpit or groin.
– DERIVATIVES **bubonic** /bjuːˈbɒnɪk/ adjective.
– ORIGIN late Middle English: from Latin, from Greek *boubōn* 'groin or swelling in the groin'.

bubonic plague ▶ noun the commonest form of plague in humans, characterized by fever, delirium, and the formation of buboes.

The plague bacterium, *Yersinia pestis*, is transmitted by rat fleas. Epidemics occurred in Europe throughout the Middle Ages (notably as the Black Death and the Great Plague of 1665–6); the disease is still endemic in parts of Asia.

bucatini /ˌbʊkəˈtiːni/ ▶ plural noun small hollow tubes of pasta.
– ORIGIN Italian.

buccal /ˈbʌk(ə)l/ ▶ adjective technical of or relating to the cheek: *the buccal side of the molars.*
■ of or relating to the mouth: *the buccal cavity.*
– ORIGIN early 19th cent.: from Latin *bucca* 'cheek' + **-AL**.

buccaneer /ˌbʌkəˈnɪə/ ▶ noun historical a pirate, originally one operating in the Caribbean.
■ a person who acts in a recklessly adventurous and often unscrupulous way, especially in business.
– ORIGIN mid 17th cent. (originally denoting European hunters in the Caribbean): from French *boucanier*, from *boucan* 'a frame on which to cook or cure meat', from Tupi *mukem*.

buccaneering ▶ adjective high-risk and adventurous (often used in a business context): *the buccaneering nature of the oil-transport industry.*

buccinator /ˈbʌksɪneɪtə/ ▶ noun Anatomy a flat thin muscle in the wall of the cheek.
– ORIGIN late 17th cent.: from Latin, from *buccinare* 'blow a trumpet', from *buccina*, denoting a kind of trumpet.

Bucephalus /bjuːˈsefələs/ the favourite horse of Alexander the Great, who tamed the horse as a boy and took it with him on his campaigns until its death, after a battle, in 326 BC.

Buchan[1] /ˈbʌx(ə)n/, Alexander (1829–1907), Scottish meteorologist. He wrote a textbook on meteorology and produced maps and tables of atmospheric circulation, and of ocean currents and temperatures, based largely on information gathered on the voyage of HMS *Challenger* in 1872–6.

Buchan[2] /ˈbʌx(ə)n/, John, 1st Baron Tweedsmuir (1875–1940), Scottish novelist. His adventure stories feature recurring heroes such as Richard Hannay. Notable works: *The Thirty-Nine Steps* (1915).

Buchanan /bjuːˈkanən/, James (1791–1868), American Democratic statesman, 15th President of the US 1857–61. His leanings towards the pro-slavery side in the developing dispute over slavery made the issue more fraught and he retired from politics in 1861.

Bucharest /ˌbuːkəˈrɛst/ the capital of Romania; pop. 2,343,800 (1993). It was founded in the 14th century on the trade route between Europe and Constantinople. Romanian name **BUCUREŞTI**.

Buchenwald /ˈbuːkənˌvald/, German /ˈbuːxnˌvalt/ a Nazi concentration camp in the Second World War, near the village of Buchenwald in eastern Germany.

Buchmanism /ˈbʌkmənɪz(ə)m, ˈbʊk-/ ▶ noun see **MORAL REARMAMENT**.
– DERIVATIVES **Buchmanite** noun & adjective.
– ORIGIN 1920s: from the name of Frank *Buchman* (1878–1961), American evangelist, + **-ISM**.

Buchner /ˈbʌknə/, German /ˈbuːxnɐ/, Eduard (1860–1917), German organic chemist. He studied the chemistry of alcoholic fermentation and identified several enzymes, notably zymase. Nobel Prize for Chemistry (1907).

buchu /ˈbʌkuː/ ▶ noun a heather-like South African shrub which is cultivated for its essential oil and as an ornamental.
● Genus *Agathosma* (or *Barosma*) and *Diosma*, family Rutaceae.
■ [mass noun] a diuretic drug made from the powdered leaves of this shrub.
– ORIGIN mid 18th cent.: from Khoikhoi.

Buck, Pearl S. (1892–1973), American writer; full name *Pearl Sydenstricker Buck*. Her upbringing and work in China inspired her earliest novels, including *The Good Earth* (Pulitzer Prize, 1931). Nobel Prize for Literature (1938).

buck[1] ▶ noun **1** the male of some horned animals, especially the fallow deer, roe deer, reindeer, and antelopes. Compare with **DOE**.
■ a male hare, rabbit, ferret, rat, or kangaroo. ■ S. African an antelope of either sex. Compare with **BUSHBUCK**, **REEDBUCK**, **WATERBUCK**.
2 another term for **VAULTING HORSE**.
3 a vertical jump performed by a horse, with the head lowered, back arched, and back legs thrown out behind.
4 archaic a fashionable and typically hellraising young man.
▶ verb **1** [no obj.] (of a horse) to perform a buck: *he's got to get his head down to buck* | [with obj.] *she bucked them off if they tried to get on her back.*
■ (of a vehicle) make sudden jerky movements.
2 [with obj.] oppose or resist (something which seems oppressive or inevitable): *the shares bucked the market trend.*
3 [with obj.] informal make (someone) more cheerful: *Bella and Jim need me to buck them up* | [no obj.] (**buck up**) *buck up, kid, it's not the end of the game.*
▶ adjective US military slang lowest of a particular rank: *a buck private.*
– PHRASES **buck up one's ideas** become more serious, energetic, and hard-working.
– ORIGIN Old English, partly from *buc* 'male deer' (of Germanic origin, related to Dutch *bok* and German *Bock*); reinforced by *bucca* 'male goat', of the same ultimate origin.

buck[2] ▶ noun N. Amer. & Austral./NZ informal a dollar: *a run-down hotel room for five bucks a night.*
■ S. African informal a rand. ■ Indian informal a rupee.
– PHRASES **big bucks** a lot of money. **a fast** (or **quick**) **buck** easily and quickly earned money: *they are itinerant traders out to make a fast buck.*
– ORIGIN mid 19th cent.: of unknown origin.

buck[3] ▶ noun an article placed as a reminder in front of a player whose turn it is to deal at poker.
– PHRASES **the buck stops here** (or **with someone**) informal the responsibility for something cannot or should not be passed to someone else. **pass the buck** informal shift the responsibility for something to someone else.
– ORIGIN mid 19th cent.: of unknown origin.

buck-and-wing ▶ noun US, chiefly historical a lively solo tap dance, performed typically in wooden-soled shoes.

buckaroo /ˌbʌkəˈruː/ ▶ noun N. Amer., dated a cowboy.

b

– ORIGIN early 19th cent.: alteration of **VAQUERO**.

buckbean ▶ noun another term for **BOGBEAN**.
– ORIGIN late 16th cent.: from Flemish *bocks boonen* 'goat's beans'.

buckboard ▶ noun N. Amer. an open horse-drawn carriage with four wheels and seating that is attached to a plank stretching between the front and rear axles.
– ORIGIN mid 19th cent.: from *buck* 'body of a cart' (perhaps a variant of obsolete *bouk* 'belly, body') + **BOARD**.

buckbrush ▶ noun [mass noun] N. Amer. coarse vegetation on which wild deer browse.

buckeen /bʌˈkiːn/ ▶ noun historical a poor but aspiring young man of the lower Anglo-Irish gentry.

bucket ▶ noun a roughly cylindrical open container, typically made of metal or plastic and having a handle, used to hold and carry liquids. ■ the contents of such a container or the amount it can contain: *she emptied a bucket of water over them.* ■ (**buckets**) informal large quantities of liquid, typically rain or tears: *I wept buckets.* ■ a compartment on the outer edge of a waterwheel. ■ the scoop of a dredger or grain elevator. ■ a scoop attached by two movable forks to the front of a loader, digger, or tractor. ■ Computing a unit of data that can be transferred from a backing store in a single operation.
▶ verb (**bucketed**, **bucketing**) [no obj.] **1** Brit. informal (**it buckets, it is bucketing**, etc.) rain heavily: *it was still bucketing down.* **2** [with adverbial of direction] informal (of a vehicle) move quickly and jerkily: *the car came bucketing out of a side road.*
– DERIVATIVES **bucketful** noun (pl. **-fuls**).
– ORIGIN Middle English: from Anglo-Norman French *buquet* 'tub, pail', perhaps from Old English *būc* 'belly, pitcher'.

bucket seat ▶ noun a seat in a car or aircraft with a rounded back to fit one person.

bucket shop ▶ noun informal, derogatory **1** an unauthorized office for speculating in stocks or currency using the funds of unwitting investors. **2** Brit. a travel agency, typically of an unregistered or unscrupulous type, that specializes in providing cheap air tickets.

bucketwheel ▶ noun a machine with a series of scoops or buckets on a rotating belt, used to excavate or move material.

buckeye ▶ noun **1** an American tree or shrub related to the horse chestnut, with showy red or white flowers. ● Genus *Aesculus*, family Hippocastanaceae: several species. **2** (also **buckeye butterfly**) an orange and brown New World butterfly with conspicuous eyespots on the wings. ● *Junonia coenia*, subfamily Nymphalinae, family Nymphalidae. **3** (**Buckeye**) US informal a native of the state of Ohio. [ORIGIN: from the nickname given to the state, with reference to the abundance of buckeye trees.] **4** (also **buckeye coupling**) a kind of automatic coupling for railway rolling stock. [ORIGIN: named after the *Buckeye* Steel Castings Company, Columbus, Ohio.]

Buckeye State informal name for **OHIO**.

buck fever ▶ noun [mass noun] N. Amer. nervousness felt by novice hunters when they first sight game.

buckhorn ▶ noun a horn of a deer. ■ [mass noun] such horn, used typically for knife handles, small containers, and rifle sights.

buck-hound ▶ noun a staghound of a small breed.

Buckingham Palace the London residence of the British sovereign since 1837, adjoining St James's Park, Westminster. It was built for the Duke of Buckingham in the early 18th century and bought by George III in 1761.

Buckinghamshire a county of central England; county town, Aylesbury.

buckjump Austral. ▶ verb [no obj.] (of a horse) jump vertically with its head lowered, back arched, and legs drawn together, typically in an attempt to unseat its rider.
▶ noun [often as modifier] an act or display of buckjumping: *a buckjump rider.*
– DERIVATIVES **buckjumper** noun.

buckjumping ▶ noun [mass noun] a rodeo event in which a rider attempts to stay in the saddle of a bucking horse for a period of eight seconds: [as modifier] *a buckjumping event.*

Buckland, William (1784–1856), English geologist. He helped to redefine geology, correlating deposits and associated fossils with former conditions, and developed the idea of an ice age. He was the first to describe and name a dinosaur (*Megalosaurus*), in 1824.

buckle ▶ noun a flat, typically rectangular or oval frame with a hinged pin, used for joining the ends of a belt or strap. ■ a similarly shaped ornament, especially on a shoe.
▶ verb **1** [with obj.] fasten or decorate with a buckle: *he buckled his belt.* ■ [no obj.] (**buckle up**) fasten one's seat belt in a car or aircraft. **2** [no obj.] bend and give way under pressure or strain: *the earth buckled under the titanic stress.* [ORIGIN: from French *boucler* 'to bulge'.] ■ [with obj.] bend (something) out of shape: *a lorry backed into the wall and buckled the gate.* ■ figurative (of a person) suffer a psychological collapse as a result of enormous stress or pressure: *a weaker person might have buckled under the strain.*
– ORIGIN Middle English: from Old French *bocle*, from Latin *buccula* 'cheek strap of a helmet', from *bucca* 'cheek'.
▶ **buckle down** tackle a task with determination: *they will buckle down to negotiations over the next few months.*
buckle to dated make a determined effort.

buckler ▶ noun historical a small round shield held by a handle or worn on the forearm.
– ORIGIN Middle English: from Old French (*escu*) *bocler*, literally '(shield) with a boss', from *bocle* 'buckle, boss' (see **BUCKLE**).

buckler fern ▶ noun a European fern with deeply divided lobes and with stalks that are typically covered with brown scales. ● Several species in the genus *Dryopteris*, family Dryopteridaceae, in particular the common **broad buckler fern** (*D. dilatata*).

Buckley's ▶ noun (in phrase (**not**) **have Buckley's** (or **Buckley's chance**)) Austral./NZ informal used to suggest that someone has little or no hope of achieving a particular aim: *the vehicle had Buckley's chance of stopping.*
– ORIGIN late 19th cent.: sometimes said to be from the name of William *Buckley* (died 1856), who, despite dire predictions as to his chances of survival, lived with the Aboriginals for many years.

buckling ▶ noun a smoked herring.
– ORIGIN early 20th cent.: from German *Bückling* 'bloater'.

buckminsterfullerene /ˌbʌkmɪnstəˈfʊləriːn/ ▶ noun [mass noun] Chemistry a form of carbon having molecules of 60 atoms arranged in a polyhedron resembling a geodesic sphere. See also **FULLERENE**.
– ORIGIN 1980s: named after Richard *Buckminster* Fuller (see **FULLER**[1]).

bucko ▶ noun (pl. **-oes** or **-os**) informal a young man (often as a form of address): *I know you, my bucko, you're a troublemaker.*
– ORIGIN late 19th cent. (originally nautical slang): from **BUCK**[1] + **-o**.

buck-passing ▶ noun [mass noun] the practice of shifting the responsibility for something to someone else.

buckra /ˈbʌkrə/ ▶ noun (pl. same or **buckras**) US & W. Indian informal, chiefly derogatory a white person, especially a man.
– ORIGIN mid 18th cent.: from Ibibio and Efik (*m*)*bakara* 'European, master'.

buckram /ˈbʌkrəm/ ▶ noun [mass noun] coarse linen or other cloth stiffened with gum or paste, and used typically as interfacing in bookbinding. ■ figurative, archaic stiffness of manner.
– PHRASES **men in buckram** archaic non-existent people. [ORIGIN: with allusion to Shakespeare's *1 Henry IV* II. iv. 210–50.]
– ORIGIN Middle English (denoting a kind of fine linen or cotton cloth): from Old French *boquerant*, perhaps from **BUKHORO** in central Asia.

buck rarebit ▶ noun Brit. a dish of melted cheese on toast with a poached egg on top.

Bucks ▶ abbreviation for Buckinghamshire.

Buck's Fizz ▶ noun [mass noun] Brit. champagne or sparkling white wine mixed with orange juice as a cocktail.
– ORIGIN 1930s: from the name *Buck's Club*, in London, and **FIZZ**.

buckshee /bʌkˈʃiː, ˈbʌkʃiː/ ▶ adjective informal, chiefly Brit. free of charge: *a buckshee brandy.*
– ORIGIN First World War (originally soldiers' slang): alteration of **BAKSHEESH**.

buckshot ▶ noun [mass noun] coarse lead shot used in shotgun shells.

buckskin ▶ noun **1** the skin of a male deer. ■ [mass noun] greyish leather with a suede finish, traditionally made from such skin but now more commonly made from sheepskin: [as modifier] *a pair of buckskin moccasins.* ■ (**buckskins**) clothes or shoes made from such leather. ■ thick smooth cotton or woollen fabric. **2** N. Amer. a horse of a greyish-yellow colour.
– DERIVATIVES **buckskinned** adjective.

buckthorn ▶ noun a shrub or small tree which typically bears thorns and black berries. Some kinds yield dyes and others have been used medicinally. ● Genus *Rhamnus*, family Rhamnaceae: several species, including the **common** (also **European** or **purging**) **buckthorn** (*R. cathartica*), with berries formerly used as a cathartic. See also **ALDER BUCKTHORN**.
– ORIGIN late 16th cent.: from **BUCK**[1] in the sense 'deer' + **THORN**, translating modern Latin *spina cervina*.

buck-tooth ▶ noun an upper tooth that projects over the lower lip.
– DERIVATIVES **buck-toothed** adjective.

buckwheat ▶ noun an Asian plant of the dock family, producing starchy seeds that are used for fodder and also milled into flour which is widely used in the US. ● *Fagopyrum esculentum*, family Polygonaceae.
– ORIGIN mid 16th cent.: from Middle Dutch *boecweite* 'beech wheat', its grains being shaped like beechmast.

buckyballs ▶ plural noun Chemistry, informal spherical molecules of a fullerene, especially buckminsterfullerene. Related cylindrical molecules are termed **buckytubes**.

bucolic /bjuːˈkɒlɪk/ ▶ adjective of or relating to the pleasant aspects of the countryside and country life: *the church is lovely for its bucolic setting.*
▶ noun (usu. **bucolics**) a pastoral poem.
– DERIVATIVES **bucolically** adverb.
– ORIGIN early 16th cent. (denoting a pastoral poem): via Latin from Greek *boukolikos*, from *boukolos* 'herdsman', from *bous* 'ox'.

Bucureşti /ˌbukuˈreʃti/ Romanian name for **BUCHAREST**.

bud[1] ▶ noun a compact knob-like growth on a plant which develops into a leaf, flower, or shoot. ■ Biology an outgrowth from an organism, e.g. a yeast cell, that separates to form a new individual without sexual reproduction taking place. ■ [with modifier] Zoology a rudimentary leg or other appendage of an animal which has not yet grown, or never will grow, to full size.
▶ verb (**budded**, **budding**) [no obj.] Biology (of a plant or animal) form a bud: *new blood vessels bud out from the vascular bed* | [with obj.] *tape worms bud off egg-bearing sections from their tail end.* ■ [with obj.] graft a bud of (a plant) on to another plant.
– PHRASES **in bud** (of a plant) having newly formed buds.
– ORIGIN late Middle English: of unknown origin.

bud[2] ▶ noun N. Amer. informal a friendly form of address from one boy or man to another.
– ORIGIN mid 19th cent.: abbreviation of **BUDDY**.

Budapest /ˌb(j)uːdəˈpɛst/ the capital of Hungary; pop. 2,000,000 (1990). The city was formed in 1873 by the union of the hilly city of Buda on the right bank of the River Danube with the low-lying city of Pest on the left.

Buddha /ˈbʊdə/ (often **the Buddha**) a title given to the founder of Buddhism, Siddartha Gautama (*c.*563–*c.*460 BC). Born an Indian prince, he renounced wealth and family to become an ascetic, and after achieving enlightenment while meditating, taught all who came to learn from him. ■ [as noun **a Buddha**] Buddhism a person who has attained full enlightenment. ■ a statue or picture of the Buddha.
– ORIGIN Sanskrit, literally 'enlightened', past participle of *budh* 'know'.

Buddh Gaya /ˌbʊd ɡəˈjɑː/ variant spelling of **BODHGAYA**.

Buddhism /ˈbʊdɪz(ə)m/ ▶ noun [mass noun] a

widespread Asian religion or philosophy, founded by Siddartha Gautama in NE India in the 5th century BC.

Buddhism has no god, and gives a central role to the doctrine of karma. The 'four noble truths' of Buddhism state that all existence is suffering, that the cause of suffering is desire, that freedom from suffering is nirvana, and that this is attained through the 'eightfold path' of ethical conduct, wisdom, and mental discipline (including meditation). There are two major traditions, Theravada and Mahayana.

– DERIVATIVES **Buddhist** noun & adjective, **Buddhistic** adjective.

buddhu /ˈbʊdʊ, ˈbʊdˌdə/ ▶ **noun** Indian informal an idiot.
– ORIGIN from Hindi *buddhū*.

budding ▶ **adjective** [attrib.] (of a plant) having or developing buds: *a budding chrysanthemum.*
■(of a part of the body) becoming larger as part of the process of normal growth. ■ (of a person) beginning and showing signs of promise in a particular career or field: *budding young actors.* ■ just beginning and showing promising signs of continuing: *their budding relationship.*

buddle ▶ **noun** a shallow inclined container in which ore is washed.
– ORIGIN mid 16th cent.: of unknown origin.

buddleia /ˈbʌdlɪə/ ▶ **noun** a widely cultivated shrub with clusters of fragrant lilac, white, or yellow flowers.
● Genus *Buddleia* (or *Buddleja*), family Loganiaceae: several species, especially the butterfly bush.
– ORIGIN modern Latin; named in honour of the English botanist Adam *Buddle* (died 1715), by Linnaeus, at the suggestion of Sir William Houston, who introduced the plant to Europe from South America.

buddy informal, chiefly N. Amer. ▶ **noun** (pl. **-ies**) a close friend.
■ a working companion with whom close cooperation is required. ■ a person who befriends and helps another with an incapacitating disease, typically Aids.
▶ **verb** (**-ies, -ied**) [no obj.] become friendly and spend time with: *I decided to* **buddy up** *to them.*
– ORIGIN mid 19th cent. (originally US): perhaps an alteration of **BROTHER**, or a variant of **BUTTY**[2].

buddy-buddy ▶ **adjective** informal, chiefly derogatory very friendly: *he's buddy-buddy with the Ambassador.*

buddy movie ▶ **noun** informal, chiefly N. Amer. a film portraying a close friendship between two people.

buddy system ▶ **noun** a cooperative arrangement whereby individuals are paired or teamed up and assume responsibility for one another's welfare or safety.

Budge, Don (1915–2000), American tennis player; born *John Donald Budge*. He was the first to win the four major singles championships – Australia, France, Britain, and the US – in one year (1938). In both 1937 and 1938 he won the Wimbledon singles, men's doubles, and mixed doubles.

budge ▶ **verb** [usu. with negative] make or cause to make the slightest movement: [no obj.] *the queue in the bank hasn't budged* | [with obj.] *I couldn't budge the door.*
■ [no obj.] (**budge up/over**) informal make room for another person by moving: *budge up, boys, make room for your uncle.* ■ [usu. with modal] change or make (someone) change an opinion: [no obj.] *I tried to persuade him but he wouldn't budge* | [with obj.] *neither bribe nor threat will budge him.*
– ORIGIN late 16th cent.: from French *bouger* 'to stir', based on Latin *bullire* 'to boil'.

budgerigar ▶ **noun** a small gregarious Australian parakeet which is green with a yellow head in the wild. It is popular as a cage bird and has been bred in a variety of colours.
● *Melopsittacus undulatus*, family Psittacidae.
– ORIGIN mid 19th cent.: of Aboriginal origin, perhaps an alteration of Kamilaroi *gijirrigaa* (also in related languages).

budget ▶ **noun 1** an estimate of income and expenditure for a set period of time: *keep within the household budget.*
■ (**Budget**) an annual or other regular estimate of national revenue and expenditure put forward by a finance minister, including details of changes in taxation. ■ the amount of money needed or available for a particular purpose: *they have a limited budget.*
2 archaic a quantity of material, typically that which is written or printed.
▶ **verb** (**budgeted, budgeting**) [no obj.] allow or provide for in a budget: *the university is* **budgeting for** *a deficit* | [as adj. **budgeted**] *a budgeted figure of £31,000* | [as noun **budgeting**] *corporate planning and budgeting.*
■ [with obj.] provide (a sum of money) for a particular purpose from a budget: *the council proposes to budget £100,000 to provide grants.*
▶ **adjective** [attrib.] inexpensive: *a budget guitar.*
– PHRASES **on a budget** with a restricted amount of money: *we're travelling on a budget.*
– DERIVATIVES **budgetary** adjective.
– ORIGIN late Middle English: from Old French *bougette*, diminutive of *bouge* 'leather bag', from Latin *bulga* 'leather bag, knapsack', of Gaulish origin. Compare with **BULGE**. The word originally meant a pouch or wallet, and later its contents. In the mid 18th cent., the Chancellor of the Exchequer, in presenting his annual statement, was said 'to open the budget'. In the late 19th cent. the use of the term was extended from governmental to private or commercial finances.

budget account ▶ **noun** Brit. an account with a bank, store, or public utility into which one makes regular payments to cover bills.

budgie ▶ **noun** (pl. **-ies**) informal term for **BUDGERIGAR**.

bud-graft ▶ **verb** [with obj.] graft a bud of (a plant) on to another plant.
▶ **noun** a plant grown by this method.

budstick ▶ **noun** a small piece of plant stem with a bud, prepared for grafting on to another plant.

Budweis /ˈbʊtvaɪs/ German name for **ČESKÉ BUDĚJOVICE**.

budwood ▶ **noun** [mass noun] short lengths of young branches with buds prepared for grafting on to the rootstock of another plant.

budworm ▶ **noun** a moth caterpillar that is destructive to buds. See **SPRUCE BUDWORM**.

Buenaventura /ˌbweɪnəvɛnˈtjʊərə, Spanish bwenaβenˈtura/ the chief Pacific port of Colombia; pop. 122,500 (1985).

Buenos Aires /ˌbweɪnəs ˈʌɪriːz, Spanish bwenos ˈajres/ the capital city and chief port of Argentina, on the River Plate; pop. 2,961,000 (1991).

Buerger's disease /ˈbəːgəz/ ▶ **noun** [mass noun] inflammation and thrombosis in small and medium-sized blood vessels, typically in the legs and leading to gangrene. It has been associated with smoking.
– ORIGIN early 20th cent.: named after Leo *Buerger* (1879–1943), American surgeon.

buff[1] ▶ **noun** [mass noun] **1** a yellowish-beige colour: [as modifier] *a buff envelope.*
2 a stout dull yellow leather with a velvety surface.
3 [count noun] a stick, wheel, or pad used for polishing or smoothing.
▶ **verb** [with obj.] polish (something): *he buffed the glass until it gleamed.*
■ give (leather) a velvety finish by removing the surface of the grain.
▶ **adjective** N. Amer. informal (of a person or their body) in good physical shape with well-developed muscles: *the driver was a buff blond named March.*
– PHRASES **in the buff** informal naked.
– ORIGIN mid 16th cent.: probably from French *buffle*, from Italian *bufalo*, from late Latin *bufalus* (see **BUFFALO**). The original sense in English was 'buffalo', later 'oxhide' or 'colour of oxhide'.

buff[2] ▶ **noun** [with modifier] informal a person who is enthusiastically interested in and very knowledgeable about a particular subject: *a computer buff.*
– ORIGIN early 20th cent.: from **BUFF**[1], originally applied to enthusiastic fire-watchers, because of the buff uniforms formerly worn by New York volunteer firemen.

Buffalo an industrial city in New York State; pop. 328,120 (1990). Situated at the eastern end of Lake Erie, it is a major port of the St Lawrence Seaway.

buffalo ▶ **noun** (pl. same or **-oes**) **1** a heavily built wild ox with backswept horns, found mainly in the Old World tropics:
● four species native to South Asia (genus *Bubalus*, family Bovidae). See also **WATER BUFFALO, ANOA.** ● see **AFRICAN BUFFALO.**
■ the North American bison.
2 (also **buffalo fish**) a large greyish-olive freshwater fish with thick lips, common in North America.
● Genus *Ictiobus*, family Catostomidae: several species.
▶ **verb** (**-oes, -oed**) [with obj.] (often **be buffaloed**) N. Amer. informal overawe or intimidate (someone): *she didn't like being buffaloed.*
■ baffle (someone): *the problem has buffaloed the advertising staff.*
– ORIGIN mid 16th cent.: probably from Portuguese *bufalo*, from late Latin *bufalus*, from earlier *bubalus*, from Greek *boubalos* 'antelope, wild ox'.

Buffalo Bill (1846–1917), American showman; born *William Frederick Cody*. He gained his nickname for killing 4,280 buffalo in eight months to feed the Union Pacific Railroad workers, and subsequently devoted his life to his travelling Wild West Show.

buffalo gnat ▶ **noun** North American term for **BLACKFLY** (in sense 2).

buffalo grass ▶ **noun** [mass noun] any of a number of grasses, in particular:
● a creeping grass of the North American plains (*Buchloe dactyloides*, family Gramineae). ● a grass of Australia and New Zealand (*Stenotaphrum secundatum*, family Gramineae).

buffalo thorn ▶ **noun** a tropical African shrub or small tree with glossy leaves and thorns which grow in pairs, one of each pair being straight and the other curved.
● *Ziziphus mucronata*, family Rhamnaceae.

buffalo weaver ▶ **noun** a large thickset African weaver bird with a very stout bill and plumage that is either all black or has a white head and red rump. It builds large ragged nests.
● Genera *Bubalornis* and *Dinemellia*, family Ploceidae: three species.

Buffalo wings (also **Buffalo chicken wings**) ▶ **plural noun** N. Amer. deep-fried chicken wings coated in a spicy sauce and served with blue cheese dressing.

buffed (also **buffed-out**) ▶ **adjective** another term for **BUFF**.

buffer[1] ▶ **noun 1** a person or thing that prevents incompatible or antagonistic people or things from coming into contact with or harming each other: *family and friends can provide a buffer against stress.*
■ (**buffers**) Brit. a pair of shock-absorbing pistons projecting from a cross-beam at the end of a railway track or on the front and rear of a railway vehicle to reduce the effect of an impact.
2 (also **buffer solution**) Chemistry a solution which resists changes in pH when acid or alkali is added to it. Buffers typically involve a weak acid or alkali together with one of its salts.
3 Computing a temporary memory area or queue used when transferring data between devices or programs operating at different speeds.
▶ **verb** [with obj.] **1** lessen or moderate the impact of (something): *the massage helped to buffer the strain.*
2 treat with a chemical buffer: *add organic matter to buffer the resulting alkalinity.*
– ORIGIN mid 19th cent.: probably from obsolete *buff* (verb), imitative of the sound of a blow to a soft body.

buffer[2] ▶ **noun** Brit. informal an elderly man who is considered to be foolishly old-fashioned, unworldly, or incompetent: *a distinguished* **old buffer**.
– ORIGIN mid 18th cent.: probably from obsolete *buff* (see **BUFFER**[1]), or from dialect *buff* 'stutter, splutter' (possibly the same word). In late Middle English *buffer* had the sense 'stammerer'.

buffer state ▶ **noun** a small neutral country, situated between two larger hostile countries, serving to prevent the outbreak of regional conflict.

buffer stock ▶ **noun** a reserve of a commodity that can be used to offset price fluctuations.

buffer zone ▶ **noun** a neutral area serving to separate hostile forces or nations.
■ an area of land designated for environmental protection.

buffet[1] /ˈbʊfeɪ, ˈbʌfeɪ/ ▶ **noun 1** a meal consisting of several dishes from which guests serve themselves: [as modifier] *a cold buffet lunch.*
2 a room or counter in a station, hotel, or other public building selling light meals or snacks.
■ (also **buffet car**) Brit. a railway carriage in which light meals or snacks can be purchased.
3 also /ˈbʌfɪt/ an old-fashioned piece of dining-room furniture with cupboards and open shelves for keeping crockery in.
– ORIGIN early 18th cent. (in sense 3): from French, from Old French *bufet* 'stool', of unknown origin.

buffet[2] /ˈbʌfɪt/ ▶ **verb** (**buffeted, buffeting**) [with obj.] (especially of wind or waves) strike repeatedly and

violently; batter: *rough seas buffeted the coast* | [no obj.] *the wind was buffeting at their bodies.*
■knock (someone) over or off course: *he was buffeted from side to side.* ■(often **be buffeted**) figurative (of misfortunes or difficulties) afflict or harm (someone) repeatedly or over a long period: *they were buffeted by a major recession.*
▶**noun 1** dated a blow, typically of the hand or fist.
■figurative a shock or misfortune: *the daily buffets of urban civilization.*
2 [mass noun] Aeronautics another term for **BUFFETING**.
– ORIGIN Middle English: from Old French *buffeter* (verb), *buffet* (noun), diminutive of *bufe* 'a blow'.

buffet[3] /ˈbʌfɪt/ ▶**noun** Scottish & N. English a low stool or hassock.
– ORIGIN late Middle English: from Old French *bufet*, of unknown origin.

buffeting ▶**noun** [mass noun] the action of striking someone or something repeatedly and violently: *the roofs have survived the buffeting of worse winds than this.*
■figurative the action or result of afflicting or harming someone repeatedly or over a long period: *the buffeting that people are taking in lost job status.* ■ Aeronautics irregular oscillation of part of an aircraft, caused by turbulence.

bufflehead /ˈbʌf(ə)lhɛd/ ▶**noun** a small North American diving duck related to the goldeneye, with a large puffy head. The male has white plumage with a black back.
● *Bucephala albeola*, family Anatidae.
– ORIGIN mid 17th cent. (in the sense 'simpleton'): from obsolete *buffle* 'buffalo' + **HEAD**. The current sense (mid 18th cent.) may be an independent formation because of the duck's large square-shaped head.

buffo /ˈbʊfəʊ/ ▶**noun** (pl. **-os**) a comic actor in Italian opera or a person resembling such an actor.
▶**adjective** of or typical of Italian comic opera: *a buffo character.*
– ORIGIN mid 18th cent.: Italian, 'puff of wind, buffoon', from *buffare* 'to puff', of imitative origin.

Buffon /ˈbuːfɒn, French byfɔ̃/, Georges-Louis Leclerc, Comte de (1707–88), French naturalist. A founder of palaeontology, he emphasized the unity of all living species, minimizing the apparent differences between animals and plants. He produced a compilation of the animal kingdom, the *Histoire Naturelle*, which had reached thirty-six volumes by the time of his death.

buffoon /bəˈfuːn/ ▶**noun** a ridiculous but amusing person; a clown.
– DERIVATIVES **buffoonish** adjective.
– ORIGIN mid 16th cent.: from French *bouffon*, from Italian *buffone*, from medieval Latin *buffo* 'clown'. Originally recorded as a rare Scots word for a kind of pantomime dance, the term later (late 16th cent.) denoted a professional jester.

buffoonery ▶**noun** (pl. **-ies**) [mass noun] behaviour that is ridiculous but amusing.

buff-tip ▶**noun** a European moth that has buff-coloured wing tips and thoracic hair, giving it the appearance of a twig when at rest.
● *Phalera bucephala*, family Notodontidae.

bug ▶**noun 1** a small insect.
■informal a harmful micro-organism, typically a bacterium. ■ an illness caused by such a micro-organism: *he'd just recovered from a flu bug.* ■[with modifier] figurative, informal an enthusiastic, almost obsessive, interest in something: *they* ***caught*** *the sailing* ***bug*** | *Joe was* ***bitten by the*** *showbiz* ***bug.***
2 (also **true bug**) Entomology an insect of a large order distinguished by having mouthparts that are modified for piercing and sucking.
● Order Hemiptera: see **HEMIPTERA**.
3 a miniature microphone, typically concealed in a room or telephone.
4 an error in a computer program or system.
▶**verb** (**bugged**, **bugging**) [with obj.] **1** (often **be bugged**) conceal a miniature microphone in (a room or telephone) in order to eavesdrop on or record someone's conversations illicitly: *the telephones in the presidential palace were bugged.*
■record or eavesdrop on (a conversation) in this way.
2 informal annoy or bother (someone): *a persistent reporter was bugging me.*
– ORIGIN early 17th cent.: of unknown origin. Current verb senses date from the early 20th cent.
▶**bug off** N. Amer. informal go away.
bug out N. Amer. informal **1** leave quickly: *if you see enemy troops, bug out.* **2** bulge outwards: *men's eyes bug out when she walks past.*

bugaboo /ˈbʌɡəbuː/ ▶**noun** chiefly N. Amer. an object of fear or alarm; a bogey.
– ORIGIN mid 18th cent.: probably of Celtic origin and related to Welsh *bwci bo* 'bogey, the Devil', *bwci* 'hobgoblin' and Cornish *bucca*.

Buganda /b(j)uːˈɡandə/ a former kingdom of East Africa, on the north shore of Lake Victoria, now part of Uganda.

bugbane ▶**noun** a tall plant of the buttercup family, with spikes of cream or yellow flowers and fern-like leaves, native to north temperate regions.
● Genus *Cimicifuga*, family Ranunculaceae: several species, in particular *C. foetida*.
– ORIGIN early 19th cent.: from **BUG** + **BANE**, with reference to the former use of the species *C. foetida* to drive away bedbugs.

bugbear ▶**noun** a cause of obsessive fear, irritation, or loathing.
■archaic an imaginary being invoked to frighten children, typically a sort of hobgoblin supposed to devour them.
– ORIGIN late 16th cent.: probably from obsolete *bug* 'bogey' (of unknown origin) + **BEAR**[2].

bug-eyed ▶**adjective** & **adverb** with bulging eyes: [as adj.] *a bug-eyed monster* | [as adv.] *he stared bug-eyed at John.*

bugger vulgar slang, chiefly Brit. ▶**noun 1** derogatory a person who commits buggery.
2 [with adj.] a contemptible or pitied person, typically a man.
■a person with a particular negative quality or characteristic. ■ used as a term of affection or respect, typically grudgingly. ■ an annoyingly awkward thing.
▶**verb** [with obj.] **1** penetrate the anus of (someone) during sexual intercourse.
2 cause serious damage, harm, or trouble to.
■(**bugger someone about**) cause (someone) a lot of trouble and irritation. ■[no obj.] (**bugger about/around**) act in a stupid or feckless way. ■ used to express an angrily dismissive attitude to (someone or something).
▶**exclamation** used to express annoyance or anger.
– PHRASES **bugger all** nothing. **bugger me** used to express surprise or amazement. **I'm buggered if ——** used to make the following clause negative. **not give a bugger** not care in the slightest. **play silly buggers** act in a foolish way. **well, I'm** (or **I'll be**) **buggered** used to express one's amazement at something.
– ORIGIN Middle English (originally denoting a heretic, specifically an Albigensian): from Middle Dutch, from Old French *bougre* 'heretic', from medieval Latin *Bulgarus* 'Bulgarian', particularly one belonging to the Orthodox Church and therefore regarded as a heretic by the Roman Church. The sense 'sodomite' (16th cent.) arose from an association of heresy with forbidden sexual practices; its use as a general insult dates from the early 18th cent.
▶**bugger off** [usu. in imperative] go away.

buggered ▶**adjective** [predic.] Brit. vulgar slang (of a person) extremely tired.

buggery ▶**noun** [mass noun] anal intercourse. In law the term also covers bestiality.
■Brit. vulgar slang used in various expressions as an intensifier: *drive like buggery if you know what's good for you.*
– ORIGIN Middle English (in the sense 'heresy'): from Middle Dutch *buggerie*, from Old French *bougrerie*, from *bougre* (see **BUGGER**).

Buggins' turn ▶**noun** Brit. informal a system by which appointments or awards are made in rotation rather than by merit.
– ORIGIN early 20th cent.: from *Buggins*, used to represent a typical surname.

buggy[1] ▶**noun** (pl. **-ies**) a small or light vehicle, in particular:
■a small motor vehicle, typically one with an open top: *a golf buggy.* ■ short for **BABY BUGGY**. ■ historical a light horse-drawn vehicle for one or two people, with two or (in North America) four wheels.
– ORIGIN mid 18th cent.: of unknown origin.

buggy[2] ▶**adjective** (**buggier**, **buggiest**) **1** infested with bugs.
■(of a computer program or system) faulty in operation.
2 N. Amer. informal mad; insane.

bughouse informal ▶**noun 1** chiefly US a mental hospital or asylum.
2 informal a seedy, run-down cinema.
▶**adjective** chiefly US crazy.

bugle[1] ▶**noun** (also **bugle-horn**) a brass instrument like a small trumpet, typically without valves or keys and used for military signals.
▶**verb** [no obj.] sound a bugle.
■[with obj.] sound (a note or call) on a bugle: *he bugled a warning.*
– DERIVATIVES **bugler** noun.
– ORIGIN Middle English: via Old French from Latin *buculus*, diminutive of *bos* 'ox'. The early English sense was 'wild ox', hence the compound *bugle-horn*, denoting the horn of an ox used to give signals, originally in hunting.

bugle[2] ▶**noun** [mass noun] a creeping Eurasian plant of the mint family, with blue flowers held on upright stems. Also called **BUGLEWEED** in North America.
● Genus *Ajuga*, family Labiatae: several species, especially the common *A. reptans*.
– ORIGIN Middle English: from late Latin *bugula*.

bugle[3] ▶**noun** an ornamental tube-shaped glass or plastic bead sewn on to clothing.
– ORIGIN late 16th cent.: of unknown origin.

bugleweed ▶**noun** North American term for **BUGLE**[2].

bugloss /ˈbjuːɡlɒs/ ▶**noun** a bristly plant of the borage family, with bright blue flowers.
● *Anchusa* and other genera, family Boraginaceae: several species, including the Eurasian *A. arvensis* and the widespread **viper's bugloss**.
– ORIGIN late Middle English: from Old French *buglosse* or Latin *buglossus*, from Greek *bouglōssos* 'ox-tongued', from *bous* 'ox' + *glōssa* 'tongue'.

buhl /buːl/ ▶**noun** variant spelling of **BOULLE**.

build ▶**verb** (past and past participle **built**) [with obj.] (often **be built**) construct (something, typically something large) by putting parts or material together over a period of time: *the ironworks were built in 1736.*
■commission, finance, and oversee the building of (something): *the county council plans to build a bypass.* ■(**build something in/into**) incorporate (something) and make it a permanent part of a structure, system, or situation: *engineers want to build in extra traction.* ■ Computing compile (a program, database, index, etc.). ■[no obj.] (of a program, database, index, etc.) be compiled. ■ establish and develop (a business, relationship, or situation) over a period of time: *he'd* ***built up*** *the store from nothing.* ■[no obj.] (**build on**) use as a basis for further progress or development: *Britain should build on the talents of its workforce.* ■ increase the size, intensity, or extent of: *we* ***built up*** *confidence in our abilities* | [no obj.] *the air of excited anticipation builds.*
▶**noun 1** [mass noun] the proportions of a person's or animal's body: *she was of medium height and slim build* | [in sing.] *he was an ideal build for a sprinter.*
■the style or form of construction of something, especially a vehicle.
2 Computing a compiled version of a program.
■[mass noun] the process of compiling a program.
– PHRASES **build one's hopes up** become ever more hopeful or optimistic about something. **built on sand** figurative without reliable foundations or any real substance.
– ORIGIN Old English *byldan*, from *bold*, *botl* 'dwelling', of Germanic origin; related to **BOWER**[1].

builder ▶**noun** a person who constructs something by putting parts or material together over a period of time: *a boatbuilder.*
■a person whose job is to construct or repair houses, or to contract for their construction and repair. ■[usu. in combination] a person or thing that creates or develops a particular thing: *breaking the record was a real confidence builder.*

builders' merchant ▶**noun** a supplier of construction materials.

building ▶**noun 1** a structure with a roof and walls, such as a house, school, or factory.
2 [mass noun] the process or trade of constructing something: *the building of motorways* | [as modifier] *building materials.*
■the process of commissioning, financing, or overseeing the construction of something. ■ the process of creating or developing something, typically a system or situation, over a period of time: *the building of democracy in Guatemala.* ■ the process of increasing the intensity of a feeling: *a playwright's cunning in the building of suspense.*

building block ▶ noun a child's wooden or plastic toy brick.
■ figurative a basic unit from which something is built up: *sounds are the building blocks of language.*

building line ▶ noun a limit beyond which a house must not extend into a street.

building site ▶ noun an area where a structure is being constructed or repaired.

building society ▶ noun Brit. a financial organization which pays interest on investments by its members and lends capital for the purchase or improvement of houses.

Building societies originally developed as non-profit-making cooperative societies from friendly societies. Since 1986 changes in legislation have allowed them to offer banking and other facilities, and some have become public limited companies.

build-up ▶ noun [usu. in sing.] **1** a gradual accumulation or increase, typically of something negative and typically leading to a problem or crisis: *the build-up of carbon dioxide in the atmosphere.*
2 a period of excitement and preparation in advance of a significant event: *the build-up to Christmas.*
■ a favourable description in advance; publicity: *a showbiz build-up before the album release.*

built past and past participle of **BUILD**. ▶ adjective (of a person) having a specified physical size or build: *a slightly built woman.*

built-in ▶ adjective forming an integral part of a structure: *a worktop with a built-in cooker.*
■ (of a characteristic) inherent; innate: *the system has a built-in resistance to change.*

built-up ▶ adjective **1** (of an area) densely covered by houses or other buildings.
2 increased in height by the addition of parts: *shoes with built-up heels.*
■ (of a feeling) increasing in intensity over a period of time: *built-up frustration.*

Bujumbura /ˌbuːdʒəmˈbʊərə/ the capital of Burundi, at the north-eastern end of Lake Tanganyika; pop. 235,440 (1990). It was known as Usumbura until 1962.

Bukharin /bʊˈkɑːrɪn/, Nikolai (Ivanovich) (1888–1938), Russian revolutionary activist and theorist. Editor of *Pravda* (1918–29) and *Izvestia* (1934–7), a member of the Politburo (1924–9), and chairman of Comintern from 1926, he was executed in one of Stalin's purges.

Bukhoro /buːˈkɔːrə/ (also **Bukhara**, **Bokhara**) a city in the central Asian republic of Uzbekistan; pop. 246,200 (1990). It is one of the oldest trade centres in central Asia, and is noted for the production of karakul fleeces.

Bukovina /ˌbʊkə(ʊ)ˈviːnə/ a region of SE Europe in the Carpathians, divided between Romania and Ukraine. Formerly a province of Moldavia, it was ceded to Austria by the Turks in 1775. After the First World War it was made part of Romania, the northern part being incorporated into the Ukrainian SSR in the Second World War.

Bulawayo /ˌbʊləˈweɪəʊ/ an industrial city in western Zimbabwe; pop. 620,940 (1992).

bulb ▶ noun **1** a rounded underground storage organ present in some plants, notably those of the lily family, consisting of a short stem surrounded by fleshy scale leaves or leaf bases, lying dormant over winter. Compare with **CORM**, **RHIZOME**.
■ a plant grown from an organ of this kind. ■ a similar underground organ such as a corm or a rhizome.
2 an object with a rounded or teardrop shape like a bulb, in particular:
■ short for **LIGHT BULB**. ■ an expanded part of a glass tube such as that forming the reservoir of a thermometer. ■ a hollow flexible container with an opening through which the air can be expelled by squeezing, such as that used to fill a syringe. ■ a spheroidal dilated part at the end of an anatomical structure.
– ORIGIN late Middle English: via Latin from Greek *bolbos* 'onion, bulbous root'.

bulb fibre ▶ noun [mass noun] a mixture of peat, oyster shell, and charcoal used for growing bulbs or other plants, typically in containers.

bulb fly ▶ noun a hoverfly that resembles a bumblebee, with larvae that are pests of daffodil bulbs.
• *Merodon equestris*, family Syrphidae.

bulbil /ˈbʌlbɪl/ ▶ noun Botany a small bulb-like structure, in particular one in the axil of a leaf, which may fall to form a new plant.
– ORIGIN mid 19th cent.: from modern Latin *bulbillus*, diminutive of *bulbus* 'onion, bulbous root'.

bulbous ▶ adjective **1** fat, round, or bulging: *a bulbous nose.*
2 (of a plant) growing from a bulb.

bulbul /ˈbʊlbʊl/ ▶ noun a tropical African and Asian songbird that typically has a melodious voice and drab plumage. Many kinds have a crest.
• Family Pycnonotidae: several genera and numerous species.
– ORIGIN mid 17th cent.: from Persian, of imitative origin.

Bulganin /bʊlˈɡɑːnɪn/, Nikolai (Aleksandrovich) (1895–1975), Soviet statesman, Chairman of the Council of Ministers (Premier) 1955–8. He was Vice-Premier in the government of Georgi Malenkov in 1953, and in 1955 shared the premiership with Khrushchev.

Bulgar /ˈbʌlɡɑː/ ▶ noun a member of a Slavic people who settled in what is now Bulgaria in the 7th century.
– ORIGIN from medieval Latin *Bulgarus*, from Old Church Slavonic *Blŭgarinŭ*.

bulgar /ˈbʌlɡə/ (also **bulgur**, **bulgar wheat**) ▶ noun [mass noun] a cereal food made from whole wheat partially boiled then dried, eaten especially in Turkey.
– ORIGIN 1930s: from Turkish *bulgur* 'bruised grain'.

Bulgaria /bʌlˈɡɛːrɪə/ a country in SE Europe on the western shores of the Black Sea; pop. 8,798,000 (est. 1991); official language, Bulgarian; capital, Sofia. Part of the Ottoman Empire from the 14th century, Bulgaria remained under Turkish rule until the late 19th century, becoming independent in 1908. A communist state was set up by the Soviets after the Second World War, and a multiparty democratic system was introduced in 1989.
– ORIGIN named after the Bulgars (see **BULGAR**).

Bulgarian ▶ adjective of or relating to Bulgaria, its people, or their language.
▶ noun **1** a native or national of Bulgaria, or a person of Bulgarian descent.
2 [mass noun] the Southern Slavic language spoken in Bulgaria.

bulge ▶ noun **1** a rounded swelling or protuberance which distorts a flat surface.
■ (especially in a military context) a piece of land which projects outwards from an otherwise regular line: *the advance created an eastward-facing bulge in the line.* ■ [in sing.] informal a temporary unusual increase in number or size: *a bulge in the birth rate.*
2 N. Amer. informal an advantage in the scoreline: *the Suns moved to a 61–39 bulge at half-time.*
▶ verb [no obj.] swell or protrude to an unnatural or incongruous extent: *the veins in his neck bulged* | [as adj. **bulging**] *he stared with bulging eyes.*
■ be full of and distended with: *a briefcase bulging with documents.*
– DERIVATIVES **bulgingly** adverb, **bulgy** adjective.
– ORIGIN Middle English: from Old French *boulge*, from Latin *bulga* (see **BUDGET**). The original meaning was 'wallet or bag', later 'a ship's bilge' (early 17th cent.); other senses presumably derived from association with the shape of a full bag.

Bulge, Battle of the in the Second World War, a German counteroffensive in the Ardennes aimed at preventing an Allied invasion of Germany, in late 1944–early 1945. The Germans drove a 'bulge' about 60 miles (110 km) deep in the front line, but were later forced to retreat.

bulgur ▶ noun variant spelling of **BULGAR**.

bulimarexia /bjʊˌlɪməˈrɛksɪə, bʊ-/ ▶ noun chiefly US another term for *bulimia nervosa* (see **BULIMIA**).
– DERIVATIVES **bulimarexic** adjective & noun.
– ORIGIN 1970s: blend of **BULIMIA** and **ANOREXIA**.

bulimia /bjʊˈlɪmɪə, bʊ-/ ▶ noun [mass noun] insatiable overeating as a medical condition, in particular:
■ (also **bulimia nervosa**) an emotional disorder involving distortion of body image and an obsessive desire to lose weight, in which bouts of extreme overeating are followed by depression and self-induced vomiting, purging, or fasting.
– DERIVATIVES **bulimic** adjective & noun.
– ORIGIN late Middle English (as *bolisme*, later *bulimy*): modern Latin, or from medieval Latin *bolismos*, from Greek *boulimia* 'ravenous hunger', from *bous* 'ox' + *limos* 'hunger'.

bulk ▶ noun [mass noun] the mass or magnitude of something large: *the sheer bulk of the bags.*
■ [count noun] a large mass or shape, for example of a building or a heavy body: *he moved quickly in spite of his bulk.* ■ [as modifier] large in quantity or amount: *bulk orders of over 100 copies.* ■ (**the bulk**) the majority or greater part of something: *the bulk of the traffic had passed.* ■ roughage in food: *bread and potatoes supply energy, essential protein, and bulk.* ■ cargo in an unpackaged mass such as grain, oil, or milk. ■ Printing the thickness of paper or a book.
▶ verb **1** [no obj.] be or seem to be of great size or importance: *territorial questions* ***bulked large*** *in diplomatic relations.*
2 [with obj.] treat (a product) so that its quantity appears greater than it in fact is: *traders were* ***bulking up*** *their flour with chalk.*
■ [no obj.] (**bulk up**) build up flesh and muscle, typically in training for sporting events. ■ (often **be bulked**) combine (shares or commodities for sale).
– PHRASES **in bulk 1** (of goods) in large quantities and generally at a reduced price: *retail multiples buy in bulk.* **2** (of a cargo or commodity) loose; not packaged: *sugar is imported in bulk and bagged on the island.*
– ORIGIN Middle English: the senses 'cargo as a whole' and 'heap, large quantity' (the earliest recorded) are probably from Old Norse *búlki* 'cargo'; other senses arose perhaps by alteration of obsolete *bouk* 'belly, body'.

bulk buying ▶ noun [mass noun] the purchase of goods in large amounts, typically at a discount.
– DERIVATIVES **bulk-buy** verb.

bulk carrier ▶ noun a ship that carries non-liquid cargoes such as grain or ore in bulk.

bulker ▶ noun another term for **BULK CARRIER**.

bulkhead ▶ noun a dividing wall or barrier between separate compartments inside a ship, aircraft, or other vehicle.
– ORIGIN late 15th cent.: from Old Norse *bálkr* 'partition' + **HEAD**.

bulk mail ▶ noun [mass noun] N. Amer. a category of mail for sending out large numbers of identical items at a reduced rate.

bulk modulus ▶ noun Physics the relative change in the volume of a body produced by a unit compressive or tensile stress acting uniformly over its surface.

bulky ▶ adjective (**bulkier**, **bulkiest**) taking up much space, typically inconveniently; large and unwieldy: *a bulky carrier bag.*
■ (of a person) heavily built.
– DERIVATIVES **bulkily** adverb, **bulkiness** noun.

bull[1] ▶ noun **1** an uncastrated male bovine animal: [as modifier] *bull calves.*
■ a large male animal, especially a whale or elephant.
■ (**the Bull**) the zodiacal sign or constellation Taurus.
2 Brit. the centre of a target; a bullseye.
3 Stock Exchange a person who buys shares hoping to sell them at a higher price later. Often contrasted with **BEAR**[2].
▶ adjective [attrib.] (of a part of the body, especially the neck) resembling the corresponding part of a male bovine animal in build and strength: *his bull neck and broad shoulders.*
▶ verb **1** [with obj. and adverbial of direction] push or drive powerfully or violently: *he bulled the motor cycle clear of the tunnel* | [no obj., with adverbial of direction] *he was bulling through a mob of admirers.*
2 [no obj.] (**be bulling**) (of a cow) behave in a manner characteristic of being on heat.
– PHRASES **like a bull at a gate** taking action hastily and without thought. **like a bull in a china shop** behaving recklessly and clumsily in a situation where one is likely to cause damage or injury. **(like) a red rag to a bull** see **RED**. **take the bull by the horns** deal decisively with a difficult, dangerous, or unpleasant situation.
– ORIGIN late Old English *bula* (recorded in place names), from Old Norse *boli*. Compare with **BULLOCK**.

bull[2] ▶ noun a papal edict.
– ORIGIN Middle English: from Old French *bulle*, from Latin *bulla* 'bubble, rounded object' (in medieval Latin 'seal or sealed document').

bull[3] ▶ noun [mass noun] informal stupid or untrue talk or writing; nonsense: *much of what he says is sheer bull.*
■ [count noun] US a bad blunder in speech.
– ORIGIN early 17th cent.: of unknown origin.

bulla /ˈbʊlə/ ▶ **noun** (pl. **bullae** /ˈbʊliː/) **1** Medicine a bubble-like cavity filled with air or fluid, in particular:
▪a large blister containing serous fluid. ▪an abnormal air-filled cavity in the lung.
2 Anatomy a rounded prominence.
3 a round seal attached to a papal bull, typically one made of lead.
– ORIGIN Latin, literally 'bubble'.

bullace /ˈbʊlɪs/ ▶ **noun** a thorny shrub or small tree with small purple-black plum-like fruits. The damson is probably a cultivated form.
• *Prunus domestica* subsp. *insititia* (or *P. insititia*), family Rosaceae.
– ORIGIN Middle English: from Old French *buloce* 'sloe': of unknown origin.

bull ant ▶ **noun** another term for **BULLDOG ANT**.

bullate /ˈbʊleɪt/ ▶ **adjective** Botany covered with rounded swellings like blisters.
– ORIGIN mid 18th cent.: from Latin *bullatus*, from Latin *bulla* 'bubble'.

bull-baiting ▶ **noun** [mass noun] historical the practice of setting dogs to harass a bull, popular as an entertainment in medieval Europe.

bull bar ▶ **noun** a strong metal grille fitted to the front of a motor vehicle to protect it against impact damage.

bulldike ▶ **noun** variant spelling of **BULLDYKE**.

bulldog ▶ **noun** a dog of a sturdy smooth-haired breed with a large head and powerful protruding lower jaw, a flat wrinkled face, and a broad chest.
▪a person noted for courageous or stubborn tenacity: [as modifier] *the bulldog spirit*. ▪informal (at Oxford and Cambridge Universities) an official who assists the proctors, especially in disciplinary matters.
▶**verb** (**-dogged**, **-dogging**) [with obj.] N. Amer. wrestle (a steer) to the ground by holding its horns and twisting its neck: [as noun **bulldogging**] *cowboys compete in bulldogging and bareback riding.*
– DERIVATIVES **bulldogger** noun.

bulldog ant ▶ **noun** a large Australian ant with large jaws and a powerful sting. Also called **BULL ANT**.
• Genus *Myrmecia*, family Formicidae.

bulldog bat ▶ **noun** a fish-eating bat that has long legs and very large feet with sharp claws, native to Central and South America. Also called **FISHERMAN BAT**, **MASTIFF BAT**.
• *Noctilio leporinus*, family Noctilionidae.

bulldog bond ▶ **noun** a sterling bond issued on the UK market by a foreign borrower.

bulldog clip ▶ **noun** Brit. trademark a strong sprung metal device with two flat plates that close so as to hold papers together.

bulldoze ▶ **verb** [with obj.] clear (ground) or destroy (buildings, trees, etc.) with a bulldozer: *developers are bulldozing the site.*
▪figurative, informal use force insensitively when dealing with (someone or something): *she believes that to build status you need to bulldoze everyone else.*
– ORIGIN late 19th cent. (originally US in the sense 'intimidate'): from **BULL**[1] + *-doze*, alteration of the noun **DOSE**.

bulldozer ▶ **noun** a powerful track-laying tractor with a broad curved upright blade at the front for clearing ground.
▪figurative a person, army, or other body exercising irresistible force, especially in disposing of obstacles or opposition: *the new Duke was a political bulldozer.*

bulldyke (also **bulldike**, or **bulldyker**) ▶ **noun** informal, often offensive a particularly masculine lesbian.

bullet ▶ **noun** **1** a projectile for firing from a rifle, revolver, or other small firearm, typically made of metal, cylindrical and pointed, and sometimes containing an explosive.
▪used in similes to refer to someone or something that moves very fast: *the ball sped across the grass like a bullet.* ▪US (in sporting contexts) a very fast ball. ▪(**the bullet**) informal dismissal from employment: *your record's bad, but it's doubtful they'll give you the bullet.*
2 Printing a small solid circle printed before each in a list of items, for emphasis.
– ORIGIN early 16th cent. (denoting a cannonball): from French *boulet*, *boulette* 'small ball', diminutive of *boule*, from Latin *bulla* 'bubble'.

bullet head ▶ **noun** derogatory a person's head that is small, round, and slightly pointed.
– DERIVATIVES **bullet-headed** adjective.

bulletin ▶ **noun** a short official statement or broadcast summary of news.
▪a regular newsletter or printed report issued by an organization or society.
– ORIGIN mid 17th cent. (denoting an official warrant in some European countries): from French, from Italian *bullettino*, diminutive of *bulletta* 'passport', diminutive of *bulla* 'seal, bull'.

bulletin board ▶ **noun** N. Amer. a noticeboard.
▪Computing an information storage system designed to permit any authorized user to access and add to it from a remote terminal.

bullet point ▶ **noun** each of several items in a list, typically a summary of the arguments in a presentation printed with a bullet before each for emphasis.

bulletproof ▶ **adjective** designed to resist the penetration of bullets: *a bulletproof vest.*

bullet train ▶ **noun** informal a Japanese high-speed passenger train.

bull fiddle ▶ **noun** informal, chiefly US a double bass.

bullfight ▶ **noun** a public spectacle, especially in Spain, at which a bull is baited and killed.
– DERIVATIVES **bullfighter** noun.

bullfighting ▶ **noun** [mass noun] the sport of baiting and killing a bull as a public spectacle in an outdoor arena.

> Bullfighting is the national spectator sport of Spain, and is found also in Latin America. Typically, the bull is tormented by mounted picadors who stick darts into its neck, and the matador then baits it with a red cape and attempts to kill it with a sword-blow beneath the shoulder blade.

bullfinch ▶ **noun** **1** a stocky Eurasian finch with a short thick bill, and typically with grey or pinkish plumage, dark wings, and a white rump.
• Genus *Pyrrhula*, family Fringillidae: several species, in particular the common *P. pyrrhula*, the male of which has a black face and pink breast.
2 a Caribbean songbird of the bunting family, resembling the Old World bullfinch.
• Genera *Loxigilla* and *Melopyrrha*, family Emberizidae (subfamily Emberizinae): four species.

bullfrog ▶ **noun** a very large frog which has a deep booming croak and is often a predator of smaller vertebrates.
• Genera *Rana* and *Pyxicephalus*, family Ranidae: the **North American bullfrog** (*R. catesbiana*), the **Asian bullfrog** (*R. tigrina*), and the **African bullfrog** (*P. adspersus*).

bullhead ▶ **noun** **1** a small mainly freshwater Eurasian fish of the sculpin family, with a broad flattened head and spiny fins.
• Genera *Cottus* and *Taurulus*, family Cottidae: three species, in particular the miller's thumb.
2 (also **bullhead catfish**) an American freshwater catfish.
• Genus *Ictalurus*, family Ictaluridae: several species, in particular the **brown bullhead** (*I. nebulosus*).

bullheaded ▶ **adjective** determined in an obstinate and unthinking way: *a bullheaded belief that she is right.*
– DERIVATIVES **bullheadedly** adverb, **bullheadedness** noun.

bullhorn ▶ **noun** chiefly N. Amer. a megaphone.

bull huss ▶ **noun** see **HUSS**.

bullion ▶ **noun** [mass noun] **1** gold or silver in bulk before coining, or valued by weight.
2 ornamental braid or fringing made with twists of gold or silver thread.
– ORIGIN Middle English: from Anglo-Norman French, in the sense 'a mint', variant of Old French *bouillon*, based on Latin *bullire* 'to boil'.

bullion knot ▶ **noun** a decorative stitch in embroidery made by winding the thread several times round the needle before sewing a backstitch.

bullish ▶ **adjective** **1** aggressively confident and self-assertive.
2 Stock Exchange characterized by rising share prices: *the market was bullish.*
▪(of a dealer) inclined to buy because of an anticipated rise in prices.
– DERIVATIVES **bullishly** adverb, **bullishness** noun.

bull kelp ▶ **noun** [mass noun] a very large brown seaweed found in Pacific and Antarctic waters, growing up to 50 m in length off the north-western coasts of North America.
• *Nereocystis* and other genera, class Phaeophyceae.

bull market ▶ **noun** Stock Exchange a market in which share prices are rising, encouraging buying.

bull-mastiff ▶ **noun** a dog that is a cross-breed of bulldog and mastiff.

bull-nose ▶ **noun** technical a surface or object having a rounded edge or end: [as modifier] *a bull-nose tile.*
– DERIVATIVES **bull-nosed** adjective.

bullock ▶ **noun** a male domestic bovine animal that has been castrated and is raised for beef.
▶**verb** [no obj.] Austral./NZ informal work long and hard: *people have dropped dead bullocking their guts out* | [as noun **bullocking**] *I had done all the bullocking.*
– ORIGIN late Old English *bulluc*, diminutive of *bula* (see **BULL**[1]). The verb (late 19th cent.) is by association with a bullock's use as a draught animal.

bullock's heart ▶ **noun** the edible fruit of a tropical American custard apple.
• The tree is *Annona reticulata*, family Annonaceae.

bullocky ▶ **noun** (pl. **-ies**) Austral./NZ informal a bullock driver.

bullous /ˈbʊləs/ ▶ **adjective** Medicine characterized by blisters or bullae on the skin.

bullpen ▶ **noun** chiefly N. Amer. an enclosure for bulls.
▪an exercise area for baseball pitchers. ▪the relief pitchers of a baseball team. ▪an open-plan office area. ▪a large cell in which prisoners are held before a court hearing.

bullring ▶ **noun** an arena where bullfights are held.

Bull Run a small river in eastern Virginia, scene of two Confederate victories, in 1861 and 1862, during the American Civil War.

bullrush ▶ **noun** variant spelling of **BULRUSH**.

bull session ▶ **noun** N. Amer. an informal group discussion.
– ORIGIN 1920s: *bull* from **BULL**[3].

bullseye ▶ **noun** **1** the centre of the target in sports such as archery, shooting, and darts.
▪a shot that hits the centre of such a target. ▪figurative used to refer to something that achieves exactly the intended effect: *the silence told him he'd scored a bullseye.*
2 a large, round, hard peppermint-flavoured sweet.
3 dated a hemisphere or thick disc of glass forming a small window in a ship or the glass of a lamp: [as modifier] *a bullseye lantern.*
▪a thick knob or boss of glass at the centre of a blown glass sheet.

bullshit vulgar slang ▶ **noun** [mass noun] stupid or untrue talk or writing; nonsense.
▶**verb** (**-shitted**, **-shitting**) [with obj.] talk nonsense to (someone), typically in an attempt to deceive them.
– DERIVATIVES **bullshitter** noun.
– ORIGIN early 20th cent.: from **BULL**[3] + **SHIT**.

bull snake ▶ **noun** a gopher snake of a race found commonly on the plains and prairies of North America.
• *Pituophis catenifer sayi*, family Colubridae.

bull terrier ▶ **noun** a short-haired dog of a breed that is a cross between a bulldog and a terrier.

bull trout ▶ **noun** a North American trout that resembles the Dolly Varden, found in cold rivers and lakes.
• *Salvelinus confluentus*, family Salmonidae.
▪Brit. a sea trout.

bullwhip chiefly N. Amer. ▶ **noun** a whip with a long heavy lash.
▶**verb** (**-whipped**, **-whipping**) [with obj.] strike or thrash with such a whip.

bully[1] ▶ **noun** (pl. **-ies**) a person who uses strength or influence to harm or intimidate others who are weaker.
▶**verb** (**-ies**, **-ied**) [with obj.] use superior strength or influence to intimidate (someone), typically to force them to do what one wants: *a local man was bullied into helping them.*
– ORIGIN mid 16th cent.: probably from Middle Dutch *boele* 'lover'. Original use was as a term of endearment applied to either sex; later becoming a familiar form of address to a male friend. The current sense dates from the late 17th cent.

bully[2] informal ▶ **adjective** chiefly N. Amer. very good; first-rate: *the statue really looked bully.*
▶**exclamation** (**bully for**) an expression of admiration or approval: *he got away—bully for him!*
– ORIGIN late 16th cent. (originally used of a person, meaning 'admirable, gallant, jolly'): from **BULLY**[1]. The current sense dates from the mid 19th cent.

bully[3] ▶ **noun** (pl. **-ies**) (also **bully off**) the start of play in field hockey, in which two opponents strike each

other's sticks three times and then go for the ball.
▶ verb (-ies, -ied) [no obj.] start play in this way.
– ORIGIN late 19th cent. (originally denoting a scrum in Eton football): of unknown origin.

bully⁴ (also **bully beef**) ▶ noun [mass noun] informal corned beef.
– ORIGIN mid 18th cent.: alteration of **BOUILLI**.

bully boy ▶ noun a tough or aggressive man: [as modifier] bully-boy tactics.

bully pulpit ▶ noun [in sing.] N. Amer. a public office or position of authority that provides its occupant with an opportunity to speak out on any issue: he could use the presidency as a bully pulpit to bring out the best in civic life.
– ORIGIN early 20th cent.: apparently originally used by President Theodore Roosevelt, explaining his personal view of the presidency.

bullyrag (also **ballyrag**) ▶ verb (-ragged, -ragging) [with obj.] N. Amer. informal treat (someone) in a scolding or intimidating way: he would bullyrag them around but lick up to his superiors.
– ORIGIN late 18th cent.: of unknown origin.

bulrush (also **bullrush**) ▶ noun 1 a tall reed-like water plant with strap-like leaves and a dark brown velvety cylindrical head of numerous tiny flowers. Also called **REED MACE**.
● Genus Typha, family Typhaceae: several species, in particular Typha latifolia.
2 another term for **CLUBRUSH**.
3 (in biblical use) a papyrus plant.
– ORIGIN late Middle English: probably from **BULL**¹ in the sense 'large or coarse', as in words such as bullfrog.

Bultmann /ˈbʊltmən, German ˈbʊltman/, Rudolf (Karl) (1884–1976), German Lutheran theologian. Notable works: The History of the Synoptic Tradition (1921).

bulwark /ˈbʊlwək/ ▶ noun a defensive wall.
■ figurative a person, institution, or principle that acts as a defence: the security forces are a bulwark against the breakdown of society. ■ (usu. **bulwarks**) an extension of a ship's sides above the level of the deck.
– ORIGIN late Middle English: from Middle Low German and Middle Dutch bolwerk; related to **BOLE**¹ and **WORK**.

Bulwer-Lytton /ˌbʊlwə ˈlɪt(ə)n/ see **LYTTON**.

bum¹ ▶ noun Brit. informal a person's buttocks or anus.
– PHRASES **bums on seats** the audience at a theatre, cinema, or other entertainment, viewed as a source of income.
– ORIGIN late Middle English: of unknown origin.

bum² informal ▶ noun N. Amer. 1 a vagrant.
■ a lazy or worthless person: you ungrateful bum.
2 [in combination] a person who devotes a great deal of time to a specified activity: a ski bum | a dance bum.
▶ verb (**bummed**, **bumming**) 1 [no obj.] **bum around**) chiefly N. Amer. travel, with no particular purpose or destination: he bummed around Florida for a few months.
■ pass one's time idly: students bumming around at university.
2 [with obj.] get by asking or begging: they tried to bum quarters off us.
▶ adjective [attrib.] of poor quality; bad or wrong: not one bum note was played.
– PHRASES **give someone** (or **get**) **the bum's rush** chiefly N. Amer. forcibly eject someone (or be forcibly ejected) from a place or gathering. ■ abruptly dismiss someone (or be abruptly dismissed) for a poor idea or performance. **on the bum** N. Amer. travelling rough and with no fixed home; vagrant.
– ORIGIN mid 19th cent.: probably from **BUMMER**.

bumbag ▶ noun Brit. informal a small pouch on a belt, for money and other valuables, worn round the waist or hips.

bum-bailiff ▶ noun historical, derogatory a bailiff empowered to collect debts or arrest debtors for non-payment.
– ORIGIN early 17th cent.: from **BUM**¹, so named because of the association of an approach from behind.

bumble ▶ verb 1 [no obj., with adverbial of direction] move or act in an awkward or confused manner: they bumbled around the house | [as adj. **bumbling**] his bumbling interventions.
2 [no obj.] speak in a confused or indistinct way.
■ [with adverbial] (of an insect) buzz or hum: she watched a bee bumble among the flowers.
– DERIVATIVES **bumbler** noun.

– ORIGIN late Middle English (in the sense 'hum, drone'): from **BOOM**¹ + **-LE**⁴.

bumblebee ▶ noun a large hairy social bee which flies with a loud hum, living in small colonies in holes underground. Also called **HUMBLE-BEE**.
● Genus Bombus, family Apidae: many species.

bumblebee fish ▶ noun a small yellow- and black-striped goby of SE Asia, able to live in both fresh and salt water and popular in aquaria.
● Brachygobius nunus, family Gobiidae.

bumboat ▶ noun a small vessel carrying provisions for sale to moored or anchored ships.
– ORIGIN late 17th cent.: from **BUM**¹ + **BOAT**. The term originally denoted a scavenger's boat removing refuse etc. from ships, often also bringing produce for sale.

bumboy ▶ noun vulgar slang a young male homosexual, especially a prostitute.

bumf (also **bumph**) ▶ noun [mass noun] informal, chiefly Brit. useless or tedious printed information or documents.
■ dated toilet paper.
– ORIGIN late 19th cent.: abbreviation of slang bum-fodder, in the same sense.

bumfluff ▶ noun [mass noun] Brit. informal, derogatory the first beard growth of an adolescent.

bumiputra /ˌbuːmɪˈpuːtrə/ ▶ noun (pl. same or **bumiputras**) a Malaysian of indigenous Malay origin.
– ORIGIN Malay, literally 'son of the soil'.

bummalo /ˈbʌmələʊ/ ▶ noun (pl. same) a small elongated fish of South Asian coasts which is dried and used as food. Also called **BOMBAY DUCK**.
● Harpadon nehereus, family Harpadontidae.
– ORIGIN late 17th cent.: perhaps from Marathi bombīl.

bummaree /ˌbʌməˈriː/ ▶ noun a self-employed licensed porter at Smithfield meat market in London.
– ORIGIN late 18th cent.: of unknown origin.

bummer ▶ noun informal 1 (a bummer) a thing that is annoying or disappointing: the team's relegation is a real bummer.
■ an unpleasant reaction to a hallucinogenic drug.
2 N. Amer. a loafer or vagrant.
– ORIGIN mid 19th cent.: perhaps from German Bummler, from bummeln 'stroll, loaf about'.

bump ▶ noun 1 a light blow or a jolting collision: a nasty bump on the head.
■ the dull sound of such a blow or collision. ■ Aeronautics a rising air current causing an irregularity in an aircraft's motion. ■ (**the bumps**) Brit. informal the action of lifting a person by the arms and legs on their birthday and letting them down on to the ground, once for each year of their age: the children were given the bumps. ■ Rowing (in races on narrow rivers where boats make a spaced start one behind another) the point at which a boat begins to overtake or touch the boat ahead, thereby defeating it and so being started ahead of it in the next race.
2 a protuberance on a level surface: bumps in the road.
■ a swelling on the skin, especially one caused by illness or injury. ■ dated or humorous a prominence on a person's skull, formerly thought to indicate a particular mental faculty. ■ such a faculty: making the most of his bump of direction.
3 [mass noun] a loosely woven fleeced cotton fabric used in upholstery and as lining material.
▶ verb 1 [no obj.] knock or run into someone or something, typically with a jolt: I almost bumped into him | [with obj.] she bumped the girl with her hip.
■ (**bump into**) meet by chance: we might just bump into each other. ■ [with obj.] hurt or damage (something) by striking or knocking it against something else: she bumped her head on the sink. ■ [with obj.] cause to collide with something: she went through the door, bumping the bag against it. ■ [with obj.] Rowing (in a race) gain a bump against.
2 [no obj., with adverbial of direction] move or travel with much jolting and jarring: the car bumped along the rutted track.
■ [with obj. and adverbial of direction] push (something) jerkily in a specified direction: she had to bump the pushchair down the steps.
3 [with obj.] refuse (a passenger) a reserved place on an airline flight, typically because of deliberate overbooking by the airline.
■ N. Amer. cause to move from a job or position, especially in favour of someone else; displace: she was bumped for a youthful model.

– PHRASES **be bumping along the bottom** reach the lowest point in performance or ranking without improving or deteriorating further: the economy was still bumping along the bottom. **with a bump** suddenly and shockingly (especially of an unpleasant or disillusioning surprise): the scandal brought them down to earth with a bump.
– ORIGIN mid 16th cent. (as a verb): imitative, perhaps of Scandinavian origin.
▶ **bump someone off** informal murder someone.
bump something up informal make something larger: the hotel may well bump up the bill.

bumper ▶ noun 1 a horizontal bar fixed across the front or back of a motor vehicle to reduce damage in a collision or as a trim.
2 Cricket, dated another term for **BOUNCER** (in sense 2).
3 Horse Racing (also **bumper race**) a flat race for inexperienced horses which are intended for future racing in hurdles or steeplechases. [ORIGIN: said to be from an earlier racing term bumper 'amateur rider'.]
4 archaic a generous glassful of an alcoholic drink, typically one drunk as a toast.
5 Austral./NZ, informal a cigarette butt. [ORIGIN: late 19th cent.: of unknown origin.]
▶ adjective exceptionally large, fine, or successful: a bumper crop.
– PHRASES **bumper-to-bumper** very close together, as cars in a traffic jam. ■ (of an insurance policy) comprehensive; all-inclusive.

bumper car ▶ noun another term for **DODGEM**.

bumper sticker ▶ noun a label carrying a slogan or advertisement fixed to a vehicle's bumper.

bumph ▶ noun variant spelling of **BUMF**.

bumpkin ▶ noun an unsophisticated or socially awkward person from the countryside: she thought Tom a bit of a country bumpkin.
– DERIVATIVES **bumpkinish** adjective.
– ORIGIN late 16th cent.: perhaps from Dutch boomken 'little tree' or Middle Dutch bommekijn 'little barrel', used to denote a dumpy person.

bump run ▶ noun a ski run with many small mounds of snow on it, caused by skiers turning in the same places.

bump-start ▶ noun & verb another term for **PUSH-START**.

bumptious ▶ adjective self-assertive or proud to an irritating degree: these bumptious young boys today.
– DERIVATIVES **bumptiously** adverb, **bumptiousness** noun.
– ORIGIN early 19th cent.: humorously from **BUMP**, on the pattern of fractious.

bumpy ▶ adjective (**bumpier**, **bumpiest**) (of a surface) uneven, with many patches raised above the rest: the bumpy road.
■ (of a journey or other movement) involving sudden jolts and jerks, typically caused by an uneven surface: she took us all on a bumpy ride. ■ figurative fluctuating and unreliable; subject to unexpected difficulties: bumpy market conditions.
– DERIVATIVES **bumpily** adverb, **bumpiness** noun.

bum rap ▶ noun [in sing.] informal, chiefly N. Amer. a false charge, typically one leading to imprisonment: he's been handed a bum rap for handling stolen goods.
■ figurative an unfair punishment or scolding.

bum-rush ▶ verb [with obj.] US informal suddenly force or barge one's way into: fans bum-rushed record stores.

bum steer ▶ noun N. Amer. informal a piece of false information or guidance.
– ORIGIN 1920s: from **BUM**² + **STEER**¹ in the sense 'advice, guidance'.

bum-sucking ▶ noun [mass noun] Brit. vulgar slang obsequious, servile behaviour.
– DERIVATIVES **bum-sucker** noun.

bun ▶ noun 1 a small cake, typically containing dried fruit.
■ a bread roll. ■ (in Scotland and Jamaica) a rich fruit cake or currant bread.
2 a hairstyle in which the hair is drawn back into a tight coil at the back of the head.
3 (**buns**) N. Amer. informal a person's buttocks.
– PHRASES **have a bun in the oven** informal be pregnant.
– ORIGIN late Middle English: of unknown origin.

Bunbury a seaport and resort to the south of Perth in Western Australia; pop. 24,000 (1991).

bunch ▶ noun a number of things, typically of the

same kind, growing or fastened together: *a bunch of grapes.*
■ informal a group of people. ■ informal, chiefly N. Amer. a large number or quantity; a lot: *we had been watching a bunch of horrible TV.* ■ (**bunches**) a hairstyle in which the hair is tied back into two clumps at the back or on either side of the head.
▶ **verb** [with obj.] collect or fasten into a compact group: *she bunched the needles together.*
■ gather (cloth) into close folds. ■ [no obj.] (of cloth) gather into close folds: *his trousers bunched round his ankles.* ■ [no obj.] form into a tight group or crowd: *he halted, forcing the rest of the field to **bunch up** behind him.* ■ [no obj.] (of muscles) flex or bulge.
– PHRASES **the best** (or **the pick**) **of the bunch** the best in a particular group. **bunch of fives** Brit. informal a fist. ■ a punch.
– DERIVATIVES **bunchy** adjective.
– ORIGIN late Middle English: of unknown origin.

bunchberry ▶ **noun** (pl. **-ies**) a low-growing plant of the dogwood family, which produces white flowers followed by red berries and bright red autumn foliage. It is native to North America, east Asia, and Greenland.
• *Cornus canadensis*, family Cornaceae.

bunchflower ▶ **noun** a North American plant of the lily family, with yellowish-green flowers.
• *Melanthium virginicum*, family Liliaceae.

bunch grass ▶ **noun** [mass noun] N. Amer. a grass that grows in clumps.
• *Schizachyrium* and other genera, family Gramineae: several species, especially *S. scoparium*, used for grazing and in erosion control, especially on the Great Plains.

bunco N. Amer. informal ▶ **noun** (pl. **-os**) [often as modifier] a swindle or confidence trick: *a bunco artist* | [mass noun] *he was out to make a buck using fraud or bunco.*
▶ **verb** (**-oes**, **-oed**) [with obj.] dated swindle or cheat.
– ORIGIN late 19th cent.: perhaps from Spanish *banca*, the name of a card game.

buncombe ▶ **noun** variant spelling of **BUNKUM**.

bund ▶ **noun** (in India and Pakistan) an embankment or causeway.
– ORIGIN early 19th cent.: via Urdu from Persian.

Bundesbank /ˈbʊndəsˌbaŋk/ the central bank of Germany, established in 1875. Its headquarters are in Frankfurt.
– ORIGIN German, from *Bund* 'federation' + *Bank* 'bank'.

Bundesrat /ˈbʊndəzˌrɑːt/ the Upper House of Parliament in Germany or in Austria.
– ORIGIN German, from *Bund* 'federation' + *Rat* 'council'.

Bundestag /ˈbʊndəzˌtɑːg/ the Lower House of Parliament in Germany.
– ORIGIN German, from *Bund* 'federation' + *tagen* 'confer'.

bundle ▶ **noun** a collection of things, or a quantity of material, tied or wrapped up together: ***a thick bundle of** envelopes* | figurative ***a bundle of** facts.*
■ [in sing.] informal a person displaying a specified characteristic to a very high degree: *he was an enthusiastic bundle of energy.* ■ figurative a person, especially a child, huddled or wrapped up. ■ a set of nerve, muscle, or other fibres running in parallel close together. ■ Computing a set of software or hardware sold together. ■ (**a bundle**) informal a large amount of money: *the new printer **cost a bundle**.*
▶ **verb 1** [with obj.] tie or roll up (a number of things) together as though into a parcel: *she quickly **bundled up** her clothes.*
■ [with obj. and adverbial] wrap or pack (something): *the figure was bundled in furs.* ■ (usu. **be bundled up**) dress (someone) in many clothes to keep warm: *they were bundled up in thick sweaters* | [no obj.] *I bundled up in my parka.* ■ Computing sell (items of hardware and software) as a package.
2 [with obj. and adverbial of direction] (often **be bundled**) informal push or carry forcibly: *he was bundled into a van.*
■ send (someone) away hurriedly or unceremoniously: *the old man was **bundled off** into exile.* ■ [no obj., with adverbial of direction] (of a group of people) move in a disorganized way: *they bundled out into the corridor.*
3 [no obj.] sleep fully clothed with another person, as a former local custom during courtship.
– PHRASES **a bundle of fun** (or **laughs**) [often with negative] informal something extremely amusing or pleasant: *the last year hasn't been a bundle of fun.* **a bundle of nerves** see *a bag of nerves* at **BAG**. **drop one's bundle** Austral./NZ informal give up trying to succeed or achieve something; go to pieces. [ORIGIN: from obsolete *bundle* 'swag'.] **go a bundle on** [usu. with negative] Brit. informal be very keen on: *they don't really go a bundle on employing married women.*
– DERIVATIVES **bundler** noun.
– ORIGIN Middle English: perhaps originally from Old English *byndelle* 'a binding', reinforced by Low German and Dutch *bundel* (to which *byndelle* is related).

bundu /ˈbʊnduː/ ▶ **noun** [mass noun] S. African the wilds; a distant or wilderness region.
– ORIGIN probably from Shona *bundo* 'grasslands'.

bundu-bashing ▶ **noun** [mass noun] S. African the activity of making one's way through rough and difficult terrain, especially as a sport.
– DERIVATIVES **bundu-basher** noun.

bunfight ▶ **noun** Brit. informal, humorous a tea party or other function, typically of a grand or official kind.
■ a heated argument or exchange.

bun foot ▶ **noun** (pl. **bun feet**) a foot in the shape of a flattened sphere, used for chairs, tables, or other furniture in the late 17th century.

bung[1] ▶ **noun** a stopper for closing a hole in a container.
▶ **verb** [with obj.] close with a stopper: *the casks are bunged before delivery.*
■ (**bung something up**) block (something), typically by overfilling it: *you let vegetable peelings bung the sink up.*
– ORIGIN late Middle English: from Middle Dutch *bonghe* (noun).

bung[2] Austral./NZ informal ▶ **adjective** dead, ruined, or useless.
– PHRASES **go bung 1** die. **2** fail or go bankrupt.
– ORIGIN mid 19th cent. (originally Australian pidgin): from Yagara (an extinct Aboriginal language).

bung[3] ▶ **noun** Brit. informal a bribe.
– ORIGIN 1950s: of unknown origin.

bung[4] ▶ **verb** [with obj. and adverbial of direction] Brit. informal put (something) somewhere carelessly or casually: *I've bunged down a few ideas.*
■ throw, typically with violence: *they were bunging bricks through a shop window.*
– ORIGIN early 19th cent.: symbolic.

bungalow /ˈbʌŋgələʊ/ ▶ **noun** a low house having only one storey or, in some cases, upper rooms set in the roof, typically with dormer windows.
– ORIGIN late 17th cent.: from Hindi *baṅglā* 'belonging to Bengal'.

bungarotoxin /ˌbʌŋgərə(ʊ)ˈtɒksɪn/ ▶ **noun** [mass noun] Biochemistry a compound found in the venom of the krait (snake) which is a powerful neurotoxin.
– ORIGIN 1960s: from the modern Latin genus name *Bungarus* (perhaps from Sanskrit *bhaṅgura* 'bent') + **TOXIN**.

bungee /ˈbʌndʒi/ ▶ **noun** (also **bungee cord** or **bungee rope**) a long nylon-cased rubber band used for securing luggage and in the sport of bungee-jumping.
▶ **verb** [no obj.] perform a bungee jump.
– ORIGIN 1930s (denoting an elasticated cord for launching a glider): of unknown origin.

bungee-jumping ▶ **noun** [mass noun] the sport of leaping from a bridge, crane, or other high place while secured by a long nylon-cased rubber band around the ankles.
– DERIVATIVES **bungee jump** noun, **bungee-jumper** noun.

bunghole ▶ **noun** an aperture through which a cask can be filled or emptied.

bungle ▶ **verb** [with obj.] carry out (a task) clumsily or incompetently, leading to failure or an unsatisfactory outcome: *she had bungled every attempt to help* | [as adj. **bungled**] *a bungled bank raid.*
■ [no obj.] [usu. as adj. **bungling**] make or be prone to making many mistakes: *the work of a bungling amateur.*
▶ **noun** a mistake or failure, typically one resulting from mismanagement or confusion.
– DERIVATIVES **bungler** noun.
– ORIGIN mid 16th cent.: of unknown origin; compare with **BUMBLE**.

Bunin /ˈbuːnɪn/, Ivan (Alekseevich) (1870–1953), Russian poet and prose writer. An opponent of modernism, he concentrated on the themes of peasant life and love.

bunion /ˈbʌnj(ə)n/ ▶ **noun** a painful swelling on the first joint of the big toe.
– ORIGIN early 18th cent.: ultimately from Old French *buignon*, from *buigne* 'bump on the head'.

bunk[1] ▶ **noun** a narrow shelf-like bed, typically one of two or more arranged one on top of the other.
▶ **verb** [no obj.] chiefly N. Amer. sleep in a narrow berth or improvised bed, typically in shared quarters: *they bunk together in the dormitory.*
– ORIGIN mid 18th cent.: of unknown origin; perhaps related to **BUNKER**.

bunk[2] Brit. informal ▶ **verb** [no obj.] abscond or play truant from school or work: *he **bunked off** school.*
■ [with obj.] illicitly avoid paying (a fee or debtor): *he nearly got caught bunking his fare.*
▶ **noun** a hurried and furtive departure; an escape: *there was no sign of him—he'd **done a bunk**.*
– ORIGIN mid 19th cent.: of unknown origin.

bunk[3] ▶ **noun** [mass noun] informal nonsense: *anyone with a brain cell would never believe such bunk.*
– ORIGIN early 20th cent.: abbreviation of **BUNKUM**.

bunk bed ▶ **noun** a piece of furniture consisting of two beds, one above the other, that form a unit.

bunker ▶ **noun 1** a large container or compartment for storing fuel: *a coal bunker.*
2 a reinforced underground shelter, typically for use in wartime.
3 a hollow filled with sand, used as an obstacle on a golf course.
▶ **verb** [with obj.] **1** fill the fuel containers of (a ship); refuel.
2 (**be bunkered**) Golf (of a player) have one's ball lodged in a bunker: *he was bunkered at the fifth hole.*
■ [with obj.] hit (the ball) into a bunker: *he bunkered his second shot.* ■ (**be bunkered**) (of a golf course) have bunkers. ■ (usu. **be bunkered**) Brit. informal bring into difficulties; prevent the progress of: *the act was bunkered by all the showbiz flannel.*
– ORIGIN mid 16th cent. (originally Scots, denoting a seat or bench): perhaps related to **BUNK**[1].

Bunker Hill the first pitched battle (1775) of the War of American Independence (actually fought on Breed's Hill near Boston, Massachusetts). Although the British won, the good performance of the untrained Americans gave considerable impetus to the Revolution.

bunkhouse ▶ **noun** a building offering basic sleeping accommodation for workers.

bunkum (also **buncombe**) ▶ **noun** [mass noun] informal, dated nonsense: *they talk a lot of bunkum about their products.*
– ORIGIN mid 19th cent. (originally *buncombe*): named after *Buncombe* County in North Carolina, mentioned in an inconsequential speech made by its congressman solely to please his constituents (*c.*1820).

bunk-up ▶ **noun** informal a helping push or pull up.

bunny ▶ **noun** (pl. **-ies**) informal **1** a child's term for a rabbit.
■ (also **bunny girl**) a club hostess, waitress, or photographic model, wearing a skimpy costume with ears and a tail suggestive of a rabbit. ■ [with adj.] informal a person of a specified type or in a specified mood: *the dumb bunny wanted to marry me.*
2 Austral. a victim or dupe.
– ORIGIN early 17th cent. (originally used as a term of endearment to a person, later as a pet name for a rabbit): from dialect *bun* 'squirrel, rabbit', also used as a term of endearment, of unknown origin. Sense 2 dates from the early 20th cent.

bunny chow ▶ **noun** (in South Africa) a takeaway food consisting of a hollowed-out half loaf of bread filled with vegetable or meat curry.
– ORIGIN probably from Hindi *banyā*, from Gujerati *vaniya*, denoting one of a Hindu caste of merchants, + **CHOW** in the sense 'food'.

bunny-hop ▶ **verb** [no obj.] jump forward in a crouched position: *he bunny-hopped around the stage.*
■ [with obj.] move (a vehicle) forward jerkily. ■ move a bicycle forward by jumping in the air while standing on the pedals. ■ [with obj.] jump (an obstacle) on a bicycle in this way.
▶ **noun** a jump in a crouched position.
■ a short jump forwards on a bicycle. ■ an obstacle on a cycling course which is generally cleared by jumping the bicycle over it.

bunny hugger ▶ **noun** informal, derogatory an animal lover; a conservationist.

Bunsen /ˈbʌns(ə)n, German ˈbʊnzn/, Robert Wilhelm Eberhard (1811–99), German chemist. With Gustav Kirchhoff he pioneered spectroscopy, detecting new elements (caesium and rubidium) and determining the composition of many substances and of the sun and stars. He designed numerous items of chemical apparatus, notably the Bunsen burner (1855).

Bunsen burner (also **Bunsen**) ▶**noun** a small adjustable gas burner used in laboratories as a source of heat.

bunt[1] /bʌnt/ ▶**noun** the baggy centre of a fishing net or a sail.
– ORIGIN late 16th cent.: of unknown origin.

bunt[2] /bʌnt/ (also **wheat bunt**) ▶**noun** [mass noun] a disease of wheat caused by a smut fungus, the spores of which give off a smell of rotten fish. Also called **STINKING SMUT**.
• The fungus is *Tilletia caries*, class Teliomycetes.
– ORIGIN early 17th cent. (denoting the puffball fungus): of unknown origin.

bunt[3] /bʌnt/ ▶**verb** [with obj.] **1** Baseball (of a batter) gently tap (a pitched ball) without swinging so that it does not roll beyond the infield: *he can bunt the ball and get on base* | [no obj.] *Phil bunted and got to first.*
■(of a batter) help (a base-runner) to progress to a further base by tapping a ball in such a way: *he bunted him to third.*
2 (of a person or animal) butt with the head or horns: *he bunted her with his head.*
▶**noun 1** Baseball an act or result of tapping a pitched ball in such a way.
2 an act of flying an aircraft in part of an outside loop.
– ORIGIN mid 18th cent.: probably related to the noun **BUTT**[1] (the original sense). The usage in aeronautics dates from the 1930s.

buntal /ˈbʌnt(ə)l/ ▶**noun** [mass noun] [often as modifier] the straw from a talipot palm used for making hats: *a buntal hat.*
– ORIGIN early 20th cent.: from Tagalog.

Bunter /ˈbʌntə/, Billy, a schoolboy character, noted for his fatness and gluttony, in stories by Frank Richards (pseudonym of Charles Hamilton 1876–1961).

Bunting, Basil (1900–85), English poet and journalist. He was influenced by modernists including Ezra Pound and T. S. Eliot. He published his early work abroad, not really gaining recognition until *Briggflatts* (1966).

bunting[1] ▶**noun 1** an Old World seed-eating songbird related to the finches, typically having brown streaked plumage and a boldly marked head.
• Family Emberizidae, subfamily Emberizinae (the **bunting family** and **subfamily**): several genera, in particular *Emberiza*, and numerous species.
2 a small New World songbird of the cardinal subfamily, the male of which is mainly or partly bright blue in colour.
• Family Emberizidae, subfamily Cardinalinae: genera *Passerina* and *Cyanocompsa*, and several species.
– ORIGIN Middle English: of unknown origin.

bunting[2] ▶**noun** [mass noun] flags and other colourful festive decorations.
■a loosely woven fabric used for such decoration.
– ORIGIN early 18th cent.: of unknown origin.

buntline /ˈbʌntlʌɪn/ ▶**noun** a line for restraining the loose centre of a sail while it is furled.

Buñuel /buːˈnwɛl, Spanish buˈɲwel/, Luis (1900–83), Spanish film director. Influenced by surrealism, he wrote and directed his first film, *Un Chien andalou* (1928), jointly with Salvador Dali. Other notable films: *Belle de jour* (1967) and *The Discreet Charm of the Bourgeoisie* (1972).

bunya /ˈbʌnjə/ (also **bunya pine** or **bunya bunya** /ˈbʌnjəˌbʌnjə/) ▶**noun** a tall coniferous Australian tree related to the monkey puzzle, bearing large cones containing edible seeds.
• *Araucaria bidwillii*, family Araucariaceae.
– ORIGIN mid 19th cent.: from Wiradhuri.

Bunyan /ˈbʌnjən/, John (1628–88), English writer. A Nonconformist, he was imprisoned twice for unlicensed preaching and during this time wrote his spiritual autobiography *Grace Abounding* (1666), and began his major work *The Pilgrim's Progress* (1678–84).

bunyip /ˈbʌnjɪp/ ▶**noun** Austral. **1** a mythical amphibious monster said to inhabit inland waterways.
2 [often as modifier] an impostor or pretender: *Australia's bunyip aristocracy.*
– ORIGIN from an Aboriginal word.

Buonaparte /bwonaˈparte/ Italian spelling of **BONAPARTE**.

Buonarroti /ˌbwɒnəˈrɒti/, Michelangelo, see **MICHELANGELO**.

buoy /bɔɪ/ ▶**noun** an anchored float serving as a navigation mark, to show reefs or other hazards, or for mooring.
▶**verb** [with obj.] **1** keep (someone or something) afloat: *I let the water* ***buoy up*** *my weight.*
■(often **be buoyed**) cause to become or remain cheerful and confident: *the party was buoyed by an election victory.* ■ (often **be buoyed**) cause (a price) to rise to or remain at a high level: *the price is* ***buoyed up*** *by investors.*
2 mark with an anchored float: [as adj. **buoyed**] *a buoyed channel.*
– ORIGIN Middle English: probably from Middle Dutch *boye, boeie*, from a Germanic base meaning 'signal'. The verb is from Spanish *boyar* 'to float', from *boya* 'buoy'.

buoyage ▶**noun** [mass noun] the provision of buoys.

buoyancy ▶**noun** [mass noun] the ability or tendency of something to float in water or other fluid.
■the power of a liquid to keep something afloat. ■ figurative an optimistic and cheerful disposition. ■ figurative a high level of activity in an economy or stock market: *there is renewed buoyancy in the demand for steel.*

buoyancy aid ▶**noun** a sleeveless jacket lined with buoyant material, worn for water sports.

buoyant ▶**adjective** able or tending to keep afloat or rise to the top of a liquid or gas.
■(of a liquid or gas) able to keep something afloat. ■ figurative (of an economy, business, or market) involving or engaged in much activity: *car sales were buoyant.* ■ figurative cheerful and optimistic: *the conference ended with the party in a buoyant mood.*
– DERIVATIVES **buoyantly** adverb.
– ORIGIN late 16th cent.: from French *bouyant* or Spanish *boyante*, present participle of *boyar* 'to float' (see **BUOY**).

BUPA /ˈbuːpə/ ▶**abbreviation for** (in the UK) British United Provident Association, a private health insurance organization.

buppie ▶**noun** (pl. **-ies**) informal a young urban black professional; a black yuppie.

BUR ▶**abbreviation for** Burma (international vehicle registration).

bur ▶**noun** see **BURR** (senses 2, 3, 5, and 6).

burb ▶**noun** (usu. **the burbs**) informal, chiefly N. Amer. short for **SUBURB**: *the leafy burbs of Connecticut.*

Burbage /ˈbəːbɪdʒ/, Richard (*c.*1567–1619), English actor. He was the creator of most of Shakespeare's great tragic roles: Hamlet, Othello, Lear, and Richard III, and was also associated with the building of the Globe Theatre.

Burbank /ˈbəːbaŋk/ a city in southern California, on the north side of the Los Angeles conurbation; pop. 93,640 (1990). It is a centre of the film and television industries.

Burberry /ˈbəːb(ə)ri/ ▶**noun** (pl. **-ies**) trademark a kind of lightweight belted raincoat, typically beige in colour, with a distinctive tartan lining.
– ORIGIN early 20th cent.: from *Burberrys Ltd*, the name of the manufacturer.

burble ▶**verb** [no obj.] make a continuous murmuring noise: *the wind burbled at his ear.*
■speak in an unintelligible or silly way, especially at unnecessary length: *he* ***burbled on*** *about annuities* | [with obj.] *he was burbling inanities.* ■ [often as noun] Aeronautics (**burbling**) (of an airflow) break up into turbulence.
▶**noun** [mass noun] continuous murmuring noise.
■rambling speech: *an hour of boring burble.*
– DERIVATIVES **burbler** noun.
– ORIGIN Middle English (in the sense 'to bubble'): imitative. Current senses date from the late 19th cent.

burbot /ˈbəːbət/ ▶**noun** an elongated bottom-dwelling fish that is the only freshwater member of the cod family, occurring in Eurasia and North America but almost extinct in Britain.
• *Lota lota*, family Gadidae.
– ORIGIN Middle English: from Old French *borbete*, probably from *borbe* 'mud, slime'.

burden ▶**noun 1** a load, typically a heavy one.
■figurative a duty or misfortune that causes hardship, anxiety, or grief; a nuisance: *the burden of mental illness.* ■the main responsibility for achieving a specified aim or task: *the burden of establishing that the cost was unreasonable.* ■a ship's carrying capacity; tonnage: *the schooner Wyoming, of about 6,000 tons burden.*
2 (**the burden**) the main theme or gist of a speech, book, or argument: *the burden of his views.*
▶**verb** [with obj.] (usu. **be burdened**) load heavily.
■figurative cause (someone) worry, hardship, or distress: *they were not yet burdened with adult responsibility.*
– PHRASES **burden of proof** the obligation to prove one's assertion.
– DERIVATIVES **burdensome** adjective.
– ORIGIN Old English *byrthen*, of West Germanic origin; related to **BEAR**[1].

burdock /ˈbəːdɒk/ ▶**noun** a large herbaceous Old World plant of the daisy family. The hook-bearing flowers become woody burrs after fertilization and cling to animals' coats to aid seed dispersal.
• Genus *Arctium*, family Compositae: several species, including the large-leaved **great burdock** (*A. lappa*), which has edible roots and is used in herbal medicine.
– ORIGIN late 16th cent.: from **BUR** + **DOCK**[3].

bureau /ˈbjʊərəʊ/ ▶**noun** (pl. **bureaux** or **bureaus**) **1** Brit. a writing desk with drawers and typically an angled top opening downwards to form a writing surface.
■N. Amer. a chest of drawers.
2 an office or department for transacting particular business: *a news bureau.*
■the office in a particular place of an organization based elsewhere: *the London bureau of the Washington Post.* ■a government department: *the intelligence bureau.*
– ORIGIN late 17th cent.: from French, originally 'baize' (used to cover writing desks), from Old French *burel*, probably from *bure* 'dark brown', based on Greek *purros* 'red'.

bureaucracy /ˌbjʊ(ə)ˈrɒkrəsi/ ▶**noun** (pl. **-ies**) [mass noun] a system of government in which most of the important decisions are taken by state officials rather than by elected representatives.
■[count noun] a state or organization governed or managed according to such a system. ■ [count noun] the officials in such a system, considered as a group or hierarchy. ■excessively complicated administrative procedure, seen as characteristic of such a system: *the unnecessary bureaucracy in local government.*
– ORIGIN early 19th cent.: from French *bureaucratie*, from *bureau* (see **BUREAU**).

bureaucrat ▶**noun** an official in a government department, in particular one perceived as being concerned with procedural correctness at the expense of people's needs.
– DERIVATIVES **bureaucratic** adjective, **bureaucratically** adverb.
– ORIGIN mid 19th cent.: from French *bureaucrate*, from *bureaucratie* (see **BUREAUCRACY**).

bureaucratize (also **-ise**) ▶**verb** [with obj.] [usu. as adj. **bureaucratized**] govern (someone or something) by an excessively complicated administrative procedure: *impersonal and bureaucratized welfare systems.*
– DERIVATIVES **bureaucratization** noun.

bureau de change /ˌbjʊərəʊ də ˈʃɒʒ, French byʀo də ʃɑ̃ʒ/ ▶**noun** (pl. **bureaux de change** pronunc. same) an establishment at which customers can exchange foreign money.
– ORIGIN 1950s: French, literally 'office of exchange'.

Bureau of State Security (abbrev. **BOSS**) the former South African intelligence and security organization under apartheid.

burette /bjʊˈrɛt/ (US also **buret**) ▶**noun** a graduated glass tube with a tap at one end, for delivering known volumes of a liquid, especially in titrations.
– ORIGIN mid 19th cent.: from French, from *buire* 'jug', of Germanic origin; related to German *Bauch* 'stomach'.

burfi /ˈbəːfiː/ (also **barfi**) ▶**noun** [mass noun] an Indian sweet made from milk solids and sugar, cut into squares or diamonds, and typically flavoured with cardamom or nuts.
– ORIGIN Hindi, from Persian *barfī*, literally, 'icy, snowy', also denoting a kind of sweetmeat decorated with silver leaf.

burg /bəːg/ ▶**noun** an ancient or medieval fortress or walled town. [ORIGIN: from late Latin *burgus* (see **BURGESS**).]
■N. Amer. informal a town or city. [ORIGIN: mid 19th cent.: from German *Burg* 'castle, city'; related to **BOROUGH**.]

b

burgage /ˈbəːgɪdʒ/ ▶ **noun** [mass noun] historical (in England and Scotland) tenure of land in a town held in return for service or annual rent.
■ [count noun] a house or other property held by such tenure.
– ORIGIN late Middle English: from medieval Latin *burgagium*, from *burgus* 'fortified town', of Germanic origin.

Burgas /bʊəˈgas/ an industrial port and resort in Bulgaria, on the Black Sea; pop. 226,120 (1990).

burgee /bəːˈdʒiː/ ▶ **noun** a flag bearing the colours or emblem of a sailing club, typically triangular.
– ORIGIN mid 18th cent.: perhaps from French *bourgeois* (see **BURGESS**) in the sense 'owner, master'.

Burgenland /ˈbʊəgən,land, German ˈbʊrgn̩,lant/ a state of eastern Austria; capital, Eisenstadt.

burgeon /ˈbəːdʒ(ə)n/ ▶ **verb** [no obj.] [often as adj. **burgeoning**] begin to grow or increase rapidly; flourish: *manufacturers are keen to cash in on the burgeoning demand.*
– ORIGIN Middle English: from Old French *bourgeonner* 'put out buds', from *borjon* 'bud', based on late Latin *burra* 'wool'.

burger ▶ **noun** a flat round cake of minced beef that is fried or grilled and generally eaten in a bread roll.
■ [with modifier] a particular variation of such a cake with additional or substitute ingredients: *a nut burger.*
– ORIGIN 1930s (originally US): abbreviation of **HAMBURGER**.

burger bun ▶ **noun** a flattish soft white bread roll topped with sesame seeds, designed to be filled with a hamburger.

Burgess[1], Anthony (1917–93), English novelist and critic; pseudonym of *John Anthony Burgess Wilson*. One of his best-known novels is *A Clockwork Orange* (1962), a disturbing, futuristic vision of juvenile delinquency, violence, and high technology. Other notable works: *The Malayan Trilogy* (1956–9) and *Earthly Powers* (1980).

Burgess[2], Guy (Francis de Moncy) (1911–63), British Foreign Office official and spy. Acting as a Soviet agent from the 1930s, he worked for MI5 while ostensibly employed by the BBC. After the war he worked at the British Embassy in Washington, under Kim Philby; charged with espionage in 1951, he fled to the USSR with Donald Maclean.

burgess ▶ **noun** a person with municipal authority or privileges, in particular:
■ Brit. archaic an inhabitant of a town or borough with full rights of citizenship. ■ Brit. historical a Member of Parliament for a borough, corporate town, or university. ■ (in the US and also historically in the UK) a magistrate or member of the governing body of a town. ■ US historical a member of the assembly of colonial Maryland or Virginia.
– ORIGIN Middle English: from Anglo-Norman French *burgeis*, from late Latin *burgus* 'castle, fort' (in medieval Latin 'fortified town'); related to **BOROUGH**.

Burgess Shale a stratum of sedimentary rock exposed in the Rocky Mountains in British Columbia, Canada. The bed, dated to the Cambrian period (about 540 million years ago), is rich in well-preserved fossils of early marine invertebrates, many of which represent evolutionary lineages unknown in later times.
– ORIGIN named after the *Burgess* Pass, British Columbia, where the shale outcrops.

burgh /ˈbʌrə/ ▶ **noun** archaic or Scottish a borough or chartered town.
– DERIVATIVES **burghal** /ˈbəːg(ə)l/ adjective.
– ORIGIN late Middle English: Scots form of **BOROUGH**.

burgher /ˈbəːgə/ ▶ **noun 1** archaic or humorous a citizen of a town or city, typically a member of the wealthy bourgeoisie.
■ historical (in southern Africa) a civilian member of a local militia unit. ■ historical (in southern Africa) an Afrikaans citizen of a Boer Republic.
2 (**Burgher**) a descendant of a Dutch or Portuguese colonist in Sri Lanka.
– ORIGIN Middle English: from **BURGH**, reinforced by Dutch *burger*, from *burg* 'castle' (see **BOROUGH**).

Burghley /ˈbəːli/, William Cecil, 1st Baron (1520–98), English statesman. Secretary of State to Queen Elizabeth I 1558–72 and Lord High Treasurer 1572–98, he was the queen's most trusted councillor and minister.

burghul /bəːˈguːl/ ▶ **noun** another term for **BULGAR**.
– ORIGIN Persian.

burglar ▶ **noun** a person who commits burglary.
– DERIVATIVES **burglarious** /-ˈglɛːrɪəs/ adjective (archaic).
– ORIGIN mid 16th cent.: from legal French *burgler* or Anglo-Latin *burgulator*, *burglator*; related to Old French *burgier* 'pillage'.

burglarize (also **-ise**) ▶ **verb** North American term for **BURGLE**.

burglary ▶ **noun** (pl. **-ies**) entry into a building illegally with intent to commit a crime such as theft: [mass noun] *a two-year sentence for burglary* | [count noun] *a series of burglaries.*

In English law before 1968, burglary was a crime under statute and in common law; since 1968 it has been a statutory crime only. See also **HOUSEBREAKING**.

– ORIGIN early 16th cent.: from legal French *burglarie*, from *burgler* (see **BURGLAR**).

burgle ▶ **verb** [with obj.] (often **be burgled**) enter (a building) illegally with intent to commit a crime, especially theft: *our house in London has been burgled.*
– ORIGIN late 19th cent.: originally a humorous and colloquial back-formation from **BURGLAR**.

burgomaster /ˈbəːgə(ʊ)mɑːstə/ ▶ **noun** the mayor of a Dutch, Flemish, German, Austrian, or Swiss town.
– ORIGIN late 16th cent.: from Dutch *burgemeester*, from *burg* 'castle, citadel' (see **BOROUGH**) + *meester* 'master'. The change in the final element was due to association with **MASTER[1]**.

burgonet /ˈbəːgənɛt/ ▶ **noun** historical a kind of visored helmet.
■ a light steel cap worn by pikemen.
– ORIGIN late 16th cent.: from French *bourguignotte*, perhaps a use of the feminine of *bourgignot* 'Burgundian', the ending being assimilated to **-ET[1]**.

burgoo /bəːˈguː/ ▶ **noun** [mass noun] N. Amer. a stew or thick soup, typically one made for an outdoor meal.
■ [count noun] an outdoor meal at which a stew or thick soup is served. ■ chiefly Nautical a thick porridge.
– ORIGIN from Arabic *burġul* (see **BURGHUL**).

Burgos /ˈbʊəgɒs, Spanish ˈburɣos/ a town in northern Spain; pop. 169,280 (1991). It was the capital of Castile during the 11th century, and the official seat of Franco's Nationalist government (1936–9).

Burgoyne /bəːˈgɔɪn/, John (1722–92), English general and dramatist; known as **Gentleman Johnny**. He surrendered to the Americans at Saratoga (1777) in the War of American Independence.

burgrave /ˈbəːgreɪv/ ▶ **noun** historical the governor or hereditary ruler of a German town or castle.
– ORIGIN mid 16th cent.: from German *Burggraf*, from *Burg* 'castle' (see **BOROUGH**) + *Graf* 'count, noble'.

Burgundian /bəːˈgʌndɪən/ ▶ **noun** a native or inhabitant of Burgundy.
■ historical a member of a Germanic people that invaded Gaul from the east and established the kingdom of Burgundy in the 5th century AD.
▶ **adjective** of or relating to Burgundy or the Burgundians.

Burgundy /ˈbəːgəndi/ a region and former duchy of east central France, centred on Dijon. The region is noted for its wine. French name **BOURGOGNE**.

burgundy (also **Burgundy**) ▶ **noun** (pl. **-ies**) [mass noun] a wine from Burgundy (usually taken to be red unless otherwise specified): *a glass of Burgundy* | [count noun] *elegant red burgundies.*
■ a deep red colour like that of burgundy wine: *warm shades of brown and burgundy* | [as modifier] *burgundy leather.*

burial ▶ **noun** [mass noun] the action or practice of interring a dead body: *his remains were shipped home for burial.*
■ [count noun] a ceremony at which someone's body is interred; a funeral: [as modifier] *burial rites.* ■ [count noun] Archaeology a grave or the remains found in it.
– ORIGIN Old English *byrgels* 'place of burial, grave' (interpreted as plural in Middle English, hence the loss of the final *-s*), of Germanic origin; related to **BURY**.

burial ground ▶ **noun** an area of ground set aside for the burying of human bodies.

burin /ˈbjʊərɪn/ ▶ **noun** a hand-held steel tool used for engraving in metal or wood; a graver.
■ Archaeology a flint tool with a chisel point.
– ORIGIN mid 17th cent.: from French; perhaps related to Old High German *bora* 'boring tool'.

burk ▶ **noun** variant spelling of **BERK**.

burka /ˈbʊəkə/ (also **burkha**) ▶ **noun** a long, loose garment covering the whole body, worn in public by women in many Muslim countries.
– ORIGIN from Urdu and Persian *burḳa'*, from Arabic *burḳu'*.

Burke[1], Edmund (1729–97), British man of letters and Whig politician. Burke wrote on the issues of political emancipation and moderation, notably with respect to Roman Catholics and the American colonies.

Burke[2], John (1787–1848), Irish genealogical and heraldic writer. He compiled *Burke's Peerage* (1826), the guide to peers and baronets.

Burke[3], Robert O'Hara (1820–61), Irish explorer. He led a successful expedition from south to north across Australia in the company of William Wills and two others—the first white men to make this journey. On the return journey, however, Burke, Wills, and a third companion died of starvation.

Burke[4], William (1792–1829), Irish murderer. He was a bodysnatcher operating in Edinburgh with his accomplice **William Hare**.

burke ▶ **noun** variant spelling of **BERK**.

burkha /ˈbʊəkə/ ▶ **noun** variant spelling of **BURKA**.

Burkina /bəːˈkiːnə/ a landlocked country in western Africa, in the Sahel; pop. 9,271,000 (est. 1991); official language, French; capital, Ouagadougou. A French protectorate from 1898, it became an autonomous republic within the French Community in 1958 and a fully independent republic in 1960. Official name **BURKINA FASO** /ˈfasəʊ/; former name (until 1984) **UPPER VOLTA**.
– DERIVATIVES **Burkinan** adjective & noun.

Burkitt's lymphoma /ˈbəːkɪts/ ▶ **noun** [mass noun] Medicine cancer of the lymphatic system, caused by the Epstein–Barr virus, chiefly affecting children in central Africa.
– ORIGIN 1960s: named after Denis P. *Burkitt* (1911–93), the British surgeon who described it.

burl[1] /bəːl/ ▶ **noun** a slub or lump in wool or cloth.
■ N. Amer. a rounded knotty growth on a tree, giving an attractive figure when polished and used especially for handcrafted objects and veneers: *she used warty burls to construct her pieces* | [mass noun] *wooden coin banks made of elm burl* | [as modifier] *a burl bowl.*
– ORIGIN late Middle English: from Old French *bourle* 'tuft of wool', diminutive of *bourre* 'coarse wool', from late Latin *burra* 'wool'.

burl[2] /bəːl/ ▶ **noun** Austral./NZ an attempt: *we'll give it a burl.*
– ORIGIN early 20th cent.: regional usage of **BIRL**.

burlap /ˈbəːlap/ ▶ **noun** [mass noun] coarse canvas woven from jute, hemp, or a similar fibre, used especially for sacking.
■ lighter material of a similar kind used in dressmaking and furnishing: [as modifier] *a burlap shirt* | [count noun] *fabrics ranging from hessians to burlaps.*
– ORIGIN late 17th cent.: of unknown origin.

burlesque /bəːˈlɛsk/ ▶ **noun 1** a parody or comically exaggerated imitation of something, especially in a literary or dramatic work: *the funniest burlesque of music hall* | [as modifier] *burlesque Spenserian stanzas.*
■ [mass noun] humour that depends on comic imitation and exaggeration; absurdity: *the argument descends into burlesque.*
2 N. Amer. a variety show, typically including striptease: [as modifier] *burlesque clubs.*
▶ **verb** (**burlesques**, **burlesqued**, **burlesquing**) [with obj.] cause to appear absurd by parodying or copying in an exaggerated form: *a mock-heroic farce that burlesques the affectations of Restoration heroic drama.*
– DERIVATIVES **burlesquer** noun.
– ORIGIN mid 17th cent.: from French, from Italian *burlesco*, from *burla* 'mockery', of unknown origin.

burley /ˈbəːli/ ▶ **noun** (also **burley tobacco**) [mass noun] a tobacco of a light-coloured variety which is grown mainly in Kentucky, US.
– ORIGIN late 19th cent.: of unknown origin.

Burlington a city in southern Canada, on Lake Ontario south-west of Toronto; pop. 129,600 (1991).

burly ▶ **adjective** (**burlier**, **burliest**) (of a person) large and strong; heavily built.

– DERIVATIVES **burliness** noun.

– ORIGIN Middle English (in the sense 'dignified, imposing'): probably from an unrecorded Old English word meaning 'stately, fit for the bower' (see BOWER¹, -LY¹).

Burma /ˈbəːmə/ a country in SE Asia, on the Bay of Bengal; pop. 42,528,000 (est. 1991); official language, Burmese; capital, Rangoon. Official name (since 1989) UNION OF MYANMAR.

Annexed by the British during the 19th century, Burma was occupied by the Japanese from 1942 to 1945 and became an independent republic in 1948. In 1962 an army coup led by Ne Win overthrew the government and established an authoritarian state. The National League for Democracy (NLD) won the election held in May 1990, even though its leader Aung San Suu Kyi was under house arrest; however, the military regime did not relinquish power.

Burman ▶ noun (pl. **Burmans**) & adjective another term for BURMESE (chiefly in or with reference to sense 1 of the noun).

bur-marigold ▶ noun a plant of the daisy family with inconspicuous yellow flowers and small barbed fruit which cling to passing animals. Several kinds are widespread weeds. Also called **BEGGARTICKS**.
● Genus *Bidens*, family Compositae: several species, in particular *B. frondosa*.

Burma Road a route linking Lashio in Burma to Kunming in China, covering 1,154 km (717 miles). Completed in 1939, it was built by the Chinese in response to the Japanese occupation of the Chinese coast, to serve as a supply route to the interior.

Burmese ▶ noun (pl. same) **1** a member of the largest ethnic group of Burma (now Myanmar) in SE Asia.
2 a native or national of Burma (Myanmar).
3 [mass noun] the official language of Burma (Myanmar), which is the first language of about 22 million people (75 per cent of the population). It is a tonal Sino-Tibetan language written in an alphabet derived from that of ancient Pali.
4 (also **Burmese cat**) a cat of a short-coated breed originating in Asia.
▶ adjective of or relating to Burma, its people, or their language.

burn¹ ▶ verb (past and past participle **burned** or chiefly Brit. **burnt**) **1** [no obj.] (of a fire) flame or glow while consuming a material such as coal or wood: *a fire burned and crackled cheerfully in the grate.*
■(of a candle or other source of light) be alight: *a light was burning in the hall.* ■ be or cause to be destroyed by fire: [no obj.] *he watched his restaurant burn to the ground* | [with obj.] *he burned all the letters.* ■ [with obj.] damage or injure by heat or fire: *I burned myself on the stove.*
2 [no obj.] (of a person, the skin, or a part of the body) become red and painful through exposure to the sun: *my skin tans easily but sometimes burns.*
■feel or cause to feel sore, hot, or inflamed, typically as a result of illness or injury. ■ (of a person's face) feel hot and flushed from an intense emotion such as shame or indignation: *her face burned with the humiliation.* ■ (**be burning with**) be entirely possessed by (a desire or an emotion): *Martha was burning with curiosity.*
3 [with obj.] use (a type of fuel) as a source of heat or energy: *a diesel engine converted to burn natural gas.*
■[with obj.] (of the body of a person or animal) convert (calories) to energy.
4 [no obj., with adverbial of direction] informal drive very fast: *a despatch rider burning up the highways.*
▶ noun **1** an injury caused by exposure to heat or flame: *he was treated in hospital for burns to his hands.*
■a mark left on something as a result of being burned: *the cord carpet was covered in cigarette burns.* ■ [mass noun] a feeling of heat and discomfort on the skin caused by friction, typically from a rope or razor: *a smooth shave without razor burn.* ■ a sensation of heat experienced on swallowing hot liquid or strong liquor: *Kate felt the burn as the liquid hit her throat.* ■ Brit. informal a cigarette.
2 consumption of a type of fuel as an energy source: *natural gas produces the cleanest burn of the lot.*
■a firing of a rocket engine in flight.
3 N. Amer. & Austral./NZ an act of clearing of vegetation by burning.
■an area of land cleared in this way.
– PHRASES **be burned at the stake** historical be executed by being tied to a stake and being publicly burned alive, typically for alleged heresy or witchcraft. **burn one's boats** (or **bridges**) do something which makes it impossible to return to

an earlier state. **burn the candle at both ends** go to bed late and get up early. **burn the midnight oil** read or work late into the night. **burn** (N. Amer. also **lay**) **rubber** informal drive very quickly. **go for the burn** informal push one's body to the extremes when doing physical exercise. **a slow burn** informal a state of slowly mounting anger or annoyance: *the medical community's shrugging acceptance is fuelling a slow burn among women.* **with money burning a hole in one's pocket** having a strong urge to spend money as soon as one receives it.
– ORIGIN Old English *birnan* 'be on fire' and *bærnan* 'consume by fire', both from the same Germanic base; related to German *brennen*.
▶**burn something down** (or **burn down**) (of a building or structure) destroy or be destroyed completely by fire.
burn something in/into brand or imprint by burning: *designs are burnt into the skin* | figurative *a childhood incident that was burnt into her memory.* ■ Photography expose one area of a print more than the rest: *the sky and bottom of the picture needed substantial burning in.*
burn something off remove a substance using heat: *using a blowlamp to burn off the paint.*
burn out be completely consumed and thus no longer alight: *the candle in the saucer had burned out.* ■ cease to function as a result of excessive heat or friction: *the clutch had burned out.*
burn oneself out ruin one's health or become completely exhausted through overwork.
burn someone out make someone homeless by destroying their home by fire: *Catholics and Protestants were burned out of their homes.*
burn something out completely destroy a building or vehicle by fire, so that only a shell remains.
burn up 1 (of a fire) produce brighter and stronger flames. **2** (of an object entering the earth's atmosphere) be destroyed by heat.
burn someone up N. Amer. informal make someone very angry.

burn² ▶ noun Scottish & N. English a small stream.
– ORIGIN Old English *burna*, *burn(e)*, of Germanic origin; related to Dutch *bron* and German *Brunnen* 'well'.

burned ▶ adjective variant spelling of BURNT.

Burne-Jones, Sir Edward (Coley) (1833–98), English painter and designer. His work, which included tapestry and stained-glass window designs, is typical of the later Pre-Raphaelite style. Notable paintings: *The Golden Stairs* (1880) and *The Mirror of Venus* (1867–77).

burner ▶ noun a thing that burns, in particular:
■a part of a cooker, lamp, etc. that emits and shapes a flame. ■ an apparatus in which a fuel is used or an aromatic substance is heated. ■ [with modifier] an activity that uses something of a specified kind as energy: *uphill walking is a great calorie burner.* ■ [with adj.] a person or thing that evolves or develops at a specified speed: *the play is a slow burner.* ■ US informal, figurative a team player who can move very fast.
– PHRASES **on the back** (or **front**) **burner** informal having low (or high) priority: *he wants the matter to be put on the back burner.*

burnet /ˈbəːnɪt/ ▶ noun **1** a herbaceous plant of the rose family, with globular pinkish flower heads and leaves composed of many small leaflets.
● Genus *Sanguisorba*, family Rosaceae: several species, including the edible **salad burnet** (*S. minor*), and the spiny shrub-like **thorny burnet** (*S. spinosum*) of the eastern Mediterranean.
2 a day-flying moth that typically has greenish-black wings with crimson markings.
● *Zygaena* and other genera, family Zygaenidae.
– ORIGIN Middle English (denoting a kind of dark brown woollen cloth): from Old French *brunete*, *burnete* (denoting brown cloth or a plant with brown flowers), diminutives of *brun* 'brown'.

burnet rose ▶ noun a small wild Eurasian rose with white flowers and leaves like those of salad burnet.
● *Rosa pimpinellifolia*, family Rosaceae.

burnet saxifrage ▶ noun a slender white-flowered European plant of the parsley family.
● *Pimpinella saxifraga*, family Umbelliferae.

Burnett /bəːˈnɛt/, Frances (Eliza) Hodgson (1849–1924), British-born American novelist. She is remembered chiefly for her novels for children, including *Little Lord Fauntleroy* (1886), *A Little Princess* (1905), and *The Secret Garden* (1911).

Burney, Fanny (1752–1840), English novelist; born *Frances Burney*. Notable works: *Evelina* (1778), *Cecilia* (1782), and *Letters and Diaries* (1846).

burn-in ▶ noun [mass noun] damage to a computer or television screen, caused by being left on for an excessive period.
■[count noun] a reliability test in which a device is left switched on for a long time.

burning ▶ adjective [attrib.] on fire: *a burning building.*
■very hot or bright: *burning desert sands.* ■ figurative very keenly or deeply felt; intense: *he had a burning ambition to climb to the upper reaches of management.* ■ figurative of urgent interest and importance; exciting or calling for debate: *democracy remains a burning issue* | *the burning question of independence.*
– DERIVATIVES **burningly** adverb.

burning bush ▶ noun **1** any of a number of shrubs noted for their bright red autumn foliage, in particular:
● the kochia. ● the smoke tree.
2 any of a number of shrubs or trees with bright red leaves or fruits.
● Several plants, in particular North American spindles of the genus *Euonymus* (family Celastraceae), e.g. the wahoo (*E. atropurpurea*).
3 another term for GAS PLANT.
– ORIGIN mid 19th cent.: with biblical allusion to Exod. 3:2.

burning-ghat ▶ noun see GHAT (sense 1).

burning glass ▶ noun a lens for concentrating the sun's rays on an object so as to set fire to it.

burnish ▶ verb [with obj.] [usu. as adj. **burnished**] polish (something, especially metal) by rubbing: *highly burnished armour.*
■figurative enhance or perfect (something such as a reputation or a skill).
▶ noun [in sing.] the shine on a highly polished surface.
– DERIVATIVES **burnisher** noun.
– ORIGIN Middle English: from Old French *burniss-*, lengthened stem of *burnir*, variant of *brunir* 'make brown', from *brun* 'brown'.

burnished brass ▶ noun a European moth that has green to gold wing patches with a metallic lustre.
● Genus *Diachrisia*, family Noctuidae: several species, in particular *D. chrysitis*.

burnous /bəːˈnuːs/ (US also **burnoose**) ▶ noun a long loose hooded cloak worn by Arabs.
– ORIGIN late 16th cent.: French, from Arabic *burnus*, from Greek *birros* 'cloak'.

burnout ▶ noun [mass noun] **1** the reduction of a fuel or substance to nothing through use or combustion: *good carbon burnout* | [as modifier] *a burnout furnace.*
2 physical or mental collapse caused by overwork or stress: *high levels of professionalism which may result in burnout* | [count noun] *you'll suffer a burnout.*
■[count noun] US informal a dropout or drug abuser, especially a teenage one.
3 failure of an electrical device or component through overheating: [with modifier] *an anti-stall mechanism prevents motor burnout.*

Burns¹, George (1896–1996), American comedian; born *Nathan Birnbaum*. He won an Oscar for the film *The Sunshine Boys* (1975).

Burns², Robert (1759–96), Scottish poet, best known for poems such as 'The Jolly Beggars' (1786) and 'Tam o' Shanter' (1791), and for old Scottish songs which he collected, including 'Auld Lang Syne'. Burns Night celebrations are held in Scotland and elsewhere on his birthday, 25 January.

burnside ▶ noun (usu. **burnsides**) a moustache in combination with whiskers on the cheeks but no beard on the chin.
– ORIGIN late 19th cent.: named after General Ambrose *Burnside* (1824–81), American army officer.

burnt (also **burned**) past and past participle of BURN¹. ▶ adjective [attrib.] having been burned: *burnt wood* | *burnt shoulders and peeling noses.*
■(of a taste) like that of food that has been charred in cooking. ■ (of sugar) cooked or heated until caramelized. ■ (of a warm colour) dark or deep.

burnt ochre ▶ noun [mass noun] an opaque, deep yellow-brown pigment made by calcining ochre.
■the colour of this pigment.

burnt offering ▶ noun **1** an offering burnt on an altar as a religious sacrifice.
2 humorous overcooked or charred food.

burnt-out (also **burned-out**) ▶ adjective (of a

vehicle or building) destroyed or badly damaged by fire; gutted.
■(of an electrical device or component) having failed through overheating. ■(of a person) in a state of physical or mental collapse caused by overwork or stress: *burnt-out old hacks.* ■US informal (of a teenager or other person) having dropped out, typically through drug abuse: *a burnt-out high school case.*

burnt sienna ▶**noun** [mass noun] a deep reddish-brown pigment made by calcining raw sienna.
■the colour of this pigment.

burnt umber ▶**noun** [mass noun] a deep brown pigment made by calcining raw umber.
■the colour of this pigment.

bur oak ▶**noun** a North American oak, with large fringed acorn cups and timber that was formerly important in shipbuilding.
• *Quercus macrocarpa*, family Fagaceae.

buroo /bəˈruː/ ▶**noun** variant form for **BROO**.

burp informal ▶**verb** [no obj.] noisily release air from the stomach through the mouth; belch.
■[with obj.] make (a baby) belch after feeding, typically by patting its back.
▶**noun** a noise made by air released from the stomach through the mouth; a belch.
– ORIGIN 1930s (originally US): imitative.

burpee /ˈbəːpiː/ ▶**noun** a physical exercise consisting of a squat thrust made from and ending in a standing position.
– ORIGIN 1930s: named after Royal H. *Burpee* (born 1897), American psychologist. The original usage was *Burpee test*, in which a series of burpees are executed in rapid succession, designed to measure agility and coordination.

burp gun ▶**noun** US informal a lightweight sub-machine gun.

Burr, Aaron (1756–1836), American Democratic Republican statesman. In 1804, while Vice-President, he killed his rival Alexander Hamilton in a duel. He then plotted to form an independent administration in Mexico and was tried for treason but acquitted.

burr ▶**noun 1** [in sing.] a whirring sound, such as a telephone ringing tone or the sound of cogs turning.
■a rough pronunciation of the letter *r*, especially with a uvular trill as in a Northumberland accent. ■(loosely) a regional accent: *a soft Scottish burr.*
2 (also **bur**) a rough edge or ridge left on an object (especially of metal) by the action of a tool or machine.
■the irregular edge in a dog's ear.
3 (also **bur**) a small rotary cutting tool with a shaped end, used chiefly in woodworking and dentistry.
■a small surgical drill for making holes in bone, especially in the skull.
4 [mass noun] a siliceous rock used for millstones.
■[count noun] a whetstone.
5 (also **bur**) a prickly seed case or flower head that clings to clothing and animal fur.
■[usu. as modifier] a plant that produces burrs, for example bur-reed.
6 (also **bur**) [as modifier] denoting wood containing knots or other growths which show a pattern of dense swirls in the grain when sawn, used for veneers and other decorative woodwork: *burr walnut.*
7 the coronet of a deer's antler.
▶**verb 1** [no obj.] make a whirring sound such as a telephone dialling tone or the sound of cogs turning.
■speak with a regional accent, especially one in which the letter *r* is prominent: [with direct speech] *'I like to have a purrrpose,' she burrs.* [ORIGIN: probably imitative.]
2 [with obj.] form a rough edge on (metal).
– PHRASES **a burr under someone's saddle** N. Amer. informal a persistent source of irritation: *he had been a burr under the saddle of the government in his time.*
– ORIGIN Middle English (in sense 5): probably of Scandinavian origin and related to Danish *burre* 'bur, burdock', Swedish *kard-borre* 'burdock'.

Burra /ˈbʌrə/, Edward (1905–76), English painter, noted for his low-life subjects, as in *Harlem* (1934), and the bizarre and fantastic, as in *Dancing Skeletons* (1934).

burra /ˈbʌrə/ ▶**adjective** [attrib.] Indian big; important; *the burra sahibs.*
– ORIGIN from Hindi *baṛā* 'great, greatest'.

Burra Din /ˌbʌrə ˈdɪn/ ▶**noun** Indian Christmas.
– ORIGIN from Hindi *baṛā* 'great' and *din* 'day'.

burrawang /ˈbʌrəwaŋ/ (also **burrawong**) ▶**noun** an Australian cycad with palm-like leaves and a sunken underground trunk.
• *Macrozamia spiralis*, family Zamiaceae.
■the poisonous nut of this tree, which becomes edible after prolonged soaking.
– ORIGIN early 19th cent.: from Dharuk.

bur-reed ▶**noun** an aquatic reed-like plant with rounded flower heads. Its oily seeds are an important source of winter food for wildfowl.
• Genus *Sparganium*, family Sparganiaceae.

burrfish ▶**noun** (pl. same or **-fishes**) a porcupine fish with spines that are permanently erected, occurring in tropical waters of the Atlantic and Pacific.
• Genus *Chilomycterus*, family Diodontidae: several species, including the common *C. schoepfi* of the western Atlantic.

burrito /bʊˈriːtəʊ/ ▶**noun** (pl. **-os**) a Mexican dish consisting of a tortilla rolled round a savoury filling, typically of minced beef or beans.
– ORIGIN Latin American Spanish, diminutive of Spanish *burro*, literally 'donkey' (see **BURRO**).

burro /ˈbʊrəʊ/ ▶**noun** (pl. **-os**) chiefly US a small donkey used as a pack animal.
– ORIGIN early 19th cent.: from Spanish.

Burroughs[1] /ˈbʌrəʊz/, Edgar Rice (1875–1950), American novelist and writer of science fiction. Notable works: *Tarzan of the Apes* (1914).

Burroughs[2] /ˈbʌrəʊz/, William (Seward) (1914–97), American novelist. In the 1940s he became addicted to heroin, and his best-known writing, for example *Junkie* (1953) and *The Naked Lunch* (1959), deals with life as a drug addict in a unique, surreal style.

burrow ▶**noun** a hole or tunnel dug by a small animal, especially a rabbit, as a dwelling.
▶**verb** [no obj.] (of an animal) make a hole or tunnel, typically for use as a dwelling: *moles burrowing away underground* | [as adj. **burrowing**] *burrowing earthworms* | [with obj.] *the fish can burrow a hiding place.*
■[with adverbial of direction] advance into or through something solid by digging or making a hole: *worms that burrow through dead wood.* ■[with adverbial of direction] move underneath or press close to something in order to hide oneself or in search of comfort: *the child* ***burrowed*** *deeper* ***into*** *the bed.* ■[with obj.] move (something) in this way: *she* ***burrowed*** *her face* ***into*** *the pillow.* ■figurative make a thorough inquiry; investigate: *journalists are* ***burrowing into*** *the prime minister's business affairs.*
– DERIVATIVES **burrower** noun.
– ORIGIN Middle English: variant of **BOROUGH**.

Bursa /ˈbəːsə/ a city in NW Turkey, capital of a province of the same name; pop. 834,580 (1990). It was the capital of the Ottoman Empire from 1326 to 1402.

bursa /ˈbəːsə/ ▶**noun** (pl. **bursae** /-siː/ or **bursas**) Anatomy a fluid-filled sac or sac-like cavity, especially one countering friction at a joint.
– DERIVATIVES **bursal** adjective.
– ORIGIN early 19th cent.: from medieval Latin, 'bag, purse', from Greek *bursa* 'leather'.

bursa of Fabricius ▶**noun** Zoology a glandular sac opening into the cloaca of a bird, producing B-cells.
– ORIGIN mid 19th cent. (in the Latin form *bursa Fabricii*): from **BURSA** and a Latinized form of the name of Girolama *Fabrici* (1533–1619), Italian anatomist.

bursar ▶**noun** chiefly Brit. **1** a person who manages the financial affairs of a college or school.
2 Scottish a student who holds a bursary.
– ORIGIN late Middle English: from French *boursier* or (in sense 1) medieval Latin *bursarius*, from *bursa* 'bag, purse' (see **BURSA**).

bursary /ˈbəːsəri/ ▶**noun** (pl. **-ies**) chiefly Brit. **1** a grant, especially one awarded to someone to enable them to study at university or college.
2 the room of a bursar in a college or school.
– DERIVATIVES **bursarial** /-ˈsɛːrɪəl/ adjective, **bursarship** noun.
– ORIGIN late 17th cent. (in sense 2): from medieval Latin *bursaria*, from *bursa* 'bag, purse' (see **BURSA**).

burse /bəːs/ ▶**noun 1** a flat, square, fabric-covered case in which a folded corporal cloth is carried to and from an altar in church.
2 (**the Burse**) historical the Royal Exchange in Cornhill, London. Compare with **BOURSE**.

bursitis /bəːˈsʌɪtɪs/ ▶**noun** [mass noun] Medicine inflammation of a bursa, typically one in a shoulder joint.

burst ▶**verb** (past and past participle **burst**) [no obj.] (of a container) break suddenly and violently apart, spilling the contents, especially as a result of an impact or internal pressure: *we started to inflate our balloons and eventually one burst.*
■[with obj.] cause to break, especially by puncturing: *he burst the balloon in my face.* ■[with obj.] (of contents) break open (a container) from the inside by growing too large to be held: *the swollen river was expected to burst its banks.* ■[with obj.] suffer from the sudden breaking of (a bodily organ or vessel): *he burst a blood vessel during a fit of coughing.* ■be so full as almost to break open: *the wardrobe was* ***bursting with*** *piles of clothes.* ■feel a very strong or irrepressible emotion or impulse: *he was* ***bursting with*** *joy and excitement* | [with infinitive] *she was bursting to say something.* ■suddenly begin doing something as an expression of a strong feeling: *if anyone said anything to upset me I'd* ***burst out crying*** | *she* ***burst into*** *a fresh flood of* ***tears*** ■issue suddenly and uncontrollably, as though from a splitting container: *the words* ***burst from*** *him in an angry rush* | *an aircraft crashed and* ***burst into flames.*** ■be opened suddenly and forcibly: *a door burst open and a girl raced out.* ■[with adverbial of direction] make one's way suddenly and violently: *he burst into the room without knocking.* ■[with obj.] separate (continuous stationery) into single sheets.
▶**noun** an instance of breaking or splitting as a result of internal pressure or puncturing; an explosion.
■a sudden issuing forth: *her breath was coming in short bursts.* ■a sudden brief outbreak, typically of something violent or noisy: *a sudden burst of activity* | *he heard a burst of gunfire.* ■a period of continuous and intense effort: *he sailed 474 miles in one 24-hour burst.*
– PHRASES **burst someone's bubble** shatter someone's illusions about something or destroy their sense of well-being.
– ORIGIN Old English *berstan*, of Germanic origin; related to Dutch *bersten, barsten.*

burster ▶**noun** a thing which bursts, in particular:
■Astronomy a cosmic source of powerful short-lived bursts of X-rays or other radiation. ■a violent gale. ■a machine which separates continuous stationery into single sheets.

bursty ▶**adjective** informal or technical occurring at intervals in short sudden episodes.
■relating to or denoting the transmission of data in short separate bursts of signals.

Burt, Cyril (Lodowic) (1883–1971), English psychologist. Using studies of identical twins, he claimed that intelligence is inherited, but he was later accused of fabricating data.

burthen ▶**noun** archaic form of **BURDEN**.
– DERIVATIVES **burthensome** adjective.

Burton[1], Richard (1925–84), Welsh actor; born *Richard Jenkins.* He often co-starred with Elizabeth Taylor (to whom he was twice married). Notable films: *The Spy Who Came in from the Cold* (1966) and *Who's Afraid of Virginia Woolf?* (1966).

Burton[2], Sir Richard (Francis) (1821–90), English explorer, anthropologist, and translator. He and John Hanning Speke were the first Europeans to see Lake Tanganyika (1858). Notable translations: the *Arabian Nights* (1885–8), the *Kama Sutra* (1883), and *The Perfumed Garden* (1886).

burton[1] ▶**noun** (in phrase **go for a burton**) Brit. informal meet with disaster; be ruined, destroyed, or killed.
– ORIGIN Second World War (originally RAF slang): perhaps referring to *Burton* ale, from Burton-upon-Trent.

burton[2] (also **burton-tackle**) ▶**noun** historical a light two-block tackle for hoisting.
– ORIGIN early 18th cent.: alteration of Middle English *Breton tackle*, a nautical term in the same sense (see **BRETON**[1]).

Burton-upon-Trent a town in west central England, in Staffordshire; pop. 59,600 (1981). The town is noted for its breweries.

Burundi /bʊˈrʊndi/ a central African country on the east side of Lake Tanganyika, to the south of Rwanda; pop. 5,800,000 (est. 1991); official languages, French and Kirundi (a Bantu language); capital, Bujumbura.

Inhabited mainly by Hutu and Tutsi peoples, the area formed part of German East Africa from the 1890s until the First World War, after which it was administered by Belgium. The country became an independent monarchy in 1962 and a republic in 1966. Multiparty elections in 1993 resulted in the country being led for the first time by a member of the Hutu majority rather than the traditionally dominant Tutsis; this led within months to large-scale ethnic violence.

– DERIVATIVES **Burundian** adjective & noun.

bury ▶verb (-ies, -ied) [with obj.] put or hide underground: *he buried the box in the back garden* | [as adj. **buried**] *buried treasure.*
■(usu. **be buried**) place (a dead body) in the earth, in a tomb, or in the sea, usually with funeral rites: *he was buried in St John's churchyard.* ■ figurative lose (someone, especially a relative) through death: *she buried her sixty-year-old husband.* ■ cause to disappear or become unnoticeable: *the countryside has been buried under layers of concrete* | figurative *the warehouse was buried in the faceless sprawl of south London.* ■ move or put out of sight: *she buried her face in her hands* | *with his hands buried in the pockets of his overcoat.* ■ figurative deliberately forget; conceal from oneself: *they had buried their feelings of embarrassment and fear.* ■ informal (of a football player) put (the ball) in the goal: *he ran through to bury a right-foot shot inside the near post.* ■ overwhelm (an opponent) beyond hope of recovery: *he boasted that socialism would bury capitalism.* ■ (**bury oneself**) involve oneself deeply in something to the exclusion of other concerns: *he buried himself in work.*
– PHRASES **bury the hatchet** end a quarrel or conflict and become friendly. **bury one's head in the sand** ignore unpleasant realities.
– ORIGIN Old English *byrgan*, of West Germanic origin; related to the verb **BORROW** and to **BOROUGH**.

Buryat /ˈbʊəyat/ ▶noun **1** a member of a people living in southern Siberia, Mongolia, and northern China.
2 [mass noun] the language of this people, related to Mongolian and having over 400,000 speakers.
▶adjective of or relating to this people or their language.

Buryatia /ˌbʊəˈjɑːtɪə/ (also **Buryat Republic** /ˌbʊəˈjɑːt/) an autonomous republic in SE Russia, between Lake Baikal and the Mongolian border; pop. 1,049,000 (1990); capital, Ulan-Ude.

burying beetle ▶noun a black beetle, typically with broad orange bands on its wing cases, which buries small animal carcasses to provide a food store for its larvae. Also called **SEXTON BEETLE**.
● *Nicrophorus* and other genera, family Silphidae.

burying ground ▶noun a cemetery.

burying place ▶noun a grave or cemetery.

bus ▶noun (pl. **buses**; US also **busses**) **1** a large motor vehicle carrying passengers by road, typically one serving the public on a fixed route and for a fare: [as modifier] *a bus service.*
■informal, dated a motor car, aircraft, or other vehicle, regarded with familiarity or affection.
2 Computing a distinct set of conductors carrying data and control signals within a computer system, to which pieces of equipment may be connected in parallel.
▶verb (**buses** or **busses**, **bused** or **bussed**, **busing** or **bussing**) **1** [with obj. and adverbial of direction] (often **be bussed**) transport in a communal road vehicle: *staff were bussed in and out of the factory.*
■N. Amer. transport (a child of one race) to a school where another race is predominant, in an attempt to promote racial integration. ■ [no obj., with adverbial of direction] travel by road in a public vehicle: *the priest bussed in from a neighbouring parish.*
2 [with obj.] chiefly N. Amer. remove (dirty plates and dishes) from a table in a restaurant or cafeteria.
■remove dirty plates and dishes from (a table).
– ORIGIN early 19th cent.: shortening of **OMNIBUS**.

busbar /ˈbʌsbɑː/ ▶noun a system of electrical conductors in a generating or receiving station on which power is concentrated for distribution.

busboy /ˈbʌsbɔɪ/ ▶noun chiefly N. Amer. a young man who clears tables in a restaurant or cafe.

Busby, Sir Matt (1909–94), Scottish-born footballer and football manager. As manager of Manchester United 1945–69 he led them to win five League Championships and the European Cup in 1968.

busby /ˈbʌzbi/ ▶noun (pl. **-ies**) a tall fur hat with a coloured cloth flap hanging down on the right-hand side and in some cases a plume on the top, worn by soldiers of certain regiments of hussars and artillerymen.
■popular term for **BEARSKIN** (the cap).
– ORIGIN mid 18th cent. (denoting a large bushy wig): of unknown origin.

Bush[1], George (Herbert Walker) (b.1924), American Republican statesman, 41st President of the US 1989–93. He negotiated further arms reductions with the Soviet Union and organized international action to expel the Iraqis from Kuwait in 1990.

Bush[2], George W(alker) (b.1946), American Republican statesman, 43rd President of the US (since 2001). He is the son of George Bush.

bush[1] ▶noun a shrub or clump of shrubs with stems of moderate length: *a rose bush* | *the plant will develop into a dense bush.*
■a thing resembling such a shrub, especially a clump of thick hair or fur: *a childish face with a bush of bright hair.* ■ vulgar slang a woman's pubic hair. ■ (**the bush**) (especially in Australia and Africa) wild or uncultivated country: *they have to spend a night camping in the bush.* ■ [mass noun] the vegetation growing in such a district: *the lowland country was covered in thick bush.* ■ [as modifier] chiefly S. African uncivilized or primitive: *bush justice.* ■ historical a bunch of ivy as a vintner's sign.
▶verb [no obj.] spread out into a thick clump: *her hair bushed out like a halo.*
– PHRASES **beat about the bush** see **BEAT**. **beat the bushes** see **BEAT**. **go bush** Austral. leave one's usual surroundings; run wild. [ORIGIN: early 20th cent: by association with the phrase *take to the bush*, originally said of escaped convicts.]
– ORIGIN Middle English: from Old French *bos*, *bosc*, variants of *bois* 'wood', reinforced by Old Norse *buski*, of Germanic origin and related to Dutch *bos* and German *Busch*. The sense 'uncultivated country' is probably directly from Dutch *bos*.

bush[2] ▶noun Brit. a metal lining for a round hole, especially one in which an axle revolves.
■a bearing for a revolving shaft. ■a sleeve that protects an electric cable where it passes through a panel.
– ORIGIN late 15th cent.: from Middle Dutch *busse*.

bushbaby ▶noun (pl. **-ies**) a small nocturnal tree-dwelling African primate with very large eyes. Also called **GALAGO**.
● Genus *Galago*, family Lorisidae, suborder Prosimii: several species.

bush basil ▶noun a low-growing compact variety of basil.
● *Ocimum minimum*, family Labiatae.

bushbuck ▶noun a small antelope with a reddish-brown coat with white markings, found in southern Africa.
● *Tragelaphus scriptus*, family Bovidae.
– ORIGIN mid 19th cent.: from **BUSH**[1] + **BUCK**[1], influenced by Dutch *bosbok*.

bushchat ▶noun an Asian songbird related to the stonechat, the males of which generally have black (or grey) and white plumage.
● Genus *Saxicola*, family Turdidae: several species.

bushcraft ▶noun [mass noun] skill at living in the bush.

bush cricket ▶noun an insect related to the grasshoppers, with very long antennae. Many kinds live among shrubby vegetation, active and singing mainly at dusk and in the night. Formerly called **LONG-HORNED GRASSHOPPER**.
● Family Tettigoniidae: many genera.

bush dog ▶noun a small stocky carnivorous mammal of the dog family, with short legs and small ears. It is native to the forests of Central and South America.
● *Speothus venaticus*, family Canidae.

bushed ▶adjective informal **1** tired out; exhausted.
2 Austral./NZ lost in wild uncultivated country.
3 Canadian & Austral./NZ mad or bewildered: *unused to solitude, he went bushed.*

bushel /ˈbʊʃ(ə)l/ (abbrev.: **bu.**) ▶noun **1** Brit. a measure of capacity equal to 8 gallons (equivalent to 36.4 litres), used for corn, fruit, liquids, etc.
2 US a measure of capacity equal to 64 US pints (equivalent to 35.2 litres), used for dry goods.
– PHRASES **hide one's light under a bushel** see **HIDE**[1].
– DERIVATIVES **bushelful** noun (pl. **-fuls**).
– ORIGIN Middle English: from Old French *boissel*, perhaps of Gaulish origin.

bush fallow ▶noun [mass noun] a system of farming in which bushes and trees are cleared from virgin land, which is then allowed to lie fallow for a while before cultivation begins.

bush fire ▶noun a fire in scrub or a forest, especially one that spreads rapidly.

bush-hen ▶noun an Australasian rail with plain brown and grey plumage.
● *Amaurornis olivaceus*, family Rallidae. Alternative name: **rufous-tailed moorhen**.

bushido /ˈbuːʃɪdəʊ, bʊˈʃiːdəʊ/ ▶noun [mass noun] the code of honour and morals developed by the Japanese samurai.
– ORIGIN Japanese, from *bushi* 'samurai' + *dō* 'way'.

bushing ▶noun another term for **BUSH**[2].

bush jacket ▶noun another term for **SAFARI JACKET**.

bush lawyer ▶noun Austral./NZ informal a person claiming legal or other knowledge who is unqualified to do so.

bush league N. Amer. ▶noun a minor league of a professional sport, especially baseball: [as modifier] *their bush league image.*
▶adjective (**bush-league**) informal not of the highest quality or sophistication; second-rate.
– DERIVATIVES **bush-leaguer** noun.

Bushman ▶noun (pl. **-men**) **1** a member of any of several aboriginal peoples of southern Africa, especially of the Kalahari Desert. They are traditionally nomadic hunter-gatherers, though many are now employed by farmers. Also called **SAN**. [ORIGIN: influenced by Dutch *boschjesman*.]
2 older term for **SAN** (the languages of these people).
3 (**bushman**) a person who lives, works, or travels in the Australian bush.

bushmaster ▶noun a pit viper which is the largest venomous snake in the New World, found in Central and South America.
● *Lachesis muta*, family Viperidae.
– ORIGIN early 19th cent.: perhaps from Dutch *bosmeester*, from *bos* 'bush' + *meester* 'master'.

bush medicine ▶noun [mass noun] chiefly W. Indian traditional folk medicine, typically prepared from herbs and other plants.

bush pig (also **African bush pig**) ▶noun a wild pig that is native to the forests and savannahs of Africa and Madagascar. Also called **RED RIVER HOG**.
● *Potamochoerus porcus*, family Suidae.

bushranger ▶noun US a person living far from civilization.
■Austral. historical an outlaw living in the bush.

bush sickness ▶noun [mass noun] a deficiency disease of animals caused by a lack of cobalt in the soil (and hence in the diet).

bush tea ▶noun a tea made from dried leaves and twigs of various shrubs, especially in tropical countries.

bush telegraph ▶noun [in sing.] a rapid informal network by which information or gossip is spread.

bushtit ▶noun a small American songbird of the long-tailed tit family, with mainly pale grey plumage and sometimes a black mask.
● *Psaltriparus minimus*, family Aegithalidae (formerly Paridae); formerly regarded as two species.

bushveld /ˈbʊʃfɛlt, -vɛlt/ ▶noun (**the bushveld**) (in South Africa) an area of largely wild or uncultivated country.
– ORIGIN late 19th cent.: from **BUSH**[1] + **VELD**, influenced by Afrikaans *bosveld*.

bushwa /ˈbʊʃwɑː/ (also **bushwah**) ▶noun [mass noun] N. Amer. informal rubbish, nonsense.
– ORIGIN 1920s: apparently a euphemism for **BULLSHIT**.

bushwalking ▶noun [mass noun] chiefly Austral./NZ hiking or backpacking.
– DERIVATIVES **bushwalker** noun.

bushwhack ▶verb **1** [no obj.] [often as noun **bushwhacking**] N. Amer. live or travel in wild or uncultivated country.
■[with adverbial of direction] N. Amer. cut or push one's way through dense vegetation. ■ Austral./NZ work clearing scrub and felling trees in the country.
2 [with obj.] N. Amer. surprise (someone) by attacking them from a hidden place; ambush.

bushwhacked ▶adjective exhausted or worn out.

bushwhacker ▶noun **1** N. Amer. & Austral./NZ a person who clears woods and bush country.
■a person who lives or travels in bush country.

b

2 US a guerrilla fighter (originally in the American Civil War).

bushy[1] ▶ **adjective** (**bushier**, **bushiest**) **1** growing thickly into or so as to resemble a bush: *a dense, bushy plant | his eyebrows were thick and bushy.*
2 covered with bush or bushes: *bushy desert areas.*
– DERIVATIVES **bushily** adverb, **bushiness** noun.

bushy[2] ▶ **noun** (pl. **-ies**) Austral./NZ informal a person who lives in the bush (as distinct from in a town), typically regarded as uncultured or unsophisticated.

business ▶ **noun** [mass noun] **1** a person's regular occupation, profession, or trade: *she had to do a lot of smiling in her business | are you here* ***on business****?*
▪an activity that someone is engaged in: *what is your business here?* ▪ a person's concern: *this is none of your business | the neighbours make it their business to know all about you.* ▪ work that has to be done or matters that have to be attended to: *government business | let's get down to business.*
2 the practice of making one's living by engaging in commerce: *the world of business | who do you* ***do business with*** *in Manila?* | [as modifier] *the business community* | [with modifier] *the tea business.*
▪trade considered in terms of its volume or profitability: *how's business?* ▪ [count noun] a commercial house or firm: *a catering business.*
3 [in sing.] informal a series of events, typically a scandalous or discreditable one: *they must find out about the blackmailing business.*
▪informal a group of related or previously mentioned things: *use carrots, cauliflower, and broccoli, and serve the whole business hot.*
4 Theatre actions other than dialogue performed by actors.
5 (**the business**) informal a very enjoyable or popular person, activity, or thing: *spring skiing is the business.*
6 a difficult matter: *what a business!*
– PHRASES **business as usual** an ongoing and unchanging state of affairs despite difficulties or disturbances: *apart from being under new management, it's business as usual in the department.* **do the business** Brit. informal do what is required to achieve the desired result: *Rogers has got to do the business, score a hat trick or something.* ▪ vulgar slang have sexual intercourse. **have no business** have no right to do something: *he had no business tampering with social services.* **in business** operating, especially in commerce: *they will have to import from overseas to remain in business.* ▪ informal able to begin operations: *if you'll contact the right people, I should think we're in business.* **in the business of** engaged in or prepared to engage in: *I am not in the business of making accusations.* **like nobody's business** informal to an extraordinarily high degree or standard: *these weeds spread like nobody's business.* **mind one's own business** refrain from meddling in other people's affairs: *he was yelling at her to get out and mind her own business.* **send someone about their business** dated tell someone to go away.
– ORIGIN Old English *bisignis* 'anxiety' (see **BUSY**, **-NESS**); the sense 'state of being busy' was used from Middle English down to the 18th cent., but is now differentiated as *busyness.* The use 'appointed task' dates from late Middle English, and from it all the other current senses have developed.

business card ▶ **noun** a small card printed with one's name, professional occupation, company position, business address, etc.

business cycle ▶ **noun** a cycle or series of cycles of economic expansion and contraction. Also called **TRADE CYCLE**.

business day ▶ **noun** chiefly N. Amer. another term for **WORKING DAY**.

business double ▶ **noun** Bridge a double made with the intention of increasing the penalty points scored by a partnership if they defeat their opponents' contract. Often contrasted with **TAKE-OUT DOUBLE**.

business end ▶ **noun** informal (**the business end**) the functional part of a tool or device: *he found himself facing the business end of six lethal-looking weapons.*
▪the essential or basic part of a process or operation: *the rigs are the business end of the oil industry.*

business hours ▶ **plural noun** another term for **OFFICE HOURS**.

businesslike ▶ **adjective** (of a person) carrying out tasks efficiently without wasting time or being distracted by personal or other concerns; systematic and practical.
▪(of clothing, furniture, etc.) designed or appearing to be practical rather than decorative.

businessman ▶ **noun** (pl. **-men**) a man who works in commerce, especially at executive level.

business park ▶ **noun** an area where company offices and light industrial premises are built.

business person ▶ **noun** a man or woman who works in commerce, especially at executive level.

business process re-engineering (also **business process redesign**) (abbrev.: **BPR**) ▶ **noun** [mass noun] the process of restructuring a company's organization and methods, especially so as to exploit the capabilities of computers.

business studies ▶ **plural noun** [treated as sing.] the study of economics and management, especially as an educational topic.

businesswoman ▶ **noun** (pl. **-women**) a woman who works in commerce, especially at executive level.

busk[1] ▶ **verb** [no obj.] play music or otherwise perform for voluntary donations in the street or in a subway: *the group began by busking on Philadelphia sidewalks* | [as noun **busking**] *busking was a real means of living.*
▪(**busk it**) informal improvise.
– DERIVATIVES **busker** noun.
– ORIGIN mid 17th cent.: from obsolete French *busquer* 'seek', from Italian *buscare* or Spanish *buscar*, of Germanic origin. Originally in nautical use in the sense 'cruise about, tack', the term later meant 'go about selling things', hence 'go about performing' (mid 19th cent.).

busk[2] ▶ **noun** historical a stay or stiffening strip for a corset.
– ORIGIN late 16th cent.: from French *busc*, from Italian *busco* 'splinter' (related to French *bûche* 'log'), of Germanic origin.

buskin ▶ **noun** chiefly historical a calf-high or knee-high boot of cloth or leather.
▪a thick-soled laced boot worn by an ancient Athenian tragic actor to gain height. ▪ (**the buskin**) the style or spirit of tragic drama.
– DERIVATIVES **buskined** adjective.
– ORIGIN early 16th cent. (designating a calf-length boot): probably from Old French *bouzequin*, variant of *brousequin*, from Middle Dutch *broseken*, of unknown ultimate origin.

bus lane ▶ **noun** a division of a road marked off with painted lines for use by buses.

busman ▶ **noun** (pl. **-men**) a driver of a bus.
– PHRASES **a busman's holiday** a holiday or form of recreation that involves doing the same thing that one does at work.

Busoni /buːˈsəʊni/, Ferruccio (Benvenuto) (1866–1924), Italian composer, conductor, and pianist. As a composer he is best known for his piano works and his unfinished opera *Doktor Faust* (1925).

Buss, Frances Mary (1827–94), English educationist. She was in charge of the North London Collegiate School for Ladies (1850–94) and campaigned for higher education for women with her friend Dorothea Beale.

buss archaic or N. Amer. informal ▶ **noun** a kiss.
▶ **verb** [with obj.] kiss.
– ORIGIN late 16th cent.: alteration of late Middle English *bass* (noun and verb), probably from French *baiser*, from Latin *basiare*.

bus shelter ▶ **noun** a roofed structure for people to wait under at a bus stop.

bus station ▶ **noun** a place in a town where buses arrive and depart.

bus stop ▶ **noun** a place where a bus regularly stops, usually marked by a sign.

bust[1] ▶ **noun** **1** a woman's chest as measured around her breasts: *a 36-inch bust.*
▪a woman's breasts, especially considered in terms of their size: *if you have a big bust, you're seen as stupid.*
2 a sculpture of a person's head, shoulders, and chest.
– ORIGIN mid 17th cent. (denoting the upper part or torso of a large sculpture): from French *buste*, from Italian *busto*, from Latin *bustum* 'tomb, sepulchral monument'.

bust[2] informal ▶ **verb** (past and past participle **busted** or **bust**) [with obj.] **1** break, split, or burst (something): *they bust the tunnel wide open* | figurative *the film busts every box office record.*
▪[no obj.] come apart or split open: *laughing* ***fit to bust****.* ▪ cause to collapse; defeat utterly: *he promised to bust the mafia.* ▪ [no obj.] (**bust up**) (of a group or married couple) separate, typically after a quarrel. ▪ (**bust something up**) cause (something) to break up: *men hired to bust up union rallies.* ▪ chiefly N. Amer. strike violently: *they wanted to bust me on the mouth.* ▪ [no obj.] (**bust out**) break out; escape: *she* ***busted out of*** *prison.* ▪ [no obj.] (in blackjack and similar card games) exceed the score of 21, so losing one's stake.
2 chiefly N. Amer. raid or search (premises where illegal activity is suspected): *my flat got busted.*
▪arrest: *two roadies were* ***busted for*** *drugs.* ▪ chiefly US reduce (a soldier) to a lower rank; demote: *he was* ***busted to*** *private.*
▶ **noun** **1** a period of economic difficulty or depression: *the boom was followed by the present bust.*
2 informal a police raid: *a drug bust.*
3 a worthless thing: *as a show it was a bust.*
4 chiefly N. Amer. a punch or other hit: *a bust on the snout.*
▶ **adjective** **1** damaged or broken.
2 bankrupt: *firms will* ***go bust****.*
– ORIGIN mid 18th cent. (originally US, as a noun in the sense 'an act of bursting or splitting'): variant of **BURST**.

bustard /ˈbʌstəd/ ▶ **noun** a large, heavily built, swift-running bird, found in open country in the Old World. The males of most bustards have a spectacular courtship display.
• Family Otididae: several genera and species, including the **great bustard** (*Otis tarda*), which is the heaviest flying land bird.
– ORIGIN late 15th cent.: perhaps an Anglo-Norman French blend of Old French *bistarde* and *oustarde*, both from Latin *avis tarda* 'slow bird': the name is unexplained, as the bustards are fast runners.

bustard quail ▶ **noun** the barred button-quail. See **BUTTON-QUAIL**.

bustee /ˈbʌstiː/ ▶ **noun** Indian a slum area or shanty town.
– ORIGIN from Hindi *bastī* 'dwelling'.

buster ▶ **noun** chiefly informal **1** a person or thing that breaks, destroys, or overpowers something: [in combination] *the drug's reputation as a cold-buster.*
▪a violent gale. ▪ a heavy fall. ▪ N. Amer. short for **BRONCOBUSTER**.
2 a notable or impressive person or thing.
▪a large sturdy young child.
3 informal, chiefly N. Amer. used as a mildly disrespectful form of address to a man or boy: *your parents' decisions affect you, like it or not, buster.*

bustier /ˈbʌstɪeɪ, ˈbʊst-/ ▶ **noun** a close-fitting strapless top worn by women.
– ORIGIN 1970s: from French, from *buste* (see **BUST**[1]).

bustle[1] ▶ **verb** [no obj., with adverbial of direction] move in an energetic or noisy manner: *people clutching clipboards bustled about.*
▪[with obj. and adverbial of direction] make (someone) move hurriedly in a particular direction: *she bustled us into the kitchen.* ▪ [no obj.] (of a place) be full of activity: *the small harbour* ***bustled with*** *boats* | [as adj. **bustling**] *the bustling little town.*
▶ **noun** [mass noun] excited activity and movement: *all the noise and the traffic and the bustle.*
– ORIGIN late Middle English: perhaps a variant of obsolete *buskle*, frequentative of *busk* 'prepare', from Old Norse.

bustle[2] ▶ **noun** historical a pad or frame worn under a skirt and puffing it out behind.
– ORIGIN late 18th cent.: of unknown origin.

bust-up ▶ **noun** informal, chiefly Brit. a bad quarrel, especially one that finishes a relationship: *he has had a bust-up with his manager | the bust-up of my marriage.*
▪a fight or brawl: *a touchline bust-up.*

busty ▶ **adjective** (**bustier**, **bustiest**) informal (of a woman) having large breasts.
– DERIVATIVES **bustiness** noun.

busway ▶ **noun** a road or section of a road set apart exclusively for buses, typically one equipped with tracks or grooves for guiding them.

busy ▶ **adjective** (**busier**, **busiest**) having a great deal to do: *he had been too busy to enjoy himself | there was enough work to keep two people busy.*
▪occupied with or concentrating on a particular activity or object of attention: *the team members are busy raising money | he was* ***busy with*** *preparations.* ▪ (of a place) full of activity. ▪ excessively detailed or

decorated; fussy: *the rugs have crisp, not busy, patterns.* ■ chiefly N. Amer. (of a telephone line) engaged.
▶ **verb** (**-ies**, **-ied**) [with obj.] (**busy oneself**) keep occupied: *she **busied herself with** her new home.*
▶ **noun** (also **bizzy**) (pl. **-ies**) Brit. informal a police officer: *I was picked up by the busies for possession.*
– DERIVATIVES **busily** adverb, **busyness** noun.
– ORIGIN Old English *bisgian* (verb), *bisig* (noun); related to Dutch *bezig*, of unknown origin.

busy bee ▶ **noun** informal an industrious person.

busybody ▶ **noun** (pl. **-ies**) a meddling or prying person.

busy Lizzie ▶ **noun** (pl. **-ies**) Brit. an East African plant with abundant red, pink, or white flowers. It is widely grown as a house plant, and its many hybrids are grown as bedding plants. Called **PATIENT LUCY** in North America.
• *Impatiens walleriana*, family Balsaminaceae.

busy signal ▶ **noun** North American term for **ENGAGED TONE**.

busywork ▶ **noun** [mass noun] chiefly N. Amer. work that keeps a person busy but has little value in itself.

but[1] ▶ **conjunction 1** used to introduce a phrase or clause contrasting with what has already been mentioned:
■ nevertheless; however: *he stumbled but didn't fall | this is one principle, but it is not the only one | the food is cheap but delicious | but I digress.* ■ on the contrary; in contrast: *the problem is not that they are cutting down trees, but that they are doing it in a predatory way.*
2 [with negative or in questions] used to indicate the impossibility of anything other than what is being stated: *one **cannot but** sympathize | there was nothing they could do but swallow their pride | what could he do but forgive her?*
3 used to introduce a response expressing a feeling such as surprise or anger: *but that's an incredible saving! | but why?*
4 used after an expression of apology for what one is about to say: *I'm sorry, but I can't pay you.*
5 [with negative] archaic without it being the case that: *it never rains but it pours.*
▶ **preposition** except; apart from; other than: *we were never anything but poor | used in all but the most remote areas | the last but one.*
■ used with repetition of certain words to give emphasis: *nobody, but nobody, was going to stop her.*
▶ **adverb 1** no more than; only: *he is but a shadow of his former self | choose from a colourful array of mango, starfruit, and raspberries, to name but a few.*
2 Austral./NZ & Scottish informal (used at the end of a sentence) though, however: *he was a nice bloke but.*
▶ **noun** an argument against something; an objection: ***no buts**—just get out of here | as with all these proposals, **ifs and buts** abound.*
– PHRASES **all but** see **ALL**. **anything but** see **ANYTHING**. **but for** except for: *I walked along Broadway, deserted but for the occasional cab.* ■ if it were not for: *the game could be over but for you.* **but that** archaic other than that; except that: *who knows but that the pictures painted on air are eternal.* **but then** on the other hand; that being so: *it's a very hard match, but then they all are.*
– ORIGIN Old English *be-ūtan, būtan, būta* 'outside, without, except' (see **BY**, **OUT**).

USAGE For advice about using **but** and other conjunctions to begin a sentence, see **usage** at **AND**.

but[2] ▶ **noun** Scottish an outer room, especially in a two-roomed cottage.
– PHRASES **but and ben** a two-roomed cottage; a humble home.
– ORIGIN early 18th cent.: from **BUT**[1] in the early sense 'outside', specifically 'into the outer part of a house'.

butadiene /ˌbjuːtəˈdʌɪiːn/ ▶ **noun** [mass noun] Chemistry a colourless gaseous hydrocarbon made by catalytic dehydrogenation of butane. It is used in the manufacture of synthetic rubber.
• Chem. formula: $CH_2{=}CHCH{=}CH_2$.
– ORIGIN early 20th cent.: from **BUTANE** + **DI-**[1] + **-ENE**.

butane /ˈbjuːteɪn/ ▶ **noun** [mass noun] Chemistry a flammable hydrocarbon gas of the alkane series, present in petroleum and natural gas. It is used in bottled form as a fuel. See also **ISOBUTANE**.
• Chem. formula: $CH_3CH_2CH_2CH_3$.
– ORIGIN late 19th cent.: from **BUTYL** + **-ANE**[2].

butanoic acid /ˌbjuːtəˈnəʊɪk/ ▶ **noun** systematic chemical name for **BUTYRIC ACID**.
– DERIVATIVES **butanoate** noun.

butanol /ˈbjuːtənɒl/ ▶ **noun** [mass noun] Chemistry each of two isomeric liquid alcohols used as solvents; butyl alcohol.
• Chem. formula: $CH_3CH_2CH_2CH_2OH$ (**1-butanol**, **butan-1-ol**) and $CH_3CH_2CH(OH)CH_3$ (**2-butanol**, **butan-2-ol**).

butch informal ▶ **adjective** manlike or masculine in appearance or behaviour, often aggressively or ostentatiously so.
▶ **noun** a mannish lesbian, typically as contrasted with a more feminine partner.
– ORIGIN 1940s: perhaps an abbreviation of **BUTCHER**.

butcher ▶ **noun 1** a person whose trade is cutting up and selling meat in a shop.
■ a person who slaughters and cuts up animals for food: [with modifier] *a pork butcher.* ■ a person who kills or has people killed indiscriminately or brutally: *the Nazi death camp butcher.*
2 N. Amer. informal a person selling refreshments, newspapers, and other items on a train or in a theatre.
▶ **verb** [with obj.] (often **be butchered**) slaughter or cut up (an animal) for food.
■ kill (someone) brutally: *they rounded up and butchered 250 people.* ■ figurative ruin (something) deliberately or through incompetence: *the film was butchered by the studio that released it.*
– PHRASES **have** (or **take**) **a butcher's** Brit. informal have a look: *let's take a butcher's at those bugs.* [ORIGIN: *butcher's* from *butcher's hook*, rhyming slang for a 'look'.]
– ORIGIN Middle English: from an Anglo-Norman French variant of Old French *bochier*, from *boc* 'he-goat', probably of the same ultimate origin as **BUCK**[1].

butcher-bird ▶ **noun 1** a shrike (family Laniidae), which impales its prey on thorns.
2 a crow-like predacious Australasian songbird, with a heavy hook-tipped bill. Compare with **MAGPIE** (in sense 2).
• Family Cracticidae: three genera, in particular *Cracticus*, and several species.
– ORIGIN mid 17th cent.: from its habit of impaling its prey on thorns.

butcher block ▶ **noun** [mass noun] N. Amer. a material used to make kitchen worktops and tables, consisting of strips of wood glued together.

butcher's broom ▶ **noun** a low evergreen Eurasian shrub of the lily family, with flat shoots that give the appearance of stiff spine-tipped leaves.
• *Ruscus aculeatus*, family Liliaceae.

butcher's meat (also **butcher meat**) ▶ **noun** [mass noun] Brit. fresh uncured meat excluding game and poultry.

butchery ▶ **noun** (pl. **-ies**) [mass noun] the savage killing of large numbers of people.
■ the work of slaughtering animals and preparing them for sale as meat. ■ [count noun] Brit. a slaughterhouse. ■ [count noun] Brit. a butcher's shop.
– ORIGIN Middle English (denoting a slaughterhouse or meat market): from Old French *boucherie*, from *bouchier* 'butcher'.

Bute /bjuːt/, John Stuart, 3rd Earl of (1713–92), Scottish courtier and Tory statesman, Prime Minister 1762–3.

bute /bjuːt/ ▶ **noun** informal term for **PHENYLBUTAZONE**.

buteo /ˈbjuːtɪəʊ/ ▶ **noun** Ornithology, chiefly US a bird of prey of a group distinguished by broad wings that are used for soaring.
• *Buteo* and related genera, family Accipitridae; many species, including the buzzards and the American red-tailed and Harris' hawks.
– ORIGIN from Latin *buteo* 'buzzard, hawk'.

Buthelezi /ˌbuːtəˈleɪzi/, Chief Mangosuthu (Gatsha) (b.1928), South African politician. He became leader of the Inkatha movement in 1975 and Minister of Home Affairs in 1994.

Butler[1], Reg (1913–81), English sculptor; born *Reginald Cotterell*. Working mainly in forged or cast metal, he won an international competition in 1953 for a monument (never built) to the Unknown Political Prisoner.

Butler[2], Samuel (1612–80), English poet, most notable for his three-part satirical poem *Hudibras* (1663–78).

Butler[3], Samuel (1835–1902), English novelist. Notable works: *Erewhon* (1872), *Erewhon Revisited* (1901), and *The Way of All Flesh* (1903).

butler ▶ **noun** the chief manservant of a house.
– ORIGIN Middle English: from Old French *bouteillier* 'cup-bearer', from *bouteille* 'bottle'.

butt[1] ▶ **verb** [with obj.] (of a person or animal) hit (someone or something) with the head or horns: *she **butted** him **in** the chest with her head.*
■ strike (the head) against something: *he **butts** his head **against** a wall.*
▶ **noun** a push or blow, especially one given with the head: *he would follow up with a butt from his head.*
– ORIGIN Middle English: from Old French *boter*, of Germanic origin.
▶ **butt in** interrupt or join in a conversation or activity, or enter a room, without being invited or expected: *sorry to **butt in on** you.*
butt out N. Amer. informal stop interfering: *anyone who tries to cut across our policies should butt out.*

butt[2] ▶ **noun** the person or thing at which criticism or ridicule is directed: *his singing is the butt of dozens of jokes.*
■ (usu. **butts**) an archery or shooting target or range. ■ a mound on or in front of which a target is set up for archery or shooting. ■ a grouse-shooter's stand, screened by low turf or a stone wall.
– ORIGIN Middle English (in the archery sense): from Old French *but*, of unknown origin; perhaps influenced by French *butte* 'rising ground'.

butt[3] ▶ **noun 1** (also **butt-end**) the thicker end of something, especially a tool or a weapon: *a rifle butt.*
■ the square end of a plank or plate meeting the end or side of another, as in the side of a ship: [as modifier] *a butt joint.* ■ the thicker or hinder end of a hide used for leather.
2 (also **butt-end**) the stub of a cigar or a cigarette: *the ashtray was crammed with cigarette butts.*
3 informal, chiefly N. Amer. the buttocks or anus.
4 the trunk of a tree, especially the part just above the ground.
▶ **verb** [no obj.] adjoin or meet end to end: *the shop **butted up against** the row of houses | a garden that **butted up to** his own.*
■ [with obj.] join (pieces of stone, timber, and other building materials) with the ends or sides flat against each other: *the rail will be **butted up against** the wardrobe.*
– ORIGIN late Middle English: the noun apparently related to Dutch *bot* 'stumpy', also to **BUTTOCK**; the verb partly from **BUTT**[2], reinforced by **ABUT**.

butt[4] ▶ **noun** a cask, typically used for wine, ale, or water: *a **butt of** malmsey.*
■ US a liquid measure equal to 126 US gallons (equivalent to 477.5 litres).
– ORIGIN late Middle English: from Old French *bot*, from late Latin *buttis*.

butte /bjuːt/ ▶ **noun** N. Amer. & technical an isolated hill with steep sides and a flat top (similar to but narrower than a mesa).
– ORIGIN mid 19th cent.: from French, 'mound', from Old French *but*, of unknown origin (compare with **BUTT**[2]).

butter ▶ **noun** [mass noun] a pale yellow edible fatty substance made by churning cream and used as a spread or in cooking.
■ [with modifier] a substance of a similar consistency: *cocoa butter.*
▶ **verb** [with obj.] spread (something) with butter: *she buttered toast with a steady hand | [as adj. **buttered**] lavishly buttered bread.*
– PHRASES **look as if butter wouldn't melt in one's mouth** informal appear gentle or innocent while typically being the opposite.
– ORIGIN Old English *butere*, of West Germanic origin; related to Dutch *boter* and German *Butter*, based on Latin *butyrum*, from Greek *bouturon*.
▶ **butter someone up** informal flatter or otherwise ingratiate oneself with someone.

butter-and-eggs ▶ **noun** any of a number of plants having two shades of yellow in the flower, especially yellow toadflax.

butterball ▶ **noun** N. Amer. informal a derogatory way of addressing or referring to a fat person.
■ a plump bird, especially a turkey or bufflehead.

butter bean ▶ **noun** a lima bean, especially one of a variety with large flat white seeds.

butterbur /ˈbʌtəbəː/ ▶ **noun** a Eurasian waterside plant of the daisy family, the rounded flower heads of which are produced before the leaves. The large soft leaves were formerly used to wrap butter, and extracts are used medicinally as an anticonvulsant.

b

• Genus *Petasites*, family Compositae: several species, in particular the common *P. hybridus*.

butter cap ▶ **noun** a buff-coloured woodland toadstool with a greasy cap, found in both Eurasia and North America and typically growing in tufts and often in rings.
• *Collybia butyracea*, family Tricholomataceae, class Hymenomycetes.

buttercream ▶ **noun** [mass noun] a soft mixture of butter and icing sugar used as a filling or topping for a cake.

buttercup ▶ **noun** a herbaceous plant with bright yellow cup-shaped flowers, which is common in grassland and as a garden weed. All kinds are poisonous and generally avoided by livestock.
• Genus *Ranunculus*, family Ranunculaceae (the **buttercup family**). This large family also includes anemones, celandines, aconites, clematis, and hellebores, many of which have poisonous seeds.

buttercup squash ▶ **noun** a winter squash of a variety with dark green rind and orange flesh.

butterfat ▶ **noun** [mass noun] the natural fat contained in milk and dairy products.

Butterfield, William (1814–1900), English architect, an exponent of the Gothic revival. Notable designs: All Saints', Margaret Street, London (1850–9) and Keble College, Oxford (1867–83).

butterfingers ▶ **noun** (pl. same) informal a clumsy person, especially one who fails to hold a catch.
■ [mass noun] clumsiness in handling something: *fumbling for the ball with butterfingers*.
– DERIVATIVES **butterfingered** adjective.

butterfish ▶ **noun** (pl. same or **-fishes**) any of a number of fishes with oily flesh or slippery skin:
• a deep-bodied edible fish of temperate and tropical seas (family Stromateidae), in particular *Peprilus triacanthus* of eastern North America. • another term for **GUNNEL**[1]. • an Australasian reef fish (family Odacidae), in particular the edible *Odax pullus* of New Zealand, which has green bones and feeds on kelp. • a tropical freshwater or marine fish that is popular in aquaria (several families, including Scatophagidae).

butterfly ▶ **noun** (pl. **-flies**) an insect with two pairs of large wings that are covered with microscopic scales, typically brightly coloured and held erect when at rest. Butterflies fly by day, have clubbed or dilated antennae, and typically feed on nectar.
• Superfamilies Papilionoidea and Hesperioidea, order Lepidoptera: several families. Formerly placed in a grouping known as the Rhopalocera.
■ a showy or frivolous person: *a social butterfly*. ■ (**butterflies**) informal a fluttering and nauseous sensation felt in the stomach when one is nervous. ■ [in sing.] a stroke in swimming in which both arms are raised out of the water and lifted forwards together. ■ [as modifier] having a two-lobed shape resembling the spread wings of a butterfly: *a butterfly clip*.
▶ **verb** (**-flies**, **-flied**) [with obj.] split (a piece of meat) almost in two and spread it out flat: [as adj. **butterflied**] *butterflied shrimp*.
– ORIGIN Old English, from **BUTTER** + **FLY**[2]; perhaps from the cream or yellow colour of common species, or from an old belief that the insects stole butter.

butterfly bush ▶ **noun** a Chinese buddleia that is cultivated in the West for its large spikes of fragrant purplish-lilac or white flowers, which are highly attractive to butterflies.
• *Buddleia davidii*, family Loganiaceae.

butterfly cake ▶ **noun** Brit. a small sponge cake with its top cut off and divided into two pieces, which are then fixed to the cake with buttercream at an angle to resemble a butterfly's wings.

butterfly effect ▶ **noun** (with reference to chaos theory) the phenomenon whereby a minute localized change in a complex system can have large effects elsewhere.
– ORIGIN 1980s: from the notion that a butterfly fluttering in Rio de Janeiro could change the weather in Chicago.

butterfly fish ▶ **noun** **1** any of a number of typically brightly coloured or boldly marked fish of warm waters, in particular:
• a reef-dwelling fish that is popular in marine aquaria (*Chaetodon* and other genera, family Chaetodontidae). • a predatory marine fish that bears long venomous spines (genus *Pterois*, family Scorpaenidae).
2 a West African freshwater fish with large pectoral fins used in leaping out of the water and long fin rays used as stilts.
• *Pantodon buchholzi*, the only member of the family Pantodontidae.

butterfly knife ▶ **noun** a long broad knife used in pairs in some forms of kung fu.

butterfly net ▶ **noun** a fine-meshed bag supported on a frame at the end of a handle, used for catching butterflies.

butterfly nut ▶ **noun** another term for **WING NUT**.

butterfly orchid ▶ **noun** a wild orchid with a flower that somewhat resembles a butterfly in shape, found in both Eurasia and North America.
• Genus *Platanthera*, family Orchidaceae: many species, including two widely distributed European species with fragrant greenish-white flowers, *P. chlorantha* and the smaller *P. bifolia*.

butterfly ray ▶ **noun** a ray of warm coastal waters, typically small in size, with very broad triangular fins.
• Family Gymnuridae and genus *Gymnura*: several species, including *G. natalensis*.

butterfly valve ▶ **noun** a valve consisting of a rotating circular plate or a pair of hinged semicircular plates, attached to a transverse spindle and mounted inside a pipe in order to regulate or prevent flow.

butterfly weed ▶ **noun** [mass noun] a North American milkweed with bright orange flowers which are attractive to butterflies.
• *Asclepias tuberosa*, family Asclepiadaceae.

butterhead lettuce ▶ **noun** a class of lettuce varieties having soft leaves that grow in a loose head and are said to have the flavour of butter.

butter-icing ▶ **noun** another term for **BUTTERCREAM**.

butter knife ▶ **noun** a blunt knife used for cutting butter at table.

buttermilk ▶ **noun** [mass noun] the slightly sour liquid left after butter has been churned, used in baking or consumed as a drink.
■ a pale yellow colour (used especially to describe paint or wallpaper): [as modifier] *buttermilk paintwork*.

butter muslin ▶ **noun** [mass noun] Brit. loosely woven cotton cloth, formerly used for wrapping butter.

butternut ▶ **noun** a North American walnut tree which is cultivated as an ornamental and also for its quality timber.
• *Juglans cinerea*, family Juglandaceae.
■ the edible oily nut of this tree.

butternut squash ▶ **noun** a popular winter squash of a pear-shaped variety with light yellowish-brown rind and orange flesh.

butterscotch ▶ **noun** [mass noun] a brittle yellow-brown sweet made with butter and brown sugar.

butterwort /ˈbʌtəwəːt/ ▶ **noun** a carnivorous bog plant which has violet flowers borne above a rosette of greasy yellowish-green leaves that trap and digest small insects, found in both Eurasia and North America.
• Genus *Pinguicula*, family Lentibulariaceae: several species, in particular the **common butterwort** (*P. vulgaris*).
– ORIGIN late 16th cent.: named from the plant's supposed ability to keep cows in milk, and so maintain the supply of butter.

buttery[1] ▶ **adjective** containing or tasting like butter: *layers of flaky buttery pastry*.
■ covered with butter: *buttery fingers*.
– DERIVATIVES **butteriness** noun.

buttery[2] ▶ **noun** (pl. **-ies**) Brit. a room in a college where food is kept and sold to students.
– ORIGIN Middle English: from Anglo-Norman French *boterie* 'butt-store', from Old French *bot* (see **BUTT**[4]).

buttie ▶ **noun** (pl. **-ies**) variant spelling of **BUTTY**[1].

buttle ▶ **verb** [no obj.] humorous work as a butler: *there is no one today worth buttling for*.
– ORIGIN mid 19th cent.: back-formation from **BUTLER**.

buttock ▶ **noun** either of the two round fleshy parts of the human body that form the bottom.
– ORIGIN Old English *buttuc*, probably from the base of **BUTT**[3] + **-OCK**.

buttock line ▶ **noun** each of a series of longitudinal lines or curves marked on a plan of a ship to show its fore-and-aft sections at various distances from the centre line.

button ▶ **noun** a small disc or knob sewn on to a garment, either to fasten it by being pushed through a slit made for the purpose or for decoration.
■ a knob on a piece of electrical or electronic equipment which is pressed to operate it. ■ chiefly N. Amer. a badge bearing a design or slogan and pinned to the clothing. ■ a small round object resembling a button: *chocolate buttons*. ■ Fencing a knob fitted to the point of a foil to make it harmless. ■ used in reference to things of little worth: *he will never give away anything that is worth a button*.
▶ **verb** [with obj.] fasten (clothing) with buttons: *he buttoned up his jacket*.
■ (**button someone into**) fasten the buttons of a garment being worn by (someone): *he buttoned himself into the raincoat*. ■ [no obj.] (of a garment) be fastened with buttons: *a dress which buttoned down the front*. ■ attach buttons to: *white shiny plastic that was buttoned here and there*. ■ [often in imperative] (**button it**) informal stop talking.
– PHRASES **button one's lip** informal stop or refrain from talking. **on the button** informal, chiefly US punctually: *she would arrive on the button*. ■ exactly right: *his pond was right on the button in terms of size*. **press the button** informal initiate an action or train of events (often used to refer to the ease with which a nuclear war might be started). **push** (or **press**) **someone's buttons** informal arouse or provoke a reaction in someone: *don't allow co-workers to push your buttons*.
– DERIVATIVES **buttoned** adjective [in combination] *a gold-buttoned blazer*, **buttonless** adjective, **buttony** adjective.
– ORIGIN Middle English: from Old French *bouton*, of Germanic origin and related to **BUTT**[1].
▶ **button something up** **1** informal complete or conclude something satisfactorily: *trying to button up a deal*. **2** [often as adj. **buttoned up**] repress or contain something: *it was repressive enough to keep public opinion buttoned up*.

button-back ▶ **noun** [as modifier] denoting a chair, sofa, or other seat with a quilted back, the stitching being hidden by buttons: *a button-back antique chair*.

buttonball tree ▶ **noun** see **BUTTONWOOD** (sense 1).

buttonbush ▶ **noun** a low-growing North American shrub that grows in water, with small tubular flowers forming globular flower heads.
• *Cephalanthus occidentalis*, family Rubiaceae.

button chrysanthemum ▶ **noun** a variety of chrysanthemum with small spherical flowers.

button-down ▶ **adjective** [attrib.] (of a collar) having points which are buttoned to the garment.
■ (of a shirt) having such a collar. ■ N. Amer. (of a person) conservative or unimaginative.
▶ **noun** a shirt with a button-down collar.

button grass ▶ **noun** [mass noun] chiefly Austral. a grass or sedge with compact rounded flowering heads.
• a large tufted sedge (*Gymnoschoenus spaerocephalus*, family Cyperaceae). • an annual grass (*Dactyloctenium radulans*, family Gramineae).

buttonhole ▶ **noun** a slit made in a garment to receive a button for fastening.
■ Brit. a flower or spray worn in such a slit on the collar or lapel of a jacket.
▶ **verb** [with obj.] **1** informal attract the attention of and detain (someone) in conversation, typically against their will.
2 make slits for receiving buttons in (a garment).

buttonholer ▶ **noun** an attachment for a sewing machine used to make buttonholes.

buttonhole stitch ▶ **noun** [mass noun] a looped stitch used for edging buttonholes or pieces of material: *a row of buttonhole stitch*.

buttonhook ▶ **noun** **1** a small hook with a long handle for fastening tight buttons (often formerly on buttoned boots).
2 American Football a play in which a pass receiver runs straight downfield and then doubles back sharply towards the line of scrimmage.

button lift ▶ **noun** another term for **POMA**.

button mushroom ▶ **noun** a young unopened mushroom.

button-quail ▶ **noun** a small quail-like Old World bird related to the rails, with only three toes. Also called **HEMIPODE**.
• Family Turnicidae and genus *Turnix*: several species, including the widespread **barred button-quail** (*T. suscitator*) of Asia (also called **BUSTARD QUAIL**).

Buttons ▶ **noun** Brit. informal a nickname for a liveried pageboy, now normally only in pantomimes.
– ORIGIN mid 19th cent.: from the rows of buttons on his jacket.

button spider ▶ **noun** a highly venomous African spider which is a close relative of the American black widow.
• A subspecies of *Latrodectus mactans*, family Theridiidae.

button-through ▶ **adjective** Brit. (of clothing) fastened with buttons from top to bottom.
▶ **noun** a dress that fastens in such a way.

buttonwood ▶ **noun 1** (also **buttonwood tree**) N. Amer. an American plane tree. Also called **SYCAMORE** in North America.
• Genus *Platanus*, family Platanaceae: several species, in particular *P. occidentalis* (also called **BUTTONBALL TREE**), which is the largest deciduous tree in the US and is grown for ornament and timber.
2 either of two mangroves found mainly in tropical America, used in the production of tanbark and for charcoal.
• *Conocarpus erectus* (the button mangrove) and *Laguncularia racemosa*, family Combretaceae.

buttress /ˈbʌtrɪs/ ▶ **noun** a projecting support of stone or brick built against a wall.
■ a projecting portion of a hill or mountain. ■ figurative a source of defence or support: *there was a demand for a new stable order as a buttress against social collapse.*
▶ **verb** [with obj.] provide (a building or structure) with projecting supports built against its walls: [as adj. **buttressed**] *a buttressed wall.*
■ figurative increase the strength of or justification for; reinforce: *authority was buttressed by religious belief.*
– ORIGIN Middle English: from Old French (*ars*) *bouterez* 'thrusting (arch)', from *boter* 'to strike or thrust' (see **BUTT**[1]).

butty[1] (also **buttie**) ▶ **noun** (pl. **-ies**) informal, chiefly N. English a filled or open sandwich: *a bacon butty.*
– ORIGIN mid 19th cent.: from **BUTTER** + **-Y**[2].

butty[2] ▶ **noun** (pl. **-ies**) Brit. **1** used informally among miners to refer to a friend or workmate.
■ historical a middleman negotiating between the miners and mine owner: [as modifier] *the butty system.*
2 (also **butty boat**) an unpowered freight barge intended to be towed.
– ORIGIN late 18th cent.: probably from **BOOTY**[1] in the phrase *play booty* 'join in sharing plunder'.

butut /ˈbuːtuːt/ ▶ **noun** (pl. same or **bututs**) a monetary unit of Gambia, equal to one hundredth of a dalasi.
– ORIGIN a local word.

butyl /ˈbjuːtʌɪl, -tɪl/ ▶ **noun** [as modifier] Chemistry of or denoting an alkyl radical —C_4H_9, derived from butane: *butyl acetate.* See also **ISOBUTYL**.
■ short for **BUTYL RUBBER**.
– ORIGIN mid 19th cent.: from **BUTYRIC ACID** + **-YL**.

butyl rubber ▶ **noun** [mass noun] a synthetic rubber made by polymerizing isobutylene and isoprene.

butyric acid /bjuːˈtɪrɪk/ ▶ **noun** [mass noun] Chemistry a colourless syrupy liquid organic acid found in rancid butter and in arnica oil.
• Alternative name: **butanoic acid**; chem. formula: C_3H_7COOH.
– DERIVATIVES **butyrate** /ˈbjuːtɪreɪt/ noun.
– ORIGIN mid 19th cent.: *butyric* from Latin *butyrum* (see **BUTTER**) + **-IC**.

buxom /ˈbʌks(ə)m/ ▶ **adjective** (of a woman) plump, with a full figure and large breasts.
– DERIVATIVES **buxomness** noun.
– ORIGIN Middle English: from the stem of Old English *būgan* 'to bend' (see **BOW**[2]) + **-SOME**[1]. The original sense was 'compliant, obliging', later 'lively and good-tempered', influenced by the traditional association of plumpness and good health with an easy-going nature.

Buxtehude /ˈbʊkstəˌhuːdə/, Dietrich (*c.*1637–1707), Danish organist and composer. Working in Lübeck, he wrote mainly for the organ.

buy ▶ **verb** (**buys**, **buying**; past and past participle **bought**) [with obj.] **1** obtain in exchange for payment: *we had to find some money to buy a house | he had been able to* **buy up** *hundreds of acres* | [with two objs] *he bought me a new frock* | [no obj.] *homeowners who* **buy into** *housing developments.*
■ (**buy someone out**) pay someone to give up an ownership, interest, or share. ■ (**buy oneself out**) obtain one's release from the armed services by payment. ■ procure the loyalty and support of (someone) by bribery: *here was a man who could not be bought | I'll* **buy off** *the investigators.* ■ [often with negative] be a means of obtaining (something) through exchange or payment: *money can't buy happiness.* ■ (often **be bought**) get by sacrifice or great effort: *greatness is* **dearly bought**. ■ [no obj.] make a profession of purchasing goods for a store or firm.
2 informal accept the truth of: *I am not prepared to buy the claim that the ends justify the means* | [no obj.] *I hate to* **buy into** *stereotypes.*
3 (**bought it**) informal used to indicate that someone has died: *his friends had bought it in the jungle.*
▶ **noun** informal a purchase: *the wine is a good buy at £3.49.*
■ an act of purchasing something: *phoney drug buys.*
– PHRASES **buy the farm** N. Amer. informal die. **buy time** delay an event temporarily so as to have longer to improve one's own position.
– ORIGIN Old English *bycgan*, of Germanic origin.
▶ **buy something in 1** purchase goods for stock; stock up with something. **2** withdraw something at auction because it fails to reach the reserve price.

buy-back ▶ **noun** the buying back of goods by the original seller.
■ a form of borrowing in which shares or bonds are sold with an agreement to repurchase them at a later date: [with modifier] *a share buy-back.*

buyer ▶ **noun** a person who makes a purchase.
■ a person employed to select and purchase stock or materials for a large retail or manufacturing business etc.
– PHRASES **a buyer's market** an economic situation in which goods or shares are plentiful and buyers can keep prices down.

buy-in ▶ **noun 1** a purchase of shares by a broker after a seller has failed to deliver similar shares, the original seller being charged any difference in cost.
2 (also **management buy-in**) a purchase of shares in a company by managers who are not employed by it.
3 the buying back by a company of its own shares.

buyout ▶ **noun** the purchase of a controlling share in a company, especially by its own managers (also **management buyout**).

buzz ▶ **noun** [in sing.] a low, continuous humming or murmuring sound, made by or similar to that made by an insect: *the buzz of the bees | a buzz of conversation.*
■ the sound of a buzzer or telephone. ■ informal a telephone call: *I'll give you a buzz.* ■ informal a rumour: *there's a strong buzz that he's in Scotland.* ■ an atmosphere of excitement and activity: *there is a real buzz about the place.* ■ informal a feeling of excitement or euphoria: *I got such* **a buzz** *out of seeing the kids' faces.*
▶ **verb** [no obj.] **1** make a humming sound: *mosquitoes were buzzing all around us.*
■ [often as noun **buzzing**] (of the ears) be filled with a humming sound: *I remember a buzzing in my ears.* ■ signal with a buzzer: *the electric bell began to buzz for closing time* | [with obj.] *he buzzed the stewardesses every five minutes.* ■ [with obj.] informal telephone.
2 [with adverbial of direction] move quickly or busily: *she buzzed along the M1 back into town.*
■ [with obj.] Aeronautics, informal fly very close to (another aircraft, the ground, etc.) at high speed.
3 (of a place) have an air of excitement or purposeful activity: *the club is* **buzzing with** *excitement.*
■ (of a person's mind or head) be filled with excited or confused thoughts: *her mind was* **buzzing with** *ideas.*
4 [with obj.] informal throw hard: *some tribes buzzed a few spears at us.*
– ORIGIN late Middle English: imitative.
▶ **buzz off** [often in imperative] informal go away.

buzzard /ˈbʌzəd/ ▶ **noun** a large hawklike bird of prey with broad wings and a rounded tail, often seen soaring in wide circles.
• Family Accipitridae: several genera, in particular *Buteo*, and including the common (**Eurasian**) **buzzard** (*B. buteo*).
■ N. Amer. a vulture, especially a turkey vulture.
– ORIGIN late Middle English: from Old French *busard*, based on Latin *buteo* 'falcon'.

buzz bomb ▶ **noun** informal term for **FLYING BOMB**.

buzzer ▶ **noun** an electrical device, similar to a bell, that makes a buzzing noise and is used for signalling.
– PHRASES **at the buzzer** N. Amer. at the end of a game or period of play, especially in basketball.

buzz saw ▶ **noun** North American term for **CIRCULAR SAW**.

buzzword (also **buzz-phrase**) ▶ **noun** informal a technical word or phrase that has become fashionable, typically as a slogan.

BVDs ▶ **plural noun** N. Amer. trademark a type of boxer shorts.
– ORIGIN late 19th cent.: acronym from the name of the manufacturers; the mistaken full form in folk etymology is *babies' ventilated diapers.*

BVM ▶ **abbreviation for** Blessed Virgin Mary.

b/w ▶ **abbreviation for** black and white (used especially to describe printing, film, photographs, or television pictures).

bwana /ˈbwɑːnə/ ▶ **noun** (in East Africa) a boss or master: [as title] *Bwana Hemedi.*
■ used as a form of address: *he can't hear you, bwana.*
– ORIGIN Kiswahili.

BWR ▶ **abbreviation for** boiling-water reactor.

by ▶ **preposition 1** identifying the agent performing an action:
■ after a passive verb: *the door was opened by my cousin Annie | damage caused by fire.* ■ after a noun denoting an action: *further attacks by the Mob | a clear decision by the electorate.* ■ identifying the author of a text, idea, or work of art: *a book by Ernest Hemingway.*
2 [often with verbal noun] indicating the means of achieving something: *malaria can be controlled by attacking the parasite | substantiating their opinions by the use of precise textual reference | they plan to provide further working capital* **by means of** *borrowing.*
■ indicating a term to which an interpretation is to be assigned: *what is meant by 'fair'?* ■ indicating a name according to which a person is known: *she mostly calls me by my last name.* ■ indicating the means of transport selected for a journey: *the cost of travelling by bus | travelling by road to Aylsham.* ■ indicating the other parent of someone's child or children: *Richard is his son by his third wife.* ■ indicating the sire of a pedigree animal, especially a horse: *a black filly by Goldfuerst.* ■ (followed by a noun without a determiner) in various phrases indicating how something happens: *I heard by chance that she has married again | Anderson, by contrast, rejects this view | she ate by candlelight.*
3 indicating the amount or size of a margin: *the shot missed her by miles | the raising of VAT by 2.5%.*
■ indicating a quantity or amount: *billing is by the minute | the drunken yobbos who turned up by the cartload.* ■ in phrases indicating something happening repeatedly or progressively, typically with repetition of a unit of time: *colours changing minute by minute | the risk becomes worse by the day.* ■ identifying a parameter: *a breakdown of employment figures by age and occupation.* ■ expressing multiplication, especially in dimensions: *a map measuring 400 by 600 mm | she multiplied it by 89.*
4 indicating a deadline or the end of a particular time period: *I've got to do this report by Monday | by now Kelly needed extensive physiotherapy.*
5 indicating location of a physical object beside a place or object: *remains were discovered by the roadside | the pram was by the dresser.*
■ past and beyond: *I drove by our house.*
6 indicating the period in which something happens: *this animal always hunts* **by night**.
7 concerning; according to: *anything you do is all right by me | she had done her duty by him.*
8 used in mild oaths: *it was the least he could do, by God.* [ORIGIN: partly translating French *par* 'through the medium or agency of'.]
▶ **adverb** so as to go past: *a car flashed by on the other side of the road | he let only a moment go by.*
▶ **noun** (pl. **byes**) variant spelling of **BYE**[1].
– PHRASES **by and by** before long; eventually. **by the by** (or **bye**) incidentally; parenthetically: *where's Hector, by the by?* **by and large** on the whole; everything considered: *mammals have, by and large, bigger brains than reptiles.* [ORIGIN: originally in nautical use, describing the handling of a ship both to the wind and off it.] **by oneself 1** alone: *living in Farley Court by himself.* **2** unaided: *the patient often learns to undress by himself.* **by way of** see **WAY**.
– ORIGIN Old English *bī*, *bi*, *be*, of Germanic origin; related to Dutch *bij* and German *bei*.

by- (also **bye-**) ▶ **prefix** subordinate; incidental; secondary: *by-election | by-product.*

Byatt /ˈbʌɪət/, Dame A. S. (b.1936), English novelist and literary critic; born *Antonia Susan Byatt*. She is the elder sister of Margaret Drabble. Notable novels: *The Virgin in the Garden* (1978) and *Possession* (1990, Booker Prize).

Byblos /ˈbɪblɒs/ an ancient Mediterranean seaport, situated on the site of modern Jebeil, to the north of Beirut in Lebanon. It became a thriving Phoenician city in the 2nd millennium BC.

by-blow ▶ **noun** Brit. dated a man's illegitimate child.

by-catch ▶ **noun** the unwanted fish and other

marine creatures trapped by commercial fishing nets during fishing for a different species.

Bydgoszcz /ˈbɪdɡɒʃtʃ/ an industrial river port in north central Poland; pop. 381,530 (1990). 20,000 of its citizens were massacred by Nazis in September 1939. German name **BROMBERG**.

bye[1] ▶ **noun 1** the transfer of a competitor directly to the next round of a competition in the absence of an assigned opponent.
2 Cricket a run scored from a ball that passes the batsman without being hit (recorded as an extra, not credited to the individual batsman).
3 Golf one or more holes remaining unplayed after a match has been decided.
– PHRASES **by the bye** variant spelling of **BY THE BY** (see **BY**).
– ORIGIN mid 16th cent. (denoting a side issue or incidental matter): from **BY**.

bye[2] ▶ **exclamation** informal short for **GOODBYE**.

bye- ▶ **prefix** variant spelling of **BY-**.

bye-bye ▶ **exclamation** informal way of saying **GOODBYE**.
– ORIGIN early 18th cent.: child's reduplication.

bye-byes ▶ **noun** [mass noun] a child's word for sleep.
– ORIGIN mid 19th cent.: from the sound bye-bye, long used as a refrain in lullabies.

by-election ▶ **noun** Brit. the election of an MP in a single constituency to fill a vacancy arising during a government's term of office.

byeline ▶ **noun** variant spelling of **BYLINE** (in sense 2).

Byelorussia /ˌbjɛlə(ʊ)ˈrʊʃə/ variant spelling of **BELORUSSIA**.

Byelorussian /ˌbjɛlə(ʊ)ˈrʌʃ(ə)n/ ▶ **adjective** & **noun** variant spelling of **BELORUSSIAN**.

by-form ▶ **noun** a secondary form of a word: historically, 'inquire' is a by-form of 'enquire'.

by gad ▶ **exclamation** see **GAD**[2].

by golly ▶ **exclamation** see **GOLLY**[1].

bygone ▶ **adjective** belonging to an earlier time: relics of a bygone society.
▶ **noun** (usu. **bygones**) a thing dating from an earlier time.
– PHRASES **let bygones be bygones** forget past offences or causes of conflict and be reconciled.

by-law (also **bye-law**) ▶ **noun 1** Brit. a regulation made by a local authority or corporation.
2 a rule made by a company or society to control the actions of its members.
– ORIGIN Middle English: probably from obsolete byrlaw 'local law or custom', from Old Norse býjar, genitive singular of býr 'town', but associated with **BY**.

byline ▶ **noun 1** a line in a newspaper naming the writer of an article.
2 (also **byeline**) (chiefly in soccer) the part of the goal line to either side of the goal.

byname ▶ **noun** a sobriquet or nickname, especially one given to distinguish a person from others with the same given name.

BYOB ▶ **abbreviation** for bring your own bottle (used chiefly on party invitations).

bypass ▶ **noun** a road passing round a town or its centre to provide an alternative route for through traffic.
■ a secondary channel, pipe, or connection to allow a flow when the main one is closed or blocked. ■ an alternative passage made by surgery, typically to aid the circulation of blood. ■ a surgical operation to make such a passage: a heart bypass.
▶ **verb** [with obj.] go past or round: bypass the farm and continue to the road.
■ provide (a town) with a route diverting traffic from its centre: the town has been bypassed. ■ avoid or circumvent (an obstacle or problem): a manager might bypass formal channels of communication.

bypath ▶ **noun** an indirect route.
■ figurative a minor or obscure branch or detail of a subject: the bypaths of European political life.

byplay ▶ **noun** [mass noun] secondary or subsidiary action or involvement in a play or film.

by-product ▶ **noun** an incidental or secondary product made in the manufacture or synthesis of something else: zinc is a by-product of the glazing process.
■ a secondary result, unintended but inevitably produced in doing or producing something else: he saw poverty as the by-product of colonial prosperity.

Byrd[1], Richard (Evelyn) (1888–1957), American explorer, naval officer, and aviator. He claimed to have made the first aircraft flight over the North Pole (1926), although his actual course has been disputed. He was the first to fly over the South Pole (1929).

Byrd[2], William (1543–1623), English composer. He was joint organist of the Chapel Royal with Tallis and is famous for his Latin masses and his Anglican Great Service.

byre ▶ **noun** Brit. a cowshed.
– ORIGIN Old English býre; perhaps related to **BOWER**[1].

byroad ▶ **noun** a minor road.

Byron /ˈbʌɪərən/, George Gordon, 6th Baron (1788–1824), English poet. Byron's poetry exerted considerable influence on the romantic movement, particularly on the Continent. Having joined the fight for Greek independence, he died of malaria before seeing serious action. Notable works: Childe Harold's Pilgrimage (1812–18) and Don Juan (1819–24)

Byronic /bʌɪˈrɒnɪk/ ▶ **adjective** characteristic of Lord Byron or his poetry.
■ (of a man) alluringly dark, mysterious, and moody.

byssinosis /ˌbɪsɪˈnəʊsɪs/ ▶ **noun** [mass noun] a lung disease caused by prolonged inhalation of textile fibre dust.
– ORIGIN late 19th cent.: from Latin byssinus 'made of byssus' (from Greek bussinos) + -OSIS.

byssus /ˈbɪsəs/ ▶ **noun** (pl. **byssuses** or **byssi** /-sʌɪ/)
1 [mass noun] historical a fine textile fibre and fabric of flax.
2 [count noun] Zoology a tuft of tough silky filaments by which mussels and some other bivalves adhere to rocks and other objects: [as modifier] byssus threads.
– DERIVATIVES **byssal** adjective.
– ORIGIN late Middle English: from Latin, from Greek bussos, of Semitic origin.

bystander ▶ **noun** a person who is present at an event or incident but does not take part.

byte /bʌɪt/ ▶ **noun** Computing a group of binary digits or bits (usually eight) operated on as a unit.
■ such a group as a unit of memory size.
– ORIGIN 1960s: an arbitrary formation based on **BIT**[4] and **BITE**.

by-the-wind sailor ▶ **noun** a surface-dwelling colonial marine coelenterate of the Atlantic and Mediterranean. It has a disc-like float bearing a sail that is used to catch the wind.
● Velella velella, suborder Chondrophora, order Hydroida.

Bytom /ˈbɪtəm/ a city in southern Poland, north-west of Katowice; pop. 231,200 (1990). German name **BEUTHEN**.

bytownite /ˈbʌɪtaʊnʌɪt/ ▶ **noun** [mass noun] a mineral present in many basic igneous rocks, consisting of a calcic plagioclase feldspar.
– ORIGIN mid 19th cent.: from Bytown, the former name of Ottawa, Canada, + -ITE[1].

byway ▶ **noun** a road or track not following a main route; a minor road or path.
■ a little-known area or detail: byways of Russian music.

byword ▶ **noun** a person or thing cited as a notorious and outstanding example or embodiment of something: his name became a byword for luxury.
■ a word or expression summarizing a thing's characteristics or a person's principles: 'Small is beautiful' may be the byword for most couturiers.

Byzantine /bɪˈzantʌɪn, bʌɪ-/ ▶ **adjective** of or relating to Byzantium, the Byzantine Empire, or the Eastern Orthodox Church.
■ of an ornate artistic and architectural style which developed in the Byzantine Empire and spread to Italy, Russia, and elsewhere. The art is generally rich and stylized (as in religious icons) and the architecture is typified by many-domed, highly decorated churches. ■ (of a system or situation) excessively complicated, and typically involving a great deal of administrative detail: Byzantine insurance regulations. ■ characterized by deviousness or underhand procedure: Byzantine intrigues | he has the most Byzantine mind in politics.
▶ **noun** a citizen of Byzantium or the Byzantine Empire.
– DERIVATIVES **Byzantinism** /bɪˈzantɪnɪz(ə)m, bʌɪ-/ noun.
– ORIGIN late 16th cent.: from Latin Byzantinus, from **BYZANTIUM**.

Byzantine Empire the empire in SE Europe and Asia Minor formed from the eastern part of the Roman Empire.

The Roman Empire was divided in AD 395 by the Emperor Theodosius between his sons; Constantinople (Byzantium) became the capital of the Eastern Empire in 476, with the fall of Rome. In 1054 theological and political differences between Constantinople and Rome led to the breach between Eastern and Western Christianity (see **GREAT SCHISM** in sense 1). After about 1100 the empire gradually declined; the loss of Constantinople to the Ottoman Turks in 1453 was the end of the empire, although its rulers held Trebizond (Trabzon) until 1461.

Byzantinist /bɪˈzantɪst, bʌɪ-/ ▶ **noun** a historian or other scholar specializing in the study of the Byzantine Empire, its history, art, and culture.

Byzantium /bɪˈzantɪəm, bʌɪ-/ an ancient Greek city, founded in the 7th century BC, at the southern end of the Bosporus, site of the modern city of Istanbul. It was rebuilt by Constantine the Great in AD 324–30 as Constantinople.

Cc

C¹ (also **c**) ▶ noun (pl. **Cs** or **C's**) **1** the third letter of the alphabet.
■denoting the third in a set of items, categories, sizes, etc. ■ denoting the third of three or more hypothetical people or things. ■ the third highest class of academic mark. ■ denoting an intermediate socio-economic category for marketing purposes, including the majority of white-collar (**C1**) and skilled blue-collar personnel (**C2**). ■ (**c**) Chess denoting the third file from the left of a chessboard, as viewed from White's side of the board. ■ (usu. **c**) the third fixed constant to appear in an algebraic expression, or a known constant. ■ denoting the lowest soil horizon, comprising parent materials.
2 a shape like that of a letter C: [in combination] *C-springs*.
3 (usu. **C**) Music the first note of the diatonic scale of C major, the major scale having no sharps or flats.
■a key based on a scale with C as its keynote.
4 the Roman numeral for 100. [ORIGIN: abbreviation of Latin *centum* 'hundred'.]
5 (**C**) [mass noun] a computer programming language originally developed for implementing the UNIX operating system. [ORIGIN: formerly known as *B*, abbreviation of *BCPL*.]

C² ▶ abbreviation for ■ (**C.**) Cape (chiefly on maps): *C. Hatteras*. ■ Celsius or centigrade: *29°C*. ■ (in names of sports clubs) City: *Lincoln C*. ■ (**C.**) Brit. Command Paper (second series, 1870–99). ■ (in Britain) Conservative. ■ (©) copyright. ■ Physics coulomb(s). ■ Cuba (international vehicle registration).
▶ symbol for ■ Physics capacitance. ■ the chemical element carbon.
– PHRASES **the Big C** informal cancer.

c ▶ abbreviation for ■ Cricket (on scorecards) caught by: *ME Waugh c Lara b Walsh 19*. ■ cent(s). ■ [in combination] (in units of measurement) centi-: *centistokes* (*cS*). ■ (**c.**) century or centuries: *a watch case, 19th c*. ■ (preceding a date or amount) circa; approximately: *Isabella was born c 1759*. ■ (of water) cold: *all bedrooms have h & c*. ■ colt.
▶ symbol for Physics the speed of light in a vacuum: $E = mc^2$.

c/- Austral./NZ ▶ abbreviation for care of (used chiefly in addresses on envelopes).

CA ▶ abbreviation for ■ California (in official postal use). ■ Scottish & Canadian chartered accountant.

Ca ▶ symbol for the chemical element calcium.

ca ▶ abbreviation for (preceding a date or amount) circa.

CAA ▶ abbreviation for (in the UK) Civil Aviation Authority.

Caaba variant spelling of KAABA.

caatinga /ˈkɑːtɪŋɡə/ ▶ noun [mass noun] (in Brazil) vegetation in semi-arid country consisting of thorny shrubs and stunted trees.
– ORIGIN via Portuguese from Tupi, from *caá* 'natural vegetation' + *tinga* 'white'.

CAB ▶ abbreviation for ■ Citizens' Advice Bureau. ■ US Civil Aeronautics Board.

cab¹ ▶ noun **1** (also **taxi cab**) a taxi.
■historical a horse-drawn vehicle for public hire.
2 the driver's compartment in a lorry, bus, or train.
▶ verb (**cabbed**, **cabbing**) [no obj.] travel in a taxi: *Roger cabbed home*.

– ORIGIN early 19th cent.: abbreviation of CABRIOLET.

cab² ▶ noun informal a cabinet containing a speaker or speakers for a guitar amplifier.
– ORIGIN late 20th cent.: abbreviation.

cabal /kəˈbal/ ▶ noun a secret political clique or faction: *a cabal of dissidents*.
■historical a committee of five ministers under Charles II, whose surnames happened to begin with C, A, B, A, and L.
– ORIGIN late 16th cent. (denoting the cabbala): from French *cabale*, from medieval Latin *cabala* (see CABBALA).

Cabala ▶ noun variant spelling of KABBALAH.

cabaletta /ˌkabəˈlɛtə/ ▶ noun (pl. **cabalettas** or **cabalette**) a simple aria with a repetitive rhythm.
■the uniformly quick final section of an aria.
– ORIGIN mid 19th cent.: from Italian, variant of *coboletta* 'short stanza', diminutive of *cobola*, from Old Provençal *cobla*, from Latin *copula* 'connection'.

Caballé /kəˈbaljeɪ, ˌkabalˈjeɪ, Spanish kaβaˈʎe/, Montserrat (b.1933), Spanish operatic soprano.

caballero /ˌkabəˈljɛːrəʊ/ ▶ noun (pl. **-os**) **1** a Spanish gentleman.
2 US (in the south-western states) a horseman.
– ORIGIN mid 19th cent.: Spanish, 'gentleman, horseman', based on Latin *caballus* 'horse'. Compare with CAVALIER, CHEVALIER.

cabana /kəˈbɑːnə/ ▶ noun N. Amer. a hut, cabin, or shelter at a beach or swimming pool.
– ORIGIN late 19th cent.: from Spanish *cabaña*, from late Latin *capana*, *cavana* 'cabin'.

cabaret /ˈkabəreɪ, ˌkabəˈreɪ/ ▶ noun [mass noun] entertainment held in a nightclub or restaurant while the audience eat or drink at tables: *she was seen recently in cabaret* | [as modifier] *a cabaret act* | [count noun] *the cabaret drew to a close*.
■[count noun] a nightclub or restaurant where such entertainment is performed.
– ORIGIN mid 17th cent. (denoting a French inn): from Old French, literally 'wooden structure', via Middle Dutch from Old Picard *camberet* 'little room'. Current senses date from the early 20th cent.

cabbage ▶ noun a cultivated plant eaten as a vegetable, having thick green or purple leaves surrounding a spherical heart or head of young leaves.
● *Brassica oleracea*, family Cruciferae (or Brassicaceae; the **cabbage family**). As well as the brassicas, the members of this family (known as crucifers) include the mustards and cresses together with many ornamentals (candytuft, alyssum, stocks, nasturtiums, wallflowers).
■[mass noun] the leaves of this plant, eaten as a vegetable. ■ Brit. offensive a person whose physical or mental activity is impaired or destroyed as a result of injury or illness. ■ Brit. informal a person who leads a very dull and limited life.
– DERIVATIVES **cabbagy** adjective.
– ORIGIN late Middle English: from Old French (Picard) *caboche* 'head', variant of Old French *caboce*, of unknown origin.

cabbage lettuce ▶ noun a lettuce of a variety which has broad, rounded leaves forming a globular head close to the ground.

cabbage moth ▶ noun a brown moth whose caterpillars are pests of cabbages and related plants.
● *Mamestra brassicae*, family Noctuidae.

cabbage palm ▶ noun any of a number of palms or palm-like plants that resemble a cabbage in some way, in particular:
● a Caribbean palm with edible buds that resemble a cabbage (*Roystonea oleraceae*, family Palmae). ● an evergreen plant occurring in warm regions and grown elsewhere as a greenhouse or indoor plant (genus *Cordyline*, family Agavaceae).

cabbage root fly ▶ noun a small fly whose larvae feed on the roots and stems of cabbages and related plants and can be a serious pest.
● *Delia radicum*, family Anthomyiidae.

cabbage rose ▶ noun a kind of rose with a large, round, compact double flower.

Cabbagetown ▶ noun Canadian informal a depressed urban area; an inner-city slum.
– ORIGIN from the nickname of a depressed area of Toronto, where the inhabitants were said to exist on a diet of cabbage.

cabbage tree ▶ noun any of a number of palm-like trees that resemble a cabbage in some way, in particular:
● a New Zealand tree grown for its sugary sap or for ornament (*Cordyline australis*, family Agavaceae). ● a cabbage palm.

cabbage white ▶ noun a mainly white butterfly that has caterpillars which are pests of cabbages and related plants.
● Genus *Pieris*, family Pieridae: several species, in particular the **small white** (*P. rapae*) and the **large white** (*P. brassicae*).

cabbageworm ▶ noun N. Amer. any caterpillar that is a pest of cabbages, especially that of the cabbage white butterfly.

Cabbala ▶ noun variant spelling of KABBALAH.

cabbalistic /ˌkabəˈlɪstɪk/ ▶ adjective relating to or associated with mystical interpretation or esoteric doctrine. See also KABBALAH.
– DERIVATIVES **cabbalism** noun, **cabbalist** noun.
– ORIGIN variant of *Kabbalistic*: see KABBALAH.

cabby (also **cabbie**) ▶ noun (pl. **-ies**) informal a taxi driver.

caber /ˈkeɪbə/ ▶ noun a roughly trimmed tree trunk used in the Scottish Highland sport of **tossing the caber**. This involves holding the caber upright and running forward to toss it so that it lands on the opposite end.
– ORIGIN early 16th cent.: from Scottish Gaelic *cabar* 'pole'.

Cabernet /ˈkabəneɪ/ ▶ noun short for CABERNET FRANC or CABERNET SAUVIGNON.

Cabernet Franc /frɒ̃/ ▶ noun [mass noun] a variety of black wine grape grown chiefly in parts of the Loire Valley and NE Italy.
■a red wine made from this grape.
– ORIGIN French.

Cabernet Sauvignon /ˈsəʊvɪnjɒ̃/ ▶ noun [mass noun] a variety of black wine grape from the Bordeaux area of France, now grown throughout the world.
■a red wine made from this grape.
– ORIGIN French.

cabezon /ˈkabɪzɒn/ ▶ noun a heavy-bodied fish with

a broad tentacle above each eye and a green-brown body with white patches, found on the west coast of North America.
● *Scorpaenichthys marmoratus*, family Cottidae.
– ORIGIN Spanish.

cab-forward ▶ adjective [attrib.] denoting a design of car or truck in which the driver's or passenger compartment is placed so as to extend further forward than the standard position.

cabildo /kəˈbɪldəʊ/ ▶ noun (pl. **-os**) (in Spain and Spanish-speaking countries) a town council or local government council.
■ a town hall.
– ORIGIN Spanish, from late Latin *capitulum* 'chapter house'.

cabin ▶ noun **1** a private room or compartment on a ship.
■ the area for passengers in an aircraft.
2 a small shelter or house, made of wood and situated in a wild or remote area.
▶ verb (**cabined**, **cabining**) [with obj.] [often as adj. **cabined**] dated confine in a small place.
– ORIGIN Middle English: from Old French *cabane*, from Provençal *cabana*, from late Latin *capanna*, *cavanna*.

cabin boy ▶ noun chiefly historical a boy employed to wait on a ship's officers or passengers.

cabin class ▶ noun [mass noun] the intermediate class of accommodation on a passenger ship.

cabin crew ▶ noun [treated as sing. or pl.] the members of an aircraft crew who attend to passengers or cargo.

cabin cruiser ▶ noun a motor boat with living accommodation.

Cabinda /kəˈbɪndə/ an enclave of Angola at the mouth of the River Congo, separated from the rest of Angola by a wedge of Zaire (Democratic Republic of Congo).
■ the capital of this area; pop. 163,000 (1991).

cabinet ▶ noun **1** a cupboard with drawers or shelves for storing or displaying articles: *a cocktail cabinet*.
■ a wooden box, container, or piece of furniture housing a radio, television set, or speaker.
2 (also **Cabinet**) (in the UK, Canada, and other Commonwealth countries) the committee of senior ministers responsible for controlling government policy: [as modifier] *a cabinet meeting*.
■ (in the US) a body of advisers to the President, composed of the heads of the executive departments of the government.
3 archaic a small private room.
– ORIGIN mid 16th cent.: from **CABIN** + **-ET**[1], influenced by French *cabinet*.

cabinetmaker ▶ noun a skilled joiner who makes furniture or similar high-quality woodwork.
– DERIVATIVES **cabinetmaking** noun.

cabinet minister ▶ noun (in the UK, Canada, and other Commonwealth countries) a member of a parliamentary cabinet.

cabinet pudding ▶ noun [mass noun] a steamed suet pudding containing dried fruit.

cabinetry ▶ noun [mass noun] cabinets collectively.

cabin fever ▶ noun [mass noun] informal chiefly N. Amer. lassitude, irritability, and similar symptoms, resulting from long confinement or isolation indoors during the winter.

cable ▶ noun **1** a thick rope of wire or hemp, typically used for construction, mooring ships, and towing vehicles.
■ the chain of a ship's anchor. ■ Nautical a length of 200 yards (182.9 m) or (in the US) 240 yards (219.4 m). ■ short for **CABLE STITCH**. ■ (also **cable moulding**) Architecture a moulding resembling twisted rope.
2 an insulated wire or wires having a protective casing and used for transmitting electricity or telecommunication signals: *an underground cable* | [mass noun] *transatlantic phone calls were by cable*.
■ a cablegram. ■ short for **CABLE TELEVISION**.
▶ verb [with obj.] **1** contact or send a message to (someone) by cablegram.
■ transmit (a message) by cablegram. ■ [no obj.] send a cablegram: *have you got the drugs I cabled for?*
2 (often **be cabled**) provide (an area or community) with power lines or with the equipment necessary for cable television.
3 Architecture decorate (a structure) with rope-shaped mouldings.
– ORIGIN Middle English: from an Anglo-Norman

French variant of Old French *chable*, from late Latin *capulum* 'halter'.

cable car ▶ noun **1** a transport system, typically one travelling up and down a mountain, in which cabins are suspended on a continuous moving cable driven by a motor at one end of the route.
■ a cabin on such a system.
2 a carriage on a cable railway.

cablegram ▶ noun historical a telegraph message sent by cable: *Walter shot off a cablegram* | [mass noun] *we heard of his death by cablegram.*

cable-laid ▶ adjective (of rope) made of three triple strands.

cable railway ▶ noun a railway along which carriages are drawn by a continuous cable, in particular:
■ a tramway on which the unpowered cars are attached, for as long as they are required to move, to a continuously moving cable running in a slot in the street. ■ a funicular.

cable-ready ▶ adjective [attrib.] N. Amer. adapted for cable television.

cable release ▶ noun Photography a cable attached to the shutter release of a camera, allowing the photographer to open the shutter without touching or moving the camera.

cable-stayed bridge ▶ noun a bridge in which the weight of the deck is supported by a number of cables running directly to one or more towers.

cable stitch ▶ noun [mass noun] a combination of knitted stitches resembling twisted rope.

cable television ▶ noun [mass noun] a system in which television programmes are transmitted to the sets of subscribers by cable rather than by a broadcast signal.

cable tier ▶ noun Nautical, historical a place in a ship for stowing a coiled cable.

cableway ▶ noun a transport system in which goods are carried suspended from a continuous moving cable.

cabman ▶ noun (pl. **-men**) historical the driver of a horse-drawn hackney carriage.

caboched ▶ adjective variant spelling of **CABOSHED**.

cabochon /ˈkabəʃɒn/ ▶ noun a gem polished but not faceted: [as modifier] *a necklace of cabochon rubies.*
– PHRASES **en cabochon** (of a gem) treated in this way.
– ORIGIN mid 16th cent.: from French, diminutive of *caboche* 'head'.

caboclo /kəˈbɒkləʊ/ ▶ noun (pl. **-os**) (in Brazil) an American Indian.
■ a Brazilian of mixed white and Indian or Indian and black ancestry.
– ORIGIN Brazilian Portuguese, perhaps from Tupi *Kaa-boc* 'person having copper-coloured skin'.

caboodle (also **kaboodle**) ▶ noun (in phrase **the whole caboodle** or **the whole kit and caboodle**) informal the whole number or quantity of people or things in question.
– ORIGIN mid 19th cent. (originally US): perhaps from the phrase *kit and boodle*, in the same sense (see **KIT**[1], **BOODLE**).

caboose ▶ noun **1** N. Amer. a railway wagon with accommodation for the train crew, typically attached to the end of the train.
2 archaic a kitchen on a ship's deck.
– ORIGIN mid 18th cent.: from Dutch *kabuis*, *kombuis*, of unknown origin.

Cabora Bassa /kəˌbɔːrə ˈbasə/ a lake on the Zambezi River in western Mozambique. Its waters are impounded by a dam and massive hydroelectric complex.

caboshed /kəˈbɒʃt/ (also **cabochéd** or **cabossed** /-ˈbɒst/) ▶ adjective [usu. postpositive] Heraldry (of the head of a stag, bull, etc.) shown full face with no neck visible.
– ORIGIN late 16th cent.: from French *caboché*, in the same sense.

Cabot /ˈkabət/ the name of two Italian explorers and navigators.
■ John (*c*.1450–*c*.1498); Italian name *Giovanni Caboto*. He sailed from Bristol in 1497 in search of Asia, but in fact discovered the mainland of North America.
■ Sebastian (*c*.1475–1557), son of John. Sebastian accompanied his father on his voyage in 1497 and made further voyages after the latter's death, most notably to Brazil and the River Plate (1526).

cabotage /ˈkabətɑːʒ, -ɪdʒ/ ▶ noun [mass noun] the right to operate sea, air, or other transport services within a particular territory.
■ restriction of the operation of sea, air, or other transport services within or into a particular country to that country's own transport services.
– ORIGIN mid 19th cent.: from French, from *caboter* 'sail along a coast', perhaps from Spanish *cabo* 'cape, headland'.

cabover ▶ noun N. Amer. a truck where the driver's cab is mounted directly above the engine.

cabrio /ˈkabrɪəʊ/ ▶ noun (pl. **-os**) short for **CABRIOLET** (in sense 1).

cabriole /ˈkabrɪəʊl/ ▶ noun Ballet a jump in which one leg is extended into the air forwards or backwards, the other is brought up to meet it, and the dancer lands on the second foot.
– ORIGIN French, literally 'light leap', from *cabrioler* (earlier *caprioler*), from Italian *capriolare* 'to leap in the air' (see **CAPRIOLE**).

cabriole leg ▶ noun a kind of curved leg characteristic of Chippendale and Queen Anne furniture.
– ORIGIN late 18th cent.: so named from the resemblance to the front leg of a leaping animal (see **CABRIOLE**).

cabriolet /ˈkabrɪ(ʊ)leɪ/ ▶ noun **1** a car with a roof that folds down.
2 a light two-wheeled carriage with a hood, drawn by one horse.
– ORIGIN mid 18th cent.: from French, from *cabriole* 'goat's leap', from *cabrioler* 'to leap in the air' (see **CABRIOLE**); so named because of the carriage's motion.

ca'canny /kɑːˈkani/ ▶ noun [mass noun] Brit. dated the policy of deliberately limiting output at work.
– ORIGIN late 19th cent. (originally Scots in the sense 'proceed warily'): from *ca'* (variant of the verb **CALL**) and **CANNY**.

cacao /kəˈkɑːəʊ, -ˈkeɪəʊ/ ▶ noun (pl. **-os**) **1** [mass noun] bean-like seeds from which cocoa, cocoa butter, and chocolate are made.
2 the small tropical American evergreen tree which bears these seeds, which are contained in large oval pods that grow on the trunk, now cultivated mainly in West Africa.
● *Theobroma cacao*, family Sterculiaceae.
– ORIGIN mid 16th cent.: via Spanish from Nahuatl *cacaua*.

cacciatore /ˌkatʃəˈtɔːreɪ, -ri/ (also **cacciatora** /-rə/) ▶ adjective [postpositive] prepared in a spicy tomato sauce with mushrooms and herbs: *chicken cacciatore.*
– ORIGIN Italian, literally 'hunter' (because of the use of ingredients that a hunter might have to hand).

cachalot /ˈkaʃəlɒt/ ▶ noun another term for **SPERM WHALE**.
– ORIGIN mid 18th cent.: from French, from Spanish and Portuguese *cachalote*, from *cachola* 'big head'.

cache /kaʃ/ ▶ noun a collection of items of the same type stored in a hidden or inaccessible place: *an arms cache* | *a cache of gold coins.*
■ a hidden or inaccessible storage place for valuables, provisions, or ammunition. ■ (also **cache memory**) Computing an auxiliary memory from which high-speed retrieval is possible.
▶ verb [with obj.] store away in hiding or for future use.
■ Computing store (data) in a cache memory. ■ Computing provide (hardware) with a cache memory.
– ORIGIN late 18th cent.: from French, from *cacher* 'to hide'.

cachectic /kəˈkɛktɪk/ ▶ adjective Medicine relating to or having the symptoms of cachexia.

cachepot /ˈkaʃpəʊ, ˈkaʃpɒt/ ▶ noun (pl. pronounced same) an ornamental holder for a flowerpot.
– ORIGIN late 19th cent.: from French *cache-pot*, from *cacher* 'to hide' + *pot* 'pot'.

cache-sexe /ˈkaʃsɛks/ ▶ noun (pl. pronounced same) a covering for a person's genitals, typically worn by erotic dancers or tribal peoples.
– ORIGIN 1920s: from French, from *cacher* 'to hide' and *sexe* 'genitals'.

cachet /ˈkaʃeɪ/ ▶ noun **1** [mass noun] the state of being respected or admired; prestige: *no other shipping company had quite the cachet of Cunard.*
2 a distinguishing mark or seal.
3 a flat capsule enclosing a dose of unpleasant-tasting medicine.
– ORIGIN early 17th cent.: from French, from *cacher*

in the sense 'to press', based on Latin *coactare* 'constrain'.

cachexia /kəˈkɛksɪə/ ▶ noun [mass noun] Medicine weakness and wasting of the body due to severe chronic illness.
– ORIGIN mid 16th cent.: via late Latin from Greek *kakhexia*, from *kakos* 'bad' + *hexis* 'habit'.

cachinnate /ˈkakɪneɪt/ ▶ verb [no obj.] poetic/literary laugh loudly.
– DERIVATIVES **cachinnation** noun.
– ORIGIN early 19th cent.: from Latin *cachinnat-* 'laughed loudly', from the verb *cachinnare*, of imitative origin.

cachou /ˈkaʃuː, kəˈʃuː/ ▶ noun (pl. **cachous**) dated a pleasant-smelling lozenge sucked to mask bad breath.
– ORIGIN late 16th cent. (in the sense 'catechu'): from French, from Portuguese *cachu*, from Malay *kacu*. The current sense dates from the early 18th cent.

cachucha /kəˈtʃuːtʃə/ ▶ noun a lively Spanish solo dance in triple time, performed with castanet accompaniment.
– ORIGIN Spanish.

cacique /kəˈsiːk/ ▶ noun 1 (in Latin America or the Spanish-speaking Caribbean) a native chief.
2 (in Spain or Latin America) a local political boss.
3 a gregarious tropical American bird that has black plumage with patches of red or yellow.
● Genus *Cacicus*, family Icteridae: several species.
– ORIGIN mid 16th cent.: from Spanish or French, from Taino.

cack Brit. informal ▶ noun [mass noun] excrement; dung.
■ figurative rubbish: *he can't just churn out any old cack and expect to rake it in.*
▶ verb [with obj.] defecate in (one's clothes).
– ORIGIN Old English (as *cac-* in *cachūs* 'privy'); the verb dates from late Middle English and is related to Middle Dutch *cacken*; based on Latin *cacare* 'defecate'.

cack-handed ▶ adjective Brit. informal 1 inept; clumsy: *a great song ruined by cack-handed production.*
2 derogatory left-handed.
– DERIVATIVES **cack-handedly** adverb, **cack-handedness** noun.
– ORIGIN mid 19th cent.: from CACK, in the sense 'excrement', + HAND + -ED[2].

cackle ▶ verb [no obj.] (of a bird, typically a hen or goose) give a raucous clucking cry: *the hen was cackling as if demented* | [as adj.] **cackling** *cackling, whooping cries.*
■ make a harsh sound resembling such a cry when laughing: *she cackled with laughter* | [with direct speech] '*Ah ha!*' *he cackled.* ■ talk at length without acting on what is said: *corporate luminaries* **cackle on about** *the importance of quality.*
▶ noun the raucous clucking cry of a bird such as a hen or a goose.
■ a harsh laugh resembling such a cry: *her delighted cackle.*
– PHRASES **cut the cackle** [usu. in imperative] informal stop talking aimlessly and come to the point.
– ORIGIN Middle English: probably from Middle Low German *kākelen*, partly imitative, reinforced by *kāke* 'jaw, cheek'.

cacodemon /ˌkakə(ʊ)ˈdiːmən/ ▶ noun a malevolent spirit or person.
– ORIGIN late 16th cent.: from Greek *kakodaimōn*, from *kakos* 'bad' + *daimōn* 'spirit'.

cacodyl /ˈkakə(ʊ)dʌɪl, -dɪl/ ▶ noun [mass noun] Chemistry a malodorous, toxic, spontaneously flammable liquid compound containing arsenic.
● Chem. formula: $((CH_3)_2As)_2$.
■ [as modifier] of or denoting the radical —$As(CH_3)_2$, derived from this.
– ORIGIN mid 19th cent.: from Greek *kakōdēs* 'stinking' (from *kakos* 'bad') + -YL.

cacodylic acid /ˌkakə(ʊ)dʌɪlɪk, -dɪlɪk/ ▶ noun [mass noun] Chemistry a toxic crystalline acid containing arsenic, used as a herbicide.
● Chem. formula: $(CH_3)_2AsO(OH)$.
– DERIVATIVES **cacodylate** noun.

cacoethes /ˌkakəʊˈiːθiːz/ ▶ noun [in sing.] rare an urge to do something inadvisable.
– ORIGIN mid 16th cent.: via Latin from Greek *kakoēthes* 'ill-disposed', from *kakos* 'bad' + *ēthos* 'disposition'.

cacography /kəˈkɒɡrəfi/ ▶ noun [mass noun] archaic bad handwriting or spelling.
– DERIVATIVES **cacographer** noun.
– ORIGIN late 16th cent.: from Greek *kakos* 'bad', on the pattern of *orthography*.

cacology /kəˈkɒlədʒi/ ▶ noun [mass noun] archaic bad choice of words or poor pronunciation.
– ORIGIN late 18th cent.: via late Latin from Greek *kakologia* 'vituperation', from *kakos* 'bad'.

cacomistle /ˈkakə(ʊ)ˌmɪs(ə)l/ ▶ noun a nocturnal raccoon-like animal with a dark-ringed tail, found in North and Central America.
● Genus *Bassariscus*, family Procyonidae: two species, in particular *B. sumichrasti* of Central America. See also RINGTAILED CAT.
– ORIGIN mid 19th cent.: from Latin American Spanish *cacomixtle*, from Nahuatl *tlacomiztli*.

cacophony /kəˈkɒf(ə)ni/ ▶ noun (pl. **-ies**) a harsh discordant mixture of sounds: *a cacophony of deafening alarm bells* | figurative *a cacophony of architectural styles* | [mass noun] *songs of unrelieved cacophony.*
– DERIVATIVES **cacophonous** adjective.
– ORIGIN mid 17th cent.: from French *cacophonie*, from Greek *kakophōnia*, from *kakophōnos* 'ill-sounding', from *kakos* 'bad' + *phōnē* 'sound'.

cactus ▶ noun (pl. **cacti** /-tʌɪ/ or **cactuses**) a succulent plant with a thick fleshy stem which typically bears spines, lacks leaves, and has brilliantly coloured flowers. Cacti are native to arid regions of the New World and are cultivated elsewhere, especially as pot plants.
● Family Cactaceae: numerous genera and species.
– DERIVATIVES **cactaceous** adjective.
– ORIGIN early 17th cent. (in the sense 'cardoon'): from Latin, from Greek *kaktos* 'cardoon'.

cactus dahlia ▶ noun a dahlia of a variety which has rolled petals, giving the flower a prickly appearance.

cacuminal /kəˈkjuːmɪn(ə)l/ ▶ adjective Phonetics another term for RETROFLEX.
– ORIGIN mid 19th cent.: from Latin *cacuminare* 'make pointed' (from *cacumen, cacumin-* 'top, summit') + -AL.

CAD ▶ abbreviation for computer-aided design.

cad ▶ noun dated or humorous a man who behaves dishonourably, especially towards a woman: *her adulterous cad of a husband.*
– DERIVATIVES **caddish** adjective, **caddishly** adverb, **caddishness** noun.
– ORIGIN late 18th cent. (denoting a passenger picked up by the driver of a horse-drawn coach for personal profit): abbreviation of CADDIE or CADET.

cadastral /kəˈdastr(ə)l/ ▶ adjective (of a map or survey) showing the extent, value, and ownership of land, especially for taxation.
– ORIGIN mid 19th cent.: from French, from *cadastre* 'register of property', from Provençal *cadastro*, from Italian *catastro* (earlier *catastico*), from late Greek *katastikhon* 'list, register', from *kata stikhon* 'line by line'.

cadaver /kəˈdɑːvə, -ˈdeɪ-/ ▶ noun Medicine or poetic/literary a corpse.
– DERIVATIVES **cadaveric** adjective.
– ORIGIN late Middle English: from Latin, from *cadere* 'to fall'.

cadaverous ▶ adjective resembling a corpse in being very pale, thin, or bony: *he had a cadaverous appearance.*
– ORIGIN late Middle English: from Latin *cadaverosus*, from *cadaver* 'corpse'.

Cadbury /ˈkadb(ə)ri/, George (1839–1922) and Richard (1835–99), English cocoa and chocolate manufacturers and social reformers. As committed Quakers, they were concerned with improving their employees' working and living conditions, and established a new factory and housing estate at Bournville.

CADCAM ▶ abbreviation for computer-aided design, computer-aided manufacture.

caddie (also **caddy**) ▶ noun (pl. **-ies**) a person who carries a golfer's clubs and provides other assistance during a match.
▶ verb (**caddying**) [no obj.] work as a caddie.
– ORIGIN mid 17th cent. (originally Scots): from French CADET. The original term denoted a gentleman who joined the army without a commission, intending to learn the profession and follow a military career, later coming to mean 'odd-job man'. The current sense dates from the late 18th cent.

caddis /ˈkadɪs/ (also **caddis fly**) ▶ noun a small moth-like insect with an aquatic larva that typically builds a protective portable case of sticks, stones, and other particles. Some kinds have been traditionally used as bait by fishermen.
● Order Trichoptera: several families.
– ORIGIN mid 17th cent.: of unknown origin.

caddis worm ▶ noun the soft-bodied aquatic larva of a caddis fly, widely used as fishing bait.

Caddoan /ˈkadəʊən/ ▶ adjective relating to or denoting a group of American Indian peoples formerly inhabiting the Midwest, or their languages, now all virtually extinct.
▶ noun 1 a member of any of these peoples.
2 [mass noun] the family of languages spoken by these peoples, which includes Pawnee and may be related to Siouan and Iroquoian.
– ORIGIN from Caddo (a language of this family) *kaduhdacu*, denoting a band belonging to this group, + -AN.

caddy[1] ▶ noun (pl. **-ies**) [usu. with modifier] a small storage container, typically one with divisions: *a tool caddy.* See also TEA CADDY.
– ORIGIN late 18th cent.: from earlier *catty*, denoting a unit of weight of 1⅓ lb (0.61 kg), from Malay *kati*.

caddy[2] ▶ noun & verb variant spelling of CADDIE.

caddy spoon ▶ noun a spoon used to dispense tea from a tea caddy, typically with a wide, shallow bowl and a short handle.

Cade /keɪd/, Jack (d.1450), Irish rebel; full name *John Cade*. In 1450 he assumed the name of Mortimer and led the Kentish rebels against Henry VI. They occupied London for three days and executed the treasurer of England and the sheriff of Kent.

cadelle /kəˈdɛl/ ▶ noun a small dark beetle that is frequently found in food stores, where it scavenges and preys on other insects.
● *Tenebroides mauritanicus*, family Cleridae.
– ORIGIN mid 19th cent.: from French, based on Latin *catella, catellus* 'young (of an animal), little dog'.

cadence /ˈkeɪd(ə)ns/ ▶ noun 1 a modulation or inflection of the voice: *the measured cadences that he employed in the Senate.*
■ such a modulation in reading aloud as implied by the structure and ordering of words and phrases in written text: *the dry cadences of the essay.* ■ a fall in pitch of the voice at the end of a phrase or sentence. ■ [mass noun] rhythm: *the thumping cadence of the engines.*
2 Music a sequence of notes or chords comprising the close of a musical phrase: *the final cadences of the Prelude.*
– DERIVATIVES **cadenced** adjective.
– ORIGIN late Middle English (in the sense 'rhythm or metrical beat'): via Old French from Italian *cadenza*, based on Latin *cadere* 'to fall'.

cadency ▶ noun [mass noun] chiefly Heraldry the status of a younger branch of a family.
– ORIGIN early 17th cent. (in the sense 'rhythm or metrical beat'): based on Latin *cadent-* 'falling', from the verb *cadere*. The current sense is apparently by association with CADET.

cadential ▶ adjective of or relating to a cadenza or cadence.
– ORIGIN mid 19th cent.: from CADENCE, on the pattern of pairs such as *essence, essential*.

cadenza /kəˈdɛnzə/ ▶ noun Music a virtuoso solo passage inserted into a movement in a concerto or other work, typically near the end.
– PHRASES **have a cadenza** S. African informal be extremely agitated. [ORIGIN: said to be from Danny Kaye's *The Little Fiddle*, a humorous recording made in the 1940s.]
– ORIGIN mid 18th cent.: from Italian (see CADENCE).

cadet ▶ noun 1 a young trainee in the armed services or police force: *an air cadet.*
■ a boy or girl of 13–18 who undergoes voluntary army, navy, or air force training together with adventure training. ■ NZ a young man learning sheep farming on a sheep station.
2 formal or archaic a younger son or daughter.
■ [usu. as modifier] a junior branch of a family: *a cadet branch of the family.*
– DERIVATIVES **cadetship** noun.
– ORIGIN early 17th cent. (in sense 2): from French, from Gascon dialect *capdet*, a diminutive based on Latin *caput* 'head'. The notion 'little head' or 'inferior head' gave rise to that of 'younger, junior'.

cadge ▶verb [with obj.] informal ask for or obtain (something to which one is not strictly entitled): *he cadged fivers off old school friends* | [no obj.] *when news of our money gets in the papers people'll be round cadging.*
▶noun Falconry a padded wooden frame on which hooded hawks are carried to the field. [ORIGIN: apparently an alteration of **CAGE**, perhaps confused with the dialect verb *cadge* 'carry about'.]
– PHRASES **on the cadge** informal looking for an opportunity to obtain something without paying for it.
– DERIVATIVES **cadger** noun.
– ORIGIN early 17th cent. (in the dialect sense 'carry about'): back-formation from the noun *cadger*, which dates from the late 15th cent., denoting (in northern English and Scots) an itinerant dealer, whence the verb sense 'hawk, peddle', giving rise to the current verb senses from the early 19th cent.

cadi /ˈkɑːdi, ˈkeɪdi/ (also **kadi**) ▶noun (pl. **cadis**) (in Islamic countries) a judge.
– ORIGIN late 16th cent.: from Arabic *ḳāḍī*, from *ḳaḍā* 'to judge'.

Cadiz /kəˈdɪz/ a city and port on the coast of SW Spain; pop. 156,560 (1991). Spanish name **CÁDIZ** /ˈkaðiθ, ˈkaðis/.

Cadmean /kadˈmiːən/ ▶adjective of or relating to Cadmus.

cadmium /ˈkadmɪəm/ ▶noun [mass noun] the chemical element of atomic number 48, a silvery-white metal. (Symbol: **Cd**)

Cadmium occurs naturally in zinc ores and is obtained as a by-product of zinc smelting. It is used as a component in low melting point alloys and as a corrosion-resistant coating on other metals.

– ORIGIN early 19th cent.: from Latin *cadmia* 'calamine', so named because it is found with calamine in zinc ore. Compare with **CALAMINE**.

cadmium cell ▶noun a primary electric cell with a cathode of cadmium amalgam and an electrolyte of saturated cadmium sulphate solution, used in laboratories as a standard of electromotive force.

cadmium yellow ▶noun [mass noun] a bright yellow pigment containing cadmium sulphide. Deeper versions are called **cadmium orange**; the addition of cadmium selenide gives **cadmium red**.
■a bright yellow colour.

Cadmus /ˈkadməs/ Greek Mythology the brother of Europa and traditional founder of Thebes in Boeotia. He killed a dragon which guarded a spring, and when (on Athene's advice) he sowed the dragon's teeth there came up a harvest of armed men; he disposed of the majority by setting them to fight one another, and the survivors formed the ancestors of the Theban nobility.

cadre /ˈkɑːdə, ˈkɑːdr(ə), ˈkadrɪ/ ▶noun a small group of people specially trained for a particular purpose or profession: *a cadre of professional managers.*
■[also ˈkeɪdə] a group of activists in a communist or other revolutionary organization. ■a member of such a group.
– ORIGIN mid 19th cent.: from French, from Italian *quadro*, from Latin *quadrus* 'square'.

caduceus /kəˈdjuːsɪəs/ ▶noun (pl. **caducei** /-sɪʌɪ/) an ancient Greek or Roman herald's wand, typically one with two serpents twined round it, carried by the messenger god Hermes or Mercury.
– ORIGIN Latin, from Doric Greek *karukeion* from Greek *kērux* 'herald'.

caducity /kəˈdjuːsɪti/ ▶noun [mass noun] archaic the infirmity of old age; senility.
■poetic/literary frailty or transitory nature: *read these books and reflect on their caducity.*
– ORIGIN mid 18th cent.: from French *caducité*, from *caduc*, from Latin *caducus* 'liable to fall', from *cadere* 'to fall'.

caducous /kəˈdjuːkəs/ ▶adjective chiefly Botany (of an organ or part) easily detached and shed at an early stage.
– ORIGIN late 17th cent. (in the sense 'epileptic'): from Latin *caducus* 'liable to fall' (from *cadere* 'to fall') + -OUS.

CAE ▶abbreviation for computer-aided engineering.

caecilian /sɪˈsɪlɪən/ (also **coecilian**) ▶noun Zoology a burrowing worm-like amphibian of a tropical order distinguished by poorly developed eyes and the lack of limbs.
●Order Gymnophiona (or Apoda): five families.
– ORIGIN from modern Latin *Caecilia* (genus name), from Latin *caecilia* 'slow-worm', + -AN.

caecitis /sɪˈkʌɪtɪs/ (US **cecitis**) ▶noun Medicine inflammation of the caecum.

caecum /ˈsiːkəm/ (US **cecum**) ▶noun (pl. **caeca**) Anatomy a pouch connected to the junction of the small and large intestines.
– DERIVATIVES **caecal** adjective.
– ORIGIN late Middle English: from Latin (*intestinum*) *caecum* 'blind (gut)', translation of Greek *tuphlon enteron.*

Caedmon /ˈkadmən/ (7th century), Anglo-Saxon monk and poet, said to have been an illiterate herdsman inspired in a vision to compose poetry on biblical themes. The only authentic fragment of his work is a song in praise of the Creation, quoted by Bede.

Caelum /ˈsiːləm/ Astronomy a small and faint southern constellation (the Chisel), next to Eridanus.
■[as genitive **Caeli** /ˈsiːli/] used with preceding letter or numeral to designate a star in this constellation: *the star Beta Caeli.*
– ORIGIN Latin.

Caen /kɑːn, French kɑ̃/ an industrial city and river port in Normandy in northern France, on the River Orne, capital of the region of Basse-Normandie; pop. 115,620 (1990).

Caerdydd /ˈkaɪrdɪð/ Welsh name for **CARDIFF**.

Caerfyrddin /kaɪrˈvɪrðin/ Welsh name for **CARMARTHEN**.

Caergybi /kaɪrˈɡʌbi/ Welsh name for **HOLY ISLAND** (sense 2).

Caernarfon /kəˈnɑːv(ə)n, Welsh kaɪrˈnarvɒn/ (also **Caernarvon**) a town in NW Wales on the shore of the Menai Strait, the administrative centre of Gwynedd; pop. 9,400 (1981).

Caernarfonshire (also **Caernarvonshire**) a former county of NW Wales, part of Gwynedd from 1974.

Caerns. ▶abbreviation for Caernarfonshire.

Caerphilly /kɛːˈfɪli, kɑː-, kə-/ ▶noun [mass noun] a kind of mild white cheese, originally made in Caerphilly in Wales.

Caesar /ˈsiːzə/ ▶noun 1 a title of Roman emperors, especially those from Augustus to Hadrian.
■an autocrat.
2 Medicine, Brit. informal a Caesarean section.
– PHRASES **Caesar's wife** a person who is required to be above suspicion. [ORIGIN: with reference to Plutarch's *Caesar* (x. 6) 'I thought my wife ought not even to be under suspicion'.]
– ORIGIN Middle English: from Latin *Caesar*, family name of the Roman statesman, Gaius **JULIUS CAESAR**.

Caesarea /ˌsiːzəˈrɪə/ an ancient port on the Mediterranean coast of Israel, one of the principal cities of Roman Palestine.

Caesarea Mazaca /ˈmazəkə/ former name for **KAYSERI**.

Caesarean /sɪˈzɛːrɪən/ (also **Caesarian**) ▶adjective 1 (US also **Cesarean**) of or effected by Caesarean section: *a Caesarean delivery.*
2 of or connected with Julius Caesar or the Caesars.
▶noun a Caesarean section: *I had to have a Caesarean* | [mass noun] *two sons both born by Caesarean.*
– ORIGIN early 16th cent. (as a noun denoting a supporter of an emperor or imperial system): from Latin *Caesareus* 'of Caesar' + -AN.

Caesarean section ▶noun a surgical operation for delivering a child by cutting through the wall of the mother's abdomen.
– ORIGIN early 17th cent.: *Caesarian* from the story that Julius Caesar was delivered by this method.

Caesarea Philippi /ˈfɪlɪpʌɪ, fɪˈlɪpʌɪ/ a city in ancient Palestine, on the site of the present-day village of Baniyas in the Golan Heights.

Caesar salad ▶noun a salad consisting of cos lettuce and croutons served with a dressing of olive oil, lemon juice, raw egg, Worcester sauce, and seasoning.
– ORIGIN named after *Caesar* Cardini, the Mexican restaurateur who invented it in 1924.

caesium /ˈsiːzɪəm/ (US **cesium**) ▶noun [mass noun] the chemical element of atomic number 55, a soft, silvery, extremely reactive metal. It belongs to the alkali metal group and occurs as a trace element in some rocks and minerals. (Symbol: **Cs**)
– ORIGIN mid 19th cent.: from Latin *caesius* 'greyish-

blue' (because it has characteristic lines in the blue part of the spectrum).

caesium clock ▶noun an atomic clock that uses the vibrations of caesium atoms as a time standard.

caesura /sɪˈzjʊərə/ ▶noun (in Greek and Latin verse) a break between words within a metrical foot.
■(in modern verse) a pause near the middle of a line.
– DERIVATIVES **caesural** adjective.
– ORIGIN mid 16th cent.: from Latin, from *caes-* 'cut, hewn', from the verb *caedere.*

CAF N. Amer. ▶abbreviation for cost and freight.

cafard /kaˈfɑː/ ▶noun [mass noun] melancholia.
– ORIGIN from French.

cafe /ˈkafeɪ, ˈkafi, or informal kaf/ ▶noun 1 a small restaurant selling light meals and drinks.
2 N. Amer. a bar or nightclub.
3 S. African a shop selling sweets, cigarettes, newspapers, and perishable goods and staying open after normal hours.
– ORIGIN early 19th cent.: from French *café* 'coffee or coffee house'.

cafe au lait /ˌkafeɪ əʊ ˈleɪ, ˌkafi/ ▶noun [mass noun] coffee with milk.
■the light brown colour of this: [as modifier] *smooth cafe au lait skin.*
– ORIGIN from French *café au lait.*

cafe bar ▶noun a cafe which also serves alcoholic drinks.

cafe curtain ▶noun a curtain covering the lower half of a window.

cafe de move-on ▶noun S. African informal a small mobile canteen catering for workers at their workplaces.
– ORIGIN pseudo-French, with reference to the mobility of the cart and the order by authorities to 'move on'.

cafe noir /ˌkafeɪ ˈnwɑː, ˌkafi/ ▶noun [mass noun] black coffee.
– ORIGIN from French *café noir.*

cafe society ▶noun [in sing.] the regular patrons of fashionable restaurants and nightclubs.

cafeteria ▶noun a restaurant in which customers serve themselves from a counter and pay before eating.
– ORIGIN mid 19th cent. (originally US): from Latin American Spanish *cafetería* 'coffee shop'.

cafetière /ˌkaf(ə)ˈtjɛː/ ▶noun a coffee pot containing a plunger made of fine mesh with which the grounds are pushed to the bottom when the coffee is ready to be poured.
– ORIGIN mid 19th cent.: from French, from *café* 'coffee'.

caff ▶noun Brit. informal a cafe.

caffeinated /ˈkafɪneɪtɪd/ ▶adjective (of coffee or tea) containing the natural amount of caffeine, or with caffeine added.

caffeine /ˈkafiːn/ ▶noun [mass noun] a crystalline compound which is found especially in tea and coffee plants and is a stimulant of the central nervous system.
●An alkaloid, **1,3,7-trimethylxanthine**; chem. formula: $C_8H_{10}N_4O_2$.
– ORIGIN mid 19th cent.: from French *caféine*, from *café* 'coffee'.

caffè latte /ˌkafeɪ ˈlɑːteɪ, ˈlateɪ/ ▶noun a drink made by adding a shot of espresso coffee to a glass or cup of frothy steamed milk.
– ORIGIN Italian, literally 'milk coffee'.

CAFOD /ˈkafɒd/ ▶abbreviation for Catholic Fund for Overseas Development.

caftan ▶noun variant spelling of **KAFTAN**.

Cagayan Islands /ˌkɑːɡəˈjɑːn/ a group of seven small islands in the Sulu Sea in the western Philippines.

Cage, John (Milton) (1912–92), American composer, pianist, and writer. He was notable for his experimental approach, which included the use of aleatory music and periods of silence.

cage ▶noun a structure of bars or wires in which birds or other animals are confined: *she kept a canary in a cage* | figurative *his cage of loneliness.*
■a prison cell or camp. ■an open framework forming the compartment in a lift. ■a structure of crossing bars or wires designed to hold or support something. ■Baseball a portable backstop situated behind the batter during batting practice. ■a soccer or hockey goal made from a network frame.

▶ **verb** [with obj.] (usu. **be caged**) confine in or as in a cage: *the parrot screamed, furious at being caged* | [as adj.] **caged**] *a caged bird.*
■ informal put in prison.
– ORIGIN Middle English: via Old French from Latin *cavea.*

cage bird ▶ **noun** a bird of a kind customarily kept in a cage.

cage fungus ▶ **noun** a fetid-smelling fungus that forms a hollow latticed spherical structure, the inner surface of which bears the spores.
● Genus *Clathrus*, family Clathraceae, class Gasteromycetes.

cagey (also **cagy**) ▶ **adjective** informal reluctant to give information owing to caution or suspicion: *a spokesman was cagey about the arrangements his company had struck.*
– DERIVATIVES **cagily** adverb, **caginess** (also **cageyness**) noun.
– ORIGIN early 20th cent. (originally US): of unknown origin.

Cagliari /ˌkalɪ'ɑːri, Italian kaʎˈʎari/ the capital of Sardinia, a port on the south coast; pop. 211,720 (1990).

Cagney /'kagni/, James (1899–1986), American actor. He is chiefly remembered for playing gangster roles in films such as *The Public Enemy* (1931), but he was also a skilled dancer and comedian who received an Oscar for his part in the musical *Yankee Doodle Dandy* (1942).

cagoule /kəˈguːl/ (also **kagoul**) ▶ **noun** a lightweight, hooded, thigh-length waterproof jacket.
– ORIGIN 1950s: from French, literally 'cowl'.

cahier /'kaɪeɪ, French kaje/ ▶ **noun** (pl. pronounced same) an exercise book or notebook.
– ORIGIN mid 19th cent.: from French; compare with **QUIRE**.

cahoots /kəˈhuːts/ ▶ **plural noun** (in phrase **in cahoots**) informal colluding or conspiring together secretly: *the area is dominated by guerrillas in cahoots with drug traffickers.*
– ORIGIN early 19th cent. (originally US): of unknown origin.

cahoun ▶ **noun** variant spelling of **COHUNE**.

cahow /kəˈhaʊ/ ▶ **noun** a large Atlantic petrel which breeds in Bermuda. It is an endangered species.
● *Pterodroma cahow*, family Procellariidae.
– ORIGIN early 17th cent.: imitative of its call.

CAI ▶ **abbreviation for** computer-assisted (or -aided) instruction.

caiman /'keɪmən/ (also **cayman**) ▶ **noun** a semiaquatic reptile similar to the alligator but with a heavily armoured belly, native to tropical America.
● *Caiman* and other genera, family Alligatoridae: three species, in particular the **spectacled caiman** (*C. sclerops*).
– ORIGIN late 16th cent.: from Spanish *caimán*, Portuguese *caimão*, from Carib *acayuman.*

Cain ▶ **noun** (in the Bible) the eldest son of Adam and Eve and murderer of his brother Abel.
– PHRASES **raise Cain** informal create trouble or a commotion.

Caine, Sir Michael (b.1933), English film actor; born *Maurice Micklewhite*. He has appeared in a wide variety of films, including *The Ipcress File* (1965) and *Hannah and Her Sisters* (1986, for which he won an Oscar).

Cainozoic /ˌkaɪnə'zəʊɪk/ ▶ **adjective** variant spelling of **CENOZOIC**.

caique /kaɪˈiːk, kɑː-/ ▶ **noun 1** a light rowing boat used on the Bosporus.
2 a small eastern Mediterranean sailing ship.
– ORIGIN early 17th cent.: from French *caïque*, from Italian *caicco*, from Turkish *kayık.*

cairn ▶ **noun 1** a mound of rough stones built as a memorial or landmark, typically on a hilltop or skyline.
■ a prehistoric burial mound made of stones.
2 (also **cairn terrier**) a small terrier of a breed with short legs, a longish body, and a shaggy coat. [ORIGIN: perhaps so named from being used to hunt among cairns.]
– ORIGIN late Middle English: from Scottish Gaelic *carn.*

cairngorm /'kɛːngɔːm/ ▶ **noun** another term for **SMOKY QUARTZ**.
– ORIGIN late 18th cent.: named after the **CAIRNGORM MOUNTAINS**.

Cairngorm Mountains (also **the Cairngorms**) a mountain range in northern Scotland.
– ORIGIN from Scottish Gaelic *carn gorm* 'blue cairn'.

Cairo /'kaɪrəʊ/ the capital of Egypt, a port on the Nile near the head of its delta; pop. 13,300,000 (est. 1991). Arabic name **AL QAHIRA**.
– DERIVATIVES **Cairene** /'kaɪriːn/ adjective & noun.

caisson /'keɪs(ə)n, kə'suːn/ ▶ **noun 1** a large watertight chamber, open at the bottom, from which the water is kept out by air pressure and in which construction work may be carried out under water.
■ a floating vessel or watertight structure used as a gate across the entrance of a dry dock or basin.
2 historical a chest or wagon for holding or conveying ammunition.
– ORIGIN late 17th cent.: from French, literally 'large chest', from Italian *cassone*, the spelling having been altered in French by association with *caisse* 'case'.

caisson disease ▶ **noun** another term for **DECOMPRESSION SICKNESS**.

Caithness /keɪθ'nɛs/ a former county in the extreme north-east of Scotland. It became part of Highland region in 1975.

caitiff /'keɪtɪf/ ▶ **noun** archaic a contemptible or cowardly person: [as modifier] *a caitiff knight.*
– ORIGIN Middle English (denoting a captive or prisoner): from Old French *caitif* 'captive', based on Latin *captivus* '(person) taken captive' (see **CAPTIVE**).

cajole /kə'dʒəʊl/ ▶ **verb** [with obj.] (often **cajole someone into doing something**) persuade someone to do something by sustained coaxing or flattery: *he hoped to cajole her into selling him her house* | [no obj.] *she pleaded and cajoled as she tried to win his support.*
– DERIVATIVES **cajolement** noun, **cajolery** noun.
– ORIGIN mid 17th cent.: from French *cajoler.*

Cajun /'keɪdʒ(ə)n/ ▶ **noun** a member of any of the largely self-contained communities in the bayou areas of southern Louisiana formed by descendants of French Canadians, speaking an archaic form of French.
▶ **adjective** of or relating to the Cajuns, especially with reference to their folk music (typically featuring the concertina, accordion, and fiddle) or spicy cuisine.
– ORIGIN alteration of **ACADIAN**.

cajuput /'kadʒəpʌt/ (also **cajeput**) ▶ **noun 1** (also **cajuput oil**) [mass noun] an aromatic medicinal oil which is similar to eucalyptus oil, obtained from a tree of the myrtle family.
2 a chiefly Australasian tree related to the bottlebrushes, having papery bark and yielding an aromatic oil. Also called **PAPERBARK**.
● Genus *Melaleuca*, family Myrtaceae: *M. cajuputi*, which produces cajuput oil, and *M. quinquenervia.*
– ORIGIN late 18th cent.: from Malay *kayu putih*, literally 'white tree'.

cake ▶ **noun** an item of soft sweet food made from a mixture of flour, fat, eggs, sugar, and other ingredients, baked and typically iced or decorated: *a fruit cake* | [as modifier] *a cake shop* | [mass noun] *a mouthful of cake.*
■ an item of savoury food formed into a flat round shape, and typically baked or fried: *crab cakes.* ■ a flattish compact mass of something, especially soap: *a cake of soap.* ■ [with modifier] (**the cake**) figurative the amount of money or assets available in a particular context and regarded as something to be divided up or shared: *you have not received a fair slice of the education cake.*
▶ **verb** [with obj.] (usu. **be caked**) (of a thick or sticky substance that hardens when dry) cover and become encrusted on (the surface of an object): *a pair of boots caked with mud.*
■ [no obj.] (of a thick or sticky substance) dry or harden into a solid mass: *the blood under his nose was beginning to cake.*
– PHRASES **cakes and ale** dated merrymaking. **a piece of cake** informal something easily achieved: *I never said that training him would be a piece of cake.* **sell like hot cakes** informal be sold quickly and in large quantities. **you can't have your cake and eat it (too)** proverb you can't enjoy both of two desirable but mutually exclusive alternatives.
– ORIGIN Middle English (denoting a small flat bread roll): of Scandinavian origin; related to Swedish *kaka* and Danish *kage.*

cake flour ▶ **noun** North American term for **PLAIN FLOUR**.

cakehole ▶ **noun** Brit. informal a person's mouth.

cakewalk ▶ **noun 1** informal an absurdly or surprisingly easy task: *winning the league won't be a cakewalk for them.*
2 a strutting dance popular at the end of the 19th century, developed from an American black contest in graceful walking which had a cake as a prize.
▶ **verb** [no obj.] **1** informal achieve or win something easily: *he cakewalked to a 5–1 triumph.*
2 walk or dance in the manner of a cakewalk: *a troupe of clowns cakewalked by.*

CAL ▶ **abbreviation for** computer-assisted (or -aided) learning.

Cal ▶ **abbreviation for** large calorie(s).

Cal. ▶ **abbreviation for** California.

cal ▶ **abbreviation for** small calorie(s).

Calabar /'kaləbɑː/ a seaport in Nigeria; pop. 126,000 (1983).

Calabar bean ▶ **noun** the poisonous seed of a tropical West African climbing plant, containing physostigmine and formerly used for tribal ordeals.
● The plant is *Physostigma venosum*, family Leguminosae.
– ORIGIN late 19th cent.: named after **CALABAR**.

calabash /'kaləbaʃ/ ▶ **noun** (also **calabash tree**) an evergreen tropical American tree which bears fruit in the form of large woody gourds.
● *Crescentia cujete*, family Bignoniaceae.
■ a gourd from this tree. ■ a water container, tobacco pipe, or other object made from the dried shell of this or a similar gourd.
– ORIGIN mid 17th cent.: from French *calebasse*, from Spanish *calabaza*, perhaps from Persian *karbuz* 'melon'.

calabash milk ▶ **noun** [mass noun] S. African curdled milk prepared in a calabash.

calabaza /ˌkalə'baːzə/ ▶ **noun** West Indian and US term for **CALABASH**.

calaboose /ˌkalə'buːs/ ▶ **noun** US informal a prison.
– ORIGIN late 18th cent.: from black French *calabouse*, from Spanish *calabozo* 'dungeon'.

calabrese /'kaləbriːs, ˌkalə'briːs, -'breɪsɪ/ ▶ **noun** see **BROCCOLI**.
– ORIGIN 1930s: from Italian, literally 'Calabrian'.

Calabria /kə'labrɪə/ a region of SW Italy, forming the 'toe' of the Italian peninsula; capital, Reggio di Calabria.
– DERIVATIVES **Calabrian** adjective & noun.

caladium /kə'leɪdɪəm/ ▶ **noun** (pl. **caladiums**) a tropical South American plant of the arum family, which is cultivated for its brilliantly coloured ornamental foliage.
● Genus *Caladium*, family Araceae.
– ORIGIN modern Latin, from Malay *keladi.*

Calah /'keɪlə/ biblical name for **NIMRUD**.

Calais /'kaleɪ, French kalɛ/ a ferry port in northern France; pop. 75,840 (1990). Captured by Edward III in 1347 after a long siege, it remained an English possession until it was retaken by the French in 1558.

calamanco /ˌkalə'maŋkəʊ/ ▶ **noun** (pl. **-oes**) [mass noun] historical a glossy woollen cloth chequered on one side only.
– ORIGIN late 16th cent.: of unknown origin.

calamander /'kaləmandə/ (also **calamander wood**) ▶ **noun** another term for **COROMANDEL**.
– ORIGIN early 19th cent.: from Sinhalese *kalumadíriya*, perhaps from *Coromandel ebony* (see **COROMANDEL**), changed by association with Sinhalese *kalu* 'black'.

calamari /ˌkalə'mɑːri/ (also **calamares** /ˌkalə'mɑːreɪz/, **calamaries** /ˌkalə'mɑːrɪz/) ▶ **plural noun** squid served as food.
– ORIGIN Italian, plural of *calamaro*, from medieval Latin *calamarium* 'pen case', from Greek *kalamos* 'pen' (with reference to the squid's long tapering internal shell and its ink). The variant *calamares* is Spanish, *calamaries* being its Anglicized form.

calamine /'kaləmʌɪn/ ▶ **noun** [mass noun] a pink powder consisting of zinc carbonate and ferric oxide, used to make a soothing lotion or ointment.
■ dated smithsonite or a similar zinc ore.
– ORIGIN late Middle English: via Old French from medieval Latin *calamina*, alteration of Latin *cadmia* 'calamine', from Greek *kadmeia* (gē) 'Cadmean (earth)', from *Kadmos* 'Cadmus' (see **CADMUS**).

calamint /ˈkaləmɪnt/ ▶ **noun** an aromatic Eurasian herbaceous plant or shrub with blue or lilac flowers.
● Genus *Calamintha*, family Labiatae.
– ORIGIN Middle English: from Old French *calament*, from medieval Latin *calamentum*, from late Latin *calaminthe*, from Greek *kalaminthē*.

calamites /ˌkaləˈmʌɪtiːz/ ▶ **noun** a jointed-stemmed swamp plant of an extinct group related to the horsetails, growing to a height of 18 m (60 ft). Calamites are characteristic fossils of the Carboniferous coal measures.
● *Calamites* and other genera, family Calamitaceae, class Sphenopsida.
– ORIGIN modern Latin, from **CALAMUS**.

calamity ▶ **noun** (pl. **-ies**) an event causing great and often sudden damage or distress; a disaster.
■[mass noun] disaster and distress: *the journey had led to calamity and ruin.*
– DERIVATIVES **calamitous** adjective, **calamitously** adverb.
– ORIGIN late Middle English (in the sense 'disaster and distress'): from Old French *calamite*, from Latin *calamitas*.

Calamity Jane (*c.*1852–1903), American frontierswoman, noted for her skill at shooting and riding; born *Martha Jane Cannary*.

calamondin /ˌkaləˈmɒndɪn/ (also **calamondin orange**) ▶ **noun** a small hybrid citrus plant which bears fragrant white flowers followed by small orange-yellow fruit, native to the Philippines and widely grown as a house plant.
● × *Citrofortunella microcarpa* (formerly *Citrus mitis*), family Rutaceae.
– ORIGIN early 20th cent.: from Tagalog *kalamunding*.

calamus /ˈkaləməs/ ▶ **noun** (pl. **calami** /-mʌɪ/) **1** another term for **SWEET FLAG**.
■(also **calamus root**) [mass noun] a preparation of the aromatic root of the sweet flag.
2 Zoology the hollow lower part of the shaft of a feather, which lacks barbs; a quill.
– ORIGIN late Middle English (denoting a reed or an aromatic plant mentioned in the Bible): from Latin, from Greek *kalamos*. Sense 1 dates from the mid 17th cent.

calando /kəˈlandəʊ/ ▶ **adverb** Music (especially as a direction) gradually decreasing in speed and volume.
– ORIGIN Italian, literally 'slackening'.

calandra /kəˈlandrə/ (also **calandra lark**) ▶ **noun** a large Eurasian lark with a stout bill and a black patch on each side of the neck.
● Genus *Melanocorypha*, family Alaudidae: two species, in particular *M. calandra*.
– ORIGIN late 16th cent.: from Old French *calandre*, via medieval Latin from Greek *kalandros*.

calash /kəˈlaʃ/ ▶ **noun** another term for **CALECHE**.

calathea /ˌkaləˈθɪə/ ▶ **noun** a tropical American plant which typically has variegated and ornamental leaves, widely grown as a greenhouse or indoor plant.
● Genus *Calathea*, family Marantaceae: many species, including the zebra plant.
– ORIGIN modern Latin, from Greek *kalathos* 'basket'.

calc- ▶ **combining form** (used chiefly in geological terms) of lime or calcium: *calcalkaline*.
– ORIGIN from German *Kalk* 'lime', with spelling influenced by Latin *calx* 'lime' (see **CALX**).

calcalkaline /kalˈkalkəlʌɪn/ ▶ **adjective** Geology (chiefly of rocks) relatively rich in both calcium and alkali metals.

calcaneus /kalˈkeɪnɪəs/ (also **calcaneum** /-nɪəm/) ▶ **noun** (pl. **calcanei** /-nɪʌɪ/ or **calcanea** /-nɪə/) Anatomy the large bone forming the heel. It articulates with the cuboid bone of the foot and the talus bone of the ankle, and the Achilles tendon (or *tendo calcaneus*) is attached to it.
– ORIGIN mid 18th cent.: from Latin.

calcareous /kalˈkɛːrɪəs/ ▶ **adjective** containing calcium carbonate; chalky.
■Ecology (of vegetation) occurring on chalk or limestone.
– ORIGIN late 17th cent.: from Latin *calcarius* (from *calx, calc-* 'lime') + **-EOUS**.

calceolaria /ˌkalsɪəˈlɛːrɪə/ ▶ **noun** a South American plant which is cultivated for its brightly coloured slipper- or pouch-shaped flowers. Also called **SLIPPER FLOWER**.
● Genus *Calceolaria*, family Scrophulariaceae.
– ORIGIN late 18th cent.: modern Latin, from Latin *calceolus*, diminutive of *calceus* 'shoe'.

calces plural form of **CALX**.

calci- ▶ **combining form** relating to calcium or its compounds: *calcifuge*.
– ORIGIN from Latin *calx, calc-* 'lime'.

calcic /ˈkalsɪk/ ▶ **adjective** (chiefly of minerals) containing or relatively rich in calcium.

calcicole /ˈkalsɪkəʊl/ ▶ **noun** Botany a plant that grows best in calcareous soil, occurring chiefly on chalk and limestone: [as modifier] *a rich calcicole flora.*
– DERIVATIVES **calcicolous** adjective.
– ORIGIN late 19th cent.: from **CALCI-** + Latin *colere* 'inhabit'.

calciferol /kalˈsɪfərɒl/ ▶ **noun** [mass noun] Biochemistry one of the D vitamins, a sterol which is formed when its isomer ergosterol is exposed to ultraviolet light, and which is routinely added to dairy products. Also called **ERGOCALCIFEROL**, ***vitamin*** D_2.
– ORIGIN 1930s: from **CALCIFEROUS** + **-OL**.

calciferous /kalˈsɪf(ə)rəs/ ▶ **adjective** containing or producing calcium salts, especially calcium carbonate.

calcifuge /ˈkalsɪfjuːdʒ/ ▶ **noun** Botany a plant that is not suited to calcareous soil: [as modifier] *calcifuge plants such as heathers.*

calcify /ˈkalsɪfʌɪ/ ▶ **verb** (**-ies**, **-ied**) [with obj.] [usu. as adj. **calcified**] harden by deposition of or conversion into calcium carbonate or some other insoluble calcium compounds: *calcified cartilage.*
– DERIVATIVES **calcific** adjective, **calcification** noun.

calcimine /ˈkalsɪmʌɪn/ ▶ **noun** & **verb** variant spelling of **KALSOMINE**.

calcine /ˈkalsʌɪn, -sɪn/ ▶ **verb** [with obj.] [usu. as adj. **calcined**] reduce, oxidize, or desiccate by roasting or strong heat: *calcined bone ash.*
– DERIVATIVES **calcination** noun.
– ORIGIN late Middle English: from medieval Latin *calcinare*, from late Latin *calcina* 'lime', from Latin *calx, calc-* 'lime' (see **CALX**).

calcite /ˈkalsʌɪt/ ▶ **noun** [mass noun] a white or colourless mineral consisting of calcium carbonate. It is a major constituent of sedimentary rocks such as limestone, marble, and chalk, can occur in crystalline form (as in Iceland spar), and is deposited in caves to form stalactites and stalagmites.
– DERIVATIVES **calcitic** adjective.
– ORIGIN mid 19th cent.: coined in German from Latin *calx, calc-* 'lime' (see **CALX**).

calcitonin /ˌkalsɪˈtəʊnɪn/ ▶ **noun** [mass noun] Biochemistry a hormone secreted by the thyroid that has the effect of lowering blood calcium.
– ORIGIN 1960s: from **CALCI-** + **TONIC** + **-IN**[1].

calcium ▶ **noun** [mass noun] the chemical element of atomic number 20, a soft grey metal. (Symbol: **Ca**)

> Calcium is one of the alkaline earth metals. Its compounds occur naturally in limestone, fluorite, gypsum, and other minerals. Many physiological processes involve calcium ions, and calcium salts are an essential constituent of bone, teeth, and shells.

– ORIGIN early 19th cent.: from Latin *calx, calc-* 'lime' (see **CALX**) + **-IUM**.

calcium antagonist ▶ **noun** Medicine a compound of a type that reduces the influx of calcium into the cells of cardiac and smooth muscle, reducing the strength of contractions. Such drugs are used to treat angina and high blood pressure.

calcium carbonate ▶ **noun** [mass noun] a white insoluble solid occurring naturally as chalk, limestone, marble, and calcite, and forming mollusc shells and stony corals.
● Chem. formula: $CaCO_3$.

calcium hydroxide ▶ **noun** [mass noun] a soluble white crystalline solid commonly produced in the form of slaked lime.
● Chem. formula: $Ca(OH)_2$.

calcium oxide ▶ **noun** [mass noun] a white caustic alkaline solid, commonly produced in the form of quicklime.
● Chem. formula: CaO.

calcrete /ˈkalkriːt/ ▶ **noun** [mass noun] Geology a breccia or conglomerate cemented together by calcareous material, formed in soils in semi-arid conditions. Also called **CALICHE**.
– ORIGIN early 20th cent.: from **CALC-** + a shortened form of **CONCRETE**.

calculable ▶ **adjective** able to be measured or assessed.
– DERIVATIVES **calculability** noun, **calculably** adverb.

calculate ▶ **verb** [with obj.] **1** determine (the amount or number of something) mathematically: *pensions were to be calculated on the basis of workers' more poorly paid years* | [with clause] *local authorities have calculated that full training would cost around £5,000 per teacher.*
■[no obj.] (**calculate on**) include as an essential element in one's plans: *he may have calculated on maximizing pressure for policy revision.*
2 (usu. **be calculated to do something**) intend (an action) to have a particular effect: *his last words were calculated to wound her.*
■[with clause] US dialect suppose; believe: *I calculate it's pretty difficult to git edication down there.*
– DERIVATIVES **calculative** adjective.
– ORIGIN late Middle English: from late Latin *calculat-* 'counted', from the verb *calculare*, from *calculus* 'a small pebble (as used on an abacus)'.

calculated ▶ **adjective** (of an action) done with full awareness of the likely consequences: *victims of vicious and calculated assaults.*
■(of an amount or number) mathematically worked out or measured.
– DERIVATIVES **calculatedly** adverb.

calculating ▶ **adjective** acting in a scheming and ruthlessly determined way: *he was a coolly calculating, ruthless man.*
– DERIVATIVES **calculatingly** adverb.

calculation ▶ **noun** a mathematical determination of the size or number of something: *finding ways of saving money involves complicated calculations* | [mass noun] *calculation of depreciation.*
■(often **calculations**) an assessment of the risks, possibilities, or effects of a situation or course of action: *decisions are shaped by political calculations.*
– ORIGIN late Middle English: via Old French from late Latin *calculatio(n-)*, from the verb *calculare* (see **CALCULATE**).

calculator ▶ **noun** something used for making mathematical calculations, in particular a small electronic device with a keyboard and a visual display.

calculus /ˈkalkjʊləs/ ▶ **noun 1** (pl. **calculuses**) (also **infinitesimal calculus**) [mass noun] the branch of mathematics that deals with the finding and properties of derivatives and integrals of functions, by methods originally based on the summation of infinitesimal differences. The two main types are **differential calculus** and **integral calculus**.
2 (pl. **calculuses**) Mathematics & Logic a particular method or system of calculation or reasoning.
3 (pl. **calculi** /-lʌɪ, -liː/) Medicine a concretion of minerals formed within the body, especially in the kidney or gall bladder.
■another term for **TARTAR**.
– ORIGIN mid 17th cent.: from Latin, literally 'small pebble (as used on an abacus)'.

Calcutta /kalˈkʌtə/ a port and industrial centre in eastern India, capital of the state of West Bengal and the second largest city in India; pop. 10,916,000 (1991). It is situated on the Hooghly River near the Bay of Bengal. Official name (from 2000) **KOLKATA**.
– DERIVATIVES **Calcuttan** noun & adjective.

caldarium /kalˈdɛːrɪəm/ ▶ **noun** (pl. **caldaria** /-rɪə/) a hot room in an ancient Roman bath.
– ORIGIN Latin.

Caldecott /ˈkɔːldɪkɒt/, Randolph (1846–86), English graphic artist and watercolour painter. He is best known for his illustrations for children's books.

Calder /ˈkɔːldə/, Alexander (1898–1976), American sculptor and painter. He was one of the first artists to introduce movement into sculpture, making mobiles incorporating abstract forms. His static sculptures are known by contrast as 'stabiles'.

caldera /kɒlˈdɛːrə, -ˈdɪərə/ ▶ **noun** a large volcanic crater, especially one formed by a major eruption leading to the collapse of the mouth of the volcano.
– ORIGIN late 17th cent.: from Spanish, from late Latin *caldaria* 'boiling pot'.

Calderón de la Barca /ˌkaldəˌrɒn deɪ la ˈbɑːkə/, Pedro (1600–81), Spanish dramatist and poet. He wrote some 120 plays, more than seventy of them religious dramas.

caldron ▶ **noun** chiefly US variant spelling of **CAULDRON**.

Caldwell /ˈkɔːldwɛl/, Erskine (Preston) (1903–87),

American novelist and short-story writer. Notable novels: *Tobacco Road* (1932).

caleche /kəˈlɛʃ/ (also **calash**) ▶**noun** historical **1** a light low-wheeled carriage with a removable folding hood.
■Canadian a two-wheeled one-horse vehicle with a seat for the driver on the splashboard.
2 a woman's hooped silk hood.
– ORIGIN mid 17th cent.: from French *calèche*, via German from Polish *kołasa*, from *koło* 'wheel'.

Caledonian /ˌkalɪˈdəʊnɪən/ ▶**adjective 1** (chiefly in names or geographical terms) of or relating to Scotland or the Scottish Highlands: *the Caledonian Railway.*
2 Geology relating to or denoting a mountain-forming period (orogeny) in NW Europe and Greenland during the Lower Palaeozoic era, especially the late Silurian.
▶**noun 1** chiefly humorous or poetic/literary a person from Scotland.
2 (**the Caledonian**) Geology the Caledonian orogeny.
– ORIGIN from *Caledonia*, the Latin name for northern Britain, + **-AN**.

Caledonian Canal a system of lochs and canals crossing Scotland from Inverness on the east coast to Fort William on the west.

calefacient /ˌkalɪˈfeɪʃ(ə)nt/ ▶**noun** Medicine, archaic a drug or other agent causing a sensation of warmth.
– ORIGIN mid 17th cent.: from Latin *calefacient-* 'making warm', from the verb *calefacere*, from *calere* 'be warm' + *facere* 'make'.

calendar /ˈkalɪndə/ ▶**noun** a chart or series of pages showing the days, weeks, and months of a particular year, or giving particular seasonal information.
■a system by which the beginning, length, and subdivisions of the year are fixed. See also **JULIAN CALENDAR** and **GREGORIAN CALENDAR**. ■ a timetable of special days or events of a specified kind or involving a specified group: *the equestrian calendar.* ■ a list of people or events connected with particular dates, especially canonized saints and cases for trial.
▶**verb** [with obj.] enter (something) in a calendar or timetable.
– DERIVATIVES **calendric** /-ˈlɛndrɪk/ adjective, **calendrical** adjective.
– ORIGIN Middle English: from Old French *calendier*, from Latin *kalendarium* 'account book', from *kalendae* (see **CALENDS**).

calendar month ▶**noun** see **MONTH**.

calendar year ▶**noun** see **YEAR** (sense 2).

calender /ˈkalɪndə/ ▶**noun** a machine in which cloth or paper is pressed by rollers to glaze or smooth it.
▶**verb** [with obj.] press in such a machine.
– ORIGIN late 15th cent. (as a verb): from French *calendre* (noun), *calendrer* (verb), of unknown origin.

calends /ˈkalɪndz/ (also **kalends**) ▶**plural noun** the first day of the month in the ancient Roman calendar.
– ORIGIN Old English (denoting an appointed time): from Old French *calendes*, from Latin *kalendae, calendae* 'first day of the month' (when accounts were due and the order of days was proclaimed); related to Latin *calare* and Greek *kalein* 'call, proclaim'.

calendula /kəˈlɛndjʊlə/ ▶**noun** a Mediterranean plant of a genus that includes the common or pot marigold.
• Genus *Calendula*, family Compositae.
– ORIGIN modern Latin, diminutive of *calendae* (see **CALENDS**); perhaps because it flowers for most of the year.

calenture /ˈkal(ə)ntjʊə/ ▶**noun** [mass noun] feverish delirium supposedly caused by the heat in the tropics.
– ORIGIN late 16th cent.: from French, from Spanish *calentura* 'fever', from *calentar* 'be hot', based on Latin *calere* 'be warm'.

calf[1] ▶**noun** (pl. **calves**) **1** a young bovine animal, especially a domestic cow or bull in its first year.
■the young of some other large mammals, such as elephants, rhinoceroses, large deer and antelopes, and whales. ■ short for **CALFSKIN**.
2 a floating piece of ice detached from an iceberg.
– PHRASES **in** (or **with**) **calf** (of a cow) pregnant.
– DERIVATIVES **calf-like** adjective.
– ORIGIN Old English *cælf*, of Germanic origin; related to Dutch *kalf* and German *Kalb*.

calf[2] ▶**noun** (pl. **calves**) the fleshy part at the back of a person's leg below the knee.
– ORIGIN Middle English: from Old Norse *kálfi*, of unknown origin.

calf love ▶**noun** another term for **PUPPY LOVE**.

calfskin ▶**noun** [mass noun] leather made from the hide or skin of a calf, used chiefly in bookbinding and shoemaking.

Calgary /ˈkalgəri/ a city in southern Alberta, SW Canada; pop. 710,680 (1991).

Cali /ˈkɑːli/ an industrial city in western Colombia; pop. 1,624,400 (1992).

calibrate /ˈkalɪbreɪt/ ▶**verb** [with obj.] (often **be calibrated**) mark (a gauge or instrument) with a standard scale of readings.
■correlate the readings of (an instrument) with those of a standard in order to check the instrument's accuracy. ■ adjust (experimental results) to take external factors into account or to allow comparison with other data.
– DERIVATIVES **calibrator** noun.
– ORIGIN mid 19th cent.: from **CALIBRE** + **-ATE**[3].

calibration ▶**noun** [mass noun] the action or process of calibrating an instrument or experimental readings: *the measuring devices require calibration* | [count noun] *calibrations in the field of electronic measurements.*
■[count noun] each of a set of graduations on an instrument.

calibre /ˈkalɪbə/ (US **caliber**) ▶**noun 1** [mass noun] the quality of someone's character or the level of their ability: *they could ill afford to lose a man of his calibre.*
■the standard reached by something: *educational facilities of a very high calibre.*
2 the internal diameter or bore of a gun barrel: [in combination] *a .22 calibre repeater rifle.*
■the diameter of a bullet, shell, or rocket. ■ the diameter of a body of circular section, such as a tube, blood vessel, or fibre.
– DERIVATIVES **calibred** adjective [also in combination].
– ORIGIN mid 16th cent. (in the sense 'social standing or importance'): from French, from Italian *calibro*, perhaps from Arabic *ḳālib* 'mould', based on Greek *kalapous* 'shoemaker's last'.

caliche /kəˈliːtʃi/ ▶**noun** [mass noun] a mineral deposit of gravel, sand, and nitrates, found in dry areas of America.
■another term for **CALCRETE**.
– ORIGIN mid 19th cent.: from Latin American Spanish.

calico /ˈkalɪkəʊ/ ▶**noun** (pl. **-oes** or US also **-os**) [mass noun] Brit. a type of cotton cloth, typically plain white or unbleached: [as modifier] *a calico dress.*
■N. Amer. printed cotton fabric.
▶**adjective** N. Amer. (of an animal, typically a cat) multicoloured or piebald.
– ORIGIN mid 16th cent. (originally also *calicut*): alteration of **CALICUT**, where the fabric originated.

Calicut /ˈkalɪkʌt/ a seaport in the state of Kerala in SW India, on the Malabar Coast; pop. 420,000 (1991). Also called **KOZHIKODE**.

Calif. ▶**abbreviation for** California.

California a state of the US, on the Pacific coast; pop. 29,760,000 (1990); capital, Sacramento. Formerly part of Mexico, it was ceded to the US in 1847, and became the 31st state of the US in 1850.
– DERIVATIVES **Californian** adjective & noun.

California, Gulf of an arm of the Pacific Ocean separating the Baja California peninsula from mainland Mexico.

California Current a cold ocean current of the eastern Pacific that flows south along the west coast of North America.

California poppy (also **Californian poppy**) ▶**noun** an annual poppy native to western North America, which is cultivated for its brilliant yellow or orange flowers.
• *Eschscholtzia californica*, family Papaveraceae.

California sheepshead ▶**noun** see **SHEEPSHEAD**.

californium /ˌkalɪˈfɔːnɪəm/ ▶**noun** [mass noun] the chemical element of atomic number 98, a radioactive metal of the actinide series, first produced by bombarding curium with helium ions. (Symbol: **Cf**)
– ORIGIN 1950s: named after *California University* (where it was first made) + **-IUM**.

Caligula /kəˈlɪgjʊlə/ (AD 12–41), Roman emperor 37–41; born *Gaius Julius Caesar Germanicus*. His reign was notorious for its tyrannical excesses.

caliper /ˈkalɪpə/ (also **calliper**) ▶**noun 1** (**calipers**) an instrument for measuring external or internal dimensions, having two hinged legs resembling a pair of compasses and in-turned or out-turned points.
■(also **caliper rule**) an instrument performing a similar function but having one linear component sliding along another, with two parallel jaws and a vernier scale. ■ (also **brake caliper**) a motor-vehicle or bicycle brake consisting of two or more hinged components.
2 (also **caliper splint**) a metal support for a person's leg.
– ORIGIN late 16th cent.: apparently an alteration of **CALIBRE**.

caliph /ˈkeɪlɪf, ˈka-/ ▶**noun** historical the chief Muslim civil and religious ruler, regarded as the successor of Muhammad. The caliph ruled in Baghdad until 1258 and then in Egypt until the Ottoman conquest of 1517; the title was then held by the Ottoman sultans until it was abolished in 1924 by Atatürk.
– DERIVATIVES **caliphate** noun.
– ORIGIN late Middle English: from Old French *caliphe*, from Arabic *ḵalīfa* meaning 'deputy (of God)' (from the title *ḵalīfat Allāh*), or meaning 'successor (of Muhammad)' (from the title *ḵalīfat rasūl Allāh* 'of the Messenger of God'), from *ḵalamfa* 'succeed'.

calisthenics ▶**plural noun** US spelling of **CALLISTHENICS**.

calix ▶**noun** variant spelling of **CALYX**.

calk ▶**noun** & **verb** US spelling of **CAULK**.

call ▶**verb 1** [with obj.] cry out to (someone) in order to summon them or attract their attention: *she heard Terry calling her* | *she called the children in from the meadow* | [no obj.] *I distinctly heard you call.*
■cry out (a word or words): *he heard an insistent voice calling his name* | *Meredith was already* ***calling out*** *a greeting.* ■ shout out or chant (the steps and figures) to people performing a square dance or country dance. ■ [no obj.] (of an animal, especially a bird) make its characteristic cry. ■ telephone (a person or telephone number): *could I* ***call you back?*** ■ summon (something, especially an emergency service or a taxi) by telephone: *if you are suspicious, call the police.* ■ bring (a witness) into court to give evidence. ■ [with obj. and infinitive] archaic inspire or urge (someone) to do something: *I am called to preach the Gospel.* ■ fix a date or time for (a meeting, strike, or election). ■ Bridge make (a particular bid) during the auction: *her partner called 6♠.* ■ [no obj.] guess the outcome of tossing a coin: *'You call,' he said. 'Heads or tails?'* ■ predict the result of (a future event, especially an election or a vote): *in the Midlands the race remains too close to call.* ■ Cricket (of an umpire) no-ball (a bowler) for throwing. ■ Computing cause the execution of (a subroutine).
2 [no obj., with adverbial of place] (of a person) pay a brief visit: *I've got to call at the bank to get some cash* | *he had promised Celia he would call in at the clinic.*
■(**call for**) stop to collect (someone) at the place where they are living or working: *I'll call for you around seven.* ■ (**call at**) (of a train or coach) stop at (a specified station or stations) on a particular route: *the 8.15 service to Paddington, calling at Reading.*
3 [with obj. and complement] give (an infant or animal) a specified name: *they called their daughter Hannah.*
■address or refer to (someone) by a specified name, title, endearment, or term of abuse: *please call me Lucy.* ■ refer to, consider, or describe (someone or something) as being: *he's the only person I would call a friend.* ■ (of an umpire or other official in a game) pronounce (a ball, stroke, or other action) to be the thing specified: *the linesman called the ball wide.*
▶**noun 1** a cry made as a summons or to attract someone's attention: *in response to the call, a figure appeared.*
■the characteristic cry of a bird or other animal. ■ [with modifier] a series of notes sounded on a brass instrument as a signal to do something: *a bugle call to rise at 8.30.* ■ a telephone communication or conversation: *I'll give you a call at around five.* ■ (**a call for**) an appeal or demand for: *the call for action was welcomed.* ■ a summons: *a messenger arrived bringing news of his call to the throne.* ■ [in sing., with infinitive] a vocation: *his call to be a disciple.* ■ [in sing.] a powerful force of attraction: *walkers can't resist the call of the Cairngorms.* ■ [usu. with negative] (**a call for**) a demand or need for (goods or services): *there is little call for antique furniture.* ■ a shout by an official in a game indicating that the ball has gone out of play or that

a rule has been breached; the decision or ruling so made. ■ Bridge a bid, response, or double. ■ a direction in a square dance given by the caller. ■ a demand for payment of lent or unpaid capital. ■ Stock Exchange short for **CALL OPTION**.

2 a brief visit: *we **paid a call on** an elderly Spaniard.* ■ a visit or journey made in response to an emergency appeal for help: *the doctor was out on a call.*

– PHRASES **at call** another way of saying ***on call*** (sense 2). **call attention to** cause people to notice: *he is a seeking to call attention to himself by his crimes.* **call someone's bluff** see **BLUFF**[1]. **call collect** N. Amer. make a telephone call reversing the charges. **call something into play** cause or require something to start working so that one can make use of it: *our active participation as spectators is called into play.* **call something into** (or **in**) **question** cast doubt on something: *these findings call into question the legitimacy of the proceedings.* **call it a day** see **DAY**. **call someone names** see **NAME**. **call of nature** see **NATURE**. **call the shots** (or **tune**) take the initiative in deciding how something should be done. **call a spade a spade** see **SPADE**[1]. **call someone to account** see **ACCOUNT**. **call someone/thing to mind** cause one to think of someone or something, especially through similarity: *the still lifes call to mind certain of Cézanne's works.* ■ [with negative] remember someone or something: [with clause] *I cannot call to mind where I have seen you.* **call someone/thing to order** ask those present at a meeting to be silent so that business may proceed. **don't call us, we'll call you** informal used as a dismissive way of saying that someone has not been successful in an audition or a job application. **on call 1** (of a person) able to be contacted in order to provide a professional service if necessary, but not formally on duty: *your local GP may be on call round the clock.* **2** (of money lent) repayable on demand. **to call one's own** used to describe something that one can genuinely feel belongs to one: *I had not an item to call my own.* **within call** near enough to be summoned by calling: *she moved into the guest room, **within call of** her father's room.*

– ORIGIN late Old English *ceallian*, from Old Norse *kalla* 'summon loudly'.

▶**call for** make necessary: *desperate times call for desperate measures.* ■ draw attention to the need for: *the report calls for an audit of endangered species.*

call something forth elicit a response: *few things call forth more compassion.*

call someone/thing down 1 cause or provoke someone or something to appear or occur: *nothing called down the wrath of Nemesis quicker.* **2** dated reprimand someone.

call someone in enlist someone's aid or services.

call something in require payment of a loan or promise of money.

call someone/thing off order a person or dog to stop attacking someone.

call something off cancel an event or agreement.

call on 1 pay a visit to (someone): *he's planning to call on Katherine today.* **2** (also **call upon**) have recourse to: *we are able to call on academic staff with a wide variety of expertise.* ■ [with infinitive] demand that (someone) do something: *he called on the government to hold a plebiscite.*

call someone out 1 summon someone, especially to deal with an emergency or to do repairs. **2** order or advise workers to strike. **3** archaic challenge someone to a duel.

call something over dated read out a list of names to determine those present.

call someone up 1 informal telephone someone. **2** summon someone to serve in the army: *they have called up more than 20,000 reservists.* ■ select someone to play in a team: *he was called up for the international against Turkey.*

call something up summon for use something that is stored or kept available: *icons which allow you to call up a graphic.* ■ figurative evoke something: *the imaginative intensity with which he called up the Devon landscape.*

calla /ˈkalə/ ▶ **noun** either of two plants of the arum family:
● (also **water calla**) another term for **BOG ARUM**. ● (usu. **calla lily**) chiefly N. Amer. another term for **ARUM LILY**.
– ORIGIN early 19th cent.: modern Latin.

Callaghan /ˈkaləhan/, (Leonard) James, Baron Callaghan of Cardiff (b.1912), British Labour statesman, Prime Minister 1976–9.

callaloo /ˌkaləˈluː/ (also **callalou**) ▶ **noun 1** [mass noun] the spinach-like leaves of a tropical American plant, widely used in Caribbean cookery.
■ a soup or stew made with such leaves.
2 the plant of the arum family from which these leaves are obtained.
● Genus *Xanthosoma*, family Araceae.
– ORIGIN mid 18th cent.: from American Spanish *calalú*.

Callanetics /ˌkaləˈnɛtɪks/ ▶ **plural noun** [treated as sing. or pl.] trademark a system of physical exercises based on small repeated movements.
– ORIGIN late 20th cent.: named after *Callan* Pinckney (born 1939), American deviser of the system, perhaps on the pattern of *athletics*.

Callao /kaˈjaʊ/ the principal seaport of Peru; pop. 369,770 (1993).

Callas /ˈkaləs/, Maria (1923–77), American-born operatic soprano, of Greek parentage; born *Maria Cecilia Anna Kalageropoulos*. She was a coloratura soprano whose bel canto style of singing was especially suited to early Italian opera.

callback ▶ **noun 1** chiefly N. Amer. an invitation to return for a second audition or interview.
2 a telephone call made to return one that someone has received.
3 [mass noun] a security feature used by some computer systems accessed by telephone, in which a user must log on from a previously registered phone number, to which the system then places a return call.

call box ▶ **noun** Brit. a public telephone booth.

call boy ▶ **noun** a person in a theatre who summons actors when they are due on stage.

call changes ▶ **plural noun** Bell-ringing changes rung in response to spoken commands.

caller ▶ **noun 1** a person who pays a brief visit or makes a telephone call.
2 a person who calls out numbers in a game of bingo or directions in a dance.
■ Austral./NZ a racing or sports commentator.

caller ID ▶ **noun** [mass noun] a facility that identifies and displays the telephone numbers of incoming calls made to a particular line.

call girl ▶ **noun** a female prostitute who accepts appointments by telephone.

Callicrates /kəˈlɪkrətiːz/ (5th century BC), Greek architect. He was the leading architect in Periclean Athens, and with Ictinus designed the Parthenon (447–438 BC).

calligraph /ˈkalɪgrɑːf/ ▶ **verb** [with obj.] (usu. **be calligraphed**) write in calligraphic style: *invitations meticulously calligraphed in black ink.*
– ORIGIN mid 19th cent. (as a noun): from French *calligraphe*, via medieval Latin from Greek *kalligraphos* (see **CALLIGRAPHY**). The verb dates from the late 19th cent.

calligraphic ▶ **adjective** of or relating to calligraphy: *a calligraphic pen | calligraphic script.*
■ resembling lettering in shape.

calligraphy ▶ **noun** [mass noun] decorative handwriting or handwritten lettering.
■ the art of producing decorative handwriting or lettering with a pen or brush.
– DERIVATIVES **calligrapher** noun, **calligraphist** noun.
– ORIGIN early 17th cent.: from Greek *kalligraphia*, from *kalligraphos* 'person who writes beautifully', from *kallos* 'beauty' + *graphein* 'write'.

Callimachus /kəˈlɪməkəs/ (c.305–c.240 BC), Greek poet and scholar. He is famed for his hymns and epigrams, and was head of the library at Alexandria.

calling ▶ **noun 1** [mass noun] the loud cries or shouts of an animal or person: *the calling of a cuckoo.*
2 [in sing.] a strong urge towards a particular way of life or career; a vocation: *those who have a special calling to minister to others' needs.*
■ a profession or occupation: *he considered engineering one of the highest possible callings.*

calling bell ▶ **noun** Indian a doorbell.

calling card ▶ **noun 1** chiefly N. Amer. a visiting card or business card.
■ figurative an action or the result of an action by which someone or something can be identified: *the explosion was a taunting calling card from the terrorists.*
2 N. Amer. a phonecard or telephone charge card.

Calliope /kəˈlʌɪəpi/ Greek & Roman Mythology the Muse of epic poetry.
– ORIGIN from Greek *Kalliopē*, literally 'having a beautiful voice'.

calliope /kəˈlʌɪəpi/ ▶ **noun** chiefly historical an American keyboard instrument resembling an organ but with the notes produced by steam whistles, used chiefly on showboats and in travelling fairs.
– ORIGIN mid 19th cent.: from the Greek name *Kalliopē* (see **CALLIOPE**).

calliper /ˈkalɪpə/ ▶ **noun** variant spelling of **CALIPER**.

callipygian /ˌkalɪˈpɪdʒɪən/ (also **callipygean**) ▶ **adjective** having well-shaped buttocks.
– DERIVATIVES **callipygous** /ˌkalɪˈpɪdʒəs, ˌkalɪˈpʌɪdʒəs/ adjective.
– ORIGIN late 18th cent.: from Greek *kallipūgos* (used to describe a famous statue of Venus), from *kallos* 'beauty' + *pūgē* 'buttocks', + **-IAN**.

callistemon /ˌkalɪˈstiːmən/ ▶ **noun** a plant of a genus that comprises the bottlebrushes.
● Genus *Callistemon*, family Myrtaceae.
– ORIGIN modern Latin, from Greek *kallos* 'beauty' + *stēmōn* 'thread or stamen'.

callisthenics /ˌkalɪsˈθɛnɪks/ (US **calisthenics**) ▶ **plural noun** gymnastic exercises to achieve bodily fitness and grace of movement.
– DERIVATIVES **callisthenic** adjective.
– ORIGIN early 19th cent.: from Greek *kallos* 'beauty' + *sthenos* 'strength' + **-ICS**.

Callisto /kəˈlɪstəʊ/ **1** Greek Mythology a nymph who was changed into a bear by Zeus. See also **URSA MAJOR**.
2 Astronomy one of the Galilean moons of Jupiter, the eighth closest satellite to the planet, icy with a dark, cratered surface (diameter 4,800 km).

callitrichid /ˌkalɪˈtrʌɪkɪd/ ▶ **noun** Zoology a primate of a family (Callitrichidae or Callithricidae) that comprises the marmosets and tamarins.
– ORIGIN late 18th cent.: from modern Latin *Callitrichidae* (plural), from Greek *kallitrikhos* 'beautiful-haired'.

call letters ▶ **plural noun** chiefly US a sequence of letters used by a television or radio station as an identifying code.

call money ▶ **noun** [mass noun] money loaned by a bank or other institution which is repayable on demand.

call note ▶ **noun** the characteristic call of a particular bird.

callop /ˈkaləp/ ▶ **noun** an edible deep-bodied gold and green freshwater fish found in Australia. Also called **GOLDEN PERCH**.
● *Plectroplites ambiguus*, family Serranidae.
– ORIGIN 1920s: perhaps from an Aboriginal language of southern Australia.

call option ▶ **noun** Stock Exchange an option to buy assets at an agreed price on or before a particular date.

callosity /kəˈlɒsɪti/ ▶ **noun** (pl. **-ies**) technical a thickened and hardened part of the skin; a callus.
– ORIGIN late Middle English: from French *callosité*, from Latin *callositas*, from *callosus* 'hard-skinned', from *callum*, *callus* 'hardened skin'.

callous ▶ **adjective** showing or having an insensitive and cruel disregard for others: *his callous comments about the murder made me shiver.*
▶ **noun** variant spelling of **CALLUS**.
– DERIVATIVES **callously** adverb, **callousness** noun.
– ORIGIN late Middle English (in the Latin sense): from Latin *callosus* 'hard-skinned'.

calloused (also **callused**) ▶ **adjective** (of a part of the body) having an area of hardened skin: *a calloused palm.*

call-out ▶ **noun** an instance of being summoned, especially in order to deal with an emergency or to do repairs: [as modifier] *a call-out charge.*

call-over ▶ **noun** Brit. dated a roll-call at school.

callow ▶ **adjective** (especially of a young person) inexperienced and immature: *earnest and callow undergraduates.*
– DERIVATIVES **callowly** adverb, **callowness** noun.
– ORIGIN Old English *calu* 'bald', of West Germanic origin, probably from Latin *calvus* 'bald'. This was extended to mean 'unfledged', which led to the present sense 'immature'.

Calloway /ˈkaləweɪ/, Cab (1907–94), American jazz singer and bandleader; full name *Cabell Calloway*. He was famous for his style of scat singing, for his flamboyant appearance, and for songs such as 'Minnie the Moocher' (1931).

call sign (also **call signal**) ▶ **noun** a message, code, or tune that is broadcast by radio to identify the broadcaster or transmitter.

calluna /kəˈluːnə/ ▶ **noun** [mass noun] the common heather of Europe and Asia Minor.
– ORIGIN early 19th cent.: modern Latin, from Greek *kallunein* 'beautify, sweep clean' (from *kallos* 'beauty'). The notion of 'sweeping' is also seen in the noun **BROOM**, besoms being originally made of twigs of heather or broom.

call-up ▶ **noun** [in sing.] an act of summoning someone or of being summoned to serve in the armed forces or a sports team: [as modifier] *my call-up papers.*

callus /ˈkaləs/ (also **callous**) ▶ **noun** a thickened and hardened part of the skin or soft tissue, especially in an area that has been subjected to friction.
■ Medicine the bony healing tissue which forms around the ends of broken bone. ■ Botany a hard formation of tissue, especially new tissue formed over a wound.
– ORIGIN mid 16th cent.: from Latin *callus* (more commonly *callum*) 'hardened skin'.

callused ▶ **adjective** variant spelling of **CALLOUSED**.

call waiting ▶ **noun** [mass noun] a service whereby someone making a telephone call is notified of an incoming call on the line that they are already using, typically one that allows the first call to be placed on hold while the second is answered.

calm ▶ **adjective 1** (of a person, action, or manner) not showing or feeling nervousness, anger, or other emotions: ***keep calm,*** *she told herself* | *his voice was calm.*
■ (of a place) peaceful, especially in contrast to recent violent activity: *the city was reported to be calm, but army patrols remained.*
2 (of the weather) pleasantly free from wind: *the night was clear and calm.*
■ (of the sea) not disturbed by large waves.
▶ **noun** [mass noun] **1** the absence of violent or confrontational activity within a place or group: *the elections proceeded in an atmosphere of relative calm* | [in sing.] *an edgy calm reigned in the capital.*
■ the absence of nervousness, agitation, or excitement in a person: *his usual calm deserted him.*
2 the absence of wind: *in the centre of the storm calm prevailed.*
■ still air represented by force 0 on the Beaufort scale (less than 1 knot or 1 kph). ■ [count noun] (often **calms**) an area of the sea without wind.
▶ **verb** [with obj.] make (someone) tranquil and quiet; soothe: *I took him inside and tried to* ***calm*** *him* ***down*** | [as adj. **calming**] *a cup of tea will have a calming effect.*
■ [no obj.] (**calm down**) (of a person) become tranquil and quiet: *gradually I calmed down and lost my anxiety.*
– PHRASES **the calm before the storm** see **STORM**.
– DERIVATIVES **calmly** adverb, **calmness** noun.
– ORIGIN late Middle English: via one of the Romance languages from Greek *kauma* 'heat (of the day)'.

calmative /ˈkɑːmətɪv, ˈkal-/ ▶ **adjective** (of a drug) having a sedative effect.
▶ **noun** a calmative drug.

calmodulin /kalˈmɒdjʊlɪn/ ▶ **noun** [mass noun] Biochemistry a protein which binds calcium and is involved in regulating a variety of activities in cells.
– ORIGIN 1970s: from *cal(cium)* + *modul(ate)* + **-IN**[1].

calomel /ˈkaləmɛl/ ▶ **noun** mercurous chloride, a white powder formerly used as a purgative.
• Chem. formula: Hg_2Cl_2.
– ORIGIN late 17th cent.: modern Latin, perhaps from Greek *kalos* 'beautiful' + *melas* 'black' (perhaps because it was originally obtained from a black mixture of mercury and mercuric chloride).

Calor gas /ˈkalə/ ▶ **noun** [mass noun] Brit. trademark liquefied butane stored under pressure in portable containers, used domestically as a substitute for mains gas and in camping as a portable fuel.
– ORIGIN 1930s: *Calor* from Latin *calor* 'heat'.

caloric /kəˈlɒrɪk, ˈkalərɪk/ ▶ **adjective** chiefly N. Amer. or technical of or relating to heat; calorific: *a caloric value of 7 calories per gram.*
▶ **noun** [mass noun] Physics, historical (in the late 18th and early 19th centuries) a hypothetical fluid substance that was thought to be responsible for the phenomena of heat.
– DERIVATIVES **calorically** adverb.
– ORIGIN late 18th cent. (as a noun): from French *calorique*, from Latin *calor* 'heat'.

calorie ▶ **noun** (pl. **-ies**) either of two units of heat energy:
■ (also **small calorie**) (abbrev.: **cal**) the energy needed to raise the temperature of 1 gram of water through 1 °C (now usually defined as 4.1868 joules). ■ (also **large calorie**) (abbrev.: **Cal**) the energy needed to raise the temperature of 1 kilogram of water through 1 °C, equal to one thousand small calories and often used to measure the energy value of foods.
– ORIGIN mid 19th cent.: from French, from Latin *calor* 'heat' + French suffix *-ie* (see **-Y**[3]).

calorific ▶ **adjective** chiefly Brit. relating to the amount of energy contained in food or fuel: *she knew the calorific contents of every morsel.*
■ (of food or drink) containing many calories and so likely to be fattening: *there is fruit salad for those who can resist the more calorific concoctions.*
– DERIVATIVES **calorifically** adverb.
– ORIGIN late 17th cent.: from Latin *calorificus*, from *calor* 'heat'.

calorific value ▶ **noun** the energy contained in a fuel or food, determined by measuring the heat produced by the complete combustion of a specified quantity of it. This is now usually expressed in joules per kilogram.

calorimeter /ˌkaləˈrɪmɪtə/ ▶ **noun** an apparatus for measuring the amount of heat involved in a chemical reaction or other process.
– DERIVATIVES **calorimetric** adjective, **calorimetry** noun.
– ORIGIN late 18th cent.: from Latin *calor* 'heat' + **-METER**.

calotype /ˈkalətʌɪp/ (also **calotype process**) ▶ **noun** [mass noun] historical an early photographic process in which negatives were made using paper coated with silver iodide.
– ORIGIN mid 19th cent.: from Greek *kalos* 'beautiful' + **TYPE**.

calque /kalk/ Linguistics ▶ **noun** another term for **LOAN TRANSLATION**.
▶ **verb** (**be calqued on**) originate or function as a loan translation of.
– ORIGIN 1930s: from French, literally 'copy, tracing', from *calquer* 'to trace', via Italian from Latin *calcare* 'to tread'.

caltrop /ˈkaltrəp/ (also **caltrap**) ▶ **noun 1** a spiked metal ball thrown on the ground to impede wheeled vehicles or (formerly) cavalry horses.
2 a creeping plant with woody carpels that typically have hard spines and resemble military caltrops.
• Genus *Tribulus*, family Zygophyllaceae.
3 (also **water caltrop**) another term for **WATER CHESTNUT** (in sense 3).
– ORIGIN Old English *calcatrippe*, denoting any plant which tended to catch the feet, from medieval Latin *calcatrippa*, from *calx* 'heel' or *calcare* 'to tread' + a word related to **TRAP**[1]. Sense 1 was probably adopted from French.

calumet /ˈkaljʊmɛt/ ▶ **noun** a North American Indian peace pipe.
– ORIGIN late 17th cent.: from French, from late Latin *calamellus* 'little reed', diminutive of Latin *calamus* (referring to the pipe's reed stem).

calumniate /kəˈlʌmnɪeɪt/ ▶ **verb** [with obj.] formal make false and defamatory statements about: *he has been calumniating the Crown and all the conservative decencies.*
– DERIVATIVES **calumniation** noun, **calumniator** noun.
– ORIGIN mid 16th cent.: from Latin *calumniari*, from *calumnia* (see **CALUMNY**).

calumny /ˈkaləmni/ ▶ **noun** (pl. **-ies**) [mass noun] the making of false and defamatory statements about someone in order to damage their reputation; slander.
▶ **verb** (**-ies, -ied**) [with obj.] formal slander (someone).
– DERIVATIVES **calumnious** /kəˈlʌmnɪəs/ adjective.
– ORIGIN late Middle English: from Latin *calumnia*.

calutron /kəˈluːtrɒn/ ▶ **noun** a device that uses large electromagnets to separate uranium isotopes from uranium ore. It was developed in the 1940s to produce highly enriched weapons-grade uranium.
– ORIGIN from *Cal(ifornia) U(niversity) (cyclo)tron.*

Calvados /ˈkalvədɒs/ ▶ **noun** [mass noun] apple brandy, traditionally made in the Calvados region of Normandy.

Calvary /ˈkalv(ə)ri/ the hill outside Jerusalem on which Christ was crucified.
■ [as noun **a calvary**] a sculpture or picture representing the scene of the Crucifixion.
– ORIGIN from late Latin *calvaria* 'skull', translation of Greek *golgotha* 'place of a skull' (Matt. 27:33) (see **GOLGOTHA**).

calve ▶ **verb 1** [no obj.] (of cows and certain other large animals) give birth to a calf.
■ [with obj.] (of a person) help (a cow) give birth to a calf.
2 [with obj.] (of an iceberg or glacier) split and shed (a smaller mass of ice).
■ [no obj.] (of a mass of ice) split off from an iceberg or glacier.
– ORIGIN Old English *calfian*, from *cælf* 'calf'.

calves plural form of **CALF**[1], **CALF**[2].

Calvin[1], John (1509–64), French Protestant theologian and reformer. On becoming a Protestant he fled to Switzerland, where he attempted to reorder society on reformed Christian principles and established the first Presbyterian government, in Geneva. His *Institutes of the Christian Religion* (1536) was the first systematic account of reformed Christian doctrine.

Calvin[2], Melvin (1911–97), American biochemist, who investigated photosynthesis and discovered the cycle of reactions (the **Calvin cycle**) which constitute the dark reaction. Nobel Prize for Chemistry (1961).

Calvinism ▶ **noun** [mass noun] the Protestant theological system of John Calvin and his successors, which develops Luther's doctrine of justification by faith alone into an emphasis on the grace of God and centres on the doctrine of predestination.
– DERIVATIVES **Calvinist** noun, **Calvinistic** adjective, **Calvinistical** adjective.

Calvino /kalˈviːnəʊ/, Italo (1923–87), Italian novelist and short-story writer, born in Cuba. His later works, such as *If on a Winter's Night a Traveller* (1979), are associated with magic realism.

calx /kalks/ ▶ **noun** (pl. **calces** /ˈkalsiːz/) Chemistry, archaic a powdery metallic oxide formed when an ore or mineral has been heated.
– ORIGIN late Middle English: from Latin, 'lime', probably from Greek *khalix* 'pebble, limestone'.

Calypso /kəˈlɪpsəʊ/ Greek Mythology a nymph who kept Odysseus on her island, Ogygia, for seven years.
– ORIGIN Greek, literally 'she who conceals'.

calypso /kəˈlɪpsəʊ/ ▶ **noun** (pl. **-os**) [mass noun] a kind of West Indian (originally Trinidadian) music in syncopated African rhythm, typically with words improvised on a topical theme.
■ [count noun] a song in this style.
– DERIVATIVES **calypsonian** adjective & noun.
– ORIGIN 1930s: of unknown origin.

calyx /ˈkalɪks, ˈkeɪ-/ (also **calix**) ▶ **noun** (pl. **calyces** /-lɪsiːz/ or **calyxes**) **1** Botany the sepals of a flower, typically forming a whorl that encloses the petals and forms a protective layer around a flower in bud. Compare with **COROLLA**.
2 Zoology a cup-like cavity or structure, in particular:
■ a portion of the pelvis of a mammalian kidney. ■ the cavity in a calcareous coral skeleton that surrounds the polyp. ■ the plated body of a crinoid, excluding the stalk and arms.
– ORIGIN late 17th cent.: from Latin, from Greek *kalux* 'case of a bud, husk', related to *kaluptein* 'to hide'.

calzone /kalˈtsəʊneɪ, -ni,/ ▶ **noun** (pl. **calzoni** or **calzones**) a type of pizza that is folded in half before cooking to contain a filling.
– ORIGIN Italian dialect, probably a special use of *calzone* 'trouser leg', with reference to the shape of the pizza.

CAM ▶ **abbreviation for** computer aided manufacturing.

cam ▶ **noun** a projection on a rotating part in machinery, designed to make sliding contact with another part while rotating and impart reciprocal or variable motion to it.
■ short for **CAMSHAFT**. ■ short for **CAMERA**[1].
– ORIGIN late 18th cent.: from Dutch *kam* 'comb', as in *kamrad* 'cog wheel'.

cama /ˈcɑːmə/ ▶ **noun** a hybrid animal produced by crossing a camel with a llama, which is said to possess the best features of both animals.

camaraderie /ˌkaməˈrɑːd(ə)ri, -riː/ ▶ **noun** [mass noun] mutual trust and friendship among people who

spend a lot of time together: *the enforced camaraderie of office life.*
– ORIGIN mid 19th cent.: from French, from *camarade* 'comrade'.

Camargue /kəˈmɑːg, French kamarg/ (**the Camargue**) a region of the Rhône delta in SE France, characterized by numerous shallow salt lagoons. The region is known for its white horses and as a nature reserve.

camarilla /ˌkaməˈrɪl(j)ə/ ▶ noun a small group of people, especially a group of advisers to a ruler or politician, with a shared, typically nefarious, purpose: *Stalin and his camarilla.*
– ORIGIN mid 19th cent.: from Spanish, diminutive of *camara* 'chamber'.

camas /kəˈmas/ (also **camass** or **quamash**) ▶ noun a North American plant of the lily family, cultivated for its starry blue or purple flowers.
● Genera *Camassia* and *Zigadenus*, family Liliaceae: several species, including *C. quamash*, the large bulbs of which are used as food by some American Indians.
– ORIGIN mid 19th cent.: from Chinook Jargon *kamass*, perhaps from Nootka.

Cambay, Gulf of /kamˈbeɪ/ (also **Gulf of Khambat**) an inlet of the Arabian Sea on the Gujarat coast of western India, north of Bombay.

camber /ˈkambə/ ▶ noun a slightly convex or arched shape of a road or other horizontal surface: *a flat roof should have a slight camber to allow water to run off.*
■ Brit. a tilt built into a road at a bend or curve, enabling vehicles to maintain speed. ■ [mass noun] the slight sideways inclination of the front wheels of a motor vehicle. ■ the extent of curvature of a section of an aerofoil.
– DERIVATIVES **cambered** adjective.
– ORIGIN late Middle English: from Old French *cambre*, dialect variant of *chambre* 'arched', from Latin *camurus* 'curved inwards'.

Camberwell beauty ▶ noun Brit. a migratory butterfly with deep purple yellow-bordered wings, which is a rare visitor to Britain.
● *Nymphalis antiopa*, subfamily Nymphalinae, family Nymphalidae. North American name: **mourning cloak**.
– ORIGIN mid 19th cent.: named after *Camberwell* in London, then a village, where the first specimens were captured.

cambium /ˈkambɪəm/ ▶ noun (pl. **cambia** or **cambiums**) [mass noun] Botany a cellular plant tissue from which phloem, xylem, or cork grows by division, resulting (in woody plants) in secondary thickening.
– DERIVATIVES **cambial** adjective.
– ORIGIN late 16th cent. (denoting one of the alimentary humours once supposed to nourish the body): from medieval Latin, 'change, exchange'.

Cambodia /kamˈbəʊdɪə/ a country in SE Asia between Thailand and southern Vietnam; pop. 8,660,000 (est. 1991); official language, Khmer; capital, Phnom Penh. Also officially called the **KHMER REPUBLIC** (1970–5) and **KAMPUCHEA** (1976–89).

The country was made a French protectorate in 1863 and remained under French influence until it became fully independent in 1953. During the Vietnam War it was bombed and invaded by US forces, and then, following a civil war (1970–5), came under the control of the Khmer Rouge; more than 2 million Cambodians died before the regime was toppled by a Vietnamese invasion in 1979.

Cambodian ▶ adjective of or relating to Cambodia, its people, or their language.
▶ noun 1 a native or national of Cambodia, or a person of Cambodian descent.
2 another term for **KHMER** (the language).

cambozola /ˌkambəˈzəʊlə/ (also **cambazola**) ▶ noun [mass noun] trademark a type of German blue soft cheese with a rind like Camembert, produced using Gorgonzola blue mould.
– ORIGIN an invented name, blend of **CAMEMBERT** and **GORGONZOLA**, with the insertion of -*bo*-.

Cambrelle /kamˈbrɛl/ ▶ noun [mass noun] trademark a synthetic fabric which absorbs perspiration, used as a lining material for climbing and walking boots.

Cambrian /ˈkambrɪən/ ▶ adjective 1 (chiefly in names or geographical terms) Welsh: *the Cambrian Railway.*
2 Geology of, relating to, or denoting the first period in the Palaeozoic era, between the end of the Precambrian aeon and the beginning of the Ordovician period.
■ [as noun **the Cambrian**] the Cambrian period or the system of rocks deposited during it.

The Cambrian lasted from about 570 to 510 million years ago and was a time of widespread seas. It is the earliest period in which fossils, notably trilobites, can be used in geological dating.

– ORIGIN mid 17th cent.: from Latin *Cambria* 'Wales', variant of *Cumbria*, from Welsh *Cymry* 'Welshman' or *Cymru* 'Wales'.

cambric /ˈkambrɪk, ˈkeɪm-/ ▶ noun [mass noun] a lightweight, closely woven white linen or cotton fabric.
– ORIGIN late Middle English: from *Kamerijk*, Flemish form of *Cambrai*, a town in northern France, where it was originally made. Compare with **CHAMBRAY**.

Cambridge 1 a city in eastern England, the county town of Cambridgeshire; pop. 101,000 (1991). Cambridge University is located there.
2 a city in eastern Massachusetts, forming part of the conurbation of Boston; pop. 95,800 (1990). Harvard University and the Massachusetts Institute of Technology are located there.

Cambridge blue ▶ noun Brit. 1 [mass noun] a pale blue colour.
2 a person who has represented Cambridge University in a particular sport.

Cambridgeshire a county of eastern England; county town, Cambridge.

Cambridge University a university at Cambridge in England, founded in 1230. The university comprises a federation of thirty-one colleges.

Cambs. ▶ abbreviation for Cambridgeshire.

Cambyses /kamˈbaɪsiːz/ (d.522 BC), king of Persia 529–522 BC, son of Cyrus. He is chiefly remembered for his conquest of Egypt in 525 BC.

camcorder ▶ noun a portable combined video camera and video recorder.
– ORIGIN 1980s: blend of **CAMERA**[1] and **RECORDER**.

came[1] past tense of **COME**.

came[2] ▶ noun (usu. **cames**) each of a number of strips forming a framework for enclosing a pane of glass, especially in a leaded window.
– ORIGIN late 16th cent.: of unknown origin.

camel ▶ noun 1 a large, long-necked ungulate mammal of arid country, with long slender legs, broad cushioned feet, and either one or two humps on the back. Camels can survive for long periods without food or drink, chiefly by using up the fat reserves in their humps.
● Genus *Camelus*, family Camelidae (the **camel family**): two species (see **ARABIAN CAMEL**, **BACTRIAN CAMEL**.) The camel family also includes the llama and its relatives.
■ [mass noun] a fabric made from camel hair. ■ [mass noun] a yellowish-fawn colour like that of camel hair.
2 an apparatus for raising a sunken ship, consisting of one or more watertight chests to provide buoyancy.
– ORIGIN Old English, from Latin *camelus*, from Greek *kamēlos*, of Semitic origin.

camelback ▶ noun a back with a hump-shaped curve on a sofa or other piece of furniture: [as modifier] *a camelback sofa.*

camel cricket ▶ noun a wingless humpbacked insect related to the grasshoppers, typically living in caves or holes Also called **CAVE CRICKET**.
● Family Raphidophoridae: several genera.

cameleer /ˌkaməˈlɪə/ ▶ noun a person who controls or rides a camel.

camel hair (also **camel's hair**) ▶ noun [mass noun] 1 a fabric made from the hair of a camel: [as modifier] *a camel-hair coat.*
2 [usu. as modifier] fine, soft hair from a squirrel's tail, used in artists' brushes.

camelid /kəˈmiːlɪd, ˈkaməlɪd/ ▶ noun Zoology a mammal of the camel family (Camelidae).
– ORIGIN late 20th cent.: from modern Latin *Camelidae* (plural), from Latin *camelus* 'camel', from Greek *kamēlos*.

camellia /kəˈmiːlɪə, -ˈmɛlɪə/ ▶ noun an evergreen East Asian shrub related to the tea plant, grown for its showy flowers and shiny leaves.
● Genus *Camellia*, family Theaceae: several species, in particular the **common camellia** (*C. japonica*), which has numerous cultivars and hybrids.
– ORIGIN modern Latin, named by Linnaeus after Joseph *Kamel* (Latinized as *Camellus*), Moravian botanist (1661–1706), who described the flora of Luzon.

camelopard /ˈkaml(ə)pɑːd, kəˈmɛləpɑːd/ ▶ noun archaic a giraffe.
– ORIGIN late Middle English: via Latin from Greek *kamēlopardalis*, from *kamēlos* 'camel' + *pardalis* (see **PARD**).

Camelopardalis /kəˌmɛlə(ʊ)pɑːˈd(ə)lɪs/ Astronomy a large but inconspicuous northern constellation (the Giraffe), between the Pole Star and Perseus.
■ [as genitive **Camelopardalis**] used with preceding letter or numeral to designate a star in this constellation: *the star Alpha Camelopardalis.*
– ORIGIN via Latin from Greek *kamēlopardalis* (see **CAMELOPARD**).

Camelot /ˈkamɪlɒt/ (in Arthurian legend) the place where King Arthur held his court.
■ [as noun **a Camelot**] a place associated with glittering romance and optimism.

camel spider ▶ noun another term for **SUN SPIDER**.

camel thorn ▶ noun either of two spiny leguminous shrubs occurring in arid country.
● *Alhagi camelorum* (of the Middle East) and *Acacia giraffae* (of southern Africa), family Leguminosae.

Camembert /ˈkaməmbɛː/ ▶ noun [mass noun] a kind of rich, soft, creamy cheese with a whitish rind, originally made near Camembert in Normandy.

cameo /ˈkamɪəʊ/ ▶ noun (pl. **-os**) 1 a piece of jewellery, typically oval in shape, consisting of a portrait in profile carved in relief on a background of a different colour.
2 a short descriptive literary sketch which neatly encapsulates someone or something: *cameos of street life.*
■ a small character part in a play or film, played by a distinguished actor: [as modifier] *he played numerous cameo roles.*
– ORIGIN late Middle English: from Old French *camahieu*, *cama(h)u*; later influenced by Italian *cam(m)eo*, from medieval Latin *cammaeus*, related to the Old French word.

cameo glass ▶ noun [mass noun] decorative glass consisting of layers of different colours, the outermost being cut away to leave a design in relief.

camera[1] ▶ noun a device for recording visual images in the form of photographs, movie film, or video signals.
– PHRASES **on** (or **off**) **camera** while being filmed or televised (or not being filmed or televised): *a four-letter word he had used off camera.*
– ORIGIN mid 19th cent.: from Latin (see **CAMERA**[2], **CAMERA OBSCURA**).

camera[2] ▶ noun [in names] a chamber or round building: *the Radcliffe Camera.*
– PHRASES **in camera** chiefly Law in private, in particular taking place in the private chambers of a judge, with the press and public excluded: *judges assess the merits of such claims in camera.* [ORIGIN: late Latin, 'in the chamber'.]
– ORIGIN late 17th cent. (denoting a council or legislative chamber in Italy or Spain): from Latin, 'vault, arched chamber', from Greek *kamara* 'object with an arched cover'.

camera lucida /ˌkam(ə)rə ˈluːsɪdə/ ▶ noun an instrument in which rays of light are reflected by a prism to produce an image on a sheet of paper, from which a drawing can be made.
– ORIGIN mid 18th cent.: from Latin, 'bright chamber', on the pattern of *camera obscura.*

cameraman ▶ noun (pl. **-men**) a man whose profession is operating a video, television, or film camera.

camera obscura /ɒbsˈkjʊərə/ ▶ noun a darkened box with a convex lens or aperture for projecting the image of an external object on to a screen inside. It is important historically in the development of photography.
■ a small round building with a rotating angled mirror at the apex of the roof, projecting an image of the landscape on to a horizontal surface inside.
– ORIGIN early 18th cent.: from Latin, 'dark chamber'.

camera-ready ▶ adjective Printing (of matter to be printed) in the right form and of good enough quality to be reproduced photographically on to a printing plate: *camera-ready copy.*

camerawork ▶ noun [mass noun] the way in which

cameras are used in a film or television programme: *discreet camerawork and underplayed acting.*

Cameron /ˈkamərən/, Julia Margaret (1815–79), English photographer, credited with being the first to use soft-focus techniques. Her work often reflects the influence of contemporary painting, especially that of the Pre-Raphaelites.

Cameron Highlands a hill resort region in Pahang, Malaysia.
– ORIGIN named after the surveyor William *Cameron*, who mapped the area in 1885.

Cameroon /ˌkaməˈruːn/ a country on the west coast of Africa between Nigeria and Gabon; pop. 12,081,000 (est. 1991); languages, French (official), English (official), many local languages, pidgin; capital, Yaoundé. French name **CAMEROUN** /kamʀun/.

> The territory was a German protectorate from 1884 to 1916, after which it was administered by France and Britain, latterly under League of Nations (later UN) trusteeship. In 1960 the French part became an independent republic, to be joined in 1961 by part of the British Cameroon; the remainder became part of Nigeria. Cameroon became a member of the Commonwealth in 1995.

– DERIVATIVES **Cameroonian** adjective & noun.

cam follower ▶ **noun** the part of a machine in sliding or rolling contact with a rotating cam and given motion by it.

camiknickers ▶ **plural noun** Brit. a woman's one-piece undergarment which combines camisole and French knickers.

Camisard /ˈkamɪsɑː, ˌkamɪˈsɑː, French kamizaʀ/ ▶ **noun** a member of the French Protestant insurgents who rebelled against the persecution that followed the revocation of the Edict of Nantes.
– ORIGIN French, from Provençal *camisa*, from late Latin *camisia* 'shirt', because of the white shirts worn by the insurgents over their clothing for ease of recognition.

camisole /ˈkamɪsəʊl/ ▶ **noun** a woman's loose-fitting undergarment for the upper body, typically held up by shoulder straps and having decorative trimming.
– ORIGIN early 19th cent.: from French, either from Italian *camiciola*, diminutive of *camicia*, or from Spanish *camisola*, diminutive of *camisa*, both from late Latin *camisia* 'shirt or nightgown'.

camo /ˈkaməʊ/ ▶ **noun** informal short for **CAMOUFLAGE**: [as modifier] *a camo jacket.*

Camões /kaˈmɔɪnʃ/ (also **Camoëns** /ˈkaməʊɛns/), Luis (Vaz) de (*c.*1524–80), Portuguese poet. His most famous work, *The Lusiads* (1572), describes Vasco da Gama's discovery of the sea route to India.

camomile ▶ **noun** variant spelling of **CHAMOMILE**.

Camorra /kəˈmɒrə/ (**the Camorra**) a secret criminal society originating in Naples and Neapolitan emigrant communities in the 19th century. Some members later moved to the US and formed links with the Mafia.
– ORIGIN Italian, perhaps from Spanish *camorra* 'dispute, quarrel'.

camouflage /ˈkaməflɑːʒ/ ▶ **noun** [mass noun] the disguising of military personnel, equipment, and installations by painting or covering them to make them blend in with their surroundings: *on the trenches were pieces of turf which served for camouflage* | [as modifier] *camouflage nets.*
▪ the clothing or materials used for such a purpose: *figures dressed in army camouflage.* ▪ the natural colouring or form of an animal which enables it to blend in with its surroundings: *the whiteness of polar bears provides camouflage.* ▪ figurative actions or devices intended to disguise or mislead: *much of my apparent indifference was merely protective camouflage.*
▶ **verb** [with obj.] (often **be camouflaged**) hide or disguise the presence of (a person, animal, or object) by means of camouflage: *the caravan was camouflaged with netting and branches from trees* | figurative *grievances should be discussed, not camouflaged.*
– ORIGIN First World War: from French, from *camoufler* 'to disguise' (originally thieves' slang), from Italian *camuffare* 'disguise, deceive', perhaps by association with French *camouflet* 'whiff of smoke in the face'.

camp[1] ▶ **noun** **1** a place with temporary accommodation of huts, tents, or other structures, typically used by soldiers, refugees, or travelling people.
▪ a complex of buildings for holiday accommodation, typically with extensive recreational facilities: *a summer camp for children.* ▪ [mass noun] temporary overnight lodging in tents: *they **made camp** in a pleasant area* | *we **pitched camp** at a fine spot.* ▪ Archaeology, Brit. a prehistoric enclosed or fortified site, especially an Iron Age hill fort.
2 the supporters of a particular party or doctrine regarded collectively: *both the liberal and conservative camps were annoyed by his high-handed manner.*
3 S. African a fenced field or enclosed area for grazing.
▪ Austral./NZ a place where livestock regularly congregate or where a mustered herd is assembled.
4 S. African a short period of annual military service, several of which are usually compulsory after completion of national service.
▶ **verb** [no obj.] **1** live for a time in a tent or caravan, especially while on holiday: *holiday parks in which you can camp or stay in a chalet* | [as noun **camping**] *camping attracts people of all ages.*
▪ lodge temporarily, especially in an inappropriate or uncomfortable place: *we **camped out** for the night in a mission schoolroom.* ▪ remain persistently in one place: *the press will be camping on your doorstep once they get on to this story.*
2 Austral./NZ (of livestock) assemble together for rest.
3 [with obj.] S. African divide (land) and enclose with fences.
– PHRASES **break camp** take down a tent or the tents of an encampment ready to leave.
– ORIGIN early 16th cent.: from French *camp*, *champ*, from Italian *campo*, from Latin *campus* 'level ground', specifically applied to the *Campus Martius* in Rome, used for games, athletic practice, and military drill.

camp[2] informal ▶ **adjective** (of a man or his manner) ostentatiously and extravagantly effeminate: *a heavily made-up and highly camp actor.*
▪ deliberately exaggerated and theatrical in style, typically for humorous effect: *the movie seems more camp than shocking or gruesome.*
▶ **noun** [mass noun] deliberately exaggerated and theatrical behaviour or style: *Hollywood camp.*
▶ **verb** [no obj.] (of a man) behave in an ostentatiously effeminate way: *he **camped it up** a bit for the cameras.*
– DERIVATIVES **campily** adverb, **campiness** noun, **campy** adjective.
– ORIGIN early 20th cent.: of unknown origin.

campaign ▶ **noun** a series of military operations intended to achieve a particular objective, confined to a particular area, or involving a specified type of fighting: *a desert campaign* | *the air campaign* | [mass noun] *the army set off **on campaign**.*
▪ an organized course of action to achieve a particular goal: *an election campaign* | *the **campaign for** a full inquiry into the regime* | [with infinitive] *the campaign to reduce harmful vehicle emissions.*
▶ **verb** [no obj.] work in an organized and active way towards a particular goal, typically a political or social one: *people who campaigned against child labour* | [with infinitive] *the services he had campaigned to protect.*
– DERIVATIVES **campaigner** noun.
– ORIGIN early 17th cent. (denoting a tract of open country): from French *campagne* 'open country', via Italian from late Latin *campania*, from *campus* 'level ground' (see **CAMP**[1]). The change in sense arose from an army's practice of 'taking the field' (i.e. moving from a fortress or town to open country) at the onset of summer.

Campaign for Nuclear Disarmament (abbrev.: **CND**) a British organization which campaigns for the abolition of nuclear weapons worldwide and calls for unilateral disarmament.

Campania /kamˈpeɪnɪə, -ˈpanjə/ a region of west central Italy; capital, Naples.
– DERIVATIVES **Campanian** noun & adjective.

campanile /ˌkampəˈniːleɪ/ ▶ **noun** an Italian bell tower, especially a free-standing one.
– ORIGIN mid 17th cent.: from Italian, from *campana* 'bell'.

campanology /ˌkampəˈnɒlədʒi/ ▶ **noun** [mass noun] the art or practice of bell-ringing.
– DERIVATIVES **campanological** adjective, **campanologist** noun.
– ORIGIN mid 19th cent.: from modern Latin *campanologia*, from late Latin *campana* 'bell'.

campanula /kamˈpanjʊlə/ ▶ **noun** another term for **BELLFLOWER**.
– ORIGIN modern Latin, diminutive of late Latin *campana* 'bell'.

campanulate /kamˈpanjʊlət/ ▶ **adjective** Botany (of a flower) bell-shaped, as in a campanula.

Campari /kamˈpɑːri/ ▶ **noun** [mass noun] trademark a pinkish aperitif flavoured with bitters.
– ORIGIN named after the manufacturer.

camp bed ▶ **noun** Brit. a folding portable bed, typically made of canvas stretched over a knock-down metal frame.

Campbell[1] /ˈkamb(ə)l/ the name of two English motor-racing drivers and holders of world speed records:
▪ **Sir Malcolm** (1885–1948). In 1935 he became the first man to exceed a land speed of 300 mph (483 kph). He also achieved a water-speed record of 141.74 mph (228 kph), in 1939.
▪ **Donald (Malcolm)** (1921–67), son of Sir Malcolm. In 1964 he achieved a speed of 276.33 mph (445 kph) on water and 403 mph (649 kph) on land. He was killed attempting to break his own water speed record.

Campbell[2] /ˈkamb(ə)l/, Mrs Patrick (1865–1940), English actress; born *Beatrice Stella Tanner.* George Bernard Shaw wrote the part of Eliza Doolittle in *Pygmalion* (1914) for her.

Campbell[3] /ˈkamb(ə)l/, Roy (1901–57), South African poet; full name *Ignatius Royston Dunnachie Campbell*. His long poem *Flowering Rifle* (1939) shows strong right-wing sympathies; he fought for Franco's side in the Spanish Civil War.

Campbell[4] /ˈkamb(ə)l/, Thomas (1777–1844), Scottish poet, chiefly remembered for his patriotic lyrics such as 'The Battle of Hohenlinden' and 'Ye Mariners of England'.

Campbell-Bannerman, Sir Henry (1836–1908), British Liberal statesman, Prime Minister 1905–8.

campcraft ▶ **noun** [mass noun] knowledge and skill required for an outdoor life lacking modern conveniences.

Camp David the country retreat of the President of the US, in the Appalachian Mountains in Maryland. President Carter hosted talks there between the leaders of Israel and Egypt which resulted in the Camp David agreements (1978) and the Egypt–Israel peace treaty of 1979.

Campeche /kamˈpɛtʃeɪ/ a state of SE Mexico, on the Yucatán Peninsula.
▪ its capital, a seaport on the Gulf of Mexico; pop. 172,200 (1990).

camper ▶ **noun** **1** a person who spends a holiday in a tent or holiday camp.
2 (also **camper van**) a large motor vehicle with living accommodation.

campesino /ˌkampəˈsiːnəʊ/ ▶ **noun** (pl. **-os** /-əʊz/) (in Spain and Spanish-speaking countries) a peasant farmer.
– ORIGIN Spanish.

campfire ▶ **noun** an open-air fire in a camp, used for cooking and as a focal point for social activity.

camp follower ▶ **noun** a civilian who works in or is attached to a military camp.
▪ a person who is nominally attached to a group but is not fully committed or does not make a substantial contribution to its activities: *cynical opportunists and camp followers.*

campground ▶ **noun** North American term for **CAMPSITE**.

camphor /ˈkamfə/ ▶ **noun** [mass noun] a white volatile crystalline substance with an aromatic smell and bitter taste, occurring in certain essential oils.
• A terpenoid ketone; chem. formula: $C_{10}H_{17}O$.
– ORIGIN Middle English: from Old French *camphore* or medieval Latin *camphora*, from Arabic *kāfūr*, via Malay from Sanskrit *karpūra*.

camphorate ▶ **verb** [with obj.] [usu. as adj. **camphorated**] impregnate or treat with camphor.

camphor tree ▶ **noun** an East Asian tree of the laurel family, which is the chief natural source of camphor.
• *Cinnamomum camphora*, family Lauraceae.

campimetry /kamˈpɪmɪtri/ ▶ **noun** [mass noun] a technique for measuring or mapping the field of vision of the eye.
– ORIGIN early 20th cent.: from Latin *campus* 'field' (see **CAMP**[1]) + **-METRY**.

Campinas /kamˈpiːnəs/ a city in SE Brazil, north-west of São Paulo; pop. 835,000 (1991).

Campion[1] /ˈkampɪən/, Jane (b.1954), New Zealand film director and screenwriter. Notable works: *An*

Angel at My Table (1990) and *The Piano* (1993), for which she received an Oscar for best screenplay.

Campion² /ˈkampɪən/, St Edmund (1540–81), English Jesuit priest and martyr. He was canonized in 1970. Feast day, 1 December.

campion /ˈkampɪən/ ▶ **noun** a plant of the pink family, typically having pink or white flowers with notched petals, found in both Eurasia and North America.
• Genera *Silene* and *Lychnis*, family Caryophyllaceae.
– ORIGIN mid 16th cent.: perhaps related to **CHAMPION**. The name was originally used for the rose campion, whose name in Latin (*Lychnis coronaria*) and Greek (*lukhnis stephanōmatikē*) means 'campion fit for a crown', and which was said in classical times to have been used for victors' garlands.

camp meeting ▶ **noun** N. Amer. a religious meeting held in the open air or in a tent, often lasting several days.

campo /ˈkampəʊ/ ▶ **noun** (pl. **-os**) **1** (usu. **the campo**) (in South America, especially Brazil) a grass plain with occasional stunted trees.
2 a square in an Italian or Spanish town.
– ORIGIN from Spanish, Portuguese, and Italian *campo*, literally 'field'.

Campobasso /ˌkampəʊˈbasəʊ/ a city in central Italy, capital of Molise region; pop. 51,300 (1990).

Campo Grande /ˌkampuː ˈgrandi/ a city in SW Brazil, capital of the state of Mato Grosso do Sul; pop. 489,000 (1991).

camporee /ˈkampəriː/ ▶ **noun** chiefly N. Amer. a local or regional camping event for Scouts.
– ORIGIN late 20th cent.: blend of **CAMP**[1] and **JAMBOREE**.

campsite ▶ **noun** a place used for camping, especially one equipped for holidaymakers.

campus ▶ **noun** (pl. **campuses**) the grounds and buildings of a university or college: *for the first year I had a room on campus.*
■ N. Amer. the grounds of a university, college, school, hospital, or other institution.
– ORIGIN late 18th cent. (originally US): from Latin *campus* 'field' (see **CAMP**[1]).

campylobacter /ˈkampɪləʊˌbaktə, ˌkampɪləʊˈbaktə/ ▶ **noun** Medicine a bacterium which sometimes causes abortion in animals and food poisoning in humans.
• Genus *Campylobacter*: several species, in particular *C. jejuni*; curved or spiral Gram-negative bacteria.
– ORIGIN 1970s: modern Latin, from Greek *kampulos* 'bent' + **BACTERIUM**.

CAMRA /ˈkamrə/ Brit. ▶ **abbreviation for** Campaign for Real Ale.

camshaft /ˈkamʃɑːft/ ▶ **noun** a shaft with one or more cams attached to it, especially one operating the valves in an internal-combustion engine.

Camulodunum /ˌkamjʊlə(ʊ)ˈd(j)uːnəm/ Roman name for **COLCHESTER**.

Camus /ˈkamuː, French kamy/, Albert (1913–60), French novelist, dramatist, and essayist, closely aligned with existentialism. Notable works: *The Outsider* (novel, 1942), *The Plague* (novel, 1947), and *The Rebel* (essay, 1951). Nobel Prize for Literature (1957).

camwood ▶ **noun 1** [mass noun] the hard red timber of an African tree.
2 either of two trees of the pea family which yield this timber.
• *Baphia nitida* and (now usually) *Pterocarpus soyauxii* (the African padouk), family Leguminosae.
– ORIGIN late 17th cent.: probably from Temne *k'am* + **WOOD**.

Can. ▶ **abbreviation for** Canada or Canadian.

can¹ ▶ **modal verb** (3rd sing. present **can**; past **could**) **1** be able to: *they can run fast | I could hear footsteps | he can't afford it.*
■ be able to through acquired knowledge or skill: *I can speak Italian.* ■ have the opportunity or possibility to: *there are many ways holidaymakers can take money abroad.* ■ [with negative or in questions] used to express doubt or surprise about the possibility of something's being the case: *he can't have finished | where can she have gone?*
2 be permitted to: *you can use the phone if you want to | nobody could legally drink on the premises.*
■ used to request someone to do something: *can you open the window? | can't you leave me alone?* ■ used to make a suggestion or offer: *we can have another drink if you like.*
3 used to indicate that something is typically the case: *antique clocks can seem out of place in modern homes | he could be very moody.*
– ORIGIN Old English *cunnan* 'know' (in Middle English 'know how to'), related to Dutch *kunnen* and German *können*; from an Indo-European root shared by Latin *gnoscere* 'know' and Greek *gignōskein* 'know'.

USAGE Is there any difference between **may** and **can** when used to request or express permission, as in *may/can I ask you a few questions?* It is still widely held that using **can** for permission is somehow incorrect, and that it should be reserved for expressions denoting capability, as in *can you swim?* Although this use of **can** is not regarded as incorrect in standard English, there is a clear difference in formality between the two verbs: **may** is, generally speaking, a more polite way of asking for something and is the better choice in more formal contexts.

can² ▶ **noun 1** a cylindrical metal container: *a petrol can | a can of paint.*
■ a small steel or aluminium container in which food or drink is hermetically sealed for storage over long periods: *a beer can.* ■ the quantity of food or drink held by such a container: *he drank two cans of lager.* ■ S. African a container for wine, typically a two-litre glass bottle.
2 (**the can**) N. Amer. informal prison.
3 (**the can**) N. Amer. informal the toilet.
4 (**cans**) informal headphones.
▶ **verb** (**canned**, **canning**) [with obj.] (often **be canned**)
1 preserve (food) in a can.
2 N. Amer. informal dismiss (someone) from their job: *he was canned because of a tiff over promotion.*
■ reject (something) as inadequate: *the editorial team was so disappointed with the pictures that they canned the project.*
– PHRASES **a can of worms** a complicated matter likely to prove awkward or embarrassing: *to question the traditional model of education opens up too big a can of worms.* **in the can** informal on tape or film and ready to be broadcast or released.
– DERIVATIVES **canner** noun.
– ORIGIN Old English *canne*, related to Dutch *kan* and German *Kanne*; either of Germanic origin or from late Latin *canna*.

Cana /ˈkeɪnə/ an ancient small town in Galilee, where Christ is said to have performed his first miracle by changing water into wine during a marriage feast (John 2:1–11).

Canaan /ˈkeɪnən/ the biblical name for the area of ancient Palestine west of the River Jordan, the Promised Land of the Israelites, who conquered and occupied it during the latter part of the 2nd millennium BC.
– DERIVATIVES **Canaanite** noun & adjective.
– ORIGIN early 17th cent.: via ecclesiastical Latin from ecclesiastical Greek *Khanaan*, from Hebrew *kĕnaʻan*.

Canada the second largest country in the world, covering the entire northern half of North America with the exception of Alaska; pop. 26,832,400 (1991); official languages, English and French; capital, Ottawa.

Eastern Canada was colonized by the French in the 17th century, with the British emerging as the ruling colonial power in 1763 after the Seven Years War. Canada became a federation of provinces with dominion status in 1867, and the final step in attaining legal independence from the UK was taken with the signing of the Constitution Act of 1982; Canada remains a member of the Commonwealth. French-speakers are largely concentrated in Quebec, the focal point for the French-Canadian separatist movement.

– DERIVATIVES **Canadian** noun & adjective.

Canada balsam ▶ **noun** [mass noun] a yellowish resin obtained from the balsam fir and used for mounting preparations on microscope slides.

Canada goose ▶ **noun** a common North American goose with a black head and neck, a white chinstrap, and a loud trumpeting call. It has been introduced widely in Britain and elsewhere.
• *Branta canadensis*, family Anatidae.

Canada jay ▶ **noun** another term for **GREY JAY**.

Canada thistle ▶ **noun** N. Amer. the European creeping or field thistle, which has become naturalized as a serious weed in North America.
• *Cirsium arvense*, family Compositae.

Canadian football ▶ **noun** [mass noun] a form of football played in Canada, derived from rugby but now resembling American football. There are twelve players a side.

Canadian French ▶ **noun** [mass noun] the form of the French language written and spoken by French Canadians.

Canadian pondweed ▶ **noun** [mass noun] an invasive aquatic American plant which has become naturalized in Europe and is grown in aquaria and ponds.
• *Elodea canadensis*, family Hydrocharitaceae.

Canadian Shield a large plateau which occupies over two fifths of the land area of Canada and is drained by rivers flowing into Hudson Bay. Also called **LAURENTIAN PLATEAU**.

Canadien /ˌkanaˈdjɑ̃, French kanadjɛ̃/ Canadian ▶ **noun** a French Canadian.
▶ **adjective** French Canadian.
– ORIGIN French.

canaille /kəˈnɑːi, French kanaj/ ▶ **noun** (**the canaille**) derogatory the common people; the masses: *hunting with dogs (the canaille does not understand the word hounds) is to be banned.*
– ORIGIN French, from Italian *canaglia* 'pack of dogs', from *cane* 'dog'.

canal ▶ **noun** an artificial waterway constructed to allow the passage of boats or ships inland or to convey water for irrigation.
■ a tubular duct in a plant or animal, serving to convey or contain food, liquid, or air: *the ear canal.* ■ Astronomy any of a number of linear markings formerly reported as seen by telescope on the planet Mars. [ORIGIN: named *canali* ('channels') by G. V. Schiaparelli; the markings are now thought to have arisen from eye or lens defects.]
– ORIGIN late Middle English: from Old French, alteration of *chanel* 'channel', from Latin *canalis* 'pipe, groove, channel', from *canna* 'cane'.

canal boat ▶ **noun** a long, narrow boat used on canals.

Canaletto /ˌkanəˈlɛtəʊ/ (1697–1768), Italian painter; born *Giovanni Antonio Canale*. He is well known for his paintings of Venetian festivals and scenery.

canalize /ˈkan(ə)lʌɪz/ (also **-ise**) ▶ **verb** [with obj.] convert (a river) into a navigable canal.
■ convey (something) through a duct or channel. ■ figurative give a direction or purpose to (something): *his strategy was to canalize the enthusiasm of the diehards into party channels.*
– DERIVATIVES **canalization** noun.
– ORIGIN mid 19th cent.: from French *canaliser*, from *canal* 'channel' (see **CANAL**).

Canal Zone see **PANAMA CANAL**.

canapé /ˈkanəpeɪ/ ▶ **noun 1** a small piece of bread or pastry with a savoury topping, often served with drinks at a reception or formal party.
2 a sofa, especially a decorative French antique.
– ORIGIN French, sense 1 being a figurative extension of the sense 'sofa' (as a 'couch' on which to place toppings). See also **CANOPY**.

canard /kəˈnɑːd, ˈkanɑːd/ ▶ **noun 1** an unfounded rumour or story: *the old canard that LA is a cultural wasteland.*
2 a small wing-like projection attached to an aircraft forward of the main wing to provide extra stability or control, sometimes replacing the tail.
– ORIGIN mid 19th cent.: from French, literally 'duck', also 'hoax', from Old French *caner* 'to quack'.

Canarese ▶ **noun** & **adjective** variant spelling of **KANARESE**.

Canaries Current a cold ocean current in the North Atlantic that flows south-westwards from Spain to meet equatorial waters near the Canary Islands.

canary ▶ **noun** (pl. **-ies**) **1** a mainly African finch with a melodious song, typically having yellowish-green plumage. One kind is popular as a cage bird and has been bred in a variety of colours, especially bright yellow.
• Genus *Serinus*, family Fringillidae: several species, especially the **island canary** (*S. canaria*), which is native to the Canary Islands, the Azores, and Madeira, and from which the domestic canary was developed.
2 (also **canary yellow**) [mass noun] a bright yellow colour resembling the plumage of a canary.
3 (also **canary wine**) [mass noun] historical a sweet wine from the Canary Islands, similar to Madeira.
– ORIGIN late 16th cent.: from French *canari*, from

Spanish *canario* 'canary' or 'person from the Canary Islands' (see **Canary Islands**).

canary creeper ▶ **noun** a South American climbing plant related to the nasturtium. It has bright yellow flowers with deeply toothed petals, which give the appearance of a small bird in flight.
• *Tropaeolium peregrinum*, family Tropaeolaceae.

canary grass ▶ **noun** [mass noun] a tall grass of NW Africa and the Canary Islands, grown for its seeds which are fed to canaries and other caged finches.
• Genus *Phalaris*, family Gramineae: several species, in particular *P. canariensis*.

Canary Islands (also **the Canaries**) a group of islands in the Atlantic Ocean, off the NW coast of Africa, forming an autonomous region of Spain; capital, Las Palmas; pop. 1,557,530 (est. 1989). The group includes the islands of Tenerife, Gomera, La Palma, Hierro, Gran Canaria, Fuerteventura, and Lanzarote.
– ORIGIN from French *Canarie*, via Spanish from Latin *Canaria (insula)* '(island) of dogs', from *canis* 'dog', one of the islands being noted in Roman times for large dogs.

canasta /kəˈnastə/ ▶ **noun** [mass noun] a card game resembling rummy, using two packs. It is usually played by two pairs of partners, and the aim is to collect sets (or melds) of cards.
■[count noun] a meld of seven cards in this game.
– ORIGIN 1940s: from Spanish (of Uruguayan origin), literally 'basket', based on Latin *canistrum* 'basket' (see **canister**).

Canaveral, Cape /kəˈnavər(ə)l/ a cape on the east coast of Florida, known as Cape Kennedy from 1963 until 1973. It is the site of the John F. Kennedy Space Center, from which the Apollo space missions were launched.

Canberra /ˈkanbərə/ the capital of Australia and seat of the federal government, in Australian Capital Territory, an enclave of New South Wales; pop. 310,000 (est. 1990).

cancan ▶ **noun** a lively, high-kicking stage dance originating in 19th-century Parisian music halls and performed by women in long skirts and petticoats: *people were dancing the cancan.*
– ORIGIN mid 19th cent.: from French, child's word for *canard* 'duck', from Old French *caner* 'to quack'.

cancel ▶ **verb** (**cancelled**, **cancelling**; US also **canceled**, **canceling**) [with obj.] **1** decide or announce that (an arranged or planned event) will not take place: *he was forced to cancel his visit.*
■annul or revoke (a formal arrangement which is in effect): *his visa had been cancelled.* ■ abolish or make void (a financial obligation): *I intend to cancel your debt to me.* ■ mark, pierce, or tear (a ticket or stamp) to show that it has been used or invalidated: *cancelling stamps on registered mail.*
2 (of a factor or circumstance) neutralize or negate the force or effect of (another): *the electric fields may cancel each other out.*
■Mathematics delete (an equal factor) from both sides of an equation or from the numerator and denominator of a fraction.
▶**noun 1** a mark made on a postage stamp to show that it has been used.
2 Printing a new page or section inserted in a book to replace the original text, typically to correct an error: [as modifier] *a cancel title page.*
3 US (in music) a natural sign (♮).
– ORIGIN late Middle English (in the sense 'obliterate or delete writing by drawing or stamping lines across it'): from Old French *canceller*, from Latin *cancellare*, from *cancelli* 'crossbars'.

cancelbot /ˈkansəlbɒt/ ▶ **noun** Computing a program that searches for and deletes specified mailings from Internet newsgroups.
– ORIGIN 1990s: from **cancel** + **bot**[2].

cancellation (US also **cancelation**) ▶ **noun** [mass noun] the action of cancelling something that has been arranged or planned: *train services are subject to alteration or cancellation at short notice | the project was threatened with cancellation by the government |* [count noun] *there had been a cancellation on a ship leaving almost at once.*
■[count noun] a crossing out of something written: *all cancellations on documents must be made indelibly.* ■ [count noun] a visible or electronic mark placed on a postage stamp to show that it has been used. ■ Law the annulling of a legal document: *the debtor can procure cancellation if satisfied within one month.*

canceller ▶ **noun** a manual, mechanical, or electronic device used to cancel something, especially one that makes a cancellation on a postage stamp.

cancellous /ˈkans(ə)ləs/ ▶ **adjective** Anatomy of or denoting bone tissue with a mesh-like structure containing many pores, typical of the interior of mature bones.
– ORIGIN mid 19th cent.: from Latin *cancelli* 'crossbars' + **-ous**.

Cancer 1 Astronomy a constellation (the Crab), said to represent a crab crushed under the foot of Hercules. It is most noted for the globular star cluster of Praesepe or the Beehive.
■[as genitive **Cancri** /ˈkaŋkriː/] used with preceding letter or numeral to designate a star in this constellation: *the star Delta Cancri.*
2 Astrology the fourth sign of the zodiac, which the sun enters at the northern summer solstice (about 21 June).
■(**a Cancer**) a person born when the sun is in this sign.
– PHRASES **tropic of Cancer** see **tropic**[1].
– DERIVATIVES **Cancerian** /-ˈsɪərɪən, -ˈsɛːrɪən/ noun & adjective (only in sense 2).
– ORIGIN Latin.

cancer ▶ **noun** [mass noun] a disease caused by an uncontrolled division of abnormal cells in a part of the body: *he's got cancer | smoking is the major cause of lung cancer.*
■[count noun] a malignant growth or tumour resulting from such a division of cells: *most skin cancers are curable.* ■ [count noun] figurative a practice or phenomenon perceived to be evil or destructive and hard to contain or eradicate: *racism is a cancer sweeping across Europe.*
– DERIVATIVES **cancerous** adjective.
– ORIGIN Old English, from Latin, 'crab or creeping ulcer', translating Greek *karkinos*, said to have been applied to such tumours because the swollen veins around them resembled the limbs of a crab. **Canker** was the usual form until the 17th cent. Compare with **Cancer**.

cancer stick ▶ **noun** informal, humorous a cigarette.

Cancún /kanˈkuːn/ a resort in SE Mexico, on the NE coast of the Yucatán Peninsula; pop. 27,500 (1980).

candela /kanˈdɛlə, -ˈdiːlə, ˈkandɪlə/ (abbrev.: **cd**) ▶ **noun** Physics the SI unit of luminous intensity. One candela is the luminous intensity, in a given direction, of a source that emits monochromatic radiation of frequency 540 × 10^{12} Hz and that has a radiant intensity in that direction of 1/683 watt per steradian.
– ORIGIN 1950s: from Latin, 'candle'.

candelabra tree ▶ **noun** a tree with upward-curving boughs, giving it a shape which resembles a candelabrum:
• a tropical African tree (genus *Euphorbia*, family Euphorbiaceae). • a South American pine tree related to the monkey puzzle (*Araucaria angustifolia*, family Araucariaceae).

candelabrum /ˌkandɪˈlɑːbrəm, -ˈleɪ-/ ▶ **noun** (pl. **candelabra** /-brə/) a large branched candlestick or holder for several candles or lamps.
– ORIGIN early 19th cent.: from Latin, from *candela* (see **candle**).

USAGE Based on the Latin forms, the correct singular is **candelabrum** and the correct plural is **candelabra**. However, these forms are often not observed in practice: the singular form is assumed to be **candelabra** and hence its plural is interpreted as **candelabras**. In nearly 50 per cent of the examples in the British National Corpus the singular is incorrectly given as **candelabra**.

candid ▶ **adjective 1** truthful and straightforward; frank: *his responses were remarkably candid | a candid discussion.*
2 (of a photograph of a person) taken informally, especially without the subject's knowledge.
– DERIVATIVES **candidly** adverb, **candidness** noun.
– ORIGIN mid 17th cent. (in the Latin sense): from Latin *candidus* 'white'. Subsequent early senses were 'pure, innocent', 'unbiased', and 'free from malice', hence 'frank' (late 17th cent.). Compare with **candour**.

candida /ˈkandɪdə/ ▶ **noun** [mass noun] a yeast-like parasitic fungus that can sometimes cause thrush.
• Genus *Candida*, subdivision Deuteromycotina, especially *C. albicans*.
– ORIGIN modern Latin, feminine of Latin *candidus* 'white'.

candidate /ˈkandɪdeɪt, -dət/ ▶ **noun** a person who applies for a job or is nominated for election: *candidates applying for this position should be computer-literate | the Green Party candidate.*
■a person taking an examination: *an A-level candidate.* ■ a person or thing regarded as suitable for or likely to receive a particular fate, treatment, or position: *she was the perfect **candidate for** a biography | a leading **candidate for** the title of London's ugliest building.*
– DERIVATIVES **candidacy** noun, **candidature** noun Brit.
– ORIGIN early 17th cent.: from Latin *candidatus* 'white-robed', also denoting a candidate for office (who traditionally wore a white toga), from *candidus* 'white'.

candidiasis /ˌkandɪˈdʌɪəsɪs/ ▶ **noun** [mass noun] infection with candida, especially as causing oral or vaginal thrush.

candiru /ˌkandɪˈruː/ ▶ **noun** a minute, slender catfish of the Amazon region, feeding by sucking blood from other fishes and sometimes entering the body orifices of mammals. It is notorious for its occasional habit of entering the urethra of human bathers.
• *Vandellia cirrhosa*, family Trichomycteridae.
– ORIGIN mid 19th cent.: via Portuguese from Tupi *candirú*.

candle ▶ **noun** a cylinder or block of wax or tallow with a central wick which is lit to produce light as it burns.
■(also **international candle**) Physics a unit of luminous intensity, superseded by the candela.
▶**verb** [with obj.] (often **be candled**) (of a poultry breeder) test (an egg) for freshness or fertility by holding it to the light.
– PHRASES **be unable to hold a candle to** informal be not nearly as good as: *nobody in the final could hold a candle to her.* (**the game's**) **not worth the candle** the potential advantages to be gained from doing something do not justify the cost or trouble involved.
– DERIVATIVES **candler** noun.
– ORIGIN Old English *candel*, from Latin *candela*, from *candere* 'be white or glisten'.

candleberry ▶ **noun** (pl. **-ies**) any of a number of trees or shrubs whose berries or seeds yield a wax or oil which can be used for making candles, in particular:
• a bayberry or related North American shrub (genus *Myrica*, family Myricaceae). • the candlenut.

candlefish ▶ **noun** (pl. same or **-fishes**) a small edible marine fish with oily flesh, occurring on the west coast of North America. Also called **eulachon**.
• *Thaleichthys pacificus*, family Osmeridae.
– ORIGIN so named because the Chinook Indians formerly burnt the oily bodies of these fish as candles.

candleholder ▶ **noun** a holder or support for a candle, typically one that is small or sturdy.

candlelight ▶ **noun** [mass noun] dim light provided by a candle or candles: *we dined **by candlelight**.*

candlelit ▶ **adjective** lit by a candle or candles: *a romantic candlelit dinner.*

Candlemas /ˈkand(ə)lmas, -məs/ ▶ **noun** a Christian festival held on 2 February to commemorate the purification of the Virgin Mary (after childbirth, according to Jewish law) and the presentation of Christ in the Temple. Candles were traditionally blessed at this festival.
– ORIGIN Old English *Candelmæsse* (see **candle**, **Mass**).

candlenut ▶ **noun** an evergreen tree of the spurge family, with large seeds that yield an oil used for lighting and other purposes, native to SE Asia and the South Pacific islands. Also called **candleberry**.
• *Aleurites moluccana*, family Euphorbiaceae.

candlepower ▶ **noun** [mass noun] illuminating power expressed in candelas or candles: [as modifier] *a 16-candlepower lamp.*

candlestick ▶ **noun** a support or holder for one or more candles, typically one that is tall and thin.

candlewick ▶ **noun** [mass noun] a thick, soft cotton fabric with a raised, tufted pattern: [as modifier] *a candlewick dressing gown.*
■the yarn used to make such a fabric.

can-do ▶ **adjective** [attrib.] informal characterized by or exhibiting a determination or willingness to take action and achieve results: *I like his can-do attitude.*

Candolle /kan'dɒl, French kɑ̃dɔl/, Augustin Pyrame de (1778–1841), Swiss botanist. He introduced a new scheme of plant classification based on morphological characteristics, which prevailed for many years.

candomblé /ˌkandɒm'bleɪ/ ▶ **noun** [mass noun] a Brazilian sect of the macumba cult.
– ORIGIN Brazilian Portuguese.

candour (US **candor**) ▶ **noun** [mass noun] the quality of being open and honest in expression; frankness: *a man of refreshing candour.*
– ORIGIN late Middle English (in the Latin sense): from Latin *candor* 'whiteness'. The current sense dates from the mid 18th cent.; the development of the senses paralleled that of **CANDID**.

CANDU /'kandu:, kan'du:/ (also **Candu**) ▶ **noun** a nuclear reactor of a Canadian design in which the fuel is unenriched uranium oxide clad in zircaloy and the coolant and moderator is heavy water.
– ORIGIN from *Can(ada)* + the initial letters of **DEUTERIUM** and **URANIUM**.

C & W ▶ **abbreviation for** country and western (music).

candy ▶ **noun** (pl. **-ies**) (also **sugar candy**) [mass noun] N. Amer. sweets; confectionery: [as modifier] *a candy bar* | [count noun] *pink and yellow candies.*
■ chiefly Brit. sugar crystallized by repeated boiling and slow evaporation.
▶ **verb** (**-ies**, **-ied**) [with obj.] [often as adj. **candied**] preserve (fruit) by coating and impregnating it with a sugar syrup: *candied fruit.*
– ORIGIN mid 17th cent. (as a verb): the noun use is from late Middle English *sugar-candy*, from French *sucre candi* 'crystallized sugar', from Arabic *sukkar* 'sugar' + *ḳandī* 'candied', based on Sanskrit *khaṇḍa* 'fragment'.

candy apple ▶ **noun** N. Amer. a toffee apple.
■ (also **candy-apple red**) [mass noun] a bright red colour.

candy-ass ▶ **noun** N. Amer. informal a timid, cowardly, or despicable person.
– DERIVATIVES **candy-assed** adjective.

candy cane ▶ **noun** N. Amer. a cylindrical stick of striped sweet rock with a curved end, resembling a walking stick.

candyfloss ▶ **noun** [mass noun] Brit. a mass of pink or white fluffy spun sugar wrapped round a stick.
■ figurative something perceived as lacking in worth or substance: *it's just aural candyfloss.*

candyman ▶ **noun** (pl. **-men**) N. Amer. informal a person who sells illegal drugs.
– ORIGIN mid 19th cent.: from **CANDY** + **MAN**, an earlier sense denoting a ragman who gave toffee in exchange for goods.

candy-striped ▶ **adjective** (of material or a garment) patterned with alternating stripes of white and another colour, typically pink.
– DERIVATIVES **candy-stripe** adjective & noun.

candy-striper ▶ **noun** N. Amer. informal a female voluntary nurse in a hospital.
– ORIGIN so named because of the candy-striped uniforms of such nurses.

candytuft ▶ **noun** a European plant with small heads of white, pink, or purple flowers, grown as a garden or rockery plant.
• Genus *Iberis*, family Cruciferae.
– ORIGIN early 17th cent.: from *Candy* (obsolete form of *Candia*, former name of Crete) + **TUFT**.

cane ▶ **noun 1** the hollow jointed stem of a tall grass, especially bamboo or sugar cane, or the stem of a slender palm such as rattan.
■ any plant that produces such stems. ■ [mass noun] stems of bamboo, rattan, or wicker used as a material for making furniture or baskets: [as modifier] *a cane coffee table.* ■ short for **SUGAR CANE**. ■ a flexible woody stem of the raspberry plant or any of its relatives.
2 a length of cane or a slender stick, especially one used as a support for plants, a walking stick, or an instrument of punishment.
■ (**the cane**) a form of corporal punishment used in certain schools, involving beating with a cane: *wrong answers were rewarded by the cane.*
▶ **verb** [with obj.] **1** (often **be caned**) beat with a cane as a punishment.
2 [usu. as adj. **caned**] make or repair (furniture) with cane: *armchairs with caned seats.*
– DERIVATIVES **caner** noun.
– ORIGIN late Middle English: from Old French, via Latin from Greek *kanna, kannē*, of Semitic origin.

canebrake ▶ **noun** N. Amer. a piece of ground covered with a dense growth of canes.

cane chair ▶ **noun** a chair with a seat made of woven cane strips.

cane rat ▶ **noun** a large rat-like African rodent found in wetlands south of the Sahara. It is often a pest of sugar plantations.
• Family Thryonomyidae and genus *Thryonomys*: two species.

cane sugar ▶ **noun** [mass noun] sugar obtained from sugar cane.

Canes Venatici /ˌkeɪni:z vɪ'natɪsʌɪ/ Astronomy a small northern constellation (the Hunting Dogs), said to represent two dogs (Asterion and Chara) held on a leash by Boötes.
■ [as genitive **Canum Venaticorum** /ˌkɑ:nʊm vɪˌnatɪ'kɔ:rʊm/] used with preceding letter or numeral to designate a star in this constellation: *the star Beta Canum Venaticorum.*
– ORIGIN Latin.

cane toad ▶ **noun** a large brown toad native to tropical America. It has been introduced elsewhere as a pest control agent but can become a serious pest itself, partly because animals eating it are killed by its toxins. Also called **MARINE TOAD, GIANT TOAD**.
• *Bufo marinus*, family Bufonidae.

cane trash ▶ **noun** see **TRASH** (sense 2).

Canetti /kə'nɛti/, Elias (1905–94), Bulgarian-born British writer. Notable works: *Auto-da-Fé* (1936) and *Crowds and Power* (1960). Nobel Prize for Literature (1981).

Canfield ▶ **noun** [mass noun] chiefly N. Amer. a form of the card game patience or solitaire.
– ORIGIN early 20th cent.: named after Richard A. *Canfield* (1855–1914), an American gambler.

canid /'kanɪd/ ▶ **noun** Zoology a mammal of the dog family (Canidae).
– ORIGIN late 19th cent.: from modern Latin *Canidae* (plural), from Latin *canis* 'dog'.

canine /'keɪnʌɪn, 'ka-/ ▶ **adjective** of, relating to, or resembling a dog or dogs: *canine behavioural problems.*
■ Zoology of or relating to animals of the dog family.
▶ **noun 1** a dog.
■ Zoology another term for **CANID**.
2 (also **canine tooth**) a pointed tooth between the incisors and premolars of a mammal, often greatly enlarged in carnivores.
– ORIGIN late Middle English (in sense 2): from French, from Latin *caninus*, from *canis* 'dog'.

caning ▶ **noun** a beating with a cane as a punishment.
■ informal a resounding defeat: *the team suffered a caning at Blackburn.* ■ informal a severe reprimand: *education experts gave BBC chiefs a caning over the drama series.*

Canis Major /ˌkeɪnɪs 'meɪdʒə/ Astronomy a small constellation (the Great Dog), said to represent one of the dogs following Orion. It is just south of the celestial equator and contains the brightest star, Sirius.
■ [as genitive **Canis Majoris** /mə'dʒɔ:rɪs/] used with preceding letter or numeral to designate a star in this constellation: *the star Eta Canis Majoris.*
– ORIGIN Latin.

Canis Minor /'mʌɪnə/ Astronomy a small constellation (the Little Dog), said to represent one of the dogs following Orion. It is close to the celestial equator and contains the bright star Procyon.
■ [as genitive **Canis Minoris** /mɪ'nɔ:rɪs/] used with preceding letter or numeral to designate a star in this constellation: *the star Beta Canis Minoris.*
– ORIGIN Latin.

canister ▶ **noun** a round or cylindrical container, typically one made of metal, used for storing such things as food, chemicals, or rolls of film.
■ a cylinder of pressurized gas, typically one that explodes when thrown or fired from a gun: *riot police fired tear-gas canisters into the crowd.* ■ [mass noun] historical small bullets packed in cases that fit the bore of a gun: *another deadly volley of canister.*
– ORIGIN late 15th cent. (denoting a basket): from Latin *canistrum*, from Greek *kanastron* 'wicker basket', from *kanna* 'cane, reed' (see **CANE**).

canker ▶ **noun** [mass noun] **1** a necrotic fungal disease of apple and other trees that results in damage to the bark.
■ [count noun] an open lesion in plant tissue caused by infection or injury. ■ fungal rot in some fruits and vegetables, e.g. parsnips and tomatoes.
2 Medicine an ulcerous condition or disease, in particular:
■ (also **canker sore**) chiefly US a small ulcer of the mouth or lips. ■ another term for **THRUSH**[2] (in sense 2). ■ ulceration of the throat and other orifices of birds, typically caused by a protozoal infection. ■ (also **ear canker**) inflammation of the ear of a dog, cat, or rabbit, typically caused by a mite infestation. ■ figurative a malign and corrupting influence that is difficult to eradicate: [in sing.] *racism remains a canker at the heart of the nation.*
▶ **verb 1** [no obj.] (of woody plant tissue) become infected with canker: [as noun **cankering**] *we found some cankering of the wood.*
2 [with obj.] [usu. as adj. **cankered**] infect with a pervasive and corrupting bitterness: *he hated her with a cankered, shameful abhorrence.*
– DERIVATIVES **cankerous** adjective.
– ORIGIN Middle English (denoting a tumour): from Old French *chancre*, from Latin *cancer* 'crab' (see **CANCER**).

cankerworm ▶ **noun** the caterpillar of a North American moth that has wingless females. Cankerworms consume the buds and leaves of trees and can be a major pest.
• Several species in the family Geometridae, in particular *Paleacrita vernata* and *Alsophila pometaria*.

canna /'kanə/ (also **canna lily**) ▶ **noun** a lily-like tropical American plant with bright flowers and ornamental strap-like leaves.
• Genus *Canna*, family Cannaceae: several species, in particular forms of Indian shot (*C. indica*), which are widely naturalized.
– ORIGIN from modern Latin, from Latin *canna* 'cane, reed' (see **CANE**).

cannabinoid /'kanəbɪˌnɔɪd/ ▶ **noun** [mass noun] Chemistry any of a group of closely related compounds which include cannabinol and the active constituents of cannabis.

cannabinol /'kanəbɪˌnɒl, kə'nab-/ ▶ **noun** [mass noun] Chemistry a crystalline compound whose derivatives, especially THC, are the active constituents of cannabis.
• A polycyclic phenol; chem. formula: $C_{21}H_{26}O_2$.
– ORIGIN late 19th cent.: from **CANNABIS** + **-OL**.

cannabis ▶ **noun** [mass noun] a tall plant with a stiff upright stem, divided serrated leaves, and glandular hairs. It is used to produce hemp fibre and as a psychotropic drug. Also called **INDIAN HEMP, MARIJUANA**.
• *Cannabis sativa*, family Cannabaceae (or Cannabidaceae): two subspecies (sometimes considered two species), *C. s. sativa*, which is chiefly used for hemp, and *C. s. indica*, from which the drug is usually obtained.
■ a dried preparation of the flowering tops or other parts of this plant, or a resinous extract of it (**cannabis resin**), used (generally illegally) as a psychotropic drug, chiefly in cigarettes.
– ORIGIN from Latin, from Greek *kannabis*.

canned ▶ **adjective 1** (of food or drink) preserved or supplied in a sealed can: *canned beans.*
2 informal, often derogatory (of music, laughter, or applause) pre-recorded and therefore considered to be lacking in freshness and spontaneity.

cannel coal /'kan(ə)l/ ▶ **noun** [mass noun] a hard, compact kind of bituminous coal.
– ORIGIN mid 16th cent. (originally a northern English usage): of unknown origin.

cannellini bean /ˌkanə'li:ni/ ▶ **noun** a kidney-shaped bean of a medium-sized creamy-white variety.
– ORIGIN Italian *cannellini*, literally 'small tubes'.

cannelloni /ˌkanə'ləʊni/ ▶ **plural noun** rolls of pasta stuffed with a meat or vegetable mixture.
■ [treated as sing.] an Italian dish consisting of such rolls of pasta cooked in a cheese sauce.
– ORIGIN Italian, literally 'large tubes', from *cannello* 'tube'.

cannelure /'kan(ə)ljʊə/ ▶ **noun** a groove round the cylindrical part of a bullet.
– ORIGIN mid 18th cent.: from French, from *canneler* 'provide with a channel', from *canne* 'reed, cane'.

cannery ▶ **noun** (pl. **-ies**) a factory where food is canned.

Cannes /kan/ a resort on the Mediterranean coast of France; pop. 69,360 (1990). An international film festival is held there annually.

cannibal ▶ **noun** a person who eats the flesh of other human beings: [as modifier] *cannibal tribes.*
■ an animal that feeds on flesh of its own species.

– DERIVATIVES **cannibalism** noun, **cannibalistic** adjective, **cannibalistically** adverb.
– ORIGIN mid 16th cent.: from Spanish *Caníbales* (plural), variant (recorded by Columbus) of *Caribes*, the name of a West Indian people reputed to eat humans (see CARIB).

cannibalize (also **-ise**) ▶ verb [with obj.] **1** use (a machine) as a source of spare parts for another, similar machine.
■(of a company) reduce (the sales of one of its products) by introducing a similar, competing product.
2 (of an animal) eat (an animal of its own kind): *female spiders cannibalize courting males.*
– DERIVATIVES **cannibalization** noun.

Canning, George (1770–1827), British Tory statesman, Prime Minister 1827. After two periods as Foreign Secretary he succeeded Lord Liverpool as Prime Minister but died shortly afterwards.

Cannizzaro /ˌkanɪˈzɑːrəʊ/, Stanislao (1826–1910), Italian chemist. He revived Avogadro's hypothesis and used it to distinguish clearly between atoms and molecules, and to introduce the unified system of atomic and molecular weights.

cannon ▶ noun **1** (pl. usu. same) a large, heavy piece of artillery, typically mounted on wheels, formerly used in warfare.
■an automatic heavy gun that fires shells from an aircraft or tank.
2 Billiards & Snooker, chiefly Brit. a stroke in which the cue ball strikes two balls successively (for which two points are scored in billiards). [ORIGIN: early 19th cent.: alteration of CAROM.]
3 Engineering a heavy cylinder or hollow drum that is able to rotate independently on a shaft.
▶ verb [no obj., with adverbial of direction] chiefly Brit. collide with something forcefully or at an angle: *the couple behind almost cannoned into us | his shot cannoned off the crossbar.*
■Billiards & Snooker make a cannon shot.
– ORIGIN late Middle English: from French *canon*, from Italian *cannone* 'large tube', from *canna* 'cane, reed' (see CANE).

cannonade /ˌkanəˈneɪd/ ▶ noun a period of continuous heavy gunfire.
▶ verb [no obj.] discharge heavy guns continuously: [as noun **cannonading**] *the daily cannonading continued.*
– ORIGIN mid 16th cent.: from French, from Italian *cannonata*, from *cannone* (see CANNON).

cannonball ▶ noun a round metal or stone projectile fired from a cannon in former times.
■(also **cannonball dive**) N. Amer. a jump into water feet first with the knees clasped to the chest.

cannon bone ▶ noun a long tube-shaped bone in the lower leg of a horse or other large quadruped, between the fetlock and the knee or hock.

cannoneer ▶ noun historical an artilleryman who positioned and fired a cannon.

cannon fodder ▶ noun [mass noun] soldiers regarded merely as material to be expended in war.

cannot ▶ contraction of can not.

USAGE Both the one word form **cannot** and the two word form **can not** are acceptable, but **cannot** is far more common in all contexts.

cannula /ˈkanjʊlə/ ▶ noun (pl. **cannulae** /-liː/ or **cannulas**) Surgery a thin tube inserted into a vein or body cavity to administer medication, drain off fluid, or insert a surgical instrument.
– ORIGIN late 17th cent.: from Latin 'small reed', diminutive of *canna* (see CANE).

cannulate ▶ verb [with obj.] Surgery introduce a cannula or thin tube into (a vein or body cavity).
– DERIVATIVES **cannulation** noun.

canny ▶ adjective (**cannier**, **canniest**) **1** having or showing shrewdness and good judgement, especially in money or business matters: *canny investors will switch banks if they think they are getting a raw deal.*
2 N. English & Scottish pleasant; nice: *she's a canny lass.*
– DERIVATIVES **cannily** adverb, **canniness** noun.
– ORIGIN late 16th cent. (originally Scots): from CAN[1] (in the obsolete sense 'know') + -Y[1].

canoe ▶ noun a narrow keelless boat with pointed ends, propelled by using a paddle or paddles.
▶ verb (**-oes**, **-oed**, **-oeing**) [no obj., with adverbial of direction] travel in or paddle a canoe: *he had once canoed down the Nile.*

– DERIVATIVES **canoeist** noun.
– ORIGIN mid 16th cent.: from Spanish *canoa*, from Arawak, from Carib *canaoua*.

canoeing ▶ noun [mass noun] the sport or activity of travelling in or paddling a canoe.

canoe shell ▶ noun a marine mollusc which has a thin shell with a wide aperture.
● Family Scaphandridae, class Gastropoda: *Scaphander* and other genera.

canola /kəˈnəʊlə/ ▶ noun [mass noun] oilseed rape of a variety developed in Canada and grown in North America. It yields a valuable culinary oil.
– ORIGIN 1970s: from CANADA + -ola (based on Latin *oleum* 'oil').

canon[1] ▶ noun **1** a general law, rule, principle, or criterion by which something is judged: *the appointment violated the canons of fair play and equal opportunity.*
■a Church decree or law: *a set of ecclesiastical canons.*
2 a collection or list of sacred books accepted as genuine: *the formation of the biblical canon.*
■the works of a particular author or artist that are recognized as genuine: *the Shakespeare canon.* ■a list of literary works considered to be permanently established as being of the highest quality: *Hopkins was firmly established in the canon of English poetry.*
3 (also **canon of the Mass**) (in the Roman Catholic Church) the part of the Mass containing the words of consecration.
4 Music a piece in which the same melody is begun in different parts successively, so that the imitations overlap.
– PHRASES **in canon** Music with different parts successively beginning the same melody.
– ORIGIN Old English: from Latin, from Greek *kanōn* 'rule', reinforced in Middle English by Old French *canon.*

canon[2] ▶ noun a member of the clergy who is on the staff of a cathedral, especially one who is a member of the chapter. The position is frequently conferred as an honorary one.
■(also **canon regular** or **regular canon**) (in the Roman Catholic Church) a member of certain orders of clergy that live communally according to an ecclesiastical rule in the same way as monks.
– ORIGIN Middle English (in the sense 'canon regular'): from Old French *canonie*, from Latin *canonicus* 'according to rule' (see CANONIC). The other sense dates from the mid 16th cent.

cañon ▶ noun archaic spelling of CANYON.

canon cancrizans /ˈkanɡrɪˌzanz/ ▶ noun Music a canon in which the theme or subject is repeated backwards in the second part. Also called CRAB CANON.
– ORIGIN late 19th cent.: from CANON[1] + medieval Latin *cancrizans* 'walking backwards' (from *cancer* 'crab').

canoness /ˈkanənɪs/ ▶ noun (in the Roman Catholic Church) a member of certain religious orders of women living communally according to an ecclesiastical rule in the same way as nuns.

canonic /kəˈnɒnɪk/ ▶ adjective **1** Music in canon form.
2 another term for CANONICAL.
– DERIVATIVES **canonically** adverb.
– ORIGIN Old English (as a noun): from Old French *canonique* or Latin *canonicus* 'canonical', from Greek *kanonikos*, from *kanon* 'rule' (see CANON[1]). The adjective dates from the late 15th cent.

canonical /kəˈnɒnɪk(ə)l/ ▶ adjective **1** according to or ordered by canon law: *the canonical rites of the Roman Church.*
2 included in the list of sacred books officially accepted as genuine: *the canonical Gospels of the New Testament.*
■accepted as being accurate and authoritative: *the canonical method of comparative linguistics.* ■(of a writer or work) belonging to the literary canon: *canonical writers like Jane Austen.* ■according to recognized rules or scientific laws: *canonical nucleotide sequences.* ■Mathematics of or relating to a general rule or standard formula.
3 of or relating to a cathedral chapter or a member of it.
▶ plural noun (**canonicals**) the prescribed official dress of the clergy: *Cardinal Bea in full canonicals.*
– DERIVATIVES **canonically** adverb.
– ORIGIN late Middle English: from medieval Latin *canonicalis*, from Latin *canonicus* (see CANONIC).

canonical hours ▶ plural noun **1** the times of daily Christian prayer appointed in the breviary.
■the offices set for these times, namely matins with lauds, prime, terce, sext, nones, vespers, and compline.
2 (in the Church of England) the time during which a marriage may legally be celebrated (usually between 8 a.m. and 6 p.m.).

canonicity ▶ noun [mass noun] the fact or status of being canonical: *established standards of canonicity.*

canonist ▶ noun an expert in canon law.
– DERIVATIVES **canonistic** adjective.
– ORIGIN mid 16th cent.: from French *canoniste* or medieval Latin *canonista*, from Latin *canon* (see CANON[1]).

canonize (also **-ise**) ▶ verb [with obj.] (often **be canonized**) (in the Roman Catholic Church) officially declare (a dead person) to be a saint: *he was the last English saint to be canonized prior to the Reformation.*
■figurative regard as being above reproach or of great significance: *we have canonized freedom of speech as an absolute value overriding all others.* ■sanction by Church authority.
– DERIVATIVES **canonization** noun.
– ORIGIN late Middle English: from late Latin *canonizare* 'admit as authoritative' (in medieval Latin 'admit to the list of recognized saints'), from Latin *canon* (see CANON[1]).

canon law ▶ noun [mass noun] ecclesiastical law, especially (in the Roman Catholic Church) that laid down by papal pronouncements.

canon regular ▶ noun see CANON[2].

canonry ▶ noun (pl. **-ies**) the office or benefice of a canon.

canoodle ▶ verb [no obj.] informal kiss and cuddle amorously: *she was caught canoodling with her boyfriend.*
– ORIGIN mid 19th cent. (originally US): of unknown origin.

Canopic jar /kəˈnəʊpɪk/ (also **Canopic vase**) ▶ noun a covered urn used in ancient Egyptian burials to hold the entrails and other visceral organs from an embalmed body.
– ORIGIN late 19th cent.: *Canopic* from Latin *Canopicus*, from *Canopus*, the name of a town in ancient Egypt.

Canopus /kəˈnəʊpəs/ Astronomy the second brightest star in the sky, and the brightest in the constellation Carina. It is a supergiant, visible only to observers in the southern hemisphere.
– ORIGIN Latin, from Greek *Kanōpus*, the name of the pilot of the fleet of King Menelaus in the Trojan War.

canopy ▶ noun (pl. **-ies**) an ornamental cloth covering hung or held up over something, especially a throne or bed.
■figurative something hanging or perceived as hanging over a person or scene: *the canopy of twinkling stars.* ■Architecture a roof-like projection or shelter: *they mounted the station steps under the concrete canopy.* ■the transparent plastic or glass cover of an aircraft's cockpit. ■the expanding, umbrella-like part of a parachute, made of silk or nylon. ■[in sing.] the uppermost branches of the trees in a forest, forming a more or less continuous layer of foliage: *woolly monkeys spend hours every day sitting high in the canopy.*
▶ verb (**-ies**, **-ied**) [with obj.] [usu. as adj. **canopied**] cover or provide with a canopy: *a canopied bed | the river was canopied by overhanging trees.*
– ORIGIN late Middle English: from medieval Latin *canopeum* 'ceremonial canopy', alteration of Latin *conopeum* 'mosquito net over a bed', from Greek *kōnōpeion* 'couch with mosquito curtains', from *kōnōps* 'mosquito'.

canorous /kəˈnɔːrəs/ ▶ adjective rare (of song or speech) melodious or resonant.
– ORIGIN mid 17th cent.: from Latin *canorus* (from *canere* 'sing') + -OUS.

Canova /kəˈnəʊvə, Italian kaˈnɔva/, Antonio (1757–1822), Italian sculptor, a leading exponent of neoclassicism. Notable works: *Cupid and Psyche* (1792) and *The Three Graces* (1813–16).

canst archaic second person singular present of CAN[1].

Cant. ▶ abbreviation for Canticles (the Song of Songs) (in biblical references).

cant[1] /kant/ ▶ noun [mass noun] **1** hypocritical and sanctimonious talk, typically of a moral, religious,

or political nature: *he had no time for the cant of the priests about sin.*
2 [as modifier] denoting a phrase or catchword temporarily current or in fashion: *'herstories' rather than 'histories' as the cant phrase goes.*
■language peculiar to a specified group or profession and regarded with disparagement: *thieves' cant.*
▶**verb** [no obj.] dated talk hypocritically and sanctimoniously about something: *if they'd stop canting about 'honest work' they might get somewhere.*
– ORIGIN early 16th cent.: probably from Latin *cantare* 'to sing' (see **CHANT**). The early meaning was 'musical sound, singing'; in the mid 17th cent. this gave rise to the senses 'whining manner of speaking' and 'form of words repeated mechanically in such a manner' (for example a beggar's plea), hence 'jargon' (of beggars and other such groups).

cant² /kant/ ▶**verb** [with obj.] cause (something) to be in a slanting or oblique position; tilt: *he canted his head to look at the screen.*
■[no obj.] take or have a slanting position: *mismatched slate roofs canted at all angles.* ■ [no obj.] (of a ship) swing round: *the ship canted to starboard.*
▶**noun 1** [in sing.] a slope or tilt: *the outward cant of the curving walls.*
2 a wedge-shaped block of wood, especially one remaining after the better-quality pieces have been cut off.
– ORIGIN Middle English (denoting an edge or brink): from Middle Low German *kant, kante*, Middle Dutch *cant*, 'point, side, edge', based on a Romance word related to medieval Latin *cantus* 'corner, side'.

can't ▶**contraction of** cannot.

Cantab /'kantab/ ▶**abbreviation** of Cambridge University: *John Smith, MA (Cantab).*
– ORIGIN from Latin *Cantabrigiensis*, from *Cantabrigia* 'Cambridge'.

cantabile /kan'tɑːbɪleɪ/ Music ▶**adverb** & **adjective** in a smooth singing style.
▶**noun** a cantabile passage or movement.
– ORIGIN Italian, literally 'singable'.

Cantabria /kan'tabrɪə/ an autonomous region of northern Spain; capital, Santander.
– DERIVATIVES **Cantabrian** adjective & noun.

Cantabrigian /ˌkantə'brɪdʒɪən/ ▶**adjective** of or relating to Cambridge (in England) or Cambridge University.
▶**noun** a member of Cambridge University.
– ORIGIN mid 16th cent.: from Latin *Cantabrigia* (see sense 1 of **CAMBRIDGE**) + **-IAN**.

cantal /'kantɑːl/ ▶**noun** [mass noun] a hard, strong cheese made chiefly in the Auvergne.
– ORIGIN named after *Cantal*, a department of Auvergne, France.

cantaloupe /'kantəluːp/ (also **cantaloupe melon**) ▶**noun** a small round melon of a variety with orange flesh and ribbed skin.
– ORIGIN late 18th cent.: from French *cantaloup*, from *Cantaluppi* near Rome, where it was first grown in Europe after being introduced from Armenia.

cantankerous ▶**adjective** bad-tempered, argumentative, and uncooperative: *he can be a cantankerous old fossil at times.*
– DERIVATIVES **cantankerously** adverb, **cantankerousness** noun.
– ORIGIN mid 18th cent.: of unknown origin; perhaps a blend of Anglo-Irish *cant* 'auction' and *rancorous* (see **RANCOUR**).

cantata /kan'tɑːtə/ ▶**noun** a medium-length narrative or descriptive piece of music with vocal solos and usually a chorus and orchestra.
– ORIGIN early 18th cent.: from Italian *cantata (aria)* 'sung (air)', from *cantare* 'sing'.

cant dog ▶**noun** another term for **CANT HOOK**.

canteen ▶**noun 1** a restaurant provided by an organization such as a college, factory, or company for its students or staff.
2 Brit. a specially designed case or box containing a set of cutlery.
3 a small water bottle, as used by soldiers or campers.
– ORIGIN mid 18th cent. (originally denoting a type of shop in a barracks or garrison town): from French *cantine*, from Italian *cantina* 'cellar'. A French use of *cantine* denoting a small compartmented case for carrying bottles of wine may have given rise to sense 2.

canteen culture ▶**noun** [mass noun] informal, derogatory (in the UK) a set of conservative and discriminatory attitudes said to exist within the police force.

canter ▶**noun** [in sing.] a pace of a horse or other quadruped between a trot and a gallop, with not less than one foot on the ground at any time: *he kicked his horse into a canter | I rode away **at a canter**.*
■a ride on a horse at such a speed: *we came back from one of our canters.*
▶**verb** [no obj., with adverbial of direction] (of a horse) move at a canter in a particular direction: *they cantered down into the village.*
■[with obj.] make (a horse) move at a canter: *Katharine cantered Benji in a smaller and smaller circle.*
– PHRASES **in** (or **at**) **a canter** Brit. without much effort; easily: *they retained their leadership of the Second Division at a canter.*
– ORIGIN early 18th cent. (as a verb): short for *Canterbury pace* or *Canterbury gallop*, from the supposed easy pace of medieval pilgrims to **CANTERBURY**.

Canterbury 1 a city in Kent, SE England, the seat of the Archbishop of Canterbury; pop. 39,700 (1981). St Augustine established a church and monastery there in 597 and it became a place of medieval pilgrimage.
2 a region on the central east coast of South Island, New Zealand.

canterbury ▶**noun** (pl. **-ies**) a low open-topped cabinet with partitions for holding music or books.
– ORIGIN early 19th cent.: named after **CANTERBURY** in Kent (from a belief that the Archbishop of Canterbury ordered such a piece to be made).

Canterbury, Archbishop of ▶**noun** the archbishop of the southern province of the Church of England, who is Primate of All England and first peer of the realm, and plays a leading role in the worldwide Anglican Church.

Canterbury bell ▶**noun** a tall, sturdy cultivated bellflower with large pale blue flowers.
• *Campanula medium*, family Campanulaceae.
– ORIGIN late 16th cent.: named after the bells on Canterbury pilgrims' horses (see **CANTER**).

cantharides /kan'θarɪdiːz/ ▶**plural noun** see **SPANISH FLY**.
– ORIGIN late Middle English: from Latin, plural of *cantharis*, from Greek *kantharis* 'Spanish fly'.

cantharus /'kanθ(ə)rəs/ ▶**noun** (pl. **canthari**) (in ancient Greece and Rome) a large two-handled drinking cup.
– ORIGIN Latin, from Greek *kantharos*.

cant hook ▶**noun** a hinged metal hook at the end of a long handle, used for gripping and rolling logs.

canthus /'kanθəs/ ▶**noun** (pl. **canthi** /-θʌɪ/) the outer or inner corner of the eye, where the upper and lower lids meet.
– DERIVATIVES **canthic** adjective.
– ORIGIN mid 17th cent.: from Latin, from Greek *kanthos*.

canticle /'kantɪk(ə)l/ ▶**noun 1** a hymn or chant, typically with a biblical text, forming a regular part of a church service.
2 (**Canticles** or **Canticle of Canticles**) another name for **SONG OF SONGS** (especially in the Vulgate Bible).
– ORIGIN Middle English: from Latin *canticulum* 'little song', diminutive of *canticum*, from *canere* 'sing'.

cantilena /ˌkantɪ'leɪnə, -'liːnə/ ▶**noun** Music the part carrying the melody in a composition.
– ORIGIN mid 18th cent.: from Italian, from Latin, 'song'.

cantilever /'kantɪliːvə/ ▶**noun** a long projecting beam or girder fixed at only one end, used chiefly in bridge construction.
■a long bracket or beam projecting from a wall to support a balcony, cornice, or similar structure.
▶**verb** [with obj.] [usu. as adj. **cantilevered**] support by a cantilever or cantilevers: *a cantilevered deck.*
■[no obj., with adverbial of direction] project as or like a cantilever: *a conveyor cantilevered out over the river.*
– ORIGIN mid 17th cent.: of unknown origin.

cantilever bridge ▶**noun** a bridge in which each span is constructed from cantilevers built out sideways from piers.

cantillate /'kantɪleɪt/ ▶**verb** [with obj.] rare chant or intone (a passage of religious text).
– DERIVATIVES **cantillation** noun.
– ORIGIN mid 19th cent.: from Latin *cantillat-* 'hummed', from the verb *cantillare*, from *cantare* (see **CHANT**).

cantina /kan'tiːnə/ ▶**noun** (especially in a Spanish-speaking country or the south-western US) a bar.
■(in Italy) a wine shop.
– ORIGIN late 19th cent.: from Spanish and Italian.

canting arms ▶**plural noun** Heraldry arms containing an allusion to the name of the bearer.
– ORIGIN early 17th cent.: *canting* from **CANT¹**, in the obsolete sense 'speak, say (in a particular way)'.

cantle /'kant(ə)l/ ▶**noun** the raised curved part at the back of a horse's saddle.
– ORIGIN Middle English (in the sense 'a corner'): from Anglo-Norman French *cantel*, variant of Old French *chantel*, from medieval Latin *cantellus*, from *cantus* 'corner, side'.

canto /'kantəʊ/ ▶**noun** (pl. **-os**) one of the sections into which certain long poems are divided.
– ORIGIN late 16th cent.: from Italian, literally 'song', from Latin *cantus*.

Canton /kan'tɒn/ variant of **GUANGZHOU**.

canton ▶**noun 1** /'kantɒn, kan'tɒn/ a subdivision of a country established for political or administrative purposes.
■a state of the Swiss Confederation.
2 /'kant(ə)n/ Heraldry a square charge smaller than a quarter and positioned in the upper (usually dexter) corner of a shield.
– DERIVATIVES **cantonal** /'kantən(ə)l, kan'tɒn(ə)l/ adjective.
– ORIGIN early 16th cent.: from Old French, literally 'corner', from Provençal, based on a Romance word related to medieval Latin *cantus* (see **CANT²**). The verb was reinforced by French *cantonner* 'to quarter'.

Cantonese ▶**adjective** of or relating to Canton (Guangzhou), its inhabitants, their dialect, or their cuisine.
▶**noun** (pl. same) **1** a native or inhabitant of Canton.
2 [mass noun] a form of Chinese spoken by over 54 million people, mainly in SE China (including Hong Kong). Also called **YUE**.

cantonment /kan'tuːnm(ə)nt, -'tuːn-/ ▶**noun** a military camp, especially (historical) a permanent military station in British India.
– ORIGIN mid 18th cent.: from French *cantonnement*, from *cantonner* 'to quarter' (see **CANTON**).

Cantor /'kantɔː, German 'kantɔr/, Georg (1845–1918), Russian-born German mathematician. His work on numbers laid the foundations for the theory of sets and stimulated 20th-century exploration of number theory.

cantor /'kantɔː, -ə/ ▶**noun 1** an official who sings liturgical music and leads prayer in a synagogue. Also called **HAZZAN**.
2 (in formal Christian worship) a person who sings solo verses or passages to which the choir or congregation respond.
– ORIGIN mid 16th cent.: from Latin, 'singer', from *canere* 'sing'.

cantorial ▶**adjective** of or relating to a cantor.
■relating to or denoting the north side of the choir of a church, the side on which the cantor sits. The opposite of **DECANAL**.

cantoris /kan'tɔːrɪs/ ▶**noun** the section of a church or cathedral choir conventionally placed on the north side and taking the second or lower part in antiphonal singing. The opposite of **DECANI**.
– ORIGIN mid 17th cent.: from Latin, literally 'of the cantor' (see **CANTOR**).

cantrail /'kantreɪl/ ▶**noun** Brit. a timber or piece of metal supporting the roof of a railway carriage.
– ORIGIN late 19th cent.: from **CANT²** + **RAIL¹**.

cantrip /'kantrɪp/ ▶**noun** Scottish archaic a mischievous or playful act; a trick.
– ORIGIN late 16th cent. (also in the sense 'witch's trick'): of unknown origin.

cantus /'kantəs/ ▶**noun** the highest voice in polyphonic choral music.
– ORIGIN late 16th cent.: from Latin.

cantus firmus /ˌkantəs 'fəːməs/ ▶**noun** (pl. **cantus firmi** /ˌkantuːs 'fəːmʌɪ/) Music an existing melody used as the basis for a polyphonic composition.
– ORIGIN mid 19th cent.: from Latin, literally 'firm song'.

Canuck /kə'nʌk/ ▶**noun** informal a Canadian, especially a French Canadian (chiefly used by Canadians themselves and often derogatory in the US).
– ORIGIN apparently from **CANADA**.

Canute /kə'njuːt/ (also **Cnut** or **Knut**) (d.1035),

Danish king of England 1017–35, Denmark 1018–35, and Norway 1028–35, son of Sweyn I. He is remembered for demonstrating to fawning courtiers his inability to stop the rising tide; this has become distorted in folklore to suggest that Canute really expected to turn back the tide.

canvas ▶**noun** [mass noun] (pl. **canvases** or **canvasses**) a strong, coarse unbleached cloth made from hemp, flax, or a similar yarn, used to make items such as sails and tents and as a surface for oil painting: [as modifier] *a canvas bag*.
■[count noun] a piece of such cloth prepared for use as the surface for an oil painting. ■[count noun] an oil painting: *Turner's late canvases*. ■a variety of canvas with an open weave, used as a basis for tapestry and embroidery. ■(**the canvas**) the floor of a boxing or wrestling ring, having a canvas covering. ■[count noun] either of a racing boat's tapering ends, originally covered with canvas.
▶**verb** (**canvassed**, **canvassing**; US **canvased**, **canvasing**) [with obj.] (usually **be canvassed**) cover with canvas: *the door had been canvassed over*.
– PHRASES **by a canvas** (in boat racing) by a small margin. [ORIGIN: referring to the tapered front end of a racing boat (see above).] **under canvas 1** in a tent or tents: *the family will be living under canvas*. **2** with sails spread.
– ORIGIN late Middle English: from Old Northern French *canevas*, based on Latin *cannabis* 'hemp', from Greek.

canvasback ▶**noun** a North American diving duck with a long, sloping black bill, related (and with similar colouring) to the common pochard.
● *Aythya valisineria*, family Anatidae.
– ORIGIN late 16th cent.: so named because of the white back of the male.

canvass ▶**verb 1** [with obj.] solicit votes from (electors in a constituency): *in each ward, two workers canvassed some 2,000 voters* | [no obj.] *he's* ***canvassing for*** *the Green Party*.
■question (someone) in order to ascertain their opinion on something: *they promised to canvass all member clubs for their views*. ■ascertain (someone's opinion) by questioning them: *opinions on the merger were canvassed*. ■try to obtain; request: *they're canvassing support among shareholders*.
2 [with obj.] (often **be canvassed**) Brit. propose (an idea or plan) for discussion: *early retirement was canvassed as a solution to the problem of unemployment*.
■discuss thoroughly: *the issues that were canvassed are still unresolved*.
▶**noun** [usu. in sing.] an act or process of attempting to secure votes or ascertain opinions: *a house-to-house canvass*.
– DERIVATIVES **canvasser** noun.
– ORIGIN early 16th cent. (in the sense 'toss in a canvas sheet' (as a sport or punishment)): from **CANVAS**. Later extended senses include 'criticize, discuss' (mid 16th cent.) and 'propose for discussion'; hence 'seek support for'.

canyon ▶**noun** a deep gorge, typically one with a river flowing through it, as found in North America.
– ORIGIN mid 19th cent.: from Spanish *cañón* 'tube', based on Latin *canna* 'reed, cane'.

canyoning ▶**noun** [mass noun] the sport or activity of jumping into a fast-flowing mountain stream and allowing oneself to be carried downstream at high speed.

canzona /kanˈtsəʊnə, -z-/ ▶**noun** Music an instrumental arrangement of a French or Flemish song, typical of 16th-century Italy.
– ORIGIN late 19th cent.: from Italian, from **CANZONE**.

canzone /kanˈtsəʊneɪ, -z-/ ▶**noun** (pl. **canzoni** /-ni/) an Italian or Provençal song or ballad.
■a type of lyric resembling a madrigal.
– ORIGIN late 16th cent.: from Italian, 'song', from Latin *cantio(n-)* 'singing', from *canere* 'sing'.

canzonetta /ˌkanzəˈnɛtə, ˌkantsəˈnɛtə/ ▶**noun** (pl. **canzonettas** or **canzonette** /-ˈnɛteɪ/) a short, light vocal piece, especially in the Italian style of the 17th century.
– ORIGIN late 16th cent.: from Italian 'little song', diminutive of *canzone*, from Latin *cantio(n-)* 'singing', from *canere* 'sing'.

caoutchouc /ˈkaʊtʃʊk/ ▶**noun** [mass noun] unvulcanized natural rubber.
– ORIGIN late 18th cent.: from French, from obsolete Spanish *cauchuc*, from Quechua *kauchuk*.

CAP ▶**abbreviation for** Common Agricultural Policy.

cap ▶**noun 1** a kind of soft, flat hat without a brim and typically having a peak.
■[with adj. or noun modifier] a kind of soft, close-fitting head covering worn for a particular purpose: *a shower cap* | *a bathing cap*. ■chiefly Brit. a cap awarded as a sign of membership of a particular football, rugby, or cricket team, especially the national team in an international competition: *he has won three caps for Scotland*. ■a player to whom such a cap is awarded: *a former naval officer and rugby cap*. ■an academic mortar board: *school-leavers in cap and gown*.
2 a protective lid or cover for an object such as a bottle, the point of a pen, or a camera lens.
■Dentistry an artificial protective covering for a tooth. ■(also **Dutch cap**) Brit. informal a contraceptive diaphragm. ■the top of a bird's head when distinctively coloured. ■the broad upper part of the fruiting body of most mushrooms and toadstools, at the top of a stem and bearing gills or pores.
3 an upper limit imposed on spending or borrowing: *he raised the cap on local authority spending*.
4 short for **PERCUSSION CAP**.
▶**verb** (**capped**, **capping**) [with obj.] **1** put a lid or cover on: *he capped his pen*.
■(often **be capped**) form a covering layer or top part of: *several towers were capped by domes* | [as adj., in combination **-capped**] *snow-capped mountains*. ■put an artificial protective covering on (a tooth). ■provide a fitting climax or conclusion to: *he capped a memorable season by becoming champion of champions*. ■follow or reply to (a story, remark, or joke) by producing a better or more apposite one: *he prayed no wit would cap his remark with some repartee*.
2 (often **be capped**) place a limit or restriction on (prices, expenditure, or borrowing): *council budgets will be capped*.
3 (**be capped**) chiefly Brit. be chosen as a member of a particular soccer, rugby, or cricket team, especially a national one in an international competition: *he was capped ten times by England*.
4 Scottish & NZ confer a university degree on.
– PHRASES **cap** (or N. Amer. also **hat**) **in hand** humbly asking for a favour: *we have to* ***go cap in hand*** *begging for funds*. **if the cap** (or N. Amer. **the shoe**) **fits, wear it** used as a way of suggesting that someone should accept a generalized remark or criticism as applying to themselves. **set one's cap at** (or US **for**) dated (of a woman) try to attract (a particular man) as a suitor. **to cap it all** as the final unfortunate incident or piece of bad luck in a long series: *she was on edge, her nerves taut, and to cap it all, she could feel the beginnings of a headache*.
– DERIVATIVES **capful** noun (pl. **-fuls**).
– ORIGIN Old English *cæppe* 'hood', from late Latin *cappa*, perhaps from Latin *caput* 'head'.

cap. ▶**abbreviation for** ■capacity. ■capital (city). ■capital letter.

capability ▶**noun** (pl. **-ies**) (often **capability of doing/to do something**) the power or ability to do something: *he had an intuitive capability of bringing the best out in people* | *the capability to increase productivity*.
■(often **capabilities**) the extent of someone's or something's ability: *the job is* ***beyond*** *my* ***capabilities***. ■[usu. with noun modifier] a facility on a computer for performing a specified task: *a graphics capability*. ■[usu. with adj. or noun modifier] forces or resources giving a country or state the ability to undertake a particular kind of military action: *their nuclear weapons capability*.

Capability Brown see **BROWN**[5].

Capablanca /ˌkapəˈblaŋkə/, José Raúl (1888–1942), Cuban chess player, world champion 1921–1927.

capable ▶**adjective** [predic.] (**capable of doing something**) having the ability, fitness, or quality necessary to do or achieve a specified thing: *I'm quite capable of taking care of myself* | *the aircraft is capable of flying 5,000 miles non-stop*.
■able to achieve efficiently whatever one has to do; competent: *she looked enthusiastic and capable* | *a highly capable man*. ■open to or admitting of something: *the strange events are* ***capable of*** *rational explanation*.
– DERIVATIVES **capably** adverb.
– ORIGIN mid 16th cent. (in the sense 'able to take in', physically or mentally): from French, from late Latin *capabilis*, from Latin *capere* 'take or hold'.

capacious ▶**adjective** having a lot of space inside; roomy: *she rummaged in her capacious handbag*.
– DERIVATIVES **capaciously** adverb, **capaciousness** noun.
– ORIGIN early 17th cent.: from Latin *capax*, *capac-* 'capable' + **-IOUS**.

capacitance /kəˈpasɪt(ə)ns/ ▶**noun** [mass noun] Physics the ability of a system to store an electric charge.
■the ratio of the change in an electric charge in a system to the corresponding change in its electric potential. (Symbol: **C**)
– ORIGIN late 19th cent.: from **CAPACITY** + **-ANCE**.

capacitate ▶**verb** [with obj.] formal or archaic make (someone) capable of a particular action or legally competent to act in a particular way.
■(**be capacitated**) Physiology (of spermatozoa) undergo changes inside the female reproductive tract enabling them to penetrate and fertilize an ovum.
– DERIVATIVES **capacitation** noun.

capacitor /kəˈpasɪtə/ ▶**noun** a device used to store an electric charge, consisting of one or more pairs of conductors separated by an insulator.

capacity ▶**noun** (pl. **-ies**) **1** [in sing.] the maximum amount that something can contain: *the capacity of the freezer is 1.1 cubic feet* | *the stadium's seating capacity* | [mass noun] *the room was* ***filled to capacity***.
■[as modifier] fully occupying the available area or space: *they played to a capacity crowd*. ■the amount that something can produce: *the company aimed to double its electricity-generating capacity* | *when running* ***at full capacity***, *the factory will employ 450 people*. ■the total cylinder volume that is swept by the pistons in an internal-combustion engine. ■former term for **CAPACITANCE**.
2 the ability or power to do, experience, or understand something: *I was impressed by her* ***capacity for*** *hard work* | [with infinitive] *his capacity to inspire trust in others* | *their intellectual capacities*.
■[in sing.] a person's legal competence: *cases where a patient's testamentary capacity is in doubt*.
3 [in sing.] a specified role or position: *I was engaged in a voluntary capacity* | *writing* ***in his capacity as*** *legal correspondent*.
– DERIVATIVES **capacitive** (also **capacitative**) adjective (chiefly Physics).
– ORIGIN late Middle English: from French *capacité*, from Latin *capacitas*, from *capax*, *capac-* 'that can contain', from *capere* 'take or hold'.

cap and bells ▶**plural noun** historical the insignia of the professional jester.

caparison /kəˈparɪs(ə)n/ ▶**noun** an ornamental covering spread over a horse's saddle or harness.
▶**verb** (**be caparisoned**) (of a horse) be decked out in rich decorative coverings.
– ORIGIN early 16th cent.: from obsolete French *caparasson*, from Spanish *caparazón* 'saddlecloth', from *capa* 'hood'.

cape[1] ▶**noun** a sleeveless cloak, typically a short one.
■a part of a longer coat or cloak that falls loosely over the shoulders from the neckband. ■N. Amer. the pelt from the head and neck of an animal, for preparation as a hunting trophy.
▶**verb** [with obj.] N. Amer. skin the head and neck of (an animal) to prepare a hunting trophy.
– DERIVATIVES **caped** adjective.
– ORIGIN mid 16th cent.: from French, from Provençal *capa*, from late Latin *cappa* 'covering for the head'.

cape[2] ▶**noun** a headland or promontory.
■(**the Cape**) the Cape of Good Hope. ■(**the Cape**) the former Cape Province of South Africa.
– ORIGIN late Middle English: from Old French *cap*, from Provençal, based on Latin *caput* 'head'.

Cape Agulhas, Cape Bon, etc. see **AGULHAS, CAPE**; **BON, CAPE**, etc.

Cape Barren goose ▶**noun** a pale grey Australian goose related to the shelducks, with a short black bill that is almost covered by a waxy yellow cere, and a black tail. Also called **CEREOPSIS GOOSE**.
● *Cereopsis novaehollandiae*, family Anatidae.
– ORIGIN mid 19th cent.: named after *Cape Barren*, an island in the Bass Strait, Australia.

Cape Breton Island /ˈbrɛt(ə)n/ an island forming the north-eastern part of the province of Nova Scotia, Canada.

Cape buffalo ▶**noun** see **AFRICAN BUFFALO**.

Cape Cod a sandy peninsula in SE Massachusetts, forming a wide curve enclosing Cape Cod Bay.

Cape Colony early name (1814–1910) for the former **CAPE PROVINCE**.

Cape coloured ▶**noun** (pl. same or **Cape**

C

coloureds) (in South Africa) a person of mixed ethnic descent resident in the Western Cape Province, speaking Afrikaans or English as their first language, and typically not a follower of Islam. Compare with **CAPE MALAY**.
▶ adjective of or relating to Cape coloured people.

Cape cowslip ▶ noun a small, bulbous southern African plant of the lily family, which bears thick, typically spotted leaves and spikes of tubular or bell-shaped flowers.
● Genus *Lachenalia*, family Liliaceae.

Cape doctor ▶ noun S. African informal the strong prevailing SE wind in Western Cape Province.

Cape Dutch ▶ noun [mass noun] historical the form of Dutch spoken by the early settlers at the Cape of Good Hope, which developed into Afrikaans.
▶ adjective 1 historical of or relating to this language.
2 of or denoting a style of furniture or architecture used by early settlers in South Africa.

Cape gooseberry ▶ noun 1 a soft edible yellow berry enclosed in a husk that resembles a lantern in shape.
2 the tropical South American plant with heart-shaped leaves which bears this fruit.
● *Physalis peruviana*, family Solanaceae.

Cape hen ▶ noun the white-chinned petrel of southern oceans, with mainly dark brown plumage.
● *Procellaria aequinoctialis*, family Procellariidae.

Cape hunting dog ▶ noun see **HUNTING DOG** (sense 1).

Cape jasmine (also **jessamine**) ▶ noun a fragrant Chinese gardenia, some kinds of which have flowers that are used to perfume tea.
● Genus *Gardenia*, family Rubiaceae: several species, in particular *G. jasminoides*.

Čapek /ˈtʃapɛk/, Karel (1890–1938), Czech novelist and dramatist. He is known for *R.U.R.* (*Rossum's Universal Robots*) (1920), which introduced the word *robot* to the English language, and *The Insect Play* (1921), written with his brother **Josef** (1887–1945).

capelin /ˈkeɪplɪn, ˈkap-/ (also **caplin**) ▶ noun a small fish of the North Atlantic, resembling a smelt. It is abundant in coastal waters and provides a staple food for humans and many animals.
● *Mallotus villosus*, family Osmeridae.
– ORIGIN early 17th cent.: from French, from Provençal *capelan*, from medieval Latin *cappellanus* 'custodian' (see **CHAPLAIN**).

Capella /kəˈpɛlə/ Astronomy the sixth brightest star in the sky, and the brightest in the constellation Auriga. It is a yellow giant.
– ORIGIN Latin, 'she-goat', diminutive of *caper* 'goat'.

Cape Malay (also **Cape Muslim**) ▶ noun (in South Africa) a member of a predominantly Afrikaans-speaking and Muslim group resident mainly in the Western Cape Province. Compare with **CAPE COLOURED**.
▶ adjective of or relating to the Cape Malay people.

Cape marigold ▶ noun another term for **AFRICAN DAISY**.

Cape of Good Hope a mountainous promontory south of Cape Town, South Africa, near the southern extremity of Africa.

Cape pigeon (also **Cape petrel**) ▶ noun another term for **PINTADO PETREL**.

Cape primrose ▶ noun another term for **STREPTOCARPUS**.

Cape Province a former province of South Africa, containing the Cape of Good Hope. The area became a British colony in 1814: it was known as Cape Colony from then until 1910, when it joined the Union of South Africa. In 1994 it was divided into the provinces of Northern Cape, Western Cape, and Eastern Cape.

caper[1] ▶ verb [no obj., with adverbial of direction] skip or dance about in a lively or playful way: *children were capering about the room.*
▶ noun 1 a playful skipping movement: *she did a little caper or dance.*
2 informal an activity or escapade, typically one that is illicit or ridiculous: *I'm too old for this kind of caper | some sort of organized-crime caper.*
■ an amusing or far-fetched film or television drama: *a cop caper about intergalactic drug dealers.*
– PHRASES **cut a caper** make a playful, skipping movement.
– DERIVATIVES **caperer** noun.

– ORIGIN late 16th cent.: abbreviation of **CAPRIOLE**.

caper[2] ▶ noun 1 (usu. **capers**) the cooked and pickled flower buds of a bramble-like southern European shrub, used to flavour food.
2 the shrub from which these buds are taken.
● *Capparis spinosa*, family Capparidaceae.
– ORIGIN late Middle English: from French *câpres* or Latin *capparis*, from Greek *kapparis*; later interpreted as plural, hence the loss of the final *-s* in the 16th cent.

capercaillie /ˌkapəˈkeɪli/ (Scottish also **capercailzie** /-ˈkeɪlzi/) ▶ noun (pl. **-ies**) a large turkey-like Eurasian grouse of mature pine forests. The male has a courtship display in which it fans the tail and makes an extraordinary succession of sounds.
● Genus *Tetrao*, family Tetraonidae: two species, in particular *T. urogallus*, which has been re-established in the Scottish Highlands.
– ORIGIN mid 16th cent.: from Scottish Gaelic *capull coille*, literally 'horse of the wood'.

caper spurge ▶ noun an ornamental European spurge which has become naturalized in North America. It has poisonous seeds, but the buds can be used as a substitute for capers.
● *Euphorbia lathyris*, family Euphorbiaceae.

capeskin ▶ noun [mass noun] a soft leather made from South African sheepskin.

Cape sparrow ▶ noun a dark brown sparrow native to southern Africa.
● *Passer melanurus*, family Passeridae (or Ploceidae).

Capet /ˈkapɪt, kaˈpɛt, French kapɛ/, Hugh (938–96), king of France 987–96, founder of the Capetian dynasty.

Capetian /kəˈpiːʃ(ə)n/ ▶ adjective relating to or denoting the dynasty ruling France 987–1328.
▶ noun a member of this dynasty.

Cape Town the legislative capital of South Africa and administrative capital of the province of Western Cape; pop. 776,600 (1985).

Cape Verde Islands /vɜːd/ a country consisting of a group of islands in the Atlantic off the coast of Senegal, named after the most westerly cape of Africa; pop. 383,000 (est. 1991); languages, Portuguese (official), Creole; capital, Praia. Previously uninhabited, the islands were settled by the Portuguese from the 15th century. They remained a Portuguese colony until 1975, when an independent republic was established.
– DERIVATIVES **Cape Verdean** adjective & noun.

Cape Wrath /rɒθ, rɑːθ/ a headland at the north-western tip of the mainland of Scotland.

Cape York the northernmost point of the continent of Australia, on the Torres Strait at the tip of the sparsely populated **Cape York Peninsula** in Queensland.

capias /ˈkeɪpɪəs, ˈkap-/ ▶ noun (pl. **capiases**) Law, dated a writ ordering the arrest of a named person.
– ORIGIN late Middle English: from Latin *capias* (*ad respondendum*), literally 'you are to seize (until reply is made)', from *capere* 'take'.

capillarity ▶ noun [mass noun] the tendency of a liquid in a capillary tube or absorbent material to rise or fall as a result of surface tension. Also called **CAPILLARY ACTION**.
– ORIGIN mid 19th cent.: from French *capillarité*, from Latin *capillaris* 'like a hair' (see **CAPILLARY**).

capillary /kəˈpɪləri/ ▶ noun 1 Anatomy any of the fine branching blood vessels that form a network between the arterioles and venules.
2 (also **capillary tube**) a tube which has an internal diameter of hair-like thinness.
▶ adjective [attrib.] of or relating to capillaries or capillarity.
– ORIGIN mid 17th cent.: from Latin *capillaris*, from *capillus* 'hair', influenced by Old French *capillaire*.

capillary action ▶ noun another term for **CAPILLARITY**.

capillary joint ▶ noun a joint made between two pipes by putting their ends into a fitting that is only slightly larger than the pipes and filling the gap with molten solder.

capital[1] ▶ noun 1 (also **capital city** or **town**) the most important city or town of a country or region, usually its seat of government and administrative centre.
■ [with modifier] a place associated more than any other with a specified activity or product: *Milan is the fashion capital of the world.*

2 [mass noun] wealth in the form of money or other assets owned by a person or organization or available for or contributed for a particular purpose such as starting a company or investing: *the senior partner would provide the initial capital | rates of return on invested capital were high.*
■ the excess of a company's assets over its liabilities.
■ people who possess wealth and use it to control a society's economic activity, considered collectively: *a conflict of interest between capital and labour.* ■ [with modifier] figurative a valuable resource of a particular kind: *there is insufficient investment in human capital.*
3 (also **capital letter**) a letter of the size and form used to begin sentences and names: *he wrote the name in capitals.*
▶ adjective 1 [attrib.] (of an offence or charge) liable to the death penalty: *murder is the only capital crime in the state.*
2 [attrib.] (of a letter of the alphabet) large in size and of the form used to begin sentences and names.
3 informal, dated excellent: *he's a really capital fellow.*
▶ exclamation Brit. informal, dated used to express approval, satisfaction, or delight: *That's splendid! Capital!*
– PHRASES **make capital out of** use to one's own advantage: *trying to make political capital out of the weakness of his rival.* **with a capital ——** used to give emphasis to the word or concept in question: *she was ugly with a capital U.*
– DERIVATIVES **capitally** adverb.
– ORIGIN Middle English (as an adjective in the sense 'relating to the head or top', later 'standing at the head or beginning'): via Old French from Latin *capitalis*, from *caput* 'head'.

capital[2] ▶ noun Architecture the distinct, typically broader section at the head of a pillar or column.
– ORIGIN Middle English: from Old French *capitel*, from late Latin *capitellum* 'little head', diminutive of Latin *caput*.

capital adequacy ▶ noun [mass noun] the statutory minimum reserves of capital which a bank or other financial institution must have available.

capital consumption ▶ noun [mass noun] Economics the total depreciation of assets in an economy in a specified period.

capital gain ▶ noun (often **capital gains**) a profit from the sale of property or an investment.

capital gains tax ▶ noun [mass noun] a tax levied on profit from the sale of property or an investment.

capital goods ▶ plural noun goods that are used in producing other goods, rather than being bought by consumers. Often contrasted with **CONSUMER GOODS**.

capital-intensive ▶ adjective (of a business or industrial process) requiring the investment of large sums of money.

capitalism ▶ noun [mass noun] an economic and political system in which a country's trade and industry are controlled by private owners for profit, rather than by the state.

capitalist ▶ noun a person who uses their wealth to invest in trade and industry for profit in accordance with the principles of capitalism: *the creation of the factory system by nineteenth-century capitalists.*
▶ adjective practising, supporting, or based on the principles of capitalism: *capitalist countries | the global economy is essentially capitalist.*
– DERIVATIVES **capitalistic** adjective, **capitalistically** adverb.

capitalize (also **-ise**) ▶ verb 1 [no obj.] (**capitalize on**) take the chance to gain advantage from: *an attempt by the opposition to capitalize on the government's embarrassment.*
2 [with obj.] provide (a company or industry) with capital: [as adj. **capitalized**] *a highly capitalized industry.*
3 realize (the present value of an income); convert into capital.
■ reckon (the value of an asset) by setting future benefits against the cost of maintenance: *a trader will want to capitalize repairs expenditure.*
4 [with obj.] write or print (a word or letter) in capital letters.
■ begin (a word) with a capital letter.
– DERIVATIVES **capitalization** noun.

capital levy ▶ noun a tax by means of which the state appropriates a fixed proportion of private wealth.

capital market ▶ noun the part of a financial system concerned with raising capital by dealing in shares, bonds, and other long-term investments.

capital punishment ▶ noun [mass noun] the legally authorized killing of someone as punishment for a crime.

capital ship ▶ noun a large warship such as a battleship or aircraft carrier.

capital sum ▶ noun a lump sum of money payable to an insured person or paid as an initial fee or investment.

capital territory ▶ noun a territory containing the capital city of a country, in Australia, Nigeria, Pakistan, and elsewhere.

capital transfer tax ▶ noun [mass noun] (in the UK) a tax levied on the transfer of capital by gift or bequest (replaced in 1986 by inheritance tax).

capitano /ˌkapɪˈtɑːnəʊ/ ▶ noun (pl. **-os**) (in Italy or among Italian-speakers) a captain or chief (used chiefly as a form of address).
– ORIGIN Italian.

capitate /ˈkapɪteɪt/ ▶ adjective Botany & Zoology ending in a distinct compact head.
▶ noun (also **capitate bone**) Anatomy the largest of the carpal bones, situated at the base of the palm of the hand and articulating with the third metacarpal.
– ORIGIN mid 17th cent.: from Latin *capitatus*, from *caput, capit-* 'head'.

capitation ▶ noun [mass noun] the payment of a fee or grant to a doctor, school, or other person or body providing services to a number of people, such that the amount paid is determined by the number of patients, pupils, or customers: *the increased capitation enabled schools to offer pupils an enhanced curriculum* | [as modifier] *income from capitation fees.*
– ORIGIN early 17th cent. (denoting the counting of heads): from late Latin *capitatio* 'poll tax', from *caput* 'head'.

Capitol /ˈkapɪt(ə)l/ (usu. **the Capitol**) **1** the seat of the US Congress in Washington DC.
■ **(capitol)** US a building housing a legislative assembly: *50,000 people marched on New Jersey's state capitol.*
2 the temple of Jupiter on the Capitoline Hill in ancient Rome.
– ORIGIN from Old French *capitolie, capitoile*, later assimilated to Latin *Capitolium* (from *caput, capit-* 'head').

Capitol Hill the region around the Capitol in Washington DC (often as an allusive reference to the US Congress itself).

capitular /kəˈpɪtjʊlə/ ▶ adjective **1** of or relating to a cathedral chapter.
2 Anatomy & Biology of or relating to a capitulum.
– ORIGIN early 16th cent.: from late Latin *capitularis*, from Latin *capitulum* 'small head'.

capitulary /kəˈpɪtjʊləri/ ▶ noun (pl. **-ies**) historical a royal ordinance under the Merovingian dynasty.
– ORIGIN mid 17th cent.: from Latin *capitularius*, from Latin *capitulum* in the sense 'section of a law'.

capitulate /kəˈpɪtjʊleɪt/ ▶ verb [no obj.] cease to resist an opponent or an unwelcome demand; surrender: *the patriots had to capitulate to the enemy forces.*
– DERIVATIVES **capitulator** noun.
– ORIGIN mid 16th cent. (in the sense 'parley, draw up terms'): from French *capituler*, from medieval Latin *capitulare* 'draw up under headings', from Latin *capitulum*, diminutive of *caput* 'head'.

capitulation ▶ noun [mass noun] the action of surrendering or ceasing to resist an opponent or demand: *the victor sees it as a sign of capitulation* | [count noun] *a capitulation to wage demands.*
■ **(capitulations)** historical an agreement or set of conditions.
– ORIGIN mid 16th cent.: from late Latin *capitulatio(n-)*, from the verb *capitulare* (see **CAPITULATE**).

capitulum /kəˈpɪtjʊləm/ ▶ noun (pl. **capitula** /-lə/) Anatomy & Biology a compact head of a structure, in particular a dense flat cluster of small flowers or florets, as in plants of the daisy family.
– ORIGIN early 18th cent.: from Latin, diminutive of *caput* 'head'.

caplet (trademark **Caplet**) ▶ noun a coated oral medicinal tablet.
– ORIGIN 1930s: blend of **CAPSULE** and **TABLET**.

caplin ▶ noun variant spelling of **CAPELIN**.

cap'n /ˈkapn/ ▶ noun informal contraction of **CAPTAIN**, used in representing speech.

capo¹ /ˈkapəʊ/ (also **capo tasto**) ▶ noun (pl. **-os**) a clamp fastened across all the strings of a fretted musical instrument to raise their tuning by a chosen amount.
– ORIGIN late 19th cent.: from Italian *capo tasto*, literally 'head stop'.

capo² /ˈkapəʊ/ ▶ noun (pl. **-os**) chiefly US the head of a crime syndicate, especially the Mafia, or a branch of one.
– ORIGIN 1950s: from Italian, from Latin *caput* 'head'.

Capo di Monte /ˌkapəʊ dɪ ˈmɒnteɪ, ˈmɒnti/ ▶ noun [mass noun] a type of porcelain first produced at the Capo di Monte palace near Naples in the mid 18th century. It is usually in the form of tableware or figures, and is generally white with richly coloured rococo decoration.

capoeira /ˌkapʊˈeɪrə/ ▶ noun [mass noun] a system of physical discipline and movement originating among Brazilian slaves, treated as a martial art and dance form.
– ORIGIN Portuguese.

cap of liberty ▶ noun a conical cap given to Roman slaves on their emancipation and often used as a republican symbol in more recent times.

cap of maintenance ▶ noun a cap or hat worn as a symbol of official dignity or carried in front of a sovereign on ceremonial occasions.

capon /ˈkeɪp(ə)n/ ▶ noun a castrated domestic cock fattened for eating.
– DERIVATIVES **caponize** (also **-ise**) verb.
– ORIGIN late Old English: from Old French, based on Latin *capo, capon-*.

caponata /ˌkapə(ʊ)ˈnɑːtə/ ▶ noun [mass noun] a dish of aubergines, olives, and onions seasoned with herbs, typically served as an appetizer.
– ORIGIN Italian.

Capone /kəˈpəʊn/, Al (1899–1947), American gangster, of Italian descent; full name *Alphonse Capone*. Although he was indirectly responsible for many murders, including the St Valentine's Day Massacre, it was for federal income tax evasion that he was eventually imprisoned in 1931.

caponier /ˌkapəˈnɪə/ ▶ noun a covered passage across a ditch round a fort.
– ORIGIN late 17th cent.: from Spanish *caponera*, literally 'capon enclosure'.

capot /kəˈpɒt/ ▶ noun (in piquet) the winning of all twelve tricks in the hand by one player, for which a bonus is awarded.
▶ verb (**capotted, capotting**) [with obj.] score a capot against (one's opponent).
– ORIGIN mid 17th cent.: from French, perhaps from a dialect variant of *chapoter* 'castrate'.

capo tasto /ˌkapəʊ ˈtastəʊ/ ▶ noun (pl. **-os**) another term for **CAPO¹**.

Capote /kəˈpəʊti/, Truman (1924–84), American writer; born *Truman Streckfus Persons*. Notable works: *Breakfast at Tiffany's* (1958), *In Cold Blood* (1966).

capote /kəˈpəʊt/ ▶ noun N. Amer., historical a long cloak or coat with a hood, typically part of an army or company uniform.
– ORIGIN early 19th cent.: from French, diminutive of *cape* (see **CAPE¹**).

Capp, Al (1909–79), American cartoonist; full name *Alfred Gerald Caplin*. He is best known for his comic strip 'Li'l Abner', which appeared in the *New York Mirror* from 1934 to 1977.

Cappadocia /ˌkapəˈdəʊʃə/ an ancient region of central Asia Minor, between Lake Tuz and the Euphrates, north of Cilicia. It was an important centre of early Christianity.
– DERIVATIVES **Cappadocian** adjective & noun.

cappelletti /ˌkapəˈlɛti/ ▶ plural noun small pieces of pasta folded and stuffed with meat or cheese.
– ORIGIN Italian, literally 'little hats'.

capper ▶ noun N. Amer. informal a more surprising, upsetting, or entertaining event or situation than all others that have gone before: *the capper was him accusing her of ripping off his car.*

cappuccino /ˌkapʊˈtʃiːnəʊ/ ▶ noun (pl. **-os**) [mass noun] coffee made with milk that has been frothed up with pressurized steam.
– ORIGIN 1940s: from Italian, literally 'Capuchin', because its colour resembles that of a Capuchin's habit.

Capra /ˈkaprə/, Frank (1897–1991), Italian-born American film director. He is known for comedies such as: *It Happened One Night* (1934), *Arsenic and Old Lace* (1944), and *It's a Wonderful Life* (1946). He won six Oscars.

Capri /kəˈpriː, Italian ˈkapri/ an island off the west coast of Italy, south of Naples.

capriccio /kəˈprɪtʃɪəʊ/ ▶ noun (pl. **-os**) a lively piece of music, typically one that is short and free in form.
■ a painting or other work of art representing a fantasy or a mixture of real and imaginary features.
– ORIGIN early 17th cent. (denoting a sudden change of mind): from Italian, literally 'head with the hair standing on end', hence 'horror', later 'a sudden start' (influenced by *capra* 'goat', associated with frisky movement), from *capo* 'head' + *riccio* 'hedgehog'.

capriccioso /kəˌprɪtʃɪˈəʊzəʊ, -səʊ/ ▶ adverb & adjective Music (especially as a direction) in a free and impulsive style.
– ORIGIN Italian, literally 'capricious', from **CAPRICCIO**.

caprice /kəˈpriːs/ ▶ noun **1** a sudden and unaccountable change of mood or behaviour: *her caprices had made his life impossible* | [mass noun] *a land where men were ruled by law and not by caprice.*
2 Music another term for **CAPRICCIO**.
– ORIGIN mid 17th cent.: from French, from Italian (see **CAPRICCIO**).

capricious /kəˈprɪʃəs/ ▶ adjective given to sudden and unaccountable changes of mood or behaviour: *a capricious and often brutal administration.*
■ changing according to no discernible rules; unpredictable: *a capricious climate.*
– DERIVATIVES **capriciously** adverb, **capriciousness** noun.
– ORIGIN early 17th cent.: from French *capricieux*, from Italian (see **CAPRICCIO**).

Capricorn /ˈkaprɪkɔːn/ Astrology the tenth sign of the zodiac (the Goat), which the sun enters at the northern winter solstice (about 21 December). Compare with **CAPRICORNUS**.
■ **(a Capricorn)** a person born when the sun is in this sign.
– PHRASES **tropic of Capricorn** see **TROPIC¹**.
– DERIVATIVES **Capricornian** noun & adjective.
– ORIGIN Old English, from Latin *capricornus*, from *caper, capr-* 'goat' + *cornu* 'horn', on the pattern of Greek *aigokerōs* 'goat-horned, Capricorn'.

Capricornus /ˌkaprɪˈkɔːnəs/ Astronomy a constellation (the Goat), said to represent a goat with a fish's tail. It has few bright stars. Compare with **CAPRICORN**.
■ [as genitive **Capricorni** /ˌkaprɪˈkɔːniː/] used with preceding letter or numeral to designate a star in this constellation: *the star 41 Capricorni.*
– ORIGIN Latin (see **CAPRICORN**).

caprine /ˈkaprʌɪn/ ▶ adjective of, relating to, or resembling goats.
– ORIGIN late Middle English: from Latin *caprinus*, from *caper, capr-* 'goat'.

capriole /ˈkaprɪəʊl/ ▶ noun a movement performed in classical riding, in which the horse leaps from the ground and kicks out with its hind legs.
■ a leap or caper in dancing, especially a cabriole.
– ORIGIN late 16th cent.: from obsolete French (now *cabriole*), from Italian *capriola* 'leap', from *capriolo* 'roebuck', from Latin *capreolus*, diminutive of *caper, capr-* 'goat'.

capri pants /kəˈpriː/ (also **capris**) ▶ plural noun close-fitting tapered trousers for women.
– ORIGIN 1950s (originally US): named after the island of **CAPRI**.

Caprivi Strip /kəˈpriːvi/ a narrow strip of Namibia which extends towards Zambia from the north-eastern corner of Namibia and reaches the Zambezi River.
– ORIGIN named after Leo Graf von *Caprivi*, German imperial Chancellor (1890–4) at the time when this region became part of the colony of German South West Africa.

cap rock ▶ noun [mass noun] a layer of hard impervious rock overlying and often sealing in a deposit of oil, gas, or coal.

caproic acid /kəˈprəʊɪk/ ▶ noun [mass noun] Chemistry

a liquid fatty acid present in milk fat and coconut and palm oils.
• Alternative name: **hexanoic acid**; chem. formula: $CH_3(CH_2)_4COOH$.
– DERIVATIVES **caproate** noun.
– ORIGIN mid 19th cent.: *caproic* from Latin *caper, capr-* 'goat' (because of its smell) + **-IC**.

caprolactam /ˌkaprə(ʊ)ˈlaktam/ ▶ **noun** [mass noun] Chemistry a synthetic crystalline compound which is an intermediate in nylon manufacture.
• A lactam; chem. formula: $C_6H_{11}NO$.
– ORIGIN 1940s: from **CAPROIC ACID** + **LACTAM**.

caprylic acid /kaˈprɪlɪk/ ▶ **noun** [mass noun] Chemistry a liquid fatty acid present in butter and other fats.
• Alternative name: ***n*-octanoic acid**; chem. formula: $CH_3(CH_2)_6COOH$.
– DERIVATIVES **caprylate** noun.
– ORIGIN mid 19th cent.: from Latin *caper, capr-*, 'goat' + **-YL** + **-IC**.

caps ▶ **abbreviation for** capital letters.

capsaicin /kapˈseɪɪsɪn/ ▶ **noun** [mass noun] Chemistry a compound that is responsible for the pungency of capsicums.
• A cyclic amide; chem. formula: $C_{18}H_{27}NO_3$.
– ORIGIN late 19th cent.: alteration of *capsicine*, the name of a substance formerly thought to have the same property.

Capsian /ˈkapsɪən/ ▶ **adjective** Archaeology of, relating to, or denoting a Palaeolithic culture of North Africa and southern Europe, noted for its microliths. It is dated to *c.*8000–4500 BC.
■ [as noun **the Capsian**] the Capsian culture or period.
– ORIGIN early 20th cent.: from Latin *Capsa* (now *Gafsa* in Tunisia), where objects from this culture were found, + **-IAN**.

capsicum /ˈkapsɪkəm/ ▶ **noun** (pl. **capsicums**) a tropical American plant of the nightshade family with fruits containing many seeds. Many kinds of cultivated peppers with edible pungent fruits have been developed.
• Genus *Capsicum*, family Solanaceae: several species and varieties, in particular *C. annuum* var. *annuum*, the cultivated forms of which include the '*grossum*' group (sweet peppers) and the '*longum*' group (chilli peppers).
■ the fruit of any of these plants, varying in size, colour, and pungency.
– ORIGIN late 16th cent.: modern Latin, perhaps from Latin *capsa* (see **CASE**[2]).

capsid[1] ▶ **noun** another term for **MIRID**.
– ORIGIN late 19th cent.: from modern Latin *Capsidae* (plural), from *Capsus* (genus name).

capsid[2] ▶ **noun** Microbiology the protein coat or shell of a virus particle, surrounding the nucleic acid or nucleoprotein core.
– ORIGIN 1960s: coined in French from Latin *capsa* (see **CASE**[2]).

capsize ▶ **verb** [no obj.] (of a boat) be overturned in the water: *the craft capsized in heavy seas* | [as adj. **capsized**] *a capsized dinghy.*
■ [with obj.] cause (a boat) to overturn.
▶ **noun** [in sing.] an instance of capsizing.
– ORIGIN late 18th cent.: perhaps based on Spanish *capuzar* 'sink (a ship) by the head', from *cabo* 'head' + *chapuzar* 'to dive or duck'.

cap sleeve ▶ **noun** a sleeve extending only a short distance from the shoulder and tapering to nothing under the arm.

capstan /ˈkapst(ə)n/ ▶ **noun** a broad revolving cylinder with a vertical axis used for winding a rope or cable, powered by a motor or pushed round by levers.
■ the motor-driven spindle on a tape recorder that makes the tape travel past the head at constant speed.
– ORIGIN late Middle English: from Provençal *cabestan*, from *cabestre* 'halter', from Latin *capistrum*, from *capere* 'seize'.

capstan lathe ▶ **noun** a lathe with a revolving tool holder that enables several tools to be permanently mounted on it.

capstone ▶ **noun** a stone fixed on top of something, typically a wall.
■ Archaeology a large flat stone forming a roof over the chamber of a megalithic tomb.

capsule /ˈkapsjuːl, -sjʊl/ ▶ **noun** a small case or container, especially a round or cylindrical one.
■ a small soluble case of gelatin containing a dose of medicine, swallowed whole. ■ a top or cover for a bottle, especially the foil or plastic covering the cork of a wine bottle. ■ short for **SPACE CAPSULE**. ■ [as modifier] figurative (of a piece of writing) shortened but retaining the essence of the original; condensed: *a capsule review of the movie.* ■ Anatomy a tough sheath or membrane that encloses something in the body, such as a kidney, a lens, or a synovial joint. ■ Biology a gelatinous layer forming the outer surface of some bacterial cells. ■ Botany a dry fruit that releases its seeds by bursting open when ripe, such as a pea pod. ■ Botany the spore-producing structure of mosses and liverworts, typically borne on a stalk.
– DERIVATIVES **capsular** adjective, **capsulate** adjective.
– ORIGIN late Middle English (in the general sense 'small container'): via French from Latin *capsula*, diminutive of *capsa* (see **CASE**[2]).

capsulize (also **-ise**) ▶ **verb** [with obj.] put (information) in compact form; summarize.

Capt. ▶ **abbreviation for** Captain.

captain ▶ **noun** the person in command of a ship.
■ the pilot in command of a civil aircraft. ■ a rank of naval officer above commander and below commodore. ■ a rank of officer in the army and in the US and Canadian air forces, above lieutenant and below major. ■ (in the US) a police officer in charge of a precinct, ranking below a chief. ■ the leader of a team, especially in sports. ■ a powerful or influential person in a particular field: *a captain of industry.* ■ Brit. a head boy or girl in a school. ■ N. Amer. a supervisor of waiters or bellboys. ■ Brit. a foreman.
▶ **verb** [with obj.] be the captain of (a ship, aircraft, or sports team).
– DERIVATIVES **captaincy** noun.
– ORIGIN late Middle English (in the general sense 'chief or leader'): from Old French *capitain* (superseding earlier *chevetaigne* 'chieftain'), from late Latin *capitaneus* 'chief', from Latin *caput, capit-* 'head'.

Captain Cooker ▶ **noun** NZ a wild boar.
– ORIGIN late 19th cent.: named after Captain J. Cook (see **COOK**[1]), who brought domesticated pigs (from which the wild boar is supposedly descended) to New Zealand.

captain general ▶ **noun** an honorary rank of senior officer in the British army, most commonly in an artillery regiment.

captan /ˈkapt(ə)n/ ▶ **noun** [mass noun] a synthetic fungicide and insecticide derived from a mercaptan.

caption ▶ **noun** a title or brief explanation appended to an illustration, cartoon, or poster.
■ a piece of text appearing on a cinema or television screen as part of a film or broadcast. ■ Law the heading of a legal document.
▶ **verb** [with obj.] (usu. **be captioned**) provide (an illustration) with a title or explanation: *the drawings were captioned with humorous texts* | [with two objs] *the photograph was captioned 'Three little maids'.*
– ORIGIN late Middle English (in the sense 'seizing, capture'): from Latin *captio(n-)*, from *capere* 'take, seize'. Early senses 'arrest' and 'warrant for arrest' gave rise to 'statement of where, when, and by whose authority a warrant was issued' (late 17th cent.): this was usually appended to a legal document, hence the sense 'heading or appended wording' (late 18th cent.).

captious /ˈkapʃəs/ ▶ **adjective** formal (of a person) tending to find fault or raise petty objections.
– DERIVATIVES **captiously** adverb, **captiousness** noun.
– ORIGIN late Middle English (also in the sense 'intended to deceive someone'): from Old French *captieux* or Latin *captiosus*, from *captio(n-)* 'seizing', (figuratively) 'deceiving' (see **CAPTION**).

captivate ▶ **verb** [with obj.] attract and hold the interest and attention of; charm: *he was captivated by her beauty* | [as adj. **captivating**] *a captivating smile.*
– DERIVATIVES **captivatingly** adverb, **captivation** noun.
– ORIGIN early 16th cent.: from late Latin *captivat-* 'taken captive', from the verb *captivare*, from *captivus* (see **CAPTIVE**).

captive ▶ **noun** a person who has been taken prisoner or an animal that has been confined.
▶ **adjective** imprisoned or confined: *the farm was used to **hold** prisoners of war **captive** | a captive animal.*
■ [attrib.] having no freedom to choose alternatives or to avoid something: *advertisements at the cinema reach a captive audience.* ■ (of a facility or service) controlled by, and typically for the sole use of, an establishment or company: *a captive power plant.*
– ORIGIN late Middle English: from Latin *captivus*, from *capere* 'seize, take'.

captive balloon ▶ **noun** a lighter-than-air balloon secured by a rope to the ground, used to carry radar equipment or for parachute jumps.

captivity ▶ **noun** (pl. **-ies**) [mass noun] the condition of being imprisoned or confined: *he was released after 865 days **in captivity** | the third month of their captivity passed.*
■ (**the Captivity**) short for **BABYLONIAN CAPTIVITY**.
– ORIGIN late Middle English: from Latin *captivitas*, from *captivus* 'taken captive' (see **CAPTIVE**).

captor ▶ **noun** a person or animal that catches or confines another.
– ORIGIN mid 16th cent.: from Latin, from *capt-* 'seized, taken', from the verb *capere*.

capture ▶ **verb** [with obj.] take into one's possession or control by force: *the Russians captured 13,000 men* | figurative *the appeal captured the imagination of thousands.*
■ record or express accurately in words or pictures: *she did a series of sketches, trying to capture all his moods.* ■ Physics absorb (an atomic or subatomic particle). ■ (in chess and other board games) make a move that secures the removal of (an opposing piece) from the board. ■ Astronomy (of a star, planet, or other celestial body) bring (a less massive body) permanently within its gravitational influence. ■ (of a stream) divert the upper course of (another stream) by encroaching on its catchment area. ■ cause (data) to be stored in a computer.
▶ **noun** [mass noun] the action of capturing or of being captured: *the capture of the city marks the high point of his career | he was killed while resisting capture.*
■ [count noun] a person or thing that has been captured.
– DERIVATIVES **capturer** noun.
– ORIGIN mid 16th cent. (as a noun): from French, from Latin *captura*, from *capt-* 'seized, taken', from the verb *capere*.

Capuchin /ˈkapʊtʃɪn/ ▶ **noun 1** a friar belonging to a branch of the Franciscan order that observes a strict rule drawn up in 1529.
2 a cloak and hood formerly worn by women.
3 (**capuchin** or **capuchin monkey**) a South American monkey with a cap of hair on the head which has the appearance of a cowl.
• Genus *Cebus*, family Cebidae: four species, including the **brown capuchin** (*C. apella*).
4 (**capuchin**) a pigeon of a breed with head and neck feathers resembling a cowl.
– ORIGIN late 16th cent.: from obsolete French, earlier form of *capucin*, from Italian *cappuccino*, from *cappuccio* 'hood, cowl', from *cappa* (see **CAPE**[1]), the friars being so named because of their sharp-pointed hoods.

capybara /ˌkapɪˈbɑːrə/ ▶ **noun** (pl. same or **capybaras**) a South American mammal that resembles a giant long-legged guinea pig. It lives in groups near water and is the largest living rodent.
• *Hydrochaerus hydrochaeris*, the only member of the family Hydrochaeridae.
– ORIGIN early 17th cent.: from Spanish *capibara* or Portuguese *capivara*, from Tupi *capiuára*, from *capĩ* 'grass' + *uára* 'eater'.

car ▶ **noun** a road vehicle, typically with four wheels, powered by an internal-combustion engine and able to carry a small number of people: *we're going **by car** |* [as modifier] *a car crash.*
■ a railway carriage, especially one of a specified kind: *the first-class cars.* ■ N. Amer. any railway carriage or wagon: *a railroad car.* ■ the passenger compartment of a lift, cableway, or balloon. ■ poetic/literary a chariot.
– DERIVATIVES **carful** noun (pl. **-fuls**).
– ORIGIN late Middle English (in the general sense 'wheeled vehicle'): from Old Northern French *carre*, based on Latin *carrum, carrus*, of Celtic origin.

Cara /ˈkɑːrə/ ▶ **noun** a potato of a maincrop variety.

carabao /ˌkarəˈbeɪəʊ/ ▶ **noun** (pl. same or **-os**) another term for **WATER BUFFALO**.
– ORIGIN early 20th cent.: from Spanish, from a local word in the Philippines.

carabid /ˈkarəbɪd/ ▶ **noun** Entomology a fast-running beetle of a family (Carabidae) that comprises the predatory ground beetles.
– ORIGIN late 19th cent.: from modern Latin *Carabidae* (plural), from Latin *carabus*, denoting a kind of crab.

carabineer /ˌkarəbɪˈnɪə/ (also **carabinier**) ▶ **noun** historical a cavalry soldier whose principal weapon was a carbine.
– ORIGIN mid 17th cent.: from French *carabinier*, from *carabine* (see **CARBINE**).

carabiner ▶ noun variant spelling of **KARABINER**.

carabinero /ˌkarabɪˈnɛːrəʊ/ ▶ noun (pl. **-os** /-əʊz/) a Spanish or South American frontier guard or customs officer.
– ORIGIN Spanish, literally 'soldier armed with a carbine'.

carabiniere /ˌkarabɪˈnjɛːreɪ/ ▶ noun (pl. **carabinieri** pronunc. same) a member of the Italian paramilitary police.
– ORIGIN Italian, literally 'carabineer'.

caracal /ˈkarakal/ ▶ noun a long-legged lynx-like cat with black tufted ears and a uniform brown coat, native to Africa and western Asia. Also called **AFRICAN LYNX**.
● *Felis caracal*, family Felidae.
– ORIGIN mid 19th cent.: from French or Spanish, from Turkish *karakulak*, from *kara* 'black' + *kulak* 'ear' (because of its black ear tufts).

Caracalla /ˌkaraˈkalə/ (188–217), Roman emperor 211–17; born *Septimius Bassanius*; later called *Marcus Aurelius Severus Antoninus Augustus*. In 212 he granted Roman citizenship to all free inhabitants of the Roman Empire.

caracara /ˌkarəˈkɑːrə/ ▶ noun (pl. same or **caracaras**) a large New World bird of prey of the falcon family, with a bare face and a deep bill, feeding largely on carrion.
● Family Falconidae: four genera and several species, in particular the **common caracara** (*Polyborus plancus*).
– ORIGIN mid 19th cent.: from Spanish or Portuguese *caracará*, from Tupi-Guarani, imitating its cry.

Caracas /kəˈrakəs/ the capital of Venezuela; pop. 1,824,890 (1991).

caracole /ˈkarakəʊl/ ▶ noun a half turn to the right or left by a horse.
▶ verb [no obj., usu. with adverbial of direction] (of a horse) perform a caracole.
– ORIGIN early 17th cent.: from French *caracole*, *caracol* 'snail's shell, spiral'.

Caractacus /kəˈraktəkəs/ variant spelling of **CARATACUS**.

caracul ▶ noun variant spelling of **KARAKUL**.

carafe /kəˈraf, -ˈrɑːf/ ▶ noun an open-topped glass flask typically used for serving wine in a restaurant.
– ORIGIN late 18th cent.: from French, from Italian *caraffa*, probably based on Arabic *garafa* 'draw water'.

caragana /ˌkarəˈɡɑːnə/ ▶ noun a leguminous shrub or small tree which is native to central Asia and Siberia, widely planted as an ornamental.
● Genus *Caragana*, family Leguminosae: several species, including the pea tree of Siberia.
– ORIGIN modern Latin, of Turkic origin.

Carajás /ˌkarəˈʒɑːs/ a mining region in north Brazil, the site of one of the richest deposits of iron ore in the world.

caramba /kəˈrambə/ ▶ exclamation informal, often humorous an expression of surprise or dismay.
– ORIGIN mid 19th cent.: from Spanish.

carambola /ˌkar(ə)mˈbəʊlə/ ▶ noun 1 a golden-yellow juicy fruit with a star-shaped cross section. Also called **STARFRUIT**.
2 the small tropical tree which bears this fruit.
● *Averrhoa carambola*, family Oxalidaceae.
– ORIGIN late 16th cent.: from Portuguese, probably from Marathi *karambal*.

caramel /ˈkaram(ə)l, -mɛl/ ▶ noun [mass noun] sugar or syrup heated until it turns brown, used as a flavouring or colouring for food or drink: *a gateau frosted with caramel* | [as modifier] *caramel ice cream*.
■ the light brown colour of this substance: *the liquid turns a pale caramel* | [as modifier] *a caramel sweater*.
■ [count noun] a soft toffee made with sugar and butter that have been melted and further heated.
– ORIGIN early 18th cent.: from French, from Spanish *caramelo*.

caramelize (also **-ise**) ▶ verb [no obj.] (of sugar or syrup) be converted into caramel.
■ [with obj.] [usu. as adj. **caramelized**] cook (food) with sugar so that it becomes coated with caramel.
– DERIVATIVES **caramelization** noun.
– ORIGIN mid 19th cent.: from French *caraméliser*, from *caramel* 'caramel'.

carangid /kəˈrandʒɪd/ ▶ noun Zoology a marine fish of the jack family (Carangidae), whose members typically have a sloping forehead and two dorsal fins.

– ORIGIN late 19th cent.: from modern Latin *Carangidae* (plural), from the genus name *Caranx*.

carapace /ˈkarapeɪs/ ▶ noun the hard upper shell of a tortoise or crustacean.
– ORIGIN mid 19th cent.: from French, from Spanish *carapacho*, of unknown origin.

carat /ˈkarat/ ▶ noun 1 a unit of weight for precious stones and pearls, now equivalent to 200 milligrams: *a half-carat diamond ring*.
2 (US also **karat**) a measure of the purity of gold, pure gold being 24 carats: *an ounce of 23-carat gold*.
– ORIGIN late Middle English (in sense 2): from French, from Italian *carato*, from Arabic *ḳīrāṭ* (a unit of weight), from Greek *keration* 'fruit of the carob' (also denoting a unit of weight), diminutive of *keras* 'horn', with reference to the elongated seed pod of the carob.

Caratacus /kəˈratəkəs/ (also **Caractacus**) (1st century AD), British chieftain, son of Cymbeline. He took part in the resistance to the Roman invasion of AD 43.

Caravaggio /ˌkaraˈvadʒɪəʊ, Italian karaˈvaddʒo/, Michelangelo Merisi da (*c.*1571–1610), Italian painter. An influential figure in the transition from late mannerism to baroque, he made use of naturalistic realism and dramatic light and shade.
– DERIVATIVES **Caravaggesque** /ˌkaravaˈdʒɛsk/ adjective.

caravan ▶ noun 1 Brit. a vehicle equipped for living in, typically towed by a car and used for holidays: [as modifier] *a caravan holiday*.
■ a covered horse-drawn wagon: *a gypsy caravan*. ■ N. Amer. a covered lorry.
2 historical a group of people, especially traders or pilgrims, travelling together across a desert in Asia or North Africa.
■ any large group of people, typically with vehicles or animals travelling together, in single file: *a caravan of cars and trucks*.
– ORIGIN late 15th cent. (in sense 2): from French *caravane*, from Persian *kārwān*. The sense 'covered horse-drawn wagon' dates from the early 19th cent.

caravanette ▶ noun Brit. a motor vehicle with a rear compartment equipped for living in, used for holidays.

caravanning ▶ noun [mass noun] Brit. the activity of spending a holiday in a caravan.
– DERIVATIVES **caravanner** noun.

caravanserai /ˌkaraˈvansəraɪ, -riː/ (US also **caravansary**) ▶ noun (pl. **caravanserais** or **caravansaries**) 1 historical an inn with a central courtyard for travellers in the desert regions of Asia or North Africa.
2 a group of people travelling together; a caravan.
– ORIGIN late 16th cent.: from Persian *kārwānsarāy*, from *kārwān* 'caravan' + *sarāy* 'palace'.

caravan site (also **caravan park**) ▶ noun Brit. an area with special amenities where caravans are parked and used for holidays or as permanent homes.

caravel /ˈkaravɛl/ (also **carvel**) ▶ noun historical a small, fast Spanish or Portuguese ship of the 15th–17th centuries.
– ORIGIN early 16th cent.: from French *caravelle*, from Portuguese *caravela*, diminutive of *caravo*, via Latin from Greek *karabos* 'horned beetle' or 'light ship'.

caraway /ˈkarəweɪ/ ▶ noun [mass noun] 1 (also **caraway seed**) the seeds of a plant of the parsley family, used for flavouring and as a source of oil.
2 the white-flowered Mediterranean plant which bears these seeds.
● *Carum carvi*, family Umbelliferae.
– ORIGIN Middle English: from medieval Latin *carui*, from Arabic *alkarāwiyā*, probably from Greek *karon* 'cumin'.

carb[1] ▶ noun short for **CARBURETTOR**.

carb[2] ▶ noun short for **CARBOHYDRATE**.

carbamate /ˈkɑːbəmeɪt/ ▶ noun Chemistry a salt or ester containing the anion NH_2COO^- or the group —$OOCNH_2$, derived from the hypothetical compound **carbamic acid**.
– ORIGIN mid 19th cent.: from *carbamic* (from **CARBO-** + **AMIDE** + **-IC**) + **-ATE**[1].

carbamazepine /ˌkɑːbəˈmeɪzɪpiːn/ ▶ noun [mass noun] Medicine a synthetic compound of the benzodiazepine class, used as an anticonvulsant and analgesic drug.

– ORIGIN 1990s: from **CARBO-** + **AMIDE**, on the pattern of *benzodiazepine*.

carbanion /kɑːˈbanɪən/ ▶ noun Chemistry an organic anion in which the negative charge is located on a carbon atom.

carbaryl /ˈkɑːbərɪl/ ▶ noun [mass noun] a synthetic insecticide used to protect crops and in the treatment of fleas and lice.
● Alternative name: **1-naphthyl-N-methylcarbamate**; chem. formula: $C_{12}H_{11}NO_2$.
– ORIGIN mid 20th cent.: from **CARBAMATE** + **-YL**.

carbazole /ˈkɑːbəˈzəʊl/ ▶ noun [mass noun] Chemistry a colourless crystalline substance obtained from coal tar, used in dye production.
● A tricyclic heteroaromatic compound; chem. formula: $C_{12}H_9N$.
– ORIGIN late 19th cent.: from **CARBO-** + **AZO-** + **-OLE**.

carbene /ˈkɑːbiːn/ ▶ noun Chemistry a highly reactive molecule containing a divalent carbon atom, examples of which occur as intermediates in some organic reactions.

carbide /ˈkɑːbaɪd/ ▶ noun Chemistry a binary compound of carbon with an element of lower or comparable electronegativity.
■ [mass noun] calcium carbide (CaC_2), used to generate acetylene by reaction with water and formerly used in portable lamps: [as modifier] *a carbide lamp*.

carbine /ˈkɑːbaɪn/ ▶ noun a light automatic rifle.
■ historical a short rifle or musket used by cavalry.
– ORIGIN early 17th cent.: from French *carabine*, from *carabin* 'mounted musketeer', of unknown origin.

carbo- ▶ combining form representing **CARBON**.

carbocation /ˌkɑːbə(ʊ)ˈkatʌɪən/ ▶ noun Chemistry another term for **CARBONIUM ION**.
– ORIGIN 1950s: from **CARBO-** + **CATION**.

carbohydrate ▶ noun Biochemistry any of a large group of organic compounds occurring in foods and living tissues and including sugars, starch, and cellulose. They contain hydrogen and oxygen in the same ratio as water (2:1) and typically can be broken down to release energy in the animal body.

carbolic ▶ noun short for **CARBOLIC ACID** or **CARBOLIC SOAP**.

carbolic acid ▶ noun [mass noun] phenol, especially when used as a disinfectant.

carbolic soap ▶ noun [mass noun] disinfectant soap containing phenol.

car bomb ▶ noun a bomb concealed in or under a parked car, used especially by terrorists.
▶ verb (**car-bomb**) [with obj.] attack with such a bomb.
– DERIVATIVES **car bomber** noun.

carbon ▶ noun [mass noun] the chemical element of atomic number 6, a non-metal which has two main forms (diamond and graphite) and which also occurs in impure form in charcoal, soot, and coal. (Symbol: **C**)
■ [count noun] Chemistry an atom of this element. ■ [count noun] a rod of carbon in an arc lamp. ■ [count noun] a piece of carbon paper or a carbon copy.

Compounds of carbon (organic compounds) form the physical basis of all living organisms. Carbon atoms are able to link with each other and with other atoms to form chains and rings, and an infinite variety of carbon compounds exist.

– ORIGIN late 18th cent.: from French *carbone*, from Latin *carbo*, *carbon-* 'coal, charcoal'.

carbon-12 ▶ noun [mass noun] the commonest natural carbon isotope, of mass 12. It is the basis for the accepted scale of atomic mass units.

carbon-14 ▶ noun [mass noun] a long-lived naturally occurring radioactive carbon isotope of mass 14, used in carbon dating and as a tracer in biochemistry.

carbonaceous ▶ adjective (chiefly of rocks or sediments) consisting of or containing carbon or its compounds.

carbonado /ˌkɑːbəˈneɪdəʊ/ ▶ noun (pl. **-os**) a dark opaque diamond, used in abrasives and cutting tools.
– ORIGIN mid 19th cent.: from Portuguese.

carbonara /ˌkɑːbəˈnɑːrə/ ▶ adjective denoting a pasta sauce made with bacon or ham, egg, and cream: [postpositive] *spaghetti carbonara*.
– ORIGIN Italian, literally 'charcoal kiln', perhaps influenced by *carbonata*, a dish of charcoal-grilled salt pork.

carbonate /ˈkɑːbəneɪt/ ▶ noun a salt of the anion CO_3^{2-}, typically formed by reaction of carbon dioxide with bases.

▶**verb** [with obj.] [usu. as adj. **carbonated**] dissolve carbon dioxide in (a liquid): *a carbonated soft drink.*
■ Chemistry convert into a carbonate, typically by reaction with carbon dioxide.
– DERIVATIVES **carbonation** noun.

carbonatite /kɑːˈbɒnətʌɪt/ ▶ **noun** Geology a lava or other igneous rock composed chiefly of carbonates rather than silicates.

carbon black ▶ **noun** [mass noun] a fine carbon powder used as a pigment, made by burning hydrocarbons in insufficient air.

carbon copy ▶ **noun** a copy of written or typed material made with carbon paper.
■ figurative a person or thing identical or very similar to another: *the trip was a carbon copy of the previous one.*

carbon cycle ▶ **noun 1** the series of processes by which carbon compounds are interconverted in the environment, chiefly involving the incorporation of carbon dioxide into living tissue by photosynthesis and its return to the atmosphere through respiration, the decay of dead organisms, and the burning of fossil fuels.
2 Astronomy the cycle of thermonuclear reactions believed to occur in stars, in which carbon nuclei are repeatedly formed and broken down in the conversion of hydrogen into helium.

carbon dating ▶ **noun** [mass noun] the determination of the age of an organic object from the relative proportions of the carbon isotopes carbon-12 and carbon-14 that it contains. The ratio between them changes as radioactive carbon-14 decays and is not replaced by exchange with the atmosphere.

carbon dioxide ▶ **noun** [mass noun] a colourless, odourless gas produced by burning carbon and organic compounds and by respiration. It is naturally present in air (about 0.03 per cent) and is absorbed by plants in photosynthesis.
● Chem. formula: CO_2.

carbon disulphide ▶ **noun** [mass noun] a colourless toxic flammable liquid used as a solvent, especially for rubber and sulphur.
● Chem. formula: CS_2.

carbon fibre ▶ **noun** [mass noun] a material consisting of thin, strong crystalline filaments of carbon, used as a strengthening material, especially in resins and ceramics: [as modifier] *a carbon-fibre brake disc.*

carbon fixation ▶ **noun** [mass noun] Biology the incorporation of carbon into organic compounds by living organisms, chiefly by photosynthesis in green plants.

carbonic /kɑːˈbɒnɪk/ ▶ **adjective** of or relating to carbon or its compounds, especially carbon dioxide.

carbonic acid ▶ **noun** [mass noun] a very weak acid formed in solution when carbon dioxide dissolves in water.
● Chem. formula: H_2CO_3.

carbonic acid gas ▶ **noun** archaic term for **CARBON DIOXIDE**.

carbonic anhydrase /anˈhʌɪdreɪz/ ▶ **noun** [mass noun] Biochemistry an enzyme which catalyses the conversion of dissolved bicarbonates into carbon dioxide.

Carboniferous /ˌkɑːbəˈnɪf(ə)rəs/ ▶ **adjective** Geology of, relating to, or denoting the fifth period of the Palaeozoic era, between the Devonian and Permian periods.
■ (**the Carboniferous**) [as noun] the Carboniferous period or the system of rocks deposited during it.

The Carboniferous lasted from about 363 to 290 million years ago. During this time the first reptiles and seed-bearing plants appeared, and there were extensive coral reefs and coal-forming swamp forests.

carbonium ion /kɑːˈbəʊnɪəm/ ▶ **noun** Chemistry an organic cation in which the positive charge is located on a carbon atom.
– ORIGIN early 20th cent.: *carbonium* from **CARBO-** 'carbon', on the pattern of *ammonium.*

carbonize (also **-ise**) ▶ **verb** [with obj.] convert into carbon, typically by heating or burning, or during fossilization: *the steak was carbonized on the outside.*
■ [usu. as adj. **carbonized**] coat with carbon.
– DERIVATIVES **carbonization** noun.

carbon monoxide ▶ **noun** [mass noun] a colourless, odourless toxic flammable gas formed by incomplete combustion of carbon.
● Chem. formula: CO.

carbonnade /ˌkɑːbəˈnɑːd, -ˈneɪd/ ▶ **noun** a rich beef stew made with onions and beer.
– ORIGIN mid 17th cent. (denoting a piece of meat or fish cooked on hot coals): from French, from Latin *carbo, -onis* 'coal, charcoal'.

carbon paper ▶ **noun** [mass noun] thin paper coated with carbon or another pigmented substance, used for making copies of written or typed documents.

carbon steel ▶ **noun** [mass noun] steel in which the main alloying element is carbon, and whose properties are chiefly dependent on the percentage of carbon present.

carbon tax ▶ **noun** a tax on fossil fuels, especially those used by motor vehicles, intended to reduce the emission of carbon dioxide.

carbon tetrachloride ▶ **noun** [mass noun] a colourless toxic volatile liquid used as a solvent, especially for fats and oils.
● Chem. formula: CCl_4.

carbonyl /ˈkɑːbənʌɪl, -nɪl/ ▶ **noun** [as modifier] Chemistry of or denoting the divalent radical $=C=O$, present in such organic compounds as aldehydes, ketones, amides, and esters, and in organic acids as part of the carboxyl group: *carbonyl compounds.*
■ [count noun] a coordination compound in which one or more carbon monoxide molecules are bonded as neutral ligands to a central metal atom: [with modifier] *nickel carbonyl.*

carbonyl chloride ▶ **noun** another term for **PHOSGENE**.

car boot sale ▶ **noun** Brit. an outdoor sale at which people sell things, typically from the boots of their cars.

carborundum /ˌkɑːbəˈrʌndəm/ ▶ **noun** [mass noun] a very hard black solid consisting of silicon carbide, used as an abrasive.
– ORIGIN late 19th cent. (originally US, as a trademark): blend of **CARBON** and **CORUNDUM**.

carboxyhaemoglobin /kɑːˌbɒksɪˌhiːməˈɡləʊbɪn/ ▶ **noun** [mass noun] Biochemistry a compound formed in the blood by the binding of carbon monoxide to haemoglobin. It is stable and therefore cannot absorb or transport oxygen.

carboxyl /kɑːˈbɒksʌɪl, -sɪl/ ▶ **noun** [as modifier] Chemistry of or denoting the acid radical —COOH, present in most organic acids: *the carboxyl group.*
– ORIGIN mid 19th cent.: from **CARBO-** + **OX-** 'oxygen' + **-YL**.

carboxylase /kɑːˈbɒksɪleɪz/ ▶ **noun** Biochemistry an enzyme which catalyses the addition of a carboxyl group to a specified substrate.

carboxylate /kɑːˈbɒksɪleɪt/ Chemistry ▶ **noun** a salt or ester of a carboxylic acid.
▶ **verb** [with obj.] add a carboxyl group to (a compound): [as adj. **carboxylated**] *carboxylated polysaccharides.*
– DERIVATIVES **carboxylation** noun.

carboxylic acid /ˌkɑːbɒkˈsɪlɪk/ ▶ **noun** Chemistry an organic acid containing a carboxyl group. The simplest examples are methanoic (or formic) acid and ethanoic (or acetic) acid.

carboy ▶ **noun** a large globular glass bottle with a narrow neck, typically protected by a frame and used for holding acids or other corrosive liquids.
– ORIGIN mid 18th cent.: from Persian *karāba* 'large glass flagon'.

car bra ▶ **noun** see **BRA**.

carbuncle /ˈkɑːbʌŋk(ə)l/ ▶ **noun 1** a severe abscess or multiple boil in the skin, typically infected with staphylococcus bacteria.
2 a bright red gem, in particular a garnet cut en cabochon.
– DERIVATIVES **carbuncular** adjective.
– ORIGIN Middle English: from Old French *charbuncle*, from Latin *carbunculus* 'small coal', from *carbo* 'coal, charcoal'.

carburation /ˌkɑːbjʊˈreɪʃ(ə)n/ ▶ **noun** [mass noun] the process of mixing air with a fine spray of liquid hydrocarbon fuel, as in an internal-combustion engine.
– ORIGIN late 19th cent.: from archaic *carburet* 'combine or charge with a hydrocarbon' + **-ATION**.

carburetted (US **carbureted**) ▶ **adjective** (of a vehicle or engine) having fuel supplied through a carburettor, rather than an injector.
– ORIGIN early 19th cent.: from archaic *carburet* 'carbide' + **-ED**[2].

carburettor /kɑːbjʊˈrɛtə, -bə-/ (also **carburetter**, US **carburetor**) ▶ **noun** a device in an internal-combustion engine for mixing air with a fine spray of liquid fuel.
– ORIGIN mid 19th cent.: from archaic *carburet* 'combine or charge with a hydrocarbon' + **-OR**[1].

carburize /ˈkɑːbjʊrʌɪz, -bə-/ (also **-ise**) ▶ **verb** [with obj.] add carbon to (iron or steel), in particular by heating in the presence of carbon to harden the surface.
– DERIVATIVES **carburization** noun.
– ORIGIN mid 19th cent.: from French *carbure* 'carbide' + **-IZE**.

carcajou /ˈkɑːkədʒuː, -əʒuː/ ▶ **noun** North American term for **WOLVERINE**.
– ORIGIN early 18th cent.: from Canadian French, apparently of Algonquian origin (compare with **KINKAJOU**).

carcass (Brit. also **carcase**) ▶ **noun** the dead body of an animal.
■ the trunk of an animal such as a cow, sheep, or pig, for cutting up as meat. ■ the remains of a cooked bird after all the edible parts have been removed.
■ derogatory or humorous a person's body, living or dead: *my obsession will last while there's life in this old carcass.*
■ the structural framework of a building, ship, or piece of furniture. ■ figurative the remains of something being discarded, dismembered, or worthless: *the floor is littered with the carcasses of newspapers.*
– ORIGIN Middle English: from Anglo-Norman French *carcois*, variant of Old French *charcois*; in later use from French *carcasse*; of unknown ultimate origin.

carcass meat ▶ **noun** [mass noun] Brit. raw meat as distinct from corned or tinned meat.

Carcassonne /ˌkɑːkəˈsɒn, French karkasɔn/ a walled city in SW France; pop. 45,000 (1990).

carceral /ˈkɑːs(ə)r(ə)l/ ▶ **adjective** poetic/literary of or relating to a prison.
– ORIGIN late 16th cent.: from late Latin *carceralis*, from *carcer* 'prison'.

Carchemish /ˈkɑːkɪmɪʃ/ an ancient city on the upper Euphrates, north-east of Aleppo.

carcinogen /kɑːˈsɪnədʒ(ə)n/ ▶ **noun** a substance capable of causing cancer in living tissue.
– ORIGIN mid 19th cent.: from an abbreviation of **CARCINOMA** + **-GEN**.

carcinogenesis /ˌkɑːs(ɪ)nəˈdʒɛnɪsɪs/ ▶ **noun** [mass noun] the initiation of cancer formation.

carcinogenic /ˌkɑːs(ɪ)nəˈdʒɛnɪk/ ▶ **adjective** having the potential to cause cancer.
– DERIVATIVES **carcinogenicity** noun.

carcinoid /ˈkɑːsɪnɔɪd/ ▶ **noun** Medicine a tumour of a type occurring in the glands of the intestine (especially the appendix) or in the bronchi, and abnormally secreting hormones.
– ORIGIN late 19th cent.: from an abbreviation of **CARCINOMA** + **-OID**.

carcinoma /ˌkɑːsɪˈnəʊmə/ ▶ **noun** (pl. **carcinomas** or **carcinomata** /-mətə/) a cancer arising in the epithelial tissue of the skin or of the lining of the internal organs.
– DERIVATIVES **carcinomatous** adjective.
– ORIGIN early 18th cent.: via Latin from Greek *karkinōma*, from *karkinos* 'crab' (compare with **CANCER**).

car coat ▶ **noun** a short, square-cut style of coat designed to be worn when driving a car.

Card. ▶ **abbreviation** for Cardinal.

card[1] ▶ **noun 1** a piece of thick, stiff paper or thin pasteboard, in particular one used for writing or printing on: *some notes jotted down on a card* | [mass noun] *a piece of card.*
■ such a piece of thick paper printed with a picture and used to send a message or greeting: *a birthday card.* ■ a small piece of such paper with a person's name and other details printed on it for purposes of identification, for example a business card or a visiting card.
2 a small rectangular piece of plastic issued by a bank or building society, containing personal data in a machine-readable form and used chiefly to obtain cash or credit.
■ a similar piece of plastic used for other purposes such as paying for a telephone call or gaining entry to a room or building.
3 a playing card: *a pack of cards.*
■ (**cards**) a game played with playing cards.
4 Computing short for **EXPANSION CARD**.

5 (**cards**) Brit. informal documents relating to an employee, especially for tax and national insurance, held by the employer.
6 a programme of events at a race meeting.
■ a record of scores in a sporting event; a scorecard. ■ a list of holes on a golf course, on which a player's scores are entered.
7 informal, dated or N. Amer. a person regarded as odd or amusing: *He laughed: 'You're a card, you know'.*
▶ **verb** [with obj.] **1** write (something) on a card, especially for indexing.
2 N. Amer. check the identity card of (someone), in particular as evidence of legal drinking age.
3 informal (in golf and other sports) score (a certain number of points on a scorecard): *he carded 68 in the final round.*
4 (**be carded**) Canadian (of an amateur athlete) be in receipt of government funding to pursue training.
– PHRASES **a card up one's sleeve** Brit. a plan or asset that is kept secret until it is needed. **get one's cards** Brit. informal be dismissed from one's employment. **give someone their cards** Brit. informal dismiss someone from employment. **hold all the cards** be in a very strong or advantageous position. **on** (or N. Amer. **in**) **the cards** informal possible or likely: *our marriage has been on the cards from day one.* **play the —— card** exploit the specified issue or idea mentioned, especially for political advantage: *he saw an opportunity to play the peace card.* **play one's cards right** make the best use of one's assets and opportunities. **put** (or **lay**) **one's cards on the table** be completely open and honest in declaring one's resources, intentions, or attitude.
– ORIGIN late Middle English (in sense 3 of the noun): from Old French *carte*, from Latin *carta*, *charta*, from Greek *khartēs* 'papyrus leaf'.

card² ▶ **verb** [with obj.] comb and clean (raw wool, hemp fibres, or similar material) with a sharp-toothed instrument in order to disentangle the fibres before spinning.
▶ **noun** a toothed implement or machine for this purpose.
– DERIVATIVES **carder** noun.
– ORIGIN late Middle English: from Old French *carde*, from Provençal *carda*, from *cardar* 'tease, comb', based on Latin *carere* 'to card'.

cardamom /ˈkɑːdəməm/ (also **cardamum**) ▶ **noun** [mass noun] **1** the aromatic seeds of a plant of the ginger family, used as a spice and also medicinally.
2 the SE Asian plant which bears these seeds.
• *Elettaria cardamomum*, family Zingiberaceae.
– ORIGIN late Middle English: from Old French *cardamome* or Latin *cardamomum*, from Greek *kardamōmon*, from *kardamon* 'cress' + *amōmon*, the name of a kind of spice plant.

Cardamom Mountains a range of mountains in western Cambodia, rising to a height of 1,813 m (5,886 ft) at its highest point.

cardan joint /ˈkɑːd(ə)n/ ▶ **noun** Brit. another term for **UNIVERSAL JOINT**.
– ORIGIN early 20th cent.: named after Gerolamo *Cardano* (1501–76), Italian mathematician.

cardan shaft /ˈkɑːd(ə)n/ ▶ **noun** Brit. a shaft with a universal joint at one or both ends.
– ORIGIN early 20th cent.: named after Gerolamo *Cardano* (see **CARDAN JOINT**).

cardboard ▶ **noun** [mass noun] pasteboard or stiff paper: [as modifier] *a cardboard box.*
■ [as modifier] (of a character in a literary work) lacking depth and realism; artificial: *with its superficial, cardboard characters, the novel was typical of her work.*

cardboard city ▶ **noun** chiefly Brit. an urban area where homeless people congregate under makeshift shelters made from cardboard boxes.

card-carrying ▶ **adjective** [attrib.] registered as a member of a political party or trade union.
■ often humorous confirmed in or dedicated to a specified pursuit or outlook: *a card-carrying pessimist.*

cardholder ▶ **noun** a person who has a credit card or debit card.

cardia /ˈkɑːdɪə/ ▶ **noun** Anatomy the upper opening of the stomach, where the oesophagus enters.
– ORIGIN late 18th cent.: from Greek *kardia*.

cardiac /ˈkɑːdɪak/ ▶ **adjective** [attrib.] **1** of or relating to the heart: *a cardiac arrest.*
2 of or relating to the part of the stomach nearest the oesophagus.
▶ **noun** Medicine, informal a person with heart disease.
– ORIGIN late Middle English (as a noun denoting heart disease): from French *cardiaque* or Latin *cardiacus*, from Greek *kardiakos*, from *kardia* 'heart or upper opening of the stomach'. The adjective dates from the early 17th cent.

cardiac tamponade ▶ **noun** see **TAMPONADE** (sense 1).

Cardiff the capital of Wales, a seaport on the Bristol Channel; pop. 272,600 (1991). Welsh name **CAERDYDD**.

cardigan ▶ **noun** a knitted jumper fastening down the front, typically with long sleeves.
– ORIGIN mid 19th cent. (Crimean War): named after James Thomas Brudenel, 7th Earl of *Cardigan* (1797–1868), leader of the Charge of the Light Brigade, whose troops first wore such garments.

Cardiganshire a former county of SW Wales. It became part of Dyfed in 1974; the area became a county once more in 1996, as Ceredigion.

Cardin /ˈkɑːdã, French kardɛ̃/, Pierre (b.1922), French couturier, the first designer in the field of haute couture to show a collection of clothes for men as well as women.

cardinal ▶ **noun 1** a leading dignitary of the Roman Catholic Church. Cardinals are nominated by the Pope, and form the Sacred College which elects succeeding popes (now invariably from among their own number).
■ (also **cardinal red**) [mass noun] a deep scarlet colour like that of a cardinal's cassock.
2 a New World songbird of the bunting family, with a stout bill and typically with a conspicuous crest. The male is partly or mostly red in colour.
• Family Emberizidae, subfamily Cardinalinae (the **cardinal grosbeak subfamily**): four genera and several species, especially the **northern** (or **common**) **cardinal** (*Cardinalis cardinalis*), the male of which is scarlet with a black face. This subfamily also includes American grosbeaks, buntings, and saltators.
▶ **adjective** [attrib.] of the greatest importance; fundamental: *two cardinal points must be borne in mind.*
– DERIVATIVES **cardinalate** noun (in sense 1 of the noun), **cardinally** adverb, **cardinalship** noun (in sense 1 of the noun).
– ORIGIN Old English, from Latin *cardinalis*, from *cardo*, *cardin-* 'hinge'. Sense 1 has arisen through the notion of the important function of such priests as 'pivots' of church life.

cardinal beetle ▶ **noun** a mainly bright red beetle with feathery or comb-like antennae, which typically lives under loose bark.
• Family Pyrochroidae: several genera.

cardinal fish ▶ **noun** a small brightly coloured fish found in shallow tropical seas around reefs. The male often broods the eggs in his mouth.
• Family Apogonidae: several genera, in particular *Apogon*, and numerous species.

cardinal flower ▶ **noun** a tall scarlet-flowered lobelia found in North America.
• *Lobelia cardinalis*, family Campanulaceae.

cardinal humour ▶ **noun** see **HUMOUR** (sense 3).

cardinality ▶ **noun** (pl. **-ies**) Mathematics the number of elements in a set or other grouping, as a property of that grouping.

cardinal number ▶ **noun** a number denoting quantity (one, two, three, etc.), as opposed to an ordinal number (first, second, third, etc.).

cardinal point ▶ **noun** each of the four main points of the compass (north, south, east, and west).

cardinal virtue ▶ **noun** each of the chief moral attributes of scholastic philosophy: justice, prudence, temperance, and fortitude. Compare with **THEOLOGICAL VIRTUE**.

cardinal vowel ▶ **noun** Phonetics each of a series of vowel sounds used as a standard reference point to assist in the description and classification of vowel sounds in any language.

card index ▶ **noun** a catalogue or similar collection of information in which each item is entered on a separate card and the cards are arranged in a particular order, typically alphabetical.
▶ **verb** (**card-index**) [with obj.] list on such a set of cards.

carding wool ▶ **noun** [mass noun] short-stapled pieces of wool which result from the carding process, spun and woven to make standard-quality fabrics. Compare with **COMBING WOOL**.

cardio- /ˈkɑːdɪəʊ/ ▶ **combining form** of or relating to the heart: *cardiograph | cardiopulmonary.*
– ORIGIN from Greek *kardia* 'heart'.

cardiogram /ˈkɑːdɪə(ʊ)gram/ ▶ **noun** a record of muscle activity within the heart made by a cardiograph.

cardiograph /ˈkɑːdɪə(ʊ)grɑːf/ ▶ **noun** an instrument for recording heart muscle activity, such as an electrocardiograph.
– DERIVATIVES **cardiographer** noun, **cardiography** noun.

cardioid ▶ **noun** Mathematics a heart-shaped curve traced by a point on the circumference of a circle as it rolls around another identical circle.
■ (also **cardioid microphone**) a directional microphone with a pattern of sensitivity of this shape.
▶ **adjective** of the shape of a cardioid.
– ORIGIN mid 18th cent.: from Greek *kardioeidēs* 'heart-shaped', from *kardia* 'heart' + *eidos* 'form'.

cardiology ▶ **noun** [mass noun] the branch of medicine that deals with diseases and abnormalities of the heart.
– DERIVATIVES **cardiological** adjective, **cardiologist** noun.

cardiomegaly /ˌkɑːdɪəʊˈmɛgəli/ ▶ **noun** [mass noun] Medicine abnormal enlargement of the heart.
– ORIGIN 1960s: from **CARDIO-** + Greek *megas*, *megal-* 'great'.

cardiomyopathy /ˌkɑːdɪəʊmʌɪˈɒpəθi/ ▶ **noun** [mass noun] Medicine chronic disease of the heart muscle.

cardiopulmonary ▶ **adjective** Medicine of or relating to the heart and the lungs.

cardiorespiratory ▶ **adjective** Medicine relating to the action of both heart and lungs.

cardiovascular ▶ **adjective** Medicine of or relating to the heart and blood vessels.

carditis /kɑːˈdʌɪtɪs/ ▶ **noun** [mass noun] Medicine inflammation of the heart.

card key ▶ **noun** another term for **KEY CARD**.

cardoon /kɑːˈduːn/ ▶ **noun** a tall thistle-like southern European plant related to the globe artichoke, with leaves and roots that may be used as vegetables.
• *Cynara cardunculus*, family Compositae.
– ORIGIN early 17th cent.: from French *cardon*, from *carde* 'edible part of an artichoke', from modern Provençal *cardo*, based on Latin *carduus*, *cardus* 'thistle, artichoke'.

cardphone ▶ **noun** Brit. a public telephone operated by the insertion of a prepaid phonecard rather than coins.

card sharp (also **card sharper**) ▶ **noun** a person who cheats at cards in order to win money.

card swipe ▶ **noun** an electronic reader through which a credit or charge card or cheque guarantee card is passed in order to record the information it bears: [as modifier] *a card swipe system.*

card table ▶ **noun** a table for playing cards on, typically having legs that fold flat for storage and a baize surface.

card vote ▶ **noun** Brit. another term for **BLOCK VOTE**.

cardy (also **cardie**) ▶ **noun** (pl. **-ies**) Brit. informal short for **CARDIGAN**.

care ▶ **noun** [mass noun] **1** the provision of what is necessary for the health, welfare, maintenance, and protection of someone or something: *the care of the elderly | the child is safe* **in the care of** *her grandparents | health care.*
■ Brit. protective custody or guardianship provided by a local authority for children whose parents are dead or unable to look after them properly: *she was taken* **into care** | [as modifier] *a care order.*
2 serious attention or consideration applied to doing something correctly or to avoid damage or risk: *he planned his departure with great care.*
■ [count noun] an object of concern or attention: *the cares of family life.* ■ [count noun] a feeling of or occasion for anxiety: *she was driving along without a care in the world.*
▶ **verb** [no obj.] **1** [often with negative] feel concern or interest; attach importance to something: *they don't* **care about** *human life* | [with clause] *I don't care what she says.*
■ feel affection or liking: *you* **care** *very deeply* **for** *him.* ■ (**care for/to do something**) like or be willing to do or have something: *would you care for some tea?*

2 (**care for**) look after and provide for the needs of: *he has numerous animals to care for.*

– PHRASES **care of** at the address of: *write to me care of Ann.* **I** (or **he, she,** etc.) **couldn't** (or N. Amer. informal also **could**) **care less** informal used to express complete indifference: *he couldn't care less about football.* **for all you care** (or **he, she,** etc. **cares**) informal used to indicate that someone feels no interest or concern: *I could drown for all you care.* **have a care** [often in imperative] dated be cautious: *'Have a care!' she warned.* **take care 1** [often in imperative] be cautious; keep oneself safe: *take care if you're planning to go out tonight.* ■ said to someone on leaving them: *take care, see you soon.* **2** [with infinitive] make sure of doing something: *he would take care to provide himself with an escape clause.* **take care of 1** keep (someone or something) safe and provided for: *I can take care of myself.* **2** deal with (something): *he has the equipment to take care of my problem.*

– ORIGIN Old English *caru* (noun), *carian* (verb), of Germanic origin; related to Old High German *chara* 'grief, lament', *charon* 'grieve', and Old Norse *kǫr* 'sickbed'.

careen /kəˈriːn/ ▶ **verb 1** [with obj.] turn (a ship) on its side for cleaning, caulking, or repair.
■ [no obj.] (of a ship) tilt; lean over: *a heavy flood tide caused my vessel to careen dizzily.*
2 [no obj., with adverbial of direction] move swiftly and in an uncontrolled way in a specified direction: *an electric golf cart careened around the corner.* [ORIGIN: influenced by the verb **CAREER**.]

– ORIGIN late 16th cent. (as a noun denoting the position of a careened ship): from French *carène*, from Italian *carena*, from Latin *carina* 'a keel'.

career ▶ **noun** an occupation undertaken for a significant period of a person's life and with opportunities for progress.
■ the time spent by a person in such an occupation or profession: *the end of a distinguished career in the Royal Navy.* ■ the progress through history of an institution or organization: *the court has had a chequered career.* ■ [as modifier] working permanently in or committed to a particular profession: *a career diplomat.* ■ [as modifier] (of a woman) interested in pursuing a profession rather than devoting all her time to childcare and housekeeping.
▶ **verb** [no obj., with adverbial of direction] move swiftly and in an uncontrolled way in a specified direction: *the coach careered across the road and went through a hedge.*

– PHRASES **in full career** archaic at full speed.

– ORIGIN mid 16th cent. (denoting a road or racecourse): from French *carrière*, from Italian *carriera*, based on Latin *carrus* 'wheeled vehicle'.

careerist ▶ **noun** a person whose main concern is for advancement in their profession, especially one willing to achieve this by any means: [as modifier] *a careerist politician.*

– DERIVATIVES **careerism** noun.

career structure ▶ **noun** Brit. a recognized pattern of advancement within a job or profession.

carefree ▶ **adjective** free from anxiety or responsibility: *she changed from a carefree girl into a woman* | *the carefree days of the holidays.*

– DERIVATIVES **carefreeness** noun.

careful ▶ **adjective 1** making sure of avoiding potential danger, mishap, or harm; cautious: *I begged him to be more careful* | *be careful not to lose her address* | [as exclamation] *Careful! That stuff's worth a fortune!*
■ (**careful of/about**) anxious to protect (something) from harm or loss; solicitous: *he was very careful of his reputation.* ■ prudent in the use of something, especially money: *Ali had always been careful with money.*
2 done with or showing thought and attention: *a careful consideration of the facts.*

– DERIVATIVES **carefully** adverb, **carefulness** noun.

– ORIGIN Old English *carful* (see **CARE, -FUL**).

caregiver ▶ **noun** chiefly N. Amer. another term for **CARER**.

– DERIVATIVES **caregiving** noun & adjective.

care in the community ▶ **noun** another term for **COMMUNITY CARE**.

care label ▶ **noun** a label giving instructions for the washing and care of a fabric or garment.

careless ▶ **adjective** not giving sufficient attention or thought to avoiding harm or errors: *she had been careless and had left the window unlocked.*
■ (of an action or its result) showing or caused by a lack of attention: *he admitted careless driving* | *a careless error.* ■ [predic.] (**careless of/about**) not concerned or worried about: *he was careless of his own safety.* ■ showing no interest or effort; casual: *she gave a careless shrug.*

– DERIVATIVES **carelessly** adverb, **carelessness** noun.

– ORIGIN Old English *carlēas* 'free from care' (see **CARE, -LESS**).

careline ▶ **noun** Brit. a telephone service provided by the manufacturers of a particular product to deal with queries and complaints from consumers.

carer ▶ **noun** Brit. a family member or paid helper who regularly looks after a child or a sick, elderly, or disabled person.

caress ▶ **verb** [with obj.] touch or stroke gently or lovingly: *she caressed the girl's forehead* | figurative [as adj. **caressing**] *the caressing warmth of the sun.*
▶ **noun** a gentle or loving touch.

– DERIVATIVES **caressingly** adverb.

– ORIGIN mid 17th cent.: from French *caresser* (verb), *caresse* (noun), from Italian *carezza*, based on Latin *carus* 'dear'.

caret /ˈkarət/ ▶ **noun** a mark (^, ʎ) placed below the line to indicate a proposed insertion in a printed or written text.

– ORIGIN late 17th cent.: from Latin, 'is lacking'.

caretaker ▶ **noun 1** a person employed to look after a public building or a house in the owner's absence.
■ [as modifier] holding power temporarily: *he was to act as caretaker Prime Minister.*
2 chiefly N. Amer. a person employed to look after people or animals.

careworn ▶ **adjective** tired and unhappy because of prolonged worry: *a careworn expression.*

carex /ˈkɛːrɛks/ ▶ **noun** (pl. **carices** /-rɪsiːz/) a typical sedge of a large genus found chiefly in temperate and cold regions.
• Genus *Carex*, family Cyperaceae.

– ORIGIN modern Latin, from Latin, 'sedge'.

Carey /ˈkɛːri/, George (Leonard) (b.1935), English Anglican churchman, Archbishop of Canterbury since 1991.

carfare /ˈkɑːfɛː/ ▶ **noun** [mass noun] N. Amer. the fare for travel on a bus, underground train, or similar public transport.

cargador /ˌkɑːgəˈdɔː/ ▶ **noun** (pl. **cargadores** /ˌkɑːgəˈdɔːrɪz/) (in Spanish-speaking parts of America) a porter.

– ORIGIN early 19th cent.: Spanish, from *carga* 'load (as a measure of weight)'.

cargo ▶ **noun** (pl. **-oes** or **-os**) [mass noun] goods carried on a ship, aircraft, or motor vehicle: *transportation of bulk cargo* | [count noun] *a cargo of oil.*

– ORIGIN mid 17th cent.: from Spanish *cargo*, *carga*, from late Latin *carricare*, *carcare* 'to load', from Latin *carrus* 'wheeled vehicle'.

cargo cult ▶ **noun** (in the Melanesian Islands) a system of belief based around the expected arrival of ancestral spirits in ships bringing cargoes of food and other goods.

carhop ▶ **noun** N. Amer. informal, dated a waiter or waitress at a drive-in restaurant.

Caria /ˈkɛːrɪə/ an ancient region of SW Asia Minor, south of the Maeander River and north-west of Lycia.

– DERIVATIVES **Carian** adjective & noun.

cariama /ˌkarɪˈɑːmə, s-/ ▶ **noun** variant spelling of **SERIEMA**.

Carib /ˈkarɪb/ ▶ **noun 1** a member of an indigenous South American people living mainly in coastal regions of French Guiana, Suriname, Guyana, and Venezuela.
2 [mass noun] the language of this people, the only member of the Cariban family of languages still spoken by a substantial number of people (around 20,000). Also called **GALIBI**.
3 (also **Island Carib**) [mass noun] an unrelated Arawakan language, now extinct, formerly spoken in the Lesser Antilles. It became so called because the mainland Caribs were in the process of subjugating the Arawakan peoples of the Lesser Antilles at the time of the arrival of the Spaniards, who confused the two groups. See also **BLACK CARIB**.
▶ **adjective** of or relating to the Caribs or their language.
■ of or relating to Island Carib or Black Carib.

– ORIGIN from Spanish *caribe*, from Haitian Creole. Compare with **CANNIBAL**.

Cariban /ˈkarɪb(ə)n/ ▶ **adjective** of, belonging to, or denoting a family of South American languages scattered widely throughout Brazil, Suriname, Guyana, Venezuela, and Colombia. With the exception of Carib, they are all extinct or nearly so.
▶ **noun** [mass noun] this family of languages.

Caribbean /ˌkarɪˈbiːən, kəˈrɪbɪən/ ▶ **noun** (**the Caribbean**) the region consisting of the Caribbean Sea, its islands (including the West Indies), and the surrounding coasts.
▶ **adjective** of or relating to this region.

> **USAGE** There are two possible pronunciations of the word **Caribbean**. The first, found in the US and the Caribbean itself, puts the stress on the **-rib-**, while the second, more familiar to most British people, puts the stress on the **-be-**. In recent years the first pronunciation has gained ground in Britain as the more 'up-to-date' and, to some, the more 'correct' pronunciation. At present, both pronunciations are acceptable in standard British English.

Caribbean Community and Common Market (abbrev.: **CARICOM**) an organization established in 1973 to promote cooperation in economic affairs and social services and to coordinate foreign policy among its members, all of which are independent states of the Caribbean region.

Caribbean Sea the part of the Atlantic Ocean lying between the Antilles and the mainland of Central and South America.

caribou /ˈkarɪbuː/ ▶ **noun** (pl. same) North American term for **REINDEER**.

– ORIGIN mid 17th cent.: from Canadian French, from Micmac *yalipu*, literally 'snow-shoveller' (because the caribou scrapes away snow to feed on the vegetation underneath).

caricature /ˈkarɪkəˌtjʊə/ ▶ **noun** a picture, description, or imitation of a person in which certain striking characteristics are exaggerated in order to create a comic or grotesque effect.
■ [mass noun] the art or style of such exaggerated representation: *there are elements of caricature in the portrayal of the hero.* ■ a ludicrous or grotesque version of someone or something: *he looked a caricature of his normal self.*
▶ **verb** [with obj.] (usu. **be caricatured**) make or give a comically or grotesquely exaggerated representation of (someone): *he was famous enough to be caricatured by* Punch.

– DERIVATIVES **caricatural** adjective, **caricaturist** noun.

– ORIGIN mid 18th cent.: from French, from Italian *caricatura*, from *caricare* 'load, exaggerate', from Latin *carricare* (see **CHARGE**).

CARICOM /ˈkarɪkɒm/ ▶ **abbreviation for** Caribbean Community and Common Market.

caries /ˈkɛːriːz/ ▶ **noun** [mass noun] decay and crumbling of a tooth or bone.

– ORIGIN late 16th cent.: from Latin.

carillon /ˈkarɪljən, -lɒn, kəˈrɪljən/ ▶ **noun** a set of bells in a tower, played using a keyboard or by an automatic mechanism similar to a piano roll.
■ a tune played on such bells.

– DERIVATIVES **carillonneur** /ˌkarɪljəˈnəː, -ˈrɪlə-, kə-/ noun.

– ORIGIN late 18th cent.: from French, from Old French *quarregnon* 'peal of four bells', based on Latin *quattuor* 'four'.

Carina /kəˈrʌɪnə, -ˈriː-/ Astronomy a southern constellation (the Keel) partly in the Milky Way, originally part of Argo. It contains the second brightest star in the sky, Canopus.
■ [as genitive **Carinae** /kəˈrʌɪni, -ˈriːni, -nʌɪ/] used with preceding letter or numeral to designate a star in this constellation: *the star Beta Carinae.*

– ORIGIN Latin.

carina /kəˈrʌɪnə, -ˈriː-/ ▶ **noun** (pl. **carinae** /-niː/ or **carinas**) chiefly Biology a keel-shaped structure, in particular:
■ Zoology the ridge of a bird's breastbone, to which the main flight muscles are attached. ■ Anatomy a cartilage situated at the point where the trachea (windpipe) divides into the two bronchi.

– DERIVATIVES **carinal** adjective.

– ORIGIN early 18th cent.: from Latin, 'keel'.

carinate /ˈkarɪneɪt, -ət/ ▶ **adjective** having a keel-like ridge.

■(of a bird) having a deep ridge on the breastbone for the attachment of flight muscles. Contrasted with **RATITE**.
– DERIVATIVES **carinated** adjective, **carination** noun.
– ORIGIN late 18th cent.: from Latin *carinatus* 'having a keel', from *carina* 'keel'.

caring ▶ adjective displaying kindness and concern for others: *a caring and invaluable friend*.
▶ noun [mass noun] the work or practice of looking after those unable to care for themselves, especially the sick and the elderly: [as modifier] *the caring professions*.

Carinthia /kəˈrɪnθɪə/ an Alpine state of southern Austria; capital, Klagenfurt. German name **KÄRNTEN**.
– DERIVATIVES **Carinthian** noun & adjective.

carioca /ˌkarɪˈəʊkə/ ▶ noun 1 a native of Rio de Janeiro.
2 a Brazilian dance resembling the samba.
– ORIGIN mid 19th cent.: from Portuguese, from Tupi *kari'oka* 'house of the white man'.

cariogenic /ˌkɛːrɪəʊˈdʒɛnɪk, ˌka-/ ▶ adjective technical causing tooth decay.

cariole ▶ noun variant spelling of **CARRIOLE**.

carious /ˈkɛːrɪəs/ ▶ adjective (of bones or teeth) decayed.
– ORIGIN mid 16th cent.: from Latin *cariosus* (see **CARIES**).

caritas /ˈkarɪtaːs/ ▶ noun [mass noun] Christian love of humankind; charity.
– ORIGIN mid 19th cent.: Latin.

carjacking ▶ noun [mass noun] chiefly N. Amer. the action of violently stealing an occupied car: *carjacking is a big worry* | [count noun] *the victim of a carjacking*.
– DERIVATIVES **carjack** verb, **carjacker** noun.
– ORIGIN 1990s: blend of **CAR** and *hijacking* (see **HIJACK**).

carking ▶ adjective [attrib.] archaic causing distress or worry: *her carking doubts*.
– ORIGIN mid 16th cent.: present participle of Middle English *cark* 'worry, burden', from Old Northern French *carkier*, based on late Latin *carcare* (see **CHARGE**).

carl ▶ noun archaic a peasant or man of low birth.
■Scottish a man; a fellow.
– ORIGIN Old English (denoting a peasant or villein): from Old Norse *karl* 'man, freeman', of Germanic origin; related to **CHURL**.

Carley float /ˈkɑːli/ ▶ noun a large emergency raft carried on board ship, typically consisting of a buoyant canvas ring with a wooden grid deck inside it.
– ORIGIN early 20th cent.: named after Horace S. *Carley*, American inventor.

carline¹ /ˈkɑːlɪn/ (also **carline thistle**) ▶ noun a thistle-like European plant with flower heads that bear shiny persistent straw-coloured bracts.
● Genus *Carlina*, family Compositae: several species, in particular *C. vulgaris*.
– ORIGIN late 16th cent.: from French, from medieval Latin *carlina*, perhaps an alteration of *cardina* (from Latin *carduus* 'thistle'), by association with *Carolus Magnus* (see **CHARLEMAGNE**), to whom its medicinal properties were said to have been revealed.

carline² /ˈkɑːlɪn/ (also **carlin** or **carling**) ▶ noun (usu. **carlines**) any of the pieces of squared timber fitted fore and aft between the deck beams of a wooden ship to support the deck planking.
– ORIGIN Middle English (in the sense 'old woman, witch'): from Old Norse *karling*; the reason for nautical use of the word remains obscure.

Carling, Will (b.1965), English rugby union player; full name *William David Charles Carling*. He made his England debut and was appointed captain in 1988, a position he retired from in 1996.

Carlisle /kɑːˈlʌɪl/ a city in NW England, the county town of Cumbria; pop. 99,800 (1991).

Carlism /ˈkɑːlɪz(ə)m/ ▶ noun [mass noun] historical a Spanish conservative political movement originating in support of Don Carlos, brother of Fernando VII (died 1833), who claimed the throne in place of Fernando's daughter Isabella. The movement supported the Catholic Church and opposed centralized government; it was revived in support of the Nationalist side during the Spanish Civil War.
– DERIVATIVES **Carlist** adjective & noun.

carload ▶ noun the number of people that can travel in a motor car: *a carload of passengers*.
■N. Amer. the quantity of goods that can be carried in a railway freight car.

Carlovingian /ˌkɑːlə(ʊ)ˈvɪndʒɪən/ ▶ adjective & noun another term for **CAROLINGIAN**.
– ORIGIN from French *carlovingien*, from *Karl* 'Charles', on the pattern of *mérovingien* 'Merovingian'.

Carlow /ˈkɑːləʊ/ a county of the Republic of Ireland, in the province of Leinster.

Carlsbad plum /ˈkɑːlzbad/ ▶ noun a dessert plum of a blue-black variety, that is often crystallized.
– ORIGIN late 19th cent.: named after *Karlsbad* (now Karlovy Vary).

Carlyle /kɑːˈlʌɪl/, Thomas (1795–1881), Scottish historian and political philosopher. He established his reputation as a historian with his *History of the French Revolution* (1837). Influenced by German Romanticism, many of his works, including *Sartor Resartus* (1833–4), celebrate the force of the 'strong, just man' as against the degraded masses.

carman ▶ noun (pl. **-men** pronunc. same) dated a driver of a van or cart; a carrier.

Carmarthen /kəˈmɑːðən/ a town in SW Wales, the administrative centre of Carmarthenshire; pop. 54,800 (1991). Welsh name **CAERFYRDDIN**.

Carmarthenshire a county of South Wales; administrative centre, Carmarthen. It was part of Dyfed between 1974 and 1996.

Carmel, Mount /ˈkɑːm(ə)l/ a group of mountains near the Mediterranean coast in NW Israel, sheltering the port of Haifa. In the Bible it is the scene of the defeat of the priests of Baal by the prophet Elijah (I Kings 18).

Carmelite /ˈkɑːmɪlʌɪt/ ▶ noun a friar or nun of a contemplative Catholic order founded at Mount Carmel during the Crusades and dedicated to Our Lady.
▶ adjective of or relating to the Carmelites.

Carmichael /kɑːˈmʌɪk(ə)l/, Hoagy (1899–1981), American jazz pianist, composer, and singer; born *Howard Hoagland Carmichael*. His best-known songs include 'Stardust' (1929), 'Two Sleepy People' (1938), and 'In the Cool, Cool, Cool of the Evening' (1951).

carminative /ˈkɑːmɪnətɪv, kɑːˈmɪnətɪv/ ▶ adjective Medicine (chiefly of a drug) relieving flatulence.
▶ noun a drug of this kind.
– ORIGIN late Middle English: from Old French *carminatif*, *-ive*, or medieval Latin *carminat-* 'healed (by incantation)', from the verb *carminare*, from Latin *carmen* (see **CHARM**).

carmine /ˈkɑːmʌɪn, -mɪn/ ▶ noun [mass noun] a vivid crimson colour: [as modifier] *carmine roses*.
■a vivid crimson pigment made from cochineal.
– ORIGIN early 18th cent.: from French *carmin*, based on Arabic *ḳirmiz* (see **KERMES**). Compare with **CRIMSON**.

Carnaby Street /ˈkɑːnəbi/ a street in the West End of London. It became famous in the 1960s as a centre of the popular fashion industry.

Carnac /ˈkɑːnak/ the site in Brittany of nearly 3,000 megalithic stones dating from the Neolithic period.

carnage /ˈkɑːnɪdʒ/ ▶ noun [mass noun] the killing of a large number of people.
– ORIGIN early 17th cent.: from French, from Italian *carnaggio*, from medieval Latin *carnaticum*, from Latin *caro*, *carn-* 'flesh'.

carnal /ˈkɑːn(ə)l/ ▶ adjective relating to physical, especially sexual, needs and activities: *carnal desire*.
– DERIVATIVES **carnality** noun, **carnally** adverb.
– ORIGIN late Middle English: from Christian Latin *carnalis*, from *caro*, *carn-* 'flesh'.

carnal knowledge ▶ noun [mass noun] dated, chiefly Law sexual intercourse.

carnallite /ˈkɑːn(ə)lʌɪt/ ▶ noun a white or reddish mineral consisting of a hydrated chloride of potassium and magnesium.
– ORIGIN mid 19th cent.: named after Rudolf von *Carnall* (1804–74), German mining engineer, + **-ITE¹**.

Carnap /ˈkɑːnap/, Rudolf (1891–1970), German-born American philosopher, a founding member of the Vienna Circle. Notable works: *The Logical Structure of the World* (1928) and *The Logical Foundations of Probability* (1950).

carnassial /kɑːˈnasɪəl/ ▶ adjective Zoology denoting

the large upper premolar and lower molar teeth of a carnivore, adapted for shearing flesh.
▶ noun a tooth of this type.
– ORIGIN mid 19th cent.: from French *carnassier* 'carnivorous', based on Latin *caro*, *carn-* 'flesh'.

Carnatic /kɑːˈnatɪk/ ▶ adjective of or denoting the main style of classical music in southern India, as distinct from the Hindustani music of the north: *Carnatic music*.
– ORIGIN Anglicization of **KARNATAKA** in SW India.

carnation ▶ noun a double-flowered cultivated variety of clove pink, with grey-green leaves and showy pink, white, or red flowers.
● *Dianthus caryophyllus*, family Caryophyllaceae: many cultivars.
■[mass noun] a rosy pink colour.
– ORIGIN late 16th cent.: perhaps based on a misreading of Arabic *ḳaranful* 'clove or clove pink', from Greek *karyophyllon*. The early forms suggest confusion with a different word *carnation* 'rosy pink colour', with *incarnation*, and with *coronation*.

carnauba /kɑːˈnɔːbə, -ˈnaʊbə/ ▶ noun a NE Brazilian fan palm, the leaves of which exude a yellowish wax. Also called **WAX PALM**.
● *Copernicia cerifera*, family Palmae.
■(also **carnauba wax**) [mass noun] wax from this palm, formerly used as a polish and for making candles.
– ORIGIN mid 19th cent.: from Portuguese, from Tupi.

Carné /ˈkɑːneɪ, French karne/, Marcel (1906–96), French film director. He gained his reputation for the films he made with the poet and scriptwriter Jacques Prévert (1900–77), notably *Le Jour se lève* (1939) and *Les Enfants du paradis* (1945).

Carnegie /kɑːˈneɪgi, ˈkɑːnəgi/, Andrew (1835–1919), Scottish-born American industrialist and philanthropist. He built up a fortune in the steel industry in the US, then retired from business in 1901 and devoted his wealth to charitable purposes, in particular libraries, education, and the arts.

carnelian /kɑːˈniːlɪən/ (also **cornelian**) ▶ noun [mass noun] a semi-precious stone consisting of a dull red or reddish-white variety of chalcedony.
– ORIGIN late Middle English: from Old French *corneline*; the prefix *car-* being suggested by Latin *caro*, *carn-* 'flesh'.

carnet /ˈkɑːneɪ/ ▶ noun a permit, in particular:
■a permit allowing use of certain campsites while travelling abroad. ■ a customs permit allowing a motor vehicle to be taken across a frontier for a limited period. ■ a book of tickets for use on public transport in some countries.
– ORIGIN 1920s: from French, 'notebook'.

carnival ▶ noun 1 a period of public revelry at a regular time each year, typically during the week before Lent in Roman Catholic countries, involving processions, music, dancing, and the use of masquerade: *the culmination of the week-long carnival* | [mass noun] *Mardi Gras is the last day of carnival* | [as modifier] *a carnival parade*.
■figurative an exciting or riotous mixture of something: *the film is a visual and aural carnival*.
2 N. Amer. a travelling funfair or circus.
– DERIVATIVES **carnivalesque** adjective.
– ORIGIN mid 16th cent.: from Italian *carnevale*, *carnovale*, from medieval Latin *carnelevamen*, *carnelevarium* 'Shrovetide', from Latin *caro*, *carn-* 'flesh' + *levare* 'put away'.

Carnivora /kɑːˈnɪvərə/ Zoology an order of mammals that comprises the cats, dogs, bears, hyenas, weasels, civets, raccoons, and mongooses. They are distinguished by having powerful jaws and teeth adapted for stabbing, tearing, and eating flesh.

carnivore /ˈkɑːnɪvɔː/ ▶ noun an animal that feeds on flesh.
■Zoology a mammal of the order Carnivora.
– ORIGIN mid 19th cent.: from French, from Latin *carnivorus* (see **CARNIVOROUS**).

carnivorous /kɑːˈnɪv(ə)rəs/ ▶ adjective (of an animal) feeding on other animals.
■(of a plant) able to trap and digest small animals, especially insects.
– DERIVATIVES **carnivorously** adverb, **carnivorousness** noun.
– ORIGIN late 16th cent.: from Latin *carnivorus*, from *caro*, *carn-* 'flesh' + *-vorus* (see **-VOROUS**).

carnosaur /ˈkɑːnəsɔː/ ▶ noun a large bipedal

carnivorous dinosaur, typically one with greatly reduced forelimbs.
● Infraorder Carnosauria, suborder Theropoda, order Saurischia; includes tyrannosaurus, allosaurus, and megalosaurus.
– ORIGIN 1930s: from modern Latin, from Latin *caro*, *carn-* 'flesh' + Greek *sauros* 'lizard'.

Carnot /ˈkɑːnəʊ, French karno/, Nicolas Léonard Sadi (1796–1832), French scientist. His work in analysing the efficiency of steam engines was posthumously recognized as being of crucial importance to the theory of thermodynamics.

carnotite /ˈkɑːnətʌɪt/ ▶ noun [mass noun] a lemon-yellow radioactive mineral consisting of hydrated vanadate of uranium, potassium, and other elements.
– ORIGIN late 19th cent.: named after Marie Adolphe Carnot (1839–1920), French inspector of mines, + -ITE[1].

carny[1] (also **carney**) ▶ noun [usu. as modifier] N. Amer. informal a carnival or funfair: *a carny atmosphere*.
■ a person who works in a carnival or funfair.

carny[2] (also **carney**) ▶ adjective (**-ier, -iest**) informal or dialect artful; sly: *Finley's carny approach to baseball*.
– ORIGIN late 19th cent.: of unknown origin.

carob /ˈkarəb/ ▶ noun **1** [mass noun] a brown floury powder extracted from the carob bean, used as a substitute for chocolate.
2 (also **carob tree**) a small evergreen Arabian tree which bears long brownish-purple edible pods. Also called *locust tree*.
● *Ceratonia siliqua*, family Leguminosae.
■ (also **carob bean**) the edible pod of this tree. Also called *locust bean*.
– ORIGIN late Middle English (denoting the carob bean): from Old French *carobe*, from medieval Latin *carrubia*, from Arabic *ḵarrūba*.

carol ▶ noun a religious folk song or popular hymn, particularly one associated with Christmas: *singing carols around the Christmas tree* | [as modifier] *a carol service*.
▶ verb (**carolled, carolling**; US **caroled, caroling**) [with obj.] sing or say (something) happily: *she was cheerfully carolling the words of the song* | [with direct speech] *'Goodbye,' he carolled*.
– ORIGIN Middle English: from Old French *carole* (noun), *caroler* (verb), of unknown origin.

Carolina duck /ˌkarəˈlʌɪnə/ ▶ noun another term for **WOOD DUCK**.

Carolina parakeet ▶ noun a small long-tailed parakeet with mainly green plumage and a yellow and orange head. It was formerly common in the eastern US but was exterminated by about 1920.
● *Conuropsis* (or *Aratinga*) *carolinensis*, family Psittacidae.

Caroline /ˈkarəlʌɪn/ ▶ adjective **1** (also **Carolean** /-ˈliːən/) of or relating to the reigns of Charles I and II of England: *a Caroline poet*.
2 another term for **CAROLINGIAN**.
– ORIGIN early 17th cent.: from medieval Latin *Carolus* 'Charles'.

Caroline Islands (also **the Carolines**) a group of islands in the western Pacific Ocean, north of the equator, forming the Federated States of Micronesia.

Carolingian /ˌkarəˈlɪndʒɪən/ (also **Carlovingian**) ▶ adjective of or relating to the Frankish dynasty, founded by Charlemagne's father (Pepin III), that ruled in western Europe from 750 to 987.
■ denoting or relating to a style of minuscule script developed in France during the time of Charlemagne, on which modern lower-case letters are largely based.
▶ noun a member of the Carolingian dynasty.
– ORIGIN alteration of earlier **CARLOVINGIAN**, by association with medieval Latin *Carolus* 'Charles'.

Carolingian Renaissance a period during the reign of Charlemagne and his successors that was marked by achievements in art, architecture, learning, and music.

carolling (US **caroling**) ▶ noun [mass noun] the activity of singing Christmas carols.
– DERIVATIVES **caroller** noun.

carol-singing ▶ noun [mass noun] the singing of carols, especially by groups going from door to door at Christmas with the object of raising money.
– DERIVATIVES **carol-singer** noun.

carom /ˈkarəm/ chiefly N. Amer. ▶ noun a cannon in billiards or pool.

■ (also **carom billiards**) [mass noun] a game resembling billiards, played on a table without pockets and depending on cannons for scoring.
▶ verb [no obj.] make a carom; strike and rebound.
– ORIGIN late 18th cent.: abbreviation of *carambole*, from Spanish *carambola*, apparently from *bola* 'ball'.

carotene /ˈkarətiːn/ ▶ noun [mass noun] Chemistry an orange or red plant pigment found in carrots and many other plant structures. It is a terpenoid hydrocarbon with several isomers, of which one (**beta-carotene**) is important in the diet as a precursor of vitamin A.
– ORIGIN mid 19th cent.: coined in German from Latin *carota* (see **CARROT**).

carotenoid /kəˈrɒtɪnɔɪd/ ▶ noun Chemistry any of a class of mainly yellow, orange, or red fat-soluble pigments, including carotene, which give colour to plant parts such as ripe tomatoes and autumn leaves. They are terpenoids based on a structure having the formula $C_{40}H_{56}$.

Carothers /kəˈrʌðəz/, Wallace Hume (1896–1937), American industrial chemist. He developed the first successful synthetic rubber, neoprene, and the synthetic fibre Nylon 6.6. He committed suicide before nylon had been commercially exploited.

carotid /kəˈrɒtɪd/ ▶ adjective of, relating to, or denoting the two main arteries which carry blood to the head and neck, and their two main branches.
▶ noun each of these arteries.
– ORIGIN early 17th cent.: from French *carotide* or modern Latin *carotides*, from Greek *karōtides*, plural of *karōtis* 'drowsiness', from *karoun* 'stupefy' (because compression of these arteries was thought to cause stupor).

carouse /kəˈraʊz/ ▶ verb [no obj.] drink plentiful amounts of alcohol and enjoy oneself with others in a noisy, lively way: *they danced and caroused until the drink ran out* | [as noun **carousing**] *a night of carousing*.
▶ noun a noisy, lively drinking party: *corporate carouses*.
– DERIVATIVES **carousal** noun, **carouser** noun.
– ORIGIN mid 16th cent.: originally as an adverb meaning 'right out, completely' in the phrase *drink carouse*, from German *gar aus trinken*; hence 'drink heavily, have a drinking bout'.

carousel /ˌkarəˈsɛl, -ˈzɛl/ ▶ noun **1** a merry-go-round at a fair.
■ a rotating machine or device, in particular a conveyor system at an airport from which arriving passengers collect their luggage.
2 historical a tournament in which groups of knights took part in chariot races and other demonstrations of equestrian skills.
– ORIGIN mid 17th cent.: from French *carrousel*, from Italian *carosello*.

carp[1] ▶ noun (pl. same) a deep-bodied freshwater fish, typically with barbels around the mouth. Carp are farmed for food in some parts of the world and are widely kept in large ponds.
● Family Cyprinidae (the **carp family**): several genera and species, including the **common carp** (*Cyprinus carpio*) and **silver carp** (*Hypophthalmichthys molitrix*). The family includes the majority of freshwater fishes in Eurasia, Africa, and North and Central America.
– ORIGIN late Middle English: from Old French *carpe*, from late Latin *carpa*.

carp[2] ▶ verb [no obj.] complain or find fault continually, typically about trivial matters: *I don't want to carp about the way you did it* | *he was constantly carping at me*.
– DERIVATIVES **carper** noun.
– ORIGIN Middle English (in the sense 'talk, chatter'): from Old Norse *karpa* 'brag'; later influenced by Latin *carpere* 'pluck at, slander'.

Carpaccio /kɑːˈpatʃɪəʊ, Italian karˈpattʃo/, Vittore (c.1455–1525), Italian painter noted especially for his paintings of Venice.

carpaccio /kɑːˈpatʃɪəʊ, Italian karˈpattʃo/ ▶ noun [mass noun] an Italian hors d'oeuvre consisting of thin slices of raw beef or fish served with a sauce.
– ORIGIN Italian, named after Vittore **CARPACCIO** (from his use of red pigments, resembling raw meat).

carpal /ˈkɑːp(ə)l/ ▶ noun any of the eight small bones forming the wrist. See **CARPUS**.
■ any of the equivalent bones in an animal's forelimb.
▶ adjective of or relating to these bones.
– ORIGIN mid 18th cent.: from **CARPUS** + **-AL**.

carpal tunnel syndrome ▶ noun [mass noun] a painful condition of the hand and fingers caused by compression of a major nerve where it passes over the carpal bones through a passage at the front of the wrist, alongside the flexor tendons of the hand. It may be caused by repetitive movements over a long period, or by fluid retention, and is characterized by sensations of tingling, numbness, or burning.

car park ▶ noun chiefly Brit. an area or building where cars or other vehicles may be left temporarily.

Carpathian Mountains /kɑːˈpeɪθɪən/ (also **the Carpathians**) a mountain system extending south-eastwards from southern Poland and Slovakia into Romania.

carpe diem /ˌkɑːpeɪ ˈdiːɛm, ˈdʌɪɛm/ ▶ exclamation used to urge someone to make the most of the present time and give little thought to the future.
– ORIGIN Latin, 'seize the day!', a quotation from Horace (*Odes* I.xi).

carpel /ˈkɑːp(ə)l/ ▶ noun Botany the female reproductive organ of a flower, consisting of an ovary, a stigma, and usually a style. It may occur singly or as one of a group.
– DERIVATIVES **carpellary** adjective.
– ORIGIN mid 19th cent.: from French *carpelle* or modern Latin *carpellum*, from Greek *karpos* 'fruit'.

Carpentaria, Gulf of /ˌkɑːpənˈtɛːrɪə/ a large bay on the north coast of Australia, between Arnhem Land and the Cape York Peninsula.

carpenter ▶ noun a person who makes and repairs wooden objects and structures.
▶ verb [with obj.] (usu. **be carpentered**) make by shaping wood: *the rails were carpentered very skilfully*.
■ [no obj.] do the work of a carpenter.
– ORIGIN Middle English: from Anglo-Norman French, from Old French *carpentier, charpentier*, from late Latin *carpentarius* (*artifex*) 'carriage(-maker)', from *carpentum* 'wagon', of Gaulish origin; related to **CAR**.

carpenter ant ▶ noun a large ant which burrows into wood to make a nest.
● Genus *Camponotus*, family Formicidae: numerous species.

carpenter bee ▶ noun a large solitary black bee with purplish wings, which nests in tunnels bored in dead wood or plant stems.
● Genus *Xylocopa*, family Apidae: several species.

carpentry ▶ noun [mass noun] the activity or occupation of making or repairing things in wood.
■ the work made or done by a carpenter: *the superb carpentry of the timber roof*.
– ORIGIN late Middle English: from Anglo-Norman French *carpentrie*, Old French *charpenterie*, from *charpentier* (see **CARPENTER**).

carpet ▶ noun **1** a floor or stair covering made from thick woven fabric, typically shaped to fit a particular room: *the house has fitted carpets throughout* | [mass noun] *the floor was covered with carpet*.
■ a large rug, especially an oriental one: *priceless Persian carpets*. ■ figurative a thick or soft expanse or layer of something: *carpets of wood anemones and bluebells*. ■ informal, chiefly US a type of artificial playing surface on a tennis court or sports field.
2 [with modifier] a slender moth marked typically with undulating bands of colour across the wings.
● Many species in the family Geometridae, including the **garden carpet** (*Xanthorhoe fluctuata*).
▶ verb (**carpeted, carpeting**) [with obj.] **1** (usu. **be carpeted**) cover (a floor or stairs) with a carpet: *the stairs were carpeted in a lovely shade of red*.
■ figurative cover with a thick or soft expanse or layer of something: *the meadows are carpeted with flowers*.
2 Brit. informal reprimand severely: *the Chancellor of the Exchequer carpeted the bank bosses*.
– PHRASES **on the carpet** informal being severely reprimanded by someone in authority: *we've all been on the carpet for the chances we took*. [ORIGIN: from *carpet* in the sense 'table covering', referring to 'the carpet of the council table', before which one would be summoned for reprimand.] **sweep something under the carpet** conceal or ignore a problem or difficulty in the hope that it will be forgotten.
– ORIGIN Middle English (denoting a thick fabric used as a cover for a table or bed): from Old French *carpite* or medieval Latin *carpita*, from obsolete Italian *carpita* 'woollen counterpane', based on Latin *carpere* 'pluck, pull to pieces'.

carpet bag ▶ noun a travelling bag of a kind originally made of carpet-like material.
▶ verb (**carpet-bag**) [no obj.] N. Amer. act as a carpetbagger: [as adj. **carpet-bagging**] *carpet-bagging developers.*

carpetbagger ▶ noun derogatory, chiefly N. Amer. a political candidate who seeks election in an area where they have no local connections.
■ historical (in the US) a person from the northern states who went to the South after the Civil War to profit from the Reconstruction. ■ a person perceived as an unscrupulous opportunist: *the organization is rife with carpetbaggers.*

carpet beetle ▶ noun a small beetle whose larva (the woolly bear) is destructive to carpets, fabrics, and other materials.
● Genus *Anthrenus*, family Dermestidae.

carpet-bomb ▶ verb [with obj.] [often as noun **carpet-bombing**] bomb (an area) intensively.

carpet-fitter ▶ noun a person who lays carpets for a living.

carpeting ▶ noun 1 [mass noun] carpets collectively: *offices with wall-to-wall carpeting.*
■ the fabric from which carpets are made.
2 [in sing.] Brit. informal a severe reprimand: *I was called to her office for a carpeting.*

carpet knight ▶ noun archaic a man who avoids hard work in favour of leisure activities or philandering.
– ORIGIN late 16th cent.: with reference to a knight's exploits being restricted to a carpeted boudoir, instead of to the field of battle.

carpet python (also **carpet snake**) ▶ noun a common large Australian climbing snake that is typically brightly patterned.
● *Morelia spilota*, family Pythonidae.

carpet shark ▶ noun a relatively small shallow-water shark with barbels around the nose or mouth and typically with a conspicuous colour pattern. It is found in the Indo-Pacific region and the Red Sea.
● Family Orectolobidae: *Orectolobus* and other genera, and several species, including the wobbegong.

carpet shell ▶ noun a burrowing bivalve mollusc of temperate and warm seas, with concentric growth rings and irregular coloured markings.
● Genus *Venerupis*, family Veneriidae.

carpet slipper ▶ noun a soft slipper whose upper part is made of wool or thick cloth.

carpet snake ▶ noun 1 Indian the common wolf snake, which often enters houses.
2 the carpet python.

carpet sweeper ▶ noun a manual household implement used for sweeping carpets, having a revolving brush or brushes and a receptacle for dust and dirt.

carphology /kɑːˈfɒlədʒi/ ▶ noun [mass noun] rare plucking at the bedclothes by a delirious patient.
– ORIGIN mid 19th cent.: from Greek *karphologia*, from *karphos* 'straw' + *legein* 'collect'.

car phone ▶ noun a cellular phone designed for use in a motor vehicle.

carpology /kɑːˈpɒlədʒi/ ▶ noun [mass noun] rare the study of fruits and seeds.
– DERIVATIVES **carpological** adjective.
– ORIGIN early 19th cent.: from Greek *karpos* 'fruit' + -LOGY.

carpool chiefly N. Amer. ▶ noun an arrangement between people to make a regular journey in a single vehicle, typically with each person taking turns to drive the others.
■ a group of people with such an arrangement.
▶ verb [no obj.] form or participate in a carpool.
– DERIVATIVES **carpooler** noun.

carpophore /ˈkɑːpə(ʊ)fɔː/ ▶ noun Botany (in a flower) an elongated axis that raises the stem of the pistil above the stamens.
■ (in a fungus) the stem of the fruiting body.
– ORIGIN late 19th cent.: from Greek *karpos* 'fruit' + -PHORE.

carport ▶ noun a shelter for a car consisting of a roof supported on posts, built beside a house.

carpus /ˈkɑːpəs/ ▶ noun (pl. **carpi** /-pʌɪ/) the group of small bones between the main part of the forelimb and the metacarpus in terrestrial vertebrates. The eight bones of the human carpus form the wrist and part of the hand, and are arranged in two rows.

– ORIGIN late Middle English: from modern Latin, from Greek *karpos* 'wrist'.

carr ▶ noun [mass noun] Brit. fenland with neutral water.
■ [usu. with modifier] Ecology wet woodland, typically dominated by alder or willow: *a patch of alder carr.*
– ORIGIN Middle English: from Old Norse *kjarr* 'brushwood', in *kjarr-mýrr* 'marsh overgrown with brushwood'.

Carracci /kəˈratʃi/ the name of a family of Italian painters comprising the brothers **Annibale** (1560–1609) and **Agostino** (1557–1602) and their cousin **Ludovico** (1555–1619). Together they established a teaching academy at Bologna, while Annibale became famed for his frescoes on the ceiling of the Farnese Gallery in Rome and for his invention of the caricature.

carrack /ˈkarək/ ▶ noun a large merchant ship of a kind operating in European waters from the 14th to the 17th century.
– ORIGIN late Middle English: from Old French *caraque*; perhaps from Spanish *carraca*, from Arabic, perhaps from *ḳarāḳir*, plural of *ḳurḳūra*, a type of merchant ship.

carrageen /ˈkarəgiːn/ (also **carragheen** or **carrageen moss**) ▶ noun [mass noun] an edible red shoreline seaweed with flattened branching fronds, found in both Eurasia and North America. Also called **IRISH MOSS**.
● *Chondrus crispus*, division Rhodophyta.
– ORIGIN early 19th cent.: from Irish *carraigín*.

carrageenan /ˌkarəˈgiːnən/ ▶ noun [mass noun] a substance extracted from red and purple seaweeds, consisting of a mixture of polysaccharides. It is used as a thickening or emulsifying agent in food products.
– ORIGIN 1960s: from CARRAGEEN + -AN.

Carrara /kəˈrɑːrə, Italian karˈrara/ a town in Tuscany in NW Italy, famous for the white marble quarried there since Roman times; pop. 68,480 (1990).

Carrel /kəˈrɛl, ˈkarəl, French karɛl/, Alexis (1873–1944), French surgeon and biologist. He developed improved techniques for suturing arteries and veins, and carried out some of the first organ transplants. Nobel Prize for Physiology or Medicine (1912).

carrel /ˈkar(ə)l/ ▶ noun a small cubicle with a desk for the use of a reader or student in a library.
■ historical a small enclosure or study in a cloister.
– ORIGIN late 16th cent.: apparently related to CAROL in the old sense 'ring'.

Carreras /kəˈrɛːrəs/, José (b.1946), Spanish operatic tenor.

carriage ▶ noun 1 a means of conveyance, in particular:
■ Brit. any of the separate sections of a train that carry passengers: *the first-class carriages.* ■ a four-wheeled passenger vehicle pulled by two or more horses: *a horse-drawn carriage.* ■ a wheeled support for moving a heavy object such as a gun.
2 [mass noun] Brit. the conveying of items or merchandise from one place to another.
■ the cost of such a procedure: *only £16.95 including VAT and carriage.*
3 a moving part of a machine that carries other parts into the required position: *a typewriter carriage.*
4 [in sing.] a person's bearing or deportment: *her carriage was graceful, her movements quick and deft.*
5 [mass noun] the harbouring of a potentially disease-causing organism by a person or animal that does not contract the disease.
– ORIGIN late Middle English: from Old Northern French *cariage*, from *carier* (see CARRY).

carriage and pair ▶ noun a four-wheeled passenger carriage pulled by two horses.

carriage bolt ▶ noun North American term for COACH BOLT.

carriage clock ▶ noun Brit. a portable clock in a rectangular case with a handle on top.

carriage dog ▶ noun archaic term for DALMATIAN.
– ORIGIN early 19th cent.: because Dalmatians were formerly trained to run behind a carriage as a guard dog.

carriage paid ▶ adverb with the cost of transport and delivery borne in advance by the sender of a parcel or other item.

carriage release ▶ noun a function or lever which enables the carriage on a manual or electric typewriter to move freely, instead of only in one direction when the keys are pressed.

carriage return ▶ noun another term for RETURN (in sense 5).

carriageway ▶ noun Brit. each of the two sides of a dual carriageway or motorway, each of which usually have two or more lanes.
■ the part of a road intended for vehicles rather than pedestrians.

carrick bend ▶ noun a kind of knot used to join ropes end to end, especially so that they can go round a capstan without jamming.
– ORIGIN early 19th cent.: from BEND[2]: *carrick* perhaps an alteration of CARRACK.

Carrick-on-Shannon the county town of Leitrim in the Republic of Ireland, on the River Shannon; pop. 6,168 (1991).

carrier ▶ noun 1 a person or thing that carries, holds, or conveys something: *water carriers.*
■ Brit. a carrier bag: *a plastic carrier.*
2 a person or company that undertakes the professional conveyance of goods or people: *Pan Am was the third US carrier to cease operations in 1991.*
■ a vessel or vehicle for transporting people or things, especially goods in bulk: *the largest timber carrier ever to dock at Sharpness.* ■ an aircraft carrier. ■ a company that provides facilities for conveying telecommunications messages.
3 a person or animal that transmits a disease-causing organism to others, especially without suffering from it themselves: *the badger is a carrier of TB.*
■ a person or other organism that possesses a particular gene, especially as a single copy whose effect is masked by a dominant allele, so that the associated characteristic (such as a hereditary disease) is not displayed but may be passed to offspring.
4 a substance used to support or convey another substance such as a pigment, catalyst, or radioactive material.
■ Physics short for CHARGE CARRIER. ■ Biochemistry a molecule that transfers a specified molecule or ion within the body, especially across a cell membrane.

carrier bag ▶ noun Brit. a plastic or paper bag with handles, typically one supplied by a shop to carry goods purchased there.

carrier pigeon ▶ noun a pigeon trained to carry messages tied to its neck or leg.

carrier shell ▶ noun a mollusc of warm seas which camouflages itself by cementing shell fragments and pebbles to its shell.
● Family Xenophoridae, class Gastropoda: *Xenophora* and other genera.

carrier wave ▶ noun a high-frequency electromagnetic wave modulated in amplitude or frequency to convey a signal.

Carrington /ˈkarɪŋtən/, Dora (de Houghton) (1893–1932), English painter, a member of the Bloomsbury Group.

carriole /ˈkarɪəʊl/ (also **cariole**) ▶ noun 1 historical a small open horse-drawn carriage for one person.
■ a light covered cart.
2 (in Canada) a kind of sledge pulled by a horse or dogs and with space for one or more passengers.
– ORIGIN mid 18th cent.: from French, from Italian *carriuola*, diminutive of *carro*, from Latin *carrum* (see CAR).

carrion ▶ noun [mass noun] the decaying flesh of dead animals.
– ORIGIN Middle English: from Anglo-Norman French and Old Northern French *caroine, caroigne*, Old French *charoigne*, based on Latin *caro* 'flesh'.

carrion beetle ▶ noun a beetle that feeds on decaying animal and plant matter, frequently also eating blowfly and other insect larvae.
● Family Silphidae: many species, including the burying beetles.

carrion crow ▶ noun a medium-sized, typically all-black crow which is common throughout much of Eurasia.
● *Corvus corone*, family Corvidae. See also HOODED CROW.

carrion flower ▶ noun another term for STAPELIA.

Carroll, Lewis (1832–98), English writer; pseudonym of *Charles Lutwidge Dodgson*. He wrote the children's classics *Alice's Adventures in Wonderland* (1865) and *Through the Looking Glass* (1871), which were inspired by Alice Liddell, the young daughter of the dean at the Oxford college where Carroll was a mathematics lecturer.

carronade /ˌkarəˈneɪd/ ▶ **noun** historical a short large-calibre cannon, formerly in naval use.
– ORIGIN late 18th cent.: from *Carron*, near Falkirk in Scotland, where this kind of cannon was first made.

carrot ▶ **noun** **1** a tapering orange-coloured root eaten as a vegetable.
2 a cultivated plant of the parsley family with feathery leaves, which yields this vegetable.
• *Daucus carota*, family Umbelliferae: two subspecies and many varieties; wild forms lack the swollen root.
3 an offer of something enticing as a means of persuasion (often contrasted with the threat of something punitive or unwelcome): *carrots will promote cooperation over the environment far more effectively than sticks* | [as modifier] *the carrot and stick approach*. [ORIGIN: with allusion to the proverbial encouragement of a donkey to move by enticing it with a carrot.]
4 (**carrots**) informal, usu. derogatory a nickname for a red-haired person.
– ORIGIN late 15th cent.: from French *carotte*, from Latin *carota*, from Greek *karōton*.

carrot fly ▶ **noun** a small fly whose larvae are a widespread pest of carrots, burrowing into the roots.
• *Psila rosae*, family Psilidae.

carroty ▶ **adjective** (of a person's hair) orange-red in colour.

carry ▶ **verb** (**-ies**, **-ied**) [with obj.] **1** support and move (someone or something) from one place to another: *medics were carrying a wounded man on a stretcher.*
■ transport: *the train service carries 20,000 passengers daily.* ■ have on one's person and take with one wherever one goes: *he was killed for the money he was carrying* | figurative *she had carried the secret all her life.* ■ conduct; transmit: *nerves carry visual information from the eyes.* ■ be infected with (a disease) and liable to transmit it to others: *ticks can carry a nasty disease which affects humans.* ■ transfer (a figure) to an adjacent column during an arithmetical operation (e.g. when a column of digit adds up to more than ten).
2 support the weight of: *the bridge is capable of carrying even the heaviest loads.*
■ be pregnant with: *she was carrying twins.* ■ (**carry oneself**) stand and move in a specified way: *she carried herself straight and with assurance.* ■ assume or accept (responsibility or blame): *they must carry management responsibility for the mess they have got the company into.* ■ be responsible for the effectiveness or success of: *they relied on dialogue to carry the plot.*
3 have as a feature or consequence: *being a combat sport, karate **carries with it** the risk of injury* | *each bike carries a ten-year guarantee.*
4 take or develop (an idea or activity) to a specified point: *he carried the criticism much further.*
■ (of a gun or similar weapon) propel (a missile) to a specified distance. ■ Golf & Cricket hit the ball over and beyond (a particular point). ■ [no obj.] Cricket (of the ball hit by a batsman) reach a fielder without bouncing, offering a possible catch: *the ball **carried to** second slip.*
5 (often **be carried**) approve (a proposed measure) by a majority of votes: *the resolution was carried by a two-to-one majority.*
■ persuade (colleagues or followers) to support one's policy: *he could not carry the cabinet.* ■ N. Amer. gain (a state or district) in an election.
6 (of a newspaper or a television or radio station) publish or broadcast: *the paper carried a detailed account of the current crisis.*
■ (of a retailing outlet) keep a regular stock of (particular goods for sale): *550 off-licences carry the basic range.* ■ have visible on the surface: *the product does not carry the swallow symbol.* ■ be known by (a name): *some products carry the same names as overseas beers.*
7 [no obj.] (of a sound or a person's voice) be audible at a distance: *his voice carried clearly across the room.*
▶ **noun** (pl. **-ies**) [usu. in sing.] **1** an act of lifting and transporting something from one place to another: *we did a carry of equipment from the camp.*
■ American Football an act of running or rushing with the ball. ■ [mass noun] chiefly N. Amer. the action of keeping something, especially a gun, on one's person: *this pistol is the right choice for on-duty or off-duty carry.* ■ N. Amer. historical a place or route between navigable waters over which boats or supplies had to be carried. ■ the transfer of a figure into an adjacent column (or the equivalent part of a computer memory) during an arithmetical operation. ■ Finance the maintenance of an investment position in a securities market, especially with regard to the costs or profits accruing.
2 Golf the distance a ball travels before reaching the ground.
■ the range of a gun or similar weapon.
– PHRASES **carry all before one** overcome all opposition. **carry one's bat** Cricket (of an opening or high-order batsman) be not out at the end of a side's completed innings. **carry the can** Brit. informal take responsibility for a mistake or misdeed. **carry conviction** be convincing. **carry the day** be victorious or successful. **carry something into effect** act on a plan or proposal. **carry weight** be influential or important: *the report is expected to carry considerable **weight with** the administration.*
– ORIGIN late Middle English: from Anglo-Norman French and Old Northern French *carier*, based on Latin *carrus* 'wheeled vehicle'.
▶ **be/get carried away** lose self-control: *I got a bit carried away when describing his dreadful season.*
carry something away Nautical lose (a mast or other part of a ship) through breakage.
carry something forward transfer figures to a new page or account. ■ keep something to use or deal with at a later time: *we carried forward a reserve which allowed us to meet demands.*
carry someone/thing off take someone or something away by force: *bandits carried off his mule.* ■ (of a disease) kill someone: *Parkinson's disease carried him off in September.*
carry something off win a prize: *she failed to carry off the gold medal.* ■ succeed in doing something difficult: *he could not have carried it off without government help.*
carry on 1 continue an activity or task: *you can **carry on with** a sport as long as you feel comfortable* | *she carries on watching the telly.* ■ continue to move in the same direction: *I knew I was going the wrong way, but I just carried on.* **2** informal behave in a specified way: *they carry on in a very adult fashion.* **3** informal, chiefly Brit. be engaged in a love affair, typically one of which the speaker disapproves: *she was **carrying on with** young Adam.*
carry something on engage in an activity: *he could not carry on a logical conversation.*
carry something out perform a task or planned operation: *we're carrying out a market-research survey.*
carry over extend beyond the normal or original area of application: *his artistic practice is clearly carrying over into his social thought.*
carry something over retain something and apply or deal with it in a new context: *much of the wartime economic planning was carried over into the peace.* ■ postpone an event: *the match had to be carried over till Sunday.* ■ another way of saying ***carry something forward***.
carry something through bring a project to completion: *policy blueprints are rarely carried through perfectly.* ■ bring something safely out of difficulties: *he was the only person who could carry the country through.*

carryall ▶ **noun** **1** N. Amer. a large bag or case.
2 historical a light carriage. [ORIGIN: early 18th cent.: apparently altered by folk etymology from French *carriole*, denoting a small covered carriage.]
■ US a large car or truck with seats facing each other along the sides.

carrycot ▶ **noun** Brit. a small portable bed for a baby.

carrying capacity ▶ **noun** [mass noun] the number or quantity of people or things which can be conveyed by a vehicle or container.
■ Ecology the number of people, animals, or crops which a region can support without environmental degradation.

carrying charge ▶ **noun** **1** Finance, chiefly N. Amer. an expense or effective cost arising from unproductive assets such as stored goods or unoccupied premises.
2 a sum payable for the conveying of goods.

carrying trade ▶ **noun** the business of transporting commercial goods from one place to another by land, sea, or air.

carry-on ▶ **noun** [usu. in sing.] Brit. informal **1** a display of excitement or fuss over an unimportant matter: *I never saw such a carry-on!*
■ [mass noun] (also **carryings-on**) questionable behaviour, typically involving sexual impropriety: *the sort of carry-on that goes on behind the chintz curtains of suburbia.*
2 [usu. as modifier] a bag or suitcase suitable for taking on to an aircraft as hand luggage: *a carry-on bag.*

carry-out ▶ **adjective** & **noun** chiefly Scottish & US another term for **TAKEAWAY**.

carry-over ▶ **noun** [usu. in sing.] something transferred or resulting from a previous situation or context: *the slow trading was a carry-over from the big losses of last week.*

carse /kɑːs/ ▶ **noun** [mass noun] Scottish fertile lowland beside a river.
– ORIGIN Middle English: perhaps an alteration of *carrs*, plural of **CARR**.

carsick ▶ **adjective** affected with nausea caused by the motion of a car or other vehicle in which one is travelling.
– DERIVATIVES **carsickness** noun.

Carson[1], Rachel (Louise) (1907–64), American zoologist, a pioneer ecologist and popularizer of science. She is noted especially for *The Sea Around Us* (1951) and *Silent Spring* (1963), an attack on the indiscriminate use of pesticides.

Carson[2], Willie (b.1942), Scottish jockey; full name *William Fisher Hunter Carson*.

Carson City the state capital of Nevada; pop. 40,440 (1990).

cart ▶ **noun** a strong open vehicle with two or four wheels, typically used for carrying loads and pulled by a horse.
■ a light two-wheeled open vehicle pulled by a single horse and used as a means of transport: *he drove them in a pony and cart.* ■ a shallow open container on wheels that may be pulled or pushed by hand. ■ (also **shopping cart**) N. Amer. a supermarket trolley.
▶ **verb** [with obj.] **1** (often **be carted**) convey or put in a cart or similar vehicle: *the meat was pickled in salt and carted to El Paso.*
2 [with obj. and adverbial of direction] informal carry (a heavy or cumbersome object) somewhere with difficulty: *they carted the piano down three flights of stairs.*
■ remove or convey (someone) somewhere unceremoniously: *they carted off the refugees in the middle of the night.* ■ Cricket hit (the ball) with a powerful stroke that sends it a long way; play such a stroke against (the bowler): *he carted Sinfield for six.*
– PHRASES **in the cart** Brit. informal in trouble or difficulty. **put the cart before the horse** reverse the proper order or procedure of something.
– DERIVATIVES **carter** noun, **cartful** noun (pl. **-fuls**).
– ORIGIN Middle English: from Old Norse *kartr*, probably influenced by Anglo-Norman French and Old Northern French *carete*, diminutive of *carre* (see **CAR**).

cartage ▶ **noun** [mass noun] the conveyance of something in a cart or other vehicle.

Cartagena /ˌkɑːtəˈdʒiːnə, Spanish kartaˈxena/ **1** a port in SE Spain; pop. 172,150 (1991). Originally named Mastia, it was refounded as Carthago Nova (New Carthage) by Hasdrubal in *c.*225 BC, as a base for the Carthaginian conquest of Spain.
2 a port, resort, and oil-refining centre in NW Colombia, on the Caribbean Sea; pop. 688,300 (1992).

carte ▶ **noun** variant spelling of **QUART** (in sense 2).

carte blanche /kɑːt ˈblɑːnʃ/ ▶ **noun** **1** [mass noun] complete freedom to act as one wishes or thinks best: *we were **given carte blanche**.*
2 (in piquet) a hand containing no court cards as dealt.
– ORIGIN late 17th cent.: French, literally 'blank paper' (i.e. a blank sheet on which to write whatever one wishes, particularly one's own terms for an agreement).

carte de visite /ˌkɑːt də vɪˈziːt/ ▶ **noun** (pl. **cartes de visite** pronunc. same) historical a small photographic portrait of someone, mounted on a piece of card.
– ORIGIN mid 19th cent.: French, 'visiting card'.

cartel /kɑːˈtɛl/ ▶ **noun** an association of manufacturers or suppliers with the purpose of maintaining prices at a high level and restricting competition: *the Columbian drug cartels.*
■ chiefly historical a coalition or cooperative arrangement between political parties intended to promote a mutual interest.
– ORIGIN late 19th cent.: from German *Kartell*, from French *cartel*, from Italian *cartello*, diminutive of *carta*, from Latin *carta* (see **CARD**[1]). It was originally used to refer to the coalition of the Conservatives and National Liberal parties in Germany (1887), and

hence any political combination; later to denote a trade agreement (early 20th cent.).

cartelize /ˈkɑːtɛlaɪz, ˈkɑːtəlaɪz/ (also **-ise**) ▶ verb [with obj.] (of manufacturers or suppliers) form a cartel in (an industry or trade).

Carter[1], Angela (1940–92), English novelist and short-story writer, whose fiction is characterized by fantasy, black humour, and eroticism. Notable works: *The Magic Toyshop* (1967) and *Nights at the Circus* (1984).

Carter[2], Elliott (Cook) (b.1908), American composer. He is noted for his innovative approach to metre and his choice of sources as diverse as modern jazz and Renaissance madrigals.

Carter[3], Howard (1874–1939), English archaeologist. In 1922, while excavating in the Valley of the Kings at Thebes, he discovered the tomb of Tutankhamen.

Carter[4], Jimmy (b.1924), American Democratic statesman, 39th President of the US 1977–81; full name *James Earl Carter*. He hosted the talks which led to the Camp David agreements (1978).

Cartesian /kɑːˈtiːzɪən, -ˌʒ(ə)n/ ▶ adjective of or relating to Descartes and his ideas.
▶ noun a follower of Descartes.
– DERIVATIVES **Cartesianism** noun.
– ORIGIN mid 17th cent.: from modern Latin *Cartesianus*, from *Cartesius*, Latinized form of the name of *Descartes*.

Cartesian coordinates ▶ plural noun numbers which indicate the location of a point relative to a fixed reference point (the origin), being its shortest (perpendicular) distances from two fixed axes (or three planes defined by three fixed axes) which intersect at right angles at the origin.

Carthage /ˈkɑːθɪdʒ/ an ancient city on the coast of North Africa near present-day Tunis. Founded by the Phoenicians *c*.814 BC, Carthage became a major force in the Mediterranean, and came into conflict with Rome in the Punic Wars. It was finally destroyed by the Romans in 146 BC.
– DERIVATIVES **Carthaginian** noun & adjective.

carthorse ▶ noun Brit. a large, strong horse suitable for heavy work.

Carthusian /kɑːˈθjuːzɪən/ ▶ noun a monk or nun of an austere contemplative order founded by St Bruno in 1084.
▶ adjective of or relating to this order.
– ORIGIN from medieval Latin *Carthusianus*, from *Cart(h)usia*, Latin name of *Chartreuse*, near Grenoble, where the order was founded.

Cartier /ˈkɑːtɪeɪ, French kaʁtje/, Jacques (1491–1557), French explorer. The first to establish France's claim to North America, he made three voyages to Canada between 1534 and 1541.

Cartier-Bresson /ˌkɑːtɪeɪˈbrɛsɒ̃, French kaʁtjebʁɛsɔ̃/, Henri (b.1908), French photographer and film director. He is famed for his collection of photographs *The Decisive Moment* (1952) and his documentary film about the Spanish Civil War, *Return to Life* (1937).

Cartier Islands see ASHMORE AND CARTIER ISLANDS.

cartilage /ˈkɑːt(ɪ)lɪdʒ/ ▶ noun [mass noun] firm, whitish, flexible connective tissue found in various forms in the larynx and respiratory tract, in structures such as the external ear, and in the articulating surfaces of joints. It is more widespread in the infant skeleton, being replaced by bone during growth.
■ [count noun] a particular structure made of this tissue.
– DERIVATIVES **cartilaginoid** /-ˈladʒɪnɔɪd/ adjective.
– ORIGIN late Middle English: from French, from Latin *cartilago*, *cartilagin-*.

cartilaginous /ˌkɑːtɪˈladʒɪnəs/ ▶ adjective Anatomy (of a structure) made of cartilage.
■ Zoology (of a vertebrate animal) having a skeleton of cartilage.
– ORIGIN late Middle English: from Old French, or from Latin *cartilaginosus*, from *cartilago*, *cartilagin-* 'cartilage'.

cartilaginous fish ▶ noun a fish of a class distinguished by having a skeleton of cartilage rather than bone, including the sharks, rays, and chimaeras. Compare with BONY FISH.
● Class Chondrichthyes: subclasses Elasmobranchii (sharks and rays) and Holocephali (chimaeras).

Cartland, Dame (Mary) Barbara (Hamilton) (1901–2000), English author of light romantic fiction.

cartload ▶ noun the amount held by a cart.
■ informal a large quantity or number of people or things: *drunken yobbos who turned up by the cartload*.

cartogram /ˈkɑːtəgram/ ▶ noun a map on which statistical information is shown in diagrammatic form.
– ORIGIN late 19th cent.: from French *cartogramme*, from *carte* 'map or card' + *-gramme* (from Greek *gramma* 'thing written').

cartography /kɑːˈtɒgrəfi/ ▶ noun [mass noun] the science or practice of drawing maps.
– DERIVATIVES **cartographer** noun, **cartographic** adjective, **cartographical** adjective, **cartographically** adverb.
– ORIGIN mid 19th cent.: from French *cartographie*, from *carte* 'map, card' (see CARD[1]) + *-graphie* (see -GRAPHY).

cartomancy /ˈkɑːtə(ʊ)ˌmansi/ ▶ noun [mass noun] fortune telling by interpreting a random selection of playing cards.
– DERIVATIVES **cartomancer** noun.
– ORIGIN late 19th cent.: from French *cartomancie*, from *carte* 'card' + *-mancie* (see -MANCY).

carton ▶ noun a light box or container, typically one made of waxed cardboard or plastic in which drinks or foodstuffs are packaged.
– ORIGIN early 19th cent.: from French, from Italian *cartone* (see CARTOON).

cartonnage /ˈkɑːt(ə)nɪdʒ/ ▶ noun an ancient Egyptian mummy case made of tightly fitting layers of linen or papyrus glued together.
– ORIGIN mid 19th cent.: French.

cartoon ▶ noun 1 a simple drawing showing the features of its subjects in a humorously exaggerated way, especially a satirical one in a newspaper or magazine.
■ (also **cartoon strip**) a narrative sequence of humorous drawings in a comic, magazine, or newspaper, usually with captions. ■ figurative a simplified or exaggerated version or interpretation of something: *this film is a cartoon of public life in the US* | [as modifier] *Dolores becomes a cartoon housewife, reading glossy magazines in a bathrobe*.
2 a film using animation techniques to photograph a sequence of drawings rather than real people or objects.
3 a full-size drawing made by an artist as a preliminary design for a painting or other work of art.
▶ verb [with obj.] (usu. **be cartooned**) make a drawing of (someone) in a simplified or exaggerated way: *she has a face with enough character to be cartooned*.
– DERIVATIVES **cartoonish** adjective, **cartoonist** noun, **cartoony** adjective.
– ORIGIN late 16th cent. (in sense 3): from Italian *cartone*, from *carta*, from Latin *carta*, *charta* (see CARD[1]). Sense 1 dates from the mid 19th cent.

cartooning ▶ noun [mass noun] the activity or occupation of drawing cartoons for newspapers or magazines.

cartophily /kɑːˈtɒfɪli/ ▶ noun [mass noun] the collecting of picture cards, such as postcards or cigarette cards, as a hobby.
– DERIVATIVES **cartophilist** noun.
– ORIGIN 1930s: from French *carte* or Italian *carta* 'card' + -PHILY.

cartouche /kɑːˈtuːʃ/ ▶ noun a carved tablet or drawing representing a scroll with rolled-up ends, used ornamentally or bearing an inscription.
■ a decorative architectural feature, such as a modillion or corbel, resembling a scroll. ■ a space within a border or frame for a design or inscription, typically an oval one. ■ an ornate frame around a design or inscription: *a coat of arms in a cartouche*. ■ Archaeology an oval or oblong enclosing a group of Egyptian hieroglyphs, typically representing the name and title of a monarch.
– ORIGIN early 17th cent.: from French *cartouche* (masculine noun), earlier *cartoche*, from Italian *cartoccio*, from *carta*, from Latin *carta*, *charta* (see CARD[1]).

cartridge ▶ noun a container holding a spool of photographic film, a quantity of ink, or other item or substance, designed for insertion into a mechanism.
■ a casing containing a charge and a bullet or shot for small arms or an explosive charge for blasting. ■ a

component carrying the stylus on the pickup head of a record player.
– ORIGIN late 16th cent.: from French *cartouche* (feminine noun), from Italian *cartoccio* (see CARTOUCHE).

cartridge belt ▶ noun a belt with pockets or loops for cartridges of ammunition, typically worn over the shoulder.

cartridge paper ▶ noun [mass noun] thick, rough-textured paper used for drawing and for strong envelopes.
– ORIGIN mid 17th cent.: originally used to make cartridge cases.

cartwheel ▶ noun 1 the wheel of a cart.
2 a circular sideways handspring with the arms and legs extended.
▶ verb [no obj., with adverbial of direction] perform such a handspring or handsprings: *he cartwheeled across the room*.

Cartwright, Edmund (1743–1823), English engineer, inventor of the power loom.

cartwright ▶ noun chiefly historical a person whose job is making carts.

caruncle /ˈkarəŋk(ə)l, kəˈrʌŋ-/ ▶ noun a fleshy outgrowth, in particular:
■ a wattle of a bird such as a turkeycock. ■ the red prominence at the inner corner of the eye. ■ Botany a coloured waxy or oily outgrowth from a seed near the micropyle, attractive to ants which aid the seed's dispersal.
– DERIVATIVES **caruncular** adjective.
– ORIGIN late 16th cent.: obsolete French, from Latin *caruncula*, from *caro*, *carn-* 'flesh'.

Caruso /kəˈruːzəʊ, -səʊ, Italian kaˈruso/, Enrico (1873–1921), Italian operatic tenor. He was the first major tenor to be recorded on gramophone records.

carve ▶ verb [with obj.] 1 (often **be carved**) cut (a hard material) in order to produce an aesthetically pleasing object or design: *the wood was carved with runes* | [as adj. **carved**] *bookcases of carved oak*.
■ produce (an object) by cutting and shaping a hard material: *the altar was carved from a block of solid jade*. ■ produce (an inscription or design) by cutting into hard material: *an inscription was carved over the doorway* | figurative *the river carved a series of gorges into the plain*.
2 cut (cooked meat) into slices for eating.
■ cut (a slice of meat) from a larger piece.
3 Skiing make (a turn) by tilting one's skis on to their edges and using one's weight to bend them so that they slide into an arc.
– PHRASES **be carved on tablets of stone** see STONE.
– ORIGIN Old English *ceorfan* 'cut, carve', of West Germanic origin; related to Dutch *kerven*.
▶ **carve something out 1** take something from a larger whole, especially with difficulty: *carving out a 5 per cent share of the overall vote*. **2** establish or create something through painstaking effort: *he managed to carve out a successful photographic career for himself*. **carve someone up** informal **1** slash someone with a knife or other sharp object. **2** drive aggressively into the path of another driver travelling in the same direction. **carve something up** divide something ruthlessly into separate areas or domains: *West Africa was carved up by the Europeans*.

carvel /ˈkɑːv(ə)l/ ▶ noun variant spelling of CARAVEL.

carvel-built ▶ adjective (of a boat) having external planks which do not overlap. Compare with CLINKER-BUILT.

carven archaic past participle of CARVE.

carver ▶ noun 1 a person who carves wood or stone professionally: *an ivory carver*.
2 a knife designed for slicing meat.
■ (**carvers**) a knife and fork for slicing meat.
3 a person who cuts and serves the meat at a meal.
■ Brit. the principal chair, with arms, in a set of dining chairs, intended for the person carving meat.

carvery ▶ noun (pl. **-ies**) chiefly Brit. a buffet or restaurant where cooked joints are displayed and carved as required in front of customers.

carve-up ▶ noun [in sing.] Brit. informal a ruthless division of something into separate areas or domains: *the carve-up of the brewing industry by vested interests*.
■ a sharing-out of dishonest gains.

carving ▶ noun an object or design cut from a hard material as an artistic work.

carving knife ▶ noun a knife with a long blade used for carving cooked meat into slices.

car wash ▶ noun a building containing equipment for washing vehicles automatically.

Cary /ˈkɛːri/, (Arthur) Joyce (Lunel) (1888–1957), English novelist. Notable works: *The Horse's Mouth* (1944) and *Not Honour More* (1955).

caryatid /ˌkarɪˈatɪd/ ▶ noun (pl. **caryatides** /-diːz/ or **caryatids**) Architecture a stone carving of a draped female figure, used as pillar to support the entablature of a Greek or Greek-style building.
– ORIGIN mid 16th cent.: via French and Italian from Latin *caryatides*, from Greek *karuatides*, plural of *karuatis* 'priestess of Artemis at Caryae', from *Karuai* (Caryae) in Laconia.

caryophyllaceous /ˌkarɪə(ʊ)fɪˈleɪʃəs/ ▶ adjective Botany of, relating to, or denoting plants of the pink family (Caryophyllaceae).
– ORIGIN mid 19th cent.: from modern Latin *Caryophyllaceae* (plural), based on Greek *karuophullon* 'clove pink', + **-OUS**.

caryopsis /ˌkarɪˈɒpsɪs/ ▶ noun (pl. **caryopses** /-siːz/) Botany a dry one-seeded fruit in which the ovary wall is united with the seed coat, typical of grasses and cereals.
– ORIGIN early 19th cent.: from modern Latin, from Greek *karuon* 'nut' + *opsis* 'appearance'.

casaba /kəˈsɑːbə/ ▶ noun N. Amer. a winter melon of a variety with a wrinkled yellow rind and sweet flesh.
■ (**casabas**) informal a woman's breasts.
– ORIGIN early 20th cent.: named after *Kasaba* (now Turgutlu) in Turkey, from which the melons were first exported.

Casablanca /ˌkasəˈblaŋkə/ the largest city of Morocco, a seaport on the Atlantic coast; pop. 2,943,000 (1993).

Casals /kəˈsalz/, Pablo (1876–1973), Spanish cellist, conductor, and composer.

Casanova /ˌkasəˈnəʊvə, -z-/, Giovanni Jacopo (1725–98), Italian adventurer; full name *Giovanni Jacopo Casanova de Seingalt*. He is famous for his memoirs describing his sexual encounters and other exploits.
■ [as noun] (usu. **a Casanova**) a man notorious for seducing women.

casareep ▶ noun variant spelling of **CASSAREEP**.

casbah ▶ noun variant spelling of **KASBAH**.

cascabel /ˈkaskəb(ə)l/ ▶ noun a small red chilli pepper of a mild-flavoured variety.
– ORIGIN mid 17th cent.: from Spanish, from Catalan *cascavel*, from medieval Latin *cascabellus* 'little bell'.

cascade ▶ noun **1** a small waterfall, typically one of several that fall in stages down a steep rocky slope.
■ a mass of something that falls or hangs in copious or luxuriant quantities: *a cascade of pink bougainvillea*. ■ a large number or amount of something occurring or arriving in rapid succession: *a cascade of anti-war literature*.
2 a process whereby something, typically information or knowledge, is successively passed on: [as modifier] *the greater the number of people who are well briefed, the wider the cascade effect*.
■ a succession of devices or stages in a process, each of which triggers or initiates the next.
▶ verb **1** [no obj., with adverbial of direction] (of water) pour downwards rapidly and in large quantities: *water was* ***cascading down*** *the stairs*.
■ fall or hang in copious or luxuriant quantities: *blonde hair* ***cascaded down*** *her back*.
2 [with obj.] pass (something) on to a succession of others: *teachers who are able to cascade their experience effectively*.
3 [with obj.] arrange (a number of devices or objects) in a series or sequence.
– ORIGIN mid 17th cent.: from French, from Italian *cascata*, from *cascare* 'to fall', based on Latin *casus* (see **CASE**[1]).

Cascade Range a range of volcanic mountains in western North America, extending from southern British Columbia through Washington and Oregon to northern California.

cascara /kasˈkɑːrə/ (also **cascara sagrada** /səˈgrɑːdə/) ▶ noun **1** [mass noun] a purgative made from the dried bark of an American buckthorn.
2 the tree from which this bark is obtained, native to western North America.
• *Rhamnus purshiana*, family Rhamnaceae.
– ORIGIN late 19th cent.: from Spanish *cáscara (sagrada)*, literally '(sacred) bark'.

case[1] ▶ noun **1** an instance of a particular situation; an example of something occurring: *a case of mistaken identity* | ***in many cases*** *farmers do have a deep feeling for their land*.
■ [usu. in sing.] the situation affecting or relating to a particular person or thing; one's circumstances or position: *I'll make an exception* ***in your case***. ■ an incident or set of circumstances under official investigation by the police: *a murder case*.
2 an instance of a disease, injury, or problem: *200,000 cases of hepatitis B*.
■ a person suffering from a disease or injury: *most breast cancer cases were older women*. ■ a person or their particular problem requiring or receiving medical or welfare attention: *the local social services discussed Gemma's case*. ■ [with adj. or noun modifier] informal a person whose situation is regarded as pitiable or as having no chance of improvement: *Vicky was a very* ***sad case***.
■ informal, dated an amusing or eccentric person.
3 a legal action, especially one to be decided in a court of law: *a libel case* | *a former employee brought the case against the council*.
■ a set of facts or arguments supporting one side in such a legal action: *the case for the defence*. ■ a legal action that has been decided and may be cited as a precedent. ■ (also **case stated**) an agreed summary of the facts relating to a case, drawn up for review or decision on a point of law by a higher court. ■ a set of facts or arguments supporting one side of a debate or controversy: *the* ***case against*** *tobacco advertising*.
4 Grammar any of the inflected forms of a noun, adjective, or pronoun that express the semantic relation of the word to other words in the sentence: *the accusative case*.
■ [mass noun] such a relation whether indicated by inflection or not: *English normally expresses case by the use of prepositions*.
– PHRASES **as the case may be** according to the circumstances (used when referring to two or more possible alternatives): *the authorities will decide if they are satisfied or not satisfied, as the case may be*. **be the case** be so. **in any case** whatever happens or may have happened. ■ used to confirm or support a point or idea just mentioned: *he wasn't allowed out yet, and in any case he wasn't well enough*. **(just) in case 1** as a provision against something happening or being true: *we put on thick jumpers, in case it was cold*. **2** if it is true that: *in case you haven't figured it out, let me explain*. **in case of** in the event of (a particular situation): *instructions about what to do in case of fire*. **in no case** under no circumstances. **in that case** if that happens or has happened; if that is the situation: *'I'm free this evening.' 'In that case, why not have dinner with me?'* **on** (or **off**) **someone's case** informal continually (or no longer) criticizing or harassing someone: *teachers, you know,* ***get on your case***.
– ORIGIN Middle English: from Old French *cas*, from Latin *casus* 'fall', related to *cadere* 'to fall'; in sense 4 directly from Latin, translating Greek *ptōsis*, literally 'fall'.

case[2] ▶ noun a container designed to hold or protect something: *a silver cigarette case*.
■ the outer protective covering of a natural or manufactured object: *a seed case*. ■ Brit. an item of luggage; a suitcase. ■ a box containing twelve bottles of wine or other drink, sold as a unit: *a case of champagne*. ■ Printing a partitioned container for loose metal type. ■ each of the two forms, capital or minuscule, in which a letter of the alphabet may be written or printed. See also **UPPER CASE**, **LOWER CASE**.
▶ verb [with obj.] (usu. **be cased**) **1** surround in a material or substance: *the towers are of steel cased in granite*.
■ enclose in a protective container: [as adj. **cased**] *a cased pair of pistols*.
2 informal reconnoitre (a place) before carrying out a robbery: *I was* ***casing the joint***.
– ORIGIN late Middle English: from Old French *casse*, *chasse* (modern *caisse* 'trunk, chest', *châsse* 'reliquary, frame'), from Latin *capsa*, related to *capere* 'to hold'.

caseation /ˌkeɪsɪˈeɪʃ(ə)n/ ▶ noun [mass noun] Medicine a form of necrosis characteristic of tuberculosis, in which diseased tissue forms a firm, dry mass like cheese in appearance.
– ORIGIN mid 19th cent.: from medieval Latin *caseatio(n-)*, from Latin *caseus* 'cheese'.

casebook ▶ noun Brit. a written record of cases dealt with, especially one kept by a doctor or investigator.
■ a book containing extracts of important legal cases.
■ US a book containing a selection of source materials on a particular subject, especially one used as a reference work or in teaching.

case-bound ▶ adjective technical (of a book) hardback.

case conference ▶ noun a meeting of professionals such as teachers or social workers to discuss a particular case.

case grammar ▶ noun [mass noun] Linguistics a form of grammar in which the structure of sentences is analysed in terms of semantic case relationships.

case-harden ▶ verb [with obj.] [often as adj. **case-hardened**] harden the surface of (a material): *case-hardened sandstones*.
■ give a hard surface to (iron or steel) by carburizing it: *a case-hardened steel anvil*. ■ figurative make (someone) callous or tough: *a case-hardened politician*.

case history ▶ noun a record of a person's background or medical history kept by a doctor or social worker.

casein /ˈkeɪsiːn, -sɪɪn/ ▶ noun [mass noun] the main protein present in milk and (in coagulated form) in cheese. It is used in processed foods and in adhesives, paints, and other industrial products.
– ORIGIN mid 19th cent.: from Latin *caseus* 'cheese'.

case knife ▶ noun US term for **TABLE KNIFE**.
■ archaic a type of dagger carried in a sheath.

case law ▶ noun [mass noun] the law as established by the outcome of former cases. Compare with **COMMON LAW**, **STATUTE LAW**.

caseload ▶ noun the amount of work (in terms of number of cases) with which a doctor, lawyer, or social worker is concerned at one time.

casemate /ˈkeɪsmeɪt/ ▶ noun historical a small room in the thickness of the wall of a fortress, with embrasures from which guns or missiles can be fired.
■ an armoured enclosure for guns on a warship.
– ORIGIN mid 16th cent.: from French, from Italian *casamatta*, perhaps from Greek *khasma*, *khasmat-* (see **CHASM**).

Casement, Sir Roger (David) (1864–1916), Irish diplomat and nationalist. In 1914 he sought German support for an Irish uprising, and was subsequently hanged by the British for treason.

casement ▶ noun a window or part of a window set on a vertical hinge so that it opens like a door.
■ chiefly poetic/literary a window. ■ the sash of a sash window.
– ORIGIN late Middle English (as an architectural term denoting a hollow moulding): from Anglo-Latin *cassimentum*, from *cassa*, from Latin *capsa* (see **CASE**[2]).

caseous /ˈkeɪsɪəs/ ▶ adjective Medicine characterized by caseation.
– ORIGIN mid 17th cent.: from Latin *caseus* 'cheese' + **-OUS**.

case-sensitive ▶ adjective Computing (of a program or function) differentiating between capital and lower-case letters.
■ (of input) treated differently depending on whether it is in capitals or lower-case text.

case-shot ▶ noun [mass noun] historical bullets or pieces of metal in an iron case fired from a cannon.

case stated ▶ noun see **CASE**[1] (sense 3).

case study ▶ noun **1** a process or record of research in which detailed consideration is given to the development of a particular person, group, or situation over a period of time.
2 a particular instance of something used or analysed in order to illustrate a thesis or principle: *airline deregulation provides a case study of the effects of the internal market*.

casevac /ˈkazɪvak, ˈkaʒɪ-/ military slang ▶ noun [mass noun] evacuation of casualties by air.
▶ verb (**casevaced**, **casevacing**) [with obj.] evacuate (a casualty) by air.
– ORIGIN 1950s: blend of **CASUALTY** and **EVACUATION**.

casework[1] ▶ noun [mass noun] social work directly concerned with individuals, especially that involving a study of a person's family history and personal circumstances.
– DERIVATIVES **caseworker** noun.

casework[2] ▶ noun [mass noun] the decorative outer

case protecting the workings of a complex mechanism such as an organ or harpsichord.

Cash, Johnny (b.1932), American country music singer and songwriter. Notable songs: 'I Walk the Line' (1956) and 'A Boy Named Sue' (1969).

cash¹ ▶ noun [mass noun] money in coins or notes, as distinct from cheques, money orders, or credit: *the staff were paid in cash* | *a discount for cash*.
 ■ money in any form, especially that which is immediately available: *she was always short of cash.*
▶ verb [with obj.] give or obtain notes or coins for (a cheque or money order).
 ■ [with two objs] give (someone) notes or coins for (a cheque or money order): *haven't you a friend who would cash you a cheque?* ■ Bridge lead (a high card) so as to take the opportunity to win a trick.
 – PHRASES **cash down** with immediate and full payment at the time of purchase: *the price was £900 cash down.* **cash in one's chips** informal die. [ORIGIN: with reference to gambling in a casino.] **cash in hand** payment for goods and services in cash rather than by cheque or other means, typically as a way of avoiding the payment of tax on the amount earned: [as modifier] *a cash-in-hand job.*
 – DERIVATIVES **cashable** adjective.
 – ORIGIN late 16th cent. (denoting a box for money): from Old French *casse* or Italian *cassa* 'box', from Latin *capsa* (see CASE²).

▶ **cash in** informal take advantage of or exploit (a situation): *the breweries were cashing in on the rediscovered taste for real ales.*
 cash something in convert an insurance policy, savings account, or other investment into money. **cash up** (or **cash something up**) Brit. count and check takings at the end of a day's trading.

cash² ▶ noun (pl. same) historical a coin of low value from China, southern India, or SE Asia.
 – ORIGIN late 16th cent.: from Portuguese *caixa*, from Tamil *kāsu*, influenced by CASH¹.

cash and carry ▶ noun [mass noun] a system of wholesale trading whereby goods are paid for in full at the time of purchase and taken away by the purchaser.
 ■ [count noun] a wholesale store operating this system.

cashback ▶ noun a form of incentive offered to buyers of certain products whereby they receive a cash refund after making their purchase.
 ■ a facility offered by certain retailers whereby the customer may withdraw cash when making a debit card purchase, the amount of which is added to their bill.

cash bar ▶ noun a bar at a social function at which guests buy drinks rather than having them provided free.

cash book ▶ noun a book in which receipts and payments of money are recorded.

cash box ▶ noun a metal box with a lock for keeping cash in.

cash card ▶ noun Brit. a plastic card issued by a bank or building society which enables the holder to withdraw money from a cash dispenser.

cash cow ▶ noun informal a business or investment that provides a steady income or profit.

cash crop ▶ noun a crop produced for its commercial value rather than for use by the grower.
 – DERIVATIVES **cash cropping** noun.

cash desk ▶ noun Brit. a counter or compartment in a shop or restaurant where payments are made.

cash dispenser ▶ noun Brit. another term for AUTOMATED TELLER MACHINE.

cashew /ˈkaʃuː, kaˈʃuː/ ▶ noun 1 (also **cashew nut**) an edible kidney-shaped nut, rich in oil and protein, which is roasted and shelled before it can be eaten. Oil is extracted from the shells and used as a lubricant and insecticide and in the production of plastics.
 2 (also **cashew tree**) a bushy tropical American tree related to the mango, bearing cashew nuts singly at the tip of each swollen fruit. Also called ACAJOU.
 ● *Anacardium occidentale*, family Anacardiaceae.
 – ORIGIN late 16th cent.: from Portuguese, from Tupi *acajú, cajú.*

cashew apple ▶ noun the swollen edible fruit of the cashew tree, from which the cashew nut hangs, sometimes used to make wine.

cash flow ▶ noun the total amount of money being transferred into and out of a business, especially as affecting liquidity.

cashier¹ ▶ noun a person handling payments and receipts in a shop, bank, or business.
 – ORIGIN late 16th cent.: from Dutch *cassier* or French *caissier*, from *caisse* 'cash'.

cashier² ▶ verb [with obj.] (usu. **be cashiered**) dismiss someone from the armed forces in disgrace because of a serious misdemeanour.
 – ORIGIN late 16th cent. (in the sense 'dismiss or disband troops'): from Flemish *kasseren* 'disband (troops)' or 'revoke (a will)', from French *casser* 'revoke, dismiss', from Latin *quassare* (see QUASH).

cashless ▶ adjective characterized by the exchange of funds by cheque, debit or credit card, or various electronic methods rather than the use of cash: *the cashless society.*

cashmere ▶ noun [mass noun] fine soft wool, originally that from the Kashmir goat.
 ■ woollen material made from or resembling such wool: [as modifier] *a cashmere jumper.*
 – ORIGIN late 17th cent.: an early spelling of KASHMIR.

cash nexus ▶ noun the relationship constituted by monetary transactions.

cash on delivery (abbrev.: **COD**) ▶ noun [mass noun] the system of paying for goods when they are delivered.

cashpoint ▶ noun Brit. another term for AUTOMATED TELLER MACHINE.

cash ratio ▶ noun the ratio of the liquid assets of a company to its current liabilities.
 ■ the ratio of cash to deposits in a bank (for which minimum values are generally set officially).

cash register ▶ noun a machine used in shops that has a drawer for money and totals, displays, and records the amount of each sale.

casing ▶ noun 1 a cover or shell that protects or encloses something: *a waterproof casing.*
 2 the frame round a door or window.

casino ▶ noun (pl. **-os**) a public room or building where gambling games are played.
 – ORIGIN mid 18th cent.: from Italian, diminutive of *casa* 'house', from Latin *casa* 'cottage'.

cask ▶ noun a large barrel-like container made of wood, metal, or plastic, used for storing liquids, typically alcoholic drinks.
 ■ the quantity of liquid held in such a container: *a cask of cider.*
 – ORIGIN early 16th cent.: from French *casque* or Spanish *casco* 'helmet'. The current senses appear only in English; from the late 16th to the late 18th centuries the word also denoted a helmet (compare with CASQUE).

cask beer ▶ noun [mass noun] draught beer brewed and stored in the traditional way, maturing naturally in the cask from which it is served. Compare with KEG BEER.

cask-conditioned ▶ adjective (of beer) undergoing a secondary fermentation in the cask and not filtered, pasteurized, or further processed before serving.

casket ▶ noun a small ornamental box or chest for holding jewels, letters, or other valuable objects.
 ■ Brit. a small wooden box for cremated ashes. ■ chiefly N. Amer. a coffin.
 – ORIGIN late Middle English: perhaps an Anglo-Norman French form of Old French *cassette*, diminutive of *casse* (see CASE²).

Caslon /ˈkazlən, -lən/ ▶ noun [mass noun] a kind of roman typeface first introduced in the 18th century.
 – ORIGIN mid 19th cent.: named after William *Caslon* (1692–1766), English type founder.

Casnewydd /kasˈnewɪð/ Welsh name for NEWPORT.

Caspar /ˈkaspə, -pɑː/ one of the three Magi.

Caspian Sea /ˈkaspɪən/ a large landlocked salt lake, bounded by Russia, Kazakhstan, Turkmenistan, Azerbaijan, and Iran. It is the world's largest body of inland water. Its surface lies 28 m (92 ft) below sea level.

casque /kɑːsk/ ▶ noun 1 historical a helmet.
 2 Zoology a helmet-like structure, such as that on the bill of a hornbill or the head of a cassowary.
 – ORIGIN late 17th cent.: from French, from Spanish *casco*. Compare with CASK.

Cassandra /kəˈsandrə/ Greek Mythology a daughter of the Trojan king Priam, who was given the gift of prophecy by Apollo. When she cheated him, however, he turned this into a curse by causing her prophecies, though true, to be disbelieved.
 ■ [as noun **a Cassandra**] a prophet of disaster, especially one who is disregarded.

cassareep /ˈkasəriːp/ (also **casareep**) ▶ noun [mass noun] W. Indian a thick brown syrup made by boiling down the juice of grated cassava with sugar and spices, and typically used as a flavouring for pepper pot (see PEPPER POT sense 2).
 – ORIGIN from Arawak *casiripe.*

cassata /kəˈsɑːtə/ ▶ noun [mass noun] Neapolitan ice cream containing candied or dried fruit and nuts.
 – ORIGIN 1920s: Italian.

cassation /kaˈseɪʃ(ə)n/ ▶ noun Music an informal instrumental composition of the 18th century, similar to a divertimento and originally often for outdoor performance.
 – ORIGIN late 19th cent.: from German *Kassation* 'serenade', from Italian *cassazione.*

Cassatt /kəˈsat/, Mary (1844–1926), American painter. Her paintings display a close interest in everyday subject matter.

cassava /kəˈsɑːvə/ ▶ noun 1 [mass noun] the starchy tuberous root of a tropical tree, used as food in tropical countries but requiring careful preparation to remove traces of cyanide from the flesh.
 ■ a starch or flour obtained from such a root. Also called MANIOC.
 2 the shrubby tree from which this root is obtained, native to tropical America and cultivated throughout the tropics.
 ● Genus *Manihot*, family Euphorbiaceae: several species, in particular **bitter cassava** (*M. esculenta*) and **sweet cassava** (*M. dulcis*).
 – ORIGIN mid 16th cent.: from Taino *casávi, cazábbi*, influenced by French *cassave.*

Cassegrain telescope /ˈkasɪɡreɪn/ ▶ noun a reflecting telescope in which light reflected from a convex secondary mirror passes through a hole in the primary mirror.
 – ORIGIN late 19th cent.: named after N. *Cassegrain* (1625–1712), the French astronomer who devised it.

casserole ▶ noun a kind of stew that is cooked slowly in an oven: *a chicken casserole.*
 ■ a large covered dish, typically of earthenware or glass, used for cooking such stews.
▶ verb [with obj.] cook (food) slowly in a such a dish.
 – ORIGIN early 18th cent.: from French, diminutive of *casse* 'spoon-like container', from Old Provençal *casa*, from late Latin *cattia* 'ladle, pan', from Greek *kuathion*, diminutive of *kuathos* 'cup'.

cassette ▶ noun a sealed plastic unit containing a length of audio tape wound on a pair of spools, for insertion into a recorder or playback device.
 ■ a similar unit containing videotape, film, or other material for insertion into a machine.
 – ORIGIN late 18th cent.: from French, diminutive of *casse* (see CASE²).

cassette deck ▶ noun a unit in hi-fi equipment for playing or recording audio cassettes.

cassette player (also **cassette recorder**) ▶ noun a machine for playing back or recording audio cassettes.

cassette tape ▶ noun a cassette of audio tape or videotape.

cassia /ˈkasɪə/ ▶ noun 1 a tree, shrub, or herbaceous plant of the pea family, native to warm climates. Cassias yield a variety of products, including fodder, timber, and medicinal drugs, and many are cultivated as ornamentals. [ORIGIN: modern Latin.]
 ● Genus *Cassia*, family Leguminosae: many species, including *C. fistula*, which provides much of the commercially produced senna.
 2 (also **cassia bark**) [mass noun] the aromatic bark of an East Asian tree, yielding an inferior kind of cinnamon which is sometimes used to adulterate true cinnamon. [ORIGIN: from Latin, probably denoting the wild cinnamon, via Greek from Hebrew *qĕṣī'āh*.]
 ● *Cinnamomum aromaticum*, family Lauraceae.

cassingle /kaˈsɪŋɡ(ə)l/ ▶ noun an audio cassette with a single piece of music, especially popular music, on each side.
 – ORIGIN 1970s: blend of CASSETTE and SINGLE.

Cassini¹ /kaˈsiːni/, Giovanni Domenico (1625–1712),

Italian-born French astronomer. He discovered the gap in the rings of Saturn known as Cassini's division.

Cassini² a spacecraft launched in 1997 to explore Saturn and Titan, which it is due to reach in 2004. It consists of an orbiter and a probe (see **HUYGENS²**).

Cassiopeia /ˌkasɪə(ʊ)ˈpiːə/ **1** Greek Mythology the wife of Cepheus, king of Ethiopia, and mother of Andromeda.
2 Astronomy a constellation near the north celestial pole, recognizable by the conspicuous 'W' pattern of its brightest stars.
▪[as genitive **Cassiopeiae** /ˌkasɪə(ʊ)ˈpiːʌɪ, -ˈpiːiː/] used with preceding letter or numeral to designate a star in this constellation: *the star Delta Cassiopeiae.*

cassis¹ /kaˈsiːs, ˈkasɪs/ (also **crème de cassis**) ▶ **noun** [mass noun] a syrupy blackcurrant liqueur produced mainly in Burgundy.
– ORIGIN French, 'blackcurrant', apparently from Latin *cassia* (see **CASSIA**).

cassis² /kaˈsi/ ▶ **noun** [mass noun] a wine produced in the region of Cassis, a small town near Marseilles.

cassiterite /kəˈsɪtərʌɪt/ ▶ **noun** [mass noun] a reddish, brownish, or yellowish mineral consisting of tin dioxide. It is the main ore of tin.
– ORIGIN mid 19th cent.: from Greek *kassiteros* 'tin' + **-ITE¹**.

Cassius /ˈkasɪəs/, Gaius (d.42 BC), Roman general; full name *Gaius Cassius Longinus*. He was one of the leaders of the conspiracy in 44 BC to assassinate Julius Caesar.

cassock ▶ **noun** a full-length garment of a single colour worn by certain Christian clergy, members of church choirs, and others having some particular office or role in a church.
– DERIVATIVES **cassocked** adjective.
– ORIGIN mid 16th cent.: from French *casaque* 'long coat', from Italian *casacca* 'riding coat', probably from Turkic *kazak* 'vagabond'. Compare with **COSSACK**.

cassone /kaˈsəʊne, -ni/ ▶ **noun** (pl. **cassones** /-nɪz/ or **cassoni** /-ni/) (in Italy) a large chest, especially one used to hold a bride's trousseau.
– ORIGIN late 19th cent.: Italian, 'large chest'.

cassoulet /ˈkasʊleɪ/ ▶ **noun** [mass noun] a stew made with meat and beans.
– ORIGIN French, diminutive of dialect *cassolo* 'stew pan', from Old Provençal *cassa* 'pan'; related to **CASSEROLE**.

cassowary /ˈkasəwəri, -wɛːri/ ▶ **noun** (pl. **-ies**) a very large flightless bird related to the emu, with a bare head and neck, a tall horny crest, and one or two coloured wattles. It is native mainly to the forests of New Guinea.
• Family Casuariidae and genus *Casuarius*: three species, in particular the **double-wattled** (or **Australian**) **cassowary** (*C. casuarius*).
– ORIGIN early 17th cent.: from Malay *kesuari*.

cast¹ ▶ **verb** (past and past participle **cast**) **1** [with obj., usu. with adverbial of direction] throw (something) forcefully in a specified direction: *they cast themselves off the cliff* | figurative *individuals who do not accept the norms are **cast out** from the group.*
▪throw (something) so as to cause it to spread over an area: *the fishermen cast a large net around a school of tuna* | figurative *he cast his net far and wide in search of evidence.* ▪ direct (one's eyes or a look) at something: *she cast down her eyes* | [with two objs] *she cast him a desperate glance.* ▪ [with obj.] throw the hooked and baited end of (a fishing line) out into the water. ▪ [with obj.] register (a vote): *votes have been cast in 40 per cent of the seats.* ▪ [with obj.] Hunting let loose (hounds) on a scent. ▪ [no obj.] Hunting (of a dog) search in different directions for a lost scent: *the dog cast furiously for the vanished rabbit.* ▪ [with obj.] let down (an anchor or sounding line). ▪ [with obj.] immobilize (an animal, especially a cow) by using a rope to cause it to fall on its side.
2 [with obj. and adverbial of place] cause (light or shadow) to appear on a surface: *the moon cast a pale light over the cottages* | figurative *running costs were already **casting a shadow** over the programme.*
▪cause (uncertainty or disparagement) to be associated with something: *journalists **cast doubt on** the government's version of events* | *I do not wish to **cast aspersions on** your honesty.* ▪ cause (a magic spell) to take effect: *the witch **cast a spell on** her to turn her into a beast* | figurative *the city casts a spell on the visitor.*
3 [with obj. and adverbial of direction] discard: *he jumped in, **casting caution to the wind.***
▪shed (skin or horns) in the process of growth: *the antlers are cast each year.* ▪ (of a horse) lose (a shoe).
4 [with obj.] shape (metal or other material) by pouring it into a mould while molten.
▪make (a moulded object) in this way: *a bell was cast for the church.* ▪ arrange and present in a specified form or style: *he issued statements **cast in** tones of reason.* ▪ calculate and record details of (a horoscope).
5 [no obj., usu. with adverbial of direction] (in country dancing) change one's position by moving a certain number of places in a certain direction along the outside of the line in which one is dancing.
▶ **noun 1** an object made by shaping molten metal or similar material in a mould: *bronze casts of the sculpture.*
▪(also **plaster cast**) a mould used to make such an object. ▪ (also **plaster cast**) a bandage stiffened with plaster of Paris, moulded to the shape of a limb that is broken and used to support and protect it.
2 an act of throwing something forcefully: *he grabbed a spear for a third cast.*
▪archaic a throw or a number thrown at dice. ▪ Fishing a throw of a fishing line. ▪ Brit. the leader of a fishing line.
3 [in sing.] [with adj. or noun modifier] the form or appearance of something, especially someone's features: *she had a somewhat masculine cast of countenance.*
▪the character of something: *this question is for minds of a more philosophical cast than mine.* ▪ the overall appearance of someone's skin or hair as determined by a tinge of a particular colour: *the colours he wore emphasized the olive cast of his skin.*
4 a slight squint: *he had a cast in one eye.*
5 a convoluted mass of earth or sand ejected on to the surface by a burrowing worm.
▪a pellet regurgitated by a hawk or owl.
6 a search made by a hound or pack of hounds over a wide area to find a trail.
▪Austral./NZ a wide sweep made by a sheepdog in mustering sheep.
– PHRASES **be cast in a —— mould** be of the type specified: *he was cast in a cautious mould.* **cast adrift** see **ADRIFT**. **cast one's bread upon the waters** see **BREAD**. **cast one's eyes over** have a quick appraising look at: *he was invited to cast his eyes over the exhibition.* **cast light on** see **LIGHT¹**. **cast lots** see **LOT**. **cast one's mind back** think back to a particular event or time: *he cast his mind back to the fatal evening.*
– ORIGIN Middle English: from Old Norse *kasta* 'to cast or throw'.
▶**cast about** (or **around** or **round**) search far and wide (physically or mentally): *he is restlessly casting about for novelties.* [ORIGIN: from a hunting term meaning '(of a hound) go in all directions looking for game or a lost scent'.]
be cast away be stranded after a shipwreck.
be cast down feel depressed: *she was greatly cast down by abusive criticism of her novels.*
cast off (or **cast something off**) **1** Knitting take the stitches off the needle by looping each over the next to finish the edge. **2** set a boat or ship free from her moorings: *the boatmen cast off and rowed downriver* | *Jack cast off our moorings.* ▪ (**cast off**) (of a boat or ship) be set free from her moorings. **3** let loose a hunting hound or hawk. **4** Printing estimate the space that will be taken in print by manuscript copy.
cast someone off exclude someone from a relationship.
cast on (or **cast something on**) Knitting make the first row of a specified number of loops on the needle: *cast on and knit a few rows of stocking stitch.*
cast something up 1 (of the sea) deposit something on the shore. **2** dated add up figures.

cast² ▶ **noun** the actors taking part in a play, film, or other production: *he draws sensitive performances from his inexperienced cast.*
▶ **verb** (past and past participle **cast**) [with obj.] assign a part in a play or film to (an actor): *he was **cast as** an oriental ruler* | figurative *King John has been **cast** by tradition **as** a villain.*
▪allocate parts in (a play or film).
– ORIGIN mid 17th cent.: a special use of **CAST¹** in sense 4 of the verb.

Castalia /kaˈsteɪlɪə/ a spring on Mount Parnassus, sacred in antiquity to Apollo and the Muses.
– DERIVATIVES **Castalian** adjective.

castanets ▶ **plural noun** small concave pieces of wood, ivory, or plastic, joined in pairs by a cord and clicked together by the fingers as a rhythmic accompaniment to Spanish dancing.
– ORIGIN early 17th cent.: from Spanish *castañeta*, diminutive of *castaña*, from Latin *castanea* 'chestnut'.

castaway ▶ **noun** a person who has been shipwrecked and stranded in an isolated place.

caste ▶ **noun** each of the hereditary classes of Hindu society, distinguished by relative degrees of ritual purity or pollution and of social status: *members of the lower castes* | [mass noun] *a man of high caste.*
▪[mass noun] the system of dividing society into such classes. ▪ any class or group of people who inherit exclusive privileges or are perceived as socially distinct: *those educated in private schools belong to a privileged caste.* ▪ Entomology (in some social insects) a physically distinct individual with a particular function in the society.

There are four basic classes or varnas in Hindu society: Brahman (priest), Kshatriya (warrior), Vaisya (merchant or farmer), and Sudra (labourer).

– PHRASES **lose caste** descend in the caste system, e.g. by having contact with a person of low caste, by eating foods regarded as unclean, or by taking employment regarded as of lower status. ▪ come to be regarded with less respect; lose status: *they lost caste by moving away from the old house.*
– ORIGIN mid 16th cent. (in the general sense 'race, breed'): from Spanish and Portuguese *casta* 'lineage, race, breed', feminine of *casto* 'pure, unmixed', from Latin *castus* 'chaste'.

caste Hindu ▶ **noun** a Hindu who belongs to one of the four main castes.

casteism ▶ **noun** [mass noun] adherence to a caste system.

Castel Gandolfo /ˌkastɛl ganˈdɒlfəʊ/ the summer residence of the pope, situated on the edge of Lake Albano near Rome.

castellan /ˈkastələn/ ▶ **noun** historical the governor of a castle.
– ORIGIN late Middle English: from Old Northern French *castelain*, from medieval Latin *castellanus*, from Latin *castellum* (see **CASTLE**).

castellated /ˈkastəleɪtɪd/ ▶ **adjective** having battlements: *a castellated gatehouse.*
▪(of a nut or other mechanical part) having grooves or slots on its upper face.
– ORIGIN late 17th cent.: from medieval Latin *castellatus*, from Latin *castellum* (see **CASTLE**).

castellations /ˌkastəˈleɪʃ(ə)nz/ ▶ **plural noun** defensive or decorative parapets with regularly spaced notches; battlements.
▪(**castellation**) [mass noun] the use or building of such parapets.
– ORIGIN early 19th cent.: based on medieval Latin *castellare* 'to build castles', from *castellum* (see **CASTLE**).

Castell-Nedd /ˌkastelˈneð/ Welsh name for **NEATH**.

caste mark ▶ **noun** a symbol on the forehead denoting membership of a particular Hindu caste.

caster ▶ **noun 1** a person who casts something or a machine for casting something.
2 Fishing a fly pupa used as bait.
3 variant spelling of **CASTOR¹**.

caster sugar (also **castor sugar**) ▶ **noun** [mass noun] Brit. finely granulated white or pale golden sugar.
– ORIGIN mid 19th cent.: so named because it was suitable for use in a castor (see sense 2 of **CASTOR¹**).

castigate /ˈkastɪgeɪt/ ▶ **verb** [with obj.] formal reprimand (someone) severely: *he was castigated for not setting a good example.*
– DERIVATIVES **castigation** noun, **castigator** noun, **castigatory** adjective.
– ORIGIN early 17th cent.: from Latin *castigare* 'reprove', from *castus* 'pure, chaste'.

Castile /kaˈstiːl/ a region of central Spain, on the central plateau of the Iberian peninsula, formerly an independent Spanish kingdom.
– ORIGIN from French *Castille*, from Spanish *Castilla*.

Castile soap ▶ **noun** [mass noun] fine, hard white or mottled soap made with olive oil and soda.
– ORIGIN late Middle English: named after **CASTILE** in Spain, where it was originally made.

Castilian /kaˈstɪlɪən/ ▶ **noun 1** a native of Castile.
2 [mass noun] the language of Castile; standard spoken and literary Spanish.

▶**adjective** of or relating to Castile, Castilians, or the Castilian form of Spanish.

Castilla-La Mancha /kaˌstiːjəlaˈmantʃə, -ljə-/ an autonomous region of central Spain; capital, Toledo.

Castilla-León /kaˌstiːjəleɪˈɒn, -ljə-/ an autonomous region of northern Spain; capital, Valladolid.

casting ▶**noun** an object made by pouring molten metal or other material into a mould.

casting couch ▶**noun** informal used in reference to the supposed practice whereby actresses are awarded parts in films or plays in return for granting sexual favours to the casting director: *she was no stranger to the casting couch.*

casting director ▶**noun** the person responsible for assigning roles in a film or play.

casting vote ▶**noun** an extra vote given by a chairperson to decide an issue when the votes on each side are equal.
– ORIGIN early 17th cent.: from an obsolete sense of *cast* 'turn the scale'.

cast iron ▶**noun** [mass noun] a hard, relatively brittle alloy of iron and carbon which can be readily cast in a mould and contains a higher proportion of carbon than steel (typically 2–4.3 per cent).
■[as modifier] figurative firm and unchangeable: *there are no cast-iron guarantees.*

Castle, Barbara (Anne), Baroness of Blackburn (b.1911), British Labour politician. As Minister of Transport (1965–8) she introduced the 70 mph speed limit and the breathalyser test.

castle ▶**noun** a large building or group of buildings fortified against attack with thick walls, battlements, towers, and in many cases a moat.
■a magnificent and imposing mansion, especially one that is the home or former home of a member of the nobility: [in names] *Castle Howard.* ■ Chess, informal old-fashioned term for **ROOK**[2].
▶**verb** [no obj.] [often as noun **castling**] Chess make a special move (no more than once in a game by each player) in which the king is transferred from its original square two squares along the back rank towards a rook on its corner square which is then transferred to the square passed over by the king.
■[with obj.] move (the king) in this way.
– PHRASES **castles in the air** (or **in Spain**) visionary unattainable schemes; daydreams: *my father built castles in the air about owning a boat.*
– DERIVATIVES **castled** adjective (archaic).
– ORIGIN late Old English: from Anglo-Norman French and Old Northern French *castel*, from Latin *castellum*, diminutive of *castrum* 'fort'.

Castlebar /ˌkɑːs(ə)lˈbɑː/ the county town of Mayo, in the Republic of Ireland; pop. 6,070 (est. 1991).

Castlereagh /ˈkɑːs(ə)lreɪ/, Robert Stewart, Viscount (1769–1822), British Tory statesman. He became Foreign Secretary in 1812 and represented Britain at the Congress of Vienna (1814–15).

cast net ▶**noun** Fishing a net that is thrown out and immediately drawn in again, as opposed to one that is set up and left.

cast-off ▶**adjective** no longer wanted; abandoned or discarded: *a pile of cast-off clothes.*
▶**noun** (usu. **cast-offs**) something, especially a garment, that is no longer wanted: *I'm not going out in her cast-offs!*

Castor /ˈkɑːstə/ **1** Greek Mythology the twin brother of Pollux. See **DIOSCURI**.
2 Astronomy the second brightest star in the constellation Gemini, close to Pollux. It is a multiple star system, the three components visible in a moderate telescope being close binaries.

castor[1] /ˈkɑːstə/ (also **caster**) ▶**noun 1** each of a set of small wheels, free to swivel in any direction, fixed to the legs or base of a heavy piece of furniture so that it can be moved easily.
2 a small container with holes in the top, especially one used for sprinkling sugar or pepper.
– ORIGIN late 17th cent. (in sense 2): originally a variant of **CASTER**, in the general sense 'something that casts'.

castor[2] /ˈkɑːstə/ ▶**noun** [mass noun] a reddish-brown oily substance secreted by beavers, used in medicine and perfumes.
– ORIGIN late Middle English (in the sense 'beaver'): from Old French or Latin, from Greek *kastōr*.

castor bean ▶**noun** the seed of the castor oil plant, which contains a number of poisonous compounds, especially ricin, as well as castor oil.
■N. Amer. the castor oil plant.

castor bean tick ▶**noun** another term for **SHEEP TICK**.

castor oil ▶**noun** [mass noun] a pale yellow oil obtained from castor beans, used as a purgative, a lubricant, and in manufacturing oil-based products.
– ORIGIN mid 18th cent.: perhaps so named because it succeeded **CASTOR**[2] in medicinal use.

castor oil plant ▶**noun** an African shrub with lobed serrated leaves, yielding the seeds from which castor oil is obtained and widely naturalized in warm countries.
● *Ricinus communis*, family Euphorbiaceae.

castor sugar ▶**noun** variant spelling of **CASTER SUGAR**.

castrate ▶**verb** [with obj.] remove the testicles of (a male animal or man).
■figurative deprive of power, vitality, or vigour: *a restrictive classicism would have castrated England's literature.*
▶**noun** a man or male animal whose testicles have been removed.
– DERIVATIVES **castration** noun, **castrator** noun.
– ORIGIN mid 16th cent.: from Latin *castrare*.

castration complex ▶**noun** Psychoanalysis (in Freudian theory) an unconscious anxiety arising during psychosexual development, represented in males as a fear that the penis will be removed by the father in response to sexual interest in the mother, and in females as a compulsion to demonstrate that they have an adequate symbolic equivalent to the penis, whose absence is blamed on the mother.

castrato /kaˈstrɑːtəʊ/ ▶**noun** (pl. **castrati** /-ti/) historical a male singer castrated in boyhood so as to retain a soprano or alto voice. The practice of castration was banned in 1903.
– ORIGIN mid 18th cent.: from Italian, past participle of *castrare* (see **CASTRATE**).

Castries /kaˈstriːs/ the capital of the Caribbean island of St Lucia, a seaport on the NW coast; pop. 14,055 (est. 1994).

Castro /ˈkastrəʊ/, Fidel (b.1927), Cuban statesman, Prime Minister 1959–76 and President since 1976. After overthrowing President Batista he set up a communist regime which survived the abortive Bay of Pigs invasion, the Cuban Missile Crisis, and the collapse of the Soviet bloc.

casual /ˈkaʒjʊəl, -zj-/ ▶**adjective 1** relaxed and unconcerned: *she regarded his affairs with a casual indulgence | he tried to make his voice sound casual.*
■made or done without much thought or premeditation: *a casual remark.* ■ done or acting in a desultory way: *to the casual observer, rugby looks something like football.* ■ done or acting without sufficient care or thoroughness: *the casual way in which victims were treated.*
2 not regular or permanent: *the tent is ideal for casual outdoor use | casual jobs.*
■(of a worker) employed on a temporary or irregular basis: *casual staff.* ■ (of a sexual relationship or encounter) occurring between people who are not regular or established sexual partners.
3 [attrib.] happening by chance; accidental: *he pretended it was a casual meeting.*
4 without formality of style, manner, or procedure, in particular:
■(of clothes or a style of dress) suitable for everyday wear rather than formal occasions. ■ (of a social event) not characterized by particular social conventions. ■ (of a place or environment) relaxed and friendly: *the inn's casual atmosphere.*
▶**noun 1** a person who does something irregularly: *a number of casuals became regular customers.*
■a worker employed on an irregular or temporary basis. ■ historical a person admitted to a workhouse for a short period.
2 (**casuals**) clothes or shoes suitable for everyday wear rather than formal occasions.
3 Brit. a youth belonging to a subculture characterized by the wearing of expensive casual clothing and frequently associated with football hooliganism.
– DERIVATIVES **casually** adverb, **casualness** noun.
– ORIGIN late Middle English (in senses 2 and 3 of the adjective): from Old French *casuel* and Latin *casualis*, from *casus* 'fall' (compare with **CASE**[1]).

casualization (also **-isation**) ▶**noun** [mass noun] the practice or process of transforming a workforce from one employed chiefly on permanent contracts to one engaged on a short-term temporary basis.
– DERIVATIVES **casualize** verb.

casualty ▶**noun** (pl. **-ies**) a person killed or injured in a war or accident.
■figurative a person or thing badly affected by an event or situation: *the building industry has been one of the casualties of the recession.* ■ Brit. the casualty department of a hospital: *he went to casualty to have a cut stitched.* ■ (chiefly in insurance) an accident, mishap, or disaster: *the Insurers acquire all the Policyholder's rights in respect of the casualty which caused the loss.*
– ORIGIN late Middle English (in the sense 'chance, a chance occurrence'): from medieval Latin *casualitas*, from *casualis* (see **CASUAL**), on the pattern of words such as *penalty.*

casualty department (also **casualty ward**) ▶**noun** Brit. the department of a hospital providing immediate treatment for emergency cases.

casual ward ▶**noun** historical a ward in a workhouse providing accommodation for those temporarily unable to support themselves.

casual water ▶**noun** [mass noun] Golf water that has accumulated temporarily and does not constitute a recognized hazard of the course. A player may move a ball from casual water without penalty.

casuarina /ˌkasjʊəˈriːnə/ ▶**noun** a tree with slender, jointed, drooping twigs which resemble horsetails and bear tiny scale-like leaves. It is native to Australia and SE Asia, and is a valuable source of timber and firewood. Also called **SHE-OAK**.
● Genus *Casuarina*, family Casuarinaceae.
– ORIGIN from modern Latin *casuarius* 'cassowary' (from the resemblance of the branches to the bird's feathers).

casuist /ˈkazjʊɪst, -ʒj-/ ▶**noun** a person who uses clever but unsound reasoning, especially in relation to moral questions; a sophist.
■a person who resolves moral problems by the application of theoretical rules to particular instances.
– DERIVATIVES **casuistic** adjective, **casuistical** adjective, **casuistically** adverb.
– ORIGIN early 17th cent.: from French *casuiste*, from Spanish *casuista*, from Latin *casus* (see **CASE**[1]).

casuistry ▶**noun** [mass noun] the use of clever but unsound reasoning, especially in relation to moral questions; sophistry.
■the resolving of moral problems by the application of theoretical rules to particular instances.

casus belli /ˌkeɪsəs ˈbɛlʌɪ, ˌkɑːsʊs ˈbɛliː/ ▶**noun** (pl. same) an act or situation provoking or justifying war.
– ORIGIN Latin, from *casus* (see **CASE**[1]) and *belli*, genitive of *bellum* 'war'.

CAT ▶**abbreviation for** ■ clear air turbulence. ■ computer-assisted (or -aided) testing. ■ Medicine computerized axial tomography: [as modifier] *a CAT scan.*

cat[1] ▶**noun 1** a small domesticated carnivorous mammal with soft fur, a short snout, and retractile claws. It is widely kept as a pet or for catching mice, and many breeds have been developed.
● *Felis catus*, family Felidae (the **cat family**); probably domesticated in ancient Egypt from the local race of wildcat, and was held in great reverence there. The cat family also includes the ocelot, serval, margay, lynx, and the big cats.
■a wild animal of the cat family: *a marbled cat.* See also **BIG CAT**. ■ used in names of catlike animals of other families, e.g. **native cat**, **ring-tailed cat**. ■ informal a malicious or spiteful woman: *his mother called me an old cat.* ■ historical short for **CAT-O'-NINE-TAILS**. ■ short for **CATFISH**. ■ short for **CATHEAD**. ■ short for **CATBOAT**.
2 informal, chiefly N. Amer. (especially among jazz enthusiasts) a man.
3 historical a short tapered stick used in the game of tipcat.
▶**verb** (**catted**, **catting**) [with obj.] Nautical raise (an anchor) from the surface of the water to the cathead.
– PHRASES **all cats are grey in the dark** (or US **at night all cats are gray**) proverb the qualities that distinguish people from one another are obscured in some circumstances, and if they can't be perceived they don't matter. **cat and mouse** a series of cunning manoeuvres designed to thwart an opponent: *he continues to play cat and mouse with*

C

the UN inspection teams. **a cat may look at a king** proverb even a person of low status or importance has rights. **fight like cat and dog** informal (of two people) be continually arguing with one another. **has the cat got your tongue?** said to someone who remains silent when they are expected to speak. **let the cat out of the bag** informal reveal a secret carelessly or by mistake. **like a cat on a hot tin roof** (Brit. also **on hot bricks**) informal very agitated or anxious. **like the cat that's got** (or **who's stolen**) **the cream** informal, chiefly Brit. self-satisfied, having achieved one's objective. **look like something the cat brought in** informal (of a person) look very dirty or dishevelled. **not have a cat in hell's chance** informal have no chance at all. **put** (or **set**) **the cat among the pigeons** Brit. say or do something that is likely to cause trouble or controversy. **see which way the cat jumps** informal see what direction events are taking before committing oneself. **when** (or **while**) **the cat's away, the mice will play** proverb people will naturally take advantage of the absence of someone in authority to do as they like. **who's she—the cat's mother?** see **SHE**.
– ORIGIN Old English *catt, catte*, of Germanic origin; related to Dutch *kat* and German *Katze*; reinforced in Middle English by forms from late Latin *cattus*.

cat² ▶ noun short for **CATALYTIC CONVERTER**.

cat³ ▶ noun short for **CATAMARAN**.

cata- (also **cat-**) ▶ prefix **1** down; downwards: *catadromous.*
2 wrongly; badly: *catachresis.*
3 completely: *cataclysm.*
4 against; alongside: *catapult.*
– ORIGIN from Greek *kata* 'down'.

catabolism /kəˈtabəlɪz(ə)m/ (also **katabolism**) ▶ noun [mass noun] Biology the breakdown of complex molecules in living organisms to form simpler ones, together with the release of energy; destructive metabolism.
– DERIVATIVES **catabolic** /katəˈbɒlɪk/ adjective.
– ORIGIN late 19th cent.: from Greek *katabolē* 'throwing down', from *kata-* 'down' + *ballein* 'to throw'.

catabolite /kəˈtabəlʌɪt/ ▶ noun Biochemistry a product of catabolism.

catachresis /ˌkatəˈkriːsɪs/ ▶ noun (pl. **catachreses** /-siːz/) [mass noun] the use of a word in a way which is not correct, for example the use of *mitigate* for *militate*.
– DERIVATIVES **catachrestic** /-ˈkriːstɪk, -ˈkrɛstɪk/ adjective.
– ORIGIN mid 16th cent.: from Latin, from Greek *katakhrēsis*, from *katakhrēsthai* 'misuse', from *kata-* 'down' (expressing the sense 'wrongly') + *khrēsthai* 'use'.

cataclasis /ˌkatəˈkleɪsɪs/ ▶ noun [mass noun] Geology the fracture and breaking up of rock by natural processes.
– DERIVATIVES **cataclastic** /-ˈklastɪk/ adjective.
– ORIGIN 1950s: from **CATA-** 'completely' + Greek *klasis* 'breaking'.

cataclysm /ˈkatəˌklɪz(ə)m/ ▶ noun a large-scale and violent event in the natural world.
■ a sudden violent upheaval, especially in a political or social context: *the cataclysm of the First World War.*
– ORIGIN early 17th cent. (originally denoting the biblical Flood described in Genesis): from French *cataclysme*, via Latin from Greek *kataklusmos* 'deluge', from *kata-* 'down' + *kluzein* 'to wash'.

cataclysmic ▶ adjective relating to or denoting a violent natural event.
■ denoting something unpleasant or unsuccessful on an enormous scale: *the concert was a cataclysmic failure.*
– DERIVATIVES **cataclysmically** adverb.

catacomb /ˈkatəkuːm, -kəʊm/ ▶ noun (usu. **catacombs**) an underground cemetery consisting of a subterranean gallery with recesses for tombs, as constructed by the ancient Romans.
■ an underground construction resembling or compared to such a cemetery.
– ORIGIN Old English, from late Latin *catacumbas*, the name of the subterranean cemetery of St Sebastian near Rome.

catadioptric /ˌkatədʌɪˈɒptrɪk/ ▶ adjective Optics denoting an optical system which involves both the reflecting and refracting of light, in order to reduce aberration.

catadromous /kəˈtadrəməs/ ▶ adjective Zoology (of a fish such as the eel) migrating down rivers to the sea to spawn. The opposite of **ANADROMOUS**.
– ORIGIN late 19th cent.: from **CATA-** 'down' + Greek *dromos* 'running', on the pattern of *anadromous.*

catafalque /ˈkatəfalk/ ▶ noun a decorated wooden framework supporting the coffin of a distinguished person during a funeral or while lying in state.
– ORIGIN mid 17th cent.: from French, from Italian *catafalco*, of unknown origin. Compare with **SCAFFOLD**.

Catalan /ˈkatəlan/ ▶ noun **1** a native of Catalonia in Spain.
2 [mass noun] a Romance language closely related to Castilian Spanish and Provençal, widely spoken in Catalonia (where it has official status alongside Castilian Spanish) and in Andorra, the Balearic Islands, and parts of southern France. It has about 6 million speakers altogether.
▶ adjective of or relating to Catalonia, its people, or its language.
– ORIGIN from French, from Spanish *catalán*, related to Catalan *català* 'Catalan', *Catalunya* 'Catalonia'.

catalase /ˈkatəleɪz/ ▶ noun [mass noun] Biochemistry an enzyme that catalyses the reduction of hydrogen peroxide.
– ORIGIN early 20th cent.: from **CATALYSIS** + **-ASE**.

catalectic /ˌkatəˈlɛktɪk/ Prosody ▶ adjective (of a metrical line of verse) lacking one syllable in the last foot.
▶ noun a line lacking a syllable in the last foot.
– ORIGIN late 16th cent.: from late Latin *catalecticus*, from Greek *katalēktikos*, from *katalēgein* 'leave off'.

catalepsy /ˈkat(ə)lɛpsi/ ▶ noun [mass noun] a medical condition characterized by a trance or seizure with a loss of sensation and consciousness accompanied by rigidity of the body.
– DERIVATIVES **cataleptic** adjective & noun.
– ORIGIN late Middle English: from French *catalepsie* or late Latin *catalepsia*, from Greek *katalēpsis*, from *katalambanein* 'seize upon'.

catalogue (US also **catalog**) ▶ noun a complete list of items, typically one in alphabetical or other systematic order, in particular:
■ a list of all the books or resources in a library. ■ a publication containing details and often photographs of items for sale, especially one produced by a mail-order company. ■ a descriptive list of works of art in an exhibition or collection giving detailed comments and explanations. ■ US a list of courses offered by a university or college. ■ [in sing.] a series of unfortunate or bad things: *his life was a catalogue of dismal failures.*
▶ verb (**catalogues, catalogued, cataloguing**; US also **catalogs, cataloged, cataloging**) [with obj.] make a systematic list of (items of the same type).
■ enter (an item) in such a list. ■ list (similar situations, qualities, or events) in succession: *the report catalogues dangerous work practices in the company.*
– DERIVATIVES **cataloguer** (US also **cataloger**) noun.
– ORIGIN late Middle English: via Old French from late Latin *catalogus*, from Greek *katalogos*, from *katalegein* 'pick out or enrol'.

catalogue raisonné /ˌreɪzɒ'neɪ/ ▶ noun (pl. **catalogues raisonnés** pronunc. same) a descriptive catalogue of works of art with explanations and scholarly comments.
– ORIGIN late 18th cent.: French, 'explained catalogue'.

Catalonia /ˌkatəˈləʊnɪə/ an autonomous region of NE Spain; capital, Barcelona. The region has a strong separatist tradition; the normal language for everyday purposes is Catalan, which has also won acceptance in recent years for various official purposes. Catalan name **CATALUNYA** /ˌkatəˈluːnɪə/; Spanish name **CATALUÑA** /ˌkataˈluɲa/.
– DERIVATIVES **Catalonian** adjective & noun.

catalpa /kəˈtalpə/ ▶ noun a tree with large heart-shaped leaves, clusters of trumpet-shaped flowers, and slender bean-like seed pods, native to North America and east Asia and cultivated as an ornamental.
● Genus *Catalpa*, family Bignoniaceae: several species, in particular the Indian bean tree.
– ORIGIN from Creek.

catalufa /ˌkatəˈluːfə/ ▶ noun another term for **BIGEYE** (in sense 2).
– ORIGIN from Spanish.

catalyse /ˈkat(ə)lʌɪz/ (US **catalyze**) ▶ verb [with obj.] cause or accelerate (a reaction) by acting as a catalyst.
■ figurative cause (an action or process) to begin: *the bank was set up to catalyse investment in the former communist countries.*
– ORIGIN late 19th cent.: from **CATALYSIS**, on the pattern of *analyse.*

catalyser ▶ noun Brit. another term for **CATALYTIC CONVERTER**.

catalysis /kəˈtalɪsɪs/ ▶ noun [mass noun] Chemistry & Biochemistry the acceleration of a chemical reaction by a catalyst.
– ORIGIN mid 19th cent.: from modern Latin, from Greek *katalusis*, from *kataluein* 'dissolve', from *kata-* 'down' + *luein* 'loosen'.

catalyst ▶ noun a substance that increases the rate of a chemical reaction without itself undergoing any permanent chemical change.
■ figurative a person or thing that precipitates an event: *the prime minister's speech acted as a catalyst for debate.*
– ORIGIN early 20th cent.: from **CATALYSIS**, on the pattern of *analyst.*

catalytic ▶ adjective relating to or involving the action of a catalyst.
– DERIVATIVES **catalytically** adverb.
– ORIGIN mid 19th cent.: from **CATALYSIS**, on the pattern of pairs such as *analysis, analytic.*

catalytic converter ▶ noun a device incorporated in the exhaust system of a motor vehicle, containing a catalyst for converting pollutant gases into less harmful ones.

catalyze ▶ verb US spelling of **CATALYSE**.

catamaran ▶ noun a yacht or other boat with twin hulls in parallel.
– ORIGIN early 17th cent.: from Tamil *kaṭṭumaram*, literally 'tied wood'.

catamite /ˈkatəmʌɪt/ ▶ noun archaic a boy kept for homosexual practices.
– ORIGIN late 16th cent.: from Latin *catamitus*, via Etruscan from Greek *Ganumēdēs* (see **GANYMEDE**).

catamount /ˈkatəmaʊnt/ (also **catamountain** /ˌkatəˈmaʊntɪn/) ▶ noun a medium-sized or large wild cat, especially (N. Amer.) a puma.
– ORIGIN late Middle English (as *catamountain*): from the phrase *cat of the mountain.*

catananche /ˌkatəˈnaŋki/ ▶ noun a plant of a genus that includes cupid's dart.
● Genus *Catananche*, family Compositae.
– ORIGIN from modern Latin, from Latin *catanance*, a plant used in love potions, from Greek *katanankē*, from *kata-* 'down' + *anankē* 'compulsion'.

Catania /kəˈtɑːnɪə, -ˈteɪnɪə/ a seaport situated at the foot of Mount Etna, on the east coast of Sicily; pop. 364,180 (1990).

cataphatic /ˌkatəˈfatɪk/ ▶ adjective Theology (of knowledge of God) obtained through affirmation. The opposite of **APOPHATIC**.
– ORIGIN mid 19th cent.: from Greek *kataphatikos* 'affirmative', from *kataphasis* 'affirmation', from *kata-* (as an intensifier) + *phanai* 'speak'.

cataphor /ˈkatəfɔ, -fɔː/ ▶ noun Grammar a word or phrase that refers to or stands for a later word or phrase (e.g. in *when they saw Ruth, the men looked slightly abashed, they* is used as a cataphor for *the men*).
– ORIGIN late 20th cent.: back-formation from **CATAPHORA**.

cataphora /kəˈtaf(ə)rə/ ▶ noun [mass noun] Grammar the use of a word or phrase that refers to or stands for a later word or phrase (e.g. the pronoun *he* in *he may be approaching 37, but Jeff has no plans to retire from the sport yet*). Compare with **ANAPHORA**.
– DERIVATIVES **cataphoric** /katəˈfɒrɪk/ adjective, **cataphorically** adverb.
– ORIGIN 1970s: from **CATA-** on the pattern of *anaphora.*

cataphract /ˈkatəfrakt/ ▶ noun archaic a soldier in full armour.
– ORIGIN late 17th cent.: via Latin from Greek *kataphraktos* 'clothed in full armour'.

cataplexy /ˈkatəˌplɛksi/ ▶ noun [mass noun] a medical condition in which strong emotion or laughter causes a person to suffer sudden physical collapse though remaining conscious.
– DERIVATIVES **cataplectic** adjective.
– ORIGIN late 19th cent.: from Greek *kataplēxis* 'stupefaction', from *kataplessein*, from *kata-* 'down' + *plēssein* 'strike'.

catapult ▶**noun** a device in which accumulated tension is suddenly released to hurl an object some distance, in particular:
■chiefly Brit. a forked stick with an elastic band fastened to the two prongs, typically used by children for shooting small stones. ■historical a military machine worked by a lever and ropes for hurling large stones or other missiles. ■a mechanical device for launching a glider or other aircraft, especially from the deck of a ship.
▶**verb** [with obj. and adverbial of direction] hurl or launch (something) in a specified direction with or as if with a catapult: *the plane was refuelled and catapulted back into the air again* | *the explosion catapulted the car 30 yards along the road* | figurative *their music catapulted them to the top of the charts.*
■[no obj., with adverbial of direction] move suddenly or at great speed as though hurled by a catapult: *the horse catapulted away from the fence.*
– ORIGIN late 16th cent.: from French *catapulte* or Latin *catapulta*, from Greek *katapeltēs*, from *kata-* 'down' + *pallein* 'hurl'.

cataract /ˈkatərakt/ ▶**noun 1** a large waterfall.
■a sudden rush of water; a downpour: *the rain enveloped us in a deafening cataract.*
2 a medical condition in which the lens of the eye becomes progressively opaque, resulting in blurred vision: *she had cataracts in both eyes.*
– ORIGIN late Middle English: from Latin *cataracta* 'waterfall, floodgate', also 'portcullis' (medical sense 2 probably being a figurative use of this), from Greek *kataraktēs* 'down-rushing', from *katarassein*, from *kata-* 'down' + *arassein* 'strike, smash'.

catarrh /kəˈtɑː/ ▶**noun** [mass noun] excessive discharge or build-up of mucus in the nose or throat, associated with inflammation of the mucous membrane.
– DERIVATIVES **catarrhal** adjective.
– ORIGIN early 16th cent.: from French *catarrhe*, from late Latin *catarrhus*, from Greek *katarrhous*, from *katarrhein* 'flow down', from *kata-* 'down' + *rhein* 'flow'.

catarrhine /ˈkatərʌɪn/ Zoology ▶**adjective** of or relating to primates of a group that comprises the Old World monkeys, gibbons, great apes, and humans. They are distinguished by having nostrils that are close together and directed downwards, and do not have a prehensile tail. Compare with **PLATYRRHINE**.
▶**noun** a catarrhine primate.
● Infraorder Catarrhini, order Primates: four families.
– ORIGIN mid 19th cent.: from **CATA-** 'down' + Greek *rhis, rhin-* 'nose'.

catastrophe /kəˈtastrəfi/ ▶**noun** an event causing great and often sudden damage or suffering; a disaster: *an environmental catastrophe* | [mass noun] *leading the world to catastrophe.*
■the denouement of a drama, especially a classical tragedy.
– ORIGIN mid 16th cent. (in the sense 'denouement'): from Latin *catastropha*, from Greek *katastrophē* 'overturning, sudden turn', from *kata-* 'down' + *strophē* 'turning' (from *strephein* 'to turn').

catastrophe theory ▶**noun** [mass noun] a branch of mathematics concerned with systems displaying abrupt discontinuous change.

catastrophic ▶**adjective 1** involving or causing sudden great damage or suffering: *a catastrophic earthquake.*
■involving a sudden and large-scale alteration in the state of something: *the body undergoes catastrophic collapse towards the state of a black hole.* ■of or relating to geological catastrophism.
2 extremely unfortunate or unsuccessful: *catastrophic mismanagement of the economy.*
– DERIVATIVES **catastrophically** adverb.

catastrophism ▶**noun** [mass noun] Geology the theory that changes in the earth's crust during geological history have resulted chiefly from sudden violent and unusual events. Often contrasted with **UNIFORMITARIANISM**.
– DERIVATIVES **catastrophist** noun & adjective.

catatonia /ˌkatəˈtəʊnɪə/ ▶**noun** [mass noun] Psychiatry abnormality of movement and behaviour arising from a disturbed mental state (typically schizophrenia). It may involve repetitive or purposeless overactivity, or catalepsy, resistance to passive movement, and negativism.
■informal a state of immobility and stupor.
– ORIGIN late 19th cent.: from **CATA-** 'badly' + Greek *tonos* 'tone or tension'.

catatonic ▶**adjective** Psychiatry of, relating to, or characterized by catatonia: *catatonic schizophrenia.*
■informal of or in an immobile or unresponsive stupor.

catawba /kəˈtɔːbə/ ▶**noun** [mass noun] a North American variety of grape.
■a white wine made from this grape.
– ORIGIN named after the river *Catawba* in North and South Carolina.

cat-bear ▶**noun** another term for **RED PANDA**.

catbird ▶**noun 1** a long-tailed American songbird of the mockingbird family, with mainly dark grey or black plumage and catlike mewing calls.
● Two genera and species, family Mimidae, in particular the **grey catbird** (*Dumetella carolinensis*).
2 a thickset Australasian bird of the bowerbird family, typically with a loud call like a yowling cat. It does not generally construct bowers.
● Genus *Ailuroedus* (and *Scenopoeetes*), family Ptilonorhynchidae: several species, in particular the **green catbird** (*A. crassirostris*).
– PHRASES **in the catbird seat** N. Amer. informal in a superior or advantageous position. [ORIGIN: said to be an allusion to a baseball player in the fortunate position of having no strikes and therefore three balls still to play (a reference made in James Thurber's short story *The Catbird Seat*).]

catboat ▶**noun** a sailing boat with a single mast placed well forward and carrying only one sail.
– ORIGIN mid 19th cent.: perhaps from *cat* (denoting a type of merchant ship formerly used in the coal and timber trades in NE England) + **BOAT**.

cat burglar ▶**noun** a thief who enters a building by climbing to an upper storey.

catcall ▶**noun** a shrill whistle or shout of disapproval, typically one made at a public meeting or performance.
■a loud whistle or a comment of a sexual nature made by a man to a passing woman.
▶**verb** [no obj.] make such a whistle, shout, or comment: *they were fired for catcalling at women.*
– ORIGIN mid 17th cent.: from **CAT**[1] + **CALL**, originally denoting a kind of whistle or squeaking instrument used to express disapproval at a theatre.

catch ▶**verb** (past and past participle **caught**) [with obj.] **1** intercept and hold (something which has been thrown, propelled, or dropped): *she threw the bottle into the air and caught it again.*
■intercept the fall of (someone). ■seize or take hold of: *he* ***caught hold of*** *her arm as she tried to push past him.* ■[no obj.] (**catch at**) grasp or try to grasp: *his hands caught at her arms as she tried to turn away.* ■Cricket (often **be caught**) dismiss (a batsman) by catching the ball before it touches the ground.
2 capture (a person or animal that tries or would try to escape): *we hadn't caught a single rabbit.*
■[no obj., with adverbial of place] (of an object) accidentally become entangled or trapped in something: *a button caught in her hair.* ■[with obj. and adverbial of place] (of a person) have (a part of one's body or clothing) become entangled or trapped in something: *she caught her foot in the bedspread* | figurative *companies face increased risks of being caught in a downward spiral.* ■[with obj. and adverbial of place] (usu. **be caught**) fix or fasten in place: *her hair was caught back in a chignon.*
3 reach in time and board (a train, bus, or aircraft): *they caught the 12.15 from Oxford.*
■reach or be in a place in time to see (a person, performance, programme, etc.): *she was hurrying downstairs to catch the news.* ■come upon (someone) unexpectedly: *unexpected snow* ***caught*** *us* ***by surprise.*** ■(**be caught in**) (of a person) unexpectedly find oneself in (an unwelcome situation): *my sister was caught in a thunderstorm.* ■(**catch it**) informal be punished or told off. ■(often **be caught**) surprise (someone) in an incriminating situation or in the act of doing something wrong: *he was caught with bomb-making equipment in his home.*
4 engage (a person's interest or imagination).
■perceive fleetingly: *she* ***caught a glimpse of*** *herself in the mirror.* ■hear or understand (something said), especially with effort: *he bellowed something Jess couldn't catch.* ■succeed in evoking or representing: *the programme caught something of the flavour of Minoan culture.*
5 [with obj. and adverbial of place] strike (someone) on a part of the body: *Ben caught him on the chin with an uppercut.*
■accidentally strike (a part of one's body) against something: *she fell and caught her head on the corner of the hearth.*
6 contract (an illness) through infection or contagion.
7 [no obj.] become ignited, due to contact with flame, and start burning: *the rafters have caught.*
■(of an engine) fire and start running.
▶**noun 1** an act of catching something, typically a ball.
■Cricket a chance or act of catching the ball to dismiss a batsman: *he took a brilliant catch at deep square leg.* ■an amount of fish caught: *the UK's North Sea haddock catch.* ■[in sing.] informal a person considered attractive or prestigious and so desirable as a partner or spouse: *Giles is a good catch for any girl.*
2 a device for securing something such as a door, window, or box: *the window catch was rusty.*
3 a hidden problem or disadvantage in an apparently ideal situation: *there's a catch in it somewhere.*
4 [in sing.] an unevenness in a person's voice caused by emotion: *there was a catch in Anne's voice.*
5 Music a round, typically one with words arranged to produce a humorous effect.
– PHRASES **catch someone napping** see **NAP**[1]. **be caught short** see **SHORT**. **catch at straws** see **STRAW**. **catch one's breath 1** draw one's breath in sharply as a reaction to an emotion. **2** recover one's breath after exertion. **catch one's death (of cold)** see **DEATH**. **catch someone's eye 1** be noticed by someone: *a vase on a side table caught his eye.* **2** attract someone's attention by making eye contact with them: *he caught Eva's eye and beckoned.* **catch fire** (or **light**) become ignited and burn. **catch someone in the act** see **ACT**. **catch light** see *catch fire*. **catch the light** shine or glint in the light. **catch sight of** suddenly notice; glimpse. **catch the sun 1** be in a sunny position: *a glassed-in porch that caught the sun.* **2** Brit. become tanned or sunburnt. **you wouldn't catch —— doing something** informal used to indicate that there is no possibility of the person mentioned doing what is specified: *you wouldn't catch me walking back to the house alone at night.*
– DERIVATIVES **catchable** adjective.
– ORIGIN Middle English (also in the sense 'chase'): from Anglo-Norman French and Old Northern French *cachier*, variant of Old French *chacier*, based on Latin *captare* 'try to catch', from *capere* 'take'.
▶**catch on** informal **1** (of a practice or fashion) become popular: *the idea of linking pay to performance has caught on.* **2** understand what is meant or how to do something: *I* ***caught on to*** *what it was the guy was saying.*
catch someone out Brit. detect that someone has done something wrong or made a mistake: *his tone suggested he'd caught her out in some misdemeanour.* ■(often **be caught out**) put someone in a difficult situation for which they are unprepared: *you might get caught out by the weather.* ■Cricket dismiss a batsman by catching the ball before it touches the ground.
catch up succeed in reaching a person who is ahead of one: *O'Hara* ***caught up with*** *Stella at the bottom of the hill.* ■do work or other tasks which one should have done earlier: *he normally used the afternoons to* ***catch up on*** *paperwork.*
catch up with 1 talk to (someone) whom one has not seen for some time in order to find out what they have been doing in the interim. **2** begin to have a damaging effect on: *the physical exertions began to catch up with Sue.*
catch someone up 1 succeed in reaching a person who is ahead of one. **2** (**be/get caught up in**) become involved in (something that one had not intended to become involved in): *he had no desire to be caught up in political activities.*
catch something up pick something up hurriedly.

catch-all ▶**noun** [usu. as modifier] a term or category that includes a variety of different possibilities: *the stigmatizing catch-all term 'schizophrenia'.*

catch-as-catch-can ▶**noun** [mass noun] archaic wrestling in which all holds are permitted.
▶**adjective** [attrib.] using whatever is available: *pictures shot on mobile camera on a catch-as-catch-can basis.*

catch crop ▶**noun** Brit. a crop grown in the space between two main crops or at a time when no main crops are being grown.

catcher ▶**noun** a person or thing that catches something.

C

■Baseball a fielder positioned behind home plate to catch pitches not hit by the batter.

catchfly ▶ noun (pl. **-flies**) a campion or similar plant of the pink family, with a sticky stem.
● *Silene, Lychnis,* and other genera, family Caryophyllaceae.

catching ▶ adjective [predic.] informal (of a disease) infectious: *Huntington's chorea isn't catching* | figurative *her enthusiasm is catching.*

catch-light ▶ noun a gleam of reflected light in the eye of a person in a photograph.

catchline ▶ noun Printing, Brit. a short, eye-catching line of type, typically one at the top of a page such as a running head.
■an advertising slogan.

catchment ▶ noun [mass noun] the action of collecting water, especially the collection of rainfall over a natural drainage area.

catchment area ▶ noun **1** (also **catchment**) the area from which a hospital's patients or school's pupils are drawn.
2 the area from which rainfall flows into a river, lake, or reservoir.

catchpenny ▶ adjective [attrib.] having a cheap superficial attractiveness designed to encourage quick sales.

catchphrase ▶ noun a well-known sentence or phrase, typically one that is associated with a particular famous person.

catch points ▶ plural noun railway points positioned so as to derail any vehicle running in the wrong direction on a line, as a safety precaution.

catch-22 ▶ noun a dilemma or difficult circumstance from which there is no escape because of mutually conflicting or dependent conditions: [as modifier] *a catch-22 situation.*
– ORIGIN 1970s: title of a novel by Joseph Heller (1961), in which the main character feigns madness in order to avoid dangerous combat missions, but his desire to avoid them is taken to prove his sanity.

catchup /ˈkatʃʌp/ ▶ noun variant spelling of KETCHUP.

catch-up ▶ noun informal an act of catching someone up in a particular activity.
– PHRASES **play catch-up** N. Amer. try to equal a competitor in a sport or game.

catchweight ▶ noun [mass noun] [usu. as modifier] chiefly historical unrestricted weight in a wrestling match or other sporting contest: *a catchweight contest.*

catchword ▶ noun **1** a word or phrase, used to encapsulate a particular concept, which is briefly popular or fashionable: *'motivation' is a great catchword.*
2 a word printed or placed so as to attract attention.
■Printing, chiefly historical the first word of a page given at the foot of the previous one.

catchy ▶ adjective (**catchier, catchiest**) (of a tune or phrase) instantly appealing and memorable: *catchy pop melodies.*
– DERIVATIVES **catchily** adverb, **catchiness** noun.

cat door ▶ noun another term for CAT FLAP.

cate /keɪt/ ▶ noun (usu. **cates**) archaic a choice food; a delicacy.
– ORIGIN late Middle English (in the sense 'selling, a bargain'): from obsolete *acate* 'purchasing, things purchased', from Old French *acat, achat,* from *acater, achater* 'buy', based on Latin *captare* 'seize', from *capere* 'take'.

catechesis /ˌkatɪˈkiːsɪs/ ▶ noun [mass noun] religious instruction given to a person in preparation for Christian baptism or confirmation, typically using a catechism.
– ORIGIN mid 18th cent.: via ecclesiastical Latin from Greek *katēkhēsis* 'oral instruction'.

catechetical /ˌkatɪˈkɛtɪk(ə)l/ ▶ adjective of or relating to religious instruction given to a person in preparation for Christian baptism or confirmation.
■of or relating to religious teaching by means of questions and answers.
– DERIVATIVES **catechetic** adjective, **catechetically** adverb.
– ORIGIN early 17th cent.: from ecclesiastical Greek *katēkhētikos,* from *katēkhētēs* 'catechist', from *katēkhein* 'instruct orally' (see CATECHIZE).

catechetics /ˌkatɪˈkɛtɪks/ ▶ plural noun [treated as sing.]

the branch of theology that deals with the instruction given to Christians before baptism or confirmation.
■religious teaching in general, typically that given to children in the Roman Catholic Church.

catechin /ˈkatɪtʃɪn/ ▶ noun [mass noun] Chemistry a crystalline compound which is the major constituent of catechu.
● A phenol; chem. formula: $C_{15}H_{14}O_6$; several isomers.
– ORIGIN mid 19th cent.: from CATECHU + -IN[1].

catechism /ˈkatɪkɪz(ə)m/ ▶ noun a summary of the principles of Christian religion in the form of questions and answers, used for the instruction of Christians.
■a series of fixed questions, answers, or precepts used for instruction in other situations.
– DERIVATIVES **catechismal** adjective.
– ORIGIN early 16th cent.: from ecclesiastical Latin *catechismus,* from ecclesiastical Greek, from *katēkhizein* (see CATECHIZE).

catechist ▶ noun a teacher of the principles of Christian religion, especially one using a catechism.
– ORIGIN mid 16th cent.: via ecclesiastical Latin from ecclesiastical Greek *katēkhistēs,* from *katēkhein* 'instruct orally'.

catechize (also **-ise**) ▶ verb [with obj.] instruct (someone) in the principles of Christian religion by means of question and answer, typically by using a catechism.
■figurative put questions to or interrogate (someone).
– DERIVATIVES **catechizer** noun.
– ORIGIN late Middle English: via late Latin from ecclesiastical Greek *katēkhizein,* from *katēkhein* 'instruct orally, make hear'.

catechol /ˈkatɪtʃɒl, -kɒl/ ▶ noun [mass noun] Chemistry a crystalline compound obtained by distilling catechu.
● Alternative name: **benzene-1,2-diol**; chem. formula: $C_6H_4(OH)_2$.
– ORIGIN late 19th cent.: from CATECHU + -OL.

catecholamine /ˌkatɪˈkɒləmiːn/ ▶ noun Biochemistry any of a class of aromatic amines which includes a number of neurotransmitters such as adrenalin and dopamine.

catechu /ˈkatɪtʃuː/ ▶ noun [mass noun] a vegetable extract containing tannin, especially one (also called **CUTCH**) obtained from the heartwood of an Indian acacia tree, used chiefly for tanning and dyeing.
● The chief source of this is *Acacia catechu,* family Leguminosae.
■another term for GAMBIER.
– ORIGIN late 17th cent.: modern Latin, from Malay *kacu.* Compare with CACHOU.

catechumen /ˌkatɪˈkjuːmɛn/ ▶ noun a Christian convert under instruction before baptism.
■a young Christian preparing for confirmation.
– ORIGIN late Middle English: via ecclesiastical Latin from Greek *katēkhoumenos* 'being instructed', present participle of *katēkhein* 'instruct orally' (see CATECHIZE).

categorical ▶ adjective unambiguously explicit and direct: *a categorical assurance.*
– DERIVATIVES **categoric** adjective, **categorically** adverb.
– ORIGIN late 16th cent.: from late Latin *categoricus* (from Greek *katēgorikos,* from *katēgoria* 'statement': see CATEGORY) + -AL.

categorical imperative ▶ noun Philosophy (in Kantian ethics) an unconditional moral obligation which is binding in all circumstances and is not dependent on a person's inclination or purpose.

categorize (also **-ise**) ▶ verb [with obj.] (often be **categorized**) place in a particular class or group: *the issues can be categorized into three central questions.*
– DERIVATIVES **categorization** noun.

category ▶ noun (pl. **-ies**) **1** a class or division of people or things regarded as having particular shared characteristics: *the various categories of research.*
2 Philosophy one of a possibly exhaustive set of classes among which all things might be distributed.
■one of a priori conceptions applied by the mind to sense impressions. ■a relatively fundamental philosophical concept.
– DERIVATIVES **categorial** adjective.
– ORIGIN late Middle English (in sense 2): from French *catégorie* or late Latin *categoria,* from Greek

katēgoria 'statement, accusation', from *katēgoros* 'accuser'.

category mistake ▶ noun Logic the error of assigning to something a quality or action which can only properly be assigned to things of another category, for example treating abstract concepts as though they had a physical location.

catena /kəˈtiːnə/ ▶ noun (pl. **catenae** /-niː/ or **catenas**) technical a connected series or chain.
■a connected series of texts written by early Christian theologians.
– ORIGIN mid 17th cent.: from Latin, 'chain', originally in *catena patrum* 'chain of the (Church) Fathers'.

catenane /ˈkatəneɪn/ ▶ noun Chemistry a molecule which consists of two or more connected rings like links in a chain.
– ORIGIN 1960s: from Latin *catena* 'chain' + -ANE[2].

catenary /kəˈtiːnəri/ ▶ noun (pl. **-ies**) a curve formed by a wire, rope, or chain hanging freely from two points that are on the same horizontal level.
■a wire, rope, or chain forming such a curve.
▶ adjective [attrib.] having the form of, involving, or denoting a curve of this type.
– ORIGIN mid 18th cent.: from Latin *catenarius* 'relating to a chain', from *catena* 'chain'.

catenated /ˈkatɪneɪtɪd/ ▶ adjective technical connected in a chain or series: *catenated molecules.*
– DERIVATIVES **catenation** noun.
– ORIGIN late 19th cent.: past participle of the rare verb *catenate,* from Latin *catenat-* 'chained, fettered', from the verb *catenare,* from *catena* 'chain'.

catenative /kəˈtɪnətɪv/ Grammar ▶ adjective denoting a verb that governs a non-finite form of another verb, for example *like* in *I like swimming.*
▶ noun a catenative verb.
– ORIGIN late 20th cent.: from Latin *catena* 'chain' + -ATIVE.

catenoid /ˈkatənɔɪd/ ▶ noun Geometry the surface generated by rotating a catenary about its axis of symmetry.
– ORIGIN late 19th cent.: from Latin *catena* 'chain' + -OID.

cater ▶ verb [no obj.] (**cater for**) chiefly Brit. provide with food and drink, typically at social events and in a professional capacity: *my mother helped to cater for the party* | [as noun **catering**] *high standards of catering.*
■[with obj.] provide (food and drink) in this way: *he catered a lunch for 20 people.* ■ (**cater for/to**) provide with what is needed or required: *the school caters for children with learning difficulties.* ■ (**cater for**) take into account or make allowances for: *the scheme caters for interest rate fluctuations.* ■ (**cater to**) try to satisfy (a particular need or demand): *he catered to her every whim.*
– DERIVATIVES **caterer** noun.
– ORIGIN late 16th cent.: from obsolete *cater* 'caterer', from Old French *acateor* 'buyer', from *acater* 'buy' (see CATE).

cateran /ˈkat(ə)r(ə)n/ ▶ noun historical a warrior or raider from the Scottish Highlands.
– ORIGIN Middle English (originally in the plural or as a collective singular denoting the peasantry as fighters): from Scottish Gaelic *ceathairne* 'peasantry'.

cater-cornered /ˈkeɪtəˌkɔːnəd/ (also **cater-corner, catty-cornered, kitty-corner**) ▶ adjective & adverb N. Amer. situated diagonally opposite someone or something: [as adj.] *a restaurant cater-cornered from the movie theatre* | [as adv.] *motorcyclists cut cater-cornered across his yard.*
– ORIGIN mid 19th cent.: from dialect *cater* 'diagonally', from *cater* denoting the four on dice, from French *quatre* 'four', from Latin *quattuor.*

caterpillar ▶ noun **1** the larva of a butterfly or moth, which has a segmented worm-like body with three pairs of true legs and several pairs of leg-like appendages. Caterpillars may be hairy, have warning coloration, or be coloured to resemble their surroundings.
■(in general use) any similar larva of various insects, especially sawflies.
2 (also **caterpillar track** or **tread**) trademark an articulated steel band passing round the wheels of a vehicle for travel on rough ground.
■a vehicle with such tracks.
– ORIGIN late Middle English: perhaps from a variant of Old French *chatepelose,* literally 'hairy cat', influenced by obsolete *piller* 'ravager'. The association with 'cat' is found in other languages,

e.g. Swiss German *Teufelskatz* (literally 'devil's cat'), Lombard *gatta* (literally 'cat'). Compare with French *chaton*, English **CATKIN**, resembling hairy caterpillars.

caters ▶ **noun** Bell-ringing a system of change-ringing using nine bells, with four pairs changing places each time.
– ORIGIN late 19th cent.: from French *quatre* 'four'.

caterwaul /ˈkatəwɔːl/ ▶ **verb** [no obj.] [often as noun **caterwauling**] (of a cat) make a shrill howling or wailing noise: *the caterwauling of a pair of bobcats* | [as adj. **caterwauling**] figurative *a caterwauling guitar.*
▶ **noun** a shrill howling or wailing noise.
– ORIGIN late Middle English: from **CAT**[1] + imitative **WAUL**.

catfish ▶ **noun** (pl. same or **-fishes**) **1** a freshwater or marine fish with whisker-like barbels round the mouth, typically bottom-dwelling.
• Order Siluriformes: many families, including the Eurasian family Siluridae (see **WELS**) and the Callichthyidae (which contains a number of species that are popular in aquaria, in particular the genus *Corydoras*).
2 another term for **WOLF FISH**.
3 S. African an octopus.

cat flap (also **cat door**) ▶ **noun** a small hinged flap in an outer door, through which a cat may enter or leave a building.

catgut ▶ **noun** [mass noun] a material used for the strings of musical instruments and for surgical sutures, made of the dried twisted intestines of sheep or horses, but not cats.
– ORIGIN late 16th cent.: the association with **CAT**[1] remains unexplained.

Cath. ▶ **abbreviation for** ■ Cathedral. ■ Catholic.

Cathar /ˈkaθɑː/ ▶ **noun** (pl. **Cathars** or **Cathari** /-ri/) a member of a heretical medieval Christian sect which professed a form of Manichaean dualism and sought to achieve great spiritual purity.
– DERIVATIVES **Catharism** noun, **Catharist** noun & adjective.
– ORIGIN mid 17th cent.: from medieval Latin *Cathari* (plural), from Greek *katharoi* 'the pure'.

catharsis /kəˈθɑːsɪs/ ▶ **noun** [mass noun] **1** the process of releasing, and thereby providing relief from, strong or repressed emotions.
2 Medicine, rare purgation.
– ORIGIN early 19th cent. (in sense 2): from Greek *katharsis*, from *kathairein* 'cleanse', from *katharos* 'pure'. The notion of 'release' through drama (sense 1) derives from Aristotle's *Poetics*.

cathartic ▶ **adjective 1** providing psychological relief through the open expression of strong emotions; causing catharsis: *crying is a cathartic release.*
2 Medicine (chiefly of a drug) purgative.
▶ **noun** Medicine a purgative drug.
– DERIVATIVES **cathartically** adverb.
– ORIGIN early 17th cent. (in medical use): via late Latin from Greek *kathartikos*, from *katharsis* 'cleansing' (see **CATHARSIS**).

Cathay /kaˈθeɪ/ the name by which China was known to medieval Europe. Also called **KHITAI**.
– ORIGIN from medieval Latin *Cataya*, *Cathaya*, from Turkic *Khitāy*.

cathead ▶ **noun** a horizontal beam extending from each side of a ship's bow, used for raising and carrying an anchor.

cathectic /kəˈθɛktɪk/ ▶ **adjective** Psychoanalysis of or relating to cathexis.
– ORIGIN 1920s: from Greek *kathektikos* 'capable of holding'.

cathedral ▶ **noun** the principal church of a diocese, with which the bishop is officially associated: [in names] *St Paul's Cathedral.*
– ORIGIN Middle English (as an adjective, the noun being short for *cathedral church* 'the church which contains the bishop's throne'): from late Latin *cathedralis*, from Latin *cathedra* 'seat', from Greek *kathedra*.

Cather /ˈkaðə/, Willa (Sibert) (1876–1974), American novelist and short-story writer. Her home state of Nebraska provides the setting for some of her best writing. Notable novels: *O Pioneers!* (1913) and *Death Comes for the Archbishop* (1927).

Catherine II (1729–96), empress of Russia, reigned 1762–96; known as **Catherine the Great**. She became empress after her husband, Peter III, was deposed; her attempted social and political reforms were impeded by the aristocracy. She formed alliances with Prussia and Austria, and made territorial advances at the expense of the Turks and Tartars.

Catherine, St (died *c.*307), early Christian martyr; known as **St Catherine of Alexandria**. According to tradition she opposed the persecution of Christians under the emperor Maxentius and refused to recant or to marry the emperor. She is said to have been tortured on a spiked wheel and then beheaded. Feast day, 25 November.

Catherine de' Medici (1519–89), queen of France, wife of Henry II. She ruled as regent (1560–74) during the minority reigns of her three sons, Francis II, Charles IX, and Henry III, and it was at her instigation that Huguenots were killed in the Massacre of St Bartholomew (1572).

Catherine of Aragon (1485–1536), first wife of Henry VIII, youngest daughter of Ferdinand and Isabella of Castile, mother of Mary I. Henry's wish to annul his marriage to Catherine (due to her failure to produce a male heir) led eventually to England's break with the Roman Catholic Church.

Catherine wheel ▶ **noun** a firework in the form of a flat coil which spins when fixed to something solid and lit.
■ Heraldry a wheel with curved spikes projecting around the circumference.
– ORIGIN late 16th cent. (as a heraldic term): named after St *Catherine* (see **CATHERINE, ST**), with reference to her martyrdom.

catheter /ˈkaθɪtə/ ▶ **noun** Medicine a flexible tube inserted through a narrow opening into a body cavity, particularly the bladder, for removing fluid.
– ORIGIN early 17th cent.: from late Latin, from Greek *kathetēr*, from *kathienai* 'send or let down'.

catheterize (also **-ise**) ▶ **verb** [with obj.] Medicine insert a catheter into (a patient or body cavity).
– DERIVATIVES **catheterization** noun.

cathetometer /ˌkaθɪˈtɒmɪtə/ ▶ **noun** a telescope mounted on a graduated scale, used for accurate measurement of small vertical distances.
– ORIGIN mid 19th cent.: from Latin *cathetus* (from Greek *kathetos* 'perpendicular line', from *kathienai* 'send or let down') + **-METER**.

cathexis /kəˈθɛksɪs/ ▶ **noun** [mass noun] Psychoanalysis the concentration of mental energy on one particular person, idea, or object (especially to an unhealthy degree).
– ORIGIN 1920s: from Greek *kathexis* 'retention', translating German *Libidobesetzung*, coined by Freud.

cathiodermie /ˌkaθɪəʊˈdəmiː/ ▶ **noun** [mass noun] trademark a beauty treatment in which an electric current is passed through a gel applied to a person's face, in order to cleanse their skin.
– ORIGIN late 20th cent.: from French.

cathode /ˈkaθəʊd/ ▶ **noun** the negatively charged electrode by which electrons enter an electrical device. The opposite of **ANODE**.
■ the positively charged electrode of an electrical device, such as a primary cell, that supplies current.
– DERIVATIVES **cathodal** adjective, **cathodic** /kəˈθɒdɪk/ adjective.
– ORIGIN mid 19th cent.: from Greek *kathodos* 'way down', from *kata-* 'down' + *hodos* 'way'.

cathode ray ▶ **noun** a beam of electrons emitted from the cathode of a high-vacuum tube.

cathode ray tube (abbrev.: **CRT**) ▶ **noun** a high-vacuum tube in which cathode rays produce a luminous image on a fluorescent screen, used chiefly in televisions and computer terminals.

cathodic protection ▶ **noun** [mass noun] protection of a metal structure from corrosion under water by making it act as an electrical cathode.

cathodoluminescence /ˌkaθədə(ʊ)ˌluːmɪˈnɛs(ə)ns/ ▶ **noun** [mass noun] Physics luminescence excited by the impact of an electron beam.

catholic ▶ **adjective 1** (especially of a person's tastes) including a wide variety of things; all-embracing.
2 (**Catholic**) of the Roman Catholic faith.
■ of or including all Christians. ■ of or relating to the historic doctrine and practice of the Western Church.
▶ **noun** (**Catholic**) a member of the Roman Catholic Church.
– DERIVATIVES **catholicity** noun, **catholicly** adverb.
– ORIGIN late Middle English (in sense 2): from Old French *catholique* or late Latin *catholicus*, from Greek *katholikos* 'universal', from *kata* 'in respect of' + *holos* 'whole'.

Catholic Emancipation the granting of full political and civil liberties to Roman Catholics in Britain and Ireland. This was effected by the Catholic Emancipation Act of 1829, which repealed restrictive laws, including that which barred Catholics from holding public office.

Catholicism /kəˈθɒlɪsɪz(ə)m/ ▶ **noun** [mass noun] the faith, practice, and church order of the Roman Catholic Church.
■ adherence to the forms of Christian doctrine and practice which are generally regarded as Catholic rather than Protestant or Eastern Orthodox.

Catholicize (also **-ise**) ▶ **verb** [with obj.] make Roman Catholic; convert to Catholicism.

Catholic League see **HOLY LEAGUE**.

Catholicos /kəˈθɒlɪkɒs/ ▶ **noun** (pl. **Catholicoses** /kəˌθɒlɪˈkəʊsiːz/ or **Catholicoi** /kəˈθɒlɪkɔɪ/) the Patriarch of the Armenian or the Nestorian Church.
– ORIGIN early 17th cent.: from medieval Greek *katholikos* 'universal' (see **CATHOLIC**).

cathouse ▶ **noun** informal, chiefly N. Amer. a brothel.

cat ice ▶ **noun** [mass noun] thin ice from under which the water has receded.

Catiline /ˈkatɪlʌɪn/ (*c.*108–62 BC), Roman nobleman and conspirator; Latin name *Lucius Sergius Catilina*. In 63 BC he planned an uprising which was suppressed; his fellow conspirators were executed and he died in battle in Etruria.

cation /ˈkatʌɪən/ ▶ **noun** Chemistry a positively charged ion, i.e. one that would be attracted to the cathode in electrolysis. The opposite of **ANION**.
– DERIVATIVES **cationic** /katʌɪˈɒnɪk/ adjective.
– ORIGIN mid 19th cent.: from **CATA-** 'alongside' or from **CATHODE**, + **ION**.

catkin ▶ **noun** a flowering spike of trees such as willow and hazel. Catkins are typically downy, pendulous, composed of flowers of a single sex, and wind-pollinated.
– ORIGIN late 16th cent.: from obsolete Dutch *katteken* 'kitten'.

cat ladder ▶ **noun** a ladder used for working on a sloping roof, with a hook at one end, wheels at the other and pads to spread the load.

catlick ▶ **noun** a perfunctory wash.

catlike ▶ **adjective** resembling a cat in appearance, action, or character, especially by moving gracefully or stealthily.

catlinite /ˈkatlɪnʌɪt/ ▶ **noun** [mass noun] a red clay of the Upper Missouri region, the sacred pipe-stone of the American Indians.
– ORIGIN mid 19th cent.: from the name of George *Catlin* (1796–1872), American artist, + **-ITE**[1].

cat litter ▶ **noun** see **LITTER** (sense 3).

catmint ▶ **noun** a plant of the mint family, with downy leaves, purple-spotted white flowers, and a pungent smell attractive to cats. Also called **CATNIP**.
• Genus *Nepeta*, family Labiatae: several species, including the Eurasian *N. cataria*.

catnap ▶ **noun** a short sleep during the day, typically while sitting in a chair or at a desk.
▶ **verb** (**-napped**, **-napping**) [no obj.] have such a sleep.

catnip ▶ **noun** another term for **CATMINT**.
– ORIGIN late 18th cent. (originally US): from **CAT**[1] + *nip*, variant of dialect *nep*, *nept*, from medieval Latin *nepta*, from Latin *nepeta* 'catmint'.

Cato /ˈkeɪtəʊ/, Marcus Porcius (234–149 BC), Roman statesman, orator, and writer; known as **Cato the Elder** or **Cato the Censor**. As censor he initiated a vigorous programme of reform, and attempted to stem the growing influence of Greek culture.

cat-o'-nine-tails ▶ **noun** historical a rope whip with nine knotted cords, formerly used (especially at sea) to flog offenders.

catoptric /kaˈtɒptrɪk/ ▶ **adjective** Physics of or relating to a mirror, a reflector, or reflection.
– ORIGIN early 18th cent.: from Greek *katoptrikos*, from *katoptron* 'mirror'.

catoptrics ▶ **plural noun** [treated as sing.] Physics the branch of optics that deals with reflection.
– ORIGIN mid 16th cent. (originally *catoptric*): from Greek *katoptrikos* 'reflecting', from *katoptron* 'mirror'.

cat's cradle ▶ **noun** [mass noun] a child's game in

which a loop of string is put around and between the fingers and complex patterns are formed.
■[in sing.] a complex pattern made of string in such a game.

cat scratch fever (also **cat scratch disease**) ▶ noun [mass noun] an infectious disease occurring after a scratch by a cat's claw, a splinter, or a thorn. Symptoms include mild fever and inflammation of the injury site and of the lymph glands.

cat's ear (also **cat's ears**) ▶ noun a plant which resembles the dandelion, with yellow flowers and rosettes of leaves.
● Genus *Hypochaeris*, family Compositae.

cat's eye ▶ noun 1 a semi-precious stone, especially chalcedony, with a chatoyant lustre.
2 (**catseye**) Brit. trademark a light-reflecting stud set into a road as one of a series to mark traffic lanes or the edge of the carriageway by reflecting light from headlights.

cat's foot ▶ noun a small white-flowered creeping plant of the daisy family, which bears soft white woolly hairs on the flowering stems and undersides of the leaves. Also called **MOUNTAIN EVERLASTING**.
● *Antennaria dioica*, family Compositae.

cat shark ▶ noun a small bottom-dwelling shark that has catlike eyes and small dorsal fins set well back. It is typically strikingly marked, and lives in warmer waters.
● *Apristurus* and other genera, family Scyliorhinidae: several species, including the **brown cat shark** (*A. brunneus*).

Catskill Mountains /ˈkatskɪl/ (also **the Catskills**) a range of mountains in the state of New York, part of the Appalachian system.

cat's meow ▶ noun (**the cat's meow**) chiefly US another term for *the cat's whiskers* (see **CAT'S WHISKER**).

cat's paw ▶ noun a person who is used by another, typically to carry out an unpleasant or dangerous task.

cat's pyjamas ▶ noun (**the cat's pyjamas**) chiefly US another term for *the cat's whiskers* (see **CAT'S WHISKER**).

cat's tail (also **cattail**) ▶ noun a plant with long thin parts suggestive of cats' tails, in particular:
● the reed mace. ● (also **cat's-tail grass**) timothy grass.

catsuit ▶ noun chiefly Brit. a woman's one-piece garment with trouser legs, typically close-fitting and covering the body from the neck to the feet.

catsup /ˈkatsəp/ ▶ noun US another term for **KETCHUP**.

cat's whisker ▶ noun a fine adjustable wire in a crystal radio receiver.
– PHRASES **the cat's whiskers** informal an excellent person or thing: *this car is the cat's whiskers.*

cattery ▶ noun (pl. **-ies**) a boarding or breeding establishment for cats.

cattie ▶ noun variant spelling of **CATTY²**.

cattish ▶ adjective another term for **CATTY¹**.
– DERIVATIVES **cattishly** adverb, **cattishness** noun.

cattle ▶ plural noun 1 large ruminant animals with horns and cloven hoofs, domesticated for meat or milk, or as beasts of burden; cows and oxen.
● *Bos taurus* (including the zebu, *B. indicus*), family Bovidae; descended from the extinct aurochs.
2 similar animals of a group related to domestic cattle, including yak, bison, and buffaloes.
● Tribe Bovini, family Bovidae (the **cattle family**): four genera, in particular *Bos*. The cattle family also includes the sheep, goats, goat-antelopes, and antelopes.
– ORIGIN Middle English (also denoting personal property or wealth): from Anglo-Norman French *catel*, variant of Old French *chatel* (see **CHATTEL**).

cattle cake ▶ noun [mass noun] Brit. concentrated food for cattle in a compressed flat form.

cattle call ▶ noun N. Amer. informal an open audition for parts in a play or film.

cattle dog ▶ noun Austral./NZ a dog bred and trained to work cattle.

cattle-duff ▶ verb [no obj.] [usu. as noun **cattle-duffing**] Austral. steal cattle.
– DERIVATIVES **cattle-duffer** noun.
– ORIGIN mid 19th cent.: *duff* from **DUFFER²**.

cattle egret ▶ noun a small white heron with long buff feathers on the head, back, and chest in the breeding season, which normally feeds around grazing cattle and game herds. It is native to southern Eurasia and Africa, and has colonized

North and South America and Australasia in the 20th century.
● *Bubulcus* (or *Ardeola*) *ibis*, family Ardeidae.

cattle grid ▶ noun Brit. a metal grid covering a ditch, allowing vehicles and pedestrians to pass over but not cattle and other animals.

cattle guard ▶ noun North American term for **CATTLE GRID**.

cattle plague ▶ noun another term for **RINDERPEST**.

cattle stop ▶ noun New Zealand term for **CATTLE GRID**.

cattleya /ˈkatlɪə/ ▶ noun a tropical American orchid with brightly coloured showy flowers and thick leaves, typically growing as an epiphyte. They are popular greenhouse plants, with many hybrids.
● Genus *Cattleya*, family Orchidaceae.
– ORIGIN early 19th cent.: modern Latin, named after William *Cattley* (died 1832), English patron of botany.

cat train ▶ noun N. Amer. a crawler tractor pulling a train of sleighs across snow or ice.
– ORIGIN *cat* from **CATERPILLAR**.

catty¹ ▶ adjective (**cattier**, **cattiest**) 1 deliberately hurtful in one's remarks; spiteful.
2 of or relating to cats; catlike.
– DERIVATIVES **cattily** adverb, **cattiness** noun.

catty² (also **cattie** or **kettie**) ▶ noun S. African informal a catapult.

catty-cornered ▶ adjective another term for **CATER-CORNERED**.

Catullus /kəˈtʌləs/, Gaius Valerius (*c.*84–*c.*54 BC), Roman poet. He is best known for his love poems.

CATV ▶ abbreviation for community antenna television (cable television).

catwalk ▶ noun a narrow walkway or open bridge, especially in an industrial installation.
■a platform extending into an auditorium, along which models walk to display clothes in fashion shows.

caubeen /kɔːˈbiːn/ ▶ noun an Irish beret, typically dark green in colour.
– ORIGIN early 19th cent.: Irish, literally 'old hat', from *cáibín* 'little cape', diminutive of *cába* 'cape'.

Caucasian /kɔːˈkeɪzɪən, -ˈʒ(ə)n/ ▶ adjective 1 of or relating to one of the traditional divisions of humankind, covering a broad group of peoples from Europe, western Asia, and parts of India and North Africa. [ORIGIN: so named because the German physiologist Blumenbach believed that it originated in the Caucasus region of SE Europe.]
■white-skinned; of European origin.
2 of or relating to the Caucasus.
3 of or relating to a group of languages spoken in the region of the Caucasus, of which thirty-eight are known, many not committed to writing. The most widely spoken is Georgian, of the small **South Caucasian** family, not related to the three **North Caucasian** families.
▶ noun a Caucasian person.
■a white person; a person of European origin.

USAGE In the racial classification as developed by Blumenbach and others in the 19th century, **Caucasian** (or **Caucasoid**) included peoples whose skin colour ranged from light (in northern Europe) to dark (in parts of North Africa and India). Although the classification is outdated and the categories are now not generally accepted as scientific (see usage at **MONGOLOID**), the term **Caucasian** has acquired a more restricted meaning. It is now used, especially in the US, as a synonym for 'white or of European origin', as in the following citation: *the police are looking for a Caucasian male in his forties.*

Caucasoid /ˈkɔːkəsɔɪd/ ▶ adjective of or relating to the Caucasian division of humankind.

USAGE The term **Caucasoid** belongs to a set of terms introduced by 19th-century anthropologists attempting to categorize human races. Such terms are associated with outdated notions of racial types, and so are now potentially offensive and best avoided. See usage at **MONGOLOID**.

Caucasus /ˈkɔːkəsəs/ (also **Caucasia** /kɔːˈkeɪzɪə, -ˈkeɪʒə/) a mountainous region of SE Europe, lying between the Black Sea and the Caspian Sea, in Georgia, Armenia, Azerbaijan, and SE Russia.

Cauchy /ˈkəʊʃi, French koʃi/, Augustin Louis, Baron (1789–1857), French mathematician. He

transformed the theory of complex functions by discovering his integral theorems, founded the modern theory of elasticity, and contributed substantially to the founding of group theory and analysis.

caucus /ˈkɔːkəs/ ▶ noun (pl. **caucuses**) 1 (in North America and New Zealand) a meeting of the members of a legislative body who are members of a particular political party, to select candidates or decide policy.
■the members of such a body.
2 (in the UK) a group of people with shared concerns within a political party or larger organization.
■a meeting of such a group.
▶ verb (**caucused**, **caucusing**) [no obj.] chiefly N. Amer. hold or form such a group or meeting.
– ORIGIN mid 18th cent. (originally US): perhaps from Algonquian *cau'-cau-as'u* 'adviser'.

caudal /ˈkɔːd(ə)l/ ▶ adjective of or like a tail.
■at or near the tail or the posterior part of the body.
– DERIVATIVES **caudally** adverb.
– ORIGIN mid 17th cent.: from modern Latin *caudalis*, from Latin *cauda* 'tail'.

caudal fin ▶ noun Zoology another term for **TAIL FIN**.

Caudata /kɔːˈdeɪtə/ Zoology another term for **URODELA**.
– ORIGIN modern Latin (plural), from Latin *cauda* 'tail'.

caudate /ˈkɔːdeɪt/ ▶ adjective Anatomy relating to or denoting the caudate nucleus.
▶ noun short for **CAUDATE NUCLEUS**.
– ORIGIN early 17th cent.: from medieval Latin *caudatus*, from *cauda* 'tail'.

caudate nucleus ▶ noun Anatomy the upper of the two grey nuclei of the corpus striatum in the cerebrum of the brain.

caudex /ˈkɔːdɛks/ ▶ noun (pl. **caudices** /-dɪsiːz/) Botany the axis of a woody plant, especially a palm or tree fern, comprising the stem and root.
– ORIGIN late 18th cent.: from Latin, earlier form of **CODEX**.

caudillo /kaʊˈdiːjəʊ, -ˈdiːljəʊ/ ▶ noun (pl. **-os**) (in Spain and other Spanish-speaking countries) a military or political leader.
– ORIGIN Spanish, from late Latin *capitellum*, diminutive of *caput* 'head'. The title *El Caudillo* 'the leader' was assumed by General Franco of Spain in 1938.

caught past and past participle of **CATCH**.

caul /kɔːl/ ▶ noun 1 the amniotic membrane enclosing a fetus.
■part of this membrane occasionally found on a child's head at birth, thought to bring good luck.
2 historical a woman's close-fitting indoor headdress or hairnet.
3 Anatomy the omentum.
– ORIGIN Middle English: perhaps from Old French *cale* 'head covering', but recorded earlier.

cauldron (also **caldron**) ▶ noun a large metal pot with a lid and handle, used for cooking over an open fire.
■figurative a situation characterized by instability and strong emotions: *a cauldron of repressed anger.*
– ORIGIN Middle English: from Anglo-Norman French *caudron*, based on Latin *caldarium*, *calidarium* 'cooking-pot', from *calidus* 'hot'.

cauliflower ▶ noun a cabbage of a variety which bears a large immature flower head of small creamy-white flower buds.
■[mass noun] the flower head of this plant eaten as a vegetable.
– ORIGIN late 16th cent.: from obsolete French *chou fleuri* 'flowered cabbage', probably from Italian *cavolfiore* or modern Latin *cauliflora*. The original English form *colieflorie* or *cole-flory*, had its first element influenced by **COLE**; the second element was influenced by **FLOWER** during the 17th cent.

cauliflower cheese ▶ noun [mass noun] Brit. a savoury dish of cauliflower in a cheese sauce.

cauliflower ear ▶ noun a person's ear that has become thickened or deformed as a result of repeated blows, typically in boxing or rugby.

cauliflower fungus ▶ noun an edible fungus which forms a distinctive fruiting body with a yellowish lobed surface, growing on wood and other plant debris in both Eurasia and North America. Also called **BRAIN FUNGUS**.

• Genus *Sparassis* and family Sparassidaceae, class Hymenomycetes: several species, in particular *S. crispa*.

caulk /kɔːk/ (US also **calk**) ▶ **noun** [mass noun] a waterproof filler and sealant, used in building work and repairs.
▶ **verb** [with obj.] seal (a gap or seam) with such a substance.
■ stop up (the seams of a boat) with oakum and waterproofing material, or by driving plate-junctions together; make (a boat) watertight by this method.
– DERIVATIVES **caulker** noun.
– ORIGIN late Middle English (in the sense 'copulate', used of birds): from Old Northern French *cauquer, caukier*, variant of *cauchier* 'tread, press with force', from Latin *calcare* 'tread', from *calx, calc-* 'heel'.

causal ▶ **adjective** of, relating to, or acting as a cause: *the causal factors associated with illness.*
■ Grammar & Logic expressing or indicating a cause: *a causal conjunction.*
– DERIVATIVES **causally** adverb.
– ORIGIN late Middle English (as a noun denoting a causal conjunction or particle): from late Latin *causalis*, from Latin *causa* 'cause'.

causalgia /kɔːˈzaldʒə/ ▶ **noun** [mass noun] severe burning pain in a limb caused by injury to a peripheral nerve.
– ORIGIN mid 19th cent.: from Greek *kausos* 'heat, fever' + **-ALGIA**.

causality ▶ **noun** [mass noun] **1** the relationship between cause and effect.
2 the principle that everything has a cause.
– ORIGIN late 15th cent.: from French *causalité* or medieval Latin *causalitas*, from Latin *causa* 'cause'.

causation ▶ **noun** [mass noun] the action of causing something: *the postulated role of nitrate in the causation of cancer.*
■ the relationship between cause and effect; causality.
– PHRASES **chain of causation** Law a linked series of events leading from cause to effect, typically in the assessment of liability for damages.
– ORIGIN late 15th cent.: from Latin *causatio(n-)* 'pretext' (in medieval Latin 'the action of causing'), from *causare* 'to cause'.

causative ▶ **adjective** acting as a cause: *a causative factor.*
■ Grammar expressing causation: *a causative verb.*
▶ **noun** a causative verb.
– ORIGIN late Middle English: from Old French *causatif, -ive*, or late Latin *causativus*, from *causare* 'to cause'.

cause ▶ **noun 1** a person or thing that gives rise to an action, phenomenon, or condition: *the cause of the accident is not clear.*
■ [mass noun] reasonable grounds for doing, thinking, or feeling something: *Faye's condition had given no* **cause for concern** | [with infinitive] *the government had good cause to avoid war* | [count noun] *class size is a cause for complaint in some schools.*
2 a principle, aim, or movement to which one is deeply committed and which one is prepared to defend or advocate: *she devoted her whole adult life to the cause of deaf people.*
■ [with adj.] something deserving of one's support, typically a charity: *I'm raising money for a good cause.*
3 a matter to be resolved in a court of law.
■ an individual's case offered at law.
▶ **verb** [with obj.] make (something) happen: *this disease can cause blindness* | [with obj. and infinitive] *we have no idea what has happened to cause people to stay away.*
– PHRASES **cause and effect** the principle of causation. ■ the operation or relation of a cause and its effect. **cause of action** Law a fact or facts that enable a person to bring an action against another. **in the cause of** so as to support, promote, or defend something. **make common cause** unite in order to achieve a shared aim: *nationalist movements* **made common cause with** *the reformers.* **a rebel without a cause** a person who is dissatisfied with society but does not have a specific aim to fight for. [ORIGIN: from the title of a US film, released in 1955.]
– DERIVATIVES **causeless** adjective, **causer** noun.
– ORIGIN Middle English: from Old French, from Latin *causa* (noun), *causare* (verb).

'cause ▶ **conjunction** informal short for **BECAUSE**.

cause célèbre /ˌkɔːz seˈlɛbr(ə), French koz selɛbʀ/ ▶ **noun** (pl. **causes célèbres** pronunc. same) a controversial issue that attracts a great deal of public attention.
– ORIGIN mid 18th cent.: French, literally 'famous case'.

causerie /ˈkəʊzəri, French kozʀi/ ▶ **noun** (pl. **-ies** pronunc. same) an informal article or talk, typically one on a literary subject.
– ORIGIN French, from *causer* 'to talk'.

causeway ▶ **noun** a raised road or track across low or wet ground.
– ORIGIN late Middle English: from **CAUSEY** + **WAY**.

causewayed camp ▶ **noun** Archaeology a type of Neolithic settlement in southern Britain, visible as an oval enclosure surrounded by concentric ditches that are crossed by several causeways.

causey /ˈkɔːzi, -si/ ▶ **noun** (pl. **-eys**) archaic or dialect term for **CAUSEWAY**.
– ORIGIN Middle English: from Anglo-Norman French *causee*, based on Latin *calx* 'lime, limestone' (used for paving roads).

caustic /ˈkɔːstɪk, ˈkɒst-/ ▶ **adjective 1** able to burn or corrode organic tissue by chemical action: *a caustic cleaner.*
■ figurative sarcastic in a scathing and bitter way: *the players were making caustic comments about the refereeing.* ■ figurative (of an expression or sound) expressive of such sarcasm: *a caustic smile.*
2 Physics formed by the intersection of reflected or refracted parallel rays from a curved surface.
▶ **noun 1** a caustic substance.
2 Physics a caustic surface or curve.
– DERIVATIVES **caustically** adverb, **causticity** noun.
– ORIGIN late Middle English: via Latin from Greek *kaustikos*, from *kaustos* 'combustible', from *kaiein* 'to burn'.

caustic potash ▶ **noun** another term for **POTASSIUM HYDROXIDE**.

caustic soda ▶ **noun** another term for **SODIUM HYDROXIDE**.

cauterize /ˈkɔːtərʌɪz/ (also **-ise**) ▶ **verb** [with obj.] Medicine burn the skin or flesh of (a wound) with a heated instrument or caustic substance, typically to stop bleeding or prevent the wound becoming infected.
– DERIVATIVES **cauterization** noun.
– ORIGIN late Middle English: from Old French *cauteriser*, from late Latin *cauterizare*, from Greek *kautēriazein*, from *kautērion* 'branding iron', from *kaien* 'to burn'.

cautery /ˈkɔːt(ə)ri/ ▶ **noun** (pl. **-ies**) Medicine an instrument or a caustic substance used for cauterizing.
■ [mass noun] the action of cauterizing something.
– ORIGIN late Middle English: via Latin from Greek *kautērion* 'branding iron' (see **CAUTERIZE**).

caution ▶ **noun 1** [mass noun] care taken to avoid danger or mistakes: *anyone receiving a suspect package should exercise extreme caution.*
■ [count noun] chiefly Brit. an official or legal warning given to someone who has committed a minor offence but has not been charged, to the effect that further action will be taken if they commit another such offence: *they* **let him off with a caution**. ■ warning: *business advisers have sounded a note of caution.*
2 informal, dated an amusing or surprising person.
▶ **verb** [reporting verb] say something as a warning: [with clause] *the Chancellor cautioned that economic uncertainties remained* | [with direct speech] *'Be careful now,' I cautioned.*
■ [no obj.] (**caution against**) warn or advise against (doing something): *advisers have cautioned against tax increases.* ■ [with obj.] (often **be cautioned**) chiefly Brit. issue an official or legal warning to: *he* **was cautioned for** *possessing drugs.* ■ [with obj.] (of a police officer) advise (someone) of their legal rights when arresting them.
– PHRASES **err on the side of caution** take a comparatively safe course of action when presented with a choice. **throw caution to the wind** (or **winds**) act in a completely reckless manner. **under caution** having been told of one's legal rights when under arrest.
– ORIGIN Middle English (denoting bail or a guarantee; now chiefly Scots and US): from Latin *cautio(n-)*, from *cavere* 'take heed'.

cautionary ▶ **adjective** serving as a warning: *a cautionary tale.*

caution money ▶ **noun** [mass noun] Brit. money deposited, especially by a college student, as security for good conduct.

cautious ▶ **adjective** attentive to potential problems or dangers: *a cautious driver.*
■ (of an action) characterized by such an attitude: *the plan received a cautious welcome.*
– DERIVATIVES **cautiously** adverb, **cautiousness** noun.
– ORIGIN mid 17th cent.: from **CAUTION**, on the pattern of pairs such as *ambition, ambitious.*

Cauvery /ˈkɔːvəri/ (also **Kaveri**) a river in south India which rises in north Kerala and flows 765 km (475 miles) eastwards to the Bay of Bengal, south of Pondicherry. It is held sacred by Hindus.

cava /ˈkɑːvə/ ▶ **noun** [mass noun] a Spanish sparkling wine made in the same way as champagne.
– ORIGIN Spanish.

Cavafy /kəˈvɑːfi/, Constantine (Peter) (1863–1933), Greek poet; born *Konstantinos Petrou Kavafis*. His poems refer mainly to the Hellenistic and Graeco-Roman period of his native Alexandria.

cavalcade /ˌkav(ə)lˈkeɪd, ˈkav(ə)lkeɪd/ ▶ **noun** a formal procession of people walking, on horseback, or riding in vehicles.
– ORIGIN late 16th cent. (denoting a ride or raid on horseback): from French, from Italian *cavalcata*, from *cavalcare* 'to ride', based on Latin *caballus* 'horse'.

cavalier ▶ **noun 1** (**Cavalier**) historical a supporter of King Charles I in the English Civil War.
■ archaic or poetic/literary a courtly gentleman, especially one acting as a lady's escort. ■ archaic a horseman, especially a cavalryman.
2 (also **Cavalier King Charles**) a small spaniel of a breed with a long snout.
▶ **adjective** showing a lack of proper concern; offhand: *Anne was irritated by his cavalier attitude.*
– DERIVATIVES **cavalierly** adverb.
– ORIGIN mid 16th cent.: from French, from Italian *cavaliere*, based on Latin *caballus* 'horse': Compare with **CABALLERO** and **CHEVALIER**.

cavalry ▶ **noun** (pl. **-ies**) [usu. treated as pl.] historical soldiers who fought on horseback.
■ modern soldiers who fight in armoured vehicles.
– DERIVATIVES **cavalryman** noun (pl. **-men**).
– ORIGIN mid 16th cent.: from French *cavallerie*, from Italian *cavalleria*, from *cavallo* 'horse', from Latin *caballus*.

cavalry twill ▶ **noun** [mass noun] strong woollen twill used typically for making trousers and sportswear.

Cavan /ˈkav(ə)n/ a county of the Republic of Ireland, part of the old province of Ulster.
■ its county town; pop. 3,330 (1991).

cavatina /ˌkavəˈtiːnə/ ▶ **noun** (pl. **cavatine**) Music a short operatic aria in simple style without repeated sections.
■ a similar piece of lyrical instrumental music.
– ORIGIN early 19th cent.: from Italian.

cave[1] /keɪv/ ▶ **noun** a large underground chamber, typically of natural origin, in a hillside or cliff.
▶ **verb** [no obj.] **1** explore caves as a sport.
2 US short for *cave in* below.
– DERIVATIVES **cave-like** adjective, **caver** noun.
▶ **cave in** (or **cave something in**) (with reference to a roof or similar structure) subside or collapse or cause something to do this: *the ceiling caved in* | *Len's club would have caved his skull in.* ■ figurative yield or submit under pressure: *the manager* **caved in to** *his demands.*
– ORIGIN Middle English: from Old French, from Latin *cava*, from *cavus* 'hollow' (compare with **CAVERN**). The usage *cave in* may be from the synonymous dialect expression *calve in*, influenced by obsolete *cave* 'excavate, hollow out'.

cave[2] /keɪvi/ ▶ **exclamation** Brit. school slang, dated look out!
– PHRASES **keep cave** act as lookout.
– ORIGIN Latin, imperative of *cavere* 'beware'.

caveat /ˈkavɪat, ˈkeɪ-/ ▶ **noun** a warning or proviso of specific stipulations, conditions, or limitations.
■ Law a notice, especially in a probate, that certain actions may not be taken without informing the person who gave the notice.
– ORIGIN mid 16th cent.: from Latin, literally 'let a person beware'.

caveat emptor /ˈɛmptɔː/ ▶ **noun** the principle that the buyer alone is responsible for checking the quality and suitability of goods before a purchase is made.
– ORIGIN Latin, 'let the buyer beware'.

cave bear ▶ noun a large extinct bear of the Pleistocene epoch, whose remains are found commonly in caves throughout Europe.
● *Ursus spelaeus*, family Ursidae.

cave cricket ▶ noun another term for **CAMEL CRICKET**.

cave-dweller ▶ noun a caveman or cavewoman.

cavefish ▶ noun (pl. same or **-fishes**) a small colourless fish which lives only in limestone caves in North America. It has reduced or absent eyes, and the head and body are covered with papillae which are sensitive to vibration.
● Family Amblyopsidae: four genera, in particular *Amblyopsis* and *Typhlichthys*.

cave-in ▶ noun a collapse of a roof or similar structure, typically underground: *a mine cave-in.*
■ [in sing.] figurative an instance of yielding or submitting under pressure: *the government's cave-in to industry pressure.*

Cavell /ˈkav(ə)l/, Edith (Louisa) (1865–1915), English nurse. During the First World War she helped Allied soldiers to escape from occupied Belgium. She was subsequently executed by the Germans and became a heroine of the Allied cause.

caveman ▶ noun (pl. **-men**) a prehistoric man who lived in caves.
■ a man whose behaviour is uncivilized or violent: [as modifier] *you can't change my mind by caveman tactics.*

Cavendish /ˈkav(ə)ndɪʃ/, Henry (1731–1810), English chemist and physicist. He identified hydrogen, studied carbon dioxide, and determined their densities relative to atmospheric air. He also established that water is a compound, and determined the density of the earth.

cavendish /ˈkav(ə)ndɪʃ/ ▶ noun [mass noun] tobacco softened, sweetened, and formed into cakes.
– ORIGIN mid 19th cent.: probably from the surname *Cavendish*.

cave painting ▶ noun a prehistoric picture on the interior of a cave, often depicting animals.

cavern /ˈkav(ə)n/ ▶ noun a cave, or a chamber in a cave, typically a large one.
■ used in similes and comparisons to refer to a vast, dark space: *a dark cavern of a shop.*
– ORIGIN late Middle English: from Old French *caverne* or from Latin *caverna*, from *cavus* 'hollow'. Compare with **CAVE**[1].

cavernous ▶ adjective like a cavern in size, shape, or atmosphere: *a dismal cavernous hall.*
■ figurative giving the impression of vast, dark depths: *his cavernous eyes.*
– DERIVATIVES **cavernously** adverb.
– ORIGIN late Middle English: from Old French *caverneux* or Latin *cavernosus* (from *caverna* 'cavern').

cave salamander ▶ noun a cave-dwelling salamander with pinkish to brown skin.
● Several genera and species in the family Plethodontidae, including the North American *Eurycea lucifuga* and the European genus *Hydromantes*.

cavesson /ˈkavɪs(ə)n/ ▶ noun (also **lungeing cavesson**) a type of heavy bridle, which lacks a bit and has a thick noseband fitted with rings to which a lunge rein may be attached.
■ (also **cavesson noseband**) a simple noseband on a horse's bridle, which does not affect the action of the bit or bridle.
– ORIGIN late 16th cent.: from French *caveçon*, Italian *cavezzone*, based on Latin *caput* 'head'.

cavewoman ▶ noun (pl. **-women**) a prehistoric woman who lived in caves.

caviar /ˈkavɪɑː, ˌkavɪˈɑː/ (also **caviare**) ▶ noun [mass noun] the pickled roe of sturgeon or other large fish, eaten as a delicacy.
– PHRASES **caviar to the general** a good thing unappreciated by the ignorant.
– ORIGIN mid 16th cent.: from Italian *caviale* (earlier *caviaro*) or French *caviar*, probably from medieval Greek *khaviari*.

cavil /ˈkav(ə)l/ ▶ verb (**cavilled**, **cavilling**; US **caviled**, **caviling**) [no obj.] make petty or unnecessary objections: *they cavilled at the cost.*
▶ noun an objection of this kind.
– DERIVATIVES **caviller** noun.
– ORIGIN mid 16th cent.: from French *caviller*, from Latin *cavillari*, from *cavilla* 'mockery'.

caving ▶ noun [mass noun] the sport or pastime of exploring caves.

cavitation /ˌkavɪˈteɪʃ(ə)n/ ▶ noun [mass noun] Physics the formation of an empty space within a solid object or body.
■ the formation of bubbles in a liquid, typically by the movement of a propeller through it.

cavity ▶ noun (pl. **-ies**) an empty space within a solid object, in particular the human body: *the abdominal cavity.*
■ a decayed part of a tooth.
– DERIVATIVES **cavitary** adjective.
– ORIGIN mid 16th cent.: from French *cavité* or late Latin *cavitas*, from Latin *cavus* 'hollow'.

cavity wall ▶ noun a wall formed from two thicknesses of brickwork or blockwork with a space between them.

cavort ▶ verb [no obj.] jump or dance around excitedly: *the players cavorted about the pitch.*
■ informal apply oneself enthusiastically to sexual or disreputable pursuits: *he spent his nights cavorting with the glitterati.*
– ORIGIN late 18th cent. (originally US): perhaps an alteration of **CURVET**.

Cavour /kaˈvuə/, Camillo Benso, Conte di (1810–61), Italian statesman. A supporter of Italian unification under Victor Emmanuel II, he was Premier of Piedmont (1852–59; 1860–1), and in 1861 became the first Premier of a unified Italy.

cavy /ˈkeɪvi/ ▶ noun (pl. **-ies**) a South American rodent with a sturdy body and vestigial tail.
● Family Caviidae: five genera and several species, in particular the guinea pig. The **Patagonian cavy** is the mara.
– ORIGIN late 18th cent.: from modern Latin *cavia*, from Galibi *cabiai*.

caw ▶ noun the harsh cry of a rook, crow, or similar bird.
▶ verb [no obj.] utter such a cry.
– ORIGIN late 16th cent.: imitative.

Cawley /ˈkɔːli/, Evonne (Fay) (b.1951), Australian tennis player; born *Evonne Fay Goolagong*. She won two Wimbledon singles titles (1971; 1980) and was three times Australian singles champion (1974–6).

Cawnpore /kɔːnˈpɔː/ variant spelling of **KANPUR**.

Caxton, William (*c.*1422–91), the first English printer. He printed the first book in English in 1474 and went on to produce about eighty other texts, including editions of *Le Morte d'Arthur* and *Canterbury Tales*.

cay /keɪ, kiː/ ▶ noun a low bank or reef of coral, rock, or sand, especially one on the islands in Spanish America. Compare with **KEY**[2].
– ORIGIN late 17th cent.: from Spanish *cayo* 'shoal, reef', from French *quai* 'quay'.

Cayenne /keɪˈɛn/ the capital and chief port of French Guiana; pop. 41,600 (1990).

cayenne /keɪˈɛn/ (also **cayenne pepper**) ▶ noun [mass noun] a pungent hot-tasting red powder prepared from ground dried chilli peppers.
– ORIGIN early 18th cent.: from Tupi *kyynha*, *quiynha*, later associated with **CAYENNE**.

Cayley[1] /ˈkeɪli/, Arthur (1821–95), English mathematician and barrister. He wrote almost a thousand mathematical papers, including articles on determinants, group theory, and the algebra of matrices. The **Cayley numbers**, a generalization of complex numbers, are named after him.

Cayley[2] /ˈkeɪli/, Sir George (1773–1857), British engineer, the father of British aeronautics. He is best known for his understanding of the principles of flight and for building the first manned glider, which was flown in 1853. He was also a founder of the original Polytechnic Institution.

cayman ▶ noun variant spelling of **CAIMAN**.

Cayman Islands /ˈkeɪmən/ (also **the Caymans**) a group of three islands in the Caribbean Sea, south of Cuba; pop. 31,930 (est. 1994); official language, English; capital, George Town. The Cayman Islands are a British dependency.

Cayuga /ˈkeɪjʊɡə, ˈkʌɪ-/ ▶ noun (pl. same or **Cayugas**) 1 a member of an American Indian people, one of the five of the original Iroquois confederacy, formerly inhabiting part of New York State.
2 [mass noun] the extinct Iroquoian language of this people.
▶ adjective of or relating to this people or their language.
– ORIGIN from an Iroquoian place name.

Cayuse /ˈkʌɪjuːs/ ▶ noun (pl. same or **Cayuses**) 1 a member of an American Indian people of Washington State and Oregon.
2 [mass noun] the extinct Penutian language of this people.
3 (**cayuse**) an American Indian pony.
■ N. Amer. informal a horse.
▶ adjective of or relating to this people or their language.
– ORIGIN the name in Chinook Jargon.

CB ▶ abbreviation for ■ Citizens' Band (radio frequencies). ■ (in the UK) Companion of the Order of the Bath.

CBC ▶ abbreviation for Canadian Broadcasting Corporation.

CBE ▶ abbreviation for (in the UK) Commander of the Order of the British Empire.

CBI ▶ abbreviation for Confederation of British Industry.

CBS ▶ abbreviation for (in the US) Columbia Broadcasting System.

CC ▶ abbreviation for ■ Brit. City Council. ■ Companion of the Order of Canada. ■ Brit. County Council. ■ Brit. County Councillor. ■ Cricket Club.

cc (also **c.c.**) ▶ abbreviation for ■ carbon copy (used as an indication that a duplicate has been or should be sent to another person). ■ cubic centimetre(s).

CCD Electronics ▶ abbreviation for charge-coupled device, a high-speed semiconductor used chiefly in image detection.

CCK Biochemistry ▶ abbreviation for cholecystokinin.

CCTV ▶ abbreviation for closed-circuit television.

CD ▶ abbreviation for ■ civil defence. ■ compact disc. ■ corps diplomatique.

Cd ▶ symbol for the chemical element cadmium.

Cd. ▶ abbreviation for (in the UK) Command Paper (third series, 1900–18).

cd ▶ abbreviation for candela.

CDC ▶ abbreviation for ■ (in the US) Centers for Disease Control. ■ Commonwealth Development Corporation.

CD-I ▶ abbreviation for compact disc (interactive).

CDN ▶ abbreviation for Canada (international vehicle registration).

cDNA ▶ abbreviation for complementary DNA.

Cdr ▶ abbreviation for (in the navy or air force) Commander.

Cdre ▶ abbreviation for Commodore.

CD-ROM ▶ noun a compact disc used as a read-only optical memory device for a computer system.
– ORIGIN 1980s: acronym from *compact disc read-only memory*.

CDT ▶ abbreviation for ■ Central Daylight Time (see **CENTRAL TIME**). ■ craft, design, and technology, a subject taught in schools in the UK.

CD video (abbrev.: **CDV**) ▶ noun [mass noun] a video system in which both sound and picture are recorded on compact disc.

CE ▶ abbreviation for ■ Church of England. ■ civil engineer. ■ Common Era.

Ce ▶ symbol for the chemical element cerium.

ceanothus /ˌsiːəˈnəʊθəs/ ▶ noun a North American shrub which is cultivated for its dense clusters of small, typically blue, flowers.
● Genus *Ceanothus*, family Rhamnaceae.
– ORIGIN modern Latin, from Greek *keanōthos*, denoting a kind of thistle.

Ceará /seɪəˈrɑː/ a state in NE Brazil, on the Atlantic coast; capital, Fortaleza.

cease ▶ verb [no obj.] come to an end: *the hostilities had ceased and normal life was resumed* | [with infinitive] *on his retirement the job will cease to exist.*
■ [with obj.] bring (a specified action) to an end: *they were asked to cease all military activity.*
– PHRASES **never cease to** (in hyperbolic use) do something very frequently: *her exploits never cease to amaze me.* **without cease** without stopping.
– ORIGIN Middle English: from Old French *cesser*, from Latin *cessare* 'stop', from *cedere* 'to yield'.

ceasefire ▶ noun a temporary suspension of fighting, typically one during which peace talks take place; a truce.
■ an order or signal to stop fighting.

ceaseless ▶ adjective constant and unending: *the fort was subjected to ceaseless bombardment.*
– DERIVATIVES **ceaselessly** adverb.

Ceauşescu /tʃaʊˈʃɛskuː/, Nicolae (1918–89), Romanian communist statesman, first President of the Socialist Republic of Romania 1974–89. His regime became increasingly totalitarian and corrupt; a popular uprising in December 1989 resulted in its downfall and in his execution.

cebid /ˈsiːbɪd/ ▶ **noun** Zoology a primate of a family (Cebidae) that includes most of the New World monkeys.
– ORIGIN late 19th cent.: from modern Latin *Cebidae* (plural), from the genus name *Cebus*.

Cebu /sɪˈbuː/ an island of the south central Philippines.
■ its chief city and port; pop. 610,000 (1990).

Cecil /ˈsɛs(ə)l, ˈsɪs-/, William, see **BURGHLEY**.

Cecilia, St /sɪˈsiːljə/ (2nd or 3rd century), Roman martyr. According to legend, she took a vow of celibacy but when forced to marry converted her husband to Christianity and both were martyred. She is the patron saint of church music. Feast day, 22 November.

cecitis ▶ **noun** US spelling of **CAECITIS**.

cecropia /sɪˈkrəʊpɪə/ ▶ **noun** **1** a fast-growing tropical American tree which is typically among the first to colonize a cleared area. Many cecropias have a symbiotic relationship with ants.
● Genus *Cecropia*, family Cecropiaceae.
2 (also **cecropia moth**) a very large North American silk moth with boldly marked reddish-brown wings. The caterpillars feed on a variety of forest trees.
● *Platysamia* (or *Hyalophora*) *cecropia*, family Saturniidae.
– ORIGIN early 19th cent.: modern Latin, from the name *Cecrops*, a king of Attica.

cecum ▶ **noun** (pl. **ceca**) US spelling of **CAECUM**.

cedar ▶ **noun** any of a number of conifers which typically yield fragrant, durable timber, in particular:
● a large tree of the pine family (genus *Cedrus*, family Pinaceae), in particular the **cedar of Lebanon** (*C. libani*), with spreading branches, and the deodar. ● a tall slender North American or Asian tree (genus *Thuja*, family Cupressaceae), in particular the **western red cedar** (*T. plicata*).
– DERIVATIVES **cedarn** adjective (poetic/literary).
– ORIGIN Old English, from Old French *cedre* or Latin *cedrus*, from Greek *kedros*.

cede /siːd/ ▶ **verb** [with obj.] give up (power or territory): *they have had to **cede** ground **to** the government.*
– ORIGIN early 16th cent.: from French *céder* or Latin *cedere* 'to yield'.

cedi /ˈsiːdi/ ▶ **noun** (pl. same or **cedis**) the basic monetary unit of Ghana, equal to 100 pesewas.
– ORIGIN of Ghanaian origin, perhaps an alteration of **SHILLING**.

cedilla /sɪˈdɪlə/ ▶ **noun** a mark (̧) written under the letter *c*, especially in French, to show that it is pronounced like an *s* rather than a *k* (e.g. *façade*).
■ a similar mark under *s* in Turkish and other oriental languages.
– ORIGIN late 16th cent.: from obsolete Spanish, earlier form of *zedilla*, diminutive of *zeda* (the letter Z), from Greek *zēta*.

CEGB historical ▶ **abbreviation for** (in the UK) Central Electricity Generating Board.

ceiba /ˈsʌɪbə/ ▶ **noun** a very tall tropical American tree from which kapok is obtained, with lightweight yellowish or pinkish timber. It is pollinated by bats, and was held sacred by the Maya. Also called **KAPOK**.
● *Ceiba pentandra*, family Bombacaceae.
– ORIGIN via Spanish from Taino, literally 'giant tree'.

ceil /siːl/ ▶ **verb** [with obj.] (usu. **be ceiled**) archaic line or plaster the roof of (a building).
– ORIGIN late Middle English (in the sense 'line (the interior of a room) with plaster or panelling': perhaps related to Latin *celare*, French *céler* 'conceal'.

ceilidh /ˈkeɪli/ ▶ **noun** a social event at which there is Scottish or Irish folk music and singing, traditional dancing, and storytelling.
– ORIGIN late 19th cent.: from Scottish Gaelic *ceilidh* and Irish *céilidhe* (earlier form of *céilí*), from Old Irish *céilide* 'visit, visiting', from *céile* 'companion'.

ceiling ▶ **noun** **1** the upper interior surface of a room or other similar compartment.
■ figurative an upper limit, typically one set on prices, wages, or expenditure. See also **GLASS CEILING**. ■ the maximum altitude that a particular aircraft can reach. ■ the altitude of the base of a cloud layer.
2 the inside planking of a ship's bottom and sides.
– ORIGIN Middle English (denoting the action of lining the interior of a room with plaster or panelling): from **CEIL** + **-ING**[1]. Sense 1 dates from the mid 16th cent.

ceiling rose ▶ **noun** a circular mounting on a ceiling, through which the wiring of an electric light passes.

cel /sɛl/ ▶ **noun** a transparent sheet of celluloid or similar film material, which can be drawn on and used in the production of cartoons.
– ORIGIN mid 20th cent.: abbreviation of **CELLULOID**.

celadon /ˈsɛlədɒn/ ▶ **noun** [mass noun] a willow-green colour: [as modifier] *panelling painted in **celadon green**.*
■ a grey-green glaze used on pottery, especially that from China. ■ pottery made with this glaze.
– ORIGIN mid 18th cent.: from French *céladon*, a colour named after the hero in d'Urfé's pastoral romance *L'Astrée* (1607–27).

celandine /ˈsɛləndʌɪn/ (also **lesser celandine**) ▶ **noun** a common plant of the buttercup family which produces yellow flowers in the early spring, reproducing either by seed or by bulbils at the base of the stems. See also **GREATER CELANDINE**.
● *Ranunculus ficaria*, family Ranunculaceae.
– ORIGIN Middle English, from Old French *celidoine*, from medieval Latin *celidonia*, based on Greek *khelidōn* 'swallow' (the flowering of the plant being associated with the arrival of swallows).

-cele (also **-coele**) ▶ **combining form** Medicine denoting a swelling or hernia in a specified part: *meningocele*.
– ORIGIN from Greek *kēlē* 'tumour'.

celeb /sɪˈlɛb/ ▶ **noun** informal a celebrity: *a TV celeb.*
– ORIGIN early 20th cent. (originally US): abbreviation.

Celebes /ˈsɛlɪbiːz/ former name for **SULAWESI**.

Celebes sailfish ▶ **noun** see **SAILFISH**.

Celebes Sea a part of the western Pacific between the Philippines and Sulawesi, bounded to the west by Borneo. It is linked to the Java Sea by the Makassar Strait.

celebrant /ˈsɛlɪbr(ə)nt/ ▶ **noun** **1** a person who performs a rite, especially a priest at the Eucharist.
2 a person who celebrates something.
– ORIGIN mid 19th cent.: from French *célébrant* or Latin *celebrant-* 'celebrating', from the verb *celebrare* (see **CELEBRATE**).

celebrate ▶ **verb** [with obj.] **1** mark (a significant or happy day or event), typically with a social gathering.
■ [no obj.] do something enjoyable to mark such an occasion: *she celebrated with a glass of schnapps.* ■ reach (a birthday or anniversary).
2 perform (a religious ceremony) publicly and duly, in particular officiate at (the Eucharist): *he celebrated holy communion.*
3 honour or praise publicly: *a film celebrating the actor's career* | [as adj. **celebrated**] *a celebrated mathematician.*
– DERIVATIVES **celebrator** noun, **celebratory** adjective.
– ORIGIN late Middle English (in sense 2): from Latin *celebrat-* 'celebrated', from the verb *celebrare*, from *celeber*, *celebr-* 'frequented or honoured'.

celebration ▶ **noun** [mass noun] the action of marking one's pleasure at an important event or occasion by engaging in enjoyable, typically social, activity: *the birth of his son was a cause for celebration* | [count noun] *a birthday celebration.*
– ORIGIN early 16th cent.: from Latin *celebratio(n-)*, from the verb *celebrare* (see **CELEBRATE**).

celebrity ▶ **noun** (pl. **-ies**) a famous person.
■ [mass noun] the state of being well known: *his prestige and celebrity grew.*
– ORIGIN late Middle English (in the sense 'solemn ceremony'): from Old French *celebrite* or Latin *celebritas*, from *celeber*, *celebr-* 'frequented or honoured'.

celeriac /sɪˈlɛrɪak/ ▶ **noun** [mass noun] celery of a variety which forms a large swollen turnip-like root which can be eaten cooked or raw as a salad.
– ORIGIN mid 18th cent.: from **CELERY** + an arbitrary use of **-AC**.

celerity /sɪˈlɛrɪti/ ▶ **noun** [mass noun] archaic or poetic/literary swiftness of movement.
– ORIGIN late 15th cent.: from Old French *celerite*, from Latin *celeritas*, from *celer* 'swift'.

celery ▶ **noun** [mass noun] a cultivated plant of the parsley family, with closely packed succulent leaf stalks which are blanched and used as a salad or cooked vegetable.
● *Apium graveolens* var. *dulce*, family Umbelliferae.
– ORIGIN mid 17th cent.: from French *céleri*, from Italian dialect *selleri*, based on Greek *selinon* 'parsley'.

celery pine (also **celery-top pine**) ▶ **noun** a slow-growing evergreen tree with shoots that resemble celery leaves. It grows from Borneo to New Zealand and is used as a source of timber and red dye.
● Genus *Phyllocladus*, family Phyllocladaceae.

celery salt ▶ **noun** [mass noun] a mixture of salt and ground celery seed used for seasoning.

celesta /sɪˈlɛstə/ ▶ **noun** a small keyboard instrument in which felted hammers strike a row of steel plates suspended over wooden resonators, giving an ethereal bell-like sound.
– ORIGIN late 19th cent.: pseudo-Latin, based on French *céleste* 'heavenly'.

celeste /sɪˈlɛst/ ▶ **noun** **1** short for **VOIX CELESTE**.
2 another term for **CELESTA**.
– ORIGIN late 19th cent.: from French *céleste* 'heavenly', from Latin *caelestis*, from *caelum* 'heaven'.

celestial ▶ **adjective** [attrib.] positioned in or relating to the sky, or outer space as observed in astronomy: *a celestial body.*
■ belonging or relating to heaven: *the celestial city.* ■ supremely good: *the celestial beauty of music.*
– DERIVATIVES **celestially** adverb.
– ORIGIN late Middle English: via Old French from medieval Latin *caelestialis*, from Latin *caelestis*, from *caelum* 'heaven'.

celestial bamboo ▶ **noun** another term for **NANDINA**.

celestial equator ▶ **noun** the projection into space of the earth's equator; an imaginary circle equidistant from the celestial poles.

celestial globe ▶ **noun** a spherical representation of the sky showing the constellations.

celestial latitude ▶ **noun** Astronomy the angular distance of a point north or south of the ecliptic. Compare with **DECLINATION** (in sense 1).

celestial longitude ▶ **noun** Astronomy the angular distance of a point east of the First Point of Aries, measured along the ecliptic. Compare with **RIGHT ASCENSION**.

celestial mechanics ▶ **plural noun** [treated as sing.] the branch of theoretical astronomy that deals with the calculation of the motions of celestial objects such as planets.

celestial navigation ▶ **noun** [mass noun] the action of finding one's way by observing the sun, moon, and stars.

celestial pole ▶ **noun** Astronomy the point on the celestial sphere directly above either of the earth's geographic poles, around which the stars and planets appear to rotate during the course of the night. The north celestial pole is currently within one degree of the star Polaris.

celestial sphere ▶ **noun** an imaginary sphere of which the observer is the centre and on which all celestial objects are considered to lie.

celiac ▶ **noun** US spelling of **COELIAC**.

celibate /ˈsɛlɪbət/ ▶ **adjective** abstaining from marriage and sexual relations, typically for religious reasons: *a celibate priest.*
■ having or involving no sexual relations: *I'd rather stay single and celibate.*
▶ **noun** a person who abstains from marriage and sexual relations.
– DERIVATIVES **celibacy** noun.
– ORIGIN early 19th cent.: from *celibacy*, on the pattern of pairs such as *magistracy*, *magistrate*.

Céline /seɪˈliːn/, Louis-Ferdinand (1894–1961), French novelist; pseudonym of *Louis-Ferdinand Destouches*. He is best known for his autobiographical novel, the satirical *Voyage au bout de la nuit* (1932).

cell ▶ **noun** **1** a small room in which a prisoner is locked up or in which a monk or nun sleeps.
■ a small compartment in a larger structure such as a honeycomb. ■ historical a small monastery or nunnery dependent on a larger one.
2 Biology the smallest structural and functional unit of an organism, which is typically microscopic and

consists of cytoplasm and a nucleus enclosed in a membrane. Microscopic organisms typically consist of a single cell, which is either eukaryotic or prokaryotic.
■an enclosed cavity in an organism. ■ figurative a small group forming a nucleus of political activity, typically a secret, subversive one: *the weapons may be used to arm terrorist cells*. ■ the local area covered by one of the short-range transmitters in a cellular telephone system.
3 a device containing electrodes immersed in an electrolyte, used for current-generation or electrolysis.
■a unit in a device for converting chemical or solar energy into electricity.
– DERIVATIVES **celled** adjective [in combination] *a single-celled organism*, **cell-like** adjective.
– ORIGIN Old English, from Old French *celle* or Latin *cella* 'storeroom or chamber'.

cella /ˈkɛlə/ ▶ noun (pl. **cellae** /-liː/) the inner area of an ancient temple, especially one housing the hidden cult image in a Greek or Roman temple.
– ORIGIN Latin.

cellar ▶ noun a room below ground level in a house, typically one used for storing wine or coal.
■a stock of wine.
▶ verb [with obj.] store (wine) in a cellar.
– ORIGIN Middle English (in the general sense 'storeroom'): from Old French *celier*, from late Latin *cellarium* 'storehouse', from *cella* 'storeroom or chamber'.

cellarage ▶ noun [mass noun] cellars collectively.
■money charged for the use of a cellar or storehouse.

cellarer /ˈsɛlərə/ ▶ noun the person in a monastery who is responsible for provisioning and catering.
■a cellarman.

cellaret /ˌsɛləˈrɛt/ (US also **cellarette**) ▶ noun historical a cabinet or sideboard for keeping alcoholic drinks and glasses in a dining room.

cellarman ▶ noun (pl. **-men**) Brit. a person in charge of a wine cellar.

cell block ▶ noun a large single building or part of a complex subdivided into separate prison cells.

Cellini /tʃɛˈliːni/, Benvenuto (1500–71), Italian goldsmith and sculptor, the most renowned goldsmith of his day.

cell line ▶ noun Biology a cell culture developed from a single cell and therefore consisting of cells with a uniform genetic make-up.

cell-mediated ▶ adjective Physiology denoting the aspect of an immune response involving the action of white blood cells, rather than that of circulating antibodies. Often contrasted with **HUMORAL**.

cello /ˈtʃɛləʊ/ ▶ noun (pl. **-os**) a bass instrument of the violin family, held upright on the floor between the legs of the seated player.
– DERIVATIVES **cellist** noun.
– ORIGIN late 19th cent.: shortening of **VIOLONCELLO**.

cellophane /ˈsɛləfeɪn/ ▶ noun trademark a thin transparent wrapping material made from viscose.
– ORIGIN early 20th cent.: from **CELLULOSE** + *-phane*, from *diaphane*, a kind of semi-transparent woven silk (from medieval Latin *diaphanus* 'diaphanous').

cellphone ▶ noun another term for **MOBILE PHONE**.

cellular /ˈsɛljʊlə/ ▶ adjective **1** of, relating to, or consisting of living cells: *cellular proliferation*.
2 denoting or relating to a mobile telephone system that uses a number of short-range radio stations to cover the area that it serves, the signal being automatically switched from one station to another as the user travels about.
3 (of a fabric item, such as a blanket or vest) knitted so as to form holes or hollows that trap air and provide extra insulation.
4 consisting of small compartments or rooms: *cellular accommodation*.
– DERIVATIVES **cellularity** noun.
– ORIGIN mid 18th cent.: from French *cellulaire*, from modern Latin *cellularis*, from *cellula* 'little chamber', diminutive of *cella*.

cellular automaton ▶ noun (pl. **cellular automata**) Computing one of a set of units in a mathematical model which have simple rules governing their replication and destruction. They are used to model complex systems composed of simple units such as living things or parallel processors.

cellulase /ˈsɛljʊleɪz/ ▶ noun [mass noun] Biochemistry an enzyme that converts cellulose into glucose or a disaccharide.
– ORIGIN early 20th cent.: from **CELLULOSE** + **-ASE**.

cellulite /ˈsɛljʊlʌɪt/ ▶ noun [mass noun] persistent subcutaneous fat causing dimpling of the skin, especially on women's hips and thighs. Not in technical use.
– ORIGIN 1960s: from French, from *cellule* 'small cell'.

cellulitis ▶ noun [mass noun] Medicine inflammation of subcutaneous connective tissue.

celluloid ▶ noun [mass noun] a transparent flammable plastic made in sheets from camphor and nitrocellulose, formerly used for cinematographic film.
■the cinema as a genre: *having made the leap from theatre to celluloid, she can now make more money*.
– ORIGIN mid 19th cent.: from **CELLULOSE** + **-OID**.

cellulose /ˈsɛljʊləʊz, -s/ ▶ noun [mass noun] **1** an insoluble substance which is the main constituent of plant cell walls and of vegetable fibres such as cotton. It is a polysaccharide consisting of chains of glucose monomers.
2 paint or lacquer consisting principally of cellulose acetate or nitrate in solution.
– DERIVATIVES **cellulosic** adjective.
– ORIGIN mid 19th cent.: from French, from *cellule* 'small cell' + **-OSE**[2].

cellulose acetate ▶ noun [mass noun] Chemistry a non-flammable thermoplastic polymer made by acetylating cellulose, used as the basis of artificial fibres and plastic.

cellulose nitrate ▶ noun another term for **NITROCELLULOSE**.

cellulose triacetate ▶ noun see **TRIACETATE**.

cell wall ▶ noun Biology a rigid layer of polysaccharides lying outside the plasma membrane of the cells of plants, fungi, and bacteria. In the algae and higher plants it consists mainly of cellulose.

celosia /sɪˈləʊsɪə, -ʃə/ ▶ noun a plant of a genus that includes cockscomb.
● Genus *Celosia*, family Amarantaceae.
– ORIGIN modern Latin, from Greek *kēlos* 'burnt or dry' (from the burnt appearance of the flowers in some species).

Celsius[1] /ˈsɛlsɪəs/, Anders (1701–44), Swedish astronomer, best known for his temperature scale.

Celsius[2] /ˈsɛlsɪəs/ (abbrev.: **C**) ▶ adjective [postpositive when used with a numeral] of or denoting a scale of temperature on which water freezes at 0° and boils at 100° under standard conditions.
▶ noun (also **Celsius scale**) this scale of temperature.

USAGE **Celsius** rather than **centigrade** is the standard accepted term when giving temperatures: use *25° **Celsius*** rather than *25° **centigrade***.

Celt /kɛlt, s-/ ▶ noun a member of a group of peoples inhabiting much of Europe and Asia Minor in pre-Roman times. Their culture developed in the late Bronze Age around the upper Danube, and reached its height in the La Tène culture (5th to 1st centuries BC) before being overrun by the Romans and various Germanic peoples.
■a native of any of the modern nations or regions in which Celtic languages are (or were until recently) spoken; a person of Irish, Highland Scottish, Manx, Welsh, or Cornish descent.
– ORIGIN from Latin *Celtae* (plural), from Greek *Keltoi*; in later use from French *Celte* 'Breton' (taken as representing the ancient Gauls).

celt /sɛlt/ ▶ noun Archaeology a prehistoric stone or metal implement with a bevelled cutting edge, probably used as a tool or weapon.
– ORIGIN early 18th cent.: from medieval Latin *celtis* 'chisel'.

Celtiberian /ˌkɛltɪˈbɪərɪən, -tʌɪ-, ˌsɛlt-/ ▶ noun another term for **IBERIAN** (in sense 3 of the noun).

Celtic /ˈkɛltɪk, ˈs-/ ▶ adjective of or relating to the Celts or their languages, which constitute a branch of the Indo-European family and include Irish, Scottish Gaelic, Welsh, Breton, Manx, Cornish, and several extinct pre-Roman languages such as Gaulish.
▶ noun [mass noun] the Celtic language group. See also **P-CELTIC**, **Q-CELTIC**.
– DERIVATIVES **Celticism** /-sɪz(ə)m/ noun.
– ORIGIN late 16th cent.: from Latin *Celticus* (from *Celtae* 'Celts'), or from French *Celtique* (from *Celte* 'Breton').

USAGE **Celt** and **Celtic** can be pronounced either with an initial k- or s-, but in standard English the normal pronunciation is with a k-, except in the name of the Glaswegian football club.

Celtic Church the Christian Church in the British Isles from its foundation in the 2nd or 3rd century until its assimilation into the Roman Catholic Church (664 in England; 12th century in Wales, Scotland, and Ireland).

Celtic cross ▶ noun a Latin cross with a circle round the centre.

Celtic fringe ▶ noun the Highland Scots, Irish, Welsh, and Cornish in relation to the rest of Britain.
■the land inhabited by these peoples.

Celtic harp ▶ noun another term for **CLARSACH**. Compare with **WELSH HARP**.

Celtic Sea the part of the Atlantic Ocean between southern Ireland and SW England.

cembalo /ˈtʃɛmbaləʊ/ ▶ noun (pl. **-os**) another term for **HARPSICHORD**.
– DERIVATIVES **cembalist** noun.
– ORIGIN mid 19th cent.: from Italian, shortening of *clavicembalo*, from medieval Latin *clavicymbalum*, from Latin *clavis* 'key' + *cymbalum* 'cymbal'.

cement ▶ noun [mass noun] a powdery substance made by calcining lime and clay, mixed with water to form mortar or mixed with sand, gravel, and water to make concrete.
■a soft glue that hardens on setting: *tile cement*. ■ figurative a factor or element that unites a group of people: *traditional entertainment was a form of community cement*. ■ a substance for filling cavities in teeth. ■ (also **cementum**) Anatomy a thin layer of bony material that fixes teeth to the jaw. ■ Geology the material which binds particles together in sedimentary rock.
▶ verb [with obj.] fix with cement.
■figurative settle or establish firmly: *the two firms are expected to cement an agreement soon*. ■ Geology (of a material) bind (particles) together in sedimentary rock.
– DERIVATIVES **cementer** noun.
– ORIGIN Middle English: from Old French *ciment* (noun), *cimenter* (verb), from Latin *caementum* 'quarry stone', from *caedere* 'hew'.

cementation /ˌsiːmɛnˈteɪʃ(ə)n/ ▶ noun [mass noun] **1** chiefly Geology the binding together of particles or other things by cement.
2 Metallurgy a process of altering a metal by heating it in contact with a powdered solid, especially an old method of making steel by heating iron in contact with charcoal.

cementite /sɪˈmɛntʌɪt/ ▶ noun [mass noun] Metallurgy a hard, brittle iron carbide present in cast iron and most steels.
● Chem. formula: Fe_3C.
– ORIGIN late 19th cent.: from **CEMENT** + **-ITE**[1].

cementitious /ˌsiːmɛnˈtɪʃəs/ ▶ adjective of the nature of cement.

cement mixer (also **concrete mixer**) ▶ noun a machine with a revolving drum used for mixing cement with sand, gravel, and water to make concrete.

cemetery ▶ noun (pl. **-ies**) a burial ground, especially one not in a churchyard: *a military cemetery*.
– ORIGIN late Middle English: via late Latin from Greek *koimētērion* 'dormitory', from *koiman* 'put to sleep'.

cenacle /ˈsɛnək(ə)l/ ▶ noun **1** a group of people such as a discussion group or literary clique.
2 the room in which the Last Supper was held.
– ORIGIN late Middle English: from Old French *cenacle*, from Latin *cenaculum*, from *cena* 'dinner'.

CEng ▶ abbreviation for (in the UK) chartered engineer.

cenobite ▶ noun variant spelling of **COENOBITE**.

cenotaph /ˈsɛnətɑːf, -taf/ ▶ noun a monument to someone buried elsewhere, especially one commemorating people who died in a war.
– ORIGIN early 17th cent.: from French *cénotaphe*, from late Latin *cenotaphium*, from Greek *kenos* 'empty' + *taphos* 'tomb'.

Cenozoic /ˌsiːnəˈzəʊɪk/ (also **Cainozoic**) ▶ adjective Geology of, relating to, or denoting the most recent era, following the Mesozoic era and comprising the Tertiary and Quaternary periods.

■ [as noun **the Cenozoic**] the Cenozoic era, or the system of rocks deposited during it.

> The Cenozoic has lasted from about 65 million years ago to the present day. It has seen the rapid evolution and rise to dominance of mammals, birds, and flowering plants.

– ORIGIN mid 19th cent.: from Greek *kainos* 'new' + *zōion* 'animal' + -IC.

cense /sɛns/ ▶ verb [with obj.] ritually perfume (something) with the odour of burning incense.
– ORIGIN late Middle English: from Old French *encenser*.

censer ▶ noun a container in which incense is burnt, typically during a religious ceremony.
– ORIGIN Middle English: from Old French *censier*, from *encensier*, from *encens* (see INCENSE¹).

censor ▶ noun **1** an official who examines material that is about to be published, such as books, films, news, and art, and suppresses any parts that are considered obscene, politically unacceptable, or a threat to security.
■ Psychoanalysis an aspect of the superego which is said to prevent certain ideas and memories from emerging into consciousness. [ORIGIN: from a mistranslation of German *Zensur* 'censorship', coined by Freud.]
2 (in ancient Rome) either of two magistrates who held censuses and supervised public morals.
▶ verb [with obj.] examine (a book, film, etc.) officially and suppress unacceptable parts of it.
– DERIVATIVES **censorial** adjective.
– ORIGIN mid 16th cent. (in sense 2): from Latin, from *censere* 'assess'.

censorious /sɛnˈsɔːrɪəs/ ▶ adjective severely critical of others: *he was not censorious of other people.*
– DERIVATIVES **censoriously** adverb, **censoriousness** noun.
– ORIGIN mid 16th cent.: from Latin *censorius* (from *censor* 'magistrate') + -IOUS.

censorship ▶ noun [mass noun] the practice of officially examining books, films, etc. and suppressing unacceptable parts.

censure /ˈsɛnʃə/ ▶ verb [with obj.] (often **be censured**) express severe disapproval of (someone or something), typically in a formal statement.
▶ noun [mass noun] the expression of formal disapproval: *two MPs were singled out for censure* | [count noun] *despite episcopal censures, the practice continued.*
– DERIVATIVES **censurable** adjective.
– ORIGIN late Middle English (in the sense 'judicial sentence': from Old French *censurer* (verb), *censure* (noun), from Latin *censura* 'judgement, assessment', from *censere* 'assess'.

census ▶ noun (pl. **censuses**) an official count or survey of a population or of a class of things, typically recording various details of individuals: *a traffic census* | [as modifier] *census data.*
– ORIGIN early 17th cent. (denoting a poll tax): from Latin, applied to the registration of citizens and property in ancient Rome, usually for taxation, from *censere* 'assess'. The current sense dates from the mid 18th cent.

cent ▶ noun **1** a monetary unit in various countries, equal to one hundredth of a dollar or other decimal currency unit.
■ a coin of this value. ■ informal a small sum of money: *she saved every cent possible.* ■ [in sing.] [with negative] informal used for emphasis to denote no money at all: *he hadn't yet earned a cent.*
2 Music one hundredth of a semitone.
– ORIGIN late Middle English (in the sense 'a hundred'): from French *cent*, Italian *cento*, or Latin *centum* 'hundred'.

cent. ▶ abbreviation for century.

centas /ˈsɛntas/ ▶ noun (pl. same) a monetary unit of Lithuania, equal to one hundredth of a litas.
– ORIGIN Lithuanian.

centaur /ˈsɛntɔː/ ▶ noun Greek Mythology a member of a group of creatures with the head, arms, and torso of a man and the body and legs of a horse.
– ORIGIN via Latin from Greek *kentauros*, the Greek name for a Thessalonian tribe of expert horsemen; of unknown ultimate origin.

centaurea /sɛnˈtɔːrɪə, ˌsɛntɔːˈriːə/ ▶ noun a plant of a Eurasian genus which includes the cornflower and knapweed. Several kinds are cultivated for their bright flowers.
● Genus *Centaurea*, family Compositae.

– ORIGIN modern Latin based on Greek *kentauros* 'centaur' (see CENTAURY).

Centaurus /sɛnˈtɔːrəs/ Astronomy a large southern constellation (the Centaur). It lies in the Milky Way and contains the stars Alpha and Proxima Centauri.
■ [as genitive **Centauri** /sɛnˈtɔːriː/] used with preceding letter or numeral to designate a star in this constellation: *the star Lambda Centauri.*
– ORIGIN Latin.

centaury /ˈsɛntɔːri/ ▶ noun (pl. -ies) a widely distributed herbaceous plant of the gentian family, typically having pink flowers.
● *Centaurium* and related genera, family Gentianaceae: many species, including the **common centaury** (*C. minus*) and the cultivated ornamental *C. scilloides*.
– ORIGIN late Middle English: from late Latin *centaurea*, based on Greek *kentauros* 'centaur' (because its medicinal properties were said to have been discovered by the centaur Chiron).

centavo /sɛnˈtɑːvəʊ/ ▶ noun (pl. -os) a monetary unit of Mexico, Brazil, and certain other countries (formerly including Portugal), equal to one hundredth of the basic unit.
– ORIGIN Spanish and Portuguese, from Latin *centum* 'a hundred'.

Centcom ▶ abbreviation for Central Command.

centenarian /ˌsɛntɪˈnɛːrɪən/ ▶ noun a person who is a hundred or more years old.
▶ adjective [attrib.] a hundred or more years old.

centenary /sɛnˈtiːnəri, -ˈtɛn-/ chiefly Brit. ▶ noun (pl. -ies) the hundredth anniversary of a significant event.
■ a celebration of such an anniversary.
▶ adjective of or relating to a hundredth anniversary.
– ORIGIN early 17th cent. (denoting a century): from Latin *centenarius* 'containing a hundred', based on Latin *centum* 'a hundred'.

centennial /sɛnˈtɛnɪəl/ chiefly N. Amer. ▶ adjective of or relating to a hundredth anniversary.
▶ noun a hundredth anniversary.
– ORIGIN late 18th cent.: from Latin *centum* 'a hundred', on the pattern of *biennial*.

Centennial State informal name for COLORADO.

center ▶ noun US spelling of CENTRE.

centerboard ▶ noun US spelling of CENTREBOARD.

centerfield ▶ noun US spelling of CENTREFIELD.

centerfold ▶ noun US spelling of CENTREFOLD.

centering ▶ noun US spelling of CENTRING.

centesimal /sɛnˈtɛsɪm(ə)l/ ▶ adjective of or relating to division into hundredths.
– DERIVATIVES **centesimally** adverb.
– ORIGIN early 19th cent.: from Latin *centesimus* 'hundredth', from *centum* 'a hundred'.

centesimo /tʃɛnˈtɛsɪməʊ/ ▶ noun (pl. -os) a former monetary unit of Italy used only in calculations, worth one hundredth of a lira.
– ORIGIN Italian.

centésimo /sɛnˈtɛsɪməʊ, Spanish senˈtesimo, θen-/ ▶ noun (pl. -os) a monetary unit of Uruguay and Panama, equal to one hundredth of a peso in Uruguay, and one hundredth of a balboa in Panama.
– ORIGIN Spanish.

centi- ▶ combining form used commonly in units of measurement: **1** one hundredth: *centilitre.*
2 hundred: *centigrade* | *centipede.*
– ORIGIN from Latin *centum* 'hundred'.

centigrade ▶ adjective [postpositive when used with a numeral] another term for CELSIUS².
▶ noun (also **centigrade scale**) the Celsius scale of temperature.
– ORIGIN early 19th cent.: from French, from Latin *centum* 'a hundred' + *gradus* 'step'.

> **USAGE** In giving temperatures, use **Celsius** rather than **centigrade** in all contexts.

centigram (also **centigramme**) (abbrev.: **cg**) ▶ noun a metric unit of mass, equal to one hundredth of a gram.

centile /ˈsɛntʌɪl/ ▶ noun another term for PERCENTILE.

centilitre (US **centiliter**) (abbrev.: **cl**) ▶ noun a metric unit of capacity, equal to one hundredth of a litre.

centime /ˈsɒtiːm, French sɑ̃tim/ ▶ noun a monetary unit equal to one hundredth of a franc or some other decimal currency units (used in France,

Belgium, and Luxembourg until the introduction of the euro in 2002).
■ a coin of this value.
– ORIGIN French, from Latin *centesimus* 'hundredth', from *centum* 'a hundred'.

centimetre (US **centimeter**) (abbrev.: **cm**) ▶ noun a metric unit of length, equal to one hundredth of a metre.

centimetre-gram-second system ▶ noun a system of measurement using the centimetre, the gram, and the second as basic units of length, mass, and time respectively.

centimo /ˈsɛntɪməʊ, Spanish ˈθentimo, ˈsen-/ ▶ noun (pl. -os) a monetary unit of a number of Latin American countries (and formerly of Spain), equal to one hundredth of the basic unit.
– ORIGIN Spanish.

centimorgan /ˈsɛntɪˌmɔːɡ(ə)n/ (also **centiMorgan**) ▶ noun Genetics a map unit used to express the distance between two gene loci on a chromosome. A spacing of one centimorgan indicates a one per cent chance that two genes will be separated by crossing over.
– ORIGIN mid 20th cent.: from *centi-* (denoting a factor of one hundredth) + the name of T. H. *Morgan* (see MORGAN²).

centipede /ˈsɛntɪpiːd/ ▶ noun a predatory myriapod invertebrate with a flattened elongated body composed of many segments. Most segments bear a single pair of legs, the front pair being modified as poison fangs.
● Class Chilopoda: several orders.
– ORIGIN mid 17th cent.: from French *centipède* or Latin *centipeda*, from *centum* 'a hundred' + *pes, ped-* 'foot'.

cento /ˈsɛntəʊ/ ▶ noun (pl. -os) rare a literary work made up of quotations from other authors.
– ORIGIN early 17th cent.: Latin, 'patchwork garment', the original sense in English.

centra plural form of CENTRUM.

central ▶ adjective **1** at the point or in the area that is in the middle of something: *the station has a central courtyard* | *the apartments are very central.*
■ Phonetics (of a vowel) articulated in the centre of the mouth.
2 of the greatest importance; principal or essential: *his preoccupation with American history is central to his work.*
■ [attrib.] (of a group or organization) having supreme power over a country or another organization.
■ [attrib.] (of power or authority) in the hands of such a group: *local councils are increasingly subject to central control.*
– DERIVATIVES **centrality** noun, **centrally** adverb.
– ORIGIN mid 17th cent.: from French, or from Latin *centralis*, from *centrum* (see CENTRE).

Central African Republic a country of central Africa; pop. 3,113,000 (est. 1991); languages, French (official), Sango; capital, Bangui. Formerly a French colony, it became a republic within the French Community in 1958 and a fully independent state in 1960. Former name (until 1958) UBANGHI SHARI.

Central America the southernmost part of North America, linking the continent to South America and consisting of the countries of Guatemala, Belize, Honduras, El Salvador, Nicaragua, Costa Rica, and Panama.
– DERIVATIVES **Central American** adjective & noun.

central bank ▶ noun a national bank that provides financial and banking services for its country's government and commercial banking system, as well as implementing the government's monetary policy and issuing currency.

Central Command (abbrev.: **Centcom**) a US military strike force consisting of units from the army, air force, and navy, established in 1979 (as the Rapid Deployment Force) to operate in the Middle East and North Africa.

Central Criminal Court official name for OLD BAILEY.

Central European Time (abbrev.: **CET**) the standard time based on the mean solar time at the meridian 15° E, used in central and western continental Europe. It is one hour ahead of GMT.

central heating ▶ noun [mass noun] a system for warming a building by heating water or air in one place and circulating it through pipes and radiators or vents.

Central Intelligence Agency (abbrev.: **CIA**) a federal agency in the US responsible for coordinating government intelligence activities. Established in 1947 and originally intended to operate only overseas, it has since also operated in the US.

centralism ▶ noun [mass noun] control of disparate activities and organizations under a single authority.
– DERIVATIVES **centralist** noun & adjective.

centralize (also **-ise**) ▶ verb [with obj.] [often as adj. **centralized**] concentrate (control of an activity or organization) under a single authority: *a highly centralized country.*
■bring (activities) together in one place.
– DERIVATIVES **centralization** noun.

central limit theorem ▶ noun Statistics a theorem that states that the distribution of the mean of a very large number of random variables tends to a normal distribution.

central locking ▶ noun [mass noun] a locking system in a motor vehicle which enables the locks of all doors to be operated simultaneously.

central nervous system ▶ noun Anatomy the complex of nerve tissues that controls the activities of the body. In vertebrates it comprises the brain and spinal cord.

Central Park a large public park in the centre of Manhattan in New York City.

Central Powers the alliance of Germany, Austria–Hungary, Turkey, and Bulgaria during the First World War.
■the alliance of Germany, Austria–Hungary, and Italy between 1882 and 1914.

central processing unit (also **central processor**) (abbrev.: **CPU**) ▶ noun Computing the part of a computer in which operations are controlled and executed.

central reservation ▶ noun Brit. the strip of land between the carriageways of a motorway or other major road.

central tendency ▶ noun Statistics the tendency for the values of a random variable to cluster round its mean, mode, or median.

Central time the standard time in a zone that includes the central states of the US and parts of central Canada, specifically:
●(**Central Standard Time** abbrev.: **CST**) standard time based on the mean solar time at longitude 90° W., six hours behind GMT. ●(**Central Daylight Time** abbrev.: **CDT**) Central time during daylight saving, seven hours behind GMT.

Centre /'sõtr(ə), French sãtr/ a region of central France, including the cities of Orleans, Tours, and Chartres.

centre (US **center**) ▶ noun **1** the point that is equally distant from every point on the circumference of a circle or sphere.
■a point or part that is equally distant from all sides, ends, or surfaces of something: *the centre of the ceiling | the city centre.* ■a political party or group whose opinions avoid extremes. ■ the middle player in a line or group in certain team games. ■a kick, hit, or throw of the ball from the side to the middle of field in soccer, hockey, and other team games. ■ the filling in a chocolate: *truffles with liqueur centres.* ■a pivot or axis of rotation. ■a conical adjustable support for a workpiece in a lathe or similar machine.
2 a place or group of buildings where a specified activity is concentrated: *a centre for medical research | a conference centre.*
■a point at which an activity, process, or quality is at its most intense and from which it spreads: *the city was a centre of discontent.* ■the point to which an activity or process is directed or on which it is focused: *the director is at the centre of a row over policy.* ■ the most important place in the respect specified: *Geneva was then the centre of the international world.*
▶ verb **1** [no obj.] (**centre around/on**) have (something) as a major concern or theme: *the case centres around the couple's adopted children.*
■[with obj.] (**centre something around/on**) cause an argument or discussion to focus on (a specified issue): *he is centring his discussion on an analysis of patterns of mortality.* ■ (**be centred in**) (of an activity) occur mainly in or around (a specified place): *the textile industry was centred in Lancashire and Yorkshire.*
2 [with obj.] place in the middle: *to centre the needle, turn the knob.*
■[no obj.] (in soccer, hockey, and other team games) kick, hit, or throw the ball from the side to the

middle of the playing area. ■ [no obj.] chiefly N. Amer. play as the middle player of a line or group in certain team games.
– PHRASES **the centre of attention** a person or thing that excites everyone's interest or concern. **a centre of excellence** a place where the highest standards are maintained.
– DERIVATIVES **centremost** adjective.
– ORIGIN late Middle English: from Old French, or from Latin *centrum*, from Greek *kentron* 'sharp point, stationary point of a pair of compasses', related to *kentein* 'to prick'.

> **USAGE** The construction **centre round** or **centre around** (as opposed to **centre on**) has been denounced as incorrect since it first appeared in the middle of the 19th century. The argument is that it is illogical, since 'centre' designates a fixed point and the prepositions **around/round** are not used to refer to fixed points. The use is very well established, however, and, given the extension of the sense away from geometrical exactitude, it is difficult to sustain the argument that it is incorrect. A quarter of the citations in the Oxford Reading Programme for this sense are for the construction **centre around/round**.

centre back ▶ noun Soccer a defender who plays in the middle of the field.

centre bit ▶ noun a tool for boring cylindrical holes.

centreboard (US **centerboard**) ▶ noun a pivoted board that can be lowered through the keel of a sailing boat to reduce sideways movement.

centreboarder ▶ noun a sailing boat with a centreboard.

centred (US **centered**) ▶ adjective **1** [in combination] taking a specified subject as the most important or focal element: *a child-centred school.*
2 [in combination] (of a chocolate) having a centre or filling of a specified type: *a soft-centred chocolate.*
3 chiefly US (of a person) well balanced and confident or serene.
– DERIVATIVES **centredness** noun.

centrefield (US **centerfield**) ▶ noun Baseball the central part of the outfield.
– DERIVATIVES **centrefielder** noun.

centrefire ▶ adjective [attrib.] (of a gun cartridge) having the primer in the centre of the base.
■(of a gun) using such cartridges.
▶ noun a gun using such a cartridge.

centrefold (US **centerfold**) ▶ noun the two middle pages of a magazine, typically taken up by a single illustration or feature.
■an illustration on such pages, typically a picture of a naked or scantily clad model.

centre forward ▶ noun Soccer & Hockey an attacker who plays in the middle of the field.

centre half ▶ noun Soccer another term for **CENTRE BACK**.

centre line ▶ noun a real or imaginary line through the centre of something, especially one following an axis of symmetry.

centre of attraction ▶ noun Physics the point to which bodies tend to gravity.
■another term for **CENTRE OF ATTENTION** (see **CENTRE**).

centre of buoyancy ▶ noun Physics the centroid of the immersed part of a ship or other floating body.

centre of curvature ▶ noun Mathematics the centre of a circle which passes through a curve at a given point and has the same tangent and curvature at that point.

centre of flotation ▶ noun the centre of gravity of a floating object.

centre of gravity ▶ noun a point from which the weight of a body or system may be considered to act. In uniform gravity it is the same as the centre of mass.

centre of mass ▶ noun a point representing the mean position of the matter in a body or system.

centre of pressure ▶ noun Physics a point on a surface through which the resultant force due to pressure passes.

centrepiece ▶ noun a prominent ornament placed in the middle of a dinner table.
■an item, object, or issue intended to be a focus of attention: *the tower is the centrepiece of the park.*

centrepin ▶ noun a relatively simple type of fishing

reel with the line winding directly on to a revolving spool.

centre punch ▶ noun a tool consisting of a metal rod with a conical point for making an indentation in an object, to allow a drill to make a hole at the same spot without slipping.

centre spread ▶ noun the two facing middle pages of a newspaper or magazine.

centre stage ▶ noun [in sing.] the centre of a stage.
■the most prominent position: *finance is taking centre stage in debates on policy.*
▶ adverb at or towards the middle of a stage: *at the play's opening she stands centre stage.*
■in or towards a prominent position: *Asian countries have moved centre stage for world business.*

centrex ▶ noun [mass noun] a telephone service in which a group of phone lines can be joined by part of the local exchange acting as a private exchange.
– ORIGIN late 20th cent.: blend of **CENTRAL** and **EXCHANGE**.

centric ▶ adjective **1** in or at the centre; central: *centric and peripheral forces.*
2 Botany (of a diatom) radially symmetrical. Compare with **PENNATE**.
– DERIVATIVES **centrical** adjective, **centricity** /-'trɪsɪti/ noun.
– ORIGIN late 16th cent.: from Greek *kentrikos*, from *kentron* 'sharp point' (see **CENTRE**).

-centric ▶ combining form having a specified centre: *geocentric.*
■forming an opinion or evaluation originating from a specified viewpoint: *Eurocentric | ethnocentric.*
– DERIVATIVES **-centricity** combining form in corresponding nouns.
– ORIGIN from Greek *kentrikos*, on the pattern of words such as (con)*centric.*

centrifugal /ˌsɛntrɪ'fjuːg(ə)l, sɛn'trɪfjʊg(ə)l/ ▶ adjective Physics moving or tending to move away from a centre. The opposite of **CENTRIPETAL**.
– DERIVATIVES **centrifugally** adverb.
– ORIGIN early 18th cent.: from modern Latin *centrifugus*, from Latin *centrum* (see **CENTRE**) + *-fugus* 'fleeing' (from *fugere* 'flee').

centrifugal force ▶ noun Physics a force, arising from the body's inertia, which appears to act on a body moving in a circular path and is directed away from the centre around which the body is moving.

centrifugal pump ▶ noun a pump that uses an impeller to move water or other fluids.

centrifuge /'sɛntrɪfjuːdʒ/ ▶ noun a machine with a rapidly rotating container that applies centrifugal force to its contents, typically to separate fluids of different densities (e.g. cream from milk) or liquids from solids.
▶ verb [with obj.] (usu. **be centrifuged**) subject to the action of a centrifuge.
■separate by centrifuge: *the black liquid is centrifuged into oil and water.*
– DERIVATIVES **centrifugation** /-fjʊ'geɪʃ(ə)n/ noun.

centring (US **centering**) ▶ noun [mass noun] **1** the action or process of placing something in the middle of something else.
2 Architecture framing used to support an arch or dome while it is under construction.

centriole /'sɛntrɪəʊl/ ▶ noun Biology each of a pair of minute cylindrical organelles near the nucleus in animal cells, involved in the development of spindle fibres in cell division.
– ORIGIN late 19th cent.: from modern Latin *centriolum*, diminutive of *centrum* (see **CENTRE**).

centripetal /ˌsɛntrɪ'piːt(ə)l, sɛn'trɪpɪt(ə)l/ ▶ adjective Physics moving or tending to move towards a centre. The opposite of **CENTRIFUGAL**.
– DERIVATIVES **centripetally** adverb.
– ORIGIN early 18th cent.: from modern Latin *centripetus*, from Latin *centrum* (see **CENTRE**) + *-petus* 'seeking' (from *petere* 'seek').

centripetal force ▶ noun Physics a force which acts on a body moving in a circular path and is directed towards the centre around which the body is moving.

centrist ▶ adjective having moderate political views or policies.
▶ noun a person who holds moderate political views.
– DERIVATIVES **centrism** noun.
– ORIGIN late 19th cent.: from French *centriste*, from Latin *centrum* (see **CENTRE**).

centroid ▶ **noun** Mathematics the centre of mass of a geometric object of uniform density.

centromere /ˈsɛntrə(ʊ)mɪə/ ▶ **noun** Biology the point on a chromosome by which it is attached to a spindle fibre during cell division.
– DERIVATIVES **centromeric** adjective.
– ORIGIN 1920s: from Latin *centrum* (see CENTRE) + Greek *meros* 'part'.

centrosome /ˈsɛntrəsəʊm/ ▶ **noun** Biology an organelle near the nucleus of a cell which contains the centrioles (in animal cells) and from which the spindle fibres develop in cell division.
– ORIGIN late 19th cent.: from Latin *centrum* (see CENTRE) + Greek *sōma* 'body'.

centrum /ˈsɛntrəm/ ▶ **noun** (pl. **centrums** or **centra** /-trə/) Anatomy the solid central part of a vertebra, to which the arches and processes are attached.
– ORIGIN mid 19th cent.: from Latin.

centuple /ˈsɛntjʊp(ə)l/ ▶ **verb** [with obj.] multiply by a hundred or by a very large amount: *they were centupling the national debt.*
– ORIGIN early 17th cent.: from French, or from ecclesiastical Latin *centuplus*, alteration of Latin *centuplex*, from Latin *centum* 'hundred'.

centurion /sɛnˈtjʊərɪən/ ▶ **noun** the commander of a century in the ancient Roman army.
– ORIGIN Middle English: from Latin *centurio(n-)*, from *centuria* (see CENTURY).

century ▶ **noun** (pl. **-ies**) **1** a period of one hundred years: *a century ago most people walked to work.*
■ a period of a hundred years reckoned from the traditional date of the birth of Christ: *the fifteenth century* | [as modifier] *a twentieth-century lifestyle.*
2 a score of a hundred in a sporting event, especially a batsman's score of a hundred runs in cricket.
3 a company in the ancient Roman army, originally of a hundred men.
■ an ancient Roman political division for voting.
– DERIVATIVES **centurial** adjective.
– ORIGIN late Middle English (in sense 3): from Latin *centuria*, from *centum* 'hundred'. Sense 1 dates from the early 17th cent.

> USAGE **1** Strictly speaking, centuries run from 01 to 100, meaning that the new century begins on the first day of the year 01 (i.e. 1 January 1901, 1 January 2001, etc.). In practice and in popular perception, however, the new century is held to begin when the significant digits in the date change, i.e. on 1 January 2000, when 1999 becomes 2000.
> **2** Since the 1st century ran from the year 1 to the year 100, the ordinal number (i.e. second, third, fourth, etc.) used to denote the century will always be one digit higher than the corresponding cardinal digit(s). Thus, 1066 is a date in the 11th century, 1542 is a date in the 16th century, and so on.

century plant ▶ **noun** a large stemless agave with long spiny leaves, which produces a very tall flowering stem after many years of growth and then dies. Also called AMERICAN ALOE.
● *Agave americana*, family Agavaceae.

CEO ▶ **abbreviation for** chief executive officer.

cep /sɛp/ ▶ **noun** an edible European mushroom with a smooth brown cap, a stout white stalk, and pores rather than gills, growing in dry woodland and much sought after as a delicacy. Also called PENNY BUN.
● *Boletus edulis*, family Boletaceae, class Hymenomycetes.
– ORIGIN mid 19th cent.: from French *cèpe*, from Gascon *cep* 'tree trunk, mushroom', from Latin *cippus* 'stake'.

cephalic /sɪˈfalɪk, kɛ-/ ▶ **adjective** technical of, in, or relating to the head.
– ORIGIN late Middle English: from Old French *cephalique*, from Latin *cephalicus*, from Greek *kephalikos*, from *kephalē* 'head'.

-cephalic ▶ **combining form** equivalent to -CEPHALOUS.

cephalic index ▶ **noun** Anthropology a number expressing the ratio of the maximum breadth of a skull to its maximum length.

cephalin /ˈsɛfəlɪn, ˈkɛf-/ ▶ **noun** [mass noun] Biochemistry any of a group of phospholipids present in cell membranes, especially in the brain.
– ORIGIN late 19th cent.: from Greek *kephalē* 'brain' + -IN[1].

cephalization /ˌsɛfəlʌɪˈzeɪʃ(ə)n, ˌkɛf-/ ▶ **noun** [mass noun] Zoology the concentration of sense organs,

nervous control, etc., at the anterior end of the body, forming a head and brain, both during evolution and in the course of an embryo's development.

cephalo- /ˈsɛfələʊ, ˈkɛf-/ ▶ **combining form** relating to the head or skull: *cephalometry.*
– ORIGIN from Greek *kephalē* 'head'.

Cephalochordata /ˌsɛfələ(ʊ)kɔːˈdeɪtə, ˌkɛ-/ Zoology a small group of marine invertebrates that comprises the lancelets.
● Subphylum Cephalochordata, phylum Chordata.
– DERIVATIVES **cephalochordate** /ˌsɛfələ(ʊ)ˈkɔːdeɪt, ˌkɛ-/ noun & adjective.
– ORIGIN modern Latin (plural), from CEPHALO- 'head' + Greek *chorda* 'cord'.

cephalometry /ˌsɛfəˈlɒmɪtri, ˌkɛf-/ ▶ **noun** [mass noun] Medicine measurement and study of the proportions of the head and face, especially during development and growth.
– DERIVATIVES **cephalometric** adjective.

cephalon /ˈsɛfəlɒn, ˈkɛf-/ ▶ **noun** Zoology (in some arthropods, especially trilobites) the region of the head, composed of fused segments.
– ORIGIN late 19th cent.: from Greek *kephalē* 'head'.

Cephalonia /ˌsɛfəˈləʊnɪə, ˌkɛ-/ a Greek island in the Ionian Sea; pop. 29,400 (1991). Greek name KEFALLINÍA.

Cephalopoda /ˌsɛfəˈləʊdə, ˌkɛ-/ Zoology a large class of active predatory molluscs comprising octopuses, squids, and cuttlefish. They have a distinct head with large eyes and a ring of tentacles around a beaked mouth, and are able to release a cloud of inky fluid to confuse predators.
– DERIVATIVES **cephalopod** /ˈsɛf(ə)lə(ʊ)pɒd, ˈkɛ-/ noun.
– ORIGIN modern Latin (plural), from Greek *kephalē* 'head' + *pous, pod-* 'foot'.

cephalosporin /ˌsɛfələ(ʊ)ˈspɔːrɪn, ˌkɛ-/ ▶ **noun** any of a group of semi-synthetic broad-spectrum antibiotics resembling penicillin.
– ORIGIN 1950s: from modern Latin *Cephalosporium* (genus providing moulds for this) + -IN[1].

cephalothorax /ˌsɛf(ə)ləʊˈθɔːraks, ˌkɛf-/ ▶ **noun** (pl. **-thoraces** /-ˈθɔːrəsiːz/ or **-thoraxes**) Zoology the fused head and thorax of spiders and other chelicerate arthropods.

-cephalous ▶ **combining form** -headed (used most commonly in medical terms): *macrocephalous.*
– ORIGIN based on Greek *kephalē* 'head' + -OUS.

cepheid /ˈsiːfɪɪd, ˈsɛ-/ (also **cepheid variable**) ▶ **noun** Astronomy a variable star having a regular cycle of brightness with a frequency related to its luminosity, so allowing estimation of its distance from the earth.
– ORIGIN early 20th cent.: from the name of the variable star *Delta Cephei*, which typifies this class of stars.

Cepheus /ˈsiːfɪəs/ Astronomy a constellation near the north celestial pole, with no very bright stars.
■ [as genitive **Cephei** /ˈsiːfɪʌɪ/] used with preceding letter or numeral to designate a star in this constellation: *the star Beta Cephei.*
– ORIGIN from the name of a king of Ethiopia, the husband of Cassiopeia.

ceramic /sɪˈramɪk/ ▶ **adjective** made of clay and permanently hardened by heat: *a ceramic bowl.*
■ of or relating to the manufacture of such articles.
▶ **noun** (**ceramics**) pots and other articles made from clay hardened by heat.
■ [usu. treated as sing.] the art of making such articles. ■ [mass noun] (**ceramic**) the material from which such articles are made: *tableware in ceramic.* ■ [mass noun] (**ceramic**) any non-metallic solid which remains hard when heated.
– DERIVATIVES **ceramicist** noun.
– ORIGIN early 19th cent.: from Greek *keramikos*, from *keramos* 'pottery'.

ceramic hob ▶ **noun** an electric cooker hob made of ceramic, with heating elements fixed to its underside.

Ceram Sea /ˈseɪram/ (also **Seram Sea**) the part of the western Pacific Ocean at the centre of the Molucca Islands.

cerastes /sɪˈrastiːz/ ▶ **noun** a North African viper which has a spike over each eye.

● Genus *Cerastes*, family Viperidae: two species, in particular the horned viper.
– ORIGIN late Middle English: from Latin, from Greek *kerastēs* 'horned', from *keras* 'horn'.

cerastium /sɪˈrastɪəm/ ▶ **noun** (pl. **cerastiums**) a plant of a genus that includes chickweed and snow-in-summer.
● Genus *Cerastium*, family Caryophyllaceae.
– ORIGIN modern Latin, from Greek *kerastēs* 'horned' (with reference to the shape of many seed capsules) + -IUM.

ceratite /ˈsɛrətʌɪt, ˈsɪər-/ ▶ **noun** an ammonoid fossil of an intermediate type found chiefly in the Permian and Triassic periods, typically with partly frilled and partly lobed suture lines. Compare with AMMONITE and GONIATITE.
● Typified by the genus *Ceratites*, order Ceratida.
– ORIGIN mid 19th cent.: from modern Latin *Ceratites* (from Greek *keras, kerat-* + -ITE[1].

ceratobranchial /ˌsɛrətə(ʊ)ˈbraŋkɪəl, ˌkɛ-/ ▶ **noun** Zoology one of the paired ventral cartilaginous sections of the branchial arch in fishes.
– ORIGIN mid 19th cent.: from Greek *keras, kerat-* 'horn' + *branchial* (see BRANCHIA).

ceratopsian /ˌsɛrəˈtɒpsɪən, ˌkɛr-/ Palaeontology ▶ **noun** a gregarious quadrupedal herbivorous dinosaur of a group found in the Cretaceous period, including triceratops. It had a large beaked and horned head and a bony frill protecting the neck.
● Infraorder Ceratopsia, order Ornithischia.
▶ **adjective** of or relating to the ceratopsians.
– ORIGIN early 20th cent.: from modern Latin *Ceratopsia* (plural) (from Greek *keras, kerat-* 'horn' + *ops* 'face') + -AN.

Cerberus /ˈsəːbərəs/ Greek Mythology a monstrous watchdog with three (or in some accounts fifty) heads, which guarded the entrance to Hades.

cercaria /səːˈkɛːrɪə/ ▶ **noun** (pl. **cercariae** /-iː/) Zoology a free-swimming larval stage in which a parasitic fluke passes from an intermediate host (typically a snail) to another intermediate host or to the final vertebrate host.
– ORIGIN mid 19th cent.: modern Latin, formed irregularly from Greek *kerkos* 'tail'.

cerclage /səːˈklɑːʒ/ ▶ **noun** [mass noun] Medicine the use of a ring or loop to bind together the ends of an obliquely fractured bone or encircle the opening of a malfunctioning cervix.
– ORIGIN early 20th cent.: from French, literally 'encirclement'.

cercopithecine /ˌsəːkə(ʊ)ˈpɪθɪsiːn/ ▶ **noun** Zoology an Old World monkey of a group that includes the macaques, mangabeys, baboons, and guenons.
● Subfamily Cercopithecinae, family Cercopithecidae.
– ORIGIN from modern Latin *Cercopithecinae* (plural), based on Greek *kerkopithēkos* 'long-tailed monkey', from *kerkos* 'tail' + *pithēkos* 'ape'.

cercopithecoid /ˌsəːkə(ʊ)ˈpɪθɪkɔɪd/ Zoology ▶ **noun** a primate of a group that comprises the Old World monkeys.
● Superfamily Cercopithecoidea and family Cercopithecidae.
▶ **adjective** of or relating to monkeys of this group.
– ORIGIN late 19th cent.: from modern Latin *Cercopithecoidea*, based on Greek *kerkopithēkos*, a long-tailed monkey (from *kerkos* 'tail' + *pithēkos* 'ape').

cercus /ˈsəːkəs/ ▶ **noun** (pl. **cerci** /-kʌɪ/) Zoology either of a pair of small appendages at the end of the abdomen of some insects and other arthropods.
– ORIGIN early 19th cent.: from modern Latin, from Greek *kerkos* 'tail'.

cere /sɪə/ ▶ **noun** Ornithology a waxy fleshy covering at the base of the upper beak in some birds.
– ORIGIN late 15th cent.: from Latin *cera* 'wax'.

cereal ▶ **noun** a grain used for food, for example wheat, maize, or rye.
■ (usu. **cereals**) a grass producing such grain, grown as an agricultural crop: [as modifier] *low yields for cereal crops.* ■ [mass noun] a breakfast food made from roasted grain, typically eaten with milk: *a bowl of cereal.*
– ORIGIN early 19th cent. (as an adjective): from Latin *cerealis*, from *Ceres*, the name of the Roman goddess of agriculture.

cerebellum /ˌsɛrɪˈbɛləm/ ▶ **noun** (pl. **cerebellums** or **cerebella**) Anatomy the part of the brain at the back of the skull in vertebrates, which coordinates and regulates muscular activity.
– DERIVATIVES **cerebellar** adjective.

– ORIGIN mid 16th cent.: from Latin, diminutive of **CEREBRUM**.

cerebral /ˈsɛrɪbr(ə)l/ ▶ **adjective 1** of the cerebrum of the brain: *a cerebral haemorrhage | the cerebral cortex.*
■intellectual rather than emotional or physical: *she excelled in cerebral pursuits.*
2 Phonetics another term for **RETROFLEX**.
– DERIVATIVES **cerebrally** adverb.
– ORIGIN early 19th cent.: from Latin *cerebrum* 'brain' + **-AL**.

cerebral aqueduct ▶ **noun** another term for **AQUEDUCT OF SYLVIUS**.

cerebral dominance ▶ **noun** [mass noun] the normal tendency for one side of the brain to control particular functions, such as handedness and speech.

cerebral palsy ▶ **noun** [mass noun] a condition marked by impaired muscle coordination (spastic paralysis) and/or other disabilities, typically caused by damage to the brain before or at birth. See also **SPASTIC**.

cerebration /ˌsɛrɪˈbreɪʃ(ə)n/ ▶ **noun** [mass noun] technical or formal the working of the brain; thinking.
– DERIVATIVES **cerebrate** verb.

cerebro- ▶ **combining form** of or relating to the brain: *cerebrospinal.*
– ORIGIN from Latin *cerebrum* 'brain'.

cerebroside /ˈsɛrɪbrə(ʊ)sʌɪd/ ▶ **noun** Biochemistry any of a group of complex lipids present in the sheaths of nerve fibres.
– ORIGIN late 19th cent.: from Latin 'cerebrum' 'brain' + **-OSE**[2] + **-IDE**.

cerebrospinal /ˌsɛrɪbrə(ʊ)ˈspʌɪn(ə)l/ ▶ **adjective** Anatomy of or relating to the brain and spine.

cerebrospinal fluid ▶ **noun** [mass noun] Anatomy clear watery fluid which fills the space between the arachnoid membrane and the pia mater.

cerebrovascular /ˌsɛrɪbrə(ʊ)ˈvaskjʊlə/ ▶ **adjective** Anatomy of or relating to the brain and its blood vessels.

cerebrum /ˈsɛrɪbrəm/ ▶ **noun** (pl. **cerebra** /-brə/) Anatomy the principal and most anterior part of the brain in vertebrates, located in the front area of the skull and consisting of two hemispheres, left and right, separated by a fissure. It is responsible for the integration of complex sensory and neural functions and the initiation and coordination of voluntary activity in the body. See also **TELENCEPHALON**.
– ORIGIN early 17th cent.: from Latin, 'brain'.

cerecloth /ˈsɪəklɒθ/ ▶ **noun** [mass noun] historical waxed cloth typically used for wrapping a corpse.
– ORIGIN late Middle English: from earlier *cered cloth*, from *cere* 'to wax', from Latin *cerare*, from *cera* 'wax'.

Ceredigion /ˌkɛrəˈdɪgɪən/ a county of western mid Wales; administrative centre, Aberaeron.

cerement /ˈsɪəm(ə)nt/ ▶ **noun** (usu. **cerements**) historical waxed cloth for wrapping a corpse.
– ORIGIN early 17th cent. (first used by Shakespeare in *Hamlet*, 1602): from *cere* (see **CERECLOTH**).

ceremonial ▶ **adjective 1** relating to or used for formal religious or public events: *a ceremonial occasion.*
2 (of a post or role) conferring or involving only nominal authority or power.
▶ **noun** [mass noun] the system of rules and procedures to be observed at a formal or religious occasion: *the procedure was conducted with all due ceremonial.*
■[count noun] a rite or ceremony.
– DERIVATIVES **ceremonialism** noun, **ceremonialist** noun, **ceremonially** adverb.
– ORIGIN late Middle English: from late Latin *caerimonialis*, from *caerimonia* 'religious worship' (see **CEREMONY**).

ceremonious ▶ **adjective** relating or appropriate to grand and formal occasions: *a Great Hall where ceremonious and public appearances were made | he accepted the gifts with ceremonious dignity.*
– DERIVATIVES **ceremoniously** adverb, **ceremoniousness** noun.
– ORIGIN mid 16th cent.: from French *cérémonieux* or late Latin *caerimoniosus*, from *caerimonia* (see **CEREMONY**).

ceremony ▶ **noun** (pl. **-ies**) **1** a formal religious or public occasion, typically one celebrating a particular event, achievement, or anniversary.
■an act or series of acts performed according to a traditional or prescribed form.
2 [mass noun] the ritual observances and procedures required or performed at grand and formal occasions: *the new Queen was proclaimed with due ceremony.*
■formal polite behaviour: *he showed them to their table with great ceremony.*
– PHRASES **stand on ceremony** [usu. with negative] insist on the observance of formalities: *we don't stand on ceremony in this house.* **without ceremony** without preamble or politeness: *he was pushed without ceremony into the bathroom.*
– ORIGIN late Middle English: from Old French *ceremonie* or Latin *caerimonia* 'religious worship', (plural) 'ritual observances'.

Cerenkov, Pavel, see **CHERENKOV**.

Cerenkov radiation /tʃəˈrɛŋkɒf/ (also **Cherenkov radiation**) ▶ **noun** [mass noun] Physics electromagnetic radiation emitted by particles moving in a medium at speeds faster than that of light in the same medium.

cereology /ˌsɪərɪˈɒlədʒi/ ▶ **noun** [mass noun] the study or investigation of crop circles.
– DERIVATIVES **cereologist** noun.
– ORIGIN late 20th cent.: from **CERES** + **-LOGY**.

cereopsis goose /ˌsɛrɪˈɒpsɪs/ ▶ **noun** another term for **CAPE BARREN GOOSE**.
– ORIGIN late 19th cent.: from modern Latin *Cereopsis* (genus name), from Greek *kerinos* 'waxen' + *opsis* 'face' (because of its cere).

Ceres /ˈsɪəriːz/ **1** Roman Mythology the corn goddess. Greek equivalent **DEMETER**.
2 Astronomy the first asteroid to be discovered, found by G. Piazzi of Palermo on 1 January 1801. It is also much the largest (diameter 913 km).

ceresin /ˈsɛrɪsɪn/ ▶ **noun** [mass noun] a hard whitish paraffin wax used with or instead of beeswax.
– ORIGIN late 19th cent.: from modern Latin *ceres* (from Latin *cera* 'wax') + **-IN**[1].

cerise /səˈriːs, -z/ ▶ **noun** [mass noun] a light clear red colour: *a shade of vivid cerise.*
▶ **adjective** of a light clear red colour.
– ORIGIN mid 19th cent.: from French, literally 'cherry'.

cerium /ˈsɪərɪəm/ ▶ **noun** [mass noun] the chemical element of atomic number 58, a silvery-white metal. It is the most abundant of the lanthanide elements and is the main component of the alloy misch metal. (Symbol: **Ce**)
– ORIGIN early 19th cent.: named after the asteroid **CERES**, discovered shortly before.

cermet /ˈsəːmɛt/ ▶ **noun** any of a class of heat-resistant materials made of ceramic and sintered metal.
– ORIGIN 1950s: blend of **CERAMIC** and **METAL**.

CERN /səːn/ ▶ **abbreviation for** European Organization for Nuclear Research.
– ORIGIN initial letters of French *Conseil Européen pour la Recherche Nucléaire*, its former title.

cero /ˈsɪərəʊ/ ▶ **noun** (pl. same or **-os**) a large fish of the mackerel family, which is an important food fish in the tropical western Atlantic.
• *Scomberomorus regalis*, family Scombridae.
– ORIGIN late 19th cent.: from Spanish *sierra* 'saw or sawfish'.

cero- /ˈsɪərəʊ/ ▶ **combining form** of or relating to wax: *ceroplastic.*
– ORIGIN from Latin *cera* or Greek *kēros* 'wax'.

ceroplastic ▶ **adjective** of or relating to modelling in wax.

cert ▶ **noun** Brit. informal an event regarded as inevitable: *of course Mum would cry, it was a* ***dead cert.***
■a racehorse strongly tipped to win a race. ■a person regarded as certain to do something: *the Scottish keeper was a cert to play.*
– ORIGIN late 19th cent.: abbreviation of **CERTAINTY**.

cert. ▶ **abbreviation for** ■ certificate. ■ certified.

certain /ˈsəːt(ə)n, -tɪn/ ▶ **adjective 1** able to be firmly relied on to happen or be the case: *it's certain that more changes are in the offing | she looks certain to win an Oscar.*
■having or showing complete conviction about something: *are you absolutely* ***certain about*** *this? | to my certain knowledge, I've never set eyes on her before.*
2 [attrib.] specific but not explicitly named or stated: *he raised certain personal problems with me | the exercise was causing him a certain amount of pain.*
■used when mentioning the name of someone not known to the reader or hearer: *a certain General Percy captured the town.*
▶ **pronoun** (**certain of**) some but not all: *certain of his works have been edited.*
– PHRASES **for certain** without any doubt: *I don't know for certain.* **make certain** [with clause] take action to ensure that something happens or is the case.
■ establish whether something is definitely correct or true: *he probably knew her, but it didn't do any harm to make certain.*
– ORIGIN Middle English: from Old French, based on Latin *certus* 'settled, sure'.

certainly ▶ **adverb** [sentence adverb] used to convey the speaker's belief that what is said is true: *the prestigious address certainly adds to the firm's appeal.*
■used to indicate that a statement is made as a concession or contrasted with another: *our current revenues are certainly lower than anticipated.* ■ used to express complete agreement with something that has just been said: *'A good idea,' she agreed. 'Certainly!'*

certainty ▶ **noun** (pl. **-ies**) [mass noun] firm conviction that something is the case: *she knew* ***with*** *absolute* ***certainty*** *that they were dead.*
■the quality of being reliably true: *there is a bewildering lack of certainty and clarity in the law.* ■ a general air of confidence: *a man exuding certainty.* ■ [count noun] a fact that is definitely true or an event that is definitely going to take place: *the passing of the act made a general election a certainty.* ■ [count noun] a thing or person that may be relied on in a specified context or to do something specified: *he was expected to be a certainty for a gold medal.*
– PHRASES **for a certainty** beyond the possibility of doubt.
– ORIGIN Middle English: from Old French *certainete*, from *certain* (see **CERTAIN**).

CertEd ▶ **abbreviation for** (in the UK) Certificate in Education.

certes /ˈsəːtɪz/ ▶ **adverb** archaic assuredly; I assure you.
– ORIGIN Middle English: from Old French, based on Latin *certus* 'settled, sure'.

certifiable ▶ **adjective 1** able or needing to be officially attested or recorded: *encephalitis was a certifiable condition.*
2 officially recognized as needing treatment for mental disorder.

certificate ▶ **noun** /səˈtɪfɪkət/ **1** an official document attesting a certain fact, in particular:
■a document recording a person's birth, marriage, or death. ■ a document attesting a level of achievement in a course of study or training: *a university-accredited certificate.* ■a document attesting the fulfilment of certain legal requirements: *a certificate of motor insurance.* ■a document attesting ownership of a certain item: *a share certificate.*
2 an official classification awarded to a cinema film by a board of censors indicating its suitability for a particular age group: *an 18 certificate.*
▶ **verb** /səˈtɪfɪkeɪt/ [with obj.] (usu. **be certificated**) provide with or attest in an official document.
– DERIVATIVES **certification** noun.
– ORIGIN late Middle English (in the sense 'certification, attestation'): from French *certificat* or medieval Latin *certificatum*, from *certificare* (see **CERTIFY**).

certificate of deposit ▶ **noun** a certificate issued by a bank to a person depositing money for a specified length of time.

Certificate of Secondary Education (abbrev.: **CSE**) ▶ **noun** an examination set for secondary-school pupils in England and Wales, replaced in 1988 by the GCSE.

certified accountant ▶ **noun** an accountant holding a certificate of professional competence (in the UK, from the Chartered Association of Certified Accountants).

certified cheque ▶ **noun** a cheque which is guaranteed by a bank.

certified mail ▶ **noun** North American term for **RECORDED DELIVERY**.

certified milk ▶ **noun** [mass noun] historical milk guaranteed free from the tuberculosis bacillus.

certified public accountant ▶ **noun** N. Amer. a member of an officially accredited professional body of accountants (in the US, the Institute of Certified Public Accountants).

certified stock ▶ **noun** [mass noun] plants or plant material certified as being free from certain diseases and pests.

certify ▶ **verb** (**-ies**, **-ied**) [with obj.] (often **be**

certified) attest or confirm in a formal statement: *the profits for the year had been certified by the auditors* | [with clause] *the Law Society will certify that the sum charged is fair and reasonable.*
 ■officially recognize (someone or something) as possessing certain qualifications or meeting certain standards: *scenes of violence had to be cut before the film could be certified.* ■ officially declare insane.
 – ORIGIN Middle English: from Old French *certifier*, from late Latin *certificare*, from Latin *certus* 'certain'.

certiorari /ˌsəːtɪəˈ(ʊ)rɑːri/ ▶ noun [mass noun] Law a writ or order by which a higher court reviews a case tried in a lower court: *an order of certiorari.*
 – ORIGIN late Middle English: from Law Latin, 'to be informed', a phrase originally occurring at the start of the writ, from *certiorare* 'inform', from *certior*, comparative of *certus* 'certain'.

certitude /ˈsəːtɪtjuːd/ ▶ noun [mass noun] absolute certainty or conviction that something is the case: *the question may never be answered with certitude.*
 ■[count noun] something that someone firmly believes is true.
 – ORIGIN late Middle English: from late Latin *certitudo*, from Latin *certus* 'certain'.

cerulean /sɪˈruːlɪən/ poetic/literary ▶ adjective deep blue in colour like a clear sky.
 ▶ noun [mass noun] a deep sky-blue colour: *the background was painted in cerulean blue.*
 – ORIGIN mid 17th cent.: from Latin *caeruleus* 'sky blue', from *caelum* 'sky'.

cerumen /sɪˈruːmən/ ▶ noun technical term for EARWAX.
 – ORIGIN late 17th cent.: modern Latin, from Latin *cera* 'wax'.

ceruse /ˈsɪəruːs, sɪˈruːs/ ▶ noun archaic term for WHITE LEAD.
 – ORIGIN late Middle English: via Old French from Latin *cerussa*, perhaps from Greek *kēros* 'wax'.

Cervantes /səːˈvantiːz, Spanish θerˈβantes, ser-/, Miguel de (1547–1616), Spanish novelist and dramatist; full name *Miguel de Cervantes Saavedra*. His most famous work is *Don Quixote* (1605–15), a satire on chivalric romances that greatly influenced the development of the novel.

cervelat /ˈsəːvəlɑː, -lat/ ▶ noun [mass noun] a kind of smoked pork sausage.
 – ORIGIN early 17th cent.: from obsolete French, earlier form of *cervelas*, from Italian *cervellata*.

cervical /ˈsəːvɪk(ə)l, səːˈvʌɪk(ə)l/ ▶ adjective Anatomy **1** of or relating to the narrow neck-like passage forming the lower end of the womb: *cervical cancer.* **2** of or relating to the neck: *the fifth cervical vertebra.*
 – ORIGIN late 17th cent.: from French, or from modern Latin *cervicalis*, from Latin *cervix, cervic-* 'neck'.

cervical screening ▶ noun [mass noun] Brit. the examination of cellular material from the neck of the womb for cancer.

cervical smear ▶ noun Brit. a specimen of cellular material from the neck of the womb spread on a microscope slide for examination for cancerous cells or precancerous changes.

cervicitis /ˌsəːvɪˈsʌɪtɪs/ ▶ noun [mass noun] Medicine inflammation of the neck of the womb.

cervid /ˈsəːvɪd/ ▶ noun Zoology a mammal of the deer family (Cervidae).
 – ORIGIN late 19th cent.: from modern Latin *Cervidae* (plural), from Latin *cervus* 'deer'.

cervix /ˈsəːvɪks/ ▶ noun (pl. **cervices** /-siːz/) the narrow neck-like passage forming the lower end of the womb.
 ■technical the neck. ■ a part of other bodily organs resembling a neck.
 – ORIGIN mid 18th cent.: Latin.

Cesarean (also **Cesarian**) ▶ adjective & noun US spelling of CAESAREAN.

Cesarewitch /sɪˈzarəwɪtʃ/ ▶ noun a horse race run annually over two miles at Newmarket, England.
 – ORIGIN mid 19th cent.: from Russian *tsesarevich* 'heir to the throne', named in honour of the Russian Crown prince (later Alexander II) who attended the inaugural race in 1839.

cesium ▶ noun US spelling of CAESIUM.

České Budějovice /ˌtʃɛskeɪ ˈbuːdjejɒvɪtsə/ a city in the south of the Czech Republic, on the River Vltava; pop. 173,400 (1991). It is noted for the production of lager. German name BUDWEIS.

cess[1] /sɛs/ (also **sess**) ▶ noun (in Scotland, Ireland, and India) a tax or levy.
 – ORIGIN late 15th cent. (denoting the obligation placed on the Irish to supply the Lord Deputy's household and garrison with provisions at prices 'assessed' by the government): shortened from the obsolete noun *assess* 'assessment'.

cess[2] /sɛs/ ▶ noun (in phrase **bad cess to**) chiefly Irish a curse on: *bad cess to the day I joined that band!*
 – ORIGIN mid 19th cent. (originally Anglo-Irish): perhaps from CESS[1].

cessation /sɛˈseɪʃ(ə)n/ ▶ noun [mass noun] the fact or process of ending or being brought to an end: *the cessation of hostilities* | [count noun] *a cessation of animal testing of cosmetics.*
 – ORIGIN late Middle English: from Latin *cessatio(n-)*, from *cessare* 'cease'.

cesser /ˈsɛsə/ ▶ noun [mass noun] Law termination or cessation, especially of a period of tenure or legal liability.
 – ORIGIN mid 16th cent.: from Old French *cesser* 'cease', used as a noun.

cession /ˈsɛʃ(ə)n/ ▶ noun [mass noun] the formal giving up of rights, property, or territory by a state: *the cession of twenty important towns.*
 – ORIGIN late Middle English; from Latin *cessio(n-)*, from *cedere* 'cede'.

cesspit ▶ noun a pit for the disposal of liquid waste and sewage.
 ■figurative a disgusting or corrupt place or situation: *the affair threatened to be a cesspit of scandal.*
 – ORIGIN mid 19th cent.: from *cess* (the supposed base of CESSPOOL) + PIT[1].

cesspool ▶ noun an underground container for the temporary storage of liquid waste and sewage.
 ■figurative a disgusting or corrupt place.
 – ORIGIN late 17th cent. (denoting a trap under a drain to catch solids): probably an alteration, influenced by POOL[1], of archaic *suspiral* 'vent, water pipe, settling tank', from Old French *souspirail* 'air hole', based on Latin *sub-* 'from below' + *spirare* 'breathe'.

c'est la vie /ˌseɪ lɑːˈviː, French sɛ la vi/ ▶ exclamation used to express acceptance or resignation in the face of a difficult or unpleasant situation: *if you get thwarted, c'est la vie.*
 – ORIGIN French, literally 'that's life'.

Cestoda /sɛsˈtəʊdə/ (also **Cestoidea**) Zoology a class of parasitic flatworms that comprises the tapeworms.
 – DERIVATIVES **cestode** /ˈsɛstəʊd/ noun.
 – ORIGIN modern Latin (plural), from Latin *cestus*, from Greek *kestos*, literally 'stitched', used as a noun in the sense 'girdle'.

cestui que trust /ˌsɛti kiː ˈtrʌst/ ▶ noun [in sing.] Law the beneficiary of a trust.
 – ORIGIN mid 16th cent.: from Law French, short for *cestui a que use le trust est créé*, 'the person for whose benefit anything is given in trust to another'.

CET ▶ abbreviation for Central European Time.

Cetacea /sɪˈteɪʃə/ Zoology an order of marine mammals that comprises the whales, dolphins, and porpoises. These have a streamlined hairless body, no hindlimbs, a horizontal tail fin, and a blowhole on top of the head for breathing. See also MYSTICETI, ODONTOCETI.
 – DERIVATIVES **cetacean** noun & adjective.
 – ORIGIN modern Latin (plural), from Latin *cetus*, from Greek *kētos* 'whale'.

cetane /ˈsiːteɪn/ ▶ noun [mass noun] Chemistry a colourless liquid hydrocarbon of the alkane series, present in petroleum spirit.
 ● Alternative name: *n*-hexadecane; chem. formula: $C_{16}H_{34}$.
 – ORIGIN late 19th cent.: from Latin *cetus* 'whale', from Greek *kētos* (because related compounds were first derived from spermaceti) + -ANE[2].

cetane number ▶ noun a quantity indicating the ignition properties of diesel fuel relative to cetane as a standard.

ceteris paribus /ˌkeɪtərɪs ˈparɪbʊs, ˌsɛt-, ˌsiːt-/ ▶ adverb formal with other conditions remaining the same: *shorter hours of labour will, ceteris paribus, reduce the volume of output.*
 – ORIGIN early 17th cent.: modern Latin.

cetrimide /ˈsɛtrɪmʌɪd/ ▶ noun [mass noun] a synthetic detergent and antiseptic which is a quaternary ammonium compound derived from cetane.

– ORIGIN 1940s: from *cet(yl)trim(ethylammomium bromid)e.*

Cetshwayo /sɛˈtʃweɪəʊ/ (also **Cetewayo**) (*c*.1826–84), Zulu king. He became ruler of Zululand in 1873 and was involved in a series of battles with the Afrikaners and British; he was deposed as leader after the capture of his capital by the British in 1879.

Cetti's warbler /ˈtʃɛtɪz/ ▶ noun a chestnut-brown Eurasian warbler with a strikingly loud and abrupt song.
 ● *Cettia cetti*, family Sylviidae.
 – ORIGIN late 19th cent.: named after Francesco Cetti, 18th-cent. Italian ornithologist.

Cetus /ˈsiːtəs/ Astronomy a large northern constellation (the Whale), said to represent the sea monster which threatened Andromeda. It contains the variable star Mira, but no other bright stars.
 ■[as genitive **Ceti** /ˈsiːti/] used with preceding letter or numeral to designate a star in this constellation: *the star Tau Ceti.*
 – ORIGIN Latin.

Ceuta /ˈseɪuːtə, Spanish ˈθeuta, ˈseuta/ a Spanish enclave on the coast of North Africa, in Morocco; pop. 67,615 (1991, with Melilla).

Cévennes /seɪˈvɛn, French sevɛn/ a mountain range on the south-eastern edge of the Massif Central in France.

ceviche /sɛˈviːtʃeɪ/ (also **seviche**) ▶ noun [mass noun] a South American dish of marinaded raw fish or seafood, typically garnished and served as a starter.
 – ORIGIN South American Spanish.

Ceylon /sɪˈlɒn/ former name (until 1972) for SRI LANKA.

Ceylon moss ▶ noun [mass noun] a red seaweed of the Indian subcontinent, which is the main source of agar.
 ● *Gracilaria lichenoides*, division Rhodophyta.

Ceylon satinwood ▶ noun see SATINWOOD (sense 2).

Cézanne /seɪˈzan, French sezan/, Paul (1839–1906), French painter. He is closely identified with post-Impressionism and his later work had an important influence on cubism. Notable works: *Bathers* (sequence of paintings 1890–1905).

CF ▶ abbreviation ■ (in the UK) Chaplain to the Forces. ■ cystic fibrosis.

Cf ▶ symbol for the chemical element californium.

cf. ▶ abbreviation compare with (used to refer a reader to another written work or another part of the same written work).
 – ORIGIN from Latin *confer* 'compare'.

c.f. ▶ abbreviation for carried forward (used to refer to figures transferred to a new page or account).

CFA (also **CFA franc**) ▶ noun the basic monetary unit of Cameroon, Congo, Gabon, and the Central African Republic, equal to 100 centimes.
 – ORIGIN *CFA* from French *Communauté Financière Africaine* 'African Financial Community'.

CFC Chemistry ▶ abbreviation for chlorofluorocarbon, any of a class of compounds of carbon, hydrogen, chlorine, and fluorine, typically gases used chiefly in refrigerants and aerosol propellants. They are harmful to the ozone layer in the earth's atmosphere owing to the release of chlorine atoms on exposure to ultraviolet radiation.

CFE ▶ abbreviation for (in the UK) College of Further Education.

CFS ▶ abbreviation for chronic fatigue syndrome.

CG ▶ abbreviation for Democratic Republic of Congo (international vehicle registration).

cg ▶ abbreviation for centigram(s).

CGS ▶ abbreviation for (in the UK) Chief of General Staff.

cgs ▶ abbreviation for centimetre-gram-second.

CGT ▶ abbreviation for capital gains tax.

CH ▶ abbreviation ■ (in the UK) Companion of Honour. ■ Switzerland (international vehicle registration). [ORIGIN: from French *Confédération Helvétique* 'Swiss Confederation'.]

ch. ▶ abbreviation for ■ chapter. ■ (of a horse) chestnut in colour. ■ church.

cha ▶ noun variant spelling of CHAR[3].

chaat /tʃɑːt/ ▶ noun [mass noun] an Indian dish of boiled vegetables or raw fruit, with spices.
 – ORIGIN from Hindi *cāṭ.*

chabazite /ˈkabəzʌɪt/ ▶ **noun** [mass noun] a colourless, pink, or yellow zeolite mineral, typically occurring as rhombohedral crystals.
– ORIGIN early 19th cent.: from French *chabazie*, from Greek *khabazie*, a misreading of *khalazie*, vocative form of *khalazios* 'hailstone' (from *khalaza* 'hail', because of its form and colour), + **-ITE**[1].

Chablis /ˈʃabliː/ ▶ **noun** [mass noun] a dry white burgundy wine from Chablis in eastern France.

Chabrol /ʃaˈbrɒl, French ʃabʀɔl/, Claude (b.1930), French film director, a member of the *nouvelle vague*. His films typically combine suspense with studies of personal relationships, and include *Les Biches* (1968).

cha-cha (also **cha-cha-cha**) ▶ **noun** a ballroom dance with small steps and swaying hip movements, performed to a Latin American rhythm.
■ music for or in the rhythm of such a dance.
▶ **verb** (**cha-chas**, **cha-chaed** or **cha-cha'd**, **cha-chaing**) [no obj.] dance the cha-cha.
– ORIGIN 1950s: Latin American Spanish .

chachalaca /ˌtʃatʃəˈlakə/ ▶ **noun** a pheasant-like tree-dwelling bird of the guan family, with a loud harsh call. It is found mainly in the forests of tropical America.
● Genus *Ortalis*, family Cracidae: several species, in particular the **plain chachalaca** (*O. vetula*).
– ORIGIN late 19th cent.: via South American Spanish from Nahuatl, of imitative origin.

chacham /ˈxɑːxəm/ ▶ **noun** variant spelling of **HAHAM**.

chack ▶ **verb** [no obj.] (of a bird) make a harsh call.
▶ **noun** a harsh call made by a bird.
– ORIGIN early 16th cent.: imitative.

chacma baboon /ˈtʃakmə/ ▶ **noun** a dark grey baboon which lives on the savannah of southern Africa.
● *Papio ursinus*, family Cercopithecidae.
– ORIGIN mid 19th cent.: from Khoikhoi.

Chaco another name for **GRAN CHACO**.

chaconne /ʃəˈkɒn/ ▶ **noun** Music a composition in a series of varying sections in slow triple time, typically over a short repeated bass theme. Compare with **PASSACAGLIA**.
■ a stately dance performed to such music, popular in the 18th century. ■ a ballroom dance performed in Europe in the late 19th and early 20th centuries.
– ORIGIN late 17th cent.: from French, from Spanish *chacona*.

Chaco War /ˈtʃɑːkəʊ/ a boundary dispute in 1932–5 between Bolivia and Paraguay, in which Paraguay eventually gained most of the disputed territory.

chacun à son goût /ˌʃakəːn a sɒn ˈguː, French ʃakœ̃ a sɔ̃ gu/ ▶ **exclamation** each to their own taste.
– ORIGIN French.

Chad /tʃad/ a landlocked country in northern central Africa; pop. 5,828,000 (est. 1991); official languages, French and Arabic; capital, N'Djamena.

Much of the country lies in the Sahel and, in the north, the Sahara Desert. A French colony from 1913, Chad became autonomous within the French Community in 1958, and fully independent as a republic in 1960.

– DERIVATIVES **Chadian** adjective & noun.

chad /tʃad/ ▶ **noun** a piece of waste material removed from punched cards or tape by punching.
– ORIGIN 1950s: of unknown origin.

Chad, Lake a shallow lake on the borders of Chad, Niger, and Nigeria in north central Africa. Its size varies seasonally from *c.*10,360 sq. km (4,000 sq. miles) to *c.*25,900 sq. km (10,000 sq. miles).

Chadic /ˈtʃadɪk/ ▶ **noun** [mass noun] a group of Afro-Asiatic languages spoken in the region of Lake Chad, of which the most important is Hausa.
▶ **adjective** of or relating to this group of languages.

chador /ˈtʃɑːdɔː, ˈtʃɑːdə, ˈtʃʌdə/ (also **chadar** or **chuddar**) ▶ **noun** a large piece of dark-coloured cloth, typically worn by Muslim women, wrapped around the head and upper body to leave only the face exposed.
– ORIGIN early 17th cent.: from Urdu *chādar, chaddar*, from Persian *čādar* 'sheet or veil'.

Chadwick /ˈtʃadwɪk/, Sir James (1891–1974), English physicist. He discovered the neutron, for which he received the 1935 Nobel Prize for Physics.

chaebol /ˈtʃeɪbɒl/ ▶ **noun** (pl. same or **chaebols**) (in the Republic of Korea) a large business conglomerate, typically a family-owned one.
– ORIGIN 1980s: Korean, literally 'money clan'.

chaeta /ˈkiːtə/ ▶ **noun** (pl. **chaetae** /-tiː/) Zoology a stiff bristle made of chitin, especially in an annelid worm.
– ORIGIN mid 19th cent.: modern Latin, from Greek *khaitē* 'long hair'.

Chaetognatha /ˌkiːtəgˈnaθə, -ˈneɪθə/ Zoology a small phylum of marine invertebrates that comprises the arrow worms.
– DERIVATIVES **chaetognath** noun.
– ORIGIN modern Latin (plural), from Greek *khaitē* 'long hair' + *gnathos* 'jaw'.

chafe /tʃeɪf/ ▶ **verb 1** [with obj.] (of something restrictive or too tight) make (a part of the body) sore by rubbing against it: *the collar chafed his neck.*
■ [no obj.] (of a part of the body) be or become sore as a result of such rubbing. ■ [no obj.] (of an object) rub abrasively against another: *the grommet stops the cable chafing on the metal.*
2 [with obj.] rub (a part of the body) to restore warmth or sensation.
■ restore (warmth or sensation) in this way: *he* **chafed** *some feeling* **into** *his frozen hands.*
3 become or make annoyed or impatient because of a restriction or inconvenience: [no obj.] *the bank chafed at the restrictions imposed upon it* | [with obj.] *it chafed him to be confined like this.*
▶ **noun 1** [mass noun] wear or damage caused by rubbing: *to prevent chafe the ropes should lie flat.*
2 archaic a state of annoyance.
– ORIGIN late Middle English (in the sense 'make warm'): from Old French *chaufer* 'make hot', based on Latin *calefacere*, from *calere* 'be hot' + *facere* 'make'.

chafer /ˈtʃeɪfə/ ▶ **noun** a large flying beetle, the adult and larva of which can be very destructive to foliage and plant roots respectively.
● Several subfamilies of the family Scarabaeidae. See also **COCKCHAFER**.
– ORIGIN Old English *ceafor, cefer*, of Germanic origin; related to Dutch *kever*.

chaff[1] /tʃɑːf, tʃaf/ ▶ **noun** [mass noun] the husks of corn or other seed separated by winnowing or threshing.
■ chopped hay and straw used as fodder. ■ figurative worthless things; rubbish. ■ strips of metal foil released in the atmosphere from aircraft, or deployed as missiles, to obstruct radar detection.
– PHRASES **separate** (or **sort**) **the wheat from the chaff** distinguish valuable people or things from worthless ones.
– DERIVATIVES **chaffy** adjective.
– ORIGIN Old English *cæf, ceaf*, probably from a Germanic base meaning 'gnaw'; related to Dutch *kaf*, also to **CHAFER**.

chaff[2] /tʃɑːf, tʃaf/ ▶ **noun** [mass noun] light-hearted joking; banter.
▶ **verb** [with obj.] tease.
– ORIGIN early 19th cent.: perhaps from **CHAFE**.

chaff-cutter ▶ **noun** chiefly historical a machine for chopping hay and straw for use as fodder.

chaffer /ˈtʃafə/ ▶ **verb** [no obj.] haggle about the terms of an agreement or price of something.
▶ **noun** [mass noun] archaic haggling about the price of something.
– DERIVATIVES **chafferer** noun.
– ORIGIN Middle English (in the sense 'trade or trading'): from Old English *cēap* 'a bargain' + *faru* 'journey'; probably influenced by Old Norse *kaupfǫr*.

chaffinch ▶ **noun** a Eurasian and North African finch, typically with a bluish top to the head and dark wings and tail.
● Genus *Fringilla*, family Fringillidae: two species, in particular the widespread *F. coelebs*, which (in the male of the typical European form) has a pinkish face and breast.
– ORIGIN Old English *ceaffinc* 'chaff finch' (because it forages around barns, picking seeds out of the chaff).

chaffweed /ˈtʃafwiːd/ ▶ **noun** [mass noun] a tiny European pimpernel with pink or white flowers.
● *Anagallis minima*, family Primulaceae.
– ORIGIN mid 16th cent.: probably from the verb **CHAFE** + **WEED**.

chafing dish ▶ **noun** a cooking pot with an outer pan of hot water, used for keeping food warm.
■ a metal pan, typically one containing a spirit lamp or burning charcoal, used for cooking at table.
– ORIGIN late 15th cent.: from the original (now obsolete) sense of **CHAFE** 'become warm, warm up'.

Chagall /ʃaˈgal/, Marc (1887–1985), Russian-born French painter and graphic artist. His work was characterized by the use of rich emotive colour and dream imagery, and had a significant influence on surrealism.

Chagas' disease /ˈtʃɑːgəsɪz/ ▶ **noun** [mass noun] a disease caused by trypanosomes transmitted by bloodsucking bugs, endemic in South America and causing damage to the heart and central nervous system.
– ORIGIN early 20th cent.: named after Carlos *Chagas* (1879–1934), the Brazilian physician who first described it.

Chagos Archipelago /ˈtʃɑːgəs/ an island group in the Indian Ocean forming the British Indian Ocean Territory.

chagrin /ˈʃagrɪn, ʃəˈgrɪn/ ▶ **noun** [mass noun] annoyance or distress at having failed or been humiliated: *to my* **chagrin**, *he was nowhere to be seen.*
▶ **verb** (**be chagrined**) feel distressed or humiliated.
– ORIGIN mid 17th cent. (in the sense 'melancholy'): from French *chagrin* (noun), literally 'rough skin, shagreen', *chagriner* (verb), of unknown origin.

chai /tʃʌɪ/ ▶ **noun** [mass noun] Indian tea, especially when made by boiling the tea leaves with milk, sugar, and cardamoms.
– ORIGIN a term in various Indian languages.

Chain, Sir Ernst Boris (1906–79), German-born British biochemist. With Howard Florey he isolated and purified penicillin and in 1945 they shared a Nobel Prize with Alexander Fleming.

chain ▶ **noun 1** a connected flexible series of metal links used for fastening or securing objects and pulling or supporting loads.
■ (**chains**) such a series of links, or a set of them, used to confine a prisoner: *the drug dealer is being kept* **in chains**. ■ such a series of links worn as a decoration or badge of office. ■ figurative a force or factor which binds or restricts someone: *workers secured by the chains of the labour market.*
2 a sequence of items of the same type forming a line: *he kept the chain of buckets supplied with water.*
■ a sequence or series of connected elements: *the action would initiate a chain of events.* ■ a group of hotels or shops owned by the same company: *the agency is part of a nationwide chain.* ■ a part of a molecule consisting of a number of atoms (typically carbon) bonded together in a linear sequence. ■ a figure in a quadrille or similar dance, in which dancers meet and pass each other in a continuous sequence.
3 a jointed measuring line consisting of linked metal rods.
■ the length of such a measuring line (66 ft).
4 (**chains**) a structure of planks projecting horizontally from a sailing ship's sides abreast of the masts, used to widen the basis for the shrouds. [ORIGIN: formed earlier of iron plates.]
▶ **verb** [with obj.] fasten or secure with a chain: *she chained her bicycle to the railings.*
■ confine with a chain: *he had been* **chained up** | figurative *as an actuary you will not be chained to a desk.*
– PHRASES **pull** (or **yank**) **someone's chain** US informal tease someone, typically by leading them to believe something untrue.
– ORIGIN Middle English: from Old French *chaine, chaeine*, from Latin *catena* 'a chain'.

chain armour ▶ **noun** another term for **CHAIN MAIL**.

chain bridge ▶ **noun** a suspension bridge supported by chains rather than cables.

chain drive ▶ **noun** [mass noun] a mechanism in which power is transmitted from an engine, typically to the wheels of a vehicle or a boat's propeller, by means of a moving endless chain.
– DERIVATIVES **chain-driven** adjective.

chaîné /ˈʃeneɪ/ ▶ **noun** (pl. **chaînés** pronunc. same) Ballet a sequence of fast turns from one foot to the other, executed in a straight line.

chain gang ▶ **noun** a group of convicts chained together while working outside the prison.

chain gear ▶ **noun** a gear transmitting motion by means of a moving endless chain, especially in a bicycle.

chain gun ▶ **noun** a machine gun that uses a motor-driven chain to power all moving parts.

chain harrow ▶ **noun** a harrow consisting of a net made of chains in a metal frame.

chain letter ▶ **noun** one of a sequence of letters, each recipient in the sequence being requested to send copies to a specific number of other people.

chain-link ▶ adjective [attrib.] made of wire in a diamond-shaped mesh: *a chain-link fence.*

chain mail ▶ noun [mass noun] historical armour made of small metal rings linked together.

chainplate ▶ noun a strong link or plate on a sailing ship's side, to which the shrouds are secured.

chain reaction ▶ noun a chemical reaction or other process in which the products themselves promote or spread the reaction, which under certain conditions may accelerate dramatically.
  ■ the self-sustaining fission reaction spread by neutrons which occurs in nuclear reactors and bombs. ■ figurative a series of events, each caused by the previous one.

chainring ▶ noun a large cog carrying the chain on a bicycle, to which the pedals are attached.

chainsaw ▶ noun a mechanical power-driven cutting tool with teeth set on a chain which moves around the edge of a blade.

chain shot ▶ noun [mass noun] historical pairs of cannonballs or half balls joined by a chain, fired from cannons in sea battles in order to damage masts and rigging.

chain-smoke ▶ verb [no obj.] smoke continually, typically by lighting a cigarette from the stub of the last one smoked.
  – DERIVATIVES **chain-smoker** noun.

chain stitch ▶ noun [mass noun] an ornamental embroidery or crochet stitch resembling a chain.

chain store ▶ noun one of a series of shops owned by one firm and selling the same goods.

chain wheel ▶ noun a wheel transmitting power by means of a chain fitted to its edges.

chair ▶ noun **1** a separate seat for one person, typically with a back and four legs.
  ■ historical a sedan chair. ■ short for **CHAIRLIFT**.
  2 the person in charge of a meeting or of a commercial or political organization (used as a neutral alternative to chairman or chairwoman): *the deputy chair of the Supreme Soviet.*
  ■ an official position of authority, for example on a board of directors: *the editorial chair.*
  3 a professorship: *he held a chair in physics.*
  4 (**the chair**) US short for **ELECTRIC CHAIR**.
  5 chiefly Brit. a metal socket holding a rail in place on a railway sleeper.
  ▶ verb [with obj.] **1** act as chairperson of or preside over (an organization, meeting, or public event).
  2 Brit. carry (someone) aloft in a chair or in a sitting position to celebrate a victory.
  – PHRASES **take the chair** act as chairperson.
  – ORIGIN Middle English: from Old French *chaiere* (modern *chaire* 'bishop's throne, etc.', *chaise* 'chair'), from Latin *cathedra* 'seat', from Greek *kathedra*. Compare with **CATHEDRAL**.

chair car ▶ noun N. Amer. a railway carriage with adjustable seats in pairs either side of a central gangway.

chairlady ▶ noun (pl. **-ies**) another term for **CHAIRWOMAN**.

chairlift ▶ noun **1** a series of chairs hung from a moving cable, typically used for carrying passengers up and down a mountain.
  2 a device for carrying people in wheelchairs from one floor of a building to another.

chairman ▶ noun (pl. **-men**) **1** a person chosen to preside over a meeting.
  ■ the permanent or long-term president of a committee, company, or other organization.
  ■ (**Chairman**) (since 1949) the leading figure in the Chinese Communist Party.
  2 historical a sedan-bearer.
  – DERIVATIVES **chairmanship** noun.

chairperson ▶ noun a chairman or chairwoman (used as a neutral alternative).

chairwoman ▶ noun (pl. **-women**) a female chairperson.

chaise /ʃeɪz/ ▶ noun **1** chiefly historical a horse-drawn carriage for one or two people, typically one with an open top and two wheels.
  ■ another term for **POST-CHAISE**.
  2 US term for **CHAISE LONGUE**.
  – ORIGIN mid 17th cent.: from French, variant of *chaire* (see **CHAIR**).

chaise longue /'lɒŋ/ ▶ noun (pl. **chaises longues** pronunc. same) a sofa with a backrest at only one end.

■ N. Amer. a sunbed or other chair with a lengthened seat for reclining on.
  – ORIGIN early 19th cent.: French, literally 'long chair'.

chaise lounge /'laʊndʒ/ ▶ noun US term for **CHAISE LONGUE**.
  – ORIGIN early 20th cent.: alteration by association with **LOUNGE**.

Chaka variant spelling of **SHAKA**.

chakra /'tʃʌkrə/ ▶ noun (in Indian thought) each of the centres of spiritual power in the human body, usually considered to be seven in number.
  – ORIGIN from Sanskrit *cakra* 'wheel or circle', from an Indo-European base meaning 'turn', shared by **WHEEL**.

chal[1] /tʃal/ ▶ noun a male gypsy.
  – ORIGIN mid 19th cent.: from Romany, literally 'person, fellow'.

chal[2] ▶ noun variant spelling of **CHAWL**.

chalaza /kə'leɪzə/ ▶ noun (pl. **chalazae** /-ziː/) Zoology (in a bird's egg) each of two twisted membranous strips joining the yolk to the ends of the shell.
  – DERIVATIVES **chalazal** adjective.
  – ORIGIN early 18th cent.: modern Latin, from Greek *khalaza* 'small knot'.

Chalcedon /'kalsɪdɒn, kal'siːd(ə)n/ a former city on the Bosporus in Asia Minor, now part of Istanbul. Turkish name **KADIKÖY**.

Chalcedon, Council of the fourth ecumenical council of the Christian Church, held at Chalcedon in 451. It condemned the Monophysite position and affirmed the dual but united nature of Christ as god and man.
  – DERIVATIVES **Chalcedonian** /ˌkalsɪ'dəʊnɪən/ noun & adjective.

chalcedony /kal'sɛdəni/ ▶ noun (pl. **-ies**) [mass noun] a microcrystalline type of quartz occurring in several different forms including onyx and agate.
  – DERIVATIVES **chalcedonic** /ˌkalsɪ'dɒnɪk/ adjective.
  – ORIGIN late Middle English: from Latin *calcedonius*, *chalcedonius* (often believed to mean 'stone of Chalcedon', but this is doubtful), from Greek *khalkēdōn*.

chalcid /'kalsɪd/ (also **chalcid wasp**) ▶ noun a minute parasitic wasp of a large group whose members lay eggs inside the eggs of other insects. They typically have bright metallic coloration.
  ● Superfamily Chalcidoidea, order Hymenoptera.
  – ORIGIN late 19th cent.: from modern Latin *Chalcis* (genus name), from Greek *khalkos* 'copper, brass', + **-ID**[3].

Chalcis /'kalsɪs/ the chief town of the island of Euboea, on the coast opposite mainland Greece; pop. 44,800 (1981). Greek name **KHALKÍS**.

Chalcolithic /ˌkalkə(ʊ)'lɪθɪk/ ▶ adjective Archaeology of, relating to, or denoting a period in the 4th and 3rd millennia BC, chiefly in the Near East and SE Europe, during which some weapons and tools were made of copper. This period was still largely Neolithic in character. Also called **ENEOLITHIC**.
  ■ [as noun **the Chalcolithic**] the Chalcolithic period. Also called **COPPER AGE**.
  – ORIGIN early 20th cent.: from Greek *khalkos* 'copper' + *lithos* 'stone' + **-IC**.

chalcopyrite /ˌkalkə(ʊ)'pʌɪrʌɪt/ ▶ noun [mass noun] a yellow crystalline mineral consisting of a sulphide of copper and iron. It is the principal ore of copper. Also called **COPPER PYRITES**.
  – ORIGIN mid 19th cent.: from modern Latin *chalcopyrites*, from Greek *khalkos* 'copper' + *puritēs* (see **PYRITES**).

Chaldea /kal'diːə/ an ancient country in what is now southern Iraq, inhabited by the Chaldeans.
  – ORIGIN from Greek *Khaldaia*, from Akkadian *Kaldû*, the name of a Babylonian tribal group.

Chaldean ▶ noun **1** a member of an ancient people who lived in Chaldea c.800 BC and ruled Babylonia 625–539 BC. They were renowned as astronomers and astrologers.
  2 [mass noun] the Semitic language of the ancient Chaldeans.
  ■ a language related to Aramaic and spoken in parts of Iraq.
  3 a member of a Syrian Uniate (formerly Nestorian) Church based mainly in Iran and Iraq.
  ▶ adjective **1** of or relating to ancient Chaldea or its people or language.
  ■ poetic/literary of or relating to astrology.

2 of or relating to the East Syrian Uniate Church.

Chaldee /kal'diː, 'kaldiː/ ▶ noun **1** [mass noun] the language of the ancient Chaldeans.
  ■ dated the Aramaic language as used in some books of the Old Testament.
  2 a native of ancient Chaldea.
  – ORIGIN from Latin *Chaldaei* 'Chaldeans', from Greek *Khaldaioi*, from *Khaldaia* (see **CHALDEA**).

chalet /'ʃaleɪ/ ▶ noun a wooden house or cottage with overhanging eaves, typically found in the Swiss Alps.
  ■ a small cabin or house used by holidaymakers, typically forming a unit of a large holiday complex.
  – ORIGIN late 18th cent.: from Swiss French, diminutive of Old French *chasel* 'farmstead', based on Latin *casa* 'hut, cottage'.

Chaliapin /ʃa'ljɑːpɪn/, Fyodor (Ivanovich) (1873–1938), Russian operatic bass.

chalice ▶ noun historical a large cup or goblet, typically used for drinking wine.
  ■ the wine cup used in the Christian Eucharist.
  – ORIGIN Middle English: via Old French from Latin *calix*, *calic-* 'cup'.

chalicothere /'kalɪkə‚θɪə/ ▶ noun a large horse-like fossil mammal of the late Tertiary period, with stout claws on the toes instead of hooves.
  ● Family Chalicotheriidae, order Perissodactyla: several genera, in particular *Moropus*.
  – ORIGIN early 20th cent.: from modern Latin *Chalicotherium* (genus name), from Greek *khalix*, *khalik-* 'gravel' + *thērion* 'wild animal'.

chalk ▶ noun [mass noun] **1** a white soft earthy limestone (calcium carbonate) formed from the skeletal remains of sea creatures.
  ■ a similar substance (calcium sulphate), made into white or coloured sticks used for drawing or writing.
  ■ [count noun] Geology a series of strata consisting mainly of chalk.
  2 short for **FRENCH CHALK**.
  ▶ verb [with obj.] **1** draw or write with chalk.
  ■ draw or write on (a surface) with chalk.
  2 rub (something, especially a snooker cue) with chalk.
  3 Brit. charge (drinks bought in a pub or bar) to a person's account.
  – PHRASES **as different as** (or **like**) **chalk and cheese** Brit. fundamentally different or incompatible. **by a long chalk** Brit. by far. **chalk and talk** Brit. teaching by traditional methods focusing on the blackboard and presentation by the teacher as opposed to more informal or interactive methods. **not by a long chalk** Brit. by no means; not at all. [ORIGIN: with reference to the chalk used for marking up scores in competitive games.]
  – ORIGIN Old English *cealc* (also denoting lime), related to Dutch *kalk* and German *Kalk*, from Latin *calx* (see **CALX**).
  ▶ **chalk something out** sketch or plan something.
  chalk something up 1 draw or write something with chalk. **2** achieve something noteworthy: *he has chalked up a box office success.* **3** ascribe something to a particular cause: *I chalked my sleeplessness up to nerves.*

chalkboard ▶ noun North American term for **BLACKBOARD**.

chalkdown ▶ noun S. African informal a teachers' strike.

chalkface ▶ noun [in sing.] Brit. the day-to-day work of teaching in a school: *teachers at the chalkface.*

chalkhill blue ▶ noun a European blue butterfly of calcareous grassland, of which the male is silvery-blue with blackish markings and the female is brown.
  ● *Lysandra coridon*, family Lycaenidae.

chalkie ▶ noun (pl. **-ies**) Austral./NZ informal a schoolteacher.

chalk pit ▶ noun Brit. a quarry from which chalk is extracted.

chalk-stone ▶ noun Medicine, dated a chalky deposit of sodium urate formed in the hands and feet of sufferers from severe gout.

chalk-stripe ▶ adjective [attrib.] (of a garment or material) having a pattern of thin white stripes on a dark background.
  ▶ noun (**chalk stripe**) a pattern of this kind.
  – DERIVATIVES **chalk-striped** adjective.

chalk talk ▶ noun N. Amer. a talk or lecture in which the speaker uses blackboard and chalk.

chalky ▶ adjective (**chalkier**, **chalkiest**) **1** consisting of or rich in chalk: *chalky soil.*
2 resembling chalk in texture or paleness of colour: *a board whitened with a chalky substance.*
– DERIVATIVES **chalkiness** noun.

challah /ˈhɑːlə, xɑːˈlɑː/ ▶ noun (pl. **challahs** or **chalot(h)** /xɑːˈlɒt/) a loaf of white leavened bread, typically plaited in form, traditionally baked to celebrate the Jewish sabbath.
– ORIGIN 1920s: from Hebrew *ḥallah*.

challenge ▶ noun **1** a call to someone to participate in a competitive situation, game, or fight to decide who is superior in terms of ability or strength: *he accepted the challenge.*
■ a task or situation that tests someone's abilities: *the traverse of the ridge is a challenge for experienced climbers.* ■ an attempt to win a contest or championship in a sport.
2 an objection or query as to the truth of something, often with an implicit demand for proof: *a* ***challenge to*** *the legality of the banning order.*
■ a sentry's call for a password or other proof of identity. ■ Law an objection regarding the eligibility or suitability of a jury member.
3 [mass noun] Medicine exposure of the immune system to pathogenic organisms or antigens: *recently vaccinated calves should be protected from challenge.*
▶ verb [with obj.] **1** dispute the truth or validity of: *it is possible to challenge the report's assumptions.*
■ Law object to (a jury member). ■ (of a sentry) call on (someone) to prove their identity.
2 invite (someone) to engage in a contest: *he challenged one of my men to a duel.*
■ enter into competition with or opposition against: *organizations challenged the government in by-elections.* ■ make a rival claim to or threaten someone's hold on (a position): *they were challenging his leadership.* ■ [with obj. and infinitive] invite (someone) to do or say something that one thinks will be difficult or impossible: *I challenge the Minister to deny these accusations.* ■ [usu. as adj. **challenging**] test the abilities of: *challenging and rewarding employment.*
3 Medicine expose (the immune system) to pathogenic organisms or antigens.
– DERIVATIVES **challengeable** adjective, **challenger** noun, **challengingly** adverb.
– ORIGIN Middle English (in the senses 'accusation' and 'accuse'): from Old French *chalenge* (noun), *chalenger* (verb), from Latin *calumnia* 'calumny', *calumniari* 'calumniate'.

challenged ▶ adjective [with submodifier or in combination] used euphemistically to indicate that someone suffers impairment or disability in a specified respect: *my experience of being physically challenged.*
■ informal used to indicate that someone or something is lacking or deficient in a specified respect: *vertically challenged | today's attention-challenged teens.*

USAGE The use with a preceding adverb (e.g. **physically challenged**), originally intended to give a more positive tone than terms such as **disabled** or **handicapped**, arose in the US in the 1980s and quickly spread to the UK and elsewhere. Despite the originally serious intention the term rapidly became stalled by uses whose intention was to make fun of the attempts at euphemism and whose tone was usually clearly ironic: examples include **cerebrally challenged**, **conversationally challenged**, and **follicularly challenged**. See also usage at **DISABLED**.

Challenger Deep the deepest part (11,034 m, 36,201 ft) of the Mariana Trench in the North Pacific, discovered by HMS *Challenger II* in 1948.

challis /ˈʃalɪs, ˈʃali/ ▶ noun [mass noun] a lightweight soft clothing fabric made from silk and worsted.
– ORIGIN mid 19th cent.: origin uncertain; perhaps from the surname *Challis*.

chalone /ˈkaləʊn, ˈkeɪ-/ ▶ noun Biochemistry a substance secreted like a hormone but having the effect of inhibiting a physiological process, e.g. mitosis.
– ORIGIN early 20th cent.: from Greek *khalōn* 'slackening', present participle of *khalaein*, on the pattern of *hormone*.

chalta hai /ˌtʃʌlta ˈhʌɪ/ ▶ adjective Indian informal unconcerned; easy-going.
– ORIGIN from Hindi.

chalumeau /ˈʃaləməʊ/ ▶ noun (pl. **chalumeaux** pronunc. same) a reed instrument of the early 18th century from which the clarinet was developed.
■ (also **chalumeau register**) the lowest octave of the clarinet's range.
– ORIGIN early 18th cent.: from French, from Latin *calamellus* 'little reed', diminutive of *calamus*.

chalybeate /kəˈlɪbɪət/ ▶ adjective [attrib.] of or denoting natural mineral springs containing iron salts.
– ORIGIN mid 17th cent.: from modern Latin *chalybeatus*, from Latin *chalybs*, from Greek *khalups, khalub-* 'steel'.

Cham /tʃam/ ▶ noun (pl. same or **Chams**) **1** a member of an indigenous people of Vietnam and Cambodia, who formed an independent kingdom from the 2nd to 17th centuries AD, and whose culture is strongly influenced by that of India.
2 [mass noun] the Austronesian language of this people, with about 230,000 speakers.
▶ adjective of or relating to this people, their culture, or their language.

Chamaeleon /kəˈmiːlɪən/ Astronomy a small and faint southern constellation (the Chameleon), close to the south celestial pole.
■ [as genitive **Chamaeleontis** /kəˌmiːlɪˈɒntɪs/] used with preceding letter or numeral to designate a star in this constellation: *the star Delta Chamaeleontis.*
– ORIGIN from Greek.

chamaeleon ▶ noun variant spelling of **CHAMELEON**.

chamaephyte /ˈkamɪfʌɪt/ ▶ noun Botany a woody plant whose resting buds are on or near the ground.
– ORIGIN early 20th cent.: from Greek *khamai* 'on the ground' + **-PHYTE**.

chamber ▶ noun **1** a large room used for formal or public events: *a council chamber.*
■ one of the houses of a parliament: *the upper chamber.* ■ (**chambers**) Law, Brit. rooms used by a barrister or barristers, especially in the Inns of Court. ■ Law a judge's room used for official proceedings not required to be held in open court. ■ poetic/literary or archaic a private room, especially a bedroom.
2 an enclosed space or cavity: *a burial chamber.*
■ a large underground cavern. ■ the part of a gun bore that contains the charge. ■ Biology a cavity in a plant, animal body, or organ.
3 [as modifier] Music of or for a small group of instruments: *a chamber concert.*
▶ verb [with obj.] place (a bullet) into the chamber of a gun.
– ORIGIN Middle English (in the sense 'private room'): from Old French *chambre*, from Latin *camera* 'vault, arched chamber', from Greek *kamara* 'object with an arched cover'.

chambered ▶ adjective (especially of a gun) having a chamber of a particular kind.
■ Archaeology (of a tomb) containing a burial chamber. ■ Biology (of a plant, animal body, or organ) having one or more body cavities: [in combination] *a four-chambered heart.*

Chamberlain[1] /ˈtʃeɪmbəlɪn/, (Arthur) Neville (1869–1940), British Conservative statesman, Prime Minister 1937–40, son of Joseph Chamberlain. He pursued a policy of appeasement with Germany, signing the Munich Agreement (1938), but was forced to abandon this policy following Hitler's invasion of Czechoslovakia in 1939.

Chamberlain[2] /ˈtʃeɪmbəlɪn/, Joseph (1836–1914), British Liberal statesman. He left the Liberal party in 1886 because of Gladstone's support of Irish Home Rule. The leader of the Liberal Unionists from 1891, he played a leading role in the handling of the Second Boer War.

Chamberlain[3] /ˈtʃeɪmbəlɪn/, Owen (b.1920), American physicist. He investigated subatomic particles and in 1955 discovered the antiproton with E. G. Segrè (1905–89), for which they shared the 1959 Nobel Prize for Physics.

chamberlain /ˈtʃeɪmbəlɪn/ ▶ noun historical an officer who managed the household of a monarch or noble.
■ Brit. an officer who received revenue on behalf of a corporation or public body.
– DERIVATIVES **chamberlainship** noun.
– ORIGIN Middle English (denoting a servant in a bedchamber): via Old French from Old Saxon *kamera*, from Latin *camera* 'vault'(see **CHAMBER**).

chambermaid ▶ noun a woman who cleans bedrooms and bathrooms in a hotel.

chamber music ▶ noun [mass noun] instrumental music played by a small ensemble, with one player to a part, the most important form being the string quartet which developed in the 18th century.

Chamber of Commerce ▶ noun a local association to promote and protect the interests of the business community in a particular place.

Chamber of Deputies ▶ noun the lower legislative assembly in some parliaments.

chamber of horrors ▶ noun a place of entertainment containing instruments or scenes of torture or execution.
– ORIGIN mid 19th cent.: from the name given to a room in Madame Tussaud's waxwork exhibition.

Chamber of Trade ▶ noun a national organization representing local Chambers of Commerce.

chamber orchestra ▶ noun a small orchestra.

chamber organ ▶ noun a movable pipe organ for playing in a small concert hall, chapel, or private house.

chamber pot ▶ noun a bowl kept in a bedroom and used as a toilet, especially at night.

Chambers, Sir William (1723–96), Scottish architect. His neoclassical style is demonstrated in buildings such as Somerset House in London (1776).

Chambertin /ˈʃɒ̃bəːtã/ ▶ noun [mass noun] a dry red burgundy wine of high quality from Gevrey Chambertin in eastern France.

Chambéry /ˈʃɒ̃bəri, French ʃɑ̃beʀi/ a town in eastern France; pop. 55,600 (1990).

chambray /ˈʃambreɪ/ ▶ noun [mass noun] a linen-finished gingham cloth with a white weft and a coloured warp, producing a mottled appearance.
– ORIGIN early 19th cent. (originally US): formed irregularly from *Cambrai*, the name of a town in northern France, where it was originally made. Compare with **CAMBRIC**.

chambré /ˈʃɒmbreɪ, ˈʃɒ̃-/ ▶ adjective [predic.] (of red wine) at room temperature: *Cabernet tastes best chambré.*
– ORIGIN 1950s: French, past participle of *chambrer* 'bring to room temperature', from *chambre* 'room' (see **CHAMBER**).

chamcha /ˈtʃʌmtʃə/ ▶ noun Indian informal an obsequious person.
– ORIGIN from Hindi *camcā*, literally 'spoon'. The extended use derives from the practice of using cutlery to please British guests (the custom being to eat with the fingers).

chameleon /kəˈmiːlɪən/ (also **chamaeleon**) ▶ noun a small slow-moving Old World lizard with a prehensile tail, long extensible tongue, protruding eyes that rotate independently, and a highly developed ability to change colour.
● Family Chamaeleonidae: four genera, in particular *Chamaeleo*, and numerous species, including the **European chameleon** (*C. vulgaris*).
■ (also **American chameleon**) N. Amer. an anole. ■ figurative a changeable or inconstant person.
– DERIVATIVES **chameleonic** adjective.
– ORIGIN Middle English: via Latin *chamaeleon* from Greek *khamaileōn*, from *khamai* 'on the ground' + *leōn* 'lion'.

chameli /tʃʌˈmeɪli/ ▶ noun Indian term for **JASMINE**.
– ORIGIN from Hindi *camelī*.

chametz /hɑːˈmɛts, ˈxɑːmɛts/ (also **chometz**) ▶ noun [mass noun] Judaism leaven or food mixed with leaven, prohibited during Passover.
– ORIGIN mid 19th cent.: from Hebrew *ḥāmēṣ*.

chamfer /ˈtʃamfə/ Carpentry ▶ verb [with obj.] cut away (a right-angled edge or corner) to make a symmetrical sloping edge.
▶ noun a symmetrical sloping surface at an edge or corner.
– ORIGIN mid 16th cent. (in the sense 'flute or furrow'): back-formation from *chamfering*, from French *chamfrain*, from *chant* 'edge' (see **CANT**[2]) + *fraint* 'broken' (from Old French *fraindre* 'break', from Latin *frangere*).

chamise /ʃəˈmɪːz/ ▶ noun an evergreen shrub with small narrow leaves, common in the chaparral of California, US.
● *Adenostoma fasciculatum*, family Rosaceae.
– ORIGIN mid 19th cent.: from Mexican Spanish *chamiso*.

chamois ▶ noun **1** /ˈʃamwɑː/ (pl. same /-wɑːz/) an agile goat-antelope with short hooked horns, found in mountainous areas of Europe from Spain to the Caucasus.

● Genus *Rupicapra*, family Bovidae: *R. rupicapra* (of the Alps, East, and SE Europe), and *R. pyrenaica* (of the Pyrenees and Apennines, also called IZARD.)

2 /ˈʃami, ˈʃamwɑː/ (pl. same /-mɪz, -wɑːz/) (also **chamois leather**) [mass noun] soft pliable leather made from the skin of sheep, goats, or deer.
▪ [count noun] a piece of such leather, used typically for washing windows or cars.
– ORIGIN mid 16th cent.: from French, of unknown ultimate origin.

chamomile /ˈkaməmʌɪl/ (also **camomile**) ▶ noun an aromatic European plant of the daisy family, with white and yellow daisy-like flowers.
● The perennial **sweet** (or **Roman**) **chamomile** (*Chamaemelum nobile* (or *Anthemis nobilis*), family Compositae), used, especially formerly, for lawns and herbal medicine, the annual **German chamomile** (*Matricaria recutita*), used medicinally, and the yellow-flowered **dyer's chamomile** (*Anthemis tinctoria*), used to produce a yellow-brown dye.
– ORIGIN Middle English: from Old French *camomille*, from late Latin *chamomilla*, from Greek *khamaimēlon* 'earth-apple' (because of the apple-like smell of its flowers).

chamomile tea (also **camomile**) ▶ noun [mass noun] an infusion of dried flowers of sweet chamomile.

Chamonix /ˈʃamɒniː, French ʃamɔni/ a ski resort at the foot of Mont Blanc, in the Alps of eastern France; pop. 9,255 (1982). Full name **CHAMONIX-MONT-BLANC.**

Chamorro /tʃəˈmɒrəʊ/ ▶ noun **1** a member of the indigenous people of Guam.
2 [mass noun] the Austronesian language of this people, with about 73,000 speakers.

champ¹ ▶ verb [no obj.] **1** munch or chew enthusiastically or noisily: *he champed on his sandwich.*
▪ (of a horse) make a noisy biting or chewing action.
2 fret impatiently: *he waited, champing at her non-appearance.*
▶ noun [in sing.] a chewing noise or action.
– PHRASES **champ** (or **chafe**) **at the bit** be restlessly impatient to start doing something.
– ORIGIN late Middle English: probably imitative.

champ² ▶ noun informal a champion.
– ORIGIN mid 19th cent.: abbreviation.

Champagne /ʃamˈpeɪn, French ʃɑ̃paɲ/ a region and former province of NE France, which now corresponds to the Champagne-Ardenne administrative region. The region is noted for the white sparkling wine first produced there in about 1700.

champagne /ʃamˈpeɪn/ ▶ noun [mass noun] a white sparkling wine from Champagne, regarded as a symbol of luxury and associated with celebration.
▪ a pale cream or straw colour.

Champagne-Ardenne a region of NE France, comprising part of the Ardennes forest and the vine-growing area of Champagne.

Champagne Charlie ▶ noun informal a man noted for living a life of luxury and excess.
– ORIGIN from the name of a popular song, first performed in 1868.

champagne socialist ▶ noun Brit. derogatory a person who espouses socialist ideals while enjoying a wealthy and luxurious lifestyle.
– DERIVATIVES **champagne socialism** noun.

champaign /ˈtʃampeɪn/ ▶ noun [mass noun] poetic/literary open level countryside.
– ORIGIN late Middle English: from Old French *champagne*, from late Latin *campania*, based on Latin *campus* 'level ground'. Compare with **CAMPAIGN.**

champak /ˈtʃampək, ˈtʃam-/ (also **chempaka**) ▶ noun an Asian evergreen tree of the magnolia family, which bears fragrant orange flowers and is sacred to Hindus and Buddhists.
● *Michelia champaca*, family Magnoliaceae.
– ORIGIN from Sanskrit *campaka*.

champers ▶ noun [mass noun] informal, chiefly Brit. champagne.

champerty /ˈtʃampəːti/ ▶ noun [mass noun] Law an illegal agreement in which a person with no previous interest in a lawsuit finances it with a view to sharing the disputed property if the suit succeeds.
– DERIVATIVES **champertous** adjective.
– ORIGIN late Middle English: from Anglo-Norman French *champartie*, from Old French *champart* 'feudal lord's share of produce', from Latin *campus* 'field' + *pars* 'part'.

champignon /tʃamˈpɪnjən/ (also **fairy ring champignon**) ▶ noun a small edible mushroom with a light brown cap, growing in short grass in both Eurasia and North America and often forming fairy rings.
● *Marasmius oreades*, family Tricholomataceae, class Hymenomycetes.
– ORIGIN late 16th cent.: from French, diminutive of Old French *champagne* 'open country' (see **CHAMPAIGN**).

champion ▶ noun **1** a person who has defeated or surpassed all rivals in a competition, especially a sporting contest: [as modifier] *a champion hurdler.*
2 a person who fights or argues for a cause or on behalf of another: *a champion of financial probity.*
▪ historical a knight who fought in single combat on behalf of the monarch.
▶ verb [with obj.] support the cause of; defend: *priests who championed human rights.*
▶ adjective Brit. informal or dialect excellent: *'Thank ye, lad,' the farmer said. 'That's champion.'*
▶ adverb Brit. informal or dialect very well: *those slacks'll do champion.*
– ORIGIN Middle English (denoting a fighting man): from Old French, from medieval Latin *campio(n-)* 'fighter', from Latin *campus* (see **CAMP¹**).

Champion of England ▶ noun (in the UK) a hereditary official who offers to defend the monarch's title to the throne at coronations.

championship ▶ noun **1** a contest for the position of champion in a sport or game, typically involving a series of matches.
▪ the position or title of the winner of such a contest.
2 [mass noun] the vigorous support or defence of someone or something: *Alan's championship of his estranged wife.*

Champlain /ʃamˈpleɪn, French ʃɑ̃plɛ̃/, Samuel de (1567–1635), French explorer and colonial statesman. He established a settlement at Quebec in 1608, developing alliances with the native peoples, and was appointed Lieutenant Governor in 1612.

Champlain, Lake a lake in North America, situated to the east of the Adirondack Mountains.
– ORIGIN named after Samuel de **CHAMPLAIN**, who reached it in 1609.

champlevé /ˈʃam(p)ləˈveɪ, ʃɑ̃ˈləveɪ/ ▶ noun [mass noun] enamelwork in which hollows made in a metal surface are filled with coloured enamels.
– ORIGIN French, from *champ* 'field' + *levé* 'raised'.

Champollion /ʃɔ̃ˈpɒljɔ̃, French ʃɑ̃pɔljɔ̃/, Jean-François (1790–1832), French Egyptologist. A pioneer in the study of ancient Egypt, he is best known for his success in deciphering some of the hieroglyphic inscriptions on the Rosetta Stone in 1822.

Champs Élysées /ˌʃɒz eɪˈliːzeɪ, French ʃɑ̃z elize/ an avenue in Paris, leading from the Place de la Concorde to the Arc de Triomphe.

chana /ˈtʃʌnə/ (also **channa**) ▶ noun [mass noun] Indian chickpeas, especially when roasted and prepared as a snack.
– ORIGIN from Hindi *canā*.

chance ▶ noun **1** a possibility of something happening: *there is a chance of winning the raffle* | [mass noun] *there is little chance of his finding a job.*
▪ (chances) the probability of something happening, often with a desirable outcome: *he played down his chances of becoming chairman.* ▪ [in sing.] an opportunity to do or achieve something: *I gave her a chance to answer.*
2 [mass noun] the occurrence and development of events in the absence of any obvious design or cause: *he met his brother by chance* | [count noun] *what a lucky chance you are here.*
▪ the unplanned and unpredictable course of events regarded as a power: *chance was offering me success.*
▶ verb **1** [no obj., with infinitive] do something by accident or without design: *he was very effusive if they chanced to meet.*
▪ (chance upon/on/across) find or see by accident: *he chanced upon an interesting advertisement.*
2 [with obj.] informal do (something) despite its being dangerous or of uncertain outcome: *they chanced a late holiday.*
– PHRASES **as chance would have it** as it happened. **by any chance** possibly (used in tentative enquiries or suggestions): *were you looking for me by any chance?* **chance one's arm** (or **luck**) Brit. informal undertake something although it may be

dangerous or unsuccessful. **chance would be a fine thing** informal expressing a speaker's belief that something is desirable but the opportunity is unlikely to arise. **no chance** informal there is no possibility of that. **on the (off) chance** just in case. **stand a chance** [usu. with negative] have a prospect of success or survival: *his rivals don't stand a chance.* **take a chance** (or **chances**) behave in a way that leaves one vulnerable to danger or failure. ▪ (**take a chance on**) put one's trust in (something or someone) knowing that it may not be safe or certain. **take one's chance** do something risky with the hope of success.
– ORIGIN Middle English: from Old French *cheance*, from *cheoir* 'fall, befall', based on Latin *cadere*.

chancel /ˈtʃɑːns(ə)l/ ▶ noun the part of a church near the altar, reserved for the clergy and choir, and typically separated from the nave by steps or a screen.
– ORIGIN Middle English: from Old French, from Latin *cancelli* 'crossbars'.

chancellery /ˈtʃɑːns(ə)l(ə)ri, -sləri/ ▶ noun (pl. **-ies**) **1** the position, office, or department of a chancellor.
▪ the official residence of a chancellor.
2 chiefly US an office attached to an embassy or consulate.
– ORIGIN Middle English: from Old French *chancellerie*, from *chancelier* 'secretary' (see **CHANCELLOR**).

chancellor ▶ noun a senior state or legal official.
▪ (**Chancellor**) short for **CHANCELLOR OF THE EXCHEQUER.** ▪ (**Chancellor**) the head of the government in some European countries, such as Germany. ▪ chiefly Brit. the non-resident honorary head of a university. ▪ US the president or chief administrative officer of a university. ▪ a bishop's law officer. ▪ US the presiding judge of a chancery court. ▪ (in the UK) an officer of an order of knighthood who seals commissions.
– DERIVATIVES **chancellorship** noun.
– ORIGIN late Old English from Old French *cancelier*, from late Latin *cancellarius* 'porter, secretary' (originally a court official stationed at the grating separating public from judges), from *cancelli* 'crossbars'.

Chancellor of the Duchy of Lancaster ▶ noun (in the UK) a member of the government legally representing the Crown as Duke of Lancaster, typically a cabinet minister employed on non-departmental work.

Chancellor of the Exchequer ▶ noun the finance minister of the United Kingdom, who prepares the nation's annual budgets.

chance-medley ▶ noun [mass noun] Law, rare the killing of a person accidentally in self-defence in a fight.
– ORIGIN late 15th cent.: from Anglo-Norman French *chance medlee*, literally 'mixed chance', from *chance* 'luck' + *medlee*, feminine past participle of *medler* 'to mix' (based on Latin *miscere*).

chancer ▶ noun informal a person who exploits any opportunity to the utmost.

chancery ▶ noun (pl. **-ies**) **1** (**Chancery** or **Chancery Division**) Law (in the UK) the Lord Chancellor's court, a division of the High Court of Justice.
▪ US a court of equity. ▪ [mass noun] US equity. ▪ historical the court of a bishop's chancellor.
2 chiefly Brit. an office attached to an embassy or consulate.
3 a public record office.
– ORIGIN late Middle English: contraction of **CHANCELLERY.**

Chan Chan /tʃan ˈtʃan/ the capital of the pre-Inca civilization of the Chimu. Its extensive adobe ruins are situated on the coast of north Peru.

Chan-chiang /tʃanˈtʃjaŋ/ variant of **ZHANJIANG.**

chancre /ˈʃaŋkə/ ▶ noun Medicine a painless ulcer, particularly one developing on the genitals in venereal disease.
– ORIGIN late 16th cent.: from French, from Latin *cancer* 'creeping ulcer'.

chancroid /ˈʃaŋkrɔɪd/ ▶ noun [mass noun] a venereal infection causing ulceration of the lymph nodes in the groin. Also called **SOFT SORE.**

chancy ▶ adjective (**chancier**, **chanciest**) informal subject to unpredictable changes and circumstances.

– DERIVATIVES **chancily** adverb, **chanciness** noun.

chandelier /ˌʃandəˈlɪə/ ▶ **noun** a large, decorative hanging light with branches for several light bulbs or candles.

– ORIGIN mid 18th cent.: from French, from *chandelle* 'candle', from Latin *candela*, from *candere* 'be white, glisten'.

C

chandelle /ʃanˈdɛl/ ▶ **noun** a steep climbing turn executed in an aircraft to gain height while changing the direction of flight.

– ORIGIN 1970s: from French, literally 'candle'.

Chandigarh /ˌtʃʌndɪˈgɑː/ **1** a Union Territory of NW India, created in 1966.
2 a city in this territory; pop. 503,000 (1991). The present city was designed in 1950 by Le Corbusier as a new capital for the Punjab and is now the capital of the states of Punjab and Haryana.

Chandler /ˈtʃɑːndlə/, Raymond (Thornton) (1888–1959), American novelist. He is remembered as the creator of the private detective Philip Marlowe. Notable novels: *The Big Sleep* (1939).

chandler /ˈtʃɑːndlə/ ▶ **noun 1** (also **ship chandler**) a dealer in supplies and equipment for ships and boats.
2 historical a dealer in household items such as oil, soap, paint, and groceries.
■ a person who makes and sells candles.

– ORIGIN Middle English (denoting a candlemaker or candle seller): from Old French *chandelier*, from *chandelle* 'candle' (see **CHANDELIER**).

chandlery ▶ **noun** (pl. **-ies**) the shop or business of a chandler.
■ [mass noun] goods sold by a chandler.

Chandragupta Maurya /ˌtʃʌndrəˌgʊptə ˈmaʊrɪə/ (*c.*325–297 BC), Indian emperor. He founded the Mauryan empire and annexed provinces deep into Afghanistan from Alexander's Greek successors.

Chandrasekhar /ˌtʃʌndrəˈsiːkə, -ˈseɪkə/, Subrahmanyan (1910–95), Indian-born American astronomer. He suggested how some stars could eventually collapse to form a dense white dwarf, provided that their mass does not exceed an upper limit (the **Chandrasekhar limit**).

Chanel /ʃəˈnɛl, French ʃanɛl/, Coco (1883–1971), French couturière; born *Gabrielle Bonheur Chanel*. Her simple but sophisticated garments were a radical departure from the stiff corseted styles of the day. She also diversified into perfumes, costume jewellery, and textiles.

Chaney /ˈtʃeɪni/, Lon (1883–1930), American actor; born *Alonso Chaney*. He played a wide variety of deformed villains and macabre characters in more than 150 films, including *The Hunchback of Notre Dame* (1923).

Changan /tʃaŋˈɑːn/ former name for **XIAN**.

Chang-chiakow /ˌtʃaŋtʃjɑːˈkaʊ/ variant of **ZHANGJIAKOU**.

Changchun /tʃaŋˈtʃʊn/ an industrial city in NE China, capital of Jilin province; pop. 2,070,000 (1990).

change ▶ **verb 1** make or become different: [with obj.] *a proposal to change the law* | *filters* ***change*** *the ammonia* ***into*** *nitrate* | [no obj.] *the caterpillar begins to* ***change to*** *the chrysalis stage after two to three weeks.*
■ [no obj., with complement] alter in terms of: *the ferns began to* ***change shape***. ■ [no obj.] (of traffic lights) move from one colour of signal to another. ■ [no obj.] (of the moon) arrive at a fresh phase; become new.
2 [with obj.] take or use another instead of: *she decided to change her name.*
■ move from one to another: *she had to change trains.* ■ [no obj.] move to a different train, bus, or underground line: *we had to change at Rugby.* ■ give up or get rid of (something) in exchange for something else: *we* ***changed*** *the flagstones* ***for*** *quarry tiles.* ■ remove (something, typically something dirty or faulty) and replace it with another of the same kind: *he scarcely knew how to change a plug.* ■ put a clean nappy on (a baby or young child). ■ engage a different gear in a motor vehicle: *he changed into second* | [with obj.] *wait for a gap and then change gear* | figurative *with business concluded, the convention changes gear and a gigantic circus takes over the town.* ■ exchange (a sum of money) for the same sum in a different currency or denomination. ■ [no obj.] put different clothes on: *he changed for dinner.*
▶ **noun 1** an act or process through which something becomes different: *the* ***change from*** *a nomadic* ***to*** *an agricultural society* | [mass noun] *activities related to environmental change.*
■ the substitution of one thing for another: *we need a change of government.* ■ an alteration or modification: *a change came over Eddie's face.* ■ a new or refreshingly different experience: *couscous makes an interesting change from rice.* ■ [in sing.] a clean garment or garments as a replacement for something one is wearing: ***a change of*** *socks.* ■ (**the change** or **the change of life**) informal the menopause. ■ the moon's arrival at a fresh phase, typically at the new moon.
2 [mass noun] coins as opposed to banknotes: *a handful of loose change.*
■ money given in exchange for the same sum in larger units. ■ money returned to someone as the balance of the sum paid for something.
3 (usu. **changes**) an order in which a peal of bells can be rung.
4 (**Change** or **'Change**) historical a place where merchants met to do business.

– PHRASES **change address** move house or business premises. **change colour** blanch or flush. **change hands** (of a business or building) pass to a different owner. ■ (of money or a marketable commodity) pass to another person in the course of a business transaction. **a change is as good as a rest** proverb a change of work or occupation can be as restorative or refreshing as a period of relaxation. **change one's mind** adopt a different opinion or plan. **a change of air** a different climate, typically as means of improving one's health. **a change of heart** a move to a different opinion or attitude. **change places** exchange places or roles. **change step** alter one's step so that the opposite leg is the one that marks time when marching. **change the subject** begin talking of something different, especially to avoid embarrassment. **change one's tune** express a very different opinion or behave in a very different way, especially in response to a change in circumstances. **for a change** contrary to how things usually happen or in order to introduce variety: *it's nice to be pampered for a change.* **get no change out of** Brit. informal fail to get information or a desired reaction from. **ring the changes** vary the ways of expressing, arranging, or doing something. [ORIGIN: with allusion to bell-ringing and the different orders in which a peal of bells may be rung.]

– DERIVATIVES **changeful** adjective.

– ORIGIN Middle English: from Old French *change* (noun), *changer* (verb), from late Latin *cambiare*, from Latin *cambire* 'barter', probably of Celtic origin.

▶ **change down** Brit. engage a lower gear in a vehicle or on a bicycle.
change over 1 move from one system or situation to another: *arable farmers have to* ***change over to*** *dairy farming.* **2** swap roles or duties.
change up Brit. engage a higher gear in a vehicle or on a bicycle.

changeable ▶ **adjective 1** liable to unpredictable variation: *the weather will be changeable with rain at times.*
2 able to be altered.
■ able to be exchanged for another item of the same type.

– DERIVATIVES **changeability** noun, **changeableness** noun, **changeably** adverb.

changeless ▶ **adjective** remaining the same.

– DERIVATIVES **changelessly** adverb, **changelessness** noun.

changeling ▶ **noun** a child believed to have been secretly substituted by fairies for the parents' real child in infancy.

changement de pieds /ˌʃɒ̃(d)ʒmɒ̃ də ˈpjeɪ/ (also **changement**) ▶ **noun** (pl. **changements de pieds** pronunc. same) Ballet a leap during which a dancer changes the position of the feet.

changeover ▶ **noun** a change from one system or situation to another.

change purse ▶ **noun** N. Amer. a purse used for carrying money, especially by a woman.

changer ▶ **noun** a person or thing that changes something.
■ Computing a device that holds several disks, CDs, or other memory devices, and is able to switch between them: *a disk changer.*

change-ringing ▶ **noun** [mass noun] the ringing of sets of church bells or handbells in a constantly varying order.

– DERIVATIVES **change-ringer** noun.

change-up ▶ **noun** Baseball an unexpectedly slow pitch designed to throw off the batter's timing.

Chang Jiang /tʃaŋ dʒaŋ/ another name for **YANGTZE**.

Changsha /tʃaŋˈʃɑː/ the capital of Hunan province in east central China; pop. 1,300,000 (1990).

Chania /kɑːˈnjɑː/ a port on the north coast of Crete, capital of the island from 1841 to 1971; pop. 47,340 (1981). Greek name **KHANIÁ**.

channa /ˈtʃʌnə/ ▶ **noun** variant spelling of **CHANA**.

channel ▶ **noun 1** a length of water wider than a strait, joining two larger areas of water, especially two seas.
■ (**the Channel**) the English Channel. ■ a navigable passage in a stretch of water otherwise unsafe for vessels. ■ a hollow bed for a natural or artificial waterway. ■ Biology a tubular passage or duct for liquid. ■ a narrow gap, passage, or groove: *a channel opened up between two lines of cars.* ■ an electric circuit which acts as a path for a signal: *an audio channel.* ■ Electronics the semiconductor region in a field-effect transistor that forms the main current path between the source and the drain.
2 a band of frequencies used in radio and television transmission, especially as used by a particular station.
■ a service or station using such a band.
3 a medium for communication or the passage of information: *they didn't apply through the proper channels.*
▶ **verb** (**channelled**, **channelling**; US **channeled**, **channeling**) [with obj.] **1** direct towards a particular end or object: *the council is to channel public funds into training schemes.*
■ cause to pass along or through a specified route or medium: *many countries* ***channel*** *their aid* ***through*** *charities.* ■ (of a person) serve as a medium for (a spirit).
2 [usu. as adj. **channelled**] form channels or grooves in: *pottery with a distinctive channelled decoration.*

– ORIGIN Middle English: from Old French *chanel*, from Latin *canalis* 'pipe, groove, channel', from *canna* 'reed' (see **CANE**). Compare with **CANAL**.

channel cat (also **channel catfish**) ▶ **noun** a common North American freshwater catfish which has a pale blue to olive back with dark spots.
● *Ictalurus punctatus*, family Ictaluridae.

Channel Country an area of SW Queensland and NE South Australia, watered intermittently by natural channels, where rich grasslands produced by the summer rains provide grazing for cattle.

channel-graze ▶ **verb** US informal another term for **CHANNEL-HOP** (in sense 1).

– DERIVATIVES **channel-grazer** noun.

channel-hop ▶ **verb** [no obj.] informal **1** change frequently from one television channel to another, using a remote control device.
2 travel across the English Channel and back to Britain frequently or for only a brief trip.

– DERIVATIVES **channel-hopper** noun.

Channel Islands a group of islands in the English Channel off the NW coast of France, of which the largest are Jersey, Guernsey, and Alderney; pop. 146,000 (1991). Formerly part of the dukedom of Normandy, they have owed allegiance to England since the Norman Conquest in 1066.

channelize (also **-ise**) ▶ **verb** [with obj.] chiefly N. Amer. another term for **CHANNEL** (in sense 1).

channel-surf ▶ **verb** informal, chiefly N. Amer. another term for **CHANNEL-HOP** (in sense 1).

Channel Tunnel a railway tunnel under the English Channel, linking the coasts of England and France, opened in 1994 and 49 km (31 miles) long.

chanson /ˈʃɒ̃sɒ̃, French ʃɑ̃sɔ̃/ ▶ **noun** a French song.

– ORIGIN French, from Latin *cantio(n-)* 'singing', from *canere* 'sing'.

chanson de geste /ˌʃɒ̃sɒ̃ də ˈʒɛst, French ʃɑ̃sɔ̃də ʒɛst/ ▶ **noun** (pl. **chansons de geste** pronunc. same) a medieval French historical verse romance, typically one connected with Charlemagne.

– ORIGIN French, literally 'song of heroic deeds', from *chanson* 'song' (see **CHANSON**) and *geste* from Latin *gesta* 'actions, exploits', from *gerere* 'perform'.

chant ▶ **noun 1** a repeated rhythmic phrase, typically one shouted or sung in unison by a crowd.
■ a monotonous or repetitive song, typically an incantation or part of a ritual.
2 Music a short musical passage in two or more

phrases used for singing unmetrical words; a psalm or canticle sung to such music.
■[mass noun] the style of music consisting of such passages: *Gregorian chant.*
▶**verb** [with obj.] say or shout repeatedly in a sing-song tone: *protesters were chanting slogans* | [with direct speech] *the crowd chanted 'No violence!'*
■sing or intone (a psalm, canticle, or sacred text).
– ORIGIN late Middle English (in the sense 'sing'): from Old French *chanter* 'sing', from Latin *cantare*, frequentative of *canere* 'sing'.

chanter ▶ **noun** **1** a person who chants something. **2** Music the pipe of a bagpipe with finger holes, on which the melody is played.
– ORIGIN late Middle English: from Old French *chanteor*, from Latin *cantator*, from *cantare* (see **CHANT**).

chanterelle /ˈtʃɑːntərɛl, ˌtʃɑːntəˈrɛl/ ▶ **noun** an edible woodland mushroom which has a yellow funnel-shaped cap and a faint smell of apricots, found in both Eurasia and North America.
● *Cantharellus cibarius*, family Cantharellaceae, class Hymenomycetes.
– ORIGIN late 18th cent.: from French, from modern Latin *cantharellus*, diminutive of *cantharus*, from Greek *kantharos*, denoting a kind of drinking container.

chanteuse /ʃɑːnˈtəːz, French ʃɑ̃tøz/ ▶ **noun** a female singer of popular songs.
– ORIGIN French, from *chanter* 'sing'.

chantey /ˈʃanti/ ▶ **noun** archaic spelling of **SHANTY**[2].

chanticleer /ˈtʃɑːntɪˌklɪə/ ▶ **noun** poetic/literary a name given to a domestic cock, especially in fairy tales.
– ORIGIN Middle English: from Old French *Chantecler*, the name of the cock in the fable *Reynard the Fox*, from *chanter* 'sing, crow' (see **CHANT**) + *cler* 'clear'.

Chantilly cream /ʃanˈtɪli/ ▶ **noun** [mass noun] sweetened or flavoured whipped cream.
– ORIGIN mid 19th cent.: named after *Chantilly*, a town near Paris, where it originated.

Chantilly lace ▶ **noun** [mass noun] a delicate kind of bobbin lace.
– ORIGIN mid 19th cent.: named after *Chantilly* (see **CHANTILLY CREAM**).

chanting goshawk ▶ **noun** a long-legged African hawk with pale grey upper parts, throat, and breast, noted for its prolonged musical fluting call delivered from a treetop perch.
● Genus *Melierax*, family Accipitridae: three species.

chantry /ˈtʃɑːntri/ ▶ **noun** (pl. **-ies**) an endowment for a priest or priests to celebrate masses for the founder's soul.
■a chapel, altar, or other part of a church endowed for such a purpose.
– ORIGIN late Middle English: from Old French *chanterie*, from *chanter* 'to sing'.

chanty /ˈʃanti/ ▶ **noun** (pl. **-ies**) variant spelling of **SHANTY**[2].

Chanukkah ▶ **noun** variant spelling of **HANUKKAH**.

Chanute /tʃəˈnuːt/, Octave (1832–1910), French-born American aviation pioneer. From 1898 he produced a number of gliders, including a biplane which made over 700 flights. He assisted the Wright brothers in making the world's first controlled powered flight.

chaology /keɪˈɒlədʒi/ ▶ **noun** [mass noun] Physics the study of chaotic systems.
– DERIVATIVES **chaologist** noun.

Chao Phraya /ˌtʃaʊ prəˈjɑː/ a major waterway of central Thailand, formed by the junction of the Ping and Nan Rivers.

chaos /ˈkeɪɒs/ ▶ **noun** [mass noun] complete disorder and confusion: *snow caused chaos in the region.*
■Physics behaviour so unpredictable as to appear random, owing to great sensitivity to small changes in conditions. ■ the formless matter supposed to have existed before the creation of the universe. ■ (**Chaos**) Greek Mythology the first created being, from which came the primeval deities Gaia, Tartarus, Erebus, and Nyx.
– ORIGIN late 15th cent. (denoting a gaping void or chasm, later formless primordial matter): via French and Latin from Greek *khaos* 'vast chasm, void'.

chaotic ▶ **adjective** in a state of complete confusion and disorder: *the political situation was chaotic.*
■Physics of or relating to systems which exhibit chaos.
– DERIVATIVES **chaotically** adverb.
– ORIGIN early 18th cent.: from **CHAOS**, on the pattern of words such as *hypnotic*.

chaotic attractor ▶ **noun** Mathematics another term for **STRANGE ATTRACTOR**.

chap[1] ▶ **verb** (**chapped**, **chapping**) [no obj.] (of the skin) become cracked, rough, or sore, typically through exposure to cold weather.
■[with obj.] [usu. as adj. **chapped**] (of the wind or cold) cause (skin) to crack in this way: *chapped lips.*
▶**noun** a cracked or sore patch on the skin.
– ORIGIN late Middle English: of unknown origin.

chap[2] ▶ **noun** informal, chiefly Brit. a man or a boy.
■dated a friendly form of address between men and boys: *best of luck, old chap.*
– ORIGIN late 16th cent. (denoting a buyer or customer): abbreviation of **CHAPMAN**. The current sense dates from the early 18th cent.

chap[3] ▶ **noun** (usu. **chaps**) the lower jaw or half of the cheek, especially that of a pig used as food.
– ORIGIN mid 16th cent.: of unknown origin. Compare with **CHOPS**.

chap. ▶ abbreviation for chapter.

chaparajos /ˌʃapəˈreɪhəʊs, ˌtʃ-/ (also **chaparejos**) ▶ **plural noun** N. Amer. leather trousers without a seat, worn by a cowboy over ordinary trousers to protect the legs.
– ORIGIN mid 19th cent.: from Mexican Spanish *chaparreras*, from *chaparra* (with reference to protection from thorny vegetation: see **CHAPARRAL**); probably influenced by Spanish *aparejo* 'equipment'.

chaparral /ˌʃapəˈral, ˌtʃ-/ ▶ **noun** [mass noun] N. Amer. vegetation consisting chiefly of tangled shrubs and thorny bushes.
– ORIGIN mid 19th cent.: from Spanish, from *chaparra* 'dwarf evergreen oak'.

chapatti /tʃəˈpɑːti, -ˈpati/ (also **chupatty**) ▶ **noun** (pl. **chapattis**) (in Indian cookery) a thin pancake of unleavened wholemeal bread cooked on a griddle.
– ORIGIN from Hindi *capātī*, from *capānā* 'flatten, roll out'.

chapbook ▶ **noun** historical a small pamphlet containing tales, ballads, or tracts, sold by pedlars.
■chiefly N. Amer. a small paper-covered booklet, typically containing poems or fiction.
– ORIGIN early 19th cent.: from **CHAPMAN** + **BOOK**.

chape /tʃeɪp/ ▶ **noun** **1** historical the metal point of a scabbard.
2 the metal pin of a buckle.
– ORIGIN Middle English (in the general sense 'plate of metal overlaying or trimming something'): from Old French, literally 'cape, hood', from late Latin *cappa* 'cap'.

chapeau /ˈʃapəʊ/ ▶ **noun** (pl. **chapeaux**) Heraldry a hat or cap, typically a red one with an ermine lining, on which the crests of some peers are borne.
– ORIGIN late 15th cent.: from French, from Latin *cappellum*, diminutive of *cappa* 'cap'.

chapeau-bras /ˌʃapəʊˈbrɑː, French ʃapobʀa/ ▶ **noun** (pl. **chapeaux-bras** pronunc. same) historical a man's three-cornered flat silk hat, typically carried under the arm.
– ORIGIN French, from *chapeau* 'hat' and *bras* 'arm'.

chapel ▶ **noun** **1** a small building for Christian worship, typically one attached to an institution or private house: *attendance **at chapel** was compulsory.*
■a part of a large church or cathedral with its own altar and dedication. ■ Brit. a place of worship for Nonconformist congregations: *she went **to chapel** twice on Sunday.* ■ a room or building for funeral services. ■ chiefly US a chapel of rest.
2 Brit. the members or branch of a print or newspaper trade union at a particular place of work.
▶**adjective** Brit. informal belonging to or regularly attending a Nonconformist chapel: *they were staunch chapel folk.*
– ORIGIN Middle English: from Old French *chapele*, from medieval Latin *cappella*, diminutive of *cappa* 'cap or cape' (the first chapel being a sanctuary in which St Martin's cloak was preserved).

chapel of ease ▶ **noun** an Anglican chapel situated for the convenience of parishioners living a long distance from the parish church.

chapel of rest ▶ **noun** Brit. an undertaker's mortuary, where bodies are kept before a funeral.

chapel royal ▶ **noun** a chapel in a royal palace.
■(**the Chapel Royal**) the body of clergy, singers, and musicians employed by the English monarch for religious services, now based at St James's Palace, London.

chapelry ▶ **noun** (pl. **-ies**) a district served by an Anglican chapel.
– ORIGIN Middle English: from Old French *chapelerie*, medieval Latin *cappellaria*, from *cappella*, originally 'little cloak' (see **CHAPEL**).

chaperone /ˈʃapərəʊn/ (also **chaperon** /ˈʃapərɒn/) ▶ **noun** a person who accompanies and looks after another person or group of people, in particular:
■dated an older woman responsible for the decorous behaviour of a young unmarried girl at social occasions. ■ a person who takes charge of a child or group of children in public.
▶**verb** [with obj.] accompany and look after or supervise.
– DERIVATIVES **chaperonage** /ˈʃap(ə)r(ə)nɪdʒ/ noun.
– ORIGIN late Middle English (denoting a hood or cap, regarded as giving protection): from French, feminine of *chaperon* 'hood', diminutive of *chape* (see **CHAPE**). The current sense dates from the early 18th cent.

chaperonin /ˌʃapəˈrəʊnɪn/ ▶ **noun** Biochemistry a protein that aids the assembly and folding of other protein molecules in living cells.
– ORIGIN late 20th cent.: from **CHAPERONE** + **-IN**[1].

chap-fallen (also **chop-fallen**) ▶ **adjective** archaic with one's lower jaw hanging due to extreme exhaustion or dejection.
– ORIGIN late 16th cent.: from **CHAP**[3].

chaplain ▶ **noun** a member of the clergy attached to a private chapel, institution, ship, regiment, etc.
– DERIVATIVES **chaplaincy** noun.
– ORIGIN Middle English: from Old French *chapelain*, from medieval Latin *cappellanus*, originally denoting a custodian of the cloak of St Martin, from *cappella*, originally 'little cloak' (see **CHAPEL**).

chaplet /ˈtʃaplɪt/ ▶ **noun** **1** a garland or circlet for a person's head.
2 a string of 55 beads (one third of the rosary number) for counting prayers, or as a necklace.
3 a metal support for the core of a hollow casting mould.
– DERIVATIVES **chapleted** adjective.
– ORIGIN late Middle English: from Old French *chapelet*, diminutive of *chapel* 'hat', based on late Latin *cappa* 'cap'.

Chaplin, Charlie (1889–1977), English film actor and director; full name *Sir Charles Spencer Chaplin*. He directed and starred in many short silent comedies, mostly playing a bowler-hatted tramp, a character which was his trademark for more than twenty-five years. Notable films: *The Kid* (1921).
– DERIVATIVES **Chaplinesque** adjective.

Chapman, George (*c.*1560–1634), English poet and dramatist. He is chiefly known for his translations of Homer; the complete *Iliad* and *Odyssey* were published in 1616.

chapman ▶ **noun** (pl. **-men**) archaic a pedlar.
– ORIGIN Old English *cēapman*, from *cēap* 'bargaining, trade' (see **CHEAP**) + **MAN**.

chappal /ˈtʃap(ə)l/ ▶ **noun** Indian a sandal.
– ORIGIN from Hindi *cappal*.

Chappaquiddick Island /ˌtʃapəˈkwɪdɪk/ a small island off the coast of Massachusetts, the scene of a car accident in 1969 involving Senator Edward Kennedy in which his assistant Mary Jo Kopechne drowned.

Chappell /ˈtʃap(ə)l/, Greg (b.1948), Australian cricketer; full name *Gregory Stephen Chappell*. Captain of Australia (1975–84), he was the first Australian to score more than 7,000 test-match runs.

chappie ▶ **noun** (pl. **-ies**) Brit. informal another term for **CHAP**[2].

chaprasi /tʃʌˈprɑːsi/ ▶ **noun** (pl. **chaprasis**) Indian a person carrying out junior office duties, especially one who carries messages.
– ORIGIN from Hindi, from *caprās*, denoting a metal identity badge worn by messengers or orderlies.

chaps ▶ **plural noun** short for **CHAPARAJOS**.

chaptalization /ˌtʃaptəlʌɪˈzeɪʃ(ə)n/ ▶ **noun** [mass noun] (in winemaking) the correction or improvement of must by the addition of calcium carbonate to neutralize acid, or of sugar to increase alcoholic strength.
– DERIVATIVES **chaptalize** verb.
– ORIGIN late 19th cent.: from the name of Jean A.

Chaptal (1756–1832), the French chemist who invented the process, + *-ization* (see **-IZE**).

chapter ▶ **noun** **1** a main division of a book, typically with a number or title.
■ figurative a period of time in a person's life or the history of a nation or organization distinguished from the rest by important events or developments. ■ an Act of Parliament numbered as part of a session's proceedings. ■ a section of a treaty.
2 the governing body of a religious community, especially a cathedral, or a knightly order.
3 chiefly N. Amer. a local branch of a society.
■ a local group of Hell's Angels.
– PHRASES **chapter and verse** an exact reference or authority: *she can give chapter and verse on current legislation.* **a chapter of accidents** a series of unfortunate events.
– ORIGIN Middle English: from Old French *chapitre*, from Latin *capitulum*, diminutive of *caput* 'head'.

Chapter 11 ▶ **noun** [mass noun] US protection from creditors given to a company in financial difficulties for a limited period to allow it to reorganize.
– ORIGIN with allusion to chapter 11 of the US bankruptcy code.

chapter house ▶ **noun** a building used for the meetings of the canons of a cathedral or other religious community.
■ US a place where a college fraternity or sorority meets.

char[1] /tʃɑː/ ▶ **verb** (**charred**, **charring**) [with obj.] (usu. **be charred**) partially burn (an object) so as to blacken its surface: *their bodies were badly charred in the fire* | [as adj. **charred**] *charred remains.*
■ [no obj.] (of an object) become burnt and discoloured in such a way.
▶ **noun** [mass noun] material that has been charred.
– ORIGIN late 17th cent.: apparently a back-formation from **CHARCOAL**.

char[2] /tʃɑː/ Brit. informal ▶ **noun** a charwoman.
▶ **verb** (**charred**, **charring**) [no obj.] work as a charwoman.

char[3] /tʃɑː/ (also **cha** /tʃɑː/ or **chai** /tʃʌɪ/) ▶ **noun** [mass noun] Brit. informal tea.
– ORIGIN late 16th cent. (as *cha*; rare before the early 20th cent.): from Chinese (Mandarin dialect) *chá*.

char[4] ▶ **noun** variant spelling of **CHARR**.

charabanc /ˈʃarəbaŋ/ ▶ **noun** Brit. an early form of bus, used typically for pleasure trips.
– ORIGIN early 19th cent.: from French *char-à-bancs* 'carriage with benches' (the original horse-drawn charabancs having rows of bench seats).

characin /ˈkarəsɪn/ ▶ **noun** a small and brightly coloured freshwater fish native to Africa and tropical America.
• Family Characidae: numerous species, including the piranhas and popular aquarium fishes such as the tetras.
– ORIGIN late 19th cent.: from modern Latin *Characinus* (genus name), from Greek *kharax*, literally 'pointed stake', denoting a kind of fish.

character ▶ **noun** **1** the mental and moral qualities distinctive to an individual: *running away was not in keeping with her character.*
■ the distinctive nature of something: *gas lamps give the area its character.* ■ [mass noun] the quality of being individual, typically in an interesting or unusual way: *the island is full of character.* ■ [mass noun] strength and originality in a person's nature: *she had character as well as beauty.* ■ a person's good reputation: *to what do I owe this attack on my character?* ■ dated a written statement of someone's good qualities; a testimonial.
2 a person in a novel, play, or film.
■ a part played by an actor. ■ [with adj.] a person seen in terms of a particular aspect of their nature: *he was a larger-than-life character.* ■ informal a very individual person, typically an interesting or amusing one: *she's a right character with a will of her own.*
3 a printed or written letter or symbol.
■ Computing a symbol representing a letter or number. ■ Computing the bit pattern used to store this.
4 chiefly Biology a characteristic, especially one that assists in the identification of a species.
▶ **verb** [with obj.] archaic inscribe.
■ describe: *you have well charactered him.*
– PHRASES **in** (or **out of**) **character** in keeping (or not in keeping) with someone's usual pattern of behaviour and motives.
– DERIVATIVES **characterful** adjective, **characterfully** adverb, **characterless** adjective.
– ORIGIN Middle English: from Old French *caractere*, via Latin from Greek *kharaktēr* 'a stamping tool'. From the early sense 'distinctive mark' arose 'token, feature, or trait' (early 16th cent.), and from this 'a description, especially of a person's qualities', giving rise to 'distinguishing qualities'.

character actor ▶ **noun** an actor who specializes in playing eccentric or unusual people rather than leading roles.

character assassination ▶ **noun** [mass noun] the malicious and unjustified harming of a person's good reputation.

character code ▶ **noun** Computing the binary code used to represent a letter or number.

character dance ▶ **noun** [mass noun] a style of ballet deriving inspiration from national or folk dances, or interpreting and representing a particular profession, mode of living, or personality. The movements used tend to be less stylized than in classical ballet, allowing greater individual expression and diversity.
– DERIVATIVES **character dancer** noun.

characteristic ▶ **adjective** typical of a particular person, place, or thing: *he began with a characteristic attack on extremism.*
▶ **noun** **1** a feature or quality belonging typically to a person, place, or thing and serving to identify them.
2 Mathematics the whole number or integral part of a logarithm, which gives the order of magnitude of the original number.
– DERIVATIVES **characteristically** adverb.
– ORIGIN mid 17th cent.: from French *caractéristique* or medieval Latin *characteristicus*, from Greek *kharaktēristikos*, from *kharaktēr* 'a stamping tool'.

characteristic curve ▶ **noun** a graph showing the relationship between two variable but interdependent quantities.

characteristic function ▶ **noun** Mathematics a function whose result is unity for the members of a given set and zero for all non-members.

characteristic radiation ▶ **noun** [mass noun] radiation consisting of wavelengths which are peculiar to the element which emits them.

characterize (also **-ise**) ▶ **verb** [with obj.] **1** describe the distinctive nature or features of: *the historian characterized the period as the decade of revolution.*
2 (often **be characterized**) (of a feature or quality) be typical or characteristic of: *the disease is characterized by weakening of the immune system.*
– DERIVATIVES **characterization** noun.
– ORIGIN late 16th cent. (in the sense 'engrave, inscribe'): from French *caractériser* or medieval Latin *characterizare*, from Greek *kharaktērizein*, from *kharaktēr* 'a stamping tool'.

character part ▶ **noun** a part played by a character actor.

character recognition ▶ **noun** [mass noun] the identification by electronic means of printed or written characters.

character string ▶ **noun** a linear sequence of characters, typically one stored in or processed by a computer.

character witness ▶ **noun** a person who attests to another's good reputation in a court of law.

charade /ʃəˈrɑːd/ ▶ **noun** an absurd pretence intended to create a pleasant or respectable appearance.
■ (**charades**) a game in which players guess a word or phrase from a written or acted clue given for each syllable and for the whole item.
– ORIGIN late 18th cent.: from French, from modern Provençal *charrado* 'conversation', from *charra* 'chatter', perhaps of imitative origin.

charango /tʃəˈraŋɡəʊ/ ▶ **noun** a small Andean guitar, traditionally made from an armadillo shell.
– ORIGIN 1920s: from South American Spanish.

charas /ˈtʃɑːrəs/ ▶ **noun** [mass noun] cannabis resin.
– ORIGIN from Hindi *caras*.

charbroil ▶ **verb** [with obj.] [usu. as adj. **charbroiled**] N. Amer. grill (food, especially meat) on a rack over charcoal: *charbroiled steak.*
– ORIGIN 1950s: blend of **CHARCOAL** and **BROIL**[1].

charcoal ▶ **noun** [mass noun] a porous black solid, consisting of an amorphous form of carbon, obtained as a residue when wood, bone, or other organic matter is heated in the absence of air.
■ a substance of this kind used for drawing. ■ [count noun] a drawing made using this substance. ■ a dark grey colour: [as modifier] *a phone in* ***charcoal grey.***
– ORIGIN late Middle English: probably related to **COAL** in the early sense 'charcoal'.

charcoal burner ▶ **noun** **1** a person who makes charcoal.
2 a small stove using charcoal as fuel.

charcoal filter ▶ **noun** a filter containing charcoal to absorb impurities.

Charcot /ˈʃɑːkəʊ, French ʃarko/, Jean-Martin (1825–93), French neurologist, regarded as one of the founders of modern neurology. He established links between neurological conditions and particular lesions in the central nervous system. His work on hysteria was taken up by his pupil Sigmund Freud.

charcuterie /ʃɑːˈkuːt(ə)ri/ ▶ **noun** (pl. **-ies**) [mass noun] cold cooked meats collectively.
■ [count noun] a shop selling such meats.
– ORIGIN French, from obsolete *char* (earlier form of *chair*) 'flesh' + *cuite* 'cooked'.

chard /tʃɑːd/ ▶ **noun** (also **Swiss chard**) a beet of a variety with broad white leaf stalks which may be prepared and eaten separately from the green parts of the leaf.
■ the blanched shoots of other plants, eaten as a vegetable, e.g. globe artichoke.
– ORIGIN mid 17th cent.: from French *carde*, perhaps influenced by *chardon* 'thistle'.

Chardonnay /ˈʃɑːdəneɪ/ ▶ **noun** [mass noun] a variety of white wine grape used for making champagne and other wines.
■ a wine made from this grape.
– ORIGIN French.

charentais /ˈʃarənteɪ/ (also **charentais melon**) ▶ **noun** a melon of a small variety with a pale green rind and orange flesh.
– ORIGIN French, literally 'from the Charentes region'.

Charente /ʃaˈrɒnt, French ʃarɑ̃t/ a river of western France, which rises in the Massif Central and flows 360 km (225 miles) westwards to enter the Bay of Biscay at Rochefort.

charge ▶ **verb** [with obj.] **1** demand (an amount) as a price from someone for a service rendered or goods supplied: *the restaurant charged £15 for dinner* | [with two objs] *he charged me 20,000 lire for the postcard* | [no obj.] *museums should* ***charge for*** *admission.*
■ (**charge something to**) record the cost of something as an amount payable by (someone) or on (an account): *they charge the calls to their credit-card accounts.*
2 accuse (someone) of something, especially an offence under law: *they were* ***charged with*** *assault.*
■ [with clause] make an accusation or assertion that: *opponents* ***charged that*** *below-cost pricing would reduce safety.* ■ Law accuse someone of (an offence).
3 entrust (someone) with a task as a duty or responsibility: *the committee was* ***charged with*** *reshaping the educational system.*
4 store electrical energy in (a battery or battery-operated device): *the shaver can be* ***charged up*** *and used while travelling.*
■ [no obj.] (of a battery or battery-operated device) receive and store electrical energy. ■ technical or formal load or fill (a container, gun, etc.) to the full or proper extent: *will you see to it that your glasses are charged?* ■ (usu. **be charged with**) figurative fill or pervade (something) with a quality or emotion: *the air was charged with menace.*
5 [no obj.] rush forward in attack: *the plan is to charge headlong at the enemy.*
■ [with obj.] rush aggressively towards (someone or something) in attack. ■ [with adverbial of direction] move quickly and with impetus: *Henry charged up the staircase.*
6 (usu. **be charged with**) Heraldry place a heraldic bearing on: *a pennant argent, charged with a cross gules.*
▶ **noun** **1** a price asked for goods or services: *an admission charge.*
■ a financial liability or commitment: *an asset of some £102.7 m should have been taken as* ***a charge on*** *earnings.*
2 an accusation, typically one formally made against a prisoner brought to trial: *he appeared in court* ***on a charge of*** *attempted murder* | [mass noun] *three people were arrested but released* ***without charge.***
3 [mass noun] the responsibility of taking care or control of someone or something: *the people* ***in her charge*** *are pupils and not experimental subjects.*
■ [count noun] a person or thing entrusted to the care of

someone: *the babysitter watched over her charges.* ■ [count noun] dated a responsibility or onerous duty assigned to someone. ■ [count noun] an official instruction, especially one given by a judge to a jury regarding points of law.

4 the property of matter that is responsible for electrical phenomena, existing in a positive or negative form.

■ the quantity of this carried by a body. ■ [mass noun] energy stored chemically for conversion into electricity. ■ [mass noun] the process of storing electrical energy in a battery. ■ [in sing.] N. Amer. informal a thrill: *I get a real* ***charge out of*** *working hard.*

5 a quantity of explosive to be detonated, typically in order to fire a gun or similar weapon.

6 a headlong rush forward, typically one made by attacking soldiers in battle: *a cavalry charge.*

■ the signal or call for such a rush: *he yelled to his bugler to sound the charge.*

7 Heraldry a device or bearing placed on a shield or crest.

– PHRASES **free of charge** without any payment due. **in charge** in control or with overall responsibility: *he was* ***in charge of*** *civil aviation matters.* **lay something to someone's charge** Brit. archaic accuse someone of something. **press** (or **prefer**) **charges** accuse someone formally of a crime so that they can be brought to trial. **put someone on a charge of something** Brit. charge someone with a specified offence. **return to the charge** archaic make a further attempt at something, especially when arguing a point. **take charge** assume control or responsibility: *the candidate must* ***take charge of*** *an actual flight.*

– DERIVATIVES **chargeable** adjective.

– ORIGIN Middle English (in the general senses 'to load' and 'a load', from Old French *charger* (verb), *charge* (noun), from late Latin *carricare, carcare* 'to load', from Latin *carrus* 'wheeled vehicle'.

charge account ▶ noun an account to which goods and services may be charged on credit.

charge-cap ▶ verb [with obj.] [often as noun **charge-capping**] Brit. (of a government) subject (a local authority) to an upper limit on the charges it may levy on the public for services.

charge card ▶ noun a credit card for use with an account which must be paid in full when a statement is issued.

charge carrier ▶ noun a particle which carries an electric charge.

■ a mobile electron or hole by which electric charge passes through a semiconductor.

charge conjugation ▶ noun [mass noun] Physics replacement of a particle by its antiparticle.

charge-coupled device ▶ noun see **CCD**.

charged ▶ adjective having an electric charge.

■ figurative filled with excitement, tension, or emotion: *the highly charged atmosphere created by the boycott.*

chargé d'affaires /ˌʃɑːʒeɪ daˈfɛː, French ʃarʒe dafɛr/ (also **chargé**) ▶ noun (pl. **chargés** pronunc. same) an ambassador's deputy.

■ a state's diplomatic representative in a minor country.

– ORIGIN mid 18th cent.: French, '(a person) in charge of affairs'.

charge density ▶ noun [mass noun] Physics the electric charge per unit area of a surface, or per unit volume of a field or body.

chargehand ▶ noun Brit. a worker, ranking below a foreman, in charge of others on a particular job.

charge nurse ▶ noun Brit. a nurse in charge of a ward in a hospital.

Charge of the Light Brigade a British cavalry charge in 1854 during the Battle of Balaclava in the Crimean War. A misunderstanding between the commander of the Light Brigade and his superiors led to the British cavalry being destroyed. The charge was immortalized in verse by Alfred Tennyson.

charger[1] ▶ noun **1** a horse ridden by a knight or cavalryman.

2 a device for charging a battery or battery-powered equipment.

3 a person who charges forward.

charger[2] ▶ noun archaic a large flat dish.

– ORIGIN Middle English: from Anglo-Norman French *chargeour*, from *chargier* 'to load', from late Latin *carricare, carcare* 'to load' (see **CHARGE**).

charge sheet ▶ noun Brit. a record made in a police station of the charges against a person.

chargrill ▶ verb [usu. as adj. **chargrilled**] grill (food, typically meat or fish) quickly at a very high heat.

– ORIGIN late 20th cent.: on the pattern of *charbroil*.

chariot ▶ noun a horse-drawn wheeled vehicle, in particular:

■ a two-wheeled vehicle drawn by horses, used in ancient warfare and racing. ■ historical a four-wheeled carriage with back seats and a coachman's seat. ■ poetic/literary a stately or triumphal carriage.

▶ verb [with obj.] poetic/literary convey in or as in a chariot.

– ORIGIN late Middle English: from Old French, augmentative of *char* 'cart', based on Latin *carrus* 'wheeled vehicle'.

charioteer ▶ noun a chariot driver.

■ (**the Charioteer**) the constellation Auriga.

– ORIGIN Middle English: from Old French *charieter*, from *chariot* 'large cart' (see **CHARIOT**). The sense in astronomy dates from the early 20th cent.

charism /ˈkarɪz(ə)m/ ▶ noun Theology another term for **CHARISMA** (in sense 2).

charisma /kəˈrɪzmə/ ▶ noun **1** [mass noun] compelling attractiveness or charm that can inspire devotion in others: *she enchanted guests with her charisma.*

2 (pl. **charismata** /kəˈrɪzmətə/) a divinely conferred power or talent.

– ORIGIN mid 17th cent. (in sense 2): via ecclesiastical Latin from Greek *kharisma*, from *kharis* 'favour, grace'.

charismatic ▶ adjective **1** exercising a compelling charm which inspires devotion in others: *a charismatic leader.*

2 of or relating to the charismatic movement in the Christian Church.

■ (of a power or talent) divinely conferred: *charismatic prophecy.*

▶ noun an adherent of the charismatic movement.

■ a person who claims divine inspiration.

– DERIVATIVES **charismatically** adverb.

– ORIGIN late 19th cent.: from Greek *kharisma, kharismat-* 'charisma', + **-IC**.

charismatic movement ▶ noun a fundamentalist movement within the Roman Catholic, Anglican, and other Christian Churches that emphasizes talents held to be conferred by the Holy Spirit, such as speaking in tongues and healing of the sick.

charitable ▶ adjective **1** of or relating to the assistance of those in need: *he has spent £50,000 on charitable causes.*

■ (of an organization or activity) officially recognized as devoted to the assistance of those in need. ■ generous in giving to those in need.

2 apt to judge others leniently or favourably: *those who were less charitable called for his resignation.*

– DERIVATIVES **charitableness** noun, **charitably** adverb.

– ORIGIN Middle English (in the sense 'showing Christian love to God and man'): from Old French, from *charite* (see **CHARITY**).

charity ▶ noun (pl. **-ies**) **1** an organization set up to provide help and raise money for those in need.

■ [mass noun] such organizations viewed collectively as the object of fund-raising or of donations: *the proceeds of the sale will go to charity.*

2 [mass noun] the voluntary giving of help, typically in the form of money, to those in need.

■ help or money given in this way: *an unemployed teacher living on charity.*

3 [mass noun] kindness and tolerance in judging others: *she found it hard to look on her mother with much charity.*

■ archaic love of humankind, typically in a Christian context: *faith, hope, and charity.*

– PHRASES **charity begins at home** proverb a person's first responsibility is for the needs of their own family and friends.

– ORIGIN late Old English (in the sense 'Christian love of one's fellows'): from Old French *charite*, from Latin *caritas*, from *carus* 'dear'.

Charity Commission (in the UK) a board established to control charitable trusts.

charity school ▶ noun a school which is supported by charitable contributions.

charity shop ▶ noun Brit. a shop where second-hand goods are sold to raise money for a charity.

charity walk ▶ noun a sponsored walk to raise money for a charity.

charivari /ˌʃɑːrɪˈvɑːri/ (chiefly US also **shivaree**) ▶ noun (pl. **charivaris**) chiefly historical a cacophonous mock serenade, typically performed by a group of people in derision of an unpopular person or in celebration of a marriage.

■ a series of discordant noises.

– ORIGIN mid 17th cent.: from French, of unknown origin.

charkha /ˈtʃɔːkə/ (also **charka**) ▶ noun (in the Indian subcontinent) a domestic spinning wheel used chiefly for cotton.

– ORIGIN from Urdu *charḵa* 'spinning wheel', from Persian; related to Sanskrit *cakra* 'wheel'.

charlady ▶ noun (pl. **-ies**) Brit. a charwoman.

charlatan /ˈʃɑːlət(ə)n/ ▶ noun a person falsely claiming to have a special knowledge or skill.

– DERIVATIVES **charlatanism** noun, **charlatanry** noun.

– ORIGIN early 17th cent. (denoting an itinerant seller of supposed remedies): from French, from Italian *ciarlatano*, from *ciarlare* 'to babble'.

Charlemagne /ˈʃɑːləmeɪn/ (742–814), king of the Franks 768–814 and Holy Roman emperor (as Charles I) 800–14; Latin name *Carolus Magnus*; known as **Charles the Great**. As the first Holy Roman emperor Charlemagne promoted the arts and education, and his court became the cultural centre of the Carolingian Renaissance, the influence of which outlasted his empire.

Charleroi /ˈʃɑːləˌrwʌ, French ʃarlrwa/ an industrial city in SW Belgium; pop. 206,200 (1991).

Charles[1] the name of two kings of England, Scotland, and Ireland:

■ Charles I (1600–49), son of James I, reigned 1625–49. His reign was dominated by the deepening religious and constitutional crisis that resulted in the English Civil War 1642–9. After the battle of Naseby, Charles tried to regain power in alliance with the Scots, but his forces were defeated in 1648 and he was tried by a special Parliamentary court and beheaded.

■ Charles II (1630–85), son of Charles I, reigned 1660–85. Charles was restored to the throne after the collapse of Cromwell's regime and displayed considerable adroitness in handling the difficult constitutional situation, although continuing religious and political strife dogged his reign.

Charles[2] the name of four kings of Spain:

■ Charles I (1500–58), son of Philip I, reigned 1516–56, Holy Roman emperor (as Charles V) 1519–56. His reign was characterized by the struggle against Protestantism in Germany, rebellion in Castile, and war with France (1521–44). Exhausted by these struggles, Charles handed Naples, the Netherlands, and Spain over to his son Philip II and the imperial Crown to his brother Ferdinand, and retired to a monastery.

■ Charles II (1661–1700), reigned 1665–1700. He inherited a kingdom already in a decline which he was unable to halt. His choice of Philip of Anjou, grandson of Louis XIV of France, as his successor gave rise to the War of the Spanish Succession.

■ Charles III (1716–88), reigned 1759–88. He improved Spain's position as an international power through an increase in foreign trade, and brought Spain a brief cultural and economic revival.

■ Charles IV (1748–1819), reigned 1788–1808. During the Napoleonic Wars he suffered the loss of the Spanish fleet, destroyed along with that of France at Trafalgar in 1805. Following the French invasion of Spain in 1807, Charles was forced to abdicate.

Charles[3] the name of seven Holy Roman emperors:

■ Charles I see **CHARLEMAGNE**.

■ Charles II (823–877), reigned 875–877.

■ Charles III (839–888), reigned 881–887.

■ Charles IV (1316–1378), reigned 1355–1378.

■ Charles V Charles I of Spain (see **CHARLES**[2]).

■ Charles VI (1685–1740), reigned 1711–40. His claim to the Spanish throne instigated the War of the Spanish Succession, but he was ultimately unsuccessful. He drafted the Pragmatic Sanction in an attempt to ensure that his daughter succeeded to the Habsburg dominions; this triggered the War of the Austrian Succession after his death.

■ Charles VII (1697–1745), reigned 1742–45.

Charles[4], Ray (b.1930), American pianist and singer; born *Ray Charles Robinson*. Totally blind from the age of 6, he drew on blues, jazz, and country music for songs such as 'What'd I Say' (1959), 'Georgia On My Mind' (1960), and 'Busted' (1963).

Charles VII (1403–61), king of France 1422–61. At the time of his accession much of northern France was under English occupation. After the intervention of Joan of Arc, however, the French experienced a dramatic military revival and the defeat of the English ended the Hundred Years War.

Charles XII (also **Karl XII**) (1682–1718), king of Sweden 1697–1718. In 1700 he embarked on the Great Northern War against Denmark, Poland-Saxony, and Russia. Initially successful, in 1709 he embarked on an expedition into Russia which ended in the destruction of his army and his internment.

Charles, Prince, Charles Philip Arthur George, Prince of Wales (b.1948), heir apparent to Elizabeth II. He married Lady Diana Spencer in 1981; the couple had two children, Prince William Arthur Philip Louis (b.1982) and Prince Henry Charles Albert David (known as Prince Harry, b.1984), and were divorced in 1996.

Charles' law (also **Charles's law**) Chemistry a law stating that the volume of an ideal gas at constant pressure is directly proportional to the absolute temperature.
– ORIGIN late 19th cent.: named after Jacques A. C. Charles (1746–1823), the French physicist who first formulated it.

Charles Martel /maːˈtɛl/ (c.688–741), Frankish ruler of the eastern part of the Frankish kingdom from 715 and the whole kingdom from 719, grandfather of Charlemagne. His rule marked the beginning of Carolingian power.

Charles's Wain archaic, chiefly Brit. the Plough in Ursa Major.
– ORIGIN Old English Carles wægn 'the wain of Carl (Charlemagne)', perhaps because the star Arcturus was associated with King Arthur, with whom Charlemagne was connected in legend.

Charleston 1 the state capital of West Virginia; pop. 57,290 (1990). **2** a city and port in South Carolina; pop. 80,410 (1990). The bombardment in 1861 of Fort Sumter, in the harbour, by Confederate troops marked the beginning of the American Civil War.

charleston (also **Charleston**) ▶ noun a lively dance of the 1920s which involved turning the knees inwards and kicking out the lower legs.
▶ verb [no obj.] dance the charleston.
– ORIGIN 1920s: named after **CHARLESTON** in South Carolina, US.

charley horse ▶ noun [in sing.] N. Amer. informal a cramp or feeling of stiffness in an arm or leg.
– ORIGIN late 19th cent.: of unknown origin.

charlie ▶ noun (pl. **-ies**) **1** Brit. informal a fool. **2** (**charlies**) Brit. informal, dated a woman's breasts. **3** [mass noun] informal cocaine: taking loads of charlie. **4** a code word representing the letter C, used in radio communication. **5** US & NZ military slang, historical a member of the Vietcong or the Vietcong collectively. [ORIGIN: shortening of Victor Charlie, radio code for VC, representing Vietcong.]
– ORIGIN late 19th cent.: diminutive of the male given name Charles.

charlock /ˈtʃaːlɒk/ ▶ noun [mass noun] a wild mustard with yellow flowers, which is a common weed of cornfields.
● Sinapis arvensis, family Cruciferae.
– ORIGIN Old English cerlic, cyrlic, of unknown origin.

Charlotte a commercial city and transportation centre in southern North Carolina; pop. 395,930 (1990).

charlotte ▶ noun a pudding made of stewed fruit with a casing or covering of bread, sponge cake, biscuits, or breadcrumbs.
– ORIGIN French, from the female given name Charlotte.

Charlotte Amalie /əˈmaːlɪə/ the capital of the Virgin Islands, on the island of St Thomas; pop. 52,660 (1985).
– ORIGIN named after the wife of King Christian V of Denmark.

Charlotte Dundas /dʌnˈdas/ a paddle steamer launched in 1802 on the River Clyde, the first vessel to use steam propulsion commercially.

charlotte russe /ˈruːs/ ▶ noun a pudding consisting of custard enclosed in sponge cake or a casing of sponge fingers.
– ORIGIN French, literally 'Russian charlotte'.

Charlottetown the capital and chief port of Prince Edward Island, Canada; pop. 33,150 (1991).

Charlton the name of two brothers eminent in football:
■ Jack (b.1935), English footballer and manager; full name John Charlton. A rugged Leeds United defender, he was a member of the England side that won the World Cup in 1966. He later managed a number of teams including the Republic of Ireland national side (1986–95).
■ Bobby (b.1937), English footballer; full name Sir Robert Charlton. An outstanding Manchester United striker, he scored a record forty-nine goals for England and was a member of the side that won the World Cup in 1966.

charm ▶ noun **1** [mass noun] the power or quality of delighting, attracting, or fascinating others: he was captivated by her youthful charm.
■ [count noun] (usu. **charms**) an attractive or alluring characteristic or feature: the hidden charms of the city. **2** a small ornament worn on a necklace or bracelet. **3** an object, act, or saying believed to have magic power.
■ an object kept or worn to ward off evil and bring good luck: a good luck charm. **4** [mass noun] Physics one of six flavours of quark.
▶ verb [with obj.] **1** delight greatly: the books have charmed children the world over.
■ use one's ability to please and attract in order to influence someone or to achieve something: he charmed her into going out. **2** control or achieve by or as if by magic: a gesticulating figure endeavouring to charm a cobra | [with adverbial] she will charm your warts away.
– PHRASES **turn on the charm** use one's ability to please in a calculated way so as to influence someone or to obtain something. **work like a charm** be completely successful or effective.
– ORIGIN Middle English (in the senses 'incantation or magic spell' and 'to use spells'): from Old French charme (noun), charmer (verb), from Latin carmen 'song, verse, incantation'.

charm bracelet ▶ noun a bracelet hung with small trinkets or ornaments.

charmed ▶ adjective **1** (of a person's life or a period of this) unusually lucky or happy as though protected by magic: I felt that I had a charmed life. **2** Physics (of a particle) possessing the property charm: a charmed quark.
▶ exclamation dated expressing polite pleasure at an introduction: charmed, I'm sure.

charmer ▶ noun a person with an attractive, engaging personality.
■ a person who habitually seeks to impress or manipulate others by exploiting their power to please and attract.

charmeuse /ʃaːˈməːz/ ▶ noun [mass noun] a soft smooth silky dress fabric.
– ORIGIN early 20th cent.: from French, feminine of charmeur 'charmer', from charmer 'to charm'.

charming ▶ adjective very pleasant or attractive: a charming country cottage.
■ (of a person or their manner) very polite, friendly, and likeable: he was a charming, affectionate colleague.
▶ exclamation used as an ironic expression of displeasure or disapproval: 'I hate men.' 'Charming!' he said.
– DERIVATIVES **charmingly** adverb.

charmless ▶ adjective unattractive or unpleasant: a charmless sixties structure.
– DERIVATIVES **charmlessly** adverb, **charmlessness** noun.

charm offensive ▶ noun a campaign of flattery, friendliness, and cajolement designed to achieve the support or agreement of others: he launched a charm offensive against MPs who didn't support the government.

charmonium /tʃaːˈməʊnɪəm/ ▶ noun (pl. **charmonia**) Physics a combination of a charmed quark and antiquark.
– ORIGIN 1970s: from **CHARM** (in sense 4).

charm school ▶ noun a school where young women are taught social graces such as deportment and etiquette.

charnel /ˈtʃaːn(ə)l/ ▶ noun short for **CHARNEL HOUSE**.
▶ adjective associated with death: I gagged on the charnel stench of the place.
– ORIGIN late Middle English: from Old French, from

medieval Latin carnale, neuter (used as a noun) of carnalis 'relating to flesh' (see **CARNAL**).

charnel house ▶ noun historical a building or vault in which corpses or bones are piled.
■ figurative a place associated with violent death: Europe in the immediate post-war period had become a charnel house.
– ORIGIN mid 16th cent.: from Middle English charnel 'burying place', from Old French, from medieval Latin carnale, from late Latin carnalis 'relating to flesh', from caro, carn- 'flesh'.

Charolais /ˈʃarə(ʊ)leɪ/ ▶ noun (pl. same) an animal of a breed of large white beef cattle.
– ORIGIN late 19th cent.: named after the Monts du Charollais, hills in eastern France where the breed originated.

Charon /ˈkɛːrən/ **1** Greek Mythology an old man who ferried the souls of the dead across the Rivers Styx and Acheron to Hades. **2** Astronomy the only satellite of Pluto, discovered in 1978, with a diameter (1,190 km) that is more than half that of Pluto.

Charophyta /ˈkaːrə(ʊ)ˌfʌɪtə, ˈkarə(ʊ)-, ˈtʃarə(ʊ)-/ Botany a division of lower plants that includes the stoneworts, which are frequently treated as a class (Charophyceae) of the green algae.
– DERIVATIVES **charophyte** noun.
– ORIGIN modern Latin (plural), former name of the family Characeae, from Chara (genus name) + phuton 'a plant'.

charpoy /ˈtʃaːpɔɪ/ ▶ noun Indian a light bedstead.
– ORIGIN mid 17th cent.: from Urdu cārpāī 'four-legged', from Persian.

charr /tʃaː/ (also **char**) ▶ noun (pl. same) a trout-like freshwater or marine fish of northern countries, widely valued as a food and game fish.
● Genus Salvelinus, family Salmonidae: several species, in particular the red-bellied **Arctic charr** (S. alpinus), which occurs in Arctic waters as well as landlocked lakes, and the North American **brook charr** or brook trout (S. fontinalis), which has been introduced widely elsewhere.
– ORIGIN mid 17th cent.: perhaps of Celtic origin.

charro /ˈtʃaːrəʊ/ ▶ noun (pl. **-os**) a Mexican cowboy, typically one in elaborate traditional dress.
– ORIGIN Mexican Spanish, from Spanish, literally 'rustic'.

chart ▶ noun a sheet of information in the form of a table, graph, or diagram: the doctor recorded her blood pressure on a chart.
■ (usu. **the charts**) a weekly listing of the current best-selling pop records: she topped the charts for eight weeks. ■ a geographical map or plan, especially one used for navigation by sea or air. ■ (also **birth chart** or **natal chart**) Astrology a map, typically circular, showing the positions of the planets in the twelve houses at the time of someone's birth, from which astrologers are said to be able to deduce their character or potential.
▶ verb **1** [with obj.] make a map of (an area).
■ plot (a course) on a chart: the pilot found his craft taking a route he had not charted | figurative the poems chart his descent into madness. ■ (usu. **be charted**) record on a chart. **2** [no obj.] (of a record) sell enough copies in a particular week to enter the music charts at a particular position: the record will probably chart at about No. 74.
– ORIGIN late 16th cent.: from French charte, from Latin charta 'paper, papyrus leaf' (see **CARD**¹).

chartbuster ▶ noun informal a popular singer or group that makes a best-selling recording.
■ a best-selling recording.

charter ▶ noun **1** a written grant by the sovereign or legislative power of a country, by which a body such as a borough, company, or university is created or its rights and privileges defined.
■ a written constitution or description of an organization's functions. ■ [with modifier] (in the UK) a written statement of the rights that a specified group of people has or should have: the standard set by the patient's charter. ■ (**a charter for**) a decision or piece of legislation regarded as enabling people to engage more easily in a specified undesirable activity: he described the act as a charter for vandals. **2** [mass noun] the hiring of an aircraft, ship, or motor vehicle for a special purpose: a plane on charter to a multinational company.
■ [count noun] a ship or vehicle that is hired. ■ [count noun] a trip made by a ship or vehicle under hire: he liked to see the boat sparkling clean before each charter.
▶ verb [with obj.] **1** [usu. as adj. **chartered**] grant a charter

to (a city, university, or other body): *chartered corporations.*
2 hire (an aircraft, ship, or motor vehicle).
– ORIGIN Middle English: from Old French *chartre*, from Latin *chartula*, diminutive of *charta* 'paper' (see **CARD**[1]).

chartered ▶ **adjective** [attrib.] **1** Brit. (of an accountant, engineer, librarian, etc.) qualified as a member of a professional body that has a royal charter.
2 (of an aircraft or ship) having been hired.

charterer ▶ **noun** a person or organization that charters a ship or aircraft.

charter flight ▶ **noun** a flight by an aircraft chartered for a specific journey, not part of an airline's regular schedule.

Charter Mark ▶ **noun** (in the UK) an award granted to institutions for exceptional public service under the terms of the Citizen's Charter.

charter member ▶ **noun** chiefly N. Amer. an original or founding member of a society or organization.

charter party ▶ **noun 1** a deed between a shipowner and a merchant for the hire of a ship and the delivery of cargo.
2 a group of people using a hired aircraft or ship.
– ORIGIN late Middle English: from French *charte partie*, from medieval Latin *charta partita* 'divided charter', i.e. one written in duplicate on a single sheet, then divided in such a way that the two parts could be fitted together again as proof of authenticity.

charter school ▶ **noun 1** (in North America) a publicly funded independent school established by teachers, parents, or community groups under the terms of a charter with a local or national authority.
2 (**Charter School**) historical a school established by the Charter Society (founded for that purpose in 1733) to provide a Protestant education to poor Catholics in Ireland.

Chartism ▶ **noun** [mass noun] **1** a UK parliamentary reform movement of 1837–48, the principles of which were set out in a manifesto called *The People's Charter* and called for universal suffrage for men, equal electoral districts, voting by secret ballot, abolition of property qualifications for MPs, and annual general elections.
2 (**chartism**) the use of charts of financial data to predict future trends and to guide investment strategies.
– DERIVATIVES **Chartist** noun & adjective.

Chartres /'ʃɑːtr(ə), French ʃaʀtʀ/ a city in northern France; pop. 41,850 (1990). It is noted for its Gothic cathedral.

chartreuse /ʃɑː'trəːz/ ▶ **noun 1** [mass noun] a pale green or yellow liqueur made from brandy and aromatic herbs.
▪a pale yellow or green colour resembling this liqueur.
2 a dish made in a mould using pieces of meat, game, vegetables, or (now most often) fruit in jelly.
– ORIGIN named after *La Grande Chartreuse*, the Carthusian monastery near Grenoble, where the liqueur (sense 1) was first made; sense 2 is an extended use.

chart-topping ▶ **adjective** informal (of a popular singer, group, or recording) having reached the top of the music charts.
– DERIVATIVES **chart-topper** noun.

charwoman ▶ **noun** (pl. **-women**) Brit., dated a woman employed as a cleaner in a house or office.
– ORIGIN late 16th cent.: from obsolete *char* or *chare* 'a turn of work, an odd job, chore' (obscurely related to **CHORE**) + **WOMAN**.

chary /'tʃɛːri/ ▶ **adjective** (**charier**, **chariest**) cautiously or suspiciously reluctant to do something; wary: *most people are **chary of** allowing themselves to be photographed.*
▪cautious about the amount one gives or reveals: *he was chary with specifics about the script.*
– DERIVATIVES **charily** adverb.
– ORIGIN Old English *cearig* 'sorrowful, anxious', of West Germanic origin; related to **CARE**. The current sense arose in the mid 16th cent.

Charybdis /kə'rɪbdɪs/ Greek Mythology a dangerous whirlpool in a narrow channel of the sea, opposite the cave of the sea monster Scylla.

Chas ▶ **abbreviation for** Charles.

chase[1] ▶ **verb** [with obj.] **1** pursue in order to catch or catch up with: *police chased the stolen car through the city* | [no obj.] *the dog **chased after** the stick.*
▪seek to attain: *the team are chasing their first home win this season.* ▪ seek the company of (a member of the opposite sex) in an obvious way: *playing football by day and chasing women by night* | [no obj.] *René is always **chasing after** other women.* ▪ [with obj. and adverbial of direction] drive or cause to go in a specified direction: *she chased him **out of** the house.* ▪ [no obj., with adverbial of direction] rush or hurry in a specified direction: *he chased down the motorway.*
2 try to obtain (something owed or required): *the company employs people to **chase up** debts.*
▪try to make contact with (someone) in order to obtain something owed or required: *chasing customers who had not paid their bills.* ▪ make further investigation of (an unresolved matter): *be sure you **chase up** late invitation replies* | N. Amer. *investigators got a warrant, but they didn't have time to **chase down** the case.*
▶ **noun** an act of pursuing someone or something: *they captured the youths after a brief chase.*
▪short for **STEEPLECHASE**. ▪ (**the chase**) hunting as a sport: *she was an ardent follower of the chase.* ▪ [in place names] Brit. an area of unenclosed land formerly reserved for hunting: *Cannock Chase.* ▪ archaic a hunted animal.
– PHRASES **beast** (or **bird**) **of the chase** archaic an animal traditionally hunted for sport across open country. **chase the game** (in soccer) adopt attacking tactics, especially at the risk of being vulnerable to counter-attack. **give chase** go in pursuit. **go and chase oneself** [in imperative] informal go away.
– ORIGIN Middle English: from Old French *chacier* (verb), *chace* (noun), based on Latin *captare* 'continue to take', from *capere* 'take'.

chase[2] ▶ **verb** [with obj.] [usu. as adj. **chased**] engrave (metal, or a design on metal): *a miniature container with a delicately chased floral design.*
– ORIGIN late Middle English: apparently from earlier *enchase*, from Old French *enchasser*.

chase[3] ▶ **noun** (in letterpress printing) a metal frame for holding the composed type and blocks being printed at one time.
– ORIGIN late 16th cent.: from French *châsse*, from Latin *capsa* 'box' (see **CASE**[2]).

chase[4] ▶ **noun 1** the part of a gun enclosing the bore.
2 a groove or furrow cut in the face of a wall or other surface to receive a pipe.
– ORIGIN early 17th cent.: from French *chas* 'enclosed space', from Provençal *cas*, *caus*, from medieval Latin *capsum* 'thorax or nave of a church'.

chaser ▶ **noun 1** a person or thing that pursues someone or something: [in combination] *a woman-chaser.*
2 a horse for steeplechasing.
3 informal a drink taken after another of a different kind, typically a strong alcoholic drink after a weaker one: *drinking pints of bitter with vodka chasers.*

Chasid /'xasɪd/ ▶ **noun** variant spelling of **HASID**.

Chasidism /'xasɪdɪz(ə)m/ ▶ **noun** variant spelling of **HASIDISM**.

chasm /'kaz(ə)m/ ▶ **noun** a deep fissure in the earth, rock, or another surface.
▪figurative a profound difference between people, viewpoints, feelings, etc.: *the **chasm between** rich and poor.*
– DERIVATIVES **chasmic** adjective (rare).
– ORIGIN late 16th cent. (denoting an opening up of the sea or land, as in an earthquake): from Latin *chasma*, from Greek *khasma* 'gaping hollow'.

chasse /ʃas/ ▶ **noun** a drink taken to accompany another, especially a liqueur drunk after coffee.
– ORIGIN French, abbreviation of *chasse-café*, literally 'chase-coffee'.

chassé /'ʃaseɪ/ ▶ **noun** a gliding step in dancing in which one foot displaces the other.
▶ **verb** (**chasséd**, **chasséing**) [no obj.] make such a step.
– ORIGIN French, literally 'chased'.

Chasselas /'ʃas(ə)lɑː/ ▶ **noun** [mass noun] a variety of white grape, grown mainly in Europe and Chile as a table grape or for making wine.
▪a wine made from this grape.
– ORIGIN named after a village near Mâcon, France.

chasseur /ʃa'səː, French ʃasœʀ/ ▶ **noun** (pl. pronounced same) historical a soldier equipped and trained for rapid movement, especially in the French army.
– ORIGIN mid 18th cent.: French, from *chasser* 'to chase'.

chasseur sauce ▶ **noun** [mass noun] a rich dark sauce with wine and mushrooms, typically served with poultry or game.
– ORIGIN from French *chasseur* 'huntsman', from *chasser* 'to chase or hunt'.

Chassid /'xasɪd/ ▶ **noun** variant spelling of **HASID**.

Chassidism /'xasɪˌdɪz(ə)m/ ▶ **noun** variant spelling of **HASIDISM**.

chassis /'ʃasi, -iː/ ▶ **noun** (pl. same /-sɪz/) the base frame of a motor vehicle, carriage, or other wheeled conveyance.
▪the outer structural framework of a piece of audio, radio, or computer equipment.
– ORIGIN early 20th cent.: from French *châssis* 'frame', based on Latin *capsa* 'box' (see **CASE**[2]).

chaste ▶ **adjective** abstaining from extramarital, or from all, sexual intercourse.
▪not having any sexual nature or intention: *a chaste, consoling embrace.* ▪ without unnecessary ornamentation; simple or restrained: *the dark, chaste interior was lightened by tile-work.*
– DERIVATIVES **chastely** adverb, **chasteness** noun.
– ORIGIN Middle English: from Old French, from Latin *castus*.

chasten /'tʃeɪs(ə)n/ ▶ **verb** [with obj.] (usu. **be chastened**) (of a reproof or misfortune) have a restraining or moderating effect on: *the director was somewhat chastened by his recent flops* | [as adj. **chastening**] *a chastening experience.*
▪archaic (especially of God) discipline; punish.
– DERIVATIVES **chastener** noun.
– ORIGIN early 16th cent.: from an obsolete verb *chaste*, from Old French *chastier*, from Latin *castigare* 'castigate', from *castus* 'morally pure, chaste'.

chaste tree ▶ **noun** a southern European shrub with blue or white flowers, grown as an ornamental.
● *Vitex agnus-castus*, family Verbenaceae.
– ORIGIN mid 16th cent.: so named because of its association with chastity in sacrifices to Ceres.

chastise ▶ **verb** [with obj.] rebuke or reprimand severely: *he chastised his colleagues for their laziness.*
▪dated punish, especially by beating.
– DERIVATIVES **chastisement** noun, **chastiser** noun.
– ORIGIN Middle English: apparently formed irregularly from the obsolete verb *chaste* (see **CHASTEN**).

chastity ▶ **noun** [mass noun] the state or practice of refraining from extramarital, or especially from all, sexual intercourse: *vows of chastity.*
– ORIGIN Middle English: from Old French *chastete*, from Latin *castitas*, from *castus* 'morally pure' (see **CHASTE**).

chastity belt ▶ **noun** historical a garment or device designed to prevent the woman wearing it from having sexual intercourse.

chasuble /'tʃazjʊb(ə)l/ ▶ **noun** a sleeveless outer vestment worn by a Catholic or High Anglican priest when celebrating Mass, typically ornate and having a simple hole for the head.
– ORIGIN Middle English: from Old French *chesible*, later *chasuble*, from late Latin *casubla*, alteration of Latin *casula* 'hooded cloak or little cottage', diminutive of *casa* 'house'.

chat[1] ▶ **verb** (**chatted**, **chatting**) [no obj.] talk in a friendly and informal way: *she chatted to her mother on the phone every day.*
▶ **noun** an informal conversation: *he dropped in for a chat* | [mass noun] *that's enough chat for tonight.*
– ORIGIN Middle English: shortening of **CHATTER**.
▶ **chat someone up** informal engage someone in flirtatious conversation. ▪ talk persuasively to someone, especially with a particular motive: *I chatted up the paper's editor, feigning interest in his anecdotes.*

chat[2] ▶ **noun 1** [often in combination] a small Old World songbird of the thrush family, with a harsh call and typically with bold black, white, and buff or chestnut coloration.
● *Saxicola* and other genera, family Turdidae: numerous species. See also **BUSHCHAT**, **STONECHAT**, **WHINCHAT**.
2 [with modifier] any of a number of small songbirds with harsh calls:
● a New World warbler that typically has a yellow or pink breast (genera *Icteria* and *Granatellus*, family Parulidae). ● an Australian songbird related to the honeyeaters, the male of which is either mainly yellow or boldly marked (genera *Ephthianura* and *Ashbyia*, family Ephthianuridae).

– ORIGIN late 17th cent.: probably imitative of its call.

chateau /ˈʃatəʊ, French ʃato/ (also **château**) ▶ **noun** (pl. **chateaux** pronunc. same or /-təʊz/) a large French country house or castle, often giving its name to wine made in its neighbourhood: [in names] *Château Margaux*.
– ORIGIN mid 18th cent.: French, from Old French *chastel* (see **CASTLE**).

Chateaubriand /ˌʃatəʊˈbriːɒ̃, French ʃatobʀijɑ̃/, François-René, Vicomte de (1768–1848), French writer and diplomat. He was an important figure in early French romanticism. Notable works: *Le Génie du Christianisme* (1802) and *Mémoires d'outre-tombe* (autobiography, 1849–50).

chateaubriand /ˌʃatəʊˈbriːɒ̃/ ▶ **noun** a thick fillet of beef steak.
– ORIGIN late 19th cent.: named after François-René, Vicomte de **CHATEAUBRIAND**, whose chef is said to have created the dish.

chatelain /ˈʃatəleɪn/ ▶ **noun** another term for **CASTELLAN**.
– ORIGIN late Middle English: from Old French *chastelain*, from medieval Latin *castellanus* 'castellan', from Latin *castellum* (see **CASTLE**).

chatelaine /ˈʃatəleɪn/ ▶ **noun** dated a woman in charge of a large house.
▪ historical a set of short chains attached to a woman's belt, used for carrying keys or other items.
– ORIGIN mid 19th cent.: from French *châtelaine*, feminine of *châtelain* 'castellan', from medieval Latin *castellanus* (see **CHATELAIN**).

Chatham /ˈtʃatəm/, 1st Earl of, see **PITT**.

Chatham Islands a group of two islands, Pitt Island and Chatham Island, in the SW Pacific to the east of New Zealand.

chatline ▶ **noun** a telephone service which allows conversation among a number of people who call in to it separately.

chatoyant /ʃəˈtɔɪənt/ ▶ **adjective** (of a gem, especially when cut en cabochon) showing a band of bright lustre caused by reflection from inclusions in the stone.
– DERIVATIVES **chatoyance** noun, **chatoyancy** noun.
– ORIGIN late 18th cent.: French, present participle of *chatoyer* 'to shimmer'.

chat room ▶ **noun** an area on the Internet or other computer network where users can communicate, typically one dedicated to a particular topic.

chat show ▶ **noun** Brit. a television or radio programme in which celebrities are invited to talk informally about various topics.

chattel /ˈtʃat(ə)l/ ▶ **noun** (in general use) a personal possession.
▪ Law an item of property other than freehold land, including tangible goods (**chattels personal**) and leasehold interests (**chattels real**). See also **GOODS AND CHATTELS**.
– ORIGIN Middle English: from Old French *chatel*, from medieval Latin *capitale*, from Latin *capitalis*, from *caput* 'head'. Compare with **CAPITAL**[1] and **CATTLE**.

chattel mortgage ▶ **noun** N. Amer. a mortgage on a movable item of property.

chattel slave ▶ **noun** a human being treated as a chattel.

chatter ▶ **verb** [no obj.] talk rapidly or incessantly about trivial matters: *she was chattering about her holiday*.
▪ (of a bird, monkey, or machine) make a series of short quick high-pitched sounds. ▪ (of a person's teeth) click repeatedly together, typically from cold or fear.
▶ **noun** [mass noun] incessant trivial talk: *a stream of idle chatter*.
▪ a series of short quick high-pitched sounds: *the chatter of a typewriter*. ▪ undesirable vibration in a mechanism: *the wipers should operate without chatter*.
– PHRASES **the chattering classes** derogatory educated people, especially those in academic, artistic, or media circles, considered as a social group given to the expression of liberal opinions about society and culture.
– DERIVATIVES **chattery** adjective.
– ORIGIN Middle English: imitative.

chatterbox ▶ **noun** informal a person who talks at length about trivial matters.

chatterer ▶ **noun 1** a person who talks at length about trivial matters.
2 informal any of a number of birds with chattering calls, especially a babbler, a waxwing, or a cotinga.

Chatterton, Thomas (1752–70), English poet, chiefly remembered for his fabricated poems professing to be those of a 15th-century monk. He committed suicide at the age of 17.

chatty ▶ **adjective** (**chattier**, **chattiest**) (of a person) fond of talking in an easy, informal way.
▪ (of a conversation, letter, etc.) informal and lively.
– DERIVATIVES **chattily** adverb, **chattiness** noun.

chat-up ▶ **noun** [often as modifier] Brit. informal an act of talking flirtatiously to someone: *a chat-up line*.

Chaucer /ˈtʃɔːsə/, Geoffrey (*c*.1342–1400), English poet. His most famous work, the *Canterbury Tales* (*c*.1387–1400), is a cycle of linked tales told by a group of pilgrims. His skills of characterization, humour, and versatility established him as the first great English poet. Other notable works: *Troilus and Criseyde* (1385).
– DERIVATIVES **Chaucerian** /tʃɔːˈsɪərɪən/ adjective & noun.

chaudhuri /ˈtʃaʊˌdʌri/ ▶ **noun** (pl. **chaudhuris**) Indian a government employee who supplies and is in charge of workers and materials for public works.
– ORIGIN from Hindi *caudharī*, literally 'holder of four', or from Sanskrit *cakradhārin*, denoting the bearer of a discus as a sign of authority.

chauffeur ▶ **noun** a person employed to drive a private or hired motor car.
▶ **verb** [with obj.] (often **be chauffeured**) drive (a car or a passenger in a car), typically as part of one's job: *she insisted on being **chauffeured around***.
– ORIGIN late 19th cent. (in the general sense 'motorist'): from French, literally 'stoker' (by association with steam engines), from *chauffer* 'to heat'.

chauffeuse /ʃəʊˈfəːz/ ▶ **noun** rare a female chauffeur.

Chauliac /ˈʃəʊlɪak, French ʃoljak/, Guy de (*c*.1300–68), French physician. His *Chirurgia Magna* (1363) was the first work to describe many surgical techniques.

chaulmoogra /tʃɔːlˈmuːgrə/ ▶ **noun** a tropical Asian evergreen tree with narrow leathery leaves and oil-rich seeds.
• Genus *Hydnocarpus*, family Flacourtiaceae: several species, in particular *H. kurzii*, the main source of the oil.
▪ (also **chaulmoogra oil**) [mass noun] the oil obtained from the seeds of this tree. It is used medically and as a preservative, and was formerly widely used in the treatment of leprosy.
– ORIGIN early 19th cent.: from Bengali *cāul-mugrā*.

chausses /ʃəʊs/ ▶ **plural noun** historical pantaloons or close-fitting coverings for the legs and feet, in particular those forming part of a knight's armour.
– ORIGIN late 15th cent.: French, literally 'clothing for the legs'.

chautauqua /tʃɔːˈtɔːkwə, ʃ-/ ▶ **noun** N. Amer. an institution that provided popular adult education courses and entertainment in the late 19th and early 20th centuries.
– ORIGIN late 19th cent.: named after *Chautauqua*, a county in New York State, where such an institution was first set up.

chauvinism /ˈʃəʊv(ɪ)nɪz(ə)m/ ▶ **noun** [mass noun] exaggerated or aggressive patriotism.
▪ excessive or prejudiced support or loyalty for one's own cause, group, or sex: *a bastion of male chauvinism*.
– ORIGIN late 19th cent.: named after Nicolas *Chauvin*, a Napoleonic veteran noted for his extreme patriotism, popularized as a character by the Cogniard brothers in *Cocarde Tricolore* (1831).

chauvinist ▶ **noun** a person displaying aggressive or exaggerated patriotism.
▪ a person displaying excessive or prejudiced support or loyalty for their own cause, group, or sex: *what a male chauvinist that man is*.
▶ **adjective** showing or relating to such excessive or prejudiced support or loyalty: *don't talk such chauvinist rubbish!*
– DERIVATIVES **chauvinistic** adjective, **chauvinistically** adverb.

Chavín /tʃɑːˈviːn/ ▶ **noun** [usu. as modifier] Archaeology a civilization that flourished in Peru *c*.1000–200 BC, uniting a large part of the country's coastal region in a common culture.
– ORIGIN from the name of the town and temple complex of *Chavín* de Huantar in the northern highlands, where the civilization was centred.

chaw /tʃɔː/ informal, chiefly N. Amer. ▶ **noun** an act of chewing something, especially something not intended to be swallowed: *enjoying a good chaw*.
▪ something chewed, especially a quid of tobacco: *a chaw of tobacco*.
▶ **verb** [with obj.] chew (something, especially tobacco).
– ORIGIN late Middle English (as a verb): variant of **CHEW**.

chawl /tʃɔːl/ ▶ **noun** (in the Indian subcontinent, especially Bombay) a large lodging house, offering cheap, basic accommodation.
– ORIGIN from Marathi *cāḷ*, denoting a long narrow building.

chayote /ˈtʃeɪəʊti/ ▶ **noun 1** a succulent green pear-shaped tropical fruit which resembles cucumber in flavour.
2 the tropical American vine which yields this fruit, also producing an edible yam-like tuberous root.
• *Sechium edule*, family Cucurbitaceae.
– ORIGIN late 19th cent.: from Spanish, from Nahuatl *chayotli*.

ChB ▶ **abbreviation** Bachelor of Surgery.
– ORIGIN from Latin *Chirurgiae Baccalaureus*.

CHD ▶ **abbreviation for** coronary heart disease.

cheap ▶ **adjective** (of an item for sale) low in price, especially in comparison with its value or with the usual price of similar items: *they bought some cheap fruit in the market | local buses were reliable and cheap*.
▪ charging low prices: *a cheap restaurant*. ▪ (of prices or other charges) low: *my rent was pretty cheap*. ▪ inexpensive because of inferior quality: *cheap, shoddy goods*. ▪ of little worth because achieved in a discreditable way requiring little effort: *her moment of cheap triumph*. ▪ deserving contempt: *a cheap trick*. ▪ N. Amer. informal miserly: *she's too cheap to send me a postcard*.
▶ **adverb** at or for a low price: *a house that was **going cheap** because of the war*.
– PHRASES **cheap and cheerful** Brit. simple and inexpensive but not unattractive. **cheap and nasty** Brit. of low cost and bad quality. **cheap at the price** well worth having, regardless of the cost: *as an investment for the future, the books are cheap at the price*. **on the cheap** informal at a low cost, typically lower than should be the case.
– DERIVATIVES **cheapish** adjective, **cheaply** adverb, **cheapness** noun.
– ORIGIN late 15th cent.: from an obsolete phrase *good cheap* 'a good bargain', from Old English *cēap* 'bargaining, trade', based on Latin *caupo* 'small trader, innkeeper'.

cheapen ▶ **verb** [with obj.] reduce the price of: *the depreciation of the dollar would cheapen US exports*.
▪ degrade: *the mass media simplify and cheapen the experience of art*.

cheapjack ▶ **noun** a seller of cheap inferior goods, typically a hawker at a fair or market.
▶ **adjective** chiefly N. Amer. of inferior quality.
– ORIGIN mid 19th cent.: from **CHEAP** + **JACK**[1].

cheapo (chiefly N. Amer. also **cheapie**) ▶ **adjective** [attrib.] informal inexpensive and of poor quality: *a cheapo version of the guitar*.
▶ **noun** (pl. **-os**) an inexpensive thing of poor quality.

cheapskate ▶ **noun** informal a miserly person.
– ORIGIN late 19th cent. (originally US): from **CHEAP** + *skate* 'a worn-out horse' or 'a mean, contemptible, or dishonest person', of unknown origin.

cheat ▶ **verb 1** [no obj.] act dishonestly or unfairly in order to gain an advantage, especially in a game or examination: *she always **cheats at** cards*.
▪ [with obj.] gain an advantage over or deprive of something by using unfair or deceitful methods; defraud: *he had **cheated** her **out of** everything she had*. ▪ use different and inferior materials or methods unobtrusively, especially in order to save time or money: *the dish should be made with cream, but many restaurants cheat*. ▪ informal be sexually unfaithful: *his wife was **cheating on** him*.
2 [with obj.] avoid (something undesirable) by luck or skill: *she cheated death in a spectacular crash*.
▪ archaic help (time) pass: *the tuneless rhyme with which the warder cheats the time*.
▶ **noun** a person who behaves dishonestly in order to gain an advantage.
▪ an act of cheating; a fraud or deception. ▪ [mass noun] a children's card game, the object of which is to get rid of one's cards while making declarations about them which may or may not be truthful.

– ORIGIN late Middle English: shortening of **ESCHEAT** (the original sense).

cheater ▶ noun *chiefly N. Amer.* **1** a person who acts dishonestly in order to gain an advantage.
2 (**cheaters**) *informal, dated* a pair of glasses or sunglasses.

cheat grass ▶ noun [mass noun] *chiefly N. Amer.* a tough wild grass of open land, sometimes growing as a weed among cereal crops and in pasture.
● Genus *Bromus*, family Gramineae: several species, in particular *B. tectorum*.
– ORIGIN late 18th cent.: a local word for various wild plants, perhaps from their resemblance to the cereals among which they grew.

cheat sheet ▶ noun *N. Amer. informal* a piece of paper bearing written notes intended to aid one's memory, used surreptitiously in an examination.

Cheboksary /ˌtʃɛbək'sɑːri/ a city in west central Russia, on the River Volga, west of Kazan, capital of the autonomous republic of Chuvashia; pop. 429,000 (1990).

Chechen /'tʃɛtʃɛn/ ▶ noun (pl. same or **Chechens**) **1** a member of the largely Muslim people inhabiting Chechnya.
2 [mass noun] the North Caucasian language of this people.
▶ adjective of or relating to this people or their language.
– ORIGIN from obsolete Russian *chechen* (earlier form of *chechenets*).

Chechnya /ˌtʃɛtʃ'njɑː/ (also **Chechenia**) an autonomous republic in the Caucasus in SW Russia, on the border with Georgia; pop. 1,290,000 (1990); capital, Grozny. The republic declared itself independent of Russia in 1991 and was invaded by Russian troops (1994). A peace treaty agreed the withdrawal of troops, but Russian forces invaded again in 1999. Also called **CHECHEN REPUBLIC**.

check[1] ▶ verb [with obj.] **1** examine (something) in order to determine its accuracy, quality, or condition, or to detect the presence of something: *customs officers have the right to check all luggage* | [no obj.] *a simple blood test to check for anaemia.*
■ verify or establish to one's satisfaction: *phone us to check the availability of your chosen holiday* | [with clause] *she glanced over her shoulder to check that the door was shut.* ■ (**check against**) verify the accuracy of something by comparing it with (something else): *keep your receipt to check against your statement.* ■ N. Amer. another way of saying **check something off.** ■ N. Amer. another way of saying **check something in.** ■ S. African look at; see: *he is checking the scene like the special branch do* | [no obj.] *it's a work of art—just check at it!*
2 stop or slow down the progress of (something undesirable): *efforts were made to check the disease.*
■ curb or restrain (a feeling or emotion): *he learned to check his excitement.* ■ (**check oneself**) master an involuntary reaction: *Chris took one step backwards then checked himself.* ■ Ice Hockey hamper or neutralize (an opponent) with one's body or stick. ■ informal, dated find fault with: *I was hut orderly, and got checked for dull brass doorknobs.* ■ [no obj.] (**check against**) provide a means of preventing: *processes to check against deterioration in the quality of the data held.* ■ [no obj.] (of a hound) pause to make sure of or regain a scent. ■ [no obj.] (of a trained hawk) abandon the intended quarry and fly after other prey.
3 [with obj.] Chess move a piece or pawn to a square where it attacks (the opposing king).
4 [no obj.] (in poker) choose not to make a bet when called upon, allowing another player to do so instead.
▶ noun **1** an examination to test or ascertain accuracy, quality, or satisfactory condition: *a campaign calling for regular checks on gas appliances* | *a health check.*
2 a stopping or slowing of progress: *there was no check to the expansion of the market.*
■ a means of control or restraint: *a permanent check upon the growth or abuse of central authority.* ■ Ice Hockey an act of hampering or neutralizing an opponent with one's body or stick. ■ a temporary loss of the scent in hunting. ■ Falconry a false stoop when a hawk abandons its intended quarry and pursues other prey. ■ a part of a piano which catches the hammer and prevents it retouching the strings.
3 Chess a move by which a piece or pawn directly attacks the opponent's king. If the defending player cannot counter the attack, the king is checkmated.
■ [mass noun] the position resulting from such a move.
4 N. Amer. the bill in a restaurant.
■ (also **baggage/luggage check**) a token of

identification for left luggage. ■ a counter used as a stake in a gambling game.
5 (also **check mark**) North American term for **TICK**[1] (in sense 1).
6 a crack or flaw in timber.
▶ exclamation **1** informal, chiefly N. Amer. expressing assent or agreement.
2 used by a chess player to announce that the opponent's king has been placed in check.
– PHRASES **check someone/thing skeef** S. African give someone or something a disapproving look. **check you** S. African goodbye. **in check 1** under control: *a way of keeping inflation in check.* **2** Chess (of a king) directly attacked by an opponent's piece or pawn; (of a player) having the king in this position. **keep a check on** monitor: *keep a regular check on your score.*
– DERIVATIVES **checkable** adjective.
– ORIGIN Middle English (originally as used in the game of chess): the noun and exclamation from Old French *eschec*, from medieval Latin *scaccus*, via Arabic from Persian *šāh* 'king'; the verb from Old French *eschequier* 'play chess, put in check'. The sense 'stop, restrain, or control' arose from the use in chess, and led (in the late 17th cent.) to 'examine the accuracy of, verify'.
▶ **check in** (or **check someone in**) arrive and register at a hotel or airport: *you must check in at least one hour before take-off* | *they check in the passengers.*
check something in have one's baggage weighed and put aside for consignment to the hold of an aircraft on which one is booked to travel. ■ register and leave baggage in a left-luggage department.
check into register one's arrival at (a hotel).
check something off tick or otherwise mark an item on a list to show that it has been dealt with.
check on 1 verify, ascertain, or monitor the state or condition of: *the doctor had come to check on his patient.* **2** another way of saying **CHECK UP ON.**
check out settle one's hotel bill before leaving. ■ N. Amer. informal die.
check someone/thing out 1 establish the truth or inform oneself about someone or something: *they decided to go and check out a local restaurant.* **2** (**check something out**) chiefly N. Amer. enter the price of goods in a supermarket into a cash machine for addition and payment by a customer. ■ register something as having been borrowed.
check something over inspect or examine something thoroughly.
check through inspect or examine thoroughly.
check up on investigate in order to establish the truth about or accuracy of.

check[2] ▶ noun a pattern of small squares: *a fine black-and-white check.*
■ a garment or fabric with such a pattern: *on Wednesdays he wore the small check.*
▶ adjective [attrib.] having such a pattern: *a blue check T-shirt.*
– ORIGIN late Middle English: probably from **CHEQUER**.

check[3] ▶ noun US spelling of **CHEQUE**.

checkbox ▶ noun Computing a small area on a computer screen which when selected by the user, acquires a cross to show that the feature described alongside it has been enabled.

checked ▶ adjective (of clothes or fabric) having a pattern of small squares: *a checked shirt.*

checker[1] ▶ noun **1** a person or thing that verifies or examines something: *a spelling checker.*
2 US a cashier in a supermarket.

checker[2] ▶ noun & verb US spelling of **CHEQUER**.

checkerberry ▶ noun (pl. **-ies**) a creeping evergreen North American shrub of the heather family, with spiny scented leaves and waxy white flowers. Also called **WINTERGREEN**.
● *Gaultheria procumbens*, family Ericaceae.
■ the edible red fruit of this plant.
– ORIGIN late 18th cent.: from *checkers* or *chequers* 'berries of the service tree' (so named from their colour) + **BERRY**.

checkerboard ▶ noun US spelling of **CHEQUERBOARD**.

checkered ▶ adjective US spelling of **CHEQUERED**.

checkerspot ▶ noun a North American butterfly that resembles a fritillary, with pale markings on the wings that typically form a chequered pattern.
● *Euphydryas* and other genera, subfamily Melitaeinae, family Nymphalidae.

check-in ▶ noun [mass noun] [often as modifier] the action of reporting one's presence and registering, typically as a passenger at an airport: *the check-in counter.*
■ the point at which such registration takes place.

checking account (Canadian **chequing account**) ▶ noun N. Amer. a current account at a bank.
– ORIGIN 1920s: from **CHECK**[3].

checklist ▶ noun a list of items required, things to be done, or points to be considered, used as a reminder.

check mark ▶ noun N. Amer. a mark (✓) used to indicate that a textual item is correct or has been chosen or checked.

checkmate ▶ noun [mass noun] Chess a position in which a player's king is directly attacked by an opponent's piece or pawn and has no possible move to escape the check. The attacking player thus wins the game.
■ [as exclamation] (by a player) announcing that the opponent's king is in such a position. ■ figurative a final defeat or deadlock: *if the rebel forces succeed in cutting off the road, they will have achieved checkmate.*
▶ verb [with obj.] Chess put into checkmate.
■ figurative defeat or frustrate totally: *US aid would help them to checkmate communist invasion.*
– ORIGIN Middle English: from Old French *eschec mat*, from Arabic *šāh māta*, from Persian *šāh māt* 'the king is dead'.

checkout ▶ noun **1** a point at which goods are paid for in a supermarket or similar store.
2 [mass noun] the administrative procedure followed when a guest leaves a hotel at the end of their stay.

checkpoint ▶ noun a barrier or manned entrance, typically at a border, where security checks are carried out on travellers.
■ a place on the route in a long-distance race where the time for each competitor is recorded. ■ a location whose exact position can be verified visually or electronically, used by pilots to aid navigation.

check rein ▶ noun a bearing rein.

checkroom ▶ noun N. Amer. a cloakroom in a hotel or theatre.
■ an office for left luggage.

checks and balances ▶ plural noun counterbalancing influences by which an organization or system is regulated, typically those ensuring that power in political institutions is not concentrated in the hands of particular individuals or groups.

checksum ▶ noun a digit representing the sum of the correct digits in a piece of stored or transmitted digital data, against which later comparisons can be made to detect errors in the data.

check-up ▶ noun a thorough examination, especially a medical or dental one, to detect any problems.

check valve ▶ noun a valve that closes to prevent backward flow of liquid.

Cheddar ▶ noun [mass noun] a kind of firm smooth yellow, white, or orange cheese, originally made in Cheddar but now widely imitated.

cheder /'xɛdə/ (also **heder**) ▶ noun (pl. **chedarim** /-'dɑːrɪm/, **cheders**) a school for Jewish children in which Hebrew and religious knowledge are taught.
– ORIGIN late 19th cent.: from Hebrew *ḥeḏer* 'room'.

cheechako /tʃiː'tʃɑːkəʊ/ ▶ noun (pl. **-os**) N. Amer. informal a person newly arrived in the mining districts of Alaska or NW Canada.
– ORIGIN late 19th cent.: Chinook Jargon, 'newcomer'.

chee-chee ▶ exclamation variant spelling of **CHI-CHI**.

cheek ▶ noun **1** either side of the face below the eye: *tears rolled down her cheeks.*
■ either of the inner sides of the mouth: *Gabriel had to bite his cheeks to keep from laughing.* ■ informal either of the buttocks. ■ either of two side pieces or parts arranged in lateral pairs in a structure.
2 [in sing.] talk or behaviour that is boldly impertinent or unreasonable: *he had the cheek to complain* | *that's enough of your cheek!*
▶ verb [with obj.] speak impertinently to: *Frankie always got away with cheeking his elders.*
– PHRASES **cheek by jowl** close together; side by side: *they lived cheek by jowl in a one-room flat.*
[ORIGIN: from a use of *jowl* in the sense 'cheek'; the

phrase was originally *cheek by cheek*.] **cheek to cheek** (of two people dancing) with their heads close together in an intimate and romantic way. **turn the other cheek** refrain from retaliating when one has been attacked or insulted. [ORIGIN: with biblical allusion to Matt. 5:39.]
– DERIVATIVES **cheeked** adjective [in combination] *rosy-cheeked*.
– ORIGIN Old English *cē(a)ce, cēoce* 'cheek, jaw', of West Germanic origin; related to Dutch *kaak*.

cheekbone ▶ noun the bone below the eye.

cheekpiece ▶ noun a part of an object which covers or rests on the cheek, in particular:
▪ a smooth block fitted to the stock of a rifle or shotgun and resting against the face when aiming from the shoulder. ▪ either of the two straps of a horse's bridle joining the bit and the headpiece. ▪ a bar on a horse's bit which lies outside the mouth.

cheeky ▶ adjective (**cheekier**, **cheekiest**) impudent or irreverent, typically in an endearing or amusing way: *a cheeky grin*.
– DERIVATIVES **cheekily** adverb, **cheekiness** noun.

cheep ▶ noun a shrill squeaky cry made by a bird, typically a young one.
▪ a sound resembling such a cry: *an electronic cheep from the alarm*. ▪ [in sing.] [with negative] informal the slightest sound: *there has not been a cheep from anybody*.
▶ verb [no obj.] make a shrill squeaky sound.
– ORIGIN early 16th cent. (originally Scots): imitative (compare with **PEEP**²).

cheer ▶ verb **1** [no obj.] shout for joy or in praise or encouragement: *she cheered from the sidelines*.
▪ [with obj.] praise or encourage with shouts: *MPs rose to cheer the Chancellor* | *the cyclists were* ***cheered on*** *by the crowds*.
2 [with obj.] give comfort or support to: *he seemed greatly cheered by my arrival*.
▪ (**cheer someone up** or **cheer up**) make or become less miserable: [with obj.] *I asked her out to lunch to cheer her up* | [no obj.] *he cheered up at the sight of the food*.
▶ noun **1** a shout of encouragement, praise, or joy: *a tremendous cheer from the audience*.
2 (also **good cheer**) [mass noun] cheerfulness, optimism, or confidence: *an attempt to inject a little cheer into this gloomy season*.
▪ something that causes such feelings: *there was some cheer for the government concerning the balance of payments*. ▪ food and drink provided for a festive occasion: *they had partaken heartily of the Christmas cheer*.
– PHRASES **of good cheer** archaic cheerful; optimistic. **three cheers** three successive hurrahs shouted to express appreciation or congratulation: ***three cheers*** *for the winners!* **two cheers** qualified approval or mild enthusiasm: *larger companies gave at least two cheers for the Budget*. **what cheer?** archaic how are you?
– ORIGIN Middle English: from Old French *chiere* 'face', from late Latin *cara*, from Greek *kara* 'head'. The original sense was 'face', hence 'expression, mood', later specifically 'a good mood'.

cheerful ▶ adjective noticeably happy and optimistic: *how can she be so cheerful at six o'clock in the morning?* | *a cheerful voice*.
▪ causing happiness by its nature or appearance: *cheerful news* | *the room was painted in cheerful colours*.
– DERIVATIVES **cheerfulness** noun.

cheerfully ▶ adverb in a way that displays happiness or optimism: *he was whistling cheerfully*.
▪ in a way that inspires feelings of happiness: *a cheerfully decorated tram car*. ▪ readily and willingly: *I could cheerfully have strangled her*.

cheerio ▶ exclamation Brit. informal used as an expression of good wishes on parting; goodbye.
▪ dated used to express friendly feelings towards one's companions before drinking.

cheerleader ▶ noun a member of a team of girls who perform organized cheering, chanting, and dancing in support of a sports team at matches in the US and elsewhere.
▪ an enthusiastic and vocal supporter of someone or something: *he was a cheerleader for individual initiative*.

cheerless ▶ adjective gloomy; depressing: *the corridors were ill-lit and cheerless*.
– DERIVATIVES **cheerlessly** adverb, **cheerlessness** noun.

cheerly ▶ adverb archaic heartily (used as a cry of encouragement among sailors).

cheers ▶ exclamation informal expressing good wishes, in particular:
▪ good wishes before drinking. ▪ Brit. good wishes on parting or ending a conversation: *'Cheers, Jack, see you later.'* ▪ chiefly Brit. gratitude or acknowledgement for something: *Billy tossed him the key. 'Cheers, pal.'*

cheery ▶ adjective (**cheerier**, **cheeriest**) happy and optimistic: *a cheery smile*.
– DERIVATIVES **cheerily** adverb, **cheeriness** noun.

cheese¹ ▶ noun [mass noun] **1** a food made from the pressed curds of milk, firm and elastic or soft and semi-liquid in texture: *grated cheese* | [as modifier] *a cheese sandwich* | [count noun] *a cow's milk cheese*.
▪ [count noun] a complete cake of such food with its rind. ▪ [with modifier] Brit. a conserve having the consistency of soft cheese: *lemon cheese*. ▪ [count noun] a round flat object resembling a complete cake of cheese, such as the heavy flat wooden disc used in skittles and other games.
2 informal the quality of being too obviously sentimental: *the conversations tend too far towards cheese*.
– PHRASES **hard cheese** Brit. informal used to express sympathy over a petty matter. **say cheese** said by a photographer to encourage the subject to smile.
– ORIGIN Old English *cēse, cȳse*, of West Germanic origin; related to Dutch *kaas* and German *Käse*; from Latin *caseus*.

cheese² ▶ verb [with obj.] (usu. **be cheesed off**) Brit. informal exasperate, frustrate, or bore (someone): *I got a bit cheesed off with the movie*.
– PHRASES **cheese it!** **1** Brit. archaic used to urge someone to stop doing something. **2** dated used to urge someone to make a hasty departure from somewhere: *Cheese it, here comes Mr Madigan!*
– ORIGIN early 19th cent. (in sense 1 of *cheese it*): of unknown origin.

cheeseboard ▶ noun a selection of cheeses served as a course of a meal.
▪ a board on which cheese is served and cut.

cheeseburger ▶ noun a beefburger with a slice of cheese on it, served in a bread roll.

cheesecake ▶ noun **1** a kind of rich sweet tart made with cream and soft cheese on a biscuit base, typically topped with a fruit sauce.
2 [mass noun] informal photography, film, or art that portrays women in a manner which emphasizes idealized or stereotypical sexual attractiveness.

cheesecloth ▶ noun [mass noun] thin, loosely woven, unsized cotton cloth, used typically for light clothing and in preparing or protecting food.

cheese-cutter ▶ noun **1** an implement for cutting cheese, especially by means of a wire which can be pulled through the cheese.
2 (also **cheese-cutter cap**) informal a cap with a broad, squared peak.

cheese fly ▶ noun a small shiny black fly whose larvae frequently infest cheese. Also called **CHEESE-SKIPPER**.
• *Piophila casei*, family Piophilidae.

cheese head ▶ noun Brit. a type of screw head with vertical sides and a slightly domed top.

cheese mite ▶ noun a mite that infests cheese.
• Genus *Tyroglyphus*, order (or subclass) Acari.

cheesemonger ▶ noun Brit. a person who sells cheese, butter, and other dairy products.

cheese-paring ▶ adjective very careful or mean with money: *cheese-paring methods necessitated by desperate shortages*.
▶ noun [mass noun] meanness.

cheese plant ▶ noun see **SWISS CHEESE PLANT**.

cheese-skipper ▶ noun another term for **CHEESE FLY**.

cheese straw ▶ noun a thin strip of pastry, flavoured with cheese and eaten as a snack.

cheesewood ▶ noun a small tropical evergreen tree with white flowers and yellowish-orange fruit containing orange seeds.
• Genus *Pittosporum*, family Pittosporaceae: several species, in particular the Australian *P. undulatum*, with fragrant flowers and hard yellowish timber used in making golf clubs, and the South African *P. viridifolium*.

cheesy ▶ adjective (**cheesier**, **cheesiest**) **1** like cheese in taste, smell, or consistency: *a pungent, cheesy sauce*.
2 informal cheap, unpleasant, or blatantly inauthentic: *a big cheesy grin* | *cheesy motel rooms*.
– DERIVATIVES **cheesiness** noun.

cheetah /ˈtʃiːtə/ ▶ noun a large slender spotted cat found in Africa and parts of Asia. It is more highly adapted for running than other cats, and is the fastest animal on land.
• *Acinonyx jubatus*, family Felidae.
– ORIGIN late 18th cent.: from Hindi *cītā*, perhaps from Sanskrit *citraka* 'leopard'.

Cheever /ˈtʃiːvə/, John (1912–82), American short-story writer and novelist. His stories frequently satirize affluent suburban New Englanders. Notable novels: *The Wapshot Chronicle* (1957).

chef ▶ noun a professional cook, typically the chief cook in a restaurant or hotel.
– ORIGIN early 19th cent.: French, literally 'head'.

chef d'école /ˌʃɛf deɪˈkɒl, French ʃɛ dekɔl/ ▶ noun (pl. **chefs d'école** pronunc. same) the initiator or leader of a school or style of music, painting, or literature.
– ORIGIN mid 19th cent.: French, 'head of school'.

chef-d'œuvre /ʃeɪ ˈdəːvr(ə), French ʃɛ dœvʀ/ ▶ noun (pl. **chefs-d'œuvre** pronunc. same) a masterpiece.
– ORIGIN French, 'chief work'.

Chefoo /tʃiːˈfuː/ former name for **YANTAI**.

cheiro- ▶ combining form variant spelling of **CHIRO-**.

Cheka /ˈtʃɛkə/ an organization under the Soviet regime for the investigation of counter-revolutionary activities. It executed many real and alleged enemies of Lenin's regime from its formation in 1917 until 1922, when it was replaced by the OGPU.
– ORIGIN Russian, from *che, ka*, the initial letters of *Chrezvychaĭnaya komissiya* 'Extraordinary Commission (for combating Counter-revolution, Sabotage, and Speculation)'.

Chekhov /ˈtʃɛkɒf/, Anton (Pavlovich) (1860–1904), Russian dramatist and short-story writer. Chekhov's work, portraying upper-class life in pre-revolutionary Russia with a blend of naturalism and symbolism, had a considerable influence on 20th-century drama. Notable plays: *The Seagull* (1895), *Uncle Vanya* (1900), *The Three Sisters* (1901), and *The Cherry Orchard* (1904).
– DERIVATIVES **Chekhovian** /tʃɛˈkəʊvɪən/ adjective.

Chekiang /tʃɛˈkjaŋ/ variant of **ZHEJIANG**.

chela¹ /ˈkiːlə/ ▶ noun (pl. **chelae** /-liː/) Zoology a pincer-like claw, especially of a crab or other crustacean. Compare with **CHELICERA**.
– ORIGIN mid 17th cent.: modern Latin, from Latin *chele* or Greek *khēlē* 'claw'.

chela² /ˈtʃeɪlə/ ▶ noun a follower and pupil of a guru.
– ORIGIN from Hindi *celā*.

chelate /ˈkiːleɪt/ ▶ noun Chemistry a compound containing a ligand (typically organic) bonded to a central metal atom at two or more points.
▶ adjective Zoology (of an appendage) bearing chelae.
▶ verb [with obj.] Chemistry form a chelate with.
– DERIVATIVES **chelation** noun, **chelator** noun.

chelicera /kəˈlɪs(ə)rə/ ▶ noun (pl. **chelicerae** /-riː/) Zoology either of a pair of appendages in front of the mouth in arachnids and some other arthropods, usually modified as pincer-like claws. Compare with **CHELA**¹.
– DERIVATIVES **cheliceral** adjective.
– ORIGIN mid 19th cent.: modern Latin, from Greek *khēlē* 'claw' + *keras* 'horn'.

Chelicerata /kəˌlɪsəˈreɪtə/ Zoology a large group of arthropods that comprises the arachnids, sea spiders, and horseshoe crabs. They lack antennae, but possess a pair of chelicerae, a pair of pedipalps, and (typically) four pairs of legs.
• Subphylum Chelicerata, phylum Arthropoda.
– DERIVATIVES **chelicerate** /kəˈlɪsəreɪt, -(ə)rət/ noun & adjective.
– ORIGIN modern Latin (plural), from Greek *khēlē* 'claw' + *keras* 'horn'.

Chellean /ˈʃɛlɪən/ ▶ adjective & noun former term for **ABBEVILLIAN**.
– ORIGIN late 19th cent.: from French *Chelléen*, from *Chelles*, near Paris, where tools from this period were discovered.

Chelmsford /ˈtʃɛlmzfəd/ a cathedral city in SE England, the county town of Essex; pop. 152,418 (1991).

Chelonia /kɪˈləʊnɪə/ Zoology former term for **TESTUDINES**.
– DERIVATIVES **chelonian** noun & adjective.
– ORIGIN modern Latin (plural), from Greek *khelōnē* 'tortoise'.

Chelsea a residential district of London, on the north bank of the River Thames.

Chelsea boot ▶ noun an elastic-sided boot, typically with a high heel.

Chelsea bun ▶ noun Brit. a flat, spiral-shaped currant bun sprinkled with sugar.
– ORIGIN early 18th cent.: named after **CHELSEA**, where such buns were originally made.

Chelsea pensioner ▶ noun (in the UK) an inmate of the Chelsea Royal Hospital for old or disabled soldiers.

Chelsea ware ▶ noun [mass noun] a type of soft-paste porcelain made at Chelsea in the 18th century.

Cheltenham /'tʃɛlt(ə)nəm/ a town in western England, in Gloucestershire; pop. (1991) 85,900. It became a fashionable spa town in the 19th century.

Chelyabinsk /tʃɪl'jɑːbɪnsk/ an industrial city in southern Russia on the eastern slopes of the Ural Mountains; pop. 1,148,000 (1990).

chemi- ▶ combining form representing **CHEMICAL**. See also **CHEMO-**.

chemical ▶ adjective of or relating to chemistry, or the interactions of substances as studied in chemistry: *the chemical composition of the atmosphere.*
■of or relating to chemicals: *chemical treatments for killing fungi.* ■ relating to, involving, or denoting the use of poison gas or other chemicals as weapons of war.
▶ noun a compound or substance which has been purified or prepared, especially artificially: *never mix disinfectant with other chemicals* | [mass noun] *neat chemical is sucked into the tube.*
– DERIVATIVES **chemically** adverb.
– ORIGIN late 16th cent.: from French *chimique* or modern Latin *chimicus, chymicus*, from medieval Latin *alchymicus*, from *alchimia* (see **ALCHEMY**).

chemical bond ▶ noun see **BOND**[1] (sense 3).

chemical compound ▶ noun see **COMPOUND**[1].

chemical engineering ▶ noun [mass noun] the branch of engineering concerned with the design and operation of industrial chemical plants.
– DERIVATIVES **chemical engineer** noun.

chemical formula ▶ noun see **FORMULA** (sense 1).

chemical potential ▶ noun Chemistry a thermodynamic function expressing the ability of an uncharged atom or molecule in a chemical system to perform physical work.

chemical reaction ▶ noun a process that involves rearrangement of the molecular or ionic structure of a substance, as distinct from a change in physical form or a nuclear reaction.

chemical weathering ▶ noun [mass noun] the erosion or disintegration of rocks, building materials, etc., caused by chemical reactions (chiefly with water and substances dissolved in it) rather than by mechanical processes.

chemico- ▶ combining form representing **CHEMICAL**.

chemiluminescence ▶ noun [mass noun] the emission of light during a chemical reaction which does not produce significant quantities of heat.
– DERIVATIVES **chemiluminescent** adjective.

chemin de fer /ʃə,mã də 'fɛː, French ʃ(ə)mɛ̃ d(ə) fɛʀ/ ▶ noun [mass noun] a card game which is a variety of baccarat.
– ORIGIN late 19th cent.: French, literally 'railway'.

chemise /ʃə'miːz/ ▶ noun a dress hanging straight from the shoulders and giving the figure a uniform shape, popular in the 1920s.
■a woman's loose-fitting undergarment or nightdress, typically of silk or satin with a lace trim. ■ a priest's alb or surplice. ■ historical a smock.
– ORIGIN Middle English: from Old French, from late Latin *camisia* 'shirt or nightgown'.

chemisette /,ʃɛmɪ'zɛt/ ▶ noun a woman's undergarment similar to a camisole, typically worn so as to be visible beneath an open-necked blouse or dress.
– ORIGIN early 19th cent.: French, diminutive of *chemise*.

chemisorption /,kɛmɪ'sɔːpʃ(ə)n, -'zɔːp-/ ▶ noun [mass noun] Chemistry adsorption in which the adsorbed substance is held by chemical bonds.
– DERIVATIVES **chemisorbed** adjective.
– ORIGIN 1930s: from **CHEMI-** + a shortened form of **ADSORPTION**.

chemist ▶ noun 1 Brit. a shop where medicinal drugs are dispensed and sold, and in which toiletries and other medical goods can be purchased.

■a person who is authorized to dispense such medicinal drugs.
2 an expert in chemistry; a person engaged in chemical research or experiments.
– ORIGIN late Middle English (denoting an alchemist): from French *chimiste*, from modern Latin *chimista*, from *alchimista* 'alchemist', from *alchimia* (see **ALCHEMY**).

chemistry ▶ noun (pl. **-ies**) [mass noun] **1** the branch of science which deals with the identification of the substances of which matter is composed, the investigation of their properties and the ways in which they interact, combine and change, and the use of these processes to form new substances.
■the chemical composition and properties of a substance or body: *the chemistry of iron* | [count noun] *the chemistries of other galaxies.* ■ figurative a process or phenomenon perceived as complex or mysterious: *the chemistry of politics.*
2 the complex emotional or psychological interaction between two people, typically when experienced as a powerful mutual attraction: *their affair was triggered by intense sexual chemistry.*

Chemnitz /'kɛmnɪts/ an industrial city in eastern Germany, on the Chemnitz River; pop. 310,000 (est. 1990). Former name (from 1953) **KARL-MARX-STADT**.

chemo /'kiːməʊ/ ▶ noun [mass noun] informal chemotherapy.

chemo- ▶ combining form representing **CHEMICAL**. See also **CHEMI-**.

chemoattractant /,kiːməʊə'traktənt, ,kɛm-/ ▶ noun Biology a substance which attracts motile cells of a particular type: *a fibroblast chemoattractant.*

chemoautotroph /,kiːməʊ'ɔːtətrəʊf, -trɒf, ,kɛm-/ ▶ noun Biology an organism, typically a bacterium, which derives energy from the oxidation of inorganic compounds.
– DERIVATIVES **chemoautotrophic** /-'trəʊfɪk, -'trɒfɪk/ adjective, **chemoautotrophy** /-'trəʊfi, -'trɒfi/ noun.

chemoprophylaxis /,kiːməʊprɒfɪ'laksɪs, ,kɛm-/ ▶ noun [mass noun] the use of drugs to prevent disease.
– DERIVATIVES **chemoprophylactic** adjective.

chemoreceptor /'kiːməʊrɪ,sɛptə, ,kɛm-/ ▶ noun Physiology a sensory cell or organ responsive to chemical stimuli.
– DERIVATIVES **chemoreception** noun.

chemostat /'kiːmə(ʊ)stat, ,kɛm-/ ▶ noun a system in which the chemical composition is kept at a controlled level, especially for the culture of micro-organisms.

chemosynthesis /,kiːmə(ʊ)'sɪnθɪsɪs, ,kɛm-/ ▶ noun [mass noun] Biology the synthesis of organic compounds by bacteria or other living organisms using energy derived from reactions involving inorganic chemicals, typically in the absence of sunlight. Compare with **PHOTOSYNTHESIS**.
– DERIVATIVES **chemosynthetic** adjective.

chemotaxis /,kiːmə(ʊ)'taksɪs, ,kɛm-/ ▶ noun [mass noun] Biology movement of a motile cell or organism, or part of one, in a direction corresponding to a gradient of increasing or decreasing concentration of a particular substance.
– DERIVATIVES **chemotactic** adjective.

chemotherapy /,kiːmə(ʊ)'θɛrəpi, ,kɛm-/ ▶ noun [mass noun] the treatment of disease by the use of chemical substances, especially the treatment of cancer by cytotoxic and other drugs.
– DERIVATIVES **chemotherapist** noun.

chempaka /'tʃɛmpəkə/ ▶ noun variant spelling of **CHAMPAK**.

chemurgy /'kɛmə:dʒi/ ▶ noun [mass noun] N. Amer. the chemical and industrial use of organic raw materials.
– DERIVATIVES **chemurgic** adjective.
– ORIGIN 1930s: from **CHEMO-**, on the pattern of *metallurgy.*

Chenab /tʃɪ'nɑːb/ a river of northern India and Pakistan, which rises in the Himalayas and flows through Himachal Pradesh and Jammu and Kashmir, to join the Sutlej River in Punjab. It is one of the five rivers that gave Punjab its name.

Chennai /'tʃɪnʌɪ/ official name (since 1995) for **MADRAS**.

chenar ▶ noun variant spelling of **CHINAR**.

Chen-chiang /tʃɛn'tʃjaŋ/ variant of **ZHENJIANG**.

Chengchow /tʃɛŋ'tʃaʊ/ variant of **ZHENGZHOU**.

Chengdu /tʃɛŋ'duː/ the capital of Sichuan province in west central China; pop. 2,780,000 (1990).

chenille /ʃə'niːl/ ▶ noun [mass noun] a tufty velvety cord or yarn, used for trimming furniture, making carpets, and in clothing.
■fabric made from such yarn.
– ORIGIN mid 18th cent.: from French, literally 'hairy caterpillar', from Latin *canicula* 'small dog', diminutive of *canis.*

cheongsam /tʃɪɒŋ'sam, tʃɒŋ-/ ▶ noun a straight, close-fitting silk dress with a high neck and slit skirt, worn by Chinese and Indonesian women.
– ORIGIN Chinese (Cantonese dialect).

Cheops /'kiːɒps/ (fl. early 26th century BC), Egyptian pharaoh of the 4th dynasty; Egyptian name **Khufu**. He commissioned the building of the Great Pyramid at Giza.

cheque (US **check**) ▶ noun an order to a bank to pay a stated sum from the drawer's account, written on a specially printed form.
– ORIGIN early 18th cent. (originally denoting a counterfoil, or a form with a counterfoil): variant of **CHECK**[1], in the sense 'device for checking the amount of an item'.

chequebook ▶ noun a book of forms for writing cheques.

chequebook journalism ▶ noun [mass noun] the practice of paying a large amount of money to someone so as to acquire the exclusive right to publish their story in a particular newspaper.

cheque card (also **cheque guarantee card**) ▶ noun Brit. a card issued by a bank to guarantee the honouring of cheques up to a stated amount.

chequer (US **checker**) ▶ noun 1 (**chequers**) a pattern of squares, typically alternately coloured: *a geometric shape bordered by chequers* | [as modifier] (**chequer**) *a chequer design.*
2 (**checkers**) [treated as sing.] N. Amer. the game of draughts.
■(**checker**) a piece used in this game.
▶ verb [with obj.] (usu. **be chequered**) divide into or mark with an arrangement of squares of a different colour or character: *a great plain chequered with corn and green mosses.*
– ORIGIN Middle English: from **EXCHEQUER**. The original sense 'chessboard' gave rise to *chequered* meaning 'marked like a chessboard'; hence sense 1 (early 16th cent.).

chequerboard (US **checkerboard**) ▶ noun a board for playing checkers and similar games, having a regular pattern of squares in alternating colours, typically black and white.
■a pattern resembling such a board.

chequered (US **checkered**) ▶ adjective having a pattern consisting of alternating squares of different colours.
■figurative marked by periods of varied fortune or discreditable incidents : *the chequered history of post-war Britain.*

chequered flag ▶ noun Motor Racing a flag with a black-and-white chequered pattern, displayed to drivers at the end of a race.
– PHRASES **take the chequered flag** finish first in a race.

Chequers a Tudor mansion in Buckinghamshire which serves as a country seat of the British Prime Minister in office.

Cher /ʃɛː/ a river of central France, which rises in the Massif Central, flowing 350 km (220 miles) northwards to meet the Loire near Tours.

Cherbourg /'ʃəːbʊəɡ, French ʃɛʀbuʀ/ a seaport and naval base in Normandy, northern France; pop. 28,770 (1990).

Cheremis /'tʃɛrəmɪs/ ▶ noun former term for the Mari language (see **MARI**[2]).

Cherenkov /tʃɪ'rɛŋkɒf/, Pavel (Alekseevich) (also **Cerenkov**) (1904–90), Soviet physicist. He investigated the effects of high-energy particles and shared the 1958 Nobel Prize for Physics for discovering the cause of blue light (now called **CERENKOV RADIATION**) emitted by radioactive substances underwater.

Cherenkov radiation ▶ noun variant spelling of **CERENKOV RADIATION**.

Cherepovets /,tʃɛrɪpə'vjɛts/ a city in NW Russia, on the Rybinsk reservoir; pop. 313,000 (1990).

cherimoya /,tʃɛrɪ'mɔɪə/ (also **chirimoya**) ▶ noun 1 a

kind of custard apple with a pineapple-like flavour and scaly green skin.
2 the small tree which bears this fruit, native to the Andes of Peru and Ecuador.
• *Annona cherimola*, family Annonaceae.
– ORIGIN mid 18th cent.: from Spanish, from Quechua, from *chiri* 'cold or refreshing' + *muya* 'circle'.

cherish ▶ **verb** [with obj.] protect and care for (someone) lovingly.
▪hold (something) dear: *I cherish the letters she wrote.* ▪ keep in one's mind (a hope or ambition): *he had long cherished a secret fantasy about his future.*
– ORIGIN Middle English (in the sense 'treat with affection'): from Old French *cheriss-*, lengthened stem of *cherir*, from *cher* 'dear', from Latin *carus*.

Cherkasy /tʃəˈkasi/ a port in central Ukraine, on the River Dnieper; pop. 297,000 (1990). Russian name **CHERKASSY**.

Cherkess /tʃəˈkɛs/ ▶ **noun** another term for **CIRCASSIAN**.

Cherkessk /tʃəˈkɛsk/ a city in the Caucasus in southern Russia, capital of the republic of Karachai-Cherkessia; pop 113,000 (1990).

Chernenko /tʃəˈnjɛŋkəʊ/, Konstantin (Ustinovich) (1911–85), Soviet statesman, General Secretary of the Communist Party of the USSR and President 1984–5. He died after only thirteen months in office and was succeeded by Mikhail Gorbachev.

Chernihiv /tʃɛːˈniːhɪv/ a port in northern Ukraine, on the River Desna; pop. 301,000 (1990). Russian name **CHERNIGOV** /tʃəˈniːɡɒf/.

Chernivtsi /tʃəˈnɪvtsi/ a city in western Ukraine, in the foothills of the Carpathians, close to the border with Romania; pop. 257,000 (est. 1990). It was part of Romania between 1918 and 1940. Russian name **CHERNOVTSY** /ˌtʃernəvˈtsi/.

Chernobyl /tʃəˈnɒbɪl, -ˈnəʊbɪl/ a town near Kiev in Ukraine where, in April 1986, an accident at a nuclear power station resulted in a serious escape of radioactive material.

Chernorechye /ˌtʃɜːnəˈrɛtʃjə/ former name (until 1919) for **DZERZHINSK**.

chernozem /ˈtʃɜːnəzɛm/ ▶ **noun** Soil Science a fertile black soil rich in humus, with a lighter lime-rich layer beneath. Such soils typically occur in temperate grasslands such as the Russian steppes and North American prairies.
– ORIGIN mid 19th cent.: from Russian, from *chërnyĭ* 'black' + *zemlya* 'earth'.

Cherokee /ˌtʃɛrəˈkiː/ ▶ **noun** (pl. same or **Cherokees**)
1 a member of an American Indian people formerly inhabiting much of the southern US, now living on reservations in Oklahoma and North Carolina.
2 [mass noun] the Iroquoian language of this people, which has had its own script since 1820 and has about 11,000 speakers.
▶ **adjective** of or relating to this people or their language.
– ORIGIN from obsolete Cherokee *tsaraki*, earlier form of *tsaliki*.

Cherokee rose ▶ **noun** a climbing Chinese rose with fragrant white flowers, which has become naturalized in the southern US.
• *Rosa laevigata*, family Rosaceae.

cheroot /ʃəˈruːt/ ▶ **noun** a cigar with both ends open.
– ORIGIN late 17th cent.: from French *cheroute*, from Tamil *curuṭṭu* 'roll of tobacco'.

cherry ▶ **noun** (pl. **-ies**) **1** a small, soft round stone fruit that is typically bright or dark red. See also **MARASCHINO CHERRY**.
2 (also **cherry tree**) the tree that bears such fruit.
• Genus *Prunus*, family Rosaceae: several species, the edible kinds being derived from the **sweet** (or **wild**) **cherry** (*P. avium*) and the **sour** (or **morello**) **cherry** (*P. cerasus*).
▪used in names of unrelated plants with similar fruits, e.g. **cornelian cherry**.
3 [mass noun] a bright deep red colour: [as modifier] *her mouth was a bright cherry red.*
4 [in sing.] informal a person's virginity: *only 3 per cent of the students lost their cherry at college.*
– PHRASES **a bite at the cherry** an attempt or opportunity to do something. **a bowl of cherries** [usu. with negative] a very pleasant or enjoyable situation or experience: *being in the band isn't a bowl of cherries.* **the cherry on the cake** a desirable feature perceived as the finishing touch to something that is already inviting or worth having. **pop someone's cherry** informal have sexual intercourse with a girl or woman who is a virgin.
– ORIGIN Middle English: from Old Northern French *cherise*, from medieval Latin *ceresia*, based on Greek *kerasos* 'cherry tree, cherry'. The final *-s* was lost because *cherise* was interpreted as plural (compare with **CAPER**[2] and **PEA**).

cherry brandy ▶ **noun** [mass noun] a dark red, sweet, cherry-flavoured liqueur, typically made with brandy in which cherries have been steeped, or with crushed cherry stones.
▪rare a strong spirit distilled from fermented cherry juice. Compare with **KIRSCH**.

cherry laurel ▶ **noun** an evergreen shrub or small tree with leathery leaves, white flowers, and cherry-like fruits, native to the Balkans and widely cultivated as the common 'laurel' of gardens.
• *Prunus laurocerasus*, family Rosaceae.

cherry-pick ▶ **verb** [with obj.] selectively choose (the most beneficial or profitable items, opportunities, etc.) from what is available: *the company should buy the whole airline and not just cherry-pick its best assets.*

cherry picker ▶ **noun** informal **1** a hydraulic crane with a railed platform at the end for raising and lowering people, for instance to work on overhead cables.
2 a person who cherry-picks.

cherry pie ▶ **noun** a garden heliotrope cultivated for its fragrant blue flowers.
• Genus *Heliotropium*, family Boraginaceae: several species, in particular *H. arborescens*.

cherry plum ▶ **noun** a shrub or small tree with white flowers and small red and yellow edible fruit which do not form every year. Native to SW Asia, it is used as stock for commercial varieties of plum. Also called **MYROBALAN**.
• *Prunus cerasifera*, family Rosaceae.
▪the fruit of this tree.

cherry tomato ▶ **noun** a miniature tomato with a strong flavour.

Chersonese /ˈkəːsəniːz/ ancient name for the Gallipoli peninsula.
– ORIGIN from Latin *chersonesus*, from Greek *khersonēsos*, from *khersos* 'dry' + *nēsos* 'island'.

chert /tʃəːt/ ▶ **noun** [mass noun] a hard, dark, opaque rock composed of silica (chalcedony) with an amorphous or microscopically fine-grained texture. It occurs as nodules (flint) or, less often, in massive beds.
– DERIVATIVES **cherty** adjective.
– ORIGIN late 17th cent. (originally dialect): of unknown origin.

cherub ▶ **noun** (pl. **cherubim**) a winged angelic being described in biblical tradition as attending on God, represented in ancient Middle Eastern art as a lion or bull with eagles' wings and a human face and regarded in traditional Christian angelology as an angel of the second highest order of the ninefold celestial hierarchy.
▪(pl. **cherubim** or **cherubs**) a representation of a cherub in art, depicted as a chubby, healthy-looking child with wings. ▪ (pl. **cherubs**) a beautiful or innocent-looking child.
– ORIGIN Old English *cherubin*, ultimately (via Latin and Greek) from Hebrew *kĕrūḇ*, plural *kĕrūḇīm*. A rabbinic folk etymology, which explains the Hebrew singular form as representing Aramaic *kĕ-raḇyā* 'like a child', led to the representation of the cherub as a child.

cherubic /tʃɪˈruːbɪk/ ▶ **adjective** having the innocence or plump prettiness of a young child: *a round, cherubic face.*
– DERIVATIVES **cherubically** adverb.

Cherubini /ˌkɛrʊˈbiːni/, (Maria) Luigi (Carlo Zenobio Salvatore) (1760–1842), Italian composer. He spent most of his composing career in Paris and is principally known for his church music and operas.

chervil /ˈtʃəːvɪl/ ▶ **noun** [mass noun] a Eurasian plant of the parsley family, with small white flowers and delicate fern-like leaves which are used as a culinary herb.
• *Anthriscus cerefolium*, family Umbelliferae.
– ORIGIN Old English, from Latin *chaerephylla*, from Greek *khairephullon*.

chervonets /ˌtʃəːvɒˈnjɛts/ ▶ **noun** (pl. **chervontsy**) a pre-Revolutionary Russian gold coin, worth three roubles.
▪a currency note introduced by the Bolsheviks in 1922, worth ten roubles.
– ORIGIN Russian.

Cherwell /ˈtʃɑːwɛl/, Frederick Alexander Lindemann, 1st Viscount (1886–1957), German-born British physicist, who was Churchill's scientific and aeronautical adviser during the war.

Ches. ▶ **abbreviation for** Cheshire.

Chesapeake Bay /ˈtʃɛsəpiːk/ a large inlet of the North Atlantic on the US coast, extending 320 km (200 miles) northwards through the states of Virginia and Maryland.

Cheshire[1] /ˈtʃɛʃɪə, -ʃə/ a county of west central England; county town, Chester.

Cheshire[2] /ˈtʃɛʃə/, (Geoffrey) Leonard (1917–92), British airman and philanthropist. A bomber pilot in the Second World War, he later founded the Cheshire Foundation Homes for the disabled and incurably sick.

Cheshire[3] /ˈtʃɛʃə/ ▶ **noun** [mass noun] a kind of firm crumbly cheese, originally made in Cheshire.

Cheshire cat ▶ **noun** a cat depicted with a broad fixed grin, as popularized through Lewis Carroll's *Alice's Adventures in Wonderland* (1865).
– PHRASES **grin like a Cheshire cat** have a broad fixed smile on one's face.
– ORIGIN late 18th cent.: of unknown origin, but it is said that *Cheshire* cheeses used to be marked with the face of a smiling cat.

Chesil Beach /ˈtʃɛz(ə)l/ (also **Chesil Bank**) a shingle beach in southern England, off the Dorset coast. It is over 25 km (17 miles) long and encloses a tidal lagoon.

chess ▶ **noun** [mass noun] a board game of strategic skill for two players, played on a chequered board. Each player begins the game with a king, a queen, two bishops, two knights, two rooks (or 'castles'), and eight pawns, which are moved and capture opposing pieces according to precise rules. The object is to put the opponent's king under a direct attack from which escape is impossible (*checkmate*).
– ORIGIN Middle English: from Old French *esches*, plural of *eschec* 'a check' (see **CHECK**[1]).

chessboard ▶ **noun** a square board divided into sixty-four alternating dark and light squares (conventionally called 'black' and 'white'), used for playing chess or draughts (checkers).

chessman ▶ **noun** (pl. **-men**) a solid figure used as a chess piece.

chess set ▶ **noun** a chessboard and a set of chessmen.

chest ▶ **noun** **1** the front surface of a person's or animal's body between the neck and the stomach.
▪the whole of a person's upper trunk, especially as considered with reference to their respiratory health or to their size of clothes: *a bad chest* | *a 42-inch chest.*
2 a large strong box, typically made of wood and used for storage or transport: *an oak chest.*
▪Brit. the treasury or financial resources of some institutions: *the university chest.*
▶ **verb** [with obj. and adverbial of direction] Soccer propel (the ball) by means of one's chest.
– PHRASES **get something off one's chest** informal say something that one has wanted to say for a long time, resulting in a feeling of relief. **play** (or **keep**) **one's cards close to one's chest** (or N. Amer. **vest**) informal be extremely secretive and cautious about one's intentions.
– DERIVATIVES **chested** adjective [in combination].
– ORIGIN Old English *cest*, *cyst*, related to Dutch *kist* and German *Kiste*, based on Greek *kistē* 'box'.

Chester a city in NW England, the county town of Cheshire; pop. 115,000 (1991).

Chesterfield a town in Derbyshire; pop. 99,700 (1991).

chesterfield ▶ **noun** **1** a sofa with padded arms and back of the same height and curved outwards at the top.
2 a man's plain straight overcoat, typically with a velvet collar.
– ORIGIN mid 19th cent. (in sense 2): named after a 19th-cent. Earl of **CHESTERFIELD**.

Chesterton, G. K. (1874–1936), English essayist, novelist, and critic; full name *Gilbert Keith Chesterton*. His novels include *The Napoleon of Notting Hill* (1904) and a series of detective stories featuring Father Brown, a priest with a talent for crime detection.

Chester White ▶ noun a pig of a prolific white breed, developed in North America.

chest freezer ▶ noun a freezer with a hinged lid rather than a door.

chestnut ▶ noun **1** (also **sweet chestnut**) a glossy hard brown edible nut, which may be roasted and eaten.
■ [mass noun] a deep reddish-brown colour. ■ a horse of a reddish-brown or yellowish-brown colour, with a brown mane and tail. ■ a small horny patch on the inside of each of a horse's legs.
2 (also **chestnut tree**, **sweet chestnut**, or **Spanish chestnut**) the large European tree that produces the edible chestnut, which develops within a bristly case, with serrated leaves and heavy timber.
● *Castanea sativa*, family Fagaceae.
■ short for **HORSE CHESTNUT**. ■ used in names of trees and plants that are related to the sweet chestnut, or produce similar nuts or edible parts that resemble them, e.g. **water chestnut**.
– PHRASES **an old chestnut** a joke, story, or subject that has become tedious and uninteresting because of its age and constant repetition. **pull someone's chestnuts out of the fire** succeed in a hazardous undertaking for someone else's benefit. [ORIGIN: with reference to the fable of a monkey using a cat's paw to extract roasting chestnuts from a fire.]
– ORIGIN early 16th cent.: from Old English *chesten* (from Old French *chastaine*, via Latin from Greek *kastanea*) + **NUT**.

chestnut oak ▶ noun a North American oak which has leaves resembling those of the chestnut.
● Genus *Quercus*, family Fagaceae: several species, in particular *Q. prinus* and *Q. montana*.

chest of drawers ▶ noun a piece of furniture used for storage, consisting of an upright frame into which drawers are fitted.

chest voice ▶ noun [in sing.] the lowest register of the voice in singing or speaking.

chesty ▶ adjective informal **1** Brit. having a lot of catarrh in the lungs: *a chesty cough.*
2 (of a woman) having large or prominent breasts.
3 N. Amer. conceited and arrogant.
– DERIVATIVES **chestily** adverb, **chestiness** noun.

Chesvan /ˈxɛsv(ə)n/ variant spelling of **HESVAN**.

Chetnik /ˈtʃɛtnɪk/ ▶ noun a member of a Slavic nationalist guerrilla force in the Balkans, especially that active during the Second World War.
– ORIGIN early 20th cent.: from Serbo-Croat *četnik*, from *četa* 'band, troop'.

chetrum /ˈtʃɛtruːm/ ▶ noun (pl. same or **chetrums**) a monetary unit of Bhutan, equal to one hundredth of a ngultrum.
– ORIGIN Dzongkha.

Chetumal /ˌtʃɛtʊˈmaːl/ a port in SE Mexico, on the Yucatán Peninsula at the border with Belize, capital of the state of Quintana Roo; pop. 40,000 (1981).

cheval glass /ʃəˈval/ (also **cheval mirror**) ▶ noun a tall mirror fitted at its middle to an upright frame so that it can be tilted.
– ORIGIN mid 19th cent.: *cheval* from French, in the sense 'frame'.

Chevalier /ʃəˈvalɪɛ, French ʃ(ə)valje/, Maurice (1888–1972), French singer and actor. Notable films: *Innocents of Paris* (1929), *Love Me Tonight* (1932), and *Gigi* (1958).

chevalier /ˌʃɛvəˈlɪə/ ▶ noun historical a knight.
■ a member of certain orders of knighthood or of modern French orders such as the Legion of Honour.
■ (**Chevalier**) Brit. historical a title of the Old and Young Pretenders.
– ORIGIN late Middle English (denoting a horseman or mounted knight): from Old French, from medieval Latin *caballarius*, from Latin *caballus* 'horse'. Compare with **CABALLERO** and **CAVALIER**.

chevet /ʃəˈveɪ/ ▶ noun Architecture (in large churches) an apse with an ambulatory giving access behind the high altar to a series of chapels set in bays.
– ORIGIN early 19th cent.: from French, literally 'pillow', from Latin *capitium*, from *caput* 'head'.

Cheviot /ˈtʃɛvɪət, ˈtʃiːv-/ ▶ noun a large sheep of a breed with short thick wool.
■ (**cheviot**) [mass noun] the wool or tweed cloth obtained from this breed.

Cheviot Hills /ˈtʃɛvɪət, ˈtʃiːv-/ (also **the Cheviots**) a range of hills on the border between England and Scotland.

chèvre /ˈʃɛvr(ə)/ ▶ noun [mass noun] French cheese made with goat's milk.
– ORIGIN 1960s: French, literally 'goat, she-goat', from Latin *caper*.

chevron ▶ noun a V-shaped line or stripe, especially one on the sleeve of a uniform indicating rank or length of service.
■ Heraldry an ordinary in the form of a broad inverted V-shape.
– ORIGIN late Middle English (in heraldic use): from Old French, based on Latin *caper* 'goat'; compare with Latin *capreoli* (diminutive of *caper*) used to mean 'pair of rafters'.

chevrotain /ˈʃɛvrəteɪn/ ▶ noun a small deer-like mammal with small tusks, typically nocturnal and found in the tropical rainforests of Africa and South Asia. Also called **MOUSE DEER**.
● Family Tragulidae: genera *Tragulus* (three Asian species) and *Hyemoschus* (one African species).
– ORIGIN late 18th cent.: from French, diminutive of Old French *chevrot*, diminutive of *chèvre* 'goat'.

Chevy /ˈʃɛvi/ (also **Chevvy**) ▶ noun (pl. **chevys** or **chevvys**) informal a Chevrolet car.

chevy ▶ verb variant spelling of **CHIVVY**.

chew ▶ verb [with obj.] bite and work (food) in the mouth with the teeth, especially to make it easier to swallow: *he was chewing a mouthful of toast* | [no obj.] *he chewed for a moment, then swallowed.*
■ gnaw at (something) persistently, typically as a result of worry or anxiety: *he chewed his lip reflectively* | [no obj.] *she chewed at a fingernail.*
▶ noun a repeated biting or gnawing of something.
■ something other than food that is meant for chewing: *a dog chew* | *a chew of tobacco*. ■ a chewy sweet.
– PHRASES **chew the cud** see **CUD**. **chew the fat** (or **rag**) informal chat in a leisurely way, especially at length.
– DERIVATIVES **chewable** adjective, **chewer** noun [usu. in combination] *a tobacco-chewer.*
– ORIGIN Old English *cēowan*, of West Germanic origin; related to Dutch *kauwen* and German *kauen*.
▶ **chew someone out** N. Amer. informal reprimand someone severely: *he chewed me out for being late.*
chew something over discuss or consider something at length: *executives met to chew over the company's future.*
chew something up chew food until it is soft or in small pieces. ■ damage or destroy something by or as if by chewing: *the bikes were chewing up the paths.*

chewing gum ▶ noun [mass noun] flavoured gum for chewing, typically made from chicle.

chew stick ▶ noun **1** chiefly W. Indian the twig or bark of a plant, used to clean the teeth or chewed for its flavour or as a stimulant.
2 a Caribbean climbing plant of the buckthorn family, the twigs or bark of which are used in this way.
● *Gouania domingensis*, family Rhamnaceae.

chewy ▶ adjective (**chewier**, **chewiest**) (of food) needing to be chewed hard or for some time before being swallowed.
– DERIVATIVES **chewiness** noun.

Cheyenne[1] /ʃʌɪˈan, -ˈɛn/ the state capital of Wyoming; pop. 50,000 (1990).

Cheyenne[2] /ʃʌɪˈan/ ▶ noun (pl. same or **Cheyennes**)
1 a member of an American Indian people formerly living between the Missouri and Arkansas Rivers but now on reservations in Montana and Oklahoma.
2 [mass noun] the Algonquian language of this people, now almost extinct.
▶ adjective of or relating to the Cheyenne or their language.
– ORIGIN Canadian French, from Dakota *šahíyena*, from *šaia* 'speak incoherently', from *ša* 'red' + *ya* 'speak'.

Cheyne-Stokes breathing /tʃeɪn/ ▶ noun [mass noun] Medicine a cyclical pattern of breathing in which movement gradually decreases to a complete stop and then returns to normal. It occurs in various medical conditions, and at high altitudes.
– ORIGIN late 19th cent.: named after John Cheyne (1777–1836), Scottish physician, and William Stokes (1804–78), Irish physician.

chez /ʃeɪ/ ▶ preposition at the home of (used in conscious imitation of French, often humorously): *I spent one summer chez Grandma.*

– ORIGIN mid 18th cent.: French, from Old French *chiese*, from Latin *casa* 'cottage'.

chi[1] /kʌɪ/ ▶ noun the twenty-second letter of the Greek alphabet (Χ, χ), transliterated as 'kh' or 'ch'.
■ (**Chi**) [followed by Latin genitive] Astronomy the twenty-second star in a constellation: *Chi Ophiuchi.*
– ORIGIN Greek.

chi[2] /kiː/ (also **qi** or **ki**) ▶ noun [mass noun] the circulating life force whose existence and properties are the basis of much Chinese philosophy and medicine.
– ORIGIN from Chinese *qì*, literally 'air, breath'.

Chiang Kai-shek /ˌtʃjaŋ kʌɪˈʃɛk/ (also **Jiang Jie Shi**) (1887–1975), Chinese statesman and general, President of China 1928–31 and 1943–9 and of Taiwan 1950–75. He tried to unite China by military means in the 1930s but was defeated by the communists. Forced to abandon mainland China in 1949, he set up a separate Nationalist Chinese State in Taiwan.

Chiangmai /tʃjaŋˈmʌɪ/ a city in NW Thailand; pop. 164,900 (1990).

Chianina /ˌkjɑːˈniːnə/ ▶ noun an animal of a very large white breed of cattle, kept for its lean meat.
– ORIGIN from Italian.

Chianti /kɪˈanti/ ▶ noun (pl. **Chiantis**) [mass noun] a dry red Italian wine produced in Tuscany.
– ORIGIN named after the *Chianti* Mountains, Italy.

Chiapas /tʃɪˈɑːpəs/ a state of southern Mexico, bordering Guatemala; capital, Tuxtla Gutiérrez.

chiaroscuro /kɪˌɑːrəˈskʊərəʊ/ ▶ noun [mass noun] the treatment of light and shade in drawing and painting.
■ an effect of contrasted light and shadow created by light falling unevenly or from a particular direction on something: *the chiaroscuro of cobbled streets.*
– ORIGIN mid 17th cent.: from Italian, from *chiaro* 'clear, bright' (from Latin *clarus*) + *oscuro* 'dark, obscure' (from Latin *obscurus*).

chiasma /kʌɪˈazmə, kɪ-/ ▶ noun (pl. **chiasmata** /-tə/) Biology a point at which paired chromosomes remain in contact during the first metaphase of meiosis, and at which crossing over and exchange of genetic material occur between the strands. See also **OPTIC CHIASMA**.
– ORIGIN mid 19th cent.: modern Latin, from Greek *chiasma* 'crosspiece, cross-shaped mark', from *khiazein* 'mark with the letter chi'.

chiasmus /kʌɪˈazməs, kɪ-/ ▶ noun a rhetorical or literary figure in which words, grammatical constructions, or concepts are repeated in reverse order, in the same or a modified form.
– DERIVATIVES **chiastic** adjective.
– ORIGIN mid 17th cent. (in the general sense 'crosswise arrangement'): modern Latin, from Greek *khiasmos* 'crosswise arrangement', from *khiazein* 'mark with the letter chi', from *khi* 'chi'.

chiastolite /kʌɪˈastəlʌɪt, kɪ-/ ▶ noun [mass noun] a form of the mineral andalusite containing carbonaceous inclusions which cause some sections of the mineral to show the figure of a cross.
– ORIGIN early 19th cent.: from Greek *khiastos* 'arranged crosswise' + **-LITE**.

Chiba /ˈtʃiːbə/ a city in Japan, on the island of Honshu, east of Tokyo; pop. 829,470 (1990).

Chibcha /ˈtʃɪbtʃə/ ▶ noun (pl. same) **1** a member of a native people of Colombia whose ancient civilization was destroyed by Europeans.
2 [mass noun] the extinct Chibchan language of this people.
▶ adjective of or relating to the Chibcha or their language.
– ORIGIN American Spanish, from Chibcha *zipa* 'chief, hereditary leader'.

Chibchan /ˈtʃɪbtʃ(ə)n/ ▶ noun [mass noun] a language family of Colombia and Central America, most members of which are now extinct or nearly so.
▶ adjective of or relating to this language family.

chibol /ˈtʃɪb(ə)l/ ▶ noun dialect term for **SPRING ONION** or **WELSH ONION**.
– ORIGIN late Middle English: from an Old Northern French variant of Old French *cibole*, from late Latin *caepulla* 'onion bed', from Latin *caepa* 'onion'.

chibouk /tʃɪˈbuːk/ (also **chibouque**) ▶ noun a long Turkish tobacco pipe.
– ORIGIN early 19th cent.: French *chibouque*, from Turkish *çubuk*, literally 'tube'.

chic /ʃiːk/ ▶ adjective (**chicer, chicest**) elegantly and stylishly fashionable.
▶ noun [mass noun] stylishness and elegance, typically of a specified kind: *French chic.*
– DERIVATIVES **chicly** adverb.
– ORIGIN mid 19th cent.: from French, probably from German *Schick* 'skill'.

Chicago a city in Illinois, on Lake Michigan; pop. 2,783,730 (1990). Selected as a terminal for the new Illinois and Michigan canal, Chicago developed during the 19th century as a major grain market and food-processing centre.
– DERIVATIVES **Chicagoan** noun & adjective.

Chicago Board of Trade ▶ noun see **BOARD OF TRADE** (sense 1).

Chicana /tʃɪˈkɑːnə, ʃɪ-, -ˈkeɪn-/ ▶ noun chiefly US a female North American of Mexican origin or descent. See also **CHICANO**.
– ORIGIN Mexican Spanish, alteration of Spanish *mejicana* (feminine) 'Mexican'.

chicane /ʃɪˈkeɪn/ ▶ noun 1 a sharp double bend created to form an obstacle on a motor-racing track or a road.
2 dated (in card games) a hand without cards of one particular suit; a void.
3 [mass noun] archaic chicanery.
▶ verb [no obj.] archaic employ trickery or chicanery.
■ [with obj.] deceive or trick (someone).
– ORIGIN late 17th cent. (in the senses 'chicanery' and 'use chicanery'): from French *chicane* (noun), *chicaner* (verb) 'quibble', of unknown origin.

chicanery ▶ noun [mass noun] the use of trickery to achieve a political, financial, or legal purpose: *financial chicanery.*
– ORIGIN late 16th cent.: from French *chicanerie*, from *chicaner* 'to quibble' (see **CHICANE**).

Chicano /tʃɪˈkɑːnəʊ, ʃɪ-, -ˈkeɪn-/ ▶ noun (pl. **-os**) chiefly US a North American of Mexican origin or descent. See also **CHICANA**.
– ORIGIN Mexican Spanish, alteration of Spanish *mejicano* (masculine) 'Mexican'.

chicha /ˈtʃiːtʃə/ ▶ noun [mass noun] (in South and Central America) a kind of beer made typically from maize.
– ORIGIN American Spanish, from Kuna.

chicharron /ˌtʃiːtʃəˈrəʊn/ ▶ noun (pl. **chicharrones** /-əʊnɪz/) chiefly US (in Mexican cooking) a piece of fried pork crackling.
– ORIGIN from American Spanish *chicharrón*.

Chichén Itzá /tʃiˌtʃɛn ɪtˈsɑː/ a site in northern Yucatán, Mexico, the centre of the Mayan empire after AD 918.

Chichester[1] /ˈtʃɪtʃɪstə/ a city in southern England, the county town of West Sussex; pop. 27,200 (1981).

Chichester[2] /ˈtʃɪtʃɪstə/, Sir Francis (Charles) (1901–72), English yachtsman. In his yacht *Gipsy Moth IV* he was the first person to sail alone round the world with only one stop (1966–7).

Chichewa /tʃɪˈtʃeɪwə/ ▶ noun another term for **NYANJA** (the language).

chichi[1] /ˈʃiːʃiː/ ▶ adjective attempting stylish elegance but achieving only an over-elaborate affectedness: *the tiny chichi dining room.*
▶ noun [mass noun] pretentious and over-elaborate refinement: *the relentless chichi of late-eighties dining.*
– ORIGIN early 20th cent. (in the sense 'showiness or pretentious object'): from French, of imitative origin.

chichi[2] /ˈʃiːʃiː/ ▶ noun US informal a woman's breast.
– ORIGIN late 20th cent.: military slang, of Japanese origin.

chi-chi /ˈtʃiːtʃiː/ (also **chee-chee**) ▶ adjective dated (especially of a girl or woman) Anglo-Indian.
■ of or denoting a style of English formerly spoken by some Anglo-Indians in India.
▶ exclamation Indian expressing disgust.
– ORIGIN perhaps from Hindi *chī-chī!* 'shame on you!', said to be used by Anglo-Indians.

Chichimec /ˌtʃiːtʃɪˈmɛk/ ▶ noun (pl. same or **Chichimecs**) **1** a member of a group of native peoples, including the Toltecs and the Aztecs, dominant in central Mexico from the 10th to the 16th centuries.
2 [mass noun] a Uto-Aztecan language of these peoples, with some 5,000 surviving speakers.
– ORIGIN Spanish, from Nahuatl.

chick[1] ▶ noun **1** a young bird, especially one newly hatched.

■ a newly hatched young domestic fowl.
2 informal a young woman: *she's a great-looking chick.*
– PHRASES **neither chick nor child** N. Amer. or dialect no children at all.
– ORIGIN Middle English: abbreviation of **CHICKEN**.

chick[2] ▶ noun (in the Indian subcontinent) a screen for a doorway, made from split bamboo and twine.
– ORIGIN from Urdu *chik*, from Persian *čīgh*.

chickabiddy ▶ noun (pl. **-ies**) informal an affectionate form of address or way of referring to a small child or a loved one.
– ORIGIN late 18th cent.: from **CHICK**[1] + *-a-* (for ease of pronunciation) + **BIDDY**.

chickadee ▶ noun North American term for **TIT**[1].
– ORIGIN mid 19th cent.: imitative of its call.

chickaree ▶ noun a squirrel with red fur, found in the coniferous forests of North America.
● Genus *Tamiasciurus*, family Sciuridae: three species, including the American red squirrel (*T. hudsonicus*).
– ORIGIN early 19th cent.: imitative of its call.

Chickasaw /ˈtʃɪkəsɔː/ ▶ noun (pl. same or **Chickasaws**) **1** a member of an American Indian people formerly resident in Mississippi and Alabama, and now in Oklahoma.
2 [mass noun] the Muskogean language of this people, now all but extinct.
▶ adjective of or relating to this people or their language.
– ORIGIN the name in Chickasaw.

chicken ▶ noun **1** a domestic fowl kept for its eggs or meat, especially a young one.
■ [mass noun] meat from such a bird: *roast chicken.*
2 [mass noun] informal a game in which the first person to lose their nerve and withdraw from a dangerous situation is the loser.
■ [count noun] a coward.
▶ adjective [predic.] informal cowardly: *they were too chicken to follow the murderers into the mountains.*
▶ verb [no obj.] (**chicken out**) informal withdraw from or fail in something through lack of nerve: *the referee chickened out of giving a penalty.*
– PHRASES **don't count your chickens before they're hatched** see **COUNT**[1]. **running** (or **rushing**) **about like a headless chicken** informal acting in a panic-stricken manner and not thinking clearly about what should be done.
– ORIGIN Old English *cīcen, cȳcen*, of Germanic origin; related to Dutch *kieken* and German *Küchlein*, and probably also to **COCK**[1].

chicken à la king ▶ noun [mass noun] cooked breast of chicken in a cream sauce with mushrooms and peppers.
– ORIGIN said to be named after E. Clark *King*, proprietor of a New York hotel.

chicken-and-egg ▶ adjective [attrib.] denoting a situation in which each of two things appears to be necessary to the other. Either it is impossible to say which came first or it appears that neither could ever exist.

chicken-breasted ▶ adjective another term for *pigeon-breasted* (see **PIGEON BREAST**).

chicken brick ▶ noun Brit. an earthenware container for roasting a chicken in its own juices.

chicken cholera ▶ noun [mass noun] an infectious disease of fowls.

chicken feed ▶ noun [mass noun] food for poultry.
■ figurative, informal a paltry sum of money.

chicken-fried steak ▶ noun US a thin piece of beef which is lightly battered and fried until crisp.

chicken hawk ▶ noun N. Amer. a hawk of a type that is reputed to prey on domestic fowl.

chicken-hearted (also **chicken-livered**) ▶ adjective easily frightened; cowardly.

chickenpox ▶ noun [mass noun] an infectious disease causing a mild fever and a rash of itchy inflamed pimples which turn to blisters and then loose scabs. It is caused by the herpes zoster virus and mainly affects children, who are afterwards usually immune. Also called **VARICELLA**.
– ORIGIN early 18th cent.: probably so named because of its mildness, as compared to smallpox.

chicken run ▶ noun S. African informal the exodus of people from South Africa because of fears for the future.
– DERIVATIVES **chicken-runner** noun.

chickenshit informal, chiefly N. Amer. ▶ adjective worthless or contemptible (used as a general term of deprecation): *no more chickenshit excuses.*

■ cowardly.
▶ noun a worthless or contemptible person.
■ [mass noun] something worthless or petty: *names are chickenshit; they didn't need any names.*

chicken wire ▶ noun [mass noun] light wire netting with a hexagonal mesh.

chickling pea ▶ noun another term for **GRASS PEA**.
– ORIGIN mid 16th cent.: based on obsolete *chich* 'chickpea'.

chickpea ▶ noun **1** a round yellowish seed which is a pulse of major importance as food. Also called **GARBANZO**.
2 the leguminous Old World plant which bears these seeds.
● *Cicer arietinum*, family Leguminosae.
– ORIGIN late 18th cent. (earlier as *chiche-pease*): from late Middle English *chiche* (from Old French *chiche, cice*, from Latin *cicer* 'chickpea') + **PEASE**.

chickweed ▶ noun [mass noun] a small, widely distributed, white-flowered plant of the pink family, often growing as a garden weed, and sometimes eaten by poultry.
● *Stellaria* and other genera, family Caryophyllaceae: several species, including the common *S. media*.

chicle /ˈtʃɪk(ə)l, -kli/ ▶ noun [mass noun] the milky latex of the sapodilla tree, formerly chewed by the Aztecs and now used to make chewing gum.
■ another term for **SAPODILLA**.
– ORIGIN via Latin American Spanish, from Nahuatl *tzictli*.

chicory /ˈtʃɪk(ə)ri/ ▶ noun (pl. **-ies**) **1** a blue-flowered Mediterranean plant of the daisy family, cultivated for its edible salad leaves and carrot-shaped root.
● *Cichorium intybus*, family Compositae.
■ [mass noun] the root of this plant, which is roasted and ground for use as an additive to or substitute for coffee.
2 North American term for **ENDIVE**.
– ORIGIN late Middle English: from obsolete French *cicorée* (earlier form of *chicorée*) 'endive', via Latin from Greek *kikhorion*.

chide /tʃaɪd/ ▶ verb (past **chided** or **chid** /tʃɪd/; past participle **chided** or archaic **chidden** /ˈtʃɪd(ə)n/) [with obj.] scold or rebuke: *she chided him for not replying to her letters* | [with direct speech] *'Now, now,' he chided.*
– DERIVATIVES **chider** noun, **chidingly** adverb.
– ORIGIN Old English *cīdan*, of unknown origin.

chief ▶ noun **1** a leader or ruler of a people or clan: *the chief of the village* | *a Masai chief* | [as title] *Chief Banawi.*
■ the person with the highest rank in an organization: *a union chief* | *the chief of police.* ■ an informal form of address to a man, especially one of superior rank or status to the speaker: *it's quite simple, chief.*
2 Heraldry an ordinary consisting of a broad horizontal band across the top of the shield.
■ the upper third of the field.
▶ adjective most important: *the chief reason for the spending cuts* | *chief among her concerns is working alone at night.*
■ having or denoting the highest rank or authority: *the Queen's chief minister.*
– PHRASES **chief cook and bottle-washer** informal a person who performs a variety of important but routine tasks. **in chief** Heraldry at the top; in the upper part. See also **-IN-CHIEF**. **too many chiefs and not enough Indians** used to describe a situation where there are too many people giving orders and not enough people to carry them out.
– DERIVATIVES **chiefdom** noun.
– ORIGIN Middle English: from Old French *chief, chef*, based on Latin *caput* 'head'.

chief constable ▶ noun Brit. the head of the police force of a county or other region.

chief inspector ▶ noun Brit. a police officer ranking above inspector and below superintendent.

chiefly ▶ adverb mainly: *he is remembered chiefly for his organ sonatas.*
■ for the most part; mostly: *a faction that consisted chiefly of communists.*

chief master sergeant ▶ noun a rank of non-commissioned officer in the US air force, above senior master sergeant and below chief warrant officer.

chief of staff ▶ noun the senior staff officer of a service, command, or formation.

chief petty officer ▶ noun a rank of non-commissioned officer in a navy, above petty officer and below warrant officer or senior chief petty officer.

chief rabbi ▶**noun** (in the UK and some other countries) the pre-eminent rabbi of a national Jewish community.

chieftain ▶**noun** the leader of a people or clan.
■informal a powerful member of an organization.
– DERIVATIVES **chieftaincy** /-si/ noun (pl. **-ies**), **chieftainship** noun.
– ORIGIN Middle English and Old French *chevetaine*, from late Latin *capitaneus* (see **CAPTAIN**). The spelling was altered by association with **CHIEF**.

chief technician ▶**noun** a rank of non-commissioned officer in the RAF, above sergeant and below flight sergeant.

chief warrant officer ▶**noun** a rank in the US armed forces, above warrant officer and below the lowest-ranking commissioned officer.

chiffchaff ▶**noun** a small Eurasian and North African migratory leaf warbler with drab plumage.
● Genus *Phylloscopus*, family Sylviidae: two species, in particular the common *P. collybita*.
– ORIGIN late 18th cent.: imitative of its call.

chiffon ▶**noun** [mass noun] a light, transparent fabric typically made of silk or nylon: [as modifier] *a chiffon blouse.*
■[as modifier] (of a cake or dessert) made with beaten egg to give a light consistency: *chiffon cake.*
– ORIGIN mid 18th cent. (originally plural, denoting trimmings or ornaments on a woman's dress): from French, from *chiffe* 'rag'.

chiffonade /ˌʃɪfəˈnɑːd/ (also **chiffonnade**) ▶**noun** (pl. same) a preparation of shredded or finely cut leaf vegetables, used as a garnish for soup.
– ORIGIN French, from *chiffonner* 'to crumple'.

chiffonier /ˌʃɪfəˈnɪə/ ▶**noun 1** Brit. a low cupboard either used as a sideboard or with a raised bookshelf on top.
2 N. Amer. a tall chest of drawers.
– ORIGIN mid 18th cent.: from French *chiffonnier*, *chiffonnière*, literally 'ragpicker', also denoting a chest of drawers for odds and ends.

chifforobe /ˈʃɪfərəʊb/ ▶**noun** US a piece of furniture with drawers on one side and hanging space on the other.
– ORIGIN early 20th cent.: blend of **CHIFFONIER** and **WARDROBE**.

Chifley /ˈtʃɪfli/, Joseph Benedict (1885–1951), Australian Labor statesman, Prime Minister 1945–9.

chigger /ˈtʃɪɡə, ˈdʒ-/ (also **jigger**) ▶**noun 1** a tropical flea, the female of which burrows and lays eggs beneath the host's skin, causing painful sores. Also called **CHIGOE**, **SAND FLEA**.
● *Tunga penetrans*, family Tungidae.
2 N. Amer. a harvest mite.
– ORIGIN mid 18th cent.: variant of **CHIGOE**.

chignon /ˈʃiːnjɒ̃/ ▶**noun** a knot or coil of hair arranged on the back of a woman's head.
– ORIGIN late 18th cent.: from French, originally 'nape of the neck', based on Latin *catena* 'chain'.

chigoe /ˈtʃɪɡəʊ/ ▶**noun** another term for **CHIGGER** (in sense 1).
– ORIGIN mid 17th cent.: from French *chique*, from a West African language.

Chihli, Gulf of /ˈtʃiːliː/ another name for **BO HAI**.

Chihuahua /tʃɪˈwɑːwə/ a state of northern Mexico.
■its capital, the principal city of north central Mexico; pop. 530,490 (1990).

chihuahua /tʃɪˈwɑːwə/ ▶**noun** a very small dog of a smooth-haired large-eyed breed originating in Mexico.
– ORIGIN early 19th cent.: named after **CHIHUAHUA**.

chikan /ˈtʃɪk(ə)n/ ▶**noun** [mass noun] (in the Indian subcontinent) a type of hand embroidery using cutwork and shadow-work.
– ORIGIN from Urdu, from Persian *čikan*.

chikungunya /ˌtʃɪk(ə)nˈɡʌnjə/ (also **chikungunya fever**) ▶**noun** [mass noun] a viral disease resembling dengue, transmitted by mosquitoes and endemic in East Africa and parts of Asia.
– ORIGIN 1950s: a local word.

chilblain ▶**noun** a painful, itching swelling on the skin, typically on a hand or foot, caused by poor circulation in the skin when exposed to cold.
– DERIVATIVES **chilblained** adjective.
– ORIGIN mid 16th cent.: from **CHILL** + **BLAIN**.

child ▶**noun** (pl. **children**) a young human being below the age of full physical development.
■a son or daughter of any age. ■an immature or irresponsible person: *she's such a child!* ■a person who has little or no experience in a particular area: *he's a child in financial matters.* ■(**children**) the descendants of a family or people: *the children of Abraham.* ■(**child of**) a person or thing regarded as the product of a specified influence or environment: *a child of the Sixties.*
– PHRASES **child's play** a task which is easily accomplished. **from a child** since childhood. **with child** formal pregnant.
– DERIVATIVES **childless** adjective, **childlessness** noun.
– ORIGIN Old English *cild*, of Germanic origin. The Middle English plural *childer* or *childre* became *childeren* or *children* by association with plurals ending in *-en*, such as *brethren*.

child abuse ▶**noun** [mass noun] physical maltreatment or sexual molestation of a child.

child allowance ▶**noun** informal term for **CHILD BENEFIT**.
■historical (in the UK) a tax allowance granted to parents of dependent children.

childbearing ▶**noun** [mass noun] the process of giving birth to children: [as modifier] *women of childbearing age.*

childbed ▶**noun** archaic term for **CHILDBIRTH**.

child benefit ▶**noun** [mass noun] (in the UK) regular payment by the state to the parents of a child up to a certain age.

childbirth ▶**noun** [mass noun] the action of giving birth to a child: *she died in* **in childbirth**.

childcare ▶**noun** [mass noun] the skill or action of looking after children.
■the care of children by a crèche, nursery, or childminder while parents are working.

child-centred ▶**adjective** giving priority to the interests and needs of children: *child-centred teaching methods.*

Childe /tʃʌɪld/ ▶**noun** [in names] archaic or poetic/literary a youth of noble birth: *Childe Harold.*
– ORIGIN late Old English, variant of **CHILD**.

Childermas /ˈtʃɪldəmas/ ▶**noun** archaic the feast of the Holy Innocents, 28 December.
– ORIGIN Old English *cildramæsse*, from *cildra* 'of children', genitive plural of *cild* (see **CHILD**) + *mæsse* (see **MASS**).

Childers /ˈtʃɪldəz/, (Robert) Erskine (1870–1922), English-born Irish writer and political activist. He was shot for his involvement in the Irish civil war. Notable works: *The Riddle of the Sands* (novel, 1903). His son **Erskine Hamilton Childers** (1905–74) was President of Ireland 1973–4.

child guidance ▶**noun** [mass noun] Brit. care for psychologically or emotionally disturbed children and adolescents through counselling, and support and education for families and professionals.

childhood ▶**noun** [mass noun] the state of being a child.
■the period during which a person is a child: *he spent his childhood in Lewes* | [as modifier] *a childhood friend.*
– ORIGIN Old English *cildhād* (see **CHILD**, **-HOOD**).

childish ▶**adjective** of, like, or appropriate to a child: *childish enthusiasm.*
■silly and immature: *a childish outburst.*
– DERIVATIVES **childishly** adverb, **childishness** noun.

child labour ▶**noun** [mass noun] the use of children in industry or business, especially when illegal or considered inhumane.

childlike ▶**adjective** (of an adult) having the good qualities associated with a child: *she speaks with a childlike directness.*

childminder ▶**noun** Brit. a person who looks after children in his or her own house for payment.

childproof ▶**adjective** designed to prevent children from injuring themselves or doing damage: *disinfectants that are fitted with childproof caps.*

children plural form of **CHILD**.

children of Israel see **ISRAEL**[1] (sense 1).

Children's Crusade a crusade to the Holy Land in 1212 by tens of thousands of children, chiefly from France and Germany. Most of the children never reached their destination, and were sold into slavery.

Child Support Agency (abbrev.: **CSA**) (in the UK) a government agency responsible for the assessment and collection of compulsory child maintenance payments from absent parents.

Chile /ˈtʃɪli, Spanish ˈtʃile/ a country occupying a long coastal strip down the southern half of the west of South America; pop. 13,231,800 (1992); official language, Spanish; capital, Santiago.

Most of Chile was part of the Inca empire and became part of Spanish Peru after Pizarro's conquest. Independence was achieved in 1818 with help from Argentina. After the overthrow of the Marxist democrat Salvador Allende in 1973, Chile was ruled by the right-wing military dictatorship of General Pinochet until a democratically elected President took office in 1990.

– DERIVATIVES **Chilean** adjective & noun.

chile ▶**noun** variant spelling of **CHILLI**.

Chile pine ▶**noun** another term for **MONKEY PUZZLE**.

chile relleno /ˌtʃɪlɪ rɛˈljeɪnəʊ/ ▶**noun** (pl. **chiles rellenos**) (in Mexican cuisine) a stuffed chilli pepper, typically battered and deep-fried.
– ORIGIN Spanish, 'stuffed chilli'.

Chile saltpetre ▶**noun** another term for **SODIUM NITRATE**, especially as a commercial product mined in Chile and other arid parts of the world.

chili ▶**noun** (pl. **chilies**) US spelling of **CHILLI**.

chiliarch /ˈkɪlɪɑːk/ ▶**noun** historical (especially in ancient Greece) a commander of a thousand men.
– ORIGIN late 16th cent.: via late Latin from Greek *khiliarkhēs*, from *khilioi* 'thousand'.

chiliast /ˈkɪlɪast/ ▶**noun** another term for **MILLENARIAN**.
– DERIVATIVES **chiliasm** noun.
– ORIGIN late 16th cent.: via late Latin from Greek *khiliastēs*, from *khilias* 'a thousand years', from *khilioi* 'thousand'.

chiliastic /ˌkɪlɪˈastɪk/ ▶**adjective** another term for **MILLENARIAN**.

chili dog ▶**noun** N. Amer. a hot dog garnished with chilli con carne.

chill ▶**noun** [in sing.] an unpleasant coldness in the atmosphere, one's surroundings, or the body: *there was a chill in the air.*
■a lowered body temperature, often accompanied by shivering: *the disease begins abruptly with chills, headaches, and dizziness.* ■a feverish cold. ■figurative a coldness of manner: *the sudden chill in China's relations with the West.* ■a sudden and powerful unpleasant feeling, especially of fear: *his words sent* **a chill of** *apprehension down my spine.* ■a metal mould or part of a mould, often cooled, designed to ensure rapid or even cooling of metal during casting.
▶**verb** [with obj.] **1** (often **be chilled**) make (someone) cold: *I'm* **chilled to the bone**.
■cool (food or drink) in a refrigerator: [as adj. **chilled**] *chilled white wine.* ■Metallurgy another term for **CHILL-CAST**.
2 (often **be chilled**) horrify or frighten (someone): *the city was chilled by the violence* | [as adj. **chilling**] *a chilling account of the prisoners' fate.*
3 [no obj.] informal, chiefly N. Amer. calm down and relax: *I can lean back and chill* | **chill out**, *okay?*
■pass time without a particular aim or purpose, especially with other people: *after the show, the band* **chilled out** *in the car park.*
▶**adjective** chilly: *the chill grey dawn* | figurative *the chill winds of public censure.*
– PHRASES **chill someone's blood** horrify or terrify someone. **take the chill off** warm slightly.
– DERIVATIVES **chillingly** adverb, **chillness** noun, **chillsome** adjective (poetic/literary).
– ORIGIN Old English *cele*, *ciele* 'cold, coldness', of Germanic origin; related to **COLD**.

chill-cast ▶**verb** [with obj.] Metallurgy rapidly solidify (cast iron or other metal) by contact with a cooled metal mould or other cold surface in order to produce a hard, dense surface.

chiller ▶**noun 1** a machine for cooling something, especially a cold cabinet or refrigerator for keeping stored food a few degrees above freezing point. See also **BLAST CHILLER**.
2 short for **SPINE-CHILLER**.

chill factor ▶**noun** a quantity expressing the perceived lowering of the air temperature caused by the wind.

chilli /ˈtʃɪli/ (also **chilli pepper**, **chile**, US **chili**) ▶**noun** (pl. **chillies**, **chiles**, or US **chilies**) a small hot-tasting pod of a variety of capsicum, used chopped (and often dried) in sauces, relishes, and spice powders. There are various forms with pods of

differing size, colour, and strength of flavour, such as cascabels and jalapeños.
• *Capsicum annuum* var. *annuum*, 'longum' group (or var. *longum*).
▪short for **CHILLI POWDER**. ▪short for **CHILLI CON CARNE**.
– ORIGIN early 17th cent.: from Spanish *chile*, from Nahuatl *chilli*.

chilli-bite ▶ noun S. African a savoury fritter of pea flour containing chillies, onion, and other vegetables.

chilli con carne /kɒn 'kɑːneɪ, -ni/ ▶ noun [mass noun] a stew of minced beef and beans flavoured with chilli powder.
– ORIGIN from Spanish *chile con carne*, literally 'chilli pepper with meat'.

chilli powder ▶ noun [mass noun] a hot-tasting mixture of ground dried red chillies and other spices.

chill-out ▶ adjective [attrib.] informal denoting something intended to induce or enhance a relaxed mood, in particular a room or area in a nightclub in which dancers may relax and where quiet or ambient music is played.

chillum /'tʃɪləm/ ▶ noun (pl. **chillums**) a hookah.
▪a pipe used for smoking cannabis.
– ORIGIN from Hindi *cilam*.

chilly ▶ adjective (**chillier**, **chilliest**) uncomfortably or unpleasantly cold: *it had turned chilly | a chilly day.*
▪(of a person) feeling or sensitive to the cold: *I felt a bit chilly.* ▪ unfriendly: *a chilly reception.*
– DERIVATIVES **chilliness** noun.

Chilopoda /ˌkʌɪlə'pəʊdə/ Zoology a class of myriapod arthropods which comprises the centipedes.
– DERIVATIVES **chilopod** /'kʌɪləpɒd/ noun.
– ORIGIN modern Latin (plural), from Greek *kheilos* 'lip' + *pous*, *pod-* 'foot'.

Chilpancingo /ˌtʃɪlpan'sɪŋgəʊ/ a city in SW Mexico, capital of the state of Guerrero; pop. 120,000 (1980).

Chiltern Hills /'tʃɪlt(ə)n/ (also **the Chilterns**) a range of chalk hills in southern England, north of the River Thames and west of London.

Chiltern Hundreds (in the UK) a Crown manor, whose administration is a nominal office for which an MP applies as a way of resigning from the House of Commons. This is because stewardship of the district is legally an office of profit under the Crown, the holding of which disqualifies a person from being an MP.
– ORIGIN from **CHILTERN HILLS** and *Hundreds* (see the noun **HUNDRED**).

Chiluba /tʃɪ'luːbə/ ▶ noun another term for **LUBA** (the language).

chimaera ▶ noun variant spelling of **CHIMERA**.

Chimborazo /ˌtʃɪmbə'rɑːzəʊ/ the highest peak of the Andes in Ecuador, rising to 6,310 m (20,487 ft).

chime[1] ▶ noun (often **chimes**) a bell or a metal bar or tube, typically one of a set tuned to produce a melodious series of ringing sounds when struck.
▪a sound made by such an instrument: *the chimes of Big Ben.* ▪(**chimes**) a set of tuned bells used as a doorbell. ▪ Bell-ringing a stroke of the clapper against one or both sides of a scarcely moving bell.
▶verb [no obj.] **1** (of a bell or clock) make melodious ringing sounds, typically to indicate the time.
▪[with obj.] (of a clock) make such sounds in order to indicate (the time): *the clock chimed eight.*
2 (**chime in with**) be in agreement with: *his poem chimes with our modern experience of loss.*
– DERIVATIVES **chimer** noun.
– ORIGIN Middle English (in the senses 'cymbal' and 'ring out'): probably from Old English *cimbal* (see **CYMBAL**), later interpreted as *chime bell*.
▶**chime in** interject a remark, typically in agreement: *'Yes, you do that,' Doreen chimed in eagerly.*

chime[2] (also **chimb**) ▶ noun the projecting rim at the end of a cask.
– ORIGIN late Middle English: probably from an Old English word related to Dutch *kim* and German *Kimme*. Compare with **CHINE**[3].

chimera /kʌɪ'mɪərə, kɪ-/ (also **chimaera**) ▶ noun **1** (in Greek mythology) a fire-breathing female monster with a lion's head, a goat's body, and a serpent's tail.
▪any mythical animal with parts taken from various animals.
2 a thing which is hoped or wished for but in fact is illusory or impossible to achieve: *the economic sovereignty you claim to defend is a chimera.*
3 Biology an organism containing a mixture of genetically different tissues, formed by processes such as fusion of early embryos, grafting, or mutation: *the sheeplike goat chimera.*
▪a DNA molecule with sequences derived from two or more different organisms, formed by laboratory manipulation.
4 a cartilaginous marine fish with a long tail, an erect spine before the first dorsal fin, and typically a forward projection from the snout.
• Subclass Holocephali: three families, in particular Chimaeridae. See also **RABBITFISH**, **RATFISH**.
– DERIVATIVES **chimeric** /-'mɛrɪk/ adjective, **chimerical** adjective, **chimerically** adverb.
– ORIGIN late Middle English: via Latin from Greek *khimaira* 'she-goat or chimera'.

chimichanga /ˌtʃɪmɪ'tʃaŋgə/ ▶ noun a tortilla rolled round a savoury filling and deep-fried.
– ORIGIN Mexican Spanish, literally 'trinket'.

chimney ▶ noun (pl. **-eys**) a vertical channel or pipe which conducts smoke and combustion gases up from a fire or furnace and typically through the roof of a building.
▪a chimney stack. ▪ a glass tube protecting the flame of a lamp. ▪ a very steep narrow cleft by which a rock face may be climbed.
– ORIGIN Middle English (denoting a fireplace or furnace): from Old French *cheminee* 'chimney, fireplace', from late Latin *caminata*, perhaps from *camera caminata* 'room with a fireplace', from Latin *caminus* 'forge, furnace', from Greek *kaminos* 'oven'.

chimney breast ▶ noun a part of an interior wall that projects to surround a chimney.

chimney corner ▶ noun a warm seat within an old-fashioned fireplace.

chimney piece ▶ noun Brit. a mantelpiece.

chimney pot ▶ noun an earthenware or metal pipe at the top of a chimney, narrowing the aperture and increasing the updraught.

chimney stack ▶ noun the part of a chimney that projects above a roof.

chimney sweep ▶ noun a person whose job is cleaning out the soot from chimneys.

chimney swift ▶ noun the common swift over much of North America, with mainly dark grey plumage.
• *Chaetura pelagica*, family Apodidae.

chimonanthus /ˌkʌɪmə(ʊ)'nanθəs/ ▶ noun a shrub of the Chinese genus *Chimonanthus* (family Calycanthaceae), especially (in gardening) the wintersweet.
– ORIGIN modern Latin, from Greek *kheimōn* 'winter' + *anthos* 'flower'.

chimp ▶ noun informal term for **CHIMPANZEE**.

chimpanzee ▶ noun a great ape with large ears, mainly black coloration, and lighter skin on the face, native to the forests of west and central Africa. Chimpanzees show advanced behaviour such as the making and using of tools.
• Genus *Pan*, family Pongidae: the **common chimpanzee** (*P. troglodytes*) and the bonobo.
– ORIGIN mid 18th cent.: from French *chimpanzé*, from Kikongo.

Chimu /tʃiː'muː/ ▶ noun (pl. same or **Chimus**) **1** a member of a native people of Peru that developed the largest and most important civilization before the Incas.
2 [mass noun] the language of this people, which died out in the 19th century.
▶adjective of or relating to the Chimu or their language.
– ORIGIN from Spanish.

Chin[1] /tʃɪn/ ▶ noun **1** a member of a people of SW Burma (Myanmar) and neighbouring parts of India and Bangladesh.
2 [mass noun] the Tibeto-Burman language of this people, with about 800,000 speakers.
▶adjective of or relating to this people or their language.

Chin[2] /tʃɪn/ variant spelling of **JIN**.

Ch'in variant spelling of **QIN**.

chin ▶ noun the protruding part of the face below the mouth, formed by the apex of the lower jaw.
▶verb [with obj.] **1** informal hit or punch on the chin.
2 draw one's body up so as to bring one's chin level with or above (a horizontal bar) with one's feet off the ground, as an exercise.
– PHRASES **keep one's chin up** informal remain cheerful in difficult circumstances: *keep your chin up, we're not lost yet.* **take it on the chin** endure or accept misfortune courageously or stoically.
– DERIVATIVES **chinned** adjective [in combination] *square-chinned.*
– ORIGIN Old English *cin*, *cinn*, of Germanic origin; related to Dutch *kin*, from an Indo-European root shared by Latin *gena* 'cheek' and Greek *genus* 'jaw'.

China a country in east Asia, the third largest and most populous in the world; pop. 1,151,200,000 (est. 1991); language, Chinese (of which Mandarin is the official form); capital, Beijing. Official name **PEOPLE'S REPUBLIC OF CHINA**.

> Chinese civilization stretches back until at least the 3rd millennium BC, the country being ruled by a series of dynasties until the Qing (or Manchu) dynasty was overthrown by Sun Yat-sen in 1911; China was proclaimed a republic the following year. After the Second World War the Kuomintang government of Chiang Kai-shek was overthrown by the communists under Mao Zedong, the People's Republic of China being declared in 1949.

china ▶ noun **1** [mass noun] a fine white or translucent vitrified ceramic material: *a plate made of china* | [as modifier] *a china cup.* Also called **PORCELAIN**.
▪household tableware or other objects made from this or a similar material: *the breakfast china.*
2 Brit. informal a friend. [ORIGIN: from rhyming slang *china plate* 'mate'.]
– ORIGIN late 16th cent. (as an adjective): from Persian *chīnī* used attributively relating to China, where it was originally made.

China, Republic of official name for **TAIWAN**.

China aster ▶ noun a Chinese plant of the daisy family, which is cultivated for its bright showy flowers.
• *Callistephus chinensis*, family Compositae.

chinaberry (also **chinaberry tree** or **china tree**) ▶ noun (pl. **-ies**) a tall tree which bears fragrant lilac flowers and yellow berries, native to Asia and Australasia and naturalized in parts of North America.
• *Melia azedarach*, family Meliaceae.
▪the fruit of this tree, which has been used to make insecticides and also rosary beads.

china blue ▶ noun [mass noun] a pale greyish blue.

china clay ▶ noun another term for **KAOLIN**.

chinagraph (also **chinagraph pencil**) ▶ noun Brit. a waxy pencil used to write on china, glass, or other hard surfaces.

Chinaman ▶ noun (pl. **-men**) **1** chiefly archaic or derogatory a native of China.
2 Cricket a ball that spins from off to leg, bowled by a left-handed bowler to a right-handed batsman.

chinar /'tʃɪnɑː/ (also **chenar**) ▶ noun (also **chinar tree**) the oriental plane tree, which is native from SE Europe to northern Iran.
• *Platanus orientalis*, family Platanaceae.
– ORIGIN from Persian *chinār*.

China rose ▶ noun **1** a Chinese rose which was introduced into Europe in the 19th century.
• *Rosa chinensis*, family Rosaceae.
▪any of a number of garden rose varieties derived from crosses of this plant.
2 a tropical shrubby evergreen hibiscus, which is cultivated for its large showy flowers.
• *Hibiscus rosa-sinensis*, family Malvaceae.

China Sea the part of the Pacific Ocean off the coast of China, divided by the island of Taiwan into the **East China Sea** in the north and the **South China Sea** in the south.

china stone ▶ noun [mass noun] partly kaolinized granite containing plagioclase feldspar, which is ground and mixed with kaolin to make porcelain.

China syndrome ▶ noun [mass noun] a hypothetical sequence of events following the meltdown of a nuclear reactor, in which the core melts through its containment structure and deep into the earth.
– ORIGIN 1970s: from **CHINA** (as being on the opposite side of the earth from a reactor in the US).

China tea ▶ noun [mass noun] tea made from a small-leaved type of tea plant grown in China, typically flavoured by smoke curing or the addition of flower petals.

Chinatown ▶ noun a district of any non-Chinese town, especially a city or seaport, in which the population is predominantly of Chinese origin.

china tree ▶ noun another term for CHINABERRY.

chinch /tʃɪn(t)ʃ/ (also **chinch bug**) ▶ noun a plant-eating ground bug that forms large swarms on grasses and rushes.
- Two species in the family Lygaeidae, suborder Heteroptera: the American *Blissus leucopterus*, which is a major pest of cereal crops, and the European *Ischnodemus sabuleti*.
– ORIGIN early 17th cent. (in the sense 'bedbug'): from Spanish *chinche*, from Latin *cimex, cimic-*.

chincherinchee /ˌtʃɪntʃərɪnˈtʃiː/ ▶ noun a white-flowered South African lily.
- *Ornithogalum thyrsoides*, family Liliaceae.
– ORIGIN early 20th cent.: imitative of the squeaky sound made by rubbing its stalks together.

chinchilla /tʃɪnˈtʃɪlə/ ▶ noun a small South American rodent with soft grey fur and a long bushy tail.
- Genus *Chinchilla*, family Chinchillidae: two species, in particular *C. lanigera*.
- a cat or rabbit of a breed with silver-grey or grey fur. ■ [mass noun] the highly valued fur of the chinchilla, or of the chinchilla rabbit.
– ORIGIN early 17th cent.: from Spanish, from Aymara or Quechua.

chin-chin ▶ exclamation Brit. informal, dated used to express friendly feelings towards one's companions before drinking: *'Chin-chin,' he said, and drank.*
– ORIGIN late 18th cent.: representing a pronunciation of Chinese *qing qing*.

Chindit /ˈtʃɪndɪt/ ▶ noun a member of the Allied forces behind the Japanese lines in Burma (now Myanmar) in 1943–5.
– ORIGIN Second World War: from Burmese *chinthé*, a mythical creature.

Chindwin /tʃɪnˈdwɪn/ a river which rises in northern Burma (Myanmar) and flows southwards for 885 km (550 miles) to meet the Irrawaddy.

chine¹ /tʃʌɪn/ ▶ noun a backbone, especially that of an animal as it appears in a joint of meat.
- a joint of meat containing all or part of this. ■ a mountain ridge or arête.
▶ verb [with obj.] cut (meat) across or along the backbone.
– ORIGIN Middle English: from Old French *eschine*, based on a blend of Latin *spina* 'spine' and a Germanic word meaning 'narrow piece', related to SHIN.

chine² /tʃʌɪn/ ▶ noun (in the Isle of Wight or Dorset) a deep narrow ravine.
– ORIGIN Old English *cinu* 'cleft, chink', of Germanic origin; related to Dutch *keen*, also to CHINK¹.

chine³ /tʃʌɪn/ ▶ noun the angle where the strakes of the bottom of a boat or ship meet the side.
– ORIGIN late Middle English: variant of CHIME² (the original sense).

Chinese ▶ adjective of or relating to China or its language, culture, or people.
- belonging to or relating to the people forming the dominant ethnic group of China and also widely dispersed elsewhere. Also called HAN.
▶ noun (pl. same) 1 [mass noun] the Chinese language.
2 a native or national of China, or a person of Chinese descent.
- Brit. informal a Chinese meal. ■ Brit. informal a Chinese restaurant.

Chinese, a member of the Sino-Tibetan language family, is the world's most commonly spoken first language, with an estimated 1.2 billion native speakers worldwide. The script is logographic, using characters which originated as stylized pictographs but now also represent abstract concepts and the sounds of syllables. Though complex, it permits written communication between speakers of the many dialects, most of which are mutually incomprehensible in speech. About 8,000 characters are in everyday use, some having been simplified during the 20th century. For transliteration into the Roman alphabet, the Pinyin system is now usually used.

Chinese box ▶ noun each of a nest of boxes.

Chinese burn ▶ noun informal an act of placing both hands on a person's arm and then twisting it with a wringing motion to produce a burning sensation.

Chinese cabbage ▶ noun another term for CHINESE LEAF.

Chinese chequers (US **Chinese checkers**) ▶ plural noun [usu. treated as sing.] a board game for two to six players who attempt to move marbles or counters from one corner to the opposite one on a star-shaped board.

Chinese Chippendale ▶ noun [mass noun] a style of Chippendale furniture combining square and angular outlines with Chinese motifs.

Chinese fire drill ▶ noun N. Amer. informal a state of disorder or confusion.

Chinese gooseberry ▶ noun former term for KIWI FRUIT.

Chinese lantern ▶ noun 1 a collapsible paper lantern.
2 a Eurasian plant with white flowers and globular orange fruits enclosed in an orange-red papery calyx. The stems bearing these are dried and used for decoration.
- *Physalis alkekengi*, family Solanaceae.

Chinese layering ▶ noun another term for AIR LAYERING.

Chinese leaf (also **Chinese cabbage**) ▶ noun (often **Chinese leaves**) an oriental cabbage which does not form a firm heart.
- Genus *Brassica*, family Cruciferae: two species, pak choi (*B. chinensis*), which has smooth tapering leaves, and pe tsai (*B. pekinensis*), which resembles lettuce; they are often treated as varieties of *B. rapa*.

Chinese mitten crab ▶ noun an olive-green Asian crab with fur-covered pincers and hair on the legs. It has been introduced into Europe, living in fresh water and estuaries where it can become a pest.
- *Eriocheir sinensis*, family Grapsidae.

Chinese puzzle ▶ noun an intricate puzzle consisting of many interlocking pieces.

Chinese red ▶ noun [mass noun] a vivid orange-red.

Chinese restaurant syndrome ▶ noun [mass noun] an illness marked by short attacks of weakness, numbness, palpitations, and headaches, often attributed to overconsumption of monosodium glutamate (used as a seasoning in Chinese cooking).

Chinese wall ▶ noun an insurmountable barrier, especially to the passage of information.
– ORIGIN early 20th cent.: with allusion to the GREAT WALL OF CHINA.

Chinese water chestnut ▶ noun another term for WATER CHESTNUT (in sense 1).

Chinese water deer ▶ noun see WATER DEER.

Chinese whispers ▶ plural noun [treated as sing.] a game in which a message is distorted by being passed around in a whisper.

Chinese white ▶ noun [mass noun] white pigment consisting of zinc oxide.

Ch'ing variant spelling of QING.

ching ▶ noun an abrupt high-pitched ringing sound, typically one made by a cash register.
– ORIGIN imitative.

Chin Hills /tʃɪn/ a range of hills in western Burma (Myanmar), close to the borders with India and Bangladesh.

Chink ▶ noun informal, offensive a Chinese person.
– ORIGIN late 19th cent.: irregular formation from CHINA.

chink¹ ▶ noun a narrow opening or crack, typically one that admits light: *a chink in the curtains.*
- a narrow beam or patch of light admitted by such an opening: *I noticed a chink of light under the door.*
– PHRASES **a chink in someone's armour** a weak point in someone's character, arguments, or ideas which makes them vulnerable to attack or criticism.
– ORIGIN mid 16th cent.: related to CHINE².

chink² ▶ verb make or cause to make a light and high-pitched ringing sound, as of glasses or coins striking together: [no obj.] *the chain joining the handcuffs chinked |* [with obj.] *they chinked glasses and kissed.*
▶ noun a high-pitched ringing sound: *the chink of glasses.*
– ORIGIN late 16th cent.: imitative.

chink³ ▶ noun S. African informal short for CHINCHERINCHEE.

chinkapin ▶ noun variant spelling of CHINQUAPIN.

chinkara /tʃɪnˈkɑːrə/ ▶ noun (pl. same) (in the Indian subcontinent) the Indian gazelle, which occurs from Iran to central India.
- *Gazella bennettii* (formerly *dorcas*), family Bovidae.
– ORIGIN mid 19th cent.: from Hindi *cikārā*, from Sanskrit *chikkāra*.

Chinkiang /tʃɪnˈkjaŋ/ variant of ZHENJIANG.

chink shell ▶ noun a small marine mollusc with a conical shell that has a small chink or groove on one side, living typically in shallow water among seaweed.
- Genus *Lacuna*, family Littorinidea, class Gastropoda.

Chinky informal ▶ noun (pl. **-ies**) 1 offensive a Chinese person.
2 a Chinese restaurant.
▶ adjective offensive Chinese.

chinless ▶ adjective (of a person) lacking a well-defined chin.
- informal lacking strength of character; ineffectual.

chinless wonder ▶ noun Brit. informal an ineffectual upper-class man.

chin music ▶ noun [mass noun] informal, chiefly US idle chatter.

chino /ˈtʃiːnəʊ/ ▶ noun (pl. **-os**) [mass noun] a cotton twill fabric, typically khaki-coloured.
- [count noun] (**chinos**) casual trousers made from such fabric.
– ORIGIN 1940s: from Latin American Spanish, literally 'toasted' (referring to the typical colour).

Chino- /ˈtʃʌɪnəʊ/ ▶ combining form equivalent to SINO-.

chinoiserie /ʃɪnˈwɑːzəri/ ▶ noun (pl. **-ies**) [mass noun] the imitation or evocation of Chinese motifs and techniques in Western art, furniture, and architecture, especially in the 18th century.
- objects or decorations in this style: *a piece of chinoiserie |* [count noun] *one room has red velvet and chinoiseries.*
– ORIGIN late 19th cent.: from French, from *chinois* 'Chinese'.

Chinook /tʃɪˈnuːk, -ˈnʊk, ʃɪ-/ ▶ noun (pl. same or **Chinooks**) 1 a member of an American Indian people originally inhabiting the region around the Columbia River in Oregon.
2 [mass noun] the extinct Penutian language of this people.
▶ adjective of or relating to the Chinook or their language.
– ORIGIN from Salish *tsinúk*.

chinook /tʃɪˈnuːk, -nʊk, ʃɪ-/ ▶ noun 1 (also **chinook wind**) a warm dry wind which blows down the east side of the Rocky Mountains at the end of winter.
2 (also **chinook salmon**) a large North Pacific salmon which is an important commercial food fish.
- *Oncorhynchus tshawytscha*, family Salmonidae.
– ORIGIN mid 19th cent.: from attributive use of CHINOOK.

Chinook Jargon ▶ noun [mass noun] an extinct pidgin composed of elements from Chinook, Nootka, English, French, and other languages, formerly used in the Pacific North-West of North America.

chinquapin /ˈtʃɪŋkəpɪn/ (also **chinkapin**) ▶ noun a North American chestnut tree.
- Several species in the family Fagaceae, in particular *Castanea pumila* and *Castanopsis chrysophylla*.
- the edible nut of one of these trees.
– ORIGIN early 17th cent.: from Virginia Algonquian.

chinstrap ▶ noun a strap attached to a hat, helmet, or other headgear, designed to hold it in place by fitting under the wearer's chin.

chintz ▶ noun [mass noun] printed multicoloured cotton fabric with a glazed finish, used especially for curtains and upholstery: *a sofa upholstered in chintz |* [as modifier] *floral chintz curtains.*
– ORIGIN early 17th cent. (as *chints*, plural of *chint*, denoting a stained or painted calico cloth imported from India): from Hindi *chīṃṭ* 'spattering, stain'.

chintzy ▶ adjective (**chintzier, chintziest**) 1 of, like, or decorated with chintz: *a pretty, chintzy fabric.*
- brightly colourful but gaudy and tasteless.
2 N. Amer. informal miserly: *a chintzy salary increase.*
– DERIVATIVES **chintzily** adverb, **chintziness** noun.

chin-up ▶ noun chiefly N. Amer. another term for PULL-UP (in sense 1).

chinwag Brit. informal ▶ noun a chat.
▶ verb (**-wagged, -wagging**) [no obj.] have a chat.

chionodoxa /ˌkʌɪənəˈdɒksə/ ▶ noun a bulbous Eurasian plant of the lily family, with early blooming blue flowers. Also called GLORY-OF-THE-SNOW.
- Genus *Chionodoxa*, family Liliaceae.
– ORIGIN modern Latin, from Greek *khiōn* 'snow' + *doxa* 'glory'.

Chios /ˈkaɪɒs/ a Greek island in the Aegean Sea; pop. 52,690 (1991). Greek name KHIOS.

C

– DERIVATIVES **Chian** noun & adjective.

chip ▶ **noun** **1** a small piece of something removed in the course of chopping, cutting, or breaking something, especially a hard material such as wood or stone: *granite chips support the track.*
■ a hole or blemish left by the removal of such a piece. ■ [mass noun] Brit. wood or woody fibre split into thin strips and used for weaving hats or baskets.
2 chiefly Brit. a long rectangular piece of deep-fried potato.
■ (also **potato chip**) chiefly N. Amer. a potato crisp.
3 short for **MICROCHIP**.
4 a counter used in certain gambling games to represent money: *a poker chip.*
5 (in football, golf, and other sports) a short lofted kick or shot with the ball.
▶ **verb** (**chipped**, **chipping**) [with obj.] **1** cut or break (a small piece) from the edge or surface of a hard material: *we had to chip ice off the upper deck.*
■ [no obj.] (of a material or object) break at the edge or on the surface: *the paint had* **chipped off** *the gate.* ■ cut pieces off (a hard material) to alter its shape or break it up: *it required a craftsman to chip the blocks of flint to the required shape* | [no obj.] *she* **chipped away** *at the ground outside the door.* ■ Brit. cut (a potato or other item of food) into strips.
2 (in football, golf, and other sports) kick or strike (a ball or shot) to produce a short lobbed shot or pass: *he chipped a superb shot over the keeper.*
– PHRASES **a chip off the old block** informal someone who resembles their parent, especially in character. **a chip on one's shoulder** informal a deeply ingrained grievance, typically about a particular thing. **have had one's chips** Brit. informal be dead, dying, or out of contention. **when the chips are down** informal when a very serious and difficult situation arises.
– ORIGIN Middle English: related to Old English *forcippian* 'cut off'.
▶ **chip away** gradually and relentlessly make something smaller or weaker: *rivals may* **chip away at** *one's profits by undercutting product prices.*
chip in (or **chip something in**) **1** contribute something as one's share of a joint activity, cost, etc.: *Rollie* **chipped in with** *nine saves and five wins* | *the council will chip in a further £30,000 a year.* **2** Brit. informal join in a conversation, typically by interrupting: [with direct speech] *'He's right,' Gloria chipped in.*

chipboard ▶ **noun** [mass noun] material made in rigid sheets or panels from compressed wood chips and resin, often coated or veneered, and used in furniture, buildings, etc., where a stronger material is not required.

Chipewyan /ˌtʃɪpəˈwʌɪən/ ▶ **noun** (pl. same or **Chipewyans**) **1** a member of a Dene people of NW Canada. Compare with **CHIPPEWA**.
2 [mass noun] the Athabaskan language of this people, with about 8,000 speakers.
▶ **adjective** of or relating to this people or their language.
– ORIGIN from Cree, literally '(wearing) pointed-skin (garments)'.

chip heater ▶ **noun** Austral./NZ a domestic water heater that burns wood chips.

chipmaker ▶ **noun** a company that manufactures microchips.

chipmunk ▶ **noun** a burrowing ground squirrel with cheek pouches and light and dark stripes running down the body, found in North America and northern Eurasia.
• Genus *Tamias*, family Sciuridae: many species.
– ORIGIN mid 19th cent.: from Ojibwa.

chipolata ▶ **noun** Brit. a small thin sausage.
– ORIGIN late 19th cent.: from French, from Italian *cipollata* 'a dish of onions', from *cipolla* 'onion'.

chipotle /tʃɪˈpəʊtleɪ/ ▶ **noun** a smoked hot chilli pepper which is used in Mexican cooking.
– ORIGIN Mexican Spanish, from Nahuatl.

Chippendale[1] /ˈtʃɪp(ə)ndeɪl/, Thomas (1718–79), English furniture-maker and designer. He produced furniture in a neoclassical vein, with elements of the French rococo, chinoiserie, and Gothic revival styles, and his book of furniture designs *The Gentleman and Cabinetmaker's Director* (1754) was immensely influential.

Chippendale[2] /ˈtʃɪp(ə)ndeɪl/ ▶ **adjective** (of furniture) designed, made by, or in the style of Thomas Chippendale.

chipper[1] ▶ **adjective** informal cheerful and lively.
– ORIGIN mid 19th cent.: perhaps from northern English dialect *kipper* 'lively'.

chipper[2] ▶ **noun** **1** a person or thing that turns something into chips.
■ a machine for chipping timber.
2 Irish informal a fish-and-chip shop.

Chippewa /ˈtʃɪpəwɔː, -wɑː/ (also **Chippeway** /-weɪ/) ▶ **noun** (pl. same) chiefly US another term for **OJIBWA**. Compare with **CHIPEWYAN**.
– ORIGIN alteration of **OJIBWA**.

chippie ▶ **noun** (pl. **-ies**) variant spelling of **CHIPPY**.

chipping ▶ **noun** Brit. a small fragment of stone, wood, or similar material.
■ (**chippings**) small fragments of stone used to make road surfaces.

chipping sparrow ▶ **noun** a common American songbird related to the buntings, with a chestnut crown and a white stripe over the eye.
• *Spizella passerina*, family Emberizidae (subfamily Emberizinae).
– ORIGIN early 19th cent.: *chipping* from US *chip* 'chirp', with reference to the bird's repetitive chirping song.

chippy informal ▶ **noun** (also **chippie**) (pl. **-ies**) **1** Brit. a fish-and-chip shop.
2 Brit. a carpenter.
3 N. Amer. a promiscuous young woman, especially a prostitute.
▶ **adjective** touchy and irritable.
■ N. Amer. (of an ice-hockey game) rough and belligerent with numerous penalties.

chipset ▶ **noun** a collection of integrated circuits which form the set needed to make an electronic device such as a computer motherboard or portable telephone.

chip shot ▶ **noun** Golf a stroke at which the ball is or must be chipped into the air.

Chirac /ˈʃɪərak, French ʃiʀak/, Jacques (René) (b.1932), French statesman, Prime Minister 1974–6 and 1986–8 and President since 1995.

chiral /ˈkʌɪr(ə)l/ ▶ **adjective** Chemistry asymmetric in such a way that the structure and its mirror image are not superimposable. Chiral compounds are typically optically active; large organic molecules often have one or more **chiral centres** where four different groups are attached to a carbon atom.
– DERIVATIVES **chirality** noun.
– ORIGIN late 19th cent.: from Greek *kheir* 'hand' + **-AL**.

chi-rho ▶ **noun** a monogram of chi (X) and rho (P) as the first two letters of Greek *Khristos* Christ.

Chirico /ˈkɪrɪkəʊ/, Giorgio de (1888–1978), Greek-born Italian painter. His disconnected and unsettling dream images exerted a significant influence on surrealism.

chirimoya /ˌtʃɪrɪˈmɔɪə/ ▶ **noun** variant spelling of **CHERIMOYA**.

chiro- /ˈkʌɪrəʊ/ (also **cheiro-**) ▶ **combining form** of the hand or hands: *chiromancy.*
– ORIGIN from Greek *kheir* 'hand'.

chirography /kʌɪˈrɒɡrəfi/ ▶ **noun** [mass noun] handwriting, especially as distinct from typography.
– DERIVATIVES **chirographic** adjective.

chiromancy /ˈkʌɪrə(ʊ)mansi/ ▶ **noun** [mass noun] the prediction of a person's future from the lines on the palms of their hands; palmistry.

Chiron /ˈkʌɪərɒn/ **1** Greek Mythology a learned centaur who acted as teacher to Jason, Achilles, and many other heroes.
2 Astronomy asteroid 2060, discovered in 1977, which is unique in having an orbit lying mainly between the orbits of Saturn and Uranus. It is believed to have a diameter of 370 km.

chironomid /kʌɪˈrɒnəmɪd/ ▶ **noun** Entomology an insect of a family (Chironomidae) which comprises the non-biting midges.
– ORIGIN late 19th cent.: from modern Latin *Chironomidae* (plural), from the genus name *Chironomus*, from Greek *kheironomos* 'pantomime dancer'.

chiropody ▶ **noun** [mass noun] the treatment of the feet and their ailments.
– DERIVATIVES **chiropodist** noun.
– ORIGIN late 19th cent.: from **CHIRO-** 'hand' + Greek *pous, pod-* 'foot'.

chiropractic /ˌkʌɪrə(ʊ)ˈpraktɪk/ ▶ **noun** [mass noun] a system of complementary medicine based on the diagnosis and manipulative treatment of misalignments of the joints, especially those of the spinal column, which are held to cause other disorders by affecting the nerves, muscles, and organs.
– DERIVATIVES **chiropractor** noun.
– ORIGIN late 19th cent.: from **CHIRO-** 'hand' + Greek *praktikos* 'practical', from *prattein* 'do'.

Chiroptera /kʌɪˈrɒpt(ə)rə/ Zoology an order of mammals that comprises the bats. See also **MEGACHIROPTERA**, **MICROCHIROPTERA**.
– DERIVATIVES **chiropteran** noun & adjective.
– ORIGIN modern Latin (plural), from **CHIRO-** 'hand' + Greek *pteron* 'wing'.

chirp ▶ **verb** [no obj.] (typically of a small bird or an insect) utter a short, sharp, high-pitched sound: *outside, the crickets chirped monotonously.*
■ [with direct speech] (of a person) say something in a lively and cheerful way: *'Good morning!' chirped Alex.* ■ S. African complain: *a penalty was given and somebody chirped.* ■ [with obj.] S. African speak to (someone) in a way calculated to annoy; taunt.
▶ **noun** a short, sharp, high-pitched sound.
– DERIVATIVES **chirper** noun.
– ORIGIN late Middle English: imitative.

chirpy ▶ **adjective** (**chirpier**, **chirpiest**) informal cheerful and lively.
– DERIVATIVES **chirpily** adverb, **chirpiness** noun.

chirr /tʃəː/ (also **churr**) ▶ **verb** [no obj.] (especially of an insect) make a prolonged low trilling sound.
▶ **noun** a low trilling sound.
– ORIGIN early 17th cent.: imitative.

chirrup ▶ **verb** (**chirruped**, **chirruping**) [no obj.] (especially of a small bird) make repeated short high-pitched sounds; twitter.
■ [with direct speech] (of a person) say something in a high-pitched voice: *'Yes, Miss Honey,' chirruped eighteen voices.*
▶ **noun** a short, high-pitched sound.
– DERIVATIVES **chirrupy** adjective.
– ORIGIN late 16th cent.: alteration of **CHIRP**, by trilling the *-r-*.

chiru /ˈtʃɪruː/ ▶ **noun** (pl. same) a sandy-coloured gazelle with black horns, found on the Tibetan plateau. Also called **TIBETAN ANTELOPE**.
• *Pantholops hodgsoni*, family Bovidae.
– ORIGIN late 19th cent.: probably from Tibetan.

chisel /ˈtʃɪz(ə)l/ ▶ **noun** a long-bladed hand tool with a bevelled cutting edge and a plain handle which is struck with a hammer or mallet, used to cut or shape wood, stone, metal, or other hard materials.
▶ **verb** (**chiselled**, **chiselling**; US **chiseled**, **chiseling**) [with obj.] **1** cut or shape (something) with a chisel: *carefully chisel a recess inside the pencil line.*
2 informal, chiefly US cheat or swindle (someone) out of something: *he's chiselled me out of my dues.*
– DERIVATIVES **chiseller** noun.
– ORIGIN late Middle English: from Old Northern French, based on Latin *cis-* (as in late Latin *cisorium*), variant of *caes-*, stem of *caedere* 'to cut'. Compare with **SCISSORS**.

chiselled ▶ **adjective** (of wood or stone) shaped or cut with a chisel.
■ (of a facial feature, typically a man's) strongly and clearly defined: *the chiselled features of a male model.*

Chişinău /ˌkɪʃɪˈnaʊ/ the capital of Moldova; pop. 665,000 (est. 1989). Russian name **KISHINYOV**.

chi-squared /kʌɪ/ (also **chi-square**) ▶ **noun** [as modifier] relating to or denoting a statistical method assessing the goodness of fit between observed values and those expected theoretically. (Symbol: χ^2)

chit[1] ▶ **noun** a young woman regarded with disapproval for her immaturity or lack of respect: *she is a mere chit of a girl.*
– ORIGIN late Middle English (denoting a whelp, cub, or kitten): perhaps related to dialect *chit* 'sprout'.

chit[2] ▶ **noun** a short official note, memorandum, or voucher, typically recording a sum owed.
– ORIGIN late 18th cent.: Anglo-Indian, from Hindi *ciṭṭhī* 'note, pass'.

chit[3] ▶ **verb** (**chitted**, **chitting**) [with obj.] induce (a potato) to sprout by placing it in a cool light place.
– ORIGIN early 17th cent.: from dialect *chit* 'a shoot, sprout'.

chital /ˈtʃiːt(ə)l/ ▶ **noun** a deer that has lyre-shaped antlers and a fawn coat with white spots, native to India and Sri Lanka.
• *Cervus axis*, family Cervidae.
– ORIGIN late 19th cent.: from Hindi *cītal*, from Sanskrit *citrala* 'spotted', from *citra* 'spot, mark'.

chitarrone /ˌkɪtəˈrəʊneɪ, -ni/ ▶ noun a very large lute similar to a theorbo, used in Italy in the late 16th and early 17th centuries.
– ORIGIN Italian, literally 'large guitar'.

chit-chat informal ▶ noun [mass noun] inconsequential conversation.
▶ verb [no obj.] talk about trivial matters: *I can't stand around chit-chatting.*
– ORIGIN late 17th cent.: reduplication of **CHAT**[1].

chitin /ˈkʌɪtɪn/ ▶ noun [mass noun] Biochemistry a fibrous substance consisting of polysaccharides, which is the major constituent in the exoskeleton of arthropods and the cell walls of fungi.
– DERIVATIVES **chitinous** adjective.
– ORIGIN mid 19th cent.: from French *chitine*, formed irregularly from Greek *khitōn* (see **CHITON**).

chiton /ˈkʌɪtɒn, -t(ə)n/ ▶ noun **1** a long woollen tunic worn in ancient Greece. [ORIGIN: from Greek *khitōn* 'tunic'.]
2 a marine mollusc that has an oval flattened body with a shell of eight overlapping plates. Also called **COAT-OF-MAIL SHELL**. [ORIGIN: modern Latin (genus name).]
● Class Polyplacophora.

Chittagong /ˈtʃɪtəgɒŋ/ a seaport in SE Bangladesh, on the Bay of Bengal; pop. 1,566,070 (1991).

chitter ▶ verb [no obj.] **1** make a twittering or chattering sound.
2 Scottish & dialect shiver with cold: *they stand chittering at bus stops.*
– ORIGIN Middle English: imitative; compare with **CHATTER**.

chitterlings /ˈtʃɪtəlɪŋz/ ▶ plural noun the smaller intestines of a pig, cooked for food.
– ORIGIN Middle English: perhaps related to synonymous German *Kutteln*.

chitty ▶ noun (pl. **-ies**) Brit. informal term for **CHIT**[2].

chivalrous ▶ adjective (of a man or his behaviour) courteous and gallant, especially towards women.
■ of or relating to the historical notion of chivalry.
– DERIVATIVES **chivalrously** adverb.
– ORIGIN late Middle English (in the sense 'characteristic of a medieval knight'): from Old French *chevalerous*, from *chevalier* (see **CHEVALIER**).

chivalry ▶ noun [mass noun] the medieval knightly system with its religious, moral, and social code.
■ historical knights, noblemen, and horsemen collectively: *I fought against the cream of French chivalry.* ■ the combination of qualities expected of an ideal knight, especially courage, honour, courtesy, justice, and a readiness to help the weak. ■ courteous behaviour, especially that of a man towards women: *their relations with women were models of chivalry and restraint.*
– DERIVATIVES **chivalric** adjective.
– ORIGIN Middle English: from Old French *chevalerie*, from medieval Latin *caballerius*, for late Latin *caballarius* 'horseman' (see **CHEVALIER**).

chives ▶ plural noun a small Eurasian plant related to the onion, with purple-pink flowers and dense tufts of long tubular leaves which are used as a culinary herb: *freshly chopped chives* | [as modifier] (**chive**) *chive and garlic dressing.*
● *Allium schoenoprasum*, family Liliaceae (or Alliaceae).
■ (**chive**) a single plant of this kind; a single leaf from such a plant.
– ORIGIN Middle English: from Old French, dialect variant of *cive*, from Latin *cepa* 'onion'.

chivvy (also **chivy**) ▶ verb (**-ies, -ied**) [with obj.] tell (someone) repeatedly to do something: *an association which chivvies government into action.*
– ORIGIN late 18th cent.: probably from the ballad *Chevy Chase*, celebrating a skirmish (probably the battle of Otterburn, 1388) on the Scottish border (but often mistakenly thought to be a place name). Originally a noun denoting a hunting cry, the term later meant 'a pursuit', hence the verb 'to chase, worry' (mid 19th cent.).

Chkalov /ˈtʃkɑːlɒf/ former name (1938–57) for **ORENBURG**.

Chladni figures /ˈkladni/ (also **Chladni patterns** or **Chladni's figures**) ▶ plural noun the patterns formed when a sand-covered surface is made to vibrate. The sand collects in the regions of least motion.
– ORIGIN early 19th cent.: named after Ernst Chladni (1756–1827), German physicist.

chlamydia /kləˈmɪdɪə/ ▶ noun (pl. same or **chlamydiae** /-dɪiː/) a very small parasitic bacterium which, like a virus, requires the biochemical mechanisms of another cell in order to reproduce. Bacteria of this type cause various diseases including trachoma, psittacosis, and non-specific urethritis.
● Genus *Chlamydia* and order Chlamydiales.
– DERIVATIVES **chlamydial** adjective.
– ORIGIN 1960s: modern Latin (plural), from Greek *khlamus, khlamud-* 'cloak'.

chlamydomonas /ˌklamɪdəˈməʊnəs/ ▶ noun Biology a common single-celled green alga which typically has two flagella for swimming, living in water and moist soil.
● Genus *Chlamydomonas*, division Chlorophyta (or phylum Chlorophyta, kingdom Protista)
– ORIGIN late 19th cent.: modern Latin, from Greek *khlamus, khlamud-* 'cloak' + *monas* (see **MONAD**).

chlamydospore /ˈklamɪdə(ʊ)spɔː/ ▶ noun Botany (in certain fungi) a thick-walled hyphal cell which functions like a spore.
– ORIGIN late 19th cent.: from Greek *khlamus, khlamud-* 'mantle' + **SPORE**.

chlamys /ˈklamɪs/ ▶ noun a short cloak worn by men in ancient Greece.
– ORIGIN late 17th cent.: from Greek *khlamus* 'mantle'.

chloasma /kləʊˈazmə/ ▶ noun [mass noun] a temporary condition, typically caused by hormonal changes, in which large brown patches form on the skin, mainly on the face.
– ORIGIN mid 19th cent.: from Greek *khloazein* 'become green'.

chlor- ▶ combining form variant spelling of **CHLORO-** before a vowel (as in *chloracne*).

chloracne /klɔːˈrakni/ ▶ noun [mass noun] Medicine a skin disease resembling severe acne, caused by exposure to chlorinated chemicals.

chloral /ˈklɔːral/ ▶ noun [mass noun] Chemistry a colourless, viscous liquid made by chlorinating acetaldehyde.
● Alternative name: **trichloroethanal**; chem. formula: CCl_3CHO.
■ short for **CHLORAL HYDRATE**.
– ORIGIN mid 19th cent.: from French, blend of *chlore* 'chlorine' and *alcool* 'alcohol'.

chloral hydrate ▶ noun [mass noun] Chemistry a colourless crystalline solid made from chloral and used as a sedative.
● Chem. formula: $CCl_3CH(OH)_2$.

chlorambucil /klɔːˈrambjʊsɪl/ ▶ noun [mass noun] Medicine a cytotoxic drug used in the treatment of cancer. It belongs to the class of nitrogen mustards.
– ORIGIN 1950s: from *chlor(oethyl)am(inophenyl)bu(tyric acid)*, the systematic name, + *-cil*.

chloramine /ˈklɔːrəmiːn/ ▶ noun Chemistry an organic compound containing a chlorine atom bonded to nitrogen, especially any of a group of sulphonamide derivatives used as antiseptics and disinfectants.

chloramphenicol /ˌklɔːramˈfɛnɪkɒl/ ▶ noun [mass noun] Medicine an antibiotic used against serious infections such as typhoid fever.
● This antibiotic is obtained from the bacterium *Streptomyces venezuelae* or produced synthetically.
– ORIGIN 1940s: from **CHLORO-** (representing **CHLORINE**) + *am(ide)* + **PHENO-** + *ni(tro)-* + *(gly)col*.

chlordane /ˈklɔːdeɪn/ ▶ noun [mass noun] a synthetic viscous toxic compound used as an insecticide.
● A chlorinated derivative of indene; chem. formula: $C_{10}H_6Cl_8$.
– ORIGIN 1940s: from **CHLOR-** (representing **CHLORINE**) + *(in)dene* + **-ANE**[2].

chlordiazepoxide /ˌklɔːdʌɪazɪˈpɒksʌɪd/ ▶ noun [mass noun] Medicine a tranquillizer of the benzodiazepine group, used chiefly to treat anxiety and alcoholism. Also called **LIBRIUM** (trademark).

chlorella /kləˈrɛlə/ ▶ noun [mass noun] Biology a common single-celled green alga of both terrestrial and aquatic habitats, frequently turning stagnant water an opaque green.
● Genus *Chlorella*, division Chlorophyta (or phylum Chlorophyta, kingdom Protista).
– ORIGIN modern Latin, diminutive of Greek *khlōros* 'green'.

chlorhexidine /klɔːˈhɛksɪdiːn/ ▶ noun [mass noun] a synthetic compound used as a mild antiseptic, chiefly in skin creams and mouthwashes.
● A biguanide derivative; chem. formula: $C_{22}H_{30}Cl_2N_{10}$.
– ORIGIN mid 20th cent.: from **CHLOR-** (representing **CHLORINE**) + *hex(ane)* + *-id(e)* + *(am)ine*.

chloric acid /ˈklɔːrɪk/ ▶ noun [mass noun] Chemistry a colourless liquid acid with strong oxidizing properties.
● Chem. formula: $HClO_3$.
■ any acid containing chlorine and oxygen.
– DERIVATIVES **chlorate** noun.
– ORIGIN early 19th cent.: *chloric* from **CHLORINE** + **-IC**.

chloride /ˈklɔːrʌɪd/ ▶ noun Chemistry a compound of chlorine with another element or group, especially a salt of the anion Cl^- or an organic compound with chlorine bonded to an alkyl group.
– ORIGIN early 19th cent.: from **CHLORINE** + **-IDE**.

chlorinate /ˈklɔːrɪneɪt, ˈklɒ-/ ▶ verb [with obj.] [usu. as adj. **chlorinated**] impregnate or treat with chlorine: *chlorinated water.*
■ Chemistry introduce chlorine into (a compound).
– DERIVATIVES **chlorination** noun, **chlorinator** noun.

chlorine /ˈklɔːriːn/ ▶ noun the chemical element of atomic number 17, a toxic, irritant, pale green gas. (Symbol: **Cl**)

> A member of the halogen group, chlorine occurs in nature mainly as sodium chloride in seawater and salt deposits. The gas was used as a poison gas in the First World War. Chlorine is added to water supplies as a disinfectant.

– ORIGIN early 19th cent.: named by Sir Humphrey Davy, from Greek *khlōros* 'green' + **-INE**[4].

chlorite[1] /ˈklɔːrʌɪt/ ▶ noun [mass noun] a dark green mineral consisting of a basic hydrated aluminosilicate of magnesium and iron. It occurs as a constituent of many rocks, typically forming flat crystals resembling mica.
– DERIVATIVES **chloritic** adjective.
– ORIGIN late 18th cent.: via Latin from Greek *khlōritis*, a green precious stone.

chlorite[2] /ˈklɔːrʌɪt/ ▶ noun Chemistry a salt of chlorous acid, containing the anion ClO_2^-.
– ORIGIN mid 19th cent.: from **CHLORINE** + **-ITE**[1].

chloritoid /ˈklɔːrɪtɔɪd/ ▶ noun a greenish-grey or black mineral resembling mica, found in metamorphosed clay sediments. It consists of a basic aluminosilicate of iron, often with magnesium.

chloro- (usu. **chlor-** before a vowel) ▶ combining form **1** Biology & Mineralogy green.
2 Chemistry representing **CHLORINE**: *chloroquine.*
– ORIGIN from Greek *khlōros* 'green'.

chlorodyne /ˈklɔːrə(ʊ)dʌɪn, ˈklɒ-/ ▶ noun [mass noun] a preparation of chloroform and morphine formerly used to relieve pain.
– ORIGIN mid 19th cent.: blend of **CHLOROFORM** and **ANODYNE**.

chlorofluorocarbon /ˌklɔːrə(ʊ)ˌfluərə(ʊ)ˈkɑːb(ə)n, -ˌflɔː-/ ▶ noun see **CFC**.

chloroform ▶ noun [mass noun] a colourless, volatile, sweet-smelling liquid used as a solvent and formerly as a general anaesthetic.
● Alternative name: **trichloromethane**; chem. formula: $CHCl_3$.
▶ verb [with obj.] render (someone) unconscious with this substance.
– ORIGIN mid 19th cent.: from **CHLORO-** (representing **CHLORINE**) + *form-* from **FORMIC ACID**.

chloromelanite /ˌklɔːrə(ʊ)ˈmɛlənʌɪt, ˌklɒ-/ ▶ noun [mass noun] a greenish-black variety of jadeite containing a high proportion of iron.

chloromycetin /ˌklɔːrə(ʊ)ˈmʌɪsɪtɪn, ˌklɒ-, -mʌɪˈsiːtɪn/ ▶ noun US trademark for **CHLORAMPHENICOL**.
– ORIGIN 1940s: from **CHLORO-** 'green' + Greek *mukēs, mukēt-* 'fungus' + **-IN**[1].

chlorophyll /ˈklɔːrəfɪl, ˈklɒ-/ ▶ noun [mass noun] a green pigment, present in all green plants and in cyanobacteria, which is responsible for the absorption of light to provide energy for photosynthesis. Its molecule contains a magnesium atom held in a porphyrin ring.
– DERIVATIVES **chlorophyllous** adjective.
– ORIGIN early 19th cent.: coined in French from Greek *khlōros* 'green' + *phullon* 'leaf'.

Chlorophyta /ˈklɔːrə(ʊ)fʌɪtə, ˈklɒ-/ Botany a division of lower plants that comprises the green algae. They are frequently treated as a phylum of the kingdom Protista.
– DERIVATIVES **chlorophyte** noun.
– ORIGIN modern Latin (plural), from Greek *khlōros* 'green' + *phuton* 'plant'.

chloroplast /ˈklɔːrəplast, -plɑːst, ˈklɒ-/ ▶ noun

Botany (in green plant cells) a plastid which contains chlorophyll and in which photosynthesis takes place.
– ORIGIN late 19th cent.: coined in German from Greek *khlōros* 'green' + *plastos* 'formed'.

chloroprene /ˈklɔːrə(ʊ)priːn, ˈklɒ-/ ▶ **noun** [mass noun] Chemistry a colourless liquid made from acetylene and hydrochloric acid and polymerized to form neoprene.
• Chem. formula: CH_2=CClCH=CH_2.
– ORIGIN 1930s: from **CHLORO-** + a shortened form of **ISOPRENE**.

chloroquine /ˈklɔːrə(ʊ)kwiːn, ˈklɒ-/ ▶ **noun** [mass noun] Medicine a synthetic drug related to quinoline, chiefly used against malaria.
– ORIGIN 1940s: from **CHLORO-** + *quin(olin)e*.

chlorosis /klɒˈrəʊsɪs/ ▶ **noun** [mass noun] **1** Botany abnormal reduction or loss of the normal green coloration of leaves of plants, typically caused by iron deficiency in lime-rich soils, or by disease or lack of light.
2 Medicine anaemia caused by iron deficiency, especially in adolescent girls, causing a pale, faintly greenish complexion. It was a common diagnosis in the 19th century.
– DERIVATIVES **chlorotic** adjective.

chlorothiazide /ˌklɔːrə(ʊ)ˈθʌɪəzʌɪd, ˈklɒ-/ ▶ **noun** [mass noun] Medicine a synthetic drug used to treat fluid retention and high blood pressure. It is one of the thiazide diuretics.

chlorous acid /ˈklɔːrəs/ ▶ **noun** [mass noun] Chemistry a weak acid with oxidizing properties, formed when chlorine dioxide dissolves in water.
• Chem. formula: $HClO_2$.

chlorpromazine /klɔːˈprəʊməziːn, -ziːn/ ▶ **noun** [mass noun] Medicine a synthetic drug used as a tranquillizer, sedative, and anti-emetic. It is a phenothiazine derivative.
– ORIGIN 1950s: from **CHLORO-** + *prom(eth)azine*.

chlortetracycline /ˌklɔːtɛtrəˈsʌɪkliːn/ ▶ **noun** [mass noun] Medicine an antibiotic of the tetracycline group, active against many bacterial and fungal infections.
• This antibiotic is obtained from the bacterium *Streptomyces aureofaciens* or produced synthetically.

ChM ▶ **abbreviation** Master of Surgery.
– ORIGIN from Latin *Chirurgiae Magister*.

choanocyte /ˈkəʊənə(ʊ)sʌɪt/ ▶ **noun** Zoology a flagellated cell with a collar of protoplasm at the base of the flagellum, numbers of which line the internal chambers of sponges.
– ORIGIN late 19th cent.: from Greek *khoanē* 'funnel' + **-CYTE**.

choc ▶ **noun** Brit. informal a chocolate.
– ORIGIN late 19th cent.: abbreviation.

chocaholic ▶ **noun** variant spelling of **CHOCOHOLIC**.

chocho /ˈtʃəʊtʃəʊ/ ▶ **noun** (pl. **-os**) West Indian term for **CHOKO**.

choc ice ▶ **noun** Brit. a small block of ice cream covered with a thin coating of chocolate.

chock ▶ **noun 1** a wedge or block placed against a wheel or rounded object, to prevent it from moving.
■a support on which a rounded structure, such as a cask or the hull of a boat, may be placed to keep it steady.
2 a ring with a gap at the top, through which a rope or line is run.
▶**verb** [with obj.] (often **be chocked**) prevent the forward movement of (a wheel or vehicle) with a chock.
■Brit. support (a boat, cask, etc.) on chocks.
– ORIGIN Middle English: probably from an Old Northern French variant of Old French *çouche, çoche* 'block, log', of unknown ultimate origin.

chocka ▶ **adjective** Brit. short for **CHOCK-A-BLOCK**.

chock-a-block ▶ **adjective** [predic.] informal crammed full of people or things: *the manual is* ***chock-a-block with*** *information.*
– ORIGIN mid 19th cent. (originally in nautical use, with reference to tackle having the two blocks run close together): from *chock* (in **CHOCK-FULL**) and **BLOCK**.

chocker ▶ **adjective** [predic.] informal **1** Brit. tired of or disgusted with something: *I'm a little chocker with this place.*
2 chiefly Austral./NZ full: *the church was chocker with flowers.*
– ORIGIN Second World War (originally naval slang): from **CHOCK-A-BLOCK**.

chock-full ▶ **adjective** [predic.] informal filled to overflowing: *my case is chock-full of notes.*
– ORIGIN late Middle English: of unknown origin; later associated with **CHOCK**.

chockstone ▶ **noun** Climbing a stone that has become wedged in a vertical cleft.

chocoholic (also **chocaholic**) ▶ **noun** informal a person who is addicted to or very fond of chocolate.

chocolate ▶ **noun** [mass noun] a food preparation in the form of a paste or solid block made from roasted and ground cacao seeds, typically sweetened and eaten as confectionery: *a bar of chocolate* | [as modifier] *a chocolate biscuit.*
■[count noun] a sweet made of or covered with such confectionery: *a box of chocolates.* ■a drink made by mixing milk or water with chocolate. ■a deep brown colour: *the former Great Western colours of chocolate and cream* | [as modifier] *huge spiders, yellow and* ***chocolate brown.***
– DERIVATIVES **chocolatey** (also **chocolaty**) adjective.
– ORIGIN early 17th cent. (in the sense 'a drink made with chocolate'): from French *chocolat* or Spanish *chocolate*, from Nahuatl *chocolatl* 'food made from cacao seeds', influenced by unrelated *cacaua-atl* 'drink made from cacao'.

chocolate box ▶ **noun** a box filled with chocolates, conventionally decorated with an attractive image.
▶**adjective** [attrib.] (of a view or picture) pretty in a trite, dully conventional way.

chocolate chip ▶ **noun** [usu. as modifier] a small piece of chocolate used in making biscuits and other sweet foods: *chocolate-chip cookies.*

chocolate mousse ▶ **noun** see **MOUSSE**.

chocolate spot ▶ **noun** [mass noun] a fungal disease affecting field and broad beans, characterized by dark brown spots on all parts of the plant.
• This is caused by the fungus *Botrytis fabae* (sometimes the grey mould *B. cinerea*), subdivision Deuteromycotina (or Ascomycotina).

chocolatier /ˌtʃɒkəˈlatɪə, French ʃɔkɔlatje/ ▶ **noun** (pl. pronounced same) a maker or seller of chocolate.
– ORIGIN late 19th cent.: French.

Choctaw /ˈtʃɒktɔː/ ▶ **noun** (pl. same or **Choctaws**) **1** a member of an American Indian people now living mainly in Mississippi.
2 [mass noun] the Muskogean language of this people, closely related to Chickasaw and now almost extinct.
3 (in skating) a step from one edge of a skate to the other edge of the other skate in the opposite direction.
▶**adjective** of or relating to the Choctaw or their language.
– ORIGIN from Choctaw *čahta*.

choice ▶ **noun** an act of selecting or making a decision when faced with two or more possibilities: *the* ***choice between*** *good and evil.*
■[mass noun] the right or ability to make, or possibility of making, such a selection: *I had to do it, I had no choice.* ■a range of possibilities from which one or more may be selected: *you can have a sofa made to order in a choice of over forty fabrics.* ■a course of action, thing, or person which is selected or decided upon: *this disk drive is the perfect choice for your computer.*
▶**adjective 1** (especially of food) of very good quality: *he picked some choice early plums.*
2 (of words, phrases, or language) rude and abusive: *he had a few choice words at his command.*
– PHRASES **by choice** of one's own volition. **of choice** chiefly N. Amer. selected as one's favourite or the best: *champagne was his drink of choice.* **of one's choice** that one chooses or has chosen: *the college of her choice.*
– DERIVATIVES **choicely** adverb, **choiceness** noun.
– ORIGIN Middle English: from Old French *chois*, from *choisir* 'choose', of Germanic origin and related to **CHOOSE**.

choil /tʃɔɪl/ ▶ **noun** the end of a knife's cutting edge which is nearer to the handle.
– ORIGIN late 19th cent.: of unknown origin.

choir ▶ **noun** an organized group of singers, typically one that takes part in church services or performs regularly in public: *a church choir.*
■one of two or more subdivisions of such a group performing together: *his famous Spem in alium for eight five-part choirs.* ■the part of a cathedral or large church between the altar and the nave, used by the choir and clergy. ■a group of instruments of one family playing together: *a clarinet choir.*
– ORIGIN Middle English *quer, quere*, from Old French *quer*, from Latin *chorus* (see **CHORUS**). The spelling change in the 17th cent. was due to association with Latin *chorus* and modern French *choeur*.

choirboy ▶ **noun** a boy who sings in a church or cathedral choir.

choirgirl ▶ **noun** a girl who sings in a church or cathedral choir.

choirman ▶ **noun** (pl. **-men**) Brit. a man who sings in a church or cathedral choir.

choirmaster ▶ **noun** the conductor of a choir.

choir organ ▶ **noun** a separate division of many large organs, played using a third manual (keyboard), and typically having distinctively toned stops.

choir school ▶ **noun** a school which is attached to a cathedral or college and specializes in training choirboys.

choir stall ▶ **noun** (usu. **choir stalls**) a fixed seat for one or more people in the choir of a church or chapel.

choisya /ˈkɔɪzɪə, ˈʃwaːzɪə/ ▶ **noun** an evergreen Mexican shrub with sweet-scented white flowers, widely grown as an ornamental.
• *Choisya ternata*, family Rutaceae.
– ORIGIN named after Jacques D. *Choisy* (1799–1859), Swiss botanist.

choke[1] ▶ **verb 1** [no obj.] (of a person or animal) have severe difficulty in breathing because of a constricted or obstructed throat or a lack of air: *Willie* ***choked on*** *a mouthful of tea.*
■[with obj.] hinder or obstruct the breathing of (a person or animal) in such a way. ■[with obj.] retard the growth of or kill (a plant) by depriving it of light, air, or nourishment: *the bracken will choke the wild gladiolus.* ■[with obj.] (often **be choked with**) fill (a passage or space), especially so as to make movement difficult or impossible: *the roads were choked with traffic.* ■[with obj.] prevent or suppress (the occurrence of something): *higher rates of interest* ***choke off*** *investment demand.*
2 [with obj.] (often **be choked**) overwhelm and make (someone) speechless with a strong and typically negative feeling or emotion: *she was choked with angry emotion* | [no obj.] *I just* ***choked up*** *reading it.*
■[no obj.] informal fail to perform at a crucial point of a sporting contest owing to a failure of nerve: *we were the only team not to choke when it came to the crunch.*
3 [with obj.] enrich the fuel mixture in (a petrol engine) by reducing the intake of air.
▶**noun 1** a valve in the carburettor of a petrol engine that is used to reduce the amount of air in the fuel mixture when the engine is started.
■a knob which controls such a valve. ■a narrowed part of a shotgun bore, typically near the muzzle and serving to restrict the spread of the shot. ■informal an electrical inductor, especially an inductance coil used to smooth the variations of an alternating current or to alter its phase.
2 an action or sound of a person or animal having or seeming to have difficulty in breathing: *a little choke of laughter.*
– ORIGIN Middle English: from Old English *ācēocian* (verb), from *cēoce* (see **CHEEK**).
▶**choke something back** suppress a strong emotion or the expression of such an emotion: *Liz was choking back her anger.*
choke something down swallow something with difficulty: *I attempted to choke down supper.*

choke[2] ▶ **noun** the inedible mass of silky fibres at the centre of a globe artichoke.
– ORIGIN late 17th cent.: probably a confusion of the ending of *artichoke* with **CHOKE**[1].

chokeberry ▶ **noun** a North American shrub of the rose family, with white flowers and red autumn foliage, cultivated as an ornamental.
• Genus *Aronia*, family Rosaceae.
■the scarlet berry-like fruit of this shrub, which is bitter and unpalatable.

choke chain ▶ **noun** a chain formed into a loop by passing one end through a ring on the other, placed round a dog's neck to exert control by causing pressure on the windpipe when the dog pulls.

choke cherry ▶ **noun** a North American cherry with astringent fruit which is edible when cooked.
• *Prunus virginiana*, family Rosaceae.

choke-damp ▶ **noun** [mass noun] choking or suffocating gas, typically carbon dioxide, that is found in mines and other underground spaces.

chokehold ▶ **noun** a tight grip round a person's neck, used to restrain them by restricting their breathing: *the police have banned chokeholds* | figurative *the southern delegates had the convention in a chokehold.*

choke point ▶ **noun** N. Amer. a point of congestion or blockage: *the tunnel is a choke point at rush hour.*

choker ▶ **noun** **1** a close-fitting necklace or ornamental neckband.
■ a clerical or other high collar.
2 N. Amer. a cable looped round a log to drag it.

chokey (also **choky**) ▶ **noun** (pl. **-eys** or **-ies**) [in sing.] Brit. informal, dated prison.
■ [mass noun] imprisonment: *three months' chokey.*
– ORIGIN early 17th cent. (in the Hindi sense): Anglo-Indian, from Hindi *caukī* 'customs or toll house, police station'; influenced by **CHOKE**[1].

chokka /ˈtsɒkə/ ▶ **noun** S. African a shallow-water squid or cuttlefish, especially of a kind used as fishing bait.
– ORIGIN from Afrikaans *tjokka*, perhaps from Portuguese *choco*, denoting a species of cuttlefish.

choko /ˈtʃəʊkəʊ/ ▶ **noun** (pl. **-os**) Austral./NZ the fruit of the chayote, eaten as a vegetable in the Caribbean, Australia, and New Zealand. Called **CHOCHO** in the Caribbean.
– ORIGIN mid 18th cent.: from Spanish *chocho*, from a Brazilian Indian word. The current spelling dates from the early 20th cent.

chokra /ˈtʃəʊkrə/ ▶ **noun** chiefly derogatory (in the Indian subcontinent) a boy, especially one employed as a servant.
– ORIGIN from Hindi *chokrā*.

Chokwe /ˈtʃɒkweɪ/ ▶ **noun** (pl. same) **1** a member of a people living in Zaire (Democratic Republic of Congo) and northern Angola.
2 [mass noun] the Bantu language of this people, with over a million speakers.
▶ **adjective** of or relating to this people or their language.

choky[1] ▶ **adjective** (**chokier**, **chokiest**) having or causing difficulty in breathing: *the whole piazza was choky with tear gas.*
■ breathless and overwhelmed with emotion: *'Nick,' she said, choky suddenly.*

choky[2] ▶ **noun** variant spelling of **CHOKEY**.

chola /ˈtʃəʊlə/ ▶ **noun** a female cholo.
– ORIGIN mid 19th cent.: American Spanish (see **CHOLO**).

cholangiography /ˌkɒlandʒɪˈɒɡrəfi/ ▶ **noun** [mass noun] Medicine X-ray examination of the bile ducts, used to locate and identify an obstruction.
– DERIVATIVES **cholangiogram** noun.
– ORIGIN 1930s: coined in Spanish from Greek *kholē* 'bile' + *angeion* 'vessel' + *-graphia* (see **-GRAPHY**).

chole- /ˈkɒli/ (also **chol-** before a vowel) ▶ **combining form** Medicine & Chemistry relating to bile or the bile ducts: *cholelithiasis* | *cholesterol.*
– ORIGIN from Greek *kholē* 'gall, bile'.

cholecalciferol /ˌkɒlɪkalˈsɪf(ə)rɒl/ ▶ **noun** [mass noun] Biochemistry one of the D vitamins, a sterol which is formed by the action of sunlight on dehydrocholesterol in the skin. Deficiency of this vitamin affects calcium levels, causing rickets in children and osteomalacia in adults. Also called ***vitamin*** D_3.

cholecyst- /ˈkɒlɪsɪst/ ▶ **combining form** relating to the gall bladder: *cholecystectomy.*
– ORIGIN from modern Latin *cholecystis* 'gall bladder'.

cholecystectomy ▶ **noun** (pl. **-ies**) [mass noun] surgical removal of the gall bladder.

cholecystitis ▶ **noun** [mass noun] Medicine inflammation of the gall bladder.

cholecystography /ˌkɒlɪsɪˈstɒɡrəfi/ ▶ **noun** [mass noun] Medicine X-ray examination of the gall bladder, especially used to detect the presence of gallstones.

cholecystokinin /ˌkɒlɪˌsɪstə(ʊ)ˈkʌɪnɪn/ ▶ **noun** [mass noun] Biochemistry a hormone which is secreted by cells in the duodenum and stimulates the release of bile into the intestine and the secretion of enzymes by the pancreas.

cholelithiasis /ˌkɒlɪlɪˈθʌɪəsɪs/ ▶ **noun** [mass noun] Medicine the formation of gallstones.

cholent /ˈtʃɒl(ə)nt, ˈʃɒ-/ ▶ **noun** [mass noun] a Jewish Sabbath dish of slowly baked meat and vegetables, prepared on a Friday and cooked overnight.
– ORIGIN from Yiddish *tsholnt*.

choler /ˈkɒlə/ ▶ **noun** [mass noun] (in medieval science and medicine) one of the four bodily humours, identified with bile, believed to be associated with a peevish or irascible temperament. Also called **YELLOW BILE**.
■ poetic/literary or archaic anger or irascibility.
– ORIGIN late Middle English (also denoting diarrhoea): from Old French *colere* 'bile, anger', from Latin *cholera* 'diarrhoea' (from Greek *kholera*), which in late Latin acquired the senses 'bile or anger', from Greek *kholē* 'bile'.

cholera /ˈkɒlərə/ ▶ **noun** [mass noun] an infectious and often fatal bacterial disease of the small intestine, typically contracted from infected water supplies and causing severe vomiting and diarrhoea.
• The disease is caused by the bacterium *Vibrio cholerae*. See **VIBRIO**.
– ORIGIN late Middle English (originally denoting bile and later applied to various ailments involving vomiting and diarrhoea): from Latin (see **CHOLER**). The current sense dates from the early 19th cent.

choleraic /ˌkɒləˈreɪɪk/ ▶ **adjective** archaic infected with cholera.

choleric /ˈkɒlərɪk/ ▶ **adjective** bad-tempered or irritable.
■ historical influenced by or predominating in the humour called choler: *a choleric disposition.*
– DERIVATIVES **cholerically** adverb.
– ORIGIN Middle English (in the sense 'bilious'): from Old French *cholerique*, via Latin from Greek *kholerikos*, from *kholera* (see **CHOLER**).

cholesterol /kəˈlɛstərɒl/ ▶ **noun** [mass noun] a compound of the sterol type found in most body tissues, including the blood and the nerves. Cholesterol and its derivatives are important constituents of cell membranes and precursors of other steroid compounds, but high concentrations in the blood (mainly derived from animal fats in the diet) are thought to promote atherosclerosis.
• Chem. formula: $C_{27}H_{45}OH$.
– ORIGIN late 19th cent.: from Greek *kholē* 'bile' + *stereos* 'stiff' + **-OL**.

choli /ˈtʃəʊli/ ▶ **noun** (pl. **cholis**) a short-sleeved bodice worn under a sari by Indian women.
– ORIGIN from Hindi *colī*.

choliamb /ˈkəʊlɪam(b)/ ▶ **noun** Prosody another term for **SCAZON**.
– DERIVATIVES **choliambic** /ˌkəʊlɪˈambɪk/ adjective.
– ORIGIN mid 19th cent.: via late Latin from Greek *khōliambos*, from *khōlos* 'lame' + *iambos* (see **IAMBUS**).

cholic acid /ˈkəʊlɪk, ˈkɒl-/ ▶ **noun** [mass noun] Biochemistry a compound produced by oxidation of cholesterol. It is a steroidal fatty acid and its salts are present in bile.
– ORIGIN mid 19th cent.: from Greek *kholikos*, from *kholē* 'bile'.

choline /ˈkəʊliːn, -lɪn/ ▶ **noun** [mass noun] Biochemistry a strongly basic compound occurring widely in living tissues and important in the synthesis and transport of lipids.
• Chem. formula: $HON(CH_3)_3CH_2CH_2OH$.
– ORIGIN mid 19th cent.: coined in German from Greek *kholē* 'bile'.

cholinergic /ˌkəʊlɪˈnəːdʒɪk/ ▶ **adjective** Physiology relating to or denoting nerve cells in which acetylcholine acts as a neurotransmitter. Contrasted with **ADRENERGIC**.
– ORIGIN 1930s: from **CHOLINE** + Greek *ergon* 'work' + **-IC**.

cholinesterase /ˌkəʊlɪˈnɛstəreɪz/ ▶ **noun** [mass noun] Biochemistry an enzyme, especially acetylcholinesterase, which hydrolyses esters of choline.

cholla /ˈtʃɔɪə/ ▶ **noun** a cactus with a cylindrical stem, native to Mexico and the south-western US.
• Genus *Opuntia*, family Cactaceae.
– ORIGIN mid 19th cent.: Mexican Spanish use of Spanish *cholla* 'skull, head', of unknown origin.

cholo /ˈtʃəʊləʊ/ ▶ **noun** (pl. **-os**) a Latin American with Indian blood; a mestizo.
■ derogatory, chiefly US a lower-class Mexican, especially in an urban area.
– ORIGIN mid 19th cent.: American Spanish, from *Cholollán* (now *Cholula*), in Mexico.

chometz /hɔːˈmɛts, ˈxɔːmɛts/ ▶ **noun** variant spelling of **CHAMETZ**.

chomp ▶ **verb** another term for **CHAMP**[1] (in sense 1).
– ORIGIN mid 17th cent.: imitative.

Chomsky /ˈtʃɒmski/, (Avram) Noam (b.1928), American theoretical linguist, noted for expounding the theory of generative grammar. He also demonstrated that linguistic behaviour is innate, not learned, and that all languages share the same underlying grammatical base. Chomsky is known also for his opposition to American involvement in the Vietnam War and the Gulf War.
– DERIVATIVES **Chomskyan** (also **Chomskian**) adjective.

Chondrichthyes /kɒnˈdrɪkθɪiːz/ Zoology a class of fishes that includes those with a cartilaginous skeleton. Compare with **OSTEICHTHYES**.
– ORIGIN modern Latin, from Greek *khondros* 'cartilage' + *ikhthus* 'fish'.

chondrite /ˈkɒndrʌɪt/ ▶ **noun** a stony meteorite containing small mineral granules (chondrules).
– DERIVATIVES **chondritic** adjective.
– ORIGIN mid 19th cent.: from Greek *khondros* 'granule' + **-ITE**[1].

chondro- /ˈkɒndrə(ʊ)/ ▶ **combining form** of or relating to cartilage: *chondrocyte.*
– ORIGIN from Greek *khondros* 'grain or cartilage'.

chondrocyte /ˈkɒndrə(ʊ)sʌɪt/ ▶ **noun** Biology a cell which has secreted the matrix of cartilage and become embedded in it.

chondroitin /kɒnˈdrəʊɪtɪn/ ▶ **noun** [mass noun] Biochemistry a compound which is a major constituent of cartilage and other connective tissue. It is a mucopolysaccharide and occurs mainly in the form of sulphate esters.
– ORIGIN late 19th cent.: from **CHONDRO-** + **-ITE**[1] + **-IN**[1].

chondrule /ˈkɒndruːl/ ▶ **noun** a spheroidal mineral grain present in large numbers in some stony meteorites.

Chongjin /tʃʌŋˈdʒɪn/ a port on the NE coast of North Korea; pop. 754,100 (est. 1984).

Chongqing /tʃʊŋˈtʃɪŋ/ (also **Chungking**) a city in Sichuan province in central China; pop. 2,960,000 (1990). It was the capital of China from 1938 to 1946.

choo-choo (also **choo-choo train**) ▶ **noun** a child's word for a railway train or locomotive, especially a steam engine.
– ORIGIN early 20th cent. (originally US): imitative.

choof /tʃʊf/ ▶ **verb** [no obj., with adverbial of direction] Austral. informal go or move in a specified direction: *so away we choofed, with Mike at the wheel.*
– ORIGIN 1940s: form of **CHUFF**, used figuratively.

chook /tʃʊk/ (also **chookie**) ▶ **noun** Austral./NZ informal **1** a chicken or fowl.
2 offensive an older woman.
– ORIGIN 1920s: probably from English dialect *chuck* 'chicken', of imitative origin.

choom /tʃʊm/ ▶ **noun** Austral./NZ informal an Englishman.
– ORIGIN early 20th cent.: representing a British English dialect pronunciation of **CHUM**[1].

choose ▶ **verb** (past **chose**; past participle **chosen**) [with obj.] pick out or select (someone or something) as being the best or most appropriate of two or more alternatives: *he chose a seat facing the door* | [no obj.] *there are many versions to* ***choose from.***
■ [no obj.] decide on a course of action, typically after rejecting alternatives: [with infinitive] *he chose to go* | *I'll stay as long as I choose.*
– PHRASES **cannot choose but do something** formal have no alternative to doing something. **there is little** (or **nothing**) **to choose between** there is little or no difference between.
– DERIVATIVES **chooser** noun.
– ORIGIN Old English *cēosan*, of Germanic origin; related to Dutch *kiezen*.

choosy ▶ **adjective** (**choosier**, **choosiest**) informal overly fastidious in making a choice.
– DERIVATIVES **choosily** adverb, **choosiness** noun.

chop[1] ▶ **verb** (**chopped**, **chopping**) [with obj.] cut (something) into small pieces with repeated sharp blows using an axe or knife: *they* ***chopped up*** *the pulpit for firewood* | *finely chop 200 g of skipjack tuna.*
■ (**chop something off**) remove by cutting: *a paper guillotine chopped off all four fingers.* ■ cut through the base of (something, especially a tree) with blows from an axe or similar implement, in order to fell it: *the boy* ***chopped down*** *eight trees* | [no obj.] *the men were* ***chopping at*** *the undergrowth with machetes.* ■ strike (a

ball) with a short heavy blow, as if cutting at something. ■ (usu. **be chopped**) abolish or reduce the size or extent of (something) in a way regarded as brutally sudden: *their training courses are to be chopped.*

▶ **noun 1** a downward cutting blow or movement, typically with the hand: *an effective chop to the back of the neck.*
2 a thick slice of meat, especially pork or lamb adjacent to, and typically including, a rib.
3 [mass noun] N. Amer. crushed or ground grain used as animal feed.
4 [in sing.] the broken motion of water, typically owing to the action of the wind against the tide: *we started our run into a two-foot chop.*
– PHRASES **the chop** Brit. informal the dismissal of someone from employment: *hundreds more workers have been given the chop.* ■ the cancellation or abolition of something: *all these projects are destined for the chop.* ■ the action of killing someone or the fact of being killed: *seven men we all knew had got the chop.* **chop logic** argue in a tiresomely pedantic way; quibble. [ORIGIN: mid 16th cent.: from a dialect use of *chop* meaning 'bandy words'.]
– ORIGIN late Middle English: variant of **CHAP**[1].

chop[2] ▶ **verb** (**chopped**, **chopping**) (in phrase **chop and change**) Brit. informal change one's opinions or behaviour repeatedly and abruptly, typically for no good reason.
– ORIGIN late Middle English (in the sense 'barter, exchange'): perhaps related to Old English *cēap* 'bargaining, trade'; compare with *chap-* in **CHAPMAN**.

chop[3] ▶ **noun** Brit. archaic a trademark; a brand of goods.
– PHRASES **not much chop** informal, chiefly Austral./NZ unsatisfactory: *that veranda's not much chop in bad weather.*
– ORIGIN early 19th cent.: from Hindi *chāp* 'stamp, brand'. The original use was in the Indian subcontinent, and subsequently in China, to denote an official stamp or seal, later a licence or permit validated by such a stamp.

chop-chop ▶ **adverb** & **exclamation** quickly; quick: *'Two pints, chop-chop,' Jimmy called.*
– ORIGIN mid 19th cent.: pidgin English, based on Chinese dialect *kuài-kuài*. Compare with **CHOPSTICK**.

chop-fallen ▶ **adjective** variant spelling of **CHAP-FALLEN**.

chophouse ▶ **noun** a restaurant, especially a cheap one.

Chopin[1] /ˈʃəʊpã/, Frédéric (François) (1810–49), Polish-born French composer and pianist; Polish name *Fryderyk Franciszek Szopen*. Writing almost exclusively for the piano, he composed numerous mazurkas and polonaises inspired by Polish folk music, as well as nocturnes, preludes, and two piano concertos (1829; 1830).

Chopin[2] /ˈʃəʊpan/, Kate (O'Flaherty) (1851–1904), American novelist and short-story writer. Notable works: *Bayou Folk* (1894), *A Night in Acidie* (1897), and *The Awakening* (1899).

chopper ▶ **noun 1** Brit. a short axe with a large blade.
■ a butcher's cleaver: *a meat chopper.* ■ a machine for chopping something: *a straw chopper.* ■ a device for regularly interrupting an electric current or a beam of light or particles. ■ (**choppers**) informal teeth.
2 informal a helicopter.
3 informal a type of motorcycle with high handlebars and the front-wheel fork extended forwards.
4 vulgar slang a man's penis.

chopping block ▶ **noun** a block for chopping something on, in particular:
■ a block for chopping wood. ■ a block for chopping food such as meat, vegetables, and herbs. ■ historical an executioner's block.
– PHRASES **on the chopping block** likely to be abolished or drastically reduced.

chopping board ▶ **noun** a board on which vegetables and other types of food are chopped.

choppy ▶ **adjective** (**choppier**, **choppiest**) (of a sea or river) having many small waves.
– DERIVATIVES **choppily** adverb, **choppiness** noun.
– ORIGIN early 17th cent. (in the sense 'full of chaps or clefts'): from **CHOP**[1] + **-Y**[1].

chops ▶ **plural noun** informal **1** a person's or animal's mouth or jaws: *a smack in the chops.*
■ a person's cheeks: *his wobbling chops.*
2 the technical skill of a musician, especially one who plays jazz: *when I'm on tour my chops go down.*
– PHRASES **bust one's chops** N. Amer. informal exert oneself: **bust someone's chops** N. Amer. informal nag or criticize someone.
– ORIGIN late Middle English: variant of **CHAP**[3].

chop shop ▶ **noun** N. Amer. informal a place where stolen vehicles are dismantled so that the parts can be sold or used to repair other stolen vehicles.

chopsocky /ˈtʃɒpsɒki/ ▶ **noun** [mass noun] [usu. as modifier] N. Amer. informal kung fu or a similar martial art, especially as depicted in violent action films: *chopsocky epics from Hong Kong.*
– ORIGIN 1970s: perhaps humorously, suggested by **CHOP SUEY**.

chopstick ▶ **noun** (usu. **chopsticks**) each of a pair of small, thin, tapered sticks of wood, ivory, or plastic, held together in one hand and used as eating utensils, especially by the Chinese, the Japanese, and other people in east Asia.
– ORIGIN late 17th cent.: pidgin English, from *chop* 'quick' + **STICK**[1], translating Chinese dialect *kuàizi*, literally 'nimble ones'. Compare with **CHOP-CHOP**.

chop suey /tʃɒpˈsuːi/ ▶ **noun** [mass noun] a Chinese-style dish of meat stewed and fried with bean sprouts, bamboo shoots, and onions, and served with rice.
– ORIGIN late 19th cent.: from Chinese (Cantonese dialect) *tsaâp suì* 'mixed bits'.

choral ▶ **adjective** composed for or sung by a choir or chorus: *a choral work | choral singing.*
■ engaged in or concerned with singing: *a choral scholar.*
– DERIVATIVES **chorally** adverb.
– ORIGIN late 16th cent.: from medieval Latin *choralis*, from Latin *chorus* (see **CHORUS**).

chorale ▶ **noun 1** a musical composition (or part of one) consisting of or resembling a harmonized version of a simple, stately hymn tune.
■ a hymn tune of this kind, especially one associated with the German Lutheran church.
2 chiefly US a choir or choral society.
– ORIGIN mid 19th cent.: from German *Choral(gesang)*, translating medieval Latin *cantus choralis*.

chord[1] ▶ **noun** a group of (typically three or more) notes sounded together, as a basis of harmony: *the triumphal opening chords | a G major chord.*
▶ **verb** [no obj.] [usu. as noun **chording**] play, sing, or arrange notes in chords.
– DERIVATIVES **chordal** adjective.
– ORIGIN Middle English *cord*, from **ACCORD**. The spelling change in the 18th cent. was due to confusion with **CHORD**[2]. The original sense was 'agreement, reconciliation', later 'a musical concord or harmonious sound'; the current sense dates from the mid 18th cent.

chord[2] ▶ **noun 1** Mathematics a straight line joining the ends of an arc.
■ Aeronautics the width of an aerofoil from leading to trailing edge. ■ Engineering each of the two principal members of a truss.
2 Anatomy variant spelling of **CORD**: *spinal chord.*
3 poetic/literary a string on a harp or other instrument.
– PHRASES **strike** (or **touch**) **a chord** affect or stir someone's emotions: *the issue of food safety strikes a chord with almost everyone.* [ORIGIN: with figurative reference to the emotions being the 'strings' of the mind visualized as a musical instrument.] **strike** (or **touch**) **the right chord** skilfully appeal to or arouse a particular emotion in others: *Dickens knew how to strike the right chord in the hearts of his readers.*
– ORIGIN mid 16th cent. (in the anatomical sense): a later spelling (influenced by Latin *chorda* 'rope') of **CORD**.

Chordata /kɔːˈdeɪtə/ Zoology a large phylum of animals that includes the vertebrates together with the sea squirts and lancelets. They are distinguished by the possession of a notochord at some stage during their development.
– DERIVATIVES **chordate** /ˈkɔːdeɪt/ noun & adjective.
– ORIGIN modern Latin (plural), from Latin *chorda* (see **CHORD**[2]), on the pattern of words such as *Vertebrata.*

chord line ▶ **noun** a railway route across the outer parts of an urban area.

chordophone /ˈkɔːdəfəʊn/ ▶ **noun** Music, technical a stringed instrument.

chordotonal /ˌkɔːdə(ʊ)ˈtəʊn(ə)l/ ▶ **adjective** Entomology (in insects) denoting sense organs which are responsive to mechanical and sound vibrations.
– ORIGIN late 19th cent.: from **CHORD**[2] + **TONAL**.

chore ▶ **noun** a routine task, especially a household one.
■ an unpleasant but necessary task: *he sees interviews as a chore.*
– ORIGIN mid 18th cent. (originally dialect and US): variant of obsolete *char* or *chare* (see **CHARWOMAN**).

chorea /kɒˈrɪə/ ▶ **noun** [mass noun] Medicine a neurological disorder characterized by jerky involuntary movements affecting especially the shoulders, hips, and face. See also **HUNTINGTON'S CHOREA**, **SYDENHAM'S CHOREA**.
– ORIGIN late 17th cent.: via Latin from Greek *khoreia* 'dancing in unison', from *khoros* 'chorus'.

choreograph /ˈkɒrɪəgrɑːf/ ▶ **verb** [with obj.] compose the sequence of steps and moves for (a ballet or other performance of dance).
■ figurative plan and control (an event or operation): *the committee choreographs the movement of troops.*
– DERIVATIVES **choreographer** noun.
– ORIGIN 1940s: back-formation from **CHOREOGRAPHY**.

choreography /ˌkɒrɪˈɒgrəfi/ ▶ **noun** [mass noun] the sequence of steps and movements in dance or figure skating, especially in a ballet or other staged dance: *the rumbustious choreography reflects the themes of the original play.*
■ the art or practice of designing such sequences. ■ the written notation for such a sequence.
– DERIVATIVES **choreographic** adjective, **choreographically** adverb.
– ORIGIN late 18th cent. (in the sense 'written notation of dancing'): from Greek *khoreia* 'dancing in unison' (from *khoros* 'chorus') + **-GRAPHY**.

choreology /ˌkɒrɪˈɒlədʒi/ ▶ **noun** [mass noun] the notation of dance movement.
– DERIVATIVES **choreologist** noun.
– ORIGIN 1960s: from Greek *khoreia* 'dancing in unison' (from *khoros* 'chorus') + **-LOGY**.

choriambus /ˌkɒrɪˈambəs/ ▶ **noun** (pl. **choriambi** /-bʌɪ/) a metrical foot consisting of two short (or unstressed) syllables between two long (or stressed) ones.
– DERIVATIVES **choriambic** adjective.
– ORIGIN late 18th cent.: via late Latin from Greek *khoriambos*, from *khoreios* 'of the dance' + *iambos* (see **IAMBUS**).

choric /ˈkɒrɪk, ˈkɔːrɪk/ ▶ **adjective** belonging to, spoken by, or resembling a chorus in drama or recitation.
– ORIGIN mid 19th cent.: via late Latin from Greek *khorikos*, from *khoros* 'chorus'.

chorine /ˈkɔːriːn/ ▶ **noun** a chorus girl.
– ORIGIN 1920s (originally US): from **CHORUS** + **-INE**[3].

chorio- /ˈkɔːrɪəʊ/ ▶ **combining form** representing **CHORION** or **CHOROID**.

chorioallantoic /ˌkɔːrɪəʊˌalənˈtəʊɪk, ˌkɒrɪəʊ-/ ▶ **adjective** Embryology relating to or denoting fused chorionic and allantoic membranes around a fetus.

choriocarcinoma /ˌkɔːrɪə(ʊ)ˌkɑːsɪˈnəʊmə, ˈkɒr-/ ▶ **noun** (pl. **choriocarcinomas** or **choriocarcinomata** /-mətə/) Medicine a malignant tumour of the uterus which originates in the cells of the chorion of a fetus.

chorion /ˈkɔːrɪən/ ▶ **noun** Embryology the outermost membrane surrounding an embryo of a reptile, bird, or mammal. In mammals (including humans) it contributes to the formation of the placenta.
– DERIVATIVES **chorionic** adjective.
– ORIGIN mid 16th cent.: from Greek *khorion*.

chorionic gonadotrophin /ˌkɒrɪˈɒnɪk/ ▶ **noun** [mass noun] a hormone secreted during pregnancy by the placenta which stimulates continued production of progesterone by the ovaries. Injection of **human chorionic gonadotrophin** (**HCG**) is used to treat some disorders of the reproductive system.

chorionic villus sampling (abbrev.: **CVS**) ▶ **noun** [mass noun] Medicine a test made in early pregnancy to detect congenital abnormalities in the fetus. A tiny tissue sample is taken from the villi of the chorion, which forms the fetal part of the placenta.

chorister ▶ **noun 1** a member of a choir, especially

a child or young person singing the treble part in a church choir.

2 US a person who leads the singing of a church choir or congregation.

– ORIGIN late Middle English *queristre*, from an Anglo-Norman French variant of Old French *cueriste*, from *quer* (see **CHOIR**). The change in the first syllable in the 16th cent. was due to association with obsolete *chorist* 'member of a choir or chorus', but the older form *quirister* long survived.

chorizo /tʃəˈriːzəʊ, Spanish tʃoˈriθo, -ˈriso/ ▶ **noun** (pl. **-os**) a spicy Spanish pork sausage.

– ORIGIN Spanish.

chorography /kɔːˈrɒɡrəfi/ ▶ **noun** [mass noun] chiefly historical the systematic description and mapping of regions or districts.

– DERIVATIVES **chorographer** noun, **chorographic** adjective.

– ORIGIN mid 16th cent.: via Latin from Greek *khōrographia*, from *khōra* or *khōros* 'region'.

choroid /ˈkɔːrɔɪd, ˈkɒr-/ ▶ **adjective** resembling the chorion, particularly in containing many blood vessels.

▶ **noun** the pigmented vascular layer of the eyeball between the retina and the sclera.

– DERIVATIVES **choroidal** adjective.

– ORIGIN mid 17th cent.: from Greek *khoroeidēs* (adjective), alteration of *khorioeidēs*, from *khorion* (see **CHORION**).

choroid coat ▶ **noun** another term for **CHOROID**.

choroid plexus /ˈkɔːrɔɪd, ˈkɒr-/ ▶ **noun** (pl. same or **plexuses**) a network of blood vessels in each ventricle of the brain. It is derived from the pia mater and produces the cerebrospinal fluid.

choropleth map /ˈkɒrə(ʊ)plɛθ/ ▶ **noun** a map which uses differences in shading, colouring, or the placing of symbols within predefined areas to indicate the average values of a property or quantity in those areas. Compare with **ISOPLETH**.

– ORIGIN 1930s: *choropleth* from Greek *khōra* 'region' + *plēthos* 'multitude'.

chorten /ˈtʃɔːt(ə)n/ ▶ **noun** (chiefly in Tibet) a Buddhist shrine, typically a saint's tomb or a monument to the Buddha.

– ORIGIN Tibetan.

chortle ▶ **verb** [no obj.] laugh in a breathy, gleeful way; chuckle: *he **chortled at** his own execrable pun.*

▶ **noun** a breathy, gleeful laugh: *Thomas gave a chortle.*

– ORIGIN 1871: coined by Lewis Carroll in *Through the Looking Glass*; probably a blend of **CHUCKLE** and **SNORT**.

chorus ▶ **noun** (pl. **choruses**) **1** a large organized group of singers, especially one which performs together with an orchestra or opera company.

■ a group of singers or dancers performing together in a supporting role in a stage musical or opera. ■ a piece of choral music, especially one forming part of a larger work such as an opera or oratorio. ■ a part of a song which is repeated after each verse, typically by more than one singer. ■ a simple song for group singing, especially in informal Christian worship.

2 (in ancient Greek tragedy) a group of performers who comment on the main action, typically speaking and moving together.

■ a simultaneous utterance of something by many people: *a growing **chorus of** complaint | 'Good morning,' we replied **in chorus**.* ■ a single character who speaks the prologue and other linking parts of the play, especially in Elizabethan drama. ■ a section of text spoken by the chorus in drama. ■ a device used with an amplified musical instrument to give the impression that more than one instrument is being played: [as modifier] *a chorus pedal.*

▶ **verb** (**chorused**, **chorusing**) [with obj.] (of a group of people) say the same thing at the same time: *they chorused a noisy amen | [with direct speech] 'Morning, Sister,' the nurses chorused.*

– ORIGIN mid 16th cent. (denoting a character speaking the prologue and epilogue in a play and serving to comment on events): from Latin, from Greek *khoros*.

chorus girl ▶ **noun** a young woman who sings or dances in the chorus of a musical.

chose past of **CHOOSE**.

chosen past participle of **CHOOSE**. ▶ **adjective** [attrib.] having been selected as the best or most appropriate: *the law—his chosen profession.*

– PHRASES **chosen few** a group of people who are special or different, typically in a way thought to be unfair: *why have they kept this secret to themselves, the chosen few?* **chosen people** those selected by God for a special relationship with him, especially the people of Israel; the Jews. ■ those destined to be saved by God; believing Christians.

chota /ˈtʃəʊtə/ ▶ **adjective** Indian small: *a chota peg.*

■ lower in rank or importance: *a chota chaudhuri.*

– ORIGIN from Hindi *choṭā*.

Chou /tʃəʊ/ variant spelling of **ZHOU**.

choucroute /ˈʃuːkruːt/ ▶ **noun** [mass noun] pickled cabbage; sauerkraut.

– ORIGIN French, from German dialect *Surkrut* 'sauerkraut', influenced by French *chou* 'cabbage'.

Chou En-lai /ˌtʃəʊ ɛnˈlʌɪ/ variant of **ZHOU ENLAI**.

chough /tʃʌf/ ▶ **noun 1** a black Eurasian and North African bird of the crow family, with a downcurved bill and broad rounded wings, typically frequenting mountains and sea cliffs.

● Genus *Pyrrhocorax* (and *Pseudopodoces*), family Corvidae: three species, especially the (**red-billed**) **chough** (*P. pyrrhocorax*), with a long red bill, and the **alpine chough** (*P. graculus*), with a shorter yellow bill.

2 (also **white-winged chough**) an Australian bird of the mud-nester family, somewhat resembling the red-billed chough.

● *Corcorax melanorhamphos*, family Corcoracidae (or Grallinidae).

– ORIGIN Middle English (originally denoting the jackdaw): probably imitative.

choux pastry /ʃuː/ ▶ **noun** [mass noun] very light pastry made with egg, typically used for eclairs and profiteroles.

– ORIGIN late 19th cent.: from *choux* or *chou*, denoting a round cream-filled pastry cake (from French *chou* (plural *choux*) 'cabbage, rosette', from Latin *caulis*) + **PASTRY**.

chow /tʃaʊ/ ▶ **noun 1** [mass noun] informal, chiefly N. Amer. food.

2 (also **chow chow**) a dog of a sturdy Chinese breed with a broad muzzle, a tail curled over the back, a bluish-black tongue, and typically a dense thick coat.

– ORIGIN late 19th cent.: shortened from **CHOW CHOW**.

▶ **chow down** (or **chow something down**) N. Amer. informal eat: *he chowed down on lobster | lions chow down their kills.*

chow chow ▶ **noun 1** another term for **CHOW** (in sense 2).

2 [mass noun] a Chinese preserve of ginger, orange peel, and other ingredients, in syrup.

3 [mass noun] a mixed vegetable pickle.

– ORIGIN late 18th cent.: pidgin English, of unknown ultimate origin.

chowder ▶ **noun** [mass noun] a rich soup typically containing fish, clams, or corn with potatoes and onions: *clam chowder.*

– ORIGIN mid 18th cent.: perhaps from French *chaudière* 'stew pot', related to Old Northern French *caudron* (see **CAULDRON**).

chowderhead ▶ **noun** N. Amer. informal a stupid person.

– DERIVATIVES **chowderheaded** adjective.

– ORIGIN mid 19th cent.: probably a variant form of early 17th-cent. *jolter-head* 'thick-headed person'.

chowk /tʃaʊk/ ▶ **noun** [usu. in names] (in the Indian subcontinent) an open market area in a city at the junction of two roads: *Chandni Chowk.*

– ORIGIN from Hindi *cauk*.

chowkidar /ˈtʃəʊkɪˌdɑː/ ▶ **noun** (in the Indian subcontinent) a watchman or gatekeeper.

– ORIGIN from Urdu *caukīdār*, from *caukī* 'toll house' + *-dār* 'keeper'.

chow mein /tʃaʊ ˈmeɪn/ ▶ **noun** [mass noun] a Chinese-style dish of fried noodles with shredded meat or seafood and vegetables.

– ORIGIN late 19th cent.: from Chinese *chǎo miàn* 'fried noodles'.

CHP ▶ **abbreviation for** combined heat and power, a system in which steam produced in a power station as a by-product of electricity generation is used to heat nearby buildings.

Chr. ▶ **abbreviation for** Chronicles (in biblical references).

chrestomathy /krɛˈstɒməθi/ ▶ **noun** (pl. **-ies**) formal a selection of passages from an author or authors, designed to help in learning a language.

– ORIGIN mid 19th cent.: from Greek *khrēstomatheia*, from *khrēstos* 'useful' + *-matheia* 'learning'.

Chrétien /ˈkreɪtjã, French kretjɛ̃/, (Joseph-Jacques) Jean (b.1934), Canadian Liberal statesman, Prime Minister since 1993.

Chrétien de Troyes /ˌkreɪtjã də ˈtrwʌ, French kretjɛ̃ də trwa/ (12th century), French poet. His courtly romances on Arthurian themes include *Lancelot* (*c.*1177–81) and *Perceval* (1181–90, unfinished).

Chrimbo (also **Crimbo**) ▶ **noun** Brit. informal Christmas.

– ORIGIN 1980s: child's alteration.

chrism /ˈkrɪz(ə)m/ ▶ **noun** [mass noun] a mixture of oil and balsam, consecrated and used for anointing at baptism and in other rites of Catholic, Orthodox, and Anglican Churches.

– ORIGIN Old English, from medieval Latin *crisma*, ecclesiastical Latin *chrisma*, from Greek *khrisma* 'anointing', from *khriein* 'anoint'.

chrisom /ˈkrɪz(ə)m/ (also **chrisom-cloth**) ▶ **noun** historical a white robe put on a child at baptism, and used as its shroud if it died within the month.

– ORIGIN Middle English: alteration of **CHRISM**, representing a popular pronunciation with two syllables.

Chrissake /ˈkrʌɪseɪk/ (also **Chrissakes**) ▶ **noun** (in phrase **for Chrissake**) informal for Christ's sake (used as an exclamation, typically of annoyance or exasperation): *for Chrissake, listen to me!*

– ORIGIN 1920s: representing a pronunciation.

Chrissie (also **Chrissy**) ▶ **noun** Brit. informal Christmas.

Christ ▶ **noun** the title, also treated as a name, given to Jesus of Nazareth (see **JESUS**).

▶ **exclamation** an oath used to express irritation, dismay, or surprise.

– PHRASES **before Christ** full form of **BC**.

– DERIVATIVES **Christhood** noun, **Christlike** adjective, **Christly** adjective.

– ORIGIN Old English *Crīst*, from Latin *Christus*, from Greek *Khristos*, noun use of an adjective meaning 'anointed', from *khriein* 'anoint', translating Hebrew *māšīaḥ* 'Messiah'.

Christadelphian /ˌkrɪstəˈdɛlfɪən/ ▶ **noun** a member of a Christian sect, founded in America in 1848, which claims to return to the beliefs and practices of the earliest disciples and holds that Christ will return in power to set up a worldwide theocracy beginning at Jerusalem.

▶ **adjective** of or adhering to this sect and its beliefs.

– ORIGIN from late Greek *Khristadelphos* 'in brotherhood with Christ' (from *Khristos* 'Christ' + *adelphos* 'brother') + **-IAN**.

Christchurch a city on South Island, New Zealand; pop. 303,400 (1990).

christen ▶ **verb** [with obj.] (often **be christened**) give (a baby) a Christian name at baptism as a sign of admission to a Christian Church: [with obj. and complement] *their second daughter was christened Jeanette.*

■ give a name to (someone or something) which reflects a notable quality or characteristic: [with obj. and complement] *we have christened our regular train home the ghost train.* ■ informal use for the first time.

– DERIVATIVES **christener** noun.

– ORIGIN Old English *crīstnian* 'make Christian', from *crīsten* 'Christian', from Latin *Christianus*, from *Christus* 'Christ'.

Christendom ▶ **noun** [mass noun] dated the worldwide body or society of Christians.

■ the Christian world: *the greatest church in Christendom.*

– ORIGIN Old English *crīstendōm*, from *crīsten* (see **CHRISTEN**) + *-dōm* (see **-DOM**).

Christer /ˈkrʌɪstə/ ▶ **noun** N. Amer. informal a sanctimonious or ostentatiously pious Christian.

Christian[1] /ˈkrɪstɪən, ˈkrɪstʃən/, Fletcher (*c.*1764–*c.*1793), English seaman and mutineer. As first mate under Captain Bligh on HMS *Bounty*, in April 1789 Christian seized the ship and cast Bligh and others adrift. In 1790 the mutineers settled on Pitcairn Island, where Christian was probably killed by Tahitians.

Christian[2] /ˈkrɪstɪən, -tʃ(ə)n/ ▶ **adjective** of, relating to, or professing Christianity or its teachings: *the Christian Church.*

■ informal having or showing qualities associated with Christians, especially those of decency, kindness, and fairness.

▶ **noun** a person who has received Christian baptism or is a believer in Jesus Christ and his teachings.

– DERIVATIVES **Christianization** noun, **Christianize** (also **-ise**) verb, **Christianly** adverb.

– ORIGIN late Middle English: from Latin *Christianus*, from *Christus* 'Christ'.

Christian Aid a charity supported by most of the Christian Churches in the UK and operating chiefly in developing countries, where it works for disaster relief and supports development projects.

Christian Brothers a Roman Catholic lay teaching order founded in France in 1684.

Christian era ▸ noun (**the Christian era**) the period of time which begins with the traditional date of Christ's birth.

Christiania /ˌkrɪstɪˈɑːnɪə/ (also **Kristiania**) former name (1624–1924) for **OSLO**.

Christianity ▸ noun [mass noun] the religion based on the person and teachings of Jesus of Nazareth, or its beliefs and practices.
■ Christian quality or character: *you may know a man by his Christianity.*

Christianity is today the world's most widespread religion, with more than a billion members, mainly divided between the Roman Catholic, Protestant, and Eastern Orthodox Churches. It originated among the Jewish followers of Jesus of Nazareth, who believed that he was the promised Messiah (or 'Christ'), but the Christian Church soon became an independent organization, largely through the missionary efforts of St Paul. In 313 Constantine ended official persecution in the Roman Empire and in 380 Theodosius I recognized it as the state religion. Most Christians believe in one God in three Persons (the Father, the Son, and the Holy Spirit) and that Jesus is the Son of God who rose from the dead after being crucified; a Christian hopes to attain eternal life after death through faith in Jesus Christ and tries to live by his teachings as recorded in the New Testament.

– ORIGIN Middle English: from Old French *crestiente*, from *crestien* 'Christian', influenced by late Latin *christianitas*, from Latin *Christianus*, from *Christus* 'Christ'.

Christian name ▸ noun a name given to an individual that distinguishes them from other members of the same family and is used to address them familiarly; a forename, especially one given at baptism.

USAGE In recognition of the fact that English-speaking societies have many religions and cultures, not just Christian ones, the term **Christian name** has largely given way, at least in official contexts, to alternative terms such as **given name**, **first name**, or **forename**.

Christian Science ▸ noun [mass noun] the beliefs and practices of the Church of Christ Scientist, a Christian sect founded by Mary Baker Eddy in 1879. Members hold that only God and the mind have ultimate reality, and that sin and illness are illusions which can be overcome by prayer and faith.
– DERIVATIVES **Christian Scientist** noun.

Christie[1], Dame Agatha (1890–1976), English writer of detective fiction. Notable works: *Murder on the Orient Express* (1934), *Death on the Nile* (1937), and *The Mousetrap* (play, 1952).

Christie[2], Linford (b.1960), Jamaican-born British sprinter who won the Olympic gold medal in the 100 metres in 1992 and the world championship title at this distance in 1993.

Christie[3] ▸ noun (pl. **-ies**) Skiing, dated a sudden turn in which the skis are kept parallel, used for changing direction fast or stopping short.
– ORIGIN 1920s (earlier as *Christiania*): named after **CHRISTIANIA** in Norway.

Christingle /ˈkrɪstɪŋɡ(ə)l/ ▸ noun a lighted candle symbolizing Christ as the light of the world, held by children especially at a special Advent service originating in the Moravian Church.
– ORIGIN 1950s: probably from German dialect *Christkindl* 'Christ-child, Christmas gift'.

Christmas ▸ noun (pl. **Christmases**) the annual Christian festival celebrating Christ's birth, held on 25 December.
■ the period immediately before and after 25 December: *we had guests over Christmas.*
▸ exclamation informal expressing surprise, dismay, or despair.
– DERIVATIVES **Christmassy** adjective.
– ORIGIN Old English *Crīstes mæsse* (see **CHRIST**, **MASS**).

Christmas beètle ▸ noun S. African any of a number of cicadas whose males produce a shrill mating song during the summer.

Christmas box ▸ noun Brit. a present or gratuity given at Christmas to tradespeople and employees.

Christmas cake ▸ noun Brit. a rich fruit cake

typically covered with marzipan and icing, eaten at Christmas.

Christmas card ▸ noun a greetings card sent at Christmas.

Christmas Day ▸ noun the day on which the festival of Christmas is celebrated, 25 December.

Christmas disease ▸ noun [mass noun] a form of haemophilia caused by deficiency of a blood-clotting factor (Factor IX) different from the usual one.
– ORIGIN 1950s: *Christmas*, from the surname of the first patient examined in detail.

Christmas Eve the day or the evening before Christmas Day, 24 December.

Christmas flower ▸ noun S. African the hydrangea, which in South Africa typically blooms at Christmas.

Christmas Island 1 an island in the Indian Ocean 350 km (200 miles) south of Java, administered as an external territory of Australia since 1958; pop. 1,275 (1991).
2 former name (until 1981) for **KIRITIMATI**.

Christmas pudding ▸ noun Brit. a rich boiled pudding eaten at Christmas, made with flour, suet, and dried fruit.

Christmas rose ▸ noun **1** a small white-flowered winter-blooming hellebore, widely grown as a house plant.
● *Helleborus niger*, family Ranunculaceae.
2 S. African another term for **CHRISTMAS FLOWER**.

Christmas stocking ▸ noun a real or ornamental stocking hung up by children on Christmas Eve for Father Christmas to fill with presents.

Christmas tree ▸ noun an evergreen (typically spruce) or artificial tree set up and decorated with lights, tinsel, and other ornaments as part of Christmas celebrations.
■ NZ another term for **POHUTUKAWA**.

Christo- ▸ combining form of or relating to Christ: *Christocentric* | *Christology.*
– ORIGIN from Latin *Christus* or Greek *Khristos* 'Christ'.

Christocentric ▸ adjective having Christ as its centre: *a thoroughly Christocentric theology.*

Christology ▸ noun [mass noun] the branch of Christian theology relating to the person, nature, and role of Christ.
– DERIVATIVES **Christological** adjective, **Christologically** adverb.

Christopher, St a legendary Christian martyr, adopted as the patron saint of travellers, since it is said that he once carried Christ in the form of a child across a river.

christophine /ˈkrɪstəfiːn/ (also **christophene**) ▸ noun another term for **CHAYOTE** (in sense 1).
– ORIGIN probably based on the French given name *Christophe.*

Christ's thorn ▸ noun a thorny shrub popularly supposed to have formed Christ's crown of thorns, in particular:
● either of two shrubs related to the buckthorn (*Paliurus spina-christi* and *Ziziphus spina-christi*, family Rhamnaceae).
■ another term for **CROWN OF THORNS** (in sense 2).

chroma /ˈkrəʊmə/ ▸ noun [mass noun] purity or intensity of colour.
– ORIGIN late 19th cent.: from Greek *khrōma* 'colour'.

chromaffin /krə(ʊ)ˈmafɪn/ ▸ adjective [attrib.] Physiology denoting granules or vesicles containing adrenalin and noradrenaline, and the secretory cells of the adrenal medulla in which they are found.
– ORIGIN early 20th cent.: from **CHROMO-**[1] 'chromium' + Latin *affinis* 'akin' (because readily stained brown by chromates).

chromakey /ˈkrəʊməkiː/ ▸ noun [mass noun] a technique by which a block of a particular colour in a video image can be replaced either by another colour or by a separate image, enabling, for example, a weather forecaster to appear against a background of a computer-generated weather map.
▸ verb (**-eys**, **-eyed**) [with obj.] manipulate (an image) using this technique.

chromate /ˈkrəʊmeɪt/ ▸ noun Chemistry a salt in which the anion contains both chromium and oxygen, especially one of the anion CrO_4^{2-}.
– ORIGIN early 19th cent.: from **CHROMIC** + **-ATE**[1].

chromatic ▸ adjective **1** Music relating to or using notes not belonging to the diatonic scale of the key in which a passage is written.
■ (of a scale) ascending or descending by semitones.
■ (of an instrument) able to play all the notes of the chromatic scale.
2 of, relating to, or produced by colour.
– DERIVATIVES **chromatically** adverb, **chromaticism** noun.
– ORIGIN early 17th cent.: from French *chromatique* or Latin *chromaticus*, from Greek *khrōmatikos*, from *khrōma*, *khrōmat-* 'colour, chromatic scale'.

chromatic aberration ▸ noun [mass noun] Optics the effect produced by the refraction of different wavelengths of electromagnetic radiation through slightly different angles, resulting in a failure to focus. It causes coloured fringes in the images produced by uncorrected lenses.

chromaticity /ˌkrəʊməˈtɪsɪti/ ▸ noun [mass noun] the quality of colour, independent of brightness.

chromatid /ˈkrəʊmətɪd/ ▸ noun Biology each of the two thread-like strands into which a chromosome divides longitudinally during cell division. Each contains a double helix of DNA.
– ORIGIN early 20th cent.: from Greek *khrōma*, *khrōmat-* 'colour' + **-ID**[2].

chromatin /ˈkrəʊmətɪn/ ▸ noun [mass noun] Biology the material of which the chromosomes of organisms other than bacteria (i.e. eukaryotes) are composed. It consists of protein, RNA, and DNA.
– ORIGIN late 19th cent.: coined in German from Greek *khrōma*, *khrōmat-* 'colour'.

chromato- /ˈkrəʊmətəʊ/ (also **chromo-**) ▸ combining form colour; of or in colours: *chromatopsia* | *chromosome.*
– ORIGIN from Greek *khrōma*, *khrōmat-* 'colour'.

chromatogram /krə(ʊ)ˈmatəɡram/ ▸ noun a visible record (such as a series of coloured bands, or a graph) showing the result of separation of the components of a mixture by chromatography.

chromatograph ▸ noun an apparatus for performing chromatography.
■ another term for **CHROMATOGRAM**.

chromatography /ˌkrəʊməˈtɒɡrəfi/ ▸ noun [mass noun] Chemistry the separation of a mixture by passing it in solution or suspension through a medium in which the components move at different rates.
– DERIVATIVES **chromatographic** adjective.
– ORIGIN 1930s: from German *Chromatographie* (see **CHROMATO-**, **-GRAPHY**). The name alludes to the earliest separations when the result was displayed as a number of coloured bands or spots.

chromatopsia /ˌkrəʊməˈtɒpsɪə/ ▸ noun [mass noun] Medicine abnormally coloured vision, a rare symptom of varied cause.
– ORIGIN mid 19th cent.: from **CHROMATO-** 'colour' + Greek *-opsia* 'seeing'.

chrome ▸ noun [mass noun] chromium plate as a decorative or protective finish on motor-vehicle fittings and other objects: [as modifier] *a chrome bumper.*
■ [as modifier] denoting compounds or alloys of chromium: *chrome dyes.* ■ short for **CHROME YELLOW**.
– ORIGIN early 19th cent.: from French, from Greek *khrōma* 'colour' (because of the brilliant colours of chromium compounds).

chrome alum ▸ noun [mass noun] a reddish-purple crystalline compound used in solution in photographic processing and as a mordant in dyeing.
● Chem. formula: $K_2SO_4Cr_2(SO_4)_3.24H_2O$.

chromed ▸ adjective chromium-plated.

chrome leather ▸ noun [mass noun] leather tanned with chromium salts.

chrome steel ▸ noun [mass noun] a hard fine-grained steel containing chromium, used for making tools.

chrome yellow ▸ noun a bright yellow pigment made from lead chromate, now little used.

chromic /ˈkrəʊmɪk/ ▸ adjective Chemistry of chromium with a higher valency, usually three. Compare with **CHROMOUS**.

chromic acid ▸ noun [mass noun] Chemistry a corrosive and strongly oxidizing acid existing only in solutions of chromium trioxide.
● Chem. formula: H_2CrO_4.

chromide ▸ noun a small deep-bodied fish of India

and Sri Lanka, typically occurring in brackish water.
● Genus *Etroplus*, family Cichlidae: the **orange chromide** (*E. maculatus*) and the **green chromide** (*E. suratensis*).
– ORIGIN 1930s: from modern Latin *Chromides* (former order name), formed irregularly from *Chromis* (genus name), from Latin *chromis* 'sea fish'.

chrominance /ˈkrəʊmɪnəns/ ▶ noun [mass noun] the colorimetric difference between a given colour in a television picture and a standard colour of equal luminance.
– ORIGIN 1950s: from Greek *khrōma* 'colour', on the pattern of *luminance*.

chromite /ˈkrəʊmʌɪt/ ▶ noun [mass noun] a brownish-black mineral which consists of a mixed oxide of chromium and iron and is the principal ore of chromium.
– ORIGIN mid 19th cent.: from **CHROME** or **CHROMIUM** + **-ITE**[1].

chromium ▶ noun [mass noun] the chemical element of atomic number 24, a hard white metal used in stainless steel and other alloys. (Symbol: **Cr**)
– ORIGIN early 19th cent.: from **CHROME** + **-IUM**.

chromium plate ▶ noun [mass noun] a decorative or protective coating of metallic chromium.
■ metal with such a coating.
▶ verb (**chromium-plate**) [with obj.] coat with chromium, typically by electrolytic deposition.

chromium steel ▶ noun another term for **CHROME STEEL**.

chromo /ˈkrəʊməʊ/ ▶ noun (pl. **-os**) N. Amer. shortened form of **CHROMOLITHOGRAPH**.

chromo-[1] /ˈkrəʊməʊ/ ▶ combining form Chemistry representing **CHROMIUM**.

chromo-[2] /ˈkrəʊməʊ/ ▶ combining form variant spelling of **CHROMATO-**.

chromodynamics ▶ plural noun see **QUANTUM CHROMODYNAMICS**.

chromogen /ˈkrəʊmə(ʊ)dʒ(ə)n/ ▶ noun a substance which can be readily converted into a dye or other coloured compound.

chromogenic ▶ adjective involving the production of colour or pigments, in particular:
■ Photography denoting a modern process of developing film which uses couplers to produce black-and-white images of very high definition. ■ Photography denoting any of a number of similar developing processes. ■ Microbiology (of a bacterium) producing a pigment.

chromolithograph historical ▶ noun a coloured picture printed by lithography, especially in the late 19th and early 20th centuries.
▶ verb [with obj.] print or produce (a picture) by this process.
– DERIVATIVES **chromolithographer** noun, **chromolithographic** adjective, **chromolithography** noun.

chromoly /ˈkrəʊmɒli/ ▶ noun [mass noun] a form of steel containing chromium and molybdenum, used to make strong, lightweight components such as bicycle frames.
– ORIGIN 1980s: blend of **CHROMIUM** and **MOLYBDENUM**.

chromophore /ˈkrəʊməfɔː/ ▶ noun Chemistry an atom or group whose presence is responsible for the colour of a compound.
– DERIVATIVES **chromophoric** adjective.

chromoplast /ˈkrəʊməplast, -plɑːst/ ▶ noun Botany a coloured plastid other than a chloroplast, typically containing a yellow or orange pigment.
– ORIGIN late 19th cent.: from **CHROMO-**[2] 'colour' + Greek *plastos* 'formed'.

chromosome ▶ noun Biology a thread-like structure of nucleic acids and protein found in the nucleus of most living cells, carrying genetic information in the form of genes.

Each chromosome consists of a DNA double helix bearing a linear sequence of genes, coiled and recoiled around aggregated proteins (histones). Their number varies from species to species: humans have 22 pairs plus the two sex chromosomes (two X chromosomes in females, one X and one Y in males). During cell division each DNA strand is duplicated, and the chromosomes condense to become visible as distinct pairs of chromatids joined at the centromere. Bacteria and viruses lack a nucleus, and have a single chromosome without histones.

– DERIVATIVES **chromosomal** adjective.
– ORIGIN late 19th cent.: coined in German from Greek *khrōma* 'colour' + *sōma* 'body'.

chromosome map ▶ noun Genetics a diagram showing the relative positions of genes along the length of a chromosome.

chromosome number ▶ noun Genetics the characteristic number of chromosomes found in the cell nuclei of organisms of a particular species.

chromosphere ▶ noun Astronomy a reddish gaseous layer immediately above the photosphere of the sun or another star which, together with the corona, constitutes its outer atmosphere.
– DERIVATIVES **chromospheric** adjective.
– ORIGIN mid 19th cent.: from **CHROMO-**[2] 'colour' + **SPHERE**.

chromous ▶ adjective Chemistry of chromium with a valency of two; of chromium(II). Compare with **CHROMIC**.

Chron. ▶ abbreviation for Chronicles (in biblical references).

chronic ▶ adjective 1 (of an illness) persisting for a long time or constantly recurring: *chronic bronchitis.* Often contrasted with **ACUTE**.
■ (of a person) having such an illness: *a chronic asthmatic.* ■ (of a problem) long-lasting and difficult to eradicate: *the school suffers from chronic overcrowding.* ■ (of a person) having a particular bad habit: *a chronic liar.*
2 Brit. informal of a very poor quality: *the film was absolutely chronic.*
– DERIVATIVES **chronically** adverb, **chronicity** noun.
– ORIGIN late Middle English: from French *chronique*, via Latin from Greek *khronikos* 'of time', from *khronos* 'time'.

chronic fatigue syndrome (abbrev.: **CFS**) ▶ noun [mass noun] a medical condition of unknown cause, with fever, aching, and prolonged tiredness and depression, typically occurring after a viral infection.

chronicle ▶ noun a factual written account of important or historical events in the order of their occurrence.
■ a work of fiction or non-fiction which describes a particular series of events.
▶ verb [with obj.] record (a related series of events) in a factual and detailed way: *his work chronicles 20th-century displacement and migration.*
– DERIVATIVES **chronicler** noun.
– ORIGIN Middle English: from Anglo-Norman French *cronicle*, variant of Old French *cronique*, via Latin from Greek *khronika* 'annals', from *khronikos* (see **CHRONIC**).

Chronicles the name of two books of the Bible, recording the history of Israel and Judah until the return from Exile (536 BC). See also **PARALIPOMENA**.

chrono- /ˈkrɒnəʊ/ ▶ combining form relating to time: *chronometry.*
– ORIGIN from Greek *khronos* 'time'.

chronobiology ▶ noun [mass noun] the branch of biology concerned with natural physiological rhythms and other cyclical phenomena.
– DERIVATIVES **chronobiologist** noun.

chronograph ▶ noun an instrument for recording time with great accuracy.
■ a stopwatch.
– DERIVATIVES **chronographic** adjective.

chronological ▶ adjective relating to the establishment of dates and time sequences: *the diary provided a chronological framework for the events.*
■ (of a record of several events) starting with the earliest and following the order in which they occurred: *the entries are in chronological order.* ■ calculated in terms of the passage of time rather than some other criterion: *ratings are calculated by dividing a child's mental age by their chronological age.*
– DERIVATIVES **chronologically** adverb.

chronology /krəˈnɒlədʒi/ ▶ noun (pl. **-ies**) [mass noun] the study of historical records to establish the dates of past events.
■ the arrangement of events or dates in the order of their occurrence: *the novel abandons the conventions of normal chronology* | [count noun] *a diary recording a chronology of events.* ■ [count noun] a table or document displaying such an arrangement.
– DERIVATIVES **chronologist** noun.
– ORIGIN late 16th cent.: from modern Latin *chronologia*, from Greek *khronos* 'time' + *-logia* (see **-LOGY**).

chronometer /krəˈnɒmɪtə/ ▶ noun an instrument for measuring time, especially one designed to keep accurate time in spite of motion or variations in temperature, humidity, and air pressure.

Chronometers were first developed for marine navigation, being used in conjunction with astronomical observation to determine longitude.

chronometry ▶ noun [mass noun] the science of accurate time measurement.
– DERIVATIVES **chronometric** adjective, **chronometrical** adjective, **chronometrically** adverb.

chronostratigraphy /ˌkrɒnə(ʊ)strəˈtɪɡrəfi/ ▶ noun [mass noun] the branch of geology concerned with establishing the absolute ages of strata.
– DERIVATIVES **chronostratigraphic** adjective.

chrysalid /ˈkrɪs(ə)lɪd/ ▶ noun another term for **CHRYSALIS**.
– ORIGIN late 18th cent.: from Latin *chrysal(l)is*, *chrysal(l)id-* (see **CHRYSALIS**).

chrysalis /ˈkrɪs(ə)lɪs/ ▶ noun (pl. **chrysalises**) a quiescent insect pupa, especially of a butterfly or moth.
■ the hard outer case of this, especially after being discarded. ■ figurative a preparatory or transitional state: *she emerged from the chrysalis of self-conscious adolescence.*
– ORIGIN early 17th cent.: from Latin *chrysal(l)is*, *chrysal(l)id-*, from Greek *khrusallis*, from *khrusos* 'gold' (because of the gold colour or metallic sheen of the pupae of some species).

chrysanth ▶ noun Brit. informal a cultivated chrysanthemum.
– ORIGIN 1920s: abbreviation.

chrysanthemum /krɪˈsanθɪməm, -z-/ ▶ noun (pl. **chrysanthemums**) a popular plant of the daisy family, having brightly coloured ornamental flowers and existing in many cultivated varieties.
● Genera *Chrysanthemum* or (most cultivated species) *Dendranthema*, family Compositae.
■ a flower or flowering stem of this plant.
– ORIGIN (originally denoting the corn marigold): from Latin, from Greek *khrusanthemon*, from *khrusos* 'gold' + *anthemon* 'flower'.

chryselephantine /ˌkrɪsɛlɪˈfantʌɪn/ ▶ adjective (of ancient Greek sculpture) overlaid with gold and ivory.
– ORIGIN early 19th cent.: from Greek *khruselephantinos*, from *khrusos* 'gold' + *elephas*, *elephant-* 'elephant' or 'ivory'.

chrysoberyl /ˌkrɪsəˈbɛrɪl/ ▶ noun [mass noun] a greenish or yellowish-green mineral consisting of an oxide of beryllium and aluminium. It occurs as tabular crystals, sometimes of gem quality.
– ORIGIN mid 17th cent.: from Latin *chrysoberyllus*, from Greek *khrusos* 'gold' + *bērullos* 'beryl'.

chrysocolla /ˌkrɪsəˈkɒlə/ ▶ noun [mass noun] a greenish-blue mineral consisting of hydrated copper silicate, typically occurring as opaline crusts and masses.
– ORIGIN late 16th cent. (in the Greek sense): from Latin, from Greek *khrusokolla*, denoting a mineral used in ancient times for soldering gold.

chrysolite /ˈkrɪsəlʌɪt/ ▶ noun [mass noun] a yellowish-green or brownish variety of olivine, used as a gemstone.
– ORIGIN late Middle English: from Old French *crisolite*, from medieval Latin *crisolitus*, from Latin *chrysolithus*, based on Greek *khrusos* 'gold' + *lithos* 'stone'.

chrysomelid /ˌkrɪsə(ʊ)ˈmɛlɪd, -ˈmiːlɪd/ ▶ noun Entomology a beetle of a family (Chrysomelidae) that comprises the leaf beetles and their relatives.
– ORIGIN late 19th cent.: from modern Latin *Chrysomelidae* (plural), from *Chrysomela* (genus name), from Greek *khrusomēlon*, literally 'golden apple', influenced by *khrusomēlolonthion* 'little golden chafer'.

chrysoprase /ˈkrɪsə(ʊ)preɪz/ ▶ noun [mass noun] an apple-green variety of chalcedony containing nickel, used as a gemstone.
■ (in the New Testament) a golden-green precious stone, perhaps a variety of beryl.
– ORIGIN Middle English (in the New Testament sense): from Old French *crisopace*, via Latin from Greek *khrusoprasos*, from *khrusos* 'gold' + *prason* 'leek'.

Chrysostom, St John /ˈkrɪsəstəm/ (*c.*347–407), Doctor of the Church, bishop of Constantinople. He attempted to reform the corrupt state of the court, clergy, and people; this offended many, including the Empress Eudoxia, who banished him in 403. His name means 'golden-mouthed' in Greek. Feast day, 27 January.

chrysotile /ˈkrɪsə(ʊ)tʌɪl/ ▶ noun [mass noun] a fibrous form of the mineral serpentine. Also called **white asbestos**.
– ORIGIN mid 19th cent.: from Greek *khrusos* 'gold' + *tilos* 'fibre'.

chthonic /ˈ(k)θɒnɪk/ (also **chthonian** /ˈ(k)θəʊnɪən/) ▶ adjective concerning, belonging to, or inhabiting the underworld: *a chthonic deity.*
– ORIGIN late 19th cent.: from Greek *khthōn* 'earth' + -IC.

chub ▶ noun a thick-bodied European river fish with a grey-green back and white underparts, popular with anglers.
● *Leuciscus cephalus*, family Cyprinidae.
– ORIGIN late Middle English: of unknown origin.

Chubb (also **Chubb lock**) ▶ noun trademark a lock with a device for fixing the bolt immovably to prevent it from being picked.
– ORIGIN mid 19th cent.: named after Charles *Chubb* (1773–1845), the London locksmith who invented it.

chubby ▶ adjective (**chubbier**, **chubbiest**) plump and rounded: *a pretty child with chubby cheeks.*
– DERIVATIVES **chubbily** adverb, **chubbiness** noun.
– ORIGIN early 17th cent. (in the sense 'short and thickset, like a chub'): from CHUB.

Chubu /ˈtʃuːbuː/ a mountainous region of Japan, on the island of Honshu; capital, Nagoya.

chuck[1] informal ▶ verb [with obj.] throw (something) carelessly or casually: *someone chucked a brick through the window* | figurative *he was chucking his money about.*
■ throw (something) away: *they make a living out of stuff people chuck away.* ■ give up (a job or activity) suddenly: *Richard chucked in his cultural studies course.* ■ break off a relationship with (a partner): *Mary chucked him for another guy.* ■ (**chuck it**) dated stop doing something.
▶ noun (**the chuck**) Brit. dated a dismissal or rejection by someone.
– PHRASES **chuck it all in** (or **up**) abandon a course of action or way of life, especially for another that is radically different. **chuck it down** rain heavily.
– ORIGIN late 17th cent. (as a verb): from CHUCK[2]. The current noun sense dates from the late 19th cent.
– **chuck someone out** force someone to leave a building. **chuck up** (or **chuck something up**) vomit.

chuck[2] ▶ verb [with obj.] touch (someone) playfully or gently under the chin.
▶ noun a playful touch under the chin.
– ORIGIN early 17th cent. (as a noun): probably from Old French *chuquer*, later *choquer* 'to knock, bump', of unknown ultimate origin.

chuck[3] ▶ noun **1** a device for holding a workpiece in a lathe or a tool in a drill, typically having three or four jaws that move radially in and out.
2 [mass noun] a cut of beef that extends from the neck to the ribs, typically used for stewing.
– ORIGIN late 17th cent., as a variant of CHOCK; see also CHUNK[1].

chuck[4] ▶ noun informal, chiefly N. English used as a form of address to express friendly familiarity: *'Can I help you at all, chuck?'*
– ORIGIN late 16th cent.: alteration of CHICK[1].

chuck-a-luck ▶ noun [mass noun] N. Amer. a gambling game played with dice.

chucker ▶ noun informal a person who throws something, especially a ball.
■ Cricket, informal a bowler with an illegal arm action.

chucker out ▶ noun Brit. informal a person employed to expel troublesome people from a social event or place of entertainment.

chuckhole ▶ noun N. Amer. a hole or rut in a road or track.

chuckie stone ▶ noun Scottish a small pebble or smooth stone, especially one used in games or for skimming on water.

chuck key ▶ noun a small metal device for tightening the chuck of a drill so that it holds the drill bit securely.

chuckle ▶ verb [no obj.] laugh quietly or inwardly: *I chuckled at the astonishment on her face* | [with direct speech] *'That's a bit strong, isn't it?' he chuckled.*
▶ noun [in sing.] a quiet or suppressed laugh.
– DERIVATIVES **chuckler** noun.
– ORIGIN late 16th cent. (in the sense 'laugh convulsively'): from *chuck* meaning 'to cluck' in late Middle English.

chucklehead ▶ noun informal a stupid person.
– DERIVATIVES **chuckleheaded** adjective.
– ORIGIN mid 18th cent.: from early 18th-cent. *chuckle* 'big and clumsy', probably related to CHUCK[3] (see sense 2).

chuck wagon ▶ noun N. Amer. a wagon with cooking facilities providing food on a ranch or by a roadside.
– ORIGIN late 19th cent.: *chuck*, colloquial in the sense 'food, provisions'.

chuckwalla /ˈtʃʌkwɒlə/ ▶ noun a large dark-bodied lizard, the male of which has a light yellow tail, native to the deserts of the south-western US and Mexico. When threatened it inflates itself with air to wedge itself into a crevice.
● *Sauromalus obesus*, family Iguanidae.
– ORIGIN late 19th cent.: from Mexican Spanish *chacahuala*, from American Indian.

chuck-will's-widow ▶ noun a large nightjar native to eastern North America.
● *Caprimulgus carolinensis*, family Caprimulgidae.
– ORIGIN late 18th cent.: imitative of its call.

chuddar ▶ noun variant spelling of CHADOR.

chufa /ˈtʃuːfə/ ▶ noun an Old World sedge which yields an edible tuber. It is cultivated on a small scale, particularly in some marshy regions of Spain and Italy. Also called TIGER NUT.
● *Cyperus esculentus* var. *sativus*, family Cyperaceae.
■ [mass noun] the tuber of this plant, which may be roasted, made into flour, or turned into juice.
– ORIGIN mid 19th cent.: from Spanish.

chuff ▶ verb [no obj., with adverbial of direction] (of a steam engine) move with a regular sharp puffing sound.
– ORIGIN early 20th cent.: imitative.

chuffed ▶ adjective [predic.] Brit. informal very pleased: *I'm dead chuffed to have won.*
– ORIGIN 1950s: from dialect *chuff* 'plump or pleased'.

chug[1] ▶ verb (**chugged**, **chugging**) [no obj.] emit a series of regular muffled explosive sounds, as of an engine running slowly: *he could hear the pipes chugging.*
■ [no obj., with adverbial of direction] (of a vehicle or boat) move slowly making such sounds: *a cabin cruiser was chugging down the river.*
▶ noun a muffled explosive sound or a series of such sounds: *the chug of a motor boat.*
– ORIGIN mid 19th cent. (as a noun): imitative.

chug[2] (also **chugalug**) ▶ verb (**chugged**, **chugging**) [with obj.] N. Amer. informal consume (a drink) in large gulps without pausing: *she was chugging a Diet Pepsi.*
– ORIGIN 1980s: imitative.

Chugoku /tʃuːˈgəʊkuː/ a region of Japan, on the island of Honshu; capital, Hiroshima.

chukar /ˈtʃʊkɑː/ (also **chukor** or **chukar partridge**) ▶ noun a Eurasian partridge similar to the red-legged partridge, but with a call like a clucking domestic hen.
● Genus *Alectoris*, family Phasianidae: two species, in particular *A. chukar*.
– ORIGIN early 19th cent.: from Sanskrit *cakora*.

Chukchi /ˈtʃʊktʃiː/ (also **Chukchee**) ▶ noun (pl. same or **Chukchis**) **1** a member of an indigenous people of extreme NE Siberia.
2 [mass noun] the language of this people, which has around 10,000 speakers and belongs to a small, isolated language family also including Koryak.
▶ adjective of or relating to this people or their language.
– ORIGIN Russian (plural).

Chukchi Sea /ˈtʃʊktʃiː/ part of the Arctic Ocean lying between North America and Asia and to the north of the Bering Strait.

chukka /ˈtʃʌkə/ (US also **chukker**) ▶ noun each of a number of periods (typically six) into which play in a game of polo is divided. A chukka lasts 7½ minutes.
– ORIGIN late 19th cent.: from Hindi *cakkar*, from Sanskrit *cakra* 'circle or wheel'.

chum[1] informal, dated ▶ noun a close friend.
■ a form of address between men or boys expressing familiarity or friendliness: *it's your own fault, chum.*
▶ verb (**chummed**, **chumming**) [no obj.] be friendly to or form a friendship with someone: *his sister chummed up with Sally.*
■ [with obj.] Scottish accompany (someone) somewhere: *I'll chum you down the road.*
– DERIVATIVES **chummily** adverb, **chumminess** noun, **chummy** adjective.

chum[2] chiefly N. Amer. ▶ noun [mass noun] chopped fish, fish fluids, and other material thrown overboard as angling bait.
■ refuse from fish, especially that remaining after expressing oil.
▶ verb [no obj.] fish using chum as bait.
– ORIGIN mid 19th cent.: of unknown origin.

chum[3] (also **chum salmon**) ▶ noun (pl. same or **chums**) a large North Pacific salmon that is commercially important as a food fish.
● *Oncorhynchus keta*, family Salmonidae.
– ORIGIN early 20th cent.: from Chinook Jargon *tzum* (*samun*), literally 'spotted (salmon)'.

Chumash /ˈtʃuːmaʃ/ ▶ noun (pl. same or **Chumashes**) **1** a member of an American Indian people inhabiting coastal parts of southern California.
2 [mass noun] the extinct Hokan language of this people.
▶ adjective of or relating to this people or their language.

chumble ▶ verb [with obj.] dialect nibble; chew.
– ORIGIN early 19th cent.: probably imitative.

chump ▶ noun **1** informal a foolish person.
2 Brit. the thick end of something, especially a loin of lamb or mutton.
– PHRASES **off one's chump** Brit. informal crazy: *I was beginning to think he'd gone off his chump.*
– ORIGIN early 18th cent. (in the sense 'thick lump of wood'): probably a blend of CHUNK[1] and LUMP[1] or STUMP.

chump change ▶ noun [mass noun] N. Amer. informal a small or insignificant amount of money.
– ORIGIN 1960s: originally black English.

Chün /tʃuːn/ ▶ noun [mass noun] a type of thickly glazed, typically bluish or purplish grey stoneware originally made at Chün Chou in Honan province, China, during the Song dynasty.

chunder informal ▶ verb [no obj.] vomit.
▶ noun [mass noun] vomit.
– ORIGIN 1950s: probably from rhyming slang *Chunder Loo* 'spew', from the name of a cartoon character *Chunder Loo of Akim Foo*, devised by Norman Lindsay (1879–1969) and used in advertisements for Cobra boot polish in the Sydney *Bulletin* in the early 20th cent.

Chungking /tʃʊŋˈkɪŋ/ variant of CHONGQING.

Chung-shan /tʃʊŋˈʃan/ variant of ZHONGSHAN.

chunk[1] ▶ noun a thick, solid piece of something: *huge chunks of masonry littered the street.*
■ [in sing.] an amount or part of something: *fuel takes a large chunk of their small income.*
▶ verb [with obj.] N. Amer. divide (something) into chunks: *chunk four pounds of pears.*
■ (in psychology or linguistic analysis) group together (connected items or words) so that they can be stored or processed as single concepts.
– ORIGIN late 17th cent.: apparently an alteration of CHUCK[3].

chunk[2] ▶ verb [no obj.] chiefly N. Amer. move with or make a muffled, metallic sound: *the door chunked behind them.*
– ORIGIN late 19th cent.: imitative.

chunky ▶ adjective (**chunkier**, **chunkiest**) **1** (of a person) short and sturdy.
■ bulky and solid: *a chunky bracelet.* ■ (of wool or a woollen garment) thick and bulky.
2 (of a food which is mostly liquid) containing thick pieces: *a chunky soup.*
– DERIVATIVES **chunkily** adverb, **chunkiness** noun.

Chunnel ▶ noun informal short for CHANNEL TUNNEL.
– ORIGIN 1920s (but rare before the 1950s): blend.

chunni /ˈtʃʊni/ ▶ noun (pl. **chunnis**) another term for DUPATTA.
– ORIGIN from Punjabi.

chunter ▶ verb [no obj.] Brit. informal chatter or grumble monotonously: *they were chuntering on about the drains.*
■ [no obj., with adverbial of direction] move slowly and noisily in a particular direction: *the car came chuntering up the track.*
– ORIGIN late 17th cent.: probably imitative.

chup /tʃʊp/ ▶ exclamation Indian be quiet!
– ORIGIN from Hindi *cuprao*.

chupatty ▶ noun (pl. **-ies**) variant spelling of **CHAPATTI**.

chuppah /ˈxʊpə/ (also **chuppa**) ▶ noun (pl. **chuppot** /ˈxʊpəʊt/) a canopy beneath which Jewish marriage ceremonies are performed.
– ORIGIN late 19th cent.: from Hebrew ḥuppāh 'cover, canopy'.

Chuquisaca /ˌtʃuːkiˈsɑːkə/ former name (1539–1840) for **SUCRE**[1].

church ▶ noun a building used for public Christian worship: *they came to church with me*.
■ (usu. **Church**) a particular Christian organization, typically one with its own clergy, buildings, and distinctive doctrines: *the Church of England*. ■ (**the Church**) the hierarchy of clergy of such an organization, especially the Church of England or the Roman Catholic Church. ■ [mass noun] institutionalized religion as a political or social force: *the separation of church and state*.
▶ verb [with obj.] archaic take (a woman who has recently given birth) to church for a service of thanksgiving.
– ORIGIN Old English cir(i)ce, cyr(i)ce, related to Dutch kerk and German Kirche, based on medieval Greek kurikon, from Greek kuriakon (dōma) 'Lord's (house)', from kurios 'master or lord'. Compare with **KIRK**.

Church Army a voluntary Anglican organization concerned with social welfare. It was founded in 1882 on the model of the Salvation Army, for evangelistic purposes.

Church Commissioners a body managing the finances of the Church of England.

Churches of Christ a number of Protestant denominations, chiefly in the US, originating in the Disciples of Christ but later separated over doctrinal issues.

churchgoer ▶ noun a person who goes to church, especially one who does so regularly.
– DERIVATIVES **churchgoing** noun & adjective.

Churchill[1], Caryl (b.1938), English dramatist. She is best known for the satire *Serious Money* (1986); written in rhyming couplets, it deals with 1980s speculators and the ethics of high finance.

Churchill[2], Sir Winston (Leonard Spencer) (1874–1965), British Conservative statesman, Prime Minister 1940–5 and 1951–5.

He served as Home Secretary (1910–11) under the Liberals and as First Lord of the Admiralty 1911–15, but lost this post after the unsuccessful Allied attack on the Turks in the Dardanelles. A consistent opponent of appeasement between the wars, he replaced Neville Chamberlain as Prime Minister of the coalition government in 1940 and led Britain throughout the war, forging and maintaining the alliance which defeated the Axis Powers. His writings include *The Second World War* (1948–53) and *A History of the English-Speaking Peoples* (1956–8); he won the Nobel Prize for Literature in 1953.

– DERIVATIVES **Churchillian** adjective.

churchman ▶ noun (pl. **-men**) a male member of the Christian clergy or of a Church.

Church Militant ▶ noun (**the Church Militant**) the whole body of living Christian believers, regarded as striving to combat evil on earth.
– ORIGIN mid 16th cent.: contrasted with the *Church Triumphant* in heaven.

Church of England the English branch of the Western Christian Church, which combines Catholic and Protestant traditions, rejects the Pope's authority, and has the monarch as its titular head. The English Church was part of the Catholic Church until the Reformation of the 16th century; after Henry VIII failed to obtain a divorce from Catherine of Aragon he repudiated papal supremacy, bringing the Church under the control of the Crown.

Church of Scotland the national (Presbyterian) Christian Church in Scotland. In 1560 John Knox reformed the established Church along Presbyterian lines, but there were repeated attempts by the Stuart monarchs to impose episcopalianism, and the Church of Scotland was not finally established as Presbyterian until 1690.

church planting ▶ noun [mass noun] the practice of establishing a core of Christian worshippers in a parish, with the intention that they should develop into a thriving congregation.

church school ▶ noun (in the UK) a school founded by or associated with the Church of England.
■ (in the US) a private school supported by a particular Church or parish.

Church Slavonic ▶ noun [mass noun] the liturgical language used in the Orthodox Church in Russia, Serbia, and some other countries. It is a modified form of Old Church Slavonic.

Churchward /ˈtʃɜːtʃwəd/, George Jackson (1857–1933), English railway engineer. The standard four-cylinder 4-6-0 locomotives that he built at the Swindon works of the Great Western Railway were the basis of many later designs.

churchwarden ▶ noun 1 either of the two elected lay representatives in an Anglican parish, formally responsible for movable church property and for keeping order in church.
■ US a church administrator.
2 Brit. a long-stemmed clay pipe.

churchwoman ▶ noun (pl. **-women**) a female member of the Christian clergy or of a Church.

churchy ▶ adjective 1 (of a person) excessively pious and consequently narrow-minded or intolerant.
2 resembling a church: *Gothic design looks too churchy*.
– DERIVATIVES **churchiness** noun.

churchyard ▶ noun an enclosed area surrounding a church, especially as used for burials.

churchyard beetle ▶ noun a flightless black darkling beetle which typically lives in damp dark places and emits a foul smell when alarmed.
● *Blaps mucronata*, family Tenebrionidae.

churidars /ˈtʃʊərɪdɑːz/ (also **churidar**) ▶ plural noun tight trousers worn by people from the Indian subcontinent, typically with a kameez or kurta.
– ORIGIN from Hindi cūrīdār 'having a series of gathered rows' (i.e. at the bottom of the trouser legs, traditionally worn too long and tucked up).

churinga /tʃʌˈrɪŋgə/ ▶ noun (pl. same or **churingas**) a sacred object, typically an amulet, among the Australian Aboriginals.
– ORIGIN late 19th cent.: from Aranda, literally 'object from the dreaming'.

churl ▶ noun an impolite and mean-spirited person.
■ archaic a miser. ■ archaic a person of low birth; a peasant.
– ORIGIN Old English ceorl, of West Germanic origin; related to Dutch kerel and German Kerl 'fellow', also to **CARL**.

churlish ▶ adjective rude in a mean-spirited and surly way: *it seems churlish to complain*.
– DERIVATIVES **churlishly** adverb, **churlishness** noun.
– ORIGIN Old English cierlisc, ceorlisc (see **CHURL**, **-ISH**[1]).

churn ▶ noun a machine for making butter by agitating milk or cream.
■ Brit. a large metal milk can.
▶ verb 1 [with obj.] (often **be churned**) agitate or turn (milk or cream) in a machine in order to produce butter: *the cream is ripened before it is churned*.
■ produce (butter) in such a way.
2 [no obj.] (of liquid) move about vigorously: *the seas churned* | figurative *her stomach was churning at the thought of the ordeal*.
■ [with obj.] (often **be churned**) cause (liquid) to move in this way: *in high winds most of the loch is churned up*. ■ [with obj.] break up the surface of (an area of ground): *the earth had been churned up where vehicles had passed through*.
3 [with obj.] (of a broker) encourage frequent turnover of (investments) in order to generate commission.
– ORIGIN Old English cyrin, of Germanic origin; related to Middle Low German kerne and Old Norse kirna.
▶ **churn something out** produce something routinely or mechanically, especially in large quantities: *artists continued to churn out uninteresting works*.

churn rate ▶ noun the annual percentage rate at which customers discontinue using a service, in particular cable and satellite television.

churr ▶ verb & noun variant spelling of **CHIRR**.

churrascaria /ˌtʃʊˌraskəˈrɪə/ ▶ noun a restaurant specializing in churrasco.
– ORIGIN South American Spanish.

churrasco /tʃʊˈraskəʊ/ ▶ noun [mass noun] a South American dish consisting of steak barbecued over a wood or charcoal fire.
– ORIGIN South American Spanish, probably from Spanish dialect churrascar 'to burn', related to Spanish soccarar 'to scorch'.

Churrigueresque /ˌtʃʊərɪgəˈrɛsk/ ▶ adjective Architecture of or relating to the lavishly ornamented late Spanish baroque style: *a Churrigueresque church*.
– ORIGIN mid 19th cent.: from the name José Benito de Churriguera (1665–1725), a Spanish architect who worked in this style.

chut /tʃʊt, ʃ-/ ▶ exclamation chiefly W. Indian expressing impatience or surprise.
– ORIGIN early 19th cent.: imitative; compare with French chut, used as a warning to be silent.

chute[1] (also **shoot**) ▶ noun a sloping channel or slide for conveying things to a lower level.
■ a water slide into a swimming pool.
– ORIGIN early 19th cent. (originally a North American usage): from French, 'fall' (of water or rocks), from Old French cheoite, feminine past participle of cheoir 'to fall', from Latin cadere; influenced by **SHOOT**.

chute[2] ▶ noun informal a parachute.
■ Sailing informal term for **SPINNAKER**.
– DERIVATIVES **chutist** noun.
– ORIGIN 1920s: shortened form.

chutney ▶ noun (pl. **-eys**) [mass noun] a spicy condiment made of fruits or vegetables with vinegar, spices, and sugar, originating in India.
– ORIGIN early 19th cent.: from Hindi caṭnī.

chutzpah /ˈxʊtspə, ˈhʊ-/ ▶ noun [mass noun] informal shameless audacity; cheek.
– ORIGIN late 19th cent.: Yiddish, from Aramaic ḥu ṣpā.

Chuvash /ˈtʃuːvɑːʃ/ ▶ noun (pl. same) 1 a member of a people living mainly in Chuvashia.
2 [mass noun] the language of this people, with over a million speakers. It is a Turkic language, but rather distantly related to the other members of the family.
▶ adjective of or relating to this people or their language.

Chuvashia /tʃuːˈvɑːʃɪə/ an autonomous republic in European Russia, east of Nizhni Novgorod; pop. 1,340,000 (1990); capital, Cheboksary.

chyle /kʌɪl/ ▶ noun [mass noun] Physiology a milky fluid containing fat droplets which drains from the lacteals of the small intestine into the lymphatic system during digestion.
– DERIVATIVES **chylous** adjective.
– ORIGIN late Middle English: from late Latin chylus, from Greek khūlos 'juice' (see **CHYME**).

chylomicron /ˌkʌɪlə(ʊ)ˈmʌɪkrɒn/ ▶ noun Physiology a droplet of fat present in the blood or lymph after absorption from the small intestine.
– ORIGIN 1920s: from chylo- (combining form of **CHYLE**) + **MICRON**.

chyme /kʌɪm/ ▶ noun [mass noun] Physiology the pulpy acidic fluid which passes from the stomach to the small intestine, consisting of gastric juices and partly digested food.
– DERIVATIVES **chymous** adjective.
– ORIGIN late Middle English: from late Latin chymus, from Greek khūmos 'juice' (compare with **CHYLE**). The Greek words khūlos and khūmos are from the same root and more or less identical in sense; however, khūlos came to be used for juice in a raw or natural state, khūmos for juice produced by decoction or digestion.

chymotrypsin /ˌkʌɪmə(ʊ)ˈtrɪpsɪn/ ▶ noun [mass noun] Biochemistry a digestive enzyme which breaks down proteins in the small intestine. It is secreted by the pancreas and converted into an active form by trypsin.
– ORIGIN 1930s: from chymo- (combining form of **CHYME**) + **TRYPSIN**.

chypre /ˈʃiːpr(ə)/ ▶ noun [mass noun] a heavy perfume made from sandalwood.
– ORIGIN late 19th cent.: from French, literally 'Cyprus', perhaps where it was first made.

CI ▶ abbreviation for ■ Channel Islands. ■ Ivory Coast (international vehicle registration). [ORIGIN: from French Côte d'Ivoire.]

Ci ▶ abbreviation for curie.

CIA ▶ abbreviation for Central Intelligence Agency.

ciabatta /tʃəˈbatə/ (also **ciabatta bread**) ▶ noun [mass noun] a type of flattish, open-textured Italian bread with a floury crust, made with olive oil.
– ORIGIN Italian, literally 'slipper' (from its shape).

ciao /tʃaʊ/ ▶ exclamation informal used as a greeting at meeting or parting.
– ORIGIN 1920s: Italian, dialect alteration of schiavo

'(I am your) slave', from medieval Latin *sclavus* 'slave'.

Cibber /ˈsɪbə/, Colley (1671–1757), English comic actor, dramatist, and theatre manager. He won recognition as a dramatist with his first comedy, *Love's Last Shift* (1696). After his much-ridiculed appointment as Poet Laureate in 1730 he wrote an *Apology for the Life of Mr Colley Cibber, Comedian* (1740).

ciborium /sɪˈbɔːrɪəm/ ▶ **noun** (pl. **ciboria** /-rɪə/) **1** a receptacle shaped like a shrine or a cup with an arched cover, used in the Christian Church for the reservation of the Eucharist.
2 a canopy over an altar in a church, standing on four pillars.
– ORIGIN mid 16th cent.: via medieval Latin from Greek *kibōrion* 'seed vessel of the water lily or a cup made from it'. Sense 1 is probably influenced by Latin *cibus* 'food'.

cicada /sɪˈkɑːdə/ ▶ **noun** a large bug with long transparent wings, occurring chiefly in warm countries. The male cicada makes a loud shrill droning noise after dark by vibrating two membranes on its abdomen.
● Family Cicadidae, suborder Homoptera: many genera.
– ORIGIN late Middle English: from Latin *cicada*, *cicala*.

cicadabird ▶ **noun** a small slender cuckoo-shrike found mainly in Indonesia.
● Genus *Coracina*, family Campephagidae: several species, in particular the (**common**) **cicadabird** (*C. tenuirostris*), whose range extends to Australia.

cicatrix /ˈsɪkətrɪks/ (also **cicatrice** /ˈsɪkətrɪs/) ▶ **noun** (pl. **cicatrices** /-ˈtrʌɪsiːz/) the scar of a healed wound.
■ a scar on the bark of a tree. ■ Botany a mark on a stem left after a leaf or other part has become detached.
– DERIVATIVES **cicatricial** /sɪkəˈtrɪʃ(ə)l/ adjective.
– ORIGIN late Middle English (as *cicatrice*): from Latin *cicatrix* or Old French *cicatrice*.

cicatrize /ˈsɪkətrʌɪz/ (also **-ise**) ▶ **verb** (with reference to a wound) heal by scar formation: [with obj.] *the military required a supply to cicatrize certain types of wounds* | [no obj.] *his wound had cicatrized.*
– DERIVATIVES **cicatrization** noun.
– ORIGIN late Middle English: from Old French *cicatriser*, from *cicatrice* 'scar' (see **CICATRIX**).

cicely /ˈsɪsɪli/ (also **sweet cicely**) ▶ **noun** (pl. **-ies**) an aromatic white-flowered plant of the parsley family, with fern-like leaves.
● Genera *Myrrhis* and *Osmorhiza*, family Umbelliferae: several species, in particular the European *M. odorata*, grown as a pot herb and used in herbal medicine, and the North American *O. claytoni*.
– ORIGIN late 16th cent.: from Latin *seselis*, from Greek. The spelling change was due to association with the given name *Cicely*.

Cicero /ˈsɪsərəʊ/, Marcus Tullius (106–43 BC), Roman statesman, orator, and writer. As an orator and writer Cicero established a model for Latin prose; his surviving works include speeches, treatises on rhetoric, philosophical works, and letters. A supporter of Pompey against Julius Caesar, in the *Philippics* (43 BC) he attacked Mark Antony, who had him put to death.

cicerone /ˌtʃɪtʃəˈrəʊni, ˌsɪs-/ ▶ **noun** (pl. **ciceroni** pronunc. same) a guide who gives information about antiquities and places of interest to sightseers.
– ORIGIN early 18th cent.: from Italian, from Latin *Cicero*, *Ciceron-* (see **CICERO**), apparently alluding humorously to his eloquence and learning.

Ciceronian /ˌsɪsəˈrəʊnɪən/ ▶ **adjective** characteristic of the work and thought of Cicero.
■ (of a piece of speech or writing) in an eloquent and rhythmic style similar to that of Cicero.

cichlid /ˈsɪklɪd/ ▶ **noun** Zoology a perch-like freshwater fish of a family (Cichlidae) which is widely distributed in tropical countries and which includes the angelfishes, discuses, mouthbrooders, and tilapia. Cichlids provide a valuable source of food in some areas.
– ORIGIN late 19th cent.: from modern Latin *Cichlidae* (plural), from Greek *kikhlē*, denoting a kind of fish.

cicisbeo /ˌtʃɪtʃɪzˈbeɪəʊ/ ▶ **noun** (pl. **cicisbei** or **cicisbeos**) a married woman's male companion or lover.
– ORIGIN early 18th cent.: Italian, of unknown origin.

CID ▶ **abbreviation for** (in the UK) Criminal Investigation Department.

Cid, El /ɛl ˈsɪd, Spanish el ˈθið, ˈsið/ (also **the Cid**), Count of Bivar (*c.*1043–99), Spanish soldier; born *Rodrigo Díaz de Vivar*. A champion of Christianity against the Moors, in 1094 he captured Valencia, which he went on to rule. He is immortalized in the Spanish *Poema del Cid* (12th century) and in Corneille's play *Le Cid* (1637).

-cide ▶ **combining form 1** denoting a person or substance that kills: *insecticide* | *regicide*.
2 denoting an act of killing: *suicide*.
– ORIGIN via French; sense 1 from Latin *-cida*; sense 2 from Latin *-cidium*, both from *caedere* 'kill'.

cider ▶ **noun** [mass noun] Brit. an alcoholic drink made from fermented apple juice.
■ (also **apple cider**) N. Amer. a cloudy, typically unfermented, drink made by crushing apples.
– ORIGIN Middle English: from Old French *sidre*, via ecclesiastical Latin from ecclesiastical Greek *sikera*, from Hebrew *šēḵār* 'strong drink'.

cider apple ▶ **noun** an apple of a variety that is used in cider-making.

cider gum ▶ **noun** a fast-growing, hardy Tasmanian eucalyptus which is one of the kinds most commonly grown in northern Europe.
● *Eucalyptus gunnii*, family Myrtaceae.

cider press ▶ **noun** a press for crushing apples to make cider.

ci-devant /ˌsiːdəˈvɒ̃, French sidvɑ̃/ ▶ **adjective** [attrib.] from or in an earlier time (used to indicate that someone or something once possessed a specified characteristic but no longer does so): *her ci-devant pupil, now her lover.*
– ORIGIN French, 'heretofore'.

CIE historical ▶ **abbreviation for** Companion (of the Order) of the Indian Empire.

c.i.f. ▶ **abbreviation for** cost, insurance, freight (as included in a price).

cig ▶ **noun** informal a cigarette or cigar.
– ORIGIN late 19th cent.: abbreviation.

cigar ▶ **noun** a cylinder of tobacco rolled in tobacco leaves for smoking.
– PHRASES **close but no cigar** N. Amer. informal (of an attempt) almost but not quite successful. [ORIGIN: referring to a cigar received in congratulation.]
– ORIGIN early 18th cent.: from French *cigare*, or from Spanish *cigarro*, probably from Mayan *sik'ar* 'smoking'.

cigarette (US also **cigaret**) ▶ **noun** a thin cylinder of finely cut tobacco rolled in paper for smoking.
■ a similar cylinder containing a narcotic, herbs, or a medicated substance.
– ORIGIN mid 19th cent.: from French, diminutive of *cigare* (see **CIGAR**).

cigarette beetle ▶ **noun** a small reddish beetle that infests a variety of stored products including tobacco. Also called **TOBACCO BEETLE**.
● *Lasioderma serricorne*, family Anobiidae.

cigarette card ▶ **noun** Brit. a small collectable card with a picture on it, of a kind formerly included in packets of cigarettes.

cigarette end ▶ **noun** Brit. the unsmoked remainder of a cigarette.

cigarette machine ▶ **noun** a slot machine that dispenses cigarettes.

cigarette paper ▶ **noun** a piece of thin paper with a gummed edge for rolling tobacco in to make a cigarette.

cigarillo /ˌsɪɡəˈrɪləʊ/ ▶ **noun** (pl. **-os**) a small cigar.
– ORIGIN mid 19th cent.: from Spanish, diminutive of *cigarro* (see **CIGAR**).

ciggy ▶ **noun** (pl. **-ies**) informal a cigarette.
– ORIGIN 1960s: abbreviation.

CIGS historical ▶ **abbreviation for** Chief of the Imperial General Staff.

ciguatera /ˌsɪɡwəˈtɛːrə/ ▶ **noun** [mass noun] poisoning by neurotoxins as a result of eating the flesh of tropical marine fish that carries a toxic dinoflagellate.
● This is caused by *Gambierdiscus toxicus*, division (or phylum) Dinophyta.
– ORIGIN mid 19th cent.: from American Spanish, from *cigua* 'sea snail'.

cilantro /sɪˈlantrəʊ/ ▶ **noun** [mass noun] coriander used as a seasoning or garnish, especially the leaves as used in Mexican cuisine.
– ORIGIN 1920s: from Spanish, from Latin *coliandrum* 'coriander'.

cilia plural form of **CILIUM**.

ciliary /ˈsɪlɪəri/ ▶ **adjective 1** Biology of, relating to, or involving cilia: *ciliary action*.
2 Anatomy of or relating to the eyelashes or eyelids.
■ of or relating to the ciliary body of the eye.

ciliary body ▶ **noun** Anatomy the part of the eye that connects the iris to the choroid. It consists of the **ciliary muscle** (which alters the curvature of the lens), a series of radial **ciliary processes** (from which the lens is suspended by ligaments), and the **ciliary ring** (which adjoins the choroid).

ciliate /ˈsɪlɪeɪt/ ▶ **noun** Zoology a single-celled animal of a phylum distinguished by the possession of cilia or ciliary structures. The ciliates are a large and diverse group of advanced protozoans.
● Phylum Ciliophora, kingdom Protista (formerly class Ciliata, phylum Protozoa).
▶ **adjective** Zoology (of an organism, cell, or surface) bearing cilia.
■ Botany (of a margin) having a fringe of hairs.
– DERIVATIVES **ciliated** adjective.

cilice /ˈsɪlɪs/ ▶ **noun** [mass noun] haircloth.
■ [count noun] a garment made of such cloth.
– ORIGIN late 16th cent.: from French, from Latin *cilicium*, from Greek *kilikion*, from *Kilikia*, the Greek name for **CILICIA** in Asia Minor (because the cloth was originally made of Cilician goats' hair).

Cilicia /sɪˈlɪʃə/ an ancient region on the coast of SE Asia Minor, corresponding to the present-day province of Adana, Turkey.
– DERIVATIVES **Cilician** adjective & noun.

Cilician Gates a mountain pass in the Taurus Mountains of southern Turkey, historically forming part of a route linking Anatolia with the Mediterranean coast.

cilium /ˈsɪlɪəm/ ▶ **noun** (usu. in pl. **cilia** /-lɪə/) Biology & Anatomy a short microscopic hair-like vibrating structure. Cilia occur in large numbers on the surface of certain cells, either causing currents in the surrounding fluid, or, in some protozoans and other small organisms, providing propulsion.
■ an eyelash, or a delicate hair-like structure that resembles one.
– DERIVATIVES **ciliated** adjective, **ciliation** noun.
– ORIGIN early 18th cent. (in the sense 'eyelash'): from Latin.

cill chiefly Building ▶ **noun** variant spelling of **SILL**.

cimbalom /ˈsɪmb(ə)l(ə)m/ ▶ **noun** a large Hungarian dulcimer.
– ORIGIN late 19th cent.: from Hungarian, from Italian *cembalo*, *cimbalo*, from Latin *cymbalum* (see **CYMBAL**).

cimetidine /sʌɪˈmɛtɪdiːn/ ▶ **noun** [mass noun] Medicine an antihistamine drug which is used to treat stomach acidity and peptic ulcers. It is a sulphur-containing derivative of imidazole.
– ORIGIN 1970s: from *ci-* (alteration of *cy-* in *cyano-*) + *met(hyl)* + **-IDE** + **-INE**[4].

Cimmerian /sɪˈmɪərɪən/ ▶ **adjective 1** relating to or denoting members of an ancient nomadic people who overran Asia Minor in the 7th century BC.
2 Greek Mythology relating to or denoting members of a mythical people who lived in perpetual mist and darkness near the land of the dead.
▶ **noun** a member of the historical or mythological Cimmerian people.
– ORIGIN via Latin from Greek *Kimmerios* + **-AN**.

C.-in-C. ▶ **abbreviation for** Commander-in-Chief.

cinch ▶ **noun 1** informal an extremely easy task: *the program was a cinch to use.*
■ a sure thing; a certainty: *he was a cinch to take a prize.*
2 chiefly N. Amer. a girth for a Western saddle or pack of a type used mainly in Mexico and the western US.
▶ **verb** [with obj.] chiefly N. Amer. **1** secure (a garment) with a belt.
■ fix (a saddle) securely by means of a girth; girth up (a horse).
2 informal make certain of: *his advice cinched her decision to accept the offer.*
– ORIGIN mid 19th cent. (in sense 2 of the noun): from Spanish *cincha* 'girth'.

cinchona /sɪŋˈkəʊnə/ ▶ **noun** an evergreen South American tree or shrub with fragrant flowers, cultivated for its bark.
● Genus *Cinchona*, family Rubiaceae: several species.
■ (also **cinchona bark**) [mass noun] the dried bark of this tree, which is a source of quinine and other medicinal alkaloids. ■ [mass noun] a drug made from

this bark, formerly used as a tonic and to stimulate the appetite.
– ORIGIN mid 18th cent.: modern Latin, named after the Countess of *Chinchón* (died 1641), who introduced the drug into Spain.

cinchonine /ˈsɪŋkəniːn/ ▶ noun [mass noun] Chemistry a compound with antipyretic properties which occurs with quinine in cinchona bark.
● An alkaloid; chem. formula: $C_{19}H_{22}ON_2$.

Cincinnati /ˌsɪnsɪˈnati/ an industrial city in Ohio, on the Ohio River; pop. 364,000 (1990).

cincture /ˈsɪŋktʃə/ ▶ noun 1 poetic/literary a girdle or belt.
2 Architecture a ring at either end of a column shaft.
– ORIGIN late 16th cent. (in the sense 'encircling or enclosure'): from Latin *cinctura*, from *cinct-* 'encircled', from the verb *cingere*.

cinder ▶ noun a small piece of partly burnt coal or wood that has stopped giving off flames but still has combustible matter in it.
– PHRASES **burnt to a cinder** completely burnt.
– DERIVATIVES **cindery** adjective.
– ORIGIN Old English *sinder* 'slag', of Germanic origin; related to German *Sinter*. The similar but unconnected French *cendre* (from Latin *cinis* 'ashes') has influenced both the sense development and the spelling. Compare with **SINTER**.

cinder block ▶ noun North American term for **BREEZE BLOCK**.

cinder cone ▶ noun a cone formed round a volcanic vent by fragments of lava thrown out during eruptions.

Cinderella a girl in various traditional European fairy tales. In the version by Charles Perrault she is exploited as a servant by her family but enabled by a fairy godmother to attend a royal ball. She meets and captivates Prince Charming but has to flee at midnight, leaving the prince to identify her by the glass slipper which she leaves behind.
■ [as noun] a person or thing of unrecognized or disregarded merit or beauty. ■ [as noun] a neglected aspect of something: *is research into breast cancer to remain the Cinderella of medicine?*
– ORIGIN from **CINDER** + the diminutive suffix *-ella*, on the pattern of French *Cendrillon*, from *cendre* 'cinders'.

cinder track (also **cinder path**) ▶ noun a footpath or running track laid with fine cinders.

cine ▶ adjective cinematographic: *a cine camera.*

cine- ▶ combining form representing *cinematographic* (see **CINEMATOGRAPHY**).

cineaste /ˈsɪnɪast/ (also **cinéaste** or **cineast**) ▶ noun an enthusiast for or devotee of the cinema.
– ORIGIN 1920s: from French *cinéaste*, from *ciné* (from *cinéma*), on the pattern of *enthousiaste* 'enthusiast'.

cinema ▶ noun chiefly Brit. a theatre where films are shown for public entertainment.
■ [mass noun] the production of films as an art or industry: *one of the giants of British cinema.*
– ORIGIN early 20th cent.: from French *cinéma*, abbreviation of *cinématographe* (see **CINEMATOGRAPH**).

cinema organ ▶ noun Music an organ which has extra stops and special effects.

CinemaScope ▶ noun [mass noun] trademark a cinematographic process in which special lenses are used to compress a wide image into a standard frame and then expand it again during projection. It results in an image that is almost two and a half times as wide as it is high.

cinematheque /ˌsɪnɪməˈtɛk/ ▶ noun 1 a film library or archive.
2 a small cinema.
– ORIGIN 1960s: from French *cinémathèque*, from *cinéma* 'cinema', on the pattern of *bibliothèque* 'library'.

cinematic ▶ adjective of or relating to the cinema: *cinematic output.*
■ having qualities characteristic of films: *the cinematic feel of their video.*
– DERIVATIVES **cinematically** adverb.

cinematograph /ˌsɪnɪˈmatəgrɑːf/ (also **kinematograph**) ▶ noun historical, chiefly Brit. an apparatus for showing motion-picture films.
– ORIGIN late 19th cent.: from French *cinématographe*, from Greek *kinēma, kinēmat-* 'movement', from *kinein* 'to move'.

cinematography /ˌsɪnɪməˈtɒgrəfi/ ▶ noun [mass noun] the art of making motion-picture films.
– DERIVATIVES **cinematographer** noun, **cinematographic** adjective, **cinematographically** adverb.

cinéma-vérité /ˌsɪnɪməˈvɛriteɪ, French sinemaveʀite/ ▶ noun [mass noun] a style of film-making characterized by realistic, typically documentary films which avoid artificiality and artistic effect and are generally made with simple equipment.
■ films of this style collectively.
– ORIGIN French, literally 'cinema truth'.

cinephile ▶ noun a person who is fond of the cinema.

cineplex (also **Cineplex**) ▶ noun trademark, chiefly N. Amer. a cinema with several separate screens; a multiplex.
– ORIGIN 1970s: blend of **CINEMA** and **COMPLEX**.

cineraria /ˌsɪnəˈrɛːrɪə/ ▶ noun a plant of the daisy family with compact masses of bright flowers, cultivated as a winter-flowering pot plant.
● Genus *Pericallis* (formerly *Senecio* or *Cineraria*), family Compositae.
– ORIGIN modern Latin, feminine of Latin *cinerarius* 'of ashes', from *cinis, ciner-* 'ashes' (because of the ash-coloured down on the leaves).

cinerarium /ˌsɪnəˈrɛːrɪəm/ ▶ noun (pl. **cinerariums**) a place where a cinerary urn is kept.
– ORIGIN late 19th cent.: from late Latin, neuter (used as a noun) of *cinerarius* 'of ashes'.

cinerary urn /ˈsɪnərəri/ ▶ noun an urn for holding a person's ashes after cremation, especially as used by Classical and prehistoric cultures.
– ORIGIN mid 18th cent.: *cinerary* from Latin *cinerarius* 'of ashes'.

cinereous /sɪˈnɪərɪəs/ ▶ adjective (especially of hair or feathers) ash-grey.
– ORIGIN late Middle English: from Latin *cinereus* 'similar to ashes' (from *cinis, ciner-* 'ashes') + **-OUS**.

cinereous vulture ▶ noun another term for **BLACK VULTURE** (in sense 1).

ciné-vérité /ˌsɪnɪˈvɛriteɪ, French sineverite/ ▶ noun another term for **CINÉMA-VÉRITÉ**.

Cingalese /ˌsɪŋɡəˈliːz/ ▶ noun & adjective archaic spelling of **SINHALESE**.
– ORIGIN late 16th cent.: from French *Cinghalais*, from Sanskrit *Siṃhala* 'Sri Lanka' + **-ESE**.

cingulum /ˈsɪŋɡjʊləm/ ▶ noun (pl. **cingula** /-lə/) Anatomy an encircling structure, in particular:
■ a curved bundle of nerve fibres in each hemisphere of the brain. ■ a ridge of enamel on the base or margin of the crown of a tooth.
– DERIVATIVES **cingulate** adjective.
– ORIGIN mid 19th cent.: from Latin, 'belt', from *cingere* 'gird'.

cinnabar /ˈsɪnəbɑː/ ▶ noun 1 [mass noun] a bright red mineral consisting of mercury sulphide. It is the only important ore of mercury and is sometimes used as a pigment.
■ the bright red colour of this; vermilion: [as modifier] *the blood coagulated in cinnabar threads.*
2 (also **cinnabar moth**) a day-flying moth with black and red wings. Its black and yellow caterpillars feed on groundsel and ragwort.
● *Tyria jacobaeae*, family Arctiidae.
– ORIGIN Middle English: from Latin *cinnabaris*, from Greek *kinnabari*, of oriental origin.

cinnamon ▶ noun 1 [mass noun] an aromatic spice made from the peeled, dried, and rolled bark of a SE Asian tree: [as modifier] *a cinnamon stick.*
■ a yellowish-brown colour resembling that of this spice.
2 the tree which yields this spice.
● Genus *Cinnamomum*, family Lauraceae: several species, in particular *C. zeylanicum*, native to South India and Sri Lanka.
– ORIGIN late Middle English: from Old French *cinnamome* (from Greek *kinnamōmon*), and Latin *cinnamon* (from Greek *kinnamon*), both from a Semitic language and perhaps based on Malay.

cinnamon bear ▶ noun a North American black bear of a variety with reddish-brown hair.

cinnamon fern ▶ noun a large North American fern that typically has cinnamon-coloured fronds.
● *Osmunda cinnamomea*, family Osmundaceae.

cinnamon toast ▶ noun [mass noun] N. Amer. buttered toast spread with ground cinnamon and sugar.

cinque /sɪŋk/ (also **cinq**) ▶ noun the five on dice.
■ (**cinques**) Bell-ringing a system of change-ringing using

eleven bells, with five pairs changing places each time.
– ORIGIN late Middle English: from Old French *cinc, cink*, from Latin *quinque* 'five'.

cinquecento /ˌtʃɪŋkwɪˈtʃɛntəʊ/ ▶ noun (**the cinquecento**) the 16th century as a period of Italian art, architecture, or literature, with a reversion to classical forms.
– ORIGIN Italian, literally '500' (shortened from *milcinquecento* '1500') used with reference to the years 1500–99.

cinquefoil /ˈsɪŋkfɔɪl/ ▶ noun 1 a widely distributed herbaceous plant of the rose family, with compound leaves of five leaflets and five-petalled yellow flowers.
● Genus *Potentilla*, family Rosaceae.
2 Art an ornamental design of five lobes arranged in a circle, e.g. in architectural tracery or heraldry.
– ORIGIN Middle English: from Latin *quinquefolium*, from *quinque* 'five' + *folium* 'leaf'.

Cinque Ports /sɪŋk/ a group of medieval ports in Kent and East Sussex in SE England, which were formerly allowed trading privileges in exchange for providing the bulk of England's navy. The five original Cinque Ports were Hastings, Sandwich, Dover, Romney, and Hythe; later Rye and Winchelsea were added.
– ORIGIN from Old French *cink porz*, from Latin *quinque portus* 'five ports'.

Cintra variant spelling of **SINTRA**.

Cinzano /tʃɪnˈzɑːnəʊ/ ▶ noun [mass noun] trademark a type of vermouth produced in Italy.
– ORIGIN from the name of the producers.

CIO ▶ abbreviation for Congress of Industrial Organizations.

cion ▶ noun US variant spelling of **SCION** (in sense 1).

cipher[1] /ˈsaɪfə/ (also **cypher**) ▶ noun 1 a secret or disguised way of writing; a code: *he wrote cryptic notes in a cipher* | [mass noun] *the information may be given in cipher.*
■ something written in such a code. ■ a key to such a code.
2 dated a zero; a figure 0.
■ figurative a person or thing of no importance, especially a person who does the bidding of others and seems to have no will of their own.
3 a monogram.
▶ verb 1 [with obj.] put (a message) into secret writing; encode.
2 [no obj.] archaic do arithmetic.
– ORIGIN late Middle English (in the senses 'symbol for zero' and 'arabic numeral'): from Old French *cifre*, based on Arabic *ṣifr* 'zero'.

cipher[2] ▶ noun a continuous sounding of an organ pipe, caused by a mechanical defect.
▶ verb [no obj.] (of an organ pipe) sound continuously.
– ORIGIN late 18th cent.: perhaps from **CIPHER**[1].

cipolin /ˈsɪpəlɪn/ ▶ noun [mass noun] an Italian marble interfoliated with veins of talc, mica, or quartz, showing alternating white and green streaks.
– ORIGIN late 18th cent.: from French, from Italian *cipollino*, from *cipolla* 'onion' (because its structure, having thin veins of other minerals, resembles onion skin).

circa /ˈsəːkə/ ▶ preposition (often preceding a date) approximately: *built circa 1935.*
– ORIGIN mid 19th cent.: Latin.

circadian /səːˈkeɪdɪən/ ▶ adjective Physiology (of biological processes) recurring naturally on a twenty-four-hour cycle, even in the absence of light fluctuations: *a circadian rhythm.*
– ORIGIN 1950s: formed irregularly from Latin *circa* 'about' + *dies* 'day'.

Circassian /səːˈkasɪən/ ▶ adjective relating to or denoting a group of mainly Sunni Muslim peoples of the NW Caucasus.
▶ noun 1 a member of this people.
2 [mass noun] either of two North Caucasian languages of these peoples, Adyghe and Kabardian. Also called **CHERKESS**.
– ORIGIN from *Circassia*, Latinized form of Russian *Cherkes*, denoting a district in the northern Caucasus.

Circe /ˈsəːsi/ Greek Mythology an enchantress who lived with her wild animals on the island of Aeaea. When Odysseus visited the island his companions were changed into pigs by her potions, but he

protected himself with the mythical herb *moly* and forced her to restore his men into human form.
– ORIGIN via Latin from Greek *Kirkē*.

circinate /ˈsəːsɪnət, -eɪt/ ▶ **adjective** Botany rolled up with the tip in the centre, for example the young frond of a fern.
▪ Medicine circular in appearance.
– ORIGIN early 19th cent.: from Latin *circinatus*, past participle of *circinare* 'make round', from *circinus* 'pair of compasses'.

C

Circinus /ˈsəːsɪnəs/ Astronomy a small and faint southern constellation (the Compasses), in the Milky Way next to Centaurus.
▪ [as genitive **Circini** /ˈsəːsɪni/] used with preceding letter or numeral to designate a star in this constellation: *the star Alpha Circini.*
– ORIGIN Latin.

circle ▶ **noun 1** a round plane figure whose boundary (the circumference) consists of points equidistant from a fixed point (the centre).
▪ the line enclosing such a figure. ▪ something in the shape of such a figure: *the lamp spread a circle of light.* ▪ a group of people or things arranged to form such a figure: *they all sat round in a circle.* ▪ a movement or series of movements which follows the approximate circumference of such a figure: *describing a large circle, she arrived back at the camp.* ▪ a dark circular mark below each eye, typically caused by illness or tiredness. ▪ a curved upper tier of seats in a theatre or cinema. See also **DRESS CIRCLE**. ▪ Archaeology short for **STONE CIRCLE**. ▪ Hockey short for **STRIKING CIRCLE**.
2 a group of people with a shared profession, interests, or acquaintances: *she did not normally move in such exalted circles.*
▶ **verb** [with obj.] move all the way around (someone or something), especially more than once and in the air: *they were circling Athens airport* | [as adj. **circling**] *a circling helicopter* | [no obj.] *we circled round the island.*
▪ [no obj.] (**circle back**) move in a wide loop back towards one's starting point. ▪ (often **be circled**) form a ring around: *the abbey was circled by a huge wall.* ▪ draw a line around: *circle the correct answers.*
– PHRASES **circle the wagons** N. Amer. informal (of a group) unite in defence of a common interest. [ORIGIN: with reference to the defensive position of a wagon train under attack.] **come** (or **turn**) **full circle** return to a past position or situation, especially in a way considered to be inevitable. **go round in circles** informal do something for a long time without achieving anything but purposeless repetition: *the discussion went round and round in circles.* **run round in circles** informal be fussily busy with little result. **the wheel has turned** (or **come**) **full circle** the situation has returned to what it was in the past, as if completing a cycle. [ORIGIN: with reference to Shakespeare's *King Lear*, by association with the wheel fabled to be turned by Fortune and representing mutability.]
– ORIGIN Old English, from Old French *cercle*, from Latin *circulus* 'small ring', diminutive of *circus* 'ring'.

circle dance ▶ **noun** a country dance or folk dance, typically following a traditional set of steps, in which dancers form a circle.

circlet ▶ **noun** a circular band, typically one made of precious metal, worn on the head as an ornament.
▪ a small circular arrangement or object.
– ORIGIN late Middle English: from **CIRCLE** + **-ET**[1], perhaps reinforced by archaic French *cerclet*.

circlip /ˈsəːklɪp/ ▶ **noun** Brit. a metal ring sprung into a slot or groove in a bar to hold something in place.
– ORIGIN early 20th cent.: blend of **CIRCLE** or **CIRCULAR** and **CLIP**[1].

circs ▶ **plural noun** Brit. informal circumstances: *anyone would have done the same under the circs.*
– ORIGIN mid 19th cent.: abbreviation.

circuit ▶ **noun 1** a roughly circular line, route, or movement that starts and finishes at the same place: *I ran a circuit of the village.*
▪ Brit. a track used for motor racing, horse racing, or athletics. ▪ a complete and closed path around which a circulating electric current can flow. ▪ a system of electrical conductors and components forming such a path.
2 an established itinerary of events or venues used for a particular activity, typically involving public performance: *the alternative cabaret circuit.*
▪ a series of sporting events in which the same players regularly take part: *his first season on the professional circuit.* ▪ a series of athletic exercises performed consecutively in one training session: [as modifier] *circuit training.* ▪ (in the UK) a regular journey made by a judge around a particular district to hear cases in court: [as modifier] *a circuit judge.* ▪ a district of this type. ▪ a group of local Methodist Churches forming an administrative unit. ▪ a chain of theatres or cinemas under a single management.
▶ **verb** [with obj.] move all the way around (a place or thing): *the trains will follow the Northern line, circuiting the capital.*
– ORIGIN late Middle English: via Old French from Latin *circuitus*, from *circuire*, variant of *circumire* 'go round', from *circum* 'around' + *ire* 'go'.

circuit board ▶ **noun** a thin rigid board containing an electric circuit; a printed circuit.

circuit-breaker ▶ **noun** an automatic device for stopping the flow of current in an electric circuit as a safety measure.

circuitous ▶ **adjective** (of a route or journey) longer than the most direct way: *the canal followed a circuitous route* | figurative *a circuitous line of reasoning.*
– DERIVATIVES **circuitously** adverb, **circuitousness** noun.
– ORIGIN mid 17th cent.: from medieval Latin *circuitosus*, from *circuitus* 'a way around'(see **CIRCUIT**).

circuit rider ▶ **noun** N. Amer. historical a clergyman who travelled on horseback from church to church, especially within a rural Methodist circuit.

circuitry ▶ **noun** (pl. **-ies**) [mass noun] electric circuits collectively: *solid state circuitry.*
▪ a circuit or system of circuits performing a particular function in an electronic device: *switching circuitry.*

circular ▶ **adjective 1** having the form of a circle: *the building features a circular atrium.*
▪ (of a movement or journey) starting and finishing at the same place and often following roughly the circumference of an imaginary circle: *a circular walk.*
2 Logic (of an argument) already containing an assumption of what is to be proved, and therefore fallacious.
3 [attrib.] (of a letter or advertisement) for distribution to a large number of people.
▶ **noun** a letter or advertisement which is distributed to a large number of people.
– DERIVATIVES **circularity** noun, **circularly** adverb.
– ORIGIN late Middle English: from Old French *circulier*, from late Latin *circularis*, from Latin *circulus* 'small ring' (see **CIRCLE**).

circular breathing ▶ **noun** [mass noun] a technique of inhaling through the nose while blowing air through the lips from the cheeks, used to maintain constant exhalation especially by players of certain wind instruments.

circularize (also **-ise**) ▶ **verb** [with obj.] **1** distribute a large number of letters, leaflets, or questionnaires to (a group of people) in order to advertise something or canvas opinion.
2 Biochemistry make (a stretch of DNA) into a circular loop.
– DERIVATIVES **circularization** noun.

circular polarization ▶ **noun** [mass noun] Physics polarization of an electromagnetic wave in which either the electric or the magnetic vector executes a circle perpendicular to the path of propagation with a frequency equal to that of the wave. It is frequently used in satellite communications.

circular saw ▶ **noun** a power saw with a rapidly rotating toothed disc.

circulate ▶ **verb 1** move or cause to move continuously or freely through a closed system or area: [no obj.] *antibodies circulate in the bloodstream* | [with obj.] *the fan circulates hot air around the oven.*
▪ [no obj.] move around a social function in order to talk to many different people.
2 pass or cause to pass from place to place or person to person: [no obj.] *rumours of his arrest circulated* | [with obj.] *they were circulating the list to conservation groups.*
▪ [with obj.] (often **be circulated**) send copies of a letter or leaflet to (a group of people): *tutors were circulated with the handout.*
– DERIVATIVES **circulative** adjective, **circulator** noun.
– ORIGIN late 15th cent. (as an alchemical term meaning 'distil something in a closed container, allowing condensed vapour to return to the original liquid'): from Latin *circulat-* 'moved in a circular path', from the verb *circulare*, from *circulus* 'small ring' (see **CIRCLE**). Sense 1 dates from the mid 17th cent.

circulating library ▶ **noun** historical a small library with books lent for a small fee to subscribers.

circulating medium ▶ **noun** a commodity used in commercial exchange, especially coins or gold.

circulation ▶ **noun** [mass noun] **1** movement to and fro or around something, especially that of fluid in a closed system: *an extra pump for good water circulation.*
▪ the continuous motion by which the blood travels through all parts of the body under the action of the heart. ▪ the movement of sap through a plant.
2 the public availability or knowledge of something: *his music has achieved wide circulation.*
▪ the movement, exchange, or availability of money in a country: *the new-look 10p coins go into circulation today.* ▪ [in sing.] the number of copies sold of a newspaper or magazine: *the magazine had a large circulation.*
– PHRASES **in** (or **out of**) **circulation** available (or unavailable) to the public; in (or not in) general use: *there is a huge volume of video material in circulation.* ▪ used of a person who is seen (or not seen) in public: *Anne had made a good recovery and was back in circulation.*
– ORIGIN late Middle English (denoting continuous distillation of a liquid): from Latin *circulatio(n-)*, from the verb *circulare* (see **CIRCULATE**).

circulatory ▶ **adjective** of or relating to the circulation of blood or sap.

circum- /ˈsəːkəm/ ▶ **prefix** about; around. (functioning within the word as an adverb as in *circumambulate*, or as a preposition as in *circumpolar*).
– ORIGIN from Latin *circum* 'round'.

circumambient /ˌsəːkəmˈambɪənt/ ▶ **adjective** chiefly poetic/literary surrounding: *he could not see them clearly by reason of the circumambient water.*
– DERIVATIVES **circumambience** noun, **circumambiency** noun.

circumambulate /ˌsəːkəmˈambjʊleɪt/ ▶ **verb** [with obj.] formal walk all the way round: *they used to circumambulate the perimeter wall.*
– DERIVATIVES **circumambulation** noun, **circumambulatory** adjective.

circumcircle ▶ **noun** Geometry a circle touching all the vertices of a triangle or polygon.

circumcise /ˈsəːkəmsʌɪz/ ▶ **verb** [with obj.] cut off the foreskin of (a young boy or man, especially a baby) as a religious rite, especially in Judaism and Islam, or as a medical treatment.
▪ cut off the clitoris, and sometimes the labia, of (a girl or young woman) as a traditional practice among some peoples.
– ORIGIN Middle English: from Old French *circonciser*, or from Latin *circumcis-* 'cut around', from the verb *circumcidere*, from *circum* 'around, about' + *caedere* 'to cut'.

circumcision ▶ **noun** [mass noun] the action or practice of circumcising a young boy or man. See also **FEMALE CIRCUMCISION**.
▪ (**Circumcision**) (in church use) the feast of the Circumcision of Christ, 1 January.
– ORIGIN Middle English: from late Latin *circumcisio(n-)*, from the verb *circumcidere* (see **CIRCUMCISE**).

circumference /səˈkʌmf(ə)r(ə)ns/ ▶ **noun** the enclosing boundary of a curved geometric figure, especially a circle.
▪ the distance around something: *babies who have small head circumferences* | [mass noun] *two inches in circumference.* ▪ the edge or region which entirely surrounds something: *petals on the circumference are larger than those in the centre.*
– DERIVATIVES **circumferential** adjective, **circumferentially** adverb.
– ORIGIN late Middle English: from Old French *circonference*, from Latin *circumferentia*, from *circum* 'around, about' + *ferre* 'carry, bear'.

circumflex /ˈsəːkəmflɛks/ ▶ **noun** (also **circumflex accent**) a mark (ˆ) placed over a vowel in some languages to indicate contraction, length, or a particular quality.
▶ **adjective** Anatomy bending round something else; curved: *circumflex coronary arteries.*
– ORIGIN late 16th cent.: from Latin *circumflexus* (from *circum* 'around, about' + *flectere* 'to bend'), translating Greek *perispōmenos* 'drawn around'.

circumfluent /səːˈkʌmflʊənt/ ▶ **adjective** flowing round; surrounding.
– DERIVATIVES **circumfluence** noun.

– ORIGIN late 16th cent.: from Latin *circumfluent-* 'flowing around', from the verb *circumfluere*, from *circum* 'around, about' + *fluere* 'to flow'.

circumfuse /ˌsəːkəmˈfjuːz/ ▶ **verb** [with obj.] (usu. **be circumfused**) archaic pour (a liquid) so as to cause it to surround something: *Earth with her nether Ocean circumfused.*
– ORIGIN late 16th cent.: from Latin *circumfus-* 'poured around', from the verb *circumfundere*, from *circum* 'around' + *fundere* 'pour'.

circumjacent /ˌsəːkəmˈdʒeɪs(ə)nt/ ▶ **adjective** archaic surrounding.
– ORIGIN late 15th cent.: from Latin *circumjacent-* 'lying round about, bordering upon', from the verb *circumjacere*, from *circum* 'around' + *jacere* 'to lie'.

circumlocution /ˌsəːkəmləˈkjuːʃ(ə)n/ ▶ **noun** [mass noun] the use of many words where fewer would do, especially in a deliberate attempt to be vague or evasive: *his admission came after years of circumlocution* | [count noun] *he used a number of poetic circumlocutions.*
– DERIVATIVES **circumlocutory** /-ˈlɒkjʊt(ə)ri/ adjective.
– ORIGIN late Middle English: from Latin *circumlocutio(n-)* (translating Greek *periphrasis*), from *circum* 'around' + *locutio(n-)* from *loqui* 'speak'.

circumlunar ▶ **adjective** moving or situated around the moon: *a circumlunar flight.*

circumnavigate ▶ **verb** [with obj.] sail all the way around (something, especially the world).
■ humorous go around or across (something): *he helped her to circumnavigate a frozen puddle.*
– DERIVATIVES **circumnavigation** noun, **circumnavigator** noun.

circumpolar /səːkəmˈpəʊlə/ ▶ **adjective** situated around or inhabiting one of the earth's poles: *a strong circumpolar vortex.*
■ Astronomy (of a star or motion) above the horizon at all times in a given latitude: *the Plough is circumpolar from Britain.*

circumscribe ▶ **verb** [with obj.] (often **be circumscribed**) **1** restrict (something) within limits: *their movements were strictly monitored and circumscribed.*
2 Geometry draw (a figure) round another, touching it at points but not cutting it. Compare with **INSCRIBE**.
– DERIVATIVES **circumscriber** noun, **circumscription** noun.
– ORIGIN late Middle English: from Latin *circumscribere*, from *circum* 'around' + *scribere* 'write'.

circumsolar /ˌsəːkəmˈsəʊlə/ ▶ **adjective** moving or situated around the sun.

circumspect ▶ **adjective** wary and unwilling to take risks: *the officials were very circumspect in their statements.*
– DERIVATIVES **circumspection** noun, **circumspectly** adverb.
– ORIGIN late Middle English: from Latin *circumspectus*, from *circumspicere* 'look around', from *circum* 'around, about' + *specere* 'look'.

circumstance ▶ **noun 1** (usu. **circumstances**) a fact or condition connected with or relevant to an event or action: *we wanted to marry but circumstances didn't permit.*
■ an event or fact that causes or helps to cause something to happen, typically something undesirable: *he was found dead but there were no suspicious circumstances* | [mass noun] *they were thrown together by circumstance.*
2 one's state of financial or material welfare: *the artists are living in reduced circumstances.*
– PHRASES **circumstances alter cases** proverb one's opinion or treatment of someone or something may vary according to the prevailing circumstances. **under** (or **in**) **the circumstances** given the difficult nature of the situation: *she had every right to be cross under the circumstances.* **under** (or **in**) **no circumstances** never, whatever the situation is or might be: *under no circumstances may the child be identified.*
– DERIVATIVES **circumstanced** adjective.
– ORIGIN Middle English: from Old French *circonstance* or Latin *circumstantia*, from *circumstare* 'encircle, encompass', from *circum* 'around' + *stare* 'stand'.

circumstantial ▶ **adjective 1** (of evidence or a legal case) pointing indirectly towards someone's guilt but not conclusively proving it.
2 (of a description) containing full details: *the picture was so circumstantial that it began to be convincing.*
– DERIVATIVES **circumstantiality** noun, **circumstantially** adverb.
– ORIGIN late 16th cent.: from Latin *circumstantia* (see **CIRCUMSTANCE**) + **-AL**.

circumterrestrial ▶ **adjective** moving or situated around the earth: *circumterrestrial space.*

circumvallate /ˌsəːkəmˈvaleɪt/ ▶ **verb** [with obj.] poetic/literary surround or surrounding with or as if with a rampart: *the walls were circumvallated with a ditch.*
▶ **adjective** poetic/literary surrounded or surrounding as if by a rampart: *we looked at the circumvallate mountains.*
■ Anatomy denoting certain papillae near the back of the tongue, surrounded by taste receptors.
– ORIGIN mid 17th cent. (as an adjective): from Latin *circumvallat-* 'surrounded with a rampart', from the verb *circumvallare*, from *circum* 'around' + *vallare*, from *vallum* 'rampart'. The verb dates from the early 19th cent.

circumvent /səːkəmˈvɛnt/ ▶ **verb** [with obj.] find a way around (an obstacle).
■ overcome (a problem or difficulty), typically in a clever and surreptitious way: *terrorists found the airport checks easy to circumvent.* ■ archaic deceive; outwit: *he's circumvented her with some of his stories.*
– DERIVATIVES **circumvention** noun.
– ORIGIN late Middle English: from Latin *cirumvent-* 'skirted around', from the verb *circumvenire*, from *circum* 'around' + *venire* 'come'.

circumvolution /ˌsəːkəmvəˈluːʃ(ə)n/ ▶ **noun** a winding movement, especially of one thing round another.
– ORIGIN late Middle English: from Latin *circumvolut-* 'rolled around', from the verb *circumvolvere*, from *circum* 'around' + *volvere* 'roll'.

circus ▶ **noun** (pl. **circuses**) **1** a travelling company of acrobats, trained animals, and clowns which gives performances, typically in a large tent, in a series of different places: [as modifier] *a circus elephant.*
■ (in ancient Rome) a rounded or oval arena lined with tiers of seats, used for equestrian and other sports and games. ■ informal a group of people involved in a particular sport who travel around to compete against one another in a series of different places: *the Formula One grand prix circus.* ■ informal a public scene of frenetic and noisily intrusive activity: *a media circus.*
2 [in place names] Brit. a rounded open space in a town where several streets converge: *Piccadilly Circus.*
– ORIGIN late Middle English (with reference to the arena of Roman antiquity): from Latin, 'ring or circus'. The sense 'travelling company of performers' dates from the late 18th cent.

ciré /ˈsiːreɪ/ (also **cire** /siːə/) ▶ **noun** [mass noun] a fabric with a smooth shiny surface obtained by waxing and heating.
– ORIGIN 1920s: French, literally 'waxed'.

Cirencester /ˈsʌɪrənˌsɛstə/ a town in Gloucestershire; pop. 14,000 (1981). It was a major town in Roman Britain, when it was known as Corinium Dobunorum.

cire perdue /ˌsɪə pəːˈdjuː/ ▶ **noun** [mass noun] a method of bronze casting using a clay core and a wax coating placed in a mould. The wax is melted in the mould and drained out, and bronze poured into the space left, producing a hollow bronze figure when the core is discarded. Also called **LOST WAX**.
– ORIGIN French, 'lost wax'.

cirl bunting /səːl/ ▶ **noun** an Old World bunting related to the yellowhammer, now rare in Britain. The male has a distinctive facial pattern and a black throat.
• *Emberiza cirlus*, family Emberizidae (subfamily Emberizinae).
– ORIGIN late 18th cent.: *cirl* from Italian *cirlo*, probably from *zirlare* 'whistle as a thrush'.

cirque /səːk/ ▶ **noun 1** Geology a half-open steep-sided hollow at the head of a valley or on a mountainside, formed by glacial erosion. Also called **CORRIE** or **CWM**.
2 poetic/literary a ring, circlet, or circle.
– ORIGIN late 17th cent. (in sense 2): from French, from Latin *circus*.

cirrhosis /sɪˈrəʊsɪs/ ▶ **noun** [mass noun] a chronic disease of the liver marked by degeneration of cells, inflammation, and fibrous thickening of tissue. It is typically a result of alcoholism or hepatitis.
– DERIVATIVES **cirrhotic** /sɪˈrɒtɪk/ adjective.
– ORIGIN early 19th cent.: modern Latin, from Greek *kirrhos* 'tawny' (because this is the colour of the liver in many cases).

Cirripedia /ˌsɪrɪˈpiːdɪə/ Zoology a class of crustaceans that comprises the barnacles.
– DERIVATIVES **cirriped** noun, **cirripede** noun.
– ORIGIN modern Latin (plural), from Latin *cirrus* 'a curl' (because of the form of the legs) + *pes, ped-* 'foot'.

cirrocumulus /ˌsɪrəʊˈkjuːmjʊləs/ ▶ **noun** [mass noun] cloud forming a broken layer of small fleecy clouds at high altitude (usually 5 to 13 km, 16,500 to 45,000 ft), typically with a rippled or granulated appearance (as in a mackerel sky).

cirrostratus /ˌsɪrəʊˈstrɑːtəs, -ˈstreɪtəs/ ▶ **noun** [mass noun] cloud forming a thin, more or less uniform semi-translucent layer at high altitude (usually 5 to 13 km, 16,500 to 45,000 ft).

cirrus /ˈsɪrəs/ ▶ **noun** (pl. **cirri** /-rʌɪ/) **1** [mass noun] cloud forming wispy filamentous tufted streaks or 'mare's tails' at high altitude (usually 5 to 13 km, 16,500 to 45,000 ft).
2 Zoology a slender tendril or hair-like filament, such as the appendage of a barnacle, the barbel of a fish, or the intromittent organ of an earthworm.
■ Botany a tendril.
– ORIGIN early 18th cent. (in the sense 'tendril'): from Latin, literally 'a curl'.

CIS ▶ **abbreviation for** Commonwealth of Independent States.

cis /sɪs/ ▶ **adjective** Chemistry denoting or relating to a molecular structure in which two particular atoms or groups lie on the same side of a given plane in the molecule, in particular denoting an isomer in which substituents at opposite ends of a carbon–carbon double bond are on the same side of the bond: *the cis isomer of stilbene.* Compare with **TRANS**.
– ORIGIN independent usage of **CIS-**.

cis- ▶ **prefix 1** on this side of; on the side nearer to the speaker: *cisatlantic* | *cislunar.*
■ historical on the side nearer to Rome: *cisalpine.* ■ (of time) closer to the present: *cis-Elizabethan.* Often contrasted with **TRANS-** or **ULTRA-**.
2 Chemistry (usu. ***cis-***) denoting molecules with cis arrangements of substituents: *cis-1,2-dichloroethene.*
– ORIGIN from Latin *cis* 'on this side of'.

cisalpine /sɪsˈalpʌɪn/ ▶ **adjective** on the southern side of the Alps.
– ORIGIN mid 16th cent.: from Latin *cisalpinus*.

Cisalpine Gaul see **GAUL**[1].

cisatlantic /sɪsətˈlantɪk/ ▶ **adjective** on the same side of the Atlantic as the speaker.

cisco /ˈsɪskəʊ/ ▶ **noun** (pl. **-oes**) a freshwater whitefish of northern countries. Most species are migratory and are important food fishes.
• Genus *Coregonus*, family Salmonidae: several species, including the **lake cisco** (*C. artedii*) of North America, and the **Arctic cisco** (*C. autumnalis*) of northern Eurasia and northern North America (see also **POLLAN**).
– ORIGIN mid 19th cent.: of unknown origin.

Ciskei /sɪsˈkʌɪ/ a former homeland established in South Africa for the Xhosa people, now part of the province of Eastern Cape. See also **HOMELAND**.

cislunar /sɪsˈluːnə/ ▶ **adjective** between the earth and the moon: *the darkness of cislunar space.*

cisplatin /sɪsˈplatɪn/ ▶ **noun** [mass noun] Medicine a cytotoxic drug used in cancer chemotherapy.
• A coordination compound of platinum; chem. formula: $Pt(NH_3)_2Cl_2$.
– ORIGIN late 20th cent.: from **CIS-** (in sense 2) + **PLATINUM**.

cispontine /sɪsˈpɒntʌɪn/ ▶ **adjective** archaic on the north side of the Thames bridges in London (originally the better known side).
– ORIGIN mid 19th cent.: from **CIS-** 'on this side' + Latin *pons, pont-* 'bridge'.

cissing /ˈsɪsɪŋ/ ▶ **noun** [mass noun] the cracking that sometimes occurs in a top coat of paint.
– ORIGIN late 19th cent.: of unknown origin.

cissus /ˈsɪsəs/ ▶ **noun** a woody climbing vine of a genus that includes the kangaroo vine.
• Genus *Cissus*, family Vitaceae.
– ORIGIN modern Latin: from Greek *kissos* 'ivy'.

cissy ▶ **noun & adjective** variant spelling of **SISSY**.

cist[1] /sɪst/ (also **kist**) ▶ **noun** Archaeology a coffin or burial chamber made from stone or a hollowed tree.
– ORIGIN Welsh, literally 'chest'.

C

cist² /sɪst/ ▶ **noun** a box used in ancient Greece for sacred utensils.
– ORIGIN mid 19th cent.: from Latin *cista*, from Greek *kistē* 'box'.

Cistercian /sɪˈstəːʃ(ə)n/ ▶ **noun** a monk or nun of an order founded in 1098 as a stricter branch of the Benedictines. The monks are now divided into two observances, the strict observance, whose adherents are known popularly as Trappists, and the common observance, which has certain relaxations.
▶ **adjective** of or relating to this order: *a Cistercian abbey*.
– ORIGIN from French *cistercien*, from *Cistercium*, the Latin name of *Cîteaux* near Dijon in France, where the order was founded.

cistern ▶ **noun** a tank for storing water, especially one supplying taps or as part of a flushing toilet.
▪ an underground reservoir for rainwater.
– ORIGIN Middle English: from Old French *cisterne*, from Latin *cisterna*, from *cista* 'box' (see **CIST²**).

cisticola /sɪsˈtɪkələ, ˌsɪstɪˈkəʊlə/ ▶ **noun** a small Old World warbler, typically with brownish streaked plumage and secretive habits, found mainly in Africa.
● Genus *Cisticola*, family Sylviidae: numerous species. See also **FAN-TAILED WARBLER**.
– ORIGIN modern Latin, from Greek *kistos* 'flowering shrub' + Latin *-col-* 'dwelling in' (from the verb *colere*).

cistron /ˈsɪstrɒn/ ▶ **noun** Biochemistry a section of a DNA or RNA molecule that codes for a specific polypeptide in protein synthesis.
– ORIGIN 1950s: from **CIS-** (in sense 2) + **TRANS-** (because of the possibility of two genes being on the same or different chromosomes) + **-ON**.

cistus /ˈsɪstəs/ ▶ **noun** a southern European shrub with large white or red flowers. The resin ladanum is extracted by boiling the twigs. Also called **ROCK ROSE**.
● Genus *Cistus*, family Cistaceae.
– ORIGIN modern Latin, from Greek *kistos*.

citadel /ˈsɪtəd(ə)l, -dɛl/ ▶ **noun** **1** a fortress, typically on high ground protecting or dominating a city.
2 a meeting hall of the Salvation Army.
– ORIGIN mid 16th cent.: from French *citadelle*, or from Italian *cittadella*, based on Latin *civitas* 'city' (see **CITY**).

citation /sʌɪˈteɪʃ(ə)n/ ▶ **noun** **1** a quotation from or reference to a book, paper, or author, especially in a scholarly work: *the majority of the citations are to work published during the past 20 years* | [mass noun] *recognition through citation is one of the principal rewards in science*.
▪ a mention of a praiseworthy act or achievement in an official report, especially that of a member of the armed forces in wartime. ▪ a note accompanying an award, describing the reasons for it: *the Nobel citation noted that his discovery would be useful for energy conversion technology*. ▪ Law a reference to a former tried case, used as guidance in the trying of comparable cases or in support of an argument.
2 Law, chiefly N. Amer. a summons: *a traffic citation*.
– ORIGIN Middle English (in sense 2): from Old French, from Latin *citatio(n-)*, from *citare* 'cite'.

cite /sʌɪt/ ▶ **verb** [with obj.] (often **be cited**) **1** quote (a passage, book, or author) as evidence for or justification of an argument or statement, especially in a scholarly work.
▪ mention as an example: *medics have been cited as a key example of a modern breed of technical expert*. ▪ praise (someone, typically a member of the armed forces) for a courageous act in an official dispatch.
2 Law summon (someone) to appear in a law court: *the writ cited only four of the signatories of the petition*.
▶ **noun** US a citation.
– DERIVATIVES **citable** adjective.
– ORIGIN late Middle English (in sense 2, originally with reference to a court of ecclesiastical law): from Old French *citer*, from Latin *citare*, from *ciere*, *cire* 'to call'.

CITES /ˈsʌɪtiːz/ ▶ **abbreviation for** Convention on International Trade in Endangered Species.

citified (also **cityfied**) ▶ **adjective** chiefly derogatory characteristic of or adjusted to an urban environment: *rainbow-colour shirted, citified cowboys*.

citizen ▶ **noun** a legally recognized subject or national of a state or commonwealth, either native or naturalized: *a British citizen*.
▪ an inhabitant of a particular town or city: *the citizens of Edinburgh*.
– PHRASES **citizen of the world** a person who is at home in any country.
– DERIVATIVES **citizenry** noun, **citizenship** noun.
– ORIGIN Middle English: from Anglo-Norman French *citezein*, alteration (probably influenced by *deinzein* 'denizen') of Old French *citeain*, based on Latin *civitas* 'city' (see **CITY**).

Citizen Force ▶ **noun** the reserve force of the South African Defence Force, comprised of civilians who have completed a period of national service but have to serve additional short periods annually for several years.

Citizens' Advice Bureau ▶ **noun** (in the UK) an office at which the public can receive free advice and information on civil matters.

citizen's arrest ▶ **noun** an arrest by an ordinary person without a warrant, allowable in certain cases.

Citizens' Band (abbrev.: **CB**) ▶ **noun** [mass noun] a range of radio frequencies which are allocated for local communication by private individuals, especially by hand-held or vehicle radio.

Citizen's Charter ▶ **noun** a document setting out the rights of citizens, especially a British government document of 1991, guaranteeing citizens the right of redress where a public service fails to meet certain standards.

Citlaltépetl /ˌsiːtlalˈteɪpɛt(ə)l/ the highest peak in Mexico, in the east of the country, north of the city of Orizaba. It rises to a height of 5,699 m (18,503 ft) and is an extinct volcano. Spanish name **PICO DE ORIZABA**.
– ORIGIN Aztec, literally 'star mountain'.

citole /sɪˈtəʊl/ ▶ **noun** a lute-like medieval stringed instrument, forerunner of the cittern.
– ORIGIN late Middle English: from Old French, based on Latin *cithara* (see **CITTERN**).

citral /ˈsɪtral/ ▶ **noun** [mass noun] Chemistry a fragrant liquid occurring in citrus and lemon grass oils and used in flavourings and perfumes.
● A terpene; chem. formula: $C_{10}H_{16}O$.

citric ▶ **adjective** derived from or related to citrus fruit: *lemon grass gives a slightly sweet citric flavour*.
– ORIGIN late 18th cent.: from Latin *citrus* 'citron tree' + **-IC**.

citric acid ▶ **noun** [mass noun] Chemistry a sharp-tasting crystalline acid present in the juice of lemons and other sour fruits. It is made commercially by the fermentation of sugar and used as a flavouring and setting agent.
● A tribasic acid; chem. formula: $C_6H_8O_7$.
– DERIVATIVES **citrate** noun.

citriculture /ˈsɪtrɪˌkʌltʃə/ ▶ **noun** [mass noun] the cultivation of citrus fruit trees.

citril /ˈsɪtrɪl/ (also **citril finch**) ▶ **noun** a small European and African finch related to the canary, with generally yellowish-green plumage.
● Genus *Serinus*, family Fringillidae: two species, in particular *S. citrinella*, which has grey on the head and back.
– ORIGIN late 17th cent.: apparently from Italian *citrinella*, diminutive of *citrina* 'citrine-coloured (bird)'.

citrine /ˈsɪtrɪn/ ▶ **noun** (also **citrine quartz**) [mass noun] a glassy yellow variety of quartz.
▪ a light greenish-yellow.
– ORIGIN late Middle English: from Old French *citrin* 'lemon-coloured', from medieval Latin *citrinus*, from Latin *citrus* 'citron tree'.

citron /ˈsɪtr(ə)n/ ▶ **noun** a shrubby Asian tree which bears large lemon-like fruits, but with less acid flesh and thick fragrant peel.
● *Citrus medica*, family Rutaceae; one of the ancestors of modern commercial citrus fruits.
▪ the fruit of this tree.
– ORIGIN early 16th cent. (denoting the fruit): from French, from Latin *citrus* 'citron tree', on the pattern of *limon* 'lemon'.

citronella ▶ **noun** **1** (also **citronella oil**) [mass noun] a fragrant natural oil used as an insect repellent and in perfume and soap manufacture.
2 the South Asian grass from which this oil is obtained.
● *Cymbopogon nardus*, family Gramineae.
– ORIGIN mid 19th cent.: modern Latin, from **CITRON** + the diminutive suffix *-ella*.

citrus ▶ **noun** (pl. **citruses**) a tree of a genus that includes citron, lemon, lime, orange, and grapefruit. Native to Asia, citrus trees are widely cultivated in warm countries for their fruit, which has juicy flesh and pulpy rind.
● Genus *Citrus*, family Rutaceae.
▪ (also **citrus fruit**) a fruit from such a tree.
– DERIVATIVES **citrous** adjective, **citrusy** adjective.
– ORIGIN Latin, 'citron tree, thuja'.

cittern /ˈsɪt(ə)n/ ▶ **noun** a stringed instrument similar to a lute, with a flattened back and wire strings, used in 16th- and 17th-century Europe.
– ORIGIN mid 16th cent.: from Latin *cithara*, from Greek *kithara*, denoting a kind of harp. The spelling has been influenced by **GITTERN**.

city ▶ **noun** (pl. **-ies**) **1** a large town: [as modifier] *the city centre*.
▪ Brit. a town created a city by charter and containing a cathedral. ▪ N. Amer. a municipal centre incorporated by the state or province.
2 (**the City**) short for **CITY OF LONDON**.
▪ the financial and commercial institutions located in this part of London: *the Budget got a stony reception from the City* | [as modifier] *a City analyst*.
– DERIVATIVES **cityward** adjective & adverb, **citywards** adverb.
– ORIGIN Middle English: from Old French *cite*, from Latin *civitas*, from *civis* 'citizen'. Originally denoting a town, and often used as a Latin equivalent to Old English *burh* 'borough', the term was later applied to foreign and ancient cities and to the more important English boroughs. The connection between city and cathedral grew up under the Norman kings, as the episcopal sees (many had been established in villages) were removed to the chief borough of the diocese.

City and Guilds Institute (in the UK) an institute based in London which is responsible for courses and examinations in technical and craft subjects, generally at a lower level than university degrees.

City Company ▶ **noun** (in the UK) a corporation descended from an ancient trade guild of London.

city desk ▶ **noun** Brit. the department of a newspaper dealing with business news.
▪ N. Amer. the department of a newspaper dealing with local news.

City editor ▶ **noun** Brit. an editor dealing with financial news in a newspaper or magazine.
▪ (**city editor**) N. Amer. an editor dealing with local news in a newspaper or magazine.

city farm ▶ **noun** chiefly Brit. a farm established within an urban area for educational purposes.

city father ▶ **noun** (usu. **city fathers**) a person concerned with or experienced in the administration of a city: *the city fathers decided to build a museum*.

cityfied ▶ **adjective** variant spelling of **CITIFIED**.

city gent ▶ **noun** Brit. informal a businessman, as typified by those working in the financial district of the City of London.

city hall ▶ **noun** [treated as sing.] N. Amer. municipal offices or officers collectively.

city manager ▶ **noun** N. Amer. (in some cities) an official directing the administration of a city.

City of God Paradise, perceived as an ideal community in Heaven.
▪ the Christian Church. [ORIGIN: from *The City of God* by St Augustine.]

City of London the part of London situated within the ancient boundaries and governed by the Lord Mayor and the Corporation.

city page ▶ **noun** Brit. the part of a newspaper or magazine that deals with the financial news.

city planning ▶ **noun** US term for **TOWN PLANNING**.

cityscape ▶ **noun** the visual appearance of a city or urban area; a city landscape: *shades of red brick which once coloured the cityscape*.
▪ a picture of a city.

city slicker ▶ **noun** a person with the sophistication and tastes or values generally associated with urban dwellers, typically regarded as unprincipled and untrustworthy.

city state ▶ **noun** chiefly historical a city that with its surrounding territory forms an independent state.

City Technology College (abbrev.: **CTC**) ▶ **noun** (in the UK) a type of secondary school set up through partnerships between the government and business to teach technology and science in inner-city areas.

Ciudad Bolívar /sjuːˌdad bɒˈliːvɑː, Spanish sjuˈðað boˈliβar, θjuˈðað/ a city in SE Venezuela, on the Orinoco River; pop. 225,850 (1991). Formerly called Angostura, its name was changed in 1846 to honour the country's liberator, Simón Bolívar.

Ciudad Trujillo /truːˈhiːjəʊ, -ˈhiːljəʊ/ former name (1936–61) for **SANTO DOMINGO**.

Ciudad Victoria /vɪkˈtɔːrɪə, Spanish βikˈtorja/ a city in NE Mexico, capital of the state of Tamaulipas; pop. 207,830 (1990).

civet /ˈsɪvɪt/ ▶ **noun** (also **civet cat**) a slender nocturnal carnivorous mammal with a barred and spotted coat and well-developed anal scent glands, native to Africa and Asia.
• Family Viverridae (the **civet family**): several genera and species, in particular the **African civet** (*Viverra civetta*). The civet family also includes the genets, linsang, and fossa, and formerly included the mongooses.
■ [mass noun] a strong musky perfume obtained from the secretions of these scent glands. ■ (**civet cat**) [mass noun] an American commercial term for the fur of the ring-tailed cat.
– ORIGIN mid 16th cent.: from French *civette*, from Italian *zibetto*, from medieval Latin *zibethum*, from Arabic *zabād*, denoting the perfume.

civic ▶ **adjective** [attrib.] of or relating to a city or town, especially its administration; municipal: *civic and business leaders*.
■ of or relating to the duties or activities of people in relation to their town, city, or local area: *he was active in the civic life of Swindon*.
▶ **noun** informal (in South Africa) an elected, community-based body concerned with local government in a black township.
– DERIVATIVES **civically** adverb.
– ORIGIN mid 16th cent.: from French *civique* or Latin *civicus*, from *civis* 'citizen'. The original use was in *civic garland, crown*, etc., translating Latin *corona civica*, denoting a garland of oak leaves and acorns given in ancient Rome to a person who saved a fellow citizen's life.

civic centre ▶ **noun** the area in the centre of a town where municipal offices and other public buildings are situated.
■ a building containing municipal offices.

civics ▶ **plural noun** [usu. treated as sing.] the study of the rights and duties of citizenship.

civil ▶ **adjective 1** [attrib.] of or relating to ordinary citizens and their concerns, as distinct from military or ecclesiastical matters: *civil aviation*.
■ (of disorder or conflict) occurring between citizens of the same country. ■ Law relating to private relations between members of a community; non-criminal: *a civil action*.
2 courteous and polite: *they were comparatively civil to their daughter*.
3 (of time measurement or a point in time) fixed by custom or law rather than being natural or astronomical: *civil twilight*.
– DERIVATIVES **civilly** adverb.
– ORIGIN late Middle English: via Old French from Latin *civilis*, from *civis* 'citizen'.

civil commotion ▶ **noun** English Law a riot or similar disturbance.

civil court ▶ **noun** a court dealing with non-criminal cases.

civil defence ▶ **noun** [mass noun] the organization and training of civilians for the protection of lives and property during and after attacks in wartime.

civil disobedience ▶ **noun** [mass noun] the refusal to comply with certain laws or to pay taxes and fines, as a peaceful form of political protest.

civil engineer ▶ **noun** an engineer who designs and maintains roads, bridges, dams, and similar structures.
– DERIVATIVES **civil engineering** noun.

civilian ▶ **noun** a person not in the armed services or the police force.
▶ **adjective** of, denoting, or relating to a person not belonging to the armed services or police: *military agents in civilian clothes*.
– ORIGIN late Middle English (denoting a practitioner of civil law): from Old French *civilien*, in the phrase *droit civilien* 'civil law'. The current sense arose in the early 19th cent.

civilianize (also **-ise**) ▶ **verb** [with obj.] make (something) non-military in character or function.
– DERIVATIVES **civilianization** noun.

civility ▶ **noun** (pl. **-ies**) [mass noun] formal politeness and courtesy in behaviour or speech: *I hope we can treat each other with civility and respect*.
■ (**civilities**) polite remarks used in formal conversation: *she was exchanging civilities with his mother*.
– ORIGIN late Middle English: from Old French *civilite*, from Latin *civilitas*, from *civilis* 'relating to citizens' (see **CIVIL**). In early use the term denoted the state of being a citizen and hence good citizenship or orderly behaviour. The sense 'politeness' arose in the mid 16th cent.

civilization (also **-isation**) ▶ **noun** [mass noun] the stage of human social development and organization which is considered most advanced: *the Victorians equated the railways with progress and civilization*.
■ the process by which a society or place reaches this stage. ■ the society, culture, and way of life of a particular area: *the great books of Western civilization* | [count noun] *the early civilizations of Mesopotamia and Egypt*. ■ the comfort and convenience of modern life, regarded as available only in towns and cities: *in the UK nowhere is very far from civilization*.

civilize (also **-ise**) ▶ **verb** [with obj.] [usu. as adj. **civilized**] bring (a place or people) to a stage of social, cultural, and moral development considered to be more advanced: *a civilized society*.
■ [as adj. **civilized**] polite and good-mannered: *such an affront to civilized behaviour will no longer be tolerated*.
– DERIVATIVES **civilizable** adjective, **civilizer** noun.
– ORIGIN early 17th cent.: from French *civiliser*, from *civil* 'civil'.

civil law ▶ **noun** [mass noun] the system of law concerned with private relations between members of a community rather than criminal, military, or religious affairs. Contrasted with **CRIMINAL LAW**.
■ the system of law predominant on the European continent, historically influenced by that of ancient Rome. Compare with **COMMON LAW**.

civil liberty ▶ **noun** [mass noun] the state of being subject only to laws established for the good of the community, especially with regard to freedom of action and speech.
■ (**civil liberties**) a person's rights to be only so subject.
– DERIVATIVES **civil libertarian** noun.

Civil List ▶ **noun** (in the UK) an annual allowance voted by Parliament for the royal family's household expenses.

civil marriage ▶ **noun** a marriage solemnized as a civil contract without religious ceremony.

civil parish ▶ **noun** see **PARISH**.

civil rights ▶ **plural noun** the rights of citizens to political and social freedom and equality.

civil servant ▶ **noun** a member of the civil service.

civil service ▶ **noun** the permanent professional branches of a state's administration, excluding military and judicial branches and elected politicians.
– ORIGIN late 18th cent.: originally applied to the part of the service of the British East India Company conducted by staff who did not belong to the army or navy.

civil war ▶ **noun** a war between citizens of the same country.

civil wrong ▶ **noun** Law an infringement of a person's rights, such as a tort of breach of contract.

civil year ▶ **noun** see **YEAR** (sense 2).

civvy informal ▶ **noun** (pl. **-ies**) a civilian, as distinct from a member of the police force or armed services.
■ (**civvies**) civilian clothes, as opposed to uniform: *the Chief Constable came along in civvies*.
▶ **adjective** [attrib.] of or relating to civilians: *fliers who left the services for civvy airlines*.
– PHRASES **Civvy Street** Brit. informal civilian life: *ex-Service people starting life on Civvy Street*.
– ORIGIN late 19th cent.: abbreviation.

CJ ▶ **abbreviation for** Chief Justice.

CJD ▶ **abbreviation for** Creutzfeldt–Jakob disease.

CL ▶ **abbreviation for** ■ chemiluminescence. ■ Sri Lanka (international vehicle registration). [ORIGIN: from *Ceylon*.]

Cl ▶ **symbol for** the chemical element chlorine.

cl ▶ **abbreviation for** centilitre: *70 cl bottles*.

clabber chiefly US ▶ **noun** [mass noun] milk that has naturally clotted on souring.
▶ **verb** curdle or cause to curdle.
– ORIGIN early 19th cent.: shortening of **BONNY CLABBER**.

clachan /ˈklax(ə)n/ ▶ **noun** (in Scotland or Northern Ireland) a small village or hamlet.
– ORIGIN late Middle English: from Scottish Gaelic and Irish *clachán*.

clack ▶ **verb** make or cause to make a sharp sound or series of such sounds as a result of a hard object striking another: [no obj.] *he heard the sound of her heels clacking across flagstones* | [with obj.] *he clacked the bones in fine syncopation*.
■ [no obj.] archaic chatter loudly: *he will sit clacking for hours*.
▶ **noun** a sharp sound or series of sounds made in such a way: *the clack of her high heels*.
■ [mass noun] archaic loud chatter: *her clack would go all day*.
– DERIVATIVES **clacker** noun.
– ORIGIN Middle English: imitative.

clacket /ˈklakɪt/ ▶ **verb** (**clacketed**, **clacketing**) [no obj.] make a series of sharp sounds as a result of a hard object striking another.
– ORIGIN late 16th cent.: from French *claquet*, from *claquer* 'to clack'.

Clackmannan /klakˈmanən/ (also **Clackmannanshire**) an administrative region and former county of central Scotland; administrative centre, Alloa.

Clactonian /klakˈtəʊnɪən/ ▶ **adjective** Archaeology of, relating to, or denoting a Lower Palaeolithic culture represented by flint implements found at Clacton-on-Sea in SE England, dated to about 250,000–200,000 years ago.
■ [as noun **the Clactonian**] the Clactonian culture or period.

clad[1] archaic or poetic past participle of **CLOTHE**.
▶ **adjective 1** clothed: *they were **clad** in T-shirts and shorts* | [in combination] *glam leather-clad bad boys*.
2 provided with cladding: [in combination] *copper-clad boards*.

clad[2] ▶ **verb** (**cladding**; past and past participle **cladded** or **clad**) [with obj.] provide or encase with a covering or coating: *he cladded the concrete-frame structure in stainless steel*.
– ORIGIN mid 16th cent. (in the sense 'clothe'): apparently from **CLAD**[1].

Claddagh ring /ˈkladə/ ▶ **noun** a ring in the form of two hands clasping a heart, traditionally given in Ireland as a token of love.
– ORIGIN from the name of a small fishing village on the edge of Galway city.

cladding ▶ **noun** [mass noun] a covering or coating on a structure or material: [as modifier] *a range of roofing and cladding products*.

clade /kleɪd/ ▶ **noun** Biology a group of organisms believed to comprise all the evolutionary descendants of a common ancestor.
– ORIGIN 1950s: from Greek *klados* 'branch'.

cladistics /kləˈdɪstɪks/ ▶ **plural noun** [treated as sing.] Biology a method of classification of animals and plants that aims to identify and take account of only those shared characteristics which can be deduced to have originated in the common ancestor of a group of species during evolution, not those arising by convergence.
– DERIVATIVES **cladism** /ˈkladɪz(ə)m/ noun, **cladistic** adjective.
– ORIGIN 1960s: from **CLADE** + **-IST** + **-ICS**.

clado- /ˈkleɪdəʊ, ˈkladəʊ/ ▶ **combining form** relating to a branch or branching: *cladogram*.
– ORIGIN from Greek *klados* 'branch or shoot'.

Cladocera /kləˈdɒs(ə)rə/ Zoology an order of minute branchiopod crustaceans which includes the water fleas. They typically have a transparent shell enclosing the trunk, and large antennae which are used for swimming.
– DERIVATIVES **cladoceran** noun & adjective.
– ORIGIN modern Latin (plural), from Greek *klados* 'branch or root' + *keras* 'horn' (because of the branched antennae).

cladode /ˈkleɪdəʊd/ ▶ **noun** Botany a flattened leaf-like stem.
– ORIGIN late 19th cent.: from Greek *kladōdēs* 'with many shoots', from *klados* 'shoot'.

cladogenesis /ˌkleɪdə(ʊ)ˈdʒɛnɪsɪs, ˈkladə(ʊ)-/ ▶ **noun** [mass noun] Biology the formation of a new group of organisms or higher taxon by evolutionary divergence from an ancestral form.
– DERIVATIVES **cladogenetic** adjective.

C

cladogram /ˈkleɪdə(ʊ)gram, ˈkladə(ʊ)-/ ▶ **noun** Biology a branching diagram showing the cladistic relationship between a number of species.

claggy ▶ **adjective** Brit. dialect tending to form clots; sticky: *heavy with claggy mud.*
– ORIGIN late 16th cent.: perhaps of Scandinavian origin; compare with Danish *klag* 'sticky mud'.

claim ▶ **verb** [reporting verb] state or assert that something is the case, typically without providing evidence or proof: [with clause] *the Prime Minister* ***claimed that*** *he was concerned about Third World debt* | [with direct speech] *'I'm entitled to be conceited,' he claimed* | [with obj.] *not every employee is eligible to claim unfair dismissal.*
■ [with obj.] assert that one has gained or achieved (something): *his supporters claimed victory in the presidential elections.* ■ [with obj.] formally request or demand; say that one owns or has earned (something): *if no one claims the items, they will become Crown property.* ■ [with obj.] make a demand for (money) under the terms of an insurance policy: *she could have claimed the cost through her insurance* | [no obj.] *the premiums are reduced by fifty per cent if you don't* ***claim on*** *the policy.* ■ call for (someone's notice and thought): *a most unwelcome event* ***claimed his attention.*** ■ cause the loss of (someone's life).
▶ **noun 1** an assertion of the truth of something, typically one which is disputed or in doubt: [with clause] *he was dogged by the* ***claim that*** *he had CIA links* | *history belies statesmen's claims to be in charge of events.*
■ (also **statement of claim**) a statement of the novel features in a patent.
2 a demand or request for something considered one's due: *the court had denied their* ***claims to*** *asylum.*
■ an application for compensation under the terms of an insurance policy: ■ a right or title to something: *they have first* ***claim on*** *the assets of the trust.* ■ (also **mining claim**) a piece of land allotted to or taken by someone in order to be mined.
– PHRASES **claim to fame** a reason for being regarded as unusual or noteworthy: *the town's only claim to fame is that it is the birthplace of Elgar.*
– DERIVATIVES **claimable** adjective.
– ORIGIN Middle English: from Old French *claime* (noun), *clamer* (verb), from Latin *clamare* 'call out'.

claimant ▶ **noun** a person making a claim, especially in a lawsuit or for a state benefit.

claimer ▶ **noun** (N. Amer. also **claiming race**) Horse Racing **1** a race in which every horse may be claimed by a buyer for a predetermined price which is related to the weight that the horse carries.
2 a jockey who claims a weight allowance in a race.

claim jumper ▶ **noun** N. Amer. a person who appropriates a mining claim already taken by another.

Clair /klɛː, French klɛʀ/, René (1898–1981), French film director; born *René Lucien Chomette.* His films typically contain elements of surrealism underpinned by satire; they include *Un Chapeau de paille d'Italie* (1927), *Sous les toits de Paris* (1930), and *Les Belles de nuit* (1952).

clairaudience /klɛːrˈɔːdɪəns/ ▶ **noun** [mass noun] the supposed faculty of perceiving, as if by hearing, what is inaudible.
– DERIVATIVES **clairaudient** adjective & noun.
– ORIGIN mid 19th cent.: from French *clair* 'clear' + AUDIENCE, on the pattern of *clairvoyance.*

clair-de-lune /ˌklɛːdəˈluːn/ ▶ **noun** [mass noun] a soft white or pale blue-grey colour.
■ a Chinese porcelain glaze of this colour.
– ORIGIN late 19th cent.: French, literally 'moonlight'.

clairvoyance ▶ **noun** [mass noun] the supposed faculty of perceiving things or events in the future or beyond normal sensory contact: *she stared at the card as if she could contact its writer by clairvoyance.*
– ORIGIN mid 19th cent.: from French. from *clair* 'clear' + *voir* 'to see'.

clairvoyant ▶ **noun** a person who claims to have a supernatural ability to perceive events in the future or beyond normal sensory contact.
▶ **adjective** having or exhibiting such an ability: *he didn't tell me about it and I'm not clairvoyant.*
– DERIVATIVES **clairvoyantly** adverb.
– ORIGIN late 17th cent. (in the sense 'clear-sighted, perceptive'): from French, from *clair* 'clear' + *voyant* 'seeing' (from *voir* 'to see'). The current sense dates from the mid 19th cent.

clam[1] ▶ **noun** a marine bivalve mollusc with shells of equal size.
● Subclass Heterodonta: several families and numerous species, including the edible North American **hardshell clam** (see QUAHOG) and **softshell clam**. See also GIANT CLAM.
■ informal any of a number of edible bivalve molluscs, e.g. a scallop.
▶ **verb** (**clammed**, **clamming**) [no obj.] **1** chiefly N. Amer. dig for or collect clams.
2 (**clam up**) informal abruptly stop talking, either for fear of revealing a secret or from shyness.
– ORIGIN early 16th cent.: apparently from earlier *clam* 'a clamp', from Old English *clam, clamm* 'a bond or bondage', of Germanic origin; related to Dutch *klemme*, German *Klemme*, also to CLAMP[1].

clam[2] ▶ **noun** US informal a dollar.
– ORIGIN 1930s: of unknown origin.

clamant /ˈkleɪm(ə)nt, ˈklam-/ ▶ **adjective** forcing itself urgently on the attention: *the proper use of biotechnology has become a clamant question.*
– DERIVATIVES **clamantly** adverb.
– ORIGIN mid 17th cent.: from Latin *clamant-* 'crying out', from the verb *clamare.*

clambake ▶ **noun** N. Amer. a social gathering outdoors, especially for eating clams and other seafood.

clamber ▶ **verb** [no obj., with adverbial of direction] climb, move, or get in or out of something in an awkward and laborious way, typically using both hands and feet: *I clambered out of the trench.*
▶ **noun** [in sing.] a difficult climb or movement of this sort: *a clamber up the cliff path.*
– ORIGIN Middle English: probably from *clamb*, obsolete past tense of CLIMB.

clammy ▶ **adjective** (**clammier**, **clammiest**) unpleasantly damp and sticky or slimy to touch: *his skin felt cold and clammy.*
■ (of air or atmosphere) damp and unpleasant: *the clammy atmosphere of the cave.*
– DERIVATIVES **clammily** adverb, **clamminess** noun.
– ORIGIN late Middle English: from dialect *clam* 'to be sticky or adhere', of Germanic origin; related to CLAY.

clamour (US **clamor**) ▶ **noun** [in sing.] a loud and confused noise, especially that of people shouting vehemently: *the questions rose to a clamour.*
■ a strongly expressed protest or demand, typically from a large number of people: *the growing public* ***clamour for*** *more policemen on the beat.*
▶ **verb** [no obj.] (of a group of people) shout loudly and insistently: *the surging crowds* ***clamoured*** *for attention.*
■ make a vehement protest or demand: *scientists are* ***clamouring for*** *a ban on all chlorine substances.*
– DERIVATIVES **clamorous** adjective, **clamorously** adverb, **clamorousness** noun.
– ORIGIN late Middle English: via Old French from Latin *clamor*, from *clamare* 'cry out'.

clamp[1] ▶ **noun** a brace, band, or clasp used for strengthening or holding things together.
■ short for WHEEL CLAMP. ■ an electric circuit which serves to maintain the voltage limits of a signal at prescribed levels.
▶ **verb** [with obj. and adverbial of place] (often **be clamped**) fasten (something) in place with a clamp: *the sander is clamped on to the edge of a workbench.*
■ fasten (two things) firmly together: *the two frames are* ***clamped together.*** ■ hold (something) tightly against or in another thing: *Maggie had to clamp a hand over her mouth to stop herself from laughing.* ■ [with obj.] immobilize (an illegally parked car) by fixing a device to one of its wheels. ■ [with obj.] maintain the voltage limits of (an electrical signal) at prescribed values.
– DERIVATIVES **clamper** noun.
– ORIGIN Middle English: probably of Dutch or Low German origin and related to CLAM[1].
▶ **clamp down** suppress or prevent something, typically in an oppressive or harsh manner: *police* ***clamped down on*** *a pro-democracy demonstration.*

clamp[2] ▶ **noun** Brit. **1** a heap of potatoes or other root vegetables stored under straw or earth.
2 a three-sided structure which is used to store silage.
– ORIGIN late 16th cent. (denoting a pile of bricks for firing): probably from Dutch *klamp* 'heap'; related to CLUMP.

clampdown ▶ **noun** informal a severe or concerted attempt to suppress something: *a clampdown on crime.*

clamshell ▶ **noun** the shell of a clam, formed of two roughly equal valves with a hinge.
■ a thing with hinged parts that open and shut in a manner resembling the parts of such a shell, such as a kind of mechanical digger, a portable computer, or a box for takeaway food: *some clamshells offer full desktop power* | [as modifier] *a clamshell lid.*

clan ▶ **noun** a group of close-knit and interrelated families (especially associated with families in the Scottish Highlands).
■ a large family: *the Watts clan is one of racing's oldest families.* ■ a group of people with a strong common interest: *New York's garrulous clan of artists.*
– ORIGIN late Middle English: from Scottish Gaelic *clann* 'offspring, family', from Old Irish *cland*, from Latin *planta* 'sprout'.

clandestine /klanˈdɛstɪn, ˈklandɛstɪn/ ▶ **adjective** kept secret or done secretively, especially because illicit: *she deserved better than these clandestine meetings.*
– DERIVATIVES **clandestinely** adverb, **clandestinity** noun.
– ORIGIN mid 16th cent.: from French *clandestin* or Latin *clandestinus*, from *clam* 'secretly'.

clang ▶ **noun** a loud, resonant metallic sound or series of sounds: *the steel door slammed shut with a clang.*
▶ **verb** make or cause to make such a sound: [no obj.] *she turned the tap on and the plumbing clanged* | [with obj.] *the belfry still clangs its bell at 9 p.m.*
– ORIGIN late 16th cent.: imitative, influenced by Latin *clangere* 'resound'.

clanger ▶ **noun** informal, chiefly Brit. an absurd or embarrassing blunder.
– PHRASES **drop a clanger** see DROP.

clangour /ˈklaŋgə/ (US **clangor**) ▶ **noun** [in sing.] a continuous loud banging or ringing sound: *he went deaf because of the clangour of the steam hammers.*
– DERIVATIVES **clangorous** adjective, **clangorously** adverb.
– ORIGIN late 16th cent.: from Latin *clangor*, from *clangere* 'resound'.

clank ▶ **noun** a loud, sharp sound or series of sounds, typically made by pieces of metal meeting or being struck together: *the groan and clank of a winch.*
▶ **verb** make or cause to make such a sound: [no obj.] *I could hear the chain clanking* | [with obj.] *Cassie bounced on the bed, clanking springs.*
– DERIVATIVES **clankingly** adverb.
– ORIGIN late Middle English (but rare before the mid 17th cent.): imitative.

clannish ▶ **adjective** chiefly derogatory (of a group or their activities) tending to exclude others outside the group.
– DERIVATIVES **clannishly** adverb, **clannishness** noun.

clanship ▶ **noun** [mass noun] the system of clan membership or loyalty.

clansman ▶ **noun** (pl. **-men**) a male member of a clan.

clap[1] ▶ **verb** (**clapped**, **clapping**) [with obj.] strike the palms of (one's hands) together repeatedly, typically in order to applaud: *Agnes clapped her hands in glee* | [no obj.] *the crowd was clapping and cheering.*
■ show approval of (a person or action) in this way. ■ strike the palms of (one's hands) together once,especially as a signal: *the designer clapped his hands and the other girls exited the room.* ■ slap (someone) encouragingly on the back or shoulder: *as they parted, he clapped Owen on the back.* ■ place (a hand) briefly against or over one's mouth or forehead as a gesture of dismay or regret: *he swore and clapped a hand to his forehead.* ■ (of a bird) flap (its wings) audibly.
▶ **noun 1** an act of striking together the palms of the hands, either once or repeatedly.
■ a friendly slap or pat on the back or shoulder.
2 an explosive sound, especially of thunder: *a clap of thunder echoed through the valley.*
– PHRASES **clap eyes on** see EYE. **clap hold of** informal grab someone or something roughly or abruptly. **clap someone in jail** (or **irons**) put someone in prison (or in chains).
– ORIGIN Old English *clappan* 'throb, beat', of imitative origin. Sense 1 dates from late Middle English.
▶ **clap something on** abruptly impose a restrictive or punitive measure: *most countries clapped on tariffs to protect their farmers.*

clap[2] ▶ **noun** [mass noun] (usu. **the clap**) informal a venereal disease, especially gonorrhoea.

– ORIGIN late 16th cent.: from Old French *clapoir* 'venereal bubo'.

clapboard /ˈklapbɔːd, ˈklabəd/ ▶ **noun** chiefly N. Amer. a long, thin, flat piece of wood with edges horizontally overlapping in series, used to cover the outer walls of buildings: [as modifier] *neat clapboard houses.*
■informal a house with outer walls covered in such pieces of wood.
– DERIVATIVES **clapboarded** adjective.
– ORIGIN early 16th cent. (denoting a piece of oak used for barrel staves or wainscot): partial translation of Low German *klappholt* 'barrel stave', from *klappen* 'to crack' + *holt* 'wood'.

clapped-out ▶ **adjective** informal, chiefly Brit. (of a vehicle, machine, or person) worn out from age or heavy use and unable to work or operate: *a clapped-out old van.*

clapper ▶ **noun** the tongue or striker of a bell.
– PHRASES **like the clappers** Brit. informal very fast or very hard: *she ran off like the clappers.*

clapperboard ▶ **noun** a device of hinged boards that are struck together before filming to synchronize the starting of picture and sound machinery.

clapper bridge ▶ **noun** a simple bridge consisting of slabs of stone or planks laid across a series of rocks or piles of stones.

clapper rail ▶ **noun** a large greyish rail of American coastal marshes, which has a distinctive clattering rattle-like call.
• *Rallus longirostris*, family Rallidae.
– ORIGIN from *clapper*, denoting a device for making a loud clattering sound, with reference to the bird's cry.

Clapton, Eric (b.1945), English blues and rock guitarist, singer, and composer, known particularly for the song 'Layla' (1972) and for his group Cream (1966–8).

claptrap ▶ **noun** [mass noun] absurd or nonsensical talk or ideas: *such sentiments are just pious claptrap.*
– ORIGIN mid 18th cent. (denoting something designed to elicit applause): from **CLAP**[1] + **TRAP**[1].

claque /klak, klɑːk/ ▶ **noun** a group of people hired to applaud (or heckle) a performer or public speaker.
■a group of sycophantic followers: *the President was surrounded by a claque of scheming bureaucrats.*
– ORIGIN mid 19th cent.: French, from *claquer* 'to clap'. The practice of paying members of an audience for their support originated at the Paris opera.

claqueur /klaˈkəː, klɑː-/ ▶ **noun** a member of a claque.
– ORIGIN mid 19th cent.: French, from *claquer* 'to clap'.

clarabella /ˌklarəˈbɛlə/ ▶ **noun** an organ stop with the quality of a flute.
– ORIGIN mid 19th cent.: from the feminine forms of Latin *clarus* 'clear' and *bellus* 'pretty'.

Clare[1] a county of the Republic of Ireland, on the west coast in the province of Munster; county town, Ennis.

Clare[2], John (1793–1864), English poet, who wrote in celebration of the natural world. In 1837 he was certified insane and spent the rest of his life in an asylum. Notable works: *Poems Descriptive of Rural Life and Scenery* (1820) and *The Rural Muse* (1835).

clarence (also **Clarence**) ▶ **noun** historical a closed horse-drawn carriage with four wheels, seating four inside and two outside next to the coachman.
– ORIGIN mid 19th cent.: named in honour of the Duke of *Clarence*, later William IV.

Clarenceux /ˈklar(ə)nsuː/ ▶ **noun** Heraldry (in the UK) the title given to the second King of Arms, with jurisdiction south of the Trent. See **KING OF ARMS**.
– ORIGIN Middle English: from Anglo-Norman French, named after the dukedom of *Clarence* created for the second son of Edward II, married to the heiress of *Clare* in Suffolk.

Clarendon /ˈklarənd(ə)n/, Edward Hyde, Earl of (1609–74), English statesman and historian, chief adviser to Charles II and Chancellor of Oxford University 1660–7. Notable works: *History of the Rebellion and Civil Wars in England* (published posthumously 1702–4).

Clare of Assisi, St (1194–1253), Italian saint and abbess. With St Francis she founded the order of Poor Ladies of San Damiano ('Poor Clares'), of which she was abbess. Feast day, 11 (formerly 12) August.

claret /ˈklarət/ ▶ **noun** [mass noun] a red wine from Bordeaux, or wine of a similar character made elsewhere.
■a deep purplish-red colour. ■ Brit. archaic, informal blood.
– ORIGIN late Middle English (originally denoting a light red or yellowish wine, as distinct from a red or white): from Old French (*vin*) *claret* and medieval Latin *claratum* (*vinum*) 'clarified (wine)', from Latin *clarus* 'clear'.

clarify /ˈklarɪfʌɪ/ ▶ **verb** (**-ies**, **-ied**) [with obj.] **1** make (a statement or situation) less confused and more clearly comprehensible: *the report managed to clarify the government's position.*
2 [often as adj. **clarified**] melt (butter) in order to separate out the impurities.
– DERIVATIVES **clarification** noun, **clarificatory** adjective, **clarifier** noun.
– ORIGIN Middle English (in the senses 'set forth clearly' and 'make pure and clean'): from Old French *clarifier*, from late Latin *clarificare*, from Latin *clarus* 'clear'.

clarinet ▶ **noun** a woodwind instrument with a single-reed mouthpiece, a cylindrical tube of dark wood with a flared end, and holes stopped by keys. The most common forms are tuned in B flat, A, and E flat.
■an organ stop with a tone resembling that of a clarinet.
– DERIVATIVES **clarinettist** (US **clarinetist**) noun.
– ORIGIN mid 18th cent.: from French *clarinette*, diminutive of *clarine*, denoting a kind of bell; related to **CLARION**.

clarion /ˈklarɪən/ ▶ **noun** chiefly historical a shrill narrow-tubed war trumpet.
■an organ stop with a quality resembling that of such a trumpet.
▶ **adjective** loud and clear: *clarion trumpeters.*
– PHRASES **clarion call** a strongly expressed demand or request for action: *he issued a clarion call to young people to join the Party.*
– ORIGIN Middle English: from medieval Latin *clario(n-)*, from Latin *clarus* 'clear'.

clarity ▶ **noun** [mass noun] the quality of being clear, in particular:
■the quality of coherence and intelligibility: *for the sake of clarity, each of these strategies is dealt with separately.* ■ the quality of being easy to see or hear; sharpness of image or sound: *the clarity of the picture.* ■ the quality of being certain or definite: *it was clarity of purpose that he needed.* ■ the quality of transparency or purity: *the crystal clarity of water.*
– ORIGIN Middle English (in the sense 'glory, divine splendour'): from Latin *claritas*, from *clarus* 'clear'. The current sense dates from the early 17th cent.

Clark, William (1770–1838), American explorer. With Meriwether Lewis, he commanded an expedition (1804–6) across the North American continent.

Clarke, Sir Arthur C. (b.1917), English writer of science fiction; full name *Arthur Charles Clarke*. He co-wrote (with Stanley Kubrick) the screenplay for the film *2001: A Space Odyssey* (1968).

clarkia /ˈklɑːkɪə/ ▶ **noun** a North American plant with showy white, pink, or purple flowers, cultivated as a border plant in gardens.
• Genus *Clarkia*, family Onagraceae.
– ORIGIN modern Latin, named after W. **CLARK**, who discovered it.

clarsach /ˈklɑːrsəx, ˈklɑːsək/ ▶ **noun** a small harp with wire strings, used in the folk and early music of Scotland and Ireland. Also called **CELTIC HARP**.
– ORIGIN late 15th cent.: from Scottish Gaelic, perhaps based on *clar* 'table, board'.

clart /klɑːt/ (also **clarts**) ▶ **noun** [mass noun] Scottish & N. English sticky mud; filth.
– DERIVATIVES **clarty** adjective.
– ORIGIN late 17th cent. (as a verb in the sense 'smear, plaster'): of unknown origin.

clary /ˈklɛːri/ ▶ **noun** [mass noun] an aromatic herbaceous plant of the mint family, some kinds of which are used as culinary and medicinal herbs.
• Genus *Salvia*, family Labiatae: several species, in particular the southern European *S. sclarea*, which is used in perfumery and from which an essential oil (**clary sage**) is obtained.
– ORIGIN late Middle English: from obsolete French *clarie*, from medieval Latin *sclarea*.

clash ▶ **noun 1** a violent confrontation: *there have been minor* **clashes with** *security forces.*
■an incompatibility leading to disagreement: *a personality clash.*
2 a mismatch of colours: *a clash of tweeds and a striped shirt.*
■an inconvenient coincidence of the timing of events or activities: *it is hoped that clashes of dates will be avoided.*
3 a loud jarring sound made by or resembling that made by metal objects being struck together: *a clash of cymbals.*
▶ **verb 1** [no obj.] meet and come into violent conflict: *protestors demanding self-rule* **clashed with** *police.*
■have a forceful disagreement: *the prime minister* **clashed with** *other Commonwealth leaders.* ■ be incompatible or at odds: *his thriftiness* **clashed with** *Ross's largesse.*
2 [no obj.] (of colours) appear discordant or ugly when placed close to each other: [as adj. **clashing**] *suits in clashing colours.*
■inconveniently occur at the same time: *we play our home games when they do not* **clash with** *those of Liverpool or Everton.*
3 [with obj.] strike (cymbals) together, producing a loud discordant sound.
– DERIVATIVES **clasher** noun.
– ORIGIN early 16th cent.: imitative.

clasp ▶ **verb** [with obj.] **1** grasp (something) tightly with one's hand: *he clasped her arm.*
■place (one's arms) around something so as to hold it tightly: *Kate's arms were* **clasped around** *her knees.* ■ hold (someone) tightly: *he clasped Joanne in his arms.* ■ (**clasp one's hands**) press one's hands together with the fingers interlaced: *he lay on his back with his hands clasped behind his head.*
2 archaic fasten (something) with a small device, typically a metal one: *one modest emerald clasped her robe.*
▶ **noun 1** a device with interlocking parts used for fastening things together: *a gold bracelet with a turquoise clasp.*
■a silver bar on a medal ribbon, inscribed with the name of the battle at which the wearer was present.
2 [in sing.] an embrace.
■a grasp or handshake: *he took her hand in a firm clasp.*
– PHRASES **clasp hands** shake hands with fervour or affection.
– ORIGIN Middle English: of unknown origin.

claspers ▶ **plural noun** Zoology a pair of appendages under the abdomen of a male shark or ray, or at the end of the abdomen of a male insect, used to hold the female during copulation.
– ORIGIN mid 19th cent.: from **CLASP**.

clasp knife ▶ **noun** a knife with a blade that folds into the handle.

class ▶ **noun 1** a set or category of things having some property or attribute in common and differentiated from others by kind, type, or quality: *it was good accommodation for a hotel of this class* | *a new class of heart drug.*
■Biology a principal taxonomic grouping that ranks above order and below phylum or division, such as Mammalia or Insecta. ■ Brit. a division of candidates according to merit in a university examination: *he received a third class in literae humaniores.*
2 [mass noun] the system of ordering a society in which people are divided into sets based on perceived social or economic status: *people who are socially disenfranchised by class* | [as modifier] *the class system.*
■[count noun] a set in a society ordered in such a way: *the ruling class.* ■ (**the classes**) archaic the rich or educated. ■ informal impressive stylishness in appearance or behaviour: *she's got class—she looks like a princess.*
3 a group of students or pupils who are taught together.
■an occasion when pupils meet with their teacher for instruction; a lesson: *I was late for a class.* ■ a course of instruction: *I took classes in Indian music.* ■ N. Amer. all of the college or school students of a particular year: *the class of 1907.*
▶ **verb** [with obj.] (often **be classed as**) assign or regard as belonging to a particular category: *conduct which is classed as criminal.*
▶ **adjective** [attrib.] informal showing stylish excellence: *he's a class player.*
– PHRASES **class act** chiefly N. Amer. a person or thing displaying impressive and stylish excellence. **in a class of** (or **on**) **its** (or **one's**) **own** unequalled, especially in excellence or performance.

– ORIGIN mid 16th cent. (in sense 3): from Latin *classis* 'a division of the Roman people, a grade, or a class of pupils'.

class action ▶ **noun** Law, chiefly N. Amer. a law suit filed or defended by an individual acting on behalf of a group.

class consciousness ▶ **noun** [mass noun] awareness of one's place in a system of social class, especially (in Marxist terms) as it relates to the class struggle.
– DERIVATIVES **class-conscious** adjective.

classic ▶ **adjective** judged over a period of time to be of the highest quality and outstanding of its kind: *a classic novel | a classic car.*
■ (of a garment or design) of a simple elegant style not greatly subject to changes in fashion: *this classic navy blazer.* ■ remarkably and instructively typical: *I had all the classic symptoms of flu.*
▶ **noun 1** a work of art of recognized and established value: *his books have become classics.*
■ a garment of a simple, elegant, and long-lasting style. ■ a thing which is memorable and a very good example of its kind: *he's hoping that tomorrow's game will be a classic.*
2 (**Classics**) a subject at school or university which involves the study of ancient Greek and Latin literature, philosophy, and history.
■ (usu. **the classics**) the works of ancient Greek and Latin writers and philosophers. ■ dated a scholar of ancient Greek and Latin.
3 (**Classic**) a major sports tournament or competition, especially in golf or tennis.
– ORIGIN early 17th cent.: from French *classique* or Latin *classicus* 'belonging to a class or division', later 'of the highest class', from *classis* (see **CLASS**).

classical ▶ **adjective 1** of or relating to ancient Greek or Latin literature, art, or culture: *classical mythology.*
■ (of art or architecture) influenced by ancient Greek or Roman forms or principles. ■ (of language) having the form used by the ancient standard authors: *classical Latin.* ■ based on the study of ancient Greek and Latin: *a classical education.*
2 (typically of a form of art) regarded as representing an exemplary standard; traditional and long-established in form or style: *a classical ballet.*
3 of or relating to the first significant period of an area of study: *classical Marxism.*
■ Physics relating to or based upon concepts and theories which preceded the theories of relativity and quantum mechanics; Newtonian: *classical physics.*
– DERIVATIVES **classicalism** noun, **classicality** noun, **classically** adverb.
– ORIGIN late 16th cent. (in the sense 'outstanding of its kind'): from Latin *classicus* 'belonging to a class' (see **CLASSIC**) + **-AL**.

classical conditioning ▶ **noun** [mass noun] Psychology a learning process that occurs when two stimuli are repeatedly paired: a response which is at first elicited by the second stimulus is eventually elicited by the first stimulus alone.

classical music ▶ **noun** [mass noun] serious or conventional music following long-established principles rather than a folk, jazz, or popular tradition.
■ (more specifically) music written in the European tradition during a period lasting approximately from 1750 to 1830, when forms such as the symphony, concerto, and sonata were standardized. Often contrasted with **BAROQUE** and **ROMANTIC**.

classicism ▶ **noun** [mass noun] the following of ancient Greek or Roman principles and style in art and literature, generally associated with harmony, restraint, and adherence to recognized standards of form and craftsmanship, especially from the Renaissance to the 18th century. Often contrasted with **ROMANTICISM**.
■ the following of traditional and long-established theories or styles.

classicist ▶ **noun 1** a person who studies Classics (ancient Greek and Latin).
2 a follower of classicism in the arts.

classicize (also **-ise**) ▶ **verb** [no obj.] [usu. as adj. **classicizing**] imitate a classical style: *the classicizing strains in Guercino's art.*

Classico /ˈklasɪkəʊ/ ▶ **adjective** [postpositive] used in the classification of Italian wines to designate a wine produced in the region from which the type takes its name: *Chianti Classico.*
– ORIGIN Italian.

classic race ▶ **noun** (in the UK) each of the five main flat races of the horse-racing season, namely the Two Thousand and the One Thousand Guineas, the Derby, the Oaks, and the St Leger.

classification ▶ **noun** [mass noun] the action or process of classifying something according to shared qualities or characteristics: *the classification of disease according to symptoms.*
■ Biology the arrangement of animals and plants in taxonomic groups according to their observed similarities (including at least kingdom and phylum in animals, division in plants, and class, order, family, genus, and species). ■ another term for **TAXONOMY**. ■ [count noun] a category into which something is put.

classified ▶ **adjective** arranged in classes or categories: *a classified catalogue of books.*
■ [attrib.] (of newspaper or magazine advertisements or the pages on which these appear) organized in categories according to what is being advertised. ■ (of information or documents) designated as officially secret and to which only authorized people may have access: *classified information on nuclear experiments.* ■ Brit. (of a road) assigned to a category according to its importance within the overall system of road numbering.
▶ **noun** (**classifieds**) small advertisements placed in a newspaper and organized in categories.

classifier ▶ **noun** a person or thing that classifies something.
■ Linguistics an affix or word that indicates the semantic class to which a word belongs: *the English negative classifier 'un-'.*

classify ▶ **verb** (**-ies**, **-ied**) [with obj.] (often **be classified**) arrange (a group of people or things) in classes or categories according to shared qualities or characteristics: *mountain peaks are classified according to their shape.*
■ assign (someone or something) to a particular class or category: *elements are usually* **classified as** *metals or non-metals.* ■ designate (documents or information) as officially secret or to which only authorized people may have access: *government officials classified 6.3 million documents in 1992.*
– DERIVATIVES **classifiable** adjective, **classificatory** adjective.
– ORIGIN late 18th cent.: back-formation from **CLASSIFICATION**, from French, from *classe* 'class', from Latin *classis* 'division'.

classifying ▶ **adjective** Grammar denoting an adjective that describes the class that a head noun belongs to and characterized by not having a comparative or superlative (for example *American*, *mortal*). Contrasted with **GRADABLE**, **QUALITATIVE**.

class interval ▶ **noun** Statistics the size of each class into which a range of a variable is divided, as represented by the divisions of a histogram or bar chart.

classism ▶ **noun** [mass noun] prejudice against or in favour of people belonging to a particular social class.
– DERIVATIVES **classist** adjective & noun.

classless ▶ **adjective** (of a society) not divided into social classes.
■ not showing obvious signs of belonging to a particular social class: *his voice was classless.*
– DERIVATIVES **classlessness** noun.

class list ▶ **noun** a list of the candidates who have taken an examination, showing the class or mark achieved by each.

classmate ▶ **noun** a fellow member of a class at school, college, or university.

classroom ▶ **noun** a room, typically in a school, in which a class of pupils or students is taught.

class struggle ▶ **noun** (in Marxist ideology) the conflict of interests between the workers and the ruling class in a capitalist society, regarded as inevitably violent.

classy ▶ **adjective** (**classier**, **classiest**) informal stylish and sophisticated: *the hotel is classy but relaxed.*
– DERIVATIVES **classily** adverb, **classiness** noun.

clast /klast/ ▶ **noun** Geology a constituent fragment of a clastic rock.
– ORIGIN mid 20th cent.: back-formation from **CLASTIC**.

clastic ▶ **adjective** Geology denoting rocks composed of broken pieces of older rocks.
– ORIGIN late 19th cent.: from French *clastique*, from Greek *klastos* 'broken in pieces'.

clathrate /ˈklaθreɪt/ ▶ **noun** Chemistry a compound in which molecules of one component are physically trapped within the crystal structure of another.
– ORIGIN 1940s: from Latin *clathratus*, from *clathri* 'lattice-bars', from Greek *klēthra*.

clatter ▶ **noun** [in sing.] a continuous rattling sound as of hard objects falling or striking each other: *the horse spun round with a clatter of hooves | she dropped her knife and fork with a clatter.*
■ noisy rapid talk: *I could hear the staccato clatter of Mexican from the next table.*
▶ **verb** make or cause to make a continuous rattling sound: [no obj.] *her coffee cup clattered in the saucer |* [with obj.] *she clattered cups and saucers on to a tray.*
■ [no obj., with adverbial of direction] fall or move with such a sound: *the knife clattered to the floor.*
– ORIGIN Old English (as a verb), of imitative origin.

Claude glass /klɔːd/ ▶ **noun** a convex dark or coloured glass that reflects a small image in subdued colours, used by landscape painters to show the tonal values of a scene.

Claude Lorraine /ˌklɔːd ləˈreɪn/ (also **Lorrain**) (1600–82), French painter; born *Claude Gellée*. He is noted for the use of light in his landscapes. Notable works: *Ascanius and the Stag* (1682).

claudication /ˌklɔːdɪˈkeɪʃ(ə)n/ ▶ **noun** [mass noun] Medicine limping.
■ (also **intermittent claudication**) a condition in which cramping pain in the leg is induced by exercise, typically caused by obstruction of the arteries.
– ORIGIN late Middle English: from Latin *claudicatio(n-)*, from the verb *claudicare* 'to limp', from *claudus* 'lame'.

Claudius /ˈklɔːdɪəs/ (10 BC–AD 54), Roman emperor 41–54; full name *Tiberius Claudius Drusus Nero Germanicus*. His reign was noted for its restoration of order after Caligula's decadence and for its expansion of the Empire, in particular the invasion of Britain in AD 43. His fourth wife, Agrippina, is said to have poisoned him.

clause ▶ **noun 1** a unit of grammatical organization next below the sentence in rank and in traditional grammar said to consist of a subject and predicate. See also **MAIN CLAUSE**, **SUBORDINATE CLAUSE**.
2 a particular and separate article, stipulation, or proviso in a treaty, bill, or contract.
– DERIVATIVES **clausal** adjective.
– ORIGIN Middle English: via Old French *clause*, based on Latin *claus-* 'shut, closed', from the verb *claudere*.

Clausewitz /ˈklaʊzəvɪts/, Karl von (1780–1831), Prussian general and military theorist. His study *On War* (1833) had a marked influence on strategic studies in the 19th and 20th centuries.

Clausius /ˈklaʊzɪʊs/, Rudolf (1822–88), German physicist, one of the founders of modern thermodynamics. He was the first, in 1850, to formulate the second law of thermodynamics, developing the concept of a system's available thermal energy and coining the term *entropy* for it.

claustral /ˈklɔːstr(ə)l/ ▶ **adjective** of or relating to a cloister or religious house: *claustral buildings.*
■ figurative enveloping; confining: *this claustral heat.*
– ORIGIN late Middle English: from late Latin *claustralis*, from Latin *claustrum* 'lock, enclosed place' (see **CLOISTER**).

claustration /klɔːˈstreɪʃ(ə)n/ ▶ **noun** [mass noun] confinement as if in a cloister.
– ORIGIN mid 19th cent.: from Latin *claustrum* 'lock, bolt' + **-ATION**.

claustrophobia /klɔːstrəˈfəʊbɪə/ ▶ **noun** [mass noun] extreme or irrational fear of confined places.
– DERIVATIVES **claustrophobe** noun.
– ORIGIN late 19th cent.: modern Latin, from Latin *claustrum* 'lock, bolt' + **-PHOBIA**.

claustrophobic ▶ **adjective** (of a person) suffering from claustrophobia: *crowds made him feel claustrophobic.*
■ (of a place or situation) inducing claustrophobia: *the claustrophobic interior of the cruiser.*
▶ **noun** a person who suffers from claustrophobia.
– DERIVATIVES **claustrophobically** adverb.

clavate /ˈkleɪveɪt/ ▶ **adjective** Botany & Zoology club-shaped; thicker at the apex than the base.
– ORIGIN mid 17th cent.: from modern Latin *clavatus*, from Latin *clava* 'club'.

clave[1] /kleɪv, klɑːv/ ▶ **noun** (usu. **claves**) Music one of a pair of hardwood sticks used to make a hollow sound when struck together.

– ORIGIN 1920s: from Latin American Spanish, from Spanish *clave* 'keystone', from Latin *clavis* 'key'.

clave² archaic past of **CLEAVE²**.

clavichord /ˈklavɪkɔːd/ ▶ **noun** a small, rectangular keyboard instrument with a soft tone, used for domestic music-making from the early 15th to early 19th centuries.
– ORIGIN late Middle English: from medieval Latin *clavichordium*, from Latin *clavis* 'key' + *chorda* 'string'.

clavicle /ˈklavɪk(ə)l/ ▶ **noun** Anatomy technical term for **COLLARBONE**.
– DERIVATIVES **clavicular** /kləˈvɪkjʊlə/ adjective.
– ORIGIN early 17th cent.: from Latin *clavicula* 'small key', diminutive of *clavis* (because of its shape).

clavier /ˈklavɪə, kləˈvɪə/ ▶ **noun** Music a keyboard instrument.
– ORIGIN early 18th cent.: from German *Klavier*, from French *clavier*, from medieval Latin *claviarius* 'key-bearer', from Latin *clavis* 'key'.

claviform /ˈklavɪfɔːm/ ▶ **adjective** technical another term for **CLAVATE**.
– ORIGIN early 19th cent.: from Latin *clava* 'club' + **-IFORM**.

claw ▶ **noun** a curved pointed horny nail on each digit of the foot in birds, lizards, and some mammals.
■ either of a pair of small hooked appendages on an insect's foot. ■ the pincer of a crab, scorpion, or other arthropod. ■ a mechanical device resembling a claw, used for gripping or lifting.
▶ **verb 1** [no obj.] (of an animal or person) scratch or tear something with the claws or the fingernails: *the kitten was* **clawing at** *Lowell's trouser leg* | figurative *bitter jealousy* **clawed at** *her* | [with obj.] *her hands clawed his shoulders.*
■ clutch at something with the hands: *his fingers* **clawed** *at the air.* ■ (**claw one's way**) make one's way with difficulty by hauling oneself forward with one's hands: *he clawed his way over a pile of bricks.* ■ [with obj.] (**claw something away**) try desperately to move or remove something with the hands: *rescuers clawed away rubble with their bare hands.* ■ [with obj.] Scottish scratch gently so as to relieve itching.
2 [no obj.] (of a sailing ship) beat to windward: *the ability to* **claw off** *a lee shore.*
– PHRASES **get one's claws into** informal enter into a possessive relationship with.
– DERIVATIVES **clawed** adjective [often in combination] *a needle-clawed bushbaby*, **clawless** adjective.
– ORIGIN Old English *clawu* (noun), *clawian* (verb), of West Germanic origin; related to Dutch *klauw* and German *Klaue*.
▶ **claw something back** regain a lost advantage or position laboriously and gradually: *clawing back power from the president.* ■ (of a government) recover money paid out in the form of an allowance or benefit, typically by taxation.

clawback ▶ **noun** an act of retrieving money already paid out, typically by a government using taxation: *a clawback of tax relief* | [mass noun] *the bonds will be subject to clawback.*

clawed toad ▶ **noun** an aquatic toad with a flattened body and claws on the hind toes, related to the Suriname toad.
• *Xenopus* and other genera, family Pipidae: several species. See also **XENOPUS**.

claw foot ▶ **noun** (pl. **feet**) **1** a foot on a piece of furniture, shaped to resemble a claw.
2 Medicine an excessively arched foot with an unnaturally high instep.
■ [mass noun] a disease causing such a distortion of the foot. Also called **PES CAVUS**.

claw hammer ▶ **noun** a hammer with one side of the head split and curved, used for extracting nails.

Clay, Cassius, see **MUHAMMAD ALI²**.

clay ▶ **noun 1** [mass noun] a stiff, sticky fine-grained earth, typically yellow, red, or bluish-grey in colour and often forming an impermeable layer in the soil. It can be moulded when wet, and is dried and baked to make bricks, pottery, and ceramics.
■ technical sediment with particles smaller than silt, typically less than 0.002 mm. ■ a hardened clay surface for a tennis court. ■ poetic/literary the substance of the human body: *this lifeless clay.*
2 a European moth with yellowish-brown wings.
• Several species in the family Noctuidae, in particular **the clay** (*Mythimnia ferrago*).
– PHRASES **feet of clay** see **FOOT**.
– DERIVATIVES **clayey** adjective, **clayish** adjective, **clay-like** adjective.
– ORIGIN Old English *clǣg*, of West Germanic origin; related to Dutch *klei*, also to **CLEAVE²** and **CLIMB**.

clay mineral ▶ **noun** any of a group of minerals which occur as colloidal crystals in clay. They are all hydrated aluminosilicates having layered crystal structures.

claymore ▶ **noun 1** historical a two-edged broadsword used by Scottish Highlanders.
■ a single-edged broadsword having a hilt with a basketwork design, introduced in Scotland in the 16th century.
2 a type of anti-personnel mine.
– ORIGIN early 18th cent.: from Scottish Gaelic *claidheamh* 'sword' + *mór* 'great'.

claypan ▶ **noun** Austral. a shallow depression or hollow in the ground with an impermeable clay base which holds water after rain.

clay pigeon ▶ **noun** a saucer-shaped piece of baked clay or other material thrown up in the air from a trap as a target for shooting.

clay pipe ▶ **noun** a tobacco pipe made of hardened clay.

Clayton's ▶ **adjective** informal Austral./NZ largely illusory; existing in name only: *these Clayton's privatizations will do nothing to remove the dead hand of government.*
– ORIGIN 1980s: from the proprietary name of a soft drink marketed using the line 'It's the drink I have when I'm not having a drink'.

-cle ▶ **suffix** forming nouns such as *article, particle*, which were originally diminutives.
– ORIGIN via French from Latin *-culus, -cula, -culum*.

clean ▶ **adjective 1** free from dirt, marks, or stains: *the room was spotlessly clean* | *keep the wound clean.*
■ having been washed since last worn or used: *a clean blouse.* ■ [attrib.] (of paper) not yet marked by writing or drawing: *he copied the advert on to a clean sheet of paper.* ■ (of a person) attentive to personal hygiene: *by nature he was clean and neat.* ■ [predic.] (of a child or animal) toilet-trained or house-trained. ■ free from pollutants or unpleasant substances: *we will create a cleaner, safer environment.* ■ free from or producing relatively little radioactive contamination.
2 morally uncontaminated; pure; innocent: *clean living.*
■ not sexually offensive or obscene: *it's all* **good clean fun** | *even when clean, his verses are very funny.* ■ showing or having no record of offences or crimes: *a clean driving licence is essential for the job.* ■ played or done according to the rules: *it was a good clean fight.* ■ [predic.] informal not possessing or containing anything illegal, especially drugs or stolen goods: *I searched him and his luggage, and he was clean.* ■ [predic.] informal (of a person) not taking or having taken drugs or alcohol. ■ free from ceremonial defilement, according to Mosaic Law and similar religious codes. ■ (of an animal) not prohibited under such codes and fit to be used for food.
3 free from irregularities; having a smooth edge or surface: *a clean fracture of the leg.*
■ having a simple, well-defined, and pleasing shape: *the clean lines and pared-down planes of modernism.* ■ (of an action) smoothly and skilfully done: *I still hadn't made a clean take-off.* ■ (of a taste, sound, or smell) giving a clear and distinctive impression to the senses; sharp and fresh: *clean, fresh, natural flavours.* ■ (of timber) free from knots.
▶ **adverb 1** so as to be free from dirt, marks, or unwanted matter: *the room had been washed clean.*
2 informal used to emphasize the completeness of a reported action, condition, or experience: *he was knocked clean off his feet* | *I clean forgot her birthday.*
▶ **verb** [with obj.] make (something or someone) free of dirt, marks, or mess, especially by washing, wiping, or brushing: *clean your teeth properly after meals* | *chair covers should be easy to clean* | *we cleaned Uncle Jim up and made him presentable* | [no obj.] *he always expected other people to* **clean up after** *him* | [as noun **cleaning**] *Anne will help with the cleaning.*
■ remove the innards of (fish or poultry) prior to cooking.
▶ **noun** [in sing.] chiefly Brit. an act of cleaning something: *he* **gave** *the room* **a clean.**
– PHRASES **(as) clean as a whistle** see **WHISTLE**. **clean bill of health** see **BILL OF HEALTH**. **clean someone's clock** N. Amer. informal give someone a beating. ■ defeat or surpass someone decisively. **clean house** N. Amer. do housework. ■ eliminate corruption or inefficiency. **clean one's plate** eat up all the food put on one's plate. **clean up one's act** informal begin to behave in a better way, especially by giving up alcohol, drugs, or illegal activities. **come clean** informal be completely honest; keep nothing hidden: *the Chancellor must come clean about his plans for increasing taxation.* **have clean hands** be uninvolved and blameless with regard to an immoral act: *no one involved in the conflict has clean hands.* **keep one's hands clean** not involve oneself in an immoral act. **keep one's nose clean** see **NOSE**. **make a clean breast of something** (or **make a clean breast of it**) confess fully one's mistakes or wrongdoings. **make a clean job of something** informal do something thoroughly. **make a clean sweep 1** remove all unwanted people or things ready to start afresh. **2** win all of a group of similar or related sporting competitions, events, or matches. **wipe the slate clean** see **WIPE**.
– DERIVATIVES **cleanable** adjective, **cleanish** adjective, **cleanness** noun.
– ORIGIN Old English *clǣne*, of West Germanic origin; related to Dutch and German *klein* 'small'.
▶ **clean someone out** informal use up or take all someone's money: *they were cleaned out by the Englishman at the baccarat table.*
clean up informal make a substantial gain or profit.
■ win all the prizes available in a sporting competition or series of events.
clean something up restore order or morality to: *the police chief was given the job of cleaning up a notorious district.*

clean and jerk ▶ **noun** [in sing.] a weightlifting exercise in which a weight is raised above the head following an initial lift to shoulder level.

clean-cut ▶ **adjective** sharply outlined: *the normally clean-cut edge between sea and land has become blurred.*
■ (of a person, especially a man) appearing neat and respectable: *the part called for a clean-cut, conventional actor.*

cleaner ▶ **noun** a person or thing that cleans something, in particular:
■ a person employed to clean the interior of a building: *she's one of the office cleaners.* ■ (**the cleaners**) a shop where clothes and fabrics are dry-cleaned: *my suit's at the cleaners.* ■ a device for cleaning, such as a vacuum cleaner. ■ a chemical substance used for cleaning: *an oven cleaner.*
– PHRASES **take someone to the cleaners** informal take all someone's money or possessions in a dishonest or unfair way. ■ inflict a crushing defeat on someone: *his team were taken to the cleaners by the Australians in the first Test.*

cleaner fish ▶ **noun** a small fish, especially a striped wrasse, that is permitted to remove parasites from the skin, gills, and mouth of larger fishes, to their mutual benefit.
• Genus *Labroides*, family Labridae: several species, in particular *L. dimidiatus*.

clean-limbed ▶ **adjective** (especially of the human figure) slim; well formed and shapely.

clean-living ▶ **adjective** not indulging in anything considered unhealthy or immoral.

cleanly /ˈkliːnli/ ▶ **adverb 1** in a way that produces no dirt, noxious gases, or other pollutants: *the engine burns very cleanly.*
2 without difficulty or impediment; smoothly and efficiently: *he vaulted cleanly through the open window.* [ORIGIN: Old English *clǣnlīce* (see **CLEAN**, **-LY²**).]
▶ **adjective** /ˈklɛnli/ (**cleanlier**, **cleanliest**) archaic (of a person or animal) habitually clean and careful to avoid dirt. [ORIGIN: Old English *clǣnlīc* (see **CLEAN**, **-LY¹**).]
– DERIVATIVES **cleanliness** noun.

cleanse ▶ **verb** [with obj.] make (something, especially the skin) thoroughly clean: *this preparation will cleanse and tighten the skin* | [as adj. **cleansing**] *a cleansing cream.*
■ rid (a person, place, or thing) of something seen as unpleasant, unwanted, or defiling: *the mission to cleanse America of subversives.* ■ free (someone) from sin or guilt. ■ archaic (in biblical translations) cure (a leper).
▶ **noun** [in sing.] an act of cleansing something, especially the skin.
– ORIGIN Old English *clǣnsian* (verb), from *clǣne* (see **CLEAN**).

cleanser ▶ **noun** [often with adj. or noun modifier] a substance that cleanses something, especially a cosmetic product for cleansing the skin.

clean-shaven ▶ **adjective** (of a man) without a beard or moustache.

clean sheet ▶ **noun** an absence of existing

restraints or commitments: *no government starts with a clean sheet.*

– PHRASES **keep a clean sheet** (in a football match or tournament) prevent the opposing side from scoring.

cleansing department ▶ noun Brit. an organization controlled by local government that collects refuse or rubbish.

cleanskin ▶ noun Austral. an unbranded animal.
■ figurative, informal a person without a police record.

clean slate ▶ noun another term for CLEAN SHEET.

clean-up ▶ noun 1 an act of making a place clean or tidy: *an environmental clean-up.*
■ an act of removing or putting an end to disorder, immorality, or crime.
2 (also **cleanup**) [usu. as modifier] Baseball the fourth position in a team's batting order, usually reserved for a strong batter whose hits are likely to enable any runner who is on base to score.

clear ▶ adjective 1 easy to perceive, understand, or interpret: *the voice on the telephone was clear and strong | clear and precise directions | her handwriting was clear | am I making myself clear?*
■ leaving no doubt; obvious or unambiguous: *it was clear that they were in a trap | a clear case of poisoning.*
■ having or feeling no doubt or confusion: *every pupil must be clear about what is expected.*
2 free of anything that marks or darkens something, in particular:
■ (of a substance) transparent: *the clear glass of the French windows | a stream of clear water.* ■ free of cloud, mist, or rain: *the day was fine and clear.* ■ (of a person's skin) free from blemishes. ■ (of a person's eyes) unclouded; shining: *I looked into her clear gray eyes.* ■ (of a colour) pure and intense: *clear blue delphiniums.* ■ archaic (of a fire) burning with little smoke: *a bright, clear flame.*
3 free of any obstructions or unwanted objects: *with a clear road ahead he shifted into high gear | I had a clear view in both directions | his desktop was almost clear.*
■ (of a period of time) free of any appointments or commitments: *the following Saturday, Mattie had a clear day.* ■ [predic.] (of a person) free of something undesirable or unpleasant: *after 18 months of treatment he was clear of TB.* ■ (of a person's mind) free of something which impairs logical thought: *in the morning, with a clear head, she would tackle all her problems.* ■ (of a person's conscience) free of guilt.
4 [predic.] (**clear of**) not touching; away from: *the lorry was wedged in the ditch, one wheel clear of the ground.*
5 [attrib.] complete; full: *you must give seven clear days' notice of the meeting.*
■ (of a sum of money) net: *a clear profit of £1,100.*
6 Phonetics denoting a palatalized form of the sound of the letter *l* (as in *leaf* in south-eastern English speech). Often contrasted with DARK.
▶ adverb 1 so as to be out of the way of or away from: *he leapt clear of the car | stand clear, I'll start the plane up.*
■ so as not to be obstructed or cluttered: *the floor had been swept clear of litter.*
2 with clarity; distinctly: *she had to toss her head to see the lake clear again.*
3 completely: *he had time to get clear away.*
■ (**clear to**) chiefly N. Amer. all the way to: *you could see clear to the bottom of the lagoon.*
▶ verb 1 [no obj.] become free of something that marks, darkens, obstructs, or covers something, in particular:
■ (of the sky or weather) become free of cloud or rain: *we'll go out if the weather clears.* ■ (of a liquid) become transparent: *a wine that refuses to clear.* ■ become free of obstructions: *the boy's lungs cleared and he began to breathe more easily.* ■ gradually go away or disappear: *the fever clears in two to four weeks | the mist had cleared away.* ■ (of a person's face or expression) assume a happier aspect following previous confusion or distress: *for a moment, Sam was confused; then his expression cleared.* ■ (of a person's mind) regain the capacity for logical thought; become free of confusion: *his mind cleared and he began to reflect.*
2 [with obj.] make (something) free of marks, obstructions, or unwanted items, in particular:
■ remove an obstruction or unwanted item or items from: *the drive had been cleared of snow | Carolyn cleared the table and washed up.* ■ free (land) for cultivation or building by removing vegetation or existing structures. ■ free (one's mind) of unpleasantness or confusion: *the swift understanding cleared his mind.* ■ cause people to leave (a building or place): *the wardens shouted a warning and cleared the streets.*

3 [with obj.] remove (an obstruction or unwanted item) from somewhere: *the sludge was cleared from the colliery | park staff cleared away dead trees.*
■ chiefly Soccer send (the ball) away from the area near one's goal. ■ discharge (a debt).
4 [with obj.] get past or over (something) safely or without touching it: *the plane rose high enough to clear the trees.*
■ jump (a specified height) in a competition: *she cleared 1.50 metres in the high jump.*
5 [with obj.] show or declare (someone) officially to be innocent: *his sport's ruling body had cleared him of cheating.*
6 [with obj.] give official approval or authorization to: *I cleared him to return to his squadron.*
■ get official approval for (something): *the press releases had to be cleared with the White House.* ■ (of a person or goods) satisfy the necessary requirements to pass through (customs): *I can help her to clear customs quickly.* ■ pass (a cheque) through a clearing house so that the money goes into the payee's account: *the cheque could not be cleared until Monday.* ■ [no obj.] (of a cheque) pass through a clearing house in such a way.
7 [with obj.] earn or gain (an amount of money) as a net profit: *I would hope to clear £50,000 profit from each match.*

– PHRASES **as clear as mud** see MUD. **clear the air** make the air less sultry. ■ defuse or clarify an angry, tense, or confused situation by frank discussion: *it's time a few things were said to clear the air.* (**as**) **clear as a bell** see BELL[1]. (**as**) **clear as day** very easy to see or understand. **clear the decks** prepare for a particular event or goal by dealing with anything beforehand that might hinder progress. **clear one's lines** chiefly Rugby make a kick sending the ball well upfield from near one's own goal line. **clear the name of** show to be innocent: *the spokesman released a statement attempting to clear his client's name.* **clear one's throat** cough slightly so as to speak more clearly, attract attention, or to express hesitancy before saying something awkward. **clear the way** remove an obstacle or hindrance to allow progress: *the ruling could be enough to clear the way for impeachment proceedings.* ■ [in imperative] stand aside: *Stand back, there! Clear the way!* **in clear** not in code: *the Russian staff practice of sending radio messages and orders in clear.* **in the clear 1** no longer in danger or suspected of something: *Charles was relieved that the information put her in the clear.* **2** with nothing to hinder one in achieving something. **out of a clear sky** as a complete surprise: *his moods blew up suddenly out of a clear sky.*
– DERIVATIVES **clearable** adjective, **clearness** noun.
– ORIGIN Middle English: from Old French *cler*, from Latin *clarus.*

▶ **clear away** remove the remains of a meal from the table: *Adam cleared away and washed up.*
clear off [usu. in imperative] informal go away: '*Clear off!*' *he yelled.*
clear out informal leave quickly.
clear something out remove the contents from something so as to tidy it or free it for alternative use: *they told her to clear out her desk by the next day.*
clear up 1 (of an illness or other medical condition) become cured: *all my health problems cleared up.* **2** (of the weather) become brighter. ■ (of rain) stop.
clear something up 1 (also **clear up**) tidy something up by removing rubbish or other unwanted items: *he decided to clear up his cottage | I keep meaning to come down here and clear up.* ■ remove rubbish or other unwanted items to leave something tidy: *he asked the youths to clear up their litter.* **2** solve or explain something: *he wanted to clear up some misconceptions.* **3** cure an illness or other medical condition: *folk customs prescribed sage tea to clear up measles.*

clearance ▶ noun [mass noun] 1 the action or process of removing or getting rid of something or of something's dispersing: *cleaning of the machine should include clearance of blockages | there will be sunny intervals after clearance of any early mist.*
■ [often with adj. or noun modifier] the removal of buildings, people, or trees from land so as to free it for alternative uses: *slum clearance accelerated during the 1960s* | [count noun] *forest clearances.* ■ (also **house clearance**) the removal of contents from a house: *the sheriff's officers supervised the house clearance* | [count noun] *antiques wanted and clearances undertaken.* ■ the discharge of a debt. ■ [count noun] (in soccer and other games) a kick or hit that sends the ball out of a

defensive zone. ■ [count noun] Snooker the potting of all the balls remaining on the table in a single break.
2 official authorization for something to proceed or take place: *there was a delay in obtaining diplomatic clearance to overfly Israel.*
■ (also **security clearance**) official permission for someone to have access to classified information: *these people don't have clearance.* ■ permission for an aircraft to take off or land at an airport: *he took off without air traffic clearance.* ■ (also **customs clearance**) the clearing of a person or ship by customs. ■ [count noun] a certificate showing that such clearance has been granted. ■ the process of clearing cheques through a clearing house.
3 clear space allowed for a thing to move past or under another: *always give cyclists plenty of clearance.*

clearance sale ▶ noun a sale of goods at reduced prices to get rid of superfluous stock or because the shop is closing down.

clearcole /ˈklɪəkəʊl/ ▶ noun [mass noun] historical a mixture of size and whiting or white lead, formerly used as a primer for distemper.
– ORIGIN early 19th cent.: from French *claire colle* 'clear glue'.

clear-cut ▶ adjective 1 sharply defined; easy to perceive or understand: *we now had a clear-cut objective.*
2 (of an area) from which every tree has been cut down and removed.
▶ verb [with obj.] cut down and remove every tree from (an area): *colonizers who clear-cut large jungle tracts.* Also called CLEAR-FELL.

clearer ▶ noun 1 Brit. a clearing bank.
2 a person or thing that removes obstructions from something: *a chemical drain clearer.*

clear-eyed ▶ adjective having unclouded, bright eyes: *a handsome, clear-eyed young man.*
■ figurative having a shrewd understanding and no illusions: *clear-eyed about human nature.*

clear-fell ▶ verb another term for CLEAR-CUT.

clear-headed ▶ adjective alert and thinking logically and coherently.

clearing ▶ noun an open space in a forest, especially one cleared for cultivation.

clearing bank ▶ noun Brit. a bank which is a member of a clearing house.

clearing house ▶ noun a bankers' establishment where cheques and bills from member banks are exchanged, so that only the balances need be paid in cash.
■ an agency or organization which collects and distributes something, especially information.

clearly ▶ adverb in such a way as to allow easy and accurate perception or interpretation: *the ability to write clearly* | [as submodifier] *on white paper, the seeds are clearly visible.*
■ [sentence adverb] without doubt; obviously: *clearly, there have been disasters and reversals here.*

clear-out ▶ noun a removal and disposal of unwanted items or material.
■ a removal or dismissal of a person or people from an organization: *a staff clear-out is being planned.*

clear-sighted ▶ adjective thinking clearly and sensibly; perspicacious and discerning: *a clear-sighted sense of what is possible and appropriate.*

clearstory ▶ noun (pl. **-ies**) US spelling of CLERESTORY.

clear-up ▶ noun [often as modifier] a removal and tidying away of rubbish or obstructions: *a massive clear-up operation.*
■ [mass noun] the solving of crimes by the police: *Welsh police had one of the most successful clear-up rates.*

clearway ▶ noun Brit. a main road other than a motorway on which vehicles are not normally permitted to stop.

clearwing (also **clearwing moth**) ▶ noun a day-flying moth which has narrow mainly transparent wings and mimics a wasp or bee in appearance.
● Family Sesiidae: several genera and many species, including the hornet moth.

cleat /kliːt/ ▶ noun a T-shaped piece of metal or wood on a boat or ship, to which ropes are attached.
■ one of a number of projecting pieces of metal, rubber, or other material on the sole of a shoe, designed to prevent someone losing their footing. ■ a projecting wedge on a spar or other part of a ship, to prevent slipping. ■ a small wedge, especially one on a plough or scythe.
– DERIVATIVES **cleated** adjective.

– ORIGIN Middle English (in the sense 'wedge'): of West Germanic origin; related to Dutch *kloot* 'ball, sphere' and German *Kloss* 'clod, dumpling', also to **CLOT** and **CLOUT**.

cleavage ▶ noun a sharp division; a split: *a system dominated by the class cleavage.*
■ the hollow between a woman's breasts when supported, especially as exposed by a low-cut garment. ■ [mass noun] Biology cell division, especially of a fertilized egg cell. ■ [mass noun] the splitting of rocks or crystals in a preferred plane or direction.

cleave[1] ▶ verb (past **clove** or **cleft** or **cleaved**; past participle **cloven** or **cleft** or **cleaved**) [with obj.] split or sever (something), especially along a natural line or grain: *the large chopper his father used to cleave wood for the fire.*
■ split (a molecule) by breaking a particular chemical bond. ■ make a way through (something) forcefully, as if by splitting it apart: *they watched a coot cleave the smooth water | Stan was away,* ***cleaving a path through*** *the traffic | [no obj.] an unstoppable warrior* ***clove through*** *their ranks.* ■ [no obj.] Biology (of a cell) divide: *the egg cleaves to form a mulberry-shaped cluster of cells.*
– DERIVATIVES **cleavable** adjective.
– ORIGIN Old English *clēofan*, of Germanic origin; related to Dutch *klieven* and German *klieben*.

cleave[2] ▶ verb [no obj.] (**cleave to**) poetic/literary stick fast to: *Rose's mouth was dry, her tongue cleaving to the roof of her mouth.*
■ adhere strongly to (a particular pursuit or belief): *part of why we cleave to sports is that excellence is so measurable.* ■ become very strongly involved with or emotionally attached to (someone): *it was his choice to cleave to the Brownings.*
– ORIGIN Old English *cleofian, clifian, clīfan*, of West Germanic origin; related to Dutch *kleven* and German *kleben*, also to **CLAY** and **CLIMB**.

cleaver ▶ noun a tool with a heavy broad blade, used by butchers for chopping meat.

cleavers ▶ plural noun [treated as sing. or pl.] another term for **GOOSEGRASS**.
– ORIGIN Old English *clīfe*, related to **CLEAVE**[2].

Cleese /kliːz/, John (Marwood) (b.1939), English comic actor and writer, famous for *Monty Python's Flying Circus* (1969–74) and the situation comedy *Fawlty Towers* (1975–9).

clef ▶ noun Music any of several symbols placed at the left hand end of a stave, indicating the pitch of the notes written on it.
– ORIGIN late 16th cent.: from French, from Latin *clavis* 'key'.

cleft[1] past participle of **CLEAVE**[1]. ▶ adjective split, divided, or partially divided into two: *a cleft chin.*
– PHRASES **be** (or **be caught**) **in a cleft stick** chiefly Brit. be in a situation in which any action one takes will have adverse consequences.

cleft[2] ▶ noun a fissure or split, especially one in rock or the ground.
■ a vertical indentation in the middle of a person's forehead or chin. ■ a deep division between two parts of the body.
– ORIGIN Middle English *clift*: of Germanic origin; related to Dutch *kluft* and German *Kluft*, also to **CLEAVE**[1]. The form of the word was altered in the 16th cent. by association with **CLEFT**[1].

cleft lip ▶ noun a congenital split in the upper lip on one or both sides of the centre, often associated with a cleft palate.

USAGE **Cleft lip** is the standard accepted term and should be used instead of **harelip**, which can cause offence.

cleft palate ▶ noun a congenital split in the roof of the mouth.

cleft sentence ▶ noun Grammar a sentence in which an element is emphasized by being put in a separate clause, with the use of an empty introductory word such as *it* or *that*, e.g. *it's money we want; it was today that I saw him; that was the King you were talking to.*

cleg /klɛɡ/ ▶ noun Brit. another term for **HORSEFLY**.
– ORIGIN late Middle English: from Old Norse *kleggi*.

Cleisthenes /ˈklʌɪsθəniːz/ (*c.*570 BC–*c.*508 BC), Athenian statesman. His reforms consolidated the Athenian democratic process begun by Solon and influenced the policies of Pericles.

cleistogamy /klʌɪˈstɒɡəmi/ ▶ noun [mass noun] Botany self-fertilization that occurs within a permanently closed flower.
– DERIVATIVES **cleistogamous** adjective.
– ORIGIN late 19th cent.: from Greek *kleistos* 'closed' + *-gamy* (from *gamos* 'marriage').

clematis /ˈklɛmətɪs, kləˈmeɪtɪs/ ▶ noun a climbing plant of the buttercup family which bears white, pink, or purple flowers and feathery seeds. Several kinds are cultivated as ornamentals.
• Genus *Clematis*, family Ranunculaceae.
– ORIGIN Latin (also denoting the periwinkle), from Greek *klēmatis*, from *klēma* 'vine branch'.

Clemenceau /ˈklɛmənsəʊ, French klɛmɑ̃so/, Georges (Eugène Benjamin) (1841–1929), French statesman, Prime Minister 1906–9 and 1917–20.

clemency ▶ noun [mass noun] mercy; lenience: *an appeal for clemency.*
– ORIGIN late Middle English: from Latin *clementia*, from *clemens, clement-* 'clement'.

Clemens /ˈklɛmənz/, Samuel Langhorne, see **TWAIN**.

clement ▶ adjective **1** (of weather) mild.
2 (of a person or their actions) merciful.
– ORIGIN late Middle English (in sense 2): from Latin *clemens, clement-*.

Clement, St (1st century AD), pope (bishop of Rome) *c.*88–*c.*97, probably the third after St Peter; known as **St Clement of Rome**. Feast day, 23 November.

clementine /ˈklɛm(ə)ntʌɪn, -tiːn/ ▶ noun a tangerine of a deep orange-red North African variety which is grown around the Mediterranean and in South Africa.
– ORIGIN 1920s: from French *clémentine*, from the male given name *Clément*.

Clement of Alexandria, St (*c.*150–*c.*215), Greek theologian; Latin name *Titus Flavius Clemens*. His main contribution to theological scholarship was to relate the ideas of Greek philosophy to the Christian faith. Feast day, 5 December.

clenbuterol /klɛnˈbjuːtərɒl/ ▶ noun [mass noun] Medicine a synthetic drug used in the treatment of asthma and respiratory diseases and also in veterinary obstetrics. It also promotes the growth of muscle and has been used illegally by athletes to enhance performance.
– ORIGIN 1970s: from *c(h)l(oro-)* + *(ph)en(yl)* + *but(yl)* + *er* + **-OL**.

clench ▶ verb (with reference to the fingers or hand) close into a tight ball, especially when feeling extreme anger: [with obj.] *she clenched her fists, struggling for control* | [no obj.] *Ian's right hand clenched into a fist* | [as adj. **clenched**] *he struck the wall with his clenched fist.*
■ (with reference to the teeth) press or be pressed tightly together, especially with anger or determination or so as to suppress a strong emotion: [no obj.] *her teeth clenched in anger.* ■ [with obj.] grasp (something) tightly and firmly, especially with the hands or between the teeth: *he clenched the steering wheel so hard that the car wobbled.* ■ [no obj.] (of a muscular part of the body) tighten or contract sharply, especially with strong emotion: *Mark felt his stomach clench in alarm.*
▶ noun [in sing.] a contraction or tightening of part of the body: *she saw the anger rise, saw the clench of his fists.*
■ the state of being tightly closed or contracted.
– ORIGIN Old English (in the sense of *clinch* 'fix securely'): of Germanic origin; related to **CLING**.

cleome /klɪˈəʊmi/ ▶ noun a plant of a chiefly tropical genus which includes the spider flower. Cleomes are noted for their long stamens.
• Genus *Cleome*, family Capparidaceae.
– ORIGIN modern Latin, from Greek, denoting a different plant.

Cleopatra /ˌkliːəˈpatrə/ (also **Cleopatra VII**) (69–30 BC), queen of Egypt 47–30, the last Ptolemaic ruler. After a brief liaison with Julius Caesar she formed a political and romantic alliance with Mark Antony. Their ambitions ultimately brought them into conflict with Rome, and she and Antony were defeated at the battle of Actium in 31. She is reputed to have committed suicide by allowing herself to be bitten by an asp.

cleopatra /ˌkliːəˈpatrə/ ▶ noun a European butterfly related to the brimstone, with wings that vary from pale cream to orange-yellow.
• *Gonepteryx cleopatra*, family Pieridae.

Cleopatra's Needles a pair of granite obelisks erected at Heliopolis by Tuthmosis III *c.*1475 BC. They were taken from Egypt in 1878, one being set up on the Thames Embankment in London and the other in Central Park, New York. They have no known historical connection with Cleopatra.

clepsydra /ˈklɛpsɪdrə/ ▶ noun (pl. **clepsydras** or **clepsydrae** /-driː/) an ancient time-measuring device worked by a flow of water.
– ORIGIN late Middle English: via Latin from Greek *klepsudra*, based on *kleptein* 'steal' + *hudōr* 'water'.

clerestory /ˈklɪəˌstɔːri/ (US also **clearstory**) ▶ noun (pl. **-ies**) the upper part of the nave, choir, and transepts of a large church, containing a series of windows. It is clear of the roofs of the aisles and admits light to the central parts of the building.
■ such a series of windows in a church or similar windows in another building. ■ a raised section of roof running down the centre of a railway carriage, with small windows or ventilators.
– ORIGIN late Middle English: from **CLEAR** + **STOREY**.

clerestory window ▶ noun one of a series of windows in a clerestory.
■ a window with no crosspiece dividing the light.

clergy /ˈkləːdʒi/ ▶ noun (pl. **-ies**) [usu. treated as pl.] the body of all people ordained for religious duties, especially in the Christian Church: *all marriages were to be solemnized by* ***the clergy****.*
– ORIGIN Middle English: from Old French, based on ecclesiastical Latin *clericus* 'clergyman' (see **CLERIC**).

clergyman ▶ noun (pl. **-men**) a male priest or minister of a Christian church.

clergywoman ▶ noun (pl. **-women**) a female priest or minister of a Christian church.

cleric ▶ noun a priest or minister of a Christian church.
■ a priest or religious leader in any religion.
– ORIGIN early 17th cent.: from ecclesiastical Latin *clericus* 'clergyman', from Greek *klērikos* 'belonging to the Christian clergy', from *klēros* 'lot, heritage' (Acts 1:26).

clerical ▶ adjective **1** (of a job or person) concerned with or relating to work in an office, especially routine documentation and administrative tasks: *temps are always needed for clerical work.*
2 of or relating to the clergy: *he was still attired in his clerical outfit.*
– DERIVATIVES **clericalism** noun (only in sense 2), **clericalist** noun (only in sense 2), **clerically** adverb.
– ORIGIN late 15th cent. (in sense 2): from ecclesiastical Latin *clericalis*, from *clericus* 'clergyman' (see **CLERIC**).

clerical collar ▶ noun a stiff upright white collar which fastens at the back, worn by the clergy in some churches.

clerical error ▶ noun a mistake made in copying or writing out a document.

clerihew /ˈklɛrɪhjuː/ ▶ noun a short comic or nonsensical verse, typically in two rhyming couplets with lines of unequal length and referring to a famous person.
– ORIGIN 1920s: named after Edmund *Clerihew* Bentley (1875–1956), the English writer who invented it.

clerisy /ˈklɛrɪsi/ ▶ noun [usu. treated as pl.] a distinct class of learned or literary people: *the clerisy are those who read for pleasure.*
– ORIGIN early 19th cent.: apparently influenced by German *Klerisei*, based on Greek *klēros* 'heritage' (see **CLERIC**).

clerk ▶ noun **1** a person employed in an office or bank to keep records, accounts, and undertake other routine administrative duties: *a bank clerk.*
■ an official in charge of the records of a local council or court: *a clerk to the magistrates.* ■ a senior official in Parliament. ■ a lay officer of a cathedral, parish church, college chapel, etc.: *a chapter clerk.*
2 (also **desk clerk**) N. Amer. a receptionist in a hotel.
■ an assistant in a shop; a sales clerk.
3 (also **clerk in holy orders**) formal a member of the clergy.
▶ verb [no obj.] N. Amer. work as a clerk: *eleven of those who left college this year are clerking in auction stores.*
– PHRASES **Clerk of the Closet** (in the UK) the sovereign's principal chaplain. **clerk of the course** an official who assists the judges in horse racing or motor racing. **clerk of (the) works** Brit. a person who oversees building work in progress.
– DERIVATIVES **clerkess** noun (chiefly Scottish), **clerkish** adjective.
– ORIGIN Old English *cleric, clerc* (in the sense 'ordained minister, literate person'), from

ecclesiastical Latin *clericus* 'clergyman' (see **CLERIC**); reinforced by Old French *clerc*, from the same source. Sense 1 dates from the early 16th cent.

clerkly ▶ **adjective** archaic of, relating to, or appropriate to a clerk: *a list drawn up in a clerkly hand.*
■ scholarly; learned.

clerkship ▶ **noun** dated the position or status of a clerk, especially in the legal profession.

Clermont-Ferrand /ˌklɛːmɒ̃ fɛˈrɒ̃, French klɛrmɔ̃ fɛrɑ̃/ an industrial city in central France, capital of the Auvergne region, at the centre of the Massif Central; pop. 140,170 (1990).

Cleveland[1] /ˈkliːvlənd/ **1** a former county on the North Sea coast of NE England, formed in 1974 from parts of Durham and North Yorkshire and replaced in 1996 by the unitary councils of Middlesbrough, Hartlepool, Stockton-on-Tees, and Redcar and Cleveland.
2 a major port and industrial city in NE Ohio, situated on Lake Erie; pop 505,600 (1990).

Cleveland[2] /ˈkliːvlənd/, (Stephen) Grover (1837–1908), American Democratic statesman, 22nd and 24th President of the US 1885–9 and 1893–7.

Cleveland bay ▶ **noun** a bay horse of a strong breed originating in the north of England. Cleveland bays were formerly popular carriage horses.

clever ▶ **adjective** (**cleverer**, **cleverest**) **1** quick to understand, learn, and devise or apply ideas; intelligent: *she was an extremely clever and studious young woman | how* ***clever of*** *him to think of this!*
■ skilled at doing or achieving something; talented: *he was very* ***clever at*** *getting what he wanted | both Grandma and Mother were* ***clever with*** *their hands.* ■ (of a thing, action, or idea) showing intelligence or skill; ingenious: *a simple but clever idea for helping people learn computing | he taught the dog to perform some very clever tricks.* ■ [usu. with negative] informal sensible; well advised: *Joe had a feeling it wasn't too clever, leaving Dolly alone.*
2 [predic.] [with negative] Brit. informal healthy or well: *I was up and about by this time though still not too clever.*
– PHRASES **too clever by half** informal used to express one's belief that a person is annoyingly proud of their intelligence or skill, and that they might overreach themselves.
– DERIVATIVES **cleverly** adverb, **cleverness** noun.
– ORIGIN Middle English (in the sense 'quick to catch hold', only recorded in this period): perhaps of Dutch or Low German origin, and related to **CLEAVE**[2]. In the late 16th cent. the term came to mean (probably through dialect use) 'manually skilful'; the sense 'possessing mental agility' dates from the early 18th cent.

clever-clever ▶ **adjective** derogatory excessively anxious to appear impressively clever or intelligent: *her silly little clever-clever theories of love and marriage.*

clever clogs ▶ **noun** informal, chiefly Brit. another term for **CLEVER DICK**.

clever Dick ▶ **noun** informal, chiefly Brit. a person who is irritatingly and ostentatiously knowledgeable or intelligent.

clevis /ˈklɛvɪs/ ▶ **noun** a U-shaped or forked metal connector within which another part can be fastened by means of a bolt or pin passing through the ends of the connector.
– ORIGIN late 16th cent.: perhaps related to **CLEAVE**[1].

clew /kluː/ ▶ **noun 1** the lower or after corner of a sail.
2 (**clews**) Nautical the cords by which a hammock is suspended.
■ (**clew**) a ball of thread (used especially with reference to the thread supposedly used by Theseus to mark his way out of the Cretan labyrinth).
3 archaic variant of **CLUE**.
▶ **verb** [with obj.] (**clew a sail up**) Sailing draw the lower ends of a sail to the upper yard or the mast ready for furling.
■ (**clew a sail down**) let down a sail by the clews in unfurling.
– ORIGIN Old English *cliwen*, *cleowen* (denoting a rounded mass, also a ball of thread), of Germanic origin; related to Dutch *kluwen*. All senses are also recorded for the form **CLUE**.

clianthus /klʌɪˈanθəs, klɪ-/ ▶ **noun** an Australasian plant of the pea family, which bears drooping clusters of large scarlet flowers. Also called **GLORY PEA**.
• Genus *Clianthus*, family Leguminosae.
– ORIGIN modern Latin, apparently from Greek *kleos*, *klei-* 'glory' + *anthos* 'flower'.

cliché /ˈkliːʃeɪ/ (also **cliche**) ▶ **noun 1** a phrase or opinion that is overused and betrays a lack of original thought.
■ a very predictable or unoriginal thing or person.
2 Printing, chiefly Brit. a stereotype or electrotype.
– ORIGIN mid 19th cent.: French, past participle (used as a noun) of *clicher* 'to stereotype'.

clichéd (also **cliché'd** or **cliched**) ▶ **adjective** showing a lack of originality; based on frequently repeated phrases or opinions: *people have a very clichéd view of the Middle East.*

click ▶ **noun** a short sharp sound as of a switch being operated or of two hard objects coming smartly into contact: *she heard the click of the door | at a click of his fingers, they were supplied with a plate of olives.*
■ a speech sound produced as a type of plosive by sudden withdrawal of the tongue from the soft palate, front teeth, or back teeth and hard palate, occurring in some southern African and other languages. ■ Computing an act of pressing one of the buttons on a mouse.
▶ **verb 1** make or cause to make a short sharp sound: [no obj.] *the key clicked in the lock and the door opened |* [with obj.] *she clicked off the light | Martha clicked her tongue |* [as adj. **clicking**] *the clicking cameras outside the church.*
■ [no obj., with adverbial] move with such a sound: *Louise turned on her three-inch heels and clicked away.* ■ [with obj.] Computing press (one of the buttons on a mouse): *click the left mouse button twice.* ■ [no obj.] (**click on**) Computing select (an item represented on the screen or a particular function) by pressing one of the buttons on the mouse when the cursor is over the appropriate symbol.
2 [no obj.] informal become suddenly clear or understandable: *I wasn't used to such good treatment, then* ***it clicked****: we were wearing suits.*
■ become friendly with someone, especially someone of the opposite sex, at the first meeting: *I couldn't help notice how pretty and intelligent she was and we just clicked.* ■ become successful or popular: *a jockey who never quite* ***clicked with*** *the racing public.*
– PHRASES **click one's fingers** see **FINGER**. **click into place** (of an object, especially part of a mechanism) fall smoothly into its allotted position. ■ figurative become suddenly clear and understandable: *given this info, everything soon clicks into place.*
– DERIVATIVES **clicky** adjective.
– ORIGIN late 16th cent. (as a verb): imitative.

clickable ▶ **adjective** Computing (of text or images on a computer screen) such that clicking on them with a mouse will produce a reaction.

click beetle ▶ **noun** a long, narrow beetle which can spring up with a click as a means of startling predators and escaping. Its larva is the wireworm. Also called **SKIPJACK**.
• Family Elateridae: numerous genera.

click-clack ▶ **noun** a repeated clicking sound as of shoe heels on a hard surface.
▶ **verb** [no obj., with adverbial of direction] move with such a sound: *a woman in high heels click-clacked past.*

clicker ▶ **noun** a device which clicks.
■ chiefly N. Amer. a remote control keypad.

click language ▶ **noun** a language in which clicks are used.

click stop ▶ **noun** a control for the aperture of a camera lens which clicks into position at certain standard settings.

client ▶ **noun 1** a person or organization using the services of a lawyer or other professional person or company: *insurance tailor-made to a client's specific requirements.*
■ a person being dealt with by social or medical services: *a client referred for counselling.*
2 Computing (in a network) a desktop computer or workstation that is capable of obtaining information and applications from a server.
■ (also **client application** or **program**) a program that is capable of obtaining a service provided by another program.
3 (in ancient Rome) a plebeian under the protection of a patrician.
■ archaic a dependant; a hanger-on.
– DERIVATIVES **clientship** noun.
– ORIGIN late Middle English: from Latin *cliens*, *client-*, variant of *cluens* 'heeding', from *cluere* 'hear or obey'. The term originally denoted a person under the protection and patronage of another, hence a person 'protected' by a legal adviser (sense 1).

clientele /ˌkliːɒnˈtɛl/ ▶ **noun** [treated as sing. or pl.] clients collectively: *the solicitor's clientele.*
■ the customers of a shop, bar, or place of entertainment: *the dancers don't mix with the clientele.*
– ORIGIN mid 16th cent. (in the sense 'clientship, patronage'): via French from Latin *clientela* 'clientship', from *cliens*, *client-* (see **CLIENT**).

clientelism /ˌkliːɒnˈtɛlɪz(ə)m/ (also **clientism** /ˈklʌɪəntɪz(ə)m/) ▶ **noun** [mass noun] a social order which depends upon relations of patronage, especially as a political approach which emphasizes or exploits such relations.
– DERIVATIVES **clientelistic** adjective.
– ORIGIN 1970s: from Italian *clientelismo* 'patronage system'.

client-server ▶ **adjective** Computing denoting a computer system in which a central server provides data to a number of networked workstations.

Clifden nonpareil ▶ **noun** a large European moth of mostly subdued coloration, with a pale blue band on the underwing.
• *Catocala fraxini*, family Noctuidae.
– ORIGIN mid 18th cent.: from *Clifden* (now *Cliveden*), the name of a village in Buckinghamshire, England, and **NONPAREIL**.

cliff ▶ **noun** a steep rock face, especially at the edge of the sea: *a coast path along the top of rugged cliffs |* [as modifier] *the cliff face.*
– DERIVATIVES **cliff-like** adjective, **cliffy** adjective.
– ORIGIN Old English *clif*, of Germanic origin; related to Dutch *klif*.

cliffhanger ▶ **noun** a dramatic and exciting ending to an episode of a serial, leaving the audience in suspense and anxious not to miss the next episode.
■ a story or event with a strong element of suspense: *the match was a cliffhanger right up to the final whistle.*

cliffhanging ▶ **adjective** [attrib.] very exciting and dramatic; full of suspense: *he emerged miraculously intact at the end of each cliffhanging episode.*

Clift, (Edward) Montgomery (1920–66), American actor. He received four Oscar nominations for films that included *From Here to Eternity* (1953).

climacteric /klʌɪˈmakt(ə)rɪk, ˌklʌɪmakˈtɛrɪk/ ▶ **noun** a critical period or event: *the first major climacteric in twentieth-century poetry.*
■ Medicine the period of life when fertility and sexual activity are in decline; (in women) menopause. ■ Botany the ripening period of certain fruits such as apples, involving increased metabolism and only possible while still on the tree.
▶ **adjective** having extreme and far-reaching implications or results; critical: *Britain must possess so climacteric a weapon in order to deter an atomically armed enemy.*
■ Medicine occurring at, characteristic of, or undergoing the climacteric; (in women) menopausal. ■ Botany (of a fruit) undergoing a climacteric.
– ORIGIN mid 16th cent. (in the sense 'constituting a critical period in life'): from French *climactérique* or via Latin from Greek *klimaktērikos*, from *klimaktēr* 'critical period', from *klimax* 'ladder, climax'.

climactic /klʌɪˈmaktɪk/ ▶ **adjective** (of an action, event, or scene) exciting or thrilling and acting as a culmination or resolution to a series of events: *the film's climactic scenes.*
– DERIVATIVES **climactically** adverb.
– ORIGIN late 19th cent.: formed irregularly from **CLIMAX** + **-IC**, probably influenced by **CLIMACTERIC**.

climate ▶ **noun** the weather conditions prevailing in an area in general or over a long period: *our cold, wet climate |* [mass noun] *agricultural development is constrained by climate.*
■ a region with particular prevailing weather conditions: *holidaying in a hot climate.* ■ the prevailing trend of public opinion or of another aspect of public life: *the current economic climate.*
– DERIVATIVES **climatic** adjective, **climatical** adjective, **climatically** adverb.
– ORIGIN late Middle English: from Old French *climat* or late Latin *clima*, *climat-*, from Greek *klima* 'slope, zone', from *klinein* 'to slope'. The term originally denoted a zone of the earth between two lines of latitude, then any region of the earth, and later, a region considered with reference to its atmospheric conditions. Compare with **CLIME**.

climate control ▶ **noun** another term for **AIR CONDITIONING**.

climatology ▶ **noun** [mass noun] the scientific study of climate.
– DERIVATIVES **climatological** adjective, **climatologist** noun.

climax ▶ **noun** the most intense, exciting, or important point of something; a culmination or apex: *she was nearing the climax of her speech* | *a thrilling climax to the game.*
■ an orgasm. ■ Ecology the final stage in a succession in a given environment, at which a plant community reaches a state of equilibrium: [as modifier] *a mixed hardwood climax forest.* ■ Rhetoric a sequence of propositions or ideas in order of increasing importance, force, or effectiveness of expression.
▶ **verb** [no obj.] culminate in an exciting or impressive event; reach a climax: *the day* ***climaxed with*** *a gala concert.*
■ [with obj.] bring (something) to a climax: *three goals in the last two minutes climaxed a thrilling game.* ■ have an orgasm.
– ORIGIN mid 16th cent. (in rhetoric): from late Latin, from Greek *klimax* 'ladder, climax'. The sense 'culmination' arose in the late 18th cent.

climb ▶ **verb 1** [with obj.] go or come up a (slope, incline, or staircase); ascend: *we began to climb the hill* | [no obj.] *the air became colder as they climbed higher* | *he* ***climbed up*** *the steps slowly.*
■ [no obj.] (of an aircraft or the sun) go upwards: *we decided to climb to 6,000 feet.* ■ [no obj.] (of a road or track) slope upwards or up: *the track climbed steeply up a narrow, twisting valley.* ■ (of a plant) grow up (a wall, tree, or trellis) by clinging with tendrils or by twining: *when ivy climbs a wall it infiltrates any crack* | [no obj.] *there were roses* ***climbing up*** *the walls.* ■ [no obj.] increase in scale, value, or power: *deer numbers have been climbing steadily* | *the stock market climbed 23.9 points.* ■ move to a higher position in (a chart or table): *Wrexham's bid to climb the second division table.* ■ [no obj.] informal (in sports journalism) leap into the air to reach or deliver the ball: *Kernaghan climbed to head in Putney's corner.*
2 [no obj., with adverbial of direction] move with effort, especially into or out of a confined space; clamber: *Howard started to climb out of the front seat.*
■ (**climb into**) put on (clothes): *he climbed into his suit.*
▶ **noun** an ascent, especially of a mountain or hill, by climbing: *this walk involves a long moorland climb* | figurative *the climb out of recession.*
■ a mountain, hill, or slope that is climbed or is to be climbed: *he was too full of alcohol to negotiate the climb safely.* ■ a recognized route up a mountain or cliff: *this may be the hardest rock climb in the world.* ■ an aircraft's flight upwards: *we levelled out from the climb at 600 feet* | [mass noun] *rate of climb.* ■ a rise or increase in value, rank, or power: *an above-average climb in prices.*
– PHRASES **be climbing the walls** informal feel frustrated, helpless, and trapped: *his job soon had him climbing the walls.* **have a mountain to climb** be facing a very difficult task.
– DERIVATIVES **climbable** adjective.
– ORIGIN Old English *climban*, of West Germanic origin; related to Dutch and German *klimmen*, also to **CLAY** and **CLEAVE**[2].
▶ **climb down** withdraw from a position taken up in argument or negotiation: *he was forced to climb down over the central package in the bill.*

climbdown ▶ **noun** a withdrawal from a position taken up in argument or negotiation, typically by admitting that one was wrong: *a humiliating climbdown by the government over economic policy.*

climber ▶ **noun** a person or animal that climbs: *leopards are great tree climbers.*
■ a mountaineer. ■ a climbing plant. ■ a social climber.

climbing ▶ **noun** [mass noun] the sport or activity of ascending mountains or cliffs.

climbing frame ▶ **noun** Brit. a structure of joined bars or logs for children to climb on.

climbing irons ▶ **plural noun** a set of spikes attached to boots for climbing trees or ice slopes.

climbing perch ▶ **noun** a small edible freshwater fish which is able to breathe air and move over land, native to Africa and Asia.
• Family Anabantidae: three genera and several species, including *Anabas testudinens*.

climbing wall ▶ **noun** a wall at a sports centre or in a gymnasium fitted with attachments to simulate a rock face for climbing practice.

climb-out ▶ **noun** the part of a flight of an aircraft after take-off and before it reaches a level altitude.

clime /klʌɪm/ ▶ **noun** (usu. **climes**) chiefly poetic/literary a region considered with reference to its climate: *the Continent and its sunnier climes.*
– ORIGIN late Middle English: from late Latin *clima* 'zone' (see **CLIMATE**).

clinch ▶ **verb** [with obj.] **1** confirm or settle (a contract or bargain): *the Texan wanted to impress him to clinch a business deal.*
■ conclusively settle (an argument or debate): *these findings clinched the matter.* ■ confirm the winning or achievement of (a match, competition, or victory): *Johnson scored the goals which clinched victory.* ■ secure (a nail or rivet) by driving the point sideways when it has penetrated. ■ fasten (a rope or angling line) with a clinch knot.
2 [no obj.] grapple at close quarters, especially (of boxers) so as to be too closely engaged for full-arm blows.
■ (of two people) embrace.
▶ **noun 1** a struggle or scuffle at close quarters, especially (in boxing) one in which the fighters become too closely engaged for full-arm blows.
■ an embrace, especially an amorous one: *we went into a passionate clinch on the sofa.*
2 (also **clinch knot**) a knot used to fasten ropes or angling lines, using a half hitch with the end seized back on its own part.
– ORIGIN late 16th cent. (in the senses 'something that grips' and 'fix securely'): variant of **CLENCH**.

clincher ▶ **noun** a fact, argument, or event that settles a matter conclusively: *this latter piece of logic was the clincher.*

Cline /klʌɪn/, Patsy (1932–63), American country singer; born *Virginia Petterson Hensley.* She had hits with 'Crazy' (1961) and 'Sweet Dreams of You' (1963) before dying in an air crash.

cline /klʌɪn/ ▶ **noun** a continuum with an infinite number of gradations from one extreme to the other: *a point along a cline of activity.*
■ Biology a gradation in one or more characteristics within a species or other taxon, especially between different populations. See also **ECOCLINE**.
– DERIVATIVES **clinal** adjective.
– ORIGIN 1930s: from Greek *klinein* 'to slope'.

cling ▶ **verb** (past and past participle **clung**) [no obj.] (**cling to/on to/on**) (of a person or animal) hold on tightly to: *she clung to Joe's arm* | *we sat on the sofa clinging on to one another* | *they clung together* | figurative *she clung on to life.*
■ (**cling to**) adhere or stick firmly or closely to; be hard to part or remove from: *the smell of smoke clung to their clothes* | *the fabric clung to her smooth skin.* ■ (**cling to**) remain very close to: *the fish cling to the line of the weed.* ■ remain persistently or stubbornly faithful to something: *she clung resolutely to her convictions.* ■ be overly dependent on someone emotionally: *you are clinging to him for security.*
▶ **noun** (also **cling peach**) a clingstone peach.
– DERIVATIVES **clinger** noun.
– ORIGIN Old English *clingan* 'stick together', of Germanic origin; related to Middle Dutch *klingen* 'adhere', Middle High German *klingen* 'climb', also to **CLENCH**.

cling film ▶ **noun** [mass noun] Brit. a thin transparent plastic film that adheres to surfaces and to itself, used chiefly as a wrapping or covering for food.

clingfish ▶ **noun** (pl. same or **-fishes**) a small fish occurring mainly in shallow or intertidal water, with a sucker for attachment to rocks and other surfaces.
• Family Gobiesocidae: several genera and species, including the **shore clingfish** (*Lepadogaster lepadogaster*) of Europe and West Africa.

clinging ▶ **adjective 1** (of a garment) fitting closely to the body and showing its shape: *she was wearing a clinging black dress.*
2 overly dependent on someone emotionally: *she wasn't the clinging type.*

clingstone ▶ **noun** a peach or nectarine of a variety in which the flesh adheres to the stone. Contrasted with **FREESTONE** (in sense 2).

clingy ▶ **adjective** (**clingier**, **clingiest**) (of a person or garment) liable to cling; clinging: *at about 18 months my son became very clingy* | *clingy leggings.*
– DERIVATIVES **clinginess** noun.

clinic ▶ **noun 1** a place or hospital department where outpatients are given medical treatment or advice, especially of a specialist nature: *an antenatal clinic.*
■ an occasion or time when such treatment or advice is given: *we're now holding regular clinics.* ■ a gathering at a hospital bedside for the teaching of medicine or surgery.
2 chiefly N. Amer. a conference or short course on a particular subject: *a drum clinic.*
– ORIGIN mid 19th cent. (in the sense 'teaching of medicine at the bedside'): from French *clinique*, from Greek *klinikē (tekhnē)* 'bedside (art)', from *klinē* 'bed'.

clinical ▶ **adjective 1** of or relating to the observation and treatment of actual patients rather than theoretical or laboratory studies: *clinical medicine* | *clinical drug trials.*
■ (of a disease or condition) causing observable and recognizable symptoms.
2 very efficient and without feeling; coldly detached: *nothing was left to chance—everything was clinical.*
■ (of a room or building) bare, functional, and clean.
– ORIGIN late 18th cent.: from Greek *klinikē* 'bedside' (see **CLINIC**) + **-AL**.

clinical death ▶ **noun** [mass noun] death as judged by the medical observation of cessation of vital functions. It is typically identified with the cessation of heartbeat and respiration, though modern resuscitation methods and life-support systems have required the introduction of the alternative concept of brain death.

clinically ▶ **adverb 1** as regards clinical medicine; in clinical terms: *the first clinically useful antibiotics* | *clinically dead.*
2 very efficiently and coldly: *Goodman clinically finished off the move.*
■ [usu. as submodifier] in a very functional and clean manner: *a clinically clean kitchen.*

clinical psychology ▶ **noun** [mass noun] the branch of psychology concerned with the assessment and treatment of mental illness and handicap.
– DERIVATIVES **clinical psychologist** noun.

clinical thermometer ▶ **noun** a small medical thermometer with a short but finely calibrated range, for taking a person's temperature.

clinician ▶ **noun** a doctor having direct contact with and responsibility for patients, rather than one involved with theoretical or laboratory studies.

clink[1] ▶ **noun** a sharp ringing sound, such as that made when metal or glass are struck: *a clink of keys* | *the clink of ice in tall glasses.*
▶ **verb** [no obj.] make such a sound: *his ring clinked against the crystal* | [as noun **clinking**] *the clinking of glasses* | [as adj. **clinking**] *clinking chains.*
■ [with obj.] cause (something) to make such a sound: *I heard Suzie clink a piece of crockery.* ■ [with obj.] strike (a glass or glasses) with another to express friendly feelings towards one's companions before drinking: *she* ***clinked*** *her glass* ***on*** *mine.*
– ORIGIN Middle English (as a verb): probably from Middle Dutch *klinken*.

clink[2] ▶ **noun** [in sing.] informal prison: *he was put in the clink for six days* | *some bloke he'd met* ***in clink****.*
– ORIGIN early 16th cent. (originally denoting a prison in Southwark, London): of unknown origin.

clinker[1] ▶ **noun** [mass noun] the stony residue from burnt coal or from a furnace.
■ (also **clinker brick**) [count noun] a brick with a vitrified surface.
– ORIGIN mid 17th cent.: from obsolete Dutch *klinckaerd* (earlier form of *klinker*), from *klinken* 'to clink'.

clinker[2] ▶ **noun** informal **1** N. Amer. something that is unsatisfactory, of poor quality, or a failure: *marketing couldn't save such clinkers as these films.*
■ a wrong musical note.
2 Brit. dated something or someone excellent or outstanding: *she was a real clinker.*
– ORIGIN late 17th cent. (denoting a person or thing that clinks): from **CLINK**[1] + **-ER**[1]. Sense 2 dates from the mid 19th cent., sense 1 (with depreciatory reference) from the 1930s.

clinker-built ▶ **adjective** (of a boat) having external planks which overlap downwards and are secured with clinched nails. Compare with **CARVEL-BUILT**.
– ORIGIN mid 18th cent.: *clinker* from *clink* (northern English variant of **CLINCH**).

clinometer /klʌɪˈnɒmɪtə, klɪ-/ ▶ **noun** Surveying an instrument used for measuring the angle or elevation of slopes.
– ORIGIN early 19th cent.: from Greek *klinein* 'to slope' + **-METER**.

clinopyroxene /ˌklʌɪnə(ʊ)pʌɪˈrɒksiːn/ ▶ **noun** [mass

noun] a mineral of the pyroxene group crystallizing in the monoclinic system.
– ORIGIN early 20th cent.: from *clino-* in the sense 'monoclinic' + **PYROXENE**.

clint ▶ **noun** a block forming part of a natural limestone pavement, typically one of a number separated by fissures or grikes.
– ORIGIN Middle English: of Scandinavian origin; related to Danish *klint* 'cliff' and Swedish *klint* 'summit, cliff'.

Clinton, Bill (b.1946), American Democratic statesman, 42nd President of the US 1993–2001; full name *William Jefferson Clinton*. Re-elected in 1996, he was impeached in 1998 on charges of perjury and obstruction of justice, but was acquitted.

Clio /ˈklʌɪəʊ/ Greek & Roman Mythology the Muse of history.
– ORIGIN from Greek *kleiein* 'celebrate'.

cliometrics /ˌklʌɪə(ʊ)ˈmɛtrɪks/ ▶ **plural noun** [treated as sing.] a technique for the interpretation of economic history, based on the statistical analysis of large-scale numerical data from population censuses, parish registers, and similar sources.
– DERIVATIVES **cliometric** adjective, **cliometrician** noun.
– ORIGIN 1960s (originally US): from **CLIO**, on the pattern of words such as *econometrics*.

clip[1] ▶ **noun** a device, typically flexible or worked by a spring, for holding an object or objects together or in place.
■ a device such as this used to hold banknotes. ■ a piece of jewellery fastened by a clip. ■ a metal holder containing cartridges for an automatic firearm.
▶ **verb** (**clipped**, **clipping**) [with adverbial of place] fasten or be fastened with a clip or clips: [with obj.] *she clipped on a pair of diamond earrings* | [no obj.] *the panels simply clip on to the framework.*
– ORIGIN Old English *clyppan* (verb), of West Germanic origin. The noun use dates from the late 15th cent.

clip[2] ▶ **verb** (**clipped**, **clipping**) [with obj.] **1** cut short or trim (hair, wool, nails, or vegetation) with shears or scissors: *I was clipping the hedge.*
■ trim or remove the hair or wool of (an animal). ■ (**clip something off**) cut off a thing or part of a thing with shears or scissors: *Philip clipped off another piece of wire* | figurative *she clipped nearly two seconds off the old record.* ■ cut (a section) from a newspaper or periodical: *a photograph clipped from a magazine.* ■ pare the edge of (a coin), especially illicitly: *they clipped the edges of gold coins and melted the clippings down.* ■ Brit. remove a small piece of (a bus or train ticket) to show that it has been used. ■ speak (words) in a quick, precise, staccato manner: *'Yes?' The word was clipped short* | [as adj. **clipped**] *cold clipped tones.* ■ Computing process (an image) so as to remove the parts outside a certain area. ■ Electronics truncate the amplitude of (a signal) above or below predetermined levels.
2 strike smartly or with a glancing blow: *the car clipped the kerb* | *he'll clip your ear.*
■ [with obj. and adverbial of direction] strike or kick (something, especially a ball) smartly in a specified direction: *he clipped the ball into the net.*
3 informal, chiefly N. Amer. swindle or rob: *in all the years he ran the place, he was clipped only three times.*
4 [no obj., with adverbial of direction] informal, chiefly US move quickly in a specified direction: *we clip down the track.*
▶ **noun 1** an act of clipping or trimming something: *I gave him a full clip.*
■ a short sequence taken from a film or broadcast: *clips from earlier shows.* ■ (also **wool clip**) the quantity of wool clipped from a sheep or flock.
2 informal a smart or glancing blow: *I'd give him **a clip round the ear**.*
3 [in sing.] informal a specified speed or rate of movement, especially when rapid: *we crossed the dance floor at an amazingly fast clip.*
– PHRASES **at a clip** US informal at a time; all at once: *I spent several days with him, eight hours at a clip.* **clip the wings of** trim the feathers of (a bird) so as to disable it from flight. ■ prevent (someone) from acting freely; check the aspirations of: *he finally clipped the wings of his high-flying chief of staff.*
– ORIGIN Middle English: from Old Norse *klippa*, probably imitative.

clip art ▶ **noun** [mass noun] Computing pre-drawn pictures and symbols that computer users can add to their documents, often provided with word-processing software and drawing packages.

clipboard ▶ **noun** a small board with a spring clip at the top, used for holding papers and providing support for writing.
■ Computing a temporary storage area where text or other data cut or copied from a file is kept until it is pasted into another file.

clip-clop ▶ **noun** [in sing.] the sound of a horse's hoofs beating on a hard surface.
▶ **verb** [no obj., with adverbial of direction] move with such a sound: *the horses clip-clopped slowly along the street.*
– ORIGIN late 19th cent.: imitative.

clip joint ▶ **noun** informal a nightclub or bar that charges exorbitant prices.

clip-on ▶ **adjective** attached by a clip so as to be easy to fasten or remove: *a clip-on bow tie.*
▶ **noun** (usu. **clip-ons**) things, especially sunglasses or earrings, that are attached by clips.

clipper ▶ **noun 1** (usu. **clippers**) an instrument for cutting or trimming small pieces off things.
2 Electronics another term for **LIMITER**.
3 (also **clipper ship**) a fast sailing ship, especially one of 19th-century design with concave bows and raked masts.

clippie ▶ **noun** (pl. **-ies**) Brit. informal a bus conductress.

clipping ▶ **noun** (often **clippings**) a small piece trimmed from something: *hedge clippings and grass cuttings.*
■ an article cut from a newspaper or magazine.

clique /kliːk/ ▶ **noun** a small group of people, with shared interests or other features in common, who spend time together and do not readily allow others to join them.
– DERIVATIVES **cliquish** adjective, **cliquishness** noun.
– ORIGIN early 18th cent.: from French, from Old French *cliquer* 'make a noise'; the modern sense is related to **CLAQUE**.

cliquey ▶ **adjective** (**cliquier**, **cliquiest**) (of a group or place) tending to form or hold exclusive groups and so not welcoming to outsiders: *a cliquey school.*
■ (of music or art) appealing only to a small group or minority: *the band sound a bit too elite and cliquey.*

CLit ▶ **abbreviation for** (in the UK) Companion of Literature.

clit ▶ **noun** vulgar slang short for **CLITORIS**.

clitic /ˈklɪtɪk/ ▶ **noun** Grammar an unstressed word that normally occurs only in combination with another word, for example *'m* in *I'm*.
– DERIVATIVES **cliticization** /ˌklɪtɪkʌɪˈzeɪʃ(ə)n/ noun.
– ORIGIN 1940s: from (*en*)*clitic* and (*pro*)*clitic*.

clitoridectomy /ˌklɪt(ə)rɪˈdɛktəmi/ ▶ **noun** (pl. **-ies**) [mass noun] excision of the clitoris; female circumcision.

clitoris /ˈklɪt(ə)rɪs/ ▶ **noun** a small sensitive and erectile part of the female genitals at the anterior end of the vulva.
– DERIVATIVES **clitoral** adjective.
– ORIGIN early 17th cent.: modern Latin, from Greek *kleitoris*.

clitter ▶ **verb** [no obj.] make a thin vibratory rattling sound: *a coded message clittered over the radio speakers.*
– ORIGIN early 16th cent.: imitative.

Clive, Robert, 1st Baron Clive of Plassey (1725–74), British general and colonial administrator; known as **Clive of India**. In 1757 he recaptured Calcutta, following the Black Hole incident, and gained control of Bengal. He served as governor of Bengal 1765–7, but was implicated in the East India company's corruption scandals and committed suicide.

clivia /ˈklʌɪvɪə/ ▶ **noun** a southern African plant of the lily family, with dark green strap-like leaves and trumpet-shaped orange, red, or yellow flowers. Also called **KAFFIR LILY**.
● Genus *Clivia*, family Liliaceae (or Amaryllidaceae).
– ORIGIN modern Latin, from *Clive*, the maiden name of Charlotte, Duchess of Northumberland (1787–1866).

Cllr ▶ **abbreviation for** (in the UK) Councillor.

cloaca /kləʊˈeɪkə/ ▶ **noun** (pl. **cloacae** /-siː, -kiː/) Zoology a common cavity at the end of the digestive tract for the release of both excretory and genital products in vertebrates (except most mammals) and certain invertebrates.
■ archaic a sewer.
– DERIVATIVES **cloacal** adjective.
– ORIGIN late 16th cent. (in the sense 'sewer'): from Latin, related to *cluere* 'cleanse'. The current sense dates from the mid 19th cent.

cloak ▶ **noun 1** an outdoor overgarment, typically sleeveless, that hangs loosely from the shoulders.
■ figurative something serving to hide or disguise something: *lifting **the cloak of secrecy** on the arms trade.*
2 (**cloaks**) Brit. a cloakroom.
▶ **verb** [with obj.] dress in a cloak: *she was an introverted soul who cloaked herself in black* | *they sat cloaked and hooded.*
■ figurative hide, cover, or disguise (something): *she cloaked her embarrassment by rushing into speech.*
– ORIGIN Middle English: from Old French *cloke*, dialect variant of *cloche* 'bell, cloak' (from its bell shape), from medieval Latin *clocca* 'bell'. Compare with **CLOCK**[1].

cloak-and-dagger ▶ **adjective** involving or characteristic of mystery, intrigue, or espionage: *a cloak-and-dagger operation.*

cloakroom ▶ **noun 1** a room in a public building where outdoor clothes or luggage may be left.
2 Brit. a room in the living area of a home that contains a toilet or a room in a public place that contains a number of toilets.

clobber[1] ▶ **noun** [mass noun] Brit. informal clothing, personal belongings, or equipment, especially in inconveniently large quantities: *I found all his clobber in the locker* | *looking cool in casual clobber.*
– ORIGIN late 19th cent.: of unknown origin.

clobber[2] ▶ **verb** [with obj.] informal hit (someone) hard: *if he does that I'll clobber him!*
■ treat or deal with harshly: *the recession clobbered other parts of the business.* ■ defeat heavily: [with obj. and complement] *the Braves clobbered the Cubs 23–10.*
– ORIGIN Second World War (apparently air force slang): of unknown origin.

clobber[3] ▶ **verb** [with obj.] add enamelled decoration to (porcelain).
– ORIGIN late 19th cent.: of unknown origin.

clochard /ˈklɒʃɑː, French klɔʃaʀ/ ▶ **noun** (pl. pronounced same) (in France) a beggar; a vagrant.
– ORIGIN French, from *clocher* 'to limp'.

cloche /klɒʃ, kləʊʃ/ ▶ **noun** a small translucent cover for protecting or forcing outdoor plants.
■ (also **cloche hat**) a woman's close-fitting bell-shaped hat.
– ORIGIN late 19th cent.: from French, literally 'bell' (see **CLOAK**).

clock[1] ▶ **noun 1** a mechanical or electrical device for measuring time, indicating hours, minutes, and sometimes seconds, typically by hands on a round dial or by displayed figures.
■ (**the clock**) time taken as a factor in an activity, especially in competitive sports: *this stage is played **against the clock**.* ■ informal a measuring device resembling a clock for recording things other than time, such as a speedometer, taximeter, or milometer: *a car with over 82,000 miles **on the clock**.*
2 Brit. a downy spherical seed head, especially that of a dandelion.
3 Brit. informal a person's face.
▶ **verb** [with obj.] informal **1** attain or register (a specified time, distance, or speed): *Thomas has **clocked up** forty years service* | [no obj.] *this is a generous CD, **clocking in at** more than 60 minutes.*
■ achieve (a victory): *he **clocked up** his first win of the year.* ■ record as attaining a specified time or rate: *the tower operators clocked a gust at 185 mph.*
2 Brit. informal notice or watch: *I noticed him clocking her in the mirror.*
3 informal, chiefly Brit. hit (someone), especially on the head: *someone clocked him for no good reason.*
4 Brit. informal wind back the milometer of (a car) illegally in order to make the vehicle appear to have travelled fewer miles than it really has.
– PHRASES **round** (or **around**) **the clock** all day and all night: *I've got a team working around the clock.* **turn** (or **put**) **back the clock** return to the past or to a previous way of doing things. **watch the clock** another way of saying **CLOCK-WATCH**.
– ORIGIN late Middle English: from Middle Low German and Middle Dutch *klocke*, based on medieval Latin *clocca* 'bell'.
▶ **clock in** (or Brit. **on**) register one's arrival at work, especially by means of an automatic recording clock: *staff should clock in on arrival.*
clock out (or Brit. **off**) register one's departure from work in a similar way: *she clocks off to go home.*

clock[2] ▶ **noun** dated an ornamental pattern woven or embroidered on the side of a stocking or sock near the ankle.
– ORIGIN mid 16th cent.: of unknown origin.

clocker ▶ **noun 1** Brit. informal a person who illegally winds back the milometer of a car.
2 US informal a drug dealer, especially one who sells cocaine or crack.

clock golf ▶ **noun** [mass noun] a lawn game in which the players putt to a hole in the centre of a circle from successive points on its circumference.

clock radio ▶ **noun** a combined bedside radio and alarm clock, which can be set so that the radio will come on at the desired time.

clock speed ▶ **noun** the operating speed of a computer or its microprocessor, defined as the rate at which it performs internal operations and expressed in cycles per second (megahertz).

clock tower ▶ **noun** a tower, typically forming part of a church or civic building, with a large clock at the top.

clock-watch ▶ **verb** [no obj.] (of an employee) be overly strict or zealous about not working more than one's allotted hours: [as noun **clock-watching**] *you'll not find any mention of clock-watching in my references.*
– DERIVATIVES **clock-watcher** noun.

clockwise ▶ **adverb** & **adjective** in a curve corresponding in direction to the movement of the hands of a clock: [as adv.] *turn the knob clockwise* | [as adj.] *a clockwise direction.*

clockwork ▶ **noun** [mass noun] a mechanism with a spring and toothed gearwheels, used to drive a mechanical clock, toy, or other device.
▶ **adjective** [attrib.] driven by clockwork: *a clockwork motor* | *a clockwork train.*
■ very smooth and regular: *the clockwork precision of the galaxy.* ■ repetitive and predictable: *it was a clockwork existence for the children.*
– PHRASES **as regular as clockwork** very regularly; repeatedly and predictably. **like clockwork** very smoothly and easily: *the event ran like clockwork.* ■ with mechanical regularity: *these hens lay like clockwork.*

clod ▶ **noun 1** a lump of earth or clay.
2 informal a stupid person (often used as a general term of abuse).
3 [mass noun] Brit. a coarse cut of meat from the lower neck of an ox.
– ORIGIN late Middle English: variant of **CLOT**.

cloddish ▶ **adjective** foolish, awkward, or clumsy.
– DERIVATIVES **cloddishly** adverb, **cloddishness** noun.

clodhopper ▶ **noun** informal **1** a large, heavy shoe.
2 a foolish, awkward, or clumsy person.

clodhopping ▶ **adjective** informal foolish, awkward, or clumsy.

clodpole ▶ **noun** archaic, informal a foolish, awkward, or clumsy person.

clog ▶ **noun 1** a shoe with a thick wooden sole.
2 an encumbrance or impediment: *they found the tax to be an unacceptable* ***clog on** the market.*
▶ **verb** (**clogged**, **clogging**) [with obj.] fill or block with an accumulation of thick, wet matter: *the gutters were clogged up with leaves* | [as adj. **clogged**] *clogged drains.*
■ [no obj.] become blocked in this way: *too much fatty food makes your arteries clog up.* ■ fill up or crowd (something) so as to obstruct passage: *tourists' cars clog the roads into Cornwall.*
– ORIGIN Middle English (in the sense 'block of wood to impede an animal's movement'): of unknown origin.

clog dance ▶ **noun** a dance performed in clogs with rhythmic beating of the feet, especially as a traditional dance in Ireland, Scotland, and the North of England.
■ a North American country tap dance of similar style.
– DERIVATIVES **clog dancer** noun, **clog dancing** noun.

clogger ▶ **noun 1** a person who makes clogs.
2 Brit. informal a footballer who habitually fouls when tackling someone.

clogging ▶ **noun** [mass noun] N. Amer. clog dancing.

cloggy ▶ **adjective** (**cloggier**, **cloggiest**) thick and sticky: *cloggy mud.*

cloisonné /'klwɑːzɒneɪ, -'zɒneɪ/ (also **cloisonné enamel**) ▶ **noun** [mass noun] enamel work in which the different colours are separated by strips of flattened wire placed edgeways on a metal backing.
– ORIGIN mid 19th cent.: French, literally 'partitioned', past participle of *cloisonner*, from *cloison* 'a partition or division'.

cloister /'klɔɪstə/ ▶ **noun** a covered walk in a convent, monastery, college, or cathedral, typically with a wall on one side and a colonnade open to a quadrangle on the other.
■ (**the cloister**) monastic life: *he was inclined more to the cloister than the sword.* ■ a convent or monastery.
▶ **verb** [with obj.] seclude or shut up in a convent or monastery: *the monastery was where the Brothers would cloister themselves to meditate.*
– DERIVATIVES **cloistral** adjective.
– ORIGIN Middle English (in the sense 'place of religious seclusion'): from Old French *cloistre*, from Latin *claustrum*, *clostrum* 'lock, enclosed place', from *claudere*, 'to close'.

cloistered ▶ **adjective 1** kept away from the outside world; sheltered: *a cloistered upbringing.*
2 having or enclosed by a cloister, as in a monastery: *a cloistered walkway bordered the courtyard.*

clomiphene /'kləʊmɪfiːn/ ▶ **noun** [mass noun] Medicine a synthetic non-steroidal drug used to treat infertility in women by stimulating ovulation.

clomp ▶ **verb** [no obj., with adverbial of direction] walk with a heavy tread: *she clomped down the steps.*
▶ **noun** [in sing.] the sound of a heavy tread: *the clomp of booted feet.*
– ORIGIN early 19th cent.: imitative; compare with **CLUMP**.

clompy ▶ **adjective** variant spelling of **CLUMPY** (in sense 1).

clone ▶ **noun** Biology a group of organisms or cells produced asexually from one ancestor or stock, to which they are genetically identical.
■ an individual organism or cell so produced. ■ a person or thing regarded as identical with another: *guitarists who are labelled Hendrix clones.* ■ a microcomputer designed to simulate exactly the operation of another, typically more expensive, model: *an IBM PC clone.* ■ informal (within gay culture) a homosexual man who adopts an exaggeratedly macho appearance and style of dress.
▶ **verb** [with obj.] propagate (an organism or cell) as a clone: *of the hundreds of new plants cloned the best ones are selected.*
■ make an identical copy of. ■ Biochemistry replicate (a fragment of DNA placed in an organism) so that there is sufficient to analyse or use in protein production. ■ illegally copy the security codes from (a mobile phone) to one or more others as a way of obtaining free calls.
– DERIVATIVES **clonal** adjective.
– ORIGIN early 20th cent.: from Greek *klōn* 'twig'.

clonk ▶ **noun** [in sing.] an abrupt, heavy sound of impact.
▶ **verb 1** [no obj.] move with or make such a sound: *the horses clonked and snorted softly.*
2 [with obj.] informal hit: *I'll clonk you on the head.*
– DERIVATIVES **clonky** adjective.
– ORIGIN mid 19th cent.: imitative.

Clonmel /klɒn'mɛl/ the county town of Tipperary, in the Republic of Ireland; pop. 14,500 (1991).

clonus /'kləʊnəs/ ▶ **noun** [mass noun] Medicine muscular spasm involving repeated, often rhythmic, contractions.
– DERIVATIVES **clonic** adjective.
– ORIGIN early 19th cent.: from Greek *klonos* 'turmoil'.

clop ▶ **noun** [in sing.] a sound or series of sounds made by a horse's hooves on a hard surface.
▶ **verb** (**clopped**, **clopping**) [no obj., with adverbial of direction] (of a horse) move with such a sound: *the animal clopped on at a steady pace.*
– ORIGIN mid 19th cent.: imitative.

cloqué /'kləʊkeɪ/ ▶ **noun** [mass noun] a fabric with an irregularly raised or embossed surface.
– ORIGIN French, literally 'blistered'. It was first recorded (1920s) in the Anglicized form *cloky*; use of the French form dates from the 1950s.

close[1] /kləʊs/ ▶ **adjective 1** only a short distance away or apart in space or time: *the hotel is* ***close to** the sea* | *her birthday and her wedding date were close together* | *why don't we go straight to the shops, as we're so close?* | *the months of living* ***in close proximity to** her were taking their toll.*
■ with very little or no space in between; dense: *cloth with a closer weave* | *this work occupies over 1,300 pages of close print.* ■ [predic.] (**close to**) very near to (being or doing something): *on a good day the climate in LA is close to perfection* | *she was close to tears.* ■ (of a competitive situation) won or likely to be won by only a small amount or distance: *the race will be a close contest.* ■ [attrib.] (of a final position in a competition) very near to the competitor immediately in front: *she finished a close second.* ■ Phonetics another term for **HIGH** (sense 7).
2 [attrib.] denoting a family member who is part of a person's immediate family, typically a parent or sibling: *the family history of cancer in close relatives.*
■ (of a person or relationship) on very affectionate or intimate terms: *they had always been very close, with no secrets at all.* ■ (of a connection or resemblance) strong: *the college has close links with many other institutions.*
3 (of observation, examination, etc.) done in a careful and thorough way: *we need to* ***keep a close eye on** this project* | ***pay close attention to** what your body is telling you about yourself.*
■ carefully guarded: *his whereabouts are a close secret.* ■ not willing to give away money or information; secretive: *you're very close about your work, aren't you?*
4 uncomfortably humid or airless: *a close, hazy day* | *it was very close in the dressing room.*
▶ **adverb** in a position so as to be very near to someone or something; with very little space between: *they stood close to the door* | *he was holding her close.*
▶ **noun** an enclosed space, in particular:
■ [often in names] Brit. a residential street without through access: *she lives at 12 Goodwood Close.* ■ Brit. the precinct surrounding a cathedral. ■ Brit. a playing field at certain traditional English public schools. ■ Scottish an entry from the street to a common stairway or to a court at the back of a building.
– PHRASES **close by** very near; nearby: *her father lives quite close by.* **close on** (or **close to**) (of an amount) almost; very nearly: *he spent close to 30 years in jail.* **close to the bone** see **BONE**. **close to one's heart** see **HEART**. **close to home** see **HOME**. **close up** very near: *close up she was no less pretty.* **come close** almost achieve or do: *he* ***came close to** calling the Prime Minister a liar.* **run someone close** almost match the standards or level of achievement of someone else: *the Germans ran Argentina close in the 1986 World Cup final.* **too close for comfort** dangerously or uncomfortably near: figurative *an issue being discussed with a sufferer may be too close for comfort to the counsellor's personal experience.*
– DERIVATIVES **closely** adverb, **closeness** noun, **closish** adjective.
– ORIGIN Middle English: from Old French *clos* (as noun and adjective), from Latin *clausum* 'enclosure' and *clausus* 'closed', past participle of *claudere*.

close[2] /kləʊz/ ▶ **verb 1** move or cause to move so as to cover an opening: [no obj.] *she jumped on to the train just as the doors were closing* | [with obj.] *they had to close the window because of the insects.*
■ [with obj.] block up (a hole or opening): *glass doors* ***close off** the living room from the hall* | figurative *Stephen closed his ears to the sound.* ■ [with obj.] bring two parts of (something) together so as to block its opening or bring it into a folded state: *Loretta closed her mouth* | *Rex closed the book.* ■ [no obj.] gradually get nearer to someone or something: *he tried to walk faster, but each time the man* ***closed up on** him again.* ■ [no obj.] (**close around/over**) come into contact with (something) so as to encircle and hold it: *my fist closed around the weapon.* ■ [with obj.] make (an electric circuit) continuous: *this will cause a relay to operate and close the circuit.*
2 bring or come to an end: [with obj.] *the members were thanked for attending and the meeting was closed* | [no obj.] *the concert* ***closed with** 'Silent Night'* | [as adj. **closing**] *the closing stages of the election campaign.*
■ [no obj.] (of a business, organization, or institution) cease to be in operation or accessible to the public, either permanently or at the end of a working day or other period of time: *the factory is to close with the loss of 150 jobs* | [with obj.] *a hoax call which closed the city's stations for 4 hours.* ■ [no obj.] finish speaking or writing: *we* ***close with** a point about truth* | [as adj. **closing**] *Nellie's closing words.* ■ [with obj.] bring (a business transaction) to a satisfactory conclusion: *he closed a deal with a metal dealer and walked away with millions of francs.* ■ [with obj.] remove all the funds from (a bank or building society account) and cease to use it. ■ [with obj.] Computing make (a data file) inaccessible after use, so that it is securely stored until required again.
▶ **noun** [in sing.] **1** the end of an event or of a period of time or activity: *the afternoon* ***drew to a close.***
■ (**the close**) the end of a day's trading on a stock market: *by the close the Dow Jones average was down 13.52 points at 2,759.84.* ■ (**the close**) the end of a day's play

C

in a cricket match. ■ Music the conclusion of a phrase; a cadence.
2 the shutting of something, especially a door: *the door jerked to a close behind them.*
– PHRASES **close the door on** (or **to**) see **DOOR**. **close one's eyes to** see **EYE**. **close one's mind to** see **MIND**. **close ranks** see **RANK**[1].
– DERIVATIVES **closable** adjective, **closer** noun.
– ORIGIN Middle English: from Old French *clos-*, stem of *clore*, from Latin *claudere* 'to shut'.
▶**close something down** (or **close down**) cause to cease or cease business or operation, especially permanently: *the government promised to close down the nuclear plants within twenty years.* ■ (**close down**) Brit. (of a broadcasting station) end transmission until the next day.
close in come nearer to someone being pursued: *the police were* ***closing in on*** *them.* ■ gradually surround, especially with the effect of hindering movement or vision: *the weather has now closed in so an attempt on the summit is unlikely.* ■ (of days) get successively shorter with the approach of the winter solstice: *November was closing in.*
close something out N. Amer. bring something to an end: *Steve tried to close out the conversation.*
close up (of a person's face) become blank and emotionless or hostile: *he didn't like her laughter and his face closed up angrily.*
close something up (or **close up**) **1** cause to cease or cease operation or being used: *the solicitor advised me to close the house up for the time being.* **2** (**close up**) (of an opening) grow smaller or become blocked by something: *she felt her throat close up.*
close with come near, especially so as to engage with (an enemy force).

close call ▶ noun another term for **CLOSE SHAVE** (in sense 2).

close-coupled ▶ adjective chiefly Brit. (of two parts of a structure or thing) attached or fixed close together.

close-cropped ▶ adjective (typically of hair or grass) cut very short.

closed ▶ adjective not open: *rooms with closed doors lined the hallway | he sat with his eyes closed.*
■ (of a business) having ceased trading, especially for a short period: *he put the 'Closed' sign up on the door.* ■ (of a society or system) not communicating with or influenced by others. ■ limited to certain people; not open or available to all: *the UN Security Council met* ***in closed session.*** ■ unwilling to accept new ideas: *you're facing the situation with a closed mind.* ■ Mathematics (of a set) having the property that the result of a specified operation on any element of the set is itself a member of the set. ■ Mathematics (of a set) containing all its limit points. ■ Geometry (of a curve or figure) formed from a single unbroken line.
– PHRASES **behind closed doors** taking place secretly or without public knowledge. **closed book** a subject or person about which one knows nothing: *accounting has always been* ***a closed book*** *to me.*

closed-circuit television (abbrev.: **CCTV**) ▶ noun [mass noun] a television system in which the video signals are transmitted from one or more cameras by cable to a restricted set of monitors.

closed-end ▶ adjective having a predetermined and fixed extent: *a closed-end contract.*
■ N. Amer. denoting an investment trust or company that issues a fixed number of shares.

closed-in ▶ adjective oppressively enclosed or lacking in space: *her distress at being in closed-in places.*

close-down ▶ noun [in sing.] a cessation of work or business, especially on a permanent basis.
■ Brit. the end of broadcasting on television or radio until the next day.

closed season ▶ noun chiefly N. Amer. another term for **CLOSE SEASON**.

closed shop ▶ noun a place of work where all employees must belong to an agreed trade union. Compare with **UNION SHOP**.
■ [in sing.] a system whereby such an arrangement applies: *the outlawing of the closed shop.*

closed syllable ▶ noun a syllable ending in a consonant.

closed universe ▶ noun Astronomy the condition in which there is sufficient matter in the universe to halt the expansion driven by the big bang and cause eventual re-collapse. The amount of visible matter is only a tenth of that required for closure, but there may be large quantities of dark matter.

close-fisted ▶ adjective unwilling to spend money; mean.

close-fitting ▶ adjective (of a garment) fitting tightly and showing the contours of the body.

close-grained ▶ adjective (of wood, stone, or other material) having tightly packed fibres, crystals, or other structural elements.

close harmony ▶ noun [mass noun] Music harmony in which the notes of the chord are close together, typically in vocal music.

close-hauled ▶ adjective & adverb Sailing (of a ship) with the sails hauled aft to sail close to the wind.

close-in ▶ adjective only a short distance away: *a close-in shot.*
■ N. Amer. near to the centre of a town or city: *close-in parking.*

close-knit ▶ adjective (of a group of people) united or bound together by strong relationships and common interests: *a close-knit community.*

close-mouthed ▶ adjective reticent; discreet: *the candidates have been close-mouthed about their fund-raising goals.*

close quarters ▶ plural noun a situation of being very or uncomfortably close to someone or something: *living in close quarters with people | engaging the enemy* ***at close quarters.***

close range ▶ noun a short distance between someone or something and a target: *Wilkinson scored* ***from close range*** *| they were shot at close range.*

close-ratio ▶ adjective (of a vehicle's gearbox) having gear ratios that are set at values which are not very different from each other.

close reach Sailing ▶ noun a point of sailing in which the wind blows from slightly in front of the beam: *we sailed* ***on a close reach*** *directly for Sharp's Island.*
▶ verb (**close-reach**) [no obj.] sail with the wind in this position.

close-run ▶ adjective (of a contest, election, or objective) won or lost by a very small margin: *the motion failed to obtain an absolute majority of 249 but it was* ***a close-run thing.***

close season ▶ noun (also chiefly N. Amer. **closed season**) a period between specified dates when fishing or the killing of particular game is officially forbidden.
■ Brit. a part of the year when a particular sport is not played.

close-set ▶ adjective (of two or more things) placed or occurring with little space in between: *her eyes were too close-set for beauty.*

close shave ▶ noun **1** a shave in which the hair is cut very short.
2 informal a narrow escape from danger or disaster.

close-stool ▶ noun a covered chamber pot enclosed in a wooden stool, used in former times.

closet ▶ noun **1** chiefly N. Amer. a cupboard or wardrobe, especially one tall enough to walk into.
■ a small room, especially one used for storing things.
2 archaic a toilet.
3 (**the closet**) used to refer to a state of secrecy or concealment, especially about one's homosexuality: *lesbians who had* ***come out of the closet.***
▶ adjective [attrib.] secret; covert: *a closet socialist.*
▶ verb (**closeted**, **closeting**) [with obj.] (often **be closeted**) shut (someone) away, especially in private conference or study: *he was closeted with the king | he returned home and closeted himself in his room.*
– ORIGIN late Middle English (denoting a private or small room): from Old French, diminutive of *clos* 'closed' (see **CLOSE**[1]).

closeted ▶ adjective keeping something secret, especially the fact of being homosexual: *among those who voted against it were some closeted gays.*

closet play (also **closet drama**) ▶ noun a play to be read rather than acted.

close-up ▶ noun a photograph, film, or video taken at close range and showing the subject on a large scale: *a close-up of her face | they see themselves* ***in close-up*** *|* [as modifier] *a close-up view.*
■ an intimate and detailed description or study: [as modifier] *the book's close-up account of the violence.*

closing date ▶ noun the last date by which something must be submitted for consideration, especially a job application.

closing order ▶ noun English Law an order by a local authority prohibiting the use of premises for specified purposes.

closing price ▶ noun the price of a security at the end of the day's business in a financial market.

closing time ▶ noun the regular time at which a public house, shop, or other place closes to the public each day.

clostridium /klɒˈstrɪdɪəm/ ▶ noun (pl. **clostridia** /-dɪə/) Biology an anaerobic bacterium of a large genus that includes many pathogenic species, e.g. those causing tetanus, gas gangrene, botulism, and other forms of food poisoning.
● Genus *Clostridium*: typically rod-shaped and Gram-positive.
– DERIVATIVES **clostridial** adjective.
– ORIGIN modern Latin, based on Greek *klōstēr* 'spindle'.

closure ▶ noun **1** an act or process of closing something, especially an institution, thoroughfare, or frontier, or of being closed: *road closures |* [mass noun] *hospitals that face closure.*
■ a thing that closes or seals something, such as a cap or tie.
2 [mass noun] (in a legislative assembly) a procedure for ending a debate and taking a vote: [as modifier] *a closure motion.*
▶ verb [with obj.] apply the closure to (a debate or speaker) in a legislative assembly.
– ORIGIN late Middle English: from Old French, from late Latin *clausura*, from *claus-* 'closed', from the verb *claudere*.

clot ▶ noun **1** a thick mass of coagulated liquid, especially blood, or of material stuck together: *a blood clot | a flat, wet* ***clot of*** *dead leaves.*
2 Brit. informal a foolish or clumsy person: *'Watch where you're going, you clot!'*
▶ verb (**clotted**, **clotting**) form or cause to form into clots: [no obj.] *drugs that help blood to clot |* [with obj.] *a blood protein known as factor VIII clots blood.*
■ [with obj.] cover (something) with sticky matter: *its nostrils were clotted with blood.*
– ORIGIN Old English *clott*, *clot*, of Germanic origin; related to German *Klotz*.

clotbur /ˈklɒtbəː/ ▶ noun a herbaceous plant of the daisy family, with burred fruits. It originated in tropical America but is now cosmopolitan. See also **COCKLEBUR**.
● Genus *Xanthium*, family Compositae: two or three species, in particular **spiny clotbur** (*X. spinosum*).
■ chiefly N. Amer. a burdock.
– ORIGIN mid 16th cent.: from dialect *clote* 'burdock' + **BUR**.

cloth ▶ noun (pl. **cloths**) **1** [mass noun] woven or felted fabric made from wool, cotton, or a similar fibre: *a broad piece of pleated cloth |* [as modifier] *a cloth bag.*
■ [count noun] a piece of cloth for a particular purpose, such as a dishcloth or a tablecloth: *wipe clean with a damp cloth.* ■ [count noun] a variety of cloth.
2 (**the cloth**) the clergy; the clerical profession: *has he given up all ideas of the cloth?*
– ORIGIN Old English *clāth*, related to Dutch *kleed* and German *Kleid*, of unknown ultimate origin.

cloth cap Brit. ▶ noun a man's flat woollen cap with a peak.
▶ adjective [attrib.] relating to or associated with the working class: *Labour's traditional cloth-cap image.*

clothe ▶ verb (past and past participle **clothed** or archaic or poetic/literary **clad**) [with obj.] (often **be clothed in**) put clothes on (oneself or someone); dress: *Francesca was clothed all in white | she took off her shoes and lay down* ***fully clothed*** *|* [as adj., with submodifier] (**clothed**) *a partially clothed body.*
■ provide (someone) with clothes: *they already had eight children to feed and clothe.* ■ figurative cover (something) as if with clothes: *luxuriant tropical forests clothed the islands.* ■ figurative endow (someone) with a particular quality: *he is clothed with the personality and character of Jesus.*
– ORIGIN Old English (only recorded in the past participle *geclāded*), from *clāth* (see **CLOTH**).

cloth-eared ▶ adjective Brit. informal, derogatory unable to hear or understand clearly.

clothes ▶ plural noun **1** items worn to cover the body: *he stripped off his clothes | baby clothes |* [as modifier] *a clothes shop.*
2 bedclothes.
– ORIGIN Old English *clāthas*, plural of *clāth* (see **CLOTH**).

clothes hoist ▶ noun Austral. a rotary clothes drier consisting of a square frame between the arms of which run lengths of clothes line, turning about a central pole and adjustable in height.

clothes horse ▶ noun a frame on which washed clothes are hung to air indoors.
■ informal, often derogatory a person, typically a woman, with a good enough figure to wear or model fashionable clothes.

clothes line ▶ noun a rope or wire on which washed clothes are hung to dry.
▶ verb (**clothesline**) [with obj.] N. Amer. (chiefly in football and other games) knock down (a runner) by placing one's outstretched arm in their path at neck level.

clothes moth ▶ noun a small drab moth whose larvae feed on a range of animal fibres and can be destructive to clothing and other domestic textiles.
● Family Tineidae: several species, in particular the **common clothes moth** (Tineola bisselliella).

clothes peg (also N. Amer. **clothespin**) ▶ noun Brit. a wooden or plastic clip for securing clothes to a clothes line.

cloth head ▶ noun informal a stupid person.

clothier /ˈkləʊðɪə/ ▶ noun a person or company that makes, sells, or deals in clothes or cloth.
– ORIGIN Middle English clother, from **CLOTH**. The change in the ending was due to association with **-IER**.

clothing ▶ noun [mass noun] clothes collectively: an item of clothing | [as modifier] the clothing trade.

Clotho /ˈkləʊθəʊ/ Greek Mythology one of the three Fates.
– ORIGIN Greek, literally 'she who spins'.

cloth of gold ▶ noun [mass noun] fabric made of gold threads interwoven with silk or wool.

clotted cream ▶ noun [mass noun] chiefly Brit. thick cream obtained by heating milk slowly and then allowing it to cool while the cream content rises to the top in coagulated lumps.

clotting factor ▶ noun Physiology any of a number of substances in blood plasma which are involved in the clotting process, such as factor VIII.

cloture /ˈkləʊtjʊə/ ▶ noun & verb US term for **CLOSURE** (in sense 2 of the noun and as a verb).
– ORIGIN late 19th cent.: from French clôture, from Old French closure (see **CLOSURE**).

clou /kluː/ ▶ noun the chief attraction, point of greatest interest, or central idea of a thing.
– ORIGIN French, literally 'nail'.

cloud ▶ noun **1** a visible mass of condensed watery vapour floating in the atmosphere, typically high above the general level of the ground: the sun had disappeared behind a cloud | [mass noun] the sky was almost free of cloud.
■ an indistinct or billowing mass, especially of smoke or dust: a cloud of dust. ■ a large number of insects or birds moving together: clouds of orange butterflies. ■ a vague patch of colour in or on a liquid or transparent surface.
2 figurative used to refer to a state or cause of gloom, suspicion, trouble, or worry: the only cloud on the immediate horizon is raising a mortgage | a black cloud hung over their lives.
■ a frowning or depressed look: a cloud passed over Jessica's face.
▶ verb **1** [no obj.] (of the sky) become overcast or gloomy: the blue skies clouded over abruptly.
■ [with obj.] (usu. **be clouded**) darken (the sky) with cloud: the western sky was still clouded. ■ make or become less clear or transparent: [with obj.] blood pumped out, clouding the water | [no obj.] her eyes clouded with tears.
2 figurative make or become darkened or overshadowed, in particular:
■ [no obj.] (of someone's face or eyes) show worry, sorrow, or anger: his expression clouded over. ■ [with obj.] (of such an emotion) show in (someone's face): suspicion clouded her face. ■ [with obj.] make (a matter or mental process) unclear or uncertain; confuse: don't allow your personal feelings to cloud your judgement. ■ [with obj.] spoil or mar (something): the general election was clouded by violence.
– PHRASES **every cloud has a silver lining** see **SILVER**. **in the clouds** out of touch with reality: this clergyman was in the clouds. **on cloud nine** (or **seven**) extremely happy. [ORIGIN: with reference to a ten-part classification of clouds in which 'nine' was next to the highest.] **under a cloud** under suspicion; discredited: he left under something of a cloud, accused of misappropriating funds. **with one's**

head in the clouds (of a person) out of touch with reality; daydreaming.
– DERIVATIVES **cloudless** adjective, **cloudlessly** adverb, **cloudlet** noun.
– ORIGIN Old English clūd 'mass of rock or earth'; probably related to **CLOT**. Sense 1 dates from Middle English.

cloud base ▶ noun [in sing.] the level or altitude of the lowest part of a general mass of clouds.

cloudberry ▶ noun (pl. **-ies**) a dwarf bramble with white flowers and edible orange fruit, which grows on the mountains and moorlands of northern Eurasia and northern North America.
● Rubus chamaemorus, family Rosaceae.
– ORIGIN late 16th cent.: apparently from the noun **CLOUD** in the obsolete sense 'hill' + **BERRY**.

cloudburst ▶ noun a sudden violent rainstorm.

cloud chamber ▶ noun Physics a device containing air or gas supersaturated with water vapour, used to detect charged particles, X-rays, and gamma rays by the condensation trails which they produce.

cloud cover ▶ noun [in sing.] a mass of cloud covering all or most of the sky.

cloud cuckoo land ▶ noun [mass noun] a state of unrealistic or absurdly over-optimistic fantasy: anyone who believes that the Bill will be effective is living in cloud cuckoo land.
– ORIGIN late 19th cent.: translation of Greek Nephelokokkugia, the name of the city built by the birds in Aristophanes' comedy Birds, from nephelē 'cloud' + kokkux 'cuckoo'.

clouded leopard ▶ noun a large spotted cat which hunts in trees at twilight, found in forests in SE Asia.
● Neofelis nebulosa, family Felidae.

clouded yellow ▶ noun a migratory Old World butterfly which has yellowish wings with black margins.
● Genus Colias, family Pieridae: several species, in particular C. croceus.

cloud hopping ▶ noun [mass noun] the flying of an aircraft from cloud to cloud, typically for concealment.

cloudscape ▶ noun a large cloud formation considered in terms of its visual effect.
– ORIGIN mid 19th cent.: from the noun **CLOUD**, on the pattern of words such as landscape.

cloud seeding ▶ noun [mass noun] the dropping of crystals into clouds to cause rain.

cloud street ▶ noun a line of cumulus clouds formed parallel to the wind direction.

cloudy ▶ adjective (**cloudier**, **cloudiest**) **1** (of the sky or weather) covered with or characterized by clouds; overcast: next morning was cloudy.
2 (of a liquid) not transparent or clear: the pond water is slightly cloudy.
■ (of a colour) opaque; having white as a constituent: cloudy reds and blues and greens. ■ (of someone's eyes) misted with tears: she stared at him, her eyes cloudy. ■ uncertain; unclear: the issue becomes more cloudy.
– DERIVATIVES **cloudily** adverb, **cloudiness** noun.

Clouet /ˈkluːeɪ, French klwɛ/ two French court portrait painters, **Jean** (c.1485–1541) and his son **François** (c.1516–72).

Clough /klʌf/, Arthur Hugh (1819–61), English poet. Notable poems: Amours de Voyage (1858).

clough /klʌf/ ▶ noun N. English a steep valley or ravine.
– ORIGIN Old English clōh (recorded in place names), of Germanic origin; related to German dialect Klinge.

clout ▶ noun **1** informal a heavy blow with the hand or a hard object: a clout round the ear.
2 [mass noun] informal influence or power, especially in politics or business: I knew he carried a lot of clout.
3 archaic a piece of cloth or clothing, especially one used as a patch.
4 Archery a target twelve times the usual size, used in long-distance shooting. It is placed flat on the ground with a flag marking its centre.
■ a shot that hits such a target.
5 short for **CLOUT NAIL**.
▶ verb [with obj.] **1** informal hit hard with the hand or a hard object: I clouted him round the head.
2 archaic mend with a patch.
– PHRASES **ne'er cast a clout till May be out** proverb a warning not to discard one's winter clothes until the end of May. [ORIGIN: clout in sense 3.]
– ORIGIN Old English clūt (in the sense 'a patch or

metal plate'); related to Dutch kluit 'lump, clod', also to **CLEAT** and **CLOT**. The shift of sense to 'heavy blow', which dates from late Middle English, is difficult to explain; possibly the change occurred first in the verb (from 'put a patch on' to 'hit hard').

clout nail ▶ noun a nail with a large flat head, typically galvanized for use outdoors in securing roofing felt.

clove¹ ▶ noun **1** the dried flower bud of a tropical tree, used as a pungent aromatic spice.
■ (**oil of cloves**) [mass noun] aromatic analgesic oil extracted from these buds and used medicinally, especially for the relief of dental pain.
2 the Indonesian tree from which these buds are obtained.
● Syzygium aromaticum (also called Eugenia caryophyllus), family Myrtaceae.
3 (also **clove pink** or **clove gillyflower**) a clove-scented pink which is the original type from which the carnation and other double pinks have been bred.
● Dianthus caryophyllus, family Caryophyllaceae.
– ORIGIN Middle English: from Old French clou de girofle, literally 'nail of gillyflower' (from its shape), **GILLYFLOWER** being originally the name of the spice and later applied to the similarly scented pink.

clove² ▶ noun any of the small bulbs making up a compound bulb of garlic, shallot, etc.
– ORIGIN Old English clufu, of Germanic origin, corresponding to the first element of German Knoblauch (altered from Old High German klovolouh), and the base of **CLEAVE**¹.

clove³ past of **CLEAVE**¹.

clove hitch ▶ noun a knot by which a rope is secured by passing it twice round a spar or another rope that it crosses at right angles in such a way that both ends pass under the loop of rope at the front.
– ORIGIN mid 18th cent.: clove, past tense of **CLEAVE**¹ (because the rope appears as separate parallel lines at the back of the knot).

cloven past participle of **CLEAVE**¹. ▶ adjective split or divided in two.

cloven hoof (also **cloven foot**) ▶ noun the divided hoof or foot of ruminants such as cattle, sheep, goats, antelopes, and deer.
■ a similar foot ascribed to a satyr, the god Pan, or to the Devil, sometimes used as a symbol or mark of the latter.
– DERIVATIVES **cloven-footed** adjective, **cloven-hoofed** adjective.

clove pink ▶ noun see **CLOVE**¹ (sense 3).

clover ▶ noun [mass noun] a herbaceous plant of the pea family, which has dense globular flower heads and leaves which are typically three-lobed. It is an important and widely grown fodder and rotational crop.
● Genus Trifolium, family Leguminosae: many species, in particular **red clover** (T. pratense) and **white** (or **Dutch**) **clover** (T. repens).
– PHRASES **in clover** in ease and luxury: if your sister married the old codger we could be in clover.
– ORIGIN Old English clāfre, of Germanic origin; related to Dutch klaver and German Klee.

cloverleaf ▶ noun chiefly N. Amer. a junction of roads intersecting at different levels with connecting sections forming the pattern of a four-leaved clover.

Clovis¹ /ˈkləʊvɪs/ (465–511), king of the Franks 481–511. He extended Merovingian rule to Gaul and Germany, making Paris his capital. After his conversion to Christianity he championed orthodoxy against the Arian Visigoths, finally defeating them in the battle of Poitiers (507).

Clovis² /ˈkləʊvɪs/ ▶ noun [usu. as modifier] Archaeology a Palaeo-Indian culture of Central and North America, dated to about 11,500–11,000 years ago and earlier. The culture is distinguished by heavy leaf-shaped stone spearheads (**Clovis points**), often found in conjunction with the bones of mammoths. Compare with **FOLSOM**.
– ORIGIN first found near Clovis in eastern New Mexico, US.

clown ▶ noun **1** a comic entertainer, especially one in a circus, wearing a traditional costume and exaggerated make-up.
■ a playful, extrovert person: with his willingness to play the clown he became a great favourite. ■ a foolish or

incompetent person: *we need a serious government, not a bunch of clowns.*
2 archaic an unsophisticated country person; a rustic.
▶**verb** [no obj.] behave in a comical way; act playfully: *Harvey **clowned around** pretending to be a dog.*
■[with obj.] perform (a part or action) in a comical and exaggerated way: *they clowned the singing of the words.*
– DERIVATIVES **clownish** adjective, **clownishly** adverb, **clownishness** noun.
– ORIGIN mid 16th cent. (in sense 2): perhaps of Low German origin.

clownfish ▶**noun** (pl. same or **-fishes**) a small tropical marine fish with bold vertical stripes or other bright coloration. It lives in close association with anemones and is protected from their stings by mucus. Also called **ANEMONE FISH**.
• Genera *Amphiprion* and *Premnas*, family Pomacentridae: several species, including *A. percula*.

cloy ▶**verb** [with obj.] [usu. as adj. **cloying**] disgust or sicken (someone) with an excess of sweetness, richness, or sentiment: *a romantic, rather cloying story | a curious bitter-sweetness that cloyed her senses* | [no obj.] *the first long sip gives a malty taste that never cloys.*
– DERIVATIVES **cloyingly** adverb.
– ORIGIN late Middle English: shortening of obsolete *accloy* 'stop up, choke', from Old French *encloyer* 'drive a nail into', from medieval Latin *inclavare*, from *clavus* 'a nail'.

clozapine /ˈkləʊzəpiːn/ ▶**noun** [mass noun] Medicine a sedative drug of the benzodiazepine group, used to treat schizophrenia.
– ORIGIN mid 20th cent.: from *c(h)lo(ro)-* + elements of **BENZODIAZEPINE**.

cloze test /kləʊz/ ▶**noun** a procedure in which a subject is asked to supply words that have been removed from a passage as a test of their ability to comprehend text.
– ORIGIN 1950s: *cloze* representing a spoken abbreviation of **CLOSURE**.

club[1] ▶**noun** [treated as sing. or pl.] an association or organization dedicated to a particular interest or activity: *I belong to a photographic club* | [as modifier] *the club secretary.*
■the premises of such an association. ■an organization or premises offering members social amenities, meals, and temporary residence: *dinner at his club.* ■a nightclub, especially one playing fashionable dance music. ■[treated as sing. or pl.] an organization constituted to play matches in a particular sport: *a football club* | [as modifier] *the club captain.* ■[usu. with modifier] a commercial organization offering subscribers special benefits: *a shopping club.* ■[usu. with adj. or noun modifier] a group of people, organizations, or nations having something in common: *the wild man of the movies refused to join the teetotal club.*
▶**verb** (**clubbed**, **clubbing**) [no obj.] **1** (**club together**) combine with others to do something, especially so as to collect a sum of money for a particular purpose: *friends and colleagues clubbed together to buy him a present.*
2 informal go out to nightclubs: *she enjoys **going clubbing** in Oxford.*
– PHRASES **in the club** (or **the pudding club**) Brit. informal pregnant. **join the club** [in imperative] informal, often humorous used as an observation that someone else is in a similar difficult or unwelcome situation to oneself: *if you're confused, join the club!*
– DERIVATIVES **clubber** noun (usu. in sense 2 of the verb).
– ORIGIN early 17th cent. (as a verb): formed obscurely from **CLUB**[2].

club[2] ▶**noun 1** a heavy stick with a thick end, especially one used as a weapon.
■short for **GOLF CLUB**.
2 (**clubs**) one of the four suits in a conventional pack of playing cards, denoted by a black trefoil.
■a card of such a suit.
▶**verb** (**clubbed**, **clubbing**) [with obj.] beat (a person or animal) with a club or similar implement: *the islanders clubbed whales to death.*
– ORIGIN Middle English: from Old Norse *clubba*, variant of *klumba*; related to **CLUMP**.

clubbable ▶**adjective** suitable for membership of a club because of one's sociability or popularity.
– DERIVATIVES **clubbability** noun.

clubby ▶**adjective** (**clubbier**, **clubbiest**) informal friendly and sociable with fellow members of a group or organization but not with outsiders.

club car ▶**noun** chiefly N. Amer. a railway carriage equipped with a lounge and other amenities.

club class ▶**noun** [mass noun] Brit. the intermediate class of seating on an aircraft, designed especially for business travellers.

club foot ▶**noun 1** a deformed foot which is twisted so that the sole cannot be placed flat on the ground. It is typically congenital or a result of polio. Also called **TALIPES**.
2 a woodland toadstool with a greyish-brown cap, primrose-yellow gills, and a stem with a swollen woolly base, found in both Eurasia and North America.
• *Clitocybe clavipes*, family Tricholomataceae, class Hymenomycetes.
– DERIVATIVES **club-footed** adjective.

clubhouse ▶**noun** a building used by a sports club, especially a golf club.

clubland ▶**noun** [mass noun] Brit. an area of a town or city with many nightclubs.
■the world of nightclubs and nightclubbers.

clubman ▶**noun** (pl. **-men**) a man who is a member of one or more clubs, especially a member of a gentleman's club.

clubmate ▶**noun** a fellow member of a sports club.

clubmoss ▶**noun** a low-growing green plant that resembles a large moss, having branching stems with undivided leaves. Relatives of the clubmosses were the first plants to colonize the land during the Silurian period.
• Class Lycopsida, division Pteridophyta: three living families, in particular Lycopodiaceae and Selaginellaceae (the **lesser clubmosses**).

clubroot ▶**noun** [mass noun] a fungal disease of cabbages, turnips, and related plants, in which the root becomes swollen and distorted by a single large gall or groups of smaller ones.
• The fungus is *Plasmodiophora brassicae*, subdivision Mastigomycotina.

clubrush ▶**noun** a tall rush-like water or marsh plant of the sedge family. Also called **BULRUSH**.
• *Scirpus* and related genera, family Cyperaceae, in particular the common *S.* (or *Schoenoplectus*) *lacustris*, which is widely used for weaving.

club sandwich ▶**noun** a sandwich of meat (usually chicken and bacon), tomato, lettuce, and dressing, with two layers of filling between three slices of toast or bread.

club soda ▶**noun** trademark North American term for **SODA** (in sense 1).

cluck ▶**noun 1** the characteristic short, guttural sound made by a hen.
■a similar sound made by a person to express annoyance: *Loretta gave a cluck of impatience.*
2 N. Amer. informal a silly or foolish person.
▶**verb** [no obj.] (of a hen) make a short, guttural sound.
■[with obj.] (of a person) make such a sound with (one's tongue) to express concern or disapproval: *Carmichael clucked his tongue irritably.* ■[no obj.] (**cluck over/around**) express fussy concern about: *Pauline became worried about her health and constantly clucked over her.*
– ORIGIN late 15th cent. (as a verb): imitative, corresponding to Danish *klukke*, Swedish *klucka*.

clucky ▶**adjective** Austral. informal (of a hen) sitting or ready to sit on eggs.
■(of a woman) broody: *Mum's gone clucky.*

clue ▶**noun 1** a piece of evidence or information used in the detection of a crime or solving of a mystery: *police officers are still searching for clues.*
■a fact or idea that serves as a guide or aid in a task or problem: *archaeological evidence can give clues about the past.*
2 a verbal formula giving an indication as to what is to be inserted in a particular space in a crossword.
▶**verb** (**clues**, **clued**, **clueing**) [with obj.] (**clue someone in**) informal inform someone about a particular matter: *Stella had clued her in about Peter.*
– PHRASES **not have a clue** informal know nothing about something or about how to do something.
– ORIGIN late Middle English: variant of **CLEW**. The original sense was 'a ball of thread'; hence one used to guide a person out of a labyrinth (literally or figuratively). Sense 1 dates from the early 17th cent.

clued-up (also chiefly N. Amer. **clued-in**) ▶**adjective** informal well informed about a particular subject.

clueless ▶**adjective** informal having no knowledge, understanding, or ability: *you're clueless about how to deal with the world.*
– DERIVATIVES **cluelessly** adverb, **cluelessness** noun.

Cluj–Napoca /kluːʒˈnɑːpɒkə/ a city in west central Romania; pop. 321,850 (1993). The city was founded by 12th-century German-speaking colonists; by the 19th century it belonged to Hungary and was the cultural centre of Transylvania. The name was changed from Cluj in the mid 1970s to incorporate the name of a nearby ancient settlement. Also called **CLUJ**; Hungarian name **KOLOZSVÁR**; original name **KLAUSENBURG**.

Clumber spaniel /ˈklʌmbə/ ▶**noun** a spaniel of a slow, heavily built breed.
– ORIGIN mid 19th cent.: from the name of *Clumber* Park, Nottinghamshire.

clump ▶**noun 1** a small group of trees or plants growing closely together: ***a clump of** ferns.*
■a small, compact group of people: *they sat on the wall in **clumps of** two and three.* ■a compacted mass or lump of something: ***clumps of** earth.* ■Physiology an agglutinated mass of blood cells or bacteria, especially as an indicator of the presence of an antibody to them.
2 a thick extra sole on a boot or shoe.
3 another term for **CLOMP**.
▶**verb** [no obj.] **1** form into a clump or mass: *the particles tend to **clump together**.*
2 another term for **CLOMP**.
– ORIGIN Middle English (denoting a heap or lump): partly imitative, reinforced by Middle Low German *klumpe* and Middle Dutch *klompe*; related to **CLUB**[2].

clumpy ▶**adjective** (**clumpier**, **clumpiest**) **1** (also **clompy**) (of shoes or boots) heavy and inelegant.
2 forming or showing a tendency to form clumps.

clumsy ▶**adjective** (**clumsier**, **clumsiest**) awkward in movement or in handling things: *a terribly clumsy fellow | the cold made his fingers clumsy.*
■done awkwardly or without skill: *a very clumsy attempt to park | a clumsy remake of an old movie.* ■difficult to handle or use; unwieldy: *clumsy devices | the legal procedure is far too clumsy.* ■lacking social skills; tactless: *his choice of words was clumsy.*
– DERIVATIVES **clumsily** adverb, **clumsiness** noun.
– ORIGIN late 16th cent.: from obsolete *clumse* 'make numb, be numb', probably of Scandinavian origin and related to Swedish *klumsig*.

clunch ▶**noun** [mass noun] Brit. soft limestone capable of being easily worked.
– ORIGIN early 19th cent.: perhaps from dialect *clunch* 'lumpy, thickset'.

clung past and past participle of **CLING**.

Cluniac /ˈkluːnɪak/ ▶**adjective** of or relating to a reformed Benedictine monastic order founded at Cluny in eastern France in 910.
▶**noun** a monk of this order.

clunk ▶**noun 1** a dull sound such as that made by thick pieces of metal striking together.
2 US informal a stupid or foolish person.
▶**verb** [no obj., with adverbial] move with or make such a sound: *the machinery clunked into life.*
– ORIGIN late 18th cent. (originally Scots, as a verb): imitative; compare with **CLANK**, **CLINK**[1], and **CLONK**.

clunker ▶**noun** N. Amer. informal a dilapidated vehicle or machine.
■a thing that is totally unsuccessful: *novel after novel and not a clunker among them.*

clunky ▶**adjective** (**clunkier**, **clunkiest**) informal **1** chiefly N. Amer. solid, heavy, and old-fashioned: *even last year's laptops look clunky.*
■(of shoes) clumpy: *clunky Dr Martens.*
2 making a clunking sound: *clunky conveyor belts.*

clupeoid /ˈkluːpɪɔɪd/ Zoology ▶**noun** a marine fish of a group that includes the herring family together with the anchovies and related fish.
• Order Clupeiformes or suborder Clupeoidei.
▶**adjective** of or relating to fish of this group.
– ORIGIN mid 19th cent.: from modern Latin *Clupeoidei* (plural), from Latin *clupea*, the name of a river fish.

cluster ▶**noun** a group of similar things growing closely together: ***clusters of** creamy-white flowers.*
■a group of people or similar things positioned or occurring close together: ***a cluster of** antique shops.* ■Astronomy a group of stars or galaxies forming a relatively close association. ■Linguistics (also **consonant cluster**) a group of consonants pronounced in immediate succession, as *str* in *strong.*

■a natural subgroup of a population, used for statistical sampling or analysis. ■Chemistry a group of atoms of the same element, typically a metal, bonded closely together in a molecule.
▶**verb** [no obj.] be or come into a cluster or close group; congregate: *the children **clustered round** her skirts.*
■Statistics (of data points) have similar numerical values: *students tended to have marks clustering around 70 per cent.*
– ORIGIN Old English *clyster*; probably related to **CLOT**.

cluster bean ▶**noun** another term for **GUAR**.

cluster bomb ▶**noun** a bomb which releases a number of projectiles on impact to injure or damage personnel and vehicles.

clustered ▶**adjective** [attrib.] growing or situated in a group: *the spires and clustered roofs of the old town.*
■Architecture (of pillars, columns, or shafts) positioned close together, or disposed round or half-detached from a pier.

cluster fly ▶**noun** a fly which often enters buildings in large numbers during the autumn while looking for a place to overwinter.
• *Pollenia rudis* (family Calliphoridae), whose larvae parasitize earthworms, and the smaller *Thaumatomyia notata* (family Chloropidae).

cluster headache ▶**noun** a type of severe headache which tends to recur over a period of several weeks and in which the pain is usually limited to one side of the head.

cluster pine ▶**noun** another term for **MARITIME PINE**.

clutch[1] ▶**verb** [with obj.] grasp or seize (something) tightly or eagerly: *he stood clutching a microphone* | [no obj.] figurative *Mrs Longhill clutched at the idea.*
▶**noun** **1** a tight grasp or an act of grasping something: *she made a **clutch at** his body.*
■(**someone's clutches**) a person's power or control, especially when perceived as cruel or inescapable: *he had narrowly escaped the clutches of the Nazis.*
2 a mechanism for connecting and disconnecting a vehicle engine and its transmission system.
■the pedal operating such a mechanism. ■an arrangement for connecting and disconnecting the working parts of any machine.
– PHRASES **clutch at straws** see **STRAW**.
– ORIGIN Middle English (in the sense 'bend, crook'): variant of obsolete *clitch* 'close the hand', from Old English *clyccan* 'crook, clench', of Germanic origin.

clutch[2] ▶**noun** a group of eggs fertilized at the same time, typically laid in a single session and (in birds) incubated together.
■a brood of chicks. ■a small group of people or things: *a **clutch of** brightly painted holiday homes.*
– ORIGIN early 18th cent.: probably a southern variant of northern English dialect *cletch*, related to Middle English *cleck* 'to hatch', from Old Norse *klekja*.

clutch bag ▶**noun** a slim, flat handbag without handles or a strap.

Clutha /ˈkluːθə/ a gold-bearing river at the southern end of South Island, New Zealand. It flows 338 km (213 miles) to the Pacific Ocean.

clutter ▶**noun** [mass noun] a collection of things lying about in an untidy mass: *the attic is full of clutter.*
■[in sing.] an untidy state: *the room was in a clutter of smelly untidiness.*
▶**verb** [with obj.] crowd (something) untidily; fill with clutter: *all of the surfaces were cluttered with an assortment of equipment* | *luggage **cluttered up** the hallway.*
– ORIGIN late Middle English (as a verb): variant of dialect *clotter* 'to clot', influenced by **CLUSTER** and **CLATTER**.

Clwyd /ˈkluːɪd/ a former county of NE Wales, replaced in 1996 by Denbighshire and Flintshire.

Clyde a river in western central Scotland which flows 170 km (106 miles) from the Southern Uplands to the Firth of Clyde, formerly famous for the shipbuilding industries along its banks.

Clyde, Firth of the estuary of the River Clyde in western Scotland which separates southern Scotland to the east from the southern extremities of the Highlands to the north-west.

Clydesdale ▶**noun** **1** a horse of a heavy, powerful breed, used for pulling heavy loads.
2 a dog of a small breed of terrier.
– ORIGIN from the name of the area around the river **CLYDE** in Scotland, where they were originally bred.

clypeus /ˈklɪpɪəs/ ▶**noun** (pl. **clypei** /-pɪʌɪ/) Entomology a broad plate at the front of an insect's head.
– DERIVATIVES **clypeal** adjective.
– ORIGIN mid 19th cent.: from Latin, literally 'round shield'.

clyster /ˈklɪstə/ ▶**noun** archaic term for **ENEMA**.
– ORIGIN late Middle English: from Old French *clystere* or Latin *clyster*, from Greek *klustēr* 'syringe', from *kluzein* 'wash out'.

Clytemnestra /ˌklʌɪtɪmˈnɛstrə/ Greek Mythology wife of Agamemnon. She conspired with her lover Aegisthus to murder Agamemnon on his return from the Trojan War, and was murdered in retribution by her son Orestes and her daughter Electra.

CM ▶**abbreviation for** ■command module. ■common metre. ■Member of the Order of Canada.

Cm ▶**symbol for** the chemical element curium.

Cm. ▶**abbreviation for** (in the UK) Command Paper (sixth series, 1986–).

cm ▶**abbreviation for** centimetre(s).

Cmd. ▶**abbreviation for** (in the UK) Command Paper (fourth series, 1918–56).

Cmdr ▶**abbreviation for** Commander.

Cmdre ▶**abbreviation for** Commodore.

CMEA ▶**abbreviation for** Council for Mutual Economic Assistance.

CMG ▶**abbreviation for** (in the UK) Companion (of the Order) of St Michael and St George.

Cmnd. ▶**abbreviation for** (in the UK) Command Paper (fifth series, 1956–86).

CMOS ▶**noun** [often as modifier] Electronics a technology for making low power integrated circuits.
■a chip built using such technology.
– ORIGIN 1980s: from *Complementary Metal Oxide Semiconductor.*

CMSgt ▶**abbreviation for** Chief Master Sergeant.

CMV ▶**abbreviation for** cytomegalovirus.

CNAA ▶**abbreviation for** (in the UK) Council for National Academic Awards.

CND ▶**abbreviation for** (in the UK) Campaign for Nuclear Disarmament.

cnemial crest /ˈ(k)niːmɪəl/ ▶**noun** Zoology (in the legs of many mammals, birds, and dinosaurs) a ridge at the front of the head of the tibia or tibiotarsus to which the main extensor muscle of the thigh is attached. It is particularly well developed in running species.
– ORIGIN late 19th cent.: *cnemial*, from Greek *knēmē* 'tibia' + **-AL**.

CNG ▶**abbreviation for** compressed natural gas.

Cnidaria /(k)nʌɪˈdɛːrɪə/ Zoology a phylum of aquatic invertebrate animals that comprises the coelenterates.
– DERIVATIVES **cnidarian** noun & adjective.
– ORIGIN modern Latin (plural), from Greek *knidē* 'nettle'.

CNN ▶**abbreviation for** Cable News Network.

CNR historical ▶**abbreviation for** Canadian National Railways.

cnr ▶**abbreviation for** corner.

CNS ▶**abbreviation for** central nervous system.

CN Tower a tower in Toronto, Canada, the tallest self-supporting man-made structure in the world when it was completed in 1976. It stands 553 m (1,815 ft) high including a 100 m (328 ft) communications mast.
– ORIGIN CN from Canadian National (Railways).

Cnut variant of **CANUTE**.

CO ▶**abbreviation for** ■Colombia (international vehicle registration). ■Colorado (in official postal use). ■Commanding Officer. ■conscientious objector.

Co ▶**symbol for** the chemical element cobalt.

Co. ▶**abbreviation for** ■company: *the Consett Iron Co.* ■county: *Co. Cork.*
– PHRASES **and Co.** /kəʊ/ used as part of the titles of commercial businesses to designate the partner or partners not named. ■(also **and co.**) informal and the rest of them: *I got there at 12.30 and waited for Mark and Co. to arrive.*

c/o ▶**abbreviation for** care of.

co- /kəʊ/ ▶**prefix** **1** (forming nouns) joint; mutual; common: *co-driver* | *co-education.*
2 (forming adjectives) jointly; mutually: *coequal.*
3 (forming verbs) together with another or others: *co-produce* | *co-own.*
4 Mathematics of the complement of an angle: *cosine.*
■the complement of: *co-latitude* | *coset.*
– ORIGIN from Latin, originally a form of **COM-**.

CoA Biochemistry ▶**abbreviation for** coenzyme A.

coacervate /kəʊˈasəveɪt/ ▶**noun** Chemistry a colloid-rich viscous liquid phase which may separate from a colloidal solution on addition of a third component.
– ORIGIN early 20th cent.: back-formation from *coacervation*, based on Latin *cum* '(together) with' + *acervus* 'heap'.

coach[1] ▶**noun** **1** chiefly Brit. a single-decker bus, especially one that is comfortably equipped and used for longer journeys: [as modifier] *a coach trip.*
2 a railway carriage:
■[as modifier] N. Amer. denoting economy class seating in an aircraft or train: *the cheapest coach-class fare.*
3 a horse-drawn carriage, especially a closed one.
▶**verb** [no obj., with adverbial of direction] travel by coach: *fly or coach to the shores of the Mediterranean.*
▶**adverb** N. Amer. in economy class accommodation in an aircraft or train.
– PHRASES **drive a coach and horses through** Brit. cause (something) to be useless or ineffective: *he's driving a coach and horses through our environmental legislation.*
– ORIGIN mid 16th cent. (in sense 3): from French *coche*, from Hungarian *kocsi* (*szekér*) '(wagon) from *Kocs*', a town in Hungary.

coach[2] ▶**noun** **1** an instructor or trainer in sport.
■a tutor who gives private or specialized teaching.
2 Austral. a docile cow or bullock used as a decoy to attract wild cattle.
▶**verb** [with obj.] train or instruct (a team or player): *he moved on to coach the England team.*
■give (someone) extra or private teaching: *she was **coached for** stardom by her mother.* ■teach (a subject or sport) as a coach: *he teaches history and coaches rugby.* ■prompt or urge (someone) with instructions: *she was being coached by the off-camera voice of her mother.*
– ORIGIN early 18th cent. (as a verb): figuratively from **COACH**[1]. Sense 2 dates from the late 19th cent.

coach bolt (N. Amer. **carriage bolt**) ▶**noun** Brit. a large bolt with a round head, used chiefly for fixing wooden panels to masonry or to one another.

coach-built ▶**adjective** Brit. (of a vehicle) having specially or individually built bodywork.
– DERIVATIVES **coachbuilder** noun.

coach house ▶**noun** an outhouse in which a carriage is or was kept.

coaching inn ▶**noun** historical an inn along a route followed by horse-drawn coaches, at which horses could be changed.

coachload ▶**noun** a group of people travelling in a coach: *coachloads of tourists trudging round Oxford.*

coachman ▶**noun** (pl. **-men**) a driver of a horse-drawn carriage.

coachroof ▶**noun** a raised part of the cabin roof of a yacht.

coach station ▶**noun** an area or building from or at which coaches leave or arrive on a regular basis.

coachwhip ▶**noun** **1** (also **coachwhip snake**) a harmless fast-moving North American snake. The pattern of scales on its slender body is said to resemble a braided whip.
• *Masticophis flagellum*, family Colubridae.
2 (also **coachwhip bird**) Austral. the whipbird.

coachwood ▶**noun** a slender tree of the rainforests of Australia and New Guinea, with close-grained timber that has a characteristic caramel scent and is used for cabinetmaking and veneers.
• *Ceratopetalum apetalum*, family Cunoniaceae.

coachwork ▶**noun** [mass noun] the bodywork of a road or railway vehicle.

coadjutor /kəʊˈadʒʊtə/ ▶**noun** a bishop appointed to assist a diocesan bishop, and often also designated as their successor.
– ORIGIN late Middle English: via Old French from late Latin *coadjutor*, from *co-* (from Latin *cum* 'together with') + *adjutor* 'assistant' (from *adjuvare* 'to help').

coagulant /kəʊˈagjʊlənt/ ▶**noun** a substance that causes blood or another liquid to coagulate.
– ORIGIN late 18th cent.: from Latin *coagulant-* 'curdling', from the verb *coagulare* (see **COAGULATE**).

coagulase /kəʊˈagjʊleɪz, -s/ ▶ **noun** [mass noun] Biochemistry a bacterial enzyme which brings about the coagulation of blood or plasma and is produced by disease-causing forms of staphylococcus.

coagulate /kəʊˈagjʊleɪt/ ▶ **verb** [no obj.] (of a fluid, especially blood) change to a solid or semi-solid state: *blood had coagulated round the edges of the gash.*
■ [with obj.] cause (a fluid) to change to a solid or semi-solid state: *adrenalin coagulates the blood.*
– DERIVATIVES **coagulable** adjective, **coagulation** noun, **coagulative** adjective, **coagulator** noun.
– ORIGIN late Middle English: from Latin *coagulat-* 'curdled', from the verb *coagulare*, from *coagulum* 'rennet'.

coagulum /kəʊˈagjʊləm/ ▶ **noun** (pl. **coagula** /-lə/) a mass of coagulated matter.
– ORIGIN mid 16th cent. (denoting a coagulant): from Latin, literally 'rennet'.

Coahuila /ˌkəʊəˈwiːlə/ a state of northern Mexico, on the border with the US; capital, Saltillo.

coal ▶ **noun** [mass noun] a combustible black or dark brown rock consisting mainly of carbonized plant matter, found mainly in underground seams and widely used as fuel: [as modifier] *a coal fire.*
■ [count noun] Brit. a piece of coal for burning: *loading coals into a wagon.* ■ [count noun] a red-hot piece of coal or other material in a fire: *the glowing coals.*
▶ **verb** [with obj.] provide with a supply of coal: [as noun **coaling**] *the coaling and watering of the engine.*
■ [no obj.] mine or extract coal: *we have now finished coaling at the site.*
– PHRASES **coals to Newcastle** something brought or sent to a place where it is already plentiful. **haul someone over the coals** reprimand someone severely.
– DERIVATIVES **coaly** adjective.
– ORIGIN Old English *col* (in the senses 'glowing ember' and 'charred remnant'), of Germanic origin; related to Dutch *kool* and German *Kohle*. The sense 'combustible mineral used as fuel' dates from Middle English.

coal-black ▶ **adjective** as black as coal; utterly black: *a woman with coal-black eyes.*

coal bunker ▶ **noun** a place for storing coal, especially for private use.

coaler ▶ **noun 1** a ship that transports coal.
2 a large mechanized structure for loading coal on to a ship, railway wagon, or steam locomotive.

coalesce /ˌkəʊəˈlɛs/ ▶ **verb** [no obj.] come together and form one mass or whole: *the puddles had* ***coalesced into*** *shallow streams* | [with infinitive] *the separate details coalesce to form a single body of scientific thought.*
■ [with obj.] combine (elements) in a mass or whole: *the problem of* ***coalescing*** *disparate information sources* ***into*** *a practical form.*
– DERIVATIVES **coalescence** noun, **coalescent** adjective.
– ORIGIN mid 16th cent. (in the sense 'bring together, unite'): from Latin *coalescere*, from *co-* (from *cum* 'with') + *alescere* 'grow up' (from *alere* 'nourish').

coalface ▶ **noun** an exposed surface of coal in a mine.
– PHRASES **at the coalface** engaged in the practical work in a particular field: *academics should work closely alongside the clinicians at the coalface.*

coalfield ▶ **noun** an extensive area containing a number of underground coal strata.

coal-fired ▶ **adjective** heated, driven, or produced by the burning of coal: *a coal-fired power station.*

coalfish ▶ **noun** (pl. same or **-fishes**) another term for **SAITHE**.

coal gas ▶ **noun** [mass noun] a mixture of gases (chiefly hydrogen, methane, and carbon monoxide) obtained by the destructive distillation of coal and formerly used for lighting and heating.

coal-hole ▶ **noun** Brit. a compartment or small cellar used for storing coal.

coalhouse ▶ **noun** a building used for storing coal.

Coalite /ˈkəʊlʌɪt/ ▶ **noun** [mass noun] trademark a kind of smokeless fuel made by refining coal.

coalition /ˌkəʊəˈlɪʃ(ə)n/ ▶ **noun** a temporary alliance for combined action, especially of political parties forming a government or of states: *a coalition between Liberals and Conservatives* | [mass noun] *the SPD was* ***in coalition with*** *the CDU* | [as modifier] *a coalition government.*
– DERIVATIVES **coalitionist** noun.
– ORIGIN early 17th cent. (in the sense 'fusion'): from medieval Latin *coalitio(n-)*, from the verb *coalescere* (see **COALESCE**). Usage in politics dates from the late 18th cent.

coalman ▶ **noun** (pl. **-men**) a man who delivers coal to people's houses.

coal measures ▶ **plural noun** Geology a series of strata of the Carboniferous period, including coal seams.

coal owner ▶ **noun** chiefly historical the owner or lessee of a colliery.

Coalport ▶ **noun** [mass noun] a kind of porcelain, frequently decorated with floral designs, produced at Coalport in Shropshire, England, from the late 18th century.

coal pot ▶ **noun** chiefly W. Indian a cooking device consisting of an iron grid over a raised iron bowl that holds burning charcoal.

Coalsack (**the Coalsack**) Astronomy a dark nebula of dust near the Southern Cross that gives the appearance of a gap in the stars of the Milky Way.

coal scuttle ▶ **noun** a metal container with a sloping lid used to carry and hold coal for a domestic fire.

coal tar ▶ **noun** [mass noun] a thick black liquid produced by the destructive distillation of bituminous coal. It contains benzene, naphthalene, phenols, aniline, and many other organic chemicals.

coal tit (also **cole tit**) ▶ **noun** a small Eurasian and North African tit (songbird) with a grey back, black cap and throat, and white cheeks.
• *Parus ater*, family Paridae.

coaming /ˈkəʊmɪŋ/ (also **coamings**) ▶ **noun** a raised border round the cockpit or hatch of a yacht or other boat to keep out water.
– ORIGIN early 17th cent.: of unknown origin.

coaptation /ˌkəʊapˈteɪʃ(ə)n/ ▶ **noun** [mass noun] the adaptation or adjustment of things, parts, or people to each other.
■ Medicine the drawing together of the separated tissue in a wound or fracture.
– ORIGIN mid 16th cent.: from late Latin *coaptatio(n-)*, from the verb *coaptare*, from *co-* (from Latin *cum* 'with, together') + *aptare* (from *aptus* 'apt').

coarctate /kəʊˈɑːkteɪt/ ▶ **adjective** chiefly Anatomy & Biology pressed close together; contracted; confined.
■ Entomology (of the pupa of certain flies) formed within and remaining concealed by the larval cuticle or puparium.
– ORIGIN late Middle English: from Latin *coarctatus*, past participle of *coarctare* 'press or draw together'.

coarctation ▶ **noun** [mass noun] Medicine congenital narrowing of a short section of the aorta.
– ORIGIN late Middle English: from Latin *coarctatio(n-)*, from the verb *coarctare* (see **COARCTATE**).

coarse ▶ **adjective 1** rough or loose in texture or grain: *a coarse woollen cloth.*
■ made of large grains or particles: *a coarse white powder.* ■ (of grains or particles) large. ■ (of a person's features) not elegantly formed or proportioned. ■ (of food or drink) of inferior quality.
2 (of a person or their speech) rude, crude, or vulgar.
3 Brit. relating to the sport of angling for coarse fish: *coarse fishing* | *coarse anglers.*
– DERIVATIVES **coarseness** noun, **coarsish** adjective.
– ORIGIN late Middle English (in the sense 'ordinary or inferior'): origin uncertain; until the 17th cent. identical in spelling with **COURSE**, and possibly derived from the latter in the sense 'habitual or ordinary manner'.

coarse fish ▶ **noun** (pl. same) Brit. any freshwater fish other than salmon and trout. Compare with **GAME FISH**.

coarse-grained ▶ **adjective 1** coarse in texture or grain: *a coarse-grained flour.*
■ (of photographic film) having a noticeably grainy appearance.
2 coarse in manner or speech: *a coarse-grained man.*

coarsely ▶ **adverb 1** in a coarse manner: *Carter laughed coarsely.*
2 into large and irregularly shaped pieces: *chop the mushrooms coarsely* | *coarsely grated cheese.*

coarsen ▶ **verb** make or become rough: [with obj.] *her hands were coarsened by outside work* | [no obj.] *his facial features appeared to coarsen with age.*
■ make or become crude, vulgar, or unpleasant: [no obj.] *the voice coarsened.*

coarticulation /ˌkəʊɑːtɪkjʊˈleɪʃ(ə)n/ ▶ **noun** [mass noun] Phonetics the articulation of two or more speech sounds together, so that one influences the other.

coast ▶ **noun 1** the part of the land near the sea; the edge of the land: *the west coast of Africa* | *they sailed further up the coast* | [as modifier] *the coast road.*
■ (**the Coast**) N. Amer. the Pacific coast of North America.
2 a run or movement in or on a vehicle without use of power.
▶ **verb 1** [no obj., with adverbial of direction] (of a person or vehicle) move easily without using power: *they were coasting down a long hill.*
■ [no obj.] act or make progress without making much effort: *Colchester* ***coasted to*** *victory.*
2 [no obj., with adverbial of direction] sail along the coast, especially in order to carry cargo: [as adj. **coasting**] *a West Country coasting ketch.*
– PHRASES **the coast is clear** there is no danger of being observed or caught.
– ORIGIN Middle English (in the sense 'side of the body'), from Old French *coste* (noun), *costeier* (verb), from Latin *costa* 'rib, flank, side'. Sense 1 arose from the phrase *coast of the sea* 'side of the sea'.

coastal ▶ **adjective** of, relating to, or near a coast: *coastal erosion* | *coastal waters.*

coaster ▶ **noun 1** a ship used to carry cargo along the coast from port to port.
■ [with adj.] a person who inhabits a specified coast: *a West coaster.*
2 a small tray or mat for a bottle or glass.
3 N. Amer. a toboggan.
■ short for **ROLLER COASTER**.

coastguard ▶ **noun** (**the coastguard**) an organization keeping watch on the sea near a coast in order to assist people or ships in danger and to prevent smuggling.
■ a member of this organization.

coastland ▶ **noun** (usu. **coastlands**) an expanse of land near the sea.

coastline ▶ **noun** [mass noun] the outline of a coast, especially with regard to its shape and appearance: *the hotel has wonderful views of the rugged coastline.*

coast to coast ▶ **adjective** & **adverb** all the way across an island or continent: [as adv.] *this was the first year the game was telecast coast to coast* | [as adj. **coast-to-coast**] *a coast-to-coast journey.*

coastwise ▶ **adjective** & **adverb** along, following, or connected with the coast: [as adj.] *a small coastwise steamer* | [as adv.] *the cargo was ferried coastwise.*

coat ▶ **noun 1** a thick outer garment worn outdoors, having sleeves and typically extending below the hips: *a winter coat* | [as modifier] *his coat pocket.*
■ a similar item worn indoors as a protective garment: *a laboratory coat.* ■ a man's jacket or tunic, especially as worn when hunting or by soldiers. ■ a woman's tailored jacket, typically worn with a skirt.
2 an animal's covering of fur or hair.
■ a structure, especially a membrane, enclosing or lining an organ. ■ a skin, rind, or husk. ■ a layer of a plant bulb. ■ [with modifier] an outer layer or covering of a specified kind: *the protein coat of the virus.*
3 a covering of paint or similar material laid on a surface at one time: *apply a final top coat of varnish.*
▶ **verb** [with obj.] (often **be coated**) provide with a layer or covering of something; apply a coat to: *her right leg was* ***coated in*** *plaster* | *coat each part with a thin oil* | [as adj., in combination **-coated**] *plastic-coated wire.*
■ (of a substance) form a covering to: *a film of dust coated the floor.*
– DERIVATIVES **coated** adjective [in combination] *shaggy-coated cattle.*
– ORIGIN Middle English: from Old French *cote*, of unknown ultimate origin.

coat armour ▶ **noun** [mass noun] heraldic arms.

coat check ▶ **noun** N. Amer. a cloakroom with an attendant.

coat checker ▶ **noun** N. Amer. a cloakroom attendant.

coat dress ▶ **noun** a woman's tailored dress, typically fastening down the front and resembling a coat.

coatee /kəʊˈtiː/ ▶ **noun** Brit. a woman's or infant's short coat.
■ archaic a close-fitting short-tailed military-style coat.

coat hanger ▶ **noun** see **HANGER**[1] (sense 2).

coati /kəʊˈɑːti/ ▶ noun (pl. **coatis**) a raccoon-like animal found mainly in Central and South America, with a long flexible snout and a ringed tail. Also called **COATIMUNDI**.
- ● Genera *Nasua* and *Nasuella*, family Procyonidae: three or four species, in particular *Nasua nasua*, whose range reaches the southern US.
- – ORIGIN early 17th cent.: from Spanish and Portuguese, from Tupi *kua'ti*, from *cua* 'belt' + *tim* 'nose'.

coatimundi /kəʊˌɑːtɪˈmʌndi/ ▶ noun (pl. **coatimundis**) another term for **COATI**.
- – ORIGIN late 17th cent.: from Portuguese, from Tupi *kuatimu'ne*, from *kua'ti* (see **COATI**) + *mu'ne* 'snare or trick'. The *coatimundi* was originally thought to be a different species from the coati, but then discovered to be the male of the same species.

coating ▶ noun a thin layer or covering of something: *a coating of paint*.
- ■[mass noun] material used for making coats.

coat of arms ▶ noun the distinctive heraldic bearings or shield of a person, family, corporation, or country.

coat of mail ▶ noun historical a jacket covered with or composed of metal rings or plates, serving as armour.

coat-of-mail shell ▶ noun another term for **CHITON** (in sense 2).

coatroom ▶ noun N. Amer. another term for **CLOAKROOM** (in sense 1).

Coats Land a region of Antarctica, to the east of the Antarctic Peninsula.

coat-tail ▶ noun (usu. **coat-tails**) each of the flaps formed by the back of a tailcoat.
- – PHRASES **on someone's coat-tails** undeservedly benefiting from another's success: *he was elected on the coat-tails of his predecessor*.

co-author ▶ noun a joint author.
▶ verb [with obj.] be a joint author of (a book, paper, or report).

coax¹ /kəʊks/ ▶ verb [with obj.] persuade (someone) gradually or by flattery to do something: *the trainees were coaxed into doing hard, boring work* | [with direct speech] *'Come on now,' I coaxed*.
- ■(**coax something from/out of**) use such persuasion to obtain something from: *we coaxed our fare money out of my father* | figurative *coaxing more speed from the car*. ■ [with obj. and adverbial] manipulate (something) carefully into a particular shape or position: *her lovely hair had been coaxed into ringlets*.
- – DERIVATIVES **coaxer** noun, **coaxingly** adverb.
- – ORIGIN late 16th cent.: from obsolete *cokes* 'simpleton', of unknown origin. The original sense was 'pet, fondle', hence 'persuade by caresses or flattery', the underlying sense being 'make a simpleton of'.

coax² /ˈkəʊaks/ informal ▶ noun [mass noun] coaxial cable.
▶ adjective coaxial: *coax connectors*.

coaxial /kəʊˈaksɪəl/ ▶ adjective having a common axis.
- ■(of a cable or line) transmitting by means of two concentric conductors separated by an insulator.
- – DERIVATIVES **coaxially** adverb.

cob¹ ▶ noun **1** Brit. a loaf of bread.
2 (also **corn cob**) the central cylindrical woody part of the maize ear to which the grains are attached.
3 (also **cobnut**) a hazelnut or filbert, especially one of a large variety.
- ■ a hazel or filbert bush.
4 a powerfully built, short-legged horse.
5 a male swan.
6 a roundish lump of coal.
- – ORIGIN late Middle English (denoting a strong man or leader): of unknown origin. The underlying general sense appears to be 'stout, rounded, sturdy'.

cob² ▶ noun [mass noun] Brit. a mixture of compressed clay and straw used, especially in former times, for building walls: [as modifier] *cob and thatch cottages*.
- – ORIGIN early 17th cent.: of unknown origin.

cob³ ▶ noun (in phrase **have** or **get a cob on**) Brit. informal be or get annoyed or in a bad mood.
- – ORIGIN 1930s: of unknown origin.

cob⁴ ▶ noun variant spelling of **KOB²**.

cobalamin /kə(ʊ)ˈbaləmɪn/ ▶ noun Biochemistry any of a group of cobalt-containing substances including cyanocobalamin (vitamin B$_{12}$).

- – ORIGIN 1950s: blend of **COBALT** and **VITAMIN**.

cobalt /ˈkəʊbɔːlt, -ɒlt/ ▶ noun [mass noun] the chemical element of atomic number 27, a hard silvery-white magnetic metal. (Symbol: **Co**)
- ■ short for **COBALT BLUE**: [as modifier] *a cobalt sky*.

Cobalt is chiefly obtained as a by-product from nickel and copper ores. It is a transition metal similar in many respects to nickel. Its main use is as a component of magnetic alloys and those designed for use at high temperatures.

- – DERIVATIVES **cobaltic** /kə(ʊ)ˈbɔːltɪk, -ˈbɒlt-/ adjective, **cobaltous** /kə(ʊ)ˈbɔːltəs, -ˈbɒlt-/ adjective.
- – ORIGIN late 17th cent.: from German *Kobalt* 'imp, demon' (from the belief that cobalt was harmful to the ores with which it occurred).

cobalt blue ▶ noun [mass noun] a deep blue pigment containing cobalt and aluminium oxides.
- ■ the deep blue colour of this.

cobber ▶ noun Austral./NZ informal a companion or friend (often used as a form of address between men): *G'day cobbers!*
- – ORIGIN late 19th cent.: perhaps related to English dialect *cob* 'take a liking to'.

Cobbett, William (1763–1835), English writer and political reformer. He started his political life as a Tory, but later became a radical and in 1802 founded the periodical *Cobbett's Political Register*. Notable works: *Rural Rides* (1830).

cobble¹ ▶ noun (usu. **cobbles**) a small round stone of a kind formerly used to cover road surfaces; a cobblestone.
- ■(**cobbles**) Brit. coal in lumps of such a size.
- – ORIGIN late Middle English: from **COB¹** + **-LE²**.

cobble² ▶ verb [with obj.] **1** dated repair (shoes).
2 (**cobble something together**) roughly assemble or put together something from available parts or elements: *the film was imperfectly cobbled together from two separate stories*.
- – ORIGIN late 15th cent.: back-formation from **COBBLER**.

cobbled ▶ adjective (of an area or roadway) paved with cobbles: *a cobbled courtyard*.

cobbler ▶ noun **1** a person who mends shoes as a job.
2 [mass noun] an iced drink made with wine or sherry, sugar, and lemon.
3 chiefly US a fruit pie with a rich, thick, cake-like crust.
4 (**cobblers**) Brit. informal a man's testicles. [ORIGIN: from rhyming slang *cobbler's awls* 'balls'.]
- ■ nonsense: *I thought it was a load of cobblers*.
5 Austral./NZ informal the last sheep to be shorn. [ORIGIN: late 19th cent.: pun in allusion to the cobbler's last.]
- – PHRASES **let the cobbler stick to his last** proverb people should only concern themselves with things they know something about. [ORIGIN: translating Latin *ne sutor ultra crepidam*.]
- – ORIGIN Middle English: of unknown origin.

cobbler's pegs ▶ plural noun [treated as sing. or pl.] Australian term for **BLACKJACK** (in sense 2).
- – ORIGIN so named because of the appearance of the seeds.

cobblestone ▶ noun another term for **COBBLE¹**.

cobby ▶ adjective (of horses, dogs, and other animals) shortish and thickset; stocky.

Cobden /ˈkɒbd(ə)n/, Richard (1804–65), English political reformer, one of the leading spokesmen of the free-trade movement in Britain. From 1838, together with John Bright, he led the Anti-Corn Law League in its successful campaign for the repeal of the Corn Laws (1846).

COBE /ˈkəʊbi/ a NASA satellite launched in 1989 to map the background microwave radiation in a search for evidence of the big bang.
- – ORIGIN abbreviation of *Cosmic Background Explorer*.

co-belligerent ▶ noun any of two or more nations engaged in war as allies.
- – DERIVATIVES **co-belligerence** noun.

cobia /ˈkəʊbɪə/ ▶ noun (pl. same) a large edible game fish that lives in open waters of the Atlantic, Indian, and West Pacific oceans. Also called **SERGEANT FISH**.
- ● *Rachycentron canadum*, family Rachycentridae.
- – ORIGIN mid 19th cent.: of unknown origin.

coble /ˈkəʊb(ə)l/ ▶ noun a flat-bottomed fishing boat of a type used in Scotland and NE England.
- – ORIGIN Old English, perhaps of Celtic origin and related to Welsh *ceubal* 'ferry boat, skiff'.

cobnut ▶ noun see **COB¹** (sense 3).

COBOL /ˈkəʊbɒl/ ▶ noun [mass noun] a computer programming language designed for use in commerce.
- – ORIGIN 1960s: from *co(mmon) b(usiness) o(riented) l(anguage)*.

cobra /ˈkəʊbrə, ˈkɒbrə/ ▶ noun a highly venomous snake that spreads the skin of its neck into a hood when disturbed, native to Africa and Asia.
- ● *Naja* and two other genera, family Elapidae: several species, in particular the **spectacled cobra**.
- – ORIGIN mid 17th cent.: from Portuguese *cobra de capello*, literally 'snake with hood', based on Latin *colubra* 'snake'.

cobweb ▶ noun (usu. **cobwebs**) a spider's web, especially when old and covered with dust.
- ■ Zoology a tangled three-dimensional spider's web. ■ something resembling a cobweb in delicacy or intricacy: *white cobwebs of frost*.
- – PHRASES **blow** (or **clear**) **away the cobwebs** banish a state of lethargy; enliven or refresh oneself.
- – DERIVATIVES **cobwebbed** adjective, **cobwebby** adjective.
- – ORIGIN Middle English *coppeweb, copweb*, from obsolete *coppe* 'spider' + **WEB**.

cobweb spider ▶ noun a spider that builds tangled three-dimensional webs.
- ● Family Theridiidae: many species.

coca /ˈkəʊkə/ ▶ noun a tropical American shrub that is widely grown for its leaves, which are the source of cocaine.
- ● *Erythroxylum coca*, family Erythroxylaceae.
- ■ [mass noun] the dried leaves of this shrub, which are mixed with lime and chewed as a stimulant by the native people of western South America.
- – ORIGIN late 16th cent.: from Spanish, from Aymara *kuka* or Quechua *koka*.

Coca-Cola ▶ noun [mass noun] trademark a carbonated non-alcoholic drink.
- – ORIGIN late 19th cent.: from **COCA** and **COLA**.

cocaine /kə(ʊ)ˈkeɪn/ ▶ noun [mass noun] an addictive drug derived from coca or prepared synthetically, used as an illegal stimulant and sometimes medicinally as a local anaesthetic.
- ● An alkaloid; chem. formula: $C_{17}H_{21}NO_4$.
- – ORIGIN mid 19th cent.: from **COCA** + **-INE⁴**.

coccidia /kɒkˈsɪdɪə/ ▶ plural noun Biology parasitic protozoa of a group that includes those that cause diseases such as coccidiosis and toxoplasmosis.
- ● Suborder Eimeriorina (formerly order or subclass Coccidia), phylum Sporozoa.
- – DERIVATIVES **coccidian** adjective & noun.

coccidioidomycosis /kɒkˌsɪdɪˌɔɪdəʊmʌɪˈkəʊsɪs/ ▶ noun [mass noun] a serious fungal disease of the lungs and other tissues, endemic in the warmer, arid regions of America.
- ● The fungus is *Coccidioides immitis*, subdivision Deuteromycotina.
- – ORIGIN 1930s: from modern Latin *Coccidioides* (part of the binomial of the fungus) + **MYCOSIS**.

coccidiosis /kɒkˌsɪdɪˈəʊsɪs/ ▶ noun [mass noun] a disease of birds and mammals that chiefly affects the intestines, caused by coccidia.
- ● The coccidia belong to the genera *Eimeria*, *Isopora*, and others.
- – ORIGIN late 19th cent.: from *coccidium* (singular of modern Latin *Coccidia*, from Greek *kokkis*, diminutive of *kokkos* 'berry') + **-OSIS**.

coccidiostat /kɒkˈsɪdɪə(ʊ)stat/ ▶ noun Veterinary Medicine a substance administered to poultry or cattle to retard the growth and reproduction of coccidian parasites.

coccinellid /ˌkɒksɪˈnɛlɪd/ ▶ noun Entomology a beetle of a family (Coccinellidae) that includes the ladybirds.
- – ORIGIN late 19th cent.: from modern Latin *Coccinelidae* (plural), from the genus name *Coccinella*, from Latin *coccineus* 'scarlet'.

coccolith /ˈkɒkəlɪθ/ ▶ noun Biology a minute rounded calcareous platelet, numbers of which form the spherical shells of coccolithophores.
- – ORIGIN mid 19th cent.: from Greek *kokkos* 'grain or berry' + *lithos* 'stone'.

coccolithophore /ˌkɒkə(ʊ)ˈlɪθəfɔː/ ▶ noun Biology a single-celled marine flagellate that secretes a calcareous shell, forming an important constituent of the phytoplankton.
- ● Order Coccolithophorida, phylum Haptophyta.

– DERIVATIVES **coccolithophorid** noun & adjective.

coccus /'kɒkəs/ ▶ noun (pl. **cocci** /'kɒk(s)ʌɪ, 'kɒk(s)iː/) Biology any spherical or roughly spherical bacterium.
– DERIVATIVES **coccal** adjective, **coccoid** adjective.
– ORIGIN mid 18th cent. (denoting a scale insect): modern Latin, from Greek *kokkos* 'berry'. Compare with **COCHINEAL**.

coccyx /'kɒksɪks/ ▶ noun (pl. **coccyges** /-ɪdʒiːz/ or **coccyxes**) a small triangular bone at the base of the spinal column in humans and some apes, formed of fused vestigial vertebrae.
– DERIVATIVES **coccygeal** /kɒk'sɪdʒɪəl/ adjective.
– ORIGIN late 16th cent.: via Latin from Greek *kokkux* 'cuckoo' (because the shape of the human bone resembles the cuckoo's bill).

Cochabamba /ˌkɒtʃə'bambə/ a city in Bolivia, situated at the centre of a rich agricultural region; pop. 404,100 (1992).

co-chair ▶ noun a person who chairs a meeting jointly with another or others.
▶ verb [with obj.] chair (a meeting) in this way.

Cochin[1] /'kəʊtʃɪn, 'kɒtʃɪn/ a seaport and naval base on the Malabar Coast of SW India, in the state of Kerala; pop. 504,000 (1991).

Cochin[2] /'kəʊtʃɪn, 'kɒtʃɪn/ (also **Cochin China**) ▶ noun a chicken of an Asian breed with feathery legs.

Cochin-China /'kəʊtʃɪn, 'kɒtʃɪn/ the former name for the southern region of what is now Vietnam. Part of French Indo-China from 1862, in 1946 it became a French overseas territory, then merged officially with Vietnam in 1949.

cochineal /ˌkɒtʃɪ'niːl, 'kɒtʃɪniːl/ ▶ noun 1 [mass noun] a scarlet dye used chiefly for colouring food.
■ the dried bodies of a female scale insect, which are crushed to yield this dye. ■ a similar dye or preparation made from the oak kermes insect (see **KERMES**).
2 (**cochineal insect**) the scale insect that is used for cochineal, native to Mexico and formerly widely cultivated on cacti.
● *Dactylopius coccus*, family Dactylopiidae, suborder Homoptera.
– ORIGIN late 16th cent.: from French *cochenille* or Spanish *cochinilla*, from Latin *coccinus* 'scarlet', from Greek *kokkos* 'berry' (because the insect bodies were originally mistaken for grains or berries). Compare with **COCCUS** and **KERMES**.

cochlea /'kɒklɪə/ ▶ noun (pl. **cochleae** /-klɪiː/) the spiral cavity of the inner ear containing the organ of Corti, which produces nerve impulses in response to sound vibrations.
– DERIVATIVES **cochlear** adjective.
– ORIGIN mid 16th cent. (used to denote spiral objects such as a spiral staircase and an Archimedean screw): from Latin, 'snail shell or screw', from Greek *kokhlias*. The current sense dates from the late 17th cent.

cochoa /'kəʊʃəʊə, kə'tʃəʊə/ ▶ noun an Asian thrush of evergreen forests, typically with predominantly purplish or green plumage and a pale blue crown.
● Genus *Cochoa*, family Turdidae: four species, including the **purple cochoa** (*C. purpurea*).
– ORIGIN modern Latin, from a Nepali name for the purple cochoa.

Cochran[1] /'kɒkrən/, Sir Charles Blake (1872–1951), English theatrical producer, noted for musical revues including Noël Coward's *Bitter Sweet* (1929) and *Cavalcade* (1931). He was also agent for Houdini.

Cochran[2] /'kɒkrən/, Eddie (1938–60), American rock-and-roll singer and songwriter; born *Edward Cochrane*. He was killed in a car crash during a British tour. Notable songs: 'Summertime Blues' (1958), 'Three Steps to Heaven' (1960).

Cochran[3] /'kɒkrən/, Jacqueline (1910–80), American aviator, the first woman to break the sound barrier (1953).

cock[1] ▶ noun 1 a male bird, especially of a domestic fowl.
■ [in combination] used in names of birds, especially game birds, e.g. **snowcock**, **watercock**. ■ Brit. a male lobster, crab, or salmon. ■ Brit. informal a friendly form of address among men: *please yourself, cock*.
2 vulgar slang a man's penis.
3 [mass noun] Brit. informal nonsense: *that's all a lot of cock*.
4 a firing lever in a gun which can be raised to be released by the trigger.

5 a stopcock.
▶ verb [with obj.] 1 tilt (something) in a particular direction: *she cocked her head slightly to one side*.
■ bend a (limb or joint) at an angle: *Madge threw herself into the armchair and cocked her legs over the side*. ■ (of a male dog) lift (a back leg) in order to urinate.
2 raise the cock of (a gun) in order to make it ready for firing.
– PHRASES **at full cock** (of a gun) with the cock lifted to the position at which the trigger will act. **cock one's ear** (of a dog) raise its ears to an erect position. ■ (of a person) listen attentively to or for something. **cock one's eye** glance in a quizzical or knowing manner with a raised eyebrow. **cock of the walk** someone who dominates others within a group. **cock a snook** see **SNOOK**[1].
– ORIGIN Old English *cocc*, from medieval Latin *coccus*; reinforced in Middle English by Old French *coq*.
▶ **cock something up** (or **cock up**) Brit. informal spoil or ruin something as a result of incompetence or inefficiency: *the party cocked up the Euro-elections*.

cock[2] ▶ noun dated a small pile of hay, straw, or other material, with vertical sides and a rounded top.
▶ verb [with obj.] archaic pile (hay, straw, or other material) into such a shape.
– ORIGIN late Middle English: perhaps of Scandinavian origin and related to Norwegian *kok* 'heap, lump', Danish *kok* 'haycock', and Swedish *koka* 'clod'.

cockabully /'kɒkəbʊli/ ▶ noun (pl. **-ies**) NZ a small blunt-nosed freshwater fish related to the sleepers.
● Genus *Gobiomorphus*, family Gobiidae (or Eleotridae).
– ORIGIN late 19th cent.: from Maori *kokopu*.

cockade /kɒ'keɪd/ ▶ noun a rosette or knot of ribbons worn in a hat as a badge of office or party, or as part of a livery.
– DERIVATIVES **cockaded** adjective.
– ORIGIN mid 17th cent.: from French *cocarde*, originally in *bonnet à la coquarde*, from the feminine of obsolete *coquard* 'saucy'.

cock-a-doodle-doo ▶ noun used to represent the sound made by a cock when it crows.

cock-a-hoop ▶ adjective [predic.] extremely and obviously pleased, especially about a triumph or success.
– ORIGIN mid 17th cent.: from the phrase *set cock a hoop*, of unknown origin, apparently denoting the action of turning on the tap and allowing liquor to flow (prior to a drinking session).

cock-a-leekie ▶ noun [mass noun] a soup traditionally made in Scotland with chicken and leeks.
– ORIGIN mid 18th cent.: from **COCK**[1] and **LEEK**.

cockalorum /ˌkɒkə'lɔːrəm/ ▶ noun (pl. **cockalorums**) informal, dated a self-important little man.
– ORIGIN early 18th cent.: an arbitrary formation from **COCK**[1].

cockamamie /'kɒkəˌmeɪmi/ (also **cockamamy**) ▶ adjective informal, chiefly N. Amer. ridiculous; implausible: *a cockamamie theory*.
– ORIGIN 1940s (originally denoting a design left by a transfer): probably an alteration of **DECALCOMANIA**.

cock and bull story ▶ noun informal a ridiculous and implausible story.

cockatiel /ˌkɒkə'tiːl/ ▶ noun a slender long-crested Australian parrot related to the cockatoos, with a mainly grey body, white shoulders, and a yellow and orange face. Also called **QUARRION** in Australia.
● *Nymphicus hollandicus*, family Cacatuidae (or Psittacidae).
– ORIGIN late 19th cent.: from Dutch *kaketielje*, probably a diminutive of *kaketoe* 'cockatoo'.

cockatoo /kɒkə'tuː/ ▶ noun 1 a parrot with an erectile crest, found in Australia, eastern Indonesia, and neighbouring islands.
● Family Cacatuidae (or Psittacidae): several genera and numerous species, e.g. the **sulphur-crested cockatoo** (*Cacatua galerita*).
2 Austral./NZ informal a small farmer. [ORIGIN: mid 19th cent.: originally with reference to tenant farmers brought from Sydney and settled in the Port Fairy district, from the name of Cockatoo Island (a former prison for convicts) in Sydney Harbour.]
3 Austral./NZ informal a lookout posted by those engaged in illegal activity. [ORIGIN: late 19th cent.: by association with the characteristic wariness of a cockatoo.]

– ORIGIN mid 17th cent.: from Dutch *kaketoe*, from Malay *kakatua*, the spelling influenced by **COCK**[1]. Senses 2 and 3 date from the 19th cent.

cockatrice /'kɒkətrʌɪs, -trɪs/ ▶ noun another term for **BASILISK** (in sense 1).
■ Heraldry a mythical animal depicted as a two-legged dragon (or wyvern) with a cock's head.
– ORIGIN late Middle English: from Old French *cocatris*, from Latin *calcatrix* 'tracker' (from *calcare* 'to tread or track'), translating Greek *ikhneumōn* (see **ICHNEUMON**).

cock-bead ▶ noun a projecting wooden moulding used to decorate furniture.
– DERIVATIVES **cock-beaded** adjective, **cock-beading** noun.

cockboat ▶ noun a small boat towed behind a larger vessel, especially along a coast or river.
– ORIGIN late Middle English: from obsolete *cock* 'small boat' (from Old French *cogue*, based on Latin *caudex, codex* 'block of wood') + **BOAT**.

cockchafer /'kɒkˌtʃeɪfə/ ▶ noun a large brown European beetle which flies at dusk and often crashes into lighted windows. The adults are damaging to foliage and flowers, and the larvae are a pest of cereal and grass roots. Also called **MAY BUG**.
● *Melolontha melolontha*, family Scarabaeidae.
– ORIGIN early 18th cent.: from **COCK**[1] (expressing size or vigour) + **CHAFER**.

Cockcroft, Sir John Douglas (1897–1967), English physicist. In 1932 he succeeded with E. T. S. Walton) in splitting the atom, ushering in the whole field of nuclear and particle physics. Nobel Prize for Physics (1951, shared with Walton).

cockcrow ▶ noun poetic/literary dawn.

cocked hat ▶ noun a brimless triangular hat pointed at the front, back, and top.
■ historical a hat with a wide brim permanently turned up towards the crown, such as a tricorne.
– PHRASES **knock something into a cocked hat** utterly defeat or outdo something.

cocker (also **cocker spaniel**) ▶ noun a small spaniel of a breed with a silky coat.
– ORIGIN early 19th cent.: from **COCK**[1] + **-ER**[1] (because the dog was bred to flush game birds such as woodcock, for shooting).

cockerel ▶ noun a young domestic cock.
– ORIGIN Middle English: diminutive of **COCK**[1].

Cockerell, Sir Christopher Sydney (1910–99), English engineer, the inventor of the hovercraft.

cockeye bob (also **cockeyed bob**) ▶ noun Austral./NZ informal a cyclone; a thunderstorm.
– ORIGIN late 19th cent.: probably an alteration of an Aboriginal word.

cock-eyed ▶ adjective informal crooked or askew; not level: *cock-eyed camera angles*.
■ absurd; impractical: *do you expect us to believe a cock-eyed story like that?* ■ drunk: *I got cock-eyed.* ■ (of a person or their eyes) having a squint.
– ORIGIN early 19th cent.: apparently from the verb **COCK**[1] and **EYE**. The sense 'drunk' (originally US) dates from the 1920s.

cockfighting ▶ noun [mass noun] the sport (illegal in the UK and some other countries) of setting two cocks to fight each other.
– DERIVATIVES **cockfight** noun.

cockle[1] ▶ noun 1 an edible burrowing bivalve mollusc with a strong ribbed shell.
● Genus *Cardium*, family Cardiidae.
2 (also **cockleshell**) poetic/literary a small shallow boat.
– PHRASES **warm the cockles of one's heart** give one a comforting feeling of pleasure or contentment.
– ORIGIN Middle English: from Old French *coquille* 'shell', based on Greek *konkhulion*, from *konkhē* 'conch'.

cockle[2] ▶ verb [no obj.] (of paper) bulge out in certain places so as to present a wrinkled or creased surface; pucker.
– ORIGIN mid 16th cent.: from French *coquiller* 'blister (bread in cooking)', from *coquille* 'shell' (see **COCKLE**[1]).

cocklebur ▶ noun a herbaceous plant of the daisy family, with broad leaves and burred fruits. It originated in tropical America but is now cosmopolitan. See also **CLOTBUR**.

● Genus *Xanthium*, family Compositae: two or three species, in particular *X. strumarium*.

– ORIGIN mid 19th cent.: from **COCKLE**[2] + **BUR**.

cockling ▸ noun [mass noun] Brit. the activity or occupation of gathering cockles.

– DERIVATIVES **cockler** noun.

cock loft ▸ noun a small loft or attic.

cockney /ˈkɒkni/ ▸ noun (pl. **-eys**) **1** a native of East London, traditionally one born within hearing of Bow Bells.
- ■ [mass noun] the dialect or accent typical of such people.
- **2** Austral. a young snapper fish (*Chrysophrys auratus*). [ORIGIN: late 19th cent.: of unknown origin.]
▸ adjective of or characteristic of cockneys or their dialect or accent: *cockney humour*.

– ORIGIN late Middle English (denoting a pampered child): origin uncertain; it is apparently not the same word as Middle English *cokeney* 'cock's egg', denoting a small misshapen egg (probably from **COCK**[1] + obsolete *ey* 'egg'). A later sense was 'a town-dweller regarded as affected or puny', from which the current sense arose in the early 17th cent.

cockneyism ▸ noun a feature or style of speech or idiom characteristic of cockneys.

cock-of-the-rock ▸ noun (pl. **cocks-of-the-rock**) a crested cotinga found in the tropical forests of South America. The male has brilliant orange or red plumage used in communal display.
- ● Genus *Rupicola*, family Cotingidae: two species.

cockpit ▸ noun **1** a compartment for the pilot, and sometimes also the crew, in an aircraft or spacecraft.
- ■ a similar compartment for the driver in a racing car. ■ a space for the helmsman in some small yachts.
- **2** a place where a battle or other conflict takes place.
- ■ a place where cockfights are held.

– ORIGIN late 16th cent. (in sense 2): from **COCK**[1] + **PIT**[1]. In the early 18th cent. the term was in nautical use, denoting an area in the aft lower deck of a man-of-war where the wounded were taken, later coming to mean 'the pit' or well in a sailing yacht from which it was steered'; hence the place housing the controls of other vehicles (sense 1, early 20th cent.).

cockroach /ˈkɒkrəʊtʃ/ ▸ noun a beetle-like insect with long antennae and legs, feeding by scavenging. Several tropical kinds have become established worldwide as pests in homes and catering establishments.
- ● Suborder Blattodea, order Dictyoptera: many genera and species, including the **common cockroach** (*Blatta orientalis*) and the **American cockroach** (*Periplaneta americana*); some, especially in the genus *Ectobius*, are small temperate species that live outdoors.

– ORIGIN early 17th cent. (as *cacaroch*): from Spanish *cucaracha*. The spelling change was due to association with **COCK**[1] and **ROACH**[1].

cockscomb ▸ noun **1** the crest or comb of a domestic cock.
- **2** a tropical plant with a crest or plume of tiny yellow, orange, or red flowers, widely grown as a pot plant.
- ● *Celosia cristata*, family Amaranthaceae.
- **3** an orchid related to the coralroots but with more colourful flowers, native to southern North America. Also called **CORALROOT**.
- ● Genus *Hexalectris*, family Orchidaceae.

cocksfoot ▸ noun chiefly Brit. a pasture grass with broad leaves and green or purplish flowering spikes.
- ● *Dactylis glomerata*, family Gramineae.

cockshy /ˈkɒkʃaɪ/ ▸ noun (pl. **-ies**) Brit. dated a target for throwing sticks or stones at as a game.
- ■ an act of throwing something at such a target. ■ figurative an object of ridicule or criticism.

– ORIGIN from the original use of a replica of a cockerel as a target.

cocksman ▸ noun (pl. **-men**) US vulgar slang a man who is reputed to be extremely virile or sexually accomplished.

– DERIVATIVES **cocksmanship** noun.

cock sparrow ▸ noun Brit. archaic a lively quarrelsome person.

cockspur ▸ noun **1** the spur on the leg of a cock.
- **2** any of a number of spiny plants, in particular (Austral.) a European plant of the daisy family with yellow thistle-like flower heads that has become naturalized in Australia.

● *Centaurea melitensis*, family Compositae.

cockspur thorn ▸ noun a North American hawthorn which is widely planted for its rich orange autumn foliage.
- ● *Crataegus crus-galli*, family Rosaceae.
- ■ any of a number of trees bearing long spiny thorns.

cocksucker ▸ noun vulgar slang a fellator.
- ■ chiefly US a generalized term of abuse.

cocksure ▸ adjective presumptuously or arrogantly confident.

– DERIVATIVES **cocksurely** adverb, **cocksureness** noun.

– ORIGIN early 16th cent.: from archaic *cock* (a euphemism for *God*) + **SURE**; later associated with **COCK**[1].

cocktail ▸ noun **1** an alcoholic drink consisting of a spirit or several spirits mixed with other ingredients, such as fruit juice, lemonade, or cream: [as modifier] *cocktail parties* | *a cocktail bar*.
- ■ a mixture of substances or factors, especially when dangerous or unpleasant in its effects: *financial pressure plus isolation can be a deadly cocktail for some people*.
- **2** a dish consisting of small pieces of food, typically served cold at the beginning of a meal as an hors d'oeuvre: *a prawn cocktail*.

– ORIGIN early 17th cent.: from **COCK**[1] + **TAIL**[1]. The original use was as an adjective describing a creature with a tail like that of a cock, specifically a horse with a docked tail; hence (because hunters and coach-horses were generally docked) a racehorse which was not a thoroughbred, having a cock-tailed horse in its pedigree (early 19th cent.). Sense 1 (originally US, also early 19th cent.) is perhaps analogous, from the idea of an adulterated spirit.

cocktail dress ▸ noun a smart dress suitable for formal social occasions.

cocktail stick ▸ noun Brit. a small pointed stick on which olives, cherries, or similar items of food may be served.

cock-teaser /ˈkɒktiːzə/ (also **cock-tease**) ▸ noun vulgar slang a woman who leads a man to the mistaken belief that she is likely to have sexual intercourse with him.

cock-up ▸ noun Brit. informal something done badly or inefficiently: *we've made a total cock-up of it*.

cocky[1] ▸ adjective (**cockier**, **cockiest**) conceited or arrogant, especially in a bold or cheeky way.

– DERIVATIVES **cockily** adverb, **cockiness** noun.

– ORIGIN mid 16th cent. (in the sense 'lecherous'): from **COCK**[1] + **-Y**[1].

cocky[2] ▸ noun (pl. **-ies**) Austral./NZ informal term for **COCKATOO** (in sense 2).

coco ▸ noun (pl. **-os**) **1** [usu. as modifier] coconut: *coco matting* | *coco palm*.
- **2** [mass noun] W. Indian the root of the taro.

– ORIGIN mid 16th cent. (originally denoting the nut): from Spanish and Portuguese, literally 'grinning face' (because of the appearance of the base of the coconut).

cocoa ▸ noun [mass noun] a powder made from roasted and ground cacao seeds.
- ■ a hot drink made from such a powder mixed with milk or water.

– ORIGIN early 18th cent. (denoting cacao seed): alteration of **CACAO**.

cocoa bean ▸ noun a cacao seed.

cocoa butter ▸ noun [mass noun] a fatty substance obtained from cocoa beans and used especially in the manufacture of confectionery and cosmetics.

cocobolo /ˌkəʊkə(ʊ)ˈbəʊləʊ/ ▸ noun (pl. **-os**) a tropical American tree with hard reddish timber that is used chiefly to make cutlery handles.
- ● *Dalbergia retusa*, family Leguminosae.

– ORIGIN mid 19th cent.: via Spanish from Arawak *kakabali*.

coco de mer /ˌkəʊkəʊdəˈmɛː/ ▸ noun a tall palm tree native to the Seychelles, having an immense nut in a hard woody shell which is the largest known seed. Also called **DOUBLE COCONUT**.
- ● *Lodoicea maldivica*, family Palmae.
- ■ the large nut of this plant.

– ORIGIN early 19th cent.: from French *coco-de-mer*, literally 'coco from the sea' (because the tree was first known from nuts found floating in the sea).

coconut (also **cocoanut**) ▸ noun **1** the large oval brown seed of a tropical palm, consisting of a hard

shell lined with edible white flesh and containing a clear liquid. It grows inside a woody husk, surrounded by fibre.
- ■ [mass noun] the flesh of a coconut, especially when used as food.
- **2** (also **coconut palm** or **tree**) the tall palm tree that yields this nut, which grows mainly by coastal beaches and has become naturalized throughout the tropics. Many tropical economies are dependent upon its products, which include copra and coir.
- ● *Cocos nucifera*, family Palmae.

coconut butter ▸ noun [mass noun] a solid fat obtained from the flesh of the coconut, and used in the manufacture of soap, candles, ointment, etc.

coconut crab ▸ noun another term for **ROBBER CRAB**.

– ORIGIN so named because it climbs trees to reach coconuts.

coconut ice ▸ noun [mass noun] Brit. a sweet made from sugar and desiccated coconut.

coconut matting ▸ noun [mass noun] matting made of fibre from coconut husks.

coconut milk ▸ noun [mass noun] the watery white liquid found inside a coconut.

coconut palm ▸ noun see **COCONUT** (sense 2).

coconut shy ▸ noun Brit. a fairground sideshow where balls are thrown at coconuts in an attempt to knock them off stands.

cocoon /kəˈkuːn/ ▸ noun a silky case spun by the larvae of many insects for protection as pupae.
- ■ a similar structure made by other animals. ■ a covering that prevents the corrosion of metal equipment. ■ something that envelops or surrounds, especially in a protective or comforting way: *a cocoon of bedclothes* | figurative *a warm cocoon of love*.
▸ verb [with obj.] (usu. **be cocooned**) envelop or surround in a protective or comforting way: *we began to feel cold even though we were cocooned in our sleeping bags*.
- ■ spray with a protective coating. ■ [no obj.] N. Amer. retreat from the stressful conditions of public life into the cosy private world of the family: *the movers and shakers of the eighties are now cocooning*.

– DERIVATIVES **cocooner** noun (only in the last sense of the verb).

– ORIGIN late 17th cent.: from French *cocon*, from medieval Provençal *coucoun* 'eggshell, cocoon', diminutive of *coca* 'shell'. The verb dates from the mid 19th cent.

Cocos Islands /ˈkəʊkəs/ a group of twenty-seven small coral islands in the Indian Ocean, administered as an external territory of Australia since 1955; pop. 603 (1990). The islands were discovered in 1609 by Captain William Keeling of the East India Company. Also called **KEELING ISLANDS**.

cocotte /kɒˈkɒt/ ▸ noun **1** (usu. **en cocotte** /ɒ̃ kɒˈkɒt/) a heatproof dish or small casserole in which individual portions of food can be both cooked and served. [ORIGIN: early 20th cent.: from French *cocasse*, from Latin *cucuma* 'cooking container'.]
- **2** dated a fashionable prostitute. [ORIGIN: mid 19th cent.: French, from a child's name for a hen.]

co-counselling ▸ noun [mass noun] a form of personal or psychological counselling in which two or more people alternate the roles of therapist and patient.

cocoyam /ˈkəʊkəʊjam/ ▸ noun (in West Africa) either of two plants of the arum family with edible corms, i.e. taro (also **old cocoyam**) and tannia (also **new cocoyam**).

– ORIGIN early 20th cent.: probably from sense 2 of **COCO** + **YAM**.

Cocteau /ˈkɒktəʊ/, Jean (1889–1963), French dramatist, novelist, and film director. His plays are noted for their striking blend of poetry, irony, and fantasy. Notable works: *La Machine infernale* (play, 1934), *La Belle et la bête* (film, 1946), and *Les Enfants terribles* (novel, 1929).

cocus wood /ˈkəʊkəs/ ▸ noun [mass noun] hard, heavy timber which blackens with age and is used for musical instruments.
- ● This timber is obtained from the Jamaican ebony (*Brya ebenus*, family Leguminosae).

– ORIGIN mid 17th cent.: *cocus*, of unknown origin.

COD ▸ abbreviation for ■ cash on delivery. ■ N. Amer. collect on delivery.

C

cod[1] (also **codfish**) ▶ **noun** (pl. same) a large marine fish with a small barbel on the chin.
• Family Gadidae (the **cod family**): many genera and species, in particular the North Atlantic *Gadus morhua*, of great commercial importance as a food fish and as a source of cod liver oil. The cod family also includes the haddock, ling, pollack, whiting, and other food fishes.
■ used in names of similar or related fishes, e.g. **rock cod, tomcod**.
– ORIGIN Middle English: of unknown origin; one suggestion is that the word is the same as Old English *cod(d)* 'bag', because of the fish's appearance.

cod[2] Brit. informal ▶ **adjective** [attrib.] not authentic; fake: *a cod Mittel-European accent.*
▶ **noun** a joke or hoax: *I suppose it could all be a cod.*
▶ **verb** (**codded, codding**) [with obj.] play a joke or trick on (someone): *he was definitely codding them.*
– ORIGIN late 19th cent. (as a verb): perhaps from slang *cod* 'a fool'.

cod[3] ▶ **noun** [mass noun] Brit. informal, dated nonsense.
– ORIGIN 1960s: abbreviation of **CODSWALLOP**.

coda /ˈkəʊdə/ ▶ **noun** Music the concluding passage of a piece or movement, typically forming an addition to the basic structure.
■ the concluding section of a dance, especially of a pas de deux or the finale of a ballet in which the dancers parade before the audience. ■ a concluding event, remark, or section: *his new novel is a kind of* **coda to** *his previous books.*
– ORIGIN mid 18th cent.: Italian, from Latin *cauda* 'tail'.

coddle ▶ **verb** [with obj.] **1** treat in an indulgent or overprotective way: *I was coddled and cosseted.*
2 cook (an egg) in water below boiling point.
– DERIVATIVES **coddler** noun.
– ORIGIN late 16th cent. (in the sense 'boil (fruit) gently)': origin uncertain; sense 1 is probably a dialect variant of obsolete *caudle* 'administer invalids' gruel', based on Latin *caldum* 'hot drink', from *calidus* 'warm'.

code ▶ **noun 1** a system of words, letters, figures, or symbols used to represent others, especially for the purposes of secrecy: *the Americans cracked their diplomatic code* | [mass noun] *sending messages* **in code**.
■ a word, phrase, or concept used to represent another in a euphemistic or indirect way: *researching 'the family' is usually a* **code for** *studying women.* ■ a series of letters, numbers, or symbols assigned to something for the purposes of classification or identification. ■ a sequence of numbers dialled to connect a telephone with the exchange of the telephone being called.
2 [mass noun] Computing program instructions: *segments of code* | *assembly code.*
3 a systematic collection of laws or statutes: *a revision of the penal code.*
■ a set of conventions governing behaviour or activity in a particular sphere: *a strict dress code.* ■ a set of moral principles and standards adhered to by a society, class, or individual: *a stern code of honour.*
▶ **verb 1** [with obj.] (usu. **be coded**) convert (the words of a message) into a particular code in order to convey a secret meaning: *only Mitch knew how to read the message—even the name was coded.*
■ express the meaning of (a statement or communication) in an indirect or euphemistic way: [as adj. **coded**] *the speech was a coded acknowledgement of the barely suppressed rage of Tory MPs.* ■ assign a code to (something) for purposes of classification, analysis, or identification: *she coded the samples and sent them down for dissection.*
2 [no obj.] (**code for**) Biochemistry be the genetic code for (an amino acid or protein): *genes that code for human growth hormone.*
■ be the genetic determiner of (a characteristic): *one pair of homologous chromosomes that codes for eye colour.*
– PHRASES **bring something up to code** N. Amer. renovate an old building or update its features in line with the latest building regulations.
– DERIVATIVES **coder** noun.
– ORIGIN Middle English: via Old French from Latin *codex, codic-* (see **CODEX**). The term originally denoted a systematic collection of statutes made by one of the later Roman emperors, particularly that of Justinian; compare with sense 3 (mid 18th cent.), the earliest modern sense.

codec /ˈkəʊdɛk/ ▶ **noun** Electronics a microchip that compresses data to enable faster transmission or decompresses received data.
– ORIGIN 1960s: blend of *coder* (see **CODE**) and **DECODER**.

codeine /ˈkəʊdiːn, -dɪiːn/ ▶ **noun** [mass noun] Medicine a sleep-inducing and analgesic drug derived from morphine.
• An alkaloid; chem. formula: $C_{18}H_{21}NO_3$.
– ORIGIN mid 19th cent.: from Greek *kōdeia* 'poppy head' + **-INE**[4].

code name ▶ **noun** a word used for secrecy or convenience instead of the usual name.
– DERIVATIVES **code-named** adjective.

codependency ▶ **noun** [mass noun] chiefly N. Amer. excessive emotional or psychological reliance on a partner, typically one with an illness or addiction who requires support.
– DERIVATIVES **codependence** noun, **codependent** adjective & noun.

code-sharing ▶ **noun** [mass noun] agreement between two or more airlines to list certain flights in a reservation system under each other's names.

co-determination ▶ **noun** [mass noun] cooperation between management and workers in decision-making, especially by the representation of workers on management boards.
– ORIGIN 1950s: from **CO-** 'together' + **DETERMINATION**.

codex /ˈkəʊdɛks/ ▶ **noun** (pl. **codices** /ˈkəʊdɪsiːz, ˈkɒd-/ or **codexes**) an ancient manuscript text in book form.
■ an official list of medicines, chemicals, etc.
– ORIGIN late 16th cent. (denoting a collection of statutes or set of rules): from Latin, literally 'block of wood', later denoting a block split into leaves or tablets for writing on, hence a book.

codfish ▶ **noun** (pl. same or **-fishes**) another term for **COD**[1].

codger ▶ **noun** informal an elderly man, especially one who is old-fashioned or eccentric: *old codgers harping on about yesteryear.*
– ORIGIN mid 18th cent.: perhaps a variant of *cadger* (see **CADGE**).

codices plural form of **CODEX**.

codicil /ˈkɒdɪsɪl, ˈkəʊ-/ ▶ **noun** an addition or supplement that explains, modifies, or revokes a will or part of one.
– DERIVATIVES **codicillary** /ˌkɒdɪˈsɪləri/ adjective.
– ORIGIN late Middle English: from Latin *codicillus*, diminutive of *codex, codic-* (see **CODEX**).

codicology /ˌkəʊdɪˈkɒlədʒi/ ▶ **noun** [mass noun] the study of manuscripts and their interrelationships.
– DERIVATIVES **codicological** adjective, **codicologically** adverb.
– ORIGIN 1950s: from French *codicologie*, from Latin *codex, codic-* (see **CODEX**).

codify /ˈkəʊdɪfʌɪ/ ▶ **verb** (**-ies, -ied**) [with obj.] arrange (laws or rules) into a systematic code.
■ arrange according to a plan or system: *this would codify existing intergovernmental cooperation on drugs.*
– DERIVATIVES **codification** noun, **codifier** noun.

coding ▶ **noun** [mass noun] the process of assigning a code to something for the purposes of classification or identification.
■ [count noun] a code assigned for such a purpose: *PAYE codings.* ■ Biochemistry the process of coding genetically for an amino acid, protein, or characteristic.

codling[1] ▶ **noun** an immature cod.

codling[2] ▶ **noun** any of several varieties of cooking apple having a long tapering shape.
– ORIGIN late Middle English: from Anglo-Norman French *quer de lion* 'lion-heart'.

codling moth (also **codlin moth**) ▶ **noun** a small greyish moth whose larva feeds on apples.
• *Cydia pomonella*, family Tortricidae.

codlings-and-cream ▶ **noun** Brit. the great hairy willowherb. See **WILLOWHERB**.

cod liver oil ▶ **noun** [mass noun] oil pressed from the liver of cod, which is rich in vitamins D and A.

codomain /ˈkəʊdə(ʊ)meɪn/ ▶ **noun** Mathematics a set that includes all the possible values of a given function.

codon /ˈkəʊdɒn/ ▶ **noun** Biochemistry a sequence of three nucleotides which together form a unit of genetic code in a DNA or RNA molecule.
– ORIGIN 1960s: from **CODE** + **-ON**.

codpiece ▶ **noun** a pouch, especially a conspicuous and decorative one, attached to a man's breeches or close-fitting hose to cover the genitals, worn in the 15th and 16th centuries.
– ORIGIN from earlier *cod* 'scrotum' (from Old English *codd* 'bag, pod') + **PIECE**.

co-driver ▶ **noun** a person who shares the driving of a vehicle with another, especially in a race or rally.

codswallop ▶ **noun** [mass noun] Brit. informal nonsense.
– ORIGIN 1960s: sometimes said to be named after Hiram *Codd*, who invented a bottle for fizzy drinks (1875); the derivation remains unconfirmed.

cod war ▶ **noun** informal any of several disputes between Britain and Iceland in the period 1958–76, concerning fishing rights in waters around Iceland.

Cody /ˈkəʊdi/, William Frederick, see **BUFFALO BILL**.

Coe, Sebastian, Baron Coe of Ranmore (b.1956), British middle-distance runner and Conservative politician, an Olympic gold medal winner in the 1,500 metres in 1980 and 1984.

coecilian ▶ **noun** variant spelling of **CAECILIAN**.

coed /ˈkəʊɛd, kəʊˈɛd/ informal ▶ **noun** N. Amer. dated a female student at a co-educational institution.
▶ **adjective** (of an institution or system) co-educational.
– ORIGIN late 19th cent.: abbreviation.

co-education ▶ **noun** [mass noun] the education of pupils of both sexes together.

co-educational ▶ **adjective** (of an institution or system) educating both sexes together.

coefficient /ˌkəʊɪˈfɪʃ(ə)nt/ ▶ **noun 1** Mathematics a numerical or constant quantity placed before and multiplying the variable in an algebraic expression (e.g. 4 in $4x^y$).
2 Physics a multiplier or factor that measures some property: *coefficients of elasticity* | *the drag coefficient.*
– ORIGIN mid 17th cent. (in the sense 'cooperating to produce a result'): from modern Latin *coefficient-*, from *com-* 'together' + *efficient-* 'accomplishing' (see **EFFICIENT**).

coelacanth /ˈsiːləkanθ/ ▶ **noun** a large bony marine fish with a three-lobed tail fin and fleshy pectoral fins, found chiefly around the Comoro Islands near Madagascar. It is thought to be related to the ancestors of land vertebrates and was known only from fossils until one was found alive in 1938.
• *Latimeria chalumnae*, family Latimeriidae (or Coelacanthidae), subclass Crossopterygii.
– ORIGIN mid 19th cent.: from modern Latin *Coelacanthus* (genus name), from Greek *koilos* 'hollow' + *akantha* 'spine' (because its fins have hollow spines).

-coele ▶ **combining form** variant spelling of **-CELE**.

coelenterate /siːˈlɛnt(ə)rət, -reɪt/ ▶ **noun** Zoology an aquatic invertebrate animal of a phylum that includes jellyfishes, corals, and sea anemones. They are distinguished by having a tube- or cup-shaped body and a single opening ringed with tentacles that typically bear stinging cells (nematocysts). Also called ***cnidarian***.
• Phylum Cnidaria (formerly Coelenterata): four classes.
– ORIGIN late 19th cent.: from modern Latin *Coelenterata*, from Greek *koilos* 'hollow' + *enteron* 'intestine'.

coeliac /ˈsiːlɪak/ (US **celiac**) ▶ **adjective 1** Anatomy of or relating to the abdomen.
2 Medicine of, relating to, or affected by coeliac disease: *a coeliac child.*
▶ **noun** a person with coeliac disease.
– ORIGIN mid 17th cent.: from Latin *coeliacus*, from Greek *koiliakos*, from *koilia* 'belly'.

coeliac disease ▶ **noun** [mass noun] a disease in which chronic failure to digest food is triggered by hypersensitivity of the small intestine to gluten.

coelom /ˈsiːləm/ ▶ **noun** (pl. **-oms** or **-omata** /-ˈləʊmətə/) Zoology the principal body cavity in most animals, located between the intestinal canal and the body wall.
– DERIVATIVES **coelomate** adjective & noun.
– ORIGIN late 19th cent.: from Greek *koilōma* 'cavity'.

coelostat /ˈsiːlə(ʊ)stat/ ▶ **noun** Astronomy an instrument with a rotating mirror that continuously reflects the light from the same area of sky, allowing the path of a celestial object to be monitored.
– ORIGIN late 19th cent.: formed irregularly from Latin *caelum* 'sky' + **-STAT**.

coelurosaur /sɪˈljʊərəsɔː/ ▶ **noun** a small slender bipedal carnivorous dinosaur with long forelimbs, from which the birds are believed to have evolved.
• Infraorder Coelurosauria, suborder Theropoda, order Saurischia: many genera.

- ORIGIN 1950s: from Greek *koilos* 'hollow' + *oura* 'tail' + *sauros* 'lizard'.

coenobite /ˈsiːnəbʌɪt/ (also **cenobite**) ▶ noun a member of a monastic community.
- DERIVATIVES **coenobitic** /-ˈbɪtɪk/ adjective, **coenobitical** adjective.
- ORIGIN late Middle English: from Old French *cenobite* or ecclesiastical Latin *coenobita*, via late Latin from Greek *koinobion* 'convent', from *koinos* 'common' + *bios* 'life'.

coenocyte /ˈsiːnəsʌɪt/ ▶ noun Botany a body of algal or fungal cytoplasm containing several nuclei, enclosed in a single membrane.
- DERIVATIVES **coenocytic** /-ˈsɪtɪk/ adjective.
- ORIGIN early 20th cent.: from Greek *koinos* 'common' + -CYTE.

coenzyme /ˈkəʊˌɛnzʌɪm/ ▶ noun Biochemistry a non-protein compound that is necessary for the functioning of an enzyme.

coenzyme A ▶ noun [mass noun] Biochemistry a coenzyme derived from pantothenic acid, important in respiration and many other biochemical reactions.
- ORIGIN *A* from *acylation* (see ACYLATE).

coenzyme Q ▶ noun another term for UBIQUINONE.
- ORIGIN *Q* from QUINONE.

coequal ▶ adjective equal with one another; having the same rank or importance: *coequal partners*.
▶ noun a person or thing equal with another.
- DERIVATIVES **coequality** /kəʊiːˈkwɒlɪti/ noun.
- ORIGIN late Middle English: from Latin *coaequalis* 'of the same age', from *co-* 'jointly' + *aequalis* (see EQUAL).

coerce /kəʊˈəːs/ ▶ verb [with obj.] persuade (an unwilling person) to do something by using force or threats: *he was coerced into giving evidence.*
■ obtain (something) by such means: *their confessions were allegedly coerced by torture.*
- DERIVATIVES **coercible** adjective, **coercion** noun.
- ORIGIN late Middle English: from Latin *coercere* 'restrain', from *co-* 'jointly, together' + *arcere* 'restrain'.

coercive ▶ adjective relating to or using force or threats: *coercive measures*.
- DERIVATIVES **coercively** adverb, **coerciveness** noun.

coercive force ▶ noun Physics another term for COERCIVITY.

coercivity /ˌkəʊəːˈsɪvɪti/ ▶ noun [mass noun] Physics the resistance of a magnetic material to changes in magnetization.
■ the field intensity necessary to demagnetize it when fully magnetized.

coeternal ▶ adjective equally eternal; existing with something else eternally: *creation is not coeternal with God*.
- DERIVATIVES **coeternally** adverb.

Coetzee /kʊtˈsɪə/, J. M. (b.1940), South African novelist; full name *John Maxwell Coetzee*. He won the Booker Prize with *Life and Times of Michael K* (1983) and *Disgrace* (1999), becoming the first author to win the prize twice.

coeval /kəʊˈiːv(ə)l/ ▶ adjective having the same age or date of origin; contemporary: *these lavas were coeval with the volcanic activity*.
▶ noun a person of roughly the same age as oneself; a contemporary.
- DERIVATIVES **coevality** noun, **coevally** adverb.
- ORIGIN early 17th cent. (as a noun): from late Latin *coaevus*, from *co-* 'jointly, in common' + Latin *aevum* 'age'.

co-evolution ▶ noun [mass noun] Biology the influence of closely associated species on each other in their evolution.
- DERIVATIVES **co-evolutionary** adjective, **co-evolve** verb.

coexist ▶ verb [no obj.] exist at the same time or in the same place: *traditional and modern values coexist in Africa*.
■ (of nations or peoples) exist in mutual tolerance despite different ideologies or interests: *the task of diplomacy was to help different states to coexist*.
- DERIVATIVES **coexistence** noun, **coexistent** adjective.
- ORIGIN mid 17th cent.: from late Latin *coexistere*, from *co-* 'together' + *existere* 'exist', from *ex-* 'out' + *sister* 'take a stand'.

coextensive ▶ adjective extending over the same space or time; corresponding exactly in extent.
■ (of a term) denoting the same referent as another.

cofactor ▶ noun 1 a contributory cause of a disease.
2 Biochemistry a substance (other than the substrate) whose presence is essential for the activity of an enzyme.
3 Mathematics the quantity obtained from a determinant or a square matrix by removal of the row and column containing a specified element.

C. of E. ▶ abbreviation for Church of England.

coffee ▶ noun [mass noun] 1 a hot drink made from the roasted and ground bean-like seeds of a tropical shrub: *a cup of coffee* | [as modifier] *a coffee pot*.
■ [count noun] a cup of this drink: *we went out for a coffee*.
■ these seeds raw, roasted and ground, or processed into a powder that dissolves in hot water: *a jar of instant coffee*. ■ a pale brown colour like that of coffee mixed with milk: *coffee-coloured skin*.
2 the shrub which yields these seeds, two of which are contained in each red berry. Native to the Old World tropics, most coffee is grown in tropical America.
● Genus *Coffea*, family Rubiaceae: several species. See also ARABICA and ROBUSTA.
- ORIGIN late 16th cent.: from Turkish *kahveh*, from Arabic *ḳahwa*, probably via Dutch *koffie*.

coffee bar ▶ noun a bar or cafe serving coffee and light refreshments from a counter.

coffee bean ▶ noun a bean-like seed of the coffee shrub.

coffee cake ▶ noun 1 N. Amer. a cake or sweet bread flavoured with cinnamon or topped or filled with cinnamon sugar, eaten usually with coffee.
2 a coffee-flavoured cake.

coffee cup ▶ noun a cup, typically a small one, in which coffee is served.

coffee essence ▶ noun [mass noun] Brit. a concentrated extract of coffee, usually also containing chicory.

coffee grinder ▶ noun a small machine for grinding roasted coffee beans.

coffee house ▶ noun a place serving coffee and other refreshments.

coffee mill ▶ noun another term for COFFEE GRINDER.

coffee morning ▶ noun Brit. a morning social gathering at which coffee is served, typically one held in someone's house to raise money for charity.

coffee shop ▶ noun a small, informal restaurant, found especially in a hotel or department store.

coffee table ▶ noun a small, low table.

coffee-table book ▶ noun a large, expensive, lavishly illustrated book, especially one regarded as intended only for casual reading.

coffer ▶ noun 1 a strongbox or small chest for holding valuables.
■ (coffers) the funds or financial reserves of a group or institution: *there is not enough money in the coffers to finance the reforms*.
2 a sunken panel in a ceiling.
- DERIVATIVES **coffered** adjective (in sense 2).
- ORIGIN Middle English: from Old French *coffre* 'chest', via Latin from Greek *kophinos* 'basket'.

cofferdam ▶ noun a watertight enclosure pumped dry to permit construction work below the waterline, as when building bridges or repairing a ship.

cofferer ▶ noun historical one of the treasurers of the royal household.

coffin ▶ noun a long, narrow box, typically of wood, in which a dead body is buried or cremated.
■ informal an old and unsafe aircraft or vessel.
▶ verb (**coffined**, **coffining**) [with obj.] put (a dead body) in a coffin.
- ORIGIN Middle English (in the general sense 'box, chest, casket'): from Old French *cofin* 'little basket or case', from Latin *cophinus* (see COFFER).

coffin bone ▶ noun the terminal bone in a horse's hoof (the distal phalanx).

coffin nail ▶ noun informal a cigarette.

coffle /ˈkɒf(ə)l/ ▶ noun a line of animals or slaves fastened or driven along together.
- ORIGIN mid 18th cent.: from Arabic *ḳāfila* 'caravan'.

coffret /ˈkɒfrɪt/ ▶ noun a small container, especially one holding a selection of cosmetics or toiletries offered for sale.
- ORIGIN late 15th cent.: from Old French, 'small chest', diminutive of *coffre* (see COFFER).

co-founder ▶ noun a joint founder.
- DERIVATIVES **co-found** verb.

cog[1] ▶ noun a wheel or bar with a series of projections on its edge, which transfers motion by engaging with projections on another wheel or bar: figurative *she was only a very small cog in a big machine*.
■ each of such a series of projections.
- DERIVATIVES **cogged** adjective.
- ORIGIN Middle English: probably of Scandinavian origin and related to Swedish *kugge* and Norwegian *kug*.

cog[2] ▶ noun a broadly built medieval ship with a rounded prow and stern.
- ORIGIN Middle English: related to Middle Dutch *kogge*, Old French *cogue*.

cogeneration ▶ noun [mass noun] the generation of electricity and useful heat jointly, especially the utilization of the steam left over from electricity generation for heating.

cogent /ˈkəʊdʒ(ə)nt/ ▶ adjective (of an argument or case) clear, logical, and convincing.
- DERIVATIVES **cogency** noun, **cogently** adverb.
- ORIGIN mid 17th cent.: from Latin *cogent-* 'compelling', from the verb *cogere*, from *co-* 'together' + *agere* 'drive'.

cogitable ▶ adjective rare able to be grasped by the mind; conceivable.
- ORIGIN late Middle English: from Latin *cogitabilis*, from the verb *cogitare* (see COGITATE).

cogitate /ˈkɒdʒɪteɪt/ ▶ verb [no obj.] formal or humorous think deeply about something; meditate or reflect: *he stroked his beard and retired to cogitate*.
- DERIVATIVES **cogitation** noun, **cogitative** adjective, **cogitator** noun.
- ORIGIN late 16th cent.: from Latin *cogitat-* 'considered', from the verb *cogitare*, from *co-* 'together' + *agitare* 'turn over, consider'.

cogito /ˈkɒɡɪtəʊ, -dʒɪ-/ ▶ noun (usu. **the cogito**) Philosophy the principle establishing the existence of a being from the fact of its thinking or awareness.
- ORIGIN Latin, 'I think', in Descartes's formula (1641) *cogito, ergo sum* 'I think therefore I am'.

cognac /ˈkɒnjak/ ▶ noun [mass noun] a high-quality brandy, properly that distilled in Cognac in western France.

cognate /ˈkɒɡneɪt/ ▶ adjective 1 Linguistics (of a word) having the same linguistic derivation as another; representing the same original word or root (e.g. English *father*, German *Vater*, Latin *pater*): *the term is obviously cognate with the Malay segan*.
2 formal related; connected: *cognate subjects such as physics and chemistry*.
■ related to or descended from a common ancestor. Compare with AGNATE.
▶ noun 1 Linguistics a cognate word.
2 Law a blood relative.
- DERIVATIVES **cognately** adverb, **cognateness** noun.
- ORIGIN early 17th cent.: from Latin *cognatus*, from *co-* 'together with' + *natus* 'born'.

cognate object ▶ noun Grammar a direct object that has the same linguistic derivation as the verb which governs it, as in 'sing a song', 'live a good life'.
■ a direct object that makes explicit a semantic concept that is already wholly present in the semantics of the verb which governs it, as in 'ask a question', 'eat some food'.

cognition /kɒɡˈnɪʃ(ə)n/ ▶ noun [mass noun] the mental action or process of acquiring knowledge and understanding through thought, experience, and the senses.
■ [count noun] a result of this; a perception, sensation, notion, or intuition.
- DERIVATIVES **cognitional** adjective.
- ORIGIN late Middle English: from Latin *cognitio(-)*, from *cognoscere* 'get to know'.

cognitive /ˈkɒɡnɪtɪv/ ▶ adjective of or relating to cognition.
- DERIVATIVES **cognitively** adverb.
- ORIGIN late 16th cent.: from medieval Latin *cognitivus*, from *cognit-* 'known', from the verb *cognoscere*.

cognitive dissonance ▶ noun [mass noun] Psychology the state of having inconsistent thoughts, beliefs, or attitudes, especially as relating to behavioural decisions and attitude change.

cognitive grammar ▶ noun [mass noun] a theory of grammar that seeks to characterize, in a psychologically realistic way, those structures and abilities that constitute a speaker's grasp of linguistic convention, and to relate them to other cognitive processes.

cognitive map ▶ noun a mental representation of one's physical environment.

cognitive science ▶ noun [mass noun] the study of thought, learning, and mental organization, which draws on aspects of psychology, linguistics, philosophy, and computer modelling.
– DERIVATIVES **cognitive scientist** noun.

cognitive therapy ▶ noun [mass noun] a type of psychotherapy in which negative patterns of thought about the self and the world are challenged in order to alter unwanted behaviour patterns or treat mood disorders such as depression.

cognitivist ▶ noun a person who believes or works in cognitive grammar.
▶ adjective of or relating to cognitive grammar.
– DERIVATIVES **cognitivism** noun.

cognizable /ˈkɒɡnɪzəb(ə)l/ (also **-isable**) ▶ adjective **1** formal perceptible; clearly identifiable. **2** Law within the jurisdiction of a court.
– ORIGIN late 17th cent.: from COGNIZANCE + -ABLE.

cognizance /ˈkɒ(ɡ)nɪz(ə)ns/ (also **cognisance**) ▶ noun **1** [mass noun] formal knowledge, awareness, or notice: *he was deputed to bring the affair to the cognizance of the court.*
■ Law the action of taking judicial notice. **2** Heraldry a distinctive device or mark, especially an emblem or badge formerly worn by retainers of a noble house.
– PHRASES **take cognizance of** formal attend to; take account of.
– ORIGIN Middle English *conisance*, from Old French *conoisance*, based on Latin *cognoscere* 'get to know'. The spelling with *g*, influenced by Latin, arose in the 15th cent. and gradually affected the pronunciation.

cognizant /ˈkɒ(ɡ)nɪz(ə)nt/ (also **cognisant**) ▶ adjective [predic.] formal having knowledge or being aware of: *statesmen must be cognizant of the political boundaries within which they work.*
– ORIGIN early 19th cent.: probably directly from COGNIZANCE.

cognize /kɒɡˈnʌɪz/ ▶ verb [with obj.] formal perceive, know, or become aware of.
– ORIGIN early 19th cent.: from COGNIZANCE, on the pattern of words such as *recognize*.

cognomen /kɒɡˈnəʊmən/ ▶ noun an extra personal name given to an ancient Roman citizen, functioning rather like a nickname and typically passed down from father to son:
■ a name; a nickname.
– ORIGIN Latin, from *co-* 'together with' + *gnomen*, *nomen* 'name'.

cognoscenti /ˌkɒnjəˈʃɛnti/ ▶ plural noun people who are considered to be especially well informed about a particular subject: *it was hailed by the cognoscenti as one of the best golf courses in Europe.*
– ORIGIN late 18th cent.: Italian, literally 'people who know', from Latin *cognoscent-* 'getting to know', from the verb *cognoscere*.

cog railway ▶ noun another term for RACK RAILWAY.

cogwheel ▶ noun another term for COG[1].

cohabit ▶ verb (**cohabited**, **cohabiting**) [no obj.] live together and have a sexual relationship without being married:
■ coexist: *animals that can cohabit with humans thrive.*
– DERIVATIVES **cohabitant** noun, **cohabitation** /-ˈteɪʃ(ə)n/ noun, **cohabitee** /-ˈtiː/ noun, **cohabiter** noun.
– ORIGIN mid 16th cent.: from Latin *cohabitare*, from *co-* 'together' + *habitare* 'dwell'.

cohen ▶ noun variant spelling of KOHEN.

cohere /kə(ʊ)ˈhɪə/ ▶ verb [no obj.] **1** be united; form a whole: *he made the series of fictions cohere into a convincing sequence.*
2 (of an argument or theory) be logically consistent: *this view does not cohere with their other beliefs.*
– ORIGIN mid 16th cent.: from Latin *cohaerere*, from *co-* 'together' + *haerere* 'to stick'.

coherent ▶ adjective **1** (of an argument, theory, or policy) logical and consistent: *they failed to develop a coherent economic strategy.*
■ (of a person) able to speak clearly and logically: *she was lucid and coherent and did not appear to be injured.*
2 united as or forming a whole: *divided into a number of geographically coherent kingdoms.*
3 Physics (of waves) having a constant phase relationship.
– DERIVATIVES **coherence** noun, **coherency** noun (rare), **coherently** adverb.
– ORIGIN mid 16th cent. (in the sense 'logically related to'): from Latin *cohaerent-* 'sticking together', from the verb *cohaerere* (see COHERE).

coherer /kə(ʊ)ˈhɪːrə/ ▶ noun an early form of radio detector, typically consisting of a glass tube loosely filled with metal filings whose bulk electrical resistance decreased in the presence of radio waves.

cohesion /kə(ʊ)ˈhiːʒ(ə)n/ ▶ noun [mass noun] the action or fact of forming a united whole: *the work at present lacks cohesion.*
■ Physics the sticking together of particles of the same substance.
– ORIGIN mid 17th cent.: from Latin *cohaes-* 'cleaved together', from the verb *cohaerere* (see COHERE), on the pattern of *adhesion*.

cohesive ▶ adjective characterized by or causing cohesion.
– DERIVATIVES **cohesively** adverb, **cohesiveness** noun.

Cohn /kəʊn/, Ferdinand Julius (1828–98), German botanist, a founder of bacteriology and the first to devise a systematic classification of bacteria into genera and species.

coho /ˈkəʊhəʊ/ (also **coho salmon** or **cohoe**) ▶ noun (pl. same, **-os**, or **-oes**) a deep-bodied North Pacific salmon with small black spots. Also called SILVER SALMON.
● *Oncorhynchus kisutch*, family Salmonidae.
– ORIGIN mid 19th cent.: probably from Salish.

cohort /ˈkəʊhɔːt/ ▶ noun **1** [treated as sing. or pl.] an ancient Roman military unit, comprising six centuries, equal to one tenth of a legion.
2 [treated as sing. or pl.] a group of people banded together or treated as a group: *a cohort of civil servants patiently drafting and redrafting legislation.*
■ a group of people with a common statistical characteristic: *the 1940–4 birth cohort of women.*
3 derogatory, chiefly N. Amer. a supporter or companion.
– ORIGIN late Middle English: from Old French *cohorte*, or from Latin *cohors*, *cohort-* 'yard, retinue'. Compare with COURT.

USAGE The earliest sense of **cohort** is 'a unit of men within the Roman army'. In the mid 20th century a new sense developed in the US, meaning 'a companion or colleague', as in *young Jack arrived with three of his cohorts*. Although this use is well established (it accounts for the majority of the total citations for this word in the Oxford Reading Programme), there are still some people who object to it on the grounds that **cohort** should only be used for groups of people (as in its first sense), never for individuals.

cohosh /kəˈhɒʃ/ ▶ noun either of two medicinal plants native to North America:
● (also **black cohosh**) a plant of the buttercup family, with small white flowers (*Cimicifuga racemosa*, family Ranunculaceae). ● (also **blue cohosh**) a plant of the barberry family (*Caulophyllum thalictroides*, family Berberidaceae).
– ORIGIN late 18th cent.: from Eastern Abnaki.

cohune /kəˈhuːn/ (also **cahoun**) ▶ noun a Central American palm which is a valuable source of oil.
● *Orbignya cohune*, family Palmae.
■ (also **cohune nut**) the oil-rich nut of this palm.
– ORIGIN mid 18th cent.: from Miskito.

COI ▶ abbreviation for (in the UK) Central Office of Information.

coif /kɔɪf/ ▶ noun **1** a woman's close-fitting cap, now only worn under a veil by nuns.
■ historical a protective metal skullcap worn under armour.
2 /also kwɑːf/ informal, chiefly N. Amer. short for COIFFURE.
▶ verb /kwɑːf, kwɒf/ (**coiffed**, **coiffing**; US also **coifed**, **coifing**) [with obj.] style or arrange (someone's hair), typically in an elaborate way.

■ style or arrange the hair of (someone).
– ORIGIN Middle English: from Old French *coife* 'headdress', from late Latin *cofia* 'helmet'.

coiffeur /kwaˈfəː, kwɒ-/ ▶ noun a hairdresser.
– ORIGIN mid 19th cent.: French, from *coiffer* 'arrange the hair', in Old French 'cover with a coif' (see COIF).

coiffeuse /kwaˈfəːz, kwɒ-/ ▶ noun a female hairdresser.

coiffure /kwaˈfjʊə, kwɒ-/ ▶ noun a person's hairstyle, typically an elaborate one.
– DERIVATIVES **coiffured** adjective.
– ORIGIN mid 17th cent.: French, from *coiffer* 'arrange the hair', in Old French 'cover with a coif' (see COIF).

coign /kɔɪn/ ▶ noun a projecting corner or angle of a wall or building.
– PHRASES **coign of vantage** a favourable position for observation or action.
– ORIGIN late Middle English: variant of COIN. The phrase *coign of vantage* was first used by Shakespeare (*Macbeth* I. iv. 7), and later popularized by Sir Walter Scott.

coil[1] ▶ noun a length of something wound or arranged in a joined sequence of concentric circles or rings: *a coil of rope.*
■ a single ring or loop in such a sequence: *the snake wrapped its coils around her.* ■ a roll of postage stamps, especially one for use in a vending machine. ■ a slow-burning spiral made with the dried paste of pyrethrum powder, which produces a smoke that inhibits mosquitoes from biting. ■ (often **the coil**) an intrauterine contraceptive device in the form of a coil. ■ an electrical device consisting of a length of wire arranged in a coil for converting the level of a voltage, producing a magnetic field, or adding inductance to a circuit: *a relay coil.* ■ such a device used for transmitting high voltage to the spark plugs of an internal-combustion engine.
▶ verb [with obj.] arrange or wind (something long and flexible) into a joined sequence of concentric circles or rings: *he began to coil up the heavy ropes* | *she coiled a lock of her hair around his finger.*
■ [no obj., with adverbial] move or twist into such an arrangement or shape: *smoke coiled lazily towards the ceiling.*
– ORIGIN early 16th cent. (as a verb): from Old French *coillir*, from Latin *colligere* 'gather together' (see COLLECT[1]).

coil[2] ▶ noun archaic or dialect a confusion or turmoil.
– PHRASES **shuffle off this mortal coil** chiefly humorous die. [ORIGIN: from Shakespeare's *Hamlet* (III. i. 67).]
– ORIGIN mid 16th cent.: of unknown origin.

coil spring ▶ noun a helical spring made from metal wire.

Coimbatore /ˌkɔɪmbəˈtɔː/ a city in the state of Tamil Nadu, in southern India; pop. 853,000 (1991).

Coimbra /kəʊˈɪmbrə, ˈkɔɪmbrə/ a university city in central Portugal; pop. 96,140 (1991).

coin ▶ noun a flat, typically round piece of metal with an official stamp, used as money.
■ [mass noun] money in the form of coins: *large amounts of coin and precious metal.* ■ (**coins**) one of the suits in some tarot packs, corresponding to pentacles in others.
▶ verb [with obj.] **1** make (coins) by stamping metal.
■ make (metal) into coins. ■ Brit. informal earn a lot of (money) quickly and easily: *the company was coining it at the rate of £90 a second.*
2 invent or devise (a new word or phrase): *he coined the term 'desktop publishing'.*
– PHRASES **the other side of the coin** the opposite or contrasting aspect of a matter. **pay someone back in their own coin** retaliate by similar behaviour. **to coin a phrase** said ironically when introducing a banal remark or cliché: *I had to find out the hard way—to coin a phrase.* ■ said when introducing a new expression or a variation on a familiar one.
– ORIGIN Middle English: from Old French *coin* 'wedge, corner, die', *coigner* 'to mint', from Latin *cuneus* 'wedge'. The original sense was 'cornerstone', later 'angle or wedge' (senses now spelled QUOIN); in late Middle English the term denoted a die for stamping money, or a piece of money produced by such a die.

coinage ▶ noun [mass noun] **1** coins collectively: *the volume of coinage in circulation.*
■ the action or process of producing coins from metal. ■ [count noun] a system or type of coins in use: *decimal coinage.*

2 the invention of a new word or phrase.
■[count noun] a newly invented word or phrase.
– ORIGIN late Middle English: from Old French *coigniage*, from *coignier* 'to mint' (see **COIN**).

coin box ▶ **noun** Brit. a public telephone operated by inserting coins.
■a receptacle for such coins.

coincide /ˌkəʊɪnˈsʌɪd/ ▶ **verb** [no obj.] occur at or during the same time: *publication is timed to* ***coincide with*** *a major exhibition* | *the two events coincided.*
■be present at the same place and at the same time: *on Friday afternoons we generally coincided.* ■ correspond in nature; tally: *the interests of employers and employees do not always coincide.* ■ correspond in position; meet or intersect: *the two long-distance walks briefly coincide here.* ■ be in agreement: *the members of the College* ***coincide in*** *this opinion.*
– ORIGIN early 18th cent. (in the sense 'occupy the same space'): from medieval Latin *coincidere*, from *co-* 'together with' + *incidere* 'fall upon or into'.

coincidence ▶ **noun** **1** a remarkable concurrence of events or circumstances without apparent causal connection: *it was a coincidence that she was wearing a jersey exactly like Laura's* | [mass noun] *they met* ***by coincidence***.
2 [mass noun] correspondence in nature or in time of occurrence: *the coincidence of interest between the mining companies and certain politicians.*
3 Physics the presence of ionizing particles or other objects in two or more detectors simultaneously, or of two or more signals simultaneously in a circuit.
– ORIGIN early 17th cent. (in the sense 'occupation of the same space'): from medieval Latin *coincidentia*, from *coincidere* 'coincide, agree' (see **COINCIDE**). Sense 3 dates from the 1930s.

coincident ▶ **adjective** occurring together in space or time: *the swinging sixties, a time* ***coincident with*** *the Club's finances stabilizing.*
■in agreement or harmony: *the stake of defence attorneys is not always* ***coincident with*** *that of their clients.*
– DERIVATIVES **coincidently** adverb.
– ORIGIN mid 16th cent.: from medieval Latin *coincident-* 'coinciding, agreeing', from the verb *coincidere* (see **COINCIDE**).

coincidental ▶ **adjective** **1** resulting from a coincidence; done or happening by chance: *any resemblance between their reports is purely coincidental* | *it cannot be* ***coincidental that*** *these years were a time of important new developments.*
2 happening or existing at the same time: *it's convenient that his plan is* ***coincidental with*** *the group's closure.*
– DERIVATIVES **coincidentally** adverb [sentence adverb] *coincidentally, we had both left our previous jobs on the same day.*

coiner ▶ **noun** **1** historical a person who coins money, in particular a maker of counterfeit coins.
2 a person who invents or devises a new word, sense, or phrase.

coin-op ▶ **noun** a machine which can be used only when coins are inserted.

Cointreau /ˈkwʌntrəʊ/ ▶ **noun** [mass noun] trademark a colourless orange-flavoured liqueur.
– ORIGIN named after the *Cointreau* family, liqueur producers based in Angers, France.

coir /ˈkɔɪə/ ▶ **noun** [mass noun] fibre from the outer husk of the coconut, used in potting compost and for making ropes and matting.
– ORIGIN late 16th cent.: from Malayalam *kayaṟu* 'cord, coir'.

coition /kəʊˈɪʃ(ə)n/ ▶ **noun** another term for **COITUS**.
– ORIGIN mid 16th cent. (in the sense 'meeting or uniting'): from Latin *coitio(n-)*, from the verb *coire*, from *co-* 'together' + *ire* 'go'.

coitus /ˈkəʊɪtəs/ ▶ **noun** [mass noun] formal sexual intercourse.
– DERIVATIVES **coital** adjective.
– ORIGIN mid 19th cent.: from Latin, from *coire* 'go together' (see **COITION**).

coitus interruptus /ˌɪntəˈrʌptəs/ ▶ **noun** [mass noun] sexual intercourse in which the penis is withdrawn before ejaculation.
– ORIGIN from **COITUS** + Latin *interruptus* 'interrupted'.

coitus reservatus /ˌrɛzəˈvɑːtəs/ ▶ **noun** [mass noun] the postponement or avoidance of ejaculation, to prolong sexual intercourse.
– ORIGIN from **COITUS** + Latin *reservatus* 'reserved, kept'.

cojones /kəˈhəʊneɪz/ ▶ **plural noun** informal, chiefly US a man's testicles.
■figurative courage; guts: *big-wave riders had to have more cojones than the average human being.*
– ORIGIN Spanish.

Coke ▶ **noun** trademark short for **COCA-COLA**.

coke[1] ▶ **noun** [mass noun] a solid fuel made by heating coal in the absence of air so that the volatile components are driven off.
■carbon residue left after the incomplete combustion of petrol or other fuels.
▶ **verb** [with obj.] [usu. as noun **coking**] convert (coal) into coke.
– ORIGIN late Middle English (in the sense 'charcoal'): of unknown origin. The current sense dates from the mid 17th cent.

coke[2] ▶ **noun** informal term for **COCAINE**.
– ORIGIN early 20th cent.: abbreviation.

Coke-bottle ▶ **noun** [as modifier] N. Amer. informal denoting very thick lenses for spectacles or spectacles with such lenses.

coking coal ▶ **noun** [mass noun] coal suitable for making into coke.

Col. ▶ **abbreviation for** ■ Colonel. ■ the Epistle to the Colossians (in biblical references).

col ▶ **noun** the lowest point of a ridge or saddle between two peaks, typically affording a pass from one side of a mountain range to another.
■Meteorology a region of slightly elevated pressure between two anticyclones.
– ORIGIN mid 19th cent.: from French, literally 'neck', from Latin *collum*.

col. ▶ **abbreviation for** column.

col- ▶ **prefix** variant spelling of **COM-** assimilated before *l* (as in *collocate, collude*).

COLA ▶ **abbreviation for** cost-of-living adjustment, an increase made to wages in line with inflation.

cola ▶ **noun** **1** [mass noun] a brown carbonated drink that is flavoured with an extract of cola nuts, or with a similar flavouring. [ORIGIN: shortening of **COCA-COLA**.]
2 (also **kola**) a small evergreen African tree which is cultivated in the tropics for its seeds (cola nuts). [ORIGIN: from Temne *k'ola* 'cola nut'.]
● Genus *Cola*, family Sterculiaceae: several species, in particular *C. acuminata*.

colander /ˈkʌləndə, ˈkɒl-/ ▶ **noun** a perforated bowl used to strain off liquid from food, especially after cooking.
– ORIGIN Middle English: based on Latin *colare* 'to strain'.

cola nut (also **kola nut**) ▶ **noun** the seed of the cola tree, which contains caffeine and is chewed or made into a drink.

co-latitude ▶ **noun** Astronomy the complement of the latitude; the difference between latitude and 90°.

Colbert /ˈkɒlbɛː, French kɔlbɛʀ/, Jean Baptiste (1619–83), French statesman, chief minister to Louis XIV 1665–83. He was responsible for reforming the country's finances and the navy, and for boosting industry and commerce.

colcannon /kɒlˈkanən/ ▶ **noun** [mass noun] an Irish and Scottish dish of cabbage and potatoes boiled and pounded.
– ORIGIN late 18th cent.: from **COLE**; the origin of the second element is uncertain but it is said that cannonballs were used to pound such vegetables as spinach.

Colchester /ˈkəʊltʃɪstə/ a town in Essex; pop. 82,000 (1981). It was a prominent town in Roman Britain, when it was known as Camulodunum.

colchicine /ˈkɒltʃɪsiːn, ˈkɒlk-/ ▶ **noun** [mass noun] Chemistry a yellow compound present in the corms of colchicums, used to relieve pain in cases of gout.
● An alkaloid; chem. formula: $C_{22}H_{25}NO_6$.

colchicum /ˈkɒltʃɪkəm, ˈkɒlk-/ ▶ **noun** (pl. **colchicums**) a plant of a genus that includes the autumn crocuses.
● Genus *Colchicum*, family Liliaceae.
■[mass noun] the dried corm or seed of meadow saffron, which has analgesic properties and is used medicinally, especially as a tincture.
– ORIGIN from Latin, from Greek *kolkhikon* 'of Colchis' (see **COLCHIS**), alluding to the skills as a poisoner of the sorceress Medea of Colchis in classical mythology.

Colchis /ˈkɒlkɪs/ an ancient region south of the Caucasus mountains at the eastern end of the Black Sea. In classical mythology it was the goal of Jason's expedition for the Golden Fleece. Greek name **KOLKHIS**.

cold ▶ **adjective** **1** of or at a low or relatively low temperature, especially when compared with the human body: *a freezing cold day* | *it's cold outside* | *a sharp, cold wind.*
■(of food or drink) served or consumed without being heated or after cooling: *a cold drink* | *serve hot or cold.* ■ (of a person) feeling uncomfortably cold: *she was cold, and I put some more wood on the fire.* ■ feeling or characterized by fear or horror: *he suddenly went cold with a dreadful certainty* | *a cold shiver of fear.* ■ [as complement] informal unconscious: *she was* ***out cold***. ■ dead: *lying cold and stiff in a coffin.*
2 lacking affection or warmth of feeling; unemotional: *how cold and calculating he was* | *cold black eyes* | *cold politeness.*
■not affected by emotion; objective: *cold statistics.* ■ sexually unresponsive; frigid. ■ depressing or dispiriting; not suggestive of warmth: *the cold, impersonal barrack-room* | *a cold light streamed through the window.* ■ (of a colour) containing pale blue or grey.
3 (of the scent or trail of a hunted person or animal) no longer fresh and easy to follow: *the trail went cold.*
■[predic.] (in children's games) far from finding or guessing what is sought.
4 [as complement] without preparation or rehearsal; unawares: *going into the test cold.*
■informal at one's mercy: *they had him cold.*
▶ **noun** **1** [mass noun] a low temperature, especially in the atmosphere; cold weather; a cold environment: *my teeth chattered with* ***the cold*** | *they nearly died of cold.*
2 a common infection in which the mucous membrane of the nose and throat becomes inflamed, typically causing running at the nose, sneezing, a sore throat, and other similar symptoms.
▶ **adverb** informal, chiefly US completely; entirely: *we stopped cold behind a turn in the staircase.*
– PHRASES **as cold as ice** (or **stone** or **the grave** etc.) very cold. **catch a cold** (also **catch cold**) become infected with a cold. ■ encounter trouble or difficulties. **cold comfort** poor or inadequate consolation: *another drop in the inflation rate was cold comfort for the 2.74 million jobless.* **cold feet** loss of nerve or confidence: *I began to* ***get cold feet***, *but the other two guys were totally positive.* **the cold light of day** the objective realities of a situation: ***in the cold light of day*** *it all seemed so ridiculous.* **the cold shoulder** a show of intentional unfriendliness; rejection: *the new England manager* ***gave him the cold shoulder***. **cold-shoulder someone** reject or be deliberately unfriendly to someone. **cold steel** weapons such as swords or knives collectively. **in cold blood** without feeling or mercy; ruthlessly: *the government forces killed them in cold blood.* **out in the cold** ignored; neglected: *the talks* ***left*** *the French* ***out in the cold***. **throw** (or **pour**) **cold water on** be discouraging or negative about.
– DERIVATIVES **coldish** adjective, **coldness** noun.
– ORIGIN Old English *cald*, of Germanic origin; related to Dutch *koud* and German *kalt*, also to Latin *gelu* 'frost'.

cold-blooded ▶ **adjective** **1** (of a kind of animal) having a body temperature varying with that of the environment; poikilothermic.
2 without emotion or pity; deliberately cruel or callous: *a cold-blooded murder.*
– DERIVATIVES **cold-bloodedly** adverb, **cold-bloodedness** noun.

cold-call ▶ **verb** [with obj.] make an unsolicited call on (someone), by telephone or in person, in an attempt to sell goods or services: [as noun **cold-calling**] *severe new regulations against cold-calling.*
▶ **noun** (**cold call**) an unsolicited call of this kind.

cold cash ▶ **noun** North American term for **HARD CASH**.

cold cathode ▶ **noun** Electronics a cathode that emits electrons without being heated.

cold chisel ▶ **noun** a chisel used for cutting metal.

cold cream ▶ **noun** [mass noun] a cosmetic preparation used for cleansing and softening the skin.

cold cuts ▶ **plural noun** slices of cold cooked meats.

cold dark matter ▶ **noun** see **DARK MATTER**.

cold deck ▶ noun **1** US informal a deck of cards which has been dishonestly arranged beforehand.
2 N. Amer. a pile of logs stored away from the immediate area where logging is taking place.

cold-drawn ▶ adjective (of metal) drawn out into a wire or bar while cold.
– DERIVATIVES **cold-drawing** noun.

cold frame ▶ noun a frame with a glass top in which small plants are grown and protected without artificial heat.

cold front ▶ noun Meteorology the boundary of an advancing mass of cold air, in particular the trailing edge of the warm sector of a low-pressure system.

cold fusion ▶ noun [mass noun] nuclear fusion occurring at or close to room temperature. Claims for its discovery in 1989 are generally held to have been mistaken.

cold-hearted ▶ adjective lacking affection or warmth; unfeeling.
– DERIVATIVES **cold-heartedly** adverb, **cold-heartedness** noun.

coldie ▶ noun (pl. **-ies**) Austral. informal a chilled can or bottle of beer.

Colditz /ˈkəʊldɪts, ˈkɒl-/ a medieval castle near Leipzig, used as a top-security camp for Allied prisoners in the Second World War.

cold light ▶ noun [mass noun] Physics light accompanied by little or no heat; luminescence.

coldly ▶ adverb without affection or warmth of feeling; unemotionally: *Doyle looked at her coldly* | [as submodifier] *a coldly contemptuous tone.*

cold-moulded ▶ adjective (of an object) moulded from a resin that hardens without being heated.
– DERIVATIVES **cold-moulding** noun.

cold-rolled ▶ adjective Metallurgy (of metal) having been rolled into sheets while cold, resulting in a smooth hard finish.
– DERIVATIVES **cold-rolling** noun.

cold-short ▶ adjective (of a metal) brittle in its cold state.
– ORIGIN early 17th cent.: from Swedish *kallskör*, from *kall* 'cold' + *skör* 'brittle', later associated with **SHORT** in the same sense.

cold snap ▶ noun a sudden brief spell of cold weather.

cold sore ▶ noun an inflamed blister in or near the mouth, caused by infection with the herpes simplex virus.

cold start ▶ noun an act of starting an internal-combustion engine or other machine at the ambient temperature.
▶ verb (**cold-start**) [with obj.] start (an engine or machine) at the ambient temperature.

cold storage ▶ noun [mass noun] the keeping of something in a refrigerator or other cold place for preservation.
■ figurative the temporary postponement of something: *the project went into cold storage.*

cold store ▶ noun a large refrigerated room for preserving food stocks at very low temperatures.

cold sweat ▶ noun a state of sweating induced by fear, nervousness, or illness: *the very thought of being alone brought her out in a cold sweat.*

cold table ▶ noun Brit. a selection of dishes of cold food in a restaurant or at a formal meal.

cold turkey informal ▶ noun [mass noun] the abrupt and complete cessation of taking a drug to which one is addicted: *I had to go cold turkey.*
■ the symptoms caused by this: *suddenly stopping the drug may result in cold turkey.*
▶ adverb chiefly N. Amer. in a sudden and abrupt manner: *many banks have cut commercial builders off cold turkey.*

cold war ▶ noun (**the cold war**) a state of political hostility existing between the Soviet bloc countries and the Western powers after the Second World War, characterized by threats, violent propaganda, subversive activities, and other measures short of open warfare. It ended in 1990.

cold wave ▶ noun **1** a spell of cold weather over a wide area.
2 a kind of permanent wave for the hair created by applying chemicals at room temperature.

cold-weld ▶ verb [with obj.] join (a piece of metal) to another without the use of heat, by forcing them together so hard that the surface oxide films are disrupted and adhesion occurs.

cold-work ▶ verb [with obj.] shape (metal) while it is cold.
▶ noun (**cold work**) [mass noun] the shaping of metal while it is cold.

Cole, Nat King (1919–65), American singer and pianist; born *Nathaniel Adams Coles*. He became the first black man to have his own radio (1948–9) and television (1956–7) series. Notable songs: 'Mona Lisa' (1950), 'Ramblin' Rose' (1962).

cole ▶ noun chiefly archaic a brassica, especially cabbage, kale, or rape.
– ORIGIN Old English *cāwel*, *caul*, related to Dutch *kool* and German *Kohl*, from Latin *caulis* 'stem, cabbage'; reinforced in Middle English by forms from Old Norse *kál*. Compare with **KALE**.

colectomy /kəˈ(ʊ)lɛktəmi/ ▶ noun (pl. **-ies**) [mass noun] surgical removal of all or part of the colon.

Coleman, Ornette (b.1930), American jazz saxophonist, trumpeter, violinist, and composer, whose music is noted for its lack of harmony and chordal structure.

colemanite /ˈkəʊlmənʌɪt/ ▶ noun [mass noun] a white crystalline mineral, typically occurring as glassy prisms, consisting of hydrated calcium borate.
– ORIGIN named after William T. *Coleman* (1824–93) + **-ITE**[1].

Coleman lantern (also **Coleman lamp**) ▶ noun N. Amer. trademark a type of bright gasoline lamp used by campers.

Coleoptera /ˌkɒlɪˈɒpt(ə)rə/ Entomology an order of insects that comprises the beetles (including weevils), forming the largest order of animals on the earth.
■ [as plural noun **coleoptera**] insects of this order; beetles.
– DERIVATIVES **coleopteran** noun & adjective, **coleopterous** adjective.
– ORIGIN modern Latin (plural), from Greek *koleopteros*, from *koleos* 'sheath' + *pteron* 'wing'.

coleopterist /ˌkɒlɪˈɒptərɪst/ ▶ noun a person who studies or collects beetles.
– ORIGIN mid 19th cent.: from **COLEOPTERA** + **-IST**.

coleoptile /ˌkɒlɪˈɒptʌɪl/ ▶ noun Botany a sheath protecting a young shoot tip in a grass or cereal.
– ORIGIN mid 19th cent.: from Greek *koleon* 'sheath' + *ptilon* 'feather'.

coleorhiza /ˌkɒlɪə(ʊ)ˈrʌɪzə/ ▶ noun (pl. **coleorhizae** /-ˈrʌɪziː/) Botany a sheath protecting the root of a germinating grass or cereal grain.
– ORIGIN mid 19th cent.: from *koleos* 'sheath' + *rhiza* 'root'.

Coleraine /kəʊlˈreɪn/ a town in the north of Northern Ireland, on the River Bann in County Londonderry; pop. 16,000 (1981).

Coleridge /ˈkəʊlərɪdʒ/, Samuel Taylor (1772–1834), English poet, critic, and philosopher. His *Lyrical Ballads* (1798), written with William Wordsworth, marked the start of English romanticism and included 'The Rime of the Ancient Mariner'. Other notable poems: 'Christabel' and 'Kubla Khan' (both 1816).

coleseed ▶ noun old-fashioned term for **RAPE**[2].
– ORIGIN late 17th cent.: from Dutch *koolzaad* 'cabbage or rape seed'.

coleslaw ▶ noun [mass noun] sliced raw cabbage mixed with mayonnaise and other vegetables, eaten as a salad dish.
– ORIGIN late 18th cent. (originally US): from Dutch *koolsla*, from *kool* 'cabbage' + *sla* (see **SLAW**).

cole tit ▶ noun variant spelling of **COAL TIT**.

Colette /kɒˈlɛt/ (1873–1954), French novelist; born *Sidonie Gabrielle Claudine*. Notable novels *Chéri* (1920) and *La Fin de Chéri* (1926).

coleus /ˈkəʊlɪəs/ ▶ noun a tropical SE Asian plant of the mint family, having brightly coloured variegated leaves and popular as a house plant.
● Genus *Solenostemon* (formerly *Coleus*), family Labiatae.
– ORIGIN modern Latin, from Greek *koleos* 'sheath' (because of the way the stamens are joined together, resembling a sheath).

colewort /ˈkəʊlwəːt/ ▶ noun chiefly archaic another term for **COLE**.

coley /ˈkəʊli/ ▶ noun (pl. **-eys**) another term for **SAITHE**.
– ORIGIN 1960s: perhaps from **COALFISH**.

colic ▶ noun [mass noun] severe, often fluctuating pain in the abdomen caused by wind or obstruction in the intestines and suffered especially by babies.
– DERIVATIVES **colicky** adjective.
– ORIGIN late Middle English: from Old French *colique*, from late Latin *colicus*, from *colon* (see **COLON**[2]).

colicin /ˈkɒlɪsɪn/ ▶ noun Biology a bacteriocin produced by a coliform bacterium.
– ORIGIN 1940s: from French *colicine* (from *coli*, denoting a bacterium) + **-IN**[1].

colic root ▶ noun a North American plant of the lily family, with a rosette of leaves and a spike of small goblet-shaped white or cream flowers. It was formerly used in the treatment of colic.
● *Aletris farinosa*, family Liliaceae.

coliform /ˈkɒlɪfɔːm/ ▶ adjective Biology belonging to a group of rod-shaped bacteria typified by *E. coli*.
– ORIGIN early 20th cent.: from modern Latin *coli*, specific epithet in the sense 'of the colon' + **-IFORM**.

Colima /kɒˈliːmə/ **1** a state of SW Mexico, on the Pacific coast.
2 the capital city of this state; pop. 58,000 (est. 1984).

coliseum /ˌkɒlɪˈsiːəm/ (also **colosseum**) ▶ noun [in names] a large theatre, cinema, or stadium: *the London Coliseum.*
– ORIGIN late 19th cent.: from medieval Latin, alteration of Latin *colosseum* (see **COLOSSEUM**).

colitis /kəˈlʌɪtɪs/ ▶ noun [mass noun] Medicine inflammation of the lining of the colon.

Coll an island in the Inner Hebrides, to the west of the isle of Mull.

Coll. abbreviation for ■ Collected or Collection (used in written references to published works or sources: *source: Suss. Arch. Coll. xvii, 124.* ■ College.

collaborate /kəˈlabəreɪt/ ▶ verb [no obj.] work jointly on an activity, especially to produce or create something: *he collaborated with a distinguished painter on the designs.*
■ cooperate traitorously with an enemy: *during the last war they collaborated with the Nazis.*
– DERIVATIVES **collaborator** noun.
– ORIGIN late 19th cent.: from Latin *collaborat-* 'worked with', from the verb *collaborare*, from *col-* 'together' + *laborare* 'to work'.

collaboration ▶ noun [mass noun] **1** the action of working with someone to produce or create something: *he wrote on art and architecture in collaboration with John Betjeman.*
■ [count noun] something produced or created in this way: *his recent opera was a collaboration with Lessing.*
2 traitorous cooperation with an enemy: *he faces charges of collaboration.*
– DERIVATIVES **collaborationist** noun & adjective (in sense 2).
– ORIGIN mid 19th cent.: from Latin *collaboratio(n-)*, from *collaborare* 'work together'.

collaborative ▶ adjective produced or conducted by two or more parties working together: *collaborative research.*
– DERIVATIVES **collaboratively** adverb.

collage /ˈkɒlɑːʒ, kəˈlɑːʒ/ ▶ noun [mass noun] a form of art in which various materials such as photographs and pieces of paper or fabric are arranged and stuck to a backing.
■ [count noun] a composition made in this way. ■ [count noun] a combination or collection of various things.
– DERIVATIVES **collagist** noun.
– ORIGIN early 20th cent.: from French, literally 'gluing'.

collagen /ˈkɒlədʒ(ə)n/ ▶ noun [mass noun] Biochemistry the main structural protein found in animal connective tissue, yielding gelatin when boiled.
– ORIGIN mid 19th cent.: from French *collagène*, from Greek *kolla* 'glue' + French *-gène* (see **-GEN**).

collapsar /kəˈlapsɑː/ ▶ noun Astronomy an old star that has collapsed under its own gravity to form a white dwarf, neutron star, or black hole.
– ORIGIN late 20th cent.: from **COLLAPSE**, on the pattern of words such as *pulsar*.

collapse ▶ verb [no obj.] **1** (of a structure) fall down or in; give way: *the roof collapsed on top of me.*
■ [with obj.] cause (something) to fall in or give way: *it feels as if the slightest pressure would collapse it* | figurative *many people tend to collapse the distinction between the two concepts.* ■ (of a lung or blood vessel) fall inwards and become flat and empty: [as adj. **collapsed**] *a collapsed lung.* ■ [with obj.] cause (a lung or blood vessel)

to do this. ▪ fold or be foldable into a small space: [no obj.] *some cots collapse down to fit into a bag or holdall.*
2 (of a person) fall down and become unconscious, typically through illness or injury: *he collapsed from loss of blood.*
▪informal sit or lie down as a result of tiredness or prolonged exertion: *exhausted, he collapsed on the bed.*
3 (of an institution or undertaking) fail suddenly and completely: *in the face of such resolve his opposition finally collapsed.*
▪(of a price or currency) drop suddenly in value.
▶**noun** an instance of a structure falling down or in: *the collapse of a railway bridge* | [mass noun] *the church roof is in danger of collapse.*
▪a sudden failure of an institution or undertaking: *the collapse of communism.* ▪a physical or mental breakdown: *he suffered a collapse from overwork* | [mass noun] *she's lying there in a state of collapse.*
– ORIGIN early 17th cent. (as *collapsed*): from medical Latin *collapsus*, past participle of *collabi*, from *col-* 'together' + *labi* 'to slip'.

collapsible ▶**adjective** (of an object) able to be folded into a small space: *a collapsible bed.*
– DERIVATIVES **collapsibility** noun.

collar ▶**noun 1** a band of material around the neck of a shirt or other garment, either upright or turned over and generally an integral part of the garment.
▪a band put around the neck of a domestic animal.
2 a restraining or connecting band, ring, or pipe in machinery.
3 Brit. a piece of meat rolled up and tied.
▪a cut of bacon taken from the neck of a pig.
4 the part of a plant where the stem joins the roots.
▶**verb** [with obj.] informal seize, grasp, or apprehend (someone): *police collared the culprit.*
▪accost (someone): *he collared a departing guest for some last words.* ▪ take (something), especially illicitly: *he collared a couple of samosas.*
– DERIVATIVES **collared** adjective [in combination] *a fur-collared jacket*, **collarless** adjective.
– ORIGIN Middle English: from Old French *colier*, from Latin *collare* 'band for the neck, collar', from *collum* 'neck'.

collar beam ▶**noun** a horizontal piece of squared timber connecting two rafters and forming with them an A-shaped roof truss.

collarbone ▶**noun** either of the pair of bones joining the breastbone to the shoulder blades. Also called **CLAVICLE**.

collard /ˈkɒlɑːd/ (also **collards** or **collard greens**) ▶**noun** chiefly dialect or US a cabbage of a variety that does not develop a heart.
– ORIGIN mid 18th cent.: reduced form of *colewort*, in the same sense, from **COLE** + **WORT**.

collared dove ▶**noun** an Old World dove related to the turtle dove, with buff, grey, or brown plumage and a narrow black band around the back of the neck.
• Genus *Streptopelia*, family Columbidae: several species, in particular the sandy grey *S. decaocto*, which has spread from Asia to Europe in recent years.

collared lizard ▶**noun** a lizard which is typically marked with spots and bands and has a distinctive black-and-white collar. It is found in dry rocky areas in the southern US and Mexico.
• *Crotaphytus collaris*, family Iguanidae.

collar stud ▶**noun** a stud used to fasten a detachable collar to a shirt.

collate /kɒˈleɪt/ ▶**verb** [with obj.] **1** collect and combine (texts, information, or sets of figures).
▪compare and analyse (two or more sources of information): *these accounts he* **collated with** *his own experience.* ▪ Printing verify the order of (sheets of a book) by their signatures.
2 appoint (a clergyman) to a benefice.
– DERIVATIVES **collator** noun.
– ORIGIN mid 16th cent. (in the sense 'confer (a benefice) upon'): from Latin *collat-* 'brought together', from the verb *conferre* (see **CONFER**).

collateral /kɒˈlat(ə)r(ə)l/ ▶**noun 1** [mass noun] something pledged as security for repayment of a loan, to be forfeited in the event of a default.
2 a person having the same descent as another but by a different line.
▶**adjective 1** descended from the same stock but by a different line: *a collateral descendant of Robert Burns.*
2 additional but subordinate; secondary: *the collateral meanings of a word.*
▪situated side by side; parallel: *collateral veins.*
– DERIVATIVES **collaterality** noun, **collaterally** adverb.
– ORIGIN late Middle English (as an adjective): from medieval Latin *collateralis*, from *col-* 'together with' + *lateralis* (from *latus, later-* 'side'). Sense 1 (originally US) is from the phrase *collateral security*, denoting something pledged in addition to the main obligation of a contract.

collateral contract ▶**noun** Law a subsidiary contract which induces a person to enter into a main contract or which depends upon the main contract for its existence.

collateral damage ▶**noun** [mass noun] used euphemistically to refer to inadvertent casualties and destruction in civilian areas in the course of military operations.

collateralize (also **-ise**) ▶**verb** [with obj.] provide something as collateral for (a loan): *these loans are collateralized by property.*

collation /kəˈleɪʃ(ə)n/ ▶**noun 1** [mass noun] the action of collating something: *data management and collation.*
2 a light informal meal.
▪(in the Roman Catholic Church) a light meal allowed during a fast.
– ORIGIN Middle English: via Old French from Latin *collatio(n-)*, from *conferre* (see **CONFER**). Originally (in the plural) the term denoted John Cassian's *Collationes Patrum in Scetica Eremo Commorantium* 'Conferences of, or with, the Egyptian Hermits' (AD 415–20), from which a reading would be given in Benedictine communities prior to a light meal (see sense 2).

colleague ▶**noun** a person with whom one works, especially in a profession or business.
– ORIGIN early 16th cent.: from French *collègue*, from Latin *collega* 'partner in office', from *col-* 'together with' + *legare* 'depute'.

collect[1] /kəˈlɛkt/ ▶**verb** [with obj.] **1** bring or gather together (things, typically when scattered or widespread): *he went round the office collecting old coffee cups* | *he* **collected up** *all his clothing.*
▪accumulate and store over a period of time: *collect rainwater to use on the garden.* ▪ systematically seek and acquire (items of a particular kind) as a hobby: *I've started collecting stamps.* ▪ [no obj.] come together and form a group or mass: *worshippers* **collected together** *in centres* | *dust and dirt collect so quickly.*
2 call for and take away; fetch: *the children were collected from school.*
▪go somewhere and accept or receive (something), especially as a right or due: *she came to Oxford to collect her honorary degree.* ▪ solicit and receive (donations), especially for charity: *collecting money for the war effort* | [no obj.] *I* **collect for** *Oxfam.* ▪ [no obj.] informal receive money that is due; be paid: *he'd come to collect.*
3 (**collect oneself**) regain control of oneself, typically after a shock.
▪bring together and concentrate (one's thoughts).
4 archaic conclude; infer: [with clause] *by all best conjectures, I collect Thou art to be my fatal enemy.*
5 cause (a horse) to bring its hind legs further forward as it moves, thereby shortening the stride and increasing balance and impulsion.
6 Austral./NZ informal collide with: *he lost control of the truck and collected two cats and a cow.*
▶**adverb** & **adjective** N. Amer. (with reference to a telephone call) to be paid for by the person receiving it: [as adv.] *I called my mother collect* | [as adj.] *a collect call.*
▶**noun** Austral./NZ informal a winning bet.
– ORIGIN late Middle English: from Old French *collecter* or medieval Latin *collectare*, from Latin *collect-* 'gathered together', from the verb *colligere*, from *col-* 'together' + *legere* 'choose or collect'.

collect[2] /ˈkɒlɛkt, -lɪkt/ ▶**noun** (in church use) a short prayer, especially one assigned to a particular day or season.
– ORIGIN Middle English: from Old French *collecte*, from Latin *collecta* 'gathering', feminine past participle of *colligere* 'gather together' (see **COLLECT**[1]).

collectable /kəˈlɛktəb(ə)l/ (also **collectible**) ▶**adjective 1** (of an item) worth collecting; of interest to a collector.
2 able to be collected: *a hire car, collectable on your arrival.*
▶**noun** (usu. **collectables**) an item valued and sought by collectors.
– DERIVATIVES **collectability** /-ˈbɪlɪti/ noun.

collectanea /kɒlɛkˈtɑːnɪə, -ˈteɪn-/ ▶**plural noun** [also treated as sing.] passages, remarks, and other pieces of text collected from various sources.
– ORIGIN mid 17th cent.: Latin, neuter plural of *collectaneus* 'gathered together', used as an adjective in Caesar's *Dicta collectanea* and as a noun in Solinus' *Collectanea*.

collected ▶**adjective 1** (of a person) not perturbed or distracted: *outwardly they are cool, calm, and collected.*
2 [attrib.] (of individual works) brought together in one volume or edition: *Lenin's collected works.*
▪(of a volume or edition) containing all the works of a particular person or category.
3 (of a horse) moving with a shortened stride and with its hind legs correctly placed to achieve balance and impulsion.
– DERIVATIVES **collectedly** adverb (only in sense 1).

collection ▶**noun 1** [mass noun] the action or process of collecting someone or something: *the collection and recycling of paper* | *tax collection* | *she left the envelope in the office* **for collection**.
▪[count noun] a regular removal of mail for dispatch or of refuse for disposal. ▪ [count noun] an instance of collecting money in a church service or for a charitable cause. ▪ [count noun] a sum collected in this way.
2 a group of things or people: *a rambling* **collection of** *houses.*
▪an assembly of items such as works of art, pieces of writing, or natural objects, especially one systematically ordered: *a record collection.* ▪ a book or recording containing various texts, poems, songs, etc.: *a collection of essays.* ▪ a range of new clothes produced by a fashion house: *a preview of their autumn collection.*
3 (**collections**) Brit. college examinations held at the beginning or end of a term, especially at Oxford University.
– ORIGIN late Middle English: via Old French from Latin *collectio(n-)*, from *colligere* 'gather together' (see **COLLECT**[1]).

collective ▶**adjective** done by people acting as a group: *a collective protest.*
▪belonging or relating to all the members of a group: *ministers who share collective responsibility.* ▪ (especially of feelings or memories) common to the members of a group: *the collective wrath of the villagers.* ▪ taken as a whole; aggregate: *the collective power of the workforce.*
▶**noun** a cooperative enterprise.
▪a collective farm.
– DERIVATIVES **collectively** adverb, **collectiveness** noun, **collectivity** noun.
– ORIGIN late Middle English (in the sense 'representing many individuals'): from Old French *collectif, -ive* or Latin *collectivus*, from *collect-* 'gathered together', from the verb *colligere* (see **COLLECT**[1]).

collective bargaining ▶**noun** [mass noun] negotiation of wages and other conditions of employment by an organized body of employees.

collective farm ▶**noun** a jointly operated amalgamation of several smallholdings, especially one owned by the state.

collective memory ▶**noun** [mass noun] the memory of a group of people, typically passed from one generation to the next.

collective noun ▶**noun** Grammar a count noun that denotes a group of individuals (e.g. *assembly, family, crew*).

> **USAGE** A **collective noun** can be used with either a singular verb (*my family* **was** *always hard-working*) or a plural verb (*his family* **were** *disappointed in him*). Generally speaking, in Britain it is more usual for collective nouns to be followed by a plural verb while in the US the opposite is true. Notice that, if the verb is singular, any following pronouns must be too: *the government* **is** *prepared to act, but not until* **it** *knows the outcome of the latest talks* (not … *until* **they** *know the outcome* …).

collective ownership ▶**noun** [mass noun] ownership of something, typically land or industrial assets, by all members of a group for the mutual benefit of all.

collective security ▶**noun** [mass noun] the cooperation of several countries in an alliance to strengthen the security of each.

collective unconscious ▶**noun** (in Jungian psychology) the part of the unconscious mind which is derived from ancestral memory and experience and is common to all humankind, as distinct from the individual's unconscious.

collectivism ▶ **noun** [mass noun] the practice or principle of giving a group priority over each individual in it.
■ the theory and practice of the ownership of land and the means of production by the people or the state.
– DERIVATIVES **collectivist** adjective & noun, **collectivistic** adjective.

collectivize (also **-ise**) ▶ **verb** [with obj.] [usu. as adj. **collectivized**] organize (something) on the basis of ownership by the people or the state, abolishing private ownership or involvement: *collectivized agriculture.*
– DERIVATIVES **collectivization** noun.

collector /kəˈlɛktə/ ▶ **noun** a person or thing that collects something, in particular:
■ a person who collects things of a specified type, professionally or as a hobby: *an art collector.* ■ an official who is responsible for collecting money owed to an organization or body: *a tax collector.* ■ an official who collects tickets from bus or train passengers. ■ Electronics the region in a bipolar transistor that absorbs charge carriers.

collector's item (also **collector's piece**) ▶ **noun** an object of interest to collectors, especially because it is rare, beautiful, or associated with someone famous.

colleen /kɒˈliːn, ˈkɒliːn/ ▶ **noun** an Irish term for a girl or young woman.
■ an Irish girl or young woman.
– ORIGIN early 19th cent.: from Irish *cailín*, diminutive of *caile* 'countrywoman'.

college ▶ **noun** **1** an educational institution or establishment, in particular:
■ one providing higher education or specialized professional or vocational training: *my brother wanted to go to college | I'm at college, studying graphic design.* ■ (in Britain) any of a number of independent institutions within certain universities, each having its own teaching staff, students, and buildings. ■ Brit. a private secondary school: [in names] *Eton College.* ■ US a university offering a limited curriculum or teaching only to a bachelor's degree. ■ the teaching staff and students of such an institution considered collectively: *the college was shocked by his death.*
2 an organized group of professional people with particular aims, duties, and privileges: [in names] *the Royal College of Physicians.*
– ORIGIN late Middle English: from Old French, from Latin *collegium* 'partnership, association', from *collega* 'partner in office', from *col-* 'together with' + *legare* 'depute'.

College of Arms (also **College of Heralds**) (in the UK) a corporation which officially records and grants armorial bearings. Formed in 1484, it comprises three Kings of Arms, six heralds, and four pursuivants. Also called **HERALDS' COLLEGE**.

College of Cardinals the body of cardinals of the Roman Catholic Church, founded in the 11th century and since 1179 responsible for the election of the Pope. Also called **SACRED COLLEGE**.

college of education ▶ **noun** an institution where schoolteachers are trained.

collegia plural form of **COLLEGIUM**.

collegial /kəˈliːdʒɪəl, -dʒ(ə)l/ ▶ **adjective** **1** another term for **COLLEGIATE** (in sense 1).
2 relating to or involving shared responsibility, as among a group of colleagues.
– DERIVATIVES **collegiality** noun.
– ORIGIN late Middle English: from Old French *collegial* or late Latin *collegialis*, from *collegium* 'partnership, association' (see **COLLEGE**).

collegian /kəˈliːdʒɪən, -dʒ(ə)n/ ▶ **noun** a member of a college, especially within a university.
– ORIGIN late Middle English: from medieval Latin *collegianus*, from *collegium* 'partnership, association' (see **COLLEGE**).

collegiate /kəˈliːdʒ(ɪ)ət/ ▶ **adjective** **1** belonging or relating to a college or its students: *collegiate life.*
2 (of a university) composed of different colleges.
– ORIGIN late Middle English: from late Latin *collegiatus*, from *collegium* 'partnership, association' (see **COLLEGE**).

collegiate church ▶ **noun** a church endowed for a chapter of canons but without a bishop's see.
■ US & Scottish a church or group of churches established under two or more pastors.

collegiate Gothic N. Amer. ▶ **noun** [mass noun] a style of neo-Gothic architecture used for some US university buildings.
▶ **adjective** of or built in such a style.

collegium /kəˈliːdʒɪəm/ ▶ **noun** (pl. **collegia** /kəˈliːdʒɪə, -dʒə/) **1** (in full **collegium musicum**) (pl. **collegia musica**) a society of amateur musicians, especially one attached to a German or US university.
2 historical an advisory or administrative board in Russia.
– ORIGIN late 19th cent.: from Latin, literally 'association'.

col legno /kɒl ˈlɛnjəʊ/ ▶ **adverb** (of a passage of music for a bowed instrument) played by hitting the strings with the back of the bow.
– ORIGIN Italian, 'with the wood (of the bow)'.

Collembola /kəˈlɛmbələ/ Entomology an order of insects that comprises the springtails.
■ [as plural noun **collembola**] insects of this order; springtails.
– DERIVATIVES **collembolan** noun & adjective.
– ORIGIN modern Latin (plural), from Greek *kolla* 'glue' + *embolon* 'peg, stopper' (with reference to the sticky substance secreted by the ventral tube of the insects).

collenchyma /kəˈlɛŋkɪmə/ ▶ **noun** [mass noun] Botany tissue strengthened by the thickening of cell walls, as in young shoots.
– ORIGIN mid 19th cent.: from Greek *kolla* 'glue' + *enkhuma* 'infusion'.

Colles' fracture /ˈkɒlɪs/ ▶ **noun** Medicine a fracture of the lower end of the radius in the wrist with a characteristic backward displacement of the hand.
– ORIGIN late 19th cent.: named after Abraham *Colles* (1773–1843), Irish surgeon.

collet /ˈkɒlɪt/ ▶ **noun** a ring or lining that holds something, in particular:
■ a segmented band or sleeve put round a shaft or spindle and tightened so as to grip it. ■ a small collar in a clock to which the inner end of a balance spring is attached. ■ a flange or socket for setting a gem in jewellery.
– ORIGIN late Middle English (denoting a piece of armour to protect the neck): from Old French, diminutive of *col* 'neck', from Latin *collum*.

colliculus /kəˈlɪkjʊləs/ ▶ **noun** (pl. **colliculi** /-lʌɪ, -liː/) Anatomy a small protuberance, especially one of two pairs in the roof of the midbrain, involved respectively in vision and hearing.
– DERIVATIVES **collicular** adjective.
– ORIGIN mid 19th cent.: from Latin, diminutive of *collis* 'hill'.

collide ▶ **verb** [no obj.] hit by accident when moving: *she collided with someone | two suburban trains collided.*
■ come into conflict or opposition: *in his work, politics and metaphysics collide.*
– ORIGIN early 17th cent. (in the sense 'cause to collide'): from Latin *collidere*, from *col-* 'together' + *laedere* 'to strike or damage'.

collider ▶ **noun** Physics an accelerator in which two beams of particles are made to collide.

collie ▶ **noun** (pl. **-ies**) a sheepdog of a breed originating in Scotland, having a long, pointed nose and thick long hair.
– ORIGIN mid 17th cent.: perhaps from **COAL** (the breed originally being black).

collier /ˈkɒlɪə/ ▶ **noun** chiefly Brit. **1** a coal miner.
2 a ship carrying coal.
– ORIGIN Middle English: from **COAL** + **-IER**. The original sense (surviving in US use) was 'maker of charcoal', who usually brought it to market, hence 'person selling charcoal', later 'person selling coal', whence current senses.

colliery ▶ **noun** (pl. **-ies**) a coal mine and the buildings and equipment associated with it.

colligate /ˈkɒlɪgeɪt/ ▶ **verb** Linguistics be or cause to be juxtaposed or grouped in a syntactic relation: [no obj.] *the two grammatical items are said to colligate* | [with obj.] *pronouns are regularly colligated with verbal forms.*
– DERIVATIVES **colligation** noun.
– ORIGIN mid 16th cent. (in the literal Latin sense): from Latin *colligat-* 'bound together', from the verb *colligare*, from *col-* 'together' + *ligare* 'bind'. The current sense dates from the 1960s.

colligative /kəˈlɪgətɪv/ ▶ **adjective** Chemistry of or relating to the binding together of molecules: *the colligative properties of dilute solutions.*

collimate /ˈkɒlɪmeɪt/ ▶ **verb** [with obj.] make (rays of light or particles) accurately parallel: [as adj. **collimated**] *a collimated electron beam.*
■ accurately set the alignment of (an optical or other system).
– DERIVATIVES **collimation** noun.
– ORIGIN mid 19th cent.: from Latin *collimare*, an erroneous reading (in some editions of Cicero) of *collineare* 'align or aim', from *col-* 'together with' + *linea* 'line'.

collimator ▶ **noun** a device for producing a parallel beam of rays or radiation.
■ a small fixed telescope used for adjusting the line of sight of an astronomical telescope.

collinear /kɒˈlɪnɪə/ ▶ **adjective** Geometry (of points) lying in the same straight line.
– DERIVATIVES **collinearity** noun.

Collins[1], Joan (Henrietta) (b.1933), English actress, a sex symbol in films such as *Our Girl Friday* (1953) and known more recently for the television series *Dynasty* (1981–9).

Collins[2], Michael (1890–1922), Irish nationalist leader and politician. A member of Parliament for Sinn Fein, he was one of the negotiators of the Anglo-Irish Treaty of 1921. He commanded the Irish Free State forces in the civil war and became head of state but was assassinated ten days later.

Collins[3], (William) Wilkie (1824–89), English novelist, noted for his detective stories *The Woman in White* (1860) and *The Moonstone* (1868).

Collins[4] ▶ **noun** short for **TOM COLLINS**.

collision ▶ **noun** **1** an instance of one moving object or person striking violently against another: *a mid air **collision between** two aircraft* | [mass noun] *his car was **in collision with** a lorry.*
■ an instance of conflict between opposing ideas, interests, or factions: *a **collision between** two mutually inconsistent ideas | the LP is a collision of different styles.*
2 Computing an event of two or more records being assigned the same location in memory.
■ an instance of simultaneous transmission by more than one node of a network.
– PHRASES **on (a) collision course** going in a direction that will lead to a collision with another moving object or person. ■ adopting an approach that is certain to lead to conflict with another person or group: *nurses are on a collision course with the government.*
– DERIVATIVES **collisional** adjective.
– ORIGIN late Middle English: from late Latin *collisio(n-)*, from Latin *collidere* 'strike together' (see **COLLIDE**).

collocate ▶ **verb** /ˈkɒləkeɪt/ **1** [no obj.] Linguistics (of a word) be habitually juxtaposed with another with a frequency greater than chance: *'maiden' collocates with 'voyage'.*
2 [with obj.] rare place side by side or in a particular relation: [as adj. **collocated**] *McAndrew was a collocated facility with Argentia Naval Station.*
▶ **noun** /ˈkɒləkət/ Linguistics a word that is habitually juxtaposed with another with a frequency greater than chance: *collocates for the word 'mortgage' include 'lend' and 'property'.*
– ORIGIN early 16th cent. (in sense 2): from Latin *collocat-* 'placed together', from the verb *collocare*, from *col-* 'together' + *locare* 'to place'. Sense 1 dates from the 1950s.

collocation ▶ **noun** [mass noun] **1** Linguistics the habitual juxtaposition of a particular word with another word or words with a frequency greater than chance: *the words have a similar range of collocation.*
■ [count noun] a pair or group of words that are juxtaposed in such a way: *'strong tea' and 'heavy drinker' are typical English collocations.*
2 the action of placing things side by side or in position: *the collocation of the two pieces.*
– ORIGIN late Middle English: from Latin *collocatio(n-)*, from *collocare* 'place together' (see **COLLOCATE**).

collocutor /ˈkɒləˌkjuːtə, kəˈlɒkjʊtə/ ▶ **noun** rare a person who takes part in a conversation.
– ORIGIN mid 16th cent.: from late Latin, from *collocut-* 'conversed', from the verb *colloqui*.

collodion /kəˈləʊdɪən/ ▶ **noun** [mass noun] a syrupy solution of nitrocellulose in a mixture of alcohol and ether, used for coating things, chiefly in surgery and in a former photographic process.
– ORIGIN mid 19th cent.: from Greek *kollōdēs* 'glue-like', from *kolla* 'glue'.

collogue /kɒˈləʊg/ ▶ **verb** (**collogues**, **collogued**,

collouging) [no obj.] archaic talk confidentially or conspiratorially.
– ORIGIN early 17th cent. (in the sense 'flatter, pretend to agree with or believe'): probably an alteration of obsolete *colleague* 'conspire', by association with Latin *colloqui* 'to converse'.

colloid /ˈkɒlɔɪd/ ▶ noun a homogeneous non-crystalline substance consisting of large molecules or ultramicroscopic particles of one substance dispersed through a second substance. Colloids include gels, sols, and emulsions; the particles do not settle, and cannot be separated out by ordinary filtering or centrifuging like those in a suspension. ■[mass noun] Anatomy & Medicine a substance of gelatinous consistency.
▶ adjective [attrib.] of the nature of, relating to, or characterized by a colloid or colloids.
– DERIVATIVES **colloidal** adjective.
– ORIGIN mid 19th cent.: from Greek *kolla* 'glue' + -OID.

collop /ˈkɒləp/ ▶ noun a slice of meat: *three collops of bacon*.
– ORIGIN late Middle English: of Scandinavian origin and related to Swedish *kalops* 'meat stew'.

colloquial /kəˈləʊkwɪəl/ ▶ adjective (of language) used in ordinary or familiar conversation; not formal or literary.
– DERIVATIVES **colloquially** adverb.
– ORIGIN mid 18th cent.: from Latin *colloquium* 'conversation' + -AL.

colloquialism ▶ noun a word or phrase that is not formal or literary, typically one used in ordinary or familiar conversation. ■[mass noun] the use of such words or phrases.

colloquium /kəˈləʊkwɪəm/ ▶ noun (pl. **colloquiums** or **colloquia** /-kwɪə/) an academic conference or seminar.
– ORIGIN late 16th cent. (denoting a conversation or dialogue): from Latin, from *colloqui* 'to converse', from *col-* 'together' + *loqui* 'to talk'.

colloquy /ˈkɒləkwi/ ▶ noun (pl. **-ies**) **1** formal a conversation: *they broke off their colloquy at once* | [mass noun] *he found her in earnest colloquy with the postman.* **2** a gathering for discussion of theological questions.
– ORIGIN late Middle English: from Latin *colloquium* 'conversation'.

collotype /ˈkɒlətaɪp/ ▶ noun [mass noun] Printing a process for making high-quality prints from a sheet of light-sensitive gelatin exposed photographically to the image without using a screen: [as modifier] *collotype printing.* ■[count noun] a print made by such a process.
– ORIGIN late 19th cent.: from Greek *kolla* 'glue' + TYPE.

collude /kəˈl(j)uːd/ ▶ verb [no obj.] come to a secret understanding; conspire: *certain officials were colluding in the avoidance of drugs tests* | *the president accused his opponents of colluding with foreigners.*
– DERIVATIVES **colluder** noun.
– ORIGIN early 16th cent.: from Latin *colludere* 'have a secret agreement', from *col-* 'together' + *ludere* 'to play'.

collusion ▶ noun [mass noun] secret or illegal cooperation or conspiracy, especially in order to cheat or deceive others: *the armed forces were working in collusion with drug traffickers* | *collusion between media owners and political leaders.* ■Law such cooperation or conspiracy between ostensible opponents in a lawsuit.
– DERIVATIVES **collusive** adjective, **collusively** adverb.
– ORIGIN late Middle English: from Latin *collusio(n-)*, from *colludere* 'have a secret agreement' (see COLLUDE).

colluvium /kəˈl(j)uːvɪəm/ ▶ noun [mass noun] Geology material which accumulates at the foot of a steep slope.
– DERIVATIVES **colluvial** adjective.
– ORIGIN mid 20th cent.: from Latin *colluvies* 'confluence or collection of matter', from *colluere* 'to rinse', from *col-* 'together' + *luere* 'to wash'.

collyrium /kəˈlɪrɪəm/ ▶ noun (pl. **collyria** /-rɪə/) a medicated eyewash. ■[mass noun] a kind of dark eyeshadow, used especially in Eastern countries.
– ORIGIN late Middle English: Latin, from Greek *kollurion* 'poultice', from *kollura* 'coarse bread roll'.

collywobbles ▶ plural noun informal, chiefly humorous stomach pain or queasiness: *an attack of collywobbles.* ■intense anxiety or nervousness, especially with such symptoms: *such organizations give him the collywobbles.*
– ORIGIN early 19th cent.: fanciful formation from COLIC and WOBBLE.

Colo ▶ abbreviation for Colorado.

colobine /ˈkɒləbaɪn/ ▶ noun Zoology an Old World monkey of a mainly leaf-eating group that includes the colobus monkeys, langurs, and leaf monkeys. ● Subfamily Colobinae, family Cercopithicidae.
– ORIGIN 1950s: from modern Latin *Colobinae*, based on Greek *kolobos* 'curtailed'.

coloboma /ˌkɒləˈbəʊmə/ ▶ noun [mass noun] Medicine a congenital malformation of the eye causing defects in the lens, iris, or retina.
– ORIGIN mid 19th cent.: modern Latin, from Greek *kolobōma* 'part removed in mutilation', from *kolobos* 'cut short'.

colobus /ˈkɒləbəs/ (also **colobus monkey**) ▶ noun (pl. same) a slender leaf-eating African monkey with silky fur, a long tail, and very small or absent thumbs. ● Genera *Colobus* and *Procolobus*, family Cercopithecidae: several species.
– ORIGIN modern Latin, from Greek *kolobos* 'curtailed'.

co-locate ▶ verb (be co-located) share a location or facility with something else: *a United Kingdom battalion would be co-located with the home-base battalion.*

colocynth /ˈkɒləsɪnθ/ ▶ noun a tropical Old World climbing plant of the gourd family, which bears a pulpy fruit and has long been cultivated. Also called BITTER APPLE. ● *Citrullus colocynthis*, family Curcurbitaceae. ■the fruit of this plant. ■[mass noun] a bitter purgative drug obtained from this fruit.
– ORIGIN mid 16th cent.: via Latin from Greek *kolokunthis.*

Cologne /kəˈləʊn/ an industrial and university city in western Germany, in North Rhine-Westphalia; pop. 956,690 (1991). Founded by the Romans and situated on the River Rhine, Cologne is notable for its medieval cathedral. German name KÖLN.

cologne /kəˈləʊn/ ▶ noun [mass noun] eau de cologne or similarly scented toilet water.
– ORIGIN early 19th cent.: named after COLOGNE in Germany.

Colombia /kəˈlɒmbɪə/ a country in the extreme NW of South America, having a coastline on both the Atlantic and the Pacific Ocean; pop. 34,479,000 (est. 1994); official language, Spanish; capital, Bogotá. Colombia was conquered by the Spanish in the early 16th century and achieved independence in the early 19th century.
– DERIVATIVES **Colombian** adjective & noun.

Colombo /kəˈlʌmbəʊ/ the capital and chief port of Sri Lanka; pop. 615,000 (1990).

Colón /kɒˈlɒn/ the chief port of Panama, at the Caribbean end of the Panama Canal; pop. 140,900 (1990). It was founded in 1850 by the American William Aspinwall (1807–55), after whom it was originally named.

colon[1] /ˈkəʊlən/ ▶ noun a punctuation mark (:) indicating: ■that a writer is introducing a quotation or a list of items. ■that a writer is separating two clauses of which the second expands or illustrates the first. ■a statement of proportion between two numbers: *10:1.* ■the separation of hours from minutes (and minutes from seconds) in a statement of time given in numbers: *4:30pm.* ■the number of the chapter and verse respectively in biblical references: *Exodus 3:2.*
– ORIGIN mid 16th cent. (as a term in rhetoric denoting a section of a complex sentence, or a pause before it): via Latin from Greek *kōlon* 'limb, clause'.

colon[2] /ˈkəʊlən, -lɒn/ ▶ noun Anatomy the main part of the large intestine, which passes from the caecum to the rectum and absorbs water and electrolytes from food which has remained undigested. Its parts are called the ascending, transverse, descending, and sigmoid colon.
– ORIGIN late Middle English: via Latin from Greek *kolon.*

colón /kɒˈlɒn/ ▶ noun (pl. **colones** /-ˈlɒnɛz/) the basic monetary unit of Costa Rica and El Salvador, equal to 100 centimos in Costa Rica and 100 centavos in El Salvador.
– ORIGIN from Cristóbal *Colón*, the Spanish name of Christopher Columbus (see COLUMBUS[2]).

colonel /ˈkɜːn(ə)l/ ▶ noun a rank of officer in the army and in the US air force, above a lieutenant colonel and below a brigadier or brigadier general. ■informal short for LIEUTENANT COLONEL.
– DERIVATIVES **colonelcy** noun (pl. **-ies**).
– ORIGIN mid 16th cent.: from obsolete French *coronel* (earlier form of *colonel*), from Italian *colonnello* 'column of soldiers', from *colonna* 'column', from Latin *columna*. The form *coronel*, source of the modern pronunciation, was usual until the mid 17th cent.

Colonel Blimp ▶ noun another term for BLIMP (in sense 1).

colonel-in-chief ▶ noun (pl. **colonels-in-chief**) a title given to the honorary head of a regiment in the British army.

colonial ▶ adjective **1** of, relating to, or characteristic of a colony or colonies: *British colonial rule* | *colonial expansion.* ■(especially of architecture or furniture) made during or in the style of the period of the British colonies in America before independence. **2** (of animals or plants) living in colonies.
▶ noun **1** a native or inhabitant of a colony. **2** a house built in colonial style.
– DERIVATIVES **colonially** adverb.

colonial goose ▶ noun Austral./NZ dated a boned and stuffed roast leg of mutton.

colonialism ▶ noun [mass noun] the policy or practice of acquiring full or partial political control over another country, occupying it with settlers, and exploiting it economically.
– DERIVATIVES **colonialist** noun & adjective.

colonic /kəˈlɒnɪk/ ▶ adjective Anatomy of, relating to, or affecting the colon.
▶ noun informal an act or instance of colonic irrigation, performed for its supposed therapeutic benefits.

colonic irrigation ▶ noun [mass noun] the application of water via the anus to flush out the colon.

colonist ▶ noun a settler in or inhabitant of a colony.

colonize (also **-ise**) ▶ verb [with obj.] (of a country or its citizens) send a group of settlers to (a place) and establish political control over it: *the Greeks colonized Sicily and southern Italy.* ■come to settle among and establish political control over (the indigenous people of an area): [as plural noun **the colonized**] *an organization seeking to protect the rights of the newly colonized.* ■appropriate (a place or domain) for one's own use. ■Ecology (of a plant or animal) establish itself in (an area).
– DERIVATIVES **colonization** noun, **colonizer** noun.

colonnade /ˌkɒləˈneɪd/ ▶ noun a row of columns supporting a roof, an entablature, or arches. ■a row of trees or other tall objects.
– DERIVATIVES **colonnaded** adjective.
– ORIGIN early 18th cent.: from French, from *colonne* 'column', from Latin *columna.*

colonoscope /kəˈlɒnəskəʊp/ ▶ noun (pl. **-ies**) Medicine a flexible fibre optic instrument inserted through the anus in order to examine the colon.
– DERIVATIVES **colonoscopy** noun.

colony ▶ noun (pl. **-ies**) **1** a country or area under the full or partial political control of another country, typically a distant one, and occupied by settlers from that country. ■a group of people living in such a country or area, consisting of the original settlers and their descendants and successors. ■(the colonies) all the foreign countries or areas formerly under British political control. ■(the colonies) the thirteen areas on the east coast of North America that gained independence from Britain and founded the United States of America. **2** a group of people of one nationality or race living in a foreign city or country: *the British colony in New York.* ■a place where a group of people with the same occupation or interest live together: *a nudist colony.* **3** Biology a community of animals or plants of one kind living close together or forming a physically connected structure: *a colony of seals.* ■a group of fungi or bacteria grown from a single spore or cell on a culture medium.
– ORIGIN late Middle English (denoting a settlement formed mainly of retired soldiers, acting as a garrison in newly conquered territory in the

Roman Empire): from Latin *colonia* 'settlement, farm', from *colonus* 'settler, farmer', from *colere* 'cultivate'.

colony-stimulating factor ▶ **noun** Biochemistry a substance secreted by bone marrow which promotes the growth and differentiation of stem cells into colonies of specific blood cells.

colophon /ˈkɒləf(ə)n/ ▶ **noun** a publisher's emblem or imprint, especially one on the title page of a book.
■ historical a statement at the end of a book, typically with a printer's emblem, giving information about its authorship and printing.
– ORIGIN early 17th cent. (denoting a finishing touch): via late Latin from Greek *kolophōn* 'summit or finishing touch'.

colophony /kəˈlɒfəni, ˈkɒləˌfəʊni/ ▶ **noun** another term for **ROSIN**.
– ORIGIN Middle English: from Latin *colophonia (resina)* '(resin) from Colophon', a town in Lydia, Asia Minor.

color ▶ **noun** & **verb** US spelling of **COLOUR**.

Colorado /ˌkɒləˈrɑːdəʊ/ **1** a river which rises in the Rocky Mountains of northern Colorado and flows generally south-westwards for 2,333 km (1,468 miles) to the Gulf of California, passing through the Grand Canyon.
2 a state in the central US; pop. 3,294,400 (1990); capital, Denver. Colorado extends from the Great Plains in the east to the Rocky Mountains in the west. Part of it was acquired by the Louisiana Purchase in 1803 and the rest ceded by Mexico in 1848. It became the 38th state in 1876.
– DERIVATIVES **Coloradan** noun & adjective.

Colorado beetle ▶ **noun** a yellow- and black-striped leaf beetle that is native to America. The larvae are highly destructive to potato plants and have occurred in many countries.
● *Leptinotarsa decemlineata*, family Chrysomelidae.
– ORIGIN late 19th cent.: named after the state of **COLORADO**.

coloration (also **colouration**) ▶ **noun** **1** a visual appearance with regard to colour: *some bacterial structures take on a purple coloration.*
■ the natural colour or variegated markings of animals or plants: *the red coloration of many maples* | [mass noun] *many insects have bright coloration.* ■ a scheme or method of applying colour.
2 a specified pervading character or tone of something: *the movement has taken on a fundamentalist coloration.*
■ a variety of musical or vocal expression: *the subtle colorations of big-box speakers* | [mass noun] *a skilful singer can do much with coloration.*
– ORIGIN early 17th cent.: from late Latin *coloratio(n-)*, from *colorare* 'to colour'.

coloratura /ˌkɒlərəˈtjʊərə/ ▶ **noun** [mass noun] elaborate ornamentation of a vocal melody, especially in operatic singing by a soprano.
■ (also **coloratura soprano**) [count noun] a soprano skilled in such singing.
– ORIGIN Italian, literally 'colouring', from Latin *colorare* 'to colour'.

colorectal /ˌkəʊləʊˈrɛkt(ə)l/ ▶ **adjective** relating to or affecting the colon and the rectum.

colorific /ˌkʌləˈrɪfɪk, ˌkɒl-/ (also **colourific**) ▶ **adjective** rare having much colour: *the colorific radiance of costume.*
– ORIGIN late 17th cent.: from French *colorifique* or modern Latin *colorificus*, from Latin *color* 'colour'.

colorimeter /ˌkʌləˈrɪmɪtə, ˌkɒl-/ ▶ **noun** an instrument for measuring the intensity of colour.
– DERIVATIVES **colorimetric** adjective, **colorimetry** noun.
– ORIGIN mid 19th cent.: from Latin *color* 'colour' + **-METER**.

colorize (Brit. also **colourize**) ▶ **verb** [with obj.] add colour to (a black-and-white film) by means of a computer.
– DERIVATIVES **colorization** noun (trademark in the US), **colorizer** noun (trademark in the US).

colossal ▶ **adjective** extremely large: *a colossal amount of mail* | *a colossal mistake.*
■ Architecture (of an order) having more than one storey of columns. ■ Sculpture (of a statue) at least twice life size.
– DERIVATIVES **colossally** adverb.
– ORIGIN early 18th cent.: from French, from *colosse*, from Latin *colossus* (see **COLOSSUS**).

Colosseum /ˌkɒləˈsiːəm/ ▶ **noun** the name since medieval times of the *Amphitheatrum Flavium*, a vast amphitheatre in Rome, begun *c.*75 AD.
– ORIGIN from Latin, neuter of *colosseus* 'gigantic', from *colossus* (see **COLOSSUS**).

colosseum ▶ **noun** variant spelling of **COLISEUM**.

Colossians, Epistle to the /kəˈlɒʃ(ə)nz/ a book of the New Testament, an epistle of St Paul to the Church at Colossae in Phrygia.

colossus /kəˈlɒsəs/ ▶ **noun** (pl. **colossi** /-sʌɪ/ or **colossuses**) a statue that is much bigger than life size.
■ figurative a person or thing of enormous size, importance, or ability: *the Russian Empire was the colossus of European politics.*
– ORIGIN late Middle English: via Latin from Greek *kolossos* (applied by Herodotus to the statues of Egyptian temples).

Colossus of Rhodes a huge bronze statue of the sun god Helios, one of the Seven Wonders of the World. Built *c.*292–280 BC, it stood beside the harbour entrance at Rhodes for about fifty years.

colostomy /kəˈlɒstəmi/ ▶ **noun** (pl. **-ies**) a surgical operation in which the colon is shortened to remove a damaged part and the cut end diverted to an opening in the abdominal wall.
■ an opening so formed: [as modifier] *a colostomy bag.*
– ORIGIN late 19th cent.: from **COLON**[2] + Greek *stoma* 'mouth'.

colostrum /kəˈlɒstrəm/ ▶ **noun** [mass noun] the first secretion from the mammary glands after giving birth, rich in antibodies.
– ORIGIN late 16th cent.: from Latin.

colour (US **color**) ▶ **noun** **1** [mass noun] the property possessed by an object of producing different sensations on the eye as a result of the way it reflects or emits light: *the lights flickered and changed colour.*
■ [count noun] one, or any mixture, of the constituents into which light can be separated in a spectrum or rainbow, sometimes including (loosely) black and white: *a rich brown colour* | *a range of bright colours.* ■ the use of all colours, not only black and white, in photography or television: *he has shot the whole film in colour* | [as modifier] *colour television.* ■ a substance used to give something a particular colour: *lip colour.* ■ [count noun] Heraldry any of the major conventional colours used in coats of arms (gules, vert, sable, azure, purpure), especially as opposed to the metals, furs, and stains. ■ [count noun] figurative a shade of meaning: *many events in her past had taken on a different colour.* ■ [count noun] Snooker any of the balls other than the white cue ball and the reds.
2 [mass noun] the appearance of someone's skin, in particular:
■ pigmentation of the skin, especially as an indication of someone's race: *discrimination on the basis of colour.* ■ [count noun] a group of people considered as being distinguished by skin pigmentation: *all colours and nationalities.* ■ rosiness of the complexion, especially as an indication of someone's health: *there was some colour back in his face.* ■ redness of the face as a manifestation of an emotion, especially embarrassment or anger: *colour flooded her skin as she realized what he meant.*
3 [mass noun] vividness of visual appearance resulting from the juxtaposition of many bright things: *for colour, plant groups of winter-flowering pansies.*
■ figurative picturesque or exciting features that lend a particularly interesting quality to something: *a town full of colour and character.* ■ figurative variety of musical tone or expression: *orchestral colour.*
4 (**colours**) chiefly Brit. an item or items of a particular colour worn to identify or distinguish an individual or a member of a group, in particular:
■ the clothes or accoutrements worn by a jockey or racehorse to indicate the horse's owner. ■ the clothes worn by the members of sports team while they are playing. ■ (also **school colours**) a badge, cap, or other item in the distinctive colours of a particular school, awarded to a pupil to denote selection to represent the school in a competitive sport. ■ the flag of a regiment or ship. ■ a national flag.
5 [mass noun] Physics a quantized property of quarks which can take three values (designated blue, green, and red) for each flavour.
▶ **verb** **1** [with obj.] change the colour of (something) by painting or dyeing it with crayons, paints, or dyes.
■ [no obj.] take on a different colour: *the foliage will not colour well if the soil is too rich.* ■ use crayons to fill (a particular shape or outline) with colour: *he hated finger-painting and* ***colouring in*** *pictures.* ■ figurative make vivid or picturesque: *he has coloured the dance with gestures from cabaret and vaudeville.*
2 [no obj.] (of a person or their skin) show embarrassment or shame by becoming red; blush: *she coloured slightly* | *she* ***coloured up*** *with embarrassment.*
■ [with obj.] cause (a person or their skin) to change in colour: *rage coloured his pale complexion.* ■ [with obj.] (of a particular colour) imbue (a person's skin): *a faint pink flush coloured her cheeks.* ■ [with obj.] figurative (of an emotion) imbue (a person's voice) with a particular tone: *surprise coloured her voice.*
3 [with obj.] influence, especially in a negative way; distort: *the experiences had coloured her whole existence.*
■ misrepresent by distortion or exaggeration: *witnesses might colour evidence to make a story saleable.*
– PHRASES **lend** (or **give**) **colour to** make something seem true or probable: *this lent colour and credibility to his defence.* **sail under false colours** disguise one's true nature or intentions. **show one's true colours** reveal one's real character or intentions, especially when these are disreputable or dishonourable. **under colour of** under the pretext of. **with flying colours** see **FLYING**.
– ORIGIN Middle English: from Old French *colour* (noun), *colourer* (verb), from Latin *color* (noun), *colorare* (verb).

colourable (US **colorable**) ▶ **adjective** **1** apparently correct or justified: *a colourable legal claim.*
■ counterfeit.
2 capable of being coloured: *colourable illustrations.*

colourant (US **colorant**) ▶ **noun** a dye, pigment, or other substance that colours something.

colouration ▶ **noun** variant spelling of **COLORATION**.

colour bar ▶ **noun** **1** a social system in which black people are denied access to the same rights, opportunities, and facilities as white people.
2 a strip on printed material or a screen display showing a range of colours, used to ensure that all colours are printed or displayed correctly.

colour-blind ▶ **adjective** unable to distinguish certain colours, or (rarely in humans) any colours at all. See **PROTANOPIA**.
– DERIVATIVES **colour blindness** noun.

colour code ▶ **noun** a system of marking things with different colours as a means of identification.
▶ **verb** (**colour-code**) [with obj.] (usu. **be colour-coded**) mark (things) with different colours as a means of identification: *each unit is colour-coded for clarity.*
■ mark different features of (something) with different colours: *the map is colour-coded.*

coloured (US **colored**) ▶ **adjective** **1** having or having been given a colour or colours, especially as opposed to being black, white, or neutral: *brightly coloured birds are easier to see* | [in combination] *a peach-coloured sofa.*
■ figurative imbued with an emotive or exaggerated quality: ***highly coloured*** *examples were used by both sides.*
2 (also **Coloured**) wholly or partly of non-white descent (now usually offensive, except in South African use).
■ S. African used as an official ethnic label for people of mixed ethnic origin, including Khoisan, African slave, Malay, Chinese, and white. ■ relating to people who are wholly or partly of non-white descent: *a coloured club.*
▶ **noun** **1** (also **Coloured**) dated or offensive a person who is wholly or partly of non-white descent.
■ S. African a person of mixed descent speaking Afrikaans or English as their mother tongue.
2 (**coloureds**) clothes, sheets, etc. that are any colour but white (used especially in the context of washing and colour fastness).

USAGE **Coloured** referring to skin colour is first recorded in the early 17th century and was adopted in the US by emancipated slaves as a term of racial pride after the end of the American Civil War. In Britain it was the accepted term until the 1960s, when it was superseded (as in the US) by **black**. The term **coloured** lost favour among blacks during this period and is now widely regarded as offensive except in historical contexts.
In South Africa, the term **coloured** (normally written **Coloured**) has a different history. It is used to refer to people of mixed-race parentage rather than, as

elsewhere, to refer to African peoples and their descendants (i.e. as a synonym for **black**). In modern use in this context the term is not considered offensive or derogatory.

colour fast ▶ **adjective** dyed in colours that will not fade or be washed out.
– DERIVATIVES **colour fastness** noun.

colour-field painting ▶ **noun** [mass noun] a style of American abstract painting prominent from the late 1940s to the 1960s which features large expanses of unmodulated colour covering the greater part of the canvas. Barnett Newman and Mark Rothko were considered its chief exponents.

colour filter ▶ **noun** a photographic filter that absorbs light of certain colours.

colourful (US **colorful**) ▶ **adjective 1** having much or varied colour; bright: *a colourful array of fruit.*
2 full of interest; lively and exciting: *a controversial and colourful character | a colourful account.*
■ (of a person's life or background) involving variously disreputable activities: *the financier had had a colourful career in the more maverick corners of the Euromarkets.* ■ (of language) vulgar or rude: *she made it clear, in colourful language, that she did not wish to talk to the police.*
– DERIVATIVES **colourfully** adverb, **colourfulness** noun.

colouring (US **coloring**) ▶ **noun** [mass noun] **1** the process or skill of applying a substance to something so as to change its original colour.
■ the process of filling in a particular shape or outline with crayons: [as modifier] *a colouring book.* ■ [count noun] a drawing produced in this way.
2 visual appearance with regard to colour, in particular:
■ the arrangement of colours and markings on an animal. ■ the natural hues of a person's skin, hair, and eyes: *her fair colouring.* ■ figurative the pervading character or tone of something: *the chorus is given oriental colouring by the use of exotic instruments.*
3 matter used to give a particular colour to something, especially food.

colourist (US **colorist**) ▶ **noun** an artist or designer who uses colour in a special or skilful way.
■ a person who tints black-and-white prints, photographs, or films. ■ a hairdresser who specializes in dyeing people's hair.

colouristic (US **coloristic**) ▶ **adjective** showing or relating to a special use of colour: *his great colouristic wallpapers.*
■ having or showing a variety of musical or vocal expression: *the choir's colouristic resources.*
– DERIVATIVES **colouristically** adverb.

colourize ▶ **verb** Brit. variant spelling of **COLORIZE**.

colourless (US **colorless**) ▶ **adjective 1** (especially of a gas or liquid) without colour.
■ dull or pale in hue: *colourless cheeks.*
2 lacking distinctive character or interest; dull: *the book is rather colourless, like its author.*
– DERIVATIVES **colourlessly** adverb.

colour phase ▶ **noun** a genetic or seasonal variation in the colour of the skin, pelt, or feathers of an animal.

colourpoint ▶ **noun** a cat of a long-haired breed having a pale coat with dark points, and blue eyes, developed by crossing Persian and Siamese cats.

colour prejudice ▶ **noun** [mass noun] prejudice against people on the basis of their skin colour.

colour reversal ▶ **noun** [mass noun] [usu. as modifier] Photography the process of producing a positive image directly from another positive: *colour reversal films.*

colour saturation ▶ **noun** see **SATURATION**.

colour scheme ▶ **noun** an arrangement or combination of colours, especially one used in interior decoration: *a brown or gold colour scheme.*
– DERIVATIVES **colour scheming** noun.

colour separation ▶ **noun** Photography & Printing any of three negative images of the same subject taken through green, red, and blue filters and combined to reproduce the full colour of the original.
■ [mass noun] the production of such images.

colour sergeant ▶ **noun** a rank of non-commissioned officer in the Royal Marines, above sergeant and below warrant officer.
– ORIGIN with reference to the sergeant's responsibility for carrying one of the regiment's colours in an honour guard.

colour supplement ▶ **noun** Brit. a magazine printed in colour and issued with a newspaper, especially at weekends.

colour temperature ▶ **noun** Astronomy & Physics the temperature at which a black body would emit radiation of the same colour as a given object.

colour therapy ▶ **noun** [mass noun] a system of alternative medicine based on the use of colour, especially projected coloured light.

colour wash ▶ **noun** [mass noun] coloured distemper.
▶ **verb** (**colour-wash**) [with obj.] paint (something) with coloured distemper.

colourway (US **colorway**) ▶ **noun** any of a range of combinations of colours in which a style or design is available: *our sweater comes in two colourways.*

colour wheel ▶ **noun** a circle with different coloured sectors used to show the relationship between colours.

colporteur /ˈkɒlˌpɔːtə, ˌkɒlpɔːˈtəː/ ▶ **noun** a pedlar of books, newspapers, and similar literature.
■ someone employed by a religious society to distribute bibles and other religious tracts.
– DERIVATIVES **colportage** /ˈkɒlˌpɔːtɪdʒ/ noun.
– ORIGIN late 18th cent.: French, from the verb *colporter*, probably an alteration of *comporter*, from Latin *comportare* 'carry with one'.

colposcope /ˈkɒlpəskəʊp/ ▶ **noun** a surgical instrument used to examine the vagina and the cervix of the womb.
– DERIVATIVES **colposcopy** /kɒlˈpɒskəpi/ noun.
– ORIGIN mid 20th cent.: from Greek *kolpos* 'womb' + **-SCOPE**.

Colt[1] /kəʊlt/, Samuel (1814–62), American inventor. He is remembered chiefly for the revolver named after him, which he patented in 1836.

Colt[2] /kəʊlt/ ▶ **noun** trademark a type of revolver.

colt /kəʊlt/ ▶ **noun** a young uncastrated male horse, in particular one less than four years old.
■ a member of a junior sports team: *England Colts.*
– ORIGIN Old English; perhaps related to Swedish *kult*, applied to boys or half-grown animals.

colter ▶ **noun** US spelling of **COULTER**.

coltish ▶ **adjective** energetic but awkward in one's movements or behaviour.
– DERIVATIVES **coltishly** adverb, **coltishness** noun.

Coltrane /kɒlˈtreɪn/, John (William) (1926–67), American jazz saxophonist. He was a leading figure in avant-garde jazz, bridging the gap between the harmonically dense jazz of the 1950s and the free jazz that evolved in the 1960s.

coltsfoot ▶ **noun** (pl. **coltsfoots**) a Eurasian plant of the daisy family, with yellow flowers which appear in the early spring before the large heart-shaped leaves. It is used in herbal medicine for the treatment of coughs and respiratory disorders.
● *Tussilago farfara*, family Compositae.
– ORIGIN mid 16th cent.: translating medieval Latin *pes pulli* 'foal's foot', with reference to the shape of the leaves.

colubrid /ˈkɒljʊbrɪd/ ▶ **noun** Zoology a snake of a very large family (Colubridae) which includes the majority of harmless species, such as grass snakes and garter snakes. The few venomous species have grooved fangs in the rear of the upper jaw.
– ORIGIN late 19th cent.: from modern Latin *Colubridae* (plural), from Latin *coluber* 'snake'.

colubrine /ˈkɒljʊbrʌɪn/ ▶ **adjective** chiefly figurative of or belonging to a snake; snake-like: *he had played a game of subtle, colubrine misdirection.*
– ORIGIN early 16th cent.: from Latin *colubrinus*, from *coluber* 'snake'.

colugo /kəˈluːgəʊ/ ▶ **noun** (pl. **-os**) another term for **FLYING LEMUR**.
– ORIGIN late 18th cent.: of unknown origin.

Columba /kəˈlʌmbə/ Astronomy a small and faint southern constellation (the Dove), near Canis Major. It is sometimes said to represent the dove that Noah sent out from the Ark.
■ [as genitive **Columbae** /kəˈlʌmbi, -bʌɪ/] used with preceding letter or numeral to designate a star in this constellation: *the star Beta Columbae.*
– ORIGIN Latin.

Columba, St /kəˈlʌmbə/ (*c.*521–97), Irish abbot and missionary. He established the monastery at Iona in *c.*563 and converted the Picts to Christianity. Feast day, 9 June.

columbarium /ˌkɒl(ə)mˈbɛːrɪəm/ ▶ **noun** (pl. **columbaria**) a room or building with niches for funeral urns to be stored.
– ORIGIN mid 18th cent.: from Latin, literally 'pigeon-house', from *columba* 'pigeon'.

Columbia /kəˈlʌmbɪə/ **1** a river in NW North America which rises in the Rocky Mountains of SE British Columbia, Canada, and flows 1,953 km (1,230 miles) generally southwards into the US, where it turns westwards to enter the Pacific south of Seattle.
2 the state capital of South Carolina; pop. 98,000 (1990).

Columbia, District of see **DISTRICT OF COLUMBIA**.

Columbia University a university in New York City, one of the most prestigious in the US. It was founded in 1754.

Columbine /ˈkɒl(ə)mbʌɪn/ a character in Italian *commedia dell'arte*, the mistress of Harlequin.
– ORIGIN from French *Colombine*, from Italian *Colombina*, feminine of *colombino* 'dovelike', from *colombò* 'dove'.

columbine /ˈkɒl(ə)mbʌɪn/ ▶ **noun** an aquilegia which has long-spurred flowers that are typically purplish-blue.
● Genus *Aquilegia*, family Ranunculaceae, especially *A. vulgaris* and its hybrids.
– ORIGIN late Middle English: from Old French *colombine*, from medieval Latin *colombina* (*herba*) 'dovelike (plant)', from Latin *columba* 'dove' (from the supposed resemblance of the flower to a cluster of five doves).

columbite /kəˈlʌmbʌɪt/ ▶ **noun** [mass noun] a black mineral, typically occurring as dense tabular crystals, consisting of an oxide of iron, manganese, niobium, and tantalum. It is the chief ore of niobium.
– ORIGIN early 19th cent.: from **COLUMBIUM** + **-ITE**[1].

columbium /kəˈlʌmbɪəm/ ▶ **noun** old-fashioned term for **NIOBIUM**.
– ORIGIN early 19th cent.: modern Latin, from *Columbia*, a poetic name for America from the name of Christopher *Columbus* (see **COLUMBUS**[2]).

Columbus[1] the state capital of Ohio; pop. 632,900 (1990).

Columbus[2], Christopher (1451–1506), Italian-born Spanish explorer; Spanish name *Cristóbal Colón*.

Columbus persuaded the Spanish monarchs, Ferdinand and Isabella, to sponsor an expedition to sail across the Atlantic in search of Asia and to prove that the world was round. In 1492 he set sail with three small ships and discovered the New World (in fact various Caribbean islands). He made three further voyages between 1493 and 1504, in 1498 discovering the South American mainland.

Columbus Day ▶ **noun** (in the US) a legal holiday commemorating the discovery of the New World by Christopher Columbus in 1492. It is observed by most states on the second Monday of October.

columella /ˌkɒljʊˈmɛlə/ ▶ **noun** (pl. **columellae** /-liː/) Biology a structure resembling a small column, typically forming a central axis, in particular:
■ Zoology the axis of a spiral shell. ■ Zoology an ossicle of the middle ear of birds, reptiles, and amphibians. ■ Anatomy the pillar around which the cochlea spirals. ■ Botany the axis of the spore-producing body of some lower plants.
– DERIVATIVES **columellar** adjective.
– ORIGIN late 16th cent.: from Latin, 'small column'.

column ▶ **noun 1** an upright pillar,typically cylindrical and made of stone or concrete, supporting an arch, entablature, or other structure or standing alone as a monument.
■ a similar vertical, roughly cylindrical thing: *a great column of smoke.* ■ an upright shaft forming part of a machine and typically used for controlling it: *a Spitfire control column.*
2 a vertical division of a page or text.
■ a vertical arrangement of figures or other information. ■ a section of a newspaper or magazine regularly devoted to a particular subject or written by a particular person.
3 one or more lines of people or vehicles moving in the same direction: *a column of tanks moved north-west | we walked in a column.*
■ Military a narrow-fronted deep formation of troops in successive lines. ■ a military force which might deploy in such a formation. ■ a similar formation of ships in a fleet or convoy.
– DERIVATIVES **columnar** adjective, **columned** adjective [often in combination] *a four-columned portico.*

– ORIGIN late Middle English: partly from Old French *columpne*, reinforced by its source, Latin *columna* 'pillar'.

columnated /ˈkɒl(ə)mneɪtɪd/ ▶ **adjective** supported on or having columns: *a columnated church interior.*

column inch ▶ **noun** a one-inch length of a column in a newspaper or magazine.

columnist /ˈkɒl(ə)m(n)ɪst/ ▶ **noun** a journalist contributing regularly to a newspaper or magazine.

colure /kəˈljʊə/ ▶ **noun** Astronomy either of two great circles intersecting at right angles at the celestial poles and passing through the ecliptic at either the equinoxes or the solstices.

– ORIGIN late Middle English: from late Latin *coluri* (plural), from Greek *kolourai* (*grammai*) 'truncated (lines)', from *kolouros* 'truncated', so named because the lower part is permanently cut off from view.

coly /ˈkəʊli/ ▶ **noun** (pl. **-ies**) another term for **MOUSEBIRD**.

– ORIGIN mid 19th cent.: from modern Latin *Colius*, from Greek *kolios*, denoting a type of woodpecker.

colza /ˈkɒlzə/ ▶ **noun** another term for **RAPE**[2].

– ORIGIN early 18th cent.: from Walloon French *kolza*, from Low German *kōlsāt*, Dutch *koolzaad*, from *kool* 'cole' + *zaad* 'seed'.

COM ▶ **abbreviation** for computer output on microfilm or microfiche.

com- (also **co-**, **col-**, **con-**, or **cor-**) ▶ **prefix** with; together; jointly; altogether: *combine* | *command* | *collude.*

– ORIGIN from Latin *cum* 'with'.

USAGE **Com-** is used before **b**, **m**, **p**, also occasionally before vowels and **f**. The following variant forms occur: **co-** especially before vowels, **h**, and **gn**; **col-** before **l**; **cor-** before **r**; and **con-** before other consonants.

coma[1] /ˈkəʊmə/ ▶ **noun** a state of deep unconsciousness that lasts for a prolonged or indefinite period, caused especially by severe injury or illness: *a road crash left him in a coma.*

■ humorous a state of extreme exhaustion, lethargy, or sleepiness.

– ORIGIN mid 17th cent.: modern Latin, from Greek *kōma* 'deep sleep'; related to *koitē* 'bed' and *keisthai* 'lie down'.

coma[2] /ˈkəʊmə/ ▶ **noun** (pl. **comae** /-miː/) Astronomy a diffuse cloud of gas and dust surrounding the nucleus of a comet.

■ [mass noun] Optics aberration which causes the image of an off-axis point to be flared like a comet.

– ORIGIN early 17th cent. (as a botanical term): via Latin from Greek *komē* 'hair of the head'.

Coma Berenices /ˌkəʊmə ˌbɛrɪˈnʌɪsiːz/ Astronomy a small inconspicuous northern constellation (Berenice's Hair), said to represent the tresses of Queen Berenice. It contains a large number of galaxies.

■ [as genitive **Comae Berenices** /ˌkəʊmiː ˌbɛrɪˈnʌɪsiːz/ or **Comae**] used with preceding letter or numeral to designate a star in this constellation: *the star Beta Comae Berenices.*

– ORIGIN Latin.

Comanche /kəˈmantʃi/ ▶ **noun** (pl. same or **Comanches**) **1** a member of an American Indian people of the south-western US. The Comanche were among the first to acquire horses (from the Spanish) and resisted white settlers fiercely.

2 [mass noun] the Uto-Aztecan language of this people, now virtually extinct.

▶ **adjective** of or relating to this people or their language.

– ORIGIN Spanish, from Comanche.

Comaneci /ˌkɒməˈnɛtʃ/, Nadia (b.1961), Romanian-born American gymnast. In 1976 she became the first Olympic competitor to be awarded the maximum score of 10.00.

comatose /ˈkəʊmətəʊs, -z/ ▶ **adjective** of or in a state of deep unconsciousness for a prolonged or indefinite period, especially as a result of severe injury or illness: *she had been comatose for seven months* | *lying in a comatose state.*

■ humorous (of a person or thing) extremely exhausted, lethargic, or sleepy, typically as a result of overdrinking or taking drugs.

– ORIGIN late 17th cent.: from Greek *kōma*, *kōmat-* 'deep sleep' + **-OSE**[1].

comb ▶ **noun** **1** a strip of plastic, metal, or wood with a row of narrow teeth, used for untangling or arranging the hair.

■ [in sing.] an instance of untangling or arranging the hair with such a device: *she gave her hair a comb.* ■ a short curved type of this device, worn by women to hold the hair in place or as an adornment.

2 something resembling a comb in function or structure, in particular:

■ a device for separating and dressing textile fibres. ■ a row of brass points for collecting the electricity in an electrostatic generator. ■ Austral./NZ the lower, fixed cutting-piece of a sheep-shearing machine.

3 the red fleshy crest on the head of a domestic fowl, especially a cock.

4 short for **HONEYCOMB** (sense 1).

▶ **verb** [with obj.] **1** untangle or arrange (the hair) by drawing a comb through it: [as adj., with submodifier] (**combed**) *neatly combed hair.*

■ (**comb something out**) remove something in the hair by drawing a comb through it: *she combed the burrs out of the dog's coat.* ■ (**comb something through**) use a comb to work a conditioning or styling preparation through (the hair).

2 prepare (wool, flax, or cotton) for manufacture with a comb.

■ [usu. as adj. **combed**] treat (a fabric) in such a way: *the socks are made of soft combed cotton.*

3 search carefully and systematically: *police combed the area for the murder weapon* | [no obj.] *his mother* ***combed through*** *the cardboard boxes.*

– DERIVATIVES **comb-like** adjective.

– ORIGIN Old English *camb*, of Germanic origin; related to Dutch *kam* and German *Kamm*.

combat ▶ **noun** [mass noun] fighting between armed forces: *five Hurricanes were shot down* ***in combat*** | [count noun] *pilots re-enacted the aerial combats of yesteryear* | [as modifier] *a combat zone.*

■ non-violent conflict or opposition: *electoral combat.*

▶ **verb** (**combated** or **combatted**, **combating** or **combatting**) [with obj.] take action to reduce, destroy, or prevent (something bad or undesirable): *an effort to combat drug trafficking.*

■ archaic engage in a fight with; oppose in battle: [no obj.] *your men combated against the first of ours.*

– ORIGIN mid 16th cent. (originally denoting a fight between two persons or parties): from French *combattre* (verb), from late Latin *combattere*, from *com-* 'together with' + *battere*, variant of Latin *batuere* 'to fight'.

combatant /ˈkɒmbət(ə)nt, ˈkʌm-/ ▶ **noun** a person engaged in fighting during a war.

■ a nation at war with another. ■ a person engaged in conflict or competition with another.

▶ **adjective** engaged in fighting during a war: *all the combatant armies went to war with machine guns.*

– ORIGIN late Middle English (as an adjective used in heraldry to describe two lions facing one another with raised forepaws): from Old French, present participle of *combatre* 'to fight' (see **COMBAT**).

combat dress ▶ **noun** [mass noun] uniform of a type intended to be worn by soldiers in actual combat.

combat fatigue ▶ **noun** **1** more recent term for **SHELL SHOCK**.

2 (**combat fatigues**) combat dress.

combative /ˈkɒmbətɪv, ˈkʌm-/ ▶ **adjective** ready or eager to fight or argue: *he made some enemies with his combative style.*

– DERIVATIVES **combatively** adverb, **combativeness** noun.

comb-back ▶ **noun** a high-backed Windsor chair with a straight top rail: [as modifier] *a comb-back rocker.*

combe /kuːm/ (also **coomb** or **coombe**) ▶ **noun** Brit. a short valley or hollow on a hillside or coastline, especially in southern England.

■ Geology a dry valley in a limestone or chalk escarpment.

– ORIGIN Old English *cumb*, occurring in charters in the names of places in southern England, many of which survive; of Celtic origin, related to **CWM**. The current general use dates from the late 16th cent.

comber[1] /ˈkəʊmə/ ▶ **noun** **1** a long curling sea wave.

2 a person or machine that prepares cotton or wool for manufacture by separating and straightening the fibres.

comber[2] /ˈkɒmbə/ ▶ **noun** a small fish that gapes when dead, occurring in shallow waters from the western English Channel to the Mediterranean. Also called **GAPER**.

● *Serranus cabrilla*, family Serranidae.

– ORIGIN mid 18th cent.: of unknown origin.

combfish ▶ **noun** (pl. same or **-fishes**) a fish of the NE Pacific, with small rough scales and long spines in the comblike dorsal fin.

● Family Zaniolepididae and genus *Zaniolepis*: several species.

combi ▶ **noun** a machine or appliance with two or more functions: [as modifier] *a combi oven.*

– ORIGIN 1960s: abbreviation of **COMBINATION**.

combination ▶ **noun** **1** [mass noun] the joining or uniting of two or more different things or qualities in such a way that their individual distinctness is retained: *the combination of recession and falling property values proved fatal to the business community.*

■ [as modifier] denoting an object or process that unites different uses, functions, or ingredients: *combination remedies contain painkiller, decongestant, and cough soother.* ■ the state of being joined or united in such a way: *these four factors work together* ***in combination.*** ■ Chemistry the joining of substances in a compound with new properties. ■ Chemistry the state of being in a compound.

2 a union or conjunction of different features, qualities, or parts, in which the component elements are individually distinct: *a magnificent combination of drama, dance, and music* | *this colour combination is stunningly effective.*

■ a union or arrangement of different elements resulting from selection among a larger number: *the canvases may be arranged in any number of combinations.* ■ a sequence of numbers or letters used to open a combination lock. ■ (in various sports and games) a coordinated and effective sequence of moves: *a good uppercut/hook combination.* ■ (in equestrian sports) a jump consisting of two or more elements. ■ Brit. a motorcycle with a sidecar attached. ■ (**combinations**) dated a single undergarment covering the body and legs.

3 Mathematics a selection of a given number of elements from a larger number without regard to their arrangement.

– DERIVATIVES **combinational** adjective, **combinative** adjective, **combinatorial** adjective (Mathematics), **combinatorially** adverb (Mathematics), **combinatory** adjective.

– ORIGIN late Middle English: from late Latin *combinatio(n-)*, from the verb *combinare* 'join two by two' (see **COMBINE**[1]).

combinational circuit ▶ **noun** Electronics a circuit whose output is dependent only on the state of its inputs. Compare with **SEQUENTIAL CIRCUIT**.

combination lock ▶ **noun** a lock that is opened by rotating a set of dials, marked with letters or numbers, to show a specific sequence.

combination oven ▶ **noun** an oven operating by both conventional heating and microwaves.

combination skin ▶ **noun** [mass noun] a type of facial skin characterized by an oily forehead, nose, and chin and relatively dry cheeks.

combination therapy ▶ **noun** [mass noun] treatment in which a patient is given two or more drugs (or other therapeutic agents) for a single disease.

combinatorics /ˌkɒmbɪnəˈtɒrɪks/ ▶ **plural noun** [treated as sing.] the branch of mathematics dealing with combinations of objects belonging to a finite set in accordance with certain constraints, such as those of graph theory.

– ORIGIN 1940s: from *combinatorial* (see **COMBINATION**), influenced by German *Kombinatorik*.

combine[1] ▶ **verb** /kəmˈbʌɪn/ [with obj.] unite; merge: *a new product which combines the benefits of a hairspray and a gel* | ***combine*** *the flour* ***with*** *the margarine and salt* | [no obj., with infinitive] *high tides and winds combined to bring chaos to the east coast.*

■ [no obj.] Chemistry unite to form a compound: *oxygen and hydrogen do not combine at room temperatures* | *oxygen* ***combines with*** *haemoglobin.* ■ [no obj.] unite for a common purpose: [with infinitive] *groups of teachers combined to tackle a variety of problems.* ■ engage in simultaneously: *combine shopping and sightseeing.*

▶ **noun** /ˈkɒmbʌɪn/ a group of people or companies acting together for a commercial purpose: *one of the world's biggest food and personal products combines.*

– DERIVATIVES **combinable** adjective.

– ORIGIN late Middle English: from Old French *combiner* or late Latin *combinare* 'join two by two', from *com-* 'together' + Latin *bini* 'two together'.

combine[2] /ˈkɒmbʌɪn/ ▶ **verb** [with obj.] harvest (a crop) by means of a combine harvester.

▶ **noun** a combine harvester.

– ORIGIN early 20th cent.: short for **COMBINE HARVESTER**.

combined pill ▶ **noun** an oral contraceptive containing both an oestrogen and a progestogen.

combine harvester ▶**noun** an agricultural machine that reaps, threshes, and cleans a cereal crop in one operation.

combings ▶**plural noun** hairs that come out when someone combs their hair.

combing wool ▶**noun** long-stapled wool with straight, parallel fibres, suitable for combing and making into high-quality fabrics, in particular worsted. Compare with **CARDING WOOL**.

combining form ▶**noun** Grammar a form of a word normally used in compounds in combination with another element to form a word (e.g. *Anglo-* 'English' in *Anglo-Irish*, *bio-* 'life' in *biology*, *-graphy* 'writing' in *biography*).

> **USAGE** In this dictionary, **combining form** is used to denote an element that contributes to the particular sense of words (as with **bio-** and **-graphy** in **biography**), as distinct from a prefix or suffix that adjusts the sense of or determines the function of words (as with **un-**, **-able**, and **-ation**).

comb jelly ▶**noun** a marine animal with a jellyfish-like body bearing rows of fused cilia for propulsion. They are typically small planktonic animals and are noted for their luminescence. Also called ***ctenophore***.
• Phylum Ctenophora: two classes.

combo ▶**noun** (pl. **-os**) informal **1** a small jazz, rock, or pop band.
2 chiefly N. Amer. a combination, typically of different foods: [as modifier] *combo meals.*
■a guitar amplifier with an integral speaker rather than a separate one.
– ORIGIN 1920s (originally US): abbreviation of **COMBINATION** + **-O**.

comb-out ▶**noun** an act of combing something out.

combs ▶**plural noun** Brit. informal, dated a single undergarment covering the body and legs.
– ORIGIN 1930s: abbreviation of *combination garments.*

combust /kəmˈbʌst/ ▶**verb** [with obj.] consume or destroy by fire.
■[no obj.] be consumed or destroyed by fire.
– ORIGIN late 15th cent.: from obsolete *combust* 'burnt, calcined', from Latin *combustus*, past participle of *comburere* 'burn up'.

combustible /kəmˈbʌstɪb(ə)l/ ▶**adjective** able to catch fire and burn easily.
■figurative excitable; easily annoyed.
▶**noun** a combustible substance.
– DERIVATIVES **combustibility** noun.
– ORIGIN early 16th cent.: from Old French, from late Latin *combustibilis*, from Latin *combust-* 'burnt up', from the verb *comburere*.

combustion ▶**noun** [mass noun] the process of burning something: *the combustion of fossil fuels* | [as modifier] *a large combustion plant.*
■Chemistry rapid chemical combination of a substance with oxygen, involving the production of heat and light.
– DERIVATIVES **combustive** adjective.
– ORIGIN late Middle English: from late Latin *combustio(n-)*, from Latin *comburere* 'burn up'.

combustion chamber ▶**noun** an enclosed space in which combustion takes place, especially in an engine or furnace.

come ▶**verb** (past **came**; past participle **come**) **1** [no obj., usu. with adverbial of direction] move or travel towards or into a place thought of as near or familiar to the speaker: *Jess came into the kitchen* | *they came here as immigrants* | *he came rushing out.*
■arrive at a specified place: *we walked along till we **came to** a stream* | *it was very late when she **came back*** | *my trunk hasn't come yet.* ■(of a thing) reach or extend to a specified point: *women in slim dresses that came all the way to their shoes* | *the path comes straight down.* ■(**be coming**) approach: *someone was coming* | *she heard the train coming.* ■travel in order to be with a specified person, to do a specified thing, or to be present at an event: *the police came* | ***come and** live with me* | [with infinitive] *the electrician came to mend the cooker* | figurative *we have certainly come a long way since Aristotle.* ■[with present participle] join someone in participating in a specified activity or course of action: *do you want to come fishing tomorrow?* ■(**come along/on**) make progress; develop: *he's coming along nicely* | *she asked them how their garden was coming on.* ■[in imperative] (also **come, come!**) said to someone when correcting, reassuring, or urging them on: *'Come, come, child, don't thank me.'*
2 [no obj.] occur; happen; take place: *twilight had not yet come* | *waiting for a crash that never came* | *a chance like this doesn't **come along** every day.*
■be heard, perceived, or experienced: *a voice came from the kitchen* | *'Nay,' came the reply* | *it **came as** a great shock.* ■[with adverbial] (of a quality) become apparent or noticeable through actions or performance: *as an actor your style and personality must **come through**.* ■(**come across** or Brit. **over** or US **off**) (of a person) appear or sound in a specified way; give a specified impression: *he'd always **come across as** a decent sort.* ■(of a thought or memory) enter one's mind: *the basic idea **came to** me while reading an article* | *a passage from a novel **came back to** Adam.*
3 [no obj., with complement] take or occupy a specified position in space, order, or priority: *prisons come well down the list of priorities* | *I make sure my kids come first.* ■achieve a specified place in a race or contest: *she came second among sixty contestants.*
4 [no obj., with complement] pass into a specified state, especially one of separation or disunion: *his shirt had come undone.*
■(**come to/into**) reach or be brought to a specified situation or result: *you will come to no harm* | *staff who come into contact with the public.* ■[with infinitive] reach eventually a certain condition or state of mind: *he had come to realize she was no puppet.*
5 [no obj., with adverbial] be sold, available, or found in a specified form: *the cars **come with** a variety of extras* | *they **come in** three sizes.*
6 [no obj.] informal have an orgasm.
▶**preposition** informal when a specified time is reached or event happens: *I don't think that they'll be far away from honours come the new season.*
▶**noun** [mass noun] informal semen ejaculated at an orgasm.
– PHRASES **as —— as they come** used to describe someone or something that is a supreme example of the quality specified: *Smith is as tough as they come.* **come again?** informal used to ask someone to repeat or explain something they have said. **come and go** arrive and then depart again; move around freely. ■exist or be present for a limited time; be transitory: *kings and queens may come and go, but the Crown goes on forever.* **come from behind** win after lagging. **come off it** [in imperative] informal said when vigorously expressing disbelief. **come right** informal have a good outcome; end well. **come the ——** informal play the part of; behave like: *don't come the innocent with me.* **come to nothing** have no significant or successful result in the end. **come to pass** chiefly poetic/literary happen; occur: *it **came to pass that** she had two sons.* **come to rest** eventually cease moving. **come to that** (or **if it comes to that**) informal in fact (said to introduce an additional point): *there isn't a clock on the mantelpiece—come to that, there isn't a mantelpiece!* **come to think of it** on reflection (said when an idea or point occurs to one while one is speaking). **come what may** no matter what happens. **have it coming** (**to one**) informal be due for retribution on account of something bad that one has done: *his uppity sister-in-law had it coming to her.* **how come?** informal said when asking how or why something happened or is the case: *how come you never married, Jimmy?* **to come** (following a noun) in the future: *films that would inspire generations to come* | *in years to come.* **where someone is coming from** informal someone's meaning, motivation, or personality.
– ORIGIN Old English *cuman*, of Germanic origin; related to Dutch *komen* and German *kommen*.

> **USAGE** The use of **come** followed by **and**, as in ***come and see for yourself***, dates back to Old English, but is seen by some as incorrect or only suitable for informal English: for more details see **usage** at **AND**.

▶**come about 1** happen; take place: *the relative speed with which emancipation came about.* **2** (of a ship) change direction.
come across 1 meet or find by chance: *I came across these old photos recently.* **2** informal hand over or provide what is wanted: *she has **come across with** some details.* ■(of a woman) agree to have sexual intercourse with a man.
come along [in imperative] said when encouraging someone or telling them to hurry up.
come around see *come round.*
come at launch oneself at (someone); attack.
come away be left with a specified feeling, impression, or result after doing something: *she came away feeling upset.*
come back 1 (in sport) recover from a deficit: *the Mets **came back from** a 3–0 deficit.* **2** chiefly N. Amer. reply or respond to someone, especially vigorously: *he **came back at** Judy with a vengeance.*
come before be dealt with by (a judge or court): *it is the most controversial issue to come before the Supreme Court.*
come between interfere with or disturb the relationship of (two people): *I let my stupid pride come between us.*
come by 1 chiefly N. Amer. call casually and briefly as a visitor: *his friends came by* | *she came by the house.* **2** manage to acquire or obtain (something).
come down 1 (of a building or other structure) collapse or be demolished. ■(of an aircraft) crash or crash-land. **2** be handed down by tradition or inheritance: *the name has **come down from** the last century.* **3** reach a decision or recommendation in favour of one side or another: *advisers and inspectors came down on our side.* **4** Brit. leave a university, especially Oxford or Cambridge, after finishing one's studies. **5** informal experience the lessening of an excited or euphoric feeling, especially one produced by a narcotic drug. **6** S. African (of a river) rise in flood.
come down on criticize or punish (someone) harshly: *she came down on me like a ton of bricks.*
come down to (of a situation or outcome) be dependent on (a specified factor): *it came down to her word against Guy's.*
come down with begin to suffer from (a specified illness): *I came down with influenza.*
come for 1 (of police or other officials) arrive to arrest or detain (someone). **2** launch oneself at (someone) to attack them: *he came for me with his fists.*
come forward volunteer oneself for a task or post or to give evidence about a crime.
come from originate in; have as its source: *the word caviar comes from the Italian caviale.* ■be the result of: *a dignity that comes from being in control.* ■have as one's place of birth or residence: *I come from Sheffield.* ■be descended from: *she comes from a family of Muslim scholars.*
come in 1 join or become involved in an enterprise: *that's where Jack comes in* | *I agreed to **come in on** the project.* ■have a useful role or function: *this is where grammar comes in.* ■[with complement] prove to have a specified good quality: *the boots also came in handy for kicking policemen.* **2** [with complement] finish a race in a specified position: *the favourite came in first.* **3** (of money) be earned or received regularly. **4** [in imperative] begin speaking or make contact, especially in radio communication: *come in, London.* **5** (of a tide) rise; flow.
come in for receive or be the object of (a reaction),typically a negative one: *he has come in for a lot of criticism.*
come into suddenly receive (money or property), especially by inheriting it.
come of result from: *no good will come of it.* ■be descended from: *she came of Dorset stock.*
come off 1 (of an action) succeed; be accomplished. ■fare in a specified way in a contest: *Geoffrey always came off worse in an argument.* **2** become detached or be detachable from something. ■Brit. fall from a horse or cycle that one is riding. **3** stop taking or being addicted to (a drug or form of medication). **4** Brit. informal have an orgasm.
come on 1 (of a state or condition) start to arrive or happen: *she felt a mild case of the sniffles coming on* | [with infinitive] *it was coming on to rain.* **2** (also **come upon**) meet or find by chance. **3** [in imperative] said when encouraging someone to do something or to hurry up or when one feels that someone is wrong or foolish: *Come on! We must hurry!* ■said or shouted to express support, for example for a sports team.
come on to informal make sexual advances towards.
come out 1 (of a fact) emerge; become known: *it **came out that** the accused had illegally registered to vote.* ■happen as a result: *something good can **come out of** something that went wrong.* ■(of a photograph) be produced satisfactorily or in a specified way: *I hope my photographs come out all right.* ■be satisfactorily visible in a photograph or present in a specified way. ■(of the result of a calculation or measurement) emerge at a specified figure: *rough cider usually **comes out at** about eight per cent alcohol.* ■(of patience or a similar card game) be played to a finish with all cards dealt with. **2** (of a book or other work) appear; be released or published. **3** declare oneself as being for or against something: *residents have **come out against** the proposals.* **4** [with complement] achieve a specified placing in an

C

examination or contest: *he deservedly came out the winner on points* | *she came out victorious.* ■ acquit oneself in a specified way: *surprisingly, it's Penn who comes out best.* **5** (of a stain) be removed or able to be removed. **6** Brit. go on strike. **7** informal openly declare that one is homosexual. [ORIGIN: from the phrase *come out of the closet* (see **CLOSET** (sense 3)).] **8** Brit. dated (of a young upper-class woman) make one's debut in society.

come out in Brit. (of a person's skin) break out in (spots or a similar condition).

come out with say (something) in a sudden, rude, or incautious way.

come over 1 (of a feeling or manner) begin to affect (someone). ■ [with complement] Brit. informal (of a person) suddenly start to feel a specified way: *they come over all misty-eyed with nostalgia.* **2** change to another side or point of view.

come round chiefly Brit. (chiefly US also **come around**) **1** recover consciousness: *I'd just come round from a drunken stupor.* **2** be converted to another person's opinion: *I came round to her point of view.* **3** (of a date or regular occurrence) recur; be imminent again: *Friday had come round so quickly.*

come through 1 succeed in surviving or dealing with (an illness or ordeal): *she's come through the operation very well.* **2** (of a message) be sent and received. ■ (of an official decree) be processed and notified.

come to 1 (also **come to oneself**) recover consciousness. **2** (of an expense) reach in total; amount to: *he hasn't the least idea of how much it will come to.* **3** (of a ship) come to a stop.

come under 1 be classified as or among: *they all come under the general heading of opinion polls.* **2** be subject to (an influence or authority). ■ be subjected to (pressure or aggression): *his vehicle came under mortar fire.*

come up 1 (of an issue, situation, or problem) occur or present itself, especially unexpectedly. ■ (of a specified time or event) approach or draw near: *she's got exams coming up.* ■ (of a legal case) reach the time when it is scheduled to be dealt with. **2** become brighter in a specified way as a result of being polished or cleaned. **3** Brit. begin one's studies at a university, especially Oxford or Cambridge.

come up against be faced with or opposed by (something such as an enemy or problem).

come up with produce (something), especially when pressured or challenged.

come upon 1 attack by surprise. **2** see *come on* (sense 2).

come-along ▶ **noun** N. Amer. informal a hand-operated winch.

comeback ▶ **noun 1** a return by a well-known person, especially an entertainer or sports player, to the activity in which they have formerly been successful: *the heavyweight champion is set to **make his comeback** in England* | [as modifier] *a comeback tour.* ■ a return to fashion of an item, activity, or style: *trouser suits are **making a comeback**.* **2** informal a quick reply to a critical remark. ■ [mass noun] [usu. with negative] the opportunity to seek redress: *there's no comeback if he messes up your case.* **3** Austral./NZ a sheep bred from cross-bred and pure-bred parents for both wool and meat.

Comecon /ˈkɒmɪkɒn/ an economic association of east European countries founded in 1949 and analogous to the European Economic Community. With the collapse of communism in eastern Europe, the association was dissolved in 1991.
– ORIGIN contraction of **COUNCIL FOR MUTUAL ECONOMIC ASSISTANCE**.

comedian ▶ **noun** an entertainer on stage or television whose act is designed to make an audience laugh. ■ often ironic a person who is or thinks themselves to be amusing or entertaining. ■ a comic actor.
– ORIGIN late 16th cent. (denoting a comic playwright): from French *comédien*, from Old French *comedie* (see **COMEDY**). The sense 'entertainer' dates from the late 19th cent.

Comédie Française /ˌkɒmedi: frɒ̃ˈseɪz, French kɔmedi fʀɑ̃sɛz/ the French national theatre (used for both comedy and tragedy), in Paris, founded in 1680 by Louis XIV.

comedienne /kəˌmi:dɪˈɛn, -ˌmɛ-/ ▶ **noun** a female comedian.
– ORIGIN mid 19th cent.: from French *comédienne*, feminine of *comédien* (see **COMEDIAN**).

comedo /ˈkɒmɪdəʊ, kəˈmi:dəʊ/ ▶ **noun** (pl. **comedones** /-ˈdəʊni:z/) technical term for **BLACKHEAD** (in sense 1).
– ORIGIN mid 19th cent.: from Latin, literally 'glutton', from *comedere* 'eat up', from *com-* 'altogether' + *edere* 'eat'. Used formerly as a name for parasitic worms, the term here alludes to the worm-like matter which can be squeezed from a blackhead.

comedogenic /ˌkɒmɪdə(ʊ)ˈdʒɛnɪk/ ▶ **adjective** tending to cause blackheads by blocking the pores of the skin.

comedown ▶ **noun** informal **1** a loss of status or importance: *Patrol duty? Bit of a **comedown for** a sergeant.* **2** a feeling of disappointment or depression. ■ [in sing.] a lessening of the sensations generated by a narcotic drug as its effects wear off.

comedy ▶ **noun** (pl. **-ies**) [mass noun] professional entertainment consisting of jokes and satirical sketches, intended to make an audience laugh. ■ [count noun] a film, play, or broadcast programme intended to make an audience laugh: [as modifier] *a comedy film.* ■ the style or genre of such types of entertainment. ■ the humorous or amusing aspects of something: *advertising people see the comedy in their work.* ■ [count noun] a play characterized by its humorous or satirical tone and its depiction of amusing people or incidents, in which the characters ultimately triumph over adversity. ■ the dramatic genre represented by such plays: *satiric comedy.* Compare with **TRAGEDY** (in sense 2).
– DERIVATIVES **comedic** /kəˈmi:dɪk, -ˈmɛ-/ adjective.
– ORIGIN late Middle English (as a genre of drama, also denoting a narrative poem with a happy ending, as in Dante's *Divine Comedy*): from Old French *comedie*, via Latin from Greek *kōmōidia*, from *kōmōidos* 'comic poet', from *kōmos* 'revel' + *aoidos* 'singer'.

comedy of manners ▶ **noun** a play, novel, or film that gives a satirical portrayal of behaviour in a particular social group.

come-hither informal, dated ▶ **adjective** suggesting that one finds someone sexually attractive; flirtatious: *nymphs with come-hither looks.*
▶ **noun** [in sing.] a flirtatious or enticing manner.

comely ▶ **adjective** (**comelier**, **comeliest**) archaic or humorous (typically of a woman) pleasant to look at; attractive. ■ archaic agreeable; suitable.
– DERIVATIVES **comeliness** noun.
– ORIGIN Middle English: probably shortened from *becomely* 'fitting, becoming', from **BECOME**.

come-on ▶ **noun** informal a thing that is intended to lure or entice. ■ a gesture or remark that is intended to attract someone sexually: *she was **giving** me **the come-on**.* ■ a marketing ploy, such as a free or cheap offer: [as modifier] *introductory come-on rates.*

come-outer ▶ **noun** US chiefly historical a person who dissociates himself or herself from an organization.

comer ▶ **noun 1** [with adj.] a person of a specified kind who arrives somewhere: *feeding every comer is still a sacred duty.* See also ***all comers*** at **ALL**, **LATECOMER**, **NEWCOMER**. **2** [in sing.] N. Amer. informal a person or thing likely to succeed: *many in the party see tax relief as a comer.*

comess /kɒˈmɛs/ ▶ **noun** W. Indian a confused or noisy situation.
– ORIGIN from French Creole *commece* 'confusion', from French *commerce* 'commerce'.

comestible /kəˈmɛstɪb(ə)l/ formal or humorous ▶ **noun** (usu. **comestibles**) an item of food: *a fridge groaning with comestibles.*
▶ **adjective** edible.
– ORIGIN late 15th cent.: from Old French, from medieval Latin *comestibilis*, from Latin *comest-* 'eaten up', from the verb *comedere*, from *com-* 'altogether' + *edere* 'eat'.

comet /ˈkɒmɪt/ ▶ **noun** a celestial object consisting of a nucleus of ice and dust and, when near the sun, a 'tail' of gas and dust particles pointing away from the sun.

Originating in the remotest regions of the solar system, most comets follow regular eccentric orbits and appear in the inner solar system as periodic comets, some of which break up and can be the origin of annual meteor showers. They were formerly considered to be supernatural omens.

– DERIVATIVES **cometary** adjective.
– ORIGIN late Old English, from Latin *cometa*, from Greek *komētēs* 'long-haired (star)', from *komē* 'hair'; reinforced by Old French *comete*.

comeuppance ▶ **noun** [usu. in sing.] informal a punishment or fate that someone deserves: *he got his comeuppance* | [mass noun] *a dose of comeuppance.*

comfit /ˈkʌmfɪt/ ▶ **noun** dated a sweet consisting of a nut, seed, or other centre coated in sugar.
– ORIGIN Middle English: from Old French *confit*, from Latin *confectum* 'something prepared', neuter past participle of *conficere* 'put together' (see **CONFECT**).

comfort ▶ **noun** [mass noun] **1** a state of physical ease and freedom from pain or constraint: *room for four people to travel in comfort.* ■ (**comforts**) things that contribute to physical ease and well-being: *the low upholstered chair was one of the room's few comforts.* ■ prosperity and the pleasant lifestyle secured by it: *my father left us enough to live in comfort.* **2** consolation for grief or anxiety: *a few words of comfort* | *they should **take comfort** that help is available.* ■ [in sing.] a person or thing that gives consolation or alleviates a difficult situation: *his friendship was a great comfort.* **3** US dialect a warm quilt.
▶ **verb** [with obj.] cause to feel less unhappy; console: [as adj. **comforting**] *his comforting presence.*
– PHRASES **too —— for comfort** causing physical or mental unease by an excess of the specified quality: *changes are happening too rapidly for comfort.*
– DERIVATIVES **comfortingly** adverb.
– ORIGIN Middle English (as a noun, in the senses 'strengthening, support, consolation'; as a verb, in the senses 'strengthen, give support, console'): from Old French *confort* (noun), *conforter* (verb), from late Latin *confortare* 'strengthen', from *com-* (expressing intensive force) + Latin *fortis* 'strong'. The sense 'something producing physical ease' arose in the mid 17th cent.

comfortable ▶ **adjective 1** (especially of clothes or furnishings) providing physical ease and relaxation. ■ (of a person) physically relaxed and free from constraint: *he would not be comfortable in any other clothes.* ■ not in pain (used especially in an official report of the condition of a hospital patient). ■ free from stress or fear: *they appear very comfortable in each other's company* | *few of us are **comfortable with** confrontations.* ■ free from financial worry; having an adequate standard of living. **2** as large as is needed or wanted: *a comfortable income.* ■ with a wide margin: *a comfortable victory.*
▶ **noun** US dialect a warm quilt.
– DERIVATIVES **comfortableness** noun, **comfortably** adverb.
– ORIGIN Middle English (in the sense 'pleasant, pleasing'): from Anglo-Norman French *confortable*, from *conforter* 'to comfort' (see **COMFORT**).

comforter ▶ **noun 1** a person or thing that provides consolation. ■ Brit. a baby's dummy. **2** dated a woollen scarf. **3** N. Amer. a warm quilt.
– ORIGIN late Middle English: from Old French *comforteor*, from *conforter* 'to comfort' (see **COMFORT**).

comfort food ▶ **noun** [mass noun] food that provides consolation or a feeling of well-being, typically any with a high sugar or carbohydrate content and associated with childhood or home cooking.

comfortless ▶ **adjective 1** offering no means of relaxation and pleasure: *the prison was comfortless.* **2** having or offering no consolation: *a fierce and comfortless play.*

comfort station ▶ **noun** N. Amer. used euphemistically to refer to a public toilet.

comfort zone ▶ **noun** a place or situation where one feels safe or at ease: *outside my comfort zone.* ■ a settled method of working that requires little effort and yields only barely acceptable results: *if you stay within your comfort zone you will never improve.*

comfrey /ˈkʌmfri/ ▶ **noun** (pl. **-eys**) a Eurasian plant of the borage family, which has large hairy leaves and clusters of purplish or white bell-shaped flowers.
● Genus *Symphytum*, family Boraginaceae: several species, in particular the **common comfrey** (*S. officinale*), which is used in herbal medicine (see **BONESET**).

– ORIGIN Middle English: from Anglo-Norman French *cumfirie*, based on Latin *conferva*, from *confervere* 'heal' (literally 'boil together', referring to the plant's medicinal use).

comfy ▶ adjective (**comfier**, **comfiest**) informal comfortable.
– DERIVATIVES **comfily** adverb, **comfiness** noun.
– ORIGIN early 19th cent.: abbreviation.

comic ▶ adjective causing or meant to cause laughter: *comic and fantastic exaggeration.*
■[attrib.] relating to or in the style of comedy: *a comic actor | comic drama.*
▶ noun **1** a comedian, especially a professional one.
2 a children's periodical, containing mainly comic strips.
■a similar publication intended for adults. ■ (**comics**) N. Amer. comic strips.
– ORIGIN late 16th cent.: via Latin from Greek *kōmikos*, from *kōmos* 'revel'.

comical ▶ adjective amusing: *a series of comical misunderstandings.*
– DERIVATIVES **comicality** noun (archaic), **comically** adverb.
– ORIGIN late Middle English (in the sense 'relating to or in the style of comedy'): from Latin *comicus* (see **COMIC**) + **-AL**.

Comice /ˈkɒmɪs/ ▶ noun a large yellow dessert pear of a late-fruiting variety that is cultivated commercially.
– ORIGIN mid 19th cent.: from French, literally 'association, cooperative', referring to the *Comice Horticole* of Angers, France, where this variety was developed.

comic opera ▶ noun an opera that portrays humorous situations and characters, enhanced by much spoken dialogue.
■[mass noun] the genre of such opera.

comic relief ▶ noun [mass noun] humour conveyed in comic episodes in a dramatic or literary work in order to offset more serious portions.
■a character or characters providing this. ■ the humour of comical episodes which serve to release tension in real life.

comic strip ▶ noun a sequence of drawings in boxes that tell an amusing story, typically printed in a newspaper or magazine.

coming ▶ adjective [attrib.] **1** due to happen or just beginning: *work is due to start in the coming year.*
2 likely to be important or successful in the future: *he was the coming man of French racing.*
▶ noun [in sing.] an arrival or an approach: *the coming of a new age.*
– PHRASES **coming and going** (or **comings and goings**) the busy, active movements of a person or group of people,especially in and out of a place. **not know if one is coming or going** informal be confused, especially as a result of being very busy.

Comino /kɒˈmiːnəʊ/ the smallest of the three main islands of Malta.

COMINT /ˈkɒmɪnt/ ▶ abbreviation for communications intelligence.

Comintern /ˈkɒmɪntəːn/ the Third International, a communist organization (1919–43). See **INTERNATIONAL** (sense 2).
– ORIGIN from Russian *Komintern*, blend of *kom(munisticheskiĭ)* 'communist' and *intern(atsional)* 'international'.

comital /ˈkɒmɪt(ə)l/ ▶ adjective chiefly historical of or relating to a count or earl.
– ORIGIN mid 19th cent.: from medieval Latin *comitalis*, from *comes*, *comit-* 'a count'.

comity /ˈkɒmɪti/ ▶ noun (pl. **-ies**) **1** an association of nations for their mutual benefit.
■(also **comity of nations**) [mass noun] the mutual recognition by nations of the laws and customs of others.
2 [mass noun] courtesy and considerate behaviour towards others.
– ORIGIN mid 16th cent. (in sense 2): from Latin *comitas*, from *comis* 'courteous'.

comm ▶ noun short for **COMMUNICATION**: [as modifier] *a comm link.* See also **COMMS**.

comma ▶ noun **1** a punctuation mark (,) indicating a pause between parts of a sentence or separating items in a list. See also **INVERTED COMMA**.
2 Music a minute interval or difference of pitch.
3 (also **comma butterfly**) a widespread butterfly that has orange and brown wings with ragged edges, and a white comma-shaped mark on the underside of the hindwing. Also called **HOP MERCHANT** in North America.
● *Polygonia c-album*, subfamily Nymphalinae, family Nymphalidae. See also **ANGLE WINGS**.
– ORIGIN late 16th cent. (originally as a term in rhetoric denoting a group of words shorter than a colon; see **COLON**[1]): via Latin from Greek *komma* 'piece cut off, short clause', from *koptein* 'cut'.

command ▶ verb **1** [reporting verb] give an authoritative or peremptory order: [with obj. and infinitive] *a gruff voice commanded us to enter* | [with direct speech] *'Stop arguing!' he commanded* | [with clause] *he commanded that work should cease* | [with obj.] *my mother commands my presence.*
■[with obj.] Military have authority over; be in charge of (a unit). ■ [with obj.] dominate (a strategic position) from a superior height: *the fortress commands the shortest Channel crossing.* ■ [with obj.] archaic control or restrain (oneself or one's feelings): *he commanded himself with an effort.*
2 [with obj.] be in a strong enough position to have or secure: *they command a majority in Parliament | signed bindings by superb craftsmen command a high price.*
■deserve and get (something such as sympathy or respect): *he commanded considerable personal loyalty.*
▶ noun an authoritative order.
■Computing an instruction or signal causing a computer to perform one of its basic functions. ■ [mass noun] authority, especially over armed forces: *an officer **took command** | who's **in command**?* ■ [in sing.] the ability to use or control something: *he had a brilliant command of English.* ■ [treated as sing. or pl.] Military a group of officers exercising control over a particular group or operation. ■ Military a body of troops or a district under the control of a particular officer.
– PHRASES **at someone's command** at someone's disposal to use or instruct: *I shall defend myself with all the eloquence at my command.* **by someone's command** in accordance with someone's orders. **word of command** Military an order for a movement in a drill. ■ a pre-arranged spoken signal for the start of an operation.
– ORIGIN Middle English: from Old French *comander* 'to command', from late Latin *commandare*, from *com-* (expressing intensive force) + *mandare* 'commit, command'. Compare with **COMMEND**.

command and control ▶ noun [mass noun] [usu. as modifier] chiefly Military the running of an armed force or other organization: *a command-and-control bunker.*

commandant /ˌkɒmənˈdant, ˈkɒmənˌdant, -dɑːnt/ ▶ noun an officer in charge of a particular force or institution: *the camp commandant.*
■a former rank of officer in the South African army or air force, above major and below colonel.
– ORIGIN late 17th cent.: from French *commandant*, or Italian or Spanish *commandante*, all from late Latin *commandare* 'to command' (see **COMMAND**).

command-driven ▶ adjective Computing (of a program or computer) operated by means of commands keyed in by the user or issued by another program or computer.

command economy ▶ noun another term for **PLANNED ECONOMY**.

commandeer /ˌkɒmənˈdɪə/ ▶ verb [with obj.] officially take possession or control of (something), especially for military purposes.
■take possession of (something) by force. ■ [with obj. and infinitive] enlist (someone) to help in a task, typically against their will: *he commandeered the men to find a table.*
– ORIGIN early 19th cent.: from Afrikaans *kommandeer*, from Dutch *commanderen*, from French *commander* 'to command' (see **COMMAND**).

commander ▶ noun **1** a person in authority, especially over a body of troops or a military operation: *the commander of a paratroop regiment.*
■a rank of naval officer, above lieutenant commander and below captain. ■ an officer in charge of a Metropolitan Police district in London.
2 a member of a higher class in some orders of knighthood. See also **KNIGHT COMMANDER**.
– DERIVATIVES **commandership** noun.
– ORIGIN Middle English: from Old French *comandeor*, from late Latin *commandare* 'to command' (see **COMMAND**).

commander-in-chief ▶ noun (pl. **commanders-in-chief**) an officer in charge of all of the armed forces of a country, a major subdivision of them, or all its forces in a particular area.
■a politician or head of state in supreme command of a country's armed forces.

Commander of the Faithful ▶ noun one of the titles of a caliph.

commanding ▶ adjective [attrib.] (in military contexts) having a position of authority: *a commanding officer.*
■possessing or giving superior strength: *a commanding 13–6 lead.* ■ indicating or expressing authority; imposing: *a man of commanding presence | her style is commanding.* ■ (of a place or position) dominating physically; giving a wide view.
– DERIVATIVES **commandingly** adverb.

command language ▶ noun Computing a source language composed chiefly of a set of commands or operators, used especially for communicating with the operating system of a computer.

commandment ▶ noun a divine rule, especially one of the Ten Commandments.
■humorous a rule to be observed as strictly as one of the Ten Commandments.
– ORIGIN Middle English: from Old French *comandement*, from *comander* 'to command' (see **COMMAND**).

command module (abbrev.: **CM**) ▶ noun the detachable control compartment of a manned spacecraft.

commando ▶ noun (pl. **-os**) a soldier specially trained for carrying out raids.
■a unit of such troops. ■ a group forming part of a larger organization, typically an illegal or secret one, and carrying out attacks on its behalf.
– ORIGIN late 18th cent. (denoting a militia, originally consisting of Boers in South Africa): from Portuguese (earlier form of *comando*), from *commandar* 'to command', from late Latin *commandare* (see **COMMAND**).

commando knife ▶ noun a long, slender knife suitable for hand-to-hand combat.

Command Paper ▶ noun (in the UK) a document laid before Parliament by order of the Crown, though in practice by the government.

command performance (also **Royal Command Performance**) ▶ noun (in the UK) a presentation of a play, concert, film, or other show at the request of royalty, who usually attend.

command post ▶ noun the place from which a unit commander controls a military unit.

comme ci, comme ça /kɒm ˌsiː kɒm ˈsɑː, French kɔm si kɔm sa/ ▶ adverb used, especially in answer to a question, to convey that something is neither very good nor very bad.
– ORIGIN French, literally 'like this, like that'.

commedia dell'arte /kɒˈmeɪdɪə dɛlˈɑːteɪ, Italian komˈmɛdja delˈlarte/ ▶ noun [mass noun] an improvised kind of popular comedy in Italian theatres in the 16th–18th centuries, based on stock characters. Actors adapted their comic dialogue and action according to a few basic plots (commonly love intrigues) and to topical issues.
– ORIGIN Italian, 'comedy of art'.

comme il faut /ˌkɒm iːl ˈfəʊ, French kɔm il fo/ ▶ adjective [predic.] correct in behaviour or etiquette.
– ORIGIN French, literally 'as is necessary'.

commemorate ▶ verb [with obj.] recall and show respect for (someone or something) in a ceremony: *a wreath-laying ceremony to commemorate the war dead.*
■serve as a memorial to: *a stone commemorating a boy who died at sea.* ■ mark (a significant event): *his centenary is commemorated by several exhibitions of his work.* ■ (often **be commemorated**) celebrate (an event, a person, or a situation) by doing or building something: *the victory was commemorated in songs.*
– DERIVATIVES **commemorator** noun.
– ORIGIN late 16th cent.: from Latin *commemorat-* 'brought to remembrance', from the verb *commemorare*, from *com-* 'altogether' + *memorare* 'relate' (from *memor* 'mindful').

commemoration ▶ noun [mass noun] remembrance, typically expressed in a ceremony: *local martyrs received public commemoration.*
■[count noun] a ceremony or celebration in which a person or event is remembered.
– PHRASES **in commemoration** as a reminder, especially a ritual or official one: *the window was ordered by the duchess in commemoration of her son.*
– ORIGIN late Middle English: from Latin *commemoratio(n-)*, from the verb *commemorare* 'bring to remembrance' (see **COMMEMORATE**).

commemorative ▶ adjective acting as a mark or memorial of an event or person.

▶ **noun** an object such as a stamp, a coin, or a piece of pottery made to mark an event or honour a person. Compare with **DEFINITIVE**.

commence ▶ **verb** begin: [with obj.] *his design team commenced work* | [no obj.] *a public inquiry is due to commence on the 16th.*
– ORIGIN Middle English: from Old French *commencier, comencier*, based on Latin *com-* (expressing intensive force) + *initiare* 'begin'.

commencement ▶ **noun 1** [usu. in sing.] the time, action, or process of beginning: *at the commencement of training* | [mass noun] *the date of commencement.*
■ the first part or earliest stage: *the commencement of this chapter.*
2 N. Amer. a ceremony in which degrees or diplomas are conferred on university or high-school students: [as modifier] *a commencement address.*
– ORIGIN Middle English: from Old French, from the verb *commencier* (see **COMMENCE**).

commend ▶ **verb** [with obj.] **1** (often **be commended**) praise formally or officially: *he was commended by the judge for his courageous actions.*
■ present as suitable for approval or acceptance; recommend: *I commend her to you without reservation.* ■ cause to be acceptable or pleasing: *the emphasis on peace will commend itself to all* | *most one-roomed flats have little to commend them.*
2 (**commend someone/thing to**) archaic or formal entrust someone or something to: *as they set out on their journey I commend them to your care.*
– PHRASES **commend me to** archaic remember me kindly to (someone). **highly commended** Brit. failing to win a prize but nevertheless considered meritorious.
– ORIGIN Middle English: from Latin *commendare*, from *com-* (expressing intensive force) + *mandare* 'commit, entrust'. Compare with **COMMAND**.

commendable ▶ **adjective** deserving praise: *commendable restraint.*
– DERIVATIVES **commendably** adverb.
– ORIGIN late Middle English: via Old French from Latin *commendabilis*, from *commendare* (see **COMMEND**).

commendation ▶ **noun** [mass noun] praise: *the film deserved the highest commendation* | [count noun] *the book gives commendations for initiative.*
■ [count noun] an award involving the giving of special praise: *the detectives received commendations for bravery.* ■ a very good result or high place in an examination or competition: [mass noun] *completion of the course with commendation.*
– ORIGIN Middle English: from Old French, from Latin *commendatio(n-)*, from *commendare* 'commit to the care of' (see **COMMEND**). Originally (in the plural) the term denoted a liturgical office ending with a prayer commending the souls of the dead to God.

Commendatore /kɒˌmɛndəˈtɔːreɪ/ ▶ **noun** (pl. **Commendatori** /-ri/) a knight of an Italian order of chivalry.
– ORIGIN Italian, from Latin *commendator*, based on *commendare* 'entrust'.

commendatory /kɒˈmɛndət(ə)ri/ ▶ **adjective** archaic serving to present something as suitable for approval or acceptance.
– ORIGIN mid 16th cent.: from late Latin *commendatorius*, from Latin *commendare* 'commit to the care of' (see **COMMEND**).

commensal /kəˈmɛns(ə)l/ ▶ **adjective** Biology of, relating to, or exhibiting commensalism.
▶ **noun** Biology a commensal organism, such as many bacteria.
– DERIVATIVES **commensality** /kɒmənˈsalɪti/ noun.
– ORIGIN late 19th cent.: from medieval Latin *commensalis*, from *com-* 'sharing' + *mensa* 'a table'.

commensalism ▶ **noun** [mass noun] Biology an association between two organisms in which one benefits and the other derives neither benefit nor harm.

commensurable /kəˈmɛnʃ(ə)rəb(ə)l, -sjə-/ ▶ **adjective 1** measurable by the same standard: *the finite is not commensurable with the infinite.*
2 [predic.] (**commensurable to**) rare proportionate to.
3 Mathematics (of numbers) in a ratio equal to a ratio of integers.
– DERIVATIVES **commensurability** noun, **commensurably** adverb.
– ORIGIN mid 16th cent.: from late Latin *commensurabilis*, from *com-* 'together' + *mensurabilis*, from *mensurare* 'to measure'.

commensurate /kəˈmɛnʃ(ə)rət, -sjə-/ ▶ **adjective** corresponding in size or degree; in proportion: *salary will be commensurate with age and experience* | *such heavy responsibility must receive commensurate reward.*
– DERIVATIVES **commensurately** adverb.
– ORIGIN mid 17th cent.: from late Latin *commensuratus*, from *com-* 'together' + *mensuratus*, past participle of *mensurare* 'to measure'.

comment ▶ **noun** a remark expressing an opinion or reaction: *you asked for comments on the new proposals* | [mass noun] *the plans were not sent to the council for comment.*
■ [mass noun] discussion, especially of a critical nature, of an issue or event: *the exhibition has aroused comment.* ■ an indirect expression of the views, especially critical ones, of the writer of a play, book, film, or similar work: *their second single is a comment on the commercial nature of raves.* ■ an explanatory note in a book or other written text. ■ archaic a written explanation or commentary. ■ Computing a piece of text placed within a program to help other users to understand it, which the computer ignores when running the program.
▶ **verb** [reporting verb] express an opinion or reaction in speech or writing: [with clause] *the review commented that the book was agreeably written* | [no obj.] *the company would not comment on the venture* | [with direct speech] *'She's an independent soul,' she commented.*
■ [with obj.] Computing place a piece of explanatory text within (a program) to assist other users. ■ [with obj.] Computing turn (part of a program) into a comment so that the computer ignores it when running the program: *you could try commenting out that line.*
– PHRASES **no comment** used in refusing to answer a question, especially in a sensitive situation.
– DERIVATIVES **commenter** noun.
– ORIGIN late Middle English (in the senses 'expository treatise' and 'explanatory note'): from Latin *commentum* 'contrivance' (in late Latin also 'interpretation'), neuter past participle of *comminisci* 'devise'.

commentary ▶ **noun** (pl. **-ies**) [mass noun] the expression of opinions or offering of explanations about an event or situation: *narrative overlaid with commentary* | [count noun] *an editorial commentary.*
■ [count noun] a descriptive spoken account (especially on radio or television) of an event or a performance as it happens. ■ [count noun] a set of explanatory or critical notes on a text: *a commentary on the Old Testament.*
– ORIGIN late Middle English: from Latin *commentarius, commentarium* (adjective, used as a noun), from *commentari*, frequentative of *comminisci* 'devise'.

commentate ▶ **verb** [no obj.] report on an event as it occurs, especially for a news or sports broadcast; provide a commentary: *they commentate on live Monday matches.*
– ORIGIN mid 19th cent.: back-formation from **COMMENTATOR**.

commentator ▶ **noun** a person who comments on events, especially in the media, or on a text.
■ a person who commentates on a sports match or other event.

commerce ▶ **noun** [mass noun] **1** the activity of buying and selling, especially on a large scale: *the changes in taxation are of benefit to commerce.*
2 dated social dealings between people.
3 archaic sexual intercourse.
– ORIGIN mid 16th cent. (in sense 2): from French, or from Latin *commercium* 'trade, trading', from *com-* 'together' + *mercium* (from *merx, merc-* 'merchandise').

commercial ▶ **adjective 1** concerned with or engaged in commerce: *a commercial agreement.*
2 making or intended to make a profit: *commercial products.*
■ having profit, rather than artistic or other value, as a primary aim: *their work is too commercial.*
3 [attrib.] (of television or radio) funded by the revenue from broadcast advertisements.
4 (of chemicals) supplied in bulk and not of the highest purity.
▶ **noun 1** a television or radio advertisement.
2 Brit. archaic a travelling sales representative.
– DERIVATIVES **commerciality** noun, **commercially** adverb.

commercial art ▶ **noun** [mass noun] art used in advertising and selling.

commercial bank ▶ **noun** a bank that offers services to the general public and to companies.

commercial bill ▶ **noun** a bill of exchange issued by a commercial organization to raise money for short-term needs.

commercial break ▶ **noun** an interruption in the transmission of a broadcast programme, or an intermission between programmes, during which advertisements are broadcast.

commercialism ▶ **noun** [mass noun] emphasis on the maximizing of profit: *political concern with state enterprise deficits prompted efforts for greater commercialism.*
■ derogatory practices and attitudes that are concerned with the making of profit at the expense of quality: *the cut-throat commercialism of the Paris art world.*

commercialize (also **-ise**) ▶ **verb** [with obj.] (usu. **be commercialized**) start to manage (an organization or an activity) in a way designed to make a profit: *the museum has been commercialized.*
■ exploit or spoil for the purpose of gaining profit: [as adj. **commercialized**] *commercialized resort areas.*
– DERIVATIVES **commercialization** noun.

commercial paper ▶ **noun** [mass noun] short-term unsecured promissory notes issued by companies.

commercial space ▶ **noun** see **SPACE** (sense 1).

commercial traveller ▶ **noun** Brit., dated a travelling sales representative.

commercial vehicle ▶ **noun** a vehicle used for carrying goods or fare-paying passengers.

commère /ˈkɒmɛː/ ▶ **noun** Brit. a female compère.
– ORIGIN early 20th cent.: French, feminine of **COMPÈRE**.

Commie informal, derogatory ▶ **noun** (pl. **-ies**) a communist.
▶ **adjective** communist.
– ORIGIN 1940s: abbreviation.

commination /ˌkɒmɪˈneɪʃ(ə)n/ ▶ **noun** [mass noun] the action of threatening divine vengeance.
■ the recital of divine threats against sinners in the Anglican Liturgy for Ash Wednesday. ■ [count noun] the service that includes this.
– ORIGIN late Middle English: from Latin *comminatio(n-)*, from the verb *comminari*, from *com-* (expressing intensive force) + *minari* 'threaten'.

comminatory /ˈkɒmɪnəˌt(ə)ri/ ▶ **adjective** rare threatening, punitive, or vengeful.
– ORIGIN early 16th cent.: from medieval Latin *comminatorius*, from *comminat-* 'threatened', from the verb *comminari* (see **COMMINATION**).

commingle /kɒˈmɪŋg(ə)l/ ▶ **verb** poetic/literary mix; blend: [no obj.] *the part of the brain where the senses commingle* | [with obj.] *his humanitarian stance was commingled with a desire for survival.*
– ORIGIN early 17th cent.: from **COM-** 'together' + **MINGLE**.

comminuted /ˈkɒmɪnjuːtɪd/ ▶ **adjective** technical reduced to minute particles or fragments.
■ Medicine (of a fracture) producing multiple bone splinters.
– ORIGIN early 17th cent.: past participle of *comminute*, from Latin *comminut-* 'broken into pieces', from the verb *comminuere*, from *com-* 'together' + *minuere* 'lessen'.

comminution /ˌkɒmɪˈnjuːʃ(ə)n/ ▶ **noun** [mass noun] technical the action of reducing a material, especially a mineral ore, to minute particles or fragments.

commis /ˈkɒmi/ (also **commis chef**) ▶ **noun** (pl. same /ˈkɒmi, ˈkɒmɪz/) a junior chef.
– ORIGIN 1930s: from French, 'deputy, clerk', past participle of *commettre* 'entrust', from Latin *committere* (see **COMMIT**).

commiserate /kəˈmɪzəreɪt/ ▶ **verb** [no obj.] express or feel sympathy or pity; sympathize: *she went over to commiserate with Rose on her unfortunate circumstances.*
■ [with obj.] archaic feel, show, or express pity for (someone): *she did not exult in her rival's fall, but, on the contrary, commiserated her.*
– DERIVATIVES **commiseration** noun, **commiserative** adjective.
– ORIGIN late 16th cent.: from Latin *commiserat-* 'commiserated', from the verb *commiserari*, from *com-* 'with' + *miserari* 'to lament' (from *miser* 'wretched').

commish /kəˈmɪʃ/ ▶ **noun** informal **1** N. Amer. short for **COMMISSIONER**.
2 short for **COMMISSION**: *out of commish.*

commissaire /ˌkɒmɪˈsɛː, French kɔmisɛʀ/ ▶ **noun** a senior police officer in France.

■(in France) an official at a cycle race or other sporting event.
– ORIGIN French.

commissar /ˌkɒmɪˈsɑː/ ▶noun an official of the Communist Party, especially in the former Soviet Union or present-day China, responsible for political education and organization.
■a head of a government department in the former Soviet Union before 1946. ■figurative a strict or prescriptive figure of authority: *our academic commissars.*
– ORIGIN early 20th cent. (Russian Revolution): from Russian *komissar*, from French *commissaire*, from medieval Latin *commissarius* (see **COMMISSARY**).

commissariat /ˌkɒmɪˈsɛːrɪət/ ▶noun **1** chiefly Military a department for the supply of food and equipment.
2 a government department of the USSR before 1946.
– ORIGIN late 16th cent. (as a Scots legal term denoting the jurisdiction of a commissary, often spelled *commissariot*): from French *commissariat*, reinforced by medieval Latin *commissariatus*, both from medieval Latin *commissarius* 'person in charge', from Latin *committere* 'entrust'.

commissary /ˈkɒmɪs(ə)ri/ ▶noun (pl. **-ies**) **1** a deputy or delegate.
■a representative or deputy of a bishop.
2 N. Amer. a restaurant in a film studio, military base, prison, or other institution.
■a store for the supply of food and drink to soldiers or other members of an organization.
– DERIVATIVES **commissarial** /-ˈsɛːrɪəl/ adjective.
– ORIGIN late Middle English: from medieval Latin *commissarius* 'person in charge', from Latin *commiss-* 'joined, entrusted', from the verb *committere* (see **COMMIT**).

commission ▶noun **1** an instruction, command, or role given to a person or to a specially constituted group: *one of his first commissions was to redesign the Great Exhibition building* | [with infinitive] *he received a commission to act as an informer.*
■an order for something, especially a work of art, to be produced specially. ■a work produced in response to such an order. ■[mass noun] archaic the authority to perform a task or certain duties: *the divine Commission of Christ.*
2 a group of people entrusted by a government or other official body with authority to do something.
3 a sum, typically a set percentage of the value involved, paid to an agent in a commercial transaction: *foreign banks may charge a commission* | [mass noun] *he sold cosmetics* ***on commission.***
4 a warrant conferring the rank of officer in an army, navy, or air force.
5 [mass noun] the action of committing a crime or offence.
▶verb [with obj.] **1** give an order for or authorize the production of (something such as a building, piece of equipment, or work of art).
■[with obj. and infinitive] order or authorize (a person or organization) to do or produce something: *they commissioned an architect to manage the building project.* ■[with obj. and infinitive] give (an artist) an order for a piece of work: *he was commissioned to do a series of drawings.*
2 bring (something newly produced, such as a factory or machine) into working condition: *we had a few hiccups getting the heating equipment commissioned.*
■bring (a warship) into readiness for active service: *the aircraft carrier* Midway *was commissioned in 1945.*
3 (usu. **be commissioned**) appoint (someone) to the rank of officer in an army, navy, or air force: *he was* ***commissioned into*** *the Royal Fusiliers* | [as adj. **commissioned**] *a commissioned officer.*
– PHRASES **in commission** (of a ship, vehicle, machine, etc.) in use or in service. **out of commission** not in service; not in working order.
■(of a person) unable to work or function normally, especially through illness or injury.
– ORIGIN Middle English: via Old French from Latin *commissio(n-)*, from *committere* 'entrust' (see **COMMIT**).

commission agent ▶noun Brit. a person who transacts business on commission, typically on behalf of a principal from another country.

commissionaire /kəˌmɪʃəˈnɛː/ ▶noun chiefly Brit. a uniformed door attendant at a hotel, theatre, or other building.
– ORIGIN mid 17th cent.: from French, from medieval Latin *commissarius* 'person in charge', from Latin *committere* 'entrust' (see **COMMIT**).

commissioner ▶noun a person appointed to a role on or by a commission, in particular:
■a representative of the supreme authority in an area. ■the head of the Metropolitan Police in London. ■N. Amer. a person appointed to regulate a particular sport: *a baseball commissioner.*
– ORIGIN late Middle English: from medieval Latin *commissionarius*, from Latin *commissio* (see **COMMISSION**).

commissioner for oaths ▶noun Brit. a solicitor authorized to administer an oath to a person making an affidavit.

commission of the peace ▶noun Brit., chiefly historical the Justices of the Peace in a particular jurisdiction considered collectively.

commissure /ˈkɒmɪsjʊə/ ▶noun technical a junction, joint, or seam, in particular:
■Anatomy the joint between two bones. ■Anatomy a band of nerve tissue connecting the hemispheres of the brain, the two sides of the spinal cord, etc. ■Anatomy the line where the upper and lower lips or eyelids meet.
– DERIVATIVES **commissural** /ˌkɒmɪˈsjʊər(ə)l/ adjective.
– ORIGIN late Middle English: from Latin *commissura* 'junction', from *committere* 'join' (see **COMMIT**).

commit ▶verb (**committed**, **committing**) [with obj.] **1** perpetrate or carry out (a mistake, crime, or immoral act): *he committed an uncharacteristic error.*
2 pledge or bind (a person or an organization) to a certain course or policy: *they were reluctant to* ***commit themselves to*** *an opinion* | [with obj. and infinitive] *the treaty commits each party to defend the other* | [no obj.] *try it out before you* ***commit to*** *a purchase.*
■pledge or set aside (resources) for future use: *manufacturers will have to commit substantial funds to developing new engines.* ■(**commit oneself to**) resolve to remain in a long-term emotional relationship with (someone): *she didn't love him enough to commit herself to him.* ■(**be committed to**) be in a long-term emotional relationship with (someone). ■(**be committed to**) be dedicated to (something): *it is a modern Marxist party committed to democratic socialism.*
3 send, entrust, or consign, in particular:
■consign (someone) officially to prison, especially on remand: *he was* ***committed to*** *prison for contempt of court.* ■send (a person or case) for trial in a higher court: *the magistrate decided to* ***commit*** *him* ***for trial.*** ■send (someone) to be confined in a psychiatric hospital. ■(**commit something to**) transfer something to (a state or place where it can be kept or preserved): *he composed a letter but didn't commit it to paper* | *she committed each tiny feature to memory.* ■refer (a parliamentary or legislative bill) to a committee.
– PHRASES **commit suicide** kill oneself.
– DERIVATIVES **committable** adjective, **committer** noun.
– ORIGIN late Middle English: from Latin *committere* 'join, entrust' (in medieval Latin 'put into custody'), from *com-* 'with' + *mittere* 'put or send'.

commitment ▶noun **1** [mass noun] the state or quality of being dedicated to a cause or activity: *the company's* ***commitment to*** *quality* | *I could not fault my players for commitment.*
■[count noun] a pledge or undertaking: *I cannot make such a commitment at the moment.* ■[count noun] an act of pledging or setting aside something: *there must be a major commitment of money and time.*
2 (usu. **commitments**) an engagement or obligation that restricts freedom of action: *business commitments.*

committal ▶noun [mass noun] **1** the action of sending a person to an institution, especially prison or a psychiatric hospital: *his* ***committal to prison*** | [count noun] *seeking to reduce the number of committals* | [as modifier] *committal proceedings.*
2 the burial of a corpse.

committed ▶adjective feeling great dedication and loyalty to a cause, activity, or job; wholeheartedly dedicated: *a committed Christian.*

committee /kəˈmɪti/ ▶noun **1** [treated as sing. or pl.] a group of people appointed for a specific function by a larger group and typically consisting of members of that group: *the housing committee* | [as modifier] *a committee meeting.*
■(in the UK) a group of this kind appointed by Parliament to consider the details of proposed legislation: *there was much scrutiny* ***in committee.*** ■(**Committee of the whole House**) (in the UK) the whole House of Commons when sitting as a committee.
2 /ˌkɒmɪˈtiː/ Law, Brit. a person entrusted with the charge of another person or another person's property.
■chiefly US a person who has been judicially committed to the charge of another because of insanity or mental retardation.
– ORIGIN late 15th cent. (in the general sense 'person to whom something has been entrusted'): from **COMMIT** + **-EE**.

committeeman ▶noun (pl. **-men**) (in the US) a male local political party leader.

Committee of Public Safety a French governing body set up in April 1793, during the Revolution. Under the influence of Robespierre it initiated the Terror but it was dissolved in 1795.

committee stage ▶noun Brit. the third of five stages of a bill's progress through Parliament when it may be debated and amended.

committeewoman ▶noun (pl. **-women**) (in the US) a female local political party leader.

commix /kɒˈmɪks/ ▶verb [with obj.] archaic mix; mingle: *beat them till they be thoroughly commixed.*
– DERIVATIVES **commixture** noun.
– ORIGIN late Middle English (as the past participle *commixt*): from Latin *commixtus*, from *com-* 'together with' + *mixtus* 'mixed'.

Commo Austral./NZ informal, derogatory ▶noun (pl. **-os**) a communist.
▶adjective communist.
– ORIGIN 1940s: abbreviation.

commo ▶noun US informal communication, especially as a departmental function in an organization.

commode ▶noun **1** a piece of furniture containing a concealed chamber pot.
■N. Amer. a toilet. ■N. Amer. historical a movable washstand.
2 a chest of drawers or chiffonier of a decorative type popular in the 18th century.
– ORIGIN mid 18th cent. (in sense 2): from French, literally 'convenient, suitable', from Latin *commodus*. Sense 1 dates from the early 19th cent.

commodify /kəˈmɒdɪfʌɪ/ ▶verb (**-ies**, **-ied**) [with obj.] turn into or treat as a mere commodity: [as adj. **commodified**] *art has become commodified.*
– DERIVATIVES **commodification** noun.
– ORIGIN 1980s: from **COMMODITY** + **-FY**.

commodious /kəˈməʊdɪəs/ ▶adjective **1** formal (especially of furniture or a building) roomy and comfortable.
2 archaic convenient.
– DERIVATIVES **commodiously** adverb, **commodiousness** noun.
– ORIGIN late Middle English (in the sense 'beneficial, useful'): from French *commodieux* or medieval Latin *commodiosus*, based on Latin *commodus* 'convenient'.

commoditize ▶verb another term for **COMMODIFY**.
– DERIVATIVES **commoditization** noun.

commodity /kəˈmɒdɪti/ ▶noun (pl. **-ies**) a raw material or primary agricultural product that can be bought and sold, such as copper or coffee.
■a useful or valuable thing, such as water or time.
– ORIGIN late Middle English: from Old French *commodite* or Latin *commoditas*, from *commodus* (see **COMMODIOUS**).

commodore /ˈkɒmədɔː/ ▶noun a naval rank above captain and below rear admiral, generally given temporarily to an officer commanding a squadron or division of a fleet.
■the president of a yacht club. ■the senior captain of a shipping line.
– ORIGIN late 17th cent.: probably from Dutch *komandeur*, from French *commandeur* 'commander'.

common ▶adjective (**commoner**, **commonest**) **1** occurring, found, or done often; prevalent: *salt and pepper are the two most common seasonings* | *it's* ***common for*** *a woman to be depressed after giving birth.*
■(of an animal or plant) found or living in relatively large numbers; not rare. ■ordinary; of ordinary qualities; without special rank or position: *the dwellings of common people* | *a common soldier.* ■(of a quality) of a sort or level to be generally expected: *common decency.* ■of the most familiar type: *the common or vernacular name.* ■denoting the most widespread or typical species of an animal or plant: *the common gull.*

2 showing a lack of taste and refinement supposedly typical of the lower classes; vulgar: *she's so common.*
3 shared by, coming from, or done by two or more people, groups, or things: *the two republics' common border* | *problems common to both communities.*
■belonging to, open to, or affecting the whole of a community or the public at large: *common land.* ■ Mathematics belonging to two or more quantities.
4 Grammar (in Latin, Dutch, and certain other languages) of or denoting a gender of nouns that are conventionally regarded as masculine or feminine, contrasting with neuter.
■(in English) denoting a noun that refers to individuals of either sex (e.g. *teacher*).
5 Prosody (of a syllable) able to be either short or long.
6 Law (of a crime) of lesser importance: *common assault.*
▶noun **1** a piece of open land for public use, especially in a village or town.
2 Brit. informal common sense.
3 (in the Christian Church) a form of service used for each of a group of occasions.
4 (also **right of common**) English Law a person's right over another's land, e.g. for pasturage or mineral extraction.
– PHRASES **the common good** the benefit or interests of all: *it is time our elected officials stood up for the common good.* **common ground** a point accepted or shared by each of two or more conflicting or differing parties: *artists from different cultural backgrounds found common ground.* **common knowledge** something known by most people. **common or garden** Brit. informal of the usual or ordinary type: *Britain's common or garden house sparrow.* **common property** a thing or things held jointly. ■ something known by most people. **the common touch** the ability to get on with or appeal to ordinary people. **have something in common** have a specified amount or degree of shared interests or characteristics: *the two men had little in common.* **in common** in joint use or possession; shared: *a sect that had wives in common.* **in common with** in the same way as: *in common with other officers I had to undertake guard duties.* **out of the common** Brit. rarely occurring; unusual.
– DERIVATIVES **commonness** noun.
– ORIGIN Middle English: from Old French *comun* (adjective), from Latin *communis.*

commonable ▶ adjective Brit., chiefly historical (of land) allowed to be jointly used or owned.
■(of an animal) allowed to be pastured on common land: *these Acts exclude the deer and commonable cattle.*
– ORIGIN early 17th cent.: from obsolete *common* 'to exercise right of common' + -ABLE.

commonage ▶ noun [mass noun] **1** chiefly Brit. the right of pasturing animals on common land.
■land held in common.
2 the common people; the commonalty.

Common Agricultural Policy (abbrev.: **CAP**) the system in the EU for establishing common prices for most agricultural products within the European Union, a single fund for price supports, and levies on imports.

commonality ▶ noun (pl. -ies) **1** [in sing.] the state of sharing features or attributes: *a commonality of interest ensures cooperation* | [mass noun] *the explanations show a high degree of commonality in their reasoning.*
■[count noun] a shared feature or attribute.
2 (the commonality) another term for COMMONALTY.
– ORIGIN late Middle English (in sense 2): variant of COMMONALTY. Sense 1 dates from the mid 16th cent., but was rarely used before the 1950s.

commonalty /ˈkɒmən(ə)lti/ ▶ noun [treated as pl.] (**the commonalty**) chiefly historical people without special rank or position, usually viewed as an estate of the realm: *a petition by the earls, barons, and commonalty of the realm.*
■the general body of a group: *uptalk seems to be spreading from teenagers to the broad commonalty.*
– ORIGIN Middle English: from Old French *comunalte,* from medieval Latin *communalitas,* from Latin *communis* 'common, general' (see COMMON).

common carrier ▶ noun a person or company undertaking to transport any goods or passengers on regular routes at agreed rates.
■N. Amer. a company providing public telecommunications facilities.

common chord ▶ noun Music a triad containing a root, a major or minor third, and a perfect fifth.

common cold ▶ noun (**the common cold**) another term for COLD (in sense 2).

common council ▶ noun a town or city council, now only in London and some parts of Canada and the US.

common denominator ▶ noun Mathematics a common multiple of the denominators of several fractions. See also LOWEST COMMON DENOMINATOR, LEAST COMMON DENOMINATOR.
■figurative a feature shared by all members of a group.

Common Entrance ▶ noun Brit. an examination taken, usually at 13, by pupils wishing to enter public schools.

commoner ▶ noun **1** one of the ordinary or common people, as opposed to the aristocracy or to royalty.
2 a person who has the right of common.
3 (at some British universities) an undergraduate who does not have a scholarship.
– ORIGIN Middle English (denoting a citizen or burgess): from medieval Latin *communarius,* from *communa, communia* 'community', based on Latin *communis* (see COMMON).

Common Era ▶ noun (**the Common Era**) another term for CHRISTIAN ERA.

common gull ▶ noun a migratory gull with greenish-grey legs, found locally in northern and eastern Eurasia and NW North America.
● *Larus canus,* family Laridae. North American name: **mew gull.**

commonhold ▶ noun [mass noun] Brit. the proposed system of freehold tenure of a unit within a multi-occupancy building, but with shared responsibility for common services; condominium.

common jury ▶ noun Brit. historical a jury for which no qualification of property or social standing was required. Compare with SPECIAL JURY.

common law ▶ noun [mass noun] the part of English law that is derived from custom and judicial precedent rather than statutes. Often contrasted with STATUTE LAW.
■the body of English law as adopted and adapted by the different States of the US. Compare with CIVIL LAW. ■ [as modifier] denoting a partner in a marriage recognized in some jurisdictions (excluding the UK) as valid by common law, though not brought about by a civil or ecclesiastical ceremony: *a common-law husband.* ■ [as modifier] denoting a partner in a relationship in which a man and woman cohabit for a period long enough to suggest stability.

common logarithm ▶ noun a logarithm to the base 10.

commonly ▶ adverb very often; frequently: *a commonly used industrial chemical* | *shift workers commonly complain of not getting enough sleep.*

common market ▶ noun a group of countries imposing few or no duties on trade with one another and a common tariff on trade with other countries.
■(the Common Market) a name for the European Economic Community or European Union, used especially in the 1960s and 1970s.

common metre (abbrev.: **CM**) ▶ noun [mass noun] a metrical pattern for hymns in which the stanzas have four lines containing eight and six syllables alternately.

common noun ▶ noun Grammar a noun denoting a class of objects or a concept as opposed to a particular individual. Often contrasted with PROPER NOUN.

commonplace ▶ adjective not unusual; ordinary: *unemployment was commonplace in his trade.*
■not interesting or original; trite: *the usual commonplace remarks.*
▶noun **1** a usual or ordinary thing: *bombing has become almost a commonplace of public life there.*
■a trite saying or topic; a platitude: *it is a commonplace to talk of the young being alienated.*
2 a notable passage in a work copied into a commonplace book.
– DERIVATIVES **commonplaceness** noun.
– ORIGIN mid 16th cent. (originally *common place*): translation of Latin *locus communis,* rendering Greek *koinos topos* 'general theme'.

commonplace book ▶ noun a book into which notable extracts from other works are copied for personal use.

Common Pleas (in full **Court of Common Pleas**) Law, historical a court for hearing civil cases between subjects or citizens not involving Crown or state.

Common Prayer the Church of England liturgy, originally set forth in the *Book of Common Prayer* of Edward VI (1549) and revised in 1662.

common rat ▶ noun another term for BROWN RAT.

common room ▶ noun chiefly Brit. a room in a school, college, or other educational institution for use of students or staff outside teaching hours.

commons ▶ plural noun **1** (**the Commons**) short for HOUSE OF COMMONS.
■historical the common people regarded as a part of a political system, especially in Britain.
2 [treated as sing.] land or resources belonging to or affecting the whole of a community.
3 archaic provisions shared in common; rations.
– PHRASES **short commons** archaic insufficient allocation of food: *a life of short commons.*
– ORIGIN Middle English: plural of COMMON.

common salt ▶ noun see SALT (sense 1).

common seal[1] ▶ noun a seal with a mottled grey-brown coat and a concave profile, found along North Atlantic and North Pacific coasts.
● *Phoca vitulina,* family Phocidae. North American name: **harbour seal.**

common seal[2] ▶ noun an official seal of a corporate body.

common sense ▶ noun [mass noun] good sense and sound judgement in practical matters: *it is all a matter of common sense* | [as modifier] *a common-sense approach.*
– DERIVATIVES **commonsensical** adjective.

Common Serjeant ▶ noun (in the UK) a circuit judge of the Central Criminal Court with duties in the City of London.

common soldier ▶ noun see SOLDIER (sense 1).

common stock ▶ plural noun (also **common stocks**) [mass noun] N. Amer. ordinary shares.

common time ▶ noun [mass noun] Music a rhythmic pattern in which there are two or four beats, especially four crotchets, in a bar.

commonweal /ˈkɒmənwiːl/ ▶ noun (**the commonweal**) archaic the welfare of the public.

commonwealth ▶ noun **1** an independent state or community, especially a democratic republic.
■an aggregate or grouping of states or other bodies. ■ a community or organization of shared interests in a non-political field: *the Christian commonwealth* | *the commonwealth of letters.* ■ a self-governing unit voluntarily grouped with the US, such as Puerto Rico. ■ a formal title of some of the states of the US, especially Kentucky, Massachusetts, Pennsylvania, and Virginia. ■ the title of the federated Australian states. ■ (**the Commonwealth**) the republican period of government in Britain between the execution of Charles I in 1649 and the Restoration of Charles II in 1660.
2 (**the Commonwealth**) (in full **the Commonwealth of Nations**) an international association consisting of the UK together with states that were previously part of the British Empire, and dependencies. The British monarch is the symbolic head of the Commonwealth.
3 (**the commonwealth**) archaic the general good.
– ORIGIN late Middle English (originally as two words, denoting public welfare; compare with COMMONWEAL): from COMMON + WEALTH.

Commonwealth Day ▶ noun the second Monday in March, celebrating the British Commonwealth. It was instituted to commemorate assistance given to Britain by the colonies during the Boer War (1899–1902). Formerly called EMPIRE DAY.

Commonwealth Games an amateur sports competition held every four years between member countries of the Commonwealth.

Commonwealth of Independent States (abbrev.: **CIS**) a confederation of independent states, formerly constituent republics of the Soviet Union, established in 1991. The member states are Armenia, Belarus, Kazakhstan, Kyrgyzstan, Moldova, Russia, Tajikistan, Turkmenistan, Ukraine, and Uzbekistan.

commotion ▶ noun a state of confused and noisy disturbance: *she was distracted by a commotion across the street* | [mass noun] *they set off firecrackers to make a lot of commotion.*
■[mass noun] civil insurrection: *damage caused by civil commotion.*

– ORIGIN late Middle English: from Latin *commotio(n-)*, from *com-* 'altogether' + *motio* (see **MOTION**).

comms ▶ **plural noun** [usu. as modifier] communications: *comms software.*
– ORIGIN late 20th cent.: abbreviation.

communal /ˈkɒmjʊn(ə)l, kəˈmjuː-/ ▶ **adjective** **1** shared by all members of a community; for common use: *a communal bathroom and kitchen.*
■ of, relating to, or done by a community: *communal pride in impressive local buildings.* ■ involving the sharing of work and property: *communal living.*
2 (of conflict) between different communities, especially those having different religions or ethnic origins: *violent communal riots.*
– DERIVATIVES **communality** noun, **communally** adverb.
– ORIGIN early 19th cent. (in the sense 'relating to a commune, especially the Paris Commune'): from French, from late Latin *communalis*, from *communis* (see **COMMON**).

communalism ▶ **noun** [mass noun] **1** a principle of political organization based on federated communes.
■ the principle or practice of living together and sharing possessions and responsibilities.
2 allegiance to one's own ethnic group rather than to the wider society.
– DERIVATIVES **communalist** adjective & noun, **communalistic** adjective.

communalize (also **-ise**) ▶ **verb** [with obj.] rare organize (something) on the basis of shared ownership: *attempts to communalize farming.*
– DERIVATIVES **communalization** noun.

communard /ˈkɒmjʊnɑːd/ ▶ **noun** a member of a commune.
■ (**Communard**) historical a supporter of the Paris Commune.
– ORIGIN late 19th cent.: from French, from **COMMUNE**[1].

commune[1] /ˈkɒmjuːn/ ▶ **noun** **1** a group of people living together and sharing possessions and responsibilities.
■ a communal settlement in a communist country.
2 the smallest French territorial division for administrative purposes.
■ a similar division elsewhere.
3 (**the Commune**) the group which seized the municipal government of Paris in the French Revolution and played a leading part in the Reign of Terror until suppressed in 1794.
■ (also **the Paris Commune**) the municipal government organized on communalistic principles elected in Paris in 1871. It was soon brutally suppressed by government troops.
– ORIGIN late 17th cent. (in sense 2): from French, from medieval Latin *communia*, neuter plural of Latin *communis* (see **COMMON**).

commune[2] /kəˈmjuːn/ ▶ **verb** [no obj.] (**commune with**) share one's intimate thoughts or feelings with (someone or something), especially when the exchange is on a spiritual level: *the purpose of praying is to **commune with** God.*
■ feel in close spiritual contact with: *he spent an hour **communing with** nature on the bank of a stream.*
– ORIGIN Middle English: from Old French *comuner* 'to share', from *comun* (see **COMMON**).

communicable ▶ **adjective** able to be communicated to others: *the value of the product must be communicable to the potential consumers.*
■ (of a disease) able to be transmitted from one sufferer to another; contagious or infectious.
– DERIVATIVES **communicability** noun, **communicably** adverb.
– ORIGIN late Middle English (in the sense 'communicating, having communication'): from Old French, from late Latin *communicabilis*, from the verb *communicare* 'to share' (see **COMMUNICATE**).

communicant ▶ **noun** **1** a person who receives Holy Communion.
2 archaic a person who imparts information.
– ORIGIN mid 16th cent.: from Latin *communicant-* 'sharing', from the verb *communicare* (see **COMMUNICATE**).

communicate ▶ **verb** **1** [no obj.] share or exchange information, news, or ideas: *the prisoner was forbidden to **communicate with** his family.*
■ [with obj.] impart or pass on (information, news, or ideas): *he **communicated** his findings **to** the inspector.* ■ [with obj.] convey or transmit (an emotion or feeling) in a non-verbal way: *the ability of good teachers to communicate their own enthusiasm | his sudden fear **communicated itself**.* ■ succeed in conveying one's ideas or in evoking understanding in others: *a politician must have the ability to communicate.* ■ (of two people) be able to share and understand each other's thoughts and feelings. ■ [with obj.] (usu. **be communicated**) pass on (an infectious disease) to another person or animal. ■ [with obj.] transmit (heat or motion): *the heat is communicated through a small brass grating.* ■ [often as adj. **communicating**] (of two rooms) have a common connecting door: *he went into the communicating room to pick up the phone.*
2 [no obj.] receive Holy Communion.
– DERIVATIVES **communicator** noun, **communicatory** adjective.
– ORIGIN early 16th cent.: from Latin *communicat-* 'shared', from the verb *communicare*, from *communis* (see **COMMON**).

communication ▶ **noun** **1** [mass noun] the imparting or exchanging of information by speaking, writing, or by using some other medium: *direct communication between the two countries will produce greater understanding | at the moment I am **in communication with** London.*
■ [count noun] a letter or message containing such information or news. ■ the successful conveying or sharing of ideas and feelings: *there was a lack of **communication between** Pamela and her parents.* ■ social contact: *she gave him some hope of her return, or at least of their future communication.*
2 (**communications**) means of connection between people or places, in particular:
■ the means of sending or receiving information, such as telephone lines or computers: *satellite communications | [as modifier] a communications network.* ■ the means of travelling or of transporting goods, such as roads or railways: *a city providing excellent road and rail communications.* ■ [treated as sing.] the field of study concerned with the transmission of information by various means.
– PHRASES **line of communications** the connections between an army in the field and its bases.
– DERIVATIVES **communicational** adjective.
– ORIGIN late Middle English: from Old French *comunicacion*, from Latin *communicatio(n-)*, from the verb *communicare* 'to share' (see **COMMUNICATE**).

communication cord ▶ **noun** Brit. another term for **EMERGENCY CORD**.

communications satellite (also **communication satellite**) ▶ **noun** a satellite placed in orbit round the earth in order to relay television, radio, and telephone signals.

communication theory (also **communications theory**) ▶ **noun** [mass noun] the branch of knowledge dealing with the principles and methods by which information is conveyed.

communicative ▶ **adjective** willing, eager, or able to talk or impart information: *Lew was a very communicative chap.*
■ relating to the conveyance or exchange of information: *the communicative process in literary texts.*
– DERIVATIVES **communicatively** adverb.
– ORIGIN late Middle English: from late Latin *communicativus*, from *communicat-* 'shared', from the verb *communicare* (see **COMMUNICATE**).

communion ▶ **noun** **1** [mass noun] the sharing or exchanging of intimate thoughts and feelings, especially when the exchange is on a mental or spiritual level: *in this churchyard **communion with** the dead was almost palpable | [count noun] for a moment there was a blessed **communion between** them.*
■ the common participation in a mental or spiritual experience: *the Coronation marked a high spot of national communion.*
2 (often **Communion** or **Holy Communion**) the service of Christian worship at which bread and wine are consecrated and shared. See **EUCHARIST**.
■ the consecrated bread and wine so administered and received: *the priests gave him Holy Communion.* ■ reception of the consecrated bread and wine at such a service.
3 a relationship of recognition and acceptance between Christian Churches or denominations, or between individual Christians or Christian communities and a Church (signified by a willingness to give or receive the Eucharist): *the Eastern Churches are not **in communion with** Rome.*
■ [count noun] a group of Christian communities or Churches which recognize one another's ministries or that of a central authority. See also **ANGLICAN COMMUNION**.
– PHRASES **make one's communion** receive bread and wine which has been consecrated at a Eucharist, as a sacramental, spiritual, or symbolic act of receiving the presence of Christ.
– ORIGIN late Middle English: from Latin *communio(n-)*, from *communis* (see **COMMON**).

communion of saints ▶ **noun** [in sing.] a fellowship between Christians living and dead.

communiqué /kəˈmjuːnɪkeɪ/ (also **communique**) ▶ **noun** an official announcement or statement, especially one made to the media.
– ORIGIN mid 19th cent.: from French, past participle of *communiquer* 'communicate'.

communism (often **Communism**) ▶ **noun** [mass noun] a theory or system of social organization in which all property is vested in the community and each person contributes and receives according to their ability and needs. See also **MARXISM**.

The most familiar form of communism is that established by the Bolsheviks after the Russian Revolution of 1917, and it has generally been understood in terms of the system practised by the former USSR and its allies in eastern Europe, in China since 1949, and in some developing countries such as Cuba, Vietnam, and North Korea. Communism embraced a revolutionary ideology in which the state would wither away after the overthrow of the capitalist system. In practice, however, the state grew to control all aspects of communist society. Communism in eastern Europe collapsed in the late 1980s and early 1990s against a background of failure to meet people's economic expectations, a shift to more democracy in political life, and increasing nationalism such as that which led to the break-up of the USSR.

– DERIVATIVES **communist** noun & adjective, **communistic** adjective.
– ORIGIN mid 19th cent.: from French *communisme*, from *commun* (see **COMMON**).

Communism Peak one of the principal peaks in the Pamir Mountains of Tajikistan, rising to 7,495 m (24,590 ft). It was the highest mountain in the Soviet Union. Former names **MOUNT GARMO** (until 1933) and **STALIN PEAK** (until 1962).

communitarianism ▶ **noun** [mass noun] a theory or system of social organization based on small self-governing communities.
■ an ideology which emphasizes the responsibility of the individual to the community and the social importance of the family unit.
– DERIVATIVES **communitarian** adjective & noun.
– ORIGIN mid 19th cent.: from **COMMUNITY** + **-ARIAN**, on the pattern of words such as *unitarian*.

community ▶ **noun** (pl. **-ies**) **1** a group of people living together in one place, especially one practising common ownership: *a community of nuns.*
■ all the people living in a particular area or place: *local communities.* ■ a particular area or place considered together with its inhabitants: *a rural community.* ■ (**the community**) the people of a district or country considered collectively, especially in the context of social values and responsibilities; society: *preparing prisoners for life back in the community.* ■ [as modifier] denoting a worker or resource designed to serve the people of a particular area: *community health services.*
2 [usu. with modifier] a group of people having a religion, race, profession, or other particular characteristic in common: *Bangkok's Chinese community | the scientific community.*
■ a body of nations or states unified by common interests: [in names] *the African Economic Community.* ■ (**the Community**) short for **EUROPEAN COMMUNITY**.
3 [mass noun] the condition of sharing or having certain attitudes and interests in common: *the sense of community that organized religion can provide.*
■ [in sing.] a similarity or identity: *the law presupposes a community of interest between an employer and employees.* ■ joint ownership or liability: *the community of goods.*
4 Ecology a group of interdependent plants or animals growing or living together in natural conditions or occupying a specified habitat: *communities of insectivorous birds.*
– PHRASES **the international community** the countries of the world considered collectively.
– ORIGIN late Middle English: from Old French *comunete*, reinforced by its source, Latin *communitas*, from *communis* (see **COMMON**).

community architect ▶ **noun** an architect working in consultation with local inhabitants in designing housing and other amenities.
– DERIVATIVES **community architecture** noun.

community care (also **care in the community**) ▶ **noun** [mass noun] long-term care for the mentally ill,

C

the elderly, and people with disabilities which is provided within the community rather than in hospitals or institutions, especially as implemented in the UK under the National Health Service and Community Care Act of 1990.

community centre ▶ **noun** a place where people from a particular neighbourhood can meet for social events, education classes, or recreational activities.

community charge ▶ **noun** [mass noun] (in the UK) a tax, introduced by the Conservative government in 1990 (1989 in Scotland), levied locally on every adult in a community. It was replaced in 1993 by the council tax. Informally called POLL TAX.

community chest ▶ **noun** a fund for charitable activities among the people in a particular area.

community college ▶ **noun 1** chiefly N. Amer. a college providing further and higher education for people living in a particular area.
2 Brit. a secondary school whose educational and recreational facilities are available to adults in the local community.

community home ▶ **noun** Brit. a centre for housing young offenders and other young people in need of custodial care.

community hospital ▶ **noun** a non-specialized hospital serving a local area.

community of property ▶ **noun** [mass noun] (in South Africa) a marriage contract in which the possessions of the partners are merged in a joint estate and disposed of by means of a joint will.

community policing ▶ **noun** [mass noun] the system of allocating police officers to particular areas so that they become familiar with the local inhabitants.

community service ▶ **noun** [mass noun] voluntary work intended to help people in a particular area.
■English Law unpaid work, intended to be of social use, that an offender is required to do instead of going to prison: [as modifier] *a community-service order.*

community singing ▶ **noun** [mass noun] singing by a large crowd or group, especially of old popular songs or hymns.

community worker ▶ **noun** a person who works among the people of a particular area to promote their welfare.

communize /'kɒmjʊnʌɪz/ (also **-ise**) ▶ **verb** [with obj.] rare cause (a country, people, or economic activity) to be organized on the principles of communism.
– DERIVATIVES **communization** noun.
– ORIGIN late 19th cent.: from Latin *communis* (see COMMON) + -IZE.

commutable /kə'mju:təb(ə)l/ ▶ **adjective 1** (of a place or home) sufficiently close to one's place of work that one can travel between the two on a regular basis.
■(of a journey or distance between home and work) sufficiently short that it can be travelled on a regular basis. [ORIGIN: 1970s (originally US): from sense 1 of COMMUTE.]
2 rare capable of being exchanged or converted.
– DERIVATIVES **commutability** noun.
– ORIGIN mid 17th cent.: from Latin *commutabilis*, from *commutare* 'exchange, interchange' (see COMMUTE).

commutate /'kɒmjʊteɪt/ ▶ **verb** [with obj.] regulate or reverse the direction of (an alternating electric current), especially to make it a direct current.
– ORIGIN late 19th cent.: from Latin *commutat-* 'changed altogether, exchanged, interchanged', from the verb *commutare* (see COMMUTE).

commutation ▶ **noun** [mass noun] **1** the action or process of commuting a judicial sentence.
■the conversion of a legal obligation or entitlement into another form, e.g. the replacement of an annuity or series of payments by a single payment.
2 the process of commutating an electric current.
3 Mathematics the property of having a commutative relation.
– ORIGIN late Middle English (in the sense 'exchange, barter', later 'alteration'): from Latin *commutatio(n-)*, from *commutare* 'exchange, interchange' (see COMMUTE). Sense 1 dates from the late 16th cent.

commutative /kə'mju:tətɪv, 'kɒmjʊˌteɪtɪv/ ▶ **adjective** Mathematics involving the condition that a group of quantities connected by operators gives the same result whatever the order of the quantities involved, e.g. $a \times b = b \times a$.
■rare (generally) relating to or involving substitution or exchange.
– ORIGIN mid 16th cent. (in the sense 'relating to transactions between people'): from French *commutatif, -ive* or medieval Latin *commutativus*, from *commutat-* 'exchanged', from the verb *commutare* (see COMMUTE).

commutator /'kɒmjʊˌteɪtə/ ▶ **noun** an attachment, connected with the armature of a motor or dynamo, through which electrical connection is made and which ensures the current flows as direct current.
■a device for reversing the direction of flow of electric current.

commute ▶ **verb 1** [no obj.] travel some distance between one's home and place of work on a regular basis: *he* **commuted from** *Corby* **to** *Kentish Town.*
2 [with obj.] reduce (a judicial sentence, especially a sentence of death) to another less severe one: *the head of state* **commuted** *the sentence* **to** *fifteen years' imprisonment.*
■(**commute something for/into**) change one kind of payment or obligation for (another): *tithes were commuted into an annual sum varying with the price of corn.* ■replace (an annuity or other series of payments) with a single payment: *if he had commuted some of his pension he would have received £330,000.*
3 [no obj.] Mathematics (of two operations or quantities) have a commutative relation: *operators which do not commute with each other.*
▶ **noun** a regular journey of some distance to and from one's place of work.
– DERIVATIVES **commuter** noun (only in sense 1).
– ORIGIN late Middle English (in the sense 'interchange (two things)'): from Latin *commutare*, from *com-* 'altogether' + *mutare* 'to change'. Sense 1 originally meant to buy and use a *commutation ticket*, the US term for a season ticket (because the daily fare is commuted to a single payment).

commuter belt ▶ **noun** the area surrounding a city from which a large number of people travel to work each day.

Como, Lake /'kəʊməʊ/ a lake in the foothills of the Alps in northern Italy.

Comodoro Rivadavia /ˌkɒməˌdɔːrəʊ ˌriːvə'dɑːvɪə, Spanish komoˌðoro riβa'ðaβja/ a port in Argentina situated on the Atlantic coast of Patagonia; pop. 124,000 (1991).

Comorin, Cape /'kɒmərɪn/ a cape at the southern tip of India, in the state of Tamil Nadu.

Comoros /'kɒmərəʊz/ a country consisting of a group of islands in the Indian Ocean north of Madagascar; pop. 492,000 (est. 1991); languages, French (official), Arabic (official), Comoran Swahili; capital, Moroni. The islands were first visited by the English at the end of the 16th century. At that time and for long afterwards Arab influence was dominant. In the mid 19th century they came under French protection, until in 1974 all but one of the four major islands voted for independence.
– DERIVATIVES **Comoran** adjective & noun.

comp informal ▶ **noun** short for:
■Brit. a competition. ■Brit. a comprehensive school. ■Brit. a compositor. ■a composition. ■a compilation. ■N. Amer. a complimentary ticket or voucher. ■[mass noun] N. Amer. compensation. ■a musical accompaniment.
▶ **verb** [with obj.] **1** play (music) as an accompaniment, especially in jazz or blues: *if someone is comping chord changes, there are more textured harmonies* | [no obj.] *he comps with an open, jangly sound.*
2 N. Amer. give (something) away free, especially as part of a promotion: *the management did graciously comp our wine selection.*
3 short for COMPOSITE.
▶ **adjective** [attrib.] N. Amer. complimentary; free: *the average fan was unable to get comp press tickets.*

compact[1] ▶ **adjective** /kəm'pakt/ **1** closely and neatly packed together; dense: *a compact cluster of houses.*
■having all the necessary components or features neatly fitted into a small space: *this compact car has plenty of boot space.* ■(of a person or animal) small, solid, and well proportioned. ■(of speech or writing) concise in expression: *a compact summary of the play.*
2 [predic.] (**compact of**) archaic composed or made up of: *towns compact of wooden houses.*
▶ **verb** /kəm'pakt/ [with obj.] (often **be compacted**) exert force on (something) so that it becomes more dense; compress: *the rubbish was taken to the depot to be compacted* | [as adj. **compacted**] *compacted earth.*
■[no obj.] (of a substance) become compressed in this way: *the snow hardened and compacted.* ■archaic form (something) by pressing its component parts firmly together: *the foundation of the walls,* **compacted of** *Moorstone and Lime.* ■express in fewer words; condense: *the ideas are* **compacted into** *two sentences.*
▶ **noun** /'kɒmpakt/ **1** a small flat case containing face powder, a mirror, and a powder puff.
2 something that is a small and conveniently shaped example of its kind, in particular:
■N. Amer. short for COMPACT CAR. ■short for COMPACT CAMERA.
3 Metallurgy a mass of powdered metal compacted together in preparation for sintering.
– DERIVATIVES **compaction** noun, **compactly** adverb, **compactness** noun, **compactor** noun.
– ORIGIN late Middle English: from Latin *compact-* 'closely put together, joined', from the verb *compingere*, from *com-* 'together' + *pangere* 'fasten'.

compact[2] /'kɒmpakt/ ▶ **noun** a formal agreement or contract between two or more parties.
▶ **verb** [with obj.] make or enter into (a formal agreement) with another party or parties: *the Democratic Party compacted an alliance with dissident groups.*
– ORIGIN late 16th cent.: from Latin *compactum*, past participle of *compacisci*, from *com-* 'with' + *pacisci* 'make a covenant'. Compare with PACT.

compact camera ▶ **noun** a small and simple 35 mm camera with automatic focusing and exposure.

compact car ▶ **noun** N. Amer. a medium-sized car.

compact disc (abbrev.: **CD**) ▶ **noun** a small plastic disc on which music or other digital information is stored in the form of a pattern of metal-coated pits from which it can be read using laser light reflected off the disc. See also CD-ROM.

compadre /kɒm'pɑːdreɪ/ ▶ **noun** (pl. **compadres**) informal, chiefly US a way of addressing or referring to a friend or companion.
– ORIGIN Spanish, literally 'godfather', hence 'benefactor, friend'. Compare with COMPÈRE and GOSSIP.

compand /kɒm'pand/ ▶ **verb** [with obj.] reduce the signal-to-noise ratio of (a signal) using a compander.
– ORIGIN 1950s: back-formation from COMPANDER.

compander (also **compandor**) ▶ **noun** a device that improves the signal-to-noise ratio of an electrical signal by compressing the range of amplitudes of the signal before transmission, and then expanding it on reproduction or reception.
– ORIGIN 1930s: blend of COMPRESSOR and *expander* (see EXPAND).

companion[1] ▶ **noun 1** a person or animal with whom one spends a lot of time or with whom one travels: *his travelling companion* | figurative *fear became my constant companion.*
■a person who shares the experiences of another, especially when these are unpleasant or unwelcome: *my* **companions in** *misfortune.* ■a person with similar tastes and interests to one's own and with whom one has an enjoyable, friendly relationship: *they were drinking companions.* ■used euphemistically to denote a person's long-term sexual partner outside marriage. ■a person, especially an unmarried or widowed woman, employed to live with and assist another. ■Astronomy a star, galaxy, or other celestial object that is close to or associated with another.
2 one of a pair of things intended to complement or match each other: [as modifier] *a companion volume.*
■[usu. in names] a book that provides information about a particular subject: *the Oxford Companion to English Literature.* ■Brit. dated a piece of equipment containing several objects used in a particular activity: *a traveller's companion.*
3 (**Companion**) a member of the lowest grade of certain orders of knighthood: *a Companion of the Order of Canada.*
▶ **verb** [with obj.] formal accompany: *he is companioned by a pageboy.*
– ORIGIN Middle English: from Old French *compaignon*, literally 'one who breaks bread with another', based on Latin *com-* 'together with' + *panis* 'bread'.

companion[2] ▶ **noun** a covering over the hatchway leading to a ship's companionway.
■archaic a raised frame with windows on the quarterdeck of a ship to allow light into the decks below. ■short for COMPANIONWAY.

– ORIGIN mid 18th cent.: from obsolete Dutch *kompanje* (earlier form of *kampanje*) 'quarterdeck', from Old French *compagne*, from Italian (*camera della*) *compagna* '(storeroom for) provisions'.

companionable ▶ **adjective** (of a person) friendly and sociable: *a companionable young man.*
■(of a situation) relaxed and pleasant because shared with friends or friendly people: *they walked in companionable silence.*
– DERIVATIVES **companionableness** noun, **companionably** adverb.
– ORIGIN early 17th cent.: alteration of obsolete *companiable*, influenced by **COMPANION**[1].

companion animal ▶ **noun** a pet or other domestic animal.

USAGE **Companion animal** is a somewhat more 'official' and formal term for **pet** and is generally restricted to larger animals such as dogs and cats.

companionate /kəmˈpanjənət/ ▶ **adjective** formal (of a marriage or relationship) between partners or spouses as equal companions.
■(of a person) acting as a companion.

companion-in-arms ▶ **noun** a fellow soldier.

companion ladder ▶ **noun** another term for **COMPANIONWAY**.

Companion of Honour (abbrev.: **CH**) ▶ **noun** (in the UK) a member of an order of knighthood founded in 1917.

Companion of Literature ▶ **noun** (in the UK) a holder of an honour awarded by the Royal Society of Literature and founded in 1961.

companion-planting ▶ **noun** [mass noun] the close planting of different plants that enhance each other's growth or protect each other from pests.
– DERIVATIVES **companion plant** noun, **companion-plant** verb.

companion set ▶ **noun** Brit. a collection of fireside implements on a stand.

companionship ▶ **noun** [mass noun] a feeling of fellowship or friendship.

companionway ▶ **noun** a set of steps leading from a ship's deck down to a cabin or lower deck.

company ▶ **noun** (pl. **-ies**) **1** a commercial business: *a shipping company* | [in names] *the Ford Motor Company* | [as modifier] *a company director.*
2 [mass noun] the fact or condition of being with another or others, especially in a way that provides friendship and enjoyment: *I could do with some company.*
■a person or people seen as a source of a specified kind of such friendship and enjoyment: *she is excellent company.* ■ the person or group of people whose society someone is currently sharing: *he was silent among such distinguished company.* ■ a visiting person or group of people: *I'm expecting company.*
3 a number of individuals gathered together, especially for a particular purpose: *the Mayor addressed the assembled company.*
■a body of soldiers, especially the smallest subdivision of an infantry battalion, typically commanded by a major or captain: *B Company of the Cheshire Regiment.* ■ a group of actors, singers, or dancers who perform together: *a national opera company.* ■ Brit. a group of Guides.
▶ **verb** (**-ies**, **-ied**) [no obj.] (**company with**) poetic/literary associate with; keep company with: *these men which have companied with us all this time.*
■[with obj.] archaic accompany (someone): *the fair dame, companied by Statius and myself.*
– PHRASES **and company** used after a person's name to denote those people usually associated with them. **be in good company** be in the same situation as someone important or respected. **in company** with another person or a group of people: *he feels at ease in company.* **in company with** together with: *the US dollar went through a bad patch in 1986, in company with the oil market.* **keep** (or archaic **bear**) **someone company** accompany or spend time with someone in order to prevent them feeling lonely or bored. ■ engage in the same activity as someone else in order to be sociable: *I'll have a drink myself, just to keep you company.* **keep company with** associate with habitually: *she began keeping company with a real estate developer.* **part company** see **PART**.
– ORIGIN Middle English (in senses 2 and 3): from Old French *compainie*; related to *compaignon* (see **COMPANION**[1]).

company car ▶ **noun** a car provided by a firm for the business and private use of an employee.

company officer ▶ **noun** an army officer serving within an infantry company.

company promoter ▶ **noun** see **PROMOTER**.

company sergeant major ▶ **noun** the highest-ranking non-commissioned officer of an infantry company.

comparable /ˈkɒmp(ə)rəb(ə)l/ ▶ **adjective** (of a person or thing) able to be likened to another; similar: *the situation in Holland is* **comparable to** *that in England.*
■of equivalent quality; worthy of comparison: *nobody is comparable with this athlete.*
– DERIVATIVES **comparability** noun.
– ORIGIN late Middle English: from Old French, from Latin *comparabilis*, from the verb *comparare* (see **COMPARE**).

USAGE The correct pronunciation in standard English is with the stress on the first syllable rather than the second: **com**parable, not com**par**able.

comparably /ˈkɒmp(ə)rəbli/ ▶ **adverb** in a similar way or to a similar degree: *a comparably priced CD player.*

comparatist /kəmˈparətɪst/ ▶ **noun** a person who carries out comparative study, especially of language or literature.
– ORIGIN 1930s: from **COMPARATIVE** + **-IST**.

comparative /kəmˈparətɪv/ ▶ **adjective 1** measured or judged by estimating the similarity or dissimilarity between one thing and another; relative: *he returned to the comparative comfort of his own home.*
2 of or involving the systematic observation of the similarities or dissimilarities between two or more branches of science or subjects of study: *comparative religion.*
3 Grammar (of an adjective or adverb) expressing a higher degree of a quality, but not the highest possible (e.g. *braver; more fiercely*). Contrasted with **POSITIVE**, **SUPERLATIVE**.
■(of a clause) involving comparison (e.g. *he's not as good as he was*).
▶ **noun** Grammar a comparative adjective or adverb.
■(**the comparative**) the middle degree of comparison.
– ORIGIN late Middle English (in sense 3): from Latin *comparativus*, from *comparare* 'to pair, match' (see **COMPARE**).

comparative advantage ▶ **noun** Economics the ability of an individual or group to carry out a particular economic activity (such as making a specific product) more efficiently than another activity.

comparative linguistics ▶ **plural noun** [treated as sing.] the study of similarities and differences between languages, in particular the comparison of related languages with a view to reconstructing forms in their lost parent languages.

comparatively ▶ **adverb** [as submodifier] to a moderate degree as compared to something else; relatively: *inflation was comparatively low.*

comparator /kəmˈparətə/ ▶ **noun** a device for comparing a measurable property or thing with a reference or standard.
■an electronic circuit for comparing two electrical signals. ■ something used as a standard for comparison.
– ORIGIN late 19th cent.: from Latin *comparat-* 'paired, matched', from the verb *comparare* (see **COMPARE**), + **-OR**[1].

compare ▶ **verb** [with obj.] **1** estimate, measure, or note the similarity or dissimilarity between: *individual schools* **compared** *their facilities* **with** *those of others in the area* | *the survey compares prices in different countries* | *total attendance figures were 28,000,* **compared to** *40,000 at last year's event.*
■(**compare something to**) point out or describe the resemblances with; liken to: *her novel was compared to the work of Daniel Defoe.* ■ (**compare something to**) draw an analogy between one thing and (another) for the purposes of explanation or clarification: *he compared the religions to different paths towards the peak of the same mountain.* ■ [no obj., with adverbial] have a specified relationship with another thing or person in terms of nature or quality: *salaries compare favourably* **with** *those of other professions.* ■ [no obj., usu. with negative] be of an equal or similar nature or quality: *sales were modest and cannot* **compare with** *the glory days of 1989.*
2 (usu. **be compared**) Grammar form the comparative and superlative degrees of (an adjective or an adverb): *words of one syllable are usually compared by '-er' and '-est'.*
– PHRASES **beyond** (or **without**) **compare** of a quality or nature surpassing all others of the same kind: *a diamond beyond compare.* **compare notes** (of two or more people) exchange ideas, opinions, or information about a particular subject.
– ORIGIN late Middle English: from Old French *comparer*, from Latin *comparare*, from *compar* 'like, equal', from *com-* 'with' + *par* 'equal'.

USAGE Is there any difference between **compare with** and **compare to**, and is one more correct than the other? There is a slight difference, in that it is usual to use **to** rather than **with** when describing the resemblance, by analogy, of two quite different things, as in *critics* **compared** *Ellington's music* **to** *the music of Beethoven and Brahms.* In the sense 'estimate the similarity or dissimilarity between', it is traditionally held that **with** is more correct than **to**, as in *schools* **compared** *their facilities* **with** *those of others in the area.* However, in practice the distinction is not clear-cut and both **compare with** and **compare to** can be used in either context.

comparison ▶ **noun 1** a consideration or estimate of the similarities or dissimilarities between two things or people: *they* **drew a comparison between** *Gandhi's teaching and that of other teachers* | [mass noun] *the two books invite comparison with one another.*
■an analogy: *perhaps the best comparison is that of seasickness.* ■ [mass noun] the quality of being similar or equivalent: *when it comes to achievements this season,* **there's no comparison between** *Linfield and Bangor.*
2 [mass noun] Grammar the formation of the comparative and superlative forms of adjectives and adverbs.
– PHRASES **bear** (or **stand**) **comparison** be of sufficient quality to be likened favourably to someone or something of the same kind. **beyond comparison** another way of saying ***beyond compare*** (see **COMPARE**). **by/in comparison** when compared: *the Prime Minister's support staff is tiny* **in comparison with** *that of a US President.*
– ORIGIN Middle English: from Old French *comparesoun*, from Latin *comparatio(n-)*, from *comparare* 'to pair, match' (see **COMPARE**).

compartment ▶ **noun 1** a separate section or part of something, in particular:
■a division of a railway carriage marked by partitions: *a first-class compartment.* ■ a section of a container in which certain items can be kept separate from others: *there's some ice cream in the freezer compartment.* ■ a division of a ship's hull: *the aft cargo compartment.* ■ figurative an area in which something can be considered in isolation from other things: *religion and politics should be kept in different compartments.*
2 Heraldry a grassy mound or other support depicted below a shield.
▶ **verb** [with obj.] (usu. **be compartmented**) divide (something) into separate parts or sections: *the buildings are to be compartmented by fire walls.*
– DERIVATIVES **compartmentation** noun.
– ORIGIN mid 16th cent.: from French *compartiment*, from Italian *compartimento*, from *compartire*, from late Latin *compartiri* 'divide'.

compartmental ▶ **adjective** characterized by division into separate sections: *the compartmental interior of the church.*
– DERIVATIVES **compartmentally** adverb.

compartmentalize (also **-ise**) ▶ **verb** [with obj.] divide into discrete sections or categories: *he had the ability to compartmentalize his life.*
– DERIVATIVES **compartmentalism** noun, **compartmentalization** noun.

compass ▶ **noun 1** an instrument containing a magnetized pointer which shows the direction of magnetic north and bearings from it.
2 (also **compasses** or **a pair of compasses**) an instrument for drawing circles and arcs and measuring distances between points, consisting of two arms linked by a movable joint, one arm ending in a point and the other usually carrying a pencil or pen.
3 [in sing.] the range or scope of something: *the event had political repercussions which are* **beyond the compass** *of this book* | *goods and services which fall* **within the compass of** *the free market.*
■the enclosing limits of an area: *this region had within its compass many types of agriculture.* ■ the range of

notes that can be produced by a voice or a musical instrument: *the cellos were playing in a rather sombre part of their compass.*
▶**verb** [with obj.] archaic **1** go round (something) in a circular course: *the ship wherein Magellan compassed the world.*
■surround or hem in on all sides: *we were compassed round by a thick fog.*
2 contrive to accomplish (something): *he compassed his end only by the exercise of gentle violence.*
– ORIGIN Middle English: from Old French *compas* (noun), *compasser* (verb), based on Latin *com-* 'together' + *passus* 'a step or pace'. Several senses ('measure', 'artifice', 'circumscribed area', and 'pair of compasses') which appeared in Middle English are also found in Old French, but their development and origin are uncertain. The transference of sense to the magnetic compass is held to have occurred in the related Italian word *compasso*, from the circular shape of the compass box.

compass card ▶**noun** a circular rotating card showing the 32 principal bearings, forming the indicator of a magnetic compass.

compassion ▶**noun** [mass noun] sympathetic pity and concern for the sufferings or misfortunes of others: *the victims should be treated with compassion.*
– ORIGIN Middle English: via Old French from ecclesiastical Latin *compassio(n-)*, from *compati* 'suffer with'.

compassionate ▶**adjective** feeling or showing sympathy and concern for others.
– DERIVATIVES **compassionately** adverb.
– ORIGIN late 16th cent.: from **COMPASSION** + **-ATE**[2], influenced by archaic French *compassioné* 'feeling pity'.

compassionate leave ▶**noun** [mass noun] a period of absence from work granted to someone as the result of particular personal circumstances, especially the death of a close relative.

compassion fatigue ▶**noun** [mass noun] indifference to charitable appeals on behalf of those who are suffering, experienced as a result of the frequency or number of such appeals.

compass rose ▶**noun** a graduated circle printed on a map or chart from which bearings can be taken.

compass saw ▶**noun** a handsaw with a narrow blade for cutting curves.

compass window ▶**noun** a bay window with a semicircular curve.

compatible ▶**adjective** (of two things) able to exist or occur together without problems or conflict: *the careers structure here is not compatible with having a family.*
■(of two people) able to have a harmonious relationship; well suited: *it's a pity we're not compatible.* ■(of one thing) consistent with another: *the symptoms were compatible with gastritis or a peptic ulcer.* ■(of a computer, a peripheral, or a piece of software) able to be used with a specified piece of equipment or software without special adaptation or modification: *the printer is fully compatible with all leading software.*
▶**noun** a computer that can use software designed for another make or type.
– DERIVATIVES **compatibility** noun, **compatibly** adverb.
– ORIGIN late Middle English: from French, from medieval Latin *compatibilis*, from *compati* 'suffer with'.

compatriot /kəmˈpatrɪət, -ˈpeɪt-/ ▶**noun** a fellow citizen or national of a country.
– ORIGIN late 16th cent.: from French *compatriote*, from late Latin *compatriota* (translating Greek *sumpatriōtēs*), from *com-* 'together with' + *patriota* (see **PATRIOT**).

compeer /kəmˈpɪə/ ▶**noun** formal a person of equal rank, status, or ability.
■archaic a companion or associate.
– ORIGIN Middle English: from Old French *comper*, from *com-* 'with' + *per*, from Latin *par* 'equal' (compare with **PEER**[2]).

compel ▶**verb** (**compelled**, **compelling**) [with obj. and infinitive] force or oblige (someone) to do something: *a sense of duty compelled Harry to answer her questions.*
■[with obj.] bring about (something) by the use of force or pressure: *they may compel a witness's attendance at court by issue of a summons | his striking appearance compelled attention.* ■[with obj. and adverbial of direction] poetic/literary force to come or go in a particular direction: *by heav'n's high will compell'd from shore to shore.*
– ORIGIN late Middle English: from Latin *compellere*, from *com-* 'together' + *pellere* 'drive'.

compellable ▶**adjective** Law (of a witness) able to be made to attend court or give evidence.

compelling ▶**adjective** evoking interest, attention, or admiration in a powerfully irresistible way: *his eyes were strangely compelling | a compelling film.*
■not able to be refuted; inspiring conviction: *there is compelling evidence that the recession is ending. | a compelling argument.* ■not able to be resisted; overwhelming: *the temptation to give up was compelling.*
– DERIVATIVES **compellingly** adverb.

compendious ▶**adjective** formal containing or presenting the essential facts of something in a comprehensive but concise way: *a compendious study.*
– DERIVATIVES **compendiously** adverb, **compendiousness** noun.
– ORIGIN late Middle English: from Old French *compendieux*, from Latin *compendiosus* 'advantageous, brief', from *compendium* 'profit, saving, abbreviation'.

compendium ▶**noun** (pl. **compendiums** or **compendia** /-dɪə/) chiefly Brit. a collection of concise but detailed information about a particular subject, especially in a book or other publication.
■a collection of things, especially one systematically gathered: *the programme is a compendium of out-takes from our archives.* ■a collection of similar items in one container. ■a package of stationery for writing letters.
– ORIGIN late 16th cent.: from Latin, 'profit, saving' (literally 'what is weighed together'), from *compendere*, from *com-* 'together' + *pendere* 'weigh'.

compensable /kəmˈpɛnsəb(ə)l/ ▶**adjective** (of a loss or hardship) for which compensation can be obtained.
– ORIGIN mid 17th cent.: French, from *compenser*, from Latin *compensare* 'weigh (something) against (another)'.

compensate ▶**verb** **1** [with obj.] recompense (someone) for loss, suffering, or injury, typically by the award of a sum of money: *payments were made to farmers to **compensate** them **for** cuts in subsidies.*
2 [no obj.] (**compensate for**) make up for (something unwelcome or unpleasant) by exerting an opposite force or effect: *the manager is hoping for victory to compensate for the team's dismal league campaign.*
■act so as to neutralize or correct (a deficiency or abnormality in a physical property or effect): *the output voltage rises, compensating for the original fall.* ■attempt to conceal or offset (a disability or frustration) by development in another direction: *they identified with radical movements to compensate for their inability to relate to individual human beings.*
– DERIVATIVES **compensative** adjective, **compensator** noun.
– ORIGIN mid 17th cent. (in the sense 'counterbalance'): from Latin *compensat-* 'weighed against', from the verb *compensare*, from *com-* 'together' + *pensare* (frequentative of *pendere* 'weigh').

compensation ▶**noun** [mass noun] something, typically money, awarded to someone as a recompense for loss, injury, or suffering: *seeking compensation for injuries suffered at work* | [as modifier] *a compensation claim.*
■the action or process of making such an award: *the compensation of victims.* ■something that counterbalances or makes up for an undesirable or unwelcome state of affairs: *the grey streets of London were small compensation for the loss of her beloved Africa* | [count noun] *getting older has some compensations.* ■chiefly N. Amer. the money received by an employee from an employer as a salary or wages. ■the process of concealing or offsetting a psychological difficulty by developing in another direction.
– DERIVATIVES **compensational** adjective.
– ORIGIN late Middle English: via Old French from Latin *compensatio(n-)*, from the verb *compensare* 'weigh against' (see **COMPENSATE**).

compensation pendulum ▶**noun** Physics a pendulum constructed from metals with differing coefficients of expansion in order to neutralize the effects of temperature variation.

compensation water ▶**noun** [mass noun] water supplied from a reservoir to a stream in time of drought.

compensatory ▶**adjective** providing, effecting, or aiming at compensation, in particular:
■(of a payment) intended to recompense someone who has experienced loss, suffering, or injury: *$50 million in compensatory damages.* ■reducing or offsetting the unpleasant or unwelcome effects of something: *the government is taking compensatory actions to keep the interest rate constant.*

compère /ˈkɒmpɛː/ Brit. ▶**noun** a person who introduces the performers or contestants in a variety show.
▶**verb** [with obj.] act as a compère for (such a show).
– ORIGIN early 20th cent.: French, literally 'godfather', from medieval Latin *compater*, from *com-* 'together with' + Latin *pater* 'father'.

compete ▶**verb** [no obj.] strive to gain or win something by defeating or establishing superiority over others who are trying to do the same: *universities are **competing for** applicants | he **competed with** a number of other candidates* | [as adj. **competing**] *competing political ideologies.*
– ORIGIN early 17th cent.: from Latin *competere*, in its late sense 'strive or contend for (something)', from *com-* 'together' + *petere* 'aim at, seek'.

competence (also **competency**) ▶**noun** **1** [mass noun] the ability to do something successfully or efficiently: *courses to improve the competence of staff | the players displayed varying degrees of competence.*
■the scope of a person or group's knowledge or ability: *the music is within the competence of an average choir.* ■[count noun] a skill or ability. ■the legal authority of a court or other body to deal with a particular matter: *the court's competence has been accepted to cover these matters.* ■(also **linguistic** or **language competence**) Linguistics a person's subconscious knowledge of the rules governing the formation of speech in their first language. Often contrasted with **PERFORMANCE**. ■Biology & Medicine effective performance of the normal function.
2 dated an income large enough to live on, typically unearned: *he found himself with an ample competence and no obligations.*

competent ▶**adjective** having the necessary ability, knowledge, or skill to do something successfully: *a highly competent surgeon | make sure the firm **is competent to** carry out the work.*
■(of a person) efficient and capable: *an infinitely competent mother of three.* ■acceptable and satisfactory, though not outstanding: *she spoke quite competent French.* ■(chiefly of a court or other body) accepted as having legal authority to deal with a particular matter: *the London Stock Exchange is the **competent authority** under the Financial Services Act.* ■Biology & Medicine capable of performing the normal function effectively.
– DERIVATIVES **competently** adverb.
– ORIGIN late Middle English (in the sense 'suitable, adequate'): from Latin *competent-*, from the verb *competere* in its earlier sense 'be fit or proper' (see **COMPETE**).

competition ▶**noun** [mass noun] the activity or condition of striving to gain or win something by defeating or establishing superiority over others engaged in the same attempt: *there is fierce **competition between** banks | the **competition for** university places is greater than ever this year.*
■[count noun] an event or contest in which people take part in order to establish superiority or supremacy in a particular area: *a beauty competition.* ■the action of participating in such an event or contest: *the team was banned from European competition.* ■[in sing.] the person or people over whom one is attempting to establish one's supremacy or superiority, especially in a commercial or sporting arena; the opposition: *I walked round to check out the competition.* ■Ecology interaction between animal or plant species, or individual organisms, in which their population levels, reproductive success, etc. depend upon their gaining a share of a limited environmental resource.
– ORIGIN early 17th cent.: from late Latin *competitio(n-)* 'rivalry', from *competere* 'strive for' (see **COMPETE**).

competitive ▶**adjective** **1** of, relating to, or characterized by competition: *a competitive sport | the intensely competitive newspaper industry.*
■having or displaying a strong desire to be more successful than others: *she had a competitive streak.*
2 as good as or better than others of a comparable nature: *a car industry competitive with any in the world.*
■(of prices) low enough to compare well with those of rival traders: *we offer prompt service at competitive rates.*
– DERIVATIVES **competitiveness** noun.

– ORIGIN early 19th cent.: from Latin *competit-* 'striven for', from the verb *competere* (see **COMPETE**), + **-IVE**.

competitive exclusion ▶ **noun** [mass noun] Ecology the inevitable elimination from a habitat of one of two different species with identical needs for resources.

competitively ▶ **adverb** in a competitive way, in particular:
■ in a way that strives to gain or win something by defeating others engaged in the same attempt: *he has been driving competitively since he was young.* ■ (of a product) priced in a way that compares favourably with others of the same nature: *our exports remained competitively priced.*

competitor ▶ **noun** an organization or country that is engaged in commercial or economic competition with others: *our main industrial competitors.*
■ a person who takes part in a sporting contest.

compilation ▶ **noun 1** [mass noun] the action or process of producing something, especially a list, book, or report, by assembling information collected from other sources: *great care has been taken in the compilation of this guidebook.*
2 a thing, especially a book, record, or broadcast programme, that is put together by assembling previously separate items: *there are thirty-three stories in this compilation* | [as modifier] *a compilation album.*
– ORIGIN late Middle English: via Old French from Latin *compilatio(n-)*, from *compilare* 'to plunder' (see **COMPILE**).

compile ▶ **verb** [with obj.] **1** produce (a list, report, or book) by assembling information collected from other sources: *the local authority must compile a list of the names and addresses of taxpayers.*
■ collect (information) in order to produce such a list, report, or book: *the figures were compiled from a survey of 2,000 schoolchildren.* ■ accumulate (a specified score): *the world champion compiled a break of 101.*
2 Computing (of a computer) convert (a program) into a machine-code or lower-level form in which the program can be executed.
– DERIVATIVES **compiler** noun.
– ORIGIN Middle English: from Old French *compiler* or its apparent source, Latin *compilare* 'plunder or plagiarize'.

comping ▶ **noun** [mass noun] **1** Brit. informal the practice of entering competitions, especially those promoting consumer products.
2 the action of playing a musical accompaniment, especially in jazz or blues.
3 the process of making composite images, especially electronically.
– DERIVATIVES **comper** noun Brit. (only in sense 1).

complacency (also **complacence**) ▶ **noun** [mass noun] a feeling of smug or uncritical satisfaction with oneself or one's achievements: *the figures are better, but there are no grounds for complacency.*
– ORIGIN mid 17th cent.: from medieval Latin *complacentia*, from Latin *complacere* 'to please'.

complacent /kəmˈpleɪs(ə)nt/ ▶ **adjective** showing smug or uncritical satisfaction with oneself or one's achievements: *you can't afford to be complacent about security.*
– DERIVATIVES **complacently** adverb.
– ORIGIN mid 17th cent. (in the sense 'pleasant'): from Latin *complacent-* 'pleasing', from the verb *complacere.*

> **USAGE** **Complacent** and **complaisant** are two words which are similar in pronunciation and which both come from the Latin verb *complacere* 'to please', but which in English do not mean the same thing. **Complacent** is the commoner word and means 'smug and self-satisfied'. **Complaisant**, on the other hand, means 'willing to please', as in *the local people proved* ***complaisant*** *and cordial.* Writers occasionally use **complaisant** when they mean **complacent**: just under half of the citations for **complaisant** in the British National Corpus exhibit this confusion.

complain ▶ **verb 1** [reporting verb] express dissatisfaction or annoyance about a state of affairs or an event: [with clause] *local authorities complained that they lacked sufficient resources* | [with direct speech] *'You never listen to me,' Larry complained* | [no obj.] *we all complained bitterly about the food.*
■ [no obj.] (**complain of**) state that one is suffering from (a pain or other symptom of illness): *her husband began to complain of headaches.* ■ [no obj.] poetic/literary make a mournful sound: *let the warbling flute complain.* ■ [no obj.] (of a structure or mechanism) groan or creak under strain.
– DERIVATIVES **complainer** noun, **complainingly** adverb.
– ORIGIN late Middle English: from Old French *complaindre*, from medieval Latin *complangere* 'bewail', from *com-* (expressing intensive force) + *plangere* 'to lament'.

complainant ▶ **noun** Law a plaintiff in certain lawsuits.
– ORIGIN late Middle English: from French *complaignant*, present participle of *complaindre* 'to lament' (see **COMPLAIN**).

complaint ▶ **noun 1** a statement that a situation is unsatisfactory or unacceptable or that someone has done something wrong: *I intend to make an official complaint* | *there were complaints that the building was an eyesore.*
■ a reason for dissatisfaction: *I have no complaints about the hotel.* ■ [mass noun] the expression of dissatisfaction: *a letter of complaint* | *he hasn't any cause for complaint.* ■ Law the plaintiff's reasons for proceeding in a civil action.
2 [often with modifier] an illness or medical condition, especially one considered as relatively minor: *she is receiving treatment for her skin complaint.*
– ORIGIN late Middle English: from Old French *complainte*, feminine past participle of *complaindre* 'to lament' (see **COMPLAIN**).

complaisant /kəmˈpleɪz(ə)nt/ ▶ **adjective** willing to please others or to accept what they do or say without protest: *he went to join his apparently complaisant wife for Christmas.*
– DERIVATIVES **complaisance** noun.
– ORIGIN mid 17th cent.: French, from *complaire* 'acquiesce in order to please', from Latin *complacere* 'to please'.

> **USAGE** **Complaisant** does not mean the same as **complacent**. See usage at **COMPLACENT**.

compleat ▶ **adjective** & **verb** archaic spelling of **COMPLETE**.

complected /kəmˈplɛktɪd/ ▶ **adjective** [in combination] N. Amer. having a specified complexion: *lighter-complected invaders from the north.*
– ORIGIN early 19th cent.: apparently from **COMPLEXION**.

complement ▶ **noun** /ˈkɒmplɪm(ə)nt/ **1** a thing that contributes extra or contrasting features to something else in such a way as to improve or emphasize its quality: *local ales provide the perfect complement to fine food.*
2 [in sing.] a number or quantity of something, especially that required to make a group complete: *at the moment we have* ***a full complement of*** *staff.*
■ the number of people required to crew a ship: *almost half the ship's complement of 322 were wounded.* ■ Geometry the amount in degrees by which a given angle is less than 90°. ■ Mathematics the members of a set or class that are not members of a given subset.
3 Grammar one or more words, phrases, or clauses governed by a verb (or by a nominalization or a predicative adjective) that complete the meaning of the predicate. In generative grammar, all the constituents of a sentence that are governed by a verb form the complement.
■ (in systemic grammar) an adjective or noun that has the same reference as either the subject (as *mad* in *he is mad*) or the object (as *mad* in *he drove her mad* or *manager* in *they appointed him manager*).
4 [mass noun] Physiology a group of proteins present in blood plasma and tissue fluid which combine with an antigen–antibody complex to bring about the lysis of foreign cells.
▶ **verb** /ˈkɒmplɪmɛnt/ [with obj.] contribute extra or contrasting features to (someone or something) in such a way as to improve or enhance their qualities: *a classic blazer complements a look that's smart or casual.*
■ add to or make complete: *the proposals complement the incentives already available.*
– PHRASES **in her complement** Heraldry (of the moon) depicted as full.
– DERIVATIVES **complemental** adjective.
– ORIGIN late Middle English (in the sense 'completion'): from Latin *complementum*, from *complere* 'fill up' (see **COMPLETE**). Compare with **COMPLIMENT**.

> **USAGE** **Complement** and **compliment** (together with related words such as **complementary** and **complimentary**) are frequently confused. They are pronounced in the same way but have quite different meanings: as a verb **complement** means 'add to (something) in a way that enhances or improves', as in *a classic blazer* ***complements*** *a look that's smart or casual*, while **compliment** means 'admire and praise (someone) for something', as in *he* ***complimented*** *her on her appearance.* Mistakes are common, particularly where **complimentary** is meant but **complementary** is written, as in *honeymooners receive* ***complementary*** *fruit and flowers.*

complementarity ▶ **noun** (pl. **-ies**) [mass noun] a relationship or situation in which two or more different things enhance or emphasize each other's qualities or form a balanced whole: *a culture based on the complementarity of men and women.*
■ Physics the concept that two contrasted theories, such as the wave and particle theories of light, may be able to explain a set of phenomena, although each separately only accounts for some aspects.

complementary ▶ **adjective 1** (of two or more different things) combining in such a way as to form a complete whole or to enhance or emphasize each other's qualities: *the second TV network was* ***complementary to*** *the BBC.*
■ Biochemistry (of gene sequences, nucleotides, etc.) related by the rules of base pairing.
2 [attrib.] of or relating to complementary medicine.
– DERIVATIVES **complementarily** adverb, **complementariness** noun.

complementary angle ▶ **noun** either of two angles whose sum is 90°.

complementary colour ▶ **noun** a colour that combined with a given colour makes white or black.

complementary distribution ▶ **noun** [mass noun] the occurrence of phenomena such as speech sounds in mutually exclusive contexts.

complementary DNA ▶ **noun** [mass noun] synthetic DNA in which the sequence of bases is complementary to that of a given example of DNA.

complementary function ▶ **noun** Mathematics the part of the general solution of a linear differential equation which is the general solution of the associated homogeneous equation obtained by substituting zero for the terms not containing the dependent variable.

complementary medicine ▶ **noun** [mass noun] any of a range of medical therapies that fall beyond the scope of scientific medicine but may be used alongside it in the treatment of disease and ill health. Examples include acupuncture and osteopathy. See also **ALTERNATIVE MEDICINE**.

complementation ▶ **noun** [mass noun] the action of complementing something.
■ Grammar all the clause constituents that are governed by a verb, nominalization, or adjective. ■ Genetics the phenomenon by which the effects of two different non-allelic mutations in a gene are partly or entirely cancelled out when they occur together.

complement fixation test ▶ **noun** Medicine a test for infection with a micro-organism which involves measuring the amount of complement available in serum to bind with an antibody–antigen complex.

complementizer (also **complementiser**) ▶ **noun** Grammar a word or morpheme that marks an embedded clause as functioning as a complement, typically a subordinating conjunction or infinitival *to.*

complete ▶ **adjective 1** having all the necessary or appropriate parts: *a complete list of courses offered by the university* | *no wardrobe is complete without this pretty top.*
■ (of all the works of a particular author) collected together in one volume or edition: *the complete works of Shakespeare.* ■ entire; full: *I only managed one complete term at school.* ■ [predic.] having run its full course; finished: *the restoration of the chapel is complete.*
2 [attrib.] (often used for emphasis) to the greatest extent or degree; total: *a complete ban on smoking* | *their marriage came as a complete surprise to me.*
■ (also **compleat**) chiefly humorous skilled at every aspect of a particular activity; consummate: *his range of skills made him the complete footballer.* [ORIGIN: the spelling *compleat* is a revival of the 17th cent. use as in Walton's *The Compleat Angler.*]

▶**verb** [with obj.] **1** finish making or doing: *he completed his PhD in 1983.*
■[no obj.] Brit. conclude the sale of a property. ■American Football (of a quarterback) successfully throw (a forward pass) to a receiver.
2 provide with the item or items necessary to make a (set or group) full or entire: *complete your collection of Britain's brightest gardening magazine.*
■make (something) whole or perfect: *quarry tiles and faded rugs complete the look.* ■write the required information on (a form or questionnaire): *please complete the attached forms.*
– PHRASES **complete with** having something as an additional part or feature: *the house* ***comes complete with*** *gas central heating and double glazing.*
– DERIVATIVES **completeness** noun.
– ORIGIN late Middle English: from Old French *complet* or Latin *completus*, past participle of *complere* 'fill up, finish, fulfil', from *com-* (expressing intensive force) + *plere* 'fill'.

USAGE On the question of the use of adjectives like **complete**, **equal**, and **unique** with submodifiers such as **very** or **more**, see **usage** at **UNIQUE**.

completely ▶**adverb** totally; utterly: *the fire completely destroyed the building* | [as submodifier] *you must be completely mad!*

completion ▶**noun** [mass noun] the action or process of finishing something: *funds for the completion of the new building.*
■the state of being finished: *work on the new golf course is nearing completion* | [as modifier] *the completion date is early next year.* ■Law the final stage in the sale of a property, at which point it legally changes ownership: *the risk stays with the seller until completion.* ■the action of writing the required information on a form.
– ORIGIN late 15th cent.: from Latin *completio(n-)*, from *complere* 'fill up' (see **COMPLETE**).

completist ▶**noun** an obsessive, typically indiscriminate, collector or fan of something.

completive ▶**noun** Grammar a word or morpheme which adds a sense of completeness to a word or phrase (e.g. in the phrase *break up, up* is a completive).

complex ▶**adjective 1** consisting of many different and connected parts: *a complex network of water channels.*
■not easy to analyse or understand: complicated or intricate: *a complex personality* | *the situation is more complex than it appears.*
2 Mathematics denoting or involving numbers or quantities containing both a real and an imaginary part.
3 Chemistry denoting an ion or molecule in which one or more groups are linked to a metal atom by coordinate bonds.
▶**noun 1** a group of similar buildings or facilities on the same site: *a leisure complex* | *a complex of hotels.*
■a group or system of different things that are linked in a close or complicated way; a network: *a complex of mountain roads.*
2 Psychoanalysis a related group of repressed or partly repressed emotionally significant ideas which cause psychic conflict leading to abnormal mental states or behaviour.
■informal a strong or disproportionate concern or anxiety about something: *there's no point having a* ***complex about*** *losing your hair.*
3 Chemistry an ion or molecule in which one or more groups are linked to a metal atom by coordinate bonds.
■any loosely bonded species formed by the association of two molecules: *cross-linked protein–DNA complexes.*
▶**verb** [with obj.] (usu. **be complexed**) Chemistry make (an atom or compound) form a complex with another: *the DNA was* ***complexed with*** *the nuclear extract* | [as adj. **complexed**] *the complexed metal ion.*
■[no obj.] form a complex: *these proteins are capable of complexing with VP16.*
– DERIVATIVES **complexation** noun (Chemistry), **complexly** adverb.
– ORIGIN mid 17th cent. (in the sense 'group of related elements'): from Latin *complexus*, past participle (used as a noun) of *complectere* 'embrace, comprise', later associated with *complexus* 'plaited'; the adjective is partly via French *complexe*.

complex conjugate ▶**noun** Mathematics each of two complex numbers having their real parts identical and their imaginary parts of equal magnitude but opposite sign.

complexion ▶**noun 1** the natural colour, texture, and appearance of a person's skin, especially of the face: *an attractive girl with a pale complexion.*
2 the general aspect or character of something: *the complexion of the game changed* | *successive governments of all complexions.*
– DERIVATIVES **complexioned** adjective [often in combination] *they were both fair-complexioned.*
– ORIGIN Middle English: via Old French from Latin *complexio(n-)* 'combination' (in late Latin 'physical constitution'), from *complectere* 'embrace, comprise'. The term originally denoted physical constitution or temperament determined by the combination of the four bodily humours, hence sense 1 (late 16th cent.) as a visible sign of this.

complexity ▶**noun** (pl. **-ies**) [mass noun] the state or quality of being intricate or complicated: *an issue of great complexity.*
■[count noun] (usu. **complexities**) a factor involved in a complicated process or situation: *the complexities of family life.*

complex sentence ▶**noun** a sentence containing a subordinate clause or clauses.

compliance /kəmˈplʌɪəns/ ▶**noun** [mass noun] **1** the action or fact of complying with a wish or command: *the ways in which the state maintains order and compliance.*
■(**compliance with**) the state or fact of according with or meeting rules or standards: *all imports of timber are* ***in compliance with*** *regulations.* ■unworthy or excessive acquiescence: *the appalling compliance with government views shown by the commission.*
2 Physics the property of a material of undergoing elastic deformation or (of a gas) change in volume when subjected to an applied force. It is equal to the reciprocal of stiffness.
■Medicine the ability of an organ to distend in response to applied pressure.

compliance officer ▶**noun** a person who is employed to ensure that a company does not contravene any statutes or regulations which apply to its activities.

compliant ▶**adjective 1** disposed to agree with others or obey rules, especially to an excessive degree; acquiescent: *a compliant labour force.*
■meeting or in accordance with rules or standards: *food which is compliant with safety regulations.*
2 Physics & Medicine having the property of compliance.
– DERIVATIVES **compliantly** adverb.

complicate /ˈkɒmplɪkeɪt/ ▶**verb** [with obj.] make (something) more difficult or confusing by causing it to be more complex: *increased choice will complicate matters for the consumer* | [as adj. **complicating**] *a complicating factor.*
■Medicine introduce complications in (an existing condition): *smoking may complicate pregnancy* | [as adj. **complicating**] *patients with complicating biliary calculi.*
– ORIGIN early 17th cent. (in the sense 'combine, entangle, intertwine'): from Latin *complicat-* 'folded together', from the verb *complicare*, from *com-* 'together' + *plicare* 'to fold'.

complicated ▶**adjective 1** consisting of many interconnecting parts or elements; intricate: *a complicated stereo system.*
■involving many different and confusing aspects: *a long and complicated saga.*
2 Medicine involving complications: *complicated appendicitis.*
– DERIVATIVES **complicatedly** adverb.

complication ▶**noun 1** a circumstance that complicates something; a difficulty: *there is a complication concerning ownership of the site.*
■[mass noun] an involved or confused condition or state: *to add further complication, English-speakers use a different name.*
2 Medicine a secondary disease or condition aggravating an already existing one: *she developed complications after the surgery.*
– ORIGIN late Middle English: from late Latin *complicatio(n-)*, from Latin *complicare* 'fold together' (see **COMPLICATE**).

complicit /kəmˈplɪsɪt/ ▶**adjective** involved with others in an illegal activity: *the careers of those* ***complicit in*** *the cover-up were blighted.*
– ORIGIN 1940s: back-formation from **COMPLICITY**.

complicity ▶**noun** [mass noun] the fact or condition of being involved with others in an illegal activity: *they were accused of* ***complicity in*** *the attempt to overthrow the government.*
– ORIGIN mid 17th cent.: from Middle English *complice* 'an associate', from Old French, from late Latin *complex, complic-* 'allied', from Latin *complicare* 'fold together' (see **COMPLICATE**). Compare with **ACCOMPLICE**.

compliment ▶**noun** /ˈkɒmplɪm(ə)nt/ a polite expression of praise or admiration: *she paid me an enormous compliment.*
■an act or circumstance that implies praise or respect: *it's a compliment to the bride to dress up on her special day.* ■(**compliments**) congratulations or praise expressed to someone: ***my compliments on*** *your cooking.* ■(**compliments**) formal greetings, especially when sent as a message: *carry my compliments to your kinsmen.*
▶**verb** /ˈkɒmplɪmɛnt/ [with obj.] politely congratulate or praise (someone) for something: *he* ***complimented*** *Erika* ***on*** *her appearance.*
■praise (something) politely: *complimenting the other team's good play.* ■(**compliment someone with**) archaic present someone with (something) as a mark of courtesy: *Prince George expected to be complimented with a seat in the royal coach.*
– PHRASES **compliments of the season** used as a seasonal greeting at Christmas or the New Year. **pay one's compliments** send or express formal greetings. **return the compliment** give a compliment in return for another. ■retaliate or respond in kind. **with someone's compliments** (or **the compliments of**) used to express the fact that what one is giving is free: *all drinks will be supplied with our compliments.*
– ORIGIN mid 17th cent.: from French *compliment* (noun), *complimenter* (verb), from Italian *complimento* 'fulfilment of the requirements of courtesy', from Latin *complementum* 'completion, fulfilment' (reflected in the earlier English spelling *complement*, gradually replaced by the French form between 1655 and 1715).

USAGE **Compliment** (together with **complimentary**) is quite different in meaning from **complement** (and **complementary**). See **usage** at **COMPLEMENT**.

complimentary ▶**adjective 1** expressing a compliment; praising or approving: *Jennie was very complimentary about Kath's riding* | *complimentary remarks.*
2 given or supplied free of charge: *a complimentary bottle of wine.*

compliments slip (also **compliment slip**) ▶**noun** Brit. a small piece of paper on which a company's name, address, and logo are printed and which is sent out with goods or information, typically in place of a covering letter.

compline /ˈkɒmplɪn, -ʌɪn/ ▶**noun** a service of evening prayers forming part of the Divine Office of the Western Christian Church, traditionally said (or chanted) before retiring for the night.
– ORIGIN Middle English: from Old French *complie*, feminine past participle of obsolete *complir* 'to complete', from Latin *complere* 'fill up' (see **COMPLETE**). The ending *-ine* was probably influenced by Old French *matines* 'matins'.

comply /kəmˈplʌɪ/ ▶**verb** (**-ies, -ied**) [no obj.] (of a person or group) act in accordance with a wish or command: *we are unable to* ***comply with*** *your request.*
■(of an article) meet specified standards: *all second-hand furniture must* ***comply with*** *the new regulations.*
– ORIGIN late 16th cent.: from Italian *complire*, Catalan *complir*, Spanish *cumplir*, from Latin *complere* 'fill up, fulfil' (see **COMPLETE**). The original sense was 'fulfil, accomplish', later 'fulfil the requirements of courtesy', hence 'to be agreeable, to oblige or obey'. Compare with **COMPLIMENT**.

compo[1] ▶**noun** (pl. **-os**) [mass noun] **1** a material made up of a mixture of different substances.
2 (also **compo rations**) Brit. a supply of food designed to last a specified number of man-days and made up of various tinned items carried in a large pack.
– ORIGIN early 19th cent.: abbreviation.

compo[2] ▶**noun** [mass noun] Austral./NZ informal money paid to an employee as compensation for an industrial injury.
– ORIGIN 1940s: abbreviation of **COMPENSATION**.

component /kəmˈpəʊnənt/ ▶**noun** a part or element of a larger whole, especially a part of a machine or vehicle.
■each of two or more forces, velocities, or other vectors acting in different directions which are together equivalent to a given vector.
▶**adjective** [attrib.] constituting part of a larger whole;

constituent: *the component elements of the armed forces.*
– ORIGIN mid 17th cent.: from Latin *component-* 'putting together', from the verb *componere*, from *com-* 'together' + *ponere* 'put'. Compare with **COMPOUND**[1].

componential analysis /ˌkɒmpəˈnɛnʃ(ə)l/ ▶ **noun** [mass noun] Linguistics the analysis of the meaning of a word or other linguistic unit into discrete semantic components.

compony /kɒmˈpɒni/ ▶ **adjective** [usu. postpositive] Heraldry divided into a single row of squares in alternating tinctures: *a bordure compony.*
– ORIGIN late 16th cent.: from French *componé*, from Old French *compondre*, from Latin *componere* 'put together'.

comport[1] /kəmˈpɔːt/ ▶ **verb 1** (**comport oneself**) formal conduct oneself; behave: *articulate students who comported themselves well in television interviews.*
2 [no obj.] (**comport with**) archaic accord with; agree with: *they do all that nature and art can do to comport with his will.*
– ORIGIN late Middle English (in the sense 'tolerate'): from Latin *comportare*, from *com-* 'together' + *portare* 'carry, bear'.

comport[2] /ˈkɒmpɔːt/ ▶ **noun** another term for **COMPOTE** (in sense 2).
– ORIGIN late 19th cent.: apparently an abbreviation of French *comportier*, variant of *compotier* 'dessert dish'.

comportment ▶ **noun** [mass noun] behaviour; bearing.
– ORIGIN late 16th cent.: from French *comportement*, from the verb *comporter*, from Latin *comportare* (see **COMPORT**[1]).

compose ▶ **verb** [with obj.] **1** write or create (a work of art, especially music or poetry): *he composed the First Violin Sonata four years earlier.*
■ write or phrase (a letter or piece of writing) with great care and thought: *the first sentence is so hard to compose.* ■ form (a whole) by ordering or arranging the parts, especially in an artistic way: *compose and draw a still life.* ■ order or arrange (parts) to form a whole, especially in an artistic way: *make an attempt to compose your images.*
2 (usu. **be composed**) (of elements) constitute or make up (a whole): *the National Congress is* ***composed of*** *ten senators.*
■ be (a specified number or amount) of a whole: *Christians compose 40 per cent of the state's population.*
3 calm or settle (oneself or one's features or thoughts): *she tried to* ***compose herself.***
■ archaic settle (a dispute): *the king, with some difficulty, composed this difference.*
4 prepare (a text) for printing by manually, mechanically, or electronically setting up the letters and other characters in the order to be printed.
■ set up (letters and characters) in this way.
– ORIGIN late Middle English (in the general sense 'put together, construct'): from Old French *composer*, from Latin *componere* (see **COMPONENT**), but influenced by Latin *compositus* 'composed' and Old French *poser* 'to place'.

USAGE For an explanation of the differences between **compose** and **comprise**, see **usage** at **COMPRISE**.

composed ▶ **adjective** having one's feelings and expression under control; calm.
– DERIVATIVES **composedly** adverb.

composer ▶ **noun** a person who writes music, especially as a professional occupation.

composite /ˈkɒmpəzɪt/ ▶ **adjective 1** made up of various parts or elements.
■ (especially of a constructional material) made up of recognizable constituents: *modern composite materials.* ■ (of a railway carriage) having compartments of more than one class or function. ■ Mathematics (of an integer) being the product of two or more factors greater than unity; not prime.
2 (**Composite**) relating to or denoting a classical order of architecture consisting of elements of the Ionic and Corinthian orders.
3 /usu. ˈkɒmpəzʌɪt/ Botany of, relating to, or denoting plants of the daisy family (Compositae).
▶ **noun 1** a thing made up of several parts or elements: *the English legal system is a composite of legislation and judicial precedent.*
■ a composite constructional material. ■ /ˈkɒmpəzʌɪt/ a motion for debate composed of two or more related resolutions.
2 /usu. ˈkɒmpəzʌɪt/ Botany a plant of the daisy family (Compositae).
3 (**Composite**) [mass noun] the Composite order of architecture.
▶ **verb** [with obj.] [usu. as noun **compositing**] combine (two or more images) to make a single picture, especially electronically: *photographic compositing by computer.*
– DERIVATIVES **compositely** adverb, **compositeness** noun.
– ORIGIN late Middle English (describing a number having more than one digit): via French from Latin *compositus*, past participle of *componere* 'put together'.

composition ▶ **noun 1** [mass noun] the nature of something's ingredients or constituents; the way in which a whole or mixture is made up: *the social composition of villages.*
■ the action of putting things together; formation or construction: *the composition of a new government was announced in November.* ■ [count noun] a thing composed of various elements: *a theory is a composition of interrelated facts.* ■ archaic mental constitution; character: *persons who have a touch of madness in their composition.* ■ [often as modifier] a compound artificial substance, especially one serving the purpose of a natural one: *composition tiles.* ■ Mathematics the successive application of functions to a variable, the value of the first function being the argument of the second, and so on: *composition of functions, when defined, is associative.* ■ Physics the process of finding the resultant of a number of forces.
2 a work of music, literature, or art: *Chopin's most romantic compositions.*
■ [mass noun] the action or art of producing such a work: *the technical aspects of composition.* ■ an essay, especially one written by a school or college student. ■ the artistic arrangement of the parts of a picture: *lightly sketching in the compositions for his paintings.*
3 [mass noun] the preparing of text for printing by setting up the characters in order. See **COMPOSE** (sense 4).
4 a legal agreement to pay a sum in lieu of a larger debt or other obligation: *he had been released by deed on* ***making a composition with*** *the creditors.*
■ a sum paid in this way.
– DERIVATIVES **compositional** adjective, **compositionally** adverb.
– ORIGIN late Middle English: via Old French from Latin *compositio(n-)*, from *componere* 'put together'.

compositor /kəmˈpɒzɪtə/ ▶ **noun** Printing a person who arranges type for printing or keys text into a composing machine.
– ORIGIN late Middle English (originally Scots, denoting an umpire or arbiter): from Anglo-Norman French *compositour*, from Latin *compositor*, from *composit-* 'put together', from the verb *componere* (see **COMPOSITION**).

compos mentis /ˌkɒmpɒs ˈmɛntɪs/ ▶ **adjective** [predic.] having full control of one's mind: *are you sure he was totally compos mentis?*
– ORIGIN early 17th cent.: Latin.

compossible ▶ **adjective** rare (of one thing) compatible or possible in conjunction with another.
– ORIGIN mid 17th cent.: from Old French, from medieval Latin *compossibilis*, from *com-* 'together with' + *possibilis* (see **POSSIBLE**).

compost ▶ **noun** [mass noun] decayed organic material used as a fertilizer for growing plants.
■ a mixture of this or similar material with loam soil and/or other ingredients, used as a growing medium.
▶ **verb** [with obj.] make (vegetable matter or manure) into compost: *don't compost heavily infested plants.*
■ treat (soil) with compost: *we turned clay soil into almost workable soil by composting it.*
– ORIGIN late Middle English: from Old French *composte*, from Latin *composita*, *compositum* 'something put together', feminine and neuter past participle of *componere*.

compost heap (N. Amer. also **compost pile**) ▶ **noun** a pile of garden and organic kitchen refuse which decomposes to produce compost.

composure ▶ **noun** [mass noun] the state or feeling of being calm and in control of oneself: *she was struggling to regain her composure.*
– ORIGIN late 16th cent. (in the sense 'composing, composition'): from **COMPOSE** + **-URE**.

compote /ˈkɒmpəʊt, -ɒt/ ▶ **noun 1** [mass noun] fruit preserved or cooked in syrup.
2 a bowl-shaped dessert dish with a stem.
– ORIGIN late 17th cent.: from French, from Old French *composte* 'mixture' (see **COMPOST**).

compound[1] ▶ **noun** /ˈkɒmpaʊnd/ a thing that is composed of two or more separate elements; a mixture of two or more things: *the air smelled like a compound of diesel and petrol fumes.*
■ (also **chemical compound**) a substance formed from two or more elements chemically united in fixed proportions: *a compound of hydrogen and oxygen | lead compounds.* ■ a word made up of two or more existing words.
▶ **adjective** /ˈkɒmpaʊnd/ [attrib.] made up or consisting of several parts or elements, in particular:
■ (of a word) made up of two or more existing words or elements: *a compound noun.* ■ (of interest) payable on both capital and the accumulated interest: *compound interest.* Compare with **SIMPLE**. ■ Biology (especially of a leaf, flower, or eye) consisting of two or more simple parts or individuals in combination.
▶ **verb** /kəmˈpaʊnd/ [with obj.] **1** (often **be compounded**) make up (a composite whole); constitute: *a dialect* ***compounded of*** *Spanish and Dutch.*
■ mix or combine (ingredients or constituents): *the groundnuts were compounded into cattle food.* ■ reckon (interest) on previously accumulated interest: *the yield at which the interest is compounded.*
2 make (something bad) worse; intensify the negative aspects of: *prisoners' lack of contact with the outside world compounds their problems.*
3 Law forbear from prosecuting (a felony) in exchange for money or other consideration.
■ settle (a debt or other matter) in this way: *he compounded the case with the defendant for a cash payment.*
– DERIVATIVES **compoundable** adjective.
– ORIGIN late Middle English *compoune* (verb), from Old French *compoun-*, present tense stem of *compondre*, from Latin *componere* 'put together'. The final *-d* was added in the 16th cent. on the pattern of *expound* and *propound*.

USAGE The sense of the verb **compound** which means 'make (something bad) worse', as in *this* ***compounds*** *their problems*, has an interesting history. It arose through a misinterpretation of the phrase **compound a felony**, which, strictly speaking, means 'forbear from prosecuting a felony in exchange for money or other consideration'. The 'incorrect' sense has become the usual one in legal uses and, by extension, in general senses too, and is now accepted as part of standard English.

compound[2] /ˈkɒmpaʊnd/ ▶ **noun** an area enclosed by a fence, in particular:
■ an open area in which a factory or large house stands. ■ an open area in a prison, prison camp, or work camp. ■ S. African a fenced area containing single-sex living quarters for migrant workers, especially miners. ■ another term for **POUND**[3].
– ORIGIN late 17th cent. (referring to such an area in SE Asia): from Portuguese *campon* or Dutch *kampoeng*, from Malay *kampong* 'enclosure, hamlet'; compare with **KAMPONG**.

compounder ▶ **noun** a person who mixes or combines ingredients in order to produce an animal feed, medicine, or other substance.

compound eye ▶ **noun** an eye consisting of an array of numerous small visual units, as found in insects and crustaceans. Contrasted with **SIMPLE EYE**.

compound fracture ▶ **noun** an injury in which a broken bone pierces the skin, causing a risk of infection.

compound interval ▶ **noun** Music an interval greater than an octave.

compound sentence ▶ **noun** a sentence with more than one subject or predicate.

compound time ▶ **noun** [mass noun] Music musical rhythm or metre in which each beat in a bar is subdivided into three smaller units, so having the value of a dotted note. Compare with **SIMPLE TIME**.

comprador /ˌkɒmprəˈdɔː/ (also **compradore**) ▶ **noun** a person within a country who acts as an agent for foreign organizations engaged in investment, trade, or economic or political exploitation.
– ORIGIN early 17th cent. (denoting a local person employed in a European household in SE Asia or India to make small purchases and keep the household accounts): from Portuguese, 'buyer', from late Latin *comparator*, from Latin *comparare* 'to purchase', from *com-* 'with' + *parare* 'provide'.

comprehend /kɒmprɪˈhɛnd/ ▶ **verb** [with obj.] **1** [often with negative] grasp mentally; understand: *he couldn't comprehend her reasons for marrying Lovat* | [with clause] *I simply couldn't comprehend what had happened.*
2 formal include, comprise, or encompass: *a divine order comprehending all men.*
– ORIGIN Middle English: from Old French *comprehender*, or Latin *comprehendere*, from *com-* 'together' + *prehendere* 'grasp'.

comprehensible ▶ **adjective** able to be understood; intelligible: *clear and comprehensible English.*
– DERIVATIVES **comprehensibility** noun, **comprehensibly** adverb.
– ORIGIN late 15th cent.: from French *compréhensible* or Latin *comprehensibilis*, from *comprehens-* 'seized, comprised', from the verb *comprehendere* (see **COMPREHEND**).

comprehension ▶ **noun** [mass noun] **1** the action or capability of understanding something: *some won't have the least comprehension of what I'm trying to do* | *the comprehension of spoken language.*
■ Brit. the setting or answering of questions on a set text to test understanding, especially as a school exercise.
2 archaic inclusion.
■ historical the inclusion of Nonconformists within the Established Church of England (as proposed in the 17th to 19th centuries but not adopted).
– ORIGIN late Middle English: from French *compréhension* or Latin *comprehensio(n-)*, from the verb *comprehendere* 'seize, comprise' (see **COMPREHEND**).

comprehensive ▶ **adjective** **1** including or dealing with all or nearly all elements or aspects of something: *a comprehensive list of sources.*
■ of large content or scope; wide-ranging: *a comprehensive collection of photographs.* ■ (of a victory or defeat) achieved by a large margin: *a comprehensive victory for Swansea.* ■ (of motor-vehicle insurance) providing cover for most risks, including damage to the policyholder's own vehicle.
2 Brit. relating to or denoting a system of secondary education in which children of all abilities from a particular area are educated in one school: *a comprehensive school.*
3 archaic of or relating to understanding.
▶ **noun** Brit. a comprehensive school.
– DERIVATIVES **comprehensively** adverb, **comprehensiveness** noun.
– ORIGIN early 17th cent.: from French *compréhensif, -ive*, from late Latin *comprehensivus*, from the verb *comprehendere* 'grasp mentally'.

compresence ▶ **noun** [mass noun] chiefly Philosophy the simultaneous presence together of properties or experienced qualities.
– DERIVATIVES **compresent** adjective.

compress ▶ **verb** /kəmˈprɛs/ [with obj.] (often **be compressed**) flatten by pressure; squeeze; press: *the skirt can be folded and **compressed into** a relatively small bag* | [as adj. **compressed**] *compressed gas.*
■ [no obj.] be squeezed or pressed together or into a smaller space: *her face **compressed into** a frown.* ■ [as adj. **compressed**] chiefly Biology having a narrow shape as if flattened, especially sideways: *most sea snakes have a compressed tail.* ■ squeeze or press (two things) together: *Viola compressed her lips together grimly.* ■ express in a shorter form; abridge: *in this chapter we **compress into** summary form the main findings.* ■ Computing alter the form of (data) to reduce the amount of storage necessary.
▶ **noun** /ˈkɒmprɛs/ a pad of lint or other absorbent material pressed on to part of the body to relieve inflammation or stop bleeding: *a cold compress.*
– DERIVATIVES **compressibility** /-ˈbɪlɪti/ noun, **compressible** /kəmˈprɛsɪb(ə)l/ adjective, **compressive** /kəmˈprɛsɪv/ adjective.
– ORIGIN late Middle English: from Old French *compresser* or late Latin *compressare*, frequentative of Latin *comprimere*, from *com-* 'together' + *premere* 'to press'; or directly from *compress-* 'pressed together', from the verb *comprimere*.

compressed air ▶ **noun** [mass noun] air that is at more than atmospheric pressure.

compression ▶ **noun** [mass noun] the action of compressing or being compressed.
■ the reduction in volume (causing an increase in pressure) of the fuel mixture in an internal-combustion engine before ignition.
– DERIVATIVES **compressional** adjective.
– ORIGIN late Middle English: via Old French from Latin *compressio(n-)*, from *comprimere* 'press together' (see **COMPRESS**).

compression joint ▶ **noun** a joint between two pipes made by tightening a threaded nut on to a metal ring, the compression thus caused creating the seal.

compression ratio ▶ **noun** the ratio of the maximum to minimum volume in the cylinder of an internal-combustion engine.

compressive strength ▶ **noun** the resistance of a material to breaking under compression. Compare with **TENSILE STRENGTH**.

compressor ▶ **noun** an instrument or device for compressing something.
■ a machine used to supply air or other gas at increased pressure, e.g. to power a gas turbine. ■ an electrical amplifier which reduces the dynamic range of a signal. ■ a computer program which compresses data.

comprise ▶ **verb** [with obj.] consist of; be made up of: *the country comprises twenty states.*
■ make up; constitute: *this single breed comprises 50 per cent of the Swiss cattle population* | (**be comprised of**) *documents are comprised of words.*
– ORIGIN late Middle English: from French, 'comprised', feminine past participle of *comprendre*, from Old French *comprehender* (see **COMPREHEND**).

USAGE 1 According to traditional usage, **comprise** means 'consist of', as in *the country **comprises** twenty states*, and should not be used to mean 'constitute or make up (a whole)', as in *this single breed **comprises** 50 per cent of the Swiss cattle population*. But confusion has arisen because of uses in the passive, which have been formed by analogy with words like **compose**: when **comprise** is used in the active (as in *the country **comprises** twenty states*) it is, oddly, more or less synonymous with the passive use of the second sense (as in *the country **is comprised of** twenty states*). Such passive uses of **comprise** are common and are fast becoming part of standard English. Other erroneous forms, such as *the property **comprises of** bedroom, bathroom, and kitchen*, should not be used in standard English.
2 On the differences between **comprise** and **include**, see usage at **INCLUDE**.

compromise ▶ **noun** an agreement or settlement of a dispute that is reached by each side making concessions: *eventually they reached a compromise* | [mass noun] *the secret of a happy marriage is compromise.*
■ an intermediate state between conflicting opinions or actions reached by mutual concession or modification: *a **compromise between** the freedom of the individual and the need to ensure orderly government.* ■ [mass noun] the expedient acceptance of standards that are lower than is desirable: *sexism should be tackled without compromise.*
▶ **verb** **1** [no obj.] settle a dispute by mutual concession: *in the end we compromised and deferred the issue.*
■ [with obj.] archaic settle (a dispute) by mutual concession: *I should compromise the matter with my father.*
2 [with obj.] weaken (a reputation or principle) by accepting standards that are lower than is desirable: *commercial pressures could compromise safety.*
■ [no obj.] expediently accept standards that are lower than is desirable: *we were not prepared to **compromise on** safety.* ■ bring into disrepute or danger by indiscreet, foolish, or reckless behaviour: *situations in which his troops could be compromised.*
– DERIVATIVES **compromiser** noun.
– ORIGIN late Middle English (denoting mutual consent to arbitration): from Old French *compromis*, from late Latin *compromissum* 'a consent to arbitration', neuter past participle of *compromittere*, from *com-* 'together' + *promittere* (see **PROMISE**).

compromising ▶ **adjective** (of information or a situation) revealing an embarrassing or incriminating secret about someone.

compte rendu /ˌkɔ̃t rɑ̃ˈdjuː, French kɔ̃t rɑ̃dy/ ▶ **noun** (pl. **comptes rendus** pronunc. same) a formal report or review.
■ (usu. **Comptes Rendus**) the published proceedings of a French academy.
– ORIGIN early 19th cent.: French, literally 'account rendered'.

Compton[1], Arthur Holly (1892–1962), American physicist. He observed the Compton effect and thus demonstrated the dual particle and wave properties of electromagnetic radiation and matter, as predicted by quantum theory. Nobel Prize for Physics (1927).

Compton[2], Denis (Charles Scott) (1918–97), English cricketer. He played for Middlesex and England, and also played football for Arsenal and England.

Compton-Burnett /ˌkɒmptənbəːˈnɛt, -ˈbəːnɪt/, Dame Ivy (1884–1969), English novelist. Notable novels: *Brothers and Sisters* (1929), *A Family and a Fortune* (1939), and *Manservant and Maidservant* (1947).

Compton effect ▶ **noun** [mass noun] Physics an increase in wavelength of X-rays or gamma rays that occurs when they are scattered.
– ORIGIN early 20th cent.: named after A. H. *Compton* (see **COMPTON**[1]).

comptroller /kənˈtrəʊlə, kɒmp-/ ▶ **noun** a controller (used in the title of some financial officers).
– ORIGIN late 15th cent.: variant of **CONTROLLER**, by erroneous association with French *compte* 'calculation' or its source, late Latin *computus*.

compulsion ▶ **noun** **1** [mass noun] the action or state of forcing or being forced to do something: constraint: *the payment was made **under compulsion**.*
2 an irresistible urge to behave in a certain way, especially against one's conscious wishes: *he felt a compulsion to babble on about what had happened.*
– ORIGIN late Middle English: via Old French from late Latin *compulsio(n-)*, from *compellere* 'to drive, force' (see **COMPEL**).

compulsive ▶ **adjective** **1** resulting from or relating to an irresistible urge, especially one that is against one's conscious wishes: *compulsive eating.*
■ [attrib.] (of a person) acting as a result of such an urge: *a compulsive liar.*
2 irresistibly interesting or exciting; compelling: *this play is compulsive viewing.*
– DERIVATIVES **compulsively** adverb, **compulsiveness** noun.
– ORIGIN late 16th cent. (in the sense 'compulsory'): from medieval Latin *compulsivus*, from *compuls-* 'driven, forced', from the verb *compellere* (see **COMPEL**). Sense 1 (originally a term in psychology) dates from the early 20th cent.

compulsory ▶ **adjective** required by law or a rule; obligatory: *compulsory military service* | *it was compulsory to attend mass.*
■ involving or exercising compulsion; coercive: *the abuse of compulsory powers.*
– DERIVATIVES **compulsorily** adverb, **compulsoriness** noun.
– ORIGIN early 16th cent. (as a noun denoting a legal mandate which had to be obeyed): from medieval Latin *compulsorius*, from *compuls-* 'driven, forced', from the verb *compellere* (see **COMPEL**).

compulsory purchase ▶ **noun** [mass noun] [usu. as modifier] Brit. the officially enforced purchase of privately owned land or property for public use: *the City Council has applied for a compulsory purchase order.*

compunction ▶ **noun** [mass noun] [usu. with negative] a feeling of guilt or moral scruple that prevents or follows the doing of something bad: *they used their tanks **without compunction**.*
– DERIVATIVES **compunctious** adjective, **compunctiously** adverb.
– ORIGIN Middle English: from Old French *componction*, from ecclesiastical Latin *compunctio(n-)*, from Latin *compungere* 'prick sharply', from *com-* (expressing intensive force) + *pungere* 'to prick'.

compurgation /ˌkɒmpəːˈgeɪʃ(ə)n/ ▶ **noun** [mass noun] Law, historical acquittal from a charge or accusation obtained by statements of innocence given by witnesses under oath.
– ORIGIN mid 17th cent.: from medieval Latin *compurgatio(n-)*, from Latin *compurgare*, from *com-* (expressing intensive force) + *purgare* 'purify' (from *purus* 'pure').

compurgator /ˈkɒmpəːgeɪtə/ ▶ **noun** Law, historical a sworn witness to the innocence or good character of an accused person.
– ORIGIN mid 16th cent.: medieval Latin, from Latin *com-* 'together with' + *purgator*, from *purgare* 'purify' (see **COMPURGATION**).

computation ▶ **noun** [mass noun] the action of mathematical calculation: *methods of computation* | [count noun] *statistical computations.*
■ the use of computers, especially as a subject of research or study.
– ORIGIN late Middle English: from Latin *computatio(n-)*, from the verb *computare* (see **COMPUTE**).

computational ▶ *adjective* using computers: *the computational analysis of English.*
▪of or relating to computers: *computational power.* ▪ of or relating to the process of mathematical calculation: *the exam only really tested computational ability.*
– DERIVATIVES **computationally** adverb.

computational linguistics ▶ *plural noun* [treated as sing.] the branch of linguistics in which the techniques of computer science are applied to the analysis and synthesis of language and speech.

compute ▶ *verb* [with obj.] (usu. **be computed**) reckon or calculate (a figure or amount): *the hire charge is computed on a daily basis.*
▪[no obj., with negative] informal seem reasonable; make sense: *the idea of a woman alone in a pub did not compute.* [ORIGIN: from the phrase *does not compute*, once used as an error message in computing.]
– DERIVATIVES **computability** noun, **computable** adjective.
– ORIGIN early 17th cent.: from French *computer* or Latin *computare*, from *com-* 'together' + *putare* 'to settle (an account)'.

computer ▶ *noun* a device which is capable of receiving information (data) in a particular form and of performing a sequence of operations in accordance with a predetermined but variable set of procedural instructions (program) to produce a result in the form of information or signals. Most computers operate electronically and manipulate data in digital form.
▪a person who makes calculations, especially with a calculating machine.

computer animation ▶ *noun* see **ANIMATION**.

computerate /kəm'pjuːtərət/ ▶ *adjective* informal another term for **COMPUTER-LITERATE**.

computer conferencing ▶ *noun* [mass noun] the use of computer and telecommunication technology to hold discussions between three or more people operating computers in separate locations.

computer dating ▶ *noun* [mass noun] the use of computer databases to identify potentially compatible partners for people.

computer-friendly ▶ *adjective* **1** suitable for use with computers; compatible with computers.
2 (of a person) well disposed towards computers.

computer game ▶ *noun* a game played using a computer, typically a video game.

computer graphics ▶ *plural noun* another term for **GRAPHICS** (in sense 3).

computerize (also **-ise**) ▶ *verb* [with obj.] [often as adj. **computerized**] convert to a system which is operated or controlled by computer: *the advantages of computerized accounting.*
▪convert (information) to a form which is stored or processed by computer: *a computerized register of dogs.*
– DERIVATIVES **computerization** noun.

computer-literate ▶ *adjective* (of a person) having sufficient knowledge and skill to be able to use computers; familiar with the operation of computers.
– DERIVATIVES **computer literacy** noun.

computer science ▶ *noun* [mass noun] the study of the principles and use of computers.

computer virus ▶ *noun* see **VIRUS**.

computing ▶ *noun* [mass noun] the use or operation of computers: *developments in mathematics and computing* | [as modifier] *computing facilities.*

comrade ▶ *noun* (among men) a companion who shares one's activities or is a fellow member of an organization.
▪(also **comrade-in-arms**) a fellow soldier or serviceman. ▪ a fellow socialist or communist (often as a form of address): [as title] *Comrade Petrova.* ▪ (in South Africa) a young militant supporter of the African National Congress.
– DERIVATIVES **comradely** adjective, **comradeship** noun.
– ORIGIN mid 16th cent. (originally also *camerade*): from French *camerade, camarade* (originally feminine), from Spanish *camarada* 'room-mate', from Latin *camera* 'chamber'. Compare with **CHUM**[1].

Comsat ▶ *noun* trademark a communications satellite.
– ORIGIN 1960s: blend.

Comte /kɒmt, French kɔ̃t/, Auguste (1798–1857), French philosopher, one of the founders of sociology. Comte's positivist philosophy attempted to define the laws of social evolution and to found a genuine social science that could be used for social reconstruction.

Con Brit. ▶ *abbreviation for* ▪ Conservative (denoting the political affiliation of a Member of Parliament): *Teddy Taylor, MP (Con).* ▪ constable (as part of a police officer's title): *Deputy Chief Con Tony Burden.*

con[1] informal ▶ *verb* (**conned**, **conning**) [with obj.] persuade (someone) to do or believe something by telling them something that is not true: *I conned him* ***into*** *giving me your home number* | *she was jailed for* ***conning*** *her aunt* ***out of*** *£500,000* | *a bogus social worker* ***conned her way into*** *the pensioner's home.*
▶ *noun* an instance of deceiving or tricking someone, especially by persuading them to believe something that is not true: *the Charter is a glossy public relations con* | [as modifier] *a big con trick.*
– ORIGIN late 19th cent. (originally US): abbreviation of **CONFIDENCE**, as in *confidence trick.*

con[2] ▶ *noun* a disadvantage: *borrowers have to weigh up* ***the pros and cons of*** *each mortgage offer.*
– ORIGIN late 16th cent.: from Latin *contra* 'against'.

con[3] ▶ *noun* informal a convict.
– ORIGIN late 19th cent.: abbreviation.

con[4] (US also **conn**) Nautical ▶ *verb* (**conned**, **conning**) [with obj.] direct the steering of (a ship): *he hadn't conned anything bigger than a Boston whaler.*
▶ *noun* (**the con**) the action or post of conning a ship.
– ORIGIN early 17th cent.: apparently a weakened form of obsolete *cond* 'conduct, guide', from Old French *conduire*, from Latin *conducere* (see **CONDUCE**).

con[5] ▶ *verb* (**conned**, **conning**) [with obj.] archaic study attentively or learn by heart (a piece of writing): *the girls conned their pages with a great show of industry.*
– ORIGIN Middle English *cunne, conne, con*, variants of **CAN**[1].

con[6] ▶ *noun* informal a convention, especially one for science-fiction enthusiasts.
– ORIGIN 1970s: abbreviation.

con- ▶ *prefix* variant spelling of **COM-** assimilated before *c, d, f, g, j, n, q, s, t, v*, and sometimes before vowels (as in *concord, condescend, confide*, etc.).
– ORIGIN Latin variant of *com-*.

conacre /'kɒneɪkə/ ▶ *noun* [mass noun] (in Ireland) the letting by a tenant of small portions of land prepared for crops or grazing.
– ORIGIN early 19th cent.: from **CORN**[1] + **ACRE**.

Conakry /'kɒnəkri/ the capital and chief port of Guinea; pop. 950,000 (1992).

con amore /ˌkɒn a'mɔːreɪ/ ▶ *adverb* Music (especially as a direction) with tenderness.
– ORIGIN Italian, 'with love'.

Conan Doyle /'kəʊnən/ see **DOYLE**.

conation /kə'neɪʃ(ə)n/ ▶ *noun* [mass noun] Philosophy & Psychology the mental faculty of purpose, desire, or will to perform an action; volition.
– ORIGIN early 17th cent. (denoting an attempt or endeavour): from Latin *conatio(n-)*, from *conari* 'to try'.

conative /'kɒnətɪv/ ▶ *adjective* **1** of or involving conation.
2 Grammar denoting a word or structure that expresses attempted action as opposed to action itself, for example *at* in *he was kicking at the bicycle.*
– ORIGIN late 19th cent.: from Latin *conat-* 'endeavoured' (from the verb *conari*) + **-IVE**.

con brio /kɒn 'briːəʊ/ ▶ *adverb* Music (especially as a direction) with vigour.
– ORIGIN Italian.

concatenate /kən'katɪneɪt/ ▶ *verb* [with obj.] formal or technical link (things) together in a chain or series: *some words may be concatenated, such that certain sounds are omitted.*
– ORIGIN late 15th cent. (as an adjective): from late Latin *concatenat-* 'linked together', from the verb *concatenare*, from *con-* 'together' + *catenare*, from *catena* 'chain'.

concatenation ▶ *noun* a series of interconnected things or events: *a concatenation of events which had finally led to the murder.*
▪[mass noun] the action of linking things together in a series or the condition of being linked in such a way.

concave /'kɒnkeɪv/ ▶ *adjective* having an outline or surface that curves inwards like the interior of a circle or sphere. Compare with **CONVEX** (in sense 1).
– DERIVATIVES **concavely** adverb, **concavity** noun.
– ORIGIN late Middle English: from Latin *concavus*, from *con-* 'together' + *cavus* 'hollow'.

concavity /kɒn'kavɪti/ ▶ *noun* (pl. **-ies**) [mass noun] the state or quality of being concave.
▪[count noun] a concave surface or thing.

concavo-concave /kɒn'keɪvəʊ/ ▶ *adjective* another term for **BICONCAVE**.

concavo-convex ▶ *adjective* (of a lens) concave on one side and convex on the other and thickest at the periphery.

conceal ▶ *verb* [with obj.] not allow to be seen; hide: *a line of sand dunes concealed the distant sea* | [as adj. **concealed**] *he pressed a concealed button.*
▪keep (something) secret; prevent from being known or noticed: *love that they had to* ***conceal from*** *others.*
– DERIVATIVES **concealment** noun.
– ORIGIN Middle English: from Old French *conceler*, from Latin *concelare*, from *con-* 'completely' + *celare* 'hide'.

concealer ▶ *noun* a flesh-toned cosmetic stick used to cover spots, blemishes, and dark under-eye circles.

concede ▶ *verb* **1** [reporting verb] admit or agree that something is true or valid after first denying or resisting it: [with clause] *I had to concede that I'd overreacted* | [with direct speech] *'All right then,' she conceded* | [with obj.] *that principle now seems to have been conceded.*
▪[with obj.] admit (defeat) in a match or contest: *he conceded defeat* | [no obj.] *reluctantly, Ellen conceded.* ▪ [with obj.] admit defeat in (a match or contest): *they conceded the match to their opponents.*
2 [with obj.] surrender or yield (something that one possesses): *in 475 the emperor* ***conceded*** *the Auvergne* ***to*** *Euric.*
▪grant (a right, privilege, or demand): *the government conceded a key demand.* ▪ (in sport) fail to prevent the scoring of (a goal or point) by an opponent: *they have conceded only one goal in seven matches.* ▪ allow (a lead or advantage) to slip: *he took an early lead which he never conceded.*
– DERIVATIVES **conceder** noun.
– ORIGIN late 15th cent.: from French *concéder* or Latin *concedere*, from *con-* 'completely' + *cedere* 'yield'.

conceit ▶ *noun* **1** [mass noun] excessive pride in oneself: *he was puffed up with conceit.*
2 a fanciful or ingenious expression in writing or speech; an elaborate metaphor: *the idea of the wind's singing is a prime romantic conceit.*
▪an artistic effect or device: *the director's brilliant conceit was to film this tale in black and white.* ▪ a fanciful notion: *he is alarmed by the widespread conceit that he spent most of the 1980s drunk.*
– ORIGIN late Middle English (in the sense 'idea or notion', also 'quaintly decorative article'): from **CONCEIVE**, on the pattern of pairs such as *deceive, deceit.*

conceited ▶ *adjective* excessively proud of oneself; vain.
– DERIVATIVES **conceitedly** adverb, **conceitedness** noun.

conceivable ▶ *adjective* capable of being imagined or grasped mentally: *a mass uprising was entirely conceivable* | *in every conceivable way that action was entirely wrong* | *it was photographed from every conceivable angle.*
– DERIVATIVES **conceivability** noun.

conceivably ▶ *adverb* [sentence adverb] it is conceivable or imaginable that: *it may conceivably cause liver disease.*

conceive ▶ *verb* [with obj.] (often **be conceived**) **1** cause (an embryo) to come into being by fertilizing an egg: *she was conceived when her father was 49.*
▪[no obj.] (of a woman) become pregnant: *five months ago Wendy conceived.*
2 form or devise (a plan, idea, or work) in the mind: *the dam project was originally conceived in 1977* | [as adj., with submodifier] (**conceived**) *a brilliantly conceived and executed robbery.*
▪form a mental representation of; imagine: *without society an individual cannot be* ***conceived as*** *having rights* | [no obj.] *we could not* ***conceive of*** *such things happening to us.* ▪ become affected by (a feeling): *I had conceived a passion for another.*
– ORIGIN Middle English: from Old French *concevoir*, from Latin *concipere*, from *com-* 'together' + *capere* 'take'.

concelebrate /kɒn'sɛlɪbreɪt/ ▶ *verb* [with obj.] Christian

Church officiate jointly at (a Mass): *the pro-nuncio will concelebrate Mass with bishops from Wales.*
– DERIVATIVES **concelebrant** noun, **concelebration** noun.
– ORIGIN late 19th cent.: from Latin *concelebrat-* 'celebrated together', from the verb *concelebrare*, from *con-* 'together' + *celebrare* (see **CELEBRATE**).

concentrate ▶ **verb 1** [no obj.] focus all one's attention or mental effort on a particular object or activity: *she couldn't concentrate on the film* | [with obj.] *a threatened tax rise concentrates the mind wonderfully.*
■ (**concentrate on/upon**) do or deal with (one particular thing) above all others: *Luke wants to concentrate on his film career.*
2 [with obj.] (often **be concentrated**) gather (people or things) together in numbers or a mass to one point: *power was concentrated in the hands of the ruling Politburo.*
■ [no obj.] come together in this way: *troops were concentrating at the western front.* ■ increase the strength or proportion of (a substance or solution) by removing or reducing the water or other diluting agent or by selective accumulation of atoms or molecules: *plants and micro-organisms can concentrate metals from the environment.*
▶ **noun** [mass noun] a substance made by removing water or other diluting agent; a concentrated form of something, especially food: *apple juice concentrate.*
– DERIVATIVES **concentrative** adjective, **concentrator** noun.
– ORIGIN mid 17th cent. (in the sense 'bring towards a centre'): Latinized form of **CONCENTRE**, or from French *concentrer* 'to concentrate'. Sense 1 dates from the early 20th cent.

concentrated ▶ **adjective 1** wholly directed to one thing; intense: *a concentrated campaign.*
2 (of a substance or solution) present in a high proportion relative to other substances; having had water or other diluting agent removed or reduced: *pure concentrated fruit juice.*
– DERIVATIVES **concentratedly** adverb.

concentration ▶ **noun 1** [mass noun] the action or power of focusing one's attention or mental effort: *frowning in concentration* | *the worker needs total concentration.*
■ (**concentration on/upon**) dealing with one particular thing above all others: *concentration on the needs of the young can mean that the elderly are forgotten.*
2 a close gathering of people or things: *the island has the greatest concentration of seabirds in the north-west.*
■ [mass noun] the action of gathering together closely: *the concentration of power in the hands of nobles.*
3 the relative amount of a particular substance contained within a solution or mixture or in a particular volume of space; the amount of solute per unit volume of solution: *the gas can collect in dangerous concentrations.*
■ [mass noun] the action of strengthening a solution by the removal of water or other diluting agent or by the selective accumulation of atoms or molecules.

concentration camp ▶ **noun** a place in which large numbers of people, especially political prisoners or members of persecuted minorities, are deliberately imprisoned in a relatively small area with inadequate facilities, sometimes to provide forced labour or to await mass execution. The term is most strongly associated with the several hundred camps established by the Nazis in Germany and occupied Europe 1933–45, among the most infamous being Dachau, Belsen, and Auschwitz.

concentre (US **concenter**) ▶ **verb** [with obj.] concentrate (something) in a small space or area: *the property of this country is concentred in a very few hands.*
■ [no obj.] come together or collect at a common centre: *here the produce of this extensive territory concentres.* ■ archaic bring or draw (two or more things) towards a common centre: *a passion in which soul and body were concentred.*
– ORIGIN late 16th cent.: from French *concentrer*, from Latin *con-* 'together' + *centrum* 'centre'.

concentric ▶ **adjective** of or denoting circles, arcs, or other shapes which share the same centre, the larger often completely surrounding the smaller.
– DERIVATIVES **concentrically** adverb, **concentricity** noun.
– ORIGIN late Middle English: from Old French *concentrique* or medieval Latin *concentricus*, from *con-* 'together' + *centrum* 'centre'.

Concepción /kɒn,sɛpsɪ'ɒn, Spanish konsep'sjon, -θep'θjon/ an industrial city in south central Chile; pop. 294,000 (est. 1987).

concept ▶ **noun** an abstract idea; a general notion: *structuralism is a difficult concept* | *the concept of justice.*
■ a plan or intention; a conception: *the centre has kept firmly to its original concept.* ■ an idea or invention to help sell or publicize a commodity: *a new concept in corporate hospitality.* ■ Philosophy an idea or thought which corresponds to some distinct entity or class of entities, or to its essential features, or determines the application of a term (especially a predicate), and thus plays a part in the use of reason or language.
■ [as modifier] (of a car or other vehicle) produced as an experimental model to test the viability of innovative design features.
– ORIGIN mid 16th cent. (in the sense 'thought, frame of mind, imagination'): from Latin *conceptum* 'something conceived', from Latin *concept-* 'conceived', from *concipere* (see **CONCEIVE**).

concept album ▶ **noun** a rock album featuring a cycle of songs expressing a particular theme or idea.

conception ▶ **noun 1** [mass noun] the action of conceiving a child or of one being conceived: *an unfertilized egg before conception* | [count noun] *a rise in premarital conceptions.*
■ the forming or devising of a plan, idea, or work: *the time between a product's conception and its launch.*
2 the way in which something is perceived or regarded: *our conception of how language relates to reality.*
■ a general notion; an abstract idea: *the conception of a balance of power.* ■ a plan or intention: *reconstructing Bach's original conceptions.* ■ [mass noun] understanding; ability to imagine: *the administration had no conception of women's problems.*
– DERIVATIVES **conceptional** adjective.
– ORIGIN Middle English: via Old French from Latin *conceptio(n-)*, from the verb *concipere* (see **CONCEIVE**).

conceptual ▶ **adjective** of, relating to, or based on mental concepts: *philosophy deals with conceptual difficulties.*
– ORIGIN mid 17th cent.: from medieval Latin *conceptualis*, from Latin *concept-* 'conceived', from the verb *concipere* (see **CONCEPT**).

conceptual art ▶ **noun** [mass noun] art in which the idea or concept presented by the artist is considered more important than the finished product, if any such exists.

conceptualism ▶ **noun** [mass noun] Philosophy the theory that universals can be said to exist, but only as concepts in the mind.
– DERIVATIVES **conceptualist** noun.

conceptualize (also **-ise**) ▶ **verb** [with obj.] form a concept or idea of (something): *sex was conceptualized as an overpowering force in the individual.*
– DERIVATIVES **conceptualization** noun.

conceptually ▶ **adverb** in terms of a concept or abstract idea: [sentence adverb] *conceptually, this is a complex process* | *a conceptually simple task.*

conceptus /kən'sɛptəs/ ▶ **noun** (pl. **conceptuses**) technical the embryo in the womb, especially during the early stages of pregnancy.
– ORIGIN mid 18th cent.: from Latin, 'conception, embryo', from *concept-* 'conceived', from the verb *concipere.*

concern ▶ **verb** [with obj.] **1** relate to; be about: *the story concerns a friend of mine* | (**be concerned with**) *the report is mainly concerned with 1984 onwards.*
■ be relevant or important to; affect or involve: *she was prying into that which did not concern her* | *many thanks to all concerned.* ■ (**be concerned**) regard it as important or interesting to do something: *I was mainly concerned with making something that children could enjoy.* ■ (**be concerned in**) formal have a specific connection with or responsibility for: *those concerned in industry, academia, and government.* ■ (**concern oneself with**) interest or involve oneself in: *it is not necessary for us to concern ourselves with this point.*
2 worry (someone); make anxious: *the roof of the barn concerns me because eventually it will fall in* | *'Don't concern yourself, old boy—my lips are sealed'*
▶ **noun 1** [mass noun] anxiety; worry: *such unsatisfactory work gives cause for concern.*
■ [count noun] a cause of anxiety or worry: *environmental concerns.*
2 a matter of interest or importance to someone: *housing is the concern of the Housing Executive* | [mass noun] *the prospect should be of concern to us all.*
■ (**concerns**) affairs; issues: *public awareness of Aboriginal concerns.*
3 a business; a firm.
4 informal, dated a complicated or awkward object or structure.
– PHRASES **as** (or **so**) **far as —— is concerned** as regards the interests or case of ——: *the measures are irrelevant as far as inflation is concerned.* **have no concern with** formal have nothing to do with: *drama seemed to have no concern with 'truth' at all.* **to whom it may concern** a formula placed at the beginning of a letter, notice, or testimonial when the identity of the reader or readers is unknown.
– ORIGIN late Middle English: from French *concerner* or late Latin *concernere* (in medieval Latin 'be relevant to'), from *con-* (expressing intensive force) + *cernere* 'sift, discern'.

concerned ▶ **adjective** worried, troubled, or anxious: *the villagers are concerned about burglaries.*
– DERIVATIVES **concernedly** adverb.

concerning ▶ **preposition** on the subject of or in connection with; about: *further revelations concerning his role in the affair.*

concernment ▶ **noun** [mass noun] archaic importance: *matters of great public concernment.*
■ [count noun] a matter of interest or importance to someone; a concern: *if the captain has a family or any absorbing concernment of that sort.*

concert ▶ **noun** /'kɒnsət/ **1** a musical performance given in public, typically by several performers or of several separate compositions: *a pop concert* | [as modifier] *a concert pianist.*
■ [as modifier] of, relating to, or denoting the performance of music written for opera, ballet, or theatre on its own without the accompanying dramatic action: *the concert version of the fourth interlude from the opera.* See also **CONCERT PERFORMANCE**.
2 [mass noun] formal agreement, accordance, or harmony: *critics' inability to describe with any precision and concert the characteristics of literature.*
■ Law joint action, especially in the committing of a crime: *they found direct evidence of concert of action.*
▶ **verb** /kən'sɔːt/ [with obj.] formal arrange (something) by mutual agreement or coordination: *they started meeting regularly to concert their parliamentary tactics.*
– PHRASES **in concert 1** acting jointly: *we must take stronger action in concert with our European partners.*
2 (of music or a performer) giving a public performance; live: *they saw Pink Floyd in concert.*
– ORIGIN late 16th cent. (in the sense 'unite, cause to agree'): from French *concerter*, from Italian *concertare* 'harmonize'. The noun use, dating from the early 17th cent. (in the sense 'a combination of voices or sounds'), is from French *concert*, from Italian *concerto*, from *concertare.*

concertante /,kɒntʃə'tanteɪ, -'tanti/ ▶ **adjective 1** denoting a piece of music containing one or more solo parts, typically of less prominence or weight than in a concerto. See also **SINFONIA CONCERTANTE**.
2 chiefly historical denoting prominent instrumental parts present throughout a piece of music, especially in baroque and early classical compositions.
– ORIGIN Italian, 'harmonizing', from *concertare* 'harmonize'.

concert band ▶ **noun** another term for **MILITARY BAND**.

concerted ▶ **adjective 1** [attrib.] jointly arranged, planned, or carried out; coordinated: *a concerted attempt to preserve religious unity.*
■ strenuously carried out; done with great effort: *you must make a concerted effort to curb this.*
2 (of music) arranged in several parts of equal importance: *concerted secular music for voices.*

concert grand ▶ **noun** the largest size of grand piano, up to 2.75 m long, used for concerts.

concertina /,kɒnsə'tiːnə/ ▶ **noun** a small musical instrument, typically polygonal in form, played by stretching and squeezing between the hands to work a central bellows which blows air over reeds, each note being sounded by a button. Compare with **ACCORDION**.
■ [as modifier] opening or closing in multiple folds: *concertina doors.*
▶ **verb** (**concertinas**, **concertinaed** or **concertina'd**, **concertinaing**) [with obj.] extend, compress, or collapse in folds like those of a concertina: [as adj. **concertinaed**] *big rolls of concertinaed wire* | figurative *a*

request that the negotiations be concertinaed into a week-long session.
– ORIGIN mid 19th cent.: from **CONCERT** + **-INA**.

concertino /ˌkɒntʃəˈtiːnəʊ/ ▶ **noun** (pl. **-os**) **1** a simple or short concerto.
2 a solo instrument or solo instruments playing with an orchestra.
– ORIGIN late 18th cent.: Italian, diminutive of *concerto* (see **CONCERTO**).

concertize /ˈkɒnsətʌɪz/ ▶ **verb** [no obj.] N. Amer. give a concert or concerts.

concertmaster ▶ **noun** chiefly N. Amer. the leading first-violin player in some orchestras.

concerto /kənˈtʃəːtəʊ, -ˈtʃɛːtəʊ/ ▶ **noun** (pl. **concertos** or **concerti**) a musical composition for a solo instrument or instruments accompanied by an orchestra, especially one conceived on a relatively large scale.
– ORIGIN early 18th cent.: Italian, from *concertare* 'harmonize'.

concerto grosso /ˈgrɒsəʊ/ ▶ **noun** (pl. **concerti grossi** /-si/) a musical composition for a group of solo instruments accompanied by an orchestra. The term is used mainly of baroque works.
– ORIGIN early 18th cent.: Italian, literally 'big concerto'.

concert overture ▶ **noun** a piece of music in the style of an overture but intended for independent performance.

concert party ▶ **noun** a group of variety performers.
■ a show staged by such a group. ■ Stock Exchange a number of parties who separately invest in a company with the concealed intention of using their holdings as a single block.

concert performance ▶ **noun** **1** Brit. a performance of a piece of music written for an opera, ballet, piece of theatre, religious service, etc., at a concert without the accompanying dramatic action, dance, or liturgy.
2 a performance of a piece of music at a live concert.

concert pitch ▶ **noun** [mass noun] Music a standard for the tuning of musical instruments, internationally agreed in 1960, in which the note A above middle C has a frequency of 440 Hz.
■ figurative a state of readiness, efficiency, and keenness: *slightly unnerved by the contretemps, I was not at concert pitch.*

concession ▶ **noun** **1** a thing that is granted, especially in response to demands; a thing conceded: *the government was unwilling to make any further concessions.*
■ [mass noun] the action of conceding, granting, or yielding something: *this strict rule was relaxed by concession.* ■ (**a concession to**) a gesture, especially a token one, made in recognition of a demand or prevailing standard: *her only concession to fashion was her ornate silver ring.*
2 a preferential allowance or rate given by an organization: *tax concessions.*
■ a reduction in the price of something, especially a fare or ticket, for a certain category of person.
3 the right to use land or other property for a specified purpose or to conduct specified commercial operations in a particular area, granted by a government, company, or other controlling body: *new logging concessions.*
■ a commercial operation set up by agreement within the premises of a larger concern. ■ Canadian a piece of land into which surveyed land is divided.
– ORIGIN late Middle English: from Latin *concessio(n-)*, from the verb *concedere* (see **CONCEDE**).

concessionaire /kənˌsɛʃəˈnɛː/ (also **concessionnaire**) ▶ **noun** the holder of a concession or grant, especially for the use of land or commercial premises or for trading rights.
– ORIGIN mid 19th cent.: from French *concessionnaire*, from Latin *concessio* (see **CONCESSION**).

concessional ▶ **adjective** [attrib.] (of a rate or allowance) constituting a concession: *a concessional interest rate.*

concessionary ▶ **adjective** of, relating to, or constituting a concession or reduced rate: *concessionary bus passes.*

concession road (also **concession line**) ▶ **noun** Canadian a rural road separating concessions.

concessive ▶ **adjective** **1** of, characterized by, or tending to concession: *we must look for a more concessive approach.*
2 Grammar (of a preposition or conjunction) introducing a phrase or clause denoting a circumstance which might be expected to preclude the action of the main clause, but does not (e.g. *in spite of*, *although*).
■ (of a phrase or clause) introduced by a concessive preposition or conjunction.
– ORIGIN early 18th cent. (in sense 2): from late Latin *concessivus*, from *concess-* 'withdrawn, yielded' (see **CONCESSION**).

conch /kɒŋk, kɒn(t)ʃ/ ▶ **noun** (pl. **conchs** /kɒŋks/ or **conches** /ˈkɒntʃɪz/) **1** (also **conch shell**) a tropical marine mollusc with a robust spiral shell which may bear long projections and have a flared lip.
● *Strombus* and other genera, family Strombidae, class Gastropoda.
■ a shell of this kind blown like a trumpet to produce a hollow-sounding musical note, often depicted as played by Tritons and other mythological figures.
2 Architecture the roof of a semicircular apse, shaped like half a dome.
3 another term for **CONCHA**.
– ORIGIN late Middle English: from Latin *concha* 'shellfish, shell', from Greek *konkhē* 'mussel, cockle, or shell-like cavity'.

concha /ˈkɒŋkə/ ▶ **noun** (pl. **conchae** /-kiː/) Anatomy & Zoology a part resembling a spiral shell, in particular:
■ the depression in the external ear leading to its central opening. ■ (also **nasal concha**) any of several thin, scroll-like (turbinate) bones in the sides of the nasal cavity.
– ORIGIN late 16th cent.: from Latin (see **CONCH**).

conchie /ˈkɒnʃi/ ▶ **noun** (pl. **-ies**) Brit. informal, derogatory a conscientious objector.
– ORIGIN First World War: abbreviation.

conchiolin /ˈkɒntʃɪə(ʊ)lɪn/ ▶ **noun** [mass noun] Zoology a tough, insoluble protein secreted by molluscs, forming the organic matrix of the shell within which calcium carbonate is deposited.
– ORIGIN late 19th cent.: from Latin *concha* 'shell' + the diminutive suffix *-iola* + **-IN**[1].

conchoid /ˈkɒŋkɔɪd/ ▶ **noun** Mathematics a plane quartic curve consisting of two separate branches either side of and asymptotic to a central straight line (the asymptote), such that if a line is drawn from a fixed point (the pole) to intersect both branches, the part of the line falling between the two branches is of constant length and is exactly bisected by the asymptote.
● Such curves are represented by the general equation $(x - a)^2(x^2 + y^2) = b^2x^2$, where a is the distance between the pole and the asymptote, and b is the constant length. The branch on the same side of the asymptote as the pole typically has a cusp or loop.
– ORIGIN early 18th cent.: from **CONCH** + **-OID**.

conchoidal /kɒŋˈkɔɪd(ə)l/ ▶ **adjective** chiefly Mineralogy denoting a type of fracture in a solid (such as flint) which results in a smooth rounded surface resembling the shape of a scallop shell.

conchology /kɒŋˈkɒlədʒi/ ▶ **noun** [mass noun] the scientific study or collection of mollusc shells. Compare with **MALACOLOGY**.
– DERIVATIVES **conchological** adjective, **conchologist** noun.
– ORIGIN late 18th cent.: from Greek *konkhē* 'shell' + **-LOGY**.

concierge /ˈkɒnsɪɛːʒ/ ▶ **noun** **1** (especially in France) a caretaker of a block of flats or a small hotel, typically one living on the premises.
2 a hotel employee whose job is to assist guests by booking tours, making theatre and restaurant reservations, etc.
– ORIGIN mid 16th cent. (denoting the warden of a house, castle, prison, or royal palace): French, probably based on Latin *conservus* 'fellow slave'.

conciliar /kənˈsɪlɪə/ ▶ **adjective** of, relating to, or proceeding from a council, especially an ecclesiastical one: *conciliar decrees.*
– ORIGIN late 17th cent.: from medieval Latin *consiliarius* 'counsellor', from Latin *concilium* (see **COUNCIL**).

conciliate /kənˈsɪlɪeɪt/ ▶ **verb** [with obj.] **1** stop (someone) being angry or discontented; placate; pacify: *concessions were made to conciliate the peasantry.*
■ [no obj.] act as a mediator: *he sought to conciliate in the dispute.* ■ formal reconcile; make compatible: *all complaints about charges will be conciliated if possible.*
2 archaic gain (esteem or goodwill): *the arts which conciliate popularity.*
– DERIVATIVES **conciliation** noun, **conciliative** adjective, **conciliator** noun, **conciliatoriness** noun.
– ORIGIN mid 16th cent. (in sense 2): from Latin *conciliat-* 'combined, gained', from the verb *conciliare*, from *concilium* (see **COUNCIL**).

conciliatory ▶ **adjective** intended or likely to placate or pacify: *a conciliatory approach.*

concinnity /kənˈsɪnɪti/ ▶ **noun** [mass noun] rare the skilful and harmonious arrangement or fitting together of the different parts of something.
■ studied elegance of literary or artistic style.
– ORIGIN mid 16th cent.: from Latin *concinnitas*, from *concinnus* 'skilfully put together'.

concise ▶ **adjective** giving a lot of information clearly and in a few words; brief but comprehensive: *a concise account of the country's history.*
– DERIVATIVES **concisely** adverb, **conciseness** noun, **concision** noun.
– ORIGIN late 16th cent.: from French *concis* or Latin *concisus*, past participle of *concidere* 'cut up, cut down', from *con-* 'completely' + *caedere* 'to cut'.

conclave /ˈkɒŋkleɪv/ ▶ **noun** a private meeting.
■ (in the Roman Catholic Church) the assembly of cardinals for the election of a pope. ■ the meeting place for such an assembly.
– ORIGIN late Middle English (denoting a private room): via French from Latin *conclave* 'lockable room', from *con-* 'with' + *clavis* 'key'.

conclude ▶ **verb** **1** [with obj.] bring (something) to an end: *they conclude their study with these words* | [no obj.] *we concluded by singing carols.*
■ [no obj.] come to an end: *the talk concluded with slides.* ■ formally and finally settle or arrange (a treaty or agreement): *an attempt to conclude a ceasefire.*
2 [with clause] arrive at a judgement or opinion by reasoning: *the doctors concluded that Esther had suffered a stroke* | *what do you conclude from all this?*
■ [with direct speech] say in conclusion: *'It's a wicked old world,' she concluded.* ■ [with infinitive] US dated decide to do something: *we found some bread, which we concluded to eat.*
– ORIGIN Middle English (in the sense 'convince'): from Latin *concludere*, from *con-* 'completely' + *claudere* 'to shut'.

conclusion ▶ **noun** **1** the end or finish of an event or process: *the conclusion of World War Two.*
■ the summing-up of an argument or text. ■ [mass noun] the settling or arrangement of a treaty or agreement: *the conclusion of a free-trade accord.*
2 a judgement or decision reached by reasoning: *each research group came to a similar conclusion.*
■ Logic a proposition that is reached from given premises.
– PHRASES **in conclusion** lastly; to sum up: *in conclusion, it is clear that the market is maturing.* **jump** (or **leap**) **to conclusions** (or **the conclusion that**) make a hasty judgement before learning or considering all the facts. **try conclusions with** formal engage in a trial of skill or argument with.
– ORIGIN late Middle English: from Latin *conclusio(n-)*, from the verb *concludere* (see **CONCLUDE**).

conclusive ▶ **adjective** (of evidence or argument) having or likely to have the effect of proving a case; decisive or convincing: *conclusive evidence* | *the findings were by no means conclusive.*
■ (of a victory) achieved easily or by a large margin.
– DERIVATIVES **conclusively** adverb, **conclusiveness** noun.
– ORIGIN late 16th cent. (in the sense 'summing up, concluding'): from late Latin *conclusivus*, from Latin *conclus-* 'closed up', from the verb *concludere* (see **CONCLUSION**).

concoct /kənˈkɒkt/ ▶ **verb** [with obj.] make (a dish or meal) by combining various ingredients: *she began to concoct a dinner likely to appeal to him.*
■ create or devise (a story or plan): *his cronies concocted a simple plan.*
– DERIVATIVES **concocter** noun.
– ORIGIN mid 16th cent.: from Latin *concoct-*, literally 'cooked together', from *concoquere*. The original sense was 'refine or purify metals or minerals by heating', later 'cook'.

concoction ▶ **noun** a mixture of various ingredients or elements: *the facade is a strange concoction of northern Mannerism and Italian Baroque.*
■ an elaborate story, especially a fabricated one: *her*

story is an improbable concoction. ■ an elaborate or showy garment or hat.

concomitance /kən'kɒmɪt(ə)ns/ ▶ **noun** (also **concomitancy**) [mass noun] the fact of existing or occurring together with something else.
■ Theology the doctrine that the body and blood of Christ are each present in both the bread and the wine of the Eucharist.
– ORIGIN mid 16th cent.: from medieval Latin *concomitantia*, from the verb *concomitari* 'accompany' (see **CONCOMITANT**).

concomitant /kən'kɒmɪt(ə)nt/ formal ▶ **adjective** naturally accompanying or associated: *she loved travel, with all its concomitant worries* | ***concomitant with** his obsession with dirt was a desire for order.*
▶ **noun** a phenomenon that naturally accompanies or follows something: *some of us look on pain and illness as concomitants of the stresses of living.*
– DERIVATIVES **concomitantly** adverb.
– ORIGIN early 17th cent.: from late Latin *concomitant-* 'accompanying', from *concomitari*, from *con-* 'together with' + *comitari*, from Latin *comes* 'companion'.

Concord[1] **1** the state capital of New Hampshire; pop. 36,000 (1990).
2 a town in NE Massachusetts; pop. 17,080 (1990). Battles there and at Lexington in April 1775 marked the start of the War of American Independence.

Concord[2] /'kɒŋkɔːd/ ▶ **noun** [mass noun] a variety of dessert grape developed at Concord, Massachusetts.

concord ▶ **noun** [mass noun] **1** formal agreement or harmony between people or groups: *a pact of peace and concord.*
■ [count noun] a treaty.
2 Grammar agreement between words in gender, number, case, person, or any other grammatical category which affects the forms of the words.
3 [count noun] Music a chord that is pleasing or satisfactory in itself.
– ORIGIN Middle English: from Old French *concorde*, from Latin *concordia*, from *concors* 'of one mind', from *con-* 'together' + *cor, cord-* 'heart'.

concordance /kən'kɔːd(ə)ns/ ▶ **noun 1** an alphabetical list of the words (especially the important ones) present in a text or body of texts, usually with citations of the passages concerned or with the context displayed on a computer screen: *a concordance to the Bible.*
2 [mass noun] formal agreement: *the concordance between the teams' research results.*
■ Medicine the inheritance by two related individuals (especially twins) of the same genetic characteristic, such as susceptibility to a disease.
▶ **verb** [with obj.] [often as adj. **concordanced**] make a concordance of: *the value of concordanced information.*
– ORIGIN late Middle English: from Old French, from medieval Latin *concordantia*, from *concordant-* 'being of one mind' (see **CONCORDANT**).

concordant ▶ **adjective** in agreement; consistent: *the answers were roughly concordant.*
■ Geology corresponding in direction with the planes of adjacent or underlying strata. ■ Medicine (of twins) inheriting the same genetic characteristic, such as susceptibility to a disease. ■ Music in harmony.
– DERIVATIVES **concordantly** adverb.
– ORIGIN late 15th cent.: via Old French from Latin *concordant-* 'being of one mind', from the verb *concordare* (see **CONCORD**).

concordat /kən'kɔːdat/ ▶ **noun** an agreement or treaty, especially one between the Vatican and a secular government relating to matters of mutual interest.
– ORIGIN early 17th cent.: from French, or from Latin *concordatum* 'something agreed upon', neuter past participle of *concordare* 'be of one mind' (see **CONCORD**).

concours /'kõkuə/ (also **concours d'élégance** /ˌdeleɪ'gɒ̃s/) ▶ **noun** (pl. same) an exhibition or parade of vintage or classic motor vehicles in which prizes are awarded for those in the best or most original condition.
– ORIGIN French, 'contest (of elegance)'.

concourse ▶ **noun 1** a large open central area inside or in front of a public building: *a station concourse.*
2 formal a crowd or assembly of people: *a vast **concourse of** onlookers.*
■ [mass noun] the action of coming together or meeting: *the concourse of bodies.* ■ another term for **CONCOURS**.
– ORIGIN late Middle English (in sense 2): from Old French *concours*, from Latin *concursus*, from *concurs-* 'run together, met', from the verb *concurrere* (see **CONCUR**). Sense 1 (originally US) dates from the mid 19th cent.

concrescence /kən'krɛs(ə)ns/ ▶ **noun** [mass noun] Biology the coalescence or growing together of parts originally separate.
– DERIVATIVES **concrescent** adjective.
– ORIGIN early 17th cent. (in the senses 'growth by assimilation' and 'a concretion'): from **CON-** 'together' + *-crescence*, on the pattern of words such as *excrescence*. The current sense dates from the late 19th cent.

concrete ▶ **adjective** /'kɒŋkriːt/ existing in a material or physical form; real or solid; not abstract: *concrete objects like stones* | *it exists as a physically concrete form.*
■ specific; definite: *I haven't got any concrete proof.* ■ (of a noun) denoting a material object as opposed to an abstract quality, state, or action.
▶ **noun** [mass noun] a heavy, rough building material made from a mixture of broken stone or gravel, sand, cement, and water, which can be spread or poured into moulds and forms a stone-like mass on hardening: *slabs of concrete* | [as modifier] *concrete blocks.*
▶ **verb** [with obj.] (often **be concreted**) **1** /'kɒŋkriːt/ cover (an area) with concrete: *the precious English countryside may soon be **concreted over**.*
■ [with obj. and adverbial of place] fix in position with concrete: *the post is concreted into the ground.*
2 /kən'kriːt/ archaic form (something) into a mass; solidify: *the juices of the plants are concreted upon the surface.*
■ make real or concrete instead of abstract: *concreting God into actual form of man.*
– PHRASES **be set in concrete** (of a policy or idea) be fixed and unalterable: *I do not regard the constitution as set in concrete.* **in the concrete** formal in reality or in practice.
– DERIVATIVES **concretely** adverb, **concreteness** noun.
– ORIGIN late Middle English (in the sense 'formed by cohesion, solidified'): from French *concret* or Latin *concretus*, past participle of *concrescere* 'grow together'. Early use was also as a grammatical term designating a quality belonging to a substance (usually expressed by an adjective such as *white* in *white paper*) as opposed to the quality itself (expressed by an abstract noun such as *whiteness*); later *concrete* came to be used to refer to nouns embodying attributes (e.g. *fool, hero*), as opposed to the attributes themselves (e.g. *foolishness, heroism*), and this is the basis of the modern use as the opposite of 'abstract'. The noun sense 'building material' dates from the mid 19th cent.

concrete jungle ▶ **noun** a city or an area of a city with a high density of large, unattractive, modern buildings and which is perceived as an unpleasant living environment.

concrete mixer ▶ **noun** a cement mixer.

concrete music ▶ **noun** another term for **MUSIQUE CONCRÈTE**.

concrete poetry ▶ **noun** [mass noun] poetry in which the meaning or effect is conveyed partly or wholly by visual means, using patterns of words or letters and other typographical devices.

concrete universal ▶ **noun** (in idealist philosophy) an abstraction which is manifest in a developing or organized set of instances, so having the qualities of both the universal and the particular.

concretion ▶ **noun** a hard solid mass formed by the local accumulation of matter, especially within the body or within a mass of sediment.
■ [mass noun] the formation of such a mass.
– DERIVATIVES **concretionary** adjective.
– ORIGIN mid 16th cent.: from Latin *concretio(n-)*, from *concrescere* 'grow together'.

concretize /'kɒŋkrɪtʌɪz/ (also **-ise**) ▶ **verb** [with obj.] make (an idea or concept) real; give specific or definite form to: *the theme park is an attempt to concretize our fantasies about America.*
– DERIVATIVES **concretization** noun.

concubinage /kɒn'kjuːbɪnɪdʒ/ ▶ **noun** [mass noun] chiefly historical the practice of keeping or the state of being a concubine.
– ORIGIN late Middle English: from French, from Old French *concubine* (see **CONCUBINE**).

concubine /'kɒŋkjʊbʌɪn/ ▶ **noun** chiefly historical (in polygamous societies) a woman who lives with a man but has lower status than his wife or wives.
■ archaic a mistress.
– DERIVATIVES **concubinary** /kən'kjuːbɪn(ə)ri/ adjective.
– ORIGIN Middle English: from Old French, from Latin *concubina*, from *con-* 'with' + *cubare* 'to lie'.

concupiscence /kən'kjuːpɪs(ə)ns/ ▶ **noun** [mass noun] formal strong sexual desire; lust.
– ORIGIN Middle English: via Old French from late Latin *concupiscentia*, from Latin *concupiscent-* 'beginning to desire', from the verb *concupiscere*, from *con-* (expressing intensive force) + *cupere* 'to desire'.

concupiscent ▶ **adjective** formal filled with sexual desire; lustful: *concupiscent dreams.*

concur ▶ **verb** (**concurred**, **concurring**) [no obj.] **1** be of the same opinion; agree: *the authors **concurred with** the majority* | *they **concurred in** the creation of the disciplinary procedures* | [with direct speech] *'That's right,' the chairman concurred.*
■ (**concur with**) agree with (a decision, opinion, or finding): *we strongly concur with this recommendation.*
2 happen or occur at the same time; coincide: *in tests, cytogenetic determination has been found to **concur with** enzymatic determination.*
– ORIGIN late Middle English (also in the senses 'collide' and 'act in combination'): from Latin *concurrere* 'run together, assemble in crowds', from *con-* 'together with' + *currere* 'to run'.

concurrent ▶ **adjective** existing, happening, or done at the same time: *there are three concurrent art fairs around the city.*
■ (of two or more prison sentences) to be served at the same time: [postpositive] *she was given nine months concurrent for each offence.* ■ Mathematics (of three or more lines) meeting at or tending towards one point.
– DERIVATIVES **concurrence** noun, **concurrently** adverb.
– ORIGIN late Middle English: from Latin *concurrent-* 'running together, meeting', from the verb *concurrere* (see **CONCUR**).

concuss /kən'kʌs/ ▶ **verb** [with obj.] [usu. as adj. **concussed**] hit the head of (a person or animal), causing them to become temporarily unconscious or confused: *Michael was a bit concussed.*
– DERIVATIVES **concussive** adjective.
– ORIGIN late 16th cent. (in the sense 'shake violently'): from Latin *concuss-* 'dashed together, violently shaken', from the verb *concutere*, from *con-* 'together' + *quatere* 'shake'.

concussion ▶ **noun 1** [mass noun] temporary unconsciousness caused by a blow on the head. The term is also used loosely of the after-effects such as confusion or temporary incapacity.
2 a violent shock as from a heavy blow: *the ground shuddered with the concussion of the blast.*
– ORIGIN late Middle English: from Latin *concussio(n-)*, from the verb *concutere* 'dash together, shake' (see **CONCUSS**).

condemn ▶ **verb** [with obj.] **1** express complete, typically public, disapproval of; censure: *the plan was condemned by campaigners.*
2 sentence (someone) to a particular punishment, especially death: *the rebels had been **condemned to** death* | [as adj. **condemned**] *the condemned men.*
■ (usu. **be condemned**) officially declare (something, especially a building) to be unfit for use: *the pool has been condemned as a health hazard.* ■ prove or show the guilt of: *she could see in his eyes that her stumble had condemned her.* ■ (of circumstances) force (someone) to endure or do something that is unpleasant or undesirable: *the physical ailments that **condemned** him **to** a lonely childhood.*
– DERIVATIVES **condemnable** adjective, **condemnation** noun, **condemnatory** adjective.
– ORIGIN Middle English (in sense 2): from Old French *condemner*, from Latin *condemnare*, from *con-* (expressing intensive force) + *damnare* 'inflict loss on' (see **DAMN**).

condemned cell ▶ **noun** Brit. historical a prison cell in which a prisoner who has received a death sentence is kept.

condensate /'kɒnd(ə)nseɪt/ ▶ **noun** [mass noun] liquid collected by condensation.
■ [count noun] Chemistry a compound produced by a condensation reaction.

condensation ▶ **noun 1** [mass noun] water which

collects as droplets on a cold surface when humid air is in contact with it.
2 [mass noun] the process of becoming more dense, in particular:
▪the conversion of a vapour or gas to a liquid. ▪ (also **condensation reaction**) [count noun] Chemistry a reaction in which two molecules combine to form a larger molecule, producing a small molecule such as H_2O as a by-product. ▪ Psychology the fusion of two or more images, ideas, or symbolic meanings into a single composite or new image, as a primary process in unconscious thought exemplified in dreams.
3 [count noun] a concise version of something, especially a text: *a readable condensation of the recent literature.*
– ORIGIN early 17th cent.: from late Latin *condensatio(n-)*, from *condensare* 'press close together' (see **CONDENSE**).

condense ▶**verb 1** [with obj.] make (something) denser or more concentrated: *on the Dorset coast the limestones of the Jurassic age are condensed into a mere 11 feet* | [as adj. **condensed**] *check that your printer can cope with wide text or condensed characters.*
▪[usu. as adj. **condensed**] thicken (a liquid) by heating it to reduce the water content: *condensed soup.* ▪ express (a piece of writing or speech) in fewer words; make concise: *he **condensed** the three plays **into** a three-hour drama.*
2 [no obj.] be changed from a gas or vapour to a liquid: *the moisture vapour in the air **condenses into** droplets of water.*
▪[with obj.] cause (a gas or vapour) to be changed to a liquid: *the cold air was condensing his breath.*
– DERIVATIVES **condensable** adjective.
– ORIGIN late Middle English: from Old French *condenser* or Latin *condensare*, from *condensus* 'very thick', from *con-* 'completely' + *densus* 'dense'.

condensed milk ▶**noun** [mass noun] milk that has been thickened by evaporation and sweetened, sold in tins.

condenser ▶**noun** a person or thing that condenses something, in particular:
▪an apparatus or container for condensing vapour. ▪ a lens or system of lenses for collecting and directing light. ▪ another term for **CAPACITOR**.

condescend ▶**verb** [no obj.] show that one feels superior; patronize: *take care not to **condescend to** your reader.*
▪[with infinitive] do something in such a way as to emphasize that one clearly regards it as below one's dignity or level of importance: *we'll be waiting for twenty minutes before she condescends to appear.*
– DERIVATIVES **condescension** noun.
– ORIGIN Middle English (in the sense 'give way, defer'): from Old French *condescendre*, from ecclesiastical Latin *condescendere*, from *con-* 'together' + *descendere* 'descend'.

condescending ▶**adjective** acting in a way that betrays a feeling of patronizing superiority towards someone: *she thought the teachers were arrogant and condescending.*
▪(of an action) demonstrating such an attitude: *a condescending smile.*
– DERIVATIVES **condescendingly** adverb.

condign /kən'dʌɪn/ ▶**adjective** formal (of punishment or retribution) appropriate to the crime or wrongdoing; fitting and deserved.
– DERIVATIVES **condignly** adverb.
– ORIGIN late Middle English (in the general sense 'worthy, appropriate'): from Old French *condigne*, from Latin *condignus*, from *con-* 'altogether' + *dignus* 'worthy'.

condiment ▶**noun** a substance such as salt or pepper that is used to add flavour to food.
– ORIGIN late Middle English: from Latin *condimentum*, from *condire* 'to pickle'.

condition ▶**noun 1** [mass noun] [usu. with adj.] the state of something, especially with regard to its appearance, quality, or working order: *the wiring is in good condition* | [in sing.] *the bridge is in an extremely dangerous condition.*
▪a person's or animal's state of health or physical fitness: *he is in fairly good condition considering what he has has been through* | [in sing.] *she was in a serious condition.* ▪ [count noun] [often with modifier] an illness or other medical problem: *a heart condition.* ▪ [in sing.] a particular state of existence: *a condition of misery.* ▪ archaic social position or rank: *those of humbler condition.*
2 (**conditions**) [often with adj.] the circumstances or factors affecting the way in which people live or work, especially with regard to their safety or well-being: *harsh working and living conditions.*
▪the factors or prevailing situation influencing the performance or the outcome of a process: *present market conditions.* ▪ the prevailing state of the weather, ground, sea, or atmosphere at a particular time, especially as it affects a sporting event: *the appalling conditions determined the style of play.*
3 [count noun] a state of affairs that must exist or be brought about before something else is possible or permitted: *for a member to borrow money, three conditions have to be met* | *all personnel should comply with this policy as **a condition of** employment* | *I'll accept your offer **on one condition**.*
▪US an unsatisfactory grade indicating that a student must pass an examination or undertake additional work within a stated time to receive credit for a course.
▶**verb** [with obj.] **1** (often **be conditioned**) have a significant influence on or determine (the manner or outcome of something): *national choices are conditioned by the international political economy.*
▪train or accustom (someone or something) to behave in a certain way or to accept certain circumstances: *we could be **conditioned into** mistaken views* | [with obj. and infinitive] *the child is conditioned to dislike food* | [as noun **conditioning**] *the programme examines aspects of social conditioning.*
2 bring (something) into the desired state for use: *a product for conditioning leather.*
▪[often as adj. **conditioned**] bring (beer or stout) to maturation after fermentation while the yeast is still present: [in combination] *cask-conditioned real ales.* ▪ [no obj.] (of a beer or stout) undergo such a process: *brews that are allowed to condition in the bottle.* ▪ apply something to (the skin or hair) to give it a healthy or attractive look or feel: *I condition my hair regularly.* ▪ [often as adj. **conditioned**] make (a person or animal) fit and healthy: *he was six feet two of perfectly conditioned muscle and bone.*
3 set prior requirements on (something) before it can occur or be done: *Congressmen have sought to limit and condition military and economic aid.*
▪US give (a student) an unsatisfactory grade indicating that an examination must be passed or additional work undertaken before credit for a course can be received.
– PHRASES **in** (or **out of**) **condition** in a fit (or unfit) physical state. **in no condition to do something** certainly not fit or well enough to do something: *you're in no condition to tackle the stairs.* **on condition that** with the stipulation that: *I got three years' probation, on condition that I stay at the hostel for a year.*
– ORIGIN Middle English: from Old French *condicion* (noun), *condicionner* (verb), from Latin *condicio(n-)* 'agreement', from *condicere* 'agree upon', from *con-* 'with' + *dicere* 'say'.

conditional ▶**adjective 1** subject to one or more conditions or requirements being met; made or granted on certain terms: *Western aid was only granted conditional on further reform* | *the consortium have made a conditional offer.*
2 Grammar (of a clause, phrase, conjunction, or verb form) expressing a condition.
▶**noun 1** Grammar & Philosophy a conditional clause or conjunction.
▪a statement or sentence containing a conditional clause.
2 [mass noun] Grammar the conditional mood of a verb, for example *should* in *if I should die.*
– DERIVATIVES **conditionality** noun, **conditionally** adverb.
– ORIGIN late Middle English: from Old French *condicionel* or late Latin *condicionalis*, from *condicio(n-)* 'agreement' (see **CONDITION**).

conditional discharge ▶**noun** an order made by a criminal court whereby an offender will not be sentenced for an offence unless a further offence is committed within a stated period.

conditional probability ▶**noun** Statistics the probability of an event (*A*), given that another (*B*) has already occurred.

conditional sale ▶**noun** the sale of goods according to a contract under which ownership does not pass to the buyer until after a set time, usually after payment of the last instalment of the purchase price, although the buyer has possession and is committed to acquiring ownership.

condition code ▶**noun** Computing a group of bits indicating the condition of something inside a computer, often used to decide which instructions the computer will subsequently execute.

conditioned response (also **conditioned reflex**) ▶**noun** Psychology an automatic response established by training to an ordinarily neutral stimulus. See also **CLASSICAL CONDITIONING**.

conditioner ▶**noun** a substance or appliance used to improve or maintain something's condition: *add a water conditioner to neutralize chlorine.*
▪a liquid applied to the hair after shampooing to improve its condition: *to prevent static, always use a conditioner* | [mass noun] *I have to use a lot of conditioner.*

condo /'kɒndəʊ/ ▶**noun** (pl. **-os**) N. Amer. informal short for **CONDOMINIUM** (in sense 2): *a high-rise condo.*

condole /kən'dəʊl/ ▶**verb** [no obj.] (**condole with**) express sympathy for (someone); grieve with: *the priest came to condole with Madeleine.*
– ORIGIN late 16th cent.: from Christian Latin *condolere*, from *con-* 'with' + *dolere* 'grieve, suffer'.

condolence ▶**noun** (usu. **condolences**) an expression of sympathy, especially on the occasion of the death of a person's relative or close friend: *we offer our sincere condolences to his widow* | [mass noun] *letters of condolence.*
– ORIGIN early 17th cent.: from **CONDOLE**, influenced by French *condoléance*.

condom ▶**noun** a thin rubber sheath worn on a man's penis during sexual intercourse as a contraceptive or as a protection against infection. See also **FEMALE CONDOM**.
– ORIGIN early 18th cent.: of unknown origin; often said to be named after a physician who invented it, but no such person has been traced.

condominium /ˌkɒndə'mɪnɪəm/ ▶**noun** (pl. **condominiums**) **1** [mass noun] the joint control of a state's affairs by other states.
▪[count noun] a state so governed.
2 N. Amer. a building or complex of buildings containing a number of individually owned flats (apartments) or houses.
▪each of the individual flats or houses in such a building. ▪ [mass noun] the system of ownership by which these operate, in which owners have full title to the individual flat or house and an undivided interest in the shared parts of the property.
– ORIGIN early 18th cent.: modern Latin, from *con-* 'together with' + *dominium* 'right of ownership' (see **DOMINION**). Sense 2 dates from the 1960s.

condone /kən'dəʊn/ ▶**verb** [with obj.] [often with negative] accept and allow (behaviour that is considered morally wrong or offensive) to continue: *the college cannot condone any behaviour that involves illicit drugs.*
▪approve or sanction (something), especially with reluctance: *those arrested were released and the exhibition was officially condoned a few weeks later.*
– DERIVATIVES **condonation** /kɒndə'neɪʃ(ə)n/ noun, **condoner** noun.
– ORIGIN mid 19th cent.: from Latin *condonare* 'refrain from punishing', from *con-* 'altogether' + *donare* 'give'.

condor ▶**noun** a very large New World vulture with a bare head and mainly black plumage, living in mountainous country and spending much time soaring on massive outstretched wings.
• Two species in the family Cathartidae: the **Andean condor** (*Vultur gryphus*) of South America, and the **California** (or **Californian**) **condor** (*Gymnogyps californianus*), which is probably extinct in the wild.
– ORIGIN early 17th cent.: from Spanish *cóndor*, from Quechua *kuntur.*

condottiere /ˌkɒndɒ'tjɛːreɪ, -ri/ ▶**noun** (pl. **condottieri** pronunc. same) historical a leader or a member of a troop of mercenaries, especially in Italy.
– ORIGIN Italian, from *condotto* 'troop under contract', from *condotta* 'a contract', from *condurre* 'conduct', from Latin *conducere* (see **CONDUCT**).

conduce ▶**verb** [no obj.] (**conduce to**) formal help to bring about (a particular situation or outcome): *nothing would conduce more to the unity of the nation.*
– ORIGIN late Middle English (in the sense 'lead or bring'): from Latin *conducere* 'bring together' (see **CONDUCT**).

conducive ▶**adjective** making a certain situation or outcome likely or possible: *the harsh lights and cameras were hardly **conducive to** a relaxed atmosphere.*
– ORIGIN mid 17th cent.: from **CONDUCE**, on the pattern of words such as *conductive.*

conduct ▶**noun** /'kɒndʌkt/ [mass noun] **1** the manner in which a person behaves, especially on a particular occasion or in a particular context: *the*

conduct of the police during the riot | *a code of conduct for directors of listed companies.*
2 the action or manner of directing or managing an activity or organization: *the conduct of the elections.*
■archaic the action of leading; guidance: *travelling through the world under the conduct of chance.*
▶**verb** /kən'dʌkt/ **1** [with obj.] organize and carry out: *in the second trial he conducted his own defence* | *surveys conducted among students.*
■direct the performance of (a piece of music or an orchestra, choir, etc.): *my first attempt to conduct a great work* | [no obj.] *Toscanini is coming to conduct.* ■ [with obj. and adverbial of direction] lead or guide (someone) to or around a particular place: *he conducted us through his personal gallery of the American Civil War* | [as adj. **conducted**] *a conducted tour.* ■ Physics transmit (a form of energy such as heat or electricity) by conduction: *heat is conducted to the surface.*
2 (**conduct oneself**) behave in a specified way: *he conducted himself with the utmost propriety.*
– DERIVATIVES **conductible** /kən'dʌktɪb(ə)l/ adjective.
– ORIGIN Middle English: from Old French, from Latin *conduct-* 'brought together', from the verb *conducere*. The term originally denoted some provision for safe passage, such as an escort or pass, surviving in **SAFE CONDUCT**; later the verb sense 'lead, guide' arose, hence 'manage' and 'management' (late Middle English), later 'management of oneself, behaviour' (mid 16th cent.). The original form of the word was *conduit*, which was preserved only in the sense 'channel' (see **CONDUIT**); in all other uses the spelling was influenced by Latin.

conductance ▶**noun** the degree to which an object conducts electricity, calculated as the ratio of the current which flows to the potential difference present. This is the reciprocal of the resistance, and is measured in siemens or mhos.

conduct disorder ▶**noun** [mass noun] chiefly US a range of antisocial types of behaviour displayed in childhood or adolescence.

conduction ▶**noun** [mass noun] the process by which heat or electricity is directly transmitted through the material of a substance when there is a difference of temperature or of electrical potential between adjoining regions, without movement of the material.
■the process by which sound waves travel through a medium. ■the transmission of impulses along nerves. ■ the conveying of fluid through a pipe or other channel.
– ORIGIN mid 16th cent. (in the senses 'provision for safe passage' and 'leadership': from Latin *conductio(n-)*, from the verb *conducere* (see **CONDUCT**).

conduction band ▶**noun** Physics a delocalized band of energy levels in a crystalline solid which is partly filled with electrons. These electrons have great mobility and are responsible for electrical conductivity.

conductive ▶**adjective** having the property of conducting something (especially heat or electricity): *a conductive material.*
■of or relating to conduction.
– DERIVATIVES **conductively** adverb.

conductive education ▶**noun** [mass noun] Brit. a system of training for people with motor disorders, especially children, which aims to reduce their dependence on artificial aids and facilitate active participation in society.

conductivity ▶**noun** (pl. **-ies**) [mass noun] (also **electrical conductivity**) the degree to which a specified material conducts electricity, calculated as the ratio of the current density in the material to the electric field which causes the flow of current. It is the reciprocal of the resistivity.
■(also **thermal conductivity**) the rate at which heat passes through a specified material, expressed as the amount of heat that flows per unit time through a unit area with a temperature gradient of one degree per unit distance.

conductor ▶**noun** **1** a person who directs the performance of an orchestra or choir.
2 a person who collects fares and sells tickets on a bus.
■N. Amer. an official in charge of a train; a guard.
3 Physics a material or device that conducts or transmits heat or electricity, especially when regarded in terms of its capacity to do this: *most polymers are poor conductors.*
■short for **LIGHTNING CONDUCTOR**.
4 Brit. a person who is trained to provide conductive education.
– DERIVATIVES **conductorship** noun (only in sense 1).
– ORIGIN late Middle English (denoting a military leader): via Old French from Latin *conductor*, from *conducere* 'bring together' (see **CONDUCT**).

conductor rail ▶**noun** a rail transmitting current to an electric train or other vehicle.

conductress ▶**noun** a female conductor, especially in a bus or other passenger vehicle.

conduct sheet ▶**noun** a military form designed to record someone's offences and punishments.

conductus /kən'dʌktəs/ ▶**noun** (pl. **conducti** /-tʌɪ/) a musical setting of a metrical Latin text, of the 12th or 13th century.
– ORIGIN from medieval Latin, from Latin *conducere* 'bring together' (see **CONDUCT**).

conduit /'kɒndɪt, -djʊɪt/ ▶**noun** a channel for conveying water or other fluid: figurative *the office acts as a conduit for ideas to flow throughout the organization.*
■a tube or trough for protecting electric wiring.
– ORIGIN Middle English: from Old French, from medieval Latin *conductus*, from Latin *conducere* 'bring together' (see **CONDUCT**).

condylarth /'kɒndɪlɑːθ/ ▶**noun** a fossil herbivorous mammal of the early Tertiary period, ancestral to the ungulates.
• Order Condylarthra: several families.
– ORIGIN late 19th cent.: from modern Latin *Condylarthra* (plural), from Greek *kondulos* 'knuckle' + *arthron* 'joint'.

condyle /'kɒndɪl, -dʌɪl/ ▶**noun** Anatomy a rounded protuberance at the end of some bones, forming an articulation with another bone.
– DERIVATIVES **condylar** adjective, **condyloid** adjective.
– ORIGIN mid 17th cent.: from French, from Latin *condylus*, from Greek *kondulos* 'knuckle'.

condyloma /ˌkɒndɪ'ləʊmə/ ▶**noun** (pl. **condylomas** or **condylomata** /-mətə/) Medicine a raised growth on the skin resembling a wart, typically in the genital region, caused by viral infection or syphilis and transmissible by contact.
– DERIVATIVES **condylomatous** adjective.
– ORIGIN late Middle English: via Latin from Greek *kondulōma* 'callous lump', from *kondulos* 'knuckle'.

cone ▶**noun** **1** a solid or hollow object which tapers from a circular or roughly circular base to a point.
■Mathematics a surface or solid figure generated by the straight lines which pass from a circle or other closed curve to a single point (the vertex) not in the same plane as the curve. A cone with the vertex perpendicularly over the centre of a circular base is a **right circular cone**. ■(also **traffic cone**) a plastic cone-shaped object that is used to separate off or close sections of a road. ■ a wafer container shaped like a cone in which ice cream is served. ■ a conical mountain or peak, especially one of volcanic origin. ■(also **pyrometric cone**) a ceramic pyramid that melts at a known temperature and is used to indicate the temperature of a kiln. ■ short for **CONE SHELL**.
2 the dry fruit of a conifer, typically tapering to a rounded end and formed of a tight array of overlapping scales on a central axis which separate to release the seeds.
■a flower resembling a pine cone, especially that of the hop plant.
3 Anatomy a light-sensitive cell of one of the two types present in large numbers in the retina of the eye, responding mainly to bright light and responsible for sharpness of vision and colour perception. Compare with **ROD** (in sense 5).
▶**verb** [with obj.] (**cone something off**) Brit. separate off or mark a road with traffic cones: *part of the road has been coned off.*
– ORIGIN late Middle English (denoting an apex or vertex): from French *cône*, via Latin from Greek *kōnos*.

coned ▶**adjective** conical.
■wound on a cone: *a coned yarn.*

coneflower ▶**noun** a North American plant of the daisy family, which has flowers with cone-like centres.
• *Rudbeckia*, *Echinacea*, and other genera, family Compositae.

Conegliano /ˌkɒnɛ'ljɑːnəʊ/, Emmanuele, see **DA PONTE**.

conehead ▶**noun** a small bush cricket that is mostly active by day and sings for long periods without a break.
• Genus *Conocephalus*, family Tettigoniidae.

cone shell ▶**noun** a predatory mollusc of warm seas, with a conical, typically intricately patterned, shell. It captures prey by injecting venom, which can be lethal to humans, and the shells are popular with collectors.
• Genus *Conus*, family Conidae, class Gastropoda: numerous species.

Conestoga wagon /ˌkɒnɪ'stəʊgə/ ▶**noun** N. Amer. historical a large wagon used for long-distance travel.
– ORIGIN early 18th cent.: named after *Conestoga*, a town in Pennsylvania, US.

coney /'kəʊni/ (also **cony**) ▶**noun** (pl. **-eys**) **1** Brit. & Heraldry a rabbit.
■N. Amer. a pika. ■ (in biblical use) a hyrax.
2 a small grouper (fish) found on the coasts of the tropical western Atlantic, with variable coloration.
• *Epinephelus fulvus*, family Serranidae.
– ORIGIN Middle English: from Old French *conin*, from Latin *cuniculus*.

Coney Island a resort and amusement park on the Atlantic coast in Brooklyn, New York City, on the south shore of Long Island.

confab informal ▶**noun** an informal private conversation or discussion.
■N. Amer. a meeting or conference of members of a particular group.
▶**verb** (**confabbed**, **confabbing**) [no obj.] engage in informal private conversation: *Peter was confabbing with a curly-haired guy.*
– ORIGIN early 18th cent.: abbreviation of *confabulation* (see **CONFABULATE**).

confabulate /kən'fabjʊleɪt/ ▶**verb** [no obj.] **1** formal engage in conversation; talk: *she could be heard on the telephone confabulating with someone.*
2 Psychiatry fabricate imaginary experiences as compensation for loss of memory.
– DERIVATIVES **confabulation** noun, **confabulatory** adjective.
– ORIGIN early 17th cent.: from Latin *confabulat-* 'chatted together', from the verb *confabulari*, from *con-* 'together' + *fabulari* (from *fabula* 'fable').

confect /kən'fɛkt/ ▶**verb** [with obj.] make (something elaborate or dainty) from various elements: *a trifle confected from angelica and piped cream.*
– ORIGIN late Middle English: from Latin *confect-* 'put together', from the verb *conficere*, from *con-* 'together' + *facere* 'make'.

confection ▶**noun** **1** an elaborate dish or delicacy made with sweet ingredients: *a fruit confection.*
■an elaborately constructed thing, especially a frivolous one: *his elaborate pop confections.* ■ a fashionable or elaborate article of women's dress: *Therese was magnificent in a swirling confection of crimson.*
2 [mass noun] the action of mixing or compounding something: *the confection of a syllabub.*
– ORIGIN Middle English (in the general sense 'something made by mixing', especially a medicinal preparation): via Old French from Latin *confectio(n-)*, from *conficere* 'put together' (see **CONFECT**).

confectioner ▶**noun** a person whose trade is making or selling confectionery.

confectioner's custard ▶**noun** [mass noun] thick sweet custard used as a filling for cakes and pastries.

confectioner's sugar ▶**noun** US term for **ICING SUGAR**.

confectionery ▶**noun** (pl. **-ies**) [mass noun] sweets and chocolates considered collectively.
■[count noun] a shop that sells such items.

confederacy ▶**noun** (pl. **-ies**) a league or alliance, especially of confederate states.
■(**the Confederacy**) another term for **CONFEDERATE STATES**. ■ a league formed for an unlawful purpose.
– ORIGIN late Middle English: from Old French *confederacie*, based on Latin *confoederare* 'join together in league' (see **CONFEDERATION**).

confederal ▶**adjective** relating to or denoting a confederation.
– ORIGIN late 18th cent.: from **CONFEDERATION**, on the pattern of *federal*.

confederate ▶**adjective** /kən'fɛd(ə)rət/ [attrib.] joined by an agreement or treaty: *some local groups united to form confederate councils.*
■(**Confederate**) of or relating to the Confederate States of the southern US: *the Confederate flag.*
▶**noun** /kən'fɛd(ə)rət/ **1** a person one works with,

especially in something secret or illegal; an accomplice.
2 (**Confederate**) a supporter of the Confederate States of the southern US.
▶**verb** /kənˈfɛdəreɪt/ [with obj.] [usu. as adj. **confederated**] bring (states or groups of people) into an alliance: *Switzerland is a model for the new confederated Europe.*
– ORIGIN late Middle English: from late (ecclesiastical) Latin *confoederatus*, from *con-* 'together' + *foederatus* (see **FEDERATE**).

Confederate States (also **the Confederacy**) the eleven Southern states (Alabama, Arkansas, Florida, Georgia, Louisiana, Mississippi, North Carolina, South Carolina, Tennessee, Texas, Virginia) which seceded from the United States in 1860–1, thus precipitating the American Civil War.

confederation ▶**noun** an organization which consists of a number of parties or groups united in an alliance or league: *a confederation of trade unions.*
■a more or less permanent union of states with some or most political power vested in a central authority. ■ [mass noun] the action of confederating or the state of being confederated: *a referendum on confederation.*
– ORIGIN late Middle English: from Old French *confederacion* or late Latin *confederatio(n-)*, from Latin *confoederare*, from *con-* 'together' + *foederare* 'join in league with' (from *foedus* 'league, treaty').

Confederation of British Industry (abbrev.: **CBI**) (in the UK) an organization to promote the prosperity of British business.

confer /kənˈfəː/ ▶**verb** (**conferred**, **conferring**) **1** [with obj.] grant (a title, degree, benefit, or right): *moves were made to* ***confer*** *an honorary degree* ***on*** *her.*
2 [no obj.] have discussions; exchange opinions: *the officials were* ***conferring with*** *allies.*
– DERIVATIVES **conferment** noun (only in sense 1), **conferrable** adjective, **conferral** noun (only in sense 1).
– ORIGIN late Middle English (in the general sense 'bring together', also in sense 2): from Latin *conferre*, from *con-* 'together' + *ferre* 'bring'.

conferee ▶**noun 1** a person who attends a conference.
2 a person on whom something is conferred.

Conference ▶**noun** a dessert pear of a firm-fleshed variety.

conference ▶**noun 1** a formal meeting which typically takes place over a number of days and involves people with a shared interest, especially one held regularly by an association or organization: *an international conference on the environment | the Labour Party Conference.*
■a formal meeting for discussion. ■ [usu. as modifier] a linking of several telephones or computers, so that each user may communicate with the others simultaneously: *a conference call.*
2 an association for the regulation of a sphere of activity or the mutual exchange of information.
■an association of sports teams or athletic clubs which play each other. ■ the governing body of some Christian Churches, especially Methodist Churches.
▶**verb** [no obj.] [usu. as noun **conferencing**] take part in a conference or conference call: *video conferencing.*
– PHRASES **in conference** in a meeting; engaged in discussions.
– ORIGIN early 16th cent. (in the general sense 'conversation, talk'): from French *conférence* or medieval Latin *conferentia*, from Latin *conferre* 'bring together' (see **CONFER**).

Conference on Disarmament a committee with forty nations as members that seeks to negotiate multilateral disarmament.

confess ▶**verb** [reporting verb] admit or state that one has committed a crime or is at fault in some way: [with clause] *he confessed that he had attacked the old man* | [no obj.] *he wants to* ***confess to*** *Caroline's murder* | [with direct speech] *'I damaged your car,' she confessed* | [with obj.] *once apprehended, they would confess their guilt.*
■admit or acknowledge something reluctantly, typically because one feels slightly ashamed or embarrassed: [with clause] *I must confess that I was slightly surprised* | [no obj.] *he* ***confessed to*** *a lifelong passion for food* | [with direct speech] *'I needed to see you, too,' he confessed.* ■ declare one's sins formally to a priest: [with obj.] *I could not confess all my sins to the priest* | [no obj.] *he gave himself up after* ***confessing to*** *a priest.* ■ [with obj.] (of a priest) hear the confession of (someone) in such a way: *St Ambrose would weep bitter tears when confessing a sinner.*
– ORIGIN late Middle English: from Old French *confesser*, from Latin *confessus*, past participle of *confiteri* 'acknowledge', from *con-* (expressing intensive force) + *fateri* 'declare, avow'.

confessant ▶**noun** a person who confesses to a priest; a penitent.

confessedly ▶**adverb** by one's own admission: *many therapists have had clients who, confessedly or otherwise, have fallen in love with them.*

confession ▶**noun 1** a formal statement admitting that one is guilty of a crime: *he signed a confession to both the murders* | [mass noun] *proof of this crime must be established by confession.*
■an admission or acknowledgement that one has done something about which one is ashamed or embarrassed: *by his own confession, he had strayed perilously close to alcoholism.* ■ a formal admission of one's sins with repentance and desire of absolution, especially privately to a priest as a religious duty: *she still had not been* ***to confession.*** See also **SACRAMENT OF RECONCILIATION**. ■ (**confessions**) often humorous intimate revelations about a person's private life or occupation, especially as presented in a sensationalized form in a book, newspaper, or film: *confessions of a driving instructor.*
2 (also **confession of faith**) a statement setting out essential religious doctrine.
■(also **Confession**) the religious body or church sharing a confession of faith. ■ a statement of one's principles: *his words are a political confession of faith.*
– DERIVATIVES **confessionary** adjective.
– ORIGIN late Middle English: via Old French from Latin *confessio(n-)*, from *confiteri* 'acknowledge' (see **CONFESS**).

confessional ▶**noun 1** an enclosed stall in a church divided by a screen or curtain in which a priest sits to hear people confess their sins.
2 an admission or acknowledgement that one has done something about which one is ashamed or embarrassed; a confession.
▶**adjective 1** (especially of speech or writing) in which a person reveals or admits to private thoughts or incidents in their past, especially ones about which they feel ashamed or embarrassed: *the autobiography is remarkably confessional | his confessional outpourings.*
■of or relating to religious confession: *the priest leaned forward in his best confessional manner.*
2 of or relating to confessions of faith or doctrinal systems: *the confessional approach to religious education.*
– ORIGIN late Middle English (as an adjective): the adjective from **CONFESSION** + **-AL**; the noun via French from Italian *confessionale*, from medieval Latin, neuter of *confessionalis*, from Latin *confessio(n-)*, from *confiteri* 'acknowledge' (see **CONFESS**).

confessor ▶**noun 1** a priest who hears confessions and gives absolution and spiritual counsel.
■a person to whom another confides personal problems.
2 a person who avows religious faith in the face of opposition, but does not suffer martyrdom.
3 a person who makes a confession.
– ORIGIN Old English (in sense 2): from Old French *confessour*, from ecclesiastical Latin *confessor*, from Latin *confess-* 'acknowledged' (see **CONFESS**).

confetti ▶**noun** [mass noun] small pieces of coloured paper traditionally thrown over a bride and bridegroom by their wedding guests after the marriage ceremony has taken place.
– ORIGIN early 19th cent. (originally denoting the real or imitation sweets thrown during Italian carnivals): from Italian, literally 'sweets', from Latin *confectum* 'something prepared', neuter past participle of *conficere* 'put together' (see **CONFECT**).

confidant /ˈkɒnfɪdant, ˌkɒnfɪˈdant, -dɑːnt/ ▶**noun** (fem. **confidante** pronunc. same) a person with whom one shares a secret or private matter, trusting them not to repeat it to others.
– ORIGIN mid 17th cent.: alteration of **CONFIDENT** (as a noun in the same sense in the early 17th cent.), probably to represent the pronunciation of French *confidente* 'having full trust'.

confide /kənˈfʌɪd/ ▶**verb** [reporting verb] tell someone about a secret or private matter while trusting them not to repeat it to others: [with obj.] *he* ***confided*** *his fears* ***to*** *his mother* | [with direct speech] *'I have been afraid,' she confided* | [with clause] *he confided that stress had caused him to lose a stone in weight.*
■[no obj.] (**confide in**) trust (someone) enough to tell them of such a secret or private matter: [with clause] *he confided in friends that he and his wife planned to separate.* ■ [with obj.] (**confide something to**) dated entrust something to (someone) in order for them to look after it: *the property of others confided to their care was unjustifiably risked.*
– DERIVATIVES **confidingly** adverb.
– ORIGIN late Middle English (in the sense 'place trust (in)'): from Latin *confidere* 'have full trust'. The sense 'impart as a secret' dates from the mid 18th cent.

confidence ▶**noun** [mass noun] the feeling or belief that one can have faith in or rely on someone or something: *we had every* ***confidence in*** *the staff* | *he had gained the young man's confidence.*
■the state of feeling certain about the truth of something: *it is not possible to say with confidence how much of the increase in sea levels is due to melting glaciers.* ■ a feeling of self-assurance arising from one's appreciation of one's own abilities or qualities: *she's brimming with confidence* | [in sing.] *he would walk up those steps with a confidence he didn't feel.* ■ the telling of private matters or secrets with mutual trust: *someone with whom you may raise your suspicions* ***in confidence*** | *opinions were expressed without any* ***breach of confidence.*** ■ [count noun] (often **confidences**) a secret or private matter told to someone under such a condition of trust: *the girls exchanged confidences about their parents.*
– PHRASES **in someone's confidence** in a position of trust with someone. **take someone into one's confidence** tell someone one's secrets.
– ORIGIN late Middle English: from Latin *confidentia*, from *confidere* 'have full trust' (see **CONFIDENT**).

confidence interval ▶**noun** Statistics a range of values so defined that there is a specified probability that the value of a parameter lies within it.

confidence level ▶**noun** Statistics the probability that the value of a parameter falls within a specified range of values.

confidence limit ▶**noun** Statistics either of the extreme values of a confidence interval.

confidence man ▶**noun** old-fashioned term for **CON MAN**.

confidence trick (N. Amer. also **confidence game**) ▶**noun** an act of cheating or tricking someone by gaining their trust and persuading them to believe something that is not true.

confidence trickster ▶**noun** a person who sets out to defraud or deceive people by persuading them to believe something that is not true.

confident ▶**adjective** feeling or showing confidence in oneself or one's abilities or qualities: *a confident smile* | *people who are* ***confident in*** *their identity.*
■feeling or showing certainty about something: *this time they're* ***confident of*** *a happy ending* | *I am not very* ***confident about*** *tonight's game.*
▶**noun** archaic a confidant.
– DERIVATIVES **confidently** adverb.
– ORIGIN late 16th cent.: from French *confident(e)*, from Italian *confidente*, from Latin *confident-* 'having full trust', from the verb *confidere*, from *con-* (expressing intensive force) + *fidere* 'trust'.

confidential ▶**adjective** intended to be kept secret: *confidential information* | *we won't name the informant because it's confidential.*
■(of a person's tone of voice) indicating that what one says is private or secret: *he dropped his voice to a confidential whisper.* ■ [attrib.] entrusted with private or restricted information: *a confidential secretary.*
– DERIVATIVES **confidentiality** noun, **confidentially** adverb.

configuration /kənˌfɪgəˈreɪʃ(ə)n, -gjʊ-/ ▶**noun** an arrangement of parts or elements in a particular form, figure, or combination: *the broad configuration of the economy remains capitalist.*
■Chemistry the fixed three-dimensional relationship of the atoms in a molecule, defined by the bonds between them. Compare with **CONFORMATION**. ■ Psychology another term for **GESTALT**.
– DERIVATIVES **configurational** adjective.
– ORIGIN mid 16th cent. (denoting the relative position of celestial objects): from late Latin *configuratio(n-)*, from Latin *configurare* 'shape after a pattern' (see **CONFIGURE**).

configure ▶**verb** [with obj.] (often **be configured**) shape or put together in a particular form or configuration: *two of the aircraft will be configured as VIP transports.*
■Computing arrange or order (a computer system or an element of it) so as to fit it for a designated task: *memory can be configured as a virtual drive.*
– DERIVATIVES **configurable** adjective.
– ORIGIN late Middle English (in the Latin sense):

from Latin *configurare* 'shape after a pattern', from *con-* 'together' + *figurare* 'to shape' (from *figura* 'shape or figure').

confine ▶ **verb** /kən'fʌɪn/ [with obj.] (**confine someone/thing to**) keep or restrict someone or something within certain limits of (space, scope, quantity, or time): *he does not confine his message to high politics | your boating will mostly be confined to a few hours at weekends | you've* ***confined yourself to*** *what you know.*
■(**confine someone to/in**) restrain or forbid someone from leaving (a place): *the troops were confined to their barracks.* ■ (**be confined to**) (of a person) be unable to leave (one's bed, home, or a wheelchair) because of illness or disability: *he had been confined to a wheelchair for some time.* ■ (**be confined**) dated (of a woman) remain in bed for a period before, during, and after the birth of a child: *she was confined for nearly a month.*
▶ **noun** /'kɒnfʌɪn/ (**confines**) the borders or boundaries of a place, especially with regard to their restricting freedom of movement: *within* ***the confines of*** *the hall escape was difficult.*
■figurative the limits or restrictions of something abstract, especially a subject or sphere of activity: *the narrow confines of political life.*
– DERIVATIVES **confinement** noun.
– ORIGIN late Middle English (as a noun): from French *confins* (plural noun), from Latin *confinia*, from *confinis* 'bordering', from *con-* 'together' + *finis* 'end, limit' (plural *fines* 'territory'). The verb senses are from French *confiner*, based on Latin *confinis*.

confined ▶ **adjective** (of a space) restricted in area or volume; cramped: *her fear of confined spaces.*

confirm ▶ **verb** [with obj.] **1** establish the truth or correctness of (something previously believed, suspected, or feared to be the case): *if these fears are confirmed, the outlook for the economy will be dire |* [with clause] *the report confirms that a diet rich in vitamin C can help to prevent cataracts.*
■[reporting verb] state with assurance that a report or fact is true: [with clause] *he confirmed that the general was in the hands of the rebels |* [with direct speech] *'It is indeed proper coffee,' I confirmed |* [with obj.] *his story was confirmed by former colleagues.* ■ (**confirm someone in**) reinforce someone in (an opinion, belief, or feeling): *he fuelled his misogyny by cultivating women who confirmed him in this view.* ■ make (a provisional arrangement or appointment) definite: *Mr Baker's assistant telephoned to confirm his appointment with the chairman.* ■ make (something, especially a person's appointment to a post or an agreement) formally valid; ratify: *the organization has confirmed the appointment of Mr Collins as managing director.* ■ declare (someone) formally to be appointed to a particular post: *he was* ***confirmed as*** *the new EC peace envoy.*
2 administer the religious rite of confirmation to: *he had been baptized and confirmed.*
– DERIVATIVES **confirmative** adjective, **confirmatory** adjective.
– ORIGIN Middle English: from Old French *confermer*, from Latin *confirmare*, from *con-* 'together' + *firmare* 'strengthen' (from *firmus* 'firm').

confirmand /'kɒnfəmand/ ▶ **noun** a person who is to undergo the religious rite of confirmation.

confirmation ▶ **noun** [mass noun] **1** the action of confirming something or the state of being confirmed: *the greens took it as confirmation that industrial society is not sustainable.*
2 (in the Christian Church) the rite at which a baptized person, especially one baptized as an infant, affirms Christian belief and is admitted as a full member of the Church.
■the Jewish ceremony of bar mitzvah.
– ORIGIN Middle English: via Old French from Latin *confirmatio(n-)*, from *confirmare* 'make firm, establish' (see **CONFIRM**).

confirmed ▶ **adjective** (of a person) firmly established in a particular habit, belief, or way of life and unlikely to change their ways: *a confirmed bachelor | a confirmed teetotaller.*

confiscate /'kɒnfɪskeɪt/ ▶ **verb** [with obj.] take or seize (someone's property) with authority: *the guards confiscated his camera |* [as adj. **confiscated**] *confiscated equipment.*
■appropriate (something, especially land) to the public treasury as a penalty.
– DERIVATIVES **confiscation** noun, **confiscator** noun, **confiscatory** adjective.
– ORIGIN mid 16th cent.: from Latin *confiscat-* 'put away in a chest, consigned to the public treasury', from the verb *confiscare*, based on *con-* 'together' + *fiscus* 'chest, treasury'.

confit /'kɒnfi/ ▶ **noun** [mass noun] duck or other meat cooked very slowly in its own fat.
– ORIGIN French, 'conserved', from *confire* 'prepare'.

Confiteor /kɒn'fɪtɪɔː/ ▶ **noun** a form of prayer confessing sins, used in the Roman Catholic Mass and some other sacraments.
– ORIGIN Latin, 'I confess', from the formula *Confiteor Deo Omnipotenti* 'I confess to Almighty God'.

conflab ▶ **noun** & **verb** informal another term for **CONFAB**.
– ORIGIN late 19th cent.: alteration.

conflagration /ˌkɒnflə'greɪʃ(ə)n/ ▶ **noun** an extensive fire which destroys a great deal of land or property.
– ORIGIN late 15th cent. (denoting consumption by fire): from Latin *conflagratio(n-)*, from the verb *conflagrare*, from *con-* (expressing intensive force) + *flagrare* 'to blaze'.

conflate ▶ **verb** [with obj.] combine (two or more sets of information, texts, ideas, etc.) into one: *the urban crisis conflates a number of different economic, political, and social issues.*
– DERIVATIVES **conflation** noun.
– ORIGIN late Middle English (in the sense 'fuse or melt down metal'): from Latin *conflat-* 'kindled, fused', from the verb *conflare*, from *con-* 'together' + *flare* 'to blow'.

conflict ▶ **noun** /'kɒnflɪkt/ a serious disagreement or argument, typically a protracted one: *the eternal* ***conflict between*** *the sexes |* [mass noun] *doctors often* ***come into conflict with*** *politicians.*
■a prolonged armed struggle: *regional conflicts.* ■ [mass noun] a state of mind in which a person experiences a clash of opposing wishes or needs: *bewildered by her own inner conflict, she could only stand there feeling vulnerable.* ■ a serious incompatibility between two or more opinions, principles, or interests: *there was a* ***conflict between*** *his business and domestic life.*
▶ **verb** /kən'flɪkt/ [no obj.] be incompatible or at variance; clash: *parents' and children's interests sometimes conflict | the date for the match* ***conflicted with*** *a religious festival |* [as adj. **conflicting**] *there are conflicting accounts of what occurred.*
■[as adj. **conflicted**] N. Amer. having or showing confused and mutually inconsistent feelings: *he remains a little conflicted about Marlene.*
– DERIVATIVES **conflictual** adjective.
– ORIGIN late Middle English: from Latin *conflict-* 'struck together, fought', from the verb *confligere*, from *con-* 'together' + *fligere* 'to strike'; the noun is via Latin *conflictus* 'a contest'.

confluence /'kɒnflʊəns/ ▶ **noun** the junction of two rivers, especially rivers of approximately equal width.
■an act or process of merging: *a major confluence of the world's financial markets.*
– ORIGIN late Middle English: from late Latin *confluentia*, from Latin *confluere* 'flow together' (see **CONFLUENT**).

confluent ▶ **adjective** flowing together or merging.
– ORIGIN late 15th cent.: from Latin *confluent-* 'flowing together', from *confluere*, from *con-* 'together' + *fluere* 'to flow'.

conflux /'kɒnflʌks/ ▶ **noun** another term for **CONFLUENCE**.
– ORIGIN early 17th cent.: from late Latin *confluxus*, from *con-* 'together' + *fluxus* (see **FLUX**).

confocal /kɒn'fəʊk(ə)l/ ▶ **adjective** having a common focus or foci: *confocal ellipses.*
■denoting or using a microscope whose imaging system only collects light from a small spot on the specimen, giving greater resolution.

conform ▶ **verb** [no obj.] comply with rules, standards, or laws: *the kitchen does not* ***conform to*** *hygiene regulations | the changes were introduced to* ***conform with*** *international classifications.*
■(of a person) behave according to socially acceptable conventions or standards: *the pressure to conform.* ■ be similar in form or type; agree: *the countryside should* ***conform to*** *a certain idea of the picturesque.*
– ORIGIN Middle English (in the sense 'make (something) like another thing'): from Old French *conformer*, from Latin *conformare*, from *con-* 'together' + *formare* 'to form'.

conformable ▶ **adjective** (usu. **conformable to**) (of a person) disposed or accustomed to conform to what is acceptable or expected.
■similar in form or nature; consistent: *the human adoption of practices which are conformable to biological constraints.* ■ Geology (of strata in contact) deposited in a continuous sequence, and typically having the same direction of stratification.
– DERIVATIVES **conformability** noun, **conformably** adverb.
– ORIGIN late 15th cent. (in the sense 'compliant (to) or tractable'): from medieval Latin *conformabilis*, from Latin *conformare* 'to form, fashion' (see **CONFORM**).

conformal ▶ **adjective** (of a map or a mathematical mapping) preserving the correct angles between directions within small areas (though distorting distances).
– DERIVATIVES **conformally** adverb.
– ORIGIN mid 17th cent. (in the sense 'conformable'): from late Latin *conformalis*, from *con-* 'together' + *formalis* 'formal'. The current sense was coined in German.

conformance ▶ **noun** another term for **CONFORMITY**.

conformation ▶ **noun** the shape or structure of something, especially an animal.
■Chemistry any of the spatial arrangements which the atoms in a molecule may adopt and freely convert between, especially by rotation about individual single bonds. Compare with **CONFIGURATION**.
– DERIVATIVES **conformational** adjective.
– ORIGIN early 16th cent. (in the sense 'conforming, adaptation'): from Latin *conformatio(n-)*, from *conformare* 'to shape, fashion' (see **CONFORM**).

conformer ▶ **noun** Chemistry a form of a compound having a particular molecular conformation.
– ORIGIN 1960s: blend of *conformational* (see **CONFORMATION**) and **ISOMER**.

conformist ▶ **noun** a person who conforms to accepted behaviour or established practices.
■Brit., chiefly historical a person who conforms to the practices of the Church of England.
▶ **adjective** (of a person or activity) conforming to accepted behaviour or established practices; conventional.
– DERIVATIVES **conformism** noun.

conformity ▶ **noun** [mass noun] compliance with standards, rules, or laws: ***conformity to*** *regulations | the goods were* ***in conformity*** *with the contract.*
■behaviour in accordance with socially accepted conventions or standards: *loyalty to one's party need not imply unquestioning conformity.* ■ Brit., chiefly historical compliance with the practices of the Church of England. ■ similarity in form or type; agreement in character: *these changes are intended to ensure* ***conformity between*** *all schemes.*
– ORIGIN late Middle English: from Old French *conformite* or late Latin *conformitas*, from *conformare* 'to form, fashion' (see **CONFORM**).

confound ▶ **verb** [with obj.] **1** cause surprise or confusion in (someone), especially by not according with their expectations: *the inflation figure confounded economic analysts.*
■prove (a theory, expectation, or prediction) wrong: *the rise in prices confounded expectations.* ■ defeat (a plan, aim, or hope): *we will confound these tactics by the pressure groups.* ■ archaic overthrow (an enemy).
2 (often **be confounded with**) mix up (something) with something else so that the individual elements become difficult to distinguish.
▶ **exclamation** dated used to express anger or annoyance: *oh confound it, where is the thing?*
– ORIGIN Middle English: from Old French *confondre*, from Latin *confundere* 'pour together, mix up'. Compare with **CONFUSE**.

confounded ▶ **adjective** [attrib.] informal, dated used for emphasis, especially to express anger or annoyance: *he was a confounded nuisance.*
– DERIVATIVES **confoundedly** adverb.

confraternity ▶ **noun** (pl. **-ies**) a brotherhood, especially with a religious or charitable purpose.
– ORIGIN late Middle English: from Old French *confraternite*, from medieval Latin *confraternitas*, from *confrater* (see **CONFRÈRE**).

confrère /'kɒnfrɛː/ ▶ **noun** a fellow member of a profession: *Pooley's police confrères.*
– ORIGIN mid 18th cent.: French, from medieval Latin *confrater*, from *con-* 'together with' + *frater* 'brother'.

confront ▶ **verb** [with obj.] stand or meet (someone) face to face with hostile or argumentative intent: *300 policemen confronted an equal number of union supporters.*
■(often **be confronted**) (of a problem, difficulty, etc.) present itself to (someone) so that dealing with it

cannot be avoided: *the new government was* ***confronted with*** *many profound difficulties.* ■ (usu. **be confronted**) appear or be placed in front of (someone) so as to unsettle or threaten them: *we were* ***confronted with*** *pictures of moving skeletons.* ■ face up to and deal with (a problem or difficult situation): *we knew we couldn't ignore the race issue and decided we'd confront it head on.* ■ compel (someone) to face or consider something, especially by way of accusation: *Merrill* ***confronted*** *him* ***with*** *her suspicions.*

– ORIGIN mid 16th cent.: from French *confronter*, from medieval Latin *confrontare*, from Latin *con-* 'with' + *frons, front-* 'face'.

confrontation ▶ **noun** a hostile or argumentative situation or meeting between two or more opposing parties: *a* ***confrontation with*** *the legislature* | [mass noun] *four months of violent confrontation between government and opposition forces.*

– DERIVATIVES **confrontational** adjective.

Confucian /kən'fjuːʃ(ə)n/ ▶ **adjective** of or relating to Confucius or Confucianism.

▶ **noun** an adherent of Confucianism.

Confucianism /kən'fjuːʃənɪz(ə)m/ ▶ **noun** [mass noun] a system of philosophical and ethical teachings founded by Confucius and developed by Mencius.

– DERIVATIVES **Confucianist** noun & adjective.

Confucius /kən'fjuːʃəs/ (551–479 BC), Chinese philosopher; Latinized name of *Kongfuze* (*K'ung Fu-tzu*) 'Kong the master'. His ideas about the importance of practical moral values, collected by his disciples in the *Analects*, formed the basis of the philosophy of Confucianism.

confusable ▶ **adjective** able or liable to be confused with something else: *convocation was by 1327 no longer* ***confusable with*** *parliament.*

▶ **noun** a word or phrase that is easily confused with another in meaning or usage, such as *mitigate*, which is often confused with *militate*.

– DERIVATIVES **confusability** noun.

confuse ▶ **verb** [with obj.] cause (someone) to become bewildered or perplexed: *past and present blurred together, confusing her still further.*

■ make (something) more complex or less easy to understand: *the points made by the authors confuse rather than clarify the issue.* ■ identify wrongly; mistake: *a lot of people* ***confuse*** *a stroke* ***with*** *a heart attack* | *purchasers might confuse the two products.*

– DERIVATIVES **confusingly** adverb.

– ORIGIN Middle English (in the sense 'rout, bring to ruin'): from Old French *confus*, from Latin *confusus*, past participle of *confundere* 'mingle together' (see **CONFOUND**). Originally all senses of the verb were passive, and therefore appeared only as the past participle *confused*; the active voice occurred rarely until the 19th cent. when it began to replace *confound*.

confused ▶ **adjective** (of a person) unable to think clearly; bewildered: *she was utterly* ***confused about*** *what had just happened* | *a very confused and unhappy boy.*

■ showing bewilderment: *a confused expression crossed her face.* ■ not in possession of all one's mental faculties, especially because of old age: *interviewing confused old people does take longer.* ■ lacking order and so difficult to understand: *the confused information supplied by authorities* | *reports about the incident were rather confused.* ■ lacking clear distinction of elements; jumbled: *the sound of a sort of confused hammering and shouting.*

– DERIVATIVES **confusedly** adverb.

confusion ▶ **noun** [mass noun] **1** uncertainty about what is happening, intended, or required: *there seems to be some* ***confusion about*** *which system does what* | *he cleared up the* ***confusion over*** *the party's policy.* ■ a situation of panic; a breakdown of order: *the guaranteed income bond market was* ***thrown into confusion.*** ■ a disorderly jumble: *all I can see is a* ***confusion of*** *brown cardboard boxes.*

2 the state of being bewildered or unclear in one's mind about something: *she looked about her* ***in confusion.***

■ the mistaking of one person or thing for another: *there is some confusion between 'unlawful' and 'illegal'* | [count noun] *most of the errors are reasonable confusions between similar words or sequences of words.*

– ORIGIN Middle English: from Latin *confusio(n-)*, from the verb *confundere* 'mingle together' (see **CONFUSE**).

confute ▶ **verb** [with obj.] formal prove (a person or an assertion or accusation) to be wrong: *restorers who sought to confute this view were accused of ignorance.*

– DERIVATIVES **confutation** noun.

– ORIGIN early 16th cent.: from Latin *confutare* 'restrain, answer conclusively', from *con-* 'altogether' + the base of *refutare* 'refute'.

conga /'kɒŋgə/ ▶ **noun 1** a Latin American dance of African origin, usually with several people in a single line, one behind the other.

2 (also **conga drum**) a tall, narrow, low-toned drum beaten with the hands.

▶ **verb** (**congas**, **congaed** or **conga'd**, **congaing**) [no obj.] perform the conga.

– ORIGIN 1930s: from Latin American Spanish, from Spanish, feminine of *congo* 'Congolese'.

congé /'kɒ̃ʒeɪ/ ▶ **noun** [in sing.] an unceremonious dismissal or rejection of someone.

– ORIGIN late Middle English (in the general sense 'permission to do something'): from Old French *congie*, from Latin *commeatus* 'leave of absence', from *commeare* 'go and come'. The word is now usually treated as equivalent to modern French.

congeal /kən'dʒiːl/ ▶ **verb** [no obj.] become semi-solid, especially on cooling: *the blood had* ***congealed into*** *blobs* | [as adj. **congealed**] *a lump of congealed moussaka.*

■ figurative take shape or coalesce, especially to form a satisfying whole: *the ballet failed to congeal as a single oeuvre.*

– DERIVATIVES **congealable** adjective, **congealment** noun (archaic).

– ORIGIN late Middle English: from Old French *congeler*, from Latin *congelare*, from *con-* 'together' + *gelare* 'freeze' (from *gelu* 'frost').

congee /'kɒndʒiː/ ▶ **noun** [mass noun] (in Chinese cookery) broth or porridge made from rice.

– ORIGIN from Tamil *kañci*.

congelation /ˌkɒndʒə'leɪʃ(ə)n/ ▶ **noun** [mass noun] the process of congealing or the state of being congealed: *the component of metals that causes their congelation.*

– ORIGIN late Middle English: from Latin *congelatio(n-)*, from the verb *congelare* 'freeze together' (see **CONGEAL**).

congener /'kɒndʒɪnə, kən'dʒiːnə/ ▶ **noun 1** a thing or person of the same kind or category as another.

■ an animal or plant of the same genus as another: *these birds or their congeners may be found in East Africa.*

2 a minor chemical constituent, especially one which gives a distinctive character to a wine or spirit or is responsible for some of its physiological effects.

– ORIGIN mid 18th cent.: from Latin, from *con-* 'together with' + *genus, gener-* 'race, stock'.

congeneric /ˌkɒndʒɪ'nɛrɪk/ ▶ **adjective** Biology (of an animal or plant species) belonging to the same genus: *this animal is* ***congeneric with*** *the later species.*

■ of a related nature or origin: *the two sets were congeneric.*

– DERIVATIVES **congenerous** /kən'dʒɛn(ə)rəs/ adjective.

– ORIGIN mid 17th cent.: from Latin *congener* (see **CONGENER**) + **-IC**.

congenial /kən'dʒiːnɪəl/ ▶ **adjective** (of a person) pleasant because of a personality, qualities, or interests that are similar to one's own: *his need for some congenial company.*

■ (of a thing) pleasant or agreeable because suited to one's taste or inclination: *he went back to a climate more* ***congenial to*** *his cold stony soul.*

– DERIVATIVES **congeniality** noun, **congenially** adverb.

congenital /kən'dʒɛnɪt(ə)l/ ▶ **adjective** (especially of a disease or physical abnormality) present from birth: *a congenital malformation of the heart.*

■ (of a person) having a particular trait from birth or by firmly established habit: *a congenital liar.*

– DERIVATIVES **congenitally** adverb.

– ORIGIN late 18th cent.: from Latin *congenitus*, from *con-* 'together' + *genitus* (past participle of *gignere* 'beget') + **-AL**.

conger /'kɒŋgə/ (also **conger eel**) ▶ **noun** a large edible predatory eel of shallow coastal waters.

● *Conger* and other genera, family Congridae: several species, in particular the European *C. conger* and the American *C. oceanica*.

– ORIGIN Middle English: from Old French *congre*, via Latin from Greek *gongros*.

congeries /kɒn'dʒɪəriːz, -ɪz/ ▶ **noun** (pl. same) a disorderly collection; a jumble: *a congeries of European states.*

– ORIGIN mid 16th cent.: from Latin *congeries* 'heap, pile', from *congerere* 'heap up'.

congested ▶ **adjective** blocked up with or too full of something, in particular:

■ (of a road or place) so crowded with traffic or people as to hinder or prevent freedom of movement: *the congested roads of south-east England* | *the road was* ***congested with*** *refugees.* ■ (of a part of the body) abnormally full of blood: *congested arteries.* ■ (of the respiratory tract) blocked with mucus so as to hinder breathing: *his nose was congested.*

– ORIGIN mid 19th cent.: past participle of *congest*, from Latin *congest-* 'heaped up', from the verb *congerere*, from *con-* 'together' + *gerere* 'bring'.

congestion /kən'dʒɛstʃ(ə)n/ ▶ **noun** [mass noun] the state of being congested: *the new bridge should ease congestion in the area.*

– ORIGIN late Middle English: via Old French from Latin *congestio(n-)*, from *congere* 'heap up', from *con-* 'together' + *gerere* 'bring'.

congestive ▶ **adjective** Medicine involving or produced by congestion of a part of the body: *congestive heart failure.*

– ORIGIN mid 19th cent.: from *congest* (see **CONGESTED**) + **-IVE**.

congius /'kɒndʒɪəs/ ▶ **noun** (pl. **congii** /'kɒndʒɪʌɪ/) an ancient Roman liquid measure of one eighth of an amphora, equal in modern terms to about 6 imperial pints.

– ORIGIN Latin.

conglobulate /kɒn'glɒbjʊleɪt/ ▶ **verb** [no obj.] rare join closely together: *these people's feeble sense of self-respect prompts them to conglobulate in collectives.*

– ORIGIN mid 18th cent.: from Latin *globulus* 'globule', on the pattern of earlier *conglobate* 'make into a ball'.

conglomerate ▶ **noun** /kən'glɒm(ə)rət/ **1** a number of different things or parts that are put or grouped together to form a whole but remain distinct entities: *the Earth is a specialized conglomerate of organisms.*

■ [often with adj. or noun modifier] a large corporation formed by the merging of separate and diverse firms: *a media conglomerate.*

2 [mass noun] Geology a coarse-grained sedimentary rock composed of rounded fragments embedded in a matrix of cementing material such as silica: *the sediments vary from coarse conglomerate to fine silt and clay* | [count noun] *the zone is associated with conglomerates and chert.*

▶ **adjective** /kən'glɒm(ə)rət/ of or relating to a conglomerate, especially a large corporation: *conglomerate firms.*

▶ **verb** /kən'glɒməreɪt/ [no obj.] gather together into a compact mass: *atoms which conglomerate at the centre.*

■ form a conglomerate by merging diverse firms.

– DERIVATIVES **conglomeration** noun.

– ORIGIN late Middle English (as an adjective describing something gathered up into a rounded mass): from Latin *conglomeratus*, past participle of *conglomerare*, from *con-* 'together' + *glomus, glomer-* 'ball'. The geological sense dates from the early 19th cent.; the other noun senses are later.

Congo /'kɒŋgəʊ/ **1** a major river of central Africa, which rises as the Lualaba to the south of Kisangani in northern Zaire (Democratic Republic of Congo) and flows 4,630 km (2,880 miles) in a great curve westwards, turning south-westwards to form the border with the Congo before emptying into the Atlantic. Also called **ZAIRE RIVER**.

2 (often **the Congo**) an equatorial country in Africa, with a short Atlantic coastline; pop. 2,351,000 (est. 1991); languages, French (official), Kikongo, and other Bantu languages; capital, Brazzaville.

> The region was colonized in the 19th century by France, and as Middle Congo formed part of the larger territory of French Congo (later, French Equatorial Africa). After becoming independent in 1960, the Congo was the scene of civil war for nearly two decades.

Congo, Democratic Republic of official name (since 1997) for **ZAIRE**.

Congolese /ˌkɒŋgə'liːz/ ▶ **adjective** of or relating to the Congo or the Democratic Republic of Congo (formerly Zaire).

▶ **noun** (pl. same) **1** a native or inhabitant of the Congo or the Democratic Republic of Congo (formerly Zaire).

2 [mass noun] any of the Bantu languages spoken in the Congo region, in particular Kikongo.

– ORIGIN from French *Congolais*.

Congo red ▶ **noun** [mass noun] a red-brown azo

dyestuff which becomes blue in acidic conditions, used as a chemical indicator and as a stain in histology.

congrats ▶ **plural noun** informal congratulations: [as exclamation] *'Congrats on your exams, Cal!'*
– ORIGIN late 19th cent.: abbreviation.

congratulate ▶ **verb** [with obj.] give (someone) one's good wishes when something special or pleasant has happened to them: *he had taken the chance to* ***congratulate*** *him* ***on*** *his marriage.*
■ praise (someone) for a particular achievement: *the operators are to be* ***congratulated for*** *the excellent service that they now provide.* ■ (**congratulate oneself**) feel pride or satisfaction: *she* ***congratulated herself on*** *her powers of deduction* | [with clause] *the Director was congratulating himself that nothing could go wrong.*
– DERIVATIVES **congratulator** noun, **congratulatory** adjective.
– ORIGIN mid 16th cent.: from Latin *congratulat-* 'congratulated', from the verb *congratulari*, from *con-* 'with' + *gratulari* 'show joy' (from *gratus* 'pleasing').

congratulation ▶ **noun** (**congratulations**) words expressing one's praise for an achievement or good wishes on a special occasion: *our congratulations to the winners* | [as exclamation] *congratulations on a job well done!*
■ [mass noun] the expression of such praise or good wishes: *he began pumping the hand of his son in congratulation.*
– ORIGIN late Middle English: from Latin *congratulatio(n-)*, from the verb *congratulari* (see **CONGRATULATE**).

congregant /ˈkɒŋgrɪg(ə)nt/ ▶ **noun** a member of a congregation, especially that of a church or synagogue.
– ORIGIN late 19th cent.: from Latin *congregant-* 'collecting (into a flock), uniting', from the verb *congregare* (see **CONGREGATE**).

congregate ▶ **verb** [no obj.] gather into a crowd or mass: *some 4000 demonstrators had congregated at a border point.*
– ORIGIN late Middle English: from Latin *congregat-* 'collected (into a flock), united', from the verb *congregare*, from *con-* 'together' + *gregare* (from *grex, greg-* 'a flock').

congregation ▶ **noun** **1** a group of people assembled for religious worship.
■ a group of people regularly attending a particular place of worship: *he was a member of the Emmanuel Chapel congregation.*
2 a gathering or collection of people, animals, or things: *large congregations of birds may cause public harm.*
■ [mass noun] the action of gathering together in a crowd: *drought conditions lead to congregation of animals around watering points.*
3 (often **Congregation**) a council or deliberative body.
■ (in the Roman Catholic Church) a permanent committee of the College of Cardinals: *the Congregation for the Doctrine of the Faith.* ■ Brit. (in some universities) a general assembly of resident senior members.
4 a group of people obeying a common religious rule but under less solemn vows than members of the older religious orders: *the sisters of the Congregation of Our Lady.*
■ a group of communities within a religious order sharing particular historical or regional links.
– ORIGIN late Middle English (in senses 2, 3, and 4): from Latin *congregatio(n-)*, from *congregare* 'collect (into a flock)' (see **CONGREGATE**).

congregational ▶ **adjective** **1** of or relating to a congregation: *congregational singing.*
2 (**Congregational**) of or adhering to Congregationalism: *the Congregational Church.*

Congregationalism ▶ **noun** [mass noun] a system of organization among Christian churches whereby individual local churches are largely self-governing.
– DERIVATIVES **Congregationalist** noun & adjective.

congress ▶ **noun** **1** a formal meeting or series of meetings for discussion between delegates, especially those from a political party, trade union, or from within a particular sphere of activity: *an international congress of mathematicians.*
2 (**Congress**) a national legislative body, especially that of the US. The US Congress, which meets at the Capitol in Washington DC, was established by the Constitution of 1787 and is composed of the Senate and the House of Representatives.
3 a society or organization, especially a political one.
4 [mass noun] the action of coming together: *sexual congress.*
– DERIVATIVES **congressional** adjective.
– ORIGIN late Middle English (denoting an encounter during battle): from Latin *congressus*, from *congredi* 'meet', from *con-* 'together' + *gradi* 'walk'.

congressman ▶ **noun** (pl. **-men**) a male member of the US Congress (also used as a form of address).

Congress of Industrial Organizations (abbrev.: **CIO**) a federation of North American trade unions, organized largely by industry rather than craft. In 1955 it merged with the American Federation of Labor to form the AFL-CIO.

congresswoman ▶ **noun** (pl. **-women**) a female member of the US Congress (also used as a form of address).

Congreve /ˈkɒŋgriːv/, William (1670–1729), English dramatist. A close associate of Swift, Pope, and Steele, he wrote plays such as *Love for Love* (1695) and *The Way of the World* (1700), which epitomize the wit and satire of Restoration comedy.

congruent /ˈkɒŋgrʊənt/ ▶ **adjective** **1** in agreement or harmony: *institutional and departmental objectives are very largely congruent* | *the rules may not be* ***congruent with*** *the requirements of the law.*
2 Geometry (of figures) identical in form; coinciding exactly when superimposed.
– DERIVATIVES **congruence** noun, **congruency** noun, **congruently** adverb.
– ORIGIN late Middle English: from Latin *congruent-* 'agreeing, meeting together', from the verb *congruere*, from *con-* 'together' + *ruere* 'fall or rush'.

congruous /ˈkɒŋgrʊəs/ ▶ **adjective** in agreement or harmony: *this explanation is* ***congruous with*** *earlier observations.*
– DERIVATIVES **congruity** /-ˈgruːɪti/ noun, **congruously** adverb.
– ORIGIN late 16th cent.: from Latin *congruus*, from *congruere* 'agree' (see **CONGRUENT**), + **-OUS**.

conic /ˈkɒnɪk/ chiefly Mathematics ▶ **adjective** of a cone.
▶ **noun** short for **CONIC SECTION**. See also **CONICS**.
– ORIGIN late 16th cent.: from modern Latin *conicus*, from Greek *kōnikos*, from *kōnos* 'cone'.

conical ▶ **adjective** having the shape of a cone.
– DERIVATIVES **conically** adverb.

conical projection (also **conic projection**) ▶ **noun** a map projection in which an area of the earth is projected on to a cone, of which the vertex is usually above one of the poles.

conics ▶ **plural noun** [treated as sing.] the branch of mathematics concerned with conic sections.

conic section ▶ **noun** a figure formed by the intersection of a plane and a circular cone. Depending on the angle of the plane with respect to the cone, a conic section may be a circle, an ellipse, a parabola, or a hyperbola.

conidiophore /kəʊˈnɪdɪə(ʊ)fɔː/ ▶ **noun** Botany (in certain fungi) a conidium-bearing hypha or filament.
– ORIGIN late 19th cent.: from *conidio-* (combining form of **CONIDIUM**) + **-PHORE**.

conidium /kəʊˈnɪdɪəm/ ▶ **noun** (pl. **conidia** /-dɪə/) Botany a spore produced asexually by various fungi at the tip of a specialized hypha.
– ORIGIN late 19th cent.: modern Latin, from Greek *konis* 'dust' + the diminutive suffix *-idium*.

conifer /ˈkɒnɪfə, ˈkəʊn-/ ▶ **noun** a tree which bears cones and evergreen needle-like or scale-like leaves. Conifers are of major importance as the source of softwood, and also supply resins and turpentine.
● Order Coniferales, class Coniferopsida, subdivision Gymnospermae: several families, including the pines and firs (Pinaceae) and the cypresses (Cupressaceae).
– DERIVATIVES **coniferous** adjective.
– ORIGIN mid 19th cent.: from Latin, literally 'cone-bearing', from *conus* (see **CONE**).

coniform /ˈkəʊnɪfɔːm/ ▶ **adjective** rare having the shape of a cone.
– ORIGIN late 18th cent.: from Latin *conus* 'cone' + **-IFORM**.

coniine /ˈkəʊniːn/ ▶ **noun** [mass noun] Chemistry a volatile poisonous compound found in hemlock and other plants. It affects the motor nerves, causing paralysis and asphyxia.
● An alkaloid, 2-propylpiperidine; chem. formula: $C_8H_{17}N$.
– ORIGIN mid 19th cent.: from Latin *conium* (from Greek *kōneion* 'hemlock') + **-INE**[4].

conjectural ▶ **adjective** based on or involving conjecture: *the evidence was deemed too conjectural.*
– DERIVATIVES **conjecturally** adverb.
– ORIGIN mid 16th cent.: via French from Latin *conjecturalis*, from *conjectura* 'inference' (see **CONJECTURE**).

conjecture /kənˈdʒɛktʃə/ ▶ **noun** an opinion or conclusion formed on the basis of incomplete information: ***conjectures about*** *the newcomer were many and varied* | [mass noun] *a matter for conjecture.*
■ an unproven mathematical or scientific theorem. ■ [mass noun] (in textual criticism) the suggestion or reconstruction of a reading of a text not present in the original source.
▶ **verb** [with obj.] form an opinion or supposition about (something) on the basis of incomplete information: *he conjectured the existence of an otherwise unknown feature* | [with clause] *many conjectured that she had a second husband in mind.*
■ (in textual criticism) propose (a reading).
– DERIVATIVES **conjecturable** adjective.
– ORIGIN late Middle English (in the senses 'to divine' and 'divination'): from Old French, or from Latin *conjectura*, from *conicere* 'put together in thought', from *con-* 'together' + *jacere* 'throw'.

conjoin ▶ **verb** [with obj.] formal join; combine: *an approach which conjoins theory and method.*
– ORIGIN late Middle English: from Old French *conjoindre*, from Latin *conjungere*, from *con-* 'together' + *jungere* 'to join'.

conjoint ▶ **adjective** [attrib.] combining all or both people or things involved.
– DERIVATIVES **conjointly** adverb.
– ORIGIN Middle English: from Old French, past participle of *conjoindre* (see **CONJOIN**).

conjugal /ˈkɒndʒʊg(ə)l/ ▶ **adjective** of or relating to marriage or the relationship between husband and wife: *conjugal loyalty.*
– DERIVATIVES **conjugality** noun, **conjugally** adverb.
– ORIGIN early 16th cent.: from Latin *conjugalis*, from *conjux, conjug-* 'spouse', from *con-* 'together'+ *jugum* 'a yoke'.

conjugal rights ▶ **plural noun** the rights, especially to sexual relations, regarded as exercisable in law by each partner in a marriage.

conjugate ▶ **verb** /ˈkɒndʒʊgeɪt/ **1** [with obj.] Grammar give the different forms of (a verb in an inflected language such as Latin) as they vary according to voice, mood, tense, number, and person.
2 [no obj.] Biology (of bacteria or unicellular organisms) become temporarily united in order to exchange genetic material: *E. coli only conjugate when one of the cells possesses fertility genes.*
■ (of gametes) become fused.
3 [with obj.] Chemistry be combined with or joined to reversibly: *bilirubin is then conjugated by liver enzymes and excreted in the bile.*
▶ **adjective** /ˈkɒndʒʊgət/ coupled, connected, or related, in particular:
■ Chemistry (of an acid or base) related to the corresponding base or acid by loss or gain of a proton. ■ Mathematics joined in a reciprocal relation, especially having the same real parts and equal magnitudes but opposite signs of imaginary parts. ■ Geometry (of angles) adding up to 360°; (of arcs) combining to form a complete circle. ■ Biology (especially of gametes) fused.
▶ **noun** /ˈkɒndʒʊgət/ a thing which is conjugate or conjugated, in particular:
■ chiefly Biochemistry a substance formed by the reversible combination of two or more others. ■ a mathematical value or entity having a reciprocal relation with another. See also **COMPLEX CONJUGATE**.
– DERIVATIVES **conjugacy** noun.
– ORIGIN late 15th cent. (as an adjective): from Latin *conjugat-* 'yoked together', from the verb *conjugare*, from *con-* 'together' + *jugum* 'yoke'.

conjugated ▶ **adjective** [attrib.] another term for **CONJUGATE**, in particular:
■ Chemistry relating to or denoting double or triple bonds in a molecule which are separated by a single bond, across which some sharing of electrons occurs. ■ (of a substance) reversibly combined with another: *conjugated bile salts.*

conjugate diameter ▶ **noun** Anatomy the distance between the front and rear of the pelvis.

conjugation ▶ **noun** **1** [mass noun] the formation or

existence of a link or connection between things, in particular:
■Biology the temporary union of two bacteria or unicellular organisms for the exchange of genetic material. ■Biology the fusion of two gametes, especially when they are of a similar size. ■chiefly Biochemistry the combination of two substances: *toxic compounds eliminated from the body by conjugation with glutathione.* ■Chemistry the sharing of electron density between nearby multiple bonds in a molecule. ■Mathematics the solution of a problem by transforming it into an equivalent problem of a different form, solving this, and then reversing the transformation.
2 [mass noun] Grammar the variation of the form of a verb in an inflected language such as Latin, by which are identified the voice, mood, tense, number, and person.
■[count noun] the class in which a verb is put according to the manner of this variation: *a past participle of the first conjugation.*
– DERIVATIVES **conjugational** adjective.
– ORIGIN late Middle English (in sense 2): from Latin *conjugatio(n-)*, from *conjugare* 'join together' (see **CONJUGATE**).

conjunct ▶ **adjective** /kən'dʒʌŋ(k)t/ joined together, combined, or associated.
■Music of or relating to the movement of a melody between adjacent notes of the scale. ■Astrology in conjunction with.
▶ **noun** /'kɒndʒʌŋ(k)t/ each of two or more things which are joined or associated.
■Logic each of the terms of a conjunctive proposition. ■Grammar an adverbial whose function is to join two sentences or other discourse units (e.g. *however, anyway, in the first place*).
– ORIGIN late Middle English: from Latin *conjunctus*, past participle of *conjungere* 'join together' (see **CONJOIN**).

conjunction ▶ **noun 1** Grammar a word used to connect clauses or sentences or to coordinate words in the same clause (e.g. *and, but, if*).
2 an instance of two or more events or things occurring at the same point in time or space: *a conjunction of favourable political and economic circumstances.*
■Astronomy & Astrology an alignment of two planets or other celestial objects so that they appear to be in the same, or nearly the same, place in the sky.
– PHRASES **in conjunction** together: *herbal medicine was used* ***in conjunction with*** *acupuncture and massage.*
– DERIVATIVES **conjunctional** adjective.
– ORIGIN late Middle English: via Old French from Latin *conjunctio(n-)*, from the verb *conjungere* (see **CONJOIN**).

conjunctiva /ˌkɒndʒʌŋ(k)'tʌɪvə, kən'dʒʌŋ(k)tɪvə/ ▶ **noun** Anatomy the mucous membrane that covers the front of the eye and lines the inside of the eyelids.
– DERIVATIVES **conjunctival** adjective.
– ORIGIN late Middle English: from medieval Latin *(membrana) conjunctiva* 'conjunctive (membrane)', from late Latin *conjunctivus*, from *conjungere* 'join together' (see **CONJOIN**).

conjunctive ▶ **adjective** relating to or forming a connection or combination of things: *the conjunctive tissue.*
■involving the combination or co-occurrence of two or more conditions or properties. ■Grammar of the nature of or relating to a conjunction.
▶ **noun** Grammar a word or expression acting as a conjunction.
– DERIVATIVES **conjunctively** adverb.
– ORIGIN late Middle English: from late Latin *conjunctivus*, from *conjungere* 'join together' (see **CONJUNCT**).

conjunctivitis /kənˌdʒʌŋ(k)tɪ'vʌɪtɪs/ ▶ **noun** [mass noun] Medicine inflammation of the conjunctiva of the eye.

conjuncture ▶ **noun** a combination of events: *it was due to the happy conjuncture of two facts.*
■a state of affairs: *the wider political conjuncture.*
– ORIGIN early 17th cent.: from **CONJUNCTION**, by substitution of the suffix; influenced by obsolete French *conjuncture*, from Italian *congiuntura*, based on Latin *conjungere* 'join together' (see **CONJOIN**).

conjuration /ˌkʌndʒə'reɪʃ(ə)n, ˌkɒndʒʊ(ə)-/ ▶ **noun** a magic incantation or spell.
■[mass noun] the performance of something supernatural by means of a magic incantation or spell.
– ORIGIN late Middle English (also in the sense 'conspiracy, the swearing of an oath together'): via Old French from Latin *conjuratio(n-)*, from *conjurare* (see **CONJURE**).

conjure /'kʌndʒə/ ▶ **verb 1** [with obj.] make (something) appear unexpectedly or seemingly from nowhere as if by magic: *Anne* ***conjured up*** *a most delicious home-made hot pot.*
■call (an image) to the mind: *she had forgotten how to* ***conjure up*** *the image of her mother's face.* ■(of a word, sound, smell, etc.) cause someone to feel or think of (something): *a special tune that* ***conjures up*** *a particular time and place.* ■call upon (a spirit or ghost) to appear by means of a magic ritual: *they hoped to* ***conjure up*** *the spirit of their dead friend.*
2 /kən'dʒʊə/ [with obj. and infinitive] archaic implore (someone) to do something.
– PHRASES **a name to conjure with** used to indicate that one believes a person to be important within a particular sphere of activity: *on the merger scene his is a name to conjure with.*
– ORIGIN Middle English (also in the sense 'oblige by oath'): from Old French *conjurer* 'to plot or exorcize', from Latin *conjurare* 'band together by an oath, conspire' (in medieval Latin 'invoke'), from *con-* 'together' + *jurare* 'swear'.

conjure woman ▶ **noun** US & W. Indian a sorceress, especially one who practises voodoo.

conjuring ▶ **noun** [mass noun] [often as modifier] the performance of tricks which are seemingly magical, typically involving sleight of hand: *a conjuring trick.*

conjuror (also **conjurer**) ▶ **noun** a performer of conjuring tricks.
– ORIGIN Middle English: partly from **CONJURE**, partly from Old French *conjureor, conjurere*, from medieval Latin *conjurator*, from Latin *conjurare* 'conspire' (see **CONJURE**).

conk[1] ▶ **verb** [no obj.] (**conk out**) informal (of a machine) break down: *my car conked out.*
■(of a person) faint or go to sleep: *he conked out on the rear seat.* ■die: *most creatures conk out smartly once they have passed on their genes.*
– ORIGIN First World War: of unknown origin.

conk[2] informal ▶ **noun** Brit. a person's nose.
■dated a person's head.
▶ **verb** [with obj.] chiefly US hit (someone) on the head: *the clown conked him.*
– ORIGIN early 19th cent.: perhaps an alteration of **CONCH**.

conker ▶ **noun** Brit. the hard shiny dark brown nut of a horse chestnut tree.
■(**conkers**) [treated as sing.] a children's game in which each has a conker on the end of a string and takes turns in trying to break another's with it.
– ORIGIN mid 19th cent. (a dialect word denoting a snail shell, with which the game, or a similar form of it, was originally played): perhaps from **CONCH**, but associated with (and frequently spelled) **CONQUER** in the 19th and early 20th cents: an alternative name was *conquerors.*

con man ▶ **noun** informal a man who cheats or tricks someone by means of a confidence trick.

con moto /kɒn 'məʊtəʊ/ ▶ **adverb** Music (especially as a direction) with movement: *andante con moto.*
– ORIGIN Italian.

Conn. ▶ **abbreviation for** Connecticut.

conn ▶ **verb** US spelling of **CON**[4].

Connacht /'kɒnɔːt/ (also **Connaught**) a province in the south-west of the Republic of Ireland.

connate /'kɒneɪt/ ▶ **adjective 1** (especially of ideas or principles) existing in a person or thing from birth; innate: *are our ethical values connate?*
2 Biology (of parts) united so as to form a single part.
3 Geology (of water) trapped in sedimentary rock during its deposition.
– ORIGIN mid 17th cent.: from late Latin *connatus*, past participle of *connasci*, from *con-* 'together' + *nasci* 'be born'.

connatural ▶ **adjective** belonging naturally; innate.
– DERIVATIVES **connaturally** adverb.
– ORIGIN late 16th cent.: from late Latin *connaturalis*, from *con-* 'together'+ Latin *naturalis* 'natural'.

Connaught variant spelling of **CONNACHT**.

connect ▶ **verb** [with obj.] (often **be connected**) bring together or into contact so that a real or notional link is established: *the electrodes were* ***connected to*** *a recording device | a computer network that* ***connects*** *all the PC terminals* ***together.***
■join together so as to provide access and communication: *all the buildings are connected by underground passages |* [no obj.] *the motorway* ***connects with*** *major routes from all parts of the country.* ■link to a power or water supply: *by 1892 most of the village had been* ***connected to*** *the mains.* ■put (someone) into contact by telephone: *I was quickly* ***connected to*** *the police.* ■[no obj.] (of a train, bus, aircraft, etc.) be timed to arrive at its destination just before another train, aircraft, etc., departs so that passengers can transfer from one to the other: *the bus* ***connects with*** *trains from Windermere station.* ■associate or relate in some respect: *employees are rewarded with bonuses* ***connected to*** *their firm's performance | the issues* ***connected with*** *female criminality.* ■think of as being linked or related: *I didn't connect the two incidents at the time.* ■(of a thing) provide or have a link or relationship with (someone or something): *there was no evidence to* ***connect*** *Jefferson* ***with*** *the theft.* ■[no obj.] form a relationship or feel an affinity: *he can't* ***connect with*** *anyone any more.* ■[no obj.] informal (of a blow) hit the intended target: *the blow connected and he felt a burst of pain.*
– DERIVATIVES **connectable** adjective, **connectedly** adverb, **connectedness** noun.
– ORIGIN late Middle English (in the sense 'be united physically'; rare before the 18th cent.): from Latin *connectere*, from *con-* 'together' + *nectere* 'bind'.

Connecticut /kə'nɛtɪkət/ **1** a state in the north-eastern US, on the Atlantic coast; capital, Hartford; pop. 3,287,100 (1990). It was one of the original thirteen states of the Union and ratified the draft US Constitution in 1788.
2 the longest river in New England, rising in northern New Hampshire and flowing south for 655 km (407 miles) to enter Long Island Sound.

connecting rod ▶ **noun** a rod connecting two moving parts in a mechanism, especially that between the piston and the crankpin (or equivalent parts) in an engine or pump.

connection (Brit. also **connexion**) ▶ **noun 1** a relationship in which a person, thing, or idea is linked or associated with something else: *the* ***connections between*** *social attitudes and productivity | sufferers deny that their problems have any* ***connection with*** *drugs.*
■[mass noun] the action of linking one thing with another: *connection to the Internet.* ■[mass noun] the placing of parts of an electric circuit in contact so that a current may flow. ■a link between electrical components or pipes: *it is important to ensure that all connections between the wires are properly made.* ■a link between two telephones: *she replaced the receiver before the connection was made.* ■an arrangement or opportunity for catching a connecting train, bus, aircraft, etc.: *ferry connections are sporadic in the low season.* ■such a train, bus, etc.: *we had to wait for our connection to Frankfurt.* ■(**connections**) people with whom one has social or professional contact or to whom one is related, especially those with influence and able to offer one help: *he had connections with the music industry.*
2 informal, chiefly US a supplier of narcotics.
■a narcotics sale or purchase.
3 chiefly historical an association of Methodist churches.
– PHRASES **in connection with** with reference to; concerning: *detectives are questioning two men in connection with alleged criminal damage.* **in this** (or **that**) **connection** with reference to this (or that): *the local Marine Surveyor should be able to assist in this connection.*
– DERIVATIVES **connectional** adjective.
– ORIGIN late Middle English: from Latin *connexio(n-)*, from *connectere* (see **CONNECT**). The spelling *-ct* (18th cent.) is from *connect*, on the pattern of pairs such as *collect, collection.*

connectionism ▶ **noun** [mass noun] an artificial intelligence approach to cognition in which multiple connections between nodes (equivalent to brain cells) form a massive interactive network in which many processes take place simultaneously and certain processes, operating in parallel, are grouped together in hierarchies that bring about results such as thought or action. Also called **PARALLEL DISTRIBUTED PROCESSING**.

connective ▶ **adjective** connecting: *connective words and phrases.*
▶ **noun** something that connects, in particular:
■Grammar a word or phrase whose function is to link other linguistic units. ■Anatomy a bundle of nerve fibres connecting two nerve centres or ganglia, especially in invertebrate animals.

■archaic showing careful thought: *be considerate over your handwriting.*
– DERIVATIVES **considerately** adverb, **considerateness** noun.
– ORIGIN late 16th cent. (in the sense 'showing careful thought'): from Latin *consideratus*, past participle of *considerare* 'examine' (see CONSIDER).

consideration ▶ noun 1 [mass noun] careful thought, typically over a period of time.
■[count noun] a fact or a motive taken into account in deciding or judging something: *the idea was motivated by political considerations.* ■ thoughtfulness and sensitivity towards others: *companies should show more consideration for their employees.*
2 a payment or reward: *you can buy the books for a small consideration.*
■Law (in a contractual agreement) anything given or promised or forborne by one party in exchange for the promise or undertaking of another.
3 archaic importance; consequence.
– PHRASES **in consideration of** in return for; on account of: *he paid them in consideration of their services.* **take into consideration** take into account. **under consideration** being thought about: *the abolition of the House of Lords was under consideration.*
– ORIGIN late Middle English : via Old French from Latin *consideratio(n-)*, from *considerare* 'examine'.

considering ▶ preposition & conjunction taking into consideration: [as prep.] *considering the conditions it's very good* | [as conjunction] **considering that** *he was the youngest on the field he played well.*
▶ adverb informal taking everything into account: *they weren't feeling too bad, considering.*

consign /kənˈsʌɪn/ ▶ verb [with obj.] deliver (something) to a person's custody, typically in order for it to be sold: *he consigned three paintings to Sotheby's.*
■send (goods) by a public carrier. ■ (**consign someone/thing to**) put someone or something in (a place) in order to be rid of it or them: *she consigned the letter to the waste-paper basket.*
– DERIVATIVES **consignee** noun, **consignor** noun.
– ORIGIN late Middle English (in the sense 'mark with the sign of the cross', especially at baptism or confirmation, as a sign of dedication to God): from French *consigner* or Latin *consignare* 'mark with a seal'.

consignment ▶ noun a batch of goods destined for or delivered to someone: *a consignment of drugs.*
■[mass noun] the action of consigning or delivering something.

consist ▶ verb /kənˈsɪst/ [no obj.] 1 (**consist of**) be composed or made up of: *the crew consists of five men.*
■(**consist in**) have as an essential feature: *his poetry consisted in the use of emotive language.*
2 (**consist with**) archaic be consistent with: *the information perfectly consists with our friend's account.*
▶ noun /ˈkɒnsɪst/ Railways the set of vehicles forming a complete train: *to turn an entire consist requires a wye.*
– ORIGIN late Middle English (in the sense 'be located or inherent in'): from Latin *consistere* 'stand firm or still, exist', from *con-* 'together' + *sistere* 'stand (still)'.

consistency (also **consistence**) ▶ noun (pl. **-ies**) [mass noun] **1** conformity in the application of something, typically that which is necessary for the sake of logic, accuracy, or fairness: *the consistency of measurement techniques.*
■the achievement of a level of performance which does not vary greatly in quality over time.
2 the way in which a substance, typically a liquid, holds together; thickness or viscosity: *the sauce has the consistency of creamed butter.*
– ORIGIN late 16th cent. (denoting permanence of form): from late Latin *consistentia*, from *consistent-* 'standing firm' (see CONSISTENT).

consistent ▶ adjective (of a person, behaviour, or process) unchanging in achievement or effect over a period of time: *manufacturing processes require a consistent approach.*
■[predic.] compatible or in agreement with something: *the injuries are consistent with falling from a great height.* ■ (of an argument or set of ideas) not containing any logical contradictions: *a consistent explanation.*
– DERIVATIVES **consistently** adverb.
– ORIGIN late 16th cent. (in the sense 'consisting or composed of'): from Latin *consistent-* 'standing firm or still, existing', from the verb *consistere* (see CONSIST).

consistory /kənˈsɪst(ə)ri/ ▶ noun (pl. **-ies**) a church council or court, in particular:

■(in the Roman Catholic Church) the council of cardinals, with or without the Pope. ■ (also **consistory court**) (in the Church of England) a court presided over by a bishop, for the administration of ecclesiastical law in a diocese. ■ (in other Churches) a local administrative body.
– DERIVATIVES **consistorial** /ˌkɒnsɪˈstɔːrɪəl/ adjective.
– ORIGIN Middle English (originally denoting a non-ecclesiastical council): from Anglo-Norman French *consistorie*, from late Latin *consistorium*, from *consistere* 'stand firm' (see CONSIST).

consociation ▶ noun 1 a group or association of a distinctive type, in particular:
■a political system formed by the cooperation of different, especially antagonistic, social groups on the basis of shared power. ■ Ecology a small climax community or division of a plant association having a characteristic dominant species. ■ Zoology a group of animals of the same species which interact more or less equally with each other.
2 [mass noun] dated close association or fellowship.
– DERIVATIVES **consociational** adjective, **consociationalism** noun.
– ORIGIN late 16th cent. (in the sense 'associating, combination'): from Latin *consociatio(n-)*, from the verb *consociare*, from *con-* 'together' + *sociare* 'to associate' (from *socius* 'fellow').

consolation /ˌkɒnsəˈleɪʃ(ə)n/ ▶ noun [mass noun] the comfort received by a person after a loss or disappointment: *there was consolation in knowing that others were worse off.*
■[count noun] a person or thing providing such comfort: *the church was the main consolation in a short and hard life.*
– DERIVATIVES **consolatory** /kənˈsɒlət(ə)ri, -ˈsəʊl-/ adjective.
– ORIGIN late Middle English: via Old French from Latin *consolatio(n-)*, from the verb *consolari* (see CONSOLE¹).

consolation prize ▶ noun a prize given to a competitor who just fails to win or who has come last.

console¹ /kənˈsəʊl/ ▶ verb [with obj.] comfort (someone) at a time of grief or disappointment: *she tried to console him but he pushed her gently away* | *you can console yourself with the thought that you did your best.*
– DERIVATIVES **consolable** adjective, **consoler** noun, **consolingly** adverb.
– ORIGIN mid 17th cent. (replacing earlier *consolate*): from French *consoler*, from Latin *consolari*, from *con-* 'with' + *solari* 'soothe'.

console² /ˈkɒnsəʊl/ ▶ noun **1** a panel or unit accommodating a set of controls for electronic or mechanical equipment.
■a cabinet for television or radio equipment. ■ (also **games console**) a small machine for playing computerized video games, normally requiring connection to a television set. ■ the cabinet or enclosure containing the keyboards, stops, pedals, etc., of an organ.
2 an ornamented bracket or corbel supporting a shelf or table top.
– ORIGIN mid 17th cent. (in sense 2): from French, perhaps from *consolider*, from Latin *consolidare* (see CONSOLIDATE).

console table ▶ noun a table top supported by ornamented brackets against a wall.

consolidate /kənˈsɒlɪdeɪt/ ▶ verb [with obj.] make (something) physically stronger or more solid: *the first phase of the project is to consolidate the outside walls.*
■reinforce or strengthen (one's position or power): *the company consolidated its position in the international market.* ■ combine (a number of things) into a single more effective or coherent whole: *all manufacturing activities have been consolidated in new premises.* ■ combine (a number of financial accounts or funds) into a single overall account or set of accounts. ■ chiefly Brit. combine (separate pieces of legislation) into a single legislative act.
– DERIVATIVES **consolidation** noun, **consolidator** noun.
– ORIGIN early 16th cent. (in the sense 'combine into a single whole'): from Latin *consolidare*, from *con-* 'together' + *solidare* 'make firm' (from *solidus* 'solid').

Consolidated Fund the account held by the Exchequer of the British government at the Bank of England into which public monies (such as tax receipts) are paid and from which major payments

are made, other than those dependent on periodic parliamentary approval.

Consols /ˈkɒns(ə)lz/ ▶ plural noun British government securities without redemption date and with fixed annual interest.
– ORIGIN late 18th cent.: contraction of *consolidated annuities.*

consommé /kənˈsɒmeɪ/ ▶ noun [mass noun] a clear soup made with concentrated stock.
– ORIGIN French, past participle of *consommer* 'consume or consummate', from Latin *consummare* 'make complete' (see CONSUMMATE).

consonance /ˈkɒns(ə)nəns/ ▶ noun [mass noun] agreement or compatibility between opinions or actions: *consonance between conservation measures and existing agricultural practice* | *a constitution in consonance with the people's customs.*
■the recurrence of similar sounds, especially consonants, in close proximity (chiefly as used in prosody). ■ Music the combination of notes which are in harmony with each other due to the relationship between their frequencies.
– ORIGIN late Middle English: from Old French, or from Latin *consonantia*, from *consonant-* 'sounding together', from the verb *consonare* (see CONSONANT).

consonant /ˈkɒns(ə)nənt/ ▶ noun a basic speech sound in which the breath is at least partly obstructed and which can be combined with a vowel to form a syllable. Contrasted with VOWEL.
■a letter representing such a sound.
▶ adjective **1** [attrib.] denoting or relating to such a sound or letter: *a consonant phoneme.*
2 [predic.] (**consonant with**) in agreement or harmony with: *the findings are consonant with other research.*
■Music making a harmonious interval or chord: *the bass is consonant with all the upper notes.*
– DERIVATIVES **consonantal** adjective, **consonantly** adverb.
– ORIGIN Middle English (in the sense 'letter representing a consonantal sound'): via Old French from Latin *consonare* 'sound together', from *con-* 'with' + *sonare* 'to sound' (from *sonus* 'sound').

con sordino /ˌkɒn sɔːˈdiːnəʊ/ ▶ adverb Music (especially as a direction) with the use of a mute.
– ORIGIN Italian.

consort¹ ▶ noun /ˈkɒnsɔːt/ a wife, husband, or companion, in particular the spouse of a reigning monarch.
■a ship sailing in company with another.
▶ verb /kənˈsɔːt/ [no obj.] (**consort with**) habitually associate with (someone), typically with the disapproval of others: *you chose to consort with the enemy.*
■(**consort with/to**) archaic agree or be in harmony with.
– ORIGIN late Middle English (denoting a companion or colleague): via French from Latin *consors* 'sharing, partner', from *con-* 'together with' + *sors*, *sort-* 'lot, destiny'. The verb senses are probably influenced by similar senses (now obsolete) of the verb *sort*.

consort² /ˈkɒnsɔːt/ ▶ noun a small group of musicians performing together, typically playing instrumental music of the Renaissance period.
– ORIGIN late 16th cent.: earlier form of CONCERT.

consortium /kənˈsɔːtɪəm/ ▶ noun (pl. **consortia** /-tɪə/ or **consortiums**) **1** an association, typically of several business companies.
2 [mass noun] Law the right of association and companionship with one's husband or wife.
– ORIGIN early 19th cent. (in the sense 'partnership'): from Latin, from *consors* 'sharing, partner' (see CONSORT¹).

conspecific /ˌkɒnspəˈsɪfɪk/ Biology ▶ adjective (of animals or plants) belonging to the same species.
▶ noun (usu. **conspecifics**) a member of the same species: *the rabbit was isolated from male conspecifics.*
– DERIVATIVES **conspecificity** noun.

conspectus /kənˈspɛktəs/ ▶ noun a summary or overview of a subject.
– ORIGIN mid 19th cent.: from Latin, past participle (used as a noun) of *conspicere* 'look at attentively'.

conspicuous /kənˈspɪkjʊəs/ ▶ adjective standing out so as to be clearly visible: *he was very thin, with a conspicuous Adam's apple.*
■attracting notice or attention: *he showed conspicuous bravery.*
– PHRASES **conspicuous by one's absence** obviously not present in a place where one or it should be. [ORIGIN: from a speech made by Lord

b **b**ut | d **d**og | f **f**ew | g **g**et | h **h**e | j **y**es | k **c**at | l **l**eg | m **m**an | n **n**o | p **p**en | r **r**ed | s **s**it | t **t**op | v **v**oice | w **w**e | z **z**oo | ʃ **sh**e | ʒ deci**s**ion | θ **th**in | ð **th**is | ŋ ri**ng** | x lo**ch** | tʃ **ch**ip | dʒ **j**ar

John Russell in an address to electors (1859): taken from Tacitus (*Annals* iii. 76).]
– DERIVATIVES **conspicuity** noun, **conspicuously** adverb, **conspicuousness** noun.
– ORIGIN mid 16th cent.: from Latin *conspicuus* (from *conspicere* 'look at attentively', from *con-* (expressing intensive force) + *spicere* 'look at') + **-OUS**.

conspiracist ▶ noun a person who supports a conspiracy theory.

conspiracy ▶ noun (pl. **-ies**) a secret plan by a group to do something unlawful or harmful: *a conspiracy to destroy the government.*
■ [mass noun] the action of plotting or conspiring: *they were cleared of conspiracy to pervert the course of justice.*
– PHRASES **a conspiracy of silence** an agreement to say nothing about an issue that should be generally known.
– ORIGIN late Middle English: from Anglo-Norman French *conspiracie*, alteration of Old French *conspiration*, based on Latin *conspirare* 'agree, plot' (see **CONSPIRE**).

conspiracy theory ▶ noun a belief that some covert but influential organization is responsible for an unexplained event.

conspirator ▶ noun a person who takes part in a conspiracy.
– DERIVATIVES **conspiratorial** adjective, **conspiratorially** adverb.
– ORIGIN late Middle English: from Old French *conspirateur*, from Latin *conspirator*, from *conspirat-* 'agreed, plotted', from the verb *conspirare* (see **CONSPIRE**).

conspire ▶ verb [no obj.] make secret plans jointly to commit an unlawful or harmful act: *they **conspired against** him* | [with infinitive] *they deny conspiring to defraud the Inland Revenue.*
■ [with infinitive] (of events or circumstances) seem to be working together to bring about a particular result, typically to someone's detriment: *everything conspires to exacerbate the situation.*
– ORIGIN late Middle English: from Old French *conspirer*, from Latin *conspirare* 'agree, plot', from *con-* 'together with' + *spirare* 'breathe'.

Const. ▶ abbreviation for constable.

Constable /ˈkʌnstəb(ə)l, ˈkɒn-/, John (1776–1837), English painter. Among his best-known works are early paintings like *Flatford Mill* (1817) and *The Hay Wain* (1821), inspired by the landscape of his native Suffolk.

constable /ˈkʌnstəb(ə)l, ˈkɒn-/ ▶ noun **1** Brit. a police officer.
■ (also **police constable**) a police officer of the lowest rank.
2 the governor of a royal castle.
■ historical the highest-ranking official in a royal household.
– ORIGIN Middle English (in sense 2): from Old French *conestable*, from late Latin *comes stabuli* 'count (head officer) of the stable'. Sense 1 dates from the mid 19th cent.

constabulary /kənˈstabjʊləri/ ▶ noun (pl. **-ies**) chiefly Brit. a police force covering a particular area or city: *the Royal Irish Constabulary.*
– ORIGIN late 15th cent. (denoting the district under the charge of a constable): from medieval Latin *constabularia (dignitas)* '(rank) of constable', from *constabulus*, based on Latin *comes stabuli* (see **CONSTABLE**).

Constance, Lake a lake in SE Germany on the north side of the Swiss Alps, at the meeting point of Germany, Switzerland, and Austria, forming part of the course of the River Rhine. German name **BODENSEE**.

constancy ▶ noun [mass noun] the quality of being faithful and dependable.
■ the quality of being enduring and unchanging: *the constancy of the tradition.*
– ORIGIN late 15th cent.: from Latin *constantia*, from *constant-* 'standing firm' (see **CONSTANT**).

constant ▶ adjective occurring continuously over a period of time: *the pain is constant.*
■ remaining the same over a period of time: *the company has kept its prices fairly constant.* ■ (of a person) unchangingly faithful and dependable.
▶ noun a situation or state of affairs that does not change: *the condition of struggle remained a constant.*
■ Mathematics a quantity or parameter that does not change its value whatever the value of the variables, under a given set of conditions. ■ Physics a number expressing a relation or property which remains the same in all circumstances, or for the same substance under the same conditions.
– DERIVATIVES **constantly** adverb.
– ORIGIN late Middle English (in the sense 'staying resolute or faithful'): from Old French, from Latin *constant-* 'standing firm', from the verb *constare*, from *con-* 'with' + *stare* 'stand'. The noun senses date from the mid 19th cent.

Constanța /kɒnˈstantsə/ (also **Constanza**) the chief port of Romania, on the Black Sea; pop. 349,000 (1993). Founded in the 7th century BC by the Greeks, it was under Roman rule from 72 BC. Formerly called Tomis, it was renamed after Constantine I in the 4th century.

constantan /ˈkɒnst(ə)ntan/ ▶ noun [mass noun] a copper–nickel alloy used in electrical work for its high resistance.
– ORIGIN early 20th cent.: from **CONSTANT** + **-AN**.

Constantine[1] /ˈkɒnstəntʌɪn/ a city in NE Algeria; pop. 449,000 (1989). The capital of the Roman province of Numidia, it was destroyed in 311 but rebuilt by Constantine the Great and given his name.

Constantine[2] /ˈkɒnstəntʌɪn/ (*c.*274–337), Roman emperor; known as **Constantine the Great**. He was the first Roman emperor to be converted to Christianity and in 324 made Christianity a state religion. In 330 he moved his capital from Rome to Byzantium, renaming it Constantinopolis (Constantinople). In the Orthodox Church he is venerated as a saint.

Constantinople /ˌkɒnstantɪˈnəʊp(ə)l/ the former name for Istanbul from AD 330 (when it was given its name by Constantine the Great) to the capture of the city by the Turks in 1453.

Constanza variant spelling of **CONSTANȚA**.

constative /ˈkɒnstətɪv, kənˈsteɪtɪv/ Linguistics ▶ adjective denoting a speech act or sentence that is a statement declaring something to be the case. Often contrasted with **PERFORMATIVE**.
▶ noun a constative speech act or sentence.
– ORIGIN early 20th cent.: from Latin *constat-* 'established' (from the verb *constare*) + **-IVE**.

constellate /ˈkɒnstəleɪt/ ▶ verb poetic/literary form or cause to form into a cluster or group; gather together: [no obj.] *the towns and valleys where people constellate* | [with obj.] *their stories were never constellated.*
– ORIGIN mid 17th cent.: from late Latin *constellatus*, from *con-* 'together' + *stellatus* 'arranged like a star'.

constellation ▶ noun a group of stars forming a recognizable pattern that is traditionally named after its apparent form or identified with a mythological figure. Modern astronomers divide the sky into eighty-eight constellations with defined boundaries.
■ figurative a group of associated or similar people or things: *no two patients ever show exactly the same **constellation** of symptoms.*
– ORIGIN Middle English (as an astrological term denoting the relative positions of the 'stars' (planets), supposed to influence events): via Old French from late Latin *constellatio(n-)*, based on Latin *stella* 'star'.

consternate /ˈkɒnstəneɪt/ ▶ verb [with obj.] fill (someone) with anxiety: [as adj. **consternated**] *'Oh dear' said Georgiana, looking a little consternated.*
– ORIGIN mid 17th cent.: from Latin *consternat-* 'terrified, prostrated', from the verb *consternare*.

consternation ▶ noun [mass noun] feelings of anxiety or dismay, typically at something unexpected: ***to her consternation** her car wouldn't start.*
– ORIGIN early 17th cent.: from Latin *consternatio(n-)*, from the verb *consternare* 'lay prostrate, terrify' (see **CONSTERNATE**).

constipate /ˈkɒnstɪpeɪt/ ▶ verb [with obj.] (usu. **be constipated**) affect (a person or animal) with constipation: *regular heroin users can become constipated.*
– ORIGIN mid 16th cent.: from Latin *constipat-* 'crowded or pressed together', from the verb *constipare*, from *con-* 'together' + *stipare* 'press, cram'.

constipation ▶ noun [mass noun] a condition in which there is difficulty in emptying the bowels, usually associated with hardened faeces.
■ figurative a high level of constraint or restriction; a pronounced lack of ease: *literary constipation.*
– ORIGIN late Middle English (in the sense 'contraction of body tissues'): from late Latin *constipatio(n-)*, from the verb *constipare* (see **CONSTIPATE**).

constituency /kənˈstɪtjʊənsi/ ▶ noun (pl. **-ies**) a body of voters in a specified area who elect a representative to a legislative body: *most politicians are more interested in the voice of their constituency.*
■ chiefly Brit. the area represented in this way: *a parliamentary candidate in the Hampstead and Highgate constituency.* ■ a body of customers or supporters: *a constituency of racing fans.*

constituent ▶ adjective [attrib.] **1** being a part of a whole: *the constituent minerals of the rock.*
2 being a voting member of an organization and having the power to appoint or elect: *the constituent body has a right of veto.*
■ able to make or change a political constitution: *a constituent assembly.*
▶ noun **1** a member of an area which elects a representative to a legislative body.
2 a component part of something: *the essential constituents of the human diet.*
– ORIGIN late 15th cent. (in the legal sense of the noun): from Latin *constituent-* (partly via French *constituant*) 'establishing, appointing', from the verb *constituere* (see **CONSTITUTE**).

constitute /ˈkɒnstɪtjuːt/ ▶ verb [with obj.] **1** be (a part) of a whole: *lone parents constitute a great proportion of the poor.*
■ (of people or things) combine to form (a whole): *there were enough members present to constitute a quorum.* ■ be or be equivalent to (something): *his failure to act constituted a breach of duty.*
2 (usu. **be constituted**) give legal or constitutional form to (an institution); establish by law.
– ORIGIN late Middle English: from Latin *constitut-* 'established, appointed', from the verb *constituere*, from *con-* 'together' + *statuere* 'set up'.

constitution ▶ noun **1** a body of fundamental principles or established precedents according to which a state or other organization is acknowledged to be governed.
■ historical a decree, ordinance, or law. ■ (**the Constitution**) the basic written set of principles and precedents of federal government in the US, which came into operation in 1789 and has since been modified by twenty-six amendments.
2 [mass noun] the composition of something: *the genetic constitution of a species.*
■ the forming or establishing of something: *the constitution of a police authority.*
3 a person's physical state as regards vitality, health, and strength: *pregnancy had weakened her constitution.*
■ a person's mental or psychological make-up.
– ORIGIN Middle English (denoting a law, or a body of laws or customs): from Latin *constitutio(n-)*, from *constituere* 'establish, appoint' (see **CONSTITUTE**).

constitutional ▶ adjective **1** of or relating to an established set of principles governing a state: *a constitutional amendment.*
■ in accordance with or allowed by such principles: *a constitutional monarchy.*
2 of or relating to someone's physical or mental condition: *a constitutional weakness.*
▶ noun dated a walk, typically one taken regularly to maintain or restore good health.
– DERIVATIVES **constitutionality** noun, **constitutionally** adverb.

constitutionalism ▶ noun [mass noun] constitutional government.
■ adherence to such a system of government.
– DERIVATIVES **constitutionalist** noun.

constitutionalize (also **-ise**) ▶ verb [with obj.] US make subject to the provisions of a country's constitution: *divorce is not constitutionalized.*

Constitution State informal name for **CONNECTICUT**.

constitutive ▶ adjective **1** having the power to establish or give organized existence to something: *the state began to exercise a new and constitutive function.*
2 forming a part or constituent of something; component: *poverty is a constitutive element of a particular form of economic growth.*
■ forming an essential element of something: *language **is constitutive of** thought.*
3 Biochemistry relating to an enzyme or enzyme system that is continuously produced in an organism, regardless of the needs of cells.

– DERIVATIVES **constitutively** adverb.

constrain ▶ verb [with obj.] (often **be constrained**) compel or force (someone) towards a particular course of action: [with obj. and infinitive] *children are constrained to work in the way the book dictates.* ■ archaic bring about (something) by compulsion: *Calypso in her caves constrained his stay.* ■ [usu. as adj. **constrained**] cause to appear unnaturally forced, typically because of embarrassment: *he was acting in a constrained manner.* ■ severely restrict the scope, extent, or activity of: *agricultural development is considerably constrained by climate.* ■ poetic/literary confine forcibly; imprison.
– DERIVATIVES **constrainedly** adverb.
– ORIGIN Middle English: from Old French *constraindre*, from Latin *constringere* 'bind tightly together'.

constraint ▶ noun a limitation or restriction: *the availability of water is the main constraint on food production* | [mass noun] *remove any clips to allow the pipe to expand without constraint.* ■ [mass noun] stiffness of manner and inhibition in relations between people: *they would be able to talk without constraint.*
– ORIGIN late Middle English (in the sense 'coercion'): from Old French *constreinte*, feminine past participle of *constraindre* (see **CONSTRAIN**).

constrict ▶ verb [with obj.] make narrower, especially by encircling pressure: *chemicals that constrict the blood vessels* | [as adj. **constricted**] *constricted air passages.* ■ [no obj.] become narrower: *he felt his throat constrict.* ■ (of a snake) coil round (prey) in order to asphyxiate it. ■ figurative restrict: *the fear and the reality of crime constrict many people's lives.*
– DERIVATIVES **constriction** noun, **constrictive** adjective.
– ORIGIN mid 18th cent.: from Latin *constrict-* 'bound tightly together', from the verb *constringere* (see **CONSTRAIN**).

constrictor ▶ noun 1 a snake that kills by coiling round its prey and asphyxiating it.
● Families Boidae and Pythonidae, and some members of other families (in particular Colubridae).
2 (also **constrictor muscle**) Anatomy a muscle whose contraction narrows a vessel or passage. ■ each of the muscles which constrict the pharynx.
– ORIGIN early 18th cent.: modern Latin, from *constrict-* 'bound tightly together', from the verb *constringere* (see **CONSTRAIN**).

construct ▶ verb /kən'strʌkt/ [with obj.] build or erect (something, typically a building, road, or machine): *a company that constructs oil rigs.* ■ form (an idea or theory) by bringing together various conceptual elements, typically over a period of time: *poetics should construct a theory of literary discourse.* ■ Grammar form (a sentence) according to grammatical rules. ■ Geometry draw or delineate (a geometrical figure) accurately to given conditions.
▶ noun /'kɒnstrʌkt/ an idea or theory containing various conceptual elements, typically one considered to be subjective and not based on empirical evidence: *history is largely an ideological construct.* ■ Linguistics a group of words forming a phrase. ■ a physical thing which is deliberately built or formed.
– DERIVATIVES **constructor** noun.
– ORIGIN late Middle English: from Latin *construct-* 'heaped together, built', from the verb *construere*, from *con-* 'together' + *struere* 'pile, build'.

construction ▶ noun [mass noun] the building of something, typically a large structure: *there was a skyscraper under construction.* ■ such activity considered as an industry. ■ the style or method used in the building of something: *the mill is of brick construction.* ■ [count noun] a building or other structure. ■ the creation or formation of an abstract entity: *language plays a large part in our construction of reality.* ■ [count noun] an interpretation or explanation: *you could put an honest construction upon their conduct.* ■ Grammar the arrangement of words according to syntactical rules: *sentence construction.*
– DERIVATIVES **constructional** adjective, **constructionally** adverb.
– ORIGIN late Middle English: via Old French from Latin *constructio(n-)*, from *construere* 'heap together' (see **CONSTRUCT**).

constructionism ▶ noun another term for **CONSTRUCTIVISM**.

constructionist ▶ noun 1 another term for *constructivist* (see **CONSTRUCTIVISM**).
2 US a person who puts a particular construction

upon a legal document, especially the US Constitution.

construction site ▶ noun a building site.
– DERIVATIVES **constructionism** noun.

constructive ▶ adjective 1 serving a useful purpose: *constructive advice.*
2 Law derived by inference; not obvious or stated explicitly: *constructive liability.*
3 Mathematics relating to, based on, or denoting mathematical proofs which show how an entity may in principle be constructed or arrived at in a finite number of steps.
– DERIVATIVES **constructively** adverb, **constructiveness** noun.
– ORIGIN mid 17th cent. (in sense 2): from late Latin *constructivus*, from Latin *construct-* 'heap together', from the verb *construere* (see **CONSTRUCT**).

constructive dismissal ▶ noun [mass noun] the changing of an employee's job or working conditions with the aim of forcing resignation.

constructivism ▶ noun [mass noun] 1 Art a style or movement in which assorted mechanical objects are combined into abstract mobile structural forms. The movement originated in Russia in the 1920s and has influenced many aspects of modern architecture and design. |ORIGIN: transliterating Russian *konstruktivizm*.]
2 Mathematics a view which admits as valid only constructive proofs and entities demonstrable by them, implying that the latter have no independent existence.
– DERIVATIVES **constructivist** noun.

construe ▶ verb (**construes**, **construed**, **construing**) [with obj.] (often **be construed**) interpret (a word or action) in a particular way: *his words could hardly be construed as an apology.* ■ dated analyse the syntax of (a text, sentence, or word): *both verbs can be construed with either infinitive.* ■ dated translate (a passage or author) word for word, typically aloud.
– DERIVATIVES **construable** adjective, **construal** noun.
– ORIGIN late Middle English: from Latin *construere* (see **CONSTRUCT**), in late Latin 'analyse the construction of a sentence'.

consubstantial ▶ adjective of the same substance or essence (used especially of the three persons of the Trinity in Christian theology): *Christ is consubstantial with the Father.*
– DERIVATIVES **consubstantiality** noun.
– ORIGIN late Middle English: from ecclesiastical Latin *consubstantialis* (translating Greek *homoousios* 'of one substance'), from *con-* 'with' + *substantialis* (see **SUBSTANTIAL**).

consubstantiation /ˌkɒnsəbstanʃɪ'eɪʃ(ə)n, -sɪ-/ ▶ noun [mass noun] Christian Theology the doctrine, especially in Lutheran belief, that the substance of the bread and wine coexists with the body and blood of Christ in the Eucharist. Compare with **TRANSUBSTANTIATION**.
– ORIGIN late 16th cent.: from modern Latin *consubstantiatio(n-)*, from *con-* 'together', on the pattern of *transubstantiatio(n-)* 'transubstantiation'.

consuetude /'kɒnswɪtjuːd/ ▶ noun chiefly Scottish a custom, especially one having legal force.
– DERIVATIVES **consuetudinary** /-'tjuːdɪn(ə)ri/ adjective.
– ORIGIN late Middle English: from Old French, or from Latin *consuetudo* (see **CUSTOM**).

consul /'kɒns(ə)l/ ▶ noun 1 an official appointed by a state to live in a foreign city and protect the state's citizens and interests there.
2 (in ancient Rome) one of the two annually elected chief magistrates who jointly ruled the republic. ■ any of the three chief magistrates of the first French republic (1799–1804).
– DERIVATIVES **consular** /'kɒnsjʊlə/ adjective, **consulship** noun.
– ORIGIN late Middle English (denoting an ancient Roman magistrate): from Latin, related to *consulere* 'take counsel'.

consulate ▶ noun 1 the place or building in which a consul's duties are carried out. ■ [treated as sing. or pl.] the staff assigned the duties associated with this.
2 historical the period of office of a Roman consul. ■ (**the consulate**) the system of government by consuls in ancient Rome.
3 (**the Consulate**) the government of the first French republic (1799–1804) by three consuls.

– ORIGIN late Middle English (denoting the government of Rome by consuls, or their office or dignity): from Latin *consulatus*, from *consul* (see **CONSUL**).

consul general ▶ noun (pl. **consuls general**) a consul of the highest status.

consult ▶ verb [with obj.] seek information or advice from (someone with expertise in a particular area): *she had consulted Doctor Staples.* ■ have discussions or confer with (someone), typically before undertaking a course of action: *patients are entitled to be consulted about their treatment* | [no obj.] *the government must consult with interested bodies.* ■ refer for information to (a book, diary, or watch) in order to ascertain something.
– DERIVATIVES **consultative** adjective.
– ORIGIN early 16th cent. (in the sense 'deliberate together, confer'): from French *consulter*, from Latin *consultare*, frequentative of *consulere* 'take counsel'.

consultancy ▶ noun (pl. **-ies**) a professional practice that gives expert advice within a particular field, especially business: [as modifier] *a management consultancy firm.* ■ [mass noun] the work of giving such advice.

consultant ▶ noun 1 a person who provides expert advice professionally.
2 [usu. as modifier] Brit. a hospital doctor of senior rank within a specific field: *a consultant paediatrician.*
– ORIGIN late 17th cent. (in the sense 'a person who consults'): probably from French, from Latin *consultare* (see **CONSULT**).

consultation ▶ noun [mass noun] the action or process of formally consulting or discussing: *they improved standards in consultation with consumer representatives* | [count noun] *consultations between all sections of the party.* ■ [count noun] a meeting with an expert or professional, such as a medical doctor, in order to seek advice.
– ORIGIN late Middle English: from Latin *consultatio(n-)*, from the verb *consultare* (see **CONSULT**).

consultee ▶ noun a person who is formally consulted or asked for advice on a matter.

consulting ▶ adjective [attrib.] (of a senior person in a professional or technical field) engaged in the business of giving advice to others working in the same field: *a consulting engineer.* ■ (of a business or company) giving specialist advice.
▶ noun [mass noun] the business of giving specialist advice to other professionals, typically in financial and business matters.

consulting room ▶ noun a room in which a doctor or other therapeutic practitioner examines patients.

consumable ▶ adjective (of an item for sale) intended to be used up and then replaced.
▶ noun (usu. **consumables**) a commodity that is intended to be used up relatively quickly: *drugs and other medical consumables.*

consume ▶ verb [with obj.] eat, drink, or ingest (food or drink): *people consume a good deal of sugar in drinks.* ■ buy (goods or services). ■ use up (a resource): *there has been a doubling in the amount of gas consumed by electricity generators.* ■ (especially of a fire) completely destroy: *the fire spread rapidly, consuming many homes.* ■ (usu. **be consumed**) (of a feeling) absorb all of the attention and energy of (someone): *Carolyn was consumed with guilt* | [as adj. **consuming**] *a consuming passion.*
– DERIVATIVES **consumingly** adverb.
– ORIGIN late Middle English: from Latin *consumere*, from *con-* 'altogether' + *sumere* 'take up'; reinforced by French *consumer*.

consumer ▶ noun a person who purchases goods and services for personal use: [as modifier] *consumer demand.* ■ a person or thing that eats or uses something.

consumer durable ▶ noun (usu. **consumer durables**) a manufactured item, typically a car or household appliance, that is expected to have a relatively long useful life after purchase.

consumer goods ▶ plural noun goods bought and used by consumers, rather than by manufacturers for producing other goods. Often contrasted with **CAPITAL GOODS**.

consumerism ▶ noun [mass noun] 1 the protection or promotion of the interests of consumers.
2 often derogatory the preoccupation of society with the acquisition of consumer goods.

– DERIVATIVES **consumerist** adjective & noun, **consumeristic** adjective.

consumer research ▶ noun [mass noun] the investigation of the needs and opinions of consumers, especially as regards a particular product or service.

consumer society ▶ noun chiefly derogatory a society in which the buying and selling of goods and services is the most important social and economic activity.

consumer unit ▶ noun an apparatus in the electrical supply at the point it enters a domestic property, which contains devices such as a switch and circuit-breakers.

consummate ▶ verb /ˈkɒnsəmeɪt, -sjʊ-/ [with obj.] make (a marriage or relationship) complete by having sexual intercourse: *his first wife refused to consummate their marriage.*
■ complete (a transaction): *the property sale is consummated.*
▶ adjective /kənˈsʌmət, ˈkɒnsəmət/ showing a high degree of skill and flair: *she dressed with consummate elegance.*
– DERIVATIVES **consummately** adverb, **consummator** noun.
– ORIGIN late Middle English (as an adjective in the sense 'completed, accomplished'): from Latin *consummat-* 'brought to completion', from the verb *consummare*, from *con-* 'altogether' + *summa* 'sum total', feminine of *summus* 'highest, supreme'.

consummation ▶ noun [mass noun] the point at which something is complete or finalized: *the consummation of a sale.*
■ the action of making a marriage or relationship complete by having sexual intercourse: *the eager consummation that follows a long and passionate seduction.*
– ORIGIN late Middle English: from Latin *consummatio(n-)*, from the verb *consummare* (see **CONSUMMATE**).

consumption ▶ noun [mass noun] **1** the using up of a resource: *industrialized countries should reduce their energy consumption.*
■ the eating, drinking, or ingesting of something: *liquor is sold for consumption off the premises.* ■ [in sing.] an amount of something which is used up or ingested: *a daily consumption of 15 cigarettes.* ■ the purchase and use of goods and services by the public. ■ the reception of information or entertainment, especially by a mass audience: *his confidential speech was not meant for public consumption.*
2 dated a wasting disease, especially pulmonary tuberculosis.
– ORIGIN late Middle English: from Latin *consumptio(n-)*, from the verb *consumere* (see **CONSUME**).

consumptive ▶ adjective **1** dated affected with a wasting disease, especially pulmonary tuberculosis: *from birth he was sickly and consumptive.*
2 chiefly derogatory of or relating to the using up of resources: *tourism represents an insidious form of consumptive activity.*
▶ noun dated a person with a wasting disease, especially pulmonary tuberculosis.
– DERIVATIVES **consumptively** adverb.
– ORIGIN mid 17th cent.: from medieval Latin *consumptivus*, from Latin *consumpt-* 'consumed', from the verb *consumere* (see **CONSUME**).

cont. ▶ abbreviation for ■ contents. ■ continued.

contact ▶ noun /ˈkɒntakt/ **1** [mass noun] the state or condition of physical touching: *his head made contact with one of the bollards.*
■ the state or condition of communicating or meeting: *he had lost contact with his friends.* ■ [as modifier] caused or activated by or operating through physical touch: *contact dermatitis.* ■ [count noun] a connection for the passage of an electric current from one thing to another, or a part or device by which such a connection is made: *the sliding contact of the potentiometer.* ■ (**contacts**) contact lenses.
2 a meeting, communication, or relationship with someone: *they have forged contacts with key people in business.*
■ a person who may be communicated with for information or assistance, especially with regard to one's job: *Francesca had good contacts.* ■ a person who has associated with a patient with a contagious disease (and so may carry the infection).
▶ verb /ˈkɒntakt, kənˈtakt/ [with obj.] communicate with (someone), typically in order to give or receive specific information.

– DERIVATIVES **contactable** adjective.
– ORIGIN early 17th cent.: from Latin *contactus*, from *contact-* 'touched, grasped, bordered on', from the verb *contingere*, from *con-* 'together with' + *tangere* 'to touch'.

contact-breaker ▶ noun another term for **CIRCUIT-BREAKER**.

contact clause ▶ noun Grammar a relative clause appended without a relative pronoun to the noun phrase that governs it, as in *the man I saw yesterday.*

contactee ▶ noun a person who claims to have been contacted by alien beings, especially through an abduction.

contact flight (also **contact flying**) ▶ noun [mass noun] navigation of an aircraft by the observation of landmarks.

contact lens ▶ noun a thin plastic lens placed directly on the surface of the eye to correct visual defects.

contact man ▶ noun a man who provides a link for information or representation between two parties.

contact metamorphism ▶ noun [mass noun] Geology metamorphism due to contact with or proximity to an igneous intrusion.

contact print ▶ noun a photographic print made by placing a negative directly on to sensitized paper, glass, or film and illuminating it.
▶ verb (**contact-print**) [with obj.] make a photograph from (a negative) in this way.

contact process ▶ noun the major industrial process used to make sulphuric acid, by oxidizing sulphur dioxide in the presence of a solid catalyst and absorbing the resulting sulphur trioxide in water.

contact sheet ▶ noun a piece of photographic paper on to which several or all of the negatives on a film have been contact printed.

contact sport ▶ noun a sport in which the participants necessarily come into bodily contact with one another.

contadina /ˌkɒntəˈdiːnə/ ▶ noun (pl. **contadine** /-neɪ/ or **contadinas**) an Italian peasant girl or peasant woman.
– ORIGIN Italian.

contadino /ˌkɒntəˈdiːnəʊ/ ▶ noun (pl. **contadini** /-ni/ or **contadinos**) an Italian peasant or countryman.
– ORIGIN Italian, from *contado*, denoting the peasant population around a city.

contagion /kənˈteɪdʒ(ə)n/ ▶ noun [mass noun] the communication of disease from one person to another by close contact: *the rooms held no risk of contagion.*
■ [count noun] dated a disease spread in such a way. ■ figurative the spreading of a harmful idea or theory: *the contagion of disgrace.*
– ORIGIN late Middle English (denoting a contagious disease): from Latin *contagio(n-)*, from *con-* 'together with' + the base of *tangere* 'to touch'.

contagious ▶ adjective (of a disease) spread from one person or organism to another by direct or indirect contact.
■ (of a person) likely to transmit a disease by contact with other people. ■ figurative (of an emotion, feeling, or attitude) likely to spread to and affect others: *her enthusiasm is contagious.*
– DERIVATIVES **contagiously** adverb, **contagiousness** noun.
– ORIGIN late Middle English: from late Latin *contagiosus*, from *contagio* (see **CONTAGION**).

USAGE In practice, there is little or no difference in meaning between **contagious** and **infectious** when applied to disease: both mean, roughly, 'communicable'. There is, however, a difference in emphasis or focus between the two words. **Contagious** tends to be focused on the person or animal affected by the disease (*precautions are taken with anyone who seems contagious*), while **infectious** emphasizes the agent or organism which carries the disease: there are, for example, plenty of examples in the British National Corpus of *infectious agent* but none of *contagious agent*.

contagious abortion ▶ noun [mass noun] a type of brucellosis which causes spontaneous abortion in cattle.

contain ▶ verb [with obj.] **1** have or hold (someone or

something) within: *the cigarettes were thought to contain cannabis.*
■ be made up of (a number of things); consist of: *documents containing both text and simple graphics can be created.* ■ (of a number) be divisible by (a factor) without a remainder.
2 control or restrain (oneself or a feeling): *he could barely contain himself from jumping up to exclaim.*
■ prevent (a severe problem) from increasing in extent or intensity: *a new western policy to contain the conflict in Bosnia.*
– DERIVATIVES **containable** adjective.
– ORIGIN Middle English: from Old French *contenir*, from Latin *continere*, from *con-* 'altogether' + *tenere* 'to hold'.

container ▶ noun an object which can be used to hold or transport something.
■ a large metal box of a standard design and size used for the transport of goods by road, rail, sea, or air: [as modifier] *a container lorry.*

container-grown ▶ adjective (of a plant) grown in a container rather than in the ground.

containerize (also **-ise**) ▶ verb [with obj.] [usu. as adj. **containerized**] pack into or transport by container.
– DERIVATIVES **containerization** noun.

container port ▶ noun a port which specializes in handling goods transported in containers.

container ship ▶ noun a ship which is designed to carry goods stored in containers.

containment ▶ noun [mass noun] the action of keeping something harmful under control or within limits: *the containment of the Aids epidemic.*
■ the action or policy of preventing the expansion of a hostile country or influence: *the US government saw the containment of communism as a global task.*

contaminate ▶ verb [with obj.] (often **be contaminated**) make (something) impure by exposure to or addition of a poisonous or polluting substance: *the site was found to be contaminated by radioactivity* | figurative *the entertainment industry is able to contaminate the mind of the public* | [as adj. **contaminated**] *contaminated blood products.*
– DERIVATIVES **contaminant** noun, **contamination** noun, **contaminator** noun.
– ORIGIN late Middle English: from Latin *contaminat-* 'made impure', from the verb *contaminare*, from *contamen* 'contact, pollution', from *con-* 'together with' + the base of *tangere* 'to touch'.

contango /kənˈtaŋɡəʊ/ ▶ noun [mass noun] Stock Exchange Brit. the normal situation in which the spot or cash price of a commodity is lower than the forward price. Often contrasted with **BACKWARDATION**.
■ historical a percentage paid by a buyer of stock to postpone transfer to a future settling day.
– ORIGIN mid 19th cent.: probably an arbitrary formation on the pattern of Latin verb forms ending in *-o* in the first person singular, perhaps with the idea 'I make contingent' (see **CONTINGENT**).

Conté /ˈkɒnteɪ/ ▶ noun [mass noun] a kind of hard, grease-free crayon used as a medium for artwork: [as modifier] *Conté pastels.*
– ORIGIN mid 19th cent.: named after Nicolas J. *Conté* (1755–1805), the French inventor who developed it.

conte /kɒnt, French kɔ̃t/ ▶ noun a short story as a form of literary composition.
■ a medieval narrative tale.
– ORIGIN French, based on Latin *computare* 'reckon, sum up'.

contemn /kənˈtɛm/ ▶ verb [with obj.] archaic treat or regard with contempt.
– DERIVATIVES **contemner** /-ˈtɛmə, -ˈtɛmnə/ noun.
– ORIGIN late Middle English: from Latin *contemnere*, from *con-* (expressing intensive force) + *temnere* 'despise'.

contemplate /ˈkɒntɛmpleɪt, -təm-/ ▶ verb [with obj.] look thoughtfully for a long time at: *he sat on the carpet contemplating his image in the mirrors.*
■ think about: *the results of a trade war are too horrifying to contemplate.* ■ [no obj.] think profoundly and at length; meditate: *he sat morosely contemplating.* ■ have in view as a probable though not certain intention: *he was contemplating action for damages.*
– DERIVATIVES **contemplator** noun.
– ORIGIN late 16th cent.: from Latin *contemplat-* 'surveyed, observed, contemplated', from the verb *contemplari*, based on *templum* 'place for observation'.

contemplation ▶ noun [mass noun] the action of

looking thoughtfully at something for a long time: *the road is too busy for leisurely contemplation of the scenery.*
■deep reflective thought: *he would retire to his room for study or contemplation.* ■ the state of being thought about or planned: *substantial fitting work is* ***in contemplation.*** ■ religious meditation. ■ (in Christian spirituality) a form of prayer or meditation in which a person seeks to pass beyond mental images and concepts to a direct experience of the divine.
– ORIGIN Middle English: from Old French, from Latin *contemplatio(n-)*, from the verb *contemplari* (see **CONTEMPLATE**).

contemplative /kən'tɛmplətɪv/ ▶ **adjective** expressing or involving prolonged thought: *she regarded me with a contemplative eye.*
■involving or given to deep silent prayer or religious meditation: *contemplative knowledge of God.*
▶ **noun** a person whose life is devoted primarily to prayer, especially in a monastery or convent.
– DERIVATIVES **contemplatively** adverb.

contemporaneous /kən,tɛmpə'reɪnɪəs, kɒn-/ ▶ **adjective** existing or occurring in the same period of time: *Pythagoras was* ***contemporaneous with*** *Buddha.*
– DERIVATIVES **contemporaneity** noun, **contemporaneously** adverb, **contemporaneousness** noun.
– ORIGIN mid 17th cent.: from Latin, from *con-* 'together with' + *temporaneus* (from *tempus, tempor-* 'time') + **-OUS**.

contemporary /kən'tɛmp(ə)r(ər)i/ ▶ **adjective** **1** living or occurring at the same time: *the event was recorded by a contemporary historian.*
■dating from the same time: *this series of paintings is* ***contemporary with*** *other works in an early style.*
2 belonging to or occurring in the present. *the tension and complexities of our contemporary society.*
■following modern ideas or fashion in style or design: *contemporary art.*
▶ **noun** (pl. **-ies**) a person or thing living or existing at the same time as another: *he was a contemporary of Darwin.*
■a person of roughly the same age as another: *my contemporaries at school.*
– DERIVATIVES **contemporarily** adverb, **contemporariness** noun.
– ORIGIN mid 17th cent.: from medieval Latin *contemporarius*, from *con-* 'together with' + *tempus, tempor-* 'time' (on the pattern of Latin *contemporaneus* and late Latin *contemporalis*).

contempt ▶ **noun** [mass noun] the feeling that a person or a thing is beneath consideration, worthless, or deserving scorn: *he showed his contempt for his job by doing it very badly.*
■disregard for something that should be taken into account: *this action displays an arrogant* ***contempt for*** *the wishes of the majority.* ■ (also **contempt of court**) the offence of being disobedient to or disrespectful of a court of law and its officers: *several unions were held to be* ***in contempt*** *and were fined.*
– PHRASES **beneath contempt** utterly worthless or despicable. **hold someone in contempt** judge someone to have committed the offence of contempt of court: *the advocate was held in contempt for subpoenaing the judge.* **hold someone/thing in contempt** consider someone or something to be unworthy of respect or attention: *he wouldn't answer a woman he held in such contempt.*
– ORIGIN late Middle English: from Latin *contemptus*, from *contemnere* (see **CONTEMN**).

contemptible ▶ **adjective** deserving contempt; despicable: *a display of contemptible cowardice.*
– DERIVATIVES **contemptibly** adverb.
– ORIGIN late Middle English: from Old French, or from late Latin *contemptibilis*, from Latin *contemnere* (see **CONTEMN**).

contemptuous ▶ **adjective** showing contempt; scornful: *she was intolerant and* ***contemptuous of*** *the majority of the human race.*
– DERIVATIVES **contemptuously** adverb, **contemptuousness** noun.
– ORIGIN mid 16th cent. (in the sense 'despising law and order'): from medieval Latin *contemptuosus*, from Latin *contemptus* 'contempt', from *contemnere* (see **CONTEMN**).

contend ▶ **verb** **1** [no obj.] (**contend with/against**) struggle to surmount (a difficulty or danger): *she had to contend with his uncertain temper.*
■(**contend for**) engage in a struggle or campaign in order to achieve (something): *factions within the government were contending for the succession to the presidency* | [as adj. **contending**] *disputes continued between the contending parties.*
2 [with clause] assert something as a position in an argument: *he contends that the judge was wrong.*
– DERIVATIVES **contender** noun.
– ORIGIN late Middle English (in the sense 'compete for (something)'): from Old French *contendre* or Latin *contendere*, from *con-* 'with' + *tendere* 'stretch, strive'.

content[1] /kən'tɛnt/ ▶ **adjective** [attrib.] in a state of peaceful happiness: *he seemed more content, less bitter.*
■satisfied with a certain level of achievement, good fortune, etc., and not wishing for more: *he had to be* ***content with*** *third place* | [with infinitive] *the duke was content to act as Regent.*
▶ **verb** [with obj.] satisfy (someone): *nothing would content her but we should go off to Barcelona.*
■(**content oneself with**) accept as adequate despite wanting more or better: *we contented ourselves with a few small purchases.*
▶ **noun** **1** [mass noun] a state of satisfaction: *the greater part of the century was a time of content.*
2 a member of the British House of Lords who votes for a particular motion.
– PHRASES **to one's heart's content** to the full extent of one's desires: *the children could run and play to their heart's content.*
– ORIGIN late Middle English: via Old French from Latin *contentus* 'satisfied', past participle of *continere* (see **CONTAIN**).

content[2] /'kɒntɛnt/ ▶ **noun** **1** (usu. **contents**) the things that are held or included in something: *he unscrewed the top of the flask and drank the contents* | *he picked up the correspondence and scanned the contents.*
■[usu. in sing.] [with modifier] the amount of a particular constituent occurring in a substance: *soya milk has a low fat content.* ■ (**contents** or **table of contents**) a list of the titles of chapters or sections given at the front of a book or periodical: [as modifier] *the contents page.*
2 [mass noun] the substance or material dealt with in a speech, literary work, etc. as distinct from its form or style.
– DERIVATIVES **contentless** adjective.
– ORIGIN late Middle English: from medieval Latin *contentum* (plural *contenta* 'things contained'), neuter past participle of *continere* (see **CONTAIN**).

contented ▶ **adjective** happy and at ease: *I felt warm and contented.*
■expressing happiness and satisfaction: *she gave a contented little smile.* ■ willing to accept something; satisfied: *I was never* ***contented with*** *half measures.*
– DERIVATIVES **contentedly** adverb, **contentedness** noun.

contention ▶ **noun** **1** [mass noun] heated disagreement: *the captured territory was one of the main areas of contention between the two countries* | [count noun] *a long-standing contention among geographers.*
2 [count noun] an assertion, especially one maintained in argument: *they dispute the contention that changes in interest rates directly affect the price level.*
– PHRASES **in contention** having a good chance of success in a contest.
– ORIGIN late Middle English: from Latin *contentio(n-)*, from *contendere* 'strive with' (see **CONTEND**).

contentious ▶ **adjective** causing or likely to cause an argument; controversial: *a contentious issue.*
■involving heated argument: *the socio-economic plan had been the subject of contentious debate.* ■ Law of, relating to, or involving differences between contending parties. ■ (of a person) given to arguing or provoking argument.
– DERIVATIVES **contentiously** adverb, **contentiousness** noun.
– ORIGIN late Middle English: from Old French *contentieux*, from Latin *contentiosus*, from *content-* 'striven', from the verb *contendere*.

contentment ▶ **noun** [mass noun] a state of happiness and satisfaction: *he found contentment in living a simple life in the country.*
– ORIGIN late Middle English (denoting the payment of a claim): from French *contentement*, from Latin *contentus* (see **CONTENT**[1]).

conterminous /kɒn'tə:mɪnəs/ ▶ **adjective** sharing a common boundary: *the forty-eight conterminous United States.*
■having the same area, context, or meaning: *a genealogy conterminous with the history of the USA.*
– DERIVATIVES **conterminously** adverb.
– ORIGIN mid 17th cent.: from Latin *conterminus* (from *con-* 'with' + *terminus* 'boundary') + **-OUS**. Compare with **COTERMINOUS**.

contessa /kɒn'tɛsə/ ▶ **noun** an Italian countess.
– ORIGIN Italian, from late Latin *comitissa* (see **COUNTESS**).

contest ▶ **noun** /'kɒntɛst/ an event in which people compete for supremacy in a sport or other activity, or in a quality: *a tennis contest.*
■a competition for a political position: *a leadership contest.* ■ a dispute or conflict: *a contest between traditional and liberal views.*
▶ **verb** /kən'tɛst/ [with obj.] **1** engage in competition to attain (a position of power): *she declared her intention to contest the presidency.*
■take part in (a competition or election): *a coalition was formed to contest the presidential elections.*
2 oppose (an action, decision, or theory) as mistaken or wrong: *the former chairman contests his dismissal.*
■engage in dispute about: *the issues have been hotly contested.*
– PHRASES **no contest** **1** chiefly US another term for **NOLO CONTENDERE**: *he pleaded no contest to two misdemeanor counts.* **2** a decision by the referee to declare a boxing match invalid on the grounds that one or both of the boxers are not making serious efforts. ■ a competition, comparison, or choice of which the outcome is a foregone conclusion: *when the two teams faced each other it was no contest.*
– DERIVATIVES **contestable** adjective, **contester** noun.
– ORIGIN late 16th cent. (as a verb in the sense 'swear to, attest'): from Latin *contestari* 'call upon to witness, initiate an action (by calling witnesses)', from *con-* 'together' + *testare* 'to witness'. The senses 'wrangle, strive, struggle for' arose in the early 17th cent., whence the current noun and verb senses.

contestant ▶ **noun** a person who takes part in a contest or competition.
– ORIGIN mid 17th cent.: from French, present participle of *contester*, from Latin *contestari* 'call upon to witness' (see **CONTEST**).

contestation ▶ **noun** [mass noun] formal the action or process of disputing or arguing.
– ORIGIN mid 16th cent. (in the sense 'solemn appeal or protest'): from Latin *contestatio(n-)*, from *contestari* 'call upon to witness' (see **CONTEST**); reinforced by French *contestation*.

context /'kɒntɛkst/ ▶ **noun** the circumstances that form the setting for an event, statement, or idea, and in terms of which it can be fully understood and assessed: *the proposals need to be considered in the context of new European directives.*
■the parts of something written or spoken that immediately precede and follow a word or passage and clarify its meaning.
– PHRASES **in context** considered together with the surrounding words or circumstances: *the complex meaning of irony is only graspable in context.* **out of context** without the surrounding words or circumstances and so not fully understandable: *the article portrayed her as domineering by dropping quotes from her out of context.*
– DERIVATIVES **contextual** adjective, **contextually** adverb.
– ORIGIN late Middle English (denoting the construction of a text): from Latin *contextus*, from *con-* 'together' + *texere* 'to weave'.

contextualism ▶ **noun** [mass noun] Philosophy a doctrine which emphasizes the importance of the context of enquiry in a particular question.
– DERIVATIVES **contextualist** noun.

contextualize (also **-ise**) ▶ **verb** [with obj.] place or study in context: *some Christians fail to contextualize the words of Jesus.*
– DERIVATIVES **contextualization** noun.

contiguity /,kɒntɪ'gju:ɪti/ ▶ **noun** [mass noun] the state of bordering or being in direct contact with something: *nations bound together by geographical contiguity.*
■Psychology the sequential occurrence or proximity of stimulus and response, causing their association in the mind.
– ORIGIN early 16th cent.: from late Latin *contiguitas*, from Latin *contiguus* 'touching' (see **CONTIGUOUS**).

contiguous /kən'tɪgjʊəs/ ▶ **adjective** sharing a common border; touching: *the Southern Ocean is* ***contiguous with*** *the Atlantic.*
■next or together in sequence.
– DERIVATIVES **contiguously** adverb.

– ORIGIN early 16th cent.: from Latin *contiguus* 'touching', from the verb *contingere* 'be in contact, befall' (see **CONTINGENT**), + **-OUS**.

continent[1] ▶ **noun** any of the world's main continuous expanses of land (Europe, Asia, Africa, North and South America, Australia, Antarctica).
■ (also **the Continent**) the mainland of Europe as distinct from the British Isles. ■ a mainland contrasted with islands: *the maritime zone is richer in varieties of plant than the continent.*
– ORIGIN mid 16th cent. (denoting a continuous tract of land): from Latin *terra continens* 'continuous land'.

continent[2] ▶ **adjective 1** able to control movements of the bowels and bladder.
2 exercising self-restraint, especially sexually.
– DERIVATIVES **continence** noun, **continently** adverb.
– ORIGIN late Middle English (in the sense 'characterized by self-restraint'): from Latin *continent-* 'holding together, restraining oneself', from *continere* (see **CONTAIN**).

continental ▶ **adjective 1** [attrib.] forming or belonging to a continent: *continental Antarctica.*
2 (also **Continental**) coming from or characteristic of mainland Europe.
▶ **noun** an inhabitant of mainland Europe.
– DERIVATIVES **continentally** adverb.

Continental Army (in the US) the army raised by the Continental Congress of 1775, with George Washington as commander.

continental breakfast ▶ **noun** a light breakfast, typically consisting of coffee and bread rolls with butter and jam.

continental climate ▶ **noun** a relatively dry climate with very hot summers and very cold winters, characteristic of the central parts of Asia and North America.

Continental Congress (in the US) each of the three congresses held by the American colonies in revolt against British rule in 1774, 1775, and 1776 respectively. The second Congress, convened in the wake of the battles at Lexington and Concord, created a Continental Army, which fought and eventually won the American War of Independence.

continental crust ▶ **noun** Geology the relatively thick part of the earth's crust which forms the large land masses. It is generally older and more complex than the oceanic crust.

continental day ▶ **noun** Brit. a school day lasting from early morning to early afternoon.

Continental Divide the main series of mountain ridges in North America, chiefly the crests of the Rocky Mountains, which form a watershed separating the rivers flowing eastwards into the Atlantic Ocean or the Gulf of Mexico from those flowing westwards into the Pacific. Also called **GREAT DIVIDE**.

continental drift ▶ **noun** [mass noun] the gradual movement of the continents across the earth's surface through geological time.

The reality of continental drift was confirmed in the 1960s, leading to the theory of plate tectonics. It is believed that a single supercontinent called Pangaea broke up to form Gondwana and Laurasia, which further split to form the present-day continents. South America and Africa, for example, are moving apart at a rate of a few centimetres per year.

continental quilt ▶ **noun** British term for **DUVET**.

Continental roast ▶ **noun** [mass noun] dark-roasted coffee beans with a taste associated with mainland Europe.

continental shelf ▶ **noun** the area of seabed around a large land mass where the sea is relatively shallow compared with the open ocean. The continental shelf is geologically part of the continental crust.

continental slope ▶ **noun** the slope between the outer edge of the continental shelf and the deep ocean floor.

Continental System Napoleon's strategy of blockading Britain (1806–13), by which British ships were prohibited from entering the ports of France and her allies.

contingency /kən'tɪndʒ(ə)nsi/ ▶ **noun** (pl. **-ies**) a future event or circumstance which is possible but cannot be predicted with certainty: *a detailed contract which attempts to provide for all possible contingencies.*
■ a provision for such an event or circumstance: *stores were kept as a contingency against a blockade.* ■ an incidental expense: *allow an extra fifteen per cent on the budget for contingencies.* ■ [mass noun] the absence of certainty in events: *the island's public affairs can occasionally be seen to be invaded by contingency.* ■ [mass noun] Philosophy the absence of necessity; the fact of being so without having to be so.
– ORIGIN mid 16th cent. (in the philosophical sense): from late Latin *contingentia* (in its medieval Latin sense 'circumstance'), from *contingere* 'befall' (see **CONTINGENT**).

contingency fund ▶ **noun** a reserve of money set aside to cover possible unforeseen future expenses.

contingency plan ▶ **noun** a plan designed to take account of a possible future event or circumstance.

contingency table ▶ **noun** Statistics a table showing the distribution of one variable in rows and another in columns, used to study the correlation between the two variables.

contingent /kən'tɪndʒ(ə)nt/ ▶ **adjective 1** subject to chance: *the contingent nature of the job.*
■ (of losses, liabilities, etc.) that can be anticipated to arise if a particular event occurs. ■ true by virtue of the way things in fact are and not by logical necessity.
2 [predic.] (**contingent on/upon**) occurring or existing only if (certain other circumstances) are the case; dependent on: *resolution of the conflict was contingent on the signing of a ceasefire agreement.*
▶ **noun** a group of people united by some common feature, forming part of a larger group.
■ a body of troops or police sent to join a larger force in an operation.
– DERIVATIVES **contingently** adverb.
– ORIGIN late Middle English (in the sense 'of uncertain occurrence'): from Latin *contingere* 'befall', from *con-* 'together with' + *tangere* 'to touch'. The noun sense was originally 'something happening by chance', then 'a person's share resulting from a division, a quota'; the current sense dates from the early 18th cent.

continual ▶ **adjective** forming a sequence in which the same action or event is repeated frequently: *his plane went down after continual attacks.*
■ having no interruptions: *some patients need continual safeguarding.*
– DERIVATIVES **continually** adverb.
– ORIGIN Middle English: from Old French *continuel*, from *continuer* 'continue', from Latin *continuare*, from *continuus* (see **CONTINUOUS**).

USAGE For an explanation of the difference between **continual** and **continuous**, see **usage** at **CONTINUOUS**.

continuance ▶ **noun 1** [mass noun] formal the state of remaining in existence or operation: *his interests encouraged him to favour the continuance of war.*
■ the time for which a situation or action lasts: *the trademarks shall be used only during the continuance of this agreement.* ■ the state of remaining in a particular position or condition: *the king's ministers depended on his favour for their continuance in office.*
2 US Law a postponement or an adjournment.
– ORIGIN late Middle English: from Old French, from *continuer* 'continue', from Latin *continuare*, from *continuus* (see **CONTINUOUS**).

continuant ▶ **noun 1** Phonetics a consonant which is sounded with the vocal tract only partly closed, allowing the breath to pass through and the sound to be prolonged (as with *f, l, m, n, r, s, v*).
2 Philosophy & Psychology a thing that retains its identity even though its states and relations may change.
▶ **adjective** of, relating to, or denoting a continuant.
– ORIGIN early 17th cent. (as an adjective in the general sense 'continuing') : from French, from *continuer*, reinforced by Latin *continuant-* 'continuing', from the verb *continuare*, from *continuus* (see **CONTINUOUS**). Current senses date from the 19th cent.

continuation ▶ **noun** [mass noun] the action of carrying something on over a period of time or the state of being carried on: *the continuation of discussions about a permanent peace.*
■ the state of remaining in a particular position or condition. ■ [count noun] [usu. in sing.] a part that is attached to and an extension of something else: *once a separate village, it is now a continuation of the suburbs.*
– ORIGIN late Middle English: via Old French from Latin *continuatio(n-)*, from *continuare* 'continue', from *continuus* (see **CONTINUOUS**).

continuative /kən'tɪnjʊətɪv/ Linguistics ▶ **adjective** (of a word or phrase) having the function of moving a discourse or conversation forward.
▶ **noun** a word or phrase of this type (e.g. *yes, well, as I was saying*).
– ORIGIN mid 16th cent. (as a noun denoting something which brings about continuity): from late Latin *continuativus*, from *continuat-* 'continued', from the verb *continuare* (see **CONTINUE**).

continuator ▶ **noun** a person or thing that continues something or maintains continuity.
■ a person who writes a continuation of another's work.

continue ▶ **verb** (**continues**, **continued**, **continuing**) **1** [no obj.] persist in an activity or process: *he was unable to continue with his job* | [with infinitive] *prices continued to fall during April.*
■ remain in existence or operation: *discussions continued throughout the year.* ■ [with obj.] carry on with (something that one has begun): *the Archive has continued its programme of research* | [as adj. **continued**] *he asked for their continued support.* ■ remain in a specified position or state: *they have indicated their willingness to continue in office* | [with complement] *the weather continued warm and pleasant.* ■ [with adverbial of direction] carry on travelling in the same direction: *he hummed to himself as they continued northwards.*
2 recommence or resume after interruption: [with obj.] *we continue the story from the point reached in Chapter 1* | [no obj.] *the trial continues tomorrow.*
■ [no obj.] carry on speaking after a pause or interruption: *I told him he was obstructing the enquiry and he let me continue* | [with direct speech] *'Pleased to make your acquaintance,' he continued.* ■ [with obj.] US Law postpone or adjourn (a legal proceeding): *the case was continued without a finding until August 2.*
– DERIVATIVES **continuer** noun.
– ORIGIN Middle English: from Old French *continuer*, from Latin *continuare*, from *continuus* (see **CONTINUOUS**).

continued fraction ▶ **noun** Mathematics a fraction of infinite length whose denominator is a quantity plus a fraction, which latter fraction has a similar denominator, and so on.

continuing education ▶ **noun** [mass noun] education provided for adults after they have left the formal education system, consisting typically of short or part-time courses.

continuity /ˌkɒntɪ'njuːɪti/ ▶ **noun** (pl. **-ies**) [mass noun] **1** the unbroken and consistent existence or operation of something over a period of time: *a consensus favouring continuity of policy.*
■ a state of stability and the absence of disruption: *they have provided the country with a measure of continuity.* ■ (often **continuity between/with**) a connection or line of development with no sharp breaks: *a firm line of continuity between pre-war and post-war Britain.*
2 the maintenance of continuous action and self-consistent detail in the various scenes of a film or broadcast: [as modifier] *a continuity error.*
■ the linking of broadcast items, especially by a spoken commentary: [as modifier] *the BBC continuity announcer.*
– ORIGIN late Middle English: from Old French *continuite*, from Latin *continuitas*, from *continuare* 'continue', from *continuus* (see **CONTINUOUS**).

continuo /kən'tɪnjʊəʊ/ (also **basso continuo**) ▶ **noun** (pl. **-os**) [mass noun] (in baroque music) an accompanying part which includes a bass line and harmonies, typically played on a keyboard instrument and with other instruments such as cello or lute.
– ORIGIN early 18th cent.: Italian *basso continuo* 'continuous bass'.

continuous ▶ **adjective 1** forming an unbroken whole; without interruption: *the whole performance is enacted in one continuous movement.*
■ forming a series with no exceptions or reversals: *there are continuous advances in design and production.* ■ Mathematics (of a function) of which the graph is a smooth unbroken curve, i.e. one such that as the value of *x* approaches any given value *a*, the value of *f*(*x*) approaches that of *f*(*a*) as a limit.
2 Grammar another term for **PROGRESSIVE** (in sense 3).
– DERIVATIVES **continuously** adverb, **continuousness** noun.
– ORIGIN mid 17th cent.: from Latin *continuus*

'uninterrupted', from *continere* 'hang together' (from *con-* 'together with' + *tenere* 'hold') + **-ous**.

USAGE There is some overlap in meaning between **continuous** and **continual**, but the two words are not wholly synonymous. Both can mean roughly 'without interruption' (*a long and **continual** war; five years of **continuous** warfare*), but **continuous** is much more prominent in this sense and, unlike **continual**, can be used to refer to space as well as time, as in *the development forms a **continuous** line along the coast.* **Continual**, on the other hand, typically means 'happening frequently, with intervals between', as in *the bus service has been disrupted by **continual** breakdowns.* Overall, **continuous** occurs much more frequently than **continual** (around six times more often in the citations for the British National Corpus) and is found in many technical and specialist uses ranging from grammar and education to mathematics.

continuous assessment ▶ **noun** [mass noun] Brit. the evaluation of a pupil's progress throughout a course of study, as distinct from by examination.

continuous creation ▶ **noun** [mass noun] the creation of matter as a continuing process throughout time, especially as postulated in steady state theories of the universe.

continuous spectrum ▶ **noun** Physics an emission spectrum that consists of a continuum of wavelengths.

continuous stationery ▶ **noun** [mass noun] Brit. stationery, such as invoices and letterheads, printed on a long strip of paper that is often folded zigzag and is perforated to form sheets.

continuous wave ▶ **noun** an electromagnetic wave, especially a radio wave, having a constant amplitude.

continuum ▶ **noun** (pl. **continua**) [usu. in sing.] a continuous sequence in which adjacent elements are not perceptibly different from each other, but the extremes are quite distinct.
– ORIGIN mid 17th cent.: from Latin, neuter of *continuus* (see **CONTINUOUS**).

contort /kən'tɔːt/ ▶ **verb** twist or bend out of its normal shape: [with obj.] *a spasm of pain contorted his face* | [no obj.] *her face contorted with anger* | [as adj. **contorted**] *contorted limbs* | figurative *a contorted version of the truth.*
– DERIVATIVES **contortion** noun.
– ORIGIN late Middle English: from Latin *contort-* 'twisted round, brandished', from the verb *contorquere*, from *con-* 'together' + *torquere* 'twist'.

contortionist ▶ **noun** an entertainer who twists and bends their body into strange and unnatural positions.

contour ▶ **noun** (usu. **contours**) an outline, especially one representing or bounding the shape or form of something: *she traced the contours of his face with her finger* | figurative *the orchestra tend to smooth the music's contours.*
■ an outline of a natural feature such as a hill or valley: *cliffs with grassy rounded contours.* ■ short for **CONTOUR LINE**. ■ a line joining points on a diagram at which some property has the same value: *the figure shows contours of 21-cm line emission of atomic hydrogen.* ■ a way in which something varies, especially the pitch of music or the pattern of tones in an utterance.
▶ **verb** [with obj.] **1** (usu. **be contoured**) mould into a specific shape, typically one designed to fit into something else: *the compartment has been contoured with smooth rounded corners* | [as adj. **contoured**] *the contoured leather seats.*
2 mark (a map or diagram) with contour lines: [as adj. **contoured**] *a huge contoured map.*
3 (of a road or railway) follow the outline of (a topographical feature), especially along a contour line: *the road contours the hillside* | [no obj.] *the road rises sharply before contouring along the side of the fell.*
– ORIGIN mid 17th cent.: from French, from Italian *contorno*, from *contornare* 'draw in outline', from *con-* 'together'+ *tornare* 'to turn'.

contour feather ▶ **noun** any of the mainly small feathers which form the outline of an adult bird's plumage.

contour line ▶ **noun** a line on a map joining points of equal height above or below sea level.

contour map ▶ **noun** a map marked with contour lines.

contour ploughing ▶ **noun** [mass noun] ploughing along the contours of the land in order to minimize soil erosion.

contra /'kɒntrə/ (also **Contra**) ▶ **noun** a member of a guerrilla force in Nicaragua which opposed the left-wing Sandinista government 1979–90, and was supported by the US for much of that time. It was officially disbanded in 1990, after the Sandinistas' electoral defeat.
– ORIGIN abbreviation of Spanish *contrarevolucionario* 'counter-revolutionary'.

contra- /'kɒntrə/ ▶ **prefix 1** against; opposite: *contraception* | *contraflow.*
2 Music (of instruments or organ stops) pitched an octave below: *contrabass.*
– ORIGIN from Latin *contra* 'against'.

contraband /'kɒntrəband/ ▶ **noun** [mass noun] goods that have been imported or exported illegally: *customs men had searched the carriages for contraband.*
■ trade in smuggled goods: *the salt trade (and contraband in it) were very active in the town.* ■ (also **contraband of war**) goods forbidden to be supplied by neutrals to those engaged in war.
▶ **adjective** imported or exported illegally, either in defiance of a total ban or without payment of duty: *contraband brandy.*
■ relating to traffic in illegal goods: *the contraband market.*
– DERIVATIVES **contrabandist** noun.
– ORIGIN late 16th cent.: from Spanish *contrabanda*, from Italian *contrabando*, from *contra-* 'against' + *bando* 'proclamation, ban'.

contrabass ▶ **noun** another term for **DOUBLE BASS**.
▶ **adjective** [attrib.] denoting a musical instrument with a range an octave lower than the normal bass range: *a contrabass clarinet.*
– ORIGIN late 18th cent.: from Italian *contrabasso*, from *contra-* 'pitched an octave below' + *basso* (see **BASS**[1]).

contrabassoon ▶ **noun** another term for **DOUBLE BASSOON**.

contraception ▶ **noun** [mass noun] the deliberate use of artificial methods or other techniques to prevent pregnancy as a consequence of sexual intercourse. The major forms of artificial contraception are: barrier methods, of which the commonest is the condom or sheath; the contraceptive pill, which contains synthetic sex hormones which prevent ovulation in the female; intrauterine devices, such as the coil, which prevent the fertilized ovum from implanting in the uterus; and male or female sterilization.
– ORIGIN late 19th cent.: from **CONTRA-** 'against' + a shortened form of **CONCEPTION**.

contraceptive ▶ **adjective** (of a method or device) serving to prevent pregnancy: *the contraceptive pill.*
■ of or relating to contraception: *a book popularizing contraceptive knowledge.*
▶ **noun** a device or drug serving to prevent pregnancy.

contract ▶ **noun** /'kɒntrakt/ a written or spoken agreement, especially one concerning employment, sales, or tenancy, that is intended to be enforceable by law: *the company retained its £25 million catering contract* | [mass noun] *much of the produce is grown **under contract**.*
■ [mass noun] the branch of law concerned with the making and observation of such agreements. ■ informal an arrangement for someone to be killed by a hired assassin: *smuggling bosses routinely put out contracts on witnesses* | [as modifier] *a contract killer.* ■ Bridge the declarer's undertaking to win the number of tricks bid with a stated suit as trumps: *South can **make the contract** with correct play.* ■ dated a formal agreement to marry.
▶ **verb** /kən'trakt/ **1** [no obj.] decrease in size, number, or range: *glass contracts as it cools.*
■ (of a muscle) become shorter and tighter in order to effect movement of part of the body: *the heart is a muscle which contracts about seventy times a minute* | [with obj.] *the exercises contract the muscles working through the knee.* ■ [with obj.] shorten (a word or phrase) by combination or elision.
2 [no obj.] enter into a formal and legally binding agreement: *the local authority will **contract with** a wide range of agencies to provide services.*
■ (**contract in/into**) Brit. choose to be involved in (a scheme or commitment): *politically committed members contract into paying the levy.* ■ (**contract out**) Brit. choose to withdraw from or not become involved in a scheme or commitment: *plans to encourage people to **contract out of** the pension scheme.* ■ secure specified rights or undertake specified obligations in a formal and legally binding agreement: *a buyer may **contract for** the right to withhold payment* | [with infinitive] *the paper had contracted to publish extracts from the diaries.* ■ [with obj. and infinitive] impose an obligation on (someone) to do something by means of a formal agreement: *health authorities contract a hospital to treat a specific number of patients.* ■ [with obj.] (**contract something out**) arrange for work to be done by another organization: *local authorities will have to contract out waste management.* ■ [with obj.] dated formally enter into (a marriage): *kings obtained dispensations to enable them to contract politically advantageous matches.* ■ [with obj.] enter into (a friendship or other relationship): *the patterns of social relationships contracted by men and women differ.*
3 [with obj.] catch or develop (a disease or infectious agent): *three people contracted a killer virus.*
4 [with obj.] become liable to pay (a debt): *he contracted a debt of £3,300.*
– DERIVATIVES **contractive** adjective.
– ORIGIN Middle English: via Old French from Latin *contractus*, from *contract-* 'drawn together, tightened', from the verb *contrahere*, from *con-* 'together' + *trahere* 'draw'.

contractable ▶ **adjective** (of a disease) able to be caught.

contract bridge ▶ **noun** [mass noun] the standard form of the card game bridge, in which only tricks bid and won count towards the game, as opposed to auction bridge.

contractible ▶ **adjective** able to be shrunk or capable of contracting.

contractile /kən'traktʌɪl/ ▶ **adjective** Biology & Physiology capable of or producing contraction: *the contractile activity of the human colon.*
– DERIVATIVES **contractility** noun.

contractile vacuole ▶ **noun** Zoology a vacuole in some protozoans which expels excess liquid on contraction.

contraction ▶ **noun** [mass noun] the process of becoming smaller: *the general contraction of the industry did further damage to morale* | [count noun] *the manufacturing sector suffered a severe contraction.*
■ the process in which a muscle becomes or is made shorter and tighter: *neurons control the contraction of muscles* | [count noun] *repeat the exercise, holding each contraction for one second.* ■ [count noun] (usu. **contractions**) a shortening of the uterine muscles occurring at intervals before and during childbirth. ■ the process of shortening a word by combination or elision. ■ [count noun] a word or group of words resulting from shortening an original form: *'goodbye' is a contraction of 'God be with you'.*
– ORIGIN late Middle English: via Old French from Latin *contractio(n-)*, from *contrahere* 'draw together' (see **CONTRACT**).

contract note ▶ **noun** a certificate confirming the terms of a sale of specified assets or securities between two parties.

contractor ▶ **noun** a person or firm that undertakes a contract to provide materials or labour to perform a service or do a job.

contractorization (also **-isation**) ▶ **noun** [mass noun] Brit. the provision of a service, especially a public one, by an external contractor rather than by the employees of the body responsible for the service.
– DERIVATIVES **contractorize** verb.

contractual ▶ **adjective** agreed in a contract: *a contractual obligation.*
■ having similar characteristics to a contract: *the contractual nature of the shareholder's rights.*
– DERIVATIVES **contractually** adverb.

contractural ▶ **adjective 1** Medicine relating to or involving contracture.
2 another term for **CONTRACTUAL**. [ORIGIN: formed by erroneous insertion of *-r-*.]

contracture /kən'traktʃə/ ▶ **noun** [mass noun] Medicine a condition of shortening and hardening of muscles, tendons, or other tissue, often leading to deformity and rigidity of joints: *adduction contracture of the hip in cerebral palsy* | [count noun] *the contractures had been caused by intramuscular injections.*
– ORIGIN mid 17th cent.: from French, or from Latin *contractura*, from Latin *contract-* 'drawn together', from the verb *contrahere*.

contradance ▶ **noun** a country dance in which the couples form lines facing each other.
– ORIGIN early 19th cent.: variant of **CONTREDANSE**.

contradict ▶ **verb** [with obj.] deny the truth of (a

statement), especially by asserting the opposite: *the survey appears to contradict the industry's claims.* | [with clause] *he did not contradict what he said last week.*
■assert the opposite of a statement made by (someone): *he did not contradict her but just said nothing* | *within five minutes he had contradicted himself twice.* ■ be in conflict with: *the existing layout of the city contradicted the logic of the new centre.*
– DERIVATIVES **contradictor** noun.
– ORIGIN late 16th cent.: from Latin *contradict-* 'spoken against', from the verb *contradicere*, originally *contra dicere* 'speak against'.

contradiction ▶noun a combination of statements, ideas, or features of a situation which are opposed to one another: *the proposed new system suffers from a set of internal contradictions.*
■a person, thing, or situation in which inconsistent elements are present: *the paradox of using force to overcome force is a real contradiction.* ■ [mass noun] the statement of a position opposite to one already made: *the second sentence appears to be in flat contradiction of the first* | [count noun] *the experiment provides a contradiction of the hypothesis.*
– PHRASES **contradiction in terms** a statement or group of words associating objects or ideas which are incompatible.
– ORIGIN late Middle English: via Old French from Latin *contradictio(n-)*, from the verb *contradicere* (see **CONTRADICT**).

contradictory ▶adjective mutually opposed or inconsistent: *the two attitudes are contradictory.*
■containing elements which are inconsistent or in conflict: *the committee rejected the policy as too vague and internally contradictory.* ■ Logic (of two propositions) so related that one and only one must be true. Compare with **CONTRARY**.
▶noun (pl. **-ies**) Logic a contradictory proposition.
– DERIVATIVES **contradictorily** adverb, **contradictoriness** noun.
– ORIGIN late Middle English (as a term in logic denoting a proposition or principle which contradicts another): from late Latin *contradictorius*, from Latin *contradict-* 'spoken against', from the verb *contradicere* (see **CONTRADICT**).

contradistinction ▶noun [mass noun] distinction made by contrasting the different qualities of two things.

contradistinguish ▶verb [with obj.] (often **be contradistinguished**) archaic distinguish between (two things) by contrasting them.

contrafactive ▶adjective Linguistics denoting a verb that assigns to its object (normally a clausal object) the status of not being true, e.g. *pretend* and *wish.* Contrasted with **FACTIVE, NON-FACTIVE**.

contrafactual /kɒntrəˈfaktʃʊəl, -tjʊəl/ ▶adjective another term for **COUNTERFACTUAL**.

contraflow ▶noun Brit. a temporary arrangement where traffic on a road is transferred from its usual side to share the other half of the carriageway with traffic moving in the opposite direction.

contrail /ˈkɒntreɪl/ ▶noun chiefly US another term for **VAPOUR TRAIL**.
– ORIGIN 1940s: abbreviation of *condensation trail.*

contraindicate ▶verb [with obj.] (usu. **be contraindicated**) Medicine (of a condition or circumstance) suggest or indicate that (a particular technique or drug) should not be used in the case in question.
– DERIVATIVES **contraindication** noun.

contralateral /ˌkɒntrəˈlat(ə)r(ə)l/ ▶adjective Medicine relating to or denoting the side of the body opposite to that on which a particular structure or condition occurs: *the symptom develops in the hand contralateral to the lesion.*

contralto /kənˈtraltəʊ/ ▶noun (pl. **-os**) the lowest female singing voice: *she sang in a high contralto.*
■a singer with such a voice. ■ a part written for such a voice.
– ORIGIN mid 18th cent.: Italian, from *contra-* (in the sense 'counter to') + **ALTO**. Compare with **COUNTERTENOR**.

contra mundum /ˌkɒntrə ˈmʌndəm/ ▶adverb defying or opposing everyone else.
– ORIGIN Latin, 'against the world'.

contraposition ▶noun [mass noun] Logic conversion of a proposition from *all A is B* to *all not-B is not-A.*
– DERIVATIVES **contrapositive** adjective & noun.
– ORIGIN mid 16th cent.: from late Latin *contrapositio(n-)*, from the verb *contraponere*, from *contra-* 'against' + *ponere* 'to place'.

contrapposto /ˌkɒntrəˈpɒstəʊ/ ▶noun (pl. **contrapposti** /-ti/) Sculpture an asymmetrical arrangement of the human figure in which the line of the arms and shoulders contrasts with, while balancing, those of the hips and legs.
– ORIGIN Italian, past participle of *contrapporre*, from Latin *contraponere* 'place against'.

contra proferentem /ˌkɒntrə prɒfəˈrɛntɛm/ ▶adverb Law (of the interpretation of a contract) against the party which proposes or adduces the contract or a condition in the contract.
– ORIGIN Latin, 'against (the person) mentioning'.

contraption ▶noun a machine or device that appears strange or unnecessarily complicated, and often badly made or unsafe.
– ORIGIN early 19th cent.: perhaps from **CONTRIVE** (on the pattern of pairs such as *conceive, conception*), by association with **TRAP**[1].

contrapuntal /ˌkɒntrəˈpʌnt(ə)l/ ▶adjective Music of or in counterpoint.
– DERIVATIVES **contrapuntally** adverb, **contrapuntist** noun.
– ORIGIN mid 19th cent.: from Italian *contrapunto* (see **COUNTERPOINT**) + **-AL**.

contrarian /kənˈtrɛːrɪən/ ▶noun a person who opposes or rejects popular opinion, especially in stock exchange dealing.
▶adjective opposing or rejecting popular opinion; going against current practice: *the comment came more from a contrarian disposition than moral conviction.*
– DERIVATIVES **contrarianism** noun.

contrariety /ˌkɒntrəˈrʌɪəti/ ▶noun [mass noun] **1** Logic contrary opposition.
2 opposition or inconsistency between two things.
– ORIGIN late Middle English: from Old French *contrariete*, from late Latin *contrarietas*, from *contrarius* (see **CONTRARY**).

contrariwise /kənˈtrɛːrɪwʌɪz, ˈkɒntrərɪˌwʌɪz/ ▶adverb in the opposite way or order: *to act contrariwise would make him marginal to his occupational role.*
■[sentence adverb] in contrast to something that has just been stated or mentioned: *contrariwise, a registered person may vote, even if not entitled to be registered.*

contra-rotating ▶adjective rotating in the opposite direction or in opposite directions, especially about the same shaft.

contrary /ˈkɒntrəri/ ▶adjective **1** opposite in nature, direction, or meaning: *he ignored contrary advice and agreed on the deal.*
■(of two or more statements, beliefs, etc.) opposed to one another: *his mother had given him contrary messages.* ■ (of a wind) blowing in the opposite direction to one's course; unfavourable. ■ Logic (of two propositions) so related that one or neither but not both must be true. Compare with **CONTRADICTORY**.
2 /kənˈtrɛːri/ perversely inclined to disagree or to do the opposite of what is expected or desired: *she is sulky and contrary where her work is concerned.*
▶noun (pl. **-ies**) **1** (**the contrary**) the opposite: *an Act applies only to the United Kingdom unless the contrary is expressed.*
2 Logic a contrary proposition.
– PHRASES **contrary to** conflicting with or running counter to: *contrary to his expectations, he found the atmosphere exciting.* **on** (or **quite**) **the contrary** used to intensify a denial of what has just been implied or stated by suggesting that the opposite is the case: *there was no malice in her; on the contrary, she was very kind.* **to the contrary** with the opposite meaning or implication: *he continued to drink despite medical advice to the contrary.*
– DERIVATIVES **contrarily** /ˈkɒntrərɪli, kənˈtrɛːrɪli/ adverb, **contrariness** /ˈkɒntrərɪnɪs, kənˈtrɛːrɪnɪs/ noun.
– ORIGIN Middle English: from Anglo-Norman French *contrarie*, from Latin *contrarius*, from *contra* 'against'.

contrast ▶noun /ˈkɒntrɑːst/ [mass noun] the state of being strikingly different from something else, typically something in juxtaposition or close association: *the day began cold and blustery, **in contrast to** almost two weeks of uninterrupted sunshine* | [count noun] *a **contrast between** rural and urban trends.*
■the degree of difference between tones in a television picture, photograph, or other image. ■ enhancement of the apparent brightness or clarity of a design provided by the juxtaposition of different colours or textures. ■ the action of calling attention to notable differences: *use knowledge of other languages for **contrast** and comparison **with** English.* ■ [in sing.] a thing or person having qualities noticeably different from another: *the castle is quite a **contrast to** other places where the singer has performed.*
▶verb /kənˈtrɑːst/ [no obj.] differ strikingly: *his friend's success **contrasted with** his own failure* | [as adj. **contrasting**] *a contrasting view.*
■[with obj.] compare in such a way as to emphasize differences: *people **contrasted** her **with** her sister.*
– DERIVATIVES **contrastingly** adverb, **contrastive** adjective.
– ORIGIN late 17th cent. (as a term in fine art, in the sense 'juxtapose so as to bring out differences in form and colour'): from French *contraste* (noun), *contraster* (verb), via Italian from medieval Latin *contrastare*, from Latin *contra-* 'against' + *stare* 'stand'.

contrast medium ▶noun Medicine a substance introduced into a part of the body in order to improve the visibility of internal structure during radiography.

contrasty ▶adjective informal (of a photograph, film, or television picture) showing a high degree of contrast.

contra-suggestible ▶adjective tending to respond to a suggestion by believing or doing the contrary.

contrate wheel /ˈkɒntreɪt/ ▶noun another term for **CROWN WHEEL**.
– ORIGIN late 17th cent.: *contrate* (a rare adjective meaning 'opposed, contrary') from medieval Latin *contrata* 'lying opposite', from Latin *contra* 'against'.

contravene /ˌkɒntrəˈviːn/ ▶verb [with obj.] offend against the prohibition or order of (a law, treaty, or code of conduct): *he contravened the Official Secrets Act.*
■conflict with (a right, principle, etc.), especially to its detriment: *the Privy Council held that the prosecution contravened the rights of the individual.*
– DERIVATIVES **contravener** noun.
– ORIGIN mid 16th cent.: from late Latin *contravenire*, from Latin *contra-* 'against' + *venire* 'come'.

contravention ▶noun an action which offends against a law, treaty, or other ruling: *the publishing of misleading advertisements was a contravention of the Act* | [mass noun] *contravention of parking restrictions.*
– PHRASES **in contravention of** in a manner contrary and disobedient to (a law or other ruling).
– ORIGIN mid 16th cent.: via French from medieval Latin *contraventio(n-)*, from late Latin *contravenire* (see **CONTRAVENE**).

contredanse /ˈkɒntrədɑːns, -dɒ̃s/ ▶noun (pl. same) a French form of country dance, originating in the 18th century and related to the quadrille.
■a piece of music for such a dance. ■ another term for **CONTRADANCE**.
– ORIGIN French, alteration of English **COUNTRY DANCE**, by association with *contre* 'against, opposite'.

contre-jour /ˈkɒ̃trəˌʒʊə, French kɔ̃trəʒuʀ/ ▶adjective & adverb Photography having or involving the sun or other light source behind the subject: [as adj.] *a glorious contre-jour effect* | [as adv.] *it is recommended not to use the film contre-jour.*
– ORIGIN early 20th cent.: French, from *contre* 'against' + *jour* 'daylight'.

contretemps /ˈkɒntrətɒ̃/ ▶noun (pl. same /-tɒ̃z/) a minor dispute or disagreement: *she had occasional contretemps with her staff.*
■an unexpected and unfortunate occurrence.
– ORIGIN late 17th cent. (originally as a fencing term, denoting a thrust made at an inopportune moment): French, originally 'motion out of time', from *contre-* 'against' + *temps* 'time'.

contribute /kənˈtrɪbjuːt, ˈkɒntrɪbjuːt/ ▶verb [with obj.] give (something, especially money) in order to help achieve or provide something: *taxpayers had **contributed** £141.8 million **towards** the cost of local services* | [no obj.] *he **contributed to** a private pension.*
■[no obj.] (**contribute to**) help to cause or bring about: *the government imposed a tax on fuels which contributed to global warming.* ■ supply (an article) for publication: *he **contributed** articles **to** the magazine* | [no obj.] *the staff who **contribute to** your sports pages are doing a splendid job.* ■ [no obj.] give one's views in a discussion: *he did not **contribute to** the meetings.*
– DERIVATIVES **contributive** /kənˈtrɪb-/ adjective.
– ORIGIN mid 16th cent.: from Latin *contribut-* 'brought together, added', from the verb *contribuere*, from *con-* 'with' + *tribuere* 'bestow'.

USAGE There are two possible pronunciations of the word **contribute**, one which puts the stress on the **-tri-** and one which puts it on the **con-**. The first is held to be the standard, correct pronunciation even though the pronunciation with stress on the **con-** is older.

C

contribution ▶ **noun** a gift or payment to a common fund or collection: *the agency is mainly financed from voluntary contributions.*
■ the part played by a person or thing in bringing about a result or helping something to advance: *the major contribution of social scientists to the understanding of political life.* ■ an article or other piece of writing submitted for publication in a collection.
– ORIGIN late Middle English (denoting a tax or levy): from late Latin *contributio(n-)*, from Latin *contribuere* 'bring together, add' (see **CONTRIBUTE**).

contributor ▶ **noun** a person or thing that contributes something, in particular:
■ a person who writes articles for a magazine or newspaper. ■ a person who donates to a cause. ■ a causal factor in the existence or occurrence of something.

contributory ▶ **adjective 1** playing a part in bringing something about: *smoking may be a contributory cause of lung cancer.*
2 (of a pension or insurance scheme) operated by means of a fund into which people pay: *contributory benefits.*
▶ **noun** (pl. **-ies**) Law, Brit. a person liable to give money towards the payment of a wound-up company's debts.
– ORIGIN late Middle English (in the sense 'contributing to a fund'): from medieval Latin *contributorius*, from Latin *contribut-* 'added' (see **CONTRIBUTION**).

contributory negligence ▶ **noun** [mass noun] Law failure of an injured party to act prudently, considered to be a contributory factor in the injury which he or she has suffered.

con trick ▶ **noun** informal term for **CONFIDENCE TRICK**.

contrite /'kɒntrʌɪt/ ▶ **adjective** feeling or expressing remorse at the recognition that one has done wrong: *a contrite tone.*
– DERIVATIVES **contritely** adverb, **contriteness** noun.
– ORIGIN Middle English: from Old French *contrit*, from Latin *contritus*, past participle of *conterere* 'grind down, wear away', from *con-* 'together' + *terere* 'rub'.

contrition ▶ **noun** [mass noun] the state of feeling remorseful and penitent.
■ (in the Roman Catholic Church) the repentance of past sins during or after confession: *prayers of contrition.*
– ORIGIN Middle English: via Old French from late Latin *contritio(n-)*, from *contrit-* 'ground down', from the verb *conterere* (see **CONTRITE**).

contrivance ▶ **noun** [mass noun] the use of skill to bring something about or create something, especially when this results in a sense of strain and artificiality: *the story is told with an absence of contrivance or literary device.*
■ [count noun] a thing which is created skilfully and inventively to serve a particular purpose: *an assortment of electronic equipment and mechanical contrivances.* ■ [count noun] a device, especially in literary or artistic composition, which gives a sense of artificiality.

contrive /kən'trʌɪv/ ▶ **verb** [with obj.] create or bring about (an object or a situation) by deliberate use of skill and artifice: *his opponents contrived a cabinet crisis* | [with infinitive] *you contrived to be alone with me despite the supervision.*
■ [with infinitive] manage to do something foolish or create an undesirable situation: *he contrived to flood the flat three times.*
– DERIVATIVES **contrivable** adjective, **contriver** noun.
– ORIGIN Middle English: from Old French *contreuve-*, stressed stem of *controver* 'imagine, invent', from medieval Latin *contropare* 'compare'.

contrived ▶ **adjective** deliberately created rather than arising naturally or spontaneously: *the carefully contrived image of party unity.*
■ giving a sense of artificiality: *the ending of the novel is too pat and contrived.*

control ▶ **noun 1** [mass noun] the power to influence or direct people's behaviour or the course of events: *the whole operation is* ***under the control of*** *a production manager* | *the situation was slipping* ***out of*** *her control.*
■ the restriction of an activity, tendency, or phenomenon: *crime control.* ■ the power to restrain something, especially one's own emotions or actions: *she was goaded beyond control.* ■ [count noun] (often **controls**) a means of limiting or regulating something: *growing* ***controls on*** *local spending.* ■ [count noun] a switch or other device by which a machine is regulated: *the volume control.* ■ [with modifier] the place where a particular item is verified: *passport control.* ■ the base from which a system or activity is directed: *communications could be established with central control.* ■ [count noun] Bridge a high card that will prevent the opponents from establishing a particular suit. ■ Computing short for **CONTROL KEY**.
2 a group or individual used as a standard of comparison for checking the results of a survey or experiment: *platelet activity was higher in patients with the disease than in the controls.*
3 [count noun] a member of an intelligence organization who personally directs the activities of a spy.
▶ **verb** (**controlled**, **controlling**) **1** [with obj.] determine the behaviour or supervise the running of: *he was appointed to control the company's marketing strategy.*
■ maintain influence or authority over: *there were never enough masters to control the unruly mobs of boys.* ■ limit the level, intensity, or numbers of: *he had to control his temper.* ■ (**control oneself**) remain calm and reasonable despite provocation. ■ regulate (a mechanical or scientific process): *the airflow is controlled by a fan.* ■ [as adj. **controlled**] (of a drug) restricted by law in respect of use and possession: *a sentence for possessing controlled substances.*
2 [no obj.] (**control for**) take into account (an extraneous factor that might affect the results of an experiment): *no attempt was made to control for variations* | [as adj. **controlled**] *a controlled trial.*
– PHRASES **in control** able to direct a situation, person, or activity. **out of control** no longer possible to manage. **under control** (of a danger or emergency) such that people are able to deal with it successfully and competently: *it took two hours to bring the blaze under control.*
– DERIVATIVES **controllability** noun, **controllable** adjective, **controllably** adverb.
– ORIGIN late Middle English (as a verb in the sense 'check or verify accounts', especially by referring to a duplicate register): from Anglo-Norman French *contreroller* 'keep a copy of a roll of accounts', from medieval Latin *contrarotulare*, from *contrarotulus* 'copy of a roll', from *contra-* 'against' + *rotulus* 'a roll'. The noun is perhaps via French *contrôle*.

control account ▶ **noun** an account used to record the balances on a number of subsidiary accounts and to provide a cross-check on them.

control character ▶ **noun** Computing a character that does not represent a printable character but serves to initiate a particular action.

control key ▶ **noun** Computing a key which alters the function of another key if they are pressed at the same time.

controller ▶ **noun** a person or thing that directs or regulates something: *the Controller of BBC Television Programmes* | *a temperature controller.*
■ a person in charge of an organization's finances.
– DERIVATIVES **controllership** noun.
– ORIGIN Middle English (denoting a person who kept a duplicate register of accounts): from Anglo-Norman *contrerollour*, from *contreroller* 'keep a copy of a roll of accounts' (see **CONTROL**). Compare with **COMPTROLLER**.

controlling interest ▶ **noun** the holding by one person or group of a majority of the stock of a business, giving the holder a means of exercising control: *the purchase of a* ***controlling interest*** *in a company in California.*

control rod ▶ **noun** a rod of a neutron-absorbing substance used to vary the output power of a nuclear reactor.

control tower ▶ **noun** a tall building at an airport from which the movements of air traffic are controlled.

controversial ▶ **adjective** giving rise or likely to give rise to public disagreement: *years of wrangling over a controversial bypass.*
– DERIVATIVES **controversialist** noun, **controversially** adverb.
– ORIGIN late 16th cent.: from late Latin *controversialis*, from *controversia* (see **CONTROVERSY**).

controversy /'kɒntrəvəːsi, kən'trɒvəsi/ ▶ **noun** (pl. **-ies**) [mass noun] disagreement, typically when prolonged, public, and heated: *security laws passed to tackle terrorism caused controversy* | [count noun] *the announcement ended a protracted controversy.*
– ORIGIN late Middle English: from Latin *controversia*, from *controversus* 'turned against, disputed', from *contro-* (variant of *contra-* 'against') + *versus*, past participle of *vertere* 'to turn'.

USAGE There are two possible pronunciations of the word **controversy**: one puts the stress on the **con-** and the other puts it on the **-trov-**. The second pronunciation, though common, is still widely held to be incorrect in standard English.

controvert ▶ **verb** [with obj.] deny the truth of (something): *subsequent work from the same laboratory controverted these results.*
■ argue about (something): *the views in the article have been controverted.*
– DERIVATIVES **controvertible** adjective.
– ORIGIN mid 16th cent.: from Latin *controversus* (see **CONTROVERSY**), on the pattern of pairs such as *adversus* (see **ADVERSE**), *advertere* (see **ADVERT**[2]).

contumacious /ˌkɒntjʊ'meɪʃəs/ ▶ **adjective** archaic or Law (especially of a defendant's behaviour) stubbornly or wilfully disobedient to authority.
– DERIVATIVES **contumaciously** adverb.
– ORIGIN late 16th cent.: from Latin *contumax*, *contumac-* (perhaps from *con-* 'with' + *tumere* 'to swell') + **-IOUS**.

contumacy /'kɒntjʊməsi/ ▶ **noun** [mass noun] archaic or Law stubborn refusal to obey or comply with authority, especially disobedience to a court order or summons.
– ORIGIN Middle English: from Latin *contumacia* 'inflexibility', from *contumax* (see **CONTUMACIOUS**).

contumelious /ˌkɒntjʊ'miːlɪəs/ ▶ **adjective** archaic (of behaviour) scornful and insulting; insolent.
– DERIVATIVES **contumeliously** adverb.
– ORIGIN late Middle English: from Old French *contumelieus*, from Latin *contumeliosus*, from *contumelia* 'abuse, insult' (see **CONTUMELY**).

contumely /'kɒntjuːmɪli, -tjuːmli/ ▶ **noun** (pl. **-ies**) [mass noun] archaic insolent or insulting language or treatment: *the church should not be exposed to gossip and contumely.*
– ORIGIN late Middle English: from Old French *contumelie*, from Latin *contumelia*, perhaps from *con-* 'with' + *tumere* 'to swell'.

contuse /kən'tjuːz/ ▶ **verb** [with obj.] (usu. **be contused**) Medicine injure (a part of the body) without breaking the skin, forming a bruise.
– ORIGIN late Middle English: from Latin *contus-* 'bruised, crushed', from the verb *contundere*, from *con-* 'together' + *tundere* 'beat, thump'.

contusion /kən'tjuːʒ(ə)n/ ▶ **noun** a region of injured tissue or skin in which blood capillaries have been ruptured; a bruise.
– ORIGIN late Middle English: from French, from Latin *contusio(n-)*, from the verb *contundere* (see **CONTUSE**).

conundrum /kə'nʌndrəm/ ▶ **noun** (pl. **conundrums**) a confusing and difficult problem or question: *one of the most difficult conundrums for the experts.*
■ a question asked for amusement, typically one with a pun in its answer; a riddle.
– ORIGIN late 16th cent.: of unknown origin, but first recorded in a work by Thomas Nashe, as a term of abuse for a crank or pedant, later coming to denote a whim or fancy, also a pun. Current senses date from the late 17th cent.

conurbation /ˌkɒnə'beɪʃ(ə)n/ ▶ **noun** an extended urban area, typically consisting of several towns merging with the suburbs of a central city.
– ORIGIN early 20th cent.: from **CON-** 'together' + Latin *urbs*, *urb-* 'city' + **-ATION**.

conure /'kɒnjʊə/ ▶ **noun** a Central and South American parakeet that typically has green plumage with patches of other colours.
● *Aratinga*, *Pyrrhura*, and other genera, family Psittacidae: numerous species.
– ORIGIN mid 19th cent.: from modern Latin *conurus* (former genus name), from Greek *kōnos* 'cone' + *oura* 'tail'.

conus /'kəʊnəs/ ▶ **noun** (pl. **coni** /-nʌɪ/) Anatomy **1** (in full **conus arteriosus** /ɑːˌtɪərɪ'əʊsəs/) the upper front part of the right ventricle of the heart.
2 (in full **conus medullaris** /ˌmɛdə'lɑːrɪs/) the conical lower extremity of the spinal cord.
– ORIGIN late 19th cent.: from Latin, literally 'cone'.

convalesce /ˌkɒnvəˈlɛs/ ▶ verb [no obj.] recover one's health and strength over a period of time after an illness or medical treatment: *he spent eight months convalescing after the stroke.*
– ORIGIN late 15th cent.: from Latin *convalescere*, from *con-* 'altogether' + *valescere* 'grow strong' (from *valere* 'be well').

convalescent ▶ adjective (of a person) recovering from an illness or medical treatment.
■ [attrib.] relating to convalescence: *a convalescent home.*
▶ noun a person who is recovering after an illness or medical treatment.
– DERIVATIVES **convalescence** noun.
– ORIGIN mid 17th cent.: from Latin *convalescent-* 'growing strong, recovering', from the verb *convalescere* (see **CONVALESCE**).

convect /kənˈvɛkt/ ▶ verb [with obj.] transport (heat or material) by convection: *this gas fire convects heat efficiently* | [as adj. **convected**] *convected warmth.*
■ [no obj.] (of a fluid or fluid body) undergo convection: *the fluid starts to convect* | [as adj. **convecting**] *the convecting layer.*
– ORIGIN late 19th cent.: back-formation from **CONVECTION**.

convection ▶ noun [mass noun] the movement caused within a fluid by the tendency of hotter and therefore less dense material to rise, and colder, denser material to sink under the influence of gravity, which consequently results in transfer of heat.
– DERIVATIVES **convectional** adjective, **convective** adjective.
– ORIGIN mid 19th cent.: from late Latin *convectio(n-)*, from Latin *convehere*, from *con-* 'together' + *vehere* 'carry'.

convection cell ▶ noun a self-contained convective zone in a fluid in which upward motion of warmer fluid in the centre is balanced by downward motion of cooler fluid at the periphery.

convection current ▶ noun a current in a fluid that results from convection.

convector ▶ noun a heating appliance that circulates warm air by convection.

convenance /ˈkɒnvəˌnɑːns/ ▶ noun [mass noun] (also **convenances**) archaic conventional propriety.
– ORIGIN French, from *convenir* 'be fitting', from Latin *convenire* (see **CONVENE**).

convene /kənˈviːn/ ▶ verb [with obj.] call people together for (a meeting): *he had convened a secret meeting of military personnel.*
■ assemble or cause to assemble for a common purpose: [with obj.] *the head convened an informal working party* | [no obj.] *the committee had convened for its final plenary session.*
– DERIVATIVES **convenable** adjective.
– ORIGIN late Middle English: from Latin *convenire* 'assemble, agree, fit', from *con-* 'together' + *venire* 'come'.

convener (also **convenor**) ▶ noun a person whose job it is to call people together for meetings of a committee.
■ Brit. a senior trade union official at a workplace. ■ the chairman and civic head of some regional Scottish councils.

convenience ▶ noun 1 [mass noun] the state of being able to proceed with something with little effort or difficulty: *the sequence has been simplified for convenience.*
■ the quality of contributing to such a state: *the success of the food halls in large stores is due to their convenience.* ■ [count noun] a thing that contributes to an easy and effortless way of life: *voicemail was seen as one of the desktop conveniences of the electronic office.*
2 [count noun] Brit. a public toilet.
– PHRASES **at one's convenience** at a time or place that suits one. **at one's earliest convenience** as soon as one can without difficulty.
– ORIGIN late Middle English: from Latin *convenientia*, from *convenient-* 'assembling, agreeing', from the verb *convenire* (see **CONVENE**).

convenience food ▶ noun a food, typically a complete meal, that has been pre-prepared commercially and so requires minimum further preparation by the consumer.

convenience store ▶ noun chiefly N. Amer. a shop with extended opening hours, stocking a limited range of household goods and groceries.

conveniency ▶ noun rare term for **CONVENIENCE** (in sense 1).

convenient ▶ adjective fitting in well with a person's needs, activities, and plans: *I phoned your office to confirm that this date is convenient.*
■ involving little trouble or effort: *the new car park will make shopping much more convenient.* ■ [predic.] (**convenient for**) situated so as to allow easy access to: *the site would have to be convenient for London.* ■ occurring in a place or at a time that is useful: *guests were relaxing beneath a convenient palm tree.*
– DERIVATIVES **conveniently** adverb [sentence adverb] *he lived, conveniently, in Paris.*
– ORIGIN late Middle English (in the sense 'befitting, becoming, suitable'): from Latin *convenient-* 'assembling, agreeing, fitting', from the verb *convenire* (see **CONVENE**).

convenor ▶ noun variant spelling of **CONVENER**.

convent ▶ noun a Christian community under monastic vows, especially one of nuns.
■ (also **convent school**) a school, especially one for girls, attached to and run by such a community. ■ the building or buildings occupied by such a community.
– ORIGIN Middle English: from Old French, from Latin *conventus* 'assembly, company', from the verb *convenire* (see **CONVENE**). The original spelling was *covent* (surviving in the place name *Covent Garden*); the modern form dates from the 16th cent.

conventicle /kənˈvɛntɪk(ə)l/ ▶ noun historical a secret or unlawful religious meeting, typically of people with nonconformist views.
– ORIGIN late Middle English (in the general sense 'assembly, meeting', particularly a clandestine or illegal one): from Latin *conventiculum* '(place of) assembly', diminutive of *conventus* 'assembly, company', from the verb *convenire* (see **CONVENE**).

convention ▶ noun 1 a way in which something is usually done, especially within a particular area or activity: *the pictorial conventions of mass-media imagery.*
■ [mass noun] behaviour that is considered acceptable or polite to most members of a society: *he was an upholder of convention and correct form* | [count noun] *the law is felt to express social conventions.* ■ Bridge a bid or system of bidding by which the bidder tries to convey specific information about the hand to their partner, as opposed to seeking to win the auction.
2 an agreement between states covering particular matters, especially one less formal than a treaty.
3 a large meeting or conference, especially of members of a political party or a particular profession: *the party held its biennial convention.*
■ N. Amer. an assembly of the delegates of a political party to select candidates for office. ■ an organized meeting of enthusiasts for a television programme, film, or literary genre: *a Star Trek convention.* ■ a body set up by agreement to deal with a particular issue. ■ historical a meeting of Parliament without a summons from the sovereign.
– ORIGIN late Middle English (in sense 3): via Old French from Latin *conventio(n-)* 'meeting, covenant', from the verb *convenire* (see **CONVENE**). Sense 1 dates from the late 18th cent.

conventional ▶ adjective based on or in accordance with what is generally done or believed: *a conventional morality had dictated behaviour.*
■ (of a person) concerned with what is generally held to be acceptable at the expense of individuality and sincerity. ■ (of a work of art or literature) following traditional forms and genres rather than drawn directly from nature: *conventional love poetry.* ■ (of weapons or power) non-nuclear: *agreement on reducing conventional forces in Europe.* ■ Bridge (of a bid) intended to convey a particular meaning according to an agreed convention. Often contrasted with **NATURAL**.
– DERIVATIVES **conventionalism** noun, **conventionalist** noun, **conventionality** noun, **conventionalize** (also **-ise**) verb, **conventionally** adverb.
– ORIGIN late 15th cent. (in the sense 'relating to a formal agreement or convention'): from French *conventionnel* or late Latin *conventionalis*, from Latin *conventio(n-)* 'meeting, covenant', from the verb *convenire* (see **CONVENE**).

conventional memory ▶ noun [mass noun] Computing (in a personal computer running DOS) the first 640 k of memory where programs to be run must be loaded.

conventioneer ▶ noun N. Amer. a person attending a convention.

conventual /kənˈvɛntʃʊəl/ ▶ adjective relating or belonging to a convent: *the conventual life.*
■ relating to the less strict order of the Franciscans, living in large convents.
▶ noun a person who lives in or is a member of a convent.
– ORIGIN late Middle English: from medieval Latin *conventualis*, from Latin *conventus* 'assembly, company' (see **CONVENT**).

converge /kənˈvəːdʒ/ ▶ verb [no obj.] (of several people or things) come together from different directions so as eventually to meet: *convoys from America and the UK traversed thousands of miles to converge in the Atlantic* | figurative *two separate people whose lives converge briefly from time to time.*
■ (**converge on/upon**) come from different directions and meet at (a place): *half a million sports fans will converge on the capital for the London Marathon.* ■ (of a number of things) gradually change so as to become similar or develop something in common: *the aims of the two developments can and should converge.* ■ (of lines) tend to meet at a point: *a pair of lines of longitude are parallel at the equator but converge toward the poles.* ■ Mathematics (of a series) approximate in the sum of its terms towards a definite limit: *the powers of E therefore converge very slowly indeed.*
– ORIGIN late 17th cent.: from late Latin *convergere*, from *con-* 'together' + Latin *vergere* 'incline'.

convergence (also **convergency**) ▶ noun [mass noun] the process or state of converging: *the convergence of lines in the distance.*
■ Biology the tendency of unrelated animals and plants to evolve superficially similar characteristics under similar environmental conditions. ■ (also **convergence zone**) a location where airflows or ocean currents meet, characteristically marked by upwelling (of air) or downwelling (of water).

convergent ▶ adjective coming closer together, especially in characteristics or ideas: *there are a number of convergent reasons for the growth of interest in pragmatics.*
■ relating to convergence: *a convergent boundary.* ■ Mathematics (of a series) approaching a definite limit as more of its terms are added. ■ Biology relating to or denoting evolutionary convergence. ■ (of thought) tending to follow well-established patterns.
– ORIGIN early 18th cent.: from late Latin *convergent-* 'inclining together', from the verb *convergere* (see **CONVERGE**).

conversant ▶ adjective [predic.] familiar with or knowledgeable about something: *he was fully conversant with the principles of word processing.*
– DERIVATIVES **conversance** noun, **conversancy** noun.
– ORIGIN Middle English: from Old French, present participle of *converser* (see **CONVERSE**¹). The original sense was 'habitually spending time in a particular place or with a particular person'.

conversation ▶ noun a talk, especially an informal one, between two or more people, in which news and ideas are exchanged: *she picked up the phone and held a conversation in French* | [mass noun] *the two men were deep in conversation.*
– PHRASES **make conversation** talk for the sake of politeness without having anything to say.
– ORIGIN Middle English (in the sense 'living among, familiarity, intimacy'): via Old French from Latin *conversatio(n-)*, from the verb *conversari* (see **CONVERSE**¹).

conversational ▶ adjective appropriate to an informal conversation: *his tone was casual and conversational.*
■ consisting of or relating to conversation: *conversational skills.*
– DERIVATIVES **conversationally** adverb.

conversationalist ▶ noun a person who is good at or fond of engaging in conversation.

conversation piece ▶ noun 1 a type of genre painting in which a group of figures are posed in a landscape or domestic setting, popular especially in the 18th century.
2 an object whose unusual quality makes it a topic of conversation.

conversazione /ˌkɒnvəsatsɪˈəʊneɪ/ ▶ noun (pl. **conversaziones** or **conversazioni** pronunc. same) a scholarly social gathering held for discussion of literature and the arts.
– ORIGIN Italian, from Latin *conversatio* (see **CONVERSATION**).

converse¹ ▶ verb /kənˈvəːs/ [no obj.] engage in conversation: *she was withdrawn and preoccupied, hardly able to converse with her mother.*
▶ noun /ˈkɒnvəːs/ [mass noun] archaic conversation.

– DERIVATIVES **converser** noun.
– ORIGIN late Middle English (in the sense 'live among, be familiar with'): from Old French *converser*, from Latin *conversari* 'keep company (with)', from *con-* 'with' + *versare*, frequentative of *vertere* 'to turn'. The current sense of the verb dates from the early 17th cent.

converse[2] /ˈkɒnvəːs/ ▶ **noun** a situation, object, or statement that is the reverse of another or corresponds to it but with certain terms transposed: *if spirituality is properly political, the converse is also true: politics is properly spiritual.*
■ Mathematics a theorem whose hypothesis and conclusion are the conclusion and hypothesis of another.
▶ **adjective** having characteristics which are the reverse of something else already mentioned: *the only mode of change will be the slow process of growth and the converse process of decay.*
– ORIGIN late Middle English: from Latin *conversus* 'turned about', past participle of *convertere* (see **CONVERT**).

conversely ▶ **adverb** introducing a statement or idea which reverses one that has just been made or referred to: *he would have preferred his wife not to work, although conversely he was also proud of what she did.*

conversion ▶ **noun 1** [mass noun] the process or action of changing or causing something to change from one form to another: *the conversion of food into body tissues.*
■ the fact of changing one's religion or beliefs or the action of persuading someone else to change theirs. ■ Christian Theology repentance and change to a godly life. ■ the adaptation of a building for a new purpose: *the conversion of a house into flats* | [count noun] *they were carrying out a loft conversion.* ■ [count noun] Brit. a building or part of a building that has been adapted in this way: *the modern landscape, where barn conversions harbour computer hardware.* ■ Law the changing of real property into personalty, or of joint into separate property, or vice versa. ■ Psychiatry the manifestation of a mental disturbance as a physical disorder or disease: [as modifier] *conversion disorders.* ■ Logic the transposition of the subject and predicate of a proposition according to certain rules to form a new proposition by inference.
2 Rugby a successful kick at goal after a try, scoring two points.
■ American Football the act of converting a touchdown or a down.
3 [mass noun] Law the action of wrongfully dealing with goods in a manner inconsistent with the owner's rights: *he was found guilty of the* ***fraudulent conversion*** *of clients' monies.*
– ORIGIN Middle English (in the sense 'turning of sinners to God'): via Old French from Latin *conversio(n-)*, from *convers-* 'turned about', from the verb *convertere* (see **CONVERT**).

conversion factor ▶ **noun 1** an arithmetical multiplier for converting a quantity expressed in one set of units into an equivalent expressed in another.
2 Economics the manufacturing cost of a product relative to the cost of raw materials.

convert ▶ **verb** /kənˈvəːt/ **1** [with obj.] cause to change in form, character, or function: *modernization has* ***converted*** *the country* ***from*** *a primitive society* ***to*** *a near-industrial one*
■ [no obj.] change or be able to change from one form to another: *the seating* ***converts to*** *a double or two single beds.* ■ [no obj.] change one's religious faith or other beliefs: *at sixteen he* ***converted to*** *Catholicism.* ■ persuade (someone) to do this: *he was* ***converted*** *in his later years* ***to*** *the socialist cause.* ■ change (money, stocks, or units in which a quantity is expressed) into others of a different kind. ■ adapt (a building) to make it suitable for a new purpose: *the company converted a disused cinema to house twelve machinists* | [as adj. **converted**] *a converted Victorian property.* ■ Logic transpose the subject and predicate of (a proposition) according to certain rules to form a new proposition by inference.
2 [with obj.] score from (a penalty kick, pass, or other opportunity) in a sport or game.
■ Rugby score extra points after (a try) by a successful kick at goal. ■ American Football advance the ball far enough after (a down) to get another try for a first down. ■ American Football make an extra score after (a touchdown) by kicking a goal (one point) or running another play into the end zone (two points).
▶ **noun** /ˈkɒnvəːt/ a person who has been persuaded to change their religious faith or other beliefs: *he is a recent* ***convert to*** *the church.*
– PHRASES **convert something to one's own use** Law wrongfully make use of another's property.
– ORIGIN Middle English (in the sense 'turn round, send in a different direction'): from Old French *convertir*, based on Latin *convertere* 'turn about', from *con-* 'altogether' + *vertere* 'turn'.

converted rice ▶ **noun** [mass noun] N. Amer. (trademark in the US) white rice prepared from brown rice that has been soaked, steamed under pressure, and then dried and milled.

converter (also **convertor**) ▶ **noun** a person or thing that converts something: *the would-be converter of a building to domestic use.*
■ a device for altering the nature of an electric current or signal, especially from AC to DC or vice versa, or from analogue to digital or vice versa. ■ a retort used in steel-making. ■ short for **CATALYTIC CONVERTER**. ■ Computing a program that converts data from one format to another. ■ a camera lens which changes the focal length of another lens by a set amount: *a camera fitted with a x2 converter.*

converter reactor ▶ **noun** a nuclear reactor that converts fertile material into fissile material.

convertible ▶ **adjective** able to be changed in form, function, or character: *a convertible sofa* | *nationalism is too easily* ***convertible into*** *bitterness and selfishness.*
■ (of currency) able to be converted into other forms, especially into gold or US dollars. ■ (of a bond or stock) able to be converted into ordinary or preference shares. ■ (of a car) having a folding or detachable roof. ■ Logic (of terms) synonymous.
▶ **noun 1** a car with a folding or detachable roof.
2 (usu. **convertibles**) a convertible security.
– DERIVATIVES **convertibility** noun.
– ORIGIN late Middle English (in the sense 'interchangeable'): from Old French, from Latin *convertibilis*, from *convertere* 'turn about' (see **CONVERT**).

convex /ˈkɒnvɛks/ ▶ **adjective 1** having an outline or surface curved like the exterior of a circle or sphere. Compare with **CONCAVE**.
2 (of a polygon) not having any interior angles greater than 180°.
– DERIVATIVES **convexity** noun, **convexly** adverb.
– ORIGIN late 16th cent.: from Latin *convexus* 'vaulted, arched'.

convexo-concave /kənˈvɛksəʊ/ ▶ **adjective** (of a lens) convex on one side and concave on the other and thickest in the centre.

convexo-convex ▶ **adjective** another term for **BICONVEX**.

convey /kənˈveɪ/ ▶ **verb** [with obj.] transport or carry to a place: *pipes were laid to* ***convey*** *water* ***to*** *the house.*
■ make (an idea, impression, or feeling) known or understandable to someone: *the real virtues and diversity of America had never been conveyed in the movies* | [with clause] *it's impossible to convey how lost I felt.* ■ communicate (a message or information): *Mr Harvey and his daughter have asked me to convey their very kind regards.* ■ Law transfer the title to (property).
– DERIVATIVES **conveyable** adjective.
– ORIGIN Middle English (in the sense 'escort'; compare with **CONVOY**): from Old French *conveier*, from medieval Latin *conviare*, from *con-* 'together' + Latin *via* 'way'.

conveyance ▶ **noun** [mass noun] **1** the action or process of transporting or carrying someone or something from one place to another: *a busy centre for the conveyance of agricultural produce from the Billingshurst area.*
■ [count noun] formal or humorous a means of transport; a vehicle: *adventurers attempt the trail using all manner of conveyances, including mountain bikes and motorcycles.* ■ the action of making an idea, feeling, or impression known or understandable to someone: *art's conveyance of meaning is complicated.*
2 Law the legal process of transferring property from one owner to another: *protective measures that might be taken before the conveyance is concluded.*
■ [count noun] a legal document effecting such a process in the case of an unregistered title.

conveyancing ▶ **noun** [mass noun] the branch of law concerned with the preparation of documents for the conveyance of property.
■ the action of preparing documents for the conveyance of property.
– DERIVATIVES **conveyancer** noun.

conveyor (also **conveyer**) ▶ **noun** a person or thing that transports or communicates something: *a conveyor of information.*
■ a conveyor belt.

conveyor belt ▶ **noun** a continuous moving band of fabric, rubber, or metal used for transporting objects from one place to another.

convict ▶ **verb** /kənˈvɪkt/ [with obj.] (often **be convicted**) declare (someone) to be guilty of a criminal offence by the verdict of a jury or the decision of a judge in a court of law: *her former boyfriend was* ***convicted of*** *assaulting her* | [as adj. **convicted**] *a convicted murderer.*
▶ **noun** /ˈkɒnvɪkt/ a person found guilty of a criminal offence and serving a sentence of imprisonment.
– ORIGIN Middle English: from Latin *convict-* 'demonstrated, refuted, convicted', from the verb *convincere* (see **CONVINCE**). The noun is from obsolete *convict* 'convicted'.

conviction ▶ **noun 1** a formal declaration by the verdict of a jury or the decision of a judge in a court of law that someone is guilty of a criminal offence: *she had a previous conviction for a similar offence* | [mass noun] *the Crown Prosecution Service had to consider whether there was a proper chance of conviction.*
2 a firmly held belief or opinion: [with clause] *his conviction that the death was no accident was stronger* | *she takes pride in stating her political convictions.*
■ [mass noun] the quality of showing that one is firmly convinced of what one believes or says: *his voice lacked conviction.*
– ORIGIN late Middle English: from Latin *convictio(n-)*, from the verb *convincere* (see **CONVINCE**).

convince ▶ **verb** [with obj.] cause (someone) to believe firmly in the truth of something: *Robert's expression had obviously* ***convinced*** *her* ***of*** *his innocence* | [with obj. and clause] *she needed to find a way to convince Michel he was wrong.*
■ [with obj. and infinitive] persuade (someone) to do something: *she convinced my father to branch out on his own.*
– DERIVATIVES **convincer** noun, **convincible** adjective.
– ORIGIN mid 16th cent. (in the sense 'overcome, defeat in argument'): from Latin *convincere*, from *con-* 'with' + *vincere* 'conquer'. Compare with **CONVICT**.

USAGE **Convince** used (with an infinitive) as a synonym for **persuade** first became common in the 1950s in the US, as in *she* ***convinced*** *my father* ***to*** *branch out on his own.* Some traditionalists deplore the blurring of distinction between **convince** and **persuade**, maintaining that **convince** should be reserved for situations in which someone's belief is changed but no action is taken as a result (*he* ***convinced*** *me that he was right*) while **persuade** should be used for situations in which action results (*he* ***persuaded*** *me* rather than *he* ***convinced*** *me to seek more advice*). In practice the newer use is well established and used by well-respected writers: around 10 per cent of citations for **convince** in the Oxford Reading Programme relate to this use.

convinced ▶ **adjective** completely certain about something: *she was not entirely* ***convinced of*** *the soundness of his motives* | [with clause] *I am convinced the war will be over in a matter of months.*
■ [attrib.] firm in one's belief, especially with regard to a particular cause or issue: *a convinced pacifist.*

convincing ▶ **adjective** capable of causing someone to believe that something is true or real: *there is no convincing evidence that advertising influences total alcohol consumption* | *to make the detective's character convincing, she did extensive research with the CID.*
■ (of a victory or a winner) leaving no margin of doubt; clear: *Wales cruised to a convincing win over Ireland.*
– DERIVATIVES **convincingly** adverb.

convivial /kənˈvɪvɪəl/ ▶ **adjective** (of an atmosphere or event) friendly, lively, and enjoyable.
■ (of a person) cheerful and friendly; jovial.
– DERIVATIVES **conviviality** noun, **convivially** adverb.
– ORIGIN mid 17th cent. (in the sense 'fit for a feast, festive'): from Latin *convivialis*, from *convivium* 'a feast', from *con-* 'with' + *vivere* 'live'.

convocation /ˌkɒnvəˈkeɪʃ(ə)n/ ▶ **noun 1** a large formal assembly of people, in particular:
■ (in the church of England) a representative assembly of clergy of the province of Canterbury or York. ■ Brit. a legislative or deliberative assembly of a university. ■ N. Amer. a formal ceremony for the conferment of university awards.
2 [mass noun] the action of calling people together for a large formal assembly.
– DERIVATIVES **convocational** adjective.
– ORIGIN late Middle English: from Latin *convocatio(n-)*, from the verb *convocare* (see **CONVOKE**).

convoke /kən'vəʊk/ ▶ verb [with obj.] formal call together or summon (an assembly or meeting): *she sent messages convoking a Council of Ministers.*
– ORIGIN late 16th cent.: from Latin *convocare*, from *con-* 'together' + *vocare* 'call'.

convoluted /ˌkɒnvə'l(j)uːtɪd/ ▶ adjective (especially of an argument, story, or sentence) extremely complex and difficult to follow: *the film is let down by a convoluted plot in which nothing really happens.* ■chiefly technical intricately folded, twisted, or coiled: *walnuts come in hard and convoluted shells.*
– DERIVATIVES **convolutedly** adverb.
– ORIGIN late 18th cent.: past participle of *convolute*, from Latin *convolutus*, past participle of *convolvere* 'roll together, intertwine' (see **CONVOLVE**).

convolution ▶ noun 1 (often **convolutions**) a coil or twist, especially one of many: *crosses adorned with elaborate convolutions.* ■a thing that is complex and difficult to follow: *the convolutions of farm policy.* ■a sinuous fold in the surface of the brain. ■ [mass noun] the state of being or process of becoming coiled or twisted: *the flexibility of the polymer chain allows extensive convolution.* 2 (also **convolution integral**) Mathematics a function derived from two given functions by integration which expresses how the shape of one is modified by the other. ■a method of determination of the sum of two random variables by integration or summation.
– DERIVATIVES **convolutional** adjective.
– ORIGIN mid 16th cent.: from medieval Latin *convolutio(n-)*, from *convolvere* 'roll together' (see **CONVOLVE**).

convolve /kən'vɒlv/ ▶ verb [with obj.] rare roll or coil together; entwine. ■Mathematics combine (one function or series) with another by forming their convolution.
– ORIGIN late 16th cent. (in the sense 'enclose in folds'): from Latin *convolvere* 'roll together', from *con-* 'together' + *volvere* 'roll'.

convolvulus /kən'vɒlvjʊləs/ ▶ noun (pl. **convolvuluses**) a twining plant with trumpet-shaped flowers, some kinds of which are invasive weeds (see also **BINDWEED**), and others are cultivated for their bright flowers. ●Genus *Convolvulus*, family Convolvulaceae.
– ORIGIN Latin, 'bindweed', from *convolvere* 'roll together' (see **CONVOLVE**).

convoy /'kɒnvɔɪ/ ▶ noun a group of ships or vehicles travelling together, typically one accompanied by armed troops, warships, or other vehicles for protection. ▶ verb [with obj.] (of a warship or armed troops) accompany (a group of ships or vehicles) for protection.
– PHRASES **in convoy** (of travelling vehicles) as a group; together: *the army trucks had passed through in convoy the previous evening.*
– ORIGIN late Middle English (originally Scots, as a verb in the senses 'convey', 'conduct', and 'act as escort'): from French *convoyer*, from medieval Latin *conviare* (see **CONVEY**).

convulsant ▶ adjective (chiefly of drugs) producing sudden and involuntary muscle contractions. ▶ noun a convulsant drug.
– ORIGIN late 19th cent.: from French, from *convulser*, from Latin *convuls-* 'pulled violently, wrenched', from the verb *convellere* (see **CONVULSE**).

convulse /kən'vʌls/ ▶ verb [no obj.] (of a person) suffer violent involuntary contraction of the muscles, producing contortion of the body or limbs: *she convulsed, collapsing to the floor with the pain.* ■ [with obj.] (usu. **be convulsed**) (of an emotion, laughter, or physical stimulus) cause (someone) to make sudden, violent, uncontrollable movements: *Harry was convulsed by a second bout of sneezing* | *she rocked backwards and forwards, **convulsed with** helpless mirth.* ■ [with obj.] figurative throw (a country) into violent social or political upheaval: *a wave of mass strikes convulsed the Ruhr, Berlin, and central Germany.*
– ORIGIN mid 17th cent.: from Latin *convuls-* 'pulled violently, wrenched', from the verb *convellere*, from *con-* 'together' + *vellere* 'to pull'.

convulsion ▶ noun (often **convulsions**) a sudden, violent, irregular movement of a limb or limbs or the body, caused by involuntary contraction of muscles and associated especially with brain disorders such as epilepsy, the presence of certain toxins or other agents in the blood, or fever in children. ■ (**convulsions**) uncontrollable laughter: *the audience collapsed in convulsions.* ■ an earthquake or other violent or major movement of the earth's crust: *the violent convulsions of tectonic plates.* ■ figurative a violent social or political upheaval: *the convulsions of 1939–45.*
– ORIGIN mid 16th cent. (originally in the sense 'cramp, spasm'): from Latin *convulsio(n-)*, from the verb *convellere* (see **CONVULSE**).

convulsive ▶ adjective producing or consisting of sudden, violent, and uncontrollable body movements: *a convulsive disease* | *she gave a convulsive sob.*
– DERIVATIVES **convulsively** adverb.

Conwy /'kɒnwi/ (also **Conway**) a market town and county in north Wales, on the River Conwy; town pop. 12,950 (1981). A railway bridge built by Stephenson in 1848 and a suspension bridge built by Telford in 1826 span the river here.

cony ▶ noun (pl. **-ies**) variant spelling of **CONEY**.

coo[1] ▶ verb (**coos, cooed**) [no obj.] (of a pigeon or dove) make a soft murmuring sound: *ringdoves cooed among the branches.* ■ (of a baby) make a soft murmuring sound similar to this, expressing contentment: *he gurgled and cooed in her arms.* ■ (of a person) speak in a soft gentle voice, typically to express affection: *all eyes are upon her, when they are not **cooing over** her daughter* | [with direct speech] *'I knew I could count on you,' she cooed.* ▶ noun [in sing.] a soft murmuring sound made by a dove or pigeon.
– PHRASES **bill and coo** see **BILL**[2].
– ORIGIN mid 17th cent.: imitative.

coo[2] ▶ exclamation Brit. informal used to express surprise: *'Coo, ain't it high!' Mary squeaked.*
– ORIGIN early 20th cent.: imitative.

co-occur ▶ verb [no obj.] occur together or simultaneously.
– DERIVATIVES **co-occurrence** noun.

cooee informal ▶ exclamation used to attract attention, especially at a distance: *'Cooee!' The call brought all three heads round.* ▶ noun such a call or cry. ▶ verb (**cooees, cooeed, cooeeing**) [no obj.] make such a call to attract attention.
– PHRASES **within cooee** Austral./NZ within reach; near: *there's loads of cheap accommodation **within cooee** of the airport.*
– ORIGIN late 18th cent.: imitative of a signal used by Australian Aboriginals and copied by settlers.

Cook[1], Captain James (1728–79), English explorer. On his first expedition to the Pacific (1768–71), he charted the coasts of New Zealand and New Guinea as well as exploring the east coast of Australia and claiming it for Britain. He made two more voyages to the Pacific before being killed in a skirmish with native people in Hawaii.

Cook[2], Peter (Edward) (1937–95), English comedian and actor. A writer and performer of the revue *Beyond the Fringe* (1959–64), he is remembered also for his television partnership with Dudley Moore. He had a long association with the satirical magazine *Private Eye*.

Cook[3], Thomas (1808–92), English founder of the travel firm Thomas Cook. In 1841 he organized the first publicly advertised excursion train in England; the success of this venture led him to organize further excursions both in Britain and abroad, laying the foundations for the tourist and travel-agent industry.

cook ▶ verb 1 [with obj.] prepare (food, a dish, or a meal) by mixing, combining, and heating the ingredients in various ways: *shall I cook dinner tonight?* | [with two objs] *she cooked me eggs and bacon* | [as adj. **cooked**] *a cooked breakfast* | [no obj.] *I told you I could cook.* ■ [no obj.] (of food) be heated so that the state or condition required for eating is reached: *while the rice is cooking, add the saffron to the stock.* ■ (**cook something down**) heat food and cause it to thicken and reduce in volume: *cooking down the chutney can take up to 45 minutes.* ■ [no obj.] (**cook down**) (of food being cooked) be reduced in volume in this way. ■ (**be cooking**) informal be happening or planned: *what's cooking on the alternative fuels front?* 2 [with obj.] informal alter dishonestly; falsify: *a narcotics team who cooked the evidence.* ■ (**be cooked**) be in an inescapably bad situation: *if I can't talk to him I'm cooked.* 3 [no obj.] N. Amer. informal perform or proceed vigorously or very well: *the band used to get up on the bandstand and really cook.* ▶ noun [often with adj. or noun modifier] a person who prepares and cooks food, especially as a job or in a specified way: *Susan was a school cook* | *I'm a good cook.*
– PHRASES **cook the books** informal alter facts or figures dishonestly or illegally. **cook someone's goose** informal spoil someone's plans; cause someone's downfall. **too many cooks spoil the broth** proverb if too many people are involved in a task or activity, it will not be done well.
– DERIVATIVES **cookable** adjective.
– ORIGIN Old English *cōc* (noun), from popular Latin *cocus*, from Latin *coquus*.
▶ **cook something up** concoct a story, excuse, or plan, especially an ingenious or devious one.

Cook, Mount the highest peak in New Zealand, in the Southern Alps on South Island, rising to a height of 3,764 m (12,349 ft). It is named after Captain James Cook. Maori name **AORANGI**.

cookbook ▶ noun a cookery book.

cook-chill ▶ adjective [attrib.] Brit. relating to or denoting a procedure whereby food is cooked and refrigerated by the manufacturer ready for reheating by the consumer: *cook-chill food* | *cook-chill processes.*

Cooke, Sir William Fothergill (1806–79), English inventor. With Sir Charles Wheatstone he invented the electric telegraph alarm.

cooker ▶ noun 1 chiefly Brit. an appliance used for cooking food, typically consisting of an oven, hob, and grill and powered by gas or electricity. 2 Brit. informal a fruit, especially an apple, that is more suitable for cooking than for eating raw.

cookery ▶ noun (pl. **-ies**) 1 [mass noun] the practice or skill of preparing and cooking food. 2 N. Amer. a place in which food is cooked; a kitchen.

cookery book ▶ noun chiefly Brit. a book containing recipes and other information about the preparation and cooking of food.

cookhouse ▶ noun a place where food is prepared and cooked, in particular: ■a kitchen in a military camp. ■ an outdoor kitchen in a warm country.

cookie ▶ noun (pl. **-ies**) 1 N. Amer. a sweet biscuit. 2 [with adj.] informal a person of a specified kind: *a tough cookie with one eye on her bank account.* 3 Scottish a plain bun. 4 Computing a packet of data sent by an Internet server to a browser, which is returned by the browser each time it subsequently accesses the same server, used to identify the user or track their access to the server.
– PHRASES **that's the way the cookie crumbles** informal, chiefly N. Amer. that's how things turn out (often used of an undesirable but unalterable situation).
– ORIGIN early 18th cent.: from Dutch *koekje* 'little cake', diminutive of *koek*.

cookie cutter ▶ noun N. Amer. a device with sharp edges for cutting biscuit dough into a particular shape. ■ [as modifier] denoting something mass-produced or lacking any distinguishing characteristics: *a cookie-cutter apartment in a high-rise building.*

cookie jar ▶ noun N. Amer. a jar for biscuits or small cakes.
– PHRASES **with one's hand in the cookie jar** engaged in surreptitious theft from one's employer: *they got caught with their hands in the cookie jar.*

cookie sheet ▶ noun N. Amer. a flat metal tray on which biscuits or cakes may be cooked.

cooking ▶ noun [mass noun] the process of preparing food by heating it: *he developed an interest in cooking.* ■food that has been prepared in this way: *authentic Italian cooking.* ■ [as modifier] suitable for or used in cooking: *cooking oil* | *cooking chocolate.*

Cook Islands a group of fifteen islands in the SW Pacific Ocean between Tonga and French Polynesia, which have the status of a self-governing territory in free association with New Zealand; pop. 18,000 (1992); languages, English (official), Rarotongan (a Polynesian language); capital, Avarua, on Rarotonga.
– ORIGIN named after Captain J. Cook (see **COOK**[1]), who visited them in 1773.

cookout ▶ noun chiefly US a party or gathering where a meal is cooked and eaten outdoors.

cookshop ▶ noun 1 archaic a shop where cooked food is sold.
■ NZ a sheep station's kitchen.
2 Brit. a shop or section of a department store in which cooking equipment is sold.

Cookson /ˈkʊks(ə)n/, Dame Catherine (Anne) (1906–98), English writer, a prolific author of light romantic fiction.

Cook's tour ▶ noun informal a rapid tour of many places: figurative *he then took me on a Cook's tour of his neuroscientific theories.*
– ORIGIN early 20th cent.: from the name of the travel agent Thomas Cook (see **COOK**[3]).

Cook Strait the strait separating the North and South Islands of New Zealand. It was named after Captain James Cook, who visited it in 1770.

cooktop ▶ noun N. Amer. a cooking unit, usually with hot plates or burners, built into or fixed on the top of a cabinet or other surface.

cookware ▶ noun [mass noun] pots, pans, or dishes in which food can be cooked: *cast-iron cookware.*

cool ▶ adjective 1 of or at a fairly low temperature: *it'll be a cool afternoon | the wind kept them cool.*
■ soothing or refreshing because of its low temperature: *a long, cool glass of orange juice |* figurative *the bathroom was all glass and cool, muted blues.* ■ (especially of clothing) keeping one from becoming too hot: *people planning a holiday in the sun and looking for cool tops to pack.* ■ showing no friendliness towards a person or enthusiasm for an idea or project: *he gave a cool reception to the suggestion for a research centre.* ■ free from excitement or anxiety: *he prided himself on **keeping a cool head** | she seems **cool, calm, and collected**.* ■ calmly audacious: *such an expensive strategy requires cool nerves.* ■ (of jazz, especially modern jazz) restrained and relaxed.
2 informal fashionably attractive or impressive: *youngsters are turning to smoking because they think it makes them appear cool.*
■ excellent: [as exclamation] *our office was a sunny room with a computer you didn't even have to plug in. Cool!*
3 (**a cool ——**) informal used to emphasize a specified quantity or amount, especially of money: *research for a new drug can cost a cool £50 million.*
▶ noun [mass noun] 1 (**the cool**) a fairly low temperature: *the cool of the night air.*
■ a time or place at which the temperature is pleasantly low: *the cool of the day.*
2 the quality of being fashionably attractive or impressive: *all the cool of high fashion.*
▶ verb become or cause to become less hot: [no obj.] *we dived into the river to **cool off** |* figurative *his feelings for her took a long time to cool |* [with obj.] *cool the pastry for five minutes.*
■ become or cause to become calm or less excited: [no obj.] *after I'd **cooled off**, I realized I was being irrational |* [with obj.] *George was trying to **cool** him **down**.* ■ [usu. in imperative] (**cool it**) informal behave in a less excitable manner: *'Cool it and tell me why you're so ecstatic.'*
– PHRASES **cool one's heels** see **HEEL**[1]. **keep** (or **lose**) **one's cool** informal maintain (or fail to maintain) a calm and controlled attitude.
– DERIVATIVES **cooled** adjective [in combination] *a water-cooled engine*, **coolish** adjective, **coolly** adverb, **coolness** noun.
– ORIGIN Old English *cōl* (noun), *cōlian* (verb), of Germanic origin; related to Dutch *koel*, also to **COLD**.

coolabah /ˈkuːləbɑː/ ▶ noun variant spelling of **COOLIBAH**.

coolant ▶ noun a liquid or gas that is used to remove heat from something.
– ORIGIN 1930s: from **COOL**, on the pattern of *lubricant*.

cool bag ▶ noun Brit. a soft insulated container for keeping food and drink cool.

cool box (also **cool bag**) ▶ noun Brit. a rigid insulated container for keeping food and drink cool.

cooldrink ▶ noun S. African a soft drink.

cooler ▶ noun 1 a device or container for keeping things cool, in particular:
■ a tall plastic or earthenware container for keeping bottles cool. ■ a cool box or cool bag. ■ N. Amer. a refrigerator.
2 a long drink, especially a mixture of wine, fruit juice, and soda water.
3 (**the cooler**) informal prison or a prison cell.

Cooley's anaemia /ˈkuːlɪz/ ▶ noun another term for **THALASSAEMIA**.
– ORIGIN 1930s: named after Thomas B. *Cooley* (1871–1945), American paediatrician.

Coolgardie safe /kuːlˈgɑːdi/ ▶ noun Austral. a food safe cooled by strips of wetted fabric.
– ORIGIN 1940s: named after *Coolgardie*, a town in Western Australia.

cool-headed ▶ adjective not easily worried or excited.

coolibah /ˈkuːlɪbɑː/ (also **coolabah**) ▶ noun a North Australian gum tree which typically grows near watercourses and yields very strong, hard timber.
• *Eucalyptus microtheca*, family Myrtaceae.
– ORIGIN late 19th cent.: from Kamilaroi (and related languages) *gulubaa*.

Coolidge /ˈkuːlɪdʒ/, (John) Calvin (1872–1933), American Republican statesman, 30th President of the US 1923–9.

coolie /ˈkuːli/ ▶ noun (pl. **-ies**) an unskilled native labourer in India, China, and some other Asian countries.
■ offensive a person from the Indian subcontinent; a person of Indian descent.
– ORIGIN mid 17th cent.: from Hindi and Telugu *kūlī* 'day-labourer', probably associated with Urdu *ḳulī* 'slave'.

coolie hat ▶ noun a broad conical hat as worn by labourers in some Asian countries.

cooling-off period ▶ noun an interval during which two people or groups who are in disagreement can try to settle their differences before taking further action.
■ an interval after a sale contract is agreed during which the purchaser can decide to cancel without loss.

cooling tower ▶ noun a tall, open-topped, cylindrical concrete tower, used for cooling water or condensing steam from an industrial process.

coolth /kuːlθ/ ▶ noun [mass noun] 1 pleasantly low temperature: *the coolth of the evening.*
2 informal articles, activities, or people perceived as fashionable: *the pinnacle of 1960s coolth.*
– ORIGIN mid 16th cent. (but rare before the 20th cent.): from **COOL** + **-TH**[2].

coombe (also **coomb**) ▶ noun variant spelling of **COMBE**.

coon ▶ noun 1 N. Amer. short for **RACCOON**.
2 offensive a black person. [ORIGIN: slang use of sense 1, from an earlier sense '(sly) fellow'.]
– PHRASES **for** (or **in**) **a coon's age** N. Amer. informal, dated a very long time.

cooncan /ˈkuːnkan/ ▶ noun [mass noun] a card game for two players, originally from Mexico, similar to rummy.
– ORIGIN late 19th cent.: probably from Spanish *con quién* 'with whom?'

coonhound ▶ noun a dog of a black-and-tan American breed, used to hunt raccoons.

coonskin ▶ noun the pelt of a raccoon.

coop ▶ noun a cage or pen for confining poultry.
■ Brit. a basket used in catching fish.
▶ verb [with obj.] (usu. **be cooped up**) confine in a small space: *being cooped up indoors all day makes him fidgety.*
■ put or keep (a fowl) in a cage or pen.
– ORIGIN Middle English *cowpe*; related to Dutch *kuip* 'vat' and German *Kufe* 'cask', based on Latin *cupa*. Compare with **COOPER**.

co-op /ˈkəʊɒp/ ▶ noun informal a cooperative society, shop, business, or farm.
– ORIGIN mid 19th cent.: abbreviation.

Cooper[1], Gary (1901–61), American actor; born *Frank James Cooper*. He is noted for his performances in such westerns as *The Virginian* (1929) and *High Noon* (1952).

Cooper[2], Sir Henry (b.1934), English boxer, the only man to win a Lonsdale belt outright three times. He beat Muhammad Ali (then Cassius Clay) in 1963, but a bad cut inflicted by the same opponent in 1966 in his only world title fight hastened his retirement in 1971.

Cooper[3], James Fenimore (1789–1851), American novelist. He is renowned for his tales of American Indians and frontier life, in particular *The Last of the Mohicans* (1826).

Cooper[4], Susie (1902–95), English ceramic designer and manufacturer; full name *Susan Vera Cooper*. Her work was noted for its functional shapes and simple, vivid designs.

cooper ▶ noun a maker or repairer of casks and barrels.
▶ verb [with obj.] make or repair (a cask or barrel).
– ORIGIN Middle English *cowper*, from Middle Dutch, Middle Low German *kūper*, from *kūpe* 'tub, vat', based on Latin *cupa*. Compare with **COOP**.

cooperage ▶ noun a cooper's business or premises.
■ [mass noun] the making of barrels and casks.

cooperate /kəʊˈɒpəreɪt/ (also **co-operate**) ▶ verb [no obj.] act jointly; work towards the same end: *the leaders promised to **cooperate in** ending the civil war | staff need to **cooperate with each other**.*
■ assist someone or comply with their requests: *his captor threatened to kill him if he didn't cooperate.*
– DERIVATIVES **cooperant** noun, **cooperator** noun.
– ORIGIN late 16th cent.: from ecclesiastical Latin *cooperat-* 'worked together', from the verb *cooperari*, from *co-* 'together' + *operari* 'to work'.

cooperation (also **co-operation**) ▶ noun [mass noun] the process of working together to the same end: *they worked **in close cooperation with** the British Tourist Authority.*
■ assistance, especially by complying readily with requests: *we should like to ask for your cooperation in the survey.* ■ Economics the formation and operation of cooperatives.
– ORIGIN late Middle English: from Latin *cooperatio(n-)*, from the verb *cooperari* (see **COOPERATE**); later reinforced by French *coopération*.

cooperative (also **co-operative**) ▶ adjective involving mutual assistance in working towards a common goal: *every member has clearly defined tasks in a cooperative enterprise.*
■ willing to be of assistance: *they have been extremely considerate, polite, and cooperative.* ■ (of a farm, business, etc.) owned and run jointly by its members, with profits or benefits shared among them.
▶ noun a farm, business, or other organization which is owned and run jointly by its members, who share the profits or benefits.
– DERIVATIVES **cooperatively** adverb, **cooperativeness** noun.
– ORIGIN early 17th cent.: from late Latin *cooperativus*, from Latin *cooperat-* 'worked together', from the verb *cooperari* (see **COOPERATE**).

cooperative movement ▶ noun a movement originating in the industrial areas of northern England and Scotland in the late 18th century, based on the belief that industries and commercial concerns should be owned and controlled by the people working in them, for joint economic benefit.

Cooper pair ▶ noun Physics a loosely bound pair of electrons with opposite spins and moving with the same speed in opposite directions, held to be responsible for the phenomenon of superconductivity.
■ a similar bound pair of atoms in a superfluid.
– ORIGIN 1960s: named after Leon N. *Cooper* (born 1930), American physicist.

coopery ▶ noun (pl. **-ies**) another term for **COOPERAGE**.

co-opt ▶ verb [with obj.] (often **be co-opted**) appoint to membership of a committee or other body by invitation of the existing members.
■ divert to or use in a role different from the usual or original one: [with obj. and infinitive] *social scientists were co-opted to work with the development agencies.* ■ adopt (an idea or policy) for one's own use: *the green parties have had most of their ideas co-opted by bigger parties.*
– DERIVATIVES **co-optation** noun, **co-option** noun, **co-optive** adjective.
– ORIGIN mid 17th cent.: from Latin *cooptare*, from *co-* 'together' + *optare* 'choose'.

coordinate (also **co-ordinate**) ▶ verb /kəʊˈɔːdɪneɪt/ 1 [with obj.] bring the different elements of (a complex activity or organization) into a relation that will ensure efficiency or harmony: *he had responsibility for coordinating London's transport services.*
■ [no obj.] negotiate with others in order to work together effectively: *you will coordinate with consultants and other departments on a variety of projects.* ■ [no obj.] match or harmonize attractively: *the stud fastenings are coloured to coordinate with the shirt |* [as adj. **coordinating**] *a variety of coordinating colours.*
2 Chemistry form a coordinate bond to (an atom or

molecule): *the sodium atom is coordinated to two oxygen atoms.*
▶**adjective** /kəʊˈɔːdɪnət/ **1** equal in rank or importance: *cross references in the catalogue link subjects which may be coordinate.*
■Grammar (of parts of a compound sentence) equal in rank and fulfilling identical functions.
2 Chemistry denoting a type of covalent bond in which one atom provides both the shared electrons.
▶**noun** /kəʊˈɔːdɪnət/ **1** Mathematics each of a group of numbers used to indicate the position of a point, line, or plane.
2 (**coordinates**) matching items of clothing.
– DERIVATIVES **coordinative** adjective, **coordinator** noun.
– ORIGIN mid 17th cent. (in the senses 'of the same rank' and 'place in the same rank'): from **CO-** 'together' + Latin *ordinare* (from *ordo* 'order'), on the pattern of *subordinate*.

Coordinated Universal Time (abbrev.: **UTC**) another term for **GREENWICH MEAN TIME**.

coordinating conjunction ▶**noun** a conjunction placed between words, phrases, clauses, or sentences of equal rank, e.g. *and, but, or.* Contrasted with **SUBORDINATING CONJUNCTION**.

coordination /kəʊˌɔːdɪˈneɪʃ(ə)n/ ▶**noun** [mass noun] **1** the organization of the different elements of a complex body or activity so as to enable them to work together effectively: *both countries agreed to intensify efforts at economic policy coordination.*
■cooperative effort resulting in an effective relationship: *action groups work **in coordination with** local groups to end rainforest destruction.* ■ the ability to use different parts of the body together smoothly and efficiently: *changing from one foot position to another requires coordination and balance.*
2 Chemistry the linking of atoms by coordinate bonds.
– ORIGIN mid 17th cent. (in the sense 'placing in the same rank'): from French or from late Latin *coordinatio(n-)*, based on Latin *ordo, ordin-* 'order'.

coordination number ▶**noun** Chemistry the number of atoms or ions immediately surrounding a central atom in a complex or crystal.

coot ▶**noun** **1** (pl. same) an aquatic bird of the rail family, with blackish plumage, lobed feet, and a bill that extends back on to the forehead as a horny shield.
• Genus *Fulica*, family Rallidae: several species, in particular the widespread *F. atra*, which has a white bill and frontal shield.
2 (usu. **old coot**) informal, chiefly N. Amer. a stupid or eccentric person, typically an old man.
– ORIGIN Middle English: probably of Dutch or Low German origin and related to Dutch *koet*.

cooter ▶**noun** a North American river turtle with a dull brown shell and typically having yellow stripes on the head.
• Genus *Pseudemys*, family Emydidae: several species, in particular *P. concinna*, some races of which are known as sliders.
– ORIGIN early 19th cent.: of unknown origin.

cootie /kuːti/ ▶**noun** N. Amer. informal a body louse.
– ORIGIN First World War: perhaps from Malay *kutu*, denoting a parasitic biting insect.

co-own ▶**verb** [with obj.] own (something) jointly.
– DERIVATIVES **co-owner** noun, **co-ownership** noun.

cop[1] informal ▶**noun** a police officer.
▶**verb** (**copped**, **copping**) [with obj.] **1** catch or arrest (an offender): *he was copped for speeding.*
■incur (something unwelcome): *England's captain copped most of the blame.* ■ (**cop it**) Brit. get into trouble: *will you cop it from your dad if you get back late?* ■ (**cop it**) chiefly Brit. be killed: *he almost copped it in a horrific accident.* ■ US obtain (an illegal drug): *he copped some hash for me.* ■ receive or attain (something welcome): *she copped an award for her role in the film.*
2 N. Amer. strike (an attitude or pose): *I copped an attitude—I acted real tough.*
– PHRASES **cop a feel** N. Amer. informal fondle someone sexually, especially in a surreptitious way or without their permission. **cop hold of** [usu. in imperative] Brit. take hold of: *cop hold of the suitcase, I'm off.* **cop a plea** N. Amer. engage in plea bargaining. **it's a fair cop** see **FAIR**[1]. **not much cop** Brit. not very good: *they say he's not much cop as a coach.*
– ORIGIN early 18th cent. (as a verb): perhaps from obsolete *cap* 'arrest', from Old French *caper* 'seize', from Latin *capere*. The noun is from **COPPER**[2].
▶**cop off** have a sexual encounter: *loads of girls think that guys just want to cop off with any girl.*
cop out avoid doing something that one ought to do: *he copped out at the last moment.*
cop to US accept or admit to: *there are a lot of people in the world who don't cop to their past.*

cop[2] ▶**noun** a conical mass of thread wound on to a spindle.
– ORIGIN late 18th cent.: possibly from Old English *cop* 'summit, top'.

Copacabana Beach /ˌkɒpəkəˈbanə/ a resort on the Atlantic coast of Brazil near Rio de Janeiro.

copacetic /ˌkəʊpəˈsɛtɪk, -ˈsiːt-/ ▶**adjective** N. Amer. informal in excellent order.
– ORIGIN early 20th cent.: of unknown origin.

copal /ˈkəʊp(ə)l/ ▶**noun** [mass noun] resin from any of a number of tropical trees, used to make varnish.
• The resin is obtained from trees in the families Leguminosae (genera *Guibourtia*, *Copaifera*, and *Trachylobium*) and Araucariaceae (genus *Agathis*).
– ORIGIN late 16th cent.: via Spanish from Nahuatl *copalli* 'incense'.

Copán /kəʊˈpan/ an ancient Mayan city, in western Honduras near the Guatemalan frontier, the southernmost point of the Mayan empire.

coparcenary /kəʊˈpɑːs(ə)n(ə)ri/ ▶**noun** (pl. **-ies**) [mass noun] English Law joint heirship; the status of a coparcener.
– ORIGIN early 16th cent.: from **CO-** 'together' + *parcenary*, legal term in the same sense, from Anglo-Norman French *parcenarie*, from *parcener* 'coparcener' (see **COPARCENER**).

coparcener /kəʊˈpɑːs(ə)nə/ ▶**noun** English Law a person who shares equally with others in the inheritance of an undivided estate or in the rights to it (in the UK now as equitable interests).
– ORIGIN late Middle English: from **CO-** 'together' + *parcener*, legal term in the same sense (see **PARTNER**).

co-partner ▶**noun** a partner or associate, especially an equal partner in a business.
– DERIVATIVES **co-partnership** noun.

COPD Medicine ▶**abbreviation for** chronic obstructive pulmonary disease, involving constriction of the airways and difficulty or discomfort in breathing.

cope[1] ▶**verb** [no obj.] (of a person) deal effectively with something difficult: *his ability to **cope with** stress | it all got too much for me and I couldn't cope.*
■(of a machine or system) have the capacity to deal successfully with: *the roads are barely adequate to **cope with** the present traffic.*
– DERIVATIVES **coper** noun.
– ORIGIN Middle English (in the sense 'meet in battle, come to blows'): from Old French *coper*, *colper*, from *cop*, *colp* 'a blow', via Latin from Greek *kolaphos* 'blow with the fist'.

cope[2] ▶**noun** a long, loose cloak worn by a priest or bishop on ceremonial occasions.
■technical or poetic/literary a thing resembling or likened to a cloak: *the bay and the square were a seamless cope.*
▶**verb** [with obj.] [usu. as adj. **coped**] (in building) cover (a joint or structure) with a coping.
– ORIGIN Middle English (denoting a long outdoor cloak): from medieval Latin *capa*, variant of late Latin *cappa* (see **CAP** and **CAPE**[1]).

copeck ▶**noun** variant spelling of **KOPEK**.

Copenhagen /ˌkəʊpənˈheɪɡ(ə)n, -ˈhɑːɡ(ə)n/ the capital and chief port of Denmark, a city occupying the eastern part of Zealand and northern part of the island of Amager; pop. 466,700 (1990). Danish name **København**.

Copepoda /ˌkəʊpɪˈpəʊdə/ Zoology a large class of small aquatic crustaceans, many of which occur in plankton and some of which are parasitic on larger aquatic animals.
– DERIVATIVES **copepod** /ˈkəʊpɪpɒd/ noun.
– ORIGIN modern Latin, from Greek *kōpē* 'handle, oar' + *pous, pod-* 'foot' (because of its paddle-like feet).

Copernican system /kəˈpəːnɪk(ə)n/ (also **Copernican theory**) ▶**noun** Astronomy the theory that the sun is the centre of the solar system, with the planets (including the earth) orbiting round it. Compare with **PTOLEMAIC SYSTEM**.
– ORIGIN mid 17th cent.: named after **COPERNICUS**.

Copernicus /kəˈpəːnɪkəs/, Nicolaus (1473–1543), Polish astronomer; Latinized name of *Mikolaj Kopernik*. He proposed a model of the solar system in which the planets orbited in perfect circles around the sun and his work ultimately led to the overthrow of the established geocentric cosmology. He published his astronomical theories in *De Revolutionibus Orbium Coelestium* (1543).
– DERIVATIVES **Copernican** adjective.

copestone ▶**noun** old-fashioned term for **COPING STONE**.
– ORIGIN mid 16th cent.: from **COPE**[2] + **STONE**.

copiable ▶**adjective** able to be copied, especially legitimately.

copier ▶**noun** a machine that makes exact copies of something, especially documents, video or audio recordings, or software.

co-pilot ▶**noun** a second pilot in an aircraft.
▶**verb** [with obj.] act as the co-pilot of (an aircraft).

coping ▶**noun** the top, typically sloping, course of a brick or stone wall.
– ORIGIN mid 16th cent.: from the verb **COPE**[2], originally meaning 'dress in a cope', hence 'to cover'.

coping saw ▶**noun** a saw with a very narrow blade stretched across a D-shaped frame, used for cutting curves in wood.
– ORIGIN 1920s: *coping* from **COPE**[2], used to describe likeness to a vault, arch, canopy, etc., based on Latin *cappa* 'cap or cape'.

coping stone ▶**noun** a flat stone forming part of a coping.
■figurative a finishing touch or crowning achievement.

copious ▶**adjective** abundant in supply or quantity: *she took copious notes.*
■archaic profuse in speech or ideas: *I had been a little too copious in talking of my country.*
– DERIVATIVES **copiously** adverb, **copiousness** noun.
– ORIGIN late Middle English: from Old French *copieux* or Latin *copiosus*, from *copia* 'plenty'.

copita /kəˈpiːtə/ ▶**noun** a slim stemmed glass that narrows slightly towards the top, used for sherry.
– ORIGIN mid 19th cent.: from Spanish, diminutive of *copa* 'cup', from popular Latin *cuppa* (see **CUP**).

coplanar /kəʊˈpleɪnə/ ▶**adjective** Geometry in the same plane.
– DERIVATIVES **coplanarity** noun.

Copland /ˈkəʊplənd/, Aaron (1900–90), American composer, pianist, and conductor, of Lithuanian descent. He established a distinctive American style in his compositions, borrowing from jazz, folk, and other traditional music. Notable works: *Music for the Theater* (1925), *Appalachian Spring* (1944), *Fanfare for the Common Man* (1942).

Copley /ˈkɒpli/, John Singleton (1738–1815), American painter. He is noted for his portraits and for paintings such as *The Death of Chatham* (1779–80), one of the first large-scale paintings of contemporary events.

copolymer /kəʊˈpɒlɪmə/ ▶**noun** Chemistry a polymer made by reaction of two different monomers, with units of more than one kind.

copolymerize (also **-ise**) ▶**verb** [with obj.] Chemistry polymerize together to form a copolymer.
– DERIVATIVES **copolymerization** noun.

cop-out ▶**noun** informal an instance of avoiding a commitment or responsibility.

copper[1] ▶**noun** **1** [mass noun] a red-brown metal, the chemical element of atomic number 29. (Symbol: **Cu**)

Copper was the earliest metal to be used by humans, first by itself and then later alloyed with tin to form bronze. A ductile easily worked metal, it is a very good conductor of heat and electricity and is used especially for electrical wiring.

2 (**coppers**) Brit. brown coins of low value made of copper or bronze.
■dated a large container made of copper or iron for boiling or washing.
3 [mass noun] a reddish-brown colour like that of copper.
4 [with modifier] a small butterfly with bright reddish-brown wings.
• Genus *Lycaena*, family Lycaenidae: many species.
▶**verb** [with obj.] cover or coat (something) with copper.
– ORIGIN Old English *copor, coper* (related to Dutch *koper* and German *Kupfer*), based on late Latin *cuprum*, from Latin *cyprium aes* 'Cyprus metal' (so named because Cyprus was the chief source).

copper[2] ▶**noun** Brit. informal a police officer.
– ORIGIN mid 19th cent.: from **COP**[1] + **-ER**[1].

Copper Age Archaeology the Chalcolithic period, especially in SE Europe.

copperas /ˈkɒp(ə)rəs/ ▶**noun** [mass noun] green

crystals of hydrated ferrous sulphate, especially as an industrial product.
– ORIGIN late Middle English *coperose*, from Old French *couperose*, from medieval Latin *cuperosa*, literally 'flower of copper', from late Latin *cuprum* (see **COPPER**[1]) + *rosa* 'rose', translating Greek *khalkanthon*.

copper beech ▶ **noun** a beech tree of a variety with purplish-brown leaves.

Copperbelt a mining region of central Zambia with rich deposits of copper, cobalt, and uranium; chief town, Ndola.

copper-bottomed ▶ **adjective** Brit. thoroughly reliable; certain not to fail: *a copper-bottomed guarantee.* [ORIGIN: figuratively, from earlier usage referring to the copper sheathing of the bottom of a ship.]

copper-fasten ▶ **verb** [with obj.] make (an undertaking or agreement) firm or binding.

copperhead ▶ **noun** any of a number of stout-bodied venomous snakes with coppery-pink or reddish-brown coloration, in particular:
• a North American pit viper (*Agkistrodon contortrix*, family Viperidae). Also called **HIGHLAND MOCCASIN**. • an Australian snake of the cobra family (genus *Austrelaps*, family Elapidae, in particular *A. superbus*).

coppering ▶ **noun** [mass noun] Brit. informal the work of a police officer: *he doesn't do his coppering by the book.*

coppernob ▶ **noun** informal a red-haired person.

copperplate ▶ **noun** 1 a polished copper plate with a design engraved or etched into it.
■ a print made from such a plate.
2 [mass noun] a style of neat, round handwriting, usually slanted and looped, the thick and thin strokes being made by pressure with a flexible metal nib. [ORIGIN: the copybooks for this round hand were originally printed from copperplates.]
▶ **adjective** of or in copperplate writing.

copper pyrites ▶ **noun** another term for **CHALCOPYRITE**.

coppersmith ▶ **noun** 1 a person who makes things out of copper.
2 (also **coppersmith barbet**) the crimson-breasted barbet of SE Asia, which has a red breast band, a streaked belly, and a repetitive metallic call.
• *Megalaima hemacephala*, family Capitonidae.

copper sulphate ▶ **noun** [mass noun] a blue crystalline solid used in electroplating and as a fungicide.
• Chem. formula: $CuSO_4.5H_2O$.

coppery ▶ **adjective** like copper, especially in colour: *his hair was fine and coppery.*

coppice ▶ **noun** an area of woodland in which the trees or shrubs are, or formerly were, periodically cut back to ground level to stimulate growth and provide firewood or timber.
▶ **verb** [with obj.] cut back (a tree or shrub) to ground level periodically to stimulate growth: [as adj. **coppiced**] *coppiced timber.*
– ORIGIN late Middle English: from Old French *copeiz*, based on medieval Latin *colpus* 'a blow' (see **COPE**[1]). Compare with **COPSE**.

coppice with standards ▶ **noun** [mass noun] chiefly historical managed woodland consisting of coppiced shrubs or trees, with scattered trees that are allowed to reach full height.

Coppola /ˈkɒpələ/, Francis Ford (b.1939), American film director, writer, and producer. Notable films: *The Godfather* (1972) and its two sequels; *Apocalypse Now* (1979).

copra /ˈkɒprə/ ▶ **noun** [mass noun] dried coconut kernels, from which oil is obtained.
– ORIGIN late 16th cent.: via Portuguese and Spanish from Malayalam *koppara* 'coconut'.

co-precipitation ▶ **noun** [mass noun] Chemistry the simultaneous precipitation of more than one compound from a solution.
– DERIVATIVES **co-precipitate** verb.

copro- ▶ **combining form** of or relating to dung or faeces: *coprophagous* | *coprophilia.*
– ORIGIN from Greek *kopros* 'dung'.

coprocessor ▶ **noun** Computing a microprocessor designed to supplement the capabilities of the primary processor.

co-produce ▶ **verb** [with obj.] produce (a theatrical work or a radio or television programme) jointly.
– DERIVATIVES **co-producer** noun, **co-production** noun.

coprolalia /ˌkɒprə(ʊ)ˈleɪlɪə/ ▶ **noun** [mass noun] Psychiatry the involuntary and repetitive use of obscene language, as a symptom of mental illness or organic brain disease.
– ORIGIN late 19th cent.: from Greek *kopros* 'dung' + *lalia* 'speech, chatter'.

coprolite /ˈkɒprə(ʊ)lʌɪt/ ▶ **noun** Palaeontology a piece of fossilized dung.

coprophagy /kɒˈprɒfədʒi/ (also **coprophagia** /ˌkɒprə(ʊ)ˈfeɪdʒɪə/) ▶ **noun** [mass noun] Zoology the eating of faeces or dung.
– DERIVATIVES **coprophagic** adjective, **coprophagous** adjective (chiefly Zoology).

coprophilia /ˌkɒprə(ʊ)ˈfɪlɪə/ ▶ **noun** [mass noun] abnormal interest and pleasure in faeces and defecation.

copse ▶ **noun** a small group of trees.
– ORIGIN late 16th cent.: shortened from **COPPICE**.

cop shop ▶ **noun** informal a police station.

Copt /kɒpt/ ▶ **noun** 1 a native Egyptian in the Hellenistic and Roman periods.
2 a member of the Coptic Church.
– ORIGIN from French *Copte* or modern Latin *Coptus*, from Arabic *al-ķibṭ, al-ķubṭ* 'Copts', from Coptic *Gyptios*, from Greek *Aiguptios* 'Egyptian'.

copter ▶ **noun** informal term for **HELICOPTER**.

Coptic ▶ **noun** [mass noun] the language of the Copts, which represents the final stage of ancient Egyptian. It now survives only as the liturgical language of the Coptic Church.
▶ **adjective** of or relating to the Copts or their language.

Coptic Church the native Christian Church in Egypt, traditionally founded by St Mark, and adhering to the Monophysite doctrine rejected by the Council of Chalcedon. Long persecuted after the Muslim Arab conquest of Egypt in the 7th century, the Coptic community now make up about 5 per cent of Egypt's population.

copula /ˈkɒpjʊlə/ ▶ **noun** Logic & Grammar a connecting word, in particular a form of the verb *be* connecting a subject and complement.
– DERIVATIVES **copular** adjective.
– ORIGIN early 17th cent.: from Latin, 'connection, linking of words', from *co-* 'together' + *apere* 'fasten'.

copulate /ˈkɒpjʊleɪt/ ▶ **verb** [no obj.] have sexual intercourse.
– DERIVATIVES **copulation** noun, **copulatory** adjective.
– ORIGIN late Middle English (in the sense 'join'): from Latin *copulat-* 'fastened together', from the verb *copulare*, from *copula* (see **COPULA**).

copulative ▶ **adjective** 1 Grammar (of a word) connecting words or clauses linked in sense. Compare with **DISJUNCTIVE**.
■ connecting a subject and predicate.
2 of or relating to sexual intercourse.
– DERIVATIVES **copulatively** adverb.
– ORIGIN late Middle English: from Old French *copulatif, -ive* or late Latin *copulativus*, from *copulat-* 'coupled', from the verb *copulare* (see **COPULATE**).

copy ▶ **noun** (pl. **-ies**) 1 a thing made to be similar or identical to another: *the problem is telling which is the original document and which the copy.*
2 a single specimen of a particular book, record, or other publication or issue: *the record has sold more than a million copies.*
3 [mass noun] matter to be printed: *copy for the next issue must be submitted by the beginning of the month.*
■ material for a newspaper or magazine article: *it is an unfortunate truth of today's media that bad news makes good copy.* ■ the text of an advertisement: *'No more stubble—no more trouble,' trumpeted their ad copy.*
▶ **verb** (**-ies, -ied**) [with obj.] make a similar or identical version of; reproduce: *each form had to be copied and sent to a different department.*
■ Computing reproduce (data stored in one location) in another location: *the command will* **copy** *a file* **from** *one disc* **to** *another.* ■ write out information that one has read or heard: *he copied the details into his notebook* | *I began to* **copy out** *the addresses.* ■ behave in a similar way to; do the same as: *she was such fun that everybody wanted to copy her.* ■ imitate or reproduce (an idea or style) rather than creating something original: *lifestyles* **copied from** *Miami and Fifth Avenue* | [no obj.] *art students* **copied from** *approved old masters.* ■ (**copy something to**) send a copy of a letter to (a third party).
– ORIGIN Middle English (denoting a transcript or copy of a document): from Old French *copie* (noun), *copier* (verb), from Latin *copia* 'abundance' (in medieval Latin 'transcript', from such phrases as *copiam describendi facere* 'give permission to transcribe').

copybook ▶ **noun** a book containing models of handwriting for learners to imitate.
▶ **adjective** [attrib.] exactly in accordance with established criteria; perfect.
■ tritely conventional: *out come the copybook maxims.*

copycat ▶ **noun** informal, derogatory (especially in children's use) a person who copies another's behaviour, dress, or ideas.
■ [as modifier] denoting an action, typically a crime, carried out in imitation of another: *copycat killings.*

copydesk ▶ **noun** N. Amer. a desk in a newspaper office at which copy is edited for printing.

copy-edit ▶ **verb** [with obj.] edit (text to be printed) by checking its consistency and accuracy.
– DERIVATIVES **copy editor** noun.

copyhold ▶ **noun** [mass noun] Brit. historical tenure of land based on manorial records.

copyholder ▶ **noun** 1 Brit. historical a person who held land in copyhold.
2 a clasp or stand for holding sheets of text while it is keyed or typed.

copyist ▶ **noun** a person who makes copies, especially of handwritten documents or music.
■ a person who imitates the styles of others, especially in art.
– ORIGIN mid 17th cent.: from **COPY** + **-IST**; replacing earlier *copist*, from French *copiste* or medieval Latin *copista*, from *copiare* 'to copy', from *copia* (see **COPY**).

copyread ▶ **verb** [with obj.] read and edit (text) for a newspaper, magazine, or book.
– DERIVATIVES **copyreader** noun.

copyright ▶ **noun** [mass noun] the exclusive legal right, given to the originator or their assignee for a fixed number of years, to print, publish, perform, film, or record literary, artistic, or musical material, and to authorize others to do the same.
▶ **verb** [with obj.] secure copyright for (such material).

copyright library ▶ **noun** a library entitled to a free copy of each book published in the UK. The copyright libraries in the British Isles are the British Library, the Bodleian Library, Cambridge University Library, the National Library of Wales, the National Library of Scotland, and the library of Trinity College, Dublin.

copy typist ▶ **noun** a person whose job is to type transcripts of written or dictated material.

copywriter ▶ **noun** a person who writes the text of advertisements or publicity material.
– DERIVATIVES **copywriting** noun.

coq au vin /ˌkɒk əʊ ˈvã/ ▶ **noun** [mass noun] a casserole of chicken pieces cooked in red wine.
– ORIGIN French, literally 'cock in wine'.

coquelicot /ˈkəʊklɪkəʊ/ ▶ **noun** [mass noun] a brilliant orange-red like the colour of a red poppy.
– ORIGIN late 18th cent.: French, 'red poppy'.

coquetry /ˈkɒkɪtri, ˈkəʊ-/ ▶ **noun** [mass noun] flirtatious behaviour or a flirtatious manner.
– ORIGIN mid 17th cent.: from French *coquetterie*, from *coqueter* 'to flirt', from *coquet* 'wanton' (see **COQUETTE**).

coquette /kɒˈkɛt/ ▶ **noun** 1 a woman who flirts.
2 a crested Central and South American hummingbird, typically with green plumage, a reddish crest, and elongated cheek feathers.
• *Lophornis* and two other genera, family Trochilidae: several species.
– DERIVATIVES **coquettish** adjective, **coquettishly** adverb, **coquettishness** noun.
– ORIGIN mid 17th cent.: French, feminine of *coquet* 'wanton', diminutive of *coq* 'cock'.

coquina /kɒˈkiːnə/ ▶ **noun** 1 [mass noun] a soft limestone of broken shells, used in road-making in the Caribbean and Florida.
2 (also **coquina clam**) a small bivalve mollusc with a wedge-shaped shell which has a wide variety of colours and patterns.
• Genus *Donax*, family Donacidae: several species, including the edible **American coquina** (*D. variabilis*).
– ORIGIN mid 19th cent.: from Spanish, literally 'cockle', based on Latin *concha* (see **CONCH**).

coquito /kɒˈkiːtəʊ/ ▶ **noun** (pl. **-os**) a thick-trunked Chilean palm tree which yields large amounts of sweet sap (palm honey) and fibre.
• *Jubaea chilensis*, family Palmae.

– ORIGIN mid 19th cent.: from Spanish, diminutive of *coco* 'coconut'.

Cor. ▶ **abbreviation for** ■ US coroner. ■ Epistle to the Corinthians (in biblical references).

cor ▶ **exclamation** Brit. informal expressing surprise, excitement, admiration, or alarm: *'Cor! That's a beautiful black eye you've got!'*
– PHRASES **cor blimey** see **BLIMEY**.
– ORIGIN 1930s: alteration of **GOD**.

cor- ▶ **prefix** variant spelling of **COM-** assimilated before *r* (as in *corrode, corrugate*).

Cora /ˈkɔːrə/ ▶ **noun 1** a member of an American Indian people of western Mexico.
2 [mass noun] the Uto-Aztecan language of this people, with about 15,000 speakers.
▶ **adjective** of or relating to this people or their language.

coracle /ˈkɒrək(ə)l/ ▶ **noun** (especially in Wales and Ireland) a small, round boat made of wickerwork covered with a watertight material, propelled with a paddle.
– ORIGIN mid 16th cent.: from Welsh *corwgl, cwrwgl*, related to Scottish Gaelic and Irish *curach* 'small boat'; compare with **CURRACH**.

coracoid /ˈkɒrəkɔɪd/ ▶ **noun** (also **coracoid process**) Anatomy a short projection from the shoulder blade in mammals, to which part of the biceps is attached.
– ORIGIN mid 18th cent.: from modern Latin *coracoides*, from Greek *korakoeidēs* 'raven-like', from *korax* 'raven' (because of the resemblance to a raven's beak).

coral ▶ **noun 1** [mass noun] a hard stony substance secreted by certain marine coelenterates as an external skeleton, typically forming large reefs in warm seas: [as modifier] *a coral reef*
■ precious red coral, used in jewellery. ■ the pinkish-red colour of red coral.
2 a sedentary coelenterate of warm and tropical seas, with a calcareous, horny, or soft skeleton. Most corals are colonial and many rely on the presence of green algae in their tissues to obtain energy from sunlight.
• Several orders in the class Anthozoa, including the 'true' or **stony corals** (order Scleractinia or Madreporaria), which form reefs, the **soft corals** (order Alcyonacea), and the **horny corals** (order Gorgonacea).
3 [mass noun] the unfertilized roe of a lobster or scallop, which is used as food and becomes reddish when cooked.
– DERIVATIVES **coralloid** adjective (chiefly Biology & Zoology).
– ORIGIN Middle English: via Old French from Latin *corallum*, from Greek *korallion, kouralion*.

coralberry ▶ **noun** (pl. **-ies**) an evergreen North American shrub of the honeysuckle family, which has fragrant white flowers followed by deep red berries.
• *Symphoricarpos orbiculatus*, family Caprifoliaceae.

coral fungus ▶ **noun** a fungus which produces a fruiting body composed of upright branching finger-like projections which resemble coral, found in both Eurasia and North America.
• Genus *Clavulina*, family Clavariaceae, class Hymenomycetes.

Corallian /kɒˈralɪən/ ▶ **adjective** & **noun** another term for **OXFORDIAN** (in sense 1).
– ORIGIN from Latin *corallium* 'coral' (with reference to the coral-derived limestone deposits) + **-AN**.

coralline /ˈkɒrəlʌɪn/ ▶ **noun** (also **coralline alga** or **coralline seaweed**) a branching reddish seaweed with a calcareous jointed stem.
• Family Corallinaceae, division Rhodophyta, in particular *Corallina officinalis*, which is common on the coasts of the North Atlantic.
■ (in general use) a sedentary colonial marine animal, especially a bryozoan.
▶ **adjective** chiefly Geology derived or formed from coral: *the islands were volcanic rather than coralline in origin.*
■ of the pinkish-red colour of precious red coral.
■ resembling coral: *coralline sponges.*
– ORIGIN mid 16th cent.: the noun from Italian *corallina*, diminutive of *corallo* 'coral', the adjective (mid 17th cent.) from French *corallin* or late Latin *corallinus*, both based on Latin *corallum* 'coral'.

corallita /ˌkɒrəˈliːtə/ (also **coralita**) ▶ **noun** a pink-flowered climbing vine native to Mexico and the Caribbean, grown as an ornamental.
• *Antigonon leptopus*, family Polygonaceae.
– ORIGIN late 19th cent.: from American Spanish *coralito*, diminutive of Spanish *coral* 'coral'.

corallite /ˈkɒrəlʌɪt/ ▶ **noun** Palaeontology the cup-like calcareous skeleton of a single coral polyp.
■ a fossil coral.
– ORIGIN early 19th cent.: from Latin *corallum* 'coral' + **-ITE**[1].

coral rag ▶ **noun** [mass noun] rubbly limestone composed chiefly of petrified coral.

coralroot ▶ **noun 1** (also **coralroot orchid**) a leafless orchid which has inconspicuous flowers and lacks chlorophyll. It has a pale knobbly rhizome which obtains nourishment from decaying organic matter.
• Genus *Corallorhiza*, family Orchidaceae: several species, including the widespread *C. trifida*.
■ another term for **COCKSCOMB** (in sense 3).
2 (also **coralroot bittercress**) a Eurasian woodland plant with purple flowers and bud-like swellings (bulbils) at the base of the stem.
• *Cardamine bulbifera*, family Cruciferae.

Coral Sea a part of the western Pacific lying between Australia, New Guinea, and Vanuatu, the scene of a naval battle between US and Japanese carriers in 1942.

coral snake ▶ **noun** a brightly coloured venomous snake of the cobra family, typically having conspicuous bands of red, yellow, white, and black. Compare with **FALSE CORAL SNAKE**.
• *Micrurus* and other genera in the family Elapidae: numerous species.

coral spot (also **coral spot disease**) ▶ **noun** [mass noun] a common fungal disease of trees and shrubs, appearing as numerous minute pink or dark red cushion-like bodies on the twigs and branches and causing dieback.
• *Nectria cinnabarina*, family Hypocreaceae, subdivision Ascomycotina.

coral tree ▶ **noun** a tropical or subtropical thorny shrub or tree with showy red or orange flowers that are pollinated by birds.
• Genus *Erythrina*, family Leguminosae.

cor anglais /kɔːr ˈɑːŋgleɪ, ˈɒŋgleɪ/ ▶ **noun** (pl. **cors anglais** pronunc. same) Music an alto woodwind instrument of the oboe family, having a bulbous bell and sounding a fifth lower than the oboe. Also called **ENGLISH HORN**.
– ORIGIN late 19th cent.: French, literally 'English horn'.

corbeil /ˈkɔːbeɪl/ ▶ **noun** Architecture a representation in stone of a basket of flowers.
– ORIGIN early 18th cent.: from French *corbeille* 'basket', from late Latin *corbicula* 'small basket', diminutive of *corbis*.

corbeille /kɔːˈbeɪ/ ▶ **noun** an elegant basket of flowers or fruit.
– ORIGIN early 19th cent.: French, 'basket' (see also **CORBEIL**).

corbel /ˈkɔːb(ə)l/ ▶ **noun** a projection jutting out from a wall to support a structure above it.
▶ **verb** (**corbelled**, **corbelling**; US **corbeled**, **corbeling**) [with obj.] (often **be corbelled out**) support (a structure such as an arch or balcony) on corbels.
– ORIGIN late Middle English: from Old French, diminutive of *corp* 'crow', from Latin *corvus* 'raven' (perhaps because of the shape of a corbel, resembling a crow's beak).

corbel table ▶ **noun** a projecting course of bricks or stones resting on corbels.

corbicula /kɔːˈbɪkjʊlə/ ▶ **noun** (pl. **corbiculae** /-liː/) Entomology another term for **POLLEN BASKET**.
– ORIGIN early 19th cent.: from late Latin.

corbie /ˈkɔːbi/ ▶ **noun** (pl. **-ies**) Scottish a raven, crow, or rook.
– ORIGIN late Middle English: from Old French *corb*, variant of *corp* 'crow' (see **CORBEL**).

corbie steps ▶ **plural noun** Scottish term for **CROW STEPS**

Corcovado /ˌkɔːkəˈvɑːdəʊ/ a peak rising to 711 m (2,310 ft) on the south side of Rio de Janeiro. A gigantic statue of Christ, 40 m (131 ft) high, named 'Christ the Redeemer', stands on its summit.

Corcyra /kɔːˈsʌɪərə/ ancient Greek name for **CORFU**.

cord ▶ **noun 1** [mass noun] long thin flexible string or rope made from several twisted strands: *hang the picture from a rail on a length of cord.*
■ [count noun] a length of such material, typically one used to fasten or move a specified object: *a dressing-gown cord.* ■ [count noun] an anatomical structure resembling a length of cord (e.g. the spinal cord, the umbilical cord): *the baby was still attached to its mother by the cord.* ■ [count noun] an electric flex.
2 [mass noun] ribbed fabric, especially corduroy: [as modifier] *cord jackets.*
■ (**cords**) corduroy trousers: *he was dressed in faded black cords.* ■ a cord-like rib on fabric.
3 a measure of cut wood (usually 128 cu.ft, 3.62 cubic metres).
▶ **verb** [with obj.] [usu. as adj. **corded**] attach a cord to: *a corded curtain track.*
– PHRASES **cut the (umbilical) cord** figurative cease to rely on someone or something protective or supportive and begin to act independently.
– DERIVATIVES **cord-like** adjective.
– ORIGIN Middle English: from Old French *corde*, from Latin *chorda*, from Greek *khordē* 'gut, string of a musical instrument'.

cordage ▶ **noun** [mass noun] cords or ropes, especially in a ship's rigging.
– ORIGIN late 15th cent.: from Old French, from *corde* 'rope' (see **CORD**).

cordate /ˈkɔːdeɪt/ ▶ **adjective** Botany & Zoology heart-shaped.
– ORIGIN mid 17th cent. (in the sense 'wise, prudent'): from Latin *cordatus* 'wise' (in modern Latin 'heart-shaped'), from *cor, cord-* 'heart'.

Corday /kɔːˈdeɪ/, Charlotte (1768–93), French political assassin; full name *Marie Anne Charlotte Corday d'Armont*. She became involved with the Girondists and in 1793 assassinated the revolutionary leader Jean Paul Marat in his bath; she was found guilty of treason and guillotined.

corded ▶ **adjective 1** (of cloth) ribbed.
■ (of a tensed muscle) standing out so as to resemble a piece of cord.
2 equipped with a cord or flex: *corded and cordless phones.*

Cordelier /ˌkɔːdəˈlɪə/ ▶ **noun** a Franciscan Observant.
– ORIGIN late Middle English: from Old French, from *cordelle* 'small rope', diminutive of *corde* (see **CORD**). The name derives from the knotted cord worn by the Cordeliers around the waist.

cordgrass ▶ **noun** [mass noun] a coarse wiry coastal grass which is sometimes used to stabilize mudflats.
• Genus *Spartina*, family Gramineae.

cordial ▶ **adjective** warm and friendly: *the atmosphere was cordial and relaxed.*
■ strongly felt: *I earned his cordial loathing.*
▶ **noun 1** Brit. a sweet fruit-flavoured drink, usually sold as a concentrate and diluted with water before being drunk.
■ chiefly N. Amer. another term for **LIQUEUR**.
2 a comforting or pleasant-tasting medicine.
– DERIVATIVES **cordiality** noun, **cordially** adverb.
– ORIGIN Middle English (also in the sense 'belonging to the heart') : from medieval Latin *cordialis*, from Latin *cor, cord-* 'heart'.

cordierite /ˈkɔːdɪərʌɪt/ ▶ **noun** [mass noun] a dark blue mineral occurring chiefly in metamorphic rocks. It consists of an aluminosilicate of magnesium and iron, and also occurs as a dichroic gem variety.
– ORIGIN early 19th cent.: named after Pierre L. A. *Cordier* (1777–1861), French geologist, + **-ITE**[1].

cordillera /ˌkɔːdɪˈljɛːrə/ ▶ **noun** a system or group of parallel mountain ranges together with the intervening plateaux and other features, especially in the Andes or the Rockies.
– ORIGIN early 18th cent.: from Spanish, from *cordilla*, diminutive of *cuerda* 'cord', from Latin *chorda* (see **CORD**).

cording ▶ **noun** [mass noun] cord or braid, especially that used as a decorative fabric trimming.

cordite ▶ **noun** [mass noun] a smokeless explosive made from nitrocellulose, nitroglycerine, and petroleum jelly, used in ammunition.
– ORIGIN late 19th cent.: from **CORD** (because of its string-like appearance) + **-ITE**[1].

cordless ▶ **adjective** (of an electrical appliance or telephone) working without connection to a mains supply or central unit.
▶ **noun** a cordless telephone.

Cordoba /ˈkɔːdəbə/ (also **Cordova**) **1** a city in Andalusia, southern Spain; pop. 309,200 (1991). Founded by the Carthaginians, it was under Moorish rule from 711 to 1236, and was renowned for its architecture, particularly the Great Mosque. Spanish name **CÓRDOBA** /ˈkorðoβa/.

C

2 a city in central Argentina; pop. 1,198,000 (1990).

cordoba /ˈkɔːdəbə/ ▶ **noun** the basic monetary unit of Nicaragua, equal to 100 centavos.
– ORIGIN named after F. Fernández de *Córdoba*, a 16th-cent. Spanish governor of Nicaragua.

cordon /ˈkɔːd(ə)n/ ▶ **noun 1** a line or circle of police, soldiers, or guards preventing access to or from an area or building: *troops threw a cordon around the headquarters.*
2 a fruit tree trained to grow as a single stem.
3 Architecture another term for **STRING COURSE**.
▶ **verb** [with obj.] (**cordon something off**) prevent access to or from an area or building by surrounding it with police or other guards: *the city centre was cordoned off after fires were discovered in two stores.*
– ORIGIN late Middle English (denoting an ornamental braid worn on the person): from Italian *cordone*, augmentative of *corda*, and French *cordon*, diminutive of *corde*, both from Latin *chorda* 'string, rope' (see **CORD**). Sense 3, the earliest of the current noun senses, dates from the early 18th cent.

cordon bleu /ˌkɔːdɒ̃ ˈbləː/ ▶ **adjective** Cookery of the highest class: *a cordon bleu chef.*
■ [postpositive] denoting a dish consisting of an escalope of veal or chicken rolled, filled with cheese and ham, and then fried in breadcrumbs.
▶ **noun 1** a cook of the highest class.
2 (**cordon-bleu**) (also **cordon-bleu finch**) (pl. **cordon-bleus**) an African waxbill that is popular as a cage bird. The male has a blue face, breast, and tail, a brown back, and a red bill.
● Genus *Uraeginthus*, family Estrildidae: three species.
– ORIGIN mid 18th cent. (as a noun, often specifically denoting a first-class cook): French, literally 'blue ribbon'. The blue ribbon once signified the highest order of chivalry in the reign of the Bourbon kings.

cordon sanitaire /sanɪˈtɛː/ ▶ **noun** (pl. **cordons sanitaires** pronunc. same) a guarded line preventing anyone from leaving an area infected by a disease and thus spreading it.
■ a measure designed to prevent communication or the spread of undesirable influences: *these rules help to reinforce the cordon sanitaire around Whitehall.*
– ORIGIN mid 19th cent.: French, from *cordon* 'line, border' (see **CORDON**) + *sanitaire* 'sanitary'.

Cordova /ˈkɔːdəvə/ English name for **CORDOBA**.

cordovan /ˈkɔːdəv(ə)n/ ▶ **noun** [mass noun] a kind of soft leather made originally from goatskin and now from horsehide.
– ORIGIN late 16th cent.: from Spanish *cordován*, former spelling of *cordobán* 'of Cordoba' (see sense 1 of **CORDOBA**), where it was originally made.

Cordtex ▶ **noun** [mass noun] trademark fuse cable consisting of a core of explosive material in a plastic and textile sheath.
– ORIGIN 1930s: from the noun **CORD** + **TEXTILE**.

Cordura /kɔːˈdjʊərə/ ▶ **noun** [mass noun] trademark a durable synthetic fabric.

corduroy /ˈkɔːdərɔɪ, -djʊ-/ ▶ **noun** [mass noun] a thick cotton fabric with velvety ribs.
■ (**corduroys**) trousers made of corduroy.
– ORIGIN late 18th cent.: probably from **CORD** 'ribbed fabric' + *duroy*, denoting a kind of lightweight worsted formerly made in the West of England; of unknown origin.

corduroy road ▶ **noun** historical a road made of tree trunks laid across a swamp.

cordwainer /ˈkɔːdweɪnə/ ▶ **noun** Brit. archaic a shoemaker (still used in the names of guilds): *the Cordwainers' Company.*
– ORIGIN Middle English: from Anglo-Norman French *cordewaner*, from Old French *cordewan*, 'of Cordoba' (see **CORDOVAN**).

cordwood ▶ **noun** [mass noun] wood that has been cut into uniform lengths, used especially as firewood or for building.

CORE ▶ **abbreviation for** (in the US) Congress of Racial Equality.

core ▶ **noun 1** the tough central part of various fruits, containing the seeds: *an apple core.*
2 the central or most important part of something, in particular:
■ [often as modifier] the part of something that is central to its existence or character: *managers can concentrate on their core activities | the plan has the interests of children at its core.* ■ an important or unchanging group of people forming the central part of a larger body. ■ the dense central region of a planet, especially the nickel-iron inner part of the earth. ■ the central part of a nuclear reactor, which contains the fissile material. ■ a tiny ring of magnetic material used in a computer memory to store one bit of data, now superseded by semiconductor memories. ■ the inner strand of an electric cable or rope. ■ a piece of soft iron forming the centre of an electromagnet or an induction coil. ■ an internal mould filling a space to be left hollow in a casting. ■ a cylindrical sample of rock, ice, or other material obtained by boring with a hollow drill. ■ Archaeology a piece of flint from which flakes or blades have been removed.
▶ **verb** [with obj.] remove the tough central part and seeds from (a fruit): *peel and core the pears.*
– PHRASES **to the core** to the depths of one's being: *she was shaken to the core by his words.* ■ used to indicate that someone possesses a characteristic to a very high degree: *he is a politician to the core.*
– DERIVATIVES **corer** noun.
– ORIGIN Middle English: of unknown origin.

-core ▶ **combining form** (used as the second element of various compounds) denoting types of rock or dance music that have an aggressive presentation: *queercore.*
– ORIGIN from **CORE**, on the pattern of *hard-core*.

core dump ▶ **noun** Computing a dump of the contents of main memory, carried out typically as an aid to debugging.

coreferential ▶ **adjective** Linguistics (of two elements or units) having the same reference.
– DERIVATIVES **coreference** noun.

co-religionist (also **coreligionist**) ▶ **noun** an adherent of the same religion as another person.

corella /kəˈrɛlə/ ▶ **noun** a white Australasian cockatoo with some pink feathers on the face, bare blue skin around the eye, and typically a long bill.
● Genus *Cacatua*, family Cacatuidae (or Psittacidae): three species, in particular the widespread **little corella** (*C. sanguinea*).
– ORIGIN late 19th cent.: from Wiradhuri.

Corelli[1] /kəˈrɛli/, Arcangelo (1653–1713), Italian violinist and composer. His best-known works are his trio and solo sonatas for the violin and his concerti grossi (published posthumously in 1714), especially the 'Christmas' concerto.

Corelli[2] /kəˈrɛli/, Marie (1855–1924), English writer of romantic fiction; pseudonym of *Mary Mackay*. The sales of her novels *Thelma* (1887), *Barabbas* (1893), and *The Sorrows of Satan* (1895) broke all existing records for book sales, although popularity was not matched by critical acclaim.

coreopsis /ˌkɒrɪˈɒpsɪs/ ▶ **noun** a plant of the daisy family, which is cultivated for its rayed, typically yellow, flowers. Also called **TICKSEED**.
● Genus *Coreopsis*, family Compositae.
– ORIGIN modern Latin, from Greek *koris* 'bug' + *opsis* 'appearance' (because of the shape of the seed).

co-respondent (also **corespondent**) ▶ **noun** a person cited in a divorce case as having committed adultery with the respondent.

co-respondent shoes (also **co-respondents**) ▶ **plural noun** dated, humorous men's two-toned shoes.

core time ▶ **noun** [mass noun] Brit. the central part of the working day in a flexitime system, when an employee must be present.

corf /kɔːf/ ▶ **noun** (pl. **corves**) Brit. a wagon or large basket, formerly used for bringing coal out of a mine.
– ORIGIN late Middle English (in the general sense 'basket'): from Middle Low German and Middle Dutch *korf*, from Latin *corbis* 'basket'.

Corfu /kɔːˈf(j)uː/ a Greek island, one of the largest of the Ionian Islands, off the west coast of mainland Greece. It was known in ancient times as Corcyra; pop. 105,350 (1991). Greek name **KÉRKIRA**.

corgi (also **Welsh corgi**) ▶ **noun** (pl. **corgis**) a dog of a short-legged breed with a foxlike head.
– ORIGIN 1920s: from Welsh, from *cor* 'dwarf' + *ci* 'dog'.

coriaceous /ˌkɒrɪˈeɪʃəs/ ▶ **adjective** technical resembling or having the texture of leather: *coriaceous leaves.*
– ORIGIN late 17th cent.: from late Latin *coriaceus* (from Latin *corium* 'leather') + **-OUS**.

coriander /ˌkɒrɪˈandə/ ▶ **noun** [mass noun] an aromatic Mediterranean plant of the parsley family, the leaves and seeds of which are used as culinary herbs.
● *Coriandrum sativum*, family Umbelliferae.
– ORIGIN Middle English: from Old French *coriandre*, from Latin *coriandrum*, from Greek *koriannon*.

Corinth /ˈkɒrɪnθ/ a city on the north coast of the Peloponnese, Greece; pop. 27,400 (1991). The modern city, built in 1858, is a little to the north-east of the site of an ancient city of the same name, which was a prominent city state in ancient Greece. Greek name **KÓRINTHOS**.

Corinth, Gulf of an inlet of the Ionian Sea extending between the Peloponnese and central Greece. Also called **GULF OF LEPANTO**.

Corinth, Isthmus of a narrow neck of land linking the Peloponnese with central Greece and separating the Gulf of Corinth from the Saronic Gulf.

Corinth Canal a man-made shipping channel across the narrowest part of the Isthmus of Corinth (a distance of 6.4 km, or 4 miles). Opened in 1893, it links the Gulf of Corinth and the Saronic Gulf.

Corinthian /kəˈrɪnθɪən/ ▶ **adjective 1** belonging or relating to Corinth, especially the ancient city.
■ relating to or denoting the lightest and most ornate of the classical orders of architecture (used especially by the Romans), characterized by flared capitals with rows of acanthus leaves.
2 involving or displaying the highest standards of sportsmanship: *a club embodying the Corinthian spirit.*
▶ **noun 1** a native of Corinth.
■ historical a wealthy amateur of sport.
2 [mass noun] the Corinthian order of architecture.

Corinthians, Epistle to the either of two books of the New Testament, epistles of St Paul to the Church at Corinth.

Coriolanus /ˌkɒrɪəˈleɪnəs/, Gaius (or Gnaeus) Marcius (5th century BC), Roman general, who got his name from the capture of the Volscian town of Corioli. According to legend, after his banishment from Rome he led a Volscian army against the city and was only turned back by the pleas of his mother and wife.

Coriolis effect /ˌkɒrɪˈəʊlɪs/ ▶ **noun** [mass noun] Physics an effect whereby a mass moving in a rotating system experiences a force (the **Coriolis force**) acting perpendicular to the direction of motion and to the axis of rotation. On the earth, the effect tends to deflect moving objects to the right in the northern hemisphere and to the left in the southern and is important in the formation of cyclonic weather systems.
– ORIGIN early 20th cent.: named after Gaspard *Coriolis* (1792–1843), French engineer.

corium /ˈkɔːrɪəm/ ▶ **noun** chiefly Zoology another term for **DERMIS**.
– ORIGIN early 19th cent.: from Latin, 'skin'.

Cork a county of the Republic of Ireland, on the south coast in the province of Munster.
■ its county town, a port on the River Lee; pop. 127,000 (1991).

cork ▶ **noun** [mass noun] the buoyant, light brown substance obtained from the outer layer of the bark of the cork oak: [as modifier] *cork tiles.*
■ [count noun] a bottle stopper, especially one made of cork. ■ [count noun] a piece of cork used as a float for a fishing line or net. ■ Botany a protective layer of dead cells immediately below the bark of woody plants.
▶ **verb** [with obj.] (often **be corked**) **1** close or seal (a bottle) with a cork.
■ [as adj. **corked**] (of wine) spoilt by tannin from the cork.
2 draw with burnt cork.
3 illicitly hollow out (a baseball bat) and fill it with cork to make it lighter.
– DERIVATIVES **cork-like** adjective.
– ORIGIN Middle English: from Dutch and Low German *kork*, from Spanish *alcorque* 'cork-soled sandal', from Arabic *al-* 'the' and (probably) Spanish Arabic *ḳurḳ*, *ḳorḳ*, based on Latin *quercus* 'oak, cork oak'.

corkage ▶ **noun** [mass noun] a charge made by a restaurant or hotel for serving wine that has been brought in by a customer.

cork cambium ▶ **noun** [mass noun] Botany tissue in the stem of a plant that gives rise to cork on its outer surface and a layer of cells containing chlorophyll on its inner.

corker ▶ **noun** dated, informal an excellent or astonishing person or thing: *it was the season's first goal, and a corker.*

corking ▶ **adjective** Brit. informal, dated, excellent: *cars in corking condition.*

cork oak ▶ **noun** an evergreen Mediterranean oak, the outer layer of the bark of which is the source of cork, which can be stripped without harming the tree.
• *Quercus suber*, family Fagaceae.

corks ▶ **exclamation** Brit. informal, dated expressing astonishment or dismay: *corks—he's old!*
– ORIGIN early 20th cent.: alteration of archaic *cock* 'God', used in oaths and exclamations, or a blend of this and **LAWKS**.

corkscrew ▶ **noun** a device for pulling corks from bottles, consisting of a spiral metal rod that is inserted into the cork and a handle that extracts it.
■ [usu. as modifier] a thing with a spiral shape or movement: *a girl with corkscrew curls.*
▶ **verb** [no obj.] move or twist in a spiral motion: *the plane was corkscrewing towards the earth.*

cork-tipped ▶ **adjective** Brit. (of a cigarette) having a filter made of cork-like material.

corkwood ▶ **noun** a shrub or tree which yields light porous timber, in particular:
• a small American tree which produces timber used for fishing floats (*Leitneria floridana*, family Leitneriaceae). • a similar tree native to New Zealand (*Entelea arborescens*, family Tiliaceae).

corky ▶ **adjective** (**corkier**, **corkiest**) **1** cork-like.
2 (of wine) corked.

corm ▶ **noun** a rounded underground storage organ present in plants such as crocuses, gladioli, and cyclamens, consisting of a swollen stem base covered with scale leaves. Compare with **BULB** (in sense 1), **RHIZOME**.
– ORIGIN mid 19th cent.: from modern Latin *cormus*, from Greek *kormos* 'trunk stripped of its boughs'.

cormel /ˈkɔːm(ə)l/ ▶ **noun** a small corm growing at the side of a mature corm.

cormlet ▶ **noun** a small corm growing at the base of a mature corm.

cormorant /ˈkɔːm(ə)r(ə)nt/ ▶ **noun** a rather large diving bird with a long neck, long hooked bill, short legs, and mainly dark plumage. It typically breeds on coastal cliffs.
• Genus *Phalacrocorax* (and *Nannopterum*), family Phalacrocoracidae: numerous species, in particular the widespread (**great**) **cormorant** (*P. carbo*).
– ORIGIN Middle English: from Old French *cormaran*, from medieval Latin *corvus marinus* 'sea-raven'. The final *-t* is on the pattern of words such as *peasant*.

corn[1] ▶ **noun** [mass noun] **1** chiefly Brit. the chief cereal crop of a district, especially (in England) wheat or (in Scotland) oats.
■ the grain of such a crop. ■ informal the grain of any cereal, especially as fed to livestock. ■ North American, Australian, and New Zealand term for **MAIZE**.
2 informal something banal or sentimental: *the film is pure corn.*
– PHRASES **corn on the cob** maize when cooked and eaten straight from the cob.
– ORIGIN Old English, of Germanic origin; related to Dutch *koren* and German *Korn*.

corn[2] ▶ **noun** a small, painful area of thickened skin on the foot, especially on the toes, caused by pressure.
– ORIGIN late Middle English: via Anglo-Norman French from Latin *cornu* 'horn'.

cornball N. Amer. informal ▶ **adjective** trite and sentimental: *a cornball movie.*
▶ **noun** a person with trite or sentimental ideas.

corn beef ▶ **noun** [mass noun] corned beef.

corn borer ▶ **noun** a moth whose larvae feed upon and bore into maize.
• Several species in the family Pyralidae, in particular the **European corn borer** (*Ostrinia nubilalis*), which was accidentally introduced into North America, and *Diatraea* (or *Zeadiatraea*) *grandiosella* of the southern US.

cornbrash ▶ **noun** [mass noun] Geology an earthy fossiliferous limestone occurring widely in England in a thin formation of Jurassic age.
– ORIGIN early 19th cent.: from **CORN**[1] + **BRASH**[2].

cornbread ▶ **noun** [mass noun] a type of bread made from maize meal.

corn bunting ▶ **noun** a large thickset Eurasian bunting with brown streaked plumage and a jangling song, inhabiting open grassland and arable land.
• *Emberiza* (or *Miliaria*) *calandra*, family Emberizidae (subfamily Emberizinae).

corn circle ▶ **noun** another term for **CROP CIRCLE**.

corn cob ▶ **noun** see **COB**[1] (sense 2).

corn-cob pipe ▶ **noun** US a tobacco pipe with a bowl made from a dried corn cob.

corncockle ▶ **noun** a pink-flowered Mediterranean plant introduced into Britain, where it became a cornfield weed. It has since been almost eradicated because its poisonous seeds contaminate flour.
• *Agrostemma githago*, family Caryophyllaceae.
– ORIGIN early 18th cent.: from **CORN**[1] + *cockle* (from Old English *coccul* 'corncockle', perhaps via Latin from Greek *kokkos* 'berry').

corncrake ▶ **noun** a secretive Eurasian crake inhabiting coarse grasslands, with mainly brown streaked plumage and a distinctive double rasping call. Due to changes in agricultural practices it is now much rarer in the British Isles than formerly. Also called **LANDRAIL**.
• *Crex crex*, family Rallidae.

corn crib ▶ **noun** N. Amer. a bin or ventilated building for storing maize.

corn dog ▶ **noun** N. Amer. a hot dog covered in maize-flour batter, fried, and served on a stick.

corn dolly ▶ **noun** Brit. a symbolic or decorative model of a human figure, made of plaited straw.

cornea /ˈkɔːnɪə/ ▶ **noun** the transparent layer forming the front of the eye.
– DERIVATIVES **corneal** adjective.
– ORIGIN late Middle English: from medieval Latin *cornea tela* 'horny tissue', from Latin *cornu* 'horn'.

corn earworm ▶ **noun** an American moth caterpillar which is a pest of both maize and cotton. Also called **BOLLWORM**, ***cotton bollworm***.
• *Heliothis zea*, family Noctuidae.

corned ▶ **adjective** [attrib.] (of food) preserved in salt water: *a tin of corned beef | corned ham.*

Corneille /kɔːˈneɪ, French kɔʀnɛj/, Pierre (1606–84), French dramatist, generally regarded as the founder of classical French tragedy. Notable plays: *Le Cid* (1637), *Cinna* (1641), and *Polyeucte* (1643).

cornel /ˈkɔːn(ə)l/ ▶ **noun** a dogwood, especially of a dwarf variety.
• Genus *Cornus*, family Cornaceae: several species, including the dwarf *C. suecica*.
– ORIGIN late Middle English (denoting the wood of the cornelian cherry): from Old French *corneille*, from Latin *cornus*.

cornelian /kɔːˈniːlɪən/ ▶ **noun** variant spelling of **CARNELIAN**.

cornelian cherry ▶ **noun** a Eurasian flowering shrub or small tree of the dogwood family, cultivated as an ornamental.
• *Cornus mas*, family Cornaceae.
■ the edible oval red berry of this plant.
– ORIGIN early 17th cent.: *cornelian* from **CORNEL** + **-IAN**.

corneous /ˈkɔːnɪəs/ ▶ **adjective** formal horn-like; horny: *the skeleton is formed of a corneous substance.*
– ORIGIN mid 17th cent.: from Latin *corneus* (from *cornu* 'horn') + **-OUS**.

corner ▶ **noun 1** a place or angle where two or more sides or edges meet: *Jan sat at one corner of the table.*
■ an area inside a room, box, or square-shaped space, near the place where two or more edges or surfaces meet: *he drove the ball into the corner of the net.* ■ figurative a difficult or awkward situation: *he found himself backed into a now—or never—corner.* ■ a place where two streets meet: *the pub stood on the corner of Page Street.* ■ a sharp bend in a road. ■ Brit. a triangular cut from the hind end of a side of bacon. ■ Climbing, Brit. a place where two planes of rock meet at an angle of between 60° and 120°.
2 a part, region, or area, especially one regarded as secluded or remote: *they descended on the college* ***from all corners of the world*** | figurative *she couldn't bear journalists prying into every corner of her life.*
■ a position in which one dominates the supply of a particular commodity.
3 (also **corner kick**) Soccer a free kick taken by the attacking side from a corner of the field after the ball has been sent over the byline by a defender.
■ a similar free hit in field hockey.
4 Boxing & Wrestling each of the diagonally opposite ends of the ring, where a contestant rests between rounds.
■ a contestant's supporters or seconds: *Hodkinson was encouraged by his corner.*
▶ **verb** [with obj.] **1** (often **be cornered**) force (a person or animal) into a place or situation from which it is hard to escape: *the man was eventually cornered by police dogs.*
■ detain (someone) in conversation, typically against their will: *I managed to corner Gary for fifteen minutes.*
2 control (a market) by dominating the supply of a particular commodity: *whether they will* ***corner the market*** *in graphics software remains to be seen.*
■ establish a corner in (a commodity): *you cornered vanadium and made a killing.*
3 [no obj.] (of a vehicle or driver) go round a bend in a road: *no squeal is evident from the tyres when cornering fast.*
– PHRASES (**just**) **around** (or **round**) **the corner** very near: *there's a chemist round the corner.* **fight one's corner** defend one's position or interests: *we need someone in the cabinet to fight our corner.* **in someone's corner** on someone's side; giving someone support and encouragement. **on** (or **at** or **in**) **every corner** everywhere: *there are Gaultier shops on every corner.* **see someone/thing out of** (or **from**) **the corner of one's eye** see someone or something at the edge of one's field of vision.
– ORIGIN Middle English: from Anglo-Norman French, based on Latin *cornu* 'horn, tip, corner'.

cornerback ▶ **noun** American Football a defensive back positioned to the outside of the linebackers.

corner boy ▶ **noun** chiefly Irish a disreputable man or youth who spends his time loitering on the street.

cornered ▶ **adjective** [in combination] having a specified number of places or angles where the edges or sides meet: *young boys in six-cornered hats.*
■ having a specified number of parties involved: *a three-cornered meeting was being arranged in Hong Kong.*

corner forward ▶ **noun** (in hurling) a player in an attacking position on the wing.

corner kick ▶ **noun** another term for **CORNER** (in sense 3).

cornerman ▶ **noun** (pl. **-men**) a person whose job is to assist a boxer or wrestler at the corner between rounds.

corner shop ▶ **noun** Brit. a small shop selling groceries and general goods in a mainly residential area.

cornerstone ▶ **noun** a stone that forms the base of a corner of a building, joining two walls.
■ an important quality or feature on which a particular thing depends or is based: *a national minimum wage remained the cornerstone of policy.*

cornerwise ▶ **adverb** at an angle of approximately 45°; diagonally: *he laid the cloth cornerwise on the polished table.*

cornet[1] /ˈkɔːnɪt/ ▶ **noun 1** Music a brass instrument resembling a trumpet but shorter and wider, played chiefly in bands.
■ a compound organ stop with a powerful treble sound.
2 Brit. a cone-shaped wafer, especially one filled with ice cream.
– DERIVATIVES **cornetist** /kɔːˈnɛtɪst/ (also **cornettist**) noun.
– ORIGIN late Middle English (originally denoting a wind instrument made of a horn): from Old French, diminutive of a variant of Latin *cornu* 'horn'.

cornet[2] /ˈkɔːnɪt/ ▶ **noun** chiefly historical the fifth grade of commissioned officer in a cavalry troop, who carried the colours. It is still used in some British cavalry regiments for officers of the rank of second lieutenant.
– DERIVATIVES **cornetcy** noun (pl. **-ies**).
– ORIGIN mid 16th cent.: from French *cornette*, diminutive of *corne* (originally a collective term), based on Latin *cornua* 'horns'. The word originally denoted a kind of woman's headdress, or a strip of lace hanging down from a headdress against the cheeks; later the pennon of a cavalry troop, hence the officer who carried the colours.

cornetfish ▶ **noun** (pl. same or **-fishes**) a large marine fish with a long, narrow, flute-like snout, an elongated body, and a whip-like extension to the tail. It is common in shallow tropical waters of the Atlantic and Indo-Pacific region.
• Family Fistulariidae and genus *Fistularia*: several species.

cornetto /kɔːˈnɛtəʊ/ (also **cornett** /ˈkɔːnɪt, kɔːˈnɛt/) ▶ **noun** (pl. **cornetti** or **cornetts**) a woodwind instrument of the 16th and 17th centuries, typically curved, with finger holes and a cup-shaped mouthpiece.

C

– ORIGIN late 19th cent.: from Italian, diminutive of *corno* 'horn', from Latin *cornu*. Compare with **CORNET**[1].

corn exchange ▶ noun (in the UK) a building where corn is or was traded, typically a hall now converted for other public use.

corn-fed ▶ adjective fed on grain, especially maize: *corn-fed chickens.*
■US informal plump; well fed. ■ US informal provincial; unsophisticated: *a backward, corn-fed Heartland town.*

cornflakes ▶ plural noun a breakfast cereal consisting of toasted flakes made from maize flour.

cornflour ▶ noun [mass noun] Brit. finely ground maize flour, used for thickening sauces.

cornflower ▶ noun a slender Eurasian plant related to the knapweeds, with flowers that are typically a deep, vivid blue.
● Genus *Centaurea*, family Compositae: several species, including the annual *Centaurea cyaneus* (also called **BLUEBOTTLE**), formerly a common weed of cornfields, and the perennial *C. montana*, grown in gardens.
■(also **cornflower blue**) [mass noun] a deep, vivid blue colour.

Cornhusker State informal name for **NEBRASKA**.

cornice /ˈkɔːnɪs/ ▶ noun 1 an ornamental moulding round the wall of a room just below the ceiling.
■a horizontal moulded projection crowning a building or structure, especially the uppermost member of the entablature of an order, surmounting the frieze.
2 an overhanging mass of hardened snow at the edge of a mountain precipice.
– DERIVATIVES **corniced** adjective, **cornicing** noun.
– ORIGIN mid 16th cent.: from French *corniche*, from Italian *cornice*, perhaps from Latin *cornix* 'crow' (compare with **CORBEL**), but influenced by Greek *korōnis* 'coping stone'.

corniche /ˈkɔːniʃ, kɔːˈniːʃ/ ▶ noun a road cut into the edge of a cliff, especially one running along a coast.
– ORIGIN mid 19th cent.: from French (see **CORNICE**).

Cornish ▶ adjective of or relating to Cornwall, or its people or language.
▶ noun 1 [as plural noun **the Cornish**] the people of Cornwall collectively.
2 [mass noun] the ancient Celtic language of Cornwall, belonging to the Brythonic branch of the Celtic language group. It gradually died out in the 17th and 18th centuries, although attempts have been made to revive it.
– DERIVATIVES **Cornishman** noun (pl. **-men**), **Cornishwoman** noun (pl. **-women**).
– ORIGIN late Middle English: from the first element of **CORNWALL** + **-ISH**[1].

Cornish cream ▶ noun [mass noun] Brit. clotted cream.

Cornish hen (also **Cornish game hen**) ▶ noun another term for **ROCK CORNISH**.

Cornish pasty ▶ noun Brit. a pasty containing seasoned meat and vegetables, especially potato.

Corn Laws (in the UK) a series of 19th-century laws introduced to protect British farmers from foreign competition by allowing grain to be imported only after the price of home-grown wheat had risen above a certain level. They had the unintended effect of forcing up bread prices and were eventually repealed in 1846.

corn marigold ▶ noun a daisy-like yellow-flowered Eurasian plant which was formerly a common weed of cornfields.
● *Chrysanthemum segetum*, family Compositae.

cornmeal ▶ noun [mass noun] meal made from corn, especially (in the US) maize flour or (in Scotland) oatmeal.

corn oil ▶ noun [mass noun] an oil obtained from the germ of maize, used in cookery and salad dressings.

corn pone ▶ noun N. Amer. unleavened maize bread.
▶ adjective rustic; unsophisticated.

corn roast ▶ noun Canadian a party at which green maize is roasted and eaten.

cornrows ▶ plural noun (especially among black people) a style of braiding and plaiting the hair in narrow strips to form geometric patterns on the scalp.

corn salad ▶ noun another term for **LAMB'S LETTUCE**.

corn snake ▶ noun a long North American rat snake with a spear-shaped mark between the eyes.
● *Elaphe guttata*, family Colubridae.
– ORIGIN late 17th cent.: so named because often found in cornfields.

corn snow ▶ noun [mass noun] chiefly N. Amer. snow with a rough granular surface resulting from alternate thawing and freezing.
– ORIGIN from *corn* in the dialect sense 'granule'.

cornstarch ▶ noun North American term for **CORNFLOUR**.

cornstone ▶ noun [mass noun] Geology a mottled red and green limestone characteristic of the Old and the New Red Sandstone in Britain.

corn syrup ▶ noun [mass noun] chiefly US glucose syrup, especially when made from cornflour.

cornu /ˈkɔːnjuː/ ▶ noun (pl. **cornua** /ˈ-njʊə/) Anatomy a structure with a shape likened to a horn, in particular:
■a horn-shaped projection of the thyroid cartilage or of certain bones (such as the hyoid and the coccyx). ■ either of the two lateral cavities of the womb, into which the Fallopian tubes pass. ■ each of three elongated parts of the lateral ventricles of the brain.
– DERIVATIVES **cornual** adjective.
– ORIGIN late 17th cent.: from Latin, 'horn'.

cornucopia /ˌkɔːnjʊˈkəʊpɪə/ ▶ noun a symbol of plenty consisting of a goat's horn overflowing with flowers, fruit, and corn.
■an ornamental container shaped like such a horn. ■ an abundant supply of good things of a specified kind: *the festival offers a cornucopia of pleasures.*
– DERIVATIVES **cornucopian** adjective.
– ORIGIN early 16th cent.: from late Latin, from Latin *cornu copiae* 'horn of plenty' (a mythical horn able to provide whatever is desired).

cornus /ˈkɔːnəs/ ▶ noun a plant of a genus that comprises the dogwoods.
● Genus *Cornus*, family Cornaceae.
– ORIGIN modern Latin, from Latin, 'dogwood'.

Cornwall a county occupying the extreme south-western peninsula of England; county town, Truro.

Cornwall, Duchy of an estate vested in the Prince of Wales, consisting of properties in Cornwall and elsewhere in SW England.

corny ▶ adjective (**cornier**, **corniest**) informal trite, banal, or mawkishly sentimental: *it sounds corny, but as soon as I saw her I knew she was the one.*
– DERIVATIVES **cornily** adverb, **corniness** noun.
– ORIGIN 1930s: from an earlier sense 'rustic', appealing to country folk'.

corolla /kəˈrɒlə/ ▶ noun Botany the petals of a flower, typically forming a whorl within the sepals and enclosing the reproductive organs. Compare with **CALYX**.
– ORIGIN late 17th cent. (in the sense 'little crown'): from Latin, diminutive of *corona* 'wreath, crown, chaplet'.

corollary /kəˈrɒləri/ ▶ noun (pl. **-ies**) a proposition that follows from (and is often appended to) one already proved.
■a direct or natural consequence or result: *the huge increases in unemployment were the corollary of expenditure cuts.*
▶ adjective forming a proposition that follows from one already proved.
■associated; supplementary.
– ORIGIN late Middle English: from Latin *corollarium* 'money paid for a garland or chaplet; gratuity' (in late Latin 'deduction'), from *corolla*, diminutive of *corona* 'wreath, crown, chaplet'.

coromandel /ˌkɒrəˈmand(ə)l/ ▶ noun 1 (also **coromandel wood** or **coromandel ebony**) [mass noun] a fine-grained, greyish-brown ebony streaked with black, used in furniture. Also called **CALAMANDER**.
2 the Sri Lankan tree that yields this timber.
● *Diospyros quaesita*, family Ebenaceae.
▶ adjective denoting a form of oriental lacquerware with intaglio designs.
– ORIGIN from **COROMANDEL COAST**, from which oriental lacquerware was originally trans-shipped.

Coromandel Coast /ˌkɒrəˈmand(ə)l/ the southern part of the east coast of India, from Point Calimere to the mouth of the Krishna River.

corona[1] /kəˈrəʊnə/ ▶ noun (pl. **coronae** /-niː/)
1 Astronomy the rarefied gaseous envelope of the sun and other stars. The sun's corona is normally visible only during a total solar eclipse, when it is seen as an irregularly shaped pearly glow surrounding the darkened disc of the moon.
■(also **corona discharge**) Physics the glow around a conductor at high potential. ■ a small circle of light seen round the sun or moon, due to diffraction by water droplets.
2 Anatomy a crown or crown-like structure.
■Botany the cup-shaped or trumpet-shaped outgrowth at the centre of a daffodil or narcissus flower.
3 a circular chandelier in a church.
4 Architecture a part of a cornice having a broad vertical face.
– ORIGIN mid 16th cent. (in sense 4): from Latin, 'wreath, crown'.

corona[2] /kəˈrəʊnə/ ▶ noun a long, straight-sided cigar.
– ORIGIN late 19th cent.: from Spanish *La Corona*, literally 'the crown', originally a proprietary name.

Corona Australis /kəˌrəʊnə ɒˈstreɪlɪs/ Astronomy a small southern constellation (the Southern Crown), with no bright stars.
■[as genitive **Coronae Australis** /kəˌrəʊniː ɒˈstreɪlɪs, -nʌɪ/] used with preceding letter or numeral to designate a star in this constellation: *the star Theta Coronae Australis.*
– ORIGIN Latin.

Corona Borealis /ˌbɔːrɪˈeɪlɪs/ Astronomy a northern constellation (the Northern Crown), in which the main stars form a small but prominent arc.
■[as genitive **Coronae Borealis** /kəˌrəʊni, -nʌɪ/ or **Coronae**] used with preceding letter or numeral to designate a star in this constellation: *the star R Coronae Borealis.*
– ORIGIN Latin.

coronach /ˈkɒrənək, -x/ ▶ noun (in Scotland or Ireland) a funeral song.
– ORIGIN early 16th cent. (originally Scots, denoting the outcry of a crowd): from Scottish Gaelic *corranach* (Irish *coranach*), from *comh-* 'together' + *rànach* 'outcry'.

corona discharge ▶ noun see **CORONA**[1] (sense 1).

coronagraph ▶ noun an instrument that blocks out light emitted by the sun's actual surface so that the corona can be observed.

coronal[1] /kəˈrəʊn(ə)l, ˈkɒr(ə)n(ə)l/ ▶ adjective 1 of or relating to the crown or corona of something, in particular:
■Astronomy of or relating to the corona of the sun or another star. ■ Anatomy of or relating to the crown of the head.
2 Anatomy of or in the coronal plane: *coronal imaging.*
3 Phonetics (of a consonant) formed by raising the tip or blade of the tongue towards the hard palate.
▶ noun Phonetics a coronal consonant.
– ORIGIN late Middle English (in the sense 'relating to the crown of the head'): from Latin *coronalis*, from *corona* 'crown'.

coronal[2] /ˈkɒr(ə)n(ə)l/ ▶ noun a garland or wreath for the head: *her eyes sparkled beneath a coronal of flowers.*
■poetic/literary a small crown; a coronet.
– ORIGIN Middle English: apparently from Anglo-Norman French, from *corune* 'crown, wreath' (see **CROWN**).

coronal bone ▶ noun former term for **FRONTAL BONE**.

coronal plane ▶ noun Anatomy an imaginary plane dividing the body into dorsal and ventral parts.

coronal suture ▶ noun Anatomy the transverse suture in the skull separating the frontal bone from the parietal bones.

coronary ▶ adjective Anatomy relating to or denoting the arteries which surround and supply the heart.
■relating to or denoting a structure which encircles a part of the body.
▶ noun (pl. **-ies**) short for **CORONARY THROMBOSIS**.
– ORIGIN mid 17th cent. (in the sense 'resembling a crown'): from Latin *coronarius*, from *corona* 'wreath, crown'.

coronary thrombosis ▶ noun a blockage of the flow of blood to the heart, caused by a blood clot in a coronary artery.

coronation ▶ noun the ceremony of crowning a sovereign or a sovereign's consort.
– ORIGIN late Middle English: via Old French from medieval Latin *coronatio(n-)*, from *coronare* 'to crown', adorn with a garland', from *corona* (see **CROWN**).

coronation chicken ▶ noun [mass noun] a cold dish of cooked chicken served in a sauce flavoured with apricots and curry powder.

– ORIGIN so named because the dish was created for the coronation of Queen Elizabeth II in 1953.

Coronation stone another term for **STONE OF SCONE**.

coronavirus /kəˈrəʊnəˌvʌɪrəs/ ▶ noun Medicine any of a group of RNA viruses that cause a variety of diseases in humans and other animals.

coroner /ˈkɒrənə/ ▶ noun an official who holds inquests into violent, sudden, or suspicious deaths, and (in Britain) inquiries into cases of treasure trove.
■ historical an official responsible for safeguarding the private property of the Crown.
– DERIVATIVES **coronership** noun.
– ORIGIN Middle English: from Anglo-Norman French *coruner*, from *corune* 'a crown' (see **CROWN**); reflecting the Latin title *custos placitorum coronae* 'guardian of the pleas of the crown'.

coronet /ˈkɒr(ə)nɪt/ ▶ noun 1 a small or relatively simple crown, especially as worn by lesser royalty and peers or peeresses.
■ a circular decoration for the head, especially one made of flowers.
2 a ring of bone at the base of a deer's antler.
■ the band of tissue on the lowest part of a horse's pastern, containing the horn-producing cells from which the hoof grows.
– DERIVATIVES **coroneted** adjective.
– ORIGIN late Middle English: from Old French *coronete* 'small crown or garland', diminutive of *corone* (see **CROWN**).

coronoid process ▶ noun Anatomy 1 a flattened triangular projection above the angle of the jaw where the temporalis muscle is attached.
2 a projection from the front of the ulna forming part of the articulation of the elbow.
– ORIGIN mid 18th cent.: *coronoid* from Greek *korōnē* (denoting something hooked) + **-OID**.

Corot /ˈkɒrəʊ, French kɔʁo/, (Jean-Baptiste) Camille (1796–1875), French landscape painter, who worked in an essentially classical style despite his contact with the Barbizon School. Corot had a significant influence on the Impressionists.

Corp. ▶ abbreviation for ■ **(Corp)** informal Corporal: *been abroad before, Corp?* ■ N. Amer. Corporation: *IBM Corp.*

corpora plural form of **CORPUS**.

corporal[1] ▶ noun 1 a rank of non-commissioned officer in the army, above lance corporal or private first class and below sergeant.
2 (also **ship's corporal**) Brit. historical a petty officer who attended solely to police matters, under the master-at-arms.
3 North American term for **FALLFISH**.
– ORIGIN mid 16th cent.: from French, obsolete variant of *caporal*, from Italian *caporale*, probably based on Latin *corpus*, *corpor-* 'body (of troops)', with a change of spelling in Italian due to association with *capo* 'head'.

corporal[2] ▶ adjective of or relating to the human body.
– DERIVATIVES **corporally** adverb.
– ORIGIN late Middle English: via Old French from Latin *corporalis*, from *corpus*, *corpor-* 'body'.

corporal[3] ▶ noun a cloth on which the chalice and paten are placed during the celebration of the Eucharist.
– ORIGIN Middle English: from medieval Latin *corporale* (*pallium*) 'body (cloth)', from Latin *corpus*, *corpor-* 'body'.

corporality ▶ noun [mass noun] rare material or corporeal existence.
– ORIGIN late Middle English: from late Latin *corporalitas*, from Latin *corporalis* 'relating to the body' (see **CORPORAL**[2]).

corporal punishment ▶ noun [mass noun] physical punishment, such as caning or flogging.

corporate ▶ adjective of or relating to a large company or group: *airlines are very keen on their corporate identity.*
■ Law (of a large company or group) authorized to act as a single entity and recognized as such in law. ■ of or shared by all the members of a group: *the service emphasizes the corporate responsibility of the congregation.*
▶ noun a corporate company or group.
– DERIVATIVES **corporately** adverb.
– ORIGIN late 15th cent.: from Latin *corporatus*, past participle of *corporare* 'form into a body', from *corpus*, *corpor-* 'body'.

corporate hospitality ▶ noun [mass noun] the entertaining of clients by companies in order to promote business, especially at sporting or other public events.

corporate raider ▶ noun a financier who makes a practice of making hostile takeover bids for companies, either to control their policies or to resell them for a profit.

corporate state ▶ noun a state governed by representatives not of geographical areas but of vocational corporations of the employers and employees in each trade, profession, or industry.

corporation ▶ noun a large company or group of companies authorized to act as a single entity and recognized as such in law.
■ Brit. a group of people elected to govern a city, town, or borough. ■ dated, humorous a paunch.
– ORIGIN late Middle English: from late Latin *corporatio(n-)*, from Latin *corporare* 'combine in one body' (see **CORPORATE**).

corporation tax ▶ noun [mass noun] tax levied on companies' profits.

corporatism ▶ noun [mass noun] the control of a state or organization by large interest groups.
– DERIVATIVES **corporatist** adjective & noun.

corporative ▶ adjective relating to or denoting a state, typically a fascist one, organized into corporations representing both employers and employed in various spheres.
– DERIVATIVES **corporativism** noun, **corporativist** adjective & noun.

corporatize (also **-ise**) ▶ verb [with obj.] convert (a state organization) into an independent commercial company.

corporeal /kɔːˈpɔːrɪəl/ ▶ adjective of or relating to a person's body, especially as opposed to their spirit: *he was frank about his corporeal appetites.*
■ having a body: *a corporeal God.* ■ Law consisting of material objects: *in Scotland 'goods' includes all corporeal movables except money.*
– DERIVATIVES **corporeality** /-ˈalɪti/ noun, **corporeally** adverb.
– ORIGIN late Middle English (in the sense 'material'): from late Latin *corporealis*, from Latin *corporeus* 'bodily, physical', from *corpus*, *corpor-* 'body'.

corporeity /ˌkɔːpəˈriːɪti, -ˈreɪti/ ▶ noun [mass noun] rare the quality of having a physical body or existence.
– ORIGIN early 17th cent.: from French *corporéité* or medieval Latin *corporeitas*, from Latin *corporeus* 'composed of flesh', from *corpus*, *corpor-* 'body'.

corposant /ˈkɔːpəzant/ ▶ noun archaic an appearance of St Elmo's fire on a mast, rigging, or other structure.
– ORIGIN mid 16th cent.: from Old Spanish, Portuguese, and Italian *corpo santo* 'holy body'.

corps /kɔː/ ▶ noun (pl. **corps** /kɔːz/) [often in names] a main subdivision of an army in the field, consisting of two or more divisions: *the 5th Army Corps.*
■ a branch of an army assigned to a particular kind of work: *the Royal Army Medical Corps.* ■ [with adj. or noun modifier] a body of people engaged in a particular activity: *the press corps.* ■ short for **CORPS DE BALLET**.
– ORIGIN late 16th cent.: from French, from Latin *corpus* 'body'.

corps de ballet /ˌkɔː də ˈbaleɪ/ ▶ noun [treated as sing. or pl.] the members of a ballet company who dance together as a group.
■ the members of the lowest rank of dancers in a ballet company.
– ORIGIN early 19th cent.: French.

corps d'elite /ˌkɔː deɪˈliːt/ ▶ noun a select group of people.
– ORIGIN French.

corpse ▶ noun a dead body, especially of a human being rather than an animal.
▶ verb [no obj.] theatrical slang spoil a piece of acting by forgetting one's lines or laughing uncontrollably.
■ [with obj.] cause (an actor) to do this.
– ORIGIN Middle English (denoting the living body of a person or animal): alteration of **CORSE** by association with Latin *corpus*, a change which also took place in French (Old French *cors* becoming *corps*). The *p* was originally silent, as in French; the final *e* was rare before the 19th cent., but now distinguishes *corpse* from *corps*.

corpse-candle ▶ noun a lambent flame seen just above the ground in a churchyard or over a grave, superstitiously regarded as an omen of death.

corpulent /ˈkɔːpjʊl(ə)nt/ ▶ adjective (of a person) fat.
– DERIVATIVES **corpulence** noun, **corpulency** noun.
– ORIGIN late Middle English: from Latin *corpulentus*, from *corpus* 'body'.

cor pulmonale /ˌkɔː pʌlməˈnɑːli, -ˈeɪli/ ▶ noun [mass noun] Medicine abnormal enlargement of the right side of the heart as a result of disease of the lungs or the pulmonary blood vessels.
– ORIGIN mid 19th cent.: from Latin *cor* 'heart' and modern Latin *pulmonalis* (from Latin *pulmo(n-)* 'lung').

corpus /ˈkɔːpəs/ ▶ noun (pl. **corpora** or **corpuses**)
1 a collection of written texts, especially the entire works of a particular author or a body of writing on a particular subject: *the Darwinian corpus.*
■ a collection of written or spoken material in machine-readable form, assembled for the purpose of studying linguistic structures, frequencies, etc.
2 Anatomy the main body or mass of a structure.
■ the central part of the stomach, between the fundus and the antrum.
– ORIGIN late Middle English (denoting a human or animal body): from Latin, literally 'body'. Sense 1 dates from the early 18th cent.

corpus callosum /kəˈləʊsəm/ ▶ noun (pl. **corpora callosa**) Anatomy a broad band of nerve fibres joining the two hemispheres of the brain.
– ORIGIN early 18th cent.: from **CORPUS** and Latin *callosum*, neuter of *callosus* 'tough'.

corpus cavernosum /ˌkavəˈnəʊsəm/ ▶ noun (pl. **corpora cavernosa** /-sə/) Anatomy either of two masses of erectile tissue forming the bulk of the penis and the clitoris.
– ORIGIN from **CORPUS** and Latin *cavernosum*, neuter of *cavernosus* 'containing hollows'.

Corpus Christi[1] /ˌkɔːpəs ˈkrɪsti/ a city and port in southern Texas; pop. 257,400 (1990). It is situated on Corpus Christi Bay, an inlet of the Gulf of Mexico.

Corpus Christi[2] /ˌkɔːpəs ˈkrɪsti/ a feast of the Western Christian Church commemorating the institution of the Eucharist, observed on the Thursday after Trinity Sunday.
– ORIGIN Latin, literally 'body of Christ'.

corpuscle /ˈkɔːpʌs(ə)l/ ▶ noun Biology a minute body or cell in an organism, especially a red or white cell in the blood of vertebrates.
■ historical a minute particle regarded as the basic constituent of matter or light.
– DERIVATIVES **corpuscular** /kɔːˈpʌskjʊlə/ adjective.
– ORIGIN mid 17th cent.: from Latin *corpusculum* 'small body', diminutive of *corpus*.

corpus delicti /dɪˈlɪktʌɪ/ ▶ noun Law the facts and circumstances constituting a breach of a law.
– ORIGIN Latin, literally 'body of offence'.

corpus luteum /ˈluːtɪəm/ ▶ noun (pl. **corpora lutea** /ˈluːtɪə/) Anatomy a hormone-secreting structure that develops in an ovary after an ovum has been discharged but degenerates after a few days unless pregnancy has begun.
– ORIGIN late 18th cent.: from **CORPUS** and Latin *luteum*, neuter of *luteus* 'yellow'.

corpus spongiosum /ˌspʌndʒɪˈəʊsəm/ ▶ noun (pl. **corpora spongiosa** /-sə/) Anatomy a mass of erectile tissue alongside the corpora cavernosa of the penis and terminating in the glans.
– ORIGIN from **CORPUS** and Latin *spongiosum*, neuter of *spongiosus* 'porous'.

corpus striatum /strʌɪˈeɪtəm/ ▶ noun (pl. **corpora striata** /-tə/) Anatomy part of the basal ganglia of the brain, comprising the caudate and lentiform nuclei.
– ORIGIN from **CORPUS** and Latin *striatum*, neuter of *striatus* 'grooved'.

corral /kəˈrɑːl/ ▶ noun N. Amer. a pen for livestock, especially cattle or horses, on a farm or ranch.
■ historical a defensive enclosure of wagons in an encampment.
▶ verb (**corralled**, **corralling**) [with obj.] chiefly N. Amer. put or keep (livestock) in a corral.
■ figurative gather (a group of people or things) together: *the organizers were corralling the crowd into marching formation.* ■ N. Amer. historical form (wagons) into a corral.
– ORIGIN late 16th cent.: from Spanish and Old Portuguese (now *curral*), perhaps based on Latin *currere* 'to run'. Compare with **KRAAL**.

correct ▶ adjective free from error; in accordance

with fact or truth: *make sure you have been given the correct information.*
■[predic.] not mistaken in one's opinion or judgement; right: [with infinitive] *the government was correct to follow a course of defeating inflation.* ■(of a thing or course of action) meeting the requirements of or most appropriate for a particular situation or activity: *cut the top and bottom tracks to the correct length with a hacksaw.* ■(of a person or their appearance or behaviour) conforming to accepted social standards; proper: *he was a polite man, invariably correct and pleasant with Mrs Collins.* ■ chiefly N. Amer. conforming to a particular political or ideological orthodoxy. See also **POLITICALLY CORRECT**.
▶**verb** [with obj.] put right (an error or fault): *the Council issued a statement correcting some points in the press reports.*
■mark the errors in (a written or printed text): *he corrected Dixon's writing for publication.* ■tell (someone) that they are mistaken: *he had assumed she was married and she had not corrected him* | [as adj. **corrected**] *sorry, I stand corrected.* ■counteract or rectify: *the problem of diminished sight can be reduced or corrected by using spectacles.* ■adjust (an instrument) to function accurately or accord with a standard: *motorists can have their headlights tested and corrected at a reduced price on Saturday.* ■adjust (a numerical result or reading) to allow for departure from standard conditions: *data were **corrected** for radionuclide decay.*
– DERIVATIVES **correctable** adjective, **correctly** adverb, **correctness** noun.
– ORIGIN Middle English (as a verb): from Latin *correct-* 'made straight, amended', from the verb *corrigere*, from *cor-* 'together' + *regere* 'guide'. The adjective is via French.

correction ▶**noun** [mass noun] the action or process of correcting something: *I checked the typing for errors and sent it back for correction.*
■[count noun] a change that rectifies an error or inaccuracy: *he made a few corrections to my homework.* ■used to introduce an amended version of something one has just said: *after today—correction, she thought grimly, after tonight—she'd never see him again.* ■[count noun] a quantity adjusting a numerical result to allow for a departure from standard conditions. ■N. Amer. or dated punishment, especially that of criminals in prison intended to rectify their behaviour.
– ORIGIN Middle English: via Old French from Latin *correctio(n-)*, from *corrigere* 'make straight, bring into order' (see **CORRECT**).

correctional ▶**adjective** chiefly N. Amer. of or relating to the punishment of criminals in a way intended to rectify their behaviour: *a correctional institution.*

correction fluid ▶**noun** [mass noun] an opaque liquid painted over a typed or written error so as to leave a blank space for the insertion of the correct character.

correctitude /kəˈrɛktɪtjuːd/ ▶**noun** [mass noun] correctness, especially conscious correctness in one's behaviour.
– ORIGIN late 19th cent.: blend of **CORRECT** and **RECTITUDE**.

corrective ▶**adjective** designed to correct or counteract something harmful or undesirable: *management were informed so that corrective action could be taken.*
▶**noun** a thing intended to correct or counteract something else: *the move might be a **corrective to** some inefficient practices within hospitals.*
– DERIVATIVES **correctively** adverb.
– ORIGIN mid 16th cent.: from French *correctif, -ive* or late Latin *correctivus*, from Latin *correct-* 'brought into order' from the verb *corrigere* (see **CORRECT**).

corrector ▶**noun** a person or thing that corrects something, especially a computer program or electronic device with a specified function: *a spelling corrector.*

Correggio /kɒˈrɛdʒɪəʊ/, Antonio Allegri da (*c.*1494–1534), Italian painter; born *Antonio Allegri*. The soft, sensual style of his devotional and mythological paintings influenced the rococo of the 18th century. He is best known for his frescoes in Parma cathedral.

correlate /ˈkɒrəleɪt, -rɪ-/ ▶**verb** [no obj.] have a mutual relationship or connection, in which one thing affects or depends on another: *the study found that success in the educational system **correlates** highly **with** class.*
■[with obj.] establish such a relationship or connection between: *we should **correlate** general trends in public opinion **with** trends in the content of television news.*
▶**noun** each of two or more related or complementary things: *strategies to promote health should pay greater attention to financial hardship and other correlates of poverty.*
– ORIGIN mid 17th cent. (as a noun): back-formation from **CORRELATION** and **CORRELATIVE**.

correlation ▶**noun** a mutual relationship or connection between two or more things: *research showed a clear **correlation between** recession and levels of property crime.*
■[mass noun] Statistics interdependence of variable quantities. ■ Statistics a quantity measuring the extent of such interdependence. ■[mass noun] the process of establishing a relationship or connection between two or more things.
– DERIVATIVES **correlational** adjective.
– ORIGIN mid 16th cent.: from medieval Latin *correlatio(n-)*, from *cor-* 'together' + *relatio* (see **RELATION**).

correlation coefficient ▶**noun** Statistics a number between +1 and −1 calculated so as to represent the linear interdependence of two variables or sets of data. (Symbol: **r**.)

correlative /kəˈrɛlətɪv/ ▶**adjective** having a mutual relationship; corresponding: *rights, whether moral or legal, can involve correlative duties.*
■Grammar (of words such as *neither* and *nor*) corresponding to each other and regularly used together.
▶**noun** a word or concept that has a mutual relationship with another word or concept: *the child's right to education is a correlative of the parent's duty to send the child to school.*
– DERIVATIVES **correlatively** adverb, **correlativity** noun.
– ORIGIN mid 16th cent.: from medieval Latin *correlativus*, from *cor-* 'together' + late Latin *relativus* (see **RELATIVE**).

correspond ▶**verb** [no obj.] **1** have a close similarity; match or agree almost exactly: *the carved heads described in the poem **correspond to** a drawing of Edgcote House* | *communication is successful when the ideas in the minds of the speaker and hearer correspond.*
■be analogous or equivalent in character, form, or function: *the rank of Feldwebel in the German forces nominally **corresponded to** the British rank of sergeant.*
2 communicate by exchanging letters: *Margaret **corresponded with** him until his death* | *the doctor and I corresponded for more than two decades.*
– DERIVATIVES **correspondingly** adverb.
– ORIGIN late Middle English: from Old French *correspondre*, from medieval Latin *correspondere*, from *cor-* 'together' + Latin *respondere* (see **RESPOND**).

correspondence ▶**noun** **1** a close similarity, connection, or equivalence: *there is a simple **correspondence between** the distance of a focused object from the eye and the size of its image on the retina.*
2 [mass noun] communication by exchanging letters with someone: *the organization engaged in detailed **correspondence with** local MPs.*
■letters sent or received: *his wife dealt with his private correspondence.*
– ORIGIN late Middle English: via Old French from medieval Latin *correspondentia*, from *correspondent-* 'corresponding' (see **CORRESPONDENT**).

correspondence college (also **correspondence school**) ▶**noun** a college offering correspondence courses.

correspondence column ▶**noun** Brit. the part of a newspaper, magazine, or journal that contains letters from readers.

correspondence course ▶**noun** a course of study in which student and tutors communicate by post.

correspondence principle Physics ▶**noun** the principle that states that for very large quantum numbers the laws of quantum theory merge with those of classical physics.

correspondence school ▶**noun** another term for **CORRESPONDENCE COLLEGE**.

correspondence theory Philosophy ▶**noun** the theory that states that the definition or criterion of truth is that true propositions correspond to the facts.

correspondent ▶**noun** a person who writes letters to a person or a newspaper, especially on a regular basis: *she wasn't much of a correspondent.*
■[often with adj. or noun modifier] a person employed to report for a newspaper or broadcasting organization, typically on a particular subject or from a particular country: *a cricket correspondent.*
▶**adjective** corresponding.
– ORIGIN late Middle English (as an adjective): from Old French *correspondant* or medieval Latin *correspondent-* 'corresponding', from the verb *correspondere* (see **CORRESPOND**).

corresponding angles ▶**plural noun** Mathematics the angles which occupy the same relative position at each intersection where a straight line crosses two others. If the two lines are parallel, the corresponding angles are equal.

corresponding member ▶**noun** an honorary member of a learned society who has no voice in the society's affairs, especially one living some distance from the its headquarters.

corrida /kɒˈriːdə/ ▶**noun** a bullfight.
– ORIGIN late 19th cent.: from Spanish *corrida de toros* 'running of bulls'.

corridor ▶**noun** a long passage in a building from which doors lead into rooms.
■Brit. a passage along the side of a railway carriage, from which doors lead into compartments. ■[often with adj. or noun modifier] a belt of land between two other areas, typically having a particular feature or giving access to a particular area: *the valley provides the principal wildlife corridor between the uplands and the central urban area.* ■[with adj. or noun modifier] a belt of land following a road, river, or other route of communication: *the electronics industry in the M4 Corridor.*
– PHRASES **the corridors of power** the senior levels of government or administration, where covert influence is regarded as being exerted and significant decisions are made. [ORIGIN: from the name of C. P. Snow's novel *The Corridors of Power* (1964).]
– ORIGIN late 16th cent. (as a military term denoting a strip of land along the outer edge of a ditch, protected by a parapet): from French, from Italian *corridore*, alteration (by association with *corridore* 'runner') of *corridoio* 'running-place', from *correre* 'to run', from Latin *currere*. The current sense dates from the early 19th cent.

corrie /ˈkɒri/ ▶**noun** (pl. **-ies**) a cirque, especially one in the mountains of Scotland.
– ORIGIN mid 16th cent.: from Scottish Gaelic and Irish *coire* 'cauldron, hollow'.

Corriedale /ˈkɒrɪdeɪl/ ▶**noun** a sheep of a New Zealand breed kept for both wool and meat.
– ORIGIN early 20th cent.: named after an estate in northern Otago, New Zealand.

corrigendum /ˌkɒrɪˈdʒɛndəm/ ▶**noun** (pl. **corrigenda** /-də/) a thing to be corrected, typically an error in a printed book.
– ORIGIN early 19th cent.: Latin, neuter gerundive of *corrigere* 'bring into order' (see **CORRECT**).

corrigible /ˈkɒrɪdʒɪb(ə)l/ ▶**adjective** capable of being corrected, rectified, or reformed.
– DERIVATIVES **corrigibility** noun.
– ORIGIN late Middle English (in the sense 'liable to or deserving punishment'): via French from medieval Latin *corrigibilis*, from Latin *corrigere* 'to correct'.

corroborate /kəˈrɒbəreɪt/ ▶**verb** [with obj.] confirm or give support to (a statement, theory, or finding): *the witness had corroborated the boy's account of the attack.*
– DERIVATIVES **corroboration** noun, **corroborative** adjective, **corroborator** noun, **corroboratory** adjective.
– ORIGIN mid 16th cent. (in the sense 'make physically stronger'): from Latin *corroborat-* 'strengthened', from the verb *corroborare*, from *cor-* 'together' + *roborare*, from *robur* 'strength'.

corroboree /kəˈrɒbəri/ ▶**noun** an Australian Aboriginal dance ceremony which may take the form of a sacred ritual or an informal gathering.
■chiefly Austral. a party or other social gathering, especially a lively one.
– ORIGIN from Dharuk *garaabara*, denoting a style of dancing.

corrode /kəˈrəʊd/ ▶**verb** [with obj.] destroy or damage (metal, stone, or other materials) slowly by chemical action: *acid rain poisons fish and corrodes buildings.*
■[no obj.] (of metal or other materials) be destroyed or damaged in this way: *over the years copper pipework corrodes.* ■ figurative destroy or weaken (something)

gradually: *the self-centred climate corrodes ideals and concerns about social justice.*
– DERIVATIVES **corrodible** adjective.
– ORIGIN late Middle English: from Latin *corrodere*, from *cor-* (expressing intensive force) + *rodere* 'gnaw'.

corrody /'kɒrədi/ ▶ noun (pl. **-ies**) historical a pension or provision for maintenance, especially as given regularly by a religious house.
– ORIGIN late Middle English: from Anglo-Norman French *corodie*, from a Romance word meaning 'preparation'.

corrosion ▶ noun [mass noun] the process of corroding metal, stone, or other materials: *each aircraft part is sprayed with oil to prevent corrosion.*
■ damage caused by such a process: *engineers found the corrosion when checking the bridge.*
– ORIGIN late Middle English: from Old French, or from late Latin *corrosio(n-)*, from Latin *corrodere* 'gnaw through' (see CORRODE).

corrosive ▶ adjective tending to cause corrosion.
▶ noun a corrosive substance.
– DERIVATIVES **corrosively** adverb, **corrosiveness** noun.
– ORIGIN late Middle English: from Old French *corosif, -ive*, from medieval Latin *corrosivus*, from Latin *corros-* 'gnawed through', from the verb *corrodere* (see CORRODE).

corrosive sublimate ▶ noun old-fashioned term for MERCURIC CHLORIDE.

corrugate /'kɒrʊgeɪt/ ▶ verb contract or cause to contract into wrinkles or folds: [no obj.] *Micky's brow corrugated in a simian frown.*
– ORIGIN late Middle English: from Latin *corrugat-* 'wrinkled', from the verb *corrugare*, from *cor-* (expressing intensive force) + *rugare* (from *ruga* 'a wrinkle').

corrugated ▶ adjective (of a material, surface, or structure) shaped into alternate ridges and grooves: *the roof was made of corrugated iron.*
– DERIVATIVES **corrugation** noun.

corrugated paper ▶ noun [mass noun] packaging material made from layers of thick paper, the top layer of which is alternately grooved and ridged for added strength and rigidity.

corrupt ▶ adjective **1** having or showing a willingness to act dishonestly in return for money or personal gain: *unscrupulous logging companies assisted by corrupt officials.*
■ evil or morally depraved: *the play can do no harm since its audience is already corrupt.* ■ archaic (of organic or inorganic matter) in a state of decay; rotten or putrid: *a corrupt and rotting corpse.*
2 (of a text or manuscript) debased or made unreliable by errors or alterations.
■ (of a computer database or program) having had errors introduced.
▶ verb [with obj.] **1** cause to act dishonestly in return for money or personal gain: *there is a continuing fear of firms corrupting politicians in the search for contracts.*
■ cause to become morally depraved: *he has corrupted the boy.* ■ archaic infect; contaminate: [as adj. **corrupting**] *the corrupting smell of death.*
2 (often **be corrupted**) change or debase by making errors or unintentional alterations: *Epicurus's teachings have since been much corrupted.*
■ cause errors to appear in (a computer program or database): *a program that has somehow corrupted your system files.*
– DERIVATIVES **corrupter** noun, **corruptibility** noun, **corruptible** adjective, **corruptive** adjective, **corruptly** adverb.
– ORIGIN Middle English: from Latin *corruptus*, past participle of *corrumpere* 'mar, bribe, destroy', from *cor-* 'altogether' + *rumpere* 'to break'.

corruption ▶ noun [mass noun] **1** dishonest or fraudulent conduct by those in power, typically involving bribery: *the journalist who wants to expose corruption in high places.*
■ the action of making someone or something morally depraved or the state of being so: *the word 'addict' conjures up evil and corruption.* ■ archaic decay; putrefaction: *the potato turned black and rotten with corruption.*
2 the process by which something, typically a word or expression, is changed from its original state to one that is regarded as erroneous or debased.
■ the process of causing errors to appear in a computer program or database.
– ORIGIN Middle English: via Old French from Latin

corruptio(n-), from *corrumpere* 'mar, bribe, destroy' (see CORRUPT).

corsac fox /'kɔːsak/ ▶ noun a russet-grey fox found on the steppes of central Asia.
● *Vulpes corsac*, family Canidae.
– ORIGIN mid 19th cent.: *corsac* from Russian *korsak*, from Turkic *karsak*.

corsage /kɔː'sɑːʒ, 'kɔːsɑːʒ/ ▶ noun **1** a spray of flowers worn pinned to a woman's clothes.
2 the upper part of a woman's dress.
– ORIGIN early 19th cent. (in sense 2): French, from Old French *cors* 'body', from Latin *corpus*.

corsair /kɔː'sɛː, 'kɔːsɛː/ ▶ noun archaic a pirate.
■ a privateer, especially one operating along the southern shore of the Mediterranean in the 17th century.
– ORIGIN mid 16th cent.: from French *corsaire*, from medieval Latin *cursarius*, from *cursus* 'a raid, plunder', special use of Latin *cursus* 'course', from *currere* 'to run'.

Corse /kɔːs/ French name for CORSICA.

corse /kɔːs/ ▶ noun archaic a corpse.
– ORIGIN Middle English: from Old French *cors* 'body', from Latin *corpus*. Compare with CORPSE.

corselet ▶ noun **1** /'kɔːs(ə)lɪt/ historical a piece of armour covering the trunk.
2 variant spelling of CORSELETTE.
– ORIGIN late 15th cent.: from Old French *corslet*, diminutive of *cors* 'body'.

corselette /kɔːs(ə)lɛt, 'kɔːs(ə)lɛt/ (also **corselet**) ▶ noun a woman's foundation garment combining corset and brassière.
– ORIGIN 1920s: from *corselet* (see CORSELET).

corset ▶ noun a woman's tightly fitting undergarment extending from below the chest to the hips, worn to shape the figure.
■ a similar garment worn by men or women to support a weak or injured back. ■ historical a tightly laced or stiffened outer bodice or dress. ■ informal a control or restriction placed on something: *the removal of the corset on banks.*
– DERIVATIVES **corseted** adjective, **corsetry** noun.
– ORIGIN Middle English: from Old French, diminutive of *cors* 'body', from Latin *corpus*. The sense 'close-fitting undergarment' dates from the late 18th cent., by which time the sense 'bodice' had mainly historical reference.

corsetière /'kɔːsɪtjɛː/ ▶ noun a woman who makes or fits corsets.
– ORIGIN mid 19th cent.: French, feminine of *corsetier*, from *corset* (see CORSET).

Corsica /'kɔːsɪkə/ a mountainous island off the west coast of Italy, forming an administrative region of France; pop. 249,740 (1990); chief towns, Bastia (northern department) and Ajaccio (southern department). It was the birthplace of Napoleon I. French name CORSE.

Corsican ▶ adjective of or relating to Corsica, its people, or their language.
▶ noun **1** a native of Corsica.
2 [mass noun] the language of Corsica, which originated as a dialect of Italian.

Cort /kɔːt/, Henry (1740–1800), English ironmaster. He patented a process for producing iron bars by passing iron through grooved rollers, thus avoiding a hammering stage.

cortège /kɔː'teɪʒ, -'tɛʒ/ ▶ noun a solemn procession, especially for a funeral.
■ a person's entourage or retinue.
– ORIGIN mid 17th cent.: from French, from Italian *corteggio*, from *corteggiare* 'attend court', from *corte* 'court', from Latin *cohors, cohort-* 'retinue'.

Cortes /'kɔːtɛs, -z, Spanish 'kortes/ the legislative assembly of Spain and formerly of Portugal.
– ORIGIN Spanish and Portuguese, plural of *corte* 'court', from Latin *cohors, cohort-* 'yard, retinue'.

Cortés /'kɔːtɛz, Spanish kor'tes/ (also **Cortez**), Hernando (1485–1547), first of the Spanish conquistadores. Cortés overthrew the Aztec empire, conquering its capital, Tenochtitlán, in 1519 and deposing the emperor, Montezuma. In 1521 he destroyed Tenochtitlán completely and established Mexico City as the new capital of Mexico (then called New Spain).

cortex /'kɔːtɛks/ ▶ noun (pl. **cortices** /-tɪˌsiːz/) Anatomy the outer layer of the cerebrum (the **cerebral cortex**), composed of folded grey matter and playing an important role in consciousness.

■ an outer layer of another organ or body part such as a kidney (the **renal cortex**), the cerebellum, or a hair. ■ Botany an outer layer of tissue immediately below the epidermis of a stem or root.
– DERIVATIVES **cortical** adjective.
– ORIGIN late Middle English: from Latin, literally 'bark'.

corticate /'kɔːtɪkeɪt/ ▶ adjective Botany having a cortex, bark, or rind.
– DERIVATIVES **cortication** noun.
– ORIGIN mid 19th cent.: from Latin *corticatus*, from *cortex, cortic-* 'bark'.

cortico- ▶ combining form representing CORTEX, used especially with reference to the adrenal and cerebral cortices.
– ORIGIN from Latin *cortex, cortic-* 'bark'.

corticofugal /ˌkɔːtɪkəʊ'fjuːg(ə)l/ (also **corticifugal** /ˌkɔːtɪ'sɪfjuːg(ə)l/) ▶ adjective Anatomy (of a nerve fibre) originating in and running from the cerebral cortex.
– ORIGIN late 19th cent.: from CORTICO- 'cortex' + Latin *fugere* 'run from'.

corticosteroid /ˌkɔːtɪkəʊ'stɪərɔɪd, -'stɛrɔɪd/ ▶ noun Biochemistry any of a group of steroid hormones produced in the adrenal cortex or made synthetically. There are two kinds: glucocorticoids and mineralocorticoids. They have various metabolic functions and some are used to treat inflammation.

corticosterone /ˌkɔːtɪkəʊ'stɛrəʊn/ ▶ noun [mass noun] Biochemistry a hormone secreted by the adrenal cortex, one of the glucocorticoids.

corticotrophin /ˌkɔːtɪkə(ʊ)'trəʊfɪn/ (also **corticotropin** /-pɪn/) ▶ noun Biochemistry another term for ADRENOCORTICOTROPHIC HORMONE.

cortile /kɔː'tiːleɪ, Italian kor'tile/ ▶ noun (pl. **cortili** /-li/ or **cortiles**) (in Italy) an enclosed area, typically roofless and arcaded, within or attached to a building.
– ORIGIN Italian, derivative of *corte* 'court'.

cortina /kɔː'tʌɪnə, -'tiːnə/ ▶ noun Botany (in some toadstools) a thin web-like veil extending from the edge of the cap to the stalk.
– DERIVATIVES **cortinate** adjective.
– ORIGIN mid 19th cent.: from late Latin, literally 'curtain'.

cortisol /'kɔːtɪsɒl/ ▶ noun Biochemistry another term for HYDROCORTISONE.

cortisone /'kɔːtɪzəʊn/ ▶ noun [mass noun] Biochemistry a hormone produced by the adrenal cortex. One of the glucocorticoids, it is also made synthetically for use as an anti-inflammatory and anti-allergy agent.
– ORIGIN 1940s: from elements of its chemical name *17-hydroxy-11-dehydrocorticosterone*.

corundum /kə'rʌndəm/ ▶ noun [mass noun] extremely hard crystallized alumina, used as an abrasive. Ruby and sapphire are varieties of corundum.
– ORIGIN early 18th cent.: from Tamil *kuruntam* and Telugu *kuruvindam*.

Corunna /kə'rʌnə/ a port in NW Spain; pop. 251,300 (1991). It was the point of departure for the Armada in 1588 and the site of a battle in 1809 in the Peninsular War, at which British forces under Sir John Moore defeated the French. Spanish name LA CORUÑA.

coruscant /kɒ'rʌsk(ə)nt/ ▶ adjective poetic/literary glittering; sparkling.
– ORIGIN late 15th cent.: from Latin *coruscant-* 'vibrating, glittering', from the verb *coruscare*.

coruscate /'kɒrəskeɪt/ ▶ verb [no obj.] poetic/literary (of light) flash or sparkle: *the light was coruscating through the walls.*
– DERIVATIVES **coruscation** noun.
– ORIGIN early 18th cent.: from Latin *coruscat-* 'glittered', from the verb *coruscare*.

corvée /'kɔːveɪ/ ▶ noun historical a day's unpaid labour owed by a vassal to his feudal lord.
■ [mass noun] forced labour exacted in lieu of taxes, in particular that on public roads in France before 1776.
– ORIGIN Middle English: from Old French, based on Latin *corrogare* 'ask for, collect'. Rare in English before the late 18th cent.

corves plural form of CORF.

corvette /kɔː'vɛt/ ▶ noun a small warship designed for convoy escort duty.
■ historical a flush-decked sailing warship with one tier of guns.
– ORIGIN mid 17th cent.: from French, from Dutch

korf, denoting a kind of ship, + the diminutive suffix *-ette*.

corvid /ˈkɔːvɪd/ ▶ **noun** Ornithology a bird of the crow family (Corvidae); a crow.
– ORIGIN mid 20th cent.: from modern Latin *Corvidae* (plural), from Latin *corvus* 'raven'.

corvina[1] /kɔːˈviːnə/ ▶ **noun** [mass noun] a variety of wine grape native to the Veneto region of NE Italy, used to make Valpolicella and Bardolino.
– ORIGIN Italian (feminine adjective), literally 'raven-black'

corvina[2] /kɔːˈviːnə/ ▶ **noun** a marine food and game fish of the drum family, found on the Pacific coasts of California and Mexico and sometimes living in fresh water.
● Genus *Cynoscion*, family Sciaenidae: two species, in particular the **shortfin corvina** (*C. parvipennis*).
– ORIGIN late 18th cent.: from Spanish and Portuguese.

corvine /ˈkɔːvʌɪn/ ▶ **adjective** of or like a raven or crow, especially in colour.
– ORIGIN mid 17th cent.: from Latin *corvinus*, from *corvus* 'raven'.

Corvus /ˈkɔːvəs/ Astronomy a small southern constellation (the Crow or Raven), south of Virgo.
■ [as genitive **Corvi** /ˈkɔːvi, ˈkɔːvʌɪ/] used with preceding letter or numeral to designate a star in this constellation: *the star Gamma Corvi*.
– ORIGIN Latin.

corybantic /ˌkɒrɪˈbantɪk/ ▶ **adjective** wild; frenzied.
– ORIGIN mid 17th cent.: from *Corybantes*, Latin name of the priests of Cybele, a Phrygian goddess of nature who performed wild dances, from Greek *Korubantes* + **-IC**.

corydalis /kəˈrɪdəlɪs/ ▶ **noun** a herbaceous plant with spurred tubular flowers, found in north temperate regions.
● Genus *Corydalis*, family Fumariaceae: many species, including **yellow corydalis** (*C. lutea*), a garden escape which has become naturalized in Britain.
– ORIGIN modern Latin, from Greek *korudallis* 'crested lark', alluding to a similarity between the flower and the bird's spur.

corymb /ˈkɒrɪmb/ ▶ **noun** Botany a flower cluster whose lower stalks are proportionally longer so that the flowers form a flat or slightly convex head.
– DERIVATIVES **corymbose** adjective.
– ORIGIN early 18th cent.: from French *corymbe* or Latin *corymbus*, from Greek *korumbos* 'cluster'.

corynebacterium /ˌkɒrɪnɪbakˈtɪərɪəm, kəˌrɪn-/ ▶ **noun** (pl. **corynebacteria** /-rɪə/) a bacterium which sometimes causes disease in humans and other animals, including diphtheria.
● Genus *Corynebacterium*; Gram-positive non-motile club-shaped rods.
– ORIGIN modern Latin, from Greek *korunē* 'club' + **BACTERIUM**.

coryphée /ˈkɒrɪfeɪ/ ▶ **noun** a leading dancer in a corps de ballet.
– ORIGIN French, via Latin from Greek *koruphaios* 'leader of a chorus', from *koruphē* 'head'.

coryza /kəˈrʌɪzə/ ▶ **noun** [mass noun] Medicine catarrhal inflammation of the mucous membrane in the nose, caused especially by a cold or by hay fever.
– ORIGIN early 16th cent.: from Latin, from Greek *koruza* 'nasal mucus'.

Cos variant spelling of **Kos**.

cos[1] /kɒs/ (also **cos lettuce**) ▶ **noun** a lettuce of a variety with crisp narrow leaves that form a tall head.
– ORIGIN late 17th cent.: named after the Aegean island of **Cos**, where it originated.

cos[2] /kɒz/ ▶ **abbreviation for** cosine.

cos[3] /kɒz, kəz/ (also **'cos** or **coz**) ▶ **conjunction** informal short for **BECAUSE**.

Cosa Nostra /ˌkəʊzə ˈnɒstrə/ a US criminal organization resembling and related to the Mafia.
– ORIGIN Italian, literally 'our affair'.

coscoroba swan /ˌkɒskəˈrəʊbə/ ▶ **noun** a small South American swan with white plumage and bright pink legs and feet.
● *Coscoroba coscoroba*, family Anatidae.
– ORIGIN early 19th cent.: *coscoroba* from the modern Latin taxonomic name, of unknown origin.

cosec /ˈkəʊsɛk/ ▶ **abbreviation for** cosecant.

cosecant /kəʊˈsiːk(ə)nt, -ˈsɛk-/ ▶ **noun** Mathematics the ratio of the hypotenuse (in a right-angled triangle)

to the side opposite an acute angle; the reciprocal of sine.
– ORIGIN early 18th cent.: from modern Latin *cosecant-*, from **CO-** 'mutually' + Latin *secant-* 'cutting' (from the verb *secare*). Compare with **SECANT**.

coset /ˈkəʊsɛt/ ▶ **noun** Mathematics a set composed of all the products obtained by multiplying each element of a subgroup in turn by one particular element of the group containing the subgroup.

cosh[1] Brit. informal ▶ **noun** a thick heavy stick or bar used as a weapon.
▶ **verb** [with obj.] hit (someone) on the head with a cosh.
– ORIGIN mid 19th cent.: of unknown origin.

cosh[2] Mathematics ▶ **abbreviation for** hyperbolic cosine.
– ORIGIN from **cos**[2] + *-h* for *hyperbolic*. Compare with **COTH**.

COSHH Brit. ▶ **abbreviation for** control of substances hazardous for health, a body of regulations introduced in Britain by the Health and Safety Executive in 1989 to govern the storage and use of such substances.

co-signatory (also **cosignatory**) ▶ **noun** a person or state signing a treaty or other document jointly with others.

Cosimo de' Medici /ˈkɒzɪməʊ/ (1389–1464), Italian statesman and banker; known as **Cosimo the Elder**. He laid the foundations for the Medici family's power in Florence, becoming the city's ruler in 1434 and using his considerable wealth to promote the arts and learning.

cosine /ˈkəʊsʌɪn/ ▶ **noun** Mathematics the trigonometric function that is equal to the ratio of the side adjacent to an acute angle (in a right-angled triangle) to the hypotenuse.

cosmetic ▶ **adjective** involving or relating to treatment intended to restore or improve a person's appearance: *cosmetic surgery.*
■ designed or serving to improve the appearance of the body, especially the face: *lens designs can improve the cosmetic effect of your glasses.* ■ affecting only the appearance of something rather than its substance: *the reform package was merely a cosmetic exercise.*
▶ **noun** (usu. **cosmetics**) a product applied to the body, especially the face, to improve its appearance.
– DERIVATIVES **cosmetically** adverb.
– ORIGIN early 17th cent. (as a noun denoting the art of beautifying the body): from French *cosmétique*, from Greek *kosmētikos*, from *kosmein* 'arrange or adorn', from *kosmos* 'order or adornment'.

cosmetician /ˌkɒzmɪˈtɪʃ(ə)n/ ▶ **noun** N. Amer. a person who sells or applies cosmetics as an occupation.

cosmetology /ˌkɒzmɪˈtɒlədʒi/ ▶ **noun** [mass noun] the professional skill or practice of beautifying the face, hair, and skin.
– DERIVATIVES **cosmetological** adjective, **cosmetologist** noun.

cosmic ▶ **adjective** of or relating to the universe or cosmos, especially as distinct from the earth: *cosmic matter.*
– DERIVATIVES **cosmical** adjective, **cosmically** adverb.

cosmic dust ▶ **noun** [mass noun] small particles of matter distributed throughout space.

cosmic radiation ▶ **noun** [mass noun] radiation consisting of cosmic rays.

cosmic ray ▶ **noun** a highly energetic atomic nucleus or other particle travelling through space at a speed approaching that of light.

cosmic string ▶ **noun** another term for **STRING** (in sense 5).

cosmo- /ˈkɒzməʊ/ ▶ **combining form** of or relating to the world or the universe: *cosmodrome | cosmography.*
– ORIGIN from Greek *kosmos* 'order, world'.

cosmodrome /ˈkɒzmədrəʊm/ ▶ **noun** (in the countries of the former USSR) a launching site for spacecraft.
– ORIGIN 1950s: from **COSMO-** + **DROME**, on the pattern of *aerodrome*.

cosmogenesis /ˌkɒzmə(ʊ)ˈdʒɛnɪsɪs/ ▶ **noun** the origin or evolution of the universe.
– DERIVATIVES **cosmogenetic** adjective, **cosmogenic** adjective.

cosmogony /kɒzˈmɒɡəni/ ▶ **noun** (pl. **-ies**) [mass noun] the branch of science that deals with the origin of the universe, especially the solar system.

■ [count noun] a theory regarding this: *in their cosmogony, the world was thought to be a square, flat surface.*
– DERIVATIVES **cosmogonic** /-məˈɡɒnɪk/ adjective, **cosmogonical** /-məˈɡɒnɪk(ə)l/ adjective, **cosmogonist** noun.
– ORIGIN late 17th cent.: from Greek *kosmogonia*, from *kosmos* 'order or world' + *-gonia* '-begetting'.

cosmography ▶ **noun** (pl. **-ies**) [mass noun] the branch of science which deals with the general features of the universe, including the earth.
■ [count noun] a description or representation of the universe or the earth.
– DERIVATIVES **cosmographer** noun, **cosmographic** adjective, **cosmographical** adjective.
– ORIGIN late Middle English: from French *cosmographie*, or via late Latin from Greek *kosmographia*, from *kosmos* (see **COSMOS**[1]) + *-graphia* 'writing'.

cosmological argument ▶ **noun** Philosophy an argument for the existence of God which claims that all things in nature depend on something else for their existence (i.e. are contingent), and that the whole cosmos must therefore itself depend on a being which exists independently or necessarily. Compare with **ONTOLOGICAL ARGUMENT** and **TELEOLOGICAL ARGUMENT**.

cosmological constant ▶ **noun** Physics an arbitrary constant in the field equations of general relativity.

cosmology ▶ **noun** (pl. **-ies**) [mass noun] the science of the origin and development of the universe. Modern astronomy is dominated by the big bang theory which brings together observational astronomy and particle physics.
■ [count noun] an account or theory of the origin of the universe.
– DERIVATIVES **cosmological** adjective, **cosmologist** noun.
– ORIGIN mid 17th cent.: from French *cosmologie* or modern Latin *cosmologia*, from Greek *kosmos* 'order or world' + *-logia* 'discourse'.

cosmonaut ▶ **noun** a Russian astronaut.
– ORIGIN 1950s: from **COSMOS**[1], on the pattern of *astronaut* and Russian *kosmonavt*.

cosmopolis /kɒzˈmɒp(ə)lɪs/ ▶ **noun** a city inhabited by people from many different countries.
– ORIGIN mid 19th cent.: from Greek *kosmos* 'world' + *polis* 'city'.

cosmopolitan /ˌkɒzməˈpɒlɪt(ə)n/ ▶ **adjective** familiar with and at ease in many different countries and cultures: *his knowledge of French, Italian, and Spanish made him genuinely cosmopolitan.*
■ including people from many different countries: *immigration transformed the city into a cosmopolitan metropolis.* ■ having an exciting and glamorous character associated with travel and a mixture of cultures: *their designs became a byword for cosmopolitan chic.* ■ (of a plant or animal) found all over the world.
▶ **noun** a cosmopolitan person.
■ a cosmopolitan plant or animal.
– DERIVATIVES **cosmopolitanism** noun, **cosmopolitanize** (also **-ise**) verb.
– ORIGIN mid 17th cent. (as a noun): from **COSMOPOLITE** + **-AN**.

cosmopolite /kɒzˈmɒp(ə)lʌɪt/ ▶ **noun** a cosmopolitan person.
– ORIGIN early 17th cent.: from French, from Greek *kosmopolitēs*, from *kosmos* 'world' + *politēs* 'citizen'.

cosmos[1] ▶ **noun** (**the cosmos**) the universe seen as a well-ordered whole: *he sat staring deep into the void, reminding himself of man's place in the cosmos.*
■ a system of thought: *the new gender-free intellectual cosmos.*
– ORIGIN Middle English: from Greek *kosmos* 'order or world'.

cosmos[2] ▶ **noun** an ornamental plant of the daisy family, which bears single dahlia-like flowers and is native to Mexico and warm regions of America.
● Genus *Cosmos*, family Compositae.
– ORIGIN from Greek *kosmos* in the sense 'ornament'.

COSPAR /ˈkəʊspɑː/ ▶ **abbreviation for** Committee on Space Research.

Cossack /ˈkɒsak/ ▶ **noun** a member of a people of southern Russia, Ukraine, and Siberia, noted for their horsemanship and military skill.
■ a member of a Cossack military unit.

The Cossacks had their origins in the 15th century when refugees from religious persecution, outlaws, adventurers, and escaped serfs banded together in settlements for protection. Under the tsars they were allowed considerable autonomy in return for protecting the frontiers; with the collapse of Soviet rule Cossack groups have reasserted their identity in both Russia and Ukraine.

▶ **adjective** of, relating to, or characteristic of the Cossacks.
– ORIGIN from Russian *kazak* from Turkic, 'vagabond, nomad'; later influenced by French *Cosaque* (see also **KAZAKH**).

cosset ▶ **verb** (**cosseted**, **cosseting**) [with obj.] care for and protect in an overindulgent way: *all her life she'd been cosseted by her family.*
– ORIGIN mid 16th cent. (as a noun denoting a lamb brought up by hand, later a spoiled child): probably from Anglo-Norman French *coscet* 'cottager', from Old English *cotsǣta* 'cottar'.

cossie (also **cozzie**) ▶ **noun** (pl. **-ies**) informal a swimming costume or a pair of swimming trunks.
– ORIGIN early 20th cent.: alteration of the first element of **COSTUME**.

Cossyra /kə'sʌɪrə/ Roman name for **PANTELLERIA**.

cost ▶ **verb** (past and past participle **cost**) [with obj.] **1** (of an object or an action) require the payment of (a specified sum of money) before it can be acquired or done: *each issue of the magazine costs £1.*
■ cause the loss of: [with two objs] *driving at more than double the speed limit cost the woman her driving licence.* ■ [with two objs] involve (someone) in (an effort or unpleasant action): *the accident cost me a visit to the doctor.* ■ informal be expensive for (someone): *if you want to own an island, it'll cost you.*
2 (past and past participle **costed**) estimate the price of: *it is their job to plan and cost a media schedule for the campaign.*
▶ **noun** an amount that has to be paid or spent to buy or obtain something: *we are able to cover the cost of the event* | *health care costs* | [mass noun] *the tunnel has been built at no cost to the state.*
■ the effort, loss, or sacrifice necessary to achieve or obtain something: *she averted a train accident at the cost of her life.* ■ (**costs**) legal expenses, especially those allowed in favour of the winning party or against the losing party in a suit.
– PHRASES **at all costs** (or **at any cost**) regardless of the price to be paid or the effort needed: *he was anxious to avoid war at all costs.* **at cost** at cost price; without profit to the seller. **cost an arm and a leg** see **ARM**[1]. **cost someone dear** (or **dearly**) involve someone in a serious loss or a heavy penalty: *they were really bad mistakes on my part and they cost us dear.* **to someone's cost** with loss or disadvantage to someone: *without programmes to play on it, the cleverest machine is useless—as some hardware manufacturers already know to their cost.*
– ORIGIN Middle English: from Old French *coust* (noun), *couster* (verb), based on Latin *constare* 'stand firm, stand at a price'.

Costa /'kɒstə/, Lúcio (1902–63), French-born Brazilian architect, town planner, and architectural historian. He achieved a worldwide reputation with his design for Brazil's new capital, Brasilia, which was chosen by an international jury in 1956.

costa ▶ **noun** (pl. **costae** /'kɒsti:/) Botany & Zoology a rib, midrib, or rib-like structure.
■ Entomology the main vein running along the leading edge of an insect's wing.
– ORIGIN mid 19th cent.: from Latin.

Costa Blanca /ˌkɒstə 'blaŋkə/ a resort region on the Mediterranean coast of SE Spain.
– ORIGIN Spanish, literally 'white coast'.

Costa Brava /'brɑːvə, Spanish 'braβa/ a resort region to the north of Barcelona, on the Mediterranean coast of NE Spain.
– ORIGIN Spanish, literally 'wild coast'.

cost accounting ▶ **noun** [mass noun] the recording of all the costs incurred in a business in a way that can be used to improve its management.
– DERIVATIVES **cost accountant** noun.

Costa del Sol /dɛl 'sɒl/ a resort region on the Mediterranean coast of southern Spain.
– ORIGIN Spanish, 'coast of the sun'.

costal /'kɒst(ə)l/ ▶ **adjective** of or relating to the ribs.
■ Anatomy & Zoology of or relating to a costa.
– ORIGIN mid 17th cent.: from French, from modern Latin *costalis*, from Latin *costa* 'rib'.

co-star ▶ **noun** a cinema or stage star appearing with another or others of equal importance.
▶ **verb** [no obj.] appear in a production as a co-star: *Rickman co-starred with Bruce Willis in the movie.*
■ [with obj.] (of a production) include as a co-star: *his new TV show co-stars John Schneider.*

Costard /'kɒstəd, 'kʌst-/ ▶ **noun** Brit. a cooking apple of a large ribbed variety.
■ archaic, humorous a person's head.
– ORIGIN Middle English: from Anglo-Norman French, from *coste* 'rib', from Latin *costa*.

Costa Rica /'riːkə/ a republic in Central America on the Isthmus of Panama; pop. 3,301,210 (est. 1995); official language, Spanish; capital, San José.

Colonized by Spain in the early 16th century, Costa Rica achieved independence in 1823 and emerged as a separate country in 1838 after fourteen years within the United Provinces of Central America.

– DERIVATIVES **Costa Rican** adjective & noun.
– ORIGIN Spanish, 'rich coast'.

costate /'kɒsteɪt/ ▶ **adjective** Botany & Zoology ribbed; possessing a costa.
– ORIGIN early 19th cent.: from Latin *costatus*, from *costa* 'rib'.

cost–benefit ▶ **adjective** [attrib.] relating to or denoting a process that assesses the relation between the cost of an undertaking and the value of the resulting benefits: *a cost–benefit analysis.*

cost-cutting ▶ **noun** [mass noun] the reduction of costs, especially in a business.

cost-effective ▶ **adjective** effective or productive in relation to its cost: *the most cost-effective way to invest in the stock market.*
– DERIVATIVES **cost-effectively** adverb, **cost-effectiveness** noun.

cost-efficient ▶ **adjective** another term for **COST-EFFECTIVE**.
– DERIVATIVES **cost-efficiency** noun.

coster ▶ **noun** Brit. short for **COSTERMONGER**.

costermonger /'kɒstəmʌŋgə/ ▶ **noun** Brit. dated a person who sells goods, especially fruit and vegetables, from a handcart in the street.
– ORIGIN early 16th cent. (denoting an apple seller): from **COSTARD** + **-MONGER**.

costing ▶ **noun** (often **costings**) the proposed or estimated cost of producing or undertaking something: *he obtained costings for manual keyboarding of the records.*
■ [mass noun] the process of determining such a cost: *detailed costing can make the difference between an excellent idea and a ruinous one.*

costive /'kɒstɪv/ ▶ **adjective** constipated.
■ slow or reluctant in speech or action; unforthcoming: *if he did ask her she would become costive.*
– DERIVATIVES **costively** adverb, **costiveness** noun.
– ORIGIN late Middle English: via Old French from Latin *constipatus* 'pressed together' (see **CONSTIPATE**).

costly ▶ **adjective** (**costlier**, **costliest**) costing a lot; expensive: *major problems requiring costly repairs.*
■ causing suffering, loss, or disadvantage: *the government's biggest and most costly mistake.*
– DERIVATIVES **costliness** noun.

costmary /'kɒstmɛːri/ ▶ **noun** (pl. **-ies**) an aromatic plant of the daisy family, formerly used in medicine and for flavouring ale prior to the use of hops. Also called **ALECOST**.
● *Balsamita major*, family Compositae.
– ORIGIN late Middle English: from obsolete *cost* (via Latin from Greek *kostos*, via Arabic from Sanskrit *kuṣṭha*, denoting an aromatic plant) + *Mary*, the mother of Christ (with whom it was associated in medieval times because of its medicinal qualities).

cost-of-carry ▶ **noun** Finance the difference between the cost and the financial benefit of holding a particular asset for a specified period.

cost of living ▶ **noun** the level of prices relating to a range of everyday items.

cost-of-living index ▶ **noun** another term for **RETAIL PRICE INDEX**.

cost-plus ▶ **adjective** [attrib.] relating to or denoting a method of pricing a service or product in which a fixed profit factor is added to the costs.

cost price ▶ **noun** the price at which goods are or have been bought by a merchant or retailer.

cost-push ▶ **adjective** relating to or denoting inflation caused by increased labour or raw material costs.

costume ▶ **noun** a set of clothes in a style typical of a particular country or historical period: *authentic Elizabethan costumes* | [mass noun] *a Chinese woman in national costume.*
■ a set of clothes worn by an actor or performer for a particular role: *a nun's costume.* ■ Brit. a swimming costume. ■ Brit. dated a woman's matching jacket and skirt: *a chic black costume and white fur wrap.*
▶ **verb** [with obj.] dress (someone) in a particular set of clothes: *an all-woman troupe elaborately costumed in clinging silver lame.*
– ORIGIN early 18th cent.: from French, from Italian *custume* 'custom, fashion, habit', from Latin *consuetudo* (see **CUSTOM**).

costume drama (also **costume play**) ▶ **noun** a television or cinema production set in a particular historical period, in which the actors wear costumes typical of that period.

costume jewellery ▶ **noun** [mass noun] jewellery made with inexpensive materials or imitation gems.

costumier /kɒ'stjuːmɪə/ (US also **costumer** /-mə/) ▶ **noun** a person or company that makes or supplies theatrical or fancy-dress costumes.
– ORIGIN mid 19th cent.: French, from *costumer* 'dress in a costume' (see **COSTUME**).

cosy (US **cozy**) ▶ **adjective** (**cosier**, **cosiest**) giving a feeling of comfort, warmth, and relaxation: *the flickering lamp gave the room a cosy lived-in air.*
■ (of a relationship or conversation) intimate and relaxed. ■ avoiding or not offering challenge or difficulty; complacent: *a rather cosy assumption among audit firms that they would never actually go bust.* ■ (of a transaction or arrangement) working to the mutual advantage of those involved (used to convey a suspicion of corruption): *a cosy deal.*
▶ **noun** (pl. **-ies**) **1** a cover to keep a teapot or a boiled egg hot.
2 Brit. a canopied corner seat for two.
▶ **verb** (**-ies**, **-ied**) [with obj.] informal make (someone) feel comfortable or complacent: *she cosied him and made out she found him irresistibly attractive.*
■ [no obj.] (**cosy up to**) snuggle up to: *he cosied up to the heater.* ■ [no obj.] (**cosy up to**) ingratiate oneself with: *he decided to resign rather than cosy up to hardliners in the party.*
– DERIVATIVES **cosily** adverb, **cosiness** noun.
– ORIGIN early 18th cent. (originally Scots): of unknown origin.

cot[1] ▶ **noun** a type of bed, in particular:
■ Brit. a small bed with high barred sides for a baby or very young child. ■ a hospital bed. ■ N. Amer. a camp bed. ■ a plain narrow bed. ■ Nautical a bed resembling a hammock hung from deck beams, formerly used by officers.
– ORIGIN mid 17th cent. (originally Anglo-Indian, denoting a light bedstead): from Hindi *khāṭ* 'bedstead, hammock'.

cot[2] ▶ **noun** a small shelter for livestock.
■ archaic a small, simple cottage.
– ORIGIN Old English, of Germanic origin; compare with Old Norse *kytja* 'hovel'; related to **COTE**.

cot[3] Mathematics ▶ **abbreviation for** cotangent.

cotangent /kəʊ'tandʒ(ə)nt/ ▶ **noun** Mathematics (in a right-angled triangle) the ratio of the side (other than the hypotenuse) adjacent to a particular acute angle to the side opposite the angle.

cot-case ▶ **noun** Austral./NZ informal a person who is too ill to leave their bed.
■ a person who is incapacitated by alcohol.

cot death ▶ **noun** Brit. the unexplained death of a baby in its sleep.

cote ▶ **noun** a shelter for mammals or birds, especially pigeons.
– ORIGIN Old English (in the sense 'cottage'), of Germanic origin; related to **COT**[2].

Côte d'Ivoire /kot divwaʀ/ French name for **IVORY COAST**.

cote-hardie /'kəʊt,hɑːdi/ ▶ **noun** (pl. **cote-hardies**) historical a medieval close-fitting tunic with sleeves, worn by both sexes.
– ORIGIN Middle English: from Old French, from *cote* 'coat' + *hardie* (feminine) 'bold'.

coterie /'kəʊt(ə)ri/ ▶ **noun** (pl. **-ies**) a small group of people with shared interests or tastes, especially one that is exclusive of other people: *a coterie of friends and advisers.*
– ORIGIN early 18th cent.: from French, earlier denoting an association of tenants, based on Middle Low German *kote* 'cote'.

coterminous /kəʊ'təːmɪnəs/ ▶ **adjective** having the

same boundaries or extent in space, time, or meaning: *the coterminous Borough and Parliamentary Constituency of Blyth Valley.*
– ORIGIN late 18th cent.: alteration of **CONTERMINOUS**.

coth /kɒθ, kɒˈeɪtʃ/ ▶ abbreviation for hyperbolic cotangent.
– ORIGIN from **COT**³ + -h for *hyperbolic.*

co-tidal line ▶ noun a line on a map connecting points at which a tidal level, especially high tide, occurs simultaneously.

cotillion /kəˈtɪljən/ ▶ noun 1 a dance with elaborate steps and figures, in particular:
■ an 18th-century French dance based on the contredanse. ■ US a quadrille.
2 US a formal ball, especially one at which debutantes are presented.
– ORIGIN early 18th cent.: from French *cotillon*, literally 'petticoat dance', diminutive of *cotte*, from Old French *cote*.

cotinga /kəˈtɪŋɡə/ ▶ noun a perching bird found in the forests of Central and South America, the male of which is frequently brilliantly coloured.
● Family Cotingidae (the **cotinga family**): several genera, especially *Cotinga*, and numerous species. The cotinga family also includes the bellbirds, umbrellabirds, and cocks-of-the-rock, and is sometimes placed within the family Tyrannidae.
– ORIGIN via French from Tupi *cutinga.*

Cotman /ˈkɒtmən/, John Sell (1782–1842), English watercolourist and landscape painter, regarded as one of the leading figures of the Norwich School.

cotoneaster /kəˌtəʊnɪˈastə/ ▶ noun a small-leaved shrub of the rose family, cultivated as a hedging plant or for its bright red berries which often remain on the plant throughout the winter.
● Genus *Cotoneaster*, family Rosaceae.
– ORIGIN mid 18th cent.: modern Latin, from Latin *cotoneum* (see **QUINCE**) + -**ASTER**.

Cotonou /ˌkɒtəˈnuː/ the largest city, chief port, and chief commercial and political centre of Benin, on the coast of West Africa; pop. 536,830 (1992)

Cotopaxi /ˌkɒtəˈpaksi/ the highest active volcano in the world, rising to 5,896 m (19,142 ft) in the Andes of central Ecuador. Its name is Quechuan and means 'shining peak'.

co-trimoxazole /ˌkəʊtrʌɪˈmɒksəzəʊl/ ▶ noun [mass noun] Medicine a mixture of the drugs sulphamethoxazole and trimethoprim, used to treat bacterial infections synergistically.

Cotswold /ˈkɒtswəʊld/ ▶ noun 1 a sheep of a breed with fine wool, often used to produce cross-bred lambs.
2 [mass noun] Double Gloucester cheese containing chives and onions.
▶ adjective of or relating to the Cotswolds.

Cotswold Hills (also **the Cotswolds**) a range of limestone hills in SW England, largely in the county of Gloucestershire.

cotta /ˈkɒtə/ ▶ noun a short garment resembling a surplice, worn typically by Catholic priests and servers.
– ORIGIN mid 19th cent.: from Italian; ultimately related to **COAT**.

cottage ▶ noun a small simple house, typically one in the country.
■ a dwelling forming part of a farm establishment, used by a worker: *farm cottages.* ■ informal (in the context of casual homosexual encounters) a public toilet.
▶ verb [no obj.] [usu. as noun **cottaging**] informal perform homosexual acts in a public toilet.
– DERIVATIVES **cottagey** adjective.
– ORIGIN late Middle English: from Anglo-Norman French *cotage* and Anglo-Latin *cotagium*, from **COT**² or **COTE**.

cottage cheese ▶ noun [mass noun] soft, lumpy white cheese made from the curds of skimmed milk.

cottage garden ▶ noun an informal garden stocked typically with colourful flowering plants.

cottage hospital ▶ noun Brit. & Canadian a small hospital in a country area.

cottage industry ▶ noun a business or manufacturing activity carried on in people's homes.

cottage loaf ▶ noun Brit. a loaf consisting of two round pieces of bread, the smaller of which is on top of the larger.

cottage pie ▶ noun Brit. a dish of minced meat topped with browned mashed potato.

cottager ▶ noun a person living in a cottage.
■ N. Amer. a person holidaying in a cottage.

cottar /ˈkɒtə/ (also **cotter**) ▶ noun historical (in Scotland and Ireland) a farm labourer or tenant occupying a cottage in return for labour.
– ORIGIN late Old English, from **COT**² + -**AR**⁴.

Cottbus /ˈkɒtbʊs/ an industrial city in SE Germany, in Brandenburg, on the River Spree; pop. 123,320 (1991).

cotter pin (also **cotter**) ▶ noun a metal pin used to fasten two parts of a mechanism together.
■ a split pin that is opened out after being passed through a hole.
– ORIGIN mid 17th cent.: of unknown origin.

cottier /ˈkɒtɪə/ ▶ noun 1 Brit. archaic a rural labourer living in a cottage.
2 historical an Irish peasant holding land by cottier tenure.
– ORIGIN Middle English: from Old French *cotier*, ultimately of Germanic origin and related to **COT**².

cottier tenure ▶ noun [mass noun] historical (in Ireland) the letting of land in small portions direct to the labourers, at a rent fixed by competition.

cottise /ˈkɒtɪs/ (also **cotise**) ▶ noun Heraldry a narrow band adjacent and parallel to an ordinary such as a bend or chevron.
– DERIVATIVES **cottised** adjective.
– ORIGIN late 16th cent.: from French *cotice* 'leather thong'.

cotton ▶ noun [mass noun] 1 a soft white fibrous substance which surrounds the seeds of a tropical and subtropical plant and is used as textile fibre and thread for sewing: *a cargo of cotton and wheat* | [as modifier] *a white cotton blouse* | [count noun] *an Indian hammock woven in coloured cottons.*
■ [count noun] a thread of this fibre. ■ N. Amer. cotton wool.
2 (also **cotton plant**) the plant which is commercially grown for this product. Oil and a protein-rich flour are also obtained from the seeds.
● Genus *Gossypium*, family Malvaceae: many species and forms, including *G. barbadense*, which is grown in the southern US.
▶ verb [no obj.] informal 1 (**cotton on**) begin to understand: *he cottoned on to what I was trying to say.*
2 (**cotton to**) N. Amer. have a liking for: *his rivals didn't cotton to all the attention he was getting.*
– DERIVATIVES **cottony** adjective.
– ORIGIN late Middle English: from Old French *coton*, from Arabic *ḳuṭn*.

cotton batting ▶ noun North American term for **COTTON WOOL** (in sense 1).

cotton belt ▶ noun the cotton-producing region of the southern US.

cotton bud ▶ noun Brit. a small wad of cotton wool on a short thin stick, used for cosmetic purposes or cleaning the ears.

cotton cake ▶ noun [mass noun] compressed cotton seed, used as food for cattle.

cotton candy ▶ noun North American term for **CANDYFLOSS**.

cotton gin ▶ noun a machine for separating cotton from its seeds.

cotton grass ▶ noun [mass noun] a sedge which typically grows on wet moorlands in the northern hemisphere, producing tufts of long white silky hairs which aid in the dispersal of the seeds. Also called **BOG COTTON**.
● Genus *Eriophorum*, family Cyperaceae.

cotton lavender ▶ noun a small aromatic shrubby plant of the daisy family, with silvery or greenish lavender-like foliage and yellow button flowers. Native to the Mediterranean area, it has insecticidal properties.
● Genus *Santolina*, family Compositae: several species, in particular *S. chamaecyparissus*.

cotton-leaf worm ▶ noun the larva of a migratory tropical moth which feeds on the leaves of the cotton plant and was formerly a major pest in North America.
● *Alabama argillacea*, family Noctuidae.

cottonmouth (also **cottonmouth moccasin**) ▶ noun a large, dangerous semiaquatic pit viper which inhabits lowland swamps and waterways of the south-eastern US. When threatening it opens

its mouth wide to display the white interior. Also called **WATER MOCCASIN**.
● *Agkistrodon piscivorus*, family Viperidae.

cotton-picking ▶ adjective [attrib.] N. Amer. informal used for emphasis: *just a cotton-picking minute!*

cotton rat ▶ noun a short-tailed rat found in grassland and scrub from North America to Guyana.
● Genus *Sigmodon*, family Muridae: several species.

cotton spinner ▶ noun a dark sea cucumber of shallow seas which ejects long sticky threads from the anus when disturbed.
● *Holothuria forskali*, class Holothuroidea.

cotton stainer ▶ noun a North American bug which feeds on cotton bolls, causing reddish staining of the fibres.
● Genus *Dysdercus*, family Pyrrhocoridae, suborder Heteroptera: several species, in particular *D. suturellus*.

cotton state ▶ noun any of the states of the southern US of which cotton is or was a major product.
■ (**Cotton State**) informal name for **ALABAMA**.

cotton swab ▶ noun North American term for **COTTON BUD**.

cottontail ▶ noun an American rabbit which has a speckled brownish coat and a white underside to the tail.
● Genus *Sylvilagus*, family Leporidae: several species.

cotton-top tamarin ▶ noun a rare tamarin found in Central America, with brown and cream fur and a crest of white hair.
● *Saguinus oedipus*, family Callitrichidae.

cotton waste ▶ noun [mass noun] scraps of waste cotton yarn, used typically to clean machinery.

cottonweed ▶ noun [mass noun] a yellow-flowered aromatic plant of the daisy family, with silvery felted leaves and stems. It grows on sandy beaches, chiefly in southern and western Europe.
● *Otanthus maritimus*, family Compositae.

cottonwood ▶ noun 1 a North American poplar with seeds covered in white cottony hairs.
● Genus *Populus*, family Salicaceae: several species, including *P. deltoides*, which has become naturalized in parts of Europe.
2 any of a number of downy-leaved Australasian shrubs.
● an evergreen shrub of the buckthorn family (*Pomaderris phylicifolia*, family Rhamnaceae). ● a shrub of the daisy family (*Bedfordia salicina*, family Compositae).

cotton wool ▶ noun [mass noun] 1 Brit. fluffy wadding of a kind originally made from raw cotton, used especially for cleaning the skin or bathing wounds.
2 US raw cotton.
– PHRASES **wrap someone in cotton wool** be overprotective towards someone.

cottony-cushion scale ▶ noun [mass noun] an Australian scale insect with a large fluted cottony egg sac, infesting citrus trees. It threatened to destroy the Californian citrus industry until it was controlled by the introduction of the Australian vedalia beetle.
● *Icerya purchasi*, family Margarodidae, suborder Homoptera.

cotyledon /ˌkɒtɪˈliːd(ə)n/ ▶ noun 1 Botany an embryonic leaf in seed-bearing plants, one or more of which are the first leaves to appear from a germinating seed.
2 a succulent plant of the stonecrop family, some kinds of which are grown as ornamentals.
● Genus *Cotyledon* and related genera, family Crassulaceae: several species, in particular the South African *C. orbiculata* and the European wall pennywort.
– DERIVATIVES **cotyledonary** adjective.
– ORIGIN mid 16th cent. (denoting a patch of villi on the placenta of mammals): from Latin, 'navelwort' (which has cup-shaped leaves), from Greek *kotulēdōn* 'cup-shaped cavity', from *kotulē* 'cup'.

coucal /ˈkuːk(ə)l, ˈkuːkɑːl/ ▶ noun an ungainly long-tailed Old World bird that is a large ground-dwelling member of the cuckoo family.
● Genus *Centropus* (and *Coua*), family Cuculidae: numerous species, including the Australasian **pheasant coucal** (*Centropus phasianinus*).
– ORIGIN early 19th cent.: from French, perhaps a blend of *coucou* 'cuckoo' and *alouette* 'lark'.

couch¹ /kaʊtʃ/ ▶ noun a long upholstered piece of furniture for several people to sit on.
■ a reclining seat with a headrest at one end on which a psychoanalyst's subject or doctor's patient lies while undergoing treatment.
▶ verb [with obj.] 1 (usu. **be couched in**) express

(something) in language of a specified style: *the assurances were couched in general terms.*
2 [no obj.] poetic/literary lie down: *two fair creatures, couched side by side in deepest grass.*
3 archaic lower (a spear) to the position for attack.
4 [usu. as noun **couching**] chiefly historical treat (a cataract) by pushing the lens of the eye downwards and backwards, out of line with the pupil.
5 (in embroidery) fix (a thread) to a fabric by stitching it down flat with another thread: *gold and silver threads couched by hand.*
– PHRASES **on the couch** undergoing psychoanalysis or psychiatric treatment.
– ORIGIN Middle English (as a noun denoting something to sleep on; as a verb in the sense 'lay something down'): from Old French *couche* (noun), *coucher* (verb), from Latin *collocare* 'place together' (see **COLLOCATE**).

couch[2] /kaʊtʃ, kuːtʃ/ (also **couch grass**) ▶ **noun** [mass noun] a coarse grass with long creeping roots, which can be a serious weed in gardens.
• Genera *Elymus* and *Agropyron*, family Gramineae: several species, in particular the Eurasian **common couch** (*E. repens*).
– ORIGIN late 16th cent.: variant of **QUITCH**.

couchant /ˈkaʊtʃ(ə)nt/ ▶ **adjective** [usu. postpositive] Heraldry (of an animal) lying with the body resting on the legs and the head raised: *two lions couchant.*
– ORIGIN late Middle English: French, 'lying', present participle of *coucher* (see **COUCH**[1]).

couchette /kuːˈʃɛt/ ▶ **noun** a railway carriage with seats convertible into sleeping berths.
■ a berth in such a carriage.
– ORIGIN 1920s: French, literally 'little bed', diminutive of *couche* 'a couch'.

couch potato ▶ **noun** informal a person who takes little or no exercise and watches a lot of television.

cou-cou /ˈkuːkuː/ ▶ **noun** [mass noun] W. Indian a dish of boiled maize flour and okra, rolled into balls and typically served with fish.
– ORIGIN of unknown origin.

coudé /kuːˈdeɪ/ ▶ **adjective** relating to or denoting a telescope in which the rays are bent to a focus at a fixed point off the axis.
▶ **noun** a telescope constructed in this way.
– ORIGIN late 19th cent.: French, literally 'bent at right angles', past participle of *couder*, from *coude* 'elbow', from Latin *cubitum*.

cougar /ˈkuːɡə/ ▶ **noun** North American term for **PUMA**.
– ORIGIN late 18th cent.: from French *couguar*, abbreviation of modern Latin *cuguarcarana*, from Guarani *guaçuarana*.

cough ▶ **verb** [no obj.] expel air from the lungs with a sudden sharp sound.
■ (of an engine) make a sudden harsh noise, especially as a sign of malfunction. ■ [with obj.] force (something, especially blood) out of the lungs or throat by coughing: *he **coughed up** bloodstained fluid.* ■ [with obj.] (**cough something out**) say something in a harsh, abrupt way: *he coughed out his orders.* ■ Brit. informal reveal information; confess: *once he realized we knew he was ready to cough fast enough.*
▶ **noun** an act or sound of coughing: *she gave a discreet cough.*
■ a condition of the respiratory organs causing coughing: *he looked feverish and had a bad cough.*
– ORIGIN Middle English: of imitative origin; related to Dutch *kuchen* 'to cough' and German *keuchen* 'to pant'.
▶ **cough something up** (or **cough up**) give something reluctantly, especially money or information that is due or required.

cough drop (also **cough sweet**) ▶ **noun** a medicated lozenge sucked to relieve a cough.

cough mixture ▶ **noun** [mass noun] Brit. liquid medicine taken to relieve a cough.

could ▶ **modal verb** past of **CAN**[1].
■ used to indicate possibility: *they could be right | I would go if I could afford it.* ■ used in making polite requests: *could I use the phone?* ■ used in making suggestions: *you could always ring him up.* ■ used to indicate annoyance because of something that has not been done: *they could have told me!* ■ used to indicate a strong inclination to do something: *he irritates me so much that I could scream.*

couldn't ▶ **contraction** of could not.

coulee /ˈkuːli/ ▶ **noun** N. Amer. a deep ravine.
– ORIGIN early 19th cent.: from French *coulée* '(lava) flow', from *couler* 'to flow', from Latin *colare* 'to strain or flow', from *colum* 'strainer'.

coulibiac /ˌkuːlɪˈbjak/ (also **koulibiac**) ▶ **noun** a Russian pie of fish or meat, cabbage or other vegetables, and herbs.
– ORIGIN from Russian *kulebyaka*.

coulis /ˈkuːli/ ▶ **noun** (pl. same) a thin fruit or vegetable purée, used as a sauce.
– ORIGIN French, from *couler* 'to flow'.

coulisse /kuːˈliːs/ ▶ **noun** a flat piece of scenery at the side of the stage in a theatre.
■ (**the coulisses**) the spaces between these pieces of scenery; the wings.
– ORIGIN early 19th cent.: French, feminine of *coulis* 'sliding', based on Latin *colare* 'to flow'.

couloir /ˈkuːlwɑː/ ▶ **noun** a steep, narrow gully on a mountainside.
– ORIGIN early 19th cent.: French, 'gully or corridor', from *couler* 'to flow'.

coulomb /ˈkuːlɒm/ (abbrev.: **C**) ▶ **noun** Physics the SI unit of electric charge, equal to the quantity of electricity conveyed in one second by a current of one ampere.
– ORIGIN late 19th cent.: named after Charles-Augustin de *Coulomb* (1736–1806), French military engineer.

Coulomb's law /ˈkuːlɒmz/ Physics a law stating that like charges repel and opposite charges attract, with a force proportional to the product of the charges and inversely proportional to the square of the distance between them.
– ORIGIN late 18th cent.: named after C.-A. de *Coulomb* (see **COULOMB**).

coulter /ˈkəʊltə/ (US **colter**) ▶ **noun** a vertical cutting blade fixed in front of a ploughshare.
■ the part of a seed drill that makes the furrow for the seed.
– ORIGIN Old English, from Latin *culter* 'knife or ploughshare'.

coumarin /ˈkuːmərɪn/ ▶ **noun** [mass noun] Chemistry a vanilla-scented compound found in many plants, formerly used for flavouring food.
• A bicyclic ketone; chem. formula: $C_9H_6O_2$.
■ [count noun] any derivative of this.
– ORIGIN mid 19th cent.: from French *coumarine*, from *coumarou*, via Portuguese and Spanish from Tupi *cumarú* 'tonka bean'.

coumarone /ˈkuːmərəʊn/ ▶ **noun** [mass noun] Chemistry an organic compound present in coal tar, used to make thermoplastic resins chiefly for paints and varnishes.
• A bicyclic compound with fused benzene and furan rings; chem. formula: C_8H_6O.
– ORIGIN late 19th cent.: from **COUMARIN** + **-ONE**.

council ▶ **noun** an advisory, deliberative, or administrative body of people formally constituted and meeting regularly: *an official human rights council.*
■ a body of people elected to manage the affairs of a city, county, or other municipal district. ■ [as modifier] Brit. denoting housing provided by such a body at a subsidized rent: *a council flat.* ■ an ecclesiastical assembly. ■ an assembly or meeting for consultation or advice: *that evening, she held a family council.*
– ORIGIN Old English (in the sense 'ecclesiastical assembly'): from Anglo-Norman French *cuncile*, from Latin *concilium* 'convocation, assembly', from *con-* 'together' + *calare* 'summon'. Compare with **COUNSEL**.

council estate ▶ **noun** Brit. an area of houses built and rented out to tenants by a local council.

Council for Mutual Economic Assistance historical fuller form of **COMECON**.
– ORIGIN translating Russian *Sovet ékonomicheskoĭ vzaimopomoshchi*.

councillor (US also **councilor**) ▶ **noun** a member of a council.
– DERIVATIVES **councillorship** noun.
– ORIGIN late Middle English: alteration of **COUNSELLOR**, by association with **COUNCIL**.

councilman ▶ **noun** (pl. **-men**) chiefly US a male member of a council, especially a municipal one.

Council of Chalcedon, Council of Europe, etc. see **CHALCEDON, COUNCIL OF; EUROPE, COUNCIL OF,** etc.

council of war ▶ **noun** a gathering of military officers in wartime.
■ a meeting held to plan a response to an emergency.

council tax ▶ **noun** [mass noun] a tax levied on households by local authorities in the UK, based on the estimated value of a property and the number of people living in it.

councilwoman ▶ **noun** (pl. **-women**) chiefly US a female member of a council, especially a municipal one.

C

counsel ▶ **noun 1** [mass noun] advice, especially that given formally.
■ archaic consultation, especially to seek or give advice.
2 (pl. same) a barrister or other legal adviser conducting a case: *the counsel for the defence.*
▶ **verb** (**counselled**, **counselling**; US **counseled**, **counseling**) [with obj.] give advice to (someone): [with obj. and infinitive] *he was counselled by his supporters to return to Germany.*
■ give professional psychological help and advice to (someone): *he was being counselled for depression.* ■ recommend (a course of action): *the athlete's coach counselled caution.*
– PHRASES **a counsel of despair** an action to be taken when all else fails. **a counsel of perfection** advice that is ideal but not feasible. **keep one's own counsel** say nothing about what one believes, knows, or plans: *she doubted what he said but kept her own counsel.* **take counsel** discuss a problem: *the party leader and chairman took counsel together.*
– ORIGIN Middle English: via Old French *counseil* (noun), *conseiller* (verb), from Latin *consilium* 'consultation, advice', related to *consulere* (see **CONSULT**). Compare with **COUNCIL**.

counselling (US **counseling**) ▶ **noun** [mass noun] the provision of assistance and guidance in resolving personal, social, or psychological problems and difficulties, especially by a trained person on a professional basis: *bereavement counselling.*

counsellor (US **counselor**) ▶ **noun 1** a person trained to give guidance on personal, social, or psychological problems: *a marriage counsellor.*
■ [often with modifier] a person who gives advice on a specified subject: *a debt counsellor.*
2 a senior officer in the diplomatic service.
3 (also **counselor-at-law**) US & Irish a barrister.
– ORIGIN Middle English (in the general sense 'adviser'): from Old French *conseiller*, from Latin *consiliarius*, and Old French *conseillour*, from Latin *consiliator*, both from *consilium* 'consultation or advice'.

Counsellor of State ▶ **noun** (in the UK) a temporary regent during a sovereign's absence.

count[1] ▶ **verb 1** [with obj.] determine the total number of (a collection of items): *I started to count the stars I could see | they **counted up** their change.*
■ [no obj.] recite numbers in ascending order, usually starting at the number one: *hold the position as you **count to** five.* ■ [no obj.] (**count down**) recite or display numbers backwards to zero to indicate the time remaining before the launch of a rocket or the start of an operation: *the floor manager pointed at the camera and counted down.* ■ [no obj.] (**count down**) prepare for a significant event in the short time remaining before it: *with more orders expected, the company is **counting down** to a bumper Christmas.*
2 [with obj.] take into account; include: *the staff has shrunk to four, or five if you count the European director.*
■ (**count someone in**) include someone in an activity or the plans for it: *if the project gets started, count me in.* ■ consider (someone or something) to possess a specified quality or fulfil a specified role: *she met some rebuffs from people she had **counted as** her friends* | [with obj. and complement] *I count myself fortunate to have known him.* ■ [no obj.] be regarded as possessing a specified quality or fulfilling a specified role: *results which are consistent with all models cannot **count as** evidence for any of them.*
3 [no obj.] be significant: *it did not matter what the audience thought—it was the critics that counted.*
■ (of a factor) play a part in influencing opinion for or against someone or something: *he hopes his sporting attitude will **count in his favour**.* ■ (**count for**) be worth (a specified amount): *he has no power base and his views count for little.* ■ (**count towards**) be included in an assessment of (a final result or amount): *reduced rate contributions do not count towards your pension.* ■ (**count on/upon**) rely on: *whatever you're doing, you can count on me.*
▶ **noun 1** an act of determining the total number of something: ***at the last count**, fifteen applications were still outstanding | the party's only candidate was eliminated at the first count.*
■ the total determined by such an action: *there was a moderate increase in the white cell count in both patients.*

2 an act of reciting numbers in ascending order, up to the specified number: *hold the position for five counts* | *hold it for a count of seven.*

■ an act of reciting numbers up to ten by the referee when a boxer is knocked down, the boxer being considered knocked out if still down when ten is reached.

3 a point for discussion or consideration: *the programme remained vulnerable* **on a number of counts.** ■ Law a separate charge in an indictment: *he pleaded guilty to five counts of murder.*

4 the measure of the fineness of a yarn expressed as the weight of a given length or the length of a given weight.

■ a measure of the fineness of a woven fabric expressed as the number of warp or weft threads in a given length.

– PHRASES **beat the count** (of a boxer who has been knocked down) get up before the referee counts to ten. **count one's blessings** be grateful for what one has. **count the cost** calculate the consequences of something, typically a careless or foolish action. **count the days** (or **hours**) be impatient for time to pass: *they counted the days until they came home on leave.* **count something on the fingers of one hand** used to emphasize the small number of a particular thing: *I could count on the fingers of one hand the men I know who are desperate to experience fatherhood.* **count the pennies** see **PENNY**. **count sheep** see **SHEEP**. **don't count your chickens before they're hatched** proverb don't be too confident in anticipating success or good fortune before it is certain: *I wouldn't count your chickens—I've agreed to sign the contract but that's all I've agreed to.* **keep count** (or **a count**) take note of the number or amount of something: *you can protect yourself by keeping a count of what you drink.* **lose count** forget how many of something there are, especially because the number is so high: *I've lost count of the hundreds of miles I've covered.* **out** (or N. Amer. also **down**) **for the count** Boxing defeated by being knocked to the ground and unable to rise within ten seconds. ■ unconscious or soundly asleep. ■ defeated. **take the count** Boxing be knocked out.

– ORIGIN Middle English (as a noun): from Old French *counte* (noun), *counter* (verb), from the verb *computare* 'calculate' (see **COMPUTE**).

▶ **count someone out 1** complete a count of ten seconds over a fallen boxer to indicate defeat. **2** informal exclude someone from an activity or the plans for it: *if this is a guessing game you can count me out.* **3** (in children's games) select a player for dismissal or a special role by using a counting rhyme. **count something out 1** take items one by one from a stock of something, especially money, keeping a note of how many one takes: *opening the wallet I counted out 19 dollars.* **2** Brit. procure the adjournment of the House of Commons when fewer than 40 members are present.

count² ▶ noun a foreign nobleman whose rank corresponds to that of an earl.

– DERIVATIVES **countship** noun.

– ORIGIN late Middle English: from Old French *conte*, from Latin *comes*, *comit-* 'companion, overseer, attendant' (in late Latin 'person holding a state office'), from *com-* 'together with' + *it-* 'gone' (from the verb *ire* 'go').

countable ▶ adjective able to be counted.

countable noun ▶ noun another term for **COUNT NOUN.**

countback ▶ noun a method of deciding the winner of a tied game or competition by awarding it to the contestant with the better score in the later part.

countdown ▶ noun [usu. in sing.] an act of counting numerals in reverse order to zero, especially to time the last seconds before the launching of a rocket or missile: *the missiles' launch crews would begin their final countdown.*

■ (often **countdown to**) the final moments before a significant event and the procedures carried out during this time: *it is hard to imagine the countdown to war continuing without an intensification of diplomacy.* ■ a digital display that counts down.

countenance /ˈkaʊnt(ə)nəns, -tɪn-/ ▶ noun **1** a person's face or facial expression: *his impenetrable eyes and inscrutable countenance give little away.*
2 [mass noun] support: *she was giving her specific countenance to the occasion.*

▶ verb [with obj.] admit as acceptable or possible: *he was reluctant to countenance the use of force.*

– PHRASES **keep one's countenance** maintain one's composure, especially by refraining from laughter. **keep someone in countenance** help someone to remain calm and confident: *to keep herself in countenance she opened her notebook.* **out of countenance** disconcerted or unpleasantly surprised: *I put him clean out of countenance just by looking at him.*

– ORIGIN Middle English: from Old French *contenance* 'bearing, behaviour', from *contenir* (see **CONTAIN**). The early sense was 'bearing, demeanour', also 'facial expression', hence 'the face'.

counter¹ ▶ noun **1** a long flat-topped fitment in a shop or bank across which business is conducted with customers.

■ a similar structure used for serving food and drinks in a cafeteria or bar. ■ North American term for **WORKTOP.**
2 a small disc used as a place marker or for keeping the score in board games.

■ a token representing a coin. ■ a factor used to give one party an advantage in negotiations: *the proposal has become a crucial bargaining counter over prices.*
3 an apparatus used for counting: *the counter tells you how many pictures you have taken.*

■ a person who counts something, for example votes in an election. ■ Physics an apparatus used for counting individual ionizing particles or events.

– PHRASES **behind the counter** serving in a shop or bank. **over the counter** by ordinary retail purchase, with no need for a prescription or licence: [as modifier] *over-the-counter medicines.* ■ (of share transactions) taking place outside the stock exchange system. **under the counter** (or **table**) (with reference to goods bought or sold) surreptitiously and typically illegally: *hard porn is legally banned, but still available under the counter* | [as modifier] *an under-the-counter deal.*

– ORIGIN Middle English (in sense 2): from Old French *conteor*, from medieval Latin *computatorium*, from Latin *computare* (see **COMPUTE**).

counter² ▶ verb [with obj.] speak or act in opposition to: *the second argument is more difficult to counter.*

■ [no obj.] respond to hostile speech or action: [with direct speech] *'What would you like me to do about it?' she countered.* ■ [no obj.] Boxing give a return blow while parrying: *he countered with a left hook.*

▶ adverb (**counter to**) in the opposite direction to or in conflict with: *some actions by the authorities ran counter to the call for leniency.*

▶ adjective responding to something of the same kind, especially in opposition: *after years of argument and counter argument there is no conclusive answer to the question.* See also **COUNTER-.**

▶ noun **1** [usu. in sing.] a thing which opposes or prevents something else: *the stimulus to employers' organization was partly a counter to growing union power.*

■ an answer to an argument or criticism: *he anticipates an objection and plans his counter.* ■ Boxing a blow given while parrying; a counterpunch.
2 the curved part of the stern of a ship projecting aft above the waterline.
3 Printing the white space enclosed by a letter such as O or c.

– PHRASES **go** (or Brit. **hunt** or **run**) **counter** run or ride against the direction taken by a quarry.

– ORIGIN late Middle English: from Old French *contre*, from Latin *contra* 'against', or directly from **COUNTER-.**

counter³ ▶ noun the back part of a shoe or boot, enclosing the heel.

– ORIGIN mid 19th cent.: abbreviation of *counterfort* 'buttress', from French *contrefort.*

counter- ▶ prefix denoting opposition, retaliation, or rivalry: *counter-attack* | *counter-espionage.*

■ denoting movement or effect in the opposite direction: *counterpoise.* ■ denoting correspondence, duplication, or substitution: *counterpart.*

– ORIGIN from Anglo-Norman French *countre-*, Old French *contre*, from Latin *contra* 'against'.

counteract ▶ verb [with obj.] act against (something) in order to reduce its force or neutralize it: *should we deliberately intervene in the climate system to counteract global warming?*

– DERIVATIVES **counteraction** noun, **counteractive** adjective.

counter-attack ▶ noun an attack made in response to one by an enemy or opponent.

▶ verb [no obj.] attack in response: *as deputies tried to*

---

dislodge him, he counter-attacked by forcing through elections.

– DERIVATIVES **counter-attacker** noun.

counter-attraction ▶ noun a rival attraction.

counterbalance ▶ noun /ˈkaʊntəˌbal(ə)ns/ a weight that balances another weight.

■ a factor having the opposite effect to that of another and so preventing it from exercising a disproportionate influence: *his restoration to power was intended as a counterbalance to his rival's influence.*
▶ verb /ˌkaʊntəˈbal(ə)ns/ [with obj.] (of a weight) balance (another weight).

■ neutralize or cancel by exerting an opposite influence: *the extra cost of mail order may be counterbalanced by its convenience.*

counterblast ▶ noun a strongly worded reply to someone else's views: *a counterblast to the growing propaganda of the Left.*

counterbore ▶ noun a drilled hole that has a flat-bottomed enlargement at its mouth.

■ a drill whose bit has a uniform smaller diameter near the tip, for drilling counterbores in one operation.
▶ verb [with obj.] drill a counterbore in (an object).

counterchange ▶ verb [with obj.] poetic/literary chequer with contrasting colours.

■ Heraldry interchange the tinctures of (a charge) with that of a divided field.
▶ noun [mass noun] **1** change that is equivalent in degree but opposite in effect to a previous change.
2 patterning in which a dark motif on a light ground alternates with the same motif light on a dark ground.

– ORIGIN late Middle English (as a heraldic term): from French *contrechanger*, from *contre* (expressing substitution) + *changer* 'to change'.

countercharge ▶ noun an accusation made in turn by someone against their accuser: *charges and countercharges concerning producers, quotas, and affidavits.*

■ a charge by police or an armed force in response to one made against them.

countercheck ▶ noun **1** a second check for security or accuracy.
2 archaic a restraint.
3 archaic a sharp or incisive reply; a retort.
▶ verb [with obj.] archaic stop (something) by acting to cancel or counteract it: *His Majesty with his own hand wrote to countercheck his former Warrant.*

counterclaim ▶ noun a claim made to rebut a previous claim.

■ Law a claim made by a defendant against the plaintiff.
▶ verb [no obj.] chiefly Law make a counterclaim for something.

counterclockwise ▶ adverb & adjective North American term for **ANTICLOCKWISE.**

counter-conditioning ▶ noun [mass noun] a technique employed in animal training and the treatment of phobias and similar conditions in humans, in which behaviour incompatible with a habitual undesirable pattern is induced. Compare with **DECONDITION** (in sense 2).

counterculture ▶ noun a way of life and set of attitudes opposed to or at variance with the prevailing social norm: *the idealists of the 60s counterculture.*

countercurrent ▶ noun a current flowing in an opposite direction to another.

▶ adverb in or with opposite directions of flow.

counter-espionage ▶ noun [mass noun] activities designed to prevent or thwart spying by an enemy.

counterfactual Philosophy ▶ adjective relating to or expressing what has not happened or is not the case.

▶ noun a counterfactual conditional statement (e.g. *If kangaroos had no tails, they would topple over*).

counterfeit ▶ adjective made in exact imitation of something valuable or important with the intention to deceive or defraud: *two men were remanded on bail on a charge of passing counterfeit £10 notes.*

■ archaic pretended; sham: *the counterfeit and the worthless Poor do a world of mischief to the cause of beneficence.*
▶ noun a fraudulent imitation of something else; a forgery: *he knew the tapes to be counterfeits.*
▶ verb [with obj.] imitate fraudulently: *my signature is extremely hard to counterfeit.*

■ pretend to feel or possess (an emotion or quality): *no*

---

pretence could have counterfeited such terror. ■ poetic/literary resemble closely: *sleep counterfeited Death so well.*
– DERIVATIVES **counterfeiter** noun.
– ORIGIN Middle English (as a verb): from Anglo-Norman French *countrefeter*, from Old French *contrefait*, past participle of *contrefaire*, from Latin *contra-* 'in opposition' + *facere* 'make'.

counterfoil ▶ noun chiefly Brit. the part of a cheque, receipt, ticket, or other document that is torn off and kept as a record by the person issuing it.

counter-insurgency ▶ noun [mass noun] [usu. as modifier] military or political action taken against the activities of guerrillas or revolutionaries: *a counter-insurgency force.*

counter-intelligence ▶ noun another term for COUNTER-ESPIONAGE.

counter-intuitive ▶ adjective contrary to intuition or to common-sense expectation.
– DERIVATIVES **counter-intuitively** adverb.

counterirritant ▶ noun chiefly historical something such as heat or an ointment that is used to produce surface irritation of the skin, thereby counteracting underlying pain or discomfort.
– DERIVATIVES **counterirritation** noun.

counter-jumper ▶ noun informal, derogatory a shop assistant.

countermand /ˌkaʊntəˈmɑːnd/ ▶ verb [with obj.] revoke (an order): *an order to arrest the strike leaders had been countermanded.*
■ cancel an order for (goods): *she decided she had been extravagant and countermanded the cream.* ■ revoke an order issued by (another person): *he was already countermanding her.* ■ declare (voting) invalid: *the election commission has countermanded voting on the grounds of intimidation.*
– ORIGIN late Middle English: from Old French *contremander* (verb), *contremand* (noun), from medieval Latin *contramandare*, from *contra-* 'against' + *mandare* 'to order'.

countermarch ▶ verb [no obj.] march in the opposite direction or back along the same route.
▶ noun an act or instance of marching in this way.

countermark ▶ noun an additional mark placed on something already marked, typically for increased security.
■ a second watermark.

countermeasure ▶ noun an action taken to counteract a danger or threat.

countermelody ▶ noun (pl. **-ies**) a subordinate melody accompanying a principal one.

countermine Military ▶ noun an excavation dug to intercept another dug by an enemy.
▶ verb [with obj.] dig a countermine against.

countermove ▶ noun a move or other action made in opposition to another.
– DERIVATIVES **countermovement** noun.

counteroffensive ▶ noun an attack made in response to one from an enemy, typically on a large scale or for a prolonged period.

counter-offer ▶ noun an offer made in response to another.

counterpane ▶ noun dated a bedspread.
– ORIGIN early 17th cent.: alteration of COUNTERPOINT, from Old French *contrepointe*, based on medieval Latin *culcitra puncta* 'quilted mattress' (*puncta*, literally meaning 'pricked', from the verb *pungere*). The change in the ending was due to association with PANE in an obsolete sense 'cloth'.

counterpart ▶ noun **1** a person or thing holding a position or performing a function that corresponds to that of another person or thing in a different area: *the minister held talks with his French counterpart.* **2** Law one of two copies of a legal document.

counterpart fund ▶ noun a sum of money accrued in a local currency arising from goods or services received from abroad.

counterparty ▶ noun an opposite party in a contract or financial transaction.

counterplot ▶ noun a plot intended to thwart another plot.
▶ verb (**-plotted, -plotting**) [no obj.] devise a counterplot.

counterpoint ▶ noun **1** [mass noun] Music the art or technique of setting, writing, or playing a melody or melodies in conjunction with another, according to fixed rules.

■ [count noun] a melody played in conjunction with another.
2 an argument, idea, or theme used to create a contrast with the main element: *I have used my interviews with parents as a counterpoint to a professional judgement*
▶ verb [with obj.] **1** Music add counterpoint to (a melody): *the orchestra counterpoints the vocal part.*
2 (often **be counterpointed**) emphasize by contrast: *the cream walls and maple floors are counterpointed by black accents.*
■ compensate for: *the yarn's fanciful excesses are counterpointed with some sharp and unsentimental dialogue.*
– ORIGIN late Middle English: from Old French *contrepoint*, from medieval Latin *contrapunctum* '(song) pricked or marked over against (the original melody)', from *contra-* 'against' + *punctum*, from *pungere* 'to prick'.

counterpoise ▶ noun a factor, force, or influence that balances or neutralizes another: *the organization sees the power of Brussels as a counterpoise to that of London.*
■ [mass noun] archaic a state of equilibrium. ■ a counterbalancing weight.
▶ verb [with obj.] have an opposing and balancing effect on: *our ideal of what God can do in our lives is counterpoised by the actual human condition we are in.*
■ bring into contrast: *the stories counterpoise a young recruit with an old-timer.*
– ORIGIN late Middle English: from Old French *contrepois*, from *contre* 'against' + *pois* from Latin *pensum* 'weight'. Compare with POISE¹. The verb, originally *counterpeise*, from Old French *contrepeser*, was altered under the influence of the noun in the 16th cent.

counterpose ▶ verb [with obj.] set against or in opposition to.
– DERIVATIVES **counterposition** noun.

counterproductive ▶ adjective having the opposite of the desired effect: *they believe they are helping animals but in fact their extremist behaviour is actually counterproductive.*

counterpunch Boxing ▶ noun a punch thrown in return for one received.
▶ verb [no obj.] throw a counterpunch.
– DERIVATIVES **counterpuncher** noun.

Counter-Reformation the reform of the Church of Rome in the 16th and 17th centuries which was stimulated by the Protestant Reformation.

Measures to oppose the spread of the Reformation were resolved on at the Council of Trent (1545–63) and the Jesuit order became the spearhead of the Counter-Reformation, both within Europe and abroad. Although most of northern Europe remained Protestant, southern Germany and Poland were brought back to the Roman Catholic Church.

counter-revolution ▶ noun a revolution opposing a former one or reversing its results.
– DERIVATIVES **counter-revolutionary** adjective & noun.

counterrotate ▶ verb [no obj.] rotate in opposite directions, especially about the same axis.
– DERIVATIVES **counterrotation** noun.

counterscarp ▶ noun the outer wall of a ditch in a fortification.
– ORIGIN late 16th cent.: from French *contrescarpe*, from Italian *controscarpa*; compare with SCARP.

countershading ▶ noun [mass noun] Zoology protective coloration used by some animals in which parts normally in shadow are light and those exposed to the sky are dark.
– DERIVATIVES **countershaded** adjective.

countershaft ▶ noun a machine driveshaft that transmits motion from the main shaft to where it is required, such as the drive axle in a vehicle.

countersign ▶ verb [with obj.] add a signature to (a document already signed by another person): *each cheque had to be signed and countersigned.*
▶ noun archaic a signal or password given in reply to a soldier on guard.
– DERIVATIVES **countersignature** noun.
– ORIGIN late 16th cent. (as a noun): from French *contresigner* (verb), *contresigne* (noun), from Italian *contrassegno*, based on Latin *signum* 'sign'.

countersink ▶ verb (past and past participle **-sunk**) [with obj.] enlarge and bevel the rim of (a drilled hole) so that a screw, nail, or bolt can be inserted flush with the surface.
■ drive (a screw, nail, or bolt) into such a hole.

counterspy /ˈkaʊntəspʌɪ/ ▶ noun (pl. **-ies**) a spy engaged in counter-espionage.

counterstain Biology ▶ noun an additional dye used in a microscopy specimen to produce a contrasting background or to make clearer the distinction between different kinds of tissue.
▶ verb [with obj.] treat (a specimen) with a counterstain.

counterstroke ▶ noun an attack carried out in retaliation.

countersubject ▶ noun Music a second or subsidiary subject, especially accompanying the subject or its answer in a fugue.

counter-tenor ▶ noun Music the highest male adult singing voice (sometimes distinguished from the male alto voice by its strong, pure tone).
■ a singer with such a voice.
– ORIGIN late Middle English: from French *contreteneur*, from obsolete Italian *contratenore*, based on Latin *tenor* (see TENOR¹). Compare with CONTRALTO.

countertop ▶ noun North American term for WORKTOP.

countertrade ▶ noun [mass noun] international trade by exchange of goods rather than by currency purchase.

counter-transference ▶ noun [mass noun] Psychoanalysis the emotional reaction of the analyst to the subject's contribution.

countervail /ˌkaʊntəˈveɪl/ ▶ verb [with obj.] [usu. as adj. **countervailing**] offset the effect of (something) by countering it with something of equal force: *the dominance of the party was mediated by a number of countervailing factors.*
– ORIGIN late Middle English (in the sense 'be equivalent to in value, compensate for'): from Anglo-Norman French *contrevaloir*, from Latin *contra valere* 'be of worth against'.

countervailing duty ▶ noun an import tax imposed on certain goods in order to prevent dumping or counter export subsidies.

countervalue ▶ noun Brit. an equivalent or equal, especially in military strategy: [as modifier] *countervalue weapons.*

counterweight ▶ noun another term for COUNTERBALANCE.

countess ▶ noun the wife or widow of a count or earl.
■ a woman holding the rank of count or earl in her own right.
– ORIGIN Middle English: from Old French *contesse*, from late Latin *comitissa*, feminine of *comes* (see COUNT²).

countian ▶ noun [with modifier] chiefly US an inhabitant of a particular county.

counting ▶ preposition taking account of when reaching a total; including: *there were three of us in the family, or four counting my pet rabbit* | *the college had 139 employees, not counting those engaged in routine clerical work.*

counting house ▶ noun historical an office or building in which the accounts and money of a person or company were kept.

countless ▶ adjective too many to be counted; very many: *she'd apologized countless times before.*

count noun ▶ noun Grammar a noun that can form a plural and, in the singular, can be used with the indefinite article (e.g. *books*, *a book*). Contrasted with MASS NOUN.

Count Palatine ▶ noun historical a feudal lord having royal authority within a region of a kingdom.
■ a high official of the Holy Roman Empire with royal authority within his domain.
– ORIGIN see PALATINE¹.

countrified (also **countryfied**) ▶ adjective reminiscent or characteristic of the country, especially in being unsophisticated: *a countrified cottage garden* | *her tweeds were far too countrified.*
– ORIGIN mid 17th cent.: past participle of *countrify* 'make rural'.

country ▶ noun (pl. **-ies**) **1** a nation with its own government, occupying a particular territory: *the country's increasingly precarious economic position.*
■ (**the country**) the people of a nation: *the whole country took to the streets.* ■ the land of a person's birth or citizenship: *both my native and adopted countries are at war with yours.*
2 (often **the country**) districts and small

settlements outside large towns, cities, or the capital: *the airfield is right out in the country* | [as modifier] *a country lane.*
3 [mass noun] an area or region with regard to its physical features: *a tract of wild country.*
■ a region associated with a particular person, especially a writer, or with a particular work: *an old mansion in Stevenson's 'Kidnapped' country.*
– PHRASES **across country** not keeping to roads: *their route was across country, through fields of corn.* **go** (or **appeal**) **to the country** Brit. test public opinion by dissolving Parliament and holding a general election. **line of country** Brit. a subject in which a person is skilled or knowledgeable.
– ORIGIN Middle English: from Old French *cuntree*, from medieval Latin *contrata (terra)* '(land) lying opposite', from Latin *contra* 'against, opposite'.

country and western ▶ noun another term for **COUNTRY MUSIC**.

country blues ▶ noun [mass noun] a simple form of blues in which the singer is accompanied by an acoustic guitar.

country club ▶ noun a club with sporting and social facilities, set in a rural area.

country cousin ▶ noun a person with an unsophisticated and provincial appearance or manners.

country dance ▶ noun a traditional type of social English dance, in particular one performed by couples facing each other in long lines.

countryfied ▶ adjective variant spelling of **COUNTRIFIED**.

country gentleman ▶ noun a rich man of good social standing who owns and lives on an estate in a rural area.

country house ▶ noun a large house in the country, typically the seat of a wealthy or aristocratic family.

countryman ▶ noun (pl. **-men**) **1** a person living or born in a rural area, especially one engaged in a typically rural occupation.
2 a person from the same country or district as someone else: *she followed in the tradition of her countrymen* | *they trust a fellow countryman.*

country mile ▶ noun informal a very long way: *he hit the ball a country mile.*

country music ▶ noun [mass noun] a form of popular music originating in the rural southern US. It is a mixture of ballads and dance tunes played characteristically on fiddle, banjo, guitar, and pedal steel guitar. Also called **COUNTRY AND WESTERN**.

country party ▶ noun historical a political party supporting agricultural rather than manufacturing interests.

country rock[1] ▶ noun [mass noun] Geology the rock which encloses a mineral deposit, igneous intrusion, or other feature.

country rock[2] ▶ noun [mass noun] a type of popular music that is a blend of rock and country music.

country seat ▶ noun a large country house and estate belonging to an aristocratic family.

countryside ▶ noun [mass noun] the land and scenery of a rural area: *they explored the surrounding countryside.*
■ the inhabitants of such an area: *the political influence of the countryside remains strong.*

countrywide ▶ adjective & adverb extending throughout a nation: [as adj.] *a countrywide tour* | [as adv.] *travelling countrywide.*

countrywoman ▶ noun (pl. **-women**) **1** a woman living or born in a rural area, especially one engaged in a typically rural occupation.
2 a woman from the same country or district as someone else: *a fellow countrywoman from Ohio.*

county ▶ noun (pl. **-ies**) a territorial division of some countries, forming the chief unit of local administration.
■ [treated as sing. or pl.] the people of such a territorial division collectively, especially the leading families. ■ Brit. a sporting team playing for such a territorial division. ■ US a political and administrative division of a state.
▶ adjective Brit. having the social status or characteristics of a county family: *a county grande dame.*
– ORIGIN Middle English: from Old French *conte*, from Latin *comitatus*, from *comes, comit-* (see **COUNT**[2]). The word seems earliest to have denoted a meeting held periodically to transact the business of a shire.

county borough ▶ noun (in England, Wales, and Northern Ireland) a large town formerly having the administrative status of a county.

county commissioner ▶ noun Brit. a justice of the peace on the commission of the peace of a county.

county corporate ▶ noun Brit. historical a city or town ranking as an administrative county.

county council ▶ noun (in the UK) the elected governing body of an administrative county.
– DERIVATIVES **county councillor** noun.

county court ▶ noun (in England and Wales) a judicial court for civil cases.
■ US a court for civil and criminal cases.

county cricket ▶ noun [mass noun] first-class cricket played in the UK between the eighteen professional teams contesting the County Championship.

County Durham see **DURHAM**.

county family ▶ noun Brit. an aristocratic family with an ancestral seat in a county.

County Palatine historical (in England and Ireland) a county in which royal privileges and exclusive rights of jurisdiction were held by its earl or lord.
– ORIGIN see **PALATINE**[1].

county school ▶ noun (in the UK) a school that is established and funded by the local education authority.

county town (US **county seat**) ▶ noun the town that is the administrative capital of a county.

coup /kuː/ ▶ noun (pl. **coups** /kuːz/) **1** (also **coup d'état**) a sudden, violent, and illegal seizure of power from a government: *he was overthrown in an army coup.*
2 a notable or successful stroke or move: *it was a major coup to get such a prestigious contract.*
■ an unusual or unexpected but successful tactic in card play.
3 Billiards a direct pocketing of the cue ball, which is a foul stroke.
4 historical (among North American Indians) an act of touching an enemy, as a deed of bravery, or an act of first touching an item of the enemy's in order to claim it.
– ORIGIN late 18th cent.: from French, from medieval Latin *colpus* 'blow' (see **COPE**[1]).

coup de foudre /ˌkuː də ˈfuːdr(ə), French ku də fudʀ/ ▶ noun (pl. **coups de foudre** pronunc. same) a sudden unforeseen event, in particular an instance of love at first sight.
– ORIGIN French, literally 'stroke of lightning'.

coup de grâce /ˌkuː də ˈɡrɑːs, French ku də ɡʀɑs/ ▶ noun (pl. **coups de grâce** pronunc. same) a final blow or shot given to kill a wounded person or animal: *he administered the* coup de grâce *with a knife* | figurative *the party won another term and delivered the* coup de grâce *to socialism.*
– ORIGIN French, literally 'stroke of grace'.

coup de main /ˌkuː də ˈmã, French ku də mɛ̃/ ▶ noun (pl. **coups de main** pronunc. same) a sudden surprise attack, especially one made by an army during war.
– ORIGIN French, literally 'stroke of hand'.

coup de maître /ˌkuː də ˈmɛːtr(ə), French ku də mɛtʀ/ ▶ noun (pl. **coups de maître** pronunc. same) a master stroke.
– ORIGIN French.

coup d'état /ˌkuː deɪˈtɑː, French ku deta/ ▶ noun (pl. **coups d'état** pronunc. same) another term for **COUP** (in sense 1).
– ORIGIN French, literally 'blow of state'.

coup de théâtre /ˌkuː də teɪˈɑːtr(ə), French ku də teɑtʀ/ ▶ noun (pl. **coups de théâtre** pronunc. same) **1** a sensational or dramatically sudden action or turn of events, especially in a play.
2 a theatrical hit.
– ORIGIN French, literally 'blow of theatre'.

coup d'œil /kuː ˈdəːɪ, French ku dœj/ ▶ noun (pl. **coups d'œil** pronunc. same) a glance that takes in a comprehensive view.
– ORIGIN French, literally 'stroke of eye'.

coupe /kuːp/ ▶ noun a shallow glass or glass dish, typically with a stem, in which desserts or champagne are served.
■ a dessert served in such a dish.
– ORIGIN French, 'goblet'.

coupé /ˈkuːpeɪ/ (also **coupe** /kuːp/) ▶ noun **1** a car with a fixed roof, two doors, and a sloping rear.
2 historical a four-wheeled enclosed carriage for two passengers and a driver.
3 (in South Africa) an end compartment in a railway carriage, with seats on only one side.
– ORIGIN mid 19th cent. (in sense 2): from French *carrosse coupé*, literally 'cut carriage'. Sense 1 dates from the early 20th cent.

couped /kuːpt/ ▶ adjective [usu. postpositive] Heraldry cut off or truncated in a straight line.
– ORIGIN early 16th cent.: from French *couper* 'to cut' + **-ED**[2].

Couperin /ˈkuːpərã, French kupʀɛ̃/, François (1668–1733), French composer, organist, and harpsichordist. A composer at the court of Louis XIV, he is principally known for his harpsichord works.

couple ▶ noun **1** two individuals of the same sort considered together: ***a couple of*** *girls were playing marbles.*
■ informal an indefinite small number: [as pronoun] *he hoped she'd be better in* ***a couple of*** *days* | *we got some eggs—would you like a couple?* | [as determiner] *just a couple more questions* | N. Amer. *clean the stains with a couple squirts dishwashing liquid.*
2 [treated as sing. or pl.] two people who are married, engaged, or otherwise closely associated romantically or sexually.
■ a pair of partners in a dance or game. ■ (pl. **couple**) a pair of hunting dogs. ■ (**couples**) two collars joined together and used for holding hounds together. ■ a pair of rafters. ■ Mechanics a pair of equal and parallel forces acting in opposite directions, and tending to cause rotation about an axis perpendicular to the plane containing them.
▶ verb [with obj.] (often **be coupled to/with**) combine: *a sense of hope is coupled with a palpable sense of loss.*
■ connect (a railway vehicle or a piece of equipment) to another: *a cable is* ***coupled up*** *to one of the wheels.* ■ [no obj.] (**couple up**) join to form a pair. ■ [no obj.] dated have sexual intercourse. ■ connect (two electrical components) using electromagnetic induction, electrostatic charge, or an optical link: [as adj. **coupled**] *networks of coupled oscillators.*
– DERIVATIVES **coupledom** noun.
– ORIGIN Middle English: from Old French *cople* (noun), *copler* (verb), from Latin *copula* (noun), *copulare* (verb), from *co-* 'together' + *apere* 'fasten'. Compare with **COPULA** and **COPULATE**.

coupler ▶ noun a thing that connects two things, especially mechanical components or systems: *a hydraulic coupler* | [as modifier] *coupler rod.*
■ Music a device in an organ for connecting two manuals, or a manual with pedals, so that they both sound when only one is played. ■ Music (also **octave coupler**) a similar device for connecting notes with their octaves above or below. ■ Photography a compound in a developer or an emulsion which combines with the products of development to form an insoluble dye, part of the image. ■ (also **acoustic coupler**) a modem which converts digital signals from a computer into audible sound signals and vice versa, so that the former can be transmitted and received over telephone lines.

couplet ▶ noun a pair of successive lines of verse, typically rhyming and of the same length.
– ORIGIN late 16th cent.: from French, diminutive of *couple*, from Old French *cople* (see **COUPLE**).

coupling ▶ noun **1** a device for connecting parts of machinery.
■ a fitting on the end of a railway vehicle for connecting it to another.
2 [mass noun] the pairing of two items: *the coupling of tribunals with ministerial enquiries.*
■ sexual intercourse. ■ the arrangement of items on a musical recording: *this coupling of two of the greatest works of Haydn.* ■ [count noun] each such item: *one of the more interesting couplings for the B minor Sonata.* ■ an interaction between two electrical components by electromagnetic induction, electrostatic charge, or optical link.

coupling constant ▶ noun Physics a constant representing the strength of the interaction between a particle and a field.

coupling rod ▶ noun a rod which couples the driving wheels of a locomotive, enabling them to act as a unit.

coupon ▶ noun **1** a voucher entitling the holder to a discount off a particular product.
■ a detachable ticket entitling the holder to a ration of

food, clothes, or other goods, especially in wartime. ■ a detachable portion of a bond which is given up in return for a payment of interest. ■ the nominal rate of interest on a fixed-interest security.

2 a form in a newspaper or magazine which may be filled in and sent as an application for a purchase or information.

■ Brit. an entry form for a football pool or other competition.

3 Scottish & Irish a person's face: *he had a big beaming smile on his coupon.*

– ORIGIN early 19th cent. (denoting a detachable portion of a stock certificate to be given up in return for payment of interest): from French, literally 'piece cut off', from *couper* 'cut', from Old French *colper* (see **COPE**[1]).

coupon-clipper ▶ **noun** N. Amer. informal a person with a large number of interest-bearing bonds.

coup stick ▶ **noun** (among North American Indians) a stick used to touch the enemy in a coup.

courage ▶ **noun** [mass noun] the ability to do something that frightens one: *she called on all her courage to face the ordeal.*

■ strength in the face of pain or grief: *he fought his illness with great courage.*

– PHRASES **have the courage of one's convictions** act on one's beliefs despite danger or disapproval. **pluck up** (or **screw up** or **take**) **courage** make an effort to do something that frightens one. **take one's courage in both hands** nerve oneself to do something that frightens one.

– ORIGIN Middle English (denoting the heart, as the seat of feelings): from Old French *corage*, from Latin *cor* 'heart'.

courageous ▶ **adjective** not deterred by danger or pain; brave: *her courageous human rights work.*

– DERIVATIVES **courageously** adverb, **courageousness** noun.

– ORIGIN Middle English: from Old French *corageus*, from *corage* (see **COURAGE**).

courant /kʊˈrant/ ▶ **adjective** [usu. postpositive] Heraldry represented as running.

– ORIGIN early 17th cent.: French, 'running', present participle of *courir*.

courante /kʊˈrɒ̃t, -rɑːnt/ ▶ **noun** a 16th-century court dance consisting of short advances and retreats, later developed into a rapid gliding dance in quick triple time.

■ a piece of music written for or in the style of such a dance, typically one forming a movement of a suite.

– ORIGIN late 16th cent.: French, literally 'running', feminine present participle of *courir*.

Courbet /ˈkʊəbeɪ, French kuʀbɛ/, Gustave (1819–77), French painter. A leader of the 19th-century realist school of painting, he favoured an unidealized choice of subject matter that did not exclude the ugly or vulgar. Notable works: *Burial at Ornans* (1850) and *Painter in his Studio* (1855).

courbette /kʊəˈbɛt/ ▶ **noun** (in classical riding) a movement in which the horse performs a series of jumps on the hind legs without the forelegs touching the ground.

– ORIGIN mid 17th cent.: French, from Italian *corvetta* 'little curve' based on Latin *curvus* 'curved'.

coureur de bois /kuːˌrəː də ˈbwʌ/ ▶ **noun** (pl. **coureurs de bois** pronunc. same) historical (in Canada and the northern US) a woodsman or trader of French origin.

– ORIGIN French, literally 'wood-runner'.

courgette /kʊəˈʒɛt/ ▶ **noun** Brit. the immature fruit of a vegetable marrow, in particular, one of a variety developed for harvesting and eating at an early stage of growth. Called **ZUCCHINI** in North America.

– ORIGIN 1930s: from French, diminutive of *courge* 'gourd', from Latin *cucurbita*.

courier /ˈkʊrɪə/ ▶ **noun 1** a messenger who transports goods or documents, in particular:

■ a company or employee of a company that transports commercial packages and documents: *the cheque was dispatched by courier* | [as modifier] *a courier service.* ■ a messenger for an underground or espionage organization.

2 a person employed to guide and assist a group of tourists.

▶ **verb** [with obj.] (often **be couriered**) send or transport (goods or documents) by courier.

– ORIGIN late Middle English (denoting a person sent to run with a message): originally from Old French *coreor*; later from French *courier* (now *courrier*), from Italian *corriere*; based on Latin *currere* 'to run'.

courol /ˈkuːrɒl/ ▶ **noun** another term for **CUCKOO-ROLLER**.

– ORIGIN contraction.

Courrèges /kʊəˈreɪʒ, -ˈrɛʒ, French kuʀɛʒ/, André (b.1923), French fashion designer. He is famous for his futuristic and youth-oriented styles, in particular the use of plastic and metal and unisex fashion such as trouser suits for women.

course ▶ **noun 1** [in sing.] the route or direction followed by a ship, aircraft, road, or river: *the road adopts a tortuous course along the coast* | *the new fleet **changed course** to join the other ships.*

■ the way in which something progresses or develops: *the course of history.* ■ a procedure adopted to deal with a situation: *the wisest **course of action** is to tackle the problem at source.* ■ the route of a race or similar sporting event. ■ [count noun] an area of land set aside and prepared for racing, golf, or another sport.

2 a dish, or a set of dishes served together, forming one of the successive parts of a meal: *guests are offered a choice of main course* | [in combination] *a four-course meal.*

3 a series, in particular:

■ a series of lectures or lessons in a particular subject, typically leading to a qualification: *a business studies course.* ■ Medicine a series of repeated treatments or doses of medication: *the doctor prescribed a course of antibiotics.* ■ Bell-ringing a series of changes which brings the bells back to their original order, or the changes of a particular bell.

4 Architecture a continuous horizontal layer of brick, stone, or other material in a building.

5 a pursuit of game (especially hares) with greyhounds by sight rather than scent.

6 a sail on the lowest yards of a square-rigged ship.

▶ **verb 1** [no obj., with adverbial of direction] (of liquid) move without obstruction; flow: *tears were coursing down her cheeks* | figurative *exultation coursed through him.*

2 [with obj.] pursue (game, especially hares) with greyhounds using sight rather than scent: *many of the hares coursed escaped unharmed* | [no obj.] *she would course for hares with her greyhounds.*

– PHRASES **a matter of course** see **MATTER**. **the course of nature** events or processes which are normal and to be expected: *each man would, in the course of nature, have his private opinions.* **in course of —— 1** undergoing the specified process: *a new text book was in course of preparation.* **2** during the specified period: *he was a friend to many people in the course of his life.* ■ during and as a part of the specified activity: *they became friends in the course of their long walks.* **in the course of time** as time goes by. **in due course** see **DUE**. **of course** used to introduce an idea or turn of events as being obvious or to be expected: *the point is of course that the puzzle itself is misleading.* ■ used to give or emphasize agreement or permission: *'Can I see you for a minute?' 'Of course.'* ■ introducing a qualification or admission: *of course we've been in touch by phone, but I wanted to see things for myself.* **off course** not following the intended route: *the car went careering off course.* **on course** following the intended route: *he battled to keep the ship on course* | figurative *to get back on course, I relied on one of my stock questions.* ■ (**on course for/to do something**) likely to achieve something: *he was on course for victory.* **run** (or **take**) **its course** complete its natural development without interference: *his illness had to run its course to the crisis.*

– ORIGIN Middle English: from Old French *cours*, from Latin *cursus*, from *curs-* 'run', from the verb *currere*.

coursebook ▶ **noun** Brit. a textbook designed for use on a particular course of study.

courser[1] ▶ **noun** poetic/literary a swift horse.

– ORIGIN Middle English: from Old French *corsier*, based on Latin *cursus* (see **COURSE**).

courser[2] ▶ **noun** a fast-running plover-like bird related to the pratincoles, typically found in open country in Africa and Asia.

● Genera *Cursorius* and *Rhinoptilus*, family Glareolidae: several species, in particular the desert-dwelling **cream-coloured courser** (*C. cursor*).

– ORIGIN mid 18th cent.: from modern Latin *Cursorius* 'adapted for running', from *cursor* 'runner', from the verb *currere* (see **COURSE**).

courser[3] ▶ **noun** a person who hunts animals such as hares with greyhounds using sight rather than scent.

– ORIGIN early 17th cent.: from **COURSER**[1].

courseware ▶ **noun** [mass noun] computer programs or other material designed for use in an educational or training course.

coursework ▶ **noun** [mass noun] written or practical work done by a student during a course of study, usually assessed in order to count towards a final mark or grade.

coursing ▶ **noun** [mass noun] the sport of hunting game animals such as hares with greyhounds using sight rather than scent.

court ▶ **noun 1** (also **court of law**) a body of people presided over by a judge, judges, or a magistrate, and acting as a tribunal in civil and criminal cases: *a settlement was reached during the first sitting of the court* | *she will **take** the matter **to court*** | [as modifier] *a court case.*

■ the place where such a body meets.

2 a quadrangular area, either open or covered, marked out for ball games such as tennis or squash: *a squash court.*

■ a quadrangular area surrounded by a building or group of buildings. ■ (**Court**) used in the names of large houses or blocks of flats: *Hampton Court.*

3 the establishment, retinue, and courtiers of a sovereign: *the emperor is shown with his court.*

■ a sovereign and his or her councillors, constituting a ruling power: *relations between the king and the imperial court.* ■ a sovereign's residence.

4 the qualified members of a company or a corporation.

■ a meeting of such a body.

▶ **verb** [with obj.] dated be involved with romantically, typically with the intention of marrying: *he was courting a girl from the neighbouring farm* | [no obj.] *we went to the cinema when we were courting.*

■ (of a male bird or other animal) try to attract (a mate). ■ pay special attention to (someone) in an attempt to win their support or favour: *Western politicians courted the leaders of the newly independent states.* ■ go to great lengths to win (favourable attention): *he never had to court the approval of the political elite.* ■ risk incurring (misfortune) because of the way one behaves: *he has often courted controversy.*

– PHRASES **go to court** take legal action. **in court** appearing as a party or an advocate in a court of law. **out of court 1** before a legal hearing can take place: *they are trying to settle the squabble out of court* | [as modifier] *an out-of-court settlement.* **2** treated as impossible or not worthy of consideration: *the price would put it out of court for most private buyers.* **pay court to** pay flattering attention to someone in order to win favour.

– ORIGIN Middle English: from Old French *cort*, from Latin *cohors, cohort-* 'yard or retinue'. The verb is influenced by Old Italian *corteare*, Old French *courtoyer*. Compare with **COHORT**.

Courtauld /ˈkɔːtəʊld/, Samuel (1876–1947), English industrialist. He was a director of his family's silk firm and a collector of French Impressionist and post-Impressionist paintings. He presented his collection to the University of London, endowed the Courtauld Institute of Art, and bequeathed to it his house in Portman Square, London.

court bouillon /kɔːt ˈbuːjɒn/ ▶ **noun** [mass noun] a stock made from wine and vegetables, typically used in fish dishes.

– ORIGIN French, from *court* 'short' and **BOUILLON**.

court card ▶ **noun** Brit. a playing card that is a king, queen, or jack of a suit.

– ORIGIN mid 17th cent.: alteration of 16th-cent. *coat card*, so named because of the decorative dress of the figures depicted.

court circular ▶ **noun** (usu. **the Court Circular**) Brit. a daily report of the activities and public engagements of royal family members, published in some newspapers.

court cupboard ▶ **noun** a 16th- or 17th-century sideboard for displaying plate and other decorative objects, especially one consisting of three open shelves and sometimes a small cupboard in the upper half.

court dress ▶ **noun** [mass noun] **1** historical formal clothing worn at a royal court.

2 official clothing worn in a court of law by those in the legal profession.

courteous /ˈkəːtjəs/ ▶ **adjective** polite, respectful, or considerate in manner.

– DERIVATIVES **courteously** adverb, **courteousness** noun.

– ORIGIN Middle English (meaning 'having manners fit for a royal court'): from Old French *corteis*, based on Latin *cohors* 'yard, retinue' (see **COURT**). The change in the ending in the 16th cent. was due to association with words ending in **-EOUS**.

courtesan /ˌkɔːtɪˈzan, ˈkɔːtɪ-/ ▶ **noun** chiefly poetic/literary a prostitute, especially one with wealthy or upper-class clients.
– ORIGIN mid 16th cent.: from French *courtisane*, from obsolete Italian *cortigiana*, feminine of *cortigiano* 'courtier', from *corte* (see **COURT**).

courtesy /ˈkɔːtɪsi/ ▶ **noun** (pl. **-ies**) [mass noun] the showing of politeness in one's attitude and behaviour towards others: *he had been treated with a degree of courtesy not far short of deference.*
■ [count noun] (often **courtesies**) a polite speech or action, especially one required by convention: *the superficial courtesies of diplomatic exchanges.* ■ [as modifier] (especially of transport) supplied free of charge to people who are already paying for another service: *he travelled from the hotel in a courtesy car.* ■ [count noun] archaic a curtsy.
– PHRASES **by courtesy** as a favour rather than by right: *he was not at the conference only by courtesy.* (**by**) **courtesy of** given or allowed by: *photograph courtesy of the Evening Star.* ■ informal as a result of; thanks to.
– ORIGIN Middle English: from Old French *cortesie*, from *corteis* (see **COURTEOUS**).

courtesy light ▶ **noun** a small light in a car, automatically switched on when one of the doors is opened.

courtesy title ▶ **noun** a title given to someone, especially the son or daughter of a peer, that has no legal validity.

court hand ▶ **noun** a notoriously illegible style of handwriting used in English law courts until banned in 1731.

courthouse ▶ **noun 1** a building in which a judicial court is held.
2 US a building containing the administrative offices of a county.

courtier /ˈkɔːtɪə/ ▶ **noun** a person who attends a royal court as a companion or adviser to the king or queen.
– ORIGIN Middle English: via Anglo-Norman French from Old French *cortoyer* 'be present at court', from *cort* (see **COURT**).

court leet ▶ **noun** (pl. **courts leet**) see **LEET**[1].

courtly ▶ **adjective** (**courtlier**, **courtliest**) polished or refined, as befitting a royal court: *he gave a courtly bow.*
– DERIVATIVES **courtliness** noun.

courtly love ▶ **noun** a highly conventionalized medieval tradition of love between a knight and a married noblewoman, first developed by the troubadours of Southern France and extensively employed in European literature of the time. The love of the knight for his lady was regarded as an ennobling passion and the relationship was typically unconsummated.

court martial ▶ **noun** (pl. **courts martial** or **court martials**) a judicial court for trying members of the armed services accused of offences against military law: *they appeared before a court martial* | [mass noun] *he was found guilty by court martial.*
▶ **verb** (**court-martial**) (**-martialled**, **-martialling**; US **-martialed**, **-martialing**) [with obj.] try (someone) by such a court.

Court of Appeal ▶ **noun** (in England and Wales) a court of law that hears appeals against both civil and criminal judgements from the Crown Courts, High Court, and County Courts.
■ (**court of appeals**) US a court of law in a federal circuit or state to which appeals are taken.

Court of Claims ▶ **noun** US a federal court in which claims against the government are adjudicated.

Court of Exchequer Chamber ▶ **noun** English Law see **EXCHEQUER CHAMBER**.

court of first instance ▶ **noun** a court in which legal proceedings are begun or first heard.

court of inquiry ▶ **noun** a tribunal appointed in the armed forces to investigate a matter and decide whether a court martial is called for.

court of law ▶ **noun** see **COURT** (sense 1).

Court of Protection (in the UK) the department of the Supreme Court attending to the affairs of the mentally unfit.

court of record ▶ **noun** a court whose proceedings are recorded and available as evidence of fact.

court of review ▶ **noun** a court before which sentences previously imposed come for revision.

Court of St James's the British sovereign's court.

Court of Session the supreme civil court in Scotland.

court of summary jurisdiction ▶ **noun** Brit. a court, especially a magistrate's court, that tries summary offences without a jury.

court order ▶ **noun** a direction issued by a court or a judge requiring a person to do or not do something.

court plaster ▶ **noun** [mass noun] historical sticking plaster made of silk or other cloth with an adhesive such as isinglass.
– ORIGIN late 18th cent.: so named because it was formerly used by ladies at court for beauty spots.

Courtrai /kuːrtrɛ/ French name for **KORTRIJK**.

court record ▶ **noun** see **RECORD** (sense 1).

court roll ▶ **noun** Brit. historical the record kept by a manorial court of rent paid and property held by tenants.

courtroom ▶ **noun** the place or room in which a court of law meets.

courtship ▶ **noun** a period during which a couple develop a romantic relationship, especially with a view to marriage.
■ [mass noun] behaviour designed to persuade someone to marry one. ■ [mass noun] the behaviour of male birds and other animals aimed at attracting a mate. ■ [mass noun] the process of attempting to win a person's favour or support: *the country's courtship of foreign investors.*

court shoe ▶ **noun** Brit. a woman's plain, lightweight shoe that has a low-cut upper, no fastening, and typically a medium heel.

court tennis ▶ **noun** North American term for **REAL TENNIS**.

courtyard ▶ **noun** an unroofed area that is completely or partially enclosed by walls or buildings, typically one forming part of a castle or large house.

couscous /ˈkʊskʊs, ˈkuːskuːs/ ▶ **noun** [mass noun] a type of North African semolina in granules made from crushed durum wheat.
■ a spicy dish made by steaming or soaking such granules and adding meat, vegetables, or fruit.
– ORIGIN early 17th cent.: from French, from Arabic *kuskus*, from *kaskasa* 'to pound', probably of Berber origin.

cousin ▶ **noun** (also **first cousin**) a child of one's uncle or aunt.
■ a person belonging to the same extended family. ■ a thing related or analogous to another: *the new motorbikes are not proving as popular as their four-wheeled cousins.* ■ (usu. **cousins**) a person of a kindred race or nation: *our American cousins.* ■ historical a title formerly used by a sovereign in addressing another sovereign or a noble of their own country.
– PHRASES **first cousin once removed 1** a child of one's first cousin. **2** one's parent's first cousin. **first cousin twice removed 1** a grandchild of one's first cousin. **2** one's grandparent's first cousin. **second cousin** a child of one's parent's first cousin. **second cousin once removed 1** a child of one's second cousin. **2** one's parent's second cousin. **third cousin** a child of one's parent's second cousin.
– DERIVATIVES **cousinhood** noun, **cousinly** adjective, **cousinship** noun.
– ORIGIN Middle English: from Old French *cosin*, from Latin *consobrinus* 'mother's sister's child', from *con-* 'with' + *sobrinus* 'second cousin' (from *soror* 'sister').

cousin german ▶ **noun** (pl. **cousins german**) old-fashioned term for **COUSIN**.
– ORIGIN Middle English: from French *cousin germain* (see **COUSIN**, **GERMAN**).

Cousteau /ˈkuːstəʊ, French kusto/, Jacques-Yves (1910–97), French oceanographer and film director. He devised the scuba apparatus, but is known primarily for several feature films and popular television series on marine life.

couth /kuːθ/ ▶ **adjective** [predic.] humorous cultured, refined, and well mannered: *it is more couth to hold your shrimp genteelly by the tail when eating.*
– ORIGIN late 19th cent.: back-formation from **UNCOUTH**.

couthy /ˈkuːθi/ (also **couthie**) ▶ **adjective** Scottish (of a person) warm and friendly.
■ (of a place) cosy and comfortable: *a couthy wee tavern.*
– ORIGIN early 18th cent.: apparently from Old English *cūth* 'known' + **-Y**[1] (also **-IE**).

couture /kuːˈtjʊə/ ▶ **noun** [mass noun] the design and manufacture of fashionable clothes to a client's specific requirements and measurements. See also **HAUTE COUTURE**.
■ such clothes: *they were dressed in size eight printed-silk couture.*
– ORIGIN 1920s: French, 'sewing, dressmaking'.

couturier /kuːˈtjʊərɪeɪ/ ▶ **noun** a fashion designer who manufactures and sells clothes that have been tailored to a client's specific requirements and measurements.
– ORIGIN late 19th cent.: French, from **COUTURE**.

couturière /kuːˈtjʊərɛː/ ▶ **noun** a female couturier.

couvade /kuːˈvɑːd/ ▶ **noun** [mass noun] the custom in some cultures in which a man takes to his bed and goes through certain rituals when his child is being born, as though he were physically affected by the birth.
– ORIGIN mid 19th cent.: French, from *couver* 'to hatch', from Latin *cubare* 'lie down'. The adoption of the term in French was due to a misunderstanding of the phrase *faire la couvade* 'sit doing nothing', used by earlier writers.

couvert /kuːˈvɛː/ ▶ **noun** another term for **COVER** (in sense 4).
– ORIGIN mid 18th cent.: French, past participle (used as a noun) of *couvrir* 'to cover'.

couverture /ˈkuːvətjʊə/ ▶ **noun** [mass noun] chocolate made with extra cocoa butter to give a high gloss, used for covering sweets and cakes.
– ORIGIN 1930s: French, literally 'covering', from *couvrir* 'to cover'.

covalent /kəʊˈveɪl(ə)nt/ ▶ **adjective** Chemistry of, relating to, or denoting chemical bonds formed by the sharing of electrons between atoms. Often contrasted with **IONIC**.
– DERIVATIVES **covalence** noun, **covalency** noun, **covalently** adverb.

covariance /kəʊˈvɛːrɪəns/ ▶ **noun 1** [mass noun] Mathematics the property of a function of retaining its form when the variables are linearly transformed.
2 Statistics the mean value of the product of the deviations of two variates from their respective means.

covariant Mathematics ▶ **noun** a function of the coefficients and variables of a given function which is invariant under a linear transformation except for a factor equal to a power of the determinant of the transformation.
▶ **adjective** changing in such a way that mathematical interrelations with another simultaneously changing quantity or set of quantities remain unchanged.
■ of, having the properties of, or relating to a covariant.

covariation ▶ **noun** [mass noun] Mathematics correlated variation.

cove[1] ▶ **noun 1** a small sheltered bay.
2 Architecture a concave arch or arched moulding, especially one formed at the junction of a wall with a ceiling.
▶ **verb** [with obj.] [usu. as adj. **coved**] Architecture provide (a room, ceiling, etc.) with a cove.
– ORIGIN Old English *cofa* 'chamber, cave', of Germanic origin; related to German *Koben* 'pigsty, pen'. Sense 1 dates from the late 16th cent.

cove[2] ▶ **noun** Brit. informal, dated a man: *he is a perfectly amiable cove.*
– ORIGIN mid 16th cent.: perhaps from Romany *kova* 'thing or person'.

covelline /kəʊˈvɛlɪn/ ▶ **noun** another term for **COVELLITE**.

covellite /kəʊˈvɛlaɪt/ ▶ **noun** [mass noun] a blue mineral consisting of copper sulphide, typically occurring as a coating on other copper minerals.
– ORIGIN mid 19th cent.: named after Nicolò *Covelli* (1790–1829), Italian chemist, + **-ITE**[1].

coven /ˈkʌv(ə)n/ ▶ **noun** a group or gathering of witches who meet regularly.

■ figurative, often derogatory a secret or close-knit group of associates: *covens of militants within the party.*
– ORIGIN mid 17th cent.: variant of **COVIN**.

covenant /ˈkʌv(ə)nənt/ ▶ **noun** an agreement.
■ Law a contract drawn up by deed, especially one undertaking to make regular payments to a charity. ■ Law a clause in such a contract. ■ Theology an agreement which brings about a relationship of commitment between God and his people. The Jewish faith is based on the biblical covenants made with Abraham, Moses, and David. See also **ARK OF THE COVENANT**.
▶ **verb** [no obj.] agree, especially by lease, deed, or other legal contract: [with infinitive] *the landlord covenants to repair the property.*
■ [with obj.] Brit. undertake to give (a sum of money) regularly, especially to charity, by means of a deed of covenant.
– PHRASES **Old Covenant** Christian Theology the covenant between God and Israel in the Old Testament. **New Covenant** Christian Theology the covenant between God and the followers of Christ.
– DERIVATIVES **covenantal** adjective, **covenantor** noun.
– ORIGIN Middle English: from Old French, present participle of *covenir* 'agree', from Latin *convenire* (see **CONVENE**).

Covenanter /ˈkʌv(ə)nəntə/ ▶ **noun** an adherent of the National Covenant (1638) or of the Solemn League and Covenant (1643), upholding the organization of the Scottish Presbyterian Church.

covenant of grace ▶ **noun** (in Reformation theology) the covenant between God and humanity which was established by Christ at the Atonement.

covenant of works ▶ **noun** (in Reformation theology) the covenant between God and humanity which was broken by Adam's sin at the Fall.

Covent Garden a district in central London, originally the convent garden of the Abbey of Westminster. It was the site for 300 years of London's chief fruit and vegetable market, which in 1974 was moved to Nine Elms, Battersea. The first Covent Garden Theatre was opened in 1732; since 1946 it has been the home of the national opera and ballet companies, based at the Royal Opera House (built 1888).

Coventry /ˈkɒv(ə)ntri, ˈkʌv-/ an industrial city in the west Midlands of England; pop. 292,600 (1991).
– PHRASES **send someone to Coventry** chiefly Brit. refuse to associate with or speak to someone. [ORIGIN: sometimes said to stem from the extreme unpopularity of soldiers stationed in *Coventry*, who were cut off socially by the citizens, or because Royalist prisoners were sent there during the English Civil war, the city being staunchly Parliamentarian.]

cover ▶ **verb** [with obj.] **1** (often **be covered**) put something such as a cloth or lid on top of or in front of (something) in order to protect or conceal it: *the table had been* **covered with** *a checked tablecloth | she* **covered** *her face* **with** *a pillow.*
■ envelop in a layer of something, especially dirt: *he was covered in mud |* figurative *she was covered in confusion.* ■ scatter a layer of loose material over (a surface, especially a floor), leaving it completely obscured: *the barn floor was covered in straw.* ■ lie over or adhere to (a surface), as decoration or to conceal something: *masonry paint will cover hairline cracks.* ■ protect (someone) with a garment or hat: [as adj. **covered**] *keep children covered with T-shirts.* ■ extend over (an area): *the grounds covered eight acres.* ■ travel (a specified distance): *it took them four days to cover 150 miles.*
2 deal with (a subject) by describing or analysing its most important aspects or events: *a sequence of novels that will cover the period from 1968 to the present.*
■ investigate, report on, or publish or broadcast pictures of (an event): *Channel 4 are covering the match.* ■ work in, have responsibility for, or provide services to (a particular area): *development officers whose work would cover a large area.* ■ (of a rule or law) apply to (a person or situation).
3 (of a sum of money) be enough to pay (a bill or cost): *there are grants to cover the cost of materials for loft insulation.*
■ (of insurance) protect against a liability, loss, or accident involving financial consequences: *your contents are now* **covered against** *accidental loss or damage in transit.* ■ (**cover oneself**) take precautionary measures so as to protect oneself against future blame or liability: *one reason doctors take temperatures is to* **cover** *themselves* **against** *negligence claims.*
4 disguise the sound or fact of (something) with another sound or action: *Louise laughed to cover her embarrassment.*
■ [no obj.] (**cover for**) disguise the illicit absence or wrongdoing of (someone) in order to spare them punishment: *if the sergeant wants to know where you are, I'll cover for you.* ■ [no obj.] (**cover for**) temporarily take over the job of (a colleague) in their absence: *during August ministers cover for other ministers.*
5 aim a gun at (someone) in order to prevent them from moving or escaping.
■ protect (an exposed person) by shooting at an enemy: [as adj. **covering**] *the jeeps retreated behind spurts of* **covering fire**. ■ (of a fortress, gun, or cannon) have (an area) within range. ■ chiefly Cricket stand behind (another player) to stop any missed balls. ■ (in team games) take up a position ready to defend against (an opposing player). ■ Baseball be in position at (a base) ready to catch the ball.
6 Bridge play a higher card on (a high card) in a trick: *the ploy will fail if the ten is covered |* [no obj.] *East covered with his queen.*
7 record or perform a new version of (a song) originally performed by someone else: *other artists who have covered the song include U2.*
8 (of a male animal, especially a stallion) copulate with (a female animal), especially as part of a commercial transaction between the owners of the animals.
▶ **noun 1** a thing which lies on, over, or around something, especially in order to protect or conceal it: *a seat cover | a duvet cover.*
■ a thin solid object that seals a container or hole; a lid: *a manhole cover.* ■ a thick protective outer part or page of a book or magazine: *the year that Crime and Punishment appeared in hard covers.* ■ (**the covers**) bedclothes: *she burrowed down beneath the covers.*
2 [mass noun] physical shelter or protection sought by people in danger: *the sirens wailed and people ran for cover.*
■ undergrowth, trees, or other vegetation used as a shelter by hunted animals: *the standing crops of game cover |* [count noun] *a landscape bare of woodland except for neat little fox covers.* See also **COVERT** (sense 1). ■ an activity or organization used as a means of concealing an illegal or secret activity: *the organizations often use their philanthropy as a* **cover for** *subsidies to terrorists.* ■ [in sing.] an identity or activity adopted by a person, typically a spy, to conceal their true activities: *he was worried that their cover was blown.* ■ military support given when someone is in danger from or being attacked by an enemy: *they agreed to provide additional naval cover.* ■ Ecology the amount of ground covered by a vertical projection of the vegetation, usually expressed as a percentage.
3 [mass noun] Brit. protection by insurance against a liability, loss, or accident involving financial consequences: *your policy already provides* **cover against** *damage by subsidence.*
4 a place setting at a table in a restaurant. [ORIGIN: rendering French *couvert*.]
5 Cricket short for **COVER POINT**: *an easy catch by Hick at cover.*
■ (**the covers**) an area of the field consisting of cover point and extra cover.
6 (also **cover version**) a recording or performance of a previously recorded song made especially to take advantage of the original's success.
– PHRASES **break cover** suddenly leave a place of shelter, especially vegetation, when being hunted or pursued. **cover one's back** (or N. Amer. **ass**) informal foresee and avoid the possibility of attack or criticism. **cover a multitude of sins** conceal or gloss over many problems or defects: *stucco could cover a multitude of sins, including poor brickwork.* **cover one's position** purchase securities in order to be able to fulfil a commitment to sell. **cover one's tracks** conceal evidence of what one has done. **cover the waterfront** N. Amer. informal include a wide range of things; cover every aspect of something: *while half the dishes are Italian, the kitchen covers the waterfront from Greece to Morocco.* **from cover to cover** from beginning to end of a book or magazine. **take cover** protect oneself from attack by ducking down into or under a shelter: *if the bombing starts, take cover in the basement.* **under cover** under a roof or other shelter: *store seats under cover before the bad weather sets in.* **under cover of** concealed by: *the yacht made landfall under cover of darkness.* ■ while pretending to do something: *Moran watched every move under cover of reading the newspaper.* **under plain cover** in an envelope or parcel without any marks to identify the sender. **under separate cover** in a separate envelope.
– DERIVATIVES **coverable** adjective.
– ORIGIN Middle English: from Old French *covrir*, from Latin *cooperire*, from *co-* (expressing intensive force) + *operire* 'to cover'. The noun is partly a variant of **COVERT**.
▶ **cover something up** put something on, over, or around something, especially in order to conceal or disguise it. ■ try to hide or deny the fact of an illegal or illicit action or activity.

C

coverage ▶ **noun** [mass noun] the extent to which something deals with or applies to something else: *the grammar did not offer total coverage of the language.*
■ the treatment of an issue by the media: *the programme won an award for its news coverage.* ■ the amount of protection given by an insurance policy. ■ the area reached by a particular broadcasting station or advertising medium: *a network of eighty transmitters would give nationwide coverage.* ■ the area that can be covered by a specified volume or weight of a substance: *coverage is 6.5 square metres per litre.* ■ American Football the manner in which a defender or a defensive team cover a player, an area, or a play.

coverall ▶ **noun** (usu. **coveralls**) a full-length protective outer garment often zipped up the front.
■ [as modifier] inclusive: *a coverall term.*

cover charge ▶ **noun** a flat fee paid for admission to a restaurant, bar, club, etc.

cover crop ▶ **noun** a crop grown for the protection and enrichment of the soil.

Coverdale /ˈkʌvədeɪl/, Miles (1488–1568), English biblical scholar. He translated the first complete printed English Bible (1535), published in Zurich while he was in exile for preaching against confession and images. He also edited the Great Bible of 1539.

cover drive ▶ **noun** Cricket a drive past cover point.

cover girl ▶ **noun** a female model whose picture appears on magazine covers.

cover glass ▶ **noun** another term for **COVERSLIP**.

covering ▶ **noun** a thing used to cover something else, typically in order to protect or conceal it: *a vinyl floor covering.*
■ [usu. in sing.] a layer of something that covers something else: *the sky was obscured by a covering of cloud.*

covering letter (also **covering note**) ▶ **noun** a letter sent with, and explaining the contents of, another document or a parcel of goods.

coverlet ▶ **noun** a bedspread.
– ORIGIN Middle English: from Anglo-Norman French *covrelet*, from Old French *covrir* 'to cover' + *lit* 'bed'.

cover letter ▶ **noun** North American term for **COVERING LETTER**.

cover note ▶ **noun** Brit. a temporary certificate showing that a person has a current insurance policy.

cover point ▶ **noun** Cricket a fielding position a little in front of the batsman on the off side and halfway to the boundary.
■ a fielder at this position.

coverslip ▶ **noun** a small, thin piece of glass used to cover and protect a specimen on a microscope slide.

cover story ▶ **noun 1** a magazine article that is illustrated or advertised on the front cover.
2 a fictitious account invented to conceal a person's identity or reasons for doing something.

covert ▶ **adjective** /ˈkʌvət, ˈkəʊvəːt/ not openly acknowledged or displayed: *covert operations against the dictatorship.*
▶ **noun** /ˈkʌvət, ˈkʌvə/ **1** a thicket in which game can hide.
2 Ornithology any of the feathers covering the bases of the main flight or tail feathers of a bird.
– DERIVATIVES **covertly** adverb, **covertness** noun.
– ORIGIN Middle English (in the general senses 'covered' and 'a cover'): from Old French, 'covered', past participle of *covrir* (see **COVER**).

covert coat ▶ **noun** Brit. a short, light overcoat designed to be worn for outdoor sports such as shooting and riding.

coverture /ˈkʌvətjʊə/ ▶ **noun 1** [mass noun] poetic/literary protective or concealing covering.
2 Law, historical the legal status of a married woman,

considered to be under her husband's protection and authority.
– ORIGIN Middle English: from Old French, from *covrir* 'to cover'. It originally denoted a coverlet or a garment, later various kinds of covering or shelter.

cover-up ▶ noun an attempt to prevent people discovering the truth about a serious mistake or crime.

cover version ▶ noun see COVER (sense 6).

covet /ˈkʌvɪt/ ▶ verb (**coveted**, **coveting**) [with obj.] yearn to possess or have (something): *I covet one of their bubblejet printers.*
– DERIVATIVES **covetable** adjective.
– ORIGIN Middle English: from Old French *cuveitier*, based on Latin *cupiditas* (see CUPIDITY).

covetous ▶ adjective having or showing a great desire to possess something, typically something belonging to someone else: *she fingered the linen with covetous hands.*
– DERIVATIVES **covetously** adverb, **covetousness** noun.
– ORIGIN Middle English: from Old French *coveitous*, based on Latin *cupiditas* (see CUPIDITY).

covey /ˈkʌvi/ ▶ noun (pl. **-eys**) a small party or flock of birds, especially partridge.
■ figurative a small group of people or things: *coveys of actors rushed through the rooms.*
– ORIGIN Middle English: from Old French *covee*, feminine past participle of *cover*, from Latin *cubare* 'lie down'.

covin /ˈkʌvɪn/ (also **covine**) ▶ noun [mass noun] archaic fraud; deception.
– ORIGIN Middle English (denoting a company or band): from Old French, from medieval Latin *convenium*, from Latin *convenire* (see CONVENE). Compare with COVEN.

coving ▶ noun another term for COVE[1] (in sense 2).

cow[1] ▶ noun 1 a fully grown female animal of a domesticated breed of ox, used as a source of milk or beef: *a dairy cow.* See CATTLE.
■ (loosely) a domestic bovine animal, regardless of sex or age. ■ (in farming) a female domestic bovine animal which has borne more than one calf. Compare with HEIFER. ■ the female of certain other large animals, for example elephant, rhinoceros, whale, seal, or reindeer.
2 informal, derogatory a woman.
■ Austral./NZ an unpleasant person, thing, or situation.
– PHRASES **have a cow** N. Amer. informal become angry, excited, or agitated: *don't have a cow—it's no big deal.* **till the cows come home** informal for an indefinitely long time: *those two could talk till the cows came home.*
– ORIGIN Old English *cū*, of Germanic origin; related to Dutch *koe* and German *Kuh*, from an Indo-European root shared by Latin *bos* and Greek *bous*.

cow[2] ▶ verb [with obj.] (usu. **be cowed**) cause (someone) to submit to one's wishes by intimidation: *the intellectuals had been cowed into silence.*
– ORIGIN late 16th cent.: probably from Old Norse *kúga* 'oppress'.

cowabunga /ˌkaʊəˈbʌŋɡə, ˌkɑːwə-/ ▶ exclamation informal used to express delight or satisfaction: *Cowabunga! It's an actor's dream.*
– ORIGIN 1960s: fanciful, popularized by cartoons and the films *Teenage Mutant Ninja Turtles*, also recently used as surfers' slang.

Coward, Sir Noel (Pierce) (1899–1973), English dramatist, actor, and composer. He is remembered for witty, satirical plays, such as *Hay Fever* (1925) and *Private Lives* (1930), as well as revues and musicals featuring songs such as 'Mad Dogs and Englishmen' (1932).

coward ▶ noun a person who lacks the courage to do or endure dangerous or unpleasant things.
▶ adjective 1 poetic/literary excessively afraid of danger or pain.
2 Heraldry (of an animal) depicted with the tail between the hind legs.
– ORIGIN Middle English: from Old French *couard*, based on Latin *cauda* 'tail', possibly with reference to a frightened animal with its tail between its legs, reflected in sense 2 (early 16th cent.).

cowardice ▶ noun [mass noun] lack of bravery.
– ORIGIN Middle English: from Old French *couardise*, from *couard* (see COWARD).

cowardly ▶ adjective lacking courage.
■ (of an action) carried out against a person who is unable to retaliate: *a cowardly attack on a helpless victim.*
▶ adverb archaic in a way which shows a lack of courage.
– DERIVATIVES **cowardliness** noun.

cowardy ▶ adjective (in phrase **cowardy custard**) Brit. informal a cowardly person (often used as a taunt by children).

cowbane ▶ noun any of a number of tall poisonous plants of the parsley family, growing in swampy or wet habitats:
● another term for WATER HEMLOCK. ● a North American plant (*Oxypolis rigidior*, family Umbelliferae).
– ORIGIN late 18th cent.: from COW[1] + BANE, because it is poisonous to grazing cattle.

cowbell ▶ noun a bell hung round a cow's neck in order to help locate the animal by the noise it makes.
■ a similar bell used as a percussion instrument, typically without a clapper and struck with a stick.

cowberry ▶ noun (pl. **-ies**) a low-growing evergreen dwarf shrub of the heather family, which bears dark red berries and grows in upland habitats in the north. See also LINGONBERRY.
● *Vaccinium vitis-idaea*, family Ericaceae.
■ the edible acid berry of this plant, which may be used as a cranberry substitute.

cowbird ▶ noun a New World songbird with dark plumage and a relatively short bill, typically laying its eggs in other birds' nests.
● Genus *Molothrus* (and *Scaphidura*), family Icteridae: several species, in particular the widespread **brown-headed** (or **common**) **cowbird** (*M. ater*).

cowboy ▶ noun 1 a man, typically a mounted one, who herds and tends cattle, especially in the western US and as represented in westerns and novels: *they are always playing cowboys and Indians.*
2 informal a dishonest or careless person in business, especially an unqualified one.

cow camp ▶ noun N. Amer. a seasonal camp apart from the main buildings of a ranch, used during a cattle round-up.

cowcatcher ▶ noun a metal frame at the front of a locomotive for pushing aside cattle or other obstacles on the line.

cow chip ▶ noun N. Amer. a dried cowpat.

cow-cocky ▶ noun (pl. **-ies**) Austral./NZ informal a small dairy farmer.
– ORIGIN from COW[1] + COCKY[2].

cower ▶ verb [no obj.] crouch down in fear: *children cowered in terror as the shoot-out erupted.*
– ORIGIN Middle English: from Middle Low German *kūren* 'lie in wait', of unknown ultimate origin.

Cowes /kaʊz/ a town on the Isle of Wight, southern England; pop. 16,300 (1981). It is internationally famous as a yachting centre.

cowfish ▶ noun (pl. same or **-fishes**) 1 a boxfish which has spines that resemble horns on the head, and typically with other spines on the back and sides.
● Several genera and species in the family Ostraciontidae, in particular *Lactoria diaphana*.
2 a marine mammal, especially a manatee.

cow flop (also **cow flap**) ▶ noun informal, chiefly N. Amer. a cowpat.

cowgirl ▶ noun a female equivalent of a cowboy, especially as represented in westerns and novels.

cowherd ▶ noun a person who tends grazing cattle.
– ORIGIN Old English, from COW[1] + obsolete *herd* 'herdsman'.

cowhide ▶ noun a cow's hide.
■ [mass noun] leather made from such a hide. ■ a whip made from such leather.

cow-house ▶ noun Brit. a shed or shelter for cows.

Cowichan sweater /ˈkaʊɪtʃən/ ▶ noun (in Canada) a thick sweater made with unbleached wool and decorated with symbols taken from the mythology of the Cowichan Indians of southern Vancouver Island.

cowl ▶ noun a large loose hood, especially one forming part of a monk's habit.
■ a monk's hooded, sleeveless habit. ■ a cloak with wide sleeves worn by members of Benedictine orders. ■ the hood-shaped covering of a chimney or ventilation shaft. ■ another term for COWLING.
– DERIVATIVES **cowled** adjective.
– ORIGIN Old English *cugele*, *cūle*, from ecclesiastical Latin *cuculla*, from Latin *cucullus* 'hood of a cloak'.

cowlick ▶ noun a lock of hair hanging or projecting over a person's forehead.

cowling ▶ noun the removable cover of a vehicle or aircraft engine.

cowl neck ▶ noun a neckline on a woman's garment that hangs in draped folds: [as modifier] *a cowl-neck sweater.*

cowman ▶ noun (pl. **-men**) a person who is employed to tend grazing cattle.
■ N. Amer. a cowboy.

co-worker ▶ noun a fellow worker.

cow parsley ▶ noun a European hedgerow plant of the parsley family, which has fern-like leaves and large heads of tiny white flowers, giving the appearance of lace. Also called QUEEN ANNE'S LACE.
● *Anthriscus sylvestris*, family Umbelliferae.

cow parsnip ▶ noun another term for HOGWEED.

cowpat ▶ noun a flat, round piece of cow dung.

cowpea ▶ noun a plant of the pea family native to the Old World tropics. It is an important pulse for animal feed and human consumption, both the pod and the seed being edible.
● *Vigna unguiculata*, family Leguminosae.
■ the seed of this plant as food.

Cowper /ˈkuːpə/, William (1731–1800), English poet, best known for his long poem *The Task* (1785) and the comic ballad *John Gilpin* (1782). With the evangelical minister John Newton he wrote *Olney Hymns* (1779), which includes 'Oh! for a Closer Walk with God'.

Cowper's gland ▶ noun Anatomy either of a pair of small glands which open into the urethra at the base of the penis and secrete a constituent of seminal fluid.
– ORIGIN mid 18th cent.: named after William Cowper (1666–1709), English anatomist.

cowpoke ▶ noun N. Amer. informal a cowboy.

cowpox ▶ noun [mass noun] a viral disease of cows' udders which, when contracted by humans through contact, resembles mild smallpox, and was the basis of the first smallpox vaccines.

cowpuncher ▶ noun N. Amer. informal a cowboy.

cowrie /ˈkaʊ(ə)ri/ (also **cowry**) ▶ noun (pl. **-ies**) a marine mollusc which has a smooth, glossy, domed shell with a long narrow opening, typically brightly patterned and popular with collectors.
● Genus *Cypraea*, family Cypraeidae, class Gastropoda: numerous species, including the small **money cowrie** (*C. moneta*).
■ the flattened yellowish shell of the money cowrie, formerly used as money in parts of Africa and the Indo-Pacific area.
– ORIGIN mid 17th cent.: from Hindi *kaurī*.

co-write ▶ verb [with obj.] write (something) together with another person.
– DERIVATIVES **co-writer** noun.

cow shark ▶ noun a dull grey or brown shark that lives mainly in deep water, especially in the North Atlantic and Mediterranean.
● *Hexanchus griseus*, family Hexanchidae.

cowshed ▶ noun a farm building in which cattle are kept when not at pasture, or in which they are milked.

cowslip ▶ noun 1 a European primula with clusters of drooping fragrant yellow flowers in spring, growing on dry grassy banks and in pasture.
● *Primula veris*, family Primulaceae.
2 any of a number of herbaceous plants, in particular:
● North American term for MARSH MARIGOLD. ● (also **Virginia cowslip**) a North American plant with blue flowers (*Mertensia virginica*, family Boraginaceae).
– ORIGIN Old English *cūslyppe*, from *cū* 'cow' + *slipa*, *slyppe* 'slime', i.e. cow slobber or dung.

cow town ▶ noun N. Amer. a town or city in a cattle-raising area of western North America.
■ figurative a small, isolated, or unsophisticated town.

cow tree ▶ noun a tropical American tree yielding a juice which looks and tastes like cow's milk.
● Several species, in particular the Venezuelan *Brosimum utile* (family Moraceae).

cow wheat ▶ noun a yellowish-flowered plant of the figwort family, partly parasitic on the roots of other plants and found in both Eurasia and North America.
● Genus *Melampyrum*, family Scrophulariaceae: several species, including **common cow wheat** (*M. pratense*).

---

b **b**ut | d **d**og | f **f**ew | ɡ **g**et | h **h**e | j **y**es | k **c**at | l **l**eg | m **m**an | n **n**o | p **p**en | r **r**ed | s **s**it | t **t**op | v **v**oice | w **w**e | z **z**oo | ʃ **sh**e | ʒ deci**s**ion | θ **th**in | ð **th**is | ŋ ri**ng** | x lo**ch** | tʃ **ch**ip | dʒ **j**ar

Cox (in full **Cox's orange pippin**) ▶ noun an English eating apple of a variety with a red-tinged green skin.
– ORIGIN mid 19th cent.: named after R. *Cox* (died 1845), the English amateur fruit grower who first grew it (1825).

cox ▶ noun a coxswain, especially of a racing boat.
▶ verb [with obj.] act as a coxswain for (a racing boat or crew): *the winning eight was coxed by a woman* | [as adj.] **coxed** *the coxed pairs* | [no obj.] *he once coxed for Oriel.*
– DERIVATIVES **coxless** adjective.
– ORIGIN mid 19th cent.: abbreviation.

coxa /ˈkɒksə/ ▶ noun (pl. **coxae** /-siː/) Anatomy the hip bone or hip joint.
■ Entomology the first or basal segment of the leg of an insect.
– DERIVATIVES **coxal** adjective.
– ORIGIN late 17th cent.: from Latin, 'hip'.

coxcomb /ˈkɒkskəʊm/ ▶ noun **1** archaic a vain and conceited man; a dandy.
2 variant spelling of **COCKSCOMB** (in sense 2).
– DERIVATIVES **coxcombry** /-kəmri/ noun (pl. **-ies**) (only in sense 1).
– ORIGIN mid 16th cent. (denoting a simpleton): variant of **COCKSCOMB**, in the sense 'jester's cap' (resembling a cock's comb), hence 'a jester, a fool'.

coxopodite /kɒkˈsɒpədʌɪt/ ▶ noun Zoology the segment nearest the body in the leg of an arthropod, especially a crustacean.
– ORIGIN late 19th cent.: from Latin *coxa* 'hip' + Greek *pous, pod-* 'foot' + **-ITE**[1].

Coxsackie virus /kɒkˈsaki, kʊk-/ ▶ noun Medicine any of a group of enteroviruses which cause various respiratory, neurological, and muscular diseases in humans.
– ORIGIN 1940s: named after *Coxsackie*, New York State, where the first cases were diagnosed.

Cox's Bazar a port and resort town on the Bay of Bengal, near Chittagong, southern Bangladesh; pop. 29,600 (1981).

Cox's orange pippin ▶ noun see **COX**.

coxswain /ˈkɒks(ə)n/ ▶ noun the steersman of a ship's boat, lifeboat, racing boat, or other boat.
■ the senior petty officer in a small ship or submarine in the Royal Navy.
– DERIVATIVES **coxswainship** noun.
– ORIGIN Middle English: from obsolete *cock* (see **COCKBOAT**) + **SWAIN**. Compare with **BOATSWAIN**.

Coy chiefly Military ▶ abbreviation for Company.

coy ▶ adjective (**coyer, coyest**) (especially of a woman) making a pretence of shyness or modesty which is intended to be alluring but is often regarded as irritating: *she treated him to a coy smile of invitation.*
■ reluctant to give details, especially about something regarded as sensitive: *he is coy about his age.*
– DERIVATIVES **coyly** adverb, **coyness** noun.
– ORIGIN Middle English: from Old French *coi, quei,* from Latin *quietus* (see **QUIET**). The original sense was 'quiet, still' (especially in behaviour), later 'modestly retiring', and hence (of a woman) 'affecting to be unresponsive to advances'.

coydog ▶ noun N. Amer. a hybrid between a coyote and a dog.

coyote /ˈkɔɪəʊt, kɔɪˈəʊti/ ▶ noun (pl. same or **coyotes**) a wolf-like wild dog native to North America. Also called **BRUSH WOLF** or **PRAIRIE WOLF** in North America.
● *Canis latrans,* family Canidae.
– ORIGIN mid 18th cent.: from Mexican Spanish, from Nahuatl *coyotl.*

Coyote State informal name for **SOUTH DAKOTA**.

coypu /ˈkɔɪpuː/ ▶ noun (pl. **coypus**) a large semiaquatic beaver-like rodent, native to South America. It is kept in captivity for its fur and has become naturalized in many other areas.
● *Myocastor coypus,* the only member of the family Myocastoridae.
– ORIGIN late 18th cent.: from Araucanian.

coz[1] /kʌz/ ▶ noun archaic or N. Amer. an informal word for 'cousin', used especially as a term of address.
– ORIGIN mid 16th cent.: abbreviation.

coz[2] /kɒz, kəz/ ▶ conjunction variant spelling of **COS**[3].

cozen /ˈkʌz(ə)n/ ▶ verb [with obj.] poetic/literary trick or deceive: *do not think to cozen your contemporaries.*
■ obtain by deception: *he was able to cozen a profit.*
– DERIVATIVES **cozenage** noun, **cozener** noun.
– ORIGIN late 16th cent.: perhaps from obsolete Italian *cozzonare* 'to cheat', from *cozzone* 'middleman, broker', from Latin *cocio* 'dealer'.

Cozumel /ˌkɒzʊˈmɛl/ a resort island in the Caribbean, off the NE coast of the Yucatán Peninsula of Mexico.

cozy ▶ adjective US spelling of **COSY**.

cozzie ▶ noun (pl. **-ies**) variant spelling of **COSSIE**.

CP ▶ abbreviation for ■ cerebral palsy. ■ Finance commercial paper. ■ Law historical (Rolls of the Court of) Common Pleas. ■ Communist Party. ■ (in South Africa) Conservative Party.

cp. ▶ abbreviation for compare.

c.p. ▶ abbreviation for candlepower.

CPA N. Amer. ▶ abbreviation for certified public accountant.

CPI ▶ abbreviation for (in the US) consumer price index.

Cpl ▶ abbreviation for Corporal.

CPO ▶ abbreviation for Chief Petty Officer.

CPR ▶ abbreviation for ■ Canadian Pacific Railway. ■ cardiopulmonary resuscitation.

CPS ▶ abbreviation for (in the UK) Crown Prosecution Service.

cps (also **c.p.s.**) ▶ abbreviation for ■ Computing characters per second. ■ cycles per second.

CPU ▶ abbreviation for Computing central processing unit.

CPVC ▶ abbreviation for chlorinated polyvinyl chloride, a plastic material used to make water pipes.

CPVE (in the UK) Certificate of Pre-Vocational Education, a qualification introduced in 1986 for students aged 16 or over who complete a one-year course of preparation for work or for further vocational study or training.

CR ▶ abbreviation for ■ Community of the Resurrection. ■ Costa Rica (international vehicle registration).

Cr[1] ▶ symbol for the chemical element chromium.

Cr[2] ▶ abbreviation for ■ Councillor. ■ credit.

crab[1] ▶ noun **1** a crustacean with a broad carapace, stalked eyes, and five pairs of legs, the first pair of which are modified as pincers. Crabs are abundant on many shores, especially in the tropics where some have become adapted to life on land.
● Many families in the order Decapoda, class Malacostraca.
■ [mass noun] the flesh of a crab as food. ■ (the Crab) the zodiacal sign or constellation Cancer.
2 (also **crab louse**) a louse that infests human body hair, especially in the genital region, causing extreme irritation.
● *Phthirus pubis,* family Pediculidae, order Anoplura.
■ **(crabs)** informal an infestation of crab lice.
3 a machine for picking up and lifting heavy weights.
▶ verb **1** [no obj., with adverbial of direction] move sideways or obliquely: *he began crabbing sideways across the roof.*
■ [with obj.] steer (an aircraft or ship) slightly sideways to compensate for a crosswind or current.
2 [no obj.] fish for crabs.
– PHRASES **catch a crab** Rowing effect a faulty stroke in which the oar is jammed under water or misses the water altogether.
– DERIVATIVES **crabber** noun, **crablike** adjective & adverb.
– ORIGIN Old English *crabba,* of Germanic origin; related to Dutch *krabbe,* and more distantly to Dutch *kreeft* and German *Krebs;* also to **CRAB**[3].

crab[2] ▶ noun short for **CRAB APPLE**.

crab[3] ▶ verb (**crabbed, crabbing**) informal **1** [no obj.] grumble, typically about something petty: *on picnics, I would crab about sand in my food.*
2 [with obj.] act so as to spoil: *you're trying to crab my act.*
– ORIGIN late 16th cent. (referring to hawks, meaning 'claw or fight each other'): from Low German *krabben;* related to **CRAB**[1].

crab apple ▶ noun (also **crab**) **1** a small sour apple.
2 (also **crab tree** or **crab-apple tree**) the small tree that bears this fruit.
● Genus *Malus,* family Rosaceae: several species and hybrids, in particular the wild **Eurasian crab apple** (*M. sylvestris*), which grows in woods and hedgerows and is one of the possible ancestors of cultivated apples.
– ORIGIN late Middle English: *crab* perhaps an alteration (influenced by **CRAB**[1] or **CRABBED**) of

Scots and northern English *scrab,* in the same sense, probably of Scandinavian origin.

Crabbe /krab/, George (1754–1832), English poet, best known for grimly realistic narrative poems, such as 'The Village' (1783) and 'The Borough' (1810); the latter included tales of Peter Grimes and Ellen Orford and later provided the subject matter for Benjamin Britten's opera *Peter Grimes* (1945).

crabbed ▶ adjective **1** (of handwriting) ill-formed and hard to decipher.
■ (of style) contorted and difficult to understand: *crabbed legal language.*
2 ill-humoured: *a crabbed, unhappy middle age.*
– DERIVATIVES **crabbedly** adverb, **crabbedness** noun.
– ORIGIN Middle English (in the sense 'perverse, wayward'): from **CRAB**[1], because of the crab's sideways gait and habit of snapping, thought to suggest a perverse or irritable disposition.

crabby ▶ adjective (**crabbier, crabbiest**) **1** irritable.
2 another term for **CRABBED** (in sense 1).
– DERIVATIVES **crabbily** adverb, **crabbiness** noun.

crab canon ▶ noun another term for **CANON CANCRIZANS**.

crabeater seal ▶ noun a slender grey antarctic seal which lives on the pack ice, feeding mainly on krill.
● *Lobodon carcinophagus,* family Phocidae.

crabgrass ▶ noun [mass noun] N. Amer. a creeping grass that can become a serious weed.
● *Digitaria* and other genera, family Gramineae: several species, in particular *D. sanguinalis* and *D. ciliaris.*

crab louse ▶ noun see **CRAB**[1] (sense 2).

crabmeat ▶ noun [mass noun] the flesh of a crab as food.

Crab Nebula Astronomy an irregular patch of luminous gas in the constellation Taurus, believed to be the remnant of a supernova explosion seen by Chinese astronomers in 1054. At its centre is the first pulsar to be observed visually, and the nebula is a strong source of high-energy radiation.

crab plover ▶ noun a thickset wading bird with mainly white plumage and a heavy black bill, found on the coasts of the Indian Ocean where it feeds on crabs.
● *Dromas ardeola,* the only member of the family Dromadidae.

crab pot ▶ noun a wicker trap for crabs.

crab spider ▶ noun a spider with long front legs, moving with a crablike sideways motion and typically lying in wait in vegetation and flowers for passing prey.
● Family Thomisidae: several genera.

crab stick ▶ noun a stick of mixed compressed fish pieces, rectangular in section, and including and flavoured with crab.

crab tree ▶ noun see **CRAB APPLE** (sense 2).

crabwise ▶ adverb & adjective (of movement) sideways, typically in an awkward way: [as adv.] *supermarket trolleys that only go crabwise* | [as adj.] *crabwise steps.*

crack ▶ noun **1** a line on the surface of something along which it has split without breaking into separate parts: *a hairline crack down the middle of the glass.*
■ a narrow space between two surfaces, especially ones which have broken or been moved apart: *he climbed into a crack between two rocks* | *the door opened a tiny crack.* ■ figurative a vulnerable point; a flaw: *the company spotted a crack in their rival's defences.*
2 a sudden sharp or explosive noise: *a loud crack of thunder.*
■ a sharp blow, especially one which makes a noise: *she gave the thief a crack over the head with her rolling pin.* ■ a sudden harshness or change in pitch in a person's voice: *the boy's voice had an uncertain crack in it.*
3 informal a joke, typically a critical or unkind one.
■ Scottish & N. English a conversation: *they are having a great crack about shooting.*
4 (also **craic**) [mass noun] Irish enjoyable entertainment or activity; a good time: *he loved the crack, the laughing.*
5 [in sing.] informal an attempt to gain or achieve something: *I fancy having a crack at winning a fourth title.*
■ a chance to attack or compete with someone: *he wanted to have a crack at the enemy.*
6 (also **crack cocaine**) [mass noun] a potent hard

crystalline form of cocaine broken into small pieces and inhaled or smoked.
▶**verb 1** break or cause to break without a complete separation of the parts: [no obj.] *the ice all over the bog had cracked* | [with obj.] *take care not to crack the glass.*
■break or cause to break open or apart: [no obj., with adverbial] *a chunk of the cliff had* **cracked off** *in a storm* | figurative *his face cracked into a smile* | [with obj.] *she cracked an egg into the frying pan.* ■ [with obj.] break (wheat or corn) into coarse pieces. ■ figurative give way or cause to give way under torture, pressure, or strain: [no obj.] *the witnesses cracked and the truth came out* | [with obj.] *no one can crack them—they believe their cover story.* ■ [no obj.] (**crack up**) informal suffer an emotional breakdown under pressure. ■ [no obj.] (**crack up**) informal burst into laughter.
2 make or cause to make a sudden sharp or explosive sound: [no obj.] *a shot cracked across the ridge* | [with obj.] *he* **cracked** *his* **whip** *and galloped away.*
■[no obj.] knock against something, making a noise on impact: *she winced as her knees cracked against metal.* ■ [with obj.] hit (someone or something) hard, making a sharp noise: *she cracked him across the forehead.* ■ [no obj.] (of a person's voice, especially that of an adolescent boy or a person under strain) suddenly change in pitch: *'I want to get away,' she said, her voice cracking.*
3 [with obj.] informal find a solution to; decipher or interpret: *the code will help you crack the messages.*
■break into (a safe). ■ succeed in achieving: *he cracked a brilliant goal.*
4 [with obj.] decompose (hydrocarbons) by heat and pressure with or without a catalyst to produce lighter hydrocarbons, especially in oil refining: [as noun **cracking**] *catalytic cracking.*
▶**adjective** [attrib.] very good, especially at a specified activity or in a specified role: *he is a crack shot* | *crack troops.*
– PHRASES **crack a book** N. Amer. informal open a book and read it; study. **crack a bottle** open a bottle, especially of wine, and drink it. **crack a crib** Brit. archaic, informal break into a house. **crack of dawn** a time very early in the morning; daybreak. **crack of doom** a thunder peal announcing the Day of Judgement. **crack of the whip** Brit. informal a chance to try one's hand at or participate in something: *individuals who feel that they have not had a fair crack of the whip.* **cracked up to be** [with negative] informal asserted to be (used to indicate that someone or something has been described too favourably): *life on tour is not as glamorous as it's cracked up to be.* **crack wise** N. Amer. informal make jokes. **get cracking** informal act quickly and energetically: *most tickets have been snapped up, so get cracking if you want one.* **slip** (or **fall**) **through the cracks** N. Amer. another way of saying ***slip through the net*** (see **NET**[1]).
– ORIGIN Old English *cracian* 'make an explosive noise'; of Germanic origin; related to Dutch *kraken* and German *krachen.*
▶**crack down on** informal take severe measures against: *we need to crack down hard on workplaces that break safety regulations.*
crack on informal proceed or progress quickly: *we'll crack on with the second half of the job this month.*

crackbrained ▶**adjective** informal extremely foolish; crazy: *a crackbrained idea.*

crackdown ▶**noun** [usu. in sing.] severe measures to restrict or discourage undesirable or illegal people or behaviour: *a* **crackdown on** *car crime.*

cracked ▶**adjective 1** damaged and showing lines on the surface from having split without coming apart: *the old pipes were cracked and leaking.*
■(of a person's voice) having an unusual harshness or pitch, often due to distress.
2 [predic.] informal crazy; insane: *you must think my family are cracked.*

cracked wheat ▶**noun** [mass noun] grains of wheat that have been crushed into small pieces.

cracker ▶**noun 1** a paper cylinder which is pulled apart at Christmas or other celebrations, making a sharp noise and releasing a small toy or other novelty.
■a firework exploding with a sharp noise.
2 a thin dry biscuit typically eaten with cheese or other savoury toppings.
■a light crisp made of rice or tapioca flour: *prawn crackers.*
3 Brit. informal a fine example of something: *don't miss this* **cracker of a** *CD.*
■an attractive person, especially a woman.
4 US offensive another term for **POOR WHITE.**
5 an installation for cracking hydrocarbons: *a catalytic cracker.*

cracker-barrel ▶**adjective** [attrib.] N. Amer. (especially of a philosophy) plain, simple, and unsophisticated: *his cracker-barrel fascism.*
– ORIGIN late 19th cent.: with reference to the barrels of soda crackers once found in country stores, around which informal discussions would take place between customers.

crackerjack informal, chiefly N. Amer. ▶**adjective** exceptionally good: *a crackerjack eye surgeon.*
▶**noun** an exceptionally good person or thing.

crackers ▶**adjective** [predic.] informal, chiefly Brit. insane: *if Luke wasn't here I'd go crackers.*
■extremely annoyed or angry: *when he saw the mess he went crackers.*

crackhead ▶**noun** informal a person who habitually takes or is addicted to crack cocaine.

cracking Brit. informal ▶**adjective** [attrib.] excellent: *he is in cracking form to win this race* | [as submodifier] *a cracking good story.*
■fast and exciting: *the story rips along* **at a cracking pace.**

crack-jaw ▶**adjective** archaic, informal (of a word) difficult to pronounce.

crackle ▶**verb** [no obj.] make a rapid succession of slight cracking noises: *the fire suddenly crackled and spat sparks.*
■figurative give a sense of great tension or animation: *attraction and antagonism were crackling between them.*
▶**noun 1** a sound made up of a rapid succession of slight cracking sounds: *there was a crackle and a whine from the microphone.*
2 [mass noun] a pattern of minute surface cracks on paintwork, varnish, glazed ceramics, or glass.
– DERIVATIVES **crackly** adjective.
– ORIGIN late Middle English: from **CRACK** + **-LE**[4].

crackling ▶**noun** [mass noun] **1** the crisp fatty skin of roast pork.
2 Brit. informal, offensive attractive women regarded collectively as objects of sexual desire.

cracknel /ˈkrakn(ə)l/ ▶**noun 1** a light, crisp, savoury biscuit.
2 a brittle sweet made from set melted sugar, typically containing or flavoured with nuts.
– ORIGIN late Middle English: alteration of Old French *craquelin,* from Middle Dutch *krākelinc,* from *krāken* 'to crack'.

crackpot informal ▶**noun** an eccentric or foolish person.
▶**adjective** [attrib.] eccentric; impractical: *his head's full of crackpot ideas.*

cracksman ▶**noun** (pl. **-men**) informal, dated a burglar, especially a safe-breaker.

crack-up ▶**noun** [usu. in sing.] informal **1** a collapse under strain: *he had a complete mental crack-up.*
2 an act of breaking up or splitting apart.

crack willow ▶**noun** a large Eurasian willow with long glossy leaves, growing typically in damp or riverside habitats. The brittle branches break off easily, often taking root and producing new growth.
• *Salix fragilis*, family Salicaceae.

cracky ▶**adjective** (of a surface) covered with lines or splits: *his face was all dry and cracky.*

Cracow /ˈkrakaʊ/ an industrial and university city in southern Poland, on the River Vistula; pop 750,540. (1990). It was the capital of Poland from 1320 until replaced by Warsaw in 1609. Polish name **KRAKÓW.**

-cracy ▶**combining form** denoting a particular form of government, rule, or influence: *autocracy* | *democracy.*
– ORIGIN from French *-cratie,* via medieval Latin from Greek *-kratia* 'power, rule'.

cradle ▶**noun 1** a very young child's bed or cot, typically one mounted on rockers.
■figurative a place, process, or event in which something originates or flourishes: *he saw Greek art as the cradle of European civilization.* ■ (**the cradle**) figurative infancy; childhood: *the welfare state was set up to provide care* **from the cradle to the grave.**
2 a framework resembling a cradle, in particular:
■a framework on which a ship or boat rests during construction or repairs. ■ a framework on which a worker is suspended to work on a ceiling, ship, or the vertical side of a building. ■ the part of a telephone on which the receiver rests when not in use.
▶**verb** [with obj.] **1** hold gently and protectively: *she cradled his head in her arms.*
■figurative be the place of origin of: *the north-eastern states cradled an American industrial revolution.*
2 place (a telephone receiver) in its cradle.
– ORIGIN Old English *cradol,* of uncertain origin; perhaps related to German *Kratte* 'basket'.

cradleboard ▶**noun** (among North American Indians) a board to which an infant is strapped.

cradle cap ▶**noun** [mass noun] a skin condition sometimes seen in babies caused by excessive production of sebum, characterized by areas of yellowish or brownish scales on the top of the head.

cradle-snatcher ▶**noun** derogatory a person who marries or has a sexual relationship with a much younger person.

cradle song ▶**noun** a lullaby.

cradling ▶**noun** Architecture a wooden or iron framework, typically one used as a structural support in a ceiling.

craft ▶**noun 1** an activity involving skill in making things by hand: *the craft of cobbling* | [mass noun] *art and craft.*
■(**crafts**) work or objects made by hand: *the shop sells local crafts* | [as modifier] (**craft**) *a craft fair.* ■ a skilled activity or profession: *the historian's craft.* ■ [mass noun] skill in carrying out one's work: *a player with plenty of craft.* ■ [mass noun] skill used in deceiving others: *her cousin was not her equal in guile and evasive craft.* ■ the members of a skilled profession. ■ (**the Craft**) the brotherhood of Freemasons.
2 (pl. same) a boat or ship: *sailing craft.*
■an aeroplane or spaceship.
▶**verb** [with obj.] exercise skill in making (something): *he crafted the chair lovingly* | [as adj., with submodifier] (**crafted**) *a beautifully crafted object.*
– DERIVATIVES **crafter** noun.
– ORIGIN Old English *cræft* 'strength, skill', of Germanic origin; related to Dutch *kracht,* German *Kraft,* and Swedish *kraft* 'strength' (the change of sense to 'skill' occurring only in English). Sense 2, originally in the expression *small craft* 'small trading vessels or lighters', may be elliptical, referring to vessels requiring a small amount of 'craft' or skill to handle, as opposed to large ocean-going ships.

craft beer (also **craft brew**) ▶**noun** US a beer with a distinctive flavour, produced and distributed in a particular region.

craft guild ▶**noun** historical an association of workers of the same trade for mutual benefit.

craft knife ▶**noun** another term for **UTILITY KNIFE.**

craftsman ▶**noun** (pl. **-men**) a male worker skilled in a particular craft.
■[usu. as title] (in the UK) a qualified private soldier in the Royal Electrical and Mechanical Engineers: *Craftsman Browne.*
– DERIVATIVES **craftsmanship** noun.

craftsperson ▶**noun** (pl. **craftspeople**) a person who is skilled at making things by hand (used as a neutral alternative).

craftswoman ▶**noun** (pl. **-women**) a female worker skilled in a particular craft.
– DERIVATIVES **craftswomanship** noun.

craft union ▶**noun** a trade union of people of the same skilled craft.

craftwork ▶**noun** [mass noun] the making of things, especially decorative objects, by hand as a profession or leisure activity.
■work produced in such a way.
– DERIVATIVES **craftworker** noun.

crafty ▶**adjective** (**craftier, craftiest**) **1** clever at achieving one's aims by indirect or deceitful methods: *a crafty crook faked an injury to escape from prison.*
■of, involving, or relating to indirect or deceitful methods: *he sneaked off to a toilet for a crafty fag.*
2 informal of, involving, or relating to the making of decorative objects and other things by hand: *a market full of crafty pots and interesting earrings.*
– DERIVATIVES **craftily** adverb, **craftiness** noun.
– ORIGIN Old English *cræftig* 'strong, powerful', later 'skilful' (see **CRAFT, -Y**[1]).

crag ▶**noun 1** a steep or rugged cliff or rock face.
2 [mass noun] Geology a shelly sandstone occurring in eastern England.
– ORIGIN Middle English: of Celtic origin. Sense 2, dating from the mid 18th cent., may have been a different word originally.

crag and tail ▶ **noun** Geology a rocky outcrop with a tapering ridge of glacial deposits extending to one side.

craggy ▶ **adjective** (**craggier**, **craggiest**) (of a landscape) having many crags: *a craggy coastline.*
■ (of a cliff or rock face) rough and uneven. ■ (of a person's face, typically a man's) rugged and rough-textured in an attractive way.
– DERIVATIVES **craggily** adverb, **cragginess** noun.

cragsman ▶ **noun** (pl. **-men**) a skilled rock climber.

craic ▶ **noun** variant spelling of **CRACK** (in sense 4).

Craiova /krəˈjəʊvə/ a city in SW Romania; pop. 300,030 (1989).

crake ▶ **noun** a bird of the rail family, especially one with a short bill like the corncrake.
• Family Rallidae: several genera, in particular *Porzana*, and numerous species.
■ the rasping cry of the corncrake.
– ORIGIN Middle English (originally denoting a crow or raven): from Old Norse *kráka*, *krákr*, of imitative origin.

cram ▶ **verb** (**crammed**, **cramming**) [with obj.] (often **be crammed**) completely fill (a place or container) to the point that it appears to be overflowing: *the ashtray by the bed was* ***crammed with*** *cigarette butts | it's amazing how you've managed to* ***cram*** *everyone* ***in****.*
■ [no obj.] (of a number of people) enter a place or space that is or seems to be too small to accommodate all of them: *they all crammed into the car.* ■ put (something) quickly or roughly into something which is or appears to be too small to contain it: *he crammed the sandwiches* ***into*** *his mouth* | figurative *he had crammed so much* ***into*** *his short life.* ■ [no obj.] study intensively over a short period of time just before an examination: *lectures were called off so students could cram for the semester finals.* ■ [with obj.] make (someone) study in such a way.
– ORIGIN Old English *crammian*, of Germanic origin; related to Dutch *krammen* 'to cramp or clamp'.

crambo ▶ **noun** [mass noun] a game in which a player gives a word or line of verse to which each of the other players must find a rhyme.
– ORIGIN early 17th cent. (denoting a particular fashion in drinking): from earlier *crambe* 'cabbage', used figuratively to denote something distasteful that is repeated, apparently from Latin *crambe repetita* 'cabbage served up again', applied by Juvenal to any distasteful repetition.

cram-full ▶ **adjective** [predic.] very full; packed: *all the roads were cram-full of cars.*

crammer ▶ **noun** Brit. a person or institution that prepares pupils for an examination intensively over a short period of time.

cramp ▶ **noun 1** [mass noun] painful involuntary contraction of a muscle or muscles, typically caused by fatigue or strain: *an attack of cramp* | [count noun] *he suffered severe cramps in his foot.*
■ (**cramps**) N. Amer. abdominal pain caused by menstruation.
2 a tool, typically shaped like a capital G, for clamping two objects together for gluing or other work.
■ (also **cramp-iron**) a metal bar with bent ends for holding masonry together.
▶ **verb 1** [with obj.] restrict or inhibit the development of: *tighter rules will cramp economic growth.*
2 [with obj.] fasten with a cramp or cramps: *cramp the gates to the posts.*
3 [no obj.] suffer from sudden and painful contractions of a muscle or muscles.
– PHRASES **cramp someone's style** informal prevent a person from acting freely or naturally.
– ORIGIN late Middle English: from Middle Low German and Middle Dutch *krampe*; sense 1 of the noun is via Old French *crampe*.

cramp balls ▶ **plural noun** a European fungus which produces a shiny spherical black fruiting body on dead or dying wood, especially ash. Also called **KING ALFRED'S CAKES**.
• *Daldinia concentrica*, family Xylariaceae, subdivision Ascomycotina.
– ORIGIN so named because it was once believed to be a charm against cramp and ague.

cramped ▶ **adjective 1** suffering from cramp: *rest your cramped arms for a moment.*
2 feeling or causing someone to feel uncomfortably confined or hemmed in by lack of space: *staff had to work in cramped conditions.*
■ restricting or inhibiting the development of someone or something: *he felt cramped in a large organization.* ■ (of handwriting) small and difficult to read.

crampon /ˈkrampɒn, -pən/ ▶ **noun** (usu. **crampons**) **1** a metal plate with spikes fixed to a boot for walking on ice or rock climbing.
2 archaic term for **GRAPPLING HOOK**.
– ORIGIN Middle English (in sense 2): from Old French, of Germanic origin.

cran ▶ **noun** historical a measure of fresh herrings, equivalent to 37½ gallons.
– ORIGIN late 18th cent.: from Scottish Gaelic *crann*, perhaps the same word as *crann* 'lot', denoting the share of fish given to each member of the crew.

Cranach /ˈkranək, German ˈkra:nax/ two German painters. **Lucas** (1472–1553, known as **Cranach the Elder**) was a member of the Danube School who was noted for his early religious pictures, such as *The Rest on the Flight into Egypt* (1504). He also painted portraits, including several of Martin Luther. His son **Lucas** (1515–86, known as **Cranach the Younger**) continued working in the same tradition as his father.

cranage /ˈkreɪnɪdʒ/ ▶ **noun** [mass noun] the use of a crane or cranes.
■ fees paid for using a crane or cranes.

cranberry ▶ **noun** (pl. **-ies**) **1** a small red acid berry used in cooking.
2 the evergreen dwarf shrub of the heather family which yields this fruit.
• Genus *Vaccinium*, family Ericaceae: several species, in particular, the European *V. oxycoccos* and the North American *V. macrocarpon*.
– ORIGIN mid 17th cent. (originally North American): from German *Kranbeere* or Low German *kranebeere* 'crane-berry'.

cranberry bush ▶ **noun** chiefly N. Amer. a shrub of the honeysuckle family, with round clusters of white flowers followed by red berries.
• Genus *Viburnum*, family Caprifoliaceae: the **American cranberry bush** (*V. trilobum*), with edible berries, and the guelder rose or **European cranberry bush**.

Crane[1], (Harold) Hart (1899–1932), American poet. He published only two books before committing suicide: the collection *White Buildings* (1926) and *The Bridge* (1930), a mystical epic poem concerned with American life and consciousness.

Crane[2], Stephen (1871–1900), American writer. His reputation rests on his novel *The Red Badge of Courage* (1895), a study of an inexperienced soldier in the American Civil War. It was hailed as a masterpiece of psychological realism, even though Crane himself had no personal experience of war.

crane[1] ▶ **noun** a large, tall machine used for moving heavy objects, typically by suspending them from a projecting arm or beam.
■ a moving platform supporting a television or film camera.
▶ **verb 1** [no obj., with adverbial of direction] stretch out one's neck in order to see something: *she craned forward to look more clearly.*
■ [with obj.] stretch out (one's neck) in this way.
2 [with obj. and adverbial] move (a heavy object) with a crane: *the wheelhouse module is craned into position on the hull.*
– ORIGIN Middle English: figuratively from **CRANE**[2] (the same sense development occurred in the related German *Kran* and Dutch *kraan* (see **CRANE**[2]), and in French *grue*). The verb dates from the late 16th cent.

crane[2] ▶ **noun** a tall, long-legged, long-necked bird, typically with white or grey plumage and often with tail plumes and patches of bare red skin on the head. Cranes are noted for their elaborate courtship dances.
• Family Gruidae: four genera, in particular *Grus*, and several species, including the Eurasian **common crane** (*G. grus*).
– ORIGIN Old English, of Germanic origin; related to Dutch *kraan* and German *Kran*, from an Indo-European root shared by Latin *grus* and Greek *geranos*.

crane fly ▶ **noun** a slender two-winged fly with very long legs. The larva of some kinds is the leatherjacket. Also called **DADDY-LONG-LEGS** in Britain.
• Family Tipulidae: many genera and species, in particular the large and common *Tipula maxima*.

cranesbill ▶ **noun** a herbaceous plant which typically has lobed leaves and purple, violet, or pink five-petalled flowers.
• Genus *Geranium*, family Geraniaceae: several species, including the common bluish-purple flowered **meadow cranesbill** (*G. pratense*).
– ORIGIN mid 16th cent.: so named because of the long spur on the fruit, thought to resemble a crane's beak.

cranial /ˈkreɪnɪəl/ ▶ **adjective** Anatomy of or relating to the skull or cranium.
– ORIGIN early 19th cent.: from **CRANIUM** + **-AL**.

cranial index ▶ **noun** another term for **CEPHALIC INDEX**.

cranial nerve ▶ **noun** Anatomy each of twelve pairs of nerves which arise directly from the brain, not from the spinal cord, and pass through separate apertures in the skull.

> They are (with conventional roman numbering) the olfactory (I), optic (II), oculomotor (III), trochlear (IV), trigeminal (V), abducens (VI), facial (VII), vestibulocochlear (VIII), glossopharyngeal (IX), vagus (X), accessory (XI), and hypoglossal (XII) nerves.

craniate /ˈkreɪnɪət/ Zoology ▶ **noun** an animal that possesses a skull. Compare with **VERTEBRATE**.
• Subphylum Craniata, phylum Chordata; used instead of Vertebrata in some classification schemes.
▶ **adjective** of or relating to the craniates.
– ORIGIN late 19th cent.: from modern Latin *craniatus*, from medieval Latin *cranium* (see **CRANIUM**).

cranio- /ˈkreɪnɪəʊ/ ▶ **combining form** relating to the cranium: *craniotomy.*
– ORIGIN from Greek *kranion* 'skull'.

craniology /ˌkreɪnɪˈɒlədʒi/ ▶ **noun** [mass noun] historical the scientific study of the shape and size of the skulls of different human races.
■ another term for **PHRENOLOGY**.
– DERIVATIVES **craniological** adjective, **craniologist** noun.

craniometry /ˌkreɪnɪˈɒmɪtri/ ▶ **noun** [mass noun] historical the scientific measurement of skulls, especially in relation to craniology.
– DERIVATIVES **craniometric** adjective.

craniosacral therapy /ˌkreɪnɪəʊˈseɪkr(ə)l, -ˈsak-/ ▶ **noun** [mass noun] a system of alternative medicine intended to relieve pain and tension by gentle manipulations of the skull regarded as harmonizing with a natural rhythm in the central nervous system.

craniotomy /ˌkreɪnɪˈɒtəmi/ ▶ **noun** [mass noun] surgical removal of a portion of the skull.
■ surgical perforation of the skull of a dead fetus to ease delivery.

cranium /ˈkreɪnɪəm/ ▶ **noun** (pl. **craniums** or **crania** /-nɪə/) Anatomy the skull, especially the part enclosing the brain.
– ORIGIN late Middle English: via medieval Latin from Greek *kranion* 'skull'.

crank[1] ▶ **verb** [with obj.] **1** turn the crankshaft of (an internal-combustion engine), typically in order to start the engine.
■ turn (a handle), typically in order to start an engine. ■ (**crank something up**) informal increase the intensity of something: *the volume is cranked up a notch.* ■ (**crank something out**) informal, derogatory produce something regularly and routinely: *an army of researchers cranked out worthy studies.*
2 [usu. as adj. **cranked**] give a bend to (a shaft, bar, etc.).
3 [no obj.] informal inject a narcotic drug: *he's been cranking up on smack.*
▶ **noun** a part of an axle or shaft bent out at right angles, for converting reciprocal to circular motion and vice versa.
– ORIGIN Old English *cranc* (recorded in *crancstæf*, denoting a weaver's implement), related to *crincan* (see **CRINGE**).

crank[2] ▶ **noun 1** an eccentric person, especially one who is obsessed by a particular subject or theory.
■ N. Amer. a bad-tempered person. [ORIGIN: mid 19th cent.: back-formation from **CRANKY**.]
2 poetic/literary a fanciful turn of speech. [ORIGIN: late 16th cent.: perhaps from a base meaning 'bent together, curled up', shared by Old English *cranc* (see **CRANK**[1]).]

crank[3] ▶ **adjective** Nautical, archaic (of a sailing ship) liable to heel over.
– ORIGIN early 17th cent.: perhaps from dialect *crank* 'weak, shaky' (compare with **CRANKY** or **CRANK**[1]).

crankcase ▶ **noun** a case or covering enclosing a crankshaft.

crankpin ▶ **noun** a pin by which a connecting rod is attached to a crank.

crankshaft ▶ **noun** a shaft driven by a crank.

cranky ▶ **adjective** (**crankier**, **crankiest**) informal eccentric or strange, typically because highly unorthodox: *a cranky scheme to pipe ground-level ozone into the stratosphere.*
■ chiefly N. Amer. ill-tempered; irritable: *he was bored and cranky after eight hours of working.* ■ (of a machine) working badly; shaky: *after a juddering landing the cranky plane eased up the runway.*
– DERIVATIVES **crankily** adverb, **crankiness** noun.
– ORIGIN late 18th cent. (in the sense 'sickly, in poor health'): perhaps from obsolete (*counterfeit*) *crank* 'a rogue feigning sickness', from Dutch or German *krank* 'sick'.

Cranmer /ˈkranmə/, Thomas (1489–1556), English Protestant cleric and martyr. After helping to negotiate Henry VIII's divorce from Catherine of Aragon, he was appointed the first Protestant Archbishop of Canterbury in 1532. He was responsible for liturgical reform and the compilation of the Book of Common Prayer (1549). In the reign of Mary Tudor Cranmer was tried for treason and heresy and burnt at the stake.

crannog /ˈkranəɡ/ ▶ **noun** an ancient fortified dwelling constructed in a lake or marsh in Scotland or Ireland.
– ORIGIN early 17th cent.: from Irish *crannóg*, Scottish Gaelic *crannag* 'timber structure', from *crann* 'tree, beam'.

cranny ▶ **noun** (pl. **-ies**) a small, narrow space or opening.
– DERIVATIVES **crannied** adjective.
– ORIGIN late Middle English: from Old French *crane* 'notched', from *cran*, from popular Latin *crena* 'notch'.

crap[1] vulgar slang ▶ **noun** [mass noun] **1** something which is of extremely poor quality.
■ nonsense; rubbish.
2 excrement.
■ [in sing.] an act of defecation.
▶ **verb** (**crapped**, **crapping**) [no obj.] defecate.
▶ **adjective** extremely poor in quality.
– ORIGIN Middle English: related to Dutch *krappe*, from *krappen* 'pluck or cut off', and perhaps also to Old French *crappe* 'siftings', Anglo-Latin *crappa* 'chaff'. The original sense was 'chaff', later 'residue from rendering fat', also 'dregs of beer'. Current senses date from the late 19th cent.
▶ **crap on** talk at length in a foolish or boring way.

crap[2] N. Amer. ▶ **noun** a losing throw of 2, 3, or 12 in craps.
▶ **verb** [no obj.] (**crap out**) informal make a losing throw at craps.
■ withdraw from or give up on a game or activity because of fear or fatigue: *when entrepreneurs get to $1 billion they crap out and turn their companies over to others.* ■ be unsuccessful in what one is attempting to do: *the Rams almost crapped out late in the game.* ■ (of a machine) break down: *his teleprompter crapped out.*
– ORIGIN early 20th cent.: from **CRAPS**.

crape ▶ **noun** [mass noun] **1** variant spelling of **CRÊPE**.
2 black silk or imitation silk, formerly used for mourning clothes.
■ [count noun] a band of such fabric formerly worn round a person's hat as a sign of mourning.
– DERIVATIVES **crapy** adjective.
– ORIGIN early 16th cent.: from French *crêpe* (see **CRÊPE**).

crape fern ▶ **noun** a tall New Zealand fern with dark green fronds.
• *Leptopteris superba*, family Osmundaceae.

crape hair ▶ **noun** [mass noun] Brit. artificial hair used by actors, chiefly for false beards and moustaches.

crape myrtle (also **crepe myrtle**) ▶ **noun** an ornamental Chinese shrub or small tree with pink, white, or purplish crinkled petals.
• *Lagerstroemia indica*, family Lythraceae.

crap game ▶ **noun** N. Amer. a game of craps.

crap hat ▶ **noun** vulgar slang (in the British army) a term used by paratroopers and commandos to refer to a soldier from a regiment in the rest of the army.
– ORIGIN probably with derogatory reference to the standard khaki-coloured (now dark blue) berets, in contrast to the prized red and green berets of the special regiments.

crapper ▶ **noun** vulgar slang a toilet.

crappie ▶ **noun** (pl. **-ies**) a North American freshwater fish of the sunfish family, the male of which builds a nest and guards the eggs and young.
• Genus *Pomoxis*, family Centrarchidae: several species, including the **white crappie** (*P. annularis*).
– ORIGIN mid 19th cent.: of unknown origin.

crappy ▶ **adjective** (**crappier**, **crappiest**) vulgar slang of extremely poor quality.
■ worthless; disgusting.

craps ▶ **plural noun** [treated as sing.] a gambling game played with two dice, chiefly in North America. A throw of 7 or 11 is a winning throw, 2, 3, or 12 is a losing throw; any other throw must be repeated. See also **CRAP**[2].
– ORIGIN early 19th cent.: perhaps from **CRAB**[1] or *crab's eyes*, denoting the lowest throw (two ones) at dice.

crapshoot ▶ **noun** N. Amer. a crap game.
■ informal a risky or uncertain matter: *skiing here can be a bit of a crapshoot at any time.*
– DERIVATIVES **crapshooter** noun.

crapulent /ˈkrapjʊl(ə)nt/ ▶ **adjective** poetic/literary of or relating to the drinking of alcohol or drunkenness.
– DERIVATIVES **crapulence** noun, **crapulous** adjective.
– ORIGIN mid 17th cent.: from late Latin *crapulentus* 'very drunk', from Latin *crapula* 'inebriation', from Greek *kraipalē* 'drunken headache'.

craquelure /ˈkrakljʊə, krakˈljʊə/ ▶ **noun** [mass noun] a network of fine cracks in the paint or varnish of a painting.
– ORIGIN early 20th cent.: French, from *craqueler* 'to crackle'.

crash[1] ▶ **verb 1** [no obj.] (of a vehicle) collide violently with an obstacle or another vehicle: *a racing car had crashed, wrecking a safety barrier.*
■ [with obj.] cause (a vehicle) to collide in this way. ■ (of an aircraft) fall from the sky and violently hit the land or sea: *a jet crashed 200 yards from the school.* ■ [with obj.] cause (an aircraft) to fall from the sky in this way. ■ informal (of a company's shares) fall suddenly and disastrously in value: *the shares crashed to 329p.* ■ Computing (of a machine, system, or software) fail suddenly: *the project was postponed because the computer crashed.* ■ informal go to sleep, especially suddenly or in an improvised setting: *what was it you said just before I crashed out?*
2 [no obj., with adverbial of direction] move with force, speed, and sudden loud noise: *huge waves crashed down on to us.*
■ [with obj. and adverbial of direction] move (something) in this way: *she crashed down the telephone receiver.* ■ make a sudden loud, deep noise: *the thunder crashed.*
3 [with obj.] informal enter (a party) without an invitation or permission; gatecrash.
■ illegally pass (a red traffic light), especially at high speed.
▶ **noun 1** a violent collision, typically of one vehicle with another or with an object: *a car crash.*
■ an instance of an aircraft falling from the sky to hit the land or sea. ■ a sudden loud noise as of something breaking or hitting another object: *he slammed the phone down with a crash.*
2 a sudden disastrous drop in the value or price of something, especially shares: *a stock market crash | the crash of 1987.*
■ the sudden collapse of a business. ■ Computing a sudden failure which puts a system out of action.
▶ **adjective** [attrib.] done rapidly or urgently and involving a concentrated effort: *a crash course in Italian | a crash diet.*
▶ **adverb** with a sudden loud sound: *crash went the bolt.*
– PHRASES **crash and burn** N. Amer. informal come to grief or fail spectacularly.
– ORIGIN late Middle English: imitative, perhaps partly suggested by **CRAZE** and **DASH**.

crash[2] ▶ **noun** [mass noun] dated a coarse plain linen, woollen, or cotton fabric.
– ORIGIN early 19th cent.: from Russian *krashenina* 'dyed coarse linen'.

crash barrier ▶ **noun** Brit. a strong fence at the side of a road or in the middle of a dual carriageway or motorway, intended to reduce the risk of serious accidents.

crash-dive ▶ **verb** [no obj.] (of a submarine) dive rapidly and steeply to a deeper level in an emergency.
■ (of an aircraft) plunge steeply downwards into a crash.
▶ **noun** (**crash dive**) a steep dive of this kind by a submarine or aircraft.

crash helmet ▶ **noun** a helmet worn by a motorcyclist to protect the head in case of a crash.

crashing ▶ **adjective** informal complete; total (used for emphasis): *a crashing bore.*
– DERIVATIVES **crashingly** adverb.

crash-land ▶ **verb** [no obj.] (of an aircraft) land roughly in an emergency, typically without lowering the undercarriage: [as noun **crash-landing**] *his plane made a crash-landing on a motorway.*

crash pad ▶ **noun 1** informal a place to sleep, especially for a single night or in an emergency.
2 a thick piece of shock-absorbing material for the protection of the occupants of an aircraft cockpit or motor vehicle.

crash-test ▶ **verb** [with obj.] deliberately crash (a new vehicle) under controlled conditions in order to evaluate and improve its ability to withstand impact.
▶ **noun** (**crash test**) a test of this kind.

crashworthiness ▶ **noun** [mass noun] the degree to which a vehicle will protect its occupants from the effects of an accident.

crasis /ˈkreɪsɪs/ ▶ **noun** (pl. **crases** /-siːz/) a contraction of two adjacent vowels into one long vowel or diphthong, for example the reduction of words in ancient Greek from three syllables to two.
– ORIGIN mid 16th cent. (as a medical term denoting the blending of physical qualities giving rise to a particular state of health): from Greek *krasis* 'mixture'.

crass ▶ **adjective** showing a grossly insensitive lack of intelligence: *the crass assumptions that men make about women | an act of crass stupidity.*
– DERIVATIVES **crassitude** noun, **crassly** adverb, **crassness** noun.
– ORIGIN late 15th cent. (in the sense 'dense or coarse (in constitution or texture)'): from Latin *crassus* 'solid, thick'.

Crassus /ˈkrasəs/, Marcus Licinius (*c.*115–53 BC), Roman politician. After defeating Spartacus in 71 BC, Crassus joined Caesar and Pompey in the First Triumvirate in 60. In 55 he was made consul and given a special command in Syria, where, after some successes, he was defeated and killed.

-crat ▶ **combining form** denoting a member or supporter of a particular form of government or rule: *plutocrat | technocrat.*
– ORIGIN from French *-crate*, from adjectives ending in *-cratique* (see **-CRATIC**).

cratch ▶ **noun** dialect a long open trough or rack used for holding food for farm animals out of doors.
– ORIGIN Middle English: from Old French *creche*; ultimately of Germanic origin and related to **CRIB**.

crate ▶ **noun 1** a slatted wooden case used for transporting goods: *a crate of bananas.*
■ a square metal or plastic container divided into small individual units, used for transporting or storing bottles: *a milk crate | a crate of beer.*
2 informal, dated an old and dilapidated vehicle.
▶ **verb** [with obj.] (often **be crated**) pack (something) in a crate for transportation.
– DERIVATIVES **crateful** noun (pl. **-fuls**).
– ORIGIN late Middle English: perhaps related to Dutch *krat* 'tailboard of a wagon', earlier 'box of a coach', of unknown origin.

Crater /ˈkreɪtə/ Astronomy a small and faint southern constellation (the Cup), between Hydra and Leo, said to represent the goblet of Apollo.
■ [as genitive **Crateris** /krəˈtɛrɪs/] used with preceding letter or numeral to designate a star in this constellation: *the star Delta Crateris.*
– ORIGIN Latin, from Greek, 'mixing bowl'.

crater ▶ **noun 1** a large bowl-shaped cavity in the ground or a planet, typically one caused by an explosion or the impact of a meteorite or other celestial body.
■ a large pit or hollow forming the mouth of a volcano. ■ a cavity or hole in any surface.
2 a large bowl used in ancient Greece for mixing wine.
▶ **verb** [with obj.] form a crater in (the ground or a planet): *pilots returned to the airfields to crater the runways* | [as adj. **cratered**] *the heavily cratered areas of the moon.*
– ORIGIN early 17th cent. (denoting the hollow forming the mouth of a volcano): via Latin from Greek *kratēr* 'mixing-bowl', from *krasis* 'mixture'.

Crater Lake a lake filling a volcanic crater in the Cascade mountains of SW Oregon. With a depth of more than 600 m (1,968 ft) it is the deepest lake in the US.

b **but** | d **dog** | f **few** | g **get** | h **he** | j **yes** | k **cat** | l **leg** | m **man** | n **no** | p **pen** | r **red** | s **sit** | t **top** | v **voice** | w **we** | z **zoo** | ʃ **she** | ʒ **decision** | θ **thin** | ð **this** | ŋ **ring** | x **loch** | tʃ **chip** | dʒ **jar**

-cratic ▶ combining form relating to a particular kind of government or rule: *bureaucratic* | *democratic*.
– DERIVATIVES **-cratically** combining form in corresponding adverbs.
– ORIGIN from French *-cratique*, from *-cratie* (see **-CRACY**).

C rations ▶ plural noun N. Amer. a type of tinned food formerly used by American soldiers.
– ORIGIN C for *combat*.

craton /ˈkratɒn/ ▶ noun Geology a large stable block of the earth's crust forming the nucleus of a continent.
– DERIVATIVES **cratonic** adjective.
– ORIGIN 1930s: alteration of *kratogen* in the same sense, from Greek *kratos* 'strength'.

cratur /ˈkreɪtʃə/ ▶ noun non-standard spelling of **CREATURE**, used in representing Irish speech: *choked to death on her dentures, poor cratur*.

cravat ▶ noun a short, wide strip of fabric worn by men round the neck and tucked inside an open-necked shirt.
– DERIVATIVES **cravatted** adjective.
– ORIGIN mid 17th cent.: from French *cravate*, from *Cravate* 'Croat' (from German *Krabat*, from Serbo-Croat *Hrvat*), because of the scarf worn by Croatian mercenaries in France.

crave ▶ verb [with obj.] feel a powerful desire for (something): *if only she had shown her daughter the love she craved* | [no obj.] *Will craved for family life.*
■ dated ask for (something): *I must crave your indulgence*.
– DERIVATIVES **craver** noun.
– ORIGIN Old English *crafian* (in the sense 'demand, claim as a right'), of Germanic origin; related to Swedish *kräva*, Danish *kræve* 'demand'. The current sense dates from late Middle English.

craven ▶ adjective contemptibly lacking in courage; cowardly: *a craven abdication of his moral duty*.
▶ noun archaic a cowardly person.
– DERIVATIVES **cravenly** adverb, **cravenness** noun.
– ORIGIN Middle English *cravant* 'defeated', perhaps via Anglo-Norman French from Old French *cravante*, past participle of *cravanter* 'crush, overwhelm', based on Latin *crepare* 'burst'. The change in the ending in the 17th cent. was due to association with past participles ending in *-en* (see **-EN**[3]).

craving ▶ noun a powerful desire for something: *a craving for chocolate*.

craw ▶ noun dated the crop of a bird or insect.
– PHRASES **stick in one's craw** see **STICK**[2].
– ORIGIN late Middle English: from or related to Middle Dutch *crāghe* or Middle Low German *krage* 'neck, throat'.

crawdad /ˈkrɔːdad/ ▶ noun N. Amer. a freshwater crayfish.
– ORIGIN early 20th cent.: fanciful alteration of **CRAWFISH**.

crawfish ▶ noun (pl. same or **-fishes**) another term for SPINY LOBSTER.
■ chiefly N. Amer. a freshwater crayfish.
▶ verb [no obj.] US informal retreat from a position.
– ORIGIN early 17th cent.: variant of **CRAYFISH**.

Crawford[1] /ˈkrɔːfəd/, Joan (1908–77), American actress; born *Lucille le Sueur*. Her film career lasted for over forty years, during which she played the female lead in films such as *Mildred Pierce* (1945), and later appearing in mature roles, such as her part in the horror film *Whatever Happened to Baby Jane?* (1962).

Crawford[2] /ˈkrɔːfəd/, Osbert Guy Stanhope (1886–1957), British archaeologist. He pioneered the use of aerial photography in the detection of previously unlocated or buried archaeological sites and monuments.

crawl ▶ verb 1 [no obj., with adverbial of direction] (of a person) move forward on the hands and knees or by dragging the body close to the ground: *they crawled from under the table*.
■ (of an insect or small animal) move slowly along a surface: *the tiny spider was crawling up Nicky's arm.* ■ (of a vehicle) move at an unusually slow pace: *the traffic was crawling along.* ■ swim using the crawl. ■ [no obj.] informal behave obsequiously or ingratiatingly in the hope of gaining someone's favour: *a reporter's job can involve crawling to objectionable people.* ■ technical (of paint or other liquid) move after application to form an uneven layer over the surface below: *glazes can crawl away from a crack in the piece.*
2 (**be crawling with**) be covered or crowded with

insects or people, to an extent that is disgusting or objectionable: *the place was crawling with soldiers.*
■ [no obj.] feel an unpleasant sensation resembling something moving over the skin as a symptom of fear or disgust: *a person dying in a fire—doesn't it make your skin crawl?*
▶ noun [in sing.] 1 an act of moving on one's hands and knees or dragging one's body along the ground: *they began the crawl back to their own lines.*
■ a slow rate of movement, typically that of a vehicle: *he reduced his speed to a crawl.*
2 a swimming stroke involving alternate overarm movements and rapid kicks of the legs.
– DERIVATIVES **crawlingly** adverb, **crawly** adjective.
– ORIGIN Middle English: of unknown origin; possibly related to Swedish *kravla* and Danish *kravle*.

crawlboard ▶ noun a board used as a means of access to a confined space.

crawler ▶ noun 1 a thing that crawls or moves at a slow pace, especially an insect or a slow-moving vehicle.
■ a tractor or other vehicle moving on an endless caterpillar track. ■ Computing a program that searches the World Wide Web, typically in order to create an index of data.
2 Brit. informal a person who behaves obsequiously in the hope of advantage or advancement.

crawling peg ▶ noun a point on a scale of exchange rates in which a currency's value is allowed to go up or down frequently by small amounts within overall limits.

crawl space ▶ noun an area of limited height under a floor or roof, giving access to wiring and plumbing.

cray ▶ noun Austral./NZ a freshwater crayfish.
– ORIGIN early 20th cent.: abbreviation.

crayfish ▶ noun (pl. same or **-fishes**) (also **freshwater crayfish**) a nocturnal freshwater crustacean that resembles a small lobster and inhabits streams and rivers. Also called **LOBSTER** in Australia and New Zealand.
● Several genera in the infraorder Astacidea, class Malacostraca, including *Astacus* of Europe and *Cambarus* of North America.
■ (also **marine crayfish**) another term for SPINY LOBSTER.
– ORIGIN Middle English: from Old French *crevice*, of Germanic origin and related to German *Krebs* (see **CRAB**[1]). In the 16th cent. or earlier the second syllable was altered by association with **FISH**[1].

crayon ▶ noun a pencil or stick of coloured chalk or wax, used for drawing.
▶ verb [with obj.] draw with a crayon or crayons: *Will crayoned a picture on a legal pad* | [no obj.] *a child crayoning in a colouring book.*
– ORIGIN mid 17th cent.: from French, from *craie* 'chalk', from Latin *creta*.

craze ▶ noun an enthusiasm for a particular activity or object whichtypically appears suddenly and achieves widespread but short-lived popularity: *the new craze for step aerobics.*
▶ verb [with obj.] 1 [usu. as adj. **crazed**] cause (someone) to be or appear to be wildly insane: *a crazed killer.*
2 (often **be crazed**) produce a network of fine cracks on (a surface): *the loch was frozen over but crazed with cracks.*
■ [no obj.] develop such cracks.
– ORIGIN late Middle English (in the sense 'break, shatter, produce cracks'): perhaps of Scandinavian origin and related to Swedish *krasa* 'crunch'.

crazy informal ▶ adjective (**crazier**, **craziest**) 1 mad, especially as manifested in a wild or aggressive way: *Stella went crazy and assaulted a visitor* | *a crazy grin.*
■ extremely annoyed or angry: *the noise they made was driving me crazy.* ■ foolish: *it was crazy to hope that good might come out of this mess.*
2 extremely enthusiastic: *I'm crazy about Cindy* | [in combination] *a football-crazy bunch of boys.*
3 (of an angle) appearing absurdly out of place or in an unlikely position: *the monument leant at a crazy angle.*
■ archaic (of a ship or building) full of cracks or flaws; unsound or shaky.
▶ noun (pl. **-ies**) chiefly N. Amer. a mad person.
– PHRASES **like crazy** to a great degree: *I was laughing like crazy.*
– DERIVATIVES **crazily** adverb, **craziness** noun.

crazy bone ▶ noun US term for **FUNNY BONE**.

Crazy Horse (*c*.1849–77), Sioux chief; Sioux name

Ta-Sunko-Witko. A leading figure in the resistance to white settlement on American Indian land, he was at the centre of the confederation that defeated General Custer at Little Bighorn (1876). He surrendered in 1877 and was killed in custody.

crazy paving ▶ noun [mass noun] Brit. paving made of irregular pieces of flat stone.

crazy quilt ▶ noun a patchwork quilt of a type traditionally made in North America, with patches of randomly varying sizes, shapes, colours, and fabrics.

CRC ▶ abbreviation for ■ (in printing) camera-ready copy. ■ (in computing) cyclic redundancy check or code.

creak ▶ verb [no obj.] (of an object, typically a wooden one) make a harsh high-pitched sound when being moved or when pressure or weight is applied: *the stairs creaked as she went up them* | [with complement] *the garden gate creaked open.*
■ figurative show weakness or frailty under strain: *the system started to creak.*
▶ noun a harsh scraping or squeaking sound: *the creak of a floorboard broke the silence.*
– DERIVATIVES **creakingly** adverb.
– ORIGIN Middle English (as a verb in the sense 'croak'): imitative.

creaky ▶ adjective (**creakier**, **creakiest**) (of an object, typically a wooden one) making or liable to make a harsh high-pitched sound when being moved or when pressure or weight is applied: *I climbed the creaky stairs.*
■ (of a voice) producing such a sound. ■ figurative appearing old-fashioned; decrepit: *the country's creaky legal system.*
– DERIVATIVES **creakily** adverb, **creakiness** noun.

cream ▶ noun [mass noun] 1 the thick white or pale yellow fatty liquid which rises to the top when milk is left to stand and which can be eaten as an accompaniment to desserts or used as a cooking ingredient: *strawberries and cream* | [as modifier] *a cream cake.*
■ the part of a liquid that gathers at the top. ■ figurative the very best of a group of people or things: *the paper's readership is the cream of American society.* ■ a sauce, soup, dessert, or similar food containing cream or milk or having the consistency of cream: *a tin of cream of mushroom soup.* ■ [count noun] a sweet of a specified flavour which is creamy in texture, typically covered with chocolate: *a peppermint cream.* ■ [count noun] a biscuit with a creamy filling: *a custard cream.*
2 a thick liquid or semi-solid cosmetic or medical preparation applied to the skin: *shaving cream* | [count noun] *moisturizing creams.*
3 a very pale yellow or off-white colour: *the dress is available in white or cream* | [as modifier] *a cream linen jacket.*
▶ verb [with obj.] 1 work (butter, typically with sugar) to form a smooth soft paste.
■ [usu. as adj. **creamed**] mash (a cooked vegetable) and mix with milk or cream: *creamed turnips.* ■ add cream to (coffee).
2 rub a cosmetic cream into (the skin): *Madge was creaming her face in front of the mirror.*
3 informal, chiefly N. Amer. defeat (someone) heavily, especially in a sporting contest.
■ (often **be creamed**) hit or collide heavily and violently with (someone), especially in a car: *she got creamed by a speeding car.*
4 [no obj.] vulgar slang (of a person) be sexually aroused, especially to the point of producing sexual secretions.
■ [with obj.] moisten (one's underpants) due to such arousal.
– ORIGIN Middle English: from Old French *cresme*, from a blend of late Latin *cramum* (probably of Gaulish origin) and ecclesiastical Latin *chrisma* (see **CHRISM**).
▶ **cream something off** take the best of a group of people or things, especially in a way that is considered unfair: *the schools cream off some of the more able pupils.* ■ make a disproportionate or excessive profit on a transaction.

cream bun ▶ noun Brit. a bun filled or topped with cream.

cream cheese ▶ noun [mass noun] soft, rich cheese made from unskimmed milk and cream.

cream cracker ▶ noun Brit. a dry unsweetened biscuit, typically eaten with cheese or other savoury toppings.

creamer ▶ **noun** **1** [mass noun] a cream or milk substitute for adding to coffee or tea.
2 N. Amer. a jug for cream.
3 historical a flat dish used for skimming the cream off milk.
■ a machine used for separating cream from milk.

creamery ▶ **noun** (pl. **-ies**) a factory that produces butter and cheese.
■ dated a shop where dairy products are sold.
– ORIGIN mid 19th cent.: from **CREAM**, on the pattern of French *crémerie*.

cream horn ▶ **noun** a pastry shaped like a horn and filled with cream and jam.

cream of tartar ▶ **noun** [mass noun] a white crystalline acidic compound obtained as a by-product of wine fermentation and used chiefly in baking powder.
• Alternative name: **potassium hydrogen tartrate**; chem. formula: $HOOC(CHOH)_2COOK$.

cream puff ▶ **noun** **1** a cake made of puff pastry filled with cream.
2 informal a weak or ineffectual person.
■ derogatory a male homosexual. ■ US [as modifier] denoting something of little consequence or difficulty: *a cream-puff assignment.*
3 N. Amer. informal a second-hand car or other item maintained in excellent condition.

cream sherry ▶ **noun** [mass noun] a full-bodied mellow sweet sherry.

cream soda ▶ **noun** [mass noun] a carbonated vanilla-flavoured soft drink.

cream tea ▶ **noun** Brit. a meal taken in the afternoon consisting of tea to drink with scones, jam, and cream.

creamware ▶ **noun** [mass noun] glazed earthenware pottery of a rich cream colour, developed by Josiah Wedgwood in about 1760.

creamy ▶ **adjective** (**creamier**, **creamiest**) resembling cream in consistency or colour: *beat the sugar and egg yolks together until thick and creamy | creamy white flowers.*
■ containing a lot of cream: *a thick, creamy dressing.*
– DERIVATIVES **creamily** adverb, **creaminess** noun.

creance /ˈkriːəns/ ▶ **noun** Falconry a long fine cord attached to a hawk's leash to prevent escape during training.
– ORIGIN late 15th cent.: from French *créance* 'faith', also denoting a cord to retain a bird of *peu de créance* ('of little faith' i.e. which cannot yet be relied upon).

crease ▶ **noun** **1** a line or ridge produced on paper or cloth by folding, pressing, or crushing it: *khaki trousers with knife-edge creases.*
■ a wrinkle or furrow in the skin, typically of the face, caused by age or a particular facial expression.
2 Cricket any of a number of lines marked on the pitch at specified places. See **POPPING CREASE**, **BOWLING CREASE**, and **RETURN CREASE**.
■ (**the crease**) the position of a batsman during their innings: *England were 15 for 3 overnight, with Stewart and Russell at the crease.* ■ (**the crease**) an area around the goal in ice hockey or lacrosse which the players may not enter unless the puck or the ball has already done so.
▶ **verb** [with obj.] **1** make a crease in (cloth or paper): *he sank into the chair, careful not to crease his dinner jacket* | [as adj. **creased**] *a creased piece of paper.*
■ cause a crease to appear temporarily in (the face or its features), typically as a result of the expression of an emotion or feeling: *a small frown creased her forehead.* ■ [no obj.] (of a feature of the face) be marked by creases in such a way: *his eyes creased in amusement.*
2 (of a bullet) graze (someone or something), causing little damage: *a bullet creased his thigh.*
■ Brit. informal hit or punch (someone) hard: *clap or I'll crease you.*
– ORIGIN late 16th cent.: probably a variant of **CREST**.
▶ **crease up** (or **crease someone up**) Brit. informal burst out or cause to burst out laughing: *Jo could imitate anybody and always made him crease up.*

create ▶ **verb** **1** [with obj.] bring (something) into existence: *he created a thirty-acre lake | over 170 jobs were created.*
■ cause (something) to happen as a result of one's actions: *divorce created only problems for children.* ■ (of an actor) originate (a role) by playing a character for the first time. ■ [with obj. and complement] invest (someone) with a title of nobility: *he was created a baronet.*
2 [no obj.] Brit. informal make a fuss; complain: *little kids create because they hate being ignored.*
– ORIGIN late Middle English (in the sense 'form out of nothing', used of a divine or supernatural being): from Latin *creat-* 'produced', from the verb *creare.*

creatine /ˈkriːətiːn/ ▶ **noun** [mass noun] Biochemistry a compound formed in protein metabolism and present in much living tissue. It is involved in the supply of energy for muscular contraction.
• A guanidine derivative, usually present as a phosphate; chem. formula: $C_4H_9N_3O_2$.
– ORIGIN mid 19th cent.: formed irregularly from Greek *kreas* 'meat' + **-INE**[4].

creatinine /krɪˈatɪniːn/ ▶ **noun** [mass noun] Biochemistry a compound which is produced by metabolism of creatine and excreted in the urine.
• An anhydride of creatine; chem. formula: $C_7H_4N_3O$.

creation ▶ **noun** [mass noun] **1** the action or process of bringing something into existence: *creation of a coalition government | job creation.*
■ [count noun] a thing which has been made or invented, especially something showing artistic talent: *she treats fictional creations as if they were real people.*
2 (**the Creation**) the bringing into of existence of the universe, especially when regarded as an act of God.
■ [mass noun] everything so created; the universe: *our alienation from the rest of Creation.*
3 the action or process of investing someone with a title of nobility.
– ORIGIN late Middle English: via Old French from Latin *creatio(n-)*, from the verb *creare* (see **CREATE**).

creationism ▶ **noun** [mass noun] the belief that the universe and living organisms originate from specific acts of divine creation, as in the biblical account, rather than by natural processes such as evolution.
■ another term for **CREATION SCIENCE**.
– DERIVATIVES **creationist** noun & adjective.

creation science ▶ **noun** [mass noun] the reinterpretation of scientific knowledge in accord with belief in the literal truth of the Bible, especially regarding the origin of matter, life, and humankind.

creative ▶ **adjective** relating to or involving the imagination or original ideas, especially in the production of an artistic work: *change unleashes people's creative energy | creative writing.*
■ (of a person) having good imagination or original ideas: *a creative team of designers and make-up artists.*
▶ **noun** a person who is creative, typically in a professional context.
– DERIVATIVES **creatively** adverb, **creativeness** noun, **creativity** noun.

creative accountancy (also **creative accounting**) ▶ **noun** [mass noun] informal the exploitation of loopholes in financial regulation in order to gain advantage or present figures in a misleadingly favourable light.

creator ▶ **noun** a person or thing that brings something into existence.
■ (**the Creator**) used as a name for God.

creature ▶ **noun** an animal, as distinct from a human being: *night sounds of birds and other creatures.*
■ an animal or person: *as fellow creatures on this planet, animals deserve respect.* ■ a fictional or imaginary being, typically a frightening one: *a creature from outer space.* ■ archaic anything living or existing: *dress, jewels, and other transitory creatures.* ■ [with adj.] a person of a specified kind, typically one viewed with pity, contempt, or desire: *you heartless creature!* ■ a person or organization considered to be under the complete control of another: *the village teacher was expected to be the creature of his employer.*
– PHRASES **creature of habit** a person who follows an unvarying routine.
– DERIVATIVES **creaturely** adjective.
– ORIGIN Middle English (in the sense 'something created'): via Old French from late Latin *creatura*, from the verb *creare* (see **CREATE**).

creature comforts ▶ **plural noun** material comforts that contribute to physical ease and well-being, such as good food and accommodation.

crèche /krɛʃ, kreɪʃ/ ▶ **noun** **1** Brit. a nursery where babies and young children are cared for during the working day.
2 N. Amer. a representation of the nativity scene.
– ORIGIN late 18th cent. (in sense 2): French (see also **CRATCH**).

Crécy, Battle of /ˈkrɛsi/ a battle between the English and the French in 1346 near the village of Crécy-en-Ponthieu in Picardy, at which the forces of Edward III defeated those of Philip VI. It was the first major English victory of the Hundred Years War.

cred ▶ **noun** informal term for **STREET CREDIBILITY**.

credal /ˈkriːd(ə)l/ (also **creedal**) ▶ **adjective** of or relating to a statement of Christian or other religious belief.

credence /ˈkriːd(ə)ns/ ▶ **noun** **1** [mass noun] belief in or acceptance of something as true: *psychoanalysis finds little credence among laymen.*
■ the likelihood of something being true; plausibility: *being called upon by the media as an expert **lends credence** to one's opinions.*
2 [usu. as modifier] a small side table, shelf, or niche in a church for holding the elements of the Eucharist before they are consecrated: *a credence table.*
– PHRASES **give credence to** accept as true.
– ORIGIN Middle English: via Old French from medieval Latin *credentia*, from Latin *credent-* 'believing', from the verb *credere.*

credential /krɪˈdɛnʃ(ə)l/ ▶ **noun** (usu. **credentials**) a qualification, achievement, personal quality, or aspect of a person's background, typically when used to indicate that they are suitable for something: *recruitment is based mainly on academic credentials.*
■ a document or certificate proving a person's identity or qualifications. ■ a letter of introduction given by a government to an ambassador before a new posting.
– ORIGIN late Middle English: from medieval Latin *credentialis*, from *credentia* (see **CREDENCE**). The original use was as an adjective in the sense 'giving credence to, recommending', frequently in *credential letters* or *papers*, hence *credentials* (mid 17th cent.).

credenza /krɪˈdɛnzə/ ▶ **noun** a sideboard or cupboard.
– ORIGIN late 19th cent.: Italian, from medieval Latin *credentia* (see **CREDENCE**).

credibility ▶ **noun** [mass noun] the quality of being trusted and believed in: *the government's loss of credibility.*
■ the quality of being convincing or believable: *the book's anecdotes have scant regard for credibility.* ■ another term for **STREET CREDIBILITY**.
– ORIGIN mid 16th cent.: from medieval Latin *credibilitas*, from Latin *credibilis* (see **CREDIBLE**).

credibility gap ▶ **noun** an apparent difference between what is said or promised and what happens or is true.

credible ▶ **adjective** able to be believed; convincing: *few people found his story credible | a credible witness.*
■ capable of persuading people that something will happen or be successful: *a credible threat.*
– DERIVATIVES **credibly** adverb.
– ORIGIN late Middle English: from Latin *credibilis*, from *credere* 'believe'.

credit ▶ **noun** **1** [mass noun] the ability of a customer to obtain goods or services before payment, based on the trust that payment will be made in the future: *I've got unlimited credit.*
■ the money lent or made available under such an arrangement: *the bank refused to extend their credit* | [as modifier] *he was exceeding his credit limit.*
2 an entry recording a sum received, listed on the right-hand side or column of an account. The opposite of **DEBIT**.
■ a payment received: *you need to record debits or credits made to your account.*
3 [mass noun] public acknowledgement or praise, typically that given or received when a person's responsibility for an action or idea becomes or is made apparent: *the Prime Minister was quick to claim the credit for abolishing the tax.*
■ [in sing.] a source of pride, typically someone or something that reflects well on another person or organization: *the fans are **a credit to** the club.* ■ (also **credit title**) [count noun] (usu. **credits**) an acknowledgement of a contributor's services to a film or television programme, typically one of a list which is scrolled down the screen at the beginning or end of a film or programme: *the closing credits finished rolling.*
4 [mass noun] chiefly N. Amer. the acknowledgement of a

student's completion of a course or activity that counts towards a degree or diploma as maintained in a school's records: *a student can earn one unit of academic credit*.
■ [count noun] a unit of study counting towards a degree or diploma: *the National Certificate consists of twelve credits*. ■ [count noun] Brit. a grade above a pass in an examination. ■ acknowledgement of merit in an examination which is reflected in the marks awarded: *candidates will receive credit for accuracy and style*.
5 [mass noun] archaic the quality of being believed or credited: *the abstract philosophy of Cicero has lost its credit*.
■ favourable estimation; good reputation: *John Gilpin was a citizen of credit and renown*.
▶ **verb** (**credited**, **crediting**) [with obj.] (often **be credited**) **1** publicly acknowledge someone as a participant in the production of (something published or broadcast): *the screenplay is credited to one American and two Japanese writers*.
■ (**credit someone with**) ascribe (an achievement or good quality) to someone: *he is credited with painting one hundred and twenty-five canvases*.
2 add (an amount of money) to an account: *this deferred tax can be credited to the profit and loss account*.
3 [often with modal] believe (something surprising or unlikely): *you would hardly credit it—but it was true*.
– PHRASES **be in credit** (of an account) have money in it. **credit where credit is due** praise given when it is deserved, even if one is reluctant to give it. **do someone credit** (or **do credit to someone**) make someone worthy of praise or respect: *your concern does you credit*. **give someone credit for** commend someone for (a quality or achievement), especially with reluctance or surprise: *please give me credit for some sense*. **have something to one's credit** have achieved something notable: *he has 65 Tournament wins to his credit*. **on credit** with an arrangement to pay later. **on the credit side** as a good aspect of the situation: *on the credit side, the text is highly readable*. **to one's credit** used to indicate that something praiseworthy has been achieved, especially despite difficulties: *to their credit, both sides managed to overcome the elements and produce an exciting match*.
– ORIGIN mid 16th cent. (originally in the senses 'belief', 'credibility'): from French *crédit*, probably via Italian *credito* from Latin *creditum*, neuter past participle of *credere* 'believe, trust'.

creditable ▶ **adjective** (of a performance, effort, or action) deserving public acknowledgement and praise but not necessarily outstanding or successful: *a very creditable 2–4 defeat*.
– DERIVATIVES **creditability** noun, **creditably** adverb.

credit account ▶ **noun** Brit. another term for **CHARGE ACCOUNT**.

credit agency ▶ **noun** see **CREDIT REFERENCE AGENCY**.

credit analyst ▶ **noun** a person employed to assess the credit rating of people or companies.

credit card ▶ **noun** a small plastic card issued by a bank, building society, etc., allowing the holder to purchase goods or services on credit.

credit insurance ▶ **noun** [mass noun] insurance taken out to protect against bad debts.

credit line ▶ **noun** another term for *line of credit* (see **LINE**¹).

credit note ▶ **noun** Brit. a receipt given by a shop to a customer who has returned goods, which can be offset against future purchases.

creditor ▶ **noun** a person or company to whom money is owing.

credit rating ▶ **noun** an estimate of the ability of a person or organization to fulfil their financial commitments, based on previous dealings. ■ [mass noun] the process of assessing this.

credit reference agency (also **credit agency**) ▶ **noun** a company which collects information relating to the credit ratings of individuals and makes it available to hire-purchase companies, finance houses, etc.

credit standing ▶ **noun** the reputation of a person or organization with regard to capability and promptness in meeting financial obligations.

credit title ▶ **noun** see **CREDIT** (sense 3).

credit transfer ▶ **noun** [mass noun] **1** a system whereby successfully completed units of study

contributing towards a degree or diploma can be transferred from one course to another.
2 Brit. a direct payment of money from one bank account to another.

credit union ▶ **noun** a non-profit-making money cooperative whose members can borrow from pooled deposits at low interest rates.

creditworthy ▶ **adjective** (of a person or company) considered suitable to receive credit, especially because of being reliable in paying money back in the past.
– DERIVATIVES **creditworthiness** noun.

credo /ˈkriːdəʊ, ˈkreɪ-/ ▶ **noun** (pl. **-os**) a statement of the beliefs or aims which guide someone's actions: *he announced his credo in his first editorial*.
■ (**Credo**) a creed of the Christian Church in Latin. ■ (**Credo**) a musical setting of the Nicene Creed, typically as part of a mass.
– ORIGIN Middle English: Latin, 'I believe'. Compare with **CREED**.

credulity /krɪˈdjuːlɪti/ ▶ **noun** [mass noun] a tendency to be too ready to believe that something is real or true.

credulous /ˈkrɛdjʊləs/ ▶ **adjective** having or showing too great a readiness to believe things.
– DERIVATIVES **credulously** adverb, **credulousness** noun.
– ORIGIN late 16th cent. (in the general sense 'inclined to believe'): from Latin *credulus* (from *credere* 'believe') + **-OUS**.

Cree /kriː/ ▶ **noun** (pl. same or **Crees**) **1** a member of an American Indian people living in a vast area of central Canada.
2 [mass noun] the Algonquian language of this people, closely related to Montagnais. It has about 60,000 speakers.
▶ **adjective** of or relating to the Cree or their language.
– ORIGIN from Canadian French *Cris*, abbreviation of *Cristinaux*, from Algonquian.

creed ▶ **noun** a system of Christian or other religious belief; a faith: *people of many creeds and cultures*.
■ (often **the Creed**) a formal statement of Christian beliefs, especially the Apostles' Creed or the Nicene Creed. ■ a set of beliefs or aims which guide someone's actions: *liberalism was more than a political creed*.
– ORIGIN Old English, from Latin **CREDO**.

creedal ▶ **adjective** variant spelling of **CREDAL**.

Creek /kriːk/ ▶ **noun** (pl. same) **1** a member of a confederacy of American Indian peoples of the south-eastern US in the 16th to 19th centuries. The power of the Creek Indians was broken in 1814; their descendants now live mainly in Oklahoma.
2 [mass noun] the Muskogean language that was spoken by members of this confederacy.
▶ **adjective** of, relating to, or denoting this confederacy.
– ORIGIN from **CREEK**, because they lived beside the waterways of the flatlands of Georgia and Alabama.

creek ▶ **noun** an inlet in a shoreline, channel in a marsh, or other narrow, sheltered waterway.
■ N. Amer. & Austral./NZ a stream, brook, or minor tributary of a river.
– PHRASES **be up the creek** informal **1** (also **be up the creek without a paddle**) be in severe difficulty or trouble, especially with no means of extricating oneself from it. **2** Brit. be stupid or misguided. **be up shit creek** see **SHIT**.
– ORIGIN Middle English: from Old French *crique* or from Old Norse *kriki* 'nook'; perhaps reinforced by Middle Dutch *krēke*; of unknown ultimate origin.

creel ▶ **noun** **1** a large wicker basket for carrying fish.
■ an angler's fishing basket. ■ a lobster pot made of wickerwork.
2 a rack holding bobbins or spools when spinning.
– ORIGIN Middle English (in sense 1; originally Scots and northern English): of unknown origin. Sense 2 (perhaps the same word) dates from the mid 19th cent.

creep ▶ **verb** (past and past participle **crept** /krɛpt/) [no obj.] **1** [usu. with adverbial of direction] move slowly and carefully, especially in order to avoid being heard or noticed: *he crept downstairs, hardly making any noise* | *they were taught how to creep up on an enemy*.
■ (of a thing) move very slowly at an inexorably steady pace: *the fog was creeping up from the marsh*. ■ (of a plant) grow along the ground or other surface by

means of extending stems or branches: [as adj. **creeping**] *tufts of fine leaves grow on creeping rhizomes*. ■ (of a plastic solid) undergo gradual deformation under stress.
2 (**creep in/into**) (of an unwanted and negative characteristic or fact) occur or develop gradually and almost imperceptibly: *errors crept into his game* | [as adj. **creeping**] *the creeping privatization of the health service*.
■ (**creep up**) increase slowly but steadily in number or amount: *interest rates have been creeping up in the past few weeks*. ■ (**creep to**) informal behave towards (someone) in an obsequious way in the hope of advancement.
▶ **noun 1** informal a detestable person.
■ a person who behaves in an obsequious way in the hope of advancement.
2 [mass noun] slow movement, especially at a steady but almost imperceptible pace: *an attempt to prevent this slow creep of costs*.
■ the tendency of a car with automatic transmission to move when in gear without the accelerator being pressed. ■ the gradual downward movement of disintegrated rock or soil due to gravitational forces: *stones and earth slowly slip down the slopes by soil creep*. ■ the gradual deformation of a plastic solid under stress. ■ gradual bulging of the floor of a mine owing to pressure on the pillars.
3 Brit. an opening in a hedge or wall for an animal to pass through.
■ a feeding enclosure with a long narrow entrance designed to admit only young animals. ■ [mass noun] Brit. solid food given to young farm animals in order to wean them.
– PHRASES **give someone the creeps** informal induce a feeling of revulsion or fear in someone. **make one's flesh creep** cause one to feel disgust or revulsion and have a sensation like that of something crawling over the skin.
– ORIGIN Old English *crēopan* 'move with the body close to the ground', of Germanic origin; related to Dutch *kruipen*. Sense 1 of the verb dates from Middle English.

creeper ▶ **noun 1** Botany any plant that grows along the ground, around another plant, or up a wall by means of extending stems or branches.
2 [with modifier] any of a number of small birds that creep around in trees, vegetation, etc.:
● (**brown creeper**) N. Amer. the American treecreeper (*Certhia americana*, family Certhiidae). ● (**brown creeper**) NZ a New Zealand songbird (*Mohoua* (or *Finschia*) *novaeseelandiae*, family Pachycephalidae or Acanthizidae). ● a Philippine songbird (family Rhabdornithidae and genus *Rhabdornis*: two species). ● a Hawaiian honeycreeper (genus *Paroreomyza*, family Drepanididae: three species).
3 informal (**creepers**) short for **BROTHEL CREEPERS**.

creepie ▶ **noun** (pl. **-ies**) chiefly Scottish a low stool.
– ORIGIN mid 17th cent.: from the verb **CREEP** + **-IE**.

creeping Jenny ▶ **noun** a trailing evergreen European plant with round glossy leaves and yellow flowers, growing in damp places and by water. Also called **MONEYWORT**.
● *Lysimachia nummularia*, family Primulaceae.

creeping Jesus ▶ **noun** Brit. informal a person who is obsequious or hypocritically pious.

creeping paralysis ▶ **noun** less technical term for **LOCOMOTOR ATAXIA**.

creepy ▶ **adjective** (**creepier**, **creepiest**) informal causing an unpleasant feeling of fear or unease: *the creepy feelings one often gets in a strange house*.
– DERIVATIVES **creepily** adverb, **creepiness** noun.

creepy-crawly informal ▶ **noun** (pl. **-ies**) a spider, worm, or other small flightless creature, especially when considered unpleasant or frightening.
▶ **adjective** causing an unpleasant feeling of fear or unease: *creepy-crawly stories*.

creese ▶ **noun** archaic spelling of **KRIS**.

cremaster /krɪˈmastə/ ▶ **noun 1** (also **cremaster muscle**) Anatomy the muscle of the spermatic cord, by which the testicle can be partially raised.
2 Entomology the hook-like tip of a butterfly pupa, serving as an anchorage point.
– ORIGIN late 17th cent.: from Greek *kremastēr*, from *krema-* 'hang'.

cremate ▶ **verb** [with obj.] (usu. **be cremated**) dispose of (a dead person's body) by burning it to ashes, typically after a funeral ceremony.
– DERIVATIVES **cremation** noun, **cremator** noun.
– ORIGIN late 19th cent. (as *cremation*): from Latin *cremare* 'burn'.

crematorium /ˌkrɛməˈtɔːrɪəm/ ▶ **noun** (pl.

crematoria or **crematoriums**) a place where a dead person's body is cremated.
– ORIGIN late 19th cent.: modern Latin, from *cremare* 'burn'.

crematory /ˈkrɛmət(ə)ri/ ▶ **adjective** of or relating to cremation.
▶ **noun** (pl. **-ies**) North American term for **CREMATORIUM**.

crème anglaise /ˌkrɛm ɒ̃ˈɡleɪz/ ▶ **noun** [mass noun] a rich egg custard.
– ORIGIN French, literally 'English cream'.

crème brûlée /ˌkrɛm bruːˈleɪ/ ▶ **noun** (pl. **crèmes brûlées** pronunc. same or **crème brûlées** /-ˈleɪz/) [mass noun] a dessert of custard topped with caramelized sugar.
– ORIGIN French, literally 'burnt cream'.

crème caramel /krɛm ˌkarəˈmɛl, ˈkarəmɛl/ ▶ **noun** (pl. **crèmes caramel** pronunc. same or **crème caramels**) [mass noun] a custard dessert made with whipped cream and eggs and topped with caramel.
– ORIGIN French.

crème de cacao /ˌkrɛm də kəˈkeɪəʊ, -ˈkaʊ/ ▶ **noun** [mass noun] a chocolate-flavoured liqueur.
– ORIGIN French, literally 'cream of cacao'.

crème de cassis /ˌkrɛm də kaˈsiːs/ ▶ **noun** see **CASSIS**[1].
– ORIGIN French, literally 'cream of blackcurrant'.

crème de la crème /ˌkrɛm də la ˈkrɛm, French krɛm də la krɛm/ ▶ **noun** the best person or thing of a particular kind: *the crème de la crème of the dancers have left the country.*
– ORIGIN French, literally 'cream of the cream'.

crème de menthe /ˌkrɛm də ˈmɒnθ, ˈmɒ̃t/ ▶ **noun** [mass noun] a peppermint-flavoured liqueur.
– ORIGIN French, literally 'cream of mint'.

crème fraiche /krɛm ˈfrɛʃ/ ▶ **noun** [mass noun] a type of thick cream made from double cream with the addition of buttermilk, sour cream, or yogurt.
– ORIGIN from French *crème fraîche*, literally 'fresh cream'.

Cremona /krɪˈməʊnə, krɛ-/ a city in Lombardy, in northern Italy; pop. 75,160 (1990). Between the 16th and the 18th century the city was home to three renowned families of violin-makers: the Amati, the Guarneri, and the Stradivari.

crenate /ˈkriːneɪt/ ▶ **adjective** Botany & Zoology (especially of a leaf of shell) having a round-toothed or scalloped edge. Compare with **CRENULATE**.
– DERIVATIVES **crenated** adjective, **crenation** noun.
– ORIGIN late 18th cent. (earlier as *crenated*): from modern Latin *crenatus*, from popular Latin *crena* 'notch'.

crenel /ˈkrɛn(ə)l/ (also **crenelle** /krɪˈnɛl/) ▶ **noun** an indentation in the battlements of a fort or castle, used for shooting or firing missiles through.
– ORIGIN late 15th cent.: from Old French, based on popular Latin *crena* 'notch'.

crenellate /ˈkrɛn(ə)leɪt/ (also **crenelate**) ▶ **verb** [with obj.] [usu. as adj. **crenellated**] chiefly historical provide (a wall of a building) with battlements.
– ORIGIN early 19th cent.: from French *créneler*, from Old French *crenel* (see **CRENEL**).

crenellations ▶ **plural noun** the battlements of a castle or other building.

crenulate /ˈkrɛnjʊleɪt/ ▶ **adjective** technical (especially of a leaf, shell, or shoreline) having a finely scalloped or notched outline or edge. Compare with **CRENATE**.
– DERIVATIVES **crenulated** adjective, **crenulation** noun.
– ORIGIN late 18th cent.: from modern Latin *crenulatus*, from *crenula*, diminutive of *crena* 'notch'.

creodont /ˈkriːədɒnt/ ▶ **noun** a fossil carnivorous mammal of the early Tertiary period, ancestral to modern carnivores.
• Order Creodonta: several families.
– ORIGIN late 19th cent.: from modern Latin *Creodonta* (plural), from Greek *kreas* 'flesh' + *odous, odont-* 'tooth'.

Creole /ˈkriːəʊl/ (also **creole**) ▶ **noun 1** a person of mixed European and black descent, especially in the Caribbean.
■ a descendant of Spanish or other European settlers in the Caribbean or Central or South America. ■ a white descendant of French settlers in Louisiana and other parts of the southern US.
2 a mother tongue formed from the contact of a European language (especially English, French, Spanish, or Portuguese) with local languages (especially African languages spoken by slaves in the W. Indies), usually through an earlier pidgin stage: *a Portuguese-based Creole.*
▶ **adjective** of or relating to a Creole or Creoles.
– ORIGIN from French *créole, criole*, from Spanish *criollo*, probably from Portuguese *crioulo* 'black person born in Brazil, home-born slave', from *criar* 'to breed', from Latin *creare* 'produce, create'.

creolize /ˈkriːə(ʊ)lʌɪz, ˈkriɒl-/ (also **-ise**) ▶ **verb** [with obj.] form (a Creole language) from the contact of a European language with a local language: [as adj. **creolized**] *a creolized variety of French.*
– DERIVATIVES **creolization** /-ˈzeɪʃ(ə)n/ noun.

creosol /ˈkriːəsɒl/ ▶ **noun** [mass noun] Chemistry a colourless liquid which is the chief constituent of wood-tar creosote.
• Alternative name: **2-methoxy-4-methylphenol**; chem. formula: $C_8H_{10}O_2$.
– ORIGIN mid 19th cent.: from **CREOSOTE** + **-OL**.

creosote ▶ **noun** (also **creosote oil**) [mass noun] a dark brown oil distilled from coal tar and used as a wood preservative. It contains a number of phenols, cresols, and other organic compounds.
■ a colourless, pungent, oily liquid, containing creosol and other compounds, distilled from wood tar and used as an antiseptic.
▶ **verb** [with obj.] treat (wood) with creosote.
– ORIGIN mid 19th cent.: coined in German from Greek *kreas* 'flesh' + *sōtēr* 'preserver', with reference to its antiseptic properties.

creosote bush ▶ **noun** a shrub native to arid parts of Mexico and the western US. Its leaves smell of creosote and when steeped in boiling water they yield an antiseptic lotion.
• *Larrea tridentata*, family Zygophyllaceae.

crêpe /kreɪp/ ▶ **noun 1** [mass noun] a light, thin fabric with a wrinkled surface: [as modifier] *a crêpe bandage.*
■ (also **crêpe rubber**) hard-wearing wrinkled rubber, used especially for the soles of shoes.
2 also /krɛp/ a thin pancake.
– DERIVATIVES **crêpey** (also **crêpy**) adjective.
– ORIGIN late 18th cent.: French, from Old French *crespe* 'curled, frizzed', from Latin *crispus*.

crêpe de Chine /də ˈʃiːn/ ▶ **noun** [mass noun] a fine crêpe of silk or similar fabric.
– ORIGIN late 19th cent.: French, literally 'crêpe of China'.

crepe myrtle ▶ **noun** variant spelling of **CRAPE MYRTLE**.

crêpe paper ▶ **noun** [mass noun] thin, crinkled paper resembling crêpe, used especially for making decorations.

crêperie /ˈkreɪpəri, ˈkrɛp-, French krɛpri/ ▶ **noun** (pl. **-ies**) a small restaurant, typically one in France, in which a variety of crêpes are served.
– ORIGIN French.

crêpe Suzette ▶ **noun** (pl. **crêpes Suzette** pronunc. same) a thin dessert pancake flamed and served in alcohol.

crépinette /ˌkreɪpɪˈnɛt, French krepinɛt/ ▶ **noun** a flat sausage consisting of minced meat and savoury stuffing wrapped in pieces of pork caul.
– ORIGIN French, diminutive of *crépine* 'caul'.

crepitate /ˈkrɛpɪteɪt/ ▶ **verb** [no obj.] make a crackling sound: *the night crepitates with an airy whistling cacophony* | [as adj. **crepitating**] *spidery fingers of crepitating electricity.*
– DERIVATIVES **crepitant** adjective.
– ORIGIN early 17th cent. (in the sense 'break wind'): from Latin *crepitat-* 'crackled, rustled', from the verb *crepitare*, from *crepare* 'to rattle'.

crepitation ▶ **noun** a crackling or rattling sound: *pistol-like crepitations.*
■ Medicine a crackling sound made when breathing with an inflamed lung, detected using a stethoscope. ■ [mass noun] Entomology the explosive ejection of irritant fluid from the abdomen of a bombardier beetle.
– ORIGIN mid 17th cent.: from French *crépitation* or Latin *crepitatio(n-)*, from the verb *crepitare* (see **CREPITATE**).

crepitus /ˈkrɛpɪtəs/ ▶ **noun** [mass noun] Medicine a grating sound or sensation produced by friction between bone and cartilage or the fractured parts of a bone.
■ the production of crepitations in the lungs; rale.
– ORIGIN early 19th cent.: from Latin, from *crepare* 'rattle'.

crépon /ˈkreɪpɒn/ ▶ **noun** [mass noun] a fabric resembling crêpe, but heavier and with a more pronounced crinkled effect.
– ORIGIN late 19th cent.: French.

crept past and past participle of **CREEP**.

crepuscular /krɪˈpʌskjʊlə, krɛ-/ ▶ **adjective** of, resembling, or relating to twilight.
■ Zoology (of an animal) appearing or active in twilight.
– ORIGIN mid 17th cent.: from Latin *crepusculum* 'twilight' + **-AR**[1].

Cres. ▶ **abbreviation for** crescent.

cresc. (also **cres.**) Music ▶ **abbreviation for** crescendo.

crescendo /krɪˈʃɛndəʊ/ ▶ **noun 1** (pl. **crescendos** or **crescendi** /-di/) Music a gradual increase in loudness in a piece of music.
■ Music a passage of music marked or performed in this way. ■ the loudest point reached in a gradually increasing sound: *the port engine revs rose **to a crescendo.*** ■ a progressive increase in force or intensity: *a crescendo of misery.* ■ the most intense point reached in this; a climax: *the hysteria **reached a crescendo** around the spring festival.*
▶ **adverb** & **adjective** Music with a gradual increase in loudness: [as adj.] *a short crescendo kettledrum roll.*
▶ **verb** (**-oes, -oed**) [no obj.] increase in loudness or intensity: *the reluctant cheers began to crescendo.*
– ORIGIN late 18th cent.: Italian, present participle of *crescere* 'to increase', from Latin *crescere* 'grow'.

crescent /ˈkrɛz(ə)nt, -s-/ ▶ **noun 1** the curved sickle shape of the waxing or waning moon.
■ a representation of such a shape used as an emblem of Islam or of Turkey. ■ (**the Crescent**) chiefly historical the political power of Islam or of the Ottoman Empire.
2 a thing which has the shape of a single curve, especially one that is broad in the centre and tapers to a point at each end: *a three-mile crescent of golden sand* | [in combination] *a crescent-shaped building.*
■ [usu. in names] chiefly Brit. a street or terrace of houses forming an arc: *we lived at Westway Crescent.* ■ Heraldry a charge in the form of a crescent,typically with the points upward (also a mark of cadency for a second son).
3 a moth or butterfly which bears crescent-shaped markings on the wings, in particular:
• an orange or brown American butterfly with a silvery mark on the underside of the hindwing (genus *Phyciodes*, subfamily Melitaeinae, family Nymphalidae). • a brownish European moth with a pale mark on the forewing (several species in the family Noctuidae, in particular *Celaena leucostigma*).
▶ **adjective 1** [attrib.] having the shape of a crescent: *a crescent moon.*
2 poetic/literary growing, increasing, or developing.
– DERIVATIVES **crescentic** /-ˈsɛntɪk/ adjective.
– ORIGIN late Middle English *cressant*, from Old French *creissant*, from Latin *crescere* 'grow'. The spelling change in the 17th century was due to the influence of the Latin.

crescent wrench ▶ **noun** N. Amer. an adjustable spanner designed to grip hexagonal nuts, with an adjusting screw fitted in the crescent-shaped head of the spanner.

cresol /ˈkriːsɒl/ ▶ **noun** Chemistry each of three isomeric crystalline compounds present in coal-tar creosote, used as disinfectants.
• The *ortho-*, *meta-*, and *para-*methyl derivatives of phenol; chem. formula: $CH_3C_6H_4OH$.
– ORIGIN mid 19th cent.: from **CREOSOTE** + **-OL**.

cress ▶ **noun** [mass noun] a plant of the cabbage family, typically having small white flowers and pungent leaves. Some kinds are edible and are eaten raw as salad.
• *Barbarea* and other genera, family Cruciferae: several species, including **garden cress** (used in mustard and cress) and **watercress**.
– ORIGIN Old English *cresse, cærse*, of West Germanic origin; related to Dutch *kers* and German *Kresse*.

cresset /ˈkrɛsɪt/ ▶ **noun** historical a metal container of oil, grease, wood, or coal set alight for illumination and typically mounted on a pole.
– ORIGIN late Middle English: from Old French, from *craisse*, variant of *graisse* 'oil, grease'.

Cressida /ˈkrɛsɪdə/ (in medieval legends of the Trojan War) the daughter of Calchas, a priest. She was faithless to her lover Troilus, a son of Priam.

Crest (in the UK) a computer system for buying and selling shares, introduced in 1996.
– ORIGIN an arbitrary formation.

crest ▶ **noun 1** a comb or tuft of feathers, fur, or skin on the head of a bird or other animal.

■a thing resembling such a tuft, especially a plume of feathers on a helmet.
2 the top of something, especially a mountain or hill: *she reached the crest of the hill.*
■the curling foamy top of a wave. ■ Anatomy a ridge along the surface of a bone. ■ the upper line of the neck of a horse or other mammal.
3 Heraldry a distinctive device borne above the shield of a coat of arms (originally as worn on a helmet), or separately reproduced, for example on writing paper or silverware, to represent a family or corporate body.
▶**verb** [with obj.] reach the top of (something such as a hill or wave).
■[no obj.] (of a wave) form a curling foamy top. ■ (**be crested with**) have attached or affixed at the top: *his helmet was crested with a fan of spikes.*
– PHRASES **on the crest of a wave** at a very successful point: *his career is on the crest of a wave at present.*
– DERIVATIVES **crestless** adjective.
– ORIGIN Middle English: from Old French *creste*, from Latin *crista* 'tuft, plume'.

Cresta Run a hazardously winding, steeply banked channel of ice built each year at the Cresta Valley, St Moritz, Switzerland, as a tobogganing course, on which competitors race on light toboggans in a characteristic head-first position. Such a run was first built in 1884.

crested ▶**adjective** **1** (of a bird or other animal) having a comb or tuft of feathers, fur, or skin on the head: *the crested drake mandarin duck* | [in combination] *a plush-crested jay.*
2 emblazoned with a coat of arms or other emblem: *crested notepaper.*

crested newt (also **great crested newt**) ▶**noun** a large Eurasian newt, the male of which has a tall crest along the back and tail during the breeding season. Also called **WARTY NEWT**.
● *Triturus cristatus*, family Salamandridae.

crested tit ▶**noun** a small European tit (songbird) with a short crest, living chiefly in coniferous woodland.
● *Parus cristatus*, family Paridae.

crested wood ibis ▶**noun** see **WOOD IBIS** (sense 2).

crestfallen ▶**adjective** sad and disappointed: *he came back empty-handed and crestfallen.*
– ORIGIN late 16th cent.: figuratively, from the original use referring to a mammal or bird having a fallen or drooping crest.

crestfish ▶**noun** (pl. same or **-fishes**) a very elongated silvery marine fish with a crimson dorsal fin running the full length of its body and a forehead that projects forward into a long filament.
● *Lophotus lacepedei*, family Lophotidae.

cresting ▶**noun** [mass noun] an ornamental decoration at the ridge of a roof or top of a wall.

cresyl /ˈkriːsʌɪl, -sɪl/ ▶**noun** [as modifier] Chemistry of or denoting a radical $—OC_6H_4CH_3$, derived from a cresol.

Cretaceous /krɪˈteɪʃəs/ ▶**adjective** Geology of, relating to, or denoting the last period of the Mesozoic era, between the Jurassic and Tertiary periods.
■[as noun **the Cretaceous**] the Cretaceous period or the system of rocks deposited during it.

> The Cretaceous lasted from about 146 to 65 million years ago. The climate was warm and the sea level rose; the period is characterized especially in NW Europe by the deposition of chalk. The first flowering plants emerged and the domination of the dinosaurs continued, although they died out quite abruptly towards the end of it.

– ORIGIN late 17th cent.: from Latin *cretaceus* (from *creta* 'chalk') + **-OUS**.

Cretaceous–Tertiary boundary (also **K/T boundary**) Geology the division between the Cretaceous and Tertiary periods, about 65 million years ago.

> A widespread layer of sediment dating from this time has been shown since 1980 to be enriched in iridium and other elements and to contain minerals showing evidence of thermal shock and carbon deposits indicative of extensive fires. This appears to indicate the catastrophic impact of one or more large meteorites, and geologists have identified a formation at Chicxulub in the Yucatán Peninsula, Mexico, as a probable impact site. A resulting drastic climate change has been suggested as the cause of the extinction of dinosaurs and many other organisms at this time, but this remains controversial.

Crete /kriːt/ a Greek island in the eastern Mediterranean; pop. 536,980 (1991); capital, Heraklion. It is noted for the remains of the Minoan civilization which flourished there in the 2nd millennium BC. It fell to Rome in 67 BC and was subsequently ruled by Byzantines, Venetians, and Turks. Crete played an important role in the Greek struggle for independence from the Turks in the late 19th and early 20th centuries, becoming administratively part of an independent Greece in 1913. Greek name **KRÍTI**.
– DERIVATIVES **Cretan** adjective & noun.

cretic /ˈkriːtɪk/ ▶**noun** Prosody a metrical foot containing one short or unstressed syllable between two long or stressed ones.
– ORIGIN late 16th cent.: from Latin *Creticus*, from Greek *Krētikos*, from *Krētē* 'Crete'.

cretin /ˈkrɛtɪn/ ▶**noun** a stupid person (used as a general term of abuse).
■Medicine, dated a person who is deformed and mentally handicapped because of congenital thyroid deficiency.
– DERIVATIVES **cretinism** noun, **cretinous** adjective.
– ORIGIN late 18th cent.: from French *crétin*, from Swiss French *crestin* 'Christian' (from Latin *Christianus*), here used to mean 'human being', apparently as a reminder that, though deformed, cretins were human and not beasts.

cretonne /krɛˈtɒn, ˈkrɛtɒn/ ▶**noun** [mass noun] a heavy cotton fabric, typically with a floral pattern printed on one or both sides, used for upholstery.
– ORIGIN late 19th cent.: from French, of unknown origin.

Creutzfeldt–Jakob disease /ˌkrɔɪtsfɛltˈjakɒb/ ▶**noun** [mass noun] a fatal degenerative disease affecting nerve cells in the brain, causing mental, physical, and sensory disturbances such as dementia and seizures. It is believed to be caused by prions and hence to be related to BSE and other spongiform encephalopathies such as kuru and scrapie.
– ORIGIN 1930s: named after H. G. *Creutzfeldt* (1885–1964) and A. *Jakob* (1882–1927), the German neurologists who first described cases of the disease in 1920–1. Creutzfeldt is credited with the first description of the disease in 1920, although the case is atypical by current diagnostic criteria; a year later Jakob described four cases, at least two of whom had clinical features suggestive of CJD as it is currently described.

crevasse /krɪˈvas/ ▶**noun** a deep open crack, especially one in a glacier.
■N. Amer. a breach in the embankment of a river or canal.
– ORIGIN early 19th cent.: from French, from Old French *crevace* (see **CREVICE**).

crevice /ˈkrɛvɪs/ ▶**noun** a narrow opening or fissure, especially in a rock or wall.
– ORIGIN Middle English: from Old French *crevace*, from *crever* 'to burst', from Latin *crepare* 'to rattle, crack'.

crew¹ ▶**noun** [treated as sing. or pl.] a group of people who work on and operate a ship, boat, aircraft, or train.
■such a group other than the officers: *the ship's captain and crew may be brought to trial.* ■ a group of people who work closely together, in a job that is technically difficult or dangerous: *an ambulance crew.* ■ informal, often derogatory a group of people associated in some way: *a crew of assorted computer geeks.* ■ informal, chiefly US a group of rappers, break dancers, or graffiti artists performing or operating together. ■ N. Amer. informal a criminal gang.
▶**verb** [with obj.] (often **be crewed**) provide (a craft or vehicle) with a group of people to operate it: *normally the boat is crewed by 5 people.*
■[no obj.] act as a member of a crew, subordinate to a captain: *I've never* **crewed for** *a world-famous yachtsman before.*
– DERIVATIVES **crewman** noun (pl. **-men**).
– ORIGIN late Middle English: from Old French *creue* 'augmentation, increase', feminine past participle of *croistre* 'grow', from Latin *crescere*. The original sense was 'band of soldiers serving as reinforcements'; hence it came to denote any organized armed band or, generally, a company of people (late 16th cent.).

crew² past of **CROW**².

crew cut ▶**noun** a very short haircut for men and boys.
– ORIGIN 1940s: apparently first adopted as a style by boat crews of Harvard and Yale universities.

Crewe /kruː/ a town and major railway junction in Cheshire; pop. 47,800 (1981).

crewel /ˈkruːəl/ ▶**noun** a thin, loosely twisted, worsted yarn used for tapestry and embroidery.
– ORIGIN late 15th cent.: of unknown origin.

crewel work ▶**noun** [mass noun] embroidery or tapestry worked in crewels on linen or cloth.

crew neck ▶**noun** a close-fitting round neckline, especially on a sweater or T-shirt: [as modifier] *a crew-neck sweater.*
■a sweater with such a neckline.

crib ▶**noun** **1** chiefly N. Amer. a child's bed with barred or latticed sides; a cot.
■a barred container or rack for animal fodder: a manger. ■ Brit. a model of the Nativity of Christ, with a manger as a bed.
2 informal a translation of a text for use by students, especially in a surreptitious way: *an English crib of Caesar's Gallic Wars.*
■a thing that has been plagiarized: *is the song a crib from Mozart's 'Don Giovanni'?*
3 informal, chiefly N. Amer. an apartment or house.
4 [mass noun] short for **CRIBBAGE**.
■[count noun] the cards discarded by the players at cribbage, counting to the dealer.
5 (also **cribwork**) a heavy timber framework used in foundations for a building or to line a mineshaft.
6 Austral./NZ a light meal; a snack. [ORIGIN: late 19th cent.: originally dialect.]
▶**verb** (**cribbed**, **cribbing**) [with obj.] **1** informal copy (another person's work) illicitly or without acknowledgement: *he was doing an exam and didn't want anybody to crib the answers from him* | [no obj.] *he often* **cribbed from** *other researchers.*
■archaic steal.
2 archaic restrain: *he had been so cabined, cribbed, and confined by office.*
3 Brit. dated grumble.
– DERIVATIVES **cribber** noun.
– ORIGIN Old English (in the sense 'manger'), of Germanic origin; related to Dutch *krib*, *kribbe* and German *Krippe*.

cribbage ▶**noun** [mass noun] a card game, usually for two players, in which the objective is to play so that the pip value of one's cards played reaches exactly 15 or 31. Points are also scored for various card combinations.
– ORIGIN mid 17th cent.: related to **CRIB**; according to John Aubrey, the game was invented by the English poet Sir John Suckling; it seems to have been developed from an older game called Noddy.

cribbage board ▶**noun** a board with pegs and holes, used for scoring at cribbage.

crib-biting ▶**noun** [mass noun] a repetitive habit of some horses which involves biting and chewing of wood, especially that of doors and mangers, in the stable, causing excessive wear to the front teeth.

crib death ▶**noun** North American term for **COT DEATH**.

cribellum /krɪˈbɛləm/ ▶**noun** (pl. **cribella** /-lə/) Zoology (in some spiders) an additional spinning organ with numerous fine pores, situated in front of the spinnerets.
– DERIVATIVES **cribellate** adjective.
– ORIGIN late 19th cent.: from late Latin, diminutive of *cribrum* 'sieve'.

cribo /ˈkriːbəʊ, ˈkrʌɪbəʊ/ ▶**noun** (pl. **-os**) another term for **INDIGO SNAKE**.
– ORIGIN late 19th cent.: of unknown origin.

cribriform /ˈkrɪbrɪfɔːm/ ▶**adjective** Anatomy denoting an anatomical structure that is pierced by numerous small holes, in particular the plate of the ethmoid bone through which the olfactory nerves pass.
– ORIGIN mid 18th cent.: from Latin *cribrum* 'sieve' + **-IFORM**.

cribwork ▶**noun** see **CRIB** (sense 5).

Crichton /ˈkrʌɪt(ə)n/, James (1560–c.1585), Scottish adventurer; known as **the Admirable Crichton**. Crichton was an accomplished swordsman, poet, and scholar. He served in the French army and made a considerable impression on French and Italian universities with his skills as a polyglot orator.

Crick, Francis Harry Compton (b.1916), English

biophysicist. Together with J. D. Watson he proposed the double helix structure of the DNA molecule, thus broadly explaining how genetic information is carried in living organisms and how genes replicate. Nobel Prize for Physiology or Medicine: 1962, shared with Watson and M. H. F. Wilkins.

crick ▶ **noun** a painful stiff feeling in the neck or back.
▶ **verb** [with obj.] twist or strain (one's neck or back), causing painful stiffness: [as adj. **cricked**] *he suffered a cricked neck during tackling practice.*
– ORIGIN late Middle English: of unknown origin.

cricket[1] ▶ **noun** [mass noun] an open-air game played on a large grass field with ball, bats, and two wickets, between teams of eleven players, the object of the game being to score more runs than the opposition.

Cricket is played mainly in Britain and in territories formerly under British rule, such as Australia, South Africa, the West Indies, New Zealand, and the Indian subcontinent. The full game with two innings per side can last several days; shorter single-innings matches are usual at amateur level and have become popular at professional level since the 1960s.

– PHRASES **not cricket** Brit. informal a thing contrary to traditional standards of fairness or rectitude.
– DERIVATIVES **cricketer** noun, **cricketing** adjective.
– ORIGIN late 16th cent.: of unknown origin.

cricket[2] ▶ **noun** an insect related to the grasshoppers but with shorter legs. The male produces a characteristic musical chirping sound.
• Family Gryllidae: many genera and species, including the **field cricket** and the **house cricket**.
■used in names of insects of related families, e.g. **bush cricket, mole cricket**.
– ORIGIN Middle English: from Old French *criquet*, from *criquer* 'to crackle', of imitative origin.

cricket bag ▶ **noun** a long bag used for carrying a cricketer's bat and other equipment.

cricoid /ˈkrʌɪkɔɪd/ ▶ **noun** (also **cricoid cartilage**) Anatomy the ring-shaped cartilage of the larynx.
– ORIGIN mid 18th cent.: from modern Latin *cricoides* 'ring-shaped', from Greek *krikoeidēs*, from *krikos* 'ring'.

cri de cœur /ˌkriː də ˈkəː, French kʀi də kœʀ/ ▶ **noun** (pl. **cris de cœur** pronunc. same) a passionate appeal, complaint, or protest.
– ORIGIN French, 'cry from the heart'.

cried past and past participle of **CRY**.

crier ▶ **noun** an officer who makes public announcements in a court of justice.
■short for **TOWN CRIER**.
– ORIGIN late Middle English: from Old French *criere*, from *crier* 'to shout'.

crikey ▶ **exclamation** Brit. informal an expression of surprise: *Crikey! I never thought I'd see you again.*
– ORIGIN mid 19th cent.: euphemism for **CHRIST**.

crim ▶ **noun** & **adjective** informal, chiefly Austral. short for **CRIMINAL**.

Crimbo ▶ **noun** variant spelling of **CHRIMBO**.

crime ▶ **noun** an action or omission which constitutes an offence and is punishable by law: *shoplifting was a serious crime.*
■[mass noun] illegal activities: *the victims of crime.* ■ an action or activity which, although not illegal, is considered to be evil, shameful, or wrong: *they condemned apartheid as a **crime against** humanity* | [with infinitive] *it's a crime to keep a creature like Willy in a tank.*
▶ **verb** [with obj.] Brit. informal (especially in the army) charge with or find guilty of an offence: *they found the note and I got crimed for it.*
– ORIGIN Middle English (in the sense 'wickedness, sin'): via Old French from Latin *crimen* 'judgement, offence', based on *cernere* 'to judge'.

Crimea /krʌɪˈmiːə/ (usu. **the Crimea**) a peninsula of Ukraine lying between the Sea of Azov and the Black Sea. It was the scene of the Crimean War in the 1850s. The majority of the population is Russian.
– DERIVATIVES **Crimean** adjective.

Crimean War a war (1853–6) between Russia and an alliance of Great Britain, France, Sardinia, and Turkey. Russian aggression against Turkey led to war, with Turkey's European allies intervening to destroy Russian naval power in the Black Sea in 1854 and eventually capture the fortress city of Sebastopol in 1855 after a lengthy siege.

crime-fighting ▶ **noun** [mass noun] the action of working to reduce the incidence of crime.
– DERIVATIVES **crime-fighter** noun.

crimen injuria /ˌkrʌɪmən ɪnˈdʒuːrɪə/ ▶ **noun** S. African Law a wilful injury to someone's dignity, caused by the use of obscene or racially offensive language or gestures.
– ORIGIN Latin, from *crimen* 'accusation' + *injuria* 'indignity'.

crime passionnel /ˌkriːm pasjəˈnɛl/ ▶ **noun** (pl. **crimes passionnels** pronunc. same) a crime, typically a murder, committed in a fit of sexual jealousy.
– ORIGIN French, 'crime of passion'.

crime sheet ▶ **noun** Brit. a form on which police record details of a reported crime.
■(in the armed forces) a record of someone's offences and punishments under military law.

crime wave ▶ **noun** a sudden increase in the number of crimes committed in a country or area.

crime writer ▶ **noun** a writer of detective stories or thrillers.

criminal ▶ **noun** a person who has committed a crime: *these men are dangerous criminals.*
▶ **adjective** of or relating to crime: *he is charged with conspiracy to commit criminal damage.*
■Law of or relating to crime as opposed to civil matters: *a criminal court.* ■ informal (of an action or situation) deplorable and shocking: *he may never fulfil his potential, and that would be a criminal waste.*
– DERIVATIVES **criminality** /-ˈnalɪti/ noun, **criminally** adverb.
– ORIGIN late Middle English (as an adjective): from late Latin *criminalis*, from Latin *crimen*, *crimin-* (see **CRIME**).

criminal conversation ▶ **noun** [mass noun] historical adultery, especially as formerly constituting grounds for the recovery of legal damages by a husband from his wife's adulterous partner.

criminalistics ▶ **plural noun** [treated as sing.] another term for **FORENSICS**.

criminalize (also **-ise**) ▶ **verb** [with obj.] turn (an activity) into a criminal offence by making it illegal: *the law that criminalizes assisted suicide.*
■turn (someone) into a criminal by making their activities illegal: *these punitive measures would further criminalize travellers for their way of life.*
– DERIVATIVES **criminalization** /-ˈzeɪʃ(ə)n/ noun.

criminal law ▶ **noun** [mass noun] a system of law concerned with the punishment of offenders. Contrasted with **CIVIL LAW**.
■[count noun] a law belonging to this system.

criminal libel ▶ **noun** [mass noun] Law a malicious defamatory statement in a permanent form, rendering the maker liable to criminal prosecution.

criminal record ▶ **noun** a list of a person's previous criminal convictions: *the caution wouldn't go on his criminal record.*
■a history of being convicted for crime: *he admits he has a criminal record.*

criminogenic /ˌkrɪmɪnəˈdʒɛnɪk/ ▶ **adjective** (of a system, situation, or place) causing or likely to cause criminal behaviour: *the criminogenic nature of homelessness.*

criminology /ˌkrɪmɪˈnɒlədʒi/ ▶ **noun** [mass noun] the scientific study of crime and criminals.
– DERIVATIVES **criminological** adjective, **criminologist** noun.
– ORIGIN late 19th cent.: from Latin *crimen*, *crimin-* 'crime' + **-LOGY**.

crimp ▶ **verb** [with obj.] compress (something) into small folds or ridges: *she crimped the edge of the pie.*
■squeeze (metal) so as to bend or corrugate it. ■ connect (a wire or cable) in this way. ■ [often as adj. **crimped**] make waves in (someone's hair) with a hot iron: *crimped blonde hair.* ■ N. Amer. informal have a limiting or adverse effect on (something): *his zeal about his career can crimp the rest of his life.*
▶ **noun** a curl, wave, or folded or compressed edge: *this cascade of delicate crimps depends on a perm* | [mass noun] *the wool had too much crimp to be used in weaving.*
■a small connecting piece for crimping wires or lines together. ■ N. Amer. informal a restriction or limitation: *the crimp on take-home pay has been even tighter since taxes were raised.*
– PHRASES **put a crimp in** N. Amer. informal have an adverse effect on: *well, that puts a crimp in my theory.*
– DERIVATIVES **crimper** noun, **crimpy** adjective.
– ORIGIN Old English *gecrympan*, of Germanic origin; related to Dutch *krimpen* 'shrink, wrinkle'. Of rare occurrence before the 18th cent., the word was perhaps reintroduced from Low German or Dutch.

crimplene /ˈkrɪmpliːn/ ▶ **noun** [mass noun] trademark a synthetic crease-resistant fibre and fabric.
– ORIGIN 1950s: probably from the noun **CRIMP** + a shortened form of **TERYLENE**.

crimson /ˈkrɪmz(ə)n/ ▶ **adjective** of a rich deep red colour inclining to purple: *she blushed crimson with embarrassment.*
▶ **noun** [mass noun] a rich deep red colour inclining to purple.
▶ **verb** [no obj.] (of a person's face) become flushed,especially through embarrassment: *my face crimsoned and my hands began to shake.*
– ORIGIN late Middle English: from obsolete French *cramoisin* or Old Spanish *cremesin*, based on Arabic *ḳirmizī*, from *ḳirmiz* (see **KERMES**). Compare with **CARMINE**.

cringe /krɪn(d)ʒ/ ▶ **verb** (**cringing**) [no obj.] bend one's head and body in fear or apprehension or in a servile or obsequious manner: *he **cringed away** from the blow* | [as adj. **cringing**] *we are surrounded by cringing yes-men and sycophants.*
■experience an inward shiver of embarrassment or disgust: *I **cringed at** the fellow's stupidity.*
▶ **noun** an act of cringing in fear or apprehension.
■a feeling of embarrassment or disgust.
– DERIVATIVES **cringer** noun.
– ORIGIN Middle English *crenge*, *crenche*, related to Old English *cringan*, *crincan* 'bend, yield, fall in battle', of Germanic origin and related to Dutch *krengen* 'heel over' and German *krank* 'sick', also to **CRANK**[1].

cringe-making ▶ **adjective** another term for **CRINGEWORTHY**.

cringeworthy ▶ **adjective** informal causing feelings of embarrassment or awkwardness: *the play's cast was excellent, but the dialogue was unforgivably cringeworthy.*

cringle ▶ **noun** Sailing a ring of rope containing a thimble, for another rope to pass through.
– ORIGIN early 17th cent.: from Low German *kringel*, diminutive of *kring* 'ring'.

crinkle ▶ **verb** [no obj.] form small creases or wrinkles in the surface of something, especially the skin of the face as the result of a facial expression: *Rose's face crinkled in bewilderment* | *his face **crinkled up** in a smile* | [as adj. **crinkled**] *a skirt in crinkled fabric.*
■[with obj.] cause to form such creases or wrinkles: *Burney crinkled his eyes in a smile.*
▶ **noun** a wrinkle or crease found on the surface of something: *there was a crinkle of suspicion on her forehead.*
– DERIVATIVES **crinkly** adjective.
– ORIGIN late Middle English: related to Old English *crincan* (see **CRINGE**).

crinkle-cut ▶ **adjective** (especially of chips) cut with wavy edges.

crinkum-crankum /krɪŋkəmˈkraŋkəm/ ▶ **noun** [mass noun] archaic elaborate decoration or detail.
– ORIGIN mid 17th cent.: fanciful reduplication of the nouns **CRANK**[1] and **CRANK**[2].

Crinoidea /krʌɪˈnɔɪdɪə/ Zoology a class of echinoderms that comprises the sea lilies and feather stars. They have slender feathery arms and (in some kinds) a stalk for attachment, and were abundant in the Palaeozoic era.
– DERIVATIVES **crinoid** /ˈkrʌɪnɔɪd/ noun & adjective, **crinoidal** /-ˈnɔɪd(ə)l/ adjective.
– ORIGIN modern Latin (plural), from Greek *krinoeidēs* 'lily-like', from *krinon* 'lily'.

crinoline /ˈkrɪn(ə)lɪn/ ▶ **noun 1** historical a stiffened or hooped petticoat worn to make a long skirt stand out.
2 [mass noun] a stiff fabric made of horsehair and cotton or linen thread, typically used for stiffening petticoats or as a lining.
– ORIGIN mid 19th cent. (originally in sense 2, early crinolines being made of such material): from French, formed irregularly from Latin *crinis* 'hair' + *linum* 'thread'.

criollo /krɪˈɒləʊ, -ɒljəʊ/ (also **Criollo**) ▶ **noun** (pl. **-os**)
1 a person from Spanish South or Central America, especially one of pure Spanish descent.
■a horse or other domestic animal of a South or Central American breed.
2 (also **criollo tree**) a cacao tree of a variety producing thin-shelled beans of high quality.

– ORIGIN late 19th cent.: Spanish, literally 'native to the locality' (see **CREOLE**).

crip ▶ **noun** informal, chiefly N. Amer. **1** offensive a disabled person. [ORIGIN: early 20th cent.: abbreviation of **CRIPPLE**.]
2 (usu. **Crip**) a member of a Los Angeles street gang.

cripes /krʌɪps/ ▶ **exclamation** informal used as a euphemism for Christ.
– ORIGIN early 20th cent.: alteration of **CHRIST**.

Crippen /ˈkrɪpɪn/, Hawley Harvey (1862–1910), American-born British murderer; known as **Doctor Crippen**. Crippen poisoned his wife at their London home and sailed to Canada with his former secretary. His arrest in Canada was achieved through the intervention of radio-telegraphy, the first case of its use in apprehending a criminal; Crippen was later hanged.

cripple ▶ **noun** archaic or offensive a person who is unable to walk or move properly through disability or because of injury to their back or legs.
▶ **verb** [with obj.] (often **be crippled**) cause (someone) to become unable to move or walk properly: *a young student was crippled for life* | [as adj. **crippling**] *a crippling disease.*
■ cause severe and disabling damage to (a machine): [as adj. **crippled**] *the pilot displayed skill and nerve in landing the crippled plane.* ■ cause a severe and almost insuperable problem for: *developing countries are crippled by their debts.*
– DERIVATIVES **crippledom** noun, **crippler** noun.
– ORIGIN Old English: from two words, *crypel* and *crēopel*, both of Germanic origin and related to **CREEP**.

USAGE The word **cripple** has long been in use to refer to 'a person unable to walk through illness or disability' and is recorded (in the *Lindisfarne Gospels*) as early as AD 950. In the 20th century the term has acquired offensive connotations and has now been largely replaced by broader terms such as 'disabled person'.

crise de nerfs /ˌkriːz də ˈnɛː(f), French kriz də nɛʀf/ ▶ **noun** (pl. **crises de nerfs** pronunc. same) dated an attack of anxiety: *I had a crise de nerfs before the first performance.*
– ORIGIN French, literally 'crisis of nerves'.

crisis ▶ **noun** (pl. **crises**) a time of intense difficulty or danger: *the current economic crisis* | [mass noun] *the monarchy was in crisis.*
■ a time when a difficult or important decision must be made: [as modifier] *the situation has reached crisis point.* ■ the turning point of a disease when an important change takes place, indicating either recovery or death.
– ORIGIN late Middle English (denoting the turning point of a disease): medical Latin, from Greek *krisis* 'decision', from *krinein* 'decide'. The general sense 'decisive point' dates from the early 17th cent.

crisis management ▶ **noun** [mass noun] the practice of taking managerial action only when a crisis has developed.

crisp ▶ **adjective** **1** (of a substance) firm, dry, and brittle, especially in a way considered pleasing or attractive: *crisp bacon* | *the snow is lovely and crisp.*
■ (of a fruit or vegetable) firm, indicating freshness: *a crisp lettuce.* ■ (of the weather) cool, fresh, and invigorating: *a crisp autumn day.* ■ (of paper or cloth) smoothly and attractively stiff and uncreased: *£65 in crisp new notes.* ■ (of hair) having tight curls, giving an impression of rigidity.
2 (of a way of speaking) briskly decisive and matter-of-fact, without hesitation or unnecessary detail: *her answer was crisp.*
▶ **noun** (also **potato crisp**) Brit. a wafer-thin slice of potato fried until crisp and eaten as a snack or appetizer.
▶ **verb** [with obj.] give (something, especially food) a crisp surface by placing it in an oven or grill: *crisp the pitta in the oven.*
■ [no obj.] (of food) acquire a crisp surface in this way: *open the foil so that the bread browns and crisps.* ■ archaic curl into short, stiff, wavy folds or crinkles.
– PHRASES **burn something to a crisp** burn something completely, leaving only a charred remnant.
– DERIVATIVES **crisply** adverb, **crispness** noun.
– ORIGIN Old English (referring to hair in the sense 'curly'): from Latin *crispus* 'curled'. Other senses may result from symbolic interpretation of the sound of the word.

crispate ▶ **adjective** Botany (especially of a leaf) having a wavy or curly edge.
– ORIGIN mid 19th cent.: from Latin *crispatus*, past participle of *crispare* 'to curl'.

crispbread ▶ **noun** a thin crisp biscuit made from crushed rye or wheat.

crisper ▶ **noun** a compartment at the bottom of a refrigerator for storing fruit and vegetables.

crispy ▶ **adjective** (**crispier**, **crispiest**) (of food, typically that which has been cooked) having a pleasingly firm, dry, and brittle surface or texture: *crispy fried bacon.*
– DERIVATIVES **crispiness** noun.

crissal thrasher /ˈkrɪs(ə)l/ ▶ **noun** a large grey thrasher (songbird) with a red patch under the tail, found in the south-western US and Mexico.
• *Toxostoma dorsale* (or *crissale*), family Mimidae.
– ORIGIN late 19th cent.: *crissal* from modern Latin *crissum* (denoting the vent region of a bird) + **-AL**.

criss-cross ▶ **noun** a pattern of intersecting straight lines or paths: *the blotting paper was marked with a criss-cross of different inks.*
▶ **adjective** (of a pattern) containing a number of straight lines or paths which intersect each other: *the streets ran in a regular criss-cross pattern.*
▶ **adverb** in a pattern of intersecting straight lines: *the swords were strung criss-cross on his back.*
▶ **verb** [with obj.] (usu. **be criss-crossed**) form a pattern of intersecting lines or paths on (a place): *the green hill was criss-crossed with a network of sheep tracks.*
■ [no obj.] (of straight lines or paths) intersect repeatedly: *the smaller streets criss-crossed in a grid pattern.* ■ move or travel around (a place) by going back and forth repeatedly: *the President criss-crossed America.*
– ORIGIN early 17th cent. (denoting a figure of a cross preceding the alphabet in a hornbook): from *Christ-cross* (in the same sense in late Middle English), from *Christ's cross*. The form was later treated as a reduplication of **CROSS**.

crista /ˈkrɪstə/ ▶ **noun** (pl. **cristae** /-tiː/) **1** Anatomy & Zoology a ridge or crest.
2 Biology each of the partial partitions in a mitochondrion formed by infolding of the inner membrane.
– DERIVATIVES **cristate** adjective.
– ORIGIN mid 19th cent.: from Latin, 'tuft, plume, crest'.

cristobalite /krɪˈstəʊbəlʌɪt/ ▶ **noun** [mass noun] a form of silica which is the main component of opal and also occurs as small octahedral crystals.
– ORIGIN late 19th cent.: named after *Cerro San Cristóbal* in Mexico, where it was discovered, + **-ITE**[1].

crit ▶ **noun** informal, chiefly Brit. a review of a literary or artistic work or production.
■ informal short for **CRITICISM** or **CRITIC**.

criterion /krʌɪˈtɪərɪən/ ▶ **noun** (pl. **criteria** /-rɪə/) a principle or standard by which something may be judged or decided: *they award a green label to products that meet certain environmental criteria.*
– DERIVATIVES **criterial** adjective.
– ORIGIN early 17th cent.: from Greek *kritērion* 'means of judging', from *kritēs* (see **CRITIC**).

USAGE Strictly speaking, the singular form (following the original Greek) is **criterion** and the plural form is **criteria**. It is a common mistake, however, to use **criteria** as if it were a singular, as in ***a further criteria** needs to be considered.*

critic ▶ **noun** **1** a person who expresses an unfavourable opinion of something: *critics of the new legislation say it is too broad.*
2 a person who judges the merits of literary, artistic, or musical works, especially one who does so professionally: *a film critic.*
– ORIGIN late 16th cent.: from Latin *criticus*, from Greek *kritikos*, from *kritēs* 'a judge', from *krinein* 'judge, decide'.

critical ▶ **adjective** **1** expressing adverse or disapproving comments or judgements: *I was very **critical of** the previous regime.*
2 expressing or involving an analysis of the merits and faults of a work of literature, music, or art: *she never won the critical acclaim she sought.*
■ (of a published literary or musical text) incorporating a detailed and scholarly analysis and commentary: *a critical edition of a Bach sonata.*
3 (of a situation or problem) having the potential to become disastrous; at a point of crisis: *the flood waters had not receded and the situation was still critical.*
■ (of a person) extremely ill and at risk of death: *she was critical but stable in Middlesbrough General Hospital.*
■ having a decisive or crucial importance in the success or failure of something: *temperature is a critical factor in successful fruit storage.*
4 [attrib.] Mathematics & Physics relating to or denoting a point of transition from one state to another.
■ (of a nuclear reactor or fuel) maintaining a self-sustaining chain reaction: *the reactor is due to **go critical** in October.*
– DERIVATIVES **criticality** noun (only in senses 3 and 4), **critically** adverb [as submodifier] *he's critically ill*, **criticalness** noun.
– ORIGIN mid 16th cent. (in the sense 'relating to the crisis of a disease'): from late Latin *criticus* (see **CRITIC**).

critical angle ▶ **noun** Optics the angle of incidence beyond which rays of light passing through a denser medium to the surface of a less dense medium are no longer refracted but totally reflected.

critical apparatus ▶ **noun** see **APPARATUS** (sense 3).

critical damping ▶ **noun** [mass noun] Physics damping just sufficient to prevent oscillations.

critical list ▶ **noun** [in sing.] a list of those who are critically ill in hospital.

critical mass ▶ **noun** Physics the minimum amount of fissile material needed to maintain a nuclear chain reaction.
■ figurative the minimum size or amount of resources required to start or maintain a venture: *a communication system is of no value unless there is a critical mass of users.*

critical path ▶ **noun** the sequence of stages determining the minimum time needed for an operation, especially when analysed on a computer for a large organization.

critical path analysis ▶ **noun** [mass noun] the mathematical network analysis technique of planning complex working procedures with reference to the critical path of each alternative system.

critical period ▶ **noun** Psychology a period during someone's development in which a particular skill or characteristic is believed to be most readily acquired.

critical point ▶ **noun** **1** Chemistry a point on a phase diagram at which both the liquid and gas phases of a substance have the same density, and are therefore indistinguishable.
2 Mathematics US term for **STATIONARY POINT**.

critical pressure ▶ **noun** Chemistry the pressure of a gas or vapour in its critical state.

critical state ▶ **noun** [mass noun] Chemistry the state of a substance when it is at the critical point, i.e. at critical temperature and pressure.

critical temperature ▶ **noun** Chemistry the temperature of a gas or vapour in its critical state. Above this temperature, a gas cannot be liquefied by pressure alone.

critical theory ▶ **noun** [mass noun] a philosophical approach to culture, and especially to literature, that seeks to confront the social, historical, and ideological forces and structures which produce and constrain it. The term is applied particularly to the work of the Frankfurt School.

critical volume ▶ **noun** Chemistry the volume occupied by a unit mass of a gas or vapour in its critical state.

criticaster /ˌkrɪtɪˈkastə, ˈkrɪtɪˌkastə/ ▶ **noun** rare a minor or inferior critic.
– ORIGIN late 17th cent.: from **CRITIC** + **-ASTER**.

criticism ▶ **noun** [mass noun] **1** the expression of disapproval of someone or something based on perceived faults or mistakes: *he received a lot of criticism* | [count noun] *he ignored the criticisms of his friends.*
2 the analysis and judgement of the merits and faults of a literary or artistic work: *alternative methods of criticism supported by well-developed literary theories.*
– ORIGIN early 17th cent.: from **CRITIC** or Latin *criticus* + **-ISM**.

criticize (also **-ise**) ▶ **verb** [with obj.] **1** indicate the faults of (someone or something) in a disapproving way: *the opposition criticized the government's failure to consult adequately* | *technicians were **criticized for** defective workmanship.*
2 form and express a sophisticated judgement of (a

literary or artistic work): *a literary text may be criticized on two grounds: the semantic and the expressive.*
– DERIVATIVES **criticizable** adjective, **criticizer** noun.

critique /krɪ'tiːk/ ▶**noun** a detailed analysis and assessment of something, especially a literary, philosophical, or political theory.
▶**verb** (**critiques**, **critiqued**, **critiquing**) [with obj.] evaluate (a theory or practice) in a detailed and analytical way: *the authors critique the methods and practices used in the research.*
– ORIGIN mid 17th cent. (as a noun): from French, based on Greek *kritikē tekhnē* 'critical art'.

critter ▶**noun** informal or dialect, chiefly US a living creature; an animal.
■[usu. with adj.] a person of a particular kind: *the old critter used to live in a shack.*
– ORIGIN early 19th cent.: variant of **CREATURE**.

croak ▶**noun** a deep hoarse sound made by a frog or a crow.
■a sound resembling this, especially one made by a person: *Lorton tried to laugh—it came out as a croak.*
▶**verb** [no obj.] **1** (of a frog or crow) make a characteristic deep hoarse sound.
■(of a person) make a similar sound when speaking or laughing: [with direct speech] *'Thank you,' I croaked.* ■ archaic prophesy evil or misfortune,especially unjustifiably and to the irritation of others: *without croaking, it may be observed that our government is upon a dangerous experiment.*
2 informal die: *the dog finally croaked in 1987.*
■[with obj.] kill (someone): *she got croaked by a killer sex pervert.*
– ORIGIN Middle English (as a verb): imitative.

croaker ▶**noun** **1** an animal or fish that makes a deep, hoarse sound.
■another term for **DRUM**³.
2 archaic a person who habitually prophesies evil or misfortune unjustifiably and to the irritation of others.

croaky ▶**adjective** (**croakier**, **croakiest**) (of a person's voice) deep and hoarse.
– DERIVATIVES **croakily** adverb.

Croat /'krəʊat/ ▶**noun** **1** a native or national of Croatia, or a person of Croatian descent.
2 [mass noun] the Southern Slavic language of the Croats, almost identical to Serbian but written in the Roman alphabet. See **SERBO-CROAT**.
▶**adjective** of or relating to the Croats or their language.
– ORIGIN from modern Latin *Croatae* (plural), from Serbo-Croat *Hrvat*.

Croatia /krəʊ'eɪʃə/ a country in SE Europe, formerly a constituent republic of Yugoslavia; pop. 4,760,000 (est. 1991); language, Croatian; capital, Zagreb. Croatian name **HRVATSKA**.

Apart from a period of Turkish rule in the 16th–17th centuries, Croatia largely remained linked with Hungary until 1918, when it joined the Kingdom of the Serbs, Croats, and Slovenes (later Yugoslavia). After a period in the Second World War as a Nazi puppet state (1941–5), Croatia became part of Yugoslavia once more and remained a constituent republic until it declared itself independent in 1991. The secession of Croatia led to war between Croats and the Serb minority, and with Serbia; a ceasefire was called in 1992.

Croatian ▶**noun** & **adjective** another term for **CROAT**.

croc ▶**noun** informal a crocodile.
– ORIGIN late 19th cent.: abbreviation.

Croce /'krəʊtʃeɪ, Italian 'krotʃe/, Benedetto (1866–1952), Italian philosopher and politician. In his 'Philosophy of Spirit' he denied the physical reality of a work of art and identified philosophical endeavour with a methodological approach to history. A former Minister of Education, he helped to rebuild democracy in Italy after the fall of Mussolini.

crochet /'krəʊʃeɪ, -ʃi/ ▶**noun** [mass noun] a handicraft in which yarn is made up into a patterned fabric by means of a hooked needle: [as modifier] *a crochet hook.*
■fabric or items made in such a way: *the bikini is tiny, three triangles of cotton crochet.*
▶**verb** (**crocheted** /-ʃeɪd/, **crocheting** /-ʃeɪɪŋ/) [with obj.] make (a garment or piece of fabric) in such a way: *she had crocheted the shawl herself* | [no obj.] *her mother had stopped crocheting.*
– DERIVATIVES **crocheter** /'krəʊʃeɪə/ noun.
– ORIGIN mid 19th cent.: from French, diminutive of *croc* 'hook', from Old Norse *krókr*.

croci plural form of **CROCUS**.

crocidolite /krə(ʊ)'sɪdəlʌɪt/ ▶**noun** [mass noun] a fibrous blue or green mineral consisting of a silicate of iron and sodium. Also called ***blue asbestos***.
– ORIGIN mid 19th cent.: from Greek *krokis, krokid-* 'nap of cloth' + **-LITE**.

crock¹ informal ▶**noun** an old person who is considered to be feeble and useless.
■Brit. an old and worn-out vehicle.
▶**verb** [with obj.] Brit. cause an injury to (a person or part of the body): *he crocked a shoulder in the test against South Africa.*
■[as adj. **crocked**] N. Amer. informal drunk: *his party guests were pretty crocked.*
– ORIGIN late Middle English: perhaps from Flemish, and probably related to **CRACK**. Originally a Scots term for an old ewe, it came in the late 19th cent. to denote an old or broken-down horse.

crock² ▶**noun** **1** an earthenware pot or jar.
■a broken piece of earthenware. ■ a plate, cup, or other item of crockery.
2 (also vulgar slang **crock of shit**) chiefly N. Amer. a thing that is considered to be complete nonsense.
– ORIGIN Old English *croc, crocca*, of Germanic origin; related to Old Norse *krukka* and probably to Dutch *kruik* and German *Krug*.

crockery ▶**noun** [mass noun] plates, dishes, cups, and other similar items, especially ones made of earthenware or china.
– ORIGIN early 18th cent.: from obsolete *crocker* 'potter', from **CROCK**².

crocket /'krɒkɪt/ ▶**noun** (in Gothic architecture) a small carved ornament,typically a bud or curled leaf, on the inclined side of a pinnacle or gable.
– ORIGIN Middle English (denoting a curl or roll of hair): from Old Northern French, variant of Old French *crochet* (see **CROTCHET**). The current sense dates from the late 17th cent., but *crotchet* was used in the same sense from late Middle English until the 19th cent.

Crockett /'krɒkɪt/, Davy (1786–1836), American frontiersman, soldier, and politician; full name *David Crockett*. He was a member of the House of Representatives 1827–35 and cultivated the image of a rough backwoods legislator. On leaving politics he returned to the frontier, where he took up the cause of Texan independence and was killed at the siege of the Alamo.

Crockford Crockford's Clerical Directory, a reference book of Anglican clergy in the British Isles first issued in 1860.
– ORIGIN named after John *Crockford* (1823–65), its first publisher.

Crockpot ▶**noun** N. Amer. trademark a large electric cooking pot, used to cook stews and other dishes slowly.

crocodile ▶**noun** **1** a large predatory semiaquatic reptile with long jaws, long tail, short legs, and a horny textured skin, using submersion and stealth to approach prey unseen. The crocodile has been extensively hunted for its valuable skin.
● Family Crocodylidae: three genera, in particular *Crocodylus*, and several species.
■[mass noun] leather made from crocodile skin, used especially to make bags and shoes.
2 Brit. informal a line of schoolchildren walking in pairs.
– ORIGIN Middle English *cocodrille, cokadrill*, from Old French *cocodrille*, via medieval Latin from Latin *crocodilus*, from Greek *krokodilos* 'worm of the stones', from *krokē* 'pebble' + *drilos* 'worm'. The spelling was changed in the 16th cent. to conform with the Latin and Greek forms.

crocodile bird ▶**noun** the Egyptian plover, which is said to feed on insects parasitic on crocodiles.

crocodile clip ▶**noun** chiefly Brit. a sprung metal clip with long, serrated jaws, used attached to an electric cable for making a temporary connection to a battery or other component.

crocodile tears ▶**plural noun** tears or expressions of sorrow that are insincere.
– ORIGIN mid 16th cent.: said to be so named from a belief that crocodiles wept while devouring or luring their prey.

crocodilian /ˌkrɒkə'dɪlɪən/ ▶**noun** Zoology a large predatory semiaquatic reptile of an order that comprises the crocodiles, alligators, caimans, and gharial. Crocodilians are distinguished by long jaws, short legs, and a powerful tail.
● Order Crocodylia: three families.
▶**adjective** of or relating to such reptiles.

crocoite /'krəʊkəʊʌɪt/ ▶**noun** [mass noun] a rare bright orange mineral consisting of lead chromate.
– ORIGIN mid 19th cent.: originally as French *crocoise*, from Greek *krokoeis* 'saffron-coloured', from *krokos* 'crocus'. The spelling was altered to *crocoisite*, then *crocoite*.

crocosmia /krə(ʊ)'kɒzmɪə/ ▶**noun** a plant of a genus that includes montbretia.
● Genus *Crocosmia*, family Iridaceae.
– ORIGIN modern Latin, from Greek *krokos* 'saffron'.

crocus /'krəʊkəs/ ▶**noun** (pl. **crocuses** or **croci** /-kʌɪ, -kiː/) a small spring-flowering Eurasian plant of the iris family, which grows from a corm and bears bright yellow, purple, or white flowers. See also **AUTUMN CROCUS**.
● Genus *Crocus*, family Iridaceae.
– ORIGIN late Middle English (also denoting saffron, obtained from a species of crocus): via Latin from Greek *krokos*, of Semitic origin and related to Hebrew *karkōm* and Arabic *kurkum*.

Croesus /'kriːsəs/ (6th century BC), last king of Lydia *c.*560–546 BC. Renowned for his great wealth, he subjugated the Greek cities on the coast of Asia Minor before being overthrown by Cyrus the Great.
■[as noun **a Croesus**] a person of great wealth.

croft Brit. ▶**noun** a small rented farm, especially one in Scotland, comprising a plot of arable land attached to a house and with a right of pasturage held in common with other such farms.
■an enclosed field used for tillage or pasture, typically attached to a house and worked by the occupier.
▶**verb** [with obj.] farm (land) as a croft or crofts.
– ORIGIN Old English: of unknown origin.

crofter ▶**noun** Brit. a person who farms a croft.

crofting ▶**noun** [mass noun] Brit. the practice or system of farming in crofts: [as modifier] *a crofting community.*

Crohn's disease /'krəʊnz/ ▶**noun** [mass noun] a chronic inflammatory disease of the intestines, especially the colon and ileum, associated with ulcers and fistulae.
– ORIGIN 1930s: named after Burrill B. *Crohn* (1884–1983), American pathologist, who was among the first to describe it.

croissant /'krwasɒ̃/ ▶**noun** a French crescent-shaped roll made of sweet flaky pastry, eaten for breakfast.
– ORIGIN late 19th cent.: French (see **CRESCENT**). The term had occasionally been recorded earlier as a variant of *crescent*.

Cro-Magnon man /krəʊ'manjɒ̃, -'magnən/ ▶**noun** [mass noun] the earliest form of modern human in Europe, associated with the Aurignacian flint industry. Their appearance *c.*35,000 years ago marked the beginning of the Upper Palaeolithic and the apparent decline and disappearance of Neanderthal man; the group persisted at least into the Neolithic period.
– ORIGIN *Cro-Magnon*, the name of a hill in the Dordogne, France, where remains were found in 1868.

Cromarty Firth /'krɒməti/ an inlet of the Moray Firth on the coast of Highland region, northern Scotland. The shipping forecast area **Cromarty** extends far beyond this, covering Scottish coastal waters roughly from Aberdeen in the south to John o'Groats in the north.

crombec /'krɒmbɛk/ ▶**noun** a small African warbler with a very short tail, and grey or green upper parts with rufous or white underparts.
● Genus *Sylvietta*, family Sylviidae: several species, in particular the (**northern**) **crombec** (*S. brachyura*).
– ORIGIN early 20th cent.: from French, from Dutch *krom* 'crooked' + *bek* 'beak'.

Crome /krəʊm/, John (1768–1821), English painter. Founder and leading member of the Norwich School, he later developed a distinctive romantic style of his own, exemplified in such landscapes as *Slate Quarries* (undated).

Cromerian /krəʊ'mɪərɪən/ ▶**adjective** Geology of, relating to, or denoting an interglacial period in the Middle Pleistocene of Britain and northern Europe, preceding the Elster (Anglian) glaciation.
■[as noun **the Cromerian**] the Cromerian interglacial or the system of fossil-rich deposits laid down during it.
– ORIGIN early 20th cent.: from *Cromer*, in Norfolk, site of an outcrop of fossil-rich deposits from this period, + **-IAN**.

cromlech /'krɒmlɛk/ ▶**noun** (in Wales) a megalithic

tomb consisting of a large flat stone laid on upright ones. Also called **DOLMEN**. [ORIGIN: Welsh, from *crom*, feminine of *crwm* 'arched' + *llech* 'flat stone'.]
■(in Brittany) a circle of standing stones. [ORIGIN: via French from Breton *krommlec'h*.]

cromoglycate /ˌkrəʊmə(ʊ)ˈɡlʌɪseɪt/ (also **sodium cromoglycate**) ▶ **noun** [mass noun] Medicine a synthetic non-steroidal anti-inflammatory drug, inhaled to prevent asthmatic attacks and allergic reactions.
– ORIGIN mid 20th cent.: from an alteration of *chromone* (a bicyclic ketone) + *glyc(erol)* + **-ATE**[1].

Crompton[1] /ˈkrɒmpt(ə)n/, Richmal (1890–1969), English writer; pseudonym of *Richmal Crompton Lamburn*. She made her name with *Just William* (1922), a collection of stories for children about a mischievous schoolboy, William Brown. She published a further thirty-seven collections based on the same character, as well as some fifty books for adults.

Crompton[2] /ˈkrɒmpt(ə)n/, Samuel (1753–1827), English inventor. Famed for his invention of the spinning mule, he lacked the means to obtain a patent and sold his rights to a Bolton industrialist for £67. The House of Commons subsequently gave him £5,000 in compensation.

Cromwell[1] /ˈkrɒmwɛl/, Oliver (1599–1658), English general and statesman, Lord Protector of the Commonwealth 1653–8. Cromwell was the leader of the victorious Parliamentary forces (or Roundheads) in the English Civil War. As head of state he styled himself Lord Protector, and refused Parliament's offer of the Crown in 1657. His rule was notable for its puritan reforms in the Church of England. He was briefly succeeded by his son **Richard** (1626–1712), who was forced into exile in 1659.

Cromwell[2] /ˈkrɒmwɛl/, Thomas (*c.*1485–1540), English statesman, chief minister to Henry VIII 1531–40. He presided over the king's divorce from Catherine of Aragon (1533) and his break with the Roman Catholic Church as well as the dissolution of the monasteries and the 1534 Act of Supremacy. He fell from favour over Henry's marriage to Anne of Cleves and was executed on a charge of treason.

crone ▶ **noun** an old woman who is thin and ugly.
– ORIGIN late Middle English: via Middle Dutch *croonje*, *caroonje* 'carcass, old ewe' from Old Northern French *caroigne* 'carrion, cantankerous woman' (see **CARRION**).

Cronin /ˈkrəʊnɪn/, A. J. (1896–1981), Scottish novelist; full name *Archibald Joseph Cronin*. His novels, including *The Citadel* (1937), often reflect his early experiences as a doctor and were successfully adapted for radio and television as *Dr Finlay's Casebook* in the 1960s and 1990s.

cronk ▶ **adjective** Austral. informal unfit, unsound, or liable to collapse.
■fraudulent.
– ORIGIN late 19th cent.: probably related to **CRANK**[3].

Cronus /ˈkrɒnəs, ˈkrəʊn-/ (also **Kronos**) Greek Mythology the supreme god until dethroned by Zeus. The youngest son of Uranus (Heaven) and Gaia (Earth), Cronus overthrew and castrated his father and then married his sister Rhea. Because he was fated to be overcome by one of his male children, Cronus swallowed all of them as soon as they were born, but when Zeus was born Rhea deceived him and hid the baby away. Roman equivalent **SATURN**.

crony /ˈkrəʊni/ ▶ **noun** (pl. **-ies**) informal, often derogatory a close friend or companion: *he went gambling with his cronies.*
– ORIGIN mid 17th cent. (originally Cambridge university slang): from Greek *khronios* 'long-lasting' (here used to mean 'contemporary'), from *khronos* 'time'. Compare with **CHUM**[1].

cronyism (also **croneyism**) ▶ **noun** [mass noun] derogatory the appointment of friends and associates to positions of authority, without proper regard to their qualifications.

crook ▶ **noun 1** the hooked staff of a shepherd.
■a bishop's crozier. ■ a bend in something, especially at the elbow in a person's arm: *her head was cradled in the crook of Luke's left arm.*
2 informal a person who is dishonest or a criminal.
▶ **verb** [with obj.] bend (something, especiallya finger as a signal): *he crooked a finger for the waitress.*
▶ **adjective** Austral./NZ informal (especially of a situation) bad, unpleasant, or unsatisfactory: *it was pretty crook on the land in the early 1970s.*
■(of a person or a part of the body) unwell or injured: *a crook knee.* ■ dishonest; illegal: *some pretty crook things went on there.* [ORIGIN: late 19th cent.: abbreviation of **CROOKED**.]
– PHRASES **be crook on** Austral./NZ informal be annoyed by: *you're crook on me because I didn't walk out with you.* **go crook** Austral./NZ informal lose one's temper. ■ become ill.
– DERIVATIVES **crookery** noun.
– ORIGIN Middle English (in the sense 'hooked tool or weapon'): from Old Norse *krókr* 'hook'. A noun sense 'deceit, guile, trickery' (compare with **CROOKED**) was recorded in Middle English but was obsolete by the 17th cent.

crookback ▶ **noun** archaic a person with a hunchback.
– DERIVATIVES **crookbacked** adjective.

crooked /ˈkrʊkɪd/ ▶ **adjective** (**crookeder**, **crookedest**) **1** bent or twisted out of shape or out of place: *his teeth were yellow and crooked.*
■(of a smile or grin) with the mouth sloping down on one side; lopsided. ■ informal dishonest; illegal: *a crooked business deal.*
2 Austral./NZ informal annoyed; exasperated: *'It's not you I'm crooked on,' he assured Vivien.* [ORIGIN: 1940s: from the phrase *go crook on* 'become angry'.]
– DERIVATIVES **crookedly** adverb, **crookedness** noun.
– ORIGIN Middle English: from **CROOK**, probably modelled on Old Norse *krókóttr* 'crooked, cunning'.

Crookes, Sir William (1832–1919), English physicist and chemist. In 1861 he discovered the element thallium. This led him indirectly to the invention of the radiometer in 1875. He later developed a vacuum tube (the precursor of the X-ray tube) and in 1903 invented the spinthariscope.

crookneck (also **crookneck squash**) ▶ **noun** N. Amer. a squash of a club-shaped variety with a curved neck and warty skin.

croon ▶ **verb** [no obj.] hum or sing in a soft, low voice,especially in a sentimental manner: *she was crooning to the child* | [with obj.] *the female vocalist crooned smoky blues into the microphone.*
■[with direct speech] say in a soft, low voice: *'Goodbye, you lovely darling,' she crooned.*
▶ **noun** [in sing.] a soft, low voice or tone: *he sang in a gentle, highly expressive croon.*
– ORIGIN late 15th cent. (originally Scots and northern English): from Middle Low German and Middle Dutch *krōnen* 'groan, lament'. The use of *croon* in standard English was probably popularized by Robert Burns.

crooner ▶ **noun** a singer, typically a male one, who sings sentimental songs in a soft, low voice.

crop ▶ **noun 1** a cultivated plant that is grown on a large scale commercially, especially a cereal, fruit, or vegetable: *the main crops were oats and barley.*
■an amount of such plants or their produce harvested at one time: *a heavy crop of fruit.* ■ an abundance of something, especially a person's hair: *he had a thick crop of wiry hair.* ■ the total number of young farm animals born in a particular year on one farm. ■ a group or amount of related people or things appearing or occurring at one time: *the current crop of politicians.* ■ the entire tanned hide of an animal.
2 a hairstyle in which the hair is cut very short.
3 short for **RIDING CROP** or **HUNTING CROP**.
4 a pouch in a bird's gullet where food is stored or prepared for digestion.
■a similar organ in an insect or earthworm.
▶ **verb** (**cropped**, **cropping**) [with obj.] **1** cut (something, especially a person's hair) very short: [as adj. **cropped**] *cropped blonde hair.*
■(of an animal) bite off and eat the tops of (plants): *the horse was gratefully cropping the grass.* ■ cut the edges of (a photograph) in order to produce a better picture or to fit a given space.
2 (often **be cropped**) harvest (plants or their produce) from a particular area: *hay would have been cropped several times through the summer.*
■sow or plant (land) with plants that will produce food or fodder, especially on a large commercial scale: *the southern areas are cropped in cotton* | [as adj., with submodifier] (**cropped**) *intensively cropped areas.* ■ [no obj.] (of land or a plant) yield a harvest of plants or produce: *the parsley will need protection to continue cropping through the winter.*
– ORIGIN Old English, of Germanic origin; related to German *Kropf*. From Old English to the late 18th cent. there existed a sense 'flower head, ear of corn', giving rise to sense 1 and senses referring to the top of something, whence sense 3.
▶**crop out** (of rock) appear or be exposed at the surface of the earth.
crop up appear, occur, or come to one's notice unexpectedly: *some urgent business had cropped up.*

crop circle ▶ **noun** an area of standing crops which has been flattened in the form of a circle or more complex pattern. No general cause of crop circles has been identified although various natural and unorthodox explanations have been put forward; many are known to have been hoaxes.

crop dusting ▶ **noun** [mass noun] the spraying of powdered insecticide or fertilizer on crops, especially from the air.

crop-eared ▶ **adjective** historical (especially of an animal) having the tops of the ears cut off.
■(especially of a Roundhead in the English Civil War) having the hair cut very short.

crop-over ▶ **noun** [mass noun] a West Indian celebration marking the end of the sugar-cane harvest.

cropper ▶ **noun 1** [usu. with adj. or noun modifier] a plant which yields a crop of a specified kind or in a specified way: *the white-fleshed varieties are the heaviest croppers.*
2 a machine or person that cuts or trims something, such as wool off a sheep or the pile of a carpet during manufacture.
3 chiefly US a person who raises a crop, especially as a sharecropper.
– PHRASES **come a cropper** informal fall heavily. ■ suffer a defeat or disaster: *the club's challenge for the championship has come a cropper.*

crop rotation ▶ **noun** see **ROTATION**.

crop top (also **cropped top**) ▶ **noun** a woman's casual sleeveless or short-sleeved garment or undergarment for the upper body, cut short so that it reveals the stomach.

croquembouche /ˌkrɒkɒmˈbuːʃ/ ▶ **noun** a decorative dessert consisting of choux pastry and crystallized fruit or other confectionery items arranged in a cone and held together by a caramel sauce.
– ORIGIN French, literally 'crunch in the mouth'.

croque-monsieur /ˌkrɒk məˈsjəː/ ▶ **noun** a fried or grilled cheese and ham sandwich.
– ORIGIN French, literally 'bite (a) man'.

croquet /ˈkrəʊkeɪ, -ki/ ▶ **noun** [mass noun] a game played on a lawn, in which wooden balls are driven through a series of square-topped hoops by means of mallets: [as modifier] *a croquet lawn.*
■[count noun] an act of croqueting a ball.
▶ **verb** (**croqueted** /-keɪd/, **croqueting** /-keɪɪŋ/) [with obj.] drive away (an opponent's ball) by holding one's own ball against it and striking this with the mallet. A player is entitled to do this after their ball has struck an opponent's.
– ORIGIN mid 19th cent.: perhaps a dialect form of French *crochet* 'hook'.

croquette /krə(ʊ)ˈkɛt/ ▶ **noun** a small ball or roll of vegetables, minced meat, or fish, fried in breadcrumbs: *a potato croquette.*
– ORIGIN French, from *croquer* 'to crunch'.

crore /krɔː/ ▶ **noun** Indian ten million; one hundred lakhs, especially of rupees, units of measurement, or people.
– ORIGIN from Hindi *karoṛ*, based on Sanskrit *koṭi* 'ten millions'.

Crosby, Bing (1904–77), American singer and actor; born *Harry Lillis Crosby*. His songs include 'White Christmas' (from the film *Holiday Inn*, 1942). He also starred in the series of *Road* films (1940–62) with Bob Hope and Dorothy Lamour.

crosier /ˈkrəʊzɪə, -ʒə/ ▶ **noun** variant spelling of **CROZIER**.

cross ▶ **noun 1** a mark, object, or figure formed by two short intersecting lines or pieces (+ or ×): *place a cross against the preferred choice.*
■Brit. a mark of this type (×) used to show that something is incorrect or unsatisfactory.
2 an upright post with a transverse bar, as used in antiquity for crucifixion.
■(**the Cross**) the cross on which Christ was crucified. ■ this, or a representation of it, as an emblem of Christianity: *she wore a cross around her neck.* ■ figurative a thing that is unavoidable and has to be endured: *she's just a cross we have to bear.*■ short for ***sign of the cross*** (see **SIGN**). ■ a staff surmounted by a cross carried in religious processions and on ceremonial occasions before an archbishop. ■ a cross-shaped decoration awarded for personal valour or indicating

rank in some orders of knighthood: *the Military Cross.* ■ (**the Cross**) the constellation Crux. Also called **SOUTHERN CROSS.**

3 an animal or plant resulting from cross-breeding; a hybrid: *a Galloway and shorthorn cross.*

■ (**a cross between**) a mixture or compromise of two things: *the system is a cross between a monorail and a conventional railway.*

4 a sideways or transverse movement or pass, in particular:

■ Soccer a pass of the ball across the field towards the centre close to one's opponents' goal. ■ Boxing a blow given with a crosswise movement of the fist: *a right cross.*

▶ **verb** [with obj.] **1** go or extend across or to the other side of (a path, track, stretch of water, or area): *he has crossed the Atlantic twice* | *two paths crossed the field* | figurative *a shadow of apprehension crossed her face* | [no obj.] *we crossed over the bridge.*

■ go across or climb over (an obstacle or boundary): *he attempted to cross the border into Jordan* | [no obj.] *we crossed over a stile.* ■ [no obj.] (**cross over**) (especially of an artist or an artistic style or work) begin to appeal to a different audience, especially a wider one: *a talented animator who crossed over to live action.*

2 [no obj.] pass in an opposite or different direction; intersect: *the two lines cross at 90°.*

■ [with obj.] cause (two things) to intersect: *cross the cables in opposing directions.* ■ [with obj.] place (something) crosswise: *Michele sat back and crossed her arms.* ■ (of a letter) be dispatched before receipt of another from the person being written to: *our letters crossed.*

3 draw a line or lines across; mark with a cross: *voters should ask one question before they cross today's ballot paper.*

■ Brit. mark or annotate (a cheque), typically by drawing a pair of parallel lines across it, to indicate that it must be paid into a named bank account. ■ (**cross someone/thing off**) delete a name or item on a list as being no longer required or involved: *Liz crossed off the days on the calendar.* ■ (**cross something out/through**) delete an incorrect or inapplicable word or phrase by drawing a line through it.

4 (**cross oneself**) (of a person) make the sign of the cross in front of one's chest as a sign of Christian reverence or to invoke divine protection.

5 Soccer pass (the ball) across the field towards the centre when attacking.

6 cause (an animal of one species, breed, or variety) to interbreed with one of another species, breed, or variety: *many animals of the breed were crossed with the closely related Guernsey* | figurative *he behaved like an old regular officer crossed with a mathematician.*

■ cross-fertilize (a plant): *a hybrid tea was crossed with a polyantha rose.*

7 oppose or stand in the way of (someone): *no one dared cross him.*

▶ **adjective** annoyed: *he seemed to be very cross about something.*

– PHRASES **as cross as two sticks** Brit. very annoyed or irritated. **at cross purposes** misunderstanding or having different aims from one another: *we had been talking at cross purposes.* **cross one's fingers** (or **keep one's fingers crossed**) put one finger across another as a sign of hoping for good luck. ■ hope that someone or something will be successful. **cross the floor** Brit. join the opposing side in Parliament. **cross my heart (and hope to die)** used to emphasize the truthfulness and sincerity of what one is saying, and sometimes reinforced by making a sign of the cross over one's chest. **cross one's mind** (of a thought) occur to one, especially transiently: *it had not crossed Flora's mind that they might need payment.* **cross someone's palm with silver** often humorous pay someone for a favour or service, especially before having one's fortune told. **cross someone's path** meet or encounter someone. **cross swords** have an argument or dispute. **crossed line** a telephone connection that has been wrongly made with the result that another call or calls can be heard. **get one's wires (or lines) crossed** become wrongly connected by telephone. ■ have a misunderstanding. **the way of the Cross** see **WAY.**

– DERIVATIVES **crosser** noun, **crossly** adverb, **crossness** noun.

– ORIGIN late Old English (in the sense 'monument in the form of a cross'): from Old Norse *kross*, from Old Irish *cros*, from Latin *crux.*

cross- ▶ **combining form 1** denoting movement or position across something: *cross-channel.*

■ denoting interaction: *cross-pollinate.* ■ passing from side to side; transverse: *crosspiece.*

2 describing the form or figure of a cross: *crossbones.*
– ORIGIN from **CROSS.**

cross-assembler ▶ **noun** Computing an assembler which can convert instructions into machine code for a computer other than that on which it is run.

crossbar ▶ **noun** a horizontal bar fixed across another bar or between two upright bars, in particular:

■ the bar between the two upright posts of a football goal. ■ the horizontal metal bar between the handlebars and saddle on a man's or boy's bicycle.

cross-beam ▶ **noun** a transverse beam.

cross-bedding ▶ **noun** [mass noun] Geology layering within a stratum and at an angle to the main bedding plane.

cross bench ▶ **noun** a seat in the House of Lords occupied by a member who is independent of any political party.

– DERIVATIVES **cross-bencher** noun.

crossbill ▶ **noun** a thickset finch with a crossed bill adapted for extracting seeds from the cones of conifers. The plumage is typically red in the male and olive green in the female.

● Genus *Loxia*, family Fringillidae: four species, in particular the widespread **red** (or **common**) **crossbill** (*L. curvirostra*).

crossbones ▶ **noun** see *skull and crossbones* at **SKULL.**

cross-border ▶ **adjective** [attrib.] passing, occurring, or performed across a border between two countries: *cross-border trade.*

crossbow ▶ **noun** a medieval bow of a kind that is fixed across a wooden support and has a groove for the bolt and a mechanism for drawing and releasing the string.

– DERIVATIVES **crossbowman** noun (pl. **-men**).

cross-breed ▶ **noun** an animal or plant produced by mating or hybridizing two different species, breeds, or varieties: [as modifier] *a cross-breed Labrador.*

▶ **verb** [with obj.] produce (an animal or plant) in this way: [as adj. **cross-bred**] *a cross-bred puppy.*

■ hybridize (a breed, species, or variety) with another. ■ [no obj.] (of an animal or plant) breed with a different breed, species, or variety.

cross-check ▶ **verb** [with obj.] **1** verify (figures or information) by using an alternative source or method: *always try to cross-check your bearings* | [as noun **cross-checking**] *no cross-checking has been done.* **2** Ice Hockey obstruct (an opponent) illegally with the stick held horizontally in both hands.

▶ **noun** an instance of verifying figures or information by using an alternative source or method: *as a cross-check they were also asked to give their date of birth.*

cross-colour (US **cross-color**) ▶ **noun** [mass noun] coloured flashes of interference in a colour television receiver caused by the misinterpretation of high-frequency luminance detail as colour information.

cross-compiler ▶ **noun** Computing a compiler which can convert instructions into machine code or low level code for a computer other than that on which it is run.

cross-connection ▶ **noun** a connection made between two or more distinct things, typically parts of different networks or circuits.

cross-correlate ▶ **verb** [with obj.] compare (a sequence of data) against another.

– DERIVATIVES **cross-correlation** noun.

cross-country ▶ **adjective 1** across fields or countryside, as opposed to on roads or tracks: *cross-country walking.*

■ [attrib.] of, relating to, or denoting the sport of running, riding, or driving along a course in the countryside, as opposed to round a track. ■ [attrib.] of, relating to, or denoting skiing over relatively flat countryside, as opposed to down mountain slopes.

2 across a region or country, in particular:

■ not keeping to main or direct roads, routes, or railway lines: *an awkward, cross-country journey by train* | [as adv.] *we drove cross-country to a family reunion.* ■ chiefly US travelling to many different parts of a country: *a whirlwind cross-country tour.*

▶ **noun** a cross-country race or competition.

■ [mass noun] the sport of cross-country running, riding, skiing, or motoring: *skiing in the Rockies is a pleasant mix of downhill and cross-country*

cross-court ▶ **adverb** & **adjective** (of a stroke in tennis and other racket sports) hit diagonally across the court: [as adj.] *a cross-court volley.*

▶ **noun** a stroke of this type.

cross cousin ▶ **noun** each of two cousins who are children of a brother and sister.

cross-cultural ▶ **adjective** [attrib.] of or relating to different cultures or comparison between them: *cross-cultural understanding.*

cross-current ▶ **noun** a current in a river or sea which flows across another.

■ figurative a process or tendency which is in conflict with another: *strong cross-currents of debate.*

cross-curricular ▶ **adjective** Brit. relating to or involving curricula in more than one educational subject.

cross-cut ▶ **verb** [with obj.] **1** cut (wood or stone) across its main grain or axis. **2** [with obj.] alternate (one sequence) with another when editing a film.

▶ **noun 1** a diagonal cut, especially one across the main grain or axis of wood or stone.

■ short for **CROSS-CUT SAW.** **2** an instance of alternating between two or more sequences when editing a film.

▶ **adjective** (of a file) having two sets of grooves crossing each other diagonally.

cross-cut saw ▶ **noun** a saw with a handle at each end, used by two people for cutting across the grain of timber.

cross-dating ▶ **noun** [mass noun] Archaeology the dating of objects by correlation with the chronology of another culture or site.

cross-dress ▶ **verb** [no obj.] wear clothing typical of the opposite sex.

– DERIVATIVES **cross-dresser** noun.

crosse /krɒs/ ▶ **noun** the stick used in women's field lacrosse.

– ORIGIN mid 19th cent.: from French, from Old French *croce* 'bishop's crook', ultimately of Germanic origin and related to **CRUTCH.**

cross-examine ▶ **verb** [with obj.] question (a witness called by the other party) in a court of law to check or extend testimony already given. Compare with **EXAMINATION-IN-CHIEF.**

■ question (someone) aggressively or in great detail: *I was cross-examined over the breakfast table.*

– DERIVATIVES **cross-examination** noun, **cross-examiner** noun.

cross-eyed ▶ **adjective** having one or both eyes turned inwards towards the nose, either from focusing on something very close, through temporary loss of control of focus, or as a permanent condition (convergent strabismus).

cross-fade ▶ **verb** [no obj.] (in sound or film editing) make a picture or sound appear or be heard gradually as another disappears or becomes silent.

▶ **noun** an act or instance of cross-fading.

cross-fertilize (also **-ise**) ▶ **verb** [with obj.] fertilize (a plant) using pollen from another plant of the same species.

■ [no obj.] (of two plants) fertilize each other. ■ figurative stimulate the development of (something) with an exchange of ideas or information: *sessions between the two groups cross-fertilize ideas and provide insights.*

– DERIVATIVES **cross-fertilization** noun.

crossfire ▶ **noun** [mass noun] gunfire from two or more directions passing through the same area, often killing or wounding non-combatants: *a photographer was killed in crossfire.*

■ figurative used to refer to a situation in which two or more groups are attacking or arguing with each other: *the sponsors are caught in the crossfire of the battle between the world champion and his team boss.*

crossflow ▶ **noun** a type of engine cylinder head where the intake ports are on the opposite side of the engine from the exhaust ports.

cross-grain ▶ **adjective** [attrib.] running across the regular grain in timber: *cross-grain swelling.*

cross-grained ▶ **adjective** (of timber) having a grain that runs across the regular grain.

■ stubbornly contrary or bad-tempered: *Bruce was a cross-grained and boastful individual.*

cross guard ▶ **noun** a guard on a sword or dagger consisting of a short transverse bar.

cross hairs ▶ **plural noun** a pair of fine wires crossing at right angles at the focus of an optical instrument or gun sight, for use in positioning, aiming, or measuring.

■ a representation of this on a computer screen.

cross-hatch ▶ **verb** [with obj.] [often as noun **cross-**

hatching (in drawing or graphics) shade (an area) with intersecting sets of parallel lines.

cross head ▶ noun **1** a bar or block between the piston rod and connecting rod in a steam engine. **2** a screw with an indented cross shape in its head. ■ a screwdriver for use with such a screw. **3** a heading to a paragraph printed across a column in the body of a newspaper article.

cross index ▶ noun a note or cross reference in a book or list which refers the reader to other material.
▶ verb [with obj.] index (something) under another heading as a cross reference: [as adj. **cross-indexed**] *a cross-indexed file.*

cross infection ▶ noun [mass noun] the transfer of infection, especially to a hospital patient with a different infection or between different species of animal or plant.

crossing ▶ noun **1** a place where two roads, two railway lines, or a road and a railway line cross. ■ [mass noun] the action of moving across or over something: *the crossing of the Pennines.* ■ a journey across water in a ship: *a short ferry crossing.* ■ a place at which one may most safely cross something, especially a street. ■ a place at which one can cross a border between countries. ■ Architecture the intersection of a church nave and the transepts. **2** [mass noun] cross-breeding.

crossing over ▶ noun [mass noun] Genetics the exchange of genes between homologous chromosomes, resulting in a mixture of parental characteristics in offspring.

cross-legged ▶ adjective & adverb (of a seated person) with the legs crossed at the ankles and the knees bent outwards: [as adv.] *John sat cross-legged on the floor.*

cross light ▶ noun a light positioned to illuminate the parts of a photographic subject which the main lighting leaves in shade.

cross link ▶ noun a chemical bond between different chains of atoms in a polymer or other complex molecule.
▶ verb (**cross-link**) make or become linked with such a bond. ■ [with obj.] connect (something) by a series of transverse links.
– DERIVATIVES **cross-linkage** noun.

crossmatch Medicine ▶ verb [with obj.] [often as noun **crossmatching**] test the compatibility of (a donor's and a recipient's blood or tissue). ▶ noun an instance of such testing.

cross member ▶ noun a transverse structural piece which adds support to a motor-vehicle chassis or other construction.

cross of Lorraine ▶ noun another term for **LORRAINE CROSS**.

crossopterygian /ˌkrɒsɒptəˈrɪdʒɪən/ Zoology ▶ noun a lobe-finned fish, such as the coelacanth.
▶ adjective of or relating to such fishes.
– ORIGIN mid 19th cent.: from modern Latin *Crossopterygii*, from Greek *krossos* 'tassel' + *pterux, pterug-* 'fin'.

crossover ▶ noun **1** a point or place of crossing from one side to the other. ■ a short length of track joining two adjacent railway lines. **2** [mass noun] the process of achieving success in a different field or style, especially in popular music: [as modifier] *a jazz-classical crossover album.* **3** a short cardigan or other garment wrapped around the body and fastened at the waist by ties. **4** [as modifier] relating to or denoting trials of medical treatment in which experimental subjects and control groups are exchanged after a set period: *a crossover study.*

crossover distortion ▶ noun [mass noun] Electronics distortion occurring where a signal changes from positive to negative or vice versa.

crossover network ▶ noun a filter in a loudspeaker unit that divides the signal and delivers different parts to bass and treble speakers.

cross ownership ▶ noun [mass noun] the ownership by one corporation of different companies with related interests or commercial aims.

crosspatch ▶ noun informal a bad-tempered person.
– ORIGIN early 18th cent.: from the adjective **CROSS**

+ obsolete *patch* 'fool, clown', perhaps from Italian *pazzo* 'madman'.

cross peen (also **cross pein**) ▶ noun a hammer having a peen that lies crossways to the length of the shaft.

crosspiece ▶ noun a beam or bar fixed or placed across something else.

cross-platform ▶ adjective Computing able to be used on different types of computers or with different software packages: *a cross-platform game.*

cross-ply ▶ adjective Brit. (of a tyre) having fabric layers with their threads running diagonally, crosswise to each other.

cross-point ▶ adjective [attrib.] (of a screwdriver) having a cross-shaped point for turning cross-head screws.

cross-pollinate ▶ verb [with obj.] pollinate (a flower or plant) with pollen from another flower or plant.
– DERIVATIVES **cross-pollination** noun.

cross-posting ▶ noun [mass noun] **1** the transfer of an employee or officer to a different department, industry, or regiment. **2** the simultaneous sending of a message to more than one newsgroup or other distribution system on the Internet in such a way that the receiving software at individual sites can detect and ignore duplicates.

cross-pressure ▶ verb [with obj.] N. Amer. expose (someone) to different, incompatible opinions: *the executive has been cross-pressured by the interests of the states and the electorate.*

cross product ▶ noun another term for **VECTOR PRODUCT**.

cross-question ▶ verb [with obj.] question (someone) in great detail: *the Chancellor was cross-questioned by the finance committee* | [as noun **cross-questioning**] *the cross-questioning of Lopez.*

cross-rate ▶ noun an exchange rate between two currencies computed by reference to a third currency, usually the US dollar.

cross reaction ▶ noun Biochemistry the reaction of an antibody with an antigen other than the one which gave rise to it.

cross-refer ▶ verb [no obj.] (of a text) refer to another text or part of a text, typically in order to elaborate on a point: *the database cross-refers to the printed book.* ■ [with obj.] refer (someone) to another text: *the entry cross-refers readers to 'Style'.* ■ (of a person) follow a cross reference from one part of a text to another, or one text to another: *pupils should be shown how to cross-refer between texts.*

cross reference ▶ noun a reference to another text or part of a text, typically given in order to elaborate on a point.
▶ verb [with obj.] (usu. **be cross-referenced**) provide with cross references to another text or part of a text: *entries are fully cross-referenced.*

cross-rhythm ▶ noun Music a rhythm used simultaneously with another rhythm or rhythms. ■ [mass noun] the use of two or more rhythms simultaneously.

crossroads ▶ noun an intersection of two or more roads. ■ a point at which a crucial decision must be made which will have far-reaching consequences: *by 1989 I was at the crossroads.* ■ (**crossroad**) N. Amer. a road that crosses a main road or joins two main roads.

cross-ruff ▶ noun a sequence of play in bridge or whist in which partners alternately trump each other's leads.
▶ verb [no obj.] alternately trump particular suits in such a way.

cross section ▶ noun a surface or shape that is or would be exposed by making a straight cut through something, especially at right angles to an axis: *the cross section of an octahedron is a square* | **in cross section** *the sailfish's body looks like a tapering spear.* ■ a thin strip of organic tissue or other material removed by making two such cuts. ■ a diagram representing what such a cut would reveal. ■ a typical or representative sample of a larger group, especially of people: *a cross section of our senior managers.* ■ Physics a quantity having the dimensions of an area which expresses the probability of a given interaction between particles.
▶ verb (**cross-section**) [with obj.] make a cross section of (something): [as noun **cross-sectioning**] *complex triangular terrain models for contour cross-sectioning.*

– DERIVATIVES **cross-sectional** adjective.

cross-sell ▶ verb [with obj.] sell (a different product or service) to an existing customer: *their database is used to cross-sell financial services.*

cross-slide ▶ noun a sliding part on a lathe or planing machine which is supported by the saddle and carries the tool in a direction at right angles to the bed of the machine.

cross stitch Needlework ▶ noun a stitch formed of two stitches crossing each other. ■ [mass noun] needlework done using such stitches.
▶ verb (**cross-stitch**) [with obj.] sew or embroider using such stitches: [as adj. **cross-stitched**] *a cross-stitched pillow.*

cross street ▶ noun chiefly N. Amer. a street crossing another or connecting two streets.

cross-subsidize (also **-ise**) ▶ verb [with obj.] subsidize (a business or activity) out of the profits of another business or activity.
– DERIVATIVES **cross-subsidization** noun, **cross-subsidy** noun.

crosstalk ▶ noun [mass noun] **1** unwanted transfer of signals between communication channels. **2** witty conversation; repartee.

cross tie ▶ noun US a railway sleeper.

cross-town ▶ adjective & adverb running or leading across a town: [as attrib. adj.] *the cross-town traffic* | [as adv.] *she drove us cross-town.*

cross-train ▶ verb [no obj.] learn another skill, especially one related to one's current job.

cross-training ▶ noun [mass noun] training in two or more sports in order to improve fitness and performance, especially in a main sport.

crosstrees ▶ plural noun a pair of horizontal struts attached to a sailing ship's mast to spread the rigging, especially at the head of a topmast.

cross-voting ▶ noun [mass noun] (especially in a parliament) voting for a party one does not belong to, or for more than one party.

crosswalk ▶ noun North American and Australian term for **PEDESTRIAN CROSSING**.

crossways ▶ adverb another term for **CROSSWISE**.

crosswind ▶ noun a wind blowing across one's direction of travel.

crosswise ▶ adverb in the form of a cross: *their arms were held out crosswise.* ■ diagonally; transversely: *wash the potatoes and halve them crosswise.*

crossword (also **crossword puzzle**) ▶ noun a puzzle consisting of a grid of squares and blanks into which words crossing vertically and horizontally are written according to clues.
– ORIGIN said to have been invented by the journalist Arthur Wynne, whose puzzle (called a 'word-cross') appeared in a Sunday newspaper, the *New York World*, on 21 December 1913.

crosswort /ˈkrɒswəːt/ ▶ noun a yellow-flowered European plant related to the bedstraws, with leaves arranged in a cross or whorl of four.
● *Cruciata laevipes*, family Rubiaceae.

crostini /krɒˈstiːni/ ▶ plural noun small pieces of toasted or fried bread served with a topping as a starter or canapé.
– ORIGIN Italian, plural of *crostino* 'little crust'.

crotal ▶ noun variant spelling of **CROTTLE**.

crotale /ˈkrɒtɑːl/ ▶ noun (usu. **crotales**) a small tuned cymbal.
– ORIGIN 1930s: French, from Latin *crotalum*, denoting an ancient type of castanet, from Greek *krotalon*.

crotch ▶ noun the part of the human body between the legs where they join the torso. ■ the part of a garment that passes between the legs. ■ a fork in a tree, road, or river.
– ORIGIN mid 16th cent. (denoting an agricultural or garden fork, also a crutch): perhaps related to Old French *croche* 'crozier, shepherd's crook', based on Old Norse *krókr* 'hook'; partly also a variant of **CRUTCH**.

crotchet /ˈkrɒtʃɪt/ ▶ noun **1** Music, chiefly Brit. a musical note having the time value of a quarter of a semibreve or half a minim, represented by a large solid dot with a plain stem. Also called **QUARTER NOTE**. **2** a perverse or unfounded belief or notion: *the natural crotchets of inveterate bachelors.*
– ORIGIN Middle English (in the sense 'hook'): from

Old French *crochet*, diminutive of *croc* 'hook', from Old Norse *krókr*.

crotchety ▶ **adjective** irritable: *he was tired and crotchety.*
– DERIVATIVES **crotchetiness** noun.
– ORIGIN early 19th cent.: from sense 2 of **CROTCHET** + **-Y**[1].

crotchless ▶ **adjective** (of a garment) having a hole cut so as to leave the genitals uncovered.

croton /ˈkrəʊt(ə)n/ ▶ **noun 1** a strong-scented tree, shrub, or herbaceous plant of the spurge family, native to tropical and warm regions. Several kinds yield timber and other commercially important products.
● Genus *Croton*, family Euphorbiaceae: numerous species, including *C. laccifer*, the host plant for the lac insect.
2 a small evergreen tree or shrub of the Indo-Pacific region, which is grown for its colourful ornamental foliage.
● Genus *Codiaeum*, family Euphorbiaceae: several species, in particular *C. variegatum*, many varieties of which are popular house plants.
– ORIGIN modern Latin, from Greek *krotōn* 'sheep tick' (from the shape of the seeds of the croton in sense 1).

croton oil ▶ **noun** [mass noun] a foul-smelling oil, formerly used as a purgative, obtained from the seeds of a tropical Asian croton tree.
● The tree is *Croton tiglium* (family Euphorbiaceae).

crottle /ˈkrɒt(ə)l/ (also **crotal**) ▶ **noun** a common lichen found on rocks, used in Scotland to make a golden-brown or reddish-brown dye for staining wool for making tweed.
● *Parmelia saxatilis* (order Parmeliales) and other species.
– ORIGIN mid 18th cent.: from Scottish Gaelic and Irish *crotal*, *crotan*.

crouch ▶ **verb** [no obj.] adopt a position where the knees are bent and the upper body is brought forward and down, typically in order to avoid detection or to defend oneself: *we crouched down in the trench* | (**be crouched**) *Leo was crouched before the fire.*
■ (**crouch over**) bend over so as to be close to (someone or something): *she was crouching over some flower bed.*
▶ **noun** [in sing.] a crouching stance or posture.
– ORIGIN late Middle English: perhaps from Old French *crochir* 'be bent', from *croche* (see **CROTCH**).

croup[1] /kruːp/ ▶ **noun** [mass noun] inflammation of the larynx and trachea in children, associated with infection and causing breathing difficulties.
– DERIVATIVES **croupy** adjective.
– ORIGIN mid 18th cent.: from dialect *croup* 'to croak', of imitative origin.

croup[2] /kruːp/ ▶ **noun** the rump or hindquarters, especially of a horse.
– ORIGIN Middle English: from Old French *croupe*, ultimately of Germanic origin and related to **CROP**.

croupade /kruˈpeɪd/ ▶ **noun** a movement performed in classical riding, in which the horse leaps from the ground with its legs tucked under its body.
– ORIGIN mid 17th cent.: French, from Italian *groppata*, from *groppa* 'croup'.

croupier /ˈkruːpɪə, -pɪeɪ/ ▶ **noun 1** the person in charge of a gaming table, gathering in and paying out money or tokens.
2 historical the assistant chairman at a public dinner, seated at the lower end of the table.
– ORIGIN early 18th cent. (denoting a person standing behind a gambler to give advice): French, from Old French *cropier* 'pillion rider, rider on the croup', related to Old French *croupe* (see **CROUP**[2]). Compare with **CRUPPER**.

croustade /kruˈstɑːd/ ▶ **noun** a crisp piece of bread or pastry hollowed to receive a savoury filling.
– ORIGIN French, from Old French *crouste* or Italian *crostata* 'tart' (from *crosta* 'crust').

croute /kruːt/ ▶ **noun** a piece of toasted bread on which savoury snacks can be served. See also **EN CROUTE**.
– ORIGIN French *croûte* (see **CRUST**).

crouton /ˈkruːtɒn/ ▶ **noun** a small piece of fried or toasted bread served with soup or used as a garnish.
– ORIGIN from French *croûton*, from *croûte* (see **CRUST**).

Crow ▶ **noun** (pl. same or **Crows**) **1** a member of an American Indian people inhabiting eastern Montana.
2 [mass noun] the Siouan language of this people, with about 5,000 speakers.
▶ **adjective** of or relating to this people or their language.
– ORIGIN suggested by French *gens de corbeaux*, translating Siouan *apsáaloke* 'crow people'.

crow[1] ▶ **noun 1** a large perching bird with mostly glossy black plumage, a heavy bill, and a raucous voice. See also **BALD CROW, FRUITCROW**.
● Genus *Corvus*, family Corvidae (the **crow family**): several species, including the **carrion crow** (*C. corone*) and the **American crow** (*C. brachyrhynchos*). The crow family also includes the ravens, jays, magpies, choughs, and nutcrackers.
2 informal a woman, especially an old or ugly one.
– PHRASES **as the crow flies** in a straight line: *Easingwold was 22 miles away as the crow flies.* **eat crow** N. Amer. informal be humiliated by having to admit one's defeats or mistakes.
– ORIGIN Old English *crāwe*, of West Germanic origin; related to Dutch *kraai* and German *Krähe*, also to **CROW**[2].

crow[2] ▶ **verb** (past **crowed** or **crew**) [no obj.] (of a cock) utter its characteristic loud cry.
■ (of a person) make a sound expressing a feeling of happiness or triumph: *Ruby crowed with delight.* ■ say something in a tone of gloating satisfaction: *avoid crowing about your success* | [with direct speech] *'I knew you 'd be back,' she crowed.*
▶ **noun** [usu. in sing.] the cry of a cock.
■ a sound made by a person expressing triumph or happiness: *she gave a little crow of triumph.*
– ORIGIN Old English *crāwan*, of West Germanic origin; related to German *krähen*, also to **CROW**[1]; ultimately imitative.

crowbait ▶ **noun** N. Amer. informal, derogatory an old horse.

crowbar ▶ **noun** an iron bar with a flattened end, used as a lever.
▶ **verb** (**-barred, -barring**) [with obj. and complement] use a crowbar to open (something): *he crowbarred the box open.*

crowberry ▶ **noun** (pl. **-ies**) a creeping heather-like dwarf shrub with small leaves and black berries, growing on moorland.
● *Empetrum nigrum*, family Empetraceae.
■ the edible but flavourless black berry of this plant.

crowd ▶ **noun** a large number of people gathered together, typically in a disorganized or unruly way: *a huge crowd gathered in the street outside.*
■ an audience, especially one at a sporting event: *they played before a 25,000 crowd* | [as modifier] *a match marred by crowd trouble.* ■ informal, often derogatory a group of people who are linked by a common interest or activity: *I've broken away from that whole junkie crowd.* ■ (**the crowd**) the mass or multitude of people, especially those considered to be drearily ordinary or anonymous: *make yourself* **stand out from the crowd**. ■ a large number of things regarded collectively: *the crowd of tall buildings.*
▶ **verb** [with obj.] (often **be crowded**) (of a number of people) fill (a space) almost completely, leaving little or no room for movement: *the dance floor was crowded with revellers* | [as adj. **crowded**] *the crowded streets of Southwark.*
■ [no obj.] (**crowd into**) (of a number of people) move into (a space,especially one that seems too small): *they crowded into the cockpit.* ■ [no obj.] (**crowd round**) (of a group of people) form a tightly packed mass around (someone or something): *photographers crowded round him.* ■ move too close to (someone), either aggressively or in a way that causes discomfort or harm: *don't crowd her, she needs air.* ■ (**crowd someone/thing out**) exclude someone or something by taking their place: *rampant plants will crowd out the less vigorous.* ■ [no obj.] (**crowd in on**) figurative overwhelm and preoccupy (someone): *as demands crowd in on you it becomes difficult to keep things in perspective.*
– DERIVATIVES **crowdedness** noun.
– ORIGIN Old English *crūdan* 'press, hasten', of Germanic origin; related to Dutch *kruien* 'push in a wheelbarrow'. In Middle English the senses 'move by pushing' and 'push one's way' arose, leading to the sense 'congregate', and hence (mid 16th cent.) to the noun.

crowdie /ˈkraʊdi/ (also **crowdy**) ▶ **noun** [mass noun] a soft Scottish cheese made from buttermilk or sour milk.
– ORIGIN early 19th cent.: from **CRUD** + **-IE**.

crowd-puller ▶ **noun** informal an event, person, or thing that attracts a large audience.

crowfoot ▶ **noun** a herbaceous plant related to the buttercups, typically having lobed or divided leaves and white or yellow flowers. Many kinds are aquatic with flowers held above the water.
● Genus *Ranunculus*, family Ranunculaceae: many species, in particular the European **water crowfoot** (*R. aquatilis*).

crow hop ▶ **noun** a short jump with both feet together.
■ N. Amer. a jump by a horse with its back arched and its legs stiffened.

crown ▶ **noun 1** a circular ornamental headdress worn by a monarch as a symbol of authority, usually made of or decorated with precious metals and jewels.
■ (**the Crown**) the reigning monarch, representing a country's government: *their loyalty to the Church came before their loyalty to the Crown.* ■ (usu. **the Crown**) the power or authority residing in the monarchy: *they claimed immunity on behalf of the Crown.* ■ an ornament, emblem, or badge shaped like a crown. ■ a wreath of leaves or flowers, especially that worn as an emblem of victory in ancient Greece or Rome. ■ an award or distinction gained by a victory or achievement, especially in sport: *the world heavyweight crown.*
2 the top or highest part of something: *the crown of the hill.*
■ the top part of a person's head or a hat. ■ the part of a plant just above and below the ground from which the roots and shoots branch out. ■ the upper branching or spreading part of a tree or other plant. ■ the upper part of a cut gem, above the girdle. ■ the part of a tooth projecting from the gum. ■ an artificial replacement or covering for the upper part of a tooth.
3 (also **crown piece**) a British coin with a face value of five shillings or 25 pence, now minted only for commemorative purposes.
■ a foreign coin with a name meaning 'crown', especially the krona or krone.
4 (in full **metric crown**) [mass noun] a paper size, 384 × 504 mm.
■ (in full **crown octavo**) a book size, 186 × 123 mm. ■ (in full **crown quarto**) a book size, 246 × 189 mm.
▶ **verb** [with obj.] **1** (usu. **be crowned**) ceremonially place a crown on the head of (someone) in order to invest them as a monarch: *he went to Rome to be crowned* | [with complement] *she was crowned queen in 1953.*
■ [with obj. and complement] declare or acknowledge (someone) as the best, especially at a sport: *he was crowned world champion last September.* ■ (in draughts) promote (a piece) to king by placing another on top of it. ■ rest on or form the top of: *the distant knoll was crowned with trees.* ■ fit a crown to (a tooth). ■ informal hit on the head: *she contained the urge to crown him.*
2 be the triumphant culmination of (an effort or endeavour, especially a prolonged one): *years of struggle were crowned by a state visit to Paris* | [as adj. **crowning**] *the crowning moment of a worthy career.*
3 [no obj.] (of a baby's head during labour) fully appear in the vaginal opening prior to emerging.
– PHRASES **crowning glory** the best and most notable aspect of something: *the scene is the crowning glory of this marvellously entertaining show.* ■ chiefly humorous a person's hair. **to crown it all** as the final event in a series of particularly fortunate or unfortunate events: *it was cold and raining, and, to crown it all, we had to walk home.*
– ORIGIN Middle English: from Anglo-Norman French *corune* (noun), *coruner* (verb), Old French *corone* (noun), *coroner* (verb), from Latin *corona* 'wreath, chaplet'.

Crown Agents ▶ **plural noun** a body appointed by the British government to provide commercial and financial services, originally to British colonies, now to foreign governments and international bodies. It is responsible to the Minister for Overseas Development and its full title (as re-established in 1979) is the Crown Agents for Overseas Governments and Administrations.

crown and anchor ▶ **noun** [mass noun] a gambling game played with three dice each bearing a crown, an anchor, and the four card suits, and played on a board similarly marked.

Crown attorney ▶ **noun** Canadian term for **CROWN PROSECUTOR**.

crown cap ▶ **noun** another term for **CROWN CORK**.

Crown Colony a British colony whose legislature and administration is controlled by the Crown, represented by a governor. Some British dependencies within the Commonwealth still retain the designation, with varying degrees of self-government.

crown cork ▶ noun a metal bottle cap with a crimped edge.

Crown Court ▶ noun (in England and Wales) a court of criminal jurisdiction, which deals with serious offences and appeals referred from the magistrates' courts.

Crown Derby ▶ noun [mass noun] a kind of soft-paste porcelain made at Derby and often marked with a crown above the letter 'D'.

crowned crane ▶ noun an African crane with a yellowish bristly crest, a mainly black or dark grey body, much white on the wings, and pink and white cheeks.
● Genus *Balearica*, family Gruidae: two species, in particular the (**black**) **crowned crane** (*B. pavonina*).

crowned head ▶ noun (usu. **crowned heads**) a king or queen.

crowned pigeon ▶ noun the largest known pigeon, which has mainly bluish plumage and a tall erect crest, found in New Guinea. Also called **GOURA**.
● Genus *Goura*, family Columbidae: three species, including the **Victoria crowned pigeon** (*G. victoria*).

crown ether ▶ noun Chemistry any of a class of organic compounds whose molecules are large rings containing a number of ether linkages.

crown fire ▶ noun a forest fire that spreads from treetop to treetop.

crown gall ▶ noun [mass noun] a bacterial disease of plants, especially fruit bushes and trees, which is characterized by large tumour-like galls on the roots and lower trunk.
● This disease is caused by the soil bacterium *Agrobacterium tumefaciens*.
■ [count noun] a gall of this type.

crown glass ▶ noun [mass noun] glass made without lead or iron, originally in a circular sheet. Formerly used in windows, it is now used as optical glass of low refractive index.

crown green ▶ noun Brit. a kind of bowling green which rises slightly towards the middle.

crown imperial ▶ noun an Asian fritillary (plant) with a cluster of bell-like flowers at the top of a tall, largely bare stem.
● *Fritillaria imperialis*, family Liliaceae.

Crown jewels ▶ plural noun the crown and other ornaments and jewellery worn or carried by the sovereign on certain state occasions.

Crown land ▶ noun [mass noun] (also **Crown lands**) land belonging to the British Crown.
■ land belonging to the state in some parts of the Commonwealth.

crown moulding ▶ noun US term for **CORNICE** (in sense 1).

Crown Office ▶ noun (in the UK) an office of the Supreme Court responsible for listing cases to be tried in the High Court.

crown of thorns ▶ noun 1 a large spiky starfish of the tropical Indo-Pacific, feeding on coral and sometimes causing great damage to reefs.
● *Acanthaster planci*, class Asteroidea.
2 a Madagascan shrub of the spurge family, with bright red flowers and many slender thorns. It is a popular house plant and is sometimes used for hedging in the tropics. Also called **CHRIST'S THORN**.
● *Euphorbia milii*, family Euphorbiaceae.
■ any of a number of other thorny plants, especially Christ's thorn (*Ziziphus spina-christi*).
– ORIGIN by association with Christ's crown of thorns.

crown piece ▶ noun see **CROWN** (sense 3).

Crown prince ▶ noun (in some countries) a male heir to a throne.

Crown princess ▶ noun the wife of a Crown prince.
■ (in some countries) a female heir to a throne.

Crown Prosecution Service (abbrev.: **CPS**) (in England and Wales) an independent organization which decides whether cases brought by the police proceed to the criminal court. Its head is the Director of Public Prosecutions, with each region having its own Chief Crown Prosecutor.

Crown prosecutor ▶ noun (in England, Wales, and Canada) a lawyer who acts for the Crown, especially a prosecutor in a criminal court. In Canada also called **CROWN ATTORNEY**.

crown roast ▶ noun a roast of rib pieces of pork or lamb arranged like a crown in a circle with the bones pointing upwards.

crown saw ▶ noun another term for **HOLE SAW**.

crown wheel ▶ noun a gearwheel or cogwheel with teeth that project from the face of the wheel at right angles, used especially in the gears of motor vehicles.

crow-pheasant ▶ noun a coucal, especially the greater coucal, which has black plumage with chestnut wings and back and is found in South Asia.
● Genus *Centropus*, family Cuculidae, especially *C. sinensis*.

crow quill ▶ noun a large feather from a crow's wing.
■ historical a quill pen for fine writing made from such a feather. ■ (also **crow-quill pen**) a small fine pen for map drawing.

Crow rate ▶ noun historical a reduced rate for transporting grain by rail from western to eastern Canada, legislated by the Crow's Nest Pass Agreement (1897), which ensured a subsidy to the Canadian Pacific Railway. This agreement was terminated in 1995.

crow's foot ▶ noun (pl. **feet**) 1 (usu. **crow's feet**) a branching wrinkle at the outer corner of a person's eye.
2 a mark, symbol, or design formed of lines diverging from a point, resembling a bird's footprint.
3 historical a military caltrop.

crowsfoot spanner ▶ noun an adjustable spanner.

crow's-nest ▶ noun a shelter or platform fixed at the masthead of a vessel as a place for a lookout to stand.

crow steps ▶ plural noun the steplike projections on the sloping part of a gable, common in Flemish architecture and 16th- and 17th-century Scottish buildings.
– DERIVATIVES **crow-stepped** adjective.

croze /krəʊz/ ▶ noun a groove at the end of a cask or barrel to receive the edge of the head.
■ a cooper's tool for making such grooves.
– ORIGIN early 17th cent.: perhaps from French *creux*, *creuse* 'hollow'.

Crozet Islands /krəʊˈzeɪ/ a group of five small islands in the southern Indian Ocean, under French administration.

crozier /ˈkrəʊzɪə/ ▶ noun a hooked staff carried by a bishop as a symbol of pastoral office.
■ the curled top of a young fern.
– ORIGIN Middle English (originally denoting the person who carried a processional cross in front of an archbishop): partly from Old French *croisier* 'cross-bearer', from *crois* 'cross', based on Latin *crux*; reinforced by Old French *crocier* 'bearer of a bishop's crook', from *croce* (see **CROSSE**).

CRT ▶ abbreviation for cathode ray tube.

cru /kruː, French kʀy/ ▶ noun (pl. **crus** pronunc. same) (in France) a vineyard or group of vineyards, especially one of recognized superior quality. See also **GRAND CRU**, **PREMIER CRU**.
– ORIGIN French, from *crû*, literally 'growth', past participle of *croître*.

cruces plural form of **CRUX**.

crucial /ˈkruːʃ(ə)l/ ▶ adjective decisive or critical, especially in the success or failure of something: *negotiations were at a crucial stage*.
■ of great importance: *this game is crucial to our survival*.
■ informal excellent.
– DERIVATIVES **cruciality** /-ʃɪˈalɪti/ noun, **crucially** adverb.
– ORIGIN early 18th cent. (in the sense 'cross-shaped'): from French, from Latin *crux*, *cruc-* 'cross'. The sense 'decisive' is from Francis Bacon's Latin phrase *instantia crucis* 'crucial instance', which he explained as a metaphor from a *crux* or finger-post marking a fork at a crossroad; Newton and Boyle took up the metaphor in *experimentum crucis* 'crucial experiment'.

crucian /ˈkruːʃ(ə)n/ (also **crucian carp**) ▶ noun a small olive-green to reddish-brown European carp of still or slow-moving waters, important as a farmed fish in eastern Europe.
● *Carassius carassius*, family Cyprinidae.
– ORIGIN mid 18th cent.: from Low German *karusse*, *karutze*, perhaps based on Latin *coracinus*, from

Greek *korax* 'raven', also denoting a black fish found in the Nile.

cruciate /ˈkruːʃɪət, -eɪt/ ▶ adjective Anatomy & Botany cross-shaped.
– ORIGIN early 19th cent.: from Latin *cruciatus*, from *crux*, *cruc-* 'cross'.

cruciate ligament ▶ noun Anatomy either of a pair of ligaments in the knee which cross each other and connect the femur to the tibia.

crucible /ˈkruːsɪb(ə)l/ ▶ noun a ceramic or metal container in which metals or other substances may be melted or subjected to very high temperatures.
■ a place or occasion of severe test or trial: *the crucible of combat*. ■ a place or situation in which different elements interact to produce something new: *the crucible of the new Romantic movement*.
– ORIGIN late Middle English: from medieval Latin *crucibulum* 'night lamp, crucible' (perhaps originally a lamp hanging in front of a crucifix), from Latin *crux*, *cruc-* 'cross'.

crucifer /ˈkruːsɪfə/ ▶ noun 1 Botany a cruciferous plant, with four petals arranged in a cross.
2 a person carrying a cross or crucifix in a procession.
– ORIGIN mid 16th cent.: from Christian Latin, from Latin *crux*, *cruc-* 'cross'.

cruciferous /kruːˈsɪf(ə)rəs/ ▶ adjective Botany of, relating to, or denoting plants of the cabbage family (Cruciferae).
– ORIGIN mid 19th cent.: from modern Latin *Cruciferae* (plural), from Latin *crux*, *cruc-* 'cross' + *-fer* 'bearing' (because the flowers have four equal petals arranged crosswise), + **-OUS**.

crucifix /ˈkruːsɪfɪks/ ▶ noun a representation of a cross with a figure of Christ on it.
– ORIGIN Middle English: via Old French from ecclesiastical Latin *crucifixus*, from Latin *cruci fixus* 'fixed to a cross'. Compare with **CRUCIFY**.

crucifixion /ˌkruːsɪˈfɪkʃ(ə)n/ ▶ noun [mass noun] chiefly historical the execution of a person by nailing or binding them to a cross.
■ (**the Crucifixion**) the killing of Jesus Christ in such a way. ■ (**Crucifixion**) [in sing.] an artistic representation or musical composition based on this event.
– ORIGIN late Middle English: from ecclesiastical Latin *crucifixio(n-)*, from the verb *crucifigere* (see **CRUCIFY**).

cruciform /ˈkruːsɪfɔːm/ ▶ adjective having the shape of a cross: *a cruciform sword*.
■ of or denoting a church having a cross-shaped plan with a nave and transepts.
▶ noun a thing shaped like a cross.
– ORIGIN mid 17th cent.: from Latin *crux*, *cruc-* 'cross' + **-IFORM**.

crucify /ˈkruːsɪfʌɪ/ ▶ verb (**-ies**, **-ied**) [with obj.] (often **be crucified**) chiefly historical put (someone) to death by nailing or binding them to a cross: *two thieves were crucified with Jesus*.
■ criticize (someone) severely and unrelentingly: *our fans would crucify us if we lost*. ■ cause anguish to (someone): *she'd been crucified by his departure*.
– DERIVATIVES **crucifier** noun.
– ORIGIN Middle English: from Old French *crucifier*, from late Latin *crucifigere*, from Latin *crux*, *cruc-* 'cross' + *figere* 'fix'. Compare with **CRUCIFIX**.

cruck /krʌk/ ▶ noun Brit. either of a pair of curved timbers extending to the ground in the roof framework of a type of medieval house: [as modifier] *a cruck barn*.
– ORIGIN late 16th cent.: variant of **CROOK**.

crud ▶ noun [mass noun] informal a substance which is considered disgusting or unpleasant, typically because of its dirtiness.
■ heavy snow on which it is difficult to ski.
■ nonsense: *they just want the simple truth without any religious crud*. ■ [count noun] a contemptible person.
– DERIVATIVES **cruddy** adjective.
– ORIGIN late Middle English: variant of **CURD** (the original sense). The earliest modern senses, 'filth' and 'nonsense' (originally US), date from the 1940s.

crude ▶ adjective 1 in a natural or raw state; not yet processed or refined: *crude oil*.
■ Statistics (of figures) not adjusted or corrected: *the crude mortality rate*. ■ (of an estimate or guess) likely to be only approximately accurate.
2 constructed in a rudimentary or makeshift way: *a relatively crude nuclear weapon*.
■ (of an action) showing little finesse or subtlety and as a result unlikely to succeed: *the measure was condemned by economists as crude and ill-conceived*.

3 (of language, behaviour, or a person) offensively coarse or rude, especially in relation to sexual matters: *a crude joke.*
▶ **noun** [mass noun] natural mineral oil: *the ship was carrying 80,000 tonnes of crude.*
– DERIVATIVES **crudely** adverb, **crudeness** noun, **crudity** noun.
– ORIGIN late Middle English: from Latin *crudus* 'raw, rough'.

crude turpentine ▶ **noun** see **TURPENTINE** (sense 1).

crudités /ˈkruːdɪteɪ/ ▶ **plural noun** mixed raw vegetables served as an hors d'oeuvre, typically with a sauce into which they may be dipped.
– ORIGIN plural of French *crudité* 'rawness, crudity', from Latin *crudus* 'raw, rough'.

cruel ▶ **adjective** (**crueller**, **cruellest** or **crueler**, **cruelest**) causing pain or suffering: *I can't stand people who are cruel to animals.*
■ having or showing a sadistic disregard for the pain or suffering of others: *the girl had a cruel face.*
▶ **verb** (**cruelled**, **cruelling**) [with obj.] Austral. informal spoil or ruin (an opportunity or a chance of success): *Ernie nearly cruelled the whole thing by laughing.* [ORIGIN: late 19th cent.: perhaps influenced by the idiom *queer someone's pitch* (see **QUEER**).]
– PHRASES **be cruel to be kind** act towards someone in a way which seems harsh but will ultimately be of benefit to them.
– DERIVATIVES **cruelly** adverb.
– ORIGIN Middle English: via Old French from Latin *crudelis*, related to *crudus* (see **CRUDE**).

cruelty ▶ **noun** (pl. **-ies**) [mass noun] callous indifference to or pleasure in causing pain and suffering: *he has treated her with extreme cruelty.*
■ behaviour which causes pain or suffering to a person or animal: *we can't stand cruelty to animals* | [count noun] *the cruelties of forced assimilation and genocide.* ■ Law behaviour which causes physical or mental harm to another, especially a spouse, whether intentionally or not.
– ORIGIN Middle English: from Old French *crualte*, based on Latin *crudelitas*, from *crudelis* (see **CRUEL**).

cruelty-free ▶ **adjective** (of cosmetics or other commercial products) manufactured or developed by methods which do not involve cruelty to animals.

cruet /ˈkruːɪt/ ▶ **noun 1** Brit. a small container for salt, pepper, oil, or vinegar for use at a dining table.
■ (also **cruet-stand**) Brit. a stand holding such containers.
2 (in church use) a small container for the wine or water to be used in the celebration of the Eucharist.
– ORIGIN Middle English (in sense 2): from Anglo-Norman French, diminutive of Old French *crue* 'pot', from Old Saxon *krūka*; related to **CROCK**[2].

Cruft /krʌft/, Charles (1852–1939), English showman. In 1886 he initiated the first dog show in London. The Cruft's shows, held annually, have helped to raise standards in dog breeding.

Cruikshank /ˈkrʊkʃaŋk/, George (1792–1878), English painter, illustrator, and caricaturist. The most eminent political cartoonist of his day, he was known for exposing the private life of the Prince Regent. His later work includes illustrations for Charles Dickens's *Sketches by Boz* (1836), and a series of etchings supporting the temperance movement.

cruise ▶ **verb** [no obj., with adverbial] sail about in an area without a precise destination, especially for pleasure: *they were cruising off the California coast* | [with obj.] *she cruised the canals of France in a barge.*
■ take a holiday on a ship or boat following a predetermined course, usually calling in at several places. ■ (of a vehicle or person) travel or move slowly around without a specific destination in mind: *a police van cruised past us* | [with obj.] *teenagers were aimlessly cruising the mall.* ■ (of a motor vehicle or aircraft) travel smoothly at a moderate or economical speed. ■ achieve an objective with ease,especially in sport: *Millwall* **cruised to** *a 2–0 win over Leicester.* ■ [with obj.] informal wander about (a place) in search of a sexual partner: *he cruised the gay bars of Los Angeles.* ■ [with obj.] informal attempt to pick up (a sexual partner): *he was cruising a pair of sailors.*
▶ **noun** a voyage on a ship or boat taken for pleasure or as a holiday and usually calling in at several places: *a cruise down the Nile* | [as modifier] *a cruise liner.*
– PHRASES **cruising for a bruising** informal, chiefly N. Amer. heading or looking for trouble.
– ORIGIN mid 17th cent. (as a verb): probably from Dutch *kruisen* 'to cross', from *kruis* 'cross', from Latin *crux*.

cruise control ▶ **noun** a device in a motor vehicle which can be switched on to maintain a selected constant speed without the use of the accelerator pedal.

cruise missile ▶ **noun** a low-flying missile which is guided to its target by an on-board computer.

cruiser ▶ **noun 1** a relatively fast warship larger than a destroyer and less heavily armed than a battleship.
2 a yacht or motor boat with passenger accommodation, designed for leisure use.
■ a person who goes on a pleasure cruise.
3 a motor car which can be driven smoothly at high speed.
■ N. Amer. a police patrol car.
– ORIGIN late 17th cent.: from Dutch *kruiser*, from *kruisen* (see **CRUISE**).

cruiserweight ▶ **noun** chiefly Brit. another term for **LIGHT HEAVYWEIGHT**.

cruisie ▶ **noun** variant spelling of **CRUSIE**.

cruising chute ▶ **noun** Sailing a type of spinnaker that is designed to be more stable but less efficient than a normal spinnaker.

cruising range ▶ **noun** the maximum distance from a base that the fuel capacity of a ship or aircraft will allow it to travel and then return safely at cruising speed.

cruising speed ▶ **noun** a speed for a particular vehicle, ship, or aircraft, usually somewhat below maximum, that is comfortable and economical.

cruller /ˈkrʌlə/ ▶ **noun** N. Amer. a small cake made of rich dough twisted or curled and fried in deep fat.
– ORIGIN early 19th cent.: from Dutch *kruller*, from *krullen* 'to curl'.

crumb ▶ **noun 1** a small fragment of bread, cake, or biscuit.
■ a very small amount of something: *the Budget provided few* **crumbs of comfort**. ■ [mass noun] the soft inner part of a loaf of bread. ■ (also **crumb rubber**) [mass noun] granulated rubber, usually made from recycled car tyres.
2 informal, chiefly N. Amer. an objectionable or contemptible person: *he's an absolute crumb.*
▶ **verb** [with obj.] cover (food) with breadcrumbs: [as adj. **crumbed**] *crispy crumbed mushrooms with garlic dip.*
– PHRASES **crumbs from someone's** (or **a rich man's**) **table** an unfair and inadequate or unsatisfactory share of something.
– ORIGIN Old English *cruma*, of Germanic origin; related to Dutch *kruim* and German *Krume*. The final *-b* was added in the 16th cent., perhaps from **CRUMBLE** but also influenced by words such as *dumb*, where the original final *-b* is retained although no longer pronounced.

crumble ▶ **verb** [no obj.] break or fall apart into small fragments, especially over a period of time as part of a process of deterioration: *the plaster started to crumble* | [as adj. **crumbling**] *their crumbling ancestral home.*
■ [with obj.] cause (something) to break apart into small fragments: *the easiest way to crumble blue cheese.* ■ (of an organization, relationship, or structure) disintegrate gradually over a period of time: *the party's fragile unity began to crumble.*
▶ **noun** Brit. a mixture of flour and fat that is rubbed to the texture of breadcrumbs and cooked as a topping for fruit.
■ [mass noun] a pudding made with such a topping and a particular fruit: *apple crumble.*
– ORIGIN late Middle English: probably from an Old English word related to **CRUMB**.

crumbly ▶ **adjective** (**crumblier**, **crumbliest**) consisting of or easily breaking into small fragments: *the cheese has a sharp flavour and is crumbly and moist.*
▶ **noun** (pl. **-ies**) informal, often humorous or derogatory an old person: *the high proportion of crumblies in the population.*
– DERIVATIVES **crumbliness** noun.

crumbs ▶ **exclamation** Brit. informal used to express dismay or surprise: *'Crumbs,' said Emily, 'how embarrassing.'*
– ORIGIN late 19th cent.: euphemism for *Christ*.

crumb structure ▶ **noun** [mass noun] the porous structure or condition of soil when its particles are moderately aggregated.

crumby ▶ **adjective** (**crumbier**, **crumbiest**) **1** like or covered in crumbs.
2 variant spelling of **CRUMMY**.

crumhorn ▶ **noun** variant spelling of **KRUMMHORN**.

crummy (also **crumby**) informal ▶ **adjective** (**crummier**, **crummiest**) dirty, unpleasant, or of poor quality: *a crummy little room.*
■ [predic.] unwell: *I'm crummy and want to get better.*
▶ **noun** N. Amer. an old or converted truck used to transport loggers to and from work.
– DERIVATIVES **crummily** adverb, **crumminess** noun.
– ORIGIN mid 19th cent. (earlier in the literal senses 'crumbly' and 'like or covered with crumbs'): variant of **CRUMBY**.

crump ▶ **noun** a loud thudding sound, especially one made by an exploding bomb or shell.
▶ **verb** [no obj.] make such a sound.
– ORIGIN mid 17th cent.: imitative. The original sense (as a verb) was 'munch, crunch', later 'hit hard' (used initially as a term in the game of cricket), hence the military sense 'bombard' (First World War).

crumpet ▶ **noun 1** a thick, flat, savoury cake with a soft, porous texture, made from a yeast mixture cooked on a griddle and eaten toasted and buttered.
2 [mass noun] Brit. informal people, especially women, regarded as objects of sexual desire: *fat chance of our running into any crumpet* | [in sing.] *he's the thinking woman's crumpet.*
3 Brit. archaic, informal a person's head.
– ORIGIN late 17th cent.: of unknown origin. Sense 2 dates from the 1930s.

crumple ▶ **verb** [with obj.] crush (something, typicallypaper or cloth) so that it becomes creased and wrinkled: *he* **crumpled up** *the paper bag* | [as adj. **crumpled**] *a crumpled sheet.*
■ [no obj.] become bent, crooked, or creased: *the bumper crumpled as it glanced off the wall.* ■ [no obj.] (of a person) suddenly flop down to the ground so that their body appears bent or broken: *she crumpled to the floor in a dead faint.* ■ [no obj.] (of a person's face) suddenly sag and show an expression of desolation: *the child's face crumpled and he began to howl.* ■ [no obj.] suddenly lose force or effectiveness: *her composure crumpled.*
▶ **noun** a crushed fold, crease, or wrinkle.
– DERIVATIVES **crumply** adjective.
– ORIGIN Middle English: from obsolete *crump* 'make or become curved', from Old English *crump* 'bent, crooked', of West Germanic origin; related to German *krumm*.

crumple zone ▶ **noun** a part of a motor vehicle, especially the extreme front and rear, designed to crumple easily in a crash and absorb the main force of an impact.

crunch ▶ **verb** [with obj.] crush (a hard or brittle foodstuff) with the teeth, making a loud but muffled grinding sound: *she paused to crunch a ginger biscuit.*
■ [no obj.] make such a sound, especially when walking or driving over gravel or an icy surface.
▶ **noun 1** [usu. in sing.] a loud muffled grinding sound made when crushing, moving over, or hitting something: *Marco's fist struck Brian's nose with a crunch.*
2 (**the crunch**) informal a crucial point or situation, typically one at which a decision with important consequences must be made: *when it comes to the crunch you chicken out.*
■ a severe shortage of money or credit: *the Fed would do what it could to ease America's* **credit crunch**.
3 a physical exercise designed to strengthen the abdominal muscles; a sit-up.
– ORIGIN early 19th cent. (as a verb): variant of 17th-cent. *cranch* (probably imitative), by association with **CRUSH** and **MUNCH**.

cruncher ▶ **noun** informal **1** a critical or vital point; a crucial or difficult question.
2 a computer, system, or person able to perform operations of great complexity or process large amounts of information: *a global information cruncher.* See also **NUMBER CRUNCHER**.

crunchie (also **crunchy**) ▶ **noun** (pl. **-ies**) informal, derogatory S. African an Afrikaner.
– ORIGIN perhaps from *mealie cruncher*, or a corruption of *kransie*, from South African Dutch slang *krantz-athlete* 'baboon'.

crunchy ▶ **adjective** (**crunchier**, **crunchiest**) **1** making a sharp noise when bitten or crushed

and (of food) pleasantly crisp: *bake until the topping is crunchy.*
2 N. Amer. informal politically liberal and environmentally aware: *a song that incorporates whale-singing seems pretty crunchy.*
– DERIVATIVES **crunchily** adverb, **crunchiness** noun.

crupper /ˈkrʌpə/ ▶ **noun** a strap buckled to the back of a saddle and looped under the horse's tail to prevent the saddle or harness from slipping forward.
– ORIGIN Middle English: from Old French *cropiere*, related to *croupe* (see **CROUP**[2]). Compare with **CROUPIER**.

crura plural form of **CRUS**.

crura cerebri plural form of **CRUS CEREBRI**.

crural /ˈkrʊər(ə)l/ ▶ **adjective** Anatomy & Zoology of or relating to the leg or the thigh.
■ of or relating to any part called 'crus', for example, the crura cerebri.
– ORIGIN late 16th cent.: from Latin *cruralis*, from *crus, crur-* 'leg'.

crus /krʌs/ ▶ **noun** (pl. **crura** /ˈkrʊərə/) Anatomy an elongated part of an anatomical structure,especially one which occurs in the body as a pair. See **CRUS CEREBRI**.
– ORIGIN early 18th cent.: from Latin, 'leg'.

crusade /kruːˈseɪd/ ▶ **noun** (often **Crusade**) a medieval military expedition, one of a series made by Europeans to recover the Holy Land from the Muslims in the 11th, 12th, and 13th centuries.
■ a war instigated by the Church for alleged religious ends. ■ an organized campaign concerning a political, social, or religious issue, typically motivated by a fervent desire for change: *a **crusade against** crime.*
▶ **verb** [no obj.] [often as adj. **crusading**] lead or take part in an energetic and organized campaign concerning a social, political, or religious issue: *a crusading stance on poverty.*
– DERIVATIVES **crusader** noun.
– ORIGIN late 16th cent. (originally as *croisade*): from French *croisade*, an alteration (influenced by Spanish *cruzado*) of earlier *croisée*, literally 'the state of being marked with the cross', based on Latin *crux, cruc-* 'cross'; in the 17th cent. the form *crusado*, from Spanish *cruzado*, was introduced; the blending of these two forms led to the current spelling, first recorded in the early 18th cent.

crus cerebri /ˈsɛrɪbrʌɪ/ ▶ **noun** (pl. **crura cerebri**) Anatomy either of two symmetrical tracts of nerve fibres at the base of the midbrain, linking the pons and the cerebral hemispheres.
– ORIGIN early 18th cent.: from Latin, literally 'leg of the brain'.

cruse /kruːz/ ▶ **noun** archaic an earthenware pot or jar.
– ORIGIN Old English *crūse*, of Germanic origin; related to Dutch *kroes* and German *Krause*; reinforced in Middle English by Low German *krūs*.

crush ▶ **verb** [with obj.] press or squeeze (someone or something) with force or violence, typically causing serious damage or injury: *a labourer was crushed to death by a lorry* | [as adj. **crushed**] *the crushed remains of a Ford Cortina.*
■ reduce (something) to a powder or pulp by exerting strong pressure on it: *you can crush a pill between two spoons.* ■ crease or crumple (cloth or paper): [as adj. **crushed**] *crushed trousers and a crumpled jacket.* ■ (of a government or state) violently subdue (opposition or a rebellion): *the government had taken elaborate precautions to crush any resistance.* ■ bring about a feeling of overwhelming disappointment or embarrassment in (someone): *his defeat crushed a lot of left-wing supporters* | [as adj. **crushing**] *the news came as a crushing blow.*
▶ **noun 1** [usu. in sing.] a crowd of people pressed closely together,especially in an enclosed space: *a number of youngsters fainted in the crush.*
2 informal a brief but intense infatuation for someone, especially someone unattainable or inappropriate: *she did **have a crush on** Dr Russell.*
3 [mass noun] a drink made from the juice of pressed fruit: *lemon crush.*
4 (also **crush-pen**) a fenced passage with one narrow end used for handling cattle or sheep.
■ a movable metal cage used for such a purpose.
– DERIVATIVES **crushable** adjective, **crusher** noun, **crushingly** adverb.
– ORIGIN Middle English: from Old French *cruissir*, 'gnash (teeth) or crack', of unknown origin.

crush bar ▶ **noun** Brit. a bar in a theatre or opera house selling drinks to the audience in the interval.

crush barrier ▶ **noun** Brit. a barrier, especially a temporary one, for restraining a crowd.

crushed velvet ▶ **noun** [mass noun] velvet which has its nap pointing in different directions in irregular patches.

crush zone ▶ **noun** another term for **CRUMPLE ZONE**.

crusie /ˈkruːzi/ (also **cruisie**) ▶ **noun** (pl. **-ies**) Scottish historical a small oil lamp with a handle.
■ a triangular candlestick.
– ORIGIN early 16th cent.: perhaps representing French *creuset* 'crucible'.

crust ▶ **noun** the tough outer part of a loaf of bread: *a sandwich with the crusts cut off* | [mass noun] *I tore off several pieces of crust from the loaf.*
■ a hard, dry scrap of bread: *a kindly old woman might give her a crust.* ■ informal a living or livelihood: *I've been **earning a crust** wherever I can.* ■ a layer of pastry covering a pie. ■ a hardened layer, coating, or deposit on the surface of something, especially something soft: *a crust of snow.* ■ the outermost layer of rock of which a planet consists, especially the part of the earth above the mantle: *the earth's crust* | [mass noun] *at the mid-ocean ridge new crust is formed.* ■ a deposit of tartrates and other substances formed in wine aged in the bottle, especially port.
▶ **verb** [no obj.] form into a hard outer layer: *the blisters eventually crust over.*
■ [with obj.] cover with a hard outer layer: *the burns crusted his cheek.*
– DERIVATIVES **crustal** adjective (only in the geological sense of the noun).
– ORIGIN Middle English: from Old French *crouste*, from Latin *crusta* 'rind, shell, crust'.

Crustacea /krʌˈsteɪʃ(ə)/ Zoology a large group of mainly aquatic arthropods which include crabs, lobsters, shrimps, woodlice, barnacles, and many minute forms. They are very diverse, but most have four or more pairs of limbs and several other appendages.
• Subphylum (or phylum) Crustacea.
■ [as plural noun **crustacea**] arthropods of this group.
– DERIVATIVES **crustacean** noun & adjective, **crustaceous** adjective.
– ORIGIN modern Latin (plural), from *crusta* (see **CRUST**).

crusted ▶ **adjective 1** having or forming a hard top layer or covering: *she washed away the crusted blood.*
■ denoting a style of unfiltered, blended port which deposits a sediment in the bottle.
2 old-fashioned; venerable: *a crusted establishment figure.*

crustose /ˈkrʌstəʊs/ ▶ **adjective** Botany (of a lichen or alga) forming or resembling a crust.
– ORIGIN late 19th cent.: from Latin *crustosus*, from *crusta* (see **CRUST**).

crusty ▶ **adjective** (**crustier**, **crustiest**) **1** having a crisp or hard outer layer or covering: *crusty bread.*
■ (of a substance) acting as a hard outer layer or covering: *Lake Manyara was ringed by crusty salt deposits.*
2 (especially of an old person) easily and often irritated: *a crusty old Scots judge.*
▶ **noun** (also **crustie**) (pl. **-ies**) informal a young person who is homeless or travels constantly, has a shabby appearance, and rejects conventional values.
– DERIVATIVES **crustily** adverb, **crustiness** noun.

crutch ▶ **noun 1** a long stick with a crosspiece at the top, used as a support under the armpit by a lame person.
■ [in sing.] figurative a thing used for support or reassurance: *they use the Internet as a crutch for their loneliness.*
2 another term for **CROTCH** (of the body or a garment).
– ORIGIN Old English *crycc, cryc*, of Germanic origin; related to Dutch *kruk* and German *Krücke*.

Crutched Friars an order of mendicant friars established in Italy by 1169, which spread to England, France, and the Low Countries in the 13th century and was suppressed in 1656.
– ORIGIN *crutched* (earlier *crouched*), from Latin *crux, cruc-* 'cross', referring to the cross worn on the top of their staves, and later on the front of their habits.

Crux /krʌks/ Astronomy the smallest constellation (the Cross or Southern Cross), but the most familiar one to observers in the southern hemisphere. It contains the bright star Acrux, the 'Jewel Box' star cluster, and most of the Coalsack nebula. Formerly called **CRUX AUSTRALIS**.
■ [as genitive **Crucis** /ˈkruːsɪs/] used with preceding letter or numeral to designate a star in this constellation: *the star Beta Crucis.*
– ORIGIN Latin.

crux /krʌks/ ▶ **noun** (pl. **cruxes** or **cruces** /ˈkruːsiːz/) (**the crux**) the decisive or most important point at issue: *the crux of the matter is that attitudes have changed.*
■ a particular point of difficulty: *both cruces can be resolved by a consideration of the manuscripts.*
– ORIGIN mid 17th cent. (denoting a representation of a cross, chiefly in *crux ansata* 'ankh', literally 'cross with a handle'): from Latin, literally 'cross'.

Cruyff /krɔɪf/, Johan (b.1947), Dutch footballer and football manager. An attacking midfielder, he was a member of the Ajax team that won three consecutive European Cup Finals (1971–3) and captained the Netherlands in their World Cup Final defeat by West Germany (1974).

cry ▶ **verb** (**-ies**, **-ied**) [no obj.] shed tears, especially as an expression of distress or pain: *don't cry—it'll be all right* | [with obj.] *you'll cry tears of joy.*
■ shout or scream, especially to express one's fear, pain, or grief: *the little girl fell down and cried for mummy.* ■ [with direct speech] say something in an excited or anguished tone of voice: *'Where will it end?' he **cried out**.* ■ (**cry out for**) figurative demand as a self-evident requirement or solution: *the scheme cries out for reform.* ■ (of a bird or other animal) make a loud characteristic call: *the wild birds **cried out** over the water.* ■ [with obj.] (of a hawker) proclaim (wares) for sale in the street.
▶ **noun** (pl. **-ies**) a spell of weeping: *I still **have a cry**, sometimes, when I realize that my mother is dead.*
■ a loud inarticulate shout or scream expressing a powerful feeling or emotion: *a cry of despair.* ■ a distinctive call of a bird or other animal. ■ a loud excited utterance of a word or words: *there was a cry of 'Silence!'* ■ the call of a hawker selling wares on the street. ■ an urgent appeal or entreaty: *fund-raisers have issued a cry for help.* ■ a demand or opinion expressed by many people: *peace became the popular cry.*
– PHRASES **cry one's eyes** (or **heart**) **out** weep bitterly and at length. **cry for the moon** ask for what is unattainable or impossible. **cry foul** protest strongly about a real or imagined wrong or injustice. **cry from the heart** a passionate and honest appeal or protest. **cry stinking fish** Brit. disparage one's own efforts or products. **cry wolf** see **WOLF**. **for crying out loud** informal used to express one's irritation or impatience: *why do you have to take everything so personally, for crying out loud?* **in full cry** used to describe hounds baying in keen pursuit. ■ used to show that someone is expressing an opinion loudly and forcefully: *the prime minister was in full cry with warnings against the plots of the Americans.* **it's no use crying over spilt milk** see **MILK**.
– ORIGIN Middle English (in the sense 'ask for earnestly or loudly'): from Old French *crier* (verb), *cri* (noun), from Latin *quiritare* 'raise a public outcry', literally 'call on the *Quirites* (Roman citizens) for help'.
▶ **cry someone/thing down** dated disparage or belittle someone or something.
cry off informal go back on a promise or fail to keep to an arrangement: *we were going to Spain together and he cried off at the last moment.*
cry someone/thing up dated praise or extol someone or something.

crybaby ▶ **noun** (pl. **-ies**) a person, especially a child, who sheds tears frequently or readily.

cryer ▶ **noun** archaic spelling of **CRIER**.

crying ▶ **adjective** [attrib.] very great: *it would be a **crying shame** to let some other woman have it.*

cryo- /ˈkrʌɪəʊ/ ▶ **combining form** involving or producing cold, especially extreme cold: *cryostat* | *cryosurgery.*
– ORIGIN from Greek *kruos* 'frost'.

cryobiology ▶ **noun** [mass noun] the branch of biology which deals with the properties of organisms and tissues at low temperatures.
– DERIVATIVES **cryobiological** adjective, **cryobiologist** noun.

cryogen /ˈkrʌɪə(ʊ)dʒ(ə)n/ ▶ **noun** a substance used to produce very low temperatures.

cryogenics /ˌkrʌɪə(ʊ)ˈdʒɛnɪks/ ▶ **plural noun** [treated as

sing.] the branch of physics dealing with the production and effects of very low temperatures.
■ another term for **CRYONICS**.
– DERIVATIVES **cryogenic** adjective.

cryoglobulin /ˌkrʌɪə(ʊ)ˈglɒbjʊlɪn/ ▶ **noun** Biochemistry a protein which occurs in the blood in certain disorders. It can be precipitated out of solution below 10°C, causing obstruction in the fingers and toes.

cryolite /ˈkrʌɪəlʌɪt/ ▶ **noun** [mass noun] a white or colourless mineral consisting of a fluoride of sodium and aluminium. It is added to bauxite as a flux in aluminium smelting.
– ORIGIN early 19th cent.: from **CRYO-** 'cold, frost' (because the main deposits are found in Greenland) + **-LITE**.

cryonics /krʌɪˈɒnɪks/ ▶ **plural noun** [treated as sing.] the practice or technique of deep-freezing the bodies of those who have died of an incurable disease, in the hope of a future cure.
– DERIVATIVES **cryonic** adjective.
– ORIGIN 1960s: contraction of **CRYOGENICS**.

cryoprecipitate /ˌkrʌɪəʊprɪˈsɪpɪtət/ ▶ **noun** chiefly Biochemistry a substance precipitated from a solution, especially from the blood, at low temperatures.
■ [mass noun] Medicine an extract rich in a blood-clotting factor obtained as a residue when frozen blood plasma is thawed.

cryopreserve ▶ **verb** [with obj.] Biology & Medicine preserve (cells or tissues) by cooling them below the freezing point of water.
– DERIVATIVES **cryopreservation** noun.

cryoprotectant ▶ **noun** Physiology a substance that prevents the freezing of tissues, or prevents damage to cells during freezing.

cryostat /ˈkrʌɪə(ʊ)stat/ ▶ **noun** an apparatus for maintaining a very low temperature.
■ an apparatus for taking very fine slices of tissue while it is kept very cold.

cryosurgery ▶ **noun** [mass noun] surgery using the local application of intense cold to destroy unwanted tissue.

cryotherapy ▶ **noun** [mass noun] the use of extreme cold in surgery or other medical treatment.

crypt ▶ **noun** **1** an underground room or vault beneath a church, used as a chapel or burial place.
2 Anatomy a small tubular gland, pit, or recess.
– ORIGIN late Middle English (in the sense 'cavern'): from Latin *crypta*, from Greek *kruptē* 'a vault', from *kruptos* 'hidden'.

cryptanalysis ▶ **noun** [mass noun] the art or process of deciphering coded messages without being told the key.
– DERIVATIVES **cryptanalyst** noun, **cryptanalytic** adjective, **cryptanalytical** adjective.
– ORIGIN 1920s: from **CRYPTO-** + **ANALYSIS**.

cryptic ▶ **adjective** **1** having a meaning that is mysterious or obscure: *he found his boss's utterances too cryptic.*
■ (of a crossword) having difficult clues which indicate the solutions indirectly.
2 Zoology (of coloration or markings) serving to camouflage an animal in its natural environment.
– DERIVATIVES **cryptically** adverb.
– ORIGIN early 17th cent.: from late Latin *crypticus*, from Greek *kruptikos*, from *kruptos* 'hidden'. Sense 2 dates from the late 19th cent.

crypto- /ˈkrɪptəʊ/ ▶ **combining form** concealed; secret: *cryptogram.*
– ORIGIN from Greek *kruptos* 'hidden'.

cryptobiont /ˌkrɪptəʊˈbʌɪɒnt/ ▶ **noun** Biology an organism capable of cryptobiosis.

cryptobiosis /ˌkrɪptə(ʊ)bʌɪˈəʊsɪs/ ▶ **noun** [mass noun] Biology a physiological state in which metabolic activity is reduced to an undetectable level without disappearing altogether. It is known in certain plant and animal groups adapted to survive periods of extremely dry conditions.

cryptobiotic ▶ **adjective** Biology **1** of, relating to, or capable of cryptobiosis.
2 of or denoting primitive organisms of the kind presumed to have existed in earlier geological periods but to have left no trace of their existence.

cryptococcosis /ˌkrɪptə(ʊ)kəˈkəʊsɪs/ ▶ **noun** [mass noun] Medicine infestation with a yeast-like fungus, resulting in tumours in the lungs and sometimes spreading to the brain. It occurs chiefly in the United States. Also called **TORULOSIS**.
● The fungus is *Cryptococcus neoformans*, subdivision Deuteromycotina (or class Teliomycetes).
– DERIVATIVES **cryptococcal** adjective.
– ORIGIN 1930s: from modern Latin *Cryptococcus* (part of the binomial of the fungus) + **-OSIS**.

cryptocrystalline ▶ **adjective** having a crystalline structure visible only when magnified.

cryptogam /ˈkrɪptə(ʊ)gam/ ▶ **noun** Botany, dated a plant that has no true flowers or seeds, including ferns, mosses, liverworts, lichens, algae, and fungi.
– DERIVATIVES **cryptogamous** adjective.
– ORIGIN mid 19th cent.: from French *cryptogame*, from modern Latin *cryptogamae (plantae)*, denoting non-flowering plants, from Greek *kruptos* 'hidden' + *gamos* 'marriage' (because the means of reproduction was not apparent).

cryptogamic ▶ **adjective** Botany of, relating to, or denoting cryptogams.
■ Ecology (of a desert soil or surface crust) covered with or consisting of a fragile black layer of cyanobacteria, mosses, and lichens, which is often important in preventing erosion.

cryptogenic /ˌkrɪptəʊˈdʒɛnɪk/ ▶ **adjective** (of a disease) of obscure or uncertain origin.

cryptogram /ˈkrɪptə(ʊ)gram/ ▶ **noun** a text written in code.

cryptography ▶ **noun** [mass noun] the art of writing or solving codes.
– DERIVATIVES **cryptographer** noun, **cryptographic** adjective, **cryptographically** adverb.

cryptology ▶ **noun** [mass noun] the study of codes, or the art of writing and solving them.
– DERIVATIVES **cryptological** adjective, **cryptologist** noun.

cryptomeria /ˌkrɪptə(ʊ)ˈmɪərɪə/ ▶ **noun** a tall conical coniferous tree with long, curved, spirally arranged leaves and short cones. Native to China and Japan, it is grown for timber in Japan. Also called **JAPANESE CEDAR**.
● *Cryptomeria japonica*, family Taxodiaceae.
– ORIGIN modern Latin, from **CRYPTO-** 'hidden' + Greek *meros* 'part' (because the seeds are concealed by scales).

cryptonym /ˈkrɪptənɪm/ ▶ **noun** a code name.
– DERIVATIVES **cryptonymous** adjective.
– ORIGIN late 19th cent.: from **CRYPTO-** 'hidden' + Greek *onuma* 'name'.

cryptorchid /ˌkrɪpˈtɔːkɪd/ ▶ **noun** Medicine a person suffering from cryptorchidism.

cryptorchidism ▶ **noun** [mass noun] Medicine a condition in which one or both of the testes fail to descend from the abdomen into the scrotum.
– ORIGIN late 19th cent.: from **CRYPTO-** 'hidden' + Greek *orkhis, orkhid-* 'testicle' + **-ISM**.

cryptosporidium /ˌkrɪptə(ʊ)spɒˈrɪdɪəm/ ▶ **noun** a parasitic coccidian protozoan found in the intestinal tract of many vertebrates, where it sometimes causes disease.
● Genus *Cryptosporidium*, phylum Sporozoa.
– ORIGIN early 20th cent.: from **CRYPTO-** 'concealed' + modern Latin *sporidium* 'small spore'.

Cryptozoic /ˌkrɪptəˈzəʊɪk/ ▶ **adjective** Geology of, relating to, or denoting the period (the Precambrian) in which rocks contain no, or only slight, traces of living organisms. Compare with **PHANEROZOIC**.
– ORIGIN early 20th cent.: from Greek *kruptos* 'hidden' + *zōē* 'life' + **-IC**.

cryptozoic /ˌkrɪptəˈzəʊɪk/ ▶ **adjective** Ecology (of small invertebrates) living on the ground but hidden in the leaf litter, under stones or pieces of wood.
– DERIVATIVES **cryptozoa** plural noun.
– ORIGIN late 19th cent.: from Greek *kruptos* 'hidden' + *zōē* 'life' + **-IC**.

cryptozoology ▶ **noun** [mass noun] the search for and study of animals whose existence or survival is disputed or unsubstantiated, such as the Loch Ness monster and the yeti.
– DERIVATIVES **cryptozoological** adjective, **cryptozoologist** noun.

crystal ▶ **noun** **1** a piece of a homogeneous solid substance having a natural geometrically regular form with symmetrically arranged plane faces.
■ Chemistry any solid consisting of a symmetrical, ordered, three-dimensional aggregation of atoms or molecules. ■ Electronics a crystalline piece of semiconductor used as an oscillator or transducer.
■ [mass noun] a clear transparent mineral, especially quartz.
2 (also **crystal glass**) [mass noun] highly transparent glass with a high refractive index: [as modifier] *a crystal chandelier.*
■ articles made of such glass: *a collection of crystal.*
■ [count noun] the glass over a watch face.
▶ **adjective** clear and transparent like crystal: *the clean crystal waters of the lake.*
– PHRASES **crystal clear** completely transparent and unclouded. ■ unambiguous; easily understood.
– ORIGIN late Old English (denoting ice or a mineral resembling it), from Old French *cristal*, from Latin *crystallum*, from Greek *krustallos* 'ice, crystal'. The chemistry sense dates from the early 17th cent.

crystal axis ▶ **noun** each of three axes used to define the edges of the unit cell of a crystal.

crystal ball ▶ **noun** a solid globe of glass or rock crystal, used by fortune tellers and clairvoyants for crystal-gazing.

crystal class ▶ **noun** each of thirty-two categories of crystals classified according to the possible combinations of symmetry elements possessed by the crystal lattice.

crystal form ▶ **noun** a set of crystal faces defined according to their relationship to the crystal axes.

crystal-gazing ▶ **noun** [mass noun] looking intently into a crystal ball with the aim of seeing images relating to future or distant events.
■ figurative attempting to forecast the future.

crystal healing (also **crystal therapy**) ▶ **noun** [mass noun] the use of the supposed healing powers of crystals in alternative medicine.

crystal lattice ▶ **noun** the symmetrical three-dimensional arrangement of atoms inside a crystal.

crystallin /ˈkrɪst(ə)lɪn/ ▶ **noun** [mass noun] Biochemistry a protein of the globulin class present in the lens of the eye.
– ORIGIN mid 19th cent.: from Latin *crystallum* 'crystal' + **-IN**[1].

crystalline /ˈkrɪst(ə)lʌɪn/ ▶ **adjective** having the structure and form of a crystal; composed of crystals: *a crystalline rock.*
■ poetic/literary very clear: *he writes a crystalline prose.*
– DERIVATIVES **crystallinity** noun.
– ORIGIN Middle English: from Old French *cristallin*, via Latin from Greek *krustallinos*, from *krustallos* (see **CRYSTAL**).

crystalline lens ▶ **noun** the transparent elastic structure behind the iris by which light is focused on to the retina of the eye.

crystalline sphere ▶ **noun** historical (in ancient and medieval astronomy) a transparent sphere of the heavens postulated to lie between the fixed stars and the *primum mobile* and to account for the precession of the equinox and other motions.

crystallite /ˈkrɪst(ə)lʌɪt/ ▶ **noun** an individual perfect crystal or region of regular crystalline structure in the substance of a material, typically of a metal or a partly crystalline polymer.
■ a very small crystal.

crystallize (also **-ise**) ▶ **verb** form or cause to form crystals: [no obj.] *when most liquids freeze they crystallize.*
■ figurative make or become definite and clear: [no obj.] *vague feelings of unrest **crystallized into** something more concrete* | [with obj.] *writing can help to crystallize your thoughts.* ■ [usu. as adj. **crystallized**] coat and impregnate (fruit or petals) with sugar as a means of preserving them. ■ Finance convert or be converted from a floating charge into a fixed charge.
– DERIVATIVES **crystallizable** adjective, **crystallization** noun.

crystallography /ˌkrɪstəˈlɒgrəfi/ ▶ **noun** [mass noun] the branch of science concerned with the structure and properties of crystals.
– DERIVATIVES **crystallographer** noun, **crystallographic** adjective, **crystallographically** adverb.

crystalloid ▶ **adjective** resembling a crystal in shape or structure.
▶ **noun** **1** Botany a small crystal-like mass of protein in a plant cell.
2 Chemistry a substance that, when dissolved, forms a true solution rather than a colloid and is able to pass through a semipermeable membrane.

crystal meth ▶ **noun** see **METH** (sense 1).

Crystal Palace a large building of prefabricated iron and glass resembling a giant greenhouse, designed by Joseph Paxton for the Great Exhibition of 1851 in Hyde Park, London, and re-erected at

Sydenham near Croydon; it was accidentally burnt down in 1936.

crystal set (also **crystal radio**) ▶ noun a simple early form of radio receiver with a crystal touching a metal wire as the rectifier (instead of a valve or transistor), and no amplifier or loudspeaker, necessitating headphones or an earphone.

crystal system ▶ noun each of seven categories of crystals (cubic, tetragonal, orthorhombic, trigonal, hexagonal, monoclinic, and triclinic) classified according to the possible relations of the crystal axes.

crystal therapy ▶ noun another term for CRYSTAL HEALING.

crystal violet ▶ noun [mass noun] a synthetic violet dye, related to rosaniline, used as a stain in microscopy and as an antiseptic in the treatment of skin infections.

CS Brit. ▶ abbreviation for ■ chartered surveyor. ■ Civil Service. ■ Court of Session.

Cs ▶ symbol for the chemical element caesium.

c/s ▶ abbreviation for cycles per second.

CSA ▶ abbreviation for Child Support Agency.

csardas /ˈtʃɑːdaʃ, ˈzɑːdəs/ (also **czardas**) ▶ noun (pl. same) a Hungarian dance with a slow introduction and a fast, wild finish.
– ORIGIN mid 19th cent.: from Hungarian *csárdás*, from *csárda* 'inn'.

CSC Brit. ▶ abbreviation for Civil Service Commission.

CSE ▶ abbreviation for Certificate of Secondary Education.

CS gas ▶ noun [mass noun] a powerful form of tear gas used particularly in the control of riots.
– ORIGIN 1960s: from the initials of Ben B. *Corson* (born 1896) and Roger W. *Stoughton* (1906–57), the American chemists who discovered the properties of the chemical in 1928.

CSIRO ▶ abbreviation for (in Australia) Commonwealth Scientific and Industrial Research Organization.

CSM ▶ abbreviation for ■ command and service modules (see COMMAND MODULE). ■ (in the UK) Committee on Safety of Medicines. ■ Company Sergeant Major.

CST ▶ abbreviation for Central Standard Time (see CENTRAL TIME).

CSU ▶ abbreviation for (in the UK) Civil Service Union.

CT ▶ abbreviation for ■ computerized (or computed) tomography. ■ Connecticut (in official postal use).

ct ▶ abbreviation for ■ carat: *18 ct gold.* ■ cent.

CTC ▶ abbreviation for ■ City Technology College. ■ (in the UK) Cyclists' Touring Club.

ctenidium /tɪˈnɪdɪəm/ ▶ noun (pl. **ctenidia** /-dɪə/) Zoology a comb-like structure, especially a respiratory organ or gill in a mollusc, consisting of an axis with a row of projecting filaments.
– ORIGIN late 19th cent.: modern Latin, from Greek *ktenidion*, diminutive of *kteis, kten-* 'comb'.

ctenoid /ˈtiːnɔɪd/ ▶ adjective Zoology (of fish scales) having many tiny projections on the edge like the teeth of a comb, as in many bony fishes. Compare with GANOID and PLACOID.
– ORIGIN mid 19th cent.: from Greek *kteis, kten-* 'comb' + -OID.

Ctenophora /tiːˈnɒfərə, tɛ-/ Zoology a small phylum of aquatic invertebrates that comprises the comb jellies.
– DERIVATIVES **ctenophore** /ˈtiːnəfɔː, ˈtɛ-/ noun.
– ORIGIN modern Latin (plural), from Greek *kteis, kten-* 'comb' + *pherein* 'to bear'.

Ctesiphon /ˈtɛsɪf(ə)n/ an ancient city on the Tigris near Baghdad, capital of the Parthian kingdom from *c*.224 and then of Persia under the Sassanian dynasty. It was taken by the Arabs in 636 and destroyed in the 8th century.

CTS ▶ abbreviation for carpal tunnel syndrome.

CTT ▶ abbreviation for capital transfer tax.

CU ▶ abbreviation for Christian Union.

Cu ▶ symbol for the chemical element copper.
– ORIGIN from late Latin *cuprum*.

cu. ▶ abbreviation for cubic (in units of measurement: for example, cu. ft. = cubic feet).

cuadrilla /kwɒˈdriːljə, -ˈdriːjə/ ▶ noun a matador's team.
– ORIGIN mid 19th cent.: Spanish.

cuatro /ˈkwatrəʊ/ ▶ noun (pl. **cuatros**) a small guitar, typically with four (or five) single or paired strings, used in Latin American and Caribbean folk music, especially in Puerto Rico.
– ORIGIN Latin American Spanish, literally 'four'.

cub ▶ noun **1** the young of a fox, bear, lion, or other carnivorous mammal.
■ archaic a young man, especially one who is awkward or ill-mannered.
2 (**Cubs**) a junior branch of the Scout Association, for boys aged about 8 to 11.
■ (also **Cub Scout**) a member of this organization.
▶ verb (**cubbed**, **cubbing**) [no obj.] **1** give birth to cubs: *both share the same earth during the first ten days after cubbing.*
2 hunt fox cubs: *members of the Grafton Hunt were out cubbing.*
– ORIGIN mid 16th cent.: of unknown origin.

Cuba /ˈkjuːbə/ a Caribbean country, the largest and furthest west of the islands of the West Indies, situated at the mouth of the Gulf of Mexico; pop. 10,977,000 (est. 1994); official language, Spanish; capital, Havana.

A Spanish colony, Cuba became nominally independent after the Spanish–American War of 1898, achieving full autonomy in 1934. Since a communist revolution in 1959, it has been under the presidency of Fidel Castro. The country has suffered under a US trade embargo, and since the collapse of the Soviet Union and the Eastern bloc has lost much of its trade.

– DERIVATIVES **Cuban** adjective & noun.

cubage ▶ noun cubic content or capacity.

Cuba libre /ˌk(j)uːbə ˈliːbreɪ/ ▶ noun (pl. **Cuba libres**) a long drink typically containing lime juice and rum.
– ORIGIN American Spanish, 'free Cuba'.

Cubango /kjuːˈbaŋɡəʊ/ another name for OKAVANGO.

Cuban heel ▶ noun a moderately high straight-sided heel on a shoe or boot.

Cuban Missile Crisis an international crisis in October 1962, the closest approach to nuclear war at any time between the US and the USSR. When the US discovered Soviet nuclear missiles on Cuba, President John F. Kennedy demanded their removal and announced a naval blockade of the island; the Soviet leader Khrushchev acceded to the US demands a week later.

cubature /ˈkjuːbətʃə/ ▶ noun [mass noun] the determination of the volume of a solid.
– ORIGIN late 17th cent.: from the verb CUBE, on the pattern of *quadrature*.

cubby ▶ noun (pl. **-ies**) chiefly N. Amer. a cubbyhole.
– ORIGIN mid 17th cent. (originally Scots, denoting a straw basket): related to dialect *cub* 'stall, pen, hutch', of Low German origin.

cubbyhole ▶ noun a small enclosed space or room.
■ S. African a glove compartment in a car.

cube ▶ noun a symmetrical three-dimensional shape, either solid or hollow, contained by six equal squares.
■ a block of something with six sides: *a sugar cube.* ■ Mathematics the product of a number multiplied by its square, represented by a superscript figure 3: *a body increasing in weight by the cube of its length.*
▶ verb [with obj.] **1** Mathematics raise (a number or value) to its cube.
2 cut (food) into small cubes: *I bought sirloin from the butcher and cubed it myself.*
– ORIGIN mid 16th cent.: from Old French, or via Latin from Greek *kubos*.

cubeb /ˈkjuːbɛb/ ▶ noun a tropical shrub of the pepper family, which bears pungent berries.
● Genus *Piper*, family Piperaceae: several species, including the Asian *P. cubeba*.
■ [mass noun] the dried unripe berries of this shrub, used medicinally and to flavour cigarettes.
– ORIGIN Middle English: from Old French *cubebe*, from Spanish Arabic *kubēba*, from Arabic *kubāba*.

cube root ▶ noun the number which produces a given number when cubed.

cubic /ˈkjuːbɪk/ ▶ adjective having the shape of a cube: *a cubic room.*
■ [attrib.] denoting a unit of measurement equal to the volume of a cube whose side is one of the linear unit specified: *15 billion cubic metres of water.* ■ measured or expressed in such units. ■ involving the cube (and no higher power) of a quantity or variable: *a cubic equation.* ■ of or denoting a crystal system or three-

dimensional geometrical arrangement having three equal axes at right angles.
▶ noun Mathematics a cubic equation, or a curve described by one.
– DERIVATIVES **cubical** adjective, **cubically** adverb.
– ORIGIN late 15th cent. (in the sense 'involving the cube (and no higher power)'): from Old French *cubique*, or via Latin from Greek *kubikos*, from *kobos* 'cube'.

cubic capacity ▶ noun the volume contained by a hollow structure, expressed in litres, cubic centimetres, or other cubic units.

cubic content ▶ noun the volume of a solid, often expressed in cubic metres.

cubicle ▶ noun a small partitioned-off area of a room, for example one containing a shower, toilet, or bed.
– ORIGIN late Middle English (in the sense 'bedroom'): from Latin *cubiculum*, from *cubare* 'lie down'.

cubiform ▶ adjective technical cube-shaped: *the columns are thick and have cubiform capitals.*

cubism ▶ noun [mass noun] an early 20th-century style and movement in art, especially painting, in which perspective with a single viewpoint was abandoned and use was made of simple geometric shapes, interlocking planes, and, later, collage.

Cubism was a reaction against traditional modes of representation and Impressionist concerns with light and colour. The style, created by Picasso and Braque and first named by the French critic Louis Vauxcelles in 1908, was inspired by the later work of Cézanne and by African sculpture.

– DERIVATIVES **cubist** noun & adjective.
– ORIGIN early 20th cent.: from French *cubisme*, from *cube* (see CUBE).

cubit /ˈkjuːbɪt/ ▶ noun an ancient measure of length, approximately equal to the length of a forearm. It was typically about 18 inches or 44 cm, though there was a **long cubit** of about 21 inches or 52 cm.
– ORIGIN Middle English: from Latin *cubitum* 'elbow, forearm, cubit'.

cubital /ˈkjuːbɪt(ə)l/ ▶ adjective **1** Anatomy of the forearm or the elbow: *the cubital vein.*
2 Entomology of the cubitus.
– ORIGIN late Middle English: from Latin *cubitalis*, from *cubitus* 'cubit'.

cubitus /ˈkjuːbɪtəs/ ▶ noun Entomology the fifth longitudinal vein from the anterior edge of an insect's wing.
– ORIGIN early 19th cent.: from Latin.

cuboid /ˈkjuːbɔɪd/ ▶ adjective more or less cubic in shape: *the school was a hideous cuboid erection of brick and glass.*
▶ noun **1** Geometry a solid which has six rectangular faces at right angles to each other.
2 (also **cuboid bone**) Anatomy a squat tarsal bone on the outer side of the foot, articulating with the heel bone and the fourth and fifth metatarsals.
– DERIVATIVES **cuboidal** adjective.
– ORIGIN early 19th cent.: from modern Latin *cuboides*, from Greek *kuboeidēs*, from *kubos* (see CUBE).

cub reporter ▶ noun informal a young or inexperienced newspaper reporter.

Cub Scout ▶ noun see CUB (sense 2).

cucking-stool /ˈkʌkɪŋstuːl/ ▶ noun historical a chair to which disorderly women were tied and then ducked into water or subjected to public ridicule as a punishment.
– ORIGIN Middle English: from obsolete *cuck* 'defecate', of Scandinavian origin; so named because a stool containing a chamber pot was often used for the purpose.

cuckold /ˈkʌk(ə)ld/ ▶ noun dated the husband of an adulteress, often regarded as an object of derision.
▶ verb [with obj.] (of a man) make (another man) a cuckold by having a sexual relationship with his wife.
■ (of a man's wife) make (her husband) a cuckold.
– DERIVATIVES **cuckoldry** noun.
– ORIGIN late Old English, from Old French *cucuault*, from *cucu* 'cuckoo' (from the cuckoo's habit of laying its egg in another bird's nest). The equivalent words in French and other languages applied to both the bird and the adulterer; *cuckold* has never been applied to the bird in English.

cuckoo ▶ noun a medium-sized long-tailed bird, typically with a grey or brown back and barred or

pale underparts. Many cuckoos lay their eggs in the nests of small songbirds.
• Family Cuculidae (the **cuckoo family**): numerous genera and species, especially the (**Eurasian**) **cuckoo** (*Cuculus canorus*), the male of which has a well-known two-note call. The cuckoo family also includes the coucals, roadrunners, malcohas, and anis.
▶ **adjective** informal crazy: *people think you're cuckoo.*
– PHRASES **cuckoo in the nest** an unwelcome intruder in a place or situation.
– ORIGIN Middle English: from Old French *cucu*, imitative of its call.

cuckoo bee ▶ **noun** a bee which lays its eggs in the nest of another kind of bee, the young being raised and fed by the host.
• *Nomada* and related genera (which parasitize solitary bees), and *Psithyrus* (which parasitize bumblebees), family Apidae.

cuckoo clock ▶ **noun** a clock that strikes the hour with a sound like a cuckoo's call and typically has a mechanical cuckoo that emerges with each note.

cuckooflower ▶ **noun** a spring-flowering herbaceous European plant with pale lilac flowers, growing in damp meadows and by streams. Also called **LADY'S SMOCK**.
• *Cardamine pratensis*, family Cruciferae.
– ORIGIN late 16th cent.: so named because it flowers at the time of year when the cuckoo is first heard calling.

cuckoo pint ▶ **noun** the common European wild arum of woodland and hedgerows, with a pale spathe and a purple or green spadix followed by bright red berries. Also called **LORDS AND LADIES** or **JACK-IN-THE-PULPIT**.
• *Arum maculatum*, family Araceae.
– ORIGIN late Middle English: from earlier *cuckoo-pintle*, from **PINTLE** in the obsolete sense 'penis' (because of the shape of the spadix).

cuckoo-roller ▶ **noun** a bird resembling a roller, with an iridescent green cap, back, wings, and tail, found only in Madagascar. Also called **COUROL**.
• *Leptosomus discolor*, the only member of the family Leptosomatidae.

cuckoo-shrike ▶ **noun** a shrike-like Old World songbird, somewhat resembling a cuckoo when in flight, and typically with grey, black, or white plumage.
• Family Campephagidae (the **cuckoo-shrike family**): several genera, especially *Coracina* and *Campephaga*, and numerous species. The cuckoo-shrike family also includes the cicadabirds, greybirds, minivets, and trillers.

cuckoo spit ▶ **noun** [mass noun] whitish froth found in compact masses on leaves and plant stems, exuded by the larvae of froghoppers.

cuckoo wasp ▶ **noun** a wasp which lays its eggs in the nest of a bee or another kind of wasp, in particular:
• a ruby-tailed wasp. • a true wasp lacking a worker caste, whose larvae are fed by the social wasp host (several species in the family Vespidae, including *Vespula austriaca*).

cucumber ▶ **noun** **1** a long, green-skinned fruit with watery flesh, usually eaten raw in salads or pickled.
2 the climbing plant of the gourd family which yields this fruit, native to the Chinese Himalayan region. It is widely cultivated but very rare in the wild. See also **SQUIRTING CUCUMBER**.
• *Cucumis sativus*, family Cucurbitaceae.
– PHRASES (**as**) **cool as a cucumber** untroubled by heat or exertion. ▪ calm and relaxed.
– ORIGIN late Middle English: from Old French *cocombre, coucombre*, from Latin *cucumis, cucumer-*.

cucumber mosaic ▶ **noun** [mass noun] a virus disease affecting plants of the gourd family, spread by beetles and aphids and causing mottling and stunting.

cucurbit /kjʊˈkəːbɪt/ ▶ **noun** chiefly US a plant of the gourd family (Cucurbitaceae), which includes melon, pumpkin, squash, and cucumber.
– DERIVATIVES **cucurbitaceous** adjective.
– ORIGIN late Middle English: from Old French *cucurbite*, from Latin *cucurbita*.

cud ▶ **noun** [mass noun] partly digested food returned from the first stomach of ruminants to the mouth for further chewing.
– PHRASES **chew the cud** **1** (of a ruminant animal) further chew partly digested food. **2** think or talk reflectively.
– ORIGIN Old English *cwidu, cudu*, of Germanic origin; related to German *Kitt* 'cement, putty' and Swedish *kåda* 'resin'.

cuddle ▶ **verb** [with obj.] hold close in one's arms as a way of showing love or affection: *he cuddles the baby close | they were cuddling each other in the back seat.* | [no obj.] *the pair have been spotted kissing and cuddling.*
▪ [no obj., with adverbial] lie or sit close and snug: *Rebecca* ***cuddled up to*** *Mum | they cuddled together to keep out the cold.* ▪ [no obj.] (**cuddle up to**) informal ingratiate oneself with: *they start cuddling up to the Liberals for support.*
▶ **noun** a prolonged and affectionate hug.
– DERIVATIVES **cuddlesome** adjective.
– ORIGIN early 16th cent. (rare before the 18th cent.): of unknown origin.

cuddly ▶ **adjective** (**cuddlier**, **cuddliest**) attractive, endearing, and pleasant to cuddle, especially as a result of being soft or plump: *she was short and cuddly.*
▪ [attrib.] Brit. (of a toy, especially a model of an animal) padded or spongy and covered in soft fabric.

cuddy ▶ **noun** (pl. **-ies**) dialect, chiefly Scottish **1** a donkey.
2 a stupid person: *you great soft cuddy!*
– ORIGIN early 18th cent.: perhaps a pet form of the given name *Cuthbert*, once popular in Scotland and northern England.

cudgel /ˈkʌdʒ(ə)l/ ▶ **noun** a short thick stick used as a weapon.
▶ **verb** (**cudgelled**, **cudgelling**; US **cudgeled**, **cudgeling**) [with obj.] beat with a cudgel.
– PHRASES **cudgel one's brain** (or **brains**) think hard about a problem. **take up the cudgels** start to defend or support someone or something strongly: *there was no one else to* ***take up the cudgels on their behalf.***
– ORIGIN Old English *cycgel*, of unknown origin.

Cudlipp /ˈkʌdlɪp/, Hugh, Baron Cudlipp of Aldingbourne (1913–98), British newspaper editor. Editorial director of the *Daily Mirror*, he conceived the formula of the sensationalized presentation of sex and crime, increasing dramatically the paper's circulation.

cudweed ▶ **noun** [mass noun] a plant of the daisy family, with hairy or downy leaves and inconspicuous flowers.
• Genera *Gnaphalium* and *Filago*, family Compositae.
– ORIGIN mid 16th cent.: from **CUD** + **WEED**, said to be given to cattle who had lost their cud.

cue[1] ▶ **noun** a thing said or done that serves as a signal to an actor or other performer to enter or to begin their speech or performance.
▪ a signal for action: *his success was the* ***cue for*** *the rest of Fleet Street to forge ahead.* ▪ a piece of information or circumstance which aids the memory in retrieving details not recalled spontaneously. ▪ Psychology a feature of something perceived that is used in the brain's interpretation of the perception: *expectancy is communicated both by auditory and visual cues.* ▪ a hint or indication about how to behave in particular circumstances: *my teacher joked about such attitudes and I followed her cue.* ▪ [mass noun] a facility for playing through an audio or video recording very rapidly until a desired starting point is reached.
▶ **verb** (**cues**, **cued**, **cueing** or **cuing**) [with obj.] give a cue to or for: *Ros and Guil, cued by Hamlet, also bow deeply.*
▪ act as a prompt or reminder: *have a list of needs and questions on paper to cue you.* ▪ set a piece of audio or video equipment in readiness to play (a particular part of the recorded material): *features make it easier to* ***cue up*** *a tape for editing.*
– PHRASES **on cue** at the correct moment: *right on cue the door opened.* **take one's cue from** follow the example or advice of: *McGee did not move and Julia took her cue from him.*
– ORIGIN mid 16th cent.: of unknown origin.

cue[2] ▶ **noun** a long straight tapering wooden rod for striking the ball in snooker, billiards, etc.
▶ **verb** (**cues**, **cued**, **cueing** or **cuing**) [no obj.] use such a rod to strike the ball.
– DERIVATIVES **cueist** noun (rare).
– ORIGIN mid 18th cent. (denoting a long plait or pigtail): variant of **QUEUE**.

cue ball ▶ **noun** the ball, usually a white one, that is to be struck with the cue in snooker, billiards, etc.

cue bid ▶ **noun** Bridge a bid intended to give specific information about the content of the hand to the bidder's partner, for example, possession of a control in the opponents' suit, rather than to advance the auction.

cueca /ˈkwɛkə/ ▶ **noun** a lively South American dance.
– ORIGIN early 20th cent.: American Spanish, from *zamacueca*, also denoting a dance performed especially in Chile.

cue card ▶ **noun** a card held beside a camera for a television broadcaster to read from while appearing as if looking into the camera.

Cuenca /ˈkwɛŋkə/ a city in the Andes in southern Ecuador; pop. 239,900 (est. 1995). Founded in 1557, it is known as the 'marble city' because of its many fine buildings.

Cuernavaca /ˌkwɛːnəˈvakə, Spanish kwernaˈβaka/ a resort town in central Mexico, at an altitude of 1,542 m (5,060 ft), capital of the state of Morelos; pop. 400,000 (est. 1990).

cuesta /ˈkwɛstə/ ▶ **noun** Geology a ridge with a gentle slope (dip) on one side and a steep slope (scarp) on the other.
– ORIGIN early 19th cent. (originally a US term for a steep slope at the edge of a plain): from Spanish, 'slope', from Latin *costa* 'rib, flank'.

cuff[1] ▶ **noun** **1** the end part of a sleeve, where the material of the sleeve is turned back or a separate band is sewn on.
▪ the part of a glove covering the wrist. ▪ chiefly N. Amer. a trouser turn-up. ▪ the top part of a boot, typically padded or turned down. ▪ an inflatable bag wrapped round the arm when blood pressure is measured.
2 (**cuffs**) informal handcuffs.
▶ **verb** [with obj.] informal secure with handcuffs: *the man's hands were cuffed behind his back.*
– PHRASES **off the cuff** informal without preparation: *they posed some difficult questions to answer off the cuff* | [as modifier] *an off-the-cuff remark.* [ORIGIN: as if from impromptu notes made on one's shirt cuffs.]
– DERIVATIVES **cuffed** adjective [in combination] *a double-cuffed striped shirt.*
– ORIGIN late Middle English (denoting a glove or mitten): of unknown origin.

cuff[2] ▶ **verb** [with obj.] strike (someone) with an open hand, especially on the head: *he cuffed him playfully on the ear.*
▶ **noun** [usu. in sing.] a blow given with an open hand.
– ORIGIN mid 16th cent.: of unknown origin.

cufflink ▶ **noun** (usu. **cufflinks**) a device for fastening together the sides of a shirt cuff, typically a pair of linked studs or a single plate connected to a short swivelling rod, passed through a hole in each side of the cuff.

Cufic ▶ **noun** & **adjective** variant spelling of **KUFIC**.

Cuiabá /ˌkuːjəˈbɑː/ **1** a river port in west central Brazil, on the Cuiabá River, capital of the state of Mato Grosso; pop. 389,070 (1990).
2 a river of western Brazil, which rises in the Mato Grosso plateau and flows for 483 km (300 miles) to join the São Lourenço River near the border with Bolivia.

cui bono? /kwiː ˈbɒnəʊ, ˈbəʊ-/ ▶ **exclamation** who stands, or stood, to gain (from a crime, and so might have been responsible for it)?
– ORIGIN Latin, 'to whom (is it) a benefit?'

cuirass /kwɪˈras/ ▶ **noun** **1** historical a piece of armour consisting of breastplate and backplate fastened together.
2 Medicine an artificial ventilator which encloses the body, leaving the limbs free, and forces air in and out of the lungs by changes in pressure.
– ORIGIN late Middle English: from Old French *cuirace*, based on late Latin *coriaceus* (adjective), from *corium* 'leather' (of which a cuirass was originally made).

cuirassier /ˌkwɪrəˈsiːə, French kɥirasje/ ▶ **noun** historical a cavalry soldier wearing a cuirass.
– ORIGIN mid 16th cent.: French, from *cuirasse*, from Old French *cuirace* (see **CUIRASS**).

cuisine /kwɪˈziːn/ ▶ **noun** [mass noun] a style or method of cooking, especially as characteristic of a particular country, region, or establishment: *much Venetian cuisine is based on seafood.*
▪ food cooked in a certain way: *we spent the evening sampling the local cuisine.*
– ORIGIN late 18th cent.: French, literally 'kitchen', from Latin *coquina*, from *coquere* 'to cook'.

cuisse /kwɪs/ (also **cuish** /kwɪʃ/) ▶ **noun** (usu. **cuisses** or **cuishes**) historical a piece of armour for the thigh.
– ORIGIN Middle English (originally in the plural): from Old French *cuisseaux*, plural of *cuissel*, from late Latin *coxale*, from *coxa* 'hip'.

cuke /kjuːk/ ▶ **noun** Brit. informal term for **CUCUMBER**.

Culbertson /ˈkʌlbəts(ə)n/, Ely (1891–1955),

American bridge player. An authority on contract bridge, he revolutionized the game by formalizing a system of bidding. This helped to establish this form of the game in preference to auction bridge.

culch ▶ noun variant spelling of CULTCH.

culchie /ˈkʌl(t)ʃi/ ▶ noun (pl. **-ies**) Irish derogatory a country bumpkin.
– ORIGIN 1950s: apparently an alteration of *Kiltimagh* (Irish *Coillte Mach*), the name of a country town in County Mayo, Ireland.

Culdee /kʌlˈdiː/ ▶ noun an Irish or Scottish monk of the 8th to 12th centuries, living as a recluse usually in a group of thirteen (on the analogy of Christ and his Apostles). The tradition ceased as the Celtic Church was brought under Roman Catholic rule.
– ORIGIN late Middle English: from medieval Latin *culdeus*, alteration, influenced by Latin *cultores Dei* 'worshippers of God', of *kelledei* (plural, found in early Scottish records), from Old Irish *céle dé*, literally 'companion of God'.

cul-de-sac /ˈkʌldəˌsak, ˈkʊl-/ ▶ noun (pl. **culs-de-sac** pronunc. same) a street or passage closed at one end.
■ figurative a route or course leading nowhere: *was the new post a career cul-de-sac?*
– ORIGIN mid 18th cent. (originally in anatomy): French, literally 'bottom of a sack'.

-cule ▶ suffix forming nouns such as *molecule*, *reticule*, which were originally diminutives.
– ORIGIN from French *-cule* or Latin *-culus*, *-cula*, *-culum*.

culex /ˈkjuːlɛks/ (also **culex mosquito**) ▶ noun (pl. **culices** /-lɪsiːz/) a mosquito of a genus which includes a number of kinds commonly found in cooler regions. They do not transmit malaria, but can pass on a variety of other parasites including those causing filariasis. Compare with ANOPHELES.
● Genus *Culex*, subfamily Culicinae, family Culicidae.
– DERIVATIVES **culicine** /ˈkjuːlɪsʌɪn, -siːn/ adjective & noun.
– ORIGIN Latin, 'gnat'.

Culiacán Rosales /ˌkʊljəˌkɑːn rəʊˈzɑːlɛz/ a city in NW Mexico, capital of the state of Sinaloa; pop. 662,110 (1990).

culinary ▶ adjective of or for cooking: *culinary skills* | *savour the culinary delights of the region.*
– DERIVATIVES **culinarily** adverb.
– ORIGIN mid 17th cent.: from Latin *culinarius*, from *culina* 'kitchen'.

cull ▶ verb [with obj.] (usu. **be culled**) select from a large quantity; obtain from a variety of sources: *anecdotes culled from Greek and Roman history.*
■ reduce the population of (a wild animal) by selective slaughter: *he sees culling deer as a necessity* | [as noun **culling**] *kangaroo culling.* ■ send (an inferior or surplus animal on a farm) to be slaughtered. ■ poetic/literary pick (flowers or fruit): [as adj. **culled**] *fresh culled daffodils.*
▶ noun a selective slaughter of wild animals.
■ [usu. as modifier] an inferior or surplus livestock animal selected for killing: *a cull cow.*
– DERIVATIVES **culler** noun.
– ORIGIN Middle English: from Old French *coillier*, based on Latin *colligere* (see COLLECT[1]).

cullet /ˈkʌlɪt/ ▶ noun [mass noun] recycled broken or waste glass used in glass-making.
– ORIGIN early 19th cent.: variant of COLLET, in the obsolete sense 'glass left on the blowing-iron when the finished article is removed'.

Culloden, Battle of /kəˈlɒd(ə)n/ the final engagement of the Jacobite uprising of 1745–6, fought on a moor near Inverness, the last pitched battle on British soil. The Hanoverian army under the Duke of Cumberland crushed the small and poorly supplied Jacobite army of Charles Edward Stuart, and a ruthless pursuit after the battle effectively prevented any chance of saving the Jacobite cause.

cully /ˈkʌli/ ▶ noun (pl. **-ies**) informal (often as a form of address) a man; a friend.
– ORIGIN mid 17th cent. (denoting a person who is imposed upon): of unknown origin.

Culm /kʌlm/ ▶ noun [mass noun] Geology a series of Carboniferous strata in SW England, mainly shale and limestone with some thin coal seams.
■ (**culm**) archaic coal dust or slack.
– ORIGIN Middle English (in the sense 'soot, smut', now only Scots): probably related to COAL.

culm /kʌlm/ ▶ noun the hollow stem of a grass or cereal plant, especially that bearing the flower.
– ORIGIN mid 17th cent.: from Latin *culmus* 'stalk'.

culmen /ˈkʌlmɛn/ ▶ noun (pl. **culmina** /-mɪnə/)
1 Ornithology the upper ridge of a bird's bill.
2 Anatomy a small region in the brain on the anterior surface of the cerebellum.
– ORIGIN mid 17th cent. (in the sense 'top, summit'): from Latin, contraction of *columen* 'top, summit'.

culminant ▶ adjective at or forming the top or highest point.

culminate /ˈkʌlmɪneɪt/ ▶ verb [no obj.] reach a climax or point of highest development: *weeks of violence* **culminated in** *the brutal murder of a magistrate.*
■ [with obj.] be the climax or point of highest development of: *her book culminated a research project on the symmetry studies of Escher.* ■ archaic or Astrology (of a celestial body) reach or be at the meridian.
– ORIGIN mid 17th cent. (in astronomy and astrology): from late Latin *culminat-* 'exalted', from the verb *culminare*, from *culmen* 'summit'.

culmination ▶ noun [in sing.] the highest or climactic point of something, especially as attained after a long time: *the deal marked the culmination of years of negotiation.*
■ archaic or Astrology the reaching of the meridian by a celestial body.

culottes /kjuːˈlɒt(s)/ ▶ plural noun women's knee-length trousers, cut with very full legs to resemble a skirt.
– ORIGIN mid 19th cent.: French, 'knee breeches', diminutive of *cul* 'rump', from Latin *culus*.

culpable ▶ adjective deserving blame: *mercy killings are less culpable than 'ordinary' murders.*
– DERIVATIVES **culpability** noun, **culpably** adverb.
– ORIGIN Middle English (in the sense 'deserving punishment'): from Old French *coupable*, *culpable*, from Latin *culpabilis*, from *culpare* 'to blame', from *culpa* 'fault, blame'.

culpable homicide ▶ noun [mass noun] Law (in some jurisdictions, including Scotland, South Africa, and India) an act which has resulted in a person's death but is held not to amount to murder.

Culpeper /ˈkʌlpɛpə/, Nicholas (1616–54), English herbalist. His *Complete Herbal* (1653) popularized herbalism and, despite embracing ideas of astrology and the doctrine of signatures, was important in the development of botany and pharmacology.

culprit ▶ noun a person who is responsible for a crime or other misdeed.
■ the cause of a problem or defect: *low-level ozone pollution is the real culprit.*
– ORIGIN late 17th cent. (originally in the formula *Culprit, how will you be tried?*, said by the Clerk of the Crown to a prisoner pleading not guilty): perhaps from a misinterpretation of the written abbreviation *cul. prist*, for Anglo-Norman French *Culpable: prest d'averrer notre bille* '(You are) guilty: (We are) ready to prove our indictment'; in later use influenced by Latin *culpa* 'fault, blame'.

cult ▶ noun a system of religious veneration and devotion directed towards a particular figure or object: *the cult of St Olaf.*
■ a relatively small group of people having religious beliefs or practices regarded by others as strange or sinister: *a network of Satan-worshipping cults.* ■ a misplaced or excessive admiration for a particular person or thing: *the* **cult of** *the pursuit of money as an end in itself.* ■ a person or thing that is popular or fashionable, especially among a particular section of society: *the series has become a bit of a cult in the UK* | [as modifier] *a cult film.*
– DERIVATIVES **cultic** adjective, **cultish** adjective, **cultishness** noun, **cultism** noun, **cultist** noun.
– ORIGIN early 17th cent. (originally denoting homage paid to a divinity): from French *culte* or Latin *cultus* 'worship', from *cult-* 'inhabited, cultivated, worshipped', from the verb *colere*.

cultch /kʌltʃ/ (also **culch**) ▶ noun [mass noun] the mass of stones, broken shells, and grit of which an oyster bed is formed.
– ORIGIN mid 17th cent.: of unknown origin.

cultigen /ˈkʌltɪdʒ(ə)n/ ▶ noun Botany a plant species or variety known only in cultivation, especially one with no known wild ancestor.
– ORIGIN early 20th cent.: from *cultivated* (past participle of CULTIVATE) + -GEN.

cultivar /ˈkʌltɪvɑː/ ▶ noun Botany a plant variety that has been produced in cultivation by selective breeding. Cultivars are usually designated in the style *Taxus baccata* 'Variegata'. See also VARIETY (sense 2).
– ORIGIN 1920s: blend of CULTIVATE and VARIETY.

cultivate ▶ verb [with obj.] **1** prepare and use (land) for crops or gardening.
■ break up (soil) in preparation for sowing or planting. ■ raise or grow (plants), especially on a large scale for commercial purposes. ■ Biology grow or maintain (living cells or tissue) in culture.
2 try to acquire or develop (a quality, sentiment, or skill): *he cultivated an air of indifference.*
■ try to win the friendship or favour of (someone): *it helps if you go out of your way to cultivate the local people.* ■ [usu. as adj. **cultivated**] apply oneself to improving or developing (one's mind or manners): *he was a remarkably cultivated and educated man.*
– DERIVATIVES **cultivable** adjective, **cultivatable** adjective, **cultivation** noun.
– ORIGIN mid 17th cent.: from medieval Latin *cultivat-* 'prepared for crops', from the verb *cultivare*, from *cultiva (terra)* 'arable (land)', from *colere* 'cultivate, inhabit'.

cultivator ▶ noun a person or thing that cultivates something: *they were herders of cattle and cultivators of corn.*
■ a mechanical implement for breaking up the ground and uprooting weeds.

cultural ▶ adjective of or relating to the ideas, customs, and social behaviour of a society: *the cultural diversity of British society.*
■ of or relating to the arts and to intellectual achievements: *a cultural festival.*
– DERIVATIVES **culturally** adverb.
– ORIGIN mid 19th cent.: from Latin *cultura* 'tillage' + -AL.

cultural anthropology ▶ noun see ANTHROPOLOGY.

cultural attaché ▶ noun an embassy official whose function is to promote cultural relations between his own country and that to which he is accredited.

Cultural Revolution a political upheaval in China 1966–8 intended to bring about a return to revolutionary Maoist beliefs. Largely carried forward by the Red Guard, it resulted in attacks on intellectuals, a large-scale purge in party posts, and the appearance of a personality cult around Mao Zedong. It led to considerable economic dislocation and was gradually brought to a halt by premier Zhou Enlai.

culture ▶ noun [mass noun] **1** the arts and other manifestations of human intellectual achievement regarded collectively: *20th century popular culture.*
■ a refined understanding or appreciation of this: *men of culture.* ■ the customs, arts, social institutions, and achievements of a particular nation, people, or other social group: *Afro-Caribbean culture* | [count noun] *people from many different cultures.* ■ [with modifier] the attitudes and behaviour characteristic of a particular social group: *the emerging drug culture.*
2 Biology the cultivation of bacteria, tissue cells, etc. in an artificial medium containing nutrients: *the cells proliferate readily* **in culture**.
■ [count noun] a preparation of cells obtained in such a way: *the bacterium was isolated in two blood cultures.* ■ the cultivation of plants: *this variety of lettuce is popular for its ease of culture.*
▶ verb [with obj.] Biology maintain (tissue cells, bacteria, etc.) in conditions suitable for growth.
– ORIGIN Middle English (denoting a cultivated piece of land): the noun from French *culture* or directly from Latin *cultura* 'growing, cultivation'; the verb from obsolete French *culturer* or medieval Latin *culturare*, both based on Latin *colere* 'tend, cultivate' (see CULTIVATE). In late Middle English the sense was 'cultivation of the soil' and from this (early 16th cent.), arose 'cultivation (of the mind, faculties, or manners)'; sense 1 dates from the early 19th cent.

culture-bound ▶ adjective restricted in character or outlook by belonging or referring to a particular culture.

cultured ▶ adjective **1** characterized by refined taste and manners and good education: *Muslim Spain was the most cultured society in western Europe.*
2 Biology (of tissue cells, bacteria, etc.) grown or propagated in an artificial medium.
■ (of a pearl) formed round a foreign body inserted into an oyster.

a cat | ɑː arm | ɛ bed | ɛː hair | ə ago | əː her | ɪ sit | i cosy | iː see | ɒ hot | ɔː saw | ʌ run | ʊ put | uː too | ʌɪ my | aʊ how | eɪ day | əʊ no | ɪə near | ɔɪ boy | ʊə poor | ʌɪə fire | aʊə sour

culture shock ▶ **noun** [mass noun] the feeling of disorientation experienced by someone when they are suddenly subjected to an unfamiliar culture, way of life, or set of attitudes.

culture vulture ▶ **noun** informal a person who is very interested in the arts, especially to an obsessive degree.

cultus /ˈkʌltəs/ ▶ **noun** technical a system or variety of religious worship.
– ORIGIN mid 19th cent.: Latin (see **CULT**).

culverin /ˈkʌlv(ə)rɪn/ ▶ **noun 1** a 16th- or 17th-century cannon with a relatively long barrel for its bore, typically about 10 to 13 feet long. **2** a kind of handgun of the 15th and 16th centuries.
– ORIGIN late 15th cent. (in sense 2): from Old French *couleuvrine*, from *couleuvre* 'snake', based on Latin *colubra*.

culvert /ˈkʌlvət/ ▶ **noun** a tunnel carrying a stream or open drain under a road or railway.
▶ **verb** [with obj.] (usu. **be culverted**) channel (a stream or drain) through a culvert.
– ORIGIN late 18th cent.: of unknown origin.

cum[1] /kʌm/ ▶ **preposition** [usu. in combination] combined with; also used as (used to describe things with a dual nature or function): *a study-cum-bedroom*.
– ORIGIN late 19th cent.: Latin.

cum[2] /kʌm/ ▶ **noun** informal variant spelling of **COME**.

cumber /ˈkʌmbə/ ▶ **verb** [with obj.] dated hamper or hinder (someone or something): *they were cumbered with greatcoats and swords.*
 ■ obstruct (a path or space): *the road was clean and dry and not still cumbered by slush.*
▶ **noun** archaic a hindrance, obstruction, or burden: *a cumber of limestone rocks.*
– ORIGIN Middle English (in the sense 'overthrow, destroy'): probably from **ENCUMBER**.

Cumberland[1] /ˈkʌmbələnd/ a former county of NW England. In 1974 it was united with Westmorland and part of Lancashire to form the county of Cumbria.

Cumberland[2] /ˈkʌmbələnd/, William Augustus, Duke of (1721–65), English military commander, third son of George II. He gained great notoriety (and his nickname 'the Butcher') for the severity of his suppression of the Jacobite clans in the aftermath of his victory at the Battle of Culloden (1746).

Cumberland sauce ▶ **noun** [mass noun] a piquant sauce served as a relish with game and cold meats. It is typically made from redcurrant jelly flavoured with orange, mustard, and port.

Cumberland sausage ▶ **noun** [mass noun] Brit. a type of coarse sausage traditionally made in a continuous strip and cooked and served as a spiral.

Cumbernauld /ˌkʌmbəˈnɔːld/ a town in central Scotland, in North Lanarkshire; pop. 48,760 (1991). It was built as a new town in 1955.

cumbersome ▶ **adjective** large or heavy and therefore difficult to carry or use; unwieldy: *cumbersome diving suits.*
 ■ slow or complicated and therefore inefficient: *organizations with cumbersome hierarchical structures.*
– DERIVATIVES **cumbersomely** adverb, **cumbersomeness** noun.
– ORIGIN late Middle English (in the sense 'difficult to get through'): from **CUMBER** + **-SOME**[1].

cumbia /ˈkʊmbɪə/ ▶ **noun** [mass noun] a kind of dance music of Colombian origin, similar to salsa.
 ■ [count noun] a dance performed to this music.
– ORIGIN 1940s: from Colombian Spanish, perhaps from Spanish *cumbé*.

Cumbria /ˈkʌmbrɪə/ a county of NW England; county town, Carlisle. Cumbria was an ancient British kingdom, and the name continued to be used for the hilly north-western region of England containing the Lake District and much of the northern Pennines. The county of Cumbria was formed in 1974, largely from the former counties of Westmorland and Cumberland.
– DERIVATIVES **Cumbrian** adjective & noun.
– ORIGIN from medieval Latin, from Welsh *Cymry* 'Welshman'.

cumbrous /ˈkʌmbrəs/ ▶ **adjective** poetic/literary term for **CUMBERSOME**.
– DERIVATIVES **cumbrously** adverb, **cumbrousness** noun.

– ORIGIN late Middle English (in the sense 'difficult to get through'): from **CUMBER** + **-OUS**.

cum dividend ▶ **adverb** (of share purchases) with a dividend about to be paid.

cumene /ˈkjuːmiːn/ ▶ **noun** [mass noun] Chemistry a liquid hydrocarbon made catalytically from benzene, chiefly as an intermediate in phenol synthesis.
 ● Alternative name: **isopropyl benzene**; chem. formula: $C_6H_5CH(CH_3)_2$.
– ORIGIN mid 19th cent.: from Latin *cuminum* 'cumin' + **-ENE**.

cum grano salis /kʌm ˌɡrɑːnəʊ ˈsɑːlɪs/ ▶ **adverb** (in phrase **take something cum grano salis**) another way of saying **take something with a pinch of salt** (see **SALT**).
– ORIGIN Latin, 'with a grain of salt'.

cumin /ˈkʌmɪn/ (also **cummin**) ▶ **noun** [mass noun] **1** the aromatic seeds of a plant of the parsley family, used as a spice, especially ground and used in curry powder. **2** the small slender plant which bears this fruit, occurring from the Mediterranean to central Asia.
 ● *Cuminum cyminum*, family Umbelliferae.
– ORIGIN Old English *cymen*, from Latin *cuminum*, from Greek *kuminon*, probably of Semitic origin and related to Hebrew *kammōn* and Arabic *kammūn*; superseded in Middle English by forms from Old French *cumon*, *comin*, also from Latin.

cummerbund /ˈkʌməbʌnd/ ▶ **noun** a sash worn around the waist, especially as part of a man's formal evening suit.
– ORIGIN early 17th cent.: from Urdu and Persian *kamar-band*, from *kamar* 'waist, loins' and *-bandi* 'band'. The sash was formerly worn in the Indian subcontinent by domestic workers and low-status office workers.

cummings, e. e. (1894–1962), American poet and novelist; full name *Edward Estlin Cummings*. His poems are characterized by their experimental typography (most notably in the avoidance of capital letters), technical skill, frank vocabulary, and the sharpness of his satire.

cummingtonite /ˈkʌmɪŋtənaɪt/ ▶ **noun** [mass noun] a mineral occurring typically as brownish fibrous crystals in some metamorphic rocks. It is a magnesium-rich iron silicate of the amphibole group.
– ORIGIN early 19th cent.: named after *Cummington*, a town in Massachusetts, US, + **-ITE**[1].

cumquat ▶ **noun** variant spelling of **KUMQUAT**.

cumulate ▶ **verb** /ˈkjuːmjʊleɪt/ [with obj.] gather together and combine: *the systems cumulate data over a period of years.*
 ■ [no obj.] be gathered together and combined: *all unpaid dividend payments cumulate and are paid when earnings are sufficient.* ■ [as adj. **cumulated**] Chemistry denoting two double bonds attached to the same carbon atom.
▶ **noun** /ˈkjuːmjʊlət/ Geology an igneous rock formed by gravitational settling of particles in a magma.
– DERIVATIVES **cumulation** noun.
– ORIGIN mid 16th cent. (as a verb in the sense 'gather in a heap'): from Latin *cumulat-* 'heaped', from the verb *cumulare*, from *cumulus* 'a heap'. Current senses date from the early 20th cent.

cumulative ▶ **adjective** increasing or increased in quantity, degree, or force by successive additions: *the cumulative effect of two years of drought.*
– DERIVATIVES **cumulatively** adverb, **cumulativeness** noun.

cumulative distribution function ▶ **noun** Statistics a function whose value is the probability that a corresponding continuous random variable has a value less than or equal to the argument of the function.

cumulative error ▶ **noun** Statistics an error that increases with the size of the sample revealing it.

cumulative preference share ▶ **noun** a preference share whose annual fixed-rate dividend, if it cannot be paid in any year, accrues until it can.

cumulative voting ▶ **noun** [mass noun] a system of voting in an election in which each voter is allowed as many votes as there are candidates and may give all to one candidate or varying numbers to several.

cumulonimbus /ˌkjuːmjʊləʊˈnɪmbəs/ ▶ **noun** (pl. **cumulonimbi** /-baɪ/) [mass noun] Meteorology cloud forming a towering mass with a flat base at fairly

low altitude and often a flat top, as in thunderstorms.

cumulus /ˈkjuːmjʊləs/ ▶ **noun** (pl. **cumuli** /-laɪ, -liː/) [mass noun] Meteorology cloud forming rounded masses heaped on each other above a flat base at fairly low altitude.
– ORIGIN mid 17th cent. (denoting a heap or an accumulation): from Latin, 'heap'.

Cuna ▶ **noun** & **adjective** variant spelling of **KUNA**.

Cunard /kjuːˈnɑːd/, Sir Samuel (1787–1865), Canadian-born British shipowner. One of the pioneers of the regular transatlantic passenger service, he founded the steamship company which still bears his name with the aid of a contract to carry the mail between Britain and Canada. The first such voyage for the company was made in 1840.

cuneate /ˈkjuːnɪət/ ▶ **adjective** chiefly Anatomy & Botany wedge-shaped.
– ORIGIN early 19th cent.: from Latin *cuneus* 'wedge' + **-ATE**[2].

cuneiform /ˈkjuːnɪfɔːm, kjuːˈneɪfɔːm/ ▶ **adjective** denoting or relating to the wedge-shaped characters used in the ancient writing systems of Mesopotamia, Persia, and Ugarit, surviving mainly impressed on clay tablets: *a cuneiform inscription.*
 ■ Anatomy denoting three bones of the tarsus (ankle) between the navicular bone and the metatarsals.
 ■ chiefly Biology wedge-shaped: *the eggs are cuneiform.*
▶ **noun** [mass noun] cuneiform writing.
– ORIGIN late 17th cent.: from French *cunéiforme* or modern Latin *cuneiformis*, from Latin *cuneus* 'wedge'.

Cunene /kjuːˈneɪnə/ a river of Angola, which rises near the city of Huambo and flows 250 km (156 miles) southwards as far as the frontier with Namibia, which then follows it westwards to the Atlantic.

cu-nim ▶ **noun** short for **CUMULONIMBUS**.

cunjevoi /ˈkʌndʒɪvɔɪ/ ▶ **noun 1** a tall Australian plant of the arum family, with edible corms.
 ● *Alocasia macrorrhiza*, family Araceae.
 2 an Australian sea squirt used as fishing bait.
 ● *Pyura praeputialis*, class Ascidiacea.
– ORIGIN late 19th cent. (in sense 1): of Aboriginal (probably Queensland) origin. Sense 2 dates from the early 20th cent.

cunner /ˈkʌnə/ ▶ **noun** an edible greenish-grey wrasse (fish) which lives along the Atlantic coast of North America.
 ● *Tautogolabrus adspersus*, family Labridae.
– ORIGIN early 17th cent.: perhaps associated with archaic *conder*, denoting a lookout who alerts the crew of fishing boats to the direction taken by shoals of herring.

cunnilingus /ˌkʌnɪˈlɪŋɡəs/ ▶ **noun** [mass noun] stimulation of the female genitals using the tongue or lips.
– ORIGIN late 19th cent.: from Latin, from *cunnus* 'vulva' + *lingere* 'lick'.

cunning ▶ **adjective 1** having or showing skill in achieving one's ends by deceit or evasion: *a cunning look came into his eyes.*
 ■ ingenious: *plants have evolved cunning defences.*
 2 N. Amer. attractive; quaint: *Baby will look too cunning for anything in that pink print.*
▶ **noun** [mass noun] skill in achieving one's ends by deceit: *a statesman to whom cunning had come as second nature.*
 ■ ingenuity: *what resources of energy and cunning it took just to survive.*
– DERIVATIVES **cunningly** adverb, **cunningness** noun.
– ORIGIN Middle English: perhaps from Old Norse *kunnandi* 'knowledge', from *kunna* 'know' (related to **CAN**[1]), or perhaps from Middle English *cunne*, an obsolete variant of **CAN**[1]. The original sense was '(possessing) erudition or skill' and had no implication of deceit; the sense 'deceitfulness' dates from late Middle English.

Cunningham /ˈkʌnɪŋəm/, Merce (b.1919), American dancer and choreographer. A dancer with the Martha Graham Dance Company (1939–45), he formed his own company in 1953 and explored new abstract directions for modern dance.

Cunobelinus /ˌkjuːnə(ʊ)bəˈlaɪnəs/ variant of **CYMBELINE**.

cunt ▶ **noun** vulgar slang a woman's genitals.
 ■ offensive an unpleasant, unkind, or stupid person.
– ORIGIN Middle English: of Germanic origin; related to Norwegian and Swedish dialect *kunta*, and

Middle Low German, Middle Dutch, and Danish dialect *kunte*.

CUP ► abbreviation for Cambridge University Press.

cup ► noun **1** a small bowl-shaped container for drinking from, typically having a handle and used with a matching saucer for hot drinks. ■ the contents of such a container: *a strong cup of tea*. ■ chiefly N. Amer. a measure of capacity used in cookery, equal to half a US pint (0.237 litre): *a cup of butter*. ■ (in church use) a chalice used at the Eucharist. ■ an ornamental trophy in the form of a cup, usually made of gold or silver and having a stem and two handles, awarded as a prize in a sports contest. ■ **(Cup)** such a contest: *playing in the Cup is the best thing ever*. ■ **(cups)** one of the suits in a tarot pack. **2** a cup-shaped thing, in particular: ■ either of the two parts of a bra shaped to contain or support one breast. ■ this as a measure of breast size: *she had grown from an A to a C cup in just six months*. ■ Golf the hole on a putting green or the metal container in it. ■ Canadian a receptacle forming part of a liquidizer. **3** [mass noun] a mixed drink served at parties, typically flavoured with fruit juices and containing wine or cider.
► verb (**cupped, cupping**) [with obj.] **1** form (one's hand or hands) into the curved shape of a cup: *'Hey!' Dad shouted, with his hands cupped around his mouth.* ■ place the curved hand or hands around: *he cupped her face in his hands.* **2** Medicine historical bleed (someone) by using a glass in which a partial vacuum is formed by heating: *Dr Ross ordered me to be cupped.*
– PHRASES **in one's cups** informal drunk. **not one's cup of tea** informal not what one likes or is interested in: *cats were not her cup of tea.*
– ORIGIN Old English: from popular Latin *cuppa*, probably from Latin *cupa* 'tub'.

cup-and-ring ► adjective denoting marks cut in megalithic monuments consisting of a circular depression surrounded by concentric rings.

cup-bearer ► noun chiefly historical or poetic/literary a person who serves wine, especially in a royal or noble household.

cupboard ► noun a piece of furniture with a door and usually shelves, used for storage: *a broom cupboard*. ■ a small room used for the same purpose.
– ORIGIN late Middle English (denoting a table or sideboard on which cups, plates, etc. were displayed): from **CUP** + **BOARD**.

cupboard love ► noun [mass noun] affection that is feigned in order to obtain something.

cupcake ► noun **1** a small cake baked in a cup-shaped foil or paper container and typically iced. **2** US an attractive woman (often as a term of address). ■ a weak or effeminate man.

cup coral ► noun a small brightly coloured solitary coral with tentacles that end in small knobs, sometimes found in colder seas.
● Genus *Caryophyllia*, order Scleractinia (or Madreporaria): several species, including the **Devonshire cup coral** (*C. smithi*), of European waters.

cupel /ˈkjuːp(ə)l/ ► noun a shallow, porous container in which gold or silver can be refined or assayed by melting with a blast of hot air which oxidizes lead or other base metals.
► verb (**cupelled, cupelling**; US **cupeled, cupeling**) [with obj.] assay or refine (a metal) in such a container.
– DERIVATIVES **cupellation** noun.
– ORIGIN early 17th cent. (as a noun): from French *coupelle*, diminutive of *coupe* 'goblet'.

Cup Final ► noun the final match in a sports competition in which the winners are awarded a cup.

cupful ► noun (pl. **-fuls**) the amount held by a cup: *a cupful of water*. ■ chiefly N. Amer. another term for **CUP** as a measure in cookery: *add 1 cupful of flour*.

cup fungus ► noun a fungus in which the spore-producing layer forms the lining of a shallow cup.
● Several families in the orders Helotiales and Pezizales, subdivision Ascomycotina.

Cupid Roman Mythology the god of love. He is represented as a naked winged boy with a bow and arrows, with which he wounds his victims. Greek equivalent **EROS**.

■ [as noun] (also **cupid**) a representation of a naked winged child, typically carrying a bow.
– ORIGIN from Latin *Cupido*, personification of *cupido* 'love, desire', from *cupere* 'to desire'.

cupidity /kjuːˈpɪdɪti/ ► noun [mass noun] greed for money or possessions.
– ORIGIN late Middle English: from Old French *cupidite* or Latin *cupiditas*, from *cupidus* 'desirous', from *cupere* 'to desire'. Compare with **COVET**.

Cupid's bow ► noun a shape like that of the double-curved bow often shown carried by Cupid, especially at the top edge of a person's upper lip.

cupid's dart ► noun a herbaceous plant of the daisy family, with white, blue, or lilac flowers.
● *Catananche caerulea*, family Compositae.

cup lichen ► noun a greenish-grey lichen with small cup-like structures arising from its spreading lobes, found typically on heathland and moorland.
● Genus *Cladonia*, order Cladoniales: many species.

cupola /ˈkjuːpələ/ ► noun a rounded dome forming or adorning a roof or ceiling. ■ a gun turret. ■ (also **cupola furnace**) a cylindrical furnace for refining metals, with openings at the bottom for blowing in air and originally with a dome leading to a chimney above.
– DERIVATIVES **cupolaed** /-ləd/ adjective.
– ORIGIN mid 16th cent.: Italian, from late Latin *cupula* 'small cask or burying vault', diminutive of *cupa* 'cask'.

cuppa Brit. informal ► noun a cup of tea: *a good strong cuppa*.
► contraction of cup of: *let's have another cuppa tea*.
– ORIGIN 1920s: alteration.

cuppy ► adjective (of ground) full of shallow depressions.

cupr- ► combining form variant spelling of **CUPRO-** shortened before a vowel (as in *cuprammonium*).

cuprammonium /ˌkjuːprəˈməʊniəm/ ► noun [as modifier] Chemistry a complex ion, $Cu(NH_3)_4^{2+}$, formed in solution when ammonia is added to copper salts. The solution is deep blue and is used to dissolve cellulose.

cupreous /ˈkjuːprɪəs/ ► adjective dated or poetic/literary of or like copper.
– ORIGIN mid 17th cent.: from late Latin *cupreus* (from *cuprum* 'copper') + **-OUS**.

cupric /ˈkjuːprɪk/ ► adjective Chemistry of copper with a valency of two; of copper(II). Compare with **CUPROUS**.
– ORIGIN late 18th cent.: from late Latin *cuprum* 'copper' + **-IC**.

cuprite /ˈkjuːprʌɪt/ ► noun [mass noun] a dark red or brownish black mineral consisting of cuprous oxide.

cupro- /ˈkjuːprəʊ/ (also **cupr-**) ► combining form of or relating to copper: *cupro-nickel*.
– ORIGIN from late Latin *cuprum*.

cupro-nickel ► noun [mass noun] an alloy of copper and nickel, especially in the proportions 3:1 as used in 'silver' coins.

cuprous /ˈkjuːprəs/ ► adjective Chemistry of copper with a valency of one; of copper(I).
– ORIGIN mid 17th cent.: partly directly from late Latin *cuprum* 'copper' (reinforced by **CUPRIC**) + **-OUS**.

cup tie ► noun Brit. a match in a competition for which the prize is a cup.

cup-tied ► adjective Brit. (of a soccer player) ineligible to play for one's club in a cup competition as a result of having played for another club in an earlier round.

cupule /ˈkjuːpjuːl/ ► noun Botany & Zoology a cup-shaped organ, structure, or receptacle in a plant or animal.
– ORIGIN late Middle English: from late Latin *cupula* (see **CUPOLA**).

cur /kəː/ ► noun an aggressive dog or one that is in poor condition, especially a mongrel. ■ informal a contemptible man.
– ORIGIN Middle English (in the general sense 'dog'): probably originally in *cur-dog*, perhaps from Old Norse *kurr* 'grumbling'.

curable ► adjective (of a disease or condition) able to be cured: *most skin cancers are completely curable.* ■ (of plastic, varnish, etc.) able to be hardened by some additive or other agent: [in combination] *a radiation-curable coating.*
– DERIVATIVES **curability** noun.
– ORIGIN late Middle English: from Old French, or

from late Latin *curabilis*, from Latin *curare* (see **CURE**).

Curaçao /ˌkjʊərəˈsəʊ, -ˈseɪəʊ/ the largest island of the Netherlands Antilles, situated in the Caribbean Sea 60 km (37 miles) north of the Venezuelan coast; pop. 144,100 (1992); chief town, Willemstad.

curaçao /ˌkjʊərəˈsəʊ/ ► noun (pl. **-os**) [mass noun] a liqueur flavoured with the peel of bitter oranges.
– ORIGIN early 19th cent.: named after **CURAÇAO**, where the oranges are grown.

curacy ► noun (pl. **-ies**) the office of a curate, or the tenure of this: *he served his curacy in Northampton.*

curandero /ˌkjʊərənˈdɛːrəʊ, Spanish kuranˈðero/ ► noun (pl. **-os**) (fem. **curandera** /-ˈdɛːrə, Spanish -ˈðɛrə/) (in Spain and Latin America) a healer who uses folk remedies.
– ORIGIN Spanish, from *curar* 'to cure', from Latin *curare*.

curare /kjʊˈrɑːri/ ► noun [mass noun] a bitter resinous substance obtained from the bark and stems of some South American plants. It paralyses the motor nerves and is traditionally used by some Indian peoples to poison their arrows and blowpipe darts.
● Curare is obtained from *Curarea* species and *Chondodendron tomentosum* (family Menispermaceae), and *Strychnos toxifera* (family Loganiaceae).
– ORIGIN late 18th cent.: from a Carib word, partly via Spanish and Portuguese.

curassow /ˈkjʊərəsəʊ/ ► noun a large crested pheasant-like bird of the guan family, found in tropical American forests. The male is typically black in colour.
● Genus *Crax* (and *Nothocrax*), family Cracidae: several species.
– ORIGIN late 17th cent.: Anglicized form of **CURAÇAO**.

curate¹ /ˈkjʊərət/ ► noun (also **assistant curate**) a member of the clergy engaged as assistant to a vicar, rector, or parish priest. ■ archaic a minister with pastoral responsibility.
– ORIGIN Middle English: from medieval Latin *curatus*, from Latin *cura* 'care'.

curate² /kjʊə(ə)ˈreɪt/ ► verb [with obj.] (usu. **be curated**) select, organize, and look after the items in (a collection or exhibition): *both exhibitions are curated by the Centre's director.*
– DERIVATIVES **curation** noun.
– ORIGIN late 19th cent.: back-formation from **CURATOR**.

curate-in-charge ► noun another term for **PRIEST-IN-CHARGE**.

curate's egg ► noun Brit. a thing that is partly good and partly bad: *this book is a bit of a curate's egg.*
– ORIGIN early 20th cent.: from a cartoon in *Punch* (1895) depicting a meek curate who, given a stale egg at the bishop's table, assures his host that 'parts of it are excellent'.

curative ► adjective able to cure something, typically disease: *the curative properties of herbs.*
► noun a medicine or agent of this type.
– DERIVATIVES **curatively** adverb.
– ORIGIN late Middle English (in the sense 'relating to cures'): from French *curatif*, -ive, from medieval Latin *curativus*, from Latin *curare* (see **CURE**).

curator ► noun a keeper or custodian of a museum or other collection.
– DERIVATIVES **curatorial** adjective, **curatorship** noun.
– ORIGIN late Middle English (denoting an ecclesiastical pastor, also (still a Scots legal term) the guardian of a minor): from Old French *curateur* or, in later use, directly from Latin *curator*, from *curare* (see **CURE**). The current sense dates from the mid 17th cent.

curb ► noun **1** a check or restraint on something: *plans to introduce tougher curbs on insider dealing.* **2** (also **curb bit**) a type of bit which is widely used in western riding. In English riding it is usually only used with a snaffle as part of a double bridle. **3** chiefly US variant spelling of **KERB**. **4** a swelling on the back of a horse's hock, caused by spraining a ligament.
► verb [with obj.] restrain or keep in check: *she promised she would curb her temper.* ■ restrain (a horse) by means of a curb.
– ORIGIN late 15th cent. (denoting a strap fastened to the bit): from Old French *courber* 'bend, bow', from Latin *curvare* (see **CURVE**).

curb chain ► noun a small chain which is attached

to a curb bit and lies in the groove on a horse's chin.

curb cut ▶ **noun** N. Amer. a small ramp built into the curb of a pavement to make it easier for cyclists or people using wheelchairs to pass from the pavement to the street.

curb roof ▶ **noun** the shallow upper slopes of a mansard roof.
■ Brit. a mansard roof.

curbside ▶ **adjective** US spelling of **KERBSIDE**.

curbstone ▶ **noun** US spelling of **KERBSTONE**.
■ [as modifier] informal unqualified; amateur: *curbstone commentators.*

curculio /kəː'kjuːlɪəʊ/ ▶ **noun** (pl. **-os**) chiefly N. Amer. a beetle of the weevil family, especially one which is a pest of fruit trees.
● Several genera and species in the family Curculionidae, including the **plum curculio** (*Conotrachelus nenuphar*).
– ORIGIN modern Latin, used as the genus name for weevils in the 18th cent., now restricted to the nut weevils.

curcuma /'kəːkjʊmə/ ▶ **noun** a tropical Asian plant of a genus that includes turmeric, zedoary, and other species that yield spices, dyes, and medicinal products.
● Genus *Curcuma*, family Zingiberaceae.
– ORIGIN modern Latin, from Arabic *kurkum* 'saffron', from Sanskrit *kuṅkuma* (so named because the colour of turmeric resembles that of saffron).

curd ▶ **noun 1** [mass noun] (also **curds**) a soft, white substance formed when milk coagulates, used as the basis for cheese.
■ a fatty substance found between the flakes of poached salmon.
2 the edible head of a cauliflower or similar plant.
– DERIVATIVES **curdy** adjective.
– ORIGIN late Middle English: of unknown origin.

curd cheese ▶ **noun** [mass noun] chiefly Brit. a mild, soft, smooth cheese made from skimmed milk curd.

curdle ▶ **verb** separate or cause to separate into curds or lumps: [no obj.] *take care not to let the soup boil or it will curdle* | [with obj.] *rennet is used for making cheese by curdling milk.*
– PHRASES **make one's blood curdle** fill one with horror.
– DERIVATIVES **curdler** noun.
– ORIGIN late 16th cent.: frequentative of obsolete *curd* 'congeal'.

cure ▶ **verb** [with obj.] **1** relieve (a person or animal) of the symptoms of a disease or condition: *he was* ***cured of*** *the disease* | figurative *she was too old to* ***cure*** *herself* ***of*** *facetious thoughts.*
■ eliminate (a disease, condition, or injury) with medical treatment: *this technology could be used to cure diabetes.* ■ solve (a problem): *a bid to trace and cure the gearbox problems.*
2 preserve (meat, fish, tobacco, or an animal skin) by various methods such as salting, drying, or smoking: *some farmers cured their own bacon* | [as adj., in combination **cured**] *home-cured ham.*
■ harden (rubber, plastic, concrete, etc.) after manufacture by a chemical process such as vulcanization. ■ [no obj.] undergo this process.
▶ **noun 1** a substance or treatment that cures a disease or condition: *the search for a cure for the common cold.*
■ [mass noun] restoration to health: *he was beyond cure.* ■ a solution to a problem: *the cure is to improve the clutch operation.*
2 [mass noun] the process of curing rubber, plastic, or other material.
3 [mass noun] a Christian minister's pastoral charge or area of responsibility for spiritual ministry: *a benefice involving the* ***cure of souls.***
■ [count noun] a parish.
– DERIVATIVES **curer** noun.
– ORIGIN Middle English (as a noun): from Old French *curer* (verb), *cure* (noun), both from Latin *curare* 'take care of', from *cura* 'care'. The original noun senses were 'care, concern, responsibility', in particular spiritual care (hence sense 3). In late Middle English the senses 'medical care' and 'successful medical treatment' arose, and hence 'remedy'.

curé /'kjʊəreɪ, French kyʀe/ ▶ **noun** a parish priest in a French-speaking country.
– ORIGIN French, from medieval Latin *curatus* (see **CURATE**[1]).

cure-all ▶ **noun** a medicine or other remedy that will supposedly cure any ailment.
■ a solution to any problem: *unfortunately, the new output circuitry is not a cure-all.*

curettage /kjʊə'rɛtɪdʒ, ˌkjʊərɪ'tɑːʒ/ ▶ **noun** [mass noun] Surgery the use of a curette, especially on the lining of the uterus. See **DILATATION AND CURETTAGE**.
– ORIGIN late 19th cent.: from French, from **CURETTE**.

curette /kjʊə'rɛt/ ▶ **noun** a small surgical instrument used to remove material by a scraping action, especially from the uterus.
▶ **verb** [with obj.] clean or scrape with a curette.
– ORIGIN mid 18th cent. (as a noun): from French, from *curer* 'cleanse', from Latin *curare* (see **CURE**).

curfew /'kəːfjuː/ ▶ **noun** a regulation requiring people to remain indoors between specified hours,typically at night: *a dusk-to-dawn curfew* | [mass noun] *the whole area was immediately placed* ***under curfew.***
■ the hour designated as the beginning of such a restriction: [mass noun] *to be abroad after curfew without permission was to risk punishment.* ■ the daily signal indicating this.
– ORIGIN Middle English (denoting a regulation requiring people to extinguish fires at a fixed hour in the evening, or a bell rung at that hour): from Old French *cuevrefeu*, from *cuvrir* 'to cover' + *feu* 'fire'. The current sense dates from the late 19th cent.

Curia /'kjʊərɪə/ the papal court at the Vatican, by which the Roman Catholic Church is governed. It comprises various Congregations, Tribunals, and other commissions and departments.
– DERIVATIVES **Curial** adjective.
– ORIGIN mid 19th cent.: from Latin *curia*, denoting a division of an ancient Roman tribe, also (by extension) the senate of cities other than Rome; later the term came to denote a feudal or Roman Catholic court of justice, whence the current sense.

Curie /'kjʊəri/, Marie (1867–1934), Polish-born French physicist, and Pierre (1859–1906), French physicist, pioneers of radioactivity. Working together on the mineral pitchblende, they discovered the elements polonium and radium, for which they shared the 1903 Nobel Prize for Physics with A.-H. Becquerel. After her husband's accidental death Marie received another Nobel Prize (for chemistry) in 1911 for her isolation of radium. She died of leukaemia, caused by prolonged exposure to radioactive materials.

curie /'kjʊəri/ (abbrev.: **Ci**) ▶ **noun** (pl. **-ies**) a unit of radioactivity, corresponding to 3.7×10^{10} disintegrations per second.
■ the quantity of radioactive substance that has this amount of activity.
– ORIGIN early 20th cent.: named after Pierre and Marie **CURIE**.

curio /'kjʊərɪəʊ/ ▶ **noun** (pl. **-os**) a rare, unusual, or intriguing object.
– ORIGIN mid 19th cent.: abbreviation of **CURIOSITY**.

curiosa /ˌkjʊərɪ'əʊsə/ ▶ **plural noun** curiosities, especially erotic or pornographic books or articles.
– ORIGIN late 19th cent.: from Latin, neuter plural of *curiosus* (see **CURIOUS**).

curiosity ▶ **noun** (pl. **-ies**) **1** [mass noun] a strong desire to know or learn something: *filled with curiosity, she peered through the window.*
2 a strange or unusual object or fact: *he showed them some of the curiosities of the house.*
– PHRASES **curiosity killed the cat** proverb being inquisitive about other people's affairs may get you into trouble.
– ORIGIN late Middle English: from Old French *curiousete*, from Latin *curiositas*, from *curiosus* (see **CURIOUS**).

curious ▶ **adjective 1** eager to know or learn something: *I began to be curious about the whereabouts of the bride and groom* | *she was* ***curious to know*** *what had happened.*
■ expressing curiosity: *a curious stare.*
2 strange; unusual: *a curious sensation overwhelmed her.*
■ used euphemistically to denote books that are erotic or pornographic.
– DERIVATIVES **curiously** adverb [sentence adverb] *curiously, I find snooker riveting*, **curiousness** noun.
– ORIGIN Middle English: from Old French *curios*, from Latin *curiosus* 'careful', from *cura* 'care'. Sense 2 dates from the early 18th cent.

Curitiba /ˌkʊərɪ'tiːbə/ a city in southern Brazil, capital of the state of Paraná; pop. 1,315,035 (1991).

curium /'kjʊərɪəm/ ▶ **noun** [mass noun] the chemical element of atomic number 96, a radioactive metal of the actinide series. Curium does not occur naturally and was first made by bombarding plutonium with helium ions. (Symbol: **Cm**)
– ORIGIN 1940s: modern Latin, from the name of Marie and Pierre **CURIE**.

curl ▶ **verb 1** form or cause to form into a curved or spiral shape: [no obj.] *her fingers curled round the microphone* | *a slice of ham had begun to* ***curl up*** *at the edges* | [with obj.] *she used to curl her hair with rags.*
■ [no obj.] (**curl up**) sit or lie with the knees drawn up: *she curled up and went to sleep.* ■ move or cause to move in a spiral or curved course: [no obj., with adverbial of direction] *a wisp of smoke curling across the sky.* ■ (with reference to one's mouth or upper lip) raise or cause to raise slightly on one side as an expression of contempt or disapproval: [no obj.] *Maria saw his lip curl sardonically.* ■ (in weight training) lift (a weight) using only the hands, wrists, and forearms.
2 [no obj.] play at the game of curling.
▶ **noun 1** a lock of hair having a spiral or coiled form: *her blonde hair was a mass of tangled curls.*
■ a thing having a spiral or inwardly curved form: *a curl of blue smoke.* ■ a curling movement: *the sneering curl of his lip.* ■ (with reference to a person's hair) a state or condition of being curled: *your hair has a natural curl* | [mass noun] *large perm rods give volume and control rather than lots of curl.* ■ see **LEAF CURL**. ■ a weightlifting exercise involving movement of only the hands, wrists, and forearms: *a dumb-bell curl.*
2 Mathematics the vector product of the operator del and a given vector.
– PHRASES **make someone's hair curl** informal shock or horrify someone.
– ORIGIN late Middle English: from obsolete *crulle* 'curly', from Middle Dutch *krul*.

curler ▶ **noun 1** (usu. **curlers**) a roller or clasp around which a lock of hair is wrapped to curl it.
2 a player in the game of curling.

curlew /'kəːl(j)uː/ ▶ **noun** (pl. same or **curlews**) a large wading bird of the sandpiper family, with a long downcurved bill, brown streaked plumage, and frequently a distinctive ascending two-note call. See also **STONE CURLEW**.
● Genus *Numenius*, family Scolopacidae: several species, in particular *N. arquata* of Eurasia.
– ORIGIN Middle English: from Old French *courlieu*, alteration (by association with *courliu* 'courier', from *courre* 'run' + *lieu* 'place') of imitative *courlis*.

curlicue /'kəːlɪkjuː/ ▶ **noun** a decorative curl or twist in calligraphy or in the design of an object.
– ORIGIN mid 19th cent.: from **CURLY** + **CUE**[2] (in the sense 'pigtail'), or *-cue* representing the letter *q*.

curling ▶ **noun** [mass noun] a game played on ice, especially in Scotland and Canada, in which large round flat stones are slid across the surface towards a mark. Members of a team use brooms to sweep the surface of the ice in the path of the stone to control its speed and direction.

curling stone ▶ **noun** a large polished circular stone, with an iron handle on top, used in the game of curling.

curling tongs (also **curling iron** or **curling pins**) ▶ **plural noun** a device incorporating a heated rod used for rolling a person's hair into curls.

curly ▶ **adjective** (**curlier**, **curliest**) made, grown, or arranged in curls or curves: *my hair is just naturally thick and curly.*
– DERIVATIVES **curliness** noun.

curly bracket ▶ **noun** another term for **BRACE** (in sense 3).

curly endive ▶ **noun** see **ENDIVE**.

curly kale ▶ **noun** [mass noun] kale of a variety with dark green tightly curled leaves.

curly-wurly ▶ **adjective** informal twisting and curling.
– ORIGIN late 18th cent.: reduplication of **CURLY**.

curmudgeon /kəː'mʌdʒ(ə)n/ ▶ **noun** a bad-tempered or surly person.
– DERIVATIVES **curmudgeonliness** noun, **curmudgeonly** adjective.
– ORIGIN late 16th cent.: of unknown origin.

currach /'kʌrə(x)/ (also **curragh**) ▶ **noun** Irish and Scottish term for **CORACLE**.
– ORIGIN late Middle English: from Irish and Scottish Gaelic *curach* 'small boat'. Compare with **CORACLE**.

curragh[1] ▶ **noun** variant spelling of **CURRACH**.

curragh[2] /ˈkʌrə(x)/ ▶ **noun** (in Ireland and the Isle of Man) a stretch of marshy waste ground.
■ (**the Curragh**) a level stretch of open ground in County Kildare, Ireland, famous for its racecourse and military camp.
– ORIGIN mid 17th cent.: from Irish *currach* 'marsh', Manx *curragh* 'bog, fen'.

currajong ▶ **noun** variant spelling of **KURRAJONG**.

currant ▶ **noun 1** a small dried fruit made from a small seedless variety of grape originally grown in the eastern Mediterranean region and much used in cookery: [as modifier] *a currant bun.*
2 a Eurasian shrub which produces small edible black, red, or white berries.
● Genus *Ribes*, family Grossulariaceae: several species, including **blackcurrant** and **redcurrant**.
■ a berry from such a shrub.
– ORIGIN Middle English *raisons of Corauntz*, translating Anglo-Norman French *raisins de Corauntz* 'grapes of *Corinth*' (the original source).

currant gall ▶ **noun** a spherical red or purple gall which forms on the leaves or male catkins of oak trees in response to the developing larva of a gall wasp. It results from eggs laid in the spring and alternates with the spangle gall.
● The wasp is *Neuroterus quercusbaccarum*, family Cynipidae

currant tomato ▶ **noun** a kind of tomato with tiny fruits, native to the Andes.
● *Lycopersicon pimpinellifolium*, family Solanaceae.

currawong /ˈkʌrəwɒŋ/ ▶ **noun** a crow-like songbird of the Australian butcher-bird family, with mainly black or grey plumage, a robust straight bill, and a resonant call. Also called **BELL MAGPIE**.
● Genus *Strepera*, family Cracticidae: three species.
– ORIGIN 1920s: from an Aboriginal word.

currency ▶ **noun** (pl. **-ies**) **1** a system of money in general use in a particular country: *the dollar was a strong currency* | [mass noun] *travellers cheques in foreign currency* | figurative *reason and persuasion will become the currency of party policy-making.*
2 [mass noun] the fact or quality of being generally accepted or in use: *since the Gulf war, the term has gained new currency.*
■ the time during which something is in use or operation: *no claim had been made during the currency of the policy.*

current ▶ **adjective** belonging to the present time; happening or being used or done now: *keep abreast of current events* | *I started my current job in 1994.*
■ in common or general use: *the other meaning of the word is still current.*
▶ **noun** a body of water or air moving in a definite direction, especially through a surrounding body of water or air in which there is less movement: *ocean currents.*
■ a flow of electricity which results from the ordered directional movement of electrically charged particles. ■ a quantity representing the rate of flow of electric charge, usually measured in amperes. ■ the general tendency or course of events or opinion: *the student movement formed a distinct current of protest.*
– ORIGIN Middle English (in the adjective sense 'running, flowing'): from Old French *corant* 'running', from *courre* 'run', from Latin *currere* 'run'.

current account ▶ **noun** Brit. an account with a bank or building society from which money may be withdrawn without notice, typically an active account catering for frequent deposits and withdrawals by cheque.

current affairs ▶ **plural noun** events of political or social interest and importance happening in the world at the present time.

current assets ▶ **plural noun** cash and other assets that are expected to be converted to cash within a year. Compare with **FIXED ASSETS**.

current cost accounting ▶ **noun** [mass noun] a method of accounting in which assets are valued on the basis of their current replacement cost, and increases in their value as a result of inflation are excluded from calculations of profit.

current density ▶ **noun** Physics the amount of electric current flowing per unit cross-sectional area of a material.

current liabilities ▶ **plural noun** amounts due to be paid to creditors within twelve months.

currently ▶ **adverb** at the present time: *the EC is currently attempting greater economic integration.*

curricle /ˈkʌrɪk(ə)l/ ▶ **noun** historical a light, open, two-wheeled carriage pulled by two horses side by side.
– ORIGIN mid 18th cent.: from Latin *curriculum* 'course, racing chariot', from *currere* 'to run'.

curriculum /kʌˈrɪkjʊləm/ ▶ **noun** (pl. **curricula** or **curriculums**) the subjects comprising a course of study in a school or college.
– DERIVATIVES **curricular** adjective.
– ORIGIN early 19th cent.: from Latin (see **CURRICLE**).

curriculum vitae /ˈviːtʌɪ, ˈvʌɪtiː/ (abbrev.: **CV**) ▶ **noun** (pl. **curricula vitae**) a brief account of a person's education, qualifications, and previous occupations, typically sent with a job application.
– ORIGIN early 20th cent.: Latin, 'course of life'.

currier /ˈkʌrɪə/ ▶ **noun** a person who curries leather.
– ORIGIN late Middle English: from Old French *corier*, from Latin *coriarius*, from *corium* 'leather'.

currish /ˈkəːrɪʃ/ ▶ **adjective 1** like a cur; snappish.
2 ignoble.
– DERIVATIVES **currishly** adverb, **currishness** noun.

Curry, John (Anthony) (1949–94), English ice skater. He won a succession of championships, including the British, European, and World titles, taking the gold medal for men's figure skating in his second winter Olympic Games in 1976.

curry[1] ▶ **noun** (pl. **-ies**) a dish of meat, vegetables, etc., cooked in an Indian-style sauce of strong spices and turmeric and typically served with rice.
▶ **verb** (**-ies**, **-ied**) [with obj.] [usu. as adj. **curried**] prepare or flavour with a sauce of hot-tasting spices: *curried chicken.*
– ORIGIN late 16th cent.: from Tamil *kaṟi*.

curry[2] ▶ **verb** (**-ies**, **-ied**) [with obj.] **1** chiefly N. Amer. groom (a horse) with a rubber or plastic curry-comb.
2 historical treat (tanned leather) to improve its properties.
■ archaic thrash; beat.
– PHRASES **curry favour** ingratiate oneself with someone through obsequious behaviour: *a wimpish attempt to **curry favour with** the new bosses.* [ORIGIN: alteration of Middle English *curry favel*, from the name (*Favel* or *Fauvel*) of a chestnut horse in a 14th-cent. French romance who became a symbol of cunning and duplicity; hence 'to rub down Favel' meant to use the cunning which he personified.]
– ORIGIN Middle English: from Old French *correier*, ultimately of Germanic origin.

curry-comb ▶ **noun** a hand-held metal device with serrated ridges, used for removing dirt from a body brush with which a horse is being groomed.
■ (also **rubber curry-comb**) a similar device of flexible rubber, used for grooming horses.

curry leaf ▶ **noun** a shrub or small tree native to India and Sri Lanka, the leaves of which are widely used in Indian cooking.
● *Murraya koenigii*, family Rutaceae.

curry plant ▶ **noun** a small shrubby plant of the daisy family, which has narrow silver-grey leaves and small yellow flowers and emits a strong smell of curry.
● *Helichrysum angustifolium*, family Compositae.

curry powder ▶ **noun** [mass noun] a mixture of finely ground spices, such as turmeric, ginger, and coriander, used for making curry.

curse ▶ **noun 1** a solemn utterance intended to invoke a supernatural power to inflict harm or punishment on someone or something: *she'd **put a curse on** him.*
■ [usu. in sing.] a cause of harm or misery: *impatience is the curse of our day and age.* ■ (**the curse**) informal menstruation.
2 an offensive word or phrase used to express anger or annoyance: *at every blow there was a curse.*
▶ **verb 1** [with obj.] invoke or use a curse against: *it often seemed as if the family had been cursed.*
■ (**be cursed with**) be afflicted with: *many owners have been cursed with a series of bankruptcies.*
2 [no obj.] utter offensive words in anger or annoyance: *drivers were cursing and sounding their horns.*
■ [with obj.] address with such words: *I **cursed myself** for my carelessness.*
– DERIVATIVES **curser** noun.
– ORIGIN Old English, of unknown origin.

cursed /ˈkəːsɪd, kəːst/ ▶ **adjective** [attrib.] informal, dated used to express annoyance or irritation: *his cursed tidy-mindedness.*
– DERIVATIVES **cursedly** adverb, **cursedness** noun.

cursillo /kəːˈsiːjəʊ, -ˈsiːljəʊ/ ▶ **noun** (pl. **-os**) a short informal spiritual retreat by a group of Roman Catholics, especially in Spain or Latin America.
– ORIGIN 1950s: Spanish, 'little course'.

cursive /ˈkəːsɪv/ ▶ **adjective** written with the characters joined: *cursive script.*
▶ **noun** [mass noun] writing with such a style.
– DERIVATIVES **cursively** adverb.
– ORIGIN late 18th cent.: from medieval Latin *cursivus*, from Latin *curs-* 'run', from the verb *currere*.

cursor ▶ **noun** a movable indicator on a computer screen identifying the point that will be affected by input from the user, for example showing where typed text will be inserted.
■ chiefly historical the transparent slide engraved with a hairline that is part of a slide rule and is used for marking a point on the rule while bringing a point on the central sliding portion up to it.
– ORIGIN Middle English (denoting a runner or running messenger): from Latin, 'runner', from *curs-* (see **CURSIVE**). The sense 'sliding part of an instrument' dates from the late 16th cent.

cursorial /kəːˈsɔːrɪəl/ ▶ **adjective** Zoology having limbs adapted for running.
– ORIGIN mid 19th cent.: from Latin *cursor* (see **CURSOR**) + **-IAL**.

cursory /ˈkəːs(ə)ri/ ▶ **adjective** hasty and therefore not thorough or detailed: *a cursory glance at the figures.*
– DERIVATIVES **cursorily** adverb, **cursoriness** noun.
– ORIGIN early 17th cent.: from Latin *cursorius* 'of a runner', from *cursor* (see **CURSOR**).

curst ▶ **adjective** archaic spelling of **CURSED**.

curt ▶ **adjective** rudely brief: *his reply was curt.*
– DERIVATIVES **curtly** adverb, **curtness** noun.
– ORIGIN late Middle English (in the sense 'short, shortened'): from Latin *curtus* 'cut short, abridged'.

curtail /kəːˈteɪl/ ▶ **verb** [with obj.] (often **be curtailed**) reduce in extent or quantity; impose a restriction on: *civil liberties were further curtailed.*
■ (**curtail someone of**) archaic deprive someone of (something): *I that am curtailed of this fair proportion.*
– DERIVATIVES **curtailment** noun.
– ORIGIN late 15th cent.: from obsolete *curtal* 'horse with a docked tail', from French *courtault*, from *court* 'short', from Latin *curtus*. The change in the ending was due to association with **TAIL**[1] and perhaps also with French *tailler* 'to cut'.

curtain ▶ **noun** a piece of material suspended at the top to form a screen, typically movable sideways along a rail, found as one of a pair at a window: *she drew the curtains and lit the fire* | figurative *through the curtain of falling snow, she could just make out gravestones.*
■ (**the curtain**) a screen of heavy cloth or other material that can be raised or lowered at the front of a stage. ■ a raising or lowering of such a screen at the beginning or end of an act or scene: *the art is to hold your audience right from the opening curtain.* ■ (**curtains**) informal a disastrous outcome: *it looked like curtains for me.*
▶ **verb** [with obj.] [often as adj. **curtained**] provide with a curtain or curtains: *a curtained window.*
■ conceal or screen with a curtain: *a **curtained-off** side room* | figurative *her unbound hair curtaining her face.*
– PHRASES **bring down the curtain on** bring to an end: *her decision brought down the curtain on a glittering 30-year career.*
– ORIGIN Middle English: from Old French *cortine*, from late Latin *cortina*, translation of Greek *aulaia*, from *aulē* 'court'.

curtain call ▶ **noun** the appearance of one or more performers on stage after a performance to acknowledge the audience's applause.

curtain fire (also chiefly US **curtain of fire**) ▶ **noun** [mass noun] Brit. rapid, continuous artillery or machine-gun fire on a designated line or area.

curtain lecture ▶ **noun** dated an instance of a wife reprimanding her husband in private.
– ORIGIN mid 17th cent.: originally a reprimand given behind bed curtains.

curtain-raiser ▶ **noun** an entertainment or other event happening just before a longer or more important one: *Bach's Sinfonia in B flat was an ideal **curtain-raiser to** Mozart's last piano concerto.*
– ORIGIN late 19th cent.: originally used in the

C

theatre to denote a short opening piece performed before a play.

curtain ring ▶ noun a ring, typically one of brass or wood, used to fasten a curtain to the rail or rod.

curtain-sider ▶ noun a lorry or trailer having fabric sides.

curtain speech ▶ noun a speech of thanks or appreciation to an audience, made after a performance by an actor playing a leading role, typically from the front of the stage with the curtains closed.

curtain-up ▶ noun [in sing.] the beginning of a stage performance: *curtain-up is at 8 p.m.*
■ figurative the beginning of any event viewed as having an element of display or drama: *it's curtain-up for this week's rugby review.*

curtain wall ▶ noun a fortified wall around a medieval castle, typically one linking towers together.
■ a wall which encloses the space within a building but does not support the roof.

curtal /ˈkəːt(ə)l/ ▶ adjective archaic shortened, abridged, or curtailed.
▶ noun historical a dulcian or bassoon of the late 16th to early 18th century.
– ORIGIN late 15th cent. (denoting a short-barrelled cannon): from French *courtault*, from *court* 'short' + the pejorative suffix *-ault*. In both English and French the noun denoted various items characterized by something short, especially an animal with a docked tail, which probably gave rise to the adjective sense.

curtana /kəːˈtɑːnə, -ˈteɪnə/ ▶ noun Brit. the unpointed sword carried in front of English sovereigns at their coronation to represent mercy.
– ORIGIN Middle English: from Anglo-Latin *curtana (spatha)* 'shortened (sword)', from Old French *cortain*, the name of the sword belonging to **ROLAND** (the point of which was damaged when it was thrust into a block of steel), from *cort* 'short', from Latin *curtus* 'cut short'.

curtilage /ˈkəːt(ɪ)lɪdʒ/ ▶ noun an area of land attached to a house and forming one enclosure with it: *the roads **within the curtilage of** the development site.*
– ORIGIN Middle English: from Anglo-Norman French, variant of Old French *courtillage*, from *courtil* 'small court', from *cort* 'court'.

Curtin /ˈkəːtɪn/, John (Joseph Ambrose) (1885–1945), Australian Labor statesman, Prime Minister 1941–5.

Curtiss /ˈkəːtɪs/, Glenn (Hammond) (1878–1930), American air pioneer and aircraft designer. In 1908 Curtiss made the first public American flight of 1.0 km (0.6 miles). He built his first aeroplane in 1909, and invented the aileron and demonstrated the first practical seaplane two years later.

curtsy (also **curtsey**) ▶ noun (pl. **-ies** or **-eys**) a woman's or girl's formal greeting made by bending the knees with one foot in front of the other: *she **bobbed a curtsy** to him.*
▶ verb (**-ies**, **-ied** or **-eys**, **-eyed**) [no obj.] perform such an action: *his sisters had curtsied to the vicar.*
– ORIGIN early 16th cent.: variant of **COURTESY**. Both forms were used to denote the expression of respect or courtesy by a gesture, especially in phrases such as *do courtesy, make courtesy*, and from this arose the current use (late 16th cent.).

curule /ˈkjʊəruːl/ ▶ adjective historical denoting or relating to the authority exercised by the senior magistrates in ancient Rome, chiefly the consul and praetor, who were entitled to use the *sella curulis* ('curule seat', a kind of folding chair).
– ORIGIN early 17th cent.: from Latin *curulis*, from *currus* 'chariot' (in which the chief magistrate was conveyed to the seat of office), from *currere* 'to run'.

curvaceous /kəːˈveɪʃəs/ ▶ adjective (especially of a woman or a woman's figure) having an attractively curved shape.
– DERIVATIVES **curvaceousness** noun.

curvature /ˈkəːvətʃə/ ▶ noun [mass noun] the fact of being curved or the degree to which something is curved: *spinal curvature | the curvature of the earth |* [count noun] *it has a distinct curvature near the middle.*
■ Geometry the degree to which a curve deviates from a straight line, or a curved surface deviates from a plane. ■ a numerical quantity expressing this.
– ORIGIN late Middle English: via Old French from Latin *curvatura*, from *curvare* (see **CURVE**).

curve ▶ noun a line or outline which gradually deviates from being straight for some or all of its length: *the parapet wall sweeps down in a bold curve.*
■ a place where a road deviates from a straight path: *the vehicle rounded a curve.* ■ (**curves**) a curving contour of a woman's figure. ■ a line on a graph (whether straight or curved) showing how one quantity varies with respect to another: *the population curve.* ■ (also **curve ball**) Baseball a delivery in which the pitcher causes the ball to deviate from a straight path by imparting spin.
▶ verb form or cause to form a curve: [no obj.] *her mouth curved in a smile |* [as adj. **curved**] *birds with long curved bills |* [with obj.] *starting with arms outstretched, curve the body sideways.*
– ORIGIN late Middle English: from Latin *curvare* 'to bend', from *curvus* 'bent'. The noun dates from the late 17th cent.

curvet /kəːˈvɛt/ ▶ noun a graceful or energetic leap.
▶ verb (**curvetted**, **curvetting** or **curveted**, **curveting**) [no obj.] rare leap gracefully or energetically.
■ (of a horse) perform a courbette.
– ORIGIN late 16th cent.: from Italian *corvetta*, diminutive of *corva*, earlier form of *curva* 'a curve', from Latin *curvus* 'bent'.

curvilinear /ˌkəːvɪˈlɪnɪə/ ▶ adjective contained by or consisting of a curved line or lines: *these designs employ flowing, curvilinear forms.*
– DERIVATIVES **curvilinearly** adverb.
– ORIGIN early 18th cent.: from **CURVI-**, on the pattern of *rectilinear.*

curvy ▶ adjective (**curvier**, **curviest**) having many curves: *a curvy stretch of road.*
■ informal (especially of a woman's figure) shapely and voluptuous.
– DERIVATIVES **curviness** noun.

cuscus /ˈkʌskʌs/ ▶ noun a tree-dwelling marsupial with a rounded head and prehensile tail, native to New Guinea and northern Australia.
● Four genera in the family Phalangeridae: several species, including the **spotted cuscus** (*Spilocuscus maculatus*) and the **grey cuscus** (*Phalanger orientalis*). See also **PHALANGER**.
– ORIGIN mid 17th cent.: via French and Dutch from a local name in the Molucca Islands.

cusec /ˈkjuːsɛk/ ▶ noun a unit of flow (especially of water) equal to one cubic foot per second.
– ORIGIN early 20th cent.: abbreviation of *cubic foot per second.*

Cush /kʊʃ/ **1** (in the Bible) the eldest son of Ham and grandson of Noah (Gen. 10:6).
2 the southern part of ancient Nubia, first mentioned in Egyptian records of the Middle Kingdom. In the Bible it is the country of the descendants of Cush.

cush /kʊʃ/ ▶ noun informal a cushion on a billiard table.
– ORIGIN late 19th cent.: abbreviation.

cushat /ˈkʌʃət/ ▶ noun dialect, chiefly Scottish a wood pigeon.
– ORIGIN Old English, of unknown origin.

cushaw /kʊˈʃɔː, ˈkuːʃɔː/ (also **cushaw squash**) ▶ noun US a large winter squash of a variety with a curved neck.
– ORIGIN late 16th cent.: of unknown origin.

cush-cush /ˈkʊʃkʊʃ/ (also **cush-cush yam**) ▶ noun a tropical American yam which produces a number of tubers on each plant.
● *Dioscorea trifida*, family Dioscoreaceae.
■ [mass noun] the edible tuber of this plant, eaten as a vegetable.
– ORIGIN late 19th cent.: perhaps ultimately of African origin.

Cushing /ˈkʊʃɪŋ/, Peter (1913–94), English actor, known particularly for his roles in Hammer horror films.

Cushing's disease ▶ noun [mass noun] Cushing's syndrome as caused by a tumour of the pituitary gland.

Cushing's syndrome ▶ noun [mass noun] Medicine a metabolic disorder caused by overproduction of corticosteroid hormones by the adrenal cortex and often involving obesity and high blood pressure.
– ORIGIN 1930s: named after Harvey W. *Cushing* (1869–1939), American surgeon.

cushion ▶ noun a bag of cloth stuffed with a mass of soft material, used as a comfortable support for sitting or leaning on.
■ something providing support or protection against impact: *underlay forms a cushion between carpet and floor |* figurative *he scored to restore Celtic's two-goal cushion.* ■ the elastic lining of the sides of a billiard table, from which the ball rebounds. ■ the layer of air supporting a hovercraft or similar vehicle.
▶ verb [with obj.] soften the effect of an impact on: *the bag cushions equipment from inevitable knocks.*
■ figurative mitigate the adverse effects of: *to **cushion the blow**, wages and pensions were increased.*
– DERIVATIVES **cushioned** adjective, **cushiony** adjective.
– ORIGIN Middle English: from Old French *cuissin*, based on a Latin word meaning 'cushion for the hip', from *coxa* 'hip, thigh'. The Romans also had a word *cubital* 'elbow-cushion', from *cubitus* 'elbow'.

cushion capital ▶ noun Architecture a capital resembling a cushion pressed down by a weight, seen particularly in Romanesque churches.

cushion star ▶ noun a small shallow-water starfish with a broad body and very short blunt arms. Also called **STARLET**.
● *Asterina* and related genera, class Asteroidea, in particular *A. gibbosa* of the NE Atlantic.

Cushitic /kʊˈʃɪtɪk/ ▶ noun [mass noun] a group of East African languages of the Afro-Asiatic family spoken mainly in Ethiopia and Somalia, including Somali and Oromo.
▶ adjective of or relating to this group of languages.
– ORIGIN early 20th cent.: from **CUSH** + **-ITIC**.

cushy ▶ adjective (**cushier**, **cushiest**) informal **1** (of a job, task, or situation) undemanding, easy, or secure: *he's got a very cushy number.*
2 N. Amer. (of furniture) comfortable.
– DERIVATIVES **cushiness** noun.
– ORIGIN First World War (originally Anglo-Indian): from Urdu *ḵušī* 'pleasure', from Persian *ḵuš*.

cusimanse /ˌkuːsɪˈmansi/ (also **kusimanse**) ▶ noun a small gregarious mongoose with a dark brown coat and a long mobile snout, native to West Africa.
● *Crossarchus obscurus*, family Herpestidae. Alternative name: **long-nosed mongoose**.
– ORIGIN mid 19th cent: probably a local word in West Africa.

cusk /kʌsk/ ▶ noun another term for **TORSK**.
– ORIGIN early 17th cent.: of unknown origin.

cusk-eel ▶ noun a small eel-like fish with a tapering body and fins that form a pointed tail, typically found in deep water.
● Family Ophidiidae: numerous genera.

cusp /kʌsp/ ▶ noun **1** a pointed end where two curves meet, in particular:
■ Architecture a projecting point between small arcs in Gothic tracery. ■ a cone-shaped prominence on the surface of a tooth, especially of a molar or premolar. ■ Anatomy a pocket or fold in the wall of the heart or a major blood vessel that fills and distends if the blood flows backwards, so forming part of a valve. ■ Mathematics a point at which the direction of a curve is abruptly reversed. ■ each of the pointed ends of a crescent, especially of the moon.
2 Astrology the initial point of an astrological sign or house: *he was Aries **on the cusp** with Taurus.*
■ figurative a point between two different situations or states, when a person or thing is poised between the two or just about to move from one to the other: *those **on the cusp of** adulthood.*
– DERIVATIVES **cuspate** adjective, **cusped** adjective, **cuspidate** adjective.
– ORIGIN late 16th cent. (in sense 2): from Latin *cuspis* 'point or apex'.

cuspid ▶ noun a tooth with a single cusp or point; a canine tooth.
– ORIGIN mid 18th cent.: from Latin *cuspis, cuspid-* 'point or apex'.

cuspidor /ˈkʌspɪdɔː/ ▶ noun N. Amer. a spittoon.
– ORIGIN mid 18th cent.: from Portuguese, 'spitter', from *cuspir* 'to spit', from Latin *conspuere.*

cuss informal ▶ noun **1** an annoying or stubborn person or animal: *he was certainly an unsociable cuss.*
2 another term for **CURSE** (in sense 2).
▶ verb another term for **CURSE** (in sense 2).

cussed /ˈkʌsɪd/ ▶ adjective informal awkward; annoying: *why do you have to be so cussed?*
– DERIVATIVES **cussedly** adverb, **cussedness** noun.
– ORIGIN mid 19th cent. (originally US): variant of **CURSED**.

cuss word ▶ noun informal a swear word.

custard ▶ noun [mass noun] a dessert or sweet sauce made with milk and eggs, or milk and a proprietary powder.

– ORIGIN late Middle English *crustarde, custarde* (denoting an open pie containing meat or fruit in a spiced or sweetened sauce thickened with eggs), from Old French *crouste* (see **CRUST**).

custard apple ▶ **noun 1** a large fleshy tropical fruit with a sweet yellow pulp. See also **CHERIMOYA, BULLOCK'S HEART**, and **SWEETSOP**.
2 the tree which bears this fruit, native to Central and South America.
• Genus *Annona*, family Annonaceae: several species.

custard marrow ▶ **noun** a summer squash of a variety which has flattened round fruits with scalloped edges.

custard pie ▶ **noun** an open pie containing cold set custard.
■ a pie of this type, or a flat container of foam, used for throwing in someone's face in slapstick comedy.

custard powder ▶ **noun** [mass noun] a preparation of flavoured cornflour for making custard.

Custer /ˈkʌstə/, George (Armstrong) (1839–76), American cavalry general. He served with distinction in the American Civil War but led his men to their deaths in a clash (popularly known as Custer's Last Stand) with the Sioux at Little Bighorn in Montana.

custodian /kʌˈstəʊdɪən/ ▶ **noun** a person who has responsibility for or looks after something: *New York City's school custodians | the custodians of pension and insurance funds.*
■ Brit. humorous a goalkeeper or wicketkeeper.
– DERIVATIVES **custodianship** noun.
– ORIGIN late 18th cent.: from **CUSTODY**, on the pattern of *guardian*.

custody /ˈkʌstədi/ ▶ **noun** [mass noun] the protective care or guardianship of someone or something: *the property was placed in the custody of a trustee.*
■ imprisonment: *my father was being* ***taken into custody.***
■ Law parental responsibility, especially as allocated to one of two divorcing parents: *he was trying to get* ***custody of*** *their child.*
– DERIVATIVES **custodial** /kʌˈstəʊdɪəl/ adjective.
– ORIGIN late Middle English: from Latin *custodia*, from *custos* 'guardian'.

custom ▶ **noun 1** a traditional and widely accepted way of behaving or doing something that is specific to a particular society, place, or time: *the old English custom of dancing round the maypole* | [mass noun] *custom demanded that a person should have gifts for the child.*
■ [in sing.] a thing that one does habitually: *it is our custom to visit the Lake District in October.* ■ Law established usage having the force of law or right.
2 [mass noun] chiefly Brit. regular dealings with a shop or business by customers: *if you keep me waiting, I will take my custom elsewhere.*
▶ **adjective** [attrib.] made or done to order for a particular customer: *a custom guitar.*
– ORIGIN Middle English: from Old French *coustume*, based on Latin *consuetudo*, from *consuetus*, past participle of *consuescere* 'accustom', from *con-* (expressing intensive force) + *suescere* 'become accustomed'.

customal /ˈkʌstəm(ə)l/ ▶ **noun** variant spelling of **CUSTUMAL**.

customary ▶ **adjective** according to the customs or usual practices associated with a particular society, place, or set of circumstances: *it is* ***customary to*** *mark an occasion like this with a toast.*
■ [attrib.] according to a person's habitual practice: *I put the kettle on for our customary cup of coffee.* ■ Law established by or based on custom rather than common law or statute. ■ (in South Africa) relating to black African traditional custom or law.
▶ **noun** (pl. **-ies**) historical another term for **CUSTUMAL**.
– DERIVATIVES **customarily** adverb, **customariness** noun.
– ORIGIN late Middle English (as a noun): from medieval Latin *custumarius*, from *custuma*, from Anglo-Norman French *custume* (see **CUSTOM**).

custom-built ▶ **adjective** made to a particular customer's order.

customer ▶ **noun 1** a person or organization that buys goods or services from a shop or business: *Mr Harrison was a regular customer at the Golden Lion* | [as modifier] *customer service.*
2 [with adj.] a person or thing of a specified kind that one has to deal with: *the fish is a slippery customer and very hard to catch | a tough customer.*

custom house (also **customs house**) ▶ **noun** chiefly historical the office at a port or frontier where customs duty is collected.

customize (also **-ise**) ▶ **verb** [with obj.] (often **be customized**) modify (something) to suit a particular individual or task: *it can be customized to the developing needs of your students.*

custom-made ▶ **adjective** another term for **CUSTOM-BUILT**.

customs ▶ **plural noun** the official department that administers and collects the duties levied by a government on imported goods: *cocaine seizures by customs have risen this year* | [as modifier] *a customs officer.*
■ the place at a port, airport, or frontier where officials check incoming goods, travellers, or luggage: *we were through customs with a minimum of formalities.* ■ (usu. **customs duties**) the duties levied by a government on imported goods.
– ORIGIN late Middle English: originally in the singular, denoting a customary due paid to a ruler, later duty levied on goods on their way to market.

customs union ▶ **noun** a group of states that have agreed to charge the same import duties as each other and usually to allow free trade between themselves.

custos rotulorum /ˌkʌstɒs ˌrəʊtjʊˈlɔːrəm/ ▶ **noun** (pl. **custodes rotulorum** /kʌˈstəʊdiːz/) (in England and Wales) the principal Justice of the Peace of a county, who has nominal custody of the records of the commission of the peace. The function is usually fulfilled by the Lord Lieutenant.
– ORIGIN Latin.

custumal /ˈkʌstjʊm(ə)l/ (also **customal**) ▶ **noun** historical a written account of the customs of a manor or other local community or large establishment.
– ORIGIN late 16th cent.: from medieval Latin *custumale* 'customs book', neuter of *custumalis*, from *custuma* 'custom'.

cut ▶ **verb** (**cutting**; past and past participle **cut**) [with obj.]
1 make an opening, incision, or wound in (something) with a sharp-edged tool or object: *he cut his big toe on a sharp stone | he* ***cut open*** *MacKay's face with the end of his hockey stick* | [no obj.] figurative *his scorn cut deeper than knives.*
2 remove (something) from something larger by using a sharp implement: *I cut his photograph* ***out of*** *the paper | some prisoners had their right hands* ***cut off.***
■ castrate (an animal, especially a horse). ■ (**cut something out**) make something by cutting: *I cut out some squares of paper.* ■ (**cut something out**) remove, exclude, or stop eating or doing something undesirable: *start today by cutting out fatty foods.* ■ (**cut something out**) separate an animal from the main herd.
3 divide into pieces with a knife or other sharp implement: ***cut*** *the beef* ***into*** *thin slices | he* ***cut*** *his food* ***up*** *into teeny pieces.*
■ make divisions in (something): *land that has been* ***cut up*** *by streams into forested areas.* ■ separate (something) into two; sever: *they cut the rope before he choked.* ■ (**cut something down**) make something, especially a tree, fall by cutting it through at the base. ■ (**cut someone down**) (of a weapon, bullet, or disease) kill or injure someone: *Barker had been cut down by a sniper's bullet.*
4 make or form (something) by using a sharp tool to remove material: *workmen* ***cut a hole in*** *the pipe.*
■ make or design (a garment) in a particular way: [as adj., with submodifier] (**cut**) *an impeccably cut chalk-stripe suit.* ■ make (a path, tunnel, or other route) by excavation, digging, or chopping: *plans to cut a road through a rainforest* | [no obj.] *investigators called for a machete to* ***cut through*** *the bush* | figurative *a large woman with a voice which* ***cut through*** *crowds.*
5 trim or reduce the length of (something, especially grass or a person's hair or fingernails) by using a sharp implement: *cutting the lawn |* ***cut back*** *all the year's growth to about four leaves.*
6 reduce the amount or quantity of: *buyers will bargain hard to* ***cut the cost of*** *the house they want | I should* ***cut down*** *my sugar intake* | [no obj.] *they've* ***cut back on*** *costs | the state passed a law to* ***cut down on*** *drunk-driving | the paper glut* ***cuts into*** *profits.*
■ abridge (a text, film, or performance) by removing material: *he had to cut unnecessary additions made to the opening scene.* ■ Computing delete (part of a text or other display) completely or so as to insert a copy of it elsewhere. See also **CUT AND PASTE**. ■ end or interrupt the provision of (something, especially power or food supplies): *we resolved to cut oil supplies to territories controlled by the rebels | if the pump develops a fault, the electrical supply is immediately* ***cut off.*** ■ (**cut something off**) block the usual means of access to a place: *the caves were* ***cut off from*** *the outside world by a landslide.* ■ chiefly N. Amer. absent oneself deliberately from (something one should normally attend, especially school): *Rodney was cutting class.* ■ switch off (an engine or a light).
7 (of a line) cross or intersect (another line): *the point where the line cuts the vertical axis.*
■ [no obj.] (**cut across**) pass or traverse, especially so as to shorten one's route: *the following aircraft cut across to join him.* ■ [no obj.] (**cut across**) have an effect regardless of (divisions or boundaries between groups): *subcultures which cut across national and political boundaries.* ■ [no obj.] (**cut along**) informal, dated leave or move hurriedly: *you can cut along now.*
8 dated ignore or refuse to recognize (someone).
9 [no obj., often in imperative] stop filming or recording.
■ [with adverbial] move to another shot in a film: ***cut to*** *a dentist's surgery.* ■ [with obj.] make (a film) into a coherent whole by removing parts or placing them in a different order.
10 make (a sound recording).
11 [no obj.] divide a pack of playing cards by lifting a portion from the top, either to reveal a card at random or to place the top portion under the bottom portion.
12 strike or kick (a ball) with an abrupt, typically downward motion: *Cook cut the ball back to him.*
■ Golf slice (the ball). ■ Cricket hit (the ball) to the off side with the bat held almost horizontally; play such a stroke against (the bowler). ■ [no obj.] Cricket (of the ball) turn sharply on pitching.
13 chiefly N. Amer. adulterate (a drug) or dilute (alcohol) by mixing it with another substance: *speed* ***cut with*** *rat poison.*
14 (**cut it**) informal, chiefly N. Amer. come up to expectations; meet requirements: *this CD player doesn't quite cut it.* [ORIGIN: shortened form of the idiom *cut the mustard*.]
▶ **noun 1** an act of cutting, in particular:
■ [in sing.] a haircut: *his hair was in need of a cut.* ■ a stroke or blow given by a sharp-edged implement or by a whip or cane: *he could skin an animal with a single cut of the knife.* ■ figurative a wounding remark or act: *his unkindest cut at Elizabeth was to call her heartless.* ■ [often with modifier] a reduction in amount or size: *she took a 20% pay cut | a* ***cut in*** *interest rates.* ■ Brit. a power cut. ■ an act of removing part of a play, film, or book, especially to shorten the work or to delete offensive material: *they would not publish the book unless the author was willing to* ***make cuts.*** ■ an immediate transition from one scene to another in a film. ■ Tennis & Cricket a stroke made with an abrupt, typically horizontal or downward action.
2 a result of cutting something, in particular:
■ a long narrow incision in the skin made by something sharp. ■ a long narrow opening or incision made in a surface or piece of material: *make a single cut along the top of each potato.* ■ a piece of meat cut from a carcass: *a good lean cut of beef.* ■ [in sing.] informal a share of the profits from something: *the directors are demanding their cut.* ■ a recording of a piece of music: *a cut from his forthcoming album.* ■ a version of a film after editing: *the director's cut.* ■ a passage cut or dug out, as a railway cutting or a new channel made for a river or other waterway.
3 [in sing.] the way or style in which something, especially a garment or someone's hair, is cut: *the elegant cut of his dinner jacket.*
– PHRASES **be cut out for** (or **to be**) [usu. with negative] informal have exactly the right qualities for a particular role, task, or job: *I'm just not cut out to be a policeman.* **a cut above** informal noticeably superior to: *she's a cut above the rest.* **cut and dried** [often with negative] (of a situation) completely settled or decided: *the championship is not as cut and dried as everyone thinks.* [ORIGIN: early 18th cent.: originally used to distinguish the herbs of herbalists' shops from growing herbs.] **cut and run** informal make a speedy or sudden departure from an awkward or hazardous situation rather than deal with it. [ORIGIN: originally a nautical phrase, meaning 'cut the anchor cable because of some emergency and make sail immediately'.] **cut and thrust** a spirited and rapid interchange of views: *the cut and thrust of political debate.* ■ a situation or sphere of activity regarded as carried out under adversarial conditions: *the ruthless cut and thrust of the business world.* [ORIGIN: originally a phrase in fencing.] **cut both ways** (of a point or statement) serve both sides of an argument. ■ (of an action or process) have both good and bad effects: *the triumphs of civilization cut both ways.* **cut the corner** take the shortest course by going across and not around a corner. **cut corners** undertake something in what

C

appears to be the easiest, quickest, or cheapest way, especially by omitting to do something important or ignoring rules. **cut the crap** [often in imperative] vulgar slang get to the point; state the real situation. **cut a dash** be stylish or impressive in one's dress or behaviour. **cut someone dead** completely ignore someone. **cut a deal** informal, chiefly N. Amer. come to an arrangement, especially in business; make a deal. **cut someone down to size** informal deflate someone's exaggerated sense of self-worth. **cut something down to size** reduce the size or power of something, for example an organization, which is regarded as having become too large or powerful. **cut a —— figure** present oneself or appear in a particular way: *David has cut a dashing figure on the international social scene.* **cut someone free** free someone from something in which they are trapped. **cut from the same cloth** of the same nature; similar: *don't assume all women are cut from the same cloth.* **cut in line** US jump the queue. **cut it fine** see **FINE**[1]. **cut it out** [usu. in imperative] informal used to ask someone to stop doing or saying something that is annoying or offensive: *I'm sick of that joke; cut it out, can't you?* **cut loose** distance oneself from a person, group, or system by which one is unduly influenced or on which one is over-dependent: *Poland **cut loose from** communism.* ■ begin to act without restraint: *when Mannion cut loose the home side collapsed to 127 all out.* **cut someone/thing loose** free someone or something from something which holds or restricts them; untie: *he'd cut loose the horses.* **cut one's losses** abandon an enterprise or course of action that is clearly going to be unprofitable or unsuccessful before one suffers too much loss or harm. **cut the mustard** informal come up to expectations; reach the required standard: *I didn't cut the mustard as a hockey player.* **cut no ice** informal have no influence or effect: *your holier-than-thou attitude **cuts no ice with** me.* **cut someone off** (or **down**) **in their prime** bring someone's life or career to an abrupt end while they are at the peak of their abilities. **cut someone/thing short** interrupt someone or something; bring an abrupt or premature end to something said or done: *Peter cut him short rudely.* **cut someone to pieces** kill or severely injure someone. ■ figurative totally defeat someone. **cut a** (or **the**) **rug** informal, chiefly N. Amer. dance, typically in an energetic or accomplished way. **cut one's teeth** acquire initial practice or experience of a particular sphere of activity or with a particular organization: *the brothers cut their professional teeth at Lusardi's before starting their own restaurant.* **cut a tooth** (of a baby) have a tooth appear through the gum. **cut to the chase** N. Amer. informal come to the point: *cut to the chase—what is it you want us to do?* [ORIGIN: *cut* in the sense 'move to another part of the film', expressing the notion of ignoring any preliminaries.] **cut up rough** Brit. informal behave in an aggressive, quarrelsome, or awkward way. **cut up well** Brit. archaic bequeath a large fortune. **cut your coat according to your cloth** proverb undertake only what you have the money or ability to do and no more. **have one's work cut out** see **WORK**. **make the cut** [usu. with negative] Golf equal or better a required score, thus avoiding elimination from the last two rounds of a four-round tournament. **miss the cut** Golf fail to equal or better a required score, thus being eliminated from the last two rounds of a four-round tournament.

– ORIGIN Middle English (probably existing, although not recorded, in Old English); probably of Germanic origin and related to Norwegian *kutte* and Icelandic *kuta* 'cut with a small knife', *kuti* 'small blunt knife'.

▶**cut in 1** interrupt someone while they are speaking: *'It's urgent,' Raoul cut in.* **2** pull in too closely in front of another vehicle after having overtaken it: *she **cut in on** a station wagon, forcing the driver to brake.* **3** (of a motor or other mechanical device) begin operating, especially when triggered automatically by an electrical signal: *emergency generators cut in.* **4** dated interrupt a dancing couple to take over from one partner.

cut someone in informal include someone in a deal and give them a share of the profits.

cut into interrupt the course of: *Victoria's words cut into her thoughts.*

cut someone off interrupt someone while they are speaking. ■ interrupt someone during a telephone call by breaking the connection: *I listened to pre-recorded messages for twenty-three minutes before being cut off.* ■ prevent someone from receiving or being provided with something, especially power or water: *consumers cut off for non-payment.* ■ reject someone as one's heir; disinherit someone: *Gabrielle's family **cut her off without a penny**.* ■ prevent someone from having access to somewhere or someone; isolate someone from something they previously had connections with: *we were cut off from reality.*

cut out 1 (of a motor or engine) suddenly stop operating. **2** N. Amer. informal (of a person) leave quickly, especially so as to avoid a boring or awkward situation.

cut someone out exclude someone: *his mother cut him out of her will.*

cut up 1 N. Amer. informal behave in a mischievous or unruly manner: *kids cutting up in a classroom.* **2** informal (of a horse race) have a particular selection of runners: *the race has **cut up badly** with no other opposition from England.*

cut someone up 1 informal (of a driver) overtake someone and pull in too closely in front of them. **2** informal, chiefly N. Amer. criticize someone severely: *my kids cut him up about his appetite all the time.*

cut-and-come-again ▶**noun** [usu. as modifier] a garden plant, especially a green vegetable or a flower, that can be repeatedly cut or harvested: *cut-and-come-again spinach.*

cut-and-cover ▶**noun** [mass noun] a method of building a tunnel by making a cutting which is then lined and covered over.

cut and paste ▶**noun** [mass noun] a process used in assembling text on a word processor or computer, in which items are removed from one part and inserted elsewhere.

▶**verb** [with obj.] move (an item of text) using this technique.

cutaneous /kjuːˈteɪnɪəs/ ▶**adjective** of, relating to, or affecting the skin: *cutaneous pigmentation.*

– ORIGIN late 16th cent.: from modern Latin *cutaneus* (from Latin *cutis* 'skin') + **-OUS**.

cutaway ▶**noun** [often as modifier] **1** a thing made or designed with a part cut out or absent, in particular:

■ a coat or jacket with the front cut away below the waist. ■ a diagram or drawing with some external parts left out to reveal the interior.

2 a shot or scene in a film which is of a different subject from those to which it is joined in editing.

cutback ▶**noun** an act or instance of reducing something, typically expenditure: ***cutbacks in** defence spending.*

cutch /kʌtʃ/ ▶**noun** see **CATECHU**.

cut-down ▶**adjective** [attrib.] reduced in scope or length: *it's a cut-down version of a DTP program.*

cute ▶**adjective 1** attractive in a pretty or endearing way: *a picture of a cute kitten.*

■ informal, N. Amer. sexually attractive.

2 informal, chiefly N. Amer. clever, especially in a shrewd or quick-witted way: *she had a real cute idea.*

– DERIVATIVES **cutely** adverb, **cuteness** noun.

– ORIGIN early 18th cent. (in the sense 'clever, shrewd'): shortening of **ACUTE**.

cutesy ▶**adjective** informal cute to a sentimental or mawkish extent: *the film's cutesy shots of children playing in the streets.*

cut glass ▶**noun** [mass noun] glass that has been ornamented by having patterns cut into it by grinding and polishing: [as modifier] *a cut-glass decanter.*

■ [as modifier] figurative characterized by careful enunciation or precise thought: *a cut-glass accent.*

Cuthbert, St (d.687), English monk. He lived as a hermit on Farne Island before becoming bishop of Lindisfarne. Feast day, 20 March.

cuticle /ˈkjuːtɪk(ə)l/ ▶**noun 1** [mass noun] the outer layer of living tissue, in particular:

■ Botany & Zoology a protective and waxy or hard layer covering the epidermis of a plant, invertebrate, or shell. ■ the outer cellular layer of a hair. ■ Zoology another term for **EPIDERMIS**.

2 the dead skin at the base of a fingernail or toenail.

– DERIVATIVES **cuticular** /-ˈtɪkjʊlə/ adjective.

– ORIGIN late 15th cent. (denoting a membrane of the body): from Latin *cuticula*, diminutive of *cutis* 'skin'.

cutie ▶**noun** (pl. **-ies**) informal an attractive or endearing person, especially a young woman.

cutin /ˈkjuːtɪn/ ▶**noun** [mass noun] Biochemistry a waxy water-repellent substance in the cuticle of plants, consisting of highly polymerized esters of fatty acids.

– ORIGIN mid 19th cent.: from **CUTIS** + **-IN**[1].

cut-in ▶**noun** a shot in a film that is edited into another shot or scene.

cutis /ˈkjuːtɪs/ ▶**noun** [mass noun] Anatomy the true skin or dermis.

– ORIGIN early 17th cent.: from Latin, 'skin'.

cutlass /ˈkʌtləs/ ▶**noun** a short sword with a slightly curved blade, formerly used by sailors.

– ORIGIN late 16th cent.: from French *coutelas*, based on Latin *cultellus* 'small knife' (see **CUTLER**).

cutlassfish ▶**noun** (pl. same or **-fishes**) a long slender marine fish with sharp teeth and a dorsal fin running the length of the back.

• Family Trichiuridae: several species, including the Atlantic *Trichiurus lepturus* (also called **SNAKEFISH**), an important food fish in the tropics.

cutler ▶**noun** a person who makes or sells cutlery.

– ORIGIN Middle English: from Old French *coutelier*, from *coutel* 'knife', from Latin *cultellus*, diminutive of *culter* 'knife, ploughshare'. Compare with **COULTER**.

cutlery ▶**noun** [mass noun] knives, forks, and spoons used for eating or serving food.

– ORIGIN Middle English: from Old French *coutellerie*, from *coutelier* (see **CUTLER**).

cutlet ▶**noun** a portion of meat, usually served grilled or fried and often covered in breadcrumbs.

■ Brit. a lamb or veal chop from just behind the neck. ■ a flat croquette of minced meat, nuts, or pulses, typically covered in breadcrumbs and shaped like a veal chop.

– ORIGIN early 18th cent.: from French *côtelette*, earlier *costelette*, diminutive of *coste* 'rib', from Latin *costa*.

cutline ▶**noun 1** N. Amer. the caption to a photograph or other illustration.

2 (in squash) the line above which a served ball must strike the front wall.

cut-off ▶**adjective** [attrib.] **1** of or constituting a limit: *the cut-off date to register is July 2.*

2 (of a device) producing an interruption or cessation of a power or fuel supply: *a cut-off button.*

3 (of an item of clothing) having been cut short: *a cut-off T-shirt.*

4 (of a person) isolated from or no longer having access to someone or something: *aid to the cut-off troops in the north.*

▶**noun 1** a point or level which is a designated limit of something: *2,500 g is the standard cut-off below which infants are categorized as 'low birthweight'.*

2 an act of stopping or interrupting the supply or provision of something: *a cut-off of aid would be a disaster.*

■ a device for producing an interruption or cessation of a power or fuel supply. ■ a sudden drop in amplification or responsiveness of an electric device at a certain frequency: [as modifier] *a cut-off frequency of 8 Hz.* ■ [mass noun] the stopping of the supply of steam to the cylinders of a steam engine when the piston has travelled a set percentage of its stroke.

3 (**cut-offs**) shorts made by cutting off the legs of a pair of jeans or other trousers and leaving the edges unhemmed.

4 chiefly US a short cut.

cut-out ▶**noun 1** a shape of a person or thing cut out of board or another material.

■ figurative a person perceived as characterless or lacking in individuality: *this film's protagonists are cardboard cut-outs.*

2 a hole cut in something for decoration or to allow the insertion of something else.

3 a device that automatically breaks an electric circuit for safety and either resets itself or can be reset.

cutover ▶**noun** a rapid transition from one phase of a business enterprise or project to another.

▶**adjective** [attrib.] (of land) having had its saleable timber felled and removed.

cut-price (chiefly US also **cut-rate**) ▶**adjective** [attrib.] for sale at a reduced or unusually low price: *cut-price footwear.*

■ offering goods at such prices: *cut-price supermarkets.*

cutpurse ▶**noun** archaic term for **PICKPOCKET**.

– ORIGIN late Middle English: with reference to stealing by cutting purses suspended from a waistband.

cutscene ▶ noun (in computer games) a scene that develops the storyline and is often shown on completion of a certain level, or when the player's character dies.

cutter ▶ noun **1** a person or thing that cuts something, in particular:
■ [often with adj. or noun modifier] a tool for cutting something, especially one intended for cutting a particular thing or for producing a particular shape: *a biscuit cutter* | (**cutters**) *a pair of bolt cutters.* ■ a person who cuts or edits film. ■ a person in a tailoring establishment who takes measurements and cuts the cloth. ■ a person who reduces or cuts down on something, especially expenditure: *a determined cutter of costs.*
2 a light, fast coastal patrol boat.
■ a ship's boat used for carrying light stores or passengers. ■ historical a small fore-and-aft rigged sailing boat with one mast, more than one headsail, and a running bowsprit, used as a fast auxiliary. ■ a yacht with one mainsail and two foresails.
3 Cricket & Baseball a ball that deviates sharply on pitching.
4 N. Amer. a light horse-drawn sleigh.
5 a pig heavier than a porker but lighter than a baconer.

cut-throat ▶ noun **1** dated a murderer or other violent criminal.
2 short for **CUT-THROAT RAZOR**.
3 (also **cut-throat trout**) a trout of western North America, with red or orange markings under the jaw.
● *Salmo clarki*, family Salmonidae.
▶ adjective (of a competitive situation or activity) fierce and intense; involving the use of ruthless measures: *cut-throat competition led to a lot of bankruptcies* | *the cut-throat world of fashion.*
■ (of a person) using ruthless methods in a competitive situation: *the greedy cut-throat manufacturers he worked for.* ■ denoting a form of whist (or other card game normally for four) played by three players.

cut-throat razor ▶ noun Brit. a razor having a long blade set in a handle, usually folding like a penknife.

cut-throat weaver (also **cut-throat** or **cut-throat finch**) ▶ noun a small finch-like African bird of the waxbill family, with speckled brown plumage, a conspicuous crimson throat band, and a rufous belly.
● *Amadina fasciata*, family Estrildidae.

cutting ▶ noun **1** (often **cuttings**) a piece cut off from something, especially what remains when something is being trimmed or prepared: *grass cuttings.*
■ Brit. an article or other piece cut from a newspaper or periodical. ■ a piece cut from a plant for propagation.
2 an open passage excavated through higher ground for a railway, road, or canal.
▶ adjective capable of cutting something: *the cutting blades of the hedge trimmer.*
■ figurative (especially of a comment) causing emotional pain; hurtful: *a cutting remark.* ■ figurative (of the wind) bitterly cold.
– DERIVATIVES **cuttingly** adverb.

cutting edge ▶ noun the edge of a tool's blade.
■ [in sing.] the latest or most advanced stage in the development of something: *researchers at the cutting edge of molecular biology.* ■ [in sing.] a person or factor that contributes a dynamic or invigorating quality to a situation and thereby puts one at an advantage over one's rivals: *the party's campaign began to lose its cutting edge.* ■ figurative a way of expressing oneself in speech or writing that is incisive and direct: *his wit retains its cutting edge.*
▶ adjective (**cutting-edge**) at the latest or most advanced stage of development; innovative or pioneering: *cutting-edge technology.*

cutting grass ▶ noun **1** [mass noun] an Australian and New Zealand sedge with sharp-edged leaves or stems.
● Genus *Gahnia*, family Cyperaceae.
2 another term for **CANE RAT**.

cutting horse ▶ noun N. Amer. a horse trained in separating cattle from a herd.

cutting room ▶ noun a room in a film studio where film is cut and edited: [as modifier] *such a scene would end up on the cutting-room floor.*

cuttle ▶ noun a cuttlefish.
– ORIGIN Old English *cudele* 'cuttlefish', of Germanic origin; related to *codd* 'bag', with reference to its ink bag.

cuttlebone ▶ noun the flattened oval internal skeleton of the cuttlefish, which is made of white lightweight chalky material. It is used as a dietary supplement for cage birds and for making casts for precious metal items.

cuttlefish ▶ noun (pl. same or **-fishes**) a swimming marine mollusc that resembles a broad-bodied squid, having eight arms and two long tentacles that are used for grabbing prey. Its internal skeleton is the familiar cuttlebone, which it uses for adjusting buoyancy.
● Order Sepioidea, class Cephalopoda: *Sepia* and other genera.
– ORIGIN late 16th cent.: from **CUTTLE** + **FISH**[1].

cutty Scottish & N. English ▶ adjective short, either naturally so or through being cut down.
▶ noun (pl. **-ies**) a short tobacco pipe.

Cutty Sark /ˌkʌtɪ ˈsɑːk/ the only survivor of the British tea clippers, launched in 1869 and now preserved as a museum ship at Greenwich, London.
– ORIGIN from Robert Burns's *Tam o' Shanter*, a poem about a Scottish farmer chased by a young witch who wore only her 'cutty sark' (= short shift).

cutty-stool ▶ noun Scottish historical a stool on which an offender was publicly rebuked during a church service.

cut-up (also **cut up**) ▶ adjective **1** divided into pieces by cutting: *cut-up vegetables.*
■ (of a soft piece of ground) having an uneven surface after the passage of heavy vehicles or animals: *the ground was deeply cut up where the cattle had strayed.*
2 [predic.] informal (of a person) very distressed: *Mr Brown's girlfriend is dying and he's really cut up about it.*
▶ noun **1** a film or sound recording made by cutting and editing material from pre-existing recordings.
2 N. Amer. informal a person who is fond of making jokes or playing the fool.
■ dated a practical joke.

cutwater ▶ noun **1** the forward edge of a ship's prow.
2 a wedge-shaped projection on the pier of a bridge, which divides the flow of water and prevents debris from becoming trapped against the pier.

cutwork ▶ noun [mass noun] embroidery or lace with parts cut out and the edges oversewn or filled with needlework designs.
■ appliqué work in which the pattern is cut out and sewn on.

cutworm ▶ noun a moth caterpillar that lives in the upper layers of the soil and eats through the stems of young plants at ground level.
● Several species in the family Noctuidae, in particular the large yellow underwing (see **YELLOW UNDERWING**).

cuvée /ˈkjuːveɪ, French kyve/ ▶ noun a type, blend, or batch of wine, especially champagne.
– ORIGIN mid 19th cent.: French, 'vatful', from *cuve* 'cask', from Latin *cupa.*

cuvette /kjuːˈvɛt/ ▶ noun Biochemistry a straight-sided optically clear container for holding liquid samples in a spectrophotometer or other instrument.
– ORIGIN early 18th cent.: from French, diminutive of *cuve* 'cask', from Latin *cupa.*

Cuvier /ˈkuːvɪeɪ, French kyvje/, Georges Léopold Chrétien Frédéric Dagobert, Baron (1769–1832), French naturalist. Cuvier founded the science of palaeontology and made pioneering studies in comparative anatomy and classification.

Cuzco /ˈkʊskəʊ, Spanish ˈkusko, ˈkuθko/ a city in the Andes in southern Peru; pop. 275,000 (1990). It was the capital of the Inca empire until the Spanish conquest in 1533.

CV ▶ abbreviation for curriculum vitae.

CV ▶ abbreviation for cultivated variety.

CVO ▶ abbreviation for (in the UK) Commander of the Royal Victorian Order.

CVS ▶ abbreviation for chorionic villus sampling.

CVT ▶ abbreviation for continuously variable transmission.

cwm /kʊm/ ▶ noun a cirque, especially one in the mountains of Wales.
– ORIGIN mid 19th cent.: Welsh; related to **COMBE**.

Cwmbran /kʊmˈbrɑːn/ a town in SE Wales,

administrative centre of Monmouthshire; pop. 44,800 (1981).

CWO ▶ abbreviation for Chief Warrant Officer.

c.w.o. ▶ abbreviation for cash with order.

cwr ▶ abbreviation for continuous welded rail, railway track laid in long unbroken strips rather than as short fixed lengths with gaps.

CWS ▶ abbreviation for Cooperative Wholesale Society.

cwt. ▶ abbreviation for hundredweight.

CY ▶ abbreviation for Cyprus (international vehicle registration).

-cy ▶ suffix **1** denoting state or condition: *bankruptcy.*
2 denoting rank or status: *baronetcy.*
– ORIGIN from Latin *-cia, -tia* and Greek *-k(e)ia, -t(e)ia.*

cyan /ˈsaɪən/ ▶ noun [mass noun] a greenish-blue colour which is one of the primary subtractive colours, complementary to red.
– ORIGIN late 19th cent.: from Greek *kuaneos* 'dark blue'.

cyanamide /saɪˈanəmaɪd/ ▶ noun [mass noun] Chemistry a weakly acidic crystalline compound made as an intermediate in the industrial production of ammonia.
● Alternative name: **cyanogen amide**; chem. formula: CH_2N_2.
■ a salt of this containing the anion CN_2^{2-}, especially the calcium salt used as a fertilizer.
– ORIGIN mid 19th cent.: blend of **CYANOGEN** and **AMIDE**.

cyanic /saɪˈanɪk/ ▶ adjective rare blue; azure.
– ORIGIN early 19th cent.: from **CYAN** + **-IC**.

cyanic acid ▶ noun [mass noun] Chemistry a colourless, poisonous, volatile, strongly acidic liquid.
● Chem. formula: HOCN. See also **FULMINIC ACID**, **ISOCYANIC ACID**.
– DERIVATIVES **cyanate** noun.
– ORIGIN early 19th cent.: from **CYANOGEN**.

cyanide /ˈsaɪənaɪd/ ▶ noun Chemistry a salt or ester of hydrocyanic acid, containing the anion CN^- or the group —CN. The salts are generally extremely toxic. Compare with **NITRILE**.
■ [mass noun] sodium or potassium cyanide used as a poison or in the extraction of gold and silver.
– ORIGIN early 19th cent.: from **CYANOGEN** + **-IDE**.

cyano- ▶ combining form **1** relating to the colour blue, especially dark blue: *cyanosis.*
2 representing **CYANIDE**.
– ORIGIN from Greek *kuan(e)os* 'dark blue'.

cyanoacrylate /ˌsaɪənəʊˈakrɪleɪt/ ▶ noun Chemistry any of a class of compounds which are cyanide derivatives of acrylates. They are easily polymerized and are used to make quick-setting adhesives.

Cyanobacteria /ˌsaɪənəʊbakˈtɪərɪə/ Biology a division of micro-organisms that are related to the bacteria but are capable of photosynthesis. They are prokaryotic and represent the earliest known form of life on the earth.
● Division Cyanobacteria, kingdom Monera.
■ [as plural noun **cyanobacteria**] micro-organisms of this division; blue-green algae.
– ORIGIN modern Latin (plural), from Greek *kuaneos* 'dark blue' + plural of **BACTERIUM**.

cyanocobalamin /ˌsaɪənəʊ(ʊ)kəˈbaləmɪn/ ▶ noun [mass noun] a vitamin found in foods of animal origin such as liver, fish, and eggs, a deficiency of which can cause pernicious anaemia. It contains a cyanide group bonded to the central cobalt atom of a cobalamin molecule. Also called *vitamin B_{12}*.
– ORIGIN 1950s: from **CYANOGEN** and *cobalamin* (blend of **COBALT** and **VITAMIN**).

cyanogen /saɪˈanədʒ(ə)n/ ▶ noun [mass noun] Chemistry a colourless flammable highly poisonous gas made by oxidizing hydrogen cyanide. One of the pseudohalogens, cyanogen is an intermediate in fertilizer manufacture.
● Chem. formula: C_2N_2.
– ORIGIN early 19th cent.: from French *cyanogène*, from Greek *kuanos* 'dark blue mineral' + *-gène* (see **-GEN**), so named because it is a constituent of Prussian blue.

cyanogenesis /ˌsaɪənə(ʊ)ˈdʒɛnɪsɪs/ ▶ noun [mass noun] Botany the production of hydrogen cyanide by certain plants, such as cherry laurel, bracken, and some legumes, as a response to wounding or a deterrent to herbivores.

cyanogenic /ˌsʌɪənəˈdʒɛnɪk/ ▶ **adjective** Botany (of a plant) capable of cyanogenesis: *cyanogenic forms.*
■Biochemistry containing a cyanide group in the molecule.

cyanohydrin /ˌsʌɪənə(ʊ)ˈhʌɪdrɪn/ ▶ **noun** Chemistry an organic compound containing a carbon atom linked to both a cyanide group and a hydroxyl group.

cyanophyte /ˈsʌɪənə(ʊ)fʌɪt/ ▶ **noun** Biology a micro-organism of the division Cyanobacteria.

cyanosis /ˌsʌɪəˈnəʊsɪs/ ▶ **noun** [mass noun] Medicine a bluish discoloration of the skin due to poor circulation or inadequate oxygenation of the blood.
– DERIVATIVES **cyanotic** adjective.
– ORIGIN mid 19th cent.: modern Latin, from Greek *kuanōsis* 'blueness', from *kuaneos* 'dark blue'.

cyathium /sʌɪˈaθɪəm/ ▶ **noun** (pl. **cyathia** /-ɪə/) Botany the characteristic inflorescence of the spurges, resembling a single flower. It consists of a cup-shaped involucre of fused bracts enclosing several greatly reduced male flowers and a single female flower.
– ORIGIN late 19th cent.: modern Latin, from Greek *kuathion*, diminutive of *kuathos* 'cup'.

Cybele /ˈsɪbɪli/ Mythology a mother goddess worshipped especially in Phrygia and later in Greece (where she was associated with Demeter), Rome, and the Roman provinces, with her consort Attis.

cyber /ˈsʌɪbə/ ▶ **adjective** of, relating to, or characteristic of the culture of computers, information technology, and virtual reality: *the cyber age.*
– ORIGIN 1980s: abbreviation of **CYBERNETICS**.

cyber- /ˈsʌɪbə/ ▶ **combining form** relating to electronic communication networks and virtual reality: *cyberpunk | cyberspace.*
– ORIGIN back-formation from **CYBERNETICS**.

cybercafe ▶ **noun** a cafe where customers can sit at computer terminals and log on to the Internet while eating and drinking.

cybernaut ▶ **noun** Computing a person who wears sensory devices in order to experience virtual reality.
■a person who uses the Internet.
– ORIGIN 1990s: from **CYBER-**, on the pattern of *astronaut* and *aeronaut.*

cybernetics ▶ **plural noun** [treated as sing.] the science of communications and automatic control systems in both machines and living things.
– DERIVATIVES **cybernetic** adjective, **cybernetician** noun, **cyberneticist** noun.
– ORIGIN 1940s: from Greek *kubernētēs* 'steersman', from *kubernan* 'to steer'.

cyberphobia ▶ **noun** [mass noun] extreme or irrational fear of computers or technology.
– DERIVATIVES **cyberphobe** noun, **cyberphobic** adjective & noun.

cyberpunk ▶ **noun** [mass noun] a genre of science fiction set in a lawless subculture of an oppressive society dominated by computer technology.
■[count noun] a writer of such science fiction. ■[count noun] a person who accesses computer networks illegally, especially with malicious intent.

cybersex ▶ **noun** [mass noun] sexual arousal using computer technology, especially by wearing virtual reality equipment or by exchanging messages with another person via the Internet.

cyberspace ▶ **noun** [mass noun] the notional environment in which communication over computer networks occurs.

cyborg /ˈsʌɪbɔːɡ/ ▶ **noun** a fictional or hypothetical person whose physical abilities are extended beyond normal human limitations by mechanical elements built into the body.
– ORIGIN 1960s: blend of **CYBER-** and **ORGANISM**.

cycad /ˈsʌɪkad/ ▶ **noun** a palm-like plant of tropical and subtropical regions, bearing large male or female cones. Cycads were abundant during the Triassic and Jurassic eras, but have since been in decline.
• Class Cycadopsida, subdivision Gymnospermae: twenty species in the genus *Cycas* and family Cycadaceae.
– ORIGIN mid 19th cent.: from modern Latin *Cycas, Cycad-* (order name), from supposed Greek *kukas*, scribal error for *koïkas*, plural of *koix* 'Egyptian palm'.

Cyclades /ˈsɪklədiːz/ a large group of islands in the southern Aegean Sea, regarded in antiquity as circling around the sacred island of Delos. The Cyclades form a department of modern Greece. Greek name **KIKLÁDHES**.
– ORIGIN Latin, based on Greek *kuklos* 'circle'.

Cycladic /sɪˈkladɪk, sʌɪ-/ ▶ **adjective** of or relating to the Cyclades.
■Archaeology of, relating to, or denoting a Bronze Age civilization that flourished in the Cyclades, dated to *c.*3000–1050 BC. ■[as noun **the Cycladic**] the Cycladic culture or period.

cyclamate /ˈsɪkləmeɪt, ˈsʌɪk-/ ▶ **noun** Chemistry a salt of a synthetic acid which is a cyclohexyl derivative of sulphamic acid. Sodium and calcium cyclamates were formerly used as artificial sweeteners.
– ORIGIN 1950s: contraction of *cyclohexylsulphamate.*

cyclamen /ˈsɪkləmən/ ▶ **noun** (pl. same or **cyclamens**) a European plant of the primrose family, having pink, red, or white flowers with backward-curving petals and widely grown as a winter-flowering pot plant.
• Genus *Cyclamen*, family Primulaceae: several species.
■[mass noun] a pinkish-purple colour.
– ORIGIN modern Latin, from Latin *cyclaminos*, from Greek *kuklaminos*, perhaps from *kuklos* 'circle', with reference to its bulbous roots.

cycle ▶ **noun 1** [often with adj. or noun modifier] a series of events that are regularly repeated in the same order: *the boom and slump periods of a trade cycle.*
■the period of time taken to complete a single sequence of such events: *the cells are shed over a cycle of twenty-eight days* ■technical a recurring series of successive operations or states, such as in the working of an internal-combustion engine, or in the alternation of an electric current or a wave: *the familiar four cycles of intake, combustion, ignition, and exhaust.* ■Biology a recurring series of events or metabolic processes in the lifetime of a plant or animal: *the storks' breeding cycle.* ■Biochemistry a series of successive metabolic reactions in which one of the products is regenerated and reused. ■Ecology the movement of a simple substance through the soil, rocks, water, atmosphere, and living organisms of the earth. See **CARBON CYCLE**, **NITROGEN CYCLE**. ■Computing a single set of hardware operations, especially that by which memory is accessed and an item is transferred to or from it, to the point at which the memory may be accessed again. ■Physics a cycle per second; one hertz.
2 a complete set or series: *the painting is one of a cycle of seven.*
■a series of songs, stories, plays, or poems composed around a particular theme, and usually intended to be performed or read in sequence: *Wagner's Ring Cycle.*
3 a bicycle or tricycle.
■[in sing.] a ride on a bicycle: *a 112-mile cycle.*
▶ **verb 1** [no obj., with adverbial of direction] ride a bicycle: *she cycled to work every day.*
2 [no obj.] move in or follow a regularly repeated sequence of events: *economies cycle regularly between boom and slump.*
– ORIGIN late Middle English: from Old French, from late Latin *cyclus*, from Greek *kuklos* 'circle'.

cycle lane ▶ **noun** a division of a road marked off with painted lines, for use by cyclists.

cycle of erosion ▶ **noun** Geology, dated an idealized course of landscape evolution, passing from youthful stages, marked by steep gradients, to old age, when the landscape is reduced to a peneplain.

cycle rickshaw (also **bicycle rickshaw**) ▶ **noun** (in the Indian subcontinent) a three-wheeled bicycle for public hire, with a covered seat for passengers behind the driver.

cycle track (also **cycleway**, **cycle path**) ▶ **noun** Brit. a path or road for bicycles and not motor vehicles.

cyclic /ˈsʌɪklɪk, ˈsɪk-/ ▶ **adjective 1** occurring in cycles; regularly repeated: *nature is replete with cyclic processes | the cyclic pattern of the last two decades.*
■Mathematics (of a group) having the property that each element of the group can be expressed as a power of one particular element. ■relating to or denoting a musical or literary composition with a recurrent theme or structural device.
2 Mathematics of or relating to a circle or other closed curve.
■Geometry (of a polygon) having all its vertices lying on a circle. ■Chemistry (of a compound) having a molecular structure containing one or more closed rings of atoms. ■Botany (of a flower) having its parts arranged in whorls.
– DERIVATIVES **cyclical** adjective (only in sense 1), **cyclically** adverb.
– ORIGIN late 18th cent.: from French *cyclique* or Latin *cyclicus*, from Greek *kuklikos*, from *kuklos* 'circle'.

cyclic AMP ▶ **noun** [mass noun] Biochemistry a cyclic form of adenosine monophosphate (adenylic acid) which plays a major role in controlling many enzyme-catalysed processes in living cells.

cyclic redundancy check (also **cyclic redundancy code**) (abbrev.: **CRC**) ▶ **noun** Computing a code added to data which is used to detect errors occurring during transmission, storage, or retrieval.

cyclin /ˈsʌɪklɪn/ ▶ **noun** Biochemistry any of a number of proteins associated with the cycle of cell division which are thought to initiate certain processes of mitosis.
– ORIGIN 1980s: from **CYCLE** + **-IN**[1].

cycling ▶ **noun** [mass noun] the sport or activity of riding a bicycle. Cycle racing has three main forms: road racing (typically over long distances), pursuit (on an oval track), and cyclo-cross (over rough, open country).

Cycliophora /sɪklɪˈɒphərə/ Zoology a new phylum that has been proposed for a minute marine invertebrate (*Symbion pandora*) that was discovered in 1995 attached to the mouthparts of lobsters. It is related to the phyla Bryozoa and Entoprocta.
– ORIGIN modern Latin (plural), from Greek *kuklios* 'circular' + *pherein* 'to bear'.

cyclist ▶ **noun** a person who rides a bicycle.

cyclize /ˈsʌɪklʌɪz/ (also **-ise**) ▶ **verb** Chemistry undergo or cause to undergo a reaction in which one part of a molecule becomes linked to another to form a closed ring.
– DERIVATIVES **cyclization** noun.

cyclo- /ˈsʌɪkləʊ/ ▶ **combining form 1** circular: *cyclorama.*
2 relating to a cycle or cycling: *cyclo-cross.*
3 cyclic: *cycloalkane.*
– ORIGIN from Greek *kuklos* 'circle', or directly from **CYCLE** or **CYCLIC**.

cycloaddition ▶ **noun** Chemistry an addition reaction in which a cyclic molecule is formed.

cycloalkane ▶ **noun** Chemistry a hydrocarbon with a molecule containing a ring of carbon atoms joined by single bonds.

cyclo-cross ▶ **noun** [mass noun] cross-country racing on bicycles.

cyclohexane ▶ **noun** [mass noun] Chemistry a colourless flammable liquid cycloalkane obtained from petroleum or by hydrogenating benzene, and used as a solvent and paint remover.
• Chem. formula: C_6H_{12}.

cyclohexyl /ˌsʌɪklə(ʊ)ˈhɛksʌɪl, -sɪl/ ▶ **noun** [as modifier] Chemistry of or denoting the cyclic hydrocarbon radical —C_6H_{11}, derived from cyclohexane.

cycloid /ˈsʌɪklɔɪd/ ▶ **noun** Mathematics a curve (resembling a series of arches) traced by a point on a circle being rolled along a straight line.
– DERIVATIVES **cycloidal** adjective.
– ORIGIN mid 17th cent.: from Greek *kukloeidēs* 'circular', from *kuklos* 'circle'.

cyclometer /sʌɪˈklɒmɪtə/ ▶ **noun 1** an instrument for measuring circular arcs.
2 an instrument attached to a bicycle for measuring the distance it travels.

cyclone /ˈsʌɪkləʊn/ ▶ **noun** Meteorology a system of winds rotating inwards to an area of low barometric pressure, with an anticlockwise (northern hemisphere) or clockwise (southern hemisphere) circulation; a depression.
■another term for **TROPICAL STORM**.
– DERIVATIVES **cyclonic** adjective, **cyclonically** adverb.
– ORIGIN mid 19th cent.: probably from Greek *kuklōma* 'wheel, coil of a snake', from *kuklos* 'circle'. The change of spelling from *-m* to *-n* is unexplained.

cycloparaffin ▶ **noun** Chemistry another term for **CYCLOALKANE**.

cyclopean /ˌsʌɪkləˈpiːən, sʌɪˈkləʊpɪən/ (also **cyclopian**) ▶ **adjective 1** denoting a type of ancient masonry made with massive irregular blocks: *cyclopean stone walls.* [ORIGIN: by association with the great size of the Cyclops.]

2 of or resembling a Cyclops: *a cyclopean eye.*

cyclopedia /ˌsʌɪklə(ʊ)ˈpiːdɪə/ (also **cyclopaedia**) ▶ **noun** archaic (except in book titles) an encyclopedia: *Bailey's Cyclopedia of Horticulture.*
– DERIVATIVES **cyclopedic** adjective.
– ORIGIN late 17th cent.: shortening of **ENCYCLOPEDIA**.

cyclophosphamide /ˌsʌɪklə(ʊ)ˈfɒsfəmʌɪd/ ▶ **noun** [mass noun] Medicine a synthetic cytotoxic drug used in treating leukaemia and lymphoma and as an immunosuppressive agent.

cyclopropane ▶ **noun** [mass noun] Chemistry a flammable gaseous synthetic compound whose molecule contains a ring of three carbon atoms. It has some use as a general anaesthetic.
• Chem. formula: C_3H_6.

Cyclops /ˈsʌɪklɒps/ ▶ **noun 1** (pl. **Cyclops** or **Cyclopses** or **Cyclopes** /sʌɪˈkləpiːz/) Greek Mythology a member of a race of savage one-eyed giants. In the Odyssey, Odysseus escaped death by blinding the Cyclops Polyphemus.
2 (**cyclops**) a minute predatory freshwater crustacean which has a cylindrical body with a single central eye.
• Genus *Cyclops* and other genera, order Cyclopoida.
– ORIGIN via Latin from Greek *Kuklōps*, literally 'round-eyed', from *kuklos* 'circle' + *ōps* 'eye'.

cyclorama /ˌsʌɪkləˈrɑːmə/ ▶ **noun** a circular picture of a 360° scene, viewed from inside.
■ a cloth stretched tight in an arc around the back of a stage set, often used to depict the sky.
– DERIVATIVES **cycloramic** /-ˈramɪk/ adjective.
– ORIGIN mid 19th cent.: from **CYCLO-**, on the pattern of words such as *panorama*.

cyclosporin /ˌsʌɪklə(ʊ)ˈspɔːrɪn/ (also **cyclosporin A**, **cyclosporine**) ▶ **noun** [mass noun] Medicine a drug with immunosuppressive properties used to prevent the rejection of grafts and transplants. A cyclic peptide, it is obtained from a fungus.
• This drug is obtained from the fungus *Trichoderma polysporum*.
– ORIGIN 1970s: from **CYCLO-** + *-sporin* (from Latin *spora* 'spore') + **-IN**[1].

cyclostome /ˈsʌɪklə(ʊ)stəʊm/ ▶ **noun** Zoology an eel-like jawless vertebrate with a round sucking mouth, of a former group that included the lampreys and hagfishes.
• Subclass Cyclostomata, now incorporated in the superclass Agnatha.
– ORIGIN mid 19th cent.: from **CYCLO-** + Greek *stoma* 'mouth'.

cyclostyle /ˈsʌɪklə(ʊ)stʌɪl/ ▶ **noun** an early device for duplicating handwriting, in which a pen with a small toothed wheel pricks holes in a sheet of waxed paper, which is then used as a stencil.
▶ **verb** [with obj.] [usu. as adj. **cyclostyled**] duplicate with such a device: *a cyclostyled leaflet.*
– ORIGIN late 19th cent.: from **CYCLO-** 'circular' + the noun **STYLE**.

cyclothymia /ˌsʌɪklə(ʊ)ˈθʌɪmɪə/ ▶ **noun** [mass noun] Psychiatry, dated a mental state characterized by marked swings of mood between depression and elation; manic-depressive tendency.
– DERIVATIVES **cyclothymic** adjective.
– ORIGIN 1920s: from **CYCLO-** + Greek *thumos* 'temper'.

cyclotron /ˈsʌɪklətrɒn/ ▶ **noun** Physics an apparatus in which charged atomic and subatomic particles are accelerated by an alternating electric field while following an outward spiral or circular path in a magnetic field.

cyder ▶ **noun** archaic spelling of **CIDER**.

cygnet /ˈsɪgnɪt/ ▶ **noun** a young swan.
– ORIGIN late Middle English: from Anglo-Norman French *cignet*, diminutive of Old French *cigne* 'swan', based on Latin *cycnus*, from Greek *kuknos*.

Cygnus /ˈsɪgnəs/ Astronomy a prominent northern constellation (the Swan), said to represent a flying swan that was the form adopted by Zeus on one occasion. It contains the bright star Deneb.
■ [as genitive **Cygni** /ˈsɪgni/] used with preceding letter or numeral to designate a star in this constellation: *the star Delta Cygni.*
– ORIGIN Latin.

cylinder /ˈsɪlɪndə/ ▶ **noun** a solid geometrical figure with straight parallel sides and a circular or oval section.
■ a solid or hollow body, object, or part with such a shape. ■ a piston chamber in a steam or internal-combustion engine. ■ a cylindrical container for liquefied gas under pressure. ■ a rotating metal roller in a printing press. ■ Archaeology a cylinder seal.
– DERIVATIVES **cylindric** adjective, **cylindrical** adjective, **cylindrically** /-ˈlɪndrɪk(ə)li/ adverb.
– ORIGIN late 16th cent.: from Latin *cylindrus*, from Greek *kulindros* 'roller', from *kulindein* 'to roll'.

cylinder block ▶ **noun** see **BLOCK** (sense 1).

cylinder head ▶ **noun** the end cover of a cylinder in an internal-combustion engine, against which the piston compresses the cylinder's contents.

cylinder liner ▶ **noun** see **LINER**[2].

cylinder lock ▶ **noun** a lock with the keyhole and tumbler mechanism contained in a cylinder.

cylinder seal ▶ **noun** Archaeology a small barrel-shaped stone object with a hole down the centre and bearing an incised design or cuneiform inscription, originally for rolling on clay when soft to indicate ownership or authenticate a document, used chiefly in Mesopotamia from the late 4th to the 1st millennium BC.

cymbal /ˈsɪmb(ə)l/ ▶ **noun** a musical instrument consisting of a slightly concave round brass plate which is either struck against another one or struck with a stick to make a ringing or clashing sound.
– DERIVATIVES **cymbalist** noun.
– ORIGIN Old English, from Latin *cymbalum*, from Greek *kumbalon*, from *kumbē* 'cup'; readopted in Middle English from Old French *cymbale*.

Cymbeline /ˈsɪmbəliːn/ (also **Cunobelinus**) (died *c.*42 AD), British chieftain. A powerful ruler, he made Camulodunum (Colchester) his capital, and established a mint there. He was the subject of a medieval fable used by Shakespeare for his play *Cymbeline*.

cymbidium /sɪmˈbɪdɪəm/ ▶ **noun** (pl. **cymbidiums**) a tropical orchid with long narrow leaves and arching stems bearing several flowers, growing chiefly as an epiphyte from Asia to Australasia and widely grown for buttonholes.
• Genus *Cymbidium*, family Orchidaceae.
– ORIGIN modern Latin, from Greek *kumbē* 'cup'.

cyme /sʌɪm/ ▶ **noun** Botany a flower cluster with a central stem bearing a single terminal flower that develops first, the other flowers in the cluster developing as terminal buds of lateral stems. Compare with **RACEME**.
– DERIVATIVES **cymose** adjective.
– ORIGIN early 18th cent. (denoting the unopened head of a plant): from French, literally 'summit', from a popular variant of Latin *cyma*.

Cymric /ˈkɪmrɪk/ ▶ **adjective** Welsh in language or culture.
▶ **noun** [mass noun] the Welsh language.
– ORIGIN mid 19th cent.: from Welsh *Cymru* 'Wales', *Cymry* 'the Welsh', + **-IC**.

Cymru /ˈkʌmri/ Welsh name for **WALES**.

Cynewulf /ˈkɪnɪwʊlf/ (late 8th–9th centuries), Anglo-Saxon poet. Modern scholarship attributes four poems to him: *Juliana*, *Elene*, *The Fates of the Apostles*, and *Christ II*.

cynic /ˈsɪnɪk/ ▶ **noun 1** a person who believes that people are motivated purely by self-interest rather than acting for honourable or unselfish reasons: *some cynics thought that the controversy was all a publicity stunt.*
■ a person who questions whether something will happen or whether it is worthwhile: *the cynics were silenced when the factory opened.*
2 (**Cynic**) a member of a school of ancient Greek philosophers founded by Antisthenes, marked by an ostentatious contempt for ease and pleasure. The movement flourished in the 3rd century BC and revived in the 1st century AD.
– DERIVATIVES **cynicism** noun.
– ORIGIN mid 16th cent. (in sense 2): from Latin *cynicus*, from Greek *kunikos*; probably originally from *Kunosarges*, the name of a gymnasium where Antisthenes taught, but popularly taken to mean 'doglike, churlish', *kuōn*, *kun-*, 'dog' becoming a nickname for a Cynic.

cynical ▶ **adjective 1** believing that people are motivated purely by self-interest; distrustful of human sincerity or integrity: *her cynical attitude.*
■ doubtful as to whether something will happen or whether it is worthwhile: *most residents are* **cynical about** *efforts to clean mobsters out of their city.* ■ contemptuous; mocking: *he gave a cynical laugh.*
2 concerned only with one's own interests and typically disregarding accepted or appropriate standards in order to achieve them: *Stalin had struck a cynical deal with Hitler | a cynical professional foul.*
– DERIVATIVES **cynically** adverb.

cyno- /ˈsʌɪnəʊ/ ▶ **combining form** of or relating to dogs: *cynodont*.
– ORIGIN from Greek *kuōn*, *kun-* 'dog'.

C

cynodont /ˈsʌɪnə(ʊ)dɒnt/ ▶ **noun** a fossil carnivorous mammal-like reptile of the late Permian and Triassic periods, with well-developed specialized teeth.
• Suborder Cynodontia, order Therapsida: several families.
– ORIGIN late 19th cent.: from Greek *kuōn*, *kun-* 'dog' + *odous*, *odont-* 'tooth'.

cynosure /ˈsɪnəzjʊə, ˈsʌɪn-, -sjʊə/ ▶ **noun** [in sing.] a person or thing that is the centre of attention or admiration: *Kirk was the cynosure of all eyes.*
– ORIGIN late 16th cent.: from French, or from Latin *cynosura*, from Greek *kunosoura* 'dog's tail' (also 'Ursa Minor'), from *kuōn*, *kun-* 'dog' + *oura* 'tail'. The term originally denoted the constellation Ursa Minor, or the pole star which it contains, long used as a guide by navigators.

cyphel /ˈsʌɪf(ə)l/ (also **mossy cyphel**) ▶ **noun** a European mountain plant of the pink family, which forms cushion-like mounds and bears small greenish flowers.
• *Minuartia sedoides*, family Caryophyllaceae.
– ORIGIN late Middle English (denoting the houseleek): apparently from Greek *kuphella* 'hollows of the ears'.

cypher ▶ **noun** variant spelling of **CIPHER**[1].

cypherpunk ▶ **noun** a person who uses encryption when accessing a computer network in order to ensure privacy, especially from government authorities.
– ORIGIN 1990s: on the pattern of *cyberpunk*.

cy-pres /siː ˈpreɪ/ ▶ **adverb** & **adjective** Law as near as possible to the testator's or donor's intentions when these cannot be precisely followed.
– ORIGIN early 19th cent.: from a late Anglo-Norman French variant of French *si près* 'so near'.

cypress ▶ **noun** (also **cypress tree**) an evergreen coniferous tree with small rounded woody cones and flattened shoots bearing small scale-like leaves.
• *Cupressus*, *Chamaecyparis*, and other genera, family Cupressaceae: many species, including the columnar **Italian cypress** (*Cupressus sempervirens*), common throughout southern Europe. See also **LAWSON'S CYPRESS**.
■ a tree of this type, or branches from it, as a symbol of mourning. ■ used in names of similar coniferous trees of other families, e.g. **swamp cypress**.
– ORIGIN Middle English: from Old French *cipres*, from late Latin *cypressus*, from Greek *kuparissos*.

Cyprian, St /ˈsɪprɪən/ (d.258), Carthaginian bishop and martyr. The author of a work on the nature of true unity in the Church in its relation to the episcopate, he was martyred in the reign of the Roman emperor Valerian. Feast day, 16 or 26 September.

cyprinid /ˈsɪprɪnɪd/ ▶ **noun** Zoology a fish of the carp family (Cyprinidae).
– ORIGIN late 19th cent.: from modern Latin *Cyprinidae* (plural), based on Greek *kuprinos* 'carp'.

cyprinoid /ˈsɪprɪnɔɪd/ Zoology ▶ **noun** a fish of a large group which includes the carps, suckers, and loaches, and (in some classification schemes) the characins.
• Order Cypriniformes or superfamily Cyprinoidea.
▶ **adjective** of or relating to fish of this group.
– ORIGIN mid 19th cent.: from modern Latin *Cyprinoidea*, based on Latin *cyprinus* 'carp' (from Greek *kuprinos*).

Cypriot ▶ **noun 1** a native or national of Cyprus.
2 [mass noun] the dialect of Greek used in Cyprus.
▶ **adjective** of or relating to Cyprus or its people or the Greek dialect used there.
■ denoting an ancient syllabic script related to the Minoan and Mycenaean scripts, which was used to write the Cypriot dialect of Greek from the 6th to the 3rd centuries BC.
– ORIGIN from Greek *Kupriōtes*, from *Kupros* 'Cyprus'.

cypripedium /ˌsɪprɪˈpiːdɪəm/ ▶ **noun** (pl. **cypripediums**) an orchid of a genus which comprises the lady's slippers.
• Genus *Cypripedium*, family Orchidaceae.
– ORIGIN modern Latin, from Greek *Kupris* 'Aphrodite' + *pedilon* 'slipper'.

c

Cyprus /ˈsʌɪprəs/ an island lying in the eastern Mediterranean about 80 km (50 miles) south of the Turkish coast; pop. 708,000 (est. 1991); official languages, Greek and Turkish; capital, Nicosia.

A Greek colony in ancient times, Cyprus was held by the Turks from 1571 until 1878, when it was placed under British administration. After virtual civil war between the Greek Cypriots (some of whom favour enosis or union with Greece) and the Turkish Cypriots, Cyprus became an independent Commonwealth republic in 1960. In 1974 Turkish forces took over the northern part of the island, which proclaimed itself the independent Turkish Republic of Northern Cyprus in 1983 but has not received international recognition.

cypsela /ˈsɪpsɪlə/ ▶ noun (pl. **cypselae** /-liː/) Botany a dry single-seeded fruit formed from a double ovary of which only one develops into a seed, as in the daisy family.
– ORIGIN late 19th cent.: modern Latin, from Greek *kupselē* 'hollow vessel'.

Cyrano de Bergerac /ˌsɪrənəʊ də ˈbɛːʒərak, French siranɔ də bɛrʒərak/, Savinien (1619–55), French soldier, duellist, and writer. He is chiefly remembered for the large number of duels that he fought (many on account of his proverbially large nose), as immortalized in a play by Edmond Rostand (*Cyrano de Bergerac*, 1897).

Cyrenaic /ˌsʌɪrɪˈneɪɪk/ ▶ adjective of or denoting the hedonistic school of philosophy founded *c.*400 BC by Aristippus the Elder of Cyrene which holds that pleasure is the highest good and that virtue is to be equated with the ability to enjoy.
▶ noun a follower of this school of philosophy.
– DERIVATIVES **Cyrenaicism** noun.

Cyrenaica /ˌsʌɪrɪˈneɪɪkə/ a region of NE Libya, bordering on the Mediterranean Sea, settled by the Greeks *c.*640 BC.

Cyrene /sʌɪˈriːni/ an ancient Greek city in North Africa, near the coast in Cyrenaica. From the 4th century BC it was a great intellectual centre with a noted medical school.

Cyril, St (826–69), Greek missionary. The invention of the Cyrillic alphabet is ascribed to him. Feast day (in the Eastern Church) 11 May; (in the Western Church) 14 February.

Cyrillic /sɪˈrɪlɪk/ ▶ adjective denoting the alphabet used by many Slavic peoples, chiefly those with a historical allegiance to the Orthodox Church. Ultimately derived from Greek uncials, it is now used for Russian, Bulgarian, Serbian, Ukrainian, and some other Slavic languages.
▶ noun [mass noun] the Cyrillic alphabet.
– ORIGIN early 19th cent.: named after St *Cyril* (see **CYRIL, ST**).

Cyril of Alexandria, St (d.444), Doctor of the Church and patriarch of Alexandria. A champion of orthodoxy, he is best known for his vehement opposition to the views of the patriarch of Constantinople, Nestorius, whose condemnation he secured at the Council of Ephesus in 431. Feast day, 9 February.

Cyrus¹ /ˈsʌɪrəs/ (died *c.*530 BC), king of Persia 559–530 BC and founder of the Achaemenid dynasty, father of Cambyses; known as **Cyrus the Great.** He defeated the Median empire in 550 BC and went on to conquer Asia Minor, Babylonia, Syria, Palestine, and most of the Iranian plateau.

Cyrus² /ˈsʌɪrəs/ (d.401 BC), Persian prince; known as **Cyrus the Younger.** On the death of his father, Darius II, in 405 BC, Cyrus led an army of mercenaries against his elder brother, who had succeeded to the throne as Artaxerxes II. His campaign is recounted by the historian Xenophon.

cyst /sɪst/ ▶ noun Biology a thin-walled hollow organ or cavity in an animal or plant, containing a liquid secretion; a sac, vesicle, or bladder.
■ Medicine a membranous sac or cavity of abnormal character in the body, containing fluid. ■ a tough protective capsule enclosing the larva of a parasitic worm or the resting stage of an organism.
– ORIGIN early 18th cent.: from late Latin *cystis*, from Greek *kustis* 'bladder'.

cystectomy /sɪsˈtɛktəmi/ ▶ noun 1 (pl. **-ies**) a surgical operation to remove the urinary bladder. 2 a surgical operation to remove an abnormal cyst: *an ovarian cystectomy.*

cysteine /ˈsɪstiːiːn, -tɪn, -teɪn, -tiːn/ ▶ noun [mass noun] Biochemistry a sulphur-containing amino acid which occurs in keratins and other proteins, often in the form of cystine, and is a constituent of many enzymes.

● Chem. formula: $HSCH_2CH(NH_2)COOH$.
– ORIGIN late 19th cent.: from **CYSTINE** + *-eine* (variant of **-INE⁴**).

cystic ▶ adjective 1 chiefly Medicine of, relating to, or characterized by cysts.
■ Zoology (of a parasite or other organism) enclosed in a cyst.
2 of or relating to the urinary bladder or the gall bladder: *the cystic artery.*
– ORIGIN mid 17th cent. (originally referring to the gall bladder): from French *cystique* or modern Latin *cysticus*, from late Latin *cystis* (see **CYST**).

cysticercus /ˌsɪstɪˈsəːkəs/ ▶ noun (pl. **cysticerci** /-sʌɪ/) Zoology a larval tapeworm at a stage in which the scolex is inverted in a sac, typically found encysted in the muscle tissue of the host.
– DERIVATIVES **cysticercoid** adjective & noun.
– ORIGIN mid 19th cent.: modern Latin (originally the name of a supposed genus), from Greek *kustis* 'bladder' + *kerkos* 'tail'.

cystic fibrosis ▶ noun [mass noun] a hereditary disorder affecting the exocrine glands. It causes the production of abnormally thick mucus, leading to the blockage of the pancreatic ducts, intestines, and bronchi and often resulting in respiratory infection.

cystine /ˈsɪstiːn, -tɪn/ ▶ noun [mass noun] Biochemistry a compound which is an oxidized dimer of cysteine and is the form in which cysteine often occurs in organic tissue.
● Chem. formula: $C_6H_{12}N_2O_4S_2$.
– ORIGIN mid 19th cent.: from Greek *kustis* 'bladder' (because it was first isolated from urinary calculi) + **-INE⁴**.

cystitis /sɪˈstʌɪtɪs/ ▶ noun [mass noun] Medicine inflammation of the urinary bladder. It is often caused by infection and is usually accompanied by frequent painful urination.

cysto- /ˈsɪstəʊ/ ▶ combining form of or relating to the urinary bladder: *cystotomy.*
– ORIGIN from Greek *kustis* 'bladder'.

cystoscope /ˈsɪstəskəʊp/ ▶ noun Medicine an instrument inserted into the urethra for examining the urinary bladder.
– DERIVATIVES **cystoscopic** adjective, **cystoscopy** noun.

cystotomy /sɪˈstɒtəmi/ ▶ noun (pl. **-ies**) a surgical incision into the urinary bladder.

-cyte ▶ combining form Biology denoting a mature cell: *lymphocyte.* Compare with **-BLAST**.
– ORIGIN from Greek *kutos* 'vessel'.

Cytherea /ˌsɪθəˈriːə/ ▶ noun another name for **APHRODITE**.
– ORIGIN from Latin *Cythera* 'Kithira', the name of an Ionian island.

Cytherean /ˌsɪθəˈriːən/ ▶ adjective Astronomy of or relating to the planet Venus: *the Cytherean atmosphere.*
■ of or relating to the goddess Cytherea.

cytidine /ˈsʌɪtɪdiːn/ ▶ noun [mass noun] Biochemistry a nucleoside composed of cytosine linked to ribose, obtained from RNA by hydrolysis.
– ORIGIN early 20th cent.: from **CYTO-** + **-IDE** + **-INE⁴**.

cytisus /ˈsʌɪtɪsəs, ˈsɪtɪsəs/ ▶ noun a plant of a large genus of shrubs, mostly native to southern Europe, which includes some brooms.
● Genus *Cytisus*, family Leguminosae.
– ORIGIN modern Latin, from Greek *kutisos*.

cyto- /ˈsʌɪtəʊ/ ▶ combining form Biology of a cell or cells: *cytology | cytoplasm.*
– ORIGIN from Greek *kutos* 'vessel'.

cytoarchitectonics /ˌsʌɪtəʊˌɑːkɪtɛkˈtɒnɪks/ ▶ plural noun [treated as sing. or pl.] another term for **CYTOARCHITECTURE**.
– DERIVATIVES **cytoarchitectonic** adjective.

cytoarchitecture /ˌsʌɪtəʊˈɑːkɪtɛktʃə/ ▶ noun [mass noun] Anatomy the arrangement of cells in a tissue, especially in specific areas of the cerebral cortex characterized by the arrangement of their cells and each associated with particular functions. Also called **CYTOARCHITECTONICS**.
■ the study of this.
– DERIVATIVES **cytoarchitectural** adjective, **cytoarchitecturally** adverb.

cytocentrifuge /ˌsʌɪtəʊˈsɛntrɪfjuːdʒ/ Biology ▶ noun a centrifuge used for depositing cells suspended in a liquid on a slide for microscopic examination.

▶ verb [with obj.] deposit (cells) on a slide using such a centrifuge.

cytochrome ▶ noun [mass noun] Biochemistry any of a number of compounds consisting of haem bonded to a protein. Cytochromes function as electron transfer agents in many metabolic pathways, especially cellular respiration.

cytogenetics /ˌsʌɪtəʊdʒəˈnɛtɪks/ ▶ plural noun [treated as sing.] Biology the study of inheritance in relation to the structure and function of chromosomes.
– DERIVATIVES **cytogenetic** adjective, **cytogenetical** adjective, **cytogenetically** adverb, **cytogeneticist** noun.

cytokine /ˈsʌɪtə(ʊ)kʌɪn/ ▶ noun Physiology any of a number of substances, such as interferon, interleukin, and growth factors, which are secreted by certain cells of the immune system and have an effect on other cells.

cytokinesis /ˌsʌɪtə(ʊ)kʌɪˈniːsɪs/ ▶ noun [mass noun] Biology the cytoplasmic division of a cell at the end of mitosis or meiosis, bringing about the separation into two daughter cells.

cytokinin /ˌsʌɪtə(ʊ)ˈkʌɪnɪn/ ▶ noun another term for **KININ** (in sense 2).

cytology /sʌɪˈtɒlədʒi/ ▶ noun [mass noun] the branch of biology concerned with the structure and function of plant and animal cells.
– DERIVATIVES **cytological** adjective, **cytologically** adverb, **cytologist** noun.

cytolysis /sʌɪˈtɒlɪsɪs/ ▶ noun [mass noun] Biology the dissolution or disruption of cells, especially by an external agent.
– DERIVATIVES **cytolytic** adjective.

cytomegalic /ˌsʌɪtə(ʊ)mɪˈɡalɪk/ ▶ adjective Medicine characterized by enlarged cells, especially with reference to a disease caused by a cytomegalovirus.

cytomegalovirus /ˌsʌɪtə(ʊ)ˈmɛɡ(ə)lə(ʊ)ˌvʌɪrəs/ (abbrev.: **CMV**) ▶ noun Medicine a kind of herpesvirus which usually produces very mild symptoms in an infected person but may cause severe neurological damage in people with weakened immune systems and in the newborn.

cytophotometry /ˌsʌɪtə(ʊ)fə(ʊ)ˈtɒmɪtri/ ▶ noun [mass noun] Biology the investigation of the contents of cells by measuring the light they allow through after staining.
– DERIVATIVES **cytophotometer** noun, **cytophotometric** adjective.

cytoplasm /ˈsʌɪtə(ʊ)plaz(ə)m/ ▶ noun [mass noun] Biology the material or protoplasm within a living cell, excluding the nucleus.
– DERIVATIVES **cytoplasmic** adjective.

cytosine /ˈsʌɪtəsiːn/ ▶ noun [mass noun] Biochemistry a compound found in living tissue as a constituent base of DNA. It is paired with guanine in double-stranded DNA.
● A pyrimidine derivative; chem. formula: $C_4H_5N_3O$.

cytoskeleton ▶ noun Biology a microscopic network of protein filaments and tubules in the cytoplasm of many living cells, giving them shape and coherence.
– DERIVATIVES **cytoskeletal** adjective.

cytosol /ˈsʌɪtə(ʊ)sɒl/ ▶ noun [mass noun] Biology the aqueous component of the cytoplasm of a cell, within which various organelles and particles are suspended.
– DERIVATIVES **cytosolic** adjective.

cytotoxic ▶ adjective toxic to living cells.
– DERIVATIVES **cytotoxicity** noun.

czar etc. ▶ noun variant spelling of **TSAR** etc.

czardas ▶ noun variant spelling of **CSARDAS**.

Czech /tʃɛk/ ▶ noun 1 a native or national of the Czech Republic or (formerly) Czechoslovakia, or a person of Czech descent. 2 [mass noun] the Western Slavic language spoken in the Czech Republic, closely related to Slovak. It has over 10 million speakers.
▶ adjective of or relating to the Czechs or their language.
– ORIGIN Polish spelling of Czech *Čech*.

Czechoslovakia /ˌtʃɛkə(ʊ)sləˈvakɪə/ a former country in central Europe, now divided between the Czech Republic and Slovakia; capital, Prague.

Czechoslovakia was created out of the northern part of the Austro-Hungarian empire at the end of the First World War. It was crushed by the Nazi takeover of the Sudetenland in 1938 and the rest of the country in 1939. After the Second World War Czechoslovakia fell under Soviet domination, an attempt at liberalization being crushed by military intervention in 1968, until the 'velvet revolution' of 1989. The two parts separated on 1 January 1993.

– DERIVATIVES **Czechoslovak** /-'sləʊvak/ noun &

adjective, **Czechoslovakian** adjective & noun.

Czech Republic a country in central Europe; pop. 10,298,700 (1991); official language, Czech; capital, Prague.

Formerly one of the two constituent republics of Czechoslovakia, the Czech Republic became independent on the partition of that country on 1 January 1993. It comprises the former provinces of Bohemia, Silesia, and Moravia.

Czerny /'tʃɛːni/, Karl (1791–1857), Austrian pianist, teacher, and composer. The bulk of his output is made up of more than 1,000 exercises and studies for the piano.

Częstochowa /ˌtʃɛnstə'kəʊvə/ an industrial city in south central Poland; pop. 258,000 (1990). It is famous for the painting of the black Madonna in its church.

Dd

D[1] (also **d**) ▶ noun (pl. **Ds** or **D's**) **1** the fourth letter of the alphabet.
■denoting the fourth in a set of items, categories, sizes, etc. ■ the fourth highest category of academic mark. ■ **(d)** Chess denoting the fourth file from the left, as viewed from White's side of the board. ■ denoting the second-lowest-earning socio-economic category for marketing purposes, including semi-skilled and unskilled personnel.
2 (**D**) (also **dee**) a shape like that of a capital D: [in combination] the D-shaped handle.
■a loop or ring of this shape. ■ (**D**) a semicircle marked on a billiard table in the baulk area, with its diameter part of the baulk line, within which a player must place the cue ball when breaking off or restarting from hand.
3 (usu. **D**) Music the second note of the diatonic scale of C major.
■a key based on a scale with D as its keynote.
4 the Roman numeral for 500. [ORIGIN: understood as half of CIƆ, an earlier form of M (= 1,000).]

D[2] ▶ abbreviation for ■ (in the US) Democrat or Democratic. ■ depth (in the sense of the dimension of an object from front to back). ■ Chemistry dextrorotatory: D-glucose. ■ (with a numeral) dimension(s) or dimensional: a 3-D model. ■ (in tables of sports results) drawn. ■ (on an automatic gear shift) drive. ■ Germany (international vehicle registration). [ORIGIN: from German Deutschland.]
▶ symbol for ■ Physics electric flux density. ■ Chemistry the hydrogen isotope deuterium.

d ▶ abbreviation for ■ (in genealogies) daughter. ■ day(s): orbital period (Mars): 687.0d. ■ [in combination] (in units of measurement) deci-. ■ (in travel timetables) departs. ■ (**d.**) died (used to indicate a date of death): Barents, Willem (d.1597). ■ Brit. penny or pence (of pre-decimal currency): £20 10s 6d. [ORIGIN: from Latin denarius 'penny'.] ■ Chemistry denoting electrons and orbitals possessing two units of angular momentum: d-electrons. [ORIGIN: d from diffuse, originally applied to lines in atomic spectra.]
▶ symbol for ■ Mathematics diameter. ■ Mathematics denoting a small increment in a given variable: dy/dx.

'd ▶ contraction of ■ had: they'd already gone. ■ would: I'd expect that.

DA ▶ abbreviation for ■ US district attorney. ■ informal duck's arse.

D/A Electronics ▶ abbreviation for digital to analogue.

da ▶ abbreviation for [in combination] (in units of measurement) deca-.

dab[1] ▶ verb (**dabbed**, **dabbing**) [with obj.] **1** press against (something) lightly several times with a piece of absorbent material in order to clean or dry it or to apply a substance: he dabbed his mouth with his napkin | [no obj.] she dabbed at her eyes with a handkerchief.
■apply (a substance) with light quick strokes: she dabbed disinfectant on the cut.
2 dialect aim at or strike with a light blow.
▶ noun **1** a small amount of something: she licked a dab of chocolate from her finger.
■a brief application of a piece of absorbent material to a surface: apply concealer with light dabs.
2 (**dabs**) Brit. informal fingerprints.

– ORIGIN Middle English: symbolic of a light striking movement; compare with **DABBLE** and **DIB**.

dab[2] ▶ noun a small, commercially important flatfish that is found chiefly in the North Atlantic.
● Limanda and other genera, family Pleuronectidae (several species, in particular the European L. limanda), and genus Citharichthys, family Bothidae (see also **SAND DAB**).
– ORIGIN late Middle English: of unknown origin.

dabber ▶ noun a rounded pad used in printing to apply ink to a surface.

dabberlocks /'dabəlɒks/ ▶ noun variant spelling of **BADDERLOCKS**.

dabble ▶ verb [with obj.] immerse (one's hands or feet) partially in water and move them around gently: they dabbled their feet in the rock pools.
■[no obj.] (of a duck or other water bird) move the bill around in shallow water while feeding: teal dabble in the shallows. ■ [no obj.] figurative take part in an activity in a casual or superficial way: he dabbled in left-wing politics.
– DERIVATIVES **dabbler** noun.
– ORIGIN mid 16th cent.: from obsolete Dutch dabbelen, or a frequentative of the verb **DAB**[1].

dabbling duck ▶ noun a freshwater duck which typically feeds in shallow water by dabbling and upending, such as the mallard, teal, shoveler, and pintail. Compare with **DIVING DUCK**.
● Tribe Anatini, family Anatidae: genus Anas (numerous species), and perhaps some other genera.

dabchick ▶ noun a small grebe, especially the little grebe.
● Genera Tachybaptus and Podilymbus, family Podicipedidae: several species.
– ORIGIN mid 16th cent. (as dapchick or dopchick): the first element is perhaps related to **DIP** and **DEEP**.

dab hand ▶ noun Brit. informal a person who is an expert at a particular activity: Liam is a dab hand at golf.
– ORIGIN early 19th cent.: of unknown origin.

DAC Electronics ▶ abbreviation for digital to analogue converter.

da capo /dɑːˈkɑːpəʊ/ Music ▶ adverb (especially as a direction) repeat from the beginning. Compare with **DAL SEGNO**.
▶ adjective [attrib.] including the repetition of a passage at the beginning: da capo arias.
– ORIGIN Italian, literally 'from the head'.

Dacca variant spelling of **DHAKA**.

dace /deɪs/ ▶ noun (pl. same) a small freshwater fish related to the carp, typically living in running water.
● Leuciscus and other genera, family Cyprinidae: several species, in particular the widely distributed L. leuciscus of northern Eurasia.
– ORIGIN late Middle English: from Old French dars (see **DART**).

dacha /'datʃə/ (also **datcha**) ▶ noun a country house or cottage in Russia, typically used as a second or holiday home.
– ORIGIN Russian, originally 'grant (of land)'.

Dachau /'dakaʊ, German 'daxaʊ/ a Nazi concentration camp in southern Bavaria, from 1933 to 1945.

dachshund /'dakshʊnd, -s(ə)nd/ ▶ noun a dog of a very short-legged, long-bodied breed.
– ORIGIN late 19th cent.: from German, literally

'badger dog' (the breed being originally used to dig badgers out of their setts).

Dacia /'deɪʃə, 'deɪsɪə/ an ancient country of SE Europe in what is now NW Romania. It was annexed by Trajan in AD 106 as a province of the Roman Empire.
– DERIVATIVES **Dacian** adjective & noun.

dacite /'deɪsʌɪt/ ▶ noun [mass noun] Geology a volcanic rock resembling andesite but containing free quartz.
– DERIVATIVES **dacitic** adjective.
– ORIGIN late 18th cent.: from the name of the Roman province of **DACIA** (as it was first found in the Carpathian Mountains) + -**ITE**[1].

dacoit /dəˈkɔɪt/ ▶ noun (in India or Burma (Myanmar)) a member of a band of armed robbers.
– ORIGIN from Hindi ḍakait, from ḍakaitī 'robbery by a gang'.

dacoity /dəˈkɔɪti/ ▶ noun (pl. -**ies**) (in India or Burma (Myanmar)) an act of violent robbery committed by an armed gang.
– ORIGIN from Hindi ḍakaitī.

Dacron /'dakrɒn/ ▶ noun [mass noun] trademark a synthetic polyester (polyethylene terephthalate) with tough, elastic properties, used as a textile fabric.
– ORIGIN 1950s: an invented name.

dactyl /'daktɪl/ ▶ noun Prosody a metrical foot consisting of one stressed syllable followed by two unstressed syllables or (in Greek and Latin) one long syllable followed by two short syllables.
– ORIGIN late Middle English: via Latin from Greek daktulos, literally 'finger' (the three bones of the finger corresponding to the three syllables).

dactylic Prosody ▶ adjective of or using dactyls: dactylic rhythm.
▶ noun (usu. **dactylics**) dactylic verse.
– ORIGIN late 16th cent.: via Latin from Greek daktulikos, from daktulos, literally 'finger' (see **DACTYL**).

dactylic hexameter ▶ noun Prosody a hexameter consisting of five dactyls and either a spondee or trochee, in which any of the first four dactyls, and sometimes the fifth, may be replaced by a spondee.

dad ▶ noun informal one's father.
– ORIGIN mid 16th cent.: perhaps imitative of a young child's first syllables da, da.

Dada /'dɑːdɑː/ ▶ noun an early 20th-century international movement in art, literature, music, and film, repudiating and mocking artistic and social conventions and emphasizing the illogical and absurd.

Dada was launched in Zurich in 1916 by Tristan Tzara and others, soon merging with a similar group in New York. It favoured montage, collage, and the ready-made. Leading figures: Jean Arp, André Breton, Max Ernst, Man Ray, and Marcel Duchamp.

– DERIVATIVES **Dadaism** noun, **Dadaist** noun & adjective, **Dadaistic** adjective.
– ORIGIN French, literally 'hobby horse', the title of a review which appeared in Zurich in 1916.

dada[1] /'dadə/ ▶ noun informal one's father.
– ORIGIN late 17th cent.: perhaps imitative of a young child's first syllables (see **DAD**).

dada² /'dɑːdɑː/ ▶ noun Indian an older brother or male cousin.
■ a respectful form of address for any familiar older male.
– ORIGIN from Hindi *dādā*.

Dadd, Richard (1817–86), English painter. After killing his father while suffering a mental breakdown, he was confined in asylums, where he produced a series of visionary paintings.

daddy ▶ noun (pl. **-ies**) informal one's father.
■ the oldest, best, or biggest example of something: *the daddy of all potholes.*
– ORIGIN early 16th cent.: from DAD + -Y².

daddy-long-legs ▶ noun informal an insect or arachnid with very long thin legs, in particular:
■ Brit. a crane fly. ■ N. Amer. a harvestman.

dado /'deɪdəʊ/ ▶ noun (pl. **-os**) the lower part of the wall of a room, below about waist height, if it is a different colour or has a different covering from the upper part.
■ short for DADO RAIL. ■ N. Amer. a groove cut in the face of a board, into which the edge of another board is fixed. ■ Architecture the part of a pedestal between the base and the cornice.
– ORIGIN mid 17th cent. (denoting the main part of a pedestal, above the base): from Italian, literally 'dice or cube', from Latin *datum* 'something given, starting point' (see DATUM).

dado rail ▶ noun a moulding round the wall of a room, about waist-high, which provides a decorative feature and protects the wall from damage.

Dadra and Nagar Haveli /'dɑːdrə, ˌnɑːgə hə'veɪli/ a Union Territory in western India, on the Arabian Sea; pop. 138,500 (1991); capital, Silvassa.

Daedalic /diː'dælɪk/ ▶ adjective relating to or denoting an ancient Greek (chiefly Dorian) sculptural style of the 7th century BC.
– ORIGIN from the name DAEDALUS + -IC.

Daedalus /'diːdələs/ Greek Mythology a craftsman, considered the inventor of carpentry, who is said to have built the labyrinth for Minos, king of Crete. Minos imprisoned him and his son Icarus, but they escaped using wings which Daedalus made and fastened with wax. Icarus, however, flew too near the sun and was killed.

daemon¹ /'diːmən/ (also **daimon**) ▶ noun 1 (in ancient Greek belief) a divinity or supernatural being of a nature between gods and humans.
■ an inner or attendant spirit or inspiring force.
2 archaic spelling of DEMON¹.
– DERIVATIVES **daemonic** adjective.
– ORIGIN mid 16th cent.: common spelling of DEMON¹ until the 19th cent.

daemon² /'diːmən/ (also **demon**) ▶ noun Computing a background process that handles requests for services such as print spooling and file transfers, and is dormant when not required.
– ORIGIN 1980s: perhaps from *d(isk) a(nd) e(xecution) mon(itor)* or from *de(vice) mon(itor)*, or merely a transferred use of DEMON¹.

daff ▶ noun informal term for DAFFODIL.

daffodil ▶ noun a bulbous European plant which typically bears bright yellow flowers with a long trumpet-shaped centre (corona).
● Genus *Narcissus*, family Liliaceae (or Amaryllidaceae): several species, in particular the common *Narcissus pseudonarcissus* and its varieties. See also LENT LILY, NARCISSUS.
– ORIGIN mid 16th cent.: from late Middle English *affodill*, from medieval Latin *affodilus*, variant of Latin *asphodilus* (see ASPHODEL). The initial *d-* is unexplained.

daffodil yellow ▶ noun [mass noun] a shade of pale yellow.

daffy ▶ adjective (**daffier**, **daffiest**) informal silly; mildly eccentric: *you must both be daffy.*
– DERIVATIVES **daffiness** noun.
– ORIGIN late 19th cent.: from northern English dialect *daff* 'simpleton' + -Y¹; perhaps related to DAFT.

daft ▶ adjective informal, chiefly Brit. silly; foolish: *don't ask such daft questions.*
■ [predic.] (**daft about**) infatuated with: *we were all daft about him.*
– ORIGIN Old English *gedæfte* 'mild, meek', of Germanic origin; related to Gothic *gabadan* 'become or be fitting'.

dag ▶ noun 1 (usu. **dags**) a lock of wool matted with dung hanging from the hindquarters of a sheep.
2 Austral./NZ informal a socially conservative person.
▶ verb (**dagged**, **dagging**) [with obj.] cut dags from (a sheep): *we failed to have the ewes dagged.*
– PHRASES **rattle one's dags** informal hurry up.
– ORIGIN late Middle English (denoting a hanging pointed part of something, such as ornamental edging on the bottom of a garment): possibly related to TAG¹. Sense 1 dates from the early 17th cent.; sense 2 is a tranferred use of English dialect meaning 'a challenge or dare'.

da Gama /də 'gɑːmə/, Vasco (c.1469–1524), Portuguese explorer. He led the first European expedition round the Cape of Good Hope in 1497, sighting and naming Natal on Christmas Day before crossing the Indian Ocean and arriving in Calicut in 1498. He also established colonies in Mozambique.

Dagestan /ˌdɑːgɪ'stɑːn, -'stan/ an autonomous republic in SW Russia, on the western shore of the Caspian Sea; pop. 1,823,000 (1990); capital, Makhachkala.

Dagestanian /ˌdɑːgɪ'stɑːnɪən, -'stanɪən/ ▶ adjective 1 of or relating to Dagestan or its inhabitants.
2 of, relating to, or denoting a family of North Caucasian languages spoken in Dagestan, of which the principal member is Avar. None has more than a few thousand speakers.
▶ noun 1 a native or inhabitant of Dagestan.
2 [mass noun] the family of languages spoken in Dagestan.

dagga /'daxə/ ▶ noun [mass noun] chiefly S. African cannabis.
– ORIGIN late 17th cent.: from Afrikaans, from Khoikhoi *dachab*.

dagger ▶ noun 1 a short knife with a pointed and edged blade, used as a weapon.
■ Printing another term for OBELUS.
2 a moth with a dark dagger-shaped marking on the forewing.
● Genus *Acronicta*, family Noctuidae: several species.
– PHRASES **at daggers drawn** in bitter enmity. **look daggers at** glare angrily or venomously at.
– ORIGIN late Middle English: perhaps from obsolete *dag* 'pierce, stab', influenced by Old French *dague* 'long dagger'.

daggerboard ▶ noun a kind of centreboard which slides vertically through the keel of a sailing boat.

daggertooth ▶ noun a large surface-living predatory fish of temperate and sub-polar seas, with an elongated body and large jaws containing many teeth.
● *Anotopterus pharao*, the only member of the family Anotopteridae.

daggy ▶ adjective (**daggier**, **daggiest**) Austral./NZ informal (especially of clothes) scruffy.
■ not stylish; unfashionable: *a daggy disco track.*

dago /'deɪgəʊ/ ▶ noun (pl. **-os** or **-oes**) informal, offensive a Spanish, Portuguese, or Italian-speaking person.
– ORIGIN mid 19th cent.: from the Spanish given name *Diego* (equivalent to *James*).

Dagon /'deɪgɒn/ (in the Bible) a national deity of the ancient Philistines, represented as a fish-tailed man.
– ORIGIN via Latin and Greek from Hebrew *dāgōn*, perhaps from *dāgān* 'corn', but said (according to folk etymology) to be from *dāg* 'fish'.

dago red ▶ noun [mass noun] N. Amer. offensive, dated cheap red wine, typically from Italy.

Daguerre /də'gɛː, French dagɛʁ/, Louis-Jacques-Mandé (1789–1851), French physicist, painter, and inventor of the first practical photographic process. He went into partnership with Joseph-Nicéphore Niépce (1765–1833) to improve the latter's heliography process, and in 1839 he presented his daguerreotype process to the French Academy of Sciences.

daguerreotype /də'gɛrətʌɪp/ (also **daguerrotype**) ▶ noun a photograph taken by an early photographic process employing an iodine-sensitized silvered plate and mercury vapour.
– ORIGIN mid 19th cent.: from French *daguerréotype*, named after L.-J.-M. DAGUERRE, its French inventor.

Dagwood (also **Dagwood sandwich**) ▶ noun N. Amer. a thick sandwich with a variety of different fillings.
– ORIGIN 1970s: named after *Dagwood* Bumstead, a comic-strip character who makes and eats this type of sandwich.

dah /dɑː/ ▶ noun (in the Morse system) another term for DASH.
– ORIGIN Second World War: imitative.

dahabeeyah /ˌdɑːhə'biːjə/ (also **dahabeah**) ▶ noun a large passenger boat used on the Nile, typically with lateen sails.
– ORIGIN mid 19th cent.: from Arabic, literally 'golden', denoting the gilded state barge formerly used by the Muslim rulers of Egypt.

dahi /'dɑːhi/ ▶ noun Indian term for YOGURT.
– ORIGIN from Hindi *dahī* 'curds'.

dahi vada /'vɑːdɑː/ ▶ noun [mass noun] an Indian dish consisting of balls made from ground lentils, which are deep-fried and served in a yogurt sauce.
– ORIGIN from Hindi *dahī* 'curds' and *vaḍā* 'ball of ground lentils'.

Dahl /dɑːl/, Roald (1916–90), British writer, of Norwegian descent. His fiction and drama, such as the short-story collection *Tales of the Unexpected* (1979), typically include macabre plots and unexpected outcomes. Notable works for children: *Charlie and the Chocolate Factory* (1964), *The BFG* (1982).

dahlia /'deɪlɪə/ ▶ noun a tuberous-rooted Mexican plant of the daisy family, which is cultivated for its brightly coloured single or double flowers.
● Genus *Dahlia*, family Compositae.
– ORIGIN modern Latin, named in honour of Andreas *Dahl* (1751–89), Swedish botanist.

Dahomey /də'həʊmi/ former name (until 1975) for BENIN.

dai /dʌɪ/ ▶ noun (pl. **dais**) Indian a midwife or wet nurse.
– ORIGIN from Urdu, from Persian *dāyah*.

daikon /'dʌɪkən, -kɒn/ ▶ noun another term for MOOLI.
– ORIGIN Japanese, from *dai* 'large' + *kon* 'root'.

Dáil /dɔɪl, Irish daːlʲ/ (in full **Dáil Éireann** /'ɛːrən/) the lower House of Parliament in the Republic of Ireland, composed of 166 members (called **Teachtaí Dála**). It was first established in 1919, when Irish republicans proclaimed an Irish state.
– ORIGIN Irish, 'assembly (of Ireland)'.

daily ▶ adjective [attrib.] done, produced, or occurring every day or every weekday: *a daily newspaper.*
■ relating to the period of a single day: *boats can be hired for a daily rate.*
▶ adverb every day: *the museum is open daily.*
▶ noun (pl. **-ies**) informal 1 a newspaper published every day except Sunday.
2 (also **daily help**) Brit., dated a woman who is employed to clean someone else's house each day.
3 (**dailies**) the first prints from cinematographic takes, made rapidly for film producers or editors; the rushes.
– PHRASES **daily life** the activities and experiences that constitute a person's normal existence.
– ORIGIN late Middle English: from DAY + -LY¹, -LY².

daily double ▶ noun Horse Racing a single bet on the winners of two named races in a day.

daily dozen ▶ noun [in sing.] informal, dated regular exercises, especially those done first thing in the morning.

Daimler /'deɪmlə, German 'daɪmlɐ/, Gottlieb (1834–1900), German engineer and motor manufacturer. An employee of Nikolaus Otto, he produced a small engine using the Otto cycle in 1884 and made it propel a bicycle using petrol vapour. He founded the Daimler motor company in 1890.

daimon /'dʌɪməʊn/ ▶ noun variant spelling of DAEMON¹.
– DERIVATIVES **daimonic** /-'məʊnɪk, -'mɒnɪk/ adjective.

daimyo /'dʌɪmɪəʊ, 'dʌɪmjəʊ/ (also **daimio**) ▶ noun (pl. **-os**) historical (in feudal Japan) one of the great lords who were vassals of the shogun.
– ORIGIN Japanese, from *dai* 'great' + *myō* 'name'.

dainty ▶ adjective (**daintier**, **daintiest**) 1 delicately small and pretty: *a dainty lace handkerchief.*
■ (of a person) delicate and graceful in build or movement. ■ (of food) particularly good to eat: *a dainty morsel.*
2 fastidious or difficult to please, typically concerning food: *a dainty appetite.*
▶ noun (pl. **-ies**) (usu. **dainties**) something good to eat; a delicacy.
– DERIVATIVES **daintily** adverb, **daintiness** noun.

– ORIGIN Middle English (in the sense 'titbit, (something) pleasing to the palate'): from Old French *daintie*, *deintie* 'choice morsel, pleasure', from Latin *dignitas* 'worthiness or beauty', from *dignus* 'worthy'.

daiquiri /ˈdʌɪkɪri, ˈdak-/ ▶ noun (pl. **daiquiris**) a cocktail containing rum and lime juice.
– ORIGIN named after *Daiquiri*, a rum-producing district in Cuba.

Dairen /dʌɪˈrɛn/ former name for **DALIAN**.

dairy ▶ noun (pl. **-ies**) a building or room for the storage, processing, and distribution of milk and milk products.
■ a shop where milk and milk products are sold.
▶ adjective [attrib.] containing or made from milk: *dairy products.*
■ concerned with or involved in the production of milk: *a dairy farmer.*
– ORIGIN Middle English *deierie*, from *deie* 'dairymaid' (in Old English *dæge* 'female servant'), of Germanic origin; related to Old Norse *deigja*, also to **DOUGH** and to the second element of Old English *hlǣfdige* (see **LADY**).

dairying ▶ noun [mass noun] the business of producing, storing, and distributing milk and its products.

dairymaid ▶ noun archaic a woman employed in a dairy.

dairyman ▶ noun (pl. **-men**) a man who is employed in a dairy or sells dairy products.

dais /ˈdeɪs, deɪs/ ▶ noun a low platform for a lectern or throne.
– ORIGIN Middle English (originally denoting a raised table for distinguished guests): from Old French *deis*, from Latin *discus* 'disc or dish' (later 'table'). Little used after the Middle English period, the word was revived by antiquarians in the early 19th cent. with the disyllabic pronunciation.

daisy ▶ noun (pl. **-ies**) a small European grassland plant which has flowers with a yellow disc and white rays. It has given rise to many ornamental garden varieties.
● *Bellis perennis*, family Compositae (or Asteraceae; the **daisy family**). The plants of this large family (known as composites) are distinguished by having composite flower heads consisting of numerous disc florets, ray florets, or both; they include many weeds (dandelions, thistles, ragworts) and garden flowers (asters, chrysanthemums, dahlias, marigolds).
■ used in names of other plants of this family with similar flowers, e.g. **Michaelmas daisy**, **Shasta daisy**.
– PHRASES (as) **fresh as a daisy** healthy and full of energy. **pushing up (the) daisies** informal dead and buried.
– ORIGIN Old English *dæges ēage* 'day's eye' (because the flower opens in the morning and closes at night).

daisy bush ▶ noun a shrubby evergreen Australasian plant of the daisy family, which typically has grey-green leaves and bears fragrant flower heads.
● Genus *Olearia*, family Compositae.

daisy chain ▶ noun a string of daisies threaded together by their stems.
■ figurative a string of associated people or things.
■ informal a group sexual activity in which participants act as partners to different people simultaneously.
▶ verb (**daisy-chain**) [with obj.] Computing connect (several devices) together in a linear series.
– DERIVATIVES **daisy-chainable** adjective.

daisy-cutter ▶ noun (in cricket and baseball) a ball hit or bowled so as to roll along the ground.

daisy wheel ▶ noun a device used as a printer in word processors and typewriters, consisting of a disc of spokes extending radially from a central hub, each terminating in a printing character.

Dak. ▶ abbreviation for Dakota.

dak /dɑːk, dɔːk/ ▶ noun [mass noun] the postal service in the Indian subcontinent, originally delivered by a system of relay runners.
– ORIGIN from Hindi *ḍāk.*

Dakar /ˈdakɑː/ the capital of Senegal, a port on the Atlantic coast of West Africa; pop. 1,641,350 (est. 1994).

dak bungalow /dɑːk, dɔːk/ ▶ noun a travellers' rest house in the Indian subcontinent, originally on a dak route.

Dakota¹ /dəˈkəʊtə/ a former territory of the US, organized in 1889 into the states of North Dakota and South Dakota.
– DERIVATIVES **Dakotan** noun & adjective.

Dakota² /dəˈkəʊtə/ ▶ noun (pl. same or **Dakotas**) **1** a member of a North American Indian people of the northern Mississippi valley and the surrounding plains.
2 [mass noun] the Siouan language of this people, spoken by about 15,000 people. Also called **SIOUX**.
▶ adjective of or relating to this people or their language.
– ORIGIN the name in Dakota, literally 'allies'.

daks ▶ plural noun Austral. informal trousers.
– ORIGIN a proprietary name.

dal¹ ▶ abbreviation for decalitre(s).

dal² ▶ noun variant spelling of **DHAL**.

Dalai Lama /ˌdalʌɪ ˈlɑːmə/ ▶ noun the spiritual head of Tibetan Buddhism and, until the establishment of Chinese communist rule, the spiritual and temporal ruler of Tibet.

Each Dalai Lama is believed to be the reincarnation of the bodhisattva Avalokitesvara, reappearing in a child when the incumbent Dalai Lama dies. The present Dalai Lama, the fourteenth incarnation, escaped to India in 1959 following the invasion of Tibet by the Chinese and was awarded the Nobel Peace Prize in 1989.

– ORIGIN from Tibetan, literally 'ocean monk', so named because he is regarded as 'the ocean of compassion'.

dalasi /dɑːˈlɑːsiː/ ▶ noun (pl. same or **dalasis**) the basic monetary unit of Gambia, equal to 100 butut.
– ORIGIN a local word.

Dalcroze see **JAQUES-DALCROZE**.

Dale, Sir Henry Hallett (1875–1968), English physiologist and pharmacologist. He investigated the role of histamine in anaphylactic shock and allergy, and the role of acetylcholine as a natural neurotransmitter. Nobel Prize for Physiology or Medicine (1936).

dale ▶ noun a valley, especially in northern England.
– ORIGIN Old English *dæl*, of Germanic origin; related to Old Norse *dalr*, Dutch *dal*, and German *Tal*, also to **DELL**.

dalek /ˈdɑːlɛk/ ▶ noun (in science fiction) a member of a race of hostile alien machine-organisms which appeared in the BBC television serial *Dr Who* from 1963.
– ORIGIN an invented word, coined by the author Terry Nation after a volume of an encyclopedia covering the alphabetical sequence *dal–lek.*

d'Alembert /ˈdaləmbɛː, French dalɑ̃bɛʁ/, Jean le Rond (1717–83), French mathematician, physicist, and philosopher. His most famous work was the *Traité de dynamique* (1743), in which he developed his own laws of motion. From 1746 to 1758 he was Diderot's chief collaborator on the *Encyclopédie*.

Dalesman ▶ noun (pl. **-men**) an inhabitant of the Yorkshire Dales in northern England.

Dales pony ▶ noun a large stocky pony of a breed which is typically black.

Dalglish /dalˈɡliːʃ/, Kenny (b.1951), Scottish footballer and manager; full name *Kenneth Mathieson Dalglish*. An attacker for Celtic, Liverpool, and Scotland, he has managed Liverpool, Blackburn Rovers, and Newcastle.

Dalhousie /dalˈhaʊzi/, James Andrew Broun Ramsay, 1st Marquess of (1812–60), British colonial administrator, a progressive Governor General of India 1847–56.

Dali /ˈdɑːli/, Salvador (1904–89), Spanish painter. A surrealist, he portrayed dream images with almost photographic realism against backgrounds of arid Catalan landscapes. Dali also collaborated with Buñuel in the production of the film *Un Chien andalou* (1928). Notable works: *The Persistence of Memory* (1931).
– DERIVATIVES **Daliesque** adjective.

Dalian /ˌdɑːlɪˈan/ a port and shipbuilding centre on the Liaodong Peninsula in NE China, now part of the urban complex of Luda. Former name **DAIREN**.

Dalit /ˈdɑːlɪt/ ▶ noun (in the traditional Indian caste system) a member of the lowest caste. See also **UNTOUCHABLE**, **SCHEDULED CASTE**.
– ORIGIN via Hindi from Sanskrit *dalita* 'oppressed'.

Dallapiccola /ˌdaləˈpɪkələ/, Luigi (1904–75), Italian composer. He combined serialism with lyrical polyphonic writing. Notable works: *Songs of Prison* (1938–41).

Dallas /ˈdaləs/ a city in NE Texas, noted as a centre of the oil industry; pop. 1,006,900 (1990).

dalliance /ˈdalɪəns/ ▶ noun [mass noun] the action of engaging in a casual romantic or sexual relationship.
■ brief or casual involvement with something: *Berkeley was my last dalliance with the education system.*
– ORIGIN Middle English (in the sense 'conversation'): from **DALLY** + **-ANCE**.

Dall sheep /dɑːl/ (also **Dall's sheep**) ▶ noun a wild North American sheep found in mountainous country from Alaska to British Columbia. Also called **WHITE SHEEP**.
● *Ovis dalli*, family Bovidae.
– ORIGIN early 20th cent.: named after William H. *Dall* (1845–1927), American naturalist.

dally ▶ verb (**-ies**, **-ied**) [no obj.] **1** act or move slowly: *'Come in,' he said. 'Don't dally.'*
2 have a casual romantic or sexual liaison with someone: *he should stop dallying with film stars.*
■ show a casual interest in something, without committing oneself seriously: *the company has been dallying with the idea of opening a new office.*
– ORIGIN Middle English: from Old French *dalier* 'to chat' (commonly used in Anglo-Norman French), of unknown origin.

Dalmatia /dalˈmeɪʃə/ an ancient region in what is now SW Croatia, comprising mountains and a narrow coastal plain along the Adriatic, together with offshore islands. It once formed part of the Roman province of Illyricum.

Dalmatian ▶ noun **1** a dog of a large, white short-haired breed with dark spots.
2 a native or inhabitant of Dalmatia.
– ORIGIN late 16th cent. (in sense 2): the dog is believed to have originated in Dalmatia in the 18th cent.

dalmatic /dalˈmatɪk/ ▶ noun a wide-sleeved long, loose vestment open at the sides, worn by deacons and bishops, and by monarchs at their coronation.
– ORIGIN late Middle English: from Old French *dalmatique* or late Latin *dalmatica*, from *dalmatica (vestis)* '(robe) of (white) Dalmatian wool', from *Dalmaticus* 'of Dalmatia'.

dal moth /ˈdɑːl ˌmɒt/ ▶ noun [mass noun] an Indian snack consisting of a mixed variety of lentils and spices.
– ORIGIN from Hindi *dāl* 'lentils' + *moth*, denoting a type of grain.

Dalradian /dalˈrɑːdɪən/ ▶ adjective Geology relating to or denoting a series of metamorphosed sedimentary and volcanic rocks formed at the end of the Precambrian aeon, occurring in Scotland and Ireland.
■ [as noun **the Dalradian**] the Dalradian series of rocks.
– ORIGIN late 19th cent.: from *Dalrad-*, from **DALRIADA** (by alteration), + **-IAN**.

Dalriada /dalˈrɪədə/ an ancient Gaelic kingdom in northern Ireland whose people (the Scots) established a colony in SW Scotland from about the late 5th century. By the 9th century Irish Dalriada had declined but the people of Scottish Dalriada gradually acquired dominion over the whole of Scotland.

dal segno /dal ˈsɛnjəʊ/ ▶ adverb Music (especially as a direction) repeat from the point marked by a sign. Compare with **DA CAPO**.
– ORIGIN Italian, 'from the sign'.

Dalton /ˈdɔːlt(ə)n/, John (1766–1844), English chemist, father of modern atomic theory. He defined an atom as the smallest part of a substance that could participate in a chemical reaction and argued that elements are composed of atoms. He stated that elements combine in definite proportion and produced the first table of comparative atomic weights.

dalton /ˈdɔːlt(ə)n/ ▶ noun Chemistry a unit used in expressing the molecular weight of proteins, equivalent to atomic mass unit.
– ORIGIN 1930s: named after J. **DALTON**.

daltonism ▶ noun another term for **PROTANOPIA**, a form of colour blindness.
– ORIGIN mid 19th cent.: from the name of J. **DALTON** + **-ISM**.

Dalton plan ▶ noun [mass noun] a system of education in which pupils are made responsible for the completion of assignments over fairly long periods.
– ORIGIN early 20th cent.: named after *Dalton*,

Massachusetts, where the first school used the plan.

Dalton's law Chemistry a law stating that the pressure exerted by a mixture of gases in a fixed volume is equal to the sum of the pressures that would be exerted by each gas alone in the same volume.

dam¹ ▶ abbreviation for decametre(s).

dam² ▶ noun a barrier, typically of concrete, constructed to hold back water and raise its level, the resulting reservoir being used in the generation of electricity or as a water supply.
■ chiefly S. African an artificial pond or reservoir where rain or spring water is collected for storage. ■ a barrier of branches in a stream, constructed by a beaver to provide a deep pool and a lodge. ■ chiefly N. Amer. a rubber sheet used to keep saliva from the teeth during dental operations.
▶ verb (**dammed, damming**) [with obj.] build a dam across (a river or lake).
■ hold back or obstruct (something): *the closed lock gates dammed up the canal.*
– ORIGIN Middle English: from Middle Low German or Middle Dutch; related to Dutch *dam* and German *Damm*, also to Old English *fordeman* 'close up'.

dam³ ▶ noun the female parent of an animal, especially a domestic mammal.
– ORIGIN late Middle English (denoting a human mother): alteration of **DAME**.

dama gazelle /ˈdɑːmə/ ▶ noun a large long-legged gazelle with a mainly whitish coat, native to the southern and western Sahara (where it is now very rare). Also called **ADDRA GAZELLE**.
● *Gazella dama*, family Bovidae.
– ORIGIN modern Latin *dama* 'fallow deer', specific epithet.

damage ▶ noun 1 [mass noun] physical harm caused to something in such a way as to impair its value, usefulness, or normal function.
■ unwelcome and detrimental effects: *the damage to his reputation was considerable.*
2 (**damages**) a sum of money claimed or awarded in compensation for a loss or an injury: *she was awarded $284,000 in damages.*
▶ verb [with obj.] inflict physical harm on (something) so as to impair its value, usefulness, or normal function: *the car was badly damaged in the accident* | [as adj. **damaged**] *damaged ligaments* | [as adj. **damaging**] *new cars are less damaging to the environment.*
■ have a detrimental effect on: *the scandal could seriously damage his career.*
– PHRASES **the damage is done** used to indicate that it is too late to prevent the occurrence of something unfortunate or undesirable. **what's the damage?** informal, humorous used to ask the cost of something.
– DERIVATIVES **damagingly** adverb.
– ORIGIN Middle English: from Old French, from *dam, damne* 'loss or damage', from Latin *damnum* 'loss or hurt'; compare with **DAMN**.

damage control ▶ noun chiefly N. Amer. another term for **DAMAGE LIMITATION**.

damaged goods ▶ plural noun merchandise which has deteriorated in quality.
■ figurative, derogatory a person who is regarded as inadequate or impaired in some way.

damage feasant /ˈfiːz(ə)nt/ English Law ▶ noun [mass noun] damage done on one person's land by animals or goods of another, which would justify the landowner in retaining them until compensated.
▶ adverb on grounds of damage caused to land or property.
– PHRASES **distress damage feasant** the right of a landowner to seize straying livestock which have caused actual damage to land, replaced by provisions of the Animals Act (1971).
– ORIGIN late 16th cent.: from Old French *damage fesant* 'doing damage'.

damage limitation ▶ noun [mass noun] action taken to alleviate or limit the damaging effects of an accident or error.

Daman and Diu /dəˈmɑːn, ˈdiːuː/ a Union Territory in India, on the west coast north of Bombay; pop. 101,400 (1991); capital, Daman. It consists of the district of Daman and the island of Diu, and until 1987 was administered with Goa.

damar /ˈdamə/ ▶ noun & adjective variant spelling of **DAMMAR**.

Damara /dəˈmɑːrə/ ▶ noun (pl. same or **Damaras**) a member of a people inhabiting mountainous parts of Namibia and speaking the Nama language.
▶ adjective of or relating to the Damara.
– ORIGIN the name in Nama.

Damaraland /dəˈmɑːrəland/ a plateau region of central Namibia inhabited chiefly by the Damara and Herero peoples.

Damascene /ˈdaməsiːn, ˌdaməˈsiːn/ ▶ adjective of or relating to the city of Damascus.
■ of, relating to, or resembling the conversion of St Paul on the road to Damascus: *a transformation of Damascene proportions.* ■ historical of or relating to Damascus steel or its manufacture. ■ (often **damascene**) relating to or denoting a process of inlaying a metal object with gold or silver decoration.
▶ noun a native or inhabitant of Damascus.
– ORIGIN late Middle English (as a noun): via Latin from Greek *Damaskēnos* 'of Damascus'.

damascened /ˈdaməsiːnd, ˌdaməˈsiːnd/ ▶ adjective (of iron or steel) given a wavy pattern by hammer-welding and repeated heating and forging.
■ (of a metal object) inlaid with gold or silver decoration.

Damascus /dəˈmɑːskəs, -ˈmaskəs/ the capital of Syria since the country's independence in 1946; pop. 1,497,000 (est. 1993). It has existed as a city for over 4,000 years.

Damascus steel ▶ noun [mass noun] historical steel made with a wavy surface pattern produced by hammer-welding strips of steel and iron followed by repeated heating and forging, used chiefly for knife and sword blades. Such items were often marketed, but not necessarily made, in Damascus during the medieval period.

damask /ˈdaməsk/ ▶ noun 1 [mass noun] a figured, lustrous woven fabric, with a pattern visible on both sides, typically used for table linen and upholstery.
■ [count noun] a tablecloth made of this material.
2 short for **DAMASK ROSE**.
3 (also **damask steel**) [mass noun] historical another term for **DAMASCUS STEEL**.
▶ adjective poetic/literary having the velvety pink or light red colour of a damask rose.
▶ verb [with obj.] poetic/literary decorate with or as if with a variegated pattern: *flowers damask the fragrant seat.*
– ORIGIN late Middle English: from *Damaske*, early form of the name of Damascus, where the fabric was first produced.

damask rose ▶ noun a sweet-scented rose of an old variety (or hybrid) that is typically pink or light red in colour. The petals are very soft and velvety and are used to make attar.
● *Rosa damascena*, family Rosaceae.

dame ▶ noun 1 (**Dame**) (in the UK) the title given to a woman with the rank of Knight Commander or holder of the Grand Cross in the Orders of Chivalry.
■ N. Amer. informal a woman. ■ archaic or humorous an elderly or mature woman. ■ (also **pantomime dame**) Brit. a comic middle-aged female character in modern pantomime, usually played by a man.
– ORIGIN Middle English (denoting a female ruler): via Old French from Latin *domina* 'mistress'.

dame school ▶ noun historical a small primary school run by elderly women, especially in their own homes.

damfool informal, dated ▶ adjective [attrib.] (of a person) thoroughly foolish and stupid.
▶ noun a stupid or foolish person.

Damietta /ˌdamiˈɛtə/ the eastern branch of the Nile delta. Arabic name **DUMYAT**.
■ a port at the mouth of this delta; pop. 113,000 (1991).

dammar /ˈdamə/ (also **damar**) ▶ noun [mass noun] resin obtained from any of a number of tropical and mainly Indo-Malaysian trees, used to make varnish.
● The resin is obtained from trees in the families Araucariaceae (genus *Agathis*), Dipterocarpaceae (genera *Hopea, Shorea*, and *Vatica*), and Burseraceae (genus *Canarium*).
– ORIGIN late 17th cent.: from Malay *damar* 'resin'.

damn /dam/ ▶ verb [with obj.] (**be damned**) (in Christian belief) be condemned by God to suffer eternal punishment in hell.
■ be doomed to misfortune or failure: *the enterprise was damned.* ■ condemn, especially by the public expression of disapproval: *the book damns her husband.* ■ curse (someone or something): *she cleared her throat, damning it for its huskiness.*
▶ exclamation informal expressing anger, surprise, or frustration: *Damn! I completely forgot!*
▶ adjective [attrib.] informal used for emphasis, especially to express anger or frustration: *turn that damn thing off!* | [as submodifier] *don't be so damn silly!*
– PHRASES **as near as damn it** as close to being accurate as makes no difference. —— **be damned** used to express defiance or rejection of someone or something previously mentioned: *'Glory be damned!'* **damn all** Brit. informal nothing at all. **damn someone/thing with faint praise** praise someone or something so unenthusiastically as to imply condemnation. **I'm (or I'll be) damned if** informal used to express a strong negative: *I'm damned if I know.* **not be worth a damn** informal have no value or validity at all. **not give a damn** see **GIVE**. **well I'll be (or I'm) damned** informal used as an expression of surprise.
– ORIGIN Middle English: from Old French *dam(p)ner*, from Latin *dam(p)nare* 'inflict loss on', from *damnum* 'loss, damage'.

damna /ˈdamnə/ plural form of **DAMNUM**.

damnable /ˈdamnəb(ə)l/ ▶ adjective 1 very bad or unpleasant: *leave this damnable place behind.*
2 subject to or worthy of divine condemnation: *suicide was thought damnable in the Middle Ages.*
– DERIVATIVES **damnably** adverb.
– ORIGIN Middle English (in the sense 'worthy of condemnation'): from Old French *dam(p)nable*, from Latin *dam(p)nabilis*, from *dam(p)nare* 'inflict loss on' (see **DAMN**).

damnation /damˈneɪʃ(ə)n/ ▶ noun [mass noun] condemnation to eternal punishment in hell.
▶ exclamation expressing anger or frustration.
– ORIGIN Middle English: via Old French from Latin *dam(p)natio(n-)*, from the verb *dam(p)nare* 'inflict loss on' (see **DAMN**).

damnatory /ˈdamnə(t(ə)ri/ ▶ adjective conveying or causing censure or damnation.
– ORIGIN late 17th cent.: from Latin *damnatorius*, from *dam(p)nat-* 'caused to suffer loss', from the verb *dam(p)nare* (see **DAMN**).

damned /damd/ ▶ adjective 1 (in Christian belief) condemned by God to suffer eternal punishment in hell: [as plural noun **the damned**] *the spirits of the damned.*
2 [attrib.] informal used for emphasis, especially to express anger or frustration: *it's none of your damned business* | [as submodifier] *she's too damned arrogant.*
■ (**damnedest**) used to emphasize the surprising nature or degree of something: *the damnedest thing I ever saw.*
– PHRASES **do (or try) one's damnedest** do or try one's utmost.

damnify /ˈdamnɪfʌɪ/ ▶ verb (**-ies, -ied**) [with obj.] English Law, rare cause injury to.
– DERIVATIVES **damnification** noun.
– ORIGIN early 16th cent.: from Old French *damnefier, dam(p)nifier*, from late Latin *damnificare* 'injure, condemn', from Latin *damnificus* 'hurtful', from *damnus* 'loss, damage'.

damning ▶ adjective (of a circumstance or piece of evidence) strongly suggesting guilt or error.
■ extremely critical: *a damning indictment of the government's record.*
– DERIVATIVES **damningly** adverb.

damnum /ˈdamnəm/ ▶ noun (pl. **damna** /-nə/) Law a loss.
– ORIGIN Latin, 'hurt, harm, or damage'.

Damocles /ˈdaməkliːz/ a legendary courtier who extravagantly praised the happiness of Dionysius I, ruler of Syracuse. To show him how precarious this happiness was, Dionysius seated him at a banquet with a sword hung by a single hair over his head.
– PHRASES **sword of Damocles** used to refer to a precarious situation.

Damon /ˈdeɪmən/ a legendary Syracusan of the 4th century BC whose friend Pythias (also called Phintias) was sentenced to death by Dionysius I. Damon stood bail for Pythias, who returned just in time to save him, and was himself reprieved.

damp ▶ adjective slightly wet.
▶ noun [mass noun] 1 moisture diffused through the air or a solid substance or condensed on a surface, typically with detrimental or unpleasant effects.
■ (**damps**) archaic damp air or atmosphere.
2 [count noun] archaic a check or discouragement: *shame gave a damp to her triumph.*
3 short for **FIREDAMP**.

▶ **verb** [with obj.] **1** make (something) slightly wet: *damp a small area with water.*
2 control or restrain (a feeling or a state of affairs): *she tried to* **damp down** *her feelings of despair.*
■ make (a fire) burn less strongly by reducing the flow of air to it.
3 restrict the amplitude of (a vibrating string of a piano or other musical instrument) so as to reduce the volume of sound.
■ Physics progressively reduce the amplitude of (an oscillation or vibration).
– DERIVATIVES **dampish** adjective, **damply** adverb, **dampness** noun.
– ORIGIN Middle English (in the noun sense 'noxious inhalation'): of West Germanic origin; related to a Middle Low German word meaning 'vapour, steam, smoke'.

damp course (also **damp-proof course**) ▶ **noun** a layer of waterproof material in the wall of a building near the ground, to prevent rising damp.

damp-dry ▶ **verb** [with obj.] dry (something) until it is only damp: *damp-dry the fish with kitchen paper.*

dampen ▶ **verb** [with obj.] **1** make slightly wet: *the fine rain dampened her face.*
2 make less strong or intense: *nothing could dampen her enthusiasm.*
■ reduce the amplitude of (a sound source): *slider switches on the mixers can dampen the drums.*

dampener ▶ **noun** a thing that dampens, especially something that has a restraining or subduing effect: *his vegetarianism was no dampener of his drinking.*
– PHRASES **put a dampener on** another way of saying *put a damper on* (see **DAMPER**).

damper ▶ **noun 1** a person or thing that has a depressing, subduing, or inhibiting effect.
■ Music a pad silencing a piano string except when removed by means of a pedal or by the note being struck. ■ a device for reducing mechanical vibration, in particular a shock absorber on a motor vehicle. ■ a conductor used to reduce hunting in an electric motor or generator. ■ a movable metal plate in a flue or chimney, used to regulate the draught and so control the rate of combustion.
2 chiefly Austral./NZ an unleavened loaf or cake of flour and water baked in wood ashes. [ORIGIN: in the sense 'something that takes the edge off the appetite'.]
– PHRASES **put a** (or **the**) **damper on** have a depressing, subduing, or inhibiting effect on: *he put a damper on her youthful excitement.*

Dampier /ˈdampɪə/, William (1652–1715), English explorer and adventurer. He is notable for having sailed round the world twice. In 1683 he set out from Panama, crossing the Pacific and reaching England again in 1691; in 1699 the government commissioned him to explore the NW coast of Australia.

damping ▶ **noun** [mass noun] **1** technical a decrease in the amplitude of an oscillation as a result of energy being drained from the system to overcome frictional or other resistive forces.
■ a mechanism or system for bringing about such a decrease. ■ a method of bringing about a decrease in oscillatory peaks in an electric current or voltage using an energy-absorbing or resistance circuit.
2 (**damping off**) a plant disease occurring in excessively damp conditions, in particular the collapse and death of young seedlings as a result of a fungal infection.
• The disease is commonly caused by fungi of the genera *Pythium* (subdivision Mastigomycotina) or *Fusarium* (subdivision Deuteromycotina).

damp-proof ▶ **adjective** impervious to damp.
▶ **verb** (usu. **be damp-proofed**) make impervious to damp by using a damp course.

damp squib ▶ **noun** [in sing.] Brit. a situation or event which is much less impressive than expected.

damsel /ˈdamz(ə)l/ ▶ **noun** archaic or poetic/literary a young unmarried woman.
– PHRASES **damsel in distress** often humorous a young woman in trouble.
– ORIGIN Middle English: from Old French *dameisele*, *damisele*, based on Latin *domina* 'mistress'.

damsel bug ▶ **noun** a slender long-legged bug that is a predator of other insects.
• Family Nabidae, suborder Heteroptera: several genera.

damselfish ▶ **noun** (pl. same or **-fishes**) a small brightly coloured tropical marine fish that lives in or near coral reefs.
• *Chromis* and other genera, family Pomacentridae: numerous species, in particular *C. chromis*.

damselfly ▶ **noun** (pl. **-flies**) a slender insect related to the dragonflies, having weak flight and typically resting with the wings folded back along the body.
• Suborder Zygoptera, order Odonata: several families.

damson /ˈdamz(ə)n/ ▶ **noun 1** a small purple-black plum-like fruit.
■ [mass noun] a dark purple colour.
2 (also **damson tree**) the small deciduous tree which bears this fruit, probably derived from the bullace.
• *Prunus domestica* subsp. *insititia* (or *P. damascena*), family Rosaceae.
– ORIGIN late Middle English *damascene*, from Latin *damascenum* (*prunum*) '(plum) of Damascus'. Compare with **DAMASCENE** and **DAMASK**.

damson cheese ▶ **noun** [mass noun] a solid preserve of damsons and sugar.

Dan (in the Bible) a Hebrew patriarch, son of Jacob and Bilhah (Gen. 30:6).
■ the tribe of Israel traditionally descended from him. ■ an ancient town in the north of Canaan, where the tribe of Dan settled. It marked the northern limit of the ancient Hebrew kingdom of Israel (Judges 20).

Dan. ▶ **abbreviation for** Daniel (in biblical references).

dan[1] ▶ **noun** any of ten degrees of advanced proficiency in judo or karate.
■ a person who has achieved such a degree.
– ORIGIN 1940s: from Japanese.

dan[2] (also **dan buoy**) ▶ **noun** a small temporary marker buoy with a lightweight flagpole.
– ORIGIN late 17th cent.: of unknown origin.

Dana[1] /ˈdeɪnə/, James Dwight (1813–95), American naturalist, geologist, and mineralogist. He founded an important classification of minerals based on chemistry and physics. His view of the earth as a unit was an evolutionary one, but he was slow to accept Darwin's theory of evolution.

Dana[2] /ˈdeɪnə/, Richard Henry (1815–82), American adventurer, lawyer, and writer, known for his account of his voyage from Boston round Cape Horn to California, *Two Years before the Mast* (1840).

Danae /ˈdaneɪiː/ Greek Mythology the daughter of Acrisius, king of Argos. An oracle foretold that she would bear a son who would kill her father. Attempting to evade this Acrisius imprisoned her, but Zeus visited her in the form of a shower of gold and she conceived Perseus, who killed Acrisius by accident.

danaid /ˈdaneɪɪd/ ▶ **noun** Entomology a large strikingly marked butterfly of a group that includes the monarch (milkweed) and plain tiger, found chiefly in the tropics of Africa and the Far East.
• Subfamily Danainae, family Nymphalidae (formerly family Danaidae).
– ORIGIN late 19th cent.: from modern Latin *Danaidae*, arbitrary use of the Latin name of the daughters of Danaus.

Danaids /ˈdaneɪɪdz/ Greek Mythology the daughters of Danaus, king of Argos, who were compelled to marry the sons of his brother Aegyptus but murdered their husbands on the wedding night, except for one, Hypermnestra, who helped her husband to escape. The remaining Danaids were punished in Hades by being set to fill a leaky jar with water.

Danakil /ˈdanəkɪl, dəˈnɑːk(ə)l/ ▶ **noun** & **adjective** another term for **AFAR**.
– ORIGIN from Arabic *danākil*, plural of *dankalī*.

Danakil Depression a long low-lying desert region of NE Ethiopia and northern Djibouti, between the Red Sea and the Great Rift Valley.

Da Nang /dɑː ˈnaŋ/ a port and city in central Vietnam, on the South China Sea; pop. 382,670 (est. 1992). During the Vietnam War it was used as a US military base. Former name **TOURANE**.

dance ▶ **verb** [no obj.] **1** move rhythmically to music, typically following a set sequence of steps: *all the men wanted her to dance with them.*
■ [with obj.] perform (a particular dance or a role in a ballet): *they danced a tango.* ■ [with obj. and adverbial of direction] lead (someone) in a particular direction while dancing with them: *I danced her out of the room.*
2 [with adverbial of direction] (of a person) move in a quick and lively way as an expression of pleasure or excitement: *Sheila danced in gaily.*
■ [with adverbial of place] move up and down lightly and quickly in the air: *midges danced over the stream.* ■ (of someone's eyes) sparkle brightly with pleasure or excitement.
▶ **noun** a series of steps and movements that match the speed and rhythm of a piece of music.
■ a particular sequence of steps and movements constituting a particular form of dancing. ■ [mass noun] steps and movements of this type considered as an activity or art form: *national theatre of dance.* ■ a social gathering at which people dance. ■ a set of lively movements resembling a dance: *he gesticulated comically and did a little dance.* ■ a piece of music for dancing to: *the last dance had been played.* ■ (also **dance music**) [mass noun] music for dancing to, especially in a club.
– PHRASES **dance attendance on** do one's utmost to please someone by attending to all their needs or requests. **dance to someone's tune** comply completely with someone's demands and wishes. **lead someone a dance** (or **a merry dance**) Brit. cause someone a great deal of trouble or worry.
– DERIVATIVES **danceable** adjective.
– ORIGIN Middle English: from Old French *dancer* (verb), *dance* (noun), of unknown origin.

dance band ▶ **noun** a band that plays music suitable for dancing to, especially swing.

dance card ▶ **noun** dated a card bearing the names of a woman's prospective partners at a formal dance.

dance floor ▶ **noun** an area of uncarpeted floor, typically in a nightclub or restaurant, reserved for dancing.
■ [as modifier] denoting a record or type of music particularly popular as an accompaniment to dancing.

dance hall ▶ **noun 1** a large public hall or building where people pay to enter and dance.
2 (**dancehall**) [mass noun] an uptempo style of dance music originating in Jamaica and derived from reggae, in which a DJ improvises lyrics over a recorded instrumental backing track or to the accompaniment of live musicians.

dance of death ▶ **noun** a medieval allegorical representation in which a personified Death leads people to the grave, designed to emphasize the equality of all before death.

dancer ▶ **noun** a person who dances or whose profession is dancing.

dancercise (also **-ize**) ▶ **noun** [mass noun] a system of aerobic exercise using dance movements.
– ORIGIN 1960s: blend of **DANCE** and **EXERCISE**.

dancetté /ˈdɑːnsəteɪ/ (also **dancetty**) ▶ **adjective** [usu. postpositive] Heraldry having large, deep zigzag indentations.
– ORIGIN early 17th cent.: alteration of French *denché*, based on Latin *dens*, *dent-* 'tooth'.

dancing ▶ **noun** [mass noun] the activity of dancing for pleasure or in order to entertain others.

dancing dervish ▶ **noun** see **DERVISH**.

dancing girl ▶ **noun** a female professional dancer, especially an erotic dancer or a member of the chorus in a musical.

danda /ˈdʌndə/ ▶ **noun** (in the Indian subcontinent) a large stick used as a weapon by a policeman or guard.
– ORIGIN from Hindi *ḍaṇḍā*, from Sanskrit *daṇḍa*.

D and C ▶ **abbreviation for** dilatation and curettage.

dandelion ▶ **noun** a widely distributed weed of the daisy family, with a rosette of leaves, large bright yellow flowers followed by globular heads of seeds with downy tufts, and stems containing a milky latex.
• Genus *Taraxacum*, family Compositae: several species, in particular the common *T. officinale*, which has edible leaves.
– ORIGIN late Middle English: from French *dent-de-lion*, translation of medieval Latin *dens leonis* 'lion's tooth' (because of the jagged shape of the leaves).

dandelion clock ▶ **noun** see **CLOCK**[1] (sense 2).

dandelion coffee ▶ **noun** [mass noun] a hot drink made from dried and powdered dandelion roots.

dandelion greens ▶ **plural noun** N. Amer. fresh dandelion leaves used as a salad vegetable or herb.

dander[1] ▶ **noun** (in phrase **get/have one's dander up**) informal lose one's temper.
– ORIGIN mid 19th cent. (originally US): of unknown origin.

dander[2] ▶ **noun** [mass noun] skin flakes in an animal's fur or hair.
– ORIGIN late 18th cent.: related to **DANDRUFF**.

dander[3] chiefly Scottish ▶ **noun** a stroll.
▶ **verb** [no obj., with adverbial of direction] stroll: *he dandered in to change his coat.*
– ORIGIN late 16th cent.: frequentative form; perhaps related to dialect *dadder* 'quake' and *daddle* 'dawdle'.

dandiacal /dan'dʌɪək(ə)l/ ▶ **adjective** dated or humorous relating to or characteristic of a dandy.
– ORIGIN mid 19th cent.: from **DANDY**, on the pattern of words such as *hypochondriacal.*

Dandie Dinmont /ˌdandɪ 'dɪnmənt/ ▶ **noun** a terrier of a breed from the Scottish Borders, with short legs, a long body, and a rough coat.
– ORIGIN early 19th cent.: named after a farmer who owned a special breed of terriers, portrayed in Sir Walter Scott's *Guy Mannering.*

dandified ▶ **adjective** (of a man) showing excessive concern about his clothes or appearance.
■ self-consciously sophisticated or elaborate: *he writes a dandified prose.*

dandiprat ▶ **noun** archaic, informal a small boy.
■ an insignificant person.
– ORIGIN early 16th cent. (denoting a coin worth three halfpence): of unknown origin.

dandle ▶ **verb** [with obj.] move (a baby or young child) up and down in a playful or affectionate way.
■ move (something) lightly up and down: *dandling the halter rope, he gently urged the pony's head up.*
– ORIGIN mid 16th cent.: of unknown origin.

Dandong /dan'dʊŋ/ a port in Liaoning province, NE China, near the mouth of the Yalu River, on the border with North Korea; pop. 660,500 (1990). Former name **ANTUNG**.

dandruff ▶ **noun** [mass noun] small pieces of dead skin among a person's hair.
– DERIVATIVES **dandruffy** adjective.
– ORIGIN mid 16th cent.: the first element is unknown; the second (*-ruff*) is perhaps related to Middle English *rove* 'scurfiness'.

dandy ▶ **noun** (pl. **-ies**) **1** a man unduly devoted to style, smartness, and fashion in dress and appearance.
2 informal, dated an excellent thing of its kind.
▶ **adjective** (**dandier**, **dandiest**) **1** informal, chiefly N. Amer. excellent: *things are all* ***fine and dandy.***
2 relating to or characteristic of a dandy.
– DERIVATIVES **dandyish** adjective, **dandyism** noun.
– ORIGIN late 18th cent.: perhaps a shortened form of 17th-cent. *Jack-a-dandy* 'conceited fellow' (the last element representing *Dandy*, a pet form of the given name *Andrew*).

dandy brush ▶ **noun** a coarse brush used for grooming a horse.

Dane ▶ **noun** a native or national of Denmark, or a person of Danish descent.
■ historical one of the Viking invaders of the British Isles in the 9th–11th centuries.
– ORIGIN Old English *Dene*; superseded in Middle English by forms influenced by Old Norse *Danir* and late Latin *Dani* (both plural).

Danegeld /'deɪngɛld/ ▶ **noun** [mass noun] historical a land tax levied in Anglo-Saxon England during the reign of King Ethelred to raise funds for protection against Danish invaders.
■ taxes collected for national defence by the Norman kings until 1162.
– ORIGIN late Old English, from Old Norse *Danir* 'Danes' + *gjald* 'payment'.

Danelaw /'deɪnlɔː/ the part of northern and eastern England occupied or administered by Danes from the late 9th century until after the Norman Conquest.
– ORIGIN late Old English *Dena lagu* 'Danes' law'.

danewort /'deɪnwəːt/ ▶ **noun** a dwarf Eurasian elder with a strong, unpleasant smell and berries yielding a blue dye that was formerly used to colour leather.
● *Sambucus ebulus*, family Caprifoliaceae.
– ORIGIN early 16th cent.: so named from the folklore that the plant sprang up where Danish blood was spilt in battle.

Danforth anchor /'danfəθ/ ▶ **noun** a type of lightweight anchor with flat flukes.

dang ▶ **adjective, exclamation, & verb** informal, chiefly N. Amer. euphemism for **DAMN**: [as adj.] *just get the dang car started!*

danger ▶ **noun** [mass noun] the possibility of suffering harm or injury: *his life was* ***in danger.***
■ [count noun] a person or thing that causes or is likely to cause harm or injury. ■ the possibility of something unwelcome or unpleasant: *there was no danger of the champagne running out.* ■ Brit. the status of a railway signal indicating that the line is not clear and that a train should not proceed.
– PHRASES **in danger of** likely to incur or to suffer from: *the animal is in danger of extinction.* **out of danger** (of a person who has suffered a serious injury or illness) not expected to die.
– ORIGIN Middle English: from Old French *dangier*, based on Latin *dominus* 'lord'. The original sense was 'jurisdiction or power', specifically 'power to harm', hence the current meaning 'liability to be harmed'.

danger-close ▶ **adjective** Military denoting or involving artillery fire which is liable to hit friendly forces because of their proximity to an enemy target.

danger list ▶ **noun** Brit. a list of those who are dangerously ill in a hospital.

danger man ▶ **noun** a man perceived as posing a particular threat.

danger money (US **danger pay**) ▶ **noun** [mass noun] extra payment for working under dangerous conditions.

dangerous ▶ **adjective** able or likely to cause harm or injury: *a dangerous animal.*
■ likely to have adverse or unfortunate consequences; risky: *it is dangerous to convict on his evidence.* ■ likely to cause problems or difficulty: *our most dangerous opponents in the World Cup.* ■ (of a drug) addictive or otherwise harmful or illegal.
– DERIVATIVES **dangerousness** noun.
– ORIGIN Middle English (in the senses 'arrogant', 'fastidious', and 'difficult to please'): from Old French *dangereus*, from *dangier* (see **DANGER**).

dangerously ▶ **adverb** in a way likely to cause harm or injury: *he was driving dangerously.*
■ in a way involving risk: *she liked to live dangerously.*
■ [as submodifier] to a degree likely to result in adverse or extremely unfortunate consequences: *your father is dangerously ill.*

dangle ▶ **verb** [no obj., with adverbial of place] hang or swing loosely: *saucepans dangled from a rail* | [with obj.] *they were dangling their legs over the water.*
■ [with obj.] figurative offer (an enticing incentive) to someone: *the defence portfolio could be the carrot to* ***dangle before*** *him.*
– PHRASES **keep someone dangling** keep someone in an uncertain position.
– DERIVATIVES **dangler** noun, **dangly** adjective.
– ORIGIN late 16th cent.: symbolic of something loose and pendulous, corresponding to Danish *dangle*, Swedish *dangla*, but the origin is not clear.

dangling participle ▶ **noun** Grammar a participle intended to modify a noun which is not actually present in the text.

USAGE A **participle** is a word formed as an inflection of the verb, such as *arriving* or *arrived*. A **dangling participle** is one which is left 'hanging' because, in the grammar of the clause, it does not relate to the noun it should. In the sentence ***arriving*** *at the station,* ***she*** *picked up her case* the construction is correct because the participle **arriving** and the subject **she** relate to each other (**she** is the one doing the **arriving**). But in the following sentence, a **dangling participle** has been created: ***arriving*** *at the station,* ***the sun*** *came out.* We know, logically, that it is not **the sun** which is **arriving** but grammatically that is exactly the link which has been created. Such errors are frequent, even in written English, and can give rise to genuine confusion.

Daniel a Hebrew prophet (6th century BC), who spent his life as a captive at the court of Babylon. In the Bible he interpreted the dreams of Nebuchadnezzar and was delivered by God from the lions' den into which he had been thrown as the result of a trick; in the apocryphal Book of Susanna he is portrayed as a wise judge (Sus. 45–64).
■ a book of the Bible containing his prophecies. It was probably written at the outbreak of persecution of the Jews under Seleucid rule *c.*167 BC.

Daniell cell /'danjəl/ ▶ **noun** a primary voltaic cell with a copper anode and a zinc-amalgam cathode, giving a standard electromotive force when either copper sulphate or sulphuric acid is used as the electrolyte.
– ORIGIN mid 19th cent.: named after John Daniell (1790–1845), the British physicist who invented it.

danio /'deɪnɪəʊ/ ▶ **noun** (pl. **-os**) a small, typically brightly coloured freshwater fish which is native to the Indian subcontinent and SE Asia.
● Genera *Danio* and *Brachydanio*, family Cyprinidae: several species.
– ORIGIN modern Latin (genus name).

Danish /'deɪnɪʃ/ ▶ **adjective** of or relating to Denmark or its people or language.
▶ **noun 1** [mass noun] the Scandinavian language spoken in Denmark, which is also the official language of Greenland and the Faroes. It is spoken by over 5 million people.
2 [as plural noun **the Danish**] the people of Denmark.
3 informal short for **DANISH PASTRY**.
– ORIGIN Old English *Denisc*, of Germanic origin; superseded in Middle English by forms influenced by Old French *daneis* and medieval Latin *Danensis* (from late Latin *Dani* 'Danes').

Danish blue ▶ **noun** [mass noun] a soft, salty, strong-flavoured white cheese with blue veins.

Danish oil ▶ **noun** [mass noun] a mixture of tung oil, other vegetable oils, and chemicals to quicken drying, used to treat wood.

Danish pastry ▶ **noun** a cake of sweetened yeast pastry with toppings or fillings such as icing, fruit, or nuts.

dank ▶ **adjective** disagreeably damp, cold, and musty.
– DERIVATIVES **dankly** adverb, **dankness** noun.
– ORIGIN Middle English: probably of Scandinavian origin and related to Swedish *dank* 'marshy spot'.

Danmark /'danmarg/ Danish name for **DENMARK**.

Dannebrog /'danəbrɒg/ ▶ **noun** the Danish national flag.
– ORIGIN Danish, literally 'Danish cloth'.

d'Annunzio /da'nʊntsɪəʊ/, Gabriele (1863–1938), Italian novelist, dramatist, and poet. He is best known for his 'Romances of the Rose' trilogy, including *The Triumph of Death* (1894), which shows the influence of Nietzsche.

Dano-Norwegian /ˌdeɪnəʊnɔː'wiːdʒ(ə)n/ ▶ **noun** another term for **BOKMÅL**.

danse macabre /ˌdɑːns mə'kɑːbr(ə)/ ▶ **noun** another term for **DANCE OF DEATH**.
– ORIGIN French, recorded from late Middle English in Anglicized forms such as *dance of Machabray*, *dance of Macaber* (see also **MACABRE**).

danseur /dɑ̃'səː/ ▶ **noun** a male ballet dancer.
– ORIGIN French, from *danser* 'to dance'.

danseur noble /dɑ̃ˌsəː 'nɒbl(ə)/ ▶ **noun** a principal male ballet dancer, especially one who is particularly suited by bearing or physique to princely roles.
– ORIGIN French, literally 'noble dancer'.

danseuse /dɑ̃'səːz/ ▶ **noun** a female ballet dancer.
– ORIGIN French, 'female dancer'.

Dante /'dantɛɪ/ (1265–1321), Italian poet; full name *Dante Alighieri*. His reputation rests chiefly on *The Divine Comedy* (*c.*1309–20), an epic poem describing his spiritual journey through Hell and Purgatory and finally to Paradise. His love for Beatrice Portinari is described in *Vita nuova* (*c.*1290–4).

Dantean /'dantɪən, dan'tiːən/ ▶ **adjective** of or reminiscent of the poetry of Dante, especially in invoking his vision of hell in *The Divine Comedy.*
▶ **noun** an admirer or student of Dante or his writing.

Dantesque /ˌdantɪ'ɛsk/ (also **Dante-esque**) ▶ **adjective** another term for **DANTEAN**.

danthonia /dan'θəʊnɪə/ ▶ **noun** [mass noun] a widely distributed tufted grass that typically grows on poor soils and is of low palatability to grazing animals.
● Genus *Danthonia*, family Gramineae.
– ORIGIN modern Latin, named after Étienne *Danthoine*, 19th-cent. French botanist.

Danton /'dantən, French dɑ̃tɔ̃/, Georges (Jacques) (1759–94), French revolutionary. A noted orator, he won great popularity in the early days of the French Revolution. He was initially an ally of Robespierre but later revolted against the severity of the Revolutionary Tribunal and was executed on Robespierre's orders.

Danube /'danjuːb/ a river which rises in the Black Forest in SW Germany and flows about 2,850 km (1,770 miles) into the Black Sea. It is the second longest river in Europe after the Volga; the cities of Vienna, Budapest, and Belgrade are situated on it. German name **DONAU**.

– DERIVATIVES **Danubian** /da'nju:bɪən/ adjective.

Danube School a group of landscape painters working in the Danube region in the early 16th century. Its members included Altdorfer and Cranach the Elder.

Danubian principalities the former European principalities of Moldavia and Wallachia. In 1861 they united to form the state of Romania.

Danzig /'dantsɪç/ German name for **GDAŃSK**.

dap ▶ **verb** (**dapped**, **dapping**) [no obj.] fish by letting the fly bob lightly on the water without letting the line touch the water.
▶ **noun 1** (usu. **the dap**) a fishing fly used in this way.
2 (usu. **daps**) dialect a rubber-soled shoe.
– ORIGIN mid 17th cent. (as a verb): symbolic of a flicking movement, similar to **DAB**[1].

Daphne /'dafni/ Greek Mythology a nymph who was turned into a laurel bush to save her from the amorous pursuit of Apollo.

daphne /'dafni/ ▶ **noun** a small Eurasian shrub with sweet-scented flowers and, typically, evergreen leaves.
• Genus *Daphne*, family Thymelaeaceae: several species, including mezereon and spurge laurel.
– ORIGIN late Middle English (denoting the laurel or bay tree): from Greek *daphnē*, from the name of the nymph **DAPHNE**.

daphnia /'dafnɪə/ ▶ **noun** (pl. same) a minute semi-transparent freshwater crustacean with long antennae and a prominent single eye, often used as food for aquarium fish. Also called **WATER FLEA**.
• Genus *Daphnia*, order Cladocera.
– ORIGIN modern Latin, from Greek *Daphnē*, from the name of the nymph **DAPHNE**.

Daphnis /'dafnɪs/ Greek Mythology a Sicilian shepherd who, according to one version of the legend, was struck with blindness for his infidelity to the nymph Echenaïs. He consoled himself with pastoral poetry, of which he was the inventor.

Da Ponte /dɑ: 'pɒnteɪ/, Lorenzo (1749–1838), Italian poet and librettist; born *Emmanuele Conegliano*. He became poet to the Court Opera in Vienna in 1784 and wrote the libretti for Mozart's *Marriage of Figaro* (1786), *Don Giovanni* (1787), and *Così fan tutte* (1790).

dapper ▶ **adjective** (typically of a man) neat and trim in dress, appearance, or bearing.
– DERIVATIVES **dapperly** adverb, **dapperness** noun.
– ORIGIN late Middle English: probably from a Middle Low German or Middle Dutch word meaning 'strong, stout'.

dapple ▶ **verb** [with obj.] (usu. **be dappled**) mark with spots or rounded patches: *the floor was dappled with pale moonlight* | [as adj. **dappled**] *the horse's dappled flank*.
▶ **noun** a patch or spot of colour or light.
■ an animal whose coat is marked with patches or spots.
– ORIGIN late 16th cent. (earlier as an adjective): perhaps related to Old Norse *depill* 'spot'.

dapple grey ▶ **adjective** (of a horse) grey or white with darker ring-like markings.
▶ **noun** a horse of this type.

Dapsang /dʌp'sʌŋ/ another name for **K2**.

dapsone /'dapsəʊn/ ▶ **noun** [mass noun] Medicine a sulphur compound with bacteriostatic action, used chiefly in the treatment of leprosy.
• Alternative name: **bis(4-aminophenyl)sulphone**; chem. formula: $(H_2NC_6H_4)_2SO_2$.
– ORIGIN 1950s: from elements of its alternative systematic name *dipara-aminophenyl sulphone*.

Daqing /dɑ:'tʃɪŋ/ (also **Taching**) a major industrial city in NE China, in Heilongjiang province; pop. 996,800 (1990).

DAR ▶ **abbreviation for** Daughters of the American Revolution.

darbies /'dɑ:bɪz/ ▶ **plural noun** Brit. archaic, informal handcuffs.
– ORIGIN late 17th cent.: allusive use of *Father Darby's bands*, a rigid form of agreement which put debtors in the power of moneylenders, possibly from the name of a 16th-cent. usurer.

Darby and Joan ▶ **noun** often humorous, chiefly Brit. a devoted old married couple, living in placid domestic harmony.
– ORIGIN late 18th cent.: from a poem (1735) in the *Gentleman's Magazine*, which contained the lines 'Old Darby, with Joan by his side ... They're never happy asunder.'

Darby and Joan club ▶ **noun** Brit. a club for senior citizens.

Dard /dɑ:d/ ▶ **noun 1** a member of a group of peoples inhabiting eastern Afghanistan, northern Pakistan, and Kashmir.
2 [mass noun] the group of Indic languages spoken by these people, including Kashmiri.
▶ **adjective** of or relating to the Dards or their languages.
– DERIVATIVES **Dardic** noun & adjective.
– ORIGIN the name in Dard.

Dardanelles /ˌdɑ:də'nɛlz/ a narrow strait between Europe and Asiatic Turkey (called the Hellespont in classical times), linking the Sea of Marmara with the Aegean Sea. It is 60 km (38 miles) long. In 1915 it was the scene of an unsuccessful attack on Turkey by Allied troops (see **GALLIPOLI**).

dare ▶ **verb** (3rd sing. present usu. **dare** before an expressed or implied infinitive without **to**) **1** [as modal] [usu. with infinitive with or without **to**] [often with negative] have the courage to do something: *a story he dare not write down* | *she leaned forward as far as she dared*.
■ (**how dare you**) used to express indignation at something that someone has done: *how dare you talk to me like that!* ■ (**don't you dare**) used to order someone threateningly not to do something: *don't you dare touch me*.
2 [with obj. and infinitive] defy or challenge (someone) to do something: *she was daring him to disagree* | [with obj.] *swap with me, I dare you*.
3 [with obj.] poetic/literary take the risk of; brave: *few dared his wrath*.
▶ **noun** a challenge, especially to prove courage: *she ran across a main road* ***for a dare***.
– PHRASES **I dare say** (or **daresay**) used to indicate that one believes something is probable: *I dare say you've heard about her*.
– DERIVATIVES **darer** noun.
– ORIGIN Old English *durran*, of Germanic origin; related to Gothic *gadaursan*, from an Indo-European root shared by Greek *tharsein* and Sanskrit *dhṛṣ-* 'be bold'.

daredevil ▶ **noun** a reckless person who enjoys doing dangerous things.
▶ **adjective** [attrib.] reckless and daring.
– DERIVATIVES **daredevilry** noun.

Dar es Salaam /ˌdɑ:r ɛs sə'lɑ:m/ the chief port and former capital of Tanzania; pop. 1,360,850 (1988). It was founded in 1866 by the sultan of Zanzibar. Its Arabic name means 'haven of peace'.

Darfur /dɑ:'fʊə/ a region in the west of Sudan. Until 1874 it was an independent kingdom.

darg /dɑ:g/ ▶ **noun** dialect or Austral./NZ an allotted or fixed amount of work, such as a quota to be fulfilled in one day.
– ORIGIN late Middle English: alteration of northern English dialect *daywork* 'a day's work'.

dargah /'dɑ:gə/ ▶ **noun** the tomb or shrine of a Muslim holy man.
– ORIGIN from Urdu, from Persian.

Dari /'dɑ:ri:/ ▶ **noun** [mass noun] the form of Persian spoken in Afghanistan.

Darien /'dɛ:rɪən, 'dar-/ a sparsely populated province of eastern Panama. The name was formerly applied to the whole of the Isthmus of Panama.

Darien, Gulf of part of the Caribbean Sea between Panama and Colombia.

daring ▶ **adjective** (of a person or action) adventurous or audaciously bold: *a daring crime*.
■ causing outrage or surprise by being boldly unconventional: *a pretty girl in daring clothes*.
▶ **noun** [mass noun] adventurous courage.
– DERIVATIVES **daringly** adverb.

dariole /'darɪəʊl/ (also **dariole mould**) ▶ **noun** (in French cooking) a small, round metal mould in which an individual sweet or savoury dish is cooked and served.
– ORIGIN late Middle English: from Old French.

Darius I /də'rʌɪəs/ (c.550–486 BC), king of Persia 521–486 BC; known as **Darius the Great**. After a revolt by the Greek cities in Ionia (499–494 BC) he invaded Greece but was defeated at Marathon (490 BC).

Darjeeling[1] /dɑ:'dʒi:lɪŋ/ (also **Darjiling**) a hill station at an altitude of 2,150 m (7,054 ft) in West Bengal, NE India, near the Sikkim border; pop. 73,090 (1991).

Darjeeling[2] /dɑ:'dʒi:lɪŋ/ ▶ **noun** [mass noun] a high-quality tea grown in the mountainous regions of northern India.

dark ▶ **adjective 1** with little or no light: *it's too dark to see much*.
■ hidden from knowledge; mysterious: *a dark secret*. ■ (**darkest**) humorous (of a region) most remote, inaccessible, or uncivilized: *he lives somewhere in darkest Essex*. ■ archaic ignorant; unenlightened: *he is dark on certain points of scripture*. ■ (of a theatre) closed; not in use.
2 (of a colour or object) not reflecting much light; approaching black in shade: *dark green*.
■ (of someone's skin, hair, or eyes) brown or black in colour. ■ (of a person) having such skin, hair, or eyes. ■ figurative (of a sound or taste) having richness or depth: *a distinctive dark, sweet flavour*.
3 (of a period of time or situation) characterized by tragedy, unhappiness, or unpleasantness: *the dark days of the war*.
■ gloomily pessimistic: *a dark vision of the future*. ■ (of an expression) angry; threatening. ■ suggestive of or arising from evil characteristics or forces; sinister: *so many dark deeds had been committed*.
4 Phonetics denoting a velarized form of the sound of the letter *l* (as in *pull* in south-eastern English speech). Often contrasted with **CLEAR**.
▶ **noun 1** (**the dark**) the absence of light in a place: *Carolyn was sitting in the dark* | *he's scared of the dark*.
■ [mass noun] nightfall: *I'll be home before dark*.
2 a dark colour or shade, especially in a painting.
– PHRASES **the darkest hour is just before the dawn** proverb when things seem to be at their worst they are about to start improving. **in the dark** in a state of ignorance about something. **keep something dark** keep something secret from other people. **a shot** (or **stab**) **in the dark** an act whose outcome cannot be foreseen; a mere guess.
– DERIVATIVES **darkish** adjective, **darksome** adjective (poetic/literary).
– ORIGIN Old English *deorc*, of Germanic origin, probably distantly related to German *tarnen* 'conceal'.

dark adaptation ▶ **noun** [mass noun] the adjustment of the eye to low light intensities, involving reflex dilation of the pupil and activation of the rod cells in preference to the cone cells.
– DERIVATIVES **dark-adapted** adjective.

Dark Ages 1 the period in western Europe between the fall of the Roman Empire and the high Middle Ages, c.500–1100 AD, during which Germanic tribes swept through Europe and North Africa, often attacking and destroying towns and settlements. It was judged to have been a time of relative unenlightenment, though scholarship was kept alive in the monasteries and learning was encouraged at the courts of Charlemagne and Alfred the Great.
■ a period of supposed unenlightenment: ***the dark ages** of racism*. ■ (**the dark ages**) humorous or derogatory an obscure or little-regarded period in the past, especially as characterizing an outdated attitude or practice: *the judge is living in the dark ages*.
2 Archaeology a period in Greece and the Aegean from the end of the Bronze Age until the beginning of the historical period. There was no building of palaces and fortresses, and the art of writing was apparently lost.

dark chocolate ▶ **noun** another term for **PLAIN CHOCOLATE**.

Dark Continent historical a name given to Africa at a time when it was little known to Europeans.

dark current ▶ **noun** the residual electric current flowing in a photoelectric device when there is no incident illumination.

darken ▶ **verb 1** make or become dark or darker: [no obj.] *the sky was darkening rapidly* | [with obj.] *darken the eyebrows with black powder* | [as adj. **darkened**] *a darkened room*.
■ [with obj.] figurative (of an unpleasant event or state of affairs) cast a shadow over something; spoil: *the abuse darkened the rest of their lives*.
2 make or become gloomy, angry, or unhappy: [no obj.] *his mood darkened*.
■ [no obj.] (of someone's eyes or expression) show anger or another strong negative emotion. ■ [with obj.] (of such an emotion) show in (someone's eyes or expression): *misery darkened her gaze*.
– PHRASES **never darken someone's door** keep away from someone's home permanently.
– DERIVATIVES **darkener** noun.

dark-field microscopy ▶ **noun** [mass noun] a type

of light microscopy which produces brightly illuminated objects on a dark background.

dark glasses ▶ **plural noun** glasses with tinted lenses, worn to protect or conceal a person's eyes.

Darkhan /dɑːˈkɑːn/ an industrial and mining city in northern Mongolia, established in 1961; pop. 80,100 (1990).

dark horse ▶ **noun** a person about whom little is known, especially someone whose abilities or potential for success is concealed.
– ORIGIN early 19th cent.: originally racing slang.

darkie (also **darky**) ▶ **noun** (pl. **-ies**) offensive, informal a person with black or dark skin.

dark line ▶ **noun** Physics an absorption line in an electromagnetic spectrum, appearing as a black line at visible wavelengths.

darkling ▶ **adjective** poetic/literary of or relating to growing darkness: *the darkling sky.*

darkling beetle ▶ **noun** a dark-coloured nocturnal beetle, typically with reduced or absent wings.
• Family Tenebrionidae: numerous genera and species, including the flour, meal, and churchyard beetles, and many desert species.

darkly ▶ **adverb 1** in a threatening, mysterious, or slightly ominous way.
■ in a depressing or pessimistic way: *I wondered darkly if I was wasting my time.*
2 with a dark colour: *a figure silhouetted darkly against the trees.*

dark matter ▶ **noun** [mass noun] Astronomy (in some cosmological theories) non-luminous material which is postulated to exist in space and which could take either of two forms: weakly interacting particles (**cold dark matter**) or high-energy randomly moving particles created soon after the big bang (**hot dark matter**).

dark nebula ▶ **noun** Astronomy a non-luminous nebula of dust and gas which is observable because it obscures light from other sources.

darkness ▶ **noun** [mass noun] **1** the partial or total absence of light: *the office was in darkness.*
■ night: *they began to make camp before darkness fell.* ■ the quality of being dark in colour: *the darkness of his jacket.*
2 wickedness or evil: *the forces of darkness.*
■ unhappiness, distress, or gloom: *moments of darkness were rare.* ■ secrecy or mystery: *they drew a veil of darkness across the proceedings.* ■ lack of spiritual or intellectual enlightenment; ignorance: *his accomplishments shone in a world of darkness.*

dark night of the soul (also **dark night**) ▶ **noun** a period of spiritual aridity suffered by a mystic in which all sense of consolation is removed.
– ORIGIN mid 19th cent.: translating Spanish *noche oscura* (St John of the Cross).

dark reaction ▶ **noun** Biochemistry the cycle of reactions (the Calvin cycle) which occurs in the second phase of photosynthesis and does not require the presence of light. It involves the fixation of carbon dioxide and its reduction to carbohydrate and the dissociation of water, using chemical energy stored in ATP.

darkroom ▶ **noun** a room for developing photographs, in which normal light is excluded.

dark star ▶ **noun** Astronomy a starlike object which emits little or no visible light. Its existence is inferred from other evidence, such as the eclipsing of other stars.

darky ▶ **noun** variant spelling of **DARKIE**.

Darling, Grace (1815–42), English heroine. The daughter of a lighthouse keeper on the Farne Islands off the coast of Northumberland, she came to fame in September 1838 when she and her father rowed through a storm to rescue the survivors of the wrecked ship *Forfarshire*.

darling ▶ **noun** used as an affectionate form of address to a beloved person: *good night, my darling.*
■ a lovable or endearing person: *he's such a darling.* ■ a person who is particularly popular with a certain group: *he is the darling of Labour's left wing.*
▶ **adjective** [attrib.] beloved: *his darling wife.*
■ (especially in affected use) pretty; charming: *a darling little pillbox hat.*
– PHRASES **be a darling** used as a friendly or encouraging preface to a request: *be a darling and don't mention I'm here.*
– ORIGIN Old English *dēorling* (see **DEAR**, **-LING**).

Darling River a river of SE Australia, flowing 2,757 km (1,712 miles) in a generally south-westward course to join the Murray River.

Darlington an industrial town in NE England; pop. 96,700 (1991).

Darmstadt /ˈdɑːmʃtat, German ˈdarmʃtat/ an industrial town in Hesse, western Germany; pop. 140,040 (1991).

darn[1] ▶ **verb** [with obj.] mend (knitted material or a hole in this) by interweaving yarn across the hole with a needle: *I don't expect you to darn my socks.*
■ embroider (material) with a large running stitch.
▶ **noun** a place in a garment that has been mended in such a way.
– ORIGIN early 17th cent.: perhaps from dialect *dern* 'to hide', which is from Old English *diernan*, of West Germanic origin; compare with Middle Dutch *dernen* 'stop holes in (a dyke)'.

darn[2] (US also **durn**) ▶ **verb**, **adjective**, & **exclamation** informal euphemism for **DAMN**: [as verb] *darn it all, Poppa* | [as adj.] *he was a darn sight younger than Jill.*

darned (US also **durned**) ▶ **adjective** informal, chiefly N. Amer. euphemism for **DAMNED**: *you have to work a darned sight harder* | [as submodifier] *a darned expensive guitar.*
– DERIVATIVES **darnedest** adjective.

darnel /ˈdɑːn(ə)l/ ▶ **noun** a Eurasian ryegrass.
• Genus *Lolium*, family Gramineae: several species, in particular *L. temulentum*.
– ORIGIN Middle English: of unknown origin; apparently related to French (Walloon dialect) *darnelle*.

darner ▶ **noun 1** a darning needle.
2 N. Amer. a large slender-bodied dragonfly. Also called **DARNING NEEDLE**, **DEVIL'S DARNING NEEDLE**. [ORIGIN: said to be so named because of a former belief that the dragonfly sews up the lips and eyelids of people sleeping.]
• Family Aeshnidae: several genera.

darning ▶ **noun** [mass noun] the skill or activity of darning.
■ articles being darned or needing to be darned.

darning mushroom (also **darning egg**) ▶ **noun** a mushroom-shaped (or egg-shaped) piece of wood or other smooth hard material used to stretch and support material being darned.

darning needle ▶ **noun** a long sewing needle with a large eye, used in darning.
■ N. Amer. another term for **DARNER** (in sense 2).

Darnley /ˈdɑːnli/, Henry Stewart (or Stuart), Lord (1545–67), Scottish nobleman, second husband of Mary, Queen of Scots and father of James I of England. He was implicated in the murder of his wife's secretary Rizzio in 1566, and was later killed in a mysterious gunpowder explosion in Edinburgh.

darshan /ˈdɑːʃən/ ▶ **noun** Hinduism an opportunity or occasion of seeing a holy person or the image of a deity.
– ORIGIN via Hindi from Sanskrit *darśana* 'sight or seeing'.

Dart, Raymond Arthur (1893–1988), Australian-born South African anthropologist and anatomist. In 1925 he found the first specimen of a hominid for which he coined the genus name *Australopithecus*.

dart ▶ **noun 1** a small pointed missile that can be thrown or fired.
■ a small pointed missile with a feather or plastic flight, used in the game of darts. ■ Zoology a dart-like calcareous organ of a snail forming part of the reproductive system, exchanged during copulation. ■ figurative a sudden, intense pang of a particular emotion: *a dart of panic.* ■ an act of running somewhere suddenly and rapidly: *the cat **made a dart** for the door.*
2 a tapered tuck stitched in a garment in order to shape it.
▶ **verb** [no obj., with adverbial of direction] move or run somewhere suddenly or rapidly: *she darted across the street.*
■ [with obj. and adverbial of direction] cast (a look or one's eyes) suddenly and rapidly in a particular direction: *she darted a glance across the table.* ■ [with obj.] archaic throw (a missile). ■ [with obj.] shoot (an animal) with a dart, typically in order to administer a drug.
– ORIGIN Middle English: from Old French, accusative of *darz*, *dars*, from a West Germanic word meaning 'spear, lance'.

dartboard ▶ **noun** a circular board marked with numbered segments, used as a target in the game of darts.

darter ▶ **noun 1** a long-necked fish-eating bird related to the cormorants, typically found in fresh water. Darters spear fish with their long pointed bill and frequently swim submerged to the neck. Also called **ANHINGA**, **SNAKEBIRD**.
• Family Anhingidae and genus *Anhinga*: four species.
2 a small North American freshwater fish, the male of which may develop bright coloration during the breeding season.
• Genera *Etheostoma* and *Percina*, family Percidae: numerous species.
3 (also **darter dragonfly**) a broad-bodied dragonfly that spends long periods on a perch, from which it darts out to grab prey. Called **SKIMMER** in North America.
• Libellulidae and related families: several genera.

d

Dartford warbler /ˈdɑːtfəd/ ▶ **noun** a long-tailed non-migratory warbler with grey upper parts and purplish-brown underparts, found in western Europe and North Africa.
• *Sylvia undata*, family Sylviidae.
– ORIGIN late 18th cent.: from *Dartford* in Kent, England, where the bird was first seen.

Dartmoor /ˈdɑːtmɔː, -mʊə/ a moorland district in Devon that was a royal forest in Saxon times, now a national park.

Dartmoor pony ▶ **noun** a pony of a small hardy breed with a long shaggy coat in winter.

Dartmouth /ˈdɑːtməθ/ a port in Devon; pop. 6,210 (1981). It is the site of the Royal Naval College.

darts ▶ **plural noun** [usu. treated as sing.] an indoor game in which small pointed missiles with feather or plastic flights are thrown at a circular target marked with numbers in order to score points.

Darwin[1] /ˈdɑːwɪn/ the capital of Northern Territory, Australia; pop. 73,300 (1990).

Darwin[2] /ˈdɑːwɪn/, Charles (Robert) (1809–82), English natural historian and geologist, proponent of the theory of evolution by natural selection. Darwin was the naturalist on HMS *Beagle* for her voyage around the southern hemisphere (1831–6), during which he collected the material which became the basis for his ideas on natural selection. His works *On the Origin of Species* (1859) and *The Descent of Man* (1871) had a fundamental effect on our concepts of nature and humanity's place within it.

Darwin[3] /ˈdɑːwɪn/, Erasmus (1731–1802), English physician, scientist, inventor, and poet. Darwin is chiefly remembered for his scientific and technical writing, much of which appeared in the form of long poems. These include *Zoonomia* (1794–96), which proposed a Lamarckian view of evolution. He was the grandfather of Charles Darwin and Francis Galton.

Darwinian ▶ **adjective** of or relating to Darwinism.
▶ **noun** an adherent of Darwinism.

Darwinism ▶ **noun** [mass noun] the theory of the evolution of species by natural selection advanced by Charles Darwin.

> Darwin argued that since offspring tend to vary slightly from their parents, mutations which make an organism better adapted to its environment will be encouraged and developed by the pressures of natural selection, leading to the evolution of new species differing widely from one another and from their common ancestors. Darwinism was later developed by the findings of Mendelian genetics (see **NEO-DARWINIAN**).

– DERIVATIVES **Darwinist** noun & adjective.

Darwin's finches ▶ **plural noun** a group of songbirds related to the buntings and found on the Galapagos Islands, discovered by Charles Darwin and used by him to illustrate his theory of natural selection. They are believed to have evolved from a common ancestor and have developed a variety of bills to suit various modes of life. Also called **GALAPAGOS FINCHES**.
• Family Emberizidae (subfamily Emberizinae): four to six genera, especially *Geospiza* (the **ground finches**) and *Camarhynchus* (the **tree finches**).

Dasehra /ˈdaʃərə/ ▶ **noun** variant spelling of **DUSSEHRA**.

Dasein /ˈdɑːzʌɪn/ ▶ **noun** [mass noun] Philosophy (in Hegelianism), existence or determinate being; (in existentialism) human existence.
– ORIGIN mid 19th cent.: German, from *dasein* 'exist', from *da* 'there' + *sein* 'be'.

dash ▶ **verb 1** [no obj., with adverbial of direction] run or

travel somewhere in a great hurry: *I dashed into the garden | I must dash, I'm late.*
2 [with obj. and adverbial of direction] strike or fling (something) somewhere with great force, especially so as to have a destructive effect; hurl: *the ship was dashed upon the rocks.*
■ [no obj., with adverbial of direction] strike forcefully against something: *a gust of rain dashed against the bricks.* ■ [with obj.] destroy or frustrate (a person's hopes or expectations): *the budget dashed hopes of an increase in funding.* ■ [with obj.] cause (someone) to lose confidence; dispirit: *I won't tell Stuart—I think he'd be dashed.*
▶ **exclamation** Brit. informal, dated used to express mild annoyance: *'Dash it all, I am in charge.'*
▶ **noun 1** [in sing.] an act of running somewhere suddenly and hastily: *she **made a dash for** the door.*
■ a journey or period of time characterized by urgency or eager haste: *a 20-mile dash to the airport.* ■ chiefly N. Amer. a short fast race run in one heat; a sprint.
2 a small quantity of a particular substance, especially a liquid, added to something else: *whisky with **a dash of** soda.*
■ figurative a small amount of a particular quality adding piquancy or distinctiveness to something else: *a casual atmosphere with a dash of sophistication.*
3 a horizontal stroke in writing or printing to mark a pause or break in sense or to represent omitted letters or words.
■ the longer signal of the two used in Morse code. Compare with **DOT**[1]. ■ Music a short vertical mark placed above or beneath a note to indicate that it is to be performed in a very staccato manner.
4 [mass noun] impetuous or flamboyant vigour and confidence; panache.
5 short for **DASHBOARD**.
– ORIGIN Middle English (in the sense 'strike forcibly against'): probably symbolic of forceful movement and related to Swedish and Danish *daska*.
▶ **dash something off** write something hurriedly and without much premeditation.

dashboard ▶ **noun** the panel facing the driver of a vehicle or the pilot of an aircraft, containing instruments and controls.
■ historical a board of wood or leather in front of a carriage, to keep out mud.

dashed ▶ **adjective** [attrib.] **1** Brit. informal, dated used for emphasis: *it's a dashed shame | [as submodifier] she was dashed rude.*
2 (of a line on a piece of paper) composed of dashes.

dasheen /daˈʃiːn/ ▶ **noun** another term for **TARO**.
– ORIGIN late 19th cent. (originally West Indian): of unknown origin.

dasher ▶ **noun 1** informal a person who dresses or acts flamboyantly or stylishly.
2 a plunger for agitating cream in a churn.

dashiki /ˈdɑːʃɪki/ ▶ **noun** (pl. **dashikis**) a loose brightly coloured shirt or tunic, originally from West Africa.
– ORIGIN from Yoruba or Hausa.

dashing ▶ **adjective** (of a man) attractive in a romantic, adventurous way.
■ stylish or fashionable: *a dashing S-type Jaguar.*
– DERIVATIVES **dashingly** adverb, **dashingness** noun.

dashpot ▶ **noun** a device for damping shock or vibration.

dassie /ˈdasi/ ▶ **noun** (pl. **-ies**) **1** a hyrax, especially the rock hyrax of southern Africa. [ORIGIN: late 18th cent.: from Afrikaans, from South African Dutch *dasje*, diminutive of Dutch *das* 'badger'.]
• Family Procaviidae, in particular *Procavia capensis*.
2 S. African a silvery marine fish with dark fins and a black spot on the tail. It lives around the coasts of Africa and the Mediterranean. [ORIGIN: late 19th cent.: said to have been named by early Dutch colonists, who saw a resemblance (in its habit of frequenting rocks, or from its shy nature, etc.) with the rock hyrax.]
• *Diplodus sargus*, family Sparidae.

dastard /ˈdastəd, ˈdɑː-/ ▶ **noun** dated or humorous a dishonourable or despicable person.
– ORIGIN late Middle English (in the sense 'stupid person'): probably from *dazed*, influenced by *dotard* and *bastard*.

dastardly ▶ **adjective** dated or humorous wicked and cruel: *pirates and their dastardly deeds.*
– DERIVATIVES **dastardliness** noun.
– ORIGIN mid 16th cent. (in the sense 'dull or stupid'): from **DASTARD** in the obsolete sense 'base coward'.

dastur /dəˈstʊə/ (also **dastoor** or **dustoor**) ▶ **noun** Indian a chief priest of the Parsees.
– ORIGIN Persian, from Old Persian *dastōbār*, denoting a Zoroastrian high priest.

dasyure /ˈdasɪjʊə/ ▶ **noun** another term for **QUOLL**.
– ORIGIN mid 19th cent.: from French, from modern Latin *dasyurus*, from Greek *dasus* 'rough, hairy' + *oura* 'tail'.

DAT ▶ **abbreviation for** digital audiotape.

data /ˈdeɪtə/ ▶ **noun** [mass noun] facts and statistics collected together for reference or analysis. See also **DATUM**.
■ the quantities, characters, or symbols on which operations are performed by a computer, which may be stored and transmitted in the form of electrical signals and recorded on magnetic, optical, or mechanical recording media. ■ Philosophy things known or assumed as facts, making the basis of reasoning or calculation.
– ORIGIN mid 17th cent. (as a term in philosophy): from Latin, plural of **DATUM**.

USAGE In Latin, **data** is the plural of **datum** and, historically and in specialized scientific fields, it is also treated as a plural in English, taking a plural verb, as in *the **data were** collected and classified.* In modern non-scientific use, however, despite the complaints of traditionalists, it is often not treated as a plural. Instead, it is treated as a mass noun, similar to a word like **information**, which cannot normally have a plural and which takes a singular verb. Sentences such as ***data was*** (as well as ***data were***) *collected over a number of years* are now widely accepted in standard English.

databank ▶ **noun** Computing a large repository of data on a particular topic, sometimes formed from more than one database, and accessible by many users.

database ▶ **noun** a structured set of data held in a computer, especially one that is accessible in various ways.

database management system (abbrev.: **DBMS**) ▶ **noun** Computing software that handles the storage, retrieval, and updating of data in a computer system.

datable (also **dateable**) ▶ **adjective** able to be dated to a particular time.

data capture ▶ **noun** [mass noun] Computing the action or process of gathering data from an automatic device, control system, or sensor.

datacomms (also **datacoms**) ▶ **plural noun** data communications.
– ORIGIN late 20th cent.: abbreviation.

data dictionary ▶ **noun** Computing a set of information describing the contents, format, and structure of a database and the relationship between its elements, used to control access to and manipulation of the database.

dataglove ▶ **noun** Computing a device worn like a glove, which allows the manual manipulation of images in virtual reality.

data mining ▶ **noun** [mass noun] Computing the practice of examining large pre-existing databases in order to generate new information.

data processing ▶ **noun** [mass noun] a series of operations on data, especially by a computer, to retrieve, transform, or classify information.
– DERIVATIVES **data processor** noun.

data protection ▶ **noun** [mass noun] Brit. legal control over access to and use of data stored in computers.

data set ▶ **noun** Computing a collection of related sets of information that is composed of separate elements but can be manipulated as a unit by a computer.

data terminal ▶ **noun** Computing a terminal at which a person can enter data into a computer-based system or receive data from one.

data type ▶ **noun** Computing a particular kind of data item, as defined by the values it can take, the programming language used, or the operations that can be performed on it.

data warehouse ▶ **noun** Computing a large store of data accumulated from a wide range of sources within a company and used to guide management decisions.
– DERIVATIVES **data warehousing** noun.

datcha /ˈdatʃə/ ▶ **noun** variant spelling of **DACHA**.

date[1] ▶ **noun 1** the day of the month or year as specified by a number: *what's the date today? | they've set a date for the wedding.*
■ a particular day or year when a given event occurred or will occur: *1066 is the most famous date in English history.* ■ (**dates**) the years of a particular person's birth and death or of the beginning and end of a particular period or event. ■ the period of time to which an artefact or structure belongs: *the church is the largest of its date.* ■ a written, printed, or stamped statement on a document or as an inscription giving the day, month, and year of writing, publication, or manufacture: *these Roman coins bear an explicit date.*
2 informal a social or romantic appointment or engagement.
■ a person with whom one has such an engagement: *my date isn't going to show, it seems.* ■ a musical or theatrical engagement or performance, especially as part of a tour.
▶ **verb** [with obj.] **1** establish or ascertain the date of (an object or event): *they **date** the paintings **to** 1460–70.*
■ mark with a date: *sign and date the document.* ■ [no obj.] originate at a particular time; have existed since: *the controversy **dates back to** 1986.*
2 indicate or expose as being old-fashioned: *jazzy—does that word date me?*
■ [no obj.] seem old-fashioned: *the coat may be pricey but it will never date* | [as adj. **dated**] *a dated expression.*
3 informal, chiefly N. Amer. go out with (someone in whom one is romantically or sexually interested): *my sister's pretty judgemental about the girls I date* | [no obj.] *they have been dating for more than a year.*
– PHRASES **to date** until now: *their finest work to date.*
– ORIGIN Middle English: via Old French from medieval Latin *data*, feminine past participle of *dare* 'give'; from the Latin formula used in dating letters, *data (epistola)* '(letter) given or delivered', to record a particular time or place.

date[2] ▶ **noun 1** a sweet, dark brown, oval fruit containing a hard stone, usually eaten dried.
2 (also **date palm**) a tall palm tree which bears clusters of this fruit, native to western Asia and North Africa.
• *Phoenix dactylifera*, family Palmae.
– ORIGIN Middle English: from Old French, via Latin from Greek *daktulos* 'finger' (because of the finger-like shape of its leaves).

dateable ▶ **adjective** variant spelling of **DATABLE**.

datebook ▶ **noun** N. Amer. an engagement diary.

dateless ▶ **adjective** not clearly belonging to any particular period, therefore not likely to go out of date: *a dateless dress.*
■ (of a document or stamp) having no date mark.

Date Line (also **International Date Line**) an imaginary North–South line through the Pacific Ocean, adopted in 1884, to the east of which the date is a day earlier than it is to the west. It lies chiefly along the meridian furthest from Greenwich (i.e. longitude 180°), with diversions to pass around some island groups.

date line ▶ **noun** a line at the head of a dispatch or special article in a newspaper showing the date and place of writing.

date mussel ▶ **noun** a brown, cigar-shaped bivalve mollusc which bores into limestone and coral.
• Genus *Lithophaga*, family Mytilidae.

date plum ▶ **noun** another term for **PERSIMMON**.

date rape ▶ **noun** [mass noun] rape by a person that the victim is dating, or with whom he or she has gone on a date.

date stamp ▶ **noun** a stamped mark indicating a date, typically used on food packaging or posted envelopes.
■ an adjustable stamp used to make such a mark.
▶ **verb** (**date-stamp**) [with obj.] mark (something) with a date stamp.

dating agency ▶ **noun** a service which arranges introductions for people seeking romantic partners or friends with similar interests.

dative /ˈdeɪtɪv/ Grammar ▶ **adjective** (in Latin, Greek, German, and some other languages) denoting a case of nouns and pronouns, and words in grammatical agreement with them, indicating an indirect object or recipient.
▶ **noun** a noun or other word of this type.
■ (**the dative**) the dative case.
– ORIGIN late Middle English: from Latin (*casus*) *dativus* '(case) of giving', from *dat-* 'given', from the verb *dare*.

Datong /dɑːˈtʊŋ/ a city in northern China in Shanxi province; pop. 1,090,000 (1990).

Datuk /'dɑːtək/ ▶ noun (in Malaysia) a title of respect denoting membership of a high order of chivalry.
– ORIGIN Malay.

datum /'deɪtəm/ ▶ noun (pl. **data**) See also **DATA**. **1** a piece of information.
■ an assumption or premise from which inferences may be drawn. See **SENSE DATUM**.
2 a fixed starting point of a scale or operation.
■ short for **ORDNANCE DATUM**.
– ORIGIN mid 18th cent.: from Latin, literally 'something given', neuter past participle of *dare* 'give'.

datum line (also **datum level**) ▶ noun a standard of comparison or point of reference.
■ Surveying an assumed surface used as a reference for the measurement of heights and depths. ■ a line to which dimensions are referred on engineering drawings, and from which measurements are calculated.

datura /də'tjʊərə/ ▶ noun a shrubby annual plant with large erect trumpet-shaped flowers, native to southern North America. They contain toxic or narcotic alkaloids and are used as hallucinogens by some American Indian peoples. See also **ANGEL'S TRUMPET**.
● Genus *Datura*, family Solanaceae: several species, including the thorn apple or jimson weed.
– ORIGIN modern Latin, from Hindi *dhatūrā*.

daub /dɔːb/ ▶ verb [with obj.] coat or smear (a surface) with a thick or sticky substance in a carelessly rough or liberal way: *she daubed her face with night cream.*
■ spread (a thick or sticky substance) on a surface in such a way: *a canvas with paint daubed on it.* ■ paint (words or drawings) on a surface in such a way: *they daubed graffiti on the walls.*
▶ noun **1** [mass noun] plaster, clay, or another substance used for coating a surface, especially when mixed with straw and applied to laths or wattles to form a wall: *wattle and daub.*
■ a patch or smear of a thick or sticky substance: *a daub of paint.*
2 a painting executed without much skill.
– ORIGIN late Middle English: from Old French *dauber*, from Latin *dealbare* 'whiten, whitewash', based on *albus* 'white'.

daube /dəʊb/ ▶ noun a stew of meat, typically beef, braised slowly in wine.
– PHRASES **en daube** (of meat) cooked in this way.
– ORIGIN French; compare with Italian *addobbo* 'seasoning'.

Daubenton's bat /'dɔːbəntənz, dɔː'bɛntənz/ ▶ noun a small brown myotis bat that typically flies low over water, found throughout Eurasia.
● *Myotis daubentonii*, family Vespertilionidae.
– ORIGIN late 19th cent.: named after Louis-Jean-Marie *Daubenton* (1716–1800), French naturalist and physician.

dauber ▶ noun a crude or inartistic painter.
■ an implement used for daubing.

Daubigny /'dəʊbɪnji, French dobiɲi/, Charles François (1817–78), French landscape painter. He was a member of the Barbizon School and is often regarded as a linking figure between this group and the Impressionists.

Daudet /'dəʊdeɪ, French dodɛ/, Alphonse (1840–97), French novelist and dramatist. He is best known for his sketches of life in his native Provence, particularly the *Lettres de mon moulin* (1869).

daughter ▶ noun a girl or woman in relation to either or both of her parents.
■ a female offspring of an animal. ■ a female descendant: *we are the sons and daughters of Adam.* ■ a woman considered as the product of a particular person, influence, or environment: *she was a daughter of the vicarage in manner and appearance.* ■ archaic used as a term of affectionate address to a woman or girl, typically by an older person. ■ poetic/literary a thing personified as a daughter in relation to its origin or source: *Italian, the eldest daughter of ancient Latin.* ■ Physics a nuclide formed by the radioactive decay of another.
– DERIVATIVES **daughterhood** noun, **daughterly** adjective.
– ORIGIN Old English *dohtor*, of Germanic origin; related to Dutch *dochter* and German *Tochter*, from an Indo-European root shared by Greek *thugatēr*.

daughterboard ▶ noun Electronics a small printed circuit board that attaches to a larger one.

daughter cell ▶ noun Biology a cell formed by the division or budding of another.

daughter-in-law ▶ noun (pl. **daughters-in-law**) the wife of one's son.

Daughters of the American Revolution (abbrev.: **DAR**) (in the US) a patriotic society whose aims include encouraging education and the study of US history and which tends to be politically conservative. Membership is limited to female descendants of those who aided the cause of independence.

Daumier /'dəʊmɪeɪ, French domje/, Honoré (1808–78), French painter and lithographer. From the 1830s he worked as a cartoonist for periodicals such as *Charivari*, where he produced lithographs satirizing French society and politics.

daunorubicin /ˌdɔːnə(ʊ)'ruːbɪsɪn/ ▶ noun [mass noun] Medicine a synthetic antibiotic that interferes with DNA synthesis and is used in the treatment of acute leukaemia and other cancers.
– ORIGIN 1960s: from *Daunia*, in southern Italy where it was developed, + *-rubi-* 'red' + **-MYCIN**.

daunt /dɔːnt/ ▶ verb [with obj.] (usu. **be daunted**) make (someone) feel intimidated or apprehensive: *some people are daunted by technology.*
– PHRASES **nothing daunted** without having been made fearful or apprehensive: *nothing daunted, the committee set to work.*
– ORIGIN Middle English: from Old French *danter*, from Latin *domitare*, frequentative of *domare* 'to tame'.

daunting ▶ adjective seeming difficult to deal with in prospect; intimidating: *a daunting task.*
– DERIVATIVES **dauntingly** adverb.

dauntless ▶ adjective showing fearlessness and determination: *dauntless bravery.*
– DERIVATIVES **dauntlessly** adverb, **dauntlessness** noun.

dauphin /'dɔːfɪn, 'dəʊfã, French dofɛ̃/ ▶ noun historical the eldest son of the King of France.
– ORIGIN French, from the family name of the lords of the Dauphiné (first used in this way in the 14th cent.), ultimately a nickname meaning 'dolphin'.

Dauphiné /'dəʊfɪneɪ, French dofine/ a region and former province of SE France. Its capital was Grenoble.

dauphinois /ˌdəʊfɪ'nwʌ/ (also **dauphinoise** /-'nwʌz/) ▶ adjective (of potatoes or other vegetables) sliced and cooked in milk, typically with a topping of cheese.
– ORIGIN French, 'from the province of Dauphiné'.

Davao /daː'vaːəʊ/ a seaport in the southern Philippines, on the island of Mindanao; pop. 850,000 (1990). Founded in 1849, it is the largest city on the island and the third largest city in the Philippines.

daven /'dɑːv(ə)n/ ▶ verb (**davened, davening**) [no obj.] (in Judaism) recite the prescribed liturgical prayers.
– ORIGIN Yiddish.

davenport /'dav(ə)npɔːt/ ▶ noun **1** Brit. an ornamental writing desk with drawers and a sloping surface for writing. [ORIGIN: probably named after Captain *Davenport*, for whom early examples of this type of desk were made in the late 18th cent.]
2 N. Amer. a large heavily upholstered sofa, typically able to be converted into a bed. [ORIGIN: perhaps from a manufacturer's name.]

David[1] /'deɪvɪd/ (died c.962 BC), king of Judah and Israel c.1000–c.962 BC. In the biblical account he was the youngest son of Jesse who killed the Philistine Goliath and, on Saul's death, became king, making Jerusalem his capital. He is traditionally regarded as the author of the Psalms, though this has been disputed.

David[2] /'deɪvɪd/ the name of two kings of Scotland:
■ David I (c.1084–1153), sixth son of Malcolm III, reigned 1124–53. In 1136 he invaded England in support of his niece Matilda's claim to the throne, but was defeated at the Battle of the Standard in 1138.
■ David II (1324–71), son of Robert the Bruce, reigned 1329–71. His reign witnessed a renewal of fighting with England, with Edward III supporting the pretender Edward de Baliol. His death without issue left the throne to the Stuarts.

David[3] /'deɪvɪd/, Elizabeth (1913–92), British cookery writer. She played a leading role in introducing

David[4] /da'viːd, French david/, Jacques-Louis (1748–1825), French painter, famous for neoclassical paintings such as *The Oath of the Horatii* (1784). He became actively involved in the French Revolution, voting for the death of Louis XVI and supporting Robespierre.

David, St (6th century), Welsh monk; Welsh name **Dewi**. Since the 12th century he has been regarded as the patron saint of Wales. Little is known of his life, but it is generally accepted that he transferred the centre of Welsh ecclesiastical administration from Caerleon to Mynyw (now St David's). Feast day, 1 March.

Davies[1], Sir Peter Maxwell (b.1934), English composer and conductor, influenced particularly by serialism and early English music. Notable works: *Eight Songs for a Mad King* (1969) and *Taverner* (1970).

Davies[2], W. H. (1871–1940), English poet; full name *William Henry Davies*. He emigrated to the US and lived as a vagrant and labourer, writing *The Autobiography of a Super-Tramp* (1908) about his experiences.

Davies[3], (William) Robertson (1913–95), Canadian novelist, dramatist, and journalist. He won international recognition with his Deptford trilogy of novels, comprising *Fifth Business* (1970), *The Manticore* (1972), and *World of Wonders* (1975).

da Vinci, Leonardo, see **LEONARDO DA VINCI**.

Davis[1], Bette (1908–89), American actress; born *Ruth Elizabeth Davis*. She established her Hollywood career playing a number of strong, independent female characters in such films as *Dangerous* (1935). Her flair for suggesting the macabre and menacing emerged in later films, such as *Whatever Happened to Baby Jane?* (1962).

Davis[2], the name of two English billiards and snooker players. **Joe** (1901–78) held the world championship from 1927 until his retirement in 1946. He was also world billiards champion 1928–32. His brother **Fred** (1913–98) was world snooker champion (1948–9; 1951–6) and world billiards champion (1980).

Davis[3], Miles (Dewey) (1926–91), American jazz trumpeter, composer, and bandleader. In the 1950s he played and recorded arrangements in a new style which became known as 'cool' jazz, heard on albums such as *Kind of Blue* (1959). In the 1960s he pioneered the fusion of jazz and rock.

Davis[4], Steve (b.1957), English snooker player. He was UK Professional Champion (1980–1; 1984–7) and World Professional Champion (1981; 1983–4; 1987–9).

Davis Cup an annual tennis championship for men, first held in 1900, between teams from different countries.
– ORIGIN named after Dwight F. *Davis* (1879–1945), the American doubles champion who donated the trophy.

Davisson /'deɪvɪs(ə)n/, Clinton Joseph (1881–1958), American physicist. Davisson, together with L. H. Germer (1896–1971), discovered electron diffraction, thus confirming de Broglie's theory of the wave nature of electrons. Nobel Prize for Physics (1937).

Davis Strait a sea passage 645 km (400 miles) long separating Greenland from Baffin Island and connecting Baffin Bay with the Atlantic Ocean.
– ORIGIN named after John *Davis* (1550–1605), the English explorer who sailed through it in 1587.

davit /'davɪt, 'deɪv-/ ▶ noun a small crane on board a ship, especially one of a pair for suspending or lowering a lifeboat.
– ORIGIN late 15th cent.: from Old French *daviot*, diminutive of *david*, denoting a kind of carpenter's tool.

Davos /daː'vɒs/ a resort and winter-sports centre in eastern Switzerland; pop. 10,500 (1990).

Davy, Sir Humphry (1778–1829), English chemist, a pioneer of electrochemistry. He discovered nitrous oxide (laughing gas) and the elements sodium, potassium, magnesium, calcium, strontium, and barium. He also identified and named the element chlorine, determined the properties of iodine, and demonstrated that diamond was a form of carbon. In 1815 he invented the miner's safety lamp.

Davy Jones's locker ▶ **noun** informal the bottom of the sea, especially regarded as the grave of those drowned at sea.
– ORIGIN extension of early 18th-cent. nautical slang *Davy Jones*, denoting the evil spirit of the sea.

Davy lamp ▶ **noun** a miner's portable safety lamp with the flame enclosed by wire gauze to reduce the risk of an explosion of gas.

daw ▶ **noun** another term for **JACKDAW**.
– ORIGIN late Middle English: of Germanic origin; related to German *Dohle*.

d

dawdle ▶ **verb** [no obj.] waste time; be slow: *I couldn't dawdle over my coffee any longer.*
■ [with adverbial of direction] move slowly and idly in a particular direction: *Ruth dawdled back through the wood.*
– DERIVATIVES **dawdler** noun.
– ORIGIN mid 17th cent.: related to dialect *daddle*, *doddle* 'dally'.

Dawkins, Richard (b.1941), English biologist. Dawkins's book *The Selfish Gene* (1976) did much to popularize the theory of sociobiology. In *The Blind Watchmaker* (1986) Dawkins discussed evolution by natural selection and suggested that the theory could answer the fundamental question of why life exists.

dawn ▶ **noun** the first appearance of light in the sky before sunrise: *he set off **at dawn**.*
■ figurative the beginning of a phenomenon or period of time, especially one perceived as auspicious: *the dawn of civilization.*
▶ **verb** [no obj.] **1** (of a day) begin: [with complement] *Thursday dawned bright and sunny.*
■ figurative come into existence: *a new age was dawning in the Tory party.*
2 become evident to the mind; be perceived or understood: *the awful truth was beginning to **dawn on** him* | [as adj. **dawning**] *he smiled with dawning recognition.*
– ORIGIN late 15th cent. (as a verb): back-formation from Middle English **DAWNING**.

dawn chorus ▶ **noun** [in sing.] the singing of a large number of birds before dawn each day, particularly during the breeding season.

dawning ▶ **noun** poetic/literary dawn.
■ the beginning or first appearance of something: *the dawnings of civilization.*
– ORIGIN Middle English: alteration of earlier *dawing*, from Old English *dagian* 'to dawn', of Germanic origin; related to Dutch *dagen* and German *tagen*, also to **DAY**.

dawn raid ▶ **noun** a surprise visit at dawn, especially by police searching for criminals or illicit goods.
■ Stock Exchange, Brit. an attempt to acquire a substantial portion of a company's shares at the start of a day's trading, typically as a preliminary to a takeover bid.

dawn redwood ▶ **noun** a coniferous tree with deciduous needles, known only as a fossil until it was found growing in SW China in 1941.
• *Metasequoia glyptostroboides*, family Taxodiaceae.

Day, Doris (b.1924), American actress and singer; born *Doris Kappelhoff*. She became a film star in the 1950s with roles in light-hearted musicals, comedies, and romances such as *Calamity Jane* (1953) and *Pillow Talk* (1959).

day ▶ **noun 1** one of the twenty-four-hour periods, reckoned from one midnight to the next, into which a week, month, or year is divided, and corresponding to a rotation of the earth on its axis.
■ the part of this period when it is light; the time between sunrise and sunset: *the animals hunt **by day**.* ■ the time spent working during such a period: *he works an eight-hour day.* ■ Astronomy a single rotation of a planet in relation to its primary. ■ Astronomy the period on a planet when its primary star is above the horizon. ■ [mass noun] archaic daylight: *by the time they had all gone it was broad day.*
2 (usu. **days**) a particular period of the past; an era: *the laws were very strict in those days.*
■ (**the day**) the present time: *the political issues of the day.* ■ [usu. with modifier] (**days**) a particular period in a person's life or career: *my student days.* ■ (**one's day**) the successful, fortunate, or influential period of a person's life or career: *he had been a matinée idol in his day.* ■ (**one's days**) the remaining period of someone's life: *she cared for him for **the rest of his days**.*
▶ **adjective** [attrib.] carried out during the day as opposed to the evening or at night: *my day job.*
■ (of a person) working during the day as opposed to at night: *a day nurse.*
– PHRASES **all in a** (or **the**) **day's work** (of something unusual or difficult) accepted as part of someone's normal routine or as a matter of course: *dodging sharks is all in a day's work for some scientists.* **any day** informal at any time: *they could outfight the police any day.* ■ (used to express one's strong preference for something) under any circumstances: *I'd rather have Ruth than you, any day.* ■ very soon: *she's expected to give birth **any day now**.* **at the end of the day** see **END**. **by the day** gradually and steadily: *the campaign is growing by the day.* **call it a day** decide or agree to stop doing something. **day after day** on each successive day, especially over a long period: *the rain poured down day after day.* **day and night** all the time: *the district is patrolled day and night.* **day by day** on each successive day; gradually and steadily: *day by day I grew worse.* **day in, day out** continuously or repeatedly over a long period of time. **day of reckoning** the time when past mistakes or misdeeds must be punished or paid for; a testing time when the degree of one's success or failure will be revealed. [ORIGIN: with allusion to Judgement Day, on which (in some beliefs) the judgement of mankind is expected to take place.] **don't give up the day job** informal used as a humorous way of recommending someone not to pursue something at which they are unlikely to be successful. **from day one** from the very beginning: *children need a firm hand from day one.* **have had one's** (or **its**) **day** be no longer popular, successful, or influential: *power dressing has had its day.* **if he** (or **she** etc.) **is a day** at least (appended to a statement about a person's age): *he must be seventy if he's a day.* **in this day and age** at the present time. **not someone's day** used to convey that someone has experienced a day of successive misfortunes. —— **of the day** a thing currently considered to be particularly interesting or important: *the big news story of the day.* **one day** (or **some day** or **one of these days**) at some time in the future: *our wishes will come true one of these days.* **one of those days** a day when several things go wrong. **that will be the day** informal that is very unlikely. **these days** at present: *he was drinking far too much these days.* **those were the days** used to assert that a particular past time was better in comparison with the present. **to the day** exactly: *it's four years to the day since he was killed.* **to this day** at the present time as in the past; still: *the tradition continues to this day.*
– ORIGIN Old English *dæg*, of Germanic origin; related to Dutch *dag* and German *Tag*.

Dayak /ˈdʌɪak/ (also **Dyak**) ▶ **noun** (pl. same or **Dayaks**) **1** a member of a group of indigenous peoples inhabiting parts of Borneo, including the Iban (or **Sea Dayak**) of the north, the **Land Dayak** of the south-west, and the Punan. They live in traditional longhouse communities, hunting, fishing, and growing rice.
2 [mass noun] the group of Austronesian languages spoken by these peoples.
▶ **adjective** of or relating to these peoples or their languages.
– ORIGIN Malay, literally 'up-country'.

Dayan /daˈjɑːn/, Moshe (1915–81), Israeli statesman and general. As Minister of Defence he oversaw Israel's victory in the Six Day War and as Foreign Minister he played a prominent role in negotiations towards the Camp David agreements of 1979.

dayan /daˈjɑːn/ (also **Dayan**) ▶ **noun** (pl. **dayanim** /daˈjɑːnɪm/) Judaism a senior rabbi, especially one who acts as a religious judge in a Jewish community.
– ORIGIN from Hebrew *dayyān*, from *dān* 'to judge'.

daybed ▶ **noun** a bed for daytime rest.
■ N. Amer. a couch that can be made up into a bed.

dayboat ▶ **noun** another term for **DAYSAILOR**.

daybook ▶ **noun** an account book in which a day's transactions are entered for later transfer to a ledger.
■ N. Amer. a diary.

day boy ▶ **noun** Brit. a boy who lives at home but attends a school where other pupils board.

daybreak ▶ **noun** the time in the morning when daylight first appears; dawn: *she set off **at daybreak**.*

day care ▶ **noun** [mass noun] daytime care for the needs of people who cannot be fully independent, such as children or the elderly.
■ [count noun] (**daycare**) N. Amer. a day-care centre: *just about every good daycare has a water-play table.*

day centre (also **day-care centre**) ▶ **noun** a place providing care and recreation facilities for those who cannot be fully independent.

day coach (also **day car**) ▶ **noun** N. Amer. an ordinary railway carriage, as opposed to a sleeping car.

day-dawn ▶ **noun** poetic/literary daybreak.

daydream ▶ **noun** a series of pleasant thoughts that distract one's attention from the present.
▶ **verb** [no obj.] indulge in such a series of thoughts: *stop daydreaming and pay attention.*
– DERIVATIVES **daydreamer** noun.

day flower ▶ **noun** a plant related to the spiderwort, with short-lived flowers that are typically blue, and found in warm climates.
• Genus *Commelina*, family Commelinaceae.

day girl ▶ **noun** Brit. a girl who lives at home but attends a school where other pupils board.

Day-Glo ▶ **noun** [mass noun] trademark a fluorescent paint or other colouring.
▶ **adjective** (also **dayglo**) of or denoting very bright or fluorescent colouring.
– ORIGIN 1950s: blend of **DAY** and **GLOW**.

day hospital ▶ **noun** Brit. a hospital offering psychiatric or other therapeutic facilities, which patients attend during the day, going home or to another hospital at night.

day labourer ▶ **noun** an unskilled labourer paid by the day.

Day Lewis, C. (1904–72), English poet and critic; full name *Cecil Day Lewis*. His early verse, such as *Transitional Poems* (1929), reflects the influence of revolutionary thinking. After 1940, however, he increasingly became an Establishment figure and was Poet Laureate 1968–72.

daylight ▶ **noun** [mass noun] **1** the natural light of the day: [as modifier] *the daylight hours.*
■ the first appearance of light in the morning; dawn: *I returned at daylight.* ■ figurative visible distance between one person or thing and another: *the growing daylight between himself and the leading jockey.*
2 (**daylights**) used to emphasize the severity or thoroughness of an action: *my father beat the living daylights out of them.*
– PHRASES **see daylight** begin to understand what was previously puzzling or unclear.

daylighting ▶ **noun** [mass noun] the illumination of buildings by natural light.

daylight robbery ▶ **noun** [mass noun] Brit. informal blatant and unfair overcharging.

daylight saving time (also **daylight time**) ▶ **noun** [mass noun] chiefly N. Amer. time as adjusted to achieve longer evening daylight, especially in summer, by setting the clocks an hour ahead of the standard time. Compare with **SUMMER TIME**.

day lily ▶ **noun** a Eurasian lily which bears large yellow, red, or orange flowers, each flower lasting only one day.
• Genus *Hemerocallis*, family Liliaceae.

day-long ▶ **adjective** of a day's duration: *a day-long seminar.*
■ capable of lasting all day: *day-long protection.*

daymare ▶ **noun** a frightening or oppressive trance or hallucinatory condition experienced while awake.
– ORIGIN mid 17th cent.: from **DAY**, on the pattern of *nightmare*.

day nursery ▶ **noun** see **NURSERY**.

Day of Atonement another term for **YOM KIPPUR**.

day off ▶ **noun** (pl. **days off**) a day's holiday from work or school, on what would normally be a working day.

Day of Judgement another term for **JUDGEMENT DAY**.

day of rest ▶ **noun** a day in the week set aside from normal work or activity, typically Sunday on religious grounds.

day out ▶ **noun** (pl. **days out**) Brit. a trip or excursion for a day.

day owl ▶ **noun** an owl that hunts by day, in particular the short-eared owl.

daypack ▶ **noun** chiefly N. Amer. a small rucksack.

day patient ▶ **noun** a patient who attends a hospital for treatment without staying there overnight.

day release ▶ **noun** [mass noun] Brit. a system of allowing employees days off work to go on educational courses: *she goes to college on day release.*

day return ▶ **noun** Brit. a fare or ticket at a reduced rate for a journey on public transport out and back in one day.

day room ▶ **noun** a room, especially a communal room in an institution, used during the day.

daysack ▶ **noun** Brit. another term for **DAYPACK**.

daysail ▶ **verb** [no obj.] sail a yacht for a single day: [as noun **daysailing**] *an outstanding boat for daysailing.*

daysailor (US also **daysailer**) ▶ **noun** a sailing boat without a cabin, designed for use during the day only.

day school ▶ **noun** a non-residential school, typically a fee-paying one.
■ a short educational course on a particular subject.

day shift ▶ **noun** a period of time worked during the daylight hours in a hospital, factory, etc., as opposed to the night shift.
■ [treated as sing. or pl.] the employees who work during this period.

dayside ▶ **noun** Astronomy the side of a planet that is facing its primary star.

Days of Awe ▶ **plural noun** another term for **HIGH HOLIDAYS**.

dayspring ▶ **noun** poetic/literary term for **DAWN**.

day surgery ▶ **noun** [mass noun] minor surgery that does not require the patient to stay in hospital overnight.

daytime ▶ **noun** the time of the day between sunrise and sunset: *she was alone **in the daytime*** | [as modifier] *a daytime telephone number.*

day-to-day ▶ **adjective** [attrib.] happening regularly every day: *the day-to-day management of the classroom.*
■ ordinary; everyday: *our day-to-day domestic life.* ■ short-term; without consideration for the future: *the struggle for day-to-day survival.*
▶ **noun** [in sing.] an ordinary, everyday routine: *they have come to escape the day-to-day.*
▶ **adverb** on a daily basis: *the information to be traded is determined day-to-day.*

Dayton /ˈdeɪt(ə)n/ a city in western Ohio; pop. 182,000 (1990). It was the home of the aviation pioneers the Wright brothers and is still a centre of aerospace research.

day trip ▶ **noun** a journey or excursion completed in one day.
– DERIVATIVES **day tripper** noun.

daywear ▶ **noun** [mass noun] articles of casual clothing suitable for informal or everyday occasions.

daywork ▶ **noun** [mass noun] casual work paid for on a daily basis.
– DERIVATIVES **dayworker** noun.

daze ▶ **verb** [with obj.] (usu. **be dazed**) (especially of an emotional or physical shock) make (someone) unable to think or react properly: *she was dazed by his revelations* | [as adj. **dazed**] *a dazed expression.*
▶ **noun** [in sing.] a state of stunned confusion or bewilderment: *he was walking around **in a daze**.*
– DERIVATIVES **dazedly** /-zɪdli/ adverb.
– ORIGIN Middle English: back-formation from *dazed* (adjective), from Old Norse *dasathr* 'weary'; compare with Swedish *dasa* 'lie idle'.

dazibao /ˈdɑːdzəbaʊ/ ▶ **noun** (pl. same) (in the People's Republic of China) a wall poster written in large characters. expressing a political opinion.
– ORIGIN Chinese, from *dà* 'big' + *zì* 'character' + *bào* 'newspaper or poster'.

dazzle ▶ **verb** [with obj.] (of a bright light) blind (a person or their eyes) temporarily: *she was dazzled by the headlights.*
■ [no obj.] archaic (of the eyes) be affected in such a way: *my eyes dazzled and I could not move.* ■ figurative amaze or overwhelm (someone) with a particular impressive quality: *I was dazzled by the beauty and breadth of the exhibition.*
▶ **noun** [mass noun] brightness that confuses someone's vision temporarily: *I screwed my eyes up against the dazzle* | [in sing.] *a dazzle of green and red spotlights.*
– DERIVATIVES **dazzlement** noun.
– ORIGIN late 15th cent. (in the sense 'be dazzled'): frequentative of the verb **DAZE**.

dazzler ▶ **noun** a person or thing that dazzles, in particular a person who is overwhelmingly impressive or skilful.

dazzling ▶ **adjective** extremely bright, especially so as to blind the eyes temporarily: *the sunlight was dazzling* | figurative *a dazzling smile.*
■ figurative extremely impressive, beautiful, or skilful: *a dazzling display of football.*
– DERIVATIVES **dazzlingly** adverb.

Db ▶ **symbol for** the chemical element dubnium.

dB ▶ **abbreviation for** decibel(s).

DBE ▶ **abbreviation for** (in the UK) Dame Commander of the Order of the British Empire.

DBMS ▶ **abbreviation for** database management system.

DBS ▶ **abbreviation for** ■ direct broadcasting by satellite. ■ direct-broadcast satellite.

dbx ▶ **noun** [mass noun] trademark electronic circuitry designed to increase the dynamic range of reproduced sound and reduce noise in the system.
– ORIGIN 1970s: from **DB** 'decibel' + *x* (representing *expander*).

DC ▶ **abbreviation for** ■ Music da capo. ■ direct current. ■ District of Columbia: *Washington DC.* ■ District Commissioner.

DCB ▶ **abbreviation for** (in the UK) Dame Commander of the Order of the Bath.

DCC ▶ **abbreviation for** digital compact cassette, a format for tape cassettes similar to ordinary audio cassettes but with digital rather than analogue recording.

DCL ▶ **abbreviation for** (in the UK) Doctor of Civil Law.

DCM ▶ **abbreviation for** (in the UK) Distinguished Conduct Medal, awarded for bravery.

DCMG ▶ **abbreviation for** (in the UK) Dame Commander of the Order of St Michael and St George.

DCVO ▶ **abbreviation for** (in the UK) Dame Commander of the Royal Victorian Order.

DD ▶ **abbreviation for** Doctor of Divinity.

D-Day ▶ **noun** the day (6 June 1944) in the Second World War on which Allied forces invaded northern France by means of beach landings in Normandy.
■ the day on which an important operation is to begin or a change to take effect.
– ORIGIN from *D* for *day* + **DAY**. Compare with **H-HOUR**.

DDC ▶ **abbreviation for** dideoxycytidine.

DDE ▶ **noun** Computing a standard allowing data to be shared between different programs.
– ORIGIN 1980s: abbreviation of *Dynamic Data Exchange*.

DDI ▶ **abbreviation for** ■ dideoxyinosine. ■ divisional detective inspector.

DDR ▶ **abbreviation for** German Democratic Republic.
– ORIGIN abbreviation of German *Deutsche Demokratische Republik*.

DDT ▶ **abbreviation for** dichlorodiphenyltrichloroethane, a synthetic organic compound introduced in the 1940s and used as an insecticide. Like other chlorinated aromatic hydrocarbons, DDT tends to persist in the environment and become concentrated in animals at the head of the food chain. Its use is now banned in many countries.
• Chem. formula: $CCl_3CH(C_6H_4Cl)_2$.

DE ▶ **abbreviation for** ■ Delaware (in official postal use). ■ (in the UK) Department of Employment.

de- ▶ **prefix 1** (forming verbs and their derivatives) down; away: *descend* | *deduct.*
■ completely: *denude* | *derelict.*
2 (added to verbs and their derivatives) denoting removal or reversal: *deaerate* | *de-ice.*
3 denoting formation from: *deverbal.*
– ORIGIN from Latin *de* 'off, from'; sense 2 via Old French *des-* from Latin *dis-*.

deaccession /ˌdiːəkˈsɛʃ(ə)n/ ▶ **verb** [with obj.] officially remove (an item) from the listed holdings of a library, museum, or art gallery, typically in order to sell it to raise funds.
▶ **noun** [mass noun] the disposal of books, works of art, or other items in this way.

deacon /ˈdiːk(ə)n/ ▶ **noun** (in Catholic, Anglican, and Orthodox Churches) an ordained minister of an order ranking below that of priest (now, except in the Orthodox Church, typically in training for the priesthood).
■ (in some Protestant Churches) a lay officer appointed to assist a minister, especially in secular affairs. ■ historical (in the early Church) an appointed minister of charity.
▶ **verb** [with obj.] appoint or ordain as a deacon.
– DERIVATIVES **deaconship** noun.
– ORIGIN Old English *diacon*, via ecclesiastical Latin from Greek *diakonos* 'servant' (in ecclesiastical Greek 'Christian minister').

deaconess /ˌdiːkəˈnɛs, ˈdiːk(ə)nɪs/ ▶ **noun** (in the early Church and some modern Churches) a woman with duties similar to those of a deacon.

deactivate ▶ **verb** [with obj.] make (something, typically technical equipment or a virus) inactive by disconnecting or destroying it: *the switch deactivates the alarm.*
– DERIVATIVES **deactivation** noun, **deactivator** noun.

dead ▶ **adjective 1** no longer alive: *a dead body* | [as complement] *he was shot dead by terrorists.*
■ (of a part of the body) having lost sensation; numb. ■ having or displaying no emotion, sympathy, or sensitivity: *a cold, dead voice.* ■ no longer current, relevant, or important: *pollution had become a dead issue.* ■ devoid of living things: *a dead planet.* ■ (of a place or time) characterized by a lack of activity or excitement: *Brussels isn't dead after dark, if you know where to look.* ■ (of money) not financially productive. ■ (of sound) without resonance; dull. ■ (of a colour) not glossy or bright. ■ (of a piece of equipment) no longer functioning, especially because of a fault: *the phone had gone dead.* ■ (of an electric circuit or conductor) carrying or transmitting no current: *the batteries are dead.* ■ no longer alight: *the fire had been dead for some days.* ■ (of a glass or bottle) empty or no longer being used. ■ (of the ball in a game) out of play. See also **DEAD BALL**. ■ (of a cricket pitch or other surface) lacking springiness or bounce.
2 [attrib.] complete; absolute: *we sat in dead silence.*
▶ **adverb** [often as submodifier] absolutely; completely: *you're dead right* | *he was dead against the idea.*
■ exactly: *they arrived dead on time.* ■ straight; directly: *red flares were seen dead ahead.* ■ Brit. informal very: *omelettes are dead easy to prepare.*
▶ **noun** [as plural noun **the dead**] those who have died.
– PHRASES **dead and buried** over; finished: *the incident is dead and buried.* **(as) dead as a** (or **the**) **dodo** see **DODO**. **(as) dead as a doornail** see **DOORNAIL**. **(as) dead as mutton** see **MUTTON**. **dead from the neck up** informal stupid. **dead in the water** (of a ship) unable to move. ■ figurative unable to function effectively: *the economy is dead in the water.* **dead meat** informal in serious trouble: *if anyone finds out, you're dead meat.* **the dead of night** the quietest, darkest part of the night. **the dead of winter** the coldest part of winter. **dead on** exactly right: *her judgement was dead on.* **dead on one's feet** informal extremely tired. **dead to the world** informal fast asleep. **from the dead** from a state of death: *Christ rose from the dead.* ■ figurative from a period of obscurity or inactivity: *the cartoon brought animation back from the dead.* **make a dead set at** see **SET**[2]. **over my dead body** see **BODY**. **wouldn't be seen** (or **caught**) **dead in** (or **with**, **at**, etc.) informal used to express strong dislike for a particular thing: *I wouldn't be seen dead in a navy suit.*
– DERIVATIVES **deadness** noun.
– ORIGIN Old English *dēad*, of Germanic origin: related to Dutch *dood* and German *tot*, also to **DIE**[1].

dead-alive ▶ **adjective** Brit. lacking animation and vitality.

dead ball ▶ **noun** (in ball games) a ball that has gone out of play or is declared to be out of play.
■ [as modifier] Soccer involving a restart of the game by kicking a stationary ball, e.g. by a free kick: *dead-ball situations.*

dead-ball line ▶ **noun** Rugby a line behind the goal line, beyond which the ball is out of play.

dead bat ▶ **noun** Cricket a bat held loosely so that the ball falls to the ground immediately when struck.

deadbeat ▶ **adjective 1** [predic.] (**dead beat**) informal completely exhausted: *I must go to bed—I'm dead beat.*
2 (of a clock escapement or other mechanism) without recoil.
▶ **noun** informal an idle, feckless, or disreputable person.
■ N. Amer. a person who tries to evade paying debts.

deadbolt ▶ **noun** a bolt engaged by turning a knob or key, rather than by spring action.

dead cat bounce ▶ **noun** Stock Exchange a temporary recovery in share prices after a substantial fall, caused by speculators buying in order to cover their positions.

dead centre ▶ noun **1** Baseball the area of the field directly ahead of the pitcher.
2 the position of a crank when it is in line with the connecting rod and not exerting torque.

dead duck ▶ noun informal a person or thing that is defunct or has no chance of success: *the idea of a third TV channel is now a dead duck.*
– ORIGIN from the old saying 'never waste powder on a dead duck'.

deaden ▶ verb [with obj.] make (a noise or sensation) less strong or intense: *ether was used to deaden the pain.*
■ deprive of the power of sensation: *diabetes can deaden the nerve endings.* ■ deprive of force or vitality; stultify: *the syllabus has deadened the teaching process* | [as adj. **deadening**] *a deadening routine.* ■ make (someone) insensitive to something: *laughter might deaden us to the moral issue.*
– DERIVATIVES **deadener** noun.

dead end ▶ noun **1** an end of a road or passage from which no exit is possible.
■ a road or passage having such an end. ■ a situation offering no prospects of progress or development: [as modifier] *a dead-end job.*
▶ verb [no obj.] (**dead-end**) N. Amer. (of a road or passage) come to a dead end: *he kept walking, until the corridor dead-ended.*

deadeye ▶ noun **1** Sailing a circular wooden block with a groove round the circumference to take a lanyard, used singly or in pairs to tighten a shroud.
2 informal, chiefly US an expert marksman.

deadfall ▶ noun N. Amer. **1** a trap consisting of a heavy weight positioned to fall on and kill or disable an animal.
2 [mass noun] a tangled mass of fallen trees and brush.
■ [count noun] a fallen tree.
3 informal a disreputable drinking place.

dead hand ▶ noun an undesirable persisting influence: *the dead hand of state control.*

deadhead ▶ noun **1** a faded flower head.
2 informal a boring or unenterprising person.
■ chiefly N. Amer. a passenger or member of an audience with a free ticket.
3 a sunken or partially submerged log.
▶ verb **1** [with obj.] chiefly Brit. remove dead flower heads from (a plant): *deadhead and spray rose bushes* | [as noun **deadheading**] *there is endless deadheading to be done.*
2 [no obj.] US informal drive or travel in a train or other vehicle with no passengers or cargo: *they deadhead back to Denver on eastbound trains.*

dead heat ▶ noun a situation in or result of a race in which two or more competitors are exactly level.
▶ verb [no obj.] (**dead-heat**) run or finish a race exactly level.

dead language ▶ noun a language which is no longer in everyday spoken use, such as Latin.

dead leg ▶ noun **1** an injury caused by a numbing blow with the knee to a person's upper leg.
2 a length of pipe running from a storage cylinder to the hot taps.
▶ verb [with obj.] (**dead-leg**) informal give (someone) a numbing blow to the upper leg with one's knee.

dead letter ▶ noun **1** a law or treaty which has not been repealed but is ineffectual or defunct in practice.
■ figurative a thing which is impractical or obsolete: *theoretical reasoning is a dead letter to a child.*
2 an unclaimed or undelivered piece of mail.

dead letter box ▶ noun a place where messages can be left and collected without the sender and recipient meeting.

dead lift ▶ noun Weightlifting a lift made from a standing position, without the use of a bench or other equipment.

deadlight ▶ noun **1** a protective cover or shutter fitted over a porthole or window on a ship.
2 US a skylight designed not to be opened.

deadline ▶ noun **1** the latest time or date by which something should be completed.
2 historical a line drawn around a prison beyond which prisoners were liable to be shot.

dead load ▶ noun the intrinsic weight of a structure or vehicle, excluding the weight of passengers or goods. Often contrasted with **LIVE LOAD**.

deadlock ▶ noun **1** [in sing.] a situation, typically one involving opposing parties, in which no progress can be made.

2 Brit. a type of lock requiring a key to open and close it, as distinct from a spring lock.
▶ verb [with obj.] **1** [no obj.] (usu. **be deadlocked**) cause (a situation or opposing parties) to come to a point where no progress can be made because of fundamental disagreement: *the meeting is deadlocked.*
2 Brit. secure (a door) with a deadlock.

dead loss ▶ noun a venture or situation which produces no profit whatsoever.
■ informal a person or thing that is completely useless.

deadly ▶ adjective (**deadlier, deadliest**) causing or able to cause death: *a deadly weapon.*
■ filled with hate: *his voice was cold and deadly.* ■ (typically in the context of shooting or sport) extremely accurate, effective, or skilful: *his aim is deadly.* ■ informal extremely boring: *he's well meaning, but so utterly deadly.* ■ [attrib.] complete; total: *she was in deadly earnest.*
▶ adverb [as submodifier] in a way resembling or suggesting death; as if dead: *her skin was deadly pale.*
■ extremely: *a deadly serious remark.*
– DERIVATIVES **deadliness** noun.
– ORIGIN Old English *dēadlic* 'mortal, in danger of death' (see **DEAD**, **-LY**[1]).

deadly nightshade ▶ noun a poisonous bushy Eurasian plant with drooping purple flowers and black cherry-like fruit. Also called **BELLADONNA**.
● *Atropa belladonna*, family Solanaceae.

deadly sin ▶ noun (in Christian tradition) a sin regarded as leading to damnation, especially one of a traditional list of seven. See **SEVEN DEADLY SINS**.

dead man ▶ noun **1** informal a bottle after the contents have been drunk.
2 (usu. **deadman**) an object buried in or secured to the ground for the purpose of providing anchorage or leverage.

dead man's fingers ▶ plural noun **1** a European colonial soft coral which has spongy lobes stiffened by calcareous spines. When found washed up on the beach it is said to resemble the fingers from a corpse.
● *Alcyonium digitatum*, order Alcyonacea.
2 a fungus that produces clumps of dull black, irregular, finger-like fruiting bodies at the bases of dead tree stumps in both Eurasia and North America.
● *Xylaria polymorpha*, family Xylariaceae, subdivision Ascomycotina.
3 informal the finger-like divisions of a lobster's or crab's gills.

dead man's handle (also **dead man's pedal**) ▶ noun (especially in a diesel or electric train) a lever which acts as a safety device by shutting off power when not held in place by the driver.

dead march ▶ noun a slow, solemn piece of music suitable to accompany a funeral procession.

dead-nettle ▶ noun a Eurasian and North African plant of the mint family, with leaves that resemble those of a nettle but lack stinging hairs.
● *Lamium* and related genera, family Labiatae: several species, including the common **white dead-nettle** (*L. album*).

deadpan ▶ adjective deliberately impassive or expressionless: *a deadpan expression.*
▶ adverb in a deadpan manner: *'That's all right then,' Claire said, deadpan.*
▶ verb (**-panned, -panning**) [with direct speech] say something amusing while affecting a serious manner: *'I'm an undercover dentist,' he deadpanned.*

dead reckoning ▶ noun [mass noun] the process of calculating one's position, especially at sea, by estimating the direction and distance travelled rather than by using landmarks or astronomical observations.

dead ringer ▶ noun a person or thing that seems very like someone or something else: *he is a dead ringer for his late papa.*

deadrise ▶ noun the vertical distance between a line horizontal to the keel of a boat and its chine.

Dead Sea a salt lake or inland sea in the Jordan valley, on the Israel–Jordan border. Its surface is 400 m (1,300 ft) below sea level.

Dead Sea scrolls a collection of Hebrew and Aramaic manuscripts discovered in pottery storage jars in caves near Qumran between 1947 and 1956. Thought to have been hidden by the Essenes or a similar Jewish sect shortly before the revolt against Roman rule AD 66–70, the scrolls include texts of

many books of the Old Testament; they are some 1,000 years older than previously known versions.

dead set ▶ noun see **SET**[2] (sense 2).

dead shot ▶ noun an extremely accurate marksman or markswoman.

deadstick landing ▶ noun an unpowered landing of an aircraft.

deadstock ▶ noun [mass noun] the machinery used on a farm, as opposed to the livestock.
– ORIGIN mid 19th cent.: from **DEAD**, on the pattern of *livestock*.

dead time ▶ noun [mass noun] time in which someone or something is inactive or unable to act productively.
■ Physics the period after the recording of a particle or pulse when a detector is unable to record another.

dead water ▶ noun [mass noun] chiefly N. Amer. still water without any current.

deadweight ▶ noun the weight of an inert person or thing.
■ a heavy or oppressive burden. ■ the total weight of cargo, stores, etc. which a ship carries or can carry. ■ another term for **DEAD LOAD**. ■ [mass noun] Farming animals sold by the estimated weight of saleable meat that they will yield. ■ [usu. as modifier] Economics losses incurred because of the inefficient allocation of resources, especially through taxation or restriction: *a deadweight burden.* ■ [usu. as modifier] a debt not covered by assets.

dead white ▶ noun [mass noun] a flat, lustreless white, especially one reminiscent of the appearance of a corpse.

dead white European male (also **dead white male**) ▶ noun informal, chiefly US a writer, philosopher, or other significant figure whose importance and talents may have been exaggerated by virtue of his belonging to a historically dominant gender and ethnic group.

dead wood ▶ noun [mass noun] a branch or part of a tree which is dead.
■ figurative people or things that are no longer useful or productive.

deaerate /diːˈɛːreɪt/ ▶ verb [with obj.] (usu. **be deaerated**) partially or completely remove dissolved air from (something): *the electrolyte was deaerated by purging it with argon.*
– DERIVATIVES **deaeration** noun.

deaf ▶ adjective lacking the power of hearing or having impaired hearing: [as plural noun **the deaf**] *subtitles for the deaf.*
■ unwilling or unable to hear or pay attention to something: *she is deaf to all advice.*
– PHRASES (**as**) **deaf as a post** completely or extremely deaf. **fall on deaf ears** (of a statement or request) be ignored by others. **turn a deaf ear** refuse to listen or respond to a statement or request.
– DERIVATIVES **deafness** noun.
– ORIGIN Old English *dēaf*, of Germanic origin; related to Dutch *doof* and German *taub*, from an Indo-European root shared by Greek *tuphlos* 'blind'.

deaf aid ▶ noun Brit. a hearing aid.

deaf-blind ▶ adjective having a severe impairment of both hearing and vision.

deafen ▶ verb [with obj.] (usu. **be deafened**) cause (someone) to lose the power of hearing permanently or temporarily: *we were deafened by the explosion.*
■ (of a loud noise) overwhelm (someone) with sound: *the roar of the water deafened them.* ■ (**deafen someone to**) (of a sound) cause someone to be unaware of (other sounds): *the noise deafened him to Ron's approach.*

deafening ▶ adjective (of a noise) so loud as to make it impossible to hear anything else: *the music reached a deafening crescendo.*
– DERIVATIVES **deafeningly** adverb.

deafferentation /diːˌaf(ə)r(ə)nˈteɪʃ(ə)n/ ▶ noun [mass noun] Biology the interruption or destruction of the afferent connections of nerve cells, performed especially in animal experiments to demonstrate the spontaneity of locomotor movement.
– DERIVATIVES **deafferented** adjective.

deaf mute ▶ noun a person who is both deaf and unable to speak.
▶ adjective (of a person) both deaf and unable to speak.
■ of or relating to such people.

USAGE In modern use **deaf mute** has acquired offensive connotations (implying, wrongly, that such people are without the capacity for communication). It should be avoided in favour of other terms such as **profoundly deaf**.

Deakin /ˈdiːkɪn/, Alfred (1856–1919), Australian Liberal statesman, Prime Minister 1903–4, 1905–8, and 1909–10.

deal[1] ▶ **verb** (past and past participle **dealt**) **1** [with obj.] distribute (cards) in an orderly rotation to the players for a game or round: *the cards were dealt for the last hand* | [with two objs] figurative *fate dealt her a different hand* | [no obj.] *he shuffled and dealt.*
■(**deal someone in**) include a new player in a card game by giving them cards. ■ distribute or mete out (something) to a person or group: *the funds raised were* **dealt out to** *the needy.*
2 [no obj.] take part in commercial trading of a particular commodity: *directors were prohibited from* **dealing in** *the company's shares.*
■figurative be concerned with: *journalism that* **deals in** *small-town chit-chat.* ■ informal buy and sell illegal drugs: [with obj.] *many of the men are dealing drugs.*
3 [no obj.] (**deal with**) take measures concerning (someone or something), especially with the intention of putting something right: *the government had been unable to deal with the economic crisis.*
■cope with (a difficult person or situation): *you'll have to find a way of dealing with those feelings.* ■ [with adverbial] treat (someone) in a particular way: *life had dealt very harshly with her.* ■ have relations with (a person or organization), especially in a commercial context: *the bank deals directly with the private sector.* ■ take or have as a subject; discuss: *the novel deals with several different topics.*
4 [with two objs] inflict (a blow) on (someone or something): *hopes of an economic recovery were dealt another blow.*
▶ **noun 1** an agreement entered into by two or more parties for their mutual benefit, especially in a business or political context: *the government was ready to do a deal with the opposition.*
■a set of things offered as a whole that is intended to constitute an attractive commercial arrangement for a purchaser: *an excellent deal from a tour operator.* ■ [with adj.] a particular form of treatment given or received: *working mothers get a bad deal.*
2 [in sing.] the process of distributing the cards to players in a card game.
■a player's turn to distribute cards. ■ the round of play following this. ■ the set of hands dealt to the players.
– PHRASES **a big deal** informal [usu. with negative] a thing considered important: *they don't make a big deal out of minor irritations.* ■ (**big deal**) used to express one's contempt for something regarded as impressive or important by another person. **a raw** (or **rough**) **deal** informal a situation in which someone receives unfair or harsh treatment. **a deal of** dated a large amount of: *he lost a deal of blood.* **a good** (or **great**) **deal** a large amount: *I don't know a great deal about politics.* ■ to a considerable extent: *she had got to know him a good deal better.* **a square deal** a fair bargain or treatment. **it's a deal** informal used to express one's assent to an agreement.
– ORIGIN Old English *dǣlan* 'divide', 'participate', of Germanic origin; related to Dutch *deel* and German *Teil* 'part' (noun), also to **DOLE**[1]. The sense 'divide' gave rise to 'distribute', hence senses 1 and 4 of the verb; the sense 'participate' gave rise to 'have dealings with', hence senses 2 and 3 of the verb.

deal[2] ▶ **noun** [mass noun] fir or pine wood, especially when sawn into planks of a standard size.
■[count noun] a plank of such wood.
– ORIGIN Middle English: from Middle Low German and Middle Dutch *dele* 'plank'.

de-alcoholize (also **-ise**) ▶ **verb** [with obj.] [usu. as adj. **de-alcoholized**] remove the alcohol from (a normally alcoholic drink): *de-alcoholized beer.*

dealer ▶ **noun 1** a person or business that buys and sells goods: *an antique dealer.*
■a person who buys and sells shares, securities, or other financial assets as a principal (rather than as a broker or agent). See also **BROKER-DEALER**.
2 the player who distributes the cards at the start of a game.
– DERIVATIVES **dealership** noun (only in sense 1).

dealfish ▶ **noun** (pl. same or **-fishes**) a long slender silvery fish with a dorsal fin running the length of the body, living in the NE Atlantic.
● *Trachipterus arcticus*, family Trachipteridae.
– ORIGIN mid 19th cent.: from **DEAL**[2] in the sense 'board' (with reference to its shape) + **FISH**[1].

dealign ▶ **verb** [no obj.] (of a voter) withdraw allegiance to a political party.
– DERIVATIVES **dealignment** noun.

dealing ▶ **noun 1** (usu. **dealings**) a business relation or transaction: *they had dealings with an insurance company.*
■a personal connection or association with someone: *my dealings with the gentler sex.* ■ the activity of buying and selling a particular commodity: *share dealings* | *drug dealing.*
2 [mass noun] the particular way in which someone behaves towards others: *fair dealing came naturally to him.*

dealt past participle of **DEAL**[1].

deamination /diːˌamɪˈneɪʃ(ə)n/ ▶ **noun** [mass noun] Biochemistry the removal of an amino group from an amino acid or other compound.
– DERIVATIVES **deaminated** adjective.

Dean[1], Christopher, see **TORVILL AND DEAN**.

Dean[2], James (1931–55), American actor; born *James Byron*. Although he starred in only three films before dying in a car accident, he became a cult figure closely identified with the title role of *Rebel Without a Cause* (1955), symbolizing for many the disaffected youth of the post-war era.

dean[1] ▶ **noun 1** the head of the chapter of a cathedral or collegiate church.
■(also **rural dean**) Brit. a member of the clergy exercising supervision over a group of parochial clergy within a division of an archdeaconry.
2 the head of a university faculty or department or of a medical school.
■(in a college or university, especially Oxford or Cambridge) a fellow with disciplinary and advisory functions. ■ the leader or senior member of a body.
– ORIGIN Middle English: from Old French *deien*, from late Latin *decanus* 'chief of a group of ten', from *decem* 'ten'. Compare with **DOYEN**.

dean[2] ▶ **noun** variant spelling of **DENE**[1].

deanery ▶ **noun** (pl. **-ies**) **1** Brit. the group of parishes presided over by a rural dean.
2 the official residence of a dean.
■the position or office of a dean.

de-Anglicize (also **-ise**) ▶ **verb** [with obj.] remove English characteristics or influence from.
– DERIVATIVES **de-Anglicization** noun.

Dean of Faculty ▶ **noun** the president of the Faculty of Advocates in Scotland.

dean's list ▶ **noun** N. Amer. a list of students recognized for academic achievement during a term by the dean of the college they attend.

dear ▶ **adjective 1** regarded with deep affection; cherished by someone: *a dear friend* | *he is very* **dear to** *me.*
■used in speech as a way of addressing a person in a polite way: *Martin, my dear fellow.* ■ used as part of the polite introduction to a letter: *Dear Sir or Madam.* ■ endearing; sweet: *a* **dear little** *puppy.*
2 expensive: *five pounds—that's a bit dear!*
■(of money) available as a loan only at a high rate of interest.
▶ **noun** used as an affectionate or friendly form of address: *don't you worry, dear.*
■a sweet or endearing person.
▶ **adverb** at a high cost: *they buy property cheaply and sell dear.*
▶ **exclamation** used in expressions of surprise, dismay, or sympathy: *oh dear, I've upset you.*
– PHRASES **for dear life** see **LIFE**.
– DERIVATIVES **dearness** noun.
– ORIGIN Old English *dēore*, of Germanic origin; related to Dutch *dier* 'beloved', also to Dutch *duur* and German *teuer* 'expensive'.

dearest ▶ **adjective 1** most loved or cherished: *one of my dearest friends.*
2 most expensive: *beer is dearest in Germany.*
▶ **noun** used as an affectionate form of address to a much-loved person: *you make me so happy, dearest.*
■a much-loved person: *I was going to miss my dearest.*

dearie ▶ **noun** (pl. **-ies**) informal, chiefly Brit. used as a friendly or condescending form of address.
– PHRASES **dearie me!** used to express surprise or dismay.

Dear John letter (also **Dear John**) ▶ **noun** informal a letter from a woman to a man, terminating a personal relationship.

dearly ▶ **adverb 1** very much: *he loved his parents dearly.*
2 with much loss or suffering; at great cost: *freedom to worship our religion has been bought dearly.*

dearth /dəːθ/ ▶ **noun** [in sing.] a scarcity or lack of something: *there is* **a dearth of** *evidence* | [mass noun] *times of dearth.*
– ORIGIN Middle English *derthe* (originally in the sense 'shortage and dearness of food') (see **DEAR**, **-TH**[2]).

deasil /ˈdɛs(ə)l, ˈdjɛʃ(ə)l/ (also **deisal**) ▶ **adverb** dated, chiefly Scottish in the direction of the sun's apparent course, considered as lucky; clockwise.
– ORIGIN late 18th cent.: from Scottish Gaelic *deiseil*.

death ▶ **noun** [mass noun] the action or fact of dying or being killed; the end of the life of a person or organism: *I don't believe in life after death* | [as modifier] *a death sentence.*
■an instance of a person or an animal dying: *there's been a death in his family.* ■ the state of being dead: *even in death, she was beautiful.* ■ the permanent ending of vital processes in a cell or tissue. ■ (**Death**) [in sing.] the personification of the power that destroys life, often represented in art and literature as a skeleton or an old man holding a scythe. ■ [in sing.] figurative the destruction or permanent end of something: *the death of her hopes.* ■ figurative a damaging or destructive state of affairs: *to be driven to a dance by one's father would be social death.*
– PHRASES **as sure as death** quite certain. **at death's door** (especially in hyperbolic use) so ill that one may die. **be the death of** (often used hyperbolically or humorously) cause someone's death: *you'll be the death of me with all your questions.* **be in at the death** be present when a hunted animal is caught and killed. ■ be present when something fails or comes to an end. **catch one's death** (**of cold**) informal catch a severe cold or chill. **die a** (or **the**) **death** come to an end; cease or fail to be popular or successful: *the craze for cycling shorts is dying a death.* **do someone to death** kill someone. **do something to death** perform or repeat something so frequently that it becomes tediously familiar: *a subject that has been done to death by generations of painters.* **a fate worse than death** a terrible experience, especially that of seduction or rape. **like death warmed up** (or N. Amer. **over**) informal extremely tired or ill. **a matter of life and death** see **LIFE**. **put someone to death** kill someone, especially with official sanction. **till** (or **until**) **death us do part** for as long as each of a couple live. [ORIGIN: from the marriage service in the *Book of Common Prayer*.] **to death** used of a particular action or process that results in someone's death: *he was stabbed to death.* ■ used to emphasize the extreme nature of a specific action, feeling, or state of mind: *I'm sick to death of you.* **to the death** until dead: *a fight to the death.*
– DERIVATIVES **deathlike** adjective.
– ORIGIN Old English *dēath*, of Germanic origin; related to Dutch *dood* and German *Tod*, also to **DIE**[1].

death adder ▶ **noun** a venomous Australian snake which has a thin worm-like tail that it uses to lure birds and other prey.
● Genus *Acanthophis*, family Elapidae: three species, in particular *A. antarcticus.*

deathbed ▶ **noun** the bed where someone is dying or has died.
■used in reference to the time when someone is dying: *she visited him on his deathbed.*

death blow ▶ **noun** an impact or stroke which causes death.
■figurative an event, circumstance, or action which abruptly ends something: *this feature of quantum mechanics* **dealt a death blow to** *the theory.*

death camp ▶ **noun** a prison camp, especially one for political prisoners or prisoners of war, in which many die from poor conditions and treatment or from mass execution.

death cap ▶ **noun** a deadly poisonous toadstool with a pale olive-green cap and white gills, growing in broadleaved woodland in both Eurasia and North America.
● *Amanita phalloides*, family Amanitaceae, class Hymenomycetes.

death cell ▶ **noun** a cell occupied by a prisoner condemned to death, especially that in which they await execution.

death certificate ▶ **noun** an official statement,

signed by a doctor, of the cause, date, and place of a person's death.

death-dealing ▶ adjective capable of causing death: *death-dealing drugs*.

death duty ▶ noun [mass noun] (in the UK) a tax levied on property after the owner's death (replaced officially in 1975 by capital transfer tax and in 1986 by inheritance tax).

death futures ▶ plural noun US informal life insurance policies of terminally ill people, purchased by a third party at less than their mature value as a form of short-term investment. See also **VIATICAL SETTLEMENT**.

death grant ▶ noun (in the UK) a state grant towards funeral expenses (abolished under the Social Security Act 1986).

death house ▶ noun a house in which someone has died.
■ a place for storing bodies prior to burial or cremation. ■ US informal the building in which prisoners are kept in preparation for execution.

death instinct ▶ noun Psychoanalysis an innate desire for self-annihilation, thought to be manifest in the conservative and regressive tendency of the psyche to reduce tension. Compare with **LIFE INSTINCT**.

death knell ▶ noun [in sing.] the tolling of a bell to mark someone's death.
■ figurative an event that heralds the end or destruction of something: *the chaos may sound the death knell for the peace plan*.

deathless ▶ adjective chiefly poetic/literary or humorous immortal: *he died before his song could be recorded, but his compositions are deathless*.
– DERIVATIVES **deathlessness** noun.

deathly ▶ adjective (**deathlier**, **deathliest**) resembling or suggestive of death: *a deathly hush fell over the breakfast table* | [as submodifier] *she felt deathly cold*.
■ archaic or poetic/literary of, relating to, or causing death: *an eagle carrying a snake in its deathly grasp*.

death mask ▶ noun a plaster cast taken of a dead person's face, used to make a mask or model.

death-or-glory ▶ adjective brave to the point of foolhardiness; reckless: *a death-or-glory approach to political problems*.

death penalty ▶ noun the punishment of executing someone legally convicted of a crime.

death rate ▶ noun the ratio of deaths to the population of a particular area during a particular period of time, usually calculated as the number of deaths per one thousand people per year.

death rattle ▶ noun a gurgling sound heard in a dying person's throat.

death ray ▶ noun an imaginary beam or ray capable of killing, typically featured in science fiction.

death roll ▶ noun Brit. old-fashioned term for **DEATH TOLL**.

death row ▶ noun (especially with reference to the US) a prison block or section for prisoners sentenced to death: *a convicted killer on death row*.

death's head ▶ noun a human skull as a symbol of mortality.

death's head hawkmoth ▶ noun a large dark European hawkmoth which has a skull-like marking on the thorax and a very large caterpillar.
● *Acherontia atropos*, family Sphingidae.

death song ▶ noun a song sung before or after someone's death or to commemorate the dead.

death squad ▶ noun an armed paramilitary group formed to kill particular people, especially political opponents.

death tax ▶ noun US term for **INHERITANCE TAX**.

death toll ▶ noun the number of deaths resulting from a particular cause, especially an accident, battle, or natural disaster.

death trap ▶ noun a place, structure, or vehicle that is potentially very dangerous.

Death Valley a deep arid desert basin below sea level in SE California and SW Nevada, the hottest and driest part of North America.

death warrant ▶ noun an official order for the execution of a condemned person.

death-watch beetle ▶ noun a small beetle

whose larvae bore into dead wood and structural timbers, causing considerable damage. The adult makes a tapping sound like a watch ticking, formerly believed to portend death.
● *Xestobium rufovillosum*, family Anobiidae.

death wish ▶ noun a desire for someone's death, especially an unconscious desire for one's own death. Compare with **DEATH INSTINCT**.

deattribute /ˌdiːəˈtrɪbjuːt/ ▶ verb [with obj.] cease to attribute (a work of art) to a particular artist.
– DERIVATIVES **deattribution** noun.

deb ▶ noun informal short for **DEBUTANTE**.

debacle /deɪˈbɑːk(ə)l/ ▶ noun a sudden and ignominious failure; a fiasco.
– ORIGIN early 19th cent.: from French *débâcle*, from *débâcler* 'unleash', from *dé-* 'un-' + *bâcler* 'to bar' (from Latin *baculum* 'staff').

debag /diːˈbaɡ/ ▶ verb (**debagged**, **debagging**) [with obj.] Brit. informal remove the trousers of (someone) as a joke or punishment.

deballast ▶ verb [with obj.] remove ballast from (a ship) in order to increase its buoyancy.

debar ▶ verb (**debarred**, **debarring**) [with obj.] (usu. **be debarred**) exclude or prohibit (someone) officially from doing something: *first-round candidates were debarred from standing*.
– DERIVATIVES **debarment** noun.
– ORIGIN late Middle English: from French *débarrer*, from Old French *desbarrer* 'unbar', from *des-* (expressing reversal) + *barrer* 'to bar'.

debark¹ ▶ verb [no obj.] leave a ship or aircraft.
■ [with obj.] unload (cargo or troops) from a ship or aircraft.
– DERIVATIVES **debarkation** noun.
– ORIGIN mid 17th cent.: from French *débarquer*.

debark² ▶ verb [with obj.] remove (the bark) from a tree.

debase /dɪˈbeɪs/ ▶ verb [with obj.] reduce (something) in quality or value; degrade: *the love episodes debase the dignity of the drama* | [as adj. **debased**] *the debased traditions of sportsmanship*.
■ lower the moral character of (someone): *war debases people*. ■ historical lower the value of (coinage) by reducing the content of precious metal.
– DERIVATIVES **debasement** noun, **debaser** noun.
– ORIGIN mid 16th cent. (in the sense 'humiliate, belittle'): from **DE-** 'down' + the obsolete verb *base* (compare with **ABASE**), expressing the notion 'bring down completely'.

debatable ▶ adjective open to discussion or argument: *it is debatable whether the country is coming out of recession*.
■ historical (of land) on the border between two countries and claimed by each.
– DERIVATIVES **debatably** adverb.

debate ▶ noun a formal discussion on a particular matter in a public meeting or legislative assembly, in which opposing arguments are put forward and which usually ends with a vote.
■ an argument about a particular subject, especially one in which many people are involved: *the national debate on abortion* | [mass noun] *there has been much debate about prices*.
▶ verb [with obj.] argue about (a subject), especially in a formal manner: *MPs debated the issue in the Commons* | [no obj.] *members of the society debated for five nights*.
■ [with clause] consider a possible course of action in one's mind before reaching a decision: *he debated whether he should have the matter alone or speak to her*.
– PHRASES **be open to debate** be unproven and requiring further discussion. **under debate** being discussed or disputed.
– DERIVATIVES **debater** noun.
– ORIGIN Middle English: via Old French from Latin *dis-* (expressing reversal) + *battere* 'to fight'.

debating point ▶ noun an extraneous proposition or inessential piece of information used to gain advantage in a debate.

debauch /dɪˈbɔːtʃ/ ▶ verb [with obj.] destroy or debase the moral purity of; corrupt.
■ dated seduce (a woman): *he debauched sixteen schoolgirls*.
▶ noun a bout of excessive indulgence in sensual pleasures, especially eating and drinking.
■ [mass noun] the habit or practice of such indulgence; debauchery: *his life had been spent in debauch*.
– DERIVATIVES **debaucher** noun.
– ORIGIN late 16th cent.: from French *débaucher* (verb)

'turn away from one's duty', from Old French *desbaucher*, of uncertain ultimate origin.

debauched ▶ adjective indulging in or characterized by sensual pleasures to a degree perceived to be morally harmful; dissolute: *a debauched lifestyle*.

debauchee /ˌdiːbɔːˈtʃiː, -ˈʃiː/ ▶ noun a person given to excessive indulgence in sensual pleasures.
– ORIGIN mid 17th cent.: from French *débauché* 'turned away from duty', past participle of *débaucher* (see **DEBAUCH**).

debauchery ▶ noun [mass noun] excessive indulgence in sensual pleasures.

debby ▶ adjective informal characteristic of a debutante: *a debby girlfriend*.

debeak ▶ verb [with obj.] remove the upper part of the beak of (a bird) to prevent it injuring other birds: [as noun **debeaking**] *debeaking is thought to cause chickens chronic pain*.

de Beauvoir /də ˈbəʊvwɑː, French də bovwaʀ/, Simone (1908–86), French existentialist philosopher, novelist, and feminist. Her best-known work is *The Second Sex* (1949), a central book of the 'second wave' of feminism. She is strongly associated with Jean-Paul Sartre, with whom she had a lifelong association.

debenture /dɪˈbɛntʃə/ ▶ noun Brit. a long-term security yielding a fixed rate of interest, issued by a company and secured against assets.
■ (also **debenture bond**) N. Amer. an unsecured loan certificate issued by a company.
– ORIGIN late Middle English (denoting a voucher issued by a royal household, giving the right to claim payment for goods or services): from Latin *debentur* 'are owing' (from *debere* 'owe'), used as the first word of a certificate recording a debt. The current sense dates from the mid 19th cent.

debilitate /dɪˈbɪlɪteɪt/ ▶ verb [with obj.] [often as adj. **debilitating**] make (someone) very weak and infirm: *a debilitating disease* | [as adj. **debilitated**] *a debilitated patient*.
■ hinder, delay, or weaken: *the debilitating effects of underinvestment*.
– DERIVATIVES **debilitatingly** adverb, **debilitation** noun, **debilitative** adjective.
– ORIGIN mid 16th cent.: from Latin *debilitat-* 'weakened', from the verb *debilitare*, from *debilitas* (see **DEBILITY**).

debility ▶ noun [mass noun] physical weakness, especially as a result of illness.
– ORIGIN late Middle English: from Old French *debilite*, from Latin *debilitas*, from *debilis* 'weak'.

debit ▶ noun an entry recording a sum owed, listed on the left-hand side or column of an account. The opposite of **CREDIT**.
■ a payment made or owed.
▶ verb (**debited**, **debiting**) [with obj.] (usu. **be debited**) (of a bank or other financial organization) remove (an amount of money) from a customer's account, typically as payment for services or goods: *$10,000 was debited from their account*.
■ remove an amount of money from (a bank account): *cash terminals automatically debit a customer's bank account*.
– PHRASES **be in debit** (of an account) show a net balance of money owed to others. **on the debit side** as an unsatisfactory aspect of the situation: *on the debit side they predict a rise in book prices*.
– ORIGIN late Middle English (in the sense 'debt'): from French *débit*, from Latin *debitum* 'something owed' (see **DEBT**). The verb sense dates from the 17th cent.; the current noun sense from the late 18th cent.

debitage /ˌdɛbɪˈtɑːʒ/ ▶ noun [mass noun] Archaeology waste material produced in the making of prehistoric stone implements.
– ORIGIN mid 20th cent.: from French *débitage* 'cutting of stone', from *débiter* 'discharge, dispense'.

debit card ▶ noun a card issued by a bank or building society allowing the holder to transfer money electronically to another bank account when making a purchase.

deblur ▶ verb (**deblurred**, **deblurring**) [with obj.] technical make (a blurred image) sharper.

debonair ▶ adjective (of a man) confident, stylish, and charming.
– DERIVATIVES **debonairly** adverb.
– ORIGIN Middle English (in the sense 'meek or

courteous'): from Old French *debonaire*, from *de bon aire* 'of good disposition'.

Deborah /ˈdɛbərə, ˈdɛbrə/ a biblical prophet and leader who inspired the Israelite army to defeat the Canaanites (Judges 4–5). The 'Song of Deborah', a song of victory attributed to her, is thought to be one of the oldest sections of the Bible.

debouch /dɪˈbaʊtʃ, -ˈbuːʃ/ ▶ verb [no obj., with adverbial of direction] emerge from a narrow or confined space into a wide, open area: *the stream finally debouches into a silent pool*.
– DERIVATIVES **debouchment** noun.
– ORIGIN mid 18th cent.: from French *déboucher*, from *dé-* (expressing removal) + *bouche* 'mouth' (from Latin *bucca* 'cheek').

Debrecen /ˈdɛbrɒtsɛn/ an industrial and commercial city in eastern Hungary; pop. 217,290 (1993).

Debrett /dɪˈbrɛt/, John (*c.*1750–1822), English publisher. He compiled *The Peerage of England, Scotland, and Ireland* (first issued in 1803), which is regarded as the authority on the British nobility.

debridement /deɪˈbriːdmɒ̃, dɪˈbriːdm(ə)nt/ ▶ noun [mass noun] Medicine the removal of damaged tissue or foreign objects from a wound.
– ORIGIN mid 19th cent.: from French, from *débrider*, literally 'unbridle', based on *bride* 'bridle' (of Germanic origin).

debrief ▶ verb [with obj.] question (someone, typically a soldier or spy) about a completed mission or undertaking: *together they debriefed their two colleagues* | [as noun **debriefing**] *during his debriefing he exposed two Russian spies*.
▶ noun a series of questions about a completed mission or undertaking.
– DERIVATIVES **debriefer** noun.

debris /ˈdɛbriː, ˈdeɪbriː/ ▶ noun [mass noun] scattered pieces of rubbish or remains.
■ loose natural material consisting especially of broken pieces of rock.
– ORIGIN early 18th cent.: from French *débris*, from obsolete *débriser* 'break down'.

de Broglie /də ˈbrɔʊɡli, French də brɔj/, Louis-Victor, Prince (1892–1987), French physicist. He was the first to suggest that subatomic particles can also have the properties of waves, and his name is now applied to such a wave. He further developed the study of wave mechanics, which was fundamental to the subsequent development of quantum mechanics. Nobel Prize for Physics (1929).

debruise /dɪˈbruːz/ ▶ verb [with obj.] (usu. **be debruised**) Heraldry partly obscure (another charge).

debt ▶ noun something, typically a sum of money, that is owed or due: *I paid off my debts* | [mass noun] *a way to reduce Third World debt*.
■ [mass noun] the state of owing money: *the firm is heavily in debt.* ■ [usu. in sing.] a feeling of gratitude for a service or favour: *we owe them a debt of thanks.*
– PHRASES **be in someone's debt** owe gratitude to someone for a service or favour.
– ORIGIN Middle English *dette*: from Old French, based on Latin *debitum* 'something owed', past participle of *debere* 'owe'. The spelling change in French and English was by association with the Latin word.

debt collector ▶ noun a person who is employed to collect debts for creditors.

debt counsellor ▶ noun a person who offers professional advice on methods of debt repayment.

debt of honour ▶ noun a debt that is not legally recoverable, especially a sum lost in gambling.

debtor ▶ noun a person or institution that owes a sum of money.

debt security ▶ noun a negotiable or tradable liability or loan.

debt swap (also **debt-for-nature swap**) ▶ noun a transaction in which a foreign exchange debt owed by a developing country is transferred to another organization on the condition that the country uses local currency for a designated purpose, usually environmental protection.

debug ▶ verb (**debugged**, **debugging**) [with obj.] **1** identify and remove errors from (computer hardware or software): *games are the worst to debug* | [as noun **debugging**] *software debugging*.
2 detect and remove concealed microphones from (an area).

3 N. Amer. remove insects from (something), especially with a pesticide.
▶ noun [mass noun] the process of identifying and removing errors from computer hardware or software.

debugger ▶ noun a computer program that assists in the detection and correction of errors in other computer programs.

debunk ▶ verb [with obj.] expose the falseness or hollowness of (a myth, idea, or belief): *she debunks all the usual rubbish about acting.*
■ reduce the inflated reputation of (someone), especially by ridicule: *comedy takes delight in debunking heroes.*
– DERIVATIVES **debunker** noun, **debunkery** noun.

deburr /diːˈbəː/ (also **debur**) ▶ verb (**deburred**, **deburring**) [with obj.] neaten and smooth the rough edges or ridges of (an object, typically one made of metal): *hand tools for deburring holes in metal.*

debus /diːˈbʌs/ ▶ verb (**debussed**, **debussing**) [no obj.] Brit., chiefly military slang alight from a motor vehicle: *they debussed in a tarmac-laid square.*
■ [with obj.] unload (personnel or stores) from a vehicle.

Debussy /dəˈbjuːsi, French dəbysi/, (Achille) Claude (1862–1918), French composer and critic. Debussy carried the ideas of Impressionist art and symbolist poetry into music, using melodies based on the whole-tone scale and delicate harmonies exploiting overtones. Notable works: *Prélude à l'après-midi d'un faune* (1894).

debut /ˈdeɪbjuː, -buː/ ▶ noun a person's first appearance or performance in a particular capacity or role.
■ dated the first appearance of a debutante in society. ■ [as modifier] denoting the first recording or publication of a group, singer, or writer: *a debut album.* ■ the first public appearance of a new product or presentation of a theatrical show: *the car makes its world debut next week.*
▶ verb [no obj., with adverbial] perform in public for the first time: *the Rolling Stones debuted at the Marquee.*
■ (of a new product) be launched: *the model is expected to debut at $19,000.* ■ [with obj.] (of a company) launch (a new product): *the company is to debut new software.*
– ORIGIN mid 18th cent.: from French *début*, from *débuter* 'lead off'.

debutant /ˈdɛbjuːtɒ̃, ˈdeɪ-/ ▶ noun a man making his first public appearance, especially in sport.
– ORIGIN early 19th cent.: from French *débutant* 'leading off', from the verb *débuter*.

debutante /ˈdɛbjʊtɒnt, ˈdeɪ-/ ▶ noun an upper-class young woman making her first appearance in fashionable society.
■ a woman making her first public appearance, especially in sport.
– ORIGIN early 19th cent.: from French *débutante* (feminine) 'leading off', from the verb *débuter*.

Debye /dəˈbʌɪ/, Peter Joseph William (1884–1966), Dutch-born American chemical physicist. Debye is best known for establishing the existence of permanent electric dipole moments in many molecules, demonstrating the use of these to determine molecular size and shape, and modifying Einstein's theory of specific heats as applied to solids. Nobel Prize for Chemistry (1936).

debye /dəˈbʌɪ/ (also **debye unit**) ▶ noun Chemistry a unit used to express electric dipole moments of molecules. One debye is equal to 3.336×10^{-30} coulomb metre.
– ORIGIN early 20th cent.: named after P. J. **DEBYE**.

Dec. ▶ abbreviation for December.

dec. ▶ abbreviation for ■ deceased. ■ Cricket declared.

deca- /ˈdɛkə/ (also **dec-** before a vowel) ▶ combining form (used commonly in units of measurement) ten; having ten: *decahedron* | *decane.*
– ORIGIN from Greek *deka* 'ten'.

decade /ˈdɛkeɪd, dɪˈkeɪd/ ▶ noun **1** a period of ten years.
■ a period of ten years beginning with a year ending in 0.
2 a set, series, or group of ten, in particular:
■ each of the five divisions of each chapter of the rosary. ■ a range of electrical resistances, frequencies, or other quantities spanning from one to ten times a base value: *power per decade of frequency.*
– DERIVATIVES **decadal** adjective.
– ORIGIN late Middle English (denoting each of ten parts of a literary work): via Old French and late

Latin from Greek *deka* 'ten'. Sense 1 dates from the early 17th cent.

> **USAGE** There are two possible pronunciations for **decade**: one puts the stress on the **dec-** while the other puts the stress on the **-cade** (sounds like *decayed*). The second pronunciation is disapproved of by some traditionalists but is now regarded as a standard, acceptable alternative.

decadence /ˈdɛkəd(ə)ns/ ▶ noun [mass noun] the process, period, or manifestation of moral or cultural decline: *he denounced Western decadence.*
■ behaviour reflecting such a decline: *the juvenile nature of his decadence reveals itself.* ■ luxurious self-indulgence: *cream cakes on a Wednesday—pure decadence.*
– ORIGIN mid 16th cent.: from French *décadence*, from medieval Latin *decadentia*; related to **DECAY**.

decadent ▶ adjective characterized by or reflecting a state of moral or cultural decline.
■ luxuriously self-indulgent: *a decadent soak in a scented bath.*
▶ noun a person who is luxuriously self-indulgent.
■ (often **Decadent**) a member of a group of late 19th-century French and English poets associated with the Aesthetic Movement.
– DERIVATIVES **decadently** adverb.
– ORIGIN mid 19th cent.: from French *décadent*, from medieval Latin *decadentia* (see **DECADENCE**).

decaf /ˈdiːkaf/ (also **decaff**) ▶ noun [mass noun] informal (trademark in the UK) decaffeinated coffee.
– ORIGIN 1960s: abbreviation.

decaffeinate /diːˈkafɪneɪt/ ▶ verb [with obj. (usu. as adj. **decaffeinated**)] remove most or all of the caffeine from (coffee or tea): *decaffeinated coffee.*
– DERIVATIVES **decaffeination** noun.

decagon /ˈdɛkəɡ(ə)n/ ▶ noun a plane figure with ten straight sides and angles.
– DERIVATIVES **decagonal** adjective.
– ORIGIN mid 17th cent.: via medieval Latin from Greek *dekagōnon*, neuter (used as a noun) of *dekagōnos* 'ten-angled'.

decahedron /ˌdɛkəˈhiːdr(ə)n, -ˈhɛd-/ ▶ noun (pl. **decahedra** or **decahedrons**) a solid figure with ten plane faces.
– DERIVATIVES **decahedral** adjective.
– ORIGIN early 19th cent.: from **DECA-** 'ten' + **-HEDRON**, on the pattern of words such as *polyhedron.*

decal /ˈdiːkal/ ▶ noun informal, chiefly N. Amer. a design prepared on special paper for durable transfer on to another surface such as glass or porcelain.
– ORIGIN 1950s: abbreviation of **DECALCOMANIA**.

decalcified ▶ adjective (of rock or bone) containing a reduced quantity of calcium salts: *decalcified chalk.*
– DERIVATIVES **decalcification** noun, **decalcifier** noun.

decalcomania /dɪˌkalkə(ʊ)ˈmeɪnɪə/ ▶ noun [mass noun] the process of transferring designs from prepared paper on to glass or porcelain.
■ a technique used by some surrealist artists which involves pressing paint between sheets of paper.
– ORIGIN mid 19th cent.: from French *décalcomanie*, from *décalquer* 'transfer a tracing' + *-manie* '-mania' (with reference to the enthusiasm for the process in the 1860s).

decalitre (US **decaliter**, **dekaliter**) (abbrev.: **dal**; US also **dkl**) ▶ noun a metric unit of capacity, equal to 10 litres.

Decalogue /ˈdɛkəlɒɡ/ ▶ noun (usu. **the Decalogue**) the Ten Commandments.
– ORIGIN late Middle English: via French and ecclesiastical Latin from Greek *dekalogos (biblos)* '(book of) the Ten Commandments', from *hoi deka logoi* 'the Ten Commandments' (literally 'the ten sayings').

Decameron /dɪˈkamərən/ a work by Boccaccio, written between 1348 and 1358, containing a hundred tales supposedly told in ten days by a party of ten young people who had fled from the Black Death in Florence. The work was influential on later writers such as Chaucer and Shakespeare.

decametre (US **decameter**, **dekameter**) (abbrev.: **dam**; US also **dkm**) ▶ noun a metric unit of length, equal to 10 metres.
– DERIVATIVES **decametric** adjective.

decamp ▶ verb [no obj.] depart suddenly, especially

to relocate one's business or household in another area: *now he has* **decamped to** *Hollywood.*
▪abscond hurriedly to avoid prosecution or detection: *the copyists sold the originals and decamped with the proceeds.* ▪ archaic break up or leave a military camp: *the armies of both chiefs had decamped.*
– DERIVATIVES **decampment** noun.
– ORIGIN late 17th cent.: from French *décamper*, from *dé-* (expressing removal) + *camp* 'camp'.

decan /ˈdɛk(ə)n/ ▶ **noun** Astrology each of three equal ten-degree divisions of a sign of the zodiac.
– ORIGIN late 16th cent.: from late Latin *decanus* 'chief of a group of ten' (see **DEAN**[1]).

decanal /dɪˈkeɪn(ə)l, ˈdɛk(ə)n(ə)l/ ▶ **adjective** of or relating to a dean or deanery.
▪relating to or denoting the south side of the choir of a church, the side on which the dean sits. The opposite of **CANTORIAL**.
– ORIGIN early 18th cent.: from medieval Latin *decanalis*, from late Latin *decanus* (see **DEAN**[1]).

decane /ˈdɛkeɪn/ ▶ **noun** [mass noun] Chemistry a colourless liquid hydrocarbon of the alkane series, present in petroleum spirit.
• Chem. formula: $C_{10}H_{22}$; many isomers, especially the straight-chain isomer (*n*-**decane**), which is used as a solvent and in jet fuel research.

decani /dɪˈkeɪnʌɪ/ ▶ **noun** the section of a church or cathedral choir conventionally placed on the south side and taking the first or higher part in antiphonal singing. The opposite of **CANTORIS**.
– ORIGIN mid 18th cent.: from Latin, literally 'of the dean' (see **DEAN**[1]).

decant /dɪˈkant/ ▶ **verb** [with obj.] gradually pour (wine, port, or another liquid) from one container into another, typically in order to separate the liquid from the sediment: *he decanted the rich red liquid into a pair of glasses.*
▪figurative, informal discharge or transfer (passengers) to another place: *tour coaches* **decant** *eager customers directly* **into** *the store.*
– ORIGIN mid 17th cent.: from medieval Latin *decanthare*, from Latin *de-* 'away from' + *canthus* 'edge, rim' (used to denote the angular lip of a beaker), from Greek *kanthos* 'corner of the eye'.

decanter ▶ **noun** a stoppered glass container into which wine or spirit is decanted.

decapitate /dɪˈkapɪteɪt/ ▶ **verb** [with obj.] cut off the head of (someone): [as adj. **decapitated**] *a decapitated body.*
▪cut the end or top from (something). ▪ figurative attempt to undermine (a group or organization) by removing its leaders: *the Church had been decapitated by the arrest and deportation of all its bishops.*
– DERIVATIVES **decapitation** noun, **decapitator** noun.
– ORIGIN early 17th cent.: from late Latin *decapitat-* 'decapitated', from the verb *decapitare*, from *de-* (expressing removal) + *caput, capit-* 'head'.

Decapoda /ˌdɛkəˈpəʊdə/ Zoology **1** an order of crustaceans which includes shrimps, crabs, and lobsters. They have five pairs of walking legs and are typically marine.
2 a former order of cephalopod molluscs which includes squids and cuttlefishes, which have eight arms and two long tentacles. Compare with **OCTOPODA**.
– DERIVATIVES **decapod** /ˈdɛkəpɒd/ noun & adjective.
– ORIGIN modern Latin (plural), from **DECA-** 'ten' + Greek *pous, pod-* 'foot'.

decapsulate ▶ **verb** [with obj.] Surgery remove the capsule or covering from (a kidney or other organ).
– DERIVATIVES **decapsulation** noun.

decarbonize (also **-ise**) ▶ **verb** [with obj.] remove carbon or carbonaceous deposits from (an engine or other metal object).
– DERIVATIVES **decarbonization** noun, **decarbonizer** noun.

decarboxylase /ˌdiːkɑːˈbɒksɪleɪz/ ▶ **noun** Biochemistry an enzyme that catalyses the decarboxylation of a particular organic molecule.

decarboxylate /ˌdiːkɑːˈbɒksɪleɪt/ ▶ **verb** [with obj.] Chemistry eliminate a carboxylic acid group from (an organic compound).
▪[no obj.] undergo this process.
– DERIVATIVES **decarboxylation** noun.

decarburize /diːˈkɑːbjʊrʌɪz/ (also **-ise**) ▶ **verb** [with obj.] Metallurgy remove carbon from (iron or steel).
– DERIVATIVES **decarburization** noun.
– ORIGIN mid 19th cent.: from **DE-** (expressing removal) + **CARBURIZE**, on the pattern of French *décarburer.*

decastyle /ˈdɛkəstʌɪl/ Architecture ▶ **adjective** (of a temple or portico) having ten columns.
▶ **noun** a ten-columned portico.
– ORIGIN early 18th cent.: from Greek *dekastulos* 'having ten columns', from *deka* 'ten' + *stulos* 'column'.

decasyllabic /ˌdɛkəsɪˈlabɪk/ Prosody ▶ **adjective** (of a metrical line) consisting of ten syllables.
▶ **noun** a metrical line of ten syllables.

decathlon /dɪˈkaθlɒn, -lən/ ▶ **noun** an athletic event taking place over two days, in which each competitor takes part in the same prescribed ten events (100 metres sprint, long jump, shot-put, high jump, 400 metres, 110 metres hurdles, discus, pole vault, javelin, and 1,500 metres).
– DERIVATIVES **decathlete** noun.
– ORIGIN early 20th cent.: from **DECA-** 'ten' + Greek *athlon* 'contest'.

decay ▶ **verb** [no obj.] (of organic matter) rot or decompose through the action of bacteria and fungi: *a jelly that rapidly decays into an unpleasant mush* | [as adj. **decaying**] *the odour of decaying fish.*
▪[with obj.] cause to rot or decompose: *the fungus will decay soft timber.* ▪ (of a building or area) fall into disrepair; deteriorate: *facilities decay when money is not spent on refurbishment.* ▪ decline in quality, power, or vigour: *the moral authority of the party was decaying.* ▪ Physics (of a radioactive substance, particle, etc.) undergo change to a different form by emitting radiation: *the trapped radiocarbon begins to decay at a known rate.* ▪ technical (of a physical quantity) undergo a gradual decrease: *the time taken for the current to* **decay to** *zero.*
▶ **noun** [mass noun] the state or process of rotting or decomposition: *hardwood is more resistant to decay than softwood* | *tooth decay.*
▪structural or physical deterioration: *the old barn rapidly* **fell into decay**. ▪ rotten matter or tissue: *fluoride heals small spots of decay.* ▪ the process of declining in quality, power, or vigour: *the problems of urban decay.* ▪ Physics the change of a radioactive substance, particle, etc. into another by the emission of radiation: *the gas radon is produced by the decay of uranium in rocks and soil* | [count noun] *he developed a detector for decays of carbon-14.* ▪ technical gradual decrease in the magnitude of a physical quantity: *the required time constant for current decay is 1 ms.*
– ORIGIN late Middle English: from Old French *decair*, based on Latin *decidere* 'fall down or off', from *de-* 'from' + *cadere* 'fall'.

Deccan /ˈdɛkən/ a triangular plateau in southern India, bounded by the Malabar Coast in the west, the Coromandel Coast in the east, and by the Vindhaya mountains in the north.

decease ▶ **noun** [in sing.] formal or Law death: *a doctor's sudden decease.*
▶ **verb** [no obj.] archaic die.
– ORIGIN Middle English: from Old French *deces*, from Latin *decessus* 'death', past participle (used as a noun) of *decedere* 'to die'.

deceased formal or Law ▶ **noun** (**the deceased**) the recently dead person in question.
▶ **adjective** recently dead: *the deceased Turkish ambassador* | [postpositive] *the will of Christopher Smith deceased.*

decedent /dɪˈsiːd(ə)nt/ ▶ **noun** US Law a deceased person.
– ORIGIN late 16th cent.: from Latin *decedent-* 'dying', from the verb *decedere* (see **DECEASE**).

deceit ▶ **noun** [mass noun] the action or practice of deceiving or misleading someone by concealing or misrepresenting the truth: *a web of deceit.*
▪[count noun] a dishonest act or statement. ▪ deceitful disposition or character: *I can't stand your treachery and deceit.*
– ORIGIN Middle English: from Old French, past participle (used as a noun) of *deceveir* 'deceive'.

deceitful ▶ **adjective** (of a person) deceiving or misleading others, typically on a habitual basis.
▪intended to deceive or mislead: *such an act would have been deceitful and irresponsible.*
– DERIVATIVES **deceitfully** adverb, **deceitfulness** noun.

deceive ▶ **verb** [with obj.] (of a person) cause (someone) to believe something that is not true, typically in order to gain some personal advantage: *I didn't intend to* **deceive** *people* **into** *thinking it was French champagne.*
▪(often **be deceived**) (of a thing) cause to give a mistaken impression: *the area may seem to offer nothing of interest, but don't be deceived* | [no obj.] *everything about him was intended to deceive.* ▪ (**deceive oneself**) fail to admit to oneself that something is true. ▪ be sexually unfaithful to (one's regular partner).
– DERIVATIVES **deceivable** adjective, **deceiver** noun.
– ORIGIN Middle English: from Old French *deceivre*, from Latin *decipere* 'catch, ensnare, cheat'.

decelerate /diːˈsɛləreɪt/ ▶ **verb** [no obj.] (of a vehicle, machine, or process) begin to move more slowly.
▪[with obj.] cause to move more slowly: *four steps are required to decelerate the motor.*
– DERIVATIVES **deceleration** noun, **decelerator** noun, **decelerometer** /-ˈrɒmɪtə/ noun.
– ORIGIN late 19th cent.: from **DE-** (expressing removal) + a shortened form of **ACCELERATE**.

December ▶ **noun** the twelfth month of the year, in the northern hemisphere usually considered the first month of winter: *the fuel shortage worsened during December* | [as modifier] *a December day.*
– ORIGIN Middle English: from Latin, from *decem* 'ten' (being originally the tenth month of the Roman year).

Decembrist /dɪˈsɛmbrɪst/ ▶ **noun** a member of a group of Russian revolutionaries who in December 1825 led an unsuccessful revolt against Tsar Nicholas I. The leaders were executed and later came to be regarded as martyrs by the Left.

decency ▶ **noun** (pl. **-ies**) [mass noun] behaviour that conforms to accepted standards of morality or respectability: *she* **had the decency to** *come and confess.*
▪avoidance of being shocking or obscene: *a loose dress, rather too low-cut for decency.* ▪ (**decencies**) the requirements of accepted or respectable behaviour: *an appeal to common decencies.* ▪ (**decencies**) things required for a reasonable standard of life: *I can't afford any of the decencies of life.*

decennial /dɪˈsɛnɪəl/ ▶ **adjective** recurring every ten years: *the decennial census.*
▪lasting for or relating to a period of ten years: *decennial insurance.*
– DERIVATIVES **decennially** adverb.
– ORIGIN mid 17th cent.: from Latin *decennium* 'a decade', from *decennis* 'of ten years' (from *decem* 'ten' + *annus* 'year'), + **-AL**.

decennium ▶ **noun** (pl. **decennia** or **decenniums**) a decade.
– ORIGIN late 17th cent.: from Latin, from *decem* 'ten' + *annus* 'year'.

decent ▶ **adjective 1** conforming with generally accepted standards of respectable or moral behaviour: *a decent clean-living individual.*
▪appropriate; fitting: *they would meet again after a decent interval.* ▪ not likely to shock or embarrass others: *a decent high-necked dress.* ▪ informal sufficiently clothed to see visitors: *'Hello, miss? Are you decent?'*
2 [attrib.] of an acceptable standard; satisfactory: *find me a decent cup of coffee* | *people need decent homes.*
▪good: *there's a few decent players in the team.* ▪ Brit. informal kind, obliging, or generous: *that's awfully decent of you.*
– PHRASES **do the decent thing** take the most honourable or appropriate course of action, even if is not necessarily in one's own interests: *after his defeat he should do the decent thing and step down.*
– DERIVATIVES **decently** adverb.
– ORIGIN mid 16th cent. (in the sense 'suitable, appropriate'): from Latin *decent-* 'being fitting', from the verb *decere*.

decentralize (also **-ise**) ▶ **verb** [with obj.] [often as adj. **decentralized**] transfer (authority) from central to local government: *Canada has one of the most decentralized governments in the world* | [no obj.] *European countries were trying to decentralize and devolve.*
▪move departments of (a large organization) away from a single administrative centre to other locations, usually granting them some degree of autonomy.
– DERIVATIVES **decentralist** noun & adjective, **decentralization** noun.

decentre (US **decenter**) ▶ **verb** [with obj.] displace from the centre or from a central position.
▪remove or displace (the individual human subject, such as the author of a text) from a primary place or central role: [as noun **decentring**] *the decentring of the author is paradigmatic of contemporary experimental fiction.*

deception ▶ **noun** [mass noun] the action of deceiving someone: *obtaining property by deception.*
▪[count noun] a thing that deceives: *a range of elaborate deceptions.*

– ORIGIN late Middle English: from late Latin *deceptio(n-)*, from *decipere* 'deceive'.

deceptive ▶ **adjective** giving an appearance or impression different from the true one; misleading: *he put the question with deceptive casualness.*
– DERIVATIVES **deceptiveness** noun.

deceptively ▶ **adverb** [usu. as submodifier] in a way or to an extent that gives a misleading impression:
■ to a lesser extent than appears the case: *the idea was deceptively simple.* ■ to a greater extent than appears the case: *the airy and deceptively spacious lounge.*

USAGE **Deceptively** belongs to a very small set of words whose meaning is genuinely ambiguous in that it can be used in similar contexts to mean both one thing and also its complete opposite. A ***deceptively smooth*** *surface* is one which appears smooth but in fact is not smooth at all, while a ***deceptively spacious*** *room* is one that does not look spacious but is in fact **more** spacious than it appears. But what is a ***deceptively steep*** *gradient*? Or a person who is described as ***deceptively strong***? To avoid confusion, it is probably best to reword and not to use **deceptively** in such contexts at all.

decerebrate /diːˈsɛrɪbreɪt/ ▶ **verb** [with obj.] [usu. as adj. **decerebrated**] Biology remove the cerebrum from (a laboratory animal).
– DERIVATIVES **decerebration** noun.

decertify ▶ **verb** (**-ies**, **-ied**) [with obj.] remove a certificate or certification from (someone or something), typically for failure to comply with a regulating authority's rules or standards.
– DERIVATIVES **decertification** noun.

de-Christianization (also **-isation**) ▶ **noun** [mass noun] the action or process or removing Christian influences or characteristics from something.
– DERIVATIVES **de-Christianize** verb.

deci- ▶ **combining form** (used commonly in units of measurement) one tenth: *decilitre.*
– ORIGIN from Latin *decimus* 'tenth'.

decibel /ˈdɛsɪbɛl/ (abbrev.: **dB**) ▶ **noun** a unit used to measure the intensity of a sound or the power level of an electrical signal by comparing it with a given level on a logarithmic scale.
■ (in general use) a degree of loudness: *his voice went up several decibels.*
– ORIGIN early 20th cent.: from **DECI-** 'ten' + **BEL** (the unit being one tenth of a bel).

decide ▶ **verb** come to or cause to come to a resolution in the mind as a result of consideration: [with clause] *she decided that she liked him* | [with infinitive] *I've decided to stay on a bit* | [with obj.] *this business about the letter decided me.*
■ [no obj.] make a choice from a number of alternatives: *she had* ***decided on*** *her plan of action* | *I've* ***decided against*** *having children.* ■ [no obj.] give a judgement concerning a matter or legal case: *the courts decided in favour of the New York claimants* | [with obj.] *the judge will decide the case.* ■ [with obj.] come to a decision about (something): *the council will decide the fate of the homes.* ■ resolve or settle (a question or contest): *an exciting game was decided by a 65th-minute goal.*
– DERIVATIVES **decidable** adjective.
– ORIGIN late Middle English (in the sense 'bring to a settlement'): from French *décider*, from Latin *decidere* 'determine', from *de-* 'off' + *caedere* 'cut'.

decided ▶ **adjective** [attrib.] (of a quality) definite; unquestionable: *the sunshine is a decided improvement.*
■ (of a person) having clear opinions; resolute. ■ [attrib.] (of a legal case) that has been resolved.
– DERIVATIVES **decidedness** noun.

decidedly ▶ **adverb** **1** [usu. as submodifier] undoubtedly; undeniably: *he looked decidedly uncomfortable.*
2 in a decisive and confident way: *'No,' Donna said decidedly.*

decider ▶ **noun** a person or thing that decides or settles something, in particular:
■ [in sing.] Brit. a game or race that settles a series of contests between close competitors: *a tense promotion decider against Wolves.* ■ [in sing.] Brit. a goal or point which settles the result of a game.

decidua /dɪˈsɪdjʊə/ ▶ **noun** [mass noun] Physiology the thick layer of modified mucous membrane which lines the uterus during pregnancy and is shed with the afterbirth.
– DERIVATIVES **decidual** adjective.
– ORIGIN late 18th cent.: from modern Latin *decidua* (*membrana*), literally 'falling off (membrane)'.

deciduous /dɪˈsɪdjʊəs/ ▶ **adjective** (of a tree or shrub) shedding its leaves annually. Often contrasted with **EVERGREEN**.
■ informal (of a tree or shrub) broadleaved. ■ denoting the milk teeth of a mammal, which are shed after a time.
– DERIVATIVES **deciduously** adverb, **deciduousness** noun.
– ORIGIN late 17th cent.: from Latin *deciduus* (from *decidere* 'fall down or off') + **-OUS**.

decile /ˈdɛsʌɪl/ ▶ **noun** Statistics each of ten equal groups into which a population can be divided according to the distribution of values of a particular variable: *the lowest income decile of the population.*
■ each of the nine values of the random variable which divide a population into ten such groups.
– ORIGIN late 17th cent.: from French *décile*, from a medieval Latin derivative of Latin *decem* 'ten'.

decilitre (US **-liter**) (abbrev.: **dl**) ▶ **noun** a metric unit of capacity, equal to one tenth of a litre.

decimal ▶ **adjective** relating to or denoting a system of numbers and arithmetic based on the number ten, tenth parts, and powers of ten: *decimal arithmetic.*
■ relating to or denoting a system of currency, weights and measures, or other units in which the smaller units are related to the principal units as powers of ten: *decimal coinage.*
▶ **noun** (also **decimal fraction**) a fraction whose denominator is a power of ten and whose numerator is expressed by figures placed to the right of a decimal point.
■ [mass noun] the system of decimal numerical notation.
– DERIVATIVES **decimally** adverb.
– ORIGIN early 17th cent.: from modern Latin *decimalis* (adjective), from Latin *decimus* 'tenth'.

decimalize (also **-ise**) ▶ **verb** [with obj.] convert (a system of coinage or weights and measures) to a decimal system.
– DERIVATIVES **decimalization** noun.

decimal place ▶ **noun** the position of a digit to the right of a decimal point.

decimal point ▶ **noun** a full point or dot placed after the figure representing units in a decimal fraction.

decimate /ˈdɛsɪmeɪt/ ▶ **verb** [with obj.] (often **be decimated**) **1** kill, destroy, or remove a large proportion of: *the inhabitants of the country had been decimated.*
■ drastically reduce the strength or effectiveness of (something): *public transport has been decimated.*
2 historical kill one in every ten of (a group of people) as a punishment for the whole group.
– DERIVATIVES **decimation** noun, **decimator** noun.
– ORIGIN late Middle English: from Latin *decimat-* 'taken as a tenth', from the verb *decimare*, from *decimus* 'tenth'. In Middle English the term *decimation* denoted the levying of a tithe, and later the tax imposed by Cromwell on the Royalists (1655). The verb *decimate* originally alluded to the Roman punishment of executing one man in ten of a mutinous legion.

USAGE Historically, the meaning of the word **decimate** is 'kill one in every ten of (a group of people)'. This sense has been more or less totally superseded by the later, more general sense 'kill or destroy (a large proportion of)', as in *the virus has* ***decimated*** *the population.* Some traditionalists argue that this and other later senses are incorrect, but it is clear that this is now part of standard English.

decimetre (US **-meter**) (abbrev.: **dm**) ▶ **noun** a metric unit of length, equal to one tenth of a metre.
– DERIVATIVES **decimetric** adjective.

decipher /dɪˈsʌɪfə/ ▶ **verb** [with obj.] convert (a text written in code, or a coded signal) into normal language.
■ succeed in understanding, interpreting, or identifying (something): [with clause] *visual signals help us* ***decipher*** *what is being communicated.*
– DERIVATIVES **decipherable** adjective, **decipherment** noun.
– ORIGIN early 16th cent.: from **DE-** (expressing reversal) + **CIPHER**, on the pattern of French *déchiffrer.*

decision ▶ **noun** a conclusion or resolution reached after consideration: *I'll make the decision on my own* | *the editor's decision is final.*
■ [mass noun] the action or process of deciding something or of resolving a question: *the information was used as the basis for decision.* ■ [mass noun] the ability or tendency to make decisions quickly; decisiveness: *she was a woman* ***of decision.***
– ORIGIN late Middle English: from Latin *decisio(n-)*, from *decidere* 'determine' (see **DECIDE**).

decision problem ▶ **noun** Logic the problem of finding a way to decide whether a formula or class of formulas is true or provable within a given system of axioms.
– ORIGIN 1930s: translating German *Entscheidungsproblem.*

decision support system (abbrev.: **DSS**) ▶ **noun** Computing a set of related computer programs and the data required to assist with analysis and decision-making within an organization.

decision theory ▶ **noun** [mass noun] the mathematical study of strategies for optimal decision-making between options involving different risks or expectations of gain or loss depending on the outcome. Compare with **GAME THEORY**.

decisive ▶ **adjective** settling an issue; producing a definite result: *the archers played a decisive part in the victory* | *decisive evidence.*
■ (of a person) having or showing the ability to make decisions quickly and effectively.
– DERIVATIVES **decisively** adverb, **decisiveness** noun.
– ORIGIN early 17th cent.: from French *décisif, -ive*, from medieval Latin *decisivus*, from *decis-* 'determined', from the verb *decidere* (see **DECIDE**).

Decius /ˈdiːsɪəs/, Gaius Messius Quintus Trajanus (*c.*201–51), Roman emperor 249–51. He was the first Roman emperor to promote systematic persecution of the Christians in the empire.
– DERIVATIVES **Decian** adjective.

deck ▶ **noun** **1** a floor of a ship, especially the upper, open level extending for the full length of the vessel: *he stood on the deck of his flagship.*
■ the accommodation on a particular deck of a ship: *the first-class deck.* ■ a floor or platform resembling or compared to a ship's deck: *the upper deck of the car park.* ■ a floor of a double-decker bus. ■ N. Amer. short for **SUN DECK**. ■ (**the deck**) informal the ground or floor: *there was a big thud when I* ***hit the deck.*** ■ the flat part of a skateboard or snowboard.
2 a component or unit in sound-reproduction equipment that incorporates a playing or recording mechanism for discs or tapes: *a record deck.*
3 chiefly N. Amer. a pack of cards.
■ N. Amer. informal a packet of narcotics.
▶ **verb** [with obj.] **1** (usu. **be decked**) decorate or adorn brightly or festively: *Ingrid was* ***decked out in*** *her Sunday best.*
2 informal knock (someone) to the ground with a punch.
– PHRASES **below decks** see **BELOW DECKS**. **not playing with a full deck** N. Amer. informal mentally deficient. **on deck** on or on to a ship's main deck: *she stood on deck for hours.* ■ figurative, N. Amer. ready for action or work.
– DERIVATIVES **decked** adjective [in combination] *a three-decked vessel.*
– ORIGIN late Middle English: from Middle Dutch *dec* 'covering, roof, cloak', *dekken* 'to cover'. Originally denoting canvas used to make a covering (especially on a ship), the term came to mean the covering itself, later denoting a solid surface serving as roof and floor.

deck beam ▶ **noun** a horizontal beam supporting a ship's deck.

deckchair ▶ **noun** a folding chair of wood and canvas, typically used by the sea or on the deck of passenger ships.

-decker ▶ **combining form** having a specified number of decks or layers: *double-decker.*

deckhand ▶ **noun** a member of a ship's crew whose duties include cleaning, mooring, and cargo handling.

deckhead ▶ **noun** the underside of the deck of a ship.

deckhouse ▶ **noun** a cabin on the deck of a ship or boat, used for navigation or accommodation.

deckie (also **decky**) ▶ **noun** informal short for **DECKHAND**.

decking ▶ **noun** [mass noun] **1** the material of the deck of a ship, a floor, or a platform.
2 the action of ornamenting something.

a **cat** | ɑː **arm** | ɛ **bed** | ɛː **hair** | ə **ago** | əː **her** | ɪ **sit** | i **cosy** | iː **see** | ɒ **hot** | ɔː **saw** | ʌ **run** | ʊ **put** | uː **too** | ʌɪ **my** | aʊ **how** | eɪ **day** | əʊ **no** | ɪə **near** | ɔɪ **boy** | ʊə **poor** | ʌɪə **fire** | aʊə **sour**

deckle /ˈdɛk(ə)l/ ▶ **noun** (also **deckle strap**) a device in a papermaking machine for limiting the size of the sheet, consisting of a continuous belt on either side of the wire.
■ a frame on the mould used to shape the pulp when making paper by hand.
– ORIGIN mid 18th cent.: from German *Deckel*, diminutive of *Decke* 'covering'.

deckle edge ▶ **noun** the rough uncut edge of a sheet of paper, formed by a deckle.
– DERIVATIVES **deckle-edged** adjective.

deck passenger ▶ **noun** a passenger on a ship who does not have a cabin.

deck quoits ▶ **plural noun** [treated as sing.] Brit. a game in which rope quoits are aimed at a peg, played especially on cruise ships.

deck tennis ▶ **noun** a game in which a quoit of rope or rubber is tossed to and fro over a net, played especially on cruise ships.

declaim ▶ **verb** [reporting verb] utter or deliver words or a speech in a rhetorical or impassioned way, as if to an audience: [with obj.] *she declaimed her views* | [no obj.] *a preacher declaiming from the pulpit.*
■ [no obj.] (**declaim against**) forcefully protest against or criticize (something).
– DERIVATIVES **declaimer** noun, **declamatory** adjective.
– ORIGIN late Middle English: from French *déclamer* or Latin *declamare*, from *de-* (expressing thoroughness) + *clamare* 'to shout'.

declamation ▶ **noun** [mass noun] the action or art of declaiming: *Shakespearean declamation* | [count noun] *declamations of patriotism.*
■ [count noun] a rhetorical exercise or set speech. ■ forthright or distinct projection of words set to music: *a soprano soloist with wonderfully clear declamation.*
– ORIGIN late Middle English (in the sense 'a set speech'): from Latin *declamatio(n-)*, from the verb *declamare* (see **DECLAIM**).

declarant /dɪˈklɛːr(ə)nt/ chiefly Law ▶ **noun** a person or party who makes a formal declaration.
▶ **adjective** making or having made a formal declaration.
– ORIGIN late 17th cent.: from French *déclarant*, present participle of *déclarer*, from Latin *declarare* 'make quite clear' (see **DECLARE**).

declaration ▶ **noun** a formal or explicit statement or announcement: *they issued a declaration at the close of the talks* | *declarations of love.*
■ the formal announcement of the beginning of a state or condition: *the declaration of war* | *a declaration of independence.* ■ a statement asserting or protecting a legal right. ■ a written public announcement of intentions or of the terms of an agreement. ■ Cricket an act of declaring an innings closed. ■ (also **declaration of the poll**) Brit. a public official announcement of the votes cast for candidates in an election. ■ Law a plaintiff's statement of claims in proceedings. ■ Law an affirmation made instead of taking an oath. Compare with **STATUTORY DECLARATION**. ■ the naming of trumps in bridge, whist, or a similar card game. ■ an announcement of a combination held in a card game such as piquet.
– ORIGIN late Middle English: from Latin *declaratio(n-)*, from *declarare* 'make quite clear' (see **DECLARE**).

Declaration of Independence a document declaring the US to be independent of the British Crown, signed on 4 July 1776 by the Congressional representatives of thirteen states, including Thomas Jefferson, Benjamin Franklin, and John Adams.

Declaration of Rights a statute passed by the English Parliament in 1689, which established the joint monarchy of William and Mary and which was designed to ensure that the Crown would not act without Parliament's consent. It was later incorporated in the Bill of Rights.

declarative /dɪˈklarətɪv/ ▶ **adjective** **1** of the nature of or making a declaration: *declarative statements.*
■ Grammar (of a sentence or phrase) taking the form of a simple statement.
2 Computing denoting high-level programming languages which can be used to solve problems without requiring the programmer to specify an exact procedure to be followed.
▶ **noun** a statement in the form of a declaration.
■ Grammar a declarative sentence or phrase.
– DERIVATIVES **declaratively** adverb.

declarator /dɪˈklarətə/ (also **action for declarator**) ▶ **noun** Scots Law an action whereby a legal right or status is declared but nothing further is done.

declare ▶ **verb** **1** [reporting verb] say something in a solemn and emphatic manner: [with clause] *the prime minister declared that the programme of austerity had paid off* | [with direct speech] *'I was under too much pressure,' he declared.*
■ [with obj.] formally announce the beginning of (a state or condition): *Spain **declared war on** Britain in 1796.* ■ [with obj. and complement] pronounce or assert (a person or thing) to be something specified: *the mansion was declared a fire hazard.* ■ [no obj.] (**declare for/against**) openly align oneself for or against (a party or position) in a dispute: *the president had declared for denuclearization of Europe.* ■ (**declare oneself**) reveal one's intentions or identity. ■ (**declare oneself**) archaic express feelings of love to someone: *she waited in vain for him to declare himself.* ■ [no obj.] announce oneself as a candidate for an election: *he declared last April.*
2 [with obj.] acknowledge possession of (taxable income or dutiable goods).
3 [no obj.] Cricket close an innings voluntarily before all the wickets have fallen: *Pakistan declared at 446 for four* | [with obj.] *Somerset declared their first innings.*
4 [with obj.] announce that one holds (certain combinations of cards) in a card game.
– PHRASES **well, I declare** (or **I do declare**) an exclamation of incredulity, surprise, or vexation.
– DERIVATIVES **declarable** adjective, **declaratory** adjective, **declaredly** adverb.
– ORIGIN Middle English: from Latin *declarare*, from *de-* 'thoroughly' + *clarare* 'make clear' (from *clarus* 'clear').

declarer ▶ **noun** Bridge the player whose bid establishes the suit of the contract and who must therefore play both their own hand and the exposed hand of the dummy.

declass ▶ **verb** [with obj.] (usu. **be declassed**) remove (someone) from their original social class.

déclassé /deɪˈklaseɪ/ (also **déclassée**) ▶ **adjective** having fallen in social status: *his parents were poor and déclassé.*
– ORIGIN late 19th cent.: French, 'removed from one's class, degraded', past participle of *déclasser*.

declassify ▶ **verb** (**-ies**, **-ied**) [with obj.] (often **be declassified**) officially declare (information or documents) to be no longer secret: *government documents were declassified.*
– DERIVATIVES **declassification** noun.

declension /dɪˈklɛnʃ(ə)n/ ▶ **noun** [mass noun] **1** (in the grammar of Latin, Greek, and certain other languages) the variation of the form of a noun, pronoun, or adjective, by which its grammatical case, number, and gender are identified.
■ [count noun] the class to which a noun or adjective is assigned according to the manner of this variation.
2 poetic/literary a condition of decline or moral deterioration: *the declension of the new generation.*
– DERIVATIVES **declensional** adjective.
– ORIGIN late Middle English *declinson*, from Old French *declinaison*, from *decliner* 'to decline'. The change in the ending was probably due to association with words such as *ascension*.

declination /ˌdɛklɪˈneɪʃ(ə)n/ ▶ **noun** **1** Astronomy the angular distance of a point north or south of the celestial equator. Compare with **RIGHT ASCENSION** and **CELESTIAL LATITUDE**.
■ the angular deviation of a compass needle from true north (because the magnetic north pole and the geographic north pole do not coincide).
2 Linguistics another term for **DOWNDRIFT**.
3 US formal refusal: [as modifier] *the mandatory vaccine declination form.*
– DERIVATIVES **declinational** adjective.
– ORIGIN late Middle English: from Latin *declinatio(n-)*, from the verb *declinare* (see **DECLINE**).

declination axis ▶ **noun** Astronomy the axis of an equatorially mounted telescope which is at right angles to the polar axis, about which the telescope is turned in order to view points at different declinations but at a constant right ascension.

declinature /dɪˈklʌɪnətʃə/ ▶ **noun** [mass noun] formal courteous refusal.
■ Scots Law formal refusal to accept that a court or judge has jurisdiction in a case.
– ORIGIN mid 17th cent.: alteration of obsolete *declinator*, from medieval Latin *declinatorius* 'expressing refusal'.

decline ▶ **verb** **1** [no obj.] become smaller, fewer, or less; decrease: *the birth rate continued to decline.*
■ diminish in strength or quality; deteriorate: *her health began to decline* | [as adj. **declining**] *declining industries.*
2 [with obj.] politely refuse (an invitation or offer): *Caroline declined the coffee.*
■ [with infinitive] politely refuse to do something: *the company declined to comment.*
3 [no obj.] (especially of the sun) move downwards.
■ archaic bend down; droop.
4 [with obj.] (in the grammar of Latin, Greek, and certain other languages) state the forms of (a noun, pronoun, or adjective) corresponding to cases, number, and gender.
▶ **noun** [in sing.] a gradual and continuous loss of strength, numbers, or quality: *a serious **decline in** bird numbers* | [mass noun] *a civilization **in decline**.*
■ a fall in price or value: *the decline of world coffee prices.* ■ archaic the sun's gradual setting. ■ archaic a disease in which the bodily strength gradually fails, especially tuberculosis.
– DERIVATIVES **declinable** adjective, **decliner** noun.
– ORIGIN late Middle English: from Old French *decliner*, from Latin *declinare* 'bend down, turn aside', from *de-* 'down' + *clinare* 'to bend'.

declining years ▶ **plural noun** a person's old age, especially when regarded as the time when health, vigour, and mental faculties deteriorate.
■ figurative the period leading up to the demise of something, often characterized by a loss of effectiveness: *the council's declining years.*

declivity /dɪˈklɪvɪti/ ▶ **noun** (pl. **-ies**) a downward slope: *a thickly wooded declivity.*
– DERIVATIVES **declivitous** adjective.
– ORIGIN early 17th cent.: from Latin *declivitas*, from *declivis* 'sloping down', from *de-* 'down' + *clivus* 'a slope'.

declutch ▶ **verb** [no obj.] disengage the clutch of a motor. See also **DOUBLE-DECLUTCH**.

deco ▶ **noun** **1** /ˈdɛkəʊ/ short for **ART DECO**.
2 /ˈdiːkəʊ/ (in scuba-diving) short for **DECOMPRESSION**.

decoct /dɪˈkɒkt/ ▶ **verb** [with obj.] archaic extract the essence from (something) by heating or boiling it.
– ORIGIN late Middle English (in the sense 'cook, heat up'): from Latin *decoct-* 'boiled down', from the verb *decoquere*, from *de-* 'down' + *coquere* 'cook'.

decoction ▶ **noun** the liquor resulting from concentrating the essence of a substance by heating or boiling, especially a medicinal preparation made from a plant: *a **decoction of** a root.*
■ [mass noun] the action or process of extracting the essence of something.
– ORIGIN late Middle English: from late Latin *decoctio(n-)*, from *decoquere* 'boil down' (see **DECOCT**).

decode ▶ **verb** [with obj.] convert (a coded message) into intelligible language.
■ analyse and interpret (a verbal or non-verbal communication or image): *a handbook to help parents decode street language.* ■ convert (audio or video signals) into another form, for example to analogue from digital in sound reproduction: *processors used to decode CD-quality digital audio signals.*
▶ **noun** informal a translation of a coded message.
– DERIVATIVES **decodable** adjective.

decoder ▶ **noun** a person or thing that analyses and interprets something, in particular:
■ an electronic device for analysing the information components of an audio or visual signal and feeding them to separate amplifier channels. ■ an electronic device that converts a coded signal into one that can be used by other equipment, especially a device to decode satellite television signals.

decoke Brit. informal ▶ **verb** /diːˈkəʊk/ [with obj.] remove carbon or carbonaceous material from (an internal-combustion engine).
▶ **noun** /ˈdiːkəʊk/ [in sing.] a removal of carbon or carbonaceous material from an internal-combustion engine.

decollate[1] /dɪˈkɒleɪt, ˈdɛkəleɪt/ ▶ **verb** [with obj.] archaic behead (someone).
– DERIVATIVES **decollation** noun.
– ORIGIN late Middle English: from Latin *decollat-* 'beheaded', from the verb *decollare*, from *de-* (expressing removal) + *collum* 'neck'.

decollate[2] /ˌdiːkəˈleɪt/ ▶ **verb** [no obj.] separate sheets of paper, especially of continuous stationery, mechanically into different piles.
– DERIVATIVES **decollation** noun, **decollator** noun.

– ORIGIN 1960s: from **DE-** ‘away from’ + **COLLATE**.

decollement /deɪˈkɒlmɒ̃/ ▶ **noun** [mass noun] Geology a process in which some strata become partly detached from those underneath and slide over them, causing folding and deformation.
■(also **decollement zone**) [count noun] a boundary separating deformed strata from underlying strata which are not similarly deformed.
– ORIGIN mid 19th cent.: from French, from *décoller* ‘unstick’.

décolletage /ˌdeɪkɒlˈtɑːʒ/ ▶ **noun** a low neckline on a woman’s dress or top.
– ORIGIN late 19th cent.: French, from *décolleter* ‘expose the neck’, from *dé-* (expressing removal) + *collet* ‘collar of a dress’.

décolleté /deɪˈkɒlteɪ/ ▶ **adjective** (also **décolletée**) (of a woman’s dress or top) having a low neckline.
▶ **noun** a low neckline on a woman’s dress or top.
– ORIGIN mid 19th cent.: French, past participle of *décolleter* ‘expose the neck’.

decolonize (also **-ise**) ▶ **verb** [with obj.] (of a state) withdraw from (a colony), leaving it independent: *they must decolonize French Polynesia.*
– DERIVATIVES **decolonization** noun.

decolorize (also **decolourize** or **-ise**) ▶ **verb** [with obj.] remove the colour from: *ethane decolorizes bromine water.*
– DERIVATIVES **decolorization** noun.

decommission ▶ **verb** [with obj.] withdraw (someone or something) from service, in particular:
■make (a nuclear reactor or weapon) inoperative and dismantle and decontaminate it to make it safe. ■ take (a ship) out of service.

decommunize (also **-ise**) ▶ **verb** [with obj.] remove the features or influence of communism from.
– DERIVATIVES **decommunization** noun.

decompensation ▶ **noun** [mass noun] Medicine the failure of an organ (especially the liver or heart) to compensate for the functional overload resulting from disease.
■Psychiatry the failure to generate effective psychological coping mechanisms in response to stress, resulting in personality disturbance or disintegration, especially that which causes relapse in schizophrenia.
– DERIVATIVES **decompensated** adjective.

decompose ▶ **verb** [no obj.] (of a dead body or other organic matter) decay; become rotten: *the body had begun to decompose* | [as adj. **decomposed**] *the body was badly decomposed* | [as adj. **decomposing**] *decomposing fungi.*
■[with obj.] cause (something) to decay or rot: *dead plant matter can be completely decomposed by micro-organisms.* ■(of a chemical compound) break down into component elements or simpler constituents: *many chemicals decompose rapidly under high temperature.* ■ [with obj.] break down (a chemical compound) into its component elements or simpler constituents. ■ [with obj.] Mathematics express (a number or function) as a combination of simpler components.
– DERIVATIVES **decomposable** adjective, **decomposition** noun.
– ORIGIN mid 18th cent. (in the sense ‘separate into simpler constituents’): from French *décomposer*, from *de-* (expressing reversal) + *composer*.

decomposer ▶ **noun** an organism, especially a soil bacterium, fungus, or invertebrate, that decomposes organic material.
■a device or installation that is used to break down a chemical substance.

decompress /ˌdiːkəmˈprɛs/ ▶ **verb** [with obj.] relieve of compressing forces, in particular:
■expand (compressed computer data) to its normal size so that it can be read and processed by a computer. ■ subject (a diver) to decompression. ■ [no obj.] N. Amer. informal calm down and relax: *Michael sits for a minute to decompress before walking home.*

decompression ▶ **noun** [mass noun] **1** reduction in air pressure: *decompression of the aircraft cabin.*
■a gradual reduction of air pressure on a person who has been experiencing high pressure while diving.
2 the process of expanding computer data to its normal size so that it can be read by a computer.

decompression chamber ▶ **noun** a small room in which the air pressure can be varied, used chiefly to allow deep-sea divers to adjust gradually to normal air pressure.

decompression sickness ▶ **noun** [mass noun] a condition that results when too rapid decompression causes nitrogen bubbles to form in the tissues of the body. It is suffered particularly by divers (who often call it **the bends**), and can cause pain in the muscles and joints, cramp, numbness, nausea, and paralysis. Also called **CAISSON DISEASE**.

decompressor ▶ **noun** Brit. a device for reducing pressure in the engine of a motor vehicle.

decondition ▶ **verb** [with obj.] **1** [usu. as adj. **deconditioned**] cause to lose fitness or muscle tone, especially through lack of exercise: *deconditioned muscles.*
2 [usu. as noun **deconditioning**] Psychiatry reform or reverse (previously conditioned behaviour), especially in the treatment of phobia and other anxiety disorders in which the fear response to certain stimuli is brought under control. Compare with **COUNTER-CONDITIONING**.
■informal persuade (someone) to abandon a habitual mode of thinking.

decongest ▶ **verb** [with obj.] relieve the congestion of (something).
– DERIVATIVES **decongestion** noun.

decongestant ▶ **adjective** (chiefly of a medicine) used to relieve nasal congestion.
▶ **noun** a decongestant medicine.

deconsecrate ▶ **verb** [with obj.] (usu. **be deconsecrated**) transfer (a building) from sacred to secular use: *the church was deconsecrated in the early nineteenth century.*
– DERIVATIVES **deconsecration** noun.

deconstruct /ˌdiːk(ə)nˈstrʌkt/ ▶ **verb** [with obj.] analyse (a text or linguistic or conceptual system) by deconstruction, typically in order to expose its hidden internal assumptions and contradictions and subvert its apparent significance or unity.
■(in general use) dismantle: *social forms which will have to be deconstructed before socialism can be developed.*
– DERIVATIVES **deconstructive** adjective.
– ORIGIN late 19th cent.: back-formation from **DECONSTRUCTION**.

deconstruction ▶ **noun** [mass noun] a method of critical analysis of philosophical and literary language which emphasizes the internal workings of language and conceptual systems, the relational quality of meaning, and the assumptions implicit in forms of expression.

> Deconstruction focuses on a text as such rather than as an expression of the author’s intention, stressing the limitlessness (or impossibility) of interpretation and rejecting the Western philosophical tradition of seeking certainty through reasoning by privileging certain types of interpretation and repressing others. It was effectively named and popularized by the French philosopher Jacques Derrida from the late 1960s and taken up particularly by US literary critics.

– DERIVATIVES **deconstructionism** noun, **deconstructionist** adjective & noun.
– ORIGIN late 19th cent. (originally in the general sense ‘taking to pieces’): from **DE-** (expressing reversal) + **CONSTRUCTION**.

decontaminate ▶ **verb** [with obj.] neutralize or remove dangerous substances, radioactivity, or germs from (an area, object, or person): *they tried to decontaminate nearby villages.*
– DERIVATIVES **decontamination** noun.

decontextualize (also **-ise**) ▶ **verb** [with obj.] [usu. as adj. **decontextualized**] consider (something) in isolation from its context.
– DERIVATIVES **decontextualization** noun.

decontrol ▶ **verb** (**decontrolled**, **decontrolling**) [with obj.] release (a commodity, market, etc.) from controls or restrictions: *there has been fierce debate over whether gas prices should be totally decontrolled.*
▶ **noun** [mass noun] the action of decontrolling something.

deconvolution ▶ **noun** [mass noun] a process of resolving something into its constituent elements or removing complication in order to clarify it: *the editor helped in the deconvolution of phrase and thought.*
■Mathematics the resolution of a convolution function into the functions from which it was formed in order to separate their effects. ■ (also **deconvolution analysis**) the improvement of resolution of images or other data by a mathematical algorithm designed to separate the information from artefacts which result from the method of collecting it.

decor /ˈdeɪkɔː, ˈdɛ-/ ▶ **noun** [mass noun] the furnishing and decoration of a room.
■the decoration and scenery of a stage.
– ORIGIN late 19th cent.: from French *décor*, from the verb *décorer*, from Latin *decorare* ‘embellish’ (see **DECORATE**).

decorate ▶ **verb** [with obj.] **1** make (something) look more attractive by adding ornament to it.
■apply paint or wallpaper in (a room or building): *the five bedrooms are individually decorated* | [no obj.] *we’ve just decorated.*
2 confer an award or medal on (a member of the armed forces): *he was decorated for outstanding bravery.*
– ORIGIN mid 16th cent. (in the sense ‘to grace or honour’): from Latin *decoratus* ‘embellished’ (past participle of *decorare*), from *decus*, *decor-* ‘beauty, honour, or embellishment’.

Decorated ▶ **adjective** denoting a stage of English Gothic church architecture typical of the 14th century (between Early English and Perpendicular), with increasing use of decoration and geometrical, curvilinear, and reticulated tracery.

decoration ▶ **noun 1** [mass noun] the process or art of decorating or adorning something: *the lavish decoration of cloth with gilt.*
■ornamentation: *inside there was little decoration.* ■ the application of paint or wallpaper in a room or building: *interior decoration.* ■ the paint or wallpaper applied: *an authority on English furniture and decoration.* ■ [count noun] a thing that serves as an ornament: *Christmas tree decorations.*
2 a medal or award conferred as an honour.

Decoration Day ▶ **noun** US another term for **MEMORIAL DAY**.

decorative /ˈdɛk(ə)rətɪv/ ▶ **adjective** serving to make something look more attractive; ornamental: *decorative features.*
■relating to decoration: *a decorative artist.*
– DERIVATIVES **decoratively** adverb, **decorativeness** noun.

decorative arts ▶ **plural noun** the arts concerned with the production of high-quality objects which are both useful and beautiful.

decorator ▶ **noun** a person who decorates, in particular:
■chiefly Brit. a person whose job is to decorate the interior of buildings by painting the walls and hanging wallpaper: *she became a painter and decorator.* ■ chiefly N. Amer. a person whose job is to design the interior of someone’s home, by choosing colours, carpets, materials, and furnishings.

decorous /ˈdɛk(ə)rəs/ ▶ **adjective** in keeping with good taste and propriety; polite and restrained: *Charlotte gave David a decorous kiss.*
– DERIVATIVES **decorously** adverb, **decorousness** noun.
– ORIGIN mid 17th cent. (in the sense ‘appropriate, seemly’): from Latin *decorus* ‘seemly’ + **-OUS**.

decorticate /diːˈkɔːtɪkeɪt/ ▶ **verb** [with obj.] **1** [often as adj. **decorticated**] technical remove the bark, rind, or husk from: *decorticated groundnuts.*
2 subject to surgical decortication.
▶ **adjective** Biology & Psychology of or relating to an animal that has had the cortex of the brain removed or separated.
– ORIGIN early 17th cent.: from Latin *decorticat-* ‘stripped of its bark’, from the verb *decorticare*, from *de-* (expressing removal) + *cortex*, *cortic-* ‘bark’.

decortication ▶ **noun** [mass noun] the removal of the outer layer or cortex from a structure, especially the kidney, brain, or other organ.
■Medicine, chiefly Brit. the operation of removing fibrous scar tissue that prevents expansion of the lung.
– ORIGIN early 17th cent.: from Latin *decorticatio(n-)*, from *decorticare* ‘strip of bark’ (see **DECORTICATE**).

decorum /dɪˈkɔːrəm/ ▶ **noun** [mass noun] behaviour in keeping with good taste and propriety.
■etiquette: *he had no idea of funeral decorum.* ■ [count noun] (usu. **decorums**) archaic a particular requirement of good taste and propriety. ■ archaic suitability to the requirements of a person, rank, or occasion.
– ORIGIN mid 16th cent. (as a literary term, denoting suitability of style): from Latin, neuter of the adjective *decorus* ‘seemly’.

découpage /ˌdeɪkuːˈpɑːʒ, dɪˈkuːpɑːʒ, ˈdɛkuːpɑːʒ/ ▶ **noun** [mass noun] the decoration of the surface of an object with paper cut-outs.
– ORIGIN 1960s: French, from *découper* ‘cut out’.

decouple ▶ **verb** [with obj.] separate, disengage, or dissociate (something) from something else: *the mountings effectively **decouple** movements of the engine **from** those of the wheels.*
■make the interaction between (electrical components) so weak that there is little transfer of energy between them, especially to remove

unwanted AC distortion or oscillations in circuits with a common power supply.

decoy ▶ **noun** /ˈdiːkɔɪ, dɪˈkɔɪ/ **1** a bird or mammal, or an imitation of one, used by hunters to attract other birds or mammals: [as modifier] *a decoy duck.*
■ a person or thing used to lure an animal or person into a trap. ■ a fake or non-working article, especially a weapon, used to mislead or misdirect.
2 a pond from which narrow netted channels lead, into which wild duck may be enticed for capture.
▶ **verb** /dɪˈkɔɪ, ˈdiːkɔɪ/ [with obj. and adverbial of direction] lure or entice (a person or animal) away from their intended course, typically into a trap: *they would try to decoy the enemy towards the hidden group.*
– ORIGIN mid 16th cent. (earlier as *coy*): from Dutch *de kooi* 'the decoy', from Middle Dutch *de kouw* 'the cage', from Latin *cavea* 'cage'. Sense 2 is from the practice of using tamed ducks to lead wild ones along channels into captivity.

decrease ▶ **verb** /dɪˈkriːs/ [no obj.] become smaller or fewer in size, amount, intensity, or degree: *the population of the area has decreased radically.*
■ [with obj.] make smaller or fewer in size, amount, intensity, or degree: *the aisles were decreased in height.*
▶ **noun** /ˈdiːkriːs/ an instance or example of becoming smaller or fewer: *a* **decrease in** *births.*
■ [mass noun] the action or process of becoming smaller or fewer: *the rate of decrease became greater.*
– PHRASES **on the decrease** becoming less common or widespread; decreasing.
– DERIVATIVES **decreasingly** adverb [as submodifier] *voters have proved decreasingly willing to support the party.*
– ORIGIN late Middle English: from Old French *decreis* (noun), *decreistre* (verb), based on Latin *decrescere*, from *de-* 'down' + *crescere* 'grow'.

decree ▶ **noun** an official order issued by a ruler or authority that has the force of law.
■ [mass noun] the issuing of such an order: *the king* **ruled by decree**. ■ a judgement or decision of certain law courts, especially in matrimonial cases.
▶ **verb** (**decrees**, **decreed**, **decreeing**) [with obj.] order (something) by decree: *the government decreed a ban on any contact with the guerrillas* | [with clause] *the president decreed that the military was to be streamlined.*
– ORIGIN Middle English (denoting an edict issued by an ecclesiastical council to settle a point of doctrine or discipline): from Old French *decre*, *decret*, from Latin *decretum* 'something decided', from *decernere* 'decide'.

decree absolute ▶ **noun** (pl. **decrees absolute**) English Law a final order by a court of law which officially ends a marriage, enabling either party to remarry.

decree nisi ▶ **noun** (pl. **decrees nisi**) English Law an order by a court of law that states the date on which a marriage will end, unless a good reason to prevent a divorce is produced.
– ORIGIN late 19th cent.: Latin *nisi* 'unless'.

decrement /ˈdɛkrɪm(ə)nt/ ▶ **noun** a reduction or diminution: *relaxation produces a decrement in sympathetic nervous activity.*
■ an amount by which something is reduced or diminished: *the dose was reduced by 10 mg weekly decrements.* ■ Physics the ratio of the amplitudes in successive cycles of a damped oscillation.
▶ **verb** [with obj.] chiefly Computing cause a discrete reduction in (a numerical quantity): *the instruction decrements the accumulator by one.*
– ORIGIN early 17th cent. (as a noun): from Latin *decrementum* 'diminution', from the stem of *decrescere* 'to decrease'.

decrepit /dɪˈkrɛpɪt/ ▶ **adjective** (of a person) elderly and infirm: *a rather decrepit old man.*
■ worn out or ruined because of age or neglect: *a row of decrepit houses.*
– DERIVATIVES **decrepitude** noun.
– ORIGIN late Middle English: from Latin *decrepitus*, from *de-* 'down' + *crepitus*, past participle of *crepare* 'rattle, creak'.

decrepitate /dɪˈkrɛpɪteɪt/ ▶ **verb** [no obj.] technical (of a crystal or an inclusion of something within a crystal) disintegrate audibly when heated.
– DERIVATIVES **decrepitation** noun.
– ORIGIN mid 17th cent.: from **DE-** 'away' + Latin *crepitat-* 'crackled', from the verb *crepitare*, frequentative of *crepare* 'rattle' (see **DECREPIT**).

decrescendo /ˌdiːkrɪˈʃɛndəʊ/ ▶ **noun** (pl. **-os**), **adverb**, **adjective**, & **verb** (**-os**, **-oed**) another term for **DIMINUENDO**: [as noun] *the decrescendo of distant thunder* | [as adj.] *a decrescendo heart murmur* | [as verb] *he decrescendos down to a whisper.*
– ORIGIN early 19th cent.: Italian, literally 'decreasing'.

decrescent /dɪˈkrɛs(ə)nt/ ▶ **adjective** [attrib.] (of the moon) waning.
– ORIGIN early 17th cent.: from Latin *decrescent-* 'growing less', from the verb *decrescere* (see **DECREASE**).

decretal /dɪˈkriːt(ə)l/ ▶ **noun** a papal decree concerning a point of canon law.
▶ **adjective** of the nature of a decree.
– ORIGIN Middle English: from late Latin *decretale*, neuter of *decretalis* (adjective), from Latin *decret-* 'decided', from the verb *decernere*.

Decretum /dɪˈkriːtəm/ ▶ **noun** a collection of decisions and judgements in canon law.
– ORIGIN Latin, literally 'something decreed'.

decriminalize (also **-ise**) ▶ **verb** [with obj.] cease to treat (something) as illegal: *a battle to decriminalize drugs.*
– DERIVATIVES **decriminalization** noun.

decry /dɪˈkrʌɪ/ ▶ **verb** (**-ies**, **-ied**) [with obj.] publicly denounce: *they decried human rights abuses.*
– DERIVATIVES **decrier** noun.
– ORIGIN early 17th cent. (in the sense 'decrease the value of coins by royal proclamation'): from **DE-** 'down' + **CRY**, on the pattern of French *décrier* 'cry down'.

decrypt /diːˈkrɪpt/ ▶ **verb** [with obj.] make (a coded or unclear message) intelligible: *the computer can be used to encrypt and decrypt sensitive transmissions.*
▶ **noun** a text that has been decoded.
– DERIVATIVES **decryption** noun.
– ORIGIN 1930s: from **DE-** (expressing reversal) + *crypt* as in *encrypt*.

decubitus /dɪˈkjuːbɪtəs/ ▶ **noun** [mass noun] chiefly Medicine the posture adopted by a person who is lying down: [as modifier] *lumbar puncture with the patient in the lateral decubitus position.*
– ORIGIN late 19th cent.: modern Latin, from Latin *decumbere* 'lie down', on the pattern of words such as *accubitus* 'reclining at table'.

decubitus ulcer ▶ **noun** technical term for **BEDSORE**.

decumbent /dɪˈkʌmb(ə)nt/ ▶ **adjective** Botany (of a plant or part of a plant) lying along the ground or along a surface, with the extremity curving upwards.
– ORIGIN late 18th cent.: from Latin *decumbent-* 'lying down', from the verb *decumbere*, based on *de-* 'down' + a verb related to *cubare* 'to lie'.

decumbiture /dɪˈkʌmbɪtʃə/ ▶ **noun** Astrology a chart made for the time of onset of an illness, to aid in making a prognosis and determining appropriate treatment.
■ [mass noun] archaic the action of taking to one's bed with an illness.
– ORIGIN mid 17th cent.: formed irregularly from Latin *decumbere* 'lie down' + **-URE**.

decurrent /dɪˈkʌr(ə)nt/ ▶ **adjective** Botany (of a fungus gill, leaf, etc.) extending down the stem below the point of attachment.
■ (of a shrub or the crown of a tree) having several roughly equal branches.
– ORIGIN mid 18th cent.: from Latin *decurrent-* 'running down', from the verb *decurrere*.

decurved ▶ **adjective** Biology (especially of a bird's bill) curved downwards.

decussate technical ▶ **verb** /dɪˈkʌseɪt, ˈdɛkəseɪt/ [no obj.] (of two or more things) cross or intersect each other to form an X: *the fibres decussate in the collar.*
▶ **adjective** /dɪˈkʌsət/ shaped like an X.
■ Botany (of leaves) arranged in opposite pairs, each pair being at right angles to the pair below.
– DERIVATIVES **decussation** noun.
– ORIGIN mid 17th cent. (as a verb): from Latin *decussatus*, past participle of *decussare* 'divide crosswise', from *decussis* (describing the figure X, i.e. the Roman numeral for the number 10), from *decem* 'ten'.

decyl /ˈdɛsʌɪl, -sɪl/ ▶ **noun** [as modifier] Chemistry of or denoting an alkyl radical $—C_{10}H_{21}$, derived from decane.
– ORIGIN mid 19th cent.: from Greek *deka-* 'ten' + **-YL**.

dedans /dəˈdɒ̃/ ▶ **noun** (in real tennis) an open gallery for spectators at the service side of a court.
– ORIGIN early 18th cent.: French, literally 'inside'.

Dedekind /ˈdeɪdəkɪnd, German ˈdeːdəkɪnt/, Richard (1831–1916), German mathematician, one the founders of abstract algebra and modern mathematics.

dedendum /dɪˈdɛndəm/ ▶ **noun** Engineering the radial distance from the pitch circle of a cogwheel or wormwheel to the bottom of the tooth space or groove. Compare with **ADDENDUM**.
– ORIGIN early 20th cent.: from Latin, 'thing that can be surrendered', neuter gerundive of *dedere*.

dedicate ▶ **verb** [with obj.] devote (time, effort, or oneself) to a particular task or purpose: *Joan has* **dedicated** *her life* **to** *animals.*
■ devote (something) to a particular subject or purpose: *volume four is* **dedicated to** *wasps.* ■ (usu. **be dedicated**) cite or nominate (a book or other artistic work) as being issued or performed in someone's honour: *the novel is* **dedicated to** *the memory of my mother.* ■ (usu. **be dedicated**) ceremonially assign (a church or other building) to a deity or saint: *the parish church is* **dedicated to** *St Paul.*
– DERIVATIVES **dedicatee** noun, **dedicator** noun, **dedicatory** adjective.
– ORIGIN late Middle English (in the sense 'devote to sacred use by solemn rites'): from Latin *dedicat-* 'devoted, consecrated', from the verb *dedicare*.

dedicated ▶ **adjective** (of a person) devoted to a task or purpose: *a team of dedicated doctors.*
■ (of a thing) exclusively assigned or allocated to or intended for a particular service or purpose: *a dedicated high-speed rail link from the Channel Tunnel.*
– DERIVATIVES **dedicatedly** adverb.

dedication ▶ **noun** [mass noun] **1** the quality of being dedicated or committed to a task or purpose: *his* **dedication to** *his duties.*
2 the action of dedicating a church or other building to a deity or saint: *the dedication of a new city church.*
■ [count noun] an inscription dedicating a building in this way. ■ [count noun] the words with which a book or other artistic work is dedicated.
– ORIGIN late Middle English: from Latin *dedicatio(n-)*, from *dedicare* 'devote, consecrate' (see **DEDICATE**).

de dicto /deɪ ˈdɪktəʊ, diː/ ▶ **adjective** Philosophy relating to the form of an assertion or expression itself, rather than any property of a thing it refers to. Compare with **DE RE**.
– ORIGIN Latin, 'from what is said'.

dedifferentiate /ˌdiːdɪfəˈrɛnʃɪeɪt/ ▶ **verb** [no obj.] Biology (of a cell or tissue) undergo a reversal of differentiation and lose specialized characteristics.
– DERIVATIVES **dedifferentiation** noun.

deduce ▶ **verb** [with obj.] arrive at (a fact or a conclusion) by reasoning; draw as a logical conclusion: *little can be safely* **deduced from** *these figures* | [with clause] *they* **deduced that** *the fish died because of water pollution.*
■ archaic trace the course or derivation of: *he cannot deduce his descent wholly by heirs male.*
– DERIVATIVES **deducible** adjective.
– ORIGIN late Middle English (in the sense 'lead or convey'): from Latin *deducere*, from *de-* 'down' + *ducere* 'lead'.

deduct ▶ **verb** [with obj.] subtract or take away (an amount or part) from a total: *tax has been* **deducted from** *the payments.*
– ORIGIN late Middle English: from Latin *deduct-* 'taken or led away', from the verb *deducere*. *Deduct* and *deduce* were not distinguished in sense until the mid 17th cent.

deductible ▶ **adjective** able to be deducted, especially from taxable income or tax to be paid.
▶ **noun** chiefly N. Amer. the part of an insurance claim to be paid by the insured; an excess.
– DERIVATIVES **deductibility** noun.

deduction ▶ **noun** [mass noun] **1** the action of deducting or subtracting something: *the dividend will be paid without deduction of tax.*
■ [count noun] an amount that is or may be deducted from something, especially from taxable income or tax to be paid: *tax deductions.*
2 the inference of particular instances by reference to a general law or principle: *the detective must uncover the murderer by deduction from facts.* Often contrasted with **INDUCTION**.
■ [count noun] a conclusion that has been deduced.
– ORIGIN late Middle English: from Latin *deductio(n-)*, from the verb *deducere* (see **DEDUCE**).

deductive ▶ **adjective** characterized by the

inference of particular instances from a general law: *deductive reasoning.*
■ based on reason and logical analysis of available facts: *I used my deductive powers.*
– DERIVATIVES **deductively** adverb.
– ORIGIN mid 17th cent.: from medieval Latin *deductivus*, from *deduct-* 'deduced', from the verb *deducere* (see **DEDUCE**).

de Duve /də ˈduːv, French də dyv/, Christian René (b.1917), British-born Belgian biochemist. A pioneer in the study of cell biology, he won the Nobel Prize for Physiology or Medicine in 1974.

Dee¹ 1 a river in NE Scotland, which rises in the Grampian Mountains and flows eastwards past Balmoral Castle to the North Sea at Aberdeen.
2 a river which rises in North Wales and flows past Chester and on into the Irish Sea.

Dee², John (1527–1608), English alchemist, mathematician, and geographer. He was Elizabeth I's astrologer and in later life he absorbed himself in alchemy and acquired notoriety as a sorcerer.

dee ▶ noun another way of writing the letter D (in some contexts).

deed ▶ noun **1** an action that is performed intentionally or consciously.
■ [mass noun] action or performance: *she had erred in both deed and manner.*
2 (often **deeds**) a legal document that is signed and delivered, especially one regarding the ownership of property or legal rights. See also **TITLE DEED**.
▶ verb [with obj.] N. Amer. convey or transfer (property or rights) by legal deed: *they deeded their property to their children.*
– ORIGIN Old English *dēd, dǣd*, of Germanic origin; related to Dutch *daad* and German *Tat*, from an Indo-European root shared by **DO¹**.

deed of covenant ▶ noun Brit. an agreement to pay a regular amount of money, particularly when this enables the recipient (typically a charity) to reclaim any tax paid by the donor on the amount.

deed poll ▶ noun [in sing.] English Law a legal deed made and executed by one party only, especially to formalize a change of a person's name: *he changed his name by deed poll.*
– ORIGIN late 16th cent.: so named because the parchment was 'polled' or cut even, not indented as in the case of a deed made by two parties.

deedy ▶ adjective dialect or archaic industrious, effective, or earnest.

deejay ▶ noun informal a disc jockey.
– ORIGIN 1950s (originally US): representing the pronunciation of *DJ*.

deem ▶ verb [with obj. and complement] formal regard or consider in a specified way: *the event was deemed a great success* | [with obj. and infinitive] *the strike was deemed to be illegal.*
– ORIGIN Old English *dēman* (also in the sense 'act as judge'), of Germanic origin; related to Dutch *doeman*, also to **DOOM**.

de-emphasize (also **-ise**) ▶ verb [with obj.] reduce the importance or prominence given to (something).
■ make (something) less clearly defined: *New Painting's tendency to de-emphasize individual figures.*
– DERIVATIVES **de-emphasis** noun.

deemster /ˈdiːmstə/ ▶ noun a judge (of whom there are two) in the Isle of Man judiciary.
– ORIGIN Middle English (originally a general word for a judge): from **DEEM** + **-STER**. The current sense dates from the early 17th cent.

de-energize (also **-ise**) ▶ verb [with obj.] disconnect (an electric circuit) from a power supply.
■ [no obj.] undergo loss of electrical power: *the starter relay automatically de-energizes.*

deep ▶ adjective **1** extending far down from the top or surface: *a deep gorge* | *the lake was deep and cold.*
■ extending or situated far in or down from the outer edge or surface: *a deep alcove* | **deep** in the woods. ■ [predic.] (after a measurement and in questions) extending a specified distance from the top, surface, or outer edge: *the well was 200 feet deep.* ■ [in combination] as far up or down as a specified point: *standing waist-deep in the river.* ■ [predic.] in a specified number of ranks one behind another: [in combination] *they were standing three-deep at the bar.* ■ taking in or giving out a lot of air: *she took a deep breath.* ■ Cricket (of a fielding position) relatively distant from the batsman; near the boundary: *deep midwicket.* ■ (in ball games) to or

from a position far down or across the field: *a deep cross from Neill.*
2 very intense or extreme: *she was in deep trouble* | *a deep sleep* | *a deep economic recession.*
■ (of an emotion or feeling) intensely felt: *deep disappointment.* ■ usu. **deeps** figurative a remote and mysterious region: *the deeps of her imagination.* ■ (**the deep**) Cricket the part of the field distant from the batsman.
▶ adverb far down or in; deeply: *travelling deep into the countryside* | figurative *his passion runs deep.*
■ (in sport) distant from the batsman or forward line of one's team: *he swung the ball in deep.*
– PHRASES **the deep end** the end of a swimming pool where the water is deepest. **go off** (or **go in off**) **the deep end** informal give way immediately to an emotional outburst, especially of anger. ■ chiefly US go mad; behave extremely strangely: *they looked at me as if I had gone off the deep end.* **in deep water** (or **waters**) informal in trouble or difficulty: *he landed in deep water when he began the affair.* **jump** (or **be thrown**) **in at the deep end** informal face a difficult problem or undertaking with little experience of it.
– DERIVATIVES **deepness** noun.
– ORIGIN Old English *dēop* (adjective), *dīope, dēope* (adverb), of Germanic origin; related to Dutch *diep* and German *tief*, also to **DIP**.

deep-bodied ▶ adjective (of an animal, especially a fish) having a body which is deeper (from back to belly) than it is wide.

deep breathing ▶ noun [mass noun] breathing with long breaths, especially as exercise or a method of relaxation.

deep-cycle ▶ adjective N. Amer. denoting a type of electric battery that can be totally discharged and recharged several times.

deep-discount ▶ adjective denoting financial securities carrying a low rate of interest relative to prevailing market rates and issued at a discount to their redemption value, so mainly providing capital gain rather than income.
■ N. Amer. heavily discounted; greatly reduced in price: *deep-discount pricing has kept air fares affordable.*

deep-dish ▶ adjective chiefly N. Amer. **1** (of a pie) baked in a deep dish to allow for a large filling: *deep-dish apple pie.*
■ (of a pizza) cooked in a deep dish and having a thick dough base.
2 informal extreme or thoroughgoing: *deep-dish conservatism.*

deep-drawn ▶ adjective (of metal) shaped by forcing through a die when cold.

deep-dyed ▶ adjective informal thoroughgoing; complete: *a deep-dyed Beatles fan.*

deepen ▶ verb make or become deep or deeper: [no obj.] *the crisis deepened* | [as adj. **deepening**] *a deepening depression.*

deep freeze ▶ noun (also **deep freezer**) a refrigerator in which food can be quickly frozen and kept for long periods at a very low temperature.
▶ verb (**deep-freeze**) [with obj.] [often as adj. **deep-frozen**] store (something) in a deep freeze.

deep-fry ▶ verb [with obj.] [usu. as adj. **deep-fried**] fry (food) in an amount of fat or oil sufficient to cover it completely: *deep-fried scampi.*

deep kiss ▶ noun dated a kiss involving insertion of the tongue into the partner's mouth.

deep-laid ▶ adjective (of a scheme) secret and elaborate: *a deep-laid plot.*

deep litter ▶ noun [mass noun] a deep layer of litter used to cover the floor of sheds, barns, or houses in which poultry is reared.

deeply ▶ adverb far down or in: *he breathed deeply* | *fragments of rock were deeply embedded within the wood.*

■ intensely: *Richard felt her loss very deeply* | [as submodifier] *she was deeply hurt.*

deep-mined ▶ adjective (of coal) obtained from far below the surface of the ground, not from opencast mines.

deep mourning ▶ noun [mass noun] a state of mourning, conventionally expressed by wearing only black clothing.
■ the black clothing worn by someone in deep mourning.

deep-mouthed ▶ adjective archaic (of a dog) having a deep-sounding bark.

deep-rooted ▶ adjective (of a plant) deeply implanted.
■ firmly embedded in thought, behaviour, or culture, and so having a persistent influence: *deep-rooted concern about declining values.*
– DERIVATIVES **deep-rootedness** noun.

deep sea ▶ noun [usu. as modifier] the deeper parts of the ocean, especially those beyond the edge of the continental shelf: *deep-sea diving.*

deep-seated ▶ adjective firmly established at a deep or profound level: *operations to remove deep-seated brain tumours.*

deep-set ▶ adjective embedded or positioned firmly or deeply: *the young man had deep-set eyes.*
■ long-established, ingrained, or profound: *the deep-set interrelations between religion and politics.*

deep-six ▶ verb [with obj.] N. Amer. informal destroy or dispose of (something) irretrievably: *someone had deliberately deep-sixed evidence.*
– ORIGIN 1920s (as *the deep six* 'the grave'): perhaps from the custom of burial at sea at a depth of six fathoms.

Deep South (**the Deep South**) the south-eastern region of the US regarded as embodying traditional Southern culture and traditions.

deep space ▶ noun another term for **OUTER SPACE**.

deep structure ▶ noun [mass noun] (in transformational grammar) the underlying logical relationships of the elements of a phrase or sentence. Contrasted with **SURFACE STRUCTURE**.

deer ▶ noun (pl. same) a hoofed grazing or browsing animal, with branched bony antlers that are shed annually and typically borne only by the male. See also **MOUSE DEER, MUSK DEER.**
● Family Cervidae: several genera and many species.
– ORIGIN Old English *dēor*, also originally denoting any quadruped, used in the (now archaic) phrase *small deer* meaning 'small creatures collectively'; of Germanic origin; related to Dutch *dier*, German *Tier*.

deer fly ▶ noun **1** a bloodsucking louse fly which is a parasite of deer. It loses its wings on finding a host, and the female gives birth to fully grown larvae.
● *Lipoptena cervi*, family Hippoboscidae.
2 a bloodsucking horsefly which attacks humans and other large mammals. It can transmit various diseases, including tularaemia.
● Genus *Chrysops*, family Tabanidae: several species, including *C. callidus*, widespread throughout North America.

deergrass ▶ noun a small sedge related to cotton grass, growing in tufts on wet moors and bogs.
● *Trichophorum cespitosum* (or *Scirpus cespitosus*), family Cyperaceae.

deer hair ▶ noun [mass noun] hair from a deer, particularly as used in making artificial fishing flies.

deerhound ▶ noun a large dog of a rough-haired breed, resembling the greyhound.

deer lick ▶ noun N. Amer. a place deer come to lick salt, either from a block of salt placed there, or from a natural source.

deer mouse ▶ noun a mainly nocturnal mouse found in a wide range of habitats in North and Central America.
● Genus *Peromyscus*, family Muridae: numerous species, in particular *P. maniculatus*.

deerskin ▶ noun [mass noun] leather made from deer's skin.

deerstalker ▶ noun **1** a soft cloth cap, originally worn for hunting, with peaks in front and behind and ear flaps which can be tied together over the top.
2 a person who stalks deer.

de-escalate ▶ verb [with obj.] reduce the intensity of (a conflict or potentially violent situation).

d

– DERIVATIVES **de-escalation** noun.

def ▶ **adjective** chiefly black slang excellent: *a truly def tattoo.*
– ORIGIN 1980s: probably an alteration of **DEATH** (used in Jamaican English as an intensifier), or shortened from **DEFINITIVE** or **DEFINITE**.

deface ▶ **verb** [with obj.] spoil the surface or appearance of (something), for example by drawing or writing on it: *he defaced library books.*
■ mar; disfigure: *the architects have defaced British cities.*
– DERIVATIVES **defacement** noun, **defacer** noun.
– ORIGIN Middle English: from Old French *desfacier*, from *des-* (expressing removal) + *face* 'face'.

de facto /deɪ ˈfaktəʊ, diː/ ▶ **adverb** in fact, whether by right or not: *the country was de facto divided between two states.* Often contrasted with **DE JURE**.
▶ **adjective** [attrib.] denoting someone or something that is such in fact: *a de facto one-party system.*
– ORIGIN Latin, literally 'of fact'.

defaecate ▶ **verb** Brit. variant spelling of **DEFECATE**.

defalcate /ˈdiːfalˌkeɪt/ ▶ **verb** [with obj.] formal embezzle (funds with which one has been entrusted): *the officials were charged with defalcating government money.*
– DERIVATIVES **defalcation** noun, **defalcator** noun.
– ORIGIN mid 16th cent. (in the sense 'deduct, subtract'): from medieval Latin *defalcat-* 'lopped', from the verb *defalcare*, from *de-* 'away from, off' + Latin *falx, falc-* 'sickle'.

de Falla, Manuel, see **FALLA**.

defame ▶ **verb** [with obj.] damage the good reputation of (someone); slander or libel: *he claimed that the article defamed his family.*
– DERIVATIVES **defamation** noun, **defamatory** adjective, **defamer** noun.
– ORIGIN Middle English: from Old French *diffamer*, from Latin *diffamare* 'spread evil report', from *dis-* (expressing removal) + *fama* 'report'.

defamiliarize (also **-ise**) ▶ **verb** [with obj.] render unfamiliar or strange (used especially in the context of art and literature): *art serves to defamiliarize our experience of our own present.*

defang ▶ **verb** [with obj.] [often as adj. **defanged**] render harmless or ineffectual: *the military, demoralized and defanged, gave up their campaign.*

defat ▶ **verb** (**defatted**, **defatting**) [with obj.] [usu. as adj. **defatted**] remove fat from (food).

default ▶ **noun** [mass noun] **1** failure to fulfil an obligation, especially to repay a loan or appear in a law court: *it will have to restructure its debts to avoid default.*
2 a pre-selected option adopted by a computer program or other mechanism when no alternative is specified by the user or programmer.
▶ **verb** [no obj.] **1** fail to fulfil an obligation, especially to repay a loan or to appear in a law court: *some had **defaulted on** student loans.*
■ [with obj.] declare (a party) in default and give judgement against that party: *two semi-finalists were defaulted, then reinstated.*
2 (**default to**) (of a computer program or other mechanism) revert automatically to (a pre-selected option): *when you start a fresh letter the system will default to its own style.*
– PHRASES **by default** because of a lack of opposition. ■ through lack of positive action rather than conscious choice: *he became an actor by default.* **go by default** be decided in favour of one party because of lack of opposition by the other party: *the case against us has gone by default.* **in default** guilty of failing to repay a loan or appear in a law court: *the company is already **in default on** its loans.* **in default of** in the absence of: *in default of agreement the rent was to be determined by a surveyor.*
– ORIGIN Middle English: from Old French *defaut*, from *defaillir* 'to fail', based on Latin *fallere* 'disappoint, deceive'.

defaulter ▶ **noun** a person who fails to fulfil a duty, obligation, or undertaking, especially to pay a tax or other debt.
■ a person who fails to complete a course of medical treatment. ■ chiefly Brit. a member of the armed forces guilty of a military offence.

defeasance /dɪˈfiːz(ə)ns/ ▶ **noun** [mass noun] Law the action or process of rendering something null and void.
■ [count noun] a clause or condition which, if fulfilled, renders a deed or contract null and void.
– ORIGIN late Middle English (as a legal term): from Old French *defesance*, from *defaire, desfaire* 'undo' (see **DEFEAT**).

defeasible /dɪˈfiːzɪb(ə)l/ ▶ **adjective** chiefly Law & Philosophy open in principle to revision, valid objection, forfeiture, or annulment.
– DERIVATIVES **defeasibility** noun, **defeasibly** adverb.
– ORIGIN Middle English: via Anglo-Norman French from the stem of Old French *desfesant* 'undoing' (see also **DEFEASANCE**).

defeat ▶ **verb** [with obj.] win a victory over (someone) in a battle or other contest; overcome or beat: *Garibaldi defeated the Neapolitan army.*
■ prevent (someone) from achieving an aim: *she was defeated by the last steep hill.* ■ prevent (an aim) from being achieved: *don't cheat by allowing your body to droop—this defeats the object of the exercise.* ■ reject or block (a motion or proposal): *the amendment was defeated.* ■ be impossible for (someone) to understand: *this line of reasoning defeats me, I must confess.* ■ Law render null and void; annul.
▶ **noun** an instance of defeating or being defeated: *a 1–0 defeat by Grimsby* | [mass noun] *she had still not quite admitted defeat.*
– ORIGIN late Middle English (in the sense 'undo, destroy, annul'): from Old French *desfait* 'undone', past participle of *desfaire*, from medieval Latin *disfacere* 'undo'.

defeated ▶ **adjective** having been beaten in a battle or other contest: *the defeated army.*
■ demoralized and overcome by adversity.
– DERIVATIVES **defeatedly** adverb.

defeatist ▶ **noun** a person who expects or is excessively ready to accept failure.
▶ **adjective** demonstrating expectation or acceptance of failure: *we have a duty not to be so defeatist.*
– DERIVATIVES **defeatism** noun.
– ORIGIN early 20th cent.: from French *défaitiste*, from *défaite* 'defeat'.

defecate /ˈdɛfɪkeɪt, ˈdiːf-/ (Brit. also **defaecate**) ▶ **verb** [no obj.] discharge faeces from the body.
– DERIVATIVES **defecation** noun, **defecator** noun, **defecatory** adjective.
– ORIGIN late Middle English (in the sense 'clear of dregs, purify'): from Latin *defaecat-* 'cleared of dregs', from the verb *defaecare*, from *de-* (expressing removal) + *faex, faec-* 'dregs'. The current sense dates from the mid 19th cent.

defect[1] ▶ **noun** /ˈdiːfɛkt, dɪˈfɛkt/ a shortcoming, imperfection, or lack: *genetic defects* | [mass noun] *the property is free from defect.*
– ORIGIN late Middle English (as a noun, influenced by Old French *defect* 'deficiency'): from Latin *defectus*, past participle of *deficere* 'desert or fail', from *de-* (expressing reversal) + *facere* 'do'.

defect[2] /dɪˈfɛkt/ ▶ **verb** [no obj.] abandon one's country or cause in favour of an opposing one: *he **defected to** the Soviet Union after the war.*
– DERIVATIVES **defection** noun, **defector** noun.
– ORIGIN late 16th cent.: from Latin *defect-* 'failed', from the verb *deficere* (see **DEFECT**[1]).

defective ▶ **adjective** imperfect or faulty: *complaints over defective goods.*
■ archaic or offensive mentally handicapped. ■ lacking or deficient: *dystrophin is commonly **defective in** muscle tissue.* ■ Grammar (of a word) not having all the inflections normal for the part of speech.
▶ **noun** archaic or offensive a mentally handicapped person.
– DERIVATIVES **defectively** adverb, **defectiveness** noun.

defeminize (also **-ise**) ▶ **verb** [with obj.] deprive of feminine characteristics.

defence (US **defense**) ▶ **noun** [mass noun] **1** the action of defending from or resisting attack: *they relied on missiles for the country's defence* | *she came **to the defence of** the eccentric professor.*
■ attempted justification or vindication of something: *he spoke **in defence of** a disciplined approach.* ■ [count noun] an instance of defending a title or seat in a contest or election: *his first title defence against Jones.* ■ military measures or resources for protecting a country: *the minister of defence* | [as modifier] *defence policy.* ■ a means of protecting something from attack: *wire netting is the best defence against rabbits.* ■ (**defences**) fortifications or barriers against attack: *coastal defences.* ■ (in sport) the action or role of defending one's goal or wicket against the opposition: *Wolves were pressed back into defence.* ■ (**the defence**) the players in a team who perform this role.
2 [count noun] the case presented by or on behalf of the party being accused or sued in a lawsuit.
■ (usu. **the defence**) [treated as sing. or pl.] the counsel for the defendant in a lawsuit: *the defence requested more time to prepare their case.*
– PHRASES **defence in depth** the practice of arranging defensive lines or fortifications so that they can defend each other, especially in case of an enemy incursion.
– ORIGIN Middle English: from Old French *defens*, from late Latin *defensum* (neuter), *defensa* (feminine), past participles of *defendere* 'defend'.

Defence Force the South African armed services, consisting of the army, navy, air force, and medical service.

defenceless (US **defenseless**) ▶ **adjective** without defence or protection; totally vulnerable: *attacks on defenceless civilians.*
– DERIVATIVES **defencelessness** noun.

defenceman (US **defenseman**) ▶ **noun** (pl. **-men**) (in ice hockey and lacrosse) a player in a defensive position.

defence mechanism ▶ **noun** an automatic reaction of the body against disease-causing organisms.
■ a mental process initiated, typically unconsciously, to avoid conscious conflict or anxiety.

defend ▶ **verb** [with obj.] resist an attack made on (someone or something); protect from harm or danger: *we shall defend our island, whatever the cost.*
■ speak or write in favour of (an action or person); attempt to justify: *he defended his policy of imposing high rates.* ■ conduct the case for (the party being accused or sued) in a lawsuit: *the lawyer had defended anti-communist dissidents.* ■ compete to retain (a title or seat) in a contest or election: *he won the party's nomination to defend the Welsh seat* | [as adj. **defending**] *the defending champion.* ■ [no obj.] (in sport) protect one's goal or wicket rather than attempt to score against one's opponents.
– DERIVATIVES **defendable** adjective.
– ORIGIN Middle English: from Old French *defendre*, from Latin *defendere*, from *de-* 'off' + *-fendere* 'to strike'. Compare with **OFFEND**.

defendant ▶ **noun** an individual, company, or institution sued or accused in a court of law. Compare with **PLAINTIFF**.
– ORIGIN Middle English (as an adjective in the sense 'defending'): from Old French, 'warding off', present participle of *defendre* (see **DEFEND**).

defender ▶ **noun** a person who defends someone or something: *a determined defender of British interests.*
■ (in soccer, hockey, and other games) a player whose task it is to protect their own side's goal. ■ Bridge either member of the partnership that did not win the auction. Compare with **DECLARER**.
– ORIGIN Middle English: from Old French *defendeor*.

Defender of the Faith ▶ **noun** a title conferred on Henry VIII by Pope Leo X in 1521. It was recognized by Parliament as an official title of the English monarch in 1544, and has been borne by all subsequent sovereigns.
– ORIGIN translation of Latin *Fidei Defensor*.

defenestration ▶ **noun** [mass noun] formal or humorous the action of throwing someone out of a window.
■ (**the Defenestration of Prague**) see **PRAGUE**.
– DERIVATIVES **defenestrate** verb.
– ORIGIN early 17th cent.: from modern Latin *defenestratio(n-)*, from *de-* 'down from' + Latin *fenestra* 'window'.

defense ▶ **noun** US spelling of **DEFENCE**.

defenseless ▶ **adjective** US spelling of **DEFENCELESS**.

defenseman ▶ **noun** US spelling of **DEFENCEMAN**.

defensible ▶ **adjective** **1** justifiable by argument: *a morally defensible penal system.*
2 able to be protected: *a fort with a defensible yard at its feet.*
– DERIVATIVES **defensibility** noun, **defensibly** adverb.
– ORIGIN Middle English (used of a weapon, a fortified place, etc. in the sense 'capable of giving protective defence'): from late Latin *defensibilis*, from Latin *defendere* (see **DEFEND**).

defensive ▶ **adjective** **1** used or intended to defend or protect: *defensive barriers.*
■ [attrib.] (in sport) relating to or intended as defence.
2 very anxious to challenge or avoid criticism: *he was very defensive about that side of his life.*
– PHRASES **on the defensive** expecting or resisting criticism or attack: *British forces were on the defensive.*
– DERIVATIVES **defensiveness** noun.

– ORIGIN late Middle English: from Old French *défensif, -ive*, from medieval Latin *defensivus*, from Latin *defens-* 'warded off', from the verb *defendere* (see **DEFEND**).

defensive end ▶ **noun** American Football either of the two defensive players positioned at the end of the line of the scrimmage.

defensively ▶ **adverb** in a defensive manner: *'No, I didn't,' he replied defensively.*
■ (in sport) in terms of defence: *we must tighten up defensively.*

defer[1] /dɪˈfəː/ ▶ **verb** (**deferred**, **deferring**) [with obj.] put off (an action or event) to a later time; postpone: *they deferred the decision until February.*
■ Law (of a judge) postpone (a sentence) for a period of up to six months from conviction, during which time the circumstances or conduct of the defendant are further assessed: *the judge deferred sentence until 5 April for background reports.* ■ US historical postpone the conscription of (someone): *he was no longer* ***deferred from*** *the draft.*
– DERIVATIVES **deferment** noun, **deferrable** adjective, **deferral** noun.
– ORIGIN late Middle English (also in the sense 'put on one side'): from Old French *differer* 'defer or differ', from Latin *differre*, from *dis-* 'apart' + *ferre* 'bring, carry'. Compare with **DEFER**[2] and **DIFFER**.

defer[2] /dɪˈfəː/ ▶ **verb** (**deferred**, **deferring**) [no obj.] (**defer to**) submit humbly to (a person or their wishes or qualities): *he deferred to Tim's superior knowledge.*
– DERIVATIVES **deferrer** noun.
– ORIGIN late Middle English: from Old French *deferer*, from Latin *deferre* 'carry away, refer (a matter)', from *de-* 'away from' + *ferre* 'bring, carry'. Compare with **DEFER**[1].

deference ▶ **noun** [mass noun] humble submission and respect: *he addressed her with the deference due to age.*
– PHRASES **in deference to** out of respect for; in consideration of.
– ORIGIN mid 17th cent.: from French *déférence*, from *déférer* 'refer' (see **DEFER**[2]).

deferent[1] /ˈdɛf(ə)r(ə)nt/ ▶ **adjective** another term for **DEFERENTIAL**.
– ORIGIN early 19th cent.: from **DEFER**[2] and **DEFERENCE**.

deferent[2] /ˈdɛf(ə)r(ə)nt/ ▶ **noun** (in the Ptolemaic system of astronomy) the large circular orbit followed by the centre of the small epicycle in which a planet was thought to move.
– ORIGIN late Middle English: from medieval Latin *deferent-* 'carrying away', from the verb *deferre*.

deferential ▶ **adjective** showing deference; respectful: *people were always* ***deferential to*** *him.*
– DERIVATIVES **deferentially** adverb.
– ORIGIN early 19th cent.: from **DEFERENCE**, on the pattern of pairs such as *prudence, prudential.*

deferred annuity ▶ **noun** an annuity which commences only after a lapse of some specified time after the final purchase premium has been paid.

defervescence /ˌdɪfəˈvɛs(ə)ns/ ▶ **noun** [mass noun] Medicine the abatement of a fever as indicated by a decrease in bodily temperature.
– DERIVATIVES **defervesce** verb.
– ORIGIN early 18th cent.: from Latin *defervescent-* 'ceasing to boil', from the verb *defervescere.*

defiance ▶ **noun** [mass noun] open resistance; bold disobedience: *the demonstration was held* ***in defiance of*** *official warnings.*
– ORIGIN Middle English (denoting the renunciation of an allegiance or friendship): from Old French, from *defier* 'defy'.

defiant ▶ **adjective** showing defiance: *she was in defiant mood.*
– DERIVATIVES **defiantly** adverb.
– ORIGIN late 16th cent.: from French *défiant* or directly from **DEFIANCE**.

defibrillation /ˌdiːfɪbrɪˈleɪʃ(ə)n/ ▶ **noun** [mass noun] Medicine the stopping of fibrillation of the heart by administering a controlled electric shock, to allow restoration of the normal rhythm.
– DERIVATIVES **defibrillate** verb.

defibrillator ▶ **noun** Medicine an apparatus used to control heart fibrillation by application of an electric current to the chest wall or heart.

deficiency ▶ **noun** (pl. **-ies**) a lack or shortage: ***deficiencies in*** *material resources.*
■ a failing or shortcoming: *for all its deficiencies it remains his most powerful play.* ■ the amount by which something, especially revenue, falls short; a deficit: *a budget deficiency of $96 billion.*

deficiency disease ▶ **noun** a disease caused by the lack of some essential or important element in the diet, usually a particular vitamin or mineral. See also **IMMUNE DEFICIENCY**.

deficiency payment ▶ **noun** a payment made, typically by a government body, to cover a financial deficit incurred in the course of an activity such as farming or education.

deficient /dɪˈfɪʃ(ə)nt/ ▶ **adjective** [predic.] not having enough of a specified quality or ingredient: *this diet is* ***deficient in*** *vitamin B.*
■ insufficient or inadequate: *the documentary evidence is deficient.* ■ (also **mentally deficient**) offensive having a mental handicap.
– ORIGIN late 16th cent. (originally in the theological phrase *deficient cause*, denoting a failure or deficiency that has a particular consequence): from Latin *deficient-* 'failing', from the verb *deficere* (see **DEFECT**[1]).

deficit /ˈdɛfɪsɪt, ˈdiː-/ ▶ **noun** the amount by which something, especially a sum of money, is too small.
■ an excess of expenditure or liabilities over income or assets in a given period: *an annual operating deficit* | [mass noun] *the balance of payments is again* ***in deficit.*** ■ (in sport) the amount or score by which a team or individual is losing: *a 3–0 deficit.* ■ technical a deficiency or failing, especially in a neurological or psychological function: *deficits in speech comprehension.*
– ORIGIN late 18th cent.: via French from Latin *deficit* 'it is lacking', from the verb *deficere* (see **DEFECT**[1]).

deficit financing ▶ **noun** [mass noun] government funding of spending by borrowing.

deficit spending ▶ **noun** [mass noun] government spending, in excess of revenue, of funds raised by borrowing rather than from taxation.

defilade /ˌdɛfɪˈleɪd/ Military ▶ **noun** [mass noun] the protection of a position, vehicle, or troops against enemy observation or gunfire.
▶ **verb** [with obj.] protect (a position, vehicle, or troops) against enemy observation or gunfire: [as adj. **defiladed**] *a defiladed tank.*
– ORIGIN early 19th cent.: from French *défiler* 'protect from the enemy' + **-ADE**[1].

defile[1] /dɪˈfʌɪl/ ▶ **verb** [with obj.] sully, mar, or spoil: *the land was defiled by a previous owner.*
■ desecrate or profane (something sacred): *the tomb had been defiled and looted.* ■ archaic violate the chastity of (a woman).
– DERIVATIVES **defilement** noun, **defiler** noun.
– ORIGIN late Middle English: alteration of obsolete *defoul*, from Old French *defouler* 'trample down', influenced by obsolete *befile* 'befoul, defile'.

defile[2] /dɪˈfʌɪl/ ▶ **noun** /also ˈdiːfʌɪl/ a steep-sided narrow gorge or passage (originally one requiring troops to march in single file).
▶ **verb** [no obj., with adverbial of direction] archaic (of troops) march in single file: *we emerged after defiling through the mountainsides.*
– ORIGIN late 17th cent.: from French *défilé* (noun), *défiler* (verb), from *dé* 'away from' + *file* 'column, file'.

define ▶ **verb** [with obj.] **1** state or describe exactly the nature, scope, or meaning of: *the contract will seek to define the client's obligations.*
■ give the meaning of (a word or phrase), especially in a dictionary. ■ make up or establish the character of: *for some, the football club defines their identity.*
2 mark out the boundary or limits of: [as adj. **defined**] *clearly defined boundaries.*
■ make clear the outline of; delineate: *she defined her eyes by applying eyeshadow to her eyelids.*
– DERIVATIVES **definable** adjective, **definer** noun.
– ORIGIN late Middle English (also in the sense 'bring to an end'): from Old French *definer*, from a variant of Latin *definire*, from *de-* (expressing completion) + *finire* 'finish' (from *finis* 'end').

definiendum /dɪˌfɪnɪˈɛndəm/ ▶ **noun** (pl. **definienda**) a word, phrase, or symbol which is the subject of a definition, especially in a dictionary entry, or which is introduced into a logical system by being defined. Contrasted with **DEFINIENS**.
– ORIGIN late 19th cent.: from Latin, 'that which is to be defined', from the verb *definire* (see **DEFINE**).

definiens /dɪˈfɪnɪɛnz/ ▶ **noun** (pl. **definientia**) a word, phrase, or symbolic expression used to define something, especially in a dictionary entry, or introducing a word or symbol into a logical system by providing a statement of its meaning. Contrasted with **DEFINIENDUM**.
– ORIGIN late 19th cent.: from medieval Latin, 'defining', present participle of *definire* (see **DEFINE**).

defining moment ▶ **noun** an event which typifies or determines all subsequent related occurrences.

definite ▶ **adjective** clearly stated or decided; not vague or doubtful: *we had no definite plans.*
■ clearly true or real; unambiguous: *no definite proof has emerged.* ■ [predic.] (of a person) certain or sure about something: *you're very definite about that!* ■ clear or undeniable (used for emphasis): *video is a definite asset in the classroom.* ■ having exact and discernible physical limits or form.
– DERIVATIVES **definiteness** noun.
– ORIGIN mid 16th cent.: from Latin *definitus* 'defined, set within limits', past participle of *definire* (see **DEFINE**).

> **USAGE** For an explanation of the difference between **definite** and **definitive**, see **usage** at **DEFINITIVE**.

definite article ▶ **noun** Grammar a determiner (*the* in English) that introduces a noun phrase and implies that the thing mentioned has already been mentioned, or is common knowledge, or is about to be defined (as in *the book on the table; the art of government; the famous public school in Berkshire*). Compare with **INDEFINITE ARTICLE**.

definite description ▶ **noun** chiefly Philosophy a noun phrase introduced by the definite article or its equivalent, and denoting a particular entity or phenomenon.

definite integral ▶ **noun** Mathematics an integral expressed as the difference between the values of the integral at specified upper and lower limits of the independent variable.

definitely ▶ **adverb** without doubt (used for emphasis): *I shall definitely be at the airport to meet you.*

definition ▶ **noun** **1** a statement of the exact meaning of a word, especially in a dictionary.
■ an exact statement or description of the nature, scope, or meaning of something: *our definition of what constitutes poetry.* ■ [mass noun] the action or process of defining something.
2 [mass noun] the degree of distinctness in outline of an object, image, or sound, especially of an image in a photograph or on a screen.
■ the capacity of an instrument or device for making images distinct in outline: [in combination] *high-definition television.*
– PHRASES **by definition** by its very nature; intrinsically: *it is by definition a complex object.*
– DERIVATIVES **definitional** adjective, **definitionally** adverb.
– ORIGIN late Middle English: from Latin *definitio(n-)*, from the verb *definire* 'set bounds to' (see **DEFINE**).

definitive ▶ **adjective** **1** (of a conclusion or agreement) done or reached decisively and with authority: *a definitive diagnosis.*
■ (of a book or other text) the most authoritative of its kind: *the definitive biography of Prince Charles.*
2 (of a postage stamp) for general use and typically of standard design, not special or commemorative.
▶ **noun** a definitive postage stamp.
– DERIVATIVES **definitively** adverb.
– ORIGIN late Middle English: from Old French *definitif, -ive*, from Latin *definitivus*, from *definit-* 'set within limits', from the verb *definire* (see **DEFINE**).

> **USAGE** **Definitive** is often used, rather imprecisely, when **definite** is actually intended, to mean simply 'clearly decided'. Although **definitive** and **definite** have a clear overlap in meaning, **definitive** has the additional sense of 'having an authoritative basis'. Thus, a ***definitive*** *decision* is one which is not only conclusive but also carries the stamp of authority or is a benchmark for the future, while a ***definite*** *decision* is simply one which has been made clearly and is without doubt.

definitive host ▶ **noun** Biology an organism which supports the adult or sexually reproductive form of a parasite. Compare with **INTERMEDIATE HOST**.

deflagrate /ˈdɛfləgreɪt/ ▶ **verb** Chemistry, dated burn away or cause (a substance) to burn away with a sudden flame and rapid, sharp combustion: [with obj.] *the current will deflagrate some of the particles.*
– DERIVATIVES **deflagrator** noun.
– ORIGIN early 18th cent.: from Latin *deflagrat-* 'burnt up', from the verb *deflagrare*, from *de-* 'away, thoroughly' + *flagrare* 'to burn'.

d

deflagration ▶ **noun** [mass noun] the action of heating a substance until it burns away rapidly.
■ technical combustion which propagates through a gas or across the surface of an explosive at subsonic speeds, driven by the transfer of heat. Compare with **DETONATION**.
– ORIGIN early 17th cent.: from Latin *deflagratio(n-)*, from the verb *deflagrare* (see **DEFLAGRATE**).

deflate ▶ **verb 1** [with obj.] let air or gas out of (a tyre, balloon, or similar object): *he deflated one of the tyres.*
■ [no obj.] be emptied of air or gas: *the balloon deflated.*
2 cause (someone) to suddenly lose confidence or feel less important: [as adj. **deflated**] *the news left him feeling utterly deflated.*
■ reduce the level of (an emotion or feeling): *her anger was deflated.*
3 Economics bring about a general reduction of price levels in (an economy).
– DERIVATIVES **deflator** noun.
– ORIGIN late 19th cent.: from **DE-** (expressing reversal) + *-flate* (as in *inflate*).

deflation ▶ **noun** [mass noun] **1** the action or process of deflating or being deflated: *deflation of the illusion that the 1960s were a perpetual party.*
2 Economics reduction of the general level of prices in an economy.
3 Geology the removal of particles of rock, sand, etc. by the wind.
– DERIVATIVES **deflationist** noun & adjective.
– ORIGIN late 19th cent. (in the sense 'release of air from something inflated'): from **DEFLATE**; sense 3 via German from Latin *deflat-* 'blown away', from the verb *deflare*.

deflationary ▶ **adjective** of, characterized by, or tending to cause economic deflation.

deflect ▶ **verb** [with obj., and usu. with adverbial of direction] cause (something) to change direction by interposing something; turn aside from a straight course: *the bullet was deflected harmlessly into the ceiling* | figurative *he attempted to deflect attention away from his private life.*
■ [no obj., with adverbial of direction] (of an object) change direction after hitting something: *the ball **deflected off** Knight's body.* ■ cause (someone) to deviate from an intended purpose: *she refused to be **deflected from** anything she had set her mind on.* ■ cause (something) to change orientation: *the compass needle is **deflected from** magnetic north by metal in the aircraft.*
– ORIGIN mid 16th cent.: from Latin *deflectere*, from *de-* 'away from' + *flectere* 'to bend'.

deflection (also **deflexion**) ▶ **noun** [mass noun] the action or process of deflecting or being deflected: *the deflection of the light beam.*
■ [count noun] the amount by which something is deflected: *an 11-mile deflection of the river.*
– ORIGIN early 17th cent.: from late Latin *deflexio(n-)*, from *deflectere* 'bend away' (see **DEFLECT**).

deflector ▶ **noun** a device that deflects something, in particular:
■ a plate or other attachment for deflecting a flow of air, water, heat, etc. ■ an electrode in a cathode ray tube whose magnetic field is used to deflect a beam of electrons on to a phosphor screen to form an image.

deflexed ▶ **adjective** technical (typically of plant or animal structures) bent or curving downwards or backwards: *a deflexed beak.*
– ORIGIN early 19th cent. (earlier as *deflex*): from Latin *deflexus* 'bent away' (past participle of *deflectere*) + **-ED**[1].

deflocculate /diːˈflɒkjʊleɪt/ ▶ **verb** [with obj.] Chemistry break up into fine particles the floccules of (a substance suspended in a liquid), producing a dispersion.
– DERIVATIVES **deflocculation** noun.

defloration /ˌdiːflɔːˈreɪʃ(ə)n/ ▶ **noun** [mass noun] poetic/literary the taking of a woman's virginity.
– ORIGIN late Middle English: from late Latin *defloratio(n-)*, from the verb *deflorare* (see **DEFLOWER**).

deflower ▶ **verb** [with obj.] **1** dated or poetic/literary deprive (a woman) of her virginity.
2 [usu. as adj. **deflowered**] strip (a plant or garden) of flowers: *deflowered rose bushes.*
– ORIGIN late Middle English: from Old French *desflourer*, from a variant of late Latin *deflorare*, from *de-* (expressing removal) + Latin *flos, flor-* 'a flower'.

defocus ▶ **verb** (**defocused**, **defocusing** or **defocussed**, **defocussing**) [with obj.] cause (an image, lens, or beam) to go out of focus: *the filter lets you defocus all or part of an image.*
■ [no obj.] go out of focus: *the view defocused, then resolved.* ■ take the focus of interest or activity away from (something): *defocusing the traditional contract approach in business.*

Defoe /dɪˈfəʊ/, Daniel (1660–1731), English novelist and journalist. His best-known novel, *Robinson Crusoe* (1719), is loosely based on the true story of the shipwrecked sailor Alexander Selkirk; it has a claim to being the first English novel. Other notable works: *Moll Flanders* (novel, 1722) and *A Journal of the Plague Year* (historical fiction, 1722).

defogger ▶ **noun** chiefly US another term for **DEMISTER**.

defoliant ▶ **noun** a chemical that removes the leaves from trees and plants, often used in warfare.

defoliate /diːˈfəʊlɪeɪt/ ▶ **verb** [with obj.] remove leaves from (a tree, plant, or area of land), for agricultural purposes or as a military tactic: *the area was defoliated and napalmed many times.*
– DERIVATIVES **defoliation** noun.
– ORIGIN late 18th cent.: from late Latin *defoliat-* 'stripped of leaves', from the verb *defoliare*, from *de-* (expressing removal) + *folium* 'leaf'.

defoliator ▶ **noun** an adult or larval insect which strips all the leaves from a tree or shrub.
■ a machine that removes the leaves from a root crop.

deforce /dɪˈfɔːs/ ▶ **verb** [with obj.] Law withhold (land or other property) wrongfully or forcibly from the rightful owner.
■ deprive (someone) wrongfully or forcibly of their rightful property.
– ORIGIN late Middle English: from Anglo-Norman French *deforcer*, from *de-* (expressing removal) + *forcer* 'to force'.

De Forest /də ˈfɒrɪst/, Lee (1873–1961), American physicist and electrical engineer. He designed a triode valve that was crucial to the development of radio communication, television, and computers.

deforest ▶ **verb** [with obj.] (often **be deforested**) clear (an area) of forests or trees.
– DERIVATIVES **deforestation** noun.

deform ▶ **verb** [with obj.] distort the shape or form of; make misshapen: [as adj. **deformed**] *deformed hands.*
■ [no obj.] become distorted or misshapen; undergo deformation: *the suspension deforms slightly on corners.*
– DERIVATIVES **deformable** adjective.
– ORIGIN late Middle English: from Old French *desformer*, via medieval Latin from Latin *deformare*, from *de-* (expressing reversal) + *forma* 'a shape'.

deformation /ˌdiːfɔːˈmeɪʃ(ə)n/ ▶ **noun** [mass noun] the action or process of changing in shape or distorting, especially through the application of pressure: *solid rock undergoing slow deformation.*
■ the result of such a process: *the deformation will be temporary.* ■ [count noun] an altered form of a word, especially one used to avoid overt profanity (e.g. *dang* for *damn*).
– DERIVATIVES **deformational** adjective.

deformity ▶ **noun** (pl. **-ies**) a deformed part, especially of the body; a malformation: *children born with deformities.*
■ [mass noun] the state of being deformed or misshapen: *respiratory problems caused by spinal deformity.*
– ORIGIN late Middle English: from Old French *desformite*, from Latin *deformitas*, from *deformis* 'misshapen'.

defragment /ˌdiːfragˈmɛnt/ ▶ **verb** [with obj.] Computing (of software) reduce the fragmentation of (a file) by concatenating parts stored in separate locations on a disk: *the safe way to defragment your files.*
– DERIVATIVES **defragmentation** noun, **defragmenter** noun.

defraud ▶ **verb** [with obj.] illegally obtain money from (someone) by deception: *he used a second identity to **defraud** the bank **of** thousands of pounds* | [no obj.] *conspiracy to defraud.*
– DERIVATIVES **defrauder** noun.
– ORIGIN late Middle English: from Old French *defrauder* or Latin *defraudare*, from *de-* 'from' + *fraudare* 'to cheat' (from *fraus, fraud-* 'fraud').

defray /dɪˈfreɪ/ ▶ **verb** [with obj.] provide money to pay (a cost or expense): *the proceeds from the raffle help to defray the expenses of the evening.*
– DERIVATIVES **defrayable** adjective, **defrayal** noun, **defrayment** noun.
– ORIGIN late Middle English (in the general sense 'spend money'): from French *défrayer*, from *dé-* (expressing removal) + obsolete *frai* 'cost, expenses' (from medieval Latin *fredum* 'a fine for breach of the peace').

defrock ▶ **verb** [with obj.] deprive (a person in holy orders) of ecclesiastical status.
■ [usu. as adj. **defrocked**] deprive (someone) of professional status or membership of a prestigious group: *a defrocked psychiatrist.*
– ORIGIN early 17th cent.: from French *défroquer*, from *dé-* (expressing removal) + *froc* 'frock'.

defrost ▶ **verb** [with obj.] free (the interior of a refrigerator) of accumulated ice, usually by turning it off for a period.
■ [no obj.] (of a refrigerator) become free of accumulated ice in this way: *she opened the door to let the fridge defrost.* ■ thaw (frozen food) before cooking it: *defrost the turkey slowly.* ■ [no obj.] (of frozen food) thaw before being cooked: *make sure that it has thoroughly defrosted.* ■ N. Amer. remove frost or ice from (the windscreen of a motor vehicle).
– DERIVATIVES **defroster** noun.

deft ▶ **adjective** neatly skilful and quick in one's movements: *a deft piece of footwork.*
■ demonstrating skill and cleverness: *the script was both deft and literate.*
– DERIVATIVES **deftly** adverb, **deftness** noun.
– ORIGIN Middle English: variant of **DAFT**, in the obsolete sense 'meek'.

defterdar /ˌdɛftəˈdɑː/ ▶ **noun** (in the Ottoman Empire and modern Turkey) a finance officer or treasurer, especially a provincial accountant general.
– ORIGIN Turkish, from Persian *daftardār*, from *daftar* 'register' + *-dār* 'holder'.

defunct /dɪˈfʌŋ(k)t/ ▶ **adjective** no longer existing or functioning: *the now defunct Somerset & Dorset railway line.*
– ORIGIN mid 16th cent. (in the sense 'deceased'): from Latin *defunctus* 'dead', past participle of *defungi* 'carry out, finish', from *de-* (expressing reversal) + *fungi* 'perform'.

defuse ▶ **verb** [with obj.] remove the fuse from (an explosive device) in order to prevent it from exploding: *explosives specialists tried to defuse the grenade.*
■ figurative reduce the danger or tension in (a difficult situation): *an attempt to defuse dispute.*

USAGE On the potential confusion between **defuse** and **diffuse**, see **usage at DIFFUSE**.

defy ▶ **verb** (**-ies**, **-ied**) [with obj.] openly resist or refuse to obey: *a woman who defies convention.*
■ (of a thing) make (an action or quality) almost impossible: *his actions defy belief.* ■ [with obj. and infinitive] appear to be challenging (someone) to do or prove something: *he glowered at her, defying her to mock him.* ■ archaic challenge to combat: *go now, defy him to the combat.*
– DERIVATIVES **defier** noun.
– ORIGIN Middle English (in the senses 'renounce an allegiance' and 'challenge to combat'): from Old French *desfier*, based on Latin *dis-* (expressing reversal) + *fidus* 'faithful'.

deg. ▶ **abbreviation for** degree(s).

dégagé /deɪˈgɑːʒeɪ, -ˈgaʒeɪ/ ▶ **adjective** unconcerned or unconstrained; relaxed.
▶ **noun** (pl. pronounced same) Ballet a movement in which weight is shifted from one foot to the other in preparation for the execution of a step.
– ORIGIN late 17th cent.: French, past participle of *dégager* 'set free'.

Degas /ˈdeɪgɑː, French dəga/, (Hilaire Germain) Edgar (1834–1917), French painter and sculptor. An Impressionist painter, Degas is best known for his paintings of ballet dancers.

degas /diːˈgas/ ▶ **verb** (**degassed**, **degassing**) make or become free of unwanted or excess gas: [with obj.] *the column has not been degassed* | [no obj.] *the summit craters were degassing freely.*

de Gaulle /də ˈgəʊl, French də gol/, Charles (André Joseph Marie) (1890–1970), French general and statesman, head of government 1944–6, President 1959–69. A wartime organizer of the Free French movement, he is remembered particularly for his assertive foreign policy and for quelling the student uprisings and strikes of May 1968.

degauss /diːˈgaʊs/ ▶ **verb** [with obj.] [often as noun **degaussing**] Electronics remove unwanted magnetism from (a television or monitor) in order to correct colour disturbance.
■ historical neutralize the magnetic field of (a ship) by

encircling it with a conductor carrying electric currents.
– DERIVATIVES **degausser** noun.

degeneracy ▶ noun [mass noun] the state or property of being degenerate: *the degeneracy of later Roman work.*

degenerate ▶ adjective /dɪˈdʒɛn(ə)rət/ **1** having lost the physical, mental, or moral qualities considered normal and desirable; showing evidence of decline: *a degenerate form of a higher civilization.*
2 technical lacking some property, order, or distinctness of structure previously or usually present, in particular:
■ Mathematics relating to or denoting an example of a particular type of equation, curve, or other entity that is equivalent to a simpler type, often occurring when a variable or parameter is set to zero. ■ Physics relating to or denoting an energy level which corresponds to more than one quantum state. ■ Physics relating to or denoting matter at densities so high that gravitational contraction is counteracted, either by the Pauli exclusion principle or by an analogous quantum effect between closely packed neutrons. ■ Biology having reverted to a simpler form as a result of losing a complex or adaptive structure present in the ancestral form.
▶ noun /dɪˈdʒɛn(ə)rət/ an immoral or corrupt person.
▶ verb /dɪˈdʒɛnəreɪt/ [no obj.] decline or deteriorate physically, mentally, or morally: *the quality of life had degenerated* | *the debate* **degenerated into** *a brawl.*
– DERIVATIVES **degenerately** adverb.
– ORIGIN late 15th cent.: from Latin *degeneratus* 'no longer of its kind', from the verb *degenerare*, from *degener* 'debased', from *de-* 'away from' + *genus, gener-* 'race, kind'.

degeneration ▶ noun [mass noun] the state or process of being or becoming degenerate; decline or deterioration: *overgrazing has caused serious degeneration of grassland.*
■ Medicine deterioration and loss of function in the cells of a tissue or organ: *degeneration of the muscle fibres.*

degenerative ▶ adjective (of a disease or symptom) characterized by progressive (often irreversible) deterioration and loss of function in the organs or tissues: *degenerative diseases.*
■ of or tending to decline and deterioration: *the young generation had fallen into a degenerative backslide.*

degenerescence /dɪˌdʒɛnəˈrɛs(ə)ns/ ▶ noun another term for **DEGENERATION**.
– ORIGIN mid 19th cent.: from French *dégénérescence*, from *dégénérer* 'to degenerate'.

deglaciation /ˌdiːgleɪsɪˈeɪʃ(ə)n/ ▶ noun [mass noun] Geology the disappearance of ice from a previously glaciated region.
■ [count noun] a period of geological time during which this takes place: *the last deglaciation.*

deglamorize (also **deglamourize** or **-ise**) ▶ verb [with obj.] make (someone or something) less glamorous or attractive.
– DERIVATIVES **deglamorization** noun.

deglaze ▶ verb [with obj.] dilute meat sediments in (a pan) in order to make a gravy or sauce, typically using wine: *deglaze the pan with the white wine.*
– ORIGIN late 19th cent.: from French *déglacer.*

deglutition /ˌdiːgluːˈtɪʃ(ə)n/ ▶ noun [mass noun] technical the action or process of swallowing.
– DERIVATIVES **deglutitive** adjective.
– ORIGIN mid 17th cent.: from French *déglutition* or modern Latin *deglutitio(n-)*, from *deglutire* 'swallow down'.

degradation /ˌdɛgrəˈdeɪʃ(ə)n/ ▶ noun [mass noun] the condition or process of degrading or being degraded: *a trail of human misery and degradation.*
■ Geology the wearing down of rock by disintegration.
– ORIGIN mid 16th cent. (in the sense 'deposition from an office or rank as a punishment'): from Old French, or from ecclesiastical Latin *degradatio(n-)*, from the verb *degradare* (see **DEGRADE**).

degrade ▶ verb **1** [with obj.] treat or regard (someone) with contempt or disrespect: *she thought that many supposedly erotic pictures degraded women.*
■ lower the character or quality of: *vast areas of natural habitats have been degraded.* ■ archaic reduce (someone) to a lower rank, especially as a punishment: *he was degraded from his high estate.*
2 break down or deteriorate chemically: [no obj.] *when exposed to light the materials will degrade* | [with obj.] *the bacteria will degrade hydrocarbons.*
■ [with obj.] Physics reduce (energy) to a less readily convertible form. ■ [with obj.] Geology wear down (rock) and cause it to disintegrate.
– DERIVATIVES **degradability** noun, **degradable** adjective, **degradative** adjective, **degrader** noun.
– ORIGIN late Middle English: from Old French *degrader*, from ecclesiastical Latin *degradare*, from *de-* 'down, away from' + Latin *gradus* 'step or grade'.

degrading ▶ adjective causing a loss of self-respect; humiliating: *cruel or degrading treatment.*
– DERIVATIVES **degradingly** adverb.

degranulate ▶ verb [no obj.] Physiology (of a cell) lose or release granules of a substance, typically as part of an immune reaction: *the eosinophils degranulate, releasing the toxic contents of the granules.*
– DERIVATIVES **degranulation** noun.

degrease ▶ verb [with obj.] [often as noun **degreasing**] remove excess grease or fat from (something).
– DERIVATIVES **degreasant** noun, **degreaser** noun.

degree ▶ noun **1** [in sing.] the amount, level, or extent to which something happens or is present: *a degree of caution is probably wise* | [mass noun] *a question of degree.*
2 a unit of measurement of angles, one ninetieth of a right angle or the angle subtended by one three-hundred-and-sixtieth of the circumference of a circle: *set at an angle of 45 degrees.* (Symbol: °)
3 a stage in a scale or series, in particular:
■ a unit in any of various scales of temperature, intensity, or hardness: *water boils at 100 degrees Celsius.* (Symbol: °) ■ [in combination] each of a set of grades (usually three) used to classify burns according to their severity. See **FIRST-DEGREE**, **SECOND-DEGREE**, **THIRD-DEGREE**. ■ [in combination] chiefly N. Amer. a legal grade of crime or offence, especially murder: *second-degree murder.* ■ [often in combination] a step in direct genealogical descent: *second-degree relatives.* ■ Music a position in a musical scale, counting upwards from the tonic or fundamental note: *the lowered third degree of the scale.* ■ Mathematics the class into which an equation falls according to the highest power of unknowns or variables present: *an equation of the second degree.* ■ Grammar any of the three steps on the scale of comparison of gradable adjectives and adverbs, namely positive, comparative, and superlative. ■ archaic a thing placed like a step in a series; a tier or row.
4 an academic rank conferred by a college or university after examination or after completion of a course, or conferred as an honour on a distinguished person: *a degree in zoology.*
■ [mass noun] archaic social or official rank: *persons of unequal degree.* ■ a rank in an order of freemasonry.
– PHRASES **by degrees** a little at a time; gradually: *rivalries and prejudice were by degrees fading out.* **to a degree** to some extent: *to a degree, it is possible to educate oneself.* ■ dated to a considerable extent: *the pressure you were put under must have been frustrating to a degree.*
– ORIGIN Middle English (in the senses 'step', 'tier', 'rank', or 'relative state'): from Old French, based on Latin *de-* 'down' + *gradus* 'step or grade'.

degree day ▶ noun **1** a day on which academic degrees are formally awarded.
2 a unit used to determine the heating requirements of buildings, representing a fall of one degree below a specified average outdoor temperature (usually 18°C or 65°F) for one day.

degree of freedom ▶ noun each of a number of independently variable factors affecting the range of states in which a system may exist, in particular:
■ Physics a direction in which independent motion can occur. ■ Chemistry each of a number of independent factors required to specify a system at equilibrium. ■ Statistics the number of independent values or quantities which can be assigned to a statistical distribution.

degressive /dɪˈgrɛsɪv/ ▶ adjective reducing by gradual amounts.
■ (of taxation) at successively lower rates on lower amounts.
– ORIGIN early 20th cent.: from Latin *degress-* 'descended' (from the verb *degredi*, from *de-* 'down' + *gradi* 'walk') + **-IVE**.

degu /ˈdeɪguː/ ▶ noun a rat-like rodent with a long silky coat, found in southern South America.
• Genus *Octodon*, family Octodontidae: three species.
– ORIGIN mid 19th cent.: from American Spanish, from South American Indian *deuñ.*

degust /dɪˈgʌst/ ▶ verb [with obj.] rare taste (something) carefully, so as to fully appreciate it.
– DERIVATIVES **degustation** noun.
– ORIGIN early 17th cent.: from Latin *degustare*, from *de-* 'completely' + *gustare* 'to taste'.

de haut en bas /də ˌəʊt ɒ̃ ˈbɑː, French də ot ɑ̃ bɑ/ ▶ adverb & adjective in a condescending or superior manner: [as adv.] *he never addressed his students de haut en bas* | [as adj.] *he has a certain de haut en bas style.*
– ORIGIN French, 'from above to below'.

de Havilland /də ˈhavɪlənd/, Sir Geoffrey (1882–1965), English aircraft designer and manufacturer. He designed and built many aircraft, including the Mosquito of the Second World War.

dehisce /dɪˈhɪs/ ▶ verb [no obj.] technical (of a pod or seed vessel, or of a cut or wound) gape or burst open: *after the anther lobes dehisce, the pollen is set free.*
– DERIVATIVES **dehiscence** noun, **dehiscent** adjective.
– ORIGIN mid 17th cent.: from Latin *dehiscere*, from *de-* 'away' + *hiscere* 'begin to gape' (from *hiare* 'gape').

de Hooch /də ˈhuːtʃ/ (also **de Hoogh**), Pieter (*c.*1629–*c.*1684), Dutch genre painter. He is noted for his depictions of domestic interior and courtyard scenes.

dehorn ▶ verb [with obj.] remove the horns from (an animal).

dehors /dəˈɔː, dəˈhɔː/ ▶ preposition Law other than, not including, or outside the scope of: *the plea shows that no request, dehors the letter, existed.*
– ORIGIN early 18th cent.: from an Old French usage as a preposition (in modern French functioning as an adverb and noun).

dehumanize (also **-ise**) ▶ verb [with obj.] deprive of positive human qualities: [as adj. **dehumanizing**] *the dehumanizing effects of war.*
– DERIVATIVES **dehumanization** noun.

dehumidifier ▶ noun a device which removes excess moisture from the air.

dehumidify ▶ verb (**-ies**, **-ied**) [with obj.] remove moisture from (the air or a gas).
– DERIVATIVES **dehumidification** noun.

dehydrate /diːˈhʌɪdreɪt/ ▶ verb [with obj.] [often as adj. **dehydrated**] cause (a person or their body) to lose a large amount of water: *his body temperature was high and he had become dehydrated.*
■ [no obj.] lose a large amount of water from the body. ■ remove water from (food) in order to preserve and store it: *dehydrated mashed potatoes.*
– DERIVATIVES **dehydration** noun, **dehydrator** noun.
– ORIGIN late 19th cent.: from **DE-** (expressing removal) + Greek *hudros, hudr-* 'water'.

dehydrocholesterol /diːˌhʌɪdrə(ʊ)kəˈlɛstərɒl/ ▶ noun [mass noun] Biochemistry a derivative of cholesterol present in the skin. It can be converted to cholecalciferol (vitamin D_3) by the action of ultraviolet radiation.
• Chem. formula: $C_{27}H_{44}O$. The particular isomer involved in vitamin D_3 formation is **7-dehydrocholesterol**.
– ORIGIN 1930s: from *dehydro-* 'that has lost hydrogen' + **CHOLESTEROL**.

dehydrogenase /ˌdiːhʌɪˈdrɒdʒəneɪz/ ▶ noun Biochemistry an enzyme that catalyses the removal of hydrogen atoms from a particular molecule, particularly in the electron transport chain reactions of cell respiration in conjunction with the coenzymes NAD and FAD: [with modifier] *glucose-6-phosphate dehydrogenase.*
– ORIGIN early 20th cent.: from **DE-** (expressing removal) + **HYDROGEN** + **-ASE**.

dehydrogenate ▶ verb [with obj.] Chemistry remove a hydrogen atom or atoms from (a compound).
– DERIVATIVES **dehydrogenation** noun.
– ORIGIN mid 19th cent.: from **DE-** (expressing removal) + **HYDROGEN** + **-ATE**[3].

Deianira /ˌdiːəˈnʌɪərə/ Greek Mythology the wife of Hercules, who was tricked into smearing poison on a garment which caused his death.

de-ice ▶ verb [with obj.] remove ice from: *airplanes are de-iced before take-off.*
– DERIVATIVES **de-icer** noun.

deicide /ˈdeɪɪsʌɪd, ˈdiːɪ-/ ▶ noun the killer of a god.
■ [mass noun] the killing of a god.
– DERIVATIVES **deicidal** adjective.
– ORIGIN early 17th cent.: from ecclesiastical Latin *deicida* 'killer of a god', or directly from Latin *deus* 'god' + **-CIDE**.

deictic /ˈdeɪktɪk, ˈdʌɪktɪk/ Linguistics ▶ adjective of, relating to, or denoting a word or expression whose meaning is dependent on the context in which it is used (such as *here, you, me, that one there,* or *next Tuesday*). Also called **INDEXICAL**.
▶ noun a deictic word or expression.
– DERIVATIVES **deictically** adverb.

– ORIGIN early 19th cent.: from Greek *deiktikos*, *deiktos* 'capable of proof', from *deiknunai* 'to show'.

deid /di:d/ ▶ **adjective** Scottish form of **DEAD**.

deify /'deɪfʌɪ, 'di:ɪ-/ ▶ **verb** (**-ies**, **-ied**) [with obj.] (usu. **be deified**) worship, regard, or treat (someone or something) as a god: *she was deified by the early Romans as a fertility goddess.*
– DERIVATIVES **deification** noun.
– ORIGIN Middle English (in the sense 'make godlike in character'): from Old French *deifier*, from ecclesiastical Latin *deificare*, from *deus* 'god'.

Deighton /'deɪt(ə)n/, Len (b.1929), English writer; full name *Leonard Cyril Deighton*. His reputation is based on his spy thrillers, several of which have been adapted as films and for television.

deign /deɪn/ ▶ **verb** [no obj., with infinitive] do something that one considers to be beneath one's dignity: *she did not deign to answer the maid's question.*
■[with obj.] archaic condescend to give (something): *he had deigned an apology.*
– ORIGIN Middle English: from Old French *degnier*, from Latin *dignare*, *dignari* 'deem worthy', from *dignus* 'worthy'.

Dei gratia /ˌdeɪi: 'grɑ:tɪə, -ʃɪə/ ▶ **adverb** by the grace of God.
– ORIGIN Latin.

deil /di:l/ ▶ **noun** Scottish form of **DEVIL**.

Deimos /'deɪmɒs/ Astronomy the outer of the two small satellites of Mars, discovered in 1877 (15 km long and 12 km across).
– ORIGIN named after one of the sons of Ares in Greek mythology.

de-index ▶ **verb** [with obj.] end the indexation to inflation of (pensions or other benefits).

deindustrialization (also **-isation**) ▶ **noun** [mass noun] a change from industry to other forms of activity.
■decline in industrial activity in a region or economy: *severe deindustrialization with substantial job losses.*
– DERIVATIVES **deindustrialize** (also **-ise**) verb.

deinonychus /dʌɪ'nɒnɪkəs/ ▶ **noun** a dromaeosaurid dinosaur of the mid Cretaceous period, growing up to 3.3 m (11 ft) in length.
• Genus *Deinonychus*, family Dromaeosauridae, suborder Theropoda.
– ORIGIN modern Latin, from Greek *deinos* 'terrible' + *onux*, *onukh-* 'claw'.

deinotherium /ˌdʌɪnə(ʊ)'θɪərɪəm/ (also **deinothere** /'dʌɪnə(ʊ)θɪə/) ▶ **noun** (pl. **deinotheria** or **deinotheriums**) a fossil elephant-like mammal found mainly in the Pliocene epoch, having tusks in the lower jaw that curve downward and backward.
• Genus *Deinotherium*, suborder Deinotherioidea, order Proboscidea.
– ORIGIN modern Latin, from Greek *deinos* 'terrible' + *thērion* 'wild beast'.

deinstitutionalize (also **-ise**) ▶ **verb** [with obj.] discharge (a long-term inmate) from an institution such as a mental hospital or prison: *the changes aim to deinstitutionalize mentally ill people.*
– DERIVATIVES **deinstitutionalization** noun.

deionize /di:'ʌɪənʌɪz/ (also **-ise**) ▶ **verb** [with obj.] [usu. as adj. **deionized**] remove the ions or ionic constituents from (a substance, especially water).
– DERIVATIVES **deionization** noun, **deionizer** noun.

Deirdre /'dɪədri/ Irish Mythology a tragic heroine of whom it was prophesied that her beauty would bring banishment and death to heroes. King Conchobar of Ulster wanted to marry her, but she fell in love with Naoise, son of Usnach, who with his brothers carried her off to Scotland. They were lured back by Conchobar and treacherously slain, and Deirdre took her own life.

deisal ▶ **adverb** variant spelling of **DEASIL**.

deism /'deɪɪz(ə)m, 'di:ɪ-/ ▶ **noun** [mass noun] belief in the existence of a supreme being, specifically of a creator who does not intervene in the universe. The term is used chiefly of an intellectual movement of the 17th and 18th centuries which accepted the existence of a creator on the basis of reason, but rejected belief in a supernatural deity who interacts with humankind. Compare with **THEISM**.
– DERIVATIVES **deist** noun, **deistic** adjective, **deistical** adjective.
– ORIGIN late 17th cent.: from Latin *deus* 'god' + **-ISM**.

deity /'deɪɪti, 'di:ɪ-/ ▶ **noun** (pl. **-ies**) a god or goddess (in a polytheistic religion): *a deity of ancient Greece.*
■[mass noun] divine status, quality, or nature: *a ruler driven by delusions of deity.* ■(usu. **the Deity**) the creator and supreme being (in a monotheistic religion such as Christianity). ■a representation of a god or goddess, such as a statue or carving.
– ORIGIN Middle English (denoting the divine nature of God): from Old French *deite*, from ecclesiastical Latin *deitas* (translating Greek *theotēs*), from *deus* 'god'.

deixis /'deɪksɪs, 'dʌɪksɪs/ ▶ **noun** [mass noun] Linguistics the function or use of deictic words, forms, or expressions.
– ORIGIN 1940s: from Greek, literally 'reference', from *deiknunai* 'to show'.

déjà vu /deɪʒɑ: 'vu:, French deʒa vy/ ▶ **noun** [mass noun] a feeling of having already experienced the present situation.
– ORIGIN early 20th cent.: French, literally 'already seen'.

deject ▶ **verb** [with obj.] archaic make sad or dispirited; depress: *nothing dejects a trader like the interruption of his profits.*
– ORIGIN late Middle English (also in the sense 'overthrow, abase, degrade'): from Latin *deject-* 'thrown down', from the verb *deicere*, from *de-* 'down' + *jacere* 'to throw'.

dejected ▶ **adjective** sad and depressed; dispirited: *he stood in the street looking dejected.*
– DERIVATIVES **dejectedly** adverb.

dejection ▶ **noun** [mass noun] a sad and depressed state; low spirits: *he was slumped in deep dejection.*
– ORIGIN late Middle English: from Latin *dejectio(n-)*, from *deicere* 'throw down' (see **DEJECT**).

de jure /deɪ 'jʊəreɪ, di: 'dʒʊəri/ ▶ **adverb** according to rightful entitlement or claim; by right. Often contrasted with **DE FACTO**.
▶ **adjective** denoting something or someone that is rightfully such: *he had been de jure king since his father's death.*
– ORIGIN Latin, literally 'of law'.

dekaliter ▶ **noun** US variant spelling of **DECALITRE**.

dekameter ▶ **noun** US variant spelling of **DECAMETRE**.

deke /di:k/ Ice Hockey N. Amer. ▶ **noun** a deceptive movement or feint that induces an opponent to move out of position.
▶ **verb** [with obj. and adverbial] draw (a player) out of position by such a movement.
– ORIGIN 1960s: shortened form of **DECOY**.

Dekker /'dɛkə/, Thomas (*c.*1570–1632), English dramatist, author of the revenge tragedy *The Witch of Edmonton* (1623), in which he collaborated with John Ford and William Rowley, and *The Honest Whore* (1604; 1630) with Thomas Middleton.

dekko /'dɛkəʊ/ ▶ **noun** [in sing.] Brit. informal a quick look or glance: *come and have a dekko at this.*
– ORIGIN late 19th cent. (originally used by the British army in India): from Hindi *dekho* 'look!', imperative of *dekhnā*.

de Klerk /də 'klɛ:k/, F. W. (b.1936), South African statesman, State President 1989–94; full name *Frederik Willem de Klerk*. As State President he freed Nelson Mandela in 1990, lifted the ban on membership of the ANC, and opened the negotiations that led to the first democratic elections in 1994. Nobel Peace Prize with Nelson Mandela (1993).

de Kooning /də 'ku:nɪŋ/, Willem (1904–97), Dutch-born American painter, a leading exponent of abstract expressionism. The female form became a central theme in his later work, notably in the *Women* series (1950–3).

Del. ▶ **abbreviation for** Delaware.

del ▶ **noun** Mathematics an operator used in vector analysis. (Symbol: ∇)
• del is defined as $\mathbf{i}\partial/\partial x + \mathbf{j}\partial/\partial y + \mathbf{k}\partial/\partial z$, where **i**, **j**, and **k** are vectors directed respectively along the Cartesian axes *x*, *y*, and *z*.
– ORIGIN early 20th cent.: abbreviation of **DELTA**[1], from the representation of the operator as an inverted capital delta.

Delacroix /ˌdɛlə'krwɑ:, French dəlakʀwa/, (Ferdinand Victor) Eugène (1798–1863), French painter, the chief painter of the French romantic school. He is known for his use of vivid colour, free drawing, and exotic, violent, or macabre subject matter. Notable works: *The Massacre at Chios* (1824).

de la Mare /ˌdə la 'mɛ:/, Walter (John) (1873–1956), English poet, known particularly for his verse for children. Notable works: *The Listeners* (1912).

delaminate /di:'lamɪneɪt/ ▶ **verb** divide or become divided into layers: [with obj.] *delaminating the horn into thin sheets* | [no obj.] *the plywood was starting to delaminate.*
– ORIGIN late 19th cent.: from **DE-** 'away' + Latin *lamina* 'thin plate' + **-ATE**[3].

delate /dɪ'leɪt/ ▶ **verb** [with obj.] archaic report (an offence or crime): *they may delate my slackness to my patron.*
■inform against or denounce (someone): *they deliberated together on delating her as a witch.*
– DERIVATIVES **delation** noun, **delator** noun.
– ORIGIN late 15th cent.: from Latin *delat-* 'referred, carried away', from the verb *deferre* (see **DEFER**[2]).

Delaunay /də'lɔ:neɪ, French dəlonɛ/, Robert (1885–1941), French painter. For most of his career he experimented with the abstract qualities of colour, and he painted some of the first purely abstract pictures. He was one of the founder members of Orphism together with Sonia Delaunay-Terk.

Delaunay-Terk /dəˌlɔ:neɪ'tɛ:k, French dəlonetɛʀk/, Sonia (1885–1979), Russian-born French painter and textile designer, wife of Robert Delaunay. She created abstract paintings based on harmonies of form and colour.

Delaware[1] /'dɛləwɛ:/ **1** a river of the north-eastern US. Rising in the Catskill Mountains in New York State, it flows some 450 km (280 miles) southwards to northern Delaware, where it meets the Atlantic at Delaware Bay. For much of its length it forms the eastern border of Pennsylvania.
2 a state of the US on the Atlantic coast, one of the original thirteen states of the Union (1787); pop. 666,168 (1990); capital, Dover.

Delaware[2] /'dɛləwɛ:/ ▶ **noun** (pl. same or **Delawares**) **1** a member of an American Indian people formerly inhabiting the Delaware River valley of New Jersey and eastern Pennsylvania.
2 [mass noun] either of two Algonquian languages (Munsi and Unami), both now extinct, spoken by this people.
▶ **adjective** of or relating to the Delawares or their languages.
– ORIGIN named after the River *Delaware* (see **DELAWARE**[1]).

delay ▶ **verb** [with obj.] make (someone or something) late or slow: *the train was delayed.*
■[no obj.] be late or slow; loiter: *time being of the essence, they delayed no longer.* ■postpone or defer (an action): *he may decide to delay the next cut in interest rates.*
▶ **noun** a period of time by which something is late or postponed: *a two-hour delay* | *long* ***delays in*** *obtaining passports.*
■[mass noun] the action of delaying or being delayed: *I set off without delay.* ■Electronics the time interval between the propagation of an electrical signal and its reception. ■an electronic device which introduces such an interval, especially in an audio signal.
– DERIVATIVES **delayer** noun.
– ORIGIN Middle English: from Old French *delayer* (verb).

delayed-action ▶ **adjective** [attrib.] operating or effective after a predetermined length of time: *delayed-action bombs.*
▶ **noun** (**delayed action**) [mass noun] the operation of something after a predetermined length of time.

delayering ▶ **noun** [mass noun] the action or process of reducing the number of levels in the hierarchy of employees in an organization.
– DERIVATIVES **delayer** verb.

delaying action ▶ **noun** [mass noun] action taken to gain time, especially a military engagement that delays the advance of an enemy.

delaying tactics ▶ **plural noun** tactics designed to defer or postpone something in order to gain an advantage for oneself.

delay line ▶ **noun** a device producing a specific desired delay in the transmission of a signal.
■historical a plate, wire, or mercury column used to store an electrical impulse in a valve computer. ■a set of mirrors controlling the path lengths between outlying telescopes and a central receiver.

dele /'di:li/ ▶ **verb** (**deled**, **deleing**) [with obj.] delete or mark (a part of a text) for deletion.
▶ **noun** a proof-reader's sign indicating matter to be deleted.

– ORIGIN Latin, 'blot out! efface!', imperative of *delere*.

delectable ▶ adjective (of food or drink) delicious: *delectable handmade chocolates.*
▪ chiefly humorous extremely beautiful or attractive: *the delectable Ms Davis.*
– DERIVATIVES **delectability** noun, **delectably** adverb.
– ORIGIN late Middle English: via Old French from Latin *delectabilis*, from *delectare* 'to charm' (see **DELIGHT**).

delectation /ˌdiːlɛkˈteɪʃ(ə)n/ ▶ noun [mass noun] formal, chiefly humorous pleasure and delight: *they had all manner of rock 'n' roll goodies* ***for our delectation.***
– ORIGIN late Middle English: via Old French from Latin *delectatio(n-)*, from *delectare* 'to charm' (see **DELIGHT**).

delegacy /ˈdɛlɪɡəsi/ ▶ noun (pl. **-ies**) [treated as sing. or pl.] a body of delegates; a committee or delegation.
▪ an appointment as a delegate.
– ORIGIN late Middle English: from **DELEGATE**, on the pattern of the pair *prelate, prelacy*.

delegate ▶ noun /ˈdɛlɪɡət/ a person sent or authorized to represent others, in particular an elected representative sent to a conference.
▪ a member of a committee.
▶ verb /ˈdɛlɪɡeɪt/ [with obj.] entrust (a task or responsibility) to another person, typically one who is less senior than oneself: *he delegates routine tasks* | *the power* ***delegated to*** *him must never be misused.*
▪ [with obj. and infinitive] send or authorize (someone) to do something as a representative: *Edward was delegated to meet new arrivals.*
– DERIVATIVES **delegable** /ˈdɛlɪɡəb(ə)l/ adjective, **delegator** noun.
– ORIGIN late Middle English: from Latin *delegatus* 'sent on a commission', from the verb *delegare*, from *de-* 'down' + *legare* 'depute'.

delegation ▶ noun [treated as sing. or pl.] a body of delegates or representatives; a deputation: *a delegation of teachers.*
▪ [mass noun] the act or process of delegating or being delegated: *prioritizing tasks for delegation.*
– ORIGIN early 17th cent. (denoting the act or process of delegating; also in the sense 'delegated power'): from Latin *delegatio(n-)*, from *delegare* 'send on a commission' (see **DELEGATE**).

delegitimate ▶ verb another term for **DELEGITIMIZE**.

delegitimatize ▶ verb another term for **DELEGITIMIZE**.

delegitimize (also **-ise**) ▶ verb [with obj.] withdraw legitimate status or authority from (someone or something): *political efforts to delegitimize nuclear weapons.*
– DERIVATIVES **delegitimization** noun.

de Lenclos, Ninon, see **LENCLOS**.

delete ▶ verb [with obj.] remove or obliterate (written or printed matter), especially by drawing a line through it or marking it with a delete sign: *the passage was deleted.*
▪ (usu. **be deleted**) remove (data) from a computer's memory. ▪ (**be deleted**) Genetics (of a section of genetic code, or its product) be lost or excised from a nucleic acid or protein sequence: *if one important gene is deleted from an animal's DNA, other genes can stand in.* ▪ remove (a product, especially a recording) from the catalogue of those available for purchase: *their EMI release has already been deleted.*
▶ noun a command or key on a computer which erases text.
– ORIGIN late Middle English (in the sense 'destroy'): from Latin *delet-* 'blotted out, effaced', from the verb *delere*.

deleterious /ˌdɛlɪˈtɪərɪəs/ ▶ adjective causing harm or damage: *divorce is assumed to have deleterious effects on children.*
– DERIVATIVES **deleteriously** adverb.
– ORIGIN mid 17th cent.: via medieval Latin from Greek *dēlētērios* 'noxious' + **-OUS**.

deletion ▶ noun **1** [mass noun] the action or process of deleting something: *deletion of a file.*
2 Genetics the loss or absence of a section from a nucleic acid molecule or chromosome.

delexical /diːˈlɛksɪk(ə)l/ ▶ adjective Linguistics (of a verb) having little or no meaning in its own right, for example *take* in *take a photograph.*

Delfont /ˈdɛlfɒnt/, Bernard, Baron Delfont of Stepney (1909–94), Russian-born British impresario; born *Boris Winogradsky*. From the early 1940s onwards he presented more than 200 shows in London's West End.

Delft /dɛlft/ a town in the Netherlands, in the province of South Holland; pop. 89,400 (1991). The home of the painters Pieter de Hooch and Jan Vermeer, it is noted for its pottery.
– ORIGIN originally *Delf*, from Dutch *delf* 'ditch', still the name of the town's main canal.

delft /dɛlft/ ▶ noun [mass noun] English or Dutch tin-glazed earthenware, typically decorated by hand in blue on a white background.
– DERIVATIVES **delftware** noun.
– ORIGIN late 17th cent.: (originally *Delf ware*): see **DELFT**, where the pottery originated.

Delhi /ˈdɛli/ a Union Territory in north central India, containing the cities of Old and New Delhi; pop. 7,175,000 (1991). **Old Delhi**, a walled city on the River Jumna, was made the capital of the Mogul empire in 1638 by Shah Jahan (1592–1666). **New Delhi**, the capital of India, was built 1912–29 to replace Calcutta as the capital of British India.

Delhi belly ▶ noun informal an upset stomach accompanied by diarrhoea, especially as suffered by visitors to India.
– ORIGIN 1940s: named after **DELHI**.

deli ▶ noun (pl. **delis**) informal short for **DELICATESSEN**.

Delian /ˈdiːlɪən/ ▶ adjective of or relating to Delos.
▶ noun a native or inhabitant of Delos.

Delian League an alliance of ancient Greek city states, dominated by Athens, that joined in 478–447 BC against the Persians. The league was disbanded on the defeat of Athens in the Peloponnesian War (404 BC), but again united under Athens' leadership against Spartan aggression in 377–338 BC. Also called the **ATHENIAN EMPIRE**.

deliberate ▶ adjective /dɪˈlɪb(ə)rət/ done consciously and intentionally: *a deliberate attempt to provoke conflict.*
▪ fully considered; not impulsive: *a deliberate decision.* ▪ done or acting in a careful and unhurried way: *a careful and deliberate worker.*
▶ verb /dɪˈlɪbəreɪt/ [no obj.] engage in long and careful consideration: *she* ***deliberated over*** *the menu.*
▪ [with obj.] consider (a question) carefully: *jurors deliberated the fate of those charged* | [with clause] *deliberating what she should do.*
– DERIVATIVES **deliberately** adverb, **deliberateness** noun, **deliberator** noun.
– ORIGIN late Middle English (as an adjective): from Latin *deliberatus*, 'considered carefully', past participle of *deliberare*, from *de-* 'down' + *librare* 'weigh' (from *libra* 'scales').

deliberation ▶ noun [mass noun] **1** long and careful consideration or discussion: *after much deliberation we arrived at a compromise* | [count noun] *the commission's deliberations.*
2 slow and careful movement or thought: *he replaced the glass on the table with deliberation.*
– ORIGIN late Middle English: via Old French from Latin *deliberatio(n-)*, from *deliberare* 'consider carefully' (see **DELIBERATE**).

deliberative ▶ adjective relating to or intended for consideration or discussion: *a deliberative assembly.*
– DERIVATIVES **deliberatively** adverb.

Delibes /dəˈliːb, French dəlib/, (Clément Philibert) Léo (1836–91), French composer and organist. His best-known works are the ballets *Coppélia* (1870) and *Sylvia* (1876).

delicacy ▶ noun (pl. **-ies**) **1** [mass noun] the quality of being delicate, in particular:
▪ fineness or intricacy of texture or structure: *miniature pearls of exquisite delicacy.* ▪ susceptibility to illness or adverse conditions; fragility. ▪ the quality of requiring discretion or sensitivity: *the delicacy of the situation.* ▪ tact and consideration: *I have to treat this matter with the utmost delicacy.* ▪ accuracy of perception; sensitiveness.
2 a choice or expensive food: *a Chinese delicacy.*
– ORIGIN late Middle English (in the senses 'voluptuousness' and 'luxuriousness'): from **DELICATE** + **-ACY**.

delicate ▶ adjective **1** very fine in texture or structure; of intricate workmanship or quality.
▪ (of colour) subtle and subdued: *delicate pastel shades.* ▪ (of food or drink) subtly and pleasantly flavoured: *a delicate, sweet flavour.*
2 easily broken or damaged; fragile: *delicate china.*
▪ (of a person, animal, or plant) susceptible to illness or adverse conditions: *his delicate health.* ▪ (of a state or condition) easily upset or damaged: *owls have a delicate balance with their habitat.*
3 requiring sensitive or careful handling: *delicate negotiations.*
▪ (of a person or an action) tactful and considerate: *the most delicate tact was called for.* ▪ skilful and finely judged; deft: *his delicate ball-playing skills.* ▪ (of an instrument) highly sensitive.
▶ noun informal a delicate fabric or garment made of such fabric.
– PHRASES **in a delicate condition** archaic pregnant.
– DERIVATIVES **delicately** adverb, **delicateness** noun.
– ORIGIN late Middle English (in the sense 'delightful, charming'): from French *délicat* or Latin *delicatus*, of unknown origin. Senses also expressed in Middle English (now obsolete) include 'voluptuous', 'self-indulgent', 'fastidious', and 'effeminate'.

delicatessen /ˌdɛlɪkəˈtɛs(ə)n/ ▶ noun a shop selling cooked meats, cheeses, and unusual or foreign prepared foods.
– ORIGIN late 19th cent. (originally US, denoting prepared foods for sale): from German *Delikatessen* or Dutch *delicatessen*, from French *délicatesse* 'delicateness', from *délicat* (see **DELICATE**).

delicious ▶ adjective highly pleasant to the taste: *delicious home-baked brown bread.*
▪ delightful: *a delicious irony.*
– DERIVATIVES **deliciously** adverb, **deliciousness** noun.
– ORIGIN Middle English (also in the sense 'characterized by sensuous indulgence'): via Old French from late Latin *deliciosus*, from Latin *deliciae* (plural) 'delight, pleasure'.

delict /dɪˈlɪkt, ˈdiːlɪkt/ ▶ noun Law a violation of the law; a tort: *an international delict.*
– ORIGIN late Middle English: from Latin *delictum* 'something showing fault', neuter past participle of *delinquere* (see **DELINQUENT**).

delight ▶ verb [with obj.] please (someone) greatly: *an experience guaranteed to delight both young and old.*
▪ [no obj.] (**delight in**) take great pleasure in: *they delight in playing tricks.*
▶ noun [mass noun] great pleasure: *she* ***took great delight*** *in telling your story.*
▪ [count noun] a cause or source of great pleasure: *the trees here are a delight.*
– ORIGIN Middle English: from Old French *delitier* (verb), *delit* (noun), from Latin *delectare* 'to charm', frequentative of *delicere*. The *-gh-* was added in the 16th cent. by association with **LIGHT**[1].

delighted ▶ adjective feeling or showing great pleasure: *a delighted smile* | [with infinitive] *we were delighted to see her.*
– DERIVATIVES **delightedly** adverb.

delightful ▶ adjective causing delight; charming: *a delightful secluded garden.*
– DERIVATIVES **delightfully** adverb, **delightfulness** noun.

Delilah /dɪˈlʌɪlə/ (in the Bible) a woman who betrayed Samson to the Philistines (Judges 16) by revealing to them that the secret of his strength lay in his long hair.

delimit /dɪˈlɪmɪt/ ▶ verb (**delimited**, **delimiting**) [with obj.] determine the limits or boundaries of: *agreements delimiting fishing zones.*
– DERIVATIVES **delimitation** noun, **delimiter** noun.
– ORIGIN mid 19th cent.: from French *délimiter*, from Latin *delimitare*, from *de-* 'down, completely' + *limitare* (from *limes, limit-* 'boundary, limit').

delineate /dɪˈlɪnɪeɪt/ ▶ verb [with obj.] describe or portray (something) precisely: *the law should delineate and prohibit behaviour which is socially abhorrent.*
▪ indicate the exact position of (a border or boundary).
– DERIVATIVES **delineation** /-ˈeɪʃ(ə)n/ noun, **delineator** noun.
– ORIGIN mid 16th cent. (in the sense 'trace the outline of something'): from Latin *delineat-* 'outlined', from the verb *delineare*, from *de-* 'out, completely' + *lineare* (from *linea* 'line').

delinquency ▶ noun (pl. **-ies**) [mass noun] minor crime, especially that committed by young people: *social causes of crime and delinquency.*
▪ formal neglect of one's duty: *he relayed this in such a manner as to imply grave delinquency on the host's part.*

■ [count noun] chiefly US a failure to pay an outstanding debt.
– ORIGIN mid 17th cent.: from ecclesiastical Latin *delinquentia*, from Latin *delinquent-* 'offending' (see **DELINQUENT**).

delinquent /dɪˈlɪŋkw(ə)nt/ ▶ **adjective** (typically of a young person or their behaviour) showing or characterized by a tendency to commit crime, particularly minor crime: *delinquent children.*
■ chiefly US in arrears: *delinquent accounts.* ■ formal failing in one's duty.
▶ **noun** a delinquent person: *young delinquents.*
– DERIVATIVES **delinquently** adverb.
– ORIGIN late 15th cent.: from Latin *delinquent-* 'offending', from the verb *delinquere*, from *de-* 'away' + *linquere* 'to leave'.

d

deliquesce /ˌdɛlɪˈkwɛs/ ▶ **verb** [no obj.] (of organic matter) become liquid, typically during decomposition.
■ Chemistry (of a solid) become liquid by absorbing moisture from the air.
– ORIGIN mid 18th cent.: from Latin *deliquescere* 'dissolve', from *de-* 'down' + *liquescere* 'become liquid' (from *liquere* 'be liquid').

deliquescent ▶ **adjective** becoming liquid or having a tendency to become liquid.
■ Chemistry (of a solid) tending to absorb moisture from the air and dissolve in it.
– DERIVATIVES **deliquescence** noun.
– ORIGIN late 18th cent.: from Latin *deliquescent-* 'dissolving', from the verb *deliquescere* (see **DELIQUESCE**).

delirious ▶ **adjective** in an acutely disturbed state of mind resulting from illness or intoxication and characterized by restlessness, illusions, and incoherence of thought and speech.
■ in a state of wild excitement or ecstasy: *there was a great roar from the delirious crowd.*
– DERIVATIVES **deliriant** adjective, **deliriously** adverb.

delirium /dɪˈlɪrɪəm/ ▶ **noun** [mass noun] an acutely disturbed state of mind characterized by restlessness, illusions, and incoherence of thought and speech, occurring in fever, intoxication, and other disorders.
■ wild excitement or ecstasy.
– ORIGIN mid 16th cent.: from Latin, from *delirare* 'deviate, be deranged' (literally 'deviate from the furrow'), from *de-* 'away' + *lira* 'ridge between furrows'.

delirium tremens /ˈtriːmɛnz, ˈtrɛ-/ ▶ **noun** [mass noun] a psychotic condition typical of withdrawal in chronic alcoholics, involving tremors, hallucinations, anxiety, and disorientation.
– ORIGIN early 19th cent.: from Latin, 'trembling delirium'.

delish ▶ **adjective** informal delicious.

delist ▶ **verb** [with obj.] remove (something) from a list, in particular:
■ remove (a security) from the official register of a stock exchange: *the stock collapsed and was delisted.*
■ remove (a product) from the list of those sold by a particular retailer.

Delius /ˈdiːlɪəs/, Frederick (1862–1934), English composer, of German and Scandinavian descent. He is best known for pastoral works such as *Brigg Fair* (1907), but he also wrote songs, concertos, and choral and theatre music.

deliver ▶ **verb** [with obj.] **1** bring and hand over (a letter, parcel, or ordered goods) to the proper recipient or address: *the products should be delivered on time* | [no obj.] *we'll deliver direct to your door.*
■ formally hand over (someone): *there was a reward if you were* ***delivered*** *unharmed* ***to*** *the nearest British post.* ■ obtain (a vote) in favour of a candidate or cause: *he had been able to deliver votes in huge numbers.* ■ launch or aim (a blow, a ball, or an attack): *to allow the army to deliver an early riposte to the enemy.* ■ provide (something promised or expected): *the struggle to deliver election commitments* | [no obj.] *she's waiting for him to* ***deliver on*** *his promise.* ■ (**deliver someone/thing from**) save, rescue, or set someone or something free from: *deliver us from the nightmare of junk paper.* ■ (**deliver someone/thing up**) surrender someone or something: *to deliver up to justice a member of his own family.* ■ Law acknowledge that one intends to be bound by (a deed), either explicitly by declaration or implicitly by formal handover.
2 state in a formal manner: *he will deliver a lecture on endangered species* | *he* ***delivered himself of*** *a sermon.*
■ (of a judge or court) give (a judgement or verdict): *the court was due to deliver its verdict.*
3 assist in the birth of: *the village midwife delivered the baby.*
■ give birth to: *she will deliver a child.* ■ (**be delivered of**) give birth to: *Mrs Webb—now safely delivered of her next child.* ■ assist (a woman) in giving birth.
– PHRASES **deliver the goods** informal provide that which is promised or expected.
– DERIVATIVES **deliverer** noun.
– ORIGIN Middle English: from Old French *delivrer*, based on Latin *de-* 'away' + *liberare* 'set free'.

deliverable ▶ **adjective** able to be delivered: *goods in a deliverable state.*
▶ **noun** (usu. **deliverables**) a thing able to be provided, especially as a product of a development process.

deliverance ▶ **noun 1** [mass noun] the action of being rescued or set free: *prayers for deliverance.*
2 a formal or authoritative utterance.
– ORIGIN Middle English: from Old French *delivrance*, from the verb *delivrer* (see **DELIVER**).

delivery ▶ **noun** (pl. **-ies**) [mass noun] **1** the action of delivering letters, parcels, or ordered goods: *allow up to 28 days for delivery.*
■ [count noun] a regular or scheduled occasion for this: *there will be around 15 deliveries a week.* ■ [count noun] an item or items delivered on a particular occasion: *they are getting smaller deliveries.* ■ Law the acknowledgement by the maker of a deed that they intend to be bound by it, either explicitly by declaration or implicitly by formal handover.
2 the process of giving birth: *injuries sustained during delivery* | [count noun] *practically all deliveries take place in hospital* | [as modifier] *the delivery room.*
3 [count noun] an act of throwing or bowling a ball, especially a cricket ball: *he reached 59 runs off only 42 deliveries.*
■ [mass noun] the style or manner of such an action: *they can cause him problems with the short delivery.*
4 the manner or style of giving a speech: *her delivery was stilted.*
5 the supply or provision of something: *a mechanism for rapid delivery of bile into the duodenum.*
– PHRASES **take delivery of** receive (something purchased): *we took delivery of the software in February.*
– ORIGIN late Middle English: from Anglo-Norman French *delivree*, feminine past participle of *delivrer* (see **DELIVER**).

dell ▶ **noun** poetic/literary a small valley, usually among trees: *lush green valleys and wooded dells.*
– ORIGIN Old English, of Germanic origin; related to Dutch *del* and German dialect *Telle*, also to **DALE**.

Della Cruscan /ˌdɛlə ˈkrʌsk(ə)n/ ▶ **adjective** of or relating to the Academy della Crusca in Florence, an institution established in 1582, with the purity of the Italian language as its chief interest.
■ of or relating to a late 18th-century school of English poets with an artificial style modelled on that of purist Italian writers.
▶ **noun** a member of the Academy della Crusca.
■ a Della Cruscan poet.
– ORIGIN from Italian (*Accademia*) *della Crusca* '(Academy) of the bran' (with reference to 'sifting' of the language).

della Francesca see **PIERO DELLA FRANCESCA**.

della Quercia /ˌdɛlə ˈkwɛːtʃə, Italian ˌdella ˈkwertʃa/, Jacopo (*c.*1374–1438), Italian sculptor. He is noted for his tomb of Ilaria del Carretto in Lucca cathedral (*c.*1406) and for the biblical reliefs on the portal of San Petronio in Bologna (1425–35).

della Robbia /ˈrɒbɪə/, Luca (1400–82), Italian sculptor and ceramicist. He is best known for his relief panels in Florence cathedral and his colour-glazed terracotta figures.

delocalize (also **-ise**) ▶ **verb** [with obj.] detach or remove (something) from a particular place or location: [as adj. **delocalized**] *delocalized cortical activity.*
■ not limit to a particular location: [as noun **delocalizing**] *the delocalizing of finance capital.* ■ (**be delocalized**) Chemistry (of electrons) be shared among more than two atoms in a molecule: *the pi electrons are delocalized and energetically stable.*
– DERIVATIVES **delocalization** noun.

Delors /dəˈlɔː, French dəlɔʀ/, Jacques (Lucien Jean) (b.1925), French socialist politician, president of the European Commission 1985–94. During his presidency he pressed for closer European union and oversaw the introduction of a single market within the European Community, which came into effect on 1 January 1993.

Delos /ˈdiːlɒs/ a small Greek island in the Aegean Sea, regarded as the centre of the Cyclades. Now virtually uninhabited, in classical times it was considered to be sacred to Apollo, and according to legend was the birthplace of Apollo and Artemis. Greek name **DHÍLOS**.

delouse /diːˈlaʊs/ ▶ **verb** [with obj.] treat (a person or animal) to rid them of lice and other parasitic insects.

Delphi /ˈdɛlfi, -fʌɪ/ one of the most important religious sanctuaries of the ancient Greek world, dedicated to Apollo and situated on the lower southern slopes of Mount Parnassus above the Gulf of Corinth. Thought of as the navel of the earth, it was the seat of the Delphic Oracle, whose riddling responses to a wide range of questions were delivered by the Pythia. Greek name **DHELFOÍ**.

Delphic /ˈdɛlfɪk/ (also **Delphian** /-fɪən/) ▶ **adjective** of or relating to the ancient Greek oracle at Delphi.
■ (typically of a pronouncement) deliberately obscure or ambiguous.

delphinium /dɛlˈfɪnɪəm/ ▶ **noun** (pl. **delphiniums**) a popular garden plant of the buttercup family, which bears tall spikes of blue flowers.
• Genus *Delphinium*, family Ranunculaceae.
– ORIGIN modern Latin, from Greek *delphinion* 'larkspur', from *delphin* 'dolphin' (because of the shape of the spur, thought to resemble a dolphin's back).

Delphinus /dɛlˈfʌɪnəs/ Astronomy a small constellation (the Dolphin), just north of the celestial equator near Cygnus.
■ [as genitive **Delphini** /dɛlˈfʌɪni/] used with preceding letter or numeral to designate a star in this constellation: *the star Alpha Delphini.*
– ORIGIN Latin.

del Sarto, Andrea, see **SARTO**.

delta[1] ▶ **noun 1** the fourth letter of the Greek alphabet (**Δ, δ**), transliterated as 'd'.
■ Brit. a fourth-class mark given for an essay, examination paper, or other piece of work. ■ [as modifier] the fourth in a series of items, categories, etc.: *delta hepatitis.* ■ (**Delta**) [followed by Latin genitive] Astronomy the fourth (usually fourth-brightest) star in a constellation: *Delta Cephei.*
2 a code word representing the letter D, used in radio communication.
▶ **symbol for** ■ (**δ**) Mathematics variation of a variable or function. ■ (**Δ**) Mathematics a finite increment. ■ (**δ**) Astronomy declination.
– ORIGIN Greek, from Phoenician *daleth*.

delta[2] ▶ **noun** a triangular tract of sediment deposited at the mouth of a river, typically where it diverges into several outlets.
– DERIVATIVES **deltaic** adjective.
– ORIGIN mid 16th cent.: originally specifically as *the Delta* (of the River Nile), from the shape of the Greek letter (see **DELTA**[1]).

delta connection ▶ **noun** a triangular arrangement of electrical three-phase windings in series, each of the three wires of the circuit being connected to a junction of two windings.

Delta Force an elite American military force whose main responsibilities are rescue operations and special forces work.

delta rays ▶ **plural noun** Physics rays of low penetrative power consisting of slow electrons or other particles ejected from atoms by the impact of ionizing radiation.

delta rhythm ▶ **noun** [mass noun] electrical activity of the brain at a frequency of around 1–8 Hz, typical of sleep. The resulting oscillations, detected using an electroencephalograph, are called **delta waves**.

delta-v (also **delta-vee**) ▶ **noun** [mass noun] informal acceleration: *four hundred knots of delta-v.*
– ORIGIN late 20th cent.: from **DELTA**[1] (as a mathematical symbol denoting variation) + *v* for *velocity*.

delta wing ▶ **noun** the single triangular swept-back wing on some aircraft, typically on military aircraft.
– DERIVATIVES **delta-winged** adjective.

deltiologist /ˌdɛltɪˈɒlədʒɪst/ ▶ **noun** a person who collects postcards as a hobby.
– DERIVATIVES **deltiology** noun.
– ORIGIN 1940s: from Greek *deltion* (diminutive of *deltos* 'writing tablet') + **-LOGIST**.

deltoid /ˈdɛltɔɪd/ ▶ **adjective** technical triangular: *a tree with large deltoid leaves.*

■denoting a thick triangular muscle covering the shoulder joint and used for raising the arm away from the body.
▶ noun a deltoid muscle.
■each of the three parts of a deltoid muscle, attached at the front, side, and rear of the shoulder: *the anterior deltoid.*
– ORIGIN mid 18th cent.: from French *deltoïde*, or via modern Latin from Greek *deltoeidēs.*

delude /dɪˈl(j)uːd/ ▶ verb [with obj.] impose a misleading belief upon (someone): *too many theorists have deluded the public* | [as adj. **deluded**] *the poor deluded creature.*
– DERIVATIVES **deludedly** adverb, **deluder** noun.
– ORIGIN late Middle English: from Latin *deludere* 'to mock', from *de-* (with pejorative force) + *ludere* 'to play'.

deluge /ˈdɛljuːdʒ/ ▶ noun a severe flood.
■(**the Deluge**) the biblical Flood (recorded in Genesis 6–8). ■ a heavy fall of rain: *a deluge of rain hit the plains.* ■ figurative a great quantity of something arriving at the same time: *a deluge of complaints.*
▶ verb [with obj.] (usu. **be deluged**) inundate with a great quantity of something: *he has been deluged with offers of work.*
■flood: *caravans were deluged by the heavy rains.*
– ORIGIN late Middle English: from Old French, variant of *diluve*, from Latin *diluvium*, from *diluere* 'wash away'.

delusion ▶ noun an idiosyncratic belief or impression which is firmly maintained despite being contradicted by what is generally accepted as reality or rational argument, typically a symptom of mental disorder: *the delusion of being watched.*
■[mass noun] the action of deluding someone or the state of being deluded: *what a capacity television has for delusion.*
– PHRASES **delusions of grandeur** a false impression of one's own importance.
– DERIVATIVES **delusional** adjective.
– ORIGIN late Middle English (in the sense 'act of deluding or of being deluded'): from late Latin *delusio(n-)*, from the verb *deludere* (see **DELUDE**).

delusive ▶ adjective giving a false or misleading impression: *the delusive light of Venice.*
– DERIVATIVES **delusively** adverb, **delusiveness** noun.

delusory /dɪˈl(j)uːs(ə)ri, -z-/ ▶ adjective another term for **DELUSIVE**.
– ORIGIN late 15th cent.: from late Latin *delusorius*, from *delus-* 'mocked', from the verb *deludere* (see **DELUDE**).

delustre (US **deluster**) ▶ verb [with obj.] remove lustre from (a textile), typically by chemical treatment.

de luxe /dɪ ˈlʌks, ˈlʊks/ ▶ adjective luxurious or sumptuous; of a superior kind: *a de luxe hotel.*
– ORIGIN early 19th cent.: French, literally 'of luxury'.

delve ▶ verb [no obj.] reach inside a receptacle and search for something: *she delved in her pocket.*
■research or make painstaking enquiries into something: *the society is determined to delve deeper into the matter.* ■ [with obj.] poetic/literary dig; excavate: [as adj. **delved**] *the approach from the surface above had awed her, so hugely delved were the tunnels.*
– DERIVATIVES **delver** noun.
– ORIGIN Old English *delfan* 'dig', of West Germanic origin; related to Dutch *delven.*

Dem. US ▶ abbreviation for Democrat.

demagnetize (also **-ise**) ▶ verb [with obj.] remove magnetic properties from.
– DERIVATIVES **demagnetization** noun, **demagnetizer** noun.

demagogue /ˈdɛməɡɒɡ/ ▶ noun a political leader who seeks support by appealing to popular desires and prejudices rather than by using rational argument.
■(in ancient Greece and Rome) a leader or orator who espoused the cause of the common people.
– DERIVATIVES **demagogic** /-ˈɡɒɡɪk/ adjective, **demagoguery** /-ˈɡɒɡ(ə)ri/ noun, **demagogy** noun.
– ORIGIN mid 17th cent.: from Greek *dēmagōgos*, from *dēmos* 'the people' + *agōgos* 'leading' (from *agein* 'to lead').

de Maintenon see **MAINTENON**.

demand ▶ noun an insistent and peremptory request, made as of right: *a series of demands for far-reaching reforms.*
■(**demands**) pressing requirements: *he's got enough*

demands on his time already. ■ [mass noun] Economics the desire of purchasers, consumers, clients, employers, etc. for a particular commodity, service, or other item: *a recent slump in demand* | [count noun] *a demand for specialists.*
▶ verb [reporting verb] ask authoritatively or brusquely: [with direct speech] '*Where is she?' he demanded* | [with clause] *the police demanded that he give them the names.*
■[with obj.] insist on having: *an outraged public demanded retribution* | *too much was being demanded of the top players.* ■ require; need: *a complex activity demanding detailed knowledge.*
– PHRASES **in demand** sought after: *all these skills are much in demand.* **on demand** as soon as or whenever required: *a combination boiler provides hot water on demand.*
– DERIVATIVES **demander** noun.
– ORIGIN Middle English (as a noun): from Old French *demande* (noun), *demander* (verb), from Latin *demandare* 'hand over, entrust' (in medieval Latin 'demand'), from *de-* 'formally' + *mandare* 'to order'.

demand curve ▶ noun a graph showing how the demand for a commodity or service varies with changes in its price.

demand deposit ▶ noun a deposit of money that can be withdrawn without prior notice, e.g. in a current account.

demand draft ▶ noun a financial draft payable on demand.

demand feeding ▶ noun [mass noun] the practice of feeding a baby when it cries for a feed rather than at set times.

demanding ▶ adjective (of a task) requiring much skill or effort: *she has a busy and demanding job.*
■(of a person) making others work hard or meet high standards.
– DERIVATIVES **demandingly** adverb.

demand-led (also **demand-driven**) ▶ adjective Economics caused or determined by demand from consumers or clients.

demand note ▶ noun a formal request for payment.
■N. Amer. another term for **DEMAND DRAFT**.

demand-pull ▶ adjective relating to or denoting inflation caused by an excess of demand over supply.

demantoid /dɪˈmantɔɪd/ ▶ noun [mass noun] a lustrous green variety of andradite (garnet).
– ORIGIN late 19th cent.: from German, from *Demant* 'diamond'.

demarcate /ˈdiːmɑːkeɪt/ (also **demarkate**) ▶ verb [with obj.] set the boundaries or limits of: *plots of land demarcated by barbed wire.*
■separate or distinguish from: *art was being demarcated from the more objective science.*
– ORIGIN early 19th cent.: back-formation from **DEMARCATION**.

demarcation (also **demarkation**) ▶ noun [mass noun] the action of fixing the boundary or limits of something: *the demarcation of the maritime border.*
■Brit. the practice of requiring that specific jobs be assigned to members of particular trade unions: *strikes over job demarcation.* ■ [count noun] a dividing line: *a horizontal band that produces a distinct demarcation two inches from the top.*
– DERIVATIVES **demarcator** noun.
– ORIGIN early 18th cent.: from Spanish *demarcación*, from *demarcar* 'mark the bounds of', ultimately of Germanic origin and related to **MARK**[1]. Originally used in the phrase *line of demarcation* (Spanish *linea de demarcación*, Portuguese *linha de demarcação*), the word denoted a line dividing the New World between the Spanish and Portuguese, laid down by the Pope in 1493.

demarcation dispute ▶ noun Brit. a dispute between trade unions about who does or should do a particular job.

démarche /deɪˈmɑːʃ/ ▶ noun a political step or initiative: *foreign policy démarches.*
– ORIGIN mid 17th cent.: French, from *démarcher* 'take steps'.

demark /diːˈmɑːk/ ▶ verb another term for **DEMARCATE**.
– ORIGIN mid 19th cent.: from **DEMARCATION**, on the pattern of the verb *mark.*

demassify /diːˈmasɪfʌɪ/ ▶ verb (**-ies**, **-ied**) [with obj.] divide or break up (a social or political unit) into its component parts.
– DERIVATIVES **demassification** noun.

dematerialize (also **-ise**) ▶ verb [no obj.] become free of physical substance, in particular:
■(in science fiction) disappear or cease to be physically present through some imagined technological process: *he watched the time machine dematerialize.* ■ become spiritual rather than physical: *the kiss dematerializes into a kind of spiritual rebirth.* ■ [with obj.] [usu. as adj. **dematerialized**] replace (physical records or certificates) with a paperless computerized system: *a dematerialized stock lending service.*
– DERIVATIVES **dematerialization** noun.

de Maupassant, Guy, see **MAUPASSANT**.

deme /diːm/ ▶ noun 1 a political division of Attica in ancient Greece.
■an administrative division in modern Greece.
2 Biology a subdivision of a population consisting of closely related plants, animals, or people, typically breeding mainly within the group.
– ORIGIN from Greek *dēmos* 'people'; sense 2 is an extended use dating from the 1930s.

demean[1] /dɪˈmiːn/ ▶ verb [with obj.] [often as adj. **demeaning**] cause a severe loss in the dignity of and respect for (someone or something): *the poster was not demeaning to women* | *I had demeaned the profession.*
■(**demean oneself**) do something that is beneath one's dignity.
– ORIGIN early 17th cent.: from **DE-** 'away, down' + the adjective **MEAN**[2], on the pattern of *debase.*

demean[2] /dɪˈmiːn/ ▶ verb (**demean oneself**) archaic conduct oneself in a particular way: *no man demeaned himself so honourably.*
– ORIGIN Middle English (also in the sense 'manage, control'): from Old French *demener* 'to lead', based on Latin *de-* 'away' + *minare* 'drive (animals), drive on with threats' (from *minari* 'threaten').

demeanour (US **demeanor**) ▶ noun [mass noun] outward behaviour or bearing: *his happy demeanour.*
– ORIGIN late 15th cent.: from **DEMEAN**[2], probably influenced by obsolete *havour* 'behaviour'.

de' Medici[1] see **MEDICI**.

de' Medici[2], Catherine, see **CATHERINE DE' MEDICI**.

de' Medici[3], Cosimo, see **COSIMO DE' MEDICI**.

de' Medici[4], Giovanni, the name of Pope Leo X (see **LEO**[1]).

de' Medici[5], Lorenzo, see **LORENZO DE' MEDICI**.

de Médicis, Marie, see **MARIE DE MÉDICIS**.

dement /dɪˈmɛnt/ ▶ noun archaic a person suffering from dementia.
– ORIGIN late 15th cent. (as an adjective in the sense 'demented'): from French *dément* or Latin *demens, dement-* 'insane'. The noun use dates from the late 19th cent.

demented ▶ adjective suffering from dementia.
■informal driven to behave irrationally due to anger, distress, or excitement: *the rap of a demented DJ.*
– DERIVATIVES **dementedly** adverb, **dementedness** noun.
– ORIGIN mid 17th cent.: past participle of earlier *dement* 'drive mad', from Old French *dementer* or late Latin *dementare*, from *demens* 'out of one's mind'.

démenti /deɪˈmɒti/ ▶ noun an official denial of a published statement.
– ORIGIN French, from *démentir* 'contradict or accuse of lying'.

dementia /dɪˈmɛnʃə/ ▶ noun [mass noun] Medicine a chronic or persistent disorder of the mental processes caused by brain disease or injury and marked by memory disorders, personality changes, and impaired reasoning.
– ORIGIN late 18th cent.: from Latin, from *demens, dement-* 'out of one's mind'.

dementia praecox /ˈpriːkɒks/ ▶ noun archaic term for **SCHIZOPHRENIA**.
– ORIGIN Latin, literally 'early insanity'.

Demerara /ˌdɛməˈrɛːrə, -ˈrɑːrə/ 1 a river of northern Guyana. Rising in the Guiana Highlands, it flows about 320 km (200 miles) northwards to the Atlantic.
2 a former Dutch colony in South America, now part of Guyana.

demerara /ˌdɛməˈrɛːrə, -ˈrɑːrə/ ▶ noun [mass noun] 1 (also **demerara sugar**) light brown cane sugar coming originally and chiefly from Guyana.
2 (also **demerara rum**) a dark rum fermented from molasses, made in Guyana.

– ORIGIN mid 19th cent.: named after the region of **DEMERARA**.

demerge ▶ verb [with obj.] Brit. separate (a business) from another, particularly to dissolve an earlier merger.

demerger ▶ noun Brit. the separation of a large company into two or more smaller organizations, particularly as the dissolution of an earlier merger.

demerit ▶ noun **1** a feature or fact deserving censure: *the merits and demerits of these proposals.* **2** N. Amer. a mark awarded against someone for a fault or offence.
– DERIVATIVES **demeritorious** /-ˈtɔːrɪəs/ adjective.
– ORIGIN late Middle English (also in the sense 'merit'): from Old French *desmerite* or Latin *demeritum* 'something deserved', neuter past participle of *demereri*, from *de-* 'thoroughly' (also understood in medieval Latin as denoting reversal) + *mereri* 'to merit'.

Demerol /ˈdɛmərɒl/ ▶ noun trademark for **PETHIDINE**.
– ORIGIN 1940s: of unknown origin.

demersal /dɪˈmɜːs(ə)l/ ▶ adjective (typically of fish) living close to the floor of the sea or a lake. Often contrasted with **PELAGIC**.
– ORIGIN late 19th cent.: from Latin *demersus* (past participle of *demergere* 'submerge, sink', from *de-* 'down' + *mergere* 'plunge') + *-AL*.

demesne /dɪˈmeɪn, dɪˈmiːn/ ▶ noun historical **1** land attached to a manor and retained by the owner for their own use.
■ the lands of an estate. ■ archaic a region or domain: *she may one day queen it over that fair demesne.*
2 [mass noun] Law possession of real property in one's own right.
– PHRASES **held in demesne** (of an estate) occupied by the owner, not by tenants.
– ORIGIN Middle English: from Old French *demeine* (later Anglo-Norman French *demesne*) 'belonging to a lord', from Latin *dominicus*, from *dominus* 'lord, master'. Compare with **DOMAIN**.

Demeter /dɪˈmiːtə/ Greek Mythology the corn goddess, daughter of Cronus and Rhea and mother of Persephone. She is associated with Cybele; her symbol is typically an ear of corn. The Eleusinian mysteries were held in honour of her. Roman equivalent **CERES**. See also **PERSEPHONE**.

demi- ▶ prefix **1** half; half-size: *demisemiquaver | demitasse.*
2 partially; in an inferior degree: *demigod | demi-monde.*
– ORIGIN via French from medieval Latin *dimedius* 'half', from earlier *dimidius*.

demi-caractère /ˌdɛmɪkarakˈtɛː/ ▶ noun (pl. same) [mass noun] a style of ballet having elements of character dance, but executed with steps based on the classical technique.
■ [count noun] a dancer specializing in this type of dance.
– ORIGIN French, literally 'half character'.

demi-glace /ˈdɛmɪɡlas/ (also **demi-glaze**) ▶ noun a rich, glossy, brown sauce from which the liquid has been partly evaporated, typically flavoured with wine and served with meat.
– ORIGIN French, literally 'half glaze'.

demigod ▶ noun a being with partial or lesser divine status, such as a minor deity, the offspring of a god and a mortal, or a mortal raised to divine rank.
■ figurative a person who is greatly admired or feared.
– ORIGIN mid 16th cent.: translating Latin *semideus*.

demigoddess ▶ noun a female demigod.

demijohn ▶ noun a bulbous narrow-necked bottle holding from 3 to 10 gallons of liquid, typically enclosed in a wicker cover.
– ORIGIN mid 18th cent.: probably an alteration of French *dame-jeanne* 'Lady Jane', by association with **DEMI-** 'half-sized' and the given name *John*.

demilitarize (also **-ise**) ▶ verb [with obj.] [usu. as adj. **demilitarized**] remove all military forces from (an area): *a demilitarized zone.*
– DERIVATIVES **demilitarization** noun.

de Mille /də ˈmɪl/, Cecil B. (1881–1959), American film producer and director, famous for his spectacular epics; full name *Cecil Blount de Mille.* Notable films: *The Ten Commandments* (1923; remade 1956) and *Samson and Delilah* (1949).

demilune /ˈdɛmɪluːn/ ▶ noun a crescent or half-circle, or a thing of this shape.

■ (in a fortified building) an outwork resembling a bastion, with a crescent-shaped gorge.
– ORIGIN early 18th cent.: from French *demi-lune*, literally 'half-moon'.

demi-mondaine /ˈdɛmɪmɒn‚deɪn, French dəmimɔ̃dɛn/ ▶ noun a woman considered to belong to the demi-monde.
– ORIGIN French.

demi-monde /ˌdɛmɪˈmɒnd, French dəmimɔ̃d/ ▶ noun (in 19th-century France) the class of women considered to be of doubtful social standing and morality.
■ a group of people considered to be on the fringes of respectable society: *the demi-monde of arms deals.*
– ORIGIN French, literally 'half-world'.

demineralize (also **-ise**) ▶ verb [with obj.] [often as adj. **demineralized**] remove salts from (water).
■ deprive (teeth or bones) of minerals, causing loss of tooth enamel or softening of the skeleton.
– DERIVATIVES **demineralization** noun.

demi-pension /ˌdɛmɪˈpɒ̃sjɔ̃/ ▶ noun [mass noun] hotel accommodation with bed, breakfast, and one main meal per day.
– ORIGIN French, literally 'half board'.

demirep /ˈdɛmɪrɛp/ ▶ noun archaic a woman whose chastity is considered doubtful.
– ORIGIN mid 18th cent.: abbreviation of *demi-reputable.*

demise /dɪˈmʌɪz/ ▶ noun [in sing.] **1** a person's death: *Mr Grisenthwaite's tragic demise.*
■ the end or failure of an enterprise or institution: *the demise of industry.*
2 [mass noun] Law conveyance or transfer of property or a title by demising.
▶ verb [with obj.] Law convey or grant (an estate) by will or lease.
■ transmit (a sovereign's title) by death or abdication.
– ORIGIN late Middle English (as a legal term): from Anglo-Norman French, past participle (used as a noun) of Old French *desmettre* 'dismiss', (in reflexive) 'abdicate', based on Latin *dimittere* (see **DISMISS**).

demi-sec /dɛmɪˈsɛk, French dəmisɛk/ ▶ adjective (of wine) medium dry.
– ORIGIN French, literally 'half-dry'.

demisemiquaver /ˌdɛmɪˈsɛmɪˌkweɪvə/ ▶ noun Music, chiefly Brit. a note having the time value of half a semiquaver, represented by a large dot with a three-hooked stem. Also called **THIRTY-SECOND NOTE**.

demist /diːˈmɪst/ ▶ verb [with obj.]. Brit. clear condensation from (a vehicle's windscreen).

demister ▶ noun a device on a vehicle which removes condensation from the windscreen by directing a jet of air on to it.

demit /dɪˈmɪt/ ▶ verb (**demitted**, **demitting**) [with obj.] archaic resign from (an office or position): *arguments within his congregation led to his demitting his post.*
– DERIVATIVES **demission** noun.
– ORIGIN early 16th cent. (in the sense 'dismiss'): from French *démettre*, from *dé-* 'away from' + *mettre* 'put'.

demitasse /ˈdɛmɪtas/ ▶ noun a small coffee cup.
– ORIGIN mid 19th cent.: from French, literally 'half-cup'.

demiurge /ˈdiːmɪədʒ, ˈdɛm-/ ▶ noun a being responsible for the creation of the universe, in particular:
■ (in Platonic philosophy) the Maker or Creator of the world. ■ (in Gnosticism and other theological systems) a heavenly being, subordinate to the Supreme Being, that is considered to be the controller of the material world and antagonistic to all that is purely spiritual.
– DERIVATIVES **demiurgic** /-ˈɔːdʒɪk/ adjective, **demiurgical** adjective.
– ORIGIN early 17th cent. (denoting a magistrate in certain ancient Greek states): via ecclesiastical Latin from Greek *dēmiourgos* 'craftsman', from *dēmios* 'public' (from *dēmos* 'people') + *-ergos* 'working'.

demo informal ▶ noun (pl. **-os**) **1** short for **DEMONSTRATION**: *a peace demo.*
2 a demonstration of the capabilities of something, typically computer software or a musical group: [as modifier] *a demo tape.*
▶ verb (**-os**, **-oed**) [with obj.] demonstrate the capabilities of (software or equipment).

■ record (a song) for demonstration purposes: *they've already demoed twelve new songs.*

demob /diːˈmɒb/ Brit. informal ▶ verb (**demobbed**, **demobbing**) [with obj.] (usu. **be demobbed**) demobilize.
▶ noun [mass noun] demobilization: *we were waiting for our demob.*
– ORIGIN 1920s (following the First World War): abbreviation.

demobilize /diːˈməʊbɪlʌɪz/ (also **-ise**) ▶ verb [with obj.] (usu. **be demobilized**) take (troops) out of active service, typically at the end of a war: *he was demobilized in February 1946.*
■ [no obj.] cease military operations: *Germany demanded that they demobilize within twelve hours.*
– DERIVATIVES **demobilization** noun.
– ORIGIN late 19th cent.: from French *démobiliser*, from *dé-* (expressing reversal) + *mobiliser* 'mobilize'.

democracy /dɪˈmɒkrəsi/ ▶ noun (pl. **-ies**) [mass noun] a system of government by the whole population or all the eligible members of a state, typically through elected representatives: *a capitalist system of parliamentary democracy.*
■ [count noun] a state governed in such a way: *a multiparty democracy.* ■ control of an organization or group by the majority of its members: *the intended extension of industrial democracy.* ■ the practice or principles of social equality: *demands for greater democracy.*
– ORIGIN late 16th cent.: from French *démocratie*, via late Latin from Greek *dēmokratia*, from *dēmos* 'the people' + *-kratia* 'power, rule'.

democrat ▶ noun **1** an advocate or supporter of democracy.
2 (**Democrat**) (in the US) a member of the Democratic Party.
– ORIGIN late 18th cent. (originally denoting an opponent of the aristocrats in the French Revolution of 1790): from French *démocrate*, on the pattern of *aristocrate* 'aristocrat'.

democratic ▶ adjective **1** of, relating to, or supporting democracy or its principles: *democratic reforms | democratic government.*
■ favouring or characterized by social equality; egalitarian: *cycling is a very democratic activity which can be enjoyed by anyone.*
2 (**Democratic**) (in the US) of or relating to the Democratic Party.
– DERIVATIVES **democratically** adverb.
– ORIGIN early 17th cent.: from French *démocratique*, via medieval Latin from Greek *dēmokratikos*, from *dēmokratia* (see **DEMOCRACY**).

democratic centralism ▶ noun [mass noun] the Leninist organizational system in which policy is decided centrally and is binding on all members.

Democratic Party one of the two main US political parties (the other being the Republican Party), which follows a broadly liberal programme, tending to support social reform and minority rights.

Democratic Republican Party a US political party founded in 1792 by Thomas Jefferson, a forerunner of the modern Democratic Party.

democratize /dɪˈmɒkrətʌɪz/ (also **-ise**) ▶ verb [with obj.] (often **be democratized**) introduce a democratic system or democratic principles to: *public institutions need to be democratized.*
■ make (something) accessible to everyone: *mass production has not democratized fashion.*
– DERIVATIVES **democratization** noun.
– ORIGIN late 18th cent.: from French *démocratiser.*

Democritus /dɪˈmɒkrɪtəs/ (c.460–c.370 BC), Greek philosopher. He developed the atomic theory originated by his teacher, Leucippus, which explained natural phenomena in terms of the arrangement and rearrangement of atoms moving in a void.

démodé /deɪˈməʊdeɪ/ ▶ adjective out of fashion.
– ORIGIN French, past participle of *démoder* 'go out of fashion'.

demodectic mange /ˌdiːmə(ʊ)ˈdɛktɪk/ ▶ noun [mass noun] a form of mange caused by follicle mites and tending to affect chiefly the head and foreparts. Compare with **SARCOPTIC MANGE**.
– ORIGIN late 19th cent.: *demodectic* from modern Latin *Demodex* (from Greek *dēmos* 'fat' + *dēx* 'woodworm') + *-IC*.

demodulate ▶ verb [with obj.] Electronics extract (a modulating signal) from its carrier.
■ separate a modulating signal from (its carrier).

– DERIVATIVES **demodulation** noun, **demodulator** noun.

demographic /ˌdɛməˈɡrafɪk/ ▶ adjective relating to the structure of populations: *the demographic trend is towards an older population.*
– DERIVATIVES **demographical** adjective, **demographically** adverb.

demographics ▶ plural noun statistical data relating to the population and particular groups within it: *the demographics of book buyers.*

demography /dɪˈmɒɡrəfi/ ▶ noun [mass noun] the study of statistics such as births, deaths, income, or the incidence of disease, which illustrate the changing structure of human populations.
■ the composition of a particular human population: *Europe's demography is changing.*
– DERIVATIVES **demographer** noun.
– ORIGIN late 19th cent.: from Greek *dēmos* 'the people' + -GRAPHY.

Demoi plural form of **DEMOS**.

demoiselle /ˌdɛmwɑːˈzɛl/ ▶ noun **1** (also **demoiselle crane**) a small and graceful Old World crane with a black head and breast and white ear tufts, breeding in SE Europe and central Asia.
● *Anthropoides virgo*, family Gruidae.
2 a damselfly, especially an agrion.
3 a damselfish.
4 archaic or poetic/literary a young woman.
– ORIGIN early 16th cent. (in sense 4): from French, from Old French *dameisele* 'damsel'.

de Moivre's theorem /də ˈmwɑːvr(ə)/ Mathematics a theorem which states that $(\cos \theta + i \sin \theta)^n = \cos n\theta + i \sin n\theta$, where i is the square root of -1.
– ORIGIN early 18th cent.: named after Abraham *de Moivre* (1667–1754) French-born mathematician, fellow of the Royal Society.

demolish /dɪˈmɒlɪʃ/ ▶ verb [with obj.] pull or knock down (a building).
■ comprehensively refute (an argument or its proponent): *I looked forward keenly to demolishing my opponent.* ■ informal overwhelmingly defeat (a player or team): *Arsenal demolished Coventry City 3–0.* ■ humorous eat up (food) quickly: *Brown was busy demolishing a sausage roll.*
– DERIVATIVES **demolisher** noun.
– ORIGIN mid 16th cent.: from French *démoliss-*, lengthened stem of *démolir*, from Latin *demoliri*, from *de-* (expressing reversal) + *moliri* 'construct' (from *moles* 'mass').

demolition ▶ noun [mass noun] the action or process of demolishing or being demolished: *the monument was saved from demolition.*
■ informal an overwhelming defeat.
– ORIGIN mid 16th cent.: via French from Latin *demolitio(n-)*, from the verb *demoliri* (see **DEMOLISH**).

demolition derby ▶ noun chiefly N. Amer. a competition in which cars are driven into each other until only one car is left running.

demon[1] ▶ noun **1** an evil spirit or devil, especially one thought to possess a person or act as a tormentor in hell.
■ a cruel, evil, or destructive person or thing: *I was a little demon, I can tell you.* ■ (often as modifier) a forceful, fierce, or skilful performer of a specified activity: *a friend of mine is a demon cook* | *a demon for work.* ■ [mass noun] reckless mischief; devilry: *his eyes are bursting with pure demon.*
2 another term for **DAEMON**[1] (in sense 1).
– PHRASES **like a demon** in a very forceful, fierce, or skilful way: *he worked like a demon.*
– ORIGIN Middle English: from medieval Latin, from Latin *daemon*, from Greek *daimōn* 'deity, genius'; in sense 1 also from Latin *daemonium* 'lesser or evil spirit', from Greek *daemonion*, diminutive of *daimōn*.

demon[2] ▶ noun Austral./NZ informal a police officer.
– ORIGIN late 19th cent.: apparently from Van Diemen's Land, an early name for Tasmania.

demon[3] ▶ noun variant spelling of **DAEMON**[2].

demonetize /diːˈmʌnɪtʌɪz, -mɒn-/ (also -ise) ▶ verb [with obj.] (usu. **be demonetized**) deprive (a coin or precious metal) of its status as money.
– DERIVATIVES **demonetization** noun.
– ORIGIN mid 19th cent.: from French *démonétiser*, from *dé-* (expressing reversal) + Latin *moneta* 'money'.

demoniac /dɪˈməʊnɪak/ ▶ adjective of, like, or characteristic of a demon or demons: *a goddess with both divine and demoniac qualities* | *demoniac rage.*

▶ noun a person supposedly possessed by an evil spirit.
– DERIVATIVES **demoniacal** adjective, **demoniacally** adverb.
– ORIGIN late Middle English: from Old French *demoniaque*, from ecclesiastical Latin *daemoniacus*, from *daemonium* 'lesser or evil spirit' (see **DEMON**[1]).

demonic /dɪˈmɒnɪk/ ▶ adjective of, resembling, or characteristic of demons or evil spirits: *demonic possession* | *her laughter was demonic.*
■ fiercely energetic or frenzied: *a demonic hurry.*
– DERIVATIVES **demonically** adverb.
– ORIGIN mid 17th cent.: via late Latin from Greek *daimonikos*, from *daimōn* (see **DEMON**[1]).

demonism /ˈdiːmənɪz(ə)m/ ▶ noun [mass noun] **1** belief in the power of demons.
2 action or behaviour that seems too cruel or wicked to be human: *the demonism of warfare.*

demonize (also -ise) ▶ verb [with obj.] portray as wicked and threatening: *seeking to demonize one side in the conflict.*
– DERIVATIVES **demonization** noun.

demono- /ˈdiːmənəʊ/ ▶ combining form of or relating to demons: *demonolatry.*
– ORIGIN from Greek *daimon* 'demon'.

demonolatry /ˌdiːməˈnɒlətri/ ▶ noun [mass noun] the worship of demons.

demonology ▶ noun [mass noun] the study of demons or demonic belief.
– DERIVATIVES **demonological** adjective, **demonologist** noun.

demonopolize (also -ise) ▶ verb [with obj.] introduce competition into (a market or economy) by privatizing previously nationalized assets.
– DERIVATIVES **demonopolization** noun.

demonstrable /dɪˈmɒnstrəb(ə)l, ˈdɛmən-/ ▶ adjective clearly apparent or capable of being logically proved: *the demonstrable injustices of racism.*
– DERIVATIVES **demonstrability** noun.
– ORIGIN late Middle English: from Latin *demonstrabilis*, from *demonstrare* 'point out'.

demonstrably /ˈdɛmənstrəbli/ ▶ adverb clearly and undeniably: *the situation is demonstrably unfair.*

demonstrate ▶ verb **1** [with obj.] clearly show the existence or truth of (something) by giving proof or evidence: *their shameful silence demonstrates their ineptitude.*
■ give a practical exhibition and explanation of (how a machine, skill, or craft works or is performed): *computerized design methods will be demonstrated* | [with clause] *she demonstrated how to cook chops.* ■ show or express (a feeling or quality) by one's actions: *she began to demonstrate a new-found confidence.*
2 [no obj.] take part in a public demonstration: *thousands demonstrated in favour of the government.*
– ORIGIN mid 16th cent. (in the sense 'point out'): from Latin *demonstrat-* 'pointed out', from the verb *demonstrare.*

demonstration ▶ noun **1** [mass noun] the showing of something's existence or truth by giving proof or evidence: *it is not capable of mathematical demonstration* | [count noun] *his demonstration that feature films could be both art and social treatise.*
■ the outward showing of feeling: [count noun] *physical demonstrations of affection.* ■ [count noun] a practical exhibition and explanation of how something works or is performed: *a microwave cookery demonstration.*
2 a public meeting or march protesting against something or expressing views on a political issue.
– ORIGIN late Middle English (also in the senses 'proof provided by logic' and 'sign, indication'): from Latin *demonstratio(n-)*, from *demonstrare* 'point out' (see **DEMONSTRATE**). Sense 2 dates from the mid 19th cent.

demonstrative /dɪˈmɒnstrətɪv/ ▶ adjective **1** (of a person) tending to show feelings, especially of affection, openly.
2 serving as conclusive evidence of something; giving proof: *demonstrative evidence.*
■ involving demonstration, especially by scientific means: *the possibility of a demonstrative science of ethics.*
3 Grammar (of a determiner or pronoun) indicating the person or thing referred to (e.g. *this, that, those*).
▶ noun Grammar a demonstrative determiner or pronoun.
– DERIVATIVES **demonstratively** adverb, **demonstrativeness** noun.
– ORIGIN late Middle English (in the senses 'serving as conclusive evidence of' and 'making manifest'): from Old French *demonstratif*, *-ive*, from Latin

demonstrativus, from *demonstrare* 'point out' (see **DEMONSTRATE**).

demonstrative legacy ▶ noun Law a legacy which is directed to be paid from a specified fund or pool.

demonstrator ▶ noun **1** a person who takes part in a public protest meeting or march.
2 a person who shows how a particular piece of equipment works or how a skill or craft is performed.
■ a person who teaches in this way, especially in a laboratory. ■ a piece of merchandise which can be tested by potential buyers.

de Montespan, Marquise de, see **MONTESPAN**.

de Montfort, Simon, see **MONTFORT**[1].

demoralize (also -ise) ▶ verb [with obj.] **1** (usu. as adj. **demoralized**) cause (someone) to lose confidence or hope; dispirit: *the changes leave managers angry and demoralized.*
2 archaic corrupt the morals of (someone).
– DERIVATIVES **demoralization** noun, **demoralizing** adjective, **demoralizingly** adverb.
– ORIGIN late 18th cent.: from French *démoraliser* (a word of the French Revolution), from *dé-* (expressing reversal) + *moral* 'moral', from Latin *moralis.*

de Morgan's laws Mathematics two laws in Boolean algebra and set theory which state that AND and OR, or union and intersection, are dual. They are used to simplify the design of electronic circuits.
● The laws can be expressed in Boolean logic as: NOT (*a* AND *b*) = NOT *a* OR NOT *b*; NOT (*a* OR *b*) = NOT *a* AND NOT *b*.
– ORIGIN early 20th cent.: named after Augustus *de Morgan* (1806–71), English mathematician, but already known (by logicians) as principles in the Middle Ages.

Demos /ˈdiːmɒs/ ▶ noun (pl. **Demoi** /ˈdiː-mɔɪ/) the common people of an ancient Greek state.
■ the populace as a political unit, especially in a democracy.
– ORIGIN from Greek *dēmos.*

Demosthenes /dɪˈmɒsθəniːz/ (384–322 BC), Athenian orator and statesman. He is best known for his political speeches on the need to resist the aggressive tendencies of Philip II of Macedon (the *Philippics*).

demote ▶ verb [with obj.] (often **be demoted**) give (someone) a lower rank or less senior position, usually as a punishment: *the head of the army was demoted to deputy defence secretary.*
– ORIGIN late 19th cent.: from DE- 'down' + a shortened form of **PROMOTE**.

demotic /dɪˈmɒtɪk/ ▶ adjective denoting or relating to the kind of language used by ordinary people; popular or colloquial: *a demotic idiom.*
■ relating to or denoting the form of modern Greek used in everyday speech and writing. Compare with **KATHAREVOUSA**. ■ relating to or denoting a simplified, cursive form of ancient Egyptian script, dating from *c.*650 BC and replaced by Greek in the Ptolemaic period. Compare with **HIERATIC**.
▶ noun [mass noun] ordinary colloquial speech.
■ demotic Greek. ■ demotic Egyptian script.
– ORIGIN early 19th cent. (in the sense 'relating to the Egyptian demotic'): from Greek *dēmotikos* 'popular', from *dēmotēs* 'one of the people', from *dēmos* 'the people'.

demotion ▶ noun [mass noun] reduction in rank or status: *she could remain on the staff if she accepted demotion to ordinary lecturer* | [count noun] *too many demotions would weaken morale.*
– ORIGIN early 20th cent.: from DEMOTE, on the pattern of *promotion.*

demotivate ▶ verb [with obj.] make (someone) less eager to work or study: *some children disrupt classes and demotivate pupils.*
– DERIVATIVES **demotivation** noun.

demountable ▶ adjective able to be dismantled or removed from its setting and readily reassembled or repositioned.
– DERIVATIVES **demount** verb.

Dempsey /ˈdɛmpsi/, Jack (1895–1983), American boxer; full name *William Harrison Dempsey*. He was world heavyweight champion 1919–26.

demulcent /dɪˈmʌls(ə)nt/ Medicine ▶ adjective (of a substance) relieving inflammation or irritation.
▶ noun a substance that relieves irritation of the mucous membranes in the mouth by forming a protective film.

– ORIGIN mid 18th cent.: from Latin *demulcent-* 'stroking caressingly', from the verb *demulcere*, from *de-* 'away' + *mulcere* 'soothe'.

demur /dɪˈmə:/ ▶ **verb** (**demurred**, **demurring**) [no obj.] raise doubts or objections or show reluctance: *normally she would have accepted the challenge, but she demurred.*
■ Law, dated put forward a demurrer.
▶ **noun** [mass noun] [usu. with negative] the action or process of objecting to or hesitating over something: *they accepted this ruling **without demur**.*
– ORIGIN Middle English (in the sense 'linger, delay'): from Old French *demourer* (verb), *demeure* (noun), based on Latin *de-* 'away, completely' + *morari* 'delay'.

demure /dɪˈmjʊə/ ▶ **adjective** (**demurer**, **demurest**) (of a woman or her behaviour) reserved, modest, and shy: *a demure little wife who sits at home minding the house.*
■ (of clothing) lending such an appearance.
– DERIVATIVES **demurely** adverb, **demureness** noun.
– ORIGIN late Middle English (in the sense 'sober, serious, reserved'): perhaps from Old French *demoure*, past participle of *demourer* 'remain, stay' (see **DEMUR**); influenced by Old French *mur* 'grave', from Latin *maturus* 'ripe or mature'. The sense 'reserved, shy' dates from the late 17th cent.

demurrable /dɪˈmə:rəb(ə)l/ ▶ **adjective** dated, chiefly Law open to demurrer.

demurrage /dɪˈmʌrɪdʒ/ ▶ **noun** [mass noun] Law a charge payable to the owner of a chartered ship in respect of failure to load or discharge the ship within the time agreed.
– ORIGIN mid 17th cent. (also in the general sense 'procrastination, delay'): from Old French *demourage*, from the verb *demourer* (see **DEMUR**).

demurral /dɪˈmə:r(ə)l/ ▶ **noun** [mass noun] the action of demurring: *words of demurral.*

demurrer /dɪˈmə:rə/ ▶ **noun** an objection.
■ Law, dated an objection that an opponent's point is irrelevant or invalid, while granting the factual basis of the point: ***on demurrer*** *it was held that the plaintiff's claim succeeded.*
– ORIGIN early 16th cent.: from Anglo-Norman French (infinitive used as a noun), from Old French *demourer* 'remain, stay' (see **DEMUR**).

demutualize /di:ˈmju:tʃʊəlʌɪz, -tjʊə-/ (also **-ise**) ▶ **verb** [with obj.] change (a mutual organization such as a building society) to one of a different kind.
– DERIVATIVES **demutualization** noun.

demy /dɪˈmʌɪ/ (in full **metric demy**) ▶ **noun** [mass noun] a paper size, 564 × 444 mm.
■ (in full **demy octavo**) a book size, 216 × 138 mm. ■ (in full **demy quarto**) a book size, 276 × 219 mm.
– ORIGIN late Middle English (as an adjective in the sense 'half-sized'): from **DEMI-**, or from its source, French *demi* 'half'.

demyelinate /di:ˈmʌɪəlɪneɪt/ ▶ **verb** [with obj.] [usu. as adj. **demyelinating**] Medicine cause the loss or destruction of myelin in (nerve tissue): *a chronic demyelinating disease.*
– DERIVATIVES **demyelination** noun.

demystify ▶ **verb** (**-ies**, **-ied**) [with obj.] make (a difficult or esoteric subject) clearer and easier to understand: *this book attempts to demystify technology.*
– DERIVATIVES **demystification** noun.

demythologize (also **-ise**) ▶ **verb** [with obj.] reinterpret (a subject or text) so that it is free of mythical elements.
■ reinterpret what are considered to be mythological elements of (the Bible).

den ▶ **noun** a wild mammal's lair or habitation.
■ informal a room or hideout where a person can pursue an activity in private. ■ a place where people meet in secret, typically to engage in some illicit activity: *an opium den | a den of iniquity.* ■ chiefly US a small subdivision of a Cub Scout pack.
▶ **verb** (**denned**, **denning**) [no obj.] (of a wild animal) live in or retreat to a den: *the cubs denned in the late autumn.*
– ORIGIN Old English *denn*, of Germanic origin; related to German *Tenne* 'threshing floor', also to **DENE**[1].

Denali /dɪˈnɑ:li/ another name for Mount McKinley (see **MCKINLEY, MOUNT**).

denar /ˈdi:nə/ ▶ **noun** the basic monetary unit of the former Yugoslav Republic of Macedonia.
– ORIGIN based on Latin *denarius*; compare with **DINAR**.

denarius /dɪˈnɛ:rɪəs, dɪˈnɑ:rɪəs/ ▶ **noun** (pl. **denarii** /-rɪʌɪ, -rɪi:/) an ancient Roman silver coin, originally worth ten asses.
■ a unit of weight equal to that of a silver denarius. ■ an ancient Roman gold coin worth 25 silver denarii.
– ORIGIN Latin, literally 'containing ten', from the phrase *denarius nummus* 'coin worth ten asses' (see **AS**[2]), from *deni* 'in tens', from *decem* 'ten'.

denary /ˈdi:n(ə)ri/ ▶ **adjective** relating to or based on the number ten; less common term for **DECIMAL**: *denary numbers.*
– ORIGIN mid 19th cent.: from Latin *denarius* 'containing ten' (see **DENARIUS**).

denationalize (also **-ise**) ▶ **verb** [with obj.] **1** transfer (a nationalized industry or institution) from public to private ownership.
2 deprive (a country or person) of nationality or national characteristics.
– DERIVATIVES **denationalization** noun.
– ORIGIN early 19th cent. (in sense 2): from French *dénationaliser* (a word of the French Revolution), from *dé-* (expressing reversal) + *nationaliser* 'nationalize'.

denaturalize (also **-ise**) ▶ **verb** [with obj.] **1** make (something) unnatural.
2 deprive (someone) of citizenship of a country.
– DERIVATIVES **denaturalization** noun.

denaturant /di:ˈneɪtʃər(ə)nt/ ▶ **noun** a substance which causes denaturation of proteins or other biological compounds.
■ a toxic or foul-smelling substance added to alcohol to make it unfit for drinking.

denature /di:ˈneɪtʃə/ ▶ **verb** [with obj.] [often as adj. **denatured**] take away or alter the natural qualities of: *many forms of packaged and denatured culture.*
■ make (alcohol) unfit for drinking by the addition of toxic or foul-tasting substances. ■ Biochemistry destroy the characteristic properties of (a protein or other biological macromolecule) by heat, acidity, or other effect which disrupts its molecular conformation. ■ [no obj.] (of a substance) undergo this process.
– DERIVATIVES **denaturation** noun.
– ORIGIN late 17th cent. (in the sense 'make unnatural'): from French *dénaturer*, from *dé-* (expressing reversal) + *nature* 'nature'.

Denbighshire /ˈdɛnbɪʃɪə, -ʃə/ a county of North Wales; administrative centre, Ruthin. It was divided between Clwyd and Gwynedd between 1974 and 1996.

Dench /dɛntʃ/, Dame Judi (b.1934), English actress; full name *Judith Olivia Dench*. She has performed with the Old Vic Company (1957–61) and the Royal Shakespeare Company, also appearing in numerous West End, film, and television productions.

dendrite /ˈdɛndrʌɪt/ ▶ **noun** **1** Physiology a short branched extension of a nerve cell, along which impulses received from other cells at synapses are transmitted to the cell body. Compare with **AXON**.
2 a crystal or crystalline mass with a branching, tree-like structure.
■ a natural tree-like or moss-like marking on a piece of rock or mineral.
– ORIGIN early 18th cent.: from French, from Greek *dendritēs* 'tree-like', from *dendron* 'tree'.

dendritic /dɛnˈdrɪtɪk/ ▶ **adjective** technical having a branched form resembling a tree.
■ Physiology of or relating to a dendrite or dendrites. ■ (of a solid) consisting of crystalline dendrites: *dendritic salt.*
– DERIVATIVES **dendritically** adverb.

dendro- /ˈdɛndrəʊ/ ▶ **combining form** of or relating to a tree or trees: *dendrology.*
– ORIGIN from Greek *dendron* 'tree'.

dendrochronology ▶ **noun** [mass noun] the science or technique of dating events, environmental change, and archaeological artefacts by using the characteristic patterns of annual growth rings in timber and tree trunks.
– DERIVATIVES **dendrochronological** adjective, **dendrochronologist** noun.

dendrogram /ˈdɛndrə(ʊ)gram/ ▶ **noun** a tree diagram, especially one showing taxonomic relationships.

dendroid /ˈdɛndrɔɪd/ ▶ **adjective** Biology (of a plant, marine invertebrate, or structure) tree-shaped; arborescent; branching.
■ Palaeontology denoting graptolites of a type that formed much-branched colonies, found chiefly in the Ordovician and Silurian periods.
▶ **noun** Palaeontology a graptolite of this type.
• Order Dendroidea, class Graptolithina.
– ORIGIN mid 19th cent.: from **DENDRO-** 'tree' + **-OID**.

dendrology /dɛnˈdrɒlədʒi/ ▶ **noun** [mass noun] the scientific study of trees.
– DERIVATIVES **dendrological** adjective, **dendrologist** noun.

dendron /ˈdɛndrɒn/ ▶ **noun** another term for **DENDRITE** (in sense 1).
– ORIGIN late 19th cent.: from **DENDRITE**, on the pattern of words such as *axon*.

Dene /ˈdɛneɪ, ˈdɛni/ ▶ **noun** (pl. same) **1** a member of a group of American Indian peoples of the Canadian North-West and Alaska, traditionally speaking Athabaskan languages and having collective representation in Canadian political life.
2 [mass noun] any of the languages of these peoples.
▶ **adjective** of or relating to these peoples or their languages.
– ORIGIN from French *Déné*, from an Athabaskan word meaning 'people'.

dene[1] /di:n/ (also **dean**) ▶ **noun** Brit. [usu. in place names] a vale, especially the deep, narrow, wooded valley of a small river: *Rottingdean | Deepdene.*
– ORIGIN Old English *denu*, of Germanic origin; related to **DEN**.

dene[2] /di:n/ ▶ **noun** dialect a bare sandy tract or low sandhill by the sea.
– ORIGIN Middle English: perhaps of Germanic origin and related to **DUNE**.

Deneb /ˈdɛnɛb/ Astronomy the brightest star in the constellation Cygnus, a yellow supergiant.
– ORIGIN from Arabic, literally 'tail' (i.e. of the 'swan').

Denebola /dɪˈnɛbələ/ Astronomy the second brightest star in the constellation Leo.
– ORIGIN from Arabic *dhanab al(-asad)* '(lion's) tail'.

denervate /di:ˈnə:veɪt/ ▶ **verb** [with obj.] Medicine remove or cut off the nerve supply from (an organ or other body part): [as adj. **denervated**] *the denervated muscle fibres.*
– DERIVATIVES **denervation** noun.

Deneuve /dəˈnə:v, French dənœv/, Catherine (b.1943), French actress; born *Catherine Dorléac*. Notable films: *Repulsion* (1965) and *Belle de jour* (1967).

dengue /ˈdɛŋgi/ (also **dengue fever**) ▶ **noun** [mass noun] a debilitating viral disease of the tropics, transmitted by mosquitoes, and causing sudden fever and acute pains in the joints.
– ORIGIN early 19th cent.: from West Indian Spanish, from Kiswahili *dinga* (in full *kidingapopo*), influenced by Spanish *dengue* 'fastidiousness' (with reference to the dislike of movement by affected patients).

Deng Xiaoping /ˌdɛŋ ʃaʊˈpɪŋ, ˌdʌŋ/ (also **Teng Hsiao-p'ing**) (1904–97), Chinese communist statesman, Vice-Premier 1973–6 and 1977–80; Vice-Chairman of the Central Committee of the Chinese Communist Party 1977–80. Discredited during the Cultural Revolution, he was reinstated in 1977, becoming the effective leader of China. He worked to modernize the economy and improve relations with the West, although in 1989 his orders led to the massacre of some 2,000 pro-democracy demonstrators in Beijing's Tiananmen Square.

Den Haag /Dutch dɛn ˈha:x/ Dutch name for The Hague (see **HAGUE**).

deniable ▶ **adjective** able to be denied: *the government did agree to play a limited and deniable role in the rebellion.*
– DERIVATIVES **deniability** noun, **deniably** adverb.

denial ▶ **noun** [mass noun] the action of declaring something to be untrue: *she shook her head **in denial**.*
■ the refusal of something requested or desired: *the denial of insurance to people with certain medical conditions.* ■ [count noun] a statement that something is not true: *official denials | his **denial that** he was having an affair.* ■ Psychology refusal to acknowledge an unacceptable truth or emotion or to admit it into consciousness, used as a defence mechanism. ■ short for **SELF-DENIAL**. ■ disavowal of a person as one's leader.

denier[1] /ˈdɛnɪə/ ▶ **noun** **1** a unit of weight by which the fineness of silk, rayon, or nylon yarn is measured, equal to the weight in grams of 9,000

metres of the yarn and often used to describe the thickness of hosiery: *15-denier stockings.*
2 historical a French coin, equal to one twelfth of a sou, which was withdrawn from use in the 19th century.
– ORIGIN late Middle English: via Old French from Latin *denarius* (see **DENARIUS**). Sense 1 dates from the mid 19th cent.

denier² /dɪˈnʌɪə/ ▶ **noun** a person who denies something: *a denier of God.*

denigrate /ˈdɛnɪɡreɪt/ ▶ **verb** [with obj.] criticize unfairly; disparage: *doom and gloom merchants who denigrate their own country.*
– DERIVATIVES **denigration** noun, **denigrator** noun, **denigratory** /-ˈɡreɪt(ə)ri/ adjective.
– ORIGIN late Middle English (in the sense 'blacken, make dark'): from Latin *denigrat-* 'blackened', from the verb *denigrare*, from *de-* 'away, completely' + *nigrare* (from *niger* 'black').

denim ▶ **noun** [mass noun] a hard-wearing cotton twill fabric, typically blue, used for jeans, overalls, and other clothing.
■ (**denims**) clothing made of such fabric: *a pair of denims.*
– ORIGIN late 17th cent. (as *serge denim*): from French *serge de Nimes*, denoting a kind of serge from the manufacturing town of **NÎMES**.

De Niro /də ˈnɪərəʊ/, Robert (b.1943), American actor. He has starred in many films, often playing tough characters and frequently working with director Martin Scorsese. He has won Oscars for *The Godfather Part II* (1974) and *Raging Bull* (1980).

Denis /dəˈniː, French dəni/, Maurice (1870–1943), French painter, designer, and art theorist. A member of the Nabi Group, he wrote many works on art, including *Théories* (1913) and *Nouvelles Théories* (1921).

Denis, St /ˈdɛnɪs, French dəni/ (also **Denys**) (died *c.*250), Italian-born French bishop, patron saint of France; Roman name *Dionysius*. According to tradition he was one of a group of seven missionaries sent from Rome to convert Gaul; he became bishop of Paris and was martyred in the reign of the emperor Valerian. Feast day, 9 October.

denitrify /diːˈnʌɪtrɪfʌɪ/ ▶ **verb** (**-ies**, **-ied**) [with obj.] (chiefly of bacteria) remove the nitrates or nitrites from (soil, air, or water) by chemical reduction.
– DERIVATIVES **denitrification** noun.

denizen /ˈdɛnɪz(ə)n/ ▶ **noun** formal or humorous an inhabitant or occupant of a particular place: *denizens of field and forest.*
■ Brit. historical a foreigner allowed certain rights in their adopted country.
– DERIVATIVES **denizenship** noun.
– ORIGIN late Middle English *deynseyn*, via Anglo-Norman French from Old French *deinz* 'within' (from Latin *de* 'from' + *intus* 'within') + *-ein* (from Latin *-aneus* '-aneous'). The change in the form of the word was due to association with **CITIZEN**.

Denmark a Scandinavian country consisting of the greater part of the Jutland peninsula and several neighbouring islands, between the North Sea and the Baltic; pop. 5,100,000 (est. 1991); official language, Danish; capital, Copenhagen. Danish name **DANMARK**.

Denmark emerged as a separate country during the Viking period of the 10th and 11th centuries. In the 14th century Denmark and Norway were united under a Danish king, the union being joined between 1389–97 and 1523 by Sweden; Norway was ceded to Sweden in 1814. Although neutral, Denmark was occupied by Germany for much of the Second World War. Denmark joined the EC in 1973.

den mother ▶ **noun** chiefly US the female leader of a den of Cub Scouts.

denominal /dɪˈnɒmɪn(ə)l/ ▶ **adjective** [attrib.] (of a word) derived from a noun.
▶ **noun** a verb or other word that is derived from a noun.
– ORIGIN 1930s: from **DE-** (in sense 3) + **NOMINAL**.

denominate /dɪˈnɒmɪneɪt/ ▶ **verb 1** (**be denominated**) (of sums of money) be expressed in a specified monetary unit: *the borrowings were denominated in US dollars.*
2 [with obj. and complement] formal call; name.
– ORIGIN late Middle English (in the sense 'give a name to'): from Latin *denominat-* 'named', from the verb *denominare*, from *de-* 'away, formally' + *nominare* 'to name' (from *nomen, nomin-* 'name'). Sense 1 dates from the mid 20th cent.

denomination ▶ **noun 1** a recognized autonomous branch of the Christian Church.
■ a group or branch of any religion: *Jewish clergy of all denominations.*
2 the face value of a banknote, coin, or postage stamp: [as modifier] *high-denomination banknotes.*
■ the rank of a playing card within a suit, or of a suit relative to others: *two cards of the same denomination.*
3 formal a name or designation, especially one serving to classify a set of things.
■ [mass noun] the action of naming or classifying something.
– ORIGIN late Middle English (in sense 3): from Latin *denominatio(n-)*, from the verb *denominare* (see **DENOMINATE**). Sense 1 dates from the mid 17th cent.

denominational ▶ **adjective** relating to or according to the principles of a particular religious denomination: *denominational schools.*
– DERIVATIVES **denominationalism** noun.

denominative /dɪˈnɒmɪnətɪv/ ▶ **adjective** old-fashioned term for **DENOMINAL**.
– ORIGIN late 16th cent. (as a noun in the grammatical sense): from late Latin *denominativus*, from *denominat-* 'named', from the verb *denominare* (see **DENOMINATE**).

denominator ▶ **noun** Mathematics the number below the line in a vulgar fraction; a divisor.
■ a figure representing the total population in terms of which statistical values are expressed.
– ORIGIN mid 16th cent.: from French *dénominateur* or medieval Latin *denominator*, from *denominare* 'to name' (see **DENOMINATE**).

de nos jours /ˌdə nəʊ ˈʒʊə, French də no ʒuʀ/ ▶ **adjective** [postpositive] contemporary: *he is a kind of Oscar Wilde de nos jours.*
– ORIGIN French, 'of our days'.

denotation ▶ **noun** [mass noun] the action or process of indicating or referring to something by means of a word, symbol, etc.
■ [count noun] Philosophy the object or concept to which a term refers, or the set of objects of which a predicate is true. Often contrasted with **CONNOTATION**.
– DERIVATIVES **denotational** adjective.

denote /dɪˈnəʊt/ ▶ **verb** [with obj.] be a sign of; indicate: *this mark denotes purity and quality.*
■ (often **be denoted**) stand as a name or symbol for: *the level of output per firm, denoted by X.*
– DERIVATIVES **denotative** /-tətɪv/ adjective.
– ORIGIN late 16th cent. (in the sense 'be a sign of, mark out'): from French *dénoter* or Latin *denotare*, from *de-* 'away, thoroughly' + *notare* 'observe, note' (from *nota* 'a mark').

USAGE For an explanation of the difference between **denote** and **connote**, see **usage** at **CONNOTE**.

denouement /deɪˈnuːmɒ̃/ ▶ **noun** the final part of a play, film, or narrative in which the strands of the plot are drawn together and matters are explained or resolved.
■ the climax of a chain of events, usually when something is decided or made clear: *I waited by the eighteenth green to see the denouement.*
– ORIGIN mid 18th cent.: French *dénouement*, from *dénouer* 'unknot'.

denounce ▶ **verb** [with obj.] publicly declare to be wrong or evil: *the Assembly denounced the use of violence | he was widely* **denounced as** *a traitor.*
■ inform against: *some of his own priests* **denounced** *him* **to** *the King for heresy.*
– DERIVATIVES **denouncement** noun, **denouncer** noun.
– ORIGIN Middle English (originally in the sense 'proclaim, announce', also 'proclaim someone to be wicked, cursed, a rebel, etc.'): from Old French *denoncier*, from Latin *denuntiare* 'give official information', based on *nuntius* 'messenger'.

de nouveau /ˌdə nuːˈvəʊ, French də nuvo/ ▶ **adverb** archaic starting again from the beginning; anew.
– ORIGIN French, literally 'from new'.

de novo /deɪ ˈnəʊvəʊ, diː/ ▶ **adverb & adjective** starting from the beginning; anew: [as adv.] *in a pure meritocracy, everyone must begin de novo* | [as adj.] *a general strategy for de novo protein design.*
– ORIGIN Latin, literally 'from new'.

Denpasar /dɛnˈpɑːsɑː/ the chief city of the island of Bali, a seaport on the south coast; pop. 261,200 (1980).

dense ▶ **adjective** closely compacted in substance: *this water is denser than the surrounding sea.*
■ having the constituent parts crowded closely together: *an estuary* **dense with** *marine life.* ■ figurative (of a text) hard to understand because of complexity of ideas. ■ informal (of a person) stupid.
– DERIVATIVES **densely** adverb, **denseness** noun.
– ORIGIN late Middle English: from Latin *densus*.

densify ▶ **verb** (**-ies**, **-ied**) [with obj.] [often as adj. **densified**] make (something) more dense: *densified hardboard.*
– DERIVATIVES **densification** noun.

densimeter /dɛnˈsɪmɪtə/ ▶ **noun** an instrument for measuring density, especially of liquids.
– ORIGIN mid 19th cent.: from Latin *densus* 'dense' + **-METER**.

densitometer /ˌdɛnsɪˈtɒmɪtə/ ▶ **noun 1** an instrument for measuring the photographic density of an image on a film or photographic print.
2 a device for measuring the optical density of a material by measuring the amount of light it reflects or transmits.
– DERIVATIVES **densitometric** adjective, **densitometrically** adverb, **densitometry** noun.

density ▶ **noun** (pl. **-ies**) [mass noun] the degree of compactness of a substance: *a reduction in bone density.*
■ Physics degree of consistency measured by the quantity of mass per unit volume. ■ the opacity of a photographic image. ■ the quantity of people or things in a given area or space: *areas of low population density* | [count noun] *a density of 10,000 per square mile.*
– ORIGIN early 17th cent.: from French *densité* or Latin *densitas*, from *densus* 'dense'.

density function ▶ **noun** short for **PROBABILITY DENSITY FUNCTION**.

dent ▶ **noun** a slight hollow in a hard even surface made by a blow or the exertion of pressure.
■ a diminishing effect; a reduction: *a dent in profits.*
▶ **verb** [with obj.] mark with a dent: *he hit a concrete bollard, denting the wing and spoiler.*
■ have an adverse effect on; diminish: *this neither deterred him nor dented his enthusiasm.*
– ORIGIN Middle English (as a noun designating a blow with a weapon): variant of **DINT**.

dental ▶ **adjective 1** [attrib.] of or relating to the teeth: *dental health.*
■ of or relating to dentistry: *dental councils.*
2 Phonetics (of a consonant) pronounced with the tip of the tongue against the upper front teeth (as *th*) or the alveolar ridge (as *n, d, t*).
▶ **noun** Phonetics a dental consonant.
– DERIVATIVES **dentalize** (also **-ise**) verb (Phonetics), **dentally** adverb.
– ORIGIN late 16th cent.: from late Latin *dentalis*, from Latin *dens, dent-* 'tooth'.

dental dam ▶ **noun** a thin sheet of latex used as a prophylactic device during cunnilingus and anilingus.

dental floss ▶ **noun** [mass noun] a soft thread of floss silk or similar material used to clean between the teeth.

dental formula ▶ **noun** Zoology a formula expressing the number and kinds of teeth possessed by a mammal. A dental formula is usually written in the form of four 'fractions', one for each type of tooth, with the upper and lower lines describing the upper and lower jaws respectively.

dental hygienist ▶ **noun** an ancillary dental worker specializing in scaling and polishing teeth, and giving advice on cleaning the teeth.
– DERIVATIVES **dental hygiene** noun.

dentalium /dɛnˈteɪlɪəm/ ▶ **noun** [mass noun] tusk shells used as ornaments or as a form of currency: *a white mare purchased with dentalium.*
– ORIGIN modern Latin, from late Latin *dentalis* (see **DENTAL**).

dental nurse ▶ **noun** a nurse who assists a dentist.

dental surgeon ▶ **noun** a dentist.

dental technician (also **dental mechanic**) ▶ **noun** a person who makes and repairs artificial teeth.

dentary /ˈdɛnt(ə)ri/ ▶ **noun** (pl. **-ies**) Zoology the anterior bone of the lower jaw which bears the teeth. In mammals it forms the whole of the lower jaw (or mandible).
– ORIGIN mid 19th cent.: from late Latin *dentarius*, from Latin *dens, dent-* 'tooth'.

dentate /'dɛnteɪt/ ▶ adjective Botany & Zoology having a tooth-like or serrated edge.
– ORIGIN late Middle English: from Latin *dentatus*, from *dens*, *dent-* 'tooth'.

dentelle /dɛn'tɛl/ ▶ noun (pl. pronounced same) [mass noun] ornamental tooling used in bookbinding, resembling lace edging.
– ORIGIN mid 19th cent.: from French, 'lace', from *dent* 'tooth' + the diminutive suffix *-elle*.

denticle /'dɛntɪk(ə)l/ ▶ noun Zoology a small tooth or tooth-like projection.
– ORIGIN late Middle English (denoting a pointer on an astrolabe): from Latin *denticulus*, diminutive of *dens*, *dent-* 'tooth'.

denticulate /dɛn'tɪkjʊlət/ ▶ adjective having small teeth or tooth-like projections; finely toothed.
– DERIVATIVES **denticulated** adjective.
– ORIGIN mid 17th cent.: from Latin *denticulatus*, from *denticulus* 'small tooth' (see **DENTICLE**).

dentifrice /'dɛntɪfrɪs/ ▶ noun a paste or powder for cleaning the teeth.
– ORIGIN late Middle English: from French, from Latin *dentifricium*, from *dens*, *dent-* 'tooth' + *fricare* 'to rub'.

dentil /'dɛntɪl/ ▶ noun [often as modifier] (in classical architecture) one of a number of small rectangular blocks resembling teeth, used as a decoration under the moulding of a cornice: *a dentil frieze*.
– ORIGIN late 16th cent.: from Italian *dentello* or obsolete French *dentille*, diminutive of *dent* 'tooth', from Latin *dens*, *dent-*.

dentilingual /ˌdɛntɪ'lɪŋgw(ə)l/ ▶ adjective Phonetics (of a consonant) pronounced with the teeth and the tongue; dental.
– ORIGIN late 19th cent.: from Latin *dens*, *dent-* 'tooth' + **LINGUAL**.

dentine /'dɛnti:n/ (US **dentin** /-tɪn/) ▶ noun [mass noun] hard dense bony tissue forming the bulk of a tooth, beneath the enamel.
– DERIVATIVES **dentinal** /'dɛntɪn(ə)l/ adjective.
– ORIGIN mid 19th cent.: from Latin *dens*, *dent-* 'tooth' + **-INE**⁴.

dentist ▶ noun a person who is qualified to treat the diseases and conditions that affect the teeth and gums, especially the repair and extraction of teeth and the insertion of artificial ones.
– DERIVATIVES **dentistry** noun.
– ORIGIN mid 18th cent.: from French *dentiste*, from *dent* 'tooth', from Latin *dens*, *dent-*.

dentition /dɛn'tɪʃ(ə)n/ ▶ noun [mass noun] the arrangement or condition of the teeth in a particular species or individual.
– ORIGIN late 16th cent. (denoting the process of developing of teeth): from Latin *dentitio(n-)*, from *dentire* 'teethe', from *dens*, *dent-* 'tooth'.

denture /'dɛntʃə/ ▶ noun (usu. **dentures**) a removable plate or frame holding one or more artificial teeth.
– ORIGIN late 19th cent.: from French, from *dent* 'tooth', from Latin *dens*, *dent-*.

denturist ▶ noun a person who makes dentures.

denuclearize (also **-ise**) ▶ verb [with obj.] remove nuclear weapons from.
– DERIVATIVES **denuclearization** noun.

denude ▶ verb [with obj.] (often **be denuded**) strip (something) of its covering, possessions, or assets; make bare: *almost overnight the Arctic was denuded of animals*.
– DERIVATIVES **denudation** noun.
– ORIGIN late Middle English: from Latin *denudare*, from *de-* 'completely' + *nudare* 'to bare' (from *nudus* 'naked').

denumerable /dɪ'nju:m(ə)rəb(ə)l/ ▶ adjective Mathematics able to be counted by a one-to-one correspondence with the infinite set of integers.
– DERIVATIVES **denumerability** noun, **denumerably** adverb.
– ORIGIN early 20th cent.: from late Latin *denumerare* 'count out' + **-ABLE**.

denunciation /dɪ,nʌnsɪ'eɪʃ(ə)n/ ▶ noun [mass noun] public condemnation of someone or something.
■ the action of informing against someone.
– DERIVATIVES **denunciator** noun, **denunciatory** adjective.
– ORIGIN late Middle English: from Latin *denuntiatio(n-)*, from the verb *denuntiare* (see **DENOUNCE**). The original sense was 'public

announcement', also 'formal accusation or charge'; the main sense dates from the mid 19th cent.

Denver /'dɛnvə/ the state capital of Colorado; pop. 467,600 (1990). Situated at an altitude of 1,608 m (5,280 ft) on the eastern side of the Rocky Mountains, Denver was developed in the 1870s as a silver-mining town.

deny /dɪ'naɪ/ ▶ verb (**-ies**, **-ied**) [with obj.] state one's refusal to admit the truth or existence of: *both firms deny any responsibility for the tragedy*.
■ [with two objs] refuse to give (something requested or desired) to (someone): *the inquiry was denied access to intelligence sources*. ■ archaic refuse access to (someone): *the servants are ordered to deny him*. ■ (**deny oneself**) go without: *he had denied himself sexually for years*.
– ORIGIN Middle English: from Old French *deni-*, stressed stem of *deneier*, from Latin *denegare*, from *de-* 'formally' + *negare* 'say no'.

Denys, St see **DENIS, ST**.

deoch an doris /ˌdɒx (ə)n 'dɒrɪs, dɒk/ (also **doch an dorris**) ▶ noun Scottish & Irish a final drink taken before parting.
– ORIGIN late 17th cent.: from Scottish Gaelic *deoch an doruis* 'drink at the door'.

deodar /'di:ə(ʊ)dɑː/ ▶ noun a tall, broadly conical cedar which has drooping branches and bears large barrel-shaped cones, native to the Himalayas.
● *Cedrus deodara*, family Pinaceae.
– ORIGIN early 19th cent.: from Hindi *deodār*, Sanskrit *devadāru* 'divine tree'.

deodorant /dɪ'əʊd(ə)r(ə)nt/ ▶ noun a substance which removes or conceals unpleasant smells, especially bodily odours.
– ORIGIN mid 19th cent.: from **DE-** (expressing removal) + Latin *odor* 'smell' + **-ANT**.

deodorize (also **-ise**) ▶ verb [with obj.] remove or conceal an unpleasant smell in: *people used dried flowers to deodorize their homes*.
– DERIVATIVES **deodorization** noun, **deodorizer** noun.
– ORIGIN mid 19th cent.: from **DE-** (expressing removal) + Latin *odor* 'smell' + **-IZE**.

Deo gratias /ˌdeɪəʊ 'grɑːtɪəs, -ʃɪəs/ ▶ exclamation thanks be to God.
– ORIGIN Latin.

deontic /dɪ'ɒntɪk/ ▶ adjective [attrib.] Philosophy of or relating to duty and obligation as ethical concepts.
■ Linguistics expressing duty or obligation.
– ORIGIN mid 20th cent.: from Greek *deont-* 'being right' (from *dei* 'it is right') + **-IC**.

deontology /ˌdi:ɒn'tɒlədʒi/ ▶ noun [mass noun] Philosophy the study of the nature of duty and obligation.
– DERIVATIVES **deontological** adjective, **deontologist** noun.
– ORIGIN early 19th cent.: from Greek *deont-* 'being right', (from *dei* 'it is right') + **-LOGY**.

Deo volente /ˌdeɪəʊ vɒ'lɛnteɪ/ ▶ adverb God willing; if nothing prevents it.
– ORIGIN Latin.

deoxidize /di:'ɒksɪdʌɪz/ ▶ verb [with obj.] remove combined oxygen from (a substance, usually a metal).
– DERIVATIVES **deoxidation** noun, **deoxidizer** noun.

deoxycorticosterone /di:,ɒksɪ,kɔ:tɪkəʊ'stɛrəʊn/ ▶ noun [mass noun] Biochemistry a corticosteroid hormone involved in regulating the salt and water balance.

deoxygenate /di:'ɒksɪdʒəneɪt/ ▶ verb [with obj.] [usu. as adj. **deoxygenated**] remove oxygen from: *deoxygenated air*.
– DERIVATIVES **deoxygenation** noun.

deoxyribonuclease /di:,ɒksɪrʌɪbəʊ'nju:klɪeɪz/ ▶ noun Biochemistry another term for **DNASE**.

deoxyribonucleic acid /dɪ,ɒksɪrʌɪbəʊnju:'kleɪɪk/ ▶ noun see **DNA**.
– ORIGIN 1930s: *deoxyribonucleic* from a blend of **DEOXYRIBOSE** and **NUCLEIC ACID**.

deoxyribose /dɪ,ɒksɪ'rʌɪbəʊz, -s/ ▶ noun [mass noun] Biochemistry a sugar derived from ribose by replacement of a hydroxyl group by hydrogen.
● Chem. formula: $C_5H_{10}O_4$. There are several isomers; the isomer **2-deoxyribose** is a constituent of DNA.
– ORIGIN 1930s: from **DE-** (expressing reduction) + **OXY-**² + **RIBOSE**.

dep. ▶ abbreviation for ■ departs. ■ deputy.

Depardieu /'dɛpɑːdjə:, French dəpaʁdjø/, Gérard (b.1948), French actor. Notable films: *Danton* (1982), *Jean de Florette* (1986), and *Cyrano de Bergerac* (1990).

depart ▶ verb [no obj.] leave, typically in order to start a journey: *they departed for Germany* | *a contingent was departing from Cairo*.
■ (**depart from**) deviate from (an accepted, prescribed, or traditional course of action): *he departed from the precedent set by many*.
– PHRASES **depart this life** archaic die.
– ORIGIN Middle English: from Old French *departir*, based on Latin *dispertire* 'to divide'. The original sense was 'separate', also 'take leave of each other', hence 'go away'.

departed ▶ adjective deceased: *a dear departed relative*.
▶ noun (**the departed**) a particular dead person or dead people: *the prayer for the departed*.

department ▶ noun a division of a large organization such as a government, university, business, or shop, dealing with a specific subject, commodity, or area of activity: *the council's finance department*.
■ an administrative district in France and other countries. ■ (**one's department**) informal an area of special expertise or responsibility: *that's not my department*. ■ [with modifier] informal a specified aspect or quality: *he was a few feet shy of Barry in the height department*.
– ORIGIN late Middle English: from Old French *departement*, from *departir* (see **DEPART**). The original sense was 'division or distribution', later 'separation', hence 'a separate part' (core sense, mid 18th cent.).

departmental ▶ adjective concerned with or belonging to a department of an organization: *a departmental meeting*.
– DERIVATIVES **departmentally** adverb.

departmentalism ▶ noun [mass noun] adherence to departmental methods or structure.

departmentalize (also **-ise**) ▶ verb [with obj.] (usu. **be departmentalized**) divide (an organization or its work) into departments.
– DERIVATIVES **departmentalization** noun.

department store ▶ noun a large shop stocking many varieties of goods in different departments.

departure ▶ noun [mass noun] the action of leaving, typically to start a journey: *the day of departure* | [count noun] *she made a hasty departure*.
■ [count noun] a deviation from an accepted, prescribed, or traditional course of action or thought: *a departure from their usual style*. ■ Nautical the amount of a ship's change of longitude.
– ORIGIN late Middle English: from Old French *departeure*, from the verb *departir* (see **DEPART**).

depasture ▶ verb [with obj.] Brit. put (an animal) to graze on pasture: *this right enables the commoners to depasture some 3,000 ponies*.
– DERIVATIVES **depasturage** noun.

depauperate /dɪ'pɔ:p(ə)rət/ ▶ adjective Biology (of a flora, fauna, or ecosystem) lacking in numbers or variety of species: *oceanic islands are generally depauperate in mayflies*.
■ (of a plant or animal) imperfectly developed.
– ORIGIN late Middle English (in the sense 'impoverished'): from medieval Latin *depauperatus*, past participle of *depauperare*, from *de-* 'completely' + *pauperare* 'make poor' (from *pauper* 'poor').

dépaysé /deɪ'peɪzeɪ, French depeize/ (also **dépaysée**) ▶ adjective removed from one's habitual surroundings.
– ORIGIN French, '(removed) from one's own country'.

depend ▶ verb [no obj.] **1** (**depend on/upon**) be controlled or determined by: *differences in earnings depended on a wide variety of factors*.
2 (**depend on/upon**) rely on: *the kind of person you could depend on*.
■ need or require for financial or other support: *a town which had depended heavily upon the wool industry*. ■ be grammatically dependent on.
3 archaic or poetic/literary hang down: *his tongue depended from open jaws*.
– PHRASES **depending on** according to: *makes 8–10 burgers (depending on size)* | [with clause] *the article sneered or just condescended, depending on how you read it*. **it** (or **that**) (**all**) **depends** used to express uncertainty or qualification in answering a question: *How many people use each screen? It all depends*.
– ORIGIN late Middle English (in sense 3); also in the sense 'wait or be in suspense': from Old French

dependre, from Latin *dependere*, from *de-* 'down' + *pendere* 'hang'.

USAGE In informal use, it is quite common for the **on** to be dropped in sentences such as *it all* ***depends how*** *you look at it* (rather than *it all* ***depends on how*** *you look at it*) but in well-formed written English the **on** should always be retained.

dependable ▶ **adjective** trustworthy and reliable.
– DERIVATIVES **dependability** noun, **dependably** adverb.

dependant (also **dependent**) ▶ **noun** a person who relies on another, especially a family member, for financial support.
– ORIGIN late Middle English (denoting a dependency): from Old French, literally 'hanging down from', present participle of *dependre* (see **DEPEND**).

USAGE Until recently, the correct spelling of the noun in British English was **dependant**, as in *a single man with no* ***dependants***. However, in modern British (and US) English, the variant **dependent** is now standard. The adjective is always spelled **-ent**, never **-ant**, as in *we are* ***dependent on*** *his goodwill*.

dependence ▶ **noun** [mass noun] the state of relying on or being controlled by someone or something else: *Japan's* ***dependence on*** *imported oil*.
■ reliance on someone or something for financial support: *the* ***dependence*** *of our medical schools* ***on*** *grant funds*. ■ addiction to drink or drugs: *alcohol dependence*.
– ORIGIN late Middle English (in the sense 'hanging down or something that hangs down'): from Old French *dependance*, from the verb *dependre* (see **DEPEND**).

dependency ▶ **noun** (pl. **-ies**) **1** a dependent or subordinate thing, especially a country or province controlled by another.
2 [mass noun] dependence: *the country's* ***dependency on*** *the oil industry*.

dependency culture ▶ **noun** [in sing.] a way of life characterized by dependency on state benefits.

dependent ▶ **adjective** **1** [predic.] (**dependent on/upon**) contingent on or determined by: *the various benefits will be dependent on length of service*.
2 requiring someone or something for financial, emotional, or other support: *an economy heavily* ***dependent on*** *oil exports* | *households with dependent children*.
■ unable to do without: *people* ***dependent on*** *drugs* | [in combination] *welfare-dependent families*. ■ Grammar (of a clause, phrase, or word) subordinate to another clause, phrase, or word.
▶ **noun** variant spelling of **DEPENDANT**.
– DERIVATIVES **dependently** adverb.
– ORIGIN late Middle English *dependant* 'hanging down', from Old French, present participle of *dependre* (see **DEPEND**). The spelling change in the 16th cent. was due to association with the Latin participial stem *dependent-*.

USAGE On the distinction between **dependent** and **dependant**, see **usage** at **DEPENDANT**.

dependent variable ▶ **noun** Mathematics a variable (often denoted by *y*) whose value depends on that of another. Also called **RESPONSE VARIABLE**.

depersonalization /diːˌpəːs(ə)n(ə)lʌɪˈzeɪʃ(ə)n/ (also **-isation**) ▶ **noun** [mass noun] the action of divesting someone or something of human characteristics or individuality.
■ Psychiatry a state in which one's thoughts and feelings seem unreal or not to belong to oneself, or in which one loses all sense of identity.

depersonalize (also **-ise**) ▶ **verb** [with obj.] divest of human characteristics or individuality.

dephlogisticated /ˌdiːflə'dʒɪstɪkeɪtɪd/ ▶ **adjective** Chemistry, historical deprived of 'phlogiston'. Oxygen was originally called **dephlogisticated air** by Joseph Priestley.

depict /dɪˈpɪkt/ ▶ **verb** [with obj.] show or represent by a drawing, painting, or other art form.
■ portray in words; describe: *youth is depicted as a time of vitality and good health*.
– DERIVATIVES **depicter** noun, **depiction** noun.
– ORIGIN late Middle English: from Latin *depict-* 'portrayed', from the verb *depingere*, from *de-* 'completely' + *pingere* 'to paint'.

depigment /diːˈpɪgm(ə)nt/ ▶ **verb** [with obj.] [usu. as adj. **depigmented**] reduce or remove the pigmentation of (the skin).
– DERIVATIVES **depigmentation** noun.

depilate /ˈdɛpɪleɪt/ ▶ **verb** [with obj.] remove the hair from: *they scrubbed and depilated her* | [as adj. **depilated**] *his permanently depilated and tattooed skull*.
– DERIVATIVES **depilation** noun.
– ORIGIN mid 16th cent.: from Latin *depilat-* 'stripped of hair', from the verb *depilare*, from *de-* (expressing removal) + *pilare* (from *pilus* 'hair').

depilator ▶ **noun** an instrument which removes unwanted bodily hair, typically by plucking it from the root.

depilatory /dɪˈpɪlət(ə)ri/ ▶ **adjective** used to remove unwanted hair.
▶ **noun** (pl. **-ies**) a cream or lotion for removing unwanted hair.
– ORIGIN early 17th cent.: from Latin *depilatorius*, from *depilat-* 'stripped of hair', from the verb *depilare* (see **DEPILATE**).

de Pisan /də ˈpiːzan/ (also **de Pizan**), Christine (*c.*1364–*c.*1430), Italian writer, resident in France from 1369. The first professional woman writer in France, she is best known for her works in defence of women's virtues and achievements, such as *Le Livre des trois vertus* (1406).

deplane ▶ **verb** [no obj.] chiefly N. Amer. disembark from an aircraft: *we landed and deplaned*.

deplete /dɪˈpliːt/ ▶ **verb** [with obj.] [often as adj. **depleted**] reduce the number or quantity of: *fish stocks are severely depleted*.
■ [no obj.] diminish in number or quantity: *supplies are depleting fast*. ■ exhaust: *avoid getting depleted and depressed*.
– DERIVATIVES **depletion** noun.
– ORIGIN early 19th cent.: from Latin *deplet-* 'emptied out', from the verb *deplere*, from *de-* (expressing reversal) + *plere* 'fill' (from *plenus* 'full').

depleted uranium ▶ **noun** [mass noun] uranium from which most of the fissile isotope uranium-235 has been removed.

depletion allowance ▶ **noun** N. Amer. a tax concession allowable to a company whose normal business activities (in particular oil extraction) reduce the value of its own assets.

deplorable /dɪˈplɔːrəb(ə)l/ ▶ **adjective** deserving strong condemnation: *the deplorable conditions in which most prisoners are held*.
■ shockingly bad in quality: *her spelling was deplorable*.
– DERIVATIVES **deplorably** adverb.
– ORIGIN early 17th cent.: from French *déplorable* or late Latin *deplorabilis*, from the verb *deplorare* (see **DEPLORE**).

deplore /dɪˈplɔː/ ▶ **verb** [with obj.] feel or express strong disapproval of (something): *we deplore all violence*.
– DERIVATIVES **deploringly** adverb.
– ORIGIN mid 16th cent. (in the sense 'weep for, regret deeply'): from French *déplorer* or Italian *deplorare*, from Latin *deplorare*, from *de-* 'away, thoroughly' + *plorare* 'bewail'.

deploy /dɪˈplɔɪ/ ▶ **verb** [with obj.] move (troops) into position for military action: *forces were deployed at strategic locations*.
■ [no obj.] (of troops) move into position for such action: *the air force began to deploy forward*. ■ bring into effective action; utilize: *they are not always able to deploy this skill*.
– DERIVATIVES **deployment** noun.
– ORIGIN late 18th cent.: from French *déployer*, from Latin *displicare* and late Latin *deplicare* 'unfold or explain', from *dis-*, *de-* 'un-' + *plicare* 'to fold'. Compare with **DISPLAY**.

deplume ▶ **verb** [with obj.] deprive (a bird) of feathers.
■ archaic, figurative strip or deprive of honour, status, or wealth.
– ORIGIN late Middle English: from Old French *desplumer* or medieval Latin *deplumare*, from *des-*, *de-* (expressing reversal) + Latin *pluma* 'feather'.

depolarize /diːˈpəʊlərʌɪz/ (also **-ise**) ▶ **verb** [with obj.] Physics reduce or remove the polarization of: *the threshold necessary to depolarize the membrane*.
– DERIVATIVES **depolarization** noun.

depoliticize (also **-ise**) ▶ **verb** [with obj.] remove from political activity or influence: *we have to depoliticize sex education*.
– DERIVATIVES **depoliticization** noun.

depolymerize /diːˈpɒlɪmərʌɪz/ (also **-ise**) ▶ **verb** [with obj.] Chemistry break (a polymer) down into monomers or other smaller units.
■ [no obj.] undergo this process: *the ideal disposable polymer would depolymerize naturally*.
– DERIVATIVES **depolymerization** noun.

deponent /dɪˈpəʊnənt/ ▶ **adjective** Grammar (of a verb, especially in Latin or Greek) passive or middle in form but active in meaning.
▶ **noun** **1** Grammar a deponent verb.
2 Law a person who makes a deposition or affidavit under oath.
– ORIGIN late Middle English: from Latin *deponent-* 'laying aside, putting down' (in medieval Latin 'testifying'), from the verb *deponere*, from *de-* 'down' + *ponere* 'place'. The use in grammar arose from the notion that the verb had 'laid aside' the passive sense (although in fact these verbs were originally reflexive).

d

depopulate ▶ **verb** [with obj.] substantially reduce the population of (an area): *the disease could depopulate a town the size of Bournemouth*.
– DERIVATIVES **depopulation** noun.
– ORIGIN mid 16th cent. (in the sense 'ravage, lay waste'): from Latin *depopulat-* 'ravaged', from the verb *depopulari*, from *de-* 'completely' + *populari* 'lay waste' (from *populus* 'people').

deport ▶ **verb** **1** [with obj.] expel (a foreigner) from a country, typically on the grounds of illegal status or for having committed a crime: *he was deported for violation of immigration laws*.
■ exile (a native) to another country.
2 (**deport oneself**) archaic conduct oneself in a specified manner: *he has deported himself with great dignity*.
– DERIVATIVES **deportable** adjective, **deportation** noun.
– ORIGIN late 16th cent. (in sense 2): from French *déporter*, from Latin *deportare*, from *de-* 'away' + *portare* 'carry'.

deportee /ˌdiːpɔːˈtiː/ ▶ **noun** a person who has been or is being expelled from a country.

deportment ▶ **noun** [mass noun] **1** chiefly Brit. the way a person stands and walks, particularly as an element of upper-class etiquette: *poise is directly concerned with good deportment*.
2 chiefly US a person's behaviour or manners: *there are team rules governing deportment on and off the field*.
– ORIGIN early 17th cent. (denoting behaviour in general): from French *déportement*, from the verb *déporter* (see **DEPORT**).

depose ▶ **verb** [with obj.] **1** remove from office suddenly and forcefully: *he had been deposed by a military coup*.
2 Law testify to or give (evidence) on oath, typically in a written statement: *every affidavit shall state which of the facts* ***deposed to*** *are within the deponent's knowledge*.
– ORIGIN Middle English: from Old French *deposer*, from Latin *deponere* (see **DEPONENT**), but influenced by Latin *depositus* and Old French *poser* 'to place'.

deposit ▶ **noun** **1** a sum of money placed or kept in a bank or building society account, usually to gain interest.
2 a sum payable as a first instalment on the purchase of something or as a pledge for a contract, the balance being payable later: *we've saved enough for a* ***deposit on*** *a house*.
■ a returnable sum payable on the hire or rental of something, to cover any possible loss or damage. ■ (in the UK) a sum of money lodged by an election candidate and forfeited if they fail to receive a certain proportion of the votes.
3 a layer or body of accumulated matter: *the deposits of salt on the paintwork*.
■ a natural layer of sand, rock, coal, or other material.
4 the action of placing something in a specified place.
▶ **verb** (**deposited**, **depositing**) **1** [with obj. and usu. with adverbial of place] put or set down (something or someone) in a specific place, typically unceremoniously: *he deposited a pile of school books on the kitchen table*.
■ (usu. **be deposited**) (of water, the wind, or other natural agency) lay down (matter) gradually as a layer or covering: *beds where salt is deposited by the tide*. ■ lay (an egg): *the female deposits a line of eggs*.
2 [with obj.] store or entrust with someone for safe keeping.
■ pay (a sum of money) into a bank or building society account: *the money is deposited with a bank*. ■ pay (a sum) as a first instalment or as a pledge for a contract: *I had to deposit 10% of the price of the house*.

– PHRASES **on deposit** (of money) placed in a deposit account.
– ORIGIN late 16th cent. (especially in the phrases *in deposit* or *on deposit*): from Latin *depositum* (noun), medieval Latin *depositare* (verb), both from Latin *deposit-* 'laid aside', from the verb *deponere*.

deposit account ▶ **noun** chiefly Brit. a bank account that pays interest and is usually not able to be drawn on without notice or loss of interest.

depositary (also **depository**) ▶ **noun** (pl. **-ies**) a person to whom something is lodged in trust.
– ORIGIN early 17th cent.: from late Latin *depositarius*, from the verb *deponere* (see **DEPOSIT**).

deposition /ˌdɛpəˈzɪʃ(ə)n, diː-/ ▶ **noun** [mass noun] **1** the action of deposing someone, especially a monarch: *Edward V's deposition.*
2 Law the process of giving sworn evidence: *the deposition of four expert witnesses.*
■ [count noun] a formal, usually written, statement to be used as evidence.
3 the action of depositing something: *pebbles formed by the deposition of calcium in solution.*
4 (**the Deposition**) the taking down of the body of Christ from the Cross.
– ORIGIN late Middle English: from Latin *depositio(n-)*, from the verb *deponere* (see **DEPOSIT**).

depositor ▶ **noun** a person who keeps money in a bank or building society account.

depository ▶ **noun** (pl. **-ies**) **1** a place where things are stored.
2 variant spelling of **DEPOSITARY**.
– ORIGIN mid 17th cent. (denoting a depositary): from late Latin *depositorium*, from *deposit-* 'laid aside', from the verb *deponere* (see **DEPOSIT**).

depot /ˈdɛpəʊ/ ▶ **noun** a place for the storage of large quantities of equipment, food, or some other commodity: *an arms depot.*
■ a place where buses, trains, or other vehicles are housed and maintained and from which they are dispatched for service. ■ N. Amer. a railway or bus station. ■ the headquarters of a regiment; a place where recruits or other troops are assembled.
– ORIGIN late 18th cent. (in the sense 'act of depositing'): from French *dépôt*, from Latin *depositum* 'something deposited' (see **DEPOSIT**).

depower ▶ **verb** [with obj.] Sailing adjust or alter (a sail) so that the wind no longer fills it.

deprave /dɪˈpreɪv/ ▶ **verb** [with obj.] make (someone) immoral or wicked: *this book would deprave and corrupt young children.*
– DERIVATIVES **depravation** noun.
– ORIGIN late Middle English (in the sense 'pervert the meaning or intention of something'): from Old French *depraver* or Latin *depravare*, from *de-* 'down, thoroughly' + *pravus* 'crooked, perverse'.

depraved ▶ **adjective** morally corrupt: *he was a depraved lecher | this city is depraved.*

depravity /dɪˈpravɪti/ ▶ **noun** (pl. **-ies**) [mass noun] moral corruption: *a tale of wickedness and depravity hard to credit.*
■ [count noun] a wicked or morally corrupt act. ■ Christian Theology the innate corruptness of human nature, due to original sin.
– ORIGIN mid 17th cent.: alteration (influenced by **DEPRAVE**) of obsolete *pravity*, from Latin *pravitas*, from *pravus* 'crooked, perverse'.

deprecate /ˈdɛprɪkeɪt/ ▶ **verb** [with obj.] **1** express disapproval of: [as adj. **deprecating**] *he sniffed in a deprecating way.*
2 another term for **DEPRECIATE** (in sense 2): *he deprecates the value of children's television.*
– DERIVATIVES **deprecatingly** adverb, **deprecation** noun, **deprecative** /ˈdɛprɪkətɪv/ adjective, **deprecator** noun
– ORIGIN early 17th cent. (in the sense 'pray against'): from Latin *deprecat-* 'prayed against (as being evil)', from the verb *deprecari*, from *de-* (expressing reversal) + *precari* 'pray'.

USAGE The similarity of spelling and meaning of **deprecate** and **depreciate** has led to confusions in the use, with **deprecate** being used simply as a synonym for **depreciate** in the sense 'disparage or belittle'. This use is now well established and is widely accepted in standard English.

deprecatory ▶ **adjective** expressing disapproval; disapproving.
■ apologetic or appeasing: *a deprecatory smile.*

depreciate /dɪˈpriːʃɪeɪt, -sɪ-/ ▶ **verb** **1** [no obj.] diminish in value over a period of time: *sterling is expected to **depreciate against** the dollar.*
■ [with obj.] reduce the recorded value in a company's books of (an asset) each year over a predetermined period.
2 [with obj.] disparage or belittle (something): *she was already depreciating her own aesthetic taste.*
– DERIVATIVES **depreciatory** /dɪˈpriːʃ(ɪ)ət(ə)ri/ adjective.
– ORIGIN late Middle English (in sense 2): from late Latin *depreciat-* 'lowered in price, undervalued', from the verb *depreciare*, from Latin *de-* 'down' + *pretium* 'price'.

depreciation ▶ **noun** [mass noun] a reduction in the value of an asset with the passage of time, due in particular to wear and tear.
■ decrease in the value of a currency relative to other currencies: *depreciation leads to losses for non-dollar based investors* | [count noun] *a currency depreciation.*

depredation /ˌdɛprɪˈdeɪʃ(ə)n/ ▶ **noun** (usu. **depredations**) an act of attacking or plundering: *protecting grain from the depredations of rats and mice.*
– ORIGIN late 15th cent. (in the sense 'plundering, robbery', (plural) 'ravages'): from French *déprédation*, from late Latin *depraedatio(n-)*, from *depraedari* 'plunder'.

depredator /ˈdɛprɪdeɪtə/ ▶ **noun** archaic a person or thing that makes depredations, especially a predatory animal.
– DERIVATIVES **depredatory** /ˈdɛprɪdeɪt(ə)ri, dɪˈprɛdət(ə)ri/ adjective.

depress ▶ **verb** [with obj.] **1** make (someone) feel utterly dispirited or dejected: *that first day at school depressed me.*
■ reduce the level or strength of activity in (something, especially an economic or biological system): *fear of inflation in America depressed bond markets | alcohol depresses the nervous system.*
2 push or pull (something) down into a lower position: *depress the lever.*
– DERIVATIVES **depressible** adjective.
– ORIGIN late Middle English: from Old French *depresser*, from late Latin *depressare*, frequentative of *deprimere* 'press down'.

depressant ▶ **adjective** (chiefly of a drug) reducing functional or nervous activity.
▶ **noun** a depressant drug.
■ an influence that depresses economic or other activity: *higher taxation is a depressant.*

depressed ▶ **adjective** (of a person) in a state of general unhappiness or despondency.
■ (of a person) suffering from clinical depression. ■ (of a place or economic activity) suffering the damaging effects of a lack of demand or employment: *depressed areas.* ■ (of an object or part of an object) in a physically lower position, having been pushed or forced down: *a depressed fracture of the skull.*

depressing ▶ **adjective** causing or resulting in a feeling of miserable dejection: *that thought is too depressing for words.*
■ causing a damaging reduction in economic activity: *the mortgage rate increase will have a depressing effect on the housing market.*
– DERIVATIVES **depressingly** adverb.

depression ▶ **noun** [mass noun] **1** severe despondency and dejection, typically felt over a period of time and accompanied by feelings of hopelessness and inadequacy.
■ Medicine a condition of mental disturbance characterized by such feelings to a greater degree than seems warranted by the external circumstances, typically with lack of energy and difficulty in maintaining concentration or interest in life: *clinical depression.* ■ a long and severe recession in an economy or market: *the depression in the housing market.* ■ (**the Depression** or **the Great Depression**) the financial and industrial slump of 1929 and subsequent years.
2 the lowering or reducing of something: *the depression of prices.*
■ the action of pressing down on something: *depression of the plunger delivers two units of insulin.* ■ [count noun] a sunken place or hollow on a surface: *the original shallow depressions were slowly converted to creeks.* ■ Astronomy & Geography the angular distance of an object below the horizon or a horizontal plane. ■ [count noun] Meteorology a region of lower atmospheric pressure, especially a cyclonic weather system.
– ORIGIN late Middle English: from Latin *depressio(n-)*, from *deprimere* 'press down'(see **DEPRESS**).

depressive ▶ **adjective** causing feelings of hopeless despondency and dejection.
■ Medicine relating to or tending to suffer from clinical depression: *a depressive illness.* ■ causing a reduction in strength, effectiveness, or value: *steroids have a depressive effect on the immune system.*
▶ **noun** Medicine a person suffering from or with a tendency to suffer from depression.

depressor ▶ **noun** **1** Anatomy (also **depressor muscle**) a muscle whose contraction pulls down the part of the body to which it is attached.
■ any of several specific muscles in the face: [followed by Latin genitive] *depressor anguli oris.*
2 Physiology a nerve whose stimulation results in a lowering of blood pressure.
3 an instrument for pressing something down.
– ORIGIN early 17th cent. (in the general sense 'someone or something that depresses'): from Latin, from *depress-* 'pressed down', from the verb *deprimere* (see **DEPRESS**).

depressurize (also **-ise**) ▶ **verb** [with obj.] release the pressure of the gas inside (a pressurized vehicle or container).
■ [no obj.] (of a pressurized vehicle or container) lose pressure.
– DERIVATIVES **depressurization** noun.

Deprez variant spelling of **DES PREZ**.

deprivation /dɛprɪˈveɪʃ(ə)n/ ▶ **noun** [mass noun] the damaging lack of material benefits considered to be basic necessities in a society: *low wages mean that 3.75 million people suffer serious deprivation.*
■ the lack or denial of something considered to be a necessity: *sleep deprivation.* ■ archaic the action of depriving someone of office, especially an ecclesiastical office.
– ORIGIN late Middle English (in the sense 'removal from office'): from medieval Latin *deprivatio(n-)*, from the verb *deprivare* (see **DEPRIVE**).

deprive /dɪˈprʌɪv/ ▶ **verb** [with obj.] deny (a person or place) the possession or use of something: *the city was **deprived of** its water supplies.*
■ archaic depose (someone, especially a clergyman) from office: *Archbishop Bancroft deprived a considerable number of puritan clergymen.*
– DERIVATIVES **deprival** noun.
– ORIGIN Middle English (in the sense 'depose from office'): from Old French *depriver*, from medieval Latin *deprivare*, from *de-* 'away, completely' + *privare* (see **PRIVATE**).

deprived ▶ **adjective** suffering a severe and damaging lack of basic material and cultural benefits: *the charity cares for destitute and deprived children.*
■ (of a person) suffering a lack of a specified benefit that is considered important: *the men felt sexually deprived.*

de profundis /ˌdeɪ prəˈfʊndɪs/ ▶ **adverb** used to convey that one's deepest and most heartfelt feelings of sorrow or anguish are being expressed.
▶ **noun** a heartfelt cry of appeal expressing such feelings.
– ORIGIN Latin, 'from the depths', the opening words of Psalm 130.

deprogramme (US **deprogram**) ▶ **verb** (**deprogrammed**, **deprogramming**; US **deprogramed**, **deprograming**) [with obj.] release (someone) from apparent brainwashing, typically that of a religious cult, by the systematic reindoctrination of conventional values.

deproteinize /diːˈprəʊtiːnʌɪz/ ▶ **verb** [with obj.] remove the protein from (a substance), usually as a stage in chemical purification.
– DERIVATIVES **deproteinization** noun.

Dept ▶ **abbreviation for** Department.

depth ▶ **noun** **1** [mass noun] the distance from the top or surface to the bottom of something: *shallow water of no more than 12 feet **in depth**.*
■ distance from the nearest to the farthest point of something or from the front to the back: *the depth of the wardrobe.* ■ used to specify the distance below the top or surface of something to which someone or something percolates or at which something happens: [in sing.] *loosen the soil to **a depth of** 8 inches.* ■ the apparent existence of three dimensions in a picture, photograph, or other two-dimensional representation: *texture in a picture gives it depth.*
2 [mass noun] complexity and profundity of thought: *the book has unexpected depth.*
■ extensive and detailed study or knowledge: *third-year courses typically go into more depth.* ■ intensity of

emotion, usually considered as a laudable quality: *a man of compassion and depth of feeling.*
3 (**the depths**) a point far below the surface: *he lifted the manhole cover and peered into the depths beneath.*
■ a time considered to be the worst point within a bad period: *4 am in **the depths of winter**.* ■ a time when one's negative feelings are at their most intense: *she was in **the depths of despair**.* ■ a place which is remote and inaccessible: *I wish I didn't live in the depths of Devon.*
– PHRASES **hidden depths** usually admirable but previously unnoticed qualities of a person: *solo spots reveal hidden depths.* ■ obscure or secretive aspects of a situation: *the hidden depths of marital life.* **in depth** in great detail; comprehensively and thoroughly: *research students pursue a specific aspect of a subject in depth.* See also **IN-DEPTH**. **out of one's depth** in water too deep to stand in. ■ figurative in the position of lacking the ability or knowledge to cope.
– ORIGIN late Middle English: from **DEEP** + **-TH**[2], on the pattern of pairs such as *long, length*.

depth charge ▶ **noun** an explosive charge designed to be dropped from a ship or aircraft and to explode under water at a preset depth, used for attacking submarines.

depth finder ▶ **noun** an echo sounder or other device for measuring water depth.

depth gauge ▶ **noun** a device fitted to a drill bit to ensure that the hole drilled does not exceed the required depth.

depthless ▶ **adjective** unfathomably deep: *a depthless gorge.*
■ figurative shallow and superficial.
– DERIVATIVES **depthlessly** adverb.

depth of field ▶ **noun** the distance between the nearest and the furthest objects that give an image judged to be in focus in a camera.

depth of focus ▶ **noun** **1** another term for **DEPTH OF FIELD**.
2 the distance between the two extreme axial points behind a lens at which an image is judged to be in focus.

depth psychology ▶ **noun** [mass noun] the study of unconscious mental processes and motives, especially in psychoanalytic theory and practice.

depth sounder ▶ **noun** another term for **ECHO SOUNDER**.

depurate /dɪˈpjʊəreɪt, ˈdɛpjʊreɪt/ ▶ **verb** [with obj.] rare free (something) of impurities.
– DERIVATIVES **depuration** noun, **depurative** adjective & noun, **depurator** noun.
– ORIGIN early 17th cent.: from medieval Latin *depurat-* 'purified', from the verb *depurare*, from *de-* 'completely' + *purare* 'purify' (from *purus* 'pure').

deputation ▶ **noun** a group of people appointed to undertake a mission or take part in a formal process on behalf of a larger group: *he had been a member of a deputation to Napoleon III.*
– ORIGIN late Middle English (in the sense 'appointment to an office or function'): from late Latin *deputatio(n-)*, from the verb *deputare* (see **DEPUTE**).

depute ▶ **verb** /dɪˈpjuːt/ [with obj. and infinitive] appoint or instruct (someone) to perform a task for which one is responsible: *she was deputed to look after him while Clarissa was away.*
■ [with obj.] delegate (authority or a task).
▶ **noun** /ˈdɛpjuːt/ Scottish a person appointed to act in an official capacity or as a representative of another official: [as modifier] *a depute chairman.*
– ORIGIN late Middle English: via Old French from Latin *deputare* 'consider to be, assign', from *de-* 'away'+ *putare* 'think over, consider'.

deputize /ˈdɛpjʊtʌɪz/ ▶ **verb** [no obj.] temporarily act or speak on behalf of someone else: *she got a job **deputizing for** a lecturer on maternity leave.*
■ [with obj.] N. Amer. make (someone) a deputy.

deputy ▶ **noun** (pl. **-ies**) a person whose immediate superior is a senior figure within an organization and who acts for this superior in their absence.
■ a parliamentary representative in certain countries. ■ Brit. a coal mine official responsible for safety.
– PHRASES **by deputy** historical instructing another person to act in one's stead; by proxy: *the wardens of the forests performed important duties by deputy.*
– DERIVATIVES **deputyship** noun.
– ORIGIN late Middle English: from Old French *depute*, from late Latin *deputatus*, past participle of *deputare* (see **DEPUTE**).

deputy lieutenant ▶ **noun** (in the UK) the deputy of the Lord Lieutenant of a county.

De Quincey /də ˈkwɪnsi/, Thomas (1785–1859), English essayist and critic. He achieved fame with his *Confessions of an English Opium Eater* (1822), a study of his addiction to opium and its psychological effects.

deracinate /dɪˈrasɪneɪt/ ▶ **verb** [with obj.] poetic/literary tear (something) up by the roots.
– DERIVATIVES **deracination** noun.
– ORIGIN late 16th cent.: from French *déraciner*, from *dé-* (expressing removal) + *racine* 'root' (based on Latin *radix*).

deracinated ▶ **adjective** another term for **DÉRACINÉ**.

déraciné /deɪˈrasɪneɪ, French derasine/ ▶ **adjective** uprooted or displaced from one's geographical or social environment: *the self-consciousness of déraciné Americans.*
▶ **noun** a person who has been or feels so displaced.
– ORIGIN French, 'uprooted'.

derail ▶ **verb** [with obj.] (usu. **be derailed**) cause (a train or tram) to leave its tracks accidentally: *a train was derailed after it collided with a herd of cattle.*
■ [no obj.] (of a train or tram) accidentally leave the tracks: *the trams had a tendency to derail on sharp corners.* ■ [with obj.] figurative obstruct (a process) by diverting it from its intended course: *the plot is seen by some as an attempt to derail the negotiations.*
– DERIVATIVES **derailment** noun.
– ORIGIN mid 19th cent.: from French *dérailler*, from *dé-* (expressing removal) + *rail* 'rail'.

derailleur /dɪˈreɪl(j)ə/ ▶ **noun** a bicycle gear which works by lifting the chain from one sprocket wheel to another of a different size.
– ORIGIN 1930s: from French, from *dérailler* 'derail'.

Derain /ˈdərã, French dərɛ̃/, André (1880–1954), French painter, one of the exponents of fauvism. He also designed theatre sets and costumes, notably for the Ballets Russes.

derange ▶ **verb** [with obj.] [usu. as adj. **deranged**] cause (someone) to become insane: *a deranged man.*
■ throw (something) into confusion; cause to act irregularly: *stress deranges the immune system.* ■ archaic intrude on; interrupt: *I am sorry to have deranged you for so small a matter.*
– DERIVATIVES **derangement** noun.
– ORIGIN late 18th cent.: from French *déranger*, from Old French *desrengier*, literally 'move from orderly rows'.

derate ▶ **verb** [with obj.] **1** Brit. (under the former rates system) remove part or all of the burden of rates from (a property or business).
2 reduce the power rating of (a component or device): *the engines were derated to 90 horse power.*

deration ▶ **verb** [with obj.] (usu. **be derationed**) free (a commodity) of rationing restrictions.

Derbent /dəˈbɛnt/ a city in southern Russia, in Dagestan on the western shore of the Caspian Sea; pop. 80,000 (1985).

Derby[1] /ˈdɑːbi/ a city in the Midlands of England, on the River Derwent; pop. 214,000 (1991).

Derby[2] /ˈdɑːbi/ Edward George Geoffrey Smith Stanley, 14th Earl of (1799–1869), British Conservative statesman, Prime Minister 1852, 1858–9, and 1866–8. In his last term as Prime Minister he carried the second Reform Act (1867) through Parliament.

Derby[3] /ˈdɑːbi/ ▶ **noun** (pl. **-ies**) **1** an annual flat horse race for three-year-olds, founded in 1780 by the 12th Earl of Derby. The race is run on Epsom Downs in England in late May or early June.
■ a similar race elsewhere: *the Irish Derby.* ■ [in names] an important sporting contest: *the showjumping Derby at Hickstead.* ■ (**derby**) another term for **LOCAL DERBY**.
2 (**derby**) N. Amer. a bowler hat. [ORIGIN: said to be from American demand for a hat of the type worn at the Epsom Derby.]
3 a boot or shoe having the eyelet tabs stitched on top of the vamp. [ORIGIN: so named because originally a sporting boot.]

Derby[4] /ˈdɑːbi/ ▶ **noun** [mass noun] a hard pressed cheese made from skimmed milk, chiefly in Derbyshire.

Derby Day ▶ **noun** the day on which the Derby is run.

Derbyshire /ˈdɑːbɪʃɪə, -ʃə/ a county of north central England; county town, Matlock.

Derbyshire neck ▶ **noun** [mass noun] historical goitre, formerly endemic in parts of Derbyshire.

de re /deɪ ˈreɪ, diː/ ▶ **adjective** Philosophy relating to the properties of things mentioned in an assertion or expression, rather than to the assertion or expression itself. Compare with **DE DICTO**.
– ORIGIN Latin, literally 'about the thing'.

derealization (also **-isation**) ▶ **noun** [mass noun] a feeling that one's surroundings are not real, especially as a symptom of mental disturbance.
– DERIVATIVES **derealized** adjective.

derecognize (also **-ise**) ▶ **verb** [with obj.] withdraw recognition of (an organization or country).
– DERIVATIVES **derecognition** noun.

dereference /diːˈrɛfərəns/ ▶ **verb** [with obj.] Computing obtain the address of a data item held in another location from (a pointer).

deregister ▶ **verb** [with obj.] remove from a register: *scores of patients have been deregistered by the practices.*
■ [no obj.] remove one's name from a register.
– DERIVATIVES **deregistration** noun.

de règle /də ˈrɛgl(ə), French də ʀɛgl/ ▶ **adjective** required by custom; proper: *it shall be de règle for guests to come in afternoon dresses.*
– ORIGIN French, literally 'of rule'.

deregulate ▶ **verb** [with obj.] remove regulations or restrictions from: *the trucking industry was deregulated in the early 1980s.*
– DERIVATIVES **deregulation** noun, **deregulatory** adjective.

derelict ▶ **adjective** in a very poor condition as a result of disuse and neglect: *a derelict Georgian mansion | the barge **lay derelict** for years.*
■ chiefly N. Amer. (of a person) shamefully negligent in not having done what one should have done: *he was **derelict in** his duty to his country.*
▶ **noun** a person without a home, job, or property: *derelicts who could fit all their possessions in a paper bag.*
■ a piece of property, especially a ship, abandoned by the owner and in poor condition.
– ORIGIN mid 17th cent.: from Latin *derelictus* 'abandoned', past participle of *derelinquere*, from *de-* 'completely' + *relinquere* 'forsake'.

dereliction ▶ **noun** [mass noun] the state of having been abandoned and become dilapidated: *a 15th-century farmhouse has been saved from dereliction.*
■ (usu. **dereliction of duty**) the shameful failure to fulfil one's obligations.
– ORIGIN late 16th cent.: from Latin *derelictio(n-)*, from the verb *derelinquere* (see **DERELICT**).

derepress /ˌdiːrɪˈprɛs/ ▶ **verb** [with obj.] Biochemistry & Genetics activate (enzymes, genes, etc.) from an inoperative or latent state.
– DERIVATIVES **derepression** noun.

derequisition ▶ **verb** [with obj.] dated return (requisitioned property) to its former owner.

derestrict ▶ **verb** [with obj.] remove restrictions from.
– DERIVATIVES **derestriction** noun.

deride /dɪˈrʌɪd/ ▶ **verb** [with obj.] express contempt for; ridicule: *critics derided the proposals as clumsy attempts to find a solution.*
– DERIVATIVES **derider** noun.
– ORIGIN mid 16th cent.: from Latin *deridere* 'scoff at'.

de-rig ▶ **verb** [with obj.] dismantle the rigging of (a ship, boat, or light aircraft).

de rigueur /ˌdə rɪˈɡəː/ ▶ **adjective** required by etiquette or current fashion: *it was de rigueur for bands to grow their hair long.*
– ORIGIN mid 19th cent.: French, literally 'in strictness'.

derision /dɪˈrɪʒ(ə)n/ ▶ **noun** [mass noun] contemptuous ridicule or mockery: *my stories were greeted with derision and disbelief.*
– PHRASES **hold** (or **have**) **in derision** archaic regard with mockery.
– DERIVATIVES **derisible** /dɪˈrɪzɪb(ə)l/ adjective.
– ORIGIN late Middle English: via Old French from late Latin *derisio(n-)*, from *deridere* 'scoff at'.

derisive /dɪˈrʌɪsɪv, -z-/ ▶ **adjective** expressing contempt or ridicule: *he gave a harsh, derisive laugh.*
– DERIVATIVES **derisively** adverb, **derisiveness** noun.
– ORIGIN mid 17th cent.: from **DERISION**, on the pattern of the pair *decision, decisive*.

derisory /dɪˈrʌɪs(ə)ri, -z-/ ▶ **adjective 1** ridiculously small or inadequate: *they were given a derisory pay rise.*
2 another term for **DERISIVE**: *his derisory gaze swept over her.*
– ORIGIN early 17th cent. (in the sense 'derisive'): from late Latin *derisorius*, from *deris-* 'scoffed at', from the verb *deridere* (see **DERISION**).

> **USAGE** Although the words **derisory** and **derisive** share similar roots they have different core meanings. **Derisory** usually means 'ridiculously small or inadequate', as in *a* ***derisory*** *pay offer* or *the security arrangements were* ***derisory***. **Derisive**, on the other hand, is used to mean 'showing contempt', as in *he gave a* ***derisive*** *laugh.*

derivate /ˈdɛrɪvət, -eɪt/ ▶ **noun** something derived, especially a product obtained chemically from a raw material.
– ORIGIN late Middle English: from Latin *derivat-* 'derived', from the verb *derivare* (see **DERIVE**).

derivation ▶ **noun** [mass noun] the obtaining or developing of something from a source or origin: *the* ***derivation*** *of scientific laws* ***from*** *observation.*
■ the formation of a word from another word or from a root in the same or another language. ■ Linguistics the set of stages that link a sentence in a natural language to its underlying logical form. ■ [count noun] Mathematics a sequence of statements showing that a formula, theorem, etc., is a consequence of previously accepted statements. ■ Mathematics the process of deducing a new formula, theorem, etc., from previously accepted statements.
– DERIVATIVES **derivational** adjective.
– ORIGIN late Middle English (denoting the drawing of a fluid, specifically the drawing of pus or blood; also in the sense 'formation of a word from another word'): from Latin *derivatio(n-)*, from the verb *derivare* (see **DERIVE**).

derivative /dɪˈrɪvətɪv/ ▶ **adjective** (typically of an artist or work of art) imitative of the work of another person, and usually disapproved of for that reason: *an artist who is not in the slightest bit derivative.*
■ originating from, based on, or influenced by: *Darwin's work is* ***derivative of*** *the moral philosophers.* ■ [attrib.] (of a financial product) having a value deriving from an underlying variable asset: *equity-based derivative products.*
▶ **noun** something which is based on another source: *the aircraft is a derivative of the Falcon 20G.*
■ (often **derivatives**) an arrangement or instrument (such as a future, option, or warrant) whose value derives from and is dependent on the value of an underlying asset: [as modifier] *the derivatives market.* ■ a word derived from another or from a root in the same or another language. ■ a substance that is derived chemically from a specified compound: *crack is a highly addictive cocaine derivative.* ■ Mathematics an expression representing the rate of change of a function with respect to an independent variable.
– DERIVATIVES **derivatively** adverb.
– ORIGIN late Middle English (in the adjective sense 'having the power to draw off', and in the noun sense 'a word derived from another'): from French *dérivatif, -ive*, from Latin *derivativus*, from *derivare* (see **DERIVE**).

derive /dɪˈrʌɪv/ ▶ **verb** [with obj.] (**derive something from**) obtain something from (a specified source): *they derived great comfort from this assurance.*
■ (**derive something from**) base a concept on a logical extension or modification of (another concept): *Marx derived his philosophy of history from Hegel.* ■ [no obj.] (**derive from**) (of a word) have (a specified word, usually of another language) as a root or origin: *the word 'punch' derives from the Hindustani 'pancha'* | (**be derived from**) *the word 'man' is derived from the Sanskrit 'manas'.* ■ [no obj.] (**derive from**) arise from or originate in (a specified source): *words whose spelling derives from Dr Johnson's incorrect etymology.* ■ (**be derived from**) Linguistics (of a sentence in a natural language) be linked by a set of stages to (its underlying logical form). ■ (**be derived from**) (of a substance) be formed or prepared by (a chemical or physical process affecting another substance): *strong acids are derived from the combustion of fossil fuels.* ■ Mathematics obtain (a function or equation) from another by a sequence of logical steps, for example by differentiation.
– DERIVATIVES **derivable** adjective.
– ORIGIN late Middle English (in the sense 'draw a fluid through or into a channel'): from Old French *deriver* or Latin *derivare*, from *de-* 'down, away' + *rivus* 'brook, stream'.

derived demand ▶ **noun** Economics a demand for a commodity, service, etc. which is a consequence of the demand for something else.

derived fossil ▶ **noun** a fossil redeposited in a sediment which is younger than the one in which it first occurred.

derm /dəːm/ ▶ **noun** another term for **DERMIS**.

derma[1] /ˈdəːmə/ ▶ **noun** another term for **DERMIS**.
– ORIGIN early 18th cent.: modern Latin, from Greek 'skin'.

derma[2] /ˈdəːmə/ ▶ **noun** [mass noun] beef or chicken intestine, stuffed and cooked in dishes such as kishke.
– ORIGIN from Yiddish *derme*, plural of *darm* 'intestine'; related to Old English *tharm* 'intestine'.

dermabrasion /ˌdəːməˈbreɪʒ(ə)n/ ▶ **noun** [mass noun] the removal of superficial layers of skin with a rapidly revolving abrasive tool, as a technique in cosmetic surgery.
– ORIGIN 1950s: from Greek *derma* 'skin' + **ABRASION**.

Dermaptera /dəːˈmaptərə/ Entomology an order of insects that comprises the earwigs.
– DERIVATIVES **dermapteran** noun & adjective, **dermapterous** adjective.
– ORIGIN modern Latin (plural), from Greek *derma* 'skin' + *pteron* 'wing'.

dermatitis /ˌdəːməˈtʌɪtɪs/ ▶ **noun** [mass noun] a condition of the skin in which it becomes red, swollen, and sore, sometimes with small blisters, resulting from direct irritation of the skin by an external agent or an allergic reaction to it. Compare with **ECZEMA**.
– ORIGIN late 19th cent.: from Greek *derma, dermat-* 'skin' + **-ITIS**.

dermato- /ˈdəːmətəʊ/ ▶ **combining form** of or relating to the skin: *dermatomycosis.*
– ORIGIN from Greek *derma, dermat-* 'skin, hide'.

dermatoglyphics /ˌdəːmətə(ʊ)ˈglɪfɪks/ ▶ **plural noun** [treated as sing.] the study of skin markings or patterns on fingers, hands, and feet, and its application, especially in criminology.
– DERIVATIVES **dermatoglyph** noun, **dermatoglyphic** adjective, **dermatoglyphically** adverb.
– ORIGIN 1920s: from **DERMATO-** 'skin' + Greek *gluphikos* 'carved' (from *gluphē* 'carving').

dermatology /ˌdəːməˈtɒlədʒi/ ▶ **noun** [mass noun] the branch of medicine concerned with the diagnosis and treatment of skin disorders.
– DERIVATIVES **dermatological** adjective, **dermatologically** adverb, **dermatologist** noun.

dermatome /ˈdəːmətəʊm/ ▶ **noun** Embryology the lateral wall of each somite in a vertebrate embryo, giving rise to the connective tissue of the skin. Compare with **MYOTOME, SCLEROTOME**.
■ Physiology an area of the skin supplied by nerves from a single spinal root.

dermatomycosis /ˌdəːmətə(ʊ)mʌɪˈkəʊsɪs/ ▶ **noun** (pl. **dermatomycoses** /-siːz/) [mass noun] a fungal infection of the skin, especially by a dermatophyte.

dermatomyositis /ˌdəːmətə(ʊ)mʌɪə(ʊ)ˈsʌɪtɪs/ ▶ **noun** [mass noun] Medicine inflammation of the skin and underlying muscle tissue, involving degeneration of collagen, discoloration, and swelling, typically occurring as an autoimmune condition or associated with internal cancer.

dermatophyte /ˈdəːmətə(ʊ)fʌɪt/ ▶ **noun** a pathogenic fungus that grows on skin, mucous membranes, hair, nails, feathers, and other body surfaces, causing ringworm and related diseases.
● *Trichophyton* and other genera, subdivision Deuteromycotina.
– DERIVATIVES **dermatophytic** adjective.

dermatophytosis /ˌdəːmətə(ʊ)fʌɪˈtəʊsɪs/ ▶ **noun** (pl. **dermatophytoses** /-siːz/) another term for **DERMATOMYCOSIS**.

dermatosis /ˌdəːməˈtəʊsɪs/ ▶ **noun** (pl. **dermatoses** /-siːz/) [mass noun] a disease of the skin, especially one that does not cause inflammation.

dermestid /dəːˈmɛstɪd/ ▶ **noun** Entomology a small beetle of a family (Dermestidae) that includes many kinds which are destructive (especially as larvae) to hides, skin, fur, wool, and other animal substances.
– ORIGIN late 19th cent.: from modern Latin *Dermestidae* (plural), from the genus name *Dermestes*, formed irregularly from Greek *derma* 'skin' + *esthiein* 'eat'.

dermis /ˈdəːmɪs/ ▶ **noun** [mass noun] technical the skin.
■ Anatomy the thick layer of living tissue below the epidermis which forms the true skin, containing blood capillaries, nerve endings, sweat glands, hair follicles, and other structures.
– DERIVATIVES **dermal** adjective, **dermic** adjective (rare).
– ORIGIN mid 19th cent.: modern Latin, suggested by *epidermis*.

dermoid /ˈdəːmɔɪd/ ▶ **noun** short for **DERMOID CYST**.

dermoid cyst ▶ **noun** Medicine an abnormal growth (teratoma) containing epidermis, hair follicles, and sebaceous glands, derived from residual embryonic cells.

Dermoptera /dəːˈmɒptərə/ Zoology a small order of mammals which comprises the flying lemurs or colugos.
– ORIGIN modern Latin (plural), from Greek *derma* 'skin' + *pteron* 'wing'.

dernier cri /dɛːnjeɪ ˈkriː/ ▶ **noun** (**the/le dernier cri**) the very latest fashion.
– ORIGIN late 19th cent.: French, literally 'last cry'.

derogate /ˈdɛrəgeɪt/ ▶ **verb** formal **1** [no obj.] (**derogate from**) detract from: *this does not derogate from his duty to act honestly and faithfully.*
2 [no obj.] (**derogate from**) deviate from (a set of rules or agreed form of behaviour): *one country has derogated from the Rome Convention.*
3 [with obj.] disparage (someone or something): *it is typical of him to derogate the powers of reason.*
– DERIVATIVES **derogative** adjective.
– ORIGIN late Middle English: from Latin *derogat-* 'abrogated', from the verb *derogare*, from *de-* 'aside, away' + *rogare* 'ask'.

derogation ▶ **noun 1** an exemption from or relaxation of a rule or law: *countries assuming a* ***derogation from*** *EC law.*
2 [mass noun] the perception or treatment of someone or something as being of little worth: *the derogation of women.*
– ORIGIN late Middle English (in the sense 'impairment of the force of'): from Latin *derogatio(n-)*, from the verb *derogare* (see **DEROGATE**).

derogatory /dɪˈrɒgət(ə)ri/ ▶ **adjective** showing a critical or disrespectful attitude: *she tells me I'm fat and is always making derogatory remarks.*
– DERIVATIVES **derogatorily** adverb.
– ORIGIN early 16th cent. (in the sense 'impairing in force or effect'): from late Latin *derogatorius*, from *derogat-* 'abrogated', from the verb *derogare* (see **DEROGATE**).

derrick /ˈdɛrɪk/ ▶ **noun 1** a kind of crane with a movable pivoted arm for moving or lifting heavy weights, especially on a ship.
2 the framework over an oil well or similar boring, holding the drilling machinery.
– ORIGIN early 17th cent. (denoting a hangman, also the gallows): from *Derrick*, the surname of a London hangman.

Derrida /ˈdɛrɪdə, French dɛʀida/, Jacques (b.1930), French philosopher and critic, the most important figure in deconstruction. Notable works: *Of Grammatology* (1967) and *Writing and Difference* (1967).
– DERIVATIVES **Derridean** /ˌdɛrɪˈdɪən/ adjective & noun.

derrière /ˌdɛrɪˈɛː/ ▶ **noun** informal euphemistic term for a person's buttocks.
– ORIGIN late 18th cent.: French, literally 'behind'.

derring-do /ˌdɛrɪŋˈduː/ ▶ **noun** [mass noun] dated or humorous action displaying heroic courage: *tales of derring-do.*
– ORIGIN late 16th cent.: from late Middle English *dorryng do* 'daring to do', used by Chaucer, and, in a passage by Lydgate based on Chaucer's work, misprinted in 16th-cent. editions as *derrynge do*; this was misinterpreted by Spenser to mean 'manhood, chivalry', and subsequently taken up and popularized by Sir Walter Scott.

derringer /ˈdɛrɪn(d)ʒə/ ▶ **noun** a small pistol with a large bore, which is very effective at close range.
– ORIGIN mid 19th cent.: named after Henry *Deringer* (1786–1868), the American gunsmith who invented it.

derris /ˈdɛrɪs/ ▶ **noun 1** [mass noun] an insecticide made from the powdered roots of certain tropical plants, containing rotenone. [ORIGIN: late 19th cent.: originally used in Malaya to stupefy fish.]
2 a woody climbing plant of the pea family, which bears leathery pods and has tuberous roots from which this insecticide is obtained. [ORIGIN: modern Latin, from Greek, 'leather covering' (referring to its pod).]
● Genus *Derris*, family Leguminosae.

Derry see **LONDONDERRY**.

derry ▶ **noun** (in phrase **have a derry on someone**) Austral./NZ informal be prejudiced against someone.
– ORIGIN late 19th cent.: apparently from the song refrain *derry down*.

derv (also **DERV**) ▶ **noun** [mass noun] Brit. diesel oil for road vehicles.
– ORIGIN 1940s (apparently Second World War forces' slang): acronym from *diesel-engined road-vehicle*.

dervish /ˈdəːvɪʃ/ ▶ **noun** a Muslim (specifically Sufi) religious man who has taken vows of poverty and austerity. Dervishes first appeared in the 12th century; they were noted for their wild or ecstatic rituals and were known as **dancing**, **whirling**, or **howling dervishes** according to the practice of their order.
– ORIGIN from Turkish *derviş*, from Persian *darvīš* 'poor', (as a noun) 'religious mendicant'.

DES ▶ **abbreviation for** (in the UK) Department of Education and Science (replaced in 1992 by the Department for Education).

desacralize /diːˈsakrəlʌɪz/ (also **-ise**) ▶ **verb** [with obj.] remove the religious or sacred status or significance from.
– DERIVATIVES **desacralization** noun.

de Sade, Marquis, see **SADE**.

desalinate /diːˈsalɪneɪt/ ▶ **verb** [with obj.] [usu. as adj. **desalinated**] remove salt from (seawater).
– DERIVATIVES **desalination** noun, **desalinator** noun.

desalinize ▶ **verb** US term for **DESALINATE**.
– DERIVATIVES **desalinization** noun.

desalt ▶ **verb** another term for **DESALINATE**.

desaparecido /ˌdɛzəparəˈsiːdəʊ, Spanish desapareˈsido, -ˈθido/ ▶ **noun** (pl. **-os**) (especially in South America) a person who has disappeared, presumed killed by members of the armed services or the police.
– ORIGIN Spanish, literally 'disappeared'.

desaturate ▶ **verb** [with obj.] make less saturated; cause to become unsaturated.
– DERIVATIVES **desaturation** noun.

descale ▶ **verb** [with obj.] remove deposits of scale from.
– DERIVATIVES **descaler** noun.

descamisado /dɛsˌkamɪˈsɑːdəʊ/ ▶ **noun** (pl. **-os**) (in Latin America) a very poor person.
– ORIGIN Spanish, literally 'shirtless'.

descant ▶ **noun** /ˈdɛskant/ Music an independent treble melody usually sung or played above a basic melody.
■ archaic or poetic/literary a melodious song. ■ a discourse on a theme or subject: *his descant of deprivation*.
▶ **verb** /dɪˈskant, dɛ-/ [no obj.] talk tediously or at length: *I have **descanted on** this subject before*.
– ORIGIN late Middle English: from Old French *deschant*, from medieval Latin *discantus* 'part-song, refrain'.

descant recorder ▶ **noun** the most common size of recorder (musical instrument), with a range of two octaves from the C above middle C upwards.

Descartes /ˈdeɪkɑːt, French dekaʀt/, René (1596–1650), French philosopher, mathematician, and man of science.

> Aiming to reach totally secure foundations for knowledge, he concluded that everything was open to doubt except his own conscious experience, and his existence as a necessary condition of this: *'Cogito, ergo sum'* (I think, therefore I am). From this certainty he developed a dualistic theory regarding mind and matter as separate though interacting. In mathematics Descartes developed the use of coordinates to locate a point in two or three dimensions.

descend ▶ **verb** [no obj.] **1** move or fall downwards: *the aircraft began to descend*.
■ [with obj.] move down (a slope or stairs): *the vehicle descended a ramp*. ■ (of stairs, a road or path, or a piece of land) be on a slope or incline and extend downwards: *a side road descended into the forest* | [with obj.] *a narrow flight of stairs descended a steep slope*. ■ come or go down a scale, especially from the superior to the inferior: [as adj. **descending**] *the categories are listed in descending order of usefulness*. ■ Music (of sound) become lower in pitch: [as adj. **descending**] *a passage of descending chords*. ■ (**descend to**) act in a specified shameful way that is far below one's usual standards: *he was scrupulous in refusing to descend to misrepresentation*. ■ (**descend into**) (of a situation or group of people) reach (a state considered undesirable or shameful): *the army had descended into chaos*.
2 (**descend on/upon**) make a sudden attack on: *the militia descended on Rye*.
■ (**descend on/upon**) make an unexpected and typically unwelcome visit to: *groups of visiting supporters descended on a local pub*. ■ (of a feeling or atmosphere) develop suddenly and be felt throughout a place or by a person or group of people: *an air of gloom descended on Labour party headquarters*. ■ (of night or darkness) begin to occur: *as the winter darkness descended, the fighting ceased*.
3 (**be descended from**) be a blood relative of (a specified, typically illustrious ancestor): *John Dalrymple **was descended from** an ancient Ayrshire family*.
■ (of an asset) pass by inheritance, typically from parent to child: *his lands **descended to** his eldest son*.
– DERIVATIVES **descendent** adjective.
– ORIGIN Middle English: from Old French *descendre*, from Latin *descendere*, from *de-* 'down' + *scandere* 'to climb'.

descendant ▶ **noun** a person, plant, or animal that is descended from a particular ancestor: *Shakespeare's last direct descendant*.
■ a machine, artefact, system, etc., that has developed from an earlier, more rudimentary version.
– ORIGIN late Middle English (as an adjective in the sense 'descending'): from French, present participle of *descendre* 'to descend' (see **DESCEND**). The noun dates from the early 17th cent.

descender ▶ **noun** a part of a letter that extends below the level of the base of a letter such as *x* (as in *g* and *p*).
■ a letter having such a part.

descendeur /dɪˈsɛndə/ ▶ **noun** Climbing a piece of metal around which a rope is passed, which makes use of friction to slow descent during abseiling.
– ORIGIN late 20th cent.: from French, literally 'descender'.

descendible ▶ **adjective** Law (of property) able to be inherited by a descendant.

descending colon ▶ **noun** Anatomy the part of the large intestine which passes downwards on the left side of the abdomen towards the rectum.

descent ▶ **noun** **1** [usu. in sing.] an action of moving downwards, dropping, or falling: *the plane had gone into a steep descent*.
■ a downward slope, especially a path or track: *a steep, badly eroded descent*. ■ a moral, social, or psychological decline into a specified undesirable state: *the ancient empire's slow **descent into** barbarism*.
2 [mass noun] the origin or background of a person in terms of family or nationality: *most of the settlers were **of** Cornish **descent***.
■ the transmission of qualities, property, or privileges by inheritance.
3 (**descent on**) a sudden violent attack: *a descent on the Channel ports*.
■ an unexpected visit, especially an unwelcome one.
– ORIGIN Middle English: from Old French *descente*, from *descendre* 'to descend' (see **DESCEND**).

descramble ▶ **verb** [with obj.] convert or restore (a signal) to intelligible form.
– DERIVATIVES **descrambler** noun.

describe ▶ **verb** [with obj.] **1** give an account in words of (someone or something), including all the relevant characteristics, qualities, or events: *the police said the man was **described as** white, 6 ft tall, with mousy, cropped hair*.
2 mark out or draw (a geometrical figure): *on the diameter of a circle an equilateral triangle is described*.
■ move in a way which follows the outline of (an imaginary geometrical figure): *a single light is seen to describe a circle*.
– DERIVATIVES **describable** adjective, **describer** noun.
– ORIGIN late Middle English: from Latin *describere*, from *de-* 'down' + *scribere* 'write'.

description ▶ **noun** **1** a spoken or written representation or account of a person, object, or event: *people who had seen him were able to give a description*.
■ [mass noun] the action of giving such a representation or account: *teaching by demonstration and description*.
2 a sort, kind, or class of people or things: *it is laughably easy to buy drugs **of all descriptions***.
– PHRASES **beyond description** to a great and astonishing extent: *his face was swollen beyond description*. **defy description** be so unusual or remarkable as to be impossible to describe: *the sheer scale of the Requiem defies description*.
– ORIGIN late Middle English: via Old French from Latin *descriptio(n-)*, from *describere* 'write down'.

descriptive ▶ **adjective** **1** serving or seeking to describe.
■ Grammar (of an adjective) assigning a quality rather than restricting the application of the expression modified, e.g. *blue* as distinct from *few*.
2 describing or classifying without expressing feelings or judging.
■ Linguistics denoting or relating to an approach to language analysis that describes accents, forms, structures, and usage without making value judgements. Often contrasted with **PRESCRIPTIVE**.
– DERIVATIVES **descriptively** adverb, **descriptiveness** noun.
– ORIGIN mid 18th cent.: from late Latin *descriptivus*, from *descript-* 'written down', from the verb *describere* (see **DESCRIBE**).

descriptivism ▶ **noun** [mass noun] Philosophy the doctrine that the meanings of ethical or aesthetic terms and statements are purely descriptive rather than prescriptive, evaluative, or emotive.
– DERIVATIVES **descriptivist** noun & adjective.

descriptor ▶ **noun** an element or term that has the function of describing, identifying, or indexing, in particular:
■ Linguistics a word or expression used to describe or identify something. ■ Computing a piece of stored data that indicates how other data is stored.

descry /dɪˈskrʌɪ/ ▶ **verb** (**-ies**, **-ied**) [with obj.] poetic/literary catch sight of: *she descried two figures*.
– ORIGIN Middle English: perhaps confused with obsolete *descry* 'describe', variant of obsolete *descrive* (via Old French from Latin *describere* 'write down'), which also had the meaning 'perceive'.

desecrate /ˈdɛsɪkreɪt/ ▶ **verb** [with obj.] (often **be desecrated**) treat (a sacred place or thing) with violent disrespect; violate: *more than 300 graves were desecrated*.
■ figurative spoil (something which is valued or respected): *many lanes are desecrated with yellow lines*.
– DERIVATIVES **desecration** noun, **desecrator** noun.
– ORIGIN late 17th cent.: from **DE-** (expressing reversal) + a shortened form of **CONSECRATE**.

deseed ▶ **verb** [with obj.] [usu. as adj. **deseeded**] remove the seeds from (a plant, vegetable, or fruit).
– DERIVATIVES **deseeder** noun.

desegregate ▶ **verb** [with obj.] end a policy of racial segregation in: *actions to desegregate colleges and schools*.
– DERIVATIVES **desegregation** noun.

deselect ▶ **verb** [with obj.] **1** Brit. (of a local branch of a political party) reject (an existing Member of Parliament) as a candidate in a forthcoming election.
2 turn off (a selected feature) on a list of options on a computer menu.
– DERIVATIVES **deselection** noun.

desensitize (also **-ise**) ▶ **verb** [with obj.] make less sensitive: *creams to desensitize the skin at the site of the injection*.
■ make (someone) less likely to feel shock or distress at scenes of cruelty, violence, or suffering by overexposure to such images: [as adj. **desensitized**] *people who view such movies become desensitized to violence*. ■ free (someone) from a phobia or neurosis by gradually exposing them to the thing that is feared. See **SYSTEMATIC DESENSITIZATION**.
– DERIVATIVES **desensitization** noun, **desensitizer** noun.

desert[1] /dɪˈzəːt/ ▶ **verb** [with obj.] abandon (a person, cause, or organization) in a way considered disloyal or treacherous: *he deserted his wife and daughter and went back to England*.
■ [usu. as adj. **deserted**] (of a number of people) leave (a place), causing it to appear empty: *the lobby of the hotel was virtually deserted*. ■ (of a quality or ability) fail (someone), especially at a crucial moment when most needed: *her luck deserted her*. ■ [no obj.] Military (of a soldier) illegally run away from military service.
– DERIVATIVES **desertion** noun.
– ORIGIN late Middle English: from Old French *deserter*, from late Latin *desertare*, from Latin *desertus* 'left waste' (see **DESERT**[2]).

desert[2] /ˈdɛzət/ ▶ **noun** a dry, barren area of land, especially one covered with sand, that is characteristically desolate, waterless, and without vegetation.
■ a lifeless and unpleasant place, especially one comprising or covered with a specified substance: *a*

desert of lead-mine spoil. ▪a situation or area considered dull and uninteresting: *a cultural desert.*
▶ **adjective** [attrib.] like a desert: *overgrazing has created desert conditions.*
▪uninhabited and desolate: *desert wastes.*
– ORIGIN Middle English: via Old French from late Latin *desertum* 'something left waste', neuter past participle of *deserere* 'leave, forsake'.

desert[3] /dɪˈzəːt/ ▶ **noun** (usu. **deserts**) a person's worthiness or entitlement to reward or punishment: *the penal system fails to punish offenders in accordance with their deserts.*
– PHRASES **get** (or **receive**) **one's just deserts** receive the appropriate reward or (more usually) punishment for one's actions: *those who caused great torment to others rarely got their just deserts.*
– ORIGIN Middle English: via Old French from *deservir* 'serve well' (see **DESERVE**).

desert boot ▶ **noun** a lightweight boot with the upper made from suede.

deserter ▶ **noun** a member of the armed forces who deserts: *deserters from the army.*
– ORIGIN mid 17th cent.: from **DESERT**[1], on the pattern of French *déserteur.*

desertification /dɛˌzəːtɪfɪˈkeɪʃ(ə)n/ ▶ **noun** [mass noun] the process by which fertile land becomes desert, typically as a result of drought, deforestation, or inappropriate agriculture.

desert island ▶ **noun** a remote tropical island, typically uninhabited.

desert oak ▶ **noun** an Australian casuarina tree, which typically grows in arid regions.
• *Casuarina decaisneana*, family Casuarinaceae.

desert pavement ▶ **noun** Geology a surface layer of closely packed or cemented pebbles, rock fragments, etc., from which fine material has been removed by the wind in arid regions.

desert rat ▶ **noun** informal a soldier of the 7th British armoured division (with the jerboa as a badge) in the North African desert campaign of 1941–2.

desert rose ▶ **noun** **1** a flower-like aggregate of crystals of a mineral, occurring in arid areas.
2 a succulent plant with pink tubular flowers and a swollen woody stem containing toxic milky sap that is sometimes used for arrow poison. It is native to East Africa and Arabia.
• *Adenium obesum*, family Apocynaceae.
3 (also **Sturt's desert rose**) a dense shrub with pinkish-lilac flowers and black spotted leaves and fruit. Native to arid regions of Australia, it is the floral emblem of the Northern Territory of Australia.
• *Gossypium sturtianum*, family Malvaceae.

Desert Storm syndrome ▶ **noun** another term for **GULF WAR SYNDROME**.
– ORIGIN from Operation *Desert Storm*, the name of the Allied Forces' land campaign in the 1991 Gulf War.

desert varnish ▶ **noun** [mass noun] Geology a dark hard film of oxides formed on exposed rock surfaces in arid regions.

deserve ▶ **verb** [with obj.] do something or have or show qualities worthy of (a reaction which rewards or punishes as appropriate): *the referee deserves a pat on the back for his bravery* | [with infinitive] *we didn't deserve to win, we didn't play well.*
– PHRASES **deserve a medal** have done something considered especially praiseworthy or heroic.
– DERIVATIVES **deservedly** adverb.
– ORIGIN Middle English: from Old French *deservir*, from Latin *deservire* 'serve well or zealously'.

deserving ▶ **adjective** worthy of being treated in a particular way, typically of being given assistance: *the deserving poor.*
– DERIVATIVES **deservingly** adverb, **deservingness** noun.

desex ▶ **verb** [with obj.] [usu. as adj. **desexed**] **1** deprive (someone) of sexual qualities or attraction: *Lawrence portrays feminists as shrill, humourless, and desexed.*
2 castrate or spay (an animal).

desexualize (also **-ise**) ▶ **verb** [with obj.] deprive of sexual character or the distinctive qualities of a sex.
– DERIVATIVES **desexualization** noun.

déshabillé /ˌdɛzaˈbiːjeɪ/ (also **dishabille**) ▶ **noun** [mass noun] the state of being only partly or scantily clothed: *the paintings of Venus all shared the same state of déshabillé.*
– ORIGIN French, 'undressed'.

desi /ˈdeɪsi/ (also **deshi**) ▶ **adjective** Indian local; indigenous: *desi liquor.*
▪derogatory rustic; unsophisticated.
– ORIGIN via Hindi from Sanskrit *deśa* 'country, land'.

De Sica /də ˈsiːkə/, Vittorio (1901–74), Italian film director and actor, a key figure in Italian neo-realist cinema. Notable films: *Bicycle Thieves* (1948) and *Two Women* (1960), both of which won Oscars.

desiccant ▶ **noun** a hygroscopic substance used as a drying agent.
– ORIGIN late 17th cent.: from Latin *desiccant-* 'making thoroughly dry', from the verb *desiccare.*

desiccate /ˈdɛsɪkeɪt/ ▶ **verb** [with obj.] [usu. as adj. **desiccated**] remove the moisture from (something, especially food), typically in order to preserve it: *desiccated coconut.*
▪[as adj. **desiccated**] figurative lacking interest, passion, or energy: *a desiccated history of ideas.*
– DERIVATIVES **desiccation** noun, **desiccative** adjective.
– ORIGIN late 16th cent.: from Latin *desiccat-* 'made thoroughly dry', from the verb *desiccare.*

desiccator ▶ **noun** a glass container or other apparatus holding a drying agent for removing moisture from specimens and protecting them from water vapour in the air.

desiderate /dɪˈzɪdəreɪt, -ˈsɪd-/ ▶ **verb** [with obj.] archaic feel a keen desire for (something lacking or absent): *I desiderate the resources of a family.*
– ORIGIN mid 17th cent.: from Latin *desiderat-* 'desired', from the verb *desiderare*, perhaps from *de-* 'down' + *sidus, sider-* 'star'. Compare with **CONSIDER**.

desiderative /dɪˈzɪd(ə)rətɪv, -ˈsɪd-/ ▶ **adjective** Grammar (in Latin and other inflected languages) denoting a verb formed from another and expressing a desire to do the act denoted by the root verb (such as Latin *esurire* 'want to eat', from *edere* 'eat').
▪having, expressing, or relating to desire.
▶ **noun** Grammar a desiderative verb.
– ORIGIN mid 16th cent.: from late Latin *desiderativus*, from Latin *desiderat-* 'desired', from the verb *desiderare* (see **DESIDERATE**).

desideratum /dɪˌzɪdəˈrɑːtəm, -ˈreɪtəm, -ˌsɪd-/ ▶ **noun** (pl. **desiderata** /-tə/) something that is needed or wanted: *integrity was a desideratum.*
– ORIGIN mid 17th cent.: from Latin, 'something desired', neuter past participle of *desiderare* (see **DESIDERATE**).

design ▶ **noun** **1** a plan or drawing produced to show the look and function or workings of a building, garment, or other object before it is built or made: *he has just unveiled his design for the new museum.*
▪[mass noun] the art or action of conceiving of and producing such a plan or drawing: *good design can help the reader understand complicated information* | *the cloister is of late twelfth century design.* ▪an arrangement of lines or shapes created to form a pattern or decoration: *pottery with a lovely blue and white design.*
2 [mass noun] purpose, planning, or intention that exists or is thought to exist behind an action, fact, or material object: *the appearance of design in the universe.*
▶ **verb** [with obj.] decide upon the look and functioning of (a building, garment, or other object), typically by making a detailed drawing of it: *a number of architectural students were designing a factory* | [as adj., with submodifier] (**designed**) *specially designed buildings.*
▪(often **be designed**) do or plan (something) with a specific purpose or intention in mind: [with obj. and infinitive] *the tax changes were designed to stimulate economic growth.*
– PHRASES **by design** as a result of a plan; intentionally: *I became a presenter by default rather than by design.* **have designs on** aim to obtain (something desired), typically in an underhand way: *he suspected her of having designs on the family fortune.*
– ORIGIN late Middle English (as a verb in the sense 'to designate'): from Latin *designare* 'to designate', reinforced by French *désigner.* The noun is via French from Italian.

designate ▶ **verb** /ˈdɛzɪgneɪt/ [with obj.] (often **be desigated**) appoint (someone) to a specified position: *he was* ***designated as*** *prime minister.*
▪officially assign a specified status or ascribe a specified name or quality to: [with obj. and complement] *the Wye Valley is designated an area of outstanding natural beauty* | *certain schools are designated 'science schools'.*
▶ **adjective** /ˈdɛzɪgnət/ [postpositive] appointed to an office or position but not yet installed: *the Director designate.*
– DERIVATIVES **designator** noun.
– ORIGIN mid 17th cent. (as an adjective): from Latin *designatus* 'designated', past participle of *designare*, based on *signum* 'a mark'. The verb dates from the late 18th cent.

designated hitter ▶ **noun** Baseball a non-fielding player named before the start of a game to bat instead of the pitcher anywhere in the batting order.

designation ▶ **noun** [mass noun] the choosing and naming of someone to be the holder of an official position: *a leader's designation of his own successor.*
▪the action of choosing a place for a special purpose or giving it a special status: *the designation of Stansted as the site of the third London airport.* ▪[count noun] a name, description, or title, typically one that is officially bestowed: *quality designations such as 'Premier Cru'.*
– ORIGIN late Middle English (in the sense 'the action of marking'): from Latin *designatio(n-)*, from the verb *designare* (see **DESIGNATE**).

designedly ▶ **adverb** deliberately in order to produce a specific effect: *the goblet designedly left for him.*

designer ▶ **noun** a person who plans the form, look, or workings of something prior to it being made or built, typically by drawing it in detail: *he's one of the world's leading car designers.*
▪[as modifier] made by or having the expensive sophistication of a famous and prestigious fashion designer: *a designer label.* ▪[as modifier] upmarket and fashionable: *designer food.*

designer drug ▶ **noun** chiefly N. Amer. a synthetic analogue of an illegal drug, especially one devised to circumvent drug laws.
▪a fashionable artificial drug.

designing ▶ **adjective** [attrib.] acting in a calculating, deceitful way: *a designing little minx.*

desirable ▶ **adjective** wanted or wished for as being an attractive, useful, or necessary course of action: [with infinitive] *it is desirable to exercise some social control over technology.*
▪(of a person) arousing sexual desire: *she had never looked more desirable.*
▶ **noun** a desirable person, thing, or quality: *the store sells various desirables.*
– DERIVATIVES **desirability** noun, **desirableness** noun, **desirably** adverb.
– ORIGIN late Middle English: from Old French, suggested by Latin *desiderabilis*, from *desiderare* 'to desire' (see **DESIDERATE**).

desire ▶ **noun** a strong feeling of wanting to have something or wishing for something to happen: [with infinitive] *she has no desire to become a wife and mother.*
▪[mass noun] strong sexual feeling or appetite: *they were clinging together in fierce mutual desire.*
▶ **verb** [with obj.] strongly wish for or want (something): *he never achieved the status he so desired* | [as adj. **desired**] *it failed to create the desired effect.*
▪want (someone) sexually: *there had been a time, years ago, when he had desired her.* ▪archaic express a wish to (someone); request or entreat.
– ORIGIN Middle English: from Old French *desir* (noun), *desirer* (verb), from Latin *desiderare* (see **DESIDERATE**).

Desiree /dɪˈzɪəreɪ/ ▶ **noun** a potato of a pink-skinned variety with yellow waxy flesh.

desirous /dɪˈzʌɪərəs/ ▶ **adjective** [predic.] having or characterized by desire: *the pope was* ***desirous of*** *peace in Europe.*
– ORIGIN Middle English: from Old French *desireus*, based on Latin *desiderare* 'to desire' (see **DESIDERATE**).

desist /dɪˈzɪst, dɪˈsɪst/ ▶ **verb** [no obj.] cease; abstain: *each pledged to* ***desist from*** *acts of sabotage.*
– ORIGIN late Middle English: from Old French *desister*, from Latin *desistere*, from *de-* 'down from' + *sistere* 'to stop' (reduplication of *stare* 'to stand').

desk ▶ **noun** a piece of furniture with a flat or sloped surface and typically with drawers, at which one can read, write, or do other work.
▪Music a position in an orchestra at which two players share a music stand: *an extra desk of first and second*

violins. ■ a counter in a hotel, bank, or airport at which a customer may check in or obtain information: *the reception desk.* ■ [with modifier] a specified section of a news organization, especially a newspaper: *he landed a job on the sports desk.*
– ORIGIN late Middle English: from medieval Latin *desca*, probably based on Provençal *desca* 'basket' or Italian *desco* 'table, butcher's block', both based on Latin *discus* (see **DISCUS**).

desk-bound ▶ **adjective** restricted to working in an office, rather than in an active, physical capacity: *he made no secret of his contempt for the desk-bound staff behind the lines.*

desk diary ▶ **noun** a large diary designed for use in an office.

desk dictionary ▶ **noun** chiefly N. Amer. a one-volume dictionary of medium size.

deskill ▶ **verb** [with obj.] reduce the level of skill required to carry out (a job): *advances in technology had deskilled numerous working-class jobs.*
■ make the skills of (a worker) obsolete.

desk job ▶ **noun** a job based at a desk, especially as opposed to one in active military service.

desk sergeant ▶ **noun** a sergeant in administrative charge of a police station.

desktop ▶ **noun** the working surface of a desk.
■ [as modifier] denoting a piece of equipment such as a microcomputer which is suitable for use at an ordinary desk: *a desktop machine.* ■ a computer of this type. ■ the working area of a computer screen regarded as a representation of a notional desktop and containing icons representing items such as files and a waste bin.

desktop publishing (abbreviation: **DTP**) ▶ **noun** [mass noun] the production of printed matter by means of a printer linked to a desktop computer, with special software. The system enables reports, advertising matter, company magazines, etc., to be produced cheaply with a layout and print quality similar to that of typeset books, for xerographic or other reproduction.

desman /ˈdɛzmən/ ▶ **noun** a small semiaquatic European mammal related to the mole, with a long tubular muzzle and webbed toes.
• Family Talpidae: the **Russian desman** (*Desmana moschata*) and the **Pyrenean desman** (*Galemys pyrenaicus*).
– ORIGIN late 18th cent.: via French and German from Swedish *desman-råtta* 'muskrat', from *desman* 'musk'.

desmid /ˈdɛzmɪd/ ▶ **noun** Biology a single-celled freshwater alga which appears to be composed of two rigid cells with a shared nucleus. The presence of desmids is usually an indicator of unpolluted water.
• Family Desmidiaceae, division Chlorophyta (or phylum Gamophyta, kingdom Protista).
– ORIGIN mid 19th cent.: from modern Latin *Desmidium* (genus name), from Greek *desmos* 'band, chain' (because the algae are often found united in chains or masses).

desmoid /ˈdɛzmɔɪd/ ▶ **adjective** Medicine denoting a type of fibrous tumour of muscle and connective tissue, typically in the abdomen.
– ORIGIN mid 19th cent.: from Greek *desmos* 'bond' or *desmē* 'bundle' + **-OID**.

Des Moines /dɛɪ ˈmɔɪn/ the state capital and largest city of Iowa; pop. 193,200 (1990).

desmosome /ˈdɛzməsəʊm/ ▶ **noun** Biology a structure by which two adjacent cells are attached, formed from protein plaques in the cell membranes linked by filaments.
– DERIVATIVES **desmosomal** adjective.
– ORIGIN 1930s: from Greek *desmos* 'bond, chain' + **-SOME**[3].

desolate ▶ **adjective** /ˈdɛs(ə)lət/ (of a place) uninhabited and giving an impression of bleak and dismal emptiness: *a desolate Pennine moor.*
■ feeling or showing misery, unhappiness, or loneliness: *I suddenly felt desolate and bereft.*
▶ **verb** /ˈdɛsəleɪt/ [with obj.] make (a place) appear bleakly and depressingly empty or bare: *the droughts that desolated the dry plains.*
■ (usu. **be desolated**) make (someone) feel utterly wretched and unhappy: *he was desolated by the deaths of his treasured friends.*
– DERIVATIVES **desolately** adverb, **desolateness** noun, **desolator** noun.
– ORIGIN late Middle English: from Latin *desolatus* 'abandoned', past participle of *desolare*, from *de-* 'thoroughly' + *solus* 'alone'.

desolation ▶ **noun** [mass noun] a state of complete emptiness or destruction: *the stony desolation of the desert.*
■ anguished misery or loneliness: *in choked desolation, she watched him leave.*
– ORIGIN late Middle English: from late Latin *desolatio(n-)*, from Latin *desolare* 'to abandon' (see **DESOLATE**).

desorb /diːˈsɔːb/ ▶ **verb** [with obj.] Chemistry cause the release of (an adsorbed substance) from a surface.
■ [no obj.] (of an adsorbed substance) become released.
– DERIVATIVES **desorbent** adjective & noun, **desorber** noun, **desorption** noun.
– ORIGIN 1920s: originally as *desorption* (from *de-* 'away' + *adsorption*), from which *desorb* is a back-formation.

despair ▶ **noun** [mass noun] the complete loss or absence of hope: ***driven to despair***, *he throws himself under a train* | ***in despair***, *I hit the bottle.*
▶ **verb** [no obj.] lose or be without hope: *we should not despair* | *he was beginning to* ***despair of*** *ever knowing* | [as adj. **despairing**] *he gave a despairing little shrug.*
– PHRASES **be the despair of** be the cause of a feeling of hopelessness in (someone else): *such students can be the despair of conscientious teachers.*
– DERIVATIVES **despairingly** adverb.
– ORIGIN Middle English: the noun via Anglo-Norman French from Old French *desespeir*; the verb from Old French *desperer*, from Latin *desperare*, from *de-* 'down from' + *sperare* 'to hope'.

despatch ▶ **verb** & **noun** variant spelling of **DISPATCH**.

desperado /ˌdɛspəˈrɑːdəʊ/ ▶ **noun** (pl. **-oes** or **-os**) dated a desperate or reckless person, especially a criminal.
– DERIVATIVES **desperadoism** noun.
– ORIGIN early 17th cent.: pseudo-Spanish alteration of the obsolete noun *desperate*. Both *desperate* and *desperado* originally denoted a person in despair or in a desperate situation, hence someone made reckless by despair.

desperate ▶ **adjective** feeling, showing, or involving a hopeless sense that a situation is so bad as to be impossible to deal with: *a desperate sadness enveloped Ruth.*
■ (of an act or attempt) tried in despair or when everything else has failed; having little hope of success: *drugs used in a desperate attempt to save his life.* ■ (of a situation) extremely bad, serious, or dangerous: *there is a desperate shortage of teachers.* ■ [predic.] (of a person) having a great need or desire for something: *I am* ***desperate for*** *a cigarette* | [with infinitive] *other women are desperate to get back to work.* ■ (of a person or fight) violent or dangerous: *a desperate criminal* | *a desperate struggle.*
– PHRASES **desperate diseases must have desperate remedies** proverb extreme measures are justified as a response to a difficult or dangerous situation.
– DERIVATIVES **desperateness** noun.
– ORIGIN late Middle English (in the sense 'in despair'): from Latin *desperatus* 'deprived of hope', past participle of *desperare* (see **DESPAIR**).

desperately ▶ **adverb** in a way that shows despair: *he looked around desperately.*
■ used to emphasize the extreme degree of something: *he desperately needed a drink* | [as submodifier] *I am desperately disappointed.*

desperation ▶ **noun** [mass noun] a state of despair, typically one which results in rash or extreme behaviour: *she wrote to him* ***in desperation***.
– ORIGIN late Middle English: from Old French, from Latin *desperatio(n-)*, from the verb *desperare* (see **DESPAIR**).

despicable /dɪˈspɪkəb(ə)l, ˈdɛspɪk-/ ▶ **adjective** deserving hatred and contempt: *a despicable crime.*
– DERIVATIVES **despicably** adverb.
– ORIGIN mid 16th cent.: from late Latin *despicabilis*, from *despicari* 'look down on'.

de Spinoza, Baruch, see **SPINOZA**.

despise /dɪˈspʌɪz/ ▶ **verb** [with obj.] feel contempt or a deep repugnance for: *he* ***despised*** *himself* ***for*** *being selfish.*
– DERIVATIVES **despiser** noun.
– ORIGIN Middle English: from Old French *despire*, from Latin *despicere*, from *de-* 'down' + *specere* 'look at'.

despite /dɪˈspʌɪt/ ▶ **preposition** without being affected by; in spite of: *he remains a great leader despite age and infirmity.*
▶ **noun** [mass noun] archaic or poetic/literary **1** outrage; injury: *the despite done by him to the holy relics.*
2 contempt; disdain: *the theatre only earns my despite.*
– PHRASES **despite** (or **in despite**) **of** archaic in spite of. **despite oneself** used to indicate that one did not intend or expect to do the thing mentioned: *despite herself Fran felt a ripple of appreciation for his beauty.*
– DERIVATIVES **despiteful** adjective (archaic or poetic/literary).
– ORIGIN Middle English (originally used as a noun meaning 'contempt, scorn' in the phrase *in despite of*): from Old French *despit*, from Latin *despectus* 'looking down on', past participle (used as a noun) of *despicere* (see **DESPISE**).

despoil /dɪˈspɔɪl/ ▶ **verb** [with obj.] (often **be despoiled**) steal or violently remove valuable or attractive possessions from; plunder: *the church was* ***despoiled of*** *its marble wall covering.*
– DERIVATIVES **despoiler** noun, **despoilment** noun, **despoliation** /dɪˌspəʊlɪˈeɪʃ(ə)n/ noun.
– ORIGIN Middle English: from Old French *despoillier*, from Latin *despoliare* 'rob, plunder' (from *spolia* 'spoil').

despond /dɪˈspɒnd/ ▶ **verb** [no obj.] archaic become dejected and lose confidence.
– ORIGIN mid 17th cent.: from Latin *despondere* 'give up, abandon', from *de-* 'away' + *spondere* 'to promise'. The word was originally used as a noun in **SLOUGH OF DESPOND**.

despondency ▶ **noun** [mass noun] a state of low spirits caused by loss of hope or courage: *comments spreading* ***gloom and despondency***.
– DERIVATIVES **despondence** noun.

despondent ▶ **adjective** in low spirits from loss of hope or courage.
– DERIVATIVES **despondently** adverb.

despot /ˈdɛspɒt/ ▶ **noun** a ruler or other person who holds absolute power, typically one who exercises it in a cruel or oppressive way.
– DERIVATIVES **despotic** adjective, **despotically** adverb.
– ORIGIN mid 16th cent.: from French *despote*, via medieval Latin from Greek *despotēs*, 'master, absolute ruler'. Originally (after the Turkish conquest of Constantinople) the term denoted a petty Christian ruler under the Turkish empire. The current sense dates from the late 18th cent.

despotism /ˈdɛspətɪz(ə)m/ ▶ **noun** [mass noun] the exercise of absolute power, especially in a cruel and oppressive way: *the ideology of enlightened despotism.*
■ [count noun] a country or political system where the ruler holds absolute power.
– ORIGIN early 18th cent.: from French *despotisme*, from *despote* (see **DESPOT**).

des Prez /deɪ ˈpreɪ/ (also **des Prés** or **Deprez**), Josquin (*c.*1440–1521), Flemish musician, a leading Renaissance composer.

desquamate /ˈdɛskwəmeɪt/ ▶ **verb** [no obj.] (of a layer of cells, e.g. of the skin) come off in scales or flakes: [as adj. **desquamated**] *desquamated cells.*
– DERIVATIVES **desquamation** noun, **desquamative** /-ˈskwamətɪv/ adjective.
– ORIGIN early 18th cent. (in the sense 'remove the scales from'): from Latin *desquamat-* 'scaled', from the verb *desquamare*, from *de-* 'away from' + *squama* 'a scale'.

des res /dɛz ˈrɛz/ ▶ **noun** Brit. informal a desirable residence (used as a humorous allusion to the language used in housing advertisements).
– ORIGIN 1980s: abbreviation.

Dessau /ˈdɛsaʊ/ an industrial city in Germany, on the River Mulde, in Anhalt about 112 km (70 miles) south-west of Berlin; pop. 95,100 (1991).

dessert /dɪˈzəːt/ ▶ **noun** the sweet course eaten at the end of a meal: *a dessert of chocolate mousse.*
– ORIGIN mid 16th cent.: from French, past participle of *desservir* 'clear the table', from *des-* (expressing removal) + *servir* 'to serve'.

dessertspoon ▶ **noun** a spoon used for dessert, smaller than a tablespoon and larger than a teaspoon.
■ the amount held by such a spoon, in the UK considered to be 10 millilitres when used as a measurement in cookery.
– DERIVATIVES **dessertspoonful** noun (pl. **-fuls**).

dessert wine ▶ noun a sweet wine drunk with or following dessert.

destabilize (also **-ise**) ▶ verb [with obj.] upset the stability of; cause unrest in: *the discovery of an affair can destabilize a relationship.*
– DERIVATIVES **destabilization** noun.

de Staël /də ˈstɑːl, French də stal/, Madame (1766–1817), French novelist and critic, a precursor of the French romantics, born *Anne Louise Germaine Necker*. Her best-known critical work, *De l'Allemagne* (1810), introduced late 18th-century German writers and thinkers to France.

destain ▶ verb [with obj.] Biology selectively remove stain from (a specimen for microscopy, a chromatography gel, etc.) after it has previously been stained.

De Stijl /də ˈstʌɪl/ a 20th-century Dutch art movement founded in 1917 by Theo van Doesburg (1883–1931) and Piet Mondrian. The movement favoured an abstract, economical style. It was influential on the Bauhaus and constructivist movements.
– ORIGIN Dutch, literally 'the style', originally the name of the movement's periodical.

destination ▶ noun the place to which someone or something is going or being sent: *a popular destination for holiday golfers.*
– ORIGIN late Middle English: from Latin *destinatio(n-)*, from *destinare* 'make firm, establish'. The original sense was 'the action of intending someone or something for a particular purpose', later 'being destined for a particular place', hence (from the early 19th cent.) the place itself.

destine /ˈdɛstɪn/ ▶ verb [with obj.] intend or choose (someone or something) for a particular purpose or end.
– ORIGIN Middle English (in the sense 'predetermine, decree'): from Old French *destiner*, from Latin *destinare*, 'make firm, establish'.

destined ▶ adjective [predic.] (of a person's future) regarded as developing as though according to a pre-existing plan: *she could see that he was **destined for** great things* | [with infinitive] *they were destined to become diplomats.*
■ (**destined to**) certain to meet (a particular fate): *the Act seems destined to failure.* ■ (**destined for**) intended for or travelling towards (a particular place): *a shipment of steel tubes destined for Iraq.* ■ [attrib.] preordained: *your heroine will be united with her destined mate.*

destiny ▶ noun (pl. **-ies**) the events that will necessarily happen to a particular person or thing in the future: *she was unable to control her own destiny.*
■ [mass noun] the hidden power believed to control what will happen in the future; fate: *he believes in destiny.*
– ORIGIN Middle English: from Old French *destinee*, from Latin *destinata*, feminine past participle of *destinare* 'make firm, establish'.

destitute /ˈdɛstɪtjuːt/ ▶ adjective without the basic necessities of life: *the charity cares for destitute children.*
■ [predic.] (**destitute of**) not having: *towns destitute of commerce.*
– DERIVATIVES **destitution** noun.
– ORIGIN late Middle English (in the sense 'deserted, abandoned, empty'): from Latin *destitutus*, past participle of *destituere* 'forsake', from *de-* 'away from' + *statuere* 'to place'.

destock ▶ verb [no obj.] Brit. (of a retailer) reduce the quantity of stock held.

de-stress ▶ verb [no obj.] relax after a period of work or tension.

destrier /ˈdɛstrɪə, dɛˈstriːə/ ▶ noun a medieval knight's warhorse.
– ORIGIN Middle English: from Old French, based on Latin *dextera* 'the right hand', from *dexter* 'on the right' (because the squire led the knight's horse with his right hand).

destroy ▶ verb [with obj.] put an end to the existence of (something) by damaging or attacking it: *the room had been destroyed by fire.*
■ completely ruin or spoil (something): *he had destroyed her dreams.* ■ ruin (someone) emotionally or spiritually: *he has been determined to destroy her.* ■ defeat (someone) utterly: *Northants have the batting to destroy anyone.* ■ (usu. **be destroyed**) kill (a sick, savage, or unwanted animal) by humane means: *their terrier was destroyed after the attack.*
– ORIGIN Middle English: from Old French *destruire*, based on Latin *destruere*, from *de-* (expressing reversal) + *struere* 'build'.

destroyer ▶ noun a small fast warship, especially one equipped for a defensive role against submarines and aircraft.
■ someone or something that destroys: *CFCs are the chief destroyers of the ozone layer.*

destroying angel ▶ noun a deadly poisonous white toadstool which grows in woodland, native to both Eurasia and North America.
• *Amanita virosa*, family Amanitaceae, class Hymenomycetes.

destruct ▶ verb [with obj.] cause deliberate, irreparable damage to (something, typically a rocket or missile).
▶ noun [in sing.] [usu. as modifier] the deliberate causing of terminal damage: *he had ordered him to go for the destruct button.*
– ORIGIN 1950s (originally US): back-formation from **DESTRUCTION**.

destructible ▶ adjective able to be destroyed.
– DERIVATIVES **destructibility** noun.
– ORIGIN mid 18th cent. (earlier in *indestructible*): from French, from late Latin *destructibilis*, from Latin *destruct-* 'destroyed', from the verb *destruere* (see **DESTROY**).

destruction ▶ noun [mass noun] the action or process of causing so much damage to something that it no longer exists or cannot be repaired: *the destruction of the rainforest* | *the avalanche left a trail of destruction.*
■ the action or process of killing or being killed: *weapons of mass destruction.* ■ the ruination or ending of a system or state of affairs: *the destruction of a traditional way of life.* ■ [in sing.] a cause of someone's ruin: *gambling was his destruction.*
– ORIGIN Middle English: from Latin *destructio(n-)*, from the verb *destruere* (see **DESTROY**).

destructive ▶ adjective causing great and irreparable harm or damage: *the destructive power of weapons.*
■ tending to refute or disparage; negative and unhelpful: *destructive criticism.*
– DERIVATIVES **destructively** adverb, **destructiveness** noun.

destructive distillation ▶ noun [mass noun] Chemistry decomposition of a solid by heating it in a closed container and collecting the volatile constituents given off.

destructor ▶ noun Brit. a refuse-burning furnace.

desuetude /dɪˈsjuːɪtjuːd, ˈdɛswɪ-/ ▶ noun [mass noun] formal a state of disuse: *the docks **fell into desuetude**.*
– ORIGIN early 17th cent. (in the sense 'cessation'): from French, from Latin *desuetudo*, from *desuet-* 'made unaccustomed', from the verb *desuescere*, from *de-* (expressing reversal) + *suescere* 'be accustomed'.

desulphurize (also **-ise**, US **desulfurize**) ▶ verb [with obj.] remove sulphur or sulphur compounds from (a substance).
– DERIVATIVES **desulphurization** noun, **desulphurizer** noun.

desultory /ˈdɛs(ə)lt(ə)ri, -z-/ ▶ adjective lacking a plan, purpose, or enthusiasm: *a few people were left, dancing in a desultory fashion.*
■ (of conversation or speech) going constantly from one subject to another in a half-hearted way; unfocused: *the desultory conversation faded.* ■ occurring randomly or occasionally: *desultory passengers were appearing.*
– DERIVATIVES **desultorily** adverb, **desultoriness** noun.
– ORIGIN late 16th cent. (also in the literal sense 'skipping about'): from Latin *desultorius* 'superficial' (literally 'relating to a vaulter'), from *desultor* 'vaulter', from the verb *desilire*.

desuperheater ▶ noun a container for reducing the temperature of steam to make it less superheated.

desynchronize (also **-ise**) ▶ verb [with obj.] disturb the synchronization of; put out of step or phase.
– DERIVATIVES **desynchronization** noun.

detach ▶ verb [with obj.] **1** disengage (something or part of something) and remove it: *he **detached** the front lamp **from** its bracket* | figurative *a willingness to detach comment from political allegiance.*
■ [no obj.] be easily removable: *the screen **detaches from** the keyboard.* ■ (**detach oneself from**) leave or separate oneself from (a group or place): *a figure in brown detached itself from the shadows.* ■ (**detach oneself from**) avoid or put an end to any connection or association with: *the newspaper detached itself from the political parties.*
2 (usu. **be detached**) Military send (a group of soldiers or ships) on a separate mission: *our crew were detached to Tabuk for the exercise.*
– DERIVATIVES **detachability** noun, **detachable** adjective.
– ORIGIN late 16th cent. (in the sense 'discharge a gun'): from French *détacher*, earlier *destacher*, from *des-* (expressing reversal) + *attacher* 'attach'.

detached ▶ adjective separate or disconnected, in particular:
■ (of a house or other building) not joined to another on either side: *a four-bedroomed detached house.* ■ (of a social worker or social work) operating or based in the community rather than in an office: *detached youth workers.* ■ aloof and objective: *he managed to remain **detached from** petty politics.*
– DERIVATIVES **detachedly** adverb.

detached retina ▶ noun a retina that has become separated from the underlying choroid tissue at the back of the eye, causing loss of vision in the affected area.

detachment ▶ noun **1** [mass noun] the state of being objective or aloof: *he felt a sense of detachment from what was going on.*
2 Military a group of troops, aircraft, or ships sent away on a separate mission: *a detachment of Marines* | [mass noun] *the Squadron went **on detachment** to Malta.*
■ a party of people similarly separated from a larger group: *a truck containing a detachment of villagers.*
3 [mass noun] the action or process of detaching; separation: *structural problems resulted in cracking and detachment of the wall.*
– ORIGIN mid 17th cent.: from French *détachement*, from *détacher* 'to detach' (see **DETACH**).

detail ▶ noun **1** an individual feature, fact, or item: *we shall consider every detail of the Bill* | [mass noun] *her meticulous **attention to detail**.*
■ a minor or less significant item or feature: *he didn't want them to get sidetracked on a detail of policy.* ■ a minor decorative feature of a building or work of art: *a detail on Charlemagne's tomb.* ■ [mass noun] the style or treatment of such features: *the classical French detail of the building's facade.* ■ a small part of a picture or other work of art that is reproduced separately for close study: *detail of right eye showing marks on the lids.* ■ (**details**) itemized facts or information about someone; personal particulars: *the official asked for my father's details.*
2 a small detachment of troops or police officers given a special duty: *the governor's security detail.*
■ [often with modifier] a special duty assigned to such a detachment.
▶ verb [with obj.] **1** describe item by item; give the full particulars of: *the report details the environmental and health costs of the car.*
2 [with obj. and infinitive] assign (someone) to undertake a particular task: *the ships were detailed to keep watch.*
– PHRASES **go into detail** give a full account of something. **in detail** as regards every feature or aspect; fully: *we will have to examine the proposals in detail.*
– ORIGIN early 17th cent. (in the sense 'minor items or events regarded collectively'): from French *détail* (noun), *détailler* (verb), from *dé-* (expressing separation) + *tailler* 'to cut' (based on Latin *talea* 'twig, cutting').

detailed ▶ adjective having many details or facts; showing attention to detail: *more detailed information was needed.*
■ (of a work of art) executed with many minor decorative features: *an exquisitely detailed carving.*

detailing ▶ noun [mass noun] small decorative features on a building, garment, or work of art.

detain ▶ verb [with obj.] keep (someone) in official custody, typically for questioning about a crime or in politically sensitive situations: *she was detained without trial for two years.*
■ keep (someone) from proceeding by holding them back or making claims on their attention: *she made to open the door, but he detained her.* ■ keep (a sick or injured person) in hospital for treatment. ■ officially seize and hold (goods): *customs officers may detain goods for up to two days.*
– DERIVATIVES **detainment** noun.
– ORIGIN late Middle English (in the sense 'be afflicted with sickness or infirmity'): from Old French *detenir*, from a variant of Latin *detinere*, from *de-* 'away, aside' + *tenere* 'to hold'.

detainee /ˌdɪteɪˈniː, ˌdiː-/ ▶ **noun** a person held in custody, especially for political reasons.

detainer ▶ **noun** **1** [mass noun] Law the action of detaining or withholding property.
■ the detention of a person in custody. ■ an order authorizing the continued detention of a person in custody.
2 chiefly Law a person who detains someone or something.
– ORIGIN early 17th cent.: from Anglo-Norman French *detener* 'detain' (used as a noun), variant of Old French *detenir* (see **DETAIN**).

detangle ▶ **verb** [with obj.] remove tangles from (hair).

detect ▶ **verb** [with obj.] discover or identify the presence or existence of: *cancer may soon be detected in its earliest stages.*
■ discover or investigate (a crime or its perpetrators): *the public can help the police to detect crime.* ■ discern (something intangible or barely perceptible): *Paul detected a faint note of weariness in his father's voice.*
– DERIVATIVES **detectable** adjective, **detectably** adverb.
– ORIGIN late Middle English: from Latin *detect-* 'uncovered', from the verb *detegere*, from *de-* (expressing reversal) + *tegere* 'to cover'. The original senses were 'uncover, expose' and 'give someone away', later 'expose the real or hidden nature of something or someone'; hence the current senses (partly influenced by **DETECTIVE**).

detection ▶ **noun** [mass noun] the action or process of identifying the presence of something concealed: *the early detection of fetal abnormalities.*
■ the work of a detective in investigating a crime: [as modifier] *the detection rate for murder is over 90 per cent.*
– ORIGIN late 15th cent. (in the sense 'revelation of what is concealed'): from late Latin *detectio(n-)*, from Latin *detegere* 'uncover' (see **DETECT**).

detective ▶ **noun** a person, especially a police officer, whose occupation is to investigate and solve crimes.
■ [as modifier] denoting a particular rank of police officer: *a detective chief inspector.* ■ [as modifier] concerning crime and its investigation: *detective work.*
– ORIGIN mid 19th cent.: from **DETECT**, on the pattern of pairs such as *elect, elective*. The noun was originally short for *detective policeman*, from an adjectival use of the word in the sense 'serving to detect'.

detective camera ▶ **noun** historical a hand-held camera adapted to take instant photographs.

detective story (also **detective novel**) ▶ **noun** a story whose plot revolves around the investigation and solving of a crime.

detector ▶ **noun** [often with modifier] a device or instrument designed to detect the presence of a particular object or substance and to emit a signal in response: *methane detectors.*

detectorist ▶ **noun** a person who uses a metal detector for a hobby.

detent /dɪˈtɛnt/ ▶ **noun** a catch in a machine which prevents motion until released.
■ (in a clock) a catch that regulates striking.
– ORIGIN late 17th cent. (denoting a catch in clocks and watches): from French *détente*, from Old French *destente*, from *destendre* 'slacken', from *des-* (expressing reversal) + Latin *tendere* 'to stretch'.

détente /deɪˈtɑːnt/ ▶ **noun** [mass noun] the easing of hostility or strained relations, especially between countries: *a serious effort at détente with the Eastern bloc.*
– ORIGIN early 20th cent.: French, 'loosening, relaxation'.

detention ▶ **noun** [mass noun] the action of detaining someone or the state of being detained in official custody, especially as a political prisoner: *he committed suicide while in police detention.*
■ the punishment of being kept in school after hours: *teachers were divided as to the effectiveness of detention* | [count noun] *masters gave lines or detentions.*
– ORIGIN late Middle English (in the sense 'withholding of what is claimed or due'): from late Latin *detentio(n-)*, from Latin *detinere* 'hold back' (see **DETAIN**).

detention centre ▶ **noun** an institution where people are held in detention for short periods, in particular illegal immigrants, refugees, people awaiting trial or sentence, or (formerly in the UK) young offenders.

deter /dɪˈtəː/ ▶ **verb** (**deterred**, **deterring**) [with obj.] discourage (someone) from doing something, typically by instilling doubt or fear of the consequences: *only a health problem would* ***deter*** *him* ***from*** *seeking re-election.*
■ prevent the occurrence of: *strategists think not only about how to deter war, but about how war might occur.*
– ORIGIN mid 16th cent.: from Latin *deterrere*, from *de-* 'away from' + *terrere* 'frighten'.

deterge /dɪˈtəːdʒ/ ▶ **verb** [with obj.] rare cleanse thoroughly.
– ORIGIN early 17th cent.: from French *déterger* or Latin *detergere* 'wipe away'.

detergent ▶ **noun** a water-soluble cleansing agent which combines with impurities and dirt to make them more soluble, and differs from soap in not forming a scum with the salts in hard water.
■ any additive with a similar action, e.g. an oil-soluble substance which holds dirt in suspension in lubricating oil.
▶ **adjective** of or relating to such compounds or their action: *staining that resists detergent action.*
– DERIVATIVES **detergence** noun, **detergency** noun.
– ORIGIN early 17th cent. (as an adjective): from Latin *detergent-* 'wiping away', from the verb *detergere*, from *de-* 'away from' + *tergere* 'to wipe'.

deteriorate /dɪˈtɪərɪəreɪt/ ▶ **verb** [no obj.] become progressively worse: *relations between the countries had deteriorated sharply* | [as adj. **deteriorating**] *deteriorating economic conditions.*
– DERIVATIVES **deterioration** noun, **deteriorative** adjective.
– ORIGIN late 16th cent. (used transitively in the sense 'make worse'): from late Latin *deteriorat-* 'worsened', from the verb *deteriorare*, from Latin *deterior* 'worse'.

determinable ▶ **adjective** **1** able to be firmly decided or definitely ascertained: *a readily determinable market value.*
2 Law capable of being brought to an end under given conditions.
– ORIGIN late Middle English: via Old French from late Latin *determinabilis* 'finite', from the verb *determinare* (see **DETERMINE**).

determinant /dɪˈtəːmɪnənt/ ▶ **noun** **1** a factor which decisively affects the nature or outcome of something: *pure force of will was the main determinant of his success.*
■ Biology a gene or other factor which determines the character and development of a cell or group of cells in an organism, a set of which forms an individual's idiotype.
2 Mathematics a quantity obtained by the addition of products of the elements of a square matrix according to a given rule.
▶ **adjective** serving to determine or decide something.
– ORIGIN early 17th cent.: from Latin *determinant-* 'determining', from the verb *determinare* (see **DETERMINE**).

determinate /dɪˈtəːmɪnət/ ▶ **adjective** having exact and discernible limits or form: *the longest determinate prison sentence ever upheld by English courts.*
■ Botany (of a flowering shoot) having the main axis ending in a flower bud and therefore no longer extending in length, as in a cyme.
– DERIVATIVES **determinacy** noun, **determinately** adverb, **determinateness** noun.
– ORIGIN late Middle English: from Latin *determinatus* 'limited, determined', past participle of *determinare* (see **DETERMINE**).

determination ▶ **noun** [mass noun] **1** firmness of purpose; resoluteness: *the determination of the players has been excellent.*
2 the process of establishing something exactly, typically by calculation or research: *determination of molecular structures.*
■ Law the settlement of a dispute by the authoritative decision of a judge or arbitrator. ■ [count noun] Law a judicial decision or sentence.
3 the controlling or deciding of something's nature or outcome: *genetic sex determination.*
4 Law the cessation of an estate or interest.
5 archaic a tendency to move in a fixed direction.
– ORIGIN late Middle English (in the senses 'settlement of a controversy by a judge or by reasoning' and 'authoritative opinion'): via Old French from Latin *determinatio(n-)*, from the verb *determinare* (see **DETERMINE**).

determinative /dɪˈtəːmɪnətɪv/ ▶ **adjective** [predic.] chiefly Law serving to define, qualify, or direct: *the employer's view is not determinative of the issue.*
▶ **noun** Grammar another term for **DETERMINER**.

determine /dɪˈtəːmɪn/ ▶ **verb** [with obj.] **1** cause (something) to occur in a particular way; be the decisive factor in: *it will be her mental attitude that determines her future.*
■ firmly decide: [with infinitive] *she determined to tackle Stephen the next day* | [no obj.] *he* ***determined on*** *a withdrawal of his forces.*
2 ascertain or establish exactly, typically as a result of research or calculation: *our aim is to determine the electric field* | [with clause] *the point of our study was to* ***determine what*** *is true, not what is practicable.*
■ Mathematics specify the value, position, or form of (a mathematical or geometrical object) uniquely.
3 Law, archaic bring or come to an end.
– ORIGIN late Middle English: from Old French *determiner*, from Latin *determinare* 'limit, fix', from *de-* 'completely' + *terminare* 'terminate'.

determined ▶ **adjective** having made a firm decision and being resolved not to change it: [with infinitive] *Alina was determined to be heard.*
■ possessing or displaying resolve: *Helen was a determined little girl* | *a determined effort to reduce inflation.*
– DERIVATIVES **determinedly** adverb, **determinedness** noun.

determiner ▶ **noun** **1** a person or thing that determines or decides something.
2 Grammar a modifying word that determines the kind of reference a noun or noun group has, for example *a, the, every*. See also **ARTICLE**.

determinism ▶ **noun** [mass noun] Philosophy the doctrine that all events, including human action, are ultimately determined by causes regarded as external to the will. Some philosophers have taken determinism to imply that individual human beings have no free will and cannot be held morally responsible for their actions.
– DERIVATIVES **determinist** noun & adjective, **deterministic** adjective, **deterministically** adverb.

deterrent /dɪˈtɛr(ə)nt/ ▶ **noun** a thing that discourages or is intended to discourage someone from doing something.
■ a nuclear weapon or weapons system regarded as deterring an enemy from attack.
▶ **adjective** able or intended to deter: *the deterrent effect of heavy prison sentences.*
– DERIVATIVES **deterrence** noun.
– ORIGIN early 19th cent.: from Latin *deterrent-* 'deterring', from the verb *deterrere* (see **DETER**).

detest ▶ **verb** [with obj.] dislike intensely: *she really did detest his mockery.*
– DERIVATIVES **detester** noun.
– ORIGIN late 15th cent.: from Latin *detestari*, from *de-* 'down' + *testari* 'witness, call upon to witness' (from *testis* 'a witness').

detestable ▶ **adjective** deserving intense dislike: *I found the film's violence detestable.*
– DERIVATIVES **detestably** adverb.
– ORIGIN late Middle English: from Old French, or from Latin *detestabilis*, from the verb *detestari* (see **DETEST**).

detestation /ˌdiːtɛˈsteɪʃ(ə)n/ ▶ **noun** [mass noun] intense dislike: *Wordsworth's detestation of aristocracy.*
■ [count noun] archaic a detested person or thing: *he is the detestation of the neighbourhood.*
– ORIGIN late Middle English: via Old French from Latin *detestatio(n-)*, from the verb *detestari* (see **DETEST**).

dethrone ▶ **verb** [with obj.] remove (a ruler, especially a monarch) from power.
■ figurative remove from a position of authority or dominance: *he dethroned the defending title-holder.*
– DERIVATIVES **dethronement** noun.

detinue /ˈdɛtɪnjuː/ ▶ **noun** [mass noun] Law the crime of wrongful detention of goods or personal possessions (replaced in the UK by the tort of wrongful interference of goods).
■ legal action against this.
– ORIGIN late Middle English: from Old French *detenue*, past participle (used as a noun) of *detenir* 'detain'.

detonate /ˈdɛtəneɪt/ ▶ **verb** explode or cause to explode: [no obj.] *two other bombs failed to detonate* | [with obj.] *a trigger that can detonate nuclear weapons.*
– DERIVATIVES **detonative** adjective.
– ORIGIN early 18th cent.: from Latin *detonat-*

'thundered down or forth', from the verb *detonare*, from *de-* 'down' + *tonare* 'to thunder'.

detonation ▶ noun [mass noun] the action of causing a bomb or explosive device to explode.
■ [count noun] a loud explosion: *a series of deafening detonations was heard.* ■ technical combustion of a substance which is initiated suddenly and propagates extremely rapidly giving rise to a shock wave. Compare with DEFLAGRATION. ■ the premature combustion of fuel in an internal-combustion engine, causing pinking.
– ORIGIN late 17th cent.: from French *détonation*, from the verb *détoner*, from Latin *detonare* 'thunder down' (see DETONATE).

detonator ▶ noun a device or a small sensitive charge used to detonate an explosive.
■ another term for FOG SIGNAL.

detorsion /dɪˈtɔːʃ(ə)n/ ▶ noun [mass noun] Zoology (in gastropod molluscs) the evolutionary reversion of a group to a primitive linear body plan. Compare with TORSION.

detour ▶ noun a long or roundabout route that is taken to avoid something or to visit somewhere along the way: *he had made a detour to a cafe.*
■ an alternative route for use by traffic when the usual road is temporarily closed.
▶ verb [no obj., with adverbial of direction] take a long or roundabout route: *he detoured around the walls.*
■ [with obj.] avoid or bypass by taking such a route.
– ORIGIN mid 18th cent. (as a noun): from French *détour* 'change of direction', from *détourner* 'turn away'.

detox informal ▶ noun /ˈdiːtɒks/ [mass noun] short for DETOXIFICATION: *he ended up in detox for three months.*
▶ verb /diːˈtɒks/ short for DETOXIFY.

detoxicate /diːˈtɒksɪkeɪt/ ▶ verb another term for DETOXIFY.
– DERIVATIVES **detoxication** noun.
– ORIGIN mid 19th cent.: from DE- (expressing removal) + Latin *toxicum* 'poison', on the pattern of *intoxicate.*

detoxification ▶ noun [mass noun] the process of removing toxic substances or qualities.
■ medical treatment of an alcoholic or drug addict involving abstention from drink or drugs until the bloodstream is free of toxins.

detoxify /diːˈtɒksɪfʌɪ/ ▶ verb (**-ies**, **-ied**) [with obj.] remove toxic substances or qualities from: *the process uses chemical reagents to detoxify the oil.*
■ (usu. **be detoxified**) treat (an alcoholic or drug addict) to remove the effects of drink or drugs in order to help them overcome addiction: *he was twice detoxified from heroin.* ■ [no obj.] abstain from drink and drugs until the bloodstream is free of toxins in order to overcome alcoholism or drug addiction. ■ [no obj.] become free of poisonous substances or qualities: *you can help your body detoxify by cutting down on coffee.*
– DERIVATIVES **detoxifier** noun.
– ORIGIN early 20th cent.: from DE- (expressing removal) + Latin *toxicum* 'poison' + -FY.

DETR ▶ abbreviation for (in the UK) Department of the Environment, Transport, and the Regions.

detract ▶ verb 1 [no obj.] (**detract from**) reduce or take away the worth or value of: *these quibbles in no way detract from her achievement.*
■ [with obj.] deny or qualify (a quality or achievement) so as to make its subject seem less impressive: *it is detracting nothing from his ability to say that he owed the championship to a superior car.*
2 [with obj.] (**detract someone/thing from**) divert or distract (someone or something) away from: *this CD should not detract listeners from the other two issues.*
– DERIVATIVES **detraction** noun, **detractive** adjective.
– ORIGIN late Middle English: from Latin *detract-* 'drawn away', from the verb *detrahere*, from *de-* 'away from' + *trahere* 'draw'.

detractor ▶ noun a person who disparages someone or something.

detrain ▶ verb [no obj.] leave a train.
■ [with obj.] cause or assist to leave a train: *passengers were detrained as the train was on fire.*
– DERIVATIVES **detrainment** noun.

detribalize (also **-ise**) ▶ verb [with obj.] [usu. as adj. **detribalized**] remove (someone) from a traditional tribal social structure.
■ remove a traditional tribal social structure from (a culture).
– DERIVATIVES **detribalization** noun.

detriment /ˈdɛtrɪm(ə)nt/ ▶ noun [mass noun] the state

of being harmed or damaged: *he is engrossed in his work to the detriment of his married life* | *no one could do one without detriment to the other.*
■ [count noun] a cause of harm or damage: *such tests are a detriment to good education.*
– ORIGIN late Middle English in the sense 'loss sustained by damage': from Old French, from Latin *detrimentum*, from *detri-*, stem of *deterere* 'wear away'.

detrimental ▶ adjective tending to cause harm: *recent policies have been detrimental to the interests of many old people* | *moving her could have a detrimental effect on her health.*
– DERIVATIVES **detrimentally** adverb.

detrition /dɪˈtrɪʃ(ə)n/ ▶ noun [mass noun] rare the action of wearing away by friction.
– ORIGIN late 17th cent.: from medieval Latin *detritio(n-)*, from *detri-*, stem of *deterere* 'wear away'.

detritivore /dɪˈtrɪtɪvɔː/ ▶ noun Zoology an animal which feeds on dead organic material, especially plant detritus.
– DERIVATIVES **detritivorous** /ˌdɛtrɪˈtɪv(ə)rəs/ adjective.
– ORIGIN 1960s: from DETRITUS + -vore 'eating' (see -VOROUS).

detritus /dɪˈtrʌɪtəs/ ▶ noun [mass noun] waste or debris of any kind: *the streets were foul with detritus.*
■ gravel, sand, silt, or other material produced by erosion. ■ organic matter produced by the decomposition of organisms.
– DERIVATIVES **detrital** adjective.
– ORIGIN late 18th cent. (in the sense 'detrition'): from French *détritus*, from Latin *detritus*, from *deterere* 'wear away'.

Detroit /dɪˈtrɔɪt/ a major industrial city and Great Lakes shipping centre in SE Michigan; pop. 1,028,000 (1990). It is the centre of the US automobile industry, containing the headquarters of Ford, Chrysler, and General Motors.

de trop /də ˈtrəʊ, French də tʀo/ ▶ adjective not wanted; unwelcome: *she had no grasp of the conversation and felt herself de trop.*
– ORIGIN mid 18th cent.: French, literally 'excessive'.

de Troyes, Chrétien, see CHRÉTIEN DE TROYES.

detrusor /dɪˈtruːsə/ (also **detrusor muscle**) ▶ noun Anatomy a muscle which forms a layer of the wall of the bladder.
– ORIGIN mid 18th cent.: modern Latin, from Latin *detrus-* 'thrust down', from the verb *detrudere*.

Dettol /ˈdɛtɒl, -t(ə)l/ ▶ noun [mass noun] trademark a type of surgical or household disinfectant.
– ORIGIN 1930s: an invented name.

detumescence /ˌdiːtjʊˈmɛs(ə)ns/ ▶ noun [mass noun] the process of subsiding from a state of tension, swelling, or (especially) sexual arousal.
– DERIVATIVES **detumesce** verb, **detumescent** adjective.
– ORIGIN late 17th cent.: from Latin *detumescere*, from *de-* 'down, away'+ *tumescere* 'to swell'.

detune ▶ verb [with obj.] cause (a musical instrument) to become out of tune.
■ [usu. as adj. **detuned**] reduce the performance or efficiency of (a motor vehicle or engine) by adjustment. ■ alter the wavelength of the light emitted by (a laser).

Deucalion /djuːˈkeɪlɪən/ Greek Mythology the son of Prometheus. With his wife Pyrrha he survived a flood sent by Zeus to punish human wickedness; they were then instructed to throw stones over their shoulders, and these turned into humans to repopulate the world.

deuce[1] /djuːs/ ▶ noun 1 chiefly US a thing representing, or represented by, the number two, in particular:
■ the two on dice or playing cards. ■ a throw of two at dice. ■ informal, dated a two-dollar bill.
2 Tennis the score of 40 all in a game, at which each player needs two consecutive points to win the game.
– ORIGIN late 15th cent.: from Old French *deus* 'two', from Latin *duos.*

deuce[2] /djuːs/ ▶ noun (**the deuce**) informal used as a euphemism for 'devil' in expressions of annoyance, impatience, or surprise or for emphasis: *how the deuce are we to make a profit?* | *what the deuce are you trying to do?*
– PHRASES **a** (or **the**) **deuce of a ——** used to emphasize how difficult or serious something is.
– ORIGIN mid 17th cent.: from Low German *duus*,

probably of the same origin as DEUCE[1] (two aces at dice being the worst throw).

deuced /ˈdjuːsɪd, djuːst/ informal, dated ▶ adjective [attrib.] used for emphasis, especially to express disapproval or frustration: *I sound like a deuced newspaper reporter* | [as submodifier] *I'm so deuced fond of you.*
– DERIVATIVES **deucedly** adverb [as submodifier] *they're deucedly hard to find.*

deurmekaar /ˌdjəːməˈkɑː/ ▶ adjective S. African informal in a state of muddle or confusion.
– ORIGIN Afrikaans, from Dutch dialect variants of *door elkaar*, literally 'through one another, interchangeable'.

deus ex machina /ˌdeɪʊs ɛks ˈmakɪnə, ˌdiːəs ɛks məˈʃiːnə/ ▶ noun an unexpected power or event saving a seemingly hopeless situation, especially as a contrived plot device in a play or novel.
– ORIGIN late 17th cent.: modern Latin, translation of Greek *theos ek mēkhanēs*, 'god from the machinery'. In Greek theatre, actors representing gods were suspended above the stage, the denouement of the play being brought about by their intervention.

Deut. ▶ abbreviation for Deuteronomy (in biblical references).

deuteragonist /ˌdjuːtəˈragənɪst/ ▶ noun the person second in importance to the protagonist in a drama.
– ORIGIN mid 19th cent.: from Greek *deuteragōnistēs*, from *deuteros* 'second' + *agōnistēs* 'actor'.

deuteranope /ˈdjuːt(ə)rənəʊp/ ▶ noun a person suffering from deuteranopia.

deuteranopia /ˌdjuːt(ə)rəˈnəʊpɪə/ ▶ noun [mass noun] colour blindness resulting from insensitivity to green light, causing confusion of greens, reds, and yellows. Compare with PROTANOPIA.
– ORIGIN early 20th cent.: from DEUTERO- 'second' (the colour green being regarded as the second component of colour vision) + AN-[1] + -OPIA.

deuterated /ˈdjuːtəreɪtɪd/ (also **deuteriated** /djuːˈtɪərɪeɪtɪd/) ▶ adjective Chemistry (of a compound) in which the ordinary isotope of hydrogen has been replaced with deuterium.
– DERIVATIVES **deuteration** noun.

deuteric /ˈdjuːtərɪk/ ▶ adjective Geology relating to or denoting alteration of the minerals of an igneous rock during the later stages of consolidation.
– ORIGIN early 20th cent.: from DEUTERO- 'secondary' + -IC.

deuterium /djuːˈtɪərɪəm/ ▶ noun [mass noun] Chemistry a stable isotope of hydrogen with a mass approximately twice that of the usual isotope. (Symbol: **D**)

Deuterium atoms have a neutron as well as a proton in the nucleus, and the isotope is present to about 1 part in 6,000 in naturally occurring hydrogen. It is used as a fuel in thermonuclear bombs, and heavy water (D_2O) is used as a moderator in nuclear reactors.

– ORIGIN 1930s: modern Latin, from Greek *deuteros* 'second'.

deutero- /ˈdjuːtərəʊ/ ▶ combining form second: *Deutero-Isaiah.*
■ secondary: *deuterocanonical.*
– ORIGIN from Greek *deuteros* 'second'.

deuterocanonical ▶ adjective (of sacred books or literary works) forming a secondary canon.

Deutero-Isaiah /ˌdjuːtərəʊʌɪˈzʌɪə/ the supposed later author of Isaiah 40–55.

deuteron /ˈdjuːtərɒn/ ▶ noun the nucleus of a deuterium atom, consisting of a proton and a neutron.
– ORIGIN 1930s: from Greek *deuteros* 'second', on the pattern of *proton.*

Deuteronomy /ˌdjuːtəˈrɒnəmi/ the fifth book of the Bible, containing a recapitulation of the Ten Commandments and much of the Mosaic law.

Deutschland /ˈdɔʏtʃlant/ German name for GERMANY.

Deutschmark /ˈdɔɪtʃmɑːk/ (also **Deutsche Mark** /ˈdɔɪtʃə mɑːk, German ˌdɔʏtʃə ˈmark/) ▶ noun (until the introduction of the euro in 2002) the basic monetary unit of Germany, equal to 100 pfennig.
– ORIGIN from German *deutsche Mark* 'German mark'.

deutzia /ˈdjuːtsɪə, ˈdɔɪt-/ ▶ noun an ornamental shrub with white or pinkish flowers, native to Asia and Central America.
● Genus *Deutzia*, family Hydrangeaceae.

– ORIGIN modern Latin, named after Johann van der *Deutz*, 18th-cent. Dutch patron of botany.

deva /ˈdeɪvə/ ▶ **noun** a member of a class of divine beings in the Vedic period, which in Indian religion are benevolent and in Zoroastrianism are evil. Compare with **ASURA**.
■ Indian (in general use) a god.
– ORIGIN from Sanskrit, literally 'shining one', later 'god'.

devadasi /ˌdeɪvəˈdɑːsi/ ▶ **noun** (pl. **devadasis**) a hereditary female dancer in a Hindu temple.
– ORIGIN from Sanskrit *devadāsī*, literally 'female servant of a god'.

de Valera /ˌdə vəˈlɛːrə/, Eamon (1882–1975), American-born Irish statesman, Taoiseach (Prime Minister) 1937–48, 1951–4, and 1957–9 and President of the Republic of Ireland 1959–73. He was the leader of Sinn Fein 1917–26 and the founder of the Fianna Fáil Party in 1926. As President of the Irish Free State from 1932, de Valera was largely responsible for the new constitution of 1937 which created the state of Eire.

de Valois /də ˈvalwɑː/, Dame Ninette (b.1898), Irish choreographer, ballet dancer, and teacher; born *Edris Stannus*. A former soloist with Diaghilev's Ballets Russes, she formed the Vic-Wells Ballet (which eventually became the Royal Ballet) and the Sadler's Wells ballet school.

devalorize /diːˈvalərʌɪz/ ▶ **verb** [with obj.] rare devalue.
– DERIVATIVES **devalorization** noun.
– ORIGIN early 20th cent.: from French *dévaloriser*.

devalue ▶ **verb** (**devalues**, **devalued**, **devaluing**) [with obj.] reduce or underestimate the worth or importance of: *I resent the way people seem to devalue my achievement*.
■ (often **be devalued**) Economics reduce the official value of (a currency) in relation to other currencies: *the dinar was devalued by 20 per cent*.
– DERIVATIVES **devaluation** noun.

Devanagari /ˌdeɪvəˈnɑːɡ(ə)ri, dɛv-/ ▶ **noun** [mass noun] the alphabet used for Sanskrit, Hindi, and other Indian languages.
– ORIGIN from Sanskrit, literally 'divine town script', from *deva* 'god' + *nāgarī* (from *nagara* 'town'), an earlier name of the script.

devastate /ˈdɛvəsteɪt/ ▶ **verb** [with obj.] destroy or ruin (something): *the city was devastated by a huge earthquake* | *bad weather has devastated the tourist industry*.
■ cause (someone) severe and overwhelming shock or grief: *she was devastated by the loss of Damian*.
– DERIVATIVES **devastation** noun, **devastator** noun.
– ORIGIN mid 17th cent.: from Latin *devastat-* 'laid waste', from the verb *devastare*, from *de-* 'thoroughly' + *vastare* 'lay waste'.

devastating ▶ **adjective** highly destructive or damaging: *a devastating cyclone struck Bangladesh*.
■ causing severe shock, distress, or grief: *the news came as a devastating blow*. ■ informal extremely impressive, effective, or attractive: *she had a devastating wit*.
– DERIVATIVES **devastatingly** adverb [as submodifier] *a devastatingly attractive man*.

devein ▶ **verb** [with obj.] remove the main central vein from (a shrimp or prawn).

develop ▶ **verb** (**developed**, **developing**) **1** grow or cause to grow and become more mature, advanced, or elaborate: [no obj.] *motion pictures were to* **develop into** *mass entertainment* | [as adj. **developing**] *this is a rapidly developing field* | [with obj.] *enabling individuals to develop their personal skills*.
■ [no obj.] [often as adj. **developing**] (of a poor agricultural country) become more economically and socially advanced: *the developing world*. ■ [with obj.] convert (land) to a new purpose by constructing buildings or making other use of its resources. ■ construct or convert (a building) so as to improve existing resources. ■ [with obj.] elaborate (a musical theme) by modification of the melody, harmony, or rhythm. ■ [with obj.] Chess bring (a piece) into play from its initial position on a player's back rank.
2 start to exist, experience, or possess: [no obj.] *a strange closeness developed* | [with obj.] *I developed an interest in law* | *Aids victims often develop a rare type of cancer*.
3 [with obj.] treat (a photographic film) with chemicals to make a visible image.
– ORIGIN mid 17th cent. (in the sense 'unfold, unfurl'): from French *développer*, based on Latin *dis-* 'un-' + a second element of unknown origin found also in **ENVELOP**.

developable ▶ **adjective** able to be developed, in particular:
■ (of land or property) able to be adapted or improved so as to become productive or profitable. ■ Geometry (of a curved surface) capable of being flattened into a plane without overlap or separation, as with a cylinder. ■ Mathematics (of a function or expression) capable of being expanded as a series.

developed ▶ **adjective** advanced or elaborated to a specified degree: *a fully developed system of public law*.
■ (of a person or part of the body) having specified physical proportions: *a strongman with well-developed muscles*. ■ (of a country or region) advanced economically and socially: *economic assistance to the less-developed countries* | *the developed world*.

developer ▶ **noun** a person or thing that develops something: *a property developer* | *software developers*.
■ [with adj.] a person who grows or matures at a specified time or rate: *I was a slow developer*. ■ [mass noun] a chemical agent used for treating photographic film to make a visible image.

developing country ▶ **noun** a poor agricultural country that is seeking to become more advanced economically and socially.

development ▶ **noun** [mass noun] **1** the process of developing or being developed: *she traces the development of the novel* | *the development of less invasive treatment*.
■ a specified state of growth or advancement: *the wings attain their full development several hours after birth*. ■ [count noun] a new and refined product or idea: *the latest developments in information technology*. ■ [count noun] an event constituting a new stage in a changing situation: *I don't think there have been any new developments since yesterday*. ■ the process of converting land to a new purpose by constructing buildings or making use of its resources: *land suitable for development*. ■ [count noun] an area of land with new buildings on it: *a major housing development in Essex*. ■ Chess the process of bringing one's pieces into play in the opening phase of a game.
2 the process of starting to experience or suffer from an ailment or feeling: *the development of brittle bones*.
3 the process of treating photographic film with chemicals to make a visible image.

developmental ▶ **adjective** concerned with the development of someone or something: *developmental problems* | *developmental psychology*.
■ concerned with the evolution of animals and plants: *developmental biology*.
– DERIVATIVES **developmentally** adverb.

development area ▶ **noun** (in the UK) an area in which government assistance is available to encourage business investment, in order to counteract unemployment.

development education ▶ **noun** [mass noun] education aimed at giving an understanding of developing countries and their place in the global socio-economic situation.

development system ▶ **noun** Computing a system of software and hardware designed to assist in the development of new software or products.

développé /ˌdeɪvˈlɒpeɪ/ ▶ **noun** (pl. **développés** pronunc. same) Ballet a movement in which one leg is raised and then kept in a fully extended position.

Devensian /dɪˈvɛnzɪən/ ▶ **adjective** Geology of, relating to, or denoting the most recent Pleistocene glaciation in Britain, identified with the Weichselian of northern Europe.
■ [as noun **the Devensian**] the Devensian glaciation or the system of deposits laid down during it.
– ORIGIN 1960s: from Latin *Devenses* 'people dwelling near the River Dee' (see sense 2 of **DEE**[1]) + **-IAN**.

deverbal /diːˈvəːb(ə)l/ ▶ **adjective** (of a noun or adjective) derived from a verb.
▶ **noun** a deverbal noun or adjective.

Devi /ˈdeɪvi/ Hinduism the supreme goddess, often identified with Parvati and Sakti.
■ (**devi**) Indian (in general use) a goddess. ■ Indian used after the first name of a Hindu woman as a form of respect: *Deval Devi*.

deviance ▶ **noun** [mass noun] the fact or state of diverging from usual or accepted standards, especially in social or sexual behaviour.
– DERIVATIVES **deviancy** noun.

deviant ▶ **adjective** diverging from usual or accepted standards, especially in social or sexual behaviour: *deviant behaviour* | *a deviant ideology*.
■ derogatory homosexual.
▶ **noun** a deviant person or thing.
– ORIGIN late Middle English: from late Latin *deviant-* 'turning out of the way', from the verb *deviare* (see **DEVIATE**).

deviate ▶ **verb** /ˈdiːvɪeɪt/ [no obj.] diverge from an established course: *you must not* **deviate from** *the agreed route*.
■ diverge from usual or accepted standards: *those who* **deviate from** *society's values*.
▶ **noun** & **adjective** /ˈdiːvɪət/ old-fashioned term for **DEVIANT**.
– DERIVATIVES **deviator** noun.
– ORIGIN mid 16th cent. (as an adjective in the sense 'remote'): from late Latin *deviat-* 'turned out of the way', from the verb *deviare*, from *de-* 'away from' + *via* 'way'. The verb dates from the mid 17th cent.

deviation ▶ **noun** [mass noun] **1** the action of diverging from an established course or accepted standard: **deviation from** *a norm* | *sexual deviation* | [count noun] **deviations from** *Standard English*.
2 Statistics the amount by which a single measurement differs from a fixed value such as the mean.
3 the deflection of a ship's compass needle caused by iron in the ship.
– DERIVATIVES **deviationism** noun, **deviationist** noun.
– ORIGIN late Middle English: via French from medieval Latin *deviatio(n-)*, from Latin *deviare* (see **DEVIATE**).

device ▶ **noun 1** a thing made or adapted for a particular purpose, especially a mechanical or electronic contrivance: *a measuring device*.
■ an explosive contrivance; a bomb: *an incendiary device*. ■ [mass noun] archaic the design or look of something: *works of strange device*.
2 a plan, scheme, or trick with a particular aim: *writing a public letter is a traditional device for signalling dissent*.
■ a turn of phrase intended to produce a particular effect in speech or a literary work: *a rhetorical device*.
3 a drawing or design: *the decorative device on the invitations*.
■ an emblematic or heraldic design: *their shields bear the device of the Blazing Sun*.
– PHRASES **leave someone to their own devices** leave someone to do as they wish without supervision.
– ORIGIN Middle English: from Old French *devis*, based on Latin *divis-* 'divided', from the verb *dividere*. The original sense was 'desire or intention', found now only in *leave a person to his or her own devices* (which has become associated with sense 2).

devil ▶ **noun 1** (usu. **the Devil**) (in Christian and Jewish belief) the supreme spirit of evil; Satan.
■ an evil spirit; a demon. ■ a very wicked or cruel person: *they prefer voting for devils than for decent men*. ■ a mischievously clever or self-willed person: *the cunning old devil is up to something*. ■ [with adj.] informal a person with specified characteristics: *the poor devil* | *a lucky devil*. ■ (**the devil**) fighting spirit; wildness: *he was dangerous when the devil was in him*. ■ (**the devil**) a thing that is very difficult or awkward to do or deal with: *it's going to be* **the very devil** *to disentangle*.
2 (**the devil**) expressing surprise or annoyance in various questions or exclamations: *'Where the devil is he?'*
3 an instrument or machine, especially one fitted with sharp teeth or spikes, used for tearing or other destructive work.
4 informal, dated a junior assistant of a barrister or other professional. See also **PRINTER'S DEVIL**.
5 Austral. short for **TASMANIAN DEVIL**.
▶ **verb** (**devilled**, **devilling**; US **deviled**, **deviling**) **1** [no obj.] informal, dated act as a junior assistant for a barrister or other professional.
2 [with obj.] N. Amer. harass or worry (someone): *he was deviled by a new-found fear*.
– PHRASES **be a devil!** informal said when encouraging someone to do something that they are hesitating to do: *'Go on, be a devil and stop being so staid!'* **between the devil and the deep blue sea** caught in a dilemma. [ORIGIN: alluding to two equally dangerous alternatives; also as *between the devil and the dead sea* and *between the devil and the deep sea*.] **devil a ——** archaic not even one or any: *the devil a man of you stirred himself over it*. **the devil can quote scripture for his purpose** proverb people may conceal unworthy motives by reciting words that sound morally authoritative. [ORIGIN: with

allusion to the Temptation.] **the devil finds work for idle hands to do** proverb if someone doesn't have enough work to occupy them, they are liable to cause or get into trouble. **the devil looks after his own** proverb success or good fortune often seem to come to those who least deserve it. **devil-may-care** cheerful and reckless: *light-hearted, devil-may-care young pilots*. **a devil of a ——** informal used to emphasize great size or degree: *photographic equipment costs a devil of a lot*. **the devil's dozen** thirteen. **the devil's in the detail** the details of a matter are its most problematic aspect. **the devil to pay** serious trouble to be dealt with. **the devil's own ——** informal used to emphasize the difficulty or seriousness of something: *he was in the devil's own hurry*. **every man for himself and the devil take the hindmost** see **MAN**. **give the devil his due** proverb if someone or something generally considered bad or undeserving has any redeeming features these should be acknowledged. **go to the devil!** said in angry rejection or condemnation of someone. **like the devil** with great speed or energy: *he drove like the devil*. **play the devil with** have a damaging or disruptive effect on: *this brandy plays the devil with one's emotions!* **speak** (or **talk**) **of the devil** said when a person appears just after being mentioned. [ORIGIN: from the superstition that the devil will appear if his name is spoken.]

– ORIGIN Old English *dēofol* (related to Dutch *duivel* and German *Teufel*), via late Latin from Greek *diabolos* 'accuser, slanderer' (used in the Septuagint to translate Hebrew *śāṭān* 'Satan'), from *diaballein* 'to slander', from *dia* 'across' + *ballein* 'to throw'.

devil dance ▶ **noun** a dance performed as part of Buddhist ritual in Sri Lanka and Tibet, for the invocation, propitiation, or exorcism of spirits.

– DERIVATIVES **devil dancer** noun.

devilfish ▶ **noun** (pl. same or **-fishes**) any of a number of marine creatures that are perceived as having a sinister appearance, in particular a devil ray, a stonefish, or an octopus or squid.

devilish ▶ **adjective** of, like, or appropriate to a devil in evil and cruelty: *devilish tortures*.
■ mischievous and rakish: *a wide, devilish grin*. ■ very difficult to deal with or use: *it turned out to be a devilish job*.
▶ **adverb** [as submodifier] informal, dated very; extremely: *a devilish clever chap*.

– DERIVATIVES **devilishness** noun.

devilishly ▶ **adverb** in a devilish manner.
■ [as submodifier] informal very; extremely: *I'm feeling devilishly hot!*

devilled ▶ **adjective** (of food) cooked with hot seasoning: *devilled kidneys*.

devilling float ▶ **noun** a wooden or plastic block with tips of nails just protruding through its base, used to scratch the surface of plaster lightly to enable more plaster to adhere to it.

devilment ▶ **noun** [mass noun] reckless mischief; wild spirits: *his eyes were blazing with devilment*.

devil ray ▶ **noun** a large long-tailed ray which has a fleshy horn-like projection on each side of the mouth. It occurs on or near the surface of warm seas and feeds on plankton.
● Family Mobulidae: two genera and several species, including the manta.

devilry ▶ **noun** [mass noun] wicked activity: *some devilry was afoot*.
■ reckless mischief: *a perverse sense of devilry urged her to lead him on*. ■ black magic; dealings with the devil.

devil's advocate ▶ **noun** a person who expresses a contentious opinion in order to provoke debate or test the strength of the opposing arguments: *the interviewer will need to* ***play devil's advocate****, to put the other side's case forward*.
■ historical a person appointed by the Roman Catholic Church to challenge a proposed beatification or canonization, or the verification of a miracle.

devil's bit ▶ **noun** any of a number of wild plants with a very short rootstock, said in folklore to have been bitten off by the devil, in particular:
● (also **devil's bit scabious**) a blue-flowered plant native to Eurasia and North Africa (*Succisa pratensis*, family Dipsacaceae). ● N. Amer. the blazing star (*Chamaelirium luteum*, family Liliaceae).

devil's claw ▶ **noun** a plant whose seed pods bear claw-like hooks which can harm livestock.
● Two genera in the family Pedaliaceae: genus *Proboscidea* of warm regions of America, used in basketry or grown for their fruit, and *Harpagophytum procumbens* of southern Africa and Madagascar, used in herbal medicine.

devil's club ▶ **noun** a very spiny straggling shrub of western North America.
● *Oplopanax horridus*, family Araliaceae.

devil's coach-horse ▶ **noun** Brit. a large black predatory rove beetle which raises its hind end and opens its jaws in a threatening manner when disturbed.
● *Staphylinus olens*, family Staphylinidae.

devil's darning needle ▶ **noun** N. Amer. another term for **DARNER** (in sense 2).

devil's food cake ▶ **noun** chiefly N. Amer. a rich chocolate cake.

devil's grip ▶ **noun** informal term for **BORNHOLM DISEASE**.

Devil's Island a rocky island off the coast of French Guiana, used from 1852 as a penal settlement, especially for political prisoners. The last prisoner was released in 1953.

devils on horseback ▶ **plural noun** chiefly Brit. a savoury snack of prunes individually wrapped in slices of bacon, served on toast or croutons.

devil's paintbrush ▶ **noun** N. Amer. the European orange hawkweed, which has become naturalized in North America.
● *Hieracium aurantiacum*, family Compositae.

devil's walking stick ▶ **noun** a prickly angelica tree native to the eastern US. Also called **HERCULES' CLUB**.
● *Aralia spinosa*, family Araliaceae.

deviltry ▶ **noun** archaic variant of **DEVILRY**.

devious /ˈdiːvɪəs/ ▶ **adjective 1** showing a skilful use of underhand tactics to achieve goals: *he's as devious as a politician needs to be* | *they have devious ways of making money*.
2 (of a route or journey) longer and less direct than the most straightforward way: *they arrived at the town by a devious route*.

– DERIVATIVES **deviously** adverb, **deviousness** noun.

– ORIGIN late 16th cent.: from Latin *devius* (from *de-* 'away from' + *via* 'way') + **-OUS**. The original sense was 'remote or sequestered'; the later sense 'departing from the direct route' gave rise to the figurative sense 'deviating from the straight way' and hence 'skilled in underhand tactics'.

devise /dɪˈvʌɪz/ ▶ **verb** [with obj.] **1** plan or invent (a complex procedure, system, or mechanism) by careful thought: *a training programme should be devised* | *a complicated game* ***of his own devising***.
2 Law leave (real estate) to someone by the terms of a will.
▶ **noun** Law a clause in a will leaving real estate to someone.

– DERIVATIVES **devisable** adjective, **devisee** noun (only in sense 2), **deviser** noun, **devisor** noun (only in sense 2).

– ORIGIN Middle English: the verb from Old French *deviser*, from Latin *divis-* 'divided', from the verb *dividere* (this sense being reflected in the original English sense of the verb); the noun is a variant of **DEVICE** (in the early sense 'will, desire').

devitalize (also **-ise**) ▶ **verb** [with obj.] [usu. as adj. **devitalized**] deprive of strength and vigour: *an effective product to treat devitalized skin*.

– DERIVATIVES **devitalization** noun.

devitrify ▶ **verb** (**-ies**, **-ied**) [no obj.] (of glass or vitreous rock) become hard, opaque, and crystalline.
■ [with obj.] make hard, opaque, and crystalline.

– DERIVATIVES **devitrification** noun.

devoice ▶ **verb** [with obj.] Phonetics make (a vowel or voiced consonant) voiceless.

devoid /dɪˈvɔɪd/ ▶ **adjective** [predic.] (**devoid of**) entirely lacking or free from: *Lisa kept her voice devoid of emotion*.

– ORIGIN late Middle English: past participle of obsolete *devoid* 'cast out', from Old French *devoidier*.

devoir /dəˈvwɑː/ ▶ **noun** archaic a person's duty: *you have* ***done your devoir*** *right well*.
■ (**pay one's devoirs**) pay one's respects formally.

– ORIGIN Middle English: from Old French *deveir*, from Latin *debere* 'owe'. The spelling, and subsequently the pronunciation, was changed under the influence of modern French *devoir*.

devolution /ˌdiːvəˈluːʃ(ə)n, dɛv-/ ▶ **noun** [mass noun] the transfer or delegation of power to a lower level, especially by central government to local or regional administration.
■ formal descent or degeneration to a lower or worse state: *the* ***devolution*** *of the gentlemanly ideal* ***into*** *a glorification of drunkenness*. ■ Law the legal transfer of property from one owner to another. ■ Biology evolutionary degeneration.

– DERIVATIVES **devolutionary** adjective, **devolutionist** noun.

– ORIGIN late 15th cent. (in the sense 'transference by default'): from late Latin *devolutio(n-)*, from Latin *devolvere* 'roll down' (see **DEVOLVE**).

devolve /dɪˈvɒlv/ ▶ **verb** [with obj.] transfer or delegate (power) to a lower level, especially from central government to local or regional administration: *measures to* ***devolve*** *power* ***to*** *a Scottish assembly* | [as adj. **devolved**] *devolved and decentralized government*.
■ [no obj.] (**devolve on/upon/to**) (of duties or responsibility) pass to (a body or person at a lower level): *his duties devolved on a comrade*. ■ [no obj.] (**devolve on/upon/to**) Law (of property) be transferred from one owner to (another), especially by inheritance. ■ [no obj.] (**devolve into**) formal degenerate or be split into: *the Empire devolved into separate warring states*.

– DERIVATIVES **devolvement** noun.

– ORIGIN late Middle English (in the sense 'roll down'): from Latin *devolvere*, from *de-* 'down' + *volvere* 'to roll'.

Devon[1] (also **Devonshire**) a county of SW England; county town, Exeter.

– ORIGIN from medieval Latin *Devonia* 'Devonshire'.

Devon[2] ▶ **noun** an animal of a breed of red beef cattle.

– ORIGIN mid 19th cent.: named after the county of *Devon* (see **DEVON**[1]).

Devonian /dɛˈvəʊnɪən, dɪ-/ ▶ **adjective 1** of or relating to Devon.
2 Geology of, relating to, or denoting the fourth period of the Palaeozoic era, between the Silurian and Carboniferous periods.

> The Devonian period lasted from about 409 to 363 million years ago. During this period fish became abundant, the first amphibians evolved, and the first forests appeared.

▶ **noun 1** a native or inhabitant of Devon.
2 (**the Devonian**) Geology the Devonian period or the system of rocks deposited during it.

Devonshire cream ▶ **noun** [mass noun] clotted cream.

dévot /deɪˈvəʊ, French devo/ (also **dévote** /deɪˈvɒt, French devɔt/) ▶ **noun** French term for **DEVOTEE**.

– ORIGIN French, from Old French *devot* (see **DEVOUT**).

devote ▶ **verb** [with obj.] **1** (**devote something to**) give all or a large part of one's time or resources to (a person, activity, or cause): *I wanted to devote more time to my family* | *she* ***devoted herself to*** *fund-raising*.
2 archaic invoke or pronounce a curse upon.

– ORIGIN late 16th cent. (in the sense 'dedicate formally, consecrate'): from Latin *devot-* 'consecrated', from the verb *devovere*, from *de-* 'formally' + *vovere* 'to vow'.

devoted ▶ **adjective 1** very loving or loyal: *he was a devoted husband* | *Leo was* ***devoted to*** *his job*.
2 [predic.] (**devoted to**) given over to the display, study, or discussion of: *there is a museum devoted to her work*.

– DERIVATIVES **devotedly** adverb (in sense 1), **devotedness** noun (in sense 1).

devotee /ˌdɛvə(ʊ)ˈtiː/ ▶ **noun** a person who is very interested in and enthusiastic about someone or something: *a devotee of Lewis Carroll*.
■ a strong believer in a particular religion or god: *devotees of Krishna* | *devotees thronged the temple*.

devotion ▶ **noun** [mass noun] love, loyalty, or enthusiasm for a person, activity, or cause: *Eleanor's* ***devotion to*** *her husband* | *his courage and* ***devotion to duty*** *never wavered*.
■ religious worship or observance: *the order's aim was to live a life of devotion*. ■ (**devotions**) prayers or religious observances.

– ORIGIN Middle English: from Latin *devotio(n-)*, from *devovere* 'consecrate' (see **DEVOTE**).

devotional ▶ **adjective** of or used in religious worship: *devotional books*.

devour /dɪˈvaʊə/ ▶ **verb** [with obj.] eat (food or prey) hungrily or quickly: *he devoured half of his burger in one bite*.
■ (of fire, disease, or other forces) consume (someone or something) destructively: *the hungry flames*

devoured the old house. ■ read (something) quickly and eagerly: *she spent her evenings devouring the classics.* ■ (**be devoured**) (of a person) be totally absorbed by a powerful feeling: *she was devoured by need.*
– DERIVATIVES **devourer** noun, **devouringly** adverb.
– ORIGIN Middle English: from Old French *devorer*, from Latin *devorare*, from *de-* 'down' + *vorare* 'to swallow'.

devout /dɪˈvaʊt/ ▶ adjective having or showing deep religious feeling or commitment: *she was a devout Catholic* | *a rabbi's devout prayers.*
■ totally committed to a cause or belief: *the most devout environmentalist.*
– DERIVATIVES **devoutly** adverb, **devoutness** noun.
– ORIGIN Middle English: from Old French *devot*, from Latin *devotus* 'devoted', past participle of *devovere* (see **DEVOTE**).

de Vries /də ˈvriːs/, Hugo (1848–1935), Dutch plant physiologist and geneticist. De Vries did much work on osmosis and water relations in plants, coining the term *plasmolysis*. His subsequent work on heredity and variation contributed substantially to the chromosome theory of heredity.

DEW ▶ abbreviation for distant early warning, a radar system in North America for the early detection of a missile attack.

dew ▶ noun [mass noun] tiny drops of water that form on cool surfaces at night, when atmospheric vapour condenses: *the grass was wet with dew* | [in sing.] *a cold, heavy dew dripped from the leaves.*
■ [in sing.] a beaded or glistening liquid resembling such drops: *her body had broken out in a fine dew of perspiration.*
▶ verb [with obj.] wet (a part of someone's body) with a beaded or glistening liquid: *sweat dewed her lashes.*
– ORIGIN Old English *dēaw*, of Germanic origin; related to Dutch *dauw* and German *Tau* (noun), *tauen* (verb).

dewan /dɪˈwɑːn/ ▶ noun variant spelling of **DIWAN**.

Dewar /ˈdjuːə/, Sir James (1842–1923), Scottish chemist and physicist. He is chiefly remembered for his work in cryogenics, in which he devised the vacuum flask, achieved temperatures close to absolute zero, and was the first to produce liquid oxygen and hydrogen in quantity.

dewar /ˈdjuːə/ ▶ noun a double-walled flask of metal or silvered glass with a vacuum between the walls, used to hold liquids at well below ambient temperature.
– ORIGIN late 19th cent.: named after Sir James **DEWAR**.

dewater ▶ verb [with obj.] drain (a waterlogged or flooded area).
■ remove water from (sediment or waste materials).

dewberry ▶ noun (pl. **-ies**) a trailing European bramble with soft prickles and edible blackberry-like fruit which have a dewy white bloom on the skin.
● *Rubus caesius*, family Rosaceae.
■ N. Amer. any of a number of trailing brambles. ■ the blue-black fruit of any of these plants.

dewclaw ▶ noun a rudimentary inner toe present in some dogs.
■ a false hoof on an animal such as a deer, which is formed by its rudimentary side toes.
– ORIGIN late 16th cent.: apparently from the nouns **DEW** and **CLAW**.

dewdrop ▶ noun a drop of dew.

Dewey /ˈdjuːi/, John (1859–1952), American philosopher and educationist. Working in the pragmatic tradition of William James and C. S. Pierce, he evolved the educational theory that children would learn best by doing.

Dewey decimal classification (also **Dewey system**) ▶ noun an internationally applied decimal system of library classification which uses a three-figure code from 000 to 999 to represent the major branches of knowledge, and allows finer classification to be made by the addition of further figures after a decimal point.
– ORIGIN late 19th cent.: named after Melvil *Dewey* (1851–1931), American librarian.

dewfall ▶ noun [mass noun] poetic/literary the formation of dew, or the time of the evening when dew begins to form.
■ the film of dew covering an area.

Dewi /ˈdɛwi/ Welsh name for St David (see **DAVID, ST**).

dewlap ▶ noun a fold of loose skin hanging from the neck or throat of an animal or bird, especially that present in many cattle.
– ORIGIN Middle English: from **DEW** and **LAP**[1], perhaps influenced by a Scandinavian word (compare with Danish *doglæp*).

deworm ▶ verb [with obj.] treat (an animal) to free it of worms.
– DERIVATIVES **dewormer** noun.

dew point ▶ noun the atmospheric temperature (varying according to pressure and humidity) below which water droplets begin to condense and dew can form.

dew pond ▶ noun Brit. a shallow pond, especially an artificial one, occurring on downs where the water supply from springs or surface drainage is inadequate.

Dewsbury /ˈdjuːzb(ə)ri/ a textile manufacturing town in northern England, formerly in Yorkshire; pop. 50,000 (1980).

dew worm ▶ noun N. Amer. an earthworm, in particular one that is used as fishing bait.
– ORIGIN Old English *deaw-wyrm* 'ringworm'; compare with East Frisian *dauworm*, denoting both ringworm and the earthworm.

dewy ▶ adjective (**dewier, dewiest**) wet with dew.
■ (of a person's skin) appearing soft and lustrous: *your skin will begin to feel revitalized and dewy.* ■ youthful and fresh: *the girls have yet to lose their dewy charm.*
– DERIVATIVES **dewily** adverb, **dewiness** noun.
– ORIGIN Old English *dēawig* (see **DEW, -Y**[1]).

dewy-eyed ▶ adjective having eyes that are moist with tears (used typically to indicate that a person is nostalgic, naive, or sentimental): *she gets slightly dewy-eyed as she talks about her family.*

dex ▶ noun informal short for **DEXEDRINE**.

dexamethasone /ˌdɛksəˈmɛθəsəʊn, -zəʊn/ ▶ noun [mass noun] Medicine a synthetic drug of the corticosteroid type, used especially as an anti-inflammatory agent.
– ORIGIN 1950s: from *dexa-* (blend of **DECA-** and **HEXA-**) + *meth(yl)* + *-a-* + *(cortis)one*.

Dexedrine /ˈdɛksədriːn, -drɪn/ ▶ noun trademark for *amphetamine sulphate* (see **AMPHETAMINE**).
– ORIGIN 1940s: probably from **DEXTRO-**, on the pattern of *Benzedrine*.

dexter[1] /ˈdɛkstə/ ▶ adjective [attrib.] archaic & Heraldry of, on, or towards the right-hand side (in a coat of arms, from the bearer's point of view, i.e. the left as it is depicted). The opposite of **SINISTER**.
– ORIGIN mid 16th cent.: from Latin, 'on the right'.

dexter[2] /ˈdɛkstə/ ▶ noun an animal of a small, hardy breed of Irish cattle.
– ORIGIN late 19th cent.: said to have been named after the breeder.

dexterity /dɛkˈstɛrɪti/ ▶ noun [mass noun] skill in performing tasks, especially with the hands: *her dexterity with chopsticks* | *his record testifies to a certain dexterity in politics.*
– ORIGIN early 16th cent. (in the sense 'mental adroitness'): from French *dextérité*, from Latin *dexteritas*, from *dexter* 'on the right'.

dexterous /ˈdɛkst(ə)rəs/ (also **dextrous**) ▶ adjective demonstrating neat skill, especially with the hands: *Anne was dexterous and found the tasks easy.*
– DERIVATIVES **dexterously** adverb, **dexterousness** noun.
– ORIGIN early 17th cent. (in the sense 'mentally adroit, clever'): from Latin *dexter* 'on the right' + **-OUS**.

dextral /ˈdɛkstr(ə)l/ ▶ adjective of or on the right side or the right hand (the opposite of **SINISTRAL**), in particular:
■ right-handed. ■ Geology relating to or denoting a strike-slip fault in which the motion of the block on the further side of the fault from an observer is towards the right. ■ Zoology (of a spiral mollusc shell) with whorls rising to the right and coiling in an anticlockwise direction.
▶ noun a right-handed person.
– DERIVATIVES **dextrality** /-ˈstralɪti/ noun, **dextrally** adverb.
– ORIGIN mid 17th cent.: from medieval Latin *dextralis*, from Latin *dextra* 'the right hand', from *dexter* 'on the right'.

dextran /ˈdɛkstran/ ▶ noun [mass noun] Chemistry a carbohydrate gum formed by the fermentation of sugars and consisting of polymers of glucose.
■ Medicine a solution containing a hydrolysed form of this, used as a substitute for blood plasma.

– ORIGIN late 19th cent.: from **DEXTRO-** + **-AN**.

dextrin /ˈdɛkstrɪn/ ▶ noun [mass noun] a soluble gummy substance obtained by hydrolysis of starch, used as a thickening agent and in adhesives and dietary supplements.
– ORIGIN mid 19th cent.: from **DEXTRO-** + **-IN**[1].

dextro- ▶ combining form on or to the right: *dextrorotatory.*
– ORIGIN from Latin *dexter, dextr-* 'right'.

dextrorotatory /ˌdɛkstrəʊˈrəʊtət(ə)ri/ ▶ adjective Chemistry (of a compound) having the property of rotating the plane of a polarized light ray to the right, i.e. clockwise facing the oncoming radiation. The opposite of **LAEVOROTATORY**.
– DERIVATIVES **dextrorotation** noun.

dextrose /ˈdɛkstrəʊz, -s/ ▶ noun [mass noun] Chemistry the dextrorotatory form of glucose (and the predominant naturally occurring form).
– ORIGIN mid 19th cent.: from Latin *dexter, dextr-* 'on the right' + **-OSE**[2].

dextrous ▶ adjective variant spelling of **DEXTEROUS**.

dexy /ˈdɛksi/ ▶ noun (pl. **-ies**) [mass noun] informal Dexedrine.
■ [count noun] a tablet of Dexedrine.
– ORIGIN 1950s: abbreviation.

dezincification /diːˌzɪŋkɪfɪˈkeɪʃ(ə)n/ ▶ noun [mass noun] a form of corrosion and weakening of brass objects in which zinc is dissolved out of the brass alloy.

DF ▶ abbreviation for ■ Defender of the Faith. [ORIGIN: from Latin *Defensor Fidei*.] ■ direction-finder.

DFC ▶ abbreviation for (in the UK) Distinguished Flying Cross, a decoration for distinguished active service awarded to members of the RAF, instituted in 1918.

DFE ▶ abbreviation for (in the UK) Department for Education.

Dfl ▶ abbreviation for Dutch florins.

DFM ▶ abbreviation for (in the UK) Distinguished Flying Medal, a decoration awarded to RAF personnel for acts of courage or devotion to duty when not in action against an enemy, instituted in 1918.

DG ▶ abbreviation for ■ Dei gratia, by the grace of God. ■ Deo gratias, thanks be to God. ■ (in the UK) director general.

DH Baseball ▶ abbreviation for designated hitter.
▶ verb (**DH's, DH'd, DHing**) [no obj.] act as a designated hitter.
■ [with obj.] use (a player) as a designated hitter.

dhaba /ˈdɑːbə/ ▶ noun Indian a roadside food stall.
– ORIGIN from Hindi *ḍhābā*.

Dhaka /ˈdakə/ (also **Dacca**) the capital of Bangladesh, on the Ganges delta; pop. 3,637,890 (1991).
– DERIVATIVES **Dhakai** adjective.

dhal /dɑːl/ (also **dal**) ▶ noun [mass noun] split pulses, a common foodstuff in India.
■ a dish made with these.
– ORIGIN from Hindi *dāl*.

dhamma /ˈdɑːmə, ˈdʌmə/ ▶ noun another term for **DHARMA**, especially among Theravada Buddhists.
– ORIGIN Pali, from Sanskrit *dharma* 'decree or custom'.

Dhanbad /ˈdɑːnbad/ a city in Bihar, NE India; pop. 818,000 (1991).

dhansak /ˈdʌnsaːk/ ▶ noun [mass noun] an Indian dish of meat or vegetables cooked with lentils and coriander: *chicken dhansak.*
– ORIGIN from Gujarati.

dharma /ˈdɑːmə, ˈdɑːmə/ ▶ noun [mass noun] (in Indian religion) the eternal law of the cosmos, inherent in the very nature of things.

In Hinduism, dharma is seen as the cosmic law both upheld by the gods and expressed in right behaviour by humans, including adherence to the social order. In Buddhism, it is interpreted as universal truth or law, especially as proclaimed by the Buddha. In Jainism, it is conceived both as virtue and as a kind of fundamental substance, the medium of motion.

– ORIGIN Sanskrit, literally 'decree or custom'.

dharmashala /ˈdɑːməˌʃɑːlə/ (also **dharmsala**) ▶ noun (in the Indian subcontinent) a building devoted to religious or charitable purposes, especially a rest house for travellers.
– ORIGIN from Sanskrit *dharmaśālā*, from *dharma* 'virtue' + *śālā* 'house'.

dharna /ˈdɑːnə, -ɑː/ ▶ noun [mass noun] Indian a mode of compelling payment or compliance, by sitting at the debtor's or offender's door without eating until the demand is complied with.
 ■[count noun] a peaceful demonstration.
– ORIGIN from Hindi *dharnā* 'sitting in restraint, placing'.

Dharuk /ˈdʌrʊk/ ▶ noun [mass noun] an Aboriginal language of the area around Sydney, Australia, now extinct.

Dhaulagiri /ˌdaʊləˈɡɪri/ a mountain massif in the Himalayas, in Nepal, with six peaks, rising to 8,172 m (26,810 ft) at its highest point.

Dhelfoí /ˈðɛlˈfiː/ Greek name for DELPHI.

dhikr /ˈdɪkʌr/ ▶ noun [mass noun] Islam a form of devotion, associated chiefly with Sufism, in which the worshipper is absorbed in the rhythmic repetition of the name of God or his attributes.
 ■[count noun] a Sufi ceremony in which this is practised.

Dhílos /ˈðiːlɒs/ Greek name for DELOS.

dhobi /ˈdəʊbi/ ▶ noun (pl. **dhobis**) (in the Indian subcontinent) a washerman or washerwoman.
– ORIGIN from Hindi *dhobī*, from *dhob* 'washing'.

dhobi itch ▶ noun [mass noun] informal itching inflammation of the skin, especially in the groin region, suffered particularly in the tropics and typically caused by certain types of ringworm infection or by allergic dermatitis.

Dhofar /dəʊˈfɑː/ the fertile southern province of Oman.

dhol /dəʊl/ ▶ noun a large, barrel-shaped or cylindrical wooden drum, typically two-headed, used in the Indian subcontinent.
– ORIGIN from Hindi *dhol*.

dholak /ˈdəʊlək/ ▶ noun a dhol, especially a relatively small one.
– ORIGIN Hindi, from *dhol* (see DHOL) + the diminutive suffix -*ak*.

dhole /dəʊl/ ▶ noun an Asian wild dog with a sandy coat and a black bushy tail, living in packs. Also called RED DOG.
 ● *Cuon alpinus*, family Canidae.
– ORIGIN early 19th cent.: of unknown origin.

dhoney /ˈdəʊni/ ▶ noun a small sailing vessel formerly used in southern India.
– ORIGIN from Telugu *doni*; compare with Persian *dōnī* 'yacht'.

dhoti /ˈdəʊti/ ▶ noun (pl. **dhotis**) a loincloth worn by male Hindus.
– ORIGIN from Hindi *dhotī*.

dhow /daʊ/ ▶ noun a lateen-rigged ship with one or two masts, used chiefly in the Arabian region.
– ORIGIN late 18th cent.: from Arabic *dāwa*, probably related to Marathi *dāw*.

DHSS historical ▶ abbreviation for (in the UK) Department of Health and Social Security, now replaced by the Department of Health and the Department of Social Security.

DHT ▶ abbreviation for dihydrotestosterone.

dhurrie /ˈdʌri/ (also **durrie**) ▶ noun (pl. **-ies**) a heavy cotton rug of Indian origin.
– ORIGIN from Hindi *darī*.

dhyana /dɪˈɑːnə/ ▶ noun [mass noun] (in Hindu and Buddhist practice) profound meditation which is the penultimate stage of yoga.
– ORIGIN from Sanskrit *dhyāna*.

DI ▶ abbreviation for (in the UK) Defence Intelligence.

di-¹ /dʌɪ, di/ ▶ combining form twice; two-; double: *dichromatic*.
 ■Chemistry containing two atoms, molecules, or groups of a specified kind: *dioxide*.
– ORIGIN from Greek *dis* 'twice'.

di-² /di, dʌɪ/ ▶ prefix variant spelling of DIS- shortened before l, m, n, r, s (followed by a consonant), and v; also often shortened before g, and sometimes before j.
– ORIGIN from Latin.

di-³ /dʌɪ/ ▶ prefix variant spelling of DIA- shortened before a vowel (as in *dielectric*).

dia. ▶ abbreviation for diameter.

dia- (also **di-** before a vowel) ▶ prefix **1** through; across: *diameter* | *diaphanous* | *diuretic*.
 2 apart: *diakinesis*.
– ORIGIN from Greek *dia* 'through'.

diabase /ˈdʌɪəbeɪs/ ▶ noun Geology another term for DOLERITE.

ORIGIN mid 19th cent. (originally denoting diorite): from French, formed irregularly as if from *di-* 'two' + *base* 'base' (thus 'rock with two bases', referring to the base minerals of diorite), but associated later perhaps with Greek *diabasis* 'transition'.

diabetes /ˌdʌɪəˈbiːtiːz/ ▶ noun [mass noun] a disorder of the metabolism causing excessive thirst and the production of large amounts of urine.
– ORIGIN mid 16th cent.: via Latin from Greek, literally 'siphon', from *diabainein* 'go through'.

diabetes insipidus /ɪnˈsɪpɪdəs/ ▶ noun [mass noun] a rare form of diabetes caused by a deficiency of the pituitary hormone vasopressin, which regulates kidney function.
– ORIGIN late 19th cent.: from DIABETES + Latin *insipidus* 'insipid'.

diabetes mellitus /mɪˈlʌɪtəs/ ▶ noun [mass noun] the commonest form of diabetes, caused by a deficiency of the pancreatic hormone insulin, which results in a failure to metabolize sugars and starch. Sugars accumulate in the blood and urine, and the by-products of alternative fat metabolism disturb the acid–base balance of the blood, causing a risk of convulsions and coma.
– ORIGIN late 19th cent.: from DIABETES + Latin *mellitus* 'sweet'.

diabetic ▶ adjective having diabetes.
 ■relating to or designed to relieve diabetes: *a diabetic clinic* | *a diabetic diet*.
 ▶ noun a person suffering from diabetes.

diablerie /dɪˈɑːbləri/ ▶ noun [mass noun] reckless mischief; charismatic wildness: *the beauty and diablerie of the great actor*.
 ■archaic sorcery supposedly assisted by the devil.
– ORIGIN mid 18th cent.: from French, from *diable*, from ecclesiastical Latin *diabolus* 'devil'.

diabolic /ˌdʌɪəˈbɒlɪk/ ▶ adjective relating to or characteristic of the Devil: *the darkness of a diabolic world*.
– ORIGIN late Middle English: from Old French *diabolique* or ecclesiastical Latin *diabolicus*, from *diabolus* 'devil'.

diabolical ▶ adjective characteristic of the Devil, or so evil as to recall the Devil: *his diabolical cunning*.
 ■informal disgracefully bad or unpleasant: *a singer with an absolutely diabolical voice*.
– DERIVATIVES **diabolically** adverb [as submodifier] *I am going to get diabolically drunk*.

diabolism /dʌɪˈabəlɪz(ə)m/ ▶ noun [mass noun] worship of the Devil.
– DERIVATIVES **diabolist** noun.
– ORIGIN early 17th cent.: from ecclesiastical Latin *diabolus* or Greek *diabolos* 'devil' + -ISM.

diabolize /dʌɪˈabəlʌɪz/ (also **-ise**) ▶ verb [with obj.] archaic represent as diabolical.

diabolo /dɪˈabələʊ, dʌɪ-/ ▶ noun (pl. **-os**) [mass noun] a game in which a two-headed top is thrown up and caught with a string stretched between two sticks.
 ■[count noun] the wooden top used in this game.
– ORIGIN early 20th cent.: from Italian, from ecclesiastical Latin *diabolus* 'devil'; the game was formerly called *devil on two sticks*.

diacetylmorphine /ˌdʌɪəˌsiːtʌɪlˈmɔːfiːn/ ▶ noun technical term for HEROIN.

diachronic /ˌdʌɪəˈkrɒnɪk/ ▶ adjective concerned with the way in which something, especially language, has developed and evolved through time. Often contrasted with SYNCHRONIC.
– DERIVATIVES **diachroneity** /ˌdʌɪəkrəˈniːɪti, -ˈneɪti/ noun, **diachronically** adverb, **diachronistic** /dʌɪˌakrəˈnɪstɪk/ adjective, **diachrony** /dʌɪˈakrəni/ noun.
– ORIGIN mid 19th cent.: from DIA- 'through' + Greek *khronos* 'time' + -IC.

diachronism /dʌɪˈakrənɪz(ə)m/ ▶ noun [mass noun] Geology the occurrence of a feature or phenomenon in different geological periods.
– DERIVATIVES **diachronous** adjective, **diachronously** adverb.

diaconal /dʌɪˈak(ə)n(ə)l/ ▶ adjective relating to a deacon, or to the role of a deacon.
– ORIGIN early 17th cent.: from ecclesiastical Latin *diaconalis*, from *diaconus* (see DEACON).

diaconate /dʌɪˈakəneɪt, -ət/ ▶ noun the office of deacon, or a person's tenure of it.
 ■a body of deacons collectively.
– ORIGIN early 18th cent.: from ecclesiastical Latin *diaconatus*, from *diaconus* (see DEACON).

diacritic /ˌdʌɪəˈkrɪtɪk/ ▶ noun a sign, such as an accent or cedilla, which when written above or below a letter indicates a difference in pronunciation from the same letter when unmarked or differently marked.
 ▶ adjective (of a mark or sign) indicating a difference in pronunciation.
– DERIVATIVES **diacritical** adjective, **diacritically** adverb.
– ORIGIN late 17th cent.: from Greek *diakritikos*, from *diakrinein* 'distinguish', from *dia-* 'through' + *krinein* 'to separate'.

diadelphous /ˌdʌɪəˈdɛlfəs/ ▶ adjective Botany (of stamens) united by their filaments so as to form two groups.
– ORIGIN early 19th cent.: from DI-¹ 'two' + Greek *adelphos* 'brother' + -OUS.

diadem /ˈdʌɪədɛm/ ▶ noun a jewelled crown or headband worn as a symbol of sovereignty.
 ■(the diadem) archaic the authority or dignity symbolized by a diadem: *the princely diadem*.
– DERIVATIVES **diademed** adjective.
– ORIGIN Middle English: from Old French *diademe*, via Latin from Greek *diadēma* 'the regal headband of the Persian kings', from *diadein* 'bind round'.

Diadochi /dʌɪˈadəki/ the six Macedonian generals of Alexander the Great (Antigonus, Antipater, Cassander, Lysimachus, Ptolemy, and Seleucus), among whom his empire was eventually divided after his death in 323 BC.
– ORIGIN from Greek *diadokhoi* 'successors'.

diaeresis /dʌɪˈɪərɪsɪs, -ˈɛr-/ (US **dieresis**) ▶ noun (pl. **diaereses** /-siːz/) **1** a mark (¨) placed over a vowel to indicate that it is sounded separately, as in *naïve*, *Brontë*.
 ■[mass noun] the division of a sound into two syllables, especially by sounding a diphthong as two vowels.
 2 Prosody a natural rhythmic break in a line of verse where the end of a metrical foot coincides with the end of a phrase.
– ORIGIN late 16th cent. (denoting the division of one syllable into two): via Latin from Greek *diairesis* 'separation', from *diairein* 'take apart', from *dia* 'apart' + *hairein* 'take'.

diagenesis /ˌdʌɪəˈdʒɛnɪsɪs/ ▶ noun [mass noun] Geology the physical and chemical changes occurring during the conversion of sediment to sedimentary rock.
– DERIVATIVES **diagenetic** adjective, **diagenetically** adverb.

Diaghilev /dɪˈaɡɪlɛf/, Sergei (Pavlovich) (1872–1929), Russian ballet impresario. In 1909 he formed the Ballets Russes, which he directed until his death.

diagnose /ˈdʌɪəɡnəʊz, -ˈnəʊz/ ▶ verb [with obj.] identify the nature of (an illness or other problem) by examination of the symptoms: *two doctors failed to diagnose a punctured lung*.
 ■(usu. be diagnosed) identify the nature of the medical condition of (someone): *she was finally diagnosed as having epilepsy* | *20,000 men are diagnosed with skin cancer every year*.
– DERIVATIVES **diagnosable** adjective.
– ORIGIN mid 19th cent.: back-formation from DIAGNOSIS.

diagnosis /ˌdʌɪəɡˈnəʊsɪs/ ▶ noun (pl. **diagnoses** /-siːz/) **1** the identification of the nature of an illness or other problem by examination of the symptoms: *early diagnosis and treatment are essential* | [count noun] *a diagnosis of Crohn's disease was made*.
 2 the distinctive characterization in precise terms of a genus, species, or phenomenon.
– ORIGIN late 17th cent.: modern Latin, from Greek, from *diagignōskein* 'distinguish, discern', from *dia* 'apart' + *gignōskein* 'recognize, know'.

diagnostic /dʌɪəɡˈnɒstɪk/ ▶ adjective **1** concerned with the diagnosis of illness or other problems: *a diagnostic tool*.
 ■(of a symptom) distinctive, and so indicating the nature of an illness: *there are fifteen infections which are diagnostic of Aids*.
 2 characteristic of a particular species, genus, or phenomenon: *the diagnostic character of having not one but two pairs of antennae*.
 ▶ noun **1** a distinctive symptom or characteristic.
 ■Computing a program or routine that helps a user to identify errors.
 2 (**diagnostics**) the practice or techniques of diagnosis: *advanced medical diagnostics*.
– DERIVATIVES **diagnostically** adverb, **diagnostician** /-nɒˈstɪʃ(ə)n/ noun.

– ORIGIN early 17th cent.: from Greek *diagnōstikos* 'able to distinguish', from *diagignōskein* 'distinguish'; the noun from *hē diagnōstikē tekhnē* 'the art of distinguishing (disease)'.

diagonal /dʌɪˈag(ə)n(ə)l/ ▶ **adjective** (of a straight line) joining two opposite corners of a square, rectangle, or other straight-sided shape.
■(of a line) straight and at an angle; slanting: *a tie with diagonal stripes.*
▶ **noun** a straight line joining two opposite corners of a square, rectangle, or other straight-sided shape.
■Mathematics the set of elements of a matrix that lie on a line joining two opposite corners. ■a slanting straight line: *the bars of light made diagonals across the entrance | tiles can be laid* ***on the diagonal.*** ■Chess a slanting row of squares whose colour is the same.
– DERIVATIVES **diagonally** adverb.
– ORIGIN mid 16th cent.: from Latin *diagonalis*, from Greek *diagōnios* 'from angle to angle', from *dia* 'through' + *gōnia* 'angle'.

diagonal matrix ▶ **noun** Mathematics a matrix having non-zero elements only in the diagonal running from the upper left to the lower right.

diagram /ˈdʌɪəgram/ ▶ **noun** a simplified drawing showing the appearance, structure, or workings of something; a schematic representation: *a diagram of the living room.*
■Geometry a figure composed of lines that is used to illustrate a definition or statement or to aid in the proof of a proposition. ■Brit. a graphical schedule for operating railway locomotives and rolling stock in order to provide a desired service.
▶ **verb** (**diagrammed**, **diagramming**; US **diagramed**, **diagraming**) [with obj.] represent (something) in graphic form: *the experiment is diagrammed on page fourteen.*
■Brit. schedule the operations of (a locomotive or train) according to a diagram.
– DERIVATIVES **diagrammatic** /-grəˈmatɪk/ adjective, **diagrammatically** adverb.
– ORIGIN early 17th cent.: from Latin *diagramma*, from Greek, from *diagraphein* 'mark out by lines', from *dia* 'through' + *graphein* 'write'.

diagrid /ˈdʌɪəgrɪd/ ▶ **noun** Brit. a supporting framework in a building formed with diagonally intersecting ribs of metal or concrete.
– ORIGIN 1940s: from **DIAGONAL** + **GRID**.

diakinesis /ˌdʌɪəkʌɪˈniːsɪs/ ▶ **noun** (pl. **diakineses** /-siːz/) [mass noun] Biology the fifth and last stage of the prophase of meiosis, following diplotene, when the separation of homologous chromosomes is complete and crossing over has occurred.
– ORIGIN early 20th cent.: from **DIA-** 'through, across' + Greek *kinēsis* 'motion'.

dial ▶ **noun** a face of a clock or watch that is marked to show units of time.
■a similar face or flat plate with a scale and pointer for showing measurements of weight, volume, or pressure. ■a disc with numbered holes on a telephone, enabling someone to make a call by inserting a finger in each of the holes corresponding to the number to be called and turning the disc. ■a plate or disc on a radio, cooker, washing machine, or other piece of equipment that is turned to select a wavelength or setting. ■Brit. informal a person's face: *he must be one of the new batch—I haven't seen his dial before.*
▶ **verb** (**dialled**, **dialling**; US **dialed**, **dialing**) [with obj.] call (a telephone number) by turning a disc with numbered holes or pressing a set of buttons: *she dialled 999 |* [no obj.] *company employees* ***dial out from*** *their office.*
■(**dial something up**) gain access to a service using a telephone line: *plans to enable customers to dial up videos from their living room.* ■indicate or regulate by means of a dial: *you're expected to* ***dial in*** *volume and tone settings.*
– ORIGIN Middle English (denoting a mariner's compass): from medieval Latin *diale* 'clock dial', based on Latin *dies* 'day'.

dial-a- ▶ **combining form** denoting a service available for booking by telephone: *dial-a-ride.*

dialect /ˈdʌɪəlɛkt/ ▶ **noun** a particular form of a language which is peculiar to a specific region or social group: *this novel is written in the dialect of Trinidad.*
■Computing a particular version of a programming language.
– DERIVATIVES **dialectal** /-ˈlɛkt(ə)l/ adjective.
– ORIGIN mid 16th cent. (denoting the art of investigating the truth of opinions): from French *dialecte*, or via Latin from Greek *dialektos* 'discourse, way of speaking', from *dialegesthai* 'converse with' (see **DIALOGUE**).

dialectic /ˌdʌɪəˈlɛktɪk/ Philosophy ▶ **noun** [mass noun] (also **dialectics**) [usu. treated as sing.] **1** the art of investigating or discussing the truth of opinions.
2 enquiry into metaphysical contradictions and their solutions.
■the existence or action of opposing social forces, concepts, etc.

> The ancient Greeks used the term dialectic to refer to various methods of reasoning and discussion in order to discover the truth. More recently, Kant applied the term to the criticism of the contradictions which arise from supposing knowledge of objects beyond the limits of experience, e.g. the soul. Hegel applied the term to the process of thought by which apparent contradictions (which he termed thesis and antithesis) are seen to be part of a higher truth (synthesis).

▶ **adjective** of or relating to dialectic or dialectics; dialectical.
– ORIGIN late Middle English: from Old French *dialectique* or Latin *dialectica*, from Greek *dialektikē* (*tekhnē*) '(art) of debate', from *dialegesthai* 'converse with' (see **DIALOGUE**).

dialectical ▶ **adjective** **1** relating to the logical discussion of ideas and opinions: *dialectical ingenuity.*
2 concerned with or acting through opposing forces: *a dialectical opposition between social convention and individual libertarianism.*
– DERIVATIVES **dialectically** adverb.

dialectical materialism ▶ **noun** [mass noun] the Marxist theory (adopted as the official philosophy of the Soviet communists) that political and historical events result from the conflict of social forces and are interpretable as a series of contradictions and their solutions. The conflict is seen as caused by material needs.
– DERIVATIVES **dialectical materialist** noun & adjective.

dialectician /ˌdʌɪəlɛkˈtɪʃ(ə)n/ ▶ **noun** a person skilled in philosophical debate.
– ORIGIN mid 16th cent.: from French *dialecticien*, from Latin *dialecticus*, based on Greek *dialegesthai* 'converse with'.

dialectology /ˌdʌɪəlɛkˈtɒlədʒi/ ▶ **noun** [mass noun] the branch of linguistics concerned with the study of dialects.
– DERIVATIVES **dialectological** /-təˈlɒdʒɪk(ə)l/ adjective, **dialectologist** noun.

dial-in ▶ **adjective** another term for **DIAL-UP**.

dialler (also **dialer**) ▶ **noun** a device or piece of software for calling telephone numbers automatically: *a hand-held computer phone dialler.*

dialling code ▶ **noun** Brit. a sequence of numbers dialled to connect a telephone to an exchange in another area or country.

dialling tone (N. Amer. **dial tone**) ▶ **noun** a sound produced by a telephone that indicates that a caller may start to dial.

dialog box (Brit. also **dialogue box**) ▶ **noun** Computing a small area on screen in which the user is prompted to provide information or select commands.

dialogic /ˌdʌɪəˈlɒdʒɪk/ ▶ **adjective** relating to or in the form of dialogue.
– DERIVATIVES **dialogical** adjective.
– ORIGIN mid 19th cent.: via late Latin from Greek *dialogikos*, from *dialogos* (see **DIALOGUE**).

dialogism /dʌɪˈalədʒɪz(ə)m/ ▶ **noun** [mass noun] the use in a text of different tones or viewpoints, whose interaction or contradiction are important to the text's interpretation.
– ORIGIN mid 16th cent.: from late Latin *dialogismos*, from Greek *dialogizesthai* 'to converse', from *dialogos* 'discourse' (see **DIALOGUE**).

dialogue (US also **dialog**) ▶ **noun** conversation between two or more people as a feature of a book, play, or film: *the book consisted of a series of dialogues |* [mass noun] *passages of dialogue.*
■a discussion between two or more people or groups, especially one directed towards exploration of a particular subject or resolution of a problem: *the USA would enter into a direct* ***dialogue with*** *Vietnam |* [mass noun] *interfaith dialogue.*
▶ **verb** [no obj.] chiefly N. Amer. take part in a conversation or discussion to resolve a problem: *he stated that he wasn't going to* ***dialogue with*** *the guerrillas.*
■[with obj.] provide (a film or play) with a dialogue.
– PHRASES **dialogue of the deaf** a discussion in which each party is unresponsive to what the others say.
– ORIGIN Middle English: from Old French *dialoge*, via Latin from Greek *dialogos*, from *dialegesthai* 'converse with', from *dia* 'through' + *legein* 'speak'.

dial tone ▶ **noun** North American term for **DIALLING TONE**.

dial-up ▶ **adjective** (of a computer system or service) used remotely via a telephone line.

dialysate /dʌɪˈalɪzeɪt/ (US also **dialyzate**) ▶ **noun** [mass noun] the part of a mixture which passes through the membrane in dialysis.
■the solution this forms with the fluid on the other side of the membrane. ■the fluid used on the other side of the membrane during dialysis to remove impurities.
– ORIGIN late 19th cent.: from **DIALYSIS** + **-ATE**[1]; the term originally denoted the part of the mixture which does *not* pass through the membrane.

dialyse /ˈdʌɪəlʌɪz/ (US **dialyze**) ▶ **verb** [with obj.] purify (a mixture) by means of dialysis.
■treat (a patient) by means of dialysis.
– ORIGIN mid 19th cent.: from **DIALYSIS**, on the pattern of *analyse*.

dialysis /dʌɪˈalɪsɪs/ ▶ **noun** (pl. **dialyses** /-siːz/) [mass noun] Chemistry the separation of particles in a liquid on the basis of differences in their ability to pass through a membrane.
■Medicine the clinical purification of blood by this technique, as a substitute for the normal function of the kidney.
– DERIVATIVES **dialytic** adjective.
– ORIGIN mid 19th cent.: via Latin from Greek *dialusis*, from *dialuein* 'split, separate', from *dia* 'apart' + *luein* 'set free'.

diamagnetic ▶ **adjective** Physics (of a substance or body) tending to become magnetized in a direction at 180° to the applied magnetic field.
– DERIVATIVES **diamagnet** noun, **diamagnetically** adverb, **diamagnetism** noun.
– ORIGIN 1846: coined by Faraday, from Greek *dia* 'through, across' + **MAGNETIC**.

diamanté /dɪəˈmɒnteɪ/ ▶ **adjective** decorated with artificial jewels: *a diamanté brooch.*
▶ **noun** [mass noun] artificial jewels.
■fabric or costume jewellery decorated with artificial jewels.
– ORIGIN early 20th cent.: French, literally 'set with diamonds', past participle of *diamanter*, from *diamant* 'diamond'.

diamantiferous /ˌdʌɪəmənˈtɪf(ə)rəs/ ▶ **adjective** (of a rock formation, region, etc.) producing or yielding diamonds.
– ORIGIN late 19th cent.: from French *diamantifère*, from *diamant* 'diamond' + *-fère* 'producing'.

diamantine /ˌdʌɪəˈmantɪn, -iːn/ ▶ **adjective** made from or reminiscent of diamonds.
– ORIGIN mid 16th cent. (in the sense 'hard as diamond'): from French *diamantin*, from *diamant* 'diamond'.

diameter /dʌɪˈamɪtə/ ▶ **noun** **1** a straight line passing from side to side through the centre of a body or figure, especially a circle or sphere.
■the length of this line. ■a transverse measurement of something; width or thickness.
2 a unit of linear measurement of magnifying power.
– DERIVATIVES **diametral** adjective.
– ORIGIN late Middle English: from Old French *diametre*, via Latin from Greek *diametros* (*grammē*) '(line) measuring across', from *dia* 'across' + *metron* 'measure'.

diametrical /ˌdʌɪəˈmɛtrɪk(ə)l/ ▶ **adjective** **1** used to emphasize how completely different two or more things are: *he's the diametrical opposite of Gabriel.*
2 of or along a diameter.
– DERIVATIVES **diametric** adjective, **diametrically** adverb.
– ORIGIN mid 16th cent. (in sense 2): from Greek *diametrikos* (from *diametros* 'measuring across': see **DIAMETER**) + **-AL**.

diamine /dʌɪˈeɪmiːn, dʌɪˈam-, ˈdʌɪəmiːn/ ▶ **noun** Chemistry a compound whose molecule contains two amino groups, especially when not part of amide groups.

diamond ▶ **noun** **1** a precious stone consisting of a clear and colourless crystalline form of pure carbon, the hardest naturally occurring substance.
■a tool with a small stone of such a kind for cutting

glass. ■ in extended and metaphorical use with reference to the brilliance, form, or hardness of diamonds: *the air glitters like diamonds.* ■ (**a diamond**) Brit. informal an excellent or very special person or thing: *Fred's a diamond.*

Diamonds occur in some igneous rock formations (kimberlite) and alluvial deposits. They are typically octahedral in shape but can be cut in many ways to enhance the internal reflection and refraction of light, producing jewels of sparkling brilliance. Diamonds are also used in cutting tools and abrasives.

d

2 [often as modifier] a figure with four straight sides of equal length forming two opposite acute angles and two opposite obtuse angles; a rhombus: *decorative diamond shapes.*
■ (**diamonds**) one of the four suits in a conventional pack of playing cards, denoted by a red figure of such a shape. ■ a card of this suit: *she led a losing diamond.* ■ the area delimited by the four bases of a baseball field, forming a square shape. ■ a baseball field. ■ [usu. as modifier] a railway crossing in which two tracks cross over each other at an acute angle: *diamond crossings.*
– PHRASES **diamond cut diamond** used to describe a situation in which a sharp-witted person meets their match. **diamond in the rough** North American term for **ROUGH DIAMOND**.
– DERIVATIVES **diamondiferous** /-ˈdɪf(ə)rəs/ adjective.
– ORIGIN Middle English: from Old French *diamant*, from medieval Latin *diamas, diamant-*, variant of Latin *adamans* (see **ADAMANT**).

diamondback ▶ **noun** N. Amer. **1** (also **diamondback rattlesnake**) a common large North American rattlesnake with diamond-shaped markings. Also called **DIAMOND RATTLESNAKE**.
● Genus *Crotalus*, family Viperidae: two species.
2 another term for **TERRAPIN** (in sense 2).

diamondback moth ▶ **noun** a small greyish moth which displays a pattern of diamonds along its back when the wings are folded. The caterpillar can be a pest of brassicas and other cultivated vegetables.
● *Plutella xylostella*, family Yponomeutidae.

diamond-bird ▶ **noun** Austral. a pardalote, which typically has rows of small white spots on the dark parts of its plumage.

diamond-cut ▶ **adjective 1** cut with facets like a diamond.
2 cut into the shape of a diamond.

diamond frame ▶ **noun** a bicycle frame having a diamond shape.

Diamond Head a volcanic crater overlooking the port of Honolulu on the Hawaiian island of Oahu.

diamond jubilee ▶ **noun** the sixtieth anniversary of a notable event, especially a sovereign's accession or the foundation of an organization.

diamond python ▶ **noun** a carpet python of a race occurring in the coastal areas of New South Wales.
● *Morelia spilota spilota*, family Pythonidae.

diamond rattlesnake ▶ **noun** another term for **DIAMONDBACK** (in sense 1).

Diamond State informal name for the state of **DELAWARE**[1].

diamond wedding (also **diamond wedding anniversary**) ▶ **noun** the sixtieth anniversary of a wedding.

diamond willow ▶ **noun** N. Amer. a willow with diamond-shaped depressions on the trunk as a result of fungal attack, resulting in timber with a diamond-shaped pattern of pale sapwood and darker heartwood.
● Several species in the genus *Salix* are affected, in particular *S. bebbiana*.

diamorphine /dʌɪˈmɔːfiːn/ ▶ **noun** short for **DIACETYLMORPHINE** (heroin).

Diana /dʌɪˈanə/ Roman Mythology an early Italian goddess associated with hunting, virginity, and, in later literature, with the moon. Greek equivalent **ARTEMIS**.

diana /dʌɪˈanə/ ▶ **noun** a North American fritillary (butterfly), the male of which is orange and black and the female blue and black.
● *Speyeria diana*, subfamily Argynninae, family Nymphalidae.
– ORIGIN modern Latin; associated with the goddess of the moon, because of the silvery crescents on the wings.

Diana, Princess of Wales (1961–97), former wife of Prince Charles; title before marriage *Lady Diana Frances Spencer*. The daughter of the 8th Earl Spencer, she married Prince Charles in 1981; the couple were divorced in 1996. She became a popular figure through her charity work and glamorous media appearances, and her death in a car crash in Paris gave rise to intense national mourning.

Diana monkey ▶ **noun** a West African monkey that has a black face with a white crescent on the forehead.
● *Cercopithecus diana*, family Cercopithecidae.
– ORIGIN early 19th cent.: named after the Roman moon goddess **DIANA**.

Dianetics /ˌdʌɪəˈnɛtɪks/ ▶ **plural noun** [treated as sing.] a system developed by the founder of the Church of Scientology, L. Ron Hubbard, which aims to relieve psychosomatic disorder by cleansing the mind of harmful mental images.
– ORIGIN 1950s: from Greek *dianoētikos* 'relating to thought' + **-ICS**.

dianthus /dʌɪˈanθəs/ ▶ **noun** (pl. **dianthuses**) a flowering plant of a genus that includes the pinks and carnations.
● Genus *Dianthus*, family Caryophyllaceae.
– ORIGIN from Greek *Dios* 'of Zeus' + *anthos* 'a flower'.

diapason /ˌdʌɪəˈpeɪs(ə)n, -z-/ ▶ **noun** (also **open diapason** or **stopped diapason**) an organ stop sounding a main register of flue pipes, typically of eight-foot pitch.
■ poetic/literary the entire compass, range, or scope of something. ■ figurative a grand swelling burst of harmony.
– ORIGIN late Middle English (denoting the interval of an octave): via Latin from Greek *dia pasōn (khordōn)* 'through all (notes)'.

diapause /ˈdʌɪəpɔːz/ Zoology ▶ **noun** [mass noun] a period of suspended development in an insect, other invertebrate, or mammal embryo, especially during unfavourable environmental conditions.
▶ **verb** [no obj.] [usu. as adj. **diapausing**] (of an insect or other animal) undergo such a period of suspended development.
– ORIGIN late 19th cent.: from **DIA-** 'through' + the noun **PAUSE**.

diapedesis /ˌdʌɪəpəˈdiːsɪs/ ▶ **noun** [mass noun] Medicine the passage of blood cells through the intact walls of the capillaries, typically accompanying inflammation.
– ORIGIN early 17th cent.: modern Latin, based on Greek *dia* 'through' + *pēdan* 'throb or leap'.

diaper /ˈdʌɪəpə/ ▶ **noun 1** N. Amer. a baby's nappy.
2 [mass noun] a linen or cotton fabric woven in a repeating pattern of small diamonds.
■ a repeating geometrical or floral pattern used to decorate a surface.
▶ **verb** [with obj.] **1** N. Amer. put a nappy on (a baby).
2 decorate (a surface) with a repeating geometrical or floral pattern.
– ORIGIN Middle English: from Old French *diapre*, from medieval Latin *diasprum*, from medieval Greek *diaspros* (adjective), from *dia* 'across' + *aspros* 'white'. The term seems originally to have denoted a costly fabric, but after the 15th cent. it was used as in noun sense 2; babies' nappies were originally made from pieces of this fabric, hence sense 1 (late 16th cent.).

diaphanous /dʌɪˈaf(ə)nəs/ ▶ **adjective** (especially of fabric) light, delicate, and translucent: *a diaphanous dress of pale gold.*
– ORIGIN early 17th cent.: from medieval Latin *diaphanus*, from Greek *diaphanēs*, from *dia* 'through' + *phainein* 'to show'.

diaphone /ˈdʌɪəfəʊn/ ▶ **noun** a low-pitched fog signal operated by compressed air, characterized by the 'grunt' which ends each note.
– ORIGIN early 20th cent.: from Greek *dia* 'through' + *phōnē* 'sound'.

diaphorase /dʌɪˈafəreɪz/ ▶ **noun** [mass noun] Biochemistry an enzyme of the flavoprotein type, able to oxidize a reduced form of the coenzyme NAD.
– ORIGIN 1930s: from Greek *diaphoros* 'different' + **-ASE**.

diaphoresis /ˌdʌɪəfəˈriːsɪs/ ▶ **noun** [mass noun] technical sweating, especially to an unusual degree as a symptom of disease or a side effect of a drug.
– ORIGIN late 17th cent.: via late Latin from Greek, from *diaphorein* 'carry off, sweat out', from *dia* 'through' + *phorein* 'carry'.

diaphoretic /ˌdʌɪəfəˈrɛtɪk/ ▶ **adjective** Medicine (chiefly of a drug) inducing perspiration.
■ (of a person) sweating heavily.
– ORIGIN late Middle English: via late Latin from Greek *diaphorētikos*, from *diaphorein* 'sweat out'.

diaphragm /ˈdʌɪəfram/ ▶ **noun 1** a dome-shaped muscular partition separating the thorax from the abdomen in mammals. It plays a major role in breathing, as its contraction increases the volume of the thorax and so inflates the lungs.
2 a thin sheet of material forming a partition.
■ a taut flexible membrane in mechanical or acoustic systems. ■ a thin contraceptive cap fitting over the cervix.
3 a device for varying the effective aperture of the lens in a camera or other optical system.
– DERIVATIVES **diaphragmatic** adjective.
– ORIGIN late Middle English: from late Latin *diaphragma*, from Greek, from *dia* 'through, apart' + *phragma* 'a fence'.

diaphragm pump ▶ **noun** a pump using a flexible diaphragm in place of a piston.

diaphysis /dʌɪˈafɪsɪs/ ▶ **noun** (pl. **diaphyses** /-siːz/) Anatomy the shaft or central part of a long bone. Compare with **EPIPHYSIS**.
– ORIGIN mid 19th cent.: from Greek *diaphusis* 'growing through', from *dia* 'through' + *phusis* 'growth'.

diapir /ˈdʌɪəpɪə/ ▶ **noun** Geology a domed rock formation in which a core of rock has moved upward to pierce the overlying strata.
– DERIVATIVES **diapiric** adjective, **diapirism** noun.
– ORIGIN early 20th cent.: from Greek *diapeirainein* 'pierce through', from *dia* 'through' + *peirainein* (from *peran* 'pierce').

diapositive /ˌdʌɪəˈpɒzɪtɪv/ ▶ **noun** a positive photographic slide or transparency.

diapsid /dʌɪˈapsɪd/ ▶ **noun** Zoology a reptile of a large group characterized by the presence of two temporal openings in the skull, including the lizards, snakes, crocodiles, dinosaurs, and pterosaurs.
● Sometimes placed in a subclass Diapsida.
– ORIGIN early 20th cent.: from modern Latin *Diapsida*, from **DI-**[1] 'two' + Greek *apsis, apsid-* 'arch'.

diarchy /ˈdʌɪɑːki/ (also **dyarchy**) ▶ **noun** (pl. **-ies**) [mass noun] government by two independent authorities (especially in India 1919–35).
– DERIVATIVES **diarchal** adjective, **diarchic** adjective.
– ORIGIN late 19th cent.: from **DI-**[1] 'two' + Greek *arkhia* 'rule', on the pattern of *monarchy*.

diarist ▶ **noun** a person who writes a diary.
– DERIVATIVES **diaristic** adjective.

diarize (also **-ise**) ▶ **verb** [no obj.] archaic keep a record of events in a diary.

diarrhoea /ˌdʌɪəˈrɪə/ (US **diarrhea**) ▶ **noun** [mass noun] a condition in which faeces are discharged from the bowels frequently and in a liquid form.
– DERIVATIVES **diarrhoeal** adjective, **diarrhoeic** adjective.
– ORIGIN late Middle English: via late Latin from Greek *diarrhoia*, from *diarrhein* 'flow through', from *dia* 'through' + *rhein* 'to flow'.

diary ▶ **noun** (pl. **-ies**) a book in which one keeps a daily record of events and experiences: *a useful way of assisting your learning is to **keep a diary**.*
■ a book with spaces for each day of the year in which one notes details of appointments or important information for each day. ■ a column in a newspaper or magazine giving up-to-date news or gossip on a particular topic: *the City Diary.*
– ORIGIN late 16th cent.: from Latin *diarium*, from *dies* 'day'.

Dias /ˈdiːas/ (also **Diaz**), Bartolomeu (*c.*1450–1500), Portuguese navigator and explorer. He was the first European to round the Cape of Good Hope (1488), thereby establishing a sea route from the Atlantic to Asia.

diaspora /dʌɪˈasp(ə)rə/ ▶ **noun** (**the diaspora**) Jews living outside Israel.
■ the dispersion of the Jews beyond Israel. ■ the dispersion of any people from their original homeland: *the diaspora of boat people from Asia.* ■ the people so dispersed: *the Ukrainian diaspora flocked back to Kiev.*

The main diaspora began in the 8th–6th centuries BC, and even before the sack of Jerusalem in AD 70 the number of Jews dispersed by the diaspora was greater than that living in Israel. Thereafter, Jews were dispersed even more widely throughout the Roman world and beyond.

– ORIGIN Greek, from *diaspeirein* 'disperse', from *dia*

'across'+ *speirein* 'scatter'. The term originated in the Septuagint (Deuteronomy 28:25) in the phrase *esē diaspora en pasais basileias tēs gēs* 'thou shalt be a dispersion in all kingdoms of the earth'.

diaspore /ˈdʌɪəspɔː/ ▶ **noun** Botany a spore, seed, or other structure that functions in plant dispersal; a propagule.

diastase /ˈdʌɪəsteɪz/ ▶ **noun** Biochemistry another term for **AMYLASE**.
– ORIGIN mid 19th cent.: from Greek *diastasis* 'separation', from *dia* 'apart' + *stasis* 'placing'.

diastema /ˌdʌɪəˈstiːmə, dʌɪˈastɪmə/ ▶ **noun** (pl. **diastemata**) a gap between the teeth, in particular:
■ Zoology a space separating teeth of different functions, especially that between the biting teeth (incisors and canines) and grinding teeth (premolars and molars) in rodents and ungulates. ■ a gap between a person's two upper front teeth.
– ORIGIN mid 19th cent.: via late Latin from Greek *diastēma* 'space between'.

diastereoisomer /ˌdʌɪəstɛrɪəʊˈʌɪsəmə/ ▶ **noun** Chemistry each of a pair of stereoisomeric compounds that are not mirror images of one another.
– DERIVATIVES **diastereoisomeric** adjective.

diastole /dʌɪˈastəli/ ▶ **noun** [mass noun] Physiology the phase of the heartbeat when the heart muscle relaxes and allows the chambers to fill with blood. Often contrasted with **SYSTOLE**.
– DERIVATIVES **diastolic** adjective.
– ORIGIN late 16th cent.: via late Latin from Greek, 'separation, expansion', from *diastellein*, from *dia* 'apart' + *stellein* 'to place'.

diathermy /ˈdʌɪəˌθəːmi/ ▶ **noun** [mass noun] a medical and surgical technique involving the production of heat in a part of the body by high-frequency electric currents, to stimulate the circulation, relieve pain, destroy unhealthy tissue, or cause bleeding vessels to clot.
– ORIGIN early 20th cent.: from **DIA-** 'through' + Greek *thermon* 'heat'.

diathesis /dʌɪˈaθəsɪs/ ▶ **noun** **1** [usu. with modifier] Medicine a tendency to suffer from a particular medical condition: *a bleeding diathesis*.
2 Linguistics the set of syntactic patterns with which a verb or other word is most typically associated.
– ORIGIN mid 17th cent.: modern Latin, from Greek, 'disposition', from *diatithenai* 'arrange'. Sense 2 dates from the mid 20th cent.

diatom /ˈdʌɪətəm/ ▶ **noun** Biology a single-celled alga which has a cell wall of silica. Many kinds are planktonic, and extensive fossil deposits have been found.
● Class Bacillariophyceae, division Chromophycota or Heterokontophyta (or phylum Bacillariophyta, kingdom Protista).
– DERIVATIVES **diatomaceous** adjective.
– ORIGIN mid 19th cent.: from modern Latin *Diatoma* (genus name), from Greek *diatomos* 'cut in two', from *diatemnein* 'to cut through'.

diatomaceous earth /ˌdʌɪətəˈmeɪʃəs/ ▶ **noun** [mass noun] a soft, crumbly, porous sedimentary deposit formed from the fossil remains of diatoms.

diatomic /ˌdʌɪəˈtɒmɪk/ ▶ **adjective** Chemistry consisting of two atoms.

diatomite /dʌɪˈatəmʌɪt/ ▶ **noun** [mass noun] Geology a fine-grained sedimentary rock formed from consolidated diatomaceous earth.
– ORIGIN late 19th cent.: from **DIATOM** + **-ITE**[1].

diatonic /ˌdʌɪəˈtɒnɪk/ ▶ **adjective** Music (of a scale, interval, etc.) involving only notes proper to the prevailing key without chromatic alteration.
■ (of a melody or harmony) constructed from such a scale.
– ORIGIN early 17th cent. (denoting a tetrachord divided into two tones and a lower semitone, or ancient Greek music based on this): from French *diatonique*, or via late Latin from Greek *diatonikos* 'at intervals of a tone', from *dia* 'through' + *tonos* 'tone'.

diatreme /ˈdʌɪətriːm/ ▶ **noun** Geology a long vertical pipe or plug formed when gas-filled magma forced its way up through overlying strata.
– ORIGIN early 20th cent.: from **DIA-** 'through' + Greek *trēma* 'perforation'.

diatribe /ˈdʌɪətrʌɪb/ ▶ **noun** a forceful and bitter verbal attack against someone or something: *a diatribe against the Roman Catholic Church*.
– ORIGIN late 16th cent. (denoting a disquisition): from French, via Latin from Greek *diatribē* 'spending of time, discourse', from *dia* 'through' + *tribein* 'rub'.

Diaz variant spelling of **DIAS**.

Díaz /ˈdiːaz, Spanish ˈdias, ˈdiaθ/, Porfirio (1830–1915), Mexican general and statesman, President 1877–80 and 1884–1911.

diazepam /dʌɪˈazɪpam, -ˈeɪz-/ ▶ **noun** [mass noun] a tranquillizing muscle-relaxant drug used chiefly to relieve anxiety. Also called **VALIUM** (trademark).
● A member of the benzodiazepine group; chem. formula: $C_{16}H_{13}N_2OCl$.
– ORIGIN 1960s: blend of **BENZODIAZEPINE** and **AMIDE**.

diazinon /dʌɪˈazɪnɒn/ ▶ **noun** [mass noun] an organophosphorus insecticide derived from pyrimidine.
– ORIGIN mid 20th cent.: from *diazine* (see **DI-**[1], **AZINE**) + *-on* (suffix of unknown origin).

diazo /dʌɪˈazəʊ, -ˈeɪzəʊ/ (also **diazotype**) ▶ **noun** [mass noun] a copying or colouring process using a diazo compound decomposed by ultraviolet light: [as modifier] *diazo printers*.

diazo compound ▶ **noun** Chemistry an organic compound containing two nitrogen atoms bonded together, especially a diazonium compound.
– ORIGIN late 19th cent.: *diazo* from **DIAZONIUM**.

diazomethane /dʌɪˌazəʊˈmiːθeɪn, -ˌeɪzəʊ-/ ▶ **noun** [mass noun] Chemistry a poisonous, reactive yellow gas used as a methylating agent in chemical synthesis.
● Chem. formula: CH_2N_2.
– ORIGIN late 19th cent.: from *diazo-* (indicating the presence of two nitrogen atoms) + **METHANE**.

diazonium /ˌdʌɪəˈzəʊnɪəm/ ▶ **noun** [as modifier] Chemistry an organic cation containing the group $—N_2^+$ bonded to an organic group. Aromatic diazonium compounds are typically intensely coloured and include many synthetic dyes.
– ORIGIN late 19th cent.: coined in German from *diazo-* (indicating the presence of two nitrogen atoms) + the suffix *-onium* (from **AMMONIUM**).

dib ▶ **verb** (**dibbed**, **dibbing**) another term for **DAP**.
– ORIGIN late 17th cent.: related to **DAB**[1].

dibasic /dʌɪˈbeɪsɪk/ ▶ **adjective** Chemistry (of an acid) having two replaceable hydrogen atoms.
– ORIGIN mid 19th cent.: from **DI-**[1] 'two' + **BASIC**.

dibatag /ˈdɪbətag/ ▶ **noun** a gazelle that stands on its hind legs to browse, found in semi-desert regions of Somalia and Ethiopia.
● *Ammodorcas clarkei*, family Bovidae.
– ORIGIN late 19th cent.: from Somali.

dibber ▶ **noun** British term for **DIBBLE**.

dibble ▶ **noun** a pointed hand tool for making holes in the ground for seeds or young plants.
▶ **verb** [with obj.] make (a hole) in soil with a dibble.
■ sow (a seed or plant) with a dibble.
– ORIGIN late Middle English: apparently related to **DIB** (also used in this sense in dialect).

dibbler ▶ **noun** a marsupial mouse found in SW Australia. It is very rare and possibly extinct.
● *Parantechinus apicalis*, family Dasyuridae.
– ORIGIN early 19th cent.: from **DIBBLE**.

diborane /dʌɪˈbɔːreɪn/ ▶ **noun** [mass noun] Chemistry a poisonous, reactive gas made by the action of acids on some borides. It is the simplest of the boranes and is an example of electron-deficient bonding.
● Chem. formula: B_2H_6.

dibs ▶ **plural noun** informal money.
– PHRASES **have first dibs on** N. Amer. have the first right to or choice of: *they never got first dibs on great prospects*.
– ORIGIN mid 18th cent. (denoting pebbles used in a children's game): from earlier *dib-stones*, perhaps from **DIB**.

dice ▶ **noun** (pl. same) a small cube with each side having a different number of spots on it, ranging from one to six, thrown and used in gambling and other games involving chance. See also **DIE**[2].
■ [mass noun] a game played with dice. ■ small cubes of food: *cut the meat into dice*.
▶ **verb** **1** [no obj.] play or gamble with dice: [as noun **dicing**] *prohibitions on all dancing and dicing*.
2 [with obj.] cut (food or other matter) into small cubes: *dice the peppers* | [as adj. **diced**] *add the diced onions*.
3 [with obj.] Austral. informal reject or abandon: *he'd better behave, or I'll dice him*. [ORIGIN: 1940s: extended use of *dice* 'gamble away'.]
– PHRASES **dice with death** take serious risks. **no dice** informal, chiefly N. Amer. used to refuse a request or indicate no chance of success.
– DERIVATIVES **dicer** noun.
– ORIGIN Middle English: from Old French *des*, plural of *de* (see **DIE**[2]).

USAGE Historically, **dice** is the plural of **die**, but in modern standard English **dice** is both the singular and the plural: *throw the **dice*** could mean a reference to either one or more than one dice.

dicentra /dʌɪˈsɛntrə/ ▶ **noun** a plant of the genus *Dicentra* (family Fumariaceae), especially (in gardening) a bleeding heart.
– ORIGIN modern Latin, from Greek *dikentros*, from *di-* 'two' + *kentron* 'spur, sharp point'.

dicentric /dʌɪˈsɛntrɪk/ Genetics ▶ **adjective** (of a chromosome) having two centromeres.
▶ **noun** a chromosome of this type.

dicey ▶ **adjective** (**dicier**, **diciest**) informal unpredictable and potentially dangerous: *democracy is a dicey business*.

dichasium /dʌɪˈkeɪzɪəm/ ▶ **noun** (pl. **dichasia**) Botany a cyme in which each flowering branch gives rise to two or more branches symmetrically placed.
– ORIGIN late 19th cent.: modern Latin, from **DI-**[1] 'two' + Greek *khasis* 'separation'.

dichlorvos /dʌɪˈklɔːvɒs/ ▶ **noun** Chemistry a pale yellow liquid used as an insecticide and veterinary anthelmintic.
● An organophosphorus compound; alternative name: 2,2-dichlorovinyl dimethyl phosphate; chem. formula: $(CH_3O)_2PO_2CHCCl_2$.
– ORIGIN mid 20th cent.: from elements of the systematic name (see above).

dichogamy /dʌɪˈkɒgəmi/ ▶ **noun** [mass noun] Botany the ripening of the stamens and pistils of a flower at different times, so that self-fertilization is prevented. Compare with **HOMOGAMY** (in sense 3).
– DERIVATIVES **dichogamous** adjective.
– ORIGIN mid 19th cent.: from Greek *dikho-* 'apart, in two' + *gamos* 'marriage'.

dichotic /dʌɪˈkɒtɪk/ ▶ **adjective** involving or relating to the simultaneous stimulation of the right and left ear by different sounds.
– ORIGIN mid 20th cent.: from Greek *dikho-* 'apart' + *ous, ōt-* 'ear' + **-IC**.

dichotomize /dʌɪˈkɒtəmʌɪz, dɪ-/ (also **-ise**) ▶ **verb** [with obj.] regard or represent as divided or opposed: *gender is dichotomized to give two and only two categories*.

dichotomous /dʌɪˈkɒtəməs, dɪ-/ ▶ **adjective** exhibiting or characterized by dichotomy: *a dichotomous view of the world*.
■ Botany (of branching) in which the axis is divided into two branches.
– DERIVATIVES **dichotomously** adverb.
– ORIGIN late 17th cent.: via late Latin from Greek *dikhotomos* (from *dikho-* 'in two' + *temnein* 'to cut') + **-OUS**.

dichotomy /dʌɪˈkɒtəmi, dɪ-/ ▶ **noun** (pl. **-ies**) [usu. in sing.] a division or contrast between two things that are or are represented as being opposed or entirely different: *a rigid **dichotomy between** science and mysticism*.
■ [mass noun] Botany repeated branching into two equal parts.
– ORIGIN late 16th cent.: via modern Latin from Greek *dikhotomia*, from *dikho-* 'in two, apart' + *-tomia* (see **-TOMY**).

dichroic /dʌɪˈkrəʊɪk/ ▶ **adjective** (of a crystal) showing different colours when viewed from different directions, or (more generally) having different absorption coefficients for light polarized in different directions.
– DERIVATIVES **dichroism** noun.
– ORIGIN mid 19th cent.: from Greek *dikhroos* (from *di-* 'twice' + *khrōs* 'colour') + **-IC**.

dichromate /dʌɪˈkrəʊmeɪt/ ▶ **noun** Chemistry a salt, typically red or orange, containing the anion $Cr_2O_7^{2-}$.
– ORIGIN mid 19th cent.: from **DI-**[1] 'two' + **CHROMATE**.

dichromatism /dʌɪˈkrəʊmətɪz(ə)m/ ▶ **noun** [mass noun] **1** (typically in an animal species) the occurrence of two different kinds of colouring.
2 colour blindness in which only two of the three primary colours can be discerned.
– DERIVATIVES **dichromatic** adjective.

dick[1] ▶ **noun** **1** vulgar slang a man's penis.

▶Brit. vulgar slang a stupid or contemptible person.
2 [mass noun] [with negative] US informal anything at all: *you don't know dick about this—you haven't a clue!*
▶**verb 1** [no obj.] informal handle something inexpertly; meddle: *he started **dicking around** with the controls.*
2 [with obj.] vulgar slang (of a man) have sexual intercourse with (someone).
– ORIGIN mid 16th cent. (in the general sense 'fellow'): pet form of the given name *Richard*. Sense 1 of the noun dates from the late 18th cent.

dick² ▶**noun** dated, informal, chiefly US a detective.
– ORIGIN early 20th cent.: perhaps an arbitrary shortening of **DETECTIVE**, or from obsolete slang *dick* 'look', from Romany.

dickcissel /dɪkˈsɪs(ə)l, ˈdɪksɪs(ə)l/ ▶**noun** a sparrow-like North American songbird related to the cardinals, with a black-and-white throat and bright yellow breast.
● *Spiza americana*, family Emberizidae (subfamily Cardinalinae).
– ORIGIN late 19th cent.: imitative of its call.

dicken /ˈdɪk(ə)n/ ▶**exclamation** Austral./NZ informal an expression of disgust or disbelief.
– ORIGIN late 19th cent.: abbreviation of **DICKENS**.

Dickens /ˈdɪkɪnz/, Charles (John Huffam) (1812–70), English novelist.

His novels are notable for their satirical humour and treatment of contemporary social problems, including the plight of the urban poor and the corruption and inefficiency of the legal system. Memorable characters such as Scrooge and Mr Micawber contributed to his work's popular appeal. Some of his most famous novels are *Oliver Twist* (1837–8), *Nicholas Nickleby* (1838–9), *A Christmas Carol* (1843), *David Copperfield* (1850), *Bleak House* (1852–3), and *Great Expectations* (1860–1).

dickens /ˈdɪkɪnz/ ▶**noun** [in sing.] informal, dated used for emphasis, euphemistically invoking the Devil: *they work **like the dickens** | she was in **a dickens of a** rush.*
■(**the dickens**) used when asking questions to express annoyance or surprise: *what **the dickens** is going on?*
– ORIGIN late 16th cent.: probably a use of the surname *Dickens*.

Dickensian /dɪˈkɛnzɪən/ ▶**adjective** of or reminiscent of the novels of Charles Dickens, especially in suggesting the poor social conditions or comically repulsive characters that they portray: *the backstreets of Dickensian London.*

dicker ▶**verb** [no obj.] **1** engage in petty argument or bargaining: *they have been dickering with the airline to buy a share.*
2 treat something casually or irresponsibly; toy with something: [as noun **dickering**] *there was no dickering with the lyrics.*
– DERIVATIVES **dickerer** noun.
– ORIGIN early 19th cent. (originally US): perhaps from obsolete *dicker* 'set of ten (hides)', used as a unit of trade, based on Latin *decem* 'ten'.

dickhead ▶**noun** vulgar slang a stupid, irritating, or ridiculous man.
– ORIGIN 1960s: from **DICK**¹ + **HEAD**.

Dickinson, Emily (Elizabeth) (1830–86), American poet. Her poems use an elliptical language, emphasizing assonance and alliteration rather than rhyme, reflecting the struggles of her reclusive life.

dicky¹ (also **dickey**) ▶**noun** (pl. **-ies** or **-eys**) informal
1 a false shirt front.
2 dated, chiefly Brit. a folding outside seat at the back of a vehicle.
■historical, chiefly Brit. a driver's seat in a carriage.
– ORIGIN mid 18th cent. (denoting a petticoat): each sense probably having different origins; perhaps partly from *Dicky*, pet form of the given name *Richard*.

dicky² ▶**adjective** (**dickier, dickiest**) Brit. informal (of a part of the body, a structure, or a device) not strong, healthy, or functioning reliably: *a pianist with a dicky heart.*
– ORIGIN late 18th cent. (in the sense 'almost over'): perhaps from the given name *Dick*, in the old saying *as queer as Dick's hatband.*

dicky bird ▶**noun** informal used by children to refer to a little bird. [ORIGIN: late 18th cent.: probably from *Dicky*, pet form of the given name *Richard*.]
– PHRASES **not a dicky bird** not a word; nothing at all: *'Did you hear from her?' 'Not a dicky bird.'* [ORIGIN: *dicky bird* being rhyming slang for 'word'.]

dicky bow ▶**noun** informal a bow tie.

dicot /ˈdʌɪkɒt/ ▶**noun** short for **DICOTYLEDON**.

dicotyledon /ˌdʌɪkɒtɪˈliːd(ə)n/ ▶**noun** Botany a flowering plant with an embryo that bears two cotyledons (seed leaves). Dicotyledons constitute the larger of the two great divisions of flowering plants, and typically have broad stalked leaves with net-like veins (e.g. daisies, hawthorns, oaks). Compare with **MONOCOTYLEDON**.
● Class Dicotyledoneae (or -donae, -dones; sometimes Magnoliopsida), subdivision Angiospermae.
– DERIVATIVES **dicotyledonous** adjective.
– ORIGIN early 18th cent.: from modern Latin *dicotyledones* (plural), from *di-* 'two' + *cotyledon* (see **COTYLEDON**).

dicrotic /dʌɪˈkrɒtɪk/ ▶**adjective** Medicine denoting a pulse in which a double beat is detectable for each beat of the heart.
– ORIGIN early 19th cent.: from Greek *dikrotos* 'beating twice' + **-IC**.

dicta plural form of **DICTUM**.

dictamnus /dɪkˈtamnəs/ ▶**noun 1** another term for *dittany of Crete* (see **DITTANY**).
2 another term for **GAS PLANT**.
– ORIGIN mid 16th cent.: from Latin.

Dictaphone /ˈdɪktəfəʊn/ ▶**noun** trademark a small cassette recorder used to record speech for transcription at a later time.
– ORIGIN early 20th cent.: from **DICTATE** or **DICTATION** + **-PHONE**.

dictate ▶**verb** /dɪkˈteɪt/ **1** [with obj.] lay down authoritatively; prescribe: *the tsar's attempts to dictate policy* | [no obj.] *that doesn't give you the right to **dictate to** me.*
■[with obj.] control or decisively affect; determine: *choice is often dictated by availability* | [no obj.] *a review process can be changed as circumstances dictate.*
2 say or read aloud (words to be typed, written down, or recorded on tape): *I have four letters to dictate.*
▶**noun** /ˈdɪkteɪt/ (usu. **dictates**) an order or principle that must be obeyed: *the dictates of fashion.*
– ORIGIN late 16th cent. (in sense 2): from Latin *dictat-* 'dictated', from the verb *dictare*.

dictation ▶**noun** [mass noun] **1** the action of saying words aloud to be typed, written down, or recorded on tape: *the dictation of letters.*
■the activity of taking down a passage that is read aloud by a teacher as a test of spelling, writing, or language skills: *passages for dictation.* ■ [count noun] an utterance that is typed, written down, or recorded: *the person who writes the dictation down is his agent.*
2 the action of giving orders authoritatively or categorically.
– ORIGIN mid 17th cent. (in sense 2): from late Latin *dictatio(n-)*, from the verb *dictare* (see **DICTATE**).

dictation speed ▶**noun** [mass noun] a rate of speech slow enough for someone to be able to write down what is said.

dictator ▶**noun 1** a ruler with total power over a country, typically one who has obtained power by force.
■a person who tells people what to do in an autocratic way or who determines behaviour in a particular sphere: *I'd ban coincidences, if I were a dictator of fiction.* ■ (in ancient Rome) a chief magistrate with absolute power, appointed in an emergency.
2 a machine that records words spoken into it, used for personal or administrative purposes.
– ORIGIN late Middle English: from Latin, from *dictat-* 'dictated', from the verb *dictare* (see **DICTATE**).

dictatorial ▶**adjective** of or typical of a ruler with total power: *a dictatorial regime.*
■having or showing a tendency to tell people what to do in an autocratic way: *his dictatorial manner.*
– DERIVATIVES **dictatorially** adverb.

dictatorship ▶**noun** [mass noun] government by a dictator: *the effects of forty years of dictatorship.*
■[count noun] a country governed by a dictator. ■ [mass noun] absolute authority in any sphere.

diction ▶**noun** [mass noun] **1** the choice and use of words and phrases in speech or writing: *Wordsworth campaigned against exaggerated poetic diction.*
2 the style of enunciation in speaking or singing: *she began imitating his careful diction.*
– ORIGIN mid 16th cent. (denoting a word or phrase): from Latin *dictio(n-)*, from *dicere* 'to say'.

dictionary ▶**noun** (pl. **-ies**) a book that lists the words of a language in alphabetical order and gives their meaning, or that gives the equivalent words in a different language.
■a reference book on any subject, the items of which

are arranged in alphabetical order: *a dictionary of quotations.*
– PHRASES **have swallowed a dictionary** informal (of a person) use long and obscure words when speaking.
– ORIGIN early 16th cent.: from medieval Latin *dictionarium (manuale)* or *dictionarius (liber)* 'manual or book of words', from Latin *dictio* (see **DICTION**).

dictum /ˈdɪktəm/ ▶**noun** (pl. **dicta** /-tə/ or **dictums**) a formal pronouncement from an authoritative source: *the Politburo's dictum that the party will become a 'left-wing parliamentary party'.*
■a short statement that expresses a general truth or principle: *the old dictum 'might is right'.* ■ Law short for **OBITER DICTUM**.
– ORIGIN late 16th cent.: from Latin, literally 'something said', neuter past participle of *dicere*.

dicty /ˈdɪkti/ ▶**adjective** US black slang ostentatiously stylish; pretentious: *up there in their dicty Detroit suburb living the so-called good life.*
– ORIGIN early 20th cent.: of unknown origin.

Dictyoptera /ˌdɪktɪˈɒptərə/ Entomology an order of insects that comprises the cockroaches and mantises. They have a somewhat flattened form, two pairs of wings, and long spiky legs.
– DERIVATIVES **dictyopteran** noun & adjective.
– ORIGIN modern Latin (plural), from Greek *diktuon* 'net' + *pteron* 'wing'.

dicynodont /dʌɪˈsɪnədɒnt/ ▶**noun** a fossil herbivorous mammal-like reptile of the late Permian and Triassic periods, with beaked jaws and no teeth apart from two tusks in the upper jaw of the male.
● *Dicynodon* and other genera, infra-order Dicynodontia, order Therapsida.
– ORIGIN mid 19th cent.: from modern Latin *Dicynodontia* (plural), from Greek *di-* 'two' + *kuōn* 'dog' + *odous, odont-* 'tooth'.

did past of **DO**¹.

didactic /dɪˈdaktɪk, dʌɪ-/ ▶**adjective** intended to teach, particularly in having moral instruction as an ulterior motive: *a didactic novel that set out to expose social injustice.*
■in the manner of a teacher, particularly so as to treat someone in a patronizing way: *she was speaking with a didactic severity.*
– DERIVATIVES **didactically** adverb, **didacticism** noun.
– ORIGIN mid 17th cent.: from Greek *didaktikos*, from *didaskein* 'teach'.

didanosine /dɪˈdanəʊsiːn/ ▶**noun** Medicine another term for **DIDEOXYINOSINE**.

diddicoy ▶**noun** variant spelling of **DIDICOI**.

diddle ▶**verb** informal **1** [with obj.] (usu. **be diddled**) cheat or swindle (someone) so as to deprive them of something: *he thought he'd been **diddled out of** his change.*
■deliberately falsify (something): *he diddled his income tax returns.*
2 [no obj.] chiefly US pass time aimlessly or unproductively: *why **diddle around** with slow costly tests?*
3 [with obj.] vulgar slang, chiefly US (of a man) have sexual intercourse with (a woman). [ORIGIN: originally in Scots dialect use in the sense 'jerk from side to side', apparently corresponding to dialect *didder* 'tremble'.]
– DERIVATIVES **diddler** noun.
– ORIGIN early 19th cent.: probably from the name of Jeremy *Diddler*, a character in the farce *Raising the Wind* (1803) by the Irish dramatist James Kenney (1780–1849). Diddler constantly borrowed and failed to repay small sums of money: the name may have been based on an earlier verb *diddle* 'walk unsteadily, swerve'.

diddly-squat /ˈdɪdlɪˌskwɒt/ (also **doodly-squat** or **doodly**) ▶**pronoun** [usu. with negative] N. Amer. informal anything: *Hiram didn't care diddly-squat about what Darrel thought.*
– ORIGIN late 20th cent.: probably from US slang *doodle* 'excrement' + **SQUAT** in the sense 'defecate'.

diddums /ˈdɪdəmz/ Brit. ▶**exclamation** used to express commiseration to a child.
▶**noun** used as a term of endearment: *how is my Diddums this morning?*
– ORIGIN late 19th cent.: from *did 'em*, i.e. 'did they?' (tease you, do that to you, etc.).

diddy¹ ▶**noun** (pl. **-ies**) Brit. informal a fool.
– ORIGIN late 18th cent.: alteration of **TITTY**.

diddy[2] ▶ **adjective** Brit. informal little: *a diddy word processor.*
– ORIGIN probably a child's corruption of **LITTLE**.

dideoxycytidine /ˌdʌɪdɪɒksɪˈsʌɪtɪdiːn/ (abbrev.: **DDC** or **ddC**) ▶ **noun** [mass noun] Medicine a drug which inhibits the replication of HIV and is used in the treatment of Aids, especially in combination with zidovudine. It is a synthetic analogue of a pyrimidine nucleoside.

dideoxyinosine /ˌdʌɪdɪɒksɪˈɪnəʊsiːn/ (abbrev.: **DDI** or **ddI**) ▶ **noun** [mass noun] Medicine a drug which inhibits the replication of HIV and is used in the treatment of Aids, especially in combination with zidovudine. It is a synthetic analogue of a purine nucleoside.
– ORIGIN 1970s: from **DI-**[1] 'two' + *deoxy-* (in the sense 'that has lost oxygen)' + **INOSINE**.

Diderot /ˈdiːdərəʊ, French didəʀo/, Denis (1713–84), French philosopher, writer, and critic. A leading figure of the Enlightenment in France, he was principal editor of the *Encyclopédie* (1751–76), through which he disseminated and popularized philosophy and scientific knowledge. Other notable works: *Le Rêve de D'Alembert* (1782) and *Le Neveu de Rameau* (1805).

didgeridoo /ˌdɪdʒ(ə)rɪˈduː/ (also **didjeridu**) ▶ **noun** an Australian Aboriginal wind instrument in the form of a long wooden tube, traditionally made from a hollow branch, which is blown to produce a deep resonant sound, varied by rhythmic accents of timbre and volume.
– ORIGIN 1920s: imitative; from an Aboriginal language of Arnhem Land.

didi /ˈdiːdiː/ ▶ **noun** Indian an older sister or older female cousin (often as a proper name or form of address): *'Just have a look at this luggage, didi.'*
■ a respectful form of address to any older woman familiar to the speaker.
– ORIGIN from Hindi *dīdī*.

didicoi /ˈdɪdɪkɔɪ/ (also **diddicoy**) ▶ **noun** (pl. **didicois**) dialect a gypsy; an itinerant tinker.
– ORIGIN mid 19th cent.: perhaps an alteration of Romany *dik akei* 'look here'.

didn't ▶ **contraction of** did not.

Dido /ˈdʌɪdəʊ/ (in the *Aeneid*) the queen and founder of Carthage, who fell in love with the shipwrecked Aeneas and killed herself when he deserted her.

dido /ˈdʌɪdəʊ/ ▶ **noun** (pl. **-oes** or **-os**) N. Amer. informal (in phrase **cut/cut up didoes**) perform mischievous tricks or deeds.
– ORIGIN early 19th cent.: of unknown origin.

didst archaic second person singular past of **DO**[1].

Didyma /ˈdɪdɪmə/ an ancient sanctuary of Apollo, site of one of the most famous oracles of the Aegean region, close to the west coast of Asia Minor.

didymium /dɪˈdɪmɪəm/ ▶ **noun** [mass noun] Chemistry a mixture containing the rare earth elements praseodymium and neodymium, used to colour glass for optical filters. It was originally regarded as a single element.
– ORIGIN mid 19th cent.: from Greek *didumos* 'twin' (because it was closely associated with lanthanum) + *-ium* (used as a suffix for new metals).

die[1] ▶ **verb** (**dying**) [no obj.] **1** (of a person, animal, or plant) stop living: *he* ***died of*** *Aids | trees are* ***dying from*** *acid rain* | [with obj.] *the king died a violent death.*
■ (**die for**) be killed for (a cause): *they were prepared to die for their country.* ■ [with complement] have a specified status at the time of one's death: *the inventor died a pauper.* ■ (**die out**) become extinct: *many species died out.* ■ be forgotten: *her genius has assured her name will never die.* ■ [with adverbial] become less loud or strong: *after a while, the noise* ***died down****.* ■ (of a fire or light) stop burning or gleaming. ■ informal (of a machine) stop functioning: *three toasters have* ***died on*** *me.* ■ poetic/literary have an orgasm.
2 informal used to emphasize that one wants to do or have something very much: *they must be* ***dying for*** *a drink* | [with infinitive] *he's dying to meet you.*
■ informal used to emphasize how keenly one feels something: *I'm simply* ***dying of*** *thirst.*
3 informal used to emphasize feelings of shock, embarrassment, amusement, or misery: *I* ***nearly died*** *when I saw them | we nearly died laughing when he told us.*
– PHRASES **die a** (or **the**) **death** informal see **DEATH**. **die hard** disappear or change very slowly: *old habits die hard.* **die in bed** undergo death from natural causes. **die in harness** die before retirement: *don't concern yourself with the pension fund—musicians mostly die in harness.* **die like flies** see **FLY**[2]. **die on one's feet** informal come to a sudden or premature end: *the critics said the show would die on its feet.* **die on the vine** be unsuccessful at an early stage. **die with one's boots on** see **BOOT**[1]. **never say die** used to encourage someone not to give up hope in a difficult situation. **to die for** informal extremely good or desirable: *the ice creams are to die for.*
– ORIGIN Middle English: from Old Norse *deyja*, of Germanic origin; related to **DEAD**.

die[2] ▶ **noun 1** singular form of **DICE**.
■ Architecture the cubical part of a pedestal between the base and the cornice; a dado or plinth.
2 (pl. **dies**) a device for cutting or moulding metal into a particular shape.
■ an engraved device for stamping a design on coins or medals.
– PHRASES **the die is cast** an event has happened or a decision has been taken that cannot be changed. (**as**) **straight as a die** absolutely straight. ■ entirely open and honest: *she was as straight as a die.*
– ORIGIN Middle English: from Old French *de*, from Latin *datum* 'something given or played', neuter past participle of *dare*.

> **USAGE** In modern standard English, the singular **die** (rather than **dice**) is uncommon. **Dice** is used for both the singular and the plural.

dieback ▶ **noun** [mass noun] a condition in which a tree or shrub begins to die from the tip of its leaves or roots backwards, owing to disease or an unfavourable environment.

die-cast ▶ **adjective** (of a metal object) formed by pouring molten metal into a reusable mould: *a die-cast aluminium loudspeaker chassis.*
▶ **verb** [with obj.] [usu. as noun **die-casting**] make (a metal object) in this way.

dieffenbachia /ˌdiːf(ə)nˈbakɪə/ ▶ **noun** a plant of a genus that includes dumb cane and its relatives.
• Genus *Dieffenbachia*, family Araceae.
– ORIGIN modern Latin, named after Ernst *Dieffenbach* (1811–55), German horticulturalist.

diegesis /ˌdʌɪəˈdʒiːsɪs/ ▶ **noun** (pl. **diegeses** /-siːz/) a narrative or plot, typically in a film.
– DERIVATIVES **diegetic** /-ˈdʒɛtɪk/ adjective.
– ORIGIN early 19th cent.: from Greek *diēgēsis* 'narrative'.

Diego Garcia /dɪˌeɪgəʊ gɑːˈsiːə/ the largest island of the Chagos Archipelago in the middle of the Indian Ocean, site of a strategic Anglo-American naval base established in 1973.

diehard ▶ **noun** [often as modifier] a person who strongly opposes change or who continues to support something in spite of opposition: *several hundred diehard communists shouted slogans | she was a diehard Yankees fan.*
– ORIGIN mid 19th cent.: from *die hard* (see **DIE**[1]).

die-in ▶ **noun** informal a demonstration in which people lie down as if dead.

diel /ˈdiːl/ ▶ **adjective** Biology denoting or involving a period of 24 hours: *tidal and diel cycles.*
– ORIGIN 1930s: from Latin *dies* 'day' + *-(a)l* (see **-AL**).

dieldrin /ˈdiːldrɪn/ ▶ **noun** [mass noun] a toxic insecticide produced by the oxidation of aldrin, now largely banned because of its persistence in the environment.
• A chlorinated epoxide; chem. formula: $C_{12}H_8Cl_6O$.
– ORIGIN 1940s: blend of the name *Diels* (see **DIELS–ALDER REACTION**) + **ALDRIN**.

dielectric /ˌdʌɪɪˈlɛktrɪk/ Physics ▶ **adjective** having the property of transmitting electric force without conduction; insulating.
▶ **noun** a medium or substance with such a property; an insulator.
– DERIVATIVES **dielectrically** adverb.
– ORIGIN mid 19th cent.: from **DI-**[3] + **ELECTRIC**, literally 'across which electricity is transmitted (without conduction)'.

dielectric constant ▶ **noun** Physics a quantity measuring the ability of a substance to store electrical energy in an electric field.

dielectrophoresis /dʌɪˌlɛktrəfəˈriːsɪs/ ▶ **noun** [mass noun] Physics the migration of uncharged particles towards the position of maximum field strength in a non-uniform electric field.
– ORIGIN mid 20th cent.: blend of **DIELECTRIC** and **ELECTROPHORESIS**.

die link ▶ **noun** an established connection between coins struck from the same die.
▶ **verb** [with obj.] (**die-link**) establish a connection between (coins).

Diels–Alder reaction /diːlzˈɔːldə/ ▶ **noun** Chemistry an addition reaction in which a conjugated diene reacts with a compound with a double or triple bond so as to form a six-membered ring.
– ORIGIN 1940s: named after Otto *Diels* (1876–1954), and Kurt Alder (1902–58), German chemists.

Dien Bien Phu /ˌdjɛn bjɛn ˈfuː/ a village in NW Vietnam, in 1954 the site of a French military post which was captured by the Vietminh after a 55-day siege.

diencephalon /ˌdʌɪɛnˈsɛf(ə)lɒn, -ˈkɛf-/ ▶ **noun** Anatomy the caudal (posterior) part of the forebrain, containing the epithalamus, thalamus, hypothalamus, and ventral thalamus and the third ventricle. Compare with **TELENCEPHALON**.
– DERIVATIVES **diencephalic** adjective.
– ORIGIN late 19th cent.: from **DI-**[3] 'across' + Greek *enkephalos* 'brain'.

diene /ˈdʌɪiːn/ ▶ **noun** Chemistry an unsaturated hydrocarbon containing two double bonds between carbon atoms.
– ORIGIN early 20th cent.: from **DI-**[1] 'two' + **-ENE**.

Dieppe /dɪˈɛp, French djɛp/ a channel port in northern France, from which ferries run to Newhaven and elsewhere; pop. 36,600 (1990). In August 1942 it was the scene of an unsuccessful amphibious raid by a joint force of British and Canadian troops to destroy the German-held port and airfield.

dieresis ▶ **noun** US spelling of **DIAERESIS**.

Diesel /ˈdiːz(ə)l/, Rudolf (Christian Karl) (1858–1913), French-born German engineer, inventor of the diesel engine. In 1892 he patented a design for a new, more efficient internal-combustion engine and developed it, exhibiting the prototype in 1897.

diesel /ˈdiːz(ə)l/ ▶ **noun** (also **diesel engine**) an internal-combustion engine in which heat produced by the compression of air in the cylinder is used to ignite the fuel: [as modifier] *a diesel locomotive.*
■ [mass noun] a heavy petroleum fraction used as fuel in diesel engines: *eleven litres of diesel.*
– DERIVATIVES **dieselize** (also **-ise**) verb.
– ORIGIN late 19th cent.: named after R. **DIESEL**.

diesel-electric ▶ **adjective** denoting or relating to a locomotive driven by the electric current produced by a diesel-engined generator.
▶ **noun** a locomotive of this type.

diesel-hydraulic ▶ **adjective** denoting or relating to a locomotive driven by a hydraulic transmission system powered by a diesel engine.
▶ **noun** a locomotive of this type.

die-sinker ▶ **noun** a person who engraves dies used to stamp designs on coins or medals.

Dies Irae /ˌdiːeɪz ˈɪərʌɪ, ˈɪəreɪ/ ▶ **noun** a Latin hymn sung in a Mass for the dead.
– ORIGIN Latin, 'day of wrath' (the opening words of the hymn).

dies non /ˌdiːeɪz ˈnɒn/ ▶ **noun** (pl. same) a day on which no legal business can be done, or which does not count for legal or other purposes.
– ORIGIN Latin, short for *dies non juridicus* 'non-judicial day'.

die-stamping ▶ **noun** [mass noun] a method of embossing paper or another surface using a die.
■ a method of printing using an inked die to produce raised print.

diestock ▶ **noun** a hand tool used in the cutting of external screw threads, consisting of a holder for the die which is turned using long handles.

diestrus ▶ **noun** US spelling of **DIOESTRUS**.

diet[1] ▶ **noun** the kinds of food that a person, animal, or community habitually eats: *a vegetarian diet* | [mass noun] *a specialist in diet.*
■ a special course of food to which a person restricts themselves, either to lose weight or for medical reasons: *I'm* ***going on a diet****.* ■ [as modifier] (of food or drink) with reduced fat or sugar content: *diet soft drinks.* ■ figurative a regular occupation or series of activities to which one is restricted: *youngsters are presented with a constant diet of insipid programmes.*
▶ **verb** (**dieted**, **dieting**) [no obj.] restrict oneself to small amounts or special kinds of food in order to lose weight: *it's difficult to diet.*

■[with obj.] restrict (a person or animal) to a special diet.
– DERIVATIVES **dieter** noun.
– ORIGIN Middle English: from Old French *diete* (noun), *dieter* (verb), via Latin from Greek *diaita* 'a way of life'.

diet² ▶ **noun** a legislative assembly in certain countries.
■historical a regular meeting of the states of a confederation. ■ Scots Law a meeting or session of a court.
– ORIGIN late Middle English: from medieval Latin *dieta* 'day's work, wages, etc.', also 'meeting of councillors'.

dietary ▶ **adjective** of or relating to diets or dieting: *dietary advice for healthy skin and hair.*
■provided by one's diet: *the average dietary calcium intake was 140 milligrams per day.*
▶ **noun** (pl. **-ies**) dated a regulated or restricted diet.
– ORIGIN late Middle English (as a noun): from medieval Latin *dietarium*, from Latin *diaeta* (see **DIET**[1]).

dietetic /ˌdʌɪəˈtɛtɪk/ ▶ **adjective** concerned with diet and nutrition: *experienced dietetic advice.*
– DERIVATIVES **dietetically** adverb.
– ORIGIN mid 16th cent. (as a noun in the sense 'diatetics'): via Latin from Greek *diaitētikos*, from *diaita* 'a way of life'.

dietetics ▶ **plural noun** [treated as sing.] the branch of knowledge concerned with the diet and its effects on health, especially with the practical application of a scientific understanding of nutrition.

diethylene glycol /dʌɪˈɛθɪliːn, -θ(ə)l-/ ▶ **noun** [mass noun] Chemistry a colourless soluble liquid used as a solvent and antifreeze.
• Chem. formula: $(C_2H_4OH)_2O$.

diethyl ether /dʌɪˈiːθʌɪl/ ▶ **noun** see **ETHER** (sense 1).

diethylstilboestrol /dʌɪˌiːθʌɪlstɪlˈbiːstrɒl, -ˈɛθɪl/ (US **diethylstilbestrol**) ▶ **noun** another term for **STILBOESTROL**.

dietitian /dʌɪəˈtɪʃ(ə)n/ (also **dietician**) ▶ **noun** an expert on diet and nutrition.

Diet of Worms a meeting of the Holy Roman emperor Charles V's imperial diet at Worms in 1521, at which Martin Luther was summoned to appear. Luther committed himself there to the cause of Protestant reform, and his teaching was formally condemned in the Edict of Worms.

Dietrich /ˈdiːtrɪx/, Marlene (1901–92), German-born American actress and singer; born *Maria Magdelene von Losch*. She became famous for her part as Lola in *The Blue Angel* (1930), one of many films she made with Josef von Sternberg. From the 1950s she was also successful as an international cabaret star.

Dieu et mon droit /ˌdjəː eɪ mɒ̃ ˈdrwɑː/ ▶ **noun** God and my right (the motto of the British monarch).
– ORIGIN French.

dif- ▶ **prefix** variant spelling of **DIS-** assimilated before *f* (as in *diffraction, diffuse.*).
– ORIGIN from Latin, variant of **DIS-**.

diff ▶ **noun** informal short for **DIFFERENTIAL**.

differ ▶ **verb** [no obj.] be unlike or dissimilar: *the second set of data **differed from** the first | tastes differ |* [as adj. **differing**] *widely differing circumstances.*
■disagree: *he **differed from** his contemporaries in ethical matters.*
– PHRASES **agree to differ** cease to argue about something because neither party will compromise or be persuaded. **beg to differ** politely disagree: *that's your opinion—I beg to differ.*
– ORIGIN late Middle English (also in the sense 'put off, defer'): from Old French *differer* 'differ, defer', from Latin *differre*, from *dis-* 'from, away' + *ferre* 'bring, carry'. Compare with **DEFER**[1].

difference ▶ **noun** a point or way in which people or things are not the same: *the **differences between** men and women.*
■[mass noun] the state or condition of being dissimilar or unlike: *their **difference from** one another.* ■a disagreement, quarrel, or dispute: *the couple are patching up their differences.* ■a quantity by which amounts differ; the remainder left after subtraction of one value from another: *sceptics said the marriage wouldn't last because of the age difference.* ■ Heraldry an alteration in a coat of arms to distinguish members or branches of a family.
▶ **verb** [with obj.] Heraldry alter (a coat of arms) to distinguish members or branches of a family.
– PHRASES **make a** (or **no**) **difference** have a significant effect (or no effect) on a person or situation: *the Act will **make no difference to** my business.* **with a difference** having a new or unusual feature or treatment: *a fashion show with a difference.*
– ORIGIN Middle English: via Old French from Latin *differentia* (see **DIFFERENTIA**).

difference threshold ▶ **noun** the least amount by which two sensory stimuli can differ for an individual to perceive them as different.

different ▶ **adjective 1** not the same as another or each other; unlike in nature, form, or quality: *you can play this game in different ways.* (**different from/to/than**) *the car's different from anything else on the market.*
■informal novel and unusual: *try something deliciously different.*
2 distinct; separate: *on two different occasions.*
– PHRASES **different strokes for different folks** proverb different things appeal to different people.
– DERIVATIVES **differently** adverb, **differentness** noun.
– ORIGIN late Middle English: via Old French from Latin *different-* 'carrying away, differing', from the verb *differre* (see **DIFFER**).

> **USAGE** **Different from**, **different than**, and **different to**: are there any distinctions between these three collocations, and is one more correct than the others? Since the 18th century, **different than** has been singled out by critics as incorrect. In practice, **different from** is the most common structure, both in the UK and North America, while **different than** is almost exclusively used in North America. It is difficult to sustain the view in modern standard English that one is more correct than the others, however. There is little difference in sense between the three, and all of them are used by respected writers.

differentia /ˌdɪfəˈrɛnʃɪə/ ▶ **noun** (pl. **differentiae** /-ʃɪiː/) a distinguishing mark or characteristic.
■chiefly Philosophy an attribute that distinguishes a species of thing from other species of the same genus.
– ORIGIN late 17th cent.: from Latin, literally 'difference', from *different-* 'carrying away' (see **DIFFERENT**).

differentiable /ˌdɪfəˈrɛnʃɪəb(ə)l/ ▶ **adjective** able to be differentiated.
– DERIVATIVES **differentiability** noun.
– ORIGIN mid 19th cent.: from **DIFFERENTIATE**, on the pattern of pairs such as *depreciate, depreciable.*

differential /ˌdɪfəˈrɛnʃ(ə)l/ chiefly technical ▶ **adjective** [attrib.] of, showing, or depending on a difference; differing or varying according to circumstances or relevant factors: *the differential achievements of boys and girls.*
■constituting a specific difference; distinctive: *the differential features between benign and malignant tumours.* ■ Mathematics relating to infinitesimal differences or to the derivatives of functions. ■ of or relating to a difference in a physical quantity: *a differential amplifier.*
▶ **noun** a difference between amounts of things: ***the differential between** petrol and diesel prices.*
■Brit. a difference in wages between industries or between categories of employees in the same industry: *regional differentials in pay.* ■ Mathematics an infinitesimal difference between successive values of a variable. ■ (also **differential gear**) a gear allowing a vehicle's driven wheels to revolve at different speeds in cornering.
– DERIVATIVES **differentially** adverb.
– ORIGIN mid 17th cent.: from medieval Latin *differentialis*, from Latin *differentia* 'difference' (see **DIFFERENTIA**).

differential calculus ▶ **noun** [mass noun] a branch of mathematics concerned with the determination, properties, and application of derivatives and differentials. Compare with **INTEGRAL CALCULUS**.

differential coefficient ▶ **noun** Mathematics another term for **DERIVATIVE**.

differential diagnosis ▶ **noun** Medicine the process of differentiating between two or more conditions which share similar signs or symptoms.

differential equation ▶ **noun** an equation involving derivatives of a function or functions.

differential lock ▶ **noun** a device which disables the differential of a motor vehicle in slippery conditions to improve grip.

differential operator ▶ **noun** Mathematics another term for **DEL**.

differentiate /ˌdɪfəˈrɛnʃɪeɪt/ ▶ **verb** [with obj.] **1** recognize or ascertain what makes (someone or something) different: *children can **differentiate** the past **from** the present.*
■[no obj.] (**differentiate between**) identify differences between (two or more things or people): *he is unable to differentiate between fantasy and reality.* ■make (someone or something) appear different or distinct: *little now **differentiates** the firms products **from** its rivals.*
2 technical make or become different in the process of growth or development: [with obj.] *the receptors are developed and differentiated into sense organs |* [no obj.] *the cells differentiate into a wide variety of cell types.*
3 Mathematics transform (a function) into its derivative.
– DERIVATIVES **differentiation** noun, **differentiator** noun.
– ORIGIN early 19th cent.: from medieval Latin *differentiat-* 'carried away from', from the verb *differentiare*, from *differentia* (see **DIFFERENTIA**).

differently abled ▶ **adjective** chiefly N. Amer. disabled.

> **USAGE** **Differently abled** was first proposed (in the 1980s) as an alternative to **disabled**, **handicapped**, etc. on the grounds that it gave a more positive message and so avoided discrimination towards people with disabilities. Despite this, the term has gained little currency and has been criticized as both over-euphemistic and condescending. The accepted term in general use is **disabled**.

difficult ▶ **adjective** needing much effort or skill to accomplish, deal with, or understand: *she had a difficult decision to make | the questions are too **difficult for** the children.*
■characterized by or causing hardships or problems: *a difficult economic climate.* ■(of a person) not easy to please or satisfy; awkward: *Lily could be difficult.*
– DERIVATIVES **difficultly** adverb (rare), **difficultness** noun.
– ORIGIN late Middle English: back-formation from **DIFFICULTY**.

difficulty ▶ **noun** (pl. **-ies**) [mass noun] the state or condition of being difficult: *Guy had no **difficulty in** making friends | I managed **with difficulty** to struggle upright.*
■[count noun] a thing that is hard to accomplish, deal with, or understand: *there is a practical difficulty | a club with financial difficulties.* ■ [count noun] (often **difficulties**) a situation that is difficult or dangerous: *they went for a swim but **got into difficulties**.*
– ORIGIN late Middle English (in the senses 'requiring effort or skill' and 'something difficult'): from Latin *difficultas*, from *dis-* (expressing reversal) + *facultas* 'ability, opportunity'.

diffident ▶ **adjective** modest or shy because of a lack of self-confidence: *a diffident youth.*
– DERIVATIVES **diffidence** noun, **diffidently** adverb.
– ORIGIN late Middle English (in the sense 'lacking confidence or trust in someone or something'): from Latin *diffident-* 'failing in trust', from the verb *diffidere*, from *dis-* (expressing reversal) + *fidere* 'to trust'.

diffract /dɪˈfrakt/ ▶ **verb** [with obj.] Physics cause to undergo diffraction.
– DERIVATIVES **diffractive** adjective, **diffractively** adverb.
– ORIGIN early 19th cent.: from Latin *diffract-* 'broken in pieces', from the verb *diffringere*, from *dis-* 'away, from' + *frangere* 'to break'.

diffraction ▶ **noun** [mass noun] the process by which a beam of light or other system of waves is spread out as a result of passing through a narrow aperture or across an edge, typically accompanied by interference between the wave forms produced.

diffraction grating ▶ **noun** a plate of glass or metal ruled with very close parallel lines, producing a spectrum by diffraction and interference of light.

diffractometer /ˌdɪfrakˈtɒmɪtə/ ▶ **noun** an instrument for measuring diffraction, chiefly used to determine the structure of a crystal by analysis of the diffraction of X-rays.

diffuse ▶ **verb** /dɪˈfjuːz/ spread or cause to spread over a wide area or between a large number of people: [no obj.] *technologies diffuse rapidly |* [with obj.] *the problem is how to diffuse power without creating anarchy.*

■ become or cause (a fluid, gas, individual atom, etc.) to become intermingled with a substance by movement, typically in a specified direction or at specified speed: [no obj.] *oxygen molecules **diffuse across** the membrane* | [with obj.] *gas is **diffused into** the bladder.* ■ [with obj.] cause (light) to glow faintly by dispersing it in many directions.

▶ **adjective** /dɪˈfjuːs/ spread out over a large area; not concentrated: *the diffuse community which centred on the church* | *the light is more diffuse.*

■ (of disease) not localized in the body: *diffuse hyperplasia.* ■ lacking clarity or conciseness: *the second argument is more diffuse.*

– DERIVATIVES **diffusely** /dɪˈfjuːsli/ adverb, **diffuseness** /dɪˈfjuːsnɪs/ noun.

– ORIGIN late Middle English: from Latin *diffus-* 'poured out', from the verb *diffundere*, from *dis-* 'away' + *fundere* 'pour'; the adjective via French *diffus* or Latin *diffusus* 'extensive', from *diffundere*.

> **USAGE** The verbs **diffuse** and **defuse** sound similar but have different meanings. **Diffuse** means, broadly, 'disperse', while **defuse** means 'reduce the danger or tension in'. Thus sentences such as *Cooper successfully **diffused** the situation* (taken from the British National Corpus) are wrong, while *Cooper successfully **defused** the situation* would be correct.

diffuser (also **diffusor**) ▶ **noun** a thing that diffuses something, in particular:

■ an attachment or duct for broadening an airflow and reducing its speed. ■ Photography a device which spreads the light from a light source evenly and reduces harsh shadows.

diffusible /dɪˈfjuːzɪb(ə)l/ ▶ **adjective** able to intermingle by diffusion: *diffusible factors in the cytoplasm.*

diffusion ▶ **noun** [mass noun] the spreading of something more widely: *the diffusion of Marxist ideas.*

■ the action of spreading the light from a light source evenly so as to reduce glare and harsh shadows. ■ the intermingling of substances by the natural movement of their particles: *the rate of diffusion of a gas.* ■ Anthropology the dissemination of elements of culture to another region or people.

– DERIVATIVES **diffusionism** noun (Anthropology), **diffusionist** adjective & noun (Anthropology), **diffusive** adjective (Chemistry).

– ORIGIN late Middle English (in the sense 'pouring out, effusion'): from Latin *diffusio(n-)*, from *diffundere* 'pour out'.

diffusion line (also **diffusion range**) ▶ **noun** a range of relatively inexpensive ready-to-wear garments produced for the mass market by a fashion designer.

diffusivity /ˌdɪfjuːˈsɪvɪti/ ▶ **noun** (pl. **-ies**) Physics a measure of the capability of a substance or energy to be diffused or to allow something to pass by diffusion.

dig ▶ **verb** (**digging**; past and past participle **dug**) **1** [no obj.] break up and move earth with a tool or machine, or with hands, paws, snout, etc.: *the boar had been **digging for** roots* | [with obj.] *she had to dig the garden* | *authorities cause chaos by **digging up** roads.*

■ [with obj.] make (a hole, grave, etc.) by breaking up and moving earth in such a way: *he took a spade and dug a hole* | [as adj. **dug**] *the newly dug grave.* ■ (**dig in**) (of a soldier) protect oneself by making a trench or similar ground defence. ■ [with obj. and adverbial] extract from the ground by breaking up and moving earth: *the water board came and **dug** the cable **up**.* ■ [in imperative] (**dig in**) informal used to encourage someone to start eating and have as much as they want: *I don't mind when you have the salad—dig in!* ■ [with obj.] (**dig something in/into**) push or poke something in or into: *he dug his hands into his pockets.* ■ [with obj.] excavate (an archaeological site): *apart from digging a site, recording evidence is important.* ■ [with obj.] (**dig something out**) bring out something that is hidden or has been stored for a long time: *they dug out last year's notes.* ■ (**dig into**) informal find money from (somewhere): *members must continue to dig deep into their pockets.* ■ [no obj., with adverbial] search or rummage in a specified place: *Catherine dug into her handbag and produced her card.* ■ engage in research; conduct an investigation: *a professional **digging for** information* | *he had no compunction about **digging into** her private affairs.* ■ [with obj.] (**dig something up/out**) discover information after a search or investigation: *have you **dug up** any information on the captain?*

2 [with obj.] informal, dated like, appreciate, or understand: *I really dig heavy rock.*

▶ **noun 1** [in sing.] an act or spell of digging: *a thorough dig of the whole plot.*

■ [count noun] an archaeological excavation.

2 a push or poke with one's elbow, finger, etc.: *Ginnie **gave** her sister **a dig in the ribs**.*

■ informal a remark intended to mock or criticize: *Graham **had a dig at** me in the press.*

3 (**digs**) informal, chiefly Brit. lodgings. [ORIGIN: short for *diggings*, used in the same sense, probably referring to the land where a farmer digs, i.e. works and, by extension, lives.]

– PHRASES **dig the dirt** (or **dig up dirt**) informal discover and reveal damaging information about someone. **dig a hole for oneself** (or **dig oneself into a hole**) get oneself into an awkward or restrictive situation. **dig in one's heels** (or **toes** or **feet**) resist stubbornly; refuse to give in: *officials dug their heels in on particular points.* **dig a pit for** see **PIT**[1]. **dig's one's own grave** see **GRAVE**[1].

– ORIGIN Middle English: perhaps from Old English *dīc* 'ditch'.

Digambara /dɪˈɡʌmbərə/ ▶ **noun** a member of one of two principal sects of Jainism, which was formed as a result of doctrinal schism in about AD 80 and continues today in parts of southern India. The sect's adherents reject property ownership and usually do not wear clothes. See also **SVETAMBARA**.

– ORIGIN from Sanskrit *Digāmbara*, literally 'sky-clad'.

digamma /dʌɪˈɡamə/ ▶ **noun** the sixth letter of the early Greek alphabet (Ϝ, ϝ), probably pronounced as 'w'. It became obsolete before the Classical period.

– ORIGIN late 17th cent.: via Latin from Greek, from *di-* 'twice' + **GAMMA** (because of the shape of the letter, resembling gamma (Γ) with an extra stroke).

digastric /dʌɪˈɡastrɪk/ (also **digastric muscle**) ▶ **noun** Anatomy each of a pair of muscles which run under the jaw and act to open it.

– ORIGIN late 17th cent.: from modern Latin *digastricus*, from *di-* 'twice' + Greek *gastēr* 'belly' (because the muscle has two fleshy parts or 'bellies' at an angle, connected by a tendon).

digenean /ˌdʌɪdʒɪˈniːən, dʌɪˈdʒɛnɪən/ Zoology ▶ **adjective** of or relating to a group of flukes which are internal parasites needing two to four hosts to complete their life cycle. Compare with **MONOGENEAN**.

▶ **noun** a digenean fluke; a trematode.

● Subclass Digenea, class Trematoda.

– ORIGIN 1960s: from modern Latin *Digenea* (from Greek *di-* 'twice' + *genea* 'generation, race') + **-AN**.

digerati /ˌdɪdʒəˈrɑːti/ ▶ **plural noun** people with expertise or professional involvement in information technology.

– ORIGIN 1990s: blend of **DIGITAL** and **LITERATI**.

digest ▶ **verb** /dʌɪˈdʒɛst, dɪ-/ [with obj.] break down (food) in the stomach and intestines into substances that can be used by the body.

■ understand or assimilate (new information or the significance of something) by a period of reflection. ■ arrange (something) in a systematic or convenient order, especially by reduction: *the computer **digested** your labours **into** a form understandable by a program.* ■ Chemistry treat (a substance) with heat, enzymes, or a solvent in order to decompose it or extract essential components.

▶ **noun** /ˈdʌɪdʒɛst/ **1** a compilation or summary of material or information: *a digest of their findings.*

■ a periodical consisting of condensed versions of pieces of writing or news published elsewhere. ■ a methodical summary of a body of laws. ■ (**the Digest**) the compendium of Roman law compiled in the reign of Justinian.

2 Chemistry a substance or mixture obtained by digestion: *a digest of cloned DNA.*

– ORIGIN late Middle English: from Latin *digest-* 'distributed, dissolved, digested', from the verb *digerere*, from *di-* 'apart' + *gerere* 'carry'; the noun from Latin *digesta* 'matters methodically arranged', from *digestus* 'divided', from *digerere*.

digester ▶ **noun** Chemistry a container in which substances are treated with heat, enzymes, or a solvent in order to promote decomposition or extract essential components.

digestible ▶ **adjective** (of food) able to be digested.

■ (of information) easy to understand or follow: *her books convey philosophical issues in digestible form.*

– DERIVATIVES **digestibility** noun.

– ORIGIN late Middle English: via Old French from Latin *digestibilis*, from *digest-* 'digested', from the verb *digerere* (see **DIGEST**).

digestif /dʌɪˈdʒɛstɪf, ˌdiːʒɛˈstiːf/ ▶ **noun** a drink, especially an alcoholic one, drunk before or after a meal in order to aid the digestion.

– ORIGIN French, literally 'digestive'.

digestion ▶ **noun** [mass noun] the process of breaking down food by mechanical and enzymatic action in the stomach and intestines into substances that can be used by the body.

■ [count noun] a person's capacity to break down food in such a way: *he suffered with his digestion.* ■ Chemistry the process of treating a substance by means of heat, enzymes, or a solvent to promote decomposition or extract essential components.

– ORIGIN late Middle English: via Old French from Latin *digestio(n-)*, from the verb *digerere* (see **DIGEST**).

digestive ▶ **adjective** of or relating to the process of digesting food: *stomach ulcers and other digestive disorders.*

■ (of food or medicine) aiding or promoting the process of digestion: *tubes of digestive mints.*

▶ **noun** a food or medicine that aids or promotes the digestion of food.

■ (also **digestive biscuit**) Brit. a round semi-sweet biscuit made of wholemeal flour.

– DERIVATIVES **digestively** adverb.

– ORIGIN late Middle English: from Old French *digestif, -ive* or Latin *digestivus*, from *digest-* 'digested', from the verb *digerere* (see **DIGEST**).

digestive gland ▶ **noun** Zoology a glandular organ of digestion present in crustaceans, molluscs, and certain other invertebrates.

digger ▶ **noun 1** a person, animal, or large machine that digs earth.

■ a gold-digger or other miner. ■ a person who excavates archaeological sites. ■ (**Digger**) a member of a group of radical dissenters formed in England in 1649 as an offshoot of the Levellers, believing in a form of agrarian communism in which common land would be made available to the poor.

2 Austral./NZ informal a man, especially a private soldier (often used as a friendly form of address): *how are you, Digger?* [ORIGIN: early 20th cent.: from *digger* 'miner', reinforced by association with the digging of trenches on the battlefields.]

digger wasp ▶ **noun** a solitary wasp which typically excavates a burrow in sandy soil, filling it with one or more paralysed insects or spiders for its larvae to feed on.

● Families Sphecidae (which includes sand wasps) and Pompilidae (which includes spider-hunting wasps).

diggings ▶ **plural noun 1** a site such as a mine or goldfield that has been excavated: *hills scarred with peat diggings.*

■ material that has been dug from the ground.

2 Brit. informal, dated lodgings.

digging stick ▶ **noun** a primitive digging implement consisting of a pointed stick, sometimes weighted by a stone.

dight /dʌɪt/ ▶ **adjective** archaic clothed or equipped.

▶ **verb** [with obj.] poetic/literary make ready for a use or purpose; prepare: *this Queen of the many wooers dights the wedding for us then.*

■ Scottish & N. English wipe clean or dry: *take a cloth and dight it up.* ■ Scottish & N. English winnow (corn).

– ORIGIN Middle English: past participle of archaic *dight* 'order, deal with', based on Latin *dictare* 'compose (in language), order'. The wide and varied use of the word in Middle English is reflected dialectally.

digit /ˈdɪdʒɪt/ ▶ **noun 1** any of the numerals from 0 to 9, especially when forming part of a number.

2 a finger or thumb.

■ Zoology an equivalent structure at the end of the limbs of many higher vertebrates.

– ORIGIN late Middle English: from Latin *digitus* 'finger, toe'; sense 1 arose from the practice of counting on the fingers.

digital ▶ **adjective 1** relating to or using signals or information represented by discrete values of a physical quantity such as voltage or magnetic polarization: *digital TV.* Often contrasted with **ANALOGUE**.

■ (of a clock or watch) showing the time by means of displayed digits rather than hands or a pointer.

2 of or relating to a finger or fingers.

– DERIVATIVES **digitally** adverb.

– ORIGIN late 15th cent.: from Latin *digitalis*, from *digitus* 'finger, toe'.

digital audiotape (abbrev.: **DAT**) ▶ **noun** [mass noun] magnetic tape which is used to make digital sound recordings of very high quality.

d

digital cash (also **digital money**) ▶ **noun** [mass noun] money which may be transferred electronically from one party to another during a transaction.

digitalin /ˌdɪdʒɪˈteɪlɪn/ ▶ **noun** [mass noun] a drug containing the active constituents of digitalis.
– ORIGIN mid 19th cent.: from **DIGITALIS** + **-IN**[1].

digitalis /ˌdɪdʒɪˈteɪlɪs/ ▶ **noun** [mass noun] a drug prepared from the dried leaves of foxgloves and containing substances (notably digoxin and digitoxin) that stimulate the heart muscle.
– ORIGIN late 18th cent.: from the modern Latin genus name of the foxglove, from *digitalis (herba)* '(plant) relating to the finger', from *digitus* 'finger, toe'; suggested by German *Fingerhut* 'thimble or foxglove'.

digitalize[1] (also **-ise**) ▶ **verb** another term for **DIGITIZE**.
– DERIVATIVES **digitalization** noun.

digitalize[2] (also **-ise**) ▶ **verb** [with obj.] Medicine administer digitalis or digoxin to (a patient with a heart complaint).
– DERIVATIVES **digitalization** noun.

digital to analogue converter ▶ **noun** an electronic device for converting digital signals to analogue form.

digitate /ˈdɪdʒɪtət, -eɪt/ ▶ **adjective** technical shaped like a spread hand: *digitate leaves* | *a digitate delta.*
– ORIGIN mid 17th cent.: from Latin *digitatus*, from *digitus* 'finger, toe'.

digitation ▶ **noun 1** Zoology & Botany a finger-like protuberance or division.
2 [mass noun] Computing the process of converting data to digital form.

digitigrade /ˈdɪdʒɪtɪˌɡreɪd/ ▶ **adjective** Zoology (of a mammal) walking on its toes and not touching the ground with its heels, as a dog, cat, or rodent. Compare with **PLANTIGRADE**.
– ORIGIN mid 19th cent.: from Latin *digitus* 'finger, toe' + *-gradus* '-walking'.

digitize (also **-ise**) ▶ **verb** [with obj.] [usu. as adj. **digitized**] convert (pictures or sound) into a digital form that can be processed by a computer.
– DERIVATIVES **digitization** noun, **digitizer** noun.

digitoxin /ˌdɪdʒɪˈtɒksɪn/ ▶ **noun** [mass noun] Chemistry a compound with similar properties to digoxin and found with it in the foxglove and similar plants.

diglossia /dʌɪˈɡlɒsɪə/ ▶ **noun** [mass noun] Linguistics a situation in which two languages (or two varieties of the same language) are used under different conditions within a community, often by the same speakers. The term is usually applied to languages with distinct 'high' and 'low' (colloquial) varieties, such as Arabic.
– DERIVATIVES **diglossic** adjective.
– ORIGIN 1950s: from Greek *diglōssos* 'bilingual', on the pattern of French *diglossie*.

dignified ▶ **adjective** having or showing a composed or serious manner that is worthy of respect: *she maintained a dignified silence* | *a dignified old lady.*
– DERIVATIVES **dignifiedly** adverb.

dignify ▶ **verb** (**-ies**, **-ied**) [with obj.] make (something) seem worthy and impressive: *the Americans had dignified their departure with a ceremony.*
■ (often **be dignified**) give an impressive name to (someone or something that one considers worthless): *dumps are increasingly* ***dignified as*** *landfills.*
– ORIGIN late Middle English: from Old French *dignefier*, from late Latin *dignificare*, from Latin *dignus* 'worthy'.

dignitary /ˈdɪɡnɪt(ə)ri/ ▶ **noun** (pl. **-ies**) a person considered to be important because of high rank or office.
– ORIGIN late 17th cent.: from **DIGNITY**, on the pattern of the pairs *propriety, proprietary.*

dignity ▶ **noun** (pl. **-ies**) [mass noun] the state or quality of being worthy of honour or respect: *a man of dignity and unbending principle* | *the dignity of labour.*
■ a composed or serious manner or style: *he bowed with great dignity.* ■ a sense of pride in oneself; self-respect: *it was* ***beneath his dignity*** *to shout.* ■ [count noun] a high or honourable rank or position: *he promised dignities to the nobles in return for his rival's murder.*
– PHRASES **stand on one's dignity** insist on being treated with due respect.
– ORIGIN Middle English: from Old French *dignete*, from Latin *dignitas*, from *dignus* 'worthy'.

digoxin /dɪˈdʒɒksɪn/ ▶ **noun** [mass noun] Chemistry a poisonous compound present in the foxglove and other plants. It is a steroid glycoside and is used in small doses as a cardiac stimulant.
– ORIGIN 1930s: contraction of **DIGITOXIN**.

digraph /ˈdʌɪɡrɑːf/ ▶ **noun** a combination of two letters representing one sound, as in *ph* and *ey*.
■ Printing a character consisting of two joined letters; a ligature.
– DERIVATIVES **digraphic** adjective.

digress /dʌɪˈɡrɛs/ ▶ **verb** [no obj.] leave the main subject temporarily in speech or writing: *I have* ***digressed*** *a little* ***from*** *my original plan.*
– DERIVATIVES **digresser** noun, **digression** noun, **digressive** adjective, **digressively** adverb, **digressiveness** noun.
– ORIGIN early 16th cent.: from Latin *digress-* 'stepped away', from the verb *digredi*, from *di-* 'aside' + *gradi* 'to walk'.

dihedral /dʌɪˈhiːdr(ə)l/ ▶ **adjective** having or contained by two plane faces: *a dihedral angle.*
▶ **noun** an angle formed by two plane faces.
■ [mass noun] Aeronautics inclination of an aircraft's wing from the horizontal, especially upwards away from the fuselage. Compare with **ANHEDRAL**. ■ Climbing N. Amer. a place where two planes of rock meet at an angle of between 60° and 120°.
– ORIGIN late 18th cent.: from **DI-**[1] 'two' + *-hedral* (see **-HEDRON**).

dihybrid /dʌɪˈhʌɪbrɪd/ ▶ **noun** Genetics a hybrid that is heterozygous for alleles of two different genes: [as modifier] *a dihybrid cross.*

dihydric /dʌɪˈhʌɪdrɪk/ ▶ **adjective** Chemistry (of an alcohol) containing two hydroxyl groups.
– ORIGIN late 19th cent.: from **DI-**[1] 'two' + **HYDROGEN** + **-IC**.

dihydrotestosterone /dʌɪˌhʌɪdrəʊtɛsˈtɒstərəʊn/ ▶ **noun** [mass noun] Biochemistry a male sex hormone which is the active form of testosterone, formed from testosterone in bodily tissue.
– ORIGIN 1950s: from *dihydro-* (in the sense 'containing two hydrogen atoms in the molecule') + **TESTOSTERONE**.

dihydroxyacetone /ˌdʌɪhʌɪdrɒksɪˈasɪtəʊn/ ▶ **noun** [mass noun] Chemistry a synthetic compound with strong reducing properties, used in lotions for colouring the skin in sunlight.
• Chem. formula: $(CH_2OH)CO$.
– ORIGIN late 19th cent.: from *dihydroxy-* (in the sense 'containing two hydroxyl groups in the molecule)' + **ACETONE**.

Dijon /ˈdiːʒɒ̃, French diʒɔ̃/ an industrial city in east central France, the former capital of Burgundy; pop. 151,640 (1990).

dik-dik /ˈdɪkdɪk/ ▶ **noun** a dwarf antelope found on the dry savannah of Africa, the female of which is larger than the male.
• Genus *Madoqua*, family Bovidae: several species.
– ORIGIN late 19th cent.: a local word in East Africa, imitative of its call.

dike[1] ▶ **noun** variant spelling of **DYKE**[1].

dike[2] ▶ **noun** variant spelling of **DYKE**[2].

dikkop /ˈdɪkəp/ ▶ **noun** S. African a stone curlew.
• The **Cape dikkop** is the spotted stone curlew (*Burhinus capensis*).
– ORIGIN mid 19th cent.: from Afrikaans, from *dik* 'thick' + *kop* 'head'.

diktat /ˈdɪktat/ ▶ **noun** an order or decree imposed by someone in power without popular consent: *a diktat from the Bundestag* | [mass noun] *he can disband the legislature and rule by diktat.*
– ORIGIN 1930s: from German, from Latin *dictatum* 'something dictated', neuter past participle of *dictare*.

DIL Electronics ▶ **abbreviation for** dual in-line (package). See **DIP**.

Dilantin /dʌɪˈlantɪn/ ▶ **noun** US trademark for **PHENYTOIN**.
– ORIGIN 1930s: from **DI-**[1] 'two' + *-l-* + *(hyd)ant(o)in.*

dilapidate /dɪˈlapɪdeɪt/ ▶ **verb** [with obj.] archaic cause (something) to fall into disrepair or ruin.
– ORIGIN early 16th cent. (in the sense 'waste, squander'): from Latin *dilapidat-* 'demolished, squandered', from the verb *dilapidare*, literally 'scatter as if throwing stones', from *di-* 'apart, abroad'+ *lapis, lapid-* 'stone'.

dilapidated ▶ **adjective** (of a building or object) in a state of disrepair or ruin as a result of age or neglect.

dilapidation ▶ **noun** [mass noun] the state or process of falling into decay or being in disrepair: *the mill was in a state of dilapidation.*
■ (**dilapidations**) repairs required during or at the end of a tenancy or lease. ■ (in church use) a sum charged against an incumbent for wear and tear during a tenancy.
– ORIGIN late Middle English (also in the sense 'squandering, waste'): from late Latin *dilapidatio(n-)*, from Latin *dilapidare* 'demolish, squander' (see **DILAPIDATE**).

dilatancy /dʌɪˈleɪt(ə)nsi, dɪ-/ ▶ **noun** [mass noun] Chemistry the phenomenon exhibited by some fluids, sols, and gels in which they become more viscous or solid under pressure.

dilatation /ˌdʌɪleɪˈteɪʃ(ə)n, dɪ-, -lə-/ ▶ **noun** [mass noun] chiefly Medicine & Physiology the process of becoming dilated.
■ the action of dilating a vessel or opening. ■ [count noun] a dilated part of a hollow organ or vessel.
– ORIGIN late Middle English: via Old French from late Latin *dilatatio(n-)*, from the verb *dilatare* (see **DILATE**).

dilatation and curettage (abbrev.: **D and C**) ▶ **noun** Medicine a surgical procedure involving dilatation of the cervix and curettage of the uterus, performed after a miscarriage or for the removal of cysts or tumours.

dilate /dʌɪˈleɪt, dɪ-/ ▶ **verb 1** make or become wider, larger, or more open: [no obj.] *her eyes dilated with horror* | [with obj.] *the woman dilated her nostrils.*
2 [no obj.] (**dilate on**) speak or write at length on (a subject).
– DERIVATIVES **dilatable** adjective, **dilation** noun.
– ORIGIN late Middle English: from Old French *dilater*, from Latin *dilatare* 'spread out', from *di-* 'apart' + *latus* 'wide'.

dilator ▶ **noun** a thing that dilates something, in particular:
■ (also **dilator muscle**) Anatomy a muscle whose contraction dilates an organ or aperture, such as the pupil of the eye. ■ a surgical instrument for dilating a tube or cavity in the body. ■ a vasodilatory drug.

dilatory /ˈdɪlət(ə)ri/ ▶ **adjective** slow to act: *he had been dilatory in appointing a solicitor.*
■ intended to cause delay: *they resorted to dilatory procedural tactics, forcing a postponement of peace talks.*
– DERIVATIVES **dilatorily** adverb, **dilatoriness** noun.
– ORIGIN late Middle English: from late Latin *dilatorius* 'delaying', from Latin *dilator* 'delayer', from *dilat-* 'deferred', from the verb *differre*.

dildo ▶ **noun** (pl. **-os** or **-oes**) an object shaped like an erect penis used for sexual stimulation.
■ vulgar slang a stupid or ridiculous person.
– ORIGIN late 16th cent.: of unknown origin.

dilemma /dɪˈlɛmə, dʌɪ-/ ▶ **noun** a situation in which a difficult choice has to be made between two or more alternatives, especially ones that are equally undesirable: *he wants to make money, but he also disapproves of it: Den's dilemma in a nutshell.*
■ informal a difficult situation or problem: *the insoluble dilemma of adolescence.* ■ Logic an argument forcing an opponent to choose either of two unfavourable alternatives.
– ORIGIN early 16th cent. (denoting a form of argument involving a choice between equally unfavourable alternatives): via Latin from Greek *dilēmma*, from *di-* 'twice' + *lēmma* 'premise'.

USAGE The weakened use of **dilemma** to mean 'a difficult situation or problem', as in *the insoluble* ***dilemma*** *of adolescence*, is recorded as early as the first part of the 17th century, but many regard this use as unacceptable and it should be avoided in written English. In the Oxford Reading Programme, around 10 per cent of the citations for **dilemma** are for this use.

dilettante /ˌdɪlɪˈtanteɪ, -ti/ ▶ **noun** (pl. **dilettanti** /-ti/ or **dilettantes**) a person who cultivates an area of interest, such as the arts, without real commitment or knowledge: [as modifier] *a dilettante approach.*
■ archaic a person with an amateur interest in the arts.
– DERIVATIVES **dilettantish** adjective, **dilettantism** noun.
– ORIGIN mid 18th cent.: from Italian, 'person loving the arts', from *dilettare* 'to delight', from Latin *delectare*.

Dili /ˈdiːliː/ a seaport on the Indonesian island of Timor, which was (until 1975) the capital of the former Portuguese colony of East Timor; pop. 60,150 (1980).

diligence[1] /ˈdɪlɪdʒ(ə)ns/ ▶ **noun** [mass noun] careful and persistent work or effort.
– ORIGIN Middle English (in the sense 'close attention, caution'): via Old French from Latin *diligentia*, from *diligent-* 'assiduous' (see **DILIGENT**).

diligence[2] /ˈdɪlɪdʒ(ə)ns/ ▶ **noun** historical a public stagecoach.
– ORIGIN late 17th cent.: from French, shortened from *carrosse de diligence* 'coach of speed'.

diligent ▶ **adjective** having or showing care and conscientiousness in one's work or duties: *after diligent searching, he found a parcel.*
– DERIVATIVES **diligently** adverb.
– ORIGIN Middle English: via Old French from Latin *diligens, diligent-* 'assiduous', from *diligere* 'love, take delight in'.

dill[1] (also **dill weed**) ▶ **noun** [mass noun] an aromatic annual herb of the parsley family, with fine blue-green leaves and yellow flowers. The leaves or seeds of dill are used for flavouring and for medicinal purposes.
• *Anethum graveolens*, family Umbelliferae.
– ORIGIN Old English *dile, dyle*; related to Dutch *dille* and German *Dill*; of unknown ultimate origin.

dill[2] ▶ **noun** Austral./NZ informal a naive or foolish person.
– ORIGIN 1940s: apparently a back-formation from **DILLY**[2].

dill pickle ▶ **noun** [mass noun] pickled cucumber flavoured with dill.

dill water ▶ **noun** [mass noun] an extract distilled from dill, used to relieve flatulence.

dilly[1] ▶ **noun** (pl. **-ies**) [usu. in sing.] N. Amer. informal an excellent example of a particular type of person or thing: *that's a dilly of a breakfast recipe.*
– ORIGIN late 19th cent. (as an adjective in the sense 'delightful'): alteration of the first syllable of **DELIGHTFUL** or **DELICIOUS**.

dilly[2] ▶ **adjective** (**-ier, -iest**) Austral./NZ informal, dated odd; foolish.
– ORIGIN late 19th cent.: perhaps a blend of **DAFT** and **SILLY**.

dillybag (also **dilly**) ▶ **noun** Austral. a bag or basket of traditional Aboriginal design, made from woven grass or fibre.
– ORIGIN from an Aboriginal word meaning 'coarse grass or reeds' + **BAG**.

dilly-dally ▶ **verb** (**-ies, -ied**) [no obj.] informal waste time through aimless wandering or indecision: *don't dilly-dally for too long.*
– ORIGIN early 17th cent.: reduplication of **DALLY**.

dilophosaurus /dʌɪˌləʊfə(ʊ)ˈsɔːrəs/ ▶ **noun** the earliest of the large bipedal dinosaurs, which had two long crests on the head and occurred in the early Jurassic period.
• Genus *Dilophosaurus*, infraorder Carnosauria, suborder Theropoda.
– ORIGIN modern Latin, from Greek *dilophos* 'two-crested' + *sauros* 'lizard'.

diluent /ˈdɪljʊənt/ technical ▶ **noun** a substance used to dilute something.
▶ **adjective** acting to cause dilution.
– ORIGIN early 18th cent. (denoting a medicine used to increase the proportion of water in the blood): from Latin *diluent-* 'dissolving', from the verb *diluere*.

dilute /dʌɪˈl(j)uːt, dɪ-/ ▶ **verb** [with obj.] (often **be diluted**) make (a liquid) thinner or weaker by adding water or another solvent to it: *bleach can be diluted with cold water.*
■ make (something) weaker in force, content, or value by modifying it or adding other elements to it: *the reforms have been diluted.* ■ reduce the value of (a shareholding) by issuing more shares in a company without increasing the values of its assets.
▶ **adjective** /also ˈdʌɪ-/ (of a liquid) made thinner or weaker by having had water or another solvent added to it.
■ Chemistry (of a solution) having a relatively low concentration of solute: *a dilute solution of potassium permanganate.* ■ (of colour or light) weak or low in concentration: *a short measure of dilute sun.*
– DERIVATIVES **diluter** noun.
– ORIGIN mid 16th cent.: from Latin *dilut-* 'washed away, dissolved', from the verb *diluere*.

dilution ▶ **noun** [mass noun] the action of making a liquid more dilute.
■ the action of making something weaker in force, content, or value: *he is resisting any dilution of dogma.* ■ [count noun] a liquid that has been diluted. ■ [count noun] the degree to which a solution has been diluted: *the antibody was applied* **at a dilution of** *1:50.* ■ a reduction in the value of a shareholding due to the issue of additional shares in a company without an increase in assets.
– DERIVATIVES **dilutive** adjective (chiefly Finance).

diluvial /dʌɪˈl(j)uːvɪəl, dɪ-/ ▶ **adjective** of or relating to a flood or floods, especially the biblical Flood.
– ORIGIN mid 17th cent.: from late Latin *diluvialis*, from *diluvium* 'deluge', from *diluere* 'wash away'.

diluvian /dʌɪˈl(j)uːvɪən, dɪ-/ ▶ **adjective** another term for **DILUVIAL**.

dim ▶ **adjective** (**dimmer, dimmest**) **1** (of a light, colour, or illuminated object) not shining brightly or clearly: *her face was softened by the dim light.*
■ (of an object or shape) made difficult to see by darkness, shade, or distance: *a dim figure in the dark kitchen.* ■ (of a room or space) made difficult to see in by darkness: *long dim corridors.* ■ (of the eyes) not able to see clearly: *his eyes became dim.* ■ (of a sound) indistinct or muffled: *the dim drone of their voices.* ■ (of prospects) not giving cause for hope or optimism: *their prospects for the future looked fairly dim.*
2 not clearly recalled or formulated in the mind: *she had dim memories of that time | the matter was in the dim and distant past.*
■ informal stupid or slow to understand: *you're just incredibly dim.*
▶ **verb** (**dimmed, dimming**) make or become less bright: [with obj.] *a smoky inferno that dimmed the sun |* [no obj.] *the lights dimmed and the curtains parted.*
■ [with obj.] lower the beam of (a vehicle's headlights) to avoid dazzling oncoming drivers: [as adj. **dimmed**] *the car moved slowly, its headlights dimmed.* ■ make or become less intense or favourable: [with obj.] *the difficulty in sleeping couldn't dim her happiness |* [no obj.] *the company's prospects have dimmed.* ■ make or become less able to see clearly: [with obj.] *your sight is dimmed |* [no obj.] *his eyes dimmed.* ■ make or become less clear in the mind: [with obj.] *his win dimmed the memory of the booing he'd received.*
– PHRASES **take a dim view of** regard with disapproval.
– DERIVATIVES **dimly** adverb, **dimmish** adjective, **dimness** noun.
– ORIGIN Old English *dim, dimm*, of Germanic origin; related to German dialect *timmer*.

dim. ▶ **abbreviation for** diminuendo.

DiMaggio /dɪˈmadʒɪəʊ/, Joe (1914–99), American baseball player; full name *Joseph Paul DiMaggio*. Star of the New York Yankees team 1936–51, he was renowned for his outstanding batting ability and for his outfield play. He was briefly married to Marilyn Monroe in 1954.

Dimbleby /ˈdɪmb(ə)lbi/, (Frederick) Richard (1913–65), English broadcaster. He was the BBC's first news correspondent (1936) and was particularly noted for his radio and television commentaries on royal, national, and international events. His sons **David** (b.1938) and **Jonathan** (b.1944) have both followed their father into careers in news broadcasting.

dime /dʌɪm/ ▶ **noun** N. Amer. a ten-cent coin.
■ informal a small amount of money: *he didn't have a dime.* ■ informal used to refer to something small in size, area, or degree: *Mars was now an orb the size of a dime.*
– PHRASES **a dime a dozen** informal very common and of no particular value: *experts in this field are a dime a dozen.* **drop a** (or **the**) **dime on someone** informal inform on someone. **get off the dime** informal be decisive and show initiative: *at some point you have to get off the dime and do something.* **on a dime** informal used to refer to a manoeuvre that can be performed by a moving vehicle or person within a small area or short distance: *boats that can* **turn on a dime**. ■ quickly or instantly: *he* **turned on a dime** *into a low voice.*
– ORIGIN late Middle English: from Old French *disme*, from Latin *decima pars* 'tenth part'. The word originally denoted a tithe or tenth part; the modern sense 'ten cent coin' dates from the late 18th cent.

dime bag ▶ **noun** US informal a specified amount of an illegal drug, packaged and sold for a fixed price.

dime novel ▶ **noun** dated, N. Amer. a cheap, popular novel, typically a melodramatic romance or adventure story.

dimension /dɪˈmɛnʃ(ə)n, dʌɪ-/ ▶ **noun 1** an aspect or feature of a situation, problem, or thing: *water can add a new dimension to your garden.*
2 (usu. **dimensions**) a measurable extent of some kind, such as length, breadth, depth, or height: *the final dimensions of the pond were 14 ft x 8 ft |* [mass noun] *the drawing must be precise* **in dimension**.
■ a mode of linear extension of which there are three in space and two on a flat surface, which corresponds to one of a set of coordinates specifying the position of a point. ■ Physics an expression for a derived physical quantity in terms of fundamental quantities such as mass, length, or time, raised to the appropriate power (acceleration, for example, having the dimension of *length* × *time*$^{-2}$).
▶ **verb** [with obj.] (often **be dimensioned**) cut or shape (something) to particular measurements.
■ mark (a diagram) with measurements: [as adj. **dimensioned**] *draw a dimensioned front elevation.*
– DERIVATIVES **dimensional** adjective [in combination] *multi-dimensional scaling*, **dimensionless** adjective.
– ORIGIN late Middle English (in sense 2): via Old French from Latin *dimensio(n-)*, from *dimetiri* 'measure out'. Sense 1 dates from the 1920s.

dimensional analysis ▶ **noun** Mathematics analysis using the fact that physical quantities added to or equated with each other must be expressed in terms of the same fundamental quantities (such as mass, length, or time) for inferences to be made about the relations between them.

dimer /ˈdʌɪmə/ ▶ **noun** Chemistry a molecule or molecular complex consisting of two identical molecules linked together.
– DERIVATIVES **dimeric** adjective.
– ORIGIN 1930s: from **DI-**[1] 'two', on the pattern of *polymer*.

dimercaprol /ˌdʌɪməˈkaprɒl/ ▶ **noun** [mass noun] Chemistry a colourless, oily liquid with an unpleasant smell, used as an antidote for poisoning by mercury, arsenic, lead, and other heavy metals.
• Alternative name: **2,3,-dimercapto-1-propanol**; chem. formula: $CH_2(SH)CH(SH)CH_2OH$.
– ORIGIN 1940s: from elements of the systematic name (see above).

dimerize /ˈdʌɪmərʌɪz/ (also **-ise**) ▶ **verb** [no obj.] Chemistry combine with a similar molecule to form a dimer: *ClO dimerizes to form* Cl_2O_2.
– DERIVATIVES **dimerization** noun.

dimerous /ˈdɪm(ə)rəs/ ▶ **adjective** Botany & Zoology having parts arranged in groups of two.
■ consisting of two joints or parts.
– ORIGIN early 19th cent.: from modern Latin *dimerus* (from Greek *dimerēs* 'bipartite') + **-OUS**.

dime store ▶ **noun** N. Amer. a shop selling cheap merchandise (originally one where the maximum price was a dime).
■ [as modifier] cheap and inferior: *plastic dime-store toys.* ■ [as modifier] trite; simplistic: *the dime-store moralism of yesteryear.*

dimeter /ˈdɪmɪtə/ ▶ **noun** Prosody a line of verse consisting of two metrical feet.
– ORIGIN late 16th cent.: via late Latin from Greek *dimetros* 'of two measures', from *di-* 'twice' + *metron* 'a measure'.

dimethoate /dʌɪˈmiːθəʊeɪt/ ▶ **noun** [mass noun] a crystalline synthetic organophosphorus compound used in solution as an insecticide.
– ORIGIN 1960s: from **DI-**[1] 'two' + **METHYL** + **THIO-** + **-ATE**[1].

dimethyl sulphoxide /dʌɪˌmiːθʌɪl sʌlˈfɒksʌɪd, -ˌmɛθ-, -θɪl/ (US **dimethyl sulfoxide**) (abbrev.: **DMSO**) ▶ **noun** [mass noun] Chemistry a colourless liquid used as a solvent and synthetic reagent. It is readily able to penetrate the skin and is used in medicinal preparations for skin application.
• Chem. formula: $(CH_3)_2SO$.

dimetric /dʌɪˈmɛtrɪk/ ▶ **adjective** (in technical drawing) denoting or incorporating a method of showing projection or perspective using a set of three geometrical axes of which two are of the same scale or dimension but the third is of another.
– ORIGIN mid 19th cent.: from **DI-**[1] 'two' + Greek *metron* 'measure' + **-IC**.

dimetrodon /dʌɪˈmiːtrədɒn/ ▶ **noun** a large fossil carnivorous mammal-like reptile of the Permian period, with long spines on its back supporting a sail-like crest.
• Genus *Dimetrodon*, order Pelycosauria, subclass Synapsida.
– ORIGIN modern Latin, from *di-* 'twice' + Greek *metron* 'measure' + *odous, odont-* 'tooth' (taken in the sense 'two long teeth').

dimidiate /dɪˈmɪdɪeɪt/ ▶ **verb** [with obj.] Heraldry (of a

d

coat of arms or charge) adjoin (another) so that only half of each is visible.
■[as adj. **dimidiated**] (of a charge) having only one half depicted.
– ORIGIN late 16th cent.: from Latin *dimidiat-* 'halved', from the verb *dimidiare*, from *dimidium* 'half'.

dimidiation ▶ **noun** [mass noun] Heraldry the combination of two coats of arms by juxtaposing the dexter half of one and the sinister half of the other on a single shield (a practice largely superseded by impalement).

diminish ▶ **verb** make or become less: [with obj.] *the new law is expected to diminish the government's chances* | [no obj.] *the pain will gradually diminish.*
■[with obj.] make (someone or something) seem less impressive or valuable: *the trial has aged and diminished him.*
– PHRASES **(the law of) diminishing returns** used to refer to a point at which the level of profits or benefits gained is less than the amount of money or energy invested.
– DERIVATIVES **diminishable** adjective.
– ORIGIN late Middle English: blend of archaic *minish* 'diminish' (based on Latin *minutia* 'smallness') and obsolete *diminue* 'speak disparagingly' (based on Latin *deminuere* 'lessen' (in late Latin *diminuere*), from *minuere* 'make small').

diminished ▶ **adjective 1** made smaller or less: *a diminished role for local government.*
■[predic.] made to seem less impressive or valuable: *she felt diminished by the report.*
2 [attrib.] Music denoting or containing an interval which is one semitone less than the corresponding minor or perfect interval: *a diminished fifth.*

diminished responsibility ▶ **noun** [mass noun] English Law an unbalanced mental state which is considered to make a person less answerable for murder, being recognized as grounds to reduce the charge to that of manslaughter.

diminished seventh ▶ **noun** Music **1** the interval which is a semitone less than a minor seventh, e.g. from A to G flat (which in equal tuning sounds the same as a major sixth).
2 (also **diminished seventh chord**) a chord formed by a note together with those above it at intervals of a minor third, a diminished fifth, and a diminished seventh. The resulting chord consists entirely of superimposed minor thirds, and is much used in modern music in modulating between keys.

diminuendo /dɪˌmɪnjʊˈɛndəʊ/ Music ▶ **noun** (pl. **diminuendos** or **diminuendi** /-di/) a decrease in loudness in a piece of music: *the sudden diminuendos are brilliantly effective.*
■a passage to be performed with such a decrease.
▶ **adverb** & **adjective** (especially as a direction) with a decrease in loudness: [as adj.] *the diminuendo chorus before the final tumult.*
▶ **verb** (**-os**, **-oed**) [no obj.] decrease in loudness or intensity: *the singers left and the buzz diminuendoed.*
– ORIGIN Italian, literally 'diminishing', from *diminuire*, from Latin *deminuere* 'lessen' (see **DIMINISH**).

diminution /ˌdɪmɪˈnjuːʃ(ə)n/ ▶ **noun** a reduction in the size, extent, or importance of something: *a permanent diminution in value* | [mass noun] *the disease shows no signs of diminution.*
■Music the shortening of the time values of notes in a melodic part.
– ORIGIN Middle English: via Old French from Latin *deminutio(n-)*, from the verb *deminuere* (see **DIMINISH**).

diminutive /dɪˈmɪnjʊtɪv/ ▶ **adjective** extremely or unusually small: *a diminutive figure dressed in black.*
■(of a word, name, or suffix) implying smallness, either actual or imputed in token of affection, scorn, etc. (e.g. *teeny*, *-let*, *-kins*).
▶ **noun** a smaller or shorter thing, in particular:
■a diminutive word or suffix. ■ a shortened form of a name, typically used informally: *'Nick' is a diminutive of 'Nicholas'.* ■ Heraldry a charge of the same form as an ordinary but of lesser size or width.
– DERIVATIVES **diminutively** adverb, **diminutiveness** noun.
– ORIGIN late Middle English (as a grammatical term): from Old French *diminutif, -ive*, from late Latin *diminutivus*, from Latin *deminut-* 'diminished', from the verb *deminuere* (see **DIMINISH**).

dimissory /ˈdɪmɪs(ə)ri/ ▶ **adjective** (in the Christian Church) denoting formal permission from a bishop (**letters dimissory**) for a person from one diocese to be ordained in another, or (formerly) for an ordained person to leave one diocese for another.
– ORIGIN late Middle English (as a plural noun): from late Latin *dimissorius*, from *dimiss-* 'sent away', from the verb *dimittere*. The adjective dates from the late 16th cent., the original sense being 'valedictory'.

dimity /ˈdɪmɪti/ ▶ **noun** [mass noun] a hard-wearing cotton fabric woven with stripes or checks.
– ORIGIN late Middle English: from Italian *dimito* or medieval Latin *dimitum*, from Greek *dimitos*, from *di-* 'twice' + *mitos* 'warp thread'; the origin of the final *-y* is unknown.

dimmer ▶ **noun 1** (also **dimmer switch**) a device for varying the brightness of an electric light.
2 US a headlight with a low beam.
■(**dimmers**) small parking lights on a motor vehicle.

dimorphic /dʌɪˈmɔːfɪk/ ▶ **adjective** chiefly Biology occurring in or representing two distinct forms: *in this sexually dimorphic species only the males have wings.*
– DERIVATIVES **dimorphism** noun.
– ORIGIN mid 19th cent.: from Greek *dimorphos* (from *di-* 'twice' + *morphē* 'form') + **-IC**.

dimorphotheca /ˌdʌɪmɔːfəˈθiːkə/ ▶ **noun** a southern African plant of the daisy family, sometimes grown as a border plant.
● Genus *Dimorphotheca*, family Compositae.
■(in gardening) any of a number of similar plants of the genus *Osteospermum*.
– ORIGIN modern Latin, from Greek *dimorphos* 'having two forms' + **THECA**.

dimple ▶ **noun** a small depression in the flesh, either one that exists permanently or one that forms in the cheeks when one smiles.
■[often as modifier] a slight depression in the surface of something: *a sheet of dimple foam.*
▶ **verb** [with obj.] produce a dimple or dimples in the surface of (something): *a sucking swirl dimpled the water.*
■[no obj.] (of the surface of something) form or show a dimple or dimples. ■ [no obj.] smile so as to produce a dimple or dimples: *she dimpled at Auguste.*
– DERIVATIVES **dimply** adjective.
– ORIGIN Middle English: of Germanic origin; related to German *Tümpel* 'pond'.

dim sum /dɪm ˈsʌm/ (also **dim sim** /ˈsɪm/) ▶ **noun** [mass noun] a Chinese dish of small steamed or fried savoury dumplings containing various fillings, served as a snack or course.
– ORIGIN from Chinese (Cantonese dialect) *tim sam*, from *tim* 'dot' and *sam* 'heart'.

dimwit ▶ **noun** informal a stupid or silly person.
– DERIVATIVES **dim-witted** adjective, **dim-wittedly** adverb, **dim-wittedness** noun.

DIN ▶ **noun** any of a series of technical standards originating in Germany and used internationally, especially to designate electrical connections, film speeds, and paper sizes: [as modifier] *a DIN socket.*
– ORIGIN early 20th cent.: acronym from *Deutsche Industrie-Norm* 'German Industrial Standard' (as laid down by the *Deutsches Institut für Normung* 'German Institute for Standards').

din ▶ **noun** [in sing.] a loud, unpleasant, and prolonged noise: *the fans made an awful din.*
▶ **verb** (**dinned**, **dinning**) **1** [with obj.] (**be dinned into**) (of a fact) be instilled in (someone) by constant repetition: *a runner-up, he dinned into them, was a loser.*
2 [no obj.] make a loud, unpleasant, and prolonged noise: *the sound dinning in my ears was the telephone ringing.*
– ORIGIN Old English *dyne*, *dynn* (noun), *dynian* (verb), of Germanic origin; related to Old High German *tuni* (noun) and Old Norse *dynr* (noun), *dynja* 'come rumbling down'.

dinar /ˈdiːnɑː/ ▶ **noun 1** the basic monetary unit of the states of Yugoslavia, equal to 100 paras.
2 the basic monetary unit of certain countries of the Middle East and North Africa, equal to 1000 fils in Jordan, Bahrain, and Iraq, 1000 dirhams in Libya, 100 centimes in Algeria, and 10 pounds in the Sudan.
3 a monetary unit of Iran, equal to one hundredth of a rial.
– ORIGIN from Arabic and Persian *dīnār*, Turkish and Serbo-Croat *dinar*, via late Greek from Latin *denarius* (see **DENARIUS**).

Dinaric Alps /dɪˈnarɪk/ a mountain range in the Balkans, running parallel to the Adriatic coast from Slovenia in the north-west, through Croatia, Bosnia, and Montenegro, to Albania in the south-east.

din-dins (also **din-din**) ▶ **noun** [mass noun] a child's word for dinner.

dine ▶ **verb** [no obj.] eat dinner: *we dined at a restaurant* | [as noun **dining**] *a dining area.*
■(**dine out**) eat dinner in a restaurant or the home of friends. ■ (**dine on**) eat (something) for dinner. ■ (**dine out on**) regularly entertain friends with (a humorous story or interesting piece of information). ■ [with obj.] take (someone) to dinner: *I'll dine you soon.*
– ORIGIN Middle English: from Old French *disner*, probably from *desjëuner* 'to break fast', from *des-* (expressing reversal) + *jëun* 'fasting' (from Latin *jejunus*).

diner ▶ **noun 1** a person who is eating, typically a customer in a restaurant.
2 a dining car on a train.
■chiefly N. Amer. a small roadside restaurant with a long counter and booths, originally one designed to resemble a dining car on a train.

dinero /dɪˈnɛːrəʊ/ ▶ **noun** [mass noun] N. Amer. informal money: *their pockets full of dinero.*
– ORIGIN Spanish, 'coin, money'.

Dinesen /ˈdɪnɪs(ə)n/, Isak, see **BLIXEN**.

dinette /dʌɪˈnɛt/ ▶ **noun** a small room or part of a room used for eating meals.
■N. Amer. a set of table and chairs for such an area.
– ORIGIN 1930s: formed irregularly from **DINE** + **-ETTE**.

ding[1] ▶ **verb** [no obj.] make a ringing sound: *cash registers were dinging softly.*
▶ **exclamation** used to imitate a metallic ringing sound resembling a bell.
– ORIGIN early 17th cent.: imitative.

ding[2] ▶ **noun** Austral. informal a lively party or celebration.
– ORIGIN 1950s: perhaps from **DING-DONG** or **WINGDING**.

ding[3] ▶ **noun** a deliberate or accidental blow, in particular:
■N. Amer. informal a mark or dent on the bodywork of a car, boat, or other vehicle. ■ Scottish or dialect a blow on the head.
▶ **verb** [with obj.] informal, chiefly N. Amer. dent (something).
■[no obj.] (**ding into**) Scottish bump into: *he dings into doorways like a bearing in a pinball machine.* ■ hit (someone), especially on the head: *I dinged him one.*
– ORIGIN Middle English: probably of Scandinavian origin; compare with Danish *dænge* 'beat, bang'.

ding-a-ling ▶ **noun 1** [in sing.] the ringing sound of a bell.
2 N. Amer. informal an eccentric or stupid person.
– ORIGIN late 19th cent.: imitative.

Ding an sich /ˌdɪŋ an ˈzɪx, German ˌdɪŋ an ˈzɪç/ ▶ **noun** (in Kant's philosophy) a thing as it is in itself, not mediated through perception by the senses or conceptualization, and therefore unknowable.
– ORIGIN German.

dingbat /ˈdɪŋbat/ informal ▶ **noun 1** N. Amer. & Austral./NZ a stupid or eccentric person. [ORIGIN: early 20th cent.: compare with sense 2.]
2 (**dingbats**) Austral./NZ delusions or feelings of unease, particularly those induced by delirium tremens. [ORIGIN: probably by association with *have bats in the belfry*.]
3 a typographical device other than a letter or numeral (such as an asterisk), used to signal divisions in text or to replace letters in a euphemistically presented vulgar word.
– ORIGIN mid 19th cent. (in early use applied to various vaguely specified objects): origin uncertain; perhaps based on obsolete *ding* 'to beat, deal heavy blows'.

ding-dong ▶ **noun 1** [in sing.] Brit. informal a fierce argument or fight: *they had a bit of a ding-dong.*
■dated a riotous party.
2 N. Amer. informal a silly or foolish person.
▶ **adverb** & **adjective 1** with the simple alternate chimes of or as of a bell: [as adv.] *the church bells go ding-dong* | [as adj.] *he heard the ding-dong tones on the aircraft.*
■[as adv.] Brit. energetically or wildly: *her biological clock is going ding-dong.*
2 [as adj.] Brit. informal (of a contest) evenly matched

and intensely waged: *the game was an exciting ding-dong battle.*
- ORIGIN mid 16th cent.: imitative.

dinger /ˈdɪŋə/ ▶ noun informal, chiefly US a thing outstanding of its kind: *by God, ain't that a dinger!*
  ■ Baseball a home run: *he beat the Braves twice with extra-inning dingers.*
- ORIGIN late 19th cent.: shortening of **HUMDINGER**.

dinges ▶ noun South African spelling of **DINGUS**.

dinghy /ˈdɪŋɡi, ˈdɪŋi/ ▶ noun (pl. **-ies**) a small boat for recreation or racing, especially an open boat with a mast and sails.
  ■ a small inflatable rubber boat.
- ORIGIN early 19th cent. (denoting a rowing boat used on rivers in India): from Hindi *ḍiṅgī*. The *-gh* in English serves to indicate the hard *g*.

dingle ▶ noun poetic/literary or dialect a deep wooded valley or dell.
- ORIGIN Middle English (denoting a deep abyss): of unknown origin. The current sense dates from the mid 17th cent.

dingleberry ▶ noun (pl. **-ies**) US informal a foolish or inept person.
- ORIGIN mid 20th cent.: from *dingle* of unknown origin + **BERRY**.

dingle-dangle ▶ noun informal an ornament, piece of jewellery, etc. that dangles.
- ORIGIN late 16th cent. (as an adverb): reduplication of **DANGLE**.

dingo /ˈdɪŋɡəʊ/ ▶ noun (pl. **-oes** or **-os**) **1** a wild or half-domesticated dog with a sandy-coloured coat, found in Australia. It is believed to have been introduced by early Aboriginal immigrants.
  ● *Canis dingo*, family Canidae.
  2 Austral. informal a cowardly or treacherous person.
- ORIGIN late 18th cent.: from Dharuk *din-gu* 'domesticated dingo'; sense 2 dates from the mid 19th cent. and alludes to the treachery popularly associated with the dingo.

dingus /ˈdɪŋəs/ (S. African also **dinges** pronunc. same) ▶ noun (pl. **dinguses**) N. Amer. & S. African informal used to refer to something whose name the speaker cannot remember, is unsure of, or is humorously or euphemistically omitting: *here's a doohickey—and there's the dingus.*
- ORIGIN late 19th cent.: via Afrikaans from Dutch *ding* 'thing'.

dingy /ˈdɪn(d)ʒi/ ▶ adjective (**dingier**, **dingiest**) gloomy and drab: *a dingy room.*
- DERIVATIVES **dingily** adverb, **dinginess** noun.
- ORIGIN mid 18th cent.: perhaps based on Old English *dynge* 'dung'.

dining car ▶ noun a railway carriage equipped as a restaurant.

dining hall ▶ noun a large room, typically in a school or other institution, in which people eat meals together.

dining room ▶ noun a room in a house or hotel in which meals are eaten.

dining table ▶ noun a table on which meals are served in a dining room.

dinitrogen tetroxide /daɪˈnaɪtrə(ʊ)dʒ(ə)n/ ▶ noun see **NITROGEN DIOXIDE**.

dink[1] ▶ noun another term for **DINKY**[2].

dink[2] chiefly Tennis ▶ noun a drop shot.
▶ verb [with obj.] hit (the ball) with a drop shot.
- ORIGIN 1930s (originally a North American usage): symbolic of the light action.

Dinka /ˈdɪŋkə/ ▶ noun (pl. same or **Dinkas**) **1** a member of a Sudanese people of the Nile basin.
  2 [mass noun] the Nilotic language of this people, with about 1.4 million speakers.
▶ adjective of or relating to this people or their language.
- ORIGIN from the local word *Jieng* 'people'.

dinkum /ˈdɪŋkəm/ ▶ adjective Austral./NZ informal (of an article or person) genuine: *Andy's dinkum hat from Australia* | *if you're dinkum, I'll help you.*
- PHRASES **fair dinkum** used to emphasize that or query whether something is genuine or true: *it's a fair dinkum Aussie wedding* | *'Burt's just told me he's packing up in a month.' 'Fair dinkum?'* ■ used to emphasize that behaviour complies with accepted standards: *they were asking a lot for the car, but fair dinkum considering its list price.*
- ORIGIN late 19th cent.: of unknown origin.

dinkum oil ▶ noun [mass noun] Austral./NZ informal the honest truth.

Dinky ▶ noun [as modifier] trademark denoting a miniature motor vehicle of die-cast metal.

dinky[1] ▶ adjective (**dinkier**, **dinkiest**) Brit. informal (of an object or place) small and neat in an attractive way: *the village boasts dinky shops and tea rooms.*
  ■ N. Amer. informal small; insignificant: *I can't believe the dinky salaries they pay here.*
- ORIGIN late 18th cent.: from Scots and northern English dialect *dink* 'neat, trim', of unknown origin.

dinky[2] ▶ noun (pl. **-ies**) informal a partner in a well-off working couple with no children.
- ORIGIN 1980s: acronym from *double income, no kids*, on the pattern of *yuppy*.

dinky-di /ˌdɪŋkɪˈdaɪ/ (also **dinki-di**) ▶ adjective Austral./NZ informal another term for **DINKUM**.
- ORIGIN early 20th cent.: from **DINKUM**, with a nonsensical final element.

dinna (also **dinnae**) ▶ verb non-standard spelling of **DON'T**, used in representing Scottish speech.
- PHRASES **dinna fash** see **FASH**.

dinner ▶ noun the main meal of the day, taken either around midday or in the evening.
  ■ a formal evening meal, typically one in honour of a person or event.
- PHRASES **done like (a) dinner** Austral. & Canadian informal utterly defeated or outwitted: *I had the fishing inspector wanting to see my licence—I was done like a dinner.* **more —— than someone has had hot dinners** Brit. informal used to emphasize someone's wide experience of a specified activity or phenomenon: *he's seen more battles than you've had hot dinners.*
- ORIGIN Middle English: from Old French *disner* (infinitive used as a noun: see **DINE**).

dinner dance ▶ noun a formal social event in which guests have dinner, followed by dancing.

dinner jacket ▶ noun a man's short jacket without tails, typically a black one, worn with a bow tie for formal occasions in the evening.

dinner lady ▶ noun Brit. a woman who serves meals and supervises children at mealtimes in a school.

dinner pail ▶ noun dated, chiefly US a pail in which a labourer's or schoolchild's dinner is carried and kept warm.
- PHRASES **hand in one's dinner pail** informal die.

dinner party ▶ noun a social occasion at which guests eat dinner together.

dinner service (also **dinner set**) ▶ noun a set of matching crockery for serving a meal.

dinner theatre ▶ noun N. Amer. a theatre in which a meal is included in the price of a ticket.

dinner time ▶ noun the time at which dinner is customarily eaten, either around midday or in the evening: *I'll be back at dinner time.*

dinoflagellate /ˌdaɪnə(ʊ)ˈfladʒəleɪt/ ▶ noun Biology a single-celled organism with two flagella, occurring in large numbers in marine plankton and also found in fresh water. Some produce toxins that can accumulate in shellfish, resulting in poisoning when eaten.
  ● Division Dinophyta or class Dinophyceae, division Chromophycota (or phylum Dinophyta, kingdom Protista).
- ORIGIN late 19th cent. (as an adjective): from modern Latin *Dinoflagellata* (plural), from Greek *dinos* 'whirling' + Latin *flagellum* 'small whip' (see **FLAGELLUM**).

dinosaur /ˈdaɪnəsɔː/ ▶ noun **1** a fossil reptile of the Mesozoic era, often reaching an enormous size.

> The dinosaurs are placed, according to their hip structure, in two distantly related orders (see **ORNITHISCHIAN** and **SAURISCHIAN**). Some of them may have been warm-blooded, and their closest living relatives are the birds. Dinosaurs were all extinct by the end of the Cretaceous period (65 million years ago), the most popular theory being that the extinctions were the result of the impact of a large meteorite.

  2 a person or thing that is outdated or has become obsolete because of failure to adapt to changing circumstances.
- DERIVATIVES **dinosaurian** adjective & noun.
- ORIGIN mid 19th cent.: from modern Latin *dinosaurus*, from Greek *deinos* 'terrible' + *sauros* 'lizard'.

dint ▶ noun **1** an impression or hollow in a surface: *the soft dints at the top of a coconut.*
  2 archaic a blow or stroke, typically one made with a weapon in fighting.

  ■ [mass noun] force of attack; impact: *I perceive you feel the dint of pity.*
▶ verb [with obj.] mark (a surface) with impressions or hollows: [as adj. **dinted**] *the metal was dull and dinted.*
- PHRASES **by dint of** by means of: *he had got to where he was today by dint of sheer hard work.*
- ORIGIN Old English *dynt* 'stroke with a weapon', reinforced in Middle English by the related Old Norse word *dyntr*; of unknown ultimate origin. Compare with **DENT**.

diocesan /daɪˈɒsɪs(ə)n/ ▶ adjective of or concerning a diocese.
▶ noun the bishop of a diocese.
- ORIGIN late Middle English: from French *diocésain*, from medieval Latin *diocesanus*, from Latin *dioecesis* (see **DIOCESE**).

diocesan quota ▶ noun see **QUOTA**.

diocese /ˈdaɪəsɪs/ ▶ noun (pl. **dioceses** /ˈdaɪəsiːz, -sɪzɪz/) a district under the pastoral care of a bishop in the Christian Church.
- ORIGIN Middle English: from Old French *diocise*, from late Latin *diocesis*, from Latin *dioecesis* 'governor's jurisdiction, diocese', from Greek *dioikēsis* 'administration, diocese', from *dioikein* 'keep house, administer'.

dioch /ˈdaɪɒk/ ▶ noun a quelea (weaver bird).
  ● The **black-faced** (or **Sudan**) **dioch** is the red-billed quelea (*Quelea quelea*).
- ORIGIN late 19th cent.: probably a local African name.

Diocletian /ˌdaɪəˈkliːʃ(ə)n/ (245–313), Roman emperor 284–305; full name *Gaius Aurelius Valerius Diocletianus*. Faced with mounting military problems, in 286 he divided the empire between himself in the east and Maximian in the west. Diocletian launched the final persecution of the Christians (303).

diode /ˈdaɪəʊd/ ▶ noun Electronics a semiconductor device with two terminals, typically allowing the flow of current in one direction only.
  ■ a thermionic valve having two electrodes (an anode and a cathode).
- ORIGIN early 20th cent.: from **DI**-[1] 'two' + a shortened form of **ELECTRODE**.

dioecious /daɪˈiːʃəs/ ▶ adjective Biology (of a plant or invertebrate animal) having the male and female reproductive organs in separate individuals. Compare with **MONOECIOUS**.
- DERIVATIVES **dioecy** noun.
- ORIGIN mid 18th cent.: from modern Latin *Dioecia* (a class in Linnaeus's sexual system), from **DI**-[1] 'two' + Greek *-oikos* 'house'.

dioestrus /daɪˈiːstrəs/ (US **diestrus**) ▶ noun [mass noun] Zoology (in most female mammals) a period of sexual inactivity between recurrent periods of oestrus.

Diogenes /daɪˈɒdʒɪniːz/ (*c.*400–*c.*325 BC), Greek philosopher. The most famous of the Cynics, he lived ascetically in Athens (according to legend, he lived in a tub) and was accordingly nicknamed *Kuōn* ('the dog'), from which the Cynics derived their name. He emphasized self-sufficiency and the need for natural, uninhibited behaviour, regardless of social conventions.

diogenite /daɪˈɒdʒənaɪt/ ▶ noun a stony meteorite of a kind consisting largely of pyroxenes and plagioclase.
- ORIGIN late 19th cent.: from Greek *Diogenēs* 'descended from Zeus' + **-ITE**[1].

diol /ˈdaɪɒl/ ▶ noun Chemistry an alcohol containing two hydroxyl groups in its molecule.
- ORIGIN 1920s: from **DI**-[1] 'two' + **-OL**.

Dione /daɪˈəʊni/ Astronomy a satellite of Saturn, the twelfth closest to the planet, discovered by Cassini in 1684, being icy with a partly cratered and partly smooth surface (diameter 1,120 km).
- ORIGIN named after a Titan, the mother of Aphrodite, in Greek mythology.

Dionysiac /ˌdaɪəˈnɪzɪak/ (also **Dionysian** /-zɪən/) ▶ adjective **1** Greek Mythology of or relating to the god Dionysus.
  2 of or relating to the sensual, spontaneous, and emotional aspects of human nature. Compare with **APOLLONIAN**.

Dionysius /ˌdaɪəˈnɪsɪəs/ the name of two rulers of Syracuse:
  ■ **Dionysius I** (*c.*430–367 BC), ruled 405–367; known as **Dionysius the Elder**. A tyrannical ruler, he waged three wars against the Carthaginians for control of Sicily, later becoming the principal power in Greek

Italy after the capture of Rhegium (386) and other Greek cities in southern Italy.

■**Dionysius II** (*c.*397–*c.*344 BC), son of Dionysius I, ruled 367–357 and 346–344; known as **Dionysius the Younger**. He lacked his father's military ambitions and signed a peace treaty with Carthage in 367. Despite his patronage of philosophers, he resisted the attempt by Plato to turn him into a philosopher king.

Dionysius Exiguus /ɪɡˈzɪɡjʊəs/ (died *c.*556), Scythian monk and scholar. He is famous for introducing the system of dates BC and AD that is still in use today, accepting 753 AUC as the year of the Incarnation; this has since been shown to be mistaken. He is said to have taken the nickname *Exiguus* ('little') as a sign of humility.

Dionysius of Halicarnassus (1st century BC), Greek historian, literary critic, and rhetorician. He lived in Rome from 30 BC and is best known for his detailed history of the city, written in Greek; this covers the period from the earliest times until the outbreak of the first Punic War (264 BC).

Dionysius the Areopagite /ˌarɪˈɒpəɡʌɪt/ (1st century AD), Greek churchman. His conversion by St Paul is recorded in Acts 17:34 and according to tradition he went on to become the first bishop of Athens. He was later confused with St Denis and with a mystical theologian, Pseudo-Dionysius the Areopagite, who exercised a profound influence on medieval theology.

Dionysus /ˌdʌɪəˈnʌɪsəs/ Greek Mythology a Greek god, son of Zeus and Semele; his worship entered Greece from Thrace *c.*1000 BC. Originally a god of the fertility of nature, associated with wild and ecstatic religious rites, in later traditions he is a god of wine who loosens inhibitions and inspires creativity in music and poetry. Also called **BACCHUS**.

Diophantine equation /ˌdʌɪəˈfantɪn, -tʌɪn/ ▶ noun Mathematics a polynomial equation with integral coefficients for which integral solutions are required.

– ORIGIN early 18th cent.: named after **DIOPHANTUS**.

Diophantus /ˌdʌɪəˈfantəs/ (*fl.* prob. *c.*250 AD), Greek mathematician. Diophantus was the first to attempt an algebraical notation, showing in *Arithmetica* how to solve simple and quadratic equations. His work led to Pierre de Fermat's discoveries in the theory of numbers.

diopside /dʌɪˈɒpsʌɪd/ ▶ noun [mass noun] a mineral occurring as white to pale green crystals in metamorphic and basic igneous rocks. It consists of a calcium and magnesium silicate of the pyroxene group, often also containing iron and chromium.

– ORIGIN early 19th cent.: from French, formed irregularly from **DI-**[3] 'through' + Greek *opsis* 'aspect', later interpreted as derived from Greek *diopsis* 'a view through'.

dioptase /dʌɪˈɒpteɪz/ ▶ noun [mass noun] a rare mineral occurring as emerald green or blue-green crystals. It consists of a hydrated silicate of copper.

– ORIGIN early 19th cent.: from French, formed irregularly from Greek *dioptos* 'transparent'.

dioptre /dʌɪˈɒptə/ (US **diopter**) ▶ noun a unit of refractive power, which is equal to the reciprocal of the focal length (in metres) of a given lens.

– ORIGIN late 16th cent. (originally as *diopter*, denoting an alidade): from French, from Latin *dioptra*, from Greek, from *di-* 'through' + *optos* 'visible'. The term was used in the early 17th cent. to denote an ancient form of theodolite; the current sense dates from the late 19th cent.

dioptric /dʌɪˈɒptrɪk/ ▶ adjective of or relating to the refraction of light, especially in the organs of sight or in devices which aid or improve the vision.

– ORIGIN mid 17th cent.: from Greek *dioptrikos*, from *dioptra*, a kind of theodolite (see **DIOPTRE**).

dioptrics ▶ plural noun [treated as sing.] the branch of optics that deals with refraction.

Dior /ˈdiːɔː, French djɔʀ/, Christian (1905–57), French couturier. His first collection (1947), featured narrow-waisted tightly fitted bodices and full pleated skirts; this became known as the New Look. He later created the first A-line garments and built up a range of quality accessories.

diorama /ˌdʌɪəˈrɑːmə/ ▶ noun a model representing a scene with three-dimensional figures, either in miniature or as a large-scale museum exhibit.

■chiefly historical a scenic painting, viewed through a peephole, in which changes in colour and direction of illumination simulate changes in the weather, time of day, etc. ■a miniature film set used for special effects or animation.

– ORIGIN early 19th cent.: coined in French from **DIA-** 'through', on the pattern of *panorama*.

diorite /ˈdʌɪərʌɪt/ ▶ noun [mass noun] Geology a speckled, coarse-grained igneous rock consisting essentially of plagioclase, feldspar, and hornblende or other mafic minerals.

– DERIVATIVES **dioritic** adjective.

– ORIGIN early 19th cent.: coined in French, formed irregularly from Greek *diorizein* 'distinguish' + **-ITE**[1].

Dioscuri /ˌdʌɪɒˈskʊəri, dʌɪˈɒskjʊri/ Greek & Roman Mythology the twins Castor and Pollux, born to Leda after her seduction by Zeus. Castor was mortal, but Pollux was immortal; at Pollux's request they shared his immortality between them, spending half their time below the earth in Hades and the other half on Olympus. They are often identified with the constellation Gemini.

– ORIGIN from Greek *Dioskouroi* 'sons of Zeus'.

diosgenin /dʌɪˈɒsdʒənɪn/ ▶ noun [mass noun] Chemistry a steroid compound obtained from Mexican yams and used in the synthesis of steroid hormones.

– ORIGIN 1930s: from *dios-* (from the modern Latin genus name *Dioscorea*) + *genin*, denoting steroids that occur as the non-sugar part of certain glycosides.

dioxane /dʌɪˈɒkseɪn/ (also **dioxan** /-an/) ▶ noun [mass noun] Chemistry a colourless toxic liquid used as an organic solvent.

• A heterocyclic compound with a ring of four carbon and two oxygen atoms; chem. formula: $C_4H_8O_2$.

– ORIGIN early 20th cent.: from **DI-**[1] 'two' + **OX-** 'oxygen' + **-AN** (or **-ANE**[2]).

dioxide /dʌɪˈɒksʌɪd/ ▶ noun Chemistry an oxide containing two atoms of oxygen in its molecule or empirical formula.

dioxin /dʌɪˈɒksɪn/ ▶ noun [mass noun] a highly toxic compound produced as a by-product in some manufacturing processes, notably herbicide production and paper bleaching. It is a serious and persistent environmental pollutant.

• A heterocyclic organochlorine compound; alternative name: 2,3,7,8-tetrachlorodibenzoparadioxin (abbrev.: **TCDD**); chem. formula: $C_{12}H_4O_2Cl_4$.

■[count noun] any of the class of compounds to which this belongs.

– ORIGIN early 20th cent.: from **DI-**[1] 'two' + **OX-** 'oxygen' + **-IN**[1].

DIP ▶ abbreviation for ■ Computing document image processing, a system for the digital storage and retrieval of documents as scanned images. ■ Electronics dual in-line package, a package for an integrated circuit consisting of a rectangular sealed unit with two parallel rows of downward-pointing pins.

Dip. ▶ abbreviation for diploma.

dip ▶ verb (**dipped**, **dipping**) **1** [with obj.] (**dip something in/into**) put or let something down quickly or briefly in or into (liquid): *he dipped a brush in the paint.*

■[no obj.] (**dip into**) put a hand or tool into (a bag or container) in order to take something out: *Ian dipped into his briefcase and pulled out a photograph.* ■ informal pick (someone's pocket). ■ [no obj.] (**dip into**) spend from or make use of (one's financial resources): *you won't have to dip into your savings.* ■ [no obj.] (**dip into**) read only parts of (a book) in a desultory manner. ■ immerse (sheep) in a chemical solution that kills parasites. ■ make (a candle) by immersing a wick repeatedly in hot wax: [as adj. **dipped**] *dipped candles are made using simple equipment.* ■ informal, dated baptize (someone) by immersion in water.

2 [no obj.] sink or drop downwards: *swallows dipped and soared | the sun had dipped below the horizon.*

■(of a level or amount) become lower or smaller, typically temporarily: *the president's popularity has dipped | audiences dipped below 600,000 for the match.* ■ (of a road, path, or area of land) slope downwards: *the path rose and dipped.* ■ [with obj.] lower or move (something) downwards: *the plane dipped its wings.* ■ [with obj.] Brit. lower the beam of (a vehicle's headlights).

▶ noun **1** a brief bathe: *she went for a dip in a pool.*

■a brief immersion in liquid: *a dip in hot water is prescribed to destroy fruit flies.* ■ short for **SHEEP DIP**. ■ a cursory read of part of a book: *a quick dip into this publication.*

2 [mass noun] a thick sauce in which pieces of food are dunked before eating: *tasty garlic dip.*

■a quantity that has been scooped up from a mass: *ice cream sold by the dip.*

3 a brief downward slope followed by an upward one.

■an act of sinking or dropping briefly before rising again: *a dip in the share price.*

4 [mass noun] technical the extent to which something is angled downward from the horizontal, in particular:

■(also **magnetic dip**) the angle made with the horizontal at any point by the earth's magnetic field, or by a magnetic needle in response to this. ■ Geology the angle a stratum makes with the horizontal: *the cliff profile tends to be dominated by the dip of the beds.* ■ Astronomy & Surveying the apparent depression of the horizon from the line of observation, due to the curvature of the earth.

5 informal, dated a pickpocket.

6 N. Amer. informal a stupid or foolish person.

7 archaic a candle made by immersing a wick repeatedly in hot wax.

– PHRASES **dip one's toe into** (or **in**) put one's toe briefly in (water), typically to check the temperature. ■ begin to do or test (something) cautiously: *the company has already dipped its toe into the market.*

– ORIGIN Old English *dyppan*, of Germanic origin; related to **DEEP**.

▶**dip out** Austral. informal fail: *I nearly dipped out of the course.* [ORIGIN: by association with the phrase *dip one's lid* 'raise one's hat as a mark of respect (e.g. when leaving)'.]

DipAD ▶ abbreviation for (in the UK) Diploma in Art and Design.

dip-dye ▶ verb [with obj.] immerse (a yarn or fabric) in a special solution in order to colour it.

DipEd ▶ abbreviation for (in the UK) Diploma in Education.

dipeptide /dʌɪˈpɛptʌɪd/ ▶ noun Biochemistry a peptide composed of two amino-acid residues.

DipHE ▶ abbreviation for (in the UK) Diploma of Higher Education.

diphenhydramine /ˌdʌɪfɛnˈhʌɪdrəmiːn/ ▶ noun [mass noun] Medicine an antihistamine compound used for the symptomatic relief of allergies.

• A synthetic amine, usually used as a hydrochloride salt; chem. formula: $C_{17}H_{21}NO$.

– ORIGIN 1940s: from *diphen-* (denoting the presence of two phenyl groups) + **HYDR-** + **AMINE**.

diphenylamine /dʌɪˈfiːnʌɪləˌmiːn, -ˈfɛnɪl-/ ▶ noun [mass noun] Chemistry a synthetic crystalline compound with basic properties, used in making azo dyes and as an insecticide and larvicide.

• Chem. formula: $(C_6H_5)_2NH$.

diphtheria /dɪpˈθɪərɪə, dɪf-/ ▶ noun [mass noun] an acute and highly contagious bacterial disease causing inflammation of the mucous membranes, formation of a false membrane in the throat which hinders breathing and swallowing, and potentially fatal heart and nerve damage by a bacterial toxin in the blood. It is now rare in developed countries owing to immunization.

• The disease is caused by *Corynebacterium diphtheriae*: see **KLEBS–LÖFFLER BACILLUS**.

– DERIVATIVES **diphtherial** adjective, **diphtheritic** /-θəˈrɪtɪk/ adjective.

– ORIGIN mid 19th cent.: modern Latin, from French *diphthérie* (earlier *diphthérite*), from Greek *diphthera* 'skin, hide'.

USAGE In the past, **diphtheria** was correctly pronounced with an **f** sound representing the two letters **ph** (as in **telephone**, **sulphur**, and other **ph** words derived from Greek). In recent years the pronunciation has shifted and today the most common pronunciation, no longer incorrect in standard English, is with a **p** sound.

diphtheroid /ˈdɪfθərɔɪd/ ▶ noun Microbiology any bacterium of a genus that includes the diphtheria bacillus, especially one that does not cause disease. See **CORYNEBACTERIUM**.

▶ adjective [attrib.] Medicine similar to diphtheria.

diphthong /ˈdɪfθɒŋ/ ▶ noun a sound formed by the combination of two vowels in a single syllable, in which the sound begins as one vowel and moves towards another (as in *coin*, *loud*, and *side*). Often contrasted with **MONOPHTHONG**, **TRIPHTHONG**.

■a digraph representing the sound of a diphthong or single vowel (as in *feat*). ■ a compound vowel character; a ligature (such as æ).

– DERIVATIVES **diphthongal** /-ˈθɒŋɡ(ə)l/ adjective.

– ORIGIN late Middle English: from French *diphtongue*, via late Latin from Greek *diphthongos*, from *di-* 'twice' + *phthongos* 'voice, sound'.

diphthongize /ˈdɪfθɒŋʌɪz/ (also **-ise**) ▶ **verb** [with obj.] change (a vowel) into a diphthong.

– DERIVATIVES **diphthongization** noun.

diphycercal /ˌdɪfɪˈsəːk(ə)l/ ▶ **adjective** Zoology (of a fish's tail) approximately symmetrical and with the vertebral column continuing to the tip, as in lampreys. Contrasted with **HETEROCERCAL**, **HOMOCERCAL**.

– ORIGIN mid 19th cent.: from Greek *diphu-* 'of double form' + *kerkos* 'tail' + **-AL**.

diplegia /dʌɪˈpliːdʒə/ ▶ **noun** [mass noun] Medicine paralysis of corresponding parts on both sides of the body, typically affecting the legs more severely than the arms.

– ORIGIN late 19th cent.: from **DI-**[1] 'two', on the pattern of *hemiplegia* and *paraplegia*.

diplo- ▶ **combining form 1** double: *diplococcus*.
2 diploid: *diplohaplontic*.

– ORIGIN from Greek *diplous* 'double'.

diploblastic /ˌdɪplə(ʊ)ˈblastɪk/ ▶ **adjective** Zoology having a body derived from only two embryonic cell layers (ectoderm and endoderm, but no mesoderm), as in sponges and coelenterates.

diplococcus /ˌdɪplə(ʊ)ˈkɒkəs/ ▶ **noun** (pl. **diplococci** /-k(s)ʌɪ, -k(s)iː/) a bacterium that occurs as pairs of cocci, e.g. pneumococcus.

diplodocus /dɪˈplɒdəkəs, ˌdɪplə(ʊ)ˈdəʊkəs/ ▶ **noun** a huge herbivorous dinosaur of the late Jurassic period, with a long slender neck and tail.
• Genus *Diplodocus*, infraorder Sauropoda, order Saurischia.

– ORIGIN modern Latin, from **DIPLO-** 'double' + Greek *dokos* 'wooden beam'.

diplohaplontic /ˌdɪpləʊhapˈlɒntɪk/ ▶ **adjective** Genetics (of an alga or other lower plant) having a life cycle in which full-grown haploid and diploid forms alternate. Compare with **DIPLONTIC** and **HAPLONTIC**.

diploid /ˈdɪplɔɪd/ Genetics ▶ **adjective** (of a cell or nucleus) containing two complete sets of chromosomes, one from each parent. Compare with **HAPLOID**.
▪ (of an organism or part) composed of diploid cells.
▶ **noun** a diploid cell, organism, or species.

– DERIVATIVES **diploidy** noun.

– ORIGIN late 19th cent.: from Greek *diplous* 'double' + **-OID**.

diploid number ▶ **noun** Genetics the number of chromosomes present in the body cells of a diploid organism.

diploma ▶ **noun** a certificate awarded by an educational establishment to show that someone has successfully completed a course of study.
▪ an official document or charter.

– ORIGIN mid 17th cent. (in the sense 'state paper'): via Latin from Greek *diplōma* 'folded paper', from *diploun* 'to fold', from *diplous* 'double'.

diplomacy ▶ **noun** [mass noun] the profession, activity, or skill of managing international relations, typically by a country's representatives abroad: *an extensive round of diplomacy in the Middle East*.
▪ the art of dealing with people in a sensitive and effective way: *his genius for tact and diplomacy*.

– ORIGIN late 18th cent.: from French *diplomatie*, from *diplomatique* 'diplomatic', on the pattern of *aristocratie* 'aristocracy'.

diplomat ▶ **noun** an official representing a country abroad.
▪ a person who can deal with people in a sensitive and effective way.

– ORIGIN early 19th cent.: from French *diplomate*, back-formation from *diplomatique* 'diplomatic', from Latin *diploma* (see **DIPLOMA**).

diplomate /ˈdɪpləmeɪt/ ▶ **noun** chiefly US a person who holds a diploma, especially a doctor certified as a specialist by a board of examiners.

diplomatic ▶ **adjective 1** of or concerning the profession, activity, or skill of managing international relations: *diplomatic relations with Britain were broken | their conduct caused a diplomatic incident*.
▪ having or showing an ability to deal with people in a sensitive and effective way: *that was a very diplomatic way of putting it*.
2 (of an edition or copy) exactly reproducing an original version: *a diplomatic transcription*.

– DERIVATIVES **diplomatically** adverb.

– ORIGIN early 18th cent. (in the sense 'relating to official documents'): from modern Latin *diplomaticus* and French *diplomatique*, from Latin *diploma* (see **DIPLOMA**). Sense 1 (late 18th cent.) is probably due to the publication of the *Codex Juris Gentium Diplomaticus* (1695), a collection of public documents, many of which dealt with international affairs.

diplomatic bag ▶ **noun** chiefly Brit. a container in which official mail is sent to or from an embassy, which is not subject to customs inspection.

diplomatic corps ▶ **noun** the body of diplomats representing other countries in a particular state.

diplomatic immunity ▶ **noun** [mass noun] the privilege of exemption from certain laws and taxes granted to diplomats by the state in which they are working.

diplomatic pouch ▶ **noun** US term for **DIPLOMATIC BAG**.

diplomatic service ▶ **noun** the government department concerned with the representation of a country abroad.

diplomatist ▶ **noun** old-fashioned term for **DIPLOMAT**.

diplontic /dɪpˈlɒntɪk/ ▶ **noun** Genetics (of an alga or other lower plant) having a life cycle in which the main form, except for the gametes, is diploid. Compare with **HAPLONTIC** and **DIPLOHAPLONTIC**.

– DERIVATIVES **diplont** noun.

– ORIGIN 1920s: from **DIPLO-** 'double' + Greek *on, ont-* 'being' (from *einai* 'be, exist') + **-IC**.

diplopia /dɪˈpləʊpɪə/ ▶ **noun** technical term for **DOUBLE VISION**.

Diplopoda /ˌdɪpləˈpəʊdə/ Zoology a class of myriapod arthropods that comprises the millipedes.

– DERIVATIVES **diplopod** /ˈdɪpləpɒd/ noun.

– ORIGIN modern Latin (plural), from Greek *diploos* 'double' + *pous, pod-* 'foot'.

diplotene /ˈdɪplətiːn/ ▶ **noun** [mass noun] Biology the fourth stage of the prophase of meiosis, following pachytene, during which the paired chromosomes begin to separate into two pairs of chromatids.

– ORIGIN 1920s: from **DIPLO-** 'double' + Greek *tainia* 'band'.

Diplura /dɪˈplʊərə/ Entomology an order of small primitive wingless insects which resemble the true bristletails but have two bristles at the end of the abdomen.
• Order Diplura, subclass Apterygota, class Insecta (or Hexapoda).

– DERIVATIVES **dipluran** noun & adjective.

– ORIGIN modern Latin (plural), from **DI-**[1] 'two' + Greek *pleura* 'side of the body'.

dip net chiefly N. Amer. ▶ **noun** a small fishing net with a long handle.
▶ **verb** (**dip-net**) [with obj.] catch (fish) using such a net.

dipole /ˈdʌɪpəʊl/ ▶ **noun** Physics a pair of equal and oppositely charged or magnetized poles separated by a distance.
▪ an aerial consisting of a horizontal metal rod with a connecting wire at its centre. ▪ Chemistry a molecule in which a concentration of positive electric charge is separated from a concentration of negative charge.

– DERIVATIVES **dipolar** adjective.

dipole moment ▶ **noun** Physics & Chemistry the mathematical product of the separation of the ends of a dipole and the magnitude of the charges.

dip pen ▶ **noun** a pen that has to be dipped in ink.

dipper ▶ **noun 1** a short-tailed songbird related to the wrens, frequenting fast-flowing streams and able to swim, dive, and walk under water to feed.
• Family Cinclidae and genus *Cinclus*: five species, in particular the Eurasian (**white-throated**) **dipper** (*C. cinclus*).
2 a ladle or scoop.
3 a person who immerses something in liquid.
▪ archaic an informal term for a Baptist or Anabaptist.

dippy ▶ **adjective** (**dippier**, **dippiest**) informal stupid; foolish.

– ORIGIN early 20th cent.: of unknown origin.

dipshit ▶ **noun** vulgar slang, chiefly N. Amer. a contemptible or inept person.

– ORIGIN 1970s: perhaps a blend of **DIPPY** and **SHIT**.

dip slope ▶ **noun** a gentle slope in the land that follows that of the underlying strata, especially the gentler slope of a cuesta. Often contrasted with **SCARP SLOPE**.

dipso ▶ **noun** (pl. **-os**) informal a person suffering from dipsomania; an alcoholic.

dipsomania /ˌdɪpsə(ʊ)ˈmeɪnɪə/ ▶ **noun** [mass noun] alcoholism, specifically in a form characterized by intermittent bouts of craving for alcohol.

– DERIVATIVES **dipsomaniac** noun.

– ORIGIN mid 19th cent.: from Greek *dipso-* (from *dipsa* 'thirst') + **-MANIA**.

dipstick ▶ **noun 1** a graduated rod for measuring the depth of a liquid, especially oil in a vehicle's engine.
2 informal a stupid or inept person.

DIP switch ▶ **noun** Computing an arrangement of switches in a dual in-line package used to select the operating mode of a device such as a printer.

dip switch ▶ **noun** Brit. a switch for lowering a vehicle's headlight beams.

Diptera /ˈdɪpt(ə)rə/ Entomology a large order of insects that comprises the two-winged or true flies, which have the hindwings reduced to form balancing organs (halteres). It includes many biting forms such as mosquitoes and tsetse flies that are vectors of disease.
▪ [as plural noun **diptera**] insects of this order; flies.

– DERIVATIVES **dipteran** /ˈdɪpt(ə)r(ə)n/ noun & adjective.

– ORIGIN modern Latin (plural), from Greek *diptera*, neuter plural of *dipteros* 'two-winged', from *di-* 'two' + *pteron* 'wing'.

dipteral /ˈdɪpt(ə)r(ə)l/ ▶ **adjective** Architecture having a double peristyle.

– ORIGIN early 19th cent.: from Latin *dipteros* (from Greek, from *di-* 'twice' + *pteron* 'wing') + **-AL**.

dipterist /ˈdɪpt(ə)rɪst/ ▶ **noun** a person who studies or collects flies.

– ORIGIN late 19th cent.: from **DIPTERA** + **-IST**.

dipterocarp /ˈdɪpt(ə)rə(ʊ)ˌkɑːp/ ▶ **noun** a tall forest tree from which are obtained resins and timber for the export trade, occurring mainly in SE Asia.
• Family Dipterocarpaceae: numerous species.

– ORIGIN late 19th cent.: from modern Latin *Dipterocarpus*, from Greek *dipteros* 'two-winged' + *karpos* 'fruit'.

dipterous /ˈdɪpt(ə)rəs/ ▶ **adjective 1** Entomology of or relating to flies of the order Diptera.
2 Botany having two wing-like appendages.

– ORIGIN late 18th cent.: from modern Latin *dipterus* (from Greek *dipteros* 'two-winged') + **-OUS**.

diptych /ˈdɪptɪk/ ▶ **noun 1** a painting, especially an altarpiece, on two hinged wooden panels which may be closed like a book.
2 an ancient writing tablet consisting of two hinged leaves with waxed inner sides.

– ORIGIN early 17th cent.: via late Latin from late Greek *diptukha* 'pair of writing tablets', neuter plural of Greek *diptukhos* 'folded in two', from *di-* 'twice' + *ptukhē* 'a fold'.

dipyridamole /ˌdʌɪpɪˈrɪdəməʊl/ ▶ **noun** [mass noun] Medicine a synthetic drug used as a coronary vasodilator to treat angina, and to reduce platelet aggregation and hence the chance of thrombosis.

– ORIGIN mid 20th cent.: from **DI-**[1] 'two' + *pyr(imidine)* + *(piper)id(ine)* + *am(ino-)* + **-OL**.

diquat /ˈdʌɪkwɒt/ ▶ **noun** [mass noun] a synthetic compound used in controlling plant growth, often as a non-persistent contact herbicide.
• A bromide of a quaternary amine; chem. formula: $(C_6H_4NCH_2)_2Br_2$.

– ORIGIN 1960s: from **DI-**[1] 'two' + **QUATERNARY**.

Dirac /dɪˈrak/, Paul Adrian Maurice (1902–84), English theoretical physicist. He described the behaviour of the electron, including its spin, and predicted the existence of the positron by applying Einstein's theory of relativity to quantum mechanics. Nobel Prize for Physics (1933).

dire ▶ **adjective** (of a situation or event) extremely serious or urgent: *dire consequences*.
▪ (of a warning or threat) presaging disaster: *there were dire warnings from the traffic organizations*. ▪ informal of a very poor quality: *the concert was dire*.

– DERIVATIVES **direly** adverb, **direness** noun.

– ORIGIN mid 16th cent.: from Latin *dirus* 'fearful, threatening'.

direct /dɪˈrɛkt, dʌɪ-/ ▶ **adjective** extending or moving from one place to another without changing direction or stopping: *there was no direct flight that day*.
▪ without intervening factors or intermediaries: *the complications are a direct result of bacteria spreading*. ▪ (of a person or their behaviour) going straight to

the point; frank. ■ (of evidence or proof) bearing immediately and unambiguously upon the facts at issue: *there is no direct evidence that officials accepted bribes.* ■ (of light or heat) proceeding from a source without being reflected or blocked: *ferns like a bright position out of direct sunlight.* ■ (of genealogy) proceeding in continuous succession from parent to child. ■ [attrib.] (of a quotation) taken from someone's words without being changed. ■ complete (used for emphasis): *non-violence is the direct opposite of compulsion.* ■ perpendicular to a surface; not oblique: *a direct butt joint between surfaces of steel.* ■ Astronomy & Astrology (of apparent planetary motion) proceeding from west to east in accord with actual motion.

▶ **adverb** with no one or nothing in between: *they seem reluctant to deal with me direct.*

■ by a straight route or without breaking a journey: *Austrian Airlines are flying direct to Innsbruck again.*

▶ **verb** [with obj.] **1** control the operations of; manage or govern: *an economic elite directed the nation's affairs.*

■ supervise and control (a film, play, or other production, or the actors in it). ■ (usu. **be directed**) train and conduct (a group of musicians).

2 [with obj. and adverbial of direction] aim (something) in a particular direction or at a particular person: *heating ducts to direct warm air to rear-seat passengers | his smile was directed at Lais.*

■ tell or show (someone) how to get somewhere: *can you direct me to the railway station, please?* ■ address or give instructions for the delivery of (a letter or parcel). ■ focus or concentrate (one's attention, efforts, or feelings) on: *we **direct** our anger and frustration at family.* ■ (**direct something at/to**) address a comment to or aim a criticism at: *his criticism was directed at the wastage of ammunition | I suggest that he direct his remarks to the council.* ■ (**direct something at**) target a product specifically at (someone): *the book is directed at the younger reader.* ■ archaic guide or advise (someone or their judgement) in a course or decision: *the conscience of the credulous prince was directed by saints and bishops.*

3 [with obj. and infinitive] give (someone) an official order or authoritative instruction: *the judge directed him to perform community service |* [with clause] *he **directed** that no picture from his collection could be sold.*

– DERIVATIVES **directness** noun.

– ORIGIN late Middle English: from Latin *directus*, past participle of *dirigere*, from *di-* 'distinctly' or *de-* 'down' + *regere* 'put straight'.

direct access ▶ **noun** [mass noun] the facility of retrieving data immediately from any part of a computer file, without having to read the file from the beginning. Compare with **RANDOM ACCESS** and **SEQUENTIAL ACCESS**.

direct action ▶ **noun** [mass noun] the use of strikes, demonstrations, or other public forms of protest rather than negotiation to achieve one's demands.

direct banking ▶ **noun** another term for **TELEBANKING**.

direct current (abbrev.: **DC**) ▶ **noun** an electric current flowing in one direction only. Compare with **ALTERNATING CURRENT**.

direct debit ▶ **noun** Brit. & Canadian an arrangement made with a bank that allows a third party to transfer money from a person's account on agreed dates, typically in order to pay bills.

direct dialling ▶ **noun** the facility of making a telephone call without connection by the operator.

– DERIVATIVES **direct dial** adjective.

direct discourse ▶ **noun** chiefly N. Amer. another term for **DIRECT SPEECH**.

direct-drive ▶ **adjective** [attrib.] denoting or relating to mechanical parts driven directly by a motor, without a belt or other device to transmit power.

direct examination ▶ **noun** another term for **EXAMINATION-IN-CHIEF**.

direct-grant school ▶ **noun** historical (in the UK) a fee-paying school that received funds from the government in return for the admission of non-paying pupils nominated by the local authority.

direct injection ▶ **noun** [mass noun] (in diesel engines) the use of a pump to spray fuel into the cylinder at high pressure, without the use of compressed air.

direction /dɪˈrɛkʃ(ə)n, dʌɪ-/ ▶ **noun** **1** a course along which someone or something moves: *she set off in the opposite direction |* [mass noun] *he had a terrible sense of direction.*

■ the course which must be taken in order to reach a destination: *the village is over the moors in a northerly direction.* ■ a point to or from which a person or thing moves or faces: *a house with views in all directions |* figurative *support came from an unexpected direction.* ■ a general way in which someone or something is developing: *new directions in painting and architecture | any dialogue between them is **a step in the right direction** |* [mass noun] *it is time to change direction and find a new job.* ■ [mass noun] general aim or purpose: *the campaign's lack of direction.*

2 [mass noun] the management or guidance of someone or something: *under his direction, the college has developed an international reputation.*

■ the work of supervising and controlling the actors and other staff in a film, play, or other production. ■ (**directions**) instructions on how to reach a destination or about how to do something: *Preston gave him directions to a restaurant | clear directions for creating hedges.*

– ORIGIN late Middle English (in sense 2): from Latin *directio(n-)*, from the verb *dirigere* (see **DIRECT**).

directional ▶ **adjective** **1** relating to or indicating the direction in which someone or something is situated, moving, or developing: *directional signs wherever two paths joined.*

■ relating to, influencing, or exemplifying the latest trends in fashion: *one of London's most directional second-hand shops.*

2 having a particular direction of motion, progression, or orientation: *coiling the wire permits directional flow of the magnetic flux.*

■ relating to, denoting, or designed for the projection, transmission, or reception of light, radio, or sound waves in or from a particular direction or directions: *a directional microphone.*

– DERIVATIVES **directionality** /-ˈnalɪti/ noun, **directionally** adverb.

direction-finder ▶ **noun** a system of aerials for locating the source of radio signals, used as an aid to navigation.

directionless ▶ **adjective** lacking in general aim or purpose: *music which bordered on directionless experimentalism.*

directive ▶ **noun** an official or authoritative instruction: *a new EC directive.*

▶ **adjective** involving the management or guidance of operations: *the authority is seeking a directive role in energy policy.*

– ORIGIN late Middle English (as an adjective): from medieval Latin *directivus*, from *direct-* 'guided, put straight', from the verb *dirigere* (see **DIRECT**).

direct labour ▶ **noun** [mass noun] **1** labour involved in production rather than administration, maintenance, and other support services.

2 labour employed by the authority commissioning the work, not by a contractor.

directly ▶ **adverb** **1** without changing direction or stopping: *they went directly to the restaurant.*

■ at once; immediately: *I went directly after breakfast.* ■ dated in a little while; soon: *I'll be back directly.*

2 with nothing or no one in between: *the decisions directly affect people's health | the security forces were directly responsible for the massacre.*

■ exactly in a specified position: *the ceiling directly above the door | the houses directly opposite.*

3 in a frank way: *she spoke simply and directly.*

▶ **conjunction** Brit. as soon as: *she fell asleep directly she got into bed.*

direct mail ▶ **noun** [mass noun] unsolicited commercial literature sent to prospective customers through the post.

– DERIVATIVES **direct mailing** noun.

direct marketing ▶ **noun** [mass noun] the business of selling products or services directly to the public, e.g. by mail order or telephone selling, rather than through retailers.

direct method ▶ **noun** [in sing.] a system of teaching a foreign language using only that language and without emphasis on the study of grammar.

direct object ▶ **noun** a noun phrase denoting a person or thing that is the recipient of the action of a transitive verb, for example *the dog* in *Jeremy fed the dog*. Compare with **INDIRECT OBJECT**.

Directoire /dɪˈrɛktwɑː, French dirɛktwar/ ▶ **adjective** of or relating to a neoclassical decorative style intermediate between the more ornate Louis XVI style and the Empire style, prevalent during the French Directory (1795–9).

– ORIGIN French.

Directoire drawers (also **Directoire knickers**) ▶ **plural noun** Brit. historical knickers which are straight, full, and knee-length.

director ▶ **noun** a person who is in charge of an activity, department, or organization: *he has been appointed finance director.*

■ a member of the board of people that manages or oversees the affairs of a business. ■ a person who supervises the actors, camera crew, and other staff for a film, play, television programme, or similar production. ■ short for **MUSICAL DIRECTOR**.

– DERIVATIVES **directorial** adjective, **directorship** noun.

– ORIGIN late Middle English: from Anglo-Norman French *directour*, from late Latin *director* 'governor', from *dirigere* 'to guide'.

directorate ▶ **noun** [treated as sing. or pl.] the board of directors of a company.

■ a section of a government department in charge of a particular activity: *the Food Safety Directorate.*

director-general ▶ **noun** (pl. **directors-general**) chiefly Brit. the chief executive of a large organization.

Director of Public Prosecutions (abbrev.: **DPP**) (in the UK) a senior law officer who is head of the Crown Prosecution Service.

directory ▶ **noun** (pl. **-ies**) **1** a book listing individuals or organizations alphabetically or thematically with details such as names, addresses, and telephone numbers.

■ Computing a file which consists solely of a set of other files (which may themselves be directories).

2 chiefly historical a book of directions for the conduct of Christian worship, especially in Presbyterian and Roman Catholic Churches.

3 (**the Directory**) the French revolutionary government in France 1795–9, comprising two councils and a five-member executive. It maintained an aggressive foreign policy, but could not control events at home and was overthrown by Napoleon Bonaparte.

– ORIGIN late Middle English (in the general sense 'something that directs'): from late Latin *directorium*, from *director* 'governor', from *dirigere* 'to guide'.

directory enquiries (N. Amer. **directory assistance**) ▶ **plural noun** a telephone service used to find out someone's telephone number.

direct proportion (also **direct ratio**) ▶ **noun** [mass noun] the relation between quantities whose ratio is constant: *sensors emit an electronic signal **in direct proportion to** the amount of light detected.*

directress (also **directrice**) ▶ **noun** a female director.

– ORIGIN early 17th cent.: from **DIRECTOR** + **-ESS**[1]; the variant *directrice* is an adopted French form.

directrix /dɪˈrɛktrɪks, dʌɪ-/ ▶ **noun** (pl. **directrices** /-trɪsiːz/) Geometry a fixed line used in describing a curve or surface.

– ORIGIN early 18th cent.: from medieval Latin, literally 'directress', based on Latin *dirigere* 'to guide'.

direct rule ▶ **noun** [mass noun] a system of government in which a province is controlled by a central government.

direct speech ▶ **noun** [mass noun] the reporting of speech by repeating the actual words of a speaker, for example *'I'm going', she said.* Contrasted with **REPORTED SPEECH**.

direct tax ▶ **noun** a tax, such as income tax, which is levied on the income or profits of the person who pays it, rather than on goods or services.

direful ▶ **adjective** archaic or poetic/literary extremely bad; dreadful.

– DERIVATIVES **direfully** adverb.

– ORIGIN late 16th cent.: from **DIRE** + **-FUL**.

dire wolf ▶ **noun** a large extinct wolf of the Pleistocene epoch, which preyed on large mammals.

● *Canis dirus*, family Canidae.

– ORIGIN *dire* in the sense 'threatening', translating the modern Latin taxonomic name.

dirge /dəːdʒ/ ▶ **noun** a lament for the dead, especially one forming part of a funeral rite.

■ a mournful song, piece of music, or sound: *singers chanted dirges |* figurative *the wind howled dirges around the chimney.* ■ informal a song or piece of music that is considered too slow, miserable, or boring: *after his ten-minute dirge, the audience booed.*

– DERIVATIVES **dirgeful** adjective.

– ORIGIN Middle English (denoting the Office for the Dead): from Latin *dirige!* (imperative) 'direct!', the first word of an antiphon (Ps. 5:8) used in the Latin Office for the Dead.

dirham /ˈdɪər(h)əm/ ▶ **noun** **1** the basic monetary unit of Morocco and the United Arab Emirates, equal to 100 centimes in Morocco and 100 fils in the United Arab Emirates.
2 a monetary unit of Libya and Qatar, equal to one thousandth of a dinar in Libya and one hundredth of a riyal in Qatar.
– ORIGIN from Arabic, from Greek *drakhmē*, denoting an Attic weight or coin. Compare with **DRACHMA**.

dirigible /ˈdɪrɪdʒɪb(ə)l/ ▶ **noun** an airship.
▶ **adjective** capable of being steered, guided, or directed: *a dirigible spotlight.*
– ORIGIN late 16th cent.: from Latin *dirigere* 'to direct' + **-IBLE**.

dirigisme /ˈdɪrɪʒɪz(ə)m/ ▶ **noun** [mass noun] state control of economic and social matters.
– DERIVATIVES **dirigiste** adjective.
– ORIGIN 1950s: from French, from the verb *diriger*, from Latin *dirigere* 'to direct'.

diriment impediment /ˈdɪrɪm(ə)nt/ ▶ **noun** (in ecclesiastical law) a factor which invalidates a marriage, such as the existence of a prior marriage.
– ORIGIN mid 19th cent.: *diriment* from Latin *diriment-* 'interrupting', from the verb *dirimere*.

dirk /dəːk/ ▶ **noun** a short dagger of a kind formerly carried by Scottish Highlanders.
– ORIGIN mid 16th cent.: of unknown origin.

dirndl /ˈdəːnd(ə)l/ ▶ **noun** **1** (also **dirndl skirt**) a full, wide skirt with a tight waistband.
2 a woman's dress in the style of Alpine peasant costume, with such a skirt and a close-fitting bodice.
– ORIGIN 1930s: from south German dialect, diminutive of *Dirne* 'girl'.

dirt ▶ **noun** [mass noun] a substance, such as mud or dust, that soils someone or something: *his face was covered in dirt.*
■ loose soil or earth; the ground: *the soldier sagged to the dirt.* ■ [usu. as modifier] earth used to make a surface for a road, floor, or other area of ground: *a dirt road.* ■ informal excrement: *a lawn covered in dog dirt.* ■ a state or quality of uncleanliness: *Manchester is renowned for the sweat and dirt of industry.* ■ informal information about someone's activities or private life that could prove damaging if revealed: *is there any* **dirt on** *Desmond?* ■ obscene or sordid material: *we object to the dirt that television projects into homes.* ■ informal a person or thing viewed as worthless or contemptible: *he treats her like dirt.*
– PHRASES **do someone dirt** informal harm someone's reputation maliciously. **drag the name of someone** (or **something**) **through the dirt** informal give someone or something a bad reputation through bad behaviour or damaging revelations: *he condemned players for dragging the name of football through the dirt.* **eat dirt** informal suffer insults or humiliation: *the film bombed at the box office and the critics made it eat dirt.*
– ORIGIN Middle English: from Old Norse *drit* 'excrement', an early sense in English.

dirt bike ▶ **noun** a motorcycle designed for use on rough terrain, such as unsurfaced roads or tracks, and used especially in scrambling.

dirt cheap ▶ **adverb** & **adjective** informal extremely cheap: [as adv.] *the auctioneers let us have the stuff dirt cheap* | [as adj.] *a dirt-cheap price.*

dirt farmer ▶ **noun** N. Amer. a farmer who ekes out a living from a farm on poor land, typically without the help of hired labour.
– DERIVATIVES **dirt farm** noun.

dirt poor ▶ **adverb** & **adjective** extremely poor: [as adv.] *making people dirt poor* | [as adj.] *dirt-poor villages.*

dirt track ▶ **noun** a course made of rolled cinders for motorcycle racing or of earth for flat racing.
– DERIVATIVES **dirt tracker** noun.

dirty ▶ **adjective** (**dirtier**, **dirtiest**) covered or marked with an unclean substance: *a tray of dirty cups and saucers* | *her boots were dirty.*
■ causing a person or environment to become unclean: *farming is a hard, dirty job.* ■ (of a nuclear weapon) producing considerable radioactive fallout. ■ (of a colour) not bright, clear, or pure: *the sea was a waste of dirty grey.* ■ concerned with sex in a way considered to be unpleasant or obscene: *he told a stream of dirty jokes.* ■ [attrib.] informal used to emphasize one's disgust for someone or something: *you dirty rat!* ■ (of an activity) dishonest; dishonourable: *he had a reputation for dirty dealing.* ■ (of weather) rough, stormy, and unpleasant: *the yacht was ready for dirty weather.* ■ (of popular music) having a distorted or rasping tone: *Nirvana's dirty guitar sound.*
▶ **adverb** [as submodifier] Brit. informal used for emphasis: *a dirty great slab of stone.*
▶ **verb** (**-ies**, **-ied**) [with obj.] cover or mark with an unclean substance: *she didn't like him dirtying her nice clean towels.*
■ cause to feel or appear morally tainted: *the criminals have dirtied the city.*
– PHRASES **the dirty end of the stick** informal, chiefly Brit. the difficult or unpleasant part of a task or situation. **do the dirty on someone** Brit. informal cheat or betray someone. **get one's hands dirty** (or **dirty one's hands**) do manual, menial, or other hard work: *unlike most chairmen, he gets his hands dirty working alongside the other managers.* ■ informal become involved in dishonest or dishonourable activity: *they can make a lot of money, but fat cats don't get their hands dirty.* **play dirty** informal act in a dishonest or unfair way. **talk dirty** informal speak about sex in a way considered to be coarse or obscene. **wash one's dirty linen in public** see **WASH**.
– DERIVATIVES **dirtily** adverb, **dirtiness** noun.

dirty dog ▶ **noun** informal a despicable man.

dirty look ▶ **noun** informal a facial expression of disapproval, disgust, or anger: *they were giving me dirty looks for taking up so much room at the bar.*

dirty money ▶ **noun** [mass noun] **1** money obtained unlawfully or immorally: *the bank was found to have been laundering dirty money.*
2 Brit. extra money paid to people who handle dirty materials in the course of their work.

dirty old man ▶ **noun** informal an older man who is sexually interested in younger women or girls.

dirty trick ▶ **noun** a dishonest or unkind act.
■ (**dirty tricks**) underhand political or commercial activity designed to discredit an opponent.

dirty weekend ▶ **noun** Brit. informal a weekend spent away, especially in secret, with a lover.

dirty word ▶ **noun** an offensive or indecent word.
■ figurative a thing regarded with dislike or disapproval: *VAT is a dirty word among small businesses.*

dirty work ▶ **noun** [mass noun] activities or tasks that are unpleasant or dishonest and given to someone else to undertake.

dis /dɪs/ informal, chiefly US ▶ **verb** (also **diss**) (**dissed**, **dissing**) [with obj.] act or speak in a disrespectful way towards: *he was expelled for dissing the gym teacher.*
▶ **noun** [mass noun] disrespectful talk: *the airwaves bristle with the sexual dis of shock jocks.*
– ORIGIN 1980s: abbreviation of **DISRESPECT**.

dis- /dɪs/ ▶ **prefix** **1** expressing negation: *disadvantage.*
2 denoting reversal or absence of an action or state: *diseconomy* | *disaffirm.*
3 denoting removal of something: *disbud* | *disafforest.*
■ denoting separation: *discarnate.* ■ denoting expulsion: *disbar.*
4 expressing completeness or intensification of an unpleasant or unattractive action: *disgruntled.*
– ORIGIN from Latin, sometimes via Old French *des-*.

disability ▶ **noun** (pl. **-ies**) a physical or mental condition that limits a person's movements, senses, or activities: *children with severe physical disabilities.*
■ a disadvantage or handicap, especially one imposed or recognized by the law: *the plaintiff was* **under a disability**.

disable ▶ **verb** [with obj.] (of a disease, injury, or accident) limit (someone) in their movements, senses, or activities: *it's an injury that could disable somebody for life* | [as adj. **disabling**] *a progressively disabling disease* | [no obj.] *anxiety can disrupt and disable.*
■ put out of action: *the raiders tried to disable the alarm system.* ■ (of an action or circumstance) prevent or discourage (someone) from doing something: *their choice* **disables** *them* **from** *pursuing certain avenues.*
– DERIVATIVES **disablement** noun.

disabled ▶ **adjective** (of a person) having a physical or mental condition that limits their movements, senses, or activities: *facilities for disabled people* | [as plural noun **the disabled**] *the needs of the disabled.*
■ (of an activity, organization, or facility) specifically designed for or relating to people with such a physical or mental condition.

USAGE The word **disabled** came to be used as the standard term in referring to people with physical or mental disabilities in the second half of the 20th century, and it remains the most generally accepted term in both British and US English today. It superseded outmoded, now sometimes offensive, terms such as **crippled**, **defective**, and **handicapped** and has not been overtaken itself by newer coinages such as **differently abled** or **physically challenged**.

disablist ▶ **adjective** discriminating or prejudiced against people who are disabled.

disabuse /ˌdɪsəˈbjuːz/ ▶ **verb** [with obj.] persuade (someone) that an idea or belief is mistaken: *he quickly* **disabused** *me* **of** *my fanciful notions.*

disaccharide /dʌɪˈsakərʌɪd/ ▶ **noun** Chemistry any of a class of sugars whose molecules contain two monosaccharide residues.

disaccord ▶ **noun** [mass noun] rare lack of agreement or harmony: *the disaccord remains in effect.*
▶ **verb** [no obj.] archaic disagree; be at variance: *this disaccords with the precise date.*

disadvantage ▶ **noun** an unfavourable circumstance or condition that reduces the chances of success or effectiveness: *a major disadvantage is the limited nature of the data* | [mass noun] *the impact of poverty and disadvantage on children.*
▶ **verb** [with obj.] place in an unfavourable position in relation to someone or something else: *the pension scheme tends to disadvantage women.*
– PHRASES **at a disadvantage** in an unfavourable position relative to someone or someone else: *stringent regulations have* **put** *British farmers* **at a disadvantage**. **to one's disadvantage** so as to cause harm to one's interests or standing: *his poor educational track record inevitably worked to his disadvantage.*
– ORIGIN late Middle English: from Old French *desavantage*, from *des-* (expressing reversal) + *avantage* 'advantage'.

disadvantaged ▶ **adjective** (of a person or area) in unfavourable circumstances, especially with regard to financial or social opportunities: *disadvantaged groups such as the elderly and unemployed* | [as plural noun **the disadvantaged**] *we began to help the disadvantaged.*

disadvantageous ▶ **adjective** involving or creating unfavourable circumstances that reduce the chances of success or effectiveness: *the Bill is* **disadvantageous for** *books and the reading public* | *the disadvantageous position in which some people are placed.*
– DERIVATIVES **disadvantageously** adverb.

disaffected ▶ **adjective** dissatisfied with the people in authority and no longer willing to support them: *a military plot by disaffected elements in the army.*
– DERIVATIVES **disaffectedly** adverb.
– ORIGIN mid 17th cent.: past participle of *disaffect*, originally in the sense 'dislike or disorder' from **DIS-** (expressing reversal) + **AFFECT**[2].

disaffection ▶ **noun** [mass noun] a state or feeling of being dissatisfied with the people in authority and no longer willing to support them: *there is growing* **disaffection with** *large corporations.*

disaffiliate /ˌdɪsəˈfɪlɪeɪt/ ▶ **verb** [with obj.] (of a group or organization) end its official connection with (a subsidiary group): *the party disaffiliated the Socialist League.*
■ [no obj.] (of a subsidiary group) end such a connection: *students' unions who wish to* **disaffiliate from** *the NUS.*
– DERIVATIVES **disaffiliation** noun.

disaffirm ▶ **verb** [with obj.] Law reverse (a previous decision).
■ repudiate (a settlement): *to disaffirm a contract is to say it never existed.*
– DERIVATIVES **disaffirmation** noun.

disafforest /ˌdɪsəˈfɒrɪst/ ▶ **verb** [with obj.] **1** another term for **DEFOREST**.
2 English Law, historical reduce (a district) from the legal status of forest to that of ordinary land.
– DERIVATIVES **disafforestation** noun, **disafforestment** noun (in sense 2).
– ORIGIN late Middle English (in sense 2): from Anglo-Latin *disafforestare*.

disaggregate /dɪsˈagrɪgeɪt/ ▶ **verb** [with obj.] separate (something) into its component parts: *a method for disaggregating cells.*

– DERIVATIVES **disaggregation** noun.

disagree ▶ verb (**disagrees**, **disagreed**, **disagreeing**) [no obj.] **1** have or express a different opinion: *no one was willing to* ***disagree with*** *him | historians often disagree.*
■ (**disagree with**) disapprove of: *she disagreed with the system of apartheid.*
2 (of statements or accounts) be inconsistent or fail to correspond: *results which disagree with the findings reported so far.*
■ (**disagree with**) (of food, climate, or an experience) have an adverse effect on (someone): *the North Sea crossing seemed to have disagreed with her.*
– ORIGIN late 15th cent. (in sense 2, also in the sense 'refuse to agree to'): from Old French *desagreer.*

disagreeable ▶ adjective unpleasant or unenjoyable: *another disagreeable thought came to him | some aspects of his work are* ***disagreeable to*** *him.*
■ unfriendly and bad-tempered: *Henry was always a very disagreeable boy.*
– DERIVATIVES **disagreeableness** noun, **disagreeably** adverb.
– ORIGIN late Middle English (in the sense 'discordant, incongruous'): from Old French *desagreable*, based on *agreer* 'agree'.

disagreement ▶ noun [mass noun] lack of consensus or approval: *there was some disagreement about the details | the meeting ended* ***in disagreement*** | [count noun] *disagreements between parents and adolescents.*
■ lack of consistency or correspondence: *disagreement between the results of the two assessments.*

disallow ▶ verb [with obj.] (usu. **be disallowed**) refuse to declare valid: *he was offside and the goal was disallowed.*
– DERIVATIVES **disallowance** noun.
– ORIGIN late Middle English (in the sense 'disown, refuse to accept'): from Old French *desalouer.*

disambiguate ▶ verb [with obj.] remove uncertainty of meaning from (an ambiguous sentence, phrase, or other linguistic unit).
– DERIVATIVES **disambiguation** noun.

disamenity /ˌdɪsəˈmiːnɪti, -ˈmɛnɪti/ ▶ noun (pl. **-ies**) [mass noun] unpleasant quality or character of something: *two rapidly growing sources of disamenity are air travel and tourism.*

disappear ▶ verb [no obj.] cease to be visible: *he* ***disappeared into*** *the trees | the sun had disappeared.*
■ cease to exist or be in use: *the tension had completely disappeared.* ■ (of a thing) be lost or impossible to find: *my wallet seems to have disappeared.* ■ (of a person) go missing or (in coded political language) be killed: *the family disappeared after being taken into custody.*
– ORIGIN late Middle English: from **DIS-** (expressing reversal) + **APPEAR**, on the pattern of French *disparaître.*

disappearance ▶ noun [usu. in sing.] an instance or fact of someone or something ceasing to be visible.
■ an instance or fact of someone going missing or (in coded political language) being killed: *the police were investigating her disappearance.* ■ an instance or fact of something being lost or stolen: *an investigation is being carried out into the disappearance of the money.* ■ [mass noun] the process or fact of something ceasing to exist or be in use: *the disappearance of grammar schools.*

disappearing act ▶ noun (also **disappearing trick**) informal an instance of someone being impossible to find, especially when they are required to face something difficult or unpleasant: *I don't want you* ***doing a disappearing act*** *on me.*

disapply ▶ verb (**-ies**, **-ied**) [with obj.] treat (something) as inapplicable: *British courts are under obligation to disapply Acts where they conflict with European law.*
– DERIVATIVES **disapplication** noun.

disappoint ▶ verb [with obj.] fail to fulfil the hopes or expectations of (someone): *I have no wish to disappoint everyone by postponing the visit.*
■ prevent (hopes or expectations) from being realized: *public ownership had sadly disappointed socialist hopes.*
– ORIGIN late Middle English (in the sense 'deprive of an office or position'): from Old French *desappointer.*

disappointed ▶ adjective (of a person) sad or displeased because someone or something has failed to fulfil one's hopes or expectations: *I'm* ***disappointed in*** *you, Mary | thousands of disappointed customers were kept waiting.*
■ (of hopes or expectations) prevented from being realized.
– DERIVATIVES **disappointedly** adverb.

disappointing ▶ adjective failing to fulfil someone's hopes or expectations: *the team made a disappointing start* | [with clause] *it was* ***disappointing that*** *there were relatively few possibilities.*
– DERIVATIVES **disappointingly** adverb [as submodifier] *there was disappointingly little change* | [sentence adverb] *disappointingly, my German failed to improve.*

disappointment ▶ noun [mass noun] the feeling of sadness or displeasure caused by the non-fulfilment of one's hopes or expectations: ***to her disappointment****, there was no chance to talk privately with Luke.*
■ [count noun] a person, event, or thing that causes such a feeling: *the job proved a disappointment | I was a big* ***disappointment to*** *her.*

disapprobation /dɪsˌaprəˈbeɪʃ(ə)n/ ▶ noun [mass noun] strong disapproval, typically on moral grounds: *she braved her mother's disapprobation and slipped out to enjoy herself.*

disapproval ▶ noun [mass noun] possession or expression of an unfavourable opinion: *Jill replied with a hint of disapproval in her voice.*

disapprove ▶ verb [no obj.] have or express an unfavourable opinion about something: *Bob strongly* ***disapproved of*** *drinking and driving* | [as adj. **disapproving**] *he shot a disapproving glance at her.*
■ [with obj.] officially refuse to agree to: *a company may take power to disapprove the transfer of shares.*
– DERIVATIVES **disapprover** noun, **disapprovingly** adverb.

disarm ▶ verb [with obj.] **1** take a weapon or weapons away from (a person, force, or country): *guerrillas had completely disarmed and demobilized their forces.*
■ [no obj.] (of a country or force) give up or reduce its armed forces or weapons: *the other militias had disarmed by the agreed deadline.* ■ remove the fuse from (a bomb), making it safe.
2 allay the hostility or suspicions of: *his tact and political skills will disarm critics.*
■ deprive of the power to injure or hurt: *camp humour acts to provoke rather than disarm moral indignation.*
▶ noun [in sing.] chiefly Fencing an act of taking a weapon away from someone: *a well-executed disarm.*
– ORIGIN late Middle English: from Old French *desarmer.*

disarmament /dɪsˈɑːməm(ə)nt/ ▶ noun [mass noun] the reduction or withdrawal of military forces and weapons.

disarmer ▶ noun a person who advocates or campaigns for the withdrawal of nuclear weapons.

disarming ▶ adjective (of manner or behaviour) having the effect of allaying suspicion or hostility, especially through charm: *he gave her a disarming smile.*
– DERIVATIVES **disarmingly** adverb.

disarrange ▶ verb [with obj.] (often **be disarranged**) make (something) untidy or disordered: *her hair was disarranged all round her face.*
– DERIVATIVES **disarrangement** noun.

disarray ▶ noun [mass noun] a state of disorganization or untidiness: *her grey hair was* ***in disarray*** *| his plans have been* ***thrown into disarray.***
▶ verb [with obj.] **1** throw (someone or something) into a state of disorganization or untidiness: *the inspection disarrayed the usual schedule.*
2 poetic/literary strip (someone) of clothing: *attendant damsels to help to disarray her.*
– ORIGIN late Middle English: from Anglo-Norman French *dissairay.*

disarticulate ▶ verb [with obj.] separate (bones) at the joints: *the African egg-eating snake can disarticulate its lower jaw from its upper.*
■ break up and disrupt the logic of (an argument or opinion): *novels disarticulate theories.*
– DERIVATIVES **disarticulation** noun.

disassemble ▶ verb [with obj.] (often **be disassembled**) take (something) to pieces: *the piston can be disassembled for transport.*
■ Computing translate (a program) from machine code into a symbolic language.
– DERIVATIVES **disassembly** noun.

disassembler ▶ noun Computing a program for converting machine code into a low-level symbolic language.

disassociate ▶ verb another term for **DISSOCIATE**.
– DERIVATIVES **disassociation** noun.

disaster ▶ noun a sudden event, such as an accident or a natural catastrophe, that causes great damage or loss of life: *159 people died in the disaster* | [mass noun] *disaster struck within minutes of take-off.*
■ [as modifier] denoting a genre of films that use natural or accidental catastrophe as the mainspring of plot and setting: *a disaster movie.* ■ an event or fact that has unfortunate consequences: *a string of personal disasters* | [mass noun] *reduced legal aid could spell financial disaster.* ■ informal a person, act, or thing that is a failure: *my perm is a total disaster.*
– ORIGIN late 16th cent.: from Italian *disastro* 'ill-starred event', from *dis-* (expressing negation) + *astro* 'star' (from Latin *astrum*).

disaster area ▶ noun an area in which a major disaster has recently occurred: *the vicinity of the explosion was declared a disaster area.*
■ [in sing.] informal a place, situation, person, or activity regarded as chaotic, ineffectual, or failing in some fundamental respect: *the room was a disaster area, stuff piled everywhere | she was a disaster area in fake leopard skin and stacked heels.*

disastrous ▶ adjective causing great damage: *a disastrous fire swept through the museum.*
■ informal highly unsuccessful: *United made a disastrous start to the season.*
– DERIVATIVES **disastrously** adverb.
– ORIGIN late 16th cent. (in the sense 'ill-fated'): from French *désastreux*, from Italian *disastroso*, from *disastro* 'disaster'.

disavow ▶ verb [with obj.] deny any responsibility or support for: *the union leaders resisted pressure to disavow picket-line violence.*
– DERIVATIVES **disavowal** noun.
– ORIGIN late Middle English: from Old French *desavouer.*

disband ▶ verb [with obj.] (usu. **be disbanded**) cause (an organized group) to break up.
■ [no obj.] (of an organized group) break up and stop functioning as an organization.
– DERIVATIVES **disbandment** noun.
– ORIGIN late 16th cent.: from obsolete French *desbander.*

disbar ▶ verb (**disbarred**, **disbarring**) [with obj.] **1** (usu. **be disbarred**) expel (a barrister) from the Bar, so that they no longer have the right to practise law.
2 exclude (someone) from something: *competitors wearing rings will be* ***disbarred from*** *competition.*
– DERIVATIVES **disbarment** noun.
– ORIGIN mid 16th cent. (in sense 2): from **DIS-** 'away' + **BAR**[1].

disbelief ▶ noun [mass noun] inability or refusal to accept that something is true or real: *Laura shook her head in disbelief.*
■ lack of faith in something: *I'll burn in hell for disbelief.*

disbelieve ▶ verb [with obj.] be unable to believe (someone or something): *he seemed to disbelieve her* | [as adj. **disbelieving**] *the disbelieving look in her eyes.*
■ [no obj.] have no faith in God, spiritual beings, or a religious system: *to disbelieve is as much an act of faith as belief.*
– DERIVATIVES **disbeliever** noun, **disbelievingly** adverb.

disbenefit ▶ noun Brit. a disadvantage or loss resulting from something.

disbound ▶ adjective (of a portion of a book) removed from a bound volume.

disbud ▶ verb (**disbudded**, **disbudding**) [with obj.] remove superfluous or unwanted buds from (a plant).
■ Farming remove the horn buds from (a young animal).

disburden ▶ verb [with obj.] relieve (someone or something) of a burden or responsibility: *I decided to disburden myself of the task.*
■ archaic relieve (someone's mind) of worries and anxieties.

disburse /dɪsˈbəːs/ ▶ verb [with obj.] (often **be disbursed**) pay out (money from a fund): *$6,700 million of the pledged aid had already been disbursed.*
– DERIVATIVES **disbursal** noun, **disbursement** noun, **disburser** noun.
– ORIGIN mid 16th cent.: from Old French *desbourser*, from *des-* (expressing removal) + *bourse* 'purse'.

disbursement ▶ noun [mass noun] the payment of money from a fund, e.g. to provide economic aid.
■ [count noun] a payment, especially one made by a solicitor to a third party and then claimed back from the client.

disc (US also **disk**) ▶ noun **1** a flat, thin, round object:

coins were made by striking a blank disc of metal | a man's body with an identity disc around the neck.
■(**disk**) an information storage device for a computer in the shape of a round flat plate which can be rotated to give access to all parts of the surface. The data may be stored either magnetically (in a **magnetic disk**) or optically (in an **optical disk** such as a CD-ROM). ■ short for **COMPACT DISC**. ■ dated a gramophone record. ■ (**discs**) one of the suits in some tarot packs, corresponding to coins in others.
2 a shape or surface that is round and flat in appearance: *the smudged yellow disc of the moon.*
3 a roundish, flattened part in an animal or plant, in particular:
■(also **intervertebral disc**) a layer of cartilage separating adjacent vertebrae in the spine: *he suffered a prolapsed disc.* ■ Botany (in a composite flower head of the daisy family) a close-packed cluster of disc florets in the centre, forming the yellow part of the flower head.
– ORIGIN mid 17th cent. (originally referring to the seemingly flat round form of the sun or moon): from French *disque* or Latin *discus* (see **DISCUS**).

USAGE Generally speaking, the British spelling is **disc** and the US spelling is **disk**, although there is much overlap and variation between the two. In particular, the spelling for senses relating to computers is nearly always **disk**, as in **floppy disk**, **disk drive**, and so on.

discalced /dɪsˈkalst/ ▶ **adjective** denoting or belonging to one of several strict orders of Catholic friars or nuns who go barefoot or are shod only in sandals.
– ORIGIN mid 17th cent.: variant, influenced by French *déchaux*, of earlier *discalceated*, from Latin *discalceatus*, from *dis-* (expressing removal) + *calceatus* (from *calceus* 'shoe').

discard ▶ **verb** /dɪˈskɑːd/ [with obj.] get rid of (someone or something) as no longer useful or desirable: *Hilary bundled up the clothes she had discarded.*
■(in bridge, whist, and similar card games) play (a card that is neither of the suit led nor a trump), when one is unable to follow suit.
▶ **noun** /ˈdɪskɑːd/ a person or thing rejected as no longer useful or desirable.
■(in bridge, whist, and similar card games) a card played which is neither of the suit led nor a trump, when one is unable to follow suit.
– DERIVATIVES **discardable** /dɪsˈkɑːdəb(ə)l/ adjective.
– ORIGIN late 16th cent. (originally in the sense 'reject (a playing card)'): from **DIS-** (expressing removal) + the noun **CARD**[1].

discarnate /dɪsˈkɑːnət/ ▶ **adjective** (of a person or being) not having a physical body.
– ORIGIN late 19th cent.: from **DIS-** 'without' + Latin *caro, carn-* 'flesh' or late Latin *carnatus* 'fleshy'.

disc brake ▶ **noun** a type of vehicle brake employing the friction of pads against a disc which is attached to the wheel.

disc camera ▶ **noun** a camera in which the images are formed on a disc, rather than on film.

disc drive ▶ **noun** variant spelling of **DISK DRIVE**.

discectomy /dɪsˈkɛktəmi/ ▶ **noun** [mass noun] surgical removal of the whole or a part of an intervertebral disc.

discern /dɪˈsəːn/ ▶ **verb** [with obj.] perceive or recognize (something): *I can discern no difference between the two policies* | [with clause] *pupils quickly discern what is acceptable to the teacher.*
■distinguish (someone or something) with difficulty by sight or with the other senses: *she could faintly discern the shape of a skull.*
– DERIVATIVES **discerner** noun, **discernible** adjective, **discernibly** adverb.
– ORIGIN late Middle English: via Old French from Latin *discernere*, from *dis-* 'apart' + *cernere* 'to separate'.

discerning ▶ **adjective** having or showing good judgement: *the brasserie attracts discerning customers.*
– DERIVATIVES **discerningly** adverb.

discernment ▶ **noun** [mass noun] the ability to judge well: *an astonishing lack of discernment.*

discerption /dɪˈsəːpʃ(ə)n/ ▶ **noun** [mass noun] archaic the action of pulling something apart.
■[count noun] a piece severed from something.
– DERIVATIVES **discerptibility** noun, **discerptible** adjective.
– ORIGIN mid 17th cent.: from late Latin *discerptio(n-)*, from Latin *discerpere* 'pluck to pieces'.

disc floret ▶ **noun** Botany (in a composite flower head of the daisy family) any of a number of small tubular and usually fertile florets that form the disc. In rayless plants such as the tansy the flower head is composed entirely of disc florets. Compare with **RAY FLORET**.

discharge ▶ **verb** /dɪsˈtʃɑːdʒ/ [with obj.] **1** (often **be discharged**) tell (someone) officially that they can or must leave, in particular:
■send (a patient) out of hospital because they are judged fit to go home. ■ dismiss or release (someone) from a post, especially from service in the armed forces or police. ■ release (someone) from the custody or restraint of the law: *the man was conditionally discharged for two years at Oxford Crown Court.* ■ relieve (a juror or jury) from serving in a case. ■ Law relieve (a bankrupt) of residual liability. ■ release (a party) from a contract or obligation: *the insurer is discharged from liability from the day of breach.*
2 allow (a liquid, gas, or other substance) to flow out from where it has been confined: *industrial plants **discharge** highly toxic materials **into** rivers* | [no obj.] *the overflow should discharge in an obvious place.*
■(of an orifice or diseased tissue) emit (pus, mucus, or other liquid): *the swelling will eventually break down and discharge pus* | [no obj.] *the eyes and nose began to discharge.* ■ (often **be discharged**) Physics release or neutralize the electric charge of (an electric field, battery, or other object): *the electrostatic field that builds up on a monitor screen can be discharged* | [no obj.] *batteries have a tendency to discharge slowly.* ■ (of a person) fire (a gun or missile): *when you shoot you can discharge as many barrels as you wish.* ■ [no obj.] (of a firearm) be fired: *there was a dull thud as the gun discharged.* ■ (of a person) allow (an emotion) to be released: *he discharged his resentment in the harmless form of memoirs.* ■ unload (goods or passengers) from a ship: *the ferry was discharging passengers* | [no obj.] *ninety ships were queuing to discharge.*
3 do all that is required to fulfil (a responsibility) or perform (a duty).
■pay off (a debt or other financial claim).
4 Law (of a judge or court) cancel (an order of a court).
■cancel (a contract) because of completion or breach: *an existing mortgage to be discharged on completion.*
▶ **noun** /ˈdɪstʃɑːdʒ, dɪsˈtʃɑːdʒ/ [mass noun] **1** the action of discharging someone from a hospital or from a post: *referrals can be discussed before discharge from hospital* | [count noun] *offending policemen receive a dishonourable discharge.*
■[count noun] an act of releasing someone from the custody or restraint of the law: *she was given an absolute discharge after admitting breaking a smoking ban.* See also **CONDITIONAL DISCHARGE**. ■ Law the action of relieving a bankrupt from residual liability.
2 the action of allowing a liquid, gas, or other substance to flow out from where it is confined.
■the quantity of material allowed to flow out in such a way: *industrial discharge has turned the river into an open sewer* | [count noun] *an agreement to end radioactive waste discharges into the Irish Sea.* ■ the emission of pus, mucus, or other liquid from an orifice or from diseased tissue: *those germs might lead to vaginal discharge* | [count noun] *a greeny-yellow nasal discharge.* ■ Physics the release of electricity from a charged object: *slow discharge of a condenser is fundamental to oscillatory circuits.* ■ [count noun] a flow of electricity through air or other gas, especially when accompanied by emission of light: *a sizzling discharge between sky and turret.* ■ the action of firing a gun or missile: *a police permit for discharge of an air gun* | [count noun] *sounds like discharges of artillery.* ■ the action of unloading a ship of its goods or passengers.
3 the action of doing all that is required to fulfil a responsibility or perform a duty: *directors must use skill in the discharge of their duties.*
■the payment of a debt or other financial claim: *money paid **in discharge of** a claim.*
4 Law the action of cancelling an order of a court.
– DERIVATIVES **dischargeable** adjective.
– ORIGIN Middle English (in the sense 'relieve of (an obligation)'): from Old French *descharger*, from late Latin *discarricare* 'unload', from *dis-* (expressing reversal) + *carricare* 'to load' (see **CHARGE**).

discharge lamp ▶ **noun** a lamp in which the light is produced by a discharge tube.

discharger ▶ **noun** a person or thing that allows something to flow out, in particular:
■a person or organization that allows industrial waste, sewage, or other harmful substances to be released into the environment. ■ a device that releases nerve gas, smoke, or other substances for military purposes. ■ an apparatus for releasing or neutralizing an electric charge.

discharge tube ▶ **noun** a tube containing charged electrodes and filled with a gas in which ionization is induced by an electric field. The gas molecules emit light as they return to the ground state.

disc harrow ▶ **noun** a harrow with cutting edges consisting of a row of concave discs set at an oblique angle.

disciple /dɪˈsʌɪp(ə)l/ ▶ **noun** a personal follower of Christ during his life, especially one of the twelve Apostles.
■a follower or pupil of a teacher, leader, or philosophy: *a disciple of Rousseau.*
– DERIVATIVES **discipleship** noun, **discipular** /dɪˈsɪpjʊlə/ adjective.
– ORIGIN Old English, from Latin *discipulus* 'learner', from *discere* 'learn'; reinforced by Old French *deciple*.

Disciples of Christ a Protestant denomination, originating among American Presbyterians in the early 19th century and found chiefly in the US, which rejects creeds and regards the Bible as the only basis of faith.

disciplinarian ▶ **noun** a person who believes in or practises firm discipline.

disciplinary ▶ **adjective** concerning or enforcing discipline: *a soldier will face disciplinary action after going absent without leave.*
– ORIGIN late 15th cent. (originally with reference to ecclesiastical order): from medieval Latin *disciplinarius*, from Latin *disciplina*, from *discipulus* 'learner' (see **DISCIPLE**).

discipline /ˈdɪsɪplɪn/ ▶ **noun 1** [mass noun] the practice of training people to obey rules or a code of behaviour, using punishment to correct disobedience: *a lack of proper parental and school discipline.*
■the controlled behaviour resulting from such training: *he was able to maintain discipline among his men.* ■ activity or experience that provides mental or physical training: *the tariqa offered spiritual discipline* | [count noun] *Kung fu is a discipline open to old and young.* ■ [count noun] a system of rules of conduct: *he doesn't have to submit to normal disciplines.*
2 a branch of knowledge, typically one studied in higher education: *sociology is a fairly new discipline.*
▶ **verb** [with obj.] train (someone) to obey rules or a code of behaviour, using punishment to correct disobedience: *many parents have been afraid to discipline their children.*
■(often **be disciplined**) punish or rebuke (someone) formally for an offence: *a member of staff was to be disciplined by management.* ■ (**discipline oneself to do something**) train oneself to do something in a controlled and habitual way: *every month discipline yourself to go through the file.*
– DERIVATIVES **disciplinable** adjective, **disciplinal** /ˌdɪsɪˈplʌɪn(ə)l, ˈdɪsɪplɪn(ə)l/ adjective.
– ORIGIN Middle English (in the sense 'mortification by scourging oneself'): via Old French from Latin *disciplina* 'instruction, knowledge', from *discipulus* (see **DISCIPLE**).

disciplined ▶ **adjective** showing a controlled form of behaviour or way of working: *a disciplined approach to management.*

disc jockey ▶ **noun** a person who introduces and plays recorded popular music, especially on radio or at a disco.

disclaim ▶ **verb** [with obj.] refuse to acknowledge; deny: *the school disclaimed any responsibility for his death.*
■Law renounce a legal claim to (a property or title).
– ORIGIN late Middle English (in legal contexts): from Anglo-Norman French *desclamer*, from *des-* (expressing reversal) + *clamer* 'to claim' (see **CLAIM**).

disclaimer ▶ **noun** a statement that denies something, especially responsibility: *the novel carries the usual disclaimer about the characters bearing no relation to living persons.*
■Law an act of repudiating another's claim or renouncing one's own.
– ORIGIN late Middle English (as a legal term): from Anglo-Norman French *desclamer* (infinitive used as noun: see **DISCLAIM**).

disclose ▶ **verb** [with obj.] make (secret or new information) known: *they **disclosed** her name **to** the press* | [with clause] *the magazine disclosed that he had served a prison sentence for fraud.*
■allow (something) to be seen, especially by uncovering it: *he cleared away the grass and disclosed a narrow opening descending into the darkness.*

– DERIVATIVES **discloser** noun.
– ORIGIN late Middle English: from Old French *desclos-*, stem of *desclore*, based on Latin *claudere* 'to close'.

disclosure ▶ **noun** [mass noun] the action of making new or secret information known: *a judge ordered the disclosure of the government documents.*
■ [count noun] a fact, especially a secret, that is made known: *the government's disclosures about missile programmes.*
– ORIGIN late 16th cent.: from **DISCLOSE**, on the pattern of *closure*.

disco ▶ **noun** (pl. **-os**) **1** (also **discotheque**) a club or party at which people dance to pop music.
■ the lighting and sound equipment used at such an event: *no one knows how to waltz so I've ordered a disco.*
2 short for **DISCO MUSIC**.
▶ **verb** (**-oes**, **-oed**) [no obj.] attend or dance at such a club or party: *she filled every hour of the day playing tennis, or discoing with a group of friends.*
– ORIGIN 1960s (originally US): abbreviation.

discobolus /dɪˈskɒbələs/ ▶ **noun** (pl. **discoboli** /-lʌɪ/) a discus-thrower in ancient Greece.
– ORIGIN early 18th cent.: via Latin from Greek *diskobolos*, from *diskos* 'discus' + *-bolos* '-throwing' (from *ballein* 'to throw').

discography /dɪˈskɒgrəfi/ ▶ **noun** (pl. **-ies**) a descriptive catalogue of musical recordings, particularly those of a particular performer or composer.
■ all of a performer's or composer's recordings considered as a body of work: *his discography is overwhelmingly classical.* ■ [mass noun] the study of musical recordings and compilation of descriptive catalogues.
– DERIVATIVES **discographer** noun.
– ORIGIN 1930s: from **DISC** + **-GRAPHY**, on the pattern of *biography*.

discoid /ˈdɪskɔɪd/ ▶ **adjective** technical shaped like a disc.
▶ **noun** a thing that is shaped like a disc, particularly a type of ancient stone tool.
– DERIVATIVES **discoidal** adjective.
– ORIGIN late 18th cent.: from Greek *diskoeidēs*, from *diskos* (see **DISCUS**).

discolour (US **discolor**) ▶ **verb** [no obj.] become a different, less attractive colour: *do not over-knead the dough while adding the fruit or it will discolour.*
■ [with obj.] change or spoil the colour of: *too much aluminium can discolour water* | [as adj. **discoloured**] *her beauty was marred by discoloured teeth.*
– DERIVATIVES **discoloration** (also **discolouration**) noun.
– ORIGIN late Middle English: from Old French *descolorer* or medieval Latin *discolorare*, from *des-*, *dis-* (expressing reversal) + Latin *colorare* 'to colour'.

discombobulate /ˌdɪskəmˈbɒbjʊleɪt/ ▶ **verb** [with obj.] humorous, chiefly N. Amer. disconcert or confuse (someone): [as adj. **discombobulated**] *he is looking a little pained and discombobulated.*
– ORIGIN mid 19th cent.: probably based on **DISCOMPOSE** or **DISCOMFIT**.

discomfit /dɪsˈkʌmfɪt/ ▶ **verb** (**discomfited**, **discomfiting**) [with obj.] (usu. **be discomfited**) make (someone) feel uneasy or embarrassed: *he was not noticeably discomfited by her tone.*
– DERIVATIVES **discomfiture** noun.
– ORIGIN Middle English (in the sense 'defeat in battle'): from Old French *desconfit*, past participle of *desconfire*, based on Latin *dis-* (expressing reversal) + *conficere* 'put together' (see **CONFECTION**).

USAGE The words **discomfit** and **discomfort** are etymologically unrelated but in modern use their principal meanings as a verb have collapsed into one ('make (someone) feel uneasy').

discomfort ▶ **noun** lack of physical comfort: *the discomforts of too much sun in summer.*
■ [mass noun] slight pain: *the patient complained of discomfort in the left calf.* ■ [mass noun] a state of mental unease: *his remarks caused her discomfort.*
▶ **verb** [with obj.] make (someone) feel uneasy: *the unknown leaker's purpose was to discomfort the Prime Minister.*
■ [often as adj. **discomforting**] cause (someone) slight pain: *if the patient's condition has discomforting symptoms, these should be controlled.*
– ORIGIN Middle English (as a verb in the sense 'dishearten, distress'): from Old French *desconforter* (verb), *desconfort* (noun), from *des-* (expressing reversal) + *conforter* 'to comfort' (see **COMFORT**).

discommode /ˌdɪskəˈməʊd/ ▶ **verb** [with obj.] formal cause (someone) trouble or inconvenience: *I am sorry to have discommoded you.*
– DERIVATIVES **discommodious** adjective, **discommodity** noun.
– ORIGIN early 18th cent.: from obsolete French *discommoder*, variant of *incommoder* (see **INCOMMODE**).

discompose ▶ **verb** [with obj.] [often as adj. **discomposed**] disturb or agitate (someone): *she looked a little discomposed as she spoke.*
– DERIVATIVES **discomposure** noun.

disco music ▶ **noun** [mass noun] pop music intended mainly for dancing to at discos, typically soul-influenced and melodic with a regular bass beat and popular particularly in the late 1970s.

disconcert /ˌdɪskənˈsəːt/ ▶ **verb** [with obj.] disturb the composure of; unsettle: *the abrupt change of subject disconcerted her* | [as adj. **disconcerted**] *she was amused to see a disconcerted expression on his face.*
– DERIVATIVES **disconcertedly** adverb, **disconcertion** noun, **disconcertment** noun (rare).
– ORIGIN late 17th cent. (in the sense 'upset the progress of'): from obsolete French *desconcerter*, from *des-* (expressing reversal) + *concerter* 'bring together'.

disconcerting ▶ **adjective** causing one to feel unsettled: *he had a disconcerting habit of offering jobs to people he met at dinner parties.*
– DERIVATIVES **disconcertingly** adverb.

disconfirm ▶ **verb** [with obj.] show that (a belief or hypothesis) is not or may not be true.
– DERIVATIVES **disconfirmation** /ˌdɪskɒnfəˈmeɪʃ(ə)n/ noun, **disconfirmatory** adjective.

disconformity ▶ **noun** (pl. **-ies**) **1** [mass noun] lack of conformity.
2 Geology a break in a sedimentary sequence which does not involve a difference of inclination between the strata on each side of the break. Compare with **UNCONFORMITY**.

disconnect ▶ **verb** [with obj.] break the connection of or between: *take all violence out of television drama and you* ***disconnect*** *it* ***from*** *reality.*
■ put (an electrical device) out of action by detaching it from a power supply. ■ interrupt or terminate (a telephone conversation) by breaking the connection: *I phoned them in Edinburgh but we got disconnected.* ■ (usu. **be disconnected**) terminate the connection of (a household) to water, electricity, gas, or telephone, typically because of non-payment of bills.
– DERIVATIVES **disconnection** (also **disconnexion**) noun.

disconnected ▶ **adjective** having had a connection broken: *he expected the disconnected phone to start ringing.*
■ [predic.] (of a person) lacking contact with reality: *I drove away, feeling* ***disconnected from*** *the real world.* ■ (of speech, writing, or thought) lacking a logical sequence; incoherent: *a disconnected narrative.*
– DERIVATIVES **disconnectedly** adverb, **disconnectedness** noun.

disconsolate /dɪsˈkɒns(ə)lət/ ▶ **adjective** very unhappy and unable to be comforted: *she left Fritz looking disconsolate.*
– DERIVATIVES **disconsolately** adverb, **disconsolateness** noun, **disconsolation** noun.
– ORIGIN late Middle English: from medieval Latin *disconsolatus*, from *dis-* (expressing reversal) + Latin *consolatus* (past participle of *consolari* 'to console').

discontent ▶ **noun** [mass noun] lack of contentment; dissatisfaction with one's circumstances: *popular* ***discontent with*** *the system had been general for several years* | [count noun] *the discontents and anxieties of the working class.*
■ [count noun] a person who is dissatisfied, typically with the prevailing social or political situation: *the cause attracted a motley crew of discontents and zealots.*
– DERIVATIVES **discontentment** noun.

discontented ▶ **adjective** dissatisfied, especially with one's circumstances: *I am so* ***discontented with*** *my work* | *a discontented housewife* | [as plural noun **the discontented**] *the ranks of the discontented were swelled by returning soldiers.*
– DERIVATIVES **discontentedly** adverb, **discontentedness** noun.

discontinue ▶ **verb** (**discontinues**, **discontinued**, **discontinuing**) [with obj.] cease from doing or providing (something), typically something that has been provided on a regular basis: *the ferry service was discontinued by the proprietors* | *he discontinued his visits.*
■ stop making (a particular product): *their current top-of-the-range running shoe is being discontinued* | [as adj. **discontinued**] *discontinued fabrics.* ■ cease taking (a newspaper or periodical) or paying (a subscription).
– DERIVATIVES **discontinuance** noun, **discontinuation** noun.
– ORIGIN late Middle English (in the sense 'interrupt, disrupt'): via Old French from medieval Latin *discontinuare*, from Latin *dis-* 'not' + *continuare* (see **CONTINUE**).

discontinuity ▶ **noun** (pl. **-ies**) a distinct break in physical continuity or sequence in time, or sharp difference of characteristics between parts of something: *changes in government have resulted in discontinuities in policy* | [mass noun] *there is no significant discontinuity between modern and primitive societies.*
– ORIGIN late 16th cent.: from medieval Latin *discontinuitas*, from *discontinuus* (see **DISCONTINUOUS**).

discontinuous ▶ **adjective** having intervals or gaps: *a person with a discontinuous employment record.*
■ Mathematics (of a function) having at least one discontinuity.
– DERIVATIVES **discontinuously** adverb.
– ORIGIN mid 17th cent. (in the sense 'producing discontinuity'): from medieval Latin *discontinuus*, from *dis-* 'not' + *continuus* (see **CONTINUOUS**).

discord ▶ **noun** /ˈdɪskɔːd/ [mass noun] **1** disagreement between people: *a prosperous family who showed no signs of discord.*
■ Music lack of agreement or harmony between things: *the discord between indigenous and Western cultures.*
2 lack of harmony between notes sounding together: *the music faded in discord.*
■ [count noun] a chord which (in conventional harmonic terms) is regarded as unpleasing or requiring resolution by another. ■ [count noun] any interval except unison, an octave, a perfect fifth or fourth, a major or minor third and sixth, or their octaves. ■ [count noun] a single note dissonant with another.
▶ **verb** /dɪsˈkɔːd/ [no obj.] archaic (of people) disagree: *we discorded commonly on two points.*
■ (of things) be different or in disharmony: *the party's views were apt to* ***discord with*** *those of the leading members of the government.*
– ORIGIN Middle English: from Old French *descord* (noun), *descorder* (verb), from Latin *discordare*, from *discors* 'discordant', from *dis-* (expressing negation, reversal) + *cor*, *cord-* 'heart'.

discordant ▶ **adjective** **1** disagreeing or incongruous: *the principle of meritocracy is discordant with claims of inherited worth.*
■ characterized by quarrelling and conflict: *a study of children in discordant homes.*
2 (of sounds) harsh and jarring because of a lack of harmony: *bombs, guns, and engines mingled in discordant sound.*
– PHRASES **strike a discordant note** appear strange and out of place: *the chair's modernity struck a discordant note in a room full of eighteenth-century furniture.*
– DERIVATIVES **discordance** noun, **discordancy** noun, **discordantly** adverb.
– ORIGIN late Middle English: from Old French *descordant*, present participle of *descorder* (see **DISCORD**).

discotheque /ˈdɪskətɛk/ ▶ **noun** another term for **DISCO** (in sense 1).
– ORIGIN 1950s: from French *discothèque*, originally 'record library', on the pattern of *bibliothèque* 'library'.

discount ▶ **noun** /ˈdɪskaʊnt/ a deduction from the usual cost of something, typically given to customers who pay cash or in advance: *rail commuters get a discount on season tickets* | [mass noun] *we want to introduce a standard level of discount for everyone.*
■ Finance a percentage deducted from the face value of a bill of exchange or promissory note when it changes hands before the due date.
▶ **verb** /dɪsˈkaʊnt/ [with obj.] **1** deduct an amount from (the usual price of something): *a product may carry a price which cannot easily be discounted.*
■ reduce (a product or service) in price: *one shop has discounted children's trainers* | [as adj. **discounted**] *discounted books.* ■ buy or sell (a bill of exchange) before its due date at less than its maturity value.
2 regard (a possibility, fact, or person) as being

unworthy of consideration because it lacks credibility: *I'd heard rumours, but discounted them.*
– PHRASES **at a discount** below the nominal or usual price: *a scheme which lets tenants buy their homes at a discount.* Compare with ***at a premium*** (see **PREMIUM**).
– DERIVATIVES **discountable** /dɪʃˈkaʊntəb(ə)l/ adjective, **discounter** /dɪsˈkaʊntə/ noun.
– ORIGIN early 17th cent. (denoting a reduction in the amount or value of something): from obsolete French *descompte* (noun), *descompter* (verb), or (in commercial contexts) from Italian (*di*)*scontare*, both from medieval Latin *discomputare*, from Latin *dis-* (expressing reversal) + *computare* (see **COMPUTE**).

discounted cash flow ▶ **noun** [mass noun] Finance a method of assessing investments taking into account the expected accumulation of interest.

discountenance ▶ **verb** [with obj.] (usu. **be discountenanced**) **1** refuse to approve of (something): *the best solution to alcohol abuse is a healthy family life where alcohol consumption is discountenanced.*
2 disturb the composure of: *Amanda was not discountenanced by the accusation.*

discount house ▶ **noun 1** Brit. a company that buys and sells bills of exchange.
2 N. Amer. another term for **DISCOUNT STORE**.

discount market ▶ **noun** the section of the financial market which deals in discounted bills of exchange.

discount rate ▶ **noun** Finance **1** the minimum interest rate set by the US Federal Reserve (and some other national banks) for lending to other banks.
2 a rate used for discounting bills of exchange.

discount store ▶ **noun** a shop that sells goods at less than the normal retail price.

discourage ▶ **verb** [with obj.] cause (someone) to lose confidence or enthusiasm: *I don't want to discourage you, but I don't think it's such a good idea* | [as adj. **discouraging**] *the discouraging effect of poor employment prospects.*
■ prevent or seek to prevent (something) by showing disapproval or creating difficulties: *the plan is designed to discourage the use of private cars.* ■ persuade (someone) against an action: *we want to* ***discourage*** *children* ***from*** *smoking.*
– DERIVATIVES **discouragement** noun, **discouragingly** adverb.
– ORIGIN late Middle English: from Old French *descouragier*, from *des-* (expressing reversal) + *corage* 'courage'.

discourse ▶ **noun** /ˈdɪskɔːs, -ˈkɔːs/ written or spoken communication or debate: [mass noun] *the language of political discourse* | [count noun] *an imagined discourse between two people travelling in France.*
■ [count noun] a formal discussion of a topic in speech or writing: *a discourse on critical theory.* ■ Linguistics a connected series of utterances; a text or conversation.
▶ **verb** /dɪsˈkɔːs/ [no obj.] speak or write authoritatively about a topic: *she could* ***discourse*** *at great length* ***on*** *the history of Europe.*
■ engage in conversation: *he spent an hour* ***discoursing with*** *his supporters in the courtroom.*
– ORIGIN late Middle English (denoting the process of reasoning, also in the phrase *discourse of reason*): from Old French *discours*, from Latin *discursus* 'running to and fro' (in medieval Latin 'argument'), from the verb *discurrere*, from *dis-* 'away' + *currere* 'to run'; the verb influenced by French *discourir*.

discourse marker ▶ **noun** Grammar a word or phrase whose function is to organize discourse into segments, for example *well* or *I mean*.

discourteous ▶ **adjective** showing rudeness and a lack of consideration for other people: *it would be unkind and discourteous to decline a visit.*
– DERIVATIVES **discourteously** adverb, **discourteousness** noun.

discourtesy ▶ **noun** (pl. **-ies**) [mass noun] rude and inconsiderate behaviour: *he was able to discourage visitors without obvious discourtesy.*
■ [count noun] an impolite act or remark: *the fact that MPs were not kept informed was an extraordinary discourtesy.*

discover ▶ **verb** [with obj.] **1** find (something or someone) unexpectedly or in the course of a search: *firemen discovered a body in the debris* | *she discovered her lover in the arms of another woman.*
■ become aware of (a fact or situation): *the courage to discover the truth and possibly be disappointed* | [with clause] *it was a relief to discover that he wasn't in.* ■ be the first to find or observe (a place, substance, or scientific phenomenon): *Fleming discovered penicillin early in the twentieth century.* ■ perceive the attractions of (an activity or subject) for the first time: *a teenager who has recently discovered fashion.* ■ be the first to recognize the potential of (an actor, singer, or musician): *I discovered the band back in the mid 70s.*
2 archaic divulge (a secret): *they contain some secrets which Time will discover.*
■ disclose the identity of (someone): *she at last discovered herself to me.* ■ display (a quality or feeling): *with what agility did these military men discover their skill in feats of war.*
– DERIVATIVES **discoverable** adjective, **discoverer** noun.
– ORIGIN Middle English (in the sense 'make known'): from Old French *descovrir*, from late Latin *discooperire*, from Latin *dis-* (expressing reversal) + *cooperire* 'cover completely' (see **COVER**).

discovered check ▶ **noun** Chess a check which results when a player moves a piece or pawn so as to put the opponent's king in check from another piece.

Discovery ▶ **noun** a dessert apple of a variety with crisp flesh and bright red skin.

discovery ▶ **noun** (pl. **-ies**) [mass noun] **1** the action or process of discovering or being discovered: *the discovery of the body* | [count noun] *he made some startling discoveries.*
■ [count noun] a person or thing discovered: *the drug is not a new discovery.*
2 Law the compulsory disclosure, by a party to an action, of relevant documents referred to by the other party.
– ORIGIN mid 16th cent.: from **DISCOVER**, on the pattern of the pair *recover, recovery*.

discovery well ▶ **noun** the first successful oil well in a new field.

discredit ▶ **verb** (**discredited**, **discrediting**) [with obj.] harm the good reputation of (someone or something): *his remarks were taken out of context in an effort to discredit him* | [as adj. **discredited**] *a discredited government.*
■ cause (an idea or piece of evidence) to seem false or unreliable: *his explanation for the phenomenon was soon discredited.*
▶ **noun** [mass noun] loss or lack of reputation or respect: *they committed crimes which brought discredit upon the administration.*
■ [count noun] a person or thing that is a source of disgrace: *the ships were a* ***discredit to*** *the country.*
– ORIGIN mid 16th cent.: from **DIS-** (expressing reversal) + **CREDIT**, on the pattern of Italian (*di*)*scredito* (noun), (*di*)*screditare* (verb), and French *discrédit* (noun), *discréditer* (verb).

discreditable ▶ **adjective** tending to bring harm to a reputation: *allegations of discreditable conduct.*
– DERIVATIVES **discreditably** adverb.

discreet /dɪˈskriːt/ ▶ **adjective** (**discreeter**, **discreetest**) careful and circumspect in one's speech or actions, especially in order to avoid causing offence or to gain an advantage: *we made some discreet inquiries.*
■ intentionally unobtrusive: *a discreet cough.*
– DERIVATIVES **discreetly** adverb, **discreetness** noun.
– ORIGIN Middle English: from Old French *discret*, from Latin *discretus* 'separate', past participle of *discernere* 'discern', the sense arising from late Latin *discretio* (see **DISCRETION**). Compare with **DISCRETE**.

> **USAGE** The words **discrete** and **discreet** are pronounced in the same way and share the same origin but they do not mean the same thing. **Discrete** means 'separate', as in *a finite number of* ***discrete*** *categories*, while **discreet** means 'careful and circumspect' as in *you can rely on him to be* ***discreet***. Around 10 per cent of citations in the British National Corpus for **discrete** are misspellings for **discreet**.

discrepancy /dɪsˈkrɛp(ə)nsi/ ▶ **noun** (pl. **-ies**) an illogical or surprising lack of compatibility or similarity between two or more facts: *there's a* ***discrepancy between*** *your account and his.*
– DERIVATIVES **discrepant** adjective.
– ORIGIN early 17th cent.: from Latin *discrepantia*, from *discrepare* 'be discordant', from *dis-* 'apart, away' + *crepare* 'to creak'.

discrete /dɪˈskriːt/ ▶ **adjective** individually separate and distinct: *speech sounds are produced as a continuous sound signal rather than discrete units.*
– DERIVATIVES **discretely** adverb, **discreteness** noun.
– ORIGIN late Middle English: from Latin *discretus* 'separate'; compare with **DISCREET**.

discretion ▶ **noun** [mass noun] **1** the quality of behaving or speaking in such a way as to avoid causing offence or revealing private information: *she knew she could rely on his discretion* | *I'll be* ***the soul of discretion.***
2 the freedom to decide what should be done in a particular situation: *it is up to local authorities to* ***use their discretion*** *in setting the charges* | *honorary fellowships may be awarded* ***at the discretion of*** *the council.*
– PHRASES **discretion is the better part of valour** proverb it's better to avoid a dangerous situation than to confront it.
– ORIGIN Middle English (in the sense 'discernment'): via Old French from Latin *discretio(n-)* 'separation' (in late Latin 'discernment'), from *discernere* (see **DISCERN**).

discretionary ▶ **adjective** available for use at the discretion of the user: *the criminal courts possess a discretionary power to make compensation orders* | *rules are inevitably less flexible than a discretionary policy.*
■ denoting or relating to investment funds placed with a broker or manager who has discretion to invest them on the client's behalf: *discretionary portfolios.*

discretionary income ▶ **noun** [mass noun] income remaining after deduction of taxes, other mandatory charges, and expenditure on necessary items. Compare with **DISPOSABLE INCOME**.

discretionary trust ▶ **noun** a trust in which the number of shares of each beneficiary are not fixed by the settlor in the trust deed, but at the discretion of the trustees.

discretize /dɪˈskriːtʌɪz/ ▶ **verb** [with obj.] Mathematics represent or approximate (a quantity or series) using a discrete quantity or quantities.
– DERIVATIVES **discretization** noun.

discriminable /dɪˈskrɪmɪnəb(ə)l/ ▶ **adjective** able to be discriminated; distinguishable: *the target contours will not be discriminable from their background.*
– DERIVATIVES **discriminability** noun, **discriminably** adverb.
– ORIGIN mid 18th cent.: from **DISCRIMINATE**, on the pattern of the pair *separate, separable*.

discriminant /dɪˈskrɪmɪnənt/ ▶ **noun** an agent or characteristic that enables things, people, or classes to be distinguished from one another: *anaemia is commonly present in patients with both conditions, and is therefore not a helpful discriminant.*
■ Mathematics a function of the coefficients of a polynomial equation whose value gives information about the roots of the polynomial. See also **DISCRIMINANT FUNCTION**.
– ORIGIN mid 19th cent. (in the sense 'showing discernment'): from Latin *discriminant-* 'distinguishing between', from the verb *discriminare* (see **DISCRIMINATE**).

discriminant analysis ▶ **noun** [mass noun] statistical analysis using a discriminant function to assign data to one of two or more groups.

discriminant function ▶ **noun** Statistics a function of several variates used to assign items into one of two or more groups. The function for a particular set of items is obtained from measurements of the variates of items which belong to a known group.

discriminate /dɪˈskrɪmɪneɪt/ ▶ **verb** [no obj.] **1** recognize a distinction; differentiate: *babies can* ***discriminate between*** *different facial expressions of emotion.*
■ [with obj.] perceive or constitute the difference in or between: *features that* ***discriminate*** *this species* ***from*** *other gastropods.*
2 make an unjust or prejudicial distinction in the treatment of different categories of people or things, especially on the grounds of race, sex, or age: *existing employment policies* ***discriminate against*** *women.*
– DERIVATIVES **discriminately** adverb, **discriminative** adjective.
– ORIGIN early 17th cent.: from Latin *discriminat-* 'distinguished between', from the verb *discriminare*, from *discrimen* 'distinction', from the verb *discernere* (see **DISCERN**).

discriminating ▶ **adjective** (of a person) having or showing refined taste or good judgement: *he became a discriminating collector and patron of the arts* | [as

plural noun **the discriminating**] *a fine Italian restaurant for the discriminating.*
– DERIVATIVES **discriminatingly** adverb.

discrimination ▶ **noun** [mass noun] **1** the unjust or prejudicial treatment of different categories of people or things, especially on the grounds of race, age, or sex: *victims of racial discrimination* | ***discrimination against*** *homosexuals.*
2 recognition and understanding of the difference between one thing and another: *discrimination between right and wrong* | [count noun] *young children have difficulties in making fine discriminations.*
▪ the ability to discern what is of high quality; good judgement or taste: *those who could afford to buy showed little taste or discrimination.* ▪ Psychology the ability to distinguish between different stimuli: [as modifier] *discrimination learning.*
3 Electronics the selection of a signal having a required characteristic, such as frequency or amplitude, by means of a discriminator which rejects all unwanted signals.

discriminator ▶ **noun 1** a characteristic which enables things, people, or classes to be distinguished from one another: *age should not be used as a primary discriminator in recruitment.*
2 Electronics a circuit or device which only produces an output when the input exceeds a fixed value.
▪ a circuit which converts a frequency-modulated signal into an amplitude-modulated one.

discriminatory /dɪˈskrɪmɪnət(ə)ri, dɪˌskrɪmɪˈneɪt(ə)ri/ ▶ **adjective** making or showing an unfair or prejudicial distinction between different categories of people or things, especially on the grounds of race, age, or sex: *discriminatory employment practices.*

discursive /dɪsˈkəːsɪv/ ▶ **adjective 1** digressing from subject to subject: *students often write dull, second-hand, discursive prose.*
▪ (of a style of speech or writing) fluent and expansive rather than formulaic or abbreviated: *the short story is concentrated, whereas the novel is discursive.*
2 of or relating to discourse or modes of discourse: *the attempt to transform utterances from one discursive context to another.*
3 Philosophy, archaic proceeding by argument or reasoning rather than by intuition.
– DERIVATIVES **discursively** adverb, **discursiveness** noun.
– ORIGIN late 16th cent.: from medieval Latin *discursivus*, from Latin *discurs-*, literally 'gone hastily to and fro', from the verb *discurrere* (see **DISCOURSE**).

discus /ˈdɪskəs/ ▶ **noun** (pl. **discuses**) **1** a heavy thick-centred disc thrown by an athlete, in ancient Greek games or in modern field events.
2 a small colourful freshwater fish with a rounded laterally compressed body, the young of which feed on slime produced by the parents' skin. It is native to South America and popular in aquaria.
• Genus *Symphysodon*, family Cichlidae: several species.
– ORIGIN via Latin from Greek *diskos*.

discuss ▶ **verb** [with obj.] talk about (something) with another person or group of people: *I* ***discussed*** *the matter* ***with*** *my wife* | [with clause] *they were discussing where to go for a drink.*
▪ talk or write about (a topic) in detail, taking into account different ideas and opinions: *in Chapter Six I discuss problems that arise in applying Darwin's ideas.*
– DERIVATIVES **discussable** adjective, **discusser** noun.
– ORIGIN late Middle English (in the sense 'dispel, disperse', also 'examine by argument'): from Latin *discuss-* 'dashed to pieces', later 'investigated', from the verb *discutere*, from *dis-* 'apart' + *quatere* 'shake'.

discussant ▶ **noun** a person who takes part in a discussion, especially a pre-arranged one.

discussion ▶ **noun** [mass noun] the action or process of talking about something, typically in order to reach a decision or to exchange ideas: *defence is the subject of considerable discussion in western Europe* | *the EC directive is currently* ***under discussion.***
▪ [count noun] a conversation or debate about a certain topic: *discussions about environmental improvement programmes.* ▪ [count noun] a detailed treatment of a particular topic in speech or writing.
– ORIGIN Middle English (denoting judicial examination): via Old French from late Latin *discussio(n-)*, from *discutere* 'investigate' (see **DISCUSS**).

disc wheel ▶ **noun** a bicycle wheel with a central disc in place of spokes.

disdain ▶ **noun** [mass noun] the feeling that someone or something is unworthy of one's consideration or respect; contempt: *her upper lip curled in disdain* | *an aristocratic* ***disdain for*** *manual labour.*
▶ **verb** [with obj.] consider to be unworthy of one's consideration: *gamblers disdain four-horse races.*
▪ refuse or reject (something) from feelings of pride or superiority: *she remained standing, pointedly disdaining his invitation to sit down* | [with infinitive] *he disdained to discuss the matter further.*
– ORIGIN Middle English: from Old French *desdeign* (noun), *desdeignier* (verb), based on Latin *dedignari*, from *de-* (expressing reversal) + *dignari* 'consider worthy' (from *dignus* 'worthy').

disdainful ▶ **adjective** showing contempt or lack of respect: *with a last disdainful look, she turned towards the door.*
– DERIVATIVES **disdainfully** adverb, **disdainfulness** noun.

disease ▶ **noun** a disorder of structure or function in a human, animal, or plant, especially one that produces specific signs or symptoms or that affects a specific location and is not simply a direct result of physical injury: *bacterial meningitis is quite a rare disease* | [mass noun] *a possible cause of heart disease.*
▪ figurative a particular quality, habit, or disposition regarded as adversely affecting a person or group of people: *we are suffering from the British disease of self-deprecation.*
– ORIGIN Middle English (in the sense 'lack of ease; inconvenience'): from Old French *desaise* 'lack of ease', from *des-* (expressing reversal) + *aise* 'ease'.

diseased ▶ **adjective** suffering from disease: *diseased trees.*
▪ figurative abnormal and corrupt: *I cannot bear your diseased view of mankind.*

diseconomy ▶ **noun** (pl. **-ies**) Economics an economic disadvantage such as an increase in cost arising from an increase in the size of an organization: *in an ideal world, these* ***diseconomies of scale*** *would be minimized.*

disembark ▶ **verb** [no obj.] leave a ship, aircraft, or train: *the passengers began to disembark.*
– DERIVATIVES **disembarkation** noun.
– ORIGIN late 16th cent.: from French *désembarquer*, Spanish *desembarcar*, or Italian *disimbarcare*, based on Latin *barca* 'ship's boat'.

disembarrass ▶ **verb** (**disembarrass oneself of/from**) free oneself of (a burden or nuisance): *shouldn't empires disembarrass themselves of elements which once served a purpose and no longer do?*
▪ [with obj.] rare make (someone or something) free from embarrassment.
– DERIVATIVES **disembarrassment** noun.

disembodied ▶ **adjective** separated from or existing without the body: *a disembodied ghost.*
▪ (of a sound) lacking any obvious physical source: *a disembodied voice at the end of the phone.*

disembody ▶ **verb** (**-ies**, **-ied**) [with obj.] separate or free (something) from its concrete form: *the play of light off the dome's glass further served to disembody it.*
– DERIVATIVES **disembodiment** noun.

disembogue /ˌdɪsɪmˈbəʊɡ, ˌdɪsɛm-/ ▶ **verb** (**disembogues**, **disembogued**, **disemboguing**) [no obj.] poetic/literary (of a river or stream) emerge or be discharged in quantity; pour out.
– ORIGIN late 16th cent.: from Spanish *desembocar*, from *des-* (expressing reversal) + *embocar* 'run into a creek or strait' (based on *boca* 'mouth').

disembowel /ˌdɪsɪmˈbaʊəl, ˌdɪsɛm-/ ▶ **verb** (**disembowelled**, **disembowelling**; US **disemboweled**, **disemboweling**) [with obj.] cut open and remove the internal organs of.
– DERIVATIVES **disembowelment** noun.

disembroil /ˌdɪsɪmˈbrɔɪl, ˌdɪsɛm-/ ▶ **verb** [with obj.] archaic free (someone or something) from confusion: *to disembroil a subject that seems to have perplexed even Antiquity.*

disempower ▶ **verb** [with obj.] make (a person or group) less powerful or confident: *the experience of hospital invariably disempowers women.*
– DERIVATIVES **disempowerment** noun.

disenchant ▶ **verb** [with obj.] (usu. **be disenchanted**) cause (someone) to be disappointed: *he may have been disenchanted by the loss of his huge following* | [as adj. **disenchanted**] *he became* ***disenchanted with*** *his erstwhile ally.*
– DERIVATIVES **disenchantingly** adverb, **disenchantment** noun.
– ORIGIN late 16th cent.: from French *désenchanter*, from *dés-* (expressing reversal) + *enchanter* (see **ENCHANT**).

disencumber ▶ **verb** [with obj.] free from or relieve of an encumbrance: *the sect claims to disencumber adherents of the untoward effects of past traumas.*

disendow ▶ **verb** [with obj.] deprive (someone or something) of an endowment, in particular deprive (a church) of the property and funds that it receives from the state.
– DERIVATIVES **disendowment** noun.

disenfranchise /ˌdɪsɪnˈfran(t)ʃʌɪz, ˌdɪsɛn-/ (also **disfranchise**) ▶ **verb** [with obj.] deprive (someone) of the right to vote: *the law disenfranchised some 3,000 voters on the basis of a residence qualification.*
▪ deprive (someone) of a right or privilege: *the move would disenfranchise the disabled from using the town centre.* ▪ archaic deprive (a place) of the right to send a representative to Parliament. ▪ archaic deprive (someone) of the rights and privileges of a free inhabitant of a borough, city, or country.
– DERIVATIVES **disenfranchisement** noun.

disengage /ˌdɪsɪnˈɡeɪdʒ, ˌdɪsɛn-/ ▶ **verb 1** [with obj.] separate or release (someone or something) from something to which they are attached or connected: *I* ***disengaged*** *his hand* ***from*** *mine* | *they clung together for a moment, then she* ***disengaged herself.***
▪ [no obj.] become released: *the clutch will not disengage.* ▪ remove (troops) from an area of conflict: *the ceasefire gave the commanders a chance to disengage their forces* | [no obj.] *it seemed the only means by which the Americans could* ***disengage from*** *Korea.*
2 [no obj.] Fencing pass the point of one's sword over or under the opponent's sword to change the line of attack.
▶ **noun** Fencing a disengaging movement.

disengaged ▶ **adjective** emotionally detached: *the students were oddly disengaged, as if they didn't believe they could control their lives.*

disengagement ▶ **noun** [mass noun] **1** the action or process of withdrawing from involvement in a particular activity, situation, or group: *his* ***disengagement from*** *the provisional government.*
▪ the withdrawal of military forces or the renunciation of military or political influence in a particular area. ▪ the process of separating or releasing something or of becoming separated or released: *the mechanism prevents accidental disengagement.* ▪ archaic the breaking off of an engagement to be married.
2 emotional detachment; objectivity: *contemporary criticism can afford neutral disengagement.*
3 Fencing another term for **DISENGAGE**.

disentailment ▶ **noun** [mass noun] Law the action of freeing property from entail: *the disentailment of the Church's landed property.*
– DERIVATIVES **disentail** verb.

disentangle ▶ **verb** [with obj.] free (something or someone) from something that they have become entangled with: *'I must go,' she said,* ***disentangling*** *her fingers* ***from*** *Gabriel's* | figurative *it became more and more difficult to* ***disentangle*** *fact* ***from*** *prejudice.*
▪ remove knots or tangles from (wool, rope, or hair): *Allen was on his knees disentangling a coil of rope.*
– DERIVATIVES **disentanglement** noun.

disenthral /ˌdɪsɪnˈθrɔːl, ˌdɪsɛn-/ (US **disenthrall**) ▶ **verb** (**disenthralled**, **disenthralling**) [with obj.] poetic/literary set free: *I disenthral my mind from theories.*
– DERIVATIVES **disenthralment** noun.

disentitle ▶ **verb** [with obj.] (often **be disentitled**) deprive (someone) of a right: *she was* ***disentitled to*** *a redundancy payment.*
– DERIVATIVES **disentitlement** noun.

disentomb ▶ **verb** [with obj.] remove (something) from a tomb: *a mummy which we saw disentombed* | figurative *he disentombed a great part of the early history of England.*
– DERIVATIVES **disentombment** noun.

disequilibrium /dɪsiːkwɪˈlɪbrɪəm, ˌdɪsɛk-/ ▶ **noun** [mass noun] a loss or lack of equilibrium or stability, especially in relation to supply, demand, and prices.

disestablish ▶ **verb** [with obj.] (usu. **be disestablished**) deprive (an organization, especially a national Church) of its official status.
– DERIVATIVES **disestablishment** noun.

disesteem dated ▶ **noun** [mass noun] low esteem or regard: *language is not insulting unless it is intended to show contempt or disesteem.*

▶ **verb** [with obj.] have a low opinion of: *novels and short stories have been disesteemed.*

diseuse /diːˈzəːz/ ▶ **noun** a female artiste entertaining with spoken monologues.
– ORIGIN French, literally 'talker', feminine of *diseur*, from *dire* 'to say'.

disfavour (US **disfavor**) ▶ **noun** [mass noun] disapproval or dislike: *the headmaster regarded her with disfavour.*
■ the state of being disliked: *coal fell into disfavour because steam engines are noisy and polluting.*
▶ **verb** [with obj.] put (someone or something) at a disadvantage or treat (them) as undesirable: *the system favours those who employ less labour and disfavours those who employ more.*

disfellowship ▶ **noun** [mass noun] exclusion from fellowship, especially as a form of discipline in some Protestant and Mormon Churches.
▶ **verb** (**disfellowshipped**, **disfellowshipping**) [with obj.] chiefly US exclude (someone) from fellowship.

disfigure ▶ **verb** [with obj.] spoil the attractiveness of: *litter disfigures the countryside* | [as adj. **disfiguring**] *a disfiguring birthmark.*
– DERIVATIVES **disfiguration** noun, **disfigurement** noun.
– ORIGIN late Middle English: from Old French *desfigurer*, based on Latin *figura* 'figure'.

disforest ▶ **verb** another term for **DISAFFOREST**.
– DERIVATIVES **disforestation** noun.

disfranchise ▶ **verb** another term for **DISENFRANCHISE**.

disfrock ▶ **verb** another term for **DEFROCK**.

disgorge ▶ **verb** [with obj.] **1** cause to pour out: *the combine disgorged a steady stream of grain.*
■ (of a building or vehicle) discharge (the occupants): *an aircraft disgorging paratroopers.* ■ yield or give up (funds, especially funds that have been dishonestly acquired): *they were made to disgorge all the profits made from the record.* ■ eject (food) from the throat or mouth. ■ [no obj.] (of a river) empty into a sea: *the Nile disgorges into the sea at Rashid.*
2 (usu. **be disgorged**) remove the sediment from (a sparkling wine) after fermentation: *the wine is aged in the bottle before it is disgorged.*
– DERIVATIVES **disgorgement** noun.
– ORIGIN late 15th cent.: from Old French *desgorger*, from *des-* (expressing removal) + *gorge* 'throat'.

disgorger ▶ **noun** Fishing a device for extracting a hook from a fish's throat.

disgrace ▶ **noun** [mass noun] loss of reputation or the respect of others, especially as the result of a dishonourable action: *he left the army **in disgrace** | if he'd gone back it would have brought disgrace on the family.*
■ [in sing.] a person or thing regarded as shameful and unacceptable: *he's **a disgrace to** the legal profession.*
▶ **verb** [with obj.] bring shame or discredit on (someone or something): *you have disgraced the family name | John stiffened his jaw so he wouldn't **disgrace himself** by crying.*
■ (usu. **be disgraced**) cause (someone) to fall from favour or a position of power or honour: *he has been publicly disgraced for offences for which he was not guilty.*
– ORIGIN mid 16th cent. (as a verb): via French from Italian *disgrazia* (noun), *disgraziare* (verb), from *dis-* (expressing reversal) + Latin *gratia* 'grace'.

disgraceful ▶ **adjective** shockingly unacceptable: *a disgraceful waste of money* | [with clause] *it is disgraceful that they should be denied unemployment benefits.*
– DERIVATIVES **disgracefully** adverb.

disgruntled ▶ **adjective** angry or dissatisfied: *judges receive letters from disgruntled members of the public.*
– DERIVATIVES **disgruntlement** noun.
– ORIGIN mid 17th cent.: from **DIS-** (as an intensifier) + dialect *gruntle* 'utter little grunts', from **GRUNT**.

disguise ▶ **verb** [with obj.] give (someone or oneself) a different appearance in order to conceal one's identity: *he **disguised himself as** a girl | Bryn was disguised as a priest.*
■ make (something) unrecognizable by altering its appearance, sound, taste, or smell: *does holding a handkerchief over the mouthpiece really disguise your voice?* ■ conceal the nature or existence of (a feeling or situation): *he made no effort to disguise his contempt.*
▶ **noun** a means of altering one's appearance or concealing one's identity: *his bizarre disguise drew stares from fellow shoppers | I put on dark glasses as a disguise.*
■ [mass noun] the state of having altered one's appearance in order to conceal one's identity: *I told them you were a policewoman **in disguise**.* ■ [mass noun] the concealing of one's true intentions or feelings: *rows of small children looked at her without disguise.*
– DERIVATIVES **disguisement** noun (archaic).
– ORIGIN Middle English (meaning 'change one's usual style of dress', with no implication of concealing one's identity): from Old French *desguisier*.

disgust ▶ **noun** [mass noun] a feeling of revulsion or profound disapproval aroused by something unpleasant or offensive: *the sight filled her with disgust | some of the audience walked out **in disgust**.*
▶ **verb** [with obj.] (often **be disgusted**) cause (someone) to feel revulsion or profound disapproval: *I was disgusted with myself for causing so much misery* | [as adj. **disgusted**] *a disgusted look.*
– DERIVATIVES **disgustedly** adverb.
– ORIGIN late 16th cent.: from early modern French *desgoust* or Italian *disgusto*, from Latin *dis-* (expressing reversal) + *gustus* 'taste'.

disgustful ▶ **adjective** old-fashioned term for **DISGUSTING**.

disgusting ▶ **adjective** arousing revulsion or strong indignation: *he had the most disgusting rotten teeth | I think the decision is disgusting.*
– DERIVATIVES **disgustingly** adverb, **disgustingness** noun.

dish ▶ **noun 1** a shallow, typically flat-bottomed container for cooking or serving food: *an ovenproof dish.*
■ the food contained or served in such a container: *a dish of sauté potatoes.* ■ a particular variety or preparation of food served as part of a meal: *fresh fish dishes* | figurative *films are always the main Christmas dish.* ■ (**the dishes**) all the items that have been used in the preparation, serving, and eating of a meal: *I left the children to do the dishes.* ■ [usu. with modifier] a shallow, concave receptacle, especially one intended to hold a particular substance: *a soap dish.* ■ (also **dish aerial**) a bowl-shaped radio aerial. See also **SATELLITE DISH**.
2 informal a sexually attractive person: *I gather he's quite a dish.*
■ (**one's dish**) dated a thing that one particularly enjoys or does particularly well: *as a public relations man this was my dish and the campaign was right up my street.*
3 (**the dish**) informal information which is not generally known or available: *if he has the real dish I wish he'd tell us.*
4 [mass noun] concavity of a spoked wheel resulting from a difference in spoke tension on each side and consequent sideways displacement of the rim in relation to the hub.
▶ **verb** [with obj.] **1** (**dish something out/up**) put (food) on to a plate or plates before a meal: *Steve was dishing up vegetables* | [with two objs] *she dished him out a plate of stew* | figurative *pop stars who dish up remixes of their old hits.*
■ (**dish something out**) dispense something in a casual or indiscriminate way: *the banks dished out loans to all and sundry.* ■ (**dish it out**) informal subject others to criticism or punishment: *you can dish it out but you can't take it.* ■ [no obj.] N. Amer. informal gossip or share information, especially information of an intimate or scandalous nature: *groups gather to brag about babies and dish about romances.*
2 informal, chiefly Brit. utterly destroy, confound, or defeat (someone or something): *the election interview dished Labour's chances.*
3 give concavity to (a wheel) by tensioning the spokes (see sense 4 of the noun).
– PHRASES **dish the dirt** informal reveal or spread scandalous information or gossip.
– DERIVATIVES **dishful** noun (pl. **-fuls**).
– ORIGIN Old English *disc* 'plate, bowl' (related to Dutch *dis*, German *Tisch* 'table'), based on Latin *discus* (see **DISCUS**).

dishabille /ˌdɪsaˈbiːl, -ˈbiː/ ▶ **noun** variant spelling of **DÉSHABILLÉ**.

disharmony ▶ **noun** [mass noun] lack of harmony or agreement.
– DERIVATIVES **disharmonious** adjective, **disharmoniously** adverb.

dishcloth ▶ **noun** a cloth for washing or drying dishes.

dishcloth gourd ▶ **noun** North American term for **LOOFAH**.

dishdasha /ˈdɪʃˌdaʃə/ (also **dishdash**) ▶ **noun** a long robe with long sleeves, worn by men from the Arabian peninsula.
– ORIGIN late 19th cent.: from Arabic *dišdāša*.

dishearten ▶ **verb** [with obj.] (often **be disheartened**) cause (someone) to lose determination or confidence: *the farmer was disheartened by the damage to his crops.*
– DERIVATIVES **dishearteningly** adverb, **disheartenment** noun.

dished ▶ **adjective** having the shape of a dish; concave: *overloaded timber floors are likely to sag, producing a dished or sloping floor surface.*

dishevelled /dɪˈʃɛv(ə)ld/ (US **disheveled**) ▶ **adjective** (of a person's hair, clothes, or appearance) untidy; disordered: *a man with long dishevelled hair.*
– DERIVATIVES **dishevel** verb (**dishevelled**, **dishevelling**; US **disheveled**, **disheveling**), **dishevelment** noun.
– ORIGIN late Middle English: from obsolete *dishevely*, from Old French *deschevele*, past participle of *descheveler* (based on *chevel* 'hair', from Latin *capillus*). The original sense was 'having the hair uncovered'; later, referring to the hair itself, 'hanging loose', hence 'disordered, untidy'. Compare with **UNKEMPT**.

dishonest ▶ **adjective** behaving or prone to behave in an untrustworthy or fraudulent way: *he was a dishonest hypocrite prepared to exploit his family.*
■ intended to mislead or cheat: *he gave the editor a dishonest account of events.*
– DERIVATIVES **dishonestly** adverb.
– ORIGIN late Middle English (in the sense 'dishonourable, unchaste'): from Old French *deshoneste*, Latin *dehonestus*.

dishonesty ▶ **noun** (pl. **-ies**) [mass noun] deceitfulness shown in someone's character or behaviour: *the dismissal of thirty civil servants for dishonesty and misconduct.*
■ [count noun] a fraudulent or deceitful act: *they are tackling the divisions and dishonesties on the campus.*
– ORIGIN late Middle English (in the sense 'dishonour, sexual misconduct'): from Old French *deshoneste* 'indecency' (see **DISHONEST**).

dishonour (US **dishonor**) ▶ **noun** [mass noun] a state of shame or disgrace: *the incident brought dishonour upon the police.*
▶ **verb** [with obj.] **1** bring shame or disgrace on: *you have betrayed our master's trust and dishonoured the Banner.*
■ archaic violate the chastity of (a woman); rape: *she was now unworthy of his notice, having been dishonoured by Casim.*
2 fail to observe or respect (an agreement or principle): *the community has its own principles it can itself honour or dishonour.*
■ refuse to accept or pay (a cheque or a bill of exchange).
– ORIGIN Middle English: from Old French *deshonor* (noun), *deshonorer* (verb), based on Latin *honor* 'honour'.

dishonourable (US **dishonorable**) ▶ **adjective** bringing shame or disgrace on someone or something: *his crimes are petty and dishonourable.*
– DERIVATIVES **dishonourableness** noun, **dishonourably** adverb.

dishonourable discharge ▶ **noun** the dismissal of someone from the armed forces as a result of criminal or morally unacceptable actions.

dishpan ▶ **noun** N. Amer. a bowl in which dishes are washed.

dishrag ▶ **noun** a dishcloth.

dishwasher ▶ **noun 1** a machine for washing dishes automatically.
2 a person employed to wash dishes.

dishwater ▶ **noun** [mass noun] dirty water in which dishes have been washed: figurative *I sipped the barely brown dishwater he passed off as coffee.*
– PHRASES **dull as dishwater** see **DULL**.

dishy ▶ **adjective** (**dishier**, **dishiest**) informal, chiefly Brit. sexually attractive.
■ N. Amer. informal scandalous or gossipy: *she's the perfect candidate for a dishy biography.*

disillusion /ˌdɪsɪˈl(j)uːʒ(ə)n/ ▶ **noun** [mass noun] disappointment resulting from the discovery that something is not as good as one believed it to be.
▶ **verb** [with obj.] cause (someone) to realize that a belief they hold is false: *if they think we have a magic formula to solve the problem, don't disillusion them.*

disillusioned ▶ **adjective** disappointed in someone or something that one discovers to be less good than one had believed: *the minority groups were completely **disillusioned with** the party.*

disillusionment ▶ **noun** [mass noun] a feeling of disappointment resulting from the discovery that something is not as good as one believed it to be: *the high abstention rate at the election reflected the voters' growing **disillusionment with** politics.*

disincarnate /ˌdɪsɪŋˈkɑːnət/ ▶ **adjective** another term for **DISCARNATE**.

disincentive ▶ **noun** a factor, especially a financial disadvantage, that tends to discourage people from doing something: *spiralling house prices are beginning to act as a disincentive to development.*
▶ **adjective** tending to discourage: *higher taxes have major disincentive effects on work effort.*

disinclination ▶ **noun** [in sing.] a reluctance or lack of enthusiasm: *Lucy felt a strong **disinclination to** talk about her engagement.*

disinclined ▶ **adjective** [predic., with infinitive] unwilling; reluctant: *the rural community was disinclined to abandon the old ways.*

disincorporate ▶ **verb** [with obj.] dissolve (a corporate body).

disinfect ▶ **verb** [with obj.] clean (something) with a disinfectant in order to destroy bacteria: *he disinfected and dressed the cut on his forehead.*
– DERIVATIVES **disinfection** noun.
– ORIGIN late 16th cent. (in the sense 'rid of infection'): from French *désinfecter*, from *dés-* (expressing reversal) + *infecter* 'to infect'.

disinfectant ▶ **noun** [mass noun] a chemical liquid that destroys bacteria.
▶ **adjective** causing disinfection: *cleansing and disinfectant products.*

disinfest ▶ **verb** [with obj.] rid (someone or something) of infesting vermin.
– DERIVATIVES **disinfestation** noun.

disinflation ▶ **noun** [mass noun] Economics reduction in the rate of inflation.
– DERIVATIVES **disinflationary** adjective.

disinformation ▶ **noun** [mass noun] false information which is intended to mislead, especially propaganda issued by a government organization to a rival power or the media.
– ORIGIN 1950s: formed on the pattern of Russian *dezinformatsiya*.

disingenuous /ˌdɪsɪnˈdʒɛnjʊəs/ ▶ **adjective** not candid or sincere, typically by pretending that one knows less about something than one really does.
– DERIVATIVES **disingenuously** adverb, **disingenuousness** noun.

disinherit ▶ **verb** (**disinherited**, **disinheriting**) [with obj.] change one's will or take other steps to prevent (someone) from inheriting one's property.
– DERIVATIVES **disinheritance** noun.
– ORIGIN late Middle English (superseding earlier *disherit*): from **DIS-** (expressing removal) + *inherit* in the obsolete sense 'make someone an heir'.

disinhibit ▶ **verb** (**disinhibited**, **disinhibiting**) [with obj.] make (someone or something) less inhibited: *as well as disinhibiting me, he educated me.*
– DERIVATIVES **disinhibition** noun.

disintegrate /dɪsˈɪntɪɡreɪt/ ▶ **verb** [no obj.] break up into small parts, typically as the result of impact or decay: *when the missile struck, the car disintegrated in a sheet of searing flame* | figurative *the marriage disintegrated amid allegations that she was having an affair.*
■ informal suffer from a mental breakdown: *I thought that when I finished working on the book I'd disintegrate.* ■ Physics undergo or cause to undergo disintegration at a subatomic level: [no obj.] *a meson can spontaneously disintegrate* | [with obj.] *it has become a relatively easy matter to disintegrate almost any atom.*
– DERIVATIVES **disintegrative** adjective, **disintegrator** noun.

disintegration ▶ **noun** [mass noun] the process of losing cohesion: *the twin problems of economic failure and social disintegration.*
■ the process of coming to pieces: *the disintegration of infected cells.* ■ breakdown of the personality: *loss of self-esteem leads to the disintegration of a proud man.* ■ Physics a process in which a nucleus or other subatomic particle emits a smaller particle or divides into smaller particles.

disinter /ˌdɪsɪnˈtəː/ ▶ **verb** (**disinterred**, **disinterring**) [with obj.] dig up (something that has been buried, especially a corpse).
■ discover (something that is well hidden): *he has disinterred and translated an important collection of writings.*
– DERIVATIVES **disinterment** noun.
– ORIGIN early 17th cent.: from French *désenterrer*, from *dis-* (expressing reversal) + *enterrer* 'to inter'.

disinterest ▶ **noun** [mass noun] **1** the state of not being influenced by personal involvement in something; impartiality: *I do not claim any scholarly disinterest with this book.*
2 lack of interest in something: *he chided Dennis for his **disinterest in** anything that is not his own idea.*

disinterested ▶ **adjective** **1** not influenced by considerations of personal advantage: *a banker is under an obligation to give disinterested advice.*
2 having or feeling no interest in something: *her father was so disinterested in her progress that he only visited the school once.*
– DERIVATIVES **disinterestedly** adverb, **disinterestedness** noun.
– ORIGIN early 17th cent.: past participle of the rare verb *disinterest* 'rid of interest or concern', from **DIS-** (expressing removal) + the verb **INTEREST**.

USAGE Nowhere are the battle lines more deeply drawn in usage questions than over the difference between **disinterested** and **uninterested**. According to traditional guidelines, **disinterested** should never be used to mean 'not interested' (i.e. it is not a synonym for **uninterested**) but only to mean 'impartial', as in *the judgements of **disinterested** outsiders are likely to be more useful*. Ironically, the earliest recorded sense of **disinterested** is for the disputed sense. Today, the 'incorrect' use of **disinterested** is widespread: around 20 per cent of citations on the British National Corpus for **disinterested** are for this sense.

disintermediation /ˌdɪsɪntəmiːdɪˈeɪʃ(ə)n/ ▶ **noun** [mass noun] Economics reduction in the use of banks and savings institutions as intermediaries in the borrowing and investment of money, in favour of direct involvement in the securities market.

disinvent ▶ **verb** [with obj.] undo the invention of (something): *you can't disinvent nuclear power.*

disinvest ▶ **verb** [no obj.] withdraw or reduce an investment: *the oil industry began to disinvest, and oil share prices have fallen* | [with obj.] *they opposed the move to disinvest shares.*
– DERIVATIVES **disinvestment** noun.

disinvite ▶ **verb** [with obj.] withdraw or cancel an invitation to (someone): *the White House called to disinvite him from the President's party.*

disinvoltura /ˌdɪsɪnvɒlˈtjʊərə/ ▶ **noun** [mass noun] self-assurance; lack of constraint: *a certain disinvoltura was all very well, but not as unthinkingly as this!*
– ORIGIN mid 19th cent.: from Italian, from *disinvolto* 'unembarrassed', from *disinvolgere* 'unwind'.

disjecta membra /dɪsˌdʒɛktə ˈmɛmbrə/ ▶ **plural noun** scattered fragments, especially of written work.
– ORIGIN Latin, alteration of *disjecti membra poetae* (used by Horace) 'limbs of a dismembered poet'.

disjoin ▶ **verb** [with obj.] (often **be disjoined**) separate or disunite: *they asked that their parish be disjoined from Lewis and added to Harris.*
– ORIGIN late Middle English: from Old French *desjoindre*, from Latin *disjungere*, from *dis-* (expressing reversal) + *jungere* 'to join'.

disjoint ▶ **verb** [with obj.] disturb the cohesion or organization of: *the loss of the area disjointed military plans.*
■ dated take apart at the joints: *disjoint a six-pound fowl, put in a pot, and simmer until tender.*
▶ **adjective** Mathematics (of two or more sets) having no elements in common.
– ORIGIN late Middle English (as an adjective in the sense 'disjointed'): from Old French *desjoint* 'separated', from the verb *desjoindre* (see **DISJOIN**).

disjointed ▶ **adjective** lacking a coherent sequence or connection: *piecing together disjointed fragments of information.*
– DERIVATIVES **disjointedly** adverb, **disjointedness** noun.

disjunct /ˈdɪsdʒʌŋ(k)t/ ▶ **noun** **1** Logic each of the terms of a disjunctive proposition.
2 Grammar another term for **SENTENCE ADVERB**.
▶ **adjective** disjoined and distinct from one another: *these items of evidence are just phrases and clauses, often wildly disjunct.*
– ORIGIN late Middle English: from Latin *disjunctus* 'disjoined, separated', from the verb *disjungere*.

disjunction ▶ **noun** **1** a lack of correspondence or consistency: *there is a **disjunction between** the skills taught in education and those demanded in the labour market.*
2 [mass noun] Logic the relation of two distinct alternatives.
■ [count noun] a statement expressing this relation (especially one using the word 'or').
– ORIGIN late Middle English: from Latin *disjunctio(n-)*, from *disjungere* 'disjoin' (see **DISJUNCT**).

disjunctive ▶ **adjective** **1** lacking connection: *the novel's disjunctive detail.*
2 Grammar (of a conjunction) expressing a choice between two mutually exclusive possibilities, for example *or* in *she asked if he was going or staying*. Compare with **COPULATIVE**.
■ Logic (of a proposition) expressing alternatives.
▶ **noun** Grammar a disjunctive conjunction or other word.
■ Logic a disjunctive proposition.
– DERIVATIVES **disjunctively** adverb.
– ORIGIN late Middle English (in sense 2): from Latin *disjunctivus*, from *disjunct-* 'disjoined' (see **DISJUNCT**).

disjuncture ▶ **noun** a separation or disconnection: *the monstrous disjuncture between his private and his public life.*
– ORIGIN late Middle English: from medieval Latin *disjunctura*, from Latin *disjunct-* 'disjoined' (see **DISJUNCT**).

disk ▶ **noun** US spelling of **DISC**, also widely used in computing contexts.
– DERIVATIVES **diskless** adjective.

disk drive ▶ **noun** a device which allows a computer to read from and write on to computer disks.

diskette ▶ **noun** another term for **FLOPPY**.

Disko /ˈdɪskəʊ/ an island with extensive coal deposits on the west coast of Greenland. Its chief settlement is Godhavn.

disk operating system ▶ **noun** see **DOS**.

dislike ▶ **verb** [with obj.] feel distaste for or hostility towards: *he was not distressed by the death of a man he had always disliked.*
▶ **noun** [mass noun] a feeling of distaste or hostility: *despite her dislike of publicity, she was quite a celebrated figure* | *they had **taken a dislike to** each other.*
■ [count noun] a thing to which one feels aversion: *I know all his likes and dislikes.*
– DERIVATIVES **dislikable** (also **dislikeable**) adjective.

dislocate /ˈdɪsləkeɪt/ ▶ **verb** [with obj.] disturb the normal arrangement or position of (something, typically a joint in the body): *he dislocated his shoulder in training.*
■ (often **be dislocated**) disturb the organization of; disrupt: *trade was dislocated by a famine.* ■ (often **be dislocated**) move from its proper place or position: *the symbol is dislocated from its political context.*
– ORIGIN late 16th cent.: probably a back-formation from **DISLOCATION**, but perhaps from medieval Latin *dislocatus* 'moved from a former position', from the verb *dislocare*.

dislocation /ˌdɪslə(ʊ)ˈkeɪʃ(ə)n/ ▶ **noun** [mass noun] disturbance from a proper, original, or usual place or state: *social dislocation and uncertainty do not necessarily make people turn to God* | [count noun] *massive dislocations accompany the rise of a new political force.*
■ injury or disability caused when the normal position of a joint or other part of the body is disturbed: *congenital dislocation of the hip* | [count noun] *dealing with fractures and dislocations.* ■ [count noun] Crystallography a displacement of part of a crystal lattice structure.
– ORIGIN late Middle English: from Old French, or from medieval Latin *dislocatio(n-)*, from the verb *dislocare* (see **DISLOCATE**), based on Latin *locare* 'to place'.

dislodge ▶ **verb** [with obj.] remove from an established or fixed position: *the hoofs of their horses dislodged loose stones* | figurative *this gripping race still offers the opportunity to dislodge the leader.*
– DERIVATIVES **dislodgeable** adjective, **dislodgement** noun.
– ORIGIN late Middle English: from Old French *deslogier*, from *des-* (expressing reversal) + *logier* 'encamp', from *loge* (see **LODGE**).

disloyal ▶ **adjective** failing to be loyal to a person, country, or body to which one has obligations: *she felt that inquiring into her father's past would be **disloyal to** her mother.*
■ (of an action, speech, or thought) demonstrating a lack of loyalty: *disloyal mutterings about his leadership.*

– DERIVATIVES **disloyally** adverb, **disloyalty** noun.
– ORIGIN late 15th cent.: from Old French *desloial*, from *des-* (expressing negation) + *loial* 'loyal'.

dismal /ˈdɪzm(ə)l/ ▶ **adjective** depressing; dreary: *the dismal weather made the late afternoon seem like evening.*
■(of a person or their mood) gloomy: *his dismal mood was not dispelled by finding the house empty.* ■ informal pitifully or disgracefully bad: *he shuddered as he watched his team's dismal performance.*
– PHRASES **the dismals** archaic, informal low spirits: *a fit of the dismals.*
– DERIVATIVES **dismally** adverb, **dismalness** noun.
– ORIGIN late Middle English: from earlier *dismal* (noun), denoting the two days in each month which in medieval times were believed to be unlucky, from Anglo-Norman French *dis mal*, from medieval Latin *dies mali* 'evil days'.

dismal science ▶ **noun** [in sing.] (usu. **the dismal science**) humorous economics.

Dismal Swamp another name for **GREAT DISMAL SWAMP**.

dismantle ▶ **verb** [with obj.] (often **be dismantled**) take to pieces: *the engines were dismantled and the bits piled into a heap* | figurative *the old regime was dismantled.*
– DERIVATIVES **dismantlement** noun, **dismantler** noun.
– ORIGIN late 16th cent. (in the sense 'destroy the defensive capability of (a fortification)'): from Old French *desmanteler*, from *des-* (expressing reversal) + *manteler* 'fortify' (from Latin *mantellum* 'cloak').

dismast ▶ **verb** [with obj.] break or force down the mast or masts of (a ship): [as adj. **dismasted**] *a dismasted ship wallowing in stormy seas.*

dismay ▶ **verb** [with obj.] (usu. **be dismayed**) cause (someone) to feel consternation and distress: *they were dismayed by the U-turn in policy.*
▶ **noun** [mass noun] consternation and distress, typically that caused by something unexpected: ***to his dismay**, she left him.*
– ORIGIN Middle English: from Old French, based on Latin *dis-* (expressing negation) + the Germanic base of **MAY**[1].

dismember /dɪsˈmɛmbə/ ▶ **verb** [with obj.] cut off the limbs of (a person or animal): [as adj. **dismembered**] *he buried their dismembered bodies in the back garden.*
■partition or divide up (a territory or organization): *the major European states thought Russia intended to dismember the Ottoman Empire.*
– DERIVATIVES **dismemberment** noun.
– ORIGIN Middle English: from Old French *desmembrer*, based on Latin *dis-* 'apart' + *membrum* 'limb'.

dismiss ▶ **verb** [with obj.] order or allow to leave; send away: *she dismissed the taxi at the corner of the road.*
■discharge from employment or office, typically on the grounds of unsatisfactory performance or dishonourable behaviour: *the prime minister dismissed five members of his Cabinet.* ■ [no obj.] (of a group assembled under someone's authority) disperse: *he told his company to dismiss.* ■ Law refuse further hearing to (a case): *the judge dismissed the case for lack of evidence.* ■ Cricket end the innings of (a batsman or a side): *Australia were dismissed for 118.* ■ deliberately cease to think about: *he suspected a double meaning in her words, but dismissed the thought.* ■ treat as unworthy of serious consideration: *it would be easy to **dismiss** him **as** all brawn and no brain.*
– DERIVATIVES **dismissal** noun, **dismissible** adjective.
– ORIGIN late Middle English: from medieval Latin *dismiss-*, variant of Latin *dimiss-* 'sent away', from the verb *dimittere*.

dismissive ▶ **adjective** feeling or showing that something is unworthy of consideration: *monetarist theory is dismissive of the need to control local spending* | *his dismissive attitude towards women left him isolated.*
– DERIVATIVES **dismissively** adverb, **dismissiveness** noun.

dismount ▶ **verb** **1** [no obj.] alight from a horse, bicycle, or anything that one is riding.
■[with obj.] cause to fall or alight: *his escort had dismounted a trooper.*
2 [with obj.] remove (something) from its support: *we have to dismount the pump.*
■Computing make (a disk or disk drive) unavailable for use.
– ORIGIN mid 16th cent.: from **DIS-** + **MOUNT**[1], probably on the pattern of Old French *desmonter*, medieval Latin *dismontare*.

Disney, Walt (1901–66), American animator and film producer; full name *Walter Elias Disney*. He made his name with the creation of cartoon characters such as Mickey Mouse, Donald Duck, Goofy, and Pluto. *Snow White and the Seven Dwarfs* (1937) was the first full-length cartoon feature film with sound and colour. Other notable films: *Pinocchio* (1940), *Dumbo* (1941), and *Bambi* (1942).

disobedience ▶ **noun** [mass noun] failure or refusal to obey rules or someone in authority: *disobedience to law is sometimes justified.*

disobedient ▶ **adjective** refusing to obey rules or someone in authority: *Larry was stern with disobedient employees.*
– DERIVATIVES **disobediently** adverb.
– ORIGIN late Middle English: from Old French *desobedient*, based on Latin *oboedient-* 'obeying' (see **OBEDIENT**).

disobey ▶ **verb** [with obj.] fail to obey (rules, a command, or someone in authority): *around 1,000 soldiers had disobeyed orders and surrendered.*
– DERIVATIVES **disobeyer** noun.
– ORIGIN late Middle English: from Old French *desobeir*, based on Latin *oboedire* 'obey' (see **OBEY**).

disoblige ▶ **verb** [with obj.] offend (someone) by not acting in accordance with their wishes: *one didn't disoblige them if one could help it.*
– ORIGIN late 16th cent. (in the sense 'release from an obligation'): from French *désobliger*, based on Latin *obligare* 'oblige'.

disobliging ▶ **adjective** deliberately unhelpful; uncooperative.

disomy /dʌɪˈsəʊmi/ ▶ **noun** [mass noun] Genetics the condition of having a chromosome represented twice in a chromosomal complement.
– DERIVATIVES **disomic** adjective.
– ORIGIN late 20th cent.: from **DI-**[1] 'two' + **-SOME**[3] + **-Y**[3].

disorder ▶ **noun** [mass noun] a state of confusion: *signs of disorder and decay met them at each open door.*
■the disruption of peaceful and law-abiding behaviour: *recurrent food crises led to periodic outbreaks of disorder.* ■ [count noun] Medicine a disruption of normal physical or mental functions; a disease or abnormal condition: *skin disorders* | [mass noun] *an improved understanding of mental disorder.*
▶ **verb** [with obj.] [usu. as adj. **disordered**] disrupt the systematic functioning or neat arrangement of: *she went to comb her disordered hair* | *his sleep is disordered.*
■Medicine disrupt the healthy or normal functioning of: *a patient who is mentally disordered.*
– ORIGIN late 15th cent. (as a verb in the sense 'upset the order of'): alteration, influenced by **ORDER**, of earlier *disordain*, from Old French *desordener*, ultimately based on Latin *ordinare* 'ordain'.

disorderly ▶ **adjective** lacking organization; untidy: *his life was as disorderly as ever* | *a disorderly pile of books.*
■involving or contributing to a breakdown of peaceful and law-abiding behaviour: *they had no intention of staging a disorderly protest.*
– DERIVATIVES **disorderliness** noun.

disorderly conduct ▶ **noun** [mass noun] Law unruly behaviour constituting a minor offence.

disorderly house ▶ **noun** Law or archaic a brothel.

disorganized (also **-ise**) ▶ **adjective** not properly planned and controlled: *the campaign was hopelessly disorganized.*
■(of a person) unable to plan one's activities efficiently: *she's very muddly and disorganized.*
– DERIVATIVES **disorganization** noun.

disorient /dɪsˈɔːrɪɛnt/ ▶ **verb** chiefly US another term for **DISORIENTATE**.
– ORIGIN mid 17th cent.: from French *désorienter* 'turn from the east'.

disorientate ▶ **verb** [with obj.] [often as adj. **disorientated**] make (someone) lose their sense of direction: *when he emerged into the street he was totally disorientated.*
■make (someone) feel confused: *being near him made her feel weak and disorientated.*
– DERIVATIVES **disorientation** noun.

disown ▶ **verb** [with obj.] refuse to acknowledge or maintain any connection with: *Lovell's rich family had disowned him because of his marriage.*
– DERIVATIVES **disowner** noun, **disownment** noun.

disparage /dɪˈsparɪdʒ/ ▶ **verb** [with obj.] regard or represent as being of little worth: *he never missed an opportunity to disparage his competitors* | [as adj. **disparaging**] *disparaging remarks about council houses.*
– DERIVATIVES **disparagement** noun, **disparagingly** adverb.
– ORIGIN late Middle English (in the sense 'marry someone of unequal rank', also 'bring discredit on'): from Old French *desparagier* 'marry someone of unequal rank', based on Latin *par* 'equal'.

disparate /ˈdɪsp(ə)rət/ ▶ **adjective** essentially different in kind; not allowing comparison: *they inhabit disparate worlds of thought.*
■containing elements very different from one another: *a culturally disparate country.*
▶ **noun** (**disparates**) archaic things so unlike that there is no basis for comparison.
– DERIVATIVES **disparately** adverb, **disparateness** noun.
– ORIGIN late Middle English: from Latin *disparatus* 'separated', from the verb *disparare*, from *dis-* 'apart' + *parare* 'to prepare'; influenced in sense by Latin *dispar* 'unequal'.

disparity ▶ **noun** (pl. **-ies**) a great difference: *economic **disparities between** different regions of the country* | [mass noun] *the arrangements could lead to disparity of treatment between companies.*
– ORIGIN mid 16th cent.: from French *disparité*, from late Latin *disparitas*, based on Latin *paritas* 'parity'.

dispassionate ▶ **adjective** not influenced by strong emotion, and so able to be rational and impartial: *she dealt with life's disasters in a calm, dispassionate way.*
– DERIVATIVES **dispassion** noun, **dispassionately** adverb, **dispassionateness** noun.

dispatch (also **despatch**) ▶ **verb** [with obj.] **1** send off to a destination or for a purpose: *he dispatched messages back to base* | [with obj. and infinitive] *the government dispatched 150 police to restore order.*
2 deal with (a task, problem, or opponent) quickly and efficiently: *they dispatched the opposition.*
■kill: *he dispatched the animal with one blow.*
▶ **noun** **1** [mass noun] the sending of someone or something to a destination or for a purpose: *a resolution authorizing the dispatch of a peacekeeping force.*
■speed in action: *the situation might change, so he should proceed **with dispatch**.*
2 an official report on state or military affairs: *in his battle dispatch he described the gunner's bravery.*
■a report sent in by a newspaper's correspondent from a faraway place.
3 [mass noun] the killing of someone or something: *the executioner's merciful dispatch of his victims.*
– DERIVATIVES **dispatcher** noun.
– ORIGIN early 16th cent.: from Italian *dispacciare* or Spanish *despachar* 'expedite', from *dis-*, *des-* (expressing reversal) + the base of Italian *impacciare*, Spanish *empachar* 'hinder'.

dispatch box ▶ **noun** (also **dispatch case**) a container for dispatches, especially official state or military documents.
■(**the Dispatch Box**) a box in the British House of Commons next to which Ministers stand when speaking.

dispatch rider ▶ **noun** a messenger who delivers urgent business documents or military dispatches by motor cycle or (formerly) on horseback.

dispel /dɪˈspɛl/ ▶ **verb** (**dispelled**, **dispelling**) [with obj.] make (a doubt, feeling, or belief) disappear: *the brightness of the day did nothing to dispel Elaine's dejection.*
– DERIVATIVES **dispeller** noun.
– ORIGIN late Middle English: from Latin *dispellere*, from *dis-* 'apart' + *pellere* 'to drive'.

dispensable ▶ **adjective** able to be replaced or done without; superfluous: *the captain's loss of form made him dispensable.*
■(of a law or other rule) able to be relaxed in special cases.
– DERIVATIVES **dispensability** noun.
– ORIGIN early 16th cent. (in the sense 'permissible in special circumstances'): from medieval Latin *dispensabilis*, from Latin *dispensare* (see **DISPENSE**).

dispensary /dɪˈspɛns(ə)ri/ ▶ **noun** (pl. **-ies**) **1** a room where medicines are prepared and provided.
2 a clinic provided by public or charitable funds.
– ORIGIN late 17th cent.: from medieval Latin *dispensarium*, neuter (used as a noun) of *dispensarius*, from Latin *dispensare* (see **DISPENSE**).

dispensation ▶ **noun** **1** [mass noun] exemption from a rule or usual requirement: *although she was too*

young, she was given special dispensation to play two matches before her birthday | [count noun] they were given a dispensation to take most of the first week off.
■permission to be exempted from the laws or observances of the Church: *he received papal dispensation to hold a number of benefices* | [count noun] *the pope granted Henry a dispensation to marry Elizabeth of York.*
2 a system of order, government, or organization of a nation, community, etc., especially as existing at a particular time: *scholarship is conveyed to a wider audience than under the old dispensation.*
■(in Christian theology) a divinely ordained order prevailing at a particular period of history: *the Mosaic dispensation.* ■ archaic an act of divine providence: *the laws to which the creator in all his dispensations conforms.*
3 [mass noun] the action of distributing or supplying something: *regulations controlling dispensation of medications.*
– DERIVATIVES **dispensational** adjective.
– ORIGIN late Middle English: from Latin *dispensatio(n-)*, from the verb *dispensare* (see **DISPENSE**).

dispensationalism ▶ **noun** [mass noun] Christian Theology belief in a system of historical progression, as revealed in the Bible, consisting of a series of stages in God's self-revelation and plan of salvation.
– DERIVATIVES **dispensationalist** noun.

dispense /dɪˈspɛns/ ▶ **verb** **1** [with obj.] distribute or provide (a service or information) to a number of people: *orderlies went round dispensing drinks.*
■(of a machine) supply (a product or cash): *the machines dispense a range of drinks and snacks* | [as adj. **dispensing**] *a dispensing machine.* ■(of a chemist) make up and give out (medicine) according to a doctor's prescription.
2 [no obj.] (**dispense with**) manage without; get rid of: *let's dispense with the formalities, shall we?*
■(**dispense with**) give special exemption from (a law or rule): *the Secretary of State was empowered to dispense with the nationality requirement in individual cases.* ■ grant (someone) an exemption from a religious obligation: *the pope personally nominated him as bishop, dispensing him from his impediment.*
– PHRASES **dispense with someone's services** dismiss someone from a job.
– ORIGIN late Middle English: via Old French from Latin *dispensare* 'continue to weigh out or disburse', from the verb *dispendere*, based on *pendere* 'weigh'.

dispenser ▶ **noun** a person or thing that dispenses something: *his role as protector of the weak and dispenser of justice.*
■a person who prepares medicines in a dispensary. ■ [often with modifier] an automatic machine or container which is designed to release a specific amount of something: *a paper towel dispenser.*

dispensing chemist ▶ **noun** Brit. a person qualified to make up, advise on, and dispense medicine.

dispensing optician ▶ **noun** a person qualified to prescribe and dispense as well as to make glasses and contact lenses.

dispersal ▶ **noun** [mass noun] the action or process of distributing or spreading things or people over a wide area: *the dispersal of people to increasingly distant suburbs* | [count noun] *dispersals of archaic populations.*
■the splitting up of a group or gathering of people, causing them to leave in different directions: *the dispersal of the crowd by mounted police.* ■ the splitting up and selling off of a collection of artefacts or books: *the dispersal of the John Willett Collection* | [count noun] *colleges had made large dispersals, and the shops were filled with books from their stacks.*

dispersant ▶ **noun** a liquid or gas used to disperse small particles in a medium.

disperse /dɪˈspəːs/ ▶ **verb** [with obj.] distribute or spread over a wide area: *storms can disperse seeds via high altitudes* | *caravan sites could be dispersed among trees so as to be out of sight.*
■go or cause to go in different directions or to different destinations: [no obj.] *the crowd dispersed* | [with obj.] *the police used tear gas to disperse the protesters.* ■ cause (gas, smoke, mist, or cloud) to thin out and eventually disappear: *winds dispersed the bomb's radioactive cloud high in the atmosphere.* ■ [no obj.] thin out and disappear: *the earlier mist had dispersed.* ■ Physics divide (light) into constituents of different wavelengths.
▶ **adjective** [attrib.] Chemistry denoting a phase dispersed in another phase, as in a colloid: *emulsions should be examined after storage for droplet size of the disperse phase.*
– DERIVATIVES **disperser** noun, **dispersible** adjective, **dispersive** adjective.
– ORIGIN late Middle English: from Latin *dispers-* 'scattered', from the verb *dispergere*, from *dis-* 'widely' + *spargere* 'scatter, strew'.

dispersion ▶ **noun** [mass noun] the action or process of distributing or spreading things or people over a wide area: *some seeds rely on birds for dispersion.*
■the state of being dispersed over a wide area: *the study looks at the dispersion of earnings with OECD member countries.* ■ Ecology the pattern of distribution of individuals within a habitat. ■(also **the Dispersion**) another term for **DIASPORA**. ■ [count noun] a mixture of one substance dispersed in another medium: *the virus is transmitted in the dispersion of droplets which results from sneezing or coughing.* ■ Physics the separation of white light into colours or of any radiation according to wavelength. ■ Statistics the extent to which values of a variable differ from a fixed value such as the mean.
– ORIGIN late Middle English: from late Latin *dispersio(n-)*, from Latin *dispergere* (see **DISPERSE**).

dispirit /dɪˈspɪrɪt/ ▶ **verb** [with obj.] (often **be dispirited**) cause (someone) to lose enthusiasm or hope: *the army was dispirited by the uncomfortable winter conditions* | [as adj. **dispiriting**] *it was a dispiriting occasion.*
– DERIVATIVES **dispiritedly** adverb, **dispiritedness** noun, **dispiritingly** adverb.

displace ▶ **verb** [with obj.] take over the place, position, or role of (someone or something): *in the northern states of India, Hindi has largely displaced English.*
■cause (something) to move from its proper or usual place: *he seems to have displaced some vertebrae.* ■ (usu. **be displaced**) force (someone) to leave their home, typically because of war, persecution, or natural disaster: *thousands of people have been displaced by the civil war.* ■ remove (someone) from a job or position of authority against their will: *his aides were discredited and displaced.*
– ORIGIN mid 16th cent.: from Old French *desplacer*.

displaced person ▶ **noun** a person who is forced to leave their home country because of war or persecution; a refugee.

displacement ▶ **noun** [mass noun] **1** the moving of something from its place or position: *vertical displacement of the shoreline* | [count noun] *a displacement of the vertebra at the bottom of the spine.*
■the removal of someone or something by someone or something else which takes their place: *males may be able to resist displacement by other males.* ■ the enforced departure of people from their homes, typically because of war, persecution, or natural disaster: *the displacement of farmers by guerrilla activity.* ■ [count noun] the amount by which a thing is moved from a position: *a displacement of 6.8 metres along the San Andreas fault.*
2 the occupation by a submerged body or part of a body of a volume which would otherwise be occupied by a fluid.
■the amount or weight of fluid that would fill such a volume in the case of a floating ship, used as a measure of the ship's size: *the submarine has a surface displacement of 2,185 tons.* ■ technical the volume swept by a reciprocating system, as in a pump or engine.
3 Psychoanalysis the unconscious transfer of an intense emotion from one object to another: *this phobia was linked with the displacement of fear of his father.*
4 Physics the component of an electric field due to free separated charges, regardless of any polarizing effects.
■the vector representing such a component. ■ the flux density of such an electric field.

displacement activity ▶ **noun** Psychology an animal or human activity that seems inappropriate, such as head-scratching when confused, considered to arise unconsciously when a conflict between antagonistic urges cannot be resolved.

displacement pump ▶ **noun** a pump in which liquid is moved out of the pump chamber by a moving surface or by the introduction of compressed air or gas.

displacement ton ▶ **noun** see **TON**[1] (sense 1).

display ▶ **verb** [with obj.] make a prominent exhibition of (something) in a place where it can be easily seen: *the palace used to display a series of Flemish tapestries* | *a handwritten notice was displayed in the booking office.*
■(of a computer or other device) show (information) on a screen. ■ give a conspicuous demonstration of (a quality, emotion, or skill): *a final which saw both players display a great deal of spirit.* ■ [no obj.] (of a male bird, reptile, or fish) engage in a specialized pattern of behaviour that is intended to attract a mate: *she photographed the peacock, which chose that moment to display.*
▶ **noun** **1** a performance, show, or event intended for public entertainment: *a display of fireworks* | [as modifier] *an aerobatic display team.*
■a collection of objects arranged for public viewing: *the museum houses an informative display of rocks* | [mass noun] *his plans have recently gone* **on display** *to the public.* ■ a notable or conspicuous demonstration of a particular type of behaviour, emotion, or skill: *a hint of malice underlay his display of concern.* ■ [mass noun] the conspicuous exhibition of one's wealth; ostentation: *every clansman was determined to outdo the Campbells in display, and looked to his finery.* ■ a specialized pattern of behaviour by the males of some species of birds, reptiles, and fish that is intended to attract a mate: *the teal were indulging in delightful courtship displays* | [mass noun] *the lark's song is usually uttered in aerial display.* ■ [mass noun] Printing the arrangement and choice of type in a style intended to attract attention.
2 an electronic device for the visual presentation of data: *the colour display now costs £400* | [as modifier] *the display area can be scrolled to access any remaining lines.*
■[mass noun] the process or facility of presenting data on a computer screen or other device: *the processing and display of high volumes of information.* ■ the data shown on a computer screen or other device.
– DERIVATIVES **displayer** noun.
– ORIGIN Middle English (in the sense 'unfurl, unfold'): from Old French *despleier*, from Latin *displicare* 'scatter, disperse' (in medieval Latin 'unfold'). Compare with **DEPLOY**.

display case (also **display cabinet**) ▶ **noun** a case, made all or partly of glass, for displaying items in a shop or museum for observation or inspection.

displayed ▶ **adjective** **1** (of information) shown on a computer screen or other device: *a utility designed to allow you to cut up pieces of displayed graphics.*
2 Heraldry (of a bird of prey) depicted with the wings extended.
■(of the wings of a bird of prey) extended.

display type ▶ **noun** [mass noun] large, bold, or eye-catching type used for headings or advertisements.

displease ▶ **verb** [with obj.] make (someone) feel annoyed or upset: *the tone of the letter displeased him* | [as adj. **displeasing**] *it was not entirely displeasing to be the centre of such a drama.*
– DERIVATIVES **displeasingly** adverb.
– ORIGIN late Middle English: from Old French *desplaisir*, from *des-* (expressing reversal) + *plaisir* 'to please', from Latin *placere*.

displeased ▶ **adjective** feeling or showing annoyance and displeasure: *he was* **displeased with** *your work.*

displeasure ▶ **noun** [mass noun] a feeling of annoyance or disapproval: *the striker was fined after showing his displeasure at being substituted.*
▶ **verb** [with obj.] archaic annoy; displease: *not for worlds would I do aught that might displeasure thee.*
– ORIGIN late Middle English: from Old French *desplaisir* (see **DISPLEASE**), influenced by **PLEASURE**.

disport ▶ **verb** [no obj.] archaic or humorous enjoy oneself unrestrainedly; frolic: *a painting of lords and ladies* **disporting themselves** *by a lake.*
▶ **noun** [mass noun] archaic diversion from work or serious matters; recreation or amusement: *the King and all his Court were met for solace and disport.*
■[count noun] archaic a pastime, game, or sport.
– ORIGIN late Middle English: from Old French *desporter*, from *des-* 'away' + *porter* 'carry' (from Latin *portare*).

disposable ▶ **adjective** **1** (of an article) intended to be used once and then thrown away: *disposable nappies* | *a disposable razor.*
■(of a person or idea) able to be dispensed with; easily dismissed: *the poor performer is motivated by the fear that he or she is highly disposable.*
2 (chiefly of financial assets) readily available for the owner's use as required: *he made a mental inventory of his disposable assets.*
▶ **noun** an article designed to be thrown away after use: *don't buy disposables, such as razors, cups, and plates.*

– DERIVATIVES **disposability** noun.

disposable income ▶ **noun** [mass noun] income remaining after deduction of taxes and other mandatory charges, available to be spent or saved as one wishes. Compare with **DISCRETIONARY INCOME**.

disposal ▶ **noun** [mass noun] **1** the action or process of throwing away or getting rid of something: *the disposal of radioactive waste* | [count noun] *consents for disposals at sea.*
■ [count noun] N. Amer. informal a waste disposal unit: *garbage disposals that never worked.* ■ the action of overcoming a rival or threat: *England's 4–0 disposal of Turkey.*
2 the sale of shares, property, or other assets: *the disposal of his shares in the company* | [count noun] *disposals of fixed and non-current assets.*
3 the arrangement or positioning of something: *she brushed her hair carefully, as if her success lay in the sleek disposal of each gleaming black thread.*
– PHRASES **at one's disposal** available for one to use whenever or however one wishes: *a helicopter was put at their disposal.* **at someone's disposal** ready to assist the person concerned in any way they wish: *I am at your disposal until Sunday.*

dispose ▶ **verb 1** [no obj.] (**dispose of**) get rid of by throwing away or giving or selling to someone else: *the waste is disposed of in the North Sea* | *people now have substantial assets to dispose of after their death.*
■ informal kill; destroy: *her lover came up with hundreds of schemes for disposing of her husband.* ■ overcome (a rival or threat): *the Scottish champions were buoyant after they disposed of English champions Leeds.* ■ informal consume (food or drink) quickly or enthusiastically: *she watched him dispose of a large slice of cheese.*
2 [with obj. and adverbial] arrange in a particular position: *the chief disposed his attendants in a circle.*
■ bring (someone) into a particular frame of mind: *prolactin, a calming hormone, is released,* ***disposing*** *you* ***towards*** *sleep* | [with obj. and infinitive] *if you touch the female readers' hearts, it might dispose their husbands to be charitable.* ■ [no obj.] poetic/literary determine the course of events: *the government proposed, but the trade union movement disposed.* [ORIGIN: from the proverb 'Man proposes, (but) God disposes', translating Latin *Homo proponit, sed Deus disponit* (Thomas à Kempis's *De Imitatione Christi* I. xix).]
– DERIVATIVES **disposer** noun *a waste disposer* | *a disposer of grants and subsidies.*
– ORIGIN late Middle English: from Old French *disposer*, from Latin *disponere* 'arrange', influenced by *dispositus* 'arranged' and Old French *poser* 'to place'.

disposed ▶ **adjective** [predic., usu. with infinitive] inclined or willing: *James didn't seem disposed to take the hint.*
■ [with submodifier] having a specified attitude to or towards: *it is expected that he will be favourably* ***disposed towards*** *the proposals.*

disposition ▶ **noun 1** a person's inherent qualities of mind and character: *a sweet-natured girl of a placid disposition* | *he has the disposition of a saint.*
■ [often with infinitive] an inclination or tendency: *the Prime Minister has shown a disposition to alter policies* | *the judge's* ***disposition to*** *clemency.*
2 [mass noun] the way in which something is placed or arranged, especially in relation to other things: *the plan need not be accurate so long as it shows the disposition of the rooms.*
■ the action of arranging or ordering people or things in a particular way: *the prerogative gives the state widespread powers regarding the disposition and control of the armed forces* | [count noun] *Dr Herrmann lifted a phone and began to* ***make his dispositions.*** ■ (**dispositions**) military preparations, in particular the stationing of troops ready for attack or defence: *the new strategic dispositions of our forces.*
3 [mass noun] Law the action of distributing or transferring property or money to someone, in particular by bequest: *this is a tax which affects the disposition of assets on death.*
4 the power to deal with something as one pleases: *if Napoleon had had railways* ***at his disposition,*** *he would have been invincible.*
■ archaic the determination of events, especially by divine power.
– ORIGIN late Middle English: via Old French from Latin *dispositio(n-)*, from *disponere* 'arrange' (see **DISPOSE**).

dispositive /dɪsˈpɒzətɪv/ ▶ **adjective** relating to or bringing about the settlement of an issue or the disposition of property: *such litigation will rarely be dispositive of any question.*
■ (in Scots and US law) dealing with the disposition of property by deed or will: *the testator had to make his signature after making the dispositive provisions.* ■ dealing with the settling of international conflicts by an agreed disposition of disputed territories: *a peace settlement in the nature of a dispositive treaty.*
– ORIGIN late Middle English (in the sense 'contributory, conducive'): from Old French, or from medieval Latin *dispositivus*, from Latin *disposit-* 'arranged, disposed', from the verb *disponere* (see **DISPOSE**).

dispositor /dɪˈspɒzɪtə/ ▶ **noun** Astrology the planet which rules the sign in which another planet is located in a particular chart.

dispossess ▶ **verb** [with obj.] (often **be dispossessed**) deprive (someone) of something that they own, typically land or property: *they were* ***dispossessed of*** *lands and properties at the time of the Reformation* | [as plural noun **the dispossessed**] *a champion of the poor and the dispossessed.*
■ (in sport) deprive (a player) of the ball: *he dispossessed Hendrie and set off on a solo run.*
– DERIVATIVES **dispossession** noun.
– ORIGIN late 15th cent.: from Old French *despossesser*, from *des-* (expressing reversal) + *possesser* 'possess'.

dispraise ▶ **noun** [mass noun] rare censure; criticism: *this engraving has on occasion elicited dispraise for Raphael.*
▶ **verb** [with obj.] archaic express censure or criticism of (someone): *men cannot praise Dryden without dispraising Coleridge.*
– ORIGIN Middle English: from Old French *despreisier*, based on late Latin *depreciare* (see **DEPRECIATE**).

disproof ▶ **noun** [mass noun] a set of facts that prove that something is untrue: *Rex was living disproof of the youth-preserving powers imputed to life in the college* | [count noun] *the theory also provides a disproof of the principle of closure.*
■ the action of proving that something is untrue: *the Home Secretary sought to justify placing the burden of disproof on defendants.*

disproportion ▶ **noun** an instance of being out of proportion with something else: *there is a disproportion between the scale of expenditure and any benefit that could possibly result* | [mass noun] *women undergoing Caesarean section because of feto-pelvic disproportion.*
– DERIVATIVES **disproportional** adjective, **disproportionality** noun, **disproportionally** adverb.
– ORIGIN mid 16th cent.: from **DIS-** (expressing absence) + **PROPORTION**, on the pattern of French *disproportion*.

disproportionate[1] /ˌdɪsprəˈpɔːʃ(ə)nət/ ▶ **adjective** too large or too small in comparison with something else: *people on lower incomes spend a disproportionate amount of their income on fuel* | *persistent offenders were given sentences that were disproportionate to the offences they had committed.*
– DERIVATIVES **disproportionately** adverb, **disproportionateness** noun.
– ORIGIN mid 16th cent.: from **DIS-** (expressing absence) + **PROPORTIONATE**, on the pattern of French *disproportionné*.

disproportionate[2] /ˌdɪsprəˈpɔːʃ(ə)neɪt/ ▶ **verb** [no obj.] Chemistry undergo disproportionation: *water disproportionates to oxygen and hydrogen.*

disproportionation ▶ **noun** [mass noun] Chemistry a reaction in which a substance is simultaneously oxidized and reduced, giving two different products.

disprove ▶ **verb** [with obj.] prove that (something) is false: *he has given the Department of Transport two months to disprove the allegation.*
– DERIVATIVES **disprovable** adjective.
– ORIGIN late Middle English: from Old French *desprover*.

Dispur /dɪsˈpʊə/ a city in NE India, capital of the state of Assam.

disputable ▶ **adjective** not established as a fact, and so open to question or debate: *whether it can be described as art criticism may be disputable.*
– DERIVATIVES **disputably** adverb.
– ORIGIN late 15th cent.: from Latin *disputabilis*, from the verb *disputare* 'to estimate', later 'to dispute' (see **DISPUTE**).

disputation ▶ **noun** [mass noun] debate or argument: *promoting consensus rather than disputation* | [count noun] *a lengthy disputation about the rights and wrongs of a particular request.*
■ formal academic debate: *the founding father of logical disputation* | [count noun] *scholastic disputations.*
– DERIVATIVES **disputative** adjective.
– ORIGIN late Middle English: from Latin *disputatio(n-)*, from the verb *disputare* (see **DISPUTE**).

disputatious ▶ **adjective** (of a person) fond of having heated arguments: *it's an extremely congenial hang-out for disputatious academics.*
■ (of an argument or situation) motivated by or causing strong opinions: *disputatious council meetings.*
– DERIVATIVES **disputatiously** adverb, **disputatiousness** noun.

dispute ▶ **noun** /dɪˈspjuːt, ˈdɪspjuːt/ a disagreement, argument, or debate: *a territorial dispute between the two countries* | [mass noun] *the Commission is* ***in dispute with*** *the government.*
■ a disagreement between management and employees that leads to industrial action: *an industrial dispute.*
▶ **verb** /dɪˈspjuːt/ [with obj.] argue about (something); discuss heatedly: *the point has been much disputed* | [no obj.] *he taught and* ***disputed with*** *local poets.*
■ question whether (a statement or alleged fact) is true or valid: *the accusations are not disputed* | [with clause] *the estate disputes that it is responsible for the embankment.* ■ compete for; strive to win: *the two drivers crashed while disputing the lead.* ■ archaic resist (a landing or advance): *the Sudanese chose Teb as the ground upon which to dispute the advance.*
– PHRASES **beyond** (or **past** or **without**) **dispute** certain or certainly; without doubt: *the main part of his argument was beyond dispute.* **open to dispute** not definitely decided: *such estimates are always open to dispute.*
– DERIVATIVES **disputant** noun, **disputer** noun.
– ORIGIN Middle English: via Old French from Latin *disputare* 'to estimate' (in late Latin 'to dispute'), from *dis-* 'apart' + *putare* 'reckon'.

disqualification ▶ **noun** [mass noun] the action of disqualifying or the state of being disqualified.
■ [count noun] a fact or condition that disqualifies someone from a position or activity: *such an offence is no longer a disqualification for office.*

disqualify ▶ **verb** (**-ies**, **-ied**) [with obj.] (often **be disqualified**) pronounce (someone) ineligible for an office or activity because of an offence or infringement: *he was* ***disqualified from*** *driving for six months.*
■ eliminate (someone) from a competition because of an infringement of the rules: *he was disqualified after failing a drugs test.* ■ (of a feature or characteristic) make (someone) unsuitable for an office or activity: *a heart murmur disqualified him for military service.*

disquiet ▶ **noun** [mass noun] a feeling of anxiety or worry: *public disquiet about animal testing.*
▶ **verb** [with obj.] [usu. as adj. **disquieted**] make (someone) worried or anxious: *she felt disquieted at the lack of interest the girl had shown.*

disquieting ▶ **adjective** inducing feelings of anxiety or worry: *he found Jean's gaze disquieting.*
– DERIVATIVES **disquietingly** adverb.

disquietude ▶ **noun** [mass noun] a state of uneasiness or anxiety.

disquisition /ˌdɪskwɪˈzɪʃ(ə)n/ ▶ **noun** a long or elaborate essay or discussion on a particular subject: *nothing can kill a radio show quicker than a disquisition on intertextual analysis.*
– DERIVATIVES **disquisitional** adjective (archaic).
– ORIGIN late 15th cent.: via French from Latin *disquisitio(n-)* 'investigation', based on *quaerere* 'seek'. The original sense was 'topic for investigation', whence 'discourse in which a subject is investigated' (mid 17th cent.).

Disraeli /dɪzˈreɪli/, Benjamin, 1st Earl of Beaconsfield (1804–81), British Tory statesman; Prime Minister 1868 and 1874–80. He was largely responsible for the introduction of the second Reform Act (1867). He also ensured that Britain bought a controlling interest in the Suez Canal (1875) and made Queen Victoria Empress of India.

disrate /dɪsˈreɪt/ ▶ **verb** [with obj.] (usu. **be disrated**) reduce (a sailor) to a lower rank.

disregard ▶ **verb** [with obj.] pay no attention to; ignore: *the body of evidence is too substantial to disregard.*
▶ **noun** [mass noun] the action or state of disregarding or ignoring something: *blatant* ***disregard for*** *the law.*

disrelish archaic ▶ **noun** [mass noun] a feeling of dislike or distaste: *disrelish for any pursuit is ample reason for abandoning it.*

▶ **verb** [with obj.] regard (something) with dislike or distaste: *I am not surprised that some members of the House should disrelish your report.*

disremember ▶ **verb** [with obj.] US dialect fail to remember: *mostly what you disremember ain't worth the trouble to call to mind.*

disrepair ▶ **noun** [mass noun] poor condition of a building or structure due to neglect: *the station gradually **fell into disrepair**.*

disreputable ▶ **adjective** not considered to be respectable in character or appearance: *he was heavy, grubby, and vaguely disreputable.*
– DERIVATIVES **disreputableness** noun, **disreputably** adverb.

disrepute /ˌdɪsrɪˈpjuːt/ ▶ **noun** [mass noun] the state of being held in low esteem by the public: *one of the top clubs in the country is close to bringing the game **into disrepute**.*

disrespect ▶ **noun** [mass noun] lack of respect or courtesy: *growing disrespect for the rule of law.*
▶ **verb** [with obj.] informal, chiefly US show a lack of respect for; insult: *a young brave who disrespects his elders.*
– DERIVATIVES **disrespectful** adjective, **disrespectfully** adverb.

disrobe ▶ **verb** [no obj.] take one's clothes off: *she began to disrobe.*
■ take off the clothes worn for an official ceremony: *they walked to the vestry to disrobe.* ■ [with obj.] undress (someone): *Kate remembers being disrobed.*
– ORIGIN late Middle English: from **DIS-** (expressing reversal) + **ROBE**, perhaps on the pattern of French *desrober*.

disrupt ▶ **verb** [with obj.] interrupt (an event, activity, or process) by causing a disturbance or problem: *flooding disrupted rail services.*
■ drastically alter or destroy the structure of (something): *alcohol can disrupt the chromosomes of an unfertilized egg.*
– DERIVATIVES **disrupter** (also **disruptor**) noun, **disruption** noun.
– ORIGIN late Middle English: from Latin *disrupt-* 'broken apart', from the verb *disrumpere*.

disruptive ▶ **adjective** causing or tending to cause disruption: *disruptive pupils | the hours of work are **disruptive to** home life.*
– DERIVATIVES **disruptively** adverb, **disruptiveness** noun.

diss ▶ **verb** variant spelling of **DIS**.

dissatisfaction ▶ **noun** [mass noun] lack of satisfaction: *widespread public **dissatisfaction with** incumbent politicians.*

dissatisfied ▶ **adjective** not content or happy with something: *his parents are **dissatisfied with** the quality of tuition on offer | dissatisfied customers.*
– DERIVATIVES **dissatisfiedly** adverb.

dissatisfy ▶ **verb** (**-ies**, **-ied**) [with obj.] fail to satisfy (someone).

dissaving ▶ **noun** [mass noun] chiefly N. Amer. the action of spending more than one has earned in a given period.
■ (**dissavings**) the excess amount spent.
– DERIVATIVES **dissaver** noun.

dissect /dʌɪˈsɛkt, dɪ-/ ▶ **verb** [with obj.] (often **be dissected**) methodically cut up (a body, part, or plant) in order to study its internal parts.
■ analyse (a text or idea) in minute detail.
– DERIVATIVES **dissection** noun, **dissector** noun.
– ORIGIN late 16th cent.: from Latin *dissect-* 'cut up', from the verb *dissecare*, from *dis-* 'apart' + *secare* 'to cut'.

dissected ▶ **adjective** **1** having been cut up for anatomical study.
2 having a divided form or structure, in particular:
■ Botany (of a leaf) divided into many deep lobes.
■ Geology (of a plateau or upland) divided by a number of deep valleys.

dissemble /dɪˈsɛmb(ə)l/ ▶ **verb** [no obj.] conceal one's true motives, feelings, or beliefs: *an honest, sincere person with no need to dissemble.*
■ [with obj.] disguise or conceal (a feeling or intention): *she smiled, dissembling her true emotion.*
– DERIVATIVES **dissemblance** noun, **dissembler** noun.
– ORIGIN late Middle English: alteration (suggested by **SEMBLANCE**) of obsolete *dissimule*, via Old French from Latin *dissimulare* 'disguise, conceal'.

disseminate /dɪˈsɛmɪneɪt/ ▶ **verb** [with obj.] spread or disperse (something, especially information) widely: *health authorities should foster good practice by disseminating information.*
■ [usu. as adj. **disseminated**] spread throughout an organ or the body: *disseminated colonic cancer.*
– DERIVATIVES **dissemination** noun, **disseminator** noun.
– ORIGIN late Middle English: from Latin *disseminat-* 'scattered', from the verb *disseminare*, from *dis-* 'abroad' + *semen, semin-* 'seed'.

disseminated sclerosis ▶ **noun** see **SCLEROSIS**.

disseminule /dɪˈsɛmɪnjuːl/ ▶ **noun** Botany a part of a plant that serves to propagate it, such as a seed or a fruit.
– ORIGIN early 20th cent.: formed irregularly from *dissemination* (see **DISSEMINATE**) + **-ULE**.

dissension /dɪˈsɛnʃ(ə)n/ ▶ **noun** [mass noun] disagreement that leads to discord: *this manoeuvre caused dissension within feminist ranks* | [count noun] *the mill was the cause of a dissension in 1620.*
– ORIGIN Middle English: via Old French from Latin *dissensio(n-)*, from the verb *dissentire* (see **DISSENT**).

dissensus /dɪˈsɛnsəs/ ▶ **noun** [mass noun] widespread dissent: *the 'shame' attached to being held responsible for social dissensus.*
– ORIGIN 1960s: from **DIS-** (expressing reversal) + a shortened form of **CONSENSUS**, or from Latin *dissensus* 'disagreement'.

dissent /dɪˈsɛnt/ ▶ **verb** [no obj.] hold or express opinions that are at variance with those previously, commonly, or officially expressed: *two members **dissented from** the majority* | [as adj. **dissenting**] *there were only a couple of dissenting voices.*
■ disagree with the doctrine of an established or orthodox Church.
▶ **noun** [mass noun] the holding or expression of opinions at variance with those previously, commonly, or officially held: *there was no **dissent from** this view.*
■ (also **Dissent**) refusal to accept the doctrines of an established or orthodox Church; nonconformity. ■ (in sport) the offence of expressing disagreement with the referee's decision: *he was sent off for dissent.*
– ORIGIN late Middle English: from Latin *dissentire* 'differ in sentiment'.

dissenter ▶ **noun** a person who dissents.
■ (**Dissenter**) Brit. historical a member of a non-established Church; a Nonconformist.

dissentient /dɪˈsɛnʃɪənt, -ʃ(ə)nt/ ▶ **adjective** in opposition to a majority or official opinion: *dissentient voices were castigated as 'hopeless bureaucrats'.*
▶ **noun** a person who opposes a majority or official opinion.
– ORIGIN early 17th cent.: from Latin *dissentient-* 'differing in opinion', from the verb *dissentire*.

dissepiment /dɪˈsɛpɪm(ə)nt/ ▶ **noun** Botany & Zoology a partition in a part or organ; a septum.
– ORIGIN early 18th cent.: from Latin *dissaepimentum*, from *dissaepire* 'make separate', from *dis-* (expressing separation) + *saepire* 'divide by a hedge'.

dissertation /ˌdɪsəˈteɪʃ(ə)n/ ▶ **noun** a long essay on a particular subject, especially one written for a university degree or diploma.
– DERIVATIVES **dissertational** adjective.
– ORIGIN early 17th cent. (in the sense 'discussion, debate'): from Latin *dissertatio(n-)*, from *dissertare* 'continue to discuss', from *disserere* 'examine, discuss'.

disservice ▶ **noun** [usu. in sing.] a harmful action: *you have **done a disservice to** the African people by ignoring this fact.*

dissever /dɪ(s)ˈsɛvə/ ▶ **verb** [with obj.] rare divide or sever (something): *a European tradition which had not been willing to dissever reason from the law of nature.*
– DERIVATIVES **disseverance** noun, **disseverment** noun.
– ORIGIN Middle English (in the sense 'separate'): from Old French *dessevrer*, from late Latin *disseparare*, from *dis-* (expressing intensive force) + Latin *separare* 'to separate'.

dissidence /ˈdɪsɪd(ə)ns/ ▶ **noun** [mass noun] protest against official policy.
– ORIGIN mid 17th cent.: from Latin *dissidentia*, from *dissident-* 'sitting apart' (see **DISSIDENT**).

dissident /ˈdɪsɪd(ə)nt/ ▶ **noun** a person who opposes official policy, especially that of an authoritarian state.
▶ **adjective** in opposition to official policy: *the measure was supported by dissident Tories.*
– ORIGIN mid 16th cent. (in the sense 'differing in opinion or character'): from Latin *dissident-* 'sitting apart, disagreeing', from *dis-* 'apart' + *sedere* 'sit'.

dissimilar ▶ **adjective** not the same; different: *a collection of dissimilar nations lacking overall homogeneity | the pleasures of the romance novel are **not dissimilar from** those of the chocolate bar.*
– DERIVATIVES **dissimilarity** noun, **dissimilarly** adverb.
– ORIGIN late 16th cent.: from **DIS-** (expressing reversal) + **SIMILAR**, on the pattern of Latin *dissimilis*, French *dissimilaire*.

dissimilate /dɪˈsɪmɪleɪt/ ▶ **verb** [with obj.] Linguistics change (a sound or sounds in a word) to another when the word originally had identical sounds near each other: *in 'pilgrim', from Latin 'peregrinus', the first 'r' is dissimilated to 'l'.*
■ [no obj.] (of a sound) undergo such a change: *the first 'r' dissimilates to 'l'.*
– DERIVATIVES **dissimilation** noun, **dissimilatory** /dɪˈsɪmɪlət(ə)ri/ adjective.
– ORIGIN mid 19th cent.: from **DIS-** (expressing reversal) + Latin *similis* 'like, similar', on the pattern of *assimilate*.

dissimilitude /ˌdɪsɪˈmɪlɪtjuːd/ ▶ **noun** [mass noun] formal dissimilarity or diversity.
– ORIGIN late Middle English: from Latin *dissimilitudo*, from *dissimilis* 'unlike', from *dis-* (expressing reversal) + *similis* 'like, similar'.

dissimulate /dɪˈsɪmjʊleɪt/ ▶ **verb** [with obj.] conceal or disguise (one's thoughts, feelings, or character): *a country gentleman who dissimulates his wealth beneath ragged pullovers* | [no obj.] *now that they have power, they no longer need to dissimulate.*
– DERIVATIVES **dissimulation** noun, **dissimulator** noun.
– ORIGIN late Middle English: from Latin *dissimulat-* 'hidden, concealed', from the verb *dissimulare*.

dissipate /ˈdɪsɪpeɪt/ ▶ **verb** **1** [no obj.] (of a feeling or similar thing) disappear or be dispelled: *the concern she'd felt for him had wholly dissipated.*
■ [with obj.] cause (a feeling or similar thing) to disappear or disperse: *he wanted to dissipate his anger.* ■ (of something such as a cloud or queue) disperse or scatter.
2 [with obj.] squander or fritter away (money, energy, or resources).
■ (usu. **be dissipated**) Physics cause (energy) to be lost, typically by converting it to heat.
– DERIVATIVES **dissipative** adjective, **dissipator** (also **dissipater**) noun.
– ORIGIN late Middle English: from Latin *dissipat-* 'scattered', from the verb *dissipare*, from *dis-* 'apart, widely' + *supare* 'to throw'.

dissipated ▶ **adjective** (of a person or way of life) overindulging in sensual pleasures: *dissipated behaviour.*

dissipation ▶ **noun** [mass noun] **1** dissipated living: *a descent into drunkenness and sexual dissipation.*
2 squandering of money, energy, or resources: *the dissipation of the country's mineral wealth.*
■ Physics loss of energy, especially by its conversion into heat: *energy dissipation* | [count noun] *the dissipations in the switch and diode are small.*
– ORIGIN late Middle English (in the sense 'complete disintegration'): from Latin *dissipatio(n-)*, from the verb *dissipare* (see **DISSIPATE**).

dissociable ▶ **adjective** able to be dissociated; separable: *language and cognition are not dissociable.*
– ORIGIN mid 19th cent.: from French, from Latin *dissociabilis*, from *dissociare* 'to separate'.

dissociate /dɪˈsəʊʃɪeɪt, -sɪ-/ ▶ **verb** [with obj.] **1** (especially in abstract contexts) disconnect or separate: *voices should not be **dissociated from** their social context.*
■ [no obj.] become separated or disconnected: *the area would **dissociate from** the country.* ■ (**dissociate oneself from**) declare that one is not connected with or a supporter of (someone or something): *he took pains to dissociate himself from the religious radicals.* ■ (usu. **be dissociated**) Psychiatry split off (a component of mental activity) to act as an independent part of mental life.
2 (usu. **be dissociated**) Chemistry cause (a molecule) to split into separate smaller atoms, ions, or molecules, especially reversibly: *these compounds are dissociated by solar radiation to yield atoms of chlorine.*
■ [no obj.] (of a molecule) undergo this process.
– DERIVATIVES **dissociative** adjective.
– ORIGIN mid 16th cent.: from Latin *dissociat-*

'separated', from the verb *dissociare*, from *dis-* (expressing reversal) + *sociare* 'join together' (from *socius* 'companion').

dissociated personality ▶ **noun** another term for **MULTIPLE PERSONALITY**.

dissociation /dɪˌsəʊʃɪˈeɪʃ(ə)n, -sɪ-/ ▶ **noun** [mass noun] the disconnection or separation of something from something else or the state of being disconnected: *the dissociation between the executive and the judiciary is the legacy of the Act of Settlement.*
■ Chemistry the splitting of a molecule into smaller molecules, atoms, or ions, especially by a reversible process. ■ Psychiatry separation of normally related mental processes, resulting in one group functioning independently from the rest, leading in extreme cases to disorders such as multiple personality: [count noun] *the dissociations that one can observe in neuropsychological patients.*

dissociation constant ▶ **noun** Chemistry a quantity expressing the extent to which a particular substance in solution is dissociated into ions, equal to the product of the concentrations of the respective ions divided by the concentration of the undissociated molecule.

dissoluble ▶ **adjective** able to be dissolved, loosened, or disconnected: *permitting divorce would render every marriage dissoluble.*
– DERIVATIVES **dissolubility** noun.
– ORIGIN mid 16th cent.: from Latin *dissolubilis*, from the verb *dissolvere* (see **DISSOLVE**).

dissolute /ˈdɪsəluːt/ ▶ **adjective** (of a person or a way of life) overindulging in sensual pleasures: *unfortunately, his heir was feckless and dissolute.*
– DERIVATIVES **dissolutely** adverb, **dissoluteness** noun.
– ORIGIN late Middle English: from Latin *dissolutus* 'disconnected, loose', from the verb *dissolvere* (see **DISSOLVE**).

dissolution ▶ **noun** [mass noun] **1** the closing down or dismissal of an assembly, partnership, or official body, especially a parliament: *the dissolution of their marriage* | [count noun] *the Queen would have to decide whether to grant a dissolution.*
■ technical the action or process of dissolving or being dissolved: *minerals susceptible to dissolution.* ■ disintegration; decomposition: *the dissolution of the flesh.* ■ formal death.
2 debauched living; dissipation: *an advanced state of dissolution.*
– ORIGIN late Middle English: from Latin *dissolutio(n-)*, from the verb *dissolvere* (see **DISSOLVE**).

dissolution of the monasteries the abolition of monasteries in England and Wales by Henry VIII under two Acts (1536, 1539), in order to replenish his treasury by vesting monastic assets in the Crown and to establish royal supremacy in ecclesiastical affairs.

dissolve ▶ **verb 1** [no obj.] (of a solid) become incorporated into a liquid so as to form a solution: *glucose dissolves easily in water.*
■ [with obj.] cause (a solid) to become incorporated into a liquid in this way: *dissolve a stock cube in a pint of hot water.* ■ (of something abstract, especially a feeling) disappear: *my courage dissolved.* ■ (**dissolve into/in**) subside uncontrollably into (an expression of strong feelings): *she suddenly dissolved into floods of tears.* ■ (**dissolve into/to**) (in a film) change gradually to (a different scene or picture): *the scene dissolves into a series of shots of the Morgan family.*
2 [with obj.] close down or dismiss (an assembly or official body).
■ annul or put an end to (a partnership or marriage).
▶ **noun** (in a film) an act or instance of moving gradually from one picture to another.
– DERIVATIVES **dissolvable** adjective.
– ORIGIN late Middle English (also in the sense 'break down into component parts'): from Latin *dissolvere*, from *dis-* 'apart' + *solvere* 'loosen or solve'.

dissolvent ▶ **noun** a substance that dissolves something else: *the experience of death could strengthen family ties, rather than act as a dissolvent.*
– ORIGIN mid 17th cent.: from Latin *dissolvent-* 'dissolving', from the verb *dissolvere* (see **DISSOLVE**).

dissonance /ˈdɪs(ə)nəns/ ▶ **noun** [mass noun] Music lack of harmony among musical notes: *an unusual degree of dissonance for such choral styles* | [count noun] *the harsh dissonances give a sound which is quite untypical of the Renaissance.*
■ a tension or clash resulting from the combination of two disharmonious or unsuitable elements: *the dissonance between the act of firing someone and the manager's beliefs about what is decent behaviour.*
– ORIGIN late Middle English: from Old French, from late Latin *dissonantia*, from Latin *dissonant-* 'disagreeing in sound', from the verb *dissonare*.

dissonant ▶ **adjective** Music lacking harmony: *irregular, dissonant chords.*
■ unsuitable or unusual in combination; clashing: *Jackson employs both harmonious and dissonant colour choices.*
– DERIVATIVES **dissonantly** adverb.
– ORIGIN late Middle English (in the sense 'clashing'): from Old French, or from Latin *dissonant-* 'being discordant or inharmonious', from the verb *dissonare*, from *dis-* 'apart' + *sonare* 'to sound'.

dissuade /dɪˈsweɪd/ ▶ **verb** [with obj.] persuade (someone) not to take a particular course of action: *his friends tried to **dissuade** him **from** flying.*
– DERIVATIVES **dissuader** noun, **dissuasion** noun, **dissuasive** adjective.
– ORIGIN late 15th cent. (in the sense 'advise against'): from Latin *dissuadere*, from *dis-* (expressing reversal) + *suadere* 'advise, persuade'.

dissyllable /dɪˈsɪləb(ə)l/ ▶ **noun** variant spelling of **DISYLLABLE**.
– DERIVATIVES **dissyllabic** adjective.

dissymmetry ▶ **noun** (pl. **-ies**) [mass noun] lack of symmetry.
■ technical the symmetrical relation of mirror images, the left and right hands, or crystals with two corresponding forms.
– DERIVATIVES **dissymmetric** adjective, **dissymmetrical** adjective.

distaff /ˈdɪstɑːf/ ▶ **noun** a stick or spindle on to which wool or flax is wound for spinning.
■ [as modifier] of or concerning women: *marriage is still the passport to distaff power.*
– ORIGIN Old English *distæf*: the first element is apparently related to Middle Low German *dise*, *disene* 'distaff, bunch of flax'; the second is **STAFF**[1]. The extended sense arose because spinning was traditionally done by women.

distaff side ▶ **noun** the female side of a family: *the family title could be passed down through the distaff side.* The opposite of **SPEAR SIDE**.
■ the female members of a group: *this fascination was not limited to the distaff side of society.*
– ORIGIN late 19th cent.: because spinning (see **DISTAFF**) was traditionally done by women while men did the weaving.

distal /ˈdɪst(ə)l/ ▶ **adjective** Anatomy situated away from the centre of the body or from the point of attachment: *the distal end of the tibia* | *axons **distal to** the injury will degenerate.* The opposite of **PROXIMAL**.
■ Geology relating to or denoting the outer part of an area affected by geological activity: *the distal zone is characterized by pyroclastic flow deposits.*
– DERIVATIVES **distally** adverb.
– ORIGIN early 19th cent.: from **DISTANT**, on the pattern of words such as *dorsal*.

Distalgesic /ˌdɪst(ə)lˈdʒiːzɪk, -sɪk/ ▶ **noun** [mass noun] trademark a painkiller in tablet form containing paracetamol and propoxyphene.
– ORIGIN 1950s: blend of *Distillers'* Co. Ltd (the name of the manufacturers) and **ANALGESIC**.

distance ▶ **noun 1** an amount of space between two things or people: *I cycled the short distance home* | *you may have to walk long distances.*
■ [mass noun] the condition of being far off; remoteness: *distance makes things look small.* ■ a far-off point or place: *watching them **from a distance**.* ■ (**the distance**) the more remote part of what is visible or discernible: *I heard police sirens **in the distance** | they sped off **into the distance**.* ■ an interval of time or relation: *a distance of more than twenty years.* ■ [mass noun] figurative the avoidance of familiarity; aloofness or reserve: *a mix of warmth and distance makes a good neighbour.*
2 the full length of a race: *he claimed the 10,000 m title in only his second race over the distance.*
■ (**the distance**) Boxing the scheduled length of a fight: *he has won his first five fights **inside the distance**.* ■ Horse Racing, Brit. a space of more than twenty lengths between two finishers in a race: *he stormed home by a distance in the Handicap Chase.* ■ (**the distance**) Brit. a length of 240 yards from the winning post on a racecourse. ■ N. Amer. the distance from the winning post which a horse must have reached when the winner finishes in order to qualify for a subsequent heat.
▶ **verb** [with obj.] make (someone or something) far off or remote in position or nature: *her mother wished to **distance** her **from** the rough village children.*
■ (**distance oneself from**) declare that one is not connected with or a supporter of (someone or something): *he sought to distance himself from the proposals.* ■ Horse Racing, US beat (a horse) by a distance.
– PHRASES **distance lends enchantment to the view** proverb things look better from further away. **go the distance** Boxing complete a fight without being knocked out: *he went the distance after being floored in the first round.* ■ (of a boxing match) last the scheduled length: *six of his fights went the distance.* ■ Baseball pitch for the entire length of a game. ■ last for a long time: *this amplifier system should go the distance.* **keep one's distance** stay far away: *keep your distance from birds feeding their young.* ■ maintain one's reserve: *you had to say nothing and keep your distance.* **within —— distance** near enough to reach by the means specified: *her flat is within walking distance* | *the hotel is **within** easy driving **distance of** Birmingham.* **within spitting distance** within a very short distance. **within striking distance** near enough to hit or achieve something.
– ORIGIN Middle English (in the sense 'discord, debate'): from Old French or from Latin *distantia*, from *distant-* 'standing apart', from the verb *distare* (see **DISTANT**).

distance learning ▶ **noun** [mass noun] a method of studying in which lectures are broadcast or lessons are conducted by correspondence, without the student needing to attend a school or college.

distance post ▶ **noun** N. Amer. a post placed at a specified distance before the finishing post on a racecourse, which a horse must have passed when the winner finishes in order to qualify for a subsequent heat.

distance runner ▶ **noun** an athlete who competes in long- or middle-distance races.

distant ▶ **adjective 1** far away in space or time: *distant parts of the world* | *I remember that distant afternoon.*
■ [predic.] (after a measurement) at a specified distance: *the star is 30,000 light years **distant from** Earth* | *the town lay half a mile distant.* ■ (of a sound) faint or vague because far away: *the distant bark of some farm dog.* ■ figurative remote or far apart in resemblance or relationship: *a distant acquaintance.* ■ [attrib.] (of a person) not closely related: *a distant cousin of the King.*
2 (of a person) not intimate; cool or reserved: *his children found him strangely distant* | *she and my father were **distant with** each other.*
■ remote; abstracted: *a distant look in his eyes.*
– ORIGIN late Middle English: from Latin *distant-* 'standing apart', from the verb *distare*, from *dis-* 'apart' + *stare* 'stand'.

distantiate /dɪˈstanʃɪeɪt/ ▶ **verb** [with obj.] set or keep (something) at a distance, especially mentally: *Austen's aesthetic forms distantiate ideology.*
– DERIVATIVES **distantiation** noun.
– ORIGIN 1940s: based on Latin *distantia* 'distance'.

distantly ▶ **adverb** far away: *distantly he heard shouts.*
■ not closely: *they are distantly related to the elephants.* ■ coolly or remotely: *she smiled distantly.*

distant signal ▶ **noun** a railway signal giving a warning of the condition of the next home signal.

distaste ▶ **noun** [in sing.] mild dislike or aversion: *Harry nurtured a **distaste for** all things athletic* | [mass noun] *his mouth twisted with distaste.*
– DERIVATIVES **distasteful** adjective, **distastefully** adverb, **distastefulness** noun.
– ORIGIN late 16th cent.: from **DIS-** (expressing reversal) + **TASTE**, on the pattern of early modern French *desgout*, Italian *disgusto*. Compare with **DISGUST**.

Di Stefano /dɪ ˈstɛfənəʊ/, Alfredo (b.1926), Argentinian-born Spanish footballer. He played as a forward in Argentina and Colombia, then for Spain and Real Madrid, with whom he won the European Cup in each of its first five seasons (1956–60).

distemper[1] /dɪˈstɛmpə/ ▶ **noun** [mass noun] a kind of paint using glue or size instead of an oil base, for use on walls or for scene-painting.
■ a method of mural and poster painting using this.
▶ **verb** [with obj.] [often as adj. **distempered**] paint (something) with distemper: *the distempered roof timbers.*
– ORIGIN late Middle English (originally as a verb in the senses 'dilute' and 'steep'): from Old French *destremper* or late Latin *distemperare* 'soak'.

distemper[2] /dɪˈstɛmpə/ ▶**noun** [mass noun] **1** a viral disease of some animals, especially dogs, causing fever, coughing, and catarrh.
2 archaic political disorder: *an attempt to illuminate the moral roots of the modern world's distemper.*
– ORIGIN mid 16th cent. (originally in the sense 'bad temper', later 'illness'): from Middle English *distemper* 'upset, derange', from late Latin *distemperare* 'soak, mix in the wrong proportions', from *dis-* 'thoroughly' + *temperare* 'mingle'. Compare with **TEMPER**. Sense 1 dates from the mid 18th cent.

distend /dɪˈstɛnd/ ▶**verb** [with obj.] cause (something) to swell by stretching it from inside: *air is introduced into the stomach to distend it* | [as adj. **distended**] *a distended belly.*
■[no obj.] swell out because of pressure from inside: *the abdomen distended rapidly.*
– DERIVATIVES **distensibility** noun, **distensible** adjective, **distension** noun.
– ORIGIN late Middle English: from Latin *distendere*, from *dis-* 'apart' + *tendere* 'to stretch'.

distich /ˈdɪstɪk/ ▶**noun** Prosody a pair of verse lines; a couplet.
– ORIGIN early 16th cent.: via Latin from Greek *distikhon (metron)* '(measure) of two lines', neuter of *distikhos*, from *di-* 'twice' + *stikhos* 'line'.

distichous /ˈdɪstɪkəs/ ▶**adjective** Botany (of parts) arranged alternately in two opposite vertical rows.
– DERIVATIVES **distichously** adverb.
– ORIGIN mid 18th cent.: via Latin from Greek *distikhos* (see **DISTICH**) + **-OUS**.

distil /dɪˈstɪl/ (US **distill**) ▶**verb** (**distilled**, **distilling**) [with obj.] purify (a liquid) by heating it so that it vaporizes, then condensing it by cooling the vapour, and collecting the resulting liquid: *they managed to distil a small quantity of water* | [as adj. **distilled**] *dip the slide in distilled water.*
■(usu. **be distilled**) make (something, especially spirits or an essence) in this way: *whisky is **distilled from** a mash of grains* | [as noun **distilling**] *the distilling industry.* ■extract the essence of (something) by heating it with a solvent: *distil the leaves of some agrimony.* ■remove (a volatile constituent) of a mixture by using heat: *coal tar is made by **distilling out** the volatile products in coal.* ■(often **be distilled**) figurative extract the essential meaning or most important aspects of: *my travel notes were **distilled into** a book* | [as adj. **distilled**] *the employee report is a distilled version of the main accounts.* ■[no obj.] poetic/literary emanate as a vapour or in minute drops: *she drew back from the dank breath that distilled out of the earth.*
– DERIVATIVES **distillation** noun, **distillatory** adjective.
– ORIGIN late Middle English: from Latin *distillare*, variant of *destillare*, from *de-* 'down, away' + *stillare* (from *stilla* 'a drop').

distillate /ˈdɪstɪleɪt/ ▶**noun** something formed by distillation: *petroleum distillates* | [mass noun] *natural gas mixed with distillate.*
– ORIGIN mid 19th cent.: from Latin *distillatus* 'fallen in drops', from the verb *distillare* (see **DISTIL**).

distiller ▶**noun** a person or company that manufactures spirits: *a family-owned whisky distiller.*

distillery ▶**noun** (pl. **-ies**) a place where spirits are manufactured.

distinct ▶**adjective** **1** recognizably different in nature from something else of a similar type: *the patterns of spoken language are **distinct from** those of writing* | *there are two distinct types of sickle cell disease.*
■physically separate: *the gallery is divided into five distinct spaces.*
2 readily distinguishable by the senses: *a distinct smell of nicotine.*
■[attrib.] (used for emphasis) so clearly apparent to the mind as to be unmistakable; definite: *he got the distinct impression that Melissa wasn't best pleased.*
– DERIVATIVES **distinctly** adverb, **distinctness** noun.
– ORIGIN late Middle English (in the sense 'differentiated'): from Latin *distinctus* 'separated, distinguished', from the verb *distinguere* (see **DISTINGUISH**).

distinction ▶**noun** **1** a difference or contrast between similar things or people: *there is a sharp **distinction between** domestic politics and international politics* | *I was completely unaware of class distinctions.*
■[mass noun] the separation of things or people into different groups according to their attributes or characteristics: *high interest rates strike down, without distinction, small businesses and the unemployed.*
2 [mass noun] excellence that sets someone or something apart from others: *a novelist of distinction.*
■[count noun] a decoration or honour awarded to someone: *he gained the highest distinction awarded for excellence in photography.* ■a grade in an examination denoting outstanding excellence: *she gained a distinction in her diploma.* Compare with **MERIT**.
– PHRASES **distinction without a difference** an artificially created distinction where no real difference exists.
– ORIGIN Middle English (in the sense 'subdivision, category'): via Old French from Latin *distinctio(n-)*, from the verb *distinguere* (see **DISTINGUISH**).

distinctive ▶**adjective** characteristic of one person or thing, and so serving to distinguish it from others: *juniper berries give gin its distinctive flavour.*
– DERIVATIVES **distinctively** adverb, **distinctiveness** noun.
– ORIGIN late Middle English (in the sense 'serving to differentiate'): from late Latin *distinctivus*, from Latin *distinct-* 'distinguished' (see **DISTINCT**).

distingué /dɪˈstaŋgeɪ/ ▶**adjective** (fem. **distinguée** pronunc. same) having a distinguished manner or appearance: *he was lean and distingué, with a small goatee.*
– ORIGIN French, 'distinguished', from the verb *distinguer*.

distinguish /dɪˈstɪŋgwɪʃ/ ▶**verb** [with obj.] recognize or treat (someone or something) as different: *the child is perfectly capable of **distinguishing** reality **from** fantasy.*
■[no obj.] perceive or point out a difference: *we must **distinguish between** two kinds of holiday.* ■manage to discern (something barely perceptible): *it was too dark to distinguish anything more than their vague shapes.* ■be a characteristic or identifying mark or property of: *what **distinguishes** sport **from** games?* | [as adj. **distinguishing**] *his distinguishing marks included a deformed thumb.* ■(**distinguish oneself**) make oneself prominent and worthy of respect by one's behaviour or achievements: *many distinguished themselves in the fight against Hitler.*
– DERIVATIVES **distinguishable** adjective.
– ORIGIN late 16th cent.: formed irregularly from French *distinguer* or Latin *distinguere*, from *dis-* 'apart' + *stinguere* 'put out' (from a base meaning 'prick').

distinguished ▶**adjective** very successful, authoritative, and commanding great respect: *a distinguished American educationist.*

Distinguished Flying Cross ▶**noun** see **DFC**.

Distinguished Service Order ▶**noun** see **DSO**.

distort /dɪˈstɔːt/ ▶**verb** [with obj.] pull or twist out of shape: *a grimace distorted her fine mouth* | [as adj. **distorted**] *his face was **distorted with** rage.*
■[no obj.] become twisted out of shape: *the pipe will distort as you bend it.* ■figurative give a misleading or false account or impression of: *many factors can distort the results* | [as adj. **distorted**] *his report gives a distorted view of the meeting.* ■change the form of (an electrical signal or sound wave) during transmission, amplification, or other processing: *you're distorting the sound by overdriving the amp.*
– DERIVATIVES **distortedly** adverb, **distortedness** noun, **distortion** noun, **distortional** adjective, **distortionless** adjective.
– ORIGIN late 15th cent. (in the sense 'twist to one side'): from Latin *distort-* 'twisted apart', from the verb *distorquere*, from *dis-* 'apart' + *torquere* 'to twist'.

distract /dɪˈstrakt/ ▶**verb** [with obj.] prevent (someone) from giving their full attention to something: *don't allow noise to **distract** you **from** your work* | [as adj. **distracting**] *she found his nearness distracting.*
■divert (attention) from something: *it was another attempt to **distract** attention **from** the truth.* ■(**distract oneself**) divert one's attention from something worrying or unpleasant by doing something different or more pleasurable: *I tried to distract myself by concentrating on Jane.* ■archaic perplex and bewilder: *horror and doubt distract His troubl'd thoughts.*
– ORIGIN late Middle English (also in the sense 'pull in different directions'): from Latin *distract-* 'drawn apart', from the verb *distrahere*, from *dis-* 'apart' + *trahere* 'to draw, drag'.

distracted ▶**adjective** unable to concentrate because one's mind is preoccupied by something worrying or unpleasant: *Charlotte seemed too distracted to give him much attention* | *she ran her fingers through her hair in a distracted fashion.*
– DERIVATIVES **distractedly** adverb.

distraction ▶**noun** **1** a thing that prevents someone from giving their full attention to something else: *the firm found passenger travel a **distraction from** the main business of moving freight.*
■a diversion or recreation: *there are plenty of distractions such as sailing* | [mass noun] *he roved the district in search of distraction.*
2 [mass noun] extreme agitation of the mind or emotions: *he knew she was nervous by her uncharacteristic air of distraction.*
– PHRASES **drive someone to distraction** annoy someone intensely: *he was **driven to distraction** by the pain in his shoulder.* **to distraction** (in hyperbolic use) intensely: *she loved him to distraction.*
– ORIGIN late Middle English: from Latin *distractio(n-)*, from the verb *distrahere* (see **DISTRACT**).

distractor ▶**noun** a person or thing that distracts: *the visual channel is capable of being a powerful distractor.*
■an incorrect option in a multiple choice question: *four pictures, three of which are distractors.*

distrain /dɪˈstreɪn/ ▶**verb** [with obj.] Law seize (someone's property) in order to obtain payment of rent or other money owed: *legislation has restricted the right to distrain goods found upon the premises.*
■seize the property of (someone) for this purpose: *the Crown applied political pressure by distraining debtors.*
– DERIVATIVES **distrainer** noun, **distrainment** noun.
– ORIGIN Middle English: from Old French *destreindre*, from Latin *distringere* 'stretch apart', from *dis-* 'apart' + *stringere* 'tighten'.

distraint /dɪˈstreɪnt/ ▶**noun** [mass noun] Law the seizure of someone's property in order to obtain payment of money that they owe, especially rent: *many faced heavy fines and the distraint of goods.*
– ORIGIN mid 18th cent.: from **DISTRAIN**, on the pattern of *constraint*.

distrait /dɪˈstreɪ, ˈdɪstreɪ/ ▶**adjective** (fem. **distraite** /-ˈstreɪt/) [predic.] distracted or absent-minded: *he seemed oddly distrait.*
– ORIGIN mid 18th cent.: French, from Old French *destrait*, past participle of *destraire* 'distract', from Latin *distrahere* 'pull apart' (see **DISTRACT**).

distraught /dɪˈstrɔːt/ ▶**adjective** very worried and upset: *a distraught woman sobbed and screamed for help* | *he is terribly distraught.*
– ORIGIN late Middle English: alteration of the obsolete adjective *distract* (from Latin *distractus* 'pulled apart'), influenced by *straught*, archaic past participle of **STRETCH**.

distress ▶**noun** [mass noun] **1** extreme anxiety, sorrow, or pain: *to his distress he saw that she was trembling* | *her fingers flew to her throat **in distress**.*
■the state of a ship or aircraft when in danger or difficulty and needing help: *vessels **in distress** on or near the coast* | [as modifier] *the plane sent out a distress call.* ■suffering caused by lack of money or the basic necessities of life: *the poor were helped in their distress.* ■Medicine a state of physical strain, exhaustion, or, in particular, breathing difficulty: *they said the baby was in distress.*
2 Law another term for **DISTRAINT**.
▶**verb** [with obj.] cause (someone) anxiety, sorrow, or pain: *I didn't mean to distress you* | *please don't **distress yourself*** | [with obj. and infinitive] *he was distressed to find that Anna would not talk to him* | [as adj. **distressing**] *some very distressing news.*
■give (furniture or leather) simulated marks of age and wear: *the manner in which leather jackets are industrially distressed.*
– DERIVATIVES **distressful** adjective, **distressingly** adverb.
– ORIGIN Middle English: from Old French *destresce* (noun), *destrecier* (verb), based on Latin *distringere* 'stretch apart'.

distressed ▶**adjective** suffering from extreme anxiety, sorrow, or pain: *I was distressed at the news of his death* | *the distressed relatives of his victims.*
■dated impoverished: *women in distressed circumstances.* ■(of furniture or leather) having simulated marks of age and wear: *a distressed leather jacket.*

distressed area ▶**noun** a region of high unemployment and poverty.

distress rocket ▶**noun** a rocket fired as a distress signal.

distress signal ▶**noun** a signal from a ship or aircraft that is in danger.

distress warrant ▶**noun** Law a warrant authorizing distraint: *the landlord took out a distress warrant in respect of the outstanding rent.*

distributary /dɪˈstrɪbjʊt(ə)ri/ ▶**noun** (pl. **-ies**) a branch of a river that does not return to the main stream after leaving it (as in a delta).

distribute /dɪˈstrɪbjuːt, ˈdɪstrɪbjuːt/ ▶ **verb** [with obj.] **1** give a share or a unit of (something) to each of a number of recipients: *information leaflets are being distributed to hotels and guest houses.*
■ supply (goods) to shops and other businesses that sell to consumers: *the journal is distributed worldwide.* ■ (**be distributed**) occur throughout an area: *the birds are mainly distributed in marshes and river valleys.* ■ Printing separate (metal type that has been set up) and return the characters to their separate compartments in a type case.
2 Logic use (a term) to include every individual of the class to which it refers: *the middle term must be distributed, at least once, in the premises.*
– DERIVATIVES **distributable** adjective.
– ORIGIN late Middle English: from Latin *distribut-* 'divided up', from the verb *distribuere*, from *dis-* 'apart' + *tribuere* 'assign'.

USAGE The word **distribute** is pronounced either with the stress on the **-stri-** or with the stress on the **dis-**. Until recently the latter, with the stress on the first syllable, was considered incorrect in standard British English, but now both pronunciations are standard.

distributed system ▶ **noun** a number of independent computers linked by a network.

distribution ▶ **noun** [mass noun] the action of sharing something out among a number of recipients: *the government donated 4,000 kg of coffee for distribution among refugees* | [count noun] *tax relief was extended to distributions out of settlements.*
■ the way in which something is shared out among a group or spread over an area: *changes undergone by the area have affected the distribution of its wildlife.* ■ the action or process of supplying goods to shops and other businesses that sell to consumers: *a manager has the choice of four types of distribution* | [as modifier] *an established **distribution channel**.* ■ Bridge the different number of cards of each suit in a player's hand: *strength has two ingredients, high cards and distribution.*
– DERIVATIVES **distributional** adjective.
– ORIGIN late Middle English: from Latin *distributio(n-)*, from the verb *distribuere* (see **DISTRIBUTE**).

distribution board ▶ **noun** a panel carrying the fuses, terminals, and other components of a number of subsidiary electric circuits.

distribution function ▶ **noun** short for **CUMULATIVE DISTRIBUTION FUNCTION**.

distributive /dɪˈstrɪbjʊtɪv/ ▶ **adjective** **1** concerned with the supply of goods to shops and other businesses that sell to consumers: *transport and distributive industries.*
■ concerned with the way in which things are shared between people: *the distributive effects of public expenditure* | *distributive justice.*
2 Grammar (of a determiner or pronoun) referring to each individual of a class, not to the class collectively, e.g. *each, either.*
3 Mathematics (of an operation) fulfilling the condition that, when it is performed on two or more quantities already combined by another operation, the result is the same as when it is performed on each quantity individually and the products then combined.
▶ **noun** Grammar a distributive word.
– DERIVATIVES **distributively** adverb.
– ORIGIN late Middle English: from Old French *distributif, -ive* or late Latin *distributivus*, from Latin *distribut-* 'divided up', from the verb *distribuere* (see **DISTRIBUTE**).

distributor /dɪˈstrɪbjʊtə/ ▶ **noun** **1** an agent who supplies goods to shops and other businesses that sell to consumers: *an American distributor for his records* | *a sports goods distributor.*
2 a device in a petrol engine for passing electric current to each spark plug in turn.

district ▶ **noun** an area of a country or city, especially one regarded as a distinct unit because of a particular characteristic: *a coal-mining district.*
■ [often as modifier] a region defined for an administrative purpose: *a district health authority.* ■ Brit. a division of a county or region that elects its own councillors.
▶ **verb** [with obj.] N. Amer. divide into areas: [as noun **districting**] *the province's system of electoral districting.*
– ORIGIN early 17th cent. (denoting the territory under the jurisdiction of a feudal lord): from French, from medieval Latin *districtus* '(territory of) jurisdiction', from Latin *distringere* 'draw apart'.

district attorney (abbrev.: **DA**) ▶ **noun** (in the US) a public official who acts as prosecutor for the state or the federal government in court in a particular district.

district auditor ▶ **noun** (in the UK) a civil servant responsible for auditing the accounts of local authorities.

district court ▶ **noun** (in the US) the federal or state court of first instance.

district heating ▶ **noun** [mass noun] the supply of heat or hot water from one source to a district or a group of buildings.

district nurse ▶ **noun** (in the UK) a nurse who visits and treats patients in their homes, operating in a specific area or in association with a particular general practice surgery or health centre.

District of Columbia (abbrev.: **DC**) a federal district of the US, coextensive with the city of Washington, situated on the Potomac River with boundaries on the states of Virginia and Maryland.

district surgeon ▶ **noun** (in South Africa) a doctor appointed by the government to serve a particular district in supervising vaccinations, post-mortems, and the general health care of people for whose welfare the state is responsible.

distrust ▶ **noun** [mass noun] the feeling that someone or something cannot be relied upon: *distrust of Soviet intentions soon followed.*
▶ **verb** [with obj.] doubt the honesty or reliability of; regard with suspicion: *the media were widely distrusted as agents of white power.*
– DERIVATIVES **distruster** noun, **distrustful** adjective, **distrustfully** adverb.

disturb ▶ **verb** [with obj.] interfere with the normal arrangement or functioning of: *using nails could disturb the roof covering.*
■ destroy the sleep or relaxation of: *he crept in so as not to disturb his sleeping parents.* ■ (often **be disturbed**) cause to feel anxious: *I am disturbed by the document I have just read* | [as adj. **disturbing**] *disturbing unemployment figures.* ■ interrupt or intrude on (someone) when they wish for privacy or secrecy: *I'll see my patient now and we are not to be disturbed.*
– DERIVATIVES **disturber** noun, **disturbingly** adverb.
– ORIGIN Middle English: from Old French *destourber*, from Latin *disturbare*, from *dis-* 'utterly' + *turbare* 'disturb' (from *turba* 'tumult').

disturbance ▶ **noun** [mass noun] the interruption of a settled and peaceful condition: *a helicopter landing can cause disturbance to residents.*
■ [count noun] a breakdown of peaceful and law-abiding behaviour; a riot: *the disturbances were precipitated when four men were refused bail* | [mass noun] *in court on a charge of **disturbance of the peace**.* ■ the disruption of healthy functioning: *her severe mental disturbance was diagnosed as schizophrenia.* ■ Law interference with rights or property; molestation.
– ORIGIN Middle English: from Old French *destourbance*, from *destourber* (see **DISTURB**).

disturbed ▶ **adjective** having had its normal pattern or functioning disrupted: *disturbed sleep.*
■ suffering or resulting from emotional and mental problems: *the treatment of disturbed children* | *disturbed behaviour.* ■ subject to a breakdown of peaceful and stable conditions: *the governor declared the districts a disturbed area.*

disubstituted /dʌɪˈsʌbstɪtjuːtɪd/ ▶ **adjective** Chemistry (of a molecule) having two substituent groups.

disulfiram /dʌɪˈsʌlfɪram/ ▶ **noun** [mass noun] Medicine a synthetic compound used in the treatment of alcoholics to make drinking alcohol produce unpleasant after-effects. Also called **ANTABUSE** (trademark).
• Alternative name: **tetraethylthiuram disulphide**; chem. formula: $(C_2H_5)_2NCSSCN(C_2H_5)_2$.
– ORIGIN 1940s: blend of *disulfide* (see **DISULPHIDE**) and **THIURAM**.

disulphide /dʌɪˈsʌlfʌɪd/ (US **disulfide**) ▶ **noun** Chemistry a sulphide containing two atoms of sulphur in its molecule or empirical formula.
■ an organic compound containing the group —S—S— bonded to other groups.

disunion ▶ **noun** [mass noun] the breaking up of something such as a federation: *his rejection of disunion was consistent with his nationalism.*

disunited ▶ **adjective** lacking unity: *a disunited nation.*

disunity /dɪsˈjuːnɪti/ ▶ **noun** [mass noun] disagreement and conflict within a group: *the disunity among opposition parties.*

disuse /dɪsˈjuːs/ ▶ **noun** [mass noun] the state of not being used: *his voice was croaky with disuse.*

disused ▶ **adjective** no longer being used: *they held an exhibition in a disused warehouse.*

disutility /ˌdɪsjuːˈtɪlɪti/ ▶ **noun** [mass noun] Economics the adverse or harmful effects associated with a particular activity or process, especially when carried out over a long period.

disyllabic /ˌdʌɪsɪˈlabɪk/ (also **dissyllabic**) ▶ **adjective** (of a word or metrical foot) consisting of two syllables.
■ (of a bird's characteristic call) consisting of two distinct sounds, such as the call of the cuckoo.
– ORIGIN mid 17th cent.: from French *dissyllabique*, via Latin from Greek *disullabos* 'of two syllables'.

disyllable /dʌɪˈsɪləb(ə)l, ˈdʌɪsɪl-/ (also **dissyllable** /dɪˈsɪləb(ə)l/) ▶ **noun** Prosody a word or metrical foot consisting of two syllables.
– ORIGIN late 16th cent.: alteration (influenced by **SYLLABLE**) of French *disyllabe*, via Latin from Greek *disullabos* 'of two syllables', from *di-* 'two' + *sullabē* 'syllable'.

dit ▶ **noun** (in the Morse system) another term for **DOT**[1].
– ORIGIN Second World War: imitative.

ditch ▶ **noun** a narrow channel dug in the ground, typically used for drainage alongside a road or the edge of a field.
▶ **verb** [with obj.] **1** provide with ditches: *he was praised for ditching the coastal areas.*
■ [no obj.] make or repair ditches: *we used to come across bryony while we were ditching* | [as noun **ditching**] *they would have to pay for hedging and ditching.*
2 informal get rid of; give up: *it crossed her mind to ditch her shoes and run* | *plans for the road were ditched following a public inquiry.*
■ informal end a relationship with (someone) peremptorily: *she ditched her husband to marry the window cleaner.* ■ N. Amer. informal play truant from (school): *maybe she could ditch school and run away.*
3 informal bring (an aircraft) down on the sea in an emergency: *he was picked up by a gunboat after ditching his plane in the Mediterranean.*
■ [no obj.] (of an aircraft) make a forced landing on the sea: *the aircraft was obliged to ditch in the sea off the North African coast.* ■ US derail (a train).
– DERIVATIVES **ditcher** noun.
– ORIGIN Old English *dīc*, of Germanic origin; related to Dutch *dijk* 'ditch, dyke' and German *Teich* 'pond, pool', also to **DYKE**[1].

ditchwater ▶ **noun** [mass noun] stagnant water in a ditch.
– PHRASES **dull as ditchwater** see **DULL**.

diterpene /dʌɪˈtəːpiːn/ ▶ **noun** Chemistry any of a group of terpenes found in plant gums and resins, having unsaturated molecules based on a unit with the formula $C_{20}H_{32}$.
– DERIVATIVES **diterpenoid** adjective & noun.

ditheism /ˈdʌɪθiːɪz(ə)m/ ▶ **noun** [mass noun] a belief in two gods, especially as independent and opposed principles of good and evil.
– DERIVATIVES **ditheist** noun.

dither ▶ **verb** [no obj.] **1** be indecisive: *I can't bear people who dither* | *he was dithering about the election date.*
2 [with obj.] Computing display or print (an image) without sharp edges so that there appear to be more colours in it than are really available: [as adj. **dithered**] *dithered bit maps.*
▶ **noun** **1** [mass noun] informal indecisive behaviour: *after months of dither other ministers had still not agreed.*
2 [in sing.] a state of agitation: ***all of a dither**, he prophesied instant chaos.*
– DERIVATIVES **ditherer** noun, **dithery** adjective.
– ORIGIN mid 17th cent. (in the dialect sense 'tremble, quiver'): variant of dialect *didder*; related to **DODDER**[1].

dithionite /dʌɪˈθʌɪənʌɪt/ ▶ **noun** Chemistry a salt containing the anion $S_2O_4^{2-}$.
– ORIGIN mid 20th cent.: from **DI-**[1] 'two' + Greek *theion* 'sulphur' + **-ITE**[1].

dithizone /dʌɪˈθʌɪzəʊn/ ▶ **noun** [mass noun] Chemistry a synthetic compound used as a reagent for the analysis and separation of lead and other metals.
• Alternative name: **diphenylthiocarbazone**; chem. formula: $C_{13}H_{12}N_4S$.

– ORIGIN 1920s: from elements of the systematic name (see above).

dithyramb /ˈdɪθɪram(b)/ ▶ **noun** a wild choral hymn of ancient Greece, especially one dedicated to Dionysus.
■ a passionate or inflated speech, poem, or other writing.
– DERIVATIVES **dithyrambic** adjective.
– ORIGIN early 17th cent.: via Latin from Greek *dithurambos*, of unknown ultimate origin.

ditransitive /dʌɪˈtransɪtɪv, -ˈtrɑː-, -nz-/ ▶ **adjective** Grammar denoting a verb that takes two objects, for example *give* as in *I gave her the book*.

ditsy ▶ **adjective** variant spelling of **DITZY**.

dittany /ˈdɪtəni/ ▶ **noun** [mass noun] any of a number of aromatic herbaceous or shrubby plants:
• (also **dittany of Crete**) a dwarf shrub with white woolly leaves and pink flowers, native to Crete and Greece (*Origanum dictamnus*, family Labiatae). • (also **American dittany**) an American herb used in cookery and herbal medicine (genus *Cunila*, family Labiatae). • another term for **GAS PLANT**.
– ORIGIN late Middle English: from Old French *ditain* or medieval Latin *ditaneum*, from Latin *dictamnus*, *dictamnum*, from Greek *diktamnon*, perhaps from *Diktē*, the name of a mountain in Crete.

ditto ▶ used in accounts and lists to indicate that an item is repeated (often indicated by ditto marks under the word or figure to be repeated).
■ informal used to indicate that something already said is applicable a second time: *if one folds his arms, so does the other; if one crosses his legs, ditto*.
– ORIGIN early 17th cent. (in the sense 'in the aforesaid month'): from Tuscan dialect, variant of Italian *detto* 'said', from Latin *dictus* 'said'.

dittography /dɪˈtɒɡrəfi/ ▶ **noun** (pl. **-ies**) a mistaken repetition of a letter, word, or phrase by a copyist.
– DERIVATIVES **dittographic** adjective.
– ORIGIN late 19th cent.: from Greek *dittos* 'double' + **-GRAPHY**.

ditto marks ▶ **plural noun** two apostrophes (,,) representing 'ditto'.

ditty ▶ **noun** (pl. **-ies**) a short simple song: *a lovely little music-hall ditty*.
– ORIGIN Middle English: from Old French *dite* 'composition', from Latin *dictatum* (neuter) 'something dictated', from *dictare* 'to dictate'.

ditty bag (also **ditty box**) ▶ **noun** a receptacle for odds and ends, especially one used by sailors or fishermen.
– ORIGIN mid 19th cent.: of unknown origin.

ditz ▶ **noun** N. Amer. informal a scatterbrained person.
– ORIGIN 1970s: back-formation from **DITZY**.

ditzy (also **ditsy**) ▶ **adjective** N. Amer. informal silly or scatterbrained: *don't tell me my ditzy secretary didn't send you an invitation!*
– DERIVATIVES **ditziness** noun.
– ORIGIN 1970s: of unknown origin.

diuresis /ˌdʌɪjʊ(ə)ˈriːsɪs/ ▶ **noun** [mass noun] Medicine increased or excessive production of urine. Compare with **POLYURIA**.
– ORIGIN late 17th cent.: modern Latin, from **DI-**[3] 'through' + Greek *ourēsis* 'urination'.

diuretic /ˌdʌɪjʊ(ə)ˈrɛtɪk/ Medicine ▶ **adjective** (chiefly of drugs) causing increased passing of urine.
▶ **noun** a diuretic drug.
– ORIGIN late Middle English: from Old French *diuretique*, or via late Latin from Greek *diourētikos*, from *diourein* 'urinate', from *dia* 'through' + *ouron* 'urine'.

diurnal /dʌɪˈəːn(ə)l/ ▶ **adjective** **1** of or during the day.
■ Zoology (of animals) active in the daytime. ■ Botany (of flowers) open only during the day.
2 daily; of each day: *diurnal rhythms*.
■ Astronomy of or resulting from the daily rotation of the earth: *diurnal aberration*.
– DERIVATIVES **diurnally** adverb.
– ORIGIN late Middle English (as a term in astronomy): from late Latin *diurnalis*, from Latin *diurnus* 'daily', from *dies* 'day'.

Div. ▶ **abbreviation for** Division.

div ▶ **abbreviation for** divergence (in mathematical equations).

diva /ˈdiːvə/ ▶ **noun** a famous female opera singer.
■ an admired or distinguished woman: *was it prestigious or trashy to be a disco diva?*
– ORIGIN late 19th cent.: via Italian from Latin, literally 'goddess'.

divagate /ˈdʌɪvəɡeɪt/ ▶ **verb** poetic/literary [no obj.] stray; digress: *Yeats divagated into Virgil's territory only once*.
– DERIVATIVES **divagation** noun.
– ORIGIN late 16th cent.: from Latin *divagat-* 'wandered about', from the verb *divagari*, from *di-* 'widely' + *vagari* 'wander'.

divalent /dʌɪˈveɪl(ə)nt/ ▶ **adjective** Chemistry having a valency of two.

Divali ▶ **noun** variant spelling of **DIWALI**.

divan /dɪˈvan, dʌɪˈvan, ˈdʌɪvan/ ▶ **noun** **1** (also **divan bed**) a bed consisting of a base and mattress but no footboard or headboard.
■ a long low sofa without a back or arms.
2 historical a legislative body, council chamber, or court of justice in the Ottoman Empire or elsewhere in the Middle East.
– ORIGIN late 16th cent. (in sense 2): via French or Italian from Turkish *dīvān*, from Persian *dīwān* 'anthology, register, court, or bench'; compare with **DIWAN**. As a piece of furniture, a *divan* was originally (early 18th cent.) a low bench or raised section of floor used as a long seat against the wall of a room, common in Middle Eastern countries; European imitation of this led to the sense 'low flat sofa or bed' (late 19th cent.).

divaricate /dʌɪˈvarɪkeɪt, dɪ-/ ▶ **verb** [no obj.] technical or poetic/literary stretch or spread apart; diverge widely: *her crow's feet are divaricating like deltas*.
▶ **adjective** Botany (of a branch) coming off the stem almost at a right angle.
– DERIVATIVES **divarication** noun.
– ORIGIN early 17th cent.: from Latin *divaricat-* 'stretched apart', from the verb *divaricare*, from *di-* (expressing intensive force) + *varicare* 'stretch the legs apart' (from *varicus* 'straddling').

dive ▶ **verb** (past and past participle **dived**; US also **dove** /dəʊv/) [no obj.] **1** [with adverbial of direction] plunge head first into water: *she walked to the deep end, then she dived in | he dived off the bridge for a bet*.
■ move quickly or suddenly in a specified direction: *a bullet passed close to his head and he dived for cover* | [as adj. **diving**] *he scored with a diving header*. ■ (of an aircraft or bird) plunge steeply downwards through the air: *arctic skuas which dive at your head as you walk near their territories*. ■ figurative (of prices or profits) drop suddenly: *profits before tax dived by 61 per cent*. ■ informal put one's hand quickly into something, especially a pocket or bag, in order to find something: *she **dived into** her bag and extracted a card*. ■ Soccer (of a player) deliberately fall when challenged in order to deceive the referee into awarding a foul.
2 swim under water using breathing equipment: *he had been diving in the area to test equipment*.
■ (of a fish, a submarine, or a vessel used for under water exploration) go to a deeper level in water: *the fish dive down to about 1,400 feet and then swim south-west*.
▶ **noun** **1** an act of diving, in particular:
■ a plunge head first into water: *he hit the sea in a shallow dive*. ■ an instance of swimming or exploring under water with breathing equipment: *divers should have a good intake of fluid before each dive*. ■ an act of going deeper under water by a fish, submarine, or diving vessel: *pilot whales can go to 600 metres in a dive lasting 18 minutes*. ■ a steep descent by an aircraft or bird: *the jumbo jet went into a dive*. See also **NOSEDIVE**. ■ a sudden movement in a specified direction: *she **made a dive for** the fridge to quench her raging thirst*. ■ figurative a sudden and significant fall in prices or profits: *an 11 per cent dive in profits*. ■ Soccer a deliberate fall by a player, intended to deceive the referee into awarding a foul.
2 informal a disreputable nightclub or bar: *he got into a fight in some dive*.
– PHRASES **take a dive** Boxing pretend to be knocked down or out. ■ (of prices, hopes, fortunes, etc.) fall suddenly: *profits could take a dive as easily as they could soar | her reputation took a dive from which it has not recovered*.
– ORIGIN Old English *dūfan* 'dive, sink' and *dȳfan* 'immerse', of Germanic origin; related to **DEEP** and **DIP**.

dive-bomb ▶ **verb** [with obj.] bomb (a target) while diving steeply downwards in an aircraft: *planes were dive-bombing the aerodrome*.
■ (of a bird or flying insect) attack (something) by swooping down on it: *the crow folded its wings and dive-bombed the vulture*.
– DERIVATIVES **dive-bomber** noun.

diver ▶ **noun** **1** a person or animal that dives, in particular:
■ a person who dives as a sport: *an Olympic diver*. ■ a person who wears a diving suit to work under water: *a diver at the oil terminal | a police diver*. ■ an animal that habitually dives: *dolphins are superb divers*.
2 a large diving waterbird with a sleek black or grey head, a straight pointed bill, and short legs set far back under the body. Divers breed by lakes in northern latitudes and have wailing calls. Called **LOON**[2] in North America.
• Family Gaviidae and genus *Gavia*: five species, including the **great northern diver** or common loon (*G. immer*) of both Canada and Eurasia.

diverge /dʌɪˈvəːdʒ, dɪ-/ ▶ **verb** [no obj.] **1** (of a road, route, or line) separate from another route, especially a main route, and go in a different direction: *at the square, the Lytham Road tram route **diverged from** the Promenade* | [as adj. **diverging**] *the junction of two diverging roads* | figurative *their ways had diverged at university*.
■ develop in a different direction: *English Gothic architecture began to **diverge from** that on the Continent*. ■ (of an opinion, theory, approach, etc.) differ markedly: *the coverage by the columnists **diverged from** that in the main news stories | it is here that the different theories diverge* | [as adj. **diverging**] *diverging concepts of nation-building*. ■ depart from a set course or standard: *suddenly he **diverged from** his text*.
2 Mathematics (of a series) increase indefinitely as more of its terms are added.
– ORIGIN mid 17th cent.: from medieval Latin *divergere*, from Latin *dis-* 'in two ways' + *vergere* 'to turn or incline'.

divergence ▶ **noun** [mass noun] **1** the process or state of diverging: *the divergence between primates and other groups*.
■ [count noun] a difference or conflict in opinions, interests, wishes, etc.: *a fundamental divergence of attitude*. ■ [count noun] a place where airflows or ocean currents diverge, typically marked by downwelling (of air) or upwelling (of water).
2 Mathematics the scalar product of the operator del and a given vector, which gives a measure of the quantity of flux emanating from any point of the vector field or the rate of loss of mass, heat, etc., from it.

divergent ▶ **adjective** **1** tending to be different or develop in different directions: *divergent interpretations | varieties of English can remain astonishingly **divergent from** one another*.
■ Psychology (of thought) using a variety of premises, especially unfamiliar premises, as bases for inference, and avoiding common limiting assumptions in making deductions.
2 Mathematics (of a series) increasing indefinitely as more of its terms are added.
– DERIVATIVES **divergency** noun, **divergently** adverb.

divers /ˈdʌɪvəz/ ▶ **adjective** [attrib.] archaic or poetic/literary of varying types; several: *in divers places*.
– ORIGIN Middle English: via Old French from Latin *diversus* 'diverse', from *divertere* 'turn in separate ways' (see **DIVERT**).

diverse /dʌɪˈvəːs, ˈdʌɪvəːs/ ▶ **adjective** showing a great deal of variety; very different: *a culturally diverse population | subjects as diverse as architecture, language teaching, and the physical sciences*.
– DERIVATIVES **diversely** adverb.
– ORIGIN Middle English: variant of **DIVERS**.

diversify /dʌɪˈvəːsɪfʌɪ, dɪ-/ ▶ **verb** (**-ies**, **-ied**) make or become more diverse or varied: [no obj.] *the trilobites **diversified into** a great number of species* | [with obj.] *new plants will diversify the habitat* | [as adj. **diversified**] *a diversified economy*.
■ [no obj.] (of a company) enlarge or vary its range of products or field of operation: *the company expanded rapidly and **diversified into** computers*. ■ [with obj.] [often as adj. **diversified**] enlarge or vary the range of products or the field of operation of (a company): *the rise of the diversified corporation*.
– DERIVATIVES **diversification** noun.
– ORIGIN late Middle English (in the sense 'show diversity'): via Old French from medieval Latin *diversificare* 'make dissimilar', from Latin *diversus*, past participle of *divertere* (see **DIVERT**).

diversion /dʌɪˈvəːʃ(ə)n, dɪ-/ ▶ **noun** **1** an instance of turning something aside from its course: *a diversion of resources from defence to civil research*.
■ Brit. an alternative route for use by traffic when the usual road is temporarily closed: *the road was closed and diversions put into operation*.
2 an activity that diverts the mind from tedious or serious concerns; a recreation or pastime: *our chief diversion was reading*.
■ something intended to distract someone's attention

from something more important: *a subsidiary raid was carried out on the airfield to create a diversion.*
– DERIVATIVES **diversionary** adjective.
– ORIGIN late Middle English: from late Latin *diversio(n-)*, from Latin *divertere* 'turn aside' (see **DIVERT**).

diversity /dʌɪˈvəːsɪti, dɪ-/ ▶ **noun** (pl. **-ies**) [mass noun] the state of being diverse: *there was considerable diversity in the style of the reports.*
■ [usu. in sing.] a range of different things: *newspapers were obliged to allow a diversity of views to be printed.*
– ORIGIN Middle English: from Old French *diversite*, from Latin *diversitas*, from *diversus* 'diverse', past participle of *divertere* 'turn aside' (see **DIVERT**).

divert /dʌɪˈvəːt, dɪ-/ ▶ **verb** [with obj.] **1** cause (someone or something) to change course or turn from one direction to another: *a scheme to* ***divert*** *water* ***from*** *the river to irrigate agricultural land.*
■ [no obj.] (of a vehicle or person) change course: *an aircraft has diverted and will be with you shortly.* ■ reallocate (something, especially money or resources) to a different purpose: *more of their advertising budget was* ***diverted into*** *promotions.*
2 distract (someone or their attention) from something: *she managed to* ***divert*** *Rose* ***from*** *the dangerous topic of Lady Usk.*
■ [usu. as adj. **diverting**] draw the attention of (someone) away from tedious or serious concerns; entertain or amuse: *a diverting book | playing variations on a famous passage by James Joyce to divert herself.*
– DERIVATIVES **divertingly** adverb.
– ORIGIN late Middle English: via French from Latin *divertere*, from *di-* 'aside' + *vertere* 'to turn'.

diverticula plural form of **DIVERTICULUM**.

diverticular /ˌdʌɪvəˈtɪkjʊlə/ ▶ **adjective** [attrib.] Medicine of or relating to diverticula.

diverticular disease ▶ **noun** [mass noun] a condition in which muscle spasm in the colon (lower intestine) in the presence of diverticula causes abdominal pain and disturbance of bowel function without inflammation.

diverticulitis /ˌdʌɪvətɪkjʊˈlʌɪtɪs/ ▶ **noun** [mass noun] Medicine inflammation of a diverticulum, especially in the colon, causing pain and disturbance of bowel function. Compare with **DIVERTICULOSIS**.

diverticulosis /ˌdʌɪvətɪkjʊˈləʊsɪs/ ▶ **noun** [mass noun] Medicine a condition in which diverticula are present in the intestine without signs of inflammation. Compare with **DIVERTICULITIS**.

diverticulum /ˌdʌɪvəˈtɪkjʊləm/ ▶ **noun** (pl. **diverticula** /-lə/) Anatomy & Zoology a blind tube leading from a cavity or passage.
■ Medicine an abnormal sac or pouch formed at a weak point in the wall of the alimentary tract.
– ORIGIN early 19th cent.: from medieval Latin, variant of Latin *deverticulum* 'byway', from *devertere* 'turn down or aside'.

divertimento /dɪˌvəːtɪˈmɛntəʊ, -ˌvɛːt-/ ▶ **noun** (pl. **divertimenti** /-ti/ or **divertimentos**) Music a light and entertaining composition, typically one in the form of a suite for chamber orchestra.
– ORIGIN mid 18th cent. (denoting a diversion or amusement): Italian, literally 'diversion'.

divertissement /dɪˈvəːtɪsmɒnt, ˌdiːvɛːˈtiːsmɒ̃/ ▶ **noun** a minor entertainment or diversion: *the intellectual divertissements of working men.*
■ Ballet a short dance within a ballet that displays a dancer's technical skill without advancing the plot or character development.
– ORIGIN early 18th cent. (specifically denoting a short ballet): French, from *divertiss-*, stem of *divertir*, from Latin *divertere* 'turn in separate ways'.

Dives /ˈdʌɪviːz/ ▶ **noun** poetic/literary used to refer to a typical or hypothetical rich man: *there must be rich and poor, Dives says, smacking his claret.*
– ORIGIN late Middle English: from late Latin, used in the Vulgate translation of the Bible (Luke 16).

divest /dʌɪˈvɛst, dɪ-/ ▶ **verb** [with obj.] deprive (someone) of power, rights, or possessions: *men are unlikely to be* ***divested of*** *power without a struggle.*
■ deprive (something) of a particular quality: *he has* ***divested*** *the original play* ***of*** *its charm.* ■ dated or humorous relieve (someone) of something being worn or carried: *she divested him of his coat.* ■ [no obj.] rid oneself of something which one no longer requires, such as a business interest or investment: *a situation where it appears easier to carry on in the business than to divest | the government's policy of* ***divesting itself of*** *state holdings.*
– ORIGIN early 17th cent.: alteration of *devest*, from Old French *desvestir*, from *des-* (expressing removal) + Latin *vestire* (from *vestis* 'garment').

divestiture (also **divesture**) ▶ **noun** another term for **DIVESTMENT**.
– ORIGIN early 17th cent.: from medieval Latin *divestit-* 'divested' (from the verb *divestire*) + **-URE**.

divestment ▶ **noun** [mass noun] the action or process of selling off subsidiary business interests or investments: *the importance of divestment |* [count noun] *proceeds from divestments.*

divi ▶ **noun** (pl. **divis**) variant spelling of **DIVVY**[1].

divide ▶ **verb 1** separate or be separated into parts: [with obj.] *consumer magazines can be* ***divided into*** *a number of different categories | the oak beams that* ***divided up*** *the whitewashed walls |* [no obj.] *the cell clusters began to divide rapidly.*
■ [with obj.] separate (something) into portions and distribute a share to each of a number of people: *Jack* ***divided up*** *the rest of the cash | profits from his single were to be* ***divided between*** *a number of charities.* ■ [with obj.] allocate (different parts of one's time, attention, or efforts) to different activities or places: *the last years of her life were* ***divided between*** *Bermuda and Paris.* ■ [with obj.] form a boundary between (two people or things): *a fence* ***divides off*** *the western side of the garden.* ■ (of a legislative assembly) separate or be separated into two groups for voting: [no obj.] *the House divided: Ayes 287, Noes 196 |* [with obj.] *the Party decided to put down an amendment and thus divide the House.*
2 disagree or cause to disagree: [with obj.] *the question had divided Frenchmen since the Revolution |* [as adj. **divided**] *a divided party leadership |* [no obj.] *cities where politicians frequently divide along racial lines.*
3 [with obj.] Mathematics find how many times (a number) contains another: *36* ***divided by*** *2 equals 18 |* [no obj.] *the program helps children to multiply and divide quickly and accurately.*
■ [no obj.] (of a number) be susceptible of division without a remainder: *30 does not divide by 8.* ■ find how many times (a number) is contained in another: *divide 4 into 20.* ■ [no obj.] (of a number) be contained in a number without a remainder: *3 divides into 15.*
▶ **noun** a wide divergence between two groups, typically producing tension or hostility: *there was still a profound cultural* ***divide between*** *the parties.*
■ a boundary between two things: *symbolically, the difference of sex is a divide.* ■ chiefly US a ridge or line of high ground forming the division between two valleys or river systems.
– PHRASES **divide and rule** (or **conquer**) the policy of maintaining control over one's subordinates or subjects by encouraging dissent between them, thereby preventing them from uniting to overthrow one: *the politics of divide and rule in society.* **divided against itself** (of a group which should be coherent) split by factional interests: *the regime is profoundly divided against itself.*
– ORIGIN Middle English (as a verb): from Latin *dividere* 'force apart, remove'. The noun dates from the mid 17th cent.

divided highway ▶ **noun** N. Amer. a dual carriageway.

divided skirt ▶ **noun** dated culottes.

dividend /ˈdɪvɪdɛnd/ ▶ **noun 1** a sum of money paid regularly (typically annually) by a company to its shareholders out of its profits (or reserves).
■ a payment divided among a number of people, e.g. winners in a football pool, members of a cooperative, or creditors of an insolvent estate. ■ an individual's share of a dividend. ■ (**dividends**) a benefit from an action or policy: *the club's youth policy would* ***pay dividends*** *in the future.* See also **PEACE DIVIDEND**.
2 Mathematics a number to be divided by another number.
– ORIGIN late 15th cent. (in the general sense 'portion, share'): from Anglo-Norman French *dividende*, from Latin *dividendum* 'something to be divided', from the verb *dividere* (see **DIVIDE**).

dividend cover ▶ **noun** the ratio of a company's net profits to the total sum allotted in dividends to ordinary shareholders.

dividend warrant (US **dividend check**) ▶ **noun** a document that shows that a shareholder is entitled to a dividend.

dividend yield ▶ **noun** a dividend expressed as a percentage of a current share price.

divider ▶ **noun 1** a person or thing that divides a whole into parts.
■ an issue on which opinions are divided: *on the Labour side, the big divider was still nuclear weapons.* ■ (also **room divider**) a screen or piece of furniture that divides a room into two parts.
2 (**dividers**) a measuring compass, especially one with a screw for making fine adjustments.

dividing line ▶ **noun** the boundary between two areas: ***the dividing line between*** *eastern and western zones.*
■ a distinction or set of distinctions marking the difference between two things that are or seem to be closely related: ***the dividing line between*** *what is and what is not permissible is often difficult to draw.*

divi-divi /ˈdɪvɪˌdɪvi/ ▶ **noun** (pl. **divi-divis**) a small tropical American tree of the pea family, bearing curled pods.
● *Caesalpinia coriaria*, family Leguminosae.
■ [mass noun] these pods, used as a source of tannin.
– ORIGIN mid 19th cent.: via American Spanish from Carib.

divination /ˌdɪvɪˈneɪʃ(ə)n/ ▶ **noun** [mass noun] the practice of seeking knowledge of the future or the unknown by supernatural means.
– DERIVATIVES **divinatory** adjective.
– ORIGIN late Middle English: from Latin *divinatio(n-)*, from *divinare* 'predict' (see **DIVINE**[2]).

divine[1] ▶ **adjective** (**diviner**, **divinest**) **1** of, from, or like God or a god: *heroes with divine powers | paintings of shipwrecks being prevented by divine intervention.*
■ devoted to God; sacred: *divine liturgy.*
2 informal, dated excellent; delightful: *that succulent clementine tasted divine | he had the most divine smile.*
▶ **noun 1** dated a cleric or theologian.
2 (**the Divine**) providence or God.
– DERIVATIVES **divinely** adverb, **divineness** noun.
– ORIGIN late Middle English: via Old French from Latin *divinus*, from *divus* 'godlike' (related to *deus* 'god').

divine[2] ▶ **verb** [with obj.] discover (something) by guesswork or intuition: *mum had divined my state of mind |* [with clause] *they had divined that he was a fake.*
■ have supernatural or magical insight into (future events): *frauds who claimed to divine the future in chickens' entrails.* ■ discover (water) by dowsing.
– DERIVATIVES **diviner** noun.
– ORIGIN late Middle English: from Old French *deviner* 'predict', from Latin *divinare*, from *divinus* (see **DIVINE**[1]).

Divine Office ▶ **noun** see **OFFICE** (sense 4).

divine right of kings ▶ **noun** the doctrine that kings derive their authority from God not their subjects, from which it follows that rebellion is the worst of political crimes. It was enunciated in Britain in the 16th century under the Stuarts and is also associated with the absolutism of Louis XIV of France.

divine service ▶ **noun** [mass noun] public Christian worship.

diving ▶ **noun** [mass noun] **1** the sport or activity of swimming or exploring under water.
2 the sport or activity of diving into water from a diving board.

diving beetle ▶ **noun** a predatory water beetle which has fringed back legs for swimming and which stores air under its wing cases while diving.
● Family Dytiscidae: numerous genera and species, including the **great diving beetle** (*Dytiscus marginalis*).

diving bell ▶ **noun** an open-bottomed chamber supplied with air, in which a person can be let down under water.
■ an air-filled web in which the European water spider lives under water.

diving board ▶ **noun** an elevated board projecting over a swimming pool or other body of water, from which people dive or jump in.

diving duck ▶ **noun** a duck of a type which dives under water for food, such as the pochard, scaup, tufted duck, and goldeneye. Compare with **DABBLING DUCK**.
● Tribes Aythyini and Mergini, family Anatidae: several genera, in particular *Aythya* and *Bucephala*.

diving petrel ▶ **noun** a small stocky auk-like seabird with black upper parts and white underparts, which frequents southern oceans.
● Family Pelecanoididae and genus *Pelecanoides*: four species, in particular the **common** (or **northern**) **diving petrel** (*P. urinatrix*).

diving suit ▶ **noun** a watertight suit, typically with a helmet and an air supply, worn for working or exploring deep under water.

divining rod ▶ **noun** a stick or rod used for dowsing.

divinity /dɪˈvɪnɪti/ ▶ **noun** (pl. **-ies**) [mass noun] the state or quality of being divine: *Christ's divinity.*
■ the study of religion; theology: *a doctor of divinity.* ■ [count noun] a divine being; a god or goddess: *busts of various Roman divinities.* ■ (**the Divinity**) God.
– ORIGIN Middle English: from Old French *divinite*, from Latin *divinitas*, from *divinus* 'belonging to a deity' (see **DIVINE**[1]).

divinize /ˈdɪvɪnʌɪz/ (also **-ise**) ▶ **verb** [with obj.] make (someone) divine; deify: *this brush with death seems to have divinized her.*
– ORIGIN mid 17th cent.: from French *diviniser*, from *divin* 'divine'.

divisi /dɪˈviːsi/ ▶ **adjective** a musical direction indicating that a section of players should be divided into two or more groups each playing a different part: [postpositive] *violas divisi.*
▶ **noun** (pl. same) a passage written or played in this manner.
– ORIGIN Italian, literally 'divided' (plural), from *dividere* 'to divide'.

divisible /dɪˈvɪzɪb(ə)l/ ▶ **adjective** capable of being divided, physically or mentally: *the marine environment is divisible into a number of areas.*
■ Mathematics (of a number) containing another number a number of times without a remainder: *24 is divisible by 4.*
– DERIVATIVES **divisibility** noun.
– ORIGIN late Middle English: from late Latin *divisibilis*, from *divis-* 'divided', from the verb *dividere* (see **DIVIDE**).

division ▶ **noun** [mass noun] **1** the action of separating something into parts or the process of being separated: *the division of the land into small fields | a gene that helps regulate cell division.*
■ the distribution of something separated into parts: *the* ***division*** *of his estates* ***between*** *the two branches of his family.* ■ [count noun] an instance of members of a legislative body separating into two groups to vote for or against a bill: *the new clause was agreed without a division.* ■ the action of splitting the roots of a perennial plant into parts to be replanted separately, as a means of propagation: *the plant can also be easily increased by division in autumn.* ■ Logic the action of dividing a wider class into two or more subclasses.
2 disagreement between two or more groups, typically producing tension or hostility: *a growing sense of* ***division between*** *north and south |* [count noun] *a country with ethnic and cultural divisions.*
3 the process or skill of dividing one number by another. See also **LONG DIVISION**, **SHORT DIVISION**.
■ Mathematics the process of dividing a matrix, vector, or other quantity by another under specific rules to obtain a quotient.
4 [count noun] each of the parts into which something is divided: *the main divisions of the book.*
■ a major unit or section of an organization, typically one handling a particular kind of work: *a retail division.* ■ a group of army brigades or regiments: *an infantry division.* ■ a number of teams or competitors grouped together in a sport for competitive purposes according to such characteristics as ability, weight, or size: *the club will finish in fifth place in Division One.* ■ a part of a county, country, or city defined for administrative or political purposes: *a licensing division of a district.* ■ Brit. a part of a county or borough forming a parliamentary constituency: *he was MP for the Lancaster division of North Lancashire.* ■ Botany a principal taxonomic category that ranks above class and below kingdom, equivalent to the phylum in zoology. ■ Zoology any subsidiary category between major levels of classification.
5 [count noun] a partition that divides two groups or things: *the villagers lived in a communal building and there were no solid divisions between neighbours.*
– PHRASES **division of labour** the assignment of different parts of a manufacturing process or task to different people in order to improve efficiency.
– ORIGIN late Middle English: from Old French *devisiun*, from Latin *divisio(n-)*, from the verb *dividere* (see **DIVIDE**).

divisional ▶ **adjective** of or relating to an organizational or administrative division: *a divisional manager.*
■ forming a partition: *divisional walls.*
– DERIVATIVES **divisionally** adverb.

divisionalize /dɪˈvɪʒ(ə)n(ə)lʌɪz/ (also **-ise**) ▶ **verb** [with obj.] [usu. as adj. **divisionalized**] subdivide (a company or other organization) into a number of separate divisions: *a large divisionalized Western corporation.*
■ [no obj.] undergo this process.
– DERIVATIVES **divisionalization** noun.

division bell ▶ **noun** (in Britain) a bell rung in Parliament to announce an imminent division.

divisionism ▶ **noun** another term for **POINTILLISM**.

division lobby ▶ **noun** see **LOBBY** (sense 2).

division sign ▶ **noun** the sign ÷, placed between two numbers showing that the first is to be divided by the second, as in 6 ÷ 3 = 2.

divisive /dɪˈvʌɪsɪv/ ▶ **adjective** tending to cause disagreement or hostility between people: *the highly divisive issue of abortion.*
– DERIVATIVES **divisively** adverb, **divisiveness** noun.
– ORIGIN mid 16th cent. (as a noun denoting something that divides or separates): from late Latin *divisivus*, from Latin *dividere* (see **DIVIDE**).

divisor /dɪˈvʌɪzə/ ▶ **noun** Mathematics a number by which another number is to be divided.
■ a number that divides into another without a remainder: *the greatest common divisor.*
– ORIGIN late Middle English: from French *diviseur* or Latin *divisor*, from *dividere* (see **DIVIDE**).

divorce ▶ **noun** the legal dissolution of a marriage by a court or other competent body: *her* ***divorce from*** *her first husband |* [mass noun] *one in three marriages ends in divorce |* [as modifier] *divorce proceedings.*
■ a legal decree dissolving a marriage. ■ [in sing.] a separation between things which were or ought to be connected: *a* ***divorce between*** *ownership and control in the typical large company.*
▶ **verb** [with obj.] legally dissolve one's marriage with (someone): [as adj. **divorced**] *a divorced couple |* [no obj.] *they divorced eight years later.*
■ separate or dissociate (something) from something else, typically with an undesirable effect: *religion cannot be* ***divorced from*** *morality.* ■ (**divorce oneself from**) distance or dissociate oneself from (something): *a desire to divorce myself from history.*
– DERIVATIVES **divorcement** noun.
– ORIGIN late Middle English: the noun from Old French *divorce*, from Latin *divortium*, based on *divertere* (see **DIVERT**); the verb from Old French *divorcer*, from late Latin *divortiare*, from *divortium*.

divorcee /ˌdɪvɔːˈsiː/ ▶ **noun** (US masc. **divorcé**, fem. **divorcée** /-ˈseɪ/) a divorced person.
– ORIGIN early 19th cent.: from French *divorcé(e)* 'divorced man (or woman)'.

divot /ˈdɪvət/ ▶ **noun** a piece of turf cut out of the ground by a golf club in making a stroke.
■ a small hole made in this way. ■ chiefly Scottish a piece of turf, as formerly used for roofing cottages.
– ORIGIN early 16th cent.: of unknown origin.

divulge /dʌɪˈvʌldʒ, dɪ-/ ▶ **verb** [with obj.] make known (private or sensitive information): *I am too much of a gentleman to divulge her age.*
– DERIVATIVES **divulgation** noun, **divulgence** noun.
– ORIGIN late Middle English (in the sense 'announce publicly'): from Latin *divulgare*, from *di-* 'widely' + *vulgare* 'publish' (from *vulgus* 'common people').

divvy[1] informal ▶ **noun** (also **divi**) (pl. **-ies**) Brit. a dividend or share, especially of profits earned by a cooperative: *the divvy is being held at 8.8p.*
▶ **verb** (**-ies**, **-ied**) [with obj.] share out: *they* ***divvied up*** *the proceeds.*
– ORIGIN late 19th cent.: abbreviation of **DIVIDEND**.

divvy[2] Brit. informal ▶ **noun** (pl. **-ies**) a foolish or stupid person.
▶ **adjective** foolish or stupid.
– ORIGIN 1970s: of unknown origin.

Diwali /dɪˈwɑːli/ (also **Divali**) ▶ **noun** a Hindu festival with lights, held in the period October to November, to celebrate the new season at the end of the monsoon. It is particularly associated with Lakshmi, the goddess of prosperity, and marks the beginning of the financial year in India.
– ORIGIN from Hindi *divālī*, from Sanskrit *dīpāvali* 'row of lights', from *dīpa* 'lamp' + *vali* 'row'.

diwan /dɪˈwɑːn/ (also **dewan**) ▶ **noun** **1** (in Islamic societies) a central finance department, chief administrative office, or regional governing body.
2 a chief treasury official, finance minister, or Prime Minister in some Indian states.
– ORIGIN Urdu, from Persian *dīwān* 'fiscal register'; compare with **DIVAN**.

Dixie an informal name for the Southern states of the US. It was used in the song 'Dixie' (1859), a marching song popular with Confederate soldiers in the American Civil War.
– PHRASES **whistle Dixie** US engage in unrealistic fantasies; waste one's time.

dixie ▶ **noun** (pl. **-ies**) a large iron cooking pot used by campers or soldiers.
– ORIGIN early 20th cent.: from Hindi *degcī* 'cooking pot', from Persian *degča*, diminutive of *deg* 'pot'.

Dixiecrat /ˈdɪksɪkrat/ ▶ **noun** US informal any of the Southern Democrats who seceded from the party in 1948 in opposition to its policy of extending civil rights.

Dixieland ▶ **noun** [mass noun] a kind of jazz with a strong two-beat rhythm and collective improvisation, which originated in New Orleans in the early 20th century.

DIY chiefly Brit. ▶ **noun** [mass noun] the activity of decorating, building, and making fixtures and repairs at home by oneself rather than employing a professional.
▶ **adjective** [attrib.] of or relating to DIY: *a local DIY store.*
■ done in person by someone without the relevant qualifications: *punk's DIY ethos.*
– DERIVATIVES **DIY'er** noun.
– ORIGIN 1950s: abbreviation of **DO-IT-YOURSELF**.

diya /ˈdiːjə/ ▶ **noun** Indian a small cup-shaped oil lamp made of baked clay.
– ORIGIN from Hindi *dīyā*.

Diyarbakir /dɪˈjɑːbəˌkɪə/ a city in SE Turkey, capital of a province of the same name; pop. 381,100 (1990).

dizygotic /ˌdʌɪzʌɪˈgɒtɪk/ ▶ **adjective** (of twins) derived from two separate ova, and so not identical.

dizygous /dʌɪˈzʌɪgəs/ ▶ **adjective** another term for **DIZYGOTIC**.

dizzy ▶ **adjective** (**dizzier**, **dizziest**) having or involving a sensation of spinning around and losing one's balance: *Jonathan had begun to suffer dizzy spells |* figurative *he looked around, dizzy with happiness.*
■ causing such a sensation: *a sheer, dizzy drop |* figurative *a dizzy range of hues.* ■ informal (of a woman) silly but attractive: *he only married me because he wanted a dizzy blonde.*
▶ **verb** (**-ies**, **-ied**) [with obj.] [usu. as adj. **dizzying**] make (someone) feel unsteady, confused, or amazed: *the dizzying rate of change | her nearness dizzied him.*
– PHRASES **the dizzy heights** informal a position of worldly importance: *he soon* ***reached the dizzy heights*** *of his own series.*
– DERIVATIVES **dizzily** adverb, **dizziness** noun.
– ORIGIN Old English *dysig* 'foolish', of West Germanic origin; related to Low German *dusig*, *dösig* 'giddy' and Old High German *tusic* 'foolish, weak'.

DJ[1] ▶ **noun** a disc jockey.
■ a person who uses samples of recorded music to make techno or rap music.

DJ[2] Brit. ▶ **abbreviation for** dinner jacket.

Djakarta /dʒəˈkɑːtə/ (also **Jakarta**) the capital of Indonesia, situated in NW Java; pop. 8,222,500 (1990). Former name (until 1949) **BATAVIA**.

djebel ▶ **noun** variant spelling of **JEBEL**.

djellaba /ˈdʒɛləbə/ (also **djellabah** or **jellaba**) ▶ **noun** a loose hooded woollen cloak of a kind traditionally worn by Arabs.
– ORIGIN early 19th cent.: from Moroccan Arabic *jellāba*, *jellābiyya*.

Djerba /ˈdʒəːbə/ (also **Jerba**) a resort island in the Gulf of Gabès off the coast of Tunisia.

djibba (also **djibbah**) ▶ **noun** variant spelling of **JIBBA**.

Djibouti /dʒɪˈbuːti/ (also **Jibuti**) a country on the NE coast of Africa; pop. 441,000 (est. 1991); languages, Arabic (official), French (official), Somali and other Cushitic languages.
■ the capital of Djibouti, a port at the western end of the Gulf of Aden; pop. 290,000 (est. 1988).

The territory became a French protectorate under the name of French Somaliland in 1897. It was renamed the French Territory of the Afars and Issas in 1946, the Afars and the Issas forming the two main ethnic groups. In 1977 the country achieved independence as the Republic of Djibouti.

– DERIVATIVES **Djiboutian** adjective & noun.

djinn ▶ **noun** variant spelling of **JINN**.

DK ▶ **abbreviation for** Denmark (international vehicle registration).

dkl US ▶ **abbreviation for** dekaliter(s).

dkm US ▶ **abbreviation for** dekameter(s).

DL ▶ **abbreviation for** ■ Deputy Lieutenant. ■ N. Amer. disabled list, a list of sports players who are temporarily unable to play due to an injury.

dl ▶ **abbreviation for** decilitre(s).

D-layer ▶ **noun** the lowest layer of the ionosphere, able to reflect low-frequency radio waves.
– ORIGIN 1930s: from an arbitrary use of the letter *D*.

DLitt ▶ **abbreviation for** Doctor of Letters.
– ORIGIN from Latin *Doctor Litterarum*.

DLL Computing ▶ **abbreviation for** dynamic linked library, a collection of subroutines stored on disk, which can be loaded into memory and executed when accessed by a running program.

D-lock ▶ **noun** a mechanism used to secure a bicycle or motorbike when parked, consisting of a U-shaped bar and crosspiece of solid metal.

DM (also **D-mark**) ▶ **abbreviation for** Deutschmark.

dm ▶ **abbreviation for** decimetre(s).

DMA ▶ **abbreviation for** direct memory access, a method allowing a peripheral device to transfer data to or from the memory of a computer system using operations not under the control of the central processor.

DMD ▶ **abbreviation for** Duchenne muscular dystrophy.

DMs ▶ **abbreviation for** Dr Martens.

DMSO Chemistry ▶ **abbreviation for** dimethyl sulphoxide.

dmu Brit. ▶ **abbreviation for** diesel multiple unit.

DMus ▶ **abbreviation for** Doctor of Music.

DMV ▶ **abbreviation for** (in the US) Department of Motor Vehicles.

DMZ N. Amer. ▶ **abbreviation for** demilitarized zone, an area from which warring parties agree to remove their military forces.

DNA ▶ **noun** [mass noun] Biochemistry deoxyribonucleic acid, a self-replicating material which is present in nearly all living organisms as the main constituent of chromosomes. It is the carrier of genetic information.

Each molecule of DNA consists of two strands coiled round each other to form a double helix, a structure like a spiral ladder. Each rung of the ladder consists of a pair of chemical groups called bases (of which there are four types), which combine in specific pairs so that the sequence on one strand of the double helix is complementary to that on the other: it is the specific sequence of bases which constitutes the genetic information.

DNA fingerprinting (also **DNA profiling**) ▶ **noun** another term for **GENETIC FINGERPRINTING**.

DNase /ˌdiːɛnˈeɪz/ ▶ **noun** [mass noun] Biochemistry an enzyme which catalyses the hydrolysis of DNA into oligonucleotides and smaller molecules. Also called **DEOXYRIBONUCLEASE**.
– ORIGIN 1940s: from **DNA** + **-ASE**.

DNA virus ▶ **noun** a virus in which the genetic information is stored in the form of DNA (as opposed to RNA).

DNB ▶ **abbreviation for** Dictionary of National Biography.

Dnieper /ˈdniːpə/ a river of eastern Europe, rising in Russia west of Moscow and flowing southwards some 2,200 km (1,370 miles) through Ukraine to the Black Sea. Ukrainian name **DNIPRO** /dniːˈprɒ/.

Dniester /ˈdniːstə/ a river of eastern Europe, rising in the Carpathian Mountains in western Ukraine and flowing 1,410 km (876 miles) to the Black Sea near Odessa. Russian name **DNESTR** /dnʲiˈster/, Ukrainian name **DNISTER**.

Dniprodzerzhinsk /ˌdniːprədzəːˈʒɪnsk/ an industrial city and river port in Ukraine, on the River Dnieper; pop. 283,600 (1990). Former name (until 1936) **KAMENSKOYE**.

Dnipropetrovsk /ˌdniːprəpɛˈtrɒfsk/ an industrial city and river port in Ukraine, on the River Dnieper; pop. 1,187,000 (1990). It was known as Yekaterinoslav (Ekaterinoslav) until 1926.

D notice ▶ **noun** Brit. a government notice issued to news editors requiring them not to publicize certain information for reasons of national security.
– ORIGIN Second World War: *D* for *defence*.

do[1] ▶ **verb** (**does**; past **did**; past participle **done**) **1** [with obj.] perform (an action, the precise nature of which is often unspecified): *something must be done about the city's traffic | she knew what she was doing | what can I do for you? | Brian was making eyes at the girl, and had been **doing so** for most of the hearing.*
■ perform (a particular task): *Dad always did the washing up on Sundays.* ■ work on (something) to bring it to completion or to a required state: *it takes them longer to do their hair than me | she's the secretary and does the publicity.* ■ make or have available and provide: *he's doing bistro food | many hotels don't do single rooms at all |* [with two objs] *he decided to do her a pastel sketch of himself.* ■ solve; work out: *Joe was doing sums aloud.* ■ cook (food) to completion or to a specified degree: *if a knife inserted into the centre comes out clean, then your pie is done.* ■ (often in questions) work at for a living: *what does she do?* ■ learn or study; take as one's subject: *I'm doing English, German, and History.* ■ produce or give a performance of (a particular play, opera, etc.): *the Royal Shakespeare Company are doing* Macbeth *next month.* ■ perform (a particular role, song, etc.) or imitate (a particular person) in order to entertain people: *he not only does Schwarzenegger and Groucho, he becomes them.* ■ informal take (a narcotic drug): *he doesn't smoke, drink, or do drugs.* ■ attend to (someone): *the barber said he'd do me next.* ■ vulgar slang have sexual intercourse with. ■ (**do it**) informal have sexual intercourse. ■ (**do it**) informal urinate; defecate.
2 [with obj.] achieve or complete, in particular:
■ travel (a specified distance): *one car I looked at had done 112,000 miles.* ■ travel at (a specified speed): *I was speeding, doing seventy-five.* ■ make (a particular journey): *last time I did Oxford–York return by train it was £40.* ■ achieve (a specified sales figure): *our best-selling album did about a million worldwide.* ■ informal visit as a tourist, especially in a superficial or hurried way: *the Americans are allotted only a day to do the Yorkshire Moors.* ■ spend (a specified period of time), typically in prison or in a particular occupation: *he did five years for manslaughter | Peter has done thirteen years in the RAF.* ■ [no obj.] informal finish: *you must sit there and wait till I've done |* [with present participle] *we've done arguing.* ■ (**be done**) be over: *the special formula continues to beautify your tan when the day is done.* ■ (**be/have done with**) give up concern for: have finished with: *I should sell the place and **be done with it** | we have done with history.*
3 [no obj., with adverbial] act or behave in a specified way: *they are free to do as they please | you did well to bring her back.*
■ make progress or perform in a specified way; get on: *when a team is doing badly, it's not easy for a new player to settle in | Mrs Walters, how're you doing?* ■ [with obj. and complement] have a specified effect on: *the walk will do me good.* ■ [with obj.] result in: *the years of stagnation did a lot of harm to the younger generation.*
4 [no obj.] be suitable or acceptable: *if he's anything like you, he'll do |* [with obj.] *a couple of quid'll do me.*
5 [with obj.] informal beat up; kill: *one day I'll do him.*
■ (usu. **be done**) ruin: *once you falter, you're done.* ■ rob (a place): *this would be an easy place to do and there was plenty of money lying around.* ■ swindle: *a thousand pounds for one set of photographs—Jacqui had been done.*
6 [with obj.] (usu. **be/get done for**) Brit. informal prosecute; convict: *we got done for conspiracy to cause GBH.*
▶ **auxiliary verb 1** used before a verb (except *be, can, may, ought, shall, will*) in questions and negative statements: *do you have any pets? | did he see me? | I don't smoke | it does not matter.*
■ used to make tag questions: *you write poetry, don't you? | I never seem to say the right thing, do I?* ■ used in negative commands: *don't be silly | do not forget.*
2 used to refer back to a verb already mentioned: *he looks better than he did before | you wanted to enjoy yourself, and you did | as they get smarter, so do the crooks.*
3 used to give emphasis to a positive verb: *I do want to act on this | he did look tired.*
■ used in positive commands to give polite encouragement: *do tell me! | do sit down.*
4 used with inversion of a subject and verb when an adverbial phrase begins a clause for emphasis: *only rarely did they succumb | not only did the play close, the theatre closed.*
▶ **noun** (pl. **dos** or **do's**) **1** informal, chiefly Brit. a party or other social event: *the soccer club Christmas do.*
2 (also **'do**) informal, chiefly N. Amer. short for **HAIRDO**.
3 Brit. archaic, informal a swindle or hoax.
– PHRASES **be nothing to do with** be no business or concern of: *it's my decision—it's nothing to do with you.* ■ be unconnected with: *he says his departure is nothing to do with the resignation calls.* **be to do with** be concerned or connected with: *the problems are usually to do with family tension.* **do a ——** informal behave in a manner characteristic of (a specified person): *he did a Garbo after his flop in the play.* **do battle** enter into a conflict. **do one's head** (or **nut**) **in** (or **do one's head**) Brit. informal be extremely angry, worried, or agitated. **do the honours** see **HONOUR**. **do someone/thing justice** see **JUSTICE**. **don't —— me** informal do not use the word —— to me: *'Don't morning me. Where the hell've you been all night?'* **do or die** persist, even if death is the result. ■ used to describe a critical situation where one's actions may result in victory or defeat: *the 72nd hole was do or die.* **dos and don'ts** rules of behaviour: *I have no knowledge of the political dos and don'ts.* **do well for oneself** become successful or wealthy. **do well out of** make a profit out of; benefit from: *they're doing well out of scrap metal.* **have (got) —— to do with** be connected with (someone or something) to the extent specified: *John's got nothing to do with that terrible murder.* ■ (**have nothing to do with**) have no contact or dealings with: *Billy and his father have had nothing to do with each other for nearly twenty years.* **it isn't done** Brit. used to express the speaker's opinion that something contravenes custom, opinion, or propriety: *in such a society it is not done to admit to taking religion seriously.* **it won't do** used to express the speaker's opinion that someone's behaviour is unsatisfactory and cannot be allowed to continue: *Can't have that kind of talk—I've told you before, it won't do.* **no you don't** informal used to indicate that one intends to prevent someone from doing what they were about to do: *Sharon went to get in the taxi. 'Oh no you don't', said Steve.* **that does it!** informal used to indicate that one will not tolerate something any longer: *That does it! Let's go!* **that's done it!** informal used to express dismay or anger when something has gone wrong.
– ORIGIN Old English *dōn*, of Germanic origin; related to Dutch *doen* and German *tun*, from an Indo-European root shared by Greek *tithēmi* 'I place' and Latin *facere* 'make, do'.
▶ **do away with** informal put an end to; remove: *the desire to do away with racism.* ■ kill: *he didn't have the courage to do away with her.*
do by dated treat or deal with in a specified way: *do as you would be done by | she did well by them.*
do someone/thing down Brit. informal get the better of someone, typically in an underhand way. ■ criticize someone or something: *they're always moaning and doing British industry down.*
do for 1 informal defeat, ruin, or kill: *without that contract we're done for | it was the cold that did for him in the end.* **2** Brit. informal do the cleaning for (a person or private household): *Florrie usually did for the Shermans in the mornings.* **3** suffice for: *a strip of white cotton about 20 yards long did for a fence.*
do something (or **nothing**) **for** informal enhance (or detract from) the appearance or quality of: *whatever the new forum does for industry, it certainly does something for the Minister | that scarf does nothing for you.*
do someone in informal kill someone. ■ (usu. **be done in**) informal tire someone out: *there was 1 minute 4 seconds to play and the Lions were done in.*
do something in informal injure something: *I did my back in a few years ago.*
do someone out of informal deprive someone of (something) in an underhand or unfair way.
do something out Brit. informal decorate or furnish a room or building in a particular style, colour, or material: *the basement **is done out in** limed oak.*
do someone over Brit. informal beat someone up.
do something over 1 Brit. informal ransack a place, especially in the course of a search for something worth stealing. **2** informal decorate or furnish a room or building. **3** N. Amer. informal repeat something: *to absorb the lesson, I had to do it over and over.*
do up be able to be fastened: *a shirt so tight that not all of the buttons did up.*
do someone up (usu. **be done up**) dress someone up, especially in an elaborate or impressive way: *Agnes was all done up in a slinky black number.*
do something up 1 fasten something: *she drew on her coat and did up the buttons.* ■ (usu. **be done up**) arrange one's hair in a particular way, especially so as to be pulled back from one's face or shoulders: *her dark hair was done up in a pony tail.* ■ wrap something up: *unwieldy packs all done up with string.* **2** informal renovate or redecorate a room or building: *Mrs Hamilton did the place up for letting.*
do with [with modal] would find useful or would like to have or do: *I could do with a cup of coffee.* ■ (**can't/won't be doing with**) Brit. be unwilling to tolerate or be bothered with: *she couldn't be doing with meals for one.*
do without (usu. **can do without**) manage without: *she could do without food for a day.* ■ informal would

prefer not to have: *I can do without your carping first thing in the morning.*

do² ▶ noun variant spelling of **DOH**.

do. dated ▶ abbreviation for ditto.

DOA ▶ abbreviation for dead on arrival, used to describe a person who is declared dead immediately upon their arrival at a hospital.

doable /ˈduːəb(ə)l/ ▶ adjective informal within one's powers; feasible: *none of the jobs were fun, but they were doable.*

d

dob ▶ verb (**dobbed**, **dobbing**) [with obj.] Austral./NZ informal inform against: *Helen **dobbed** me **in** to Mum.*
– ORIGIN 1950s: figurative use of dialect *dob* 'put down abruptly', later 'throw something at a target'.

dobbin ▶ noun dated a pet name for a draught horse or a farm horse.
– ORIGIN late 16th cent.: pet form of the given name *Robert*.

dobby ▶ noun (pl. **-ies**) a mechanism attached to a loom for weaving small patterns similar to but simpler than those produced by a Jacquard loom.
– ORIGIN late 19th cent.: perhaps an application of the given name *Dobbie*, from *Dob* (alteration of the given name *Rob*). The usage is probably an extension of the earlier sense 'benevolent elf' (who performed household tasks secretly).

dobby weave ▶ noun [mass noun] a style of patterned weave consisting of small geometric devices repeated frequently.

dobe /ˈdəʊbi/ ▶ noun [mass noun] US informal adobe.
– ORIGIN mid 19th cent.: abbreviation.

Dobermann /ˈdəʊbəmən/ (also **Dobermann pinscher** /ˈpɪnʃə/) (chiefly N. Amer. also **Doberman**) ▶ noun a large dog of a German breed with powerful jaws and a smooth coat, typically black with tan markings.
– ORIGIN early 20th cent.: from the name of Ludwig *Dobermann*, 19th-cent. German dog-breeder (+ German *Pinscher* 'terrier').

Dobos Torte /ˈdɒbɒʃ ˈtɔːtə/ ▶ noun a rich cake made of alternate layers of sponge and chocolate or mocha cream, with a crisp caramel topping.
– ORIGIN from German *Dobostorte*, named after József C. *Dobos* (1847–1924), Hungarian pastry cook.

dobra /ˈdɒbrə/ ▶ noun the basic monetary unit of São Tomé and Principe, equal to 100 centavos.
– ORIGIN from Portuguese *dóbra* 'doubloon'.

Dobrich /ˈdɒbrɪtʃ/ a city in NE Bulgaria, the centre for an agricultural region; pop. 115,800 (1990). It was named Tolbukhin (1949–91) after the Soviet marshal Fyodor Ivanovich Tolbukhin.

dobro /ˈdɒbrəʊ/ ▶ noun (pl. **-os**) trademark a type of acoustic guitar with steel resonating discs inside the body under the bridge.
– ORIGIN 1950s: from *Do(pěra) Bro(thers)*, the Czech-American inventors of the instrument.

Dobruja /ˈdɒbrʊjə/ a district of eastern Romania and NE Bulgaria on the Black Sea coast, bounded on the north and west by the River Danube.

dobsonfly /ˈdɒbs(ə)nflʌɪ/ ▶ noun (pl. **-flies**) a large grey North American winged insect related to the alderflies. Its predatory aquatic larva (the hellgrammite) is often used as fishing bait.
• Family Corydalidae, order Neuroptera: several genera and species, in particular *Corydalis cornutus*.
– ORIGIN early 20th cent.: of unknown origin.

Dobsonian /dɒbˈsəʊnɪən/ ▶ adjective relating to or denoting a low-cost Newtonian reflecting telescope with large aperture and short focal length, or the simple altazimuth mount used for it.
– ORIGIN late 20th cent.: from the name of John *Dobson*, American amateur astronomer, + **-IAN**.

doc informal ▶ abbreviation for ■ doctor. ■ Computing document.

docent /ˈdəʊs(ə)nt/ ▶ noun **1** (in certain US and European universities and colleges) a member of the teaching staff immediately below professorial rank.
2 a person who acts as a guide, typically on a voluntary basis, in a museum, art gallery, or zoo.
– ORIGIN late 19th cent.: via German from Latin *docent-* 'teaching', from *docere* 'teach'.

Docetism /dəˈsiːtɪz(ə)m, ˈdəʊsɪˌtɪz(ə)m/ ▶ noun [mass noun] the doctrine, important in Gnosticism, that Christ's body was not human but either a phantasm or of real but celestial substance, and that therefore his sufferings were only apparent.
– DERIVATIVES **Docetist** noun.
– ORIGIN mid 19th cent.: from medieval Latin *Docetae* (the name, based on Greek *dokein* 'seem', given to a group of 2nd-cent. Christian heretics) + **-ISM**.

doch an dorris ▶ noun variant spelling of **DEOCH AN DORIS**.

docile /ˈdəʊsʌɪl/ ▶ adjective ready to accept control or instruction; submissive: *a cheap and docile workforce.*
– DERIVATIVES **docilely** adverb, **docility** noun.
– ORIGIN late 15th cent. (in the sense 'apt or willing to learn'): from Latin *docilis*, from *docere* 'teach'.

dock¹ ▶ noun an enclosed area of water in a port for the loading, unloading, and repair of ships.
■ (**docks**) a group of such enclosed areas of water along with the wharves and buildings near them. ■ short for **DRY DOCK**. ■ N. Amer. a group of piers where a ship or boat may moor for loading and unloading. ■ (also **loading dock**) a platform for loading lorries or goods trains.
▶ verb [no obj.] (of a ship) come into an enclosed area of water in a harbour and tie up at a wharf, especially in order to load or unload passengers or cargo: *the ship docked at Southampton.*
■ [with obj.] bring (a ship or boat) into such a place: *the yard where the boats were docked and maintained.* ■ (of a spacecraft) join with a space station or another spacecraft in space. ■ attach (a piece of equipment) to another: *the user wants to dock a portable into a desktop computer.*
– PHRASES **in dock** (of a ship) moored in a dock. ■ Brit. informal (of a person) not fully fit and out of action: *he grazed my arm and put me in dock for a couple of days.* ■ (of a vehicle) in a garage for repairs.
– ORIGIN late Middle English: from Middle Dutch, Middle Low German *docke*, of unknown origin.

dock² ▶ noun (usu. **the dock**) the enclosure in a criminal court where a defendant stands or sits.
– PHRASES **in the dock** Brit. (of a defendant) on trial in court.
– ORIGIN late 16th cent.: probably originally slang and related to Flemish *dok* 'chicken coop, rabbit hutch', of unknown origin.

dock³ ▶ noun a coarse weed of temperate regions, with inconspicuous greenish or reddish flowers. The leaves are popularly used to relieve nettle stings.
• Genus *Rumex*, family Polygonaceae.
– ORIGIN Old English *docce*, of Germanic origin; related to Dutch dialect *dokke*.

dock⁴ ▶ verb [with obj.] deduct (something, especially an amount of money or a point in a game): *the agency enforce payments by **docking** money **from** the father's salary* | [with two objs] *he was docked a penalty point.*
■ [often as noun **docking**] cut short (an animal's tail): *most docking is done by breeders.* ■ cut short the tail of (an animal): *the dog had been docked.*
▶ noun the solid bony or fleshy part of an animal's tail, excluding the hair.
■ the stump left after a tail has been docked.
– ORIGIN late Middle English: perhaps related to Frisian *dok* 'bunch, ball (of string etc.)' and German *Docke* 'doll'. The original noun sense was 'the solid part of an animal's tail', whence the verb sense 'cut short (an animal's tail)', later generalized to 'reduce, deduct'.

dockage ▶ noun [mass noun] accommodation or berthing of ships in docks.

dock brief ▶ noun chiefly historical a brief given directly to a barrister selected from a panel of those present by a prisoner in the dock, without the agency of a solicitor.

docken /ˈdɒk(ə)n/ ▶ noun chiefly Scottish another term for **DOCK³** (the plant).
– ORIGIN late Middle English: apparently from Old English *doccan*, plural of *docce* (see **DOCK³**).

docker ▶ noun a person employed in a port to load and unload ships.

docket ▶ noun **1** Brit. a document or label listing the contents of a consignment or package.
■ a customs warrant certifying that duty has been paid on goods entering a country. ■ a voucher entitling the holder to receive or obtain delivery of goods ordered.
2 N. Amer. a list of cases for trial or people having cases pending.
■ an agenda or list of things to be done.
▶ verb (**docketed**, **docketing**) [with obj.] (usu. **be docketed**) mark (a consignment or package) with a document or label listing the contents.
■ figurative assign (someone or something) to a category, especially in a simplistic or reductive way: *Trollope would never have consented to being docketed as a mere entertainer.* ■ annotate (a letter or document) with a brief summary of its contents. ■ N. Amer. enter (a case or suit) on to a list of those due to be heard.
– ORIGIN late 15th cent.: perhaps from **DOCK⁴**. The word originally denoted a short summary or abstract; hence, in the early 18th cent., 'a document giving particulars of a consignment'.

dock-glass ▶ noun a large glass of a type originally used for wine tasting.

docking station ▶ noun a device to which a portable computer is connected so that it can be used like a desktop computer, with an external power supply, monitor, data transfer capability, etc.

dockland ▶ noun [mass noun] (also **docklands**) the area containing a city's docks: *an old fishing village just west of dockland* | *plans to redevelop London's docklands.*

dockominium /ˌdɒkəˈmɪnɪəm/ ▶ noun (pl. **dockominiums**) US a waterfront condominium with a private mooring.
■ a privately owned landing stage at a marina.
– ORIGIN 1980s: from **DOCK¹**, on the pattern of *condominium*.

dockside ▶ noun [in sing.] the area immediately adjacent to a dock.

dockyard ▶ noun an area or establishment with docks and equipment for repairing and maintaining ships.

Doc Martens ▶ plural noun see **DR MARTENS**.

doctor ▶ noun **1** a person who is qualified to treat people who are ill.
■ N. Amer. a qualified dentist or veterinary surgeon. ■ (in southern Africa) a person practising traditional African healing arts. ■ [with modifier] informal a person who gives advice or makes improvements: *the script doctor rewrote the original.*
2 (**Doctor**) a person who holds the highest university degree: *he was made a Doctor of Divinity.*
■ short for **DOCTOR OF THE CHURCH**. ■ archaic a teacher or learned person: *the wisest doctor is gravelled by the inquisitiveness of a child.*
3 an artificial fishing fly.
4 Austral./NZ informal a cook on board a ship or in a camp or station.
5 [with modifier] a cool onshore breeze that blows regularly in a particular warm location: *the Perth doctor blows towards evening off the Indian Ocean.* See also **CAPE DOCTOR**.
▶ verb [with obj.] **1** change the content or appearance of (a document or picture) in order to deceive; falsify: *the reports could have been doctored.*
■ alter the content of (a drink, food, or substance) by adding strong or harmful ingredients: *he denied doctoring Stephen's drinks.* ■ Cricket & Baseball tamper with (a ball) so as to affect its flight when bowled or pitched.
2 [usu. as noun **doctoring**] informal treat (someone) medically: *he contemplated giving up doctoring.*
■ (often **be doctored**) Brit. remove the sexual organs of (an animal) so that it cannot reproduce. ■ (usu. **be doctored**) repair (a machine).
– PHRASES **be (just) what the doctor ordered** informal be very beneficial or desirable under the circumstances: *a 2–0 victory is just what the doctor ordered.* **go for the doctor** Austral. informal make an all-out effort: *he will go for the doctor in Parliament next week.*
– DERIVATIVES **doctorly** adjective.
– ORIGIN Middle English (in the senses 'learned person' and 'Doctor of the Church'): via Old French from Latin *doctor* 'teacher' (from *docere* 'teach').

doctoral /ˈdɒkt(ə)r(ə)l/ ▶ adjective [attrib.] relating to or designed to achieve a doctorate: *a doctoral thesis.*

doctorate /ˈdɒkt(ə)rət/ ▶ noun the highest degree awarded by a university faculty or other approved educational organization: *a **doctorate in** art history.*
– ORIGIN mid 17th cent.: from medieval Latin *doctoratus* 'made a doctor'.

Doctor Martens ▶ plural noun see **DR MARTENS**.

Doctor of Philosophy (abbrev.: **PhD** or **DPhil**) ▶ noun a doctorate in any faculty except law, medicine, or sometimes theology.
■ a person holding such a degree.

Doctor of the Church ▶ noun one of the early Christian theologians regarded as especially authoritative in the Western Church (particularly St Augustine of Hippo, St Jerome, St Ambrose, and

St Gregory the Great) or later so designated by the Pope (e.g. St Thomas Aquinas, St Teresa of Ávila). Compare with ***Fathers of the Church*** (see **FATHER** sense 3).

doctrinaire /ˌdɒktrɪˈnɛː/ ▶**adjective** seeking to impose a doctrine in all circumstances without regard to practical considerations: *he is not a doctrinaire socialist.*
▶**noun** a person who seeks to impose a theory in such a way.
– DERIVATIVES **doctrinairism** noun.
– ORIGIN early 19th cent.: from French, from *doctrine* (see **DOCTRINE**).

doctrinal /dɒkˈtrʌɪn(ə)l/ ▶**adjective** concerned with a doctrine or doctrines: *doctrinal disputes.*
– DERIVATIVES **doctrinally** adverb.
– ORIGIN late Middle English: from late Latin *doctrinalis*, from *doctrina* 'teaching, learning' (see **DOCTRINE**).

doctrine /ˈdɒktrɪn/ ▶**noun** a belief or set of beliefs held and taught by a Church, political party, or other group: *the doctrine of predestination.*
■US a stated principle of government policy, mainly in foreign or military affairs: *the Truman Doctrine.*
– ORIGIN late Middle English: from Old French, from Latin *doctrina* 'teaching, learning', from *doctor* 'teacher', from *docere* 'teach'.

docudrama /ˈdɒkjʊˌdrɑːmə/ ▶**noun** a dramatized television film based on real events.
– ORIGIN 1960s: blend of **DOCUMENTARY** and **DRAMA**.

document ▶**noun** /ˈdɒkjʊm(ə)nt/ a piece of written, printed, or electronic matter that provides information or evidence or that serves as an official record.
▶**verb** /ˈdɒkjʊmɛnt/ [with obj.] record (something) in written, photographic, or other form: *the photographer spent years documenting the lives of miners.*
■support or accompany with documentation.
– DERIVATIVES **documentable** adjective, **documental** /-ˈmɛnt(ə)l/ adjective.
– ORIGIN late Middle English: from Old French, from Latin *documentum* 'lesson, proof' (in medieval Latin 'written instruction, official paper'), from *docere* 'teach'.

documentalist ▶**noun** a person engaged in keeping records and providing information.

documentarian /ˌdɒkjʊmɛnˈtɛːrɪən/ ▶**noun** 1 a photographer specializing in producing a factual record.
■a director or producer of documentaries.
2 an expert analyst of historical documents.

documentarist ▶**noun** another term for **DOCUMENTARIAN** (in sense 1).

documentary ▶**adjective** consisting of official pieces of written, printed, or other matter: *his book is based on documentary sources.*
■(of a film, television or radio programme, or photography) using pictures or interviews with people involved in real events to provide a factual record or report: *a documentary programme about Manchester United.*
▶**noun** (pl. **-ies**) a film or a television or radio programme that provides a factual record or report.

documentation ▶**noun** [mass noun] 1 material that provides official information or evidence or that serves as a record: *you will have to complete the relevant documentation.*
■the written specification and instructions accompanying a computer program or hardware.
2 the process of classifying and annotating texts, photographs, etc.: *she arranged the collection and documentation of photographs.*

documentative /ˌdɒkjʊˈmɛntətɪv/ ▶**adjective** employing or providing documentation.

document case ▶**noun** a lightweight, typically flexible case for carrying papers.

docutainment /ˌdɒkjʊˈteɪnmənt/ ▶**noun** [mass noun] N. Amer. entertainment provided by films or other presentations which include documentary materials, intended both to inform and entertain.
■[count noun] a film or other presentation of this kind.
– ORIGIN 1970s: blend of **DOCUMENTARY** and **ENTERTAINMENT**.

DOD ▶**abbreviation for** (in the US) Department of Defense.

dodder[1] ▶**verb** [no obj.] [often as adj. **doddering**] tremble or totter, typically because of old age: *that doddering old fool.*
– DERIVATIVES **dodderer** noun.
– ORIGIN early 17th cent.: variant of obsolete dialect *dadder*; related to **DITHER**.

dodder[2] ▶**noun** a widely distributed parasitic climbing plant of the convolvulus family, with leafless thread-like stems that are attached to the host plant by means of suckers.
• Genus *Cuscuta*, family Convolvulaceae.
– ORIGIN Middle English: related to Middle Low German *doder, dodder*, Middle High German *toter.*

doddery ▶**adjective** slow and unsteady in movement because of weakness in old age.
– DERIVATIVES **dodderiness** noun.

doddle ▶**noun** [in sing.] Brit. informal a very easy task: *this printer's a doddle to set up and use.*
– ORIGIN 1930s: perhaps from dialect *doddle* 'toddle', of unknown origin.

dodeca- /ˈdəʊdɛkə/ ▶**combining form** (used chiefly in scientific and musical terms) twelve; having twelve: *dodecahedron* | *dodecaphonic.*
– ORIGIN from Greek.

dodecagon /dəʊˈdɛkəg(ə)n/ ▶**noun** a plane figure with twelve straight sides and angles.
– ORIGIN late 17th cent.: from Greek *dōdekagōnon*, neuter (used as a noun) of *dōdekagōnos* 'twelve-angled'.

dodecahedron /ˌdəʊdɛkəˈhiːdr(ə)n, -ˈhɛd-/ ▶**noun** (pl. **dodecahedra** /-drə/ or **dedecahedrons**) a three-dimensional shape having twelve plane faces, in particular a regular solid figure with twelve equal pentagonal faces.
– DERIVATIVES **dodecahedral** adjective.
– ORIGIN late 16th cent.: from Greek *dōdekaedron*, neuter (used as a noun) of *dōdekaedros* 'twelve-faced'.

Dodecanese /ˌdəʊdɪkəˈniːz/ a group of twelve islands in the SE Aegean, of which the largest is Rhodes.

dodecaphonic /ˌdəʊdɛkəˈfɒnɪk/ ▶**adjective** Music another term for **TWELVE-NOTE**.

dodge ▶**verb** [with obj.] 1 avoid (someone or something) by a sudden quick movement: *marchers had to dodge missiles thrown by loyalists.*
■[no obj., with adverbial of direction] move quickly to one side or out of the way: *Adam dodged between the cars.* ■ avoid (something) in a cunning or dishonest way: *he'd caught her dodging fares on the underground.* ■ [no obj.] (of a bell in change-ringing) move one place contrary to the normal sequence, and then back again in the following round.
2 [often as noun **dodging**] Photography expose (one area of a print) less than the rest during processing or enlarging.
▶**noun** a sudden quick movement to avoid someone or something.
■a cunning trick or dishonest act, in particular one intended to avoid something unpleasant: *the grant system's widespread use as a tax dodge.* ■ the dodging of a bell in change-ringing.
– ORIGIN mid 16th cent. (in the senses 'dither' and 'haggle'): of unknown origin.

dodgeball ▶**noun** [mass noun] N. Amer. a game in which players, in teams, form a circle and try to hit opponents with a large ball.

Dodge City a city in SW Kansas; pop. 21,130 (1990). Established in 1872 as a railhead on the Santa Fe Trail, it rapidly gained a reputation as a rowdy frontier town.

dodgem (also **dodgem car**) ▶**noun** a small electrically powered car with rubber bumpers all round, driven in an enclosure at a funfair with the aim of bumping into other such cars.
– ORIGIN 1920s: US proprietary name (as *Dodg'em*), from the phrase *dodge them.*

dodger ▶**noun** 1 [often with modifier] a person who engages in cunning tricks or dishonest practices to avoid something unpleasant: *tax dodgers.*
2 Nautical a canvas screen on a ship giving protection from spray.
3 US & Austral. a small handbill or leaflet.
4 [mass noun] Austral. informal bread.

Dodgson, Charles Lutwidge, see **CARROLL**.

dodgy ▶**adjective** (**dodgier**, **dodgiest**) Brit. informal dishonest or unreliable: *a dodgy second-hand car salesman.*
■potentially dangerous: *activities like these could be dodgy for your heart.* ■ of low quality: *Spurs' dodgy defence had thrown away a 2–0 lead.*

dodo /ˈdəʊdəʊ/ ▶**noun** (pl. **-os** or **-oes**) a large extinct flightless bird with a stout body, stumpy wings, a large head, and a heavy hooked bill. It was found on Mauritius until the end of the 17th century.
• *Raphus cucullatus*, family Raphidae. See also **SOLITAIRE** (sense 3).
■informal an old-fashioned and ineffective person or thing.
– PHRASES **(as) dead as a** (or **the**) **dodo** informal used to emphasize that a person or animal is no longer alive. ■ no longer effective, valid, or interesting: *the campaign was as dead as a dodo.*
– ORIGIN early 17th cent.: from Portuguese *doudo* 'simpleton' (because the bird had no fear of man and was easily killed). Compare with **DOTTEREL**.

Dodoma /dəʊˈdəʊmə/ the capital of Tanzania, in the centre of the country; pop. 203,830 (1988).

DoE ▶**abbreviation for** (formerly in the UK) Department of the Environment.

doe ▶**noun** a female deer, especially a female roe, fallow deer, or reindeer.
■a female hare, rabbit, rat, ferret, or kangaroo.
– ORIGIN Old English *dā*, of unknown origin.

doe-eyed ▶**adjective** (especially of a woman) having large gentle dark eyes: *doe-eyed waifs.*

doek /dʊk/ ▶**noun** S. African a headscarf.
– ORIGIN South African Dutch, from Dutch, 'cloth'.

doer ▶**noun** the person who does something: *the doer of the action.*
■a person who acts rather than merely talking or thinking: *I'm a doer, not a moaner.* ■ (also **hard doer**) Austral./NZ a person who is admired because of their courage, toughness, and adventurousness.

does third person singular present of **DO**[1].

doeskin /ˈdəʊskɪn/ ▶**noun** [mass noun] leather made from the skin of a doe fallow deer.
■a fine satin-weave woollen cloth resembling such leather.

doesn't ▶**contraction of** does not.

doest archaic second person singular present of **DO**[1].

doeth archaic third person singular present of **DO**[1].

dof /dɒf/ ▶**adjective** S. African informal stupid; uninformed.
– ORIGIN Afrikaans.

doff ▶**verb** [with obj.] dated remove (an item of clothing, especially a hat): *the manager doffed his hat to her.*
– ORIGIN late Middle English: contraction of *do off*. Compare with **DON**[2].

dog ▶**noun** 1 a domesticated carnivorous mammal that typically has a long snout, an acute sense of smell, non-retractile claws, and a barking, howling, or whining voice. It is widely kept as a pet or for work or field sports.
• *Canis familiaris*, family Canidae (the **dog family**); probably domesticated from the wolf in the Mesolithic period. The dog family also includes the wolves, coyotes, jackals, and foxes.
■a wild animal of the dog family. ■ the male of an animal of the dog family, or of some other mammals such as the otter: [as modifier] *a dog fox.* ■ (**the dogs**) Brit. informal greyhound racing: *a night at the dogs.* ■ (in extended and metaphorical use) referring to behaviour considered to be savage, dangerous, or wildly energetic: *he attacked the PC* ***like a mad dog*** | *we* ***fought like cat and dog*** *the whole time.*
2 [often with adj.] informal a man regarded as unpleasant, contemptible, or wicked.
■[with adj.] dated used to refer to a person of a specified kind in a tone of playful reproof, commiseration, or congratulation: *your historian is a dull dog* | *you lucky dog!* ■ used in various phrases to refer to someone who is abject or miserable, especially because they have been treated harshly: *I make him* ***work like a dog*** | *Rab* ***was treated like a dog.*** ■ informal, offensive a woman regarded as unattractive. ■ informal, Austral. an informer or a traitor: *one day she's going to* ***turn dog on*** *you.* ■ informal, chiefly N. Amer. a thing of poor quality; a failure: ***a dog of a film.*** ■ informal a horse that is slow or difficult to handle.
3 used in names of dogfishes, e.g. **sandy dog**, **spurdog**.
4 a mechanical device for gripping.
5 (**dogs**) N. Amer. informal feet.
6 (**dogs**) Horse Racing, US barriers used to keep horses off a particular part of the track.
▶**verb** (**dogged**, **dogging**) [with obj.] 1 follow (someone or their movements) closely and persistently: *photographers seemed to dog her every step.*

▪(of a problem) cause continual trouble for: *the twenty-nine-year-old has constantly been dogged by controversy.*
2 (**dog it**) informal, chiefly N. Amer. act lazily; fail to try one's hardest.
3 grip (something) with a mechanical device: [with obj. and complement] *she has dogged the door shut.*
– PHRASES **dog and bone** rhyming slang a telephone. **dog eat dog** used to refer to a situation of fierce competition in which people are willing to harm each other in order to succeed: *New York is a dog-eat-dog society.* **dog in the manger** inclined to prevent others from having or using things that one does not need oneself. ▪ a person who does this. [ORIGIN: alluding to the fable of the dog that lay in a manger to prevent the ox and horse from eating the hay.] **dog-and-pony show** N. Amer. an elaborate display or presentation. **a dog's age** N. Amer. informal a very long time: *the best I've seen in a dog's age.* **dogs bark, but the caravans move on** proverb people may make a fuss, but it won't change the situation. **the dog's bollocks** Brit. vulgar slang a person or thing that is the best of its kind. **a dog's dinner** (or **breakfast**) Brit. informal a poor piece of work; a mess: *we made a real dog's breakfast of it.* **a dog's life** an unhappy existence, full of problems or unfair treatment: *he led poor Amy a dog's life.* **the dogs of war** poetic/literary the havoc accompanying military conflict. [ORIGIN: from Shakespeare's *Julius Caesar* (III. 1. 274).] **dressed (up) like a dog's dinner** Brit. informal wearing ridiculously smart or ostentatious clothes. **every dog has his** (or **its**) **day** proverb everyone will have good luck or success at some point in their lives. **give a dog a bad name and hang him** proverb it's very difficult to lose a bad reputation, even if it's unjustified. **go to the dogs** informal deteriorate shockingly: *the country is going to the dogs.* **hair of the dog** see **HAIR**. **let sleeping dogs lie** see **SLEEP**. **like a dog with two tails** used to emphasize how delighted someone is: *'Is he pleased?' 'Like a dog with two tails.'* **not a dog's chance** no chance at all. **put on the dog** N. Amer. informal behave in a pretentious or ostentatious way: *we have to put on the dog for Anne Marie.* **rain cats and dogs** see **RAIN**. **(as) sick as a dog** see **SICK**[1]. **throw someone to the dogs** discard someone as worthless: *young people look upon the older person as someone to be thrown to the dogs.* **you can't teach an old dog new tricks** proverb you cannot make people change their ways. **why keep a dog and bark yourself?** proverb why pay someone to work for you and then do the work yourself?
– DERIVATIVES **doglike** adjective.
– ORIGIN Old English *docga*, of unknown origin.

dogana /dɒ(ʊ)ˈgɑːnə/ ▶ **noun** (in Italy) a custom house.
– ORIGIN Italian, from Arabic *dīwān* (compare with **DIVAN**).

dogbane /ˈdɒgbeɪn/ ▶ **noun** a shrubby North American plant, typically having bell-shaped flowers and reputed to be poisonous to dogs.
● Genus *Apocynum*, family Apocynaceae.

dogberry ▶ **noun** (pl. **-ies**) informal the fruit of the dogwood.
▪(also **dogberry tree**) the dogwood. ▪ a fruit of poor eating quality from any of a number of other shrubs or small trees, e.g. the American rowan.

dog biscuit ▶ **noun** a hard thick biscuit for feeding to dogs.

dogbox ▶ **noun** Austral. informal a compartment in a railway carriage without a corridor.
– PHRASES **in the dogbox** NZ informal in disfavour.
– ORIGIN early 19th cent.: originally denoting a box for a dog to lie in, later denoting a railway compartment for transporting dogs.

dog cart ▶ **noun** a two-wheeled cart for driving in, with cross seats back to back, originally incorporating a box under the seat for sportsmen's dogs.

dog clutch ▶ **noun** a device for coupling two shafts in order to transmit motion, one part having teeth which engage with slots in another.

dog cockle ▶ **noun** a burrowing bivalve mollusc which has a highly convex, almost spherical, shell.
● Family Glycimeridae: many species, including the European *Glycymeris glycymeris*.

dog collar ▶ **noun** a collar for a dog.
▪informal term for **CLERICAL COLLAR**.

dog days ▶ **plural noun** chiefly poetic/literary the hottest period of the year (reckoned in antiquity from the heliacal rising of Sirius, the Dog Star).
▪a period of inactivity or decline: *these are indeed dog days for British film production.*

dogdom ▶ **noun** [mass noun] the world of dogs and dog fanciers: *the cream of British dogdom.*

doge /dəʊdʒ/ ▶ **noun** historical the chief magistrate of Venice or Genoa.
– ORIGIN mid 16th cent.: from French, from Venetian Italian *doze*, based on Latin *dux*, *duc-* 'leader'.

dog-eared ▶ **adjective** (of an object made from paper) with the corners worn or battered with use.

dog-end ▶ **noun** informal a cigarette end.
▪the last and least pleasing part of something: *the dog-end of a hard day.*

dog face ▶ **noun** **1** (also **dog face butterfly**) an American butterfly with a marking on the forewing said to resemble a dog's face, especially in the male.
● Genus *Zerene*, family Pieridae: several species.
2 (**dogface**) US informal, dated a US soldier, especially an infantryman.

dogfight ▶ **noun** a close combat between military aircraft.
▪a ferocious struggle for supremacy between interested parties: *the meeting deteriorated into a dogfight.* ▪ a fight between dogs, especially one organized illegally for public entertainment.
– DERIVATIVES **dogfighter** noun.

dogfighting ▶ **noun** [mass noun] the action of flying a fighter aircraft in close combat with an enemy.
▪the practice of making dogs fight for public entertainment, which is illegal in many countries.

dogfish ▶ **noun** (pl. same or **-fishes**) **1** a small sand-coloured bottom-dwelling shark with a long tail, common on European coasts. Also called **ROUGH HOUND**, **SANDY DOG**.
● *Scyliorhinus canicula*, family Scyliorhinidae.
2 [with modifier] a small shark that resembles or is related to the dogfish, sometimes caught for food.
● Several genera in the families Scyliorhinidae, Squalidae, and Triakidae.

dogged /ˈdɒgɪd/ ▶ **adjective** having or showing tenacity and grim persistence: *success required dogged determination.*
– DERIVATIVES **doggedly** adverb, **doggedness** noun.

dogger[1] ▶ **noun** historical a two-masted bluff-bowed Dutch sailing boat, used for fishing.
– ORIGIN Middle English: from Middle Dutch.

dogger[2] ▶ **noun** Geology a large spherical concretion occurring in sedimentary rock.
– ORIGIN late 17th cent. (originally a dialect word denoting a kind of ironstone): perhaps from **DOG**.

Dogger Bank a submerged sandbank in the North Sea, about 115 km (70 miles) off the NE coast of England. This part of the central North Sea is covered by the shipping forecast area **Dogger**.

doggerel /ˈdɒg(ə)r(ə)l/ ▶ **noun** [mass noun] comic verse composed in irregular rhythm.
▪verse or words that are badly written or expressed: *the last stanza deteriorates into doggerel.*
– ORIGIN late Middle English (as an adjective describing such verse): apparently from **DOG** (used contemptuously, as in **DOG LATIN**) + **-REL**.

Doggett's Coat and Badge /ˈdɒgɪts/ an orange livery with a silver badge offered as a trophy in an annual rowing contest among Thames watermen in London. It was instituted in 1715 by an Irish comic actor, Thomas Doggett (1620–1721).

doggie ▶ **noun** variant spelling of **DOGGY**.

doggish ▶ **adjective** of or like a dog: *her peculiar doggish smile.*
▪archaic (of a person) having the bad qualities of a dog, especially by being bad-tempered or snappish.

doggo ▶ **adverb** (in phrase **lie doggo**) Brit. informal, dated remain motionless and quiet to escape detection: *a dozen officers had been lying doggo for hours.*
– ORIGIN late 19th cent.: of obscure origin; apparently from **DOG** + **-O**.

doggone /ˈdɒgɒn/ N. Amer. informal ▶ **adjective** [attrib.] used to express feelings of annoyance, surprise, or pleasure: *now just a doggone minute* | [as submodifier] *it's doggone good to be home.*
▶ **verb** [with obj.] damn; darn (used to express surprise, irritation, or anger): *from that moment, doggone it if I didn't see a motivation in Joey!* | *I'll be doggoned if every fourth kid is affected.*
– ORIGIN early 19th cent.: probably from *dog on it*, euphemism for *God damn it*.

doggy ▶ **adjective** of or like a dog: *his doggy brown eyes.*
▪fond of dogs: *it was a doggy household.*
▶ **noun** (also **doggie**) (pl. **-ies**) a child's word for a dog.
– DERIVATIVES **dogginess** noun.

doggy bag ▶ **noun** a bag used by a restaurant customer or party guest to take home leftover food, supposedly for their dog.

doggy-paddle ▶ **noun** an elementary swimming stroke in which the swimmer beats at the water with the hands in a manner resembling a swimming dog.
▶ **verb** [no obj.] swim using this stroke.

dog handler ▶ **noun** a person who works with trained dogs: *a police dog handler.*
– DERIVATIVES **dog-handling** noun.

doghouse ▶ **noun** N. Amer. a dog's kennel.
▪humorous, informal an area or structure resembling a kennel. ▪ Sailing a raised area at the after end of a yacht's coachroof, providing standing room.
– PHRASES **(be) in the doghouse** informal (be) in disgrace or disfavour.

dogie /ˈdəʊgi/ ▶ **noun** (pl. **-ies**) N. Amer. a motherless or neglected calf.
– ORIGIN late 19th cent.: of unknown origin.

dog Latin ▶ **noun** [mass noun] a debased form of Latin.

dog-leg ▶ **noun** a thing that bends sharply, in particular a sharp bend in a road or route.
▪Golf a hole where the fairway has a bend.

dog-leg stair (also **dog-leg staircase**) ▶ **noun** a staircase which has no well and a bend of 180° in it, usually at a landing halfway between floors.

dogma /ˈdɒgmə/ ▶ **noun** a principle or set of principles laid down by an authority as incontrovertibly true: *the dogmas of faith* | [mass noun] *the rejection of political dogma.*
– ORIGIN mid 16th cent.: via late Latin from Greek *dogma* 'opinion', from *dokein* 'seem good, think'.

dogman ▶ **noun** (pl. **-men**) Austral./NZ a person giving directional signals to the operator of a crane, typically while sitting on the crane's load.
– ORIGIN 1940s: from sense 4 of **DOG** + **MAN**.

dogmatic /dɒgˈmatɪk/ ▶ **adjective** inclined to lay down principles as incontrovertibly true: *she was not tempted to be dogmatic about what she believed.*
– DERIVATIVES **dogmatically** adverb.
– ORIGIN early 17th cent. (as a noun denoting a philosopher or physician of a school based on a priori assumptions): via late Latin from Greek *dogmatikos*, from *dogma*, *dogmat-* (see **DOGMA**).

dogmatics ▶ **plural noun** [treated as sing.] a system of principles laid down by an authority, especially the Roman Catholic Church, as incontrovertibly true, without consideration of evidence or the opinions of others: *it is a work of analysis, not of dogmatics.*

dogmatism ▶ **noun** [mass noun] the tendency to lay down principles as incontrovertibly true, without consideration of evidence or the opinions of others: *a culture of dogmatism and fanaticism.*
– DERIVATIVES **dogmatist** noun.
– ORIGIN early 17th cent.: via French from medieval Latin *dogmatismus*, from Latin *dogma* (see **DOGMA**).

dogmatize /ˈdɒgmətʌɪz/ (also **-ise**) ▶ **verb** [with obj.] represent as an incontrovertible truth: *I find views dogmatized to the point of absurdity.*
– ORIGIN early 17th cent.: via French and late Latin from Greek *dogmatizein* 'lay down one's opinion', from *dogma* (see **DOGMA**).

dognap ▶ **verb** (**-napped**, **-napping**) [with obj.] informal steal (a dog), especially in order to sell it.
– DERIVATIVES **dognapper** noun.

do-gooder ▶ **noun** a well-meaning but unrealistic or interfering philanthropist or reformer.
– DERIVATIVES **do-good** adjective & noun, **do-goodery** noun, **do-goodism** noun.

dog-paddle ▶ **noun** & **verb** chiefly N. Amer. another term for **DOGGY-PADDLE**.

dog racing ▶ **noun** another term for **GREYHOUND RACING**.

Dogrib /ˈdɒgrɪb/ ▶ **noun** **1** a member of a Dene people of NW Canada.
2 [mass noun] the Athabaskan language of this people, with about 2,000 speakers.
▶ **adjective** of or relating to this people or their language.
– ORIGIN translation of Dogrib *Thlingchadinne* 'dog's flank', from the legend that the people's common ancestor was a dog.

dog-robber ▶ noun informal, chiefly US an army or navy officer's orderly.

dog rose ▶ noun a delicately scented Eurasian wild rose with pink or white flowers, which commonly grows in hedgerows.
● Genus *Rosa*, family Rosaceae: several closely related species, in particular *R. canina*.

dogsbody ▶ noun (pl. **-ies**) Brit. informal a person who is given boring, menial tasks to do, especially a junior in an office: *I got myself a job as typist and general dogsbody on a small magazine.*
– DERIVATIVES **dogsbodying** noun.

dogshore ▶ noun each of a pair of blocks of timber positioned on each side of a ship on a slipway to prevent its sliding down before launching.

dogskin ▶ noun [mass noun] leather made of or imitating dog's skin, especially as used for gloves.

dog sled ▶ noun a sled designed to be pulled by dogs.

dog's mercury ▶ noun a Eurasian plant of the spurge family, with hairy stems and small green flowers, widely found as a dominant plant of old woodland.
● *Mercurialis perennis*, family Euphorbiaceae.
– ORIGIN late 16th cent.: translating modern Latin *Mercurialis canina* (former taxonomic name); the plant is poisonous and is contrasted with *Mercurialis annua* 'annual mercury', useful in medicine.

dogstail (also **dog's-tail**) ▶ noun an Old World fodder grass with spiky flower heads.
● Genus *Cynosurus*, family Gramineae: several species, in particular **crested dogstail** (*C. cristatus*), a common pasture grass.

Dog Star the star Sirius.
– ORIGIN translating Greek *kuon* or Latin *canicula* 'small dog', both names of the star; so named as it appears to follow at the heels of Orion (the hunter).

dog's-tooth violet ▶ noun a plant of the lily family which has backward curving pointed petals. Also called **ADDER'S TONGUE** in North America.
● Genus *Erythronium*, family Liliaceae: several species, in particular the Eurasian *E. dens-canis*, with speckled leaves and pinkish-purple flowers.

dog tag ▶ noun a metal tag attached to a dog's collar, typically giving its name and owner's address.
■ informal, chiefly N. Amer. a soldier's metal identity tag.

dog-tail ▶ noun variant of **DOGSTAIL**.

dog-tired ▶ adjective extremely tired; worn out: *he'd gone to bed dog-tired.*

dog-tooth ▶ noun **1** Architecture a small pointed ornament or moulding forming one of a series radiating like petals from a raised centre, typical of Norman and Early English styles.
2 (also **dogstooth**) [mass noun] a small check pattern with notched corners suggestive of a canine tooth, typically used in cloth for jackets and suits.

dogtrot ▶ noun [in sing.] a gentle easy trot.
▶ verb [no obj.] move at such a pace.

dog violet ▶ noun a scentless wild violet, typically having purple or lilac flowers.
● Genus *Viola*, family Violaceae: several species, in particular the **common dog violet** (*V. riviniana*).

dogwatch ▶ noun either of two short watches on a ship (4–6 or 6–8 p.m.).

dog-weary ▶ adjective another term for **DOG-TIRED**.

dog whelk ▶ noun a predatory marine mollusc that typically occurs on the shore or in shallow waters.
● Family Nassariidae, class Gastropoda: *Nucella* and other genera.

dogwood ▶ noun a shrub or small tree of north temperate regions, which yields hard timber and is grown for its decorative foliage, red stems, or colourful berries.
● Genus *Cornus*, family Cornaceae: many species, including the wild **Eurasian dogwood** (*C. sanguinea*), with black berries, and the cornelian cherry.
■ used in names of trees which resemble the dogwood or yield similar hard timber.
– ORIGIN so named because the wood was formerly used to make 'dogs' (i.e. skewers).

DoH ▶ abbreviation for (in the UK) Department of Health.

doh¹ /dəʊ/ (also **do**) ▶ noun Music (in tonic sol-fa) the first and eighth note of a major scale.
■ the note C in the fixed-doh system.

– ORIGIN mid 18th cent.: from Italian *do*, an arbitrarily chosen syllable replacing *ut*, taken from a Latin hymn (see **SOLMIZATION**).

doh² /dəʊ/ ▶ exclamation informal used to comment on an action perceived as foolish or stupid: *He had approached the wrong set of supporters. Doh!*

Doha /ˈdəʊhɑ:/ the capital of Qatar; pop 300,000 (est. 1990).

DOHC ▶ abbreviation for double overhead camshaft.

doily /ˈdɔɪli/ ▶ noun (pl. **-ies**) a small ornamental mat made of lace or paper with a lace pattern, put on a plate under cakes or other sweet food.
– ORIGIN late 17th cent.: from *Doiley* or *Doyley*, the name of a 17th-cent. London draper. The word originally denoted a woollen material used for summer wear, said to have been introduced by this draper. The current sense (originally *doily napkin*) dates from the early 18th cent.

doing ▶ noun **1** (usu. **doings**) the activities in which a particular person engages: *the latest doings of television stars.*
■ informal excrement, especially that of a domestic animal. ■ [in sing.] informal a beating or scolding: *someone had given her a doing.*
2 [mass noun] used to indicate that something is considered difficult to achieve: *it would take some doing to calm him down.*
3 (**doings**) [treated as sing. or pl.] informal, chiefly Brit. used to refer to things when one has forgotten their name or when no one word easily covers them: *the drawer where he kept the doings.*
– PHRASES **be someone's doing** be the creation or fault of the person named: *he looked at Lisa as though it was all her doing.*

Doisneau /ˈdwʌnəʊ, French dwano/, Robert (1912–94), French photographer, best known for his photos of the city and inhabitants of Paris. Notable works: 'The Kiss at the Hôtel de Ville' (1950).

doit /dɔɪt/ ▶ noun [in sing.] archaic a very small amount of money.
– ORIGIN late 16th cent.: from Middle Low German *doyt*, Middle Dutch *duit*, of unknown origin.

do-it-yourself ▶ noun & adjective full form of **DIY**.
– DERIVATIVES **do-it-yourselfer** noun.

dojo /ˈdəʊdʒəʊ/ ▶ noun (pl. **-os**) a room or hall in which judo and other martial arts are practised.
– ORIGIN Japanese, from *dō* 'way, pursuit' + *jō* 'a place'.

dol. ▶ abbreviation for dollar or dollars.

Dolby /ˈdɒlbi, ˈdəʊl-/ ▶ noun [mass noun] trademark an electronic noise-reduction system used in tape recording to reduce hiss.
■ an electronic system used to provide stereophonic sound for cinemas and television sets.
– ORIGIN 1960s: named after Ray M. *Dolby* (born 1933), the American engineer who devised it.

dolce /ˈdɒltʃeɪ/ ▶ adverb & adjective Music (especially as a direction) sweetly and softly.
– ORIGIN Italian, literally 'sweet'.

dolce far niente /ˌdɒltʃeɪ fɑ: nɪˈɛnteɪ/ ▶ noun [mass noun] pleasant idleness.
– ORIGIN Italian, 'sweet doing nothing'.

Dolcelatte /ˌdɒltʃəˈlɑ:teɪ, -ˈlati/ ▶ noun [mass noun] trademark a kind of soft creamy blue-veined cheese from Italy.
– ORIGIN Italian, literally 'sweet milk'.

dolce vita /ˌdɒltʃeɪ ˈvi:tə/ ▶ noun [in sing.] (usu. **la dolce vita**) a life of heedless pleasure and luxury.
– ORIGIN Italian, literally 'sweet life'.

doldrums /ˈdɒldrəmz/ ▶ plural noun (**the doldrums**) a state or period of stagnation or depression: *the mortgage market has been in the doldrums for three years.*
■ an equatorial region of the Atlantic Ocean with calms, sudden storms, and light unpredictable winds.
– ORIGIN late 18th cent. (as *doldrum* 'dull, sluggish person'): perhaps from **DULL**, on the pattern of *tantrums*.

dole¹ ▶ noun **1** [mass noun] (usu. **the dole**) Brit. informal benefit paid by the state to the unemployed: *she is drawing the dole* | [as modifier] *my next dole cheque.*
■ [count noun] dated a charitable gift of food, clothes, or money.
2 poetic/literary a person's lot or destiny.
▶ verb [with obj.] (**dole something out**) distribute shares of something: *the scanty portions of food doled out to them.*

– PHRASES **the dole queue** the unemployed people receiving benefit from the state: *another 21,300 people joined the dole queues in May.* **on the dole** informal registered as unemployed and receiving benefit from the state.
– ORIGIN Old English *dāl* 'division, portion, or share', of Germanic origin; related to **DEAL¹**. The sense 'distribution of charitable gifts' dates from Middle English; the sense 'unemployment benefit' dates from the early 20th cent.

dole² ▶ noun [mass noun] archaic or poetic/literary sorrow; mourning.
– ORIGIN Middle English: from Old French *doel* 'mourning', from popular Latin *dolus*, from Latin *dolere* 'grieve'.

dole-bludger ▶ noun Austral. informal a person who chooses to be on the dole rather than to work.

doleful ▶ adjective expressing sorrow; mournful: *a doleful look.*
■ causing grief or misfortune: *he could be stricken off with doleful consequences.*
– DERIVATIVES **dolefully** adverb, **dolefulness** noun.

dolerite /ˈdɒlərʌɪt/ ▶ noun [mass noun] Geology a dark, medium-grained igneous rock, typically with ophitic texture, containing plagioclase, pyroxene, and olivine. It typically occurs in dykes and sills. Also called **DIABASE**.
– ORIGIN mid 19th cent.: from French *dolérite*, from Greek *doleros* 'deceptive' (because it is difficult to distinguish from diorite).

doli capax /ˌdɒlɪ ˈkapaks/ ▶ adjective Law deemed capable of having the intention to commit a crime, especially by reason of being ten years old or more.
– ORIGIN Latin, 'capable of evil'.

dolichocephalic /ˌdɒlɪkə(ʊ)sɪˈfalɪk, -kɛˈfalɪk-/ ▶ adjective Anatomy having a relatively long skull (typically with the breadth less than 80 (or 75) per cent of the length). Often contrasted with **BRACHYCEPHALIC**.
– DERIVATIVES **dolichocephaly** noun.
– ORIGIN mid 19th cent.: from Greek *dolikhos* 'long' + **-CEPHALIC**.

doli incapax /ɪnˈkapaks/ ▶ adjective Law deemed incapable of having the intention to commit a crime, especially by reason of being under ten years old.
– ORIGIN Latin, literally 'incapable of evil'.

Dolin /ˈdəʊlɪn, ˈdɒl-/, Sir Anton (1904–83), English ballet dancer and choreographer; born *Sydney Francis Patrick Chippendall Healey-Kay*. He was the first artistic director of the London Festival Ballet (1950–61), as well as first soloist.

doline /dɒˈli:n/ (also **dolina** /dɒˈli:nə/) ▶ noun Geology a hollow or basin in a karstic region, typically funnel-shaped.
– ORIGIN late 19th cent.: via German from Slovene *dolina* 'valley'.

D'Oliveira /ˌdɒlɪˈvɪərə/, Basil (Lewis) (b.1931), British cricketer and coach, born in South Africa and of Cape coloured origin. South Africa's refusal to allow him into the country led to the cancellation of England's 1968–9 tour and to South Africa's subsequent banishment from test cricket until the end of apartheid.

Doll, Sir (William) Richard (Shaboe) (b.1912), English physician. With **Sir A. Bradford Hill** (1897–1991) he was the first to show a statistical link between smoking and lung cancer.

doll¹ ▶ noun a small model of a human figure, typically one of a baby or girl, used as a child's toy.
■ informal an attractive young woman. ■ N. Amer. informal an attractive young man.
▶ verb [with obj.] (**doll someone up**) informal dress someone or oneself smartly and attractively: *I got all dolled up for a party.*
– ORIGIN mid 16th cent. (denoting a mistress): pet form of the given name *Dorothy*. The sense 'small model of a human figure' dates from the late 17th cent.

doll² Horse Racing, Brit. ▶ noun a temporary barrier on a race course or gallop.
▶ verb [with obj.] place a barrier in front of (a jump or other part of the course that is to be omitted from a race).
– ORIGIN 1940s: perhaps a variant of archaic *dool* 'boundary marker'.

dollar ▶ noun the basic monetary unit of the US, Canada, Australia, and certain countries in the

d

Pacific, Caribbean, SE Asia, Africa, and South America.
– PHRASES **dollars to doughnuts** N. Amer. informal used to emphasize one's certainty: *I'd* ***bet dollars to doughnuts*** *he's a medical student.*
– ORIGIN from early Flemish or Low German *daler*, from German *T(h)aler*, short for *Joachimsthaler*, a coin from the silver-mine of *Joachimsthal* ('Joachim's valley'), now *Jáchymov* in the Czech Republic. The term was later applied to a coin used in the Spanish-American colonies, which was also widely used in the British North American colonies at the time of the American War of Independence, hence adopted as the name of the US monetary unit in the late 18th cent.

dollar area ▶ **noun** the area of the world in which currency is linked to the US dollar.

dollarbird ▶ **noun** the eastern broad-billed roller of Asia and Australasia, which has a conspicuous white coin-like mark on the wing that is visible in flight.
• *Eyrystomus orientalis*, family Coraciidae.

dollar diplomacy ▶ **noun** [mass noun] the use of a country's financial power to extend its international influence.

dollar gap ▶ **noun** the amount by which a country's import trade with the dollar area exceeds the corresponding export trade.

dollarization (also **-sation**) ▶ **noun** [mass noun] the process of aligning a country's currency with the US dollar.
▪ the dominating effect of the US on the economy of a country.

dollar sign (also **dollar mark**) ▶ **noun** the sign $, representing a dollar.

Dollfuss /ˈdɒlfʊs/, Engelbert (1892–1934), Austrian statesman, Chancellor of Austria 1932–4. From 1933 Dollfuss attempted to block Austrian Nazi plans to force the *Anschluss* by governing without Parliament. He was assassinated by Austrian Nazis.

dollop ▶ **noun** informal a large, shapeless mass of something, especially soft food: *great* ***dollops*** *of cream* | figurative *a* ***dollop of*** *romance here and there.*
▶ **verb** (**dolloped**, **dolloping**) [with obj. and adverbial of direction] add (a large mass of something) casually and without measuring: *he stopped him from dolloping cream into his coffee.*
– ORIGIN late 16th cent. (denoting a clump of grass or weeds in a field): perhaps of Scandinavian origin and related to Norwegian dialect *dolp* 'lump'.

doll's house (N. Amer. also **dollhouse**) ▶ **noun** a miniature toy house used for playing with dolls.

dolly ▶ **noun** (pl. **-ies**) **1** a child's word for a doll.
▪ informal, dated an attractive and stylish young woman.
2 a small platform on wheels used for holding heavy objects, typically film or television cameras.
3 Cricket, informal an easy catch.
4 historical a short wooden pole for stirring clothes in a washtub.
▶ **verb** (**-ies**, **-ied**) [no obj., with adverbial of direction] (of a film or television camera) be moved on a mobile platform in a specified direction: *the camera dollies back to reveal hundreds of people.*
▶ **adjective** (**dollier**, **dolliest**) [attrib.] **1** informal (of a girl) attractive and stylish.
2 Cricket, informal denoting an easy catch.

dolly-bird ▶ **noun** Brit. informal, dated an attractive and stylish young woman, considered with reference only to her appearance.

dolly mixtures ▶ **plural noun** Brit. a mixture of small variously shaped and coloured sweets.

dolly switch ▶ **noun** an electrical on-off switch whose external operating mechanism is a short pivoted lever terminating in a rounded knob, rather than a spring-loaded rocker.

dolly tub ▶ **noun** historical a washtub.
– ORIGIN late 19th cent.: from dialect *dolly* (used as a term for various contrivances thought to resemble a doll in some way) and **TUB**.

Dolly Varden /ˈvɑːd(ə)n/ ▶ **noun 1** (also **Dolly Varden hat**) a large hat with one side drooping and with a floral trimming, formerly worn by women.
2 a brightly spotted edible charr (fish) occurring in fresh water on both sides of the North Pacific.
• *Salvelinus malma*, family Salmonidae.
– ORIGIN late 19th cent.: from the name of a character in Dickens's *Barnaby Rudge*, who wore a similar hat.

dolma /ˈdɒlmə/ ▶ **noun** (pl. **dolmas** or **dolmades** /-ˈmɑːðɛz/) a Greek and Turkish delicacy in which ingredients such as spiced rice, meat, and bread are wrapped in vine or cabbage leaves.
– ORIGIN from modern Greek *ntolmas* or its source, Turkish *dolma*, from *dolmak* 'fill, be filled'.

dolman /ˈdɒlmən/ ▶ **noun** a long Turkish robe open in front.
▪ a woman's loose cloak with cape-like sleeves.
– ORIGIN late 16th cent.: based on Turkish *dolama*, *dolaman*.

dolman sleeve ▶ **noun** a loose sleeve cut in one piece with the body of a garment.

dolmen /ˈdɒlmɛn/ ▶ **noun** a megalithic tomb with a large flat stone laid on upright ones, found chiefly in Britain and France.
– ORIGIN mid 19th cent.: from French, perhaps via Breton from Cornish *tolmen* 'hole of a stone'.

dolmus /ˈdɒlmʊʃ/ ▶ **noun** (in Turkey) a shared taxi.
– ORIGIN from Turkish *dolmuş*, literally 'filled'.

dolomite /ˈdɒləmʌɪt/ ▶ **noun** [mass noun] a translucent mineral consisting of a carbonate of calcium and magnesium, usually also containing iron.
▪ a sedimentary rock formed chiefly of this mineral.
– DERIVATIVES **dolomitic** adjective.
– ORIGIN late 18th cent.: from French, from the name of *Dolomieu* (1750–1801), the French geologist who discovered it, + **-ITE**[1].

Dolomite Mountains (also **the Dolomites**) a range of the Alps in northern Italy, so named because the characteristic rock of the region is dolomitic limestone.

dolorimeter /ˌdɒləˈrɪmɪtə/ ▶ **noun** an instrument for measuring sensitivity to, or levels of, pain.
– DERIVATIVES **dolorimetry** noun.

dolorous /ˈdɒl(ə)rəs/ ▶ **adjective** poetic/literary feeling or expressing great sorrow or distress.
– DERIVATIVES **dolorously** adverb.
– ORIGIN late Middle English: from Old French *doleros*, from late Latin *dolorosus*, from Latin *dolor* 'pain, grief'.

dolostone /ˈdɒləstəʊn/ ▶ **noun** [mass noun] Geology rock consisting of dolomite.
– ORIGIN mid 20th cent.: from **DOLOMITE** + **STONE**.

dolour /ˈdɒlə/ (US **dolor**) ▶ **noun** [mass noun] poetic/literary a state of great sorrow or distress: *they squatted, hunched in their habitual dolour.*
– ORIGIN Middle English (denoting both physical and mental pain or distress): via Old French from Latin *dolor* 'pain, grief'.

dolphin ▶ **noun 1** a small gregarious toothed whale which typically has a beak-like snout and a curved fin on the back. Dolphins have become well known for their sociable nature and high intelligence.
• Families Delphinidae (marine) and Platanistidae (the **river dolphins**): several genera and many species.
▪ a dolphin-like creature depicted in heraldry or art, typically with an arched body and fins like a fish.
2 (also **dolphinfish**) another term for **DORADO** (in sense 1).
3 a bollard, pile, or buoy for mooring.
4 a structure for protecting the pier of a bridge.
– ORIGIN late Middle English: from Old French *dauphin*, from Provençal *dalfin*, from Latin *delphinus*, from Greek *delphin*.

dolphinarium /ˌdɒlfɪˈnɛːrɪəm/ ▶ **noun** (pl. **dolphinariums** or **dolphinaria**) an aquarium in which dolphins are kept and trained for public entertainment.
– ORIGIN 1960s: from **DOLPHIN**, on the pattern of *oceanarium*.

dolt /dəʊlt/ ▶ **noun** dated a stupid person.
– DERIVATIVES **doltish** adjective, **doltishly** adverb, **doltishness** noun.
– ORIGIN mid 16th cent.: perhaps a variant of *dulled*, past participle of **DULL**.

Dom /dɒm/ ▶ **noun 1** a title prefixed to the names of some Roman Catholic dignitaries and Benedictine and Carthusian monks: *Dom Bede Griffiths.*
2 Portuguese form of **DON**[1] (in sense 2).
– ORIGIN from Latin *dominus* 'master'.

-dom ▶ **suffix** forming nouns: **1** denoting a state or condition: *freedom.*
2 denoting rank or status: *earldom.*
3 denoting a domain: *fiefdom.*
4 denoting a class of people or the attitudes associated with them, regarded collectively: *officialdom.*
– ORIGIN Old English *-dōm*, originally meaning 'decree, judgement'.

domain /də(ʊ)ˈmeɪn/ ▶ **noun** an area of territory owned or controlled by a ruler or government: *the south-western French domains of the Plantagenets.*
▪ a specified sphere of activity or knowledge: *the country's isolation in the domain of sport.* ▪ Physics a discrete region of magnetism in ferromagnetic material. ▪ Computing a distinct subset of the Internet with addresses sharing a common suffix, such as the part in a particular country or used by a particular group of users. ▪ Mathematics the set of possible values of the independent variable or variables of a function.
– ORIGIN late Middle English (denoting heritable or landed property): from French *domaine*, alteration (by association with Latin *dominus* 'lord') of Old French *demeine* 'belonging to a lord' (see **DEMESNE**).

domaine /dəˈmeɪn/ ▶ **noun** a vineyard.
– ORIGIN 1960s: from French, literally 'estate' (see **DOMAIN**).

domal /ˈdəʊm(ə)l/ ▶ **adjective** (chiefly of geological features) having the form of a dome.

domanial /dəˈmeɪnɪəl/ ▶ **adjective** of or relating to the control or ownership of an area of territory by a ruler or government.
– ORIGIN early 19th cent.: from French, from medieval Latin *domanialis*, from *domanium* 'lordship'.

dome ▶ **noun 1** a rounded vault forming the roof of a building or structure, typically with a circular base: *the dome of St Paul's Cathedral.*
▪ the revolving openable hemispherical roof of an observatory. ▪ [in names] N. Amer. a sports stadium with a domed roof.
2 a thing shaped like such a roof, in particular:
▪ the rounded summit of a hill or mountain: *the great dome of Mont Blanc.* ▪ a natural vault or canopy, such as that of the sky or trees: *the dome of the sky.* ▪ Geology a rounded uplifted landform or underground structure. ▪ informal the top of the head: *her Mohican projected from her shaved dome.*
3 poetic/literary a stately building.
▶ **verb** [no obj.] [often as noun **doming**] (of stratified rock or a surface) become rounded in formation; swell.
– DERIVATIVES **dome-like** adjective.
– ORIGIN early 16th cent. (in sense 3): from French *dôme*, from Italian *duomo* 'cathedral, dome', from Latin *domus* 'house'. Sense 3 derives directly from Latin *domus*.

domed ▶ **adjective** covered with or shaped like a rounded vault: *his domed forehead* | [in combination] *a glass-domed roof.*

dome fastener ▶ **noun** a press stud consisting of a rounded portion which clips into a socket, used especially as a fastener for gloves.

Dome of the Rock an Islamic shrine in Jerusalem, for Muslims the third most holy place after Mecca and Medina. It surrounds the sacred rock on which, according to tradition, Abraham prepared to sacrifice his son Isaac and from which the prophet Muhammad made his miraculous midnight ascent into heaven (the Night Journey).

Domesday /ˈduːmzdeɪ/ ▶ **noun 1** (also **Domesday Book**, **Doomsday Book**) a comprehensive record of the extent, value, ownership, and liabilities of land in England, made in 1086 by order of William I.
2 (also **domesday**) archaic spelling of **DOOMSDAY**.
– ORIGIN Middle English: sense 1 was apparently a popular name applied during the 12th cent. because the book was regarded as a final authority (with allusion to *doomsday* 'the Day of Judgement').

domestic ▶ **adjective 1** of or relating to the running of a home or to family relations: *domestic chores* | *domestic violence.*
▪ of or for use in the home rather than in an industrial or office environment: *domestic water supplies.* ▪ (of a person) fond of family life and running a home: *she was not at all domestic.* ▪ (of an animal) tame and kept by humans: *domestic dogs.*
2 existing or occurring inside a particular country; not foreign or international: *Korea's domestic affairs.*
▶ **noun 1** (also **domestic worker** or **domestic help**) a person who is paid to help with menial tasks such as cleaning.
2 informal a violent quarrel between family members, especially husband and wife: *they are often called to sort out a domestic.*
3 N. Amer. a product not made abroad.
– DERIVATIVES **domestically** adverb.

– ORIGIN late Middle English: from French *domestique*, from Latin *domesticus*, from *domus* 'house'.

domesticate ▶ verb [with obj.] (usu. **be domesticated**) tame (an animal) and keep it as a pet or for farm produce: *mammals were first domesticated for their milk.*
■ cultivate (a plant) for food. ■ humorous make (someone) fond of and good at home life and the tasks that it involves: *you've quite domesticated him* | [as adj. **domesticated**] *he is thoroughly domesticated.*
– DERIVATIVES **domesticable** adjective, **domestication** noun.
– ORIGIN mid 17th cent.: from medieval Latin *domesticat-* 'domesticated', from the verb *domesticare*, from Latin *domesticus* 'belonging to the house' (see **DOMESTIC**).

domestic bursar ▶ noun the person responsible for the administration of the domestic establishment of a college or university.

domesticity ▶ noun [mass noun] home or family life: *the atmosphere is one of happy domesticity.*

domestic partner ▶ noun N. Amer. a person who is living with another in a close personal and sexual relationship.
– DERIVATIVES **domestic partnership** noun.

domestic pigeon ▶ noun see **PIGEON**[1] (sense 1).

domestic science ▶ noun dated the study of household skills such as cooking or sewing, especially as taught at school; home economics.

domical /ˈdəʊmɪk(ə)l/ ▶ adjective another term for **DOMED**: *an octagonal, domical vault.*

domicile /ˈdɒmɪsʌɪl, -sɪl/ (also **domicil** /-sɪl/) ▶ noun formal or Law the country that a person treats as his or her permanent home, or lives in and has a substantial connection with: *his wife has a* ***domicile of origin*** *in Germany.* Compare with **RESIDENCE**.
■ chiefly US a person's residence or home: *the builder I've hired to renovate my new domicile.* ■ the place at which a company or other body is registered, especially for tax purposes.
▶ verb [with adverbial of place] (**be domiciled**) formal or Law treat a specified country as a permanent home: *the tenant is domiciled in the United Kingdom.* Compare with **RESIDE**.
■ chiefly US reside; be based: *he was domiciled in a frame house in the outskirts of Bogotá.*
– ORIGIN late Middle English: via Old French from Latin *domicilium* 'dwelling', from *domus* 'home'.

domiciliary /ˌdɒmɪˈsɪlɪəri/ ▶ adjective concerned with or occurring in someone's home: *a study compared domiciliary care with hospital care.*
– ORIGIN late 19th cent.: from French *domiciliaire*, from medieval Latin *domiciliarius*, from Latin *domicilium* 'dwelling' (see **DOMICILE**).

dominance ▶ noun [mass noun] power and influence over others: *the worldwide dominance of Hollywood.*
■ Genetics the phenomenon whereby, in an individual containing two allelic forms of a gene, one is expressed to the exclusion of the other. ■ Ecology the predominance of one or more species in a plant (or animal) community.
– DERIVATIVES **dominancy** noun.

dominant ▶ adjective most important, powerful, or influential: *they are now in an even more dominant position in the market.*
■ (of a high place or object) overlooking others. ■ Genetics relating to or denoting heritable characteristics which are controlled by genes that are expressed in offspring even when inherited from only one parent. Often contrasted with **RECESSIVE**. ■ Ecology denoting the predominant species in a plant (or animal) community. ■ in decision theory, (of a choice) at least as good as the alternatives in all circumstances, and better in some: *holding back is here a dominant strategy.*
▶ noun a dominant thing, in particular:
■ Genetics a dominant trait or gene. ■ Ecology a dominant species in a plant (or animal) community. ■ Music the fifth note of the diatonic scale of any key, or the key based on this, considered in relation to the key of the tonic.
– DERIVATIVES **dominantly** adverb.
– ORIGIN late Middle English: via Old French from Latin *dominant-* 'ruling, governing', from the verb *dominari* (see **DOMINATE**).

dominant seventh ▶ noun Music the common chord of the dominant note in a key, plus the diminished seventh from that note (e.g. in the key of C, a chord of G-B-D-F). It is important in conventional harmony, as it naturally resolves to the tonic or subdominant.

dominate /ˈdɒmɪneɪt/ ▶ verb [with obj.] (often **be dominated**) have a commanding influence on; exercise control over: *the company dominates the market for operating system software.*
■ be the most important or conspicuous person or thing in: *the race was dominated by the 1992 champion.* ■ (of something tall or high) have a commanding position over; overlook: *a picturesque city dominated by the cathedral tower.*
– DERIVATIVES **dominator** noun.
– ORIGIN early 17th cent.: from Latin *dominat-* 'ruled, governed', from the verb *dominari*, from *dominus* 'lord, master'.

domination ▶ noun [mass noun] **1** the exercise of control or influence over someone or something, or the state of being so controlled: *the imperial domination of India.*
2 (**dominations**) (in traditional Christian angelology) the fourth highest order of the ninefold celestial hierarchy.
– ORIGIN late Middle English: via Old French from Latin *dominatio(n-)*, from the verb *dominari* (see **DOMINATE**).

dominatrix /ˌdɒmɪˈneɪtrɪks/ ▶ noun (pl. **dominatrices** /-trɪsiːz/ or **dominatrixes**) a dominating woman, especially one who takes the sadistic role in sadomasochistic sexual activities.
– ORIGIN mid 16th cent. (rare before the late 20th cent.): from Latin, feminine of *dominator*, from *dominat-* 'ruled', from the verb *dominari* (see **DOMINATE**).

dominee /ˈduːmɪni, ˈdʊə-/ ▶ noun S. African a minister of the Dutch Reformed Church.
– ORIGIN Afrikaans and Dutch, from the Latin vocative *domine!* 'master!'

domineer /ˌdɒmɪˈnɪə/ ▶ verb [no obj.] [usu. as adj. **domineering**] assert one's will over another in an arrogant way: *Cathy had been a martyr to her gruff, domineering husband.*
– DERIVATIVES **domineeringly** adverb.
– ORIGIN late 16th cent.: from Dutch *dominieren*, from French *dominer*, from Latin *dominari* (see **DOMINATE**).

Domingo /dəˈmɪŋgəʊ/, Placido (b.1941), Spanish-born tenor. His performances in operas by Verdi and Puccini have met with particular acclaim.

Dominic, St /ˈdɒmɪnɪk/ (*c.*1170–1221), Spanish priest and friar; Spanish name *Domingo de Guzmán*. In 1216 he founded the Order of Friars Preachers at Toulouse in France; its members became known as Dominicans or Black Friars. Feast day, 8 August.

Dominica /ˌdɒmɪˈniːkə, dəˈmɪnɪkə/ a mountainous island in the Caribbean, the loftiest of the Lesser Antilles and the northernmost and largest of the Windward Islands; pop. 71,790 (1991); languages, English (official), Creole; capital, Roseau. The island came into British possession at the end of the 18th century, becoming an independent republic within the Commonwealth in 1978.
– ORIGIN named by Columbus, who discovered it on a Sunday (Latin *dies dominica* 'the Lord's day') in 1493.

dominical /dəˈmɪnɪk(ə)l/ ▶ adjective **1** of Sunday as the Lord's day.
2 of Jesus Christ as the lord.
– ORIGIN Middle English: from late Latin *dominicalis*, from Latin *dominicus*, from *dominus* 'lord, master'.

dominical letter ▶ noun any of the seven letters A–G used in church calendars to indicate the date (1–7 January) on which the first Sunday in the year falls, and hence in dating movable feasts.

Dominican[1] /dəˈmɪnɪk(ə)n/ ▶ noun a member of the Roman Catholic order of preaching friars founded by St Dominic, or of a religious order for women founded on similar principles.
▶ adjective of or relating to St Dominic or the Dominicans.
– ORIGIN late 16th cent.: from medieval Latin *Dominicanus*, from *Dominicus*, the Latin name of *Domingo de Guzmán* (see **DOMINIC, ST**).

Dominican[2] /dəˈmɪnɪk(ə)n/ ▶ adjective of or relating to the Dominican Republic or its people.
▶ noun a native or national of the Dominican Republic.
– ORIGIN from Spanish *Dominicana*, influenced by **SANTO DOMINGO**.

Dominican[3] /ˌdɒmɪˈniːk(ə)n, dəˈmɪnɪk(ə)n/ ▶ adjective of or relating to the island of Dominica or its people.
▶ noun a native or national of the island of Dominica.

Dominican Republic /dəˈmɪnɪkən/ a country in the Caribbean occupying the eastern part of the island of Hispaniola; pop. 7,770,000 (est. 1994); official language, Spanish; capital, Santo Domingo. The Dominican Republic is the former Spanish colony of Santo Domingo, the part of Hispaniola which Spain retained when it ceded the western portion (now Haiti) to France in 1697. It was proclaimed a republic in 1844.

dominie /ˈdɒmɪni/ ▶ noun (pl. **-ies**) **1** Scottish a schoolmaster.
2 chiefly US a pastor or clergyman.
– ORIGIN late 17th cent.: alteration of Latin *domine!* (vocative) 'master!, sir!', from *dominus* 'lord' (formerly used as a polite form of address to a clergyman or member of one of the professions).

dominion ▶ noun **1** [mass noun] sovereignty; control: *man's attempt to establish* ***dominion over*** *nature.*
2 (usu. **dominions**) the territory of a sovereign or government: *the Angevin dominions.*
■ (**Dominion**) historical each of the self-governing territories of the British Commonwealth.
3 (**dominions**) another term for **DOMINATION** (in sense 2).
– ORIGIN Middle English: via Old French from medieval Latin *dominio(n-)*, from Latin *dominium*, from *dominus* 'lord, master'.

dominium /dəˈmɪnɪəm/ ▶ noun [mass noun] Law, chiefly US ownership and control of property.
– ORIGIN mid 18th cent.: from Latin.

Domino /ˈdɒmɪnəʊ/, Fats (b.1928), American pianist, singer, and songwriter; born *Antoine Domino*. His music represents part of the transition from rhythm and blues to rock and roll. Notable songs: 'Ain't That a Shame' (1955) and 'Blueberry Hill' (1956).

domino /ˈdɒmɪnəʊ/ ▶ noun (pl. **-oes**) **1** any of 28 small oblong pieces marked with 0–6 pips in each half.
■ (**dominoes**) [treated as sing.] the game played with such pieces, in which they are laid down to form a line, each player in turn trying to find and lay down a domino with a value matched by that of a piece at either end of the line already formed.
2 historical a loose cloak, worn with a mask for the upper part of the face at masquerades.
– ORIGIN late 17th cent.: from French, denoting a hood worn by priests in winter, probably based on Latin *dominus* 'lord, master'.

domino effect ▶ noun the effect of the domino theory.

domino theory ▶ noun the theory that a political event in one country will cause similar events in neighbouring countries, like a falling domino causing an entire row of upended dominoes to fall.

Domitian /dəˈmɪʃ(ə)n/ (AD 51–96), son of Vespasian, Roman emperor 81–96; full name *Titus Flavius Domitianus*.

dom palm ▶ noun variant spelling of **DOUM PALM**.

Dom Pedro /dɒm ˈpɛdrəʊ/ ▶ noun S. African a drink made by mixing ice cream with whisky or a whisky liqueur.

Don /dɒn/ **1** a river in Russia which rises near Tula, south-east of Moscow, and flows for a distance of 1,958 km (1,224 miles) to the Sea of Azov.
2 a river in Scotland which rises in the Grampians and flows 131 km (82 miles) eastwards to the North Sea at Aberdeen.
3 a river in northern England which rises in the Pennines and flows 112 km (70 miles) eastwards to join the Ouse shortly before it, in turn, joins the Humber.

don[1] ▶ noun **1** a university teacher, especially a senior member of a college at Oxford or Cambridge. [ORIGIN: transferred colloquial use of the Spanish title (see below).]
2 (**Don**) a Spanish title prefixed to a male forename.
■ a Spanish gentleman; a Spaniard. ■ N. Amer. informal a high-ranking member of the Mafia.
– DERIVATIVES **donship** noun.
– ORIGIN early 16th cent. (in sense 2): from Spanish, from Latin *dominus* 'lord, master'. Compare with **DONNA**.

don[2] ▶ verb (**donned**, **donning**) [with obj.] put on (an item of clothing): *in the dressing room the players donned their football shirts.*

– ORIGIN late Middle English: contraction of *do on*. Compare with **DOFF**.

dona /'dəʊnə/ (also **donah**) ▶ noun Austral. informal, dated a woman; a sweetheart.

– ORIGIN early 17th cent. (in the sense 'donna'): from Spanish *doña* or Portuguese *dona*, from Latin *domina* 'mistress'.

donate ▶ verb [with obj.] give (money or goods) for a good cause, for example to a charity: *the proceeds will be donated to an Aids awareness charity.*
■ allow the removal of (blood or an organ) from one's body for transplantation, transfusion, or other use.
– DERIVATIVES **donator** noun.
– ORIGIN late 18th cent.: back-formation from **DONATION**.

Donatello /ˌdɒnə'tɛləʊ/ (1386–1466), Italian sculptor; born *Donato di Betto Bardi*. He was one of the pioneers of scientific perspective, and is especially famous for his lifelike sculptures, including the bronze *David* (c.1430–60).

donatio mortis causa /dəˌneɪʃɪəʊ ˌmɔːtɪs 'kɔːzə/ ▶ noun (pl. **donationes mortis causa** /dəˌneɪʃɪ'əʊniːz/) Law a gift of personal property which is made by someone who expects to die in the immediate future, and which takes full effect only after he or she dies.
– ORIGIN Latin, literally 'gift by reason of death'.

donation ▶ noun something that is given to a charity, especially a sum of money: *please send your donation of £20 to the Disaster Appeal.*
■ [mass noun] the action of donating something.
– ORIGIN late Middle English: via Old French from Latin *donatio(n-)*, from the verb *donare*, based on *donum* 'gift'.

Donatist /'dəʊnətɪst/ ▶ noun a member of a schismatic Christian group in North Africa, formed in 311, who held that only those living a blameless life belonged in the Church. They survived until the 7th century.
– DERIVATIVES **Donatism** noun.
– ORIGIN from *Donatus* (died c.355), a Christian prelate in Carthage and the group's leader, + **-IST**.

donative /'dəʊnətɪv/ rare ▶ noun a donation, especially one given formally or officially as a largesse.
▶ adjective **1** given as a donation.
■ historical (of a benefice) given directly, not presentative.
– ORIGIN late Middle English: from Latin *donativum* 'gift, largesse', from *donat-* 'given', from the verb *donare* (see **DONATION**).

Donatus /də'neɪtəs/, Aelius (4th century), Roman grammarian. The *Ars Grammatica*, containing his treatises on Latin grammar, was the sole textbook used in schools in the Middle Ages.

Donau[1] /'dɔːnaʊ/ German name for **DANUBE**.

Donau[2] /'dɔːnaʊ/ ▶ noun [usu. as modifier] Geology a series of Lower Pleistocene glaciations in the Alps, preceding the Günz.
■ the system of deposits laid down during this period.
– ORIGIN German, 'Danube'.

Donbas /dɒn'bɑːs/ Ukrainian name for **DONETS BASIN**.

Doncaster /'dɒŋkəstə/ an industrial town in northern England, a unitary council formerly in Yorkshire; pop. 284,300 (1991).

done past participle of **DO**[1]. ▶ adjective **1** carried out, completed, or treated in a particular way: *the path needed replacing and she wanted it done in asphalt.*
■ (of food) cooked thoroughly: *the turkey will be done to a turn.* ■ no longer happening or existing: *her hunting days were done.*
2 informal socially acceptable: *therapy was not the done thing then.*
▶ exclamation used to indicate that the speaker accepts the terms of an offer: *'I'll give ten to one he misses by a mile!' called Reilly. 'Done', said the conductor.*
– PHRASES **a done deal** US a plan or project that has been finalized. **done for** informal in a situation so bad that it is impossible to get out: *if the guard sees us, we're done for.* **done in** (or **up**) informal extremely tired: *you look done in.* **over and done with** see **OVER**.

donee /dəʊ'niː/ ▶ noun a person who receives a gift.
■ Law a person who is given a power of appointment.
– ORIGIN early 16th cent.: from **DONOR** + **-EE**.

Donegal[1] /ˌdɒnɪ'ɡɔːl/ a county in the extreme north-west of the Republic of Ireland, part of the old province of Ulster; capital, Lifford.

Donegal[2] (also **Donegal tweed**) ▶ noun [mass noun] a tweed characterized by bright flecks randomly distributed on a background that is typically light grey, as originally woven in County Donegal.

doner kebab /'dɒnə, 'dəʊnə/ ▶ noun a Turkish dish consisting of spiced lamb cooked on a spit and served in slices, typically with pitta bread.
– ORIGIN from Turkish *döner kebap*, from *döner* 'rotating' and *kebap* 'roast meat'.

Donets /dɒ'njɛts/ a river in eastern Europe, rising near Belgorod in southern Russia and flowing south-eastwards for some 1,000 km (630 miles) through Ukraine before re-entering Russia and joining the Don near Rostov.

Donets Basin a coal-mining and industrial region of SE Ukraine, stretching between the valleys of the Donets and lower Dnieper Rivers. Ukrainian name **DONBAS**.

Donetsk /dɒ'njɛtsk/ the leading city of the Donets Basin in Ukraine; pop. 1,117,000 (1990). The city was called Yuzovka from 1872 until 1924, and Stalin or Stalino from 1924 until 1961.

dong[1] ▶ verb **1** [no obj.] (of a bell) make a deep resonant sound.
2 [with obj.] Austral./NZ informal hit or punch (someone).
▶ noun **1** the deep resonant sound of a large bell.
2 Austral./NZ a blow; a punch.
3 vulgar slang a man's penis.
– ORIGIN late 16th cent.: imitative.

dong[2] ▶ noun the basic monetary unit of Vietnam, equal to 100 xu.
– ORIGIN from Vietnamese *đông* 'coin'.

donga /'dɒŋɡə/ ▶ noun **1** S. African & Austral./NZ a dry gully, formed by the eroding action of running water.
2 Austral./NZ a makeshift shelter or temporary dwelling.
– ORIGIN sense 1 from Xhosa and Zulu *udonga*; sense 2 is said to stem from an extended usage of the term in the Boer War.

dongle /'dɒŋɡ(ə)l/ ▶ noun Computing an electronic device which must be attached to a computer in order to use protected computer software.
– ORIGIN 1980s: an arbitrary formation.

Donizetti /ˌdɒnɪ'tsɛti/, Gaetano (1797–1848), Italian composer. His operas include tragedies such as *Lucia di Lammermoor* (1835) and comedies such as *Don Pasquale* (1843).

donjon /'dɒndʒ(ə)n, 'dʌn-/ ▶ noun the great tower or innermost keep of a castle.
– ORIGIN Middle English: variant of **DUNGEON**.

Don Juan /dɒn 'dʒʊən, 'hwɑːn/ a legendary Spanish nobleman of dissolute life, famous for seducing women.
■ [as noun **a Don Juan**] a seducer of women; a libertine.

donkey ▶ noun (pl. **-eys**) **1** a domesticated hoofed mammal of the horse family with long ears and a braying call, used as a beast of burden; an ass.
● *Equus asinus*, family Equidae, descended from the wild ass of Africa.
2 informal a stupid or foolish person.
3 informal an engine.
4 (also **donkey stool**) a low stool on which an artist sits astride, used in an art school.
5 [mass noun] a children's card game involving exchanging cards.
– PHRASES **donkey's years** informal a very long time: *we've been close friends for donkey's years.*
– ORIGIN late 18th cent. (originally pronounced to rhyme with *monkey*): perhaps from **DUN**[1], or from the given name *Duncan*.

donkey derby ▶ noun a race between competitors riding donkeys.

donkey engine ▶ noun a small auxiliary engine.

donkey jacket ▶ noun Brit. a heavy jacket which has a patch of waterproof leather or plastic across the shoulders, worn typically by building workers.

donkeyman ▶ noun (pl. **-men**) a man with responsibilities in a ship's engine room: [as modifier] *a donkeyman greaser.*

donkey work ▶ noun [mass noun] informal the boring or laborious part of a job; drudgery: *supervisors who get a research student to do the donkey work.*

Donkin /'dɒnkɪn/, Bryan (1768–1855), English engineer. He developed a method of food preservation by heat sterilization, sealing the food inside a container made of sheet steel and so producing the first tin can.

donna /'dɒnə/ ▶ noun an Italian, Spanish, or Portuguese lady.
■ (**Donna**) a courtesy title prefixed to the forename of such a lady.
– ORIGIN early 17th cent.: from Italian, from Latin *domina* 'mistress', feminine of *dominus* 'lord, master'. Compare with **DON**[1] and **DONA**.

Donnan equilibrium /'dɒn(ə)n/ ▶ noun [mass noun] Chemistry the equilibrium reached between two ionic solutions separated by a semipermeable membrane when one or more of the kinds of ion present cannot pass through the membrane. The result is a difference in osmotic pressure and electrical potential between the solutions.
– ORIGIN early 20th cent.: named after Frederick G. Donnan (1870–1956), British physical chemist.

Donne /dʌn/, John (1572–1631), English poet and preacher. A metaphysical poet, he is most famous for his *Satires* (c.1590–9), *Elegies* (c.1590–9), and love poems, which appeared in the collection *Songs and Sonnets* (undated). He also wrote religious poems and, as dean of St Paul's from 1621, was one of the most celebrated preachers of his age.

donnée /'dɒneɪ/ (also **donné**) ▶ noun **1** a subject or theme of a narrative.
2 a basic fact or assumption.
– ORIGIN French, 'given'.

donnish ▶ adjective thought to resemble or suit a college don, particularly because of a pedantic, scholarly manner.
– DERIVATIVES **donnishly** adverb, **donnishness** noun.

donnybrook /'dɒnɪbrʊk/ ▶ noun N. Amer. & Austral. a scene of uproar and disorder; a heated argument: *raucous ideological donnybrooks.*
– ORIGIN mid 19th cent.: from the name of a suburb of Dublin, Ireland, formerly famous for its annual fair.

donor /'dəʊnə, -nɔː/ ▶ noun a person who donates something, especially money to a fund or charity: *an anonymous donor has given £25* | [as modifier] *loans from rich donor countries.*
■ a person who provides blood for transfusion, semen for insemination, or an organ or tissue for transplantation. ■ Chemistry an atom or molecule that provides a pair of electrons in forming a coordinate bond. ■ Physics an impurity atom in a semiconductor which contributes a conducting electron to the material.
– ORIGIN Middle English: from Old French *doneur*, from Latin *donator*, from *donare* 'give'.

donor card ▶ noun a card which a person carries to indicate consent to the use of their organs for transplant surgery in the event of their death.

donor fatigue ▶ noun [mass noun] a lessening of public willingness to respond generously to charitable appeals, resulting from the frequency of such appeals.

Don Quixote /dɒn 'kwɪksəʊt, kiː'həʊti/ the hero of a romance (1605–15) by Cervantes, a satirical account of chivalric beliefs and conduct. The character of Don Quixote is typified by a romantic vision and naive, unworldly idealism.

don't ▶ contraction of do not.
– PHRASES **dos and don'ts** see **DO**[1].

don't-know ▶ noun a person who disclaims knowledge, especially one who is undecided when replying to an opinion poll or questionnaire.

donut ▶ noun US spelling of **DOUGHNUT**.

doodad /'duːdad/ ▶ noun North American term for **DOODAH**.
– ORIGIN early 20th cent.: of unknown origin.

doodah /'duːdɑː/ ▶ noun informal used to refer to something that the speaker cannot name precisely: *from the poshest pot pourri to the humblest dangly doodah.*
– PHRASES **all of a doodah** very agitated: *they'll be all of a doodah because of the bombs.*
– ORIGIN early 20th cent. (in the phrase *all of a doodah*): perhaps from the refrain of the song *Camptown Races*.

doodle ▶ verb [no obj.] scribble absent-mindedly: *he was only doodling in the margin.*
▶ noun a rough drawing made absent-mindedly.
– DERIVATIVES **doodler** noun.
– ORIGIN early 17th cent. (originally as a noun denoting a fool, later as a verb in the sense 'make a fool of, cheat'): from Low German *dudeltopf*, *dudeldopp* 'simpleton'. Current senses date from the 1930s.

doodlebug ▶ noun informal **1** N. Amer. the larva of an ant lion.
2 US an unscientific device for locating oil or minerals; a divining rod.
▪a prospector for oil or minerals.
3 Brit. informal term for **V-1**.
4 a midget racing car.
▪any small car, train, or other vehicle.
– ORIGIN mid 19th cent. (in sense 1): from 17th-cent. *doodle* 'ninny' + **BUG**.

doodly-squat ▶ noun another term for **DIDDLY-SQUAT**.

doo-doo ▶ noun a child's word for excrement, used euphemistically in other contexts: *when our fax machine isn't working, we're* ***in deep doo-doo.***

doofus /'du:fʌs/ (also **dufus**) ▶ noun (pl. **doofuses**) N. Amer. informal a stupid person.
– ORIGIN 1960s: perhaps an alteration of **GOOFUS**, or from Scots *doof* 'dolt'.

doohickey /'du:hɪki/ ▶ noun (pl. **-eys**) N. Amer. informal a small object or gadget, especially one whose precise name the speaker cannot recall: *a garage filled with electronic parts and other valuable doohickeys.*
– ORIGIN early 20th cent. (originally servicemen's slang): blend of **DOODAD** and **HICKEY**.

doojigger /'du:dʒɪgə/ ▶ noun US another term for **DOOHICKEY**.
– ORIGIN 1920s: blend of **DOODAD** and **JIGGER**[1].

doolally /du:'lali/ ▶ adjective informal temporarily deranged or feeble-minded: *Uncle's gone doolally again.*
▪transported with excitement or pleasure: *a return on capital employed that the City would go doolally over.*
– ORIGIN early 20th cent.: originally *doolally tap*, Indian army slang, from *Deolali* (the name of a town near Bombay) + Urdu *tap* 'fever'.

doolie /'du:li/ ▶ noun (pl. **-ies**) a simple litter, formerly used in the Indian subcontinent for transporting the wounded.
– ORIGIN from Hindi *ḍolī*, diminutive of *ḍolā* 'cradle or litter'.

Doolittle /'du:lɪt(ə)l/, Hilda (1886–1961), American poet; pseudonym H.D. Her work shows the influence of Ezra Pound and other imagist poets. Notable works: *Sea Garden* (1916).

doom ▶ noun [mass noun] death, destruction, or some other terrible fate: *the aircraft was sent crashing* ***to its doom*** *in the water.*
▪[in sing.] archaic (in Christian belief) the Last Judgement.
▶ verb [with obj.] (usu. **be doomed**) condemn to certain destruction or death: *fuel was spilling out of the damaged wing and the aircraft was doomed.*
▪cause to have an unfortunate and inescapable outcome: *her plan was* ***doomed to*** *failure* | [as adj. **doomed**] *the moving story of their doomed love affair.*
– PHRASES **doom and gloom** (also **gloom and doom**) a general feeling of pessimism or despondency: *the national feeling of doom and gloom.*
– ORIGIN Old English *dōm* 'statute, judgement', of Germanic origin, from a base meaning 'to put in place'; related to **DO**[1].

doom-laden ▶ adjective conveying a sense of tragedy: *a doom-laden speech.*

doomsayer ▶ noun a person who predicts disaster, especially in politics or economics.
– DERIVATIVES **doomsaying** noun.

doomsday (also **domesday**) ▶ noun [in sing.] the last day of the world's existence.
▪(in religious belief) the day of the Last Judgement.
▪ figurative a time or event of crisis or great danger: [as modifier] *in all the concern over greenhouse warming, one* ***doomsday scenario*** *stands out.*
– PHRASES **till doomsday** informal forever: *we'll be here till doomsday if you go blethering on.*
– ORIGIN Old English *dōmes dæg* (see **DOOM**, **DAY**).

Doomsday Book ▶ noun see **DOMESDAY**.

doomster ▶ noun another term for **DOOMSAYER**.

doomwatch ▶ noun an organized campaign of vigilance to alert people to the dangers of environmental pollution.
– DERIVATIVES **doomwatcher** noun.

doomy ▶ adjective (**-ier**, **-iest**) suggesting or predicting disaster; ominous: *doomy forecasts.*
– DERIVATIVES **doomily** adverb.

Doona /'du:nə/ ▶ noun Austral./NZ trademark a quilted eiderdown or duvet.
– ORIGIN 1970s: perhaps from Swedish *dun* (see **DOWN**[2]).

door ▶ noun a hinged, sliding, or revolving barrier at the entrance to a building, room, or vehicle, or in the framework of a cupboard.
▪a doorway: *she walked through the door.* ▪ used to refer to the distance from one building in a row to another: *they lived within three doors of each other.*
– PHRASES **as one door closes, another opens** proverb you shouldn't be discouraged by failure, as other opportunities will soon present themselves. **at the door** on admission to an event rather than in advance: *tickets will be available at the door.* **close** (or **shut**) **the door on** (or **to**) exclude the opportunity for: *she had closed the door on ever finding out what he was feeling.* (**from**) **door to door 1** from start to finish of a journey: *the trip from door to door could take more than four hours.* **2** visiting all the houses in an area to sell or publicize something: *he went from door to door selling insurance policies* | [as modifier] *a door-to-door salesman.* **lay something at someone's door** regard someone as responsible for something: *the failure is laid at the door of the government.* **leave the door open** ensure that there is still an opportunity for something: *he is leaving the door open for future change.* **on the door** monitoring admission to a building or event: *the uniformed commissionaires on the door.* **open the door to** create an opportunity for: *her research has opened the door to a deeper understanding of the subject.* **out of doors** in or into the open air: *food tastes even better out of doors.*
– DERIVATIVES **doored** adjective [in combination] *a glass-doored desk.*
– ORIGIN Old English *duru*, *dor*, of Germanic origin; related to Dutch *deur* 'door' and German *Tür* 'door', *Tor* 'gate'; from an Indo-European root shared by Latin *foris* 'gate' and Greek *thura* 'door'.

doorbell ▶ noun a bell in a building which can be rung by visitors outside to signal their arrival.

do-or-die ▶ adjective [attrib.] (of a person's attitude or a situation) showing or requiring a determination not to compromise or be deterred: *the mercenaries fought with a do-or-die fanaticism.*

door frame (also **doorcase**) ▶ noun the frame in a doorway into which a door is fitted.

door furniture ▶ noun [mass noun] the handles, lock, and other fixtures on a door.

door head ▶ noun the upper part of a door frame.

doorkeeper ▶ noun a person on duty at the entrance to a building.

doorknob ▶ noun a handle on a door that is turned to release the latch.

doorknock ▶ noun Austral./NZ a campaign of door-to-door house visits to collect for a charity or to appeal for support for a political candidate: [as modifier] *a doorknock appeal.*

doorman ▶ noun (pl. **-men**) a man such as a porter, bouncer, or janitor who is on duty at the entrance to a large building.

doormat ▶ noun a mat placed in a doorway, on which people can wipe their shoes on entering a building.
▪figurative a submissive person who allows others to dominate them: *to put up with such treatment you must be either a saint or a doormat.*

doornail ▶ noun a stud set in a door for strength or as an ornament.
– PHRASES (**as**) **dead as a doornail** quite dead.

Doornik /'do:rnɪk/ Flemish name for **TOURNAI**.

door plate ▶ noun a plate on the door of a house or room which gives information about the occupant.

doorpost ▶ noun each of the two upright parts of a door frame.

doorstep ▶ noun a step leading up to the outer door of a house.
▪Brit. informal a thick piece of something: [as modifier] *doorstep sandwiches.*
▶ verb (**-stepped**, **-stepping**) Brit. informal **1** [with obj.] (of a journalist) wait uninvited outside the home of (someone) in order to obtain an interview or photograph: *he was being doorstepped by the tabloids.*
2 [no obj.] go from door to door selling or canvassing: *he doorsteps for his church at weekends.*
– PHRASES **on one's** (or **the**) **doorstep** situated very close by: *the airport is on my doorstep so flying is easy.*

doorstop (also **doorstopper**) ▶ noun a fixed or heavy object that keeps a door open or stops it from banging against a wall.
▪figurative a heavy or bulky object (used especially in reference to a thick book): *his sixth novel is a thumping 400-page doorstop.*

doorway ▶ noun an entrance to a room or building through a door: *Beth stood there in the doorway* | figurative *the doorway to success.*

dooryard ▶ noun N. Amer. a yard or garden by the door of a house.

doo-wop /'du:wɒp/ ▶ noun [mass noun] a style of pop music marked by the use of close harmony vocals using nonsense phrases, originating in the US in the 1950s.
– DERIVATIVES **doo-wopper** noun.
– ORIGIN imitative.

doozy /'du:zi/ (also **doozie**) ▶ noun (pl. **-ies**) informal, chiefly N. Amer. something outstanding or unique of its kind: *it's gonna be a doozy of a black eye.*
– ORIGIN early 20th cent.: of unknown origin.

dop /dɒp/ ▶ noun (pl. **dops** or **doppe** /'dɒpə/) S. African **1** a rounded or spherical container.
▪a bowl-shaped object such as a shell or skull.
2 (**dops/doppe**) grape skins, especially when left as a residue after winemaking.
▪[mass noun] cheap liquor, especially the brandy formerly made from such a residue.
– ORIGIN South African Dutch, 'shell, husk'.

dopa /'dəʊpə/ ▶ noun [mass noun] Biochemistry a compound which is present in nervous tissue as a precursor of dopamine, used in the treatment of Parkinson's disease. See also **L-DOPA**.
• An amino acid; alternative name: dihydroxyphenylalanine; chem. formula: $C_9H_{11}NO_4$.
– ORIGIN early 20th cent.: from German, acronym from the systematic name.

dopamine /'dəʊpəmi:n/ ▶ noun [mass noun] Biochemistry a compound present in the body as a neurotransmitter and a precursor of other substances including adrenalin.
• Alternative name: **3,4-dihydroxyphenylethylamine**; chem. formula: $C_8H_{11}NO_2$.
– ORIGIN 1950s: blend of **DOPA** and **AMINE**.

dopant /'dəʊp(ə)nt/ ▶ noun Electronics a substance used to produce a desired electrical characteristic in a semiconductor.
– ORIGIN 1960s: from the verb **DOPE** + **-ANT**.

dope ▶ noun [mass noun] **1** informal a drug taken illegally for recreational purposes, especially cannabis or (US) heroin.
▪a drug given to a racehorse or greyhound to inhibit or enhance its performance. ▪ a drug taken by an athlete to improve performance: [as modifier] *he failed a dope test.*
2 [count noun] informal a stupid person: *though he wasn't an intellectual giant, he was no dope either.*
3 informal information about a subject, especially if not generally known: *our reviewer will give you* ***the dope on*** *hot spots around the town.*
4 a varnish applied to the fabric surface of model aircraft to strengthen them and keep them airtight.
▪a thick liquid used as a lubricant. ▪ a substance added to petrol to increase its effectiveness.
▶ verb [with obj.] **1** administer drugs to (a racehorse, greyhound, or athlete) in order to inhibit or enhance sporting performance: *the horse was doped before the race.*
▪(**be doped up**) informal be heavily under the influence of drugs, typically illegal ones: *he was so doped up that he can't remember a thing.* ▪ treat (food or drink) with drugs: *maybe they had doped her Perrier.* ▪ [no obj.] informal, dated regularly take illegal drugs.
2 smear or cover with varnish or other thick liquid: *she doped the surface with photographic emulsion.*
3 Electronics add an impurity to (a semiconductor) to produce a desired electrical characteristic.
▶ adjective black slang very good: *that suit is dope!*
– DERIVATIVES **doper** noun.
– ORIGIN early 19th cent. (in the sense 'thick liquid'): from Dutch *doop* 'sauce', from *doopen* 'to dip, mix'.
▶ **dope something out** informal, dated work out something: *they met to dope out plans for covering the event.*

dopester /'dəʊpstə/ ▶ noun N. Amer. informal a person who collects and supplies information, typically on sporting events or elections: *they are* ***inside dopesters*** *with special access to the racing world.*

dopey (also **dopy**) ▶ adjective (**dopier**, **dopiest**)

informal stupefied by sleep or a drug: *she was under sedation and a bit dopey.*
■ idiotic: *did you ever hear such dopey names?*
– DERIVATIVES **dopily** adverb, **dopiness** noun.

dopiaza /ˈdɒpɪaˌʒə/ ▶ noun [mass noun] an Indian dish consisting of meat cooked in an onion sauce: *chicken dopiaza.*
– ORIGIN from Hindi *do* 'two' + *pyāz* 'onion'.

doppelgänger /ˈdɒp(ə)lˌɡɛŋə, -ˌɡaŋə/ ▶ noun an apparition or double of a living person.
– ORIGIN mid 19th cent.: from German, literally 'double-goer'.

Dopper /ˈdɒpə/ ▶ noun (in South Africa) a member of the Gereformeerde Kerk, a strictly orthodox Calvinistic denomination.
– ORIGIN Afrikaans, of unknown origin.

doppie /ˈdɒpi/ ▶ noun S. African informal **1** a hollow object or container such as a shell or cartridge case: *lobster doppies* | *these doppies were not fired here.*
2 a tot of liquor; an alcoholic drink.
– ORIGIN Afrikaans, diminutive of *dop* (see **DOP**).

Doppler /ˈdɒplə/, Johann Christian (1803–53), Austrian physicist, famous for his discovery, in 1842, of what is now known as the Doppler effect.

Doppler broadening ▶ noun Physics the broadening of spectral lines as a result of the different velocities of the emitting atoms giving rise to different Doppler shifts.

Doppler effect ▶ noun [mass noun] Physics an increase (or decrease) in the frequency of sound, light, or other waves as the source and observer move towards (or away from) each other. The effect causes the sudden change in pitch noticeable in a passing siren, as well as the red shift seen by astronomers.

Doppler shift ▶ noun Physics a change in frequency due to the Doppler effect.

dop system ▶ noun S. African historical variant of **TOT SYSTEM**.
– ORIGIN *dop* from Afrikaans *overdop* 'extra quantity (of wine)'; compare with **DOP**.

dopy ▶ adjective variant spelling of **DOPEY**.

dor /dɔː/ (also **dor beetle**) ▶ noun a large black dung beetle that makes a droning sound in flight and excavates burrows in which its young develop.
● Family Geotrupidae: several genera and species, including the common *Geotrupes stercorarius.*
– ORIGIN Old English (denoting a bee or buzzing fly), probably imitative.

Dorado /dəˈrɑːdəʊ/ Astronomy a southern constellation (the Goldfish), containing most of the Large Magellanic Cloud.
■ [as genitive **Doradus** /dəˈrɑːdəs/] used with preceding letter or numeral to designate a star in this constellation: *the star R Doradus.*
– ORIGIN Spanish (see **DORADO**).

dorado /dəˈrɑːdəʊ/ ▶ noun (pl. **-os**) **1** an edible marine fish of warm seas, with silver and bright blue or green coloration when alive. Also called **DOLPHIN**.
● Family Coryphaenidae and genus *Coryphaena*: two species, in particular the large *C. hippurus.*
2 a South American freshwater fish with a golden body and red fins, popular as a game fish.
● *Salminus maxillosus*, family Characidae.
– ORIGIN early 17th cent.: from Spanish, literally 'gilded', from late Latin *deauratus*, from *deaurare* 'to gild over' (see also **DORY**¹).

dorcas gazelle /ˈdɔːkəs/ ▶ noun a small gazelle found on semi-desert plains in North Africa and western Asia.
● *Gazella dorcas*, family Bovidae.
– ORIGIN early 19th cent.: from modern Latin *Gazella dorcas* (from Greek *dorkas* 'gazelle').

Dorchester /ˈdɔːtʃɪstə/ a town in southern England, the county town of Dorset; pop. 14,000 (est. 1985).

Dordogne /dɔːˈdɔɪn, French dɔrdɔɲ/ a river of western France which rises in the Auvergne and flows 472 km (297 miles) westwards to meet the Garonne and form the Gironde estuary.
■ a department of SW France. It contains caves that have yielded abundant remains of early humans and their artefacts and art, such as that at Lascaux.

Dordrecht /dɔːˈdrɛxt/ an industrial city and river port in the Netherlands, near the mouth of the Rhine (there called the Waal), 20 km (12 miles)

south-east of Rotterdam; pop. 110,500 (1991). Also called **DORT**.

Doré /ˈdɔːreɪ, French dɔʁe/, Gustave (1832–83), French book illustrator, known for his woodcut illustrations of books such as Dante's *Inferno* (1861), Cervantes' *Don Quixote* (1863), and the Bible (1865–6).

doré /ˈdɔːreɪ, -riː/ ▶ noun Canadian term for *walleye* (see **WALL EYE** sense 2).
– ORIGIN late 18th cent.: French, literally 'gilded'.

Dorian /ˈdɔːrɪən/ ▶ noun a member of a Hellenic people speaking the Doric dialect of Greek, thought to have entered Greece from the north *c.*1100 BC. They settled in the Peloponnese and later colonized Sicily and southern Italy.
▶ adjective of or relating to this people or to Doris in central Greece.
– ORIGIN via Latin from Greek *Dōrios* 'of Doris' + **-IAN**.

Dorian mode ▶ noun Music the mode represented by the natural diatonic scale D–D (containing a minor 3rd and minor 7th).

Doric /ˈdɒrɪk/ ▶ adjective **1** relating to or denoting a classical order of architecture characterized by a plain, sturdy column and a thick square abacus resting on a rounded moulding.
2 relating to or denoting the ancient Greek dialect of the Dorians.
■ archaic (of a dialect) broad; rustic.
▶ noun [mass noun] **1** the Doric order of architecture.
2 the ancient Greek dialect of the Dorians.
■ a broad or rustic dialect, especially the dialect spoken in the north-east of Scotland. [ORIGIN: by association with the ancient Greek dialect, perceived as rustic.]
– ORIGIN via Latin from Greek *Dōrikos*, from *Dōrios* (see **DORIAN**).

dorje /ˈdɔːdʒeɪ/ ▶ noun (in Tibetan Buddhism) a representation of a thunderbolt in the form of a short double trident or sceptre, symbolizing the male aspect of the spirit and held during invocations and prayers. Compare with **VAJRA**.
– ORIGIN Tibetan.

dork ▶ noun informal a contemptible, socially inept person.
■ N. Amer. vulgar slang the penis.
– ORIGIN 1960s (originally US): perhaps a variant of **DIRK**, influenced by **DICK**¹.

dorm ▶ noun informal a dormitory.
– ORIGIN early 20th cent.: abbreviation.

dormant ▶ adjective (of an animal) having normal physical functions suspended or slowed down for a period of time; in or as if in a deep sleep: *dormant butterflies* | figurative *the event evoked memories that she would rather had lain dormant.*
■ (of a plant or bud) alive but not actively growing. ■ (of a volcano) temporarily inactive. ■ (of a disease) causing no symptoms but not cured and liable to recur. ■ [usu. postpositive] Heraldry (of an animal) depicted lying with its head on its paws.
– DERIVATIVES **dormancy** noun.
– ORIGIN late Middle English (in the senses 'fixed in position' and 'latent'): from Old French, 'sleeping', present participle of *dormir*, from Latin *dormire* 'to sleep'.

dormer (also **dormer window**) ▶ noun a window that projects vertically from a sloping roof.
– ORIGIN late 16th cent. (denoting the window of a dormitory or bedroom): from Old French *dormeor* 'dormitory', from *dormir* 'to sleep'.

Dormition /dɔːˈmɪʃ(ə)n/ ▶ noun (in the Orthodox Church) the passing of the Virgin Mary from earthly life.
■ the feast held in honour of this on 15 August, corresponding to the Assumption in the Western Church.
– ORIGIN late 15th cent.: from French, from Latin *dormitio(n-)* 'falling asleep', from *dormire* 'to sleep'.

dormitory /ˈdɔːmɪt(ə)ri/ ▶ noun (pl. **-ies**) a large bedroom for a number of people in a school or institution.
■ N. Amer. a university or college hall of residence or hostel. ■ [as modifier] denoting a small town or suburb providing a residential area for those who work in a nearby city.
– ORIGIN late Middle English: from Latin *dormitorium*, neuter (used as a noun) of *dormitorius*, from *dormire* 'to sleep'.

Dormobile /ˈdɔːməbiːl/ ▶ noun Brit. trademark a motor caravan that can be used for sleeping in.

– ORIGIN 1950s: blend of **DORMITORY** and **AUTOMOBILE**.

dormouse ▶ noun (pl. **dormice**) an agile mouse-like rodent with a hairy or bushy tail, found in Africa and Eurasia. Some kinds are noted for spending long periods in hibernation.
● Family Gliridae: several genera and species, including the **common** (or **hazel**) **dormouse** (*Muscardinus avellanarius*) and the **fat dormouse**.
– ORIGIN late Middle English: of unknown origin, but associated with French *dormir* or Latin *dormire* 'to sleep' and **MOUSE**.

dormy /ˈdɔːmi/ ▶ adjective [predic.] Golf (of a player in match play) ahead by a specified number of holes when the same number of holes remain to be played, and thus in a position at least to draw the match (used preceding a numeral): *he reached the 17th hole dormy two.*
– ORIGIN mid 19th cent.: of unknown origin.

doronicum /dəˈrɒnɪkəm/ ▶ noun (pl. **doronicums**) a plant of the genus *Doronicum* in the daisy family, especially (in gardening) leopard's bane.
– ORIGIN modern Latin (Linnaeus), from modern Greek *dōronikon*, from Persian *darūnak*.

dorp /dɔːp/ ▶ noun S. African a small rural town or village (often used to suggest that a place is backward or unimpressive): *dreary little dorps with an ox-wagon mentality.*
– ORIGIN Dutch, 'village' (see **THORP**).

dorsal /ˈdɔːs(ə)l/ ▶ adjective Anatomy, Zoology, & Botany of, on, or relating to the upper side or back of an animal, plant, or organ: *a dorsal view of the body* | *the dorsal aorta*. Compare with **VENTRAL**.
– DERIVATIVES **dorsally** adverb.
– ORIGIN late Middle English: from late Latin *dorsalis*, from Latin *dorsum* 'back'.

dorsal fin ▶ noun Zoology an unpaired fin on the back of a fish or whale, e.g. the tall triangular fin of a shark or killer whale.

Dorset¹ /ˈdɔːsɪt/ a county of SW England; county town, Dorchester.

Dorset² /ˈdɔːsɪt/ ▶ noun [usu. as modifier] Archaeology a prehistoric culture which flourished in the American Arctic during the 1st millennium AD and was displaced by the Thule culture.
– ORIGIN 1930s: from the name of Cape *Dorset*, Baffin Island.

Dorset Down ▶ noun a sheep of a breed with a brown face and legs.

Dorset Horn ▶ noun a sheep of a breed with a white face and horns on both the ewe and the ram.

dorsi- ▶ combining form towards or on the back: *dorsiventral.*
– ORIGIN from Latin *dorsum* 'back'.

dorsiflex /ˈdɔːsɪflɛks/ ▶ verb [with obj.] Physiology bend (something, typically the hand or foot) dorsally or towards its upper surface: *the subject dorsiflexed the ankle.*
– DERIVATIVES **dorsiflexion** noun.

dorsiflexor /ˌdɔːsɪˈflɛksə/ ▶ noun Anatomy a muscle whose contraction dorsiflexes the hand or foot.

dorsiventral /ˌdɔːsɪˈvɛntr(ə)l/ ▶ adjective chiefly Botany (of a leaf or other part of a plant) having dissimilar dorsal and ventral surfaces.
■ another term for **DORSOVENTRAL**.
– DERIVATIVES **dorsiventrality** noun, **dorsiventrally** adverb.

dorso- ▶ combining form relating to the back: *dorsoventral.*
– ORIGIN from Latin *dorsum* 'back'.

dorsolateral /ˌdɔːsə(ʊ)ˈlat(ə)r(ə)l/ ▶ adjective Anatomy & Biology of, relating to, or involving the dorsal and lateral surfaces.
– DERIVATIVES **dorsolaterally** adverb.

dorsoventral /ˌdɔːsə(ʊ)ˈvɛntr(ə)l/ ▶ adjective Anatomy & Biology extending along or denoting an axis joining the dorsal and ventral surfaces.
■ of, relating to, or involving these surfaces.
– DERIVATIVES **dorsoventrally** adverb.

dorsum /ˈdɔːsəm/ ▶ noun (pl. **dorsa**) Anatomy & Zoology the dorsal part of an organism or structure.
– ORIGIN late 18th cent. (denoting a long hill or ridge): from Latin, 'back'.

Dort /dɔːt/ another name for **DORDRECHT**.

Dortmund /ˈdɔːtmʊnd, German ˈdɔrtmʊnt/ an industrial city in NW Germany, in North Rhine-Westphalia; pop. 601,000 (1991).

---

b **b**ut | d **d**og | f **f**ew | g **g**et | h **h**e | j **y**es | k **c**at | l **l**eg | m **m**an | n **n**o | p **p**en | r **r**ed | s **s**it | t **t**op | v **v**oice | w **w**e | z **z**oo | ʃ **sh**e | ʒ deci**s**ion | θ **th**in | ð **th**is | ŋ ri**ng** | x lo**ch** | tʃ **ch**ip | dʒ **j**ar

dory[1] /ˈdɔːri/ ▶ **noun** (pl. **-ies**) a narrow deep-bodied fish with a mouth that can be opened very wide.
● Several genera and species in the families Zeidae and Oreosomatidae. See also **JOHN DORY**.
– ORIGIN late Middle English: from French *dorée*, feminine past participle of *dorer* 'gild', from late Latin *deaurare* 'gild over', based on Latin *aurum* 'gold'. Compare with **DORADO**.

dory[2] /ˈdɔːri/ ▶ **noun** (pl. **-ies**) a small flat-bottomed rowing boat with a high bow and stern, originally of a kind used for fishing in New England.
– ORIGIN early 18th cent.: perhaps from Miskito *dóri* 'dugout'.

doryphore /ˈdɒrɪfɔː/ ▶ **noun** rare a pedantic and annoyingly persistent critic.
– ORIGIN 1950s (introduced by Sir Harold Nicolson): from French, literally 'Colorado beetle', from Greek *doruphoros* 'spear-carrier'.

DOS Computing ▶ **abbreviation for** disk operating system, an operating system originally developed for IBM personal computers.

dosa /ˈdəʊsə/ ▶ **noun** (pl. **dosas** or **dosai** /ˈdəʊsʌɪ/) (in southern Indian cooking) a pancake made from rice flour, typically served with a spiced vegetable filling.
– ORIGIN from Tamil *tōcai*.

dos-à-dos /ˌdəʊzəˈdəʊ/ ▶ **adjective** (of two books) bound together with a shared central board and facing in opposite directions.
▶ **noun** (pl. same) a seat or carriage in which the occupants sit back to back. Compare with **DO-SI-DO**.
– ORIGIN French, 'back to back'.

dosage ▶ **noun** the size or frequency of a dose of a medicine or drug: *a dosage of 450 milligrams a day* | [mass noun] *there are recommendations about dosage in elderly patients.*
■ a level of exposure to or absorption of ionizing radiation.

dose ▶ **noun** a quantity of a medicine or drug taken or recommended to be taken at a particular time: *he took* ***a dose of*** *cough mixture.*
■ an amount of ionizing radiation received or absorbed at one time or over a specified period: ***a dose of*** *radiation exceeding safety limits.* ■ informal a venereal infection. ■ informal a quantity of something regarded as analogous to medicine in being necessary but unpleasant: *I wanted to give you* ***a dose of*** *the hell you put me through.*
▶ **verb** [with obj.] administer a dose to (a person or animal): *he* ***dosed*** *himself* ***with*** *vitamins.*
■ adulterate or blend (a substance) with another substance: *the petrol is* ***dosed with*** *lead.*
– PHRASES **in small doses** informal when experienced or engaged in a little at a time: *computer games are great in small doses.* **like a dose of salts** Brit. informal very fast and efficiently: *we'll go through this place like a dose of salts and scrub it from top to bottom.* [ORIGIN: from the use of Epsom salts as an aperient.]
– ORIGIN late Middle English: from French, via late Latin from Greek *dosis* 'gift', from *didonai* 'give'.

dose equivalent ▶ **noun** an estimate of the biological effect of a dose of ionizing radiation, calculated by multiplying the dose received by a factor depending on the type of radiation. It is measured in sieverts.

dosh ▶ **noun** [mass noun] Brit. informal money: *cycling saves you a heap of dosh.*
– ORIGIN 1950s: of unknown origin.

do-si-do /ˌdəʊzɪˈdəʊ, -sɪ-/ (also **do-se-do**) ▶ **noun** (pl. **-os**) (in country dancing) a figure in which two dancers pass round each other back to back and return to their original positions.
▶ **verb** [no obj.] dance a do-si-do.
– ORIGIN 1920s (originally US): alteration of **DOS-À-DOS**.

dosimeter /dəʊˈsɪmɪtə/ (also **dosemeter** /ˈdəʊsmiːtə/) ▶ **noun** a device used to measure an absorbed dose of ionizing radiation.
– DERIVATIVES **dosimetric** adjective, **dosimetry** noun.

Dos Passos /dɒs ˈpasɒs/, John (Roderigo) (1896–1970), American novelist, chiefly remembered for his portrayal of American life in such novels as *Manhattan Transfer* (1925) and *USA* (1938).

doss Brit. informal ▶ **verb** [no obj.] **1** sleep in rough accommodation or on an improvised bed: *he* ***dossed down*** *on a friend's floor.*
2 spend time idly: *all I've seen her do so far is* ***doss around.***
▶ **noun 1** an instance of sleeping in rough accommodation or on an improvised bed.
■ archaic a bed in a cheap lodging house.
2 an easy task giving the opportunity for idling: *they thought being a student was a great doss.*
– ORIGIN late 18th cent.: perhaps based on Latin *dorsum* 'back'.

dossal /ˈdɒs(ə)l/ ▶ **noun** an ornamental cloth hung behind an altar in a church or at the sides of a chancel.
– ORIGIN mid 17th cent. (denoting an ornamental cloth to cover the back of a seat): from medieval Latin *dossale*, from late Latin *dorsalis* 'on the back' (see **DORSAL**).

dosser ▶ **noun** Brit. informal, derogatory a person who sleeps rough; a tramp.

dosseret /ˈdɒsərɛt/ ▶ **noun** Architecture an additional block of stone placed above an abacus in the columns of a Byzantine or Romanesque arcade.
– ORIGIN mid 19th cent.: from French, diminutive of *dossier* 'back' (denoting a supporting structure).

dosshouse ▶ **noun** Brit. informal a cheap lodging house for homeless people and tramps.

dossier /ˈdɒsɪə, -ɪeɪ, -jeɪ/ ▶ **noun** a collection of documents about a particular person, event, or subject: *we have a* ***dossier on*** *him* | *a* ***dossier of*** *complaints.*
– ORIGIN late 19th cent.: from French, denoting a bundle of papers with a label on the back, from *dos* 'back', based on Latin *dorsum*.

dost /dʌst/ archaic second person singular present of **DO**[1].

Dostoevsky /ˌdɒstɔɪˈɛfski/ (also **Dostoyevsky**), Fyodor (Mikhailovich) (1821–81), Russian novelist. Dostoevsky's novels reveal his psychological insight, savage humour, and concern with the religious, political, and moral problems posed by human suffering. Notable novels: *Crime and Punishment* (1866), *The Idiot* (1868), and *The Brothers Karamazov* (1880).

DoT ▶ **abbreviation for** ■ (in Canada and formerly in the UK) Department of Transport. ■ (in the US) Department of Transportation.

dot[1] ▶ **noun** a small round mark or spot: *a symbol depicted in coloured dots.*
■ such a mark written or printed as part of an *i* or *j*, as one of a series of marks to signify omission, or as a full stop. ■ Music such a mark used to denote the lengthening of a note or rest by half, or to indicate staccato. ■ the shorter signal of the two used in Morse code. Compare with **DASH** (in sense 3). ■ used to refer to an object that appears tiny because it is far away: *the heath shrank figures to mere dots.*
▶ **verb** (**dotted**, **dotting**) [with obj.] **1** mark with a small spot or spots: *wet spots of rain began to dot his shirt.*
■ (of a number of items) be scattered over (an area): *churches dot the countryside* | (**be dotted**) *there appear to be a number of airfields* ***dotted about.*** ■ place a dot over (a letter): *you need to dot the i.* ■ Music mark (a note or rest) to show that the time value is increased by half: [as adj. **dotted**] *a dotted minim.*
2 Brit. informal hit (someone): *'You want to* ***dot him one,'*** *he said.*
– PHRASES **dot the i's and cross the t's** informal ensure that all details are correct. **on the dot** informal exactly on time: *he arrived on the dot at nine o'clock.* **the year dot** Brit. informal a very long time ago: *that wallpaper has been there since the year dot.*
– DERIVATIVES **dotter** noun.
– ORIGIN Old English *dott* 'head of a boil'. The word is recorded only once in Old English, then not until the late 16th cent., when it is found in the sense 'a small lump or clot', perhaps influenced by Dutch *dot* 'a knot'. The sense 'small mark or spot' dates from the mid 17th cent.

dot[2] ▶ **noun** archaic a dowry from which only the interest or annual income was available to the husband.
– ORIGIN from French, from Latin *dos*, *dot-* 'dowry' (see **DOWER**).

dotage /ˈdəʊtɪdʒ/ ▶ **noun** [in sing.] the period of life in which a person is old and weak: *you could live here and look after me* ***in my dotage.***
– ORIGIN late Middle English: from **DOTE** + **-AGE**.

dotard /ˈdəʊtəd/ ▶ **noun** an old person, especially one who has become weak or senile.
– ORIGIN late Middle English: from **DOTE** + **-ARD**.

dote ▶ **verb** [no obj.] **1** (**dote on/upon**) be extremely and uncritically fond of: *she doted on her two young children* | [as adj. **doting**] *she was spoiled outrageously by her doting father.*
2 archaic be silly or feeble-minded, especially as a result of old age: *the parson is now old and dotes.*
– DERIVATIVES **doter** noun, **dotingly** adverb.
– ORIGIN Middle English (in the sense 'act or talk foolishly'): of uncertain origin; related to Middle Dutch *doten* 'be silly'.

doth /dʌθ/ archaic third person singular present of **DO**[1].

dotish ▶ **adjective** archaic or W. Indian having or showing a lack of intelligence; stupid or silly: *dotish foreign TV programmes.*
– ORIGIN early 16th cent.: from obsolete *dote* 'folly' + **-ISH**[1].

dot matrix ▶ **noun** [usu. as modifier] a grid of dots which are filled selectively to produce an image on a screen or paper: *a dot matrix display board.*

dot matrix printer ▶ **noun** a printer which forms images of letters, numbers, etc. from a number of tiny dots.

dot plant ▶ **noun** a garden plant that is planted singly to stand out against the surrounding plants.

dot product ▶ **noun** another term for **SCALAR PRODUCT**.

dotted line ▶ **noun** a line made up of dots or dashes (often used in reference to the space left for a signature on a contract): *Adam* ***signed on the dotted line*** *with a flourish.*

dotted note ▶ **noun** Music a note written with a dot after it, which has one and a half times the length of the same note undotted.

dotted rhythm ▶ **noun** Music rhythm in which the beat is unequally subdivided into a long dotted note and a short note.

dotterel /ˈdɒt(ə)r(ə)l/ ▶ **noun** a small plover with a brown streaked back and a chestnut or buff belly with black below. Dotterels breed in mountainous areas and in the tundra.
● Genus *Eudromias*, family Charadriidae: two species, especially the Eurasian *E. morinellus*, which is noted for its tameness.
■ [with modifier] Austral./NZ any small plover, especially one of the genus *Charadrius*.
– ORIGIN Middle English: from **DOTE** (so named because it is easily caught) + **-REL**. Compare with **DODO**.

dottle /ˈdɒt(ə)l/ ▶ **noun** a remnant of tobacco left in a pipe after smoking.
– ORIGIN late Middle English (denoting a plug for a barrel or other container): from **DOT**[1] + **-LE**[1].

dotty ▶ **adjective** (**dottier**, **dottiest**) informal, chiefly Brit. (of a person, action, or idea) slightly mad or eccentric: *a dotty old lady.*
■ [predic.] (**dotty about**) infatuated with: *she's dotty about her husband.*
– DERIVATIVES **dottily** adverb, **dottiness** noun.
– ORIGIN late 19th cent.: perhaps from obsolete *dote* 'simpleton, fool', apparently from Dutch *dote* 'folly'.

Douala /duːˈɑːlə/ the chief port and largest city of Cameroon; pop. 1,200,000 (1992).

Douay Bible /ˈduːeɪ, ˈdaʊeɪ/ (also **Douay version**) ▶ **noun** an English translation of the Bible formerly used in the Roman Catholic Church, completed at Douai in France early in the 17th century.

double ▶ **adjective 1** consisting of two equal, identical, or similar parts or things: *the double doors.*
■ having twice the usual size, quantity, or strength: *she sipped a double brandy.* ■ designed to be used by two people: *a double bed.* ■ having two different roles or interpretations, especially in order to deceive or confuse: *the furtive* ***double life*** *of a terrorist.*
2 having some essential part or feature twice, in particular:
■ (of a flower variety) having more than one circle of petals: *large double blooms.* ■ (of a domino) having the same number of pips on each half. ■ used to indicate that a letter or number occurs twice in succession: *'otter' is spelled with a double t.*
3 Music lower in pitch by an octave.
▶ **predeterminer** twice as much or as many: *the jail now houses almost double the number of prisoners it was designed for* | *I'll pay double what I paid last time.*
▶ **adverb** at or to twice the amount or extent: *you have to be careful, and this counts double for older people.*
■ as two instead of the more usual one: *she thought she was seeing double.*
▶ **noun 1** a thing which is twice as large as usual or is

made up of two standard units or things: *join the two sleeping bags together to make a double.*
■ a double measure of spirits. ■ a thing designed to be used by two people: *our bed was small for a double.* ■ a system of betting in which the winnings and stake from the first bet are transferred to a second. ■ Bridge a call that will increase the penalty points won by the defenders if the declarer fails to make the contract. ■ Darts a hit on the narrow ring enclosed by the two outer circles of a dartboard, scoring double.
2 a person who looks exactly like another: *you could pass yourself off as his double.*
■ a person who stands in for an actor in a film. ■ an apparition of a living person: *she had seen her husband's double.*
3 (**doubles**) (especially in tennis and badminton) a game or competition involving sides made up of two players: *the semi-finals of the doubles.*
4 Bell-ringing a system of change-ringing using five bells, with two pairs changing places each time.
5 a pair of victories in the same sport in two different competitions: *Manchester United won the double twice.*
▶ **pronoun** a number or amount which is twice as large as a contrasting or usual number or amount: *he paid double and had a room all to himself.*
▶ **verb 1** [no obj.] become twice as much or as many: *profits doubled in one year.*
■ [with obj.] make twice as much or as many of (something): *Clare doubled her income overnight.* ■ [with obj.] archaic amount to twice as much as: *thy fifty yet doth double five and twenty.* ■ (**double up**) use the winnings from a bet as stake for another bet. ■ (of a member of the armed forces) move at twice the usual speed; run: *I doubled across the deck to join the others.* ■ (**double up**) share a room: *'Where's Jimmy going to sleep?' 'He can double up with Bertie.'* ■ Bridge make a call increasing the value of the penalty points to be scored on an opponent's bid if it wins the auction and is not fulfilled.
2 [with obj.] fold or bend (paper, cloth, or other material) over on itself: *the muslin is doubled and then laid in a sieve over the bowl.*
■ [no obj.] (**double up**) bend over or curl up, typically because one is overcome with pain or mirth: *Billy started to double up with laughter.* ■ clench (a fist): *he had one arm around her and the other fist doubled.* ■ [no obj.] (usu. **double back**) go back in the direction one has come: *he had to double back to collect them.* ■ Snooker pot (a ball) by making it rebound off a cushion. ■ Nautical sail round (a headland): *we struck out seaward to double the headland of the cape.*
3 [no obj.] (of a person or thing) be used in or play another, different role: *a laser printer doubles as a photocopier.*
■ [with obj.] (of an actor) play (two parts) in the same piece. ■ Music play two or more musical instruments. ■ [with obj.] Music add the same note in a higher or lower octave to (a note).
– PHRASES **at** (or **on**) **the double** at running speed; very fast: *he disappeared at the double.* **bend double** bend over into a stooping position. **double or nothing** (or Brit. **quits**) a gamble to decide whether a loss or debt should be doubled or cancelled.
– DERIVATIVES **doubler** noun, **doubly** adverb.
– ORIGIN Middle English: via Old French from Latin *duplus* (see **DUPLE**). The verb is from Old French *dobler*, from late Latin *duplare*, from *duplus*.

double acrostic ▶ **noun** an acrostic in which the first and last letters of each line form a hidden word or words.

double act ▶ **noun** a performance involving two people: *the best comic double act of its time.*
■ a pair of entertainers who perform a double act: *my father was part of a double act with his brother.*

double-acting ▶ **adjective** denoting a device or product which combines two different functions.
■ (of an engine) having pistons pushed from both sides alternately.

double-action ▶ **adjective** another term for **DOUBLE-ACTING**: *double-action moss killer.*
■ (of a gun) needing to be cocked and fired as two separate actions.

double agent ▶ **noun** an agent who pretends to act as a spy for one country or organization while in fact acting on behalf of an enemy.

double axe ▶ **noun** an axe with two blades.

double-bank ▶ **verb** [with obj.] chiefly Brit. arrange in two similar or parallel lines; double: *you will be double-banked with someone experienced.*

double bar ▶ **noun** a pair of closely spaced bar lines marking the end of a piece or section of music.

double-barrelled ▶ **adjective** (of a gun) having two barrels.
■ having two parts or aspects. ■ Brit. (of a surname) having two parts joined by a hyphen.

double bass ▶ **noun** the largest and lowest-pitched instrument of the violin family, providing the bass line of the orchestral string section and also much used in jazz.

double bassoon ▶ **noun** a bassoon that is larger and longer than the normal type and sounds an octave lower in pitch.

double bill ▶ **noun** a programme of entertainment with two main items: *a double bill of horror movies.*

double bind ▶ **noun** a situation in which a person is confronted with two irreconcilable demands or a choice between two undesirable courses of action.

double-bitted axe ▶ **noun** chiefly N. Amer. another term for **DOUBLE AXE**.

double-blind ▶ **adjective** [attrib.] denoting a test or trial, especially of a drug, in which any information which may influence the behaviour of the tester or the subject is withheld until after the test.

double bluff ▶ **noun** an action or statement that is intended to appear as a bluff but is in fact genuine.

double bogey Golf ▶ **noun** a score of two strokes over par for a hole.
▶ **verb** (**double-bogey**) [with obj.] complete (a hole) in two strokes over par.

double boiler ▶ **noun** a saucepan with a detachable upper compartment heated by boiling water in the lower one.

double bond ▶ **noun** a chemical bond in which two pairs of electrons are shared between two atoms.

double-book ▶ **verb** [with obj.] (usu. **be double-booked**) inadvertently reserve (something, especially a seat or a hotel room) for two different customers or parties at the same time: *the hotel was double-booked.*
■ book (someone) into a seat or room that is already reserved for another.

double-breasted ▶ **adjective** (of a jacket or coat) having a substantial overlap of material at the front and showing two rows of buttons when fastened.

double bridle ▶ **noun** a bridle which has both a curb and a snaffle bit, each with its own set of reins.

double-check ▶ **verb** [with obj.] go over (something) for a second time to ensure that it is accurate or safe: *he double-checked our credentials* | [with clause] *double-check that all windows are firmly locked.*

double chin ▶ **noun** a roll of fatty flesh below a person's chin.
– DERIVATIVES **double-chinned** adjective.

double-click ▶ **verb** [no obj.] Computing press a mouse button twice in quick succession to select a file, program, or function: *to run a window just double-click on the icon.*
■ [with obj.] select (a file) in this way.

double coconut ▶ **noun** another term for **COCO DE MER**.

double concerto ▶ **noun** a concerto for two solo instruments.

double cream ▶ **noun** [mass noun] Brit. thick cream that contains a lot of milk fat.

double-cross ▶ **verb** [with obj.] deceive or betray (a person with whom one is supposedly cooperating): *he was blackmailed into double-crossing his own government.*
▶ **noun** a betrayal of someone with whom one is supposedly cooperating.
– DERIVATIVES **double-crosser** noun.

double-cut ▶ **adjective** another term for **CROSS-CUT**.

double dagger (also **double obelus**, **double obelisk**) ▶ **noun** a symbol (‡) used in printed text to introduce an annotation.

double-dealing ▶ **noun** [mass noun] the practice of working to people's disadvantage behind their backs.
▶ **adjective** working deceitfully to injure others: *she is a back-stabbing, double-dealing twister.*
– DERIVATIVES **double-dealer** noun.

double-decker ▶ **noun** something, especially a

bus, that has two floors or levels: [as modifier] *a double-decker bus* | *double-decker sandwiches.*

double-declutch ▶ **verb** [no obj.] Brit. release and re-engage the clutch of a vehicle twice when changing gear.

double decomposition ▶ **noun** Chemistry a reaction in which two compounds exchange ions, typically with precipitation of an insoluble product.

double-density ▶ **adjective** Computing (of a disk) able to store twice as much information as other, older disks of the same physical size.

double digging ▶ **noun** [mass noun] (in gardening) digging of an area in parallel trenches two spits deep, burying the soil of each upper spit in the bottom of the next trench.

double-digit ▶ **adjective** [attrib.] (of a number or variable) between 10 and 99.
▶ **noun** (**double digits**) another term for **DOUBLE FIGURES**.

double-dip ▶ **verb** [no obj.] N. Amer. informal obtain an income from two different sources, typically in an illicit way.
– DERIVATIVES **double-dipper** noun.

double dot ▶ **noun** (in musical composition or transcription) two dots placed side by side after a note to indicate that it is to be lengthened by three quarters of its value.
▶ **verb** (**double-dot**) [with obj.] write or perform (music) with a rhythm of alternating long and short notes in a ratio of seven to one, producing a more marked effect than ordinary dotted rhythm.

double Dutch ▶ **noun** [mass noun] **1** Brit. informal language that is impossible to understand; gibberish: *instructions written in double Dutch.*
2 N. Amer. a jumping game played with two skipping ropes swung in opposite directions so that they cross rhythmically.

double-dyed ▶ **adjective** (of an item of clothing) dyed twice in order to give a very deep colour.
■ figurative (of a person) thoroughly imbued with a particular quality: *a double-dyed liberal.*

double eagle ▶ **noun 1** a representation of a two-headed eagle.
■ US a gold coin worth twenty dollars.
2 Golf a score of three strokes under par at a hole. Also called **ALBATROSS**.

double-edged ▶ **adjective** (of a knife or sword) having two cutting edges.
■ having two contradictory aspects or possible outcomes: *the consequences can be double-edged.*
– PHRASES **a double-edged sword** a situation or course of action having both positive and negative effects.

double effect ▶ **noun** [mass noun] the good and bad effect of an action, compared according to a principle which seeks to justify the action if the bad effect, though foreseen, is outweighed by the good effect.

double-ender ▶ **noun** a boat in which stern and bow are similarly tapered.

double entendre /ˌduːb(ə)l ɒ̃ˈtɒ̃dr(ə)/ ▶ **noun** (pl. **double entendres** pronunc. same) a word or phrase open to two interpretations, one of which is usually risqué or indecent.
■ [mass noun] humour using such words or phrases.
– ORIGIN late 17th cent.: from obsolete French (now *double entente*), 'double understanding'.

double-entry ▶ **adjective** [attrib.] denoting a system of bookkeeping in which each transaction is entered as a debit in one account and a credit in another.

double exposure ▶ **noun** [mass noun] the repeated exposure of a photographic plate or film to light, often producing ghost images.

double-faced ▶ **adjective** having two faces: *a double-faced clock.*
■ tending to say one thing and do another; deceitful. ■ (of a fabric or material) finished on both sides so that either may be used as the right side.

double fault ▶ **noun** Tennis an instance of two consecutive faults in serving, counting as a point against the server.
▶ **verb** (**double-fault**) [no obj.] serve a double fault.

double feature ▶ **noun** a cinema programme with two full-length films.

double figures ▶ plural noun a number or amount between 10 and 99: *inflation was in double figures.*

double first ▶ noun an achievement which represents the first place or first accomplishment of something in two respects: *they have scored a double first with top awards for two of their ships.*
- Brit. a university degree with first-class honours in two subjects or two major examinations.

double flat ▶ noun a sign (♭♭) placed before a musical note to indicate that it is to be lowered two semitones.
- a note so marked or lowered.

double-fronted ▶ adjective (of a house) with principal windows on either side of the front door.

double fugue ▶ noun Music a fugue with two subjects, each similarly treated.

double glazing ▶ noun [mass noun] windows which have two layers of glass with a space between them, designed to reduce loss of heat and exclude noise.
- DERIVATIVES **double-glaze** verb.

Double Gloucester ▶ noun [mass noun] a kind of hard cheese originally made in Gloucestershire.
- ORIGIN so named because the curd is milled twice.

double-handed ▶ adjective made to be lifted or held with two hands: *double-handed war axes.*
- using both hands: *a double-handed backhand.*

double harness ▶ noun a harness worn by two horses working together.

double-headed ▶ adjective having a double head or two heads: *a double-headed monster.*
- (of a train) pulled by two locomotives. ■ (of a weapon) having two cutting implements, typically one at each end of the shaft: *a double-headed axe.*

double-header ▶ noun **1** a train pulled by two locomotives coupled together.
2 chiefly N. Amer. a sporting event in which two games or contests are played in succession at the same venue, typically between the same teams or players.

double helix ▶ noun a pair of parallel helices intertwined about a common axis, especially that in the structure of the DNA molecule.

double-hung ▶ adjective (of a window) consisting of two sliding vertical sashes.

double indemnity ▶ noun [mass noun] chiefly N. Amer. provision for payment of double the face amount of an insurance policy under certain conditions, e.g. when death occurs as a result of an accident.

double jeopardy ▶ noun [mass noun] Law the prosecution of a person twice for the same offence.
- risk or disadvantage incurred from two sources simultaneously: *he is in double jeopardy, unable to speak either language adequately.*

double-jointed ▶ adjective (of a person) having unusually flexible joints, typically those of the fingers, arms, or legs.
- DERIVATIVES **double-jointedness** noun.

double knitting ▶ noun [mass noun] a grade of yarn of medium thickness, typically used in hand knitting.
- ORIGIN mid 19th cent.: *double* with reference to the 'doubling' of the yarn to four-ply.

double-lock ▶ verb [with obj.] fasten (a door) with two locks, or with a double lock.
▶ noun (**double lock**) a type of spring lock which may be used as a deadlock by an extra turn of the key.

double napoleon ▶ noun historical a gold forty-franc French coin.

double negation ▶ noun Philosophy the result of negating the negation of a proposition, and the principle (not admitted in intuitionist logic) that this is equivalent to the proposition itself.

double negative ▶ noun Grammar a negative statement containing two negative elements (for example *didn't say nothing*).
- a positive statement in which two negative elements are used to produce the positive force, usually for some particular rhetorical effect, for example *there is not nothing to worry about!*

USAGE According to standard English grammar, a **double negative** used to express a single negative, such as *I don't know nothing* (rather than *I don't know anything*), is incorrect. The rules dictate that the two negative elements cancel each other out to give an affirmative statement, so that *I don't know nothing* would be interpreted as *I know something.*
In practice this sort of double negative is widespread in dialect and other non-standard usage and rarely gives rise to confusion as to the intended meaning. Double negatives are standard in certain other languages such as Spanish and they have not always been unacceptable in English, either. It was normal in Old English and Middle English and did not come to be frowned upon until some time after the 16th century, when attempts were made to relate the rules of language to the rules of formal logic.
Modern (correct) uses of the double negative give an added subtlety to statements: saying *I am not unconvinced* by his argument suggests reservations in the speaker's mind that are not present in its 'logical' equivalent: *I am convinced* by his argument.

double obelus (also **double obelisk**) ▶ noun another term for **DOUBLE DAGGER**.

double-park ▶ verb [with obj.] (usu. **be double-parked**) park (a vehicle) alongside one that is already parked at the side of the road.

double play ▶ noun Baseball a defensive play in which two runners are put out.

double pneumonia ▶ noun [mass noun] pneumonia affecting both lungs.

double precision ▶ noun [mass noun] Computing the use of twice the usual number of bits to represent a number, giving greater arithmetic accuracy.

double quick ▶ adjective & adverb informal very quick or quickly: [as adj.] *I got changed in double quick time* | [as adv.] *you get upstairs double quick!*

double reed ▶ noun Music a reed with two slightly separated blades, used for playing a wind instrument such as an oboe or bassoon.

double refraction ▶ noun [mass noun] Physics division of a single incident light ray or other electromagnetic wave into two separate rays in an anisotropic medium.

double rhyme ▶ noun a rhyme involving two syllables in each rhyming line.

double salt ▶ noun Chemistry a crystalline salt having the composition of a mixture of two simple salts but with a different crystal structure from either.

double saucepan ▶ noun British term for **DOUBLE BOILER**.

double sharp ▶ noun a sign (𝄪) placed before a musical note to indicate that it is to be raised two semitones.
- a note so marked or raised.

double shuffle ▶ noun a dance in which a person makes shuffling movements twice with each foot alternately.

double-sided ▶ adjective using or able to be used on both sides: *double-sided tape.*

doublespeak ▶ noun [mass noun] deliberately euphemistic, ambiguous, or obscure language: *the art of political doublespeak.*

double standard ▶ noun a rule or principle which is unfairly applied in different ways to different people or groups: *the double standards employed to deal with ordinary people and those in the City.*

double star ▶ noun two stars actually or apparently very close together.

double steal ▶ noun Baseball a play in which two base-runners each steal or attempt to steal a base.

double-stopping ▶ noun [mass noun] the sounding of two strings at once on a violin or similar bowed instrument.
- DERIVATIVES **double stop** noun.

Double Summer Time daylight saving time in which clocks are set two hours ahead of standard time, used in Britain during the Second World War.

doublet ▶ noun **1** a pair of similar things, in particular two words of the same derivation but having different meanings, for example *fashion* and *faction*, *cloak* and *clock*.
- (**doublets**) the same number on two dice thrown at once. ■ Physics & Chemistry a pair of associated lines close together in a spectrum or electrophoretic gel. ■ a combination of two simple lenses.
2 a man's short close-fitting padded jacket, commonly worn from the 14th to the 17th century.
- ORIGIN Middle English: from Old French, 'something folded', also denoting a fur-lined coat, from *double* 'double'.

double take ▶ noun a delayed reaction to something unexpected, immediately after one's first reaction: *Tony glanced at her, then did a double take.*

doubletalk ▶ noun chiefly N. Amer. another term for **DOUBLESPEAK**.

double-team N. Amer. ▶ verb [with obj.] (in ball games) block (an opponent) with two players.
▶ noun an act of double-teaming.
- the players engaged in such play.

doublethink ▶ noun [mass noun] the acceptance of or mental capacity to accept contrary opinions or beliefs at the same time, especially as a result of political indoctrination.
- ORIGIN 1949: coined by George Orwell in his novel *Nineteen Eighty-Four*.

double time ▶ noun [mass noun] **1** a rate of pay equal to double the standard rate, sometimes paid for working on holidays or outside normal working hours.
2 Military a regulation running pace.
3 Music a rhythm that is twice as fast as an earlier one.

doubleton /ˈdʌb(ə)lt(ə)n/ ▶ noun (in card games, especially bridge) a pair of cards which are the only cards of their suit in a hand.
- [as modifier] denoting a card which is one of a doubleton: *a doubleton ace.* ■ a pair of people or things.
- ORIGIN early 20th cent.: from **DOUBLE**, on the pattern of *singleton*.

double tonguing ▶ noun [mass noun] Music the use of two alternating movements of the tongue (usually as in sounding *t* and *k*) in playing rapid passages on a wind instrument.

double top ▶ noun Darts a score of double twenty.

doubletree ▶ noun N. Amer. a crossbar in front of a wagon with a swingletree at each end, enabling two horses to be harnessed.
- ORIGIN mid 19th cent.: from **DOUBLE**, on the pattern of *singletree*.

double vision ▶ noun [mass noun] the simultaneous perception of two images, usually overlapping, of a single scene or object.

double whammy ▶ noun informal a twofold blow or setback: *a double whammy of taxation and price increases.*
- ORIGIN 1950s: originally with reference to the comic strip *Li'l Abner* (see **WHAMMY**).

double-wide ▶ noun N. Amer. a semi-permanent mobile home consisting of two separate units connected on site.

double yellow line ▶ noun (in the UK) a pair of yellow lines painted at the side of a road to indicate that parking is not permitted at most times of day.

doubloon /dʌˈbluːn/ ▶ noun historical a Spanish gold coin.
- ORIGIN from French *doublon* or its source, Spanish *doblón*, from *doble* 'double' (so named because the coin was worth double the value of a pistole).

doublure /duːˈbljʊə/ ▶ noun an ornamental lining, especially one made of leather, on the inside of a book cover.
- ORIGIN French, 'lining', from *doubler* 'to line'.

doubt ▶ noun [mass noun] a feeling of uncertainty or lack of conviction: *some doubt has been cast upon the authenticity of this account* | [count noun] *they had doubts that they would ever win.*
▶ verb **1** [with obj.] feel uncertain about: *I doubt my ability to do the job.*
- question the truth or fact of (something): *who can doubt the value and necessity of these services?* | [with clause] *I doubt if anyone slept that night.* ■ disbelieve (a person or their word): *I have no reason to doubt him.* ■ [no obj.] feel uncertain, especially about one's religious beliefs.
2 [with clause] Brit. archaic fear; be afraid: *I doubt not any ones contradicting this.*
- PHRASES **beyond doubt** allowing no uncertainty: *you've proved it beyond doubt.* **in doubt** open to question: *the outcome is no longer in doubt.* ■ feeling uncertain about something: *by the age of 14 he was in*

no doubt about his career aims. **no doubt** used to indicate the speaker's firm belief that something is true even if evidence is not given or available: *those who left were attracted, no doubt, by higher pay.* ■ used to introduce a concession which is subsequently dismissed as unimportant or irrelevant: *they no doubt did what they could to help her, but their best proved insufficient.* **without (a) doubt** indisputably: *he was without doubt the very worst kind of reporter.*
– DERIVATIVES **doubtable** adjective, **doubter** noun, **doubtingly** adverb.
– ORIGIN Middle English: from Old French *doute* (noun), *douter* (verb), from Latin *dubitare* 'hesitate', from *dubius* 'doubtful' (see **DUBIOUS**).

doubtful ▶ **adjective 1** feeling uncertain about something: *he looked doubtful, but gave a nod | I was* ***doubtful of*** *my judgement.*
2 not known with certainty: *the fire was of doubtful origin.*
■ improbable: [with clause] *it is doubtful whether these schemes have any lasting effect.* ■ not established as genuine or acceptable: *of doubtful legality.*
– DERIVATIVES **doubtfully** adverb, **doubtfulness** noun.

doubting Thomas ▶ **noun** a person who is sceptical and refuses to believe something without proof.
– ORIGIN early 17th cent.: with biblical allusion to the apostle Thomas (John 20: 24–29).

doubtless ▶ **adverb** [sentence adverb] used to indicate the speaker's belief that a statement is certain to be true given what is known about the situation: *the company would doubtless find the reduced competition to their liking.*
■ used to refer to a desirable outcome as though it were certain: *doubtless you'll solve the problem.*
– DERIVATIVES **doubtlessly** adverb.

douce /du:s/ ▶ **adjective** chiefly Scottish sober, gentle, and sedate: *stories which would have outraged their douce minds.*
– ORIGIN Middle English (in the sense 'pleasant, sweet'): from Old French *dous, douce*, from Latin *dulcis* 'sweet'.

douceur /du:'sə:, French dusœʀ/ ▶ **noun** a financial inducement; a bribe: *Pericles gave a handsome douceur to the Spartan commanders to withdraw without fighting.*
– ORIGIN French, literally 'sweetness'.

douceur de vivre /du:ˌsə: də 'vi:vr(ə), French dusœʀ də vivʀ/ (also **douceur de vie** /vi:, French vi/) ▶ **noun** [mass noun] a way of living that is pleasant and free from worries.
– ORIGIN French, literally 'sweetness of living (or life)'.

douche /du:ʃ/ ▶ **noun** a shower of water: *I felt better for taking a daily douche.*
■ a jet of liquid applied to part of the body for cleansing or medicinal purposes. ■ a device for washing out the vagina as a contraceptive measure.
▶ **verb** [with obj.] spray or shower with water.
■ [no obj.] use a douche as a method of contraception.
– ORIGIN mid 18th cent. (as a noun): via French from Italian *doccia* 'conduit pipe', from *docciare* 'pour by drops', based on Latin *ductus* 'leading' (see **DUCT**).

douche bag ▶ **noun** a small syringe for douching the vagina, especially as a contraceptive measure.
■ N. Amer. informal a loathsome or contemptible person (used as a term of abuse).

douc langur /du:k/ (also **douc monkey**) ▶ **noun** a langur with black, white, and orange fur, native to the tropical rainforests of SE Asia.
● *Pygathrix nemaeus*, family Cercopithecidae.
– ORIGIN late 18th cent.: *douc* via French from Vietnamese.

dough ▶ **noun** [mass noun] **1** a thick, malleable mixture of flour and liquid, used for baking into bread or pastry.
2 informal money: *lots of dough.*
– DERIVATIVES **doughiness** noun, **doughy** adjective (**doughier, doughiest**).
– ORIGIN Old English *dāg*, of Germanic origin; related to Dutch *deeg* and German *Teig*, from an Indo-European root meaning 'smear, knead'.

doughboy ▶ **noun 1** a boiled or deep-fried dumpling.
2 US informal a United States infantryman, especially one in the First World War. [ORIGIN: said to have been a term applied in the Civil War to the large globular brass buttons on the infantry uniform; also said to derive from the use of pipe clay 'dough' to clean the white belts worn by infantrymen.]

doughnut (also US **donut**) ▶ **noun** a small fried cake of sweetened dough, typically in the shape of a ball or ring.
■ a ring-shaped object, in particular a vacuum chamber in some types of particle accelerator.

doughty /'daʊti/ ▶ **adjective** (**doughtier, doughtiest**) archaic or humorous brave and persistent: *his doughty spirit kept him going.*
– DERIVATIVES **doughtily** adverb, **doughtiness** noun.
– ORIGIN late Old English *dohtig*, variant of *dyhtig*, of Germanic origin; related to Dutch *duchtig* and German *tüchtig*.

Douglas /'dʌgləs/ the capital of the Isle of Man; pop. 22,210 (1991).

Douglas fir ▶ **noun** a tall, slender conifer with soft foliage and, in mature trees, deeply fissured bark. It is widely planted as a timber tree.
● Genus *Pseudotsuga*, family Pinaceae: several species, in particular *P. menziesii* of western North America.
– ORIGIN mid 19th cent.: named after David Douglas (1798–1834), the Scottish botanist and explorer who introduced it to Europe from North America.

Douglas-Home /ˌdʌgləs'hju:m/, Sir Alec, Baron Home of the Hirsel of Coldstream (1903–95), British Conservative statesman, Prime Minister 1963–4; born *Alexander Frederick Douglas-Home*. When Douglas-Home became Prime Minister he relinquished his hereditary peerage.

doum palm /du:m/ (also **dom palm**) ▶ **noun** a palm tree with a forked trunk, producing edible fruit and a vegetable ivory substitute. It is native to the Nile region of Upper Egypt.
● *Hyphaene thebaica*, family Palmae.
– ORIGIN early 18th cent.: *doum* from Arabic *dawm, dūm*.

dour /'dʊə, 'daʊə/ ▶ **adjective** relentlessly severe, stern, or gloomy in manner or appearance: *a hard, dour, humourless fanatic.*
– DERIVATIVES **dourly** adverb, **dourness** noun.
– ORIGIN late Middle English (originally Scots): probably from Scottish Gaelic *dúr* 'dull, obstinate, stupid', perhaps from Latin *durus* 'hard'.

Douro /'dʊəru:/ a river of the Iberian peninsula, rising in central Spain and flowing west for 900 km (556 miles) through Portugal to the Atlantic Ocean near Oporto. Spanish name **DUERO**.

douroucouli /ˌdʊərʊ'ku:li/ ▶ **noun** (pl. **douroucoulis**) a large-eyed chiefly nocturnal monkey found in South America. Also called **NIGHT MONKEY, OWL MONKEY**.
● Genus *Aotus*, family Cebidae: two or more species.
– ORIGIN mid 19th cent.: probably a South American Indian name.

douse /daʊs/ (also **dowse**) ▶ **verb** [with obj.] pour a liquid over; drench: *he doused the car with petrol and set it on fire.*
■ extinguish (a fire or light): *stewards appeared and the fire was doused | figurative nothing could douse her sudden euphoria.* ■ Sailing lower (a sail) quickly.
– ORIGIN early 17th cent.: perhaps imitative, influenced by **SOUSE**, or perhaps from dialect *douse* 'strike, beat', from Middle Dutch and Low German *dossen*.

dout /daʊt/ (also **dowt**) chiefly Scottish ▶ **verb** [with obj.] extinguish (a fire or light).
▶ **noun** a cigarette end.
– ORIGIN early 16th cent. (as a verb): contraction of *do out*. The noun dates from the 1940s.

dove¹ /dʌv/ ▶ **noun 1** a stocky seed- or fruit-eating bird with a small head, short legs, and a cooing voice. Doves are generally smaller and more delicate than pigeons, but many kinds have been given both names.
● Family Columbidae: numerous genera and species; white doves are a variety of the domestic pigeon.
2 a person who advocates peaceful or conciliatory policies, especially in foreign affairs. Compare with **HAWK¹** (in sense 2).
3 (**Dove**) (in Christian art and poetry) the Holy Spirit (as represented in John 1:32).
– DERIVATIVES **dovelike** adjective, **dovish** adjective (in sense 2).
– ORIGIN Middle English: from Old Norse *dúfa*.

dove² /dəʊv/ chiefly N. Amer. past of **DIVE**.

dovecote /'dʌvkɒt/ (also **dovecot**) ▶ **noun** a shelter with nest holes for domesticated pigeons.
– PHRASES **flutter the dovecotes** (also **cause a flutter among the dovecotes**) startle or upset a sedate or conventionally minded community.

dove grey ▶ **noun** [mass noun] a light grey.

dovekie /'dʌvki/ ▶ **noun** chiefly N. Amer. another term for **LITTLE AUK**.
– ORIGIN early 19th cent. (originally denoting the black guillemot, *Cepphus grylle*, also formerly called the *Greenland dove*): from a Scots diminutive of **DOVE¹**.

Dover 1 a ferry port in Kent, on the coast of the English Channel; pop. 34,300 (1981). It is mainland Britain's nearest point to the Continent, being only 35 km (22 miles) from Calais.
■ a shipping forecast area covering the Strait of Dover.
2 the state capital of Delaware; pop. 23,500 (1990).

Dover, Strait of a sea passage between England and France, connecting the English Channel with the North Sea.

Dover sole ▶ **noun** either of two flatfishes which are highly valued as food:
● a true sole that is common in European waters (*Solea solea*, family Soleidae). ● N. Amer. a relative of the lemon sole found in the East Pacific (*Microstomus pacificus*, family Pleuronectidae).

dove's-foot cranesbill ▶ **noun** a European cranesbill which has white downy hairs on the leaves and spreading stems. The leaves supposedly resemble the foot of a bird.
● *Geranium molle*, family Geraniaceae.

dove shell ▶ **noun** a small mollusc with a robust shell, occurring in tropical and subtropical seas.
● Family Pyrenidae (or Columbellidae), class Gastropoda: *Pyrene* and other genera.

dovetail ▶ **noun** a joint formed by one or more tapered projections (tenons) on one piece which interlock with corresponding notches or recesses (mortises) in another.
■ a tenon used in such a joint, typically wider at its extremity.
▶ **verb** [with obj.] join together by means of a dovetail.
■ fit or cause to fit together easily and conveniently: [with obj.] *plan to enable parents to dovetail their career and family commitments* | [no obj.] *flights that* ***dovetail with*** *the working day.*

dovetail saw ▶ **noun** a tenon saw with a small blade and fine teeth, used mainly for making joints.

dove tree ▶ **noun** a slender deciduous Chinese tree with flowers that bear large white bracts said to resemble doves' wings, grown as an ornamental.
● *Davidia involucrata*, family Nyssaceae.

Dow /daʊ/ short for **DOW JONES INDEX**: *the Dow fell sharply that summer.*

dowager /'daʊədʒə/ ▶ **noun** a widow with a title or property derived from her late husband: [as modifier] *the dowager duchess* | [postpositive] *the queen dowager.*
■ informal a dignified elderly woman.
– ORIGIN mid 16th cent.: from Old French *douagiere*, from *douage* 'dower', from *douer* 'endow', from Latin *dotare* 'endow' (see **DOWER**).

dowager's hump ▶ **noun** [mass noun] forward curvature of the spine resulting in a stoop, typically in women with osteoporosis, caused by collapse of the front edges of the thoracic vertebrae.

dowd /daʊd/ ▶ **noun** a person, typically a woman, of dull, unfashionable appearance.
– ORIGIN Middle English: of unknown origin. Perhaps reintroduced in the early 19th cent. as a back-formation from **DOWDY**.

Dowding /'daʊdɪŋ/, Hugh (Caswall Tremenheere), Baron (1882–1970), British Marshal of the RAF. He was Commander-in-Chief of the British air defence forces that defeated the Luftwaffe during the Battle of Britain in 1940.

dowdy ▶ **adjective** (**dowdier, dowdiest**) (of a person, typically a woman, or their clothes) unfashionable and without style in appearance: *she could achieve the kind of casual chic which made every other woman around her look dowdy.*
▶ **noun** (pl. **-ies**) a woman who is unfashionably and unattractively dressed.
– DERIVATIVES **dowdily** adverb, **dowdiness** noun.

dowel /'daʊəl/ ▶ **noun** a peg of wood, metal, or plastic without a distinct head, used for holding together components of a structure.
▶ **verb** (**dowelled, dowelling**; US **doweled, doweling**) [with obj.] fasten with a dowel or dowels.
– ORIGIN Middle English: perhaps from Middle Low German *dovel*.

dowelling (US **doweling**) ▶ **noun** [mass noun] cylindrical rods for cutting into dowels.

dower /ˈdaʊə/ ▶ **noun** a widow's share for life of her husband's estate.
- ■ archaic a dowry.
▶ **verb** [with obj.] archaic give a dowry to.
– ORIGIN late Middle English: from Old French *douaire*, from medieval Latin *dotarium*, from Latin *dotare* 'endow', from *dos, dot-* 'dowry'; related to *dare* 'give'.

dower house ▶ **noun** Brit. a house intended as the residence of a widow, typically one near the main house on her late husband's estate.

dowitcher /ˈdaʊɪtʃə/ ▶ **noun** a wading bird of the sandpiper family, with a long straight bill, breeding in arctic and subarctic North America and east Asia.
● Genus *Limnodromus*, family Scolopacidae: three species, in particular the **short-billed dowitcher** (*L. griseus*) and the **long-billed dowitcher** (*L. scolopaceus*).
– ORIGIN mid 19th cent.: from Iroquoian.

Dow Jones index /daʊ ˈdʒəʊnz/ (also **Dow Jones average**) an index of figures indicating the relative price of shares on the New York Stock Exchange, based on the average price of selected stocks.
– ORIGIN from the name of *Dow Jones & Co, Inc.*, a financial news agency founded by Charles H. *Dow* (1851–1902) and Edward D. *Jones* (c.1855–1920), American economists whose company compiled the first average of US stock prices in 1884.

Down one of the Six Counties of Northern Ireland, formerly an administrative area; chief town, Downpatrick.

down[1] ▶ **adverb 1** towards or in a lower place or position, especially to or on the ground or another surface: *she looked down | the sun started to go down | he put his glass down | she flicked the switch up and down | he swung the axe to chop down the tree.*
- ■ at or to a specified distance below: *you can plainly see the bottom 35 feet down.* ■ downstairs: *I went down to put the kettle on.* ■ expressing movement or position away from the north: *they're living down south.* ■ to or at a place perceived as lower (often expressing casualness or lack of hurry): *I'd rather be down at the villa | I'm going down to the pub.* ■ Brit. away from the capital or major city: *there are eight trains a day, four up and four down.* ■ Brit. away from a university, especially Oxford or Cambridge. ■ (with reference to food or drink swallowed) in or into the stomach: *she couldn't keep anything down.* ■ so as to lie or be fixed flush or flat: *she stuck down a Christmas label.* ■ [as exclamation] used as a command to a person or animal to sit or lie down: *down, boy!* ■ a crossword answer which reads vertically: *how many letters in fifteen down?*
2 to or at a lower level of intensity, volume, or activity: *keep the noise down | the panic was dying down | at night it would cool down.*
- ■ to or at a lower price, value, or rank: *output was down by 20 per cent | soup is down from 59p to 49p.* ■ to a finer consistency, a smaller amount or size, or a simpler or more basic state: *I must slim down a bit | a formal statement that can't be edited down | thin down an oil-based paint with spirits.* ■ from an earlier to a later point in time or order: *buildings in England* **down** *to 1540 | everyone, from the President* **down** *to the bloke selling hot dogs, wants her dead.*
3 in or into a weaker or worse position, mood, or condition: *the scandal brought* **down** *the government |* he was **down with** the flu.
- ■ losing or at a disadvantage by a specified amount: *United were 3-0* **down.** ■ used to express progress through a series of tasks or items: *one down and only six more to go.* ■ (of a computer system) out of action or unavailable for use (especially temporarily): *the system went down yesterday.* ■ (**down with** ——) shouted to express strong dislike of a specified person or thing: *crowds chanted 'Down with America!'*
4 in or into writing: *Graham noted the numbers down carefully | taking down notes.*
- ■ on or on to a list, schedule, or record: *I'll put you* **down** *for the evening shift.*
5 (with reference to partial payment of a sum of money) made initially or on the spot: *pay £5* **down** *and the rest at the end of the month.*
6 (of sailing) with the current or the wind.
- ■ (of a ship's helm) moved round to leeward so that the rudder is to windward.
7 American Football (of the ball or a player in possession) not in play, typically through progress being stopped.
▶ **preposition 1** from a higher to a lower point of

(something): *up and down the stairs | tears streaming down her face.*
- ■ at or to a lower part of (a river or stream); nearer the sea: *a dozen miles or so down the Thames.* ■ at a point further along the course of (something): *he lived down the street.* ■ along the course or extent of: *I wandered down the road | an incision down the middle.* ■ informal at or to (a place): *tired of going down the pub every night.*
2 throughout (a period of time): *astrologers down the ages.*
▶ **adjective 1** [attrib.] directed or moving towards a lower place or position: *the down escalator | click on the down arrow.*
- ■ relating to or denoting trains travelling away from the main terminus: *we travelled on the first down train.* ■ Physics denoting a flavour of quark having a charge of −⅓. Protons and neutrons are thought to be composed of combinations of up and down quarks.
2 [predic.] (of a person) unhappy; depressed: *he's been so down lately.*
- ■ [attrib.] informal (of a period of time) causing or characterized by unhappiness or depression: *of course, there were up days and down days.*
3 [predic.] (of a computer system) temporarily out of action or unavailable: *sorry, but the computer's down.*
4 [predic.] US black slang supporting or going along with someone or something: *'You going to the movies?' 'Yo, I'm down.'*
- ■ aware of and following the latest fashion: *a seriously down, hip-hop homie.*
▶ **verb** [with obj.] informal **1** knock or bring to the ground: *175 enemy aircraft had been downed | he struck Slater on the face, downing him.*
2 consume (something, typically a drink): *he downed five pints of cider.*
- ■ (of a golfer) sink (a putt).
▶ **noun** **1** American Football a chance for a team to advance the ball, ending when the ball-carrier is tackled or the ball becomes out of play. A team must advance at least ten yards in a series of four downs in order to keep possession.
2 (**downs**) informal unwelcome experiences or events: *there had been more downs than ups during his years at Ferrari.*
3 informal a feeling or period of unhappiness or depression: *everyone gets their downs, their depressive periods.*
- ■ informal short for **DOWNER** (in sense 1).
– PHRASES **be** (or **have a**) **down on** informal disapprove of; feel hostile or antagonistic towards. **be down to 1** be attributable to (a particular factor or circumstance): *he claimed his problems were down to the media.* ■ be the responsibility of (a particular person): *it's down to you to make sure the boiler receives regular servicing.* **2** be left with only (the specified amount): *I'm down to my last few pounds.* **down in the mouth** informal (of a person or their expression) unhappy; dejected. **down on one's luck** informal experiencing a period of bad luck. **down tools** Brit. informal stop work, especially as a form of industrial action: *the union instructed its members to down tools.* **down town** into or in the centre of a town: *I went down town to do a few errands.* **have** (or **put**) **someone/thing down as** judge someone or something to be (a particular type): *I never had Jake down as a ladies' man.*
– ORIGIN Old English *dūn, dūne*, shortened from *adūne* 'downward', from the phrase of *dūne* 'off the hill' (see **DOWN**[3]).

down[2] ▶ **noun** [mass noun] soft fine fluffy feathers which form the first covering of a young bird or an insulating layer below the contour feathers of an adult bird.
- ■ such feathers taken from ducks or their nests and used for stuffing cushions, quilts, etc.; eiderdown. ■ fine soft hair on the face or body of a person: *the little girl had a covering of golden down on her head.* ■ short soft hairs on some leaves, fruit, or seeds.
– ORIGIN Middle English: from Old Norse *dúnn*.

down[3] ▶ **noun** **1** (usu. **downs**) a gently rolling hill: *the gentle green contours of the downs.*
- ■ (**the Downs**) ridges of undulating chalk and limestone hills in southern England, with few trees and used mainly for pasture.
2 (**the Downs**) a stretch of sea off the east coast of Kent, sheltered by the Goodwin Sands.
– ORIGIN Old English *dūn* 'hill' (related to Dutch *duin* 'dune'), perhaps ultimately of Celtic origin and related to Old Irish *dún* and obsolete Welsh *din* 'fort', which are from an Indo-European root shared by **TOWN**.

down-and-dirty ▶ **adjective** informal, chiefly N. Amer.

1 highly competitive or unprincipled: *back-stabbing slander and electronic harassment are freely employed in down-and-dirty hacker feuds.*
2 explicit; direct: *the sharing of down-and-dirty secrets.*

down and out ▶ **adjective 1** (of a person) without money, a job, or a place to live; destitute: *a novel about being down and out in London.*
2 (of a boxer) knocked down and unable to continue fighting.
- ■ (of a competitor) facing certain defeat.
▶ **noun** (**down-and-out**) a person without money, a job, or a place to live: *a hostel for down-and-outs.*

down at heel chiefly Brit. ▶ **adjective 1** (of a shoe) with the heel worn down.
2 (of a person or place) showing signs of neglect and deterioration; shabby: *a down-at-heel 1940s hotel.*

downbeat ▶ **adjective 1** pessimistic; gloomy: *the assessment of the UK's economic prospects is downbeat.*
2 relaxed and understated: *he responds to her enthusiasm with downbeat bemusement.*
▶ **noun** Music an accented beat, usually the first of the bar.

downcast ▶ **adjective 1** (of a person's eyes) looking downwards: *her modestly downcast eyes.*
2 (of a person) feeling despondent.
▶ **noun** a shaft dug in a mine for extra ventilation.

downchange ▶ **noun** a change to a lower gear in a motor vehicle.
▶ **verb** [with obj.] put (a vehicle) into a lower gear.
- ■ [no obj.] change to a lower gear.

downcomer ▶ **noun** a pipe for the downward transport of water or gas from the top of a furnace or boiler.

downconverter ▶ **noun** Electronics a device that converts a signal to a lower frequency, especially in television reception.
– DERIVATIVES **downconversion** noun.

downcountry ▶ **adjective** & **adverb** (in some countries, especially the United States and Australia) in, into, or relating to the low-lying and generally more densely settled part of a country as opposed to hilly regions: [as adj.] *a downcountry upstart* | [as adv.] *the land rolled away a hundred miles downcountry.*

downcurved ▶ **adjective** [attrib.] curved downwards.

downcut ▶ **verb** (**-cutting** past and past participle **-cut**) [no obj.] Geology (of a river) erode downwards through its bed.

downdraught (US **downdraft**) ▶ **noun** a downward current or draught of air.

downdrift ▶ **noun** [mass noun] a tendency in certain languages or kinds of utterance for pitch to fall near the end of a phrase, clause, or sentence.

downer ▶ **noun** informal **1** (usu. **downers**) a depressant or tranquillizing drug, especially a barbiturate.
2 a dispiriting or depressing experience or factor: *the thought of the danger his son was in put something of a downer on the situation.*
- ■ a period of consistent failure: *Birmingham City are on a real downer.*
3 a cow or other animal which has fallen down and cannot get to its feet unaided.

downfall ▶ **noun** a loss of power, prosperity, or status: *the crisis led to the downfall of the government.*
- ■ the cause of such a loss: *his intractability will prove to be his downfall.*

downfield ▶ **adverb 1** chiefly N. Amer. another term for **UPFIELD** (in sense 1).
2 Physics in a direction corresponding to decreasing field strength.

downforce ▶ **noun** a force acting on a moving vehicle having the effect of pressing it down towards the ground, giving it increased stability. Downforce is produced by a combination of air resistance and gravity.

downgrade ▶ **verb** [with obj.] (usu. **be downgraded**) reduce to a lower grade, rank, or level of importance: *some jobs had gradually been downgraded from skilled to semi-skilled.*
▶ **noun 1** an instance of reducing someone or something's rank, status, or level of importance.
2 chiefly N. Amer. a downward gradient, typically on a railway or road.
– PHRASES **on the downgrade** N. Amer. in decline: *profits are on the downgrade.*

downhaul ▶ **noun** Nautical a rope used for hauling

down a sail, spar, etc., especially in order to control a sail's shape.

downhearted ▶ adjective discouraged; in low spirits: *fans must not be downhearted even though we lost.*
– DERIVATIVES **downheartedly** adverb, **downheartedness** noun.

downhill ▶ adverb /daʊnˈhɪl/ towards the bottom of a slope: *he ran downhill* | *follow the road downhill.*
▪figurative into a steadily worsening situation: *her marriage continued to slide downhill.* ▪[predic.] figurative used to describe easy or quick progress towards an objective after initial difficulties have been overcome: *two-nil up—it should have been **downhill** all the way.*
▶ adjective leading down towards the bottom of a slope: *the route is downhill for part of the way.*
▪figurative leading to a steadily worsening situation: *the downhill road to delinquency.* ▪of or relating to the sport of skiing downhill: *the world downhill champion.*
▶ noun /ˈdaʊnhɪl/ **1** a downward slope.
2 Skiing a downhill race.
▪[mass noun] the activity of downhill skiing.
– PHRASES **go downhill** become worse; deteriorate: *the business is going downhill fast.*

downhiller ▶ noun a skier or cyclist who takes part in downhill races.

downhole ▶ adjective & adverb (in the oil industry) used, occurring, or performed in a well or borehole.

down-home ▶ adjective chiefly US connected with an unpretentious way of life, especially that of rural areas in the southern United States: *there isn't too much down-home blues coming out any more.*

Downing Street a street in Westminster, London, between Whitehall and St James's Park. No. 10 is the official residence of the Prime Minister; No. 11 is the home of the Chancellor of the Exchequer.
▪used allusively for the British government or the Prime Minister.
– ORIGIN named after the original developer of the site, Sir George *Downing* (*c.*1624–84), a diplomat under both Oliver Cromwell and Charles II.

downland ▶ noun [mass noun] (also **downlands**) gently rolling hill country, especially in southern England.

downlighter (also **downlight**) ▶ noun a light placed or designed so as to throw illumination downwards.
– DERIVATIVES **downlighting** noun.

downlink ▶ noun a telecommunications link for signals coming to the earth from a satellite, spacecraft, or aircraft.
▶ verb [with obj.] relay to the earth (a telecommunications signal or the information it conveys): *any TV station can downlink just about any game.*

download Computing ▶ verb [with obj.] copy (data) from one computer system to another or to a disk.
▶ noun [mass noun] the act or process of copying data in such a way: [as modifier] *a download and upload routine.*
▪[count noun] a computer file transferred in such a way: *a popular download from bulletin boards.*
– DERIVATIVES **downloadable** adjective.

downmarket ▶ adjective & adverb chiefly Brit. towards or relating to the cheaper or less prestigious sector of the market: [as adj.] *an interview for the downmarket tabloids* | [as adv.] *competition threatens to drive broadcasters further downmarket.*

downmost ▶ adjective & adverb chiefly Brit. the furthest down; at or towards the bottom.

down payment ▶ noun an initial payment made when something is bought on credit.

downpipe ▶ noun Brit. a pipe to carry rainwater from a roof to a drain or to ground level.

downplay ▶ verb [with obj.] make (something) appear less important than it really is: *this report downplays the seriousness of global warming.*

downpour ▶ noun a heavy fall of rain: *a sudden downpour had filled the gutters and drains.*

downrate ▶ verb [with obj.] make (someone or something) lower in value, standard, or importance: *he notched up five kills although Fighter Command downrated them to four probables.*

downright ▶ adjective **1** [attrib.] (of something bad or unpleasant) utter; complete (used for emphasis): *it's a downright disgrace.*
2 (of a person's manner or behaviour) straightforward; so direct as to be blunt: *her common sense and downright attitude to life surprised him.*
▶ adverb [as submodifier] to an extreme degree; thoroughly: *he was downright rude.*
– DERIVATIVES **downrightness** noun.

downriver ▶ adverb & adjective towards or situated at a point nearer the mouth of a river: [as adv.] *the cabin cruiser started to drift downriver* | [as adj.] *the downriver side of the bridge.*

downscale N. Amer. ▶ verb [with obj.] reduce in size, scale, or extent: *he was unable to downscale his strongly unionized workforce.*
▶ adjective at the lower end of a scale, especially a social scale; downmarket: *these brands appeal to downscale shoppers who are looking for a low price.*

downshift chiefly N. Amer. ▶ verb [no obj.] change to a lower gear in a motor vehicle or bicycle.
▪slow down; slacken off: *well before the country slipped into recession, business was downshifting.* ▪change a financially rewarding but stressful career or lifestyle for a less pressured and less highly paid but more fulfilling one: *increasing numbers of men want to downshift from full-time work.*
▶ noun a change to a lower gear in a motor vehicle or bicycle.
▪a change in quality or quantity to a lesser or lower degree: *the downshift of human position from the centre of the cosmos.* ▪an instance of changing a financially rewarding but stressful career or lifestyle for a less pressured and less highly paid but more fulfilling one.

downside ▶ noun the negative aspect of something, especially something regarded as in general good or desirable: *a magazine feature on the downside of fashion modelling.*

downsize ▶ verb [with obj.] chiefly US make (something) smaller: *I downsized the rear wheel to 26 inches.*
▪make (a company or organization) smaller by shedding staff. ▪[no obj.] (of a company) shed staff: *recession forced many companies to downsize.*

downslope ▶ noun a downward slope.
▶ adverb & adjective at or towards a lower point on a slope.

downspout ▶ noun North American term for **DOWNPIPE**.

Down's syndrome ▶ noun [mass noun] Medicine a congenital disorder arising from a chromosome defect, causing intellectual impairment and physical abnormalities including short stature and a broad facial profile. It arises from a defect involving chromosome 21, usually an extra copy (trisomy-21).
– ORIGIN 1960s: named after John L. H. *Down* (1828–96), the English physician who first described it.

USAGE Of relatively recent coinage, **Down's syndrome** is the accepted term in modern use, and former terms such as **mongol** and **mongolism**, which are likely to cause offence, should be avoided.

downstage ▶ adjective & adverb at or towards the front of a stage: [as adv.] *all four run for their lives downstage* | [as adj.] *a crowd of dancers occupies the downstage area.*

downstairs ▶ adverb down a flight of stairs: *I tripped over the cat and fell downstairs.*
▪on or to a lower floor: *we were waiting for you downstairs* | *she called him downstairs.*
▶ adjective [attrib.] situated downstairs: *the downstairs loo.*
▶ noun the ground floor or lower floors of a building: *the downstairs was hardly damaged at all.*

downstate US ▶ adjective & adverb of, in, or to a part of a state remote from its large cities, especially the southern part.
▶ noun [mass noun] such an area.
– DERIVATIVES **downstater** noun.

downstream ▶ adverb & adjective situated or moving in the direction in which a stream or river flows: [as adv.] *the bridge spanned the river just **downstream of** the rail line* | [as adj.] *deforestation could have disastrous consequences for downstream regions.*
▪Biology situated in or towards the part of a sequence of genetic material where transcription takes place later than at a given point: *a termination signal was found downstream from the coding region.* ▪at a stage in the process of gas or oil extraction and production after the raw material is ready for refining.

downstroke ▶ noun a stroke made downwards: *he writes the figure seven with a line through the downstroke* | *the blade angles back on the downstroke.*

downswing ▶ noun **1** another term for **DOWNTURN**.
2 Golf the downward movement of a club when the player is about to hit the ball.

down-the-line ▶ adjective informal thorough and uncompromising: *the party avoids down-the-line support of unions.*

downthrow Geology ▶ verb (past **-threw**; past participle **-thrown**) [with obj.] displace (a rock formation) downwards.
▶ noun a downward displacement of rock strata.

down timber ▶ noun [mass noun] N. Amer. fallen trees brought down by wind, storm, or other natural agency.

down time ▶ noun [mass noun] time during which a machine, especially a computer, is out of action or unavailable for use.
▪figurative, chiefly N. Amer. time when someone is not working or active: *everyone needs down time to unwind.*

down-to-earth ▶ adjective with no illusions or pretensions; practical and realistic: *a down-to-earth view of marriage.*
– DERIVATIVES **down-to-earthness** noun.

downtown chiefly N. Amer. ▶ adjective of, in, or characteristic of the central area or main business and commercial area of a town or city: *downtown Chicago* | *a downtown bar.*
▶ adverb in or into a such an area: *I drove downtown.*
▶ noun such an area of a town or city: *the heart of Pittsburgh's downtown.*
– DERIVATIVES **downtowner** noun.

downtrodden ▶ adjective oppressed or treated badly by people in power: *a downtrodden proletarian struggling for social justice.*

downturn ▶ noun a decline in economic, business, or other activity: *a downturn in the housing market.*
▶ verb [with obj.] [usu. as adj. **downturned**] turn (something) downwards: *his downturned mouth.*

down under informal ▶ adverb in or to Australia or New Zealand: *things are looking up down under.*
▶ noun (also **Down Under**) Australia and New Zealand: *a girl from down under.*
– ORIGIN late 19th cent.: with reference to the position of these countries on a globe.

downward ▶ adverb (also **downwards**) towards a lower place, point, or level: *he was lying face downward.*
▪used to indicate that something applies to everyone in a certain hierarchy or set: *new rules on sick leave affect employees of all grades, from managers downwards.*
▶ adjective moving or leading towards a lower place or level: *the downward curve of the stairs* | *a downward trend in inflation.*
– ORIGIN Middle English: shortening of Old English *adūnweard.*

downwardly ▶ adverb towards a lower level; in a downward direction.
– PHRASES **downwardly mobile** see **MOBILE**.

downwarp /ˈdaʊnwɔːp/ Geology ▶ noun a broad depression of the earth's surface.
▶ verb [with obj.] displace (a rock formation) downwards so as to form such a depression.

downwash ▶ noun [mass noun] the downward deflection of an airstream by an aircraft wing or helicopter rotor blade.

downwelling ▶ noun [mass noun] the downward movement of fluid, especially in the sea, the atmosphere, or deep in the earth.
▶ adjective characterized by or undergoing such movement: *downwelling mantle.*

downwind ▶ adverb & adjective in the direction in which the wind is blowing: [as adv.] *warnings were issued to people living downwind of the fire* | [as adj.] *downwind landings.*

downy ▶ adjective (**downier**, **downiest**) **1** covered with fine soft hair or feathers: *the baby's downy cheek.*
▪filled with soft feathers: *a downy pillow.* ▪soft and fluffy: *pale downy hair.*
2 informal (of a person) shrewd; sharp: *I told you she was a downy one.*
– DERIVATIVES **downily** adverb, **downiness** noun.

downy mildew ▶ noun [mass noun] mildew on a plant which is marked by a whitish down composed of spore-forming hyphae, penetrating more deeply into the plant than powdery mildew.
• Family Peronosporaceae, subdivision Mastigomycotina.

downzone ▶ verb [with obj.] N. Amer. assign (land or property) to a zoning grade under which the permitted density of housing and development is reduced.

dowry /ˈdaʊ(ə)ri/ ▶ noun (pl. **-ies**) property or money brought by a bride to her husband on their marriage.
– ORIGIN Middle English (denoting a widow's life interest in her husband's estate): from Anglo-Norman French *dowarie*, from medieval Latin *dotarium* (see **DOWER**).

dowry death ▶ noun (in the Indian subcontinent) the murder or suicide of a married woman caused by a dispute over her dowry.

dowse¹ /daʊz/ ▶ verb [no obj.] practise dowsing: *water is easy to dowse for.*
■ [with obj.] search for or discover by dowsing: *he dowsed a spiral of energy on the stone.*
– DERIVATIVES **dowser** noun.
– ORIGIN late 17th cent.: of unknown origin.

dowse² ▶ verb variant spelling of **DOUSE**.

dowsing ▶ noun [mass noun] a technique for searching for underground water, minerals, ley lines, or anything invisible, by observing the motion of a pointer (traditionally a forked stick, now often paired bent wires) or the changes in direction of a pendulum, supposedly in response to unseen influences: [as modifier] *a dowsing rod.*

Dowson /ˈdaʊs(ə)n/, Ernest (Christopher) (1867–1900), English poet, associated with the 'decadent' school of Oscar Wilde and Aubrey Beardsley. His two books of poems, *Verses* (1896) and *Decorations* (1899), deal with themes of ennui and world-weariness.

doxastic /dɒkˈsastɪk/ ▶ adjective Philosophy of or relating to an individual's beliefs: *doxastic worlds.*
– ORIGIN late 18th cent.: from Greek *doxastikos* 'conjectural', from *doxazein* 'to conjecture'.

doxology /dɒkˈsɒlədʒi/ ▶ noun (pl. **-ies**) a liturgical formula of praise to God.
– DERIVATIVES **doxological** adjective.
– ORIGIN mid 17th cent.: via medieval Latin from Greek *doxologia*, from *doxa* 'appearance, glory' (from *dokein* 'seem') + *-logia* (see **-LOGY**).

doxorubicin /ˌdɒksəʊˈruːbɪsɪn/ ▶ noun [mass noun] Medicine a bacterial antibiotic that is widely used to treat leukaemia and various other forms of cancer.
● This is produced by the streptomycete bacterium *Streptomyces peucetius caesius.*
– ORIGIN 1970s: from *deoxy-* (in the sense 'that has lost oxygen') + Latin *rubus* 'red' + **-MYCIN**.

doxy /ˈdɒksi/ ▶ noun (pl. **-ies**) archaic a lover or mistress.
■ a prostitute.
– ORIGIN mid 16th cent. (originally slang): of unknown origin.

doxycycline /ˌdɒksɪˈsaɪkliːn/ ▶ noun [mass noun] Medicine a broad-spectrum antibiotic of the tetracycline group, which has a long half-life in the body.
– ORIGIN 1960s: from *d(e)oxy-* + **TETRACYCLINE**.

doyen /ˈdɔɪɛn, ˈdwɑːjɑ̃/ ▶ noun the most respected or prominent person in a particular field: *he became the doyen of British physicists.*
– ORIGIN late 17th cent.: via French from Old French *deien* (see **DEAN**¹).

doyenne /ˈdɔɪɛn, dɔɪˈɛn, dwɑːˈjɛn/ ▶ noun a woman who is the most respected or prominent person in a particular field: *she became a doyenne of the London Irish music scene.*
– ORIGIN mid 19th cent.: from French, feminine of *doyen* (see **DOYEN**).

Doyenne du Comice /ˈdɔɪɛn d(j)uː kɒˈmiːs, dɔɪˈɛn, dwɑːˈjɛn/ ▶ noun fuller term for **COMICE**.

Doyle /dɔɪl/, Sir Arthur Conan (1859–1930), Scottish novelist and short-story writer, chiefly remembered for his creation of the private detective Sherlock Holmes. Holmes first appeared (with his friend Dr Watson, the narrator of the stories) in *A Study in Scarlet* (1887), and featured in more than fifty stories and in novels such as *The Hound of the Baskervilles* (1902).

D'Oyly Carte /ˌdɔɪlɪ ˈkɑːt/, Richard (1844–1901), English impresario and producer. He brought together the librettist Sir W. S. Gilbert and the composer Sir Arthur Sullivan, producing many of their operettas in London's Savoy Theatre, which he had established in 1881.

doz. ▶ abbreviation for dozen.

doze ▶ verb [no obj.] sleep lightly: *he found his mother dozing by the fire.*
■ (**doze off**) fall lightly asleep: *I dozed off for a few seconds.*
▶ noun [in sing.] a short light sleep.
– ORIGIN mid 17th cent. (in the sense 'stupefy, bewilder, or make drowsy'): perhaps related to Danish *døse* 'make drowsy'.

dozen ▶ noun **1** (pl. same) a group or set of twelve: *a dozen bottles of sherry.*
■ (**dozens**) informal a lot: *she has dozens of admirers.*
2 (**the dozens**) an exchange of insults engaged in as a game or ritual among black Americans.
– PHRASES **by the dozen** in large quantities. **talk nineteen to the dozen** Brit. talk incessantly.
– DERIVATIVES **dozenth** adjective.
– ORIGIN Middle English: from Old French *dozeine*, based on Latin *duodecim* 'twelve'.

dozer ▶ noun informal short for **BULLDOZER**.

dozy ▶ adjective (**dozier**, **doziest**) feeling drowsy and lazy: *he grew dozy at the end of a long day.*
■ Brit. informal sluggish and not alert; stupid: *at breakfast, a dozy waitress missing the wrong things.*
– DERIVATIVES **dozily** adverb, **doziness** noun.

DP ▶ abbreviation for ■ data processing. ■ displaced person.

dpc ▶ abbreviation for damp-proof course.

DPhil ▶ abbreviation for Doctor of Philosophy.

dpi Computing ▶ abbreviation for dots per inch, a measure of the resolution of printers, scanners, etc.

dpm ▶ abbreviation for damp-proof membrane, a sheet of material used to make a structure such as a solid concrete floor damp-proof.

DPP ▶ abbreviation for (in the UK) Director of Public Prosecutions.

DPT ▶ abbreviation for diphtheria, pertussis (whooping cough), and tetanus, a combined vaccine given to small children.

Dr ▶ abbreviation for ■ debit. [ORIGIN: formerly representing *debtor.*] ■ (as a title) Doctor: *Dr Michael Russell.* ■ (in street names) Drive.

dr. ▶ abbreviation for ■ drachm or drachms. ■ drachma or drachmas. ■ dram or drams.

drab¹ ▶ adjective (**drabber**, **drabbest**) **1** lacking brightness or interest; drearily dull: *the landscape was drab and grey* | *her drab suburban existence.*
2 of a dull light brown colour: *drab camouflage uniforms.*
▶ noun [mass noun] fabric of a dull brownish colour.
■ (**drabs**) clothes, especially trousers, made of such fabric: *a young man dressed in drabs.*
– DERIVATIVES **drably** adverb, **drabness** noun.
– ORIGIN mid 16th cent. (as a noun denoting undyed cloth): probably from Old French *drap* 'cloth' (see **DRAPE**).

drab² ▶ noun archaic **1** a slovenly woman.
2 a prostitute.
– ORIGIN early 16th cent.: perhaps related to Low German *drabbe* 'mire' and Dutch *drab* 'dregs'.

Drabble, Margaret (b.1939), English novelist, the younger sister of A. S. Byatt. Notable works: *The Millstone* (1966), *The Ice Age* (1977), and *The Radiant Way* (1987).

drabble ▶ verb archaic make or become wet and dirty by movement into or through muddy water.
– ORIGIN Middle English: from Low German *drabbelen* 'paddle in water or mire', from *drabbe* 'mire'.

dracaena /drəˈsiːnə/ ▶ noun a tropical palm-like shrub or tree with ornamental foliage, popular as a greenhouse or indoor plant.
● Genera *Dracaena* and *Cordyline*, family Agavaceae. See also **DRAGON TREE**.
– ORIGIN modern Latin, from Greek *drakaina*, feminine of *drakōn* 'serpent, dragon' (the genus *Dracaena* includes *Dracaena draco*, the dragon tree).

drachm /dram/ (abbrev.: **dr.**) ▶ noun a unit of weight formerly used by apothecaries, equivalent to 60 grains or one eighth of an ounce.
■ (also **fluid drachm**) a liquid measure formerly used by apothecaries, equivalent to 60 minims or one eighth of a fluid ounce.
– ORIGIN late Middle English (denoting the ancient Greek drachma): from Old French *dragme* or late Latin *dragma*, via Greek *drakhmē* (see **DRACHMA**).

drachma /ˈdrakmə/ ▶ noun (pl. **drachmas** or **drachmae** /-miː/) (until the introduction of the euro in 2002) the basic monetary unit of Greece, notionally equal to 100 lepta.
■ a silver coin of ancient Greece.
– ORIGIN via Latin from Greek *drakhmē*, an Attic weight and coin. Compare with **DIRHAM** and **DRACHM**.

drack /drak/ ▶ adjective Austral./NZ informal (especially of a woman) unattractive or unwelcome.
■ dreary and dull.
▶ noun an unattractive or unwelcome woman.
– ORIGIN said to be from the name of the 1930s film *Dracula's Daughter*, but possibly related to slang *dreck* 'rubbish', from Yiddish *drek* 'filth, dregs'.

Draco¹ /ˈdreɪkəʊ/ Astronomy a large northern constellation (the Dragon), stretching around the north celestial pole and said to represent the dragon killed by Hercules. It has no bright stars.
■ [as genitive **Draconis** /drəˈkəʊnɪs/] used with preceding letter or numeral to designate a star in this constellation: *the star Gamma Draconis.*
– ORIGIN Latin.

Draco² /ˈdreɪkəʊ/ (7th century BC), Athenian legislator. His codification of Athenian law was notorious for its severity in that the death penalty was imposed even for trivial crimes.

dracone /ˈdrakəʊn/ ▶ noun a large flexible sausage-shaped container used for transporting oil and other liquids on water.
– ORIGIN 1950s: from Latin *draco, dracon-*, from Greek *drakōn* 'serpent' (because of its shape).

draconian /drəˈkəʊnɪən, dreɪ-/ ▶ adjective (of laws or their application) excessively harsh and severe.
– DERIVATIVES **draconic** /-ˈkɒnɪk/ adjective.
– ORIGIN late 19th cent.: from the Greek name *Drakōn* (see **DRACO**²) + **-IAN**.

Dracula /ˈdrakjʊlə/ the Transylvanian vampire in Bram Stoker's novel *Dracula* (1897).
– ORIGIN variant of *Drakula, Dragwlya*, names given to Vlad Ţepeş (Vlad the Impaler), a 15th-cent. prince of Wallachia renowned for his cruelty.

draegerman /ˈdreɪgəmən/ ▶ noun (pl. **-men**) Canadian a member of a crew trained for underground rescue work.
– ORIGIN early 20th cent.: the first element from the name of A. B. *Dräger* (1870–1928), German inventor of a type of breathing apparatus.

draff /draf/ ▶ noun [mass noun] poetic/literary dregs or refuse.
– ORIGIN Middle English: perhaps from an unrecorded Old English word related to German *Treber, Träber* 'husks, grains', and perhaps also to **DRIVEL**.

draft ▶ noun **1** a preliminary version of a piece of writing: *the first draft of the party's manifesto* | [as modifier] *a draft document.*
■ a plan, sketch, or rough drawing. ■ [mass noun] Computing a mode of operation of a printer in which text is produced rapidly but with relatively low definition.
2 a written order to pay a specified sum.
3 (**the draft**) US compulsory recruitment for military service: *25 million men were subject to the draft.*
■ N. Amer. a procedure whereby new or existing sports players are made available for selection or reselection by the teams in a league, usually with the earlier choices being given to the weaker teams. ■ rare a group or individual selected from a larger group for a special duty, e.g. for military service.
4 US spelling of **DRAUGHT**.
▶ verb [with obj.] **1** prepare a preliminary version of (a text): *I drafted a letter of resignation.*
2 select (a person or group of people) and bring them somewhere for a certain purpose: *riot police were drafted in to break up the blockade.*
■ US conscript (someone) for military service. ■ N. Amer. select (a player) for a sports team through the draft.
– DERIVATIVES **drafter** noun.
– ORIGIN mid 16th cent.: phonetic spelling of **DRAUGHT**.

draft dodger ▶ noun N. Amer. derogatory a person who has avoided compulsory military service.
– DERIVATIVES **draft dodging** noun.

draftee ▶ noun chiefly US a person conscripted for military service.

draft pick ▶ noun N. Amer. the right of a sports team to select a player during the annual selection process.
■ a player selected during the draft.

draftsman ▶ noun (pl. **-men**) **1** a person who drafts legal documents.
2 chiefly N. Amer. variant spelling of **DRAUGHTSMAN**.

drafty ▶ adjective US spelling of **DRAUGHTY**.

drag ▶ verb (**dragged**, **dragging**) **1** [with obj. and adverbial of direction] pull (someone or something) along forcefully, roughly, or with difficulty: *we dragged the boat up the beach* | figurative *I dragged my eyes away.*
■ take (someone) to or from a place or event, despite their reluctance: *my girlfriend is dragging me off to Rhodes for a week.* ■ (**drag oneself**) go somewhere wearily, reluctantly, or with difficulty: *I have to drag myself out of bed each day.* ■ move (an icon or other image) across a computer screen using a tool such as a mouse. ■ [no obj.] (of a person's clothes or an animal's tail) trail along the ground: *the nuns walked in meditation, their habits dragging on the grassy verge.* ■ [no obj.] (**drag at**) catch hold of and pull (something): *desperately, Jinny dragged at his arm.* ■ [with obj.] (of a ship) trail (an anchor) along the seabed, causing the ship to drift. ■ [no obj.] (of an anchor) fail to hold, causing a ship or boat to drift. ■ [with obj.] search the bottom of (a river, lake, or the sea) with grapnels or nets: *frogmen had dragged the local river.*
2 [with obj.] (**drag something up**) informal deliberately mention an unwelcome or unpleasant fact: *pieces of evidence about his early life were dragged up.*
■ (**drag someone/thing into**) involve someone or something in (a situation or matter), typically when such involvement is inappropriate or unnecessary: *he had no right to drag you into this sort of thing.* ■ (**drag something in/into**) introduce an irrelevant or inappropriate subject: *politics were never dragged into the conversation.* ■ (**drag someone/thing down**) bring someone or something to a lower level or standard: *the economy will be dragged down by inefficient firms.*
3 [no obj.] (of time, events, or activities) pass slowly and tediously: *the day dragged—eventually it was time for bed.*
■ (of a process or situation) continue at tedious and unnecessary length: *the dispute between the two families **dragged on** for some years.* ■ [with obj.] (**drag something out**) protract something unnecessarily: *he dragged out the process of serving them.*
4 [no obj.] (**drag on**) informal (of a person) inhale the smoke from (a cigarette).
▶ noun **1** [mass noun] the action of pulling something forcefully or with difficulty: *the drag of the current.*
■ the longitudinal retarding force exerted by air or other fluid surrounding a moving object. ■ [in sing.] a person or thing that impedes progress or development: *Larry was turning out to be **a drag on** her career.* ■ Angling unnatural motion of a fishing fly caused by the pull of the line. ■ [count noun] archaic an iron shoe that can be applied as a brake to the wheel of a cart or wagon.
2 [in sing.] informal a boring or tiresome person or thing: *working nine to five can be a drag.*
3 informal an act of inhaling smoke from a cigarette: *he **took a** long **drag on** his cigarette.*
4 [mass noun] clothing more conventionally worn by the opposite sex, especially women's clothes worn by a man: *a fashion show, complete with men **in drag*** | [as modifier] *a live drag show.*
5 short for **DRAG RACE**.
■ informal a street or road: *the effect is like cruising along a drag in your car* | *the main drag.* ■ Brit. informal, dated a car: *a stately great drag with a smart chauffeur.* ■ historical a private vehicle like a stagecoach, drawn by four horses.
6 a thing that is pulled along the ground or through water, in particular:
■ historical a harrow used for breaking up the surface of land. ■ an apparatus for dredging a river or for recovering the bodies of drowned people from a river, a lake, or the sea. ■ another term for **DRAGNET**.
7 [mass noun] N. Amer. informal influence over other people: *they had the education but they didn't have the drag.*
8 a strong-smelling lure drawn before hounds as a substitute for a fox.
■ a hunt using such a lure.
9 Music one of the basic patterns (rudiments) of drumming, consisting of a stroke preceded by two grace notes which are usually played with the other stick. See also **RUFF**⁴.
– PHRASES **drag one's feet** walk slowly and wearily or with difficulty. ■ (also **drag one's heels**) figurative (of a person or organization) be deliberately slow or reluctant to act: *the government has dragged its heels over permanent legislation.* **drag someone/thing through the mud** make damaging allegations about someone or something: *he felt enough loyalty to his old school not to drag its name through the mud.*
– ORIGIN Middle English: from Old English *dragan* or Old Norse *draga* 'to draw'; the noun partly from Middle Low German *dragge* 'grapnel'.
▶ **drag up** informal dress up in clothes more conventionally worn by the opposite sex.
drag someone up Brit. informal bring up a child badly: *would you have her dragged up by a succession of au pairs?*

drag-anchor ▶ noun another term for **SEA ANCHOR**.

drag-and-drop Computing ▶ verb [with obj.] move (an icon or other image) to another part of the screen using a mouse or similar device, typically in order to perform some operation on a file or document.
▶ adjective of, relating to, or permitting the movement of images in this way: *drag-and-drop transfer of messages.*

drag chain ▶ noun a chain used to retard or steady the motion of a vehicle.

dragée /ˈdrɑːʒeɪ/ ▶ noun a sweet consisting of a centre covered with a coating, such as a sugared almond or a chocolate.
■ a small silver ball for decorating a cake.
– ORIGIN late 17th cent. (also denoting a mixture of spices): French, from Old French *dragie* (see **DREDGE**²).

dragger ▶ noun N. Amer. a fishing boat that uses a dragnet.

dragging brush ▶ noun another term for **FLOGGER** (in sense 2).

draggle ▶ verb [with obj.] make (something) dirty or wet, typically by trailing it through mud or water: [as adj. **draggled**] *she wore a draggled skirt.*
■ [no obj.] hang untidily: *red hairs draggled dispiritedly from her chignon.* ■ [no obj.] archaic trail behind others; lag behind: *they draggled at the heels of his troop.*
– ORIGIN early 16th cent.: diminutive and frequentative of **DRAG**.

draggle-tailed ▶ adjective archaic having untidily trailing skirts: *a draggle-tailed wench.*

draggy ▶ adjective (**draggier**, **draggiest**) informal dreary and lacking liveliness: *a long, draggy, boring Friday afternoon.*

drag hound ▶ noun a hound used to hunt with a drag.

drag lift ▶ noun a type of ski lift which pulls skiers up a slope on their skis.

dragline ▶ noun **1** a large excavator with a bucket pulled in by a wire cable.
2 a line of silk produced by a spider and acting as a safety line or (in newly hatched spiderlings) a parachute.

dragnet ▶ noun a net drawn through a river or across ground to trap fish or game.
■ figurative a systematic search for someone or something, especially criminals or criminal activity.

dragoman /ˈdragə(ʊ)mən/ ▶ noun (pl. **dragomans** or **dragomen**) an interpreter or guide, especially in countries speaking Arabic, Turkish, or Persian.
– ORIGIN late Middle English: from obsolete French, from Italian *dragomanno*, from medieval Greek *dragoumanos*, from Arabic *tarjumān* 'interpreter'.

dragon ▶ noun **1** a mythical monster like a giant reptile. In European tradition the dragon is typically fire-breathing and tends to symbolize chaos or evil, whereas in the Far East it is usually a beneficent symbol of fertility, associated with water and the heavens.
■ derogatory a fierce and intimidating woman: *his wife is a real dragon.*
2 (also **flying dragon**) another term for **FLYING LIZARD**.
■ Austral. any lizard of the agama family. ■ see **KOMODO DRAGON**.
– ORIGIN Middle English (also denoting a large serpent): from Old French, via Latin from Greek *drakōn* 'serpent'.

dragon arum ▶ noun an arum of the eastern Mediterranean, with a deep purple spathe and spadix and an unpleasant smell.
● *Dracunculus vulgaris*, family Araceae.
■ any of a number of other plants of the arum family, in particular the North American green dragon.

dragon boat ▶ noun a boat of a traditional Chinese design, typically decorated to resemble a dragon, propelled with paddles by a large crew and used for racing.

dragonet /ˈdrag(ə)nɪt/ ▶ noun a marine fish which often lies partly buried in the seabed. The male is brightly coloured.
● Two genera in the family Callionymidae: several species, in particular the European *Callionymus lyra*.
– ORIGIN Middle English (denoting a small dragon): from Old French, diminutive of *dragon* 'dragon'.

dragonfish ▶ noun (pl. same or **-fishes**) a deep-sea fish with a long slender body:
● a fish with fang-like teeth, a barbel on the chin, and luminous organs on the body (families Stomiatidae and Idiacanthidae).
● (**Antarctic dragonfish**) a fish of southern polar seas with a flattened head (family Bathydraconidae).

dragonfly ▶ noun (pl. **-flies**) a fast-flying long-bodied predatory insect with two pairs of large transparent wings which are spread out sideways at rest. The voracious aquatic larvae take up to five years to reach adulthood. Compare with **DAMSELFLY**.
● Suborder Anisoptera, order Odonata: several families.

dragonnade /ˌdragəˈneɪd/ ▶ noun one of a series of persecutions directed by Louis XIV against French Protestants, in which troops were quartered upon them.
– ORIGIN early 18th cent.: from French, from *dragon* 'dragon' (see **DRAGOON**).

dragon's blood ▶ noun [mass noun] a red gum or powder that is derived from the fruit of certain palm trees and from the stem of the dragon tree and related plants.

dragon's head ▶ noun Astrology the ascending or north node of the moon's orbit, used in drawing up an astrological chart.

dragon ship ▶ noun a Viking longship ornamented with a beaked prow.

dragon's tail ▶ noun Astrology the descending or south node of the moon's orbit, used in drawing up an astrological chart.

dragon's teeth ▶ plural noun Brit. informal concrete obstacles pointing upwards from the ground in rows, used against tanks in the Second World War.
– PHRASES **sow** (or **plant**) **dragon's teeth** take action that is intended to prevent trouble, but which actually brings it about.
– ORIGIN with allusion to the teeth of the dragon killed by Cadmus.

dragon tree ▶ noun a slow-growing palm-like tree of the agave family, which is native to the Canary Islands and yields dragon's blood.
● *Dracaena draco*, family Agavaceae.

dragoon /drəˈguːn/ ▶ noun **1** a member of any of several cavalry regiments in the household troops of the British army.
■ historical a mounted infantryman armed with a carbine.
2 a pigeon of a variety resulting from a cross between a horseman and a tumbler.
▶ verb [with obj.] coerce (someone) into doing something: *she had been **dragooned into** helping with the housework.*
– ORIGIN early 17th cent. (denoting a kind of carbine or musket, thought of as breathing fire): from French *dragon* 'dragon'.

drag queen ▶ noun a man who dresses up in women's clothes, typically for the purposes of entertainment.

drag race ▶ noun a race between two cars over a short distance, usually a quarter of a mile, as a test of acceleration.
– DERIVATIVES **drag racer** noun, **drag racing** noun.

dragster ▶ noun a car built or modified to take part in drag races.

drail /dreɪl/ ▶ noun Angling a fish-hook and line weighted with lead for dragging below the surface of the water.
– ORIGIN late 16th cent. (denoting part of a plough): from the obsolete verb *drail*, an alteration of **TRAIL**.

drain ▶ verb [with obj.] **1** cause the water or other liquid in (something) to run out, leaving it empty, dry, or drier: *we drained the swimming pool.*
■ cause or allow (liquid) to run off or out of something: *fry the pork and **drain off** any excess fat.* ■ make (land) drier by providing channels for water to flow away in: *the land was drained and the boggy ground reclaimed.* ■ (of a river) carry off the superfluous water from (a district): *the stream drains a wide moorland above the waterfall.* ■ [no obj., with adverbial of direction] (of water or another liquid) flow away from, out of, or into something: *the river drains into the Pacific* | figurative *Polly felt the blood drain from her face.* ■ [no obj.] become dry or drier as liquid runs off or

away: *dishes left to drain | the plant should be watered well and allowed to drain.* ■(of a person) drink the entire contents of (a glass or other container): *he seized the Scotch set before him and drained it.* ■[no obj., with adverbial] figurative (of a feeling or emotion) become progressively less strongly felt: *gradually the tension and stress **drained away**.*
2 deprive of strength or vitality: *his limbs were **drained of** all energy | Ruth slumped down in her seat, drained by all that had happened.*
■cause (money, energy, or another valuable resource) to be lost, wasted, or used up: *my mother's hospital bills are draining my income.* ■[no obj., with adverbial] (of such a resource) be lost, wasted, or used up: *votes and campaign funds drained away from the Republican candidate.*
3 Golf, informal (of a player) hole (a putt).
▶**noun 1** a channel or pipe carrying off surplus liquid, especially rainwater or liquid waste.
■a tube for drawing off accumulating fluid from a body cavity or an abscess. ■Electronics the part of a field-effect transistor to which the charge carriers flow after passing the gate.
2 [in sing.] a thing that uses up a particular resource: *nuclear power is **a** serious **drain on** the public purse.*
■the continuous loss or expenditure of a particular resource: *the drain of talented staff to the United States.*
– PHRASES **go down the drain** informal be totally wasted: *the government must stop public money going down the drain.*
– ORIGIN Old English *drēahnian, drēhnian* 'strain (liquid)', of Germanic origin; related to **DRY**.

drainage ▶**noun** [mass noun] the action or process of draining something: *the pot must have holes in the base for good drainage | the drainage of wetlands.*
■the means of removing surplus water or liquid waste; a system of drains.

drainboard ▶**noun** North American term for **DRAINING BOARD**.

draincock ▶**noun** a valve for draining the water from a boiler.

drainer ▶**noun** a device used to drain things, in particular a rack placed on a draining board to hold crockery while it drains.
■a draining board. ■a person who drains a flooded area.

draining board ▶**noun** Brit. a sloping grooved board or surface, on which washed dishes are left to drain into an adjacent sink.

drainpipe ▶**noun** a pipe for carrying off rainwater or liquid refuse from a building.
■(**drainpipes** or **drainpipe trousers**) trousers with very narrow legs.

Draize test ▶**noun** a pharmacological test in which a substance is introduced into the eye or applied to the skin of a laboratory animal in order to ascertain the likely effect of that substance on the corresponding human tissue.
– ORIGIN 1970s: named after John H. *Draize* (1900–92), the American pharmacologist who helped to develop this type of test.

Drake, Sir Francis (*c.*1540–96), English sailor and explorer. He was the first Englishman to circumnavigate the globe (1577–80), in his ship the *Golden Hind*. He played an important part in the defeat of the Spanish Armada.

drake[1] ▶**noun** a male duck: [as modifier] *a drake mallard.*
– ORIGIN Middle English: of West Germanic origin; related to Low German *drake* and German *Enterich*.

drake[2] ▶**noun** (in fishing) a natural or artificial mayfly, especially a subadult or a gravid female.
– ORIGIN Old English *draca*, from Latin *draco* 'dragon'.

Drake equation Astronomy a speculative equation which gives an estimate of the likelihood of discovering intelligent extraterrestrial life in the galaxy, expressed as the product of a series of factors such as the number of stars, the fraction of stars with planets, the fraction of planets on which life evolves, the average lifetime of a civilization, etc. It was formulated by the US astronomer Frank Drake in 1961.

Drakensberg Mountains /ˈdrɑːkənzˌbəːɡ/ a range of mountains in southern Africa, stretching in a NE–SW direction for a distance of 1,126 km (700 miles) through Lesotho and parts of South Africa. The highest peak is Thabana Ntlenyana (3,482 m, 11,425 ft).

Drake Passage an area of ocean, noted for its violent storms, connecting the South Atlantic with the South Pacific and separating the southern tip of South America (Cape Horn) from the Antarctic Peninsula.
– ORIGIN named after Sir Francis **DRAKE**.

Dralon /ˈdreɪlɒn/ ▶**noun** [mass noun] trademark, chiefly Brit. a synthetic textile made from acrylic fibre and used for curtains and upholstery.
– ORIGIN 1950s: on the pattern of *nylon*.

DRAM ▶**noun** Electronics a memory chip that depends upon an applied voltage to keep the stored data.
– ORIGIN acronym from *dynamic random-access memory*.

dram[1] /dram/ ▶**noun 1** a small drink of whisky or other spirits (often used in humorous imitation of Scottish speech): *a wee dram to ward off the winter chill.*
2 another term for **DRACHM**.
– ORIGIN late Middle English (in sense 2): from Old French *drame* or medieval Latin *drama*, variants of *dragme* and *dragma* (see **DRACHM**).

dram[2] /drɑːm/ ▶**noun** the basic monetary unit of Armenia, equal to 100 luma.

drama ▶**noun 1** a play for theatre, radio, or television: *a gritty urban drama about growing up in Harlem.*
■[mass noun] such works as a genre or style of literature: *Renaissance drama.*
2 an exciting, emotional, or unexpected series of events or set of circumstances: *a hostage drama |* [mass noun] *an afternoon of high drama at Wembley.*
– PHRASES **make a drama out of** informal exaggerate the importance of (a minor problem or incident).
– ORIGIN early 16th cent.: via late Latin from Greek *drama*, from *dran* 'do, act'.

drama-documentary ▶**noun** a television film based on real events.

Dramamine /ˈdraməmiːn/ ▶**noun** [mass noun] trademark an antihistamine compound used to counter nausea (especially travel sickness), also used as a recreational drug.
– ORIGIN 1940s: from *dram-* (of unknown origin) + **AMINE**.

dramatic ▶**adjective 1** [attrib.] of or relating to drama or the performance or study of drama: *the dramatic arts | a dramatic society.*
2 (of an event or circumstance) sudden and striking: *a dramatic increase in recorded crime.*
■exciting or impressive: *he recalled his dramatic escape from the building | dramatic mountain peaks.* ■(of a person or their behaviour) intending or intended to create an effect; theatrical: *with a dramatic gesture, she put a hand to her brow.*
– DERIVATIVES **dramatically** adverb.
– ORIGIN late 16th cent.: via late Latin from Greek *dramatikos*, from *drama, dramat-* (see **DRAMA**).

dramatic irony ▶**noun** see **IRONY**[1].

dramatic monologue ▶**noun** a poem in the form of a speech or narrative by an imagined person, in which the speaker inadvertently reveals aspects of their character while describing a particular situation or series of events.

dramatics ▶**plural noun 1** [often treated as sing.] the study or practice of acting in and producing plays: *amateur dramatics.*
2 theatrically exaggerated or overemotional behaviour: *cut out the dramatics.*

dramatis personae /ˌdramətɪs pəːˈsəʊnʌɪ, -niː/ ▶**plural noun** the characters of a play, novel, or narrative.
■the participants in a series of events.
– ORIGIN mid 18th cent.: from Latin, literally 'persons of the drama'.

dramatist ▶**noun** a person who writes plays.

dramatize (also **-ise**) ▶**verb** [with obj.] adapt (a novel) or present (a particular incident) as a play or film: *a thriller dramatized from the novel by Joan Smith.*
■present in a vivid or striking way: *he told his story in order to dramatize the problem of evil.* ■exaggerate the seriousness or importance of (an incident or situation): *she had a tendency to dramatize things.*
– DERIVATIVES **dramatization** /-ˈzeɪʃ(ə)n/ noun.

dramaturge /ˈdramətəːdʒ/ (also **dramaturg**) ▶**noun 1** a dramatist.
2 a literary editor on the staff of a theatre who liaises with authors and edits texts.
– ORIGIN mid 19th cent.: via French and German from Greek *dramatourgos*, from *drama, dramat-* 'drama' + *-ergos* 'worker'.

dramaturgy /ˈdraməˌtəːdʒi/ ▶**noun** [mass noun] the theory and practice of dramatic composition: *studies of Shakespeare's dramaturgy.*
– DERIVATIVES **dramaturgic** adjective, **dramaturgical** adjective, **dramaturgically** adverb.

Drambuie /dramˈbuːi, -ˈbjuːi/ ▶**noun** [mass noun] trademark a sweet Scotch whisky liqueur.
– ORIGIN from Scottish Gaelic *dram buidheach* 'satisfying drink'.

Drammen /ˈdrɑːmən/ a seaport in SE Norway, on an inlet of Oslofjord; pop. 51,900 (1991).

Drang nach Osten /ˌdraŋ nax ˈɒst(ə)n, German ˌdraŋ naːx ˈɔstn/ ▶**noun** the former German policy of eastward expansion, especially that espoused under Nazi rule.
– ORIGIN German, literally 'pressure towards the east'.

drank past of **DRINK**.

drape ▶**verb** [with obj. and adverbial] arrange (cloth or clothing) loosely or casually on or round something: *she draped a shawl around her shoulders.*
■(usu. **be draped**) adorn, cover, or wrap (someone or something) loosely with folds of cloth: *the body was draped in a blanket.* ■let (oneself or a part of one's body) rest somewhere in a casual or relaxed way: *he draped an arm around her shoulders.* ■[no obj.] (of fabric) hang or be able to hang in loose, graceful folds: *velvet drapes beautifully.*
▶**noun 1** (**drapes**) long curtains: *Katherine pulled back the heavy velvet drapes.*
■informal a man's suit consisting of a long jacket and narrow trousers, as worn by a Teddy boy. ■a cloth for covering parts of a patient's body other than that part on which a surgical operation is being performed.
2 [in sing.] the way in which a garment or fabric hangs: *by fixing the band lower down you obtain a fuller drape in the fabric.*
– ORIGIN mid 19th cent.: back-formation from **DRAPERY**, influenced by French *draper* 'to drape'. The noun senses date from the early 20th cent.

draper ▶**noun** Brit. dated a person who sells textile fabrics.
– ORIGIN late Middle English (denoting a maker of woollen cloth): from Old French *drapier*, from *drap* 'cloth', from late Latin *drappus*.

drapery ▶**noun** (pl. **-ies**) [mass noun] cloth, curtains, or clothing hanging in loose folds: *the hall of the school was hung with green drapery |* (**draperies**) *a cot swathed in draperies and blue ribbons.*
■the artistic arrangement of clothing in sculpture or painting: *the effigy is notable for its flowing drapery.*
– ORIGIN Middle English (in the sense 'cloth, fabrics'): from Old French *draperie*, from *drap* 'cloth' (see **DRAPER**).

drastic /ˈdrastɪk, ˈdrɑː-/ ▶**adjective** likely to have a strong or far-reaching effect; radical and extreme: *a drastic reduction of staffing levels.*
– DERIVATIVES **drastically** adverb.
– ORIGIN late 17th cent. (originally applied to the effect of medicine): from Greek *drastikos*, from *dran* 'do'.

drat ▶**exclamation** (often **drat someone/something**) a fairly mild expression of anger or annoyance: *'Oh, drat Feargal and his suspicions!'*
– DERIVATIVES **dratted** adjective.
– ORIGIN early 19th cent.: shortening of *od rat*, euphemism for *God rot*.

draught /drɑːft/ (US **draft**) ▶**noun 1** a current of cool air in a room or other confined space: *heavy curtains at the windows cut out draughts.*
2 a single act of drinking or inhaling: *she downed the remaining beer in one draught.*
■the amount swallowed or inhaled in one such act: *he took deep draughts of oxygen into his lungs.* ■poetic/literary or archaic a quantity of a liquid with medicinal properties: *a sleeping draught.*
3 the depth of water needed to float a particular ship: *the shallow draught enabled her to get close inshore.*
4 the drawing in of a fishing net.
■the fish taken at one drawing; a catch.
▶**verb** variant spelling of **DRAFT**.
▶**adjective** [attrib.] **1** denoting beer or other drink which is kept in and served from a barrel or tank rather than from a bottle or can, especially when cask-conditioned: *draught ale.*
2 denoting an animal used for pulling heavy loads: *draught oxen.*
– PHRASES **feel the draught** informal experience an adverse change in one's financial circumstances:

the high street shops will feel the draught most keenly. **on draught** (of beer or other drink) ready to be drawn from a barrel or tank; not bottled or canned.
– ORIGIN Middle English (in the sense 'drawing, pulling'; also 'something drawn, a load'): from Old Norse *dráttr*, of Germanic origin; related to German *Tracht*, also to **DRAW**. Compare with **DRAFT**.

draughtboard ▶ **noun** Brit. a square chequered board of 64 small squares in alternating dark and light colours (conventionally called black-and-white) identical to a chessboard and used for playing draughts.

draughtproof ▶ **adjective** sealed so as to keep out draughts.
▶ **verb** [with obj.] make (a building, door, or window) draughtproof: *they could draughtproof and insulate your home for you.*

draughts ▶ **noun** Brit. a board game for two players, played on a chequered board. Each player starts with twelve disc-shaped pieces in three rows along one side of the board, and moves them diagonally with the aim of capturing all the opponent's pieces.
– ORIGIN late Middle English: from **DRAUGHT**; related to obsolete *draught* in the sense 'move' (in chess or any similar game); compare with French *trait*, from Latin *tractus* 'a dragging'.

draughtsman ▶ **noun** (pl. **-men**) **1** a person who makes detailed technical plans or drawings.
■ an artist skilled in drawing.
2 variant spelling of **DRAFTSMAN**.
– DERIVATIVES **draughtsmanship** noun.

draughtsperson (US **draftsperson**) ▶ **noun** (pl. **-people**) a draughtsman or draughtswoman (used as a neutral alternative).

draughtswoman ▶ **noun** (pl. **-women**) a woman who makes detailed technical plans or drawings.

draughty (US **drafty**) ▶ **adjective** (**draughtier**, **draughtiest**) (of an enclosed space) cold and uncomfortable because of currents of cool air: *anyone would get pneumonia living in that draughty old house.*
■ (of a door or window) ill-fitting, and so allowing currents of cool air in.
– DERIVATIVES **draughtily** adverb, **draughtiness** noun.

Dravidian /drəˈvɪdɪən/ ▶ **adjective** of, relating to, or denoting a family of languages spoken in southern India and Sri Lanka, or the peoples who speak them.
▶ **noun 1** [mass noun] this family of languages.
2 a member of any of the peoples speaking a Dravidian language.

Dravidian languages were once spoken throughout the Indian subcontinent, but were restricted to the south following the arrival of speakers of Indic languages c.1000 BC. Those still used, by over 160 million people, include Tamil, Kannada, Malayalam, and Telugu.

– ORIGIN from Sanskrit *drāviḍa* 'relating to the Tamils' (from *Draviḍa* 'Tamil') + **-IAN**.

draw ▶ **verb** (past **drew**; past participle **drawn**) [with obj.] **1** produce (a picture or diagram) by making lines and marks, especially with a pen or pencil, on paper: *he drew a map.*
■ produce an image of (someone or something) in such a way: *I asked her to draw me* | [no obj.] *you're at art college, you must be able to draw.* ■ trace or produce (a line or mark) on a surface: *she drew a wavering line down the board* | figurative *where will we draw the outer boundaries of this Europe?*
2 pull or drag (something such as a vehicle) so as to make it follow behind: *a cart drawn by two horses.*
■ [with obj. and adverbial of direction] pull or move (something) in a specified direction: *I drew back the blanket and uncovered the body.* ■ [with obj. and adverbial of direction] gently pull or guide (someone) in a specified direction: *'David,' she whispered, **drawing him aside**.* ■ [no obj., with adverbial of direction] move in a slow steady way: *the driver slowed as he drew level with me* | *the train drew in to the station.* ■ [no obj., with adverbial] come to or arrive at a point in time or a specified point in a process: *the campaign **drew to a close*** | *the time for the parade itself is **drawing near**.* ■ pull (curtains) shut or open: *do you want me to draw the curtains?* | *she **drew back** the curtains and looked out.* ■ make (wire) by pulling a piece of metal through successively smaller holes.
3 extract (an object or liquid) from a container or receptacle: *he drew his gun and peered into the gloomy apartment* | *a donkey wheel was built to draw water from the well* | *he **drew off** a pint of bitter* | [as adj. **drawn**] *he met them with a drawn sword.*
■ run (a bath): *she drew him a hot bath.* ■ (**draw something from**) obtain something from (a particular source): *an independent panel of judges drawn from members of the public* | *he draws inspiration from ordinary scenes and simple places.* ■ (**draw on**) use (one's experience, talents, or skills) as a resource: *Sue has a lot of past experience to draw on.* ■ obtain or withdraw (money) from a bank or other source. ■ Hunting search (cover) for game. ■ Bridge (of declarer) force the defenders to play (cards in a particular suit) by leading cards in that suit: *before establishing his diamonds, declarer must draw trumps.* ■ [no obj.] suck smoke from (a cigarette or pipe). ■ [no obj.] (of a chimney, flue, or fire) allow air to flow in and upwards freely, so that a fire can burn: *failure of a fire to draw properly can have a number of causes.* ■ take in (a breath): *Mrs Feather drew a long breath and let it out.* ■ [no obj.] (of tea) be left standing so that the flavour is extracted from the leaves: *a pot of tea is allowed to draw.* ■ disembowel: *after a mockery of a trial he was **hanged, drawn, and quartered**.*
4 be the cause of (a specified response): *he drew criticism for his lavish spending.*
■ attract (someone) to come to a place or an event: *you really drew the crowds with your playing* | *customers drawn in by the reductions.* ■ (usu. **be drawn**) induce (someone) to reveal or do something: *he refused to be **drawn on** what would happen if the two failed to reach agreement.* ■ direct or attract (someone's attention) to something: *it was an outrage and we had to draw people's attention to it.* ■ reach (a conclusion) by deduction or inference from a set of circumstances: *the moral to be drawn is that spending wins votes.* ■ formulate or perceive (a comparison or distinction): *the law drew a clear distinction between innocent and fraudulent misrepresentation.*
5 finish (a contest or game) with an even score: [with obj. and complement] *Brazil had drawn a stormy match 1–1* | [no obj., with complement] *they drew 0–0 in 1974* | [as adj. **drawn**] *a run of six drawn matches.*
6 Bowls cause (a bowl) to travel in a curve determined by its bias to the desired point.
■ Golf hit (the ball) so that it travels slightly to the left (for a left-handed player, the right), usually as a result of spin given to the ball.
7 (of a ship) require (a specified depth of water) to float in: *boats that draw only a few inches of water.*
8 [no obj.] (of a sail) be filled with wind.
▶ **noun 1** an act of selecting names randomly, typically by extracting them from a bag or other container, to match competitors in a sporting contest: *the draw has been made for this year's tournament.*
■ a raffle or lottery in which the winners are chosen in such a way: *their names were the first out of the hat in our **prize draw**.*
2 a game or match that ends with the scores even: *he scored twice to force a 4–4 draw.*
■ Cricket a game which is left incomplete for lack of time, regardless of the scores. Compare with **TIE**.
3 a person or thing that is very attractive or interesting: *the big city was a powerful draw to youngsters.*
4 an act of inhaling smoke from a cigarette: *she took a long draw on her cigarette.*
■ [mass noun] informal cannabis: *they're dropping Es and smoking draw.*
5 an act of removing a gun from its holster in order to shoot.
6 Golf a shot causing the ball to deviate to the left (or, for a left-handed golfer, the right).
– PHRASES **draw a bead on** see **BEAD**. **draw a blank** see **BLANK**. **draw blood** cause someone to bleed, especially in the course of a fight: *the blow drew blood from the corner of his mouth* | figurative *she knew she'd drawn blood when the smile faded from his face.* **draw someone's fire** attract hostile criticism away from a more important target: *the concession will go some way to draw the fire of the government's critics.* **draw the line at** set a limit of what one is willing to do or accept, beyond which one will not go: *she drew the line at prostitution.* **draw lots** see **LOT**. **draw the short straw** see **STRAW**. **draw stumps** Cricket take the stumps out of the ground at close of play. **quick on the draw** very fast in taking one's gun from its holster. ■ figurative very fast in acting or reacting.
– ORIGIN Old English *dragan*, of Germanic origin; related to Dutch *dragen* and German *tragen*, also to **DRAUGHT**.
▶ **draw back** choose not to do something that one was expected to do: *the government has drawn back from attempting reform.*
draw in (of successive days) become shorter because of the changing seasons. ■ (of a day) approach its end. ■ (of successive evenings or nights) start earlier because of the changing seasons: *the nights were drawing in fast.*
draw on (of a period of time) pass by and approach its end: *he remembered sitting in silence with his grandmother as evening drew on.*
draw something on put an item of clothing on: *he drew on his dressing gown.*
draw out (of successive days) become longer because of the changing seasons.
draw someone out gently or subtly persuade someone to talk or become more expansive: *she drew me out and flattered me.*
draw something out make something last longer: *the transition was long and drawn out.*
draw up come to a halt: *drivers drew up at the lights.*
draw something up prepare a plan, proposal, agreement, or other document in detail: *they instructed an attorney to draw up a sales agreement.*
draw oneself up make oneself stand in a stiffly upright manner: *Sarah drew herself up, full of indignation that he should presume to judge her.*

drawback ▶ **noun 1** a feature that renders something less acceptable; a disadvantage or problem: *the main drawback of fitting catalytic converters is the cost.*
2 (also **duty drawback**) an amount of excise or import duty remitted on goods exported.

drawbar ▶ **noun 1** a bar on a vehicle to which something can be attached to pull it or be pulled.
2 a bar in a structure that can be removed to allow someone through or to let other parts move.
3 one of a number of bars that may be pulled out to control harmonics on an electric organ.

drawbridge ▶ **noun** historical a bridge, especially one over a castle's moat, which is hinged at one end so that it may be raised to prevent people crossing or to allow vessels to pass under it.

drawcard ▶ **noun** informal a quality or feature that evokes interest or liking; an attraction: *most described natural beauty as the country's main drawcard.*

drawcord ▶ **noun** another term for **DRAWSTRING**.

drawdown ▶ **noun** a reduction in the size or presence of a military force: *the unit is the first to leave Germany as part of the drawdown.*
■ a reduction in the volume of water in a lake or reservoir. ■ a withdrawal of oil or other commodity from stocks: *consumption grew, resulting in a 180,000-tonne drawdown in stocks.* ■ an act of drawing on available loan facilities.

drawee /drɔː(r)ˈiː/ ▶ **noun** the person or organization, typically a bank, who must pay a draft or bill.

drawer ▶ **noun 1** /drɔː/ a box-like storage compartment without a lid, made to slide horizontally in and out of a desk, chest, or other piece of furniture.
2 (**drawers**) /drɔːz/ dated or humorous knickers or underpants.
3 /ˈdrɔː(r)ə/ a person who draws something, in particular:
■ a person who writes a cheque. ■ a person who produces a drawing or design. ■ archaic another term for **TAPSTER**.
– DERIVATIVES **drawerful** noun (pl. **-fuls**).

drawing ▶ **noun** a picture or diagram made with a pencil, pen, or crayon rather than paint, especially one drawn in monochrome: *a series of charcoal drawings on white paper.*
■ [mass noun] the art or skill or making such pictures or diagrams: *she took lessons in drawing.*

drawing board ▶ **noun** a large flat board on which paper may be spread for artists or designers to work on.
– PHRASES **back to the drawing board** used to indicate that an idea, scheme, or proposal has been unsuccessful and that a new one must be devised: *the government must go back to the drawing board and review the whole issue of youth training.* **on the drawing board** (of an idea, scheme, or proposal) under consideration and not yet ready to put into practice: *there are plans to enlarge the runway, but at present all this remains on the drawing board.*

drawing paper ▶ **noun** [mass noun] thick paper for drawing and painting on.

drawing pin ▶ **noun** Brit. a short flat-headed pin,

used for fastening paper to a wall or other surface.

drawing room ▶ noun a room in a large private house in which guests can be received and entertained.
▶ adjective [attrib.] consciously refined, light-hearted, and elegant: *drawing-room small talk.*
▪(of a song or play) characterized by a polite observance of social proprieties: *a stock figure of Thirties drawing-room comedy.*
– ORIGIN mid 17th cent. (denoting a private room attached to a more public one): abbreviation of 16th-cent. *withdrawing-room* 'a room to withdraw to'.

drawknife ▶ noun (pl. **-knives**) a knife consisting of a blade with a handle at each end at right angles to it, which is drawn towards the user to remove wood from a surface.

drawl ▶ verb [no obj.] speak in a slow, lazy way with prolonged vowel sounds: [with direct speech] *'Suits me fine,' he drawled.*
▶ noun [in sing.] a slow, lazy way of speaking or an accent with unusually prolonged vowel sounds: *a strong Texan drawl.*
– DERIVATIVES **drawler** noun, **drawly** adjective.
– ORIGIN late 16th cent.: probably originally slang, from Low German or Dutch *dralen* 'delay, linger'.

drawn past participle of **DRAW**. ▶ adjective (of a person or a person's face) looking strained from illness, exhaustion, anxiety, or pain: *Cathy was pale and drawn and she looked tired out.*

drawn butter ▶ noun [mass noun] N. Amer. melted butter.

drawn-out ▶ adjective lasting or seeming to last longer than is necessary: *after the long drawn-out years of waiting the end of the war was in sight.*

drawn work (also **drawn-thread-work**) ▶ noun [mass noun] ornamental work on linen or other fabric, done by drawing out threads and usually with additional needlework.

draw-off (also **draw-off pipe**) ▶ noun a pipe which takes water from the plumbing system to a tap or other points of use.

draw reins ▶ noun a pair of reins that are attached to a horse's saddle or girth and pass through the bit rings to the rider's hands.

draw sheet ▶ noun **1** a sheet that is placed in such a way that it can be taken from under a patient or invalid without disturbing the bedclothes.
2 a list of matches to be played in a tournament.

drawstring ▶ noun a string in the seam of the material of a garment or a bag, which can be pulled to tighten or close it.

draw-well ▶ noun a deep well from which water is obtained with a bucket attached to a rope.

dray ▶ noun a truck or cart for delivering beer barrels or other heavy loads, especially a low one without sides.
▪Austral./NZ a two-wheeled cart.
– ORIGIN late Middle English (denoting a sledge): perhaps from Old English *dræge* 'dragnet', related to *dragan* 'to pull' (see **DRAW**).

drayman ▶ noun (pl. **-men**) a person who delivers beer for a brewery.

dread ▶ verb [with obj.] anticipate with great apprehension or fear: *Jane was dreading the party* | [with infinitive] *I* ***dread to think*** *what Russell will say.*
▪archaic regard with great awe or reverence.
▶ noun **1** [mass noun] great fear or apprehension: *the thought of returning to London filled her with dread* | [in sing.] *I used to have a dread of Friday afternoons.*
2 a sudden take-off and flight of a flock of gulls or other birds.
3 informal a person with dreadlocks: *the band appeals to dreads and baldheads alike.*
▪(**dreads**) dreadlocks.
▶ adjective [attrib.] greatly feared; dreadful: *he was stricken with the dread disease and died.*
▪archaic regarded with awe; greatly revered: *that dread being we dare oppose.*
– ORIGIN Old English *ādrǣdan*, *ondrǣdan*, of West Germanic origin; related to Old High German *intrātan*.

dreaded ▶ adjective [attrib.] regarded with great fear or apprehension: *the dreaded news came that Joe had been wounded* | humorous *the dreaded fax machine.*

dreadful ▶ adjective causing or involving great suffering, fear, or unhappiness; extremely bad or serious: *there's been a dreadful accident.*
▪extremely disagreeable: *the weather was dreadful.* ▪[attrib.] used to emphasize the degree to which something is the case, especially something regarded with sadness or disapproval: *you're a dreadful flirt.* ▪(of a person or their feelings) troubled: *I feel dreadful—I hate myself.* ▪(of a person or their appearance) feeling or looking ill: *she looked quite dreadful and she was struggling for breath.*
– DERIVATIVES **dreadfulness** noun.

dreadfully ▶ adverb **1** [often as submodifier] extremely: *you're dreadfully thin* | *I'm dreadfully sorry!*
▪very much: *I'll miss you dreadfully.*
2 very badly: *the company has performed dreadfully.*

dreadlocks ▶ plural noun a Rastafarian hairstyle in which the hair is washed but not combed and twisted while wet into tight braids or ringlets hanging down on all sides.
– DERIVATIVES **dreadlocked** adjective.

dreadnought /ˈdrɛdnɔːt/ ▶ noun **1** historical a type of battleship introduced in the early 20th century, larger and faster than its predecessors and equipped entirely with large-calibre guns. [ORIGIN: named after Britain's HMS *Dreadnought*, which was the first to be completed (1906).]
2 archaic a fearless person.
3 archaic a heavy overcoat for stormy weather.

dream ▶ noun a series of thoughts, images, and sensations occurring in a person's mind during sleep: *I had a recurrent dream about falling from great heights.*
▪[in sing.] a state of mind in which someone is or seems to be unaware of their immediate surroundings: *he had been walking around* ***in a dream*** *all day.* ▪a cherished aspiration, ambition, or ideal: *I fulfilled a childhood dream when I became champion* | *the girl* ***of my dreams*** | [as modifier] *they'd found their dream home.* ▪an unrealistic or self-deluding fantasy: *maybe he could get a job and earn some money—but he knew this was just a dream.* ▪a person or thing perceived as wonderful or perfect: *her new man's an absolute dream* | *it was a* ***dream of a*** *backhand* | *she's a couturier's dream.*
▶ verb (past and past participle **dreamed** /drɛmt, driːmd/ or **dreamt** /drɛmt/) [no obj.] **1** experience dreams during sleep: *I* ***dreamed about*** *her last night.*
▪[with obj.] see, hear, or feel (something) in a dream: *maybe you dreamed it* | [with clause] *I dreamed that I was going to be executed.* ▪indulge in daydreams or fantasies, typically about something greatly desired: *she had* ***dreamed of*** *a trip to America.* ▪[with obj.] (**dream time away**) waste one's time in a lazy, unproductive way.
2 [with negative] contemplate the possibility of doing something or that something might be the case: *I wouldn't* ***dream of*** *foisting myself on you* | [with clause] *I never dreamed anyone would take offence.*
– PHRASES **beyond one's wildest dreams** bigger or better than could be reasonably expected: *stockbrokers command salaries beyond the wildest dreams of most workers.* **in your dreams** used in spoken English to assert that something much desired is not likely ever to happen. **in one's wildest dreams** [with negative] used to emphasize that a situation is beyond the scope of one's imagination: *she could never in her wildest dreams have imagined the summer weather in New York.* **like a dream** informal very well or successfully: *the car is still running like a dream.*
– DERIVATIVES **dreamful** adjective (poetic/literary), **dreamless** adjective, **dreamlike** adjective.
– ORIGIN Middle English: of Germanic origin, related to Dutch *droom* and German *Traum*, and probably also to Old English *drēam* 'joy, music'.
▶ **dream on** [in imperative] informal used, especially in spoken English, as an ironic comment on the unlikely or impractical nature of a plan or aspiration: *Dean thinks he's going to get the job. Dream on, Babe.*
dream something up imagine or invent something: *he's been dreaming up new ways of attracting customers.*

dreamboat ▶ noun informal a very attractive person, especially a man.

dreamcatcher ▶ noun a small hoop containing a horsehair mesh decorated with feathers and beads, believed to give its owner good dreams. Dreamcatchers were originally made by American Indians.

dreamer ▶ noun a person who dreams or is dreaming.
▪a person who is unpractical or idealistic: *a rebellious young dreamer.*

dreamland ▶ noun [mass noun] sleep regarded as a world of dreams: *she tries to lull herself into dreamland.*
▪an imagined and unrealistically ideal world: *a digital dreamland where you'll pay bills with a click of the mouse.*

dreamscape ▶ noun a landscape or scene with the strangeness or mystery characteristic of dreams: *surrealism's popular manifestations were the dreamscapes of Salvador Dali.*

dream team ▶ noun a team of people perceived as the perfect combination for a particular purpose: *the two have been linked as the dream team that will revitalize New York Democrats.*

dream ticket ▶ noun **1** a pair of candidates standing together for political office who are ideally matched to attract widespread support.
2 an invaluable opportunity to go somewhere or do something: *a dream ticket to the Premier League.*

dreamtime ▶ noun another term for **ALCHERINGA**.

dreamwork ▶ noun [mass noun] Psychoanalysis the processes by which the unconscious mind alters the manifest content of dreams in order to conceal their real meaning from the dreamer.

dreamworld ▶ noun a fantastic or idealized view of life: *somebody who can live in a romantic dreamworld.*

dreamy ▶ adjective (**dreamier**, **dreamiest**) reflecting a preoccupation with pleasant thoughts that distract one from one's present surroundings: *a dreamy smile.*
▪(of a person) not practical; given to daydreaming: *a dreamy boy who grew up absorbed in poetry.* ▪having a magical or dreamlike quality; peacefully gentle and relaxing: *a slow dreamy melody.* ▪informal delightful; gorgeous: *I bet he was really dreamy.*
– DERIVATIVES **dreamily** adverb, **dreaminess** noun.

drear /drɪə/ ▶ adjective poetic/literary term for **DREARY**.
– ORIGIN early 17th cent.: abbreviation.

dreary ▶ adjective (**drearier**, **dreariest**) dull, bleak, and lifeless; depressing: *the dreary round of working, eating, and trying to sleep.*
– DERIVATIVES **drearily** adverb, **dreariness** noun.
– ORIGIN Old English *drēorig* 'gory, cruel', also 'melancholy', from *drēor* 'gore', of Germanic origin; related to German *traurig* 'sorrowful', also to **DROWSY**, and probably to **DRIZZLE**.

dreck /drɛk/ (also **drek**) ▶ noun [mass noun] informal rubbish; trash: *this so-called art is pure dreck.*
– DERIVATIVES **dreckish** adjective, **drecky** adjective.
– ORIGIN early 20th cent.: from Yiddish *drek* 'filth, dregs', from a Germanic base shared by Old English *threax*; probably related to Greek *skatos* 'dung'.

dredge[1] ▶ verb [with obj.] clean out the bed of (a harbour, river, or other area of water) by scooping out mud, weeds, and rubbish with a dredge.
▪bring up or clear (something) from a river, harbour, or other area of water with a dredge: *mud was dredged out of the harbour* | [no obj.] *they start to* ***dredge for*** *oysters in November.* ▪(**dredge something up**) figurative bring to people's attention an unpleasant or embarrassing fact or incident that had been forgotten: *I don't understand why you had to dredge up this story.*
▶ noun an apparatus for bringing up objects or mud from a river or seabed by scooping or dragging.
– ORIGIN late 15th cent. (as a noun; originally in *dredge-boat*): perhaps related to Middle Dutch *dregghe* 'grappling hook'.

dredge[2] ▶ verb [with obj.] sprinkle (food) with a powdered substance, typically flour or sugar: *dredge the bananas with sugar and cinnamon.*
– ORIGIN late 16th cent.: from obsolete *dredge* 'sweetmeat, mixture of spices', from Old French *dragie*, perhaps via Latin from Greek *tragēmata* 'spices'. Compare with **DRAGÉE**.

dredger ▶ noun a boat designed for dredging harbours or other bodies of water.

dree /driː/ ▶ verb (**drees**, **dreed**, **dreeing**) [with obj.] Scottish or archaic endure (something burdensome or painful): *he dreed pain and dolour.*
– PHRASES **dree one's weird** submit to one's destiny.
– ORIGIN Old English *drēogan*, of Germanic origin; related to Old Norse *drýgja* 'practise, perpetrate'.

D-region ▶ noun another term for **D-LAYER**.

dregs ▶ noun the remnants of a liquid left in a container, together with any sediment or grounds: *coffee dregs.*
▪figurative the most worthless part or parts of something: *the dregs of society.*
– DERIVATIVES **dreggy** adjective.

– ORIGIN Middle English: probably of Scandinavian origin and related to Swedish *drägg* (plural).

dreich /driːx/ (also **driech**) ▶ **adjective** Scottish dreary; bleak: *dreich weather roaring in off the sea.*

– ORIGIN Middle English (in the sense 'patient, long-suffering'): of Germanic origin, corresponding to Old Norse *drjúgr* 'enduring, lasting'.

dreidel /ˈdreɪd(ə)l/ (also **dreidl**) ▶ **noun** N. Amer. a small four-sided spinning top with a Hebrew letter on each side, used by Jewish people.
■ [mass noun] a gambling game played with such a top, especially at Hanukkah.
– ORIGIN 1930s: from Yiddish *dreydl*; compare with German *drehen* 'to turn'.

Dreiser /ˈdrʌɪsə/, Theodore (Herman Albert) (1871–1945), American novelist. His first novel, *Sister Carrie* (1900), caused controversy for its frank treatment of the heroine's sexuality and ambition. Other notable works: *America is Worth Saving* (1941).

drek ▶ **noun** variant spelling of **DRECK**.

drench ▶ **verb** [with obj.] **1** (usu. **be drenched**) wet thoroughly; soak: *I fell in the stream and was drenched* | [as noun **drenching**] *a severe drenching would kill his uncle.*
■ figurative cover (something) liberally or thoroughly: *cool patios drenched in flowers* | [as adj., in combination **-drenched**] *a sun-drenched clearing.*
2 forcibly administer a drug in liquid form orally to (an animal).
▶ **noun** a dose of medicine administered to an animal.
■ archaic a draught of a medicinal or poisonous liquid.
– ORIGIN Old English *drencan* 'force to drink', *drenc* 'a drink or draught', of Germanic origin; related to German *tränken* (verb), *Trank* (noun), also to **DRINK**.

Drenthe /ˈdrɛntə/ a sparsely populated agricultural province in the NE Netherlands; capital, Assen.

Dresden[1] /ˈdrɛzdən, German ˈdreːsdn/ a city in eastern Germany, the capital of Saxony, on the River Elbe; pop. 485,130 (1991). Famous for its baroque architecture, it was almost totally destroyed by Allied bombing in 1945.

Dresden[2] /ˈdrɛzd(ə)n/ (also **Dresden china**) ▶ **noun** [mass noun] porcelain ware with elaborate decoration and delicate colourings, made originally at Dresden and (since 1710) at nearby Meissen: [as modifier] *a fine Dresden china cup.*

dress ▶ **verb 1** [no obj.] put on one's clothes: *Graham showered and dressed quickly* | *I'll go and* **get dressed**.
■ [with adverbial] wear clothes in a particular way or of a particular type: *she's nice-looking and dresses well* | (**be dressed**) *he was dressed in jeans and a thick sweater.* ■ [with obj.] put clothes on (someone): *they dressed her in a white hospital gown.* ■ put on clothes appropriate for a formal occasion: *we* **dressed for dinner** *every night.* ■ [with obj.] design or supply clothes for (a celebrity): *for over four decades he dressed the royal family.* ■ [with obj.] decorate (something) in an artistic or attractive way: *she'd enjoyed dressing the tree when the children were little.* ■ decorate (a ship) with flags, for a special occasion. ■ (of a man) have the genitals habitually on one or the other side of the fork of the trousers: *do you dress to the left?*
2 [with obj.] treat or prepare (something) in a certain way, in particular:
■ clean, treat, or apply a dressing to (a wound). ■ clean and prepare (food, especially poultry or shellfish) for cooking or eating: [as adj. **dressed**] *dressed crab.* ■ add a dressing to (a salad). ■ apply a fertilizing substance to (a field, garden, or plant). ■ complete the preparation or manufacture of (leather or fabric) by treating its surface in some way. ■ smooth the surface of (stone): [as adj. **dressed**] *dressed Cotswold stone.* ■ arrange or style (one's own or someone else's hair), especially in an elaborate way.
3 [with obj.] Military draw up (troops) in the proper alignment.
■ [no obj.] (of troops) come into such an alignment.
4 [with obj.] make (an artificial fly) for use in fishing: [as adj. **dressed**] *a dressed wet fly.*
▶ **noun 1** a one-piece garment for a woman or girl that covers the body and extends down over the legs.
2 [mass noun] clothing of a specified kind for men or women: *traditional African dress* | figurative *the underlying theme is recognizable even when it appears in feminist dress.*
■ [as modifier] denoting military uniform or other clothing used on formal or ceremonial occasions: *a dress suit.*
– PHRASES **dressed overall** (of a ship) decorated with a continuous line of flags from bow to stern. **dressed to kill** wearing glamorous clothes intended to create a striking impression.
– ORIGIN Middle English (in the sense 'put straight'): from Old French *dresser* 'arrange, prepare', based on Latin *directus* 'direct, straight'.
▶ **dress down** dress informally: *Sue dressed down in old jeans and a white blouse.*
dress someone down informal reprimand someone.
dress up dress in smart or formal clothes. ■ dress in a special costume for fun or as part of an entertainment: *he dressed up as a gorilla.*
dress something up present something in such a way that it appears better than it really is: *the company dressed up the figures a little.*

dressage /ˈdrɛsɑː(d)ʒ/ ▶ **noun** [mass noun] the art of riding and training a horse in a manner that develops obedience, flexibility, and balance.
– ORIGIN 1930s: from French, literally 'training', from *dresser* 'to train'.

dress circle ▶ **noun** the first level of seats above the ground floor in a theatre.

dress coat ▶ **noun** a coat with long tails at the back, worn by men on very formal occasions.

dresser[1] ▶ **noun** a sideboard with shelves above for storing and displaying plates and kitchen utensils.
■ N. Amer. a dressing table or chest of drawers, typically with a mirror.
– ORIGIN late Middle English (denoting a kitchen sideboard or table on which food was prepared): from Old French *dresseur*, from *dresser* 'prepare' (see **DRESS**).

dresser[2] ▶ **noun 1** [usu. with adj.] a person who dresses in a specified way: *a snappy dresser.*
■ a person who habitually dresses in a smart or elegant way: *she's gorgeous—and she's a dresser.*
2 a person whose job is to look after theatrical costumes and help actors to dress.
3 Brit. a person who assists a surgeon during operations.
4 a person who prepares, treats, or finishes a material or piece of equipment.

dressing ▶ **noun 1** (also **salad dressing**) [mass noun] a sauce for salads, typically one consisting of oil and vinegar mixed together with herbs or other flavourings: *vinaigrette dressing.*
■ N. Amer. stuffing: *turkey with apple dressing.*
2 [count noun] a piece of material placed on a wound to protect it: *an antiseptic dressing.*
3 [mass noun] size or stiffening used in the finishing of fabrics.
4 [count noun] a fertilizing substance such as compost or manure spread over or ploughed into land.

dressing case ▶ **noun** a case used for toiletries.

dressing-down ▶ **noun** [in sing.] informal a severe reprimand: *the secretary received a public dressing-down.*

dressing gown ▶ **noun** a long loose robe, typically worn after getting out of bed or bathing.

dressing room ▶ **noun** a room in which actors or sports players change clothes before and after their performance or game.
■ a small room attached to a bedroom, used for dressing in and to store clothes.

dressing station ▶ **noun** a place for giving emergency treatment to troops injured in battle.

dressing table ▶ **noun** a table with a mirror and drawers for cosmetics, etc., used while dressing or applying make-up.

dress length ▶ **noun** a piece of material long enough to make a dress.

dressmaker ▶ **noun** a person whose job is making women's clothes.
– DERIVATIVES **dressmaking** noun.

dress parade ▶ **noun** a military parade in full dress uniform.
■ a display of clothes worn by models.

dress rehearsal ▶ **noun** the final rehearsal of a live show, in which everything is done as it would be in a real performance.

dress sense ▶ **noun** [mass noun] a good instinct for selecting garments which suit the wearer.

dress shield (also **dress preserver**) ▶ **noun** historical a piece of waterproof material fastened in the armpit of a dress to protect it from perspiration.

dress shirt ▶ **noun** a man's white shirt worn with a bow tie and a dinner jacket on formal occasions.
■ N. Amer. a man's long-sleeved shirt, suitable for wearing with a tie.

dressy ▶ **adjective** (**dressier**, **dressiest**) (of clothes) suitable for a smart or formal occasion: *wear something dressy, Kate, we've got to go to a drinks party.*
■ requiring or given to wearing such clothes.
– DERIVATIVES **dressily** adverb, **dressiness** noun.

drew past of **DRAW**.

drey /dreɪ/ ▶ **noun** (pl. **-eys**) the nest of a squirrel, typically in the form of a mass of twigs in a tree.
– ORIGIN early 17th cent.: of unknown origin.

Dreyfus /ˈdreɪfəs/, Alfred (1859–1935), French army officer, of Jewish descent. In 1894 he was falsely accused of providing military secrets to the Germans; his trial and imprisonment caused a major political crisis in France. He was eventually rehabilitated in 1906.

dribble ▶ **verb 1** [no obj. and usu. with adverbial of direction] (of a liquid) fall slowly in drops or a thin stream: *rain dribbled down the window* | figurative *refugees from central Europe dribbled into Britain.*
■ [with obj. and adverbial of direction] pour (a liquid) in such a way: *he dribbled cream into his coffee.* ■ [no obj.] allow saliva to run from the mouth: *his mouth was open and he was dribbling.*
2 [with obj. and adverbial of direction] (chiefly in soccer, hockey, and basketball) take (the ball) forwards past opponents with slight touches of the feet or the stick, or (in basketball) by continuous bouncing: *he attempted to dribble the ball from the goal area* | [no obj.] *he dribbled past a swarm of defenders.*
▶ **noun 1** a thin stream of liquid; a trickle: *a dribble of blood.*
■ [mass noun] saliva running from the mouth.
2 [mass noun] figurative foolish talk or ideas; nonsense: *don't believe a word of that dribble.*
3 (in soccer, hockey, and basketball) an act or instance of taking the ball forward with repeated slight touches or bounces.
– DERIVATIVES **dribbler** noun, **dribbly** adjective.
– ORIGIN mid 16th cent.: frequentative of obsolete *drib*, variant of **DRIP**. The original sense was 'shoot an arrow short or wide of its target', which was also a sense of *drib*. Sense 2 of the noun may have been influenced by **DRIVEL**.

driblet ▶ **noun** a thin stream or small drop of liquid: *driblets of spittle run from her mouth.*
■ a small or insignificant amount: *the prisoners were let out* **in driblets**.
– ORIGIN late 16th cent. (in the sense 'small sum of money'): from obsolete *drib* (see **DRIBBLE**) + **-LET**.

dribs and drabs ▶ **plural noun** (**in dribs and drabs**) informal in small scattered or sporadic amounts: *doing the work in dribs and drabs.*
– ORIGIN mid 19th cent.: from obsolete *drib* (see **DRIBBLE**) and *drab* (by reduplication).

driech ▶ **adjective** variant spelling of **DREICH**.

dried past and past participle of **DRY**.

drier[1] ▶ **adjective** comparative of **DRY**.

drier[2] ▶ **noun** variant spelling of **DRYER**.

drift ▶ **verb** [no obj.] **1** be carried slowly by a current of air or water: *the cabin cruiser started to drift downstream* | figurative *excited voices drifted down the hall.*
■ [with adverbial of direction] (of a person) walk slowly, aimlessly, or casually: *people began to drift away.* ■ [with adverbial] move passively, aimlessly, or involuntarily into a certain situation or condition: *I was drifting off to sleep* | *Lewis and his father drifted apart.* ■ (of a person or their attention) digress or stray to another subject: *I noticed my audience's attention drifting.*
2 (especially of snow or leaves) be blown into heaps by the wind: *fallen leaves start to drift in the gutters* | [as adj. **drifting**] *drifting snow.*
▶ **noun 1** [in sing.] a continuous slow movement from one place to another: *there was a drift to the towns.*
■ [mass noun] the deviation of a vessel, aircraft, or projectile from its intended or expected course as the result of currents or winds: *the pilot had not noticed any appreciable drift.* ■ a steady movement or development from one thing towards another, especially one that is perceived as unwelcome: *the drift towards a more repressive style of policing.* ■ [mass noun] a state of inaction or indecision: *after so much drift, any expression of enthusiasm is welcome.* ■ Motor Racing a controlled skid, used in taking bends at high speeds. ■ Brit. historical an act of driving cattle or sheep. ■ Brit. historical a herding of cattle within a forest to a particular place on an appointed day in order to determine ownership or to levy fines.
2 [in sing.] the general intention or meaning of an

argument or someone's remarks: *he didn't understand much Greek, but he got her drift.*
3 a large mass of snow, leaves, or other material piled up or carried along by the wind.
■[mass noun] Geology glacial and fluvioglacial deposits left by retreating ice sheets. ■ a large mass of flowering plants growing together: *a drift of daffodils.*
4 Mining a horizontal or inclined passage following a mineral vein or coal seam.
5 S. African a ford.
– DERIVATIVES **drifty** adjective.
– ORIGIN Middle English (in the sense 'mass of snow, leaves, etc.'): originally from Old Norse *drift* 'snowdrift, something driven'; in later use from Middle Dutch *drift* 'course, current', and (in sense 5) South African Dutch *drift* 'ford'; related to **DRIVE**.

drifter ▶ **noun 1** a person who is continually moving from place to place, without any fixed home or job.
2 a fishing boat equipped with a drift net.

driftfish ▶ **noun** (pl. same or **-fishes**) a slender-bodied bottom-dwelling fish found in the deeper waters of warm seas.
● Family Nomeidae (or Stromateidae): several genera, in particular *Ariomma*.

drift ice ▶ **noun** [mass noun] detached pieces of ice drifting with the wind or ocean currents.

drift net ▶ **noun** a large net for herring and similar fish, kept upright by weights at the bottom and floats at the top and allowed to drift with the tide.
– DERIVATIVES **drift netter** noun, **drift netting** noun.

drift pin ▶ **noun** a steel pin driven into a hole in a piece of metal to enlarge, shape, or align the hole.

drift sand ▶ **noun** [mass noun] S. African wind-blown sand.

driftway ▶ **noun** Brit. historical a broad route along which cattle or sheep used to be driven to market.

driftwood ▶ **noun** [mass noun] pieces of wood which are floating on the sea or have been washed ashore.

drill[1] ▶ **noun 1** a tool or machine with a rotating cutting tip or reciprocating hammer or chisel, used for making holes.
■such a tool used by a dentist for cutting away part of a tooth before filling it.
2 [mass noun] instruction or training in military exercises: *parade-ground drill.*
■intensive instruction or training in something, typically by means of repeated exercises: *tables can be mastered by drill and practice* | [count noun] *language-learning drills.* ■[count noun] a rehearsal of the procedure to be followed in an emergency: *air-raid drills.* ■(**the drill**) informal the correct or recognized procedure or way of doing something: *he didn't know the drill.*
3 a predatory mollusc that bores into the shells of other molluscs in order to feed on the soft tissue.
● Family Muricidae, class Gastropoda: several genera and species, in particular the American **oyster drill** (*Urosalpinx cinerea*), which is a serious pest of oyster beds.
▶ **verb** [with obj.] **1** produce (a hole) in something by or as if by boring with a drill: *drill holes through the tiles for the masonry pins.*
■make a hole in (something) by boring with a drill: *a power tool for drilling wood.* ■[no obj., with adverbial of direction] make a hole in or through something by using a drill: *do not attempt to drill through a joist* | figurative *his eyes drilled into her.* ■[no obj.] sink a borehole in order to obtain a certain substance, typically oil or water: *BP has been licensed to drill for oil in the area* | [as noun **drilling**] *drilling should begin next year.* ■(of a dentist) cut away part of (a tooth) before filling it. ■[with obj. and adverbial of direction] informal (of a sports player) hit (a shot) hard and in a straight line: *he drilled a right-foot volley into the back of the net.*
2 subject (someone) to military training exercises: *a sergeant was drilling new recruits.*
■[no obj.] (of a person) take part in such exercises: *the troops were drilling.* ■instruct (someone) in something by the means of repeated exercises or practice: *I reacted instinctively because I had been drilled to do just that.* ■(**drill something into**) cause (someone) to learn something by repeating it regularly: *his mother had drilled into him the need to pay for one's sins.*
– DERIVATIVES **driller** noun.
– ORIGIN early 17th cent.: from Middle Dutch *drillen* 'bore, turn in a circle'.

drill[2] ▶ **noun** a machine which makes small furrows, sows seed in them, and then covers the sown seed.
■a small furrow, especially one made by such a machine. ■ a ridge with such a furrow on top. ■ a row of plants sown in such a furrow: *drills of lettuces.*
▶ **verb** [with obj.] (of a person or machine) sow (seed) with a drill: *crops drilled in autumn.*
■plant (the ground) in furrows: [as noun **drilling**] *accurate ridging and drilling make hoeing much easier.*
– ORIGIN early 18th cent. (as a noun in the sense 'small furrow'): perhaps from **DRILL**[1].

drill[3] ▶ **noun** a dark brown baboon with a short tail and a naked blue or purple rump, found in the rainforests of West Africa. Compare with **MANDRILL**.
● *Mandrillus leucophaeus*, family Cercopithecidae.
– ORIGIN mid 17th cent.: probably a local word. Compare with **MANDRILL**.

drill[4] ▶ **noun** [mass noun] a coarse twilled cotton or linen fabric.
– ORIGIN early 18th cent.: abbreviation of earlier *drilling*, from German *Drillich*, from Latin *trilix* 'triple-twilled', from *tri-* 'three' + *licium* 'thread'.

drilling rig ▶ **noun** a large structure with equipment for drilling an oil well.

drill press ▶ **noun** a machine tool for drilling holes, set on a fixed stand.

drill sergeant ▶ **noun** a non-commissioned officer who trains soldiers in military parade exercises.

drill stem ▶ **noun** a rotating rod or cylinder used in drilling.

drill string ▶ **noun** a structure consisting of coupled lengths of pipe or casing, which occupies the hole made in drilling for oil or gas.

drily /ˈdrʌɪli/ (also **dryly**) ▶ **adverb 1** in a matter-of-fact or ironically humorous way: *'How very observant', he said drily.*
2 in a dry way or condition: *Evans swallowed drily.*

drink ▶ **verb** (past **drank**; past participle **drunk**) [with obj.] take (a liquid) into the mouth and swallow: *we sat by the fire, drinking our tea* | [no obj.] *he drank thirstily.*
■[no obj.] consume or be in the habit of consuming alcohol, especially to excess: *she doesn't drink or smoke* | *he drank himself into a stupor* | [as noun **drinking**] *Les was ordered to cut down his drinking.* ■[no obj.] (**drink up**) consume the rest of a drink, especially in a rapid manner. ■(**drink something in**) figurative watch or listen to something with eager pleasure or interest: *she strolled to the window to drink in the view.* ■ informal (of a plant or a porous substance) absorb (moisture). ■[no obj.] (of wine) have a specified flavour or character when drunk: *this wine is really drinking beautifully.*
▶ **noun** a liquid that can be swallowed as refreshment or nourishment: *fizzy drinks* | [mass noun] *a table covered with food and drink.*
■a quantity of liquid swallowed at one go: *he had a drink of water.* ■[mass noun] alcohol, or the habitual or excessive consumption of alcohol: *the effects of too much drink* | *they both took to drink.* ■ a glass of liquid, especially when alcoholic: *we went for a drink.* ■(**the drink**) informal the sea or another large area of water.
– PHRASES **drink and drive** drive a vehicle while under the influence of alcohol. **drink deep** take a large draught or draughts of something: figurative *he learnt to drink deep of the Catholic tradition.* **drink someone's health** express one's good wishes for someone by raising one's glass and drinking a small amount. **drink (a toast) to** celebrate or wish for the good fortune of someone or something by raising one's glass and drinking a small amount. **drink someone under the table** informal consume as much alcohol as one's drinking companion without becoming as drunk. **I'll drink to that** uttered to express one's agreement with or approval of a statement. **in drink** when intoxicated: *we've hit each other before, in drink.*
– DERIVATIVES **drinkable** adjective.
– ORIGIN Old English *drincan* (verb), *drinc* (noun), of Germanic origin; related to Dutch *drinken* and German *trinken*.

drink-driving ▶ **noun** [mass noun] Brit. the crime of driving a vehicle with an excess of alcohol in the blood.
– DERIVATIVES **drink-driver** noun.

drinker ▶ **noun 1** a person who drinks a particular drink: *coffee drinkers.*
■a person who drinks alcohol, especially to excess: *a heavy drinker.*
2 (also **drinker moth**) a large brownish European moth, the caterpillar of which bears irritant hairs and is noted for drinking dew.
● *Euthrix potatoria*, family Lasiocampidae.
3 a container from which an animal can drink.

drinking chocolate ▶ **noun** [mass noun] a mixture of cocoa powder, milk solids, and sugar, added to hot milk to make a chocolate drink.

drinking fountain ▶ **noun** a device producing a small jet of water for drinking.

drinking horn ▶ **noun** chiefly historical a drinking container carved from an animal's horn.

drinking song ▶ **noun** a hearty song, typically concerning drink and having bawdy lyrics, which is sung while drinking alcohol.

drinking-up time ▶ **noun** [mass noun] (in the UK) a short period (now twenty minutes) legally allowed for finishing drinks bought before closing time in a public house or bar.

drinking water ▶ **noun** [mass noun] water pure enough for drinking.

drip ▶ **verb 1** (**dripped**, **dripping**) [no obj.] let fall or be so wet as to shed small drops of liquid: *the tap won't stop dripping* | *his hands were dripping with blood.*
■[with adverbial] (of liquid) fall in small drops: *water dripped from her clothing.* ■[with obj.] cause or allow (a liquid) to fall in such a way: *the candle was dripping wax down one side.* ■ figurative display a copious amount or degree of a particular quality or thing: *the women were dripping with gold and diamonds* | [with obj.] *his voice dripped sarcasm.*
▶ **noun 1** a small drop of a liquid: *she put the bucket on top of the dresser to catch the drips.*
■[in sing.] the action or sound of liquid falling steadily in small drops: *the drip, drip, drip of the leak in the roof.* ■ (also **drip feed**) Medicine an apparatus which passes fluid, nutrients, or drugs drop by drop into a patient's body on a continuous basis, usually intravenously: *he had been on a drip for several days.*
2 informal a weak and ineffectual person.
3 Architecture a projection on a moulding or cornice, channelled to prevent rain from running down the wall below. Compare with **DRIPSTONE**.
– ORIGIN Old English *dryppan*, *drȳpen*, of Germanic origin; related to Danish *dryppe*, also to **DROP**.

drip-dry ▶ **adjective** (of a fabric or garment) capable of drying without creasing when hung up after washing: *drip-dry shirts.*
▶ **verb** [no obj.] (of fabric or a garment) become dry without forming creases when hung up after washing.
■[with obj.] dry (fabric or a garment) by hanging it up in this way: *it's easy to wash and simple to drip-dry.*

drip feed ▶ **noun** a device for introducing fluid drop by drop into a system, for example lubricating oil into an engine.
■a medicinal drip.
▶ **verb** (**drip-feed**) [with obj.] introduce (fluid) drop by drop: *the oiler drip-feeds oil on to all drive chains.*
■supply (a patient) with fluid, nutrients, or drugs through a drip.

drip mat ▶ **noun** Brit. a small mat placed under a glass to protect the surface on which the glass is resting.

dripping ▶ **noun** [mass noun] Brit. fat that has melted and dripped from roasting meat, used in cooking or eaten cold as a spread.
■(**drippings**) chiefly N. Amer. wax, fat, or other liquid produced from something by the effect of heat.
▶ **adjective** extremely wet: [as submodifier] *dripping wet hair.*

drippy ▶ **adjective** (**drippier**, **drippiest**) **1** informal weak, ineffectual, or sloppily sentimental: *a drippy love song.*
2 tending to drip: *drippy food.*
– DERIVATIVES **drippily** adverb, **drippiness** noun.

dripstone ▶ **noun 1** Architecture a moulding over a door or window which deflects rain and enhances the opening.
2 [mass noun] Geology rock deposited by precipitation from dripping water, such as that which forms stalactites and stalagmites.

drive ▶ **verb** (past **drove**; past participle **driven**) **1** [no obj., usu. with adverbial of direction] operate and control the direction and speed of a motor vehicle: *he got into his car and drove off* | *they drove back into town.*
■[with obj.] own or use (a specified type of motor vehicle): *Sue drives an estate car.* ■[no obj.] be licensed or competent to drive a motor vehicle: *I take it you can drive?* ■[with obj.] convey (someone) in a vehicle, especially a private car: *his wife drove him to Regent's Park.*
2 [with obj. and adverbial of direction] propel or carry along by force in a specified direction: *the wind will drive you onshore.*
■[no obj.] (of wind, water, or snow) move or fall with

great force: *the snow drove against him.* ■ [with obj.] (of a source of power) provide the energy to set and keep (an engine or piece of machinery) in motion: *turbines driven by steam.* ■ Electronics (of a device) power or operate (another device): *the interface can be used to drive a printer.* ■ [with obj.] force (a stake or nail) into place by hitting or pushing it: *nails are driven through the boards.* ■ [with obj. and adverbial] bore (a tunnel). ■ (in ball games) hit or kick (the ball) hard with a free swing of the bat, racket, or foot. ■ [with obj.] Golf strike (a ball) from the tee, typically with a driver.
3 [with obj. and adverbial of direction] urge or force (animals or people) to move in a specified direction: *they drove a flock of sheep through the centre of the city.*
■ [with obj.] urge forward and direct the course of (an animal drawing a vehicle or plough). ■ [with obj.] chase or frighten (wild animals) into nets, traps, or into a small area where they can be killed or captured: *all the clan were up on the hill before dawn, ready to drive the deer.* ■ compel to leave: *troops drove out the demonstrators* | *he wanted to drive me away.*
4 [with obj.] (usu. **be driven**) (of a fact or feeling) compel (someone) to act in a particular way, especially one that is considered undesirable or inappropriate: *he was driven by ambition* | [with obj. and infinitive] *some people are driven to murder their tormentors* | [as adj. **driven**] *my husband is a driven man.*
■ [with obj.] bring (someone) forcibly into a specified negative state: *the thought drove him to despair* | [with obj. and complement] *my laziness drives my wife crazy.* ■ [with obj.] force (someone) to work to an excessive extent: *you're driving yourself too hard.*
▶ **noun 1** a trip or journey in a car: *they went for a drive in the country.*
■ [in names] a street or road: *Hammond Drive.* ■ (also **driveway**) a short road leading from a public road to a house.
2 Psychology an innate, biologically determined urge to attain a goal or satisfy a need: *her emotional and sexual drives.*
■ [mass noun] the determination and ambition of a person to achieve something: *his drive and energy helped Leeds to four cup finals.*
3 an organized effort by a number of people to achieve a particular purpose: *a recruitment drive by the police.*
■ Brit. an organized gathering to play whist or another game, involving many players: *a whist drive.*
4 [mass noun] the transmission of power to machinery or to the wheels of a motor vehicle.
■ (in a car with automatic transmission) the position of the gear selector in which the car will move forward, changing gears automatically as required: *he threw the car into drive.* ■ [count noun] Computing short for **DISK DRIVE**.
5 (in ball games) a forceful stroke made with a free swing of the bat, racket, or foot against the ball.
■ Golf a shot from the tee.
6 an act of driving a group of animals to a particular destination.
7 Austral./NZ a line of partly cut trees on a hillside, felled when the top one topples on the others. [ORIGIN: compare with sense 2 of **DRIVE SYSTEM**.]
– PHRASES **drive something home** see **HOME**. **let drive** attack with blows, missiles, or criticism. **what someone is driving at** the point that someone is attempting to make: *I don't understand what you're driving at.*
– DERIVATIVES **drivability** (also **driveability**) noun, **drivable** (also **driveable**) adjective.
– ORIGIN Old English *drīfan* 'urge (a person or animal) to go forward', of Germanic origin; related to Dutch *drijven* and German *treiben*.

drive bay ▶ **noun** Computing a space inside a computer in which a floppy disk, hard disk, or disk drive can be accommodated.

drive belt ▶ **noun** a belt that transmits drive from a motor, engine, or line shaft to a moving part or machine tool.

drive-by ▶ **adjective** [attrib.] chiefly US (of a shooting or other act) carried out from a passing vehicle: *a drive-by shooting.*
▶ **noun** a shooting of this type.

drive-by-wire ▶ **noun** [mass noun] [usu. as modifier] a semi-automatic and normally computer-regulated system for controlling the engine, handling, suspension, and other functions of a motor vehicle.

drive chain ▶ **noun** an endless chain with links that engage with toothed wheels in order to transmit power from one shaft to another in an engine or machine tool.

drive-in chiefly N. Amer. ▶ **adjective** [attrib.] denoting a facility such as a cinema or restaurant that one can visit without leaving one's car: *a drive-in cinema.*
▶ **noun** a facility of this type.

drivel /ˈdrɪv(ə)l/ ▶ **noun** [mass noun] nonsense: *don't talk such drivel!*
▶ **verb** (**drivelled**, **drivelling**; US **driveled**, **driveling**) [no obj.] **1** talk nonsense: *he was drivelling on about the glory days.*
2 archaic let saliva or mucus flow from the mouth or nose.
– DERIVATIVES **driveller** (US **driveler**) noun.
– ORIGIN Old English *dreflian* (in sense 2), of uncertain origin; perhaps related to **DRAFF**.

driveline /ˈdrʌɪvlʌɪn/ ▶ **noun** another term for **DRIVETRAIN**.

driven past participle of **DRIVE**. ▶ **adjective 1** [in combination] operated, moved, or controlled by a specified person or source of power: *a chauffeur-driven limousine* | *wind-driven sand.*
■ motivated or determined by a specified factor or feeling: *a market-driven response to customer needs.*
2 (of snow) piled into drifts or made smooth by the wind: figurative *she was as pure as the driven snow.*

drive-on (also **drive-on/drive-off**) ▶ **adjective** [attrib.] denoting a ferry or train on to and from which motor vehicles may be driven.

driver ▶ **noun 1** a person who drives a vehicle: *a taxi driver* | *learner drivers.*
■ a person who drives a specified kind of animal: *mule drivers.*
2 a wheel or other part in a mechanism that receives power directly and transmits motion to other parts.
■ Electronics a device or part of a circuit that provides power for output. ■ Computing a program that controls the operation of a device such as a printer or scanner.
3 a golf club with a flat face and wooden head, used for driving from the tee.
– PHRASES **in the driver's seat** in control of a situation.
– DERIVATIVES **driverless** adjective.

driver ant ▶ **noun** another term for **ARMY ANT**.

driver's license ▶ **noun** North American term for **DRIVING LICENCE**.

driver's test ▶ **noun** North American term for **DRIVING TEST**.

driveshaft ▶ **noun** a rotating shaft which transmits torque in an engine.

drive system ▶ **noun 1** the part of an engine, computer, or mechanical device which brings about its dynamic movement.
2 Austral./NZ a method of felling trees in hilly country, in which one at the top of a hill is allowed to topple on to others which have been partly cut through, thus felling them in turn.

drive-through chiefly N. Amer. ▶ **adjective** [attrib.] denoting a facility through which one can drive, in particular one in which one can be served without leaving one's car: *a drive-through car wash* | *drive-through restaurants.*
▶ **noun** a place or facility of this type.

drive time ▶ **noun** (especially in broadcasting) the parts of the day when many people commute by car: [as modifier] *drive-time radio.*

drivetrain ▶ **noun** the system in a motor vehicle which connects the transmission to the drive axles.

driveway ▶ **noun** see **DRIVE** (sense 1).

driving ▶ **adjective** [attrib.] (of rain or snow) falling and being blown by the wind with great force: *driving rain.*
■ having a strong and controlling influence: *Macmillan was the driving force behind the plan* | *a driving ambition.*
▶ **noun** [mass noun] the control and operation of a motor vehicle: *he was convicted of reckless driving* | [as modifier] *a driving course.*
– PHRASES **in the driving seat** in control of a situation: *all chairmen love being in the driving seat.*

driving licence (N. Amer. **driver's license**) ▶ **noun** a document permitting a person to drive a motor vehicle: *I've got a full, clean driving licence.*

driving range ▶ **noun** an area where golfers can practise drives.

driving test (N. Amer. **driver's test**) ▶ **noun** an official test of a motorist's competence which must be passed in order to get a driving licence.

driving wheel ▶ **noun 1** any of the large wheels of a locomotive, to which power is applied either directly or via coupling rods.
2 a wheel transmitting motive power in machinery.

drizzle ▶ **noun** [mass noun] light rain falling in very fine drops: *Scotland will be cloudy with patchy drizzle* | [in sing.] *a steady drizzle has been falling since 3 a.m.*
■ [in sing.] Cookery a thin stream of a liquid ingredient trickled over something.
▶ **verb** [no obj.] (**it drizzles**, **it is drizzling**, etc.) rain lightly: *it's started to drizzle* | [as adj. **drizzling**] *the drizzling rain.*
■ [with obj.] Cookery cause a thin stream of (a liquid ingredient) to trickle over food: *drizzle the clarified butter over the top.* ■ [with obj.] cause a liquid ingredient to trickle over (food) in this way: *raspberries drizzled with melted chocolate.*
– DERIVATIVES **drizzly** adjective.
– ORIGIN mid 16th cent.: probably based on Old English *drēosan* 'to fall', of Germanic origin; probably related to **DREARY**.

Dr Martens /ˈmɑːtɪnz/ (also **Doc Martens** or **DMs**) ▶ **plural noun** trademark a type of heavy lace-up boot or shoe with an air-cushioned sole.
– ORIGIN 1970s: named after Klaus *Maertens*, German inventor of the sole.

Drogheda /ˈdrɒɪdə/ a port in the NE Republic of Ireland; pop. 23,000 (1991). In 1649 the inhabitants were massacred after refusing to surrender to Oliver Cromwell's forces.

drogue /drəʊɡ/ ▶ **noun** a device, typically conical or funnel-shaped with open ends, towed behind a boat, aircraft, or other moving object to reduce speed or improve stability.
■ a similar object used as an aerial target for gunnery practice or as a windsock. ■ (in tanker aircraft) a funnel-shaped part on the end of the hose into which a probe is inserted by an aircraft being refuelled in flight. ■ short for **DROGUE PARACHUTE**.
– ORIGIN early 18th cent. (originally a whaling term denoting a piece of stout board attached to a harpoon line, used to slow down or mark the position of a harpooned whale): perhaps related to **DRAG**.

drogue parachute ▶ **noun** a small parachute used as a brake or to pull out a larger parachute or other object from an aircraft in flight or a fast-moving vehicle.

droid /drɔɪd/ ▶ **noun** (in science fiction) a robot.
■ figurative a person regarded as lifeless or mechanical: *she will probably leave you for a sales droid.* ■ Computing a program which automatically collects information from remote systems.
– ORIGIN 1970s: shortening of **ANDROID**.

droit /drɔɪt/ ▶ **noun** Law, historical a right or due.
– ORIGIN late Middle English: from Old French, based on Latin *directus* 'straight, right, direct'.

droit de seigneur /ˌdrwʌ də senˈjəː/ ▶ **noun** [mass noun] the alleged right of a medieval feudal lord to have sexual intercourse with a vassal's bride on her wedding night.
– ORIGIN French, literally 'lord's right'.

droll /drəʊl/ ▶ **adjective** curious or unusual in a way that provokes dry amusement: *his unique brand of droll self-mockery.*
▶ **noun** archaic a jester or entertainer; a buffoon.
– DERIVATIVES **drollery** noun, **drollness** noun, **drolly** /ˈdrəʊlli/ adverb.
– ORIGIN early 17th cent. (as an adjective): from French *drôle*, perhaps from Middle Dutch *drolle* 'imp, goblin'.

dromaeosaurid /ˌdrəʊmɪə(ʊ)ˈsɔːrɪd/ (also **dromaeosaur** /ˈdrəʊmɪə(ʊ)sɔː/) ▶ **noun** a carnivorous bipedal dinosaur of a late Cretaceous family which included deinonychus and the velociraptors. They had a large slashing claw on each hind foot.
• Family Dromaeosauridae, suborder Theropoda, order Saurischia.
– ORIGIN 1970s: from modern Latin *Dromaeosauridae*, based on Greek *dromaios* 'swift-running' + *sauros* 'lizard'.

drome ▶ **noun** informal, dated an aerodrome.
– ORIGIN early 20th cent.: shortened form.

-drome ▶ **combining form 1** denoting a place for running or racing: *aerodrome.*
2 denoting something that runs or proceeds in a certain way: *palindrome.*
– ORIGIN from Greek *dromos* 'course, running' (see **DROMOS**).

dromedary /ˈdrɒmɪd(ə)ri, ˈdrʌm-/ ▶ **noun** (pl. **-ies**) an

Arabian camel, especially one of a light and swift breed trained for riding or racing.
– ORIGIN Middle English: from Old French *dromedaire* or late Latin *dromedarius (camelus)* 'swift camel', based on Greek *dromas, dromad-* 'runner'.

dromond /ˈdrɒmənd, ˈdrʌm-/ ▶ **noun** historical a large medieval ship of a kind used for war or commerce, chiefly in the Mediterranean.
– ORIGIN Middle English: via Old French and late Latin from late Greek *dromōn* 'light vessel', from Greek *dromos* 'running'.

dromos /ˈdrɒmɒs/ ▶ **noun** (pl. **dromoi** /-mɔɪ/) an avenue or passage leading into an ancient Greek temple or tomb, especially one between rows of columns or statues.
– ORIGIN Greek, 'course, running, avenue'; related to *dramein* 'to run'.

drone ▶ **verb** [no obj.] make a continuous low humming sound: *in the far distance a machine droned.*
■ speak tediously in a dull monotonous tone: *he reached for another beer while Jim* ***droned on.*** ■ [with adverbial of direction] move with a continuous humming sound: *traffic droned up and down the street.*
▶ **noun 1** a low continuous humming sound: *he nodded off to the drone of the car engine.*
■ informal a monotonous speech: *only twenty minutes of the hour-long drone had passed.* ■ a continuous musical note, typically of low pitch. ■ a musical instrument, or part of one, sounding such a continuous note, in particular (also **drone pipe**) a pipe in a bagpipe or (also **drone string**) a string in an instrument such as a hurdy-gurdy or a sitar.
2 a male bee in a colony of social bees, which does no work but can fertilize a queen.
■ figurative a person who does no useful work and lives off others.
3 a remote-controlled pilotless aircraft or missile.
– ORIGIN Old English *drān, drǣn* 'male bee', from a West Germanic verb meaning 'resound, boom'; related to Dutch *dreunen* 'to drone', German *dröhnen* 'to roar', and Swedish *dröna* 'to drowse'.

drone fly ▶ **noun** a hoverfly that resembles a honeybee. Its larva is the rat-tailed maggot.
• *Eristalis tenax*, family Syrphidae.

drongo /ˈdrɒŋgəʊ/ ▶ **noun** (pl. **-os** or **-oes**) **1** a songbird with glossy black plumage and typically a long forked tail and a crest, found in Africa, southern Asia, and Australia. [ORIGIN: mid 19th cent.: from Malagasy.]
• Family Dicruridae and genus *Dicrurus*: several species.
2 informal, chiefly Austral./NZ a stupid or incompetent person. [ORIGIN: said to be from the name of an Australian racehorse of the 1920s which consistently finished last or near last.]

droob /druːb/ ▶ **noun** Austral. informal an unprepossessing or contemptible person.
– ORIGIN 1930s: perhaps related to **DROOP**.

droog /druːg/ ▶ **noun** informal a young man belonging to a street gang.
– ORIGIN 1962: coined by Anthony Burgess in *Clockwork Orange*; alteration of Russian *drug* 'friend'.

drool ▶ **verb** [no obj.] drop saliva uncontrollably from the mouth: *the baby begins to drool, then to cough.*
■ informal make an excessive and obvious show of pleasure or desire: *I could imagine him as a schoolmaster being* ***drooled over*** *by the girls.*
▶ **noun** [mass noun] saliva falling from the mouth.
– ORIGIN early 19th cent.: contraction of **DRIVEL**.

droop ▶ **verb** [no obj.] bend or hang downwards limply: *a long black cloak drooped from his shoulders.*
■ sag down from or as if from weariness or dejection: *his eyelids drooped and he became drowsy* | figurative *the scenes are so lengthy that the reader's spirits droop.* ■ [with obj.] cause to bend or hang downwards: *James hid his face in his hands and drooped his head.*
▶ **noun** [in sing.] an act or instance of drooping; a limp or weary attitude: *the exhausted droop of her shoulders.*
– ORIGIN Middle English: from Old Norse *drúpa* 'hang the head'; related to **DRIP** and **DROP**.

droop-snoot ▶ **noun** informal a downward-sloping nose of an aircraft or motor vehicle, especially one that is of variable pitch, giving an efficient aerodynamic profile.
– DERIVATIVES **droop-snooted** adjective.

droopy ▶ **adjective** (**droopier**, **droopiest**) hanging down limply; drooping: *a droopy moustache.*
■ lacking strength or spirit: *she was a lovely girl in a rather droopy, Pre-Raphaelite way.*
– DERIVATIVES **droopily** adverb, **droopiness** noun.

drop ▶ **verb** (**dropped**, **dropping**) [with obj.] **1** let or make (something) fall vertically: *the fire was caused by someone dropping a lighted cigarette* | *they dropped bombs on Caen during the raid.*
■ deliver (supplies or troops) by parachute: *the airlift dropped food into the camp.* ■ Rugby score (a goal) by a drop kick: [as adj. **dropped**] *Botha responded with a superb dropped goal.* ■ (of an animal, especially a mare, cow, or ewe) give birth to (young). ■ informal take (a drug, especially LSD) orally: *he dropped a lot of acid in the Sixties.*
2 [no obj. and usu. with adverbial] fall vertically: *the spoon dropped with a clatter from her hand.*
■ (of a person) allow oneself to fall; let oneself down without jumping: *they escaped by climbing out of the window and dropping to the ground.* ■ (of a person or animal) sink to or towards the ground: *he dropped to his knees in the mud.* ■ informal collapse or die from exhaustion: *he looked* ***ready to drop.*** ■ (of ground) slope steeply down: *the cliff drops ninety metres to the valley below.*
3 make or become lower, weaker, or less: [with obj.] *he dropped his voice as she came into the room* | [no obj.] *pre-tax profits dropped by 37 per cent* | *tourism has* ***dropped off*** *in the last few years.*
4 abandon or discontinue (a course of action or study): *the charges against him were dropped last year* | *drop everything and get over here!*
■ discard or exclude (someone or something): *they were dropped from the team in the reshuffle.* ■ informal stop associating with: *I was under pressure from family and friends to drop Barbara.*
5 set down or unload (a passenger or goods), especially on the way to somewhere else: *he* ***dropped*** *the load* ***off*** *at a dealer's* | *his mum dropped him outside and drove off to work.*
■ [with obj. and adverbial] put or leave in a particular place without ceremony or formality: *just drop it in the post when you've got time.* ■ mention in passing, typically in order to impress: *she dropped a remark about having been included in the selection.*
6 (in sport) fail to win (a point or a match).
■ informal lose (money), especially through gambling: *he reckoned I'd dropped forty thousand pounds.*
7 Bridge be forced to play (a relatively high card) as a loser under an opponent's higher card, because it is the only card in its suit held in the hand.
■ force (an opponent's high card) to be played as a loser in this way: *declarer dropped West's queen on the second round of spades.* ■ [no obj.] (of a card) be played in this way: *the queen dropped.*
▶ **noun 1** a small round or pear-shaped portion of liquid that hangs or falls or adheres to a surface: *the first* ***drops of*** *rain splashed on the ground.*
■ [often with negative] a very small amount of liquid: *there was not a drop of water in sight.* ■ [usu. with negative] a drink of alcoholic liquor: *he doesn't touch a drop during the week.* ■ (**drops**) liquid medication to be measured or applied in very small amounts: *eye drops.*
2 [usu. in sing.] an instance of falling or dropping: *they left within five minutes of the drop of the curtain.*
■ an act of dropping supplies or troops by parachute: *the planes finally managed to make the drop.* ■ a fall in amount, quality, or rate: *a significant* ***drop in*** *consumer spending.* ■ an abrupt fall or slope: *standing on the lip of a sixty-foot drop.* ■ (**the drop**) informal the relegation of a sports team to a lower league or division. ■ (**the drop**) Bridge the playing of a high card underneath an opponent's higher card, because it is the only card in its suit held in the hand.
3 something that drops or is dropped, in particular:
■ a section of theatrical scenery lowered from the flies; a drop cloth or drop curtain. ■ a trapdoor on a gallows, the opening of which causes the prisoner to fall and thus be hanged. ■ (**the drop**) execution by hanging.
4 something resembling a drop of liquid in shape, in particular:
■ [usu. with modifier] a sweet or lozenge, especially a boiled one: *a chocolate drop.* ■ a pendant earring.
5 informal a delivery: *I got to the depot and made the drop.*
■ US a letter box. ■ a hiding place for stolen, illicit, or secret things: *the lavatory's water cistern could be used as a letter drop.*
– PHRASES **at the drop of a hat** informal without delay or good reason: *he used to be very bashful, blushing at the drop of a hat.* **drop one's aitches** omit the 'h' sound from the beginning of words (in Britain often regarded as a sign that the speaker belongs to a low social class). **drop asleep** fall gently asleep, especially without intending to. **drop the ball** N. Amer. informal make a mistake; mishandle things: *I really dropped the ball on this one.* [ORIGIN: with allusion to mishandling in baseball.] **drop a brick** Brit. informal make an indiscreet or embarrassing remark: *he dropped a brick when he admitted that he knew where we were going.* **drop a clanger** Brit. informal make an embarrassing or foolish mistake: *he admitted he might have dropped his first managerial clanger.* **drop a curtsy** Brit. make a curtsy. **drop dead** die suddenly and unexpectedly: *she had seen her father drop dead of a heart attack.* ■ [in imperative] informal used as an expression of intense scorn or dislike. **drop a** (or **the**) **dime on** US informal inform on (someone) to the police. **drop one's guard** abandon one's habitual defensive or protective stance. **drop a hint** (or **drop hints**) let fall a hint or hints, as if casually or unconsciously: *he was dropping hints that in future he would be taking a back seat in politics.* **a drop in the ocean** (or **in a bucket**) a very small amount compared with what is needed or expected: *the £550 million saving is likely to be a drop in the ocean.* **drop someone a line** send someone a note or letter in a casual manner: *drop me a line at the usual address.* **drop names** see **NAME-DROPPING**. **drop one's serve** (in tennis) lose a game in which one is serving. **drop a stitch** let a stitch fall off the end of a knitting needle. **drop one's trousers** deliberately let one's trousers fall down, especially in a public place. **have the drop on** informal have the advantage over: *if your enemy gets the drop on you he can kill you.* **have had a drop too much** informal be drunk: *obstreperous squaddies who have had a drop too much.*
– DERIVATIVES **droppable** adjective.
– ORIGIN Old English *dropa* (noun), *droppian* (verb), of Germanic origin; related to German *Tropfen* 'a drop', *tropfen* 'to drip', also to **DRIP** and **DROOP**.
▶ **drop back/behind** fall back or get left behind: *the colt was struggling to stay with the pace and started to drop back.*
drop by/in call informally and briefly as a visitor: *they would unexpectedly* ***drop in on*** *us.*
drop into 1 call casually and informally at (a place): *he'd actually considered dropping into one of the pickup bars.* **2** pass quickly and easily into (a habitual state or manner): *she couldn't help dropping into a Geordie accent.*
drop off fall asleep easily, especially without intending to: *struggle as she might, she kept dropping off.*
drop out 1 cease to participate in a race or competition. **2** abandon a course of study: *kids who had* ***dropped out of*** *college.* **3** reject conventional society to pursue an alternative lifestyle: *a child of the sixties who had temporarily dropped out.* **4** Rugby restart play with a drop kick. ■ score a drop goal.

drop capital (also **drop initial**) ▶ **noun** a large capital letter at the beginning of a section of text, occupying more than the depth of one line.

drop cloth ▶ **noun 1** another term for **DROP CURTAIN**.
2 North American term for **DUST SHEET**.

drop curtain ▶ **noun** a curtain or painted cloth lowered vertically on to a theatre stage.

drop-dead ▶ **adjective** informal used to emphasize how attractive someone or something is: *her drop-dead good looks* | [as submodifier] *a* ***drop-dead gorgeous*** *Hollywood icon.*

drop-down ▶ **adjective** [attrib.] dropping down or unfolding when required: *a drop-down bed.*
■ Computing (of a menu) appearing below a menu title when it is selected, and remaining until used or dismissed. Compare with **PULL-DOWN**.

drop-forged ▶ **adjective** (of a metal object) made by forcing hot metal into or through a die with a drop hammer.
– DERIVATIVES **drop-forging** noun.

drop goal ▶ **noun** Rugby a goal scored in open play by drop-kicking the ball over the crossbar, scoring three points (rugby union) or one point (rugby league).

drop hammer ▶ **noun** a large heavy weight raised mechanically and allowed to drop, as used in drop-forging and piledriving.

drop handlebars (also **dropped handlebars**) ▶ **plural noun** bicycle handlebars of which the handles are bent below the rest of the bar, used especially on racing cycles.

drophead ▶ **noun** Brit. a car having a fabric roof that can be folded down; a convertible.

drop-in ▶ adjective **1** visited on an informal basis without booking or appointments: *a drop-in disco.*
2 (of an object such as a chair seat) designed to drop into position.

drop-in centre ▶ noun a place run by a welfare agency or charity where people may call casually for advice or assistance.

drop initial ▶ noun another term for **DROP CAPITAL**.

drop kick ▶ noun (chiefly in rugby) a kick made by dropping the ball and kicking it as it bounces up from the ground.
▪(chiefly in martial arts) a flying kick made against an opponent while dropping to the ground.
▶ verb (**drop-kick**) [with obj.] kick using a drop kick.

drop-leaf ▶ adjective [attrib.] (of a table) having a hinged flap.

droplet ▶ noun a very small drop of a liquid: *droplets of water.*

drop-off ▶ noun **1** a decline or decrease: *a sudden drop-off in tourism.*
2 chiefly N. Amer. a sheer downward slope; a cliff: *dizzy drop-offs on either side.*
▶ adjective [attrib.] relating to or allowing the delivery or depositing of something: *the mailbags are left at drop-off points.*

dropout ▶ noun **1** a person who has abandoned a course of study or who has rejected conventional society to pursue an alternative lifestyle: *a college dropout.*
2 Rugby the restarting of play with a drop kick.
3 a momentary loss of recorded audio signal or an error in reading data on a magnetic tape or disk, usually due to a flaw in the coating.
4 (usu. **dropouts**) a U-shaped slot at the end of a fork or stay on a bicycle, made to receive the axle and enabling the wheel to be changed rapidly.

dropper ▶ noun **1** a short glass tube with a rubber bulb at one end and a tiny hole at the other, for measuring out drops of medicine or other liquids.
2 Austral./NZ & S. African a light vertical stave in a fence, especially a lath used to separate the wires of a wire fence.
3 Fishing a subsidiary line or loop of filament attached to a main line or leader.
– ORIGIN mid 17th cent. (in the sense 'a person who lets something drop'); sense 1 is first recorded in the late 19th cent.

droppings ▶ plural noun the excrement of certain animals, such as rodents, sheep, birds, and insects.

drop scene ▶ noun a drop curtain used as part of stage scenery, especially one in front of which a scene is played while the setting is changed behind.
▪the last scene of a play.

drop scone ▶ noun a small thick pancake made by dropping spoonfuls of batter on to a griddle or other heated surface.

dropseed ▶ noun [mass noun] a grass that readily drops its seeds.
● Genus *Sporobolus*, family Gramineae: several species, including the widespread North American **sand dropseed** (*S. cryptandrus*), which has a high yield of edible grain.

drop shot ▶ noun (chiefly in tennis or squash) a softly hit shot, usually with backspin, which drops abruptly to the ground.

drop shoulder (also **dropped shoulder**) ▶ noun a style of shoulder on a garment cut so that the seam is positioned on the upper arm rather than the shoulder.

dropsical /ˈdrɒpsɪk(ə)l/ ▶ adjective affected with or characteristic of dropsy; oedematous.
– ORIGIN late 17th cent.: from **DROPSY**[1], replacing earlier *hydropic(al)*, via Latin from Greek *hudrōps* 'dropsy'.

dropside ▶ adjective [attrib.] (of a cot or a truck) having a side that drops down to open.
▶ noun a side that drops down in this way.

drop-stitch ▶ adjective denoting an openwork pattern in knitted garments made by dropping a made stitch at intervals: *a drop-stitch cardigan.*

dropsy[1] /ˈdrɒpsi/ ▶ noun (pl. **-ies**) old-fashioned or less technical term for **OEDEMA**.
– ORIGIN Middle English: shortening of *idropesie*, earlier form of obsolete *hydropsy*, via Old French and Latin from Greek *hudrōps* 'dropsy', from *hudōr* 'water'.

dropsy[2] /ˈdrɒpsi/ ▶ noun (pl. **-ies**) Brit. informal a tip or bribe: *McCloy's little dropsy for services rendered.*
– ORIGIN 1930s: slang, elaborated form of slang *drop* 'a bribe'.

drop tank ▶ noun an external fuel tank on an aircraft which can be jettisoned when empty.

drop test ▶ noun a test of the strength of an object, in which it is dropped under standard conditions or a set weight is dropped on it from a given height.
– DERIVATIVES **drop-testing** noun.

drop-top ▶ noun another term for **DROPHEAD**.

drop waist (also **dropped waist**) ▶ noun a style of waistline on a dress cut so that the seam is positioned at the hips rather than the waist.

dropwort ▶ noun a Eurasian grassland plant with small white flowers and divided leaves, related to meadowsweet.
● *Filipendula vulgaris*, family Rosaceae.
– ORIGIN Middle English: so named because it has small drop-like fibrous tubers on its roots.

drop zone (also **dropping zone**) ▶ noun a designated area into which troops or supplies are dropped by parachute or in which skydivers land.

drosera /ˈdrɒs(ə)rə/ ▶ noun a sundew (insectivorous plant).
● Genus *Drosera*, family Droseraceae.
– ORIGIN modern Latin, from Greek *droseros* 'dewy' (from the appearance of the glistening hairs on the leaves).

droshky /ˈdrɒʃki/ ▶ noun (pl. **-ies**) historical a low four-wheeled open carriage of a kind formerly used in Russia.
– ORIGIN early 19th cent.: from Russian *drozhki*, diminutive of *drogi* 'wagon', from *droga* 'shaft, carriage pole'.

drosophila /drɒˈsɒfɪlə/ ▶ noun a small fruit fly, used extensively in genetic research because of its large chromosomes, numerous varieties, and rapid rate of reproduction.
● Genus *Drosophila*, family Drosophilidae: in particular *D. melanogaster.*
– ORIGIN modern Latin, from Greek *drosos* 'dew, moisture' + *philos* 'loving'.

dross ▶ noun [mass noun] something regarded as worthless; rubbish: *there are bargains if you have the patience to sift through the dross.*
▪foreign matter, dregs, or mineral waste, in particular scum formed on the surface of molten metal.
– DERIVATIVES **drossy** adjective.
– ORIGIN Old English *drōs* (in the sense 'scum on molten metal'); related to Dutch *droesem* and German *Drusen* 'dregs, lees'.

Drottningholm /ˈdrɒtnɪŋˌhəʊlm/ the winter palace of the Swedish royal family, on an island to the west of Stockholm.

drought /draʊt/ ▶ noun a prolonged period of abnormally low rainfall; a shortage of water resulting from this.
▪[usu. with modifier] figurative a prolonged absence of something specified: *he ended a five-game goal drought.* ▪ [mass noun] archaic thirst.
– DERIVATIVES **droughtiness** noun, **droughty** adjective.
– ORIGIN late Old English *drūgath* 'dryness', of Germanic origin; compare with Dutch *droogte*; related to **DRY**.

drouth /draʊθ/ ▶ noun dialect or poetic form of **DROUGHT**.
– DERIVATIVES **drouthy** adjective.

Drouzhba /ˈdruːʒbə/ a resort town on the Black Sea coast of Bulgaria. Also called **SVETI KONSTANTIN**.

drove[1] past of **DRIVE**.

drove[2] ▶ noun a herd or flock of animals being driven in a body: *a drove of cattle.*
▪a large number of people or things doing or undergoing the same thing: *tourists have stayed away in droves this summer.*
▶ verb [with obj.] [usu. as noun **droving**] historical drive (livestock, especially cattle) to market, typically as one's job: *the droving trade.*
– DERIVATIVES **drover** noun.
– ORIGIN Old English *drāf*, related to *drīfan* 'to drive'.

drove road ▶ noun an ancient roadway along which cattle were driven to market.

drown ▶ verb [no obj.] die through submersion in and inhalation of water: *a motorist drowned when her car plunged off the edge of a quay* | (**be drowned**) *two fishermen were drowned when their motor boat capsized.*
▪[with obj.] deliberately kill (a person or animal) in this way: *he killed his wife then drowned himself in a fit of despair.* ▪ [with obj.] submerge or flood (an area): *when the ice melted the valleys were drowned.* ▪ [with obj.] (of a sound) make (another sound) inaudible by being much louder: *his voice was* ***drowned out*** *by the approaching engine noise.*
– PHRASES **drown one's sorrows** forget one's problems by getting drunk. **like a drowned rat** extremely wet and bedraggled: *she arrived at the church looking like a drowned rat.*
– ORIGIN Middle English (originally northern): related to Old Norse *drukkna* 'to be drowned', also to **DRINK**.

drowned valley ▶ noun a valley partly or wholly submerged by a rise in sea level.

drowse /draʊz/ ▶ verb [no obj.] be half asleep; doze intermittently: *he was beginning to drowse in his chair.*
▪[with obj.] archaic make sleepy. ▪ archaic be sluggish or inactive: *let not your prudence drowse.*
▶ noun [in sing.] a light sleep; a condition of being half asleep.
– ORIGIN late 16th cent.: back-formation from **DROWSY**.

drowsy ▶ adjective (**drowsier**, **drowsiest**) sleepy and lethargic; half asleep: *the wine had made her drowsy.*
▪causing sleepiness: *the drowsy heat of the meadows.* ▪ (especially of a place) very peaceful and quiet: *a drowsy suburb called Surrey Hills.*
– DERIVATIVES **drowsily** adverb, **drowsiness** noun.
– ORIGIN late 15th cent.: probably from the stem of Old English *drūsian* 'be languid or slow', of Germanic origin; related to **DREARY**.

drub ▶ verb (**drubbed**, **drubbing**) [with obj.] hit or beat (someone) repeatedly.
▪informal defeat thoroughly in a match or contest: *the Cleveland Indians drubbed Baltimore 9–0.*
– ORIGIN early 17th cent.: probably from Arabic *ḍaraba* 'to beat, bastinado'. The first recorded uses in English are by travellers in the Near East referring specifically to the punishment of bastinado.

drubbing ▶ noun a beating; a thrashing: *I'll give the scoundrels a drubbing if I can!*
▪informal a resounding defeat in a match or contest.

drudge ▶ noun a person made to do hard, menial, or dull work: *she was little more than a drudge round the house.*
▶ verb [no obj.] archaic do such work.
– ORIGIN Middle English (as a noun): of unknown origin; perhaps related to **DRAG**.

drudgery ▶ noun [mass noun] hard, menial, or dull work: *domestic drudgery.*

drug ▶ noun a substance which has a physiological effect when ingested or otherwise introduced into the body, in particular:
▪a medicine, especially a pharmaceutical preparation: *a new drug aimed at sufferers from Parkinson's disease.* ▪ a substance taken for its narcotic or stimulant effects, often illegally: [as modifier] *a drug addict* | figurative *mass adoration is a highly addictive drug.*
▶ verb (**drugged**, **drugging**) [with obj.] administer a drug to (someone) in order to induce stupor or insensibility: *they were drugged to keep them quiet.*
▪add a drug to (food or drink): [as adj. **drugged**] *he offered them drugged wine.* ▪ [no obj.] informal take illegally obtained drugs: *the customers drank and drugged peacefully.*
– PHRASES **do drugs** informal take illegal drugs. **on drugs** taking medically prescribed drugs: *on drugs for high blood pressure.* ▪ under the influence of or habitually taking illegal drugs.
– ORIGIN Middle English: from Old French *drogue*, possibly from Middle Dutch *droge vate*, literally 'dry vats', referring to the contents (i.e. dry goods).

drug abuse ▶ noun [mass noun] the habitual taking of illegal drugs.

drug baron (also **drugs baron**) ▶ noun a person who controls an organization dealing in illegal drugs.

drug bust (also **drugs bust**) ▶ noun informal a seizure of illegal drugs by the police or other law-enforcement agency.

drug-free ▶ adjective (of a place) where no illegal drugs are used: *a drug-free zone.*
▪(of a person) not taking illegal drugs.

drugget /ˈdrʌgɪt/ ▶ noun [mass noun] a floor covering made of a coarse woven fabric.
– ORIGIN mid 16th cent.: from French *droguet*, from *drogue* in the sense 'poor-quality article'.

b **b**ut | d **d**og | f **f**ew | g **g**et | h **h**e | j **y**es | k **c**at | l **l**eg | m **m**an | n **n**o | p **p**en | r **r**ed | s **s**it | t **t**op | v **v**oice | w **w**e | z **z**oo | ʃ **sh**e | ʒ deci**si**on | θ **th**in | ð **th**is | ŋ ri**ng** | x lo**ch** | tʃ **ch**ip | dʒ **j**ar

druggist ▶ noun chiefly N. Amer. a pharmacist or retailer of medicinal drugs.
– ORIGIN early 17th cent.: from French *droguiste*, from *drogue* 'drug'.

druggy informal ▶ adjective caused by or involving drugs: *a druggy haze.*
■ given to taking drugs, especially illegal ones: *the druggy world of rock and roll.*
▶ noun (also **druggie**) (pl. **-ies**) a drug addict.
– ORIGIN late 16th cent. (as an adjective): from **DRUG** + **-Y**¹. The noun dates from the 1960s.

drug squad (also **drugs squad**) ▶ noun chiefly Brit. a division of a police force investigating crimes involving illegal drugs.

drugstore ▶ noun N. Amer. a pharmacy which also sells toiletries and other articles.

drugstore beetle ▶ noun another term for **BISCUIT BEETLE**.

Druid /ˈdruːɪd/ ▶ noun a priest, magician, or soothsayer in the ancient Celtic religion.
■ a member of a present-day group claiming to represent or be derived from this religion.
– DERIVATIVES **Druidic** adjective, **Druidical** adjective, **Druidism** noun.
– ORIGIN from Latin *druidae*, *druides* (plural), from Gaulish; related to Irish *draoidh* 'magician, sorcerer'.

drum¹ ▶ noun **1** a percussion instrument sounded by being struck with sticks or the hands, typically cylindrical, barrel-shaped, or bowl-shaped with a taut membrane over one or both ends.
■ (**drums**) a drum kit. ■ (**drums**) the percussion section of a band or orchestra. ■ [in sing.] a sound made by or resembling that of a drum: *the drum of their feet.* ■ historical a military drummer.
2 something resembling or likened to a drum in shape, in particular:
■ a cylindrical container or receptacle: *a drum of powdered bleach.* See also **OIL DRUM**. ■ a rotating cylindrical part in a washing machine, in which the washing is placed. ■ a similar cylindrical part in certain other appliances. ■ Architecture the circular vertical wall supporting a dome. ■ Architecture a stone block forming part of a column. ■ Austral./NZ a tramp's bundle of belongings.
3 Brit. informal a house or flat.
■ Austral. informal a brothel.
4 an evening or afternoon tea party of a kind that was popular in the late 18th and early 19th century.
5 Austral. informal a piece of reliable inside information: *he had got the drum that the police wouldn't lock us up.* [ORIGIN: early 20th cent.: perhaps by association with the musical instrument used to give a signal.]
▶ verb (**drummed**, **drumming**) **1** [no obj.] play on a drum.
■ make a continuous rhythmic noise: *she felt the blood drumming in her ears* | [as noun **drumming**] *the drumming of hooves.* ■ [with obj.] beat (the fingers, feet, etc.) repeatedly on a surface, especially as a sign of impatience or annoyance: *waiting around an empty table, drumming their fingers.* ■ (of a woodpecker) strike the bill rapidly on a dead trunk or branch, especially as a sound indicating a territorial claim. ■ (of a snipe) vibrate the outer tail feathers in a diving display flight, making a throbbing sound.
2 [with obj.] Austral. informal give (someone) reliable information or a warning: *I'm drumming you, if they come I'm going.* [ORIGIN: see sense 5 of the noun.]
– PHRASES **beat** (or **bang**) **the drum of** (or **for**) be ostentatiously in support of: *he bangs the drum of the free market.*
– ORIGIN Middle English: from Middle Dutch or Low German *tromme*, of imitative origin.
▶ **drum something into** drive a lesson into (someone) by constant repetition: *it had been drummed into them to dress correctly.*
drum someone out expel or dismiss someone with ignominy from a place or institution: *he was **drummed out of** the air force.* [ORIGIN: with allusion to the formal military drum beat accompanying dismissal from a regiment.]
drum something up attempt to obtain something by constant canvassing or soliciting: *the organizers are hoping to drum up support from local businesses.*

drum² ▶ noun Scottish & Irish a long narrow hill, especially one separating two parallel valleys.
– ORIGIN early 18th cent.: from Scottish Gaelic and Irish *druim* 'ridge'.

drum³ (also **drumfish**) ▶ noun (pl. same or **drums**) a fish that makes a drumming sound by vibrating its swim bladder, found mainly in estuarine and shallow coastal waters. Also called **CROAKER**.
• Family Sciaenidae (the **drum family**): many species, including the **black drum** (*Pogonias cromis*) of the western Atlantic. The drum family also includes the mulloway and a number of marine fishes that resemble salmon (e.g. the weakfish).

drum and bass ▶ noun [mass noun] a type of dance music characterized by bare instrumentation consisting largely of electronic drums and bass, originating in Britain during the early 1990s.

drumbeat ▶ noun a stroke or pattern of strokes on a drum: *she was aware of a constant, faint drumbeat.*

drum brake ▶ noun a type of vehicle brake in which brake shoes press against the inside of a drum on the wheel.

drumfire ▶ noun [mass noun] heavy continuous rapid artillery fire.

drumfish ▶ noun (pl. same or **-fishes**) see **DRUM**³.

drumhead ▶ noun **1** the membrane or skin of a drum.
2 a winter cabbage of a flat-topped variety.
3 chiefly historical the circular top of a ship's capstan, with holes into which bars are placed to turn it.
▶ adjective [attrib.] carried out by or as if by an army in the field; improvised or summary: *a drumhead court martial.*

drum kit ▶ noun a set of drums, cymbals, and other percussion instruments used with drumsticks in jazz and popular music. The most basic components are a foot-operated bass drum, a snare drum, a suspended cymbal, and one or more tom-toms.

drumlin /ˈdrʌmlɪn/ ▶ noun Geology a low oval mound or small hill, typically one of a group, consisting of compacted boulder clay moulded by past glacial action.
– ORIGIN mid 19th cent.: probably from **DRUM**² + *-lin* from **-LING**.

drum machine ▶ noun a programmable electronic device able to imitate the sounds of a drum kit.

drum major ▶ noun **1** a non-commissioned officer commanding the drummers of a regimental band.
2 the male leader of a marching band, who often twirls a baton.
■ a male member of a baton-twirling parading group.

drum majorette ▶ noun the female leader of a marching band, who often twirls a baton.
■ a female member of such a band.

drummer ▶ noun **1** a person who plays a drum or drums.
2 informal, chiefly US a travelling sales representative: *a drummer in electronic software.* [ORIGIN: from *drum up* (see **DRUM**¹).]
3 (also **silver drummer**) a deep-bodied marine fish with dark longitudinal stripes, found in shallow coastal waters of Australia.
• *Kyphosus sydneyanus*, family Kyphosidae.
4 Brit. informal, dated a thief or burglar.

drum pad ▶ noun an electronic device with one or more flat pads which imitate the sounds of a drum kit when struck.

drum roll ▶ noun a rapid succession of beats sounded on a drum, often used to introduce an announcement or event.

drumstick ▶ noun a stick, typically with a shaped or padded head, used for beating a drum.
■ the lower joint of the leg of a cooked chicken, turkey, or other fowl.

drumstick primrose (also **drumstick primula**) ▶ noun a Himalayan primula with a globular head of flowers on an erect stem.
• *Primula denticulata*, family Primulaceae.

drunk past participle of **DRINK**. ▶ adjective [predic.] affected by alcohol to the extent of losing control of one's faculties or behaviour: *he was so drunk he lurched from wall to wall* | ***drunk on** vodka.*
■ (**drunk with**) figurative overcome with (a strong emotion): *the crowd was high on euphoria and drunk with patriotism.*
▶ noun a person who is drunk or who habitually drinks to excess.
■ informal a drinking bout; a period of drunkenness: *he used to go on these blind drunks.*
– PHRASES **drunk and disorderly** creating a public disturbance under the influence of alcohol. (**as**) **drunk as a lord** (or **skunk**) extremely drunk.

drunkard ▶ noun a person who is habitually drunk.
– ORIGIN Middle English: from Middle Low German *drunkert*.

drunk-driving (also **drunken-driving**) ▶ noun North American term for **DRINK-DRIVING**.
– DERIVATIVES **drunk-driver** noun.

drunken ▶ adjective [attrib.] drunk or intoxicated: *gangs of drunken youths roamed the streets.*
■ habitually or frequently drunk: *his violent, drunken father.* ■ caused by or showing the effects of drink: *the man's drunken, slurred speech.*
– DERIVATIVES **drunkenly** adverb, **drunkenness** noun.
– ORIGIN Old English, archaic past participle of **DRINK**.

drunk tank ▶ noun N. Amer. informal a large prison cell for the detention of drunks.

drupe /druːp/ ▶ noun **1** Botany a fleshy fruit with thin skin and a central stone containing the seed, e.g. a plum, cherry, almond, or olive.
2 a small marine mollusc with a thick knobbly shell, found mainly in the Indo-Pacific.
• Genus *Drupa*, family Muricidae, class Gastropoda.
– DERIVATIVES **drupaceous** adjective (only in sense 1).
– ORIGIN mid 18th cent.: from Latin *drupa* 'overripe olive', from Greek *druppa* 'olive'.

drupel /ˈdruːp(ə)l/ ▶ noun Botany any of the small individual drupes forming a fleshy aggregate fruit such as a blackberry or raspberry.
– ORIGIN mid 19th cent.: from modern Latin *drupella*, diminutive of *drupa* 'overripe olive' (see **DRUPE**).

drupelet ▶ noun another term for **DRUPEL**.

Drury Lane /ˈdrʊəri/ the site in London of the Theatre Royal, one of London's most famous theatres.

druse /druːz/ ▶ noun **1** Geology a rock cavity lined with a crust of projecting crystals.
■ the crust of crystals lining such a cavity.
2 Botany a rounded cluster of calcium oxalate crystals found in some plant cells.
– DERIVATIVES **drusy** adjective (Geology).
– ORIGIN early 19th cent.: via French from German *Druse* 'weathered ore'.

druther /ˈdrʌðə/ N. Amer. informal ▶ noun (usu. **one's druthers**) a person's preference in a matter: *if I had my druthers, I would prefer to be a writer.*
▶ adverb rather; by preference.
– ORIGIN late 19th cent.: from a US regional pronunciation of *I'd rather*, contraction of *would rather*.

Druze /druːz/ (also **Druse**) ▶ noun (pl. same, **Druzes**, or **Druses**) a member of a political and religious sect of Islamic origin, living chiefly in Lebanon and Syria. The Druze broke away from the Ismaili Muslims in the 11th century; they are regarded as heretical by the Muslim community at large.
– ORIGIN from French, from Arabic *durūz* (plural), from the name of one of their founders, Muhammad ibn Ismail *al-Darazī* (died 1019).

dry ▶ adjective (**drier**, **driest**) **1** free from moisture or liquid; not wet or moist: *the jacket kept me warm and dry* | *he wiped it dry with his shirt.*
■ having lost all wetness or moisture over a period of time: *dry paint.* ■ for use without liquid: *the conversion of dry latrines into the flushing type.* ■ with little or no rainfall or humidity: *the West Coast has had two dry winters in a row.* ■ (of a river, lake, or stream) empty of water as a result of evaporation and lack of rainfall: *the river is always dry at this time of year.* ■ (of a source) not yielding a supply of water or oil: *a dry well.* ■ thirsty or thirst-making: *working in the hot sun is making me dry* | *dry work.* ■ (of a cow or other domestic animal) having stopped producing milk. ■ without grease or other moisturizer or lubricator: *cream conditioners for dry hair* | *his throat was dry and sore.* ■ (of bread or toast) without butter or other spreads: *only dry bread and water.*
2 figurative bare or lacking adornment: *the dry facts.*
■ unexciting; dull: *by current tastes the text is dry.* ■ unemotional, undemonstrative, or impassive: *Ralph gave me a dry, silent wave.* ■ (of a joke or sense of humour) subtle, expressed in a matter-of-fact way, and having the appearance of being unconscious or unintentional: *he delighted his friends with a dry, covert sense of humour.*
3 prohibiting the sale or consumption of alcoholic drink: *the country is strictly dry, in accordance with Islamic law.*
■ (of a person) no longer addicted to or drinking alcohol: *I heard much talk about how sobriety was more than staying straight or dry.*

4 (of an alcoholic drink) not sweet: *a dry, medium-bodied red wine.*
5 Brit. of or relating to political 'dries' (see sense 2 of the noun); rigidly monetarist.
▶ verb (**-ies, -ied**) [no obj.] **1** become dry: *waiting for the paint to dry* | *come in out of the rain and* **dry off** | *do not let the soil* **dry out** | *pools are left as the rivers* **dry up**.
■ [with obj.] cause to become dry: *they had washed and dried their hair.* ■ [with obj.] wipe tears from (the eyes): *she dried her eyes and blew her nose.* ■ wipe dishes dry with a cloth after they have been washed: [as noun **drying** or **drying up**] *if she washed up one day I did the drying up.* ■ [with obj.] [usu. as adj. **dried**] preserve by allowing or encouraging evaporation of moisture from: *dried flowers.* ■ [with obj.] (**dry an animal off**) cease milking and reduce the rations of a cow or other animal so that it stops producing milk.
2 theatrical slang forget one's lines: *a colleague of mine once dried in the middle of a scene.*
▶ noun (pl. **dries** or **drys**) **1** (**the dry**) chiefly Austral. the dry season: *the grass was yellowing and the dry had started.*
■ Austral. a tract of waterless country: *the forty-mile dry.*
2 (usu. **dries**) Brit. a Conservative politician in favour of strict monetarist policies (often used with reference to the politics of the 1980s).
3 US a person in favour of the prohibition of alcohol.
– PHRASES **come up dry** N. Amer. be unsuccessful: *experiments have so far come up dry.* (**as**) **dry as a bone** extremely dry. (**as**) **dry as dust** extremely dry. ■ extremely dull; lacking emotion, expression, or interest: *what the students learned was as dry as dust.* **there wasn't a dry eye (in the house)** (with reference to a play, film, or similar event) everyone in the audience was moved to tears.
– DERIVATIVES **dryish** adjective, **dryness** noun.
– ORIGIN Old English *drȳge* (adjective), *drȳgan* (verb), of Germanic origin; related to Middle Low German *dröge*, Dutch *droog*, and German *trocken*.

▶ **dry out** informal overcome alcoholism: *he intends to dry out and get his life back together again.*
dry up 1 informal cease talking: *then he dried up, and Phil couldn't get another word out of him.* **2** (of something perceived as a continuous flow or source) decrease and stop: *his commissions began to dry up.*

dryad /ˈdraɪəd, -ad/ ▶ noun **1** (in folklore and Greek mythology) a nymph inhabiting a tree, especially an oak tree, or a wood.
2 a dark brown Eurasian butterfly with two prominent bluish eyespots on each forewing.
● *Minois dryas,* subfamily Satyrinae, family Nymphalidae.
– ORIGIN via Old French and Latin from Greek *druas, druad-* 'tree nymph', from *drus* 'tree'.

dryad's saddle ▶ noun a common bracket fungus having a scaly yellowish-brown upper surface, found in both Eurasia and North America and edible when young.
● *Polyporus squamosus,* family Polyporaceae, class Hymenomycetes.

dryas /ˈdraɪəs/ ▶ noun **1** a plant of a genus that comprises the mountain avens.
● Genus *Dryas,* family Rosaceae.
2 (**Dryas**) Geology the first and third climatic stages of the late-glacial period in northern Europe, in which cold tundralike conditions prevailed and plants of the genus *Dryas* were abundant. The **Older Dryas** (about 15,000 to 12,000 years ago) followed the last ice retreat, and the **Younger Dryas** (about 10,800 to 10,000 years ago) followed the Allerød stage.
– ORIGIN modern Latin, from Greek *druas* (see **DRYAD**). The plant (sense 1) has leaves that resemble those of the oak (hence the association with dryads, being originally nymphs of the oak).

dry battery ▶ noun an electric battery consisting of one or more dry cells.

dry bulb ▶ noun an ordinary exposed thermometer bulb, especially as used in conjunction with a wet bulb.

dry cell ▶ noun an electric cell in which the electrolyte is absorbed in a solid to form a paste, preventing spillage.

dry-clean ▶ verb [with obj.] (usu. **be dry-cleaned**) clean (a garment) with an organic solvent, without using water: *I had my winter coat dry-cleaned recently* | [as noun **dry-cleaning**] *premises which offered dry-cleaning.*
– DERIVATIVES **dry-cleaner** noun.

dry cough ▶ noun a cough not accompanied by phlegm production.

dry-cure ▶ verb [with obj.] cure (meat or fish) with salt rather than in liquid.

Dryden /ˈdraɪd(ə)n/, John (1631–1700), English poet, critic, and dramatist of the Augustan Age. He is best known for *Marriage à la mode* (comedy, 1673), *All for Love* (a tragedy based on Shakespeare's *Antony and Cleopatra,* 1678), and *Absalom and Achitophel* (verse satire in heroic couplets, 1681).

dry distillation ▶ noun another term for **DESTRUCTIVE DISTILLATION**.

dry dock ▶ noun a dock which can be drained of water to allow the inspection and repair of a ship's hull.
▶ verb (**dry-dock**) [with obj.] place (a ship) in a dry dock.

dryer (also **drier**) ▶ noun **1** a machine or device for drying something, especially the hair or laundry.
2 a substance mixed with oil paint or ink to promote drying.
– ORIGIN Middle English (in the sense 'person who dries'): from the verb **DRY** + **-ER**[1].

dry eye ▶ noun [mass noun] Medicine inflammation of the conjunctiva and cornea of the eye, due to inadequate tear secretion.

dry-eyed ▶ adjective (of a person) not crying: *Jill was dry-eyed and stoical under assault.*

dry farming ▶ noun another term for **DRY-LAND FARMING**.

dry fly ▶ noun an artificial fishing fly which is made to float lightly on the water.

dry-fry ▶ verb [with obj.] fry (food) in a pan without fat or oil.

dry goods ▶ plural noun **1** solid commodities traded in bulk, such as tea, sugar, and grain.
2 chiefly N. Amer. drapery and haberdashery.

dry hole ▶ noun a well drilled for oil or gas but yielding none.

dry ice ▶ noun [mass noun] solid carbon dioxide.
■ the cold dense white mist produced by this in air, used for theatrical effects.

drying oil ▶ noun an oil that thickens or hardens on exposure to air, especially one used by artists in mixing paint.

dry land ▶ noun [mass noun] land as opposed to the sea or another body of water: *the tide came in and cut off his route to dry land.*

dry-land farming (also **dry farming**) ▶ noun [mass noun] chiefly N. Amer. a method of farming in semi-arid areas without the aid of irrigation, using drought-resistant crops and conserving moisture.

drylands ▶ plural noun chiefly N. Amer. an arid area; a region with low rainfall.

dry lease ▶ noun an arrangement covering the hire of an aircraft which does not include provision of a flight crew.
▶ verb (**dry-lease**) [with obj.] hire (an aircraft) using such an arrangement.

dry lining ▶ noun a lining to an interior wall that does not need to be plastered.

dryly ▶ adverb variant spelling of **DRILY**.

dry matter ▶ noun [mass noun] **1** the part of a foodstuff or other substance which would remain if all its water content was removed.
2 NZ feedstuff for farm animals.

dry measure ▶ noun a measure of volume for loose dry goods such as grain, tea, and sugar.

dry milk ▶ noun [mass noun] US milk that has been preserved by evaporation and reduction to powder.

dry mounting ▶ noun [mass noun] Photography a process in which a print is bonded to a mount using a layer of shellac in a hot press.

dry-nurse ▶ noun archaic a woman who looks after a baby but does not breastfeed it.

Dryopithecus /ˌdraɪəˈpɪθɪkəs/ ▶ noun a fossil anthropoid ape of the middle Miocene to early Pliocene periods, of a genus including the supposed common ancestor of gorillas, chimpanzees, and humans.
● Genus *Dryopithecus,* family Pongidae.
– DERIVATIVES **dryopithecine** /-siːn/ noun & adjective.
– ORIGIN modern Latin, from Greek *drus* 'tree' + *pithēkos* 'ape'.

dry painting ▶ noun another term for **SAND PAINTING**.

dry plate ▶ noun Photography a glass plate coated with a light-sensitive gelatin-based emulsion, used formerly as an improvement on the earlier wet plate.

dry point ▶ noun a steel needle for engraving on a bare copper plate without acid.
■ an engraving or print so produced. ■ [mass noun] engraving by this means.

dry-roasted (also **dry-roast**) ▶ adjective roasted without fat or oil: *dry-roasted peanuts.*

dry rot ▶ noun **1** [mass noun] fungal timber decay occurring in poorly ventilated conditions in buildings, resulting in cracking and powdering of the wood.
2 (also **dry rot fungus**) the fungus that causes this.
● *Serpula lacrymans,* family Corticiaceae, class Hymenomycetes.

dry run ▶ noun informal a rehearsal of a performance or procedure before the real one: *the president went through a dry run of his speech.*

dry-salt ▶ verb another term for **DRY-CURE**.

dry-salter ▶ noun Brit. historical a dealer in dyes, gums, and drugs, and sometimes also in pickles and other preserved foodstuffs.

dry shampoo ▶ noun [mass noun] a shampoo in powder form, used without the addition of water.

dry shave ▶ noun a shave without shaving foam, typically one using an electric razor.
▶ verb (**dry-shave**) [no obj.] shave in this way.
– DERIVATIVES **dry-shaver** noun.

dry-shod ▶ adjective & adverb without wetting one's shoes: [as adj.] *dry-shod evacuation involved getting into a lifeboat at deck level.*

dry sink ▶ noun N. Amer. an antique kitchen cabinet with an inset basin, now generally used as an ornament rather than for practical purposes.

dry-ski ▶ adjective [attrib.] denoting or relating to skiing on an artificial surface: *a dry-ski slope.*

dry slope (also **dry-ski slope**) ▶ noun an artificial ski slope used for practice and training.

drystone ▶ adjective [attrib.] Brit. (of a stone wall) built without using mortar.

drysuit ▶ noun a waterproof rubber suit worn for water sports and diving, under which warm clothes can be worn.

dry valley ▶ noun a valley cut by water erosion but containing no permanent surface stream, typically one occurring in an area of porous rock such as limestone.

drywall ▶ noun [mass noun] N. Amer. plasterboard.

dry wash ▶ noun US the dry bed of an intermittent stream.

dry well ▶ noun **1** a shaft or chamber constructed in the ground in order to aid drainage, sometimes containing pumping equipment.
2 another term for **DRY HOLE**.

DS ▶ abbreviation for ■ Music dal segno. ■ Military directing staff. ■ document signed.

DSC ▶ abbreviation for (in the UK) Distinguished Service Cross, a decoration for distinguished active service at sea, instituted in 1914.

DSc ▶ abbreviation for Doctor of Science.

DSM ▶ abbreviation for (in the UK) Distinguished Service Medal, a medal for distinguished service at sea, instituted in 1914.

DSO ▶ abbreviation for (in the UK) Distinguished Service Order, a decoration for distinguished service awarded to officers of the army and navy, instituted in 1886.

DSP ▶ abbreviation ■ (in genealogy) died without issue. [ORIGIN: from Latin *decessit sine prole.*] ■ (in computing and sound reproduction) digital signal processor or processing.

DSS ▶ abbreviation for ■ decision support system. ■ (in the UK) Department of Social Security. Formerly called **DHSS**.

DST ▶ abbreviation for daylight saving time.

DTI ▶ abbreviation for (in the UK) Department of Trade and Industry.

DTP ▶ abbreviation for desktop publishing.

DTp ▶ abbreviation for (in the UK) Department of Transport.

DTs ▶ plural noun (usu. **the DTs**) informal delirium tremens.
– ORIGIN mid 19th cent.: abbreviation, originally in the singular form *DT* (now rare).

dual ▶ **adjective** **1** [attrib.] consisting of two parts, elements, or aspects: *their dual role at work and home.*
▪ Grammar (in some languages) denoting an inflection that refers to exactly two people or things (as distinct from singular and plural). ▪ (in an aircraft) using dual controls: *a dual flight.*
2 (often **dual to**) Mathematics (of a theorem, expression, etc.) related to another by the interchange of particular pairs of terms, such as 'point' and 'line'.
▶ **noun** **1** Grammar a dual form of a word.
▪ [mass noun] the dual number.
2 Mathematics a theorem, expression, etc., that is dual to another.
▶ **verb** (**dualled**, **dualling**) [with obj.] Brit. convert (a road) into a dual carriageway: *dualling the A1.*
– DERIVATIVES **dualize** (also **-ise**) verb, **dually** adverb.
– ORIGIN late Middle English (as a noun denoting either of the two middle incisor teeth in each jaw): from Latin *dualis*, from *duo* 'two'.

dual carriageway ▶ **noun** Brit. a road with a dividing strip between the traffic in opposite directions and usually two or more lanes in each direction.

dual control ▶ **adjective** (of an aircraft or a vehicle) having two sets of controls, one of which is used by the instructor: *a dual-control pilot trainer.*
▶ **noun** (usu. **dual controls**) two such sets of controls in an aircraft or vehicle.

dual in-line package ▶ **noun** see **DIP**.

dualism ▶ **noun** [mass noun] **1** the division of something conceptually into two opposed or contrasted aspects, or the state of being so divided: *a dualism between man and nature.*
▪ Philosophy a theory or system of thought that regards a domain of reality in terms of two independent principles, especially mind and matter (**Cartesian dualism**). Compare with **IDEALISM**, **MATERIALISM**, and **MONISM**. ▪ the religious doctrine that the universe contains opposed powers of good and evil, especially seen as balanced equals. ▪ in Christian theology, the doctrine that Christ had two coexisting natures, human and divine.
2 the quality or condition of being dual; duality.
– DERIVATIVES **dualist** noun & adjective, **dualistic** adjective, **dualistically** adverb.
– ORIGIN late 18th cent.: from **DUAL**, on the pattern of French *dualisme*.

duality ▶ **noun** (pl. **-ies**) **1** [mass noun] the quality or condition of being dual: *this duality of purpose was discernible in the appointments.*
▪ Mathematics the property of two theorems, expressions, etc. being dual to each other. ▪ Physics the quantum-mechanical property of being regardable as both a wave and a particle.
2 an instance of opposition or contrast between two concepts or two aspects of something; a dualism: *the simple dualities of his youthful Marxism: capitalism against socialism, bourgeois against prole.*
– ORIGIN late Middle English: from late Latin *dualitas*, from *dualis* (see **DUAL**).

dual nationality ▶ **noun** [mass noun] citizenship of two countries concurrently.

dual-purpose ▶ **adjective** serving two purposes or functions: *a dual-purpose hand and nail cream.*
▪ (of a vehicle) usable for passengers or goods.

dual-use ▶ **adjective** chiefly US (of technology or equipment) designed or suitable for both civilian and military purposes.

dub[1] ▶ **verb** (**dubbed**, **dubbing**) **1** [with obj. and complement] give an unofficial name or nickname to (someone or something): *the media dubbed anorexia 'the slimming disease'.*
▪ make (someone) a knight by the ritual touching of the shoulder with a sword: *he should be dubbed Sir Hubert.*
2 [with obj.] dress (an artificial fishing fly) with strands of fur or wool or with other material.
▪ incorporate (fur, wool, or other materials) into a fishing fly.
3 [with obj.] smear (leather) with grease. Compare with **DUBBIN**.
– ORIGIN late Old English (in the sense 'make a knight'): from Old French *adober* 'equip with armour', of unknown origin. Sense 2 is from the obsolete meaning 'dress or adorn'.

dub[2] ▶ **verb** (**dubbed**, **dubbing**) [with obj.] **1** provide (a film) with a soundtrack in a different language from the original: *the film will be **dubbed into** French and Flemish.*
▪ add (sound effects or music) to a film or a recording: *background sound can be **dubbed in** at the editing stage.*
2 make a copy of (a sound or video recording).
▪ transfer (a recording) from one medium to another. ▪ combine (two or more sound recordings) into one composite soundtrack.
▶ **noun** **1** an instance of dubbing sound effects or music: *the level of the dub can be controlled manually.*
2 [mass noun] a style of popular music originating from the remixing of recorded music (especially reggae), typically with the removal of some vocals and instruments and the exaggeration of bass guitar.
– DERIVATIVES **dubby** adjective.
– ORIGIN 1920s: abbreviation of **DOUBLE**.

dub[3] informal ▶ **noun** chiefly US an inexperienced or unskilful person.
▶ **verb** (**dubbed**, **dubbing**) [with obj.] Golf misplay (a shot).
– ORIGIN late 19th cent.: perhaps from **DUB**[1] in the obsolete technical sense 'make blunt'.

dub[4] ▶ **verb** (**dubbed**, **dubbing**) [no obj.] (**dub in/up**) N. English informal pay up; make a contribution.
– ORIGIN early 19th cent.: of unknown origin.

Dubai /d(j)uːˈbʌɪ/ a member state of the United Arab Emirates; pop. 674,100 (1995).
▪ its capital city, a port on the Persian Gulf; pop. 265,700 (1980).

Du Barry /d(j)uː ˈbari, French dy baʀi/, Marie Jeanne Bécu, Comtesse (1743–93), French courtier and mistress of Louis XV. During the French Revolution she was arrested by the Revolutionary Tribunal and guillotined.

dubbin /ˈdʌbɪn/ Brit. ▶ **noun** [mass noun] prepared grease used for softening and waterproofing leather.
▶ **verb** (**dubbined**, **dubbining**) [with obj.] apply such a grease to (leather).
– ORIGIN early 19th cent.: alteration of *dubbing*, present participle of **DUB**[1] (in sense 3).

dubbing ▶ **noun** [mass noun] material used for the bodies of artificial fishing flies, especially fur or wool on waxed silk.
– ORIGIN late 17th cent.: from **DUB**[1] + **-ING**[1].

Dubček /ˈdʊbtʃɛk/, Alexander (1921–92), Czechoslovak statesman, First Secretary of the Czechoslovak Communist Party 1968–9. Dubček was the driving force behind the political reforms of 1968, which prompted the Soviet invasion of Czechoslovakia in 1968 and his removal from office. After the collapse of communism in 1989 he was elected speaker of the Federal Assembly in the new Czechoslovak parliament.

dubiety /djuːˈbʌɪɪti/ ▶ **noun** [mass noun] formal the state or quality of being doubtful; uncertainty: *his enemies made much of the dubiety of his paternity.*
– ORIGIN mid 18th cent.: from late Latin *dubietas*, from Latin *dubium* 'a doubt'.

dubious /ˈdjuːbɪəs/ ▶ **adjective** **1** hesitating or doubting: *Alex looked dubious, but complied.*
2 not to be relied upon; suspect: *extremely dubious assumptions.*
▪ morally suspect: *timeshare has been brought into disrepute by dubious sales methods.* ▪ of questionable value: *he holds the dubious distinction of being relegated with every club he has played for.*
– DERIVATIVES **dubiously** adverb, **dubiousness** noun.
– ORIGIN mid 16th cent. (in sense 2): from Latin *dubiosus*, from *dubium* 'a doubt', neuter of *dubius* 'doubtful'.

dubitable /ˈdjuːbɪtəb(ə)l/ ▶ **adjective** rare (of a belief, conclusion, etc.) open to doubt.
– DERIVATIVES **dubitability** noun.
– ORIGIN early 17th cent.: from Latin *dubitabilis*, from *dubitare* 'to doubt'.

dubitation /ˌdjuːbɪˈteɪʃ(ə)n/ ▶ **noun** [mass noun] formal doubt; hesitation: *a judgement fenced around with proper scholarly dubitation.*
– ORIGIN late Middle English: from Latin *dubitatio(n-)*, from *dubitare* 'to doubt'.

dubitative /ˈdjuːbɪtətɪv/ ▶ **adjective** formal expressing or inclined to doubt or hesitation.
– ORIGIN early 18th cent.: from French *dubitatif, -ive* or late Latin *dubitativus*, from *dubitare* 'to doubt'.

Dublin /ˈdʌblɪn/ the capital city of the Republic of Ireland, situated on the Irish Sea at the mouth of the River Liffey; pop. 477,700 (1991). It was the birthplace of many writers, including Jonathan Swift, Oscar Wilde, and James Joyce. Irish name **BAILE ÁTHA CLIATH**.
▪ a county of the Republic of Ireland, in the province of Leinster; county town, Dublin.

Dublin Bay prawn ▶ **noun** another term for **NORWAY LOBSTER**.
▪ (**Dublin Bay prawns**) scampi.

dubnium /ˈdʌbnɪəm/ ▶ **noun** [mass noun] the chemical element of atomic number 105, a very unstable element made by high-energy atomic collisions. (Symbol: **Db**) See also **HAHNIUM**, **JOLIOTIUM**.
– ORIGIN 1990s: modern Latin, from *Dubna* in Russia, site of the Joint Nuclear Institute.

Du Bois /duː ˈbɔɪz/, W. E. B. (1868–1963), American writer, sociologist, and political activist; full name *William Edward Burghardt Du Bois*. He was an important figure in campaigning for equality for black Americans and co-founded the National Association for the Advancement of Colored People in 1909.

Dubonnet /d(j)uːˈbɒneɪ/ ▶ **noun** [mass noun] trademark a sweet French red wine.
– ORIGIN from the name of a family of French wine merchants.

Dubrovnik /dʊˈbrɒvnɪk/ a port and resort on the Adriatic coast of Croatia; pop. 66,100 (1981). Italian name (until 1918) **RAGUSA**.

Dubuffet /duːˈbuːfeɪ, French dybyfɛ/, Jean (1901–85), French painter. He rejected traditional techniques, incorporating materials such as sand and plaster in his paintings and producing sculptures made from rubbish.

ducal /ˈdjuːk(ə)l/ ▶ **adjective** [attrib.] of, like, or relating to a duke or dukedom: *the ducal palace in Rouen.*
– ORIGIN late 15th cent.: from Old French, from *duc* 'duke'.

ducat /ˈdʌkət/ ▶ **noun** **1** a gold coin formerly current in most European countries.
▪ (**ducats**) informal money: *their production of Hamlet has kept the ducats pouring in.*
2 informal, chiefly US a ticket, especially an admission ticket.
– ORIGIN from Italian *ducato*, originally referring to a silver coin minted by the Duke of Apulia in 1190: from medieval Latin *ducatus* (see **DUCHY**). Sense 2 dates from the late 19th cent.

Duccio /ˈduːtʃɪəʊ, Italian ˈduttʃo/ (*c.*1255–*c.*1320), Italian painter, founder of the Sienese school of painting; full name *Duccio di Buoninsegna*. The only fully documented surviving work by him is the *Maestà* for the high altar of Siena cathedral (completed 1311).

Duce /ˈduːtʃeɪ/ (**Il Duce**) the title assumed by Benito Mussolini in 1922.
– ORIGIN Italian, literally 'leader'.

Duchamp /djuːˈʃɒ, French dyʃɑ̃/, Marcel (1887–1968), French-born artist, a US citizen from 1955. A leading figure of the Dada movement and originator of conceptual art, he invented 'ready-mades', mass-produced articles selected at random and displayed as works of art—most famously a bicycle wheel and a urinal.

Duchenne muscular dystrophy /duːˈʃɛn/ (abbrev.: **DMD**) ▶ **noun** [mass noun] a severe form of muscular dystrophy caused by a genetic defect and usually affecting boys.
– ORIGIN late 19th cent.: named after G. B. A. *Duchenne* (1806–75), the French neurologist who first described it.

duchess ▶ **noun** the wife or widow of a duke.
▪ a woman holding a rank equivalent to duke in her own right. ▪ Brit. informal (especially among cockneys) an affectionate form of address used by a man to a girl or woman he knows well.
– ORIGIN late Middle English: via Old French from medieval Latin *ducissa*, from Latin *dux, duc-* (see **DUKE**).

duchesse /duːˈʃɛs, ˈdʌtʃɪs, -ɛs/ ▶ **noun** **1** (also **duchesse satin**) [mass noun] a soft, heavy, glossy kind of satin, usually of silk.
2 a chaise longue resembling two armchairs linked by a stool.
3 (also **duchesse dressing table**) a dressing table with a pivoting mirror.
– ORIGIN late 18th cent. (in sense 2): from French, literally 'duchess'.

duchesse lace ▶ **noun** [mass noun] a kind of Brussels pillow lace characterized by bold floral patterns worked with a fine thread.

duchesse potatoes ▶ **plural noun** mashed

d

potatoes mixed with egg yolk, formed into small shapes and baked.

duchy /ˈdʌtʃi/ ▶ noun (pl. **-ies**) the territory of a duke or duchess; a dukedom.
■ **(the Duchy)** the royal dukedom of Cornwall or Lancaster.
– ORIGIN Middle English: from Old French *duche*, from medieval Latin *ducatus*, from Latin *dux, duc-* (see DUKE).

duck[1] ▶ noun (pl. same or **ducks**) **1** a waterbird with a broad blunt bill, short legs, webbed feet, and a waddling gait.
● Family Anatidae (the **duck family**); domesticated ducks are mainly descended from the mallard or **wild duck**. The duck family also includes geese and swans, from which ducks are distinguished by their generally smaller size and shorter necks.
■ the female of such a bird. Contrasted with DRAKE[1].
■ such a bird as food: *a duck for tomorrow's dinner.*
2 a pure white thin-shelled bivalve mollusc found off the Atlantic coasts of America.
● Genus *Anatina*, family Mactridae.
3 another term for DUKW.
– PHRASES **get** (or **have**) **one's ducks in a row** N. Amer. get (or have) one's facts straight; get (or have) everything organized. **take to something like a duck to water** take to something very readily: *he shows every sign of taking to University politics like a duck to water.* **water off a duck's back** a potentially hurtful or harmful remark or incident which has no apparent effect on the person mentioned: *it was like water off a duck's back to Nick, but I'm sure it upset Paul.*
– ORIGIN Old English *duce*, from the Germanic base of DUCK[2] (expressing the notion of 'diving bird').

duck[2] ▶ verb **1** [no obj.] lower the head or the body quickly to avoid a blow or missile or so as not to be seen: *spectators ducked for cover* | *she* **ducked into** *the doorway to get out of the line of fire* | [with obj.] *he ducked his head and entered.*
■ **(duck out)** depart quickly: *I thought I saw you duck out.* ■ [with obj.] avoid (a blow or missile) by moving down quickly: *he ducked a punch from an angry first baseman.* ■ [with obj.] informal evade or avoid (an unwelcome duty or undertaking): *a responsibility which a less courageous man might well have ducked* | [no obj.] *I was engaged twice and ducked out both times.*
2 [with obj.] push or plunge (someone) under water, either playfully or as a punishment: *Rufus grabbed him from behind to duck him under the surface* | [as noun **ducking**] *he got a ducking as he tried to board the canoe.*
3 [no obj.] Bridge refrain from playing a winning card on a particular trick for tactical reasons.
▶ noun [in sing.] a quick lowering of the head.
– PHRASES **duck and dive** use one's ingenuity to deal with or evade a situation.
– DERIVATIVES **ducker** noun.
– ORIGIN Middle English: of Germanic origin; related to Dutch *duiken* and German *tauchen* 'dive, dip, plunge', also to DUCK[1].

duck[3] ▶ noun Cricket a batsman's score of nought: *out for a duck.*
– PHRASES **break one's duck** Cricket score the first run of one's innings. ■ Brit. make one's first score or achieve a particular feat for the first time.
– ORIGIN mid 19th cent.: short for *duck's egg*, used for the figure 0 because of its similar outline.

duck[4] (also **ducks**) ▶ noun Brit. dear; darling (used as an informal or affectionate form of address, especially among cockneys).
– ORIGIN late 16th cent.: from DUCK[1].

duck[5] ▶ noun [mass noun] a strong untwilled linen or cotton fabric, used chiefly for work clothes and sails.
■ **(ducks)** trousers made of such a fabric.
– ORIGIN mid 17th cent.: from Middle Dutch *doek* 'linen, linen cloth'; related to German *Tuch* 'cloth'.

duckbill ▶ noun an animal with jaws resembling a duck's bill, e.g. a platypus or a duck-billed dinosaur.
▶ adjective [attrib.] shaped like a duck's bill: *duckbill pliers.*

duck-billed dinosaur ▶ noun another term for HADROSAUR.

duck-billed platypus ▶ noun see PLATYPUS.

duckboard ▶ noun (usu. **duckboards**) a board consisting of a number of wooden slats joined together, placed so as to form a path over muddy ground or in a trench.

duck-dive ▶ verb [no obj.] dive head first under the water while swimming.
▶ noun a dive of this kind.

duck-egg blue ▶ noun [mass noun] a soft, turquoise-blue shade.

duck hawk ▶ noun N. Amer., dated the peregrine falcon.

ducking stool ▶ noun historical a chair fastened to the end of a pole, used formerly to plunge offenders into a pond or river as a punishment.

duckling ▶ noun a young duck.
■ [mass noun] the flesh of a young duck as food.

duck mussel ▶ noun a freshwater bivalve mollusc that is smaller and darker than the related swan mussel, found in rivers with sandy or gravelly bottoms.
● *Anodonta anatina*, family Unionidae.

duckpin ▶ noun US a short squat bowling pin.
■ **(duckpins)** [treated as sing.] a game played with such pins.

ducks and drakes ▶ noun [mass noun] a game of throwing flat stones so that they skim along the surface of water.
– PHRASES **play ducks and drakes with** trifle with; treat frivolously.
– ORIGIN late 16th cent.: from the movement of the stone over the water.

duck's arse (N. Amer. **duck's ass**) (abbrev.: DA) ▶ noun informal a man's hairstyle, associated especially with the 1950s, in which the hair is slicked back on both sides and tapered at the nape.

duck-shove ▶ verb [with obj.] Austral./NZ informal avoid or evade (a responsibility or issue).

duck soup ▶ noun [mass noun] N. Amer. informal an easy task, or someone easy to overcome: *we had some great battles, but against me he was duck soup.*

ducktail ▶ noun North American term for DUCK'S ARSE.

duckwalk ▶ verb [no obj.] walk with the body in a squatting posture.
▶ noun a walk with the body in this posture.

duckweed ▶ noun [mass noun] a tiny aquatic flowering plant that floats in large quantities on still water, often forming an apparently continuous green layer on the surface.
● Family Lemnaceae, in particular the genus *Lemna*.

ducky informal ▶ noun (pl. **-ies**) Brit. darling; dear (used as a form of address): *come and sit down, ducky.*
▶ adjective chiefly N. Amer. charming; delightful: *everything here is just ducky.*
– ORIGIN early 19th cent.: from DUCK[4].

duct ▶ noun a channel or tube for conveying something, in particular:
■ (in a building or a machine) a tube or passageway for air, liquid, cables, etc. ■ (in the body) a vessel for conveying lymph or glandular secretions such as tears or bile. ■ (in a plant) a vessel for conveying water, sap, or air.
▶ verb [with obj.] (usu. **be ducted**) convey through a duct: *a ventilation system that must be ducted through the wall* | [as adj. **ducted**] *a ducted air system.*
– ORIGIN mid 17th cent. (in the sense 'course' or 'direction'): from Latin *ductus* 'leading, aqueduct' from *duct-* 'led', from the verb *ducere.*

ductile /ˈdʌktʌɪl/ ▶ adjective (of a metal) able to be drawn out into a thin wire.
■ able to be deformed without losing toughness; pliable, not brittle. ■ figurative (of a person) docile or gullible.
– DERIVATIVES **ductility** noun.
– ORIGIN Middle English (in the sense 'malleable'): from Latin *ductilis*, from *duct-* 'led', from the verb *ducere.*

ducting ▶ noun [mass noun] a system of ducts.
■ tubing or piping forming such a system.

ductless ▶ adjective Anatomy denoting a gland that secretes directly into the bloodstream, such as an endocrine gland or a lymph gland.

duct tape ▶ noun [mass noun] N. Amer. strong cloth-backed waterproof adhesive tape.
– ORIGIN 1970s: originally used for repairing leaks in ducted ventilation and heating systems.

ductule /ˈdʌktjuːl/ ▶ noun Anatomy a minute duct.
– DERIVATIVES **ductular** adjective.
– ORIGIN late 19th cent.: Latin, diminutive of *ductus* 'leading'.

ductus /ˈdʌktəs/ ▶ noun (pl. **ducti**) Anatomy a duct.

– ORIGIN mid 17th cent.: from Latin, literally 'leading'.

ductwork ▶ noun [mass noun] a system or network of ducts.

dud informal ▶ noun **1** a thing that fails to work properly or is otherwise unsatisfactory or worthless: *all three bombs were duds.*
■ an ineffectual person.
2 (**duds**) clothes: *buy yourself some new duds.*
▶ adjective not working or meeting standards; faulty: *a dud ignition switch.*
■ counterfeit: *charged with issuing dud cheques.*
– ORIGIN Middle English (in the sense 'item of clothing'): of unknown origin.

dude /d(j)uːd/ informal, chiefly N. Amer. ▶ noun a man; a guy: *if some dude smacked me, I'd smack him back.*
■ a stylish, fastidious man: *cool dudes.* ■ US a city-dweller, especially one holidaying on a ranch in the western US.
▶ verb [no obj.] (**dude up**) dress up elaborately: [as adj. **duded**] *my brother was all duded up in silver and burgundy.*
– DERIVATIVES **dudish** adjective.
– ORIGIN late 19th cent.: probably from German dialect *Dude* 'fool'.

dude ranch ▶ noun (in the western US) a cattle ranch converted to a holiday centre for tourists.

dudgeon /ˈdʌdʒ(ə)n/ ▶ noun a feeling of offence or deep resentment: *the manager walked out in high dudgeon.*
– ORIGIN late 16th cent.: of unknown origin.

Dudley[1] /ˈdʌdli/ an industrial town in the west Midlands of England, near Birmingham; pop. 187,000.

Dudley[2] /ˈdʌdli/, Robert, Earl of Leicester (c.1532–88), English nobleman, military commander, and favourite of Elizabeth I.

due ▶ adjective **1** [predic.] expected at or planned for at a certain time: *the baby's due in August* | *he is due back soon* | [with infinitive] *talks are due to adjourn tomorrow.*
■ (of a payment) required at a certain time: *the May instalment was due.* ■ (of a person) having reached a point where the thing mentioned is required or owed: *she was* **due** *for a rise* | *you're more than due a holiday.* ■ (of a thing) required or owed as a legal or moral obligation: *he was only taking back what was* **due** *to him* | *you must pay any income tax due.*
2 [attrib.] of the proper quality or extent; adequate: *driving without due care and attention.*
▶ noun **1** (**one's due/dues**) a person's right; what is owed to someone: *he thought it was his due.*
2 (**dues**) Brit. an obligatory payment; a fee: *he had paid trade union dues for years.*
▶ adverb (with reference to a point of the compass) exactly; directly: *we'll head due south again on the same road.*
– PHRASES **due to 1** caused by or ascribable to: *unemployment due to automation will grow steadily.* **2** because of; owing to: *he had to withdraw due to a knee injury.* **give someone their due** be fair to someone. **in due course** at the appropriate time: *the range will be extended in due course.* **pay one's dues** fulfil one's obligations: *experience difficulties before achieving success: this drummer has paid his dues with the best.*
– ORIGIN Middle English (in the sense 'payable'): from Old French *deu* 'owed', based on Latin *debitus* 'owed', from *debere* 'owe'.

USAGE Due to in the sense 'because of', as in *he had to retire due to an injury*, has been condemned as incorrect on the grounds that **due** is an adjective and should not be used as a preposition. However, the prepositional use, first recorded at the end of the 19th century, is now common in all types of literature and is regarded as part of standard English.

due date ▶ noun the date on which something falls due, especially the payment of a bill or the expected birth of a baby.

due diligence ▶ noun [mass noun] Law reasonable steps taken by a person in order to avoid committing an offence, especially in buying or selling something.

duel ▶ noun chiefly historical a pre-arranged contest with deadly weapons between two people in order to settle a point of honour.
■ (in modern use) a contest or race between two parties: *he won by a short head after a great final-furlong duel.*
▶ verb (**duelled, duelling**; US **dueled, dueling**) [no obj.]

fight a duel or duels: [as noun **duelling**] *duelling had been forbidden for serving officers.*
– DERIVATIVES **dueller** (US **dueler**) noun, **duellist** (US **duelist**) noun.
– ORIGIN late 15th cent.: from Latin *duellum*, archaic and literary form of *bellum* 'war', used in medieval Latin with the meaning 'combat between two persons', partly influenced by *dualis* 'of two'. The original sense was 'single combat used to decide a judicial dispute'; the sense 'contest to decide a point of honour' dates from the early 17th cent.

duende /du:'ɛndeɪ/ ▶ **noun** [mass noun] a quality of passion and inspiration.
■[count noun] a spirit.
– ORIGIN 1920s: from Spanish, contraction of *duen de casa*, from *dueño de casa* 'owner of the house'.

duenna /du:'ɛnə/ ▶ **noun** an older woman acting as a governess and companion in charge of girls, especially in a Spanish family; a chaperone.
– ORIGIN mid 17th cent.: earlier form of Spanish *dueña*, from Latin *domina* 'lady, mistress'.

due process (also **due process of law**) ▶ **noun** [mass noun] fair treatment through the normal judicial system, especially as a citizen's entitlement.

Duero /'dwero/ Spanish name for **DOURO**.

duet ▶ **noun** a performance by two people, especially singers, instrumentalists, or dancers.
■a musical composition for two performers.
▶ **verb** (**duetted**, **duetting**) [no obj.] perform a duet.
– DERIVATIVES **duettist** noun.
– ORIGIN mid 18th cent.: from Italian *duetto*, diminutive of *duo* 'duet', from Latin *duo* 'two'.

Dufay /dju:'fʌɪ, French dyfaj/, Guillaume (*c.*1400–74), French composer. He made a significant contribution to the development of Renaissance polyphony.

duff[1] ▶ **noun** [usu. with modifier] a flour pudding boiled or steamed in a cloth bag: *a currant duff.*
– ORIGIN mid 19th cent.: northern English form of **DOUGH**.

duff[2] ▶ **adjective** Brit. informal of very poor quality: *duff lyrics.*
■incorrect or false: *she played a couple of duff notes.*
▶ **noun** [mass noun] N. Amer. & Scottish decaying vegetable matter covering the ground under trees.
– ORIGIN late 18th cent. (denoting something worthless): of unknown origin.

duff[3] ▶ **verb** [with obj.] informal **1** (**duff someone up**) Brit. beat someone up. [ORIGIN: 1960s: of uncertain origin.]
2 Austral. steal and alter brands on (cattle). [ORIGIN: early 19th cent.: probably a back-formation from **DUFFER**[2].]
3 Golf mishit (a shot). [ORIGIN: early 19th cent.: back-formation from **DUFFER**[1].]

duff[4] ▶ **noun** N. Amer. informal a person's buttocks: *I did not get where I am today by sitting on my duff.*
– ORIGIN mid 19th cent.: of unknown origin.

duff[5] ▶ **noun** (in phrase **up the duff**) Brit. informal pregnant: *it looks like he's got her up the duff.*

duffel (also **duffle**) ▶ **noun** [mass noun] **1** a coarse woollen cloth with a thick nap.
■[count noun] short for **DUFFEL COAT**.
2 N. Amer. sporting or camping equipment.
■[count noun] short for **DUFFEL BAG**.
– ORIGIN mid 17th cent.: from *Duffel*, the name of a town in Belgium where the cloth was originally made.

duffel bag ▶ **noun** a cylindrical canvas bag closed by a drawstring and carried over the shoulder.
– ORIGIN early 20th cent. (originally US): from sense 2 of **DUFFEL**, originally denoting a bag for equipment.

duffel coat ▶ **noun** a coat made of duffel, typically hooded and fastened with toggles.

duffer[1] ▶ **noun** informal **1** an incompetent or stupid person: *a complete duffer at languages.*
2 Austral. an unproductive mine.
– ORIGIN mid 19th cent.: from Scots *dowfart* 'stupid person', from *douf* 'spiritless'.

duffer[2] ▶ **noun** Austral. informal a person who steals and alters the brands on cattle.
– ORIGIN mid 19th cent.: of unknown origin; in use earlier as thieves' slang for 'someone who sells trashy articles as if they were valuable'.

Du Fu /du:/ variant of **TU FU**.

dufus ▶ **noun** variant spelling of **DOOFUS**.

Dufy /'dju:fi, French dyfi/, Raoul (1877–1953), French painter and textile designer. His characteristic style involved calligraphic outlines sketched on brilliant background washes.

dug[1] past and past participle of **DIG**.

dug[2] ▶ **noun** (usu. **dugs**) the udder, teat, or nipple of a female animal.
■archaic a woman's breast.
– ORIGIN mid 16th cent.: possibly of Old Norse origin and related to Swedish *dägga*, Danish *dægge* 'suckle'.

dugite /'dju:gʌɪt/ ▶ **noun** a highly venomous snake found in SW Australia, similar to the related brown snakes.
• *Pseudonaja affinis*, family Elapidae.
– ORIGIN late 19th cent.: from Nyungar *dukayj*.

dugong /'du:gɒŋ, 'dju:-/ ▶ **noun** (pl. same or **dugongs**) a sea cow found on the coasts of the Indian Ocean from eastern Africa to northern Australia. It is distinguished from the manatees by its forked tail.
• *Dugong dugon*, family Dugongidae.
– ORIGIN early 19th cent.: based on Malay *duyong*.

dugout ▶ **noun** **1** a trench that is dug and roofed over as a shelter for troops.
■an underground air-raid or nuclear shelter. ■a low shelter at the side of a sports field, with seating from which a team's coaches and players not taking part can watch the game.
2 (also **dugout canoe**) a canoe made from a hollowed tree trunk.

DUI US ▶ **abbreviation for** driving under the influence (of drugs or alcohol).

duiker /'dʌɪkə/ ▶ **noun** (pl. same or **duikers**) **1** a small African antelope that typically has a tuft of hair between the horns, found mainly in the rainforest.
• *Cephalophus* and other genera, family Bovidae: several species, including the **common duiker** (*Sylvicapra grimmia*), which is unusual in occurring in open savannah, and the very small **blue duiker** (*Philantomba monticola*), prized for its skin.
2 S. African a cormorant.
• Genus *Phalacrocorax*, family Phalacrocoracidae; several species, in particular the long-tailed cormorant, *P. africanus*.
– ORIGIN late 18th cent.: from South African Dutch, from Dutch, literally 'diver', from the animal's habit of plunging through bushes when pursued; related to **DUCK**[2].

Duisburg /'dju:sbə:g, German 'dysbʊrk/ an industrial city in NW Germany, in North Rhine-Westphalia; pop. 537,440 (1991).

du jour /d(j)u: 'ʒʊə, French dy ʒuʀ/ ▶ **adjective** [postpositive] informal used to describe something that is enjoying great but probably short-lived popularity or publicity: *black comedy is the genre du jour.*
– ORIGIN French, literally 'of the day'.

duke ▶ **noun** **1** a male holding the highest hereditary title in the British and certain other peerages.
■chiefly historical (in some parts of Europe) a male ruler of a small independent state.
2 (**dukes**) informal the fists, especially when raised in a fighting attitude. [ORIGIN: from rhyming slang *Duke of Yorks* 'forks' (= fingers).]
– PHRASES **duke it out** N. Amer. informal fight it out.
– ORIGIN Old English (denoting the ruler of a duchy), from Old French *duc*, from Latin *dux*, *duc-* 'leader'; related to *ducere* 'to lead'.

duke cherry ▶ **noun** a cultivated cherry which is a hybrid between the sweet cherry and the sour cherry.
• *Prunus × gondouinii*, family Rosaceae.

dukedom ▶ **noun** a territory ruled by a duke.
■the rank of duke.

Duke of Argyll's tea tree ▶ **noun** see **TEA TREE** (sense 2).

Duke of Burgundy (also **Duke of Burgundy fritillary**) ▶ **noun** (pl. **Duke of Burgundies**) a small European butterfly resembling a fritillary, which has dark brown wings with rows of orange markings.
• *Hamearis lucina*, family Riodinidae (or Nemeobiidae); it is the only European member of this family, which includes the American metalmarks.

DUKW ▶ **noun** an amphibious transport vehicle, especially as used by the Allies during the Second World War. Also called **DUCK**.
– ORIGIN an official designation, being a combination of factory-applied letters referring to features of the vehicle.

dulcamara /ˌdʌlkə'mɛ:rə/ ▶ **noun** [mass noun] an extract of woody nightshade, used in homeopathy especially for treating skin diseases and chest complaints.
– ORIGIN late 16th cent.: from medieval Latin (used as a specific epithet in *Solanum dulcamara*), from Latin *dulcis* 'sweet' + *amara* 'bitter'.

dulcet /'dʌlsɪt/ ▶ **adjective** (especially of sound) sweet and soothing (often used ironically): *record the* **dulcet** *tones of your family and friends.*
– ORIGIN late Middle English *doucet*, from Old French *doucet*, diminutive of *doux*, from Latin *dulcis* 'sweet'. The Latin form influenced the modern spelling.

dulcian /'dʌlsɪən/ ▶ **noun** an early type of bassoon made in one piece.
■any of various organ stops, typically with 8-foot funnel-shaped flue pipes or 8- or 16-foot reed pipes.
– ORIGIN mid 19th cent.: from German *Dulzian*, or a variant of **DULCIANA**.

dulciana /ˌdʌlsɪ'ɑ:nə/ ▶ **noun** an organ stop, typically with small conical open metal pipes.
– ORIGIN late 18th cent.: via medieval Latin from Latin *dulcis* 'sweet'.

dulcify /'dʌlsɪfʌɪ/ ▶ **verb** (**-ies**, **-ied**) [with obj.] poetic/literary sweeten: *cider pap dulcified with molasses.*
■calm or soothe: *his voice dulcified the panic.*
– DERIVATIVES **dulcification** noun.
– ORIGIN late 16th cent. (in the sense 'sweeten'): from Latin *dulcificare* 'sweeten', from *dulcis* 'sweet'.

dulcimer /'dʌlsɪmə/ ▶ **noun** a musical instrument with a sounding board or box, typically trapezoid in shape, over which strings of graduated length are stretched, played by plucking or especially by being struck with hand-held hammers. The term **hammered dulcimer** is sometimes used, especially in the US, to distinguish these from plucked instruments such as the **Appalachian dulcimer**.
– ORIGIN late 15th cent.: from Old French *doulcemer*, probably from Latin *dulce melos* 'sweet melody'.

dulcitone /'dʌlsɪtəʊn/ ▶ **noun** a musical keyboard instrument in which a series of steel tuning forks are struck by hammers. It was invented in the late 19th century and was superseded by the celesta.
– ORIGIN late 19th cent.: coined by T. Machell, the instrument's inventor, from Latin *dulcis* 'sweet' + *tonus* 'tone'.

dulia /djʊ'lʌɪə/ ▶ **noun** [mass noun] (in Roman Catholic theology) the reverence accorded to saints and angels. Compare with **LATRIA**.
– ORIGIN late Middle English: via medieval Latin from Greek *douleia* 'servitude', from *doulos* 'slave'.

dull ▶ **adjective** **1** lacking interest or excitement: *your diet doesn't have to be dull and boring.*
■archaic (of a person) feeling bored and dispirited: *she said she wouldn't be dull and lonely.*
2 lacking brightness, vividness, or sheen: *his face glowed in the dull lamplight | his black hair looked dull.*
■(of the weather) overcast; gloomy: *next morning dawned dull.* ■(of sound) not clear; muffled: *a dull thud of hooves.* ■(of pain) indistinctly felt; not acute: *there was a dull pain in his lower jaw.* ■(of an edge or blade) blunt: *when cutting hard rock the edge soon became dull.*
3 (of a person) slow to understand; stupid: *the voice of a teacher talking to a rather dull child.*
■archaic (of a person's senses) not perceiving things distinctly; insensitive. ■(of activity) sluggish, slow-moving: *trading was dull and low in volume.*
▶ **verb** make or become dull or less intense: [with obj.] *time dulls the memory* | [no obj.] *Albert's eyes dulled a little.*
– PHRASES (**as**) **dull as dishwater** (or **ditchwater**) extremely dull. **dull the edge of** cause to be less keenly felt; reduce the intensity or effectiveness of: *she'd have to find something to dull the edges of the pain.*
– DERIVATIVES **dullish** adjective, **dullness** (also **dulness**) noun, **dully** /'dʌlˌli/ adverb.
– ORIGIN Old English *dol* 'stupid', of Germanic origin; related to Dutch *dol* 'crazy' and German *toll* 'mad, fantastic, wonderful'.

dullard /'dʌləd/ ▶ **noun** a slow or stupid person.
– ORIGIN Middle English: from Middle Dutch *dullaert*, from *dul* 'dull'.

Dulles /'dʌlɪs/, John Foster (1888–1959), American Republican statesman and international lawyer. He was the US adviser at the founding of the United Nations in 1945 and negotiated the peace treaty with Japan in 1951.

dullsville informal, chiefly N. Amer. ▶ **adjective** dull or monotonous: *she has transformed their dullsville life.*

▶**noun** [mass noun] a dull or monotonous place or condition.

dull-witted ▶**adjective** slow to understand; stupid.

dulosis /djʊːˈləʊsɪs/ ▶**noun** [mass noun] Entomology the practice by slave-making ants of capturing the pupae of other ant species and rearing them as workers of their own colony.
– DERIVATIVES **dulotic** adjective.
– ORIGIN early 20th cent.: from Greek *doulōsis* 'slavery', from *doulos* 'slave'.

d

dulse /dʌls/ ▶**noun** [mass noun] a dark red edible seaweed with flattened branching fronds.
● *Rhodymenia palmata*, division Rhodophyta.
– ORIGIN early 17th cent.: from Irish and Scottish Gaelic *duileasg*.

Duluth /dəˈluːθ/ a port in NE Minnesota, at the western end of Lake Superior; pop. 92,800.

duly ▶**adverb** in accordance with what is required or appropriate; following proper procedure or arrangement: *a document duly signed and authorized by the inspector | the ceremony duly began at midnight.*
■as might be expected or predicted: *I used the tent and was duly impressed.*

dum /dʌm/ ▶**adjective** Indian cooked with steam: *dum aloo.*
– ORIGIN from Hindi *dam*.

Duma /ˈduːmə/ ▶**noun** a legislative body in the ruling assembly of Russia and of some other republics of the former USSR.

'Duma' originally denoted pre-19th century advisory municipal councils in Russia. It later referred to any of four elected legislative bodies established due to popular demand in Russia between 1906 and 1917. After the collapse of communism in 1991 a new Duma was set up as the lower chamber of the Russian parliament.

Dumas /ˈdjuːmɑː, French dymɑ/ the name of two French novelists and dramatists:
■**Alexandre** (1802–70); known as **Dumas** *père*. Although he was a pioneer of the romantic theatre in France, his reputation now rests on his historical adventure novels *The Three Musketeers* (1844–5) and *The Count of Monte Cristo* (1844–5).
■**Alexandre** (1824–95), son of Dumas *père*; known as **Dumas** *fils*. He wrote the novel (and play) *La Dame aux camélias* (1848), which formed the basis of Verdi's opera *La Traviata* (1853).

Du Maurier[1] /djuː ˈmɒrɪeɪ/, Dame Daphne (1907–89), English novelist, granddaughter of George du Maurier. Many of her popular novels and period romances are set in the West Country of England, where she spent most of her life. Notable works: *Jamaica Inn* (1936) and *Rebecca* (1938).

Du Maurier[2] /djuː ˈmɒrɪeɪ/, George (Louis Palmella Busson) (1834–96), French-born novelist, cartoonist, and illustrator. He is chiefly remembered for his novel *Trilby* (1894), which included the character Svengali and gave rise to the word *Svengali*.

dumb ▶**adjective 1** (of a person) unable to speak, most typically because of congenital deafness: *he was born deaf, dumb, and blind.*
■(of animals) unable to speak as a natural state and thus regarded as helpless or deserving pity. ■ [predic.] temporarily unable or unwilling to speak: *she stood dumb while he poured out a stream of abuse.* ■ [attrib.] resulting in or expressed by speechlessness: *they stared in dumb amazement.*
2 informal, chiefly N. Amer. stupid: *a dumb question.*
■(of a computer terminal) able only to transmit data to or receive data from a computer; having no independent processing capability. Often contrasted with **INTELLIGENT**.
▶**verb** [with obj.] **1** (**dumb something down**) N. Amer. informal simplify or reduce the intellectual content of something so as to make it accessible to a larger number of people: *the producers categorically deny that they're dumbing down the show.*
■[no obj.] (**dumb down**) become less intellectually challenging: *the need to dumb down for mass audiences.*
2 poetic/literary make dumb or unheard; silence: *a splendour that dazed the mind and dumbed the tongue.*
– DERIVATIVES **dumbly** adverb, **dumbness** noun.
– ORIGIN Old English, of Germanic origin; related to Old Norse *dumbr* and Gothic *dumbs* 'mute', also to Dutch *dom* 'stupid' and German *dumm* 'stupid'.

USAGE Although **dumb** meaning 'not able to speak' is the older sense, it has been overwhelmed by the newer sense (meaning 'stupid') to such an extent that the use of the first sense is now almost certain to cause offence. Alternatives such as **speech-impaired** should be used instead.

Dumbarton /dʌmˈbɑːt(ə)n/ a town in Scotland on the Clyde west of Glasgow, in West Dunbartonshire; pop. 21,960 (1991).

Dumbartonshire variant spelling of **DUNBARTONSHIRE**.

dumb-ass ▶**adjective** [attrib.] N. Amer. informal stupid; brainless: *dumb-ass politicians.*

dumb-bell ▶**noun 1** a short bar with a weight at each end, used typically in pairs for exercise or muscle-building.
■[as modifier] shaped like a dumb-bell: *a dumb-bell molecule.*
2 informal a stupid person.
– ORIGIN early 18th cent.: originally denoting an apparatus similar to that used to ring a church bell (but without the bell, so noiseless or 'dumb'); sense 2 (dating from the 1920s) is an extended use by association with **DUMB** 'stupid'.

dumb blonde ▶**noun** informal a blonde-haired woman perceived in a stereotypical way as being attractive but unintelligent.

dumb cane ▶**noun** a thick-stemmed plant with large variegated leaves, native to tropical America and widely grown as a house plant.
● Genus *Dieffenbachia*, family Araceae: several species, in particular the Caribbean *D. seguine*, which has a poisonous sap that swells the tongue and destroys the power of speech.

dumbfound (also **dumfound**) ▶**verb** [with obj.] (usu. **be dumbfounded**) greatly astonish or amaze: *she was dumbfounded at the sight that met her eyes.*
– ORIGIN mid 17th cent.: blend of **DUMB** and **CONFOUND**.

dumbhead ▶**noun** informal, chiefly N. Amer. a stupid person.

dumb iron ▶**noun** historical a curved side piece of a vehicle chassis, to which the front springs are attached.

dumbo ▶**noun** (pl. **-os**) informal a stupid person.
– ORIGIN 1950s (originally US): from **DUMB** + **-O**, popularized by the 1941 cartoon film *Dumbo*.

dumb piano ▶**noun** a dummy piano keyboard for exercising the fingers.

dumbshow ▶**noun** [mass noun] gestures used to convey a meaning or message without speech; mime: *they demonstrated **in dumbshow** how the tea should be made.*
■[count noun] a piece of dramatic mime: *there were gags, spoofs, and dumbshows.* ■ [count noun] (especially in English drama of the 16th and 17th centuries) a part of a play acted in mime to summarize, supplement, or comment on the main action.

dumbsize ▶**verb** [no obj.] chiefly US (of a company) reduce staff numbers to levels so low that work can no longer be carried out effectively.
– ORIGIN 1990s: humorously, on the pattern of *downsize*.

dumbstruck ▶**adjective** so shocked or surprised as to be unable to speak: *he was dumbstruck with terror.*

dumb waiter ▶**noun 1** a small lift for carrying things, especially food and crockery, between the floors of a building.
2 Brit. a movable table, typically with revolving shelves, used in a dining room.

dumdum (also **dumdum bullet**) ▶**noun** a kind of soft-nosed bullet that expands on impact and inflicts laceration.
– ORIGIN late 19th cent.: from *Dum Dum*, name of a town and arsenal near Calcutta, India, where such bullets were first produced.

dum-dum ▶**noun** informal a stupid person.
– ORIGIN 1970s (originally US): reduplication of **DUMB**.

dumfound ▶**verb** variant spelling of **DUMBFOUND**.

Dumfries /dʌmˈfriːs/ a market town in SW Scotland, administrative centre of Dumfries and Galloway region; pop. 32,130 (1991).

Dumfries and Galloway an administrative region in SW Scotland, formed in 1975; administrative centre, Dumfries.

Dumfriesshire /dʌmˈfriːsʃɪə, -ʃə/ a former county of SW Scotland, which became part of Dumfries and Galloway region in 1975.

dumka /ˈdʊmkə/ ▶**noun** (pl. **dumkas** or **dumky** /ˈdʊmki/) a piece of Slavic music, originating as a folk ballad or lament, typically melancholy with contrasting lively sections.
– ORIGIN late 19th cent.: via Czech and Polish from Ukrainian.

dummy ▶**noun** (pl. **-ies**) **1** a model or replica of a human being: *a waxwork dummy.*
■a figure used for displaying or fitting clothes: *a tailor's dummy.* ■a ventriloquist's doll. ■a person taking no real part or present only for appearances; a figurehead. ■ Bridge the declarer's partner, whose cards are exposed on the table after the opening lead and played by the declarer. ■ Bridge the exposed hand of the declarer's partner. ■an imaginary fourth player in whist: [as modifier] *dummy whist.*
2 an object designed to resemble and serve as a substitute for the real or usual one: *tests using stuffed owls and wooden dummies* | [as modifier] *a dummy torpedo.*
■Brit. a rubber or plastic teat for a baby to suck on. ■a prototype or mock-up, especially of a book or the layout of a page. ■a blank round of ammunition. ■ [as modifier] Grammar denoting a word that has no semantic content but is used to maintain grammatical structure: *a dummy subject as in 'it is' or 'there are'.*
3 (chiefly in rugby and soccer) a feigned pass or kick intended to deceive an opponent.
4 informal, chiefly N. Amer. a stupid person.
▶**verb** (**-ies, -ied**) [no obj.] (chiefly in rugby and soccer) feign a pass or kick in order to deceive an opponent: *Blanco dummied past a static defence.*
– PHRASES **sell someone a dummy** (chiefly in rugby and soccer) deceive an opponent by feigning a pass or kick.
– ORIGIN late 16th cent.: from **DUMB** + **-Y**[1]. The original sense was 'a person who cannot speak', then 'an imaginary fourth player in whist' (mid 18th cent.), whence 'a substitute for the real thing' and 'a model of a human being' (mid 19th cent.).
▶**dummy up** N. Amer. informal keep quiet; give no information.

dummy run ▶**noun** a practice or trial: *do a dummy run on some scrap material.*

dumortierite /djʊˈmɔːtɪərʌɪt/ ▶**noun** [mass noun] a rare blue or violet mineral occurring typically as needles and fibrous masses in gneiss and schist. It consists of an aluminium and iron borosilicate.
– ORIGIN late 19th cent.: from the name of V.-E. *Dumortier* (1802–76), French geologist, + **-ITE**[1].

dump ▶**noun 1** a site for depositing rubbish.
■[usu. with modifier] a place where a particular kind of waste, especially dangerous waste, is left: *a nuclear waste dump.* ■a heap of rubbish left at a dump. ■ (also **mine dump**) S. African a hill of solidified crushed quartz, built up from the residue of gold-mining operations. ■ informal an unpleasant or dreary place: *she says the town has become a dump.* ■ informal, chiefly N. Amer. an act of defecation.
2 Computing a copying of stored data to a different location, performed typically as a protection against loss.
■a printout or list of the contents of a computer's memory, occurring typically after a system failure.
▶**verb** [with obj.] **1** deposit or dispose of (rubbish, waste, or unwanted material), typically in a careless or hurried way: *trucks dumped 1,900 tons of refuse here.*
■put down or abandon (something) hurriedly in order to make an escape: *the couple dumped the car and fled.* ■ put (something) down firmly or heavily and carelessly: *she dumped her knapsack on the floor.* ■ informal abandon or desert (someone): *his girlfriend dumped him for being fat.* ■send (goods unsaleable in the home market) to a foreign market for sale at a low price: *these countries have been **dumping** cheap fertilizers **on** the UK market.* ■ informal sell off (assets) rapidly: *investors dumped shares in scores of other consumer-goods firms.*
2 Computing copy (stored data) to a different location, especially so as to protect against loss.
■print out or list the contents of (a store), especially after a system failure.
– ORIGIN Middle English: perhaps from Old Norse; related to Danish *dumpe* and Norwegian *dumpa* 'fall suddenly' (the original sense in English); in later use partly imitative; compare with **THUMP**.
▶**dump on** informal, N. Amer. criticize or abuse (someone); treat badly: *you get dumped on just because of your name.*

dump bin ▶**noun** a promotional box in a shop for displaying books or other items.

dumper ▶**noun** a person or thing that dumps something.
■(also **dumper truck**) Brit. a truck with a body that tilts or opens at the back for unloading. ■ (**the dumper**) N. Amer. informal used in reference to a bad or unwanted state: *his career's **in the dumper**.* ■ chiefly Austral. a large

wave that breaks and hurls the swimmer or surfer on to the beach.

dumping ground ▶ noun a place where rubbish or unwanted material is left.

dumping syndrome ▶ noun [mass noun] Medicine a group of symptoms, including weakness, abdominal discomfort, and sometimes abnormally rapid bowel evacuation, occurring after meals in some patients who have undergone gastric surgery.

dumpling ▶ noun a small savoury ball of dough (usually made with suet) which may be boiled, fried, or baked in a casserole.
■ a pudding consisting of apple or other fruit enclosed in a sweet dough and baked. ■ humorous a small, fat person: he was a 250-pound dumpling.
– ORIGIN early 17th cent.: apparently from the rare adjective dump 'of the consistency of dough', although dumpling is recorded much earlier.

dumps ▶ plural noun (in phrase (down) in the dumps) informal (of a person) depressed or unhappy.
– ORIGIN early 16th cent. (originally singular in the sense 'a dazed or puzzled state'): probably a figurative use of Middle Dutch domp 'haze, mist'.

dumpster ▶ noun N. Amer. a very large container for rubbish; a skip.
– ORIGIN 1930s: originally Dempster Dumpster, proprietary name (based on DUMP) given by the American manufacturers, Dempster Brothers of Knoxville, Tennessee.

dump truck ▶ noun N. Amer. a dumper truck.

dumpy ▶ adjective (**dumpier, dumpiest**) (of a person) short and stout: her plain, dumpy sister.
▶ noun (pl. **-ies**) S. African informal a non-returnable beer bottle, stout in shape, holding 340 ml.
– DERIVATIVES **dumpily** adverb, **dumpiness** noun.
– ORIGIN mid 18th cent.: from DUMPLING + -Y[1].

Dumyat /dʊmˈjɑːt/ Arabic name for DAMIETTA.

dun[1] ▶ adjective of a dull greyish-brown colour: a dun cow.
■ poetic/literary dark; dusky: when the dun evening comes.
▶ noun 1 [mass noun] a dull greyish-brown colour.
2 a thing that is dun in colour, in particular:
■ a horse with a sandy or sandy-grey coat, black mane, tail, and lower legs, and a dark dorsal stripe. ■ a sub-adult mayfly, which has drab coloration and opaque wings. ■ an artificial fishing fly imitating this.
– ORIGIN Old English dun, dunn, of Germanic origin; probably related to DUSK.

dun[2] ▶ verb (**dunned, dunning**) [with obj.] (usu. be dunned) make persistent demands on (someone), especially for payment of a debt: after he left Oxford he was frequently dunned for his debts.
▶ noun archaic a debt collector or an insistent creditor.
■ a demand for payment.
– ORIGIN early 17th cent. (as a noun): from obsolete Dunkirk privateer, from the French port of DUNKIRK.

dun[3] ▶ noun Archaeology a stone-built fortified settlement in Scotland or Ireland, of a kind built from the late Iron Age to the early Middle Ages. The word is a frequent place-name element in Scotland and Ireland.
– ORIGIN late 18th cent.: from Irish dún, Scottish Gaelic dùn 'hill or hill fort'.

dunam /ˈdʊnəm/ ▶ noun a measure of land area used in parts of the former Turkish empire, including Israel (where it is equal to about 900 square metres).
– ORIGIN from modern Hebrew dûnām or Arabic dūnum, from Turkish dönüm, from dönmek 'go round'.

Dunbar /dʌnˈbɑː/, William (c.1456–c.1513), Scottish poet. He was the author of satires such as the political allegory 'The Thrissill and the Rois' ('The Thistle and the Rose', 1503) and of elegies such as 'Lament for the Makaris'.

dun-bar /dʌnˈbɑː/ ▶ noun a variable European moth with darker lines and bands on the wings, found in wooded districts.
● Cosmia trapezina, family Noctuidae.

Dunbartonshire /dʌnˈbɑːt(ə)nʃɪə, -ʃə/ (also **Dumbartonshire**) an administrative region and former county of west central Scotland, on the Clyde, divided into **East Dunbartonshire** and **West Dunbartonshire**.

Duncan, Isadora (1878–1927), American dancer and teacher. She was a pioneer of modern dance, famous for her 'free' barefoot dancing. She died through being accidentally strangled when her scarf became entangled in the wheels of a car.

Duncan I (c.1010–40), king of Scotland 1034–40. He was killed in battle by Macbeth.

dunce ▶ noun a person who is slow at learning; a stupid person.
– ORIGIN early 16th cent.: originally an epithet for a follower of John DUNS SCOTUS, whose followers were ridiculed by 16th-cent. humanists and reformers as enemies of learning.

dunce's cap (US also **dunce cap**) ▶ noun a paper cone formerly put on the head of a dunce at school as a mark of disgrace.

Dundalk /dʌnˈdɔːk/ the county town of Louth, in the Republic of Ireland, a port on the east coast; pop. 25,800 (1991).

Dundee a city in eastern Scotland, on the north side of the Firth of Tay; pop. 165,500 (1991).

Dundee cake ▶ noun chiefly Brit. a rich fruit cake, typically decorated on top with almonds.

Dundee marmalade ▶ noun [mass noun] a type of orange marmalade, originally made in Dundee.

dunderhead ▶ noun informal a stupid person.
– DERIVATIVES **dunderheaded** adjective.
– ORIGIN early 17th cent.: compare with obsolete Scots dunder, dunner 'resounding noise'; related to DIN.

dune ▶ noun a mound or ridge of sand or other loose sediment formed by the wind, especially on the sea coast or in a desert: a sand dune.
– ORIGIN late 18th cent.: from French, from Middle Dutch dūne; related to Old English dūn 'hill' (see DOWN[3]).

dune buggy ▶ noun another term for BEACH BUGGY.

Dunedin /dʌˈniːdɪn/ a city and port in South Island, New Zealand, founded in 1848 by Scottish settlers; pop. 113,900 (est. 1996).

Dunfermline /dʌnˈfəːmlɪn/ a city in Fife, Scotland, near the Firth of Forth; pop. 55,000 (1991).

dung ▶ noun [mass noun] the excrement of animals; manure.
▶ verb [no obj.] (of an animal) defecate.
– ORIGIN Old English, of Germanic origin; related to German Dung, Swedish dynga, Icelandic dyngja 'dung, dunghill, heap', and Danish dynge 'heap'.

dungaree /ˌdʌŋɡəˈriː/ ▶ noun 1 (**dungarees**) a garment consisting of trousers with a bib held up by straps over the shoulders, made of calico, denim, or a similar material and worn especially as casual or working clothes.
2 [mass noun] a kind of coarse Indian calico.
– ORIGIN late 17th cent. (in sense 2): from Hindi duṅgrī.

Dungarvan /dʌnˈɡɑːv(ə)n/ a town on the south coast of the Republic of Ireland, the administrative centre of Waterford; pop. 6,920 (1990).

dung beetle ▶ noun a beetle whose larvae feed on dung, especially a scarab. The larger kinds place the dung in a hole before the eggs are laid, and some of them roll it along in a ball.
● Superfamily Scarabaeoidea, in particular families Scarabaeidae and Geotrupidae.

Dungeness crab /ˌdʌndʒəˈnɛs/ ▶ noun a large crab found off the west coast of North America, where it is popular as food.
● Cancer magister, family Cancridae.
– ORIGIN mid 20th cent.: from Dungeness, the name of a fishing village on the coast of Washington State.

dungeon ▶ noun a strong underground prison cell, especially in a castle.
■ (in fantasy role-playing games) a labyrinthine subterranean setting. ■ archaic term for DONJON.
▶ verb [with obj.] poetic/literary imprison (someone) in a dungeon.
– ORIGIN Middle English (also with the sense 'castle keep'): from Old French (perhaps originally with the sense 'lord's tower' or 'mistress tower'), based on Latin dominus 'lord, master'. Compare with DONJON.

dung fly ▶ noun a hairy fly that lays its eggs in fresh dung.
● Families Scathophagidae and Sphaeroceridae: several species, in particular the **yellow dung fly** (Scathophaga stercoraria).

dunghill (also **dungheap**) ▶ noun a heap of dung or refuse, especially in a farmyard.

dungworm ▶ noun an earthworm found in dung or compost, used by anglers as bait.

Dunhuang /dʊnˈhwaŋ/ a town in NW China, in Gansu province, located on the old Silk Road near the site of the earliest known Buddhist cave shrines (4th century AD).

dunite /ˈdʌnʌɪt/ ▶ noun [mass noun] Geology a green to brownish coarse-grained igneous rock consisting largely of olivine.
– ORIGIN mid 19th cent.: from the name of Dun Mountain, New Zealand, + -ITE[1].

dunk ▶ verb 1 [with obj.] dip (bread or other food) into a drink or soup before eating it: she dunked a piece of bread into her coffee.
■ immerse or dip in water: [as noun **dunking**] the camera survived a dunking in a stream.
2 [no obj.] Basketball score a field goal by shooting the ball down through the basket with the hands above the rim.
▶ noun Basketball a field goal shot downwards into the basket with the hands above the rim.
– DERIVATIVES **dunker** noun.
– ORIGIN early 20th cent.: from Pennsylvanian German dunke 'dip', from German tunken 'dip or plunge'.

Dunkard /ˈdʌŋkəd/ ▶ noun another term for DUNKER.

Dunker /ˈdʌŋkə/ ▶ noun a member of the German Baptist Brethren, a sect of Baptist Christians founded in 1708 but living in the US since the 1720s.
– ORIGIN early 18th cent.: from Pennsylvanian German, from dunke (see DUNK).

Dunkirk /dʌnˈkəːk/ a port in northern France; pop. 71,070 (1990). French name **DUNKERQUE** /dœ̃kɛrk/.

Dunkirk was the scene of the evacuation of the British Expeditionary Force in 1940. Forced to retreat to the Channel by the German breakthrough at Sedan, 335,000 Allied troops were evacuated by warships, requisitioned civilian ships, and a host of small boats, under constant attack from the air.

Dun Laoghaire /dʌn ˈlɪərɪ, ˈlɛːrə, Irish duːn ˈliːrʲə/ a ferry port and resort town in the Republic of Ireland, near Dublin; pop. 54,715 (1986).

dunlin /ˈdʌnlɪn/ ▶ noun (pl. same or **dunlins**) a migratory sandpiper with a downcurved bill and (in the breeding season) a reddish-brown back and black belly. It is the commonest small wader of the northern hemisphere.
● Calidris alpina, family Scolopacidae.
– ORIGIN mid 16th cent.: probably from DUN[1] + -LING, from the greyish-brown winter colouring of its upper parts.

Dunlop[1] /ˈdʌnlɒp/, John Boyd (1840–1921), Scottish inventor. He developed the first successful pneumatic bicycle tyre (1888), manufactured by the company named after him.

Dunlop[2] /ˈdʌnlɒp, dʌnˈlɒp/ (also **Dunlop cheese**) ▶ noun [mass noun] a full-cream hard cheese originally made in Dunlop, near Ayr in Scotland.

Dunmow flitch /ˈdʌnməʊ/ a side of bacon awarded at Great Dunmow in Essex on Whit Monday to any married couple who will swear that they have not quarrelled or repented of their marriage vows for at least a year and a day.

dunnage /ˈdʌnɪdʒ/ ▶ noun [mass noun] loose wood, matting, or similar material used to keep a cargo in position in a ship's hold.
■ informal a person's belongings, especially those brought on board ship.
– ORIGIN Middle English: of unknown origin.

dunnage bag ▶ noun a kitbag.

dunnart /ˈdʌnɑːt/ ▶ noun a mouse-like insectivorous marsupial with a pointed snout and prominent eyes, found in Australia and New Guinea. Also called MARSUPIAL MOUSE.
● Genus Sminthopsis, family Dasyuridae: many species, including the **common dunnart** (S. murina).
– ORIGIN 1920s: from Nyungar danart.

Dunnet Head /ˈdʌnɪt/ a headland on the north coast of Scotland, between Thurso and John o'Groats. It is the most northerly point on the British mainland.

dunno /ˈdʌnəʊ, dəˈnəʊ/ ▶ contraction of (I) do not know.
– ORIGIN mid 19th cent.: representing an informal pronunciation.

dunnock /ˈdʌnək/ ▶ noun a small European songbird of the accentor family, with a dark grey head and a reddish-brown back. Also called HEDGE SPARROW.

• *Prunella modularis*, family Prunellidae.
– ORIGIN Middle English: apparently from **DUN**[1] (from its brown and grey plumage) + **-OCK**.

dunny /ˈdʌni/ ▶ **noun** (pl. **-ies**) **1** Scottish an underground passage or cellar, especially in a tenement.
2 informal, chiefly Austral./NZ a toilet.
– ORIGIN early 19th cent. (in the sense 'dung'): from dialect *dunnekin* 'privy', probably from **DUNG** + archaic slang *ken* 'house'. Sense 1 is perhaps a different word.

Duns Scotus /dʌnz ˈskəʊtəs/, John (*c.*1265–1308), Scottish theologian and scholar. A profoundly influential figure in the Middle Ages, he was the first major theologian to defend the theory of the Immaculate Conception, and opposed St Thomas Aquinas in arguing that faith was a matter of will rather than something dependent on logical proofs.

Dunstable /ˈdʌnstəb(ə)l/, John (*c.*1390–1453), English composer. He was a significant early exponent of counterpoint.

Dunstan, St /ˈdʌnstən/ (*c.*909–88), Anglo-Saxon prelate. As Archbishop of Canterbury he introduced the strict Benedictine rule into England and succeeded in restoring monastic life. Feast day, 19 May.

dunt /dʌnt/ chiefly N. Amer. & Scottish ▶ **verb** [with obj.] hit or knock firmly with a dull sound: *she dunted my father in the side with her elbow.*
▶ **noun** a firm dull-sounding blow.
– ORIGIN late Middle English: perhaps a variant of **DINT**.

duo ▶ **noun** (pl. **-os**) **1** a pair of people or things, especially in music or entertainment: *the comedy duo Laurel and Hardy | United's goalscoring duo.*
2 Music a duet: *he wrote two duos for violin and viola.*
– ORIGIN late 16th cent. (in sense 2): via Italian from Latin *duo* 'two'.

duo- ▶ **combining form** two; having two: *duopoly | duotone.*
– ORIGIN from Latin.

duodecimal /ˌdjuːə(ʊ)ˈdɛsɪm(ə)l/ ▶ **adjective** relating to or denoting a system of counting or numerical notation that has twelve as a base.
▶ **noun** [mass noun] the system of duodecimal notation.
– DERIVATIVES **duodecimally** adverb.
– ORIGIN late 17th cent.: from Latin *duodecimus* 'twelfth' (from *duodecim* 'twelve') + **-AL**.

duodecimo /ˌdjuːə(ʊ)ˈdɛsɪməʊ/ ▶ **noun** (pl. **-os**) a size of book in which each leaf is one twelfth of the size of the printing sheet.
■ a book of this size.
– ORIGIN mid 17th cent.: from Latin (*in*) *duodecimo* 'in a twelfth', from *duodecimus* 'twelfth'.

duodenary /ˌdjuːəˈdiːnəri/ ▶ **adjective** rare relating to or based on the number twelve.
– ORIGIN mid 19th cent.: from Latin *duodenarius* 'containing twelve', based on *duodecim* 'twelve'.

duodenitis /ˌdjuːədiːˈnʌɪtɪs/ ▶ **noun** [mass noun] Medicine inflammation of the duodenum.

duodeno- /ˌdjuːəˈdiːnəʊ/ (also **duoden-** before a vowel) ▶ **combining form** Anatomy & Medicine relating to the duodenum: *duodenitis.*

duodenum /ˌdjuːəˈdiːnəm/ ▶ **noun** (pl. **duodenums** or **duodena** /-ˈdiːnə/) Anatomy the first part of the small intestine immediately beyond the stomach, leading to the jejunum.
– DERIVATIVES **duodenal** adjective.
– ORIGIN late Middle English: from medieval Latin, from *duodeni* 'in twelves', its length being equivalent to the breadth of approximately twelve fingers.

duologue /ˈdjuːəlɒg/ ▶ **noun** a play or part of a play with speaking roles for only two actors.
– ORIGIN mid 18th cent.: from **DUO-**, on the pattern of *monologue.*

duomo /ˈdwəʊməʊ/ ▶ **noun** (pl. **-os**) an Italian cathedral.
– ORIGIN Italian, literally 'dome'.

duopoly /djʊˈɒpəli/ ▶ **noun** (pl. **-ies**) a situation in which two suppliers dominate the market for a commodity or service.
– DERIVATIVES **duopolistic** adjective.
– ORIGIN 1920s: from **DUO-**, on the pattern of *monopoly.*

duotone /ˈdjuːətəʊn/ ▶ **noun** a half-tone illustration made from a single original with two different colours at different screen angles.
■ [mass noun] the technique or process of making such illustrations: *the best images that duotone can produce.*

dupatta /dʊˈpʌtə/ ▶ **noun** a length of material worn as a scarf or head covering, typically with a salwar, by women from the Indian subcontinent.
– ORIGIN from Hindi *dupaṭṭā.*

dupe[1] ▶ **verb** [with obj.] deceive; trick: *the newspaper was duped into publishing an untrue story.*
▶ **noun** a victim of deception: *knowing accomplices or unknowing dupes.*
– DERIVATIVES **dupable** adjective, **duper** noun, **dupery** noun.
– ORIGIN late 17th cent.: from dialect French *dupe* 'hoopoe', from the bird's supposedly stupid appearance.

dupe[2] ▶ **verb** & **noun** short for **DUPLICATE**, especially in photography.

dupion /ˈdjuːpɪən/ (also **silk dupion**) ▶ **noun** [mass noun] a rough slubbed silk fabric woven from the threads of double cocoons.
■ an imitation of this with other fibres.
– ORIGIN early 19th cent. (in the sense 'double cocoon'): from French *doupion*, from Italian *doppione*, from *doppio* 'double'.

duple /ˈdjuːp(ə)l/ ▶ **adjective** Music (of rhythm) based on two main beats to the bar: *duple time.*
– ORIGIN mid 16th cent.: from Latin *duplus*, from *duo* 'two'.

duplet /ˈdjuːplɪt/ ▶ **noun** a set of two things.
■ Music a pair of equal notes to be performed in the time of three.
– ORIGIN mid 17th cent. (as a dicing term in the sense of *doublets* (see **DOUBLET**): from Latin *duplus* 'duple', on the pattern of *doublet*. Current senses date from the 1920s.

duplex /ˈdjuːplɛks/ ▶ **noun** something having two parts, in particular:
■ a flat on two floors. ■ N. Amer. a residential building divided into two apartments. ■ chiefly N. Amer. & Austral. a semi-detached house. ■ Biochemistry a double-stranded polynucleotide molecule.
▶ **adjective** **1** having two parts, in particular:
■ (of a flat or room) on two floors. ■ chiefly N. Amer. & Austral. (of a house) semi-detached. ■ (of paper or board) having two differently coloured layers or sides. ■ Biochemistry consisting of two polynucleotide strands linked side by side. ■ (of a printer or its software) capable of printing on both sides of the paper.
2 (of a communications system, computer circuit, etc.) allowing the transmission of two signals simultaneously in opposite directions.
– ORIGIN mid 16th cent. (as an adjective): from Latin *duplex, duplic-*, from *duo* 'two' + *plicare* 'to fold'. The noun dates from the 1920s.

duplicate ▶ **adjective** /ˈdjuːplɪkət/ [attrib.] **1** exactly like something else, especially through having been copied: *a duplicate licence is issued to replace a valid licence which has been lost.*
2 having two corresponding or identical parts: *a duplicate application form.*
■ twice as large or many; doubled: *duplicate computer facilities and staff.*
▶ **noun** /ˈdjuːplɪkət/ **1** one of two or more identical things: *books may be disposed of if they are duplicates.*
■ a copy of an original: *locksmiths can make duplicates of most keys.*
2 short for **DUPLICATE BRIDGE**.
3 archaic a pawnbroker's ticket.
▶ **verb** /ˈdjuːplɪkeɪt/ [with obj.] make or be an exact copy of: *a unique scent, impossible to duplicate or forget |* figurative *they have not been able to duplicate his successes.*
■ (often **be duplicated**) make or supply copies of (a document): *information sheets had to be typed and duplicated |* [as adj. **duplicating**] *a duplicating machine.* ■ multiply by two; double: *the normal amount of DNA has been duplicated thousands of times.* ■ do (something) again unnecessarily: *most of these proposals duplicated work already done.*
– PHRASES **in duplicate** consisting of two exact copies: *forms to complete in duplicate.*
– DERIVATIVES **duplicable** adjective.
– ORIGIN late Middle English (in the sense 'having two corresponding parts'): from Latin *duplicat-* 'doubled', from the verb *duplicare*, from *duplic-* 'twofold' (see **DUPLEX**).

duplicate bridge ▶ **noun** [mass noun] a competitive form of bridge in which the same hands are played successively by different partnerships.

duplication ▶ **noun** [mass noun] the action or process of duplicating something.
■ [count noun] Genetics a DNA segment in a chromosome which is a copy of another segment.
– ORIGIN late Middle English (used in the mathematical sense 'multiplication by two'): from Old French, or from Latin *duplicatio(n-)*, from *duplicare* 'to double' (see **DUPLICATE**).

duplicator ▶ **noun** a machine or device for making copies of something, in particular a machine that makes copies of documents by means of fluid ink and a stencil.

duplicitous ▶ **adjective** deceitful: *treacherous, duplicitous behaviour.*
■ Law (of a charge or plea) containing more than one allegation.

duplicity /djuːˈplɪsɪti, djʊ-/ ▶ **noun** [mass noun] **1** deceitfulness; double-dealing.
2 archaic doubleness.
– ORIGIN late Middle English: from Old French *duplicite* or late Latin *duplicitas*, from Latin *duplic-* 'twofold' (see **DUPLEX**).

dupondius /djuːˈpɒndɪəs/ ▶ **noun** (pl. **dupondii** /-dɪʌɪ/) a bronze or brass coin of the Roman Empire, equal to two asses or half a sesterce.
– ORIGIN Latin, from *duo* 'two' + *pondo* 'by weight'.

duppy /ˈdʌpi/ ▶ **noun** (pl. **-ies**) W. Indian a malevolent spirit or ghost.
– ORIGIN late 18th cent.: probably of West African origin.

du Pré /d(j)uː ˈpreɪ/, Jacqueline (1945–87), English cellist. She made her solo debut at the age of 16 and became famous for her interpretations of cello concertos. Her performing career was halted in 1972 by multiple sclerosis.

Dupuytren's contracture /djʊˈpwiːtrənz/ (also **Dupuytren's disease**) ▶ **noun** [mass noun] Medicine a condition in which there is fixed forward curvature of one or more fingers, caused by the development of a fibrous connection between the finger tendons and the skin of the palm.
– ORIGIN late 19th cent.: named after Baron Guillaume *Dupuytren* (1777–1835), the French surgeon who first described the condition.

Duque de Caxias /ˌduːkeɪ də kəˈʃiːəʃ/ a city in SE Brazil, a suburb of Rio de Janeiro; pop. 594,380 (1990).

dura[1] /ˈdjʊərə/ (in full **dura mater**) ▶ **noun** Anatomy the tough outermost membrane enveloping the brain and spinal cord.
– DERIVATIVES **dural** adjective.
– ORIGIN late 19th cent.: from medieval Latin, literally 'hard mother', translation of Arabic *al-'umm al-jāfiya* 'coarse mother'.

dura[2] ▶ **noun** variant spelling of **DURRA**.

durable ▶ **adjective** able to withstand wear, pressure, or damage; hard-wearing: *porcelain enamel is strong and durable |* figurative *a durable peace can be achieved.*
■ informal (of a person) having endurance: *the durable Smith lasted the full eight rounds.*
▶ **noun** (**durables**) short for **DURABLE GOODS**.
– DERIVATIVES **durability** noun, **durableness** noun, **durably** adverb.
– ORIGIN Middle English (in the sense 'steadfast'): via Old French from Latin *durabilis*, from *durare* 'to last' (see **DURATION**).

durable goods ▶ **plural noun** goods not for immediate consumption and able to be kept for a period of time.

Duralumin /djʊˈraljʊmɪn/ ▶ **noun** [mass noun] trademark a hard, light alloy of aluminium with copper and other elements.
– ORIGIN early 20th cent.: perhaps from Latin *durus* 'hard' + **ALUMINIUM**, but probably influenced by *Düren*, the name of the Rhineland town where such alloys were first produced.

dura mater /ˌdjʊərə ˈmeɪtə/ ▶ **noun** see **DURA**[1].

duramen /djʊˈreɪmɛn/ ▶ **noun** [mass noun] Botany the heartwood of a tree.
– ORIGIN mid 19th cent.: from Latin, literally 'hardness', from *durare* 'harden'.

durance ▶ **noun** [mass noun] archaic imprisonment or confinement.
– ORIGIN late Middle English (in the sense 'continuance'): from Old French, from *durer* 'to last', from Latin *durare* . The sense 'imprisonment' is first recorded in the early 16th cent.

b **but** | d **dog** | f **few** | g **get** | h **he** | j **yes** | k **cat** | l **leg** | m **man** | n **no** | p **pen** | r **red** | s **sit** | t **top** | v **voice** | w **we** | z **zoo** | ʃ **she** | ʒ **decision** | θ **thin** | ð **this** | ŋ **ring** | x **loch** | tʃ **chip** | dʒ **jar**

Durango /djʊˈraŋgəʊ/ a state of north central Mexico.
▪its capital city; pop. 1,352,160 (1990). Full name **VICTORIA DE DURANGO**.

Duras /ˈdjʊərɑː, French dyʀa/, Marguerite (1914–96), French novelist, film director, and dramatist; pseudonym of *Marguerite Donnadieu*. She is best known for the screenplay to Alain Resnais' film *Hiroshima mon amour* (1959) and for her semi-autobiographical novel *L'Amant* (1984).

duration ▶ **noun** the time during which something continues: *bicycle hire for the duration of your holiday | a flight of over eight hours' duration*.
– PHRASES **for the duration** until the end of something, especially a war. ▪ informal for a very long time: *some stains may be there for the duration*.
– DERIVATIVES **durational** adjective.
– ORIGIN late Middle English: via Old French from medieval Latin *duratio(n-)*, from *durare* 'to last', from *durus* 'hard'.

durative /ˈdjʊərətɪv/ ▶ **adjective** Grammar of or denoting continuing action. Contrasted with **PUNCTUAL**.

Durazzo /duˈrattso/ Italian name for **DURRËS**.

Durban a seaport and resort in South Africa, on the coast of KwaZulu/Natal; pop. 1,137,380 (1991). Former name (until 1835) **PORT NATAL**.

durbar /ˈdəːbɑː/ ▶ **noun** historical the court of an Indian ruler.
▪a public reception held by an Indian prince or a British governor or viceroy in India.
– ORIGIN Urdu, from Persian *darbār* 'court'.

durchkomponiert /ˌdʊəxˈkɒmpɒnɪət, German ˌdʊrçkɔmpoˈniːrt/ ▶ **adjective** Music (of a composition, especially a song) not based on repeated sections or verses, especially having different music for each verse. Also called **THROUGH-COMPOSED**.
– ORIGIN from German, from *durch* 'through' + *komponiert* 'composed' (because the music is different throughout).

Dürer /ˈdjʊərə, German ˈdyːrɐ/, Albrecht (1471–1528), German engraver and painter. He was the leading German artist of the Renaissance, important for his technically advanced woodcuts and copper engravings and also noted for his watercolours and drawings.

duress /djʊ(ə)ˈrɛs, ˈdjʊərɛs/ ▶ **noun** [mass noun] threats, violence, constraints, or other action brought to bear on someone to do something against their will or better judgement: *confessions extracted* ***under duress***.
▪Law constraint illegally exercised to force someone to perform an act. ▪archaic forcible restraint or imprisonment.
– ORIGIN Middle English (in the sense 'harshness, severity, cruel treatment'): via Old French from Latin *duritia*, from *durus* 'hard'.

Durex ▶ **noun** (pl. same) Brit. trademark a contraceptive sheath; a condom.
– ORIGIN 1930s: name invented by the manufacturers, probably based on Latin *durare* 'to last'.

Durey /djʊəˈreɪ, French dyʀɛ/, Louis (1888–1979), French composer. A member until 1921 of the group Les Six, he later wrote music of a deliberate mass appeal, in accordance with communist doctrines on art. Notable works: *La Longue marche* (cantata, 1949).

Durga /ˈdʊəgə/ Hinduism a fierce goddess, wife of Shiva, often identified with Kali. She is usually depicted riding a tiger or lion and slaying the buffalo demon, and with eight or ten arms.

Durgapur /ˌdʊəgəˈpʊə/ a city in NE India, in the state of West Bengal; pop. 415,990 (1991).

durgon /ˈdəːgɒn/ ▶ **noun** see **BLACK DURGON**.

Durham /ˈdʌrəm/ a city on the River Wear; pop. 85,800 (1991). It is famous for its 11th-century cathedral, which contains the tomb of the Venerable Bede, and its university.
▪(also **County Durham**) a county of NE England; county town, Durham.

Durham quilt ▶ **noun** a quilt made by sewing together a piece of fabric, an inner wad, and a lining, the stitches making decorative patterns.

durian /ˈdʊərɪən/ ▶ **noun** **1** an oval spiny tropical fruit containing a creamy pulp. Despite its fetid smell it is highly esteemed for its flavour.
2 (also **durian tree**) the large tree that bears this fruit, native to Malaysia.
• *Durio zibethinus*, family Bombaceae.
– ORIGIN late 16th cent.: from Malay *durian*, from *duri* 'thorn'.

duricrust /ˈdjʊərɪkrʌst/ ▶ **noun** Geology a hard mineral crust formed at or near the surface of soil in semi-arid regions by the evaporation of groundwater.
– ORIGIN 1920s: from Latin *durus* 'hard' + **CRUST**.

during ▶ **preposition** throughout the course or duration of (a period of time): *the restaurant is open during the day*.
▪used to indicate constant development throughout a period: *the period during which he grew to adulthood*. ▪ at a particular point in the course of: *the stabbing took place during a row at a party*.
– ORIGIN late Middle English: present participle of the obsolete verb *dure* 'last, endure, extend', via Old French from Latin *durare* 'to last' (see **DURATION**).

Durkheim /ˈdəːkhʌɪm, French dyʀkɛm/, Émile (1858–1917), French sociologist, one of the founders of modern sociology. He became the first professor of sociology at the Sorbonne (1913). Notable works: *The Division of Labour in Society* (1893) and *Suicide* (1897).

durmast oak /ˈdəːmɑːst/ ▶ **noun** another term for **SESSILE OAK**.
– ORIGIN late 18th cent.: *durmast* perhaps originally an error for *dunmast*, from **DUN**[1] + **MAST**[2].

durn ▶ **verb**, **exclamation**, **adjective**, & **adverb** US dialect form of **DARN**[2].

durned ▶ **adjective** & **adverb** US dialect form of **DARNED**.

Duroc /ˈdjʊərɒk/ ▶ **noun** a pig of a reddish breed developed in North America.
– ORIGIN early 19th cent.: from the name of a stallion that is said to have been bought by the breeder Isaac Frink on the same day as the pigs from which he developed the breed.

durra /ˈdʊrə, ˈdʊərə/ ▶ **noun** [mass noun] grain sorghum of the principal variety grown from NE Africa to India.
• *Sorghum bicolor* var. *durra*, family Gramineae; **white durra** is var. *cernuum*.
– ORIGIN late 18th cent.: from Arabic *ḏura*, *ḏurra*.

Durrell[1] /ˈdʌrəl/, Gerald (Malcolm) (1925–95), English zoologist and writer, younger brother of Lawrence Durrell. In 1958 he founded a zoo (later the Jersey Wildlife Preservation Trust) devoted to the conservation and captive breeding of endangered species. Notable works: *My Family and Other Animals* (1956).

Durrell[2] /ˈdʌrəl/, Lawrence (George) (1912–90), English novelist, poet, and travel writer, brother of Gerald Durrell. He spent much of his life abroad, particularly in the Mediterranean. Notable works: *Alexandria Quartet* (four novels, 1957–60) and *Prospero's Cell* (travel, 1945).

Durrës /ˈdʊrəs/ a port and resort in Albania, on the Adriatic coast; pop. 72,000 (1990). Italian name **DURAZZO**.

durrie ▶ **noun** (pl. **-ies**) variant spelling of **DHURRIE**.

durst archaic or regional past of **DARE**.

durum /ˈdjʊərəm/ (also **durum wheat**) ▶ **noun** [mass noun] a kind of hard wheat grown in arid regions, having bearded ears and yielding flour that is used to make pasta.
• *Triticum durum*, family Gramineae.
– ORIGIN early 20th cent.: from Latin, neuter of *durus* 'hard', used in the species name since 1798.

durzi /ˈdəːzi/ ▶ **noun** (pl. **durzis**) Indian a tailor.
– ORIGIN Urdu, from Persian *darzī*, from *darz* 'sewing'.

Duse /ˈd(j)uːzeɪ/, Eleonora (1858–1924), Italian actress, best known for her tragic roles, particularly in plays by Ibsen and Gabriele d'Annunzio.

Dushanbe /duːˈʃanbeɪ/ the capital of Tajikistan; pop. 602,000 (est. 1990). Former name (1929–61) **STALINABAD**.

dusk ▶ **noun** the darker stage of twilight: *dusk was falling rapidly | working the land* ***from dawn to dusk***.
▪[mass noun] semi-darkness: *in the dusk of an Istanbul night club*.
▶ **verb** [no obj.] poetic/literary grow dark: [as adj. **dusking**] *he saw the lights blaze in the dusking sky*.
▶ **adjective** poetic/literary shadowy, dim, or dark.
– ORIGIN Old English *dox* 'dark, swarthy' and *doxian* 'darken in colour', of Germanic origin; related to Old High German *tusin* 'darkish'; compare with **DUN**[1]. The noun dates from the early 17th cent. The change in form from *-x* to *-sk* occurred in Middle English.

dusky ▶ **adjective** (**duskier**, **duskiest**) darkish in colour: *dusky red | a dusky complexion*.
▪dated used in euphemistic or poetic reference to black or other dark-skinned people: *a dusky Moorish maiden*. ▪ poetic/literary dim: *dusky light came from a small window*. ▪ [attrib.] used in names of animals with dark coloration, e.g. **dusky dolphin**, **dusky warbler**.
– DERIVATIVES **duskily** adverb, **duskiness** noun.

dusky wing ▶ **noun** a small dark-winged butterfly of the skipper family, found in North America.
• Genus *Erynnis*, family Hesperiidae; the species are very difficult to tell apart.

Dussehra /ˈdʌʃərə/ (also **Dasehra**) ▶ **noun** the tenth and final day of the Hindu festival of Navaratri. In southern India it especially commemorates the victory of the god Rama over the demon king Ravana.
– ORIGIN from Hindi *daśahrā*, from Sanskrit *daśaharā*.

Düsseldorf /ˈdʊs(ə)ldɔːf, German ˈdʏsldɔrf/ an industrial city of NW Germany, on the Rhine, capital of North Rhine-Westphalia; pop. 577,560 (1991).

dust ▶ **noun** **1** [mass noun] fine, dry powder consisting of tiny particles of earth or waste matter lying on the ground or on surfaces or carried in the air: *the car sent up clouds of dust | they rolled and fought in the dust*.
▪[with modifier] any material in the form of tiny particles: *coal dust*. ▪ [in sing.] a fine powder: *he ground it into a fine dust*. ▪ [in sing.] a cloud of dust. ▪ poetic/literary a dead person's remains: *scatter my dust and ashes*. ▪ poetic/literary the mortal human body: *the soul, that dwells within your dust*.
2 [in sing.] an act of dusting: *a quick dust, to get rid of the cobwebs*.
▶ **verb** [with obj.] **1** remove the dust from the surface of (something) by wiping or brushing it: *I broke the vase I had been dusting | pick yourself up and* ***dust*** *yourself* ***down*** | [no obj.] *she washed and dusted and tidied*.
▪(**dust something down/off**) bring something out for use again after a long period of neglect: *a number of aircraft will be dusted off and returned to flight*.
2 (usu. **be dusted**) cover lightly with a powdered substance: *roll out on a surface dusted with icing sugar*.
▪sprinkle (a powdered substance) on to something: *orange powder was dusted over the upper body*.
3 US informal beat up or kill someone: *the officers* ***dusted*** *him* ***up*** *a little bit*.
– PHRASES **be done and dusted** informal (of a project) be completely finished or ready: *well, that's part one done and dusted*. **dust and ashes** used to convey a feeling of great disappointment or disillusion about something: *the party would be dust and ashes if he couldn't come*. **the dust settles** things quieten down: *she hoped that the dust would settle quickly and the episode be forgotten*. **eat someone's dust** N. Amer. informal fall far behind someone in a competitive situation. **gather** (or **collect**) **dust** remain unused: *some professors let their computers gather dust*. **leave someone/thing in the dust** surpass someone or something easily: *today's modems leave their predecessors in the dust*. **not see someone for dust** find that a person has made a hasty departure. **kick up a dust** (or US **kick up dust**) informal create a disturbance.
– DERIVATIVES **dustless** adjective.
– ORIGIN Old English *dūst*, of Germanic origin; related to Dutch *duist* 'chaff'.

dustball ▶ **noun** N. Amer. a ball of dust and fluff.

dust bath ▶ **noun** a bird's rolling in dust to clean its feathers.

dustbin ▶ **noun** Brit. a container for household refuse, especially one kept outside.

dustbin man ▶ **noun** (pl. **-men**) Brit. a dustman.

dust bowl ▶ **noun** an area of land where vegetation has been lost and soil reduced to dust and eroded, especially as a consequence of drought or unsuitable farming practice.
▪(**the Dust Bowl**) an area of Oklahoma and other prairie states of the US affected by severe soil erosion in the early 1930s, from which many people were obliged to move.

dust bunny ▶ **noun** N. Amer. informal a ball of dust and fluff.

dustcart ▶ noun Brit. a vehicle used for collecting household refuse.

dustcoat ▶ noun a coat worn for protection against dust.
■ another term for **DUSTER** (in sense 2).

dust cover ▶ noun a dust jacket or dust sheet.

dust devil ▶ noun a small whirlwind or air vortex over land, visible as a column of dust and debris.

duster ▶ noun **1** Brit. a cloth or pad for dusting furniture.
2 (also **duster coat**) chiefly N. Amer. a woman's loose, lightweight full-length coat without buttons, of a style originally worn in the 1920s when travelling in an open car.
3 US informal a dust storm.

dustheap ▶ noun a heap of household refuse.

dusting powder ▶ noun [mass noun] powder for dusting over something, in particular talcum powder.

dust jacket ▶ noun a removable paper cover, generally with a decorative design, used to protect a book from dirt or damage.

dustman ▶ noun (pl. **-men**) Brit. a man employed to remove household refuse from dustbins.

dustoor ▶ noun variant spelling of **DASTUR**.

dustpan ▶ noun a flat hand-held receptacle into which dust and waste can be swept from the floor.

dust sheet ▶ noun Brit. a large sheet for covering furniture or flooring to protect it from dust or while decorating.

dust shot ▶ noun [mass noun] the smallest size of gunshot.

dust storm ▶ noun a strong, turbulent wind which carries clouds of fine dust, soil, and sand over a large area.

dust trap ▶ noun something on, in, or under which dust readily gathers.

dust-up ▶ noun informal a fight; a quarrel: *he'd had a dust-up with Vera.*

dust wrapper ▶ noun another term for **DUST JACKET**.

dusty ▶ adjective (**dustier**, **dustiest**) covered with, full of, or resembling dust: *dusty old records* | *a hot, dusty road.*
■ (of a colour) dull or muted: *patches of pale gold and dusty pink.* ■ figurative staid and uninteresting: *a dusty old bore.*
– PHRASES **a dusty answer** Brit. a curt and unhelpful reply. **not so dusty** Brit. informal, dated (of a person's health or situation) fairly good.
– DERIVATIVES **dustily** adverb, **dustiness** noun.

dusty miller ▶ noun a plant of the daisy family with whitish or greyish foliage.
● Several species in the family Compositae, in particular the cultivated *Artemisia stelleriana* of North America and *Senecio cineraria* of the Mediterranean.
– ORIGIN early 19th cent.: named from the fine powder on the flowers and leaves.

Dutch ▶ adjective of or relating to the Netherlands or its people or their language.
▶ noun **1** [mass noun] the language of the Netherlands, spoken by some 20 million people.
■ S. African derogatory Afrikaans.
2 [as plural noun **the Dutch**] the people of the Netherlands collectively.

Dutch belongs to the West Germanic branch of Indo-European languages and is most closely related to German and English. It is also the official language of Suriname and the Netherlands Antilles, and is spoken in northern Belgium, where it is called Flemish.

– PHRASES **go Dutch** share the cost of something, especially a meal, equally. **in Dutch** US informal, dated in trouble: *he's been getting in Dutch at school.*
– ORIGIN from Middle Dutch *dutsch* 'Dutch, Netherlandish, German': the English word originally denoted speakers of both High and Low German, but became more specific after the United Provinces adopted the Low German of Holland as the national language on independence in 1579.

dutch ▶ noun (usu. **one's old dutch**) Brit. informal (especially among cockneys) one's wife.
– ORIGIN late 19th cent.: abbreviation of **DUCHESS**.

Dutch auction ▶ noun a method of selling in which the price is reduced until a buyer is found.

Dutch barn ▶ noun Brit. a farm building with a curved roof set over a steel, timber, or concrete frame without walls, used for storing hay.

Dutch cap ▶ noun **1** a woman's lace cap with triangular flaps on each side, worn as part of Dutch traditional dress.
2 see **CAP** (sense 2).

Dutch clover ▶ noun another term for **WHITE CLOVER**.

Dutch courage ▶ noun [mass noun] strength or confidence gained from drinking alcohol: *I'll have a couple of drinks to give me Dutch courage.*

Dutch doll ▶ noun Brit. a jointed wooden doll.

Dutch door ▶ noun N. Amer. a stable door.

Dutch East India Company a Dutch trading company founded in 1602 to protect Dutch trading interests in the Indian Ocean. It was dissolved in 1799.

Dutch East Indies former name (until 1949) for **INDONESIA**.

Dutch elm disease ▶ noun [mass noun] a fungal disease of elm trees that is spread by elm bark beetles. A virulent strain of the fungus which arose in North America has destroyed the majority of elms in southern Britain.
● The fungus is *Ceratocystis ulmi*, subdivision Ascomycotina.

Dutch Guiana former name (until 1948) for **SURINAME**.

Dutch hoe ▶ noun a hoe used with a pushing action just under the surface of the soil so as to kill weeds at this level.

Dutch interior ▶ noun a painting of the interior of a Dutch house in a style characteristic of the work of 17th-century genre painters.

Dutch light ▶ noun a cold frame in which the glass is a single large pane.
■ the pane of glass in such a cold frame.

Dutchman ▶ noun (pl. **-men**) a native or national of the Netherlands, or a person of Dutch descent.
– PHRASES **I'm a Dutchman** Brit. used to express one's disbelief or as a way of underlining an emphatic assertion: *if she's seventeen, I'm a Dutchman.*

Dutchman's breeches ▶ noun chiefly N. Amer. a plant related to bleeding heart, but typically having pale yellow flowers.
● Genus *Dicentra*, family Fumariaceae: several species, in particular *D. spectabilis*.
– ORIGIN mid 19th cent.: so named because of the shape of the spurred flower.

Dutchman's pipe ▶ noun a vigorous climbing vine with hooked tubular flowers, native to eastern North America.
● *Aristolochia durior*, family Aristolochiaceae.

Dutch metal ▶ noun [mass noun] an alloy of copper and zinc used in imitation of gold leaf.

Dutch New Guinea former name (until 1963) for **IRIAN JAYA**.

Dutch oven ▶ noun chiefly historical a large cooking pot or metal box serving as a simple oven, heated by being placed under or next to hot coals.
■ S. African a brick or clay oven traditionally built into the side of a kitchen hearth or as a free-standing structure outside a house.

Dutch Reformed Church a branch of the Protestant Church in the Netherlands, formed during the Reformation. It was disestablished in 1798 and replaced in 1816 by the Netherlands Reformed Church.
■ the dominant branch of the Protestant Church among Afrikaners in South Africa.

Dutch tile ▶ noun a kind of glazed white tile painted with traditional Dutch motifs in blue or brown.
▶ verb [with obj.] [usu. as adj. **Dutch-tiled**] decorate with such tiles: *Dutch-tiled fireplaces.*

Dutch treat ▶ noun an outing, meal, or other special occasion at which each participant pays for their share of the expenses.

Dutch uncle ▶ noun informal, chiefly US a person giving firm but benevolent advice.

Dutch West India Company a Dutch trading company founded in 1621 to develop Dutch trading interests in competition with Spain and Portugal and their colonies in western India, South America, and West Africa. It was dissolved in 1794.

Dutch wife ▶ noun a bolster used for resting the legs in bed.
– ORIGIN late 19th cent.: extended use of the term, earlier describing a rattan open frame used in the Dutch Indies to support the limbs in bed.

Dutchwoman ▶ noun (pl. **-women**) a female native or national of the Netherlands, or a woman of Dutch descent.

duteous /ˈdjuːtɪəs/ ▶ adjective archaic dutiful: *a duteous vassal.*
– DERIVATIVES **duteously** adverb, **duteousness** noun.
– ORIGIN late 16th cent.: from **DUTY**, on the pattern of words such as *bounteous.*

dutiable /ˈdjuːtɪəb(ə)l/ ▶ adjective liable to customs or other duties: *dutiable goods.*

dutiful ▶ adjective conscientiously or obediently fulfilling one's duty: *a dutiful daughter.*
■ motivated by duty rather than desire or enthusiasm: *dutiful applause* | *a dutiful visit.*
– DERIVATIVES **dutifully** adverb, **dutifulness** noun.

duty ▶ noun (pl. **-ies**) **1** a moral or legal obligation; a responsibility: *it's my duty to uphold the law* | *she was determined to do her duty as a citizen* | [mass noun] *a strong sense of duty.*
■ [as modifier] (of a visit or other undertaking) done from a sense of moral obligation rather than for pleasure: *a fifteen-minute duty visit.*
2 (often **duties**) a task or action that someone is required to perform: *the queen's official duties* | *your duties will include operating the switchboard* | [mass noun] *Juliet reported for duty.*
■ [as modifier] (of a person) engaged in their regular work: *a duty nurse.* ■ [mass noun] (also **duties**) performance of prescribed church services by a priest or minister: *he was willing to take Sunday duties.*
3 a payment due and enforced by law or custom, in particular:
■ a payment levied on the import, export, manufacture, or sale of goods: *a 6 per cent duty on imports* | [mass noun] *goods subject to excise duty.* ■ Brit. a payment levied on the transfer of property, for licences, and for the legal recognition of documents.
4 technical the measure of an engine's effectiveness in units of work done per unit of fuel.
– PHRASES **do duty as** (or **for**) serve or act as a substitute for something else: *the rusting shack which did duty as the bridge.* **on** (or **off**) **duty** engaged (or not engaged) in one's regular work: *the doorman had gone off duty and the lobby was unattended.*
– ORIGIN late Middle English: from Anglo-Norman French *duete*, from Old French *deu* (see **DUE**).

duty-bound ▶ adjective [predic., with infinitive] morally or legally obliged to do something: *legitimate news stories which the press is duty-bound to report.*

duty cycle ▶ noun the cycle of operation of a machine or other device which operates intermittently rather than continuously.
■ the time occupied by this, especially as a percentage of available time.

duty drawback ▶ noun see **DRAWBACK** (sense 2).

duty-free ▶ adjective & adverb exempt from payment of duty: [as adj.] *the permitted number of duty-free goods* | [as adv.] *most EC goods enter almost duty-free.*
■ [as adj.] (of a shop or area) selling or trading in goods that are exempt from payment of duty.
▶ noun [mass noun] (also **duty-frees**) goods that are exempt from payment of duty: *the bag of duty-free.*

duty officer ▶ noun an officer, especially in the police or armed forces, who is on duty at a particular time.

duty-paid ▶ adjective [attrib.] on which the cost of duty has been met: *limits on duty-paid goods.*

duumvir /djuːˈʌmvə/ ▶ noun (in ancient Rome) each of two magistrates or officials holding a joint office.
– ORIGIN Latin, from *duum virum* 'of the two men'.

duumvirate /djuːˈʌmvɪrət/ ▶ noun a coalition of two people having joint authority or influence.
– ORIGIN mid 17th cent.: from Latin *duumviratus.*

Duvalier /djuːˈvalɪeɪ/ François (1907–71), Haitian statesman, President 1957–71; known as **Papa Doc**. His regime was noted for its oppressive nature, opponents being assassinated or forced into exile by his security force, the Tontons Macoutes. He was succeeded by his son Jean-Claude (b.1951), known as **Baby Doc**, who was overthrown by a mass uprising in 1986.

duvet /ˈd(j)uːveɪ/ ▶ noun chiefly Brit. a soft quilt filled with down, feathers, or a synthetic fibre, used instead of an upper sheet and blankets.
■ (also **duvet jacket**) a thick down-filled jacket worn by mountaineers.
– ORIGIN mid 18th cent.: from French, literally 'down' (see **DOWN²**).

dux /dʌks/ ▸ noun (pl. **duces**) a Saxon chief or leader.
■chiefly Scottish the top pupil in a school or class.
– ORIGIN mid 18th cent. (denoting the leading voice or instrument in a fugue or canon): from Latin, 'leader'.

duxelles /'dʌks(ə)lz, dyksɛl/ ▸ noun [mass noun] a preparation of mushrooms sautéed with onions, shallots, garlic, and parsley and used to make stuffing or sauce: *chillies stuffed with duxelles.*
– ORIGIN named after the Marquis *d'Uxelles*, a 17th-cent. French nobleman.

DV formal ▸ abbreviation for Deo volente: *this time next week (DV) I shall be among the mountains.*

DVD ▸ abbreviation for digital versatile disc.

DVLA ▸ abbreviation for Driver and Vehicle Licensing Agency.

Dvořák /'dvɔːʒak, -ʒaːk/, Antonín (1841–1904), Czech composer. Combining ethnic folk elements with the Viennese musical tradition, he wrote chamber music, operas, and songs, but is probably best known for his ninth symphony ('From the New World', 1892–5).

dwaal /dwaːl/ ▸ noun S. African informal a dreamy, dazed, or absent-minded state: *you're in a real dwaal!*
– ORIGIN Afrikaans.

dwale /dweɪl/ ▸ noun [mass noun] archaic deadly nightshade or belladonna.
■a soporific drink formerly made from this.
– ORIGIN Middle English: probably of Scandinavian origin and related to Danish *dvale* 'deep sleep, stupor', *dvaledrik* 'sleeping draught'.

dwam /dwaːm/ ▸ noun chiefly Scottish a state of semi-consciousness or reverie.
– ORIGIN early 16th cent.: from the Germanic base of **DWELL**; compare with Middle Dutch *dwelm* 'stupefaction', also with Old English *dwolma* 'confusion'.

dwarf ▸ noun (pl. **dwarfs** or **dwarves**) **1** (in folklore or fantasy literature) a member of a mythical race of short, stocky human-like creatures who are generally skilled in mining and metalworking.
■an abnormally small person. ■ [as modifier] denoting something, especially an animal or plant, which is much smaller than the usual size for its type or species: *a dwarf conifer.*
2 (also **dwarf star**) Astronomy a star of relatively small size and low luminosity, including the majority of main sequence stars.
▸ verb [with obj.] cause to seem small or insignificant in comparison: *the buildings surround and dwarf All Saints church.*
■stunt the growth or development of: [as adj. **dwarfed**] *the dwarfed but solid branch of a tree.*
– DERIVATIVES **dwarfish** adjective.
– ORIGIN Old English *dweorg, dweorh*, of Germanic origin; related to Dutch *dwerg* and German *Zwerg*.

USAGE In the sense 'an abnormally small person', **dwarf** is normally considered offensive. However, there are no accepted alternatives in the general language, since terms such as **person of restricted growth** have gained little currency.

dwarfism ▸ noun [mass noun] (in medical or technical contexts) unusually or abnormally low stature or small size.

dwarf lemur ▸ noun a small Madagascan primate related to the mouse lemur, feeding primarily on fruit and gums.
● Family Cheirogaleidae: three genera and four species.

dweeb ▸ noun informal, chiefly US a boring, studious, or socially inept person.
– DERIVATIVES **dweebish** adjective, **dweeby** adjective.
– ORIGIN 1980s: perhaps a blend of **DWARF** and early 20th-cent. *feeb* 'a feeble-minded person' (from **FEEBLE**).

dwell ▸ verb (past and past participle **dwelt** or **dwelled**) [no obj.] **1** [with adverbial of place] formal live in or at a specified place: *groups of gypsies still dwell in these caves.*
2 (**dwell on/upon**) think, speak, or write at length about (a particular subject, especially one that is a source of unhappiness, anxiety, or dissatisfaction): *I've got better things to do than dwell on the past.*
■(**dwell on/upon**) (of one's eyes or attention) linger on (a particular object or place): *she let her eyes dwell on them for a moment.*
▸ noun technical a slight regular pause in the motion of a machine.

– DERIVATIVES **dweller** noun [in combination] *city-dwellers.*
– ORIGIN Old English *dwellan* 'lead astray, hinder, delay' (in Middle English 'tarry, remain in a place'), of Germanic origin; related to Middle Dutch *dwellen* 'stun, perplex' and Old Norse *dvelja* 'delay, tarry, stay'.

dwelling (also **dwelling place**) ▸ noun formal a house, flat, or other place of residence.

dwelling house ▸ noun Law a house used as a residence and not for business purposes.

DWEM ▸ abbreviation for dead white European male.

dwindle ▸ verb [no obj.] diminish gradually in size, amount, or strength: *traffic has dwindled to a trickle* | [as adj. **dwindling**] *dwindling resources.*
– ORIGIN late 16th cent.: frequentative of Scots and dialect *dwine* 'fade away', from Old English *dwīnan*, of Germanic origin; related to Middle Dutch *dwīnen* and Old Norse *dvína.*

DWM ▸ abbreviation for dead white male.

dwt ▸ abbreviation for ■ deadweight tonnage: *a 40,000 dwt slipway.* ■ pennyweight.

DY ▸ abbreviation for Benin (international vehicle registration).
– ORIGIN from **DAHOMEY**.

Dy ▸ symbol for the chemical element dysprosium.

dyad /'dʌɪad/ ▸ noun technical something that consists of two elements or parts: *the mother–child dyad.*
■Mathematics an operator which is a combination of two vectors.
– DERIVATIVES **dyadic** adjective.
– ORIGIN late 17th cent. (originally denoting the number two or a pair): from late Latin *dyas, dyad-*, from Greek *duas*, from *duo* 'two'. Current senses date from the late 19th cent.

Dyak /'dʌɪak/ ▸ noun & adjective variant spelling of **DAYAK**.

dyarchy ▸ noun (pl. **-ies**) variant spelling of **DIARCHY**.

dybbuk /'dɪbʊk/ ▸ noun (pl. **dybbuks** or **dybbukim** /-kɪm/) (in Jewish folklore) a malevolent wandering spirit that enters and possesses the body of a living person until exorcized.
– ORIGIN from Yiddish *dibek*, from Hebrew *dibbūq*, from *dābaq* 'cling'.

dye ▸ noun [mass noun] a natural or synthetic substance used to add a colour to or change the colour of something.
▸ verb (**dyeing**) [with obj.] add a colour to or change the colour of (something) by soaking it in a solution impregnated with a dye: [with complement] *I dyed my hair blonde* | [as adj. **dyed**] *dyed black hair.*
■[no obj.] take colour well or badly during such a process: *it's good material—it should dye well.*
– PHRASES **dyed in the wool** unchanging in a particular belief or opinion; inveterate: *she's a true blue dyed-in-the-wool Conservative.* [ORIGIN: with allusion to the fact that yarn was dyed in the raw state, producing a more even and permanent colour.]
– DERIVATIVES **dyeable** adjective.
– ORIGIN Old English *dēag* (noun), *dēagian* (verb). The noun is not recorded from Old English to the late 16th cent., when it was re-formed from the verb.

dye laser ▸ noun a tunable laser using the fluorescence of an organic dye.

dyeline ▸ noun another term for **DIAZO**.

dyer ▸ noun a person whose trade is the dyeing of cloth or other material.

dyer's greenweed ▸ noun [mass noun] a bushy yellow-flowered Eurasian plant of the pea family, which has become naturalized in North America. The flowers were formerly used to make a yellow or green dye.
● *Genista tinctoria*, family Leguminosae.

dyer's oak ▸ noun another term for **VALONIA**.

dyer's rocket ▸ noun another term for **WELD**[2].

dyestuff ▸ noun a substance yielding a dye or that can be used as a dye, especially when in solution.

Dyfed /'dʌvɛd/ a former county of SW Wales 1974–96, comprising the former counties of Cardiganshire, Carmarthenshire, and Pembrokeshire.

dying ▸ adjective [attrib.] on the point of death: *he visited his dying mother.*
■occurring at or connected with the time that someone dies: *he strained to catch her dying words.*

■gradually ceasing to exist or function; in decline and about to disappear: *the making of valves is a dying art* | *the dying embers of the fire.* ■(of a period of time) final; closing: *the dying moments of the match.*
– PHRASES **to one's dying day** for the rest of one's life: *I shall remember that to my dying day.*
– ORIGIN late 16th cent.: present participle of **DIE**[1].

dyke[1] (also **dike**) ▸ noun **1** a long wall or embankment built to prevent flooding from the sea.
■[often in place names] a low wall or earthwork serving as a boundary or defence: *Offa's Dyke.* ■ a causeway. ■ Geology an intrusion of igneous rock cutting across existing strata. Compare with **SILL**.
2 a ditch or watercourse.
3 Austral./NZ informal, dated a toilet.
▸ verb [with obj.] [often as adj. **dyked**] provide (land) with a wall or embankment to prevent flooding.
– PHRASES **put one's finger in the dyke** attempt to stem the advance of something undesirable. [ORIGIN: from a story of a small Dutch boy who saved his community from flooding, by placing his finger in a hole in a dyke.]
– ORIGIN Middle English (denoting a trench or ditch): from Old Norse *dík*, related to **DITCH**. Sense 1 has been influenced by Middle Low German *dīk* 'dam' and Middle Dutch *dijc* 'ditch, dam'.

dyke[2] ▸ noun informal a lesbian.
– DERIVATIVES **dykey** adjective.
– ORIGIN 1940s (earlier as **BULLDYKE**): of unknown origin.

Dylan /'dɪlən/, Bob (b.1941), American singer and songwriter; born *Robert Allen Zimmerman*. The leader of an urban folk-music revival in the 1960s, he became known for political and protest songs such as 'The Times They Are A-Changin'' (1964). Notable albums: *Highway 61 Revisited* (1965) and *Blood on the Tracks* (1975).

dyn ▸ abbreviation for dyne.

dynamic /dʌɪ'namɪk/ ▸ adjective **1** (of a process or system) characterized by constant change, activity, or progress: *a dynamic economy.*
■(of a person) positive in attitude and full of energy and new ideas: *she's dynamic and determined.* ■ (of a thing) stimulating development or progress: *the dynamic forces of nature.* ■ Physics of or relating to forces producing motion. Often contrasted with **STATIC**. ■ Linguistics (of a verb) expressing an action, activity, event, or process. Contrasted with **STATIVE**. ■ Electronics (of a memory device) needing to be refreshed by the periodic application of a voltage.
2 Music relating to the volume of sound produced by an instrument, voice, or recording: *an astounding dynamic range.*
▸ noun **1** a force that stimulates change or progress within a system or process: *evaluation is part of the basic dynamic of the project.*
2 Music another term for **DYNAMICS** (in sense 3).
– DERIVATIVES **dynamical** adjective, **dynamically** adverb.
– ORIGIN early 19th cent. (as a term in physics): from French *dynamique*, from Greek *dunamikos*, from *dunamis* 'power'.

dynamic equilibrium ▸ noun a state of balance between continuing processes.

dynamic metamorphism ▸ noun [mass noun] Geology metamorphism produced by mechanical forces.

dynamic range ▸ noun the range of acceptable or possible volumes of sound occurring in the course of a piece of music or a performance.
■the ratio of the largest to the smallest intensity of sound that can be reliably transmitted or reproduced by a particular sound system, measured in decibels.

dynamics ▸ plural noun **1** [treated as sing.] the branch of mechanics concerned with the motion of bodies under the action of forces. Compare with **STATICS**.
■[usu. with modifier] the branch of any science in which forces or changes are considered: *chemical dynamics.*
2 the forces or properties which stimulate growth, development, or change within a system or process: *the dynamics of changing social relations.*
3 Music the varying levels of volume of sound in different parts of a musical performance.
– DERIVATIVES **dynamicist** noun (only in sense 1).

dynamic viscosity ▸ noun a quantity measuring the force needed to overcome internal friction in a fluid.

dynamism ▸ noun [mass noun] **1** the quality of being

characterized by vigorous activity and progress: *the dynamism and strength of the economy.*

■the quality of being dynamic and positive in attitude: *he was known for his dynamism and strong views.*

2 Philosophy, chiefly historical the theory that phenomena of matter or mind are due to the action of forces rather than to motion or matter.

– DERIVATIVES **dynamist** noun.

– ORIGIN mid 19th cent.: from Greek *dunamis* 'power' + **-ISM**.

dynamite ▶ noun [mass noun] a high explosive consisting of nitroglycerine mixed with an absorbent material and typically moulded into sticks.

■figurative something that could generate extreme reactions or have devastating repercussions: *that roads policy is political dynamite.* ■ informal an extremely impressive or exciting person or thing: *both her albums are dynamite* | [as modifier] *a chick with a dynamite figure.* ■ informal, dated a narcotic, especially heroin.

▶ verb [with obj.] blow up (something) with dynamite.

– DERIVATIVES **dynamiter** noun.

– ORIGIN mid 19th cent.: from Greek *dunamis* 'power' + **-ITE**[1].

dynamize (also **-ise**) ▶ verb [with obj.] endow with power or energy; make dynamic.

– DERIVATIVES **dynamization** noun.

dynamo ▶ noun (pl. **-os**) chiefly Brit. a machine for converting mechanical energy into electrical energy, typically by means of rotating coils of copper wire in a magnetic field.

■informal an extremely energetic person: *she was a dynamo in London politics.*

– ORIGIN late 19th cent.: abbreviation of *dynamo-electric machine*, from Greek *dunamis* 'power'.

dynamometer /ˌdaɪnəˈmɒmɪtə/ ▶ noun an instrument which measures the power output of an engine.

– ORIGIN early 19th cent.: from French *dynamomètre*, from Greek *dunamis* 'power' + French *-mètre* '(instrument) measuring'.

dynast /ˈdɪnəst, ˈdaɪnəst, -nast/ ▶ noun a member of a powerful family, especially a hereditary ruler.

– ORIGIN mid 17th cent.: via Latin from Greek *dunastēs*, from *dunasthai* 'be able'.

dynasty /ˈdɪnəsti/ ▶ noun (pl. **-ies**) a line of hereditary rulers of a country: *the Tang dynasty.*

■a succession of people from the same family who play a prominent role in business, politics, or another field: *the Guinness dynasty.*

– DERIVATIVES **dynastic** adjective, **dynastically** adverb.

– ORIGIN late Middle English: from French *dynastie*, or via late Latin from Greek *dunasteia* 'lordship, power', from *dunastēs* (see **DYNAST**).

dyne /daɪn/ ▶ noun Physics a unit of force that, acting on a mass of one gram, increases its velocity by one centimetre per second every second along the direction that it acts.

– ORIGIN late 19th cent.: from French, from Greek *dunamis* 'force, power'.

dyno ▶ noun (pl. **-os**) **1** short for **DYNAMOMETER**. **2** Climbing a rapid move across a rock face in order to reach a hold.

▶ verb (dynos, dyno'd or dynoed) **1** [with obj.] measure (the output of an engine) with a dynamometer. **2** [no obj.] (in mountaineering) climb using dynos.

dynode /ˈdaɪnəʊd/ ▶ noun Electronics an intermediate electrode which emits additional electrons in a photomultiplier or similar amplifying device.

– ORIGIN 1930s: from Greek *dunamis* 'power' + **-ODE**[2].

dys- /dɪs/ ▶ combining form bad; difficult (used especially in medical terms): *dyspepsia* | *dysphasia.*

– ORIGIN from Greek *dus-*; related to German *zer-*, also to Old English *to-*.

dysaesthesia /ˌdɪsiːsˈθiːzɪə/ (US **dysesthesia**) ▶ noun (pl. **dysaesthesiae** /-ziː/ or **dysaesthesias**) Medicine an abnormal unpleasant sensation felt when touched, caused by damage to peripheral nerves.

– ORIGIN early 18th cent.: modern Latin, from Greek *dusaisthēsia*, from **DYS-** 'bad' + *aisthēsis* 'sensation' + **-IA**[1].

dysarthria /dɪsˈɑːθrɪə/ ▶ noun [mass noun] Medicine difficult or unclear articulation of speech that is otherwise linguistically normal.

– ORIGIN late 19th cent.: from **DYS-** 'difficult' + Greek *arthron* 'joint or articulation'.

dyscalculia /ˌdɪskalˈkjuːlɪə/ ▶ noun [mass noun] Psychiatry severe difficulty in making arithmetical calculations, as a result of brain disorder.

dyscrasia /dɪsˈkreɪzɪə/ ▶ noun [mass noun] Medicine an abnormal or disordered state of the body or of a bodily part.

– DERIVATIVES **dyscrasic** adjective.

– ORIGIN late Middle English (denoting an imbalance of physical qualities): via late Latin from Greek *duskrasia* 'bad combination', from *dus-* 'bad' + *krasis* 'mixture'.

dysentery /ˈdɪs(ə)nt(ə)ri/ ▶ noun [mass noun] infection of the intestines resulting in severe diarrhoea with the presence of blood and mucus in the faeces.

● Amoebic dysentery is caused by the protozoan *Entamoeba histolytica*, mainly in warm climates, and spread by contaminated water and food; bacterial dysentery is caused by bacteria of the genus *Shigella* and can also spread by contact (see **SHIGELLA**).

– DERIVATIVES **dysenteric** /-ˈtɛrɪk/ adjective.

– ORIGIN late Middle English: from Old French *dissenterie*, or via Latin from Greek *dusenteria*, from *dusenteros* 'afflicted in the bowels', from *dus-* 'bad' + *entera* 'bowels'.

dysesthesia ▶ noun US spelling of **dysaesthesia**.

dysfunction ▶ noun [mass noun] abnormality or impairment in the operation of a specified bodily organ or system: *bowel dysfunction.*

■disruption of normal social relations: *inner-city dysfunction.*

dysfunctional ▶ adjective not operating normally or properly: *the telephones are dysfunctional.*

■unable to deal adequately with normal social relations: *an emotionally dysfunctional businessman* | *dysfunctional families.*

– DERIVATIVES **dysfunctionally** adverb.

dysgenic /dɪsˈdʒɛnɪk/ ▶ adjective exerting a detrimental effect on later generations through the inheritance of undesirable characteristics: *dysgenic breeding.*

dysgraphia /dɪsˈɡrafɪə/ ▶ noun [mass noun] Psychiatry inability to write coherently, as a symptom of brain disease or damage.

– DERIVATIVES **dysgraphic** adjective.

– ORIGIN 1930s: from **DYS-** 'difficult' + Greek *-graphia* 'writing'.

dyskinesia /ˌdɪskɪˈniːzɪə, -kʌɪ-/ ▶ noun [mass noun] Medicine abnormality or impairment of voluntary movement.

dyslalia /dɪsˈleɪlɪə/ ▶ noun [mass noun] Medicine inability to articulate comprehensible speech, especially when associated with the use of private words or sounds.

– ORIGIN mid 19th cent.: from **DYS-** 'difficult' + Greek *lalia* 'speech'.

dyslexia /dɪsˈlɛksɪə/ ▶ noun [mass noun] a general term for disorders that involve difficulty in learning to read or interpret words, letters, and other symbols, but that do not affect general intelligence.

– DERIVATIVES **dyslectic** adjective & noun, **dyslexic** adjective & noun.

– ORIGIN late 19th cent.: coined in German from **DYS-** 'difficult' + Greek *lexis* 'speech' (apparently by confusion of Greek *legein* 'to speak' and Latin *legere* 'to read').

dysmenorrhoea /ˌdɪsmɛnəˈriːə/ (US **dysmenorrhea**) ▶ noun [mass noun] Medicine painful menstruation, typically involving abdominal cramps.

dyspareunia /ˌdɪspəˈruːnɪə/ ▶ noun [mass noun] difficult or painful sexual intercourse.

– ORIGIN late 19th cent.: from **DYS-** 'difficult' + Greek *pareunos* 'lying with'.

dyspepsia /dɪsˈpɛpsɪə/ ▶ noun [mass noun] indigestion.

– ORIGIN early 18th cent.: via Latin from Greek *duspepsia*, from *duspeptos* 'difficult to digest'.

dyspeptic ▶ adjective of or having indigestion or a consequent air of irritable bad temper or depression.

▶ noun a person who suffers from indigestion or bad temper.

dysphagia /dɪsˈfeɪdʒɪə/ ▶ noun [mass noun] Medicine difficulty or discomfort in swallowing, as a symptom of disease: *progressive dysphagia.*

dysphasia /dɪsˈfeɪzɪə/ ▶ noun [mass noun] Psychiatry language disorder marked by deficiency in the generation of speech, and sometimes also in its comprehension, due to brain disease or damage.

– DERIVATIVES **dysphasic** adjective.

to utter', from *dus-* 'difficult' + *phatos* 'spoken'.

dysphemism /ˈdɪsfɪmɪz(ə)m/ ▶ noun a derogatory or unpleasant term used instead of a pleasant or neutral one. The opposite of **EUPHEMISM**.

dysphonia /dɪsˈfəʊnɪə/ ▶ noun [mass noun] Medicine difficulty in speaking due to a physical disorder of the mouth, tongue, throat, or vocal cords.

dysphoria /dɪsˈfɔːrɪə/ ▶ noun [mass noun] Psychiatry a state of unease or generalized dissatisfaction with life. The opposite of **EUPHORIA**.

– DERIVATIVES **dysphoric** adjective & noun.

– ORIGIN mid 19th cent.: from Greek *dusphoria*, from *dusphoros* 'hard to bear'.

dysplasia /dɪsˈpleɪzɪə/ ▶ noun [mass noun] Medicine the enlargement of an organ or tissue by the proliferation of cells of an abnormal type, as a developmental disorder or an early stage in the development of cancer.

– DERIVATIVES **dysplastic** adjective.

– ORIGIN 1930s: from **DYS-** 'bad' + Greek *plasis* 'formation'.

dyspnoea /dɪspˈniːə/ (US **dyspnea**) ▶ noun [mass noun] Medicine difficult or laboured breathing.

– DERIVATIVES **dyspnoeic** adjective.

– ORIGIN mid 17th cent.: via Latin from Greek *duspnoia*, from *dus-* 'difficult' + *pnoē* 'breathing'.

dyspraxia /dɪsˈpraksɪə/ ▶ noun [mass noun] Medicine a developmental disorder of the brain in childhood causing difficulty in activities requiring coordination and movement.

– ORIGIN early 20th cent.: from Greek *dus-* 'bad or difficult' + *praxis* 'action'.

dysprosium /dɪsˈprəʊzɪəm/ ▶ noun [mass noun] the chemical element of atomic number 66, a soft silvery-white metal of the lanthanide series. (Symbol: **Dy**)

– ORIGIN late 19th cent.: from Greek *dusprositos* 'hard to get at' + **-IUM**.

dysrhythmia /dɪsˈrɪðmɪə/ ▶ noun [mass noun] Medicine abnormality in a physiological rhythm, especially in the activity of the brain or heart.

– DERIVATIVES **dysrhythmic** adjective, **dysrhythmical** adjective.

dysthymia /dɪsˈθʌɪmɪə/ ▶ noun [mass noun] Psychiatry persistent mild depression.

– DERIVATIVES **dysthymic** adjective & noun.

– ORIGIN mid 19th cent.: from Greek *dusthumia*.

dystocia /dɪsˈtəʊʃə/ ▶ noun [mass noun] Medicine & Veterinary Medicine difficult birth, typically caused by a large or awkwardly positioned fetus, by smallness of the maternal pelvis, or by failure of the uterus and cervix to contract and expand normally.

– ORIGIN early 18th cent.: from Greek *dustokia*, from *dus-* 'difficult' + *tokos* 'childbirth'.

dystonia /dɪsˈtəʊnɪə/ ▶ noun [mass noun] Medicine a state of abnormal muscle tone resulting in muscular spasm and abnormal posture, typically due to neurological disease or a side effect of drug therapy.

– DERIVATIVES **dystonic** adjective.

dystopia /dɪsˈtəʊpɪə/ ▶ noun an imagined place or state in which everything is unpleasant or bad, typically a totalitarian or environmentally degraded one. The opposite of **UTOPIA**.

– DERIVATIVES **dystopian** adjective & noun.

– ORIGIN late 18th cent.: from **DYS-** 'bad' + **UTOPIA**.

dystrophia myotonica /dɪsˌtrəʊfɪə mʌɪəˈtɒnɪkə/ ▶ noun [mass noun] Medicine a form of muscular dystrophy in which myotonia also occurs.

dystrophic /dɪsˈtrəʊfɪk, -ˈtrɒfɪk/ ▶ adjective **1** Medicine affected by or relating to dystrophy, especially muscular dystrophy. **2** Ecology (of a lake) having brown acidic water that is low in oxygen and supports little life, owing to high levels of dissolved humus. Compare with **EUTROPHIC** and **OLIGOTROPHIC**.

– ORIGIN late 19th cent.: from Greek *dus-* 'bad' + *-trophia* 'nourishment' + **-IC**.

dystrophin /dɪsˈtrəʊfɪn/ ▶ noun [mass noun] Biochemistry a protein found in skeletal muscle, which is absent in sufferers from muscular dystrophy.

dystrophy /ˈdɪstrəfi/ ▶ noun [mass noun] Medicine & Veterinary Medicine a disorder in which an organ or tissue of the body wastes away. See also **MUSCULAR DYSTROPHY**.

– ORIGIN late 19th cent.: from modern Latin *dystrophia*, from Greek *dus-* 'bad' + *-trophia* 'nourishment'.

dysuria /dɪsˈjʊərɪə/ ▶ noun [mass noun] Medicine painful or difficult urination.
– ORIGIN late Middle English: via late Latin from Greek *dusouria*, from *dus-* 'difficult' + *ouron* 'urine'.

dytiscid /dɪˈtɪskɪd, -sɪd/ ▶ noun Entomology a beetle of a family (Dytiscidae) that comprises most water beetles.
– ORIGIN mid 19th cent.: from modern Latin *Dytiscidae*, from *Dytiscus* (genus name), from Greek *dutikos* 'able to dive', from *duein* 'dive'.

DZ ▶ abbreviation for Algeria (international vehicle registration). [ORIGIN: from Arabic *Djazïr*.] ■ drop zone: *used parachutes were scattered across the DZ.*

Dzaoudzi /ˈdzaʊdzi/ the former capital of the French island of Mayotte and of the Comoros; pop. 5,675 (1985).

Dzaudzhikau /ˌdzaʊdʒɪˈkaʊ/ former name (1944–54) for VLADIKAVKAZ.

Dzerzhinsk /dzəˈʒɪnsk/ a city in west central Russia, west of Nizhni Novgorod; pop. 286,000 (1990). Former names CHERNORECHYE (until 1919) and RASTYAPINO (1919–29).

Dzerzhinsky /dzəˈʒɪnski/, Feliks (Edmundovich) (1877–1926), Russian Bolshevik leader, of Polish descent. He was the organizer and first head of the post-revolutionary Soviet security police (the Cheka, later the OGPU).

dzo /ʒəʊ, zəʊ/ (also **dzho** or **zho**) ▶ noun (pl. same or **-os**) a hybrid of a cow and a yak.
– ORIGIN mid 19th cent.: from Tibetan *mdso*.

Dzongkha /ˈzɒŋkə/ ▶ noun [mass noun] the official language of Bhutan, closely related to Tibetan.

Ee

E¹ (also **e**) ▶ noun (pl. **Es** or **E's**) **1** the fifth letter of the alphabet.
- denoting the fifth in a set of items, categories, sizes, etc. ■ the fifth highest class of academic mark. ■ (e) Chess denoting the fifth file from the left, as viewed from White's side of the board. ■ denoting the lowest-earning socio-economic category for marketing purposes.

2 (**E**) a shape like that of a capital E: [in combination] *an E-shaped stately home.*

3 (usu. **E**) Music the third note of the diatonic scale of C major.
- a key based on a scale with E as its keynote.

E² ▶ abbreviation for ■ East or Eastern: *139° E.* ■ informal the drug Ecstasy or a tablet of Ecstasy. ■ [in combination] denoting products, in particular food additives, which comply with EU regulations: *the yellow colouring tartrazine (E 102).* See also **E-NUMBER**. ■ [in combination] (in units of measurement) exa- (10^{18}). ■ Spain (international vehicle registration). [ORIGIN: from Spanish *España*.]
▶ symbol for Physics ■ electric field strength. ■ electromotive force. ■ energy: $E = mc^2$.
- PHRASES **the three Es** economy, efficiency, and effectiveness.

e ▶ symbol for ■ (also **e⁻**) Chemistry an electron. ■ (e) Mathematics the transcendental number that is the base of Napierian or natural logarithms, approximately equal to 2.71828.

e-¹ ▶ prefix variant spelling of **EX-¹** (as in *elect, emit*).

e-² ▶ prefix denoting the use of electronic data transfer in cyberspace for information exchange and financial transactions, especially through the Internet: *e-cash | e-zine.*
- ORIGIN from **ELECTRONIC**, on the pattern of *e-mail.*

ea. ▶ abbreviation for each (used especially when giving retail prices): *T-shirts for £9.95 ea.*

each ▶ determiner & pronoun used to refer to every one of two or more people or things, regarded and identified separately: [as determiner] *each battery is in a separate compartment | each one of us was asked what went on* | [as pronoun] *Derek had money from each of his five uncles | they each have their own personality.*
▶ adverb to, for, or by every one of a group (used after a noun or an amount): *they cost £35 each | Paul and Bill have a glass each.*
- PHRASES **each and every** every single (used for emphasis): *taking each and every opportunity.*
- ORIGIN Old English *ælc*; related to Dutch *elk* and German *jeglich*, based on a West Germanic phrase meaning 'ever alike' (see **AYE²**, **ALIKE**).

each other ▶ pronoun used to refer to each member of a group when each does something to or for other members: *they communicate with each other in French.*

each-way ▶ adjective & adverb Brit. (of a bet) divided into two equal wagers, one backing a horse or other competitor to win and the other backing it to finish in the first three, or (in larger races) four.
- [as adj.] to come first, second, third, or (in larger races) fourth in a race, considered from a betting point of view: *Travado has an each-way chance.*

Eadwig /ˈɛdwɪɡ/ variant spelling of **EDWY**.

eager ▶ adjective (of a person) wanting to do or have something very much: *the man was eager to please | young intellectuals eager for knowledge.*

- (of a person's expression or tone of voice) characterized by keen expectancy or interest: *small eager faces looked up and listened.*
- DERIVATIVES **eagerly** adverb, **eagerness** noun.
- ORIGIN Middle English (also in the sense 'sharp to the senses, pungent, sour'): from Old French *aigre* 'keen', from Latin *acer, acr-* 'sharp, pungent'.

eager beaver ▶ noun informal a keen and enthusiastic person who works very hard.

eagle ▶ noun **1** a large bird of prey with a massive hooked bill and long broad wings, renowned for its keen sight and powerful soaring flight.
● Family Accipitridae: several genera, in particular *Aquila.*
- a figure of an eagle, especially as a symbol of the US, or formerly as a Roman or French ensign.

2 Golf a score of two strokes under par at a hole. [ORIGIN: suggested by **BIRDIE**.]

3 US a former gold coin worth ten dollars.
▶ verb [with obj.] Golf play (a hole) in two strokes under par: *he eagled the last to share fourth place.*
- ORIGIN Middle English: from Old French *aigle*, from Latin *aquila.*

eagle eye ▶ noun a keen or close watch: *she was keeping an eagle eye on Leni.*
- DERIVATIVES **eagle-eyed** adjective.

eagle owl ▶ noun a very large Old World owl with ear tufts and a deep hoot.
● Genus *Bubo*, family Strigidae: several species, in particular the Eurasian *B. bubo.*

eagle ray ▶ noun a large marine ray with long pointed pectoral fins, a long tail, and a distinct head.
● Family Myliobatidae: genera *Myliobatis* and *Aetobatus*, and several species.

eaglet ▶ noun a young eagle.

eagre /ˈeɪɡə, ˈiː-/ ▶ noun dialect term for **BORE³**.
- ORIGIN early 17th cent.: of unknown origin.

EAK ▶ abbreviation for Kenya (international vehicle registration).
- ORIGIN from *East Africa Kenya.*

Eakins /ˈiːkɪnz/, Thomas (1844–1916), American painter and photographer noted for his portraits and genre pictures of life in Philadelphia. His picture *The Gross Clinic* (1875) aroused controversy because of its explicit depiction of surgery.

Ealing Studios a film studio in Ealing, West London, active 1929–55, but remembered chiefly for the comedies it made in the post-war decade.

-ean ▶ suffix forming adjectives and nouns such as *Antipodean* and *Pythagorean.* Compare with **-AN**.
- ORIGIN from Latin *-aeus, -eus* or Greek *-aios, -eios*, + **-AN**.

ear¹ ▶ noun the organ of hearing and balance in humans and other vertebrates, especially the external part of this.
- an organ sensitive to sound in other animals. ■ [in sing.] an ability to recognize, appreciate, and reproduce sounds, especially music or language: *an ear for rhythm and melody.* ■ used to refer to a person's willingness to listen and pay attention to something: *she offers a sympathetic ear to worried pet owners.*

The ear of a mammal is composed of three parts. The outer or external ear consists of a fleshy external flap and a tube leading to the eardrum or tympanum. The middle ear is an air-filled cavity connected to the throat, containing three small linked bones that transmit vibrations from the eardrum to the inner ear. The inner ear is a complex fluid-filled labyrinth including the spiral cochlea (where vibrations are converted to nerve impulses) and the three semicircular canals (forming the organ of balance). The ears of other vertebrates are broadly similar.

- PHRASES **be all ears** informal be listening eagerly and attentively. **bring something (down) about one's ears** bring something, especially misfortune, on oneself: *she brought her world crashing about her ears.* **one's ears are burning** one is subconsciously aware of being talked about or criticized. **grin (or smile) from ear to ear** smile broadly. **have something coming out of one's ears** informal have a substantial or excessive amount of something: *that man's got money coming out of his ears.* **have someone's ear** have access to and influence with someone: *he claimed to have the prime minister's ear.* **have (or keep) an ear to the ground** be well informed about events and trends. **in (at) one ear and out (at) the other** heard but disregarded or quickly forgotten: *whatever he tells me seems to go in one ear and out the other.* **listen with half an ear** not give one's full attention. **be out on one's ear** informal be dismissed or ejected ignominiously. **up to one's ears in** informal very busy with or deeply involved in: *I'm up to my ears in work here.*
- DERIVATIVES **eared** adjective [in combination] *long-eared*, **earless** adjective.
- ORIGIN Old English *ēare*, of Germanic origin; related to Dutch *oor* and German *Ohr*, from an Indo-European root shared by Latin *auris* and Greek *ous.*

ear² ▶ noun the seed-bearing head or spike of a cereal plant.
- N. Amer. a head of maize.
- ORIGIN Old English *ēar*, of Germanic origin; related to Dutch *aar* and German *Ähre.*

earache ▶ noun [mass noun] pain inside the ear. Also called **OTALGIA**.

earbash ▶ verb [with obj.] [usu. as noun **earbashing**] informal subject (someone) to a lengthy, tedious, or reproachful torrent of words: *I picked up the phone and gave him an earbashing.*
- DERIVATIVES **earbasher** noun.

ear defenders ▶ plural noun plugs or earmuffs which protect the eardrums from loud or persistent noise.

ear drops ▶ plural noun **1** liquid medication to be applied in small amounts to the ear.
2 hanging earrings.

eardrum ▶ noun the membrane of the middle ear, which vibrates in response to sound waves; the tympanic membrane.

eared seal ▶ noun see **SEAL²**.

ear flap ▶ noun **1** a flap of material on a hat or cap, covering the ear.
2 a part of an animal's outer ear which extends out from the head as a fleshy flap or lobe.

earful ▶ noun [in sing.] informal a loud blast of a noise: *an earful of white noise.*
- a prolonged amount of talking, typically an angry

reprimand: *executives* **got an earful** *about poor rail connections.*

Earhart /ˈɛːhɑːt/, Amelia (1898–1937), American aviator. In 1932 she became the first woman to fly across the Atlantic solo. Her aircraft disappeared over the Pacific Ocean during a subsequent round-the-world flight.

earhole ▶ **noun** the external opening of the ear.
■informal a person's ear: *a clip round the earhole.*

earl ▶ **noun** a British nobleman ranking above a viscount and below a marquess.
– ORIGIN Old English *eorl*, of Germanic origin. The word *earl* originally denoted a man of noble rank, as opposed to a churl, also specifically a hereditary nobleman directly above the rank of thane. It was later an equivalent of **JARL** and, under Canute and his successors, applied to the governor of divisions of England such as Wessex and Mercia. In the late Old English period, as the Saxon court came increasingly under Norman influence, the word was applied to any nobleman bearing the continental title of count (see **COUNT**[2]).

earldom ▶ **noun** the rank or title of an earl.
■historical the territory governed by an earl.

earless lizard ▶ **noun** a small, long-legged burrowing lizard without visible external ear openings, native to North America.
● *Holbrookia texana*, family Iguanidae.

Earl Grey ▶ **noun** [mass noun] a kind of China tea flavoured with bergamot.
– ORIGIN probably named after the 2nd *Earl Grey* (1764–1845), said to have been given the recipe by a Chinese mandarin.

Earl Marshal ▶ **noun** (in the UK) the officer presiding over the College of Arms, with ceremonial duties on various royal occasions.

ear lobe ▶ **noun** a soft, rounded fleshy part hanging from the lower margin of the ear.

earlock /ˈiːəlɒk/ ▶ **noun** a lock of hair over or above the ear.

Earl Palatine ▶ **noun** historical an earl having royal authority within his country or domain.

early ▶ **adjective** (**earlier**, **earliest**) **1** happening or done before the usual or expected time: *we ate an early lunch.*
■(of a plant or crop) flowering or ripening before other varieties: *early potatoes.*
2 happening, belonging to, or done near to the beginning of a particular time or period: *an early goal secured victory.*
■denoting or belonging to the beginning or opening stages of a historical period, cultural movement, or sphere of activity: *early Impressionism.* ■ occurring at the beginning of a sequence: *the earlier chapters of the book.*
▶ **adverb** before the usual or expected time: *I was planning to finish work early today.*
■near the beginning of a particular time or period: *we lost a couple of games early in the season.* ■ (**earlier**) before the present time or before the time one is referring to: *you met my husband earlier.*
▶ **plural noun** (**earlies**) **1** potatoes which are ready to be harvested early.
2 informal early shifts: *she is* **on earlies***.*
– PHRASES **at the earliest** not before the time or date specified. **early bird** humorous a person who rises, arrives, or acts before the usual or expected time. **the early bird catches the worm** proverb the person who takes the earliest opportunity to do something will gain the advantage over others. **an early grave** a premature or untimely death: *he worked himself into an early grave.* **the early hours** the time after midnight and before dawn. **an early night** an occasion when someone goes to bed before the usual time, especially in order to catch up on sleep. **early** (or **earlier**) **on** at an early (or earlier) stage in a particular time or period: *they discovered early on that the published data were wrong.* **it's** (or **these are**) **early days** informal, chiefly Brit. it is too soon to be sure how a situation will develop: *it's still early days for the initiative.*
– DERIVATIVES **earliness** noun.
– ORIGIN Old English (as an adverb) *ǣrlīce* (see **ERE**, **-LY**[2]), influenced by Old Norse *árliga*. The adjective use dates from Middle English.

early adopter ▶ **noun** a person who starts using a product or technology as soon as it becomes available.

early closing ▶ **noun** [mass noun] Brit. the practice of shutting business premises on a particular afternoon every week.

Early English ▶ **adjective** denoting the earliest stage of English Gothic church architecture, typical of the late 12th and 13th centuries and marked by the use of pointed arches and simple lancet windows without tracery.

early leaver ▶ **noun** a person who leaves early, in particular a person who abandons a pension plan before the expected date.

early music ▶ **noun** [mass noun] medieval, Renaissance, and early baroque music, especially as revived and played on period instruments.

early purple orchid ▶ **noun** a common Eurasian woodland orchid that produces purple flowers in the spring.
● *Orchis mascula*, family Orchidaceae.

early retirement ▶ **noun** [mass noun] the practice of leaving employment before the statutory age, especially on favourable financial terms.

earmark ▶ **noun** a mark on the ear of a domesticated animal indicating ownership or identity.
■a characteristic or identifying feature: *this car has all the earmarks of a classic.*
▶ **verb** [with obj.] **1** (usu. **be earmarked**) designate (something, typically funds or resources) for a particular purpose: *the cash had been* **earmarked for** *a big expansion of the programme.*
2 mark the ear of (an animal) as a sign of ownership or identity.

earmuffs ▶ **plural noun** a pair of soft fabric coverings, connected by a band across the top of the head, that are worn over the ears to protect them from cold or noise.

earn ▶ **verb** [with obj.] (of a person) obtain (money) in return for labour or services: *he now* **earns his living** *as a lorry driver* | [with two objs] *earn yourself a few dollars.*
■[with two objs] (of an activity or action) cause (someone) to obtain (money): *this latest win earned them $50,000 in prize money.* ■ (of capital invested) gain (money) as interest or profit. ■ gain or incur deservedly in return for one's behaviour or achievements: *through the years she has earned affection and esteem.*
– PHRASES **earn one's corn** Brit. informal put in a lot of effort to show that one deserves one's wages. **earn one's keep** work in return for food and accommodation. ■ be worth the time, money, or effort spent on one.
– ORIGIN Old English *earnian*, of West Germanic origin, from a base shared by Old English *esne* 'labourer'.

earned income ▶ **noun** [mass noun] money derived from paid work. Often contrasted with **UNEARNED INCOME**.

earned run ▶ **noun** Baseball a run scored without the aid of errors by the team in the field (i.e. by hits, walks, and outs that advance base-runners).

earner ▶ **noun** [with adj. or noun modifier] a person who obtains money, typically of a specified kind or level, in return for labour or services: *higher rates of income tax for high earners* | *a wage earner.*
■an activity or product that brings in income of a specified kind or level: *tobacco is a major foreign currency earner.*

earnest[1] /ˈəːnɪst/ ▶ **adjective** resulting from or showing sincere and intense conviction: *an earnest student* | *two girls were in earnest conversation.*
– PHRASES **in earnest** occurring to a greater extent or more intensely than before: *work began again in earnest.* ■ (of a person) sincere and serious in their behaviour or convictions.
– DERIVATIVES **earnestly** adverb, **earnestness** noun.
– ORIGIN Old English *eornoste* (adjective), *eornost* (noun), of Germanic origin; related to German *Ernst* (noun).

earnest[2] /ˈəːnɪst/ ▶ **noun** [in sing.] a thing intended or regarded as a sign or promise of what is to come: *the presence of the troops is an earnest of the world's desire not to see the conflict repeated elsewhere.*
– ORIGIN Middle English *ernes*, literally 'instalment paid to confirm a contract', based on Old French *erres*, from Latin *arra*, shortened form of *arrabo* 'a pledge'. The spelling was influenced by words ending in **-NESS**; the final *-t* is probably by association with **EARNEST**[1].

earnest money ▶ **noun** [mass noun] chiefly US money paid to confirm a contract.

earnings ▶ **plural noun** money obtained in return for labour or services.
■income derived from an investment or product: *export earnings.*

Earp /əːp/, Wyatt (Berry Stapp) (1848–1929), American gambler and marshal. He is famous for the gunfight at the OK Corral (1881), in which Wyatt with his brothers and his friend Doc Holliday fought the Clanton brothers at Tombstone, Arizona.

earphone ▶ **noun** (usu. **earphones**) an electrical device worn on the ear to receive radio or telephone communications or to listen to a radio or tape recorder without other people hearing.

earpiece ▶ **noun** **1** the part of a telephone, radio receiver, or other aural device that is applied to the ear during use.
2 the part of a pair of glasses that fits around the ear.

ear-piercing ▶ **adjective** [attrib.] loud and shrill: *the alarm emits an ear-piercing screech.*
▶ **noun** [mass noun] the practice of making holes in the lobes or edges of the ears to allow the wearing of earrings.

earplug ▶ **noun** (usu. **earplugs**) **1** a piece of wax, rubber, or cotton wool placed in the ear as protection against noise, water, or cold air.
2 historical an ornament worn in the lobe of the ear.

earring ▶ **noun** a piece of jewellery worn on the lobe or edge of the ear.

ear shell ▶ **noun** another term for **ABALONE**.

earshot ▶ **noun** [mass noun] the range or distance over which one can hear or be heard: *she waited until he was* **out of earshot** *before continuing.*

ear-splitting ▶ **adjective** extremely loud: *an ear-splitting crack of thunder.*

earth ▶ **noun** **1** (also **Earth**) the planet on which we live; the world: *the diversity of life* **on earth***.*
■the surface of the world as distinct from the sky or the sea: *it plummeted back to earth at 60 mph.* ■ the present abode of humankind, as distinct from heaven or hell: *God's will be done on earth as it is in heaven.* ■ (**the earth**) chiefly Brit. used to signify a very large amount of something: *it doesn't have to* **cost the earth** *to look good.*

The earth is the third planet from the sun in the solar system, orbiting between Venus and Mars at an average distance of 149.6 million km from the sun, and has one natural satellite, the moon. It has an equatorial diameter of 12,756 km, an average density 5.5 times that of water, and is believed to have formed about 4,600 million years ago. The earth, which is three-quarters covered by oceans and has a dense atmosphere of nitrogen and oxygen, is the only planet known to support life.

2 [mass noun] the substance of the land surface; soil: *a layer of earth.*
■one of the four elements in ancient and medieval philosophy and in astrology (considered essential to the nature of the signs Taurus, Virgo, and Capricorn): [as modifier] *an earth sign.* ■ [count noun] a stable, dense, non-volatile inorganic substance found in the ground. ■ poetic/literary the substance of the human body.
3 [mass noun] Brit. electrical connection to the ground, regarded as having zero electrical potential: *ensure metal fittings are electrically bonded to earth* | [as modifier] *an earth wire.*
4 the underground lair or habitation of a badger or fox.
▶ **verb** [with obj.] **1** (often **be earthed**) Brit. connect (an electrical device) with the ground: *the front metal panels must be soundly earthed.*
2 Hunting drive (a fox) to its underground lair.
■[no obj.] (of a fox) run to its underground lair.
3 (**earth something up**) cover the root and lower stem of a plant with heaped-up earth.
– PHRASES **bring** (or **come**) **back** (**down**) **to earth** return or cause to return to reality after a period of daydreaming or excitement. **the earth moved** (or **did the earth move for you?**) humorous one had (or did you have?) an orgasm. **go to earth** (of a hunted animal) hide in an underground burrow. ■ figurative go into hiding: *he'd gone to earth after that meeting.* **like nothing on earth** informal very strange: *they looked like nothing on earth.* **on earth** used for emphasis: *who on earth would venture out in weather like this?*
– ORIGIN Old English *eorthe*, of Germanic origin; related to Dutch *aarde* and German *Erde*.

earth ball ▶ **noun** a fungus that forms a leathery yellowish-brown warty sphere which ruptures

when mature to release the spores, growing typically on acid sandy soil in both Eurasia and North America.
● Genus *Scleroderma*, family Sclerodermataceae, class Gasteromycetes: several species, in particular *S. citrinum*.

earthbound ▶ adjective **1** attached or restricted to the earth: *a flightless earthbound bird*.
■ attached or limited to material existence as distinct from a spiritual or heavenly one: *her earthbound view of the sacrament.* ■ figurative lacking in imaginative reach or drive: *an earthbound performance.*
2 moving towards the earth: *an earthbound spaceship.*

earth closet ▶ noun Brit. a basic type of toilet with dry earth used to cover excrement.

earthen ▶ adjective [attrib.] (of a floor or structure) made of compressed earth: *earthen banks.*
■ (of a pot) made of baked or fired clay. ■ poetic/literary of, relating to, or characteristic of the earth or material existence.

earthenware ▶ noun [mass noun] [often as modifier] pottery made of clay fired to a porous state which can be made impervious to liquids by the use of a glaze: *an earthenware jug.*

earthlight ▶ noun another term for EARTHSHINE.

earthling ▶ noun (in science fiction) an inhabitant of the earth, especially as regarded by aliens.

earth loop ▶ noun an unwanted electric current path in a circuit resulting in stray signals or interference, occurring for example when two earthed points in the same circuit have different potentials.

earthly ▶ adjective **1** of or relating to the earth or human life on the earth: *water is liquid at normal earthly temperatures.*
■ of or relating to humankind's material existence as distinct from a spiritual or heavenly one: *all earthly happiness is but vanity.*
2 [with negative] informal used for emphasis: *there was no earthly reason why she should not come too.*
– PHRASES **not stand** (or **have**) **an earthly** Brit. informal have no chance at all: *she wouldn't stand an earthly if she tried to outrun him.*
– DERIVATIVES **earthliness** noun.

earth mother ▶ noun (in mythology and primitive religion) a goddess symbolizing fertility and the source of life.
■ an archetypically sensual and maternal woman.

earth mover ▶ noun a vehicle or machine designed to excavate large quantities of soil.
– DERIVATIVES **earth moving** noun.

earthnut ▶ noun **1** a Eurasian plant of the parsley family, which has an edible roundish tuber and is typically found in woodland and acid pasture. Also called PIGNUT.
● *Conopodium majus*, family Umbelliferae.
■ the almond-flavoured tuber of this plant.
2 chiefly Brit. another term for PEANUT.

earthquake ▶ noun a sudden violent shaking of the ground, typically causing great destruction, as a result of movements within the earth's crust or volcanic action.
■ figurative a great convulsion or upheaval: *a political earthquake.*

earth science ▶ noun [mass noun] the branch of science dealing with the physical constitution of the earth and its atmosphere.
■ (**earth sciences**) the various branches of this subject, e.g. geology, oceanography, or meteorology.

earth-shattering ▶ adjective (in hyperbolic use) very important, shocking, or traumatic: *tell me this earth-shattering news of yours.*
– DERIVATIVES **earth-shatteringly** adverb.

earthshine (also **earthlight**) ▶ noun [mass noun] Astronomy the glow caused by sunlight reflected by the earth, especially on the darker portion of a crescent moon.

earthstar ▶ noun a brownish woodland fungus with a spherical spore-containing fruiting body surrounded by a fleshy star-shaped structure, found in both Eurasia and North America.
● Family Geastraceae, class Gasteromycetes: *Geastrum* and other genera.

earth station ▶ noun a radio station located on the earth and used for relaying signals from satellites.

earth tremor ▶ noun see TREMOR.

earthward (also **earthwards**) ▶ adverb & adjective

towards the earth: [as adv.] *when his parachute failed to open he fell earthward at 120 mph* | [as adj.] *the bird's earthward plummet.*

earthwork ▶ noun **1** a large artificial bank of soil, especially one made as a defence in ancient times.
2 [mass noun] the process of excavating soil in civil engineering work.

earthworm ▶ noun a burrowing annelid worm that lives in the soil. Earthworms play an important role in aerating and draining the soil and in burying organic matter.
● Family Lumbricidae, class Oligochaeta: *Lumbricus, Allolobophora*, and other genera.

earthy ▶ adjective (**earthier, earthiest**) resembling or suggestive of earth or soil: *an earthy smell.*
■ (of a person or their language or humour) direct and uninhibited, especially about sexual subjects or bodily functions.
– DERIVATIVES **earthily** adverb, **earthiness** noun.

ear trumpet ▶ noun a trumpet-shaped device formerly used as a hearing aid.

ear tuft ▶ noun each of a pair of tufts of longer feathers on the top of the head of some owls. They are unconnected with the true ears.

earwax ▶ noun [mass noun] the protective yellow waxy substance secreted in the passage of the outer ear. Also called CERUMEN.

earwig ▶ noun a small elongated insect with a pair of terminal appendages that resemble pincers. The females typically care for their eggs and young until they are well grown.
● Order Dermaptera: several families.
▶ verb (**earwigged, earwigging**) [no obj.] informal eavesdrop on a conversation: *he looked behind him to see if anyone was earwigging.*
■ [with obj.] archaic influence (someone) by secret means.
– ORIGIN Old English *ēarwicga*, from *ēare* 'ear' + *wicga* 'earwig' (probably related to *wiggle*). The insect is so named because it was once thought to crawl into the human ear.

earwitness ▶ noun chiefly N. Amer. a witness whose testimony is based on what they personally heard.

ease ▶ noun [mass noun] absence of difficulty or effort: *she gave up smoking with ease* | *ease of use.*
■ freedom from worries or problems, especially about one's material situation: *a life of wealth and ease.*
▶ verb **1** [with obj.] make (something unpleasant, painful, or intense) less serious or severe: *a huge road-building programme to ease congestion.*
■ [no obj.] become less serious or severe: *the pain doesn't usually ease off for several hours.* ■ [no obj.] (**ease off/up**) relax one's efforts; do something with more moderation: *I'd ease up on the hard stuff if I were you.* ■ (**ease something away/down/off**) Nautical slacken a rope or sail slowly or gently. ■ make (something) happen more easily; facilitate: *Tokyo's dominance of government was deemed to ease efficient contact-making.* ■ [no obj.] (of share prices, interest rates, etc.) decrease in value or amount: *shares eased 6p to 224p.*
2 [no obj., with adverbial of direction] move carefully, gradually, or gently: *I eased down the slope with care* | [with obj. and adverbial of direction] *she eased off her shoes.*
■ [with obj.] (**ease someone into**) introduce someone gradually to (an activity): *he brought in someone new and eased them into the job.* ■ [with obj.] (**ease someone out**) gradually exclude someone from a post or place, especially by devious or subtle manoeuvres: *after the scandal he was eased out of his job.*
– PHRASES **at** (**one's**) **ease** free from worry, awkwardness, or problems; relaxed: *she was never quite at ease with Phil.* ■ (**at ease**) Military in a relaxed attitude with the feet apart and the hands behind the back (often as a command): *all right, stand at ease!* **ease someone's mind** alleviate someone's anxiety.
– DERIVATIVES **easer** noun.
– ORIGIN Middle English: from Old French *aise*, based on Latin *adjacens* 'lying close by', present participle of *adjacere*. The verb is originally from Old French *aisier*, from the phrase *a aise* 'at ease'; in later use from the noun.

easeful ▶ adjective poetic/literary providing or offering comfort or peace: *life was easeful at that time.*

easel /ˈiːz(ə)l/ ▶ noun a wooden frame for holding an artist's work while it is being painted or drawn.
– ORIGIN late 16th cent.: from Dutch *ezel* 'ass'. The word 'horse' is used in English in a similar way to denote a supporting frame.

easement /ˈiːzm(ə)nt/ ▶ noun **1** Law a right to cross

or otherwise use someone else's land for a specified purpose.
2 [mass noun] poetic/literary the state or feeling of comfort or peace: *time brings easement.*
– ORIGIN late Middle English: from Old French *aisement*, from *aisier* (see EASE).

easily ▶ adverb **1** without difficulty or effort: *he climbed the mountain easily* | *Bradford is easily accessible by road.*
■ in a relaxed manner: *he shrugged easily.* ■ more quickly or frequently than is usual: *they get bored easily.*
2 without doubt; by far: *English is easily the reigning language in the financial world.*
■ very probably: *the body could easily be that of an actress.*

east ▶ noun (usu. **the east**) **1** the direction towards the point of the horizon where the sun rises at the equinoxes, on the right-hand side of a person facing north, or the point on the horizon itself: *a gale was blowing from the east* | *the Atlantic Ocean to the east of Florida.*
■ the compass point corresponding to this.
2 the eastern part of the world or of a specified country, region, or town: *a factory in the east of the city.*
■ (usu. **the East**) the regions or countries lying to the east of Europe, especially China, Japan, and India: *the mysterious East.* ■ (usu. **the East**) historical the former communist states of eastern Europe.
3 (**East**) [as name] Bridge the player sitting to the left of North and partnering West.
▶ adjective [attrib.] **1** lying towards, near, or facing the east: *the hospital's east wing.*
■ (of a wind) blowing from the east. ■ situated in the part of a church containing the altar or high altar, usually the actual east.
2 of or denoting the eastern part of a specified area, city, or country or its inhabitants: *East Fife* | *East African.*
▶ adverb to or towards the east: *travelling east, he met two men* | *the river rises east of Brentford.*
– ORIGIN Old English *ēast-*, of Germanic origin; related to Dutch *oost* and German *ost*, from an Indo-European root shared by Latin *aurora*, Greek *auōs* 'dawn'.

East Africa the eastern part of the African continent, especially the countries of Kenya, Uganda, and Tanzania.

East Anglia /ˈaŋglɪə/ a region of eastern England consisting of the counties of Norfolk, Suffolk, and parts of Essex and Cambridgeshire.

East Bengal the part of the former Indian province of Bengal that was ceded to Pakistan in 1947, forming the greater part of the province of East Pakistan. It gained independence as Bangladesh in 1971.

eastbound ▶ adjective leading or travelling towards the east: *the eastbound carriageway.*

Eastbourne a town on the south coast of England, in East Sussex; pop. 78,000 (1981).

East Cape a peninsular region of North Island, New Zealand. Its tip forms the most easterly point of the island.

East China Sea see CHINA SEA.

East Coast Fever ▶ noun [mass noun] a feverish disease of cattle, prevalent mostly in Africa and usually fatal.
● This disease is caused by a parasitic protozoan of the genus *Theileria* (phylum Sporozoa, kingdom Protista), which lives in the host's blood cells and is transmitted by the bite of the tick *Rhipicephalus appendiculatus* (family Ixodidae).

East End the part of London east of the City as far as the River Lea, including the Docklands.
– DERIVATIVES **East Ender** noun.

Easter ▶ noun the most important and oldest festival of the Christian Church, celebrating the resurrection of Christ and held (in the Western Church) between 21 March and 25 April, on the first Sunday after the first full moon following the northern spring equinox.
■ the period in which this occurs, especially the weekend from Good Friday to Easter Monday.
– ORIGIN Old English *ēastre*; of Germanic origin and related to German *Ostern* and EAST. According to Bede the word is derived from *Ēastre*, the name of a goddess associated with spring.

Easter bunny ▶ noun an imaginary rabbit said to bring gifts to children at Easter.

Easter Day (also **Easter Sunday**) ▶ noun the day on which the festival of Easter is celebrated.

Easter egg ▶ noun an artificial chocolate egg or decorated hard-boiled egg given at Easter, especially to children.

Easter Eve ▶ noun the day immediately preceding Easter Day. Also called **HOLY SATURDAY**.

Easter Island an island in the SE Pacific west of Chile; pop. 2,000 (est. 1988). It has been administered by Chile since 1888. The island, first settled by Polynesians in about AD 400, is famous for its large monolithic statues of human heads, believed to date from the period 1000–1600.

Easter lily ▶ noun chiefly N. Amer. a spring-flowering lily.
● Genus *Lilium*, family Liliaceae: several species, in particular the tall, white-flowered Japanese lily *L. longiflorum*.

easterly ▶ adjective & adverb in an eastward position or direction: [as adj.] *the more easterly of the two roads* | [as adv.] *the vein could be traced up the fellside easterly of Kernal Crag*.
■ (of a wind) blowing from the east: [as adj.] *the light easterly breeze*.
▶ noun (often **easterlies**) a wind blowing from the east.

Easter Monday ▶ noun the day after Easter Sunday, a public holiday in several countries.

eastern ▶ adjective 1 [attrib.] situated in the east, or directed towards or facing the east: *the eastern slopes of the mountain* | *eastern Spain*.
■ (of a wind) blowing from the east.
2 (usu. **Eastern**) living in or originating from the east, in particular the regions or countries lying to the east of Europe: *an Eastern mystic*.
■ of, relating to, or characteristic of the east or its inhabitants: *Buddhism is no longer seen as an eastern religion*.
– DERIVATIVES **easternmost** adjective.
– ORIGIN Old English *ēasterne* (as **EAST**, **-ERN**).

Eastern bloc the countries of eastern and central Europe which were under Soviet domination from the end of the Second World War until the collapse of the Soviet communist system in 1989–91.

Eastern Cape a province of south-eastern South Africa, formerly part of Cape Province; capital, Bisho.

Eastern Church (also **Eastern Orthodox Church**) another name for **ORTHODOX CHURCH**.
■ any of the Christian Churches originating in eastern Europe and the Middle East.

Eastern Desert another name for **ARABIAN DESERT**.

Eastern Empire the eastern part of the Roman Empire, after its division in AD 395. See also **BYZANTINE EMPIRE**.

easterner ▶ noun a native or inhabitant of the east of a particular region or country, especially of Europe or the US.

Eastern Ghats see **GHATS**.

Eastern hemisphere the half of the earth containing Europe, Asia, and Africa.

Eastern time 1 the standard time in a zone including the eastern states of the US and parts of Canada, specifically:
● (**Eastern Standard Time**, abbrev: **EST**), standard time based on the mean solar time at the meridian 75° W, five hours behind GMT. ● (**Eastern Daylight Time**, abbrev: **EDT**) Eastern time during daylight saving time, six hours behind GMT.
2 the standard time in a zone including eastern Australia, based on the mean solar time at the meridian 150° E. It is ten hours ahead of GMT, or nine hours ahead when summer time is observed.

Eastern Zhou see **ZHOU**.

Easter Rising the uprising in Dublin and other cities in Ireland against British rule, Easter 1916. It ended with the surrender of the protesters, some of whose leaders were subsequently executed, but was a contributory factor in the establishment of the Irish Free State (1921).

Easter Saturday ▶ noun an informal name for the Saturday preceding Easter Day. In formal church use usually called **HOLY SATURDAY** or **EASTER EVE**.

Easter Sepulchre ▶ noun a recess in certain medieval churches for keeping the Eucharistic elements from Good Friday until the Easter festivities.

Easter Sunday ▶ noun another term for **EASTER DAY**.

Eastertide ▶ noun the Easter period.

East Flanders a province of northern Belgium; capital, Ghent. See also **FLANDERS**.

East Frisian Islands see **FRISIAN ISLANDS**.

East Germanic ▶ noun the extinct eastern group of Germanic languages, including Gothic.
▶ adjective of or relating to this group of languages.

East Germany see **GERMANY**.

East India another name for **EAST INDIES** (in sense 2).

East India Company a trading company formed in 1600 to develop commerce in the newly colonized areas of SE Asia and India. In the 18th century it took administrative control of Bengal and other areas of India, and held it until the British Crown took over in 1858 in the wake of the Indian Mutiny.

East Indiaman ▶ noun historical a trading ship belonging to the East India Company.

East Indies 1 the islands of SE Asia, especially the Malay Archipelago.
2 archaic the whole of SE Asia to the east of and including India.
– DERIVATIVES **East Indian** adjective.

easting ▶ noun [mass noun] distance travelled or measured eastward, especially at sea.
■ [count noun] a figure or line representing eastward distance on a map (expressed by convention as the first part of a grid reference, before northing).

East Kilbride /kɪlˈbrʌɪd/ a town in west central Scotland, in South Lanarkshire; pop. 81,400 (1991).

East London a port and resort in South Africa, on the Eastern Cape coast; pop. 270,130 (1991).

East Lothian an administrative region and former county of east central Scotland.

Eastman, George (1854–1932), American inventor and manufacturer of photographic equipment. He invented flexible roll film coated with light-sensitive emulsion, and, in 1888, the Kodak camera for use with it.

east-north-east ▶ noun the direction or compass point midway between east and north-east.

East Prussia the north-eastern part of the former kingdom of Prussia, on the Baltic coast, later part of Germany and divided after the Second World War between the Soviet Union and Poland.

East Riding of Yorkshire a unitary council in NE England, formerly one of the traditional ridings or divisions of the county of Yorkshire.

East River an arm of the Hudson River in New York City, separating Manhattan and the Bronx from Brooklyn and Queens.

East Siberian Sea a part of the Arctic Ocean lying between the New Siberian Islands and Wrangel Island, to the north of eastern Siberia.

East Side a part of Manhattan in New York City, lying between the East River and Fifth Avenue.

east-south-east ▶ noun the direction or compass point midway between east and south-east.

East Sussex a county of SE England; county town, Lewes.

East Timor the eastern part of the island of Timor in the southern Malay Archipelago; chief town, Dili.

> Formerly a Portuguese colony, the region declared itself independent in 1975. In 1976 it was invaded by Indonesia, which annexed and claimed it as the 27th state of Indonesia, a claim which has never been recognized by the United Nations. Since then the region has been the scene of bitter fighting and of alleged mass killings by the Indonesian government and military forces. Following a referendum in 1999, East Timor achieved independence.

– DERIVATIVES **East Timorese** noun & adjective.

eastward ▶ adjective in an easterly direction: *they followed an eastward course*.
▶ adverb (also **eastwards**) towards the east: *limestone plateaux extend eastward towards the river*.
▶ noun (**the eastward**) the direction or region towards the east: *the wind has come round to the eastward*.
– DERIVATIVES **eastwardly** adverb.

East–West ▶ adjective [attrib.] of or relating jointly to countries of eastern and western Europe (used particularly of relations before the break-up of the Soviet Union): *East–West relations*.

Eastwood, Clint (b.1930), American film actor and director. He became famous with his role in *A Fistful of Dollars* (1964), the first cult spaghetti western; other successful films include *Dirty Harry* (1971). Films directed include *Bird* (1988) and the western *Unforgiven* (1992).

easy ▶ adjective (**easier**, **easiest**) 1 achieved without great effort; presenting few difficulties: *an easy way of retrieving information*.
■ [attrib.] (of an object of attack or criticism) having no defence; vulnerable: *as a taxi driver he was vulnerable and an easy target*. ■ informal, derogatory (of a woman) open to sexual advances; sexually available: *her reputation at school for being easy*.
2 (of a period of time or way of life) free from worries or problems: *promises of an easy life in the New World*.
■ (of a person) lacking anxiety or awkwardness; relaxed: *his easy and agreeable manner* | *they didn't feel easy about what they were doing*.
▶ adverb informal chiefly archaic or US without difficulty or effort: *we all scared real easy in those days*.
▶ exclamation be careful: *easy, girl—you'll knock me over!*
– PHRASES **be easier said than done** be more easily talked about than put into practice: *going on an economy drive is easier said than done*. (**as**) **easy as pie** see **PIE**[1]. **easy come, easy go** used especially in spoken English to indicate that a relationship or possession acquired without effort or difficulty may be abandoned or lost casually and without regret. **easy does it** used especially in spoken English to advise someone to approach a task carefully and slowly. **easy on the eye** (or **ear**) informal pleasant to look at (or listen to). **go** (or **be**) **easy on someone** informal refrain from being harsh with or critical of someone. **go easy on something** informal be sparing or cautious in one's use or consumption of something: *go easy on fatty foods*. **have it easy** informal be free from difficulties; be fortunate. **I'm easy** informal said by someone when offered a choice to indicate that they have no particular preference. **of easy virtue** dated or humorous (of a woman) sexually promiscuous. **sleep** (or **rest**) **easy** go to sleep without (or be untroubled by) worries: *this insurance policy will let you rest easy*. **stand easy!** Military used to instruct soldiers standing at ease that they may relax their attitude further. **take the easy way out** extricate oneself from a difficult situation by choosing the simplest rather than the most honourable course of action. **take it easy** proceed calmly and in a relaxed manner. ■ make little effort; rest.
– DERIVATIVES **easiness** noun.
– ORIGIN Middle English (also in the sense 'comfortable, quiet, tranquil'): from Old French *aisie*, past participle of *aisier* 'put at ease, facilitate' (see **EASE**).

easy-care ▶ adjective (chiefly of man-made fabrics) requiring little effort to wash and dry, and typically no ironing.

easy chair ▶ noun a large, comfortable chair, typically an armchair.

easy-going ▶ adjective relaxed and tolerant in approach or manner: *a relaxed, easy-going atmosphere*.

easy listening ▶ noun [mass noun] popular music that is tuneful and undemanding.

easy money ▶ noun [mass noun] money obtained by dubious means or for little work.

easy-peasy ▶ adjective Brit. informal very straightforward and easy (used by or as if by children): *easy-peasy questions*.
– ORIGIN 1970s: reduplication of **EASY**.

easy street ▶ noun [mass noun] informal a state of financial comfort or security: *£50,000 a year will put one on easy street*.

EAT ▶ abbreviation for Tanzania (international vehicle registration).
– ORIGIN from *East Africa Tanzania*.

eat ▶ verb (past **ate** /ɛt, eɪt/; past participle **eaten**) [with obj.] put (food) into the mouth and chew and swallow it: *he was eating a hot dog* | *eat up all your peas* | [no obj.] *she watched her son as he ate*.
■ have (a meal): *we ate dinner in a noisy cafe*. ■ [no obj.] (**eat out**) have a meal in a restaurant. ■ [no obj.] (**eat in**) have a meal at home rather than in a restaurant.
■ vulgar slang, chiefly US perform fellatio or cunnilingus on (someone).
▶ noun (**eats**) informal light food or snacks.

– PHRASES **eat crow** see **CROW**[1]. **eat dirt** see **DIRT**. **eat someone's dust** see **DUST**. **eat one's heart out** suffer from excessive longing, especially for someone or something unattainable. ■ [in imperative] informal used to indicate that one thinks a particular person will feel great jealousy or regret: *eat your heart out, those who missed the trip*. **eat humble pie** see **HUMBLE**. **eat like a bird** (or **a horse**) informal eat very little (or a lot). **eat someone out of house and home** informal eat a lot of someone else's food. **eat one's words** retract what one has said, especially in a humiliated way: *they will eat their words when I win*. **have someone eating out of one's hand** have someone completely under one's control. **I'll eat my hat** informal used to indicate that one thinks the specified thing is extremely unlikely to happen: *if he comes back, I'll eat my hat*. **what's eating you** (or **him** or **her**)? informal what is worrying or annoying you (or him or her)?

– ORIGIN Old English *etan*, of Germanic origin; related to Dutch *eten* and German *essen*, from an Indo-European root shared by Latin *edere* and Greek *edein*.

▶**eat something away** (or **eat away at something**) erode or destroy something gradually: *the acid began to eat away at the edge of her tunic* | figurative *the knowledge of his affair still ate away at her*.

eat into another way of saying *eat away at*. ■ use up (profits, resources, or time), especially when they are intended for other purposes: *sales were hard hit by high interest rates eating into disposable income*.

eat someone up [usu. as adj. **eaten up**] dominate the thoughts of someone completely: *I'm eaten up with guilt*.

eat something up use resources or time in very large quantities: *an operating system that eats up 200Mb of disk space*. ■ encroach on something: *this is the countryside that villagers fear will be eaten up by concrete*.

eatable ▶ **adjective** fit to be consumed as food: *eatable fruits*.

▶**noun** (**eatables**) items of food: *parcels of eatables and gifts*.

eater ▶ **noun 1** [with adj. or noun modifier] a person who consumes food in a specified way or of a specified kind: *I'm still a big eater* | *they are meat eaters*.

2 Brit. informal an eating apple.

eatery ▶ **noun** (pl. **-ies**) informal a restaurant or other place where people can be served food.

eat-in ▶ **adjective** [attrib.] N. Amer. (of a kitchen) designed for eating in as well as cooking.

eating apple ▶ **noun** an apple that is suitable for eating raw.

eating disorder ▶ **noun** any of a range of psychological disorders characterized by abnormal or disturbed eating habits (such as anorexia nervosa).

EAU ▶ **abbreviation for** Uganda (international vehicle registration).

– ORIGIN from *East Africa Uganda*.

eau de cologne /ˌəʊ də kəˈləʊn/ ▶ **noun** [mass noun] a toilet water with a strong, characteristic scent, originally made in Cologne.

– ORIGIN early 19th cent.: French, literally 'water of Cologne'.

eau de Nil /ˈniːl/ ▶ **noun** [mass noun] a pale greenish colour.

– ORIGIN late 19th cent.: from French *eau-de-Nil*, literally 'water of the Nile' (from the supposed resemblance in colour).

eau de toilette /twɑːˈlɛt/ ▶ **noun** (pl. **eaux de toilette** pronunc. same) [mass noun] a dilute form of perfume; toilet water.

– ORIGIN early 20th cent.: French, 'toilet water'.

eau de vie /ˈviː/ ▶ **noun** (pl. **eaux de vie** pronunc. same) [mass noun] brandy.

– ORIGIN from French *eau-de-vie*, literally 'water of life'.

eaves ▶ **plural noun** the part of a roof that meets or overhangs the walls of a building.

– ORIGIN Old English *efes* (singular); of Germanic origin; related to German dialect *Obsen*, also probably to **OVER**.

eavesdrop ▶ **verb** (**eavesdropped**, **eavesdropping**) [no obj.] secretly listen to a conversation: *she opened the window just enough to eavesdrop on the conversation outside*.

– DERIVATIVES **eavesdropper** noun.

– ORIGIN early 17th cent.: back-formation from *eavesdropper* (late Middle English) 'a person who listens from under the eaves', from the obsolete noun *eavesdrop* 'the ground on to which water drips from the eaves', probably from Old Norse *upsardropi*, from *ups* 'eaves' + *dropi* 'a drop'.

eavestrough ▶ **noun** Canadian a gutter fixed beneath the edge of a roof.

ebb ▶ **noun** (usu. **the ebb**) the movement of the tide out to sea: *I knew the tide would be **on the ebb*** | [as modifier] *the ebb tide*.

▶**verb** [no obj.] (of tidewater) move away from the land; recede: *the tide began to ebb*. Compare with **FLOW**.

■ figurative (of an emotion or quality) gradually lessen or reduce: *my enthusiasm was ebbing away*.

– PHRASES **at a low ebb** in a poor state: *the country was at a low ebb due to the recent war*. **ebb and flow** a recurrent or rhythmical pattern of coming and going or decline and regrowth.

– ORIGIN Old English *ebba* (noun), *ebbian* (verb), of West Germanic origin; related to Dutch *ebbe* (noun), *ebben* (verb), and ultimately to **OF** which had the primary sense 'away from'.

EBCDIC /ˈɛbsɪdɪk/ ▶ **abbreviation for** Extended Binary Coded Decimal Interchange Code, a standard eight-bit character code used in computing and data transmission.

EBD ▶ **abbreviation for** emotional and behavioural difficulties (or disorder): [as modifier] *an EBD school*.

Ebla /ˈɛblə/ a city in ancient Syria, situated to the south-west of Aleppo. It became very powerful in the mid 3rd millennium BC, when it dominated a region corresponding to modern Lebanon, northern Syria, and SE Turkey.

E-boat ▶ **noun** a German torpedo boat used in the Second World War.

– ORIGIN from *E-* for *enemy* + **BOAT**.

Ebola fever /iːˈbəʊlə, əˈbəʊlə/ ▶ **noun** [mass noun] an infectious and generally fatal disease marked by fever and severe internal bleeding, spread through contact with infected body fluids by a filovirus (**Ebola virus**), whose normal host species is unknown.

– ORIGIN 1976: named after a river in Zaire (Democratic Republic of Congo), near which the disease was first observed.

ebon /ˈɛb(ə)n/ ▶ **noun** [mass noun] poetic/literary dark brown or black; ebony: [as modifier] *the ebon acid of the Styx*.

Ebonics /ɛˈbɒnɪks/ ▶ **plural noun** [treated as sing.] American black English regarded as a language in its own right rather than as a dialect of standard English.

– ORIGIN blend of **EBONY** and **PHONICS**.

ebonite ▶ **noun** another term for **VULCANITE**.

– ORIGIN mid 19th cent.: from **EBONY**+ **-ITE**[1].

ebonize (also **-ise**) ▶ **verb** [with obj.] [usu. as adj. **ebonized**] make (furniture) look like ebony: *an ebonized casket*.

ebony /ˈɛb(ə)ni/ ▶ **noun 1** [mass noun] heavy blackish or very dark brown timber from a mainly tropical tree.

■ [mass noun] a very dark brown or black colour: *his smile flashed against the ebony of his skin* | [as modifier] *his ebony hair*.

2 a tree of tropical and warm-temperate regions which produces such timber.

• Genera *Diospyros* and *Euclea*, family Ebenaceae: numerous species, in particular *D. ebenum*.

■ used in names of trees of other families which produce similar timber, e.g. **Jamaican** (or **American**) **ebony**.

– ORIGIN late Middle English: from earlier *ebon* (via Old French and Latin from Greek *ebenos* 'ebony tree'), perhaps on the pattern of *ivory*.

Eboracum /ɪˈbɔːrəkəm, ˌiːbəˈrɑːkəm/ Roman name for **YORK**.

EBRD ▶ **abbreviation for** European Bank for Reconstruction and Development (founded in 1991 to provide financial assistance to the former communist countries of eastern Europe).

Ebro /ˈiːbrəʊ, ˈɛb-/ the principal river of NE Spain, rising in the mountains of Cantabria and flowing 910 km (570 miles) south-eastwards into the Mediterranean Sea.

ebullient /ɪˈbʌljənt, -ˈbʊl-/ ▶ **adjective 1** cheerful and full of energy: *she sounded ebullient and happy*.

2 archaic or poetic/literary (of liquid or matter) boiling or agitated as if boiling: *misted and ebullient seas*.

– DERIVATIVES **ebullience** noun, **ebulliently** adverb.

– ORIGIN late 16th cent. (in the sense 'boiling'): from Latin *ebullient-* 'boiling up', from the verb *ebullire*, from *e-* (variant of *ex-*) 'out' + *bullire* 'to boil'.

ebullition /ˌɛbəˈlɪʃ(ə)n, -bʊ-/ ▶ **noun** [mass noun] technical or archaic the action of bubbling or boiling.

■ [count noun] a sudden outburst of emotion or violence: *in an ebullition of fervour*.

– ORIGIN late Middle English (used to describe a state of agitation of the bodily humours): from late Latin *ebullitio(n-)*, from *ebullire* 'boil up' (see **EBULLIENT**).

EBV ▶ **abbreviation for** Epstein-Barr virus.

EC ▶ **abbreviation for** ■ East Central (London postal district). ■ Ecuador (international vehicle registration). ■ European Commission. ■ European Community. ■ executive committee.

ecad /ˈiːkad/ ▶ **noun** Ecology an organism that is modified by its environment.

– ORIGIN early 20th cent.: from Greek *oikos* 'house' + **-AD**[1].

écarté ▶ **noun** [mass noun] **1** /eɪˈkɑːteɪ/ a card game for two players, played originally in 19th-century France, in which thirty-two cards are used and certain cards may be discarded in exchange for others.

2 /ˌeɪkɑːˈteɪ/ Ballet a position in which the dancer, facing diagonally towards the audience, extends one leg in the air to the side with the arm of the same side raised above the head and the other arm extended to the side.

– ORIGIN early 19th cent.: French, past participle of *écarter* 'discard, throw out', from *é* 'out' + *carte* 'card'.

e-cash ▶ **noun** [mass noun] electronic financial transactions conducted in cyberspace via computer networks.

ecbolic /ɛkˈbɒlɪk/ Medicine ▶ **adjective** inducing contractions of the uterus leading to expulsion of a fetus: *the ecbolic properties of Indian medicinal plants*.

▶**noun** an agent that induces such contractions.

– ORIGIN mid 18th cent.: from Greek *ekbolē* 'expulsion' + **-IC**.

Ecce Homo /ˌɛkeɪ ˈhɒməʊ, ˈhəʊməʊ/ ▶ **noun** Art a painting of Christ wearing the crown of thorns.

– ORIGIN Latin, 'behold the man', the words of Pontius Pilate to the Jews after Jesus was crowned with thorns (John 19:5).

eccentric /ɪkˈsɛntrɪk, ɛk-/ ▶ **adjective 1** (of a person or their behaviour) unconventional and slightly strange: *he noted her eccentric appearance*.

2 technical not placed centrally or not having its axis or other part placed centrally: *a servo driving an eccentric cam*.

■ (of a circle) not centred on the same point as another. ■ (of an orbit) not circular.

▶**noun 1** a person of unconventional and slightly strange views or behaviour: *he enjoys a colourful reputation as an engaging eccentric*.

2 a disc or wheel mounted eccentrically on a revolving shaft in order to transform rotation into backward-and-forward motion, e.g. a cam in an internal-combustion engine.

– DERIVATIVES **eccentrically** adverb.

– ORIGIN late Middle English (as a noun denoting a circle or orbit not having the earth precisely at its centre): via late Latin from Greek *ekkentros*, from *ek* 'out of' + *kentron* 'centre'.

eccentric anomaly ▶ **noun** Astronomy the actual anomaly of a planet in an elliptical orbit. Compare with **MEAN ANOMALY**.

eccentricity /ˌɛksɛnˈtrɪsɪti/ ▶ **noun** (pl. **-ies**) [mass noun] **1** the quality of being eccentric.

■ [count noun] (usu. **eccentricities**) an eccentric act, habit, or thing: *her eccentricities were amusing rather than irritating*.

2 technical deviation of a curve or orbit from circularity.

■ [count noun] a measure of the extent of such deviation: *Halley's Comet has an eccentricity of about 0.9675*.

ecchymosis /ˌɛkɪˈməʊsɪs/ ▶ **noun** (pl. **ecchymoses** /-siːz/) Medicine a discoloration of the skin resulting from bleeding underneath, typically caused by bruising.

– ORIGIN mid 16th cent.: modern Latin, from Greek *ekkhumōsis* 'escape of blood', from *ekkhumonathai* 'force out blood'.

Eccles /ˈɛk(ə)lz/, Sir John Carew (1903–97), Australian physiologist, who demonstrated the way in which nerve impulses are conducted by means of chemical neurotransmitters. Nobel Prize for Physiology or Medicine (1963).

Eccles. ▶ **abbreviation for** Ecclesiastes (in biblical references).

Eccles cake ▶ **noun** Brit. a round flat cake of sweetened pastry filled with currants.
– ORIGIN named after the town of *Eccles* near Manchester, England.

ecclesial /ɪˈkliːzɪ(ə)l/ ▶ **adjective** formal relating to or constituting a Church or denomination: *the modernization of ecclesial buildings*.
– ORIGIN mid 17th cent. (but rare before the 1960s): via Old French from Greek *ekklēsia* 'assembly, church' (see **ECCLESIASTIC**).

ecclesiarch /ɪkˈliːzɪɑːk/ ▶ **noun** archaic a ruler of a Church.
– ORIGIN late 18th cent.: from Greek *ekklēsia* 'church' + *arkhos* 'leader'.

Ecclesiastes /ɪˌkliːzɪˈastiːz/ a book of the Bible traditionally attributed to Solomon, consisting largely of reflections on the vanity of human life.

ecclesiastic formal ▶ **noun** a priest or clergyman.
▶ **adjective** another term for **ECCLESIASTICAL**.
– ORIGIN late Middle English: from French *ecclésiastique*, or via late Latin from Greek *ekklēsiastikos*, from *ekklēsiastēs* 'member of an assembly', from *ekklēsia* 'assembly, church', based on *ekkalein* 'summon out'.

ecclesiastical ▶ **adjective** of or relating to the Christian Church or its clergy: *the ecclesiastical hierarchy*.
– DERIVATIVES **ecclesiastically** adverb.

ecclesiasticism ▶ **noun** [mass noun] adherence or over-attention to details of Church practice: *the ecclesiasticism that so often gets in the way of the gospel*.

Ecclesiasticus /ɪˌkliːzɪˈastɪkəs/ a book of the Apocrypha containing moral and practical maxims, probably composed or compiled in the early 2nd century BC.

ecclesiology /ɪˌkliːzɪˈɒlədʒi/ ▶ **noun** [mass noun] **1** the study of churches, especially church building and decoration.
2 theology as applied to the nature and structure of the Christian Church.
– DERIVATIVES **ecclesiological** adjective, **ecclesiologist** noun.
– ORIGIN mid 19th cent.: from Greek *ekklēsia* 'assembly, church' + **-LOGY**.

Ecclus ▶ **abbreviation for** Ecclesiasticus (in biblical references).

eccrine /ˈɛkrʌɪn, -krɪn/ ▶ **adjective** Medicine relating to or denoting multicellular glands which do not lose cytoplasm in their secretions, especially the sweat glands found widely distributed on the skin. Compare with **APOCRINE**.
– ORIGIN 1930s: from Greek *ekkrinein* 'secrete', from *ek-* 'out' + *krinein* 'sift, separate'.

ecdysiast /ɛkˈdɪzɪast/ ▶ **noun** humorous a striptease performer.
– ORIGIN 1940s: from Greek *ekdusis* 'shedding', on the pattern of *enthusiast*.

ecdysis /ˈɛkdɪsɪs, ɛkˈdʌɪsɪs/ ▶ **noun** [mass noun] Zoology the process of shedding the old skin (in reptiles) or casting off the outer cuticle (in insects and other arthropods).
– DERIVATIVES **ecdysial** /ɛkˈdɪzɪəl/ adjective.
– ORIGIN mid 19th cent.: from Greek *ekdusis*, from *ekduein* 'put off', from *ek-* 'out, off' + *duein* 'put'.

ecdysone /ˈɛkdɪsəʊn, ɛkˈdʌɪsəʊn/ ▶ **noun** [mass noun] Biochemistry a steroid hormone that controls moulting in insects and other arthropods.
– ORIGIN 1950s: from Greek *ekdusis* 'shedding' + **-ONE**.

ECG ▶ **abbreviation for** electrocardiogram or electrocardiograph.

échappé /eɪˈʃapeɪ/ ▶ **adjective** [postpositive] Ballet (of a movement) progressing from a closed position (first, third, or fifth) to an open position (second or fourth) of the feet.
– ORIGIN French, literally 'escaped'.

echelon /ˈɛʃəlɒn, ˈeɪʃ-/ ▶ **noun** **1** a level or rank in an organization, a profession, or society: *the upper echelons of the business world*.
■ [often with modifier] a part of a military force differentiated by position in battle or by function: *the rear echelon*.
2 Military a formation of troops, ships, aircraft, or vehicles in parallel rows with the end of each row projecting further than the one in front.
▶ **verb** [with obj.] Military arrange in an echelon formation: [as noun **echeloning**] *the echeloning of fire teams*.
– ORIGIN late 18th cent. (in sense 2): from French *échelon*, from *échelle* 'ladder', from Latin *scala*.

echeveria /ˌɛtʃɪˈvɪərɪə/ ▶ **noun** a succulent plant with rosettes of fleshy colourful leaves, native to warm regions of America and popular as pot plants.
● Genus *Echeveria*, family Crassulaceae: numerous species and cultivars.
– ORIGIN modern Latin, named after Anastasio *Echeveri* or *Echeverría*, 19th-cent. Mexican botanical illustrator.

echidna /ɪˈkɪdnə/ ▶ **noun** a spiny insectivorous egg-laying mammal with a long snout and claws, native to Australia and New Guinea. Also called **SPINY ANTEATER**.
● Family Tachyglossidae, order Monotremata: two genera and species, in particular *Tachyglossus aculeatus*.
– ORIGIN mid 19th cent.: modern Latin, from Greek *ekhidna* 'viper', also the name of a mythical creature which gave birth to the many-headed Hydra; compare with *ekhinos* 'sea-urchin, hedgehog'.

echinacea /ˌɛkɪˈneɪsɪə/ ▶ **noun** a North American plant of the daisy family, whose flowers have a raised cone-like centre which appears to consist of soft spines. It is used in herbal medicine, largely for its antibiotic and wound-healing properties.
● Genus *Echinacea*, family Compositae: several species, in particular the purple-flowered *E. purpurea*.
– ORIGIN modern Latin, from Greek *ekhinos* 'hedgehog'.

Echinodermata /ɪˌkʌɪnə(ʊ)dəˈmɑːtə, ˌɛkɪn-, -ˈdəːmətə/ Zoology a phylum of marine invertebrates which includes starfishes, sea urchins, brittlestars, crinoids, and sea cucumbers. They have fivefold radial symmetry, a calcareous skeleton, and tube feet operated by fluid pressure.
– DERIVATIVES **echinoderm** /ɪˈkʌɪnə(ʊ)dəːm, ˈɛkɪn-/ noun.
– ORIGIN modern Latin (plural), from Greek *ekhinos* 'hedgehog, sea urchin' + *derma* 'skin'.

Echinoidea /ˌɛkɪˈnɔɪdɪə/ Zoology a class of echinoderms that comprises the sea urchins.
– DERIVATIVES **echinoid** /ˈɛkɪnɔɪd/ noun & adjective.
– ORIGIN modern Latin (plural), from **ECHINUS**.

echinus /ɪˈkʌɪnəs/ ▶ **noun** **1** Zoology a sea urchin.
● Genus *Echinus*, class Echinoidea: several species, including the common European **edible sea urchin** (*E. esculentus*).
2 Architecture a rounded moulding below an abacus on a Doric or Ionic capital.
– ORIGIN late Middle English: via Latin from Greek *ekhinos* 'hedgehog, sea urchin'.

Echiura /ˌɛkɪˈjʊ(ə)rə/ Zoology a small phylum of worm-like marine invertebrates that comprises the spoonworms.
– DERIVATIVES **echiuran** noun & adjective, **echiuroid** noun & adjective.
– ORIGIN modern Latin (earlier *Echiuroidea*), from Greek *ekhis* 'viper' + *oura* 'tail'.

Echo /ˈɛkəʊ/ Greek Mythology a nymph deprived of speech by Hera in order to stop her chatter, and left able only to repeat what others had said.

echo ▶ **noun** **1** (pl. **-oes**) a sound or series of sounds caused by the reflection of sound waves from a surface back to the listener: *the walls threw back the echoes of his footsteps*.
■ a reflected radio or radar beam. ■ [mass noun] the deliberate introduction of reverberation into a sound recording. ■ Linguistics the repetition in structure and content of one speaker's utterance by another. ■ a close parallel or repetition of an idea, feeling, style, or event: *his love for her* **found an echo in** *her own feelings*. ■ (often **echoes**) a detail or characteristic that is suggestive of something else: *the cheese has a sharp rich aftertaste with echoes of salty, earthy pastures*. ■ archaic a person who slavishly repeats the words or opinions of another. ■ used in names of newspapers: *the South Wales Echo*.
2 Bridge a play by a defender of a higher card in a suit followed by a lower one in a subsequent trick, used as a signal to request a further lead of that suit by their partner.
3 a code word representing the letter E, used in radio communication.
▶ **verb** (**-oes**, **-oed**) [no obj., with adverbial] (of a sound) be repeated or reverberate after the original sound has stopped: *their footsteps echoed on the metal catwalks*.
■ (of a place) resound with or reflect back a sound or sounds: *the house* **echoed with** *shouts and thundering feet*. ■ figurative have a continued significance or influence: *illiteracy echoed through the whole fabric of society*. ■ [with obj.] (often **be echoed**) repeat (someone's words or opinions), typically to express agreement: *these criticisms are echoed in a number of other studies* | [with direct speech] *'A trip?' she echoed*. ■ [with obj.] (of an object, movement, or event) be reminiscent of or have shared characteristics with: *a blue suit that echoed the colour of her eyes*. ■ [with obj.] Computing send a copy of (an input signal or character) back to its source or to a screen for display: *for security reasons, the password will not be echoed to the screen*. ■ Bridge (of a defender) play a higher card followed by a lower one in the same suit, as a signal to request one's partner to lead that suit.
– PHRASES **applaud** (or **cheer**) **someone to the echo** applaud (or cheer) someone enthusiastically.
– DERIVATIVES **echoer** noun, **echoey** adjective, **echoless** adjective.
– ORIGIN Middle English: from Old French or Latin, from Greek *ēkhō*, related to *ēkhē* 'a sound'.

echocardiogram /ˌɛkəʊˈkɑːdɪə(ʊ)gram/ ▶ **noun** Medicine a test of the action of the heart using ultrasound waves to produce a visual display, for the diagnosis or monitoring of heart disease.

echocardiography /ˌɛkəʊkɑːdɪˈɒgrəfi/ ▶ **noun** [mass noun] Medicine the use of ultrasound waves to investigate the action of the heart.
– DERIVATIVES **echocardiograph** noun, **echocardiographic** adjective.

echo chamber ▶ **noun** an enclosed space for producing reverberation of sound.

echogram ▶ **noun** a recording of depth or distance under water made by an echo sounder.

echograph ▶ **noun** an instrument for recording echograms; an automated echo sounder.

echoic /ɛˈkəʊɪk/ ▶ **adjective** of or like an echo.
■ Linguistics representing a sound by imitation; onomatopoeic.
– DERIVATIVES **echoically** adverb.

echolalia /ˌɛkəʊˈleɪlɪə/ ▶ **noun** [mass noun] Psychiatry meaningless repetition of another person's spoken words as a symptom of psychiatric disorder.
■ repetition of speech by a child learning to talk.
– ORIGIN late 19th cent.: modern Latin, from Greek *ēkhō* 'echo' + *lalia* 'speech'.

echolocation /ˈɛkə(ʊ)lə(ʊ),keɪʃ(ə)n/ ▶ **noun** [mass noun] the location of objects by reflected sound, in particular that used by animals such as dolphins and bats.

echopraxia /ˌɛkəʊˈpraksɪə/ ▶ **noun** [mass noun] Psychiatry meaningless repetition or imitation of the movements of others as a symptom of psychiatric disorder.
– ORIGIN early 20th cent.: modern Latin, from Greek *ēkhō* 'echo' + *praxis* 'action'.

echo sounder ▶ **noun** a device for determining the depth of the seabed or detecting objects in water by measuring the time taken for sound echoes to return to the listener.
– DERIVATIVES **echo-sounding** noun.

echo verse ▶ **noun** [mass noun] a verse form in which a line repeats the last syllables of the previous line.

echovirus (also **ECHO virus**) ▶ **noun** Medicine any of a group of enteroviruses which can cause a range of diseases including respiratory infections and a mild form of meningitis.
– ORIGIN 1950s: from *echo* (acronym from *enteric cytopathogenic human orphan*, because the virus was not originally assignable to any known disease) + **VIRUS**.

echt /ɛxt/ ▶ **adjective** authentic and typical: *an echt court bouillon*.
▶ **adverb** [as submodifier] authentically and typically: *echt-Viennese artists*.
– ORIGIN German.

eclair /eɪˈklɛː, ɪ-/ ▶ **noun** a small, soft, log-shaped cake of choux pastry filled with cream and typically topped with chocolate icing.
– ORIGIN mid 19th cent.: from French, literally 'lightning'.

éclaircissement /ˌeɪklɛːˈsiːsmɒ̃/ ▶ **noun** archaic or poetic/literary an enlightening explanation of something, typically someone's conduct, that has been hitherto inexplicable.
– ORIGIN French, from *éclaircir* 'clear up', from *é* (expressing a change of state) + *clair* (see **CLEAR**).

eclampsia /ɪˈklam(p)sɪə/ ▶ **noun** [mass noun] Medicine a condition in which one or more convulsions occur in a pregnant woman suffering from high blood pressure, often followed by coma and posing a threat to the health of mother and baby. See also **PRE-ECLAMPSIA**.

– DERIVATIVES **eclamptic** adjective.

– ORIGIN mid 19th cent.: modern Latin, from French *éclampsie*, from Greek *eklampsis* 'sudden development', from *eklampein* 'shine out'.

éclat /eɪˈklɑː/ ▶ noun [mass noun] brilliant display or effect: *he finished his recital with great éclat.*
 ▪ social distinction or conspicuous success: *such action bestows more éclat upon a warrior than success by other means.*

– ORIGIN late 17th cent.: from French, from *éclater* 'burst out'.

eclectic /ɪˈklɛktɪk/ ▶ adjective **1** deriving ideas, style, or taste from a broad and diverse range of sources: *her musical tastes are eclectic.*
 2 (**Eclectic**) Philosophy of, denoting, or belonging to a class of ancient philosophers who did not belong to or found any recognized school of thought but selected such doctrines as they wished from various schools.
 ▶ noun a person who derives ideas, style, or taste from a broad and diverse range of sources.

– DERIVATIVES **eclectically** adverb, **eclecticism** noun.

– ORIGIN late 17th cent. (as a term in philosophy): from Greek *eklektikos*, from *eklegein* 'pick out', from *ek* 'out' + *legein* 'choose'.

eclipse /ɪˈklɪps/ ▶ noun an obscuring of the light from one celestial body by the passage of another between it and the observer or between it and its source of illumination: *an eclipse of the sun.*
 ▪ figurative a loss of significance, power, or prominence in relation to another person or thing: *the election result marked the eclipse of the traditional right and centre.* ▪ Ornithology a phase during which the distinctive markings of a bird (especially a male duck) are obscured by moulting of the breeding plumage: [as modifier] *eclipse plumage.*
 ▶ verb [with obj.] (often **be eclipsed**) (of a celestial body) obscure the light from or to (another celestial body): *Jupiter was eclipsed by the Moon.*
 ▪ poetic/literary obscure or block out (light): *a sea of blue sky violently eclipsed by showers.* ▪ deprive (someone or something) of significance, power, or prominence: *the state of the economy has eclipsed the environment as the main issue.*

– PHRASES **in eclipse 1** losing or having lost significance, power, or prominence: *his political power was in eclipse.* **2** Ornithology (especially of a male duck) in its eclipse plumage.

– ORIGIN Middle English: from Old French *e(s)clipse* (noun), *eclipser* (verb), via Latin from Greek *ekleipsis*, from *ekleipein* 'fail to appear, be eclipsed', from *ek* 'out' + *leipein* 'to leave'.

eclipsing binary ▶ noun Astronomy a binary star whose brightness varies periodically as the two components pass one in front of the other.

ecliptic /ɪˈklɪptɪk/ ▶ noun Astronomy a great circle on the celestial sphere representing the sun's apparent path during the year, so called because lunar and solar eclipses can only occur when the moon crosses it.
 ▶ adjective of an eclipse or the ecliptic.

– ORIGIN late Middle English: via Latin from Greek *ekleiptikos*, from *ekleipein* 'fail to appear' (see **ECLIPSE**).

eclogite /ˈɛklədʒʌɪt/ ▶ noun [mass noun] Geology a metamorphic rock containing granular minerals, typically garnet and pyroxene.

– ORIGIN mid 19th cent.: from French, from Greek *eklogē* 'selection' (with reference to the selective content of the rock) + -ITE[1].

eclogue /ˈɛklɒg/ ▶ noun a short poem, especially a pastoral dialogue.

– ORIGIN late Middle English: via Latin from Greek *eklogē* 'selection', from *eklegein* 'pick out'.

eclose /ɪˈkləʊz/ ▶ verb [no obj.] Entomology (of an insect) emerge as an adult from the pupa or as a larva from the egg.

– DERIVATIVES **eclosion** noun.

– ORIGIN late 19th cent. (as *eclosion*): from French *éclore* 'to hatch', based on Latin *ex-* 'out' + *claudere* 'to close'.

ECM ▶ abbreviation for electronic countermeasures.

Eco /ˈɛkəʊ/, Umberto (b.1932), Italian novelist and semiotician. Notable works: *The Name of the Rose*

(novel, 1981), *Travels in Hyperreality* (writings on semiotics, 1986).

eco- /ˈiːkəʊ, ˈɛkəʊ/ ▶ combining form representing **ECOLOGY**.

ecocide ▶ noun [mass noun] destruction of the natural environment, especially when wilfully done.

ecocline ▶ noun Ecology a cline from one ecosystem to another, showing a continuous gradient between the two extremes.

ecofeminism ▶ noun [mass noun] a philosophical and political theory and movement which parallels and combines ecological concerns with feminist ones, regarding both as resulting from male domination of society.

– DERIVATIVES **ecofeminist** noun.

eco-friendly ▶ adjective not harmful to the environment: *I use only eco-friendly products.*

eco-labelling ▶ noun [mass noun] the practice of marking products with a distinctive label so that consumers know that their manufacture conforms to recognized environmental standards.

– DERIVATIVES **eco-label** noun.

E. coli /ˈkəʊlʌɪ/ ▶ noun [mass noun] a bacterium commonly found in the intestines of humans and other animals, where it usually causes no harm. Some strains can cause severe food poisoning, especially in old people and children.
 ● *Escherichia coli*; a motile Gram-negative bacillus.

ecology /ɪˈkɒlədʒi, ɛ-/ ▶ noun [mass noun] the branch of biology that deals with the relations of organisms to one another and to their physical surroundings.
 ▪ (**Ecology**) the political movement concerned with protection of the environment.

– DERIVATIVES **ecological** adjective, **ecologically** adverb, **ecologist** noun.

– ORIGIN late 19th cent. (originally as *oecology*): from Greek *oikos* 'house' + -LOGY.

econometrics /ɪˌkɒnəˈmɛtrɪks/ ▶ plural noun [treated as sing.] the branch of economics concerned with the use of mathematical methods (especially statistics) in describing economic systems.

– DERIVATIVES **econometric** adjective, **econometrical** adjective, **econometrician** noun, **econometrist** noun.

– ORIGIN 1930s: from **ECONOMY**, on the pattern of words such as *biometrics* and *cliometrics*.

economic /ˌiːkəˈnɒmɪk, ɛk-/ ▶ adjective of or relating to economics or the economy: *the government's economic policy* | *pest species of great economic importance.*
 ▪ justified in terms of profitability: *many organizations must become larger if they are to remain economic.* ▪ requiring fewer resources or costing less money: *solar power may provide a more economic solution.* ▪ (of a subject) considered in relation to trade, industry, and the creation of wealth: *economic history.*

– ORIGIN late Middle English: via Old French and Latin from Greek *oikonomikos*, from *oikonomia* (see **ECONOMY**). Originally a noun, the word denoted household management or a person skilled in this, hence the early sense of the adjective (late 16th cent.) 'relating to household management'. Modern senses date from the mid 19th cent.

economical ▶ adjective giving good value or service in relation to the amount of money, time, or effort spent: *a small, economical car.*
 ▪ (of a person or lifestyle) careful not to waste money or resources. ▪ using no more of something than is necessary: *the cast are economical with their actions.*

– PHRASES **economical with the truth** used euphemistically to describe a person or statement that lies or deliberately withholds information. [ORIGIN: from a statement given in evidence by Sir Robert Armstrong, British cabinet secretary, in the 'Spycatcher' trial (1986), conducted to prevent publication of a book by a former MI5 employee. The theological phrase *economy of truth* (i.e. sparing use of truth) has long been in use.]

economically ▶ adverb in a way that relates to economics or finance: [sentence adverb] *the region is important economically.*
 ▪ in a way that involves careful use of money or resources: *the new building was erected as economically as possible.* ▪ in a way that uses no more of something than is necessary: *a precis aims to express a passage more economically.*

Economic and Social Committee (abbrev.:

ESC) a consultative body of the European Union, set up in 1957 and composed of representatives of the member states. It meets in Brussels.

economic good ▶ noun Economics a product or service which can command a price when sold.

economic rent ▶ noun Economics the extra amount earned by a resource (e.g. land, capital, or labour) by virtue of its present use.

economics ▶ plural noun [often treated as sing.] the branch of knowledge concerned with the production, consumption, and transfer of wealth.
 ▪ the condition of a region or group as regards material prosperity: *he is responsible for the island's modest economics.*

– ORIGIN late 16th cent. (denoting the science of household management): from **ECONOMIC** + the plural suffix *-s*, originally on the pattern of Greek *ta oikonomika* (plural), the name of a treatise by Aristotle. Current senses date from the late 18th cent.

economism /ɪˈkɒnəmɪz(ə)m/ ▶ noun [mass noun] belief in the primacy of economic causes or factors.

– ORIGIN early 20th cent.: from French *économisme*, based on Greek *oikonomia* 'household management' (see **ECONOMY**).

economist ▶ noun an expert in economics.

– ORIGIN late 16th cent. (originally in the Greek sense): from Greek *oikonomos* 'household manager' (see **ECONOMY**) + -IST. The current sense dates from the early 19th cent.

economize (also **-ise**) ▶ verb [no obj.] spend less; reduce one's expenses: *I have to economize where I can* | *people on low incomes may try to economize on fuel.*

– DERIVATIVES **economization** noun.

economizer ▶ noun **1** a device designed to make a machine or system more energy-efficient.
 2 a person who reduces expenditure.

economy ▶ noun (pl. **-ies**) **1** the wealth and resources of a country or region, especially in terms of the production and consumption of goods and services.
 ▪ a particular system or stage of an economy: *the less-developed economies* | *a free-market economy.*
 2 [mass noun] careful management of available resources: *fuel economy.*
 ▪ sparing or careful use of something: *economy of words.* ▪ [count noun] (usu. **economies**) a financial saving: *there were many economies to be made by giving up our offices in central London.* ▪ (also **economy class**) the cheapest class of air or rail travel: *we flew economy.*
 ▶ adjective [attrib.] (of a product) offering the best value for money: *an economy pack of soap flakes.*
 ▪ designed to be economical to use: *a new 1.1 litre economy engine.*

– PHRASES **economy of scale** a proportionate saving in costs gained by an increased level of production. **economy of scope** a proportionate saving gained by producing two or more distinct goods, when the cost of doing so is less than that of producing each separately.

– ORIGIN late 15th cent. (in the sense 'management of material resources'): from French *économie*, or via Latin from Greek *oikonomia* 'household management', based on *oikos* 'house' + *nemein* 'manage'. Current senses date from the 17th cent.

economy-size (also **economy-sized**) ▶ adjective of a size which offers a large quantity for a proportionately lower cost: *an economy-size container.*

écorché /ˌɛkɔːˈʃeɪ/ ▶ noun (pl. pronounced same) a painting or sculpture of a human figure with the skin removed to display the musculature.

– ORIGIN French, literally 'flayed'.

ecosphere ▶ noun the biosphere of the earth or other planet, especially when the interaction between the living and non-living components is emphasized.
 ▪ Astronomy the region of space around a sun or star where conditions are such that planets are theoretically capable of sustaining life.

ecossaise /ˌɛkɒˈseɪz/ ▶ noun (pl. pronounced same) an energetic country dance in duple time in which couples form lines facing each other.

– ORIGIN mid 19th cent.: from French, feminine of *écossais* 'Scottish'; the connection with Scotland is unclear.

ecosystem ▶ noun Ecology a biological community of interacting organisms and their physical environment.

ecotage /'iːkətɑːʒ, 'ɛ-/ ▶ noun [mass noun] sabotage carried out for ecological reasons.
– ORIGIN 1970s: blend of *ecological* (see ECOLOGY) and SABOTAGE.

ecoterrorism ▶ noun [mass noun] violence carried out to further environmentalist ends.
▪ the action of causing deliberate environmental damage in order to further political ends.
– DERIVATIVES **ecoterrorist** noun.

ecotone /'iːkə(ʊ)təʊn, 'ɛk-/ ▶ noun Ecology a region of transition between two biological communities.
– DERIVATIVES **ecotonal** adjective.

ecotourism ▶ noun [mass noun] tourism directed towards exotic, often threatened, natural environments, especially to support conservation efforts and observe wildlife.
– DERIVATIVES **ecotour** noun & verb, **ecotourist** noun.

ecotoxicology ▶ noun [mass noun] the branch of science that deals with the nature, effects, and interactions of substances that are harmful to the environment.
– DERIVATIVES **ecotoxicological** adjective, **ecotoxicologist** noun.

ecotype ▶ noun Botany & Zoology a distinct form or race of a plant or animal species occupying a particular habitat.

ecru /'eɪkruː, ɛ'kruː/ ▶ noun [mass noun] the light fawn colour of unbleached linen.
– ORIGIN mid 19th cent.: from French *écru* 'unbleached'.

ECSC ▶ abbreviation for European Coal and Steel Community.

ecstasize (also **-ise**) ▶ verb [with obj.] cause (someone) to go into ecstasies.
▪ [no obj.] go into ecstasies.

ecstasy /'ɛkstəsi/ ▶ noun (pl. **-ies**) [mass noun] **1** an overwhelming feeling of great happiness or joyful excitement: *there was a look of ecstasy on his face* | [count noun] *they went into ecstasies over the view.*
2 chiefly archaic an emotional or religious frenzy or trancelike state, originally one involving an experience of mystic self-transcendence.
3 (**Ecstasy**) an illegal amphetamine-based synthetic drug with euphoric and hallucinatory effects, originally produced as an appetite suppressant. Also called MDMA.
– ORIGIN late Middle English (in sense 2): from Old French *extasie*, via late Latin from Greek *ekstasis* 'standing outside oneself', based on *ek-* 'out' + *histanai* 'to place'.

ecstatic /ɪk'statɪk, ɛk-/ ▶ adjective **1** feeling or expressing overwhelming happiness or joyful excitement: *ecstatic fans filled the stadium.*
2 involving an experience of mystic self-transcendence: *an ecstatic vision of God.*
▶ noun a person subject to mystical experiences.
– DERIVATIVES **ecstatically** adverb.

ECT ▶ abbreviation for electroconvulsive therapy.

ecto- ▶ combining form outer; external; on the outside (used commonly in scientific terms): *ectoderm* | *ectoparasite.*
– ORIGIN from Greek *ektos* 'outside'.

ectoderm /'ɛktə(ʊ)dəːm/ ▶ noun [mass noun] Zoology & Embryology the outermost layer of cells or tissue of an embryo in early development, or the parts derived from this, which include the epidermis, nerve tissue, and nephridia. Compare with ENDODERM and MESODERM.
– DERIVATIVES **ectodermal** adjective.
– ORIGIN mid 19th cent.: from ECTO- 'outside' + Greek *derma* 'skin'.

ectogenesis /ˌɛktə(ʊ)'dʒɛnɪsɪs/ ▶ noun [mass noun] (chiefly in science fiction) the development of embryos in artificial conditions outside the womb.
– DERIVATIVES **ectogene** noun, **ectogenetic** adjective, **ectogenetically** adverb.

ectomorph /'ɛktə(ʊ)mɔːf/ ▶ noun Physiology a person with a lean and delicate build of body. Compare with ENDOMORPH and MESOMORPH.
– DERIVATIVES **ectomorphic** adjective, **ectomorphy** noun.
– ORIGIN 1940s: ecto- from *ectodermal* (being the layer of the embryo giving rise to physical characteristics which predominate) + -MORPH.

-ectomy ▶ combining form denoting surgical removal of a specified part of the body: *appendectomy.*
– ORIGIN from Greek *ektomē* 'excision', from *ek* 'out' + *temnein* 'to cut'.

ectoparasite /ˌɛktə'parəsʌɪt/ ▶ noun Biology a parasite, such as a flea, that lives on the outside of its host. Compare with ENDOPARASITE.
– DERIVATIVES **ectoparasitic** adjective.

ectopic /ɛk'tɒpɪk/ ▶ adjective Medicine in an abnormal place or position.
▶ noun an ectopic pregnancy.
– ORIGIN late 19th cent.: from modern Latin *ectopia* 'presence of tissue, cells, etc. in an abnormal place' (from Greek *ektopos* 'out of place') + -IC.

ectopic beat ▶ noun another term for EXTRASYSTOLE.

ectopic pregnancy ▶ noun a pregnancy in which the fetus develops outside the womb, typically in a Fallopian tube.

ectoplasm /'ɛktə(ʊ)plaz(ə)m/ ▶ noun [mass noun] **1** Biology the more viscous, clear outer layer of the cytoplasm in amoeboid cells. Compare with ENDOPLASM.
2 a supernatural viscous substance that is supposed to exude from the body of a medium during a spiritualistic trance and form the material for the manifestation of spirits.
– DERIVATIVES **ectoplasmic** adjective.

Ectoprocta /ˌɛktə(ʊ)'prɒktə/ Zoology another term for BRYOZOA.
– DERIVATIVES **ectoproct** noun.
– ORIGIN modern Latin (plural), from *ektos* 'outside or external' + *prōktos* 'anus'.

ectotherm /'ɛktəθəːm/ ▶ noun Zoology an animal that is dependent on external sources of body heat. Often contrasted with ENDOTHERM. Compare with POIKILOTHERM.
– DERIVATIVES **ectothermic** adjective, **ectothermy** noun.

ectropion /ɛk'trəʊpɪən/ ▶ noun [mass noun] Medicine a condition, typically a consequence of advanced age, in which the eyelid is turned outwards away from the eyeball.
– ORIGIN late 17th cent.: from Greek, from *ek-* 'out' + *trepein* 'to turn'.

ecu /'ɛkjuː, 'iː-, 'eɪ-, -kuː/ (also **ECU**) ▶ noun (pl. same or **ecus**) former term for EURO.
– ORIGIN acronym from *European currency unit*.

Ecuador /'ɛkwədɔː, Spanish ekwa'ðor/ an equatorial republic in South America, on the Pacific coast; pop. 11,460,100 (est. 1995); languages, Spanish (official), Quechua; capital, Quito.

Ranges and plateaux of the Andes separate the coastal plain from the tropical forests of the Amazon basin. Formerly part of the Inca empire, Ecuador was conquered by the Spanish in 1534 and remained part of Spain's American empire until, after the first uprising against Spanish rule in 1809, independence was gained in 1822.

– DERIVATIVES **Ecuadorean** adjective & noun.

ecumenical /ˌiːkjʊ'mɛnɪk(ə)l, ɛk-/ ▶ adjective representing a number of different Christian Churches.
▪ promoting or relating to unity among the world's Christian Churches: *the ecumenical movement.*
– DERIVATIVES **ecumenically** adverb.
– ORIGIN late 16th cent. (in the sense 'belonging to the universal Church'): via late Latin from Greek *oikoumenikos* from *oikoumenē* 'the (inhabited) earth'.

Ecumenical Patriarch ▶ noun a title of the Orthodox Patriarch of Constantinople.

ecumenism /ɪ'kjuːmənɪz(ə)m/ ▶ noun [mass noun] the principle or aim of promoting unity among the world's Christian Churches.

eczema /'ɛksɪmə, 'ɛkzɪmə/ ▶ noun [mass noun] a medical condition in which patches of skin become rough and inflamed with blisters which cause itching and bleeding, sometimes resulting from a reaction to irritation (eczematous dermatitis) but more typically having no obvious external cause.
– DERIVATIVES **eczematous** /ɛk'ziːmətəs, ɛk'zɛm-/ adjective.
– ORIGIN mid 18th cent.: modern Latin from Greek *ekzema*, from *ekzein* 'boil over, break out', from *ek-* 'out' + *zein* 'boil'.

ed. ▶ abbreviation for ▪ edited by. ▪ edition. ▪ editor.

-ed¹ ▶ suffix forming adjectives: **1** (added to nouns) having; possessing; affected by: *talented* | *diseased.*
▪ (added to nouns) characteristic of: *ragged.*
2 from phrases consisting of adjective and noun: *bad-tempered* | *three-sided.*
– ORIGIN Old English *-ede.*

-ed² ▶ suffix forming: **1** the past tense and past participle of weak verbs: *landed* | *walked.*
2 participial adjectives: *wounded.*
– ORIGIN Old English *-ed, -ad, -od.*

edacious /ɪ'deɪʃəs/ ▶ adjective rare of, relating to, or given to eating.
– DERIVATIVES **edacity** noun.
– ORIGIN early 19th cent.: from Latin *edax, edac-* (from *edere* 'eat') + -IOUS.

Edam¹ /'iːdam/ a town in the Netherlands, to the north-east of Amsterdam; pop. 24,840 (1991) (with Volendam).

Edam² /'iːdam/ ▶ noun [mass noun] a round Dutch cheese, typically pale yellow with a red wax coating.

edaphic /ɪ'dafɪk/ ▶ adjective Ecology of, produced, or influenced by the soil.
– ORIGIN late 19th cent.: coined in German from Greek *edaphos* 'floor' + -IC.

edaphosaurus /ɪ'dafəsɔːrəs/ ▶ noun a large herbivorous synapsid reptile of the late Carboniferous and early Permian periods, with long knobbly spines on its back supporting a sail-like crest.
● Genus *Edaphosaurus*, order Pelycosauria, subclass Synapsida.
– ORIGIN modern Latin, from Greek *edaphos* 'floor' + *sauros* 'lizard'.

Edberg /'ɛdbəːg/, Stefan (b.1966), Swedish tennis player. He won the Australian Open in 1985 and won Wimbledon in 1990 and 1991.

Edda /'ɛdə/ either of two 13th-century Icelandic books, the **Elder** or **Poetic Edda** (a collection of Old Norse poems on Norse legends) and the **Younger** or **Prose Edda** (a handbook to Icelandic poetry by Snorri Sturluson). The Eddas are the chief source of knowledge of Scandinavian mythology.
– ORIGIN either from the name of the great-grandmother in the Old Norse poem *Rigsthul*, or from Old Norse *óthr* 'poetry'.

Eddington, Sir Arthur Stanley (1882–1944), English astronomer, considered the founder of astrophysics. He used Einstein's theory of relativity to explain the bending of light by gravity that he observed in the 1919 solar eclipse.

eddo /'ɛdəʊ/ ▶ noun (pl. **-oes**) a taro corm or plant, especially of a West Indian variety with many edible cormlets.
● *Colocasia esculenta* var. *antiquorum*, family Araceae.
– ORIGIN late 17th cent.: of West African origin.

Eddy, Mary Baker (1821–1910), American religious leader and founder of the Christian Science movement. Long a victim to various ailments, she believed herself cured by a faith healer, Phineas Quimby, and later evolved her own system of spiritual healing.

eddy ▶ noun (pl. **-ies**) a circular movement of water causing a small whirlpool.
▪ a movement of wind, fog, or smoke resembling this.
▶ verb (**-ies, -ied**) [no obj., with adverbial of direction] (of water, air, or smoke) move in a circular way: *the mists from the river eddied round the banks.*
– ORIGIN late Middle English: probably from the Germanic base of the Old English prefix *ed-* 'again, back'.

eddy current ▶ noun a localized electric current induced in a conductor by a varying magnetic field.

Eddystone Rocks /'ɛdɪstən/ a rocky reef off the coast of Cornwall, 22 km (14 miles) SW of Plymouth. The reef was the site of the earliest lighthouse (1699) built on rocks fully exposed to the sea.

edelweiss /'eɪd(ə)lvʌɪs/ ▶ noun a European mountain plant which has woolly white bracts around its small flowers and downy grey-green leaves.
● *Leontopodium alpinum*, family Compositae.
– ORIGIN mid 19th cent.: from German, from *edel* 'noble' + *weiss* 'white'.

edema ▶ noun US spelling of OEDEMA.

Eden¹ /'iːd(ə)n/, (Robert) Anthony, 1st Earl of Avon (1897–1977), British Conservative statesman, Prime Minister 1955–7. His premiership was dominated by the Suez crisis of 1956; widespread opposition to Britain's role in this led to his resignation.

Eden² /'iːd(ə)n/ (also **Garden of Eden**) the place where Adam and Eve lived in the biblical account of the Creation, from which they were expelled for disobediently eating the fruit of the tree of knowledge.

■[as noun **an Eden**] a place or state of great happiness; an unspoilt paradise: *the lost Eden of his childhood.*

– ORIGIN from late Latin (Vulgate), Greek *Ēdēn* (Septuagint), and Hebrew *ʿĒḏen*; perhaps related to Akkadian *edinu*, from Sumerian *eden* 'plain, desert' (but believed to be related to Hebrew *ʿēḏen* 'delight').

Edentata /ˌiːdənˈtɑːtə, -ˈteɪtə/ Zoology another term for **XENARTHRA**.

edentate /ˈiːdənteɪt/ ▶**noun** Zoology a mammal of an order distinguished by the lack of incisor and canine teeth. The edentates, which include anteaters, sloths, and armadillos, are all native to Central and South America.

• Order Xenarthra (or Edentata).

– ORIGIN early 19th cent.: from Latin *edentatus*, past participle of *edentare* 'make toothless', from *e-* (variant of *ex-*) 'out' + *dens, dent-* 'tooth'.

edentulous /ɪˈdɛntjʊləs/ ▶**adjective** Medicine & Zoology lacking teeth.

– ORIGIN early 18th cent.: from Latin *edentulus*, from *e-* (variant of *ex-*) 'out' + *dens, dent-* 'tooth' + **-ULOUS**.

Edgar /ˈɛdɡə/ (944–75), king of England 959–75, younger brother of Edwy. He became king of Northumbria and Mercia in 957 when these regions renounced their allegiance to Edwy, succeeding to the throne of England on Edwy's death.

edge ▶**noun 1** the outside limit of an object, area, or surface; a place or part furthest away from the centre of something: *a willow tree at the water's edge* | figurative *these measures are merely tinkering at the edges of a wider issue.*

■an area next to a steep drop: *the cliff edge.* ■[in sing.] the point or state immediately before something unpleasant or momentous occurs: *the economy was teetering on* **the edge of** *recession.*

2 the sharpened side of the blade of a cutting implement or weapon.

■the line along which two surfaces of a solid meet. ■[in sing.] an intense, sharp, or striking quality: *a flamenco singer brings a primitive edge to the music.* ■[in sing.] a quality or factor which gives superiority over close rivals or competitors: *his cars have* **the edge over** *his rivals'.*

▶**verb** [with obj.] **1** (often **be edged**) provide with a border or edge: *the pool is edged with paving.*

2 [no obj., with adverbial of direction] move gradually, carefully, or furtively in a particular direction: *she tried to edge away from him* | *Nick* **edged his way** *through the crowd.*

■[with obj. and adverbial of direction] cause to move in such a way: *Hazel quietly edged him away from the others* | figurative *she was edged out of the organization by the director.* ■[with obj.] informal defeat by a small margin: *United* **edged out** *Rovers 4–2 on penalties.*

3 figurative give an intense or sharp quality to: *the bitterness that edged her voice.*

4 Cricket strike (the ball) with the edge of the bat; strike a ball delivered by (the bowler) with the edge of the bat.

5 [no obj.] ski with one's weight on the edges of one's skis.

– PHRASES **on edge** tense, nervous, or irritable: *never had she felt so on edge before an interview.* **on the edge of one's seat** informal very excited and giving one's full attention to something. **set someone's teeth on edge** (especially of an unpleasantly harsh sound) cause someone to feel intense discomfort or irritation: *a grating that set her teeth on edge.* **take the edge off** reduce the intensity or effect of (something unpleasant or severe): *the tablets will take the edge off the pain.*

– DERIVATIVES **edged** adjective [in combination] *a black-edged handkerchief*, **edgeless** adjective, **edger** noun.

– ORIGIN Old English *ecg* 'sharpened side of a blade', of Germanic origin; related to Dutch *egge* and German *Ecke*, also to Old Norse *eggja* (see **EGG**²), from an Indo-European root shared by Latin *acies* 'edge' and Greek *akis* 'point'.

edge city ▶**noun** chiefly N. Amer. a relatively large urban area situated on the outskirts of a city, typically beside a major road.

– ORIGIN 1991 (originally US): coined by J. Garreau in a book of same name.

edge connector ▶**noun** an electrical connector with a row of contacts, fitted to the edge of a printed circuit board to facilitate connection to external circuits.

Edgehill, Battle of /ɛdʒˈhɪl/ the first pitched battle of the English Civil War (1642), fought at the village of Edgehill in the west Midlands. The Parliamentary army attempted to halt the Royalist army's march on London; the battle ended with no clear winner and with heavy losses on both sides.

edge tool ▶**noun** a handworked or machine-operated cutting tool.

edgeways (also **edgewise**) ▶**adverb** with the edge uppermost or towards the viewer.

– PHRASES **get a word in edgeways** [usu. with negative] contribute to a conversation with difficulty because the other speaker talks almost without pause.

Edgeworth /ˈɛdʒwəθ/, Maria (1767–1849), English-born Irish novelist. Notable works: *Castle Rackrent* (1800) and *Belinda* (1801).

edging ▶**noun** [mass noun] a thing forming an edge or border: *the crocheted edging of the cloth.*

■the process of providing something with an edge or border.

edgy ▶**adjective** (**edgier, edgiest**) tense, nervous, or irritable: *he became edgy and defensive.*

■(of a musical performance or a piece of writing) having an intense or sharp quality.

– DERIVATIVES **edgily** adverb, **edginess** noun.

edh /ɛð/ ▶**noun** variant spelling of **ETH**.

EDI ▶**abbreviation for** electronic data interchange (a standard for exchanging information between computer systems).

edible /ˈɛdɪb(ə)l/ ▶**adjective** fit to be eaten (often used to contrast with unpalatable or poisonous examples): *nasturtium seeds are edible.*

▶**noun** (**edibles**) items of food.

– DERIVATIVES **edibility** noun.

– ORIGIN late 16th cent.: from late Latin *edibilis*, from Latin *edere* 'eat'.

edible crab ▶**noun** a large pinkish-brown European crab with black-tipped pincers, typically found in inshore waters and often caught for food.

• *Cancer pagurus*, family Cancridae.

edible dormouse ▶**noun** another term for **FAT DORMOUSE**.

edible frog ▶**noun** a large green aquatic frog native to mainland Europe and introduced to SE Britain. It is popular as food in parts of Europe.

• *Rana esculenta*, family Ranidae.

edible-nest swiftlet ▶**noun** a small Asian swift that constructs its nest from solidified saliva. The outer part of the nest is used to make Chinese bird's-nest soup.

• Genus *Aerodramus* (or *Collocalia*), family Apodidae: two species, in particular *A. fuciphagus*.

edible snail ▶**noun** a large snail which is widely collected or cultured for food, occurring chiefly in southern Europe. Also called **ESCARGOT**.

• *Helix pomatia*, family Helicidae.

edict /ˈiːdɪkt/ ▶**noun** an official order or proclamation issued by a person in authority.

– DERIVATIVES **edictal** /ɪˈdɪkt(ə)l/ adjective.

– ORIGIN Middle English: from Latin *edictum* 'something proclaimed', neuter past participle of *edicere*, from *e-* (variant of *ex-*) 'out' + *dicere* 'say, tell'.

Edict of Nantes see **NANTES, EDICT OF**.

edification /ˌɛdɪfɪˈkeɪʃ(ə)n/ ▶**noun** [mass noun] formal the instruction or improvement of a person morally or intellectually: *an account written for edification.*

– ORIGIN late Middle English: from Latin *aedificatio(n-)*, from *aedificare* 'build' (see **EDIFY**).

edifice /ˈɛdɪfɪs/ ▶**noun** formal a building, especially a large, imposing one.

■figurative a complex system of beliefs: *the concepts on which the edifice of capitalism was built.*

– ORIGIN late Middle English: via Old French from Latin *aedificium*, from *aedis* 'dwelling' + *facere* 'make'.

edify /ˈɛdɪfʌɪ/ ▶**verb** (**-ies, -ied**) [with obj.] formal instruct or improve (someone) morally or intellectually.

– ORIGIN Middle English: from Old French *edifier*, from Latin *aedificare* 'build', from *aedis* 'dwelling' + *facere* 'make' (compare with **EDIFICE**). The word originally meant 'construct a building', also 'strengthen', hence to 'build up' morally or spiritually.

edifying ▶**adjective** providing moral or intellectual instruction: *edifying literature.*

■[with negative] used to express one's disapproval of or distaste for something: *pasty-faced Englishmen waving their Union Jacks are never an edifying sight.*

– DERIVATIVES **edifyingly** adverb.

Edinburgh /ˈɛdɪnbərə/ the capital of Scotland, lying on the southern shore of the Firth of Forth; pop. 421,200 (1991). The city grew up round the 11th-century castle built by Malcolm III on a rocky ridge which dominates the landscape.

Edinburgh, Duke of see **PHILIP, PRINCE**.

Edinburgh Festival (also **Edinburgh International Festival**) an international festival of the arts held annually in Edinburgh since 1947. In addition to the main programme a flourishing fringe festival has developed.

Edison /ˈɛdɪs(ə)n/, Thomas (Alva) (1847–1931), American inventor. He took out the first of more than a thousand patents at the age of 21. His inventions include automatic telegraph systems, the carbon microphone for telephones, the phonograph, and the carbon filament lamp.

edit ▶**verb** (**edited, editing**) [with obj.] (often **be edited**) prepare (written material) for publication by correcting, condensing, or otherwise modifying it: *Volume I was edited by J. Johnson.*

■choose material for (a film or radio or television programme) and arrange it to form a coherent whole: [as adj. **edited**] *edited highlights of the match.* ■be editor of (a newspaper or magazine). ■(**edit something out**) remove unnecessary or inappropriate words, sounds, or scenes from a text, film, or radio or television programme.

▶**noun** a change or correction made as a result of editing.

– ORIGIN late 18th cent. (as a verb): partly a back-formation from **EDITOR**, reinforced by French *éditer* 'to edit' (from *édition* 'edition').

editable ▶**adjective** (of text or software) in a format that can be edited by the user.

edition ▶**noun** a particular form or version of a published text: *a paperback edition.*

■a particular version of a text maintained by regular revision: *a first edition.* ■the total number of copies of a book, newspaper, or other published material issued at one time. ■a particular version or instance of a regular programme or broadcast: *the Monday edition will be repeated on Wednesday afternoons.* ■[in sing.] figurative a person or thing that is compared to another as a copy to an original: *the building was a simpler edition of its namesake.*

– ORIGIN late Middle English: from French *édition*, from Latin *editio(n-)*, from *edere* 'put out', from *e-* (variant of *ex-*) 'out' + *dare* 'give'.

editio princeps /ɪˌdɪʃɪəʊ ˈprɪnsɛps/ ▶**noun** (pl. **editiones principes** /ɪˌdɪʃɪˌəʊniːz ˈprɪnsɪpiːz/) the first printed edition of a book.

– ORIGIN Latin, from *editio(n-)* 'edition' and *princeps* 'chief, leader' (from *primus* 'first').

editor ▶**noun** a person who is in charge of and determines the final content of a text, particularly a newspaper or magazine: *the editor of* The Times | *a sports editor.*

■a person who works for a publishing company, commissioning or preparing material for publication. ■a computer program enabling the user to alter or rearrange online text.

– DERIVATIVES **editorship** noun.

– ORIGIN mid 17th cent.: from Latin, 'producer (of games), publisher', from *edit-* 'produced, put forth', from the verb *edere*.

editorial ▶**adjective** of or relating to the commissioning or preparing of material for publication: *the editorial team.*

■of or relating to the part of a newspaper or magazine which contains news, information, or comment as opposed to advertising.

▶**noun** a newspaper article written by or on behalf of an editor which gives an opinion on a topical issue.

■[mass noun] the parts of a newspaper or magazine which are not advertising.

– DERIVATIVES **editorialist** noun, **editorially** adverb.

editorialize (also **-ise**) ▶**verb** [no obj.] (of a newspaper, editor, or broadcasting organization) make comments or express opinions rather than just report the news.

editress ▶**noun** dated or humorous a female editor.

editrix (also **editrice**) ▶**noun** another term for **EDITRESS**.

– ORIGIN early 20th cent.: from **EDITOR** + **-TRIX**; the variant *editrice* from French *éditrice*.

edit suite ▶ **noun** a room containing equipment for electronically editing video-recorded material.

-edly ▶ **suffix** (forming adverbs) in a manner characterized by the action expressed by the formative verb: *agitatedly* | *repeatedly*.

Edmonton /ˈɛdmənt(ə)n/ the capital of Alberta, Canada; pop. 703,070 (1991).

Edmund /ˈɛdmənd/ the name of two kings of England:
▪Edmund I (921–46), reigned 939–46. After succeeding Athelstan Edmund spent much of his reign trying to win his northern lands back from Norse control.
▪Edmund II (*c.*980–1016), son of Ethelred the Unready, reigned 1016; known as **Edmund Ironside**. Edmund led the resistance to Canute's forces in 1015, but was eventually defeated and forced to divide the kingdom with Canute. On Edmund's death Canute became king of all England.

Edmund, St (*c.*1175–1240), English churchman and teacher, Archbishop of Canterbury 1234–40; born *Edmund Rich*. He was the last Primate of all England. Feast day, 16 November.

Edmund Campion, St see **CAMPION**[2].

Edmund the Martyr, St (*c.*841–70), king of East Anglia 855–70. After the defeat of his army by the invading Danes in 870, tradition holds that he was captured and shot with arrows for refusing to reject the Christian faith or to share power with his pagan conqueror. Feast day, 20 November.

Edo[1] former name for **TOKYO**.

Edo[2] /ˈɛdəʊ/ ▶ **noun** (pl. same or **-os**) **1** a member of a people inhabiting the district of Benin in Nigeria.
2 [mass noun] the Benue-Congo language of this people, with about 1 million speakers.
▶ **adjective** of or relating to this people or their language.
– ORIGIN the name of Benin City in Edo.

Edomite /ˈiːdəmʌɪt/ ▶ **adjective** of or relating to Edom, an ancient region south of the Dead Sea, or its people.
▶ **noun** a member of an ancient people living in Edom in biblical times, traditionally believed to be descended from Esau.

EDP ▶ **abbreviation for** electronic data processing.

EDT ▶ **abbreviation for** Eastern Daylight Time (see **EASTERN TIME**).

EDTA Chemistry ▶ **abbreviation for** ethylenediamine tetra-acetic acid, a crystalline acid with a strong tendency to form chelates with metal ions.
• Chem. formula: $(CH_2COOH)_2NCH_2CH_2N(CH_2COOH)_2$.

educate /ˈɛdjʊkeɪt/ ▶ **verb** [with obj.] (often **be educated**) give intellectual, moral, and social instruction to (someone, especially a child), typically at a school or university: *she was educated at a boarding school*.
▪provide or pay for instruction for (one's child), especially at a school. ▪ give (someone) training in or information on a particular field: [with obj. and infinitive] *the need to educate people to conserve water* | *a plan to educate the young* **on** *the dangers of drug-taking*.
– DERIVATIVES **educability** noun, **educable** adjective, **educative** adjective, **educator** noun.
– ORIGIN late Middle English: from Latin *educat-* 'led out', from the verb *educare*, related to *educere* 'lead out' (see **EDUCE**).

educated ▶ **adjective** having been educated: [in combination] *a Harvard-educated lawyer*.
▪resulting from or having had a good education: *educated tastes*.

educated guess ▶ **noun** a guess based on knowledge and experience and therefore likely to be correct.

education ▶ **noun** [mass noun] the process of receiving or giving systematic instruction, especially at a school or university: *a course of education*.
▪the theory and practice of teaching: *colleges of education*. ▪ [count noun] a body of knowledge acquired while being educated: *his education is encyclopedic and eclectic*. ▪ information about or training in a particular field or subject: *health education*. ▪ (**an education**) figurative an enlightening experience: *it would have been an education to have been in the House when the Minister spoke*.
– DERIVATIVES **educationist** noun.
– ORIGIN mid 16th cent.: from Latin *educatio(n-)*, from the verb *educare* (see **EDUCATE**).

educational ▶ **adjective** of or relating to the provision of education: *children with special educational needs*.
▪intended or serving to educate or enlighten.
– DERIVATIVES **educationalist** noun, **educationally** adverb.

educe /ɪˈdjuːs/ ▶ **verb** [with obj.] formal bring out or develop (something latent or potential): *out of love obedience is to be educed*.
▪infer (something) from data: *more information can be educed from these statistics*.
– DERIVATIVES **educible** adjective, **eduction** noun.
– ORIGIN late Middle English: from Latin *educere* 'lead out', from *e-* (variant of *ex-*) 'out' + *ducere* 'to lead'.

edulcorate /ɪˈdʌlkəreɪt/ ▶ **verb** [with obj.] rare make (something) more acceptable or palatable.
– DERIVATIVES **edulcoration** noun.
– ORIGIN mid 17th cent.: from medieval Latin *edulcorat-* 'sweetened', from the verb *edulcorare*, from Latin *e* (variant of *ex-*) 'out' + *dulcor* 'sweetness'.

edutainment /ˌɛdjʊˈteɪnm(ə)nt/ ▶ **noun** [mass noun] entertainment, especially computer games, with an educational aspect.
– ORIGIN 1980s: blend of **EDUCATION** and **ENTERTAINMENT**.

Edw. ▶ **abbreviation for** Edward.

Edward the name of six kings of England and also one of Great Britain and Ireland and one of the United Kingdom:
▪Edward I (1239–1307), son of Henry III, reigned 1272–1307; known as **the Hammer of the Scots**. His campaign against Prince Llewelyn ended with the annexation of Wales in 1284, but he failed to conquer Scotland, where resistance was led by Sir William Wallace and later Robert the Bruce.
▪Edward II (1284–1327), son of Edward I, reigned 1307–27. In 1314 he was defeated by Robert the Bruce at Bannockburn. In 1326 Edward's wife, Isabella of France, and her lover, Roger de Mortimer, invaded England; Edward was deposed in favour of his son and murdered.
▪Edward III (1312–77), son of Edward II, reigned 1327–77. In 1330 he took control of his kingdom, banishing Isabella and executing Mortimer. He supported Edward de Baliol, the pretender to the Scottish throne, and started the Hundred Years War.
▪Edward IV (1442–83), son of Richard, Duke of York, reigned 1461–83. He became king after defeating the Lancastrian Henry VI. Edward was briefly forced into exile in 1470–1 by the Earl of Warwick but regained his position with victory at Tewkesbury in 1471.
▪Edward V (1470–*c.*1483), son of Edward IV, reigned 1483 but not crowned. Edward and his brother Richard (known as the Princes in the Tower) were probably murdered and the throne was taken by their uncle, Richard III.
▪Edward VI (1537–53), son of Henry VIII, reigned 1547–53. His reign saw the establishment of Protestantism as the state religion.
▪Edward VII (1841–1910), son of Queen Victoria, reigned 1901–10. Although he played little part in government on coming to the throne, his popularity helped revitalize the monarchy.
▪Edward VIII (1894–1972), son of George V, reigned 1936 but not crowned. Edward abdicated eleven months after coming to the throne in order to marry the American divorcee Mrs Wallis Simpson.

Edward, Lake a lake on the border between Uganda and Zaire (Democratic Republic of Congo), linked to Lake Albert by the Semliki River.

Edward, Prince, Edward Antony Richard Louis, Earl of Wessex (b.1964), third son of Elizabeth II.

Edward, Prince of Wales see **BLACK PRINCE**.

Edwardian /ɛdˈwɔːdɪən/ ▶ **adjective** of, relating to, or characteristic of the reign of King Edward VII: *the Edwardian era* | *a fine Edwardian house*.
▶ **noun** a person who lived during this period.

Edwardiana /ɛdˌwɔːdɪˈɑːnə/ ▶ **plural noun** articles, especially collectors' items, from the reign of Edward VII.

Edwards[1], Gareth (Owen) (b.1947), Welsh rugby union player. An international from 1967 to 1978, he was the youngest-ever Welsh captain when appointed in 1968.

Edwards[2], Jonathan (David) (b.1966), English athlete. He won a gold medal in the triple jump in the 1992 World Cup and in 1995 became the first person to break the 18-metre barrier in that event.

Edward the Confessor, St (*c.*1003–66), son of Ethelred the Unready, king of England 1042–66. Famed for his piety, Edward founded Westminster Abbey, where he was eventually buried. Feast day, 13 October.

Edward the Elder (*c.*870–924), son of Alfred the Great, king of Wessex 899–924. His military successes against the Danes made it possible for his son Athelstan to become the first king of all England in 925.

Edward the Martyr, St (*c.*963–78), son of Edgar, king of England 975–8. Edward was faced by a challenge for the throne from supporters of his half-brother, Ethelred, who eventually had him murdered at Corfe Castle in Dorset. Feast day, 18 March.

Edwy /ˈɛdwi/ (also **Eadwig**) (d.959), king of England 955–7. He was probably only 15 years old when he became king; after Mercia and Northumbria renounced him in favour of his brother Edgar, he ruled over only the lands south of the Thames.

ee ▶ **exclamation** northern English form of **OH**.

-ee ▶ **suffix** forming nouns: **1** denoting the person affected directly or indirectly by the action of the formative verb: *employee* | *lessee*.
2 denoting a person described as or concerned with: *absentee* | *patentee*.
3 denoting an object of relatively smaller size: *bootee*.
– ORIGIN from Anglo-Norman French *-é*, from Latin *-atus* (past participial ending). Some forms are anglicized modern French nouns (e.g. *refugee* from *réfugié*).

EEC ▶ **abbreviation for** European Economic Community.

EEG ▶ **abbreviation for** electroencephalogram or electroencephalograph: *EEG recordings*.

eejit /ˈiːdʒɪt/ ▶ **noun** informal Irish and Scottish form of **IDIOT**.

eek ▶ **exclamation** informal used as an expression of alarm, horror, or surprise.

eel ▶ **noun** a snake-like fish with a slender elongated body and poorly developed fins, proverbial for its slipperiness.
• Order Anguilliformes: many families, in particular Anguillidae, which comprises mainly freshwater eels that breed in the sea, including the common *Anguilla anguilla* of Europe and *A. rostrata* of America.
▪used in names of unrelated fishes that resemble the true eels, e.g. **electric eel**, **moray eel**.
– DERIVATIVES **eel-like** adjective, **eely** adjective.
– ORIGIN Old English *ǣl*, of Germanic origin; related to Dutch *aal* and German *Aal*.

Eelam /ˈiːləm/ the proposed homeland of the Tamil people of Sri Lanka, for which the Tamil Tigers separatist group have been fighting since the early 1980s.

eelgrass ▶ **noun** [mass noun] **1** a marine plant with long ribbon-like leaves which grows in European coastal waters.
• *Zostera marina*, family Zosteraceae.
2 North American term for **TAPE-GRASS**.

eelpout /ˈiːlpaʊt/ ▶ **noun** a fish of cool or cold seas, having a broad head with thick lips and an elongated body with the dorsal and anal fins continuous with the tail. Called **POUT**[2] in North America.
• Family Zoarcidae: numerous genera and species, including the widely distributed northern European viviparous blenny (*Zoarces viviparus*).
– ORIGIN Old English *ǣlepūta* (see **EEL**, **POUT**[2]).

eelworm ▶ **noun** a nematode, especially a small soil nematode that can become a serious pest of crops and ornamental plants.

Eem /iːm/ ▶ **noun** [usu. as modifier] Geology the most recent interglacial period of the Pleistocene in northern Europe, preceding the Weichsel glaciation and corresponding to the Ipswichian in Britain.
▪the system of deposits laid down at this time.
– DERIVATIVES **Eemian** adjective & noun.
– ORIGIN early 20th cent.: from the name of a river in the Netherlands.

e'en[1] /iːn/ ▶ **adverb** poetic/literary form of **EVEN**[1].

e'en[2] /iːn/ ▶ **noun** Scottish form of **EVEN**[2].

-een ▶ **suffix** Irish forming diminutive nouns such as *colleen*.
– ORIGIN from the Irish diminutive suffix *-ín*.

eensy /ˈiːnsi/ (also **eensy-weensy**) ▶ **adjective** informal extremely small; tiny.

EEPROM ▶ **noun** Computing a read-only memory whose contents can be erased and reprogrammed using a pulsed voltage.
– ORIGIN acronym from *electrically erasable programmable ROM*.

e'er /ɛː/ poetic/literary ▶ **contraction of** ever.

-eer ▶ **suffix 1** (forming nouns) denoting a person concerned with or engaged in an activity: *auctioneer* | *puppeteer*.
2 (forming verbs) denoting concern or involvement with an activity: *electioneer* | *profiteer*.
– ORIGIN from French *-ier*, from Latin *-arius*; verbs (sense 2) are often back-formations (e.g. *electioneer* from *electioneering*).

eerie /ˈɪəri/ ▶ **adjective** (**eerier**, **eeriest**) strange and frightening: *an eerie green glow in the sky*.
– DERIVATIVES **eerily** adverb [as submodifier] *it was eerily quiet*, **eeriness** noun.
– ORIGIN Middle English (originally northern English and Scots in the sense 'fearful'): probably from Old English *earg* 'cowardly', of Germanic origin; related to German *arg*.

ef- ▶ **prefix** variant spelling of **EX-**[1] assimilated before *f* (as in *efface*, *effloresce*).

EFA ▶ **abbreviation for** essential fatty acid.

eff ▶ **noun** & **verb** Brit. used as a euphemism for 'fuck'.
– PHRASES **eff and blind** informal use vulgar expletives; swear. [ORIGIN: *blind* from its use in vulgar imprecations such as *blind me* (see **BLIMEY**).]
– DERIVATIVES **effing** adjective & adverb.
– ORIGIN 1950s: the letter F represented as a word.

effable /ˈɛfəb(ə)l/ ▶ **adjective** rare able to be described in words.
– ORIGIN early 17th cent.: from Latin *effabilis*, from *effari* 'utter'.

efface /ɪˈfeɪs/ ▶ **verb** [with obj.] erase (a mark) from a surface: *with time, the words are effaced by the frost and the rain* | figurative *his anger was effaced when he stepped into the open air*.
■(**efface oneself**) figurative make oneself appear insignificant or inconspicuous.
– DERIVATIVES **effacement** noun.
– ORIGIN late 15th cent. (in the sense 'pardon or be absolved from (an offence)'): from French *effacer*, from *e-* (from Latin *ex-* 'away from') + *face* 'face'.

effect ▶ **noun 1** a change which is a result or consequence of an action or other cause: *the lethal effects of hard drugs* | [mass noun] *politicians really do have some effect on the lives of ordinary people*
■[mass noun] used to refer to the state of being or becoming operative: *the ban is to* **take effect** *in six months* | *he resigned* **with effect from** *1 June*. ■[mass noun] the extent to which something succeeds or is operative: *wind power can be used to great effect*. ■[with modifier] Physics a physical phenomenon, typically named after its discoverer: *the Renner effect*. ■an impression produced in the mind of a person: *gentle music can have a soothing effect*.
2 (**effects**) the lighting, sound, or scenery used in a play, film, or broadcast: *the production relied too much on spectacular effects*.
3 (**effects**) personal belongings: *the insurance covers personal effects*.
▶ **verb** [with obj.] cause (something) to happen; bring about: *the prime minister effected a great many policy changes*.
– PHRASES **for effect** in order to impress people: *I suspect he's controversial for effect*. **in effect** in operation; in force: *a moratorium in effect since 1985 has been lifted*. ■used to convey that something is in practice the case, even if it is not formally acknowledged to be so: *the minister's powers allow him, in effect, to ban programmes*. **to the effect that** used to refer to the general sense or meaning of something written or spoken: *some comments to the effect that my essay was a little light on analysis*. **to that effect** having that result, purpose, or meaning: *she thought it a foolish rule and put a notice to that effect in a newspaper*.
– ORIGIN late Middle English: from Old French, or from Latin *effectus*, from *efficere* 'accomplish', from *ex-* 'out, thoroughly' + *facere* 'do, make'. Sense 3, 'personal belongings', arose from the obsolete sense 'something acquired on completion of an action'.

USAGE For an explanation of the difference between **effect** and **affect**, see **usage** at **AFFECT**[1].

effective ▶ **adjective 1** successful in producing a desired or intended result: *effective solutions to environmental problems*.
■(especially of a law or policy) operative: *the agreements will be* **effective from** *November*.
2 [attrib.] fulfilling a specified function in fact, though not formally acknowledged as such: *the companies were under effective Soviet control*.
■assessed according to actual rather than face value: *an effective price of £176 million*.
▶ **noun** a soldier fit and available for service.
– DERIVATIVES **effectively** adverb [sentence adverb] *effectively, this means that companies will be able to avoid regulations*, **effectiveness** noun, **effectivity** noun.
– ORIGIN late Middle English: from Latin *effectivus*, from *efficere* 'work out, accomplish' (see **EFFECT**).

effective demand ▶ **noun** Economics the level of demand that represents a real intention to purchase by people with the means to pay.

effective temperature ▶ **noun** Physics the temperature of an object calculated from the radiation it emits, assuming black-body behaviour.

effector ▶ **noun** Biology an organ or cell that acts in response to a stimulus: [as modifier] *effector cells*.

effectual /ɪˈfɛktʃʊəl, -tjʊəl/ ▶ **adjective** (typically of something inanimate or abstract) successful in producing a desired or intended result; effective: *tobacco smoke is the most effectual protection against the midge*.
■Law (of a legal document) valid or binding.
– DERIVATIVES **effectuality** noun, **effectually** adverb, **effectualness** noun.
– ORIGIN late Middle English: from medieval Latin *effectualis*, from Latin *effectus* (see **EFFECT**).

effectuate /ɪˈfɛktʃʊeɪt, -tjʊ-/ ▶ **verb** [with obj.] formal put into force or operation: *school choice would effectuate a transfer of power from government to individuals*.
– DERIVATIVES **effectuation** noun.
– ORIGIN late 16th cent.: from medieval Latin *effectuat-* 'caused to happen', from the verb *effectuare*, from Latin *effectus* (see **EFFECT**).

effeminate /ɪˈfɛmɪnət/ ▶ **adjective** derogatory (of a man) having or showing characteristics regarded as typical of a woman; unmanly.
– DERIVATIVES **effeminacy** noun, **effeminately** adverb.
– ORIGIN late Middle English: from Latin *effeminatus*, past participle of *effeminare* 'make feminine', from *ex-* (expressing a change of state) + *femina* 'woman'.

effendi /ɛˈfɛndi/ ▶ **noun** (pl. **effendis**) a man of high education or social standing in an eastern Mediterranean or Arab country.
■historical a title of respect or courtesy in Turkey.
– ORIGIN early 17th cent.: from Turkish *efendi*, from modern Greek *aphentēs*, from Greek *authentēs* 'lord, master'.

efferent /ˈɛf(ə)r(ə)nt/ ▶ **adjective** Physiology conducted or conducting outwards or away from something (for nerves, the central nervous system; for blood vessels, the organ supplied). The opposite of **AFFERENT**.
– ORIGIN mid 19th cent.: from Latin *efferent-* 'carrying out', from the verb *efferre*, from *ex-* 'out' + *ferre* 'carry'.

effervesce /ˌɛfəˈvɛs/ ▶ **verb** [no obj.] (of a liquid) give off bubbles.
■figurative (of a person) be vivacious and enthusiastic.
– ORIGIN early 18th cent.: from Latin *effervescere*, from *ex-* 'out, up' + *fervescere* 'begin to boil' (from *fervere* 'be hot, boil').

effervescent ▶ **adjective** (of a liquid) giving off bubbles; fizzy.
■figurative (of a person or their behaviour) vivacious and enthusiastic.
– DERIVATIVES **effervescence** noun.
– ORIGIN late 17th cent.: from Latin *effervescent-* 'boiling up', from the verb *effervescere* (see **EFFERVESCE**).

effete /ɪˈfiːt/ ▶ **adjective** (of a person) affected, over-refined, and ineffectual: *effete trendies from art college*.
■no longer capable of effective action: *the authority of an effete aristocracy began to dwindle*.
– DERIVATIVES **effeteness** noun.
– ORIGIN early 17th cent. (in the sense 'no longer fertile, past bearing young'): from Latin *effetus* 'worn out by bearing young', from *ex-* 'out' + *fetus* 'breeding'; related to **FETUS**.

efficacious /ˌɛfɪˈkeɪʃəs/ ▶ **adjective** formal (typically of something inanimate or abstract) successful in producing a desired or intended result; effective: *this treatment was efficacious in some cases*.
– DERIVATIVES **efficaciously** adverb, **efficaciousness** noun.
– ORIGIN early 16th cent.: from Latin *efficax*, *efficac-* (from *efficere* 'accomplish': see **EFFECT**) + **-IOUS**.

efficacy /ˈɛfɪkəsi/ ▶ **noun** [mass noun] formal the ability to produce a desired or intended result: *there is little information on the efficacy of this treatment*.
– ORIGIN early 16th cent.: from Latin *efficacia*, from *efficax*, *efficac-* (see **EFFICACIOUS**).

efficiency ▶ **noun** (pl. **-ies**) [mass noun] the state or quality of being efficient: *greater energy efficiency*.
■[count noun] an action designed to achieve this: *the reforms will lead to efficiencies and savings*. ■[count noun] technical the ratio of the useful work performed by a machine or in a process to the total energy expended or heat taken in.
– ORIGIN late 16th cent. (in the sense 'the fact of being an efficient cause'): from Latin *efficientia*, from *efficere* 'accomplish' (see **EFFECT**).

efficient ▶ **adjective** (especially of a system or machine) achieving maximum productivity with minimum wasted effort or expense: *fluorescent lamps are efficient at converting electricity into light*.
■(of a person) working in a well-organized and competent way: *an efficient administrator*. ■[in combination] preventing the wasteful use of a particular resource: *an energy-efficient heating system*.
– DERIVATIVES **efficiently** adverb.
– ORIGIN late Middle English (in the sense 'making, causing', usually in **EFFICIENT CAUSE**): from Latin *efficient-* 'accomplishing', from the verb *efficere* (see **EFFECT**). The current sense dates from the late 18th cent.

efficient cause ▶ **noun** Philosophy an agent that brings a thing into being or initiates a change.

effigy /ˈɛfɪdʒi/ ▶ **noun** (pl. **-ies**) a sculpture or model of a person: *a tomb effigy of Eleanor of Aquitaine*.
■a roughly made model of a particular person that is made in order to be damaged or destroyed as a protest or expression of anger: *the minister was* **burned in effigy**.
– ORIGIN mid 16th cent.: from Latin *effigies*, from *effingere* 'to fashion (artistically)', from *ex-* 'out' + *fingere* 'to shape'.

effleurage /ˌɛfləːˈrɑːʒ/ ▶ **noun** [mass noun] a form of massage involving a repeated circular stroking movement made with the palm of the hand.
▶ **verb** [with obj.] massage with such a circular stroking movement: *effleurage the shoulders and press gently*.
– ORIGIN late 19th cent.: from French, from *effleurer* 'skim the surface, stroke lightly', literally 'remove the flower or 'outer beauty' of (something)'.

effloresce /ˌɛfləˈrɛs/ ▶ **verb** [no obj.] **1** (of a substance) lose moisture and turn to a fine powder on exposure to air.
■(of salts) come to the surface of brickwork, rock, or other material and crystallize there. ■(of a surface) become covered with salt particles.
2 reach an optimum stage of development: *simple concepts that* **effloresce into** *testable conclusions*.
– DERIVATIVES **efflorescence** noun, **efflorescent** adjective.
– ORIGIN late 18th cent.: from Latin *efflorescere*, from *e-* (variant of *ex-*) 'out' + *florescere* 'begin to bloom' (from *florere* 'to bloom', from *flos*, *flor-* 'flower').

effluence /ˈɛflʊəns/ ▶ **noun** a substance that flows out from something.
■[mass noun] the action of flowing out.
– ORIGIN late Middle English: from medieval Latin *effluentia*, from Latin *effluere* 'flow out', from *ex-* 'out' + *fluere* 'to flow'.

effluent ▶ **noun** [mass noun] liquid waste or sewage discharged into a river or the sea: *industrial effluent* | [count noun] *contamination with trade effluents*.
– ORIGIN late Middle English (in the adjective sense 'flowing out'): from Latin *effluent-* 'flowing out', from the verb *effluere* (see **EFFLUENCE**). The noun dates from the mid 19th cent.

effluvium /ɪˈfluːvɪəm/ ▶ **noun** (pl. **effluvia** /-vɪə/) an unpleasant or harmful odour, secretion, or discharge: *smoke and effluvia from factory chimneys*.
– ORIGIN mid 17th cent.: from Latin, from *effluere*: 'flow out'.

efflux /ˈɛflʌks/ ▶ **noun** [mass noun] technical the flowing out of a particular substance or particle.
■material flowing out in this way.

– ORIGIN mid 16th cent.: from medieval Latin *effluxus*, from *effluere* 'flow out'.

effluxion /ɪˈflʌkʃ(ə)n/ ▶ **noun** [mass noun] **1** Law the passing of time, in particular when leading to the expiry of an agreement or contract.
2 archaic the action of flowing out.
– ORIGIN early 17th cent.: from French, or from late Latin *effluxio(n-)*, from *effluere* 'flow out'.

effort ▶ **noun** a vigorous or determined attempt: *in an effort to reduce inflation, the government increased interest rates.*
■ the result of an attempt: *he was a keen gardener, winning many prizes for his efforts.* ■ [mass noun] strenuous physical or mental exertion: *the doctor spared no effort in helping my father.* ■ technical a force exerted by a machine or in a process. ■ [with modifier] the activities of a group of people with a common purpose: *the war effort.*
– DERIVATIVES **effortful** adjective, **effortfully** adverb.
– ORIGIN late 15th cent.: from French, from Old French *esforcier*, based on Latin *ex-* 'out' + *fortis* 'strong'.

effortless ▶ **adjective** requiring no physical or mental exertion.
■ achieved with admirable ease: *her effortless sense of style.*
– DERIVATIVES **effortlessly** adverb, **effortlessness** noun.

effrontery /ɪˈfrʌnt(ə)ri/ ▶ **noun** [mass noun] insolent or impertinent behaviour: *one juror* **had the effrontery to** *challenge the coroner's decision.*
– ORIGIN late 17th cent.: from French *effronterie*, based on late Latin *effrons*, *effront-* 'shameless, barefaced', from *ex-* 'out' + *frons* 'forehead'.

effulgent /ɪˈfʌldʒ(ə)nt/ ▶ **adjective** poetic/literary shining brightly; radiant.
■ (of a person or their expression) emanating joy or goodness.
– DERIVATIVES **effulgence** noun, **effulgently** adverb.
– ORIGIN mid 18th cent.: from Latin *effulgent-* 'shining brightly', from the verb *effulgere*, from *ex-* 'out' + *fulgere* 'to shine'.

effuse ▶ **verb** /ɪˈfjuːz/ [with obj.] give off (a liquid, light, smell, or quality).
■ [no obj.] talk in an unrestrained, excited manner: *this was the type of material that they effused about.*
– ORIGIN late Middle English: from Latin *effusus*, past participle of *effundere* 'pour out', from *ex-* 'out' + *fundere* 'pour'.

effusion ▶ **noun** an instance of giving off something such as a liquid, light, or smell: *a massive effusion of poisonous gas* | [mass noun] *he studied the rates of effusion of gases.*
■ Medicine an escape of fluid into a body cavity. ■ an act of talking or writing in an unrestrained or heartfelt way: *literary effusions.*
– ORIGIN late Middle English: from Latin *effusio(n-)*, from *effundere* 'pour out' (see **EFFUSE**).

effusive ▶ **adjective** **1** showing or expressing feelings of gratitude, pleasure, or approval in an unrestrained or heartfelt manner: *an effusive welcome.*
2 Geology (of igneous rock) poured out when molten and later solidified.
■ of or relating to the eruption of large volumes of molten rock: *effusive volcanism.*
– DERIVATIVES **effusively** adverb, **effusiveness** noun.

Efik /ˈɛfɪk/ ▶ **noun** (pl. same) **1** a member of a people of southern Nigeria.
2 [mass noun] the Benue-Congo language of this people, closely related to Ibibio. It is used as a lingua franca and has about 3.5 million speakers.
▶ **adjective** of or relating to this people or their language.
– ORIGIN the name in Efik.

EFL ▶ **abbreviation for** English as a foreign language.

eft /ɛft/ ▶ **noun** dialect a newt.
■ Zoology the juvenile stage of a newt.
– ORIGIN Old English *efeta*, of unknown origin. Compare with **NEWT**.

EFTA ▶ **abbreviation for** European Free Trade Association.

EFTPOS /ˈɛftpɒz/ ▶ **abbreviation for** electronic funds transfer at point of sale.

e.g. ▶ **abbreviation** for example.
– ORIGIN from Latin *exempli gratia* 'for the sake of example'.

egad /ɪˈgad/ ▶ **exclamation** archaic expressing surprise, anger, or affirmation.
– ORIGIN late 17th cent.: representing earlier *A God.*

egalitarian /ɪˌgalɪˈtɛːrɪən/ ▶ **adjective** of, relating to, or believing in the principle that all people are equal and deserve equal rights and opportunities: *a fairer, more egalitarian society.*
▶ **noun** a person who advocates or supports such a principle.
– DERIVATIVES **egalitarianism** noun.
– ORIGIN late 19th cent.: from French *égalitaire*, from *égal* 'equal', from Latin *aequalis* (see **EQUAL**).

Egbert /ˈɛgbət/ (d.839), king of Wessex 802–39. In 825 he won a decisive victory that temporarily brought Mercian supremacy to an end and foreshadowed the supremacy that Wessex later secured over all England.

Eger /ˈɛgə/ a spa town in the north of Hungary, noted for the 'Bull's Blood' red wine produced in the surrounding region; pop. 63,365 (1993).

egg[1] ▶ **noun** **1** an oval or round object laid by a female bird, reptile, fish, or invertebrate, usually containing a developing embryo. The eggs of birds are enclosed in a chalky shell, while those of reptiles are in a leathery membrane.
■ an infertile egg, typically of the domestic hen, used for food. ■ Biology the female reproductive cell in animals and plants; an ovum. ■ a thing resembling a bird's egg in shape: *chocolate eggs.* ■ Architecture a decorative oval moulding, used alternately with triangular figures: [as modifier] *egg and dart moulding.*
2 [with adj.] informal, dated a person possessing a specified quality: *the biography portrays him as a thoroughly bad egg.*
– PHRASES **don't put all your eggs in one basket** proverb don't risk everything on the success of one venture. **go suck an egg** [as imperative] N. Amer. informal used as an expression of anger or scorn. **kill the goose that lays the golden eggs** destroy a reliable and valuable source of income. [ORIGIN: with allusion to one of Aesop's fables.] **lay an egg** N. Amer. informal be completely unsuccessful; fail badly. **with egg on one's face** informal appearing foolish or ridiculous: *don't underestimate this team, or you'll be left with egg on your face.*
– DERIVATIVES **eggless** adjective.
– ORIGIN Middle English (superseding earlier *ey*, from Old English *ǣg*): from Old Norse.

egg[2] ▶ **verb** [with obj.] (**egg someone on**) urge or encourage someone to do something foolish or risky.
– ORIGIN Middle English: from Old Norse *eggja* 'incite'.

egg-and-spoon race ▶ **noun** a race, typically run by children, in which each runner has to hold an egg balanced in a spoon.

eggar /ˈɛgə/ ▶ **noun** a large brownish moth which is often active during the day. The caterpillars typically bear irritant hairs and make an egg-shaped cocoon.
• Many species in the family Lasiocampidae. See **OAK EGGAR**.
– ORIGIN early 18th cent.: probably from **EGG**[1] + **-ER**[1].

egg beater ▶ **noun** a kitchen utensil used for beating ingredients such as eggs or cream.
■ N. Amer. informal a helicopter.

egg-bound ▶ **adjective** (of a hen) unable through weakness or disease to expel its eggs.

eggbutt snaffle /ˈɛgbʌt/ ▶ **noun** Riding a jointed snaffle bit, the rings of which are hinged to the mouthpiece.

egg cream ▶ **noun** US a drink consisting of milk and soda water, flavoured with syrup.

egg cup ▶ **noun** a small cup for holding a boiled egg upright while it is being eaten.

egg custard ▶ **noun** [mass noun] a custard made with milk and eggs, typically sweetened and baked.

egg-eating snake (also **egg-eater**) ▶ **noun** an Old World snake which swallows birds' eggs. It has weak teeth and the shells are broken by saw-like projections inside the gullet.
• Subfamily Dasypeltinae, family Colubridae: genus *Dasypeltis* (of Africa, in particular the widespread *D. scabra*), and *Elachistodon westermanni* (of India).

egger ▶ **noun** a collector of birds' eggs.

egghead ▶ **noun** informal a person who is highly academic or studious and very knowledgeable in a particular area.
– ORIGIN by analogy with a bald head.

egg-nog (Brit. also **egg-flip**) ▶ **noun** [mass noun] a drink consisting of hot or cold beer, cider, wine, or spirit mixed with beaten egg and milk.

eggplant ▶ **noun** chiefly N. Amer. another term for **AUBERGINE**.

egg roll ▶ **noun** N. Amer. a Chinese-style snack similar to a spring roll, consisting of diced meat or prawns and shredded vegetables encased in a dough made with egg and deep-fried.

eggs and bacon (also **egg and bacon**) ▶ **noun** [mass noun] any of a number of plants which have yellow flowers with orange, red, or brown markings, supposedly suggestive of eggs and bacon, in particular:
• bird's-foot trefoil. • a shrubby Australian bush plant (*Bossiaea* and other genera, family Leguminosae).

eggs Benedict ▶ **plural noun** a dish consisting of poached eggs and sliced ham on toasted muffins, covered with hollandaise sauce.

eggshell ▶ **noun** the thin, hard outer layer of an egg, especially a hen's egg.
■ used in similes and metaphors to refer to the fragile nature of something: *the truck would crush his car like an eggshell.* ■ (also **eggshell paint**) an oil-based paint that dries with a slight sheen: *the woodwork was painted in eggshell* | [as modifier] *an eggshell finish.* ■ [as modifier] (of china) of extreme thinness and delicacy: *eggshell porcelains.*

egg tempera ▶ **noun** [mass noun] an emulsion of pigment and egg yolk, used in tempera painting.

egg timer ▶ **noun** a device for measuring the time required to cook a boiled egg, traditionally a sealed glass container with a narrow neck in the middle through which, when the flask is inverted, sand flows for a fixed amount of time.

egg tooth ▶ **noun** a hard white protuberance on the beak or jaw of an embryo bird or reptile that is used for breaking out of the shell and is later lost.

egg white ▶ **noun** the clear, viscous substance round the yolk of an egg that turns white when cooked or beaten. Also called **ALBUMEN**.

eggy[1] ▶ **adjective** rich in or covered with egg: *many white wines go passably with eggy dishes.*

eggy[2] ▶ **adjective** Brit. informal annoyed; irritated.
– ORIGIN 1930s: from the verb **EGG**[2] + **-Y**[1].

eglantine /ˈɛgləntʌɪn/ ▶ **noun** another term for **SWEETBRIAR**.
– ORIGIN Middle English: from Old French *eglantine*, from Provençal *aiglentina*, based on Latin *acus* 'needle' or *aculeus* 'prickle'.

EGM ▶ **abbreviation** for extraordinary general meeting.

Egmont, Mount /ˈɛgmɒnt/ a volcanic peak in North Island, New Zealand, rising to a height of 2,518 m (8,260 ft). Maori name **TARANAKI**.

ego /ˈiːgəʊ, ˈɛ-/ ▶ **noun** (pl. **-os**) a person's sense of self-esteem or self-importance: *a boost to my ego.*
■ Psychoanalysis the part of the mind that mediates between the conscious and the unconscious and is responsible for reality testing and a sense of personal identity. Compare with **ID** and **SUPEREGO**. ■ Philosophy (in metaphysics) a conscious thinking subject.
– DERIVATIVES **egoless** adjective.
– ORIGIN early 19th cent.: from Latin, literally 'I'.

egocentric /ˌɛgə(ʊ)ˈsɛntrɪk, iː-/ ▶ **adjective** thinking only of oneself, without regard for or appreciation of the feelings or desires of others; self-centred: *he is childishly egocentric.*
■ centred in or arising from a person's own individual existence or perspective: *egocentric spatial perception.*
▶ **noun** an egocentric person.
– DERIVATIVES **egocentrically** adverb, **egocentricity** noun, **egocentrism** noun.
– ORIGIN early 20th cent.: from **EGO**, on the pattern of words such as *geocentric.*

ego-ideal ▶ **noun** Psychoanalysis (in Freudian theory) the part of the mind which imposes on itself concepts of ideal behaviour developed from parental and social standards.
■ (in general use) an idealized conception of oneself.

egoism /ˈɛgəʊɪz(ə)m, ˈiː-/ ▶ **noun** [mass noun] Ethics an ethical theory that treats self-interest as the foundation of morality.
■ another term for **EGOTISM**.
– DERIVATIVES **egoist** noun, **egoistic** adjective, **egoistical** adjective, **egoistically** adverb.
– ORIGIN late 18th cent.: from French *égoïsme* and modern Latin *egoismus*, from Latin *ego* 'I'.

egomania /ɛɡə(ʊ)ˈmeɪnɪə, iː-/ ▶ **noun** [mass noun] obsessive egotism or self-centredness.
– DERIVATIVES **egomaniac** noun, **egomaniacal** adjective.

ego-psychology ▶ **noun** [mass noun] Psychology a system of psychoanalytic developmental psychology concerned especially with personality.
– DERIVATIVES **ego-psychologist** noun.

egotism /ˈɛɡətɪz(ə)m, ˈiː-/ ▶ **noun** [mass noun] the practice of talking and thinking about oneself excessively because of an undue sense of self-importance: *in his arrogance and egotism, he underestimated Gill.*
– DERIVATIVES **egotist** noun, **egotistic** adjective, **egotistical** adjective, **egotistically** adverb, **egotize** (also **-ise**) verb.
– ORIGIN early 18th cent.: from French *égoïste*, from Latin *ego* 'I'.

ego trip ▶ **noun** informal an activity done in order to increase one's sense of self-importance: *driving that car was the biggest ego trip I'd ever had.*

egregious /ɪˈɡriːdʒəs/ ▶ **adjective 1** outstandingly bad; shocking: *egregious abuses of copyright.*
2 archaic remarkably good.
– DERIVATIVES **egregiously** adverb, **egregiousness** noun.
– ORIGIN mid 16th cent. (in sense 2): from Latin *egregius* 'illustrious', literally 'standing out from the flock', from *ex-* 'out' + *grex, greg-* 'flock'. The derogatory sense (late 16th cent.) probably arose as an ironical use.

egress /ˈiːɡrɛs/ ▶ **noun** [mass noun] the action of going out of or leaving a place: *direct means of access and egress for passengers.*
■ [count noun] a way out: *a narrow egress.* ■ Astronomy another term for **EMERSION**.
▶ **verb** [with obj.] chiefly US go out of or leave (a place): *they'd egress the area by heading south-west.*
– ORIGIN mid 16th cent.: from Latin *egressus* 'gone out', from the verb *egredi*, from *ex-* 'out' + *gradi* 'to step'.

egressive /ɪˈɡrɛsɪv/ ▶ **adjective** Phonetics (of a speech sound) produced using the normal outward-flowing airstream. Compare with **INGRESSIVE**.

egret /ˈiːɡrɪt, ˈɛ-/ ▶ **noun** a heron with mainly white plumage, having long plumes in the breeding season.
• Genus *Egretta* (and *Bubulcus*), family Ardeidae: several species.
– ORIGIN Middle English: from Old French *aigrette*, from Provençal *aigreta*, from the Germanic base of **HERON**.

Egypt /ˈiːdʒɪpt/ a country in NE Africa bordering on the Mediterranean Sea; pop. 53,087,000 (est. 1991); official language, Arabic; capital, Cairo.

The population of Egypt is concentrated chiefly along the fertile valley of the River Nile, the rest of the country being largely desert. Egypt's history spans 5,000 years: the ancient kingdoms of Upper and Lower Egypt were ruled successively by thirty-one dynasties, which may be divided into the Old Kingdom, the Middle Kingdom, and the New Kingdom. Egypt was a centre of Hellenistic culture and then a Roman province before coming under Islamic rule and then becoming part of the Ottoman Empire. Modern Egypt became independent in 1922. From 1958 to 1961 Egypt was united with Syria as the United Arab Republic, a title it retained until 1971. Wars with Israel were fought in 1967 (the Six Day War) and 1973 (the Yom Kippur or October War); the countries signed a peace treaty in 1979.

Egyptian ▶ **adjective** of or relating to Egypt or its people.
■ of or relating to Egyptian antiquities: *a large Egyptian collection was sold at Sotheby's.* ■ of or relating to the language of ancient Egypt.
▶ **noun 1** a native of ancient or modern Egypt, or a person of Egyptian descent.
2 [mass noun] the Afro-Asiatic language used in ancient Egypt, attested from *c.*3000 BC. It is represented in its oldest stages by hieroglyphic inscriptions and in its latest form by Coptic; it has been replaced in modern use by Arabic.
– DERIVATIVES **Egyptianization** noun, **Egyptianize** (also **-ise**) verb.

Egyptian black ▶ **noun** [mass noun] another term for **BASALT** (stoneware pottery).

Egyptian cobra ▶ **noun** a large nocturnal African cobra with a thick body and large head. Also called **ASP**.
• *Naja haje*, family Elapidae.

Egyptian goose ▶ **noun** a large African goose which has a dark patch around the eye, pink bill and legs, and either reddish-brown or greyish-brown upper parts.
• *Alopochen aegyptiacus*, family Anatidae.

Egyptian lotus ▶ **noun** see **LOTUS** (sense 1).

Egyptian mongoose ▶ **noun** a mongoose occurring over much of Africa and parts of SW Asia and Iberia, noted for its destruction of crocodile eggs. Also called **ICHNEUMON**.
• *Herpestes ichneumon*, family Herpestidae.

Egyptian plover ▶ **noun** a plover-like African bird of the courser family, with a striking pattern of black and white over a mainly bluish back and buff-coloured underparts. Also called **CROCODILE BIRD**.
• *Pluvianus aegyptius*, family Glareolidae.

Egyptian vulture ▶ **noun** a small white vulture with black wing tips, common in much of southern Eurasia and Africa.
• *Neophron percnopterus*, family Accipitridae.

Egyptology /ˌiːdʒɪpˈtɒlədʒi/ ▶ **noun** [mass noun] the study of the language, history, and culture of ancient Egypt.
– DERIVATIVES **Egyptological** adjective, **Egyptologist** noun.

eh ▶ **exclamation** used to represent a sound made in speech in a variety of situations, in particular to ask for something to be repeated or explained or to elicit agreement: *'Eh? What's this?'* | *'Let's hope so, eh?'*
– ORIGIN natural utterance: first recorded in English in the mid 16th cent.

Ehrenburg /ˈɛːrənbəːɡ/, Ilya (Grigorevich) (1891–1967), Russian novelist and journalist. He became famous during the Second World War for his anti-German propaganda in *Pravda* and *Red Star*. His novels include *The Thaw* (1954), a work criticizing Stalinism.

Ehrlich /ˈɛːlɪx, German ˈeːrlɪç/, Paul (1854–1915), German medical scientist. One of the founders of modern immunology and chemotherapy, he developed techniques for staining specific tissues, believing that a disease organism could be destroyed by an appropriate magic bullet. The effective treatment of syphilis in 1911 proved his theories.

-eian /ɪən/ ▶ **suffix** forming adjectives and nouns corresponding to nouns ending in *-ey* or *-y* (such as *Bodleian* corresponding to *Bodley*).

Eichmann /ˈʌɪxmən, German ˈaɪçman/, (Karl) Adolf (1906–62), German Nazi administrator who was responsible for administering the concentration camps. In 1960 he was traced by Israeli agents and executed after trial in Israel.

eicosapentaenoic acid /ˌʌɪkɒsəˌpɛntiːˈnəʊɪk/ ▶ **noun** [mass noun] Chemistry a polyunsaturated fatty acid found especially in fish oils. In humans it is a metabolic precursor of prostaglandins.
• Chem. formula: $C_{19}H_{29}COOH$.
– DERIVATIVES **eicosapentaenoate** noun.

Eid /iːd/ (also **Id**) ▶ **noun** a Muslim festival, in particular:
■ (in full **Eid ul-Fitr** /ˌiːdʊlˈfɪtrə/) the feast marking the end of the fast of Ramadan. ■ (in full **Eid ul-Adha** /ˌiːdʊlˈɑːdə/) the festival marking the culmination of the annual pilgrimage to Mecca and commemorating the sacrifice of Abraham.
– ORIGIN from Arabic *'īd* 'feast', from Aramaic.

eider /ˈʌɪdə/ ▶ **noun** (also **eider duck**) (pl. same or **eiders**) a northern sea duck, of which the male has mainly black-and-white plumage with a coloured head, and the brown female has soft down feathers which are used to line the nest.
• Genus *Somateria* (and *Polysticta*), family Anatidae: four species, in particular the **common eider** (*S. mollissima*).
■ (also **eider down**) [mass noun] small, soft feathers from the breast of the female eider duck.
– ORIGIN late 17th cent.: from Icelandic *æthur*, from Old Norse *æthr*.

eiderdown ▶ **noun** chiefly Brit. a quilt filled with down (originally from the eider) or some other soft material.

eidetic /ʌɪˈdɛtɪk/ ▶ **adjective** Psychology relating to or denoting mental images having unusual vividness and detail, as if actually visible.
▶ **noun** a person able to form or recall eidetic images.
– DERIVATIVES **eidetically** adverb.
– ORIGIN 1920s: coined in German from Greek *eidētikos*, from *eidos* 'form'.

eidolon /ʌɪˈdəʊlɒn/ ▶ **noun** (pl. **eidolons** or **eidola** /-lə/) **1** chiefly US an idealized person or thing.
2 archaic a spectre or phantom.
– ORIGIN early 19th cent.: from Greek *eidōlon*, from *eidos* 'form'.

eidos /ˈʌɪdɒs/ ▶ **noun** [mass noun] Anthropology the distinctive expression of the cognitive or intellectual character of a culture or social group.
– ORIGIN 1930s: from Greek, literally 'form, type, or idea', partly in contrast to **ETHOS**.

Eiffel /ˈʌɪf(ə)l, French ɛfɛl/, Alexandre Gustave (1832–1923), French engineer, best known as the designer and builder of the Eiffel Tower and architect of the inner structure of the Statue of Liberty.

Eiffel Tower a wrought-iron structure erected in Paris for the World Exhibition of 1889. With a height of 300 metres (984 ft), it was the tallest man-made structure for many years.

eigen- /ˈʌɪɡ(ə)n/ ▶ **combining form** Mathematics & Physics proper; characteristic: *eigenfunction.*
– ORIGIN from the German adjective *eigen* 'own'.

eigenfrequency ▶ **noun** (pl. **-ies**) Mathematics & Physics one of the natural resonant frequencies of a system.

eigenfunction ▶ **noun** Mathematics & Physics each of a set of independent functions which are the solutions to a given differential equation.

eigenstate ▶ **noun** Physics a quantum-mechanical state corresponding to an eigenvalue of a wave equation.

eigenvalue ▶ **noun** Mathematics & Physics **1** each of a set of values of a parameter for which a differential equation has a non-zero solution (an eigenfunction) under given conditions.
2 any number such that a given matrix minus that number times the identity matrix has zero determinant.

eigenvector ▶ **noun** Mathematics & Physics a vector which when operated on by a given operator gives a scalar multiple of itself.

Eiger /ˈʌɪɡə/ a mountain peak in the Bernese Alps in central Switzerland, which rises to 3,970 m (13,101 ft).

Eigg /ɛɡ/ an island of the Inner Hebrides, off the west coast of Scotland to the south of Skye.

eight ▶ **cardinal number 1** equivalent to the product of two and four; one more than seven, or two less than ten; 8: *a committee of eight members* | *eight were acquitted* | *eight of them were unemployed.* (Roman numeral: **viii** or **VIII**.)
■ a group or unit of eight people or things: *the win placed Canada closer to the final eight.* ■ eight years old: *children as young as eight.* ■ eight o'clock: *the play is to begin at eight.* ■ short for **FIGURE OF EIGHT**. ■ a size of garment or other merchandise denoted by eight. ■ a playing card with eight pips. ■ an eight-oared rowing boat or its crew.
2 (**the Eight**) a group of American realist painters who exhibited together in 1908, united by a concern to involve painting with the realities of contemporary, especially urban, life. The dominant member of the group was Robert Henri.
– PHRASES **have one over the eight** Brit. informal have one drink too many.
– ORIGIN Old English *ehta, eahta*, of Germanic origin; related to Dutch and German *acht*, from an Indo-European root shared by Latin *octo* and Greek *oktō*.

eight ball ▶ **noun** chiefly N. Amer. **1** (also **eight-ball pool**) [mass noun] a variety of the game of pool.
■ [count noun] the black ball, numbered eight, in such a game.
2 informal a portion of an illegal drug weighing an eighth of an ounce (3.54 g).
– PHRASES **behind the eight ball** informal at a disadvantage.

eighteen ▶ **cardinal number** equivalent to the product of two and nine; one more than seventeen, or eight more than ten; 18: *she wrote eighteen novels* | *out of sixty batches checked, eighteen were incorrect* | *eighteen of the guests were gathered.* (Roman numeral: **xviii** or **XVIII**.)
■ a set or team of eighteen individuals. ■ eighteen years old: *he was barely eighteen.* ■ a size of garment or other merchandise denoted by eighteen. ■ (**18**) Brit. (of a film) classified as suitable for people of 18 years and over.
– DERIVATIVES **eighteenth** ordinal number.
– ORIGIN Old English *e(a)htatēne* (see **EIGHT**, **-TEEN**).

eighteenmo ▶ **noun** (pl. **-os**) another term for **OCTODECIMO**.

eightfold ▶ **adjective** eight times as great or as numerous: *an eightfold increase in expenditure.*
■ having eight parts or elements: *an eightfold shape.*
▶ **adverb** by eight times; to eight times the number or amount: *claims have grown eightfold in ten years.*

eightfold path Buddhism the path to nirvana, comprising eight aspects in which an aspirant must become practised. See **BUDDHISM**.

eighth ▶ **ordinal number** constituting number eight in a sequence; 8th: *in the eighth century | the eighth of September | seven men admitted conspiracy, an eighth admitted assisting an offender.*
■ (**an eighth/one eighth**) each of eight equal parts into which something is or may be divided: *an eighth of an inch.* ■ the eighth finisher or position in a race or competition: *she finished eighth of the eleven runners.*
– DERIVATIVES **eighthly** adverb.

eighthman ▶ **noun** Rugby, S. African a number-eight forward.

eighth note ▶ **noun** Music, chiefly N. Amer. a quaver.

eights ▶ **plural noun** a race for eight-oared rowing boats: *he twice rowed in the university trial eights.*

eightsome (also **eightsome reel**) ▶ **noun** a lively Scottish dance for eight people.

8vo ▶ **abbreviation** for octavo.

eighty ▶ **cardinal number** (pl. **-ies**) equivalent to the product of eight and ten; ten less than ninety; 80: *eighty miles north | a buffet for eighty | eighty of the nurses fled.* (Roman numeral: **lxxx** or **LXXX**.)
■ (**eighties**) the numbers from 80 to 89, especially the years of a century or of a person's life: *his grandmother was in her eighties.* ■ eighty years old: *he was over eighty at the time.* ■ eighty miles an hour: *roaring down the highway doing eighty.*
– DERIVATIVES **eightieth** ordinal number, **eightyfold** adjective & adverb.
– ORIGIN Old English *hunde(a)htatig*, from *hund* (of uncertain origin) + *e(a)hta* 'eight' + *-tig* (see **-TY**[2]); the first element was lost early in the Middle English period.

Eijkman /'eɪkmən/, Christiaan (1858–1930), Dutch physician. Eijkman's work resulted in a simple cure for the disease beriberi and led to the discovery of the vitamin thiamine. Nobel Prize for Physiology or Medicine (1929).

Eilat /eɪ'lat/ (also **Elat**) the southernmost town in Israel, a port and resort at the head of the Gulf of Aqaba; pop. 19,500 (est. 1982). Founded in 1949 near the ruins of biblical Elath, it is Israel's only outlet to the Red Sea.

eina /'eɪnɑː/ S. African ▶ **noun** [mass noun] pain, trouble, or difficulty: *first aid without the eina.*
■ [count noun] a pain or wound: *have you got an eina in your leg?*
▶ **exclamation** used as an expression of pain or distress.
– ORIGIN Afrikaans, perhaps from Khoikhoi *llé*, interjection expressing pain, + *llná*, interjection expressing surprise, or perhaps from a nasalized pronunciation of Nama *llei*, also an interjection.

Eindhoven /'ʌɪnd,həʊv(ə)n/ a city in the south of the Netherlands; pop. 192,900 (1991). The city is a major producer of electrical and electronic goods.

Einfühlung /'ʌɪn,fuːləŋ, German 'aɪn,fyːlʊŋ/ ▶ **noun** [mass noun] empathy.
– ORIGIN German, from *ein-* 'into' + *Fühlung* 'feeling'.

einkorn /'ʌɪnkɔːn/ ▶ **noun** [mass noun] an old kind of wheat with small bearded ears and spikelets that each contain one slender grain, used as fodder in prehistoric times but now rarely grown. Compare with **EMMER**, **SPELT**.
• *Triticum monococcum*, family Gramineae.
– ORIGIN early 20th cent.: from German, from *ein* 'one' + *Korn* 'seed'.

Einstein /'ʌɪnstʌɪn/, Albert (1879–1955), German-born American theoretical physicist, founder of the theory of relativity.
■ [as noun **an Einstein**] a genius.

> Einstein is often regarded as the greatest scientist of the 20th century. In 1905 he published his special theory of relativity and in 1915 he succeeded in incorporating gravitation in his general theory of relativity, which was vindicated when one of its predictions was observed during the solar eclipse of 1919. However, Einstein searched without success for a unified field theory embracing electromagnetism, gravitation, relativity, and quantum mechanics. He influenced the decision to build an atom bomb but after the war he spoke out passionately against nuclear weapons.

– DERIVATIVES **Einsteinian** adjective.

einsteinium /ʌɪn'stʌɪnɪəm/ ▶ **noun** [mass noun] the chemical element of atomic number 99, a radioactive metal of the actinide series. Einsteinium does not occur naturally and was discovered in 1953 in debris from the first hydrogen bomb explosion. (Symbol: **Es**)
– ORIGIN 1950s: from the name of Albert **EINSTEIN** + **-IUM**.

Einthoven /'ʌɪnt,həʊv(ə)n/, Willem (1860–1927), Dutch physiologist. He devised the first electrocardiograph, through which he was able to identify specific muscular contractions in the heart.

Eire /'ɛːrə/ the Gaelic name for Ireland, the official name of the Republic of Ireland from 1937 to 1949.

Eirene /ʌɪ'riːni/ Greek Mythology the goddess of peace. Roman equivalent **PAX**.

eirenic ▶ **adjective** variant spelling of **IRENIC**.

eirenicon /ʌɪ'riːnɪkɒn/ (also **irenicon**) ▶ **noun** formal a proposal made as a means of achieving peace.
– ORIGIN early 17th cent. (as *irenicon*): from Greek *eirēnikon*, neuter of *eirēnikos* 'promoting peace', from *eirēnē* 'peace'. Compare with **IRENIC**.

Eisenhower /'ʌɪz(ə)n,haʊə/, Dwight David (1890–1969), American general and Republican statesman, 34th President of the US 1953–61; known as **Ike**. In the Second World War he was Supreme Commander of Allied Expeditionary Forces in western Europe 1943–5. As President, he adopted a hard line towards communism both in his domestic and foreign policy.

Eisenstadt /'ʌɪz(ə)n,ʃtat/ a city in eastern Austria, capital of the state of Burgenland; pop. 10,500 (1991).

Eisenstein /'ʌɪz(ə)n,stʌɪn/, Sergei (Mikhailovich) (1898–1948), Soviet film director, born in Latvia. He is chiefly known for *The Battleship Potemkin* (1925), a commemoration of the Russian Revolution of 1905 celebrated for its pioneering use of montage.

eisteddfod /ʌɪ'stɛdvəd, Welsh ʌɪ'stɛðvɒd/ ▶ **noun** (pl. **eisteddfods** or **eisteddfodau** /-'vɒdʌɪ/) a competitive festival of music and poetry in Wales, in particular the annual National Eisteddfod.
– DERIVATIVES **eisteddfodic** /-'vɒdɪk/ adjective.
– ORIGIN Welsh, literally 'session', from *eistedd* 'sit'.

Eiswein /'ʌɪsvʌɪn/ ▶ **noun** (pl. **Eisweine** /-nə/ or **Eisweins**) [mass noun] wine made from ripe grapes picked while covered with frost.
– ORIGIN from German, from *Eis* 'ice' + *Wein* 'wine'.

either /'ʌɪðə, 'iː-/ ▶ **conjunction** & **adverb** **1** used before the first of two (or occasionally more) alternatives that are being specified (the other being introduced by 'or'): *either I accompany you to your room or I wait here | available in either black or white.*
2 [adverb, with negative] used to indicate a similarity or link with a statement just made: *You don't like him, do you? I don't either | it won't do any harm, but won't really help either.*
■ for that matter; moreover (used to add information): *I was too tired to go. And I couldn't have paid my way, either.*
▶ **determiner** & **pronoun** one or the other of two people or things: [as determiner] *there were no children of either marriage* | [as pronoun] *they have a mortgage which will be repaid if* **either of** *them dies.*
■ [determiner] each of two: *the road was straight with fields of grass on either side.*
– PHRASES **either way** whichever of two given alternatives is the case: *I'm not sure whether he is trying to be clever or controversial, but either way, such writing smacks of racism.*
– ORIGIN Old English *ǣgther*, contracted form of *ǣg(e)hwæther*, of Germanic origin; ultimately related to **AYE**[1] and **WHETHER**.

> **USAGE** In good English writing style, it is important that **either** and **or** are correctly placed so that the structures following each word balance and mirror each other. Thus, sentences such as ***either** I accompany you **or** I wait here* and *I'm going to buy* **either** *a new camera **or** a new video* are correct, whereas sentences such as ***either** I accompany you **or** John* and *I'm **either** going to buy a new camera **or** a video* are not well-balanced sentences and should not be used in written English.

either/or ▶ **noun** [usu. as modifier] an unavoidable choice between alternatives: *an either/or situation.*

eiusdem generis ▶ **adjective** variant spelling of **EJUSDEM GENERIS**.

ejaculate ▶ **verb** /ɪ'dʒakjʊleɪt/ **1** [no obj.] (of a man or male animal) eject semen from the body at the moment of sexual climax.
2 [with direct speech] dated say something quickly and suddenly: *'That will do!' he ejaculated.*
▶ **noun** /ɪ'dʒakjʊlət/ [mass noun] semen that has been ejected from the body.
– DERIVATIVES **ejaculation** noun, **ejaculator** noun, **ejaculatory** /ɪ'dʒakjʊlət(ə)ri/ adjective.
– ORIGIN late 16th cent.: from Latin *ejaculat-* 'darted out', from the verb *ejaculari*, from *e-* (variant of *ex-*) 'out' + *jaculari* 'to dart' (from *jaculum* 'dart, javelin', from *jacere* 'to throw').

eject ▶ **verb** [with obj.] (often **be ejected**) force or throw (something) out, typically in a violent or sudden way: *many types of rock are* **ejected from** *volcanoes as solid, fragmentary material.*
■ [no obj.] (of a pilot) escape from an aircraft by being explosively propelled out of it: *he flew to open sea, put the plane in a nosedive, and ejected.* ■ compel (someone) to leave a place: *angry supporters were forcibly* **ejected from** *the court.* ■ dismiss (someone), especially from political office: *he was* **ejected from** *office in July.* ■ emit; give off: *plants utilize carbon dioxide in the atmosphere that animals eject* | [as adj. **ejected**] *ejected electrons.*
– DERIVATIVES **ejection** noun.
– ORIGIN late Middle English: from Latin *eject-* 'thrown out', from the verb *eicere*, from *e-* (variant of *ex-*) 'out' + *jacere* 'to throw'.

ejecta /ɪ'dʒɛktə/ ▶ **plural noun** [often treated as sing.] chiefly Geology & Astronomy material that is forced or thrown out, especially as a result of volcanic eruption, meteoritic impact, or stellar explosion.
– ORIGIN late 19th cent.: from Latin, 'things thrown out', neuter plural of *ejectus* 'thrown out', from *eicere* (see **EJECT**).

ejection seat ▶ **noun** a device that causes the ejection of a pilot from an aircraft, used in an emergency.

ejective /ɪ'dʒɛktɪv/ Phonetics ▶ **adjective** denoting a type of consonant in some languages (e.g. Hausa) produced by sudden release of pressure from the glottis.
▶ **noun** an ejective consonant.

ejectment ▶ **noun** [mass noun] Law, chiefly historical the action or process of evicting a tenant from property: *the landlord shall serve a* **writ in ejectment**.
■ the action or process in which a person evicted from property seeks to recover possession and damages: *he brought an* **action in ejectment** *against the rector.*

ejector ▶ **noun** a device that causes something to be removed or to drop out.

ejector seat ▶ **noun** another term for **EJECTION SEAT**.

ejido /ɛ'hiːdəʊ/ ▶ **noun** (pl. **-os**) (in Mexico) a piece of land farmed communally under a system supported by the state.
– ORIGIN Mexican Spanish, from Spanish, denoting common land on the road leading out of the village.

ejusdem generis /eɪ,(j)ʊsdɛm 'dʒɛnərɪs/ (also **eiusdem**) ▶ **adjective** & **adverb** Law of or as the same kind.
– ORIGIN Latin.

Ekaterinburg /jɛ,katə'riːnbəːg/ variant spelling of **YEKATERINBURG**.

Ekaterinodar /jə,katə'riːnədɑː/ variant spelling of **YEKATERINODAR**.

Ekaterinoslav /jə,katə'riːnəslɑːf/ variant spelling of **YEKATERINOSLAV**.

ekdam /ɛk'dʌm/ ▶ **adverb** Indian informal completely; totally: *his bravado was ekdam finished.*
– ORIGIN from Hindi *ek* 'one' + Urdu *dam* 'breath'.

eke[1] /iːk/ ▶ **verb** [with obj.] (**eke something out**) make an amount or supply of something last longer by using or consuming it frugally: *the remains of yesterday's stew could be eked out to make another meal.*
■ manage to support oneself or make a living with difficulty: *many petty traders barely eked out a living.*
– ORIGIN Old English *ēacian*, *ēcan* (in the sense 'increase'), of Germanic origin; related to Old Norse *auka*.

eke[2] /iːk/ ▶ **adverb** archaic term for **ALSO**.
– ORIGIN Old English, of Germanic origin.

ekka /'ɛkə/ ▶ **noun** Indian a small one-horse vehicle.
– ORIGIN from Hindi *ikkā*, from Sanskrit *eka* 'one'.

Ekman /'ɛkmən/, Vagn Walfrid (1874–1954), Swedish oceanographer. He recognized the importance of the Coriolis effect on ocean currents, showing that it can be responsible for surface water moving at an angle to the prevailing wind direction.

El ▶ **noun** (**the El**) (in the US) an elevated railway or section of railway, especially that in Chicago.
▪a train running on such a railway.

-el ▶ **suffix** variant spelling of **-LE**[2].

El Aaiún /ˌɛl ʌɪˈuːn/ Arabic name for **LA'YOUN**.

elaborate ▶ **adjective** /ɪˈlab(ə)rət/ involving many carefully arranged parts or details; detailed and complicated in design and planning: *elaborate security precautions | elaborate wrought-iron gates.*
▪(of an action) lengthy and exaggerated: *he made an elaborate pretence of yawning.*
▶ **verb** /ɪˈlabəreɪt/ **1** [with obj.] develop or present (a theory, policy, or system) in detail: *the key idea of the book is expressed in the title and elaborated in the text.*
▪[no obj.] add more detail concerning what has already been said: *he would not* **elaborate on** *his news.*
2 [with obj.] Biology (of a natural agency) produce (a substance) from its elements or simpler constituents.
– DERIVATIVES **elaborately** adverb, **elaborateness** noun, **elaboration** noun, **elaborative** adjective, **elaborator** noun.
– ORIGIN late 16th cent. (in the sense 'produced by effort of labour', also in sense 2 of the verb): from Latin *elaborat-* 'worked out', from the verb *elaborare*, from *e-* (variant of *ex-*) 'out' + *labor* 'work'.

Elagabalus /ˌɛləˈɡabələs/ variant spelling of **HELIOGABALUS**.

elaichi /ɪˈlʌɪtʃi/ ▶ **noun** Indian term for **CARDAMOM**.
– ORIGIN from Hindi *ilāycī*.

El Alamein, Battle of /ɛl ˈaləmeɪn/ a battle of the Second World War fought in 1942 at El Alamein in Egypt, 90 km (60 miles) west of Alexandria. The German Afrika Korps under Rommel was halted in its advance towards the Nile by the British 8th Army under Montgomery, giving a decisive British victory.

Elam /ˈiːlam/ an ancient state in SW Iran, established in the 4th millennium BC. Susa was one of its chief cities.

Elamite ▶ **noun** **1** a native or inhabitant of ancient Elam.
2 [mass noun] the agglutinative language spoken in ancient Elam from the 3rd millennium to the 4th century BC, of which a few records in pictographic and cuneiform script survive.
▶ **adjective** of or relating to the ancient Elamites or their language.

elan /eɪˈlɒ̃, eɪˈlan/ ▶ **noun** [mass noun] energy, style, and enthusiasm: *they performed with uncommon elan onstage.*
– ORIGIN mid 19th cent.: from French *élan*, from *élancer* 'to dart', from *é-* 'out' + *lancer* 'to throw'.

eland /ˈiːlənd/ ▶ **noun** a spiral-horned African antelope which lives in open woodland and grassland. It is the largest of the antelopes.
• Genus *Tragelaphus*, family Bovidae: the **giant eland** (*T. derbianus*) and the **common eland** (*T. oryx*).
– ORIGIN late 18th cent.: via Afrikaans from Dutch, 'elk', from obsolete German *Elend*, from Lithuanian *élnis*.

elapse ▶ **verb** [no obj.] (of time) pass or go by: *weeks elapsed before anyone was charged with the attack.*
– ORIGIN late 16th cent. (in the sense 'slip away'): from Latin *elaps-* 'slipped away', from the verb *elabi*, from *e-* (variant of *ex-*) 'out, away' + *labi* 'to glide, slip'.

elasipod /ɪˈlasɪpɒd/ ▶ **noun** Zoology an aberrant deep-water sea cucumber that lacks a respiratory tree. Most live on the seabed and have leg-like appendages, while some swim by means of webbed papillae.
• Order Elasipodida, class Holothuroidea.
– ORIGIN late 19th cent.: from modern Latin *Elasipoda*, from Greek *elasmos* 'beaten metal' + *pous, pod-* 'foot'.

elasmobranch /ɪˈlazmə(ʊ)braŋk/ ▶ **noun** Zoology a cartilaginous fish of a group that comprises the sharks, rays, and skates. Compare with **SELACHIAN**.
• Subclass Elasmobranchii, class Chondrichthyes.
– ORIGIN late 19th cent.: from modern Latin *Elasmobranchii* (plural), from Greek *elasmos* 'beaten metal' + *brankhia* 'gills'.

elasmosaur /ɪˈlazmə(ʊ)sɔː/ ▶ **noun** a Cretaceous plesiosaur with a long neck shaped like that of a swan.
• Family Elasmosauridae, infraorder Plesiosauria: several genera, including *Elasmosaurus*.
– ORIGIN late 19th cent.: from modern Latin *Elasmosaurus*, from Greek *elasmos* 'beaten metal' + *sauros* 'lizard'.

elastane /ɪˈlasteɪn/ ▶ **noun** [mass noun] an elastic polyurethane material, used especially for hosiery, underwear, and other close-fitting clothing.
– ORIGIN 1970s: from **ELASTIC** + **-ANE**[2].

elastase /ɪˈlasteɪz/ ▶ **noun** [mass noun] Biochemistry a pancreatic enzyme which digests elastin.
– ORIGIN 1940s: from **ELASTIC** + **-ASE**.

elastic /ɪˈlastɪk/ ▶ **adjective** (of an object or material) able to resume its normal shape spontaneously after contraction, dilatation, or distortion.
▪able to encompass much variety and change; flexible and adaptable: *the definition of nationality is elastic in this cosmopolitan country.* ▪ Economics (of demand or supply) sensitive to changes in price or income: *the labour supply is very elastic.* ▪ Physics (of a collision) involving no decrease of kinetic energy.
▶ **noun** [mass noun] cord, tape, or fabric, typically woven with strips of rubber, which returns to its original length or shape after being stretched.
– DERIVATIVES **elastically** adverb, **elasticity** /ɛlaˈstɪsɪti, iː-, ɪ-/ noun, **elasticize** (also **-ise**) verb.
– ORIGIN mid 17th cent. (originally describing a gas in the sense 'expanding spontaneously to fill the available space'): from modern Latin *elasticus*, from Greek *elastikos* 'propulsive', from *elaunein* 'to drive'.

elasticated ▶ **adjective** chiefly Brit. (of a garment or material) made elastic by the insertion of rubber thread or tape: *trousers with elasticated waists.*

elastic band ▶ **noun** a rubber band.

elastic fibre ▶ **noun** Anatomy a yellowish fibre composed chiefly of elastin and occurring in networks or sheets which give elasticity to tissues in the body.

elastic limit ▶ **noun** Physics the maximum extent to which a solid may be stretched without permanent alteration of size or shape.

elastic modulus ▶ **noun** Physics the ratio of the force exerted upon a substance or body to the resultant deformation.

elastin /ɪˈlastɪn/ ▶ **noun** [mass noun] Biochemistry an elastic, fibrous glycoprotein found in connective tissue.
– ORIGIN late 19th cent.: from **ELASTIC** + **-IN**[1].

elastomer /ɪˈlastəmə/ ▶ **noun** a natural or synthetic polymer having elastic properties, e.g. rubber.
– DERIVATIVES **elastomeric** adjective.
– ORIGIN 1930s: from **ELASTIC** + **-MER**.

Elastoplast /ɪˈlastəplast, -plɑːst/ ▶ **noun** [mass noun] trademark adhesive sticking plaster for covering cuts and wounds.
– ORIGIN 1920s: from a blend of **ELASTIC** and **PLASTER**.

Elat variant spelling of **EILAT**.

elate /ɪˈleɪt/ ▶ **verb** [with obj.] [usu. as adj. **elated**] make (someone) ecstatically happy: *I felt elated at beating Dennis.*
▶ **adjective** archaic in high spirits; exultant or proud: *the ladies returned with elate and animated faces.*
– DERIVATIVES **elatedly** adverb, **elatedness** noun.
– ORIGIN late Middle English (as an adjective): from Latin *elat-* 'raised', from the verb *efferre*, from *ex-* 'out, from' + *ferre* 'to bear'. The verb dates from the late 16th cent.

elation ▶ **noun** [mass noun] great happiness and exhilaration: *Richard's* **elation at** *regaining his health was short-lived.*
– ORIGIN late Middle English: from Old French *elacion*, from Latin *elat-* 'raised', from the verb *efferre* (see **ELATE**).

E-layer ▶ **noun** a layer of the ionosphere able to reflect medium-frequency radio waves.
– ORIGIN 1930s: arbitrary use of the letter E, + **LAYER**.

Elba /ˈɛlbə/ a small island off the west coast of Italy, famous as the place of Napoleon's first exile (1814–15).

Elbasan /ˌɛlbəˈsɑːn/ an industrial town in central Albania; pop. 70,000 (1990).

Elbe /ɛlb, ˈɛlbə/ a river of central Europe, flowing 1,159 km (720 miles) from the Czech Republic through Dresden, Magdeburg, and Hamburg to the North Sea.

El Beqa'a another name for **BEKAA**.

Elbert, Mount /ˈɛlbət/ a mountain in Colorado, to the east of the resort town of Aspen. Rising to 4,399 m (14,431 ft), it is the highest peak in the Rocky Mountains.

elbow ▶ **noun** the joint between the forearm and the upper arm: *she propped herself up on one elbow.*
▪the part of the sleeve of a garment covering the elbow. ▪ a thing resembling an elbow, in particular a piece of piping bent through an angle.
▶ **verb** [with obj. and adverbial] strike (someone) with one's elbow: *one player had elbowed another in the face.*
▪[no obj., with adverbial of direction] move by pushing past people with one's elbows: *people* **elbowed past** *each other to the door | furiously, he* **elbowed his way** *through the crush.* ▪ figurative get rid of or disregard (a person or idea) in a cursory and dismissive way: *the issues which concerned them tended to be elbowed aside by men.*
– PHRASES **at one's elbow** close at hand; nearby. **elbow-to-elbow** very close together. **give someone the elbow** informal reject or dismiss someone in a rough, almost contemptuous manner: *I tried to get her to give him the elbow |* figurative *she decided to give tradition the elbow.* **up to one's elbows in** informal with one's hands plunged in (something): *I was up to my elbows in the cheese-potato mixture.* ▪ figurative deeply involved in (a task or undertaking).
– ORIGIN Old English *elboga, elnboga*, of Germanic origin; related to Dutch *elleboog* and German *Ellenbogen* (see also **ELL**[1], **BOW**[1]).

elbow grease ▶ **noun** [mass noun] informal hard physical work, especially vigorous polishing or cleaning: *nothing would shift it however much elbow grease we used.*

elbow room ▶ **noun** [mass noun] informal adequate space to move or work in.

Elbrus /ɛlˈbruːs/ a peak in the Caucasus mountains, on the border between Russia and Georgia. Rising to 5,642 m (18,481 ft), it is the highest mountain in Europe.

Elburz Mountains /ɛlˈbʊəz/ a mountain range in NW Iran, close to the southern shore of the Caspian Sea. Damavand is the highest peak, rising to 5,604 m (18,386 ft).

Elche /ˈɛltʃeɪ/ a town in the province of Alicante in SE Spain; pop. 181,200 (1991).

el cheapo ▶ **adjective** & **noun** another way of saying **CHEAPO**.
– ORIGIN 1960s: from **CHEAP**, on the pattern of Spanish phrases such as *El Dorado* and *El Greco*.

El Cid, see **CID, EL**.

eld /ɛld/ ▶ **noun** [mass noun] poetic/literary old age.
▪former times; the past.
– ORIGIN Old English *ieldu, eldu*, of Germanic origin; related to **ELDER**[1] and **OLD**.

elder[1] ▶ **adjective** (of one or more out of a group of related or otherwise associated people) of a greater age: *my elder daughter | the elder of the two sons.*
▪(**the Elder**) used to distinguish between related famous people with the same name: *Pitt the Elder | the Elder Pliny.*
▶ **noun** (usu. **elders**) a person of greater age than someone specified: *schoolchildren were no less fascinated than their elders | take a bit of advice from your* **elders and betters**.
▪a person of advanced age. ▪ (often **elders**) a leader or senior figure in a tribe or other group: *a council of village elders.* ▪ an official in the early Christian Church, or of various Protestant Churches and sects.
– DERIVATIVES **eldership** noun.
– ORIGIN Old English *ieldra, eldra*, of Germanic origin; related to German *älter*, also to **ELD** and **OLD**.

elder[2] ▶ **noun** a small tree or shrub with pithy stems, typically having white flowers and bluish-black or red berries.
• Genus *Sambucus*, family Caprifoliaceae: numerous species, in particular the common Eurasian *S. nigra*.
▪used in names of other plants that resemble the elder in leaf or flower, e.g. **ground elder**.
– ORIGIN Old English *ellærn*; related to Middle Low German *ellern, elderne*.

elderberry ▶ **noun** the bluish-black or red berry of the elder, used especially for making jelly or wine.
▪an elder tree or shrub.

Elder Brother ▶ **noun** (pl. **Elder Brethren**) (in the UK) each of the thirteen senior members of Trinity House.

elderflower ▶ **noun** the flower of the elder, used to make wines, cordials, and other drinks.

elder hand ▶ **noun** (in card games for two players, e.g. piquet) the player who is the first to receive a complete hand, i.e. the player dealt to.

elderly ▶ **adjective** (of a person) old or ageing: *elderly*

b but | d dog | f few | g get | h he | j yes | k cat | l leg | m man | n no | p pen | r red | s sit | t top | v voice | w we | z zoo | ʃ she | ʒ decision | θ thin | ð this | ŋ ring | x loch | tʃ chip | dʒ jar

people | [as plural noun **the elderly**] *specialist services for the elderly.*
■(of a machine or similar object) showing signs of age: *a couple of elderly cars.*
– DERIVATIVES **elderliness** noun.

elder statesman ▶ noun a person who is experienced and well-respected, especially a politician.

eldest ▶ adjective (of one out of a group of related or otherwise associated people) of the greatest age; oldest: *Swift left the company to his eldest son, Charles* | *he was the eldest of the three.*
– ORIGIN Old English *ieldest, eldest*, of Germanic origin; related to German *ältest*, also to **ELD** and **OLD**.

eldest hand ▶ noun (in card games for three or more players) the player who is the first to receive a complete hand, usually the player immediately to the left of the dealer.

El Djem /ɛl ˈdʒɛm/ a town in eastern Tunisia, noted for its well-preserved Roman amphitheatre.

El Dorado /ˌɛl dəˈrɑːdəʊ/ the name of a fictitious country or city abounding in gold, formerly believed to exist somewhere in the region of the Orinoco and Amazon Rivers.
■[as noun **an El Dorado** or **eldorado**] (pl. **-os**) a place of great abundance.
– ORIGIN Spanish, literally 'the gilded one'.

eldritch /ˈɛl(d)rɪtʃ/ ▶ adjective weird and sinister or ghostly: *an eldritch screech.*
– ORIGIN early 16th cent. (originally Scots): perhaps related to **ELF**.

Eleanor Cross ▶ noun any of the stone crosses erected by Edward I to mark the stopping places of the cortège that brought the body of his queen, Eleanor of Castile (1246–90), from Nottinghamshire to London in 1290. Three of the twelve crosses survive.

Eleanor of Aquitaine (*c.*1122–1204), daughter of the Duke of Aquitaine, queen of France 1137–52 and of England 1154–89. She was married to Louis VII of France from 1137; in 1152, with the annulment of their marriage, she married the future Henry II of England.

Eleatic /ˌɛlɪˈatɪk/ ▶ adjective of or relating to Elea, an ancient Greek city in SW Italy, or the school of philosophers which flourished there in about the 5th century BC, including Xenophanes, Parmenides, and Zeno.
▶ noun an Eleatic philosopher.
– ORIGIN late 17th cent.: from Latin *Eleaticus*, from *Elea*.

elecampane /ˌɛlɪkamˈpeɪn/ ▶ noun a plant which has yellow daisy-like flowers with long slender petals and bitter aromatic roots that are used in herbal medicine, native to central Asia.
● *Inula helenium*, family Compositae.
– ORIGIN late Middle English: from medieval Latin *enula* (from Greek *helenion* 'elecampane') + *campana* probably meaning 'of the fields', (from *campus* 'field').

elect /ɪˈlɛkt/ ▶ verb [with obj.] (often **be elected**) choose (someone) to hold public office or some other position by voting: *he was* **elected as** *councillor* | *the members who were* **elected to** *the committee* | [with obj. and complement] *they elected him leader.*
■[no obj.] opt for or choose to do something: *members can* **elect for** *a voluntary audit* | [with infinitive] *more people elected to work at home.* ■ Christian Theology (of God) choose (someone) in preference to others for salvation.
▶ adjective [usu. as plural noun **the elect**] (of a person) chosen or singled out: *one of the century's elect.*
■ Christian Theology chosen by God for salvation. ■ [postpositive] elected to or chosen for a position but not yet in office: *the President Elect.*
– DERIVATIVES **electable** adjective.
– ORIGIN late Middle English: from Latin *elect-* 'picked out', from the verb *eligere*, from *e-* (variant of *ex-*) 'out' + *legere* 'to pick'.

election ▶ noun a formal and organized choice by vote of a person for a political office or other position: *the choice of when to hold an election lies with the prime minister* | [mass noun] *he has agreed to* **stand for election.**
■[mass noun] the action of choosing or the fact of being chosen in such a way: *his* **election to** *the House of Representatives.*
– ORIGIN Middle English: via Old French from Latin *electio(n-)*, from *eligere* 'pick out' (see **ELECT**).

electioneer ▶ verb [no obj.] [usu. as noun **electioneering**] (of a politician or political campaigner) take part actively and energetically in the typical activities of an election campaign: *the election will not be lost or won as the result of a few weeks of electioneering.*
▶ noun a campaigning politician during an election.

elective ▶ adjective **1** related to or working by means of election: *an elective democracy.*
■(of a person or office) appointed or filled by election: *he had never held elective office* | *the National Assembly, with 125 elective members.* ■(of a body or position) possessing or giving the power to elect: *powerful Emperors manipulated the elective body.*
2 (of a course of study) chosen by the student rather than compulsory.
■(of surgical or medical treatment) chosen by the patient rather than urgently necessary.
▶ noun chiefly N. Amer. an optional course of study.
– DERIVATIVES **electively** adverb.
– ORIGIN late Middle English: from Old French *electif, -ive*, from late Latin *electivus*, from *elect-* 'picked out', from the verb *eligere* (see **ELECT**).

elective affinity ▶ noun a correspondence with, or feeling of sympathy or attraction towards, a particular idea, attitude, or person.
– ORIGIN mid 18th cent. (as *elective attraction*): originally a technical term for the preferential combination of chemical substances, it was widely used figuratively in the 19th cent., notably by Goethe (in his novel *Die Wahlverwandschaften* 'Elective Affinities') and by Weber (in describing the correspondence between aspects of Protestantism and capitalism).

elective mutism ▶ noun see **MUTISM**.

elector ▶ noun **1** a person who has the right to vote in an election, especially one for members of a national parliament.
■(in the US) a member of the electoral college.
2 [usu. as title] historical a German prince entitled to take part in the election of the Holy Roman Emperor: *the Elector of Brandenburg.*
– DERIVATIVES **electorship** noun.

electoral ▶ adjective of or relating to elections or electors: *electoral reform.*
– DERIVATIVES **electorally** adverb.

electoral college ▶ noun a body of electors chosen or appointed by a larger group.
■(in the US) a body of people representing the states of the US, who formally cast votes for the election of the President and Vice-President.

electoral roll (also **electoral register**) ▶ noun an official list of the people in a district who are entitled to vote in an election.

electorate /ɪˈlɛkt(ə)rət/ ▶ noun **1** [treated as sing. or pl.] all the people in a country or area who are entitled to vote in an election.
2 Austral./NZ the area represented by one Member of Parliament.
■historical the office or territories of a German elector.

Electra /ɪˈlɛktrə/ Greek Mythology the daughter of Agamemnon and Clytemnestra. She persuaded her brother Orestes to kill Clytemnestra and Aegisthus (their mother's lover) in revenge for the murder of Agamemnon.

Electra complex ▶ noun Psychoanalysis old-fashioned term for the Oedipus complex as manifested in young girls.
– ORIGIN early 20th cent.: named after **ELECTRA**.

electress /ɪˈlɛktrɪs/ ▶ noun [usu. as title] historical the wife of a German elector.

electret /ɪˈlɛktrɪt/ ▶ noun Physics a permanently polarized piece of dielectric material, analogous to a permanent magnet.
– ORIGIN late 19th cent.: blend of **ELECTRICITY** and **MAGNET**.

electric /ɪˈlɛktrɪk/ ▶ adjective of, worked by, charged with, or producing electricity: *an electric cooker.*
■figurative having or producing a sudden sense of thrilling excitement: *the atmosphere was electric.*
▶ noun **1** (**electrics**) Brit. the system of electric wiring and parts in a house or vehicle: *there's something wrong with the electrics—the lights are always going out.*
2 (**electric**) an electric train or other vehicle.
– DERIVATIVES **electrically** adverb.
– ORIGIN mid 17th cent.: from modern Latin *electricus*, from Latin *electrum* 'amber', from Greek *ēlektron* (because rubbing amber causes electrostatic phenomena).

electrical ▶ adjective concerned with, operating by, or producing electricity: *an electrical transformer.*
■(of a company or shop) manufacturing or selling electrical appliances.
▶ noun (**electricals**) electrical equipment or circuitry.
■shares in companies manufacturing electrical goods.

electric-arc furnace ▶ noun a furnace which uses an electric arc as a heat source, especially for steel-making.

electric blanket ▶ noun an electrically wired blanket used for heating a bed.

electric blue ▶ noun [mass noun] a steely or brilliant light blue.

electric chair ▶ noun a chair in which convicted criminals are executed by electrocution, especially in parts of the US.

electric eel ▶ noun a large eel-like freshwater fish of South America, using pulses of electricity to kill prey, assist in navigation, and for defence.
● *Electrophorus electricus*, the only member of the family Electrophoridae.

electric eye ▶ noun informal a photoelectric cell operating a relay when the beam of light illuminating it is obscured.

electric fence ▶ noun a fence through which an electric current can be passed, giving an electric shock to any person or animal touching it.

electric field ▶ noun Physics a region around a charged particle or object within which a force would be exerted on other charged particles or objects.

electric fire ▶ noun Brit. an electrically operated incandescent or convector heater, typically a portable one for domestic use.

electric guitar ▶ noun a guitar with a built-in pickup or pickups which convert sound vibrations into electrical signals for amplification.

electric hare ▶ noun see **HARE**.

electrician ▶ noun a person who installs and maintains electrical equipment.

electricity /ˌɪlɛkˈtrɪsɪti, ˌɛl-, ˌiːl-/ ▶ noun [mass noun] a form of energy resulting from the existence of charged particles (such as electrons or protons), either statically as an accumulation of charge or dynamically as a current.
■the supply of electric current to a house or other building for heating, lighting, or powering appliances: *the electricity was back on* | [as modifier] *the regional electricity companies.* ■ figurative a state or feeling of thrilling excitement: *the atmosphere was charged with a dangerous sexual electricity.*

electric organ ▶ noun **1** Music an organ in which the sound is made electrically rather than by pipes.
2 Zoology an organ in certain fishes which is used to produce an electrical discharge for stunning prey, sense the surroundings, or as a defence.

electric ray ▶ noun a sluggish bottom-dwelling marine ray that typically lives in shallow water and can produce an electric shock for the capture of prey and for defence. Also called ***torpedo ray.***
● Family Torpedinidae: several genera, in particular *Torpedo*, and many species.

electric shaver (also **electric razor**) ▶ noun an electrical device for shaving, with oscillating or rotating blades behind a metal guard.

electric shock ▶ noun a sudden discharge of electricity through a part of the body.

electric storm ▶ noun a thunderstorm or other violent disturbance of the electrical condition of the atmosphere.

electrify /ɪˈlɛktrɪfʌɪ/ ▶ verb (**-ies**, **-ied**) [with obj.] charge with electricity; pass an electric current through: [as adj. **electrified**] *an electrified fence.*
■(often **be electrified**) convert (a machine or system, especially a railway line) to the use of electrical power. ■ [often as adj. **electrifying**] figurative cause a sudden sense of thrilling excitement in (someone): *the electrifying effect produced by Coleridge's passionate eloquence.*
– DERIVATIVES **electrification** noun, **electrifier** noun.
– ORIGIN mid 18th cent.: from **ELECTRIC** + **-FY**.

electro /ɪˈlɛktrəʊ/ ▶ noun (pl. **-os**) **1** short for **ELECTROTYPE** or **ELECTROPLATE**.
2 [mass noun] a style of dance music with a fast beat and synthesized backing track.

electro- ▶ combining form of, relating to, or caused

by electricity; involving electricity and ...: *electroconvulsive | electromagnetism*.

electro-acoustic ▶ adjective involving the direct conversion of electrical into acoustic energy or vice versa.
■ (of a guitar) having both a pickup and a reverberating hollow body.
▶ noun an electro-acoustic guitar.

electrocardiogram /ɪˌlɛktrəʊˈkɑːdɪəgram/ ▶ noun Medicine a record or display of a person's heartbeat produced by electrocardiography.

electrocardiograph /ɪˌlɛktrəʊˈkɑːdɪəgrɑːf/ ▶ noun a machine used for electrocardiography.

electrocardiography /ɪˌlɛktrəʊˌkɑːdɪˈɒgrəfi/ (abbrev.: ECG) ▶ noun [mass noun] the measurement of electrical activity in the heart and its recording as a visual trace (on paper or on an oscilloscope screen), using electrodes placed on the skin of the limbs and chest.
– DERIVATIVES **electrocardiographic** adjective.

electrocautery /ɪˌlɛktrəʊˈkɔːtəri/ ▶ noun [mass noun] cautery using a needle or other instrument that is electrically heated.

electrochemistry ▶ noun [mass noun] the branch of chemistry that deals with the relations between electrical and chemical phenomena.
– DERIVATIVES **electrochemical** adjective, **electrochemically** adverb, **electrochemist** noun.

electrochromism /ɪˌlɛktrə(ʊ)ˈkrəʊmɪz(ə)m/ ▶ noun [mass noun] Chemistry the property of certain dyes of changing colour when placed in an electric field.
– DERIVATIVES **electrochromic** adjective.

electrocoagulation /ɪˌlɛktrəʊkəʊˌagjʊˈleɪʃ(ə)n/ ▶ noun [mass noun] the coagulation of blood or other tissues by the local application of an electric current to produce concentrated heat.

electroconvulsive ▶ adjective of or relating to the treatment of mental illness by the application of electric shocks to the brain.

electrocorticogram /ɪˌlɛktrə(ʊ)ˈkɔːtɪkə(ʊ)gram/ ▶ noun Physiology a chart or record of the electrical activity of the brain made using electrodes in direct contact with it.

electrocute ▶ verb [with obj.] (often **be electrocuted**) injure or kill someone by electric shock: *a man was electrocuted on the rail track*.
– DERIVATIVES **electrocution** noun.
– ORIGIN late 19th cent.: from ELECTRO-, on the pattern of *execute*.

electrocyte /ɪˈlɛktrə(ʊ)sʌɪt/ ▶ noun Zoology a modified muscle or nerve cell that generates electricity in the electric organ of certain fishes.

electrode /ɪˈlɛktrəʊd/ ▶ noun a conductor through which electricity enters or leaves an object, substance, or region.
– ORIGIN mid 19th cent.: from ELECTRIC + Greek *hodos* 'way', on the pattern of *anode* and *cathode*.

electrodermal /ɪˌlɛktrə(ʊ)ˈdəːməl/ ▶ adjective of or relating to measurement of the electrical conductivity of the skin, especially as an indicator of someone's emotional responses.

electrodialysis /ɪˌlɛktrəʊdʌɪˈalɪsɪs/ ▶ noun [mass noun] Chemistry dialysis in which the movement of ions is aided by an electric field applied across the semipermeable membrane.

electrodynamics ▶ plural noun [usu. treated as sing.] the branch of mechanics concerned with the interaction of electric currents with magnetic fields or with other electric currents.
– DERIVATIVES **electrodynamic** adjective.

electroencephalogram /ɪˌlɛktrəʊɪnˈsɛf(ə)ləgram, -ˈkɛf-/ ▶ noun a test or record of brain activity produced by electroencephalography.

electroencephalograph /ɪˌlɛktrəʊɪnˈsɛf(ə)ləgrɑːf, -ˈkɛf-/ ▶ noun a machine used for electroencephalography.

electroencephalography /ɪˌlɛktrəʊɪnˌsɛfəˈlɒgrəfi, -ˌkɛf-/ (abbrev.: EEG) ▶ noun [mass noun] the measurement of electrical activity in different parts of the brain and its recording as a visual trace (on paper or on an oscilloscope screen).

electrofish ▶ verb [with obj.] fish (a stretch of water) using electrocution or a weak electric field.

electrogenic /ɪˌlɛktrə(ʊ)ˈdʒɛnɪk/ ▶ adjective Physiology producing a change in the electrical potential of a cell.

electrojet ▶ noun an intense electric current which occurs in a narrow belt in the lower ionosphere, especially in the region of strong auroral displays.

electrokinetic ▶ adjective of or relating to the flow of electricity.

electroless /ɪˈlɛktrəʊlɪs/ ▶ adjective relating to or denoting nickel plating using chemical means, as opposed to electroplating.

electrolier /ɪˌlɛktrəˈlɪə/ ▶ noun a chandelier in which the lights are electrical.
– ORIGIN late 19th cent.: from ELECTRO-, on the pattern of *chandelier*.

electroluminescence /ɪˌlɛktrəʊluːmɪˈnɛs(ə)ns/ ▶ noun [mass noun] Chemistry luminescence produced electrically, especially by the application of a voltage.
– DERIVATIVES **electroluminescent** adjective.

electrolyse /ɪˈlɛktrəlʌɪz/ (US **electrolyze**) ▶ verb [with obj.] subject to or treat by electrolysis.
– DERIVATIVES **electrolyser** noun.
– ORIGIN mid 19th cent.: from ELECTROLYSIS, on the pattern of *analyse*.

electrolysis /ɪˌlɛkˈtrɒlɪsɪs, ˌɛl-/ ▶ noun [mass noun]
1 Chemistry chemical decomposition produced by passing an electric current through a liquid or solution containing ions.
2 the removal of hair roots or small blemishes on the skin by the application of heat using an electric current.
– DERIVATIVES **electrolytic** /ɪˌlɛktrə(ʊ)ˈlɪtɪk/ adjective, **electrolytical** adjective, **electrolytically** adverb.

electrolyte /ɪˈlɛktrəlʌɪt/ ▶ noun a liquid or gel which contains ions and can be decomposed by electrolysis, e.g. that present in a battery.
■ (usu. **electrolytes**) Physiology the ionized or ionizable constituents of a living cell, blood, or other organic matter.
– ORIGIN mid 19th cent.: from ELECTRO- + Greek *lutos* 'released' (from *luein* 'loosen').

electromagnet ▶ noun Physics a soft metal core made into a magnet by the passage of electric current through a coil surrounding it.

electromagnetic ▶ adjective of or relating to the interrelation of electric currents or fields and magnetic fields.
– DERIVATIVES **electromagnetically** adverb.

electromagnetic radiation ▶ noun [mass noun] Physics a kind of radiation including visible light, radio waves, gamma rays, and X-rays, in which electric and magnetic fields vary simultaneously.

electromagnetic spectrum ▶ noun [mass noun] Physics the range of wavelengths or frequencies over which electromagnetic radiation extends.

electromagnetic units ▶ plural noun Physics a largely disused system of electrical units derived primarily from the magnetic properties of electric currents.

electromagnetism ▶ noun [mass noun] the phenomenon of the interaction of electric currents or fields and magnetic fields.
■ the branch of physics concerned with this.

electromechanical /ɪˌlɛktrəʊmɪˈkanɪk(ə)l/ ▶ adjective of, relating to, or denoting a mechanical device which is electrically operated.

electrometer /ɪˌlɛkˈtrɒmɪtə/ ▶ noun Physics an instrument for measuring electrical potential without drawing any current from the circuit.
– DERIVATIVES **electrometric** adjective, **electrometry** noun.

electromotive /ɪˌlɛktrəˈməʊtɪv/ ▶ adjective Physics producing or tending to produce an electric current.

electromotive force (abbrev.: emf) ▶ noun Physics a difference in potential that tends to give rise to an electric current.

electromyogram /ɪˌlɛktrə(ʊ)ˈmʌɪə(ʊ)gram/ ▶ noun Medicine a record or display produced by electromyography.

electromyography /ɪˌlɛktrə(ʊ)mʌɪˈɒgrəfi/ ▶ noun [mass noun] the recording of the electrical activity of muscle tissue, or its representation as a visual display or audible signal, using electrodes attached to the skin or inserted into the muscle.
– DERIVATIVES **electromyograph** noun, **electromyographic** adjective, **electromyographically** adverb.

electron /ɪˈlɛktrɒn/ ▶ noun Physics a stable subatomic particle with a charge of negative electricity, found in all atoms and acting as the primary carrier of electricity in solids.

The electron's mass is about 9×10^{-28}g, 1,836 times less than that of the proton. Electrons orbit the positively charged nuclei of atoms and are responsible for binding atoms together in molecules, as well as for the electrical, thermal, optical, and magnetic properties of solids. Electric currents in metals and in semiconductors consist of a flow of electrons, and light, radio waves, X-rays, and much heat radiation are all produced by accelerating and decelerating electrons.

– ORIGIN late 19th cent.: from ELECTRIC + -ON.

electron beam ▶ noun Physics a stream of electrons in a gas or vacuum.

electron diffraction ▶ noun [mass noun] Physics the diffraction of a beam of electrons by atoms or molecules, used especially for determining crystal structures.

electronegative ▶ adjective **1** Physics electrically negative.
2 Chemistry (of an element) tending to acquire electrons and form negative ions in chemical reactions.
– DERIVATIVES **electronegativity** noun (in sense 2).

electron gun ▶ noun Physics a device for producing a narrow stream of electrons from a heated cathode.

electronic ▶ adjective **1** (of a device) having or operating with the aid of many small components, especially microchips and transistors, that control and direct an electric current: *an electronic calculator | an electronic organ*.
■ (of music) produced by electronic instruments. ■ of or relating to electronics: *a degree in electronic engineering*.
2 of or relating to electrons.
3 relating to or carried out using a computer or other electronic device, especially over a network: *electronic shopping*.
– DERIVATIVES **electronically** adverb.
– ORIGIN early 20th cent.: from ELECTRON + -IC.

electronic flash ▶ noun Photography a flash from a gas-discharge tube, used in high-speed photography.

electronic mail ▶ noun another term for E-MAIL.

electronic organizer ▶ noun a pocket-sized computer used for storing and retrieving information such as addresses and appointments.

electronic publishing ▶ noun [mass noun] the issuing of books and other material in machine-readable form rather than on paper.

electronics ▶ plural noun [usu. treated as sing.] the branch of physics and technology concerned with the design of circuits using transistors and microchips, and with the behaviour and movement of electrons in a semiconductor, conductor, vacuum, or gas: *electronics is seen as a growth industry* | [as modifier] *electronics engineers*.
■ [treated as pl.] circuits or devices using transistors, microchips, and other components.

electronic tagging ▶ noun [mass noun] the attaching of electronic markers to people or goods for monitoring purposes, e.g. to track offenders under house arrest or to deter shoplifters.

electron lens ▶ noun Physics a device for focusing a stream of electrons by means of electric or magnetic fields.

electron microscope ▶ noun Physics a microscope with high magnification and resolution, employing electron beams in place of light and using electron lenses.

electron optics ▶ plural noun [treated as sing.] the branch of physics that deals with the behaviour of electrons and electron beams in magnetic and electric fields.

electron pair ▶ noun **1** Chemistry two electrons occupying the same orbital in an atom or molecule.
2 Physics an electron and a positron produced in a high-energy reaction.

electron spin resonance (abbrev.: ESR) ▶ noun [mass noun] Physics a spectroscopic method of locating electrons within the molecules of a paramagnetic substance.

electron tube ▶ noun Physics an evacuated or gas-filled tube in which a current of electrons flows between electrodes.

electronvolt (abbrev.: **eV**) ▶ **noun** Physics a unit of energy equal to the work done on an electron in accelerating it through a potential difference of one volt.

electro-oculogram /ɪˌlɛktrəʊˈɒkjələ(ʊ)gram/ ▶ **noun** a record produced by electro-oculography.

electro-oculography /ɪˌlɛktrəʊɒkjəˈlɒgrəfi/ ▶ **noun** [mass noun] the measurement of the electrical potential between electrodes placed at points close to the eye, used to investigate eye movements especially in physiological research.
– DERIVATIVES **electro-oculographic** adjective.

electro-optics ▶ **plural noun** [treated as sing.] the branch of science that deals with the effect of electric fields on light and on the optical properties of substances.
– DERIVATIVES **electro-optic** adjective, **electro-optical** adjective.

electro-osmosis ▶ **noun** [mass noun] osmosis under the influence of an electric field.
– DERIVATIVES **electro-osmotic** adjective.

electrophilic /ɪˌlɛktrə(ʊ)ˈfɪlɪk/ ▶ **adjective** Chemistry (of a molecule or group) having a tendency to attract or acquire electrons. Often contrasted with **NUCLEOPHILIC**.
– DERIVATIVES **electrophile** noun.

electrophoresis /ɪˌlɛktrə(ʊ)fəˈriːsɪs/ ▶ **noun** [mass noun] Physics & Chemistry the movement of charged particles in a fluid or gel under the influence of an electric field.
– DERIVATIVES **electrophorese** verb, **electrophoretic** adjective, **electrophoretically** adverb.
– ORIGIN early 20th cent.: from **ELECTRO-** + Greek *phorēsis* 'being carried'.

electrophorus /ˌɪlɛkˈtrɒf(ə)rəs, ɛl-/ ▶ **noun** Physics a device for repeatedly generating static electricity by induction.
– ORIGIN late 18th cent.: from **ELECTRO-** + Greek *-phoros* 'bearing'.

electrophysiology /ɪˌlɛktrəʊfɪzɪˈɒlədʒi/ ▶ **noun** [mass noun] the branch of physiology that deals with the electrical phenomena associated with nervous and other bodily activity.
– DERIVATIVES **electrophysiological** adjective, **electrophysiologically** adverb, **electrophysiologist** noun.

electroplate /ɪˈlɛktrə(ʊ)pleɪt, ɪˌlɛktrə(ʊ)ˈpleɪt/ ▶ **verb** [with obj.] [usu. as noun **electroplating**] coat (a metal object) by electrolytic deposition with chromium, silver, or another metal.
▶ **noun** [mass noun] electroplated articles.
– DERIVATIVES **electroplater** noun.

electroplax /ɪˈlɛktrəʊplaks/ (also **electroplaque** /-plak/) ▶ **noun** Zoology each of a number of flattened plates of protoplasm that make up the electric organ of certain fishes, e.g. the electric eel.

electroplexy /ɪˈlɛktrəplɛksi/ ▶ **noun** [mass noun] Brit., dated electroconvulsive therapy.
– ORIGIN 1950s: from **ELECTRO-** + **APOPLEXY**.

electropolish /ɪˈlɛktrəʊˌpɒlɪʃ/ ▶ **verb** [with obj.] [often as noun **electropolishing**] give a shiny surface to (metal) using electrolysis.

electroporation /ɪˌlɛktrə(ʊ)pəˈreɪʃ(ə)n/ ▶ **noun** [mass noun] Biology the action or process of introducing DNA or chromosomes into bacteria or other cells using a pulse of electricity to open the pores in the cell membranes briefly.
– DERIVATIVES **electroporate** verb.

electropositive ▶ **adjective** 1 Physics electrically positive.
2 Chemistry (of an element) tending to lose electrons and form positive ions in chemical reactions.

electroreception ▶ **noun** [mass noun] the detection by an aquatic animal of electric fields or currents.
– DERIVATIVES **electroreceptor** noun.

electroretinogram /ɪˌlɛktrəʊˈrɛtɪnə(ʊ)gram/ ▶ **noun** a record of the electrical activity of the retina, used in medical diagnosis and research.

electroscope ▶ **noun** Physics an instrument for detecting and measuring electricity, especially as an indication of the ionization of air by radioactivity.
– DERIVATIVES **electroscopic** adjective.

electro-selective pattern (abbrev.: **ESP**) ▶ **noun** Photography a mode of automatic light-metering in a camera which compensates for differences in the brightness of the central and peripheral portions of the image.

electroshock ▶ **adjective** [attrib.] of or relating to medical treatment by means of electric shocks: *electroshock therapy.*

electrostatic ▶ **adjective** Physics of or relating to stationary electric charges or fields as opposed to electric currents.
– ORIGIN mid 19th cent.: from **ELECTRO-** + **STATIC**, on the pattern of *hydrostatic.*

electrostatic precipitator ▶ **noun** a device that removes suspended dust particles from a gas or exhaust by applying a high-voltage electrostatic charge and collecting the particles on charged plates.

electrostatics ▶ **plural noun** [treated as sing.] Physics the study of stationary electric charges or fields as opposed to electric currents.

electrostatic units ▶ **plural noun** a system of units based primarily on the forces between electric charges.

electrosurgery ▶ **noun** [mass noun] surgery using a high-frequency electric current to heat and so cut tissue with great precision.
– DERIVATIVES **electrosurgical** adjective.

electrotechnology ▶ **noun** [mass noun] the science of the application of electricity in technology.
– DERIVATIVES **electrotechnic** adjective, **electrotechnical** adjective, **electrotechnics** noun.

electrotherapy ▶ **noun** [mass noun] the use of electric currents passed through the body to stimulate nerves and muscles, chiefly in the treatment of various forms of paralysis.
– DERIVATIVES **electrotherapeutic** adjective, **electrotherapeutical** adjective, **electrotherapist** noun.

electrothermal ▶ **adjective** Physics of or relating to heat derived from electricity.

electrotype ▶ **verb** [with obj.] [often as noun **electrotyping**] make a copy of (something) by the electrolytic deposition of copper on a mould.
▶ **noun** a copy made in such a way.
– DERIVATIVES **electrotyper** noun.

electrovalent /ɪˌlɛktrə(ʊ)ˈveɪl(ə)nt/ ▶ **adjective** Chemistry (of bonding) resulting from electrostatic attraction between positive and negative ions; ionic.
– DERIVATIVES **electrovalence** noun, **electrovalency** noun.
– ORIGIN 1920s: from **ELECTRO-** + *-valent*, on the pattern of *trivalent.*

electroweak ▶ **adjective** Physics relating to or denoting electromagnetic and weak interactions regarded as manifestations of the same interaction.

electrum /ɪˈlɛktrəm/ ▶ **noun** [mass noun] a natural or artificial alloy of gold with at least 20 per cent of silver, used for jewellery, especially in ancient times.
– ORIGIN late Middle English: via Latin from Greek *ēlektron* 'amber, electrum'.

electuary /ɪˈlɛktjʊ(ə)ri/ ▶ **noun** (pl. **-ies**) archaic a medicinal substance mixed with honey or another sweet substance.
– ORIGIN late Middle English: from late Latin *electuarium*, probably from Greek *ekleikton*, from *ekleikhein* 'lick up'.

eleemosynary /ˌɛliːˈmɒsɪnəri, -ˈmɒz-/ ▶ **adjective** formal of, relating to, or dependent on charity; charitable.
– ORIGIN late 16th cent. (as a noun denoting a place where alms were distributed): from medieval Latin *eleemosynarius*, from late Latin *eleemosyna* 'alms', from Greek *eleēmosunē* 'compassion'(see **ALMS**).

elegant ▶ **adjective** pleasingly graceful and stylish in appearance or manner: *she will look elegant in black | an elegant, comfortable house.*
■(of a scientific theory or solution to a problem) pleasingly ingenious and simple: *the grand unified theory is compact and elegant in mathematical terms.*
– DERIVATIVES **elegance** noun, **elegantly** adverb.
– ORIGIN late 15th cent. (describing a person dressing tastefully): from French, or from Latin *elegans, elegant-*, related to *eligere* 'choose, select' (see **ELECT**).

elegant variation ▶ **noun** [mass noun] the stylistic fault of studiedly finding different ways to denote the same thing in a piece of writing, merely to avoid repetition.

elegiac /ˌɛlɪˈdʒʌɪək/ ▶ **adjective** (especially of a work of art) having a pleasing quality of gentle and wistful mournfulness: *haunting and elegiac poems.*
■(of a poetic metre) used for elegies.
▶ **plural noun** (**elegiacs**) verses in an elegiac metre.
– DERIVATIVES **elegiacally** adverb.
– ORIGIN late 16th cent.: from French *élégiaque*, or via late Latin, from Greek *elegeiakos*, from *elegeia* (see **ELEGY**).

elegiac couplet ▶ **noun** a pair of lines consisting of a dactylic hexameter and a pentameter, especially in Greek and Latin verse.

elegize /ˈɛlɪdʒʌɪz/ (also **-ise**) ▶ **verb** [no obj.] write in a wistfully mournful way about someone or something.
– DERIVATIVES **elegist** noun.

elegy /ˈɛlɪdʒi/ ▶ **noun** (pl. **-ies**) 1 (in modern literature) a poem of serious reflection, typically a lament for the dead.
2 (in Greek and Roman poetry) a poem written in elegiac couplets, as notably by Catullus and Propertius.
– ORIGIN early 16th cent.: from French *élégie*, or via Latin, from Greek *elegeia*, from *elegos* 'mournful poem'.

element ▶ **noun** 1 a part or aspect of something abstract, especially one that is essential or characteristic: *the death had* **all the elements of** *a great tabloid story | there are four elements to the proposal.*
■a small but significant presence of a feeling or abstract quality: *it was the element of danger he loved in flying.* ■ (**elements**) the rudiments of a branch of knowledge: *legal training may include the elements of economics and political science.* ■ [usu. with modifier] (often **elements**) a group of people of a particular kind within a larger group or organization: *extreme right-wing elements in the army.* ■ Mathematics & Logic an entity that is a single member of a set.
2 (also **chemical element**) each of more than one hundred substances that cannot be chemically interconverted or broken down into simpler substances and are primary constituents of matter. Each element is distinguished by its atomic number, i.e. the number of protons in the nuclei of its atoms.
■any of the four substances (earth, water, air, and fire) regarded as the fundamental constituents of the world in ancient and medieval philosophy. ■ one of these substances considered as a person's or animal's natural environment: *for the islanders, the sea is their kingdom, water their element |* figurative *she* **was in her element** *with doctors and hospitals.* ■ (**the elements**) the weather, especially strong winds, heavy rain, and other kinds of bad weather: *there was no barrier against the elements.* ■ (**elements**) (in church use) the bread and wine of the Eucharist.
3 a part in an electric kettle, heater, or cooker which contains a wire through which an electric current is passed to provide heat.
– ORIGIN Middle English (denoting fundamental constituents of the world or celestial objects): via Old French from Latin *elementum* 'principle, rudiment', translating Greek *stoikheion* 'step, component part'.

elemental /ˌɛlɪˈmɛnt(ə)l/ ▶ **adjective** 1 primary or basic: *elemental features from which all other structures are compounded.*
■concerned with chemical elements or other basic components: *elemental analysis.* ■ consisting of a single chemical element; not chemically combined.
2 related to or embodying the powers of nature: *a thunderstorm is the inevitable outcome of battling elemental forces.*
■figurative (of a human emotion or action) having the primitive and inescapable character of a force of nature: *the urge for revenge was too elemental to be ignored.*
▶ **noun** a supernatural entity or force thought to be physically manifested by occult means.
– DERIVATIVES **elementalism** noun.
– ORIGIN late 15th cent.: from medieval Latin *elementalis*, from *elementum* 'principle, rudiment' (see **ELEMENT**).

elementary ▶ **adjective** of or relating to the most rudimentary aspects of a subject: *the six stages take students from elementary to advanced level.*
■easily dealt with; straightforward and uncomplicated: *it's interesting work, although quite a lot of it is elementary.* ■ not decomposable into elements or other primary constituents.
– DERIVATIVES **elementarily** adverb, **elementariness** noun.
– ORIGIN late Middle English (in the sense 'composed of the four elements, earth, air, fire, and water'): from Latin *elementarius*, from *elementum*

'principle, rudiment' (see **ELEMENT**). Current senses dates from the mid 16th cent.

elementary particle ▶ **noun** another term for **PARTICLE** (in sense 1).

elementary school ▶ **noun** N. Amer. a primary school for the first six or eight grades.
■ Brit. historical a school where children were taught between the ages of five and thirteen.

elemi /ˈɛlɪmi/ ▶ **noun** [mass noun] an oleoresin obtained from a tropical tree and used in varnishes, ointments, and aromatherapy.
● This resin is obtained from several trees in the family Burseraceae, in particular *Bursera simaruba* (producing **American elemi**) and *Canarium luzanicum* (producing **Manila elemi**).
– ORIGIN mid 16th cent.: perhaps from Arabic *al-lāmī*.

e

elenchus /ɪˈlɛŋkəs/ ▶ **noun** (pl. **elenchi** /-kʌɪ/) Logic a logical refutation. See also **IGNORATIO ELENCHI**.
■ (also **Socratic elenchus**) [mass noun] the Socratic method of eliciting truth by question and answer, especially as used to refute an argument.
– ORIGIN mid 17th cent. (superseding late Middle English *elench*): via Latin from Greek *elenkhos*.

Eleonora's falcon /ˌɛlɪəˈnɔːrəz/ ▶ **noun** a long-winged falcon that breeds on rocky islands and cliffs in the Mediterranean area, either resembling a dark hobby or with all-black plumage.
● *Falco eleonorae*, family Falconidae.
– ORIGIN mid 19th cent.: named after *Eleonora* of Arborea (*c.*1350–1404), a princess of Sardinia.

elephant ▶ **noun** (pl. same or **elephants**) **1** a heavy plant-eating mammal with a prehensile trunk, long curved ivory tusks, and large ears, native to Africa and southern Asia. It is the largest living land animal.
● Family Elephantidae, order Proboscidea: two species. See **AFRICAN ELEPHANT**, **INDIAN ELEPHANT**.
2 a size of paper, typically 28 × 23 inches (approximately 711 × 584 mm).
– DERIVATIVES **elephantoid** /ˌɛlɪˈfantɔɪd/ adjective.
– ORIGIN Middle English: from Old French *elefant*, via Latin from Greek *elephas*, *elephant-* 'ivory, elephant'.

elephant bird ▶ **noun** a heavily built, giant flightless bird, found in Madagascar until it was exterminated in about AD 1000. The eggs, which are still found occasionally, are the largest known. Also called **AEPYORNIS**.
● Family Aepyornithidae, genera *Aepyornis* and *Mullerornis*: several species, including *A. maximus*, which is the heaviest known bird.

elephant ear ▶ **noun** any of a number of plants with large heart-shaped leaves.

elephant fish ▶ **noun** a fish with a trunk-like snout or proboscis:
● a chimaera with a hook-like process on the snout (family Callorhinchidae and genus *Callorhinchus*). ● another term for **ELEPHANT-SNOUT FISH**.

elephant grass ▶ **noun** [mass noun] a tall robust tropical African grass which is used for fodder and paper.
● *Pennisetum purpureum*, family Gramineae.

elephant hawkmoth ▶ **noun** a large pinkish hawkmoth with greenish-bronze markings. The foreparts of the caterpillar have eyespots and sometimes resemble an elephant's trunk.
● Genus *Deilephila*, family Sphingidae: several species, in particular the common *D. elpenor*.

elephantiasis /ˌɛlɪf(ə)nˈtʌɪəsɪs/ ▶ **noun** [mass noun] Medicine a condition in which a limb or other part of the body becomes grossly enlarged due to obstruction of the lymphatic vessels, typically by the nematode parasites which cause filariasis.
– ORIGIN mid 16th cent.: via Latin from Greek, from *elephas*, *elephant-* 'elephant' + **-IASIS**.

elephantine /ɛlɪˈfantʌɪn/ ▶ **adjective** of, resembling, or characteristic of an elephant or elephants, especially in being large, clumsy, or awkward: *there was an elephantine thud from the bathroom.*
– ORIGIN early 17th cent.: via Latin from Greek *elephantinos*, from *elephas*, *elephant-* 'elephant'.

Elephant Pass a narrow strip of land at the north end of Sri Lanka, linking the Jaffna peninsula with the rest of the island.

elephant seal ▶ **noun** a large seal that breeds on the west coast of North America and the islands around Antarctica. The male is much larger than the female and has a very thick neck and an inflatable snout.
● Genus *Mirounga*, family Phocidae: two species.

elephant shrew ▶ **noun** a small insectivorous African mammal with a long mobile snout, long hindlimbs, and a rat-like tail.
● Family Macroscelididae and order Macroscelidea: four genera and many species; sometimes placed in the order Insectivora.

elephant-snout fish ▶ **noun** an edible African freshwater fish with a downcurved snout that is typically elongated and trunk-like. Also called **ELEPHANT FISH**.
● Family Mormyridae: several genera, in particular *Mormyrus*.

Eleusinian mysteries /ˌɛljuːˈsɪnɪən/ ▶ **plural noun** the annual rites performed by the ancient Greeks at the village of Eleusis near Athens in honour of Demeter and Persephone.

elevate /ˈɛlɪveɪt/ ▶ **verb** [with obj.] raise or lift (something) up to a higher position: *the exercise will naturally elevate your chest and head.*
■ raise to a more important or impressive level: *in the 1920s he was **elevated to** Secretary of State | the idea may be **elevated into** the rather grand status of a Theory.* ■ (of a priest) hold up (a consecrated host or chalice) for adoration. ■ increase the level or amount of (something, especially a level of a significant component of a person's blood). ■ raise the axis of (a piece of artillery) to increase its range.
– DERIVATIVES **elevatory** adjective.
– ORIGIN late Middle English: from Latin *elevat-* 'raised', from the verb *elevare*, from *e-* (variant of *ex-*) 'out, away' + *levare* 'lighten' (from *levis* 'light').

elevated ▶ **adjective** situated or placed higher than the surrounding area: *this hotel has an elevated position above the village.*
■ (of a road or railway line) raised on supports above the surrounding area: *the elevated section of the M4.* ■ (of a level or amount) higher or greater than what is considered normal: *an elevated temperature.* ■ of a high intellectual or moral standard or level: *the elevated canon of great literary texts.* ■ having a high rank or social standing: *these parish gentry were conscious of their elevated status.*

elevation ▶ **noun 1** [mass noun] the action or fact of raising or being raised to a higher or more important level, state, or position: *her sudden elevation to the cabinet.*
■ augmentation of or increase in the amount or level of something. ■ the raising of the consecrated elements for adoration at Mass.
2 [mass noun] height above a given level, especially sea level: *the area has a topography that ranges from 1,500 to 3,000 metres **in elevation**.*
■ [count noun] a high place or position: *an elevation of 300 metres.* ■ the angle of something with the horizontal, especially of a gun or of the direction of a celestial object. ■ Ballet the ability of a dancer to attain height in jumps.
3 a particular side of a building: *a burglar alarm was prominently displayed on the front elevation.*
■ a flat drawing of the front, side, or back of a house or other building: *a set of plans and elevations.* ■ a drawing or diagram, especially of a building, made by projection on a vertical plane. Compare with **PLAN** (in sense 3).
– DERIVATIVES **elevational** adjective.
– ORIGIN late Middle English: from Latin *elevatio(n-)*, from *elevare* 'raise' (see **ELEVATE**).

elevator ▶ **noun 1** a machine consisting of an endless belt with scoops attached, used typically for raising grain to be stored in an upper storey: *a grain elevator.*
■ N. Amer. a tall building used for storing large quantities of grain. ■ North American term for **LIFT** (in sense 1).
2 a hinged flap on the tailplane of an aircraft, typically one of a pair, used to control the motion of the aircraft about its lateral axis.
3 a muscle whose contraction raises a part of the body: *elevators of the upper lip.*
4 (also **elevator shoe**) trademark a shoe with a raised insole designed to make the wearer appear taller.
– ORIGIN mid 17th cent. (denoting a levator muscle): modern Latin, from Latin *elevare* 'raise'; in later use directly from **ELEVATE**.

eleven ▶ **cardinal number** equivalent to the sum of six and five; one more than ten; 11: *the room was about eleven feet wide | eighteen schools were founded, eleven of them in London.* (Roman numeral: **xi** or **XI**.)
■ eleven years old: *the eldest is only eleven.* ■ eleven o'clock: *she often worked until eleven at night.* ■ a size of garment or other merchandise denoted by eleven. ■ a group or unit of eleven people or things. ■ a sports team of eleven players: *at cricket I played in the first and second elevens.*
– DERIVATIVES **elevenfold** adjective & adverb.
– ORIGIN Old English *endleofon*, from the base of **ONE** + a second element (probably expressing the sense 'left over') occurring also in **TWELVE**; of Germanic origin and related to Dutch and German *elf*.

eleven-plus ▶ **noun** chiefly historical (in the UK) an examination taken at the age of 11–12 to determine the type of secondary school a child should enter.

elevenses ▶ **plural noun** Brit. informal a short break for light refreshments, usually with tea or coffee, taken about eleven o'clock in the morning.

eleventh ▶ **ordinal number** constituting number eleven in a sequence; 11th: *the eleventh century | February the eleventh | McGinlay scored his eleventh goal of the season on Saturday.*
■ (**an eleventh/one eleventh**) each of eleven equal parts into which something is or may be divided. ■ Music an interval or chord spanning an octave and a fourth in the diatonic scale, or a note separated from another by this interval.
– PHRASES **the eleventh hour** the latest possible moment: *the decision to send Eddie with the team was made **at the eleventh hour**.*

elevon /ˈɛlɪvɒn/ ▶ **noun** Aeronautics the movable part of the trailing edge of a delta wing.
– ORIGIN 1940s: blend of **ELEVATOR** and **AILERON** (because the elevon combines the functions of both).

ELF ▶ **abbreviation for** extremely low frequency.

elf ▶ **noun** (pl. **elves**) a supernatural creature of folk tales, typically represented as a small, delicate, elusive figure in human form with pointed ears, magical powers, and a capricious nature.
– DERIVATIVES **elfish** adjective, **elven** adjective (poetic/literary), **elvish** adjective.
– ORIGIN Old English, of Germanic origin; related to German *Alp* 'nightmare'.

elf cup (also **scarlet elf cup**) ▶ **noun** a fungus of decaying wood, producing small groups of shallow short-stemmed cups with a scarlet interior, found in both Eurasia and North America.
● *Sarcoscypha coccinea*, family Sarcosomataceae, subdivision Ascomycotina.

elfin ▶ **adjective** (of a person or their face) small and delicate, typically with an attractively mischievous or strange charm: *her black hair suited her elfin face.*
▶ **noun 1** archaic an elf.
2 a small North American butterfly that is typically brownish with markings on the wing margins that give the impression of scalloped edges.
● Genus *Incisalia*, family Lycaenidae.
– ORIGIN late 16th cent.: from **ELF**, probably suggested by Middle English *elvene* 'of elves', and by *Elphin*, the name of a character in Arthurian romance.

elf-locks ▶ **plural noun** a tangled mass of hair.

elf owl ▶ **noun** a tiny owl that nests in cacti and trees in the arid country of the southern US and Mexico.
● *Micrathene whitneyi*, family Strigidae.

Elgar /ˈɛlgɑː/, Sir Edward (William) (1857–1934), British composer. He is known particularly for the *Enigma Variations* (1899), the oratorio *The Dream of Gerontius* (1900), and for patriotic pieces such as the five *Pomp and Circumstance* marches (1901–30).

Elgin Marbles a collection of classical Greek marble sculptures and architectural fragments, chiefly from the Parthenon in Athens, brought to England by the diplomat and art connoisseur Thomas Bruce (1766–1841), the 7th Earl of Elgin.

Executed by Phidias in the 5th century BC, the sculptures were brought from Greece between 1803 and 1812, when the country was under Turkish control. They are currently housed in the British Museum, but are the subject of a repatriation request from the Greek government, who do not accept the legality of the Turkish sale.

El Giza /ɛl ˈdʒiːzə/ another name for **GIZA**.

Elgon, Mount /ˈɛlgɒn/ an extinct volcano on the border between Kenya and Uganda, rising to 4,321 m (14,178 ft).

El Greco /ɛl ˈgrɛkəʊ/ (1541–1614), Cretan-born Spanish painter; born *Domenikos Theotokopoulos*. El Greco's portraits and religious works are characterized by distorted perspective, elongated figures, and strident use of colour.
– ORIGIN Spanish, literally 'the Greek'.

Eli /ˈiːlʌɪ/ (in the Bible) a priest who acted as a teacher to the prophet Samuel (1 Sam. 1–3).

Elia /ˈiːlɪə/ the pseudonym adopted by Charles Lamb

in his *Essays of Elia* (1823) and *Last Essays of Elia* (1833).

elicit /ɪˈlɪsɪt/ ▶ **verb** (**elicited**, **eliciting**) [with obj.] evoke or draw out (a response, answer, or fact) from someone in reaction to one's own actions or questions: *taboos can elicit quite violent reactions if they are broken.*
■archaic draw forth (something that is latent or potential) into existence: *a corrupt heart elicits in an hour all that is bad in us.*
– DERIVATIVES **elicitation** noun, **elicitor** noun.
– ORIGIN mid 17th cent.: from Latin *elicit-* 'drawn out by trickery or magic', from the verb *elicere*, from *e-* (variant of *ex-*) 'out' + *lacere* 'entice, deceive'.

elide /ɪˈlʌɪd/ ▶ **verb** [with obj.] omit (a sound or syllable) when speaking: [as adj. **elided**] *the indication of elided consonants or vowels.*
■join together; merge: *whole periods of time are* **elided** *into a few seconds of screen* | [no obj.] *the two things elided in his mind.*
– ORIGIN mid 16th cent. (in the sense 'annul, do away with', chiefly as a Scots legal term): from Latin *elidere* 'crush out', from *e-* (variant of *ex-*) 'out' + *laedere* 'to dash'.

USAGE The standard meaning of the verb **elide** is 'omit', most frequently used as a term to describe the way that some sounds or syllables are dropped in speech, as for example in contractions such as **I'll** or **he's**. The result of such omission (or **elision**) is that the two surrounding syllables are merged; this fact has given rise to a new sense, with the meaning 'join together; merge', as in *the two things* **elided** *in his mind.* This new sense is now common in general use.

eligible /ˈɛlɪdʒɪb(ə)l/ ▶ **adjective** (often **eligible for/to do something**) having the right to do or obtain something; satisfying the appropriate conditions: *customers who are eligible for discounts* | *eligible candidates.*
■(of a person) desirable or suitable as a partner in marriage: *the world's most eligible bachelor.*
– DERIVATIVES **eligibility** noun, **eligibly** adverb.
– ORIGIN late Middle English: via French from late Latin *eligibilis*, from Latin *eligere* 'choose, select' (see **ELECT**).

Elijah /ɪˈlʌɪdʒə/ (9th century BC), a Hebrew prophet in the time of Jezebel who maintained the worship of Jehovah against that of Baal and other pagan gods.

eliminate /ɪˈlɪmɪneɪt/ ▶ **verb** [with obj.] completely remove or get rid of (something): *a policy that would eliminate inflation.*
■exclude (someone or something) from consideration: *the police have* **eliminated** *Lawrence* **from** *their inquiries.* ■ murder (a rival or political opponent). ■ (usu. **be eliminated**) exclude (a person or team) from further participation in a sporting competition following defeat or inadequate results: *Arbroath were* **eliminated from** *the cup in the first round.* ■ Mathematics remove (a variable) from an equation, typically by substituting another which is shown by another equation to be equivalent. ■ Chemistry generate or remove (a simple substance) as a product in the course of a reaction involving larger molecules. ■ Physiology expel (waste matter) from the body: *this diet claims to eliminate toxins from the body.*
– DERIVATIVES **eliminable** adjective, **elimination** noun, **eliminator** noun, **eliminatory** adjective.
– ORIGIN mid 16th cent. (in the sense 'drive out, expel'): from Latin *eliminat-* 'turned out of doors', from the verb *eliminare*, from *e-* (variant of *ex-*) 'out' + *limen, limin-* 'threshold'.

ELINT /ɪˈlɪnt/ ▶ **noun** [mass noun] covert intelligence-gathering by electronic means.
– ORIGIN 1960s (originally US): blend of **ELECTRONIC** and **INTELLIGENCE**.

Eliot[1] /ˈɛlɪət/, George (1819–80), English novelist; pseudonym of *Mary Ann Evans*. Her novels of provincial life are characterized by their exploration of moral problems and their development of the psychological analysis that marks the modern novel. Notable works: *Adam Bede* (1859), *The Mill on the Floss* (1860), and *Middlemarch* (1871–2).

Eliot[2] /ˈɛlɪət/, T. S. (1888–1965), American-born British poet, critic, and dramatist; full name *Thomas Stearns Eliot*. Associated with the rise of literary modernism, he was established as the voice of a disillusioned generation by *The Waste Land* (1922). *Four Quartets* (1943) revealed his increasing involvement with Christianity. Nobel Prize for Literature (1948).

ELISA /ɪˈlʌɪzə/ ▶ **noun** [mass noun] Biochemistry enzyme-linked immunosorbent assay, an immunological assay technique making use of an enzyme bonded to a particular antibody or antigen.

Elisabethville /ɪˈlɪzəbəθˌvɪl/ former name (until 1966) for **LUBUMBASHI**.

Elisha /ɪˈlʌɪʃə/ (9th century BC), a Hebrew prophet, disciple and successor of Elijah.

elision /ɪˈlɪʒ(ə)n/ ▶ **noun** [mass noun] the omission of a sound or syllable when speaking (as in *I'm, let's, e'en*).
■[count noun] an omission of a passage in a book, speech, or film: *the movie's elisions and distortions have been carefully thought out.* ■ the process of joining together or merging things, especially abstract ideas: *unease at the elision of so many vital questions.*
– ORIGIN late 16th cent.: from late Latin *elisio(n-)*, from Latin *elidere* 'crush out' (see **ELIDE**).

USAGE See usage at **ELIDE**.

Elista /ɛˈlɪstə/ a city in SW Russia, capital of the autonomous republic of Kalmykia; pop. 85,000 (1990).

elite /eɪˈliːt, ɪ-/ ▶ **noun 1** a group of people considered to be the best in a particular society or category, especially because of their power, talent, or wealth: *China's educated elite* | [as modifier] *an elite combat force.*
2 [mass noun] a size of letter in typewriting, with 12 characters to the inch (about 4.7 to the centimetre).
– ORIGIN late 18th cent.: from French *élite* 'selection, choice', from *élire* 'to elect', from a variant of Latin *eligere* (see **ELECT**). Sense 2 dates from the early 20th cent.

elitism ▶ **noun** [mass noun] the advocacy or existence of an elite as a dominating element in a system or society.
■the attitude or behaviour of a person or group who regard themselves as belonging to an elite: *he accused her of racism and white elitism.*

elitist ▶ **noun** a person who believes that a system or society should be ruled or dominated by an elite.
■a person who believes that they belong to an elite: *designers are a bunch of elitists who don't live in the real world.*
▶ **adjective** favouring, advocating, or restricted to an elite: *the old, elitist image of the string quartet.*

elixir /ɪˈlɪksə, -sɪə/ ▶ **noun** a magical or medicinal potion: *an elixir guaranteed to induce love.*
■a preparation which was supposedly able to change metals into gold, sought by alchemists. ■ (also **elixir of life**) a preparation supposedly able to prolong life indefinitely. ■ a medicinal solution of a specified type: *the cough elixir is a natural herbal expectorant.*
– ORIGIN late Middle English: via medieval Latin from Arabic *al-'iksīr*, from *al* 'the' + *'iksīr* from Greek *xērion* 'powder for drying wounds' (from *xēros* 'dry').

Elizabeth I (1533–1603), daughter of Henry VIII, queen of England and Ireland 1558–1603. Succeeding her Catholic sister Mary I, Elizabeth re-established a moderate form of Protestantism as the state religion. Her reign was dominated by the threat of a Catholic restoration and by war with Spain, culminating in the Armada of 1588. Although frequently courted, she never married.

Elizabeth II (b.1926), daughter of George VI, queen of the United Kingdom since 1952; born *Princess Elizabeth Alexandra Mary*. She married Prince Philip in 1947; they have four children, Prince Charles, Princess Anne, Prince Andrew, and Prince Edward.

Elizabeth, the Queen Mother (b.1900), wife of George VI; born *Lady Elizabeth Angela Marguerite Bowes-Lyon*. She married George VI in 1923, when he was Duke of York; they had two daughters, Elizabeth II and Princess Margaret.

Elizabethan /ɪˌlɪzəˈbiːθ(ə)n/ ▶ **adjective** of, relating to, or characteristic of the reign of Queen Elizabeth I: *an Elizabethan manor house.*
▶ **noun** a person, especially a writer, of the time of Queen Elizabeth I.

Elizavetpol /jəˌliːzəˈvjɛtpɒl/ variant spelling of **YELIZAVETPOL**.

elk /ɛlk/ ▶ **noun** (pl. same or **elks**) a large deer with palmate antlers, a sloping back, and a growth of skin hanging from the neck. It is native to northern Eurasia and northern North America. Called **MOOSE** in North America.
● *Alces alces*, family Cervidae.
■North American term for **WAPITI**.
– ORIGIN late 15th cent.: probably from Old English *elh, eolh*, with substitution of *k* for *h*. Other words which have undergone this change are dialect *selk* (Old English *seolh* 'seal') and *fark* (Old English *færh* 'farrow').

elk hound ▶ **noun** a large hunting dog of a Scandinavian breed with a shaggy grey coat.

ell[1] ▶ **noun** a former measure of length (equivalent to six hand breadths) used mainly for textiles, locally variable but typically about 45 inches in England and 37 inches in Scotland.
– ORIGIN Old English *eln*, of Germanic origin; from an Indo-European root shared by Latin *ulna* (see **ULNA**). Compare with **ELBOW** and also with **CUBIT** (the measure was originally linked to the length of the human arm or forearm).

ell[2] ▶ **noun** see **L**[1].

ellagic acid /ɛˈladʒɪk/ ▶ **noun** [mass noun] Chemistry a compound extracted from oak galls and various fruits and nuts. It has some ability to inhibit blood flow and retard the growth of cancer cells.
● A tetracyclic phenol; chem. formula: $C_{14}H_6O_8$.
– ORIGIN early 19th cent.: *ellagic* from French *ellagique* (an anagram of *galle* 'gall nut' + *-ique*), thus avoiding the form *gallique*, already in use.

Ellesmere Island /ˈɛlzmɪə/ the northernmost island of the Canadian Arctic.
– ORIGIN named after the British statesman Francis Egerton, Earl of Ellesmere (1800–57).

Ellesmere Port a port in NW England, in Cheshire, on the estuary of the River Mersey; pop. 65,800 (1981).

Ellice Islands /ˈɛlɪs/ former name for **TUVALU**.

Ellington /ˈɛlɪŋtən/, Duke (1899–1974), American jazz pianist, composer, and bandleader; born *Edward Kennedy Ellington*. Coming to fame in the early 1930s, Ellington wrote over 900 compositions and was one of the first popular musicians to write extended pieces. Notable works: *Mood Indigo* (1930).

ellipse /ɪˈlɪps/ ▶ **noun** a regular oval shape, traced by a point moving in a plane so that the sum of its distances from two other points (the foci) is constant, or resulting when a cone is cut by an oblique plane which does not intersect the base.
– ORIGIN late 17th cent.: via French from Latin *ellipsis* (see **ELLIPSIS**).

ellipsis /ɪˈlɪpsɪs/ ▶ **noun** (pl. **ellipses** /-siːz/) the omission from speech or writing of a word or words that are superfluous or able to be understood from contextual clues.
■a set of dots indicating such an omission.
– ORIGIN mid 16th cent.: via Latin from Greek *elleipsis*, from *elleipein* 'leave out'.

ellipsoid /ɪˈlɪpsɔɪd/ ▶ **noun** a three-dimensional figure symmetrical about each of three perpendicular axes, whose plane sections normal to one axis are circles and all the other plane sections are ellipses.
– DERIVATIVES **ellipsoidal** adjective.

elliptic ▶ **adjective** of, relating to, or having the form of an ellipse.
– DERIVATIVES **ellipticity** noun.
– ORIGIN early 18th cent.: from Greek *elleiptikos* 'defective', from *elleipein* 'leave out, fall short'.

elliptical ▶ **adjective 1** (of speech or writing) lacking a word or words, especially when the sense can be understood from contextual clues.
2 another term for **ELLIPTIC**.
– DERIVATIVES **elliptically** adverb.

Ellis, (Henry) Havelock (1859–1939), English psychologist and writer, remembered as the pioneer of the scientific study of sex. His major work was the six-volume *Studies in the Psychology of Sex* (1897–1910, with a seventh volume added in 1928).

Ellis Island an island in the bay of New York that from 1892 until 1943 served as an entry point for immigrants to the US, and later (until 1954) as a detention centre for people awaiting deportation.

Ellsworth /ˈɛlzwəθ/, Lincoln (1880–1951), American explorer. He participated in a number of polar expeditions and was the first person to fly over both the North (1926) and South (1935) Poles.

Ellsworth Land a plateau region of Antarctica between the Walgreen Coast and Palmer Land. It rises at the Vinson Massif, the highest point in Antarctica, to 5,140 m (16,863 ft).

elm (also **elm tree**) ▶ **noun** a tall deciduous tree which typically has rough serrated leaves and propagates from root suckers.
• Genus *Ulmus*, family Ulmaceae: several species, including the **English elm** (*U. procera*), now largely lost to Dutch Elm disease, and the **American elm** (*U. americana*).
– DERIVATIVES **elmy** adjective.
– ORIGIN Old English, of Germanic origin; related to German dialect *Ilm*, and Swedish and Norwegian *alm*.

El Niño /ɛl ˈniːnjəʊ/ ▶ **noun** (pl. **-os**) an irregularly occurring and complex series of climatic changes affecting the equatorial Pacific region and beyond every few years, characterized by the appearance of unusually warm, nutrient-poor water off northern Peru and Ecuador, typically in late December.
– ORIGIN Spanish, literally 'the (Christ) child', because of the occurrence near Christmas.

elocution /ˌɛləˈkjuːʃ(ə)n/ ▶ **noun** [mass noun] the skill of clear and expressive speech, especially of distinct pronunciation and articulation.
■ [count noun] a particular style of speaking.
– DERIVATIVES **elocutionary** adjective, **elocutionist** noun.
– ORIGIN late Middle English (denoting oratorical or literary style): from Latin *elocutio(n-)*, from *eloqui* 'speak out' (see **ELOQUENCE**).

elodea /ˌɛlə(ʊ)ˈdiːə, ɪˈləʊdɪə/ ▶ **noun** [mass noun] an aquatic plant of a genus that includes Canadian pondweed.
• Genus *Elodea*, family Hydrocharitaceae.
– ORIGIN modern Latin, from Greek *helōdēs* 'marshy'.

Elohim /ɛˈləʊhɪm, ˈɛləʊhiːm/ ▶ **noun** a name for God used frequently in the Hebrew Bible.
– ORIGIN from Hebrew *'ĕlōhīm* (plural).

Elohist /ɛˈləʊhɪst/ the postulated author or authors of parts of the Hexateuch in which God is regularly named Elohim. Compare with **YAHWIST**.
– ORIGIN from Hebrew *'ĕlōhīm* (see **ELOHIM**) + **-IST**.

elongate /ˈiːlɒŋgeɪt/ ▶ **verb** [with obj.] make (something) longer, especially unusually so in relation to its width.
■ prolong (a sound): *she can sing—notes are elongated and given fullness without a quiver.* ■ [no obj.] chiefly Biology grow longer.
▶ **adjective** chiefly Biology long in relation to width; elongated: *elongate, fishlike creatures.*
– ORIGIN late Middle English (in the sense 'move away, place at a distance'): from late Latin *elongat-* 'placed at a distance', from the verb *elongare*, from Latin *e-* (variant of *ex-*) 'away' + *longe* 'far off', *longus* 'long'.

elongated ▶ **adjective** unusually long in relation to its width: *he is tall with an elongated, finely made face.*
■ having grown or been made longer.

elongation ▶ **noun** [mass noun] the lengthening of something.
■ a part of a line formed by lengthening; a continuation. ■ the amount of extension of an object under stress, usually expressed as a percentage of the original length. ■ Astronomy the angular separation of a planet from the sun or of a satellite from a planet, as seen by an observer.
– ORIGIN late Middle English: from late Latin *elongatio(n-)*, from *elongare* 'place at a distance' (see **ELONGATE**).

elope ▶ **verb** [no obj.] run away secretly in order to get married: *later he* **eloped with** *one of the housemaids.*
– DERIVATIVES **elopement** noun, **eloper** noun.
– ORIGIN late 16th cent. (in the general sense 'abscond, run away'): from Anglo-Norman French *aloper*, perhaps related to **LEAP**.

eloquence /ˈɛləkw(ə)ns/ ▶ **noun** [mass noun] fluent or persuasive speaking or writing: *a preacher of great power and eloquence.*
– ORIGIN late Middle English: via Old French from Latin *eloquentia*, from *eloqui* 'speak out', from *e-* (variant of *ex-*) 'out' + *loqui* 'speak'.

eloquent ▶ **adjective** fluent or persuasive in speaking or writing: *an eloquent speech.*
■ clearly expressing or indicating something: *the bus journey alone is* **eloquent of** *class inequality.*
– DERIVATIVES **eloquently** adverb.
– ORIGIN late Middle English: via Old French from Latin *eloquent-* 'speaking out', from the verb *eloqui* (see **ELOQUENCE**).

El Paso /ɛl ˈpasəʊ/ a city in western Texas on the Rio Grande, on the border with Mexico; pop. 515,300 (1990).

El Qahira /ɛl ˈkɑːhɪrɑː/ variant spelling of **AL QAHIRA**.

El Salvador /ɛl ˈsalvədɔː, Spanish el salβaˈðor/ a country in Central America, on the Pacific coast; pop. 5,047,925 (est. 1992); official language, Spanish; capital, San Salvador.

The territory was conquered by the Spanish in 1524 and gained its independence in 1821. Between 1979 and 1992 the country was devastated by a civil war marked by the activities of right-wing death squads and resistance by left-wing guerrillas; a UN-brokered peace accord was agreed in 1992.

Elsan /ˈɛlsan/ ▶ **noun** Brit. trademark a type of transportable chemical toilet.
– ORIGIN 1930s: apparently from the initials of *Ephraim Louis* Jackson (its manufacturer) and **SANITATION**.

else ▶ **adverb** **1** [with indefinite pronoun or adverb] in addition; besides: ***anything else*** *you need to know?* | *I just brought basics—I wasn't sure* ***what else*** *you'd want* | *they will offer low prices but* ***little else***.
2 [with indefinite pronoun or adverb] different; instead: *isn't there* ***anyone else*** *you could ask?* | *it's fate, destiny, or* ***whatever else*** *you like to call it.*
3 short for ***or else*** below.
– PHRASES **or else** used to introduce the second of two alternatives: *she felt tempted either to shout at him or else to let his tantrums slide by.* ■ in circumstances different from those mentioned; if it were not the case: *they can't want it, or else they'd request it.* ■ used to warn what will happen if something is not carried out: *you go along with this or else you're going to jail.* ■ used after a demand as a threat: *she'd better shape up, or else.*
– ORIGIN Old English *elles*, of Germanic origin; related to Middle Dutch *els* and Swedish *eljest*.

elsewhere ▶ **adverb** in, at, or to some other place or other places: *he is seeking employment elsewhere.*
▶ **pronoun** some other place: *all Hawaiian plants originally came from elsewhere.*
– ORIGIN Old English *elles hwǣr* (see **ELSE**, **WHERE**).

Elsinore /ˈɛlsɪnɔː/ a port on the NE coast of the island of Zealand, Denmark; pop. 56,750 (1990). It is the site of the 16th-century Kronborg Castle, which is the setting for Shakespeare's *Hamlet*. Danish name **HELSINGØR**.

Elster /ˈɛlstə/ ▶ **noun** [usu. as modifier] Geology a Pleistocene glaciation in northern Europe, corresponding to the Anglian of Britain (and possibly the Mindel of the Alps).
■ the system of deposits laid down at this time.
– DERIVATIVES **Elsterian** /ɛlˈstɪərɪən/ adjective & noun.
– ORIGIN 1930s: the name of a tributary of the River Elbe in Germany.

Elton /ˈɛlt(ə)n/, Charles Sutherland (1900–91), English zoologist. Elton pioneered the study of animal ecology, and his research into rodent populations found practical application in vermin control.

eluant ▶ **noun** variant spelling of **ELUENT**.

Éluard /ˈɛlʊɑː, French elyaʀ/, Paul (1895–1952), French poet; pseudonym of *Eugène Grindel*. He was a leading figure in the surrealist movement.

eluate /ˈɛljuːət, -eɪt/ ▶ **noun** Chemistry a solution obtained by elution.
– ORIGIN 1930s: from Latin *eluere* 'wash out' + **-ATE**[1].

elucidate /ɪˈl(j)uːsɪdeɪt/ ▶ **verb** [with obj.] make (something) clear; explain: *work such as theirs will help to elucidate this matter* | [with clause] *in what follows I shall try to elucidate what I believe the problems to be.*
– DERIVATIVES **elucidation** noun, **elucidative** adjective, **elucidator** noun, **elucidatory** adjective.
– ORIGIN mid 16th cent.: from late Latin *elucidat-* 'made clear', from the verb *elucidare*, from *e-* (variant of *ex-*) 'out' + *lucidus* 'lucid'.

elude /ɪˈl(j)uːd/ ▶ **verb** [with obj.] evade or escape from (a danger, enemy, or pursuer), typically in a skilful or cunning way: *he managed to elude his pursuers by escaping into a bog.*
■ (of an idea or fact) fail to be grasped or remembered by (someone): *the logic of this eluded most people.* ■ (of an achievement, or something desired or pursued) fail to be attained by (someone): *sleep still eluded her.* ■ avoid compliance with or subjection to (a law, demand, or penalty).
– DERIVATIVES **elusion** noun.
– ORIGIN mid 16th cent. (in the sense 'delude, baffle'): from Latin *eludere*, from *e-* (variant of *ex-*) 'out, away from' + *ludere* 'to play'.

eluent /ˈɛljʊənt/ (also **eluant**) ▶ **noun** Chemistry a fluid used to elute a substance.
– ORIGIN 1940s: from Latin *eluent-* 'washing out', from the verb *eluere* (see **ELUTE**).

Elul /ˈiːlʌl, ˈɛlʌl/ ▶ **noun** (in the Jewish calendar) the twelfth month of the civil and sixth of the religious year, usually coinciding with parts of August and September.
– ORIGIN from Hebrew *'ĕlūl*.

El Uqsur /ɛl ˈʊksʊə/ (also **Al Uqsur**) Arabic name for **LUXOR**.

elusive ▶ **adjective** difficult to find, catch, or achieve: *success will become ever more elusive.*
■ difficult to remember or recall: *the elusive thought he had had moments before.*
– DERIVATIVES **elusively** adverb, **elusiveness** noun.
– ORIGIN early 18th cent.: from Latin *elus-* 'eluded' (from the verb *eludere*) + **-IVE**.

elute /ɪˈl(j)uːt/ ▶ **verb** [with obj.] Chemistry remove (an adsorbed substance) by washing with a solvent, especially in chromatography.
– DERIVATIVES **elution** noun.
– ORIGIN 1920s: from Latin *elut-* 'washed out', from the verb *eluere*, suggested by German *eluieren*.

elutriate /ɪˈl(j)uːtrɪeɪt/ ▶ **verb** [with obj.] Chemistry separate (lighter and heavier particles in a mixture) by suspension in an upward flow of liquid or gas.
– DERIVATIVES **elutriation** noun.
– ORIGIN mid 18th cent.: from Latin *elutriat-* 'washed out', from the verb *elutriare*, from *e-* (variant of *ex-*) 'out' + *lutriare* 'to wash'.

elvan /ˈɛlv(ə)n/ ▶ **noun** [mass noun] Geology hard intrusive igneous rock found in Cornwall, typically quartz porphyry.
– ORIGIN early 18th cent.: perhaps via Cornish from Welsh *elfen* 'element'.

elver /ˈɛlvə/ ▶ **noun** a young eel, especially when undergoing mass migration upriver from the sea.
– ORIGIN mid 17th cent.: variant of dialect *eel-fare* 'the passage of young eels up a river', also 'a brood of young eels', from **EEL** + **FARE** in its original sense 'a journey'.

elves plural form of **ELF**.

Ely /ˈiːli/ a cathedral city in the fenland of Cambridgeshire, on the River Ouse; pop. 9,100 (1981).

Ely, Isle of a former county of England extending over the northern part of present-day Cambridgeshire. Before widespread drainage it formed a fertile 'island' in the surrounding fenland.

Elysée Palace /eɪˈliːzeɪ/ a building in Paris which has been the official residence of the French President since 1870. It was built in 1718 and was occupied by Madame de Pompadour, Napoleon I, and Napoleon III. French name **PALAIS DE L'ELYSÉE**.

Elysian /ɪˈlɪzɪən/ ▶ **adjective** of, relating to, or characteristic of heaven or paradise: *Elysian visions.*
– PHRASES **the Elysian Fields** another name for **ELYSIUM**.

Elysium /ɪˈlɪzɪəm/ Greek Mythology the place at the ends of the earth to which certain favoured heroes were conveyed by the gods after death.
■ [as noun **an Elysium**] a place or state of perfect happiness.
– ORIGIN via Latin from Greek *Elusion (pedion)* '(plain) of the blessed'.

elytron /ˈɛlɪtrɒn/ ▶ **noun** (pl. **elytra** /-trə/) Entomology each of the two wing cases of a beetle.
– ORIGIN mid 18th cent. (denoting a sheath or covering, specifically that of the spinal cord): from Greek *elutron* 'sheath'.

Elzevir /ˈɛlzəvɪə/ a family of Dutch printers. Fifteen members were active 1581–1712; **Bonaventure** (1583–1652) and **Abraham** (1592–1652) managed the firm in its prime.

em ▶ **noun** Printing a unit for measuring the width of printed matter, equal to the height of the type size being used.
■ a unit of measurement equal to twelve points.
– ORIGIN late 18th cent.: the letter *M* represented as a word, since it is approximately this width.

em- /ɪm, ɛm/ ▶ **prefix** variant spelling of **EN-**[1], **EN-**[2] assimilated before *b*, *p* (as in *emblazon*, *emplacement*).

'em ▶ **pronoun** short for **THEM**, especially in informal use: *let 'em know who's boss.*
– ORIGIN Middle English: originally a form of *hem*, dative and accusative third person plural pronoun

in Middle English; now regarded as an abbreviation of **THEM**.

emaciated /ɪˈmeɪsɪeɪt, ɪˈmeɪʃ-/ ▶ **adjective** abnormally thin or weak, especially because of illness or a lack of food: *she was so emaciated she could hardly stand.*
– DERIVATIVES **emaciation** noun.
– ORIGIN early 17th cent.: from Latin *emaciat-* 'made thin', from the verb *emaciare*, from *e-* (variant of *ex-*, expressing a change of state) + *macies* 'leanness'.

e-mail ▶ **noun** [mass noun] messages distributed by electronic means from one computer user to one or more recipients via a network: *reading e-mail has become the first task of the morning* | [count noun] *we received thousands of e-mails* | [as modifier] *e-mail messages.*
▪the system of sending messages by such electronic means: *a contract communicated by e-mail.*
▶ **verb** [with obj.] send an e-mail to (someone).
▪send (a message) by e-mail.
– DERIVATIVES **e-mailer** noun.
– ORIGIN late 20th cent.: abbreviation of **ELECTRONIC MAIL**.

emalangeni plural form of **LILANGENI**.

emanate /ˈɛməneɪt/ ▶ **verb** [no obj.] (**emanate from**) (of something abstract but perceptible) issue or spread out from (a source): *warmth emanated from the fireplace* | *she felt an undeniable charm emanating from him.*
▪originate from; be produced by: *the proposals emanated from a committee.* ▪ [with obj.] give out or emit (something abstract but perceptible): *he emanated a powerful brooding air.*
– ORIGIN mid 18th cent.: from Latin *emanat-* 'flowed out', from the verb *emanare*, from *e-* (variant of *ex-*) 'out' + *manare* 'to flow'.

emanation ▶ **noun** an abstract but perceptible thing that issues or originates from a source: *she saw the insults as emanations of his own tortured personality.*
▪[mass noun] the action or process of issuing from a source: *the risk of radon gas emanation.* ▪ a tenuous substance or form of radiation given off by something: *vaporous emanations wreathe the mill's foundations.* ▪ Chemistry, archaic a radioactive gas formed by radioactive decay of a solid. ▪ a body or organization that has its source or takes its authority from another: *the commission is an emanation of the state.* ▪ (in various mystical traditions) a being or force which is a manifestation of God.

emancipate /ɪˈmansɪpeɪt/ ▶ **verb** [with obj.] set free, especially from legal, social, or political restrictions: *the citizen must be* **emancipated from** *the obsessive secrecy of government* | [as adj. **emancipated**] *emancipated young women.*
▪Law set (a child) free from the authority of its father or parents. ▪ free from slavery: *it is estimated that he emancipated 8,000 slaves.*
– DERIVATIVES **emancipation** noun, **emancipator** noun, **emancipatory** adjective.
– ORIGIN early 17th cent.: from Latin *emancipat-* 'transferred as property', from the verb *emancipare*, from *e-* (variant of *ex-*) 'out' + *mancipium* 'slave'.

Emancipation Proclamation (in the American Civil War) the announcement made by President Lincoln on 22 September 1862 emancipating all black slaves in states still engaged in rebellion against the Federal Union. Although implementation was strictly beyond Lincoln's powers, the declaration turned the war into a crusade against slavery.

emasculate /ɪˈmaskjʊleɪt/ ▶ **verb** [with obj.] make (a person, idea, or piece of legislation) weaker or less effective: *the refusal to allow them to testify effectively emasculated the committee.*
▪[usu. as adj. **emasculated**] deprive (a man) of his male role or identity: *he feels emasculated, because he cannot control his sons' behaviour.* ▪ archaic castrate (a man or male animal). ▪ Botany remove the anthers from a flower.
– DERIVATIVES **emasculation** noun, **emasculator** noun, **emasculatory** /-lət(ə)ri/ adjective.
– ORIGIN early 17th cent.: from Latin *emasculat-* 'castrated', from the verb *emasculare*, from *e-* (variant of *ex-*, expressing a change of state) + *masculus* 'male'.

embalm /ɪmˈbɑːm, ɛm-/ ▶ **verb** [with obj.] **1** [often as noun **embalming**] preserve (a corpse) from decay, originally with spices and now usually by arterial injection of a preservative: *the Egyptian method of embalming.*
▪figurative preserve (someone or something) in an unaltered state: *the band was all about revitalizing pop greats and embalming their legacy.*
2 archaic give a pleasant fragrance to: *the buxom air, embalm'd with odours.*
– DERIVATIVES **embalmer** noun, **embalmment** noun.
– ORIGIN Middle English: from Old French *embaumer*, from *em-* 'in' + *baume* 'balm', variant of *basme* (see **BALM**).

embank ▶ **verb** [with obj.] construct a wall or bank of earth or stone in order to confine (a river) within certain limits.
▪construct a bank of earth or stone to carry (a road or railway) over an area of low ground.

embankment ▶ **noun** a wall or bank of earth or stone built to prevent a river flooding an area.
▪a bank of earth or stone built to carry a road or railway over an area of low ground.

embargo /ɛmˈbɑːɡəʊ, ɪm-/ ▶ **noun** (pl. **-oes**) an official ban on trade or other commercial activity with a particular country: *an* **embargo on** *grain sales* | *an arms embargo.*
▪an official prohibition on any activity. ▪ historical an order of a state forbidding foreign ships to enter, or any ships to leave, its ports: *an embargo laid by our Emperor upon all vessels whatsoever.* ▪ archaic a stoppage, prohibition, or impediment.
▶ **verb** (**-oes, -oed**) [with obj.] **1** (usu. **be embargoed**) impose an official ban on (trade or a country or commodity): *the country has been virtually embargoed by most of the non-communist world.*
▪officially ban the publication of: *documents of national security importance are routinely embargoed.*
2 archaic seize (a ship or goods) for state service.
– ORIGIN early 17th cent.: from Spanish, from *embargar* 'arrest', based on Latin *in-* 'in, within' + *barra* 'a bar'.

embark ▶ **verb** [no obj.] go on board a ship or aircraft: *he* **embarked for** *India in 1817.*
▪[with obj.] put or take on board a ship or aircraft: *its passengers were ready to be embarked.* ▪ (**embark on/upon**) begin (a course of action, especially one which is important or demanding): *he embarked on a new career.*
– DERIVATIVES **embarkation** noun.
– ORIGIN mid 16th cent.: from French *embarquer*, from *em-* 'in' + *barque* 'bark, ship'.

embarras de richesses /ɒmbaˌrɑː də riːˈʃɛs/ (also **embarras de choix** /ˈʃwɑː/) ▶ **noun** more options or resources than one knows what to do with: *he had presented us with an* embarras de richesses *of history and culture.*
– ORIGIN French, 'embarrassment of riches (or choice)'.

embarrass /ɪmˈbarəs, ɛm-/ ▶ **verb** [with obj.] cause (someone) to feel awkward, self-conscious, or ashamed: *she wouldn't embarrass either of them by making a scene.*
▪(**be embarrassed**) be caused financial difficulties: *he would be embarrassed by estate duty.* ▪ archaic hamper or impede (a person, movement, or action): *the state of the rivers will embarrass the enemy in a considerable degree.* ▪ archaic make difficult or intricate; complicate.
– ORIGIN early 17th cent. (in the sense 'hamper, impede'): from French *embarrasser*, from Spanish *embarazar*, probably from Portuguese *embaraçar* (from *baraço* 'halter').

embarrassed ▶ **adjective** feeling or showing embarrassment: *he became embarrassed at his own effusiveness* | *an embarrassed silence.*
▪having or showing financial difficulties.
– DERIVATIVES **embarrassedly** adverb.

embarrassing ▶ **adjective** causing embarrassment: *an embarrassing muddle.*
– DERIVATIVES **embarrassingly** adverb.

embarrassment ▶ **noun** [mass noun] a feeling of self-consciousness, shame, or awkwardness: *I turned red with embarrassment.*
▪[count noun] a person or thing causing such feelings: *he was an embarrassment who was safely left ignored* | *her extreme views might be an* **embarrassment to** *the movement.* ▪ financial difficulty: *his temporary financial embarrassment.*

embassage /ˈɛmbəsɪdʒ/ ▶ **noun** archaic the business or message of an envoy.
▪a body of people sent as a deputation to or on behalf of a head of state.
– ORIGIN late 15th cent. (denoting the action of sending an envoy): from Old French *ambasse* 'message or embassy' + **-AGE**.

embassy ▶ **noun** (pl. **-ies**) **1** the official residence or offices of an ambassador: *the Chilean embassy in Moscow.*
2 chiefly historical a deputation or mission sent by one ruler or state to another.
– ORIGIN late 16th cent. (originally also as *ambassy* denoting the position of ambassador): from Old French *ambasse*, based on Latin *ambactus* 'servant'. Compare with **AMBASSADOR**.

embattle ▶ **verb** [with obj.] archaic set (an army) in battle array: *it was three o'clock before the king's army was embattled.*
▪fortify (a building or place) against attack.
– ORIGIN Middle English: from Old French *embataillier*.

embattled ▶ **adjective** **1** (of a place or people) involved in or prepared for war, especially because surrounded by enemy forces: *the embattled Yugoslavian republics.*
▪(of a person) beset by problems or difficulties: *the worst may not be over for the embattled Chancellor.*
2 (of a building or part of a building) having battlements: *the church has a low embattled tower.*
▪[postpositive] Heraldry divided or edged by a line of square notches like battlements in outline.

embay ▶ **verb** [with obj.] (usu. **be embayed**) (chiefly of the wind) force (a boat) into a bay: *ships were embayed between two headlands.*
▪[as adj. **embayed**] formed into bays; hollowed out by or as if by the sea: *the embayed island.* ▪ chiefly Geology enclose (something) in a recess or hollow.

embayment ▶ **noun** a recess in a coastline forming a bay.

embed (also **imbed**) ▶ **verb** (**embedded, embedding**) [with obj.] (often **be embedded**) fix (an object) firmly and deeply in a surrounding mass: *he had an operation to remove a nail* **embedded in** *his chest.*
▪figurative implant (an idea or feeling) within something else so it becomes an ingrained or essential characteristic of it: *the Victorian values* **embedded in** *Tennyson's poetry.* ▪ Linguistics place (a phrase or clause) within another clause or sentence. ▪ Computing incorporate (a text or code) within the body of a file or document. ▪ [often as adj. **embedded**] design and build (a microprocessor) as an integral part of a system or device.
– DERIVATIVES **embedment** noun.

embellish ▶ **verb** [with obj.] make (something) more attractive by the addition of decorative details or features: *blue silk embellished with golden embroidery.*
▪make (a statement or story) more interesting or entertaining by adding extra details, especially ones that are not true: *she had real difficulty telling the truth because she liked to embellish things.*
– DERIVATIVES **embellisher** noun.
– ORIGIN late Middle English: from Old French *embelliss-*, lengthened stem of *embellir*, based on *bel* 'handsome', from Latin *bellus*.

embellishment ▶ **noun** a decorative detail or feature added to something to make it more attractive: *architectural embellishments.*
▪a detail, especially one that is not true, added to a statement or story to make it more interesting or entertaining. ▪ [mass noun] the action of adding such details or features.

ember /ˈɛmbə/ ▶ **noun** (usu. **embers**) a small piece of burning or glowing coal or wood in a dying fire: *the dying embers in the grate* | figurative *the flickering embers of nationalism.*
– ORIGIN Old English *ǣmyrge*, of Germanic origin; related to Old High German *eimuria* 'pyre', Danish *emmer*, Swedish *mörja* 'embers'. The *b* was added in English for ease of pronunciation.

Ember day ▶ **noun** any of a number of days reserved for fasting and prayer in the Western Christian Church. Ember days traditionally comprise the Wednesday, Friday, and Saturday following St Lucy's Day (13 December), the first Sunday in Lent, Pentecost (Whitsun), and Holy Cross Day (14 September), though other days are observed locally.
– ORIGIN Old English *ymbren*, perhaps an alteration of *ymbryne* 'period', from *ymb* 'about' + *ryne* 'course', perhaps influenced in part by ecclesiastical Latin *quatuor tempora* 'four periods' (on which the equivalent German *Quatember* is based).

embezzle ▶ **verb** [with obj.] steal or misappropriate

(money placed in one's trust or belonging to the organization for which one works): *she had embezzled $5,600,000 in company funds.*
– DERIVATIVES **embezzlement** noun, **embezzler** noun.
– ORIGIN late Middle English (in the sense 'steal'): from Anglo-Norman French *embesiler*, from *besiler* in the same sense (compare with Old French *besillier* 'maltreat, ravage'), of unknown ultimate origin. The current sense dates from the late 16th cent.

Embioptera /ˌɛmbʌɪˈɒptərə/ Entomology a small order of insects that comprises the web-spinners.
– DERIVATIVES **embiopteran** noun & adjective.
– ORIGIN modern Latin (plural), from *Embia* (genus name) + Greek *pteron* 'wing'.

embitter ▶ verb [with obj.] [usu. as adj. **embittered**] cause (someone) to feel bitter or resentful: *he died an embittered man.*
– DERIVATIVES **embitterment** noun.

emblazon /ɪmˈbleɪz(ə)n, ɛm-/ ▶ verb [with obj. and adverbial of place] (often **be emblazoned**) conspicuously inscribe or display (a design) on something: *T-shirts **emblazoned with** the names of baseball teams.*
▪depict (a heraldic device): *the Queen's coat of arms is emblazoned on the door panel.* ▪ archaic celebrate or extol publicly: *their success was emblazoned.*
– DERIVATIVES **emblazonment** noun.

emblem /ˈɛmbləm/ ▶ noun a heraldic device or symbolic object as a distinctive badge of a nation, organization, or family: *America's national emblem, the bald eagle.*
▪(**emblem of**) a thing serving as a symbolic representation of a particular quality or concept: *our child would be a dazzling emblem of our love.*
– DERIVATIVES **emblematic** adjective, **emblematical** adjective, **emblematically** adverb.
– ORIGIN late 16th cent. (as a verb): from Latin *emblema* 'inlaid work, raised ornament', from Greek *emblēma* 'insertion', from *emballein* 'throw in, insert', from *em-* 'in' + *ballein* 'to throw'.

emblematist /ɛmˈblɛmətɪst/ ▶ noun a creator or user of emblems, especially in allegorical pictures.

emblematize /ɛmˈblɛmətʌɪz/ (also **-ise**) ▶ verb [with obj.] formal serve as a symbolic representation of (a quality or concept).

emblem book ▶ noun a book of a kind popular in medieval and Renaissance Europe, containing drawings accompanied by allegorical interpretations.

emblements /ˈɛmblɪm(ə)nts/ ▶ plural noun Law, rare the profit from growing crops that have been sown, regarded as personal property.
– ORIGIN late 15th cent.: from Old French *emblaement*, from *emblaier* 'sow with corn' (based on *blé* 'corn').

embodiment ▶ noun a tangible or visible form of an idea, quality, or feeling: *she seemed to be a living embodiment of vitality.*
▪[mass noun] the representation or expression of something in such a form: *it was in Germany alone that his hope seemed capable of embodiment.*

embody /ɪmˈbɒdi, ɛm-/ ▶ verb (**-ies**, **-ied**) [with obj.]
1 be an expression of or give a tangible or visible form to (an idea, quality, or feeling): *a national team that embodies competitive spirit and skill.*
▪provide (a spirit) with a physical form.
2 include or contain (something) as a constituent part: *the changes in law **embodied in** the Children Act.*
3 archaic form (people) into a body, especially for military purposes.
– ORIGIN mid 16th cent.: from **EM-** + **BODY**, on the pattern of Latin *incorporare*.

embolden ▶ verb [with obj.] **1** (often **be emboldened**) give (someone) the courage or confidence to do something or to behave in a certain way: *emboldened by the claret, he pressed his knee against hers.*
2 cause (a piece of text) to appear in a bold typeface: *centre, embolden, and underline the heading.*

embolectomy /ˌɛmbəˈlɛktəmi/ ▶ noun (pl. **-ies**) [mass noun] surgical removal of an embolus.

embolism /ˈɛmbəlɪz(ə)m/ ▶ noun Medicine obstruction of an artery, typically by a clot of blood or an air bubble.
– ORIGIN mid 19th cent.: via late Latin from Greek *embolismos*, from *emballein* 'insert'.

embolization /ˌɛmbəlʌɪˈzeɪʃ(ə)n/ (also **-isation**) ▶ noun [mass noun] Medicine the artificial or natural formation or development of an embolus.

embolus /ˈɛmbələs/ ▶ noun (pl. **emboli** /-lʌɪ, iː/) a blood clot, air bubble, piece of fatty deposit, or other object which has been carried in the bloodstream to lodge in a vessel and cause an embolism.
– DERIVATIVES **embolic** adjective.
– ORIGIN mid 17th cent. (denoting something inserted or moving within another, specifically the plunger of a syringe): from Latin, literally 'piston', from Greek *embolos* 'peg, stopper'. The current sense dates from the mid 19th cent.

embonpoint /ˌɒmbɒ̃ˈpwã/ ▶ noun archaic the plump or fleshy part of a person's body, in particular a woman's bosom.
– ORIGIN late 17th cent.: from French *en bon point* 'in good condition'.

embosom ▶ verb [with obj.] (usu. **be embosomed**) poetic/literary take or press to one's bosom; embrace.
▪enclose or surround (something) protectively.

emboss ▶ verb [with obj.] [usu. as adj. **embossed**] carve or mould a design on (a surface) so that it stands out in relief: *an embossed brass dish.*
– DERIVATIVES **embosser** noun.
– ORIGIN late Middle English: from the Old French base of obsolete French *embosser*, from *em-* 'into' + *boce* 'protuberance'.

embouchure /ˌɒmbʊˈʃʊə/ ▶ noun **1** Music the way in which a player applies the mouth to the mouthpiece of a brass or wind instrument.
▪the mouthpiece of a flute or a similar instrument.
2 archaic the mouth of a river or valley.
– ORIGIN mid 18th cent.: French, from *s'emboucher* 'discharge itself by the mouth', from *emboucher* 'put in or to the mouth', from *em-* 'into' + *bouche* 'mouth'.

embourgeoisement /ɒ̃ˈbʊəʒwɑːzmɒ̃, French ɑ̃buʀʒwazmɑ̃/ ▶ noun the proliferation in a society of values perceived as characteristic of the middle class, especially of materialism.
– ORIGIN 1930s: French, from *embourgeoiser* 'become or make bourgeois'.

embowed /ɪmˈbəʊd, ɛm-/ ▶ adjective poetic/literary bent, arched, or vaulted.
▪[postpositive] Heraldry (of an arm) bent at the elbow; (of a dolphin) with the body curved.

embowel /ɪmˈbaʊ(ə)l, ɛm-/ ▶ verb archaic term for **DISEMBOWEL**.
– ORIGIN early 16th cent.: from Old French *emboweler*, alteration of *esboueler*, from *es-* 'out' + *bouel* 'bowel'.

embower /ɪmˈbaʊə, ɛm-/ ▶ verb [with obj.] (usu. **be embowered**) poetic/literary surround or shelter (a place or a person), especially with trees or climbing plants: *the house stood remote, embowered in trees.*

embrace ▶ verb [with obj.] hold (someone) closely in one's arms, especially as a sign of affection: *Aunt Sophie embraced her warmly* | [no obj.] *the two embraced, holding each other tightly.*
▪accept or support (a belief, theory, or change) willingly and enthusiastically: *much of the population quickly embraced Islam.* ▪ include or contain (something) as a constituent part: *his career embraces a number of activities—composing, playing, and acting.*
▶ noun an act of holding someone closely in one's arms: *they were locked in an embrace.*
▪figurative used to refer to something which is regarded as surrounding or holding someone securely, especially in a restrictive or comforting way: *the first of the former Soviet republics to free itself from the embrace of Moscow.* ▪ [in sing.] an act of accepting or supporting something willingly or enthusiastically: *their eager embrace of foreign influences.*
– DERIVATIVES **embraceable** adjective, **embracement** noun, **embracer** noun.
– ORIGIN Middle English (in the sense 'encircle, surround, enclose'; formerly also as *imbrace*): from Old French *embracer*, based on Latin *in-* 'in' + *bracchium* 'arm'.

embrasure /ɪmˈbreɪʒə, ɛm-/ ▶ noun an opening in a wall or parapet which is bevelled or splayed out on the inside, typically one around a window or door.
– DERIVATIVES **embrasured** adjective.
– ORIGIN early 18th cent.: from French, from obsolete *embraser* (earlier form of *ébraser*) 'widen a door or window opening', of unknown ultimate origin.

embrittle ▶ verb make or become brittle.
– DERIVATIVES **embrittlement** noun.

embrocation /ˌɛmbrəˈkeɪʃ(ə)n/ ▶ noun [mass noun] a liquid used for rubbing on the body to relieve pain from sprains and strains.
– ORIGIN late Middle English: from medieval Latin *embrocatio(n-)*, from the verb *embrocare*, based on Greek *embrokhē* 'lotion'.

embroider ▶ verb [with obj.] decorate (cloth) by sewing patterns on it with thread: *she had already embroidered a dozen little nighties for the babies* | [as adj. **embroidered**] *an embroidered handkerchief* | [no obj.] *she was teaching one of the girls how to embroider.*
▪produce (a design) on cloth in this way: [as adj. **embroidered**] *a chunky knit sweater with embroidered flowers.* ▪ figurative add fictitious or exaggerated details to (an account) to make it more interesting: *she embroidered her stories with colourful detail.*
– DERIVATIVES **embroiderer** noun.
– ORIGIN late Middle English: from Anglo-Norman French *enbrouder*, from *en-* 'in, on' + Old French *brouder, broisder* 'decorate with embroidery', of Germanic origin.

embroidery ▶ noun (pl. **-ies**) [mass noun] the art or pastime of embroidering cloth.
▪cloth decorated in this way. ▪ figurative embellishment or exaggeration in the description or reporting of an event: *fanciful embroidery of the facts.*
– ORIGIN late Middle English: from Anglo-Norman French *enbrouderie*, from *enbrouder* 'embroider'.

embroil ▶ verb [with obj.] [often as adj. **embroiled**] involve (someone) deeply in an argument, conflict, or difficult situation: *she became **embroiled in** a dispute between two women she hardly knew* | *the film's about a journalist who becomes **embroiled with** a nightclub owner.*
▪archaic bring into a state of confusion or disorder.
– DERIVATIVES **embroilment** noun.
– ORIGIN early 17th cent.: from French *embrouiller* 'to muddle'.

embryo /ˈɛmbrɪəʊ/ ▶ noun (pl. **-os**) an unborn or unhatched offspring in the process of development.
▪an unborn human offspring, especially in the first eight weeks from conception, after implantation but before all the organs are developed. Compare with **FETUS**. ▪ Botany the part of a seed which develops into a plant, consisting (in the mature embryo of a higher plant) of a plumule, a radicle, and one or two cotyledons. ▪ figurative a thing at a rudimentary stage that shows potential for development: *a simple commodity economy is merely the embryo of a capitalist economy* | [as modifier] *an embryo central bank.*
– PHRASES **in embryo** at a rudimentary stage with the potential for further development.
– DERIVATIVES **embryonal** /ˈɛmbrɪən(ə)l/ adjective.
– ORIGIN late Middle English: via late Latin from Greek *embruon* 'fetus', from *em-* 'into' + *bruein* 'swell, grow'.

embryo- ▶ combining form representing **EMBRYO**.

embryogenesis /ˌɛmbrɪə(ʊ)ˈdʒɛnɪsɪs/ ▶ noun [mass noun] Biology the formation and development of an embryo.
– DERIVATIVES **embryogenic** adjective, **embryogeny** noun.

embryology /ˌɛmbrɪˈɒlədʒi/ ▶ noun [mass noun] the branch of biology and medicine concerned with the study of embryos and their development.
– DERIVATIVES **embryologic** adjective, **embryological** adjective, **embryologically** adverb, **embryologist** noun.

embryonic /ˌɛmbrɪˈɒnɪk/ ▶ adjective of or relating to an embryo.
▪figurative (of a system, idea, or organization) in a rudimentary stage with potential for further development: *the plan is still in its embryonic stages.*
– DERIVATIVES **embryonically** adverb.
– ORIGIN mid 19th cent.: from late Latin *embryo*, *embryon-* 'embryo' + **-IC**.

embus /ɪmˈbʌs, ɛm-/ ▶ verb (**embused**, **embusing** or **embussed**, **embussing**) [no obj.] chiefly Military board a bus.

emcee /ɛmˈsiː/ N. Amer. informal ▶ noun a master of ceremonies.
▶ verb (**emcees**, **emceed**, **emceeing**) [with obj.] perform such a role at (a public entertainment or a large social occasion).
– ORIGIN 1930s (originally US): representing a pronunciation of **MC**.

em dash ▶ noun another term for **EM RULE**.

-eme ▶ suffix Linguistics forming nouns denoting linguistic units that are in systemic contrast with one other: *grapheme* | *phoneme*.
– ORIGIN abstracted from **PHONEME**.

emend /ɪˈmɛnd/ ▶ verb [with obj.] make corrections and improvements to (a text).

■alter (something) in such a way as to correct it: *the year of his death might need to be emended to 652* | [with clause] *he hesitated and quickly emended what he had said.*
– DERIVATIVES **emendation** noun.
– ORIGIN late Middle English: from Latin *emendare*, from *e-* (variant of *ex-*) 'out of' + *menda* 'a fault'. Compare with AMEND.

emerald ▶ noun **1** a bright green precious stone consisting of a chromium-rich variety of beryl: [as modifier] *an emerald necklace.*
2 [mass noun] a bright green colour like that of an emerald: [as modifier] *the leaves are emerald green.*
3 (also **emerald moth**) a slender-bodied green moth, the colour of which tends to fade as the moth ages.
● Several genera in the family Geometridae.
4 a hawker dragonfly with a metallic green body.
● *Cordulia* and other genera, family Corduliidae.
5 a small hummingbird with bright metallic green plumage and darker wings and tail, found mainly in the area of the Caribbean and Central America.
● Three genera, in particular *Chlorostilbon* and *Amazilia*, family Trochilidae: numerous species.
▶ adjective bright green in colour: *beyond the airport lay emerald hills.*
– ORIGIN Middle English: from Old French *e(s)meraud*, ultimately via Latin from Greek *(s)maragdos*, via Prakrit from Semitic (compare with Hebrew *bāreqeṯ*, from *bāraq* 'flash, sparkle').

emerald-cut ▶ adjective (of a gem) cut in a square shape with stepped facets.

Emerald Isle a name for Ireland.

emerge /ɪˈmɜːdʒ/ ▶ verb [no obj.] move out of or away from something and come into view: *black ravens emerged from the fog.*
■become apparent, important, or prominent: *United have **emerged as** the bookies' clear favourite* | [as adj. **emerging**] *a world of emerging economic giants.* ■ (of facts or circumstances) become known: *reports of a deadlock emerged during preliminary discussions* | [with clause] *it emerged that the Trade Secretary and the Chancellor are still at loggerheads.* ■ recover from or survive a difficult or demanding situation: *the economy has started to **emerge from** recession.* ■ (of an insect or other invertebrate) break out from an egg, cocoon, or pupal case.
– DERIVATIVES **emergence** noun.
– ORIGIN late 16th cent. (in the sense 'become known, come to light'): from Latin *emergere*, from *e-* (variant of *ex-*) 'out, forth' + *mergere* 'to dip'.

emergency ▶ noun (pl. **-ies**) **1** a serious, unexpected, and often dangerous situation requiring immediate action: *your quick response in an emergency could be a life saver* | [mass noun] *times of emergency.*
■[as modifier] arising from or needed or used in an emergency: *an emergency exit.* ■ a person with a medical condition requiring immediate treatment. ■ N. Amer. the department in a hospital which provides immediate treatment: *a doctor in emergency cleans the wound.*
2 Austral. (in sport) a reserve, especially a reserve runner in horse racing.
– ORIGIN mid 17th cent.: from medieval Latin *emergentia*, from Latin *emergere* 'arise, bring to light' (see EMERGE).

emergency cord ▶ noun a cord or chain on a train which a passenger may pull in an emergency, causing the train to brake.

emergency room ▶ noun N. Amer. the casualty department of a hospital.

emergency services ▶ plural noun the public organizations that respond to and deal with emergencies when they occur, especially the ambulance service, the police, and the fire brigade.

emergent ▶ adjective in the process of coming into being or becoming prominent: *the emergent democracies of eastern Europe.*
■Philosophy (of a property) arising as an effect of complex causes and not analysable simply as the sum of their effects. ■ Ecology of or denoting a plant which is taller than the surrounding vegetation, especially a tall tree in a forest. ■ of or denoting a water plant with leaves and flowers that appear above the water surface.
▶ noun Philosophy an emergent property.
■Ecology an emergent tree or other plant.
– ORIGIN late Middle English (in the sense 'occurring unexpectedly'): from Latin *emergent-* 'arising from', from the verb *emergere* (see EMERGE).

emeritus /ɪˈmɛrɪtəs, iː-/ ▶ adjective (of the former

holder of an office, especially a university professor) having retired but allowed to retain their title as an honour: *emeritus professor of microbiology* | [postpositive] *the National Gallery's director emeritus.*
– ORIGIN mid 18th cent.: from Latin, past participle of *emereri* 'earn one's discharge by service', from *e-* (variant of *ex-*) 'out of, from' + *mereri* 'earn'.

emerse /ɪˈmɜːs/ ▶ adjective Botany denoting or characteristic of an aquatic plant reaching above the surface of the water. Contrasted with SUBMERSE.
– DERIVATIVES **emersed** adjective.
– ORIGIN late 17th cent. (as *emersed*): from Latin *emersus* 'arisen', past participle of *emergere* (see EMERGE).

emersion ▶ noun [mass noun] the process or state of emerging from or being out of water after being submerged.
■Astronomy the reappearance of a celestial body after its eclipse or occultation.
– ORIGIN mid 17th cent.: from late Latin *emersio(n-)*, from Latin *emergere* (see EMERGE).

Emerson /ˈɛməs(ə)n/, Ralph Waldo (1803–82), American philosopher and poet. He evolved the concept of Transcendentalism, which found expression in his essay *Nature* (1836).

emery /ˈɛm(ə)ri/ ▶ noun [mass noun] a greyish-black form of corundum containing iron oxide or other impurities, used in powdered form as an abrasive.
■[as modifier] denoting materials coated with emery for polishing, smoothing, or grinding: *emery paper.*
– ORIGIN late 15th cent.: from French *émeri*, from Old French *esmeri*, from Italian *smeriglio*, based on Greek *smuris*, *smiris* 'polishing powder'.

emery board ▶ noun a strip of thin wood or card coated with emery or another abrasive and used as a nail file.

Emesa /ˈɛməsə/ a city in ancient Syria, on the River Orontes on the site of present-day Homs. It was famous for its temple to the sun god Elah-Gabal.

emesis /ˈɛmɪsɪs/ ▶ noun [mass noun] technical the action or process of vomiting.
– ORIGIN late 19th cent.: from Greek, from *emein* 'to vomit'.

emetic /ɪˈmɛtɪk/ ▶ adjective (of a substance) causing vomiting.
■informal nauseating or revolting: *that emetic music endemic to department stores.*
▶ noun a medicine or other substance which causes vomiting.
– ORIGIN mid 17th cent.: from Greek *emetikos*, from *emein* 'to vomit'.

emetine /ˈɛmɪtiːn/ ▶ noun [mass noun] an alkaloid present in ipecacuanha and formerly used in the treatment of amoebic infections and as an emetic in aversion therapy.
– ORIGIN early 19th cent.: from Greek *emetos* 'vomiting' + -INE⁴.

EMF ▶ abbreviation for ■ electromagnetic field(s). ■ (emf) electromotive force. ■ European Monetary Fund.

EMG ▶ abbreviation for electromyogram or electromyography.

-emia ▶ combining form US spelling of -AEMIA.

emic /ˈiːmɪk/ Anthropology ▶ adjective relating to or denoting an approach to the study or description of a particular language or culture in terms of its internal elements and their functioning rather than in terms of any existing external scheme. Often contrasted with ETIC.
▶ plural noun (**emics**) [treated as sing.] study adopting this approach.
– ORIGIN 1950s: abstracted from such words as *phonemic* (see PHONEME) and SYSTEMIC.

emigrant ▶ noun a person who leaves their own country in order to settle permanently in another.
– ORIGIN mid 18th cent.: from Latin *emigrant-* 'migrating from', from the verb *emigrare* (see EMIGRATE).

emigrate /ˈɛmɪɡreɪt/ ▶ verb [no obj.] leave one's own country in order to settle permanently in another: *Rose's parents emigrated to Australia.*
– DERIVATIVES **emigration** noun.
– ORIGIN late 18th cent.: from Latin *emigrat-* 'emigrated', from the verb *emigrare*, from *e-* (variant of *ex-*) 'out of' + *migrare* 'migrate'.

émigré /ˈɛmɪɡreɪ/ ▶ noun a person who has left their

own country in order to settle in another, typically for political reasons.
– ORIGIN late 18th cent. (originally denoting a person escaping the French Revolution): French, past participle of *émigrer* 'emigrate'.

Emi Koussi /ˌɛmi ˈkuːsə/ a volcanic mountain in the Sahara, in northern Chad, the highest peak in the Tibesti Mountains.

Emilia-Romagna /ɛˌmiːljərəʊˈmɑːnjə, Italian eˈmiːlja roˈmaɲɲa/ a region of northern Italy; capital, Bologna.

eminence /ˈɛmɪnəns/ ▶ noun **1** [mass noun] fame or recognized superiority, especially within a particular sphere or profession: *her eminence in cinematography.*
■[count noun] an important, influential, or distinguished person: *the Lord Chancellor canvassed the views of various legal eminences.* ■ (**His/Your Eminence**) a title given to a Roman Catholic cardinal, or used in addressing him: *His Eminence, Cardinal Thomas Wolsey.*
2 formal or poetic/literary a piece of rising ground: *an eminence commanding the River Emme.*
■Anatomy a slight projection from the surface of a part of the body.
– ORIGIN Middle English: from Latin *eminentia*, from *eminere* 'jut, project'.

éminence grise /ˌeɪmɪnɒ̃s ˈɡriːz/ ▶ noun (pl. **éminences grises** pronunc. same) a person who exercises power or influence in a certain sphere without holding an official position.
– ORIGIN 1930s: French, literally 'grey eminence'. The term was originally applied to Cardinal Richelieu's grey-cloaked private secretary, Père Joseph (1577–1638).

eminent ▶ adjective (of a person) famous and respected within a particular sphere or profession: *one of the world's most eminent statisticians.*
■[attrib.] used to emphasize the presence of a positive quality: *the guitar's eminent suitability for recording studio work.*
– DERIVATIVES **eminently** adverb [as submodifier] *an eminently readable textbook.*
– ORIGIN late Middle English: from Latin *eminent-* 'jutting, projecting', from the verb *eminere*.

eminent domain ▶ noun [mass noun] Law the right of a government or its agent to expropriate private property for public use, with payment of compensation. In the UK it is used chiefly of international law, whereas in the US it is used of federal and state governments.

emir /ˈɛmɪə/ (also **amir**) ▶ noun a title of various Muslim (mainly Arab) rulers: *HRH the Emir of Kuwait.*
■historical a Muslim (usually Arab) military commander or local chief.
– ORIGIN late 16th cent. (denoting a male descendant of Muhammad): from French *émir*, from Arabic *'amīr* (see AMIR).

emirate /ˈɛmɪrət/ ▶ noun the rank, lands, or reign of an emir.

emissary /ˈɛmɪs(ə)ri/ ▶ noun (pl. **-ies**) a person sent as a diplomatic representative on a special mission.
– ORIGIN early 17th cent.: from Latin *emissarius* 'scout, spy', from *emittere* 'send out' (see EMIT).

emission /ɪˈmɪʃ(ə)n/ ▶ noun [mass noun] the production and discharge of something, especially gas or radiation: *the effects of lead emission on health* | [count noun] *cuts in carbon dioxide emissions.*
■[count noun] an ejaculation of semen.
– ORIGIN late Middle English (in the sense 'emanation'): from Latin *emissio(n-)*, from *emiss-* 'sent out', from the verb *emittere* (see EMIT).

emission nebula ▶ noun Astronomy a nebula that shines with its own light.

emission spectrum ▶ noun a spectrum of the electromagnetic radiation emitted by a source. Compare with ABSORPTION SPECTRUM.

emissive ▶ adjective technical having the power to radiate something, especially light, heat, or radiation.
– DERIVATIVES **emissivity** noun.
– ORIGIN mid 17th cent. (in the sense 'that is emitted'): from Latin *emiss-* 'emitted, sent out' (from the verb *emittere*) + -IVE.

emit ▶ verb (**emitted, emitting**) [with obj.] produce and discharge (something, especially gas or radiation): *coal-fired power stations continue to emit large quantities of sulphur dioxide.*
■make (a sound): *she emitted a sound like laughter.*

– ORIGIN early 17th cent.: from Latin *emittere*, from *e-* (variant of *ex-*) 'out of' + *mittere* 'send'.

emitter ▶ noun a thing which emits something.
▪ Electronics a region in a bipolar transistor producing carriers of current.

Emmanuel /ɪˈmanjʊəl/ (also **Immanuel**) the name given to Christ as the deliverer of Judah prophesied by Isaiah (Isa. 7:14, 8:8; Matt. 1:23).

emmenagogue /ɪˈmiːnəgɒg, ɛ-/ ▶ noun Medicine a substance that stimulates or increases menstrual flow.
– ORIGIN early 18th cent.: from Greek *emmēna* 'menses' + *agōgos* 'eliciting'.

Emmental /ˈɛməntɑːl/ (also **Emmenthal**) ▶ noun [mass noun] a kind of hard Swiss cheese with many holes in it, similar to Gruyère.
– ORIGIN from German *Emmentaler*, from *Emmental*, the name of a valley in Switzerland where the cheese was originally made.

emmer /ˈɛmə/ ▶ noun [mass noun] an old kind of wheat with bearded ears and spikelets that each contain two grains, now grown mainly for fodder and breakfast cereals. Compare with **EINKORN**, **SPELT**.
• *Triticum dicoccum*, family Gramineae.
– ORIGIN early 20th cent.: from German, from Old High German *amer* 'spelt'.

emmet /ˈɛmɪt/ ▶ noun dialect an ant.
▪ humorous or derogatory a holidaymaker or tourist.
– ORIGIN Old English *ǣmete* (see **ANT**).

Emmy ▶ noun (pl. **Emmys**) (in the US) a statuette awarded annually to an outstanding television programme or performer.
– ORIGIN 1940s: said to be from *Immy*, short for *image orthicon tube* (a kind of television camera tube).

emollient /ɪˈmɒlɪənt/ ▶ adjective having the quality of softening or soothing the skin.
▪ attempting to avoid confrontation or anger; soothing or calming: *the president's emollient approach to differences.*
▶ noun a preparation that softens the skin.
– DERIVATIVES **emollience** noun.
– ORIGIN mid 17th cent.: from Latin *emollient-* 'making soft', from the verb *emollire*, from *e-* (variant of *ex-* 'out') + *mollis* 'soft'.

emolument /ɪˈmɒljʊm(ə)nt, ɛ-/ ▶ noun (usu. **emoluments**) formal a salary, fee, or profit from employment or office: *the directors' emoluments.*
– ORIGIN late Middle English: from Latin *emolumentum*, originally probably 'payment to a miller for grinding corn', from *emolere* 'grind up', from *e-* (variant of *ex-*) 'out, thoroughly' + *molere* 'grind'.

Emona /ɪˈməʊnə/ Roman name for **LJUBLJANA**.

emote /ɪˈməʊt/ ▶ verb [no obj.] (especially of an actor) portray emotion in a theatrical manner.
– DERIVATIVES **emoter** noun.
– ORIGIN early 20th cent. (originally US): back-formation from **EMOTION**.

emoticon /ɪˈməʊtɪkɒn, -ˈmɒtɪ-/ ▶ noun a representation of a facial expression such as a smile or frown, formed by various combinations of keyboard characters and used in electronic communications to convey the writer's feelings or intended tone.
– ORIGIN 1990s: blend of **EMOTION** and **ICON**.

emotion ▶ noun a strong feeling deriving from one's circumstances, mood, or relationships with others: *she was attempting to control her emotions* | [mass noun] *his voice was low and shaky with emotion.*
▪ [mass noun] instinctive or intuitive feeling as distinguished from reasoning or knowledge: *responses have to be based on historical insight, not simply on emotion.*
– DERIVATIVES **emotionless** adjective.
– ORIGIN mid 16th cent. (denoting a public disturbance or commotion): from French *émotion*, from *émouvoir* 'excite', based on Latin *emovere*, from *e-* (variant of *ex-*) 'out' + *movere* 'move'. The sense 'mental agitation' dates from the mid 17th cent., the current general sense from the early 19th cent.

emotional ▶ adjective of or relating to a person's emotions: *pupils with emotional difficulties.*
▪ arousing or characterized by intense feeling: *an emotional speech.* ▪ (of a person) having feelings that are easily excited and openly displayed: *he was a strongly emotional young man.*
– DERIVATIVES **emotionalism** noun, **emotionalist** noun & adjective, **emotionality** noun, **emotionalize** (also **-ise**) verb, **emotionally** adverb.

emotive ▶ adjective arousing or able to arouse intense feeling: *animal experimentation is an emotive subject* | *the issue has proved highly emotive.*
▪ expressing a person's feelings rather than being neutrally or objectively descriptive: *the comparisons are emotive rather than analytic.*
– DERIVATIVES **emotively** adverb, **emotiveness** noun, **emotivity** /ˌiːməʊˈtɪvɪti/ noun.
– ORIGIN mid 18th cent.: from Latin *emot-* 'moved', from the verb *emovere* (see **EMOTION**).

USAGE The words **emotive** and **emotional** share similarities but are not simply interchangeable. **Emotive** is used to mean 'arousing intense feeling', while **emotional** tends to mean 'characterized by intense feeling'. Thus an ***emotive issue*** is one which is likely to arouse people's passions, while an ***emotional response*** is one which is itself full of passion. In sentences such as *we took our* ***emotive*** *farewells* (taken from the British National Corpus) the word **emotive** has been used in a context where **emotional** would be more appropriate.

emotivism ▶ noun [mass noun] Philosophy an ethical theory which regards ethical and value judgements as expressions of feeling or attitude and prescriptions of action, rather than assertions or reports of anything.
– DERIVATIVES **emotivist** noun.

empanada /ˌɛmpəˈnɑːdə/ ▶ noun a Spanish or Latin American pastry turnover filled with a variety of savoury ingredients and baked or fried.
– ORIGIN Spanish, feminine past participle (used as a noun) of *empanar* 'roll in pastry', based on Latin *panis* 'bread'.

empanel ▶ verb variant spelling of **IMPANEL**.
– DERIVATIVES **empanelment** noun.

empath /ˈɛmpaθ/ ▶ noun (chiefly in science fiction) a person with the paranormal ability to apprehend the mental or emotional state of another individual.

empathize (also **-ise**) ▶ verb [no obj.] understand and share the feelings of another: *counsellors need to be able to* ***empathize with*** *people.*

empathy /ˈɛmpəθi/ ▶ noun [mass noun] the ability to understand and share the feelings of another.
– DERIVATIVES **empathetic** adjective, **empathetically** adverb, **empathic** /ɛmˈpaθɪk/ adjective, **empathically** adverb.
– ORIGIN early 20th cent.: from Greek *empatheia* (from *em-* 'in' + *pathos* 'feeling') translating German *Einfühlung*.

Empedocles /ɛmˈpɛdəkliːz/ (*c*.493–*c*.433 BC), Greek philosopher, born in Sicily. He taught that the universe is composed of fire, air, water, and earth, which mingle and separate under the influence of the opposing principles of Love and Strife. According to legend he leapt into the crater of Mount Etna in order that he might be thought a god.

empennage /ɛmˈpɛnɪdʒ/ ▶ noun Aeronautics an arrangement of stabilizing surfaces at the tail of an aircraft.
– ORIGIN early 20th cent.: from French, from *empenner* 'to feather an arrow', from *em-* 'in' + *penne* 'a feather' (from Latin *penna*).

emperor ▶ noun **1** a sovereign ruler of great power and rank, especially one ruling an empire.
2 an orange and brown North American butterfly with a swift dodging flight, breeding chiefly on hackberries.
• Genus *Asterocampa*, subfamily Apaturinae, family Nymphalidae: several species, in particular the **tawny emperor** (*A. clyton*). See also **PURPLE EMPEROR**.
– DERIVATIVES **emperorship** noun.
– ORIGIN Middle English (especially representing the title given to the head of the Roman Empire): from Old French *emperere*, from Latin *imperator* 'military commander', from *imperare* 'to command', from *in-* 'towards' + *parare* 'prepare, contrive'.

emperor dragonfly ▶ noun a fast-flying hawker dragonfly with a bluish body, which is one of the largest dragonflies in Europe.
• *Anax imperator*, family Aeshnidae.

emperor moth ▶ noun a large moth of the silk moth family with eyespots on all four wings.
• *Saturnia* and other genera, family Saturniidae: several species, in particular the common European *S. pavonia*.

emperor penguin ▶ noun the largest penguin, which has a yellow patch on each side of the head and rears its young during the Antarctic winter.
• *Aptenodytes forsteri*, family Spheniscidae.

emphasis /ˈɛmfəsɪs/ ▶ noun (pl. **emphases** /-siːz/) [mass noun] special importance, value, or prominence given to something: *they placed great emphasis on the individual's freedom* | [count noun] *different emphases and viewpoints.*
▪ stress laid on a word or words to indicate special meaning or particular importance. ▪ vigour or intensity of expression: *he spoke with emphasis and with complete conviction.*
– ORIGIN late 16th cent.: via Latin from Greek, originally 'appearance, show', later denoting a figure of speech in which more is implied than is said (the original sense in English), from *emphainein* 'exhibit', from *em-* 'in, within' + *phainein* 'to show'.

emphasize (also **-ise**) ▶ verb [with obj.] give special importance or prominence to (something) in speaking or writing: *he jabbed a finger into the table top to emphasize his point* | [with clause] *he* ***emphasized that*** *the drug works in only 30 per cent of cases.*
▪ lay stress on (a word or phrase) when speaking. ▪ make (something) more clearly defined: *a hip-length jacket which emphasized her shape.*

emphatic ▶ adjective showing or giving emphasis; expressing something forcibly and clearly: *the children were* ***emphatic that*** *they would like to repeat the experience* | *an emphatic movement of his hand*
▪ (of an action or event or its result) definite and clear: *an emphatic World Cup win.* ▪ (of word or syllable) bearing the stress. ▪ Linguistics denoting certain Arabic consonants which are pronounced with both dental articulation and constriction of the pharynx.
▶ noun Linguistics an emphatic consonant.
– ORIGIN early 18th cent.: via late Latin from Greek *emphatikos*, from *emphasis* (see **EMPHASIS**).

emphatically ▶ adverb in a forceful way.
▪ [as submodifier] without doubt; clearly: *Jane, though born in California, feels emphatically English.* ▪ [sentence adverb] used to give emphasis to a statement: *Greg is emphatically not a slacker.*

emphysema /ˌɛmfɪˈsiːmə/ ▶ noun [mass noun] Medicine **1** (also **pulmonary emphysema**) a condition in which the air sacs of the lungs are damaged and enlarged, causing breathlessness.
2 a condition in which air is abnormally present within the body tissues.
– ORIGIN mid 17th cent. (in sense 2): via late Latin from Greek *emphusēma*, from *emphusan* 'puff up'.

empire ▶ noun an extensive group of states or countries under a single supreme authority, formerly especially an emperor or empress: [in names] *the Roman Empire.*
▪ a large commercial organization owned or controlled by one person or group: *her business empire grew.* ▪ an extensive operation or sphere of activity controlled by one person or group: *the kitchen had once been the school dinner ladies' empire.* ▪ [mass noun] supreme political power over several countries when exercised by a single authority: *he encouraged the Greeks in their dream of empire in Asia Minor.* ▪ [mass noun] archaic absolute control over a person or group.
▶ adjective (**Empire**) [attrib.] denoting a style of furniture, decoration, or dress fashionable during the First or (less commonly) the Second Empire in France. The decorative style was neoclassical but marked by an interest in Egyptian and other ancient motifs probably inspired by Napoleon's Egyptian campaigns.
▪ Brit. dated denoting produce from the Commonwealth.
– ORIGIN Middle English: via Old French from Latin *imperium*, related to *imperare* 'to command' (see **EMPEROR**).

empire builder ▶ noun a person who adds to or strengthens a state's empire.
▪ a person who seeks more power, responsibility, or staff within an organization for the purposes of self-aggrandizement.
– DERIVATIVES **empire-building** noun.

Empire Day ▶ noun former name of **COMMONWEALTH DAY**.

empire line ▶ noun [usu. as modifier] a style of women's clothing characterized by a waistline cut just under the bust and typically a low neckline, first popular during the First Empire: *empire-line dresses.*

Empire State informal name for the state of **NEW YORK**.

Empire State Building a skyscraper on Fifth Avenue, New York City, which was for several years the tallest building in the world. When first erected, in 1930–1, it measured 381 m (1,250 ft); the addition of a television mast in 1951 brought its height to 449 m (1,472 ft).

Empire State of the South informal name for the US state of **GEORGIA**.

empiric /ɛmˈpɪrɪk, ɪm-/ ▶ **adjective** another term for **EMPIRICAL**.
▶ **noun** archaic a person who, in medicine or other branches of science, relies solely on observation and experiment.
■ a quack doctor.
– ORIGIN late Middle English: via Latin from Greek *empeirikos*, from *empeiria* 'experience', from *empeiros* 'skilled' (based on *peira* 'trial, experiment').

empirical ▶ **adjective** based on, concerned with, or verifiable by observation or experience rather than theory or pure logic: *they provided considerable empirical evidence to support their argument.*
– DERIVATIVES **empirically** adverb.

empirical formula ▶ **noun** Chemistry a formula giving the proportions of the elements present in a compound but not the actual numbers or arrangement of atoms.

empiricism /ɛmˈpɪrɪsɪz(ə)m/ ▶ **noun** [mass noun] Philosophy the theory that all knowledge is derived from sense-experience. Stimulated by the rise of experimental science, it developed in the 17th and 18th centuries, expounded in particular by John Locke, George Berkeley, and David Hume. Compare with **PHENOMENALISM**.
– DERIVATIVES **empiricist** noun & adjective.

emplacement ▶ **noun 1** a structure on or in which something is firmly placed.
■ a platform or defended position where a gun is placed for firing.
2 [mass noun] chiefly Geology the process or state of setting something in place or being set in place.
– ORIGIN early 19th cent.: from French, from *em-* 'in' + *place* 'a place'.

emplane (also **enplane**) ▶ **verb** go or put on board an aircraft.

employ ▶ **verb** [with obj.] **1** give work to (someone) and pay them for it: *the firm employs 150 people* | [with obj. and infinitive] *temporary staff can be employed to undertake much of the work.*
■ keep occupied: *most of the newcomers are* **employed in** *developing the technology into a product.*
2 make use of: *the methods they have employed to collect the data.*
▶ **noun** [in sing.] the state or fact of being employed for wages or a salary: *I started work* **in the employ of** *a grocer and wine merchant.*
■ archaic employment: *her place of employ.*
– DERIVATIVES **employability** noun, **employable** adjective.
– ORIGIN late Middle English (formerly also as *imploy*): from Old French *employer*, based on Latin *implicari* 'be involved in or attached to', passive form of *implicare* (see **IMPLY**). In the 16th and 17th cent. the word also had the senses 'enfold, entangle' and 'imply', derived directly from Latin; compare with **IMPLICATE**.

employee ▶ **noun** a person employed for wages or salary, especially at non-executive level.

employer ▶ **noun** a person or organization that employs people.

employment ▶ **noun** [mass noun] the condition of having paid work: *a fall in the numbers* **in** *full-time employment.*
■ [count noun] a person's trade or profession. ■ the action of giving work to someone: *the employment of a full-time tutor.*

employment agency ▶ **noun** a business that finds employers or employees for those seeking them.

employment office ▶ **noun** (in the UK) a government employment agency.

empolder ▶ **verb** variant spelling of **IMPOLDER**.

emporium /ɛmˈpɔːrɪəm, ɪm-/ ▶ **noun** (pl. **emporia** /-rɪə/ or **emporiums**) a large retail store selling a wide variety of goods.
■ archaic a centre of commerce; a market.
– ORIGIN late 16th cent.: from Latin, from Greek *emporion*, from *emporos* 'merchant', based on a stem meaning 'to journey'.

empower ▶ **verb** [with obj. and infinitive] give (someone) the authority or power to do something: *nobody was empowered to sign cheques on her behalf.*
■ [with obj.] make (someone) stronger and more confident, especially in controlling their life and claiming their rights: *movements to empower the poor.*
– DERIVATIVES **empowerment** noun.

empress /ˈɛmprɪs/ ▶ **noun** a female emperor.
■ the wife or widow of an emperor.
– ORIGIN Middle English: from Old French *emperesse*, feminine of *emperere* (see **EMPEROR**).

empressement /ɒ̃ˈprɛsmɒ̃/ ▶ **noun** [mass noun] archaic animated eagerness or friendliness; effusion.
– ORIGIN from French, from *empresser* 'rush eagerly'.

Empson /ˈɛmps(ə)n/, Sir William (1906–84), English poet and literary critic. His influential literary criticism includes *Seven Types of Ambiguity* (1930).

empty ▶ **adjective** (**emptier**, **emptiest**) containing nothing; not filled or occupied: *he took his empty coffee cup back to the counter* | *the room was* **empty of** *furniture.*
■ figurative (of words or a gesture) having no meaning or likelihood of fulfilment. ■ figurative having no value or purpose: *after a string of unhappy love affairs, her life felt empty and meaningless.* ■ Mathematics (of a set) containing no members or elements.
▶ **verb** (**-ies**, **-ied**) [with obj.] remove all the contents of (a container): *we empty the till each night at closing time* | *pockets were* **emptied of** *loose change.*
■ remove (the contents) from a container: *he* **emptied out** *the contents of his briefcase.* ■ [no obj.] (of a place) be vacated by people in it: *the pub suddenly seemed to empty.* ■ [no obj.] (**empty into**) (of a river) discharge itself into (the sea or a lake).
▶ **noun** (pl. **-ies**) (usu. **empties**) informal a container (especially a bottle or glass) left empty of its contents.
– PHRASES **be running on empty** have exhausted all of one's resources or sustenance. **empty vessels make most noise** (or **sound**) proverb those with least wisdom or knowledge are always the most talkative. **on an empty stomach** see **STOMACH**.
– DERIVATIVES **emptily** adverb, **emptiness** noun.
– ORIGIN Old English *æmtig*, *æmetig* 'at leisure, unoccupied, empty', from *æmetta* 'leisure', perhaps from *ā* 'no, not' + *mōt* 'meeting' (see **MOOT**).

empty calories ▶ **plural noun** calories derived from food containing no nutrients.

empty-handed ▶ **adjective** [predic.] having failed to obtain or achieve what one wanted: *the burglars fled empty-handed.*

empty-headed ▶ **adjective** unintelligent and foolish: *an empty-headed bimbo.*

empty nester ▶ **noun** informal, chiefly N. Amer. a parent whose children have grown up and left home.

Empty Quarter another name for **RUB' AL KHALI**.

empty word ▶ **noun** Grammar a word which has only a grammatical function, and no meaning in itself (for example, the infinitive marker *to* in English).

empurple ▶ **verb** make or become purple: [no obj.] *his face empurpled with fury.*

empyema /ˌɛmpʌɪˈiːmə/ ▶ **noun** Medicine the collection of pus in a cavity in the body, especially in the pleural cavity.
– ORIGIN late Middle English: via late Latin from Greek *empuēma*, from *empuein* 'suppurate', from *em-* 'in' + *puon* 'pus'.

empyrean /ˌɛmpʌɪˈriːən, -pɪ-, ɛmˈpɪrɪən/ ▶ **adjective** belonging to or deriving from heaven.
▶ **noun** (**the empyrean**) heaven, in particular the highest part of heaven.
■ poetic/literary the visible heavens; the sky.
– DERIVATIVES **empyreal** /ˌɛmpʌɪˈriːəl, -pɪ-, ɛmˈpɪrɪəl/ adjective.
– ORIGIN late Middle English (as an adjective): via medieval Latin from Greek *empurios*, from *en-* 'in' + *pur* 'fire'. The noun dates from the mid 17th cent.

em rule /ˈɛm ruːl/ ▶ **noun** Brit. a long dash used in punctuation.

EMS ▶ **abbreviation for** ■ European Monetary System. ■ expanded memory system, a system for increasing the amount of memory available to a personal computer, now largely superseded by XMS.

EMU ▶ **abbreviation for** European Monetary Union.

emu¹ ▶ **noun** a large flightless fast-running Australian bird resembling the ostrich, with shaggy grey or brown plumage, bare blue skin on the head and neck, and three-toed feet.
• *Dromaius novaehollandiae*, the only member of the family Dromaiidae.
– ORIGIN early 17th cent.: from Portuguese *ema*. The word originally denoted the cassowary, later the greater rhea; current usage dates from the early 19th cent.

emu² Brit. ▶ **abbreviation for** ■ electric multiple unit. ■ electromagnetic unit(s).

emu bush ▶ **noun** an Australian shrub that typically has reddish flowers and small oval fruits which are sometimes eaten by emus.
• Genus *Eremophila*, family Myoporaceae: several species.

emulate /ˈɛmjʊleɪt/ ▶ **verb** [with obj.] match or surpass (a person or achievement), typically by imitation: *lesser men trying to emulate his greatness.*
■ imitate: *hers is not a hairstyle I wish to emulate.* ■ Computing reproduce the function or action of (a different computer or software system).
– DERIVATIVES **emulation** noun, **emulative** adjective, **emulator** noun.
– ORIGIN late 16th cent.: from Latin *aemulat-* 'rivalled, equalled', from the verb *aemulari*, from *aemulus* 'rival'.

emulous /ˈɛmjʊləs/ ▶ **adjective** (often **emulous of**) formal seeking to emulate or imitate someone or something.
■ motivated by a spirit of rivalry: *emulous young writers.*
– DERIVATIVES **emulously** adverb.
– ORIGIN late Middle English (in the sense 'resembling, imitating'): from Latin *aemulus* 'rival'. Current senses date from the mid 16th cent.

emulsifier ▶ **noun** a substance that stabilizes an emulsion, in particular a food additive used to stabilize processed foods.
■ an apparatus used for making an emulsion by stirring or shaking a substance.

emulsify /ɪˈmʌlsɪfʌɪ/ ▶ **verb** (**-ies**, **-ied**) make into or become an emulsion: [with obj.] *mustard helps to emulsify a vinaigrette.*
– DERIVATIVES **emulsifiable** adjective, **emulsification** noun.

emulsion /ɪˈmʌlʃ(ə)n/ ▶ **noun** a fine dispersion of minute droplets of one liquid in another in which it is not soluble or miscible.
■ a light-sensitive coating for photographic films and plates, containing crystals of a silver compound dispersed in a medium such as gelatin. ■ short for **EMULSION PAINT**.
▶ **verb** [with obj.] informal paint with emulsion paint.
– DERIVATIVES **emulsive** adjective.
– ORIGIN early 17th cent. (denoting a milky liquid made by crushing almonds in water): from modern Latin *emulsio(n-)*, from the verb *emulgere* 'milk out', from *e-* (variant of *ex-*) 'out' + *mulgere* 'to milk'.

emulsion paint ▶ **noun** [mass noun] a paint, used typically for walls, consisting of pigment bound in a synthetic resin which forms an emulsion with water.

emu-wren ▶ **noun** a small Australian songbird of the fairy wren family, with a very long thin cocked tail consisting of only six feathers that have a coarse open structure resembling that of emu feathers.
• Genus *Stipiturus*, family Maluridae: three species.

en ▶ **noun** Printing a unit of measurement equal to half an em and approximately the average width of typeset characters, used especially for estimating the total amount of space a text will require.
– ORIGIN late 18th cent.: the letter *N* represented as a word, since it is approximately this width.

en-¹ (also **em-**) ▶ **prefix 1** (added to nouns) forming verbs meaning 'put into or on': *engulf* | *embed.*
2 (added to nouns and adjectives) forming verbs meaning 'bring into the condition of' (as in *encrust*).
■ often forming verbs having the suffix *-en* (as in *embolden*, *enliven*).
3 (added to verbs) in; into; on: *ensnare.*
■ as an intensifier: *entangle.*
– ORIGIN from French, from Latin *in-*. See also **IN-²**, a commonly found by-form.

en-² (also **em-**) ▶ **prefix** within; inside: *empathy* | *energy* | *enthusiasm.*
– ORIGIN from Greek.

-en¹ ▶ **suffix** forming verbs: **1** (from adjectives) denoting the development, creation, or intensification of a state: *widen* | *deepen* | *loosen.*
2 from nouns (such as *strengthen* from *strength*).
– ORIGIN Old English *-nian*, of Germanic origin.

-en² ▶ **suffix** (also **-n**) forming adjectives from nouns: **1** made or consisting of: *earthen* | *woollen.*
2 resembling: *golden* | *silvern.*
– ORIGIN Old English, of Germanic origin.

-en³ (also **-n**) ▶ **suffix** forming past participles of strong verbs: **1** as a regular inflection: *spoken*.
2 as an adjective: *mistaken* | *torn*.
■often with a restricted adjectival sense: *drunken*.
– ORIGIN Old English, of Germanic origin.

-en⁴ ▶ **suffix** forming the plural of a few nouns such as *children*, *oxen*.
– ORIGIN Middle English reduction of the earlier suffix *-an*.

-en⁵ ▶ **suffix** forming diminutives of nouns (such as *chicken*, *maiden*).
– ORIGIN Old English, of Germanic origin.

-en⁶ ▶ **suffix 1** forming feminine nouns such as *vixen*.
2 forming abstract nouns such as *burden*.
– ORIGIN Old English, of Germanic origin.

enable ▶ **verb** [with obj. and infinitive] give (someone or something) the authority or means to do something: *the evidence would enable us to arrive at firm conclusions*.
■[with obj.] make possible: *a number of courses are available to enable an understanding of a broad range of issues*. ■ [with obj.] chiefly Computing make (a device or system) operational; activate.
– DERIVATIVES **enablement** noun, **enabler** noun.
– ORIGIN late Middle English (formerly also as *inable*): from EN-¹, IN-², + ABLE.

enabling act ▶ **noun** a statute empowering a person or body to take certain action, especially to make regulations, rules, or orders.

enact ▶ **verb** [with obj.] **1** (often **be enacted**) make (a bill or other proposal) law: *legislation was enacted in 1987 to attract international companies*.
■put into practice (a belief, idea, or suggestion). **2** act out (a role or play) on stage.
– DERIVATIVES **enactable** adjective, **enaction** noun, **enactor** noun.
– ORIGIN late Middle English (formerly also as *inact*): from EN-¹, IN-², + ACT, suggested by medieval Latin *inactare*, *inactitare*.

enactment ▶ **noun 1** [mass noun] the process of passing legislation.
■[count noun] a law that is passed. **2** a process of acting something out: *the story becomes an enactment of his fantasies*.
■[mass noun] Psychoanalysis the controlled expression and acceptance of repressed emotions or impulses in behaviour during therapy.
– DERIVATIVES **enactive** adjective.

enamel ▶ **noun** [mass noun] an opaque or semi-transparent glassy substance applied to metallic or other hard surfaces for ornament or as a protective coating.
■[count noun] a work of art executed in such a substance. ■ the hard glossy substance that covers the crown of a tooth. ■ (also **enamel paint**) a paint that dries to give a smooth, hard coat. ■ dated nail varnish.
▶ **verb** (**enamelled**, **enamelling**; US **enameled**, **enameling**) [with obj.] [often as adj. **enamelled**] coat or decorate (a metallic or hard object) with enamel: *an enamelled roasting tin*.
■dated apply nail varnish to (fingernails).
– DERIVATIVES **enameller** noun.
– ORIGIN late Middle English (originally as a verb; formerly also as *inamel*): from Anglo-Norman French *enamailler*, from *en-* 'in, on' + *amail* 'enamel', ultimately of Germanic origin.

enamelware ▶ **noun** [mass noun] enamelled kitchenware.

enamelwork ▶ **noun** [mass noun] the craft of inlaying or decorating metal objects with enamel.

enamour /ɪˈnamə, ɛ-/ (US **enamor**) ▶ **verb** (**be enamoured of/with/by**) be filled with a feeling of love for: *it is not difficult to see why Edward is enamoured of her*.
■have a liking or admiration for: *she was truly enamoured of New York*.
– ORIGIN Middle English (formerly also as *inamour*): from Old French *enamourer*, from *en-* 'in' + *amour* 'love'.

enanthema /ˌɛnanˈθiːmə/ ▶ **noun** Medicine an ulcer or eruption occurring on a mucus-secreting surface such as the inside of the mouth.
– ORIGIN mid 19th cent.: from EN-² 'within' + a shortened form of EXANTHEMA.

enantiodromia /ɪˌnantɪə(ʊ)ˈdrəʊmɪə, ɛ-/ ▶ **noun** [mass noun] rare the tendency of things to change into their opposites, especially as a supposed governing principle of natural cycles and of psychological development.
– ORIGIN early 20th cent.: from Greek, literally 'running in opposite ways'.

enantiomer /ɪˈnantɪə(ʊ)mə, ɛ-/ ▶ **noun** Chemistry each of a pair of molecules that are mirror images of each other.
– DERIVATIVES **enantiomeric** adjective, **enantiomerically** adverb.
– ORIGIN 1930s: from Greek *enantios* 'opposite' + -MER.

enantiomorph /ɪˈnantɪə(ʊ)mɔːf, ɛ-/ ▶ **noun** each of two crystalline or other geometrical forms which are mirror images of each other.
– DERIVATIVES **enantiomorphic** adjective, **enantiomorphism** noun, **enantiomorphous** adjective.
– ORIGIN late 19th cent.: from Greek *enantios* 'opposite' + -MORPH.

enargite /ˈɛnɑːɡʌɪt/ ▶ **noun** [mass noun] a dark grey mineral consisting of a sulphide of copper and arsenic.
– ORIGIN mid 19th cent.: from Greek *enargēs* 'clear' (referring to evident cleavage) + -ITE¹.

enarthrosis /ˌɛnɑːˈθrəʊsɪs/ ▶ **noun** (pl. **enarthroses** /-siːz/) Anatomy a ball-and-socket joint.
– ORIGIN late 16th cent.: from Greek *enarthrōsis*, from *enarthros* 'jointed', from *en-* 'inside' + *arthron* 'joint'.

enation /ɪˈneɪʃ(ə)n/ ▶ **noun** Botany an outgrowth from the surface of a leaf or other part of a plant.
– ORIGIN mid 19th cent.: from Latin *enatio(n-)*, from *enasci* 'issue forth'.

en bloc /ɒ̃ ˈblɒk/ ▶ **adverb** all together or all at the same time: *various private museums offered to purchase the trove en bloc*.
– ORIGIN mid 19th cent.: French.

en brosse /ɒ̃ ˈbrɒs/ ▶ **adjective** [postpositive] (of a person's hair) cut in a short and bristly style.
– ORIGIN French, 'in the form of a brush'.

enc. ▶ **abbreviation for** ■ enclosed. ■ enclosure.

Encaenia /ɛnˈsiːnɪə/ ▶ **noun** an annual celebration at Oxford University in memory of founders and benefactors.
– ORIGIN late 17th cent.: via Latin from Greek *enkainia* 'dedication festival' (based on *kainos* 'new').

encage ▶ **verb** [with obj.] poetic/literary confine in or as in a cage.

encamp ▶ **verb** [no obj.] settle in or establish a camp, especially a military one: *we encamped for the night by the side of a river*.

encampment ▶ **noun** a place with temporary accommodation consisting of huts or tents, typically for troops or nomads.
■a prehistoric enclosed or fortified site, especially an Iron Age hill fort. ■ [mass noun] the process of setting up a camp.

encapsidate /ɪnˈkapsɪdeɪt, ɛn-/ ▶ **verb** [with obj.] Biochemistry enclose (a gene or virus particle) in a protein shell.
– DERIVATIVES **encapsidation** noun.

encapsulate /ɪnˈkapsjʊleɪt, ɛn-/ ▶ **verb** [with obj.] enclose (something) in or as if in a capsule.
■express the essential features of (someone or something) succinctly: *the conclusion is encapsulated in one sentence*. ■ Computing enclose (a message or signal) in a set of codes which allow use by or transfer through different computer systems or networks. ■ Computing provide an interface for (a piece of software or hardware) to allow or simplify access for the user.
– DERIVATIVES **encapsulation** noun.
– ORIGIN late 19th cent. (also as *incapsulate*): from EN-¹, IN-² 'into' + Latin *capsula* (see CAPSULE).

encase (also **incase**) ▶ **verb** [with obj.] (often **be encased**) enclose or cover in a case or close-fitting surround.
– DERIVATIVES **encasement** noun.

encash ▶ **verb** [with obj.] Brit. convert (a cheque, money order, bond, etc.) into money.
– DERIVATIVES **encashable** adjective, **encashment** noun.

encaustic /ɛnˈkɔːstɪk/ ▶ **adjective** (especially in painting and ceramics) using pigments mixed with hot wax which are burned in as an inlay.
■(of bricks and tiles) decorated with differently coloured clays, which are inlaid into the surface and burnt in.
▶ **noun** [mass noun] the art or process of encaustic painting.
– ORIGIN late 16th cent.: via Latin from Greek *enkaustikos*, from *enkaiein* 'burn in', from *en-* 'in' + *kaiein* 'to burn'.

-ence ▶ **suffix** forming nouns: **1** denoting a quality or an instance of it: *impertinence*.
2 denoting an action or its result: *reference* | *reminiscence*.
– ORIGIN from French *-ence*, from Latin *-entia*, *-antia* (from present participial stems *-ent-*, *-ant-*). Since the 16th cent. many inconsistencies have occurred in the use of *-ence* and *-ance*.

enceinte¹ /ɒ̃ˈsãt/ ▶ **noun** archaic an enclosure or the enclosing wall of a fortified place.
– ORIGIN early 18th cent.: from French, from Latin *incincta*, feminine past participle of *incingere* 'gird in', from *in-* 'in' + *cingere* 'to gird'.

enceinte² /ɒ̃ˈsãt/ ▶ **adjective** archaic pregnant.
– ORIGIN early 17th cent.: from French.

Enceladus /ɛnˈsɛlədəs/ Astronomy a satellite of Saturn, the eighth closest to the planet and probably composed mainly of ice, discovered by W. Herschel in 1789 (diameter 500 km).
– ORIGIN named after a Greek mythological giant killed by Athena.

encephalic /ˌɛnsɪˈfalɪk, ɛnˈkɛf(ə)lɪk/ ▶ **adjective** Anatomy relating to, affecting, or situated in the brain.
– ORIGIN mid 19th cent.: from Greek *enkephalos* 'brain' (from *en-* 'in' + *kephalē* 'head') + -IC.

encephalin /ɛnˈsɛfəlɪn, -ˈkɛf-/ ▶ **noun** variant spelling of ENKEPHALIN.

encephalitis /ɛnˌsɛfəˈlʌɪtɪs, -ˌkɛfə-/ ▶ **noun** [mass noun] inflammation of the brain, caused by infection or an allergic reaction.
– DERIVATIVES **encephalitic** adjective.

encephalitis lethargica /lɪˈθɑːdʒɪkə/ ▶ **noun** [mass noun] a form of encephalitis caused by a virus and characterized by headache and drowsiness leading to coma. Also called SLEEPY SICKNESS.

encephalization (also **-isation**) ▶ **noun** [mass noun] Zoology an evolutionary increase in the complexity or relative size of the brain, involving a shift of function from non-cortical parts of the brain to the cortex.

encephalo- /ɛnˈsɛf(ə)ləʊ, -ˈkɛf-/ ▶ **combining form** of or relating to the brain: *encephalopathy*.
– ORIGIN from Greek *enkephalos*.

encephalogram /ɛnˈsɛf(ə)lə(ʊ)gram, -ˈkɛf-/ ▶ **noun** Medicine an image, trace, or other record of the structure or electrical activity of the brain.

encephalography /ɛnˌsɛfəˈlɒɡrəfi, -ˌkɛfə-/ ▶ **noun** [mass noun] Medicine any of various techniques for recording the structure or electrical activity of the brain.
– DERIVATIVES **encephalograph** noun, **encephalographic** adjective.

encephalomyelitis /ɛnˌsɛf(ə)ləʊmʌɪəˈlʌɪtɪs, -ˌkɛf-/ ▶ **noun** [mass noun] Medicine inflammation of the brain and spinal cord, typically due to acute viral infection.

encephalon /ɛnˈsɛfəlɒn, -ˈkɛf-/ ▶ **noun** Anatomy the brain.
– ORIGIN mid 18th cent.: from Greek *enkephalon* 'what is inside the head', from *en-* 'inside' + *kephalē* 'head'.

encephalopathy /ɛnˌsɛfəˈlɒpəθi, -ˌkɛf-/ ▶ **noun** (pl. **-ies**) Medicine a disease in which the functioning of the brain is affected by some agent or condition (such as viral infection or toxins in the blood).

enchain ▶ **verb** [with obj.] poetic/literary bind with or as with chains.
– DERIVATIVES **enchainment** noun.
– ORIGIN late Middle English: from Old French *enchainer*, based on Latin *catena* 'chain'.

enchaînement /ɒ̃ˈʃɛnmɒ̃/ ▶ **noun** (pl. pronounced same) Ballet a linked sequence of steps or movements constituting a phrase.
– ORIGIN mid 19th cent.: French, 'chaining together'.

enchant ▶ **verb** [with obj.] (often **be enchanted**) fill (someone) with great delight; charm: *Isabel was enchanted with the idea*.
■put (someone or something) under a spell: [as adj. **enchanted**] *an enchanted garden*.
– DERIVATIVES **enchantedly** adverb, **enchantment** noun.
– ORIGIN late Middle English (in the senses 'put under a spell' and 'delude'; formerly also as *inchant*): from French *enchanter*, from Latin *incantare*, from *in-* 'in' + *cantare* 'sing'.

enchanter ▶ **noun** a person who uses magic or sorcery, especially to put someone or something under a spell.

enchanter's nightshade ▶ **noun** a woodland plant with small white flowers and fruit with hooked bristles, native to Eurasia and the eastern US.
• *Circaea lutetiana*, family Onagraceae.
– ORIGIN late 16th cent.: believed by early botanists to be the herb used by Circe to charm Odysseus' companions.

enchanting ▶ **adjective** delightfully charming or attractive: *Dinah looked enchanting.*
– DERIVATIVES **enchantingly** adverb.

enchantress ▶ **noun** a woman who uses magic or sorcery, especially to put someone or something under a spell.
– ORIGIN late Middle English: from Old French *enchanteresse*, from *enchanter* (see **ENCHANT**).

enchase /ɪnˈtʃeɪs, ɛn-/ ▶ **verb** [with obj.] decorate (a piece of jewellery or work of art) by inlaying, engraving, or carving.
– ORIGIN late Middle English (in the sense 'decorate with figures in relief'): from Old French *enchasser* 'set gems, encase', from *en-* 'in' + *chasse* 'a case'.

enchilada /ˌɛntʃɪˈlɑːdə/ ▶ **noun** a tortilla served with chilli sauce and a filling of meat or cheese.
– PHRASES **the big enchilada** N. Amer. informal a person or thing of great importance. **the whole enchilada** N. Amer. informal the whole situation; everything.
– ORIGIN Latin American Spanish, feminine past participle of *enchilar* 'season with chilli'.

enchiridion /ˌɛnkʌɪˈrɪdɪən/ ▶ **noun** (pl. **enchiridions** or **enchiridia** /-dɪə/) formal a book containing essential information on a subject.
– ORIGIN late Middle English: via late Latin from Greek *enkheiridion*, from *en-* 'within' + *kheir* 'hand' + the diminutive suffix *-idion*.

encipher ▶ **verb** [with obj.] convert (a message or piece of text) into a coded form.
– DERIVATIVES **encipherment** noun.

encircle ▶ **verb** [with obj.] form a circle around; surround: *the town is encircled by fortified walls.*
– DERIVATIVES **encirclement** noun.

encl. (also **enc.**) ▶ **abbreviation for** ■ enclosed. ■ enclosure.

en clair /õ ˈklɛː/ ▶ **adjective** & **adverb** (especially of a telegram or official message) in ordinary language, rather than in code or cipher.
– ORIGIN French, literally 'in clear'.

enclasp ▶ **verb** [with obj.] formal hold tightly in one's arms.

enclave /ˈɛnkleɪv/ ▶ **noun** a portion of territory within or surrounded by a larger territory whose inhabitants are culturally or ethnically distinct.
■ figurative a place or group that is different in character from those surrounding it: *the engineering department is traditionally a male enclave.*
– ORIGIN mid 19th cent.: from French, from Old French *enclaver* 'enclose, dovetail', based on Latin *clavis* 'key'.

enclitic /ɪnˈklɪtɪk, ɛn-/ Linguistics ▶ **noun** a word pronounced with so little emphasis that it is shortened and forms part of the preceding word, for example *n't* in *can't*. Compare with **PROCLITIC**.
▶ **adjective** denoting or relating to such a word.
– DERIVATIVES **enclitically** adverb.
– ORIGIN mid 17th cent.: via late Latin from Greek *enklitikos*, from *enklinein* 'lean on', from *en-* 'in, on' + *klinein* 'to lean'.

enclose (also **inclose**) ▶ **verb** [with obj.] **1** (often **be enclosed**) surround or close off on all sides: *the entire estate was* **enclosed with** *walls* | [as adj. **enclosed**] *a dark enclosed space.*
■ historical fence in (common land) so as to make it private property. ■ [usu. as adj. **enclosed**] seclude (a religious order or other community) from the outside world.
2 place (something) in an envelope together with a letter: *I enclose a copy of the job description.*
– ORIGIN Middle English (in the sense 'shut in, imprison'): from Old French *enclos*, past participle of *enclore*, based on Latin *includere* 'shut in'.

enclosure /ɪnˈkləʊʒə, ɛn-/ (also **inclosure**) ▶ **noun** **1** an area that is sealed off with an artificial or natural barrier.
■ Brit. a section of a racecourse for a specified activity or class of people: *the members' enclosure.* ■ an artificial or natural barrier that seals off an area.
2 [mass noun] historical the process or policy of fencing in waste or common land so as to make it private property, as pursued in much of Britain in the 18th and early 19th centuries.
■ the state of being enclosed, especially in a religious community.
3 a document or object placed in an envelope together with a letter.
– ORIGIN late Middle English: from legal Anglo-Norman French and Old French, from *enclos* 'closed in' (see **ENCLOSE**).

encode ▶ **verb** [with obj.] convert into a coded form.
■ Computing convert (information or an instruction) into a digital form. ■ Biochemistry (of a gene) be responsible for producing (a substance or behaviour).
– DERIVATIVES **encoder** noun.

encomiast /ɛnˈkəʊmɪast/ ▶ **noun** formal a person who publicly praises or flatters someone else.
– DERIVATIVES **encomiastic** adjective.
– ORIGIN early 17th cent.: from Greek *enkōmiastēs*, from *enkōmiazein* 'to praise', from *enkōmion* (see **ENCOMIUM**).

encomienda /ɛnˌkɒmɪˈɛndə/ ▶ **noun** historical a grant by the Spanish Crown to a colonist in America conferring the right to demand tribute and forced labour from the Indian inhabitants of an area.
– ORIGIN Spanish, 'commission, charge'.

encomium /ɛnˈkəʊmɪəm/ ▶ **noun** (pl. **encomiums** or **encomia**) formal a speech or piece of writing that praises someone or something highly.
– ORIGIN mid 16th cent.: Latin, from Greek *enkōmion* 'eulogy', from *en-* 'within' + *komos* 'revel'.

encompass /ɪnˈkʌmpəs, ɛn-/ ▶ **verb** **1** [with obj.] surround and have or hold within: *territories encompassing high moor and upland.*
■ include comprehensively: *no studies encompass all sectors of medical care.*
2 archaic cause (something) to take place: *an act designed to encompass the death of the king.*
– DERIVATIVES **encompassment** noun.

encopresis /ˌɛnkəʊˈpriːsɪs/ ▶ **noun** [mass noun] Medicine involuntary defecation, especially associated with emotional disturbance or psychiatric disorder.

encore /ˈɒŋkɔː/ ▶ **noun** a repeated or additional performance of an item at the end of a concert, as called for by an audience.
▶ **exclamation** called out by an audience at the end of a concert to request such a performance.
▶ **verb** [with obj.] (often **be encored**) give or call for a repeated or additional performance of (an item) at the end of a concert.
– ORIGIN early 18th cent.: French, literally 'still, again'.

encounter ▶ **verb** [with obj.] unexpectedly experience or be faced with (something difficult or hostile): *we have encountered one small problem.*
■ meet unexpectedly and confront (an adversary): *the soldiers encountered a large crowd of demonstrators.* ■ meet (someone) unexpectedly.
▶ **noun** an unexpected or casual meeting with someone or something.
■ a confrontation or unpleasant struggle: *his* **close encounter with** *death.*
– ORIGIN Middle English (in the senses 'meet as an adversary' and 'a meeting of adversaries'; formerly also as *incounter*): from Old French *encontrer* (verb), *encontre* (noun), based on Latin *in-* 'in' + *contra* 'against'.

encounter group ▶ **noun** chiefly US a group of people who meet to gain psychological benefit through close contact with one another.

encourage ▶ **verb** [with obj.] give support, confidence, or hope to (someone): *we were encouraged by the success of this venture* | [as adj. **encouraging**] *the results are very encouraging* | [as adj. **encouraged**] *I feel much encouraged.*
■ give support and advice to (someone) so that they will do or continue to do something: [with obj. and infinitive] *pupils are encouraged to be creative.* ■ help or stimulate (an activity, state, or view) to develop: *the intention is to encourage new writing talent.*
– DERIVATIVES **encouragement** noun, **encourager** noun, **encouragingly** adverb [sentence adverb] *encouragingly, there is more research being done today* | [as submodifier] *the level of activity continues to be encouragingly high.*
– ORIGIN Middle English (formerly also as *incourage*): from French *encourager*, from *en-* 'in' + *corage* 'courage'.

encroach ▶ **verb** [no obj.] (**encroach on/upon**) intrude on (a person's territory or a thing considered to be a right): *rather than encroach on his privacy she might have kept to her room.*
■ advance gradually and in a way that causes damage: *the sea has encroached all round the coast.*
– DERIVATIVES **encroacher** noun, **encroachment** noun.
– ORIGIN late Middle English (in the sense 'obtain unlawfully, seize'; formerly also as *incroach*): from Old French *encrochier* 'seize, fasten upon', from *en-* 'in, on' + *crochier* (from *croc* 'hook', from Old Norse *krókr*).

en croute /õ ˈkruːt/ ▶ **adjective** & **adverb** in a pastry crust: [as postpositive adj.] *salmon en croute* | [as adv.] *goat's cheese is particularly tasty baked en croute.*
– ORIGIN French *en croûte*.

encrust /ɪnˈkrʌst, ɛn-/ (also **incrust**) ▶ **verb** [with obj.] cover or decorate (something) with a hard surface layer: *the mussels encrust navigation buoys* | [as adj. **encrusted**] *the dried and encrusted blood.*
– ORIGIN early 17th cent. (in the sense 'cause to form a crust'): from French *incruster* or *encroûter*, both from Latin *incrustare*, from *in-* 'into' + *crusta* 'a crust'.

encrustation (also **incrustation**) ▶ **noun** [mass noun] the action of encrusting or state of being encrusted.
■ [count noun] a crust or hard coating on the surface of something. ■ [count noun] Architecture a facing of marble on a building.
– ORIGIN early 17th cent. (originally as *incrustation*): from late Latin *incrustatio(n-)*, from the verb *incrustare* (see **ENCRUST**).

encrypt /ɛnˈkrɪpt/ ▶ **verb** [with obj.] convert (information or data) into a cipher or code, especially to prevent unauthorized access.
■ (**encrypt something in**) conceal information or data in something by this means.
– DERIVATIVES **encryption** noun.
– ORIGIN 1950s (originally US): from **EN-**[1] 'in' + Greek *kruptos* 'hidden'.

enculturation ▶ **noun** variant spelling of **INCULTURATION**.

encumber /ɪnˈkʌmbə, ɛn-/ ▶ **verb** [with obj.] (often **be encumbered**) restrict or burden (someone or something) in such a way that free action or movement is difficult: *she was* **encumbered by** *her heavy skirts* | *they had arrived* **encumbered with** *families.*
– ORIGIN Middle English (in the sense 'cause trouble to, entangle'; formerly also as *incumber*): from Old French *encombrer* 'block up', from *en-* 'in' + *combre* 'river barrage'.

encumbrance ▶ **noun** a burden or impediment.
■ Law a mortgage or other charge on property or assets.
■ archaic a person, especially a child, who is dependent on someone else for support.
– ORIGIN Middle English (denoting an encumbered state; formerly also as *incumbrance*): from Old French *encombrance*, from *encombrer* 'block up' (see **ENCUMBER**).

-ency ▶ **suffix** forming nouns: **1** denoting a quality: *efficiency.*
2 denoting a state: *presidency.*
– ORIGIN from Latin *-entia* (compare with **-ENCE**).

encyclical /ɛnˈsɪklɪk(ə)l, ɪn-, -ˈsʌɪk-/ ▶ **noun** a papal letter sent to all bishops of the Roman Catholic Church.
▶ **adjective** of or relating to such a letter.
– ORIGIN mid 17th cent. (as an adjective): via late Latin from Greek *enkuklios* 'circular, general', from *en-* 'in' + *kuklos* 'a circle'.

encyclopedia /ɛnˌsʌɪkləˈ(ʊ)ˈpiːdɪə, ɪn-/ (also **encyclopaedia**) ▶ **noun** a book or set of books giving information on many subjects or on many aspects of one subject and typically arranged alphabetically.
– ORIGIN mid 16th cent.: modern Latin, from pseudo-Greek *enkuklopaideia* for *enkuklios paideia* 'all-round education'.

encyclopedic /ɛnˌsʌɪklə(ʊ)ˈpiːdɪk, ɪn-/ (also **encyclopaedic**) ▶ **adjective** comprehensive in terms of information: *he has an almost encyclopedic knowledge of food.*
■ relating to or containing names of famous people and places and information about words which is not simply linguistic: *a dictionary with encyclopedic material.*

encyclopedism (also **encyclopaedism**) ▶ **noun** [mass noun] comprehensive learning or knowledge.

encyclopedist (also **encyclopaedist**) ▶ **noun** a person who writes, edits, or contributes to an encyclopedia.

encyst /ɪn'sɪst, ɛn-/ ▶ **verb** Zoology enclose or become enclosed in a cyst.
– DERIVATIVES **encystation** noun, **encystment** noun.

end ▶ **noun 1** a final part of something, especially a period of time, an activity, or a story: *the end of the year | Mario led the race* ***from beginning to end.***
▪a termination of a state or situation: *the party called for* ***an end to*** *violence | one notice will be effective to* ***bring*** *the tenancy* ***to an end.*** ▪used to emphasize that something, typically a subject of discussion, is considered finished: *you will go to church and* ***there's an end of it.*** ▪a person's death or ruin: *if she so much as makes a sound, that'll* ***be the end of*** *her.* ▪archaic (in biblical use) an ultimate state or condition: *the end of that man is peace.*
2 the furthest or most extreme part or point of something: *a length of wire with a hook at the end* | [as modifier] *the end house.*
▪a small piece that is left after something has been used: *an ashtray full of cigarette ends.* ▪a specified extreme point on a scale: *homebuyers at the lower end of the market.* ▪the part or share of an activity with which someone is concerned: *you're going to honour your end of the deal.* ▪a place that is linked to another by a telephone call, letter, or journey: *'Hello,' said a voice at the other end.* ▪the part of a sports field or court defended by one team or player.
3 a goal or result that one seeks to achieve: *each would use the other to* ***further his own ends*** *|* ***to this end,*** *schools were set up for peasant women.*
4 Bowls & Curling a session of play in one particular direction across the playing area.
5 American Football a lineman positioned nearest the sideline.
▶**verb** come or bring to a final point; finish: [no obj.] *when the war ended, policy changed | the chapter* ***ends with*** *a case study* | [with obj.] *she wanted to end the relationship.*
▪[no obj.] reach a point and go no further: *the boundary where agnosticism ends and atheism begins.* ▪[no obj.] perform a final act: *the man* ***ended by*** *attacking a police officer.* ▪[no obj.] (**end in**) have as its final part, point, or result: *one in three marriages is now likely to end in divorce.* ▪[no obj.] (**end up**) eventually reach or come to a specified place, state, or course of action: *I* ***ended up*** *in Eritrea | you could* ***end up with*** *a higher income.*
– PHRASES **all ends up** informal completely. **at the end of the day** informal, chiefly Brit. when everything is taken into consideration: *at the end of the day I'm responsible for what happens in the school.* **be at** (or **have come to**) **an end** be finished or completed. ▪(of a supply of something) become exhausted: *our patience has come to an end.* **be at the end of** be close to having no more of (something): *she was at the end of her patience.* **be the end** informal be the limit of what one can tolerate: *you really are the end!* **come to** (or **meet**) **a sticky** (or **bad**) **end** be led by one's own actions to ruin or an unpleasant death. **the end-all** a thing that is final or definitive. **end one's days** (or **life**) spend the final part of one's existence in a specified place or state: *she ended her days in London.* **an end in itself** a goal that is pursued in its own right to the exclusion of others. **end in tears** have an unhappy or painful outcome (often as a warning): *this treaty will end in tears.* **end it all** commit suicide. **the end of the road** (or **line**) the point beyond which progress or survival cannot continue: *if the damages award is not lowered it could* ***be the end of the road for*** *the publisher.* **the end of one's tether** (or N. Amer. **rope**) having no patience or energy left to cope with something: *these individuals have* ***reached the end of their tether.*** **the end of the world** the termination of life on the earth. ▪informal a complete disaster: ***it's not the end of the world*** *if we draw.* **end on** with the furthest point of an object facing towards one: *seen end on, their sharp, rocky summits point like arrows.* ▪with the furthest point of an object touching that of another: *slim stone tiles had been layered end on with incredible skill.* **end to end** in a row with the furthest point of one object touching that of another object. **get** (or **have**) **one's end away** Brit. vulgar slang have sexual intercourse. **in the end** eventually or on reflection: *in the end, I saw that she was right.* **keep** (or **hold**) **one's end up** informal perform well in a difficult or competitive situation. **make an end of** cause (someone or something) to stop existing or die. **make** (**both**) **ends meet** earn enough money to live without getting into debt. **never** (or **not**) **hear the end of** be continually reminded of (an unpleasant topic or cause of annoyance): *a criminal court which admitted such a defence would* ***never hear the end of it.*** **no end** informal to a great extent; very much: *this cheered me up no end.* **no end of** informal a vast number or amount of (something): *emotions can cause no end of problems.* **on end 1** continuing without stopping for a specified period of time: *sometimes they'll be gone for days on end.* **2** in an upright position: *he brushed his hair, leaving a tuft standing on end.* **put an end to** cause (someone or something) to stop existing or die: *injury put an end to his career | he decided to* ***put an end to himself.*** **the sharp end** informal **1** the most important or influential part of an activity or process: *Utopians are ill at ease* ***at the sharp end*** *of politics.* ▪the side of a system or activity which is the most unpleasant or suffers the chief impact: *businessmen* ***are at the sharp end of*** *the recession.* **2** Brit. humorous the bow of a ship. **a —— to end all ——s** informal used to emphasize how impressive or successful something is of its kind: *she is going to throw a party to end all parties.* **without end** without a limit or boundary: *a war without end.*
– ORIGIN Old English *ende* (noun), *endian* (verb), of Germanic origin; related to Dutch *einde* (noun), *einden* (verb) and German *Ende* (noun), *enden* (verb).

-end ▶ **suffix** denoting a person or thing to be treated in a specified way: *dividend | reverend.*
– ORIGIN from Latin *-endus*, gerundive ending.

endanger ▶ **verb** [with obj.] put (someone or something) at risk or in danger: *he was driving in a manner likely to endanger life.*
– DERIVATIVES **endangerment** noun.

endangered ▶ **adjective** (of a species) seriously at risk of extinction.

end-around ▶ **noun** American Football an offensive play in which an end carries the ball round the opposing flank.

endarterectomy /ˌɛndɑːtə'rɛktəmi/ ▶ **noun** (pl. **-ies**) [mass noun] surgical removal of part of the inner lining of an artery, together with any obstructive deposits, most often carried out on the carotid artery or on vessels supplying the legs.

endarteritis /ˌɛndɑːtə'rʌɪtɪs/ ▶ **noun** [mass noun] Medicine inflammation of the inner lining of an artery.

en dash ▶ **noun** another term for **EN RULE**.

endear /ɪn'dɪə, ɛn-/ ▶ **verb** [with obj.] cause to be loved or liked: *Flora's spirit and character* ***endeared*** *her* ***to*** *everyone who met her.*

endearing ▶ **adjective** inspiring love or affection: *an endearing little grin.*
– DERIVATIVES **endearingly** adverb.

endearment ▶ **noun** a word or phrase expressing love or affection.
▪[mass noun] love or affection: *a term of endearment.*

endeavour /ɪn'dɛvə, ɛn-/ (US **endeavor**) ▶ **verb** [no obj., with infinitive] try hard to do or achieve something: *he is endeavouring to help the Third World.*
▶**noun** an attempt to achieve a goal: [with infinitive] *an endeavour to reduce serious injury.*
▪[mass noun] earnest and industrious effort, especially when sustained over a period of time: *enthusiasm is a vital ingredient in all human endeavour.* ▪an enterprise or undertaking: *a political endeavour.*
– ORIGIN late Middle English (in the sense 'exert oneself'): from the phrase *put oneself in devoir* 'do one's utmost' (see **DEVOIR**).

endemic /ɛn'dɛmɪk/ ▶ **adjective 1** (of a disease or condition) regularly found among particular people or in a certain area: *complacency is* ***endemic in*** *industry today.*
▪[attrib.] denoting an area in which a particular disease is regularly found.
2 (of a plant or animal) native or restricted to a certain country or area: *a marsupial* ***endemic to*** *north-eastern Australia.*
▶**noun** an endemic plant or animal.
– DERIVATIVES **endemically** adverb, **endemicity** /ˌɛndɪ'mɪsɪti/ noun, **endemism** /'ɛndɪmɪz(ə)m/ noun (only in sense 2 of the adjective).
– ORIGIN mid 17th cent. (as a noun): from French *endémique* or modern Latin *endemicus*, from Greek *endēmios* 'native' (based on *dēmos* 'people').

Enderby Land /'ɛndəbi/ a part of Antarctica claimed by Australia.
– ORIGIN named by its discoverer, the English navigator John Biscoe (1794–1843), after the London whaling firm *Enderby* Brothers, where he was employed.

endergonic /ˌɛndəː'gɒnɪk/ ▶ **adjective** Biochemistry (of a metabolic or chemical process) accompanied by or requiring the absorption of energy, the products being of greater free energy than the reactants. The opposite of **EXERGONIC**.
– ORIGIN mid 20th cent.: from **ENDO-** 'within' + Greek *ergon* 'work' + **-IC**.

Enders /'ɛndəz/, John Franklin (1897–1985), American virologist. With **Frederick C. Robbins** (1916–92) and **Thomas H. Weller** (1915–92) he devised a method of growing viruses in tissue cultures which led to the development of vaccines against mumps, polio, and measles. The three scientists shared a Nobel Prize for Physiology or Medicine in 1954.

endgame ▶ **noun** the final stage of a game such as chess or bridge, when few pieces or cards remain.

endgate ▶ **noun** N. Amer. a tailboard.

end grain ▶ **noun** the grain of wood seen when it is cut across the growth rings.

ending ▶ **noun** an end or final part of something, especially a period of time, an activity, or a book or film: *the ending of the cold war.*
▪the furthest part or point of something: *a nerve ending.* ▪the final part of a word, constituting a grammatical inflection or formative element.
– ORIGIN Old English *endung* 'termination, completion' (see **END**, **-ING**[1]).

endite /'ɛndʌɪt/ ▶ **noun** Zoology an inwardly directed lobe on a limb segment of an arthropod, especially on the protopodite of a crustacean limb.
– ORIGIN late 19th cent.: from **ENDO-** 'within' + **-ITE**[1].

endive /'ɛndʌɪv, -dɪv/ ▶ **noun 1** an edible Mediterranean plant, the bitter leaves of which may be blanched and used in salads.
• *Cichorium endivia*, family Compositae. The varieties of endive are placed in two groups: **curly endive**, with curled leaves, and **Batavian endive**, with smooth leaves.
2 (also **Belgian endive**) N. Amer. a chicory crown.
– ORIGIN late Middle English (also denoting the sowthistle): via Old French from medieval Latin *endivia*, based on Greek *entubon*.

endless ▶ **adjective** having or seeming to have no end or limit: *endless ocean wastes | the list is endless.*
▪countless; innumerable: *we smoked endless cigarettes.* ▪(of a belt, chain, or tape) having the ends joined to form a loop allowing continuous action.
– DERIVATIVES **endlessly** adverb, **endlessness** noun.
– ORIGIN Old English *endelēas* (see **END**, **-LESS**).

endless screw ▶ **noun** the threaded cylinder in a worm gear.

endmember ▶ **noun** Geology a mineral or rock representing one end of a series having a range of composition.

endmost ▶ **adjective** nearest to the end.

endnote ▶ **noun** a note printed at the end of a book or section of a book.

endo- ▶ **combining form** internal; within: *endoderm | endogenous.*
– ORIGIN from Greek *endon* 'within'.

endocardial /ˌɛndə(ʊ)'kɑːdɪəl/ ▶ **adjective** Anatomy & Medicine **1** of or relating to the endocardium.
2 inside the heart.

endocarditis /ˌɛndəʊkɑː'dʌɪtɪs/ ▶ **noun** [mass noun] Medicine inflammation of the endocardium.
– DERIVATIVES **endocarditic** adjective.

endocardium /ˌɛndəʊ'kɑːdɪəm/ ▶ **noun** the thin, smooth membrane which lines the inside of the chambers of the heart and forms the surface of the valves.
– ORIGIN late 19th cent.: modern Latin, from **ENDO-** 'within' + Greek *kardia* 'heart'.

endocarp /'ɛndə(ʊ)kɑːp/ ▶ **noun** Botany the innermost layer of the pericarp which surrounds a seed in a fruit. It may be membranous (as in apples) or woody (as in the stone of a peach or cherry).
– DERIVATIVES **endocarpic** adjective.
– ORIGIN early 19th cent.: from **ENDO-** 'within' + a shortened form of **PERICARP**.

endocentric /ˌɛndəʊ'sɛntrɪk/ ▶ **adjective** Linguistics denoting or being a construction in which the whole has the same syntactic function as the head, for example *big black dogs*. Contrasted with **EXOCENTRIC**.

endocrine /'ɛndə(ʊ)krʌɪn, -krɪn/ ▶ **adjective** Physiology of, relating to, or denoting glands which secrete

hormones or other products directly into the blood: *the endocrine system.*
– ORIGIN early 20th cent.: from **ENDO-** 'within' + Greek *krinein* 'sift'.

endocrinology /ˌɛndəʊkrɪˈnɒlədʒi/ ▶ noun [mass noun] the branch of physiology and medicine concerned with endocrine glands and hormones.
– DERIVATIVES **endocrinological** adjective, **endocrinologist** noun.

endocytosis /ˌɛndəʊsaɪˈtəʊsɪs/ ▶ noun [mass noun] Biology the taking in of matter by a living cell by invagination of its membrane to form a vacuole.
– DERIVATIVES **endocytotic** adjective.

endoderm /ˈɛndə(ʊ)dəːm/ ▶ noun [mass noun] Zoology & Embryology the innermost layer of cells or tissue of an embryo in early development, or the parts derived from this, which include the lining of the gut and associated structures. Compare with **ECTODERM** and **MESODERM**.
– DERIVATIVES **endodermal** adjective.
– ORIGIN mid 19th cent.: from **ENDO-** 'within' + Greek *derma* 'skin'.

endodermis ▶ noun [mass noun] Botany an inner layer of cells in the cortex of a root and of some stems, surrounding a vascular bundle.
– ORIGIN early 20th cent.: from **ENDO-** 'within' + modern Latin *dermis* 'skin'.

endogamy /ɛnˈdɒɡəmi/ ▶ noun [mass noun] Anthropology the custom of marrying only within the limits of a local community, clan, or tribe. Compare with **EXOGAMY**.
 ■Biology the fusion of reproductive cells from related individuals; inbreeding; self-pollination.
– DERIVATIVES **endogamous** adjective.
– ORIGIN mid 19th cent.: from **ENDO-** 'within' + Greek *gamos* 'marriage', on the pattern of *polygamy.*

endogenic /ˌɛndəʊˈdʒɛnɪk/ ▶ adjective Geology formed or occurring beneath the surface of the earth. Often contrasted with **EXOGENIC**.

endogenous /ɛnˈdɒdʒɪnəs, ɪn-/ ▶ adjective having an internal cause or origin: *the expected rate of infection is endogenous to the system.* Often contrasted with **EXOGENOUS**.
 ■Biology growing or originating from within an organism: *endogenous gene sequences.* ■ chiefly Psychiatry (of a disease or symptom) not attributable to any external or environmental factor: *endogenous depression.* ■ confined within a group or society.
– DERIVATIVES **endogenously** adverb.

endolithic /ˌɛndə(ʊ)ˈlɪθɪk/ ▶ adjective Biology living in or penetrating into stone: *endolithic algae.*

endolymph /ˈɛndə(ʊ)lɪmf/ ▶ noun [mass noun] Anatomy the fluid in the membranous labyrinth of the ear.

endometriosis /ˌɛndə(ʊ)miːtrɪˈəʊsɪs/ ▶ noun [mass noun] Medicine a condition resulting from the appearance of endometrial tissue outside the womb and causing pelvic pain, especially associated with menstruation.

endometritis /ˌɛndə(ʊ)mɪˈtraɪtɪs/ ▶ noun [mass noun] Medicine inflammation of the endometrium.

endometrium /ˌɛndə(ʊ)miːtrɪəm/ ▶ noun Anatomy the mucous membrane lining the womb, which thickens during the menstrual cycle in preparation for possible implantation of an embryo.
– DERIVATIVES **endometrial** adjective.
– ORIGIN late 19th cent.: modern Latin, from **ENDO-** 'within' + Greek *mētra* 'womb'.

endomorph /ˈɛndə(ʊ)mɔːf/ ▶ noun Physiology a person with a soft round build of body and a high proportion of fat tissue. Compare with **ECTOMORPH** and **MESOMORPH**.
– DERIVATIVES **endomorphic** adjective, **endomorphy** noun.
– ORIGIN 1940s: *endo-* from *endodermal* (being the layer of the embryo giving rise to the physical characteristics which predominate) + **-MORPH**.

endonuclease /ˌɛndəʊˈnjuːklɪeɪz/ ▶ noun Biochemistry an enzyme which cleaves a polynucleotide chain by separating nucleotides other than the two end ones.

endoparasite ▶ noun Biology a parasite, such as a tapeworm, that lives inside its host. Compare with **ECTOPARASITE**.
– DERIVATIVES **endoparasitic** adjective.

endopeptidase /ˌɛndəʊˈpɛptɪdeɪz/ ▶ noun Biochemistry an enzyme which breaks peptide bonds other than terminal ones in a peptide chain.

endophora /ɛnˈdɒfərə/ ▶ noun [mass noun] Linguistics the set of relationships among words having the same reference within a text, contributing to textual cohesion; anaphora and cataphora. Compare with **EXOPHORA**.
– DERIVATIVES **endophoric** /ˌɛndəˈfɒrɪk/ adjective.
– ORIGIN late 20th cent.: from **ENDO-** 'within', on the pattern of *anaphora.*

endophyte /ˈɛndəʊfʌɪt/ ▶ noun Botany a plant, especially a fungus, which lives inside another plant.
– DERIVATIVES **endophytic** adjective.

endoplasm /ˈɛndə(ʊ)plaz(ə)m/ ▶ noun [mass noun] Biology, dated the more fluid, granular inner layer of the cytoplasm in amoeboid cells. Compare with **ECTOPLASM** (in sense 1).

endoplasmic reticulum /ˌɛndəʊˈplazmɪk/ ▶ noun [mass noun] Biology a network of membranous tubules within the cytoplasm of a eukaryotic cell, continuous with the nuclear membrane. It usually has ribosomes attached and is involved in protein and lipid synthesis.

endopodite /ɛnˈdɒpədʌɪt/ (also **endopod** /ˈɛndə(ʊ)pɒd/) ▶ noun Zoology the inner branch of the biramous limb or appendage of a crustacean. Compare with **EXOPODITE**, **PROTOPODITE**.
– ORIGIN late 19th cent.: from **ENDO-** 'within' + Greek *pous, pod-* 'foot' + **-ITE**[1].

end organ ▶ noun **1** Anatomy a specialized, encapsulated ending of a peripheral sensory nerve, which acts as a receptor for a stimulus.
2 another term for **TARGET ORGAN**.

endorphin /ɛnˈdɔːfɪn/ ▶ noun Biochemistry any of a group of hormones secreted within the brain and nervous system and having a number of physiological functions. They are peptides which activate the body's opiate receptors, causing an analgesic effect.
– ORIGIN 1970s: blend of **ENDOGENOUS** and **MORPHINE**.

endorsable ▶ adjective (in the UK) (of a driving offence) punishable by endorsement of the offender's driving licence.

endorse /ɪnˈdɔːs, ɛn-/ (US & Law also **indorse**) ▶ verb [with obj.] **1** declare one's public approval or support of: *the report was endorsed by the college.*
 ■recommend (a product) in an advertisement.
2 sign (a cheque or bill of exchange) on the back to make it payable to someone other than the stated payee or to accept responsibility for paying it.
 ■(usu. **be endorsed on**) write (a comment) on the front or back of a document.
3 (usu. **be endorsed**) Brit. enter the penalty points given as a punishment for a driving offence on (a driving licence).
4 (**endorse someone out**) historical (in South Africa) order a black person to leave an urban area for failing to meet certain requirements of the Native Laws Amendment Act.
– DERIVATIVES **endorser** noun.
– ORIGIN late 15th cent. (in the sense 'write on the back of'; formerly also as *indorse*): from medieval Latin *indorsare*, from Latin *in-* 'in, on' + *dorsum* 'back'.

endorsee /ˌɛndɔːˈsiː/ ▶ noun a person to whom a cheque or bill of exchange is made payable instead of the stated payee.

endorsement (also **indorsement**) ▶ noun **1** an act of giving one's public approval or support to someone or something.
 ■a recommendation of a product in an advertisement.
2 (in the UK) a note on a driving licence recording the penalty points incurred for a driving offence.
 ■a clause in an insurance policy detailing an exemption from or change in cover.
3 [mass noun] the action of endorsing a cheque or bill of exchange.

endoscope /ˈɛndəskəʊp/ ▶ noun Medicine an instrument which can be introduced into the body to give a view of its internal parts.
– DERIVATIVES **endoscopic** adjective, **endoscopically** adverb, **endoscopist** noun, **endoscopy** noun.

endoskeleton ▶ noun Zoology an internal skeleton, such as the bony or cartilaginous skeleton of vertebrates. Compare with **EXOSKELETON**.
– DERIVATIVES **endoskeletal** adjective.

endosperm ▶ noun [mass noun] Botany the part of a seed which acts as a food store for the developing plant embryo, usually containing starch with protein and other nutrients.

endospore ▶ noun Biology a resistant asexual spore that develops inside some bacteria cells.
 ■[mass noun] the inner layer of the membrane or wall of some spores and pollen grains.

endosymbiosis /ˌɛndəʊˌsɪmbɪˈəʊsɪs, -bʌɪ-/ ▶ noun [mass noun] Biology symbiosis in which one of the symbiotic organisms lives inside the other.
– DERIVATIVES **endosymbiont** noun, **endosymbiotic** adjective.

endothelium /ˌɛndə(ʊ)ˈθiːlɪəm/ ▶ noun [mass noun] the tissue which forms a single layer of cells lining various organs and cavities of the body, especially the blood vessels, heart, and lymphatic vessels. It is formed from the embryonic mesoderm. Compare with **EPITHELIUM**.
– DERIVATIVES **endothelial** adjective.
– ORIGIN late 19th cent.: modern Latin, from **ENDO-** 'within' + Greek *thēlē* 'nipple'.

endotherm /ˈɛndə(ʊ)θəːm/ ▶ noun Zoology an animal that is dependent on or capable of the internal generation of heat. Often contrasted with **ECTOTHERM**. Compare with **HOMEOTHERM**.
– DERIVATIVES **endothermy** noun.
– ORIGIN 1940s: from **ENDO-** 'within', on the pattern of *homoiotherm.*

endothermic ▶ adjective **1** Chemistry (of a reaction or process) accompanied by or requiring the absorption of heat. The opposite of **EXOTHERMIC**.
 ■(of a compound) requiring a net input of heat for its formation from its constituent elements.
2 Zoology (of an animal) dependent on or capable of the internal generation of heat.

endotoxin /ˈɛndəʊˌtɒksɪn/ ▶ noun Microbiology a toxin present inside a bacterial cell that is released when it disintegrates. It is sometimes responsible for the characteristic symptoms of a disease, e.g. in botulism. Compare with **EXOTOXIN**.

endotracheal /ˌɛndə(ʊ)ˈtreɪkɪəl, -trəˈkiːəl/ ▶ adjective situated or occurring within or performed by way of the trachea.
– DERIVATIVES **endotracheally** adverb.

endow /ɪnˈdaʊ, ɛn-/ ▶ verb [with obj.] give or bequeath an income or property to (a person or institution): *he endowed the church with lands.*
 ■establish (a university post, annual prize, or project) by donating the funds needed to maintain it. ■ (usu. **be endowed with**) provide with a quality, ability, or asset: *he was endowed with tremendous physical strength.*
– DERIVATIVES **endower** noun.
– ORIGIN late Middle English (also in the sense 'provide a dower or dowry'; formerly also as *indow*): from legal Anglo-Norman French *endouer*, from *en-* 'in, towards' + Old French *douer* 'give as a gift' (from Latin *dotare*: see **DOWER**).

endowment ▶ noun [mass noun] the action of endowing something or someone: *he tried to promote the endowment of a Chair of Psychiatry.*
 ■[count noun] an income or form of property given or bequeathed to someone. ■ (usu. **endowments**) a quality or ability possessed or inherited by someone. ■ [usu. as modifier] a form of life insurance involving payment of a fixed sum to the insured person on a specified date, or to their estate should they die before this date: *an endowment policy.*

endowment mortgage ▶ noun Brit. a mortgage linked to an endowment insurance policy which is intended to repay the capital sum on maturity.

endpaper ▶ noun a blank or decorated leaf of paper at the beginning or end of a book, especially that fixed to the inside of the cover.

end plate ▶ noun a flattened piece at or forming the end of something such as a motor or dynamo.
 ■Anatomy each of the discoid expansions of a motor nerve where its branches terminate on a muscle fibre.

endplay Bridge ▶ noun a way of playing in the last few tricks which forces an opponent to make a disadvantageous lead.
▶ verb [with obj.] force (an opponent) to make such a lead.

end point ▶ noun the final stage of a period or process.
 ■Chemistry the point in a titration at which a reaction is complete, often marked by a colour change.

end product ▶ noun that which is produced as the final result of an activity or process, especially the finished article in a manufacturing process.

endrin /ˈɛndrɪn/ ▶ **noun** [mass noun] a toxic insecticide which is a stereoisomer of dieldrin.
– ORIGIN mid 20th cent.: from **ENDO-** 'within' + a shortened form of **DIELDRIN**.

end run ▶ **noun** American Football an attempt by the ball-carrier to run around the end of the defensive line.
■ N. Amer. an evasive tactic or manoeuvre.
▶ **verb** (**end-run**) [with obj.] US evade; circumvent: *an attempt to end-run regulations for fire protection.*

end-scraper ▶ **noun** Archaeology a prehistoric flint tool with a single working edge at one end of a blade or flake, at right angles to the long axis.

end standard ▶ **noun** a standard of length in the form of a metal bar or block whose end faces are the standard distance apart.

end-stopped ▶ **adjective** (of verse) having a pause at the end of each line.

endue /ɪnˈdjuː, ɛn-/ (also **indue**) ▶ **verb** (**endues**, **endued**, **enduing**) [with obj.] poetic/literary endow or provide with a quality or ability: *our sight would be endued with a far greater sharpness.*
– ORIGIN late Middle English (also in the sense 'induct into an ecclesiastical living'): from Old French *enduire*, partly from Latin *inducere* 'lead in' (see **INDUCE**), reinforced by the sense of Latin *induere* 'put on clothes'.

endurance ▶ **noun** [mass noun] the fact or power of enduring an unpleasant or difficult process or situation without giving way: *she was close to the limit of her endurance.*
■ the capacity of something to last or to withstand wear and tear.
– ORIGIN late 15th cent. (in the sense 'continued existence, ability to last'; formerly also as *indurance*): from Old French, from *endurer* 'make hard' (see **ENDURE**).

endure /ɪnˈdjʊə, ɛn-/ ▶ **verb** **1** [with obj.] suffer (something painful or difficult) patiently: *it seemed impossible that anyone could endure such pain.*
■ tolerate (someone or something): *I was a fool to endure him for so long.*
2 [no obj.] remain in existence; last: *these cities have endured through time.*
– DERIVATIVES **endurable** adjective, **enduringly** adverb.
– ORIGIN Middle English: from Old French *endurer*, from Latin *indurare* 'harden', from *in-* 'in' + *durus* 'hard'.

enduro /ɪnˈdjʊərəʊ, ɛn-/ ▶ **noun** (pl. **-os**) a long-distance race for motor vehicles or bicycles, typically over rough terrain, designed to test endurance.
– ORIGIN 1950s: from **ENDURANCE** + the informal suffix **-O**.

end-user ▶ **noun** the person who actually uses a particular product.

endways (also **endwise**) ▶ **adverb** with its end facing upwards, forwards, or towards the viewer: *a little town looking endways on to the river.*
■ in a row with the end of one object touching that of another: *strips of rubber cemented endways.*

Endymion /ɛnˈdɪmɪən/ Greek Mythology a remarkably beautiful young man, loved by the Moon (Selene). According to one story, he was put in an eternal sleep by Zeus for having fallen in love with Hera, and was then visited every night by Selene.

end zone ▶ **noun** American Football the rectangular area at the end of the field into which the ball must be carried or passed to score a touchdown.

ENE ▶ **abbreviation for** east-north-east.

-ene ▶ **suffix** **1** denoting an inhabitant: *Nazarene.*
2 Chemistry forming names of unsaturated hydrocarbons containing a double bond: *benzene* | *ethylene.*
– ORIGIN from Greek *-ēnos*.

en échelon /ɒn ˈeɪʃ(ə)lɒ̃/ ▶ **adjective** & **adverb** chiefly Geology in approximately parallel formation at an oblique angle to a particular direction.
– ORIGIN French, literally 'in rung formation'.

enema /ˈɛnɪmə/ ▶ **noun** (pl. **enemas** or **enemata** /ɪˈnɛmətə/) a procedure in which liquid or gas is injected into the rectum, typically to expel its contents, but also to introduce drugs or permit X-ray imaging.
■ a quantity of fluid or a syringe used in such a procedure.
– ORIGIN late Middle English: via late Latin from Greek, from *enienai* 'send or put in', from *en-* 'in' + *hienai* 'send'.

enemy ▶ **noun** (pl. **-ies**) a person who is actively opposed or hostile to someone or something.
■ (**the enemy**) [treated as sing. or pl.] a hostile nation or its armed forces, especially in time of war: *the enemy shot down four helicopters* | [as modifier] *enemy aircraft.* ■ a thing that harms or weakens something else: *routine is the enemy of art.*
– PHRASES **be one's own worst enemy** act in a way contrary to one's own interests.
– ORIGIN Middle English: from Old French *enemi*, from Latin *inimicus*, from *in-* 'not' + *amicus* 'friend'.

Eneolithic /ˌiːnɪə(ʊ)ˈlɪθɪk/ ▶ **adjective** & **noun** another term for **CHALCOLITHIC**.
– ORIGIN early 20th cent.: from Latin *aeneus* 'of bronze or copper' + Greek *lithos* 'stone' + **-IC**.

energetic /ˌɛnəˈdʒɛtɪk/ ▶ **adjective** showing or involving great activity or vitality: *moderately energetic exercise.*
■ Physics characterized by a high level of energy (in the technical sense): *energetic X-rays.* ■ of or relating to energy (in the technical sense).
– DERIVATIVES **energetically** adverb.
– ORIGIN mid 17th cent. (in the sense 'powerfully effective'): from Greek *energētikos*, from *energein* 'operate, work in or upon' (based on *ergon* 'work').

energetics ▶ **plural noun** **1** the properties of something in terms of energy.
2 [treated as sing.] the branch of science which deals with the properties of energy and the way in which it is redistributed in physical, chemical, or biological processes.

energize (also **-ise**) ▶ **verb** [with obj.] give vitality and enthusiasm to: *people were energized by his ideas.*
■ supply energy, typically kinetic or electrical energy, to (something).
– DERIVATIVES **energizer** noun.

energumen /ˌɛnəˈgjuːmən/ ▶ **noun** archaic a person believed to be possessed by the devil or a spirit.
– ORIGIN early 18th cent. (also denoting an enthusiast or fanatic): via late Latin from Greek *energoumenos*, passive participle of *energein* 'work in or upon'.

energy ▶ **noun** (pl. **-ies**) [mass noun] **1** the strength and vitality required for sustained physical or mental activity: *changes in the levels of vitamins can affect energy and well-being.*
■ (**energies**) a person's physical and mental powers, typically as applied to a particular task or activity.
2 power derived from the utilization of physical or chemical resources, especially to provide light and heat or to work machines.
3 Physics the property of matter and radiation which is manifest as a capacity to perform work (such as causing motion or the interaction of molecules): *a collision in which no energy is transferred.*
■ [count noun] a degree or level of this capacity possessed by something or required by a process.
– ORIGIN mid 16th cent. (denoting force or vigour of expression): from French *énergie*, or via late Latin from Greek *energeia*, from *en-* 'in, within' + *ergon* 'work'.

energy audit ▶ **noun** an assessment of the energy needs and efficiency of a building or buildings.

enervate ▶ **verb** /ˈɛnəveɪt/ [with obj.] cause (someone) to feel drained of energy or vitality.
▶ **adjective** /ɪˈnəːvət/ poetic/literary lacking in energy or vitality: *the enervate slightness of his frail form.*
– DERIVATIVES **enervation** noun.
– ORIGIN early 17th cent.: from Latin *enervat-* 'weakened (by extraction of the sinews)', from the verb *enervare*, from *e-* (variant of *ex-*) 'out of' + *nervus* 'sinew'.

Enewetak variant spelling of **ENIWETOK**.

en face /ɒ̃ ˈfas/ ▶ **adverb** & **adjective** facing forwards.
– ORIGIN French.

en famille /ɒ̃ faˈmiː/ ▶ **adverb** with one's family: *when they went out en famille, Steven always drove.*
■ as or like a member or members of a family.
– ORIGIN French, literally 'in family'.

enfant gâté /ˌɒ̃fɒ̃ ˈgateɪ/ ▶ **noun** dated a person who is excessively flattered or indulged.
– ORIGIN French, literally 'spoilt child'.

enfant terrible /ˌɒ̃fɒ̃ tɛˈriːbl(ə)/ ▶ **noun** (pl. **enfants terribles** pronunc. same) a person whose unconventional or controversial behaviour or ideas shock, embarrass, or annoy others.
– ORIGIN French, literally 'terrible child'.

enfeeble ▶ **verb** [with obj.] make weak or feeble: [as adj. **enfeebled**] *trade unions are in an enfeebled state.*
– DERIVATIVES **enfeeblement** noun.
– ORIGIN Middle English: from Old French *enfeblir*, from *en-* (expressing a change of state) + *feble* 'feeble'.

enfeoff /ɪnˈfiːf, -ˈfɛf, ɛn-/ ▶ **verb** [with obj.] historical (under the feudal system) give (someone) freehold property or land in exchange for their pledged service.
■ give (property or land) in this way: *the lands were enfeoffed to the baron.*
– DERIVATIVES **enfeoffment** noun.
– ORIGIN late Middle English: from Anglo-Norman French *enfeoffer*, from Old French *en-* 'in' + *fief* 'fief'. Compare with **FEOFFMENT**.

en fête /ɒ̃ ˈfɛt/ ▶ **adverb** & **adjective** holding or prepared for a party or celebration.
– ORIGIN French, 'in festival'.

enfetter ▶ **verb** [with obj.] poetic/literary restrain (someone) with shackles.

enfevered ▶ **adjective** poetic/literary having or showing the signs of fever.

enfilade /ˌɛnfɪˈleɪd/ ▶ **noun** **1** a volley of gunfire directed along a line from end to end.
2 a suite of rooms with doorways in line with each other.
▶ **verb** [with obj.] direct a volley of gunfire along the length of (a target).
– ORIGIN early 18th cent. (denoting the position of a military post commanding the length of a line): from French, from *enfiler* 'thread on a string, pierce from end to end', from *en-* 'in, on' + *fil* 'thread'.

enflesh ▶ **verb** [with obj.] poetic/literary give bodily form to; make real or concrete.
– DERIVATIVES **enfleshment** noun.

enfleurage /ˌɒ̃fləˈrɑːʒ/ ▶ **noun** [mass noun] the extraction of essential oils and perfumes from flowers using odourless animal or vegetable fats.
– ORIGIN mid 19th cent.: French, from *enfleurer* 'saturate with the perfume from flowers'.

enflurane /ɛnˈflʊəreɪn/ ▶ **noun** [mass noun] Medicine a volatile organic liquid used as a general anaesthetic.
• A halogenated ether; chem. formula: CHF_2OCF_2CHFCl.
– ORIGIN 1970s: from *en-* (of unknown origin) + **FLUORO-** + **-ANE**[2].

enfold /ɪnˈfəʊld, ɛn-/ ▶ **verb** [with obj.] surround; envelop: *he shut off the engine and silence enfolded them.*
■ hold or clasp (someone) lovingly in one's arms.
– ORIGIN late Middle English (in the sense 'involve, entail, imply'; formerly also as *infold*): from **EN-**[1], **IN-**[2] 'within' + **FOLD**[1].

enforce ▶ **verb** [with obj.] compel observance of or compliance with (a law, rule, or obligation).
■ cause (something) to happen by necessity or force: *there is no outside agency to enforce cooperation between the players* | [as adj. **enforced**] *a period of enforced idleness.* ■ archaic press home (a demand or argument).
– DERIVATIVES **enforceability** noun, **enforceable** adjective, **enforcedly** adverb, **enforcement** noun, **enforcer** noun.
– ORIGIN Middle English (in the senses 'strive' and 'impel by force'; formerly also as *inforce*): from Old French *enforcir*, *enforcier*, based on Latin *in-* 'in' + *fortis* 'strong'.

enforcement notice ▶ **noun** English Law an official notification to remedy a breach of planning legislation.

enfranchise /ɪnˈfran(t)ʃʌɪz, ɛn-/ ▶ **verb** [with obj.] give the right to vote to: *a proposal that foreigners should be enfranchised for local elections.*
■ historical give (a town) the right to be represented in Parliament. ■ historical free (a slave).
– DERIVATIVES **enfranchisement** noun.
– ORIGIN late Middle English (formerly also as *infranchise*): from Old French *enfranchiss-*, lengthened stem of *enfranchir*, from *en-* (expressing a change of state) + *franc*, *franche* 'free'.

ENG ▶ **abbreviation for** electronic news-gathering.

engage ▶ **verb** **1** [with obj.] occupy, attract, or involve (someone's interest or attention): *he ploughed on, trying to outline his plans and engage Sutton's attention.*
■ (**engage someone in**) cause someone to become involved in (a conversation or discussion). ■ chiefly Brit. arrange to employ or hire (someone): *he was engaged as a trainee copywriter.* ■ [with infinitive] pledge or enter into a contract to do something: *he engaged to pay*

them £10,000 against a bond. ■ dated reserve (accommodation, a place, etc.) in advance.
2 [no obj.] (**engage in**) participate or become involved in: *organizations engage in a variety of activities* | (**be engaged in**) *some are actively engaged in crime.*
■(**engage with**) establish a meaningful contact or connection with: *the teams needed to engage with local communities.* ■ (of a part of a machine or engine) move into position so as to come into operation: *the clutch will not engage.* ■ [with obj.] cause (a part of a machine or engine) to do this. ■ [with obj.] (of fencers or swordsmen) bring (weapons) together preparatory to fighting. ■ [with obj.] enter into combat with (an enemy).
– ORIGIN late Middle English (formerly also as *ingage*): from French *engager*, ultimately from the base of **GAGE**[1]. The word originally meant 'to pawn or pledge something', later 'pledge oneself (to do something)', hence 'enter into a contract' (mid 16th cent.), 'involve oneself in an activity', 'enter into combat' (mid 17th cent.), giving rise to the notion 'involve someone or something else'.

engagé /ˌɒ̃gaˈʒeɪ/ ▶ **adjective** (of a writer, artist, or their works) morally committed to a particular aim or cause.
– ORIGIN French, past participle of *engager* (see **ENGAGE**).

engaged ▶ **adjective 1** [predic.] busy; occupied: *I told him I was otherwise engaged.*
■Brit. (of a telephone line) unavailable because already in use. ■ (of a toilet) already in use.
2 having formally agreed to marry.
3 Architecture (of a column) attached to or partly let into a wall.

engaged tone (also **engaged signal**) ▶ **noun** Brit. a sound indicating that a telephone line is engaged, typically a repeated single bleep.

engagement ▶ **noun 1** a formal agreement to get married.
■the duration of such an agreement: *a good long engagement to give you time to be sure.*
2 an arrangement to do something or go somewhere at a fixed time: *a dinner engagement.*
3 [mass noun] the action of engaging or being engaged: *Britain's continued **engagement in** open trading.*
4 a fight or battle between armed forces.
– ORIGIN early 17th cent. (in the general sense 'a legal or moral obligation'): French, from *engager* 'to pledge' (see **ENGAGE**).

engagement ring ▶ **noun** a ring given by a man to a woman when they agree to marry.

engaging ▶ **adjective** charming and attractive: *Sophie had a sunny personality that was very engaging.*
– DERIVATIVES **engagingly** adverb, **engagingness** noun.

Engelmann spruce /ˈɛŋg(ə)lmən/ (also **Engelmann's spruce**) ▶ **noun** a tall spruce found in the mountains of western North America and Mexico.
• *Picea engelmannii*, family Pinaceae.
– ORIGIN mid 19th cent.: named after George *Engelmann* (1809–84), American botanist.

Engels /ˈɛŋg(ə)lz/, Friedrich (1820–95), German socialist and political philosopher. He collaborated with Marx in the writing of the *Communist Manifesto* (1848) and translated and edited Marx's later work. Engels's own writings include *The Condition of the Working Classes in England in 1844* (1845).

engender /ɪnˈdʒɛndə, ɛn-/ ▶ **verb** [with obj.] cause or give rise to (a feeling, situation, or condition): *the issue engendered continuing controversy.*
■archaic (of a father) beget (offspring).
– ORIGIN Middle English (formerly also as *ingender*): from Old French *engendrer*, from Latin *ingenerare*, from *in-* 'in' + *generare* 'beget' (see **GENERATE**).

engine ▶ **noun 1** a machine with moving parts that converts power into motion.
■a thing that is the agent or instrument of a particular process: *exports used to be the engine of growth.*
2 (also **railway engine**) a locomotive.
■short for **FIRE ENGINE**. ■ historical a mechanical device or instrument, especially one used in warfare: *a siege engine.*
– DERIVATIVES **engined** adjective [in combination] *a twin-engined helicopter*, **engineless** adjective.
– ORIGIN Middle English (formerly also as *ingine*): from Old French *engin*, from Latin *ingenium* 'talent, device', from *in-* 'in' + *gignere* 'beget'; compare with **INGENIOUS**. The original sense was 'ingenuity, cunning' (surviving in Scots as *ingine*), hence 'the product of ingenuity, a plot or snare', also 'tool, weapon', later specifically denoting a large mechanical weapon; whence a machine (mid 17th cent.), used commonly later in combinations such as *steam engine, internal-combustion engine.*

engine block ▶ **noun** see **BLOCK** (sense 1).

engine driver ▶ **noun** Brit. a person who drives a railway locomotive.

engineer ▶ **noun** a person who designs, builds, or maintains engines, machines, or public works.
■a person who controls an engine, especially on an aircraft or ship. ■ N. Amer. a train driver. ■ a skilful contriver or originator of something: *the prime engineer of the approach.*
▶ **verb** [with obj.] design and build (a machine or structure): *the men who engineered the tunnel.*
■skilfully or artfully arrange for (an event or situation) to occur: *she engineered another meeting with him.* ■ modify (an organism) by manipulating its genetic material: [as adj., with submodifier] (**engineered**) *genetically engineered plants.*
– ORIGIN Middle English (denoting a designer and constructor of fortifications and weapons; formerly also as *ingineer*): in early use from Old French *engigneor*, from medieval Latin *ingeniator*, from *ingeniare* 'contrive, devise', from Latin *ingenium* (see **ENGINE**); in later use from French *ingénieur* or Italian *ingegnere*, also based on Latin *ingenium*, with the ending influenced by **-EER**.

engineering ▶ **noun** [mass noun] the branch of science and technology concerned with the design, building, and use of engines, machines, and structures.

engineering brick ▶ **noun** a brick made of semi-vitreous material, which is strong, very dense, and impervious to such things as water or frost.

engineering science (also **engineering sciences**) ▶ **noun** [mass noun] the parts of science concerned with the physical and mathematical basis of engineering and machine technology.

engine room ▶ **noun** the room containing the engines, especially in a ship.

enginery /ˈɛndʒɪn(ə)ri/ ▶ **noun** [mass noun] archaic engines collectively; machinery.

engine turning ▶ **noun** [mass noun] the decoration of metal or ceramic objects with regular engraved patterns using a lathe.
– DERIVATIVES **engine-turned** adjective.

engirdle (also **engird**) ▶ **verb** [with obj.] poetic/literary surround; encircle: *railways engirdled this tract of country.*

englacial /ɪnˈgleɪʃ(ə)l, -sɪəl, ɛn-/ ▶ **adjective** situated, occurring, or formed inside a glacier.
– DERIVATIVES **englacially** adverb.

England a country forming the largest and southernmost part of Great Britain and of the United Kingdom, and containing the capital, London; pop. 46,170,300 (1991).

England was conquered by the Romans in the first century AD, when it was inhabited by Celtic peoples, and was a Roman province until the early 5th century. During the 3rd–7th centuries Germanic-speaking tribes, traditionally known as Angles, Saxons, and Jutes, established a number of independent kingdoms. England emerged as a distinct political entity in the 9th century before being conquered by William, Duke of Normandy, in 1066.

English ▶ **adjective** of or relating to England or its people or language.
■(in South Africa) of or relating to white English-speaking South Africans.
▶ **noun 1** [mass noun] the language of England, now widely used in many varieties throughout the world.
2 [as plural noun **the English**] the people of England.
3 [mass noun] N. Amer. spin or side given to a ball, especially in pool or billiards.

English is the principal language of Great Britain, the US, Ireland, Canada, Australia, New Zealand, and many other countries. There are some 400 million native speakers, and it is the medium of communication for many millions more; it is the most widely used second language in the world. It belongs to the West Germanic group of Indo-European languages, though its vocabulary has been much influenced by Norman French and Latin.

– DERIVATIVES **Englishness** noun.
– ORIGIN Old English *Englisc* (see **ANGLE**, **-ISH**[1]). The word originally denoted the early Germanic settlers of Britain (Angles, Saxons, and Jutes), or their language (now called **OLD ENGLISH**).

English bond ▶ **noun** [mass noun] Building a bond used in brickwork consisting of alternate courses of stretchers and headers.

English breakfast ▶ **noun** a substantial breakfast including hot cooked food such as bacon and eggs.

English Canadian ▶ **noun** a Canadian whose principal language is English.
▶ **adjective** of or relating to English-speaking Canadians.

English Channel the sea channel separating southern England from northern France. It is 35 km (22 miles) wide at its narrowest point. A railway tunnel beneath it linking England and France was opened in 1994 (the Channel Tunnel).

English Civil War the war between Charles I and his Parliamentary opponents, 1642–9.

Civil war broke out after Charles refused to accede to a series of demands made by Parliament. The king's forces (the Royalists or Cavaliers) were decisively defeated by the Parliamentary forces (or Roundheads) at the Battle of Naseby (1645), and an attempt by Charles to regain power in alliance with the Scots was defeated in 1648. Charles himself was tried and executed by Parliament in 1649.

English galingale ▶ **noun** see **GALINGALE** (sense 1).

English garden snail ▶ **noun** see **GARDEN SNAIL**.

English Heritage (in the UK) a body responsible since 1983 for England's ancient monuments, listed buildings, and conservation areas.

English horn ▶ **noun** chiefly N. Amer. another term for **COR ANGLAIS**.

Englishman ▶ **noun** (pl. **-men**) a male native or national of England, or a man of English descent.
– PHRASES **an Englishman's home is his castle** Brit. proverb an English person's home is a place where they may do as they please and from which they may exclude anyone they choose.

English muffin ▶ **noun** North American term for **MUFFIN** (in sense 1).

English mustard ▶ **noun** [mass noun] a kind of mustard made from mustard seeds milled to a powder, having a very hot taste and typically bright yellow in colour.

English Pale (also **the Pale**) **1** a small area round Calais, the only part of France remaining in English hands after the Hundred Years War. It was recaptured by France in 1558.
2 that part of Ireland over which England exercised jurisdiction before the whole country was conquered. Centred on Dublin, it varied in extent at different times from the reign of Henry II until the full conquest under Elizabeth I.
– ORIGIN *Pale* from **PALE**[2].

English rose ▶ **noun** an attractive English girl with a delicate, fair-skinned complexion regarded as typically English.

English setter ▶ **noun** a setter of a breed with a long white or partly white coat.

English springer ▶ **noun** see **SPRINGER** (sense 1).

Englishwoman ▶ **noun** (pl. **-women**) a female native or national of England, or a woman of English descent.

englobe ▶ **verb** [with obj.] poetic/literary enclose in or shape into a globe.

engorge /ɪnˈgɔːdʒ, ɛn-/ ▶ **verb 1** [with obj.] cause to swell with blood, water, or another fluid: *the river was engorged by a day-long deluge.*
■[no obj.] become swollen in this way.
2 (**engorge oneself**) archaic eat to excess.
– DERIVATIVES **engorgement** noun.
– ORIGIN late 15th cent. (in the sense 'gorge; eat or fill to excess'): from Old French *engorgier* 'feed to excess', from *en-* 'into' + *gorge* 'throat'.

engraft (also **ingraft**) ▶ **verb** another term for **GRAFT**[1].
– DERIVATIVES **engraftment** noun.

engrailed ▶ **adjective** chiefly Heraldry having semicircular indentations along the edge. Compare with **INVECTED**.

engrain ▶ **verb** variant spelling of **INGRAIN**.

engrained ▶ **adjective** variant spelling of **INGRAINED**.

engram /ˈɛngram/ ▶ **noun** a hypothetical permanent change in the brain accounting for the existence of memory; a memory trace.

– DERIVATIVES **engrammatic** adjective.
– ORIGIN early 20th cent.: coined in German from Greek *en-* 'within' + *gramma* 'letter of the alphabet'.

engrave ▶ **verb** [with obj.] (usu. **be engraved**) cut or carve (a text or design) on the surface of a hard object: *my name was engraved on the ring.*
■ cut or carve a text or design on (such an object). ■ cut (a design) as lines on a metal plate for printing. ■ (**be engraved on** or **in**) be permanently fixed in (one's memory or mind): *the image would be forever engraved in his memory.*
– PHRASES **be engraved in stone** see **STONE**.
– DERIVATIVES **engraver** noun.
– ORIGIN late 15th cent. (formerly also as *ingrave*): from **EN-**[1], **IN-**[2] 'in, on' + **GRAVE**[3], influenced by obsolete French *engraver.*

engraving ▶ **noun** a print made from an engraved plate, block, or other surface.
■ [mass noun] the process or art of cutting or carving a design on a hard surface, especially so as to make a print.

engross /ɪnˈɡrəʊs, ɛn-/ ▶ **verb** [with obj.] **1** absorb all the attention or interest of: *the notes totally engrossed him.*
■ archaic gain or keep exclusive possession of (something): *the country had made the best of its position to engross trade.* [ORIGIN: from Old French *en gros,* from medieval Latin *in grosso* 'wholesale'.]
2 Law produce (a legal document) in its final or definitive form. [ORIGIN: from Anglo-Norman French *engrosser,* medieval Latin *ingrossare* (from Old French *grosse,* medieval Latin *grossa* 'large writing').]
– ORIGIN late Middle English (formerly also as *ingross*): based on **EN-**[1], **IN-**[2] 'in' + late Latin *grossus* 'large'.

engrossed ▶ **adjective** [predic.] having all one's attention or interest absorbed by someone or something: *they seemed to be* **engrossed in** *conversation.*

engrossment ▶ **noun** Law the final version of a legal document, eventually becoming the original deed.

engulf ▶ **verb** [with obj.] (often **be engulfed**) (of a natural force) sweep over (something) so as to surround or cover it completely: *the cafe was* **engulfed in flames** | figurative *Europe might be engulfed by war.*
■ eat or swallow (something) whole.
– DERIVATIVES **engulfment** noun.

enhance /ɪnˈhɑːns, -hans, ɛn-/ ▶ **verb** [with obj.] intensify, increase, or further improve the quality, value, or extent of: *his refusal does nothing to enhance his reputation.*
– DERIVATIVES **enhancement** noun, **enhancer** noun.
– ORIGIN Middle English (formerly also as *inhance*): from Anglo-Norman French *enhauncer,* based on Latin *in-* (expressing intensive force) + *altus* 'high'. The word originally meant 'elevate' (literally and figuratively), later 'exaggerate, make appear greater', also 'raise the value or price of something'. Current senses date from the early 16th cent.

enharmonic /ˌɛnhɑːˈmɒnɪk/ ▶ **adjective** Music of or relating to notes which are the same in pitch (in modern tuning) though bearing different names (e.g. F sharp and G flat or B and C flat).
■ of or having intervals smaller than a semitone (e.g. between notes such as F sharp and G flat, in systems of tuning which distinguish them).
– DERIVATIVES **enharmonically** adverb.
– ORIGIN early 17th cent. (designating ancient Greek music based on a tetrachord divided into two quarter-tones and a major third): via late Latin from Greek *enarmonikos,* from *en-* 'in' + *harmonia* 'harmony'.

enigma /ɪˈnɪɡmə/ ▶ **noun** a person or thing that is mysterious, puzzling, or difficult to understand.
– ORIGIN mid 16th cent.: via Latin from Greek *ainigma,* from *ainissesthai* 'speak allusively', from *ainos* 'fable'.

enigmatic /ˌɛnɪɡˈmatɪk/ ▶ **adjective** difficult to interpret or understand; mysterious: *he took the money with an enigmatic smile.*
– DERIVATIVES **enigmatical** adjective, **enigmatically** adverb.
– ORIGIN early 17th cent.: from French *énigmatique* or late Latin *aenigmaticus,* based on Greek *ainigma* 'riddle' (see **ENIGMA**).

enisle /ɛnˈʌɪl, ɪn-/ ▶ **verb** [with obj.] poetic/literary isolate on or as if on an island: *in the sea of life enisled, we mortal millions live alone.*

Eniwetok /ɛˈniːwəˌtɔːk, ˌɛnɪˈwiːtɔːk/ (also **Enewetak**) an uninhabited island in the North Pacific, one of the Marshall Islands. Cleared of its native population, it was used by the US as a testing ground for atom bombs from 1948 to 1954.

enjambed /ɪnˈdʒamd, ɛn-/ ▶ **adjective** (of a line, couplet, or stanza of verse) ending part-way through a sentence or clause which continues in the next.
– ORIGIN late 19th cent.: from French *enjamber* 'stride over' + **-ED**[2].

enjambement /ɪnˈdʒam(b)m(ə)nt, ɛn-, ɒ̃ˈʒɒ̃bmɒ̃/ (also **enjambment**) ▶ **noun** [mass noun] (in verse) the continuation of a sentence without a pause beyond the end of a line, couplet, or stanza.
– ORIGIN mid 19th cent.: French *enjambement,* from *enjamber* 'stride over, go beyond', from *en-* 'in' + *jambe* 'leg'.

enjoin ▶ **verb** [with obj. and infinitive] instruct or urge (someone) to do something: *the code enjoined members to trade fairly.*
■ [with obj.] prescribe (an action or attitude) to be performed or adopted: *the charitable deeds* **enjoined on** *him by religion.* ■ [with obj.] (**enjoin someone from**) Law prohibit someone from performing (a particular action) by issuing an injunction.
– DERIVATIVES **enjoinment** noun.
– ORIGIN Middle English (formerly also as *injoin*): from Old French *enjoindre,* from Latin *injungere* 'join, attach, impose', from *in-* 'in, towards' + *jungere* 'to join'.

enjoy ▶ **verb** [with obj.] **1** take delight or pleasure in (an activity or occasion): *I enjoy watching good films.*
■ (**enjoy oneself**) have a pleasant time: *I could never enjoy myself, knowing you were in your room alone.* ■ [no obj., in imperative] informal, chiefly N. Amer. used to urge someone to take pleasure in what is about happen or be done: *your love life and love for life get stronger after the 28th—enjoy!*
2 possess and benefit from: *the security forces enjoy legal immunity from prosecution.*
– DERIVATIVES **enjoyer** noun, **enjoyment** noun.
– ORIGIN late Middle English: from Old French *enjoier* 'give joy to' or *enjoïr* 'enjoy', both based on Latin *gaudere* 'rejoice'.

enjoyable ▶ **adjective** (of an activity or occasion) giving delight or pleasure: *the decision is aimed at making shopping more enjoyable.*
– DERIVATIVES **enjoyability** noun, **enjoyableness** noun, **enjoyably** adverb.

enkephalin /ɛnˈkɛf(ə)lɪn/ (also **encephalin**) ▶ **noun** Biochemistry either of two compounds which occur naturally in the brain. They are peptides related to the endorphins, with similar physiological effects.
– ORIGIN 1970s: from Greek *enkephalos* 'brain' (from *en-* 'in' + *kephalē* 'head') + **-IN**[1].

enkindle ▶ **verb** [with obj.] poetic/literary set on fire.
■ arouse or inspire (an emotion): *fresh remembrance of vexation must still enkindle rage.* ■ inflame with passion: *he confidently believed it would enkindle Clara's cold temperament.*

enlace ▶ **verb** [with obj.] poetic/literary entwine or entangle: *a web of green enlaced the thorn trees.*
– ORIGIN Middle English: from Old French *enlacier,* based on Latin *laqueus* 'noose'.

enlarge ▶ **verb** make or become bigger or more extensive: [with obj.] *recently my son enlarged our garden pond* | [no obj.] *lymph nodes enlarge and become hard* | [as adj. **enlarged**] *an enlarged spleen.*
■ [with obj.] (often **be enlarged**) develop a bigger print of (a photograph).
– ORIGIN Middle English (formerly also as *inlarge*): from Old French *enlarger,* from *en-* (expressing a change of state) + *large* 'large'.
▶ **enlarge on/upon** speak or write about (something) in greater detail: *I would like to enlarge on this theme.*

enlargement ▶ **noun** [mass noun] the action or state of enlarging or being enlarged.
■ [count noun] a photograph that is larger than the negative from which it is produced or than a print that has already been made from it.

enlarger ▶ **noun** Photography an apparatus for enlarging or reducing negatives or positives.

enlighten ▶ **verb** [with obj.] give (someone) greater knowledge and understanding about a subject or situation: *Christopher had not enlightened Francis as to their relationship.*
■ give (someone) spiritual knowledge or insight. ■ figurative illuminate or make clearer (a problem or area of study): *this will enlighten the studies of origins of myths and symbols.* ■ archaic shed light on (an object).
– DERIVATIVES **enlightener** noun.
– ORIGIN Middle English (in the sense 'make luminous'; formerly also as *inlighten*): in early use from Old English *inlīhtan* 'to shine'; later from **EN-**[1], **IN-**[2] (as an intensifier) + **LIGHTEN**[2] or the noun **LIGHT**[1].

enlightened ▶ **adjective** having or showing a rational, modern, and well-informed outlook: *the more enlightened employers offer better terms.*
■ spiritually aware.

enlightenment ▶ **noun 1** [mass noun] the action of enlightening or the state of being enlightened: *Robbie looked to me for enlightenment.*
■ the action or state of attaining or having attained spiritual knowledge or insight, in particular (in Buddhism) that awareness which frees a person from the cycle of rebirth.
2 (**the Enlightenment**) a European intellectual movement of the late 17th and 18th centuries emphasizing reason and individualism rather than tradition. It was heavily influenced by 17th-century philosophers such as Descartes, Locke, and Newton, and its prominent exponents include Kant, Goethe, Voltaire, Rousseau, and Adam Smith.

enlist ▶ **verb** enrol or be enrolled in the armed services: [no obj.] *he* **enlisted in** *the Royal Naval Air Service* | [with obj.] *hundreds of thousands of recruits had been enlisted.*
■ [with obj.] engage (a person or their help or support): *the company enlisted the help of independent consultants.*
– DERIVATIVES **enlister** noun, **enlistment** noun.
– ORIGIN mid 16th cent. (formerly also as *inlist*): from **EN-**[1], **IN-**[2] 'in, on' + **LIST**[1], perhaps suggested by Dutch *inlijsten* 'put on a list'.

enlisted man ▶ **noun** US a member of the armed forces below the rank of officer.

enliven ▶ **verb** [with obj.] make (something) more entertaining, interesting, or appealing: *the wartime routine was enlivened by a series of concerts.*
■ make (someone) more cheerful or animated: *the visit had clearly enlivened my mother.*
– DERIVATIVES **enlivener** noun, **enlivenment** noun.
– ORIGIN mid 17th cent. (in the sense 'restore to life, give life to'; formerly also as *inliven*): from 16th-cent. *enlive, inlive* (in the same sense), from **EN-**[1], **IN-**[2] (as an intensifier) + **LIFE**.

en masse /ɒ̃ ˈmas/ ▶ **adverb** in a group; all together: *the cabinet immediately resigned en masse.*
– ORIGIN late 18th cent.: French, 'in a mass'.

enmesh ▶ **verb** [with obj.] (usu. **be enmeshed in**) cause to become entangled in something: *whales enmeshed in drift nets* | figurative *he is enmeshed in an adulterous affair.*
– DERIVATIVES **enmeshment** noun.

enmity ▶ **noun** (pl. **-ies**) [mass noun] the state or feeling of being actively opposed or hostile to someone or something: *enmity between Protestants and Catholics* | [count noun] *family feuds and enmities.*
– ORIGIN Middle English: from Old French *enemi(s)tie,* based on Latin *inimicus* (see **ENEMY**).

ennead /ˈɛnɪad/ ▶ **noun** rare a group or set of nine.
– ORIGIN mid 16th cent.: from Greek *enneas, ennead-,* from *ennea* 'nine'.

enneagram /ˈɛnɪəɡram/ ▶ **noun** a nine-sided figure used in a particular system of analysis to represent the spectrum of possible personality types.
– ORIGIN from Greek *ennea* 'nine' + **-GRAM**[1].

Ennis /ˈɛnɪs/ the county town of Clare, in the Republic of Ireland; pop. 13,700 (1991).

Enniskillen /ˌɛnɪsˈkɪlɪn/ a town in Northern Ireland; pop. 10,400 (1981). The old spelling *Inniskilling* is preserved as a regimental name in the British army, commemorating the defence of Enniskillen by its townsmen against the supporters of the deposed King James II in 1689.

Ennius /ˈɛnɪəs/, Quintus (239–169 BC), Roman epic poet and dramatist. He was largely responsible for the creation of a native Roman literature based on Greek models, but only fragments of his many works survive.

ennoble ▶ **verb** [with obj.] give (someone) a noble rank or title.
■ lend greater dignity or nobility of character to: *the theatre is a moral instrument to ennoble the mind.*
– DERIVATIVES **ennoblement** noun.
– ORIGIN late 15th cent. (formerly also as *innoble*):

from French *ennoblir*, from *en-* (expressing a change of state) + *noble* 'noble'.

ennui /ɒnˈwiː/ ▶ **noun** [mass noun] a feeling of listlessness and dissatisfaction arising from a lack of occupation or excitement.
– ORIGIN mid 18th cent.: French, from Latin *in odio(n-)*, from *mihi in odio est* 'it is hateful to me'. Compare with **ANNOY**.

Enoch /ˈiːnɒk/ **1** (in the Bible) the eldest son of Cain. ■the first city, built by Cain (Gen. 4:17).
2 a Hebrew patriarch, father of Methuselah.

enology ▶ **noun** US spelling of **OENOLOGY**.

enormity ▶ **noun** (pl. **-ies**) **1** [mass noun] (**the enormity of**) the great or extreme scale, seriousness, or extent of something perceived as bad or morally wrong: *a thorough search disclosed the full enormity of the crime.*
■(in neutral use) the large size or scale of something: *the enormity of his intellect.*
2 a grave crime or sin: *the enormities of the Hitler regime.*
– ORIGIN late Middle English: via Old French from Latin *enormitas*, from *enormis*, from *e-* (variant of *ex-*) 'out of' + *norma* 'pattern, standard'. The word originally meant 'deviation from legal or moral rectitude' and 'transgression'. Current senses have been influenced by **ENORMOUS**.

USAGE It is not uncommon for **enormity** to be used as a synonym for **hugeness** or **immensity**, as in *the **enormity** of French hypermarkets.* There are some people who regard this use as wrong, arguing that **enormity** in its original sense meant 'a crime' and should therefore continue to be used only of contexts in which a negative moral judgement is implied. Between 5 and 10 per cent of uses in the British National Corpus use **enormity** in a neutral sense, however, and the use is now broadly accepted in standard English.

enormous ▶ **adjective** very large in size, quantity, or extent: *her enormous blue eyes | the possibilities are enormous.*
– DERIVATIVES **enormously** adverb [as submodifier] *she has been enormously successful*, **enormousness** noun.
– ORIGIN mid 16th cent.: from Latin *enormis* 'unusual, huge' (see **ENORMITY**) + **-OUS**.

enosis /ɪˈnəʊsɪs, ˈɛnəsɪs/ ▶ **noun** [mass noun] the political union of Cyprus and Greece, as an aim or ideal of certain Greeks and Cypriots.
– ORIGIN 1920s: from modern Greek *henōsis*, from *hena* 'one'.

enough ▶ **determiner** & **pronoun** as much or as many as required: [as determiner] *too much work and not **enough** people **to** do it | there was just **enough** room **for** two cars* | [as pronoun] *they ordered **more than enough** for five people | getting **enough of** the right things to eat* | [as postpositive adj.] *there will be time enough to tell you when we meet.*
■used to indicate that one is unwilling to tolerate any more of something undesirable: [as determiner] *we've got enough problems without that* | [as pronoun] *I've **had enough of** this arguing | **that's enough**, pack it in.*
▶ **adverb 1** to the required degree or extent (used after an adjective, adverb, or verb); adequately: *before he was old **enough to** shave | you're not big **enough for** basketball.*
2 to a moderate degree; fairly: *he can get there easily enough | he seems nice enough.*
3 [with sentence adverb] used for emphasis: *curiously enough, there is no mention of him.*
– PHRASES **enough is as good as a feast** proverb moderation is more satisfying than excess. **enough is enough** no more will be tolerated. **enough said** there is no need to say more; all is understood.
– ORIGIN Old English *genōg*, of Germanic origin; related to Dutch *genoeg* and German *genug*.

en papillote /ɒ̃ ˈpapɪjɒt/ ▶ **adjective** & **adverb** (of food) cooked and served in a paper wrapper: [as postpositive adj.] *fish en papillote .*

en passant /ɒ̃ paˈsɑːnt, ˈpasɒ̃/ ▶ **adverb** by the way; incidentally: *the singular distinction of being mentioned, en passant, in an Act of Parliament.*
■Chess by the en passant rule.
– PHRASES **en passant rule** (or **law**) Chess the rule that a pawn making a first move of two squares instead of one may nevertheless be immediately captured by an opposing pawn on the fifth rank.
– ORIGIN early 17th cent.: French, literally 'in passing'.

en pension /ɒ̃ ˈpɒ̃sjɒ̃/ ▶ **adverb** as a boarder or lodger, typically in a small hotel or private house.
– ORIGIN French (see **PENSION**[2]).

enplane ▶ **verb** variant spelling of **EMPLANE**.

en plein air /ˌɒ̃ plɛn ˈɛː/ ▶ **adverb** (chiefly with reference to painting) in the open air. See also **PLEIN AIR**.

en pointe ▶ **adjective** & **adverb** see ***on pointe*** at **POINTE**.
– ORIGIN French.

en poste /ɒ̃ pɒst/ ▶ **adverb** in an official diplomatic position at a particular place.

en primeur /ˌɒ̃ prɪˈməː, French ɑ̃ pʀimœʀ/ ▶ **adjective** & **adverb** (of wine) newly produced and made available.
– ORIGIN French, literally 'as being new'.

enprint /ˈɛnprɪnt/ ▶ **noun** Brit. a standard-sized photographic print produced by developing and printing companies, made by printing the whole of a negative to a moderate enlargement.
– ORIGIN mid 20th cent.: from *enlarged print*.

en prise /ɒ̃ ˈpriːz/ ▶ **adjective** [predic.] Chess (of a piece or pawn) in a position to be taken.
– ORIGIN early 19th cent.: French.

enquire ▶ **verb** [reporting verb] ask for information from someone: [with direct speech] *'How well do you know Berlin?' he **enquired of** Hencke* | [with clause] *I enquired where he lived* | [no obj.] *he **enquired about** cottages for sale.*
■[no obj.] (**enquire after**) ask about the health and well-being of (someone): *Angus enquired after her parents.* ■[no obj.] (**enquire for**) ask to see or speak to (someone): *that was Mr Paul enquiring for you—I told him he couldn't come in.* ■[no obj.] (**enquire into**) investigate; look into: *the task of political sociology is to enquire into the causes of political events.*
– DERIVATIVES **enquirer** noun.
– ORIGIN Middle English *enquere*, from Old French *enquerre*, based on Latin *inquirere* (based on *quaerere* 'seek').

USAGE Usage guides have traditionally drawn a distinction between **enquire** and **inquire**, implying that, in British English at least, **enquire** is used for general senses of 'ask', while **inquire** is reserved for uses meaning 'make a formal investigation'. In practice, however, **enquire** (and **enquiry**) is more common in British English while **inquire** (and **inquiry**) is more common in US English, but otherwise there is no readily discernible distinction in the way the two words are used.

enquiring ▶ **adjective** showing an interest in learning new things: *an open, enquiring mind.*
■(of a look or expression) suggesting that information is sought: *he sent her an enquiring glance.*
– DERIVATIVES **enquiringly** adverb.

enquiry ▶ **noun** (pl. **-ies**) an act of asking for information: *the police were **making enquiries** in all the neighbouring pubs* | [mass noun] *her mind was buzzing with possible lines of enquiry.*
■an official investigation.

enquiry agent ▶ **noun** Brit. a private detective.

enrage ▶ **verb** [with obj.] (usu. **be enraged**) make very angry: *the students were enraged at these new rules* | [as adj. **enraged**] *an enraged mob screamed abuse.*
– ORIGIN late 15th cent. (formerly also as *inrage*): from French *enrager*, from *en-* 'into' + *rage* 'rage, anger'.

en rapport /ɒ̃ raˈpɔː/ ▶ **adverb** having a close and harmonious relationship: *his improvisation indicates that he is **en rapport with** the rhythm of the band.*
– ORIGIN French (see **RAPPORT**).

enrapt ▶ **adjective** fascinated; enthralled: *the enrapt audience.*

enrapture ▶ **verb** [with obj.] (usu. **be enraptured**) give intense pleasure or joy to: *Ruth was enraptured by the child who was sleeping in her arms so peacefully.*

enrich ▶ **verb** [with obj.] **1** improve or enhance the quality or value of: *her exposure to museums enriched her life in France.*
■(often **be enriched**) add to the nutritive value of (food) by adding vitamins or nutrients: *porridge oats enriched with extra oat bran.* ■add to the cultural, intellectual, or spiritual wealth of: *the collection was enriched by a bequest of graphic works.* ■[usu. as adj. **enriched**] increase the proportion of a particular isotope in (an element), especially that of the fissile isotope U-235 in uranium so as to make it more powerful or explosive.
2 make (someone) wealthy or wealthier: *top party members had **enriched themselves**.*
– DERIVATIVES **enrichment** noun.
– ORIGIN late Middle English (in the sense 'make wealthy'): from Old French *enrichir*, from *en-* 'in' + *riche* 'rich'.

enrobe ▶ **verb** [with obj.] formal dress in a robe or vestment.

enrol /ɪnˈrəʊl, ɛn-/ (US **enroll**) ▶ **verb** (**enrolled**, **enrolling**) [no obj.] officially register as a member of an institution or a student on a course: *he **enrolled in** drama school.*
■[with obj.] register (someone) as a member or student: *all entrants will be **enrolled on** new-style courses.* ■[with obj.] recruit (someone) to perform a service: *a campaign to enrol more foster carers.* ■[with obj.] Law historical enter (a deed or other document) among the rolls of a court of justice. ■archaic write the name of (someone) on a list or register.
– DERIVATIVES **enrollee** noun.
– ORIGIN late Middle English (formerly also as *inroll*): from Old French *enroller*, from *en-* 'in' + *rolle* 'a roll' (names being originally written on a roll of parchment).

enrolment (US **enrollment**) ▶ **noun** [mass noun] the action of enrolling or being enrolled: *the amount due must be paid on enrolment in October* | [count noun] *enrolments for teacher training have dropped off sharply.*
■[count noun] N. Amer. the number of people enrolled, typically at a school or college.

en route /ɒn ˈruːt/ ▶ **adverb** during the course of a journey; on the way: *he stopped in Turkey en route to Geneva.*
– ORIGIN late 18th cent.: French (see **ROUTE**).

en rule /ˈɛn ruːl/ ▶ **noun** Brit. a short dash, the width of an en, used in punctuation.

ENSA /ˈɛnsə/ an organization which served to arrange variety entertainment for the British armed services during the Second World War.
– ORIGIN acronym from *Entertainments National Service Association*.

Enschede /ˈɛnskəˌdeɪ/ a city in the Netherlands; pop. 146,500 (1991).

ensconce /ɪnˈskɒns, ɛn-/ ▶ **verb** [with obj. and adverbial of place] establish or settle (someone) in a comfortable, safe, or secret place: *Agnes **ensconced herself** in their bedroom.*
– ORIGIN late 16th cent. (in the senses 'fortify' and 'shelter within or behind a fortification'; formerly also as *insconce*): from **EN-**[1], **IN-**[2] 'in' + **SCONCE**[2].

ensemble /ɒnˈsɒmb(ə)l/ ▶ **noun 1** a group of musicians, actors, or dancers who perform together: *a Bulgarian folk ensemble.*
■a scene or passage written for performance by a whole cast, choir, or group of instruments. ■[mass noun] the coordination between performers executing such a passage: *a high level of tuning and ensemble is guaranteed.*
2 a group of items viewed as a whole rather than individually: *the buildings in the square present a charming provincial ensemble.*
■[usu. in sing.] a set of clothes chosen to harmonize when worn together. ■chiefly Physics a group of similar systems, or different states of the same system, often considered statistically.
– ORIGIN late Middle English (as an adverb (long rare) meaning 'at the same time'): from French, based on Latin *insimul*, from *in-* 'in' + *simul* 'at the same time'. The noun dates from the mid 18th cent.

ensheath ▶ **verb** [with obj.] chiefly Biology enclose (an organism, tissue, structure, etc.) in or as in a sheath.
– DERIVATIVES **ensheathment** noun.

enshrine ▶ **verb** [with obj. and adverbial of place] (usu. **be enshrined**) place (a revered or precious object) in an appropriate receptacle: *relics are enshrined under altars.*
■preserve (a right, tradition, or idea) in a form that ensures it will be protected and respected: *the right of all workers to strike was **enshrined in** the new constitution.*
– DERIVATIVES **enshrinement** noun.

enshroud /ɪnˈʃraʊd, ɛn-/ ▶ **verb** [with obj.] poetic/literary envelop completely and hide from view: *heavy grey clouds enshrouded the city.*

ensiform /ˈɛnsɪfɔːm/ ▶ **adjective** chiefly Botany shaped like a sword blade; long and narrow with sharp edges and a pointed tip.
– ORIGIN mid 16th cent.: from Latin *ensis* 'sword' + **-FORM**.

ensiform cartilage ▶ noun another term for **XIPHOID PROCESS**.

ensign /ˈɛnsʌɪn/ ▶ noun **1** a flag or standard, especially a military or naval one indicating nationality.
■ archaic a sign or emblem of a particular thing: *all the ensigns of our greatness.*
2 the lowest rank of commissioned officer in the US and some other navies, above chief warrant officer and below lieutenant.
■ historical the lowest rank of commissioned infantry officer in the British army. ■ historical a standard-bearer.
– ORIGIN late Middle English: from Old French *enseigne*, from Latin *insignia* 'signs of office' (see **INSIGNIA**). Compare with **ANCIENT**².

ensilage /ˈɛnsɪlɪdʒ, ɛnˈsʌɪlɪdʒ/ ▶ noun another term for **SILAGE**.
▶ verb another term for **ENSILE**.
– ORIGIN late 19th cent.: from French, from *ensiler* (see **ENSILE**).

ensile /ɛnˈsʌɪl/ ▶ verb [with obj.] put (grass or another crop) into a silo or silage clamp in order to preserve it as silage.
– ORIGIN late 19th cent.: from French *ensiler*, from Spanish *ensilar*, from *en-* 'in' + *silo* 'silo'.

enslave ▶ verb [with obj.] make (someone) a slave.
■ cause (someone) to lose their freedom of choice or action: *they were enslaved by their need to take drugs.*
– DERIVATIVES **enslavement** noun, **enslaver** noun.
– ORIGIN early 17th cent. (in the sense 'make (a person) subject to a superstition, passion, etc.'; formerly also as *inslave*): from **EN-**¹, **IN-**² (as an intensifier) + **SLAVE**.

ensnare ▶ verb [with obj.] catch in or as in a trap: *they were ensnared in city centre traffic.*
– DERIVATIVES **ensnarement** noun.

ensnarl ▶ verb [with obj.] cause to become caught up in complex difficulties or problems.

Ensor /ˈɛnsɔː/, James (Sydney), Baron (1860–1949), Belgian painter and engraver, noted for his macabre subjects. His work is significant both for symbolism and for the development of 20th-century expressionism.

ensorcell /ɪnˈsɔːs(ə)l, ɛn-/ (US also **ensorcel**) ▶ verb (**ensorcelled**, **ensorcelling**; US **ensorceled**, **ensorceling**) [with obj.] poetic/literary enchant; fascinate.
– DERIVATIVES **ensorcellment** (US also **ensorcelment**) noun.
– ORIGIN mid 16th cent.: from Old French *ensorceler*, alteration of *ensorcerer*, from *sorcier* 'sorcerer'.

ensoul ▶ verb [with obj.] endow with a soul.
– DERIVATIVES **ensoulment** noun.

enstatite /ˈɛnstətʌɪt/ ▶ noun [mass noun] a translucent crystalline mineral of varying colours that occurs in some igneous rocks and stony meteorites. It consists of magnesium silicate and is a member of the pyroxene group.
– ORIGIN mid 19th cent.: from Greek *enstatēs* 'adversary' (because of its refractory nature) + **-ITE**¹.

ensue ▶ verb (**ensues**, **ensued**, **ensuing**) [no obj.] happen or occur afterwards or as a result: *the difficulties which* **ensued from** *their commitment to Cuba* | [as adj. **ensuing**] *there were repeated clashes in the ensuing days.*
– ORIGIN late Middle English (formerly also as *insue*): from Old French *ensivre*, from Latin *insequi*, based on *sequi* 'follow'.

en suite /ɒn ˈswiːt/ ▶ adjective & adverb (of a bathroom) immediately adjoining a bedroom and forming part of the same set of rooms.
■ [as adj.] (of a bedroom) having such a bathroom.
– ORIGIN late 18th cent. (in the sense 'in agreement or harmony'): from French, literally 'in sequence'.

ensure /ɪnˈʃʊə, ɛn-/ ▶ verb [with obj.] make certain that (something) will occur or be the case: [with clause] *the client must ensure that accurate records are kept.*
■ make certain of obtaining or providing (something): [with two objs] *she would ensure him a place in society.* ■ [no obj.] (**ensure against**) make sure that (a problem) does not occur.
– ORIGIN late Middle English (in the senses 'convince' and 'make safe'): from Anglo-Norman French *enseurer*, alteration of Old French *aseurer*, earlier form of *assurer* (see **ASSURE**). Compare with **INSURE**.

USAGE On the difference between **ensure** and **insure**, see usage at **INSURE**.

enswathe ▶ verb [with obj.] poetic/literary envelop or wrap in a garment or piece of fabric.

ENT ▶ abbreviation for ear, nose, and throat (as a department in a hospital).

-ent ▶ suffix **1** (forming adjectives) denoting an occurrence of action: *refluent.*
■ denoting a state: *convenient.*
2 (forming nouns) denoting an agent: *coefficient.*
– ORIGIN from French, or from the Latin present participial verb stem *-ent-* (see also **-ANT**).

entablature /ɛnˈtablətʃə, ɪn-/ ▶ noun Architecture the upper part of a classical building supported by columns or a colonnade, comprising the architrave, frieze, and cornice.
– ORIGIN early 17th cent. (formerly also as *intablature*): from Italian *intavolatura* 'boarding' (partly via French *entablement* 'entablement'), from *intavolare* 'board up' (based on *tavola* 'table').

entablement /ɛnˈteɪb(ə)lm(ə)nt, ɪn-/ ▶ noun Architecture a platform supporting a statue, above the dado and base.
– ORIGIN mid 17th cent. (in the sense 'entablature'): from French, based on *table* 'table'.

entail ▶ verb [with obj.] **1** involve (something) as a necessary or inevitable part or consequence: *a situation which entails considerable risks.*
■ Logic have as a logically necessary consequence.
2 Law settle the inheritance of (property) over a number of generations so that ownership remains within a particular group, usually one family: *her father's estate was* **entailed on** *a cousin.*
■ archaic cause to experience or possess in a way perceived as permanent or inescapable: *I cannot get rid of the disgrace which you have* **entailed upon** *us.*
▶ noun Law a settlement of the inheritance of property over a number of generations so that it remains within a family or other group.
■ a property that is bequeathed under such conditions.
– DERIVATIVES **entailment** noun.
– ORIGIN late Middle English (referring to settlement of property; formerly also as *intail*): from **EN-**¹, **IN-**² 'into' + Old French *taille* 'notch, tax' (see **TAIL**²).

entamoeba /ˌɛntəˈmiːbə/ (US also **entameba**) ▶ noun (pl. **entamoebae** /-biː/ or **entamoebas**) an amoeba that typically lives harmlessly in the gut, though one kind can cause amoebic dysentery.
• Genus *Entamoeba*, phylum Rhizopoda, kingdom Protista.
– ORIGIN modern Latin, from Greek *entos* 'within' + **AMOEBA**.

entangle ▶ verb [with obj.] (usu. **be entangled**) cause to become twisted together with or caught in: *fish attempt to swim through the mesh and become entangled.*
■ involve (someone) in difficulties or complicated circumstances from which it is difficult to escape: *the case of murder in which she had found herself so painfully entangled.*

entanglement ▶ noun [mass noun] the action or fact of entangling or being entangled: *many dolphins die from entanglement in fishing nets.*
■ [count noun] a complicated or compromising relationship or situation: *romantic entanglements.* ■ [count noun] an extensive barrier, typically made of interlaced barbed wire and stakes, erected to impede enemy soldiers or vehicles: *the attackers were caught up on wire entanglements.*

entasis /ˈɛntəsɪs/ ▶ noun (pl. **entases**) Architecture a slight convex curve in the shaft of a column, introduced to correct the visual illusion of concavity produced by a straight shaft.
– ORIGIN mid 17th cent.: modern Latin, from Greek, from *enteinein* 'to stretch or strain'.

Entebbe /ɛnˈtɛbi/ a town in southern Uganda, on the north shore of Lake Victoria; pop. 41,640 (1991). It was the capital of Uganda during the period of British rule, from 1894 to 1962.

entelechy /ɛnˈtɛləki, ɪn-/ ▶ noun (pl. **-ies**) [mass noun] Philosophy the realization of potential.
■ the supposed vital principle that guides the development and functioning of an organism or other system or organization. ■ [count noun] Philosophy the soul.
– ORIGIN late Middle English: via late Latin from Greek *entelekheia* (used by Aristotle), from *en-* 'within' + *telos* 'end, perfection' + *ekhein* 'be in a certain state'.

entellus /ɪnˈtɛləs, ɛn-/ (also **entellus monkey**) ▶ noun another term for **HANUMAN**.
– ORIGIN mid 19th cent.: from the name of an aged Trojan in Virgil's *Aeneid*.

entente /ɒnˈtɒnt, ɒ̃ˈtɒ̃t/ (also **entente cordiale** /ˌkɔːdɪˈɑːl/) ▶ noun a friendly understanding or informal alliance between states or factions: *the emperor hoped to bring about an entente with Russia.*
■ a group of states in such an alliance. ■ (**the Entente Cordiale**) the understanding between Britain and France reached in 1904, forming the basis of Anglo-French cooperation in the First World War.
– ORIGIN mid 19th cent.: French *entente* (*cordiale*) '(friendly) understanding'.

enter ▶ verb **1** come or go into (a place): [with obj.] *she entered the kitchen* | [no obj.] *the door opened and Karl entered* | figurative *reading the Bible, we* **enter into** *an amazing new world of thoughts.*
■ [no obj.] used as a stage direction to indicate when a character comes on stage: *enter Hamlet.* ■ [with obj.] penetrate (something): *the bullet entered his stomach.* ■ [with obj.] (of a man) insert the penis into the vagina of (a woman). ■ [with obj.] come or be introduced into: *the thought never entered my head.*
2 [with obj.] begin to be involved in: *in 1941 America entered the war.*
■ become a member of or start working in (an institution or profession): *that autumn, he entered Port Talbot Secondary School.* ■ register as a competitor or participant in (a tournament, race, or examination). ■ register (a person, animal, or thing) to compete or participate in a tournament, race, or examination. ■ start or reach (a stage or period of time) in an activity or situation: *the election campaign entered its final phase.* ■ [no obj.] (of a particular performer in an ensemble) start or resume playing or singing.
3 write or key (information) in a book, computer, etc. so as to record it: *children can* **enter** *the data* **into** *the computer.*
■ Law submit (a statement) in an official capacity, usually in a court of law: *a solicitor entered a plea of guilty on her behalf.*
▶ noun (also **enter key**) a key on a computer keyboard which is used to perform various functions, such as executing a command or selecting options on a menu.
– ORIGIN Middle English: from Old French *entrer*, from Latin *intrare*, from *intra* 'within'.
▶ **enter into** become involved in (an activity, situation, or matter): *they have entered into a relationship.* ■ undertake to bind oneself by (an agreement or other commitment): *the council entered into an agreement with a private firm.* ■ form part of or be a factor in: *medical ethics also enter into the question.*
enter on/upon 1 formal begin (an activity or job); start to pursue (a particular course in life): *he entered upon a turbulent political career.* **2** Law (as a legal entitlement) go freely into property as or as if the owner.

enteral /ˈɛntər(ə)l/ ▶ adjective Medicine (chiefly of nutrition) involving or passing through the intestine, either naturally via the mouth and oesophagus, or through an artificial opening. Often contrasted with **PARENTERAL**.
– DERIVATIVES **enterally** adverb.
– ORIGIN early 20th cent.: from Greek *enteron* 'intestine' + **-AL**, partly as a back-formation from **PARENTERAL**.

enteric /ɛnˈtɛrɪk/ ▶ adjective of, relating to, or occurring in the intestines.
– ORIGIN early 19th cent.: from Greek *enterikos*, from *enteron* 'intestine'.

enteric fever ▶ noun another term for **TYPHOID** or **PARATYPHOID**.

enteritis /ˌɛntəˈrʌɪtɪs/ ▶ noun [mass noun] Medicine inflammation of the intestine, especially the small intestine, usually accompanied by diarrhoea.

entero- ▶ combining form of or relating to the intestine: *enterovirus.*
– ORIGIN from Greek *enteron.*

enterococcus /ˌɛntərəʊˈkɒk(ə)s/ ▶ noun (pl. **enterococci** /-ˈkɒk(s)ʌɪ, -k(s)iː/) a streptococcus of a group that occurs naturally in the intestine but causes inflammation and blood infection if introduced elsewhere in the body (e.g. by injury or surgery).
• Genus *Streptococcus* (or *Enterococcus*); Gram-positive cocci.

enterocoel /ˈɛntərəʊˌsiːl/ ▶ noun Zoology a coelom or coelomic cavity, present in some invertebrates, which has developed from the wall of the archenteron.
– DERIVATIVES **enterocoelic** adjective, **enterocoely** noun.

enterocolitis /ˌɛntərəʊkəˈlʌɪtɪs/ ▶ noun [mass noun]

Medicine inflammation of both the small intestine and the colon.

enterocyte /ˈɛntərə(ʊ)sʌɪt/ ▶ **noun** Physiology a cell of the intestinal lining.

enterohepatic /ˌɛntərəʊhɪˈpatɪk/ ▶ **adjective** Physiology relating to or denoting the circulation of bile salts and other secretions from the liver to the intestine, where they are reabsorbed into the blood and returned to the liver.

enteropathy /ˌɛntəˈrɒpəθi/ ▶ **noun** (pl. **-ies**) Medicine a disease of the intestine, especially the small intestine.

enterostomy /ˌɛntəˈrɒstəmi/ ▶ **noun** (pl. **-ies**) an ileostomy or similar surgical operation in which the small intestine is diverted to an artificial opening in the abdominal wall or in another part of the intestine.
▪an opening in the abdominal wall formed in this way.

enterotomy /ˌɛntəˈrɒtəmi/ ▶ **noun** [mass noun] rare the surgical cutting open of the intestine.

enterotoxaemia /ˌɛntərəʊtɒkˈsiːmiə/ (US **enterotoxemia**) ▶ **noun** [mass noun] chiefly Veterinary Medicine blood poisoning caused by an enterotoxin.

enterotoxigenic /ˌɛntərəʊˌtɒksɪˈdʒɛnɪk/ ▶ **adjective** Medicine (of bacteria) producing an enterotoxin.

enterotoxin /ˌɛntərəʊˈtɒksɪn/ ▶ **noun** Medicine a toxin produced in or affecting the intestines, such as those causing food poisoning or cholera.

enterovirus /ˈɛntərəʊˌvʌɪrəs/ ▶ **noun** Medicine any of a group of RNA viruses (including those causing polio and hepatitis A) which typically occur in the gastrointestinal tract, sometimes spreading to the central nervous system or other parts of the body.

enterprise ▶ **noun 1** a project or undertaking, typically one that is difficult or requires effort: *a joint enterprise between French and Japanese companies.*
▪[mass noun] initiative and resourcefulness: *success came quickly, thanks to a mixture of talent, enterprise, and luck.*
2 a business or company: *a state-owned enterprise.*
▪[mass noun] entrepreneurial economic activity.
– DERIVATIVES **enterpriser** noun.
– ORIGIN late Middle English: from Old French, 'something undertaken', feminine past participle (used as a noun) of *entreprendre*, based on Latin *prendere, prehendere* 'to take'.

enterprise zone ▶ **noun** an area in which state incentives such as tax concessions are offered to encourage business investment.

enterprising ▶ **adjective** having or showing initiative and resourcefulness: *some enterprising teachers have started their own recycling programmes.*
– DERIVATIVES **enterprisingly** adverb.

entertain ▶ **verb** [with obj.] **1** provide (someone) with amusement or enjoyment: *a tremendous game that thoroughly entertained the crowd.*
▪receive (someone) as a guest and provide them with food and drink: *a private dining room where members could entertain groups of friends.*
2 give attention or consideration to (an idea, suggestion, or feeling): *Washington entertained little hope of an early improvement in relations.*
– ORIGIN late Middle English: from French *entretenir*, based on Latin *inter* 'among' + *tenere* 'to hold'. The word originally meant 'maintain, continue', later 'maintain in a certain condition, treat in a certain way', also 'show hospitality' (late 15th cent.).

entertainer ▶ **noun** a person, such as a singer, dancer, or comedian, whose job is to entertain others.

entertaining ▶ **adjective** providing amusement or enjoyment: *the magazine is both entertaining and informative.*
– DERIVATIVES **entertainingly** adverb.

entertainment ▶ **noun** [mass noun] the action of providing or being provided with amusement or enjoyment: *everyone just sits in front of the box for entertainment.*
▪[count noun] an event, performance, or activity designed to entertain others: *a theatrical entertainment.* ▪the action of receiving a guest or guests and providing them with food and drink.

enthalpy /ˈɛnθ(ə)lpi, ɛnˈθalpi/ ▶ **noun** Physics a thermodynamic quantity equivalent to the total heat content of a system. It is equal to the internal energy of the system plus the product of pressure and volume. (Symbol: **H**)
▪the change in this quantity associated with a particular chemical process.
– ORIGIN 1920s: from Greek *enthalpein* 'warm in', from *en-* 'within' + *thalpein* 'to heat'.

enthral /ɪnˈθrɔːl, ɛn-/ (US **enthrall**) ▶ **verb** (**enthralled**, **enthralling**) [with obj.] (often **be enthralled**) capture the fascinated attention of: *she had been so enthralled by the adventure that she had hardly noticed the cold* | [as adj. **enthralling**] *an enthralling best-seller.*
▪(also **inthrall**) archaic enslave.
– DERIVATIVES **enthralment** (US **enthrallment**) noun.
– ORIGIN late Middle English (in the sense 'enslave'; formerly also as *inthrall*): from **EN-**[1], **IN-**[2] (as an intensifier) + **THRALL**.

enthrone ▶ **verb** [with obj.] (usu. **be enthroned**) install (a monarch or bishop) on a throne, especially during a ceremony to mark the beginning of their rule.
▪figurative give or ascribe a position of authority to: *he was enthroned as the guru of the avant-garde.*
– DERIVATIVES **enthronement** noun.

enthuse /ɪnˈθjuːz, ɛn-/ ▶ **verb** [reporting verb] say something that expresses one's eager enjoyment, interest, or approval: [no obj.] *they both* ***enthused over*** *my new look* | [with direct speech] *'This place is superb!', she enthused.*
▪[with obj.] make (someone) interested and eagerly appreciative: *public art is a tonic that can enthuse alienated youth.*

USAGE The verb **enthuse** is formed as a back-formation from the noun **enthusiasm** and, like many verbs formed from nouns in this way (especially those originating from the US), it is regarded by traditionalists as unacceptable. It is difficult to see why: it is a perfectly respectable means for creating new words in the language (verbs like **classify**, **commentate**, and **edit** were also formed as back-formations from nouns, for example) and **enthuse** itself has now been in English over 150 years.

enthusiasm ▶ **noun** [mass noun] **1** intense and eager enjoyment, interest, or approval: *her energy and* ***enthusiasm for*** *life* | *few expressed enthusiasm about the current leaders.*
▪[count noun] a thing that arouses such feelings: *the three enthusiasms of his life were politics, religion, and books.*
2 archaic, derogatory religious fervour supposedly resulting directly from divine inspiration, typically involving speaking in tongues and wild, uncoordinated movements of the body.
– ORIGIN early 17th cent. (in sense 2): from French *enthousiasme*, or via late Latin from Greek *enthousiasmos*, from *enthous* 'possessed by a god, inspired' (based on *theos* 'god').

enthusiast ▶ **noun** a person who is highly interested in a particular activity or subject: *a sports car enthusiast.*
▪archaic, derogatory a person of intense and visionary Christian views.
– ORIGIN early 17th cent. (denoting a person believing that he or she is divinely inspired): from French *enthousiaste* or ecclesiastical Latin *enthusiastes* 'member of a heretical sect', from Greek *enthousiastēs* 'person inspired by a god', from the adjective *enthous* (see **ENTHUSIASM**).

enthusiastic ▶ **adjective** having or showing intense and eager enjoyment, interest, or approval: *the promoter was enthusiastic about the concert venue.*
– DERIVATIVES **enthusiastically** adverb.
– ORIGIN early 17th cent.: from Greek *enthousiastikos*, from *enthous* 'possessed by a god' (see **ENTHUSIASM**).

enthymeme /ˈɛnθɪmiːm/ ▶ **noun** Logic an argument in which one premise is not explicitly stated.
– ORIGIN mid 16th cent.: via Latin from Greek *enthumēma*, from *enthumeisthai* 'consider', from *en-* 'within' + *thumos* 'mind'.

entice /ɪnˈtʌɪs, ɛn-/ ▶ **verb** [with obj.] attract or tempt by offering pleasure or advantage: *a show which should* ***entice*** *a new audience* ***into*** *the theatre* | [with obj. and infinitive] *the whole purpose of bribes is to entice governments to act against the public interest* | [as adj. **enticing**] *the idea of giving up sounds enticing but would be a mistake.*
– DERIVATIVES **enticement** noun, **enticer** noun, **enticingly** adverb.
– ORIGIN Middle English (also in the sense 'incite, provoke'; formerly also as *intice*): from Old French *enticier*, probably from a base meaning 'set on fire', based on an alteration of Latin *titio* 'firebrand'.

entire /ɪnˈtʌɪə, ɛn-/ ▶ **adjective** [attrib.] with no part left out; whole: *my plans are to travel the entire world.*
▪without qualification or reservations; absolute: *an ideological system with which he is in entire agreement.*
▪(of a male horse) not castrated. ▪Botany (of a leaf) without indentations or division into leaflets.
▶ **noun** an uncastrated male horse.
– ORIGIN late Middle English (formerly also as *intire*): from Old French *entier*, based on Latin *integer* 'untouched, whole', from *in-* 'not' + *tangere* 'to touch'.

entirely ▶ **adverb** completely (often used for emphasis): *the traffic seemed to consist entirely of black cabs* | [as submodifier] *we have an entirely different outlook.*
▪solely: *eight coaches entirely for passenger transport.*

entirety ▶ **noun** [mass noun] the whole of something: *she would have to stay in her room over* ***the entirety of*** *the weekend.*
– PHRASES **in its entirety** as a whole; completely: *the poem is too long to quote in its entirety here.*
– ORIGIN Middle English: from Old French *entierete*, from Latin *integritas*, from *integer* 'untouched, whole' (see **ENTIRE**). Compare with **INTEGRITY**.

entisol /ˈɛntɪsɒl/ ▶ **noun** Soil Science a soil of an order comprising mineral soils that have not yet differentiated into distinct horizons.
– ORIGIN mid 20th cent.: from **ENTIRE** + **-SOL**.

entitle ▶ **verb** [with obj.] (usu. **be entitled**) **1** give (someone) a legal right or a just claim to receive or do something: *employees are normally* ***entitled to*** *redundancy pay* | [with obj. and infinitive] *the landlord is entitled to require references.*
2 give (something, especially a text or work of art) a particular title: *a satire entitled 'The Rise of the Meritocracy'.*
▪[with obj. and complement] archaic give (someone) a specified title expressing their rank, office, or character: *they entitled him Sultan.*
– ORIGIN late Middle English (formerly also as *intitle*): via Old French from late Latin *intitulare*, from *in-* 'in' + Latin *titulus* 'title'.

entitlement ▶ **noun** [mass noun] the fact of having a right to something: *full* ***entitlement to*** *fees and maintenance should be offered* | [count noun] *you should be fully aware of your legal entitlements.*
▪the amount to which a person has a right: *annual leave entitlement.*

entity /ˈɛntɪti/ ▶ **noun** (pl. **-ies**) a thing with distinct and independent existence: *church and empire were fused in a single entity.*
▪[mass noun] existence; being: *entity and nonentity.*
– DERIVATIVES **entitative** adjective (chiefly Philosophy).
– ORIGIN late 15th cent. (denoting a thing's existence): from French *entité* or medieval Latin *entitas*, from late Latin *ens, ent-* 'being' (from *esse* 'be').

entomb ▶ **verb** [with obj.] (usu. **be entombed**) place (a dead body) in a tomb.
▪bury or trap in or under something: *many people died, most entombed in collapsed buildings.*
– DERIVATIVES **entombment** noun.
– ORIGIN late Middle English (formerly also as *intomb*): from Old French *entomber*, from *en-* 'in' + *tombe* 'tomb'.

entomo- /ˈɛntəməʊ/ ▶ **combining form** of an insect; of or relating to insects: *entomophagous.*
– ORIGIN from Greek *entomon*, neuter (denoting an insect) of *entomos* 'cut up, segmented'.

entomology /ˌɛntəˈmɒlədʒi/ ▶ **noun** [mass noun] the branch of zoology concerned with the study of insects.
– DERIVATIVES **entomological** adjective, **entomologist** noun.
– ORIGIN mid 18th cent.: from French *entomologie* or modern Latin *entomologia*, from Greek *entomon* (denoting an insect) + *-logia* (see **-LOGY**).

entomophagy /ˌɛntəˈmɒfədʒi/ ▶ **noun** [mass noun] the practice of eating insects, especially by people.
– DERIVATIVES **entomophagist** noun, **entomophagous** adjective.

entomophilous /ˌɛntəˈmɒfɪləs/ ▶ **adjective** Botany (of a plant or flower) pollinated by insects.
– DERIVATIVES **entomophily** noun.

Entoprocta /ˌɛntə(ʊ)ˈprɒktə/ Zoology a small phylum of sedentary aquatic invertebrates that resemble moss animals. They have a rounded body on a long stalk, bearing a ring of tentacles for filtering food from the water.
– DERIVATIVES **entoproct** noun.

a cat | ɑː arm | ɛ bed | ɛː hair | ə ago | əː her | ɪ sit | i cosy | iː see | ɒ hot | ɔː saw | ʌ run | ʊ put | uː too | ʌɪ my | aʊ how | eɪ day | əʊ no | ɪə near | ɔɪ boy | ʊə poor | ʌɪə fire | aʊə sour

– ORIGIN modern Latin (plural), from Greek *entos* 'within' + *prōktos* 'anus', the anus being within the ring of tentacles.

entoptic /ɪnˈtɒptɪk, ɛn-/ ▶ **adjective** (of visual images) occurring or originating inside the eye.
– ORIGIN late 19th cent.: from Greek *entos* 'within' + **OPTIC**.

entourage /ˈɒntʊrɑːʒ, ˌɒntʊ(ə)ˈrɑːʒ/ ▶ **noun** a group of people attending or surrounding an important person: *an entourage of loyal courtiers.*
– ORIGIN mid 19th cent.: French, from *entourer* 'to surround'.

entr'acte /ˈɒntrakt, ˈɒ̃-/ ▶ **noun** an interval between two acts of a play or opera.
■ a piece of music or a dance performed during such an interval.
– ORIGIN mid 19th cent.: French, from (earlier form of *entracte*), from *entre* 'between' + *acte* 'act'.

entrails ▶ **plural noun** a person or animal's intestines or internal organs, especially when removed or exposed.
■ figurative the innermost parts of something: *digging copper out of the entrails of the earth.*
– ORIGIN Middle English: from Old French *entrailles*, from medieval Latin *intralia*, alteration of Latin *interanea* 'internal things', based on *inter* 'among'.

entrain¹ /ɪnˈtreɪn, ɛn-/ ▶ **verb** [no obj.] board a train.
■ [with obj.] put or allow on board a train.

entrain² /ɪnˈtreɪn, ɛn-/ ▶ **verb** [with obj.] **1** (of a current or fluid) incorporate and sweep along in its flow.
■ cause or bring about as a consequence: *the triumph of a revolution was measured in terms of the social revision it entrained.*
2 Biology (of a rhythm or something which varies rhythmically) cause (another) gradually to fall into synchronism with it.
■ [no obj.] (**entrain to**) fall into synchronism with (something) in such a way.
– DERIVATIVES **entrainment** noun.
– ORIGIN mid 16th cent. (in the sense 'bring on as a consequence'): from French *entraîner*, from *en-* 'in' + *traîner* 'to drag'.

entrain³ /ɒ̃ˈtrã/ ▶ **noun** [mass noun] enthusiasm or animation.
– ORIGIN French, from the phrase *être en train* 'be in the process of, be in action'.

entrammel /ɪnˈtram(ə)l, ɛn-/ ▶ **verb** (**entrammelled, entrammelling**; US **entrammeled, entrammeling**) [with obj.] poetic/literary entangle; trap.

entrance¹ /ˈɛntr(ə)ns/ ▶ **noun** an opening, such as a door, passage, or gate, that allows access to a place.
■ [usu. in sing.] an act or instance of going or coming in: *at their abrupt entrance he rose to his feet.* ■ [usu. in sing.] the coming of an actor or performer on to a stage: *her final entrance is as a triumphant princess.* ■ [usu. in sing.] an act of becoming involved in something: *their entrance into the political arena.* ■ [mass noun] the right, means, or opportunity to enter somewhere or be a member of an institution, society, or other body: *about fifty people attempted to gain entrance* | [as modifier] *an entrance examination.*
– PHRASES **make an** (or **one's**) **entrance** (of an actor or performer) come on stage. ■ enter somewhere in a conspicuous or impressive way: *she slowly counted to ten before making her entrance.*
– ORIGIN late 15th cent. (in the sense 'right or opportunity of admission'): from Old French, from *entrer* 'enter'.

entrance² /ɪnˈtrɑːns, ɛn-/ ▶ **verb** [with obj.] (often **be entranced**) fill (someone) with wonder and delight, holding their entire attention: *I was entranced by a cluster of trees which were lit up by glow-worms* | [as adj. **entrancing**] *he had never seen a more entrancing girl.*
■ cast a spell on: *Orpheus entranced the wild beasts.*
– DERIVATIVES **entrancement** noun, **entrancingly** adverb.

entrant ▶ **noun** a person or group that enters, joins, or takes part in something.
– ORIGIN early 17th cent. (denoting a person taking legal possession of land or property): from French, literally 'entering', present participle of *entrer* (see **ENTER**).

entrap ▶ **verb** (**entrapped, entrapping**) [with obj.] catch (someone or something) in or as in a trap: *she was entrapped by family expectations.*
■ trick or deceive (someone), especially by inducing them to commit a crime in order to secure their prosecution.
– DERIVATIVES **entrapment** noun.
– ORIGIN mid 16th cent.: from Old French *entraper*, from *en-* 'in' + *trappe* 'a trap'.

en travesti /ɒ̃ ˌtravɛˈstiː/ ▶ **adverb** & **adjective** dressed as a member of the opposite sex, especially for a theatrical role.
– ORIGIN French, literally '(dressed) in disguise'.

entreat ▶ **verb 1** [reporting verb] ask someone earnestly or anxiously to do something: [with obj. and infinitive] *his friends entreated him not to go.*
■ [with obj.] ask earnestly or anxiously for (something): *a message had been sent, entreating aid for the Navahos.*
2 [with obj. and adverbial] archaic treat (someone) in a specified manner: *the King, I fear, hath ill entreated her.*
– DERIVATIVES **entreatingly** adverb.
– ORIGIN late Middle English (in the sense 'treat, act towards (someone)'; formerly also as *intreat*): from Old French *entraitier*, based on *traitier* 'to treat', from Latin *tractare* 'to handle'.

entreaty ▶ **noun** (pl. **-ies**) an earnest or humble request: *the king turned a deaf ear to his entreaties.*
– ORIGIN late Middle English (in the sense 'treatment, management'; formerly also as *intreaty*): from **ENTREAT**, on the pattern of *treaty*.

entrechat /ˈɒ̃trəʃɑː/ ▶ **noun** Ballet a vertical jump during which the dancer repeatedly crosses the feet and beats them together.
– ORIGIN French, from Italian (*capriola*) *intrecciata* 'complicated (caper)'.

entrecôte /ˈɒntrəkəʊt/ ▶ **noun** a boned steak cut off the sirloin.
– ORIGIN French, from *entre* 'between' + *côte* 'rib'.

entrée /ˈɒntreɪ/ ▶ **noun 1** the main course of a meal.
■ Brit. a dish served between the fish and meat courses at a formal dinner.
2 the right to enter a domain or join a particular social group: *an actress with an entrée into the intellectual society of Berlin.*
– ORIGIN early 18th cent. (denoting a piece of instrumental music forming the first part of a suite): French, feminine past participle of *entrer* 'enter' (see **ENTRY**).

entremets /ˌɒntrəˈmeɪ/ ▶ **noun** a light dish served between two courses of a formal meal.
– ORIGIN French, from *entre* 'between' + *mets* 'dish'.

entrench (also **intrench**) ▶ **verb 1** [with obj.] (often **be entrenched**) establish (an attitude, habit, or belief) so firmly that change is very difficult or unlikely: *ageism is **entrenched in** our society.*
■ establish (a person or their authority) in a position of great strength or security: *by 1947 de Gaulle's political opponents were firmly **entrenched in** power.* ■ apply extra legal safeguards to (a right, especially a constitutional right, guaranteed by legislation). ■ establish (a military force, camp, etc.) in trenches or other fortified positions.
2 [no obj.] (**entrench on/upon**) archaic encroach or trespass upon.
– DERIVATIVES **entrenchment** noun.
– ORIGIN mid 16th cent. (in the sense 'place within a trench'): from **EN-**[1], **IN-**[2] 'into' + **TRENCH**.

entre nous /ˌɒ̃trə ˈnuː/ ▶ **adverb** between ourselves; privately: *entre nous, the old man's a bit of a case.*
– ORIGIN French.

entrepôt /ˈɒntrəpəʊ/ ▶ **noun** a port, city, or other centre to which goods are brought for import and export, and for collection and distribution.
– ORIGIN early 18th cent.: French, from *entreposer* 'to store', from *entre* 'among' + *poser* 'to place'.

entrepreneur /ˌɒntrəprəˈnəː/ ▶ **noun** a person who sets up a business or businesses, taking on greater than normal financial risks in order to do so.
■ a promoter in the entertainment industry.
– DERIVATIVES **entrepreneurial** /-ˈn(j)ɔːrɪəl, -ˈnjʊərɪəl/ adjective, **entrepreneurialism** noun, **entrepreneurially** adverb, **entrepreneurism** noun, **entrepreneurship** noun.
– ORIGIN early 19th cent. (denoting the director of a musical institution): from French, from *entreprendre* 'undertake' (see **ENTERPRISE**).

entresol /ˈɒntrəsɒl/ ▶ **noun** a low storey between the ground floor and the first floor of a building; a mezzanine floor.
– ORIGIN early 18th cent.: French, from Spanish *entresuelo*, from *entre* 'between' + *suelo* 'storey'.

entrism ▶ **noun** variant form of **ENTRYISM**.

entropion /ɪnˈtrəʊpɪən, ɛn-/ ▶ **noun** [mass noun] Medicine a condition in which the eyelid is rolled inward against the eyeball, typically caused by muscle spasm or by inflammation or scarring of the conjunctiva (as in diseases such as trachoma), and resulting in irritation of the eye by the lashes (trichiasis).
– ORIGIN late 19th cent.: from **EN-**[2] 'inside', on the pattern of *ectropion*.

entropy /ˈɛntrəpi/ ▶ **noun** [mass noun] Physics a thermodynamic quantity representing the unavailability of a system's thermal energy for conversion into mechanical work, often interpreted as the degree of disorder or randomness in the system. (Symbol: **S**)
■ figurative lack of order or predictability; gradual decline into disorder: *a marketplace where entropy reigns supreme.* ■ (in information theory) a logarithmic measure of the rate of transfer of information in a particular message or language.
– DERIVATIVES **entropic** /-ˈtrɒpɪk/ adjective, **entropically** adverb.
– ORIGIN mid 19th cent.: from **EN-**[2] 'inside' + Greek *tropē* 'transformation'.

entrust ▶ **verb** [with obj.] assign the responsibility for doing something to (someone): *I've been **entrusted with** the task of getting him safely back.*
■ put (something) into someone's care or protection: *you persuade people to **entrust** their savings **to** you.*
– DERIVATIVES **entrustment** noun.

entry ▶ **noun** (pl. **-ies**) **1** an act of going or coming in: *the door was locked, but he forced an entry.*
■ a place of entrance, such as a door or lobby. ■ [mass noun] the right, means, or opportunity to enter a place or be a member of something: *the flood of refugees seeking entry to western Europe.* ■ [mass noun] the action of undertaking something or becoming a member of something: *more young people are postponing their entry into full-time work.* ■ Bridge a card providing an opportunity to transfer the lead to a particular hand. ■ (also **entry into possession**) [mass noun] Law the action of taking up the legal right to property. ■ Music the point in a piece of music at which a particular performer in an ensemble starts or resumes playing or singing. ■ dialect a passage between buildings.
2 an item written or printed in a diary, list, account book, or reference book.
■ [mass noun] the action of recording such an item: *sophisticated features to help ensure accurate data entry.*
3 a person or thing competing in a race or competition: *from the hundreds of entries we received, twelve winners were finally chosen.*
■ [in sing.] the number of competitors in a particular race or competition. ■ [mass noun] the action of participating in a race or competition.
4 the forward part of a ship's hull below the waterline, considered in terms of breadth or narrowness.
– ORIGIN Middle English: from Old French *entree*, based on Latin *intrata*, feminine past participle of *intrare* (see **ENTER**).

entry form ▶ **noun** an application form for a competition.

entryism (also **entrism**) ▶ **noun** [mass noun] the infiltration of a political party by members of another group, with the intention of subverting its policies or objectives.
– DERIVATIVES **entrist** noun, **entryist** noun.

entry-level ▶ **adjective** (of a product) suitable for a beginner or first-time user; basic: *entry-level computers.*
■ chiefly US at the lowest level in an employment hierarchy.

entry permit ▶ **noun** an official document that authorizes a foreign citizen to enter a country.

entryphone ▶ **noun** Brit. trademark a type of intercom at the entrance to a building by which visitors may identify themselves before the door is unlocked by an internal device.

entryway ▶ **noun** N. Amer. a way in to somewhere or something; an entrance.

entry wound ▶ **noun** a wound made by a bullet or other missile at the point where it entered the body.

entwine ▶ **verb** [with obj.] (often **be entwined**) wind or twist together; interweave: *they lay entwined in each other's arms* | figurative *the nations' histories were closely entwined.*
– DERIVATIVES **entwinement** noun.

enucleate /ɪˈnjuːklɪeɪt/ ▶ **verb** [with obj.] **1** Biology remove the nucleus from (a cell).

2 surgically remove (a tumour or gland, or the eyeball) intact from its surrounding capsule.
▶**adjective** Biology (of a cell) lacking a nucleus.
– DERIVATIVES **enucleation** noun.
– ORIGIN mid 16th cent. (in the sense 'clarify, explain'): from Latin *enucleat-* 'extracted, made clear', from the verb *enucleare*, from *e-* (variant of *ex-*) 'out of' + *nucleus* 'kernel' (see **NUCLEUS**).

E-number ▶**noun** Brit. a code number preceded by the letter E, denoting food additives numbered in accordance with EU directives.
■informal a food additive.

enumerable /ɪ'nju:m(ə)rəb(ə)l/ ▶**adjective** Mathematics able to be counted by one-to-one correspondence with the set of all positive integers.

enumerate /ɪ'nju:məreɪt/ ▶**verb** [with obj.] mention (a number of things) one by one: *there is not space to enumerate all his works.*
■formal establish the number of: *the 1981 census enumerated 19,493,000 households living in the community.*
– DERIVATIVES **enumeration** noun, **enumerative** adjective.
– ORIGIN early 17th cent.: from Latin *enumerat-* 'counted out', from the verb *enumerare*, from *e-* (variant of *ex-*) 'out' + *numerus* 'number'.

enumerator ▶**noun** a person employed in taking a census of the population.

enunciate /ɪ'nʌnsɪeɪt/ ▶**verb** [with obj.] say or pronounce clearly: *she enunciated each word slowly.*
■express (a proposition or theory) in clear or definite terms: *a written document enunciating this policy.* ■ proclaim: *a prophet enunciating the Lord's wisdom.*
– DERIVATIVES **enunciation** noun, **enunciative** adjective, **enunciator** noun.
– ORIGIN mid 16th cent. (as *enunciation*): from Latin *enuntiat-* 'announced clearly', from the verb *enuntiare*, from *e-* (variant of *ex-*) 'out' + *nuntiare* 'announce' (from *nuntius* 'messenger').

enure /ɪ'njʊə/ ▶**verb 1** [no obj.] (**enure for/to**) Law (of a right or other advantage) belong or be available to.
2 variant spelling of **INURE**.

enuresis /ˌɛnjʊə'ri:sɪs/ ▶**noun** [mass noun] Medicine involuntary urination, especially by children at night.
– DERIVATIVES **enuretic** adjective & noun.
– ORIGIN early 19th cent.: modern Latin, from Greek *enourein* 'urinate in', from *en-* 'in' + *ouron* 'urine'.

enurn /ɪ'nə:n, ɛ'nə:n/ ▶**verb** variant spelling of **INURN**.

envelop /ɪn'vɛləp, ɛn-/ ▶**verb** (**enveloped**, **enveloping**) [with obj.] wrap up, cover, or surround completely: *a figure* **enveloped in** *a black cloak* | figurative *a feeling of despair enveloped him.*
■(of troops) surround (an enemy force).
– DERIVATIVES **envelopment** noun.
– ORIGIN late Middle English (formerly also as *invelop(e)*): from Old French *envoluper*, from *en-* 'in' + a second element (also found in **DEVELOP**) of unknown origin.

envelope /'ɛnvələʊp, 'ɒn-/ ▶**noun 1** a flat paper container with a sealable flap, used to enclose a letter or document.
2 a covering or containing structure or layer: *the external envelope of the swimming pool.*
■the outer metal or glass housing of a vacuum tube, electric light, etc. ■ the structure within a balloon or non-rigid airship containing the gas. ■ Microbiology a membrane which forms the outer layer of certain viruses. ■ Electronics a curve joining the successive peaks of a modulated wave. ■ Mathematics a curve or surface tangent to each of a family of curves or surfaces.
– PHRASES **the back of an envelope** used to denote calculations or plans of the most sketchy kind: *a proposal drawn up on the back of an envelope.* **push the envelope** (or **the edge of the envelope**) informal approach or extend the limits of what is possible: *these are extremely witty and clever stories that consistently push the envelope of TV comedy.* [ORIGIN: originally aviation slang, relating to graphs of aerodynamic performance.]
– ORIGIN mid 16th cent. (in the sense 'wrapper, enveloping layer'; originally as *envelope*): from French *enveloppe*, from *envelopper* 'envelop'. The sense 'covering of a letter' dates from the early 18th cent.

envenom /ɪn'vɛnəm, ɛn-/ ▶**verb** [with obj.] archaic put poison on or into; make poisonous.
■figurative infuse with hostility or bitterness: *tribal rivalries envenom the bitter civil war.*
– ORIGIN Middle English (formerly also as *invenom*): from Old French *envenimer*, from *en-* 'in' + *venim* 'venom'.

envenomate ▶**verb** [with obj.] Zoology & Medicine (of a snake, scorpion, spider, or insect) poison by biting or stinging.
– DERIVATIVES **envenomation** noun.

en ventre sa mère /ɒ̃ ˌvɒ̃trə sa 'mɛ:/ ▶**adverb** & **adjective** Law in the mother's womb.
– ORIGIN French.

Enver Pasha /ˌɛnvə 'pɑ:ʃə/ (1881–1922), Turkish political and military leader. A leader of the Young Turks in 1908, he came to power as part of a ruling triumvirate following a coup d'état in 1913.

enviable /'ɛnvɪəb(ə)l/ ▶**adjective** arousing or likely to arouse envy: *the firm is in the enviable position of having a full order book.*
– DERIVATIVES **enviably** adverb.

envious ▶**adjective** feeling or showing envy: *I'm* **envious of** *their happiness* | *an envious glance.*
– DERIVATIVES **enviously** adverb.
– ORIGIN Middle English: from Old French *envieus*, from *envie* 'envy', on the pattern of Latin *invidiosus* 'invidious'.

environ /ɪn'vʌɪrən, ɛn-/ ▶**verb** [with obj.] formal surround; enclose: *the stone circle was environed by an expanse of peat soil.*
– ORIGIN Middle English (formerly also as *inviron*): from Old French *environer*, from *environ* 'surroundings', from *en* 'in' + *viron* 'circuit' (from *virer* 'to turn, veer').

environment ▶**noun 1** the surroundings or conditions in which a person, animal, or plant lives or operates.
■[usu. with modifier] the setting or conditions in which a particular activity is carried on: *a good learning environment.* ■ [with modifier] Computing the overall structure within which a user, computer, or program operates: *a desktop development environment.*
2 (**the environment**) the natural world, as a whole or in a particular geographical area, especially as affected by human activity.

environmental ▶**adjective 1** relating to the natural world and the impact of human activity on its condition: *acid rain may have caused major environmental damage.*
■aiming or designed to promote the protection of the natural world: *environmental tourism.*
2 relating to or arising from a person's surroundings: *environmental noise.*
– DERIVATIVES **environmentally** adverb.

environmental audit ▶**noun** an assessment of the extent to which an organization is observing practices which seek to minimize harm to the environment.

environmentalist ▶**noun 1** a person who is concerned with or advocates the protection of the environment.
2 a person who considers that environment, as opposed to heredity, has the primary influence on the development of a person or group.
– DERIVATIVES **environmentalism** noun.

Environmentally Sensitive Area (abbrev.: **ESA**) ▶**noun** (in the UK) an area officially designated as containing landscapes or wildlife that would be threatened by unrestricted development.

environs ▶**plural noun** the surrounding area or district: *the picturesque environs of the loch.*
– ORIGIN mid 17th cent.: from French, plural of *environ* (see **ENVIRON**).

envisage /ɪn'vɪzɪdʒ, ɛn-/ ▶**verb** [with obj.] contemplate or conceive of as a possibility or a desirable future event: *the Rome Treaty envisaged free movement across frontiers.*
■form a mental picture of (something not yet existing or known): *he knew what he liked but had difficulty envisaging it.*
– ORIGIN early 19th cent.: from French *envisager*, from *en-* 'in' + *visage* 'face'.

envision ▶**verb** [with obj.] imagine as a future possibility; visualize: *she envisioned the admiring glances of guests seeing her home.*

envoi /'ɛnvɔɪ/ (also **envoy**) ▶**noun 1** a short stanza concluding a ballade.
2 archaic an author's concluding words.
– ORIGIN late Middle English: from Old French *envoi*, from *envoyer* 'send' (see **ENVOY**[1]).

envoy /'ɛnvɔɪ/ ▶**noun 1** a messenger or representative, especially one on a diplomatic mission.
2 (also **envoy extraordinary**) a minister plenipotentiary, ranking below ambassador and above chargé d'affaires.
– ORIGIN mid 17th cent.: from French *envoyé*, past participle of *envoyer* 'send', from *en voie* 'on the way', based on Latin *via* 'way'.

envy ▶**noun** (pl. **-ies**) [mass noun] a feeling of discontented or resentful longing aroused by someone else's possessions, qualities, or luck: *she felt a twinge of envy for the people on board.*
■(**the envy of**) a person or thing that inspires such a feeling: *our national health service is the envy of many in Europe.*
▶**verb** (**-ies**, **-ied**) [with obj.] desire to have a quality, possession, or other desirable attribute belonging to (someone else): *he envied people who did not have to work at the weekends* | [with two objs] *I envy Jane her happiness.*
■desire for oneself (something possessed or enjoyed by another): *a lifestyle which most of us would envy.*
– DERIVATIVES **envier** noun.
– ORIGIN Middle English (also in the sense 'hostility, enmity'): from Old French *envie* (noun), *envier* (verb), from Latin *invidia*, from *invidere* 'regard maliciously, grudge', from *in-* 'into' + *videre* 'to see'.

enwrap (also **inwrap**) ▶**verb** (**enwrapped**, **enwrapping**) [with obj.] wrap; envelop: *the book jacket enwraps a plain blue paper binding.*
■(usu. **be enwrapped**) engross or absorb (someone): *they were enwrapped in conversation.*

enwreathe (also **inwreathe**) ▶**verb** [with obj.] (usu. **be enwreathed**) poetic/literary surround or envelop (something): *the lofty battlements, thickly enwreathed with ivy.*

Enzed /ɛn'zɛd/ ▶**noun** Austral./NZ informal New Zealand or a New Zealander.
– DERIVATIVES **Enzedder** noun.
– ORIGIN representing a pronunciation of the initials *NZ*.

enzootic /ˌɛnzəʊ'ɒtɪk/ ▶**adjective** of, relating to, or denoting a disease that regularly affects animals in a particular district or at a particular season. Compare with **EPIZOOTIC**, **ENDEMIC** (in sense 1).
– ORIGIN late 19th cent.: from **EN-**[2] 'within' + Greek *zōion* 'animal' + **-IC**.

enzyme /'ɛnzʌɪm/ ▶**noun** Biochemistry a substance produced by a living organism which acts as a catalyst to bring about a specific biochemical reaction.

Most enzymes are proteins with large complex molecules whose action depends on their particular molecular shape. Some enzymes control reactions within cells and some, such as the enzymes involved in digestion, outside them.

– DERIVATIVES **enzymatic** adjective, **enzymic** adjective.
– ORIGIN late 19th cent.: coined in German from modern Greek *enzumos* 'leavened', from *en-* 'within' + Greek *zumē* 'leaven'.

enzymology ▶**noun** [mass noun] the branch of biochemistry concerned with enzymes.
– DERIVATIVES **enzymological** adjective, **enzymologist** noun.

EOC ▶**abbreviation for** Equal Opportunities Commission, a body appointed by the government to enforce the conditions of the Equal Pay Act and the Sex Discrimination Act.

Eocene /'i:ə(ʊ)si:n/ ▶**adjective** Geology of, relating to, or denoting the second epoch of the Tertiary period, between the Palaeocene and Oligocene epochs.
■[as noun **the Eocene**] the Eocene epoch or the system of rocks deposited during it.

The Eocene epoch lasted from 56.5 to 35.4 million years ago. It was a time of rising temperatures, and there was an abundance of mammals, including the first horses, bats, and whales.

– ORIGIN mid 19th cent.: from Greek *ēōs* 'dawn' + *kainos* 'new'.

eohippus /ˌi:əʊ'hɪpəs/ ▶**noun** (pl. **eohippuses**) former term for **HYRACOTHERIUM**.
– ORIGIN late 19th cent.: from Greek *ēōs* 'dawn' + *hippos* 'horse'.

eo ipso /ˌeɪəʊ 'ɪpsəʊ/ ▶**adverb** formal by that very act or quality; thereby: *such a grand theory would eo ipso give an account of how we communicate using language.*
– ORIGIN Latin, ablative of *id ipsum* 'the thing itself'.

EOKA /eɪ'əʊkə/ a Greek-Cypriot liberation

movement active in Cyprus in the 1950s and in the early 1970s, which fought for the independence of Cyprus from Britain and for its eventual union (enosis) with Greece.

– ORIGIN acronym from Greek *Ethnikē Organōsis Kupriakou Agōnos* 'National Organization of Cypriot Struggle'.

eolian ▶ adjective US spelling of AEOLIAN.

eolith /ˈiːə(ʊ)lɪθ/ ▶ noun Archaeology a roughly chipped flint found in Tertiary strata, originally thought to be an early artefact but probably of natural origin.
– ORIGIN late 19th cent.: from Greek *ēōs* 'dawn' + *lithos* 'stone'.

Eolithic /ˌiːə(ʊ)ˈlɪθɪk/ ▶ adjective Archaeology, dated of, relating to, or denoting a period at the beginning of the Stone Age, preceding the Palaeolithic and characterized by the earliest crude stone tools.
■ [as noun **the Eolithic**] the Eolithic period.
– ORIGIN late 19th cent.: from French *éolithique*, from Greek *ēōs* + *lithikos* (from *lithos* 'stone').

eon ▶ noun variant spelling of AEON.

Eos /ˈiːɒs/ Greek Mythology the Greek goddess of the dawn. Roman equivalent AURORA.

eosin /ˈiːə(ʊ)sɪn/ ▶ noun [mass noun] a red fluorescent dye that is a bromine derivative of fluorescein, or one of its salts or other derivatives.
– ORIGIN late 19th cent.: from Greek *ēōs* 'dawn' + -IN[1].

eosinophil /ˌiːə(ʊ)ˈsɪnəfɪl/ ▶ noun Physiology a white blood cell containing granules that are readily stained by eosin.

eosinophilia /ˌiːə(ʊ)ˌsɪnəˈfɪliə/ ▶ noun [mass noun] Medicine an increase in the number of eosinophils in the blood, occurring in response to some allergens, drugs, and parasites, and in some types of leukaemia.

eosinophilic ▶ adjective 1 Physiology (of a cell or its contents) readily stained by eosin.
2 Medicine relating to or marked by eosinophilia.

EOT ▶ abbreviation for ■ Computing end of tape. ■ Telecommunications end of transmission.

-eous ▶ suffix (forming adjectives) resembling; displaying the nature of: *aqueous | erroneous*.
– ORIGIN from the Latin suffix *-eus* + -OUS.

EP ▶ abbreviation for ■ electroplate. ■ European Parliament. ■ extended-play (of a record or compact disc): *an EP of remixes.* ■ extreme pressure (used in grading lubricants).

Ep. ▶ abbreviation for Epistle.

ep- /ɛp, ɪp, iːp/ ▶ prefix variant spelling of EPI-shortened before a vowel or h (as in *eparch, ephod*).

e.p. Chess ▶ abbreviation for en passant.

EPA ▶ abbreviation for (in the US) Environmental Protection Agency.

epact /ˈiːpakt/ ▶ noun [in sing.] the number of days by which the solar year exceeds the lunar year.
– ORIGIN mid 16th cent. (denoting the age of the moon in days at the beginning of the calendar year): from French *épacte*, via late Latin from Greek *epaktai* (*hēmerai*) 'intercalated (days)', from *epagein* 'bring in', from *epi* 'in addition' + *agein* 'bring'.

eparch /ˈɛpɑːk/ ▶ noun the chief bishop of an eparchy.
– ORIGIN mid 17th cent. (denoting the governor of an administrative division of Greece): from Greek *eparkhos*, from *epi* 'above' + *arkhos* 'ruler'.

eparchy /ˈɛpɑːki/ ▶ noun (pl. **-ies**) a province of the Orthodox Church.
– ORIGIN late 18th cent.: from Greek *eparkhia*, from *eparkhos* (see EPARCH).

épater /eɪˈpateɪ, French epate/ ▶ verb (in phrase **épater les bourgeois**) shock people who have attitudes or views perceived as conventional or complacent.
– ORIGIN French.

epaulette /ˈɛpəlɛt, -pɔːl-, ˌɛpəˈlɛt/ (US also **epaulet**) ▶ noun an ornamental shoulder piece on an item of clothing, typically on the coat or jacket of a military uniform.
– ORIGIN late 18th cent.: from French *épaulette*, diminutive of *épaule* 'shoulder', from Latin *spatula* in the late Latin sense 'shoulder blade'.

epaxial /ɛˈpaksɪəl/ ▶ adjective Anatomy & Zoology situated on the dorsal side of an axis: *epaxial muscles*.

épée /ˈeɪpeɪ, ˈɛp-/ ▶ noun a sharp-pointed duelling sword, used, with the end blunted, in fencing.
– DERIVATIVES **épéeist** noun.

– ORIGIN late 19th cent.: French, 'sword', from Old French *espee* (see SPAY).

epeirogeny /ˌɪpaɪˈrɒdʒəni/ ▶ noun [mass noun] Geology the regional uplift of an extensive area of the earth's crust.
– DERIVATIVES **epeirogenesis** noun, **epeirogenic** adjective.
– ORIGIN late 19th cent.: from Greek *ēpeiros* 'mainland' + -GENY.

ependyma /ɛˈpɛndɪmə/ ▶ noun [mass noun] Anatomy the thin membrane of glial cells lining the ventricles of the brain and the central canal of the spinal cord.
– DERIVATIVES **ependymal** adjective.
– ORIGIN late 19th cent.: from Greek *ependuma*, from *ependuein* 'put on over'.

epenthesis /ɛˈpɛnθɪsɪs/ ▶ noun (pl. **epentheses** /-siːz/) [mass noun] the insertion of a sound or an unetymological letter within a word, e.g. the *b* in *thimble*.
– DERIVATIVES **epenthetic** adjective.
– ORIGIN mid 16th cent.: via late Latin from Greek, from *epentithenai* 'insert', from *epi* 'in addition' + *en-* 'within' + *tithenai* 'to place'.

epergne /ɪˈpəːn/ ▶ noun an ornamental centrepiece for a dining table, typically used for holding fruit or flowers.
– ORIGIN early 18th cent.: perhaps an altered form of French *épargne* 'saving, economy'.

epexegesis /ɛˌpɛksɪˈdʒiːsɪs/ ▶ noun (pl. **epexegeses** /-siːz/) [mass noun] the addition of words to clarify meaning.
■ words added for such a purpose.
– DERIVATIVES **epexegetic** /-ˈdʒɛtɪk/ adjective, **epexegetical** adjective, **epexegetically** adverb.
– ORIGIN late 16th cent.: from Greek *epexēgēsis*, from *epi* 'in addition' + *exēgēsis* 'explanation' (see EXEGESIS).

Eph. ▶ abbreviation for Epistle to the Ephesians (in biblical references).

ephah /ˈiːfə/ ▶ noun an ancient Hebrew dry measure equivalent to the bath (of about 40 litres or 9 gallons).
– ORIGIN from Hebrew *'ēpāh*, probably from Egyptian.

ephebe /ɛˈfiːb, ɪ-, ˈɛfiːb/ ▶ noun (in ancient Greece) a young man of 18–20 years undergoing military training.
– DERIVATIVES **ephebic** adjective.
– ORIGIN via Latin from Greek *ephēbos*, from *epi* 'near to' + *hēbē* 'early manhood'.

ephedra /ɛˈfiːdrə/ ▶ noun an evergreen shrub of warm arid regions which has trailing or climbing stems and tiny scale-like leaves. Some kinds are a source of ephedrine and are used medicinally.
● Family Ephedraceae and genus *Ephedra*.
– ORIGIN modern Latin, from Latin, 'equisetum' (which it resembles), from Greek.

ephedrine /ˈɛfədriːn/ ▶ noun [mass noun] Medicine a crystalline alkaloid drug obtained from some ephedras. It causes constriction of the blood vessels and widening of the bronchial passages, and is used to relieve asthma and hay fever.
● Alternative name: **1-phenyl-2-methylaminopropanol**; chem. formula: $C_{10}H_{15}NO$.
– ORIGIN late 19th cent.: from EPHEDRA + -INE[4].

ephemera /ɪˈfɛm(ə)rə, -ˈfiːm-/ ▶ plural noun things that exist or are used or enjoyed for only a short time.
■ items of collectable memorabilia, typically written or printed ones, that were originally expected to have only short-term usefulness or popularity: *Mickey Mouse ephemera.*
– ORIGIN late 16th cent.: plural of *ephemeron*, from Greek, neuter of *ephēmeros* 'lasting only a day'. As a singular noun the word originally denoted a plant said by ancient writers to last only one day, or an insect with a short lifespan, and hence was applied (late 18th cent.) to a person or thing of short-lived interest. Current use has been influenced by plurals such as *trivia* and *memorabilia*.

ephemeral ▶ adjective lasting for a very short time.
■ (chiefly of plants) having a very short life cycle.
▶ noun an ephemeral plant.
– DERIVATIVES **ephemerality** noun, **ephemerally** adverb, **ephemeralness** noun.
– ORIGIN late 16th cent.: from Greek *ephēmeros* (see EPHEMERA) + -AL.

ephemeris /ɪˈfɛm(ə)rɪs, -ˈfiːm-/ ▶ noun (pl. **ephemerides** /ˌɛfɪˈmɛrɪdiːz/) Astronomy & Astrology a

table or data file giving the calculated positions of a celestial object at regular intervals throughout a period.
■ a book or set of such tables or files.
– ORIGIN early 16th cent.: from Latin, from Greek *ephēmeros* 'lasting only a day'.

ephemerist ▶ noun a person who collects ephemera.

ephemeris time ▶ noun time on a scale defined by the orbital period rather than the axial rotation of the earth.

Ephemeroptera /ɪˌfɛməˈrɒptərə, -ˌfiːm-/ Entomology an order of insects that comprises the mayflies.
■ [as plural noun **ephemeroptera**] insects of this order; mayflies.
– DERIVATIVES **ephemeropteran** noun & adjective.
– ORIGIN modern Latin (plural), from *Ephemera* (genus name) + *pteron* 'wing'.

Ephesians, Epistle to the /ɪˈfiːʒ(ə)nz/ a book of the New Testament ascribed to St Paul consisting of an epistle to the Church at Ephesus.

Ephesus /ˈɛfɪsəs/ an ancient Greek city on the west coast of Asia Minor, in present-day Turkey, site of the temple of Diana, one of the Seven Wonders of the World. It was an important centre of early Christianity; St Paul preached there and St John is traditionally said to have lived there.

ephod /ˈiːfɒd, ˈɛfɒd/ ▶ noun (in ancient Israel) a sleeveless garment worn by Jewish priests.
– ORIGIN late Middle English: from Hebrew *'ēpōd*.

ephor /ˈɛfɔː/ ▶ noun (in ancient Greece) one of five senior Spartan magistrates.
– DERIVATIVES **ephorate** noun.
– ORIGIN from Greek *ephoros* 'overseer', from *epi* 'above' + the base of *horan* 'see'.

ephyra /ˈɛfɪrə/ ▶ noun (pl. **ephyrae** /-riː/) Zoology a larval jellyfish, after separation from the scyphistoma.
– ORIGIN mid 19th cent.: modern Latin, from Greek *Ephura*, denoting a Nereid and an Oceanid.

epi- (also **ep-**) ▶ prefix 1 upon: *epigraph*.
2 above: *epicotyl | epicontinental*.
3 in addition: *epiphenomenon*.
– ORIGIN from Greek *epi* 'upon, near to, in addition'.

epibenthos /ˌɛpɪˈbɛnθɒs/ ▶ noun [mass noun] Ecology the flora and fauna living on the surface of the bottom of a sea or lake.
– DERIVATIVES **epibenthic** adjective.
– ORIGIN early 20th cent.: from Greek *epi* 'upon' + *benthos* 'depth of the sea'.

epiblast /ˈɛpɪblast/ ▶ noun Embryology the outermost layer of an embryo before it differentiates into ectoderm and mesoderm.

epic ▶ noun a long poem, typically one derived from ancient oral tradition, narrating the deeds and adventures of heroic or legendary figures or the past history of a nation.
■ [mass noun] the genre of such poems: *the romances display gentler emotions not found in Greek epic.* ■ a long film, book, or other work portraying heroic deeds and adventures or covering an extended period of time: *a Hollywood biblical epic.* ■ informal an exceptionally long and arduous task or activity: *the business of getting hospital treatment soon became an epic.*
▶ adjective of, relating to, or characteristic of an epic or epics: *our national epic poem Beowulf.*
■ heroic or grand in scale or character: *his epic journey around the world | a tragedy of epic proportions.*
– DERIVATIVES **epical** adjective, **epically** adverb.
– ORIGIN late 16th cent. (as an adjective): via Latin from Greek *epikos*, from *epos* 'word, song', related to *eipein* 'say'.

epicanthic ▶ adjective denoting a fold of skin from the upper eyelid covering the inner angle of the eye, typical in many peoples of eastern Asia and found as a congenital abnormality elsewhere.

epicardium /ˌɛpɪˈkɑːdɪəm/ ▶ noun [mass noun] Anatomy a serous membrane that forms the innermost layer of the pericardium, attached to the muscles of the wall of the heart.
– DERIVATIVES **epicardial** adjective.
– ORIGIN mid 19th cent.: from EPI- 'above' + Greek *kardia* 'heart', on the pattern of *pericardium*.

epicedium /ˌɛpɪˈsiːdɪəm/ ▶ noun (pl. **epicedia** /-dɪə/) formal a funeral ode.
– DERIVATIVES **epicedian** adjective.
– ORIGIN mid 16th cent. (originally in the Anglicized form *epicede* and the Greek form *epicedeon*): from

Latin, from Greek *epikēdeion*, neuter of *epokēdeios* 'of a funeral' (based on *kēdos* 'care, grief').

epicene /ˈɛpɪsiːn/ ▶ **adjective** having characteristics of both sexes or no characteristics of either sex; of indeterminate sex: *the sort of epicene beauty peculiar to boys of a certain age.*
■effeminate; effete: *the actor infused the role with an epicene languor.*
▶ **noun** an epicene person.
– ORIGIN late Middle English (as a grammatical term): via late Latin from Greek *epikoinos* (based on *koinos* 'common').

epicentre (US **epicenter**) ▶ **noun** the point on the earth's surface vertically above the focus of an earthquake.
■figurative the central point of something, typically a difficult or unpleasant situation: *the patient was at the epicentre of concern.*
– DERIVATIVES **epicentral** adjective.
– ORIGIN late 19th cent.: from Greek *epikentros* 'situated on a centre', from *epi* 'upon' + *kentron* 'centre'.

epicondyle /ˌɛpɪˈkɒndɪl/ ▶ **noun** Anatomy a protuberance above or on the condyle of a long bone, especially either of the two at the elbow end of the humerus.
– DERIVATIVES **epicondylar** adjective.
– ORIGIN mid 19th cent.: from French *épicondyle*, modern Latin *epicondylus* (see **EPI-**, **CONDYLE**).

epicondylitis /ˌɛpɪkɒndɪˈlʌɪtɪs/ ▶ **noun** [mass noun] Medicine a painful inflammation of tendons surrounding an epicondyle.

epicontinental ▶ **adjective** denoting those areas of sea or ocean overlying the continental shelf.

epicormic /ˌɛpɪˈkɔːmɪk/ ▶ **adjective** Botany (of a shoot or branch) growing from a previously dormant bud on the trunk or a limb of a tree.
– ORIGIN early 20th cent.: from **EPI-** 'upon' + Greek *kormos* 'tree trunk'.

epicotyl /ˌɛpɪˈkɒtɪl/ ▶ **noun** Botany the region of an embryo or seedling stem above the cotyledon.

epicritic /ˌɛpɪˈkrɪtɪk/ ▶ **adjective** Physiology relating to or denoting those sensory nerve fibres of the skin which are capable of fine discrimination of touch or temperature stimuli. Often contrasted with **PROTOPATHIC**.
– ORIGIN early 20th cent.: from Greek *epikritikos* 'giving judgement over', from *epi* 'upon or over' + *krinein* 'to judge'.

Epictetus /ˌɛpɪkˈtiːtəs/ (*c.*55–*c.*135 AD), Greek philosopher, who preached the common brotherhood of man and advocated a Stoic philosophy.

epicure /ˈɛpɪkjʊə/ ▶ **noun** a person who takes particular pleasure in fine food and drink.
– DERIVATIVES **epicurism** noun.
– ORIGIN late Middle English (denoting a disciple of **EPICURUS**): via medieval Latin from Greek *Epikouros* 'Epicurus'.

Epicurean /ˌɛpɪkjʊ(ə)ˈriːən/ ▶ **noun** a disciple or student of the Greek philosopher Epicurus.
■(**epicurean**) a person devoted to sensual enjoyment, especially that derived from fine food and drink.
▶ **adjective** of or concerning Epicurus or his ideas: *Epicurean philosophers.*
■(**epicurean**) relating to or suitable for an epicure: *epicurean feasts.*

Epicureanism /ˌɛpɪkjʊəˈriːəˌnɪz(ə)m/ ▶ **noun** [mass noun] an ancient school of philosophy, founded in Athens by Epicurus. The school rejected determinism and advocated hedonism (pleasure as the highest good), but of a restrained kind: mental pleasure was regarded more highly than physical, and the ultimate pleasure was held to be freedom from anxiety and mental pain, especially that arising from needless fear of death and of the gods.

Epicurus /ˌɛpɪˈkjʊərəs/ (341–270 BC), Greek philosopher, founder of Epicureanism. His physics is based on Democritus' theory of a materialist universe composed of indestructible atoms moving in a void, unregulated by divine providence.

epicuticle /ˈɛpɪˌkjuːtɪk(ə)l/ ▶ **noun** [mass noun] Botany & Zoology the thin, waxy protective outer layer covering the surfaces of some plants, fungi, insects, and other arthropods.
– DERIVATIVES **epicuticular** adjective.

epicycle /ˈɛpɪˌsʌɪk(ə)l/ ▶ **noun** Geometry a small circle whose centre moves round the circumference of a larger one.
■historical a circle of this type used to describe planetary orbits in the Ptolemaic system.
– DERIVATIVES **epicyclic** adjective.
– ORIGIN late Middle English: from Old French, or via late Latin from Greek *epikuklos*, from *epi* 'upon' + *kuklos* 'circle'.

epicycloid /ˌɛpɪˈsʌɪklɔɪd/ ▶ **noun** Mathematics a curve traced by a point on the circumference of a circle rolling on the exterior of another circle.
– DERIVATIVES **epicycloidal** adjective.

Epidaurus /ˌɛpɪˈdɔːrəs/ an ancient Greek city and port on the NE coast of the Peloponnese. Greek name **EPÍDHAVROS** /ɛˈpiðavrɔs/.

epideictic /ˌɛpɪˈdeɪktɪk, -ˈdʌɪktɪk/ ▶ **adjective** formal characterized by or designed to display rhetorical or oratorical skill.
– ORIGIN late 18th cent.: from Greek *epideiktikos* (based on *deiknunai* 'to show').

epidemic ▶ **noun** a widespread occurrence of an infectious disease in a community at a particular time: *a flu epidemic.*
■a disease occurring in such a way. ■a sudden, widespread occurrence of a particular undesirable phenomenon: *an epidemic of violent crime.*
▶ **adjective** of, relating to, or of the nature of an epidemic: *shoplifting has reached epidemic proportions.* Compare with **ENDEMIC**, **PANDEMIC**, **EPIZOOTIC**.
– ORIGIN early 17th cent. (as an adjective): from French *épidémique*, from *épidémie*, via late Latin from Greek *epidēmia* 'prevalence of disease', from *epidēmios* 'prevalent', from *epi* 'upon' + *dēmos* 'the people'.

epidemiology /ˌɛpɪdiːmɪˈɒlədʒi/ ▶ **noun** [mass noun] the branch of medicine which deals with the incidence, distribution, and possible control of diseases and other factors relating to health.
– DERIVATIVES **epidemiological** adjective, **epidemiologist** noun.
– ORIGIN late 19th cent.: from Greek *epidēmia* 'prevalence of disease' + **-LOGY**.

epidermis /ˌɛpɪˈdəːmɪs/ ▶ **noun** [mass noun] Biology the outer layer of cells covering an organism, in particular:
■Zoology & Anatomy the surface epithelium of the skin of an animal, overlying the dermis. ■Botany the outer layer of tissue in a plant, except where it is replaced by periderm.
– DERIVATIVES **epidermal** adjective, **epidermic** adjective, **epidermoid** adjective.
– ORIGIN early 17th cent.: via late Latin from Greek, from *epi* 'upon' + *derma* 'skin'.

epidermolysis /ˌɛpɪdəːˈmɒlɪsɪs/ (also **epidermolysis bullosa** /bʊˈləʊsə/) ▶ **noun** [mass noun] Medicine loosening of the epidermis, with extensive blistering of the skin and mucous membranes, occurring either after injury, or as a spontaneous and potentially dangerous condition, particularly in children.

epidiascope /ˌɛpɪˈdʌɪəskəʊp/ ▶ **noun** an optical projector capable of giving images of both opaque and transparent objects.
– ORIGIN early 20th cent.: from **EPI-** + **DIA-** + **-SCOPE**.

epididymis /ˌɛpɪˈdɪdɪmɪs/ ▶ **noun** (pl. **epididymides** /ˌɛpɪdɪˈdɪmɪdiːz/) Anatomy a highly convoluted duct behind the testis, along which sperm passes to the vas deferens.
– DERIVATIVES **epididymal** adjective.
– ORIGIN early 17th cent.: from Greek *epididumis*, from *epi* 'upon' + *didumos* 'testicle' (from *duo* 'two').

epidote /ˈɛpɪdəʊt/ ▶ **noun** [mass noun] a lustrous yellow-green crystalline mineral, common in metamorphic rocks. It consists of a basic, hydrated silicate of calcium, aluminium, and iron.
– ORIGIN early 19th cent.: from French *épidote*, from Greek *epididonai* 'give additionally' (because of the length of the crystals).

epidural /ˌɛpɪˈdjʊər(ə)l/ ▶ **adjective** Anatomy & Medicine on or around the dura mater, in particular, (of an anaesthetic) introduced into the space around the dura mater of the spinal cord.
▶ **noun** an epidural anaesthetic, used especially in childbirth to produce loss of sensation below the waist.
– ORIGIN late 19th cent.: from **EPI-** 'upon' + **DURA**[1] + **-AL**.

epifauna ▶ **noun** [mass noun] Ecology animals living on the surface of the seabed or a river bed, or attached to submerged objects or aquatic animals or plants. Compare with **INFAUNA**.
– DERIVATIVES **epifaunal** adjective.
– ORIGIN early 20th cent.: from **EPI-** 'upon' + **FAUNA**.

epifluorescence /ˌɛpɪflʊəˈrɛs(ə)ns, -flɔː-/ ▶ **noun** [mass noun] Optics the fluorescence of an object in an optical microscope when irradiated from the viewing side.

epigastrium /ˌɛpɪˈgastrɪəm/ ▶ **noun** (pl. **epigastria** /-rɪə/) Anatomy the part of the upper abdomen immediately over the stomach.
– DERIVATIVES **epigastric** adjective.
– ORIGIN late 17th cent.: via late Latin from Greek *epigastrion*, neuter of *epigastrios* 'over the belly', from *epi* 'upon' + *gastēr* 'belly'.

epigeal /ˌɛpɪˈdʒiːəl/ ▶ **adjective** Botany growing on or close to the ground. Compare with **HYPOGEAL**.
■(of seed germination) with one or more seed leaves appearing above the ground.
– ORIGIN mid 19th cent.: from Greek *epigeios* (from *epi* 'upon' + *gē* 'earth') + **-AL**.

epigene /ˈɛpɪdʒiːn/ ▶ **adjective** Geology taking place or produced on the surface of the earth.
– ORIGIN early 19th cent.: from French *épigène*, from Greek *epigenēs*, from *epi* 'upon' + *genēs* (see **-GEN**).

epigenesis /ˌɛpɪˈdʒɛnɪsɪs/ ▶ **noun** [mass noun] Biology the theory, now generally held, that an embryo develops progressively from an undifferentiated egg cell. Often contrasted with **PREFORMATION**.
– DERIVATIVES **epigenesist** noun & adjective.
– ORIGIN mid 17th cent.: from **EPI-** 'in addition' + **GENESIS**.

epigenetic /ˌɛpɪdʒɪˈnɛtɪk/ ▶ **adjective** Biology resulting from external rather than genetic influences: *epigenetic carcinogens.*
■Biology of, relating to, or of the nature of epigenesis. ■Geology formed later than the surrounding or underlying rock formation.
– DERIVATIVES **epigenetically** adverb, **epigeneticist** noun.

epiglottis /ˌɛpɪˈglɒtɪs/ ▶ **noun** a flap of cartilage at the root of the tongue, which is depressed during swallowing to cover the opening of the windpipe.
– DERIVATIVES **epiglottal** adjective, **epiglottic** adjective.
– ORIGIN late Middle English: from Greek *epiglōttis*, from *epi* 'upon, near to' + *glōtta* 'tongue'.

epigone /ˈɛpɪgəʊn/ ▶ **noun** (pl. **epigones** or **epigoni** /ɪˈpɪgənʌɪ, ɛ-/) a less distinguished follower or imitator of someone, especially an artist or philosopher.
– ORIGIN mid 18th cent.: plurals from French *épigones* and Latin *epigoni*, from Greek *epigonoi* 'those born afterwards' (based on *gignesthai* 'be born').

epigram /ˈɛpɪgram/ ▶ **noun** a pithy saying or remark expressing an idea in a clever and amusing way.
■a short poem, especially a satirical one, having a witty or ingenious ending.
– DERIVATIVES **epigrammatist** noun, **epigrammatize** (also **-ise**) verb.
– ORIGIN late Middle English: from French *épigramme*, or Latin *epigramma*, from Greek, from *epi* 'upon, in addition' + *gramma* (see **-GRAM**[1]).

epigrammatic /ˌɛpɪgrəˈmatɪk/ ▶ **adjective** of the nature or in the style of an epigram; concise, clever, and amusing: *an epigrammatic style.*
– DERIVATIVES **epigrammatically** adverb.
– ORIGIN early 17th cent.: from late Latin *epigrammaticus*, from Latin *epigramma* (see **EPIGRAM**).

epigraph /ˈɛpɪgrɑːf/ ▶ **noun** an inscription on a building, statue, or coin.
■a short quotation or saying at the beginning of a book or chapter, intended to suggest its theme.
– ORIGIN late 16th cent. (denoting the heading of a document or letter): from Greek *epigraphē*, from *epigraphein* 'write on'.

epigraphy /ɪˈpɪgrəfi, ɛ-/ ▶ **noun** [mass noun] the study and interpretation of ancient inscriptions.
■epigraphs collectively.
– DERIVATIVES **epigrapher** noun, **epigraphic** adjective, **epigraphical** adjective, **epigraphically** adverb, **epigraphist** noun.

epigynous /ɪˈpɪdʒɪnəs, ɛ-/ ▶ **adjective** Botany (of a plant or flower) having the ovary enclosed in the receptacle, with the stamens and other floral parts situated above. Compare with **HYPOGYNOUS**, **PERIGYNOUS**.
– DERIVATIVES **epigyny** noun.
– ORIGIN mid 19th cent.: from modern Latin

epigynus, from **EPI-** 'upon, above' + Greek *gunē* 'woman' + **-OUS**.

epilation /ˌɛpɪˈleɪʃ(ə)n/ ▶ noun [mass noun] the removal of hair by the roots.
– DERIVATIVES **epilate** verb, **epilator** noun.
– ORIGIN late 19th cent.: from French *épiler*, from *é-* (expressing removal) + Latin *pilus* 'strand of hair', on the pattern of *depilation*.

epilepsy /ˈɛpɪlɛpsi/ ▶ noun [mass noun] a neurological disorder marked by sudden recurrent episodes of sensory disturbance, loss of consciousness, or convulsions, associated with abnormal electrical activity in the brain.
– ORIGIN mid 16th cent.: from French *épilepsie*, or via late Latin from Greek *epilēpsia*, from *epilambanein* 'seize, attack', from *epi* 'upon' + *lambanein* 'take hold of'.

epileptic /ˌɛpɪˈlɛptɪk/ ▶ adjective of, relating to, or having epilepsy: *he had an epileptic fit.*
▶ noun a person who has epilepsy.
– ORIGIN early 17th cent.: from French *épileptique*, via late Latin from Greek *epilēptikos*, from *epilēpsia* (see **EPILEPSY**).

epileptogenic /ˌɛpɪlɛptə(ʊ)ˈdʒɛnɪk/ ▶ adjective Medicine capable of causing an epileptic attack.

epilimnion /ˌɛpɪˈlɪmnɪən/ ▶ noun (pl. **epilimnia** /-nɪə/) the upper layer of water in a stratified lake.
– ORIGIN early 20th cent.: from **EPI-** 'above' + Greek *limnion* (diminutive of *limnē* 'lake').

epilithic /ˌɛpɪˈlɪθɪk/ ▶ adjective Botany (of a plant) growing on the surface of rock.
– ORIGIN early 20th cent.: from **EPI-** 'upon' + Greek *lithos* 'stone' + **-IC**.

epilogue /ˈɛpɪlɒg/ (US also **epilog**) ▶ noun a section or speech at the end of a book or play that serves as a comment on or a conclusion to what has happened.
– ORIGIN late Middle English: from French *épilogue*, via Latin from Greek *epilogos*, from *epi* 'in addition' + *logos* 'speech'.

epimedium /ˌɛpɪˈmiːdɪəm/ ▶ noun (pl. **epimediums**) a creeping plant of a genus which includes barrenwort.
● Genus *Epimedium*, family Berberidaceae.
– ORIGIN modern Latin, from Greek *epimēdion*.

epimer /ˈɛpɪmə/ ▶ noun Chemistry each of two isomers with different configurations of atoms about one of several asymmetric carbon atoms present.
– DERIVATIVES **epimeric** /-ˈmɛrɪk/ adjective, **epimerism** /ɪˈpɪm-, ɛ-/ noun.

epimerize /ɪˈpɪmərʌɪz, ɛ-/ (also **-ise**) ▶ verb [with obj.] Chemistry convert from one epimeric form into the other.

epimeron /ˌɛpɪˈmɪːrən/ ▶ noun (pl. **epimerons** or **epimera**) Entomology (in insects) the posterior part of the side wall of a thoracic segment.
– ORIGIN mid 19th cent.: from **EPI-** 'near' + Greek *mēros* 'thigh'.

epimysium /ˌɛpɪˈmɪsɪəm/ ▶ noun [mass noun] Anatomy a sheath of fibrous elastic tissue surrounding a muscle.
– ORIGIN modern Latin, from **EPI-** 'upon' + Greek *mus* 'muscle'.

epinephrine /ˌɛpɪˈnɛfrɪn, -riːn/ ▶ noun Biochemistry another term for **ADRENALIN**.
– ORIGIN late 19th cent.: from **EPI-** 'above' + Greek *nephros* 'kidney' + **-INE**[4].

epinician /ˌɛpɪˈnɪsɪən/ ▶ adjective denoting an ancient Greek lyric poem celebrating a victory.
– ORIGIN early 17th cent.: from Greek *epinikion*, neuter (used as a noun) of *epinikios* 'relating to victory', + **-AN**.

Epipalaeolithic /ˌɛpɪpalɪə(ʊ)ˈlɪθɪk/ (US **Epipaleolithic**) ▶ adjective Archaeology of, relating to, or denoting a Stone Age period that shows features of both the Palaeolithic and the Mesolithic and may be transitional between them.
■[as noun **the Epipalaeolithic**] the Epipalaeolithic period.
– ORIGIN early 20th cent.: from **EPI-** 'upon, in addition' + **PALAEOLITHIC**.

epiphany /ɪˈpɪf(ə)ni, ɛ-/ ▶ noun (pl. **-ies**) (**Epiphany**) the manifestation of Christ to the Gentiles as represented by the Magi (Matthew 2: 1–12).
■the festival commemorating this on 6 January. ■a manifestation of a divine or supernatural being. ■a moment of sudden and great revelation or realization.

– DERIVATIVES **epiphanic** /ɛpɪˈfanɪk/ adjective.
– ORIGIN Middle English: from Greek *epiphainein* 'reveal'. The sense relating to the Christian festival is via Old French *epiphanie* and ecclesiastical Latin *epiphania*.

epiphenomenon /ˌɛpɪfəˈnɒmɪnən/ ▶ noun (pl. **epiphenomena** /-nə/) a secondary effect or by-product which arises from but does not causally influence a process, in particular:
■Medicine a secondary symptom, occurring simultaneously with a disease or condition but not directly related to it. ■a mental state regarded as a by-product of brain activity.
– DERIVATIVES **epiphenomenal** adjective.

epiphora /ɪˈpɪf(ə)rə/ ▶ noun [mass noun] **1** Medicine excessive watering of the eye.
2 Rhetoric another term for **EPISTROPHE**.
– ORIGIN late 16th cent. (in sense 2): via Latin from Greek *epi* 'upon' + *pherein* 'to bear or carry'. Sense 1 dates from the mid 17th cent.

epiphyllum /ˌɛpɪˈfɪləm/ ▶ noun (pl. **epiphyllums**) a cactus with flattened stems and large, fragrant red or yellow flowers.
● Genus *Epiphyllum*, family Cactaceae: several species, in particular the night-flowering cactus (*E. hookeri*).
– ORIGIN modern Latin, from **EPI-** 'upon' + Greek *phullon* 'leaf'.

epiphysis /ɪˈpɪfɪsɪs, ɛ-/ ▶ noun (pl. **epiphyses**) **1** the end part of a long bone, initially growing separately from the shaft. Compare with **DIAPHYSIS**.
2 another term for **PINEAL**.
– ORIGIN mid 17th cent.: modern Latin, from Greek *epiphusis*, from *epi* 'upon, in addition' + *phusis* 'growth'.

epiphyte /ˈɛpɪfʌɪt/ ▶ noun Botany a plant that grows on another plant, especially one that is not parasitic, such as the numerous ferns, bromeliads, air plants, and orchids growing on tree trunks in tropical rainforests.
– DERIVATIVES **epiphytal** /-ˈfʌɪt(ə)l/ adjective, **epiphytic** /-ˈfɪtɪk/ adjective.
– ORIGIN mid 19th cent.: from **EPI-** 'in addition' + Greek *phuton* 'plant'.

EPIRB ▶ abbreviation for emergency position-indicating radio beacon.

Epirus /ɪˈpʌɪərəs/ a coastal region of NW Greece; capital, Ioánnina. Greek name **IPIROS**.
■an ancient country of which the modern region of Epirus corresponds to the south-western part, extending northwards to Illyria and eastwards to Macedonia and Thessaly.

episcopacy /ɪˈpɪskəpəsi, ɛ-/ ▶ noun (pl. **-ies**) [mass noun] government of a Church by bishops.
■(**the episcopacy**) the bishops of a region or church collectively. ■another term for **EPISCOPATE**.
– ORIGIN mid 17th cent.: from ecclesiastical Latin *episcopatus* 'episcopate', on the pattern of *prelacy*.

episcopal /ɪˈpɪskəp(ə)l, ɛ-/ ▶ adjective of a bishop or bishops: *episcopal power.*
■(of a Church) governed by or having bishops.
– DERIVATIVES **episcopalism** noun, **episcopally** adverb.
– ORIGIN late Middle English: from French *épiscopal* or ecclesiastical Latin *episcopalis*, from *episcopus* 'bishop', from Greek *episkopos* 'overseer' (see **BISHOP**).

Episcopal Church the Anglican Church in Scotland and the US.

episcopalian /ɪˌpɪskəˈpeɪlɪən, ɛ-/ ▶ adjective of or advocating government of a Church by bishops.
■of or belonging to an episcopal Church. ■(**Episcopalian**) of or belonging to the Episcopal Church.
▶ noun an adherent of episcopacy.
■(**Episcopalian**) a member of the Episcopal Church.
– DERIVATIVES **episcopalianism** noun.

episcopate /ɪˈpɪskəpət, ɛ-/ ▶ noun the office or term of office of a bishop.
■(**the episcopate**) the bishops of a church or region collectively.
– ORIGIN mid 17th cent.: from ecclesiastical Latin *episcopatus* 'made a bishop', from *episcopus* 'bishop', from Greek *episkopos* 'overseer' (see **BISHOP**).

episcope /ˈɛpɪskəʊp/ ▶ noun an optical projector which gives images of opaque objects.

episematic /ˌɛpɪsɪˈmatɪk/ ▶ adjective Zoology (of coloration or markings) serving to help recognition by animals of other individuals of the same species.

– ORIGIN late 19th cent.: from **EPI-** 'upon' + Greek *sēma* 'sign' + **-ATIC**.

episiotomy /ɪˌpɪsɪˈɒtəmi, ɛ-/ ▶ noun (pl. **-ies**) a surgical cut made at the opening of the vagina during childbirth, to aid a difficult delivery and prevent rupture of tissues.
– ORIGIN late 19th cent.: from Greek *epision* 'pubic region' + **-TOMY**.

episode ▶ noun an event or a group of events occurring as part of a sequence; an incident or period considered in isolation: *one of the saddest episodes in the history of the army.*
■each of the separate instalments into which a serialized story or radio or television programme is divided. ■a finite period in which someone is affected by a specified illness: *acute psychotic episodes.* ■ Music a passage containing distinct material or introducing a new subject. ■a section between two choric songs in Greek tragedy.
– ORIGIN late 17th cent. (denoting a section between two choric songs in Greek tragedy): from Greek *epeisodion*, neuter of *epeisodios* 'coming in besides', from *epi* 'in addition' + *eisodos* 'entry' (from *eis* 'into' + *hodos* 'way').

episodic /ˌɛpɪˈsɒdɪk/ ▶ adjective containing or consisting of a series of separate parts or events: *an episodic narrative.*
■occurring occasionally and at irregular intervals: *volcanic activity is highly episodic in nature.* ■(of a television or radio programme or magazine story) broadcast or published as a series of instalments.
– DERIVATIVES **episodically** adverb.

episome /ˈɛpɪsəʊm/ ▶ noun Microbiology a genetic element inside some bacterial cells, especially the DNA of some bacteriophages, that can replicate independently of the host and also in association with a chromosome with which it becomes integrated. Compare with **PLASMID**.

epistasis /ɪˈpɪstəsɪs/ ▶ noun [mass noun] Genetics the interaction of genes that are not alleles, in particular the suppression of the effect of one such gene by another.
– DERIVATIVES **epistatic** /ˌɛpɪˈstatɪk/ adjective.
– ORIGIN early 19th cent.: from Greek, literally 'stoppage', from *ephistanai* 'to stop'.

epistaxis /ˌɛpɪˈstaksɪs/ ▶ noun [mass noun] Medicine bleeding from the nose.
– ORIGIN late 18th cent.: modern Latin, from Greek, from *epistazein* 'bleed from the nose', from *epi* 'upon, in addition' + *stazein* 'to drip'.

epistemic /ˌɛpɪˈstiːmɪk, -ˈstɛm-/ ▶ adjective of or relating to knowledge or to the degree of its validation.
– DERIVATIVES **epistemically** adverb.
– ORIGIN 1920s: from Greek *epistēmē* 'knowledge' (see **EPISTEMOLOGY**) + **-IC**.

epistemology /ɪˌpɪstɪˈmɒlədʒi, ɛ-/ ▶ noun [mass noun] Philosophy the theory of knowledge, especially with regard to its methods, validity, and scope. Epistemology is the investigation of what distinguishes justified belief from opinion.
– DERIVATIVES **epistemological** adjective, **epistemologically** adverb, **epistemologist** noun.
– ORIGIN mid 19th cent.: from Greek *epistēmē* 'knowledge', from *epistasthai* 'know, know how to do'.

episternum /ˌɛpɪˈstəːnəm/ ▶ noun (pl. **episternums** or **episterna** /-nə/) Zoology a bone between the clavicles, especially (in mammals) the upper part of the sternum.
■Entomology (in insects) the anterior part of the side wall of a thoracic segment.

epistle /ɪˈpɪs(ə)l/ ▶ noun formal or humorous a letter.
■a poem or other literary work in the form of a letter or series of letters. ■(**Epistle**) a book of the New Testament in the form of a letter from an Apostle: *St Paul's Epistle to the Romans.* ■an extract from an Epistle (or another New Testament book not a Gospel) that is read in a church service.
– ORIGIN Old English, via Latin from Greek *epistolē*, from *epistellein* 'send news', from *epi* 'upon, in addition' + *stellein* 'send'. The word was reintroduced in Middle English from Old French.

Epistle to the Colossians, Epistle to the Ephesians, etc. see **COLOSSIANS, EPISTLE TO THE; EPHESIANS, EPISTLE TO THE,** etc.

epistolary /ɪˈpɪst(ə)ləri/ ▶ adjective relating to or denoting the writing of letters or literary works in the form of letters: *an epistolary novel.*

– ORIGIN mid 17th cent.: from French *épistolaire* or Latin *epistolaris*, from *epistola* (see **EPISTLE**).

epistrophe /ɪˈpɪstrəfi, ɛ-/ ▶ **noun** [mass noun] the repetition of a word at the end of successive clauses or sentences.
– ORIGIN late 16th cent.: from Greek *epistrophē*, from *epistrephein* 'to turn around', from *epi* 'in addition' + *strephein* 'to turn'.

epistyle /ˈɛpɪstʌɪl/ ▶ **noun** Architecture an architrave.
– ORIGIN mid 16th cent. (in the Latin form *epistylium*): from French *épistyle* or via Latin, from Greek *epistulion*, from *epi* 'upon' + *stulos* 'pillar'.

epitaph /ˈɛpɪtɑːf, -taf/ ▶ **noun** a phrase or form of words written in memory of a person who has died, especially as an inscription on a tombstone.
– ORIGIN late Middle English: from Old French *epitaphe*, via Latin from Greek *epitaphion* 'funeral oration', neuter of *ephitaphios* 'over or at a tomb', from *epi* 'upon' + *taphos* 'tomb'.

epitaxy /ˈɛpɪtaksi/ ▶ **noun** [mass noun] Crystallography the natural or artificial growth of crystals on a crystalline substrate that determines their orientation.
– DERIVATIVES **epitaxial** adjective.
– ORIGIN 1930s: from French *épitaxie*, from Greek *epi* 'upon' + *taxis* 'arrangement'.

epithalamium /ˌɛpɪθəˈleɪmɪəm/ ▶ **noun** (pl. **epithalamiums** or **epithalamia**) a song or poem celebrating a marriage.
– DERIVATIVES **epithalamic** /-ˈlamɪk/ adjective.
– ORIGIN late 16th cent.: via Latin from Greek *epithalamion*, from *epi* 'upon' + *thalamos* 'bridal chamber'.

epithalamus /ˌɛpɪˈθaləməs/ ▶ **noun** (pl. **epithalami** /-mʌɪ, -miː/) Anatomy a part of the dorsal forebrain including the pineal gland and a region in the roof of the third ventricle.

epithelium /ˌɛpɪˈθiːlɪəm/ ▶ **noun** (pl. **epithelia** /-lɪə/) [mass noun] Anatomy the thin tissue forming the outer layer of a body's surface and lining the alimentary canal and other hollow structures.
■ more specifically, the part of this derived from embryonic ectoderm and endoderm, as distinct from endothelium and mesothelium.
– DERIVATIVES **epithelial** adjective.
– ORIGIN mid 18th cent.: modern Latin, from **EPI-** 'above' + Greek *thēlē* 'teat'.

epithet /ˈɛpɪθɛt/ ▶ **noun** an adjective or descriptive phrase expressing a quality or attribute regarded as characteristic of the person or thing mentioned: *old men are often unfairly awarded the epithet 'dirty'.*
– DERIVATIVES **epithetic** adjective, **epithetical** adjective, **epithetically** adverb.
– ORIGIN late 16th cent.: from French *épithète*, or via Latin from Greek *epitheton*, neuter of *epithetos* 'attributed', from *epitithenai* 'add', from *epi* 'upon' + *tithenai* 'to place'.

epitome /ɪˈpɪtəmi, ɛ-/ ▶ **noun** **1** (**the epitome of**) a person or thing that is a perfect example of a particular quality or type: *she looked the epitome of elegance and good taste.*
2 a summary of a written work; an abstract.
■ archaic a thing representing something else in miniature.
– DERIVATIVES **epitomist** noun.
– ORIGIN early 16th cent.: via Latin from Greek *epitomē*, from *epitemnein* 'abridge', from *epi* 'in addition' + *temnein* 'to cut'.

epitomize (also **-ise**) ▶ **verb** [with obj.] **1** be a perfect example of: *the company epitomized the problems faced by British industry.*
2 archaic give a summary of (a written work).
– DERIVATIVES **epitomization** noun.

epitope /ˈɛpɪtəʊp/ ▶ **noun** Biochemistry the part of an antigen molecule to which an antibody attaches itself. Also called **ANTIGENIC DETERMINANT**.
– ORIGIN 1960s: from **EPI-** 'upon' + Greek *topos* 'place'.

epizoic /ˌɛpɪˈzəʊɪk/ ▶ **adjective** Biology (of a plant or animal) growing or living non-parasitically on the exterior of a living animal.
– DERIVATIVES **epizoite** /ɛpɪˈzəʊʌɪt/ noun.
– ORIGIN mid 19th cent.: from **EPI-** 'upon' + Greek *zōion* 'animal' + **-IC**.

epizoon /ˌɛpɪˈzəʊɒn/ ▶ **noun** (pl. **epizoa** /-ˈzəʊə/) Zoology an animal that lives on the body of another animal, especially as a parasite.
– ORIGIN mid 19th cent.: from **EPI-** 'upon' + Greek *zōion* 'animal'.

epizootic /ˌɛpɪzəʊˈɒtɪk/ ▶ **adjective** of, relating to, or denoting a disease that is temporarily prevalent and widespread in an animal population. Compare with **ENZOOTIC**, **EPIDEMIC**.
▶ **noun** an outbreak of such a disease.
– ORIGIN late 18th cent. (as an adjective): from French *épizootique*, from *épizootie*, from Greek *epi* 'upon' + *zōion* 'animal'.

EPLF ▶ **abbreviation for** Eritrean People's Liberation Front, formed in 1970 to fight for independence for Eritrea.

e pluribus unum /eɪ ˌplʊərɪbʊs ˈjuːnʊm/ ▶ **noun** one out of many (the motto of the US).
– ORIGIN Latin.

EPNS ▶ **abbreviation for** electroplated nickel silver.

EPO ▶ **abbreviation for** ■ erythropoietin, especially when isolated as a drug for medical use or for illegal use by athletes. ■ European Patent Office.

epoch /ˈiːpɒk, ˈɛpɒk/ ▶ **noun** a period of time in history or a person's life, typically one marked by notable events or particular characteristics: *the Victorian epoch.*
■ the beginning of a distinctive period in the history of someone or something. ■ Geology a division of time that is a subdivision of a period and is itself subdivided into ages, corresponding to a series in chronostratigraphy: *the Pliocene epoch.* ■ Astronomy an arbitrarily fixed date relative to which planetary or stellar measurements are expressed.
– ORIGIN early 17th cent. (in the Latin form *epocha*; originally in the general sense of a date from which succeeding years are numbered): from modern Latin *epocha*, from Greek *epokhē* 'stoppage, fixed point of time', from *epekhein* 'stop, take up a position', from *epi* 'upon, near to' + *ekhein* 'stay, be in a certain state'.

epochal /ˈɛpɒk(ə)l/ ▶ **adjective** forming or characterizing an epoch; epoch-making.

epoch-making ▶ **adjective** of major importance; likely to have a significant effect on a particular period of time.

epode /ˈɛpəʊd/ ▶ **noun** **1** a form of lyric poem written in couplets, in which a long line is followed by a shorter one.
2 the third section of an ancient Greek choral ode, or of one division of such an ode.
– ORIGIN early 17th cent.: from French *épode*, or via Latin *epodos*, from Greek *epōidos*, from *epi* 'upon' + *ōidē* (see **ODE**).

eponym /ˈɛpənɪm/ ▶ **noun** a person after whom a discovery, invention, place, etc., is named or thought to be named.
■ a name or noun formed in such a way.
– ORIGIN mid 19th cent.: from Greek *epōnumos* 'given as a name, giving one's name to someone or something', from *epi* 'upon' + *onoma* 'name'.

eponymous /ɪˈpɒnɪməs/ ▶ **adjective** (of a person) giving their name to something: *the eponymous hero of the novel.*
■ (of a thing) named after a particular person or group: *their eponymous debut LP.*

EPOS /ˈiːpɒz, ˈiːpɒs/ ▶ **abbreviation for** electronic point of sale (used to describe retail outlets that record information electronically).

epoxide /ɪˈpɒksʌɪd/ ▶ **noun** Chemistry an organic compound whose molecule contains a three-membered ring involving an oxygen atom and two carbon atoms.
– ORIGIN 1930s: from **EPI-** 'in addition' + **OXIDE**.

epoxy /ɪˈpɒksi, ɛ-/ ▶ **noun** (pl. **-ies**) (also **epoxy resin**) [mass noun] an adhesive, plastic, paint, or other material made from a class of synthetic thermosetting polymers containing epoxide groups.
▶ **adjective** [attrib.] consisting of or denoting such a material: *epoxy cement.*
▶ **verb** (**-ies**, **-ied**) [with obj.] glue (something) using epoxy resin.
– ORIGIN early 20th cent.: from **EPI-** 'in addition' + **OXY-**[2].

EPROM /ˈiːprɒm/ ▶ **noun** Electronics a read-only memory whose contents can be erased by ultraviolet light or other means and reprogrammed using a pulsed voltage.
– ORIGIN 1970s: acronym from *erasable programmable ROM.*

eps ▶ **abbreviation for** earnings per share.

epsilon /ˈɛpsɪlɒn, ɛpˈsʌɪlɒn/ ▶ **noun** the fifth letter of the Greek alphabet (**Ε, ε**), transliterated as 'e'.
■ [as modifier] denoting the fifth in a series of items, categories, etc. ■ (**Epsilon**) [followed by Latin genitive] Astronomy the fifth star in a constellation: *Epsilon Carinae.*
▶ **symbol for** (**ε**) permittivity.
– ORIGIN Greek, 'bare or simple E', from *psilos* 'bare'.

Epsom /ˈɛpsəm/ a town in Surrey, SE England; pop. 68,500 (1981). The annual Derby and Oaks horse races are held at its racecourse on Epsom Downs.

Epsom salts ▶ **plural noun** crystals of hydrated magnesium sulphate used as a purgative or for other medicinal use.
• Chem. formula: $MgSO_4.7H_2O$.
– ORIGIN mid 18th cent.: named after the town of **EPSOM**, where it was first found occurring naturally.

EPSRC ▶ **abbreviation for** (in the UK) Engineering and Physical Sciences Research Council.

Epstein[1] /ˈɛpstʌɪn/, Brian (1934–67), English manager of the Beatles.

Epstein[2] /ˈɛpstʌɪn/, Sir Jacob (1880–1959), American-born British sculptor. A founder member of the vorticist group, he later had great success in his modelled portraits of the famous, in particular his *Einstein* (1933).

Epstein–Barr virus (abbrev.: **EBV**) ▶ **noun** Medicine a herpesvirus causing glandular fever and associated with certain cancers, for example Burkitt's lymphoma.
– ORIGIN 1960s: named after Michael A. *Epstein* (born 1921), British virologist, and Y. M. *Barr* (born 1932), Irish-born virologist.

epyllion /ɪˈpɪlɪən, ɛ-/ ▶ **noun** (pl. **epyllia**) a narrative poem that resembles an epic poem in style, but which is notably shorter.
– ORIGIN late 19th cent.: from Greek *epullion*, diminutive of *epos* 'word, song', from *eipein* 'say'.

equable /ˈɛkwəb(ə)l/ ▶ **adjective** not easily disturbed or angered; calm and even-tempered.
■ not varying or fluctuating greatly: *an equable climate.*
– DERIVATIVES **equability** noun, **equably** adverb.
– ORIGIN mid 17th cent. (in the sense 'fair, equitable'): from Latin *aequabilis*, from *aequare* 'make equal' (see **EQUATE**).

equal ▶ **adjective** **1** being the same in quantity, size, degree, or value: *add equal amounts of water and flour | 1 litre is roughly* **equal to** *1 quart.*
■ (of people) having the same status, rights, or opportunities. ■ uniform in application or effect; without discrimination on any grounds: *a dedicated campaigner for equal rights.* ■ evenly or fairly balanced: *it was hardly an equal contest.*
2 [predic.] (**equal to**) having the ability or resources to meet (a challenge): *the players proved equal to the task.*
▶ **noun** a person or thing considered to be the same as another in status or quality: *we all treat each other as equals | entertainment facilities* **without equal** *in the British Isles.*
▶ **verb** (**equalled**, **equalling**; US **equaled**, **equaling**) [with obj.] be the same as in number or amount: *four plus six divided by two equals five | the total debits should equal the total credits.*
■ match or rival in performance or extent: *he equalled the world record of 9.93 seconds.* ■ be equivalent to: *his work is concerned with why private property equals exploitation.*
– PHRASES (**the**) **first among equals** the person or thing having the highest status in a group. **other** (or **all**) **things being equal** provided that other factors or circumstances remain the same: *it follows that, other things being equal, the price level will rise.*
– ORIGIN late Middle English: from Latin *aequalis*, from *aequus* 'even, level, equal'.

> **USAGE** It is widely held that adjectives such as **equal** and **unique** should not be modified and that it is incorrect to say **more equal** or **very unique**, on the grounds that these are adjectives which refer to a logical or mathematical absolute. For more discussion of this question, see **usage** at **UNIQUE**.

equalitarian /ɪˌkwɒlɪˈtɛːrɪən, iː-/ ▶ **noun** another term for **EGALITARIAN**.
– DERIVATIVES **equalitarianism** noun.

equality ▶ **noun** [mass noun] the state of being equal, especially in status, rights, and opportunities: *an organization aiming to promote racial equality.*
■ Mathematics the condition of being equal in number or amount. ■ [count noun] Mathematics a symbolic expression

of the fact that two quantities are equal; an equation.
– ORIGIN late Middle English: via Old French from Latin *aequalitas*, from *aequalis* (see **EQUAL**).

Equality State informal name for **WYOMING**.

equalize (also **-ise**) ▶ **verb** [with obj.] make the same in quantity, size, or degree throughout a place or group: *the purpose is to equalize the workload among tutors.*
■ [no obj.] become equal to a specified or standard level: *cabin pressure equalized with a hiss of air.* ■ make uniform in application or effect: *Britain is required to equalize pension rights between men and women.* ■ [no obj.] level the score in a match by scoring a goal: *Morgan equalized ten minutes into the second half.*
– DERIVATIVES **equalization** noun.
– ORIGIN late 16th cent. (in the sense 'be equal to'): from **EQUAL** + **-IZE**, partly suggested by French *égaliser*.

equalizer (also **-iser**) ▶ **noun** a thing which has an equalizing effect: *education is the great equalizer.*
■ a goal that levels the score in the game. ■ N. Amer. informal a weapon, especially a gun. ■ Electronics a passive network designed to modify a frequency response, especially to compensate for distortion.

equally ▶ **adverb 1** in the same manner: *all children should be treated equally.*
■ in amounts or parts that are the same in size: *the money can be divided equally between you.*
2 to the same extent or degree: [as submodifier] *follow-up discussion is equally important.*
■ [sentence adverb] in addition and having the same importance (used to introduce a further comment on a topic): *not all who live in inner cities are poor; equally, many poor people live outside inner cities.*

> **USAGE** The construction **equally as**, as in *follow-up discussion is* ***equally as*** *important* is relatively common but is condemned on the grounds of redundancy. Either word can be used, alone, and be perfectly correct, e.g. *follow-up discussion is* ***equally*** *important* or *follow-up discussion is* ***as*** *important.*

equal opportunity ▶ **noun** [mass noun] (also **equal opportunities**) the right to be treated without discrimination, especially on the grounds of one's sex, race, or age: [as modifier] *an equal opportunity policy.*

equals sign (also **equal sign**) ▶ **noun** the symbol =.

equal temperament ▶ **noun** see **TEMPERAMENT** (sense 2).

equanimity /ˌɛkwəˈnɪmɪti, iː-/ ▶ **noun** [mass noun] mental calmness, composure, and evenness of temper, especially in a difficult situation: *she accepted both the good and the bad* ***with equanimity.***
– DERIVATIVES **equanimous** /ɪˈkwanɪməs, iː-/ adjective.
– ORIGIN early 17th cent. (also in the sense 'fairness, impartiality'): from Latin *aequanimitas*, from *aequus* 'equal' + *animus* 'mind'.

equant /ˈiːkwənt/ ▶ **noun** Astronomy, historical (in the Ptolemaic system) an imaginary circle introduced with the purpose of reconciling the planetary movements with the hypothesis of uniform circular motion.
▶ **adjective 1** Astronomy, historical relating to or denoting such an imaginary circle.
2 Geology (of a crystal or particle) having its different diameters approximately equal, so as to be roughly cubic or spherical in shape.
– ORIGIN mid 16th cent.: from Latin *aequant-* 'making equal', from the verb *aequare*.

equate /ɪˈkweɪt/ ▶ **verb** [with obj.] consider (one thing) to be the same as or equivalent to another: *customers* ***equate*** *their name* ***with*** *quality.*
■ [no obj.] (**equate to/with**) (of one thing) be the same as or equivalent to (another): *that sum equates to half a million pounds today.* ■ cause (two or more things) to be the same in quantity or value: *the level of prices will move to equate supply and demand.*
– DERIVATIVES **equatable** adjective.
– ORIGIN Middle English (in the sense 'make equal, balance'): from Latin *aequat-* 'made level or equal', from the verb *aequare*, from *aequus* (see **EQUAL**). Current senses date from the mid 19th cent.

equation /ɪˈkweɪʒ(ə)n/ ▶ **noun 1** Mathematics a statement that the values of two mathematical expressions are equal (indicated by the sign =).
2 [mass noun] the process of equating one thing with another: *the* ***equation*** *of science* ***with*** *objectivity.*
■ (**the equation**) a situation or problem in which several factors must be taken into account: *money also came into the equation.*
3 Chemistry a symbolic representation of the changes which occur in a chemical reaction, expressed in terms of the formulae of the molecules or other species involved.
– PHRASES **equation of the first** (or **second** etc.) **order** Mathematics an equation involving only the first derivative, second derivative, etc.
– ORIGIN late Middle English: from Latin *aequatio(n-)*, from *aequare* 'make equal' (see **EQUATE**).

equational ▶ **adjective** another term for **EQUATIVE**.

equation of state ▶ **noun** Chemistry an equation showing the relationship between the values of the pressure, volume, and temperature of a quantity of a particular substance.

equation of time ▶ **noun** the difference between mean solar time (as shown by clocks) and apparent solar time (indicated by sundials), which varies with the time of year.

equative /ɪˈkweɪtɪv/ ▶ **adjective** Grammar denoting a sentence or other structure in which one term is identified with another, as in *the winner is Jill.*
■ denoting a use of the verb *to be* that equates one term with another.
– DERIVATIVES **equatively** adverb.

equator /ɪˈkweɪtə/ ▶ **noun** a line notionally drawn on the earth equidistant from the poles, dividing the earth into northern and southern hemispheres and constituting the parallel of latitude 0°.
■ a corresponding line on a planet or other body. ■ Astronomy short for **CELESTIAL EQUATOR**.
– ORIGIN late Middle English: from medieval Latin *aequator*, in the phrase *circulus aequator diei et noctis* 'circle equalizing day and night', from Latin *aequare* 'make equal' (see **EQUATE**).

equatorial /ˌɛkwəˈtɔːrɪəl/ ▶ **adjective** of, at, or near the equator: *equatorial regions.*
– DERIVATIVES **equatorially** adverb.

Equatorial Guinea a small country of West Africa on the Gulf of Guinea, comprising several offshore islands and a coastal settlement between Cameroon and Gabon; pop. 426,000 (est. 1991); languages, Spanish (official), local Niger–Congo languages, pidgin; capital, Malabo (on the island of Bioko). Formerly a Spanish colony, the country became fully independent in 1968. It is the only independent Spanish-speaking state in the continent of Africa.
– DERIVATIVES **Equatorial Guinean** adjective & noun.

equatorial mount (also **equatorial mounting**) ▶ **noun** Astronomy a telescope mounting with one axis aligned to the celestial pole, which allows the movement of celestial objects to be followed by motion about this axis alone. Compare with **ALTAZIMUTH** (in sense 1).

equatorial telescope ▶ **noun** an astronomical telescope on an equatorial mount.

equerry /ɪˈkwɛri, ˈɛkwəri/ ▶ **noun** (pl. **-ies**) an officer of the British royal household who attends or assists members of the royal family.
■ historical an officer of the household of a prince or noble who had charge over the stables.
– ORIGIN early 16th cent. (formerly also as *esquiry*): from Old French *esquierie* 'company of squires, prince's stables', from Old French *esquier* 'esquire', perhaps associated with Latin *equus* 'horse'. The historical sense is apparently based on Old French *esquier d'esquierie* 'squire of stables'.

eques /ˈɛkweɪz/ singular form of **EQUITES**.

equestrian /ɪˈkwɛstrɪən, ɛ-/ ▶ **adjective** of or relating to horse riding: *his amazing equestrian skills.*
■ depicting or representing a person on horseback: *an equestrian statue.*
▶ **noun** a rider or performer on horseback.
– ORIGIN mid 17th cent. (as an adjective): from Latin *equester* 'belonging to a horseman' (from *eques* 'horseman, knight', from *equus* 'horse') + **-IAN**.

equestrianism ▶ **noun** [mass noun] the skill or sport of horse riding. As an Olympic sport it is divided into three categories: showjumping, dressage, and three-day eventing (combining showjumping, dressage, and cross-country riding).

equestrienne /ɪˌkwɛstrɪˈɛn/ ▶ **noun** a female rider or performer on horseback.
– ORIGIN mid 19th cent.: alteration of **EQUESTRIAN**, on the pattern of feminine nouns such as *Parisienne*.

equi- /ˈiːkwi, ˈɛkwi-/ ▶ **combining form** equal; equally: *equiangular* | *equidistant.*
– ORIGIN from Latin *aequi-*, from *aequus* 'equal'.

equiangular ▶ **adjective** having equal angles.

equiangular spiral ▶ **noun** Geometry a spiral such that the angle between the tangent and the radius vector is the same for all points of the spiral. Also called **LOGARITHMIC SPIRAL**.

equid /ˈɛkwɪd/ ▶ **noun** Zoology a mammal of the horse family (Equidae).
– ORIGIN late 19th cent.: from modern Latin *Equidae* (plural), from Latin *equus* 'horse'.

equidistant ▶ **adjective** at equal distances: *the line joins together all points which are* ***equidistant from*** *the two axes.*
– DERIVATIVES **equidistance** noun, **equidistantly** adverb.

equifinal /ˌɛkwɪˈfʌɪn(ə)l/ ▶ **adjective** technical having the same end or result.
– DERIVATIVES **equifinality** noun, **equifinally** adverb.

equilateral /ˌiːkwɪˈlat(ə)r(ə)l, ˌɛkwɪ-/ ▶ **adjective** having all its sides of the same length: *an equilateral triangle.*
– ORIGIN late 16th cent.: from French *équilatéral* or late Latin *aequilateralis*, from *aequilaterus* 'equal-sided' (based on Latin *latus, later-* 'side').

equilibrate /ˌiːkwɪˈlʌɪbreɪt, ɪˈkwɪlɪ-, iːˈkwɪlɪ-/ ▶ **verb** [with obj.] technical bring into or keep in equilibrium.
■ [no obj.] approach or attain a state of equilibrium.
– DERIVATIVES **equilibration** noun.
– ORIGIN mid 17th cent.: from late Latin *aequilibrat-* 'made to balance', from the verb *aequilibrare*, from *aequi-* 'equally' + *libra* 'balance'.

equilibrist /ɪˈkwɪlɪˌbrɪst, iːˈkwɪlɪ-, ˌiːkwɪˈlɪb-, ˌɛkwɪ-/ ▶ **noun** chiefly archaic an acrobat who performs balancing feats, especially a tightrope walker.
– ORIGIN mid 18th cent.: from **EQUILIBRIUM** + **-IST**.

equilibrium /ˌiːkwɪˈlɪbrɪəm, ˌɛkwɪ-/ ▶ **noun** (pl. **equilibria** /-rɪə/) [mass noun] a state in which opposing forces or influences are balanced: *the task is the maintenance of social equilibrium.*
■ a state of physical balance: *I stumbled over a rock and recovered my equilibrium.* ■ a calm state of mind: *his intensity could unsettle his equilibrium.* ■ Chemistry a state in which a process and its reverse are occurring at equal rates so that no overall change is taking place: *ice is* ***in equilibrium with*** *water.* ■ Economics a situation in which supply and demand are matched and prices stable.
– DERIVATIVES **equilibrial** adjective.
– ORIGIN early 17th cent. (in the sense 'well-balanced state of mind'): from Latin *aequilibrium*, from *aequi-* 'equal' + *libra* 'balance'.

equine /ˈiːkwʌɪn, ˈɛ-/ ▶ **adjective** of, relating to, or affecting horses or other members of the horse family: *equine infectious anaemia.*
■ resembling a horse: *her somewhat equine features.*
▶ **noun** a horse or other member of the horse family.
– ORIGIN late 18th cent.: from Latin *equinus*, from *equus* 'horse'.

equinoctial /ˌiːkwɪˈnɒkʃ(ə)l, ˌɛkwɪ-/ ▶ **adjective** happening at or near the time of an equinox.
■ of or relating to equal day and night. ■ at or near the equator.
▶ **noun** (also **equinoctial line**) another term for **CELESTIAL EQUATOR**.
– ORIGIN late Middle English (in the sense 'relating to equal periods of day and night'): via Old French from Latin *aequinoctialis*, from *aequinoctium* (see **EQUINOX**).

equinoctial point ▶ **noun** either of two points at which the ecliptic cuts the celestial equator.

equinoctial year ▶ **noun** see **YEAR** (sense 1).

equinox /ˈiːkwɪnɒks, ˌɛkwɪ-/ ▶ **noun** the time or date (twice each year) at which the sun crosses the celestial equator, when day and night are of equal length (about 22 September and 20 March).
■ another term for **EQUINOCTIAL POINT**.
– ORIGIN late Middle English: from Old French *equinoxe* or Latin *aequinoctium*, from *aequi-* 'equal' + *nox, noct-* 'night'.

equip ▶ **verb** (**equipped**, **equipping**) [with obj.] supply with the necessary items for a particular purpose: *all bedrooms are* ***equipped with*** *a colour TV* | *they* ***equipped*** *themselves* ***for*** *the campaign.*
■ prepare (someone) mentally for a particular situation or task: *I don't think he's equipped for the modern age.*
– DERIVATIVES **equipper** noun.
– ORIGIN early 16th cent.: from French *équiper*, probably from Old Norse *skipa* 'to man (a ship)', from *skip* 'ship'.

equipage /ˈɛkwɪpɪdʒ/ ▶ **noun 1** [mass noun] archaic the equipment for a particular purpose.
2 historical a carriage and horses with attendants.
– ORIGIN mid 16th cent. (denoting the crew of a ship): from French *équipage*, from *équiper* 'equip'.

equipartition /ˌiːkwɪpɑːˈtɪʃ(ə)n/ (also **equipartition of energy**) ▶ **noun** [mass noun] Physics the equal distribution of the kinetic energy of a system among its various degrees of freedom.
■ the principle that this exists for a system in thermal equilibrium.
– DERIVATIVES **equipartitioned** adjective.

equipment ▶ **noun** [mass noun] the necessary items for a particular purpose: *suppliers of office equipment.*
■ the process of supplying someone or something with such necessary items: *the construction and equipment of new harbour facilities.* ■ mental resources: *they lacked the intellectual equipment to recognize the jokes.*
– ORIGIN early 18th cent.: from French *équipement*, from *équiper* 'equip'.

equipoise /ˈɛkwɪpɔɪz, ˈiːkwɪ-/ ▶ **noun** [mass noun] balance of forces or interests: *this temporary equipoise of power.*
■ [count noun] a counterbalance or balancing force: *capital flows act as an* **equipoise to** *international imbalances in savings.*
▶ **verb** [with obj.] balance or counterbalance (something).
– ORIGIN mid 17th cent.: from **EQUI-** 'equal' + the noun **POISE**[1], replacing the phrase *equal poise*.

equipollent /ˌiːkwɪˈpɒl(ə)nt, ˌɛkwɪ-/ archaic ▶ **adjective** equal or equivalent in power, effect, or significance.
▶ **noun** a thing that has equal or equivalent power, effect, or significance.
– DERIVATIVES **equipollence** noun, **equipollency** noun.
– ORIGIN late Middle English: from Old French *equipolent*, from Latin *aequipollent-* 'of equal value', from *aequi-* 'equally' + *pollere* 'be strong'.

equipotent /ˌiːkwɪˈpəʊt(ə)nt, ˌɛkwɪ-/ ▶ **adjective** technical (chiefly of chemicals and medicines) equally powerful; having equal potencies.

equipotential ▶ **adjective** [attrib.] Physics (of a surface or line) composed of points all at the same potential.
▶ **noun** an equipotential line or surface.

equiprobable ▶ **adjective** Mathematics & Logic (of two or more things) equally likely to occur; having equal probability.
– DERIVATIVES **equiprobability** noun.

equisetum /ˌɛkwɪˈsiːtəm/ ▶ **noun** (pl. **equiseta** /-tə/ or **equisetums**) Botany a plant of a genus that comprises the horsetails.
• Genus *Equisetum*, family Equisetaceae.
– ORIGIN modern Latin, from Latin *equus* 'horse' + *saeta* 'bristle'.

equitable /ˈɛkwɪtəb(ə)l/ ▶ **adjective 1** fair and impartial: *the equitable distribution of resources.*
2 Law valid in equity as distinct from law: *the beneficiaries have an equitable interest in the property.*
– DERIVATIVES **equitability** noun, **equitableness** noun, **equitably** adverb.
– ORIGIN mid 16th cent.: from French *équitable*, from *équité* (see **EQUITY**).

equitant /ˈɛkwɪt(ə)nt/ ▶ **adjective** Botany (of a leaf) having its base folded and partly enclosing the leaf next above it, as in an iris.
– ORIGIN late 18th cent.: from Latin *equitant-* 'riding on horseback', from the verb *equitare*.

equitation /ˌɛkwɪˈteɪʃ(ə)n/ ▶ **noun** [mass noun] formal the art and practice of horsemanship and horse riding.
– ORIGIN mid 16th cent.: from French *équitation* or Latin *equitatio(n-)*, from *equitare* 'ride a horse', from *eques, equit-* 'horseman' (from *equus* 'horse').

equites /ˈɛkwɪteɪz/ ▶ **plural noun** (sing. **eques**) (in ancient Rome) a class of citizens who originally formed the cavalry of the Roman army and at a later period were a wealthy class of great political importance.
– ORIGIN Latin, plural of *eques* 'horseman'.

equity /ˈɛkwɪti/ ▶ **noun** (pl. **-ies**) [mass noun] **1** the quality of being fair and impartial: *equity of treatment.*
■ Law a branch of law that developed alongside common law in order to remedy some of its defects in fairness and justice, formerly administered in special courts. ■ (**Equity**) (in the UK, US, and several other countries) a trade union to which all professional actors must belong: [as modifier] *an Equity card.*
2 the value of the shares issued by a company: *he owns 62% of the group's equity.*
■ (**equities**) stocks and shares that carry no fixed interest.
3 the value of a mortgaged property after deduction of charges against it.
– ORIGIN Middle English: from Old French *equité*, from Latin *aequitas*, from *aequus* 'equal'.

equity of redemption ▶ **noun** [mass noun] Law the right of a mortgagor over the mortgaged property, especially the right to redeem the property on payment of the principal, interest, and costs.

equivalence class ▶ **noun** Mathematics & Logic the class of all members of a set that are in a given equivalence relation.

equivalence principle ▶ **noun** Physics a basic postulate of general relativity, stating that at any point of space-time the effects of a gravitational field cannot be experimentally distinguished from those due to an accelerated frame of reference.

equivalence relation ▶ **noun** Mathematics & Logic a relation between elements of a set which is reflexive, symmetric, and transitive. It thus defines exclusive classes whose members bear the relation to each other and not to those in other classes (e.g. 'having the same value of a measured property').

equivalent /ɪˈkwɪv(ə)l(ə)nt/ ▶ **adjective** equal in value, amount, function, meaning, etc.: *one unit is* **equivalent to** *one glass of wine.*
■ [predic.] (**equivalent to**) having the same or a similar effect as: *some regulations are equivalent to censorship.*
■ Mathematics belonging to the same equivalence class.
▶ **noun** a person or thing that is equal to or corresponds with another in value, amount, function, meaning, etc.: *the French equivalent of the Bank of England.*
■ (also **equivalent weight**) Chemistry the mass of a particular substance that can combine with or displace one gram of hydrogen or eight grams of oxygen, used in expressing combining powers, especially of elements.
– DERIVATIVES **equivalence** noun, **equivalency** noun, **equivalently** adverb.
– ORIGIN late Middle English (describing persons who were equal in power or rank): via Old French from late Latin *aequivalent-* 'being of equal worth', from the verb *aequivalere*, from *aequi-* 'equally' + *valere* 'be worth'.

equivocal /ɪˈkwɪvək(ə)l/ ▶ **adjective** open to more than one interpretation; ambiguous: *the equivocal nature of her remarks.*
■ (of a person) using ambiguous or evasive language: *politicians who are equivocal about racism.* ■ uncertain or questionable in nature: *the results of the investigation were equivocal.*
– DERIVATIVES **equivocality** noun, **equivocally** adverb, **equivocalness** noun.
– ORIGIN mid 16th cent.: from late Latin *aequivocus*, from Latin *aequus* 'equally' + *vocare* 'to call'.

equivocate /ɪˈkwɪvəkeɪt/ ▶ **verb** [no obj.] use ambiguous language so as to conceal the truth or avoid committing oneself: [with direct speech] *'Not that we are aware of,' she equivocated.*
– DERIVATIVES **equivocation** noun, **equivocator** noun, **equivocatory** adjective.
– ORIGIN late Middle English (in the sense 'use a word in more than one sense'): from late Latin *aequivocat-* 'called by the same name', from the verb *aequivocare*, from *aequivocus* (see **EQUIVOCAL**).

equivoque /ˈiːkwɪvəʊk, ˈɛkwɪ-/ (also **equivoke**) ▶ **noun** an expression capable of having more than one meaning; a pun.
■ [mass noun] the fact of having more than one meaning or possible interpretation; ambiguity.
– ORIGIN late Middle English (as an adjective in the sense 'equivocal'): from Old French *equivoque* or late Latin *aequivocus* (see **EQUIVOCAL**).

Equuleus /ɛˈkwʊlɪəs/ Astronomy a small northern constellation (the Foal or Little Horse), perhaps representing the brother of Pegasus. It has no bright stars.
■ [as genitive **Equulei** /ɛˈkwʊlɪʌɪ/] used with preceding letter or numeral to designate a star in this constellation: *the star Delta Equulei.*
– ORIGIN Latin.

ER ▶ **abbreviation for** ■ N. Amer. emergency room. ■ King Edward. [ORIGIN: from Latin *Edwardus Rex.*] ■ Queen Elizabeth. [ORIGIN: from Latin *Elizabetha Regina.*]

Er ▶ **symbol for** the chemical element erbium.

er ▶ **exclamation** expressing hesitation: *'Would you like some tea?' 'Er ... yes ... thank you.'*
– ORIGIN natural utterance: first recorded in English in the mid 19th cent.

-er[1] ▶ **suffix 1** denoting a person, animal, or thing that performs a specified action or activity: *farmer | sprinkler.*
2 denoting a person or thing that has a specified attribute or form: *foreigner | two-wheeler.*
3 denoting a person concerned with a specified thing or subject: *milliner | philosopher.*
4 denoting a person belonging to a specified place or group: *city-dweller | New Yorker.*
– ORIGIN Old English *-ere*, of Germanic origin.

-er[2] ▶ **suffix** forming the comparative of adjectives (as in *bigger*) and adverbs (as in *faster*).
– ORIGIN Old English suffix *-ra* (adjectival), *-or* (adverbial), of Germanic origin.

-er[3] ▶ **suffix** forming nouns used informally, usually by distortion of the root word: *footer | rugger.*
– ORIGIN probably an extended use of **-ER**[1]; originally Rugby School slang, later adopted at Oxford University, then extended into general use.

-er[4] ▶ **suffix** forming frequentative verbs such as *glimmer, patter.*
– ORIGIN Old English *-erian, -rian*, of Germanic origin.

-er[5] ▶ **suffix** forming nouns: **1** such as *sampler.* Compare with **-AR**[1]. [ORIGIN: ending corresponding to Latin *-aris.*]
■ such as *butler, danger.* [ORIGIN: ending corresponding to Latin *-arius, -arium.*] ■ such as *border.* [ORIGIN: ending corresponding (via Old French *-eure*) to Latin *-atura.*] ■ such as *laver.* See **LAVER**[2]. [ORIGIN: ending corresponding (via Old French *-eor*) to Latin *-atorium.*]
2 equivalent to **-OR**[1].
– ORIGIN via Old French or Anglo-Norman French (see above).

-er[6] ▶ **suffix** chiefly Law (forming nouns) denoting verbal action or a document effecting such action: *disclaimer | misnomer.*
– ORIGIN from Anglo-Norman French (infinitive ending).

era /ˈɪərə/ ▶ **noun** a long and distinct period of history with a particular feature or characteristic: *his death marked the end of an era | the era of glasnost.*
■ a system of chronology dating from a particular noteworthy event: *the dawn of the Christian era.* ■ Geology a major division of time that is a subdivision of an aeon and is itself subdivided into periods: *the Mesozoic era.* ■ archaic a date or event marking the beginning of a new and distinct period of time.
– ORIGIN mid 17th cent.: from late Latin *aera*, denoting a number used as a basis of reckoning, an epoch from which time is reckoned, plural of *aes, aer-* 'money, counter'.

eradicate /ɪˈradɪkeɪt/ ▶ **verb** [with obj.] destroy completely; put an end to: *this disease has been eradicated from the world.*
– DERIVATIVES **eradicable** adjective, **eradicant** noun, **eradication** noun, **eradicator** noun.
– ORIGIN late Middle English (in the sense 'pull up by the roots'): from Latin *eradicat-* 'torn up by the roots', from the verb *eradicare*, from *e-* (variant of *ex-*) 'out' + *radix, radic-* 'root'.

eradicated ▶ **adjective** [postpositive] Heraldry (of a tree or plant) depicted with the roots exposed.

erase /ɪˈreɪz/ ▶ **verb** [with obj.] rub out or remove (writing or marks): *graffiti had been erased from the wall.*
■ remove all traces of (a thought, feeling, or memory): *the magic of the landscape erased all else from her mind.* ■ destroy or obliterate (someone or something) so as to leave no trace: *over twenty years the last vestiges of a rural economy were erased.* ■ remove recorded material from (a magnetic tape or medium); delete (data) from a computer's memory.
– DERIVATIVES **erasable** adjective, **erasure** noun.
– ORIGIN late 16th cent. (originally as a heraldic term meaning 'represent the head or limb of an animal with a jagged edge'): from Latin *eras-* 'scraped away', from the verb *eradere*, from *e-* (variant of *ex-*) 'out' + *radere* 'scrape'.

erased ▶ **adjective** [postpositive] Heraldry (of a head or limb) depicted as cut off in a jagged line.

eraser ▶ noun an object, typically a piece of soft rubber or plastic, used to rub out something written.

Erasmus /ɪˈrazməs/, Desiderius (*c.*1469–1536), Dutch humanist and scholar; Dutch name *Gerhard Gerhards*. He was the foremost Renaissance scholar of northern Europe, paving the way for the Reformation with his satires on the Church, including the *Colloquia Familiaria* (1518). However, he opposed the violence of the Reformation and condemned Luther in *De Libero Arbitrio* (1523).

Erastianism /ɪˈrastɪəˌnɪz(ə)m/ ▶ noun [mass noun] the doctrine that the state should have supremacy over the Church in ecclesiastical matters (wrongly attributed to Erastus).
– DERIVATIVES **Erastian** noun & adjective.

Erastus /ɪˈrastəs/ (1524–83), Swiss theologian and physician; Swiss name *Thomas Lieber*; also *Liebler* or *Lüber*. Professor of medicine at Heidelberg from 1558, he opposed the imposition of a Calvinistic system of church government in the city. The doctrine of Erastianism was later wrongly attributed to him.

Erato /ˈɛrətəʊ/ Greek & Roman Mythology the Muse of lyric poetry and hymns.
– ORIGIN Greek, literally 'lovely'.

Eratosthenes /ˌɛrəˈtɒsθəniːz/ (*c.*275–194 BC), Greek scholar, geographer, and astronomer. The first systematic geographer of antiquity, he accurately calculated the circumference of the earth and attempted (less successfully) to determine the size and distance of the sun and of the moon.

erbium /ˈəːbɪəm/ ▶ noun [mass noun] the chemical element of atomic number 68, a soft silvery-white metal of the lanthanide series. (Symbol: **Er**)
– ORIGIN mid 19th cent.: modern Latin, from (*Ytt*)*erb*(*y*), in Sweden, where it was first found. Compare with **YTTERBIUM**.

ere /ɛː/ ▶ preposition & conjunction poetic/literary or archaic before (in time): [as prep.] *we hope you will return ere long* | [as conjunction] *I was driven for some half mile ere we stopped.*
– ORIGIN Old English *ǣr*, of Germanic origin; related to Dutch *eer* and German *eher*.

Erebus /ˈɛrəbəs/ Greek Mythology the primeval god of darkness, son of Chaos.

Erebus, Mount a volcanic peak on Ross Island, Antarctica. Rising to 3,794 m (12,452 ft), it is the world's most southerly active volcano.
– ORIGIN named after the *Erebus*, the ship of Sir James Ross's expedition to the Antarctic.

Erech /ˈɛrɛk/ biblical name for **URUK**.

Erechtheum /ɪˈrɛkθɪəm/ a marble temple of the Ionic order built on the Acropolis in Athens *c.*421–406 BC, with shrines to Athene, Poseidon, and Erechtheus, a legendary king of Athens.

erect ▶ adjective rigidly upright or straight: *she stood erect with her arms by her sides.*
■ (of the penis, clitoris, or nipples) enlarged and rigid, especially in sexual excitement. ■ (of hair) standing up from the skin; bristling:
▶ verb [with obj.] construct (a building, wall, or other upright structure): *the guest house was erected in the eighteenth century.*
■ put into position and set upright (a barrier, statue, or other object): *the police had erected roadblocks.* ■ create or establish (a theory or system): *the party that erected the welfare state.*
– DERIVATIVES **erectable** adjective, **erectly** adverb, **erectness** noun.
– ORIGIN late Middle English: from Latin *erect-* 'set up', from the verb *erigere*, from *e-* (variant of *ex-*) 'out' + *regere* 'to direct'.

erectile /ɪˈrɛktʌɪl/ ▶ adjective able to become erect: *erectile spines.*
■ denoting tissues which are capable of becoming of temporarily engorged with blood, particularly those of the penis or other sexual organs. ■ relating to this process: *men with erectile dysfunction.*
– ORIGIN mid 19th cent.: from French *érectile*, from Latin *erigere* 'set up' (see **ERECT**).

erection ▶ noun **1** [mass noun] the action of erecting a structure or object: *fees will be levied for the erection of monuments.*
■ [count noun] a building or other upright structure.
2 an enlarged and rigid state of the penis, typically in sexual excitement.

erector ▶ noun a person or thing that erects something.
■ a muscle which maintains an erect state of a part of the body or an erect posture of the body. ■ (**Erector**) N. Amer. trademark a construction toy consisting of components for making model buildings and vehicles.

E-region ▶ noun another term for **E-LAYER**.

eremite /ˈɛrɪmʌɪt/ ▶ noun a Christian hermit or recluse.
– DERIVATIVES **eremitic** adjective, **eremitical** adjective.
– ORIGIN Middle English: from Old French *eremite* from late Latin *eremita* (see **HERMIT**).

erethism /ˈɛrɪθɪz(ə)m/ ▶ noun [mass noun] **1** excessive sensitivity or rapid reaction to stimulation of a part of the body, especially the sexual organs.
2 a state of abnormal mental excitement or irritation.
– ORIGIN early 19th cent.: from French *éréthisme*, from Greek *erethismos*, from *erethizein* 'irritate'.

Erevan another name for **YEREVAN**.

erewhile /ɛːˈwʌɪl/ ▶ adverb archaic a while before; some time ago.
– ORIGIN Middle English: from **ERE** + **WHILE**.

erf /əːf/ ▶ noun (pl. **erfs** or **erven** /ˈəːv(ə)n/) S. African a plot of land.
– ORIGIN Dutch, originally in the sense 'inheritance'.

Erfurt /ˈɛːfʊət, German ˈɛrfʊrt/ an industrial city in central Germany, capital of Thuringia; pop. 204,910 (1991).

erg¹ /əːg/ ▶ noun Physics a unit of work or energy, equal to the work done by a force of one dyne when its point of application moves one centimetre in the direction of action of the force.
– ORIGIN late 19th cent.: from Greek *ergon* 'work'.

erg² /əːg/ ▶ noun (pl. **ergs** or **areg** /ˈɑːrɛg/) an area of shifting sand dunes in the Sahara.
– ORIGIN late 19th cent.: from French, from Arabic *'irk, 'erg.*

ergative /ˈəːgətɪv/ Grammar ▶ adjective relating to or denoting a case of nouns (in some languages, e.g. Basque and Eskimo) that identifies the doer of an action as the object rather than the subject of a verb.
■ (of a language) possessing this case. ■ (in English) denoting verbs which can be used both transitively and intransitively to describe the same action, with the object in the former case being the subject in the latter, as in *I boiled the kettle* and *the kettle boiled*. Compare with **INCHOATIVE**.
▶ noun an ergative word.
■ (**the ergative**) the ergative case.
– DERIVATIVES **ergativity** noun.
– ORIGIN 1950s: from Greek *ergatēs* 'worker' (from *ergon* 'work') + **-IVE**.

ergo /ˈəːgəʊ/ ▶ adverb [sentence adverb] therefore: *she was the sole beneficiary of the will, ergo the prime suspect.*
– ORIGIN Latin.

ergocalciferol /ˌəːgə(ʊ)kalˈsɪfərɒl/ ▶ noun Biochemistry another term for **CALCIFEROL**, ***vitamin*** D_2.
– ORIGIN 1950s: blend of **ERGOT** and **CALCIFEROL**.

ergodic /əːˈgɒdɪk/ ▶ adjective Mathematics relating to or denoting systems or processes with the property that, given sufficient time, they include or impinge on all points in a given space and can be represented statistically by a reasonably large selection of points.
– DERIVATIVES **ergodicity** noun.
– ORIGIN early 20th cent.: from German *ergoden*, from Greek *ergon* 'work' + *hodos* 'way' + **-IC**.

ergometer /əːˈgɒmɪtə/ ▶ noun an apparatus which measures work or energy expended during a period of physical exercise.

ergometrine /ˌəːgə(ʊ)ˈmɛtriːn/ ▶ noun [mass noun] Chemistry an alkaloid present in ergot. An amide of lysergic acid, it has oxytocic activity and is given to control bleeding after childbirth.
– ORIGIN 1930s: from **ERGOT** + Greek *mētra* 'womb' + **-INE**⁴.

ergonomics /ˌəːgəˈnɒmɪks/ ▶ plural noun [treated as sing.] the study of people's efficiency in their working environment.
– DERIVATIVES **ergonomic** adjective, **ergonomist** noun.
– ORIGIN 1950s: from Greek *ergon* 'work', on the pattern of *economics*.

ergosphere /ˈəːgəʊsfɪə/ ▶ noun Astronomy a postulated region round a black hole, from which energy could escape.

ergosterol /əːˈgɒstərɒl/ ▶ noun [mass noun] Biochemistry a compound present in ergot and many other fungi. A steroid alcohol, it is converted to vitamin D_2 when irradiated with ultraviolet light.
– ORIGIN early 20th cent.: from **ERGOT**, on the pattern of *cholesterol*.

ergot /ˈəːgɒt/ ▶ noun **1** [mass noun] a fungal disease of rye and other cereals in which black elongated fruiting bodies grow in the ears of the cereal. Eating contaminated food can result in ergotism.
• The fungus is *Claviceps purpurea*, subdivision Ascomycotina.
■ [count noun] a fruiting body of this fungus. ■ these fruiting bodies used as a source of certain medicinal alkaloids, especially for inducing uterine contractions or controlling post-partum bleeding.
2 a small horny protuberance on the back of each of a horse's fetlocks.
– ORIGIN late 17th cent.: from French, from Old French *argot* 'cock's spur' (because of the appearance produced by the disease).

ergotamine /əːˈgɒtəmiːn/ ▶ noun [mass noun] Medicine a compound present in some kinds of ergot. An alkaloid, it causes constriction of blood vessels and is used in the treatment of migraine.

ergotism /ˈəːgətɪz(ə)m/ ▶ noun [mass noun] poisoning produced by eating food affected by ergot, typically resulting in headache, vomiting, diarrhoea, and gangrene of the fingers and toes.

erhu /əːˈhuː/ (also **erh hu**) ▶ noun a Chinese two-stringed musical instrument held in the lap and played with a bow.
– ORIGIN early 20th cent.: from Chinese *èr* 'two' + *hú* 'bowed instrument'.

erica /ˈɛrɪkə/ ▶ noun a plant of the genus *Erica* (family Ericaceae), especially (in gardening) heather.
– ORIGIN modern Latin, from Greek *ereikē*.

ericaceous /ˌɛrɪˈkeɪʃəs/ ▶ adjective Botany of, relating to, or denoting plants of the heather family (Ericaceae).
■ (of compost) suitable for heathers and other lime-hating plants.
– ORIGIN mid 19th cent.: from modern Latin *Ericaceae* (plural), from the genus name *Erica* (see **ERICA**).

Ericsson¹ /ˈɛrɪks(ə)n/, John (1803–89), Swedish engineer whose inventions included a steam railway locomotive to rival Stephenson's *Rocket*, and the marine screw propeller (1836).

Ericsson² /ˈɛrɪks(ə)n/ (also **Ericson** or **Eriksson**), Leif, Norse explorer, son of Eric the Red. He sailed westward from Greenland (*c.*1000) and reputedly discovered land (variously identified as Labrador, Newfoundland, or New England), which he named Vinland because of the vines he claimed to have found growing there.

Eric the Red (*c.*940–*c.*1010), Norse explorer. He left Iceland in 982 in search of land to the west, exploring Greenland and establishing a Norse settlement there in 986.

Eridanus /ɛˈrɪdənəs/ Astronomy a long straggling southern constellation (the River), said to represent the river into which Phaethon fell when struck by Zeus' thunderbolt.
■ [as genitive **Eridani** /ɛˈrɪdəniː/] used with preceding letter or numeral to designate a star in this constellation: *the star Phi Eridani.*
– ORIGIN Latin.

Erie, Lake /ˈɪəri/ one of the five Great Lakes of North America, situated on the border between Canada and the US. It is linked to Lake Huron by the Detroit River and to Lake Ontario by the Welland Ship Canal and the Niagara River, which is its only natural outlet.

erigeron /ɪˈrɪdʒərɒn, ɛ-/ ▶ noun a widely distributed herbaceous plant of the daisy family, which is sometimes cultivated as an ornamental.
• Genus *Erigeron*, family Compositae.
– ORIGIN modern Latin, from Latin, 'groundsel' (the original sense in English), from Greek *ērigerōn*, from *ēri* 'early' + *gerōn* 'old man' (because the plant flowers early in the year, and some species bear grey down).

Eriksson variant spelling of **ERICSSON**².

Erin /ˈɛrɪn, ˈɪərɪn/ ▶ noun archaic or poetic/literary name for Ireland.

Erinys /ɛˈrɪnɪs/ ▶ noun (pl. **Erinyes** /ɛˈrɪniːz/) (in Greek mythology) a Fury.

b **but** | d **dog** | f **few** | g **get** | h **he** | j **yes** | k **cat** | l **leg** | m **man** | n **no** | p **pen** | r **red** | s **sit** | t **top** | v **voice** | w **we** | z **zoo** | ʃ **she** | ʒ **decision** | θ **thin** | ð **this** | ŋ **ring** | x **loch** | tʃ **chip** | dʒ **jar**

eristic /ɛˈrɪstɪk/ formal ▶ **adjective** of or characterized by debate or argument.
■(of an argument or arguer) aiming at winning rather than at reaching the truth.
▶ **noun** a person given to debate or argument.
■[mass noun] the art or practice or debate or argument.
– DERIVATIVES **eristically** adverb.
– ORIGIN mid 17th cent.: from Greek *eristikos*, from *erizein* 'to wrangle', from *eris* 'strife'.

Eritrea /ˌɛrɪˈtreɪə/ an independent state in NE Africa, on the Red Sea; pop. 3,500,000 (est. 1991); language, Tigre and Cushitic languages; capital, Asmara.

It was an Italian colony from 1890 to 1952, when it became part of Ethiopia. After a long guerrilla war it became internally self-governing in 1991 and fully independent in 1993.

– DERIVATIVES **Eritrean** adjective & noun.
– ORIGIN from Italian, from Latin *Mare Erythraeum* 'the Red Sea'.

erk /əːk/ ▶ **noun** Brit. informal a male member of the RAF of the lowest rank.
▶ **exclamation** expressing panic or dismay: *Erk! What's that?*
– ORIGIN 1920s: of unknown origin.

Erlanger /ˈəːlaŋə/, Joseph (1874–1965), American physiologist. Collaborating with Herbert Gasser, he showed that the velocity of a nerve impulse is proportional to the diameter of the fibre. Nobel Prize for Physiology or Medicine (1944, shared with Gasser).

Erlenmeyer flask /ˈəːlənˌmʌɪə/ ▶ **noun** a conical flat-bottomed laboratory flask with a narrow neck.
– ORIGIN late 19th cent.: named after Emil *Erlenmeyer* (1825–1909), German chemist.

erl-king /ˈəːlkɪŋ/ ▶ **noun** (in Germanic mythology) a bearded giant or goblin believed to lure little children to the land of death.
– ORIGIN late 18th cent.: from German *Erlkönig* 'alder-king', a mistranslation of Danish *ellerkonge* 'king of the elves'.

ERM ▶ **abbreviation for** Exchange Rate Mechanism.

ermine /ˈəːmɪn/ ▶ **noun** (pl. same or **ermines**) **1** a stoat, especially when in its white winter coat.
■[mass noun] the white fur of the stoat, used for trimming garments, especially the ceremonial robes of judges or peers. ■ [mass noun] Heraldry fur represented as black spots on a white ground, as a heraldic tincture.
2 (also **ermine moth**) a stout-bodied moth that has cream or white wings with black spots, and a very hairy caterpillar.
● Genus *Spilosoma*, family Arctiidae: several species.
– DERIVATIVES **ermined** adjective.
– ORIGIN Middle English: from Old French *hermine*, probably from medieval Latin (*mus*) *Armenius* 'Armenian (mouse)'.

ermines /ˈəːmɪnz/ ▶ **noun** [mass noun] Heraldry fur resembling ermine but with white spots on a black ground.
– ORIGIN mid 16th cent.: perhaps from Old French *hermines*, plural of *herminet*, diminutive of *hermine* 'ermine'.

erminois /ˌəːmɪˈnɔɪz/ ▶ **noun** [mass noun] Heraldry fur resembling ermine but with black spots on a gold ground.
– ORIGIN mid 16th cent.: from Old French, from *hermine* 'ermine'.

-ern ▶ **suffix** forming adjectives such as *northern*.
– ORIGIN Old English *-erne*, of Germanic origin.

erne /əːn/ ▶ **noun** poetic/literary the sea eagle.
– ORIGIN Old English *earn* 'eagle', of Germanic origin; related to Dutch *arend*.

Ernie /ˈəːni/ ▶ **noun** (in the UK) the computer that randomly selects the prizewinning numbers of Premium Bonds.
– ORIGIN 1950s: acronym from *electronic random number indicator equipment*.

Ernst /əːnst, ɛːnst/, Max (1891–1976), German artist. He was a leader of the Dada movement and developed the techniques of collage, photomontage, and frottage. He is probably best known for surrealist paintings such as *L'Eléphant de Célèbes* (1921).

erode /ɪˈrəʊd/ ▶ **verb** [with obj.] (often **be eroded**) (of wind, water, or other natural agents) gradually wear away (soil, rock, or land): *the cliffs on this coast have been eroded by the sea.*
■[no obj.] (of soil, rock, or land) be gradually worn away by such natural agents. ■ figurative gradually destroy or be gradually destroyed: [with obj.] *this humiliation has eroded what confidence Jean has* | [no obj.] *profit margins are eroding.* ■ Medicine (of a disease) gradually destroy (bodily tissue).
– DERIVATIVES **erodible** adjective.
– ORIGIN early 17th cent.: from French *éroder* or Latin *erodere*, from *e-* (variant of *ex-*) 'out, away' + *rodere* 'gnaw'.

erogenous /ɪˈrɒdʒɪnəs, ɛ-/ ▶ **adjective** (of a part of the body) sensitive to sexual stimulation: *erogenous zones.*
– ORIGIN late 19th cent.: from **EROS** + **-GENOUS**.

Eros /ˈɪərɒs/ **1** Greek Mythology the god of love, son of Aphrodite. Roman equivalent **CUPID**.
■[mass noun] sexual love or desire. ■ [mass noun] (in Freudian theory) the life instinct. Often contrasted with **THANATOS**. ■ [mass noun] (in Jungian psychology) the principle of personal relatedness in human activities, associated with the anima. Often contrasted with **LOGOS**.
2 Astronomy asteroid 433, discovered in 1898, which comes at times nearer to the earth than any celestial body except the moon.
– ORIGIN Latin, from Greek, literally 'sexual love'.

erosion /ɪˈrəʊʒ(ə)n/ ▶ **noun** [mass noun] the process of eroding or being eroded by wind, water, or other natural agents: *the problem of soil erosion.*
■figurative the gradual destruction or diminution of something: *the erosion of support for the party.* ■ Medicine the gradual destruction of tissue or tooth enamel by physical or chemical action. ■ [count noun] Medicine a place where surface tissue has been gradually destroyed: *patients with gastric erosions.*
– DERIVATIVES **erosional** adjective, **erosive** adjective.
– ORIGIN mid 16th cent.: via French from Latin *erosio(n-)*, from *erodere* 'wear or gnaw away' (see **ERODE**).

erotic /ɪˈrɒtɪk/ ▶ **adjective** of, relating to, or tending to arouse sexual desire or excitement: *Mapplethorpe's photographs are profoundly erotic.*
– DERIVATIVES **erotically** adverb.
– ORIGIN mid 17th cent.: from French *érotique*, from Greek *erōtikos*, from *erōs*, *erōt-* 'sexual love'.

erotica ▶ **noun** [mass noun] literature or art intended to arouse sexual desire.
– ORIGIN mid 19th cent.: from Greek *erōtika*, neuter plural of *erōtikos* (see **EROTIC**).

eroticism ▶ **noun** [mass noun] the quality or character or being erotic: *a disturbing blend of violence and eroticism.*
■sexual desire or excitement.

eroticize (also **-ise**) ▶ **verb** [with obj.] give (something or someone) erotic qualities: *we will explore why certain symbols and body shapes are eroticized.*
– DERIVATIVES **eroticization** noun.

erotism /ˈɛrətɪz(ə)m/ ▶ **noun** [mass noun] sexual desire or excitement; eroticism.
– ORIGIN mid 19th cent.: from Greek *erōs*, *erōt-* 'sexual love' + **-ISM**.

eroto- /ɪˈrɒtəʊ/ ▶ **combining form** relating to eroticism: *erotomania.*
– ORIGIN from Greek *erōs*, *erōt-* 'sexual love'.

erotogenic /ɪˌrɒtəˈdʒɛnɪk/ (also **erotogenous** /ˌɛrəˈtɒdʒɪnəs/) ▶ **adjective** another term for **EROGENOUS**.

erotology /ˌɛrəˈtɒlədʒi/ ▶ **noun** [mass noun] the study of sexual love and behaviour.

erotomania /ɪˌrɒtə(ʊ)ˈmeɪnɪə/ ▶ **noun** [mass noun] excessive sexual desire.
■Psychiatry a delusion in which a person (typically a woman) believes that another person (typically of higher social status) is in love with them.
– DERIVATIVES **erotomaniac** noun.

err /əː/ ▶ **verb** [no obj.] formal be mistaken or incorrect; make a mistake: *the judge had **erred in** ruling that the evidence was inadmissible.*
■[often as adj. **erring**] sin; do wrong: *he had been as solicitous as an erring husband.*
– PHRASES **err on the right side** act so that the least harmful of possible mistakes or errors is the most likely to occur. **err on the side of** display more rather than less of (a specified quality) in one's actions: *it is better to err on the side of caution.* **to err is human, to forgive divine** proverb it is human nature to make mistakes oneself while finding it hard to forgive others.
– ORIGIN Middle English (in the sense 'wander, go astray'): from Old French *errer*, from Latin *errare* 'to stray'.

errand ▶ **noun** a short journey undertaken in order to deliver or collect something, especially on someone else's behalf: *she asked Tim to **run an errand** for her.*
■archaic the purpose or object of such a journey: *she knew that if she stated her errand she would not be able to see him.*
– PHRASES **errand of mercy** a journey or mission carried out to help someone in difficulty or danger.
– ORIGIN Old English *ǣrende* 'message, mission', of Germanic origin; related to Old High German *ārunti*, and obscurely to Swedish *ärende* and Danish *ærinde*.

errand boy ▶ **noun** dated, chiefly Brit. a boy employed in a shop or office to make deliveries and run other errands.

errant /ˈɛr(ə)nt/ ▶ **adjective 1** [attrib.] chiefly formal or humorous erring or straying from the accepted course or standards: *he could never forgive his daughter's errant ways.*
■Zoology (of a polychaete worm) of a predatory kind that moves about actively and is not confined to a tube or burrow.
2 [often postpositive] archaic or poetic/literary travelling in search of adventure: *that same lady errant.* See also **KNIGHT ERRANT**.
– DERIVATIVES **errancy** noun (in sense 1), **errantry** noun (in sense 2).
– ORIGIN Middle English (in sense 2): sense 1 from Latin *errant-* 'erring', from the verb *errare*; sense 2 from Old French *errant* 'travelling', present participle of *errer*, from late Latin *iterare* 'go on a journey', from *iter* 'journey'. Compare with **ARRANT**.

erratic /ɪˈratɪk/ ▶ **adjective** not even or regular in pattern or movement; unpredictable: *her breathing was erratic.*
▶ **noun** (also **erratic block** or **boulder**) Geology a rock or boulder that differs from the surrounding rock and is believed to have been brought from a distance by glacial action.
– DERIVATIVES **erratically** adverb, **erraticism** noun.
– ORIGIN late Middle English: from Old French *erratique*, from Latin *erraticus*, from *errare* 'to stray, err'.

erratum /ɛˈrɑːtəm, -ˈreɪt-/ ▶ **noun** (pl. **errata**) an error in printing or writing.
■(**errata**) a list of corrected errors appended to a book or published in a subsequent issue of a journal.
– ORIGIN mid 16th cent.: from Latin, 'error', neuter past participle of *errare* 'err'.

Er Rif /ɛː ˈrɪf/ another name for **RIF MOUNTAINS**.

erroneous /ɪˈrəʊnɪəs, ɛ-/ ▶ **adjective** wrong; incorrect: *employers sometimes make erroneous assumptions.*
– DERIVATIVES **erroneously** adverb, **erroneousness** noun.
– ORIGIN late Middle English: from Latin *erroneus* (from *erro(n-)* 'vagabond', from *errare* 'to stray, err') + **-OUS**.

error ▶ **noun** a mistake: *spelling errors* | *an error of judgement.*
■[mass noun] the state or condition of being wrong in conduct or judgement: *goods dispatched to your branch **in error*** | *the crash was caused by human error.* ■ [mass noun] technical a measure of the estimated difference between the observed or calculated value of a quantity and its true value.
– PHRASES **see the error of one's ways** realize or acknowledge one's wrongdoing.
– DERIVATIVES **errorless** adjective.
– ORIGIN Middle English: via Old French from Latin *error*, from *errare* 'to stray, err'.

error bar ▶ **noun** Mathematics a line through a point on a graph, parallel to one of the axes, which represents the uncertainty or error of the corresponding coordinate of the point.

error correction ▶ **noun** [mass noun] Computing the automatic correction of errors that arise from the incorrect transmission of digital data.

error message ▶ **noun** Computing a message displayed on a monitor screen or printout, indicating that an incorrect instruction has been given, or that there is an error resulting from faulty software or hardware.

-ers ▶ **suffix** forming colloquial nouns and adjectives such as *Twickers* (for *Twickenham*), *brekkers* (for *breakfast*), *preggers* (for *pregnant*), etc.
– ORIGIN extension of **-ER**.

ersatz /ˈəːsats, ˈɛː-/ ▶ **adjective** (of a product) made or used as a substitute, typically an inferior one, for something else: *ersatz coffee*.
■ not real or genuine: *ersatz emotion*.
– ORIGIN late 19th cent.: from German, literally 'replacement'.

Erse /əːs/ ▶ **noun** [mass noun] the Scottish or Irish Gaelic language.
– ORIGIN early Scots form of **IRISH**.

erst /əːst/ ▶ **adverb** archaic long ago; formerly: *the friends whom erst you knew*.
– ORIGIN Old English *ǣrest*, superlative of *ǣr* (see **ERE**).

erstwhile ▶ **adjective** [attrib.] former: *the erstwhile president of the company*.
▶ **adverb** archaic formerly: *Mary Anderson, erstwhile the queen of America's stage*.

Erté /ˈɛːteɪ/ (1892–1990), Russian-born French fashion designer and illustrator; born *Romain de Tirtoff*. During the First World War his garments became internationally famous through his decorative magazine illustrations, and in the 1920s he became a noted art deco designer.

Ertebølle /ˈɛːtə,bəːlə/ ▶ **noun** [usu. as modifier] Archaeology a late Mesolithic culture in the western Baltic (4th millennium BC), the final phases of which show Neolithic influence in the form of permanent coastal fishing and collecting sites and the use of skin boats.
– ORIGIN named after *Ertebølle* in Jutland, Denmark.

erubescent /,ɛrʊˈbɛs(ə)nt/ ▶ **adjective** rare reddening; blushing.
– ORIGIN mid 18th cent.: from Latin *erubescent-* 'blushing', from the verb *erubescere*, from *e-* (variant of *ex-*) 'out' + *rubescere* 'redden' (from *rubere* 'be red').

erucic acid /ɪˈruːsɪk/ ▶ **noun** [mass noun] Chemistry a solid compound present in mustard and rape seeds.
● An unsaturated fatty acid; chem. formula: $C_{21}H_{41}COOH$.
– ORIGIN mid 19th cent.: *erucic* from Latin *eruca* 'rocket' (denoting the plant) + **-IC**.

eructation /,iːrʌkˈteɪʃ(ə)n, ɪ-, ɛ-/ ▶ **noun** formal a belch.
– ORIGIN late Middle English: from Latin *eructatio(n-)*, from the verb *eructare*, from *e-* (variant of *ex-*) 'out' + *ructare* 'belch'.

erudite /ˈɛrʊdʌɪt/ ▶ **adjective** having or showing great knowledge or learning.
– DERIVATIVES **eruditely** adverb, **erudition** noun.
– ORIGIN late Middle English: from Latin *eruditus*, past participle of *erudire* 'instruct, train' (based on *rudis* 'rude, untrained').

erupt ▶ **verb** [no obj.] (of a volcano) become active and eject lava, ash, and gases: *Mount Pinatubo began erupting in June*.
■ be ejected from an active volcano: *hot lava erupted from the crust*. ■ (of an object) explode with fire and noise resembling an active volcano: *smoke bombs erupted everywhere*. ■ break out or burst forth suddenly and dramatically: *fierce fighting erupted between the army and guerrillas | noise erupted from the drawing room*. ■ give vent to anger, enthusiasm, amusement, or other feelings in a sudden and noisy way: *the soldiers erupted in fits of laughter*. ■ (of a spot, rash, or other prominent mark) suddenly appear on the skin. ■ (of the skin) suddenly develop such a spot, rash, or mark. ■ (of a tooth) break through the gums during normal development.
– ORIGIN mid 17th cent.: from Latin *erupt-* 'broken out', from the verb *erumpere*, from *e-* (variant of *ex-*) 'out' + *rumpere* 'burst out, break'.

eruption ▶ **noun** an act or instance or erupting: *the eruption of Vesuvius* | [mass noun] *magma is stored in crustal reservoirs before eruption*.
■ a sudden outpouring of a particular substance from somewhere: *successive eruptions of lava from volcanic cones*. ■ a sudden outbreak of something, typically something unwelcome or noisy: *a sudden eruption of street violence*. ■ a spot, rash, or other prominent and reddish mark appearing suddenly on the skin.
– ORIGIN late Middle English: from Old French, or from Latin *eruptio(n-)*, from the verb *erumpere* (see **ERUPT**).

eruptive ▶ **adjective** of, relating to, or formed by volcanic activity: *a history of the eruptive activity in an area*.
■ producing or characterized by eruptions: *an acute eruptive disease*.

eruv /ˈɛrʊv/ ▶ **noun** (pl. usu. **eruvim** /ˈɛrʊvɪm/) Judaism an urban area enclosed by a wire boundary which symbolically extends the private domain of Jewish households into public areas, permitting activities within it that are normally forbidden in public on the Sabbath.
– ORIGIN from Hebrew *'ērūḇ*, from a base meaning 'mixture'.

-ery (also **-ry**) ▶ **suffix** forming nouns: **1** denoting a class or kind: *confectionery | greenery*.
2 denoting an occupation, a state, a condition, or behaviour: *archery | bravery | slavery*.
■ with depreciatory reference: *knavery | tomfoolery*.
3 denoting a place set aside for an activity or a grouping of things, animals, etc.: *orangery | rookery*.
– ORIGIN from French *-erie*, based on Latin *-arius* and *-ator*.

eryngium /ɪˈrɪndʒɪəm/ ▶ **noun** (pl. **eryngiums**) a plant of the genus *Eryngium* in the parsley family, especially (in gardening) sea holly.
– ORIGIN late 16th cent.: modern Latin, from Latin *eryngion*, from a diminutive of Greek *ērungos* 'sea holly'.

eryngo /ɪˈrɪŋgəʊ/ ▶ **noun** (pl. **-os** or **-oes**) another term for **SEA HOLLY** or **ERYNGIUM**.
– ORIGIN late 16th cent.: from Italian and Spanish *eringio*, from Latin *eryngion* (see **ERYNGIUM**).

erysipelas /,ɛrɪˈsɪpɪləs/ ▶ **noun** [mass noun] Medicine an acute, sometimes recurrent disease caused by a bacterial infection. It is characterized by large raised red patches on the skin, especially that of the face and legs, with fever and severe general illness.
● This is caused by *Streptococcus pyogenes*, a Gram-positive coccus.
– ORIGIN late Middle English: via Latin from Greek *erusipelas*; perhaps related to *eruthros* 'red' and *pella* 'skin'.

erysipeloid /,ɛrɪˈsɪpəlɔɪd/ ▶ **noun** [mass noun] Medicine dermatitis of the hands due to bacterial infection, occurring mainly among handlers of meat and fish products.
● This is caused by *Erysipelothrix rhusiopathiae*, a Gram-positive bacterium occurring either as slightly curved rods or as filaments.

erythema /,ɛrɪˈθiːmə/ ▶ **noun** [mass noun] Medicine superficial reddening of the skin, usually in patches, as a result of injury or irritation causing dilatation of the blood capillaries.
– DERIVATIVES **erythemal** adjective, **erythematous** adjective.
– ORIGIN late 18th cent.: from Greek *eruthēma*, from *eruthainein* 'be red', from *eruthros* 'red'.

erythrism /ˈɛrɪθrɪz(ə)m/ ▶ **noun** [mass noun] Zoology a congenital condition of abnormal redness in an animal's fur, plumage, or skin.
– ORIGIN late 19th cent.: from Greek *eruthros* 'red' + **-ISM**.

erythritol /ɪˈrɪθrɪtɒl/ ▶ **noun** [mass noun] Chemistry a sweet substance extracted from certain lichens and algae. It is used medicinally as a vasodilator.
● A tetrahydric alcohol; chem. formula: $C_4H_{10}O_4$.
– ORIGIN late 19th cent.: from *erythrite* (earlier name for *erythritol*) + **-OL**.

erythro- ▶ **combining form** (used commonly in zoological and medical terms) red: *erythrocyte*.
– ORIGIN from Greek *eruthros* 'red'.

erythroblast /ɪˈrɪθrə(ʊ)blast/ ▶ **noun** Physiology an immature erythrocyte, containing a nucleus.
– DERIVATIVES **erythroblastic** adjective.

erythroblastosis /ɪ,rɪθrə(ʊ)blasˈtəʊsɪs/ ▶ **noun** [mass noun] Medicine the abnormal presence of erythroblasts in the blood.
■ (also **erythroblastosis fetalis**) another term for **HAEMOLYTIC DISEASE OF THE NEWBORN**.

erythrocyte /ɪˈrɪθrə(ʊ)sʌɪt/ ▶ **noun** a red blood cell, which (in humans) is typically a biconcave disc without a nucleus. Erythrocytes contain the pigment haemoglobin, which imparts the red colour to blood, and transport oxygen and carbon dioxide to and from the tissues.
– DERIVATIVES **erythrocytic** adjective.

erythrogenic /ɪ,rɪθrə(ʊ)ˈdʒɛnɪk/ ▶ **adjective** Medicine (of a bacterial toxin) causing inflammation and reddening of the skin.

erythroid /ˈɛrɪθrɔɪd/ ▶ **adjective** Physiology of or relating to erythrocytes.

erythroleukaemia /ɪ,rɪθrə(ʊ)luːˈkiːmɪə/ (US **erythroleukemia**) ▶ **noun** [mass noun] Medicine a rare acute form of leukaemia in which there is proliferation of immature red and white blood cells.

erythromycin /ɪ,rɪθrə(ʊ)ˈmʌɪsɪn/ ▶ **noun** [mass noun] Medicine an antibiotic used in the treatment of infections caused by Gram-positive bacteria. It is similar in its effects to penicillin.
● This is obtained from the streptomycete bacterium *Streptomyces erythreus*.
– ORIGIN 1950s: from elements of the modern Latin taxonomic name (see above) + **-IN**[1].

erythronium /,ɛrɪˈθrəʊnɪəm/ ▶ **noun** (pl. **erythroniums** or **erythronia** /-ɪə/) a plant of a genus which includes dog's-tooth violet.
● Genus *Erythronium*, family Liliaceae.
– ORIGIN modern Latin, from Greek (*saturion*) *eruthronion* 'red-flowered (orchid)'.

erythropoiesis /ɪ,rɪθrə(ʊ)pɔɪˈiːsɪs/ ▶ **noun** [mass noun] Physiology the production of red blood cells.
– DERIVATIVES **erythropoietic** adjective.

erythropoietin /ɪ,rɪθrə(ʊ)pɔɪˈɛtɪn/ ▶ **noun** [mass noun] Biochemistry a hormone secreted by the kidneys that increases the rate of production of red blood cells in response to falling levels of oxygen in the tissues.

Erzgebirge /ˈɛːtsgə,bɪəgə, German ˈeːɐtsgə,bɪrgə, ˈɛrts-/ a range of mountains on the border between Germany and the Czech Republic. Also called the **ORE MOUNTAINS**.

Erzurum /ˈɛːzʊrʊm/ a city in NE Turkey, capital of a mountainous province of the same name; pop. 242,400 (1990).

ES ▶ **abbreviation for** El Salvador (international vehicle registration).

Es ▶ **symbol for** the chemical element einsteinium.

-es[1] ▶ **suffix** **1** forming plurals of nouns ending in sibilant sounds: *boxes | kisses*.
2 forming plurals of certain nouns ending in *-o*: *potatoes | heroes*.
– ORIGIN variant of **-S**[1].

-es[2] ▶ **suffix** forming the third person singular of the present tense: **1** in verbs ending in sibilant sounds: *pushes*.
2 in verbs ending in *-o* (but not *-oo*): *goes*.
– ORIGIN variant of **-S**[2].

ESA ▶ **abbreviation for** ■ (in the UK) Environmentally Sensitive Area. ■ European Space Agency.

Esaki /ɛˈzɑːki/, Leo (b.1925), Japanese physicist. He investigated and pioneered the development of quantum-mechanical tunnelling of electrons in semiconductor devices, and designed the tunnel diode (also called Esaki diode). Nobel Prize for Physics (1973).

Esau /ˈiːsɔː/ (in the Bible) the elder of the twin sons of Isaac and Rebecca, who sold his birthright to his brother Jacob and was tricked out of his father's blessing by his brother (Gen. 25, 27).

Esbjerg /ˈɛsbjəːg/ a port in Denmark, on the west coast of Jutland; pop. 81,500 (1990). It has ferry links with Britain and the Faroe Islands.

ESC ▶ **abbreviation for** Economic and Social Committee.

escadrille /,ɛskəˈdrɪl/ ▶ **noun** a French squadron of aircraft.
– ORIGIN French, literally 'flotilla, flight'.

escalade /,ɛskəˈleɪd/ ▶ **noun** [mass noun] historical the scaling of fortified walls using ladders, as a form of military attack.
– ORIGIN late 16th cent.: from French, or from Spanish *escalada*, *escalado*, from medieval Latin *scalare* 'to scale, climb', from Latin *scala* 'ladder'.

escalate /ˈɛskəleɪt/ ▶ **verb** [no obj.] increase rapidly: *the price of tickets escalated* | [as adj. **escalating**] *the escalating cost of health care*.
■ become or cause to become more intense or serious: [no obj.] *the disturbance* **escalated into** *a full-scale riot* | [with obj.] *we do not want to escalate the war*.
– DERIVATIVES **escalation** noun.
– ORIGIN 1920s (in the sense 'travel on an escalator'): back-formation from **ESCALATOR**.

escalator ▶ **noun** a moving staircase consisting of an endlessly circulating belt of steps driven by a motor, which conveys people between the floors of a public building.
– ORIGIN early 20th cent. (originally US, as a trade name): from *escalade* 'climb a wall by ladder' (from the noun **ESCALADE**), on the pattern of *elevator*.

escalator clause (also **escalation clause**) ▶ **noun** a clause in a contract that allows for a rise in wages or prices under certain conditions.

escallonia /ˌɛskəˈləʊnɪə/ ▶ noun an evergreen South American shrub with pink or white flowers.
● Genus *Escallonia*, family Grossulariaceae.
– ORIGIN modern Latin, named after *Escallon*, an 18th-cent. Spanish traveller who discovered the plants.

escallop /ɪˈskaləp, ɛ-, -ˈskɒl-/ ▶ noun **1** variant spelling of **ESCALOPE**.
2 another term for **SCALLOP** (in sense 2).
3 Heraldry a scallop shell as a charge.
▶ verb (**escalloped**, **escalloping**) another term for **SCALLOP** (in sense 3).
– ORIGIN late 15th cent. (in sense 2): from Old French *escalope* 'shell'. Compare with **ESCALOPE** and **SCALLOP**.

escalope /ɪˈskaləp, ɛ-, -ˈskɒl-, ˈɛskələʊp/ ▶ noun a thin slice of meat without any bone, typically a special cut of veal from the leg that is coated, fried, and served in a sauce. Also called **SCALLOP**.
– ORIGIN French; compare with **ESCALLOP** and **SCALLOP**.

escapade /ˈɛskəpeɪd, ˌɛskəˈpeɪd/ ▶ noun an act or incident involving excitement, daring, or adventure.
– ORIGIN mid 17th cent. (in the sense 'an escape'): from French, from Provençal or Spanish, from *escapar* 'to escape', based on medieval Latin *ex-* 'out of' + *cappa* 'cloak'. Compare with **ESCAPE**.

escape /ɪˈskeɪp/ ▶ verb [no obj.] break free from confinement or control: *two burglars have just escaped from prison* | [as adj. **escaped**] *escaped convicts*.
  ■ [with obj.] elude or get free from (someone): *he drove along the dual carriageway to escape police.* ■ succeed in avoiding or eluding something dangerous, unpleasant, or undesirable: *the driver escaped with a broken knee* | [with obj.] *a baby boy narrowly escaped death.* ■ [with obj.] fail to be noticed or remembered by (someone): *the name escaped him* | *it may have escaped your notice, but this is not a hotel.* ■ (of a gas, liquid, or heat) leak from a container. ■ [with obj.] (of words or sounds) issue involuntarily or inadvertently from (someone or their lips): *a sob escaped her lips.*
▶ noun an act of breaking free from confinement or control: *the story of his escape from a POW camp* | *the gang had made their escape* | [mass noun] *he could think of no way of escape, short of rudeness.*
  ■ an act of successfully avoiding something dangerous, unpleasant, or unwelcome: *the baby was fine, but it was a lucky escape.* ■ a means of escaping from somewhere: [as modifier] *he had planned his escape route.* ■ a form of temporary distraction from reality or routine: *romantic novels should present an escape from the dreary realities of life.* ■ a leakage of gas, liquid, or heat, from a container. ■ (also **escape key**) Computing a key on a computer keyboard which either interrupts the current operation or converts subsequent characters to a control sequence. ■ a garden plant or pet animal that has gone wild and (especially in plants) become naturalized.
– DERIVATIVES **escapable** adjective, **escaper** noun.
– ORIGIN Middle English: from Old French *eschaper*, based on medieval Latin *ex-* 'out' + *cappa* 'cloak'. Compare with **ESCAPADE**.

escape clause ▶ noun a clause in a contract which specifies the conditions under which one party can be freed from an obligation.

escapee /ɪˌskeɪˈpiː, ɪˈskeɪpiː/ ▶ noun a person who has escaped from somewhere, especially prison.

escape hatch ▶ noun a hatch for use as an emergency exit, especially from a submarine, ship, or aircraft.

escape mechanism ▶ noun Psychology a mental process which enables a person to avoid acknowledging unpleasant or threatening aspects of reality.

escapement /ɪˈskeɪpm(ə)nt, ɛ-/ ▶ noun a mechanism in a clock or watch that alternately checks and transmits a periodic impulse from the spring or weight to the balance wheel or pendulum.
  ■ a mechanism in a typewriter that shifts the carriage a small fixed amount to the left after a key is pressed and released. ■ the part of the mechanism in a piano that enables the hammer to fall back as soon as it has struck the string.
– ORIGIN late 18th cent.: from French *échappement*, from *échapper* 'to escape'.

escape road ▶ noun chiefly Brit. a slip road, especially on a racing circuit, for a vehicle to turn into if the driver is unable to negotiate a bend or slope safely.

escape velocity ▶ noun the lowest velocity which a body must have in order to escape the gravitational attraction of a particular planet or other object.

escape wheel ▶ noun a toothed wheel in the escapement of a watch or clock.

escapism ▶ noun [mass noun] the tendency to seek distraction and relief from unpleasant realities, especially by seeking entertainment or engaging in fantasy.
– DERIVATIVES **escapist** noun & adjective.

escapologist /ˌɛskəˈpɒlədʒɪst/ ▶ noun an entertainer specializing in freeing themselves from the confinement of such things as ropes, handcuffs, and chains.
– DERIVATIVES **escapology** noun.

escargot /ɛˈskɑːɡəʊ, ɪ-/ ▶ noun the edible snail, especially as an item on a menu.
– ORIGIN French, from Old French *escargol*, from Provençal *escaragol*.

escarole /ˈɛskərəʊl/ ▶ noun [mass noun] N. Amer. an endive of a variety with broad undivided leaves and a slightly bitter flavour, used in salads.
– ORIGIN early 20th cent.: from French, from Italian *scar(i)ola*, based on Latin *esca* 'food'.

escarpment /ɪˈskɑːpm(ə)nt, ɛ-/ ▶ noun a long, steep slope, especially one at the edge of a plateau or separating areas of land at different heights.
– ORIGIN early 19th cent.: from French *escarpement*, *escarpe* 'scarp', from Italian *scarpa* 'slope'. Compare with **SCARP**.

Escaut /ɛsko/ French name for **SCHELDT**.

-esce ▶ suffix forming verbs, often denoting the initiation of action: *coalesce* | *effervesce*.
– ORIGIN from or suggested by Latin verbs ending in *-escere*.

-escent ▶ suffix forming adjectives denoting a developing state or action: *coalescent* | *fluorescent*.
– DERIVATIVES **-escence** suffix forming corresponding nouns.
– ORIGIN from French, or from Latin *-escent-* (present participial stem of verbs ending in *-escere*).

eschar /ˈɛskɑː/ ▶ noun Medicine a dry, dark scab or falling away of dead skin, typically caused by a burn, or by the bite of a mite, or as a result of anthrax infection.
– ORIGIN late Middle English: from French *eschare* or late Latin *eschara* 'scar or scab', from Greek (see also **SCAR**).

eschatology /ˌɛskəˈtɒlədʒi/ ▶ noun [mass noun] the part of theology concerned with death, judgement, and the final destiny of the soul and of humankind.
– DERIVATIVES **eschatological** adjective, **eschatologist** noun.
– ORIGIN mid 19th cent.: from Greek *eskhatos* 'last' + **-LOGY**.

eschaton /ˈɛskətɒn/ ▶ noun (**the eschaton**) Theology the final event in the divine plan; the end of the world.
– ORIGIN 1930s: from Greek *eskhaton*, neuter of *eskhatos* 'last'.

escheat /ɪsˈtʃiːt, ɛs-/ chiefly historical ▶ noun [mass noun] the reversion of property to the state, or (in feudal law) to a lord, on the owner's dying without legal heirs.
  ■ [count noun] an item of property affected by this.
▶ verb [no obj.] (of land) revert to a lord or the state by escheat.
  ■ [with obj.] [usu. as adj. **escheated**] hand over (land) as an escheat.
– ORIGIN Middle English: from Old French *eschete*, based on Latin *excidere* 'fall away', from *ex-* 'out of, from' + *cadere* 'to fall'.

Escher /ˈɛʃə/, M. C. (1898–1972), Dutch graphic artist; full name *Maurits Corneille Escher*. His prints are characterized by their sophisticated use of visual illusion.

eschew /ɪsˈtʃuː, ɛs-/ ▶ verb [with obj.] deliberately avoid using; abstain from: *he appealed to the crowd to eschew violence.*
– DERIVATIVES **eschewal** noun.
– ORIGIN late Middle English: from Old French *eschiver*, ultimately of Germanic origin and related to German *scheuen* 'shun', also to **SHY**[1].

eschscholzia /ɪsˈʃɒlzɪə, ɛˈʃɒlzɪə/ (also **eschscholtzia** /-tsɪə/) ▶ noun a North American poppy which is cultivated for its bright yellow, orange, or red flowers.
● Genus *Eschscholzia*, family Papaveraceae: several species, in particular the California poppy.
– ORIGIN modern Latin, named in honour of Johann Friedrich von *Eschscholtz* (1793–1831), Russian-born botanist and traveller.

Escoffier /ɛˈskɒfɪeɪ/, Georges-Auguste (1846–1935), French chef. He gained an international reputation while working in London at the Savoy Hotel (1890–9) and later at the Carlton (1899–1919).

escolar /ˌɛskəˈlɑː/ ▶ noun a large, elongated predatory fish occurring in tropical and temperate oceans throughout the world. Also called **SNAKE MACKEREL**.
● Family Gempylidae: several genera and species.
– ORIGIN mid 19th cent.: from Spanish, literally 'scholar', so named because the ringed markings around the eyes resemble spectacles.

Escorial /ɛˌskɒrɪˈɑːl/ a monastery and palace in central Spain, near Madrid, built in the late 16th century by Philip II.

escort ▶ noun /ˈɛskɔːt/ a person, vehicle, ship, or aircraft, or a group of these, accompanying another for protection, security, or as a mark of rank: *a police escort* | [mass noun] *he was driven away under armed escort.*
  ■ a man who accompanies a woman to a particular social event. ■ a person, typically a woman, who may be hired to accompany someone socially: [as modifier] *an escort agency.*
▶ verb /ɪˈskɔːt, ɛ-/ [with obj.] accompany (someone or something) somewhere, especially for protection, security, or as a mark of rank: *Shiona escorted Janice to the door.*
– ORIGIN late 16th cent. (originally denoting a body of armed men escorting travellers): from French *escorte* (noun), *escorter* (verb), from Italian *scorta*, feminine past participle of *scorgere* 'to conduct, guide', based on Latin *ex-* 'out of' + *corrigere* 'set right' (see **CORRECT**).

escritoire /ˌɛskriˈtwɑː/ ▶ noun a small writing desk with drawers and compartments.
– ORIGIN late 16th cent.: from French, from medieval Latin *scriptorium* 'writing room' (see **SCRIPTORIUM**).

escrow /ɪˈskrəʊ, ɛ-/ Law ▶ noun a bond, deed, or other document kept in the custody of a third party, taking effect only when a specified condition has been fulfilled.
  ■ [usu. as modifier] a deposit or fund held in trust or as a security: *an escrow account.* ■ [mass noun] the state of being kept in custody or trust in this way: *the board holds funds in escrow.*
▶ verb [with obj.] chiefly US place in custody or trust in this way.
– ORIGIN late 16th cent.: from Old French *escroe* 'scrap, scroll', from medieval Latin *scroda*, of Germanic origin; related to **SHRED**.

escudo /ɛˈsk(j)uːdəʊ, ɛˈʃk-/ ▶ noun (pl. **-os**) the basic monetary unit of Portugal and the Cape Verde Islands, equal to 100 centavos (replaced in Portugal by the euro in 2002).
– ORIGIN Spanish and Portuguese, from Latin *scutum* 'shield'.

esculent /ˈɛskjʊlənt/ formal ▶ adjective fit to be eaten; edible.
▶ noun a thing, especially a vegetable, which is fit to be eaten.
– ORIGIN early 17th cent.: from Latin *esculentus*, from *esca* 'food', from *esse* 'eat'.

escutcheon /ɪˈskʌtʃ(ə)n, ɛ-/ ▶ noun **1** a shield or emblem bearing a coat of arms.
2 (also **escutcheon plate**) a flat piece of metal for protection and often ornamentation, around a keyhole, door handle, or light switch.
– PHRASES **a blot on one's escutcheon** a stain on one's reputation or character. **escutcheon of pretence** a small shield within a coat of arms, bearing another coat or device to which the bearer has a claim, especially one to which a man's wife is heiress.
– DERIVATIVES **escutcheoned** adjective.
– ORIGIN late 15th cent.: from Anglo-Norman French *escuchon*, based on Latin *scutum* 'shield'.

Esd. ▶ abbreviation for Esdras, either in the Apocrypha or the Vulgate (in biblical references).

Esdras /ˈɛzdrəs/ **1** either of two books of the Apocrypha. The first is mainly a compilation from

Chronicles, Nehemiah, and Ezra; the second is a record of angelic revelation.
2 (in the Vulgate) the books of Ezra and Nehemiah.

ESE ▶ **abbreviation for** east-south-east.

-ese ▶ **suffix** forming adjectives and nouns:
1 denoting an inhabitant or language of a country or city: *Taiwanese | Viennese.*
2 often derogatory (especially with reference to language) denoting character or style: *journalese | officialese.*
– ORIGIN from Old French *-eis*, based on Latin *-ensis*.

esemplastic /ˌɛsɛmˈplastɪk/ ▶ **adjective** rare moulding into one; unifying:
– DERIVATIVES **esemplastically** adverb.
– ORIGIN early 19th cent.: from Greek *es* 'into' + *hen* (neuter of *heis* 'one') + **-IC**; formed irregularly by Coleridge, probably suggested by German *Ineinsbildung*, in the same sense.

eserine /ˈɛsəriːn/ ▶ **noun** Chemistry another term for **PHYSOSTIGMINE**.
– ORIGIN mid 19th cent.: from French *ésérine*, from Efik *esere*.

Esfahan /ˌɛsfəˈhɑːn/ variant spelling of **ISFAHAN**.

esker /ˈɛskə/ ▶ **noun** Geology a long ridge of gravel and other sediment, typically having a winding course, deposited by meltwater from a retreating glacier or ice sheet.
– ORIGIN mid 19th cent.: from Irish *eiscir*.

Eskimo ▶ **noun** (pl. same or **-os**) **1** a member of an indigenous people inhabiting northern Canada, Alaska, Greenland, and eastern Siberia, and traditionally living by hunting seals and other Arctic animals and birds and by fishing.
2 [mass noun] either of the two main languages of this people (Inuit and Yupik), comprising a major division of the Eskimo-Aleut family.
▶ **adjective** of or relating to the Eskimos or their languages.
– ORIGIN an Algonquian word, perhaps in the sense 'people speaking a different language'.

USAGE In recent years, the word **Eskimo** has come to be regarded as offensive (partly through the associations of the now discredited folk etymology 'one who eats raw flesh'). The peoples inhabiting the regions from NW Canada to western Greenland prefer to call themselves **Inuit**: see **usage** at **INUIT**. The term **Eskimo**, however, continues to be the only term which can be properly understood as applying to the people as a whole and is still widely used in anthropological and archaeological contexts.

Eskimo-Aleut ▶ **noun** [mass noun] the family of languages comprising Inuit, Yupik, and Aleut.
▶ **adjective** of or relating to this family of languages.

Eskimo curlew ▶ **noun** a small New World curlew with a striped head, formerly common in the arctic tundra but now close to extinction.
• *Numenius borealis*, family Scolopacidae.

Eskimo pie ▶ **noun** US trademark a bar of chocolate-coated ice cream.

Eskimo roll ▶ **noun** a complete rollover in canoeing, from upright to capsized to upright.

Esky /ˈɛski/ ▶ **noun** (pl. **-ies**) Austral. trademark a portable insulated container for keeping food or drink cool.
– ORIGIN 1960s: probably from **ESKIMO**, by association with a cold climate.

ESL ▶ **abbreviation for** English as a second language.

ESN ▶ **abbreviation for** ■ dated educationally subnormal. ■ electronic serial number, a unique number programmed into a mobile phone which identifies it.

ESOL ▶ **abbreviation for** English for speakers of other languages.

esophagus etc. ▶ **noun** US spelling of **OESOPHAGUS** etc.

esoteric /ˌɛsəˈtɛrɪk, ˌiːsə-/ ▶ **adjective** intended for or likely to be understood by only a small number of people with a specialized knowledge or interest: *esoteric philosophical debates.*
– DERIVATIVES **esoterically** adverb, **esotericism** noun, **esotericist** noun.
– ORIGIN mid 17th cent.: from Greek *esōterikos*, from *esōterō*, comparative of *esō* 'within', from *es*, *eis* 'into'. Compare with **EXOTERIC**.

esoterica /ˌɛsəˈtɛrɪkə, ˌiːsə-/ ▶ **noun** [mass noun] esoteric or highly specialized subjects or publications.
– ORIGIN early 20th cent.: from Greek *esōterika*, neuter plural of *esōterikos* 'esoteric'.

ESP ▶ **abbreviation for** ■ Photography electro-selective pattern. ■ electrostatic precipitator. ■ extrasensory perception.

esp. ▶ **abbreviation for** especially.

espada /ɛˈspɑːdə/ ▶ **noun** (pl. same) a scabbardfish, especially as caught for food in Madeira and elsewhere.
– ORIGIN via Portuguese from Spanish, from Latin *spatha* 'sword'.

espadrille /ˈɛspədrɪl, ˌɛspəˈdrɪl/ ▶ **noun** a light canvas shoe with a plaited fibre sole.
– ORIGIN late 19th cent.: from French, from Provençal *espardi(l)hos*, from *espart* 'esparto', from Latin *spartum* (see **ESPARTO**).

espalier /ɪˈspaljə, ɛ-/ ▶ **noun** a fruit tree or ornamental shrub whose branches are trained to grow flat against a wall, supported on a lattice or a framework of stakes.
■ a lattice or framework of this type.
▶ **verb** [with obj.] train (a tree or shrub) in such a way.
– ORIGIN mid 17th cent.: from French, from Italian *spalliera*, from *spalla* 'shoulder', from Latin *spatula* (see **SPATULA**), in late Latin 'shoulder blade'.

España /esˈpaɲa/ Spanish name for **SPAIN**.

esparto /ɛˈspɑːtəʊ, ɪ-/ (also **esparto grass**) ▶ **noun** (pl. **-os**) a coarse grass with tough narrow leaves, native to Spain and North Africa. It is used to make ropes, wickerwork, and good-quality paper.
• *Stipa tenacissima*, family Gramineae.
– ORIGIN mid 19th cent.: from Spanish, via Latin from Greek *sparton* 'rope'.

especial /ɪˈspɛʃ(ə)l, ɛ-/ ▶ **adjective** [attrib.] better or greater than usual: special: *these traditions are of especial interest to feminists.*
■ for or belonging chiefly to one person or thing: *her outburst was for my especial benefit.*
– ORIGIN late Middle English: via Old French from Latin *specialis* 'special', from *species* (see **SPECIES**).

especially ▶ **adverb** **1** used to single out one person, thing, or situation over all others: *he despised them all, especially Sylvester | a new song, written **especially for** Jonathan.*
2 to a great extent; very much: *he didn't especially like dancing |* [as submodifier] *sleep is especially important in growing children.*

USAGE There is some overlap in the uses of **especially** and **specially**. In the broadest terms, both words mean 'particularly' and the preference for one word over the other is linked with particular conventions of use rather than with any deep difference in meaning. For example, there is little to choose between *written **especially** for Jonathan* and *written **specially** for Jonathan* and neither is more correct than the other. On the other hand, in sentences such as *he despised them all, **especially** Sylvester*, substitution of **specially** is found in informal uses but should not be used in written English, while in *the car was **specially** made for the occasion* substitution of **especially** is somewhat unusual. Overall, **especially** is by far the commoner of the two, occurring more than nine times as frequently as **specially** in the British National Corpus.

Esperanto /ˌɛspəˈrantəʊ/ ▶ **noun** [mass noun] an artificial language devised in 1887 as an international medium of communication, based on roots from the chief European languages. It retains the structure of these languages and has the advantage of grammatical regularity and ease of pronunciation.
– DERIVATIVES **Esperantist** noun.
– ORIGIN from the name *Dr Esperanto*, used as a pen-name by the inventor of the language, Ludwik L. Zamenhof (1858–1917), Polish physician; the literal sense is 'one who hopes' (based on Latin *sperare* 'to hope').

espial /ɪˈspʌɪ(ə)l, ɛ-/ ▶ **noun** [mass noun] archaic the action of watching or catching sight of something or someone or the fact of being seen: *he withdrew from his point of espial.*
– ORIGIN late Middle English (in the sense 'spying'): from Old French *espiaille*, from *espier* 'espy'.

espionage /ˈɛspɪənɑːʒ, -ɪdʒ/ ▶ **noun** [mass noun] the practice of spying or of using spies, typically by governments to obtain political and military information.
– ORIGIN late 18th cent.: from French *espionnage*, from *espionner* 'to spy', from *espion* 'a spy'.

Espírito Santo /ɛˌspɪrɪtuː ˈsantuː/ a state of eastern Brazil, on the Atlantic coast; capital, Vitória.

esplanade /ˌɛspləˈneɪd, -ˈnɑːd/ ▶ **noun** a long, open, level area, typically beside the sea, along which people may walk for pleasure.
■ an open, level space separating a fortress from a town.
– ORIGIN late 16th cent. (denoting an area of flat ground on top of a rampart): from French, from Italian *spianata*, from Latin *explanatus* 'flattened, levelled', from *explanare* (see **EXPLAIN**).

espousal /ɪˈspaʊz(ə)l, ɛ-/ ▶ **noun** **1** [in sing.] an act of adopting or supporting a cause, belief, or way of life: *his espousal of Western ideas.*
2 archaic a marriage or engagement.
– ORIGIN late Middle English: from Old French *espousaille*, from Latin *sponsalia* 'betrothal', neuter plural of *sponsalis* (adjective), from *sponsare* 'espouse, betroth' (see **ESPOUSE**).

espouse /ɪˈspaʊz, ɛ-/ ▶ **verb** [with obj.] **1** adopt or support (a cause, belief, or way of life): *the left has espoused the causes of sexual and racial equality.*
2 archaic marry: *Edward had espoused the lady Grey.*
■ (**be espoused to**) (of a woman) be engaged to (a particular man).
– DERIVATIVES **espouser** noun.
– ORIGIN late Middle English (in the sense 'take as a spouse'): from Old French *espouser*, from Latin *sponsare*, from *sponsus* 'betrothed', past participle of *spondere*.

espressivo /ˌɛsprɛˈsiːvəʊ/ ▶ **adverb** & **adjective** Music (especially as a direction) with expression of feeling.
– ORIGIN Italian, from Latin *expressus* 'distinctly presented'.

espresso /ɛˈsprɛsəʊ/ (also **expresso**) ▶ **noun** (pl. **-os**) [mass noun] strong black coffee made by forcing steam through ground coffee beans.
– ORIGIN 1940s: from Italian (*caffè*) *espresso*, literally 'pressed out (coffee)'.

esprit /ɛˈspriː, French ɛspʀi/ ▶ **noun** [mass noun] the quality of being lively, vivacious, or witty.
– ORIGIN French, from Latin *spiritus* 'spirit'.

esprit de corps /ɛˌspriː də ˈkɔː, French ɛspʀi də kɔʀ/ ▶ **noun** [mass noun] a feeling of pride, fellowship, and mutual loyalty shared by and uniting the members of a particular group.
– ORIGIN French, literally 'spirit of the body'.

esprit de l'escalier /ɛˌspriː də lɛˈskaljeɪ, French ɛspʀi də lɛskalje/ ▶ **noun** [mass noun] used to refer to the fact that a witty remark or retort often comes to mind after the opportunity to make it has passed.
– ORIGIN French, literally 'wit of the staircase' (i.e. a witty remark coming to mind on the stairs leading away from a gathering).

espy /ɪˈspʌɪ, ɛ-/ ▶ **verb** (**-ies**, **-ied**) [with obj.] poetic/literary catch sight of: *she espied her daughter rounding the corner.*
– ORIGIN Middle English: from Old French *espier*, ultimately of Germanic origin and related to Dutch *spieden* and German *spähan*. Compare with **SPY**.

Esq. ▶ **abbreviation for** Esquire.

-esque ▶ **suffix** (forming adjectives) in the style of; resembling: *carnivalesque | Dantesque.*
– ORIGIN from French, via Italian *-esco* from medieval Latin *-iscus*.

Esquimau ▶ **noun** (pl. **Esquimaux**) archaic spelling of **ESKIMO**.

Esquipulas /ˌɛskiːˈpuːlas/ a town in SE Guatemala, near the border with Honduras; pop. 18,840 (1981). Noted for the image of the 'Black Christ of Esquipulas' in its church, the town is a centre of pilgrimage.

esquire /ɪˈskwʌɪə, ɛ-/ (abbrev.: **esq.**) ▶ **noun** **1** (**Esquire**) Brit. a polite title appended to a man's name when no other title is used, typically in the address of a letter or other documents: *J. C. Pearson Esquire.*
■ N. Amer. a title appended to a lawyer's surname.
2 historical a young nobleman who, in training for knighthood, acted as an attendant to a knight.
■ an officer in the service of a king or nobleman. ■ [as title] a landed proprietor or country squire.
– PHRASES **esquire of the** (**king's**) **body** historical an officer in charge of dressing and undressing the king.
– ORIGIN late Middle English: from Old French *esquier*, from Latin *scutarius* 'shield-bearer', from

scutum 'shield'; compare with **SQUIRE**. Sense 2 was the original denotation, sense 1 being at first a courtesy title given to such a person.

ESR Physics ▶ **abbreviation for** electron spin resonance.

ESRC ▶ **abbreviation for** (in the UK) Economic and Social Research Council.

ess ▶ **noun** a thing shaped like the letter S.
– ORIGIN mid 16th cent.: the letter *S* represented as a word.

-ess¹ ▶ **suffix** forming nouns denoting female gender: *abbess | adulteress | tigress.*
– ORIGIN from French *-esse*, via late Latin from Greek *-issa*.

USAGE The suffix **-ess** has been used since the Middle Ages to form nouns denoting female persons, using a neutral or a male form as the base (as **hostess** and **actress** from **host** and **actor**, for example). Despite the apparent equivalence between the male and female pairs of forms, however, they are rarely equivalent in terms of actual use and connotation in modern English (consider the differences in meaning and use between **manager** and **manageress** or **poet** and **poetess**). In the late 20th century, as the role of women in society changed, some of these feminine forms have become problematic and are regarded as old-fashioned, sexist, and patronizing (e.g. **poetess**, **authoress**, **editress**). The 'male' form is increasingly being used as the 'neutral' form, where the gender of the person concerned is simply unspecified.

-ess² ▶ **suffix** forming abstract nouns from adjectives, such as *largess*.
– ORIGIN Middle English via French *-esse* from Latin *-itia*.

essay ▶ **noun** /ˈɛseɪ/ **1** a short piece of writing on a particular subject.
2 formal an attempt or effort: *a misjudged essay in job preservation.*
■ a trial design of a postage stamp yet to be accepted.
▶ **verb** /ɛˈseɪ/ [with obj.] formal attempt or try: *Donald essayed a smile.*
– ORIGIN late 15th cent. (as a verb in the sense 'test the quality of'): alteration of **ASSAY**, by association with Old French *essayer*, based on late Latin *exagium* 'weighing', from the base of *exigere* 'ascertain, weigh'; the noun (late 16th cent.) is from Old French *essai* 'trial'.

essayist ▶ **noun** a person who writes essays, especially as a literary genre.

essayistic ▶ **adjective** characteristic of or used in essays.

esse /ˈɛsi/ ▶ **noun** [mass noun] Philosophy essential nature or essence. See also **IN ESSE**.
– ORIGIN Latin, 'to be' (used as a noun).

Essen /ˈɛs(ə)n/ an industrial city in the Ruhr valley, in NW Germany; pop. 626,990 (1991).

essence ▶ **noun** [mass noun] the intrinsic nature or indispensable quality of something,especially something abstract, which determines its character: *conflict is the essence of drama.*
■ [count noun] Philosophy a property or group of properties of something without which it would not exist or be what it is. ■ an extract or concentrate obtained from a particular plant or other matter and used for flavouring or scent: *vanilla essence.*
– PHRASES **in essence** basically and without regard for peripheral details; fundamentally: *in detail the class system is complex but in essence it is simple.* **of the essence** critically important: *time will be of the essence during negotiations.*
– ORIGIN late Middle English: via Old French from Latin *essentia*, from *esse* 'be'.

Essene /ˈɛsiːn/ ▶ **noun** a member of an ancient Jewish ascetic sect of the 2nd century BC–2nd century AD in Palestine, who lived in highly organized groups and held property in common. The Essenes are widely regarded as the authors of the Dead Sea Scrolls.
– ORIGIN from Latin *Esseni* (plural), from Greek *Essēnoi*, perhaps from Aramaic .

essential /ɪˈsɛnʃ(ə)l/ ▶ **adjective** **1** absolutely necessary; extremely important: [with infinitive] *it is essential to keep up-to-date records | fibre is an essential ingredient of our diet.*
■ [attrib.] fundamental or central to the nature of something or someone: *the essential weakness of the plaintiff's case.* ■ (of an amino acid or fatty acid) required for normal growth but not synthesized in the body and therefore necessary in the diet.
2 Medicine (of a disease) with no known external stimulus or cause; idiopathic: *essential hypertension.*
▶ **noun** (usu. **essentials**) a thing that is absolutely necessary: *we only had the bare essentials in the way of equipment.*
■ (**essentials**) the fundamental elements or characteristics of something: *he was quick to grasp the essentials of an opponent's argument.*
– DERIVATIVES **essentiality** noun, **essentialness** noun.
– ORIGIN Middle English (in the sense 'in the highest degree'): from late Latin *essentialis*, from Latin *essentia* (see **ESSENCE**).

essentialism ▶ **noun** [mass noun] Philosophy a belief that things have a set of characteristics which make them what they are, and that the task of science and philosophy is their discovery and expression; the doctrine that essence is prior to existence. Compare with **EXISTENTIALISM**.
■ the view that all children should be taught on traditional lines the ideas and methods regarded as essential to the prevalent culture. ■ the view that categories of people, such as women and men, or heterosexuals and homosexuals, or members of ethnic groups, have intrinsically different and characteristic natures or dispositions.
– DERIVATIVES **essentialist** noun & adjective.

essentially ▶ **adverb** used to emphasize the basic, fundamental, or intrinsic nature of a person, thing, or situation: [sentence adverb] *essentially, they are amateurs.*

essential oil ▶ **noun** a natural oil typically obtained by distillation and having the characteristic odour of the plant or other source from which it is extracted.

Essequibo /ˌɛsɪˈkiːbəʊ/ a river in Guyana, rising in the Guiana Highlands and flowing about 965 km (600 miles) northwards to the Atlantic.

Essex a county of eastern England; county town, Chelmsford.

EST ▶ **abbreviation for** Eastern Standard Time (see **EASTERN TIME**).

est /ɛst/ ▶ **noun** [mass noun] a system for self-improvement aimed at developing a person's potential through intensive group awareness and training sessions.
– ORIGIN 1970s (originally US): acronym from *Erhard Seminars Training*, from the name of Werner *Erhard* (born 1935), the American businessman who devised the technique.

est. ▶ **abbreviation for** ■ established. ■ estimated.

-est¹ ▶ **suffix** forming the superlative of adjectives (such as *shortest*, *widest*), and of adverbs (such as *soonest*).
– ORIGIN Old English *-ost-*, *-ust-*, *-ast-*.

-est² (also **-st**) ▶ **suffix** archaic forming the second person singular of verbs: *canst | goest.*
– ORIGIN Old English *-est*, *-ast*, *-st*.

establish ▶ **verb** [with obj.] **1** set up (an organization, system, or set of rules) on a firm or permanent basis: *the scheme was established in 1975.*
■ initiate or bring about (contact or communication): *the two countries established diplomatic relations in 1992.*
2 achieve permanent acceptance for (a custom, belief, practice, or institution): *the principle of the supremacy of national parliaments needs to be firmly established.*
■ achieve recognition or acceptance for (someone) in a particular capacity: *he had* ***established himself*** *as a film star.* ■ [no obj.] (of a plant) take root and grow. ■ introduce (a character, set, or location) into a film or play and allow its identification: *establish the location with a wide shot.*
3 show (something) to be true or certain by determining the facts: [with clause] *the police established that the two passports were forgeries.*
4 Bridge ensure that one's remaining cards in (a suit) will be winners (if not trumped) by playing off the high cards in that suit.
– DERIVATIVES **establisher** noun.
– ORIGIN late Middle English (recorded earlier as *stablish*): from Old French *establiss-*, lengthened stem of *establir*, from Latin *stabilire* 'make firm', from *stabilis* (adjective) 'stable' .

established ▶ **adjective** **1** (of a custom, belief, practice, or institution) having been in existence for a long time and therefore recognized and generally accepted: *the ceremony was an established event in the annual calendar.*
■ (of a person) recognized and accepted in a particular capacity: *an established artist.* ■ (of a plant) having taken root; growing well.
2 (of a Church or religion) recognized by the state as the national Church or religion.
– PHRASES **the Established Church** the Church of England or of Scotland.

establishment ▶ **noun** **1** [mass noun] the action of establishing something or being established: *the establishment of a Palestinian state.*
■ [count noun] archaic a marriage.
2 a business organization, public institution, or household: *hotels or catering establishments.*
■ [usu. in sing.] the premises or staff of such an organization: *she entered this establishment as our housemaid.*
3 (usu. **the Establishment**) a group in a society exercising power and influence over matters of policy or taste, and seen as resisting change.
■ [with adj. or noun modifier] an influential group within a specified profession or area of activity: *rumblings of discontent among the medical establishment.*
4 (**the Establishment** or **the Church Establishment**) the ecclesiastical system organized by law.
■ the Church of England or of Scotland.

establishmentarian /ɪˌstablɪʃm(ə)nˈtɛːrɪən/ ▶ **adjective** adhering to, advocating, or relating to the principle of an established Church.
▶ **noun** a person adhering to or advocating this.
– DERIVATIVES **establishmentarianism** noun.

estaminet /ɛˈstamɪneɪ, French ɛstaminɛ/ ▶ **noun** a small cafe selling alcoholic drinks.
– ORIGIN French, from Walloon *staminé* 'byre', from *stamo* 'a pole for tethering a cow', probably from German *Stamm* 'stem'.

estancia /ɛˈstansɪə/ ▶ **noun** a cattle ranch in Latin America or the southern US.
– ORIGIN mid 17th cent.: from Spanish, literally 'station', from medieval Latin *stantia*, based on Latin *stare* 'to stand'.

estate ▶ **noun** **1** an area or amount of land or property, in particular:
■ Brit. an area of land and modern buildings developed for residential, industrial, or commercial purposes. ■ an extensive area of land in the country, usually with a large house, owned by one person or organization. ■ all the money and property owned by a particular person, especially at death: *in his will, he divided his estate between his wife and daughter.* ■ a property where coffee, rubber, grapes, or other crops are cultivated. ■ (in South Africa) a registered vineyard producing wines made exclusively from grapes grown within its boundaries.
2 (also **estate of the realm**) a class or order regarded as forming part of the body politic, in particular (in Britain), one of the three groups constituting Parliament, now the Lords Spiritual (the heads of the Church), the Lords Temporal (the peerage), and the Commons. They are also known as **the three estates**.
■ dated a particular class or category of people in society: *the spiritual welfare of all estates of men.*
3 archaic or poetic/literary a particular state, period, or condition in life: *programmes for the improvement of man's estate | the holy estate of matrimony.*
■ [mass noun] grandeur, pomp, or state: *a chamber without a chair of estate.*
4 Brit. short for **ESTATE CAR**.
– ORIGIN Middle English (in the sense 'state or condition'): from Old French *estat*, from Latin *status* 'state, condition', from *stare* 'to stand'.

estate agency ▶ **noun** chiefly Brit. a company or business that sells and rents out buildings and land for clients.
■ [mass noun] the activity or profession of selling and renting out buildings and land in this way.
– DERIVATIVES **estate agent** noun.

estate car ▶ **noun** Brit. a car with a longer body than usual, incorporating a large carrying area behind the seats and having an extra door at the rear for easy loading.

estate duty ▶ **noun** [mass noun] Brit. historical a former death duty levied on property from 1889. It was replaced in 1975 by capital transfer tax and in 1986 by inheritance tax.

estate of the realm ▶ **noun** see **ESTATE** (sense 2).

Estates General another term for **STATES GENERAL**.

estate tax ▶ **noun** chiefly US another term for **INHERITANCE TAX**.

esteem ▶ **noun** [mass noun] respect and admiration, typically for a person: *he was held in high esteem by colleagues.*
▶ **verb** [with obj.] (usu. **be esteemed**) respect and admire: *many of these qualities are esteemed by managers* | [as adj., with submodifier] (**esteemed**) *a highly esteemed scholar.*
■ formal consider; deem: [with two objs] *I should esteem it a favour if you could speak to them.*
– ORIGIN Middle English (as a noun in the sense 'worth, reputation'): from Old French *estime* (noun), *estimer* (verb), from Latin *aestimare* 'to estimate'. The verb was originally in the Latin sense, also 'appraise' (compare with **ESTIMATE**), used figuratively to mean 'assess the merit of'. Current senses date from the 16th cent.

ester /ˈɛstə/ ▶ **noun** Chemistry an organic compound made by replacing the hydrogen of an acid by an alkyl or other organic group. Many naturally occurring fats and essential oils are esters of fatty acids.
– DERIVATIVES **esterify** /ɛˈstɛrɪfʌɪ/ verb (**-ies**, **-ied**).
– ORIGIN mid 19th cent.: from German, probably from a blend of *Essig* 'vinegar' and *Äther* 'ether'.

esterase /ˈɛstəreɪz/ ▶ **noun** Biochemistry an enzyme which hydrolyses particular esters into acids and alcohols or phenols.

Esth. ▶ **abbreviation for** Esther (in biblical references).

Esther /ˈɛstə/ (in the Bible) a woman chosen on account of her beauty by the Persian king Ahasuerus (generally supposed to be Xerxes I) to be his queen. She used her influence with him to save the Israelites in captivity from persecution.
■ a book of the Bible containing an account of these events; a part survives only in Greek and is included in the Apocrypha.

esthetic etc. ▶ **adjective** US spelling of **AESTHETIC** etc.

Estima /ɛˈstiːmə/ ▶ **noun** a Dutch potato of a yellow-fleshed variety.

estimable /ˈɛstɪməb(ə)l/ ▶ **adjective** worthy of great respect.
– DERIVATIVES **estimably** adverb.
– ORIGIN late 15th cent. (in the sense 'able to be estimated or appraised'; earlier in *inestimable*): via Old French from Latin *aestimabilis*, from *aestimare* 'to estimate'.

estimate ▶ **verb** /ˈɛstɪmeɪt/ [with obj.] roughly calculate or judge the value, number, quantity, or extent of: *the aim is to estimate the effects of macroeconomic policy on the economy* | [with clause] *it is estimated that smoking causes 100,000 premature deaths every year* | [as adj. **estimated**] *an estimated cost of $1,000 million.*
▶ **noun** /ˈɛstɪmət/ an approximate calculation or judgement of the value, number, quantity, or extent of something: *at a rough estimate, staff are recycling a quarter of paper used.*
■ a written statement indicating the likely price that will be charged for specified work or repairs. ■ a judgement of the worth or character of someone or something: *his high estimate of the poem.*
– DERIVATIVES **estimative** /-mətɪv/ adjective.
– ORIGIN late Middle English: from Latin *aestimat-* 'determined, appraised', from the verb *aestimare*. The noun originally meant 'intellectual ability, comprehension' (only in late Middle English), later 'valuing, a valuation' (compare with **ESTIMATION**). The verb originally meant 'to think well or badly of someone or something' (late 15th cent.), later 'regard as being, consider to be' (compare with **ESTEEM**).

estimation ▶ **noun** a rough calculation of the value, number, quantity, or extent of something: *estimations of protein concentrations.*
■ [usu. in sing.] a judgement of the worth or character of someone or something: *the pop star rose in my estimation.*
– ORIGIN late Middle English (originally in the sense 'comprehension, intuition', also 'valuing, a valuation'): from Latin *aestimatio(n-)*, from *aestimare* 'determine, appraise' (see **ESTIMATE**).

estimator ▶ **noun** Statistics a rule, method, or criterion for arriving at an estimate of the value of a parameter.
■ a quantity used or evaluated as such an estimate. ■ a person who estimates the price, value, number, quantity, or extent of something.

estival ▶ **adjective** US spelling of **AESTIVAL**.

estivate ▶ **verb** US spelling of **AESTIVATE**.

estivation ▶ **noun** US spelling of **AESTIVATION**.

estoile /ɪˈstɔɪl, ɛ-/ ▶ **noun** Heraldry a star with (usually six) wavy points or rays.
– ORIGIN late 16th cent.: via Old French from Latin *stella* 'star'.

Estonia /ɪˈstəʊnɪə/ a Baltic country on the south coast of the Gulf of Finland; pop. 1,591,000 (est. 1991); languages, Estonian (official), Russian; capital, Tallinn.

> Previously ruled by the Teutonic Knights and then by Sweden, Estonia was ceded to Russia in 1721. It was proclaimed an independent republic in 1918 but was annexed by the USSR in 1940 as a constituent republic, the Estonian SSR. With the break-up of the Soviet Union Estonia regained its independence in 1991.

Estonian ▶ **adjective** of or relating to Estonia or its people or their language.
▶ **noun 1** a native or national of Estonia, or a person of Estonian descent.
2 [mass noun] the Finno-Ugric language of Estonia, which is closely related to Finnish and is spoken by about a million people.

estop /ɪˈstɒp/ ▶ **verb** (**estopped**, **estopping**) [with obj.] (usu. **be estopped from**) Law bar or preclude by estoppel.
– ORIGIN late Middle English (in the sense 'stop up, dam, plug'): from Old French *estopper* 'stop up, impede', from late Latin *stuppare*, from Latin *stuppa* 'tow, oakum'. Compare with **STOP** and **STUFF**.

estoppel /ɪˈstɒp(ə)l/ ▶ **noun** [mass noun] Law the principle which precludes a person from asserting something contrary to what is implied by a previous action or statement of that person or by a previous pertinent judicial determination.
– ORIGIN mid 16th cent.: from Old French *estouppail* 'bung', from *estopper* (see **ESTOP**).

Estoril /ˌɛʃtəˈrɪl/ a resort on the Atlantic coast of Portugal; pop. 24,850 (1991).

estovers /ɪˈstəʊvəz, ɛ-/ ▶ **plural noun** (usu. **common/right of estovers**) Brit., chiefly historical the right to take wood for fuel, repairs, or other necessary purpose from land one does not own, especially land of which one is the tenant or lessee.
– ORIGIN late 15th cent.: plural of Anglo-Norman French *estover*, noun use of a verb meaning 'be necessary', based on Latin *est opus* 'it is necessary'.

estradiol ▶ **noun** US spelling of **OESTRADIOL**.

estrange /ɪˈstreɪn(d)ʒ, ɛ-/ ▶ **verb** [with obj.] cause (someone) to be no longer close, on friendly terms, or in communication with someone: *are you deliberately seeking to estrange your readers?*
– DERIVATIVES **estrangement** noun.
– ORIGIN late 15th cent.: from Old French *estranger*, from Latin *extraneare* 'treat as a stranger', from *extraneus* 'not belonging to the family', used as a noun to mean 'stranger'. Compare with **STRANGE**.

estranged ▶ **adjective** (of a person) no longer close, on friendly terms, or in communication with someone: *Harriet felt more* ***estranged from*** *her daughter than ever* | *her estranged father.*
■ (of a wife or husband) no longer living with their spouse.

estreat /ɪˈstriːt, ɛ-/ Law, chiefly historical ▶ **verb** [with obj.] enforce the forfeit of (a surety for bail or other recognizance).
▶ **noun** a copy of a court record for use in the enforcement of a fine or forfeiture of a recognizance.
– DERIVATIVES **estreatment** noun.
– ORIGIN Middle English: from Old French *estraite*, feminine past participle of *estraire*, from Latin *extrahere* 'draw out' (see **EXTRACT**).

Estremadura /ˌɛʃtrəməˈdʊərə/ a coastal region and former province of west central Portugal.

estrogen etc. ▶ **noun** US spelling of **OESTROGEN** etc.

estrus etc. ▶ **noun** US spelling of **OESTRUS** etc.

estuary /ˈɛstjʊ(ə)ri/ ▶ **noun** (pl. **-ies**) the tidal mouth of a large river, where the tide meets the stream.
– DERIVATIVES **estuarial** adjective, **estuarine** /-rʌɪn/ adjective.
– ORIGIN mid 16th cent. (denoting a tidal inlet of any size): from Latin *aestuarium* 'tidal part of a shore', from *aestus* 'tide'.

Estuary English ▶ **noun** [mass noun] (in the UK) a type of accent identified as spreading outwards from London and containing features of both received pronunciation and London speech.

estufa /ɛˈstuːfə/ ▶ **noun 1** a heated chamber in which Madeira wine is stored and matured.
2 US an underground chamber in which a fire is kept permanently alight, used as a place of assembly by Pueblo Indians.
– ORIGIN mid 19th cent.: from Spanish, probably based on Greek *tuphos* 'steam or smoke'.

e.s.u. ▶ **abbreviation for** electrostatic unit(s).

esurient /ɪˈsjʊərɪənt, ɛ-/ ▶ **adjective** archaic or humorous hungry or greedy.
– DERIVATIVES **esuriently** adverb.
– ORIGIN late 17th cent.: from Latin *esurient-* 'being hungry', from the verb *esurire*, from *esse* 'eat'.

Esztergom /ˈɛstəgɒm/ a town and river port on the Danube in Hungary; pop. 29,730 (1993).

ET ▶ **abbreviation for** ■ (in North America) Eastern time. ■ Egypt (international vehicle registration). ■ extraterrestrial.

-et[1] ▶ **suffix** forming nouns which were originally diminutives: *baronet* | *hatchet* | *tablet.*
– ORIGIN from Old French *-et*, *-ete*.

-et[2] (also **-ete**) ▶ **suffix** forming nouns such as *comet*, and often denoting people: *athlete* | *poet.*
– ORIGIN from Greek *-ētēs*.

ETA[1] /ˌiːtiːˈeɪ/ ▶ **abbreviation for** estimated time of arrival, in particular the time at which an aircraft or ship is expected to arrive at its destination.

ETA[2] /ˈɛtə/ a Basque separatist movement in Spain, founded in 1959, which is waging a terrorist campaign for an independent Basque state.
– ORIGIN Basque acronym, from *Euzkadi ta Azkatasuna* 'Basque homeland and liberty'.

eta /ˈiːtə/ ▶ **noun** the seventh letter of the Greek alphabet (**Η**, **η**), transliterated as 'e' or 'ē'.
■ (**Eta**) [followed by Latin genitive] Astronomy the seventh star in a constellation: *Eta Carinae.*
– ORIGIN from Greek *ēta*.

etagere /ˌɛtəˈʒɛː/ ▶ **noun** (pl. same or **etageres**) a piece of furniture with a number of open shelves for displaying ornaments.
– ORIGIN French *étagère*, from *étage* 'shelf'.

et al. /ɛt ˈal/ ▶ **abbreviation** and others (used especially in referring to academic books or articles that have more than one author): *the conclusions of Gardner et al.*
– ORIGIN from Latin *et alii*.

etalon /ˈɛtəlɒn/ ▶ **noun** Physics a device consisting of two reflecting plates, for producing interfering light beams.
– ORIGIN early 20th cent.: from French *étalon*, literally 'standard of measurement'.

etc. ▶ **abbreviation for** et cetera.

et cetera /ɛtˈsɛt(ə)rə, ɪt-/ (also **etcetera**) ▶ **adverb** used at the end of a list to indicate that further, similar items are included: *we're trying to resolve problems of obtaining equipment, drugs, et cetera.*
■ indicating that a list is too tedious or clichéd to give in full: *we've all got to do our duty, pull our weight, et cetera, et cetera.*
– ORIGIN Latin, from *et* 'and' and *cetera* 'the rest' (neuter plural of *ceterus* 'left over').

> **USAGE** A common mispronunciation of **et cetera** involves replacing the **t** in **et** with a **k**. This follows a process known as *assimilation* by which sounds become made more like those that follow them—that is, they become more easy for the speaker to articulate.

etceteras ▶ **plural noun** dated unspecified or typical extra items: *she began to pack her compact, comb, and other etceteras.*

etch ▶ **verb** [with obj.] **1** engrave (metal, glass, or stone) by coating it with a protective layer, drawing on it with a needle, and then covering it with acid to attack the parts the needle has exposed, especially in order to produce prints from it: [as adj. **etched**] *etched glass windows.*
■ use such a process to produce (a print or design): *the image is* ***etched into*** *the metal plate.* ■ (of an acid or other solvent) corrode or eat away the surface of (something). ■ selectively dissolve the surface of (a semiconductor or printed circuit) with a solvent, laser, or stream of electrons.
2 (usu. **be etched**) cut or carve (a text or design) on a surface: *her initials were* ***etched on*** *the table flap* | figurative *his name is* ***etched in*** *baseball history.*
■ mark (a surface) with a carved text or design: *a Pictish stone* ***etched with*** *mysterious designs.* ■ cause to stand out or be clearly defined or visible: *Jo watched the*

outline of the town ***etched against*** *the sky* | *her face was* ***etched with*** *tiredness* | [as adj. **etched**] *her finely etched profile* | figurative *the incident was* ***etched*** *indelibly* ***in*** *her mind.*

▶**noun** [mass noun] the action or process of etching something.

– DERIVATIVES **etcher** noun.

– ORIGIN mid 17th cent.: from Dutch *etsen*, from German *ätzen*, from a base meaning 'cause to eat'; related to **EAT**.

etchant /ˈɛtʃ(ə)nt/ ▶**noun** an acid or corrosive chemical used in etching; a mordant.

etching ▶**noun** a print produced by the process of etching: *etchings of animals and wildflowers.*
■[mass noun] the art or process of producing etched plates or objects.

-ete ▶**suffix** variant spelling of **-ET**[2] (as in *athlete*).

eternal /ɪˈtəːn(ə)l, iː-/ ▶**adjective** lasting or existing forever; without end or beginning: *the secret of eternal youth* | *fear of eternal damnation.*
■(of truths, values, or questions) valid for all time; essentially unchanging: *eternal truths of art and life.* ■ informal seeming to last or persist forever, especially on account of being tedious or annoying: *eternal nagging demands* | *she is an eternal optimist.* ■ used to emphasize expressions of admiration, gratitude, or other feelings: *to his eternal credit, he maintained his dignity throughout.* ■ (**the Eternal**) used to refer to an everlasting or universal spirit, as represented by God.

– PHRASES **the Eternal City** a name for the city of Rome. **eternal triangle** a relationship between three people, typically a couple and the lover of one of them, involving sexual rivalry.

– DERIVATIVES **eternality** /ˌɪtəːˈnalɪti, iː-/ noun, **eternalize** (also **-ise**) verb, **eternally** adverb, **eternalness** noun.

– ORIGIN late Middle English: via Old French from late Latin *aeternalis*, from Latin *aeternus*, from *aevum* 'age'.

eternity ▶**noun** (pl. **-ies**) [mass noun] infinite or unending time: *their love was sealed for eternity* | *this state of affairs has lasted* ***for all eternity.***
■a state to which time has no application; timelessness. ■ Theology endless life after death: *immortal souls destined for eternity.* ■ used euphemistically to refer to death: *he could have crashed the car and taken them both to eternity.* ■ (**an eternity**) informal a period of time that seems very long, especially on account of being tedious or annoying: *a silence that lasted an eternity.*

– ORIGIN late Middle English: from Old French *eternite*, from Latin *aeternitas*, from *aeternus* 'without beginning or end' (see **ETERNAL**).

eternity ring ▶**noun** a ring given as a symbol of lasting affection, typically having an unbroken circle of gems set into it.

eternize /ɪˈtəːnʌɪz, iː-/ (also **-ise**) ▶**verb** [with obj.] poetic/literary make eternal; cause to live or last forever.

Etesian wind /ɪˈtiːʒɪən, ɪˈtiːz-, ɪˈtiːʒ(ə)n/ ▶**noun** another term for **MELTEMI**.

– ORIGIN early 17th cent.: *Etesian* from Latin *etesius* 'annual' (from Greek *etēsios*, from *etos* 'year') + **-AN**.

ETH ▶**abbreviation for** Ethiopia (international vehicle registration).

eth /ɛð/ (also **edh**) ▶**noun** an Old English letter, ð or Đ, representing the dental fricatives /ð/ and /θ/. It was superseded by the digraph *th*, but is now used as a phonetic symbol for the voiced dental fricative /ð/. Compare with **THORN** (sense 3).

– ORIGIN from Danish *edh*, perhaps representing the sound of the letter.

-eth[1] ▶**suffix** variant spelling of **-TH**[1] (as in *fiftieth*).

-eth[2] (also **-th**) ▶**suffix** archaic forming the third person singular of the present tense of verbs: *doeth* | *saith.*

– ORIGIN Old English *-eth, -ath, -th.*

ethacrynic acid /ˌɛθəˈkrɪnɪk/ ▶**noun** [mass noun] Medicine a powerful diuretic drug used in the treatment of fluid retention, especially that associated with heart, liver, and kidney disorders.
● Alternative name: **2,3-dichloro-4-(2-ethylacryloyl)phenoxy)acetic acid**; chem. formula: $C_{13}H_{12}Cl_2O_4$.

– ORIGIN 1960s: *ethacrynic* from elements of the systematic name (see above).

ethambutol /ɛˈθambjʊtɒl/ ▶**noun** [mass noun] Medicine a synthetic compound with bacteriostatic properties, used in combination with other drugs in the treatment of tuberculosis.
● A derivative of ethylenediamine; chem. formula: $C_{10}H_{24}N_2O_2$.

– ORIGIN 1960s: from *eth(yl)* + *am(ine)* + *but(an)ol.*

ethanal /ˈɛθ(ə)nal/ ▶**noun** systematic chemical name for **ACETALDEHYDE**.

– ORIGIN late 19th cent.: blend of **ETHANE** and **ALDEHYDE**.

ethanamide /ɪˈθanəmʌɪd/ ▶**noun** systematic chemical name for **ACETAMIDE**.

ethane /ˈiːθeɪn, ˈɛθ-/ ▶**noun** [mass noun] Chemistry a colourless, odourless, flammable gas which is a constituent of petroleum and natural gas. It is the second member of the alkane series.
● Chem. formula: C_2H_6.

– ORIGIN late 19th cent.: from **ETHER** + **-ANE**[2].

ethanediol /ˈiːθeɪnˌdʌɪɒl, ˈɛθ-/ ▶**noun** systematic chemical name for **ETHYLENE GLYCOL**.

ethanoic acid /ˌɛθəˈnəʊɪk/ ▶**noun** systematic chemical name for **ACETIC ACID**.

– DERIVATIVES **ethanoate** noun.

ethanol /ˈɛθənɒl/ ▶**noun** systematic chemical name for **ETHYL ALCOHOL** (see **ALCOHOL**).

– ORIGIN early 20th cent.: blend of **ETHANE** and **ALCOHOL**.

ethchlorvynol /ˌɛθklɔːˈvʌɪnɒl/ ▶**noun** another name for **PLACIDYL**.

Ethelred /ˈɛθəlrɛd/ the name of two English kings:
■**Ethelred I** (d.871), king of Wessex and Kent 865–71, elder brother of Alfred. His reign was marked by the continuing struggle against the invading Danes. Alfred joined Ethelred's campaigns and succeeded him on his death.
■**Ethelred II** (c.969–1016), king of England 978–1016; known as **Ethelred the Unready**. Ethelred's inability to confront the Danes after he succeeded his murdered half-brother St Edward the Martyr led to his payment of tribute to prevent their attacks. In 1013 he briefly lost his throne to the Danish king Sweyn I. [ORIGIN: *Unready*, later form of obsolete *unredy* 'badly advised'.]

ethene /ˈɛθiːn/ ▶**noun** systematic chemical name for **ETHYLENE**.

– ORIGIN mid 19th cent.: from **ETHER** + **-ENE**.

ether /ˈiːθə/ ▶**noun** [mass noun] **1** Chemistry a pleasant-smelling colourless volatile liquid that is highly flammable. It is used as an anaesthetic and as a solvent or intermediate in industrial processes.
● Alternative names: **diethyl ether**, ethoxyethane; chem. formula: $C_2H_5OC_2H_5$.
■[count noun] any organic compound with a similar structure to this, having an oxygen atom linking two alkyl or other organic groups: *methyl t-butyl ether.*
2 (also **aether**) chiefly poetic/literary the clear sky; the upper regions of air beyond the clouds: *nasty gases and smoke disperse into the ether.*
3 (also **aether**) Physics, archaic a very rarefied and highly elastic substance formerly believed to permeate all space, including the interstices between the particles of matter, and to be the medium whose vibrations constituted light and other electromagnetic radiation.
■(**the ether**) informal air regarded as a medium for radio: *choral evensong still wafts across the ether.*

– DERIVATIVES **etheric** /iːˈθɛrɪk, ˈiːθ(ə)rɪk/ adjective.

– ORIGIN late Middle English: from Old French, or via Latin from Greek *aithēr* 'upper air', from the base of *aithein* 'burn, shine'. Originally the word denoted a substance believed to occupy space beyond the sphere of the moon. Sense 3 arose in the mid 17th cent. and sense 1 in the mid 18th cent.

ethereal /ɪˈθɪərɪəl/ (also **etherial**) ▶**adjective** **1** extremely delicate and light in a way that seems too perfect for this world: *her ethereal beauty* | *a singer who has a weirdly ethereal voice.*
■heavenly or spiritual: *ethereal, otherworldly visions.*
2 Chemistry (of a solution) having diethyl ether as a solvent.

– DERIVATIVES **ethereality** noun, **etherealize** (also **-ise**) verb, **ethereally** adverb.

– ORIGIN early 16th cent.: via Latin from Greek *aitherios* (from *aithēr* 'ether') + **-AL**.

etherize (also **-ise**) ▶**verb** [with obj.] chiefly historical anaesthetize (a person or animal) with ether.

– DERIVATIVES **etherization** noun.

Ethernet /ˈiːθənɛt/ ▶**noun** Computing a system for connecting a number of computer systems to form a local area network, with protocols to control the passing of information and to avoid simultaneous transmission by two or more systems.
■a network using this.

– ORIGIN 1970s: blend of **ETHER** and **NETWORK**.

ethic /ˈɛθɪk/ ▶**noun** [in sing.] a set of moral principles, especially ones relating to or affirming a specified group, field, or form of conduct: *the puritan ethic was being replaced by the hedonist ethic.*

▶**adjective** rare of or relating to moral principles or the branch of knowledge dealing with these.

– ORIGIN late Middle English (denoting ethics or moral philosophy; also used attributively): from Old French *éthique*, from Latin *ethice*, from Greek (*hē*) *ēthikē* (*tekhnē*) '(the science of) morals', based on *ēthos* (see **ETHOS**).

ethical ▶**adjective** of or relating to moral principles or the branch of knowledge dealing with these: *ethical issues in nursing* | *ethical standards.*
■morally correct: *can a profitable business ever be ethical?* ■ [attrib.] (of a medicine) legally available only on a doctor's prescription and usually not advertised to the general public.

– DERIVATIVES **ethicality** noun, **ethically** adverb [sentence adverb] *is capitalism ethically justifiable?*

ethical investment ▶**noun** [mass noun] investment in companies that meet ethical criteria specified by the investor, typically excluding the armaments and tobacco industries.

ethics ▶**plural noun** **1** [usu. treated as pl.] moral principles that govern a person's behaviour or the conducting of an activity: *medical ethics also enter into the question.*
2 [usu. treated as sing.] the branch of knowledge that deals with moral principles.

Schools of ethics in Western philosophy can be divided, very roughly, into three sorts. The first, drawing on the work of Aristotle, holds that the virtues (such as justice, charity, and generosity) are dispositions to act in ways that benefit both the person possessing them and that person's society. The second, defended particularly by Kant, makes the concept of duty central to morality: humans are bound, from a knowledge of their duty as rational beings, to obey the categorical imperative to respect other rational beings. Thirdly, utilitarianism asserts that the guiding principle of conduct should be the greatest happiness or benefit of the greatest number.

– DERIVATIVES **ethicist** noun.

ethidium bromide /ɛˈθɪdɪəm/ ▶**noun** [mass noun] Chemistry a purple synthetic dye used in the treatment of trypanosome blood infection, to stain DNA, and to destroy the superhelical structure of DNA. It is a derivative of phenanthridine.

Ethiopia /ˌiːθɪˈəʊpɪə/ a country in NE Africa, on the Red Sea; pop. 45,892,000 (est. 1993); languages, Amharic (official), several other Afro-Asiatic languages; capital, Addis Ababa. Former name **ABYSSINIA**.

Ethiopia is the oldest independent country in Africa, having a recorded civilization that dates from the 2nd millennium BC. Little known to Europeans until the late 19th century, it was invaded and conquered by Italy in 1935. The emperor Haile Selassie was restored by the British in 1941 and ruled until overthrown in a Marxist coup in 1974. The subsequent period was marked by civil war, fighting against separatist guerrillas in Eritrea and Tigray, and by repeated famines; after the fall of the government in 1991 a multiparty system was adopted.

– ORIGIN via Latin from Greek *Aethiops*, from *aithein* 'to burn' + *ōps* 'the face'.

Ethiopian ▶**noun** **1** a native or national of Ethiopia, or a person of Ethiopian descent.
■archaic a black person.

▶**adjective** **1** of or relating to Ethiopia or its people.
2 Zoology of, relating to, or denoting a zoogeographical region comprising Africa south of the Sahara, together with the tropical part of the Arabian peninsula and (usually) Madagascar. Distinctive animals include the giraffes, hippopotamuses, aardvark, elephant shrews, tenrecs, and lemurs. Also called **AFROTROPICAL**.

Ethiopic /ˌiːθɪˈɒpɪk/ ▶**noun** another term for **GE'EZ**.

▶**adjective** of, in, or relating to Ge'ez.

– ORIGIN mid 17th cent. (as an adjective): via Latin from Greek *aithiopikos*, from *Aethiops* (see **ETHIOPIA**).

ethmoid /ˈɛθmɔɪd/ (also **ethmoid bone**) ▶**noun** Anatomy a square bone at the root of the nose, forming part of the cranium, and having many perforations through which the olfactory nerves pass to the nose.

– DERIVATIVES **ethmoidal** adjective.

– ORIGIN mid 18th cent.: from Greek *ēthmoeidēs*, from *ēthmos* 'a sieve'.

ethnic ▶adjective of or relating to a population subgroup (within a larger or dominant national or cultural group) with a common national or cultural tradition: *ethnic and cultural rights and traditions* | *leaders of ethnic communities.*
■ of or relating to national and cultural origins: *we recruit our employees regardless of ethnic origin.* ■ denoting origin by birth or descent rather than by present nationality: *ethnic Albanians in Kosovo.* ■ characteristic of or belonging to a non-Western cultural tradition: *cheap ethnic dresses* | *folk and ethnic music.* ■ archaic neither Christian nor Jewish; pagan or heathen.
▶noun chiefly N. Amer. a member of an ethnic minority.
– DERIVATIVES **ethnically** adverb [sentence adverb] *Denmark is ethnically Scandinavian.*
– ORIGIN late Middle English (denoting a person not of the Christian or Jewish faith): via ecclesiastical Latin from Greek *ethnikos* 'heathen', from *ethnos* 'nation'. Current senses date from the 19th cent.

ethnic cleansing ▶noun [mass noun] the mass expulsion or killing of members of one ethnic or religious group in an area by those of another.

ethnicity ▶noun (pl. **-ies**) [mass noun] the fact or state of belonging to a social group that has a common national or cultural tradition: *the interrelationship between gender, ethnicity, and class* | [count noun] *the diverse experience of women of different ethnicities.*

ethnic minority ▶noun a group within a community which has different national or cultural traditions from the main population.

ethno- /ˈɛθnəʊ/ ▶combining form ethnic; ethnological: *ethnocentric* | *ethnology.*
– ORIGIN from Greek *ethnos* 'nation'.

ethnoarchaeology ▶noun [mass noun] the study of the social organization and other ethnological features of present-day societies on the basis of their material culture, in order to draw conclusions about past societies from their material remains.
– DERIVATIVES **ethnoarchaeological** adjective, **ethnoarchaeologist** noun.

ethnobotany ▶noun [mass noun] the scientific study of the traditional knowledge and customs of a people concerning plants and their medical, religious, and other uses.
– DERIVATIVES **ethnobotanic** adjective, **ethno-botanical** adjective, **ethnobotanist** noun.

ethnocentric ▶adjective evaluating other peoples and cultures according to assumptions or preconceptions originating in the standards and customs of one's own people or culture.
– DERIVATIVES **ethnocentrically** adverb, **ethno-centricity** noun, **ethnocentrism** noun.

ethnocide /ˈɛθnə(ʊ)sʌɪd/ ▶noun [mass noun] the deliberate and systematic destruction of the culture of an ethnic group.

ethnocultural ▶adjective relating to or denoting a particular ethnic group.

ethnogenesis /ˌɛθnə(ʊ)ˈdʒɛnɪsɪs/ ▶noun the formation or emergence of an ethnic group.

ethnography /ɛθˈnɒɡrəfi/ ▶noun [mass noun] the scientific description of peoples and cultures with their customs, habits, and mutual differences.
– DERIVATIVES **ethnographer** noun, **ethnographic** adjective, **ethnographical** adjective, **ethno-graphically** adverb.

ethnohistory ▶noun [mass noun] the branch of anthropology concerned with the history of peoples and cultures, especially non-Western ones.
– DERIVATIVES **ethnohistorian** noun, **ethnohistoric** adjective, **ethnohistorical** adjective, **ethno-historically** adverb.

ethnolinguistics /ˌɛθnəʊlɪŋˈɡwɪstɪks/ ▶plural noun [treated as sing.] the branch of linguistics concerned with the relations between linguistic and cultural behaviour.
– DERIVATIVES **ethnolinguist** noun, **ethnolinguistic** adjective.

ethnology /ɛθˈnɒlədʒi/ ▶noun [mass noun] the study of the characteristics of different peoples and the differences and relationships between them.
– DERIVATIVES **ethnologic** /-nəˈlɒdʒɪk/ adjective, **ethnological** adjective, **ethnologically** adverb, **ethnologist** noun.

ethnomethodology /ˌɛθnəʊˌmɛθəˈdɒlədʒi/ ▶noun [mass noun] a method of sociological analysis that examines how individuals use everyday conversation to construct a common-sense view of the world.

– DERIVATIVES **ethnomethodological** adjective, **ethnomethodologist** noun.

ethnomusicology ▶noun [mass noun] the study of the music of different cultures, especially non-Western ones.
– DERIVATIVES **ethnomusicologic** adjective, **ethno-musicological** adjective, **ethnomusicologist** noun.

ethnoscience ▶noun [mass noun] the study of the different ways the world is perceived and categorized in different cultures.

ethogram /ˈiːθəɡram/ ▶noun Zoology a catalogue or table of all the different kinds of behaviour or activity observed in an animal.
– ORIGIN 1930s: from Greek *ēthos* 'nature, disposition' + **-GRAM**[1].

ethology /iːˈθɒlədʒi/ ▶noun [mass noun] the science of animal behaviour.
■ the study of human behaviour and social organization from a biological perspective.
– DERIVATIVES **ethological** adjective, **ethologist** noun.
– ORIGIN late 19th cent.: via Latin from Greek *ēthologia*, from *ēthos* (see **ETHOS**).

ethos /ˈiːθɒs/ ▶noun the characteristic spirit of a culture, era, or community as manifested in its attitudes and aspirations: *a challenge to the ethos of the 1960s.*
– ORIGIN mid 19th cent.: from modern Latin, from Greek *ēthos* 'nature, disposition', (plural) 'customs'.

ethoxyethane /iːˌθɒksɪˈiːθeɪn/ ▶noun systematic chemical name for **DIETHYL ETHER** (see **ETHER** (sense 1)).

ethyl /ˈɛθʌɪl, -θɪl, ˈiː-/ ▶noun [usu. as modifier] Chemistry of or denoting the hydrocarbon radical —C_2H_5, derived from ethane and present in many organic compounds: *ethyl acetate* | *an ethyl group.*
– ORIGIN mid 19th cent.: from German, from *Äther* 'ether' + **-YL**.

ethyl acetate ▶noun [mass noun] Chemistry a colourless volatile liquid with a fruity smell, used as a plastics solvent and in flavourings and perfumes.
● Chem. formula: $CH_3COOC_2H_5$.

ethyl alcohol ▶noun see **ALCOHOL**.

ethylbenzene ▶noun [mass noun] Chemistry a colourless flammable liquid hydrocarbon, used in the manufacture of styrene.
● Chem. formula: $C_6H_5C_2H_5$.

ethylene /ˈɛθɪliːn, -θ(ə)l-/ ▶noun [mass noun] Chemistry a flammable hydrocarbon gas of the alkene series, occurring in natural gas, coal gas, and crude oil and given off by ripening fruit. It is used in chemical synthesis, especially in the manufacture of polythene.
● Alternative name: **ethene**; chem. formula: C_2H_4.

ethylenediamine /ˌɛθɪliːndʌɪˈɛmiːn, -θ(ə)l-, -dʌɪˈam-, -ˈdʌɪəmiːn/ ▶noun [mass noun] Chemistry a viscous liquid used in making detergents and emulsifying agents.
● Chem. formula: $NH_2CH_2CH_2NH_2$.

ethylene glycol ▶noun [mass noun] Chemistry a colourless viscous hygroscopic liquid used as an antifreeze, in the manufacture of polyesters, and in the preservation of ancient waterlogged timbers.
● Alternative name: **ethanediol**; chem. formula: $CH_2(OH)CH_2OH$.

ethylene oxide ▶noun [mass noun] Chemistry a flammable toxic gas used as an intermediate and fumigant.
● An epoxide; chem. formula: $(CH_2)_2O$.

ethyne /ˈiːθʌɪn, ˈɛθ-/ ▶noun systematic chemical name for **ACETYLENE**.

etic /ˈɛtɪk/ Anthropology ▶adjective relating to or denoting an approach to the study or description of a particular language or culture that is general, non-structural, and objective in its perspective. Often contrasted with **EMIC**.
▶plural noun (**etics**) [treated as sing.] study adopting this approach.
– ORIGIN 1950s: abstracted from **PHONETIC**.

-etic ▶suffix forming adjectives and nouns such as *pathetic, peripatetic.*
– ORIGIN from Greek *-ētikos* or *-ētikos.*

etiolated /ˈiːtɪəleɪtɪd/ ▶adjective (of a plant) pale and drawn out due to a lack of light.
■ having lost vigour or substance; feeble: *a tone of etiolated nostalgia.*
– DERIVATIVES **etiolation** noun.

– ORIGIN late 18th cent.: from the verb *etiolate* (from French *étioler*, from Norman French *étieuler* 'grow into haulm') + **-ED**[2].

etiology ▶noun US spelling of **AETIOLOGY**.

etiquette /ˈɛtɪkɛt, ɛtɪˈkɛt/ ▶noun [mass noun] the customary code of polite behaviour in society or among members of a particular profession or group.
– ORIGIN mid 18th cent.: from French *étiquette* 'list of ceremonial observances of a court', also 'label, etiquette', from Old French *estiquette* (see **TICKET**).

Etna, Mount /ˈɛtnə/ a volcano in eastern Sicily, rising to 3,323 m (10,902 ft). It is the highest and most active volcano in Europe.

Eton collar ▶noun a broad, stiff white collar worn outside the coat collar, especially with an Eton jacket.

Eton College /ˈiːt(ə)n/ a boys' public school in southern England, on the River Thames opposite Windsor, founded in 1440 by Henry VI to prepare scholars for King's College, Cambridge.

Eton crop ▶noun a short hairstyle worn by women in the 1920s.

Etonian /iːˈtəʊnɪən/ ▶noun a past or present member of Eton College: *an Old Etonian.*
▶adjective relating to or typical of Eton College.

Eton jacket ▶noun a short jacket reaching only to the waist, typically black and having a point at the back, formerly worn by pupils of Eton College.

Eton wall game ▶noun see **WALL GAME**.

Etosha Pan /ɪˈtɒʃə/ a depression in the plateau of northern Namibia, filled with salt water and having no outlets, extending over an area of 4,800 sq. km (1,854 sq. miles).

étouffée /ˌeɪtuːˈfeɪ/ ▶noun US a spicy Cajun stew made with vegetables and seafood.

etrier /ˈeɪtrɪeɪ/ ▶noun Climbing a short rope ladder with a few rungs of wood or metal.
– ORIGIN 1950s: from French *étrier* 'stirrup'.

Etruria /ɪˈtrʊərɪə/ an ancient state of western Italy, situated between the Rivers Arno and Tiber and corresponding approximately to modern Tuscany and parts of Umbria. It was the centre of the Etruscan civilization.
– DERIVATIVES **Etrurian** noun & adjective.

Etruscan /ɪˈtrʌsk(ə)n/ ▶adjective of or relating to ancient Etruria, its people, or their language. The Etruscan civilization was at its height *c.*500 BC and was an important influence on the Romans, who had subdued the Etruscans by the end of the 3rd century BC.
▶noun 1 a native of ancient Etruria.
2 [mass noun] the language of ancient Etruria, which was written in an alphabet derived from Greek but is not related to any known language.
– ORIGIN from Latin *Etruscus* + **-AN**.

et seq. (also **et seqq.**) ▶adverb and what follows (used in page references): *see volume 35, p. 329 et seq.*
– ORIGIN from Latin *et sequens* 'and the following', or from *et sequentes, et sequentia* 'and the following things'.

-ette ▶suffix forming nouns: 1 denoting relatively small size: *kitchenette.*
2 denoting an imitation or substitute: *flannelette.*
3 denoting female gender: *suffragette.*
– ORIGIN from Old French *-ette*, feminine of **-ET**[1].

USAGE The use of **-ette** as a feminine suffix for forming new words is relatively recent: it was first recorded in the word **suffragette** at the beginning of the 20th century and has since been used to form only a handful of well-established words, including **usherette** and **drum majorette**, for example. In the modern context, where the tendency is to use words which are neutral in gender, the suffix **-ette** is not very productive and new words formed using it tend to be restricted to the deliberately flippant or humorous, as, for example, **bimbette** and **punkette**.

étude /ˈeɪtjuːd, eɪˈtjuːd/ ▶noun a short musical composition, typically for one instrument, designed as an exercise to improve the technique or demonstrate the skill of the player.
– ORIGIN mid 19th cent.: from French, literally 'study'.

etui /ɛˈtwiː/ ▶noun (pl. **etuis**) dated a small ornamental case for holding needles, cosmetics, and other articles.
– ORIGIN early 17th cent.: from French *étui*, from Old

French *estui* 'prison', from *estuier* 'shut up, keep'. Compare with **TWEEZERS**.

-etum ▶ **suffix** (forming nouns) denoting a collection or plantation of trees or other plants: *arboretum* | *pinetum*.
– ORIGIN from Latin.

etymologize (also **-ise**) ▶ **verb** [with obj.] (usu. **be etymologized**) give or trace the etymology of (a word).
– ORIGIN mid 16th cent.: from medieval Latin *etymologizare*, from Latin *etymologia* (see **ETYMOLOGY**).

etymology /ˌɛtɪˈmɒlədʒi/ ▶ **noun** (pl. **-ies**) [mass noun] the study of the origin of words and the way in which their meanings have changed throughout history.
■ [count noun] the origin of a word and the historical development of its meaning.
– DERIVATIVES **etymological** adjective, **etymologically** adverb, **etymologist** noun.
– ORIGIN late Middle English: from Old French *ethimologie*, via Latin from Greek *etumologia*, from *etumologos* 'student of etymology', from *etumon*, neuter singular of *etumos* 'true'.

etymon /ˈɛtɪmɒn/ ▶ **noun** (pl. **etymons** or **etyma**) a word or morpheme from which a later word is derived.
– ORIGIN late 16th cent. (denoting the original form of a word): via Latin from Greek *etumon* 'true thing' (see **ETYMOLOGY**).

EU ▶ **abbreviation for** European Union.

Eu ▶ **symbol for** the chemical element europium.

eu- ▶ **combining form** well; easily: *eupeptic* | *euphony*.
– ORIGIN from Greek *eu* 'well', from *eus* 'good'.

eubacterium /ˌjuːbakˈtɪərɪəm/ ▶ **noun** (pl. **eubacteria** /-rɪə/) **1** a bacterium of a large group typically having simple cells with rigid cell walls and often flagella for movement. The group comprises the 'true' bacteria and cyanobacteria, as distinct from archaea.
● Division (or subkingdom) Eubacteria, kingdom Monera; this group is sometimes taken to exclude non-rigid forms such as spirochaetes and mycoplasmas.
2 a bacterium found mainly in the intestines of vertebrates and in the soil.
● Genus *Eubacterium*; Gram-positive, anaerobic, rod-shaped bacteria.
– DERIVATIVES **eubacterial** adjective.

Euboea /juːˈbiːə/ an island of Greece in the western Aegean Sea, separated from the mainland by only a narrow channel at its capital, Chalcis. Greek name **ÉVVOIA**.

eucalyptus /ˌjuːkəˈlɪptəs/ (also **eucalypt**) ▶ **noun** (pl. **eucalyptuses** or **eucalypti** /-tʌɪ/) a fast-growing evergreen Australasian tree that has been widely introduced elsewhere. It is valued for its timber, oil, gum, resin, and as an ornamental tree. Also called **GUM**[1], **GUM TREE**.
● Genus *Eucalyptus*, family Myrtaceae: numerous species.
■ (also **eucalyptus oil**) [mass noun] the oil from eucalyptus leaves, chiefly used for its medicinal properties.
– ORIGIN modern Latin, from Greek *eu* 'well' + *kaluptos* 'covered' (from *kaluptein* 'to cover'), because the unopened flower is protected by a cap.

eucaryote ▶ **noun** variant spelling of **EUKARYOTE**.

eucatastrophe /ˌjuːkəˈtastrəfi/ ▶ **noun** rare a sudden and favourable resolution of events in a story; a happy ending.
– ORIGIN mid 20th cent.: said to have been coined by Tolkien.

Eucharist /ˈjuːk(ə)rɪst/ ▶ **noun** the Christian service, ceremony, or sacrament commemorating the Last Supper, in which bread and wine are consecrated and consumed.
■ the consecrated elements, especially the bread.

The bread and wine are referred to as the body and blood of Christ, though much theological controversy has focused on how substantially or symbolically this is to be interpreted. The service of worship is also called **Holy Communion** or (chiefly in the Protestant tradition) **the Lord's Supper** or (chiefly in the Catholic tradition) **the Mass**. See also **CONSUBSTANTIATION**, **TRANSUBSTANTIATION**.

– DERIVATIVES **Eucharistic** adjective, **Eucharistical** adjective.
– ORIGIN late Middle English: from Old French *eucariste*, based on ecclesiastical Greek *eukharistia* 'thanksgiving', from Greek *eukharistos* 'grateful', from *eu* 'well' + *kharizesthai* 'offer graciously' (from *kharis* 'grace').

euchre /ˈjuːkə/ ▶ **noun** [mass noun] a North American card game for two to four players, played with the thirty-two highest cards, the aim being to win at least three of the five tricks played.
▶ **verb** [with obj.] (in such a card game) gain the advantage over (another player) by preventing them from taking three tricks.
■ N. Amer. informal deceive, outwit, or cheat (someone): *the merchant can be euchred out of his caftan by hard bargaining.* ■ (**be euchred**) Austral. informal be exhausted or ruined.
– ORIGIN early 19th cent.: from German dialect *Jucker(spiel)*.

euchromatin /juːˈkrəʊmətɪn/ ▶ **noun** [mass noun] Genetics chromosome material which does not stain strongly except during cell division. It represents the major genes and is involved in transcription. Compare with **HETEROCHROMATIN**.
– DERIVATIVES **euchromatic** adjective.

Euclid /ˈjuːklɪd/ (*c*.300 BC), Greek mathematician. His great work *Elements of Geometry*, which covered plane geometry, the theory of numbers, irrationals, and solid geometry, was the standard work until other kinds of geometry were discovered in the 19th century.

Euclidean /juːˈklɪdɪən/ ▶ **adjective** of or relating to Euclid, in particular:
■ of or denoting the system of geometry based on the work of Euclid and corresponding to the geometry of ordinary experience. ■ of such a nature that the postulates of this system of geometry are valid. Compare with **NON-EUCLIDEAN**.

eucrite /ˈjuːkrʌɪt/ ▶ **noun** [mass noun] Geology a highly basic form of gabbro containing anorthite or bytownite with augite.
■ [count noun] a stony meteorite which contains no chondrules and consists mainly of anorthite and augite.
– ORIGIN mid 19th cent.: from Greek *eukritos* 'easily discerned', from *eu-* 'well' + *kritos* 'separated' (from *krinein* 'to separate').

eucryphia /juːˈkrɪfɪə/ ▶ **noun** a shrub or small tree with glossy dark green leaves and large white flowers, native to Australia and South America.
● Genus *Eucryphia*, family Eucryphiaceae.
– ORIGIN modern Latin, from Greek *eu* 'well' + *-kruphos* 'hidden' (with reference to its joined sepals).

eudaemonic /ˌjuːdɪˈmɒnɪk/ (also **eudemonic**) ▶ **adjective** formal conducive to happiness.
– ORIGIN mid 19th cent.: from Greek *eudaimonikos*, from *eudaimōn* 'happy' (see **EUDAEMONISM**).

eudaemonism /juːˈdiːmənɪz(ə)m/ (also **eudemonism**) ▶ **noun** [mass noun] a system of ethics that bases moral value on the likelihood of actions producing happiness.
– DERIVATIVES **eudaemonist** noun, **eudaemonistic** adjective.
– ORIGIN early 19th cent.: from Greek *eudaimonismos* 'system of happiness', from *eudaimōn* 'happy', from *eu* 'well' + *daimōn* 'guardian spirit'.

eudiometer /ˌjuːdɪˈɒmɪtə/ ▶ **noun** Chemistry a graduated glass tube in which mixtures of gases can be made to react by an electric spark, used to measure changes in volume of gases during chemical reactions.
– DERIVATIVES **eudiometric** adjective, **eudiometrical** adjective, **eudiometry** noun.
– ORIGIN late 18th cent. (denoting an instrument used to measure amounts of oxygen, thought to be greater in fine weather): from Greek *eudios* 'clear, fine' (weather), from *eu* 'well' + *dios* 'heavenly'.

eugenics /juːˈdʒɛnɪks/ ▶ **plural noun** [treated as sing.] the science of improving a population by controlled breeding to increase the occurrence of desirable heritable characteristics. Developed largely by Francis Galton as a method of improving the human race, it fell into disfavour only after the perversion of its doctrines by the Nazis.
– DERIVATIVES **eugenic** adjective, **eugenically** adverb, **eugenicist** noun & adjective, **eugenist** noun & adjective.

Eugénie /juːˈʒeɪni/ (1826–1920), Spanish empress of France 1853–70 and wife of Napoleon III; born *Eugénia María de Montijo de Guzmán*. She contributed much to her husband's court and was an important influence on his foreign policy.

eugenol /ˈjuːdʒɪnɒl/ ▶ **noun** [mass noun] Chemistry a colourless or pale yellow liquid compound present in oil of cloves and other essential oils and used in perfumery.

● Alternative name: **4-allyl-2-methoxyphenol**; chem. formula: C₁₀H₁₂O₂.
– ORIGIN late 19th cent.: from *eugenia* (genus name of the tree from which oil of cloves is obtained, named in honour of Prince *Eugene* of Savoy (1663–1736)) + **-OL**.

euglena /juːˈgliːnə/ ▶ **noun** Biology a green single-celled freshwater organism with a flagellum, sometimes forming a green scum on stagnant water.
● Genus *Euglena*, division Euglenophyta (or phylum Euglenophyta, kingdom Protista).
– ORIGIN modern Latin, from **EU-** 'well' + Greek *glēnē* 'eyeball, socket of joint'.

euglenoid /juːˈgliːnɔɪd/ Biology ▶ **noun** a flagellated single-celled organism of a group that comprises euglena and its relatives.
● Division (or phylum) Euglenophyta.
▶ **adjective** of or relating to organisms of this group.
■ (of cell locomotion) achieved by peristaltic waves that pass along the cell, characteristic of the euglenoids.

euhedral /juːˈhiːdr(ə)l/ ▶ **adjective** Geology (of a mineral crystal in a rock) bounded by faces corresponding to its regular crystal form, not constrained by adjacent minerals.

eukaryote /juːˈkarɪəʊt/ (also **eucaryote**) ▶ **noun** Biology an organism consisting of a cell or cells in which the genetic material is DNA in the form of chromosomes contained within a distinct nucleus. Eukaryotes include all living organisms other than the eubacteria and archaea. Compare with **PROKARYOTE**.
– DERIVATIVES **eukaryotic** adjective.
– ORIGIN 1960s: from **EU-** 'easily (formed)' + **KARYO-** 'kernel' + *-ote* as in *zygote*.

eulachon /ˈjuːləkɒn/ ▶ **noun** (pl. same) another term for **CANDLEFISH**.
– ORIGIN mid 19th cent.: from Lower Chinook.

Euler[1] /ˈɔɪlə/, Leonhard (1707–83), Swiss mathematician. Euler attempted to elucidate the nature of functions, and his study of infinite series led his successors, notably Abel and Cauchy, to introduce ideas of convergence and rigorous argument into mathematics.

Euler[2] /ˈɔɪlə/, Ulf Svante von (1905–83), Swedish physiologist, the son of Hans Euler-Chelpin. He was the first to discover a prostaglandin, which he isolated from semen. Euler also identified noradrenaline as the principal chemical neurotransmitter of the sympathetic nervous system. Nobel Prize for Physiology or Medicine (1970).

Euler-Chelpin /ˌɔɪləˈkɛlpɪn/, Hans Karl August Simon von (1873–1964), German-born Swedish biochemist. He worked mainly on enzymes and vitamins, and explained the role of enzymes in the alcoholic fermentation of sugar. Nobel Prize for Chemistry (1929).

Euler's constant Mathematics a constant used in numerical analysis, approximately equal to 0.577216. It represents the limit of the series $1 + \frac{1}{2} + \frac{1}{3} + \frac{1}{4} \ldots \frac{1}{n} - \ln n$ as n tends to infinity. It is not known whether this is a rational number or not.
– ORIGIN mid 19th cent.: named after L. *Euler* (see **EULER**[1]).

Euler's formula the geometrical formula $V - E + F = 2$, where V, E, and F are the numbers of vertices, edges, and faces of any simple convex polyhedron or of an equivalent topological graph.

eulogium /juːˈləʊdʒɪəm/ ▶ **noun** (pl. **eulogia** /-dʒɪə/ or **eulogiums**) another term for **EULOGY**.
– ORIGIN early 17th cent.: from medieval Latin, 'praise'.

eulogize /ˈjuːlədʒʌɪz/ (also **-ise**) ▶ **verb** [with obj.] praise highly in speech or writing: *he was eulogized as a rock star* | *a plaque that eulogizes the workers.*
– DERIVATIVES **eulogist** noun, **eulogistic** adjective, **eulogistically** adverb.

eulogy /ˈjuːlədʒi/ ▶ **noun** (pl. **-ies**) a speech or piece of writing that praises someone or something highly, typically someone who has just died: *a eulogy of Nicetas the martyr.*
– ORIGIN late Middle English (in the sense 'high praise'): from medieval Latin *eulogium*, *eulogia* (from Greek *eulogia* 'praise'), apparently influenced by Latin *elogium* 'inscription on a tomb' (from Greek *elegia* 'elegy'). The current sense dates from the late 16th cent.

Eumenides /juːˈmɛnɪdiːz/ Greek Mythology a name given to the Furies. The Eumenides probably originated as well-disposed deities of fertility, whose name was given to the Furies either by confusion or euphemistically.
– ORIGIN via Latin from Greek, from *eumenēs* 'well disposed', from *eu* 'well' + *menos* 'spirit'.

eunuch /ˈjuːnək/ ▶ noun a man who has been castrated, especially (in the past) one employed to guard the women's living areas at an oriental court.
■ an ineffectual person: *a nation of political eunuchs.*
– ORIGIN Old English, via Latin from Greek *eunoukhos*, literally 'bedroom guard', from *eunē* 'bed' + a second element related to *ekhein* 'to hold'.

eunuchoid /ˈjuːnəkɔɪd/ ▶ adjective chiefly Medicine resembling a eunuch, typically in having reduced or indeterminate sexual characteristics.
– DERIVATIVES **eunuchoidism** noun.

euonymus /juːˈɒnɪməs/ ▶ noun a shrub or small tree that is widely cultivated for its autumn colours and bright fruit.
● Genus *Euonymus*, family Celastraceae: numerous species, including the spindle tree.
– ORIGIN modern Latin (named by Linnaeus), from Latin *euonymos*, from Greek *euōnumos* 'having an auspicious or honoured name', from *eus* 'good' + *onoma* 'name'.

eupeptic /juːˈpɛptɪk/ ▶ adjective of or having good digestion or a consequent air of healthy good spirits.
– ORIGIN late 17th cent. (in the sense 'helping digestion'): from Greek *eupeptos*, from *eu* 'well, easily' + *peptein* 'to digest'.

euphausiid /juːˈfɔːzɪɪd/ ▶ noun Zoology a shrimp-like planktonic marine crustacean of an order which includes krill. Many kinds are luminescent.
● Order Euphausiacea, subclass Malacostraca.
– ORIGIN late 19th cent.: from modern Latin *Euphausia* (genus name from Greek *eu* 'well' + *phainein* 'to show' + *ousia* 'substance') + -ID².

euphemism /ˈjuːfəmɪz(ə)m/ ▶ noun a mild or indirect word or expression substituted for one considered to be too harsh or blunt when referring to something unpleasant or embarrassing: *the jargon has given us 'downsizing' as a euphemism for cuts.* The opposite of **DYSPHEMISM**.
– ORIGIN late 16th cent.: from Greek *euphēmismos*, from *euphēmizein* 'use auspicious words', from *eu* 'well' + *phēmē* 'speaking'.

euphemistic ▶ adjective using or of the nature of a euphemism: *the euphemistic terms she uses to describe her relationships.*
– DERIVATIVES **euphemistically** adverb.

euphemize (also **-ise**) ▶ verb [with obj.] refer to (something unpleasant or embarrassing) by means of a euphemism.
– ORIGIN mid 19th cent.: from Greek *euphēmizein* 'use auspicious words' (see **EUPHEMISM**).

euphonious /juːˈfəʊnɪəs/ ▶ adjective (of sound, especially speech) pleasing to the ear.
– DERIVATIVES **euphoniously** adverb.

euphonium /juːˈfəʊnɪəm/ ▶ noun a valved brass musical instrument resembling a small tuba of tenor pitch, played mainly in military and brass bands.
– ORIGIN mid 19th cent.: from Greek *euphōnos* 'having a pleasing sound' + -IUM.

euphony /ˈjuːf(ə)ni/ ▶ noun (pl. **-ies**) [mass noun] the quality of being pleasing to the ear.
■ the tendency to make phonetic change for ease of pronunciation.
– DERIVATIVES **euphonic** adjective, **euphonize** (also **-ise**) verb.
– ORIGIN late Middle English: from French *euphonie*, via late Latin from Greek *euphōnia*, from *euphōnos* 'well sounding' (based on *phōnē* 'sound').

euphorbia /juːˈfɔːbɪə/ ▶ noun a plant of a genus that comprises the spurges.
● Genus *Euphorbia*, family Euphorbiaceae.
– ORIGIN late Middle English: from Latin *euphorbea*, named after *Euphorbus*, Greek physician to the reputed discoverer of the plant, Juba II of Mauretania (1st cent. BC).

euphoria /juːˈfɔːrɪə/ ▶ noun [mass noun] a feeling or state of intense excitement and happiness: *in his euphoria, he had become convinced he could defeat them.*
– ORIGIN late 17th cent. (denoting well-being produced in a sick person by the use of drugs):

modern Latin, from Greek, from *euphoros* 'borne well, healthy', from *eu* 'well' + *pherein* 'to bear'.

euphoriant ▶ adjective (chiefly of a drug) producing a feeling of euphoria.
▶ noun a euphoriant drug.

euphoric ▶ adjective characterized by or feeling intense excitement and happiness: *a euphoric sense of freedom.*
– DERIVATIVES **euphorically** adverb.

euphrasia /juːˈfreɪzɪə/ ▶ noun a plant of the genus *Euphrasia* in the figwort family, especially eyebright.
■ [mass noun] a preparation of eyebright used in herbal medicine and homeopathy, especially for treating eye problems.
– ORIGIN early 18th cent.: via medieval Latin from Greek, literally 'cheerfulness', from *euphrainein* 'gladden the mind'.

Euphrates /juːˈfreɪtiːz/ a river of SW Asia which rises in the mountains of eastern Turkey and flows through Syria and Iraq to join the Tigris, forming the Shatt al-Arab waterway.

euphuism /ˈjuːfjʊɪz(ə)m/ ▶ noun [mass noun] formal an artificial, highly elaborate way of writing or speaking.
– DERIVATIVES **euphuist** noun, **euphuistic** adjective, **euphuistically** adverb.
– ORIGIN late 16th cent.: from *Euphues*, the name of a character in John Lyly's prose romance of the same name (1578–80), from Greek *euphuēs* 'well endowed by nature', from *eu* 'well' + the base of *phuē* 'growth'.

Eurasia /jʊ(ə)ˈreɪʒə, -ʃ(ə)/ a term used to describe the total continental land mass of Europe and Asia combined.

Eurasian ▶ adjective **1** of mixed European (or European-American) and Asian parentage.
2 of or relating to Eurasia.
▶ noun a person of mixed European (or European-American) and Asian parentage.

USAGE In the 19th century the word **Eurasian** was normally used to refer to a person of mixed British and Indian parentage. In its modern uses, however, the term is more often used to refer to a person of mixed white American and SE Asian parentage.

Euratom /jʊ(ə)ˈratəm/ ▶ abbreviation for European Atomic Energy Community.

eureka /jʊ(ə)ˈriːkə/ ▶ exclamation a cry of joy or satisfaction when one finds or discovers something.
▶ noun [mass noun] an alloy of copper and nickel used for electrical filament and resistance wire.
– ORIGIN early 17th cent.: from Greek *heurēka* 'I have found it' (from *heuriskein* 'find'), said to have been uttered by Archimedes when he hit upon a method of determining the purity of gold. The noun dates from the early 20th cent.

eurhythmic /jʊ(ə)ˈrɪðmɪk/ ▶ adjective rare (especially of architecture or art) in or relating to harmonious proportion.
– ORIGIN mid 19th cent.: based on Greek *euruthmia* 'proportion' + -IC.

eurhythmics (also **eurhythmy**; US also **eurythmics**, **eurythmy**) ▶ plural noun [treated as sing.] a system of rhythmical physical movements to music used to teach musical understanding (especially in Steiner schools) or for therapeutic purposes, evolved by Émile Jaques-Dalcroze.
– ORIGIN early 20th cent.: from EU- 'well' + RHYTHM + -ICS.

Euripides /jʊ(ə)ˈrɪpɪdiːz/ (480–c.406 BC), Greek dramatist. His nineteen surviving plays show important innovations in the handling of traditional myths, such as the introduction of realism, an interest in feminine psychology, and the portrayal of abnormal and irrational states of mind. Notable works: *Medea*, *Hippolytus*, *Electra*, *Trojan Women*, and *Bacchae*.

Euro /ˈjʊərəʊ/ ▶ adjective [attrib.] informal European, especially concerned with the European Union: *he voted with the government in the Euro debate.*
▶ noun (**euro**) the single European currency, which replaced the national currencies of France, Germany, Spain, Italy, Greece, Portugal, Luxembourg, Austria, Finland, the Republic of Ireland, Belgium, and the Netherlands in 2002.
– ORIGIN independent usage of **EURO-**.

euro ▶ noun (pl. **-os**) the common wallaroo (see **WALLAROO**).

– ORIGIN mid 19th cent.: from Adnyamadhanha *yuru*.

Euro- ▶ combining form European; European and ...: *Euro-American*.
■ relating to Europe or the European Union: *Eurocommunism | a Euro-MP*.

Eurobond ▶ noun an international bond issued in Europe or elsewhere outside the country in whose currency its value is stated (usually the US or Japan).

Eurocentric ▶ adjective focusing on European culture or history to the exclusion of a wider view of the world; implicitly regarding European culture as pre-eminent.
– DERIVATIVES **Eurocentricity** noun, **Eurocentrism** noun.

Eurocommunism ▶ noun [mass noun] a political system advocated by some communist parties in western European countries, which stresses independence from the former Soviet Communist Party and advocates the preservation of many elements of Western liberal democracy.
– DERIVATIVES **Eurocommunist** adjective & noun.

Eurocrat ▶ noun informal, chiefly derogatory a bureaucrat in the administration of the European Union.

Eurocurrency ▶ noun **1** a form of money held or traded outside the country in whose currency its value is stated (originally US dollars held in Europe).
2 [in sing.] a single currency for use by the member states of the European Union.

Eurodollar ▶ noun a US dollar held in Europe or elsewhere outside the US.

Euromarket ▶ noun **1** a financial market which deals with Eurocurrencies.
2 the European Union regarded as a single commercial or financial market.

Euro-MP ▶ noun a member of the European Parliament.

Europa /jʊ(ə)ˈrəʊpə/ **1** Greek Mythology a princess of Tyre who was courted by Zeus in the form of a bull. She was carried off by him to Crete, where she bore him three sons (Minos, Rhadamanthus, and Sarpedon).
2 Astronomy one of the Galilean moons of Jupiter, the sixth closest satellite to the planet, having a network of dark lines on a bright icy surface (diameter 3,138 km).

Europe a continent of the northern hemisphere, separated from Africa to the south by the Mediterranean Sea and from Asia to the east roughly by the Bosporus, the Caucasus Mountains, and the Ural Mountains. Europe contains approximately 20 per cent of the world's population.
■ the European Union: *the Prime Minister who took Britain into Europe.* ■ the mainland of continental Europe as distinct from the British Isles.

Europe, Council of an association of European states founded in 1949 to safeguard the political and cultural heritage of Europe and promote economic and social cooperation. One of the Council's principal achievements is the European Convention on Human Rights.

European ▶ adjective of, relating to, or characteristic of Europe or its inhabitants.
■ of or relating to the European Union: *a single European currency.*
▶ noun a native or inhabitant of Europe.
■ a national of a state belonging to the European Union. ■ a person who is committed to the European Union. ■ a person who is white or of European parentage, especially in a country with a large non-white population.
– DERIVATIVES **Europeanism** noun.
– ORIGIN from French *européen*, from Latin *europaeus*, based on Greek *Europē* 'Europe'.

European Atomic Energy Community (abbrev.: **Euratom**) an institution established in 1957 to aid the exploitation of nuclear discoveries. It is one of the communities (with the ECSC and EEC) that forms the European Community.

European Bank for Reconstruction and Development a bank established in London in 1991 to help the former communist countries of eastern Europe and the former Soviet Union make the transition to the free-market system.

European Coal and Steel Community (abbrev.: **ECSC**) an organization established in 1952 to regulate pricing, transport, and tariffs for the coal and steel industries of the member countries. It was the first of the communities which now make up the European Community (the others are Euratom and the EEC).

European Commission a group, appointed by agreement among the governments of the European Union, which initiates Union action and safeguards its treaties. It meets in Brussels.

European Commission for Human Rights an institution of the Council of Europe, set up under the European Convention on Human Rights to examine complaints of alleged breaches of the Convention. It is based in Strasbourg.

European Community (abbrev.: **EC**) an economic and political association of certain European countries, incorporated since 1993 in the European Union.

> The European Community was formed in 1967 from the European Coal and Steel Community (ECSC), the European Economic Community (EEC), and the European Atomic Energy Community (Euratom); it comprises also the European Commission, the European Parliament, and the European Court of Justice. Until 1987 it was still commonly known as the EEC. The name 'European Communities' is still used in legal contexts where the three distinct organizations are recognized. See also **EUROPEAN UNION**.

European Convention on Human Rights an international agreement set up by the Council of Europe in 1950 to protect human rights. Under the Convention were established the European Commission for Human Rights and the European Court of Human Rights.

European Council a grouping of the heads of government of the European Union countries, inaugurated in 1975, which meets two or three times a year.

European Court of Human Rights an institution of the Council of Europe to protect human rights in conjunction with the European Commission for Human Rights. The Court, based in Strasbourg, is called to give judgement in cases where the Commission has failed to secure a settlement.

European Court of Justice an institution of the European Union, with thirteen judges appointed by its member governments, meeting in Luxembourg. Established in 1958, it exists to safeguard the law in the interpretation and application of Community treaties.

European currency unit ▶ noun see **ECU**.

European Economic Community (abbrev.: **EEC**) an institution of the European Union, an economic association of western European countries set up by the Treaty of Rome (1957). The original members were France, West Germany, Italy, Belgium, the Netherlands, and Luxembourg. See also **EUROPEAN COMMUNITY** and **EUROPEAN UNION**.

European Free Trade Association (abbrev.: **EFTA**) a customs union of western European countries, established in 1960 as a trade grouping without the political implications of the European Economic Community. The original members were Austria, Denmark, Norway, Portugal, Sweden, Switzerland, and the UK.

European Investment Bank a bank set up in 1958 by the Treaty of Rome to finance capital investment projects promoting the balanced development of members of the European Community. It is based in Luxembourg.

Europeanize (also **-ise**) ▶ verb [with obj.] [often as adj. **Europeanized**] give (someone or something) a European character or scope: *the name marked him as a Europeanized Turk*.
  ▪ transfer to the control or responsibility of the European Union.
– DERIVATIVES **Europeanization** noun.

European Monetary System (abbrev.: **EMS**) a monetary system inaugurated by the European Community in 1979 to coordinate and stabilize the exchange rates of the currencies of member countries, as a prelude to monetary union. It is based on the use of the Exchange Rate Mechanism.

European Monetary Union (abbrev.: **EMU**) a European Union programme intended to work towards full economic unity in Europe based on

the phased introduction of a common currency (the euro). Announced in 1989, it was delayed by difficulties with the Exchange Rate Mechanism, but under the terms of the Maastricht Treaty the second stage came into effect on 1 January 1994.

European Parliament the Parliament of the European Community, originally established in 1952. From 1958 to 1979 it was composed of representatives drawn from the parliaments of member countries, but since 1979 direct elections have taken place every five years. Through the Single European Act (1987) it assumed a degree of sovereignty over national parliaments. The European Parliament meets in Strasbourg, and its committee is in Brussels.

European plan ▶ noun N. Amer. a system of charging for a hotel room only, without meals. Often contrasted with **AMERICAN PLAN**.

European Recovery Program official name for the **MARSHALL PLAN**.

European Space Agency (abbrev.: **ESA**) an organization set up in 1975 to coordinate the national space programmes of the collaborating countries. It is based in Paris.

European Union (abbrev.: **EU**) an economic and political association of certain European countries as a unit with internal free trade and common external tariffs.

> The European Union was created on 1 November 1993, with the coming into force of the Maastricht Treaty. It encompasses the old European Community (EC) together with two intergovernmental 'pillars' for dealing with foreign affairs and with immigration and justice. The terms **European Economic Community** (EEC) and **European Community** (EC) continue to be used loosely to refer to what is now the European Union.

europium /jʊ(ə)rˈəʊpɪəm/ ▶ noun [mass noun] the chemical element of atomic number 63, a soft silvery-white metal of the lanthanide series. Europium oxide is used with yttrium oxide as a red phosphor in colour television screens. (Symbol: **Eu**)
– ORIGIN early 20th cent.: modern Latin, based on **EUROPE**.

Europoort /ˈjʊərəʊpɔːt/ a major European port in the Netherlands, near Rotterdam.

Euro-sceptic ▶ noun a person who is opposed to increasing the powers of the European Union.
– DERIVATIVES **Euro-scepticism** noun.

Eurostar ▶ noun trademark the high-speed passenger rail service that links London with various European cities via the Channel Tunnel.

Eurotrash ▶ noun [mass noun] informal rich European socialites, especially those living or working in the United States.

Eurovision a network of European television production administered by the European Broadcasting Union.

eury- ▶ combining form denoting a wide variety or range of something specified: *eurytopic*.
– ORIGIN from Greek *eurus* 'wide'.

euryapsid /jʊərɪˈapsɪd/ ▶ noun a Mesozoic marine reptile of a group characterized by a single upper temporal opening in the skull, including the nothosaurs, plesiosaurs, and ichthyosaurs.
  ● Sometimes placed in a subclass Euryapsida, though this taxon is no longer widely recognized.
– ORIGIN from Greek *eurus* 'wide' + *apsis, apsid-* 'arch'.

Eurydice /jʊəˈrɪdɪsi/ Greek Mythology the wife of Orpheus. After she was killed by a snake Orpheus secured her release from the underworld on the condition that he did not look back at her on their way back to the world of the living. But Orpheus did look back, whereupon Eurydice disappeared.

euryhaline /jʊərɪˈheɪlʌɪn, -ˈheɪliːn/ ▶ adjective Ecology (of an aquatic organism) able to tolerate a wide range of salinity. Often contrasted with **STENOHALINE**.
– ORIGIN late 19th cent.: from Greek *eurus* 'wide' + *halinos* 'of salt'.

eurypterid /jʊˈrɪptərɪd/ ▶ noun a giant fossil marine arthropod of a group occurring in the Palaeozoic era. They are related to horseshoe crabs, and resemble large scorpions with a terminal pair of paddle-shaped swimming appendages.
  ● Subclass Eurypterida, class Merostomata, subphylum Chelicerata.
– ORIGIN late 19th cent.: from modern Latin

Eurypterus (genus name), from **EURY-** + Greek *pteron* 'wing' + **-ID**[2].

eurythermal /jʊərɪˈθəːm(ə)l/ ▶ adjective Ecology (of an organism) able to tolerate a wide range of temperatures. Often contrasted with **STENO-THERMAL**.

eurythmics ▶ plural noun US spelling of **EURHYTHMICS**.

eurythmy ▶ noun US spelling of **EURHYTHMY**.

eurytopic /jʊərɪˈtɒpɪk/ ▶ adjective Ecology (of an organism) able to tolerate a wide range of habitats or ecological conditions. Often contrasted with **STENOTOPIC**.

Eusebio /juːˈseɪbɪəʊ/ (b.1942), Mozambican-born Portuguese footballer; born *Ferraira da Silva Eusebio*. He was a forward who played largely for the Portuguese club Benfica.

Eusebius /juːˈsiːbɪəs/ (c.264–c.340 AD), bishop and Church historian; known as **Eusebius of Caesaria**. His *Ecclesiastical History* is the principal source for the history of Christianity (especially in the Eastern Church) from the age of the Apostles until 324.

Euskara /ˈjuːskərə/ ▶ noun [mass noun] the Basque language.
– ORIGIN the name in Basque.

eusocial /juːˈsəʊʃ(ə)l/ ▶ adjective Zoology (of an animal species, especially an insect) showing an advanced level of social organization, in which a single female or caste produces the offspring and non-reproductive individuals cooperate in caring for the young.
– DERIVATIVES **eusociality** noun.

eusol /ˈjuːsɒl/ ▶ noun [mass noun] an antiseptic solution of chlorinated lime and boric acid.
– ORIGIN early 20th cent.: from *E(dinburgh) U(niversity) sol(ution)*, with reference to the university's Pathology Department, where it was developed.

Eustachian tube /juːˈsteɪʃ(ə)n/ ▶ noun Anatomy a narrow passage leading from the pharynx to the cavity of the middle ear, permitting the equalization of pressure on each side of the eardrum.
– ORIGIN mid 18th cent.: named after Bartolomeo *Eustachio* (died 1574), the Italian anatomist who identified and described it.

eustasy /ˈjuːstəsi/ ▶ noun [mass noun] a change of sea level throughout the world, caused typically by movements of parts of the earth's crust or melting of glaciers.
– DERIVATIVES **eustatic** adjective.
– ORIGIN 1940s: back-formation from *eustatic*, coined in German from Greek *eu* 'well' + *statikos* 'static'.

Euston Road /ˈjuːstən/ ▶ noun [as modifier] relating to or denoting a group of English post-Impressionist realistic painters of the 1930s.
– ORIGIN from the name of a road in London, site of a former School of Drawing and Painting (1938–9).

eutectic /juːˈtɛktɪk/ Chemistry ▶ adjective relating to or denoting a mixture of substances (in fixed proportions) that melts and solidifies at a single temperature that is lower than the melting points of the separate constituents or of any other mixture of them.
  ▶ noun a eutectic mixture.
  ▪ short for **EUTECTIC POINT**.
– ORIGIN late 19th cent.: from Greek *eutēktos* 'easily melting', from *eu* 'well, easily' + *tēkein* 'melt'.

eutectic point (also **eutectic temperature**)
  ▶ noun Chemistry the temperature at which a particular eutectic mixture freezes or melts.

eutectoid /juːˈtɛktɔɪd/ Metallurgy ▶ adjective relating to or denoting an alloy which has a minimum transformation temperature between a solid solution and a simple mixture of metals.
  ▶ noun a eutectoid mixture or alloy.

Euterpe /juːˈtəːpi/ Greek & Roman Mythology the Muse of flutes.
– ORIGIN Greek, literally 'well-pleasing'.

euthanasia /juːθəˈneɪzɪə/ ▶ noun [mass noun] the painless killing of a patient suffering from an incurable and painful disease or in an irreversible coma. The practice is illegal in most countries.
– ORIGIN early 17th cent. (in the sense 'easy death'): from Greek, from *eu* 'well' + *thanatos* 'death'.

euthanize /ˈjuːθənʌɪz/ (also **-ise**) ▶ verb [with obj.]

(usu. **be euthanized**) N. Amer. put (an animal) to death humanely.
– ORIGIN 1970s: formed irregularly from **EUTHANASIA** + **-IZE**.

Eutheria /juːˈθɪərɪə/ Zoology a major group of mammals that comprises the placentals. Compare with **METATHERIA**.
• Infraclass Eutheria, subclass Theria.
– DERIVATIVES **eutherian** noun & adjective.
– ORIGIN modern Latin (plural), from **EU-** 'well, prospering' + Greek *thērion* 'wild beast'.

euthyroid /juːˈθʌɪrɔɪd/ ▶ **adjective** Medicine having a normally functioning thyroid gland.

eutrophic /juːˈtrəʊfɪk, -ˈtrɒfɪk/ ▶ **adjective** Ecology (of a lake or other body of water) rich in nutrients and so supporting a dense plant population, the decomposition of which kills animal life by depriving it of oxygen. Compare with **DYSTROPHIC** and **OLIGOTROPHIC**.
– ORIGIN early 18th cent. (denoting a medicine promoting good nutrition): from Greek *eutrophia*, from *eu* 'well' + *trephein* 'nourish'. The current sense dates from the 1930s.

eutrophication /ˌjuːtrəfɪˈkeɪʃ(ə)n/ ▶ **noun** [mass noun] excessive richness of nutrients in a lake or other body of water, frequently due to run-off from the land, which causes a dense growth of plant life.
– DERIVATIVES **eutrophicate** verb.

eV ▶ **abbreviation for** electronvolt(s).

EVA ▶ **abbreviation for** ■ ethyl vinyl acetate, a material used as cushioning in running shoes, consisting of a rubbery copolymer of ethylene and vinyl acetate. ■ (in space) extravehicular activity.

evacuant /ɪˈvakjʊənt/ ▶ **noun** a medicine that induces some kind of bodily discharge, such as an emetic, a sudorific, or especially a laxative.
▶ **adjective** (of a medicine or treatment) acting to induce some kind of bodily discharge.
– ORIGIN mid 18th cent.: from Latin *evacuant-* 'emptying (the bowels)', from the verb *evacuare*, later in the more general sense 'remove (contents)'.

evacuate /ɪˈvakjʊeɪt/ ▶ **verb** [with obj.] **1** remove (someone) from a place of danger to a safer place: *several families were evacuated from their homes.*
■ leave or cause the occupants to leave (a place of danger): *fire alarms forced staff to evacuate the building* | [no obj.] *nearly five million had to evacuate because of air terror.* ■ (of troops) withdraw from (a place): *the last British troops evacuated the Canal Zone.*
2 technical remove air, water, or other contents from (a container): *when it springs a leak, evacuate the pond* | [as adj. **evacuated**] *an evacuated bulb.*
■ empty (the bowels or another bodily organ). ■ discharge (faeces or other matter) from the body. ■ figurative deprive (something) of contents, value, or force: *he evacuated time and history of significance.*
– ORIGIN late Middle English (in the sense 'clear the contents of'): from Latin *evacuat-* '(of the bowels) emptied', from the verb *evacuare*, from *e-* (variant of *ex-*) 'out of' + *vacuus* 'empty'.

evacuation ▶ **noun** [mass noun] **1** the action of evacuating a person or a place: *there were waves of evacuation during the blitz* | [count noun] *a full-scale evacuation of the city centre.*
2 the action of emptying the bowels or another bodily organ.
■ [count noun] a quantity of matter discharged from the bowels or another bodily organ. ■ technical the action of emptying a container of air, water, or other contents.

evacuative ▶ **adjective** & **noun** another term for **EVACUANT**.

evacuee ▶ **noun** a person moved from a place of danger to somewhere safer.
– ORIGIN early 20th cent. (originally in the French form): from French *évacué*, past participle of *évacuer*, from Latin *evacuare* (see **EVACUATE**).

evade ▶ **verb** escape or avoid, especially by guile or trickery: *friends helped him to evade capture for a time* | *he tried to kiss her, but she evaded him.*
■ (of an abstract thing) elude (someone): *sleep still evaded her.* ■ avoid giving a direct answer to (a question): *he denied evading the question.* ■ avoid dealing with or accepting; contrive not to do (something morally or legally required): *difficulties to be faced and not evaded.* ■ escape paying (tax or duty), especially by illegitimate presentation of one's finances. ■ defeat the intention of (a law or rule), especially while complying with its letter.
– DERIVATIVES **evadable** adjective, **evader** noun.
– ORIGIN late 15th cent.: from French *évader*, from Latin *evadere* from *e-* (variant of *ex-*) 'out of' + *vadere* 'go'.

evaginate /ɪˈvadʒɪneɪt/ ▶ **verb** [with obj.] Biology & Physiology turn (a tubular or pouch-shaped organ or structure) inside out.
■ [no obj.] (of such a structure or organ) turn inside out.
– DERIVATIVES **evagination** noun.
– ORIGIN mid 17th cent.: from Latin *evaginat-* 'unsheathed', from the verb *evaginare*, from *e-* (variant of *ex-*) 'out of' + *vagina* 'sheath'.

evaluate ▶ **verb** [with obj.] form an idea of the amount, number, or value of; assess: *the study will assist in evaluating the impact of recent changes* | [with clause] *a system for evaluating how well the firm is performing.*
■ Mathematics find a numerical expression or equivalent for (an equation, formula, or function).
– DERIVATIVES **evaluation** noun, **evaluative** adjective, **evaluator** noun.
– ORIGIN mid 19th cent.: back-formation from *evaluation*, from French *évaluer*, from *es-* (from Latin *ex-*) 'out, from' + Old French *value* 'value'.

evanesce /ˌiːvəˈnɛs, ɛv-/ ▶ **verb** [no obj.] poetic/literary pass out of sight, memory, or existence.
– ORIGIN mid 19th cent.: from Latin *evanescere*, from *e-* (variant of *ex-*) 'out of' + *vanus* 'empty'.

evanescent ▶ **adjective** chiefly poetic/literary soon passing out of sight, memory, or existence; quickly fading or disappearing: *a shimmering evanescent bubble.*
■ Physics denoting a field or wave which extends into a region where it cannot propagate and whose amplitude therefore decreases with distance.
– DERIVATIVES **evanescence** noun, **evanescently** adverb.
– ORIGIN early 18th cent. (in the sense 'almost imperceptible'): from Latin *evanescent-* 'disappearing', from the verb *evanescere* (see **EVANESCE**).

evangel /ɪˈvan(d)ʒɛl, -(d)ʒ(ə)l/ ▶ **noun** **1** archaic the Christian gospel.
■ any of the four Gospels.
2 North American term for **EVANGELIST**.
– ORIGIN Middle English (in the sense 'gospel'): from Old French *evangile*, via ecclesiastical Latin from Greek *euangelion* 'good news', from *euangelos* 'bringing good news', from *eu-* 'well' + *angelein* 'announce'.

evangelical ▶ **adjective** of or according to the teaching of the gospel or the Christian religion.
■ of or denoting a tradition within Protestant Christianity emphasizing the authority of the Bible, personal conversion, and the doctrine of salvation by faith in the Atonement. ■ zealous in advocating something.
▶ **noun** a member of the evangelical tradition in the Christian Church.
– DERIVATIVES **evangelic** adjective, **evangelicalism** noun, **evangelically** adverb.
– ORIGIN mid 16th cent.: via ecclesiastical Latin from ecclesiastical Greek *euangelikos*, from *euangelos* (see **EVANGEL**).

evangelism ▶ **noun** [mass noun] the spreading of the Christian gospel by public preaching or personal witness.
■ zealous advocacy of a cause.

evangelist ▶ **noun** **1** a person who seeks to convert others to the Christian faith, especially by public preaching.
■ a layperson engaged in Christian missionary work. ■ a zealous advocate of something: *he is an evangelist of junk bonds.*
2 the writer of one of the four Gospels (Matthew, Mark, Luke, or John): *St John the Evangelist.*
– DERIVATIVES **evangelistic** adjective.
– ORIGIN Middle English (in sense 2): from Old French *évangéliste*, via ecclesiastical Latin from ecclesiastical Greek *euangelistēs*, from *euangelizesthai* 'evangelize'.

evangelize (also **-ise**) ▶ **verb** [with obj.] convert or seek to convert (someone) to Christianity.
■ [no obj.] preach the gospel: *the Church's Christian mission to evangelize and declare the faith.*
– DERIVATIVES **evangelization** noun, **evangelizer** noun.
– ORIGIN late Middle English: from ecclesiastical Latin *evangelizare*, from Greek *euangelizesthai*, from *euangelos* (see **EVANGEL**).

Evans[1], Sir Arthur (John) (1851–1941), English archaeologist. His excavations at Knossos (1899–1935) resulted in the discovery of the Bronze Age civilization of Crete, which he named Minoan after the legendary Cretan king Minos.

Evans[2], Dame Edith (Mary) (1888–1976), English actress. She appeared in a wide range of Shakespearean and contemporary roles but is particularly remembered as Lady Bracknell in Oscar Wilde's *The Importance of Being Earnest*.

Evans[3], Gil (1912–88), Canadian jazz pianist, composer, and arranger; born *Ian Ernest Gilmore Green*. In 1947 he began a long association with Miles Davis, producing albums such as *Porgy and Bess* (1958) and *Sketches of Spain* (1959).

Evans-Pritchard /ˌɛv(ə)nzˈprɪtʃəd/, Sir Edward (Evan) (1902–73), English anthropologist. He is noted for his studies of the Azande and Nuer peoples of the Sudan, with whom he lived in the 1920s and 1930s.

evaporate /ɪˈvapəreɪt/ ▶ **verb** turn from liquid into vapour: [no obj.] *cook until most of the liquid has evaporated* | [with obj.] *this gets the oil hot enough to evaporate any moisture.*
■ lose or cause to lose moisture or solvent as vapour: [with obj.] *the solution was evaporated to dryness.* ■ [no obj.] (of something abstract) cease to exist: *the militancy of earlier years had evaporated in the wake of defeat.*
– DERIVATIVES **evaporable** adjective, **evaporation** noun, **evaporator** noun.
– ORIGIN late Middle English: from Latin *evaporat-* 'changed into vapour', from the verb *evaporare*, from *e-* (variant of *ex-*) 'out of' + *vapor* 'steam, vapour'.

evaporated milk ▶ **noun** [mass noun] thick sweetened milk that has had some of the liquid removed by evaporation.

evaporating dish ▶ **noun** Chemistry a small ceramic dish in which liquids are heated over a flame so that they evaporate, leaving a solid residue.

evaporative /ɪˈvap(ə)rətɪv/ ▶ **adjective** relating to or involving evaporation: *evaporative water loss.*
– ORIGIN late Middle English: from late Latin *evaporativus*, from *evaporare* 'change into vapour' (see **EVAPORATE**).

evaporative cooling ▶ **noun** [mass noun] reduction in temperature resulting from the evaporation of a liquid, which removes latent heat from the surface from which evaporation takes place. This process is employed in industrial and domestic cooling systems, and is also the physical basis of sweating.

evaporite /ɪˈvapərʌɪt/ ▶ **noun** Geology a natural salt or mineral deposit left after the evaporation of a body of water.
– ORIGIN 1920s: alteration of **EVAPORATE** (see also **-ITE**[1]).

evapotranspiration /ɪˌvapəʊtranspɪˈreɪʃ(ə)n/ ▶ **noun** [mass noun] the process by which water is transferred from the land to the atmosphere by evaporation from the soil and other surfaces and by transpiration from plants.

evasion ▶ **noun** [mass noun] the action of evading something: *their adroit evasion of almost all questions.*
■ [count noun] an indirect answer; a prevaricating excuse: *the protestations and evasions of a witness.*
– ORIGIN late Middle English (in the sense 'prevaricating excuse'): via Old French from Latin *evasio(n-)*, from *evadere* (see **EVADE**).

evasive ▶ **adjective** tending to avoid commitment or self-revelation, especially by responding only indirectly: *she was evasive about her phone number.*
■ directed towards avoidance or escape: *they decided to take evasive action.*
– DERIVATIVES **evasively** adverb, **evasiveness** noun.
– ORIGIN early 18th cent.: from Latin *evas-* 'evaded' (from the verb *evadere*) + **-IVE**.

Eve (in the Bible) the first woman, companion of Adam and mother of Cain and Abel.

eve ▶ **noun** the day or period of time immediately before an event or occasion: ***on the eve of*** *her departure he gave her a little parcel.*
■ the evening or day before a religious festival: *the service for Passover eve.* ■ chiefly poetic/literary evening: *a bitter winter's eve.*
– ORIGIN late Middle English (in the sense 'close of day'): short form of **EVEN**[2].

evection /ɪˈvɛkʃ(ə)n/ ▶ **noun** [mass noun] Astronomy regular variation in the eccentricity of the moon's orbit around the earth, caused mainly by the sun's attraction.

– ORIGIN mid 17th cent. (in the sense 'elevation, exaltation'): from Latin *evectio(n-)*, from *evehere* 'carry out or up', from *e-* (variant of *ex-*) 'out' + *vehere* 'carry'.

Evelyn /'iːvlɪn/, John (1620–1706), English diarist and writer. He is remembered chiefly for his *Diary* (published posthumously in 1818), which describes such important historical events as the Great Plague and the Great Fire of London.

Even /eɪ'vɛn/ ▶ **noun** (pl. same) **1** a member of an indigenous people living in the Kamchatka peninsula of eastern Siberia.
2 [mass noun] the language of this people, a Tungusic language with about 6,000 speakers, closely related to Evenki.
▶ **adjective** of or relating to this people or their language.

even[1] ▶ **adjective** (**evener**, **evenest**) **1** flat and smooth: *prepare the site, then lay an even bed of mortar.*
■ in the same plane or line; level: *run a file along the saw to make all of the teeth* ***even with*** *each other.* ■ having little variation in quality; regular: *they travelled at an even and leisurely pace.* ■ equal in number, amount, or value: *an even gender balance among staff and students.* ■ equally balanced: *the first half of the match was fairly even.* ■ (of a person's temper or disposition) equable; calm: *she was known to have an even temper and to be difficult to rile.*
2 (of a number, such as 2, 6, or 108) divisible by two without a remainder.
■ bearing such a number: *headers can be placed on odd or even pages or both.*
▶ **verb** make or become even: [with obj.] *she cut the hair again to* ***even up*** *the ends.*
▶ **adverb** used to emphasize something surprising or extreme: *they have never even heard of the United States | they wore fur hats, even in summer.*
■ used in comparisons for emphasis: *he knows even less about it than I do.*
– PHRASES **even as** at the very same time as: *even as he spoke their baggage was being unloaded.* **an even break** informal a fair chance: *the fact is suckers never get an even break.* **even if** despite the possibility that; no matter whether: *always try everything even if it turns out to be a dud.* ■ despite the fact that: *he is a great President, even if he has many enemies.* **even now** (or **then**) **1** now (or then) as well as before: *even now, after all these years, it upsets me.* **2** in spite of what has (or had) happened: *even then he never raised his voice to me.* **3** at this (or that) very moment: *very likely you are even now picking up the telephone to ring.* **even so** in spite of that; nevertheless: *not the most exciting of places, but even so I was having a good time.* **even though** despite the fact that: *even though he was bigger, he never looked down on me.* **get** (or **be**) **even** informal inflict similar trouble or harm on someone to that which they have inflicted on oneself: *I'll get* ***even with*** *you for this.* **of even date** Law or formal of the same date. **on an even keel** (of a ship or aircraft) not listing or tilting to one side. ■ figurative (of a person or situation) functioning normally after a period of difficulty: *getting her life back on to an even keel after their break-up had been difficult.*
– DERIVATIVES **evenly** adverb, **evenness** noun.
– ORIGIN Old English *efen* (adjective), *efne* (adverb), of Germanic origin; related to Dutch *even*, *effen* and German *eben*.

even[2] ▶ **noun** archaic or poetic/literary the end of the day; evening: *bring it to my house this even.*
– ORIGIN Old English *ǣfen*, of Germanic origin; related to Dutch *avont* and German *Abend*.

even-aged ▶ **adjective** Forestry (of woodland) composed of trees of approximately the same age.
■ (of trees) of approximately the same age.

even-handed ▶ **adjective** fair and impartial in treatment or judgement: *an even-handed approach to industrial relations.*
– DERIVATIVES **even-handedly** adverb, **even-handedness** noun.

evening ▶ **noun** the period of time at the end of the day, usually from about 6 p.m. to bedtime: *it was seven o'clock* ***in the evening*** | [as modifier] *the evening meal.*
■ this time characterized by a specified type of activity or particular weather conditions: *they could have a relaxing evening.* ■ [as modifier] prescribed by fashion as suitable for relatively formal social events held in the evening: *a couple in evening dress.*
▶ **adverb** (**evenings**) informal in the evening; every evening: *Saturday evenings he invariably fell asleep.*
▶ **exclamation** informal short for **GOOD EVENING**.
– ORIGIN Old English *ǣfnung* 'dusk falling, the time around sunset', from *ǣfnian* 'approach evening', from *ǣfen* (see **EVEN**[2]).

evening class ▶ **noun** a class held in an evening, forming part of a course for adults: *evening classes in creative writing.*

eveninger /'iːv(ə)nɪŋə/ ▶ **noun** Indian informal an evening newspaper: *interviews in a Bombay eveninger.*

evening prayer ▶ **noun** a prayer said in the evening.
■ (usu. **evening prayers**) a formal act of worship held in the evening. ■ [in sing.] (in the Anglican Church) the service of evensong.

evening primrose ▶ **noun** a plant with pale yellow flowers that open in the evening and yielding seeds from which a medicinal oil is extracted.
● Genus *Oenothera*, family Onagraceae: numerous species.

evening star ▶ **noun** (**the evening star**) the planet Venus, seen shining in the western sky after sunset.

Evenki /eɪ'vɛŋki/ ▶ **noun** (pl. same or **Evenkis**) **1** a member of an indigenous people living scattered through the wastes of northern Siberia. Also called **TUNGUS**.
2 [mass noun] the Tungusic language of this people, which has about 15,000 speakers.
▶ **adjective** of or relating to this people or their language.

even money ▶ **noun** [mass noun] (in betting) odds offering an equal chance of winning or losing, with the amount won being the same as the stake: *players bet on each throw for even money* | [as modifier] *Romany King swept past the even-money favourite Paco's Boy.*
■ [as modifier] (of a chance) equally likely to happen or not; fifty-fifty: *above those engines there was an even-money chance of being heard.*

evens ▶ **plural noun** Brit. another term for **EVEN MONEY**: *the colt was 4–6 favourite after opening* ***at evens.***

evensong ▶ **noun** (in the Christian Church) a service of evening prayers, psalms, and canticles, conducted according to a set form, especially that of the Anglican Church: *choral evensong.*
– ORIGIN Old English *ǣfensang*, originally applied to the pre-Reformation service of vespers (see **EVEN**[2], **SONG**).

even-steven (also **even-stevens**) ▶ **adjective** & **adverb** informal used in reference to fair and equal competition or distribution of resources: [as adj.] *the race was an even-steven affair* | [as adv.] *I split the money with my wife even-steven.*
– ORIGIN mid 19th cent.: rhyming phrase, used as an intensive.

event ▶ **noun** a thing that happens or takes place, especially one of importance: *the media's focus on events in the Middle East.*
■ a planned public or social occasion: *staff have been holding a number of events to raise money for charity.* ■ each of several particular contests making up a sports competition: *he repeated the success in the four-lap, 600 cc event.* ■ Physics a single occurrence of a process, e.g. the ionization of one atom.
– PHRASES **in any event** (or **at all events**) whatever happens or may have happened: *in any event, I was not in a position to undertake such a task.* **in the event** as it turns (or turned) out: *he was sent on this important and, in the event, quite fruitless mission.* **in the event of ——** if —— happens: *this will reduce the chance of serious injury in the event of an accident.* **in the event that** if; should it happen that: *in the event that an attack is launched, the defenders will have been significantly weakened by air attacks.* **in that event** if that happens: *in that event, the US would incline toward a lifting of the arms embargo.*
– DERIVATIVES **eventless** adjective, **eventlessness** noun.
– ORIGIN late 16th cent.: from Latin *eventus*, from *evenire* 'result, happen', from *e-* (variant of *ex-*) 'out of' + *venire* 'come'.

even-tempered ▶ **adjective** not easily annoyed or made angry: *he was a gentle and even-tempered man.*

eventer ▶ **noun** Brit. a horse or rider that takes part in eventing.
– ORIGIN 1970s: from **EVENT**, in *three-day event* (see **EVENTING**).

eventful ▶ **adjective** marked by interesting or exciting events: *his long and eventful life.*
– DERIVATIVES **eventfully** adverb, **eventfulness** noun.

event horizon ▶ **noun** Astronomy a notional boundary around a black hole beyond which no light or other radiation can escape.

eventide ▶ **noun** archaic or poetic/literary the end of the day; evening: *the moon flower opens its white, trumpet-like flowers* ***at eventide.***
– ORIGIN Old English *ǣfentīd* (see **EVEN**[2], **TIDE**).

eventing ▶ **noun** [mass noun] an equestrian sport in which competitors must take part in each of several contests, usually cross-country, dressage, and showjumping.
– ORIGIN 1960s: from **EVENT**, in *three-day event*, horse trials held on three consecutive days. Compare with **EVENTER**.

eventive /ɪ'vɛntɪv/ ▶ **adjective** Linguistics (of the subject or object of a sentence) denoting an event.

even-toed ungulate ▶ **noun** a hoofed mammal of an order which includes the ruminants, camels, pigs, and hippopotamuses. Mammals of this group have either two or four toes on each foot. Compare with **ODD-TOED UNGULATE**.
● Order Artiodactyla: three suborders. See also **RUMINANT**, **TYLOPOD**.

eventual /ɪ'vɛn(t)ʃʊəl/ ▶ **adjective** [attrib.] occurring or existing at the end of or as a result of a process or period of time: *it's impossible to predict the eventual outcome of the competition.*
– ORIGIN early 17th cent. (in the sense 'relating to an event or events'): from Latin *eventus* (see **EVENT**), on the pattern of *actual*.

eventuality ▶ **noun** (pl. **-ies**) a possible event or outcome: *you must be prepared for all eventualities.*

eventually ▶ **adverb** [sentence adverb] in the end, especially after a long delay, dispute, or series of problems: *eventually, after midnight, I arrived at the hotel.*

eventuate /ɪ'vɛn(t)ʃʊeɪt, -tjʊ-/ ▶ **verb** [no obj.] formal occur as a result: *you never know what might eventuate.*
■ (**eventuate in**) lead to as a result: *circumstances that eventuate in crime.*
– ORIGIN late 18th cent. (originally US): from **EVENT**, on the pattern of *actuate*.
– DERIVATIVES **eventuation** noun.

ever ▶ **adverb** **1** [usu. with negative or in questions] at any time: *nothing ever seemed to ruffle her | don't you ever regret giving up all that money?*
■ used in comparisons for emphasis: *they felt better than ever before | our biggest ever range.*
2 at all times; always: *ever the man of action, he was impatient with intellectuals | it remains* ***as*** *popular* ***as ever*** *| they lived* ***happily ever after*** | [in combination] *he toyed with his ever-present cigar.*
3 [with comparative] increasingly; constantly: *having to borrow ever larger sums.*
4 used for emphasis in questions expressing astonishment or outrage: *who ever heard of a grown man being frightened of the dark? | why ever did you do it?*
– PHRASES **ever and anon** archaic occasionally: *ever and anon the stillness is rent by the scream of a gibbon.* [ORIGIN: from Shakespeare's *Love's Labour's Lost* (v. ii. 101).] **ever since** throughout the period since: *she had lived alone ever since her husband died.* **ever so/such** Brit. informal very; very much: *I am ever so grateful | ever such a pretty cat | thanks ever so.* **for ever** see **FOREVER**. **yours ever** (also **ever yours**) a formula used to end an informal letter, before the signature.
– ORIGIN Old English *ǣfre*, of unknown origin.

Everest, Mount /'ɛvərɪst/ a mountain in the Himalayas, on the border between Nepal and Tibet. Rising to 8,848 m (29,028 ft), it is the highest mountain in the world; it was first climbed in 1953 by Sir Edmund Hillary and Tenzing Norgay.
– ORIGIN named after Sir George *Everest* (1790–1866), British surveyor general of India.

Everglades a vast area of marshland and coastal mangrove in southern Florida, part of which is protected as a national park.

evergreen ▶ **adjective** of or denoting a plant that retains green leaves throughout the year: *the glossy laurel is fully hardy and evergreen | evergreen shrubs.* Often contrasted with **DECIDUOUS**.
■ having an enduring freshness, success, or popularity: *this symphony is an evergreen favourite.*
▶ **noun** a plant that retains green leaves throughout the year: *evergreens planted to cut off the east wind.*
■ a person or thing of enduring freshness, success, or popularity.

evergreen oak ▶ **noun** another term for **HOLM OAK**.

Evergreen State informal name for the state of **WASHINGTON**[1].

everlasting ▶ **adjective** lasting forever or a very long time: *the damned would suffer everlasting torment | it would be an everlasting reminder of this evening.*
▶ **noun 1** (**the everlasting**) poetic/literary eternity.
2 (also **everlasting flower**) a flower of the daisy family with a papery texture, retaining its shape and colour after being dried, especially a helichrysum. Also called **IMMORTELLE**.
– DERIVATIVES **everlastingly** adverb, **everlastingness** noun.

evermore ▶ **adverb** (chiefly used for rhetorical effect or in ecclesiastical contexts) always: *we pray that we may evermore dwell in him and he in us.*

Evert /ˈɛvət/, Chris (b.1954), American tennis player; full name *Christine Marie Evert*. She won both the US and French Open championships six times and three Wimbledon titles (1974; 1976; 1981).

evert /ɪˈvəːt/ ▶ **verb** [with obj.] Biology & Physiology turn (a structure or organ) outwards or inside out: [as adj. **everted**] *the characteristic facial appearance of full, often everted lips.*
– DERIVATIVES **eversible** adjective, **eversion** noun.
– ORIGIN mid 16th cent. (in the sense 'upset, overthrow'): from Latin *evertere*, from *e-* (variant of *ex-*) 'out' + *vertere* 'to turn'. The current sense dates from the late 18th cent.

every ▶ **determiner** (preceding a singular noun) used to refer to all the individual members of a set without exception: *the hotel assures every guest of personal attention* | [with possessive determiner] *the children hung on his every word.*
■ used before an amount to indicate something happening at specified intervals: *tours are every thirty minutes | they had every third week off.* ■ (used for emphasis) all possible; the utmost: *you have every reason to be disappointed.*
– PHRASES **every bit as** (in comparisons) quite as: *the planning should be every bit as enjoyable as the event itself.* **every inch** see **INCH**[1]. **every last** (or **every single**) used to emphasize that every member of a group is included: *unbelievers, every last one of them | they insist you weigh every single thing.* **every man has his price** proverb everyone is open to bribery if the inducement offered is large enough. **every now and again** (or **now and then**) from time to time; occasionally: *I used to see him every now and then.* **every other** each second in a series; each alternate: *I train with weights every other day.* **every so often** from time to time; occasionally: *every so often I need a laugh to stay sane.* **every time** without exception: *it brews a perfect blend of coffee every time.* **every which way** informal in all directions: *you can see cracks moving every which way.* ■ by all available means: *since then North Korea has tried every which way to avoid official contacts with the South.*
– ORIGIN Old English *ǣfre ǣlc* (see **EVER**, **EACH**).

everybody ▶ **pronoun** every person: *everybody agrees with his views | it's not everybody's cup of tea.*

everyday ▶ **adjective** [attrib.] happening or used every day; daily: *everyday chores like shopping and housework.*
■ commonplace: *everyday drugs like aspirin.*

Everyman ▶ **noun** [in sing.] an ordinary or typical human being: *it is Everyman's dream car.*
– ORIGIN early 20th cent.: the name of the principal character in a 15th-cent. morality play.

everyone ▶ **pronoun** every person: *everyone needs time to unwind | he knew everyone in the business.*

every one ▶ **pronoun** each one.

everyplace ▶ **adverb** N. Amer. informal term for **EVERYWHERE**.

everything ▶ **pronoun 1** all things; all the things of a group or class: *he taught me everything I know | herbal cures for everything from leprosy to rheumatism.*
■ all things of importance; a great deal: *I lost everything in the crash | he owed everything to his years in Munich.* ■ the most important thing or aspect: *money isn't everything.*
2 the current situation; life in general: *how's everything? | everything is going okay.*
– PHRASES **and everything** informal used to refer vaguely to other things associated with what has been mentioned: *you'll still get paid and everything.* **have everything** informal possess every attraction or advantage: *she was articulate, she was fun—it seemed to me she had everything.*

everywhere ▶ **adverb** in or to all places: *I've looked everywhere | everywhere she went she was fêted.*
■ in many places; common or widely distributed: *sandwich bars are everywhere.*
▶ **noun** [mass noun] all places or directions: *everywhere was in darkness.*
– PHRASES **everywhere else** in all other places: *they are the same machines used everywhere else in the world.*
– ORIGIN Middle English: formerly also as two words.

evict ▶ **verb** [with obj.] expel (someone) from a property, especially with the support of the law: *a single mother and her children have been evicted from their home.*
– DERIVATIVES **eviction** noun, **evictor** noun.
– ORIGIN late Middle English (in the sense 'recover property, or the title to property, by legal process'): from Latin *evict-* 'overcome, defeated', from the verb *evincere*, from *e-* (variant of *ex-*) 'out' + *vincere* 'conquer'.

evidence ▶ **noun** [mass noun] the available body of facts or information indicating whether a belief or proposition is true or valid: *the study finds little evidence of overt discrimination.*
■ Law information given personally, drawn from a document, or in the form of material objects, tending or used to establish facts in a legal investigation or admissible as testimony in a law court: *without evidence, they can't bring a charge.* ■ signs; indications: *there was no obvious evidence of a break-in.*
▶ **verb** [with obj.] (usu. **be evidenced**) be or show evidence of: *that it has been populated from prehistoric times is evidenced by the remains of Neolithic buildings.*
– PHRASES **give evidence** Law give information and answer questions formally and in person in a law court or at an inquiry. **in evidence** noticeable; conspicuous: *his dramatic flair is still very much in evidence.* **turn King's** (or **Queen's** or US **state's**) **evidence** Law (of a criminal) give information in court against one's partners in order to receive a less severe punishment oneself.
– ORIGIN Middle English: via Old French from Latin *evidentia*, from *evident-* 'obvious to the eye or mind' (see **EVIDENT**).

evident ▶ **adjective** plain or obvious; clearly seen or understood: *she ate the biscuits with evident enjoyment.*
– ORIGIN late Middle English: from Old French, or from Latin *evidens*, *evident-* 'obvious to the eye or mind', from *e-* (variant of *ex-*) 'out' + *videre* 'to see'.

evidential /ˌɛvɪˈdɛnʃ(ə)l/ ▶ **adjective** formal of or providing evidence: *the evidential value of the record.*
– DERIVATIVES **evidentiality** noun, **evidentially** adverb.
– ORIGIN early 17th cent.: from medieval Latin *evidentialis*, from Latin *evidentia* (see **EVIDENCE**).

evidentiary /ˌɛvɪˈdɛnʃ(ə)ri/ ▶ **adjective** chiefly US Law another term for **EVIDENTIAL**.

evidently ▶ **adverb 1** plainly or obviously; in a way that is clearly seen or understood: *a work so evidently laden with significance.*
2 [sentence adverb] it is plain that; it would seem that: *evidently Mrs Smith thought differently.*
■ used as an affirmative response or reply: *'Were they old pals or something?' 'Evidently.'*

evil ▶ **adjective** profoundly immoral and malevolent: *his evil deeds | no man is so evil as to be beyond redemption.*
■ (of a force or spirit) embodying or associated with the forces of the devil: *we have been driven out of the house by this evil spirit.* ■ harmful or tending to harm: *the evil effects of high taxes.* ■ (of something seen or smelt) extremely unpleasant: *a bathroom with an ineradicably evil smell.*
▶ **noun** [mass noun] profound immorality, wickedness, and depravity, especially when regarded as a supernatural force: *the world is stalked by relentless evil | good and evil in eternal opposition.*
■ [count noun] a manifestation of this, especially in people's actions: *the evil that took place last Thursday.* ■ [count noun] something which is harmful or undesirable: *sexism, racism, and all other unpleasant social evils.*
– PHRASES **the evil eye** a gaze or stare superstitiously believed to cause material harm: *he gave me the evil eye as I walked down the corridor.* **the Evil One** archaic the Devil. **put off the evil day** (or **hour**) postpone something unpleasant for as long as possible. **speak evil of** slander: *it is a sin to speak evil of the king.*
– DERIVATIVES **evilly** adverb, **evilness** noun.
– ORIGIN Old English *yfel*, of Germanic origin; related to Dutch *euvel* and German *Übel*.

evil-doer ▶ **noun** a person who commits profoundly immoral and malevolent deeds.
– DERIVATIVES **evil-doing** noun.

evince /ɪˈvɪns/ ▶ **verb** [with obj.] formal reveal the presence of (a quality or feeling): *his letters evince the excitement he felt at undertaking this journey.*
■ be evidence of; indicate: *man's inhumanity to man as evinced in the use of torture.*
– ORIGIN late 16th cent. (in the sense 'prove by argument or evidence'): from Latin *evincere* 'overcome, defeat' (see **EVICT**).

eviscerate /ɪˈvɪsəreɪt/ ▶ **verb** [with obj.] formal disembowel (a person or animal): *the goat had been skinned and neatly eviscerated.*
■ Surgery remove the contents of the (eyeball).
– DERIVATIVES **evisceration** noun.
– ORIGIN late 16th cent.: from Latin *eviscerat-* 'disembowelled', from the verb *eviscerare*, from *e-* (variant of *ex-*) 'out' + *viscera* 'internal organs'.

eviternity /ˌiːvɪˈtəːnɪti/ ▶ **noun** [mass noun] archaic or poetic/literary eternal existence; everlasting duration.
– DERIVATIVES **eviternal** adjective.
– ORIGIN late 16th cent.: from Latin *aeviternus* 'eternal' + **-ITY**.

evocative /ɪˈvɒkətɪv/ ▶ **adjective** bringing strong images, memories, or feelings to mind: *powerfully evocative lyrics | the building's cramped interiors are highly evocative of past centuries.*
– DERIVATIVES **evocatively** adverb, **evocativeness** noun.
– ORIGIN mid 17th cent.: from Latin *evocativus*, from *evocat-* 'called forth', from the verb *evocare* (see **EVOKE**).

evoke /ɪˈvəʊk/ ▶ **verb** [with obj.] **1** bring or recall to the conscious mind: *that potent tang evoking nostalgic memories of childhood holidays.*
■ elicit (a response): *the Green Paper evoked critical reactions from various bodies.*
2 invoke (a spirit or deity).
– DERIVATIVES **evocation** noun, **evoker** noun.
– ORIGIN early 17th cent. (in sense 2): from Latin *evocare*, from *e-* (variant of *ex-*) 'out of, from' + *vocare* 'to call'.

evolute /ˈiːvəl(j)uːt, ˈɛv-/ (also **evolute curve**) ▶ **noun** Mathematics a curve which is the locus of the centres of curvature of another curve (its involute).
– ORIGIN mid 18th cent.: from Latin *evolutus*, past participle of *evolvere* 'roll out' (see **EVOLVE**).

evolution /ˌiːvəˈluːʃ(ə)n, ˈɛv-/ ▶ **noun** [mass noun] **1** the process by which different kinds of living organism are thought to have developed and diversified from earlier forms during the history of the earth.

> The idea of organic evolution was proposed by some ancient Greek thinkers but was long rejected in Europe as contrary to the literal interpretation of the Bible. Lamarck proposed a theory that organisms became transformed by their efforts to respond to the demands of their environment, but he was unable to explain a mechanism for this. Lyell demonstrated that geological deposits were the cumulative product of slow processes over vast ages. This helped Darwin towards a theory of gradual evolution over a long period by the natural selection of those varieties of an organism slightly better adapted to the environment and hence more likely to produce descendants. Combined with the later discoveries of the cellular and molecular basis of genetics, Darwin's theory of evolution has, with some modification, become the dominant unifying concept of modern biology.

2 the gradual development of something, especially from a simple to a more complex form: *the forms of written languages undergo constant evolution.*
3 Chemistry the giving off of a gaseous product, or of heat.
4 [count noun] a pattern of movements or manoeuvres: *flocks of waders often perform aerial evolutions.*
5 Mathematics, dated the extraction of a root from a given quantity.
– DERIVATIVES **evolutional** adjective, **evolutionally** adverb, **evolutionarily** adverb, **evolutionary** adjective, **evolutive** adjective.
– ORIGIN early 17th cent.: from Latin *evolutio(n-)* 'unrolling', from the verb *evolvere* (see **EVOLVE**). Early senses related to physical movement, first recorded in describing a tactical 'wheeling' manoeuvre in the realignment of troops or ships. Current senses stem from a notion of 'opening out'

and 'unfolding', giving rise to a general sense of 'development'.

evolutionist ▶ noun a person who believes in the theories of evolution and natural selection.
▶ adjective of or relating to the theories of evolution and natural selection: *an evolutionist model*.
– DERIVATIVES **evolutionism** noun.

evolve ▶ verb 1 develop gradually, especially from a simple to a more complex form: [no obj.] *the company has evolved into a major chemical manufacturer* | *the Gothic style evolved steadily and naturally from the Romanesque* | [with obj.] *each school must evolve its own way of working.*
■ (with reference to an organism or biological feature) develop over successive generations, especially as a result of natural selection: [no obj.] *the populations are cut off from each other and evolve independently.*
2 [with obj.] Chemistry give off (gas or heat).
– DERIVATIVES **evolvable** adjective, **evolvement** noun.
– ORIGIN early 17th cent. (in the general sense 'make more complex, develop'): from Latin *evolvere*, from *e-* (variant of *ex-*) 'out of' + *volvere* 'to roll'.

Évros /ˈɛvrɒs/ Greek name for the **MARITSA**.

Évvoia /ˈɛvia/ Greek name for **EUBOEA**.

evzone /ˈɛvzəʊn/ ▶ noun a kilted soldier belonging to a select Greek infantry regiment.
– ORIGIN late 19th cent.: from modern Greek *euzōnos*, from Greek, 'dressed for exercise' (from *eu-* 'fine' + *zōnē* 'belt'), because of their distinctive uniform, which includes a fustanella.

Ewe /ˈeɪweɪ/ ▶ noun (pl. same) **1** a member of a West African people of Ghana, Togo, and Benin.
2 [mass noun] the language of this people, belonging to the Kwa group. It has about 3 million speakers.
▶ adjective of, relating to, or denoting this people or their language.
– ORIGIN the name in Ewe.

ewe /juː/ ▶ noun a female sheep.
– ORIGIN Old English *eowu*, of Germanic origin; related to Dutch *ooi* and German *Aue*.

ewe neck ▶ noun a horse's neck of which the upper outline curves inwards instead of outwards.
– DERIVATIVES **ewe-necked** adjective.

ewer /ˈjuːə/ ▶ noun a large jug with a wide mouth, formerly used for carrying water for someone to wash in.
– ORIGIN late Middle English: from Anglo-Norman French *ewer*, variant of Old French *aiguiere*, based on Latin *aquarius* 'of water', from *aqua* 'water'.

Ex. ▶ abbreviation for Exodus (in biblical references).

ex¹ ▶ preposition **1** (of goods) sold direct from: *carpet tiles offered at a special price, ex stock.*
2 without; excluding: *the cost is £5,000 ex VAT.*
– ORIGIN mid 19th cent. (in sense 2): from Latin, 'out of'.

ex² ▶ noun informal a former husband, wife, or partner in a relationship: *I don't want my ex to spoil what I have now.*
– ORIGIN early 19th cent.: independent usage of **EX-¹**.

ex-¹ (also **e-**) ▶ prefix **1** out: *exclude* | *excite.*
2 upward: *extol.*
3 thoroughly: *excruciate.*
4 denoting removal or release: *excommunicate* | *exculpate.*
5 forming verbs which denote inducement of a state: *exasperate.*
6 (forming nouns from titles of office, status, etc.) denoting a former state: *ex-husband* | *ex-convict.*
– ORIGIN from Latin *ex* 'out of'.

USAGE **Ex-** is also found assimilated as **ef-** before f.

ex-² ▶ prefix out: *exodus* | *exorcism.*
– ORIGIN from Greek *ex* 'out of'.

exa- ▶ combining form (used in units of measurement) denoting a factor of 10^{18}: *exajoule.*
– ORIGIN from (h)*exa-* (see **HEXA-**), based on the supposed analogy of *tera-* and *tetra-*.

exacerbate /ɪgˈzasəbeɪt, ɛkˈsas-/ ▶ verb [with obj.] make (a problem, bad situation, or negative feeling) worse: *these problems were exacerbated by central government's policies.*
– DERIVATIVES **exacerbation** noun.
– ORIGIN mid 17th cent.: from Latin *exacerbat-* 'made harsh', from the verb *exacerbare*, from *ex-* (expressing inducement of a state) + *acerbus* 'harsh, bitter'. The noun *exacerbation* (late Middle English) originally meant 'provocation to anger'.

exact ▶ adjective not approximated in any way; precise: *the exact details were still being worked out.*
■ accurate or correct in all details: *an exact replica, two feet tall, was constructed.* ■ (of a person) tending to be accurate and careful about minor details: *she was an exact, clever manager.* ■ (of a subject of study) permitting precise or absolute measurements as a basis for rigorously testable theories: *psychomedicine isn't an exact science yet.*
▶ verb [with obj.] demand and obtain (something, especially a payment) from someone: *tributes exacted from the Slav peoples* | *William's advisers exacted an oath of obedience from the clergy.*
■ inflict (revenge) on someone: *a frustrated woman bent on exacting a cruel revenge for his rejection.*
– DERIVATIVES **exactable** adjective, **exactitude** noun, **exactness** noun, **exactor** noun.
– ORIGIN late Middle English (as a verb): from Latin *exact-* 'completed, ascertained, enforced', from the verb *exigere*, from *ex-* 'thoroughly' + *agere* 'perform'. The adjective dates from the mid 16th cent. and reflects the Latin *exactus* 'precise'.

exacta /ɪgˈzaktə/ ▶ noun N. Amer. another term for **PERFECTA**.
– ORIGIN 1960s: from American Spanish *quiniela exacta* 'exact quinella'.

exacting ▶ adjective making great demands on one's skill, attention, or other resources: *living up to such exacting standards.*
– DERIVATIVES **exactingly** adverb, **exactingness** noun.

exaction ▶ noun [mass noun] formal the action of demanding and obtaining something from someone, especially a payment or service: *he supervised the exaction of tolls at various ports.*
■ [count noun] a sum of money demanded in such a way. ■ [count noun] an act of demanding unfair and exorbitant payment; an act of extortion.
– ORIGIN late Middle English: from Latin *exactio(n-)*, from *exigere* 'ascertain, perfect, enforce' (see **EXACT**).

exactly ▶ adverb **1** without discrepancy (used to emphasize the accuracy of a figure or description): *they met in 1989 and got married exactly two years later* | *fold the second strip of paper in exactly the same way.*
2 in exact terms; without vagueness: *what exactly are you looking for?*
3 used as a reply to confirm or agree with what has just been said: *'You mean that you're going to tell me the truth?' 'Exactly.'*
– PHRASES **not exactly** informal **1** not at all: *that too was not exactly convincing.* **2** not quite but close to being: *not exactly agitated, but disturbed.*

exaggerate /ɪgˈzadʒəreɪt, ɛg-/ ▶ verb [with obj.] represent (something) as being larger, greater, better, or worse than it really is: *both she and her daughter were apt to exaggerate any aches and pains* | [no obj.] *I couldn't sleep for three days—I'm not exaggerating.*
■ [as adj. **exaggerated**] enlarged or altered beyond normal or due proportions: *exaggerated features such as a massive head and beetling brows.*
– DERIVATIVES **exaggeratedly** adverb, **exaggeration** noun, **exaggerative** adjective, **exaggerator** noun.
– ORIGIN mid 16th cent.: from Latin *exaggerat-* 'heaped up', from the verb *exaggerare*, from *ex-* 'thoroughly' + *aggerare* 'heap up' (from *agger* 'heap'). The word originally meant 'pile up, accumulate', later 'intensify praise or blame', 'dwell on a virtue or fault', giving rise to current senses.

exalt /ɪgˈzɔːlt, ɛg-/ ▶ verb [with obj.] hold (someone or something) in very high regard; think or speak very highly of: *the party will continue to exalt their hero.*
■ raise to a higher rank or a position of greater power: *this naturally exalts the peasant above his brethren in the same rank of society.* ■ make noble in character; dignify: *romanticism liberated the imagination and exalted the emotions.*
– ORIGIN late Middle English: from Latin *exaltare*, from *ex-* 'out, upward' + *altus* 'high'.

exaltation ▶ noun [mass noun] **1** a feeling or state of extreme happiness: *she was in a frenzy of exaltation and terror.*
2 the action of elevating someone in rank, power, or character: *the exaltation of Jesus to the Father's right hand.*
■ the action of praising someone or something highly: *the exaltation of the army as a place for brotherhood.*
– ORIGIN late Middle English (in the sense 'the

action of raising high'): from late Latin *exaltatio(n-)*, from Latin *exaltare* 'raise aloft' (see **EXALT**).

exalté /ɪgˈzɔːlteɪ/ dated or poetic/literary ▶ noun a person who is elated or impassioned.
▶ adjective inspiring or stimulating: *in the exalté atmosphere of the Bateau Lavoir his writing flourished.*
– ORIGIN mid 19th cent.: French, 'lifted up', past participle of *exalter*.

exalted ▶ adjective **1** (of a person or their rank or status) placed at a high or powerful level; held in high regard: *it had taken her years of hard infighting to reach her present exalted rank.*
■ (of an idea) noble; lofty: *his exalted hopes of human progress.*
2 in a state of extreme happiness: *I felt exalted and newly alive.*
– DERIVATIVES **exaltedly** adverb, **exaltedness** noun.

exam ▶ noun **1** short for **EXAMINATION** (in sense 2): *he was likely to fail his exams again* | [as modifier] *exam results.*
2 [with adj. or noun modifier] N. Amer. a medical test of a specified kind: *routine eye exams.*

examen /ɛgˈzeɪmɛn/ (also **examen de conscience**) ▶ noun a formal examination of the soul or conscience, made usually daily by Jesuits and some other Roman Catholics.
– ORIGIN mid 17th cent.: from Latin, in the figurative sense 'examination' (literally 'tongue of a balance'), from *exigere* 'weigh accurately'.

examination ▶ noun **1** a detailed inspection or investigation: *an examination of marketing behaviour* | *a medical examination is conducted without delay.*
■ [mass noun] the action or process of conducting such an inspection or investigation: *the role of the planning system has come under increasing critical examination.*
2 a formal test of a person's knowledge or proficiency in a particular subject or skill: *he scraped through the examinations at the end of his first year.*
3 Law the formal questioning of a defendant or witness in court.
– ORIGIN late Middle English (also in the sense 'testing (one's conscience) by a standard'): via Old French from Latin *examinatio(n-)*, from *examinare* 'weigh, test' (see **EXAMINE**).

examination-in-chief ▶ noun [mass noun] Law the questioning of a witness by the party which has called that witness to give evidence, in order to support the case which is being made. Also called **DIRECT EXAMINATION**. Compare with **CROSS-EXAMINE**.

examination paper ▶ noun a set of printed questions used as a test of proficiency or knowledge.
■ a candidate's set of answers in such a test.

examine ▶ verb [with obj.] **1** inspect (someone or something) in detail in order to determine their nature or condition; investigate thoroughly: *a doctor examined me and said I might need a caesarean* | *this forced us to examine every facet of our business.*
2 test the knowledge or proficiency of (someone) by requiring them to answer questions or perform tasks: *the colleges set standards by examining candidates.*
■ Law formally question (a defendant or witness) in court. Compare with **CROSS-EXAMINE**.
– DERIVATIVES **examinable** adjective, **examinee** noun, **examiner** noun.
– ORIGIN Middle English: from Old French *examiner*, from Latin *examinare* 'weigh, test', from *examen* (see **EXAMEN**).

exam paper ▶ noun short for **EXAMINATION PAPER**.

example ▶ noun **1** a thing characteristic of its kind or illustrating a general rule: *it's a good example of how European action can produce results* | *some of these carpets are among the finest examples of the period.*
■ a printed or written problem or exercise designed to illustrate a rule.
2 a person or thing regarded in terms of their fitness to be imitated or the likelihood of their being imitated: *it is vitally important that parents should set an example* | *he followed his brother's example and deserted his family.*
▶ verb (**be exampled**) be illustrated or exemplified: *the extent of Allied naval support is exampled by the navigational specialists provided.*
– PHRASES **for example** used to introduce something chosen as a typical case: *many, like Hilda, for example, come from very poor backgrounds.* **make an**

example of punish as a warning or deterrent to others.
– ORIGIN late Middle English: from Old French, from Latin *exemplum*, from *eximere* 'take out', from *ex-* 'out' + *emere* 'take'. Compare with **SAMPLE**.

ex ante /ɛks 'anti/ ▶ **adjective** & **adverb** based on forecasts rather than actual results: [as adj.] *this is an ex ante estimate of the variance.*
– ORIGIN modern Latin, from Latin *ex* 'from, out of' + *ante* 'before'.

exanthema /ɪk'sanθɪmə, ˌɛksan'θiːmə/ ▶ **noun** (pl. **exanthemata**) Medicine a skin rash accompanying a disease or fever.
– DERIVATIVES **exanthematic** adjective, **exanthematous** adjective.
– ORIGIN mid 17th cent.: via late Latin from Greek *exanthēma* 'eruption', from *ex-* 'out' + *antheein* 'to blossom' (from *anthos* 'flower').

exarch /'ɛksɑːk/ ▶ **noun** **1** (in the Orthodox Church) a bishop lower in rank than a patriarch and having jurisdiction wider than the metropolitan of a diocese.
2 historical a governor of a distant province under the Byzantine emperors.
– ORIGIN late 16th cent.: via ecclesiastical Latin from Greek *exarkhos*, from *ex-* 'out of' + *arkhos* 'ruler'.

exarchate /'ɛksɑːkeɪt/ ▶ **noun** historical a distant province governed by an exarch under the Byzantine emperors.
– ORIGIN mid 16th cent.: from medieval Latin *exarchatus*, from ecclesiastical Latin *exarchus*, from Greek (see **EXARCH**).

exasperate /ɪg'zasp(ə)reɪt, ɛg-/ ▶ **verb** [with obj.] irritate intensely; infuriate: *this futile process exasperates prison officers* | [as adj. **exasperated**] *she grew exasperated with his inability to notice anything* | [as adj. **exasperating**] *they suffered a number of exasperating setbacks.*
– DERIVATIVES **exasperatedly** adverb, **exasperatingly** adverb, **exasperation** noun.
– ORIGIN mid 16th cent.: from Latin *exasperat-* 'irritated to anger', from the verb *exasperare* (based on *asper* 'rough').

Excalibur /ɛks'kalɪbə/ (in Arthurian legend) King Arthur's magic sword.

ex cathedra /ˌɛks kə'θiːdrə/ ▶ **adverb** & **adjective** with the full authority of office (especially that of the Pope, implying infallibility as defined in Roman Catholic doctrine): [as adv.] *for an encyclical to be infallible the Pope must speak ex cathedra.*
– ORIGIN Latin, 'from the (teacher's) chair', from *ex* 'from' and *cathedra* 'seat' (from Greek *kathedra*).

excavate /'ɛkskəveɪt/ ▶ **verb** [with obj.] **1** make (a hole or channel) by digging: *the cheapest way of doing this was to excavate a long trench.*
■ dig out material from (the ground): *the ground was largely excavated by hand.* ■ extract (material) from the ground by digging: *a very large amount of gravel would be excavated to form the channel.*
2 remove earth carefully and systematically from (an area) in order to find buried remains.
■ reveal or extract (buried remains) in this way: *clothing and weapons were excavated from the burial site.*
– ORIGIN late 16th cent.: from Latin *excavat-* 'hollowed out', from the verb *excavare*, from *ex-* 'out' + *cavare* 'make or become hollow' (from *cavus* 'hollow').

excavation ▶ **noun** [mass noun] the action of excavating something, especially an archaeological site: *the methods of excavation have to be extremely rigorous* | [count noun] *students often participate in excavations.*
■ [count noun] a site that is being or has been excavated.

excavator ▶ **noun** a person who removes earth carefully and systematically from an archaeological site in order to find buried remains.
■ a large machine for removing soil from the ground, especially on a building site.

exceed ▶ **verb** [with obj.] be greater in number or size than (a quantity, number, or other measurable thing): *production costs have exceeded £60,000.*
■ go beyond what is allowed or stipulated by (a set limit, especially of one's authority): *the Tribunal's decision clearly exceeds its powers under the statute.* ■ be better than; surpass: *England exceeded most people's expectations by reaching the last four.*
– ORIGIN late Middle English (in the sense 'go over (a boundary or specified point)'): from Old French *exceder*, from Latin *excedere*, from *ex-* 'out' + *cedere* 'go'.

exceeding archaic or poetic/literary ▶ **adjective** very great: *she spoke warmly of his exceeding kindness.*
▶ **adverb** [as submodifier] extremely; exceedingly: *an ale of exceeding poor quality.*

exceedingly ▶ **adverb** **1** [as submodifier] extremely: *the team played exceedingly well.*
2 archaic to a great extent: *the supply multiplied exceedingly.*

excel /ɪk'sɛl, ɛk-/ ▶ **verb** (**excelled**, **excelling**) [no obj.] be exceptionally good at or proficient in an activity or subject: *a sturdy youth who excelled at football.*
■ (**excel oneself**) perform exceptionally well; surpass one's previous performance: *the keeper excelled himself to keep out an Elliott header.*
– ORIGIN late Middle English: from Latin *excellere*, from *ex-* 'out, beyond' + *celsus* 'lofty'.

excellence ▶ **noun** [mass noun] the quality of being outstanding or extremely good: *awards for excellence* | *a centre of academic excellence.*
■ [count noun] archaic an outstanding feature or quality.
– ORIGIN late Middle English: from Latin *excellentia*, from the verb *excellere* 'surpass' (see **EXCEL**).

excellency ▶ **noun** (pl. **-ies**) **1** (**His**, **Your**, etc. **Excellency**) a title given to certain high officials of state, especially ambassadors, or of the Roman Catholic Church, or used in addressing them: *His Excellency the Indian Consul General.*
2 archaic an outstanding feature or quality.
– ORIGIN Middle English (in the sense 'excellence'): from Latin *excellentia*, from *excellere* 'surpass' (see **EXCEL**). The use of the word as a title dates from the mid 16th cent.

excellent ▶ **adjective** extremely good; outstanding: *the lorry was in excellent condition* | *their results are excellent.*
▶ **exclamation** used to indicate approval or pleasure: *'What a lovely idea! Excellent!'*
– DERIVATIVES **excellently** adverb.
– ORIGIN late Middle English (in the general sense 'excelling, outstanding', referring to either a good or bad quality): from Old French, from Latin *excellent-* 'being pre-eminent', from *excellere* (see **EXCEL**). The current appreciatory sense dates from the early 17th cent.

excelsior /ɛk'sɛlsɪɔː/ ▶ **noun** used in the names of hotels, newspapers, and manufactured products to indicate superior quality: *they stayed at the Excelsior.*
■ [mass noun] N. Amer. softwood shavings used for packing fragile goods or stuffing furniture.
– ORIGIN late 18th cent. (as an exclamation): from Latin, comparative of *excelsus*, from *ex-* 'out, beyond' + *celsus* 'lofty'.

excentric /ɪk'sɛntrɪk, ɛk-/ ▶ **adjective** chiefly Biology not centrally placed or not having its axis or other part placed centrally: *a distinct excentric nucleus.*
– DERIVATIVES **excentrically** adverb.

except ▶ **preposition** not including; other than: *naked* ***except for*** *my socks* | *they work every day except Sunday.*
▶ **conjunction** used before a statement that forms an exception to one just made: *I didn't tell him anything,* ***except that*** *I needed the money* | *our berets were the same except mine had a leather band inside.*
■ archaic unless: *she never offered advice, except it were asked of her.*
▶ **verb** [with obj.] formal specify as not included in a category or group; exclude: *from their collective guilt I except Miss Zinkeisen alone.*
– ORIGIN late Middle English: from Latin *except-* 'taken out', from the verb *excipere*, from *ex-* 'out of' + *capere* 'take'.

excepted ▶ **adjective** [postpositive] not included in the category or group specified: *most museums (the Getty excepted) have small acquisitions budgets.*

excepting ▶ **preposition** formal except for; apart from: *it was the poorest member of the Community, excepting only Ireland and Italy.*

exception ▶ **noun** a person or thing that is excluded from a general statement or does not follow a rule: *the drives between towns are a delight, and the journey to Graz is* ***no exception*** | *while he normally shies away from introducing resolutions, he* ***made an exception*** *in this case.*
– PHRASES **the exception proves the rule** proverb the fact that some cases do not follow a rule proves that the rule applies in all other cases. **take exception to** object strongly to; be offended by: *they took exception to his bohemian demeanour.* **with the exception of** except; not including. **without exception** with no one or nothing excluded.
– ORIGIN late Middle English: via Old French from Latin *exceptio(n-)*, from *excipere* 'take out' (see **EXCEPT**).

exceptionable ▶ **adjective** formal open to objection; causing disapproval or offence: *his drawings are almost the only exceptionable part of his work.*

exceptional ▶ **adjective** unusual; not typical: *no major development should take place in national parks except in exceptional circumstances.*
■ unusually good; outstanding: *from his earliest years he showed exceptional ability in mechanics.*
▶ **noun** (usu. **exceptionals**) an item in a company's accounts arising from its normal activity but much larger or smaller than usual. Compare with **EXTRAORDINARY**.
– DERIVATIVES **exceptionality** noun, **exceptionally** adverb.

excerpt ▶ **noun** /'ɛksəːpt/ a short extract from a film, broadcast, or piece of music or writing.
▶ **verb** /ɪk'səːpt, ɛk-/ [with obj.] take (a short extract) from a text: *the notes are excerpted from his forthcoming biography.*
■ take an excerpt or excerpts from (a text).
– DERIVATIVES **excerptible** adjective, **excerption** noun.
– ORIGIN mid 16th cent. (as a verb): from Latin *excerpt-* 'plucked out', from the verb *excerpere*, from *ex-* 'out of' + *carpere* 'to pluck'.

excess /ɪk'sɛs, ɛk-, 'ɛksɛs/ ▶ **noun** **1** an amount of something that is more than necessary, permitted, or desirable: *are you suffering from* ***an excess of*** *stress in your life?*
■ the amount by which one quantity or number exceeds another. ■ Brit. a part of an insurance claim to be paid by the insured.
2 [mass noun] lack of moderation in an activity, especially eating or drinking: *bouts of alcoholic excess.*
■ (**excesses**) outrageous or immoderate behaviour: *the worst excesses of the French Revolution.*
3 [mass noun] the action of exceeding a permitted limit: *there is no issue as to excess of jurisdiction.*
▶ **adjective** [attrib.] /usually 'ɛksɛs/ **1** that exceeds a prescribed or desirable amount: *trim any excess fat off the meat.*
2 Brit. required as extra payment: *the full excess fare had to be paid.*
– PHRASES **in** (or **to**) **excess** exceeding the proper amount or degree: *she insisted that he did not drink to excess.* **in excess of** more than; exceeding: *a top speed in excess of 20 knots.*
– ORIGIN late Middle English: via Old French from Latin *excessus*, from *excedere* 'go out, surpass' (see **EXCEED**).

excess baggage ▶ **noun** [mass noun] luggage weighing more than the limit allowed on an aircraft and liable to an extra charge.
■ figurative a thing that is surplus to requirements.

excessive ▶ **adjective** more than is necessary, normal, or desirable; immoderate: *he was drinking excessive amounts of brandy.*
– DERIVATIVES **excessively** adverb [as submodifier] *excessively high taxes*, **excessiveness** noun.
– ORIGIN late Middle English: from Old French *excessif, -ive*, from medieval Latin *excessivus*, from Latin *excedere* 'surpass' (see **EXCEED**).

exchange ▶ **noun** an act of giving one thing and receiving another (especially of the same type or value) in return: *negotiations should eventually lead to an* ***exchange of*** *land* ***for*** *peace* | *an exchange of prisoners of war* | [mass noun] *opportunities for the exchange of information.*
■ a visit or visits in which two people or groups from different countries stay with each other or do each other's jobs: [as modifier] *nine colleagues were away on an exchange visit to Germany.* ■ a short conversation; an argument: *there was a heated exchange.* ■ [mass noun] the giving of money for its equivalent in the money of another country. ■ a system or market in which commercial transactions involving currency, shares, commodities, etc. can be carried out within or between countries. See also **FOREIGN EXCHANGE**. ■ Chess a move or short sequence of moves in which both players capture material of comparable value, or particularly (**the exchange**) in which one captures a rook in return for a knight or bishop (and is said to *win the exchange*). ■ a building or institution used for the trading of a particular commodity or commodities: *the old Corn Exchange on Victoria Road.*
▶ **verb** [with obj.] give something and receive something

of the same kind in return: *we exchanged addresses | he* ***exchanged*** *a concerned glance* ***with*** *Stephen.*
■give or receive one thing in place of another: *we regret that tickets cannot be exchanged | he* ***exchanges*** *his cigarette ends* ***for*** *food.*
– PHRASES **in exchange** as a thing exchanged: *it would cancel its disciplinary hearing* ***in exchange for*** *Harding's dropping her lawsuit.*
– DERIVATIVES **exchangeability** noun, **exchangeable** adjective, **exchanger** noun.
– ORIGIN late Middle English: from Old French *eschange* (noun), *eschangier* (verb), based on *changer* (see **CHANGE**). The spelling was influenced by Latin *ex-* 'out, utterly' (see **EX-**[1]).

exchange control ▶ noun a governmental restriction on the movement of currency between countries.

exchange rate ▶ noun (also **rate of exchange**) the value of one currency for the purpose of conversion to another.

Exchange Rate Mechanism (abbrev.: **ERM**) an arrangement within the European Monetary System that allows the value of participating currencies to fluctuate to a defined degree in relation to each other so as to control exchange rates. Each currency is given a rate of exchange with the euro, from which it is allowed to fluctuate by no more than a specified amount; if it moves beyond this the government in question must alter its economic policies or reset the currency's rate with the euro.

exchange transfusion ▶ noun [mass noun] Medicine the simultaneous removal of a patient's blood and replacement by donated blood, used in treating serious conditions such as haemolytic disease of the newborn.

exchequer /ɪks'tʃɛkə, ɛks-/ ▶ noun a royal or national treasury.
■(**Exchequer**) Brit. the account at the Bank of England in which is held the Consolidated Fund, into which tax receipts and other public monies are paid; the funds of the British government. ■ (**Exchequer**) Brit. historical the former government office responsible for collecting revenue and making payments on behalf of the sovereign, auditing official accounts, and trying legal cases relating to revenue.
– ORIGIN Middle English: from Old French *eschequier*, from medieval Latin *scaccarium* 'chessboard', from *scaccus* (see **CHECK**[1]). The original sense was 'chessboard'. Current senses derive from the department of state established by the Norman kings to deal with the royal revenues, named *Exchequer* from the chequered tablecloth on which accounts were kept by means of counters. The spelling was influenced by Latin *ex-* 'out' (see **EX**[1]). Compare with **CHEQUER**.

Exchequer Chamber (also **Court of Exchequer Chamber**) ▶ noun English Law, historical any of a number of former courts of appeal whose functions were amalgamated in the Court of Appeal in 1873.
■an assembly of all the judges to decide points of law, defunct since the 18th century.

excimer /'ɛksɪmə/ ▶ noun Chemistry an unstable molecule which is formed in an excited state by the combination of two smaller molecules or atoms and rapidly dissociates with emission of radiation. Such species are utilized in some kinds of laser.
– ORIGIN 1960s: blend of **EXCITED** and **DIMER**.

excipient /ɛk'sɪpɪənt/ ▶ noun an inactive substance that serves as the vehicle or medium for a drug or other active substance.
– ORIGIN early 18th cent. (as an adjective in the sense 'that takes exception'): from Latin *excipient-* 'taking out', from the verb *excipere*.

excise[1] /'ɛksʌɪz/ ▶ noun [mass noun] [usu. as modifier] a tax levied on certain goods and commodities produced or sold within a country and on licences granted for certain activities: *the rate of excise duty on spirits.*
▶ verb [with obj.] [usu. as adj. **excised**] charge excise on (goods): *excised goods.*
– ORIGIN late 15th cent. (in the general sense 'a tax or toll'): from Middle Dutch *excijs, accijs*, perhaps based on Latin *accensare* 'to tax', from *ad-* 'to' + *census* 'tax' (see **CENSUS**).

excise[2] /ɪk'sʌɪz, ɛk-/ ▶ verb [with obj.] cut out surgically: *the precision with which surgeons can excise brain tumours |* [as adj. **excised**] *excised tissue.*
■remove (a section) from a text or piece of music: *the clauses were* ***excised from*** *the treaty.*
– DERIVATIVES **excision** noun.
– ORIGIN late 16th cent. (in the sense 'notch or hollow out'): from Latin *excis-* 'cut out', from the verb *excidere*, from *ex-* 'out of' + *caedere* 'to cut'.

exciseman ▶ noun (pl. **-men**) Brit. historical an official responsible for collecting excise duty and preventing infringement of the excise laws (especially by smuggling).

excitable ▶ adjective responding rather too readily to something new or stimulating; too easily excited: *Chip could be a bit wayward and excitable.*
■(of tissue or a cell) responsive to stimulation.
– DERIVATIVES **excitability** noun, **excitably** adverb.

excitant /'ɛksɪt(ə)nt, ɪk'sʌɪt(ə)nt, ɛk-/ ▶ noun Biology a substance which elicits an active physiological or behavioural response.
– ORIGIN early 17th cent.: perhaps suggested by French *excitant*.

excitation /ˌɛksɪ'teɪʃ(ə)n/ ▶ noun [mass noun] **1** technical the application of energy to a particle, object, or physical system, in particular:
■Physics the process in which an atom or other particle adopts a higher energy state when energy is supplied: *thermal excitation.* ■ Physiology the state of enhanced activity or potential activity of a cell, organism, or tissue which results from its stimulation. ■ the process of applying current to the winding of an electromagnet to produce a magnetic field. ■ the process of applying a signal voltage to the control electrode of an electron tube or the base of a transistor.
2 the action or state of exciting or being excited; excitement: *a state of sexual excitation.*
– ORIGIN late Middle English: from Old French, from late Latin *excitatio(n-)*, from *excitare* 'rouse, call forth' (see **EXCITE**).

excitative /ɪk'sʌɪtətɪv/ ▶ adjective rare causing excitation.

excitatory /ɪk'sʌɪtət(ə)ri, ɛk-/ ▶ adjective chiefly Physiology characterized by, causing, or constituting excitation: *the excitatory action of these impulses.*

excite ▶ verb [with obj.] **1** cause strong feelings of enthusiasm and eagerness in (someone): *flying still excites me | Gould was excited by these discoveries.*
■arouse (someone) sexually: *his Mediterranean vibrancy excited and stimulated her.*
2 bring out or give rise to (a feeling or reaction): *the ability to excite interest in others.*
3 produce a state of increased energy or activity in (a physical or biological system): *the energy of an electron is sufficient to excite the atom.*
– ORIGIN Middle English (in the sense 'stir someone up, incite someone to do something'): from Old French *exciter* or Latin *excitare*, frequentative of *exciere* 'call out or forth'. Sense 1 dates from the mid 19th cent.

excited ▶ adjective **1** very enthusiastic and eager: *they were excited about the prospect | the excited children.*
■sexually aroused.
2 Physics of or in an energy state higher than the normal or ground state.
– DERIVATIVES **excitedly** adverb.

excitement ▶ noun [mass noun] a feeling of great enthusiasm and eagerness: *her cheeks were flushed with excitement | the excitement of seeing a live leopard.*
■[count noun] something that arouses such a feeling; an exciting incident: *the excitements of the previous night.* ■ sexual arousal.

exciter ▶ noun a thing that produces excitation, in particular a device that provides a magnetizing current for the electromagnets in a motor or generator.

exciting ▶ adjective causing great enthusiasm and eagerness: *an exciting breakthrough.*
■sexually arousing.
– DERIVATIVES **excitingly** adverb, **excitingness** noun.

exciton /'ɛksɪtɒn, ɪk'sʌɪ-, ɛk-/ ▶ noun Physics a mobile concentration of energy in a crystal formed by an excited electron and an associated hole.
– ORIGIN 1930s: from **EXCITATION** + **-ON**.

exclaim ▶ verb [no obj.] [often with direct speech] cry out suddenly, especially in surprise, anger, or pain: *'Well I never,' she exclaimed | she looked in the mirror, exclaiming in dismay at her appearance.*
– ORIGIN late 16th cent.: from French *exclamer* or Latin *exclamare*, from *ex-* 'out' + *clamare* 'to shout'.

exclamation ▶ noun a sudden cry or remark, especially expressing surprise, anger, or pain: *Meg gave an involuntary exclamation | an exclamation of amazement.*
– ORIGIN late Middle English: from Latin *exclamatio(n-)*, from *exclamare* 'shout out' (see **EXCLAIM**).

exclamation mark (US **exclamation point**) ▶ noun a punctuation mark (!) indicating an exclamation.

exclamatory /ɪk'sklamət(ə)ri, ɛk-/ ▶ adjective of or relating to a sudden cry or remark, especially one expressing surprise, anger, or pain.

exclave /'ɛkskleɪv/ ▶ noun a portion of territory of one state completely surrounded by territory of another or others, as viewed by the home territory. Compare with **ENCLAVE**.
– ORIGIN late 19th cent.: from **EX-**[1] 'out' + a shortened form of **ENCLAVE**.

exclosure /ɪk'skləʊʒə, ɛk-/ ▶ noun Forestry an area from which unwanted animals are excluded.
– ORIGIN 1920s: from **EX-**[1] 'out' + **CLOSURE**, on the pattern of *enclosure*.

exclude ▶ verb [with obj.] deny (someone) access to or bar (someone) from a place, group, or privilege: *women had been* ***excluded from*** *many scientific societies.*
■keep (something) out of a place: *apply flux to exclude oxygen.* ■(often **be excluded**) remove from consideration; rule out: *when asset sales are excluded, earnings per share rose from 3.4p to 5p.* ■ prevent the occurrence of; preclude: *clauses seeking to exclude liability for loss or damage.*
– PHRASES **law** (or **principle**) **of the excluded middle** Logic the principle that one (and one only) of two contradictory propositions must be true.
– DERIVATIVES **excludable** adjective, **excluder** noun.
– ORIGIN late Middle English: from Latin *excludere*, from *ex-* 'out' + *claudere* 'to shut'.

excluding ▶ preposition not taking someone or something into account; apart from; except: *it cost £180, excluding accommodation.*

exclusion ▶ noun [mass noun] the process or state of excluding or being excluded: *cyclists protested at their exclusion from the zone.*
■the expulsion of a pupil from a school: *the exclusion of pupils from school |* [count noun] *an increase in pupil exclusions.* ■ [count noun] an item or eventuality specifically not covered by an insurance policy or other contract: *exclusions can be added to your policy.*
– PHRASES **to the exclusion of** so as to exclude something specified: *don't revise a few topics to the exclusion of all others.*
– DERIVATIVES **exclusionary** adjective.
– ORIGIN late Middle English: from Latin *exclusio(n-)*, from *excludere* 'shut out' (see **EXCLUDE**).

exclusion clause ▶ noun (in a contract) a clause disclaiming liability for a particular eventuality.

exclusionist ▶ adjective acting to shut out or bar someone from a place, group, or privilege: *an exclusionist foreign policy.*
▶ noun a person favouring the exclusion of someone from a place, group, or privilege.

exclusion order ▶ noun Brit. an official order excluding a person from a particular place, especially to prevent a crime being committed.

exclusion principle ▶ noun another term for **PAULI EXCLUSION PRINCIPLE**.

exclusion zone ▶ noun an area into which entry is forbidden, especially by ships or aircraft of particular nationalities.

exclusive ▶ adjective **1** excluding or not admitting other things: *the list is not exclusive.*
■unable to exist or be true if something else exists or is true: *these approaches are not exclusive; many students will combine them | mutually exclusive options.* ■ (of terms) excluding all but what is specified.
2 restricted or limited to the person, group, or area concerned: *the couple had exclusive possession of the flat | the problem isn't* ***exclusive to*** *Dublin.*
■(of an item or story) not published or broadcast elsewhere: *an exclusive interview.* ■ (of a commodity) not obtainable elsewhere.
3 catering for or available to only a few, select customers; high class and expensive: *one of Britain's most exclusive clubs.*
4 [predic.] (**exclusive of**) not including; excepting: *prices are exclusive of VAT and delivery.*
▶ noun an item or story published or broadcast by only one source.
– DERIVATIVES **exclusiveness** noun, **exclusivity** noun.
– ORIGIN late 15th cent. (as a noun denoting something that excludes or causes exclusion): from

medieval Latin *exclusivus*, from Latin *excludere* 'shut out' (see **EXCLUDE**).

Exclusive Brethren ▶ **plural noun** the more rigorous of two principal divisions of the Plymouth Brethren (the other is the Open Brethren). The Exclusive Brethren greatly restrict their contact with outsiders and modern technology.

exclusive economic zone ▶ **noun** an area of coastal water and seabed within a certain distance of a country's coastline, to which the country claims exclusive rights for fishing, drilling, and other economic activities.

exclusively ▶ **adverb** to the exclusion of others; only; solely: *paints produced exclusively for independent retailers* | [as submodifier] *exclusively female concerns.*
■ as the only source: *I can exclusively reveal that Gail shares a birthday with Rod Stewart.*

exclusive OR ▶ **noun** Electronics a Boolean operator working on two variables that has the value one if one but not both of the variables is one. Also called **XOR**.
■ (also **exclusive OR gate**) a circuit which produces an output signal when a signal is received through one and only one of its two inputs.

exclusivism ▶ **noun** [mass noun] the action or policy of excluding a person or group from a place, group, or privilege.
– DERIVATIVES **exclusivist** adjective & noun.

excogitate /ɪksˈkɒdʒɪteɪt, ɛks-/ ▶ **verb** [with obj.] formal think out, plan, or devise: *all the rubrics, forms, and functions remained to be excogitated.*
– DERIVATIVES **excogitation** noun.
– ORIGIN early 16th cent.: from Latin *excogitat-* 'found by process of thought', from the verb *excogitare*, from *ex-* 'out' + *cogitare* 'think'.

excommunicant /ˌɛkskəˈmjuːnɪk(ə)nt/ ▶ **noun** an excommunicated person.
– ORIGIN late 16th cent.: based on ecclesiastical Latin *excommunicare* (see **EXCOMMUNICATE**), with irregular use of the suffix **-ANT**.

excommunicate ▶ **verb** /ˌɛkskəˈmjuːnɪkeɪt/ [with obj.] officially exclude (someone) from participation in the sacraments and services of the Christian Church.
▶ **adjective** /ˌɛkskəˈmjuːnɪkət/ excommunicated: *all violators were to be pronounced excommunicate.*
▶ **noun** /ˌɛkskəˈmjuːnɪkət/ an excommunicated person.
– DERIVATIVES **excommunication** noun, **excommunicative** adjective, **excommunicator** noun, **excommunicatory** adjective.
– ORIGIN late Middle English: from ecclesiastical Latin *excommunicat-* 'excluded from communication with the faithful', from the verb *excommunicare*, from *ex-* 'out' + Latin *communis* 'common to all', on the pattern of Latin *communicare* (see **COMMUNICATE**).

ex-con ▶ **noun** informal an ex-convict; a former inmate of a prison.
– ORIGIN early 20th cent.: abbreviation.

excoriate /ɪkˈskɔːrɪeɪt, ɛks-/ ▶ **verb** [with obj.] **1** chiefly Medicine damage or remove part of the surface of (the skin).
2 formal censure or criticize severely: *the papers which had been excoriating him were now lauding him.*
– DERIVATIVES **excoriation** noun.
– ORIGIN late Middle English: from Latin *excoriat-* 'skinned', from the verb *excoriare*, from *ex-* 'out, from' + *corium* 'skin, hide'.

excrement /ˈɛkskrɪm(ə)nt/ ▶ **noun** [mass noun] waste matter discharged from the bowels; faeces.
– DERIVATIVES **excremental** adjective.
– ORIGIN mid 16th cent.: from French *excrément* or Latin *excrementum*, from *excernere* 'to sift out' (see **EXCRETE**).

excrescence /ɪkˈskrɛs(ə)ns, ɛks-/ ▶ **noun** a distinct outgrowth on a human or animal body or on a plant, especially one that is the result of disease or abnormality.
■ an unattractive or superfluous addition or feature: *removing the excrescences of later interpretation.*
– ORIGIN late Middle English: from Latin *excrescentia*, from *excrescere* 'grow out', from *ex-* 'out' + *crescere* 'grow'.

excrescent /ɪkˈskrɛs(ə)nt, ɛks-/ ▶ **adjective** **1** forming or constituting an excrescence.
2 (of a speech sound) added without etymological justification (e.g. the *-t* at the end of the surname *Bryant*).

excreta /ɪkˈskriːtə, ɛk-/ ▶ **noun** [treated as sing. or pl.] waste matter discharged from the body, especially faeces and urine.
– ORIGIN mid 19th cent.: from Latin, 'things sifted out', neuter plural of *excretus*, past participle of *excernere* (see **EXCRETE**).

excrete /ɪkˈskriːt, ɛk-/ ▶ **verb** [with obj.] (of a living organism or cell) separate and expel as waste (a substance, especially a product of metabolism): *excess bicarbonate is excreted by the kidney* | [no obj.] *the butterfly pupa neither feeds nor excretes.*
– DERIVATIVES **excreter** noun, **excretive** adjective.
– ORIGIN early 17th cent. (in the sense 'cause to excrete'): from Latin *excret-* 'sifted out', from the verb *excernere*, from *ex-* 'out' + *cernere* 'sift'.

excretion ▶ **noun** [mass noun] (in living organisms and cells) the process of eliminating or expelling waste matter.
■ [count noun] a product of this process: *bodily excretions.*
– ORIGIN early 17th cent.: from French *excrétion* or Latin *excretio(n-)*, from *excernere* 'sift out' (see **EXCRETE**).

excretory ▶ **adjective** of, relating to, or concerned with excretion: *the excretory organs.*

excruciate /ɪkˈskruːʃɪeɪt, ɛk-/ ▶ **verb** [with obj.] rare torment (someone) physically or mentally: *I stand back, excruciated by the possibility.*
– DERIVATIVES **excruciation** noun.
– ORIGIN late 16th cent.: from Latin *excruciat-* 'tormented', from the verb *excruciare* (based on *crux, cruc-* 'a cross').

excruciating ▶ **adjective** intensely painful: *excruciating back pain.*
■ mentally agonizing; very embarrassing, awkward, or tedious: *excruciating boredom.*
– DERIVATIVES **excruciatingly** adverb [as submodifier] *the sting can prove excruciatingly painful.*

exculpate /ˈɛkskʌlpeɪt/ ▶ **verb** [with obj.] formal show or declare that (someone) is not guilty of wrongdoing: *the article exculpated the mayor.*
– DERIVATIVES **exculpation** noun, **exculpatory** adjective.
– ORIGIN mid 17th cent.: from medieval Latin *exculpat-* 'freed from blame', from the verb *exculpare*, from *ex-* 'out, from' + Latin *culpa* 'blame'.

excurrent ▶ **adjective** chiefly Zoology (of a vessel or opening) conveying fluid outwards. The opposite of **INCURRENT**.
– ORIGIN early 17th cent.: from Latin *excurrent-* 'running out', from the verb *excurrere*.

excursion ▶ **noun** **1** a short journey or trip, especially one engaged in as a leisure activity: *an excursion to Mount Etna* | figurative *occasional* ***excursions*** *into mathematics.*
2 technical an instance of the movement of something along a path or through an angle.
■ a deviation from a regular pattern, path, or level of operation.
3 archaic a digression.
– DERIVATIVES **excursionist** noun.
– ORIGIN late 16th cent. (in the sense 'act of running out', also meaning 'sortie' in the phrase *alarums and excursions* (see **ALARUM**): from Latin *excursio(n-)*, from the verb *excurrere* 'run out', from *ex-* 'out' + *currere* 'to run'.

excursive ▶ **adjective** formal of the nature of an excursion; ranging widely; digressive.
– DERIVATIVES **excursively** adverb, **excursiveness** noun.
– ORIGIN late 17th cent.: from Latin *excurs-* 'digressed, run out' (from the verb *excurrere*) + **-IVE**, perhaps influenced by *discursive*.

excursus /ɪkˈskəːsəs, ɛk-/ ▶ **noun** (pl. same or **excursuses**) a detailed discussion of a particular point in a book, usually in an appendix.
■ a digression in a written text.
– ORIGIN early 19th cent.: from Latin, 'excursion', from *excurrere* 'run out'.

excuse ▶ **verb** /ɪkˈskjuːz, ɛk-/ [with obj.] **1** attempt to lessen the blame attaching to (a fault or offence); seek to defend or justify: *he did nothing to hide or excuse Jacob's cruelty.*
■ forgive (someone) for a fault or offence: *you must excuse my brother* | *he* ***could be excused for*** *feeling that he was born at the wrong time.* ■ overlook or forgive (a fault or offence): *sit down—excuse the mess.* ■ (of a fact or circumstance) serve in mitigation of (a person or act): *his ability excuses most of his faults.*
2 release (someone) from a duty or requirement: *it will not be possible to* ***excuse*** *you* ***from*** *attendance* | [with two objs] *may I be excused hockey?*
■ (used in polite formulas) allow (someone) to leave a room or gathering: *and now, if you'll excuse us, duty calls.* ■ (**excuse oneself**) say politely that one is leaving. ■ (**be excused**) (used especially by school pupils) be allowed to leave the room, especially to go to the toilet: *please, Miss, can I be excused?*
▶ **noun** /ɪkˈskjuːs, ɛk-/ **1** a reason or explanation put forward to defend or justify a fault or offence: *there can be no possible* ***excuse for*** *any further delay* | *the* ***excuse that*** *half the team failed to turn up.*
■ a reason put forward to conceal the real reason for an action; a pretext: *as an excuse to get out of the house she went to post a letter.*
2 (**an excuse for**) informal a poor or inadequate example of: *that pathetic excuse for a man!*
– PHRASES **excuse me** said politely in various contexts, for example when attempting to get someone's attention, asking someone to move so that one may pass, or interrupting or disagreeing with a speaker. ■ chiefly N. Amer. said when asking someone to repeat what they have just said. **make one's excuses** say politely that one is leaving or cannot be present.
– DERIVATIVES **excusable** adjective, **excusably** adverb, **excusatory** adjective.
– ORIGIN Middle English: from Old French *escuser* (verb), from Latin *excusare* 'to free from blame', from *ex-* 'out' + *causa* 'accusation, cause'.

excuse-me ▶ **noun** informal any social dance in which participants may interrupt other pairs in order to change partners.

ex-directory ▶ **adjective** Brit. (of a person or telephone number) not listed in a telephone directory or available through directory enquiries, at the wish of the subscriber.

ex div. ▶ **abbreviation for** ex dividend.

ex dividend ▶ **adjective** & **adverb** (of stocks or shares) not including the next dividend.

exeat /ˈɛksɪat/ ▶ **noun** Brit. a permission from a college, boarding school, or other institution for temporary absence, or an occasion on which this is granted.
– ORIGIN early 18th cent.: from Latin, 'let him or her go out', third person singular present subjunctive of *exire* (see **EXIT**).

exec /ɪɡˈzɛk, ɛɡ-/ ▶ **noun** informal an executive: *top execs.*
– ORIGIN late 19th cent.: abbreviation.

execrable /ˈɛksɪkrəb(ə)l/ ▶ **adjective** extremely bad or unpleasant: *execrable cheap wine.*
– DERIVATIVES **execrably** adverb.
– ORIGIN late Middle English (in the sense 'expressing or involving a curse'): via Old French from Latin *execrabilis*, from *exsecrari* 'to curse' (see **EXECRATE**).

execrate /ˈɛksɪkreɪt/ ▶ **verb** [with obj.] feel or express great loathing for: *they were execrated as dangerous and corrupt.*
■ [no obj.] archaic curse; swear.
– DERIVATIVES **execration** noun, **execrative** adjective, **execratory** adjective.
– ORIGIN mid 16th cent.: from Latin *exsecrat-* 'cursed', from the verb *exsecrari*, based on *sacrare* 'dedicate' (from *sacer* 'sacred').

executable /ɛɡˈzɛkjʊtəb(ə)l, ɪɡ-/ Computing ▶ **adjective** (of a file or program) able to be run by a computer.
▶ **noun** an executable file or program.

executant /ɪɡˈzɛkjʊt(ə)nt, ɛɡ-/ formal ▶ **noun** a person who carries something into effect: *executants of the royal will.*
■ a person who performs music or makes a work of art or craft.
▶ **adjective** of or relating to the performance of music or the making of works of art or craft: *music is both an art and an executant skill.*
– ORIGIN mid 19th cent.: from French *exécutant* 'carrying out', present participle of *exécuter* (see **EXECUTE**).

execute /ˈɛksɪkjuːt/ ▶ **verb** [with obj.] **1** carry out or put into effect (a plan, order, or course of action): *the corporation executed a series of financial deals.*
■ produce (a work of art): *not only does she execute embroideries, she designs them too.* ■ perform (an activity or manoeuvre requiring care or skill): *they had to execute their dance steps with the greatest precision.* ■ Law make (a legal instrument) valid by signing or sealing it. ■ Law carry out (a judicial sentence, the

terms of a will, or other order): *police executed a search warrant.*
2 (often **be executed**) carry out a sentence of death on (a legally condemned person): *he was convicted of treason and executed.*
▪kill (someone) as a political act.
– ORIGIN late Middle English: from Old French *executer*, from medieval Latin *executare*, from Latin *exsequi* 'follow up, carry out, punish', from *ex-* 'out' + *sequi* 'follow'.

execution ▶ noun [mass noun] **1** the carrying out or putting into effect of a plan, order, or course of action: *he was fascinated by the entire operation and its execution.*
▪the technique or style with which an artistic work is produced or carried out: *the film is entirely professional in its execution.* ▪ Law the putting into effect of a legal instrument or order. ▪ Law seizure of the property or person of a debtor in default of payment. ▪ [count noun] Law short for **WRIT OF EXECUTION**.
2 the carrying out of a sentence of death on a condemned person: *the place of execution* | [count noun] *there were mass arrests and executions.*
▪the killing of someone as a political act.

executioner ▶ noun an official who carries out a sentence of death on a legally condemned person.

executive /ɪɡˈzɛkjʊtɪv, ɛɡ-/ ▶ adjective [attrib.] having the power to put plans, actions, or laws into effect: *an executive chairman* | *executive authority.*
▪relating to managing an organization or political administration and putting into effect plans, actions, or laws: *the executive branch of government* | *the state has various executive functions.* Often contrasted with **LEGISLATIVE**.
▶ noun **1** a person with senior managerial responsibility in a business organization.
▪[as modifier] suitable or appropriate for a senior business executive: *an executive house* | *an executive jet.* ▪ an executive committee or other body within an organization: *the union executive.*
2 (**the executive**) the branch of a government responsible for putting plans, actions, or laws into effect.
– DERIVATIVES **executively** adverb.
– ORIGIN late Middle English (as an adjective): from medieval Latin *executivus*, from *exsequi* 'carry out' (see **EXECUTE**).

executive council ▶ noun a council with executive power.
▪(**Executive Council**) (in Australia) a body presided over by the Governor General or Governor and consisting of ministers of the Crown, which gives legal form to cabinet decisions.

executive officer ▶ noun an officer with executive power.
▪(in naval vessels and some other military contexts) the officer who is second in command to the captain or commanding officer.

executive privilege ▶ noun [mass noun] the privilege, claimed by the President for the executive branch of the US government, of withholding information in the public interest.

executive session ▶ noun US a meeting, especially a private one, of a legislative body for executive business.

executor /ɪɡˈzɛkjʊtə, ɛɡ-/ ▶ noun **1** Law a person or institution appointed by a testator to carry out the terms of their will.
2 a person who produces something or puts something into effect: *the makers and executors of policy.*
– DERIVATIVES **executorial** /-ˈtɔːrɪəl/ adjective (rare), **executorship** noun, **executory** adjective.
– ORIGIN Middle English: via Anglo-Norman French from Latin *execut-* 'carried out', from *exsequi* (see **EXECUTE**).

executrix /ɪɡˈzɛkjutrɪks, ɛɡ-/ ▶ noun (pl. **executrices** /-trɪsiːz/ or **executrixes**) Law a female executor of a will.
– ORIGIN late Middle English: from late Latin, from Latin *executor* (see **EXECUTOR**).

exedra /ˈɛksɪdrə, ɪkˈsiːdrə, ɛk-/ ▶ noun (pl. **exedrae** /-driː/) Architecture a room, portico, or arcade with a bench or seats where people may converse, especially in ancient Roman and Greek houses and gymnasia.
▪an outdoor recess containing a seat.
– ORIGIN Latin, from Greek *ex-* 'out of' + *hedra* 'seat'.

exegesis /ˌɛksɪˈdʒiːsɪs/ ▶ noun (pl. **exegeses** /-siːz/) [mass noun] critical explanation or interpretation of a text, especially of scripture: *the task of biblical exegesis* | [count noun] *an exegesis of Marx.*
– DERIVATIVES **exegetic** /-ˈdʒɛtɪk/ adjective, **exegetical** adjective.
– ORIGIN early 17th cent.: from Greek *exēgēsis*, from *exēgeisthai* 'interpret', from *ex-* 'out of' + *hēgeisthai* 'to guide, lead'.

exegete /ˈɛksɪdʒiːt/ ▶ noun an expounder or textual interpreter, especially of scripture.
– ORIGIN mid 18th cent.: from Greek *exēgētēs*, from *exēgeisthai* 'interpret'.

exemplar /ɪɡˈzɛmplə, ɛɡ-/ ▶ noun a person or thing serving as a typical example or appropriate model: *sociology has taken physics as the exemplar of science.*
– ORIGIN late Middle English: from Old French *exemplaire*, from late Latin *exemplarium*, from Latin *exemplum* 'sample, imitation' (see **EXAMPLE**).

exemplary ▶ adjective **1** serving as a desirable model; representing the best of its kind: *exemplary behaviour.*
2 (of a punishment) serving as a warning or deterrent: *exemplary sentencing may discourage the ultra-violent minority.*
▪Law (of damages) exceeding the amount needed for simple compensation.
– DERIVATIVES **exemplarily** adverb, **exemplariness** noun, **exemplarity** noun.
– ORIGIN late 16th cent.: from late Latin *exemplaris*, from Latin *exemplum* 'sample, imitation' (see **EXAMPLE**).

exemplify /ɪɡˈzɛmplɪfʌɪ, ɛɡ-/ ▶ verb (**-ies**, **-ied**) [with obj.] be a typical example of: *a case study of a British police operation which exemplifies current trends.*
▪give an example of; illustrate by giving an example.
– DERIVATIVES **exemplification** /-fɪˈkeɪʃ(ə)n/ noun.
– ORIGIN late Middle English (in the sense 'illustrate by examples'): from medieval Latin *exemplificare*, from Latin *exemplum* 'sample' (see **EXAMPLE**).

exemplum /ɪɡˈzɛmpləm, ɛɡ-/ ▶ noun (pl. **exempla**) an example or model, especially a moralizing or illustrative story.
– ORIGIN Latin.

exempt /ɪɡˈzɛm(p)t, ɛɡ-/ ▶ adjective free from an obligation or liability imposed on others: *these patients are **exempt from** all charges* | *they are not **exempt from** criticism.*
▶ verb [with obj.] free (a person or organization) from an obligation or liability imposed on others: *they were **exempted from** paying the tax.*
▶ noun a person who is exempt from something, especially the payment of tax.
– ORIGIN late Middle English: from Latin *exemptus* 'taken out, freed', past participle of *eximere*.

exemption ▶ noun [mass noun] the process of freeing or state of being free from an obligation or liability imposed on others: ***exemption from** prescription charges* | [count noun] *tax exemptions.*
– ORIGIN late Middle English: from Old French, or from Latin *exemptio(n-)*, from *eximere* 'take out, free'.

exenteration /ɪkˌsɛntəˈreɪʃ(ə)n, ɛk-/ ▶ noun [mass noun] Medicine complete surgical removal of the eyeball and other contents of the eye socket, usually in cases of malignant cancer.
– ORIGIN mid 17th cent. (originally in the sense 'disembowelment'): from Latin *exenterat-* 'removed', from the verb *exenterare*, (suggested by Greek *exenterizein*), from *ex-* 'out of' + *enteron* 'intestine'.

exequatur /ˌɛksɪˈkweɪtə/ ▶ noun an official recognition by a government of a consul, agent, or other representative of a foreign state, authorizing them to exercise office.
– ORIGIN Latin, literally 'let him or her perform'.

exequy /ˈɛksɪkwi/ ▶ noun (**exequies**) formal funeral rites: *he attended the exequies for the dead pope.*
▪(**exequy**) poetic/literary a funeral ode.
– ORIGIN late Middle English: via Old French from Latin *exsequias*, accusative of *exsequiae* 'funeral ceremonies', from *exsequi* 'follow after'.

exercise ▶ noun [mass noun] **1** activity requiring physical effort, carried out especially to sustain or improve health and fitness: *exercise improves your heart and lung power* | [count noun] *loosening-up exercises.*
▪[count noun] a task or activity set to practise or test a skill: *there are exercises at the end of each book to check comprehension.* ▪ [count noun] a process or activity carried out for a specific purpose, especially one concerned with a specified area or skill: *an exercise in public relations.* ▪ [count noun] (often **exercises**) a military drill or training manoeuvre. ▪ (**exercises**) N. Amer. ceremonies: *Bar Mitzvah exercises.*
2 the use or application of a faculty, right, or process: *the exercise of authority.*
▶ verb [with obj.] **1** use or apply (a faculty, right, or process): *control is exercised by the Board* | *anyone receiving a suspect package should exercise extreme caution.*
2 [no obj.] engage in physical activity to sustain or improve health and fitness; take exercise: *she still exercised every day.*
▪exert (part of the body) to promote or improve muscular strength: *raise your knee to exercise the upper leg and hip muscles.* ▪ cause (an animal) to engage in exercise: *she exercised her dogs before breakfast.*
3 occupy the thoughts of; worry or perplex: *the knowledge that a larger margin was possible still exercised him.*
– DERIVATIVES **exercisable** adjective, **exerciser** noun.
– ORIGIN Middle English (in the sense 'application of a faculty, right, or process'): via Old French from Latin *exercitium*, from *exercere* 'keep busy, practise', from *ex-* 'thoroughly' + *arcere* 'keep in or away'.

exercise bike (also **exercise bicycle**) ▶ noun a piece of exercise equipment having handlebars, pedals, and a saddle like a bicycle, on which the user replicates the movements of cycling.

exercise book ▶ noun **1** a book containing printed exercises for the use of students.
2 Brit. a booklet with blank pages for students to write school work or make notes in.

exercise price ▶ noun Stock Exchange the price per share at which the owner of a traded option is entitled to buy or sell the underlying security.

exercise yard ▶ noun an enclosed area used for physical exercise in a prison.

exercycle ▶ noun trademark an exercise bike.
– ORIGIN 1930s: blend of **EXERCISE** and **BICYCLE**.

exergonic /ˌɛksəːˈɡɒnɪk/ ▶ adjective Biochemistry (of a metabolic or chemical process) accompanied by the release of energy. The opposite of **ENDERGONIC**.
– ORIGIN mid 20th cent.: from **EX-**[2] 'out of' + Greek *ergon* 'work' + **-IC**.

exergue /ɪkˈsəːɡ, ɛkˈsəːɡ, ˈɛksəːɡ/ ▶ noun a small space or inscription below the principal emblem on a coin or medal, usually on the reverse side.
– ORIGIN late 17th cent.: from French, from medieval Latin *exergum*, from *ex-* 'out' + Greek *ergon* 'work' (probably as a rendering of French *hors d'oeuvre* 'something lying outside the work').

exert /ɪɡˈzəːt, ɛɡ-/ ▶ verb [with obj.] **1** apply or bring to bear (a force, influence, or quality): *the moon **exerts** a force **on** the Earth* | ***exerting** influence **over** the next generation.*
2 (**exert oneself**) make a physical or mental effort: *he needs to exert himself to try to find an answer.*
– ORIGIN mid 17th cent. (in the sense 'perform, practise'): from Latin *exserere* 'put forth', from *ex-* 'out' + *serere* 'bind'.

exertion ▶ noun [mass noun] **1** physical or mental effort: *she was panting with the exertion* | [count noun] *a well-earned rest after their mental exertions.*
2 the application of a force, influence, or quality: *the exertion of authority.*

Exeter /ˈɛksɪtə/ the county town of Devon, on the River Exe; pop. 101,100 (1990). Exeter was founded by the Romans, who called it Isca.

exeunt /ˈɛksɪʌnt/ ▶ verb used as a stage direction in a printed play to indicate that a group of characters leave the stage: *exeunt Hamlet and Polonius.* See also **EXIT**.
– PHRASES **exeunt omnes** used in such a way to indicate that all the actors leave the stage.
– ORIGIN late 15th cent.: Latin, literally 'they go out', third person plural present tense of *exire*.

exfiltrate ▶ verb [with obj.] withdraw (troops or spies) surreptitiously, especially from a dangerous position.
– DERIVATIVES **exfiltration** noun.
– ORIGIN late 20th cent.: back-formation from *exfiltration*, perhaps suggested by the pair *infiltration, infiltrate*.

exfoliant ▶ noun a cosmetic product designed to remove dead cells from the surface of the skin.
– ORIGIN 1980s: from **EXFOLIATE** + **-ANT**.

exfoliate /ɪksˈfəʊlɪeɪt, ɛks-/ ▶ verb [no obj.] (of a material) come apart or be shed from a surface in scales or layers: *the bark exfoliates in papery flakes.*
▪[with obj.] cause to do this: *salt solutions exfoliate rocks on*

evaporating. ■[with obj.] wash or rub (a part of the body) with a granular substance to remove dead cells from the surface of the skin: *exfoliate your legs to get rid of dead skin.* ■[with obj.] (often **be exfoliated**) shed (material) in scales or layers.
– DERIVATIVES **exfoliation** noun, **exfoliative** adjective, **exfoliator** noun.
– ORIGIN mid 17th cent.: from late Latin *exfoliat-* 'stripped of leaves', from the verb *exfoliare*, from *ex-* 'out, from' + *folium* 'leaf'.

ex gratia /ɛks ˈɡreɪʃə/ ▶ **adverb** & **adjective** (especially with reference to the paying of money) done from a sense of moral obligation rather than because of any legal requirement: [as adj.] *an ex gratia payment.*
– ORIGIN Latin, literally 'from favour', from *ex* 'from' and *gratia* (see **GRACE**).

exhalation ▶ **noun** [mass noun] the process or action of exhaling.
■[count noun] an expiration of air from the lungs: *he let his breath out in a long exhalation of relief.* ■[count noun] an amount of vapour or fumes given off.

exhale /ɪksˈheɪl, ɛks-/ ▶ **verb** breathe out in a deliberate manner: [no obj.] *she sat back and exhaled deeply* | [with obj.] *he exhaled the smoke towards the ceiling.*
■[with obj.] give off (vapour or fumes): *the jungle exhaled mists of early morning.*
– DERIVATIVES **exhalable** adjective.
– ORIGIN late Middle English (in the sense 'be given off as vapour'): from Old French *exhaler*, from Latin *exhalare*, from *ex-* 'out' + *halare* 'breathe'.

exhaust /ɪɡˈzɔːst, ɛɡ-/ ▶ **verb** [with obj.] **1** drain (someone) of their physical or mental resources; tire out: *her day out had exhausted her* | [as adj. **exhausting**] *it had been a long and exhausting day.*
2 use up (resources or reserves) completely: *the country has exhausted its treasury reserves.*
■expound on, write about, or explore (a subject or options) so fully that there is nothing further to be said or discovered: *she seemed to have exhausted all permissible topics of conversation.*
3 expel (gas or steam) from or into a particular place.
▶ **noun** [mass noun] waste gases or air expelled from an engine, turbine, or other machine in the course of its operation: *buses spewing out black clouds of exhaust* | [as modifier] *exhaust fumes.*
■[count noun] the system through which such gases are expelled: [as modifier] *an exhaust pipe.*
– DERIVATIVES **exhauster** noun, **exhaustibility** /-ˈbɪlɪti/ noun, **exhaustible** adjective, **exhaustingly** adverb.
– ORIGIN mid 16th cent. (in the general sense 'draw off or out'): from Latin *exhaust-* 'drained out', from the verb *exhaurire*, from *ex-* 'out' + *haurire* 'draw (water), drain'.

exhausted ▶ **adjective 1** drained of one's physical or mental resources; very tired: *I'm absolutely exhausted* | *she returned home,* **exhausted from** *her day in the City.*
2 (of resources or reserves) completely used up: *Kirov spat, his patience suddenly exhausted.*
– DERIVATIVES **exhaustedly** adverb.

exhaustion ▶ **noun** [mass noun] **1** a state of extreme physical or mental fatigue: *he was pale with exhaustion.*
2 the action or state of using something up or of being used up completely: *the rapid exhaustion of fossil fuel reserves.*
■Logic the process of establishing a conclusion by eliminating all the alternatives.
– ORIGIN early 17th cent.: from late Latin *exhaustio(n-)*, from Latin *exhaurire* 'drain out' (see **EXHAUST**).

exhaustive ▶ **adjective** examining, including, or considering all elements or aspects; fully comprehensive: *she has undergone exhaustive tests since becoming ill.*
– DERIVATIVES **exhaustively** adverb, **exhaustiveness** noun.

exhibit /ɪɡˈzɪbɪt, ɛɡ-/ ▶ **verb** [with obj.] **1** publicly display (a work of art or item of interest) in an art gallery or museum or at a trade fair: *only one sculpture was exhibited in the artist's lifetime.*
■[no obj.] (of an artist) display one's work to the public in an art gallery or museum: *she was invited to exhibit at several French museums.* ■(usu. **be exhibited**) publicly display the work of (an artist) in an art gallery or museum: *no foreign painters were exhibited.*
2 manifest or deliberately display (a quality or a type of behaviour): *he could exhibit a saint-like submissiveness.*
■show as a sign or symptom: *patients with alcoholic liver disease exhibit many biochemical abnormalities.*
▶ **noun** an object or collection of objects on public display in an art gallery or museum or at a trade fair: *the museum is rich in exhibits.*
■N. Amer. an exhibition: *people flocked to the exhibit in record-breaking numbers.* ■Law a document or other object produced in a court as evidence.
– ORIGIN late Middle English (in the sense 'submit for consideration', also specifically 'present a document as evidence in court'): from Latin *exhibit-* 'held out', from the verb *exhibere*, from *ex-* 'out' + *habere* 'hold'.

exhibition ▶ **noun 1** a public display of works of art or other items of interest, held in an art gallery or museum or at a trade fair: *an exhibition of French sculpture* | [mass noun] *he never lent his treasures out for exhibition.*
2 a display or demonstration of a particular skill: *fields which have been ploughed with a supreme exhibition of the farm worker's skills* | [as modifier] *an exhibition match.*
■[in sing.] an ostentatious or insincere display of a particular quality or emotion: *a false but convincing exhibition of concern for smaller nations.*
3 Brit. a scholarship awarded to a student at a school or university, usually after a competitive examination.
– PHRASES **make an exhibition of oneself** behave in a conspicuously foolish or ill-judged way in public.
– ORIGIN late Middle English (in the sense 'maintenance, support'; hence sense 3, mid 17th cent.): via Old French from late Latin *exhibitio(n-)*, from Latin *exhibere* 'hold out' (see **EXHIBIT**).

exhibitioner ▶ **noun** Brit. a student who has been awarded an exhibition (scholarship).

exhibitionism ▶ **noun** [mass noun] extravagant behaviour that is intended to attract attention to oneself.
■Psychiatry a mental condition characterized by the compulsion to display one's genitals in public.
– DERIVATIVES **exhibitionist** noun, **exhibitionistic** adjective, **exhibitionistically** adverb.

exhibitor ▶ **noun** a person who displays works of art or other items of interest at an exhibition.

exhilarate /ɪɡˈzɪləreɪt, ɛɡ-/ ▶ **verb** (usu. **be exhilarated**) make (someone) feel very happy, animated, or elated: *she was exhilarated by the day's events* | [as adj. **exhilarated**] *all this hustle and bustle makes me feel exhilarated* | [as adj. **exhilarating**] *riding was one of the most exhilarating experiences he knew.*
– DERIVATIVES **exhilaratingly** adverb, **exhilaration** noun.
– ORIGIN mid 16th cent.: from Latin *exhilarat-* 'made cheerful', from the verb *exhilarare*, from *ex-* (expressing inducement of a state) + *hilaris* 'cheerful'.

exhort /ɪɡˈzɔːt, ɛɡ-/ ▶ **verb** [with obj. and infinitive] strongly encourage or urge (someone) to do something: *the media have been exhorting people to turn out for the demonstration* | [with direct speech] *'Come on, you guys,' exhorted Linda.*
– DERIVATIVES **exhortative** adjective, **exhortatory** /-tət(ə)ri/ adjective, **exhorter** noun.
– ORIGIN late Middle English: from Old French *exhorter* or Latin *exhortari*, from *ex-* 'thoroughly' + *hortari* 'encourage'.

exhortation ▶ **noun** an address or communication emphatically urging someone to do something: *exhortations to consumers to switch off electrical appliances* | [mass noun] *no amount of exhortation had any effect.*

exhume /ɛksˈ(h)juːm, ɪɡˈzjuːm/ ▶ **verb** [with obj.] dig out (something buried, especially a corpse) from the ground.
■(usu. **be exhumed**) Geology expose (a land surface) that was formerly buried.
– DERIVATIVES **exhumation** noun.
– ORIGIN late Middle English: from medieval Latin *exhumare*, from *ex-* 'out of' + *humus* 'ground'.

ex hypothesi /ˌɛks hʌɪˈpɒθəsʌɪ/ ▶ **adverb** according to the hypothesis proposed.
– ORIGIN modern Latin, from *ex* 'from' and *hypothesi*, ablative of late Latin *hypothesis* (see **HYPOTHESIS**).

exigence /ˈɛksɪdʒ(ə)ns, ˈɛɡzɪ-/ ▶ **noun** another term for **EXIGENCY**.

exigency /ˈɛksɪdʒ(ə)nsi, ˈɛɡzɪ-, ɪɡˈzɪ-, ɛɡˈzɪ-/ ▶ **noun** (pl. **-ies**) an urgent need or demand: *women worked long hours when the exigencies of the family economy demanded it* | [mass noun] *he put financial exigency before personal sentiment.*
– ORIGIN late 16th cent.: from late Latin *exigentia*, from Latin *exigere* 'enforce' (see **EXACT**).

exigent /ˈɛksɪdʒ(ə)nt, ˈɛɡzɪ-/ ▶ **adjective** formal pressing; demanding: *the exigent demands of her contemporaries' music took a toll on her voice.*
– ORIGIN early 17th cent.: from Latin *exigent-* 'completing, ascertaining', from the verb *exigere* (see **EXACT**).

exigible /ˈɛksɪdʒɪb(ə)l, ˈɛɡzɪ-/ ▶ **adjective** (of a tax, duty, or other payment) able to be charged or levied.
– ORIGIN early 17th cent.: from French, from *exiger* 'demand, exact', from Latin *exigere* (see **EXACT**).

exiguous /ɪɡˈzɪɡjʊəs, ɛɡ-/ ▶ **adjective** formal very small in size or amount: *my exiguous musical resources.*
– DERIVATIVES **exiguity** /-ˈɡjuːɪti/ noun, **exiguously** adverb, **exiguousness** noun.
– ORIGIN mid 17th cent.: from Latin *exiguus* 'scanty' (from *exigere* 'weigh exactly') + **-OUS**.

exile ▶ **noun** [mass noun] the state of being barred from one's native country, typically for political or punitive reasons: *he knew now that he would die in exile.*
■[count noun] a person who lives away from their native country, either from choice or compulsion: *the return of political exiles.* ■(**the Exile**) another term for **BABYLONIAN CAPTIVITY**.
▶ **verb** [with obj.] (usu. **be exiled**) expel and bar (someone) from their native country, typically for political or punitive reasons: *a corrupt dictator who had been* **exiled from** *his country* | *he was* **exiled to** *Tasmania in 1849* | [as adj. **exiled**] *supporters of the exiled King.*
– ORIGIN Middle English: the noun partly from Old French *exil* 'banishment' and partly from Old French *exile* 'banished person'; the verb from Old French *exiler*; all based on Latin *exilium* 'banishment', from *exul* 'banished person'.

exilic /ɪɡˈzɪlɪk, ɪk-, ɛɡ-, ɛk-/ ▶ **adjective** of or relating to a period of exile, especially that of the Jews in Babylon in the 6th century BC.

exine /ˈɛksɪn, -ʌɪn/ ▶ **noun** Botany the decay-resistant outer coating of a pollen grain or spore. It typically bears a highly characteristic surface pattern which is used in palynology.
– ORIGIN late 19th cent.: perhaps from **EX-**[2] 'out' + Greek *is, in-* 'fibre'.

exist ▶ **verb** [no obj.] **1** have objective reality or being: *remains of these baths still exist on the south side of the Pantheon* | *there existed no organization to cope with espionage.*
■be found, especially in a particular place or situation: *two conflicting stereotypes of housework exist in popular thinking today.*
2 live, especially under adverse conditions: *how am I going to exist without you?* | *only a minority of people exist on unemployment benefit alone.*
– ORIGIN early 17th cent.: probably a back-formation from **EXISTENCE**.

existence ▶ **noun** [mass noun] the fact or state of living or having objective reality: *the plane was the oldest Boeing remaining* **in existence** | *the need to acknowledge the existence of a problem.*
■continued survival: *she helped to keep the company alive when its very existence was threatened.* ■[count noun] a way of living: *living in a city was more expensive than a rural existence.* ■[count noun] archaic a being or entity.
– ORIGIN late Middle English: from Old French, or from late Latin *existentia*, from Latin *exsistere* 'come into being', from *ex-* 'out' + *sistere* 'take a stand'.

existent ▶ **adjective** formal having reality or existence: *the technique has been existent for some years.*
– ORIGIN mid 16th cent.: from Latin *exsistent-* 'coming into being, emerging', from the verb *exsistere* (see **EXISTENCE**).

existential /ˌɛɡzɪˈstɛnʃ(ə)l/ ▶ **adjective** of or relating to existence.
■Philosophy concerned with existence, especially human existence as viewed in the theories of existentialism. ■Logic (of a proposition) affirming or implying the existence of a thing.
– DERIVATIVES **existentially** adverb.
– ORIGIN late 17th cent.: from late Latin *existentialis*, from *existentia* (see **EXISTENCE**).

existentialism ▶ **noun** [mass noun] a philosophical theory or approach which emphasizes the existence of the individual person as a free and responsible agent determining their own development through acts of the will.

Generally taken to originate with Kierkegaard and Nietzsche, existentialism tends to be atheistic, to disparage scientific knowledge, and to deny the existence of objective values, stressing instead the reality and significance of human freedom and experience. The approach was developed chiefly in 20th-century Europe, notably by Martin Heidegger, Jean-Paul Sartre, Albert Camus, and Simone de Beauvoir.

– DERIVATIVES **existentialist** noun & adjective.
– ORIGIN translating Danish *existents-forhold* 'condition of existence' (frequently used by Kierkegaard), from **EXISTENTIAL**.

existential quantifier ▶ **noun** Logic a formal expression used in asserting that something exists of which a stated general proposition can be said to be true.

existing ▶ **adjective** [attrib.] in existence or operation at the time under consideration; current: *opponents of the existing political system.*

exit ▶ **noun 1** a way out, especially of a public building, room, or passenger vehicle: *she slipped out by the rear exit | a fire exit.*
■ a place where traffic can leave a motorway, major road, or roundabout: *she slowed for a roundabout, taking the second exit.*
2 an act of going out of or leaving a place: *he made a hasty* ***exit from*** *the room.*
■ a departure of an actor from the stage: *the brief soliloquy following Clarence's exit.* ■ a departure from a particular situation: *Australia's early* ***exit from*** *the World Cup.* ■ poetic/literary a person's death.
▶ **verb** (**exited**, **exiting**) [no obj.] go out of or leave a place: *he* ***exited from*** *the changing rooms | the bullet entered her back and exited through her chest |* [with obj.] *large queues of vehicles trying to exit the airfield.*
■ (of an actor) leave the stage. ■ (**exit**) used as a stage direction in a printed play to indicate that a character leaves the stage: *exit Pamela.* See also **EXEUNT**. ■ leave a particular situation: *organizations which do not have freedom to exit from unprofitable markets.* ■ poetic/literary die. ■ Computing terminate a process or program, usually returning to an earlier or more general level of interaction: *this key enables you to temporarily exit from a LIFESPAN option.* ■ Bridge relinquish the lead.
– ORIGIN mid 16th cent. (as a stage direction): from Latin *exit* 'he or she goes out', third person singular present tense of *exire*, from *ex-* 'out' + *ire* 'go'. The noun use (late 16th cent.) is from Latin *exitus* 'going out', from the verb *exire*, and the other verb uses (early 17th cent.) are from the noun.

exit line ▶ **noun** a line spoken by an actor immediately before leaving the stage.
■ a parting remark.

exit poll ▶ **noun** an opinion poll of people leaving a polling station, asking how they voted.

exit visa (also **exit permit**) ▶ **noun** a document giving authorization to leave a particular country.

exit wound ▶ **noun** a wound made by a bullet or other missile passing out of the body.

ex libris /ɛks ˈlɪbrɪs, ˈliːbː-, ˈlʌɪb-, ˈliːbriːs/ ▶ **adverb** used as an inscription on a bookplate to show the name of the book's owner: *ex libris Edith Wharton.*
▶ **noun** (pl. same) a bookplate inscribed in such a way, especially a decorative one.
– ORIGIN Latin, literally 'out of the books or library (of someone)'.

Exmoor /ˈɛksmʊə, -mɔː/ an area of moorland in north Devon and west Somerset, SW England, rising to 520 m (1,706 ft) at Dunkery Beacon. The area is designated a national park.

Exmoor Horn ▶ **noun** a sheep of a horned, short-woolled breed.

Exmoor pony ▶ **noun** a pony of a small hardy breed, typically bay, brown, or dun in colour with a light muzzle.

ex nihilo /ɛks ˈnʌɪhɪləʊ/ ▶ **adverb** formal out of nothing: *it was created virtually ex nihilo.*
– ORIGIN Latin.

exo- ▶ **prefix** external; from outside: *exodermis.*
– ORIGIN from Greek *exō* 'outside'.

exoatmospheric ▶ **adjective** operating or taking place outside the atmosphere.

exobiology ▶ **noun** [mass noun] the branch of science that deals with the possibility and likely nature of life on other planets or in space.
– DERIVATIVES **exobiological** adjective, **exobiologist** noun.

exocarp /ˈɛksəʊkɑːp/ ▶ **noun** Botany the outer layer of the pericarp of a fruit.

exocentric /ˌɛksəʊˈsɛntrɪk/ ▶ **adjective** Linguistics denoting or being a construction which has no explicit head, for example *John slept*. Contrasted with **ENDOCENTRIC**.

Exocet /ˈɛksə(ʊ)sɛt/ ▶ **noun** trademark a French-made guided anti-ship missile.
– ORIGIN 1970s: from French, literally 'flying fish', via Latin from Greek *ekōkoitos* 'fish that comes up on the beach' (literally 'out of bed').

exocrine /ˈɛksə(ʊ)krʌɪn, -krɪn/ ▶ **adjective** Physiology relating to or denoting glands which secrete their products through ducts opening on to an epithelium rather than directly into the bloodstream. Often contrasted with **ENDOCRINE**.
– ORIGIN early 20th cent.: from **EXO-** 'outside' + Greek *krinein* 'sift'.

exocytosis /ˌɛksəʊsʌɪˈtəʊsɪs/ ▶ **noun** [mass noun] Biology a process by which the contents of a cell vacuole are released to the exterior through fusion of the vacuole membrane with the cell membrane.
– DERIVATIVES **exocytotic** adjective.

exodermis /ˌɛksə(ʊ)ˈdəːmɪs/ ▶ **noun** [mass noun] Botany a specialized layer in a root beneath the epidermis or velamen.
– ORIGIN early 20th cent.: from **EXO-** 'outside', on the pattern of *endodermis*, *epidermis*.

Exodus /ˈɛksədəs/ (abbrev.: **Exod.**) the second book of the Bible, which recounts the departure of the Israelites from slavery in Egypt, their journey across the Red Sea and through the wilderness led by Moses, and the giving of the Ten Commandments. The events have been variously dated by scholars between about 1580 and 1200 BC.
– ORIGIN Old English, via ecclesiastical Latin from Greek *exodos*, from *ex-* 'out of' + *hodos* 'way'.

exodus /ˈɛksədəs/ ▶ **noun** a mass departure of people, especially emigrants.
■ (**the Exodus**) the departure of the Israelites from Egypt.
– ORIGIN early 17th cent.: from Greek (see **EXODUS**).

exoenzyme ▶ **noun** Biochemistry an enzyme which acts outside the cell that produces it.

ex officio /ˌɛks əˈfɪʃɪəʊ/ ▶ **adverb** & **adjective** by virtue of one's position or status: [as adj.] *an ex officio member of the committee.*
– ORIGIN Latin, from *ex* 'out of, from' + *officium* 'duty'.

exogamy /ɪkˈsɒgəmi, ɛk-/ ▶ **noun** [mass noun] Anthropology the custom of marrying outside a community, clan, or tribe. Compare with **ENDOGAMY**.
■ Biology the fusion of reproductive cells from distantly related or unrelated individuals; outbreeding; cross-pollination.
– DERIVATIVES **exogamous** adjective.

exogenic /ˌɛksə(ʊ)ˈdʒɛnɪk/ ▶ **adjective** Geology formed or occurring on the surface of the earth. Often contrasted with **ENDOGENIC**.

exogenous /ɪkˈsɒdʒɪnəs, ɛk-/ ▶ **adjective** of, relating to, or developing from external factors. Often contrasted with **ENDOGENOUS**.
■ Biology growing or originating from outside an organism: *an exogenous hormone.* ■ chiefly Psychiatry (of a disease, symptom, etc.) caused by an agent or organism outside the body: *exogenous depression.* ■ relating to an external group or society: *exogenous marriage.*
– DERIVATIVES **exogenously** adverb.
– ORIGIN mid 19th cent.: from modern Latin *exogena* (denoting an exogenous plant, suggested by classical Latin *indigena* 'native') + **-OUS**.

exon[1] /ˈɛksɒn/ ▶ **noun** Biochemistry a segment of a DNA or RNA molecule containing information coding for a protein or peptide sequence. Compare with **INTRON**.
– ORIGIN late 20th cent.: from *expressed* (see **EXPRESS**[1]) + **-ON**.

exon[2] /ˈɛksɒn/ ▶ **noun** Brit. each of the four officers acting as commanders of the Yeomen of the Guard.
– ORIGIN mid 18th cent.: representing the pronunciation of French *exempt* 'free from', from Latin *exempt-* 'taken out', from the verb *eximere*, so named because these officers were exempt from normal duties.

exonerate /ɪgˈzɒnəreɪt, ɛg-/ ▶ **verb** [with obj.] **1** (especially of an official body) absolve (someone) from blame for a fault or wrongdoing, especially after due consideration of the case: *the court martial exonerated me | they should* ***exonerate*** *these men* ***from*** *this crime.*
2 (**exonerate someone from**) release someone from (a duty or obligation).
– DERIVATIVES **exoneration** noun, **exonerative** adjective.
– ORIGIN late Middle English: from Latin *exonerat-* 'freed from a burden', from the verb *exonerare*, from *ex-* 'from' + *onus*, *oner-* 'a burden'.

exonuclease /ˌɛksəʊˈnjuːklɪeɪz/ ▶ **noun** Biochemistry an enzyme which removes successive nucleotides from the end of a polynucleotide molecule.

exopeptidase /ˌɛksəʊˈpɛptɪdeɪz/ ▶ **noun** Biochemistry an enzyme which breaks the terminal peptide bond in a peptide chain.

exophora /ɪkˈsɒf(ə)rə/ ▶ **noun** [mass noun] Linguistics reference in a text or utterance to something external to it, which is only fully intelligible in terms of information about the extralinguistic situation. Compare with **ENDOPHORA**.
– DERIVATIVES **exophoric** /ˌɛksə(ʊ)ˈfɒrɪk/ adjective.

exophthalmic /ˌɛksɒfˈθalmɪk/ ▶ **adjective** Medicine having or characterized by protruding eyes.

exophthalmic goitre ▶ **noun** another term for **GRAVES' DISEASE**.

exophthalmos /ˌɛksɒfˈθalmɒs/ (also **exophthalmus** or **exophthalmia** /-mɪə/) ▶ **noun** [mass noun] Medicine abnormal protrusion of the eyeball or eyeballs.
– ORIGIN early 17th cent.: from modern Latin *exophthalmus*, from Greek *exophthalmos* 'having prominent eyes', from *ex-* 'out' + *ophthalmos* 'eye'.

exopodite /ɛkˈsɒpədʌɪt/ (also **exopod** /ˈɛksə(ʊ)pɒd/) ▶ **noun** Zoology the outer branch of the biramous limb or appendage of a crustacean. Compare with **ENDOPODITE**, **PROTOPODITE**.
– ORIGIN late 19th cent.: from **EXO-** 'outside' + Greek *pous*, *pod-* 'foot' + **-ITE**[1].

exor ▶ **abbreviation for** an executor (of a will).

exorbitant /ɪgˈzɔːbɪt(ə)nt/ ▶ **adjective** (of a price or amount charged) unreasonably high: *exclusive fabrics at exorbitant prices.*
– DERIVATIVES **exorbitance** noun, **exorbitantly** adverb.
– ORIGIN late Middle English (originally as a legal term describing a case that is outside the scope of a law): from late Latin *exorbitant-* 'going off the track', from *exorbitare*, from *ex-* 'out from' + *orbita* 'course, track'.

exorcism ▶ **noun** [mass noun] the expulsion or attempted expulsion of an evil spirit from a person or place in which it is believed to be present.
– DERIVATIVES **exorcist** noun.
– ORIGIN late Middle English: via ecclesiastical Latin from ecclesiastical Greek *exorkismos*, from *exorkizein* 'exorcize'.

exorcize /ˈɛksɔːsʌɪz/ (also **-ise**) ▶ **verb** [with obj.] drive out or attempt to drive out (an evil spirit) from a person or place in which it is believed to be present: *an attempt to exorcize an unquiet spirit |* figurative *inflation has been exorcized.*
■ (often **be exorcized**) rid (a person or place) of a supposed evil spirit: *infants were exorcized prior to baptism.*
– ORIGIN late Middle English: from French *exorciser* or ecclesiastical Latin *exorcizare*, from Greek *exorkizein*, from *ex-* 'out' + *horkos* 'oath'. The word originally meant 'conjure up or command (an evil spirit)'; the specific sense of driving out an evil spirit dates from the mid 16th cent.

exordium /ɪgˈzɔːdɪəm, ɛg-/ ▶ **noun** (pl. **exordiums** or **exordia**) formal the beginning or introductory part, especially of a discourse or treatise.
– DERIVATIVES **exordial** adjective.
– ORIGIN late 16th cent.: from Latin, from *exordiri* 'begin', from *ex-* 'out, from' + *ordiri* 'begin'.

exoskeleton ▶ **noun** Zoology a rigid external covering for the body in some invertebrate animals, especially arthropods, providing both support and protection. Compare with **ENDOSKELETON**.
– DERIVATIVES **exoskeletal** adjective.

exosphere /ˈɛksə(ʊ)sfɪə/ ▶ **noun** Astronomy the outermost region of a planet's atmosphere.
– DERIVATIVES **exospheric** adjective.

exostosis /ˌɛksɒsˈtəʊsɪs/ ▶ **noun** (pl. **exostoses** /-siːz/) Medicine a benign outgrowth of cartilaginous tissue on a bone.

– ORIGIN late 16th cent.: from Greek, from *ex-* 'out' + *osteon* 'bone'.

exoteric /ˌɛksə(ʊ)ˈtɛrɪk/ ▶ **adjective** formal (especially of a doctrine or mode of speech) intended for or likely to be understood by the general public. The opposite of **ESOTERIC**.
■ current or popular among the general public.
– ORIGIN mid 17th cent.: via Latin from Greek *exōterikos*, from *exōterō* 'outer', comparative of *exō* 'outside'.

exothermic /ˌɛksə(ʊ)ˈθəːmɪk/ ▶ **adjective** Chemistry (of a reaction or process) accompanied by the release of heat. The opposite of **ENDOTHERMIC** (in sense 1).
■ (of a compound) formed from its constituent elements with a net release of heat.
– DERIVATIVES **exothermically** adverb.
– ORIGIN late 19th cent.: from French *exothermique*.

exotic /ɪɡˈzɒtɪk, ɛɡ-/ ▶ **adjective** originating in or characteristic of a distant foreign country: *exotic birds | they loved to visit exotic places.*
■ attractive or striking because colourful or out of the ordinary: *an exotic outfit* | [as noun **the exotic**] *there was a touch of the exotic in her appearance.* ■ of a kind not used for ordinary purposes or not ordinarily encountered: *exotic elementary particles as yet unknown to science.*
▶ **noun** an exotic plant or animal: *he planted exotics in the sheltered garden.*
– DERIVATIVES **exotically** adverb, **exoticism** noun.
– ORIGIN late 16th cent.: via Latin from Greek *exōtikos* 'foreign', from *exō* 'outside'.

exotica /ɪɡˈzɒtɪkə, ɛɡ-/ ▶ **plural noun** objects considered strange or interesting because they are out of the ordinary, especially because they originated in a distant foreign country.
– ORIGIN late 19th cent.: from Latin, neuter plural of *exoticus* 'foreign' (see **EXOTIC**).

exotic dancer ▶ **noun** a striptease dancer.

exotoxin ▶ **noun** Microbiology a toxin released by a living bacterial cell into its surroundings. Compare with **ENDOTOXIN**.

exp ▶ **abbreviation for** ■ experience (usually in the context of job advertisements): *previous exp an advantage.* ■ (**Exp.**) experimental (in titles of periodicals): *J. Exp. Biol.* ■ expiry: *exp date.* ■ Mathematics the exponential function raising *e* to the power of the given quantity: *it is reduced by exp (−U).* ■ exposures (in the context of photography): *£4.45 for 24 exp.*

expand /ɪkˈspand, ɛk-/ ▶ **verb** become or make larger or more extensive: [no obj.] *their business expanded into other hotels and properties* | [with obj.] *expand the hole with a file.*
■ [no obj.] Physics (of the universe) undergo a continuous change whereby, according to theory based on observed red shifts, all the galaxies recede from one another. ■ [no obj.] (**expand on**) give a fuller version or account of: *the minister expanded on the government's proposals.* ■ [no obj.] figurative become less reserved in character or behaviour: *Alice opened and expanded in this normality.*
– DERIVATIVES **expandable** adjective, **expander** noun, **expansibility** noun, **expansible** adjective.
– ORIGIN late Middle English: from Latin *expandere* 'to spread out', from *ex-* 'out' + *pandere* 'to spread'.

expanded ▶ **noun** being or having been enlarged, extended or broadened, in particular:
■ denoting materials which have a light cellular structure: *expanded polystyrene.* ■ denoting sheet metal slit and stretched into a mesh, used to reinforce concrete and other brittle materials. ■ relatively broad in shape: *the expanded fins of the ray.*

expanse ▶ **noun** an area of something, typically land or sea, presenting a wide continuous surface: *the green expanse of the forest.*
■ the distance to which something expands or can be expanded: *the moth has a wing expanse of 20 to 24 mm.*
– ORIGIN mid 17th cent.: from modern Latin *expansum* 'something expanded', neuter past participle of *expandere* (see **EXPAND**).

expansile ▶ **adjective** Physics of, relating to, or capable of expansion.

expansion ▶ **noun** [mass noun] the action of becoming larger or more extensive: *the rapid expansion of suburban London* | [count noun] *a small expansion of industry.*
■ extension of a state's territory by encroaching on that of other nations, pursued as a political strategy: *German expansion in the 1930s.* ■ [count noun] a thing formed by the enlargement, broadening, or development of something: *the book is an expansion of a lecture given last year.* ■ the increase in the volume of fuel on combustion in the cylinder of an engine, or the piston stroke in which this occurs.
– ORIGIN early 17th cent.: from late Latin *expansio(n-)*, from Latin *expandere* (see **EXPAND**).

expansionary ▶ **adjective** (of a policy or action) intended to result in economic or political expansion: *an expansionary budget.*

expansion bolt ▶ **noun** a bolt that expands when inserted, no thread being required in the surrounding material.

expansion card (also **expansion board**) ▶ **noun** Computing a circuit board that can be inserted in a computer to give extra facilities or memory.

expansionism ▶ **noun** [mass noun] the policy of territorial or economic expansion.
– DERIVATIVES **expansionist** noun & adjective, **expansionistic** adjective.

expansion joint ▶ **noun** a joint that makes allowance for thermal expansion of the parts joined without distortion.

expansion slot ▶ **noun** Computing a place in a computer where an expansion card can be inserted.

expansive ▶ **adjective 1** covering a wide area in terms of space or scope; extensive or wide-ranging: *expansive coastal beaches.*
2 (of a person or their manner) genially frank and communicative because feeling at ease: *Miss Hatherby felt expansive and inclined to talk.*
3 tending towards economic or political expansion: *expansive domestic economic policies.*
– DERIVATIVES **expansively** adverb, **expansiveness** noun.

expansivity ▶ **noun** Physics the amount a material expands or contracts per unit length due to a one-degree change in temperature.

ex parte /ɛks ˈpɑːteɪ/ ▶ **adjective** & **adverb** Law with respect to or in the interests of one side only or of an interested outside party.
– ORIGIN Latin, 'from a side'.

expat ▶ **noun** & **adjective** informal short for **EXPATRIATE**.

expatiate /ɪkˈspeɪʃɪeɪt, ɛk-/ ▶ **verb** [no obj.] speak or write at length or in detail: *she expatiated on working-class novelists.*
– DERIVATIVES **expatiation** noun.
– ORIGIN mid 16th cent. (in the sense 'roam freely'): from Latin *exspatiari* 'move beyond one's usual bounds', from *ex-* 'out, from' + *spatiari* 'to walk' (from *spatium* 'space').

expatriate ▶ **noun** /ɪksˈpatrɪət, -ˈpeɪtrɪət, ɛks-/ a person who lives outside their native country: *American expatriates in London.*
■ archaic a person exiled from their native country.
▶ **adjective** [attrib.] (of a person) living outside their native country: *expatriate workers.*
■ archaic expelled from one's native country.
▶ **verb** /ɪksˈpatrɪeɪt, -ˈpeɪtrɪeɪt, ɛks-/ [no obj.] settle oneself abroad: *candidates should be willing to expatriate.*
– DERIVATIVES **expatriation** noun.
– ORIGIN mid 18th cent. (as a verb): from medieval Latin *expatriat-* 'gone out from one's country', from the verb *expatriare*, from *ex-* 'out' + *patria* 'native country'.

expect ▶ **verb** [with obj.] regard (something) as likely to happen: *it's as well to expect the worst* | [with obj. and infinitive] *the hearing is expected to last a week* | [with clause] *one might expect that Hollywood would adjust its approach.*
■ regard (someone) as likely to do or be something: [with obj. and infinitive] *they were not expecting him to continue.* ■ believe that (someone or something) will arrive soon: *Celia was expecting a visitor.* ■ look for (something) from someone as rightfully due or requisite in the circumstances: *we expect great things of you.* ■ require (someone) to fulfil an obligation: [with obj. and infinitive] *we expect employers to pay a reasonable salary.* ■ (**I expect**) informal used to indicate that one supposes something to be so, but has no firm evidence or knowledge: *they're just friends of his, I expect* | [with clause] *I expect you know them?*
– PHRASES **be expecting** (**a baby**) informal be pregnant. **to be expected** be completely normal: *he had a few lines about the eyes, but at forty-seven that was only to be expected.* **what can** (or **do**) **you expect?** used to emphasize that there was nothing unexpected about a person or event, however disappointed one might be.
– DERIVATIVES **expectable** adjective.
– ORIGIN mid 16th cent. (in the sense 'defer action, wait'): from Latin *exspectare* 'look out for', from *ex-* 'out' + *spectare* 'to look' (frequentative of *specere* 'see').

expectancy ▶ **noun** (pl. **-ies**) [mass noun] the state of thinking or hoping that something, especially something pleasant, will happen or be the case: *they waited with an **air of expectancy*** | [count noun] *expectancies about people.*
– ORIGIN early 17th cent.: from Latin *exspectantia*, from *exspectare* 'look out for' (see **EXPECT**).

expectant ▶ **adjective** having or showing an excited feeling that something is about to happen, especially something pleasant and interesting: *an expectant conference crowd.*
■ [attrib.] (of a woman) pregnant: *an expectant mother.*
▶ **noun** archaic a person who anticipates receiving something, especially high office.
– DERIVATIVES **expectantly** adverb.
– ORIGIN late Middle English: from Latin *exspectant-* 'expecting', from the verb *exspectare* (see **EXPECT**).

expectation ▶ **noun** a strong belief that something will happen or be the case in the future: *reality had not lived up to expectations | an **expectation that** the government will provide the resources* | [mass noun] *he drilled his men in expectation of a Prussian advance.*
■ a belief that someone will or should achieve something: *students had high expectations for their future.* ■ (**expectations**) archaic one's prospects of inheritance. ■ Mathematics another term for **EXPECTED VALUE**.

expected utility ▶ **noun** Mathematics & Economics a predicted utility value for one of several options, calculated as the sum of the utility of every possible outcome each multiplied by the probability of its occurrence.

expected value ▶ **noun** Mathematics a predicted value of a variable, calculated as the sum of all possible values each multiplied by the probability of its occurrence.

expectorant ▶ **noun** a medicine which promotes the secretion of sputum by the air passages, used especially to treat coughs.
– ORIGIN mid 18th cent.: from Latin *expectorant-* 'expelling from the chest', from the verb *expectorare* (see **EXPECTORATE**).

expectorate /ɪkˈspɛktəreɪt, ɛk-/ ▶ **verb** [with obj.] cough or spit out (phlegm) from the throat or lungs.
– DERIVATIVES **expectoration** noun.
– ORIGIN early 17th cent. (in the sense 'enable sputum to be coughed up', referring to medicine): from Latin *expectorat-* 'expelled from the chest', from the verb *expectorare*, from *ex-* 'out' + *pectus, pector-* 'breast'.

expedient /ɪkˈspiːdɪənt, ɛk-/ ▶ **adjective** (of an action) convenient and practical although possibly improper or immoral: *either side could break the agreement if it were expedient to do so.*
■ (of an action) suitable or appropriate: *holding a public enquiry into the scheme was not expedient.*
▶ **noun** a means of attaining an end, especially one that is convenient but considered improper or immoral: *the current policy is a political expedient.*
– DERIVATIVES **expedience** noun, **expediency** noun, **expediently** adverb.
– ORIGIN late Middle English: from Latin *expedient-* 'extricating, putting in order', from the verb *expedire* (see **EXPEDITE**). The original sense was neutral; the depreciatory sense, implying disregard of moral considerations, dates from the late 18th cent.

expedite /ˈɛkspɪdʌɪt/ ▶ **verb** [with obj.] make (an action or process) happen sooner or be accomplished more quickly: *he promised to expedite economic reforms.*
– DERIVATIVES **expediter** (also **expeditor**) noun.
– ORIGIN late 15th cent. (in the sense 'perform quickly'): from Latin *expedire* 'extricate (originally by freeing the feet), put in order', from *ex-* 'out' + *pes, ped-* 'foot'.

expedition ▶ **noun 1** a journey or voyage undertaken by a group of people with a particular purpose, especially that of exploration, scientific research, or war: *an expedition to the jungles of the Orinoco* | informal *a shopping expedition.*
■ the people involved in such a journey or voyage: *many of the expedition have passed rigorous courses.*
2 [mass noun] formal promptness or speed in doing

something: *the landlord shall remedy the defects with all possible expedition.*
– ORIGIN late Middle English: via Old French from Latin *expeditio(n-)*, from *expedire* 'extricate' (see **EXPEDITE**). Early senses included 'prompt supply of something' and 'setting out with aggressive intent'. The notions of 'speed' and 'purpose' are retained in current senses. Sense 1 dates from the late 16th cent.

expeditionary ▶ **adjective** [attrib.] of or forming an expedition, especially a military expedition: *an expeditionary force.*

expeditious /ˌɛkspɪˈdɪʃəs/ ▶ **adjective** done with speed and efficiency: *an expeditious investigation.*
– DERIVATIVES **expeditiously** adverb, **expeditiousness** noun.
– ORIGIN late 15th cent.: from **EXPEDITION** + **-OUS**.

expel ▶ **verb** (**expelled**, **expelling**) [with obj.] (often **be expelled**) deprive (someone) of membership of or involvement in a school or other organization: *she was* **expelled from** *school.*
■ force (someone) to leave a place, especially a country. ■ force out or eject (something), especially from the body: *she expelled a shuddering breath.*
– DERIVATIVES **expellable** adjective, **expellee** noun, **expeller** noun.
– ORIGIN late Middle English (in the general sense 'eject, force to leave'): from Latin *expellere*, from *ex-* 'out' + *pellere* 'to drive'.

expend ▶ **verb** [with obj.] spend or use up (a resource such as money, time, or energy): *the energy expended in sport could be directed into other areas.*
– ORIGIN late Middle English: from Latin *expendere*, from *ex-* 'out' + *pendere* 'weigh, pay'. Compare with **SPEND**.

expendable ▶ **adjective** (of an object) designed to be used only once and then abandoned or destroyed: *the need for unmanned and expendable launch vehicles.*
■ of little significance when compared to an overall purpose, and therefore able to be abandoned or allowed to be killed or destroyed: *the region is expendable in the wider context of national politics.*
– DERIVATIVES **expendability** noun, **expendably** adverb.

expenditure /ɪkˈspɛndɪtʃə, ɛk-/ ▶ **noun** [mass noun] the action of spending funds: *the expenditure of taxpayers' money.*
■ an amount of money spent: *cuts in public expenditure.*
– ORIGIN mid 18th cent.: from **EXPEND**, suggested by obsolete *expenditor* 'officer in charge of expenditure', from medieval Latin, from *expenditus*, irregular past participle of Latin *expendere* 'pay out' (see **EXPEND**).

expense ▶ **noun** [mass noun] the cost incurred in or required for something; the money spent on something: *we had ordered suits* **at great expense** | *the committee do not expect members to be* **put to** *any expense.*
■ (**expenses**) the costs incurred in the performance of one's job or a specific task, especially one undertaken for another person: *his hotel and travel expenses.* ■ [count noun] a thing on which one is required to spend money: *tolls are a daily expense.*
▶ **verb** [with obj.] (usu. **be expensed**) offset (an item of expenditure) as an expense against taxable income.
– PHRASES **at someone's expense** paid for by someone: *the document was printed at the taxpayer's expense.* ■ with someone as the victim, especially of a joke: *my friends all had a good laugh at my expense.* **at the expense of** so as to cause harm to or neglect of: *the pursuit of profit at the expense of the environment* | *language courses which emphasize communication skills at the expense of literature.*
– ORIGIN late Middle English: from Anglo-Norman French, alteration of Old French *espense*, from late Latin *expensa (pecunia)* '(money) spent', from Latin *expendere* 'pay out' (see **EXPEND**).

expense account ▶ **noun** an arrangement under which sums of money spent in the course of business by an employee are later reimbursed by their employer.

expensive ▶ **adjective** costing a lot of money: *keeping a horse is expensive* | *an expensive bottle of wine.*
– DERIVATIVES **expensively** adverb, **expensiveness** noun.
– ORIGIN early 17th cent. (in the sense 'lavish, extravagant'): from Latin *expens-* 'paid out', from the verb *expendere* (see **EXPEND**), + **-IVE**.

experience ▶ **noun** [mass noun] practical contact with and observation of facts or events: *he had already learned his lesson by painful experience* | *he spoke from experience.*
■ the knowledge or skill acquired by such means over a period of time, especially that gained in a particular profession by someone at work: *older men whose experience could be called upon* | *candidates with the necessary experience.* ■ [count noun] an event or occurrence which leaves an impression on someone: *for the younger players it has been a learning experience.*
▶ **verb** [with obj.] encounter or undergo (an event or occurrence): *the company is experiencing difficulties.*
■ feel (an emotion): *an opportunity to experience the excitement of New York.*
– DERIVATIVES **experienceable** adjective, **experiencer** noun (Linguistics).
– ORIGIN late Middle English: via Old French from Latin *experientia*, from *experiri* 'try'. Compare with **EXPERIMENT** and **EXPERT**.

experienced ▶ **adjective** having knowledge or skill in a particular field, especially a profession or job, gained over a period of time: *an experienced social worker* | *she was* **experienced in** *marketing.*

experiential /ɪkˌspɪərɪˈɛntʃ(ə)l, ɛk-/ ▶ **adjective** involving or based on experience and observation: *the experiential learning associated with employment.*
– DERIVATIVES **experientially** adverb.
– ORIGIN early 19th cent.: from **EXPERIENCE**, on the pattern of words such as *inferential*.

experiment ▶ **noun** a scientific procedure undertaken to make a discovery, test a hypothesis, or demonstrate a known fact: *a laboratory which carried out* **experiments on** *pigs* | [mass noun] *I have tested this by experiment.*
■ a course of action tentatively adopted without being sure of the eventual outcome: *the previous* **experiment in** *liberal democracy had ended in disaster.*
▶ **verb** [no obj.] perform a scientific procedure, especially in a laboratory, to determine something: **experimenting on** *animals causes suffering.*
■ try out new concepts or ways of doing things: *the designers* **experimented with** *new ideas in lighting.*
– DERIVATIVES **experimentation** noun, **experimenter** noun.
– ORIGIN Middle English: from Old French, or from Latin *experimentum*, from *experiri* 'try'. Compare with **EXPERIENCE** and **EXPERT**.

experimental ▶ **adjective** (of a new invention or product) based on untested ideas or techniques and not yet established or finalized: *an experimental drug.*
■ (of a work of art or an artistic technique) involving a radically new and innovative style: *experimental music.* ■ of or relating to scientific experiments: *experimental results.* ■ archaic based on experience as opposed to authority or conjecture: *an experimental knowledge of God.*
– DERIVATIVES **experimentalism** noun, **experimentalist** noun, **experimentally** adverb.
– ORIGIN late 15th cent. (in the sense 'having personal experience', also 'experienced, observed'): from medieval Latin *experimentalis*, from Latin *experimentum* (see **EXPERIMENT**).

experimental psychology ▶ **noun** [mass noun] the branch of psychology concerned with the scientific investigation of the responses of individuals to stimuli in controlled situations.

experimenter effect ▶ **noun** an influence exerted by the experimenter's expectations or other characteristics on the results of an experiment, especially in psychology.

expert ▶ **noun** a person who has a comprehensive and authoritative knowledge of or skill in a particular area: *an expert in health care* | *a financial expert.*
▶ **adjective** having or involving such knowledge or skill: *he had received expert academic advice* | *an expert witness.*
– DERIVATIVES **expertly** adverb, **expertness** noun.
– ORIGIN Middle English (as an adjective): from French, from Latin *expertus*, past participle of *experiri* 'try'. The noun use dates from the early 19th cent. Compare with **EXPERIENCE** and **EXPERIMENT**.

expertise /ˌɛkspəːˈtiːz/ ▶ **noun** [mass noun] expert skill or knowledge in a particular field: *technical expertise.*
– ORIGIN mid 19th cent.: from French, from *expert* (see **EXPERT**).

expertize /ˈɛkspətʌɪz/ (also **-ise**) ▶ **verb** [no obj.] give an expert opinion on something.

expert system ▶ **noun** Computing a piece of software programmed using artificial intelligence techniques. Such systems use databases of expert knowledge to offer advice or make decisions in such areas as medical diagnosis and dealing on the stock exchange.

expiate /ˈɛkspɪeɪt/ ▶ **verb** [with obj.] atone for (guilt or sin): *their sins must be expiated by sacrifice.*
– DERIVATIVES **expiable** adjective, **expiation** noun, **expiator** noun, **expiatory** /ˈɛkspɪət(ə)ri, ˌɛkspɪˈeɪt(ə)ri/ adjective.
– ORIGIN late 16th cent. (in the sense 'end (rage, sorrow, etc.) by suffering it to the full'): from Latin *expiat-* 'appeased by sacrifice', from the verb *expiare*, from *ex-* 'out' + *piare* (from *pius* 'pious').

expiration /ˌɛkspɪˈreɪʃ(ə)n/ ▶ **noun** [mass noun] **1** the ending of the fixed period for which a contract is valid: *the expiration of the lease.*
■ the end of a period of time: *the expiration of three years.*
2 technical exhalation of breath.
– ORIGIN late Middle English (denoting a vapour or exhalation): from Latin *exspiratio(n-)*, from the verb *exspirare* (see **EXPIRE**).

expiratory /ɛksˈpʌɪrət(ə)ri/ ▶ **adjective** of or relating to the exhalation of air from the lungs.

expire /ɪkˈspʌɪə, ɛk-/ ▶ **verb 1** [no obj.] (of a document, authorization, or agreement) cease to be valid, typically after a fixed period of time: *his driving licence expired.*
■ (of a period of time) come to an end: *the three-year period has expired.* ■ (of a person) die.
2 [with obj.] technical exhale (air) from the lung.
– ORIGIN late Middle English: from Old French *expirer*, from Latin *exspirare* 'breathe out', from *ex-* 'out' + *spirare* 'breathe'.

expiry ▶ **noun** the end of the period for which something is valid: *the expiry of the patent* | [as modifier] *an expiry date.*
■ the end of a fixed period of time: *the expiry of the six-month period.* ■ archaic death.

explain ▶ **verb** [reporting verb] make (an idea, situation, or problem) clear to someone by describing it in more detail or revealing relevant facts or ideas: [with clause] *they explained that their lives centred on the religious rituals* | [with direct speech] *'It's a mechanical device of great age,' the professor explained* | [with obj.] *he explained the situation.*
■ [with obj.] account for (an action or event) by giving a reason as excuse or justification: *Cassie found it necessary to explain her blackened eye* | [with clause] *he makes athletes explain why they made a mistake* | [no obj.] *I* **explained about** *Maureen calling round.* ■ (**explain something away**) minimize the significance of an embarrassing fact or action by giving an excuse or justification.
– PHRASES **explain oneself** expand on what one has said in order to make one's meaning clear. ■ give an account of one's motives or conduct in order to excuse or justify oneself: *he was too panicked to stay and explain himself to the policeman.*
– DERIVATIVES **explainable** adjective, **explainer** noun.
– ORIGIN late Middle English: from Latin *explanare*, based on *planus* 'plain'.

explanandum /ˌɛkspləˈnandəm/ ▶ **noun** (pl. **explananda** /-ˈnandə/) Philosophy another term for **EXPLICANDUM**.
– ORIGIN late 19th cent.: from Latin, 'something to be explained', neuter gerundive of *explanare*.

explanans /ˌɛkspləˈnanz/ ▶ **noun** (pl. **explanantia** /-ˈnantɪə/) Philosophy another term for **EXPLICANS**.
– ORIGIN 1940s: Latin, 'explaining', from the verb *explanare*.

explanation ▶ **noun** a statement or account that makes something clear: *the birth rate is central to any explanation of population trends.*
■ a reason or justification given for an action or belief: *Freud tried to make sex the explanation for everything* | [mass noun] *my application was rejected without explanation.*
– ORIGIN late Middle English: from Latin *explanatio(n-)*, from the verb *explanare* (see **EXPLAIN**).

explanatory /ɪkˈsplanəˌt(ə)ri, ɛk-/ ▶ **adjective** serving to explain something: *explanatory notes.*
– DERIVATIVES **explanatorily** adverb.

explant Biology ▶ **verb** /ɪksˈplɑːnt, ɛks-/ [with obj.] [often as adj. **explanted**] transfer (living cells, tissues, or organs) from animals or plants to a nutrient medium.

▶**noun** /ˈɛksplɑːnt/ a cell, organ, or piece of tissue which has been transferred in this way.
– DERIVATIVES **explantation** noun.
– ORIGIN early 20th cent.: from modern Latin *explantare*, from *ex-* 'out' + *plantare* 'to plant'.

expletive /ɪkˈspliːtɪv, ɛk-/ ▶**noun** an oath or swear word.
■Grammar a word or phrase used to fill out a sentence or a line of verse without adding to the sense.
▶**adjective** Grammar (of a word or phrase) serving to fill out a sentence or line of verse.
– ORIGIN late Middle English (as an adjective): from late Latin *expletivus*, from *explere* 'fill out', from *ex-* 'out' + *plere* 'fill'. The general noun sense 'word used merely to fill out a sentence' (early 17th cent.) was applied specifically to an oath or swear word in the early 19th cent.

e

explicable /ɪkˈsplɪkəb(ə)l, ɛk-, ˈɛksplɪˌkəb(ə)l/ ▶**adjective** able to be accounted for or understood: *differences in schools were not explicable in terms of differences in intake.*
– ORIGIN mid 16th cent.: from French, or from Latin *explicabilis*, from *explicare* (see **EXPLICATE**).

explicandum /ˌɛksplɪˈkandəm/ ▶**noun** (pl. **explicanda** /-ˈkandə/) Philosophy the fact, thing, or expression which is to be explained or explicated. Compare with **EXPLICANS**.
– ORIGIN mid 19th cent.: Latin, 'something to be explained', neuter gerundive of *explicare*.

explicans /ˌɛksplɪˈkanz/ ▶**noun** (pl. **explicantia** /ˌɛksplɪˈkantɪə/) Philosophy the explanation or explication given for a fact, thing, or expression. Compare with **EXPLICANDUM**.
– ORIGIN late 19th cent.: Latin, present participle of *explicare* 'explain'.

explicate /ˈɛksplɪkeɪt/ ▶**verb** [with obj.] analyse and develop (an idea or principle) in detail: *attempting to explicate the relationship between crime and economic forces.*
■analyse (a literary work) in order to reveal its meaning.
– DERIVATIVES **explication** noun, **explicative** /ɛkˈsplɪkətɪv, ˈɛksplɪkeɪtɪv/ adjective, **explicator** noun, **explicatory** /ɛkˈsplɪkət(ə)ri, ˈɛksplɪkeɪt(ə)ri/ adjective.
– ORIGIN mid 16th cent.: from Latin *explicat-* 'unfolded', from the verb *explicare*, from *ex-* 'out' + *plicare* 'to fold'.

explicit /ɪkˈsplɪsɪt, ɛk-/ ▶**adjective** stated clearly and in detail, leaving no room for confusion or doubt: *the arrangement had not been **made explicit**.*
■(of a person) stating something in such a way: *let me be explicit.* ■describing or representing sexual activity in a graphic fashion: *a sexually explicit blockbuster.*
▶**noun** the closing words of a manuscript, early printed book, or chanted liturgical text. Compare with **INCIPIT**. [ORIGIN: Middle English: late Latin, 'here ends', or abbreviation of *explicitus est liber* 'the scroll is unrolled'.]
– DERIVATIVES **explicitly** adverb, **explicitness** noun.
– ORIGIN early 17th cent. (as an adjective): from French *explicite* or Latin *explicitus*, past participle of *explicare* 'unfold' (see **EXPLICATE**).

explode ▶**verb** [no obj.] **1** burst or shatter violently and noisily as a result of rapid combustion, decomposition, excessive internal pressure, or other process, typically scattering fragments widely: *an ammunition lorry exploded with a roar.*
■[with obj.] cause (a bomb) to do this: *Britain had not yet exploded her first nuclear weapon.* ■technical undergo a violent expansion in which much energy is released as a shock wave: *lead ensures that petrol burns rather than explodes.* ■(of a person) suddenly give expression to violent and uncontainable emotion, especially anger: *he can **explode with** anger* | [with direct speech] *'This is ludicrous!' she exploded.* ■(of a violent emotion or a situation) arise or develop suddenly: *tension which could **explode into** violence at any time.* ■(**explode into**) suddenly begin to move or start a new activity: *a bird exploded into flight.* ■increase suddenly or rapidly in size, number, or extent: *the use of this drug exploded in the nineties.* ■[as adj. **exploded**] (of a diagram or drawing) showing the components of a mechanism as if separated by an explosion but in the normal relative positions: *an exploded diagram of the rifle's parts.*
2 [with obj.] (often **be exploded**) show (a belief or theory) to be false or unfounded: *the myths that link smoking with glamour need to be exploded.*
– DERIVATIVES **exploder** noun.
– ORIGIN mid 16th cent. (in the sense 'reject scornfully, discard'): from Latin *explodere* 'drive out by clapping, hiss off the stage', from *ex-* 'out' + *plaudere* 'to clap'. Sense 2 is derived from the original sense of the word. Sense 1 (late 18th cent.) evolved via an old sense 'expel with violence and sudden noise', perhaps influenced by obsolete *displode* 'burst with a noise'.

exploit ▶**verb** /ɪkˈsplɔɪt, ɛk-/ [with obj.] make full use of and derive benefit from (a resource): *500 companies sprang up to exploit this new technology.*
■make use of (a situation or opportunity) in a way considered unfair or underhand: *the company was exploiting a legal loophole.* ■benefit unjustly or unfairly from the work of (someone), typically by overworking or underpaying them: *women are exploited in the workplace.*
▶**noun** /ˈɛksplɔɪt/ a bold or daring feat.
– DERIVATIVES **exploitable** adjective, **exploitation** noun, **exploitative** adjective, **exploiter** noun, **exploitive** adjective.
– ORIGIN Middle English: from Old French *esploit* (noun), based on Latin *explicare* 'unfold' (see **EXPLICATE**). The early notion of 'success, progress' gave rise to the sense 'attempt to capture', 'military expedition', hence the current sense of the noun. Current verb senses (mid 19th cent.) are taken from modern French *exploiter*.

exploration ▶**noun** [mass noun] the action of travelling in or through an unfamiliar area in order to learn about it: *voyages of exploration* | [count noun] *an exploration of the African interior.*
■thorough analysis of a subject or theme: [count noun] *jurisprudence is an exploration of society and human nature.*
– DERIVATIVES **explorational** adjective.
– ORIGIN mid 16th cent. (denoting an investigation): from French, or from Latin *exploratio(n-)*, from the verb *explorare* (see **EXPLORE**). The current sense dates from the early 19th cent.

exploratory /ɪkˈsplɒrət(ə)ri, ɛk-/ ▶**adjective** relating to or involving exploration or investigation: *surgeons performed an exploratory operation* | *exploratory talks.*
– ORIGIN late Middle English: from Latin *exploratorius*, from Latin *explorare* (see **EXPLORE**).

explore ▶**verb** [with obj.] travel in or through (an unfamiliar country or area) in order to learn about or familiarize oneself with it: *the best way to explore Iceland's north-west* | figurative *explore the world of science and technology.*
■[no obj.] (**explore for**) search for resources such as mineral deposits: *licences to explore for petroleum.* ■inquire into or discuss (a subject or issue) in detail: *he sets out to explore fundamental questions.* ■examine or evaluate (an option or possibility): *the firm will explore joint development projects.* ■examine by touch: *her fingers explored his hair.* ■Medicine surgically examine (a wound or disordered part of the body) in detail.
– DERIVATIVES **explorative** adjective, **explorer** noun.
– ORIGIN mid 16th cent. (in the sense 'investigate (why)'): from French *explorer*, from Latin *explorare* 'search out', from *ex-* 'out' + *plorare* 'utter a cry'.

explosion ▶**noun** a violent and destructive shattering or blowing apart of something, as is caused by a bomb.
■technical a violent expansion in which energy is transmitted outwards as a shock wave. ■a sudden outburst of something such as noise, light, or violent emotion, especially anger: *an explosion of anger inside the factory.* ■a sudden political or social upheaval. ■a rapid or sudden increase in amount or extent: *an explosion in the adder population.*
– ORIGIN early 17th cent.: from Latin *explosio(n-)* 'scornful rejection', from the verb *explodere* (see **EXPLODE**).

explosive ▶**adjective** able or likely to shatter violently or burst apart, as when a bomb explodes: *an explosive device.*
■likely to cause an eruption of anger or controversy: *Marco's explosive temper* | *the idea was politically explosive.* ■of or relating to a sudden and dramatic increase in amount or extent: *the explosive growth of personal computers in the 1980s.* ■(of a vocal sound) produced with a sharp release of air.
▶**noun** (often **explosives**) a substance which can be made to explode, especially any of those used in bombs or shells.
– DERIVATIVES **explosively** adverb, **explosiveness** noun.

explosive bolt ▶**noun** a bolt that can be released by being blown out of position by an integral explosive charge.

Expo /ˈɛkspəʊ/ ▶**noun** (pl. **-os**) a large international exhibition.
– ORIGIN 1960s (referring to the World Fair held in Montreal in 1967): abbreviation of **EXPOSITION**.

exponent /ɪkˈspəʊnənt, ɛk-/ ▶**noun 1** a person who believes in and tries to explain and persuade people of the truth or benefits of an idea or theory: *an early **exponent of** the teachings of Thomas Aquinas.*
■a person who has and demonstrates a particular skill, especially to a high standard: *he's the world's leading exponent of country rock guitar.*
2 Mathematics a quantity representing the power to which a given number or expression is to be raised, usually expressed as a raised symbol beside the number or expression (e.g. 3 in $2^3 = 2 \times 2 \times 2$).
3 Linguistics a linguistic unit that realizes another, more abstract unit.
– ORIGIN late 16th cent. (as an adjective in the sense 'expounding'): from Latin *exponent-* 'putting out', from the verb *exponere* (see **EXPOUND**).

exponential /ˌɛkspəˈnɛnʃ(ə)l/ ▶**adjective** Mathematics of or expressed by a mathematical exponent: *an exponential curve.*
■(of an increase) becoming more and more rapid: *the social security budget was rising at an exponential rate.*
– DERIVATIVES **exponentially** adverb.
– ORIGIN early 18th cent.: from French *exponentiel*, from Latin *exponere* 'put out' (see **EXPOUND**).

exponential function ▶**noun** Mathematics a function whose value is a constant raised to the power of the argument, especially the function where the constant is *e*.

exponential growth ▶**noun** [mass noun] growth whose rate becomes ever more rapid in proportion to the growing total number or size.

exponentiation /ˌɛkspənɛnʃɪˈeɪʃ(ə)n/ ▶**noun** [mass noun] Mathematics the operation of raising one quantity to the power of another.
– DERIVATIVES **exponentiate** verb.

export ▶**verb** /ɪkˈspɔːt, ɛk-, ˈɛk-/ [with obj.] send (goods or services) to another country for sale: *this is the first UK field to export gas to mainland Europe.*
■spread or introduce (ideas and beliefs) to another country: *the Greeks exported Hellenic culture around the Mediterranean basin.* ■Computing transfer (data) in a format that can be used by other programs.
▶**noun** /ˈɛkspɔːt/ (usu. **exports**) a commodity, article, or service sold abroad: *wool and mohair were the principal exports.*
■(**exports**) sales of goods or services to other countries, or the revenue from such sales: *meat exports.* ■[mass noun] the selling and sending out of goods or services to other countries: *the export of Western technology.* ■[as modifier] of a high standard suitable for export: *export ales.*
– DERIVATIVES **exportability** noun, **exportable** adjective, **exportation** noun, **exporter** noun.
– ORIGIN late 15th cent. (in the sense 'take away'): from Latin *exportare*, from *ex-* 'out' + *portare* 'carry'. Current senses date from the 17th cent.

export surplus ▶**noun** the amount by which the value of a country's exports exceeds that of its imports.

expose ▶**verb** [with obj.] (often **be exposed**) make (something) visible, typically by uncovering it: *at low tide the sands are exposed.*
■[often as adj. **exposed**] leave (something) uncovered or unprotected, especially from the weather: *the coast is very exposed to the south-west.* ■subject (photographic film) to light, especially when operating a camera. ■(**expose oneself**) publicly and indecently display one's genitals. ■[usu. as adj. **exposed**] leave or put (someone) in an unprotected and vulnerable state: *Miranda felt exposed and lonely.* ■(**expose someone to**) cause someone to experience or be at risk of: *many newcomers are exposing themselves to life-threatening injury.* ■make (something embarrassing or damaging) public: *the situation appeared to expose a conflict within the government.* ■reveal the true and typically objectionable nature of (someone or something): *he has been **exposed as** a liar and a traitor.* ■leave (a child) in the open to die.
– DERIVATIVES **exposer** noun.
– ORIGIN late Middle English: from Old French *exposer*, from Latin *exponere* (see **EXPOUND**), but influenced by Latin *expositus* 'put or set out' and Old French *poser* 'to place'.

exposé /ɪkˈspəʊzeɪ, ɛk-/ ▶**noun** a report of the facts about something, especially a report in a newspaper that reveals something discreditable: *a shocking exposé of a medical cover-up.*

– ORIGIN early 19th cent.: from French, 'shown, set out', past participle of *exposer* (see **EXPOSE**).

exposition ▶ **noun 1** a comprehensive description and explanation of an idea or theory: *an exposition and defence of Marx's writings.*
■ Music the part of a movement, especially in sonata form, in which the principal themes are first presented.
2 a large public exhibition of art or trade goods.
■ [mass noun] archaic the action of making public; exposure: *the country squires dreaded the exposition of their rustic conversation.*
– DERIVATIVES **expositional** adjective.
– ORIGIN Middle English: from Latin *expositio(n-)*, from the verb *exponere* 'put out, exhibit, explain'.

expositor /ɪk'spɒzɪtə, ɛk-/ ▶ **noun** a person or thing that explains complicated ideas or theories: *a lucid expositor of difficult ideas.*
– ORIGIN Middle English: via Old French or late Latin, from Latin *exposit-* 'exposed, explained', from *exponere* (see **EXPOUND**).

expository ▶ **adjective** intended to explain or describe something: *an expository prologue.*

ex post /ɛks 'pəʊst/ ▶ **adjective** & **adverb** based on actual results rather than forecasts: [as adj.] *the ex post trade balance* | [as adv.] *the real-wage rate had fallen ex post.*
– ORIGIN modern Latin, from *ex* 'from' and *post* 'after'.

ex post facto /ˌɛks pəʊst 'faktəʊ/ ▶ **adjective** & **adverb** with retrospective action or force: [as adj.] *ex post facto laws.*
– ORIGIN erroneous division of Latin *ex postfacto* 'in the light of subsequent events'.

expostulate /ɪk'spɒstjʊleɪt, ɛk-/ ▶ **verb** [no obj.] express strong disapproval or disagreement: *he found Fox* ***expostulating with*** *a tall young man.*
– DERIVATIVES **expostulation** noun, **expostulator** noun, **expostulatory** /-lət(ə)ri/ adjective.
– ORIGIN mid 16th cent. (in the sense 'demand how or why, state a complaint'): from Latin *expostulat-* 'demanded', from the verb *expostulare*, from *ex-* 'out' + *postulare* 'demand'.

exposure ▶ **noun** [mass noun] **1** the state of having no protection from contact with something harmful: *the dangers posed by* ***exposure to*** *asbestos.*
■ a physical condition resulting from being outside in severe weather conditions without adequate protection: *suffering from exposure.* ■ experience of something: *his* ***exposure to*** *the banking system.* ■ the action of exposing a photographic film to light or other radiation: *a camera which would give a picture immediately after exposure* | [count noun] *trial exposures made with a UV filter.* ■ [count noun] the quantity of light or other radiation reaching a photographic film, as determined by shutter speed and lens aperture. ■ the action of placing oneself at risk of financial losses, e.g. through making loans, granting credit, or underwriting insurance.
2 the revelation of an identity or fact, especially one which is concealed or likely to arouse disapproval: *she took her life for fear of exposure as a spy.*
■ the publicizing of information or an event: *scientific findings receive regular exposure in the media.*
3 [count noun] the direction in which a building faces; an outlook: *the exposure is perfect—a gentle slope to the south-west.*
– ORIGIN early 17th cent.: from **EXPOSE**, on the pattern of words such as *enclosure*.

exposure meter ▶ **noun** Photography a device for measuring the strength of light, giving the correct exposure to use with a given film.

expound ▶ **verb** [with obj.] present and explain (a theory or idea) systematically and in detail: *he was expounding a powerful argument* | [no obj.] *he declined to* ***expound on*** *his decision.*
■ explain the meaning of (a literary or doctrinal work): *the abbess expounded the scriptures to her nuns.*
– DERIVATIVES **expounder** noun.
– ORIGIN Middle English *expoune* (in the sense 'explain (what is difficult)'): from Old French *espon-*, present tense stem of *espondre*, from Latin *exponere* 'expose, publish, explain', from *ex-* 'out' + *ponere* 'put'. The origin of the final *-d* (recorded from the Middle English period) is uncertain (compare with **COMPOUND**[1], **PROPOUND**).

express[1] /ɪk'sprɛs, ɛk-/ ▶ **verb** [with obj.] **1** convey (a thought or feeling) in words or by gestures and conduct: *he expressed complete satisfaction.*
■ (**express oneself**) say what one thinks or means: *with a diplomatic smile, she expressed herself more subtly.* ■ chiefly Mathematics represent (a number, relation, or property) by a figure, symbol, or formula: *constants can be* ***expressed in terms of*** *the Fourier transform.* ■ (usu. **be expressed**) Genetics cause (an inherited characteristic or gene) to appear in a phenotype.
2 squeeze out (liquid or air).
– DERIVATIVES **expresser** noun, **expressible** adjective.
– ORIGIN late Middle English (also in the sense 'press out, obtain by squeezing or wringing', used figuratively to mean 'extort'): from Old French *expresser*, based on Latin *ex-* 'out' + *pressare* 'to press'.

express[2] /ɪk'sprɛs, ɛk-/ ▶ **adjective** operating at high speed: *an express airmail service.*
■ denoting a service in which messages or goods are delivered by a special messenger to ensure speed or security: *an express letter.*
▶ **adverb** by express train or delivery service: *I got my wife to send my gloves express to the hotel.*
▶ **noun 1** (also **express train**) a train that stops at few stations and so travels quickly.
2 a special delivery service: *the books arrived* ***by express.***
■ N. Amer. a company undertaking the transport of parcels.
3 an express rifle.
▶ **verb** [with obj.] send by express messenger or delivery: *I expressed my clothes to my destination.*
– ORIGIN early 18th cent. (in the sense of the verb): extension of **EXPRESS**[3]; sense 1 from *express train*, so named because it served a particular destination without intermediate stops, reflecting an earlier sense of *express* 'done or made for a special purpose', later interpreted in the sense 'rapid'. Senses relating to *express delivery* date from the institution of this postal service in 1891.

express[3] /ɪk'sprɛs, ɛk-, 'ɛksprɛs/ ▶ **adjective** definitely stated, not merely implied: *it was his express wish that the celebration should continue.*
■ precisely and specifically identified to the exclusion of anything else: *the schools were founded for the express purpose of teaching deaf children.* ■ archaic (of a likeness) exact.
– DERIVATIVES **expressly** adverb.
– ORIGIN late Middle English: from Old French *expres*, from Latin *expressus* 'distinctly presented', past participle of *exprimere* 'press out, express', from *ex-* 'out' + *primere* 'press'.

expression ▶ **noun** [mass noun] **1** the process of making known one's thoughts or feelings: *his views* ***found expression*** *in his moral sermons* | [count noun] *she accepted his expressions of sympathy.*
■ [count noun] the look on someone's face, seen as conveying a particular emotion: *a sad expression.* ■ [count noun] a word or phrase, especially an idiomatic one, used to convey an idea: *we have an expression, 'You don't get owt for nowt.'* ■ the conveying of feeling in a work of art or in the performance of a piece of music. ■ [count noun] Mathematics a collection of symbols that jointly express a quantity: *the expression for the circumference of a circle is 2πr.* ■ Genetics the appearance in a phenotype of a characteristic or effect attributed to a particular gene. ■ (also **gene expression**) Genetics the process by which possession of a gene leads to the appearance in the phenotype of the corresponding character.
2 the production of something, especially by pressing or squeezing it out: *essential oils obtained by distillation or expression.*
– DERIVATIVES **expressional** adjective, **expressionless** adjective, **expressionlessly** adverb, **expressionlessness** noun.
– ORIGIN late Middle English: from Latin *expressio(n-)*, from *exprimere* 'press out, express'. Compare with **EXPRESS**[1].

expressionism ▶ **noun** [mass noun] a style of painting, music, or drama in which the artist or writer seeks to express emotional experience rather than impressions of the external world.

Expressionists characteristically reject traditional ideas of beauty or harmony and use distortion, exaggeration, and other non-naturalistic devices in order to emphasize and express the inner world of emotion. The paintings of El Greco and Grünewald exemplify expressionism in this broad sense, but the term is also used of a late 19th and 20th century European and specifically German movement tracing its origins to Van Gogh, Edvard Munch, and James Ensor, which insisted on the primacy of the artist's feelings and mood, often incorporating violence and the grotesque.

– DERIVATIVES **expressionist** noun & adjective, **expressionistic** adjective, **expressionistically** adverb.

expression mark ▶ **noun** Music a word or phrase on a musical score which indicates the expression required of a performer.

expressive ▶ **adjective** effectively conveying thought or feeling.
■ [predic.] (**expressive of**) conveying (the specified quality or idea): *the spires are expressive of religious aspiration.*
– DERIVATIVES **expressively** adverb, **expressiveness** noun, **expressivity** noun.
– ORIGIN late Middle English (in the sense 'tending to press out'): from French *expressif, -ive* or medieval Latin *expressivus*, from *exprimere* 'press out' (see **EXPRESS**[3]). Compare with **EXPRESS**[1].

express lift ▶ **noun** a fast-moving lift which does not stop at every floor.

expresso /ɛk'sprɛsəʊ/ ▶ **noun** variant spelling of **ESPRESSO**.

express rifle ▶ **noun** a rifle that discharges a bullet at high speed used in big-game hunting.

expressway ▶ **noun** chiefly N. Amer. an urban motorway.

expropriate /ɪks'prəʊprɪeɪt, ɛks-/ ▶ **verb** [with obj.] (especially of the state) take away (property) from its owner: *the distillery was expropriated by the communists.*
■ dispossess (someone) of property: *the measures expropriated the landlords.*
– DERIVATIVES **expropriation** noun, **expropriator** noun.
– ORIGIN late 16th cent.: from medieval Latin *expropriat-* 'taken from the owner', from the verb *expropriare*, from *ex-* 'out, from' + *proprium* 'property', neuter singular of *proprius* 'own'.

expulsion ▶ **noun** [mass noun] the action of depriving someone of membership of an organization: ***expulsion from*** *the union* | [count noun] *a rise in the number of pupil expulsions.*
■ the process of forcing someone to leave a place, especially a country: *the most brutal chapter of the expulsion of Jews from Berlin.* ■ the process of forcing something out of the body.
– DERIVATIVES **expulsive** adjective.
– ORIGIN late Middle English: from Latin *expulsio(n-)*, from *expellere* 'drive out' (see **EXPEL**).

expunge /ɪk'spʌn(d)ʒ, ɛk-/ ▶ **verb** [with obj.] erase or remove completely (something unwanted or unpleasant): *he could expunge an unsatisfactory incident from his memory.*
– DERIVATIVES **expunction** noun, **expungement** noun, **expunger** noun.
– ORIGIN early 17th cent.: from Latin *expungere* 'mark for deletion by means of points', from *ex-* 'out' + *pungere* 'to prick'.

expurgate /'ɛkspəːgeɪt/ ▶ **verb** [with obj.] [often as adj. **expurgated**] remove matter thought to be objectionable or unsuitable from (a book or account): *the expurgated* Arabian Nights.
– DERIVATIVES **expurgation** noun, **expurgator** noun, **expurgatory** /ɛk'spəːgət(ə)ri/ adjective.
– ORIGIN early 17th cent. (in the sense 'purge of excrement'): from Latin *expurgat-* 'thoroughly cleansed', from the verb *expurgare*, from *ex-* 'out' + *purgare* 'cleanse'.

exquisite /'ɛkskwɪzɪt, ɪk'skwɪzɪt, ɛk-/ ▶ **adjective** extremely beautiful and, typically, delicate: *exquisite, jewel-like portraits.*
■ intensely felt: *the most exquisite kind of agony.* ■ highly sensitive or discriminating: *her exquisite taste in painting.*
▶ **noun** a man who is affectedly concerned with his clothes and appearance; a dandy.
– DERIVATIVES **exquisitely** adverb, **exquisiteness** noun.
– ORIGIN late Middle English (in the sense 'carefully ascertained, precise'): from Latin *exquisit-* 'sought out', from the verb *exquirere*, from *ex-* 'out' + *quaerere* 'seek'.

exsanguination /ɪkˌsaŋgwɪ'neɪʃ(ə)n, ɛk-/ ▶ **noun** [mass noun] Medicine the action of draining a person, animal, or organ of blood.
■ severe loss of blood.
– DERIVATIVES **exsanguinate** verb.
– ORIGIN early 20th cent.: from Latin *exsanguinatus* 'drained of blood' (from *ex-* 'out' + *sanguis, sanguin-* 'blood') + **-ION**.

exsanguine /ɪkˈsaŋgwɪn, ɛk-/ ▶ **adjective** poetic/literary bloodless; anaemic.
– ORIGIN mid 17th cent.: from **EX-**[1] 'out' + Latin *sanguis, sanguin-* 'blood'.

exsert /ɪkˈsəːt, ɛk-/ ▶ **verb** [with obj.] Biology cause to protrude; push out: [as adj. **exserted**] *an exserted stigma.*
– ORIGIN mid 17th cent.: from Latin *exsert-* 'put forth', from the verb *exserere* (see **EXERT**).

ex-service ▶ **adjective** chiefly Brit. denoting or relating to former members of the armed forces: *ex-service personnel.*

ex-serviceman ▶ **noun** (pl. **-men**) chiefly Brit. a man who was formerly a member of the armed forces.

ex-servicewoman ▶ **noun** (pl. **-women**) chiefly Brit. a woman who was formerly a member of the armed forces.

ex silentio /ˌɛks sɪˈlɛnʃɪəʊ/ ▶ **adjective** & **adverb** by the absence of contrary evidence.
– ORIGIN Latin, 'from silence'.

exsolve /ɪkˈsɒlv, ɛk-/ ▶ **verb** [no obj.] Geology (of a mineral or other substance) separate out from solution, especially from solid solution in a rock.
■ [with obj.] [usu. as adj. **exsolved**] form (a mineral or other substance) in this way: *coarsely exsolved ilmenites.*
– DERIVATIVES **exsolution** noun.

ext. ▶ **abbreviation for** ■ extension (in a telephone number). ■ exterior. ■ external.

extant /ɪkˈstant, ɛk-, ˈɛkst(ə)nt/ ▶ **adjective** (especially of a document) still in existence; surviving: *an extant letter.*
– ORIGIN mid 16th cent. (in the sense 'accessible, able to be publicly seen or reached'): from Latin *exstant-* 'being visible or prominent, existing', from the verb *exstare*, from *ex-* 'out' + *stare* 'to stand'.

extemporaneous /ɪkˌstɛmpəˈreɪnɪəs, ɛk-/ ▶ **adjective** another term for **EXTEMPORARY**.
– DERIVATIVES **extemporaneously** adverb, **extemporaneousness** noun.

extemporary /ɪkˈstɛmp(ə)(rə)ri, ɛk-/ ▶ **adjective** spoken or done without preparation: *an extemporary prayer.*
– DERIVATIVES **extemporarily** adverb, **extemporariness** noun.
– ORIGIN late 16th cent.: from **EXTEMPORE**, on the pattern of *temporary*.

extempore /ɪkˈstɛmp(ə)ri, ɛk-/ ▶ **adjective** & **adverb** spoken or done without preparation: [as adj.] *extempore public speaking* | [as adv.] *he recited the poem extempore.*
– ORIGIN mid 16th cent.: from Latin *ex tempore* 'on the spur of the moment' (literally 'out of the time').

extemporize /ɪkˈstɛmpərʌɪz, ɛk-/ (also **-ise**) ▶ **verb** [no obj.] compose, perform, or produce something such as music or a speech without preparation; improvise: *he extemporized at the piano* | [with obj.] *she was extemporizing touching melodies.*
– DERIVATIVES **extemporization** noun.

extend ▶ **verb** [with obj.] **1** cause to cover a wider area; make larger: *the car park has been extended.*
■ cause to last longer: *they asked the government to extend its period of deliberation.* ■ straighten or spread out (the body or a limb) at full length: *hold the index finger down with the thumb extended.* ■ [no obj.] spread from a central point to cover a wider area: *the damage extended 400 yards either side of the shop.* ■ [no obj.] occupy a specified area: *the mountains* **extend over** *the western end of the island.* ■ [no obj.] (**extend to**) include within one's scope; be applicable to: *her generosity did not extend to all adults.*
2 hold (something) out towards someone: *I nod and extend my hand.*
■ offer: *she extended an invitation to her to stay.* ■ make (a resource) available to someone: *credit was extended to the country.*
– DERIVATIVES **extendability** noun, **extendable** adjective, **extendibility** noun, **extendible** adjective, **extensibility** noun, **extensible** adjective.
– ORIGIN late Middle English: from Latin *extendere* 'stretch out', from *ex-* 'out' + *tendere* 'stretch'.

extended family ▶ **noun** a family which extends beyond the nuclear family, including grandparents, aunts, uncles, and other relatives, who all live nearby or in one household.

extended-play ▶ **adjective** denoting a record that plays for longer than most singles.
■ denoting an audio or video tape that is thinner and longer than standard.

extender ▶ **noun** a person or thing that extends something.
■ a substance added to a product such as paint, ink, or glue, to dilute its colour or increase its bulk. ■ Photography another term for **EXTENSION TUBE**.

extensile /ɪkˈstɛnsʌɪl, ɛk-/ ▶ **adjective** capable of being stretched out or protruded.
– ORIGIN mid 18th cent.: from Latin *extens-* 'stretched out' (from the verb *extendere*) + **-ILE**.

extension ▶ **noun 1** a part that is added to something to enlarge or prolong it; a continuation: *the railway's southern extension.*
■ a room or set of rooms added to an existing building. ■ [mass noun] the action or process of becoming or making something larger: *the extension of the President's powers.* ■ an application of an existing system or activity to a new area: *direct marketing is an extension of telephone selling.* ■ an increase in the length of time given to someone to hold office, complete a project, or fulfil an obligation. ■ chiefly Brit. permission for the sale of alcoholic drinks until later than usual, granted to licensed premises on special occasions. ■ Computing an optional suffix to a file name, typically consisting of a full stop followed by several characters, indicating the file's content or function.
2 (also **extension lead** or **cable**) a length of electric cable which permits the use of appliances at some distance from a fixed socket.
■ a subsidiary telephone on the same line as the main one. ■ a subsidiary telephone in a set of offices or similar building, on a line leading from the main switchboard but having its own additional number.
3 [usu. as modifier] extramural instruction by a university or college: *a postgraduate extension course.*
4 [mass noun] the action of moving a limb from a bent to a straight position: *seizures with sudden rigid extension of the limbs.*
■ the muscle action controlling this: *triceps extension.* ■ Ballet the ability of a dancer to raise one leg above their waist, especially to the side: *she has amazing extension* | [count noun] *he could perform 180-degree extensions.* ■ Medicine the application of traction to a fractured or dislocated limb or to an injured or diseased spinal column to restore it to its normal position. ■ the lengthening of a horse's stride at a particular pace.
5 Logic the range of a term or concept as measured by the objects which it denotes or contains, as opposed to its internal content. Often contrasted with **INTENSION**.
■ Physics & Philosophy the property of occupying space; spatial magnitude: *nature, for Descartes, was pure extension in space.*
– PHRASES **by extension** taking the same line of argument further: *the study shows how television and, by extension, the media, alter political relationships.*
– DERIVATIVES **extensional** adjective.
– ORIGIN late Middle English: from late Latin *extensio(n-)*, from *extendere* 'stretch out' (see **EXTEND**).

extension tube ▶ **noun** Photography a tube fitted to a camera between the body and lens to shorten the distance of closest focus of an object so that close-up pictures can be taken.

extensive ▶ **adjective 1** covering or affecting a large area: *an extensive garden.*
■ large in amount or scale: *an extensive collection of silver.*
2 (of agriculture) obtaining a relatively small crop from a large area with a minimum of attention and expense: *extensive farming techniques.* Often contrasted with **INTENSIVE** (in sense 1).
– DERIVATIVES **extensively** adverb, **extensiveness** noun.
– ORIGIN late Middle English: from French *extensif, -ive* or late Latin *extensivus*, from *extens-* 'stretched out', from the verb *extendere* (see **EXTEND**).

extensometer /ˌɛkstɛnˈsɒmɪtə/ ▶ **noun** an instrument for measuring the deformation of a material under stress.
– ORIGIN late 19th cent.: from Latin *extens-* 'extended' (from the verb *extendere*) + **-METER**.

extensor /ɪkˈstɛnsə, ɛk-/ (also **extensor muscle**) ▶ **noun** Anatomy a muscle whose contraction extends or straightens a limb or other part of the body. Often contrasted with **FLEXOR**.
■ any of a number of specific muscles in the arm, hand, leg, and foot.
– ORIGIN early 18th cent.: from late Latin, from *extens-* 'stretched out', from the verb *extendere* (see **EXTEND**).

extent ▶ **noun** [in sing.] the area covered by something: *an enclosure ten acres in extent.*
■ the degree to which something has spread; the size or scale of something: *the extent of global warming.* ■ the amount to which something is or is believed to be the case: *everyone will have to compromise to some extent* | *they altered the document to such an extent that it contained little in the way of new policy.*
– ORIGIN Middle English (in the sense 'valuation of property, especially for taxation purposes'): from Anglo-Norman French *extente*, from medieval Latin *extenta*, feminine past participle of Latin *extendere* 'stretch out' (see **EXTEND**).

extenuate /ɪkˈstɛnjʊeɪt, ɛk-/ ▶ **verb** [with obj.] **1** [usu. as adj. **extenuating**] make (guilt or an offence) seem less serious or more forgivable: *hunger and poverty are not treated by the courts as* **extenuating circumstances**.
2 [usu. as adj. **extenuated**] poetic/literary make (someone) thin: *drawings of extenuated figures.*
– DERIVATIVES **extenuation** noun, **extenuatory** /-jʊət(ə)ri/ adjective.
– ORIGIN late Middle English (in the sense 'make thin, emaciate'): from Latin *extenuat-* 'made thin', from the verb *extenuare* (based on *tenuis* 'thin').

exterior ▶ **adjective** forming, situated on, or relating to the outside of something: *exterior and interior walls.*
■ coming from outside: *exterior noise.* ■ (in filming) outdoor: *exterior locations.*
▶ **noun** the outer surface or structure of something: *a jar with floral designs on the exterior.*
■ the outer structure of a building: *the museum has a modern exterior.* ■ a person's behaviour and appearance, often contrasted with their true character: *beneath that assured exterior, she's vulnerable.* ■ (in filming) an outdoor scene.
– DERIVATIVES **exteriority** noun, **exteriorize** (also **-ise**) verb, **exteriorly** adverb.
– ORIGIN early 16th cent.: from Latin, comparative of *exter* 'outer'.

exterior angle ▶ **noun** Geometry the angle between a side of a rectilinear figure and an adjacent side extended outward.

exterminate /ɪkˈstəːmɪneɪt, ɛk-/ ▶ **verb** [with obj.] (often **be exterminated**) destroy completely: *leftist ideals had not been totally exterminated.*
■ kill (a pest): *they use poison to exterminate moles.*
– DERIVATIVES **extermination** noun, **exterminator** noun, **exterminatory** /-nət(ə)ri/ adjective.
– ORIGIN late Middle English (in the sense 'drive out, banish'): from Latin *exterminat-* 'driven out, banished', from the verb *exterminare*, from *ex-* 'out' + *terminus* 'boundary'. The sense 'destroy' (mid 16th cent.) comes from the Latin of the Vulgate.

extern /ɪkˈstəːn, ɛk-/ ▶ **noun 1** N. Amer. a non-resident doctor or other worker in a hospital.
2 (in a strictly enclosed order of nuns) a sister who does not live exclusively within the enclosure and goes on outside errands.
– ORIGIN mid 16th cent. (as an adjective in the sense 'external'): from French *externe* or Latin *externus*, from *exter* 'outer'. The word was used by Shakespeare to mean 'outward appearance'; current senses date from the early 17th cent.

external ▶ **adjective 1** belonging to or forming the outer surface or structure of something: *the external walls.*
■ relating to or denoting a medicine or similar substance for use on the outside of the body: *for external application only.*
2 coming or derived from a source outside the subject affected: *for many people the church was a symbol of external authority.*
■ coming from or relating to a country or institution other than the main subject: *responsibility for defence and external affairs.* ■ outside the conscious subject: *the child learns to form conceptions of the external world.* ■ for or concerning students registered with and taking the examinations of a university but not resident there: *external degrees.* ■ Computing (of hardware) not contained in the main computer; peripheral. ■ Computing (of storage) using a disk or tape drive rather than the main memory.
▶ **noun** (**externals**) the outward features of something: *the place has all the appropriate externals, such as chimneys choked with ivy and windows with jasmine.*
■ features which are only superficial; inessentials.
– DERIVATIVES **externally** adverb.
– ORIGIN late Middle English: from medieval Latin, from Latin *exter* 'outer'.

external auditory meatus ▶ noun see **MEATUS**.

external ear ▶ noun the parts of the ear outside the eardrum, especially the pinna.

externalism ▶ noun [mass noun] **1** excessive regard for outward form in religion: *religion needs to be questioned for its negative attitudes, hypocrisy, and externalism.*
2 Philosophy the view that mental events and acts are essentially dependent on the world external to the mind, in opposition to the Cartesian separation of mental and physical worlds.
– DERIVATIVES **externalist** noun & adjective.

externality /ˌɛkstəːˈnalɪti/ ▶ noun (pl. **-ies**) **1** Economics a side effect or consequence of an industrial or commercial activity which affects other parties without this being reflected in the cost of the goods or services involved, such as the pollination of surrounding crops by bees kept for honey.
2 [mass noun] Philosophy the fact of existing outside the perceiving subject.

externalize (also **-ise**) ▶ verb [with obj.] (usu. **be externalized**) give external existence or form to: *elements of the internal construction were externalized on to the facade.*
■ express (a thought or feeling) in words or actions: *an urgent need to externalize the experience.* ■ Psychology project (a mental image or process) on to a figure outside oneself: *such neuroses are externalized as interpersonal conflicts.* ■ arrange for (work) to be carried out by a specialist outside organization: *consider externalizing local authority services.*
– DERIVATIVES **externalization** noun.

exteroceptive /ˌɛkstərə(ʊ)ˈsɛptɪv/ ▶ adjective Physiology relating to stimuli that are external to an organism. Compare with **INTEROCEPTIVE**.
– DERIVATIVES **exteroception** noun, **exteroceptivity** noun.
– ORIGIN early 20th cent.: probably a blend of **EXTERIOR** or **EXTERNAL** and **RECEPTIVE**.

exteroceptor /ˈɛkstərə(ʊ),sɛptə/ ▶ noun Physiology a sensory receptor which receives external stimuli. Compare with **INTEROCEPTOR**.

extinct ▶ adjective (of a species, family, or other larger group) having no living members: *trilobites and dinosaurs are extinct.*
■ often humorous no longer in existence: *the sort of girls' school that is now extinct.* ■ (of a volcano) not having erupted in recorded history. ■ no longer alight: *his now extinct pipe.* ■ (of a title of nobility) having no qualified claimant.
– ORIGIN late Middle English (in the sense 'no longer alight'): from Latin *exstinct-* 'extinguished', from the verb *exstinguere* (see **EXTINGUISH**).

extinction ▶ noun [mass noun] **1** the state or process of a species, family, or larger group being or becoming extinct: *the extinction of the great auk* | [count noun] *mass extinctions.*
■ the state or process of ceasing or causing something to cease to exist: *the extinction of the state.* ■ the wiping out of a debt.
2 Physics reduction in the intensity of light or other radiation as it passes through a medium or object, due to absorption, reflection, and scattering: *ultraviolet extinction.*
– ORIGIN late Middle English: from Latin *exstinctio(n-)*, from *exstinguere* 'quench' (see **EXTINGUISH**).

extinguish ▶ verb [with obj.] cause (a fire or light) to cease to burn or shine: *firemen were soaking everything to extinguish the blaze.*
■ (often **be extinguished**) put an end to; annihilate: *hope is extinguished little by little.* ■ subdue or reduce (someone) to silence: *a look which would have extinguished any man.* ■ (often **be extinguished**) cancel (a debt) by full payment: *the debt was absolutely extinguished.* ■ Law render (a right or obligation) void: *rights of common pasture were extinguished.*
– DERIVATIVES **extinguishable** adjective, **extinguishment** noun (Law).
– ORIGIN mid 16th cent.: from Latin *exstinguere*, from *ex-* 'out' + *stinguere* 'quench'. Compare with **DISTINGUISH**.

extinguisher ▶ noun short for **FIRE EXTINGUISHER**.

extirpate /ˈɛkstəːpeɪt/ ▶ verb [with obj.] root out and destroy completely: *those who tried to extirpate Christianity.*
– DERIVATIVES **extirpation** noun, **extirpator** noun.
– ORIGIN late Middle English (as *extirpation*): from Latin *exstirpare*, from *ex-* 'out' + *stirps* 'a stem'.

extol /ɪkˈstəʊl, ɛk-/ ▶ verb (**extolled**, **extolling**) [with obj.] praise enthusiastically: *he extolled the virtues of the Russian peoples.*
– DERIVATIVES **extoller** noun, **extolment** noun.
– ORIGIN late Middle English: from Latin *extollere*, from *ex-* 'out, upward' + *tollere* 'raise'.

extort /ɪkˈstɔːt, ɛk-/ ▶ verb obtain (something) by force, threats, or other unfair means: *attempts to extort money.*
– DERIVATIVES **extorter** noun, **extortive** adjective.
– ORIGIN early 16th cent.: from Latin *extort-* 'wrested', from the verb *extorquere*, from *ex-* 'out' + *torquere* 'to twist'.

extortion ▶ noun [mass noun] the practice of obtaining something,especially money, through force or threats.
– DERIVATIVES **extortioner** noun, **extortionist** noun.
– ORIGIN Middle English: from late Latin *extortio(n-)*, from Latin *extorquere* 'wrest' (see **EXTORT**).

extortionate /ɪkˈstɔːʃ(ə)nət, ɛk-/ ▶ adjective **1** (of a price) much too high; exorbitant: *£2,700 for a guitar is extortionate.*
2 using or given to extortion: *the extortionate power of the unions.*
– DERIVATIVES **extortionately** adverb [as submodifier] *lobster is extortionately expensive here.*

extra ▶ adjective added to an existing or usual amount or number: *they offered him an extra thirty-five cents an hour.*
▶ adverb **1** [as submodifier] to a greater extent than usual; especially: *he is trying to be extra good.*
2 in addition: *installation will cost about £60 extra.*
▶ noun an item in addition to what is usual or strictly necessary: *I had an education with all the extras.*
■ an item for which an additional charge is made: *the price you pay includes all major charges—there are no hidden extras.* ■ a person engaged temporarily to fill out a scene in a film or play, especially as one of a crowd. ■ Cricket a run scored other than from a hit with the bat, and credited to the batting side but not to an individual batsman. ■ dated a special issue of a newspaper.
– ORIGIN mid 17th cent. (as an adjective): probably a shortening of **EXTRAORDINARY**, suggested by similar forms in French and German.

extra- ▶ prefix outside; beyond: *extracellular* | *extraterritorial.*
■ beyond the scope of: *extra-curricular.*
– ORIGIN via medieval Latin from Latin *extra* 'outside'.

extracellular ▶ adjective Biology situated or taking place outside a cell or cells: *extracellular space in the cortex.*
– DERIVATIVES **extracellularly** adverb.

extracorporeal /ˌɛkstrəkɔːˈpɔːrɪəl/ ▶ adjective chiefly Surgery situated or occurring outside the body.
■ denoting a technique of lithotripsy using shock waves generated externally.

extra cover ▶ noun Cricket a fielding position between cover point and mid-off but further from the wicket.
■ a fielder at this position.

extract ▶ verb /ɪkˈstrakt, ɛk-/ [with obj.] (often **be extracted**) remove or take out, especially by effort or force: *the fossils are* ***extracted from*** *the chalk.*
■ obtain (something such as money or an admission) from someone in the face of initial unwillingness: *I won't let you go without trying to* ***extract*** *a promise* ***from*** *you.* ■ obtain (a substance or resource) from something by a special method: *lead was* ***extracted from*** *the copper.* ■ select (a passage from a piece of writing, music, or film) for quotation, performance, or reproduction: *the table is extracted from the report.* ■ derive (an idea or the evidence for it) from a body of information: *there are few attempts to extract generalities about the nature of the disciplines.* ■ Mathematics calculate (a root of a number).
▶ noun /ˈɛkstrakt/ **1** a short passage taken from a piece of writing, music, or film: *an extract from a historical film.*
2 [with modifier] a preparation containing the active ingredient of a substance in concentrated form: *vanilla extract.*
– DERIVATIVES **extractability** noun, **extractable** adjective.
– ORIGIN late Middle English: from Latin *extract-* 'drawn out', from the verb *extrahere*, from *ex-* 'out' + *trahere* 'draw'.

extraction ▶ noun [mass noun] **1** the action of taking out something, especially using effort or force: *mineral extraction* | [count noun] *a dental extraction.*
2 [with adj.] the ethnic origin of someone's family: *a worker of Polish extraction.*
– ORIGIN late Middle English: via Old French from late Latin *extractio(n-)*, from Latin *extrahere* 'draw out' (see **EXTRACT**).

extractive ▶ adjective of or involving extraction, especially the extensive extraction of natural resources without provision for their renewal: *extractive industry.*

extractor ▶ noun [often with modifier] a machine or device used to extract something: *a juice extractor.*
■ [as modifier] denoting a device used to ventilate and remove bad smells from an area: *the engine room's extractor fans.*

extra-curricular ▶ adjective (of an activity at a school or college) pursued in addition to the normal course of study: *extra-curricular activities include sports, drama, music, chess, and gym clubs.*
■ often humorous outside the normal routine, especially that provided by a job or marriage: *Harriet's extra-curricular sweetheart.*
– DERIVATIVES **extra-curricularly** adverb.

extraditable /ˈɛkstrəˌdʌɪtəb(ə)l/ ▶ adjective (of a crime) making a criminal liable to extradition: *possession of explosives will be an extraditable offence.*
■ (of a criminal) liable to extradition.

extradite /ˈɛkstrədʌɪt/ ▶ verb [with obj.] hand over (a person accused or convicted of a crime) to the jurisdiction of the foreign state in which the crime was committed: *they refused to* ***extradite*** *Mr Morris* ***to*** *Britain.*
– ORIGIN mid 19th cent.: back-formation from **EXTRADITION**.

extradition ▶ noun [mass noun] the action of extraditing a person accused or convicted of a crime: *they fought to prevent his extradition to the US* | [count noun] *emergency extraditions.*
– ORIGIN mid 19th cent.: from French, from *ex-* 'out, from' + *tradition* 'delivery'.

extrados /ɪkˈstreɪdɒs, ɛk-/ ▶ noun Architecture the upper or outer curve of an arch. Often contrasted with **INTRADOS**.
– ORIGIN late 18th cent.: from French, from Latin *extra* 'outside' + French *dos* 'back' (from Latin *dorsum*).

extradural /ˌɛkstrəˈdjʊər(ə)l/ ▶ adjective Medicine another term for **EPIDURAL**.

extrafamilial /ˌɛkstrəfəˈmɪljəl/ ▶ adjective outside the family.

extrafloral ▶ adjective Botany (of a nectary) situated outside a flower, especially on a leaf or stem.

extragalactic /ˌɛkstrəgəˈlaktɪk/ ▶ adjective Astronomy situated, occurring, or originating outside the Milky Way galaxy: *extragalactic radio sources.*

extrajudicial ▶ adjective Law (of a sentence) not legally authorized: *there have been reports of extrajudicial executions.*
■ (of a settlement, statement, or confession) not made in court; out-of-court.
– DERIVATIVES **extrajudicially** adverb.

extralegal ▶ adjective (of an action or situation) beyond the province of the law; not regulated by the law.

extralimital /ˌɛkstrəˈlɪmɪt(ə)l/ ▶ adjective chiefly Biology situated, occurring, or derived from outside a particular area.

extralinguistic /ˌɛkstrəlɪŋˈgwɪstɪk/ ▶ adjective not involving or beyond the bounds of language: *extralinguistic reality.*

extramarital /ˌɛkstrəˈmarɪt(ə)l/ ▶ adjective (especially of sexual relations) occurring outside marriage: *an extramarital affair.*
– DERIVATIVES **extramaritally** adverb.

extramundane /ɛkstrəˈmʌndeɪn/ ▶ adjective rare outside or beyond the physical world.

extramural /ˌɛkstrəˈmjʊər(ə)l/ ▶ adjective **1** Brit. (of a course of study) arranged for people who are not full-time members of a university or other educational establishment: *extramural education.*
■ additional to one's work or course of study and typically not connected with it: *extramural activities.*
2 outside the walls or boundaries of a town or city: *the extramural cemetery in Brighton.*
– DERIVATIVES **extramurally** adverb.
– ORIGIN mid 19th cent. (in sense 2): from Latin *extra muros* 'outside the walls' + **-AL**.

extramusical ▶ adjective extrinsic to a piece of music or outside the field of music.

extraneous /ɪkˈstreɪnɪəs, ɛk-/ ▶ **adjective** irrelevant or unrelated to the subject or matter being dealt with: *one is obliged to wade through many pages of extraneous material.*
■ of external origin: *when the transmitter pack is turned off no extraneous noise is heard.* ■ separate from the object to which it is attached: *other insects attach extraneous objects or material to themselves.*
– DERIVATIVES **extraneously** adverb, **extraneousness** noun.
– ORIGIN mid 17th cent.: from Latin *extraneus* + **-OUS**.

extraordinaire /ɪkˌstrɔːdɪˈnɛː/ ▶ **adjective** [postpositive] informal outstanding or remarkable in a particular capacity: *the noted Hollywood middleman and go-getter extraordinaire.*
– ORIGIN 1940s: French, 'extraordinary'.

extraordinary /ɪkˈstrɔːd(ə)n(ə)ri, ɛk-, ˌɛkstrəˈɔːdɪn(ə)ri/ ▶ **adjective** very unusual or remarkable: *the extraordinary plumage of the male* | [with clause] *it is extraordinary that no consultation took place.*
■ unusually great: *young children need extraordinary amounts of attention.* ■ [attrib.] (of a meeting) specially convened: *an extraordinary session of the Congress.* ■ [postpositive] (of an official) additional; specially employed: *his appointment as Ambassador Extraordinary in London.*
▶ **noun** (usu. **extraordinaries**) an item in a company's accounts not arising from its normal activities. Compare with **EXCEPTIONAL**.
– DERIVATIVES **extraordinarily** adverb [as submodifier] *an extraordinarily beautiful girl*, **extraordinariness** noun.
– ORIGIN late Middle English: from Latin *extraordinarius*, from *extra ordinem* 'outside the normal course of events'.

extraordinary general meeting (abbrev.: **EGM**) ▶ **noun** Brit. a meeting of the members or shareholders of a club, company, or other organization, held at short notice, especially in order to consider a particular matter.

extraordinary ray ▶ **noun** Optics (in double refraction) the light ray that does not obey the ordinary laws of refraction. Compare with **ORDINARY RAY**.

extrapolate /ɪkˈstrapəleɪt, ɛk-/ ▶ **verb** [with obj.] extend the application of (a method or conclusion, especially one based on statistics) to an unknown situation by assuming that existing trends will continue or similar methods will be applicable: *the results cannot be* **extrapolated to** *other patient groups* | [no obj.] *it is always dangerous to* **extrapolate from** *a sample.*
■ estimate or conclude (something) in this way: *attempts to extrapolate likely human cancers from laboratory studies.* ■ Mathematics extend (a graph, curve, or range of values) by inferring unknown values from trends in the known data: [as adj. **extrapolated**] *a set of extrapolated values.*
– DERIVATIVES **extrapolation** noun, **extrapolative** adjective, **extrapolator** noun.
– ORIGIN late 19th cent.: from **EXTRA-** 'outside' + a shortened form of **INTERPOLATE**.

extraposition /ˌɛkstrəpəˈzɪʃ(ə)n/ ▶ **noun** [mass noun] Grammar the placing of a word or group of words outside or at the end of a clause, while retaining the sense. The subject is often postponed and replaced by *it* at the start, as in *it's no use crying over spilt milk* rather than *crying over spilt milk is no use.*

extrapyramidal /ˌɛkstrəpɪˈramɪd(ə)l/ ▶ **adjective** Anatomy & Medicine relating to or denoting nerves concerned with motor activity that descend from the cortex to the spine and are not part of the pyramidal system: *extrapyramidal symptoms.*

extrasensory perception /ɛkstrəˈsɛns(ə)ri/ (abbrev.: **ESP**) ▶ **noun** [mass noun] the supposed faculty of perceiving things by means other than the known senses, e.g. by telepathy or clairvoyance.

extrasystole /ˌɛkstrəˈsɪst(ə)li/ ▶ **noun** Medicine a heartbeat outside the normal rhythm, as often occurs in normal individuals.

extraterrestrial /ˌɛkstrətəˈrɛstrɪəl/ ▶ **adjective** of or from outside the earth or its atmosphere: *searches for extraterrestrial intelligence.*
▶ **noun** a hypothetical or fictional being from outer space, especially an intelligent one.

extraterritorial /ˌɛkstrətɛrɪˈtɔːrɪəl/ ▶ **adjective** (of a law or decree) valid outside a country's territory.
■ denoting the freedom of an ambassador or other embassy staff from the jurisdiction of the territory of residence: *foreign embassies have extraterritorial rights.* ■ situated outside a country's territory: *extraterritorial industrial zones.*
– DERIVATIVES **extraterritoriality** noun.
– ORIGIN mid 19th cent.: from Latin *extra territorium* 'outside the territory' + **-AL**.

extra time ▶ **noun** [mass noun] chiefly Brit. a further period of play added on to a game if the scores are equal.

extratropical ▶ **adjective** chiefly Meteorology situated, existing, or occurring outside the tropics.

extrauterine /ˌɛkstrəˈjuːtərʌɪn/ ▶ **adjective** Medicine existing, formed, or occurring outside the uterus: *the first hour of extrauterine life.*

extravagance ▶ **noun** [mass noun] lack of restraint in spending money or use of resources: *his reckless extravagance with other people's money.*
■ [count noun] a thing on which too much money has been spent or which has used up too many resources: *salmon trout is an unnecessary extravagance.* ■ excessive elaborateness of style, speech, or action: *the extravagance of the decor.*
– DERIVATIVES **extravagancy** noun.
– ORIGIN mid 17th cent.: from French, from medieval Latin *extravagant-* 'diverging greatly', from the verb *extravagari* (see **EXTRAVAGANT**).

extravagant /ɪkˈstravəg(ə)nt, ɛk-/ ▶ **adjective** **1** lacking restraint in spending money or using resources: *it was rather extravagant to buy both.*
■ exorbitant; costing a great deal: *extravagant gifts like computer games.* ■ exceeding what is reasonable or appropriate; absurd: *extravagant claims for its effectiveness.* ■ excessively elaborate in style, speech, or action: *an extravagant collar of prickly blue bracts.*
– DERIVATIVES **extravagantly** adverb.
– ORIGIN late Middle English (in the sense 'unusual, abnormal, unsuitable'): from medieval Latin *extravagant-* 'diverging greatly', from the verb *extravagari*, from Latin *extra-* 'outside' + *vagari* 'wander'.

extravaganza /ɪkˌstravəˈganzə, ɛk-/ ▶ **noun** an elaborate and spectacular entertainment or production: *an extravaganza of dance in many forms.*
– ORIGIN mid 18th cent. (in the sense 'extravagance in language or behaviour'): from Italian *estravaganza* 'extravagance'. The change was due to association with words beginning with **EXTRA-**.

extravasate /ɪkˈstravəseɪt, ɛk-/ ▶ **verb** [with obj.] [usu. as adj. **extravasated**] chiefly Medicine let or force out (a fluid, especially blood) from the vessel that naturally contains it into the surrounding area.
– DERIVATIVES **extravasation** noun.
– ORIGIN mid 17th cent.: from **EXTRA-** 'outside' + Latin *vas* 'vessel' + **-ATE**[3].

extravascular /ˌɛkstrəˈvaskjʊlə/ ▶ **adjective** Medicine situated or occurring outside the vascular system: *extravascular fluid.*

extravehicular /ˌɛkstrəvɪˈhɪkjʊlə/ ▶ **adjective** of or relating to work performed in space outside a spacecraft.

extravert ▶ **noun** variant spelling of **EXTROVERT**.

extra virgin ▶ **adjective** denoting a particularly fine grade of olive oil made from the first pressing of the olives and containing a maximum of one per cent oleic acid.

extrema plural form of **EXTREMUM**.

Extremadura /ˌɛkstrəməˈd(j)ʊərə/ an autonomous region of western Spain, on the border with Portugal; capital, Mérida. Spanish name **ESTREMADURA** /estremaˈðura/.

extreme ▶ **adjective** **1** reaching a high or the highest degree; very great: *extreme cold.*
■ not usual; exceptional: *in extreme cases the soldier may be discharged.* ■ very severe or serious: *expulsion is an extreme sanction.* ■ (of a person or their opinions) advocating severe or drastic measures; far from moderate, especially politically: *Labour's more extreme socialist supporters.* ■ chiefly N. Amer. denoting or relating to a sport performed in a hazardous environment and involving great physical risk, such as parachuting or white-water rafting.
2 [attrib.] furthest from the centre or a given point; outermost: *the extreme north-west of Scotland.*
▶ **noun** **1** either of two abstract things that are as different from each other as possible: *ranging from free-floating at one extreme to a rigidly fixed system at the other.*
■ the highest or most extreme degree of something: *extremes of temperature.* ■ a very severe or serious measure: *the extreme of applying for poor relief.*
2 Logic the subject or predicate in a proposition, or the major or minor term in a syllogism (as contrasted with the middle term).
– PHRASES **extremes meet** proverb opposite extremes have much in common. **go** (or **take something**) **to extremes** take an extreme course of action; do something to an extreme degree: *they took a commendable anti-ageist policy to extremes.* **in the extreme** to an extreme degree: *the reasoning was convoluted in the extreme.*
– DERIVATIVES **extremely** adverb [as submodifier] *this is an extremely difficult and dangerous thing to do*, **extremeness** noun.
– ORIGIN late Middle English: via Old French from Latin *extremus* 'outermost, utmost', superlative of *exterus* 'outer'.

extreme unction ▶ **noun** (in the Roman Catholic Church) a former name for the sacrament of anointing of the sick, especially when administered to the dying.

extremist ▶ **noun** chiefly derogatory a person who holds extreme or fanatical political or religious views, especially one who resorts to or advocates extreme action: *right-wing extremists* | [as modifier] *extremist political views.*
– DERIVATIVES **extremism** noun.

extremity /ɪkˈstrɛmɪti, ɛk-/ ▶ **noun** (pl. **-ies**) **1** the furthest point or limit of something: *the peninsula's western extremity.*
■ (**extremities**) the hands and feet: *tingling and numbness in the extremities.*
2 [mass noun] the extreme degree or nature of something: *the extremity of the violence concerns us.*
■ a condition of extreme adversity or difficulty: *the terror of an animal* **in extremity**.
– ORIGIN late Middle English: from Old French *extremite* or Latin *extremitas*, from *extremus* 'utmost' (see **EXTREME**).

extremophile /ɛksˈtrɛməfʌɪl/ ▶ **noun** Biology a micro-organism, especially an archaean, that lives in conditions of extreme temperature, acidity, alkalinity, or chemical concentration.

extremum /ɪkˈstriːməm, ɛk-/ ▶ **noun** (pl. **extremums** or **extrema**) [usu. as modifier] Mathematics the maximum or minimum value of a function.
– ORIGIN early 20th cent.: from Latin, neuter of *extremus* 'utmost' (see **EXTREME**).

extricate /ˈɛkstrɪkeɪt/ ▶ **verb** [with obj.] free (someone or something) from a constraint or difficulty: *he was trying to* **extricate** *himself* **from** *official duties.*
– DERIVATIVES **extricable** adjective, **extrication** noun.
– ORIGIN early 17th cent. (in the sense 'unravel, untangle'): from Latin *extricat-* 'unravelled', from the verb *extricare*, from *ex-* 'out' + *tricae* 'perplexities'.

extrinsic /ɪkˈstrɪnsɪk, ɛk-/ ▶ **adjective** not part of the essential nature of someone or something; coming or operating from outside: *a complex interplay of extrinsic and intrinsic factors* | *reasons* **extrinsic to** *the music itself.*
■ (of a muscle, such as any of the eye muscles) having its origin some distance from the part which it moves.
– DERIVATIVES **extrinsically** adverb.
– ORIGIN mid 16th cent. (in the sense 'outward'): from late Latin *extrinsecus* 'outward', from Latin *extrinsecus* 'outwardly', based on *exter* 'outer'; the ending was altered under the influence of **-IC**.

extropy /ˈɛkstrəpi/ ▶ **noun** [mass noun] the pseudoscientific principle that life will expand indefinitely and in an orderly, progressive way throughout the entire universe by the means of human intelligence and technology.
– DERIVATIVES **extropian** adjective & noun.
– ORIGIN 1980s: from **EX-**[1] 'out' + a shortened form of **ENTROPY**.

extrorse /ɛksˈtrɔːs/ ▶ **adjective** Botany & Zoology turned outwards. The opposite of **INTRORSE**.
■ (of anthers) releasing their pollen on the outside of the flower.
– ORIGIN mid 19th cent.: from late Latin *extrorsus* 'outwards' (adverb).

extrovert /ˈɛkstrəvəːt/ (also **extravert**) ▶ **noun** an outgoing, socially confident person.
■ Psychology a person predominantly concerned with external things or objective considerations. Compare with **INTROVERT**.
▶ **adjective** of, denoting, or typical of an extrovert: *his extrovert personality made him the ideal host.*
– DERIVATIVES **extroversion** noun, **extroverted** adjective.

– ORIGIN early 20th cent.: from *extro-* (variant of **EXTRA-**, on the pattern of *intro-*) + Latin *vertere* 'to turn'.

USAGE The original spelling **extravert** is now rare in general use but is found in technical use in psychology.

extrude /ɪkˈstruːd, ɛk-/ ▶ verb [with obj.] (usu. be **extruded**) thrust or force out: *lava was being extruded from the volcano.*
■ shape (a material such as metal or plastic) by forcing it through a die.
– DERIVATIVES **extrudable** adjective, **extrusile** adjective, **extrusion** noun.
– ORIGIN mid 16th cent.: from Latin *extrudere*, from *ex-* 'out' + *trudere* 'to thrust'.

extrusive ▶ adjective Geology relating to or denoting rock that has been extruded at the earth's surface as lava or other volcanic deposits.

exuberant /ɪɡˈzjuːb(ə)r(ə)nt, ɛɡ-/ ▶ adjective (of a person or their manner or behaviour) filled with or characterized by a lively energy and excitement: *fresh-faced and youthfully exuberant.*
■ characterized by a vigorously imaginative artistic style: *exuberant, over-the-top sculptures.* ■ growing luxuriantly or profusely: *exuberant foliage.*
– DERIVATIVES **exuberance** noun, **exuberantly** adverb.
– ORIGIN late Middle English (in the sense 'overflowing, abounding'): from French *exubérant*, from Latin *exuberant-* 'being abundantly fruitful', from the verb *exuberare* (based on *uber* 'fertile').

exudate /ˈɛɡzjʊdeɪt/ ▶ noun an exuded substance, in particular:
■ Medicine a mass of cells and fluid that has seeped out of blood vessels or an organ, especially in inflammation. ■ Botany & Entomology a substance secreted by a plant or insect.
– ORIGIN late 19th cent.: from Latin *exsudat-* 'exuded', from the verb *exsudare*.

exude /ɪɡˈzjuːd, ɛɡ-/ ▶ verb [with obj.] discharge (moisture or a smell) slowly and steadily: *the beetle exudes a caustic liquid.*
■ [no obj.] (of moisture or a smell) be discharged by something in such a way: *slime exudes from the fungus.* ■ figurative (of a person) display (an emotion or quality) strongly and openly: *Sir Thomas exuded friendship and goodwill.* ■ [no obj.] figurative (of an emotion or quality) be displayed by someone in such a way: *sexuality exuded from him.* ■ figurative (of a place) have a strong atmosphere of: *the building exudes an air of tranquillity.*
– DERIVATIVES **exudation** noun, **exudative** /ɪɡˈzjuːdətɪv, ɛɡ-/ adjective.
– ORIGIN late 16th cent.: from Latin *exsudare*, from *ex-* 'out' + *sudare* 'to sweat'.

exult ▶ verb [no obj.] show or feel elation or jubilation, especially as the result of a success: *exulting in her escape, Leonora closed the door behind her.*
– DERIVATIVES **exultation** noun, **exultingly** adverb.
– ORIGIN late 16th cent.: from Latin *exsultare*, frequentative of *exsilire* 'leap up', from *ex-* 'out, upward' + *salire* 'to leap'.

exultant ▶ adjective triumphantly happy: *she felt exultant and powerful.*
– DERIVATIVES **exultancy** noun, **exultantly** adverb.
– ORIGIN mid 17th cent.: from Latin *exsultant-* 'exulting', from the verb *exsultare*.

Exuma Cays /ɪkˈsuːmə/ a group of some 350 small islands in the Bahamas.

exurb /ˈɛksəːb/ ▶ noun N. Amer. a district outside a city, especially a prosperous area beyond the suburbs.
– DERIVATIVES **exurban** adjective, **exurbanite** noun & adjective.
– ORIGIN 1955: coined by A. C. Spectorsky (1919–72), American author and editor, either from Latin *ex* 'out of' + *urbs* 'city', or as a back-formation from the earlier adjective *exurban*.

exurbia /ɛkˈsəːbɪə/ ▶ noun [mass noun] the exurbs collectively; the region beyond the suburbs.
– ORIGIN 1955 (originally US, see **EXURB**): from **EX-**¹ 'out of' + *-urbia*, on the pattern of *suburbia*.

exuviae /ɪɡˈzjuːvɪiː, ɛɡ-/ ▶ plural noun [also treated as sing.] Zoology an animal's cast or sloughed skin, especially that of an insect larva.
– DERIVATIVES **exuvial** adjective.
– ORIGIN mid 17th cent.: from Latin, literally 'animal skins, spoils of the enemy', from *exuere* 'divest oneself of'.

exuviate /ɪɡˈzjuːvɪeɪt, ɛɡ-/ ▶ verb [with obj.] technical shed (a skin or shell).

– DERIVATIVES **exuviation** noun.
– ORIGIN mid 19th cent.: from **EXUVIAE** + **-ATE**³.

ex-voto /ɛks ˈvəʊtəʊ/ ▶ noun (pl. **-os**) an offering given in order to fulfil a vow.
– ORIGIN late 18th cent.: from Latin *ex voto* 'from a vow'.

ex-works ▶ adjective & adverb Brit. direct from the factory or place of manufacture: [as adj.] *ex-works prices* | [as adv.] *all orders are shipped ex-works.*

-ey ▶ suffix variant spelling of **-Y**² (as in *Charley, Limey*).

eyas /ˈʌɪəs/ ▶ noun (pl. **eyasses**) a young hawk, especially (in falconry) an unfledged nestling taken from the nest for training.
– ORIGIN late 15th cent. (originally *nyas*): from French *niais*, based on Latin *nidus* 'nest'. The initial *n* was lost by wrong division of *a nyas*; compare with **ADDER**¹, **APRON**, and **UMPIRE**.

eye ▶ noun 1 each of a pair of globular organs in the head through which people and vertebrate animals see, the visible part typically appearing almond-shaped in animals with eyelids: *my cat is blind in one eye* | *closing her eyes, she tried to relax.*
■ the corresponding visual or light-detecting organ of many invertebrate animals. ■ the region of the face surrounding the eyes: *her eyes were swollen with crying.* ■ a person's eye as characterized by the colour of the iris: *he had piercing blue eyes.* ■ used to refer to someone's power of vision and in descriptions of the manner or direction of someone's gaze: *his sharp eyes had missed nothing* | *I couldn't take my eyes off him.* ■ used to refer to someone's opinion, point of view, or attitude towards something: *in the eyes of his younger colleagues, Mr Arnett was an eccentric* | *to European eyes, it may seem that the city is overcrowded.*

The basic components of the vertebrate eye are a transparent cornea, an adjustable iris, a lens for focusing, a sensitive retina lining the back of the eye, and a clear fluid- or jelly-filled centre. The most primitive animals only have one or two eyespots, while many other invertebrates have several simple eyes or a pair of compound eyes.

2 a thing resembling an eye in appearance, shape, or relative position, in particular:
■ the small hole in a needle through which the thread is passed. ■ a small metal loop into which a hook is fitted as a fastener on a garment. See also **HOOK AND EYE**. ■ Nautical a loop at the end of a rope, especially one at the top end of a shroud or stay. ■ a rounded eye-like marking on an animal, such as those on the tail of a peacock; an eyespot. ■ a round, dark spot on a potato from which a new shoot can grow. ■ the centre of a flower, especially when distinctively coloured. ■ the calm region at the centre of a storm or hurricane. See also **eye of the storm** below. ■ S. African the source of a spring or river. ■ (**eyes**) Nautical the extreme forward part of a ship: *it was hanging in the eyes of the ship.*
▶ verb (**eyeing** or **eying**) [with obj.] look at or watch closely or with interest: *Rose eyed him warily.*
■ (**eye someone up**) informal look at someone in a way that reveals a particular, especially sexual, interest: *Margot saw the women eyeing up her boyfriend.*
– PHRASES **all eyes** used to convey that a particular person or thing is currently the focus of public interest or attention: *over the next few weeks all eyes will be on the pound.* **be all eyes** be watching eagerly and attentively. **before** (or **in front of** or **under**) **one's** (**very**) **eyes** right in front of one (used for emphasis, especially in the context of something surprising or unpleasant): *he saw his life's work destroyed before his very eyes.* **clap** (or **lay** or **set**) **eyes on** informal see: *I'd never clapped eyes on the guy before.* **close** (or **shut**) **one's eyes to** refuse to notice or acknowledge something unwelcome or unpleasant: *he couldn't close his eyes to the truth—he had cancer.* **an eye for an eye and a tooth for a tooth** used to refer to the belief that retaliation in kind is the appropriate way to deal with an offence or crime. [ORIGIN: with biblical allusion to Exod. 21: 24.] **the eye of the storm** the calm region at the centre of a storm. ■ the most intense part of a tumultuous situation: *he was in the eye of the storm of abstract art.* **the eye of the wind** (also **the wind's eye**) the direction from which the wind is blowing. **eyes front** (or **left** or **right**) a military command to turn the head in the particular direction stated. **eyes out on stalks** used to emphasize the extreme degree of someone's eager curiosity: *when I read about his arrest my eyes popped out on stalks.* **a ——'s-eye view** a view from the position or standpoint of a ——: *a satellite's-eye view of global warming.* See also **BIRD'S-EYE VIEW, WORM'S-EYE VIEW. get** (or **keep)**

one's eye in Brit. become (or remain) able to make good judgements, especially visual ones, about a task or occupation in which one is engaged: *I've got my eye in now; I'm landing them just where I want them.* **give someone the eye** informal look at someone in a way that clearly indicates one's sexual interest in them: *this blonde was giving me the eye.* **half an eye** used in reference to a slight degree of perception or attention: *he kept half an eye on the house as he worked.* **have an eye for** be able to recognize, appreciate, and make good judgements about: *applicants should have an eye for detail.* **have** (or **keep**) **one's eye on** keep under careful observation. ■ (**have one's eye on**) hope or plan to acquire: *there was a vacant bishopric which the Dean had his eye on.* **have** (or **with**) **an eye to** have (or having) as one's objective: *with an eye to transatlantic business, he made a deal in New York.* ■ consider (or be considering) prudently; look (or be looking) ahead to: *the charity must have an eye to the future.* **have** (or **with**) **an eye to** (or **for** or **on**) **the main chance** look or be looking for an opportunity to take advantage of a situation for personal gain, typically a financial one: *a developer with an eye on the main chance.* **have eyes bigger than one's stomach** have asked for or taken more food than one can actually eat. (**only**) **have eyes for** be (exclusively) interested in or attracted to: *he has eyes for no one but you.* **have eyes in the back of one's head** know what is going on around one even when one cannot see it. **hit someone in the eye** (or **between the eyes**) informal be very obvious or impressive: *he wouldn't notice talent if it hit him right between the eyes.* **keep an eye** (or **a sharp eye**) **on** keep under careful observation: *dealers are keeping an eye on the currency markets.* **keep an eye out** (or **open**) look out for something with particular attention: *keep an eye out for his car.* **keep one's eyes open** (or **peeled** or Brit. **skinned**) be on the alert; watch carefully or vigilantly for something: *keep your eyes peeled for a phonebox.* **make eyes at someone** look at someone in a way that indicates one's sexual interest. **my eye** (or **all my eye and Betty Martin**) informal, dated used especially in spoken English to indicate surprise or disbelief. [ORIGIN: said to be originally nautical slang.] **one in the eye for** a disappointment or setback for someone or something, especially one that is perceived as being well deserved: *this success for Manchester is one in the eye for London.* **open someone's eyes** enlighten someone about certain realities; cause someone to realize or discover something: *the letter finally opened my eyes to the truth.* **see eye to eye** have similar views or attitudes to something; be in full agreement: *the headmaster and I do not always see eye to eye.* **a twinkle** (or **gleam**) **in someone's eye** something that is as yet no more than an idea or dream: *the scheme is only a gleam in the developer's eye.* **up to the** (or **one's**) **eyes** (**in**) informal extremely busy: *I'm up to my eyes this morning.* ■ used to emphasize the extreme degree of an unpleasant situation: *the council is up to its eyes in debt.* **what the eye doesn't see, the heart doesn't grieve over** proverb if you're unaware of an unpleasant fact or situation you can't be troubled by it. **with one's eyes open** fully aware of the possible difficulties or consequences: *I went into this job with my eyes open.* **with one's eyes shut** (or **closed**) **1** without having to make much effort; easily: *I could do it with my eyes shut.* **2** without considering the possible difficulties or consequences: *she didn't go to Hollywood with her eyes closed.* **with one eye on** giving some but not all one's attention to: *I sat with one eye on the clock, waiting for my turn.*
– DERIVATIVES **eyed** adjective [in combination] *a brown-eyed girl*, **eyeless** adjective.
– ORIGIN Old English *ēage*, of Germanic origin; related to Dutch *oog* and German *Auge*.

eyeball ▶ noun the round part of the eye of a vertebrate, within the eyelids and socket. In mammals it is typically a firm mobile spherical structure enclosed by the sclera and the cornea.
▶ verb [with obj.] informal, chiefly N. Amer. look or stare at closely: *we eyeballed one another.*
– PHRASES **eyeball to eyeball** face to face with someone, especially in an aggressive way: *he wheeled round to confront John eyeball to eyeball.* **up to the** (or **one's**) **eyeballs** informal used to emphasize the extreme degree of an undesirable situation or condition: *he's up to his eyeballs in debt.*

eyebath ▶ noun chiefly Brit. a small container used for applying cleansing solutions to the eye.

eyeblack ▶ noun old-fashioned term for MASCARA.

eye bolt ▶ noun a bolt or bar with an eye at the end for attaching a hook or ring to.

eyebright ▶ noun [mass noun] a small flowering plant of dry fields and heaths, traditionally used as a remedy for eye problems.
● Genus *Euphrasia*, family Scrophulariaceae: several species, in particular the European *E. officinalis*.

eyebrow ▶ noun the strip of hair growing on the ridge above a person's eye socket.
– PHRASES **raise one's eyebrows** (or **an eyebrow**) show surprise, disbelief, or mild disapproval.

eyebrow pencil ▶ noun a cosmetic pencil for defining or accentuating the eyebrows.

eye candy ▶ noun [mass noun] informal visual images that are superficially attractive and entertaining but intellectually undemanding: *the film's success rested on a promotional campaign showcasing its relentless eye candy.*

eye-catching ▶ adjective immediately appealing or noticeable; striking: *an eye-catching poster.*
– DERIVATIVES **eye-catcher** noun, **eye-catchingly** adverb.

eye contact ▶ noun [mass noun] the state in which two people are aware of looking directly into one another's eyes: *make eye contact with your interviewers.*

eyecup ▶ noun **1** a piece of an optical device such as a microscope, camera, or pair of binoculars which is contoured to provide a comfortable rest against the user's eye.
2 another term for OPTIC CUP.
3 North American term for EYEBATH.

eyeful ▶ noun [in sing.] informal a long steady look at something.
■ a visually striking person or thing: *she was quite an eyeful.* ■ a quantity or piece of something thrown or blown into the eye: *an eyeful of woodworm fluid.*

eyeglass ▶ noun a single lens for correcting or assisting defective eyesight, especially a monocle.
■ (**eyeglasses**) chiefly N. Amer. another term for GLASSES. ■ another term for EYEPIECE.

eyehole ▶ noun a hole to look through.

eyelash ▶ noun each of the short curved hairs growing on the edges of the eyelids, serving to protect the eyes from dust particles.

eyelet ▶ noun a small round hole in leather or cloth for threading a lace, string, or rope through.
■ a metal ring used to reinforce such a hole. ■ a small hole ornamented with stitching around its edge, used as a form of decoration in embroidery. ■ a small hole or slit in a wall for looking through.
▶ verb (**eyeleted**, **eyeleting**) [with obj.] make eyelets in (fabric).
– ORIGIN late Middle English *oilet*, from Old French *oillet*, diminutive of *oil* 'eye', from Latin *oculus*. The change in the first syllable in the 17th cent. was due to association with EYE.

eye level ▶ noun [mass noun] the level of the eyes looking straight ahead: *pictures hung at eye level.*

eyelid ▶ noun each of the upper and lower folds of skin which cover the eye when closed.

eyeline ▶ noun a person's line of sight.

eyeliner ▶ noun [mass noun] a cosmetic applied as a line round a woman's eyes to make them more noticeable or look bigger.

eye-opener ▶ noun informal **1** [in sing.] an event or situation that proves to be unexpectedly enlightening: *a visit to the docks can be a fascinating eye-opener.*
2 N. Amer. an alcoholic drink taken early in the day.
– DERIVATIVES **eye-opening** adjective.

eyepatch ▶ noun a patch worn to protect an injured eye.

eye pencil ▶ noun a pencil for applying make-up around the eyes.

eyepiece ▶ noun the lens or group of lenses that is closest to the eye in a microscope, telescope, or other optical instrument. Also called OCULAR.

eye-popping ▶ adjective informal astonishingly large, impressive, or blatant: *the company has doubled its assets to an eye-popping $113 billion.*

eye rhyme ▶ noun a similarity between words in spelling but not in pronunciation, for example *love* and *move.*

eyeshade ▶ noun a translucent visor used to protect the eyes from strong light.

eyeshadow ▶ noun [mass noun] a coloured cosmetic, typically in powder form, applied to the eyelids or to the skin around the eyes to accentuate them.

eyeshot ▶ noun [mass noun] the distance for which one can see: *he is within eyeshot.*

eyesight ▶ noun [mass noun] a person's ability to see: *poor eyesight ended his plans for a naval career.*

eye socket ▶ noun the cavity in the skull which encloses an eyeball with its surrounding muscles. Also called ORBIT.

eyesore ▶ noun a thing that is very ugly, especially a building that disfigures a landscape.

eye splice ▶ noun a splice made by turning the end of a rope back on itself and interlacing the strands, thereby forming a loop.

eyespot ▶ noun **1** Zoology a light-sensitive pigmented spot on the bodies of invertebrate animals such as flatworms, starfishes, and microscopic crustaceans, and also in some unicellular organisms.
2 a rounded eye-like marking on an animal, especially on the wing of a butterfly or moth.
3 [mass noun] a fungal disease of cereals, sugar cane, and other cultivated grasses, characterized by yellowish oval spots on the leaves and stems.
● The fungus is typically *Pseudocercosporella herpotrichoides*, subdivision Deuteromycotina.

eyestalk ▶ noun Zoology a movable stalk that bears an eye near its tip, especially in crabs, shrimps, and related crustaceans, and in some molluscs.

eye strain ▶ noun [mass noun] fatigue of the eyes, such as that caused by reading or looking at a computer screen for too long.

eyestripe ▶ noun a stripe on a bird's head which encloses or appears to run through the eye.

Eyetie /ˈʌɪtʌɪ/ ▶ adjective & noun (pl. **Eyeties**) Brit. informal, offensive Italian or an Italian.
– ORIGIN 1920s: abbreviation of 19th-cent. *Eyetalian*, representing a humorous pronunciation of *Italian.*

eye tooth ▶ noun a canine tooth, especially one in the upper jaw.
– PHRASES **give one's eye teeth for** (or **to be**) do anything in order to have or be something: *Mary would give her eye teeth for a cup of tea.*

eyewash ▶ noun [mass noun] **1** cleansing lotion for a person's eye.
2 informal insincere talk; nonsense: *all that stuff about blood being thicker than water was a lot of eyewash.*

eyewater ▶ noun [mass noun] poetic/literary or W. Indian water secreted by the eyes; tears.

eyewear ▶ noun [mass noun] things worn on the eyes, such as spectacles and contact lenses.

eyewitness ▶ noun [often as modifier] a person who has personally seen something happen and so can give a first-hand description of it: *eyewitness accounts of the London blitz.*

eye worm ▶ noun either of two parasitic nematode worms which affect the eyes of mammals:
● a filarial worm of equatorial Africa, infesting humans and other primates, causing loiasis and sometimes passing across the cornea (*Loa loa*, class Phasmida). ● a nematode that occurs in the region of the eyelid and tear duct, found chiefly in hoofed mammals (genus *Thelazia*, class Phasmida).

eyot /ˈeɪət/ ▶ noun another term for AIT.

eyra /ˈeɪrə/ ▶ noun a reddish-brown form of the jaguarundi (cat).
– ORIGIN early 17th cent.: from Spanish, from Tupi *eirara, irara.*

Eyre /ɛː/, Edward John (1815–1901), British-born Australian explorer and colonial statesman. He undertook explorations in the interior deserts of Australia (1840–1) and later served as Lieutenant Governor of New Zealand and Governor of Jamaica.

eyre /ɛː/ ▶ noun historical a circuit court held in medieval England by a judge (a **justice in eyre**) who rode from county to county for the purpose.
– ORIGIN Middle English: from Old French *eire*, from Latin *iter* 'journey'.

Eyre, Lake a lake in South Australia, Australia's largest salt lake.
– ORIGIN named after the explorer E. J. EYRE.

eyrie /ˈɪəri, ˈʌɪri, ˈɛːri/ (N. Amer. also **aerie**) ▶ noun a large nest of a bird of prey, especially an eagle, typically built high in a tree or on a cliff.
– ORIGIN late 15th cent.: from medieval Latin *aeria, aerea, eyria*, probably from Old French *aire*, from Latin *area* 'level piece of ground', in late Latin 'nest of a bird of prey'.

eyrir /ˈeɪriːr/ ▶ noun (pl. **aurar** /ˈøɪrar/) a monetary unit of Iceland, equal to one hundredth of a krona.

Eysenck /ˈʌɪsɛŋk/, Hans (Jürgen) (1916–97), German-born British psychologist. He was noted for his strong criticism of Freudian psychoanalysis and for his ideas concerning the assessment of intelligence and personality (published in *Race, Intelligence, and Education*, 1971).

Ezekiel /ɪˈziːkɪəl/ a Hebrew prophet of the 6th century BC who prophesied the forthcoming destruction of Jerusalem and the Jewish nation and inspired hope for the future well-being of a restored state.
■ a book of the Bible containing his prophecies.

e-zine ▶ noun a magazine only published in electronic form on a computer network.

Ezra /ˈɛzrə/ a Jewish priest and scribe who played a central part in the reform of Judaism in the 5th or 4th century BC, continuing the work of Nehemiah and forbidding mixed marriages.
■ a book of the Bible telling of Ezra, the return of the Jews from Babylon, and the rebuilding of the Temple.

Ff

F¹ (also **f**) ▶ noun (pl. **Fs** or **F's**) **1** the sixth letter of the alphabet.
■ denoting the next after E in a set of items, categories, etc. ■ the sixth highest or lowest class of academic marks (also used to represent 'Fail'). ■ (**f**) Chess denoting the sixth file from the left, as viewed from White's side of the board.
2 (usu. **F**) Music the fourth note of the diatonic scale of C major.
■ a key based on a scale with F as its keynote.

F² ▶ abbreviation for ■ Fahrenheit: *60°F.* ■ farad(s). ■ Chemistry faraday(s). ■ (in racing results) favourite. ■ female. ■ fighter (in designations of US aircraft types): *the F117 Stealth fighter.* ■ Brit. fine (used in describing grades of pencil lead): *an F pencil.* ■ (in motor racing) formula: *an F1 driver.* ■ Franc(s). ■ France (international vehicle registration). ■ (in tables of sports results) goals or points for.
▶ symbol for ■ the chemical element fluorine. ■ Physics force: *F=ma.*

f ▶ abbreviation for ■ Grammar feminine. ■ [in combination] (in units of measurement) femto- (10^{-15}). ■ (in textual references) folio. ■ Music forte. ■ (in racing results) furlong(s). ■ Chemistry denoting electrons and orbitals possessing three units of angular momentum: *f-orbitals.* [ORIGIN: *f* from *fundamental,* originally applied to lines in atomic spectra.]
▶ symbol for ■ focal length: *apertures of f/5.6 to f/11.* See also **F-NUMBER.** ■ Mathematics a function of a specified variable: *the value of f(x).* ■ Electronics frequency.

F₁ (also **F1**) Biology ▶ abbreviation for the first filial generation, i.e. the generation of hybrids arising from a first cross. The second filial generation is designated **F₂** (or **F2**), and so on.

FA ▶ abbreviation for ■ Fanny Adams (in sense 1): *sweet FA seems to have been done.* ■ (in the UK) Football Association.

fa ▶ noun variant spelling of **FAH.**

FAA ▶ abbreviation for ■ (in the US) Federal Aviation Administration. ■ (in the UK) Fleet Air Arm.

fab¹ ▶ adjective informal fabulous; wonderful.
– DERIVATIVES **fabbo** adjective, **fabby** adjective.
– ORIGIN 1960s: abbreviation.

fab² ▶ noun Electronics a microchip fabrication plant.
■ a particular fabrication process in such a plant.
– ORIGIN late 20th cent.: abbreviation of *fabrication* (see **FABRICATE**).

faba bean /ˈfɑːbə/ ▶ noun variant spelling of **FAVA BEAN.**

Fabergé /ˈfabəʒeɪ/, Peter Carl (1846–1920), Russian goldsmith and jeweller, of French descent. He is famous for the intricate Easter eggs that he made for Tsar Alexander III and other royal households.

Fabian /ˈfeɪbɪən/ ▶ noun a member or supporter of the Fabian Society, an organization of socialists aiming at the gradual rather than revolutionary achievement of socialism.
▶ adjective relating to or characteristic of the Fabians: *the Fabian movement.*
■ employing a cautiously persistent and dilatory strategy to wear out an enemy: *Fabian tactics.*
– DERIVATIVES **Fabianism** noun, **Fabianist** noun.
– ORIGIN late 18th cent.: from the name of *Quintus Fabius Maximus Verrucosus* (see **FABIUS**), after whom the Fabian Society is also named.

Fabius /ˈfeɪbɪəs/ (d.203 BC), Roman general and statesman; full name *Quintus Fabius Maximus Verrucosus;* known as **Fabius Cunctator.** After Hannibal's defeat of the Roman army at Cannae in 216 BC, Fabius successfully pursued a strategy of caution and delay in order to wear down the Carthaginian invaders. This earned him his nickname, which means 'delayer'.

fable /ˈfeɪb(ə)l/ ▶ noun a short story, typically with animals as characters, conveying a moral.
■ a story, typically a supernatural one incorporating elements of myth and legend. ■ [mass noun] myth and legend: *the unnatural monsters of fable.* ■ a false statement or belief.
▶ verb [no obj.] archaic tell fictitious tales: *I do not dream nor fable.*
■ [with obj.] fabricate or invent (an incident, person, or story).
– DERIVATIVES **fabler** noun.
– ORIGIN Middle English: from Old French *fable* (noun), from Latin *fabula* 'story', from *fari* 'speak'.

fabled ▶ adjective [attrib.] well known for being of great quality or rarity; famous: *a fabled art collection.*
■ mythical; imaginary: *the fabled kingdom.*

fabliau /ˈfablɪəʊ/ ▶ noun (pl. **fabliaux** /-əʊz/) a metrical tale, typically a bawdily humorous one, of a type found chiefly in early French poetry.
– ORIGIN from Old French (Picard dialect) *fabliaux,* plural of *fablel* 'short fable', diminutive of *fable.*

Fablon ▶ noun [mass noun] trademark flexible self-adhesive plastic sheeting used for covering table tops and working surfaces.

Fabre /ˈfabrə, French fabʀ/, Jean Henri (1823–1915), French entomologist. Fabre became well known for his meticulous observations of insect behaviour, notably the life cycles of dung beetles, oil beetles, and solitary bees and wasps.

Fabriano, Gentile da, see **GENTILE DA FABRIANO.**

fabric ▶ noun [mass noun] **1** cloth, typically produced by weaving or knitting textile fibres: *heavy cream fabric* | [count noun] *stitch seams on stretch fabrics.*
2 the walls, floor, and roof of a building.
■ the body of a car or aircraft. ■ figurative the essential structure of a society, way of life, or other product of the interaction of different elements: *the fabric of society.*
– ORIGIN late 15th cent.: from French *fabrique,* from Latin *fabrica* 'something skilfully produced', from *faber* 'worker in metal, stone, etc.' The word originally denoted a building, later a machine or appliance, the general sense being 'something made', hence sense 1 (mid 18th cent., originally denoting any manufactured material). Sense 2 dates from the mid 17th cent.

fabricate ▶ verb [with obj.] invent or concoct (something), typically with deceitful intent: *officers fabricated evidence.*
■ construct or manufacture (something, especially an industrial product), especially from prepared components: *you will have to fabricate an exhaust system.*
– DERIVATIVES **fabrication** noun, **fabricator** noun.
– ORIGIN late Middle English: from Latin *fabricat-* 'manufactured', from the verb *fabricare,* from *fabrica* 'something skilfully produced' (see **FABRIC**).

fabric conditioner ▶ noun [mass noun] liquid used to soften clothes when they are being washed.

Fabricius /faˈbrɪʃəs/, Johann Christian (1745–1808), Danish entomologist. Fabricius studied for two years under Linnaeus, and named and described some 10,000 new species of insect.

Fabry–Pérot interferometer /ˌfabrɪˈpɛrəʊ/ ▶ noun an interferometer that incorporates an etalon, used chiefly in astronomy.
– ORIGIN early 20th cent.: named after Charles *Fabry* (1867–1945) and Alfred *Pérot* (1863–1925), French physicists.

fabulate /ˈfabjʊleɪt/ ▶ verb [with obj.] relate (an event or events) as a fable or story.
■ [no obj.] relate untrue or invented stories.
– DERIVATIVES **fabulation** noun, **fabulator** noun.
– ORIGIN early 17th cent.: from Latin *fabulat-* 'narrated as a fable', from the verb *fabulari,* from *fabula* (see **FABLE**).

fabulist ▶ noun a person who composes or relates fables.
■ a liar, especially a person who invents elaborate dishonest stories.
– ORIGIN late 16th cent.: from French *fabuliste,* from Latin *fabula* (see **FABLE**).

fabulous ▶ adjective extraordinary, especially extraordinarily large: *fabulous riches.*
■ informal amazingly good; wonderful: *a fabulous two-week holiday.* ■ having no basis in reality; mythical: *fabulous creatures.*
– DERIVATIVES **fabulosity** noun, **fabulously** adverb, **fabulousness** noun.
– ORIGIN late Middle English (in the sense 'known through fable, unhistorical'): from French *fabuleux* or Latin *fabulosus* 'celebrated in fable', from *fabula* (see **FABLE**).

facade /fəˈsɑːd/ ▶ noun the face of a building, especially the principal front that looks on to a street or open space.
■ figurative an outward appearance that is maintained to conceal a less pleasant or creditable reality: *her flawless public facade masked private despair.*
– ORIGIN mid 17th cent.: from French *façade,* from *face* 'face', on the pattern of Italian *facciata.*

face ▶ noun **1** the front part of a person's head from the forehead to the chin, or the corresponding part in an animal.
■ the face as expressing emotion; an expression shown on the face: *the happy faces of these children.* ■ a manifestation or aspect of something: *the unacceptable face of social drinking.* ■ [with adj.] a person conveying a particular quality or association: *this season's squad has a lot of old faces in it.*
2 the surface of a thing, especially one that is presented to the view or has a particular function, in particular:
■ Geometry each of the surfaces of a solid. ■ a vertical or sloping side of a mountain or cliff: *the north face of the Eiger.* ■ short for **COALFACE.** ■ the side of a planet or moon facing the observer. ■ the front of a building. ■ the plate of a clock or watch bearing the digits or hands. ■ the distinctive side of a playing card. ■ short for **TYPEFACE.** ■ the obverse of a coin.
▶ verb [with obj.] **1** be positioned with the face or front towards (someone or something): *he turned to face her.*
■ [no obj., with adverbial of direction] have the face or front

pointing in a specified direction: *the house faces due east.* ■ [no obj., with adverbial of direction] (of a soldier) turn in a particular direction: *the men had faced about to the front.*
2 confront and deal with or accept: *honesty forced her to **face facts** | [no obj.] we must **face up to** the global impacts of our extravagant lifestyles.*
■ (**face someone/thing down**) overcome someone or something by a show of determination: *he climbed atop a tank to face down a coup.* ■ have (a difficult event or situation) in prospect: *each defendant faced a maximum sentence of 10 years.* ■ (of a problem or difficult situation) present itself to and require action from (someone): *if you were suddenly **faced with** an emergency, would you know how to cope?*
3 (usu. **be faced with**) cover the surface of (a thing) with a layer of a different material: *the external basement walls **were faced with** granite slabs.*
– PHRASES **face down** (or **downwards**) with the face or surface turned towards the ground: *he lay face down on his bed.* **someone's face fits** Brit. someone has the necessary qualities for something: *if your face didn't fit they could get rid of you within twelve months.* **face the music** be confronted with the unpleasant consequences of one's actions. **the face of the earth** used for emphasis or exaggeration, to refer to the existence or disappearance of someone or something: *he's just disappeared **off the face of the earth** | the most gruelling training **on the face of the earth**.* **face up** (or **upwards**) with the face or surface turned upwards to view: *place the panel face up before cutting.* **get out of someone's face** [usu. as imperative] N. Amer. informal stop harassing or annoying someone. **have the face to do something** dated have the effrontery to do something. **in one's face** directly at or against one; as one approaches: *she slammed the door in my face.* **in face** (or **the face**) **of** when confronted with: *her resolution in the face of the enemy.* ■ despite: *reform had been introduced in the face of considerable opposition.* **in your face** see **IN-YOUR-FACE**. **lose face** suffer a loss of respect; be humiliated. **loss of face** a loss of respect; humiliation: *he could step aside now without loss of face.* **make** (or **pull**) **a face** (or **faces**) produce an expression on one's face that shows dislike, disgust, or some other negative emotion, or that is intended to be amusing: *Anna pulled a funny face at the girl.* **off one's face** informal very drunk or under the influence of illegal drugs: *I had a great time going out clubbing and getting off my face.* **on the face of it** without knowing all of the relevant facts; at first glance: *on the face of it, these improvements look to be insignificant.* **put a brave** (or **bold** or **good**) **face on something** act as if something unpleasant or upsetting is not as bad as it really is: *he was putting a brave face on it but she knew he was shattered.* **put one's face on** informal apply make-up to one's face. **save face** retain respect; avoid humiliation. **save someone's face** enable someone to retain respect or avoid humiliation. **set one's face against** oppose or resist with determination: *the Council had set its face against planning consent for a heliport.* **throw something back in someone's face** reject something in a brusque or ungracious manner: *she'd given him her trust and he'd thrown it back in her face.* **to one's face** openly in one's presence: *accusing me to my face of having chickened out.*
– DERIVATIVES **faced** adjective [in combination] *red-faced.*
– ORIGIN Middle English: from Old French, based on Latin *facies* 'form, appearance, face'.
▶ **face off** chiefly N. Amer. take up an attitude of confrontation, especially at the start of a fight or game: *close to a million soldiers face off in the desert.* ■ Ice Hockey start play with a face-off.

faceache ▶ **noun 1** informal an ugly or miserable-looking person.
2 archaic term for **NEURALGIA**.

face card ▶ **noun** chiefly N. Amer. another term for **COURT CARD**.

face-centred ▶ **adjective** denoting a crystal structure in which there is an atom at each vertex and at the centre of each face of the unit cell.

facecloth ▶ **noun** a cloth for washing one's face, typically made of towelling or other absorbent material.
■ [mass noun] smooth-surfaced woollen cloth.

face cream ▶ **noun** [mass noun] cosmetic cream applied to the face to improve the complexion.

face flannel ▶ **noun** Brit. a facecloth.

faceless ▶ **adjective** (of a person) remote and impersonal; anonymous: *the faceless bureaucrats who made the rules.*
■ (of a building or place) characterless and dull.
– DERIVATIVES **facelessness** noun.

facelift ▶ **noun** a cosmetic surgical operation to remove unwanted wrinkles by tightening the skin of the face.
■ figurative a procedure carried out to improve the appearance of something: *the station has undergone a multimillion pound facelift.*

face mask ▶ **noun** a protective mask covering the nose and mouth or nose and eyes.
■ another term for **FACE PACK**.

face-off ▶ **noun** chiefly N. Amer. a direct confrontation between two people or groups: *a face-off for the championship title.*
■ Ice Hockey the start of play, in which the puck is dropped by the referee between two opposing players.

face pack ▶ **noun** chiefly Brit. a cosmetic preparation spread over the face and left for some time to cleanse and improve the skin.

face paint ▶ **noun** [mass noun] bold-coloured paint used to decorate the face.
– DERIVATIVES **face-painter** noun, **face-painting** noun.

faceplate ▶ **noun 1** an enlarged end or attachment on the end of the mandrel on a lathe, with slots and holes on which work can be mounted.
■ a plate protecting a piece of machinery. ■ the part of a cathode ray tube that carries the phosphor screen.
2 the transparent window of a diver's or astronaut's helmet.

face powder ▶ **noun** [mass noun] flesh-tinted cosmetic powder used to improve the appearance of the face by reducing shine and concealing blemishes.

facer ▶ **noun** informal, chiefly Brit. a blow to the face.
■ a sudden difficulty or obstacle.

face-saving ▶ **noun** [mass noun] the preserving of one's reputation, credibility, or dignity.
– DERIVATIVES **face-saver** noun.

facet /ˈfasɪt, -ɛt/ ▶ **noun** one side of something many-sided, especially of a cut gem.
■ a particular aspect or feature of something: *different viewpoints manifesting different facets of the truth.* ■ Zoology any of the individual units (ommatidia) that make up the compound eye of an insect or crustacean.
– DERIVATIVES **faceted** adjective [in combination] *multifaceted.*
– ORIGIN early 17th cent.: from French *facette*, diminutive of *face* 'face, side' (see **FACE**).

facetiae /fəˈsiːʃɪiː/ ▶ **plural noun 1** dated pornographic literature.
2 archaic humorous or witty sayings.
– ORIGIN early 16th cent.: from Latin, plural of *facetia* 'jest', from *facetus* 'witty'.

face time ▶ **noun** [mass noun] N. Amer. informal time spent in face-to-face contact with someone, especially one's employer.
■ time spent being filmed or photographed by the media.

facetious /fəˈsiːʃəs/ ▶ **adjective** treating serious issues with deliberately inappropriate humour; flippant.
– DERIVATIVES **facetiously** adverb, **facetiousness** noun.
– ORIGIN late 16th cent. (in the general sense 'witty, amusing'): from French *facétieux*, from *facétie*, from Latin *facetia* 'jest', from *facetus* 'witty'.

face-to-face ▶ **adjective** & **adverb** with the people involved being close together and looking directly at each other: [as adj.] *a face-to-face conversation* | [as adv.] *the two men stood face-to-face.*
■ [as adv.] in direct confrontation: ***coming face to face with** a burglar.*

face validity ▶ **noun** [mass noun] the degree to which a procedure, especially a psychological test or assessment, appears effective in terms of its stated aims.

face value ▶ **noun** the value printed or depicted on a coin, banknote, postage stamp, ticket, etc., especially when less than the actual or intrinsic value.
■ figurative the superficial appearance or implication of something: *she felt the lie was unconvincing, but he seemed to **take it at face value**.*

faceworker ▶ **noun** a miner who works at the coalface.

facia ▶ **noun** chiefly Brit. variant spelling of **FASCIA** (in sense 1).

facial /ˈfeɪʃ(ə)l/ ▶ **adjective** of or affecting the face: *facial expressions.*
▶ **noun** a beauty treatment for the face.
– DERIVATIVES **facially** adverb.
– ORIGIN early 17th cent. (as a theological term meaning 'face to face, open'): from medieval Latin *facialis*, from *facies* (see **FACE**). The current sense of the adjective dates from the early 19th cent.

facial nerve ▶ **noun** Anatomy each of the seventh pair of cranial nerves, supplying the facial muscles and the tongue.

-facient ▶ **combining form** producing a specified action or state: *abortifacient.*
– ORIGIN from Latin *facient-* 'doing, making'.

facies /ˈfeɪʃɪiːz/ ▶ **noun** (pl. same) **1** Medicine the appearance or facial expression of an individual that is typical of a particular disease or condition.
2 Geology the character of a rock expressed by its formation, composition, and fossil content.
– ORIGIN early 17th cent. (denoting the face): from Latin, 'form, appearance, face'.

facile /ˈfasʌɪl, -sɪl/ ▶ **adjective 1** (especially of a theory or argument) appearing neat and comprehensive only by ignoring the true complexities of an issue; superficial.
■ (of a person) having a superficial or simplistic knowledge or approach: *a man of facile and shallow intellect.*
2 (of success, especially in sport) easily achieved; effortless: *a facile seven lengths victory.*
– DERIVATIVES **facilely** adverb, **facileness** noun.
– ORIGIN late 15th cent. (in the sense 'easily accomplished'): from French, or from Latin *facilis* 'easy', from *facere* 'do, make'.

facilitate /fəˈsɪlɪteɪt/ ▶ **verb** [with obj.] make (an action or process) easy or easier: *schools were located in the same campus to facilitate the sharing of resources.*
– DERIVATIVES **facilitative** adjective, **facilitator** noun, **facilitatory** adjective.
– ORIGIN early 17th cent.: from French *faciliter*, from Italian *facilitare*, from *facile* 'easy', from Latin *facilis* (see **FACILE**).

facilitation ▶ **noun** [mass noun] the action of facilitating something.
■ Physiology the enhancement of the response of a neuron to a stimulus following prior stimulation.

facility ▶ **noun** (pl. **-ies**) **1** space or equipment necessary for doing something: *cooking facilities | facilities for picnicking and car parking.*
■ a service offered by an organization, or a feature of a piece of equipment, which gives the opportunity to do or benefit from something: *an overdraft facility.* ■ an amenity or resource, especially one connected with leisure or hygiene: *facilities include two swimming pools.* ■ an establishment set up to fulfil a particular function or provide a particular service, typically an industrial or medical one: *a manufacturing facility.*
2 [usu. in sing.] an ability to do or learn something well and easily; a natural aptitude: *he had **a facility for** languages.*
■ [mass noun] absence of difficulty or effort: *the pianist played with great facility.*
– ORIGIN early 16th cent. (denoting the means or unimpeded opportunity for doing something): from French *facilité* or Latin *facilitas*, from *facilis* 'easy' (see **FACILE**).

facing ▶ **noun 1** a layer of material covering part of a garment for contrast, decoration, or strength.
■ (**facings**) the cuffs, collar, and lapels of a military jacket, contrasting in colour with the rest of the garment.
2 an outer layer covering the surface of a wall.
▶ **adjective** [attrib.] positioned with the front towards a certain direction; opposite: *view one full page or two facing pages* | [in combination] *a south-facing garden.*

facsimile /fakˈsɪmɪli/ ▶ **noun** an exact copy, especially of written or printed material.
■ another term for **FAX**[1].
▶ **verb** (**facsimiled**, **facsimileing**) [with obj.] make a copy of: *the ride was facsimiled for another theme park.*
– PHRASES **in facsimile** as an exact copy.
– ORIGIN late 16th cent. (originally as *fac simile*, denoting the making of an exact copy, especially of writing): modern Latin, from Latin *fac!* (imperative of *facere* 'make') and *simile* (neuter of *similis* 'like').

fact ▶ **noun** a thing that is indisputably the case: *she*

lacks political experience—a fact that becomes clear when she appears in public | [mass noun] *a body of fact.*
■ (**the fact that**) used in discussing the significance of something that is the case: *the real problem facing them is the fact that their funds are being cut.* ■ (usu. **facts**) a piece of information used as evidence or as part of a report or news article. ■ [mass noun] chiefly Law the truth about events as opposed to interpretation: *there was a question of fact as to whether they had received the letter.*
– PHRASES **before** (or **after**) **the fact** before (or after) the committing of a crime: *an accessory before the fact.* **a fact of life** something that must be accepted as true and unchanging, even if it is unpleasant: *it is a fact of life that young girls write horrible things about people in their diaries.* **facts and figures** precise details. **the facts of life** information about sexual functions and practices, especially as given to children. **the fact of the matter** the truth. **in** (**point of**) **fact** used to emphasize the truth of an assertion, especially one contrary to what might be expected or what has been asserted: *the subjects appear off-guard, but the photographer has in fact got them to pose.*
– ORIGIN late 15th cent.: from Latin *factum*, neuter past participle of *facere* 'do'. The original sense was 'an act or feat', later 'bad deed, a crime', surviving in the phrase *before (or after) the fact*. The earliest of the current senses ('truth, reality') dates from the late 16th cent.

fact-finding ▶ **adjective** [attrib.] (especially of a committee or its activity) having the purpose of discovering and establishing the facts of an issue: *a fact-finding mission.*
▶ **noun** [mass noun] the discovery and establishment of the facts of an issue.
– DERIVATIVES **factfinder** noun.

facticity /fak'tɪsɪti/ ▶ **noun** [mass noun] the quality or condition of being fact: *the facticity of death.*

faction[1] ▶ **noun** a small organized dissentient group within a larger one, especially in politics: *the left-wing faction of the party.*
■ [mass noun] a state of dissension within an organization.
– ORIGIN late 15th cent. (denoting the action of doing or making something): via French from Latin *factio(n-)*, from *facere* 'do, make'.

faction[2] ▶ **noun** [mass noun] a literary and cinematic genre in which real events are used as a basis for a fictional narrative or dramatization.
– ORIGIN 1960s: blend of **FACT** and **FICTION**.

-faction ▶ **combining form** in nouns of action derived from verbs ending in *-fy* (such as *torrefaction* from *torrefy*).
– ORIGIN from Latin *factio(n)-*, from *facere* 'do, make'.

factional ▶ **adjective** relating or belonging to a faction: *factional leaders.*
■ characterized by dissent: *factional conflicts.*
– DERIVATIVES **factionalism** noun, **factionally** adverb.

factionalize (also **-ise**) ▶ **verb** [no obj.] (especially of a political party or other organized group) split or divide into factions: *there was a tendency for students to factionalize.*

factious /'fakʃəs/ ▶ **adjective** relating or inclined to dissension: *a factious country.*
– DERIVATIVES **factiously** adverb, **factiousness** noun.
– ORIGIN mid 16th cent.: from French *factieux* or Latin *factiosus*, from *factio* (see **FACTION**[1]).

factitious /fak'tɪʃəs/ ▶ **adjective** artificially created or developed: *a largely factitious national identity.*
– DERIVATIVES **factitiously** adverb, **factitiousness** noun.
– ORIGIN mid 17th cent. (in the general sense 'made by human skill or effort'): from Latin *facticius* 'made by art', from *facere* 'do, make'.

factitive /'faktɪtɪv/ ▶ **adjective** Linguistics (of a verb) having a sense of causing a result and taking a complement as well as an object, as in *he appointed me captain.*
– ORIGIN mid 19th cent.: from modern Latin *factitivus*, formed irregularly from Latin *factitare*, frequentative of *facere* 'do, make'.

factive ▶ **adjective** Linguistics denoting a verb that assigns the status of an established fact to its object (normally a clausal object), e.g. *know, regret, resent.* Contrasted with **CONTRAFACTIVE**, **NON-FACTIVE**.

factoid ▶ **noun** an assumption or speculation that is reported and repeated so often that it becomes accepted as fact.
■ N. Amer. a brief or trivial item of news or information.
▶ **adjective** containing a mixture of fact and fiction or supposition presented as fact: *a historical factoid novel.*

factor ▶ **noun 1** a circumstance, fact, or influence that contributes to a result or outcome: *his skill was a factor in ensuring that so much was achieved* | *she worked fast, conscious of the time factor.*
■ Biology a gene that determines a hereditary characteristic: *the Rhesus factor.*
2 a number or quantity that when multiplied with another produces a given number or expression.
■ Mathematics a number or algebraic expression by which another is exactly divisible.
3 Physiology any of a number of substances in the blood, mostly identified by numerals, which are involved in coagulation. See **FACTOR VIII**.
4 a business agent; a merchant buying and selling on commission.
■ a company that buys a manufacturer's invoices at a discount and takes responsibility for collecting the payments due on them. ■ chiefly Scottish a land agent or steward. ■ archaic an agent, deputy, or representative.
▶ **verb** [with obj.] **1** Mathematics another term for **FACTORIZE**.
2 sell (one's receivable debts) to a factor.
– PHRASES **the —— factor** used to indicate that something specified will have a powerful, though unpredictable, influence on a result or outcome: *the feel-good factor.*
– DERIVATIVES **factorable** adjective.
– ORIGIN late Middle English (meaning 'doer, perpetrator', also in the Scots sense 'agent'): from French *facteur* or Latin *factor*, from *fact-* 'done', from the verb *facere*.
▶ **factor something in** (or **out**) include (or exclude) something as a relevant element when making a calculation or decision: *when the psychological costs are factored in, a different picture will emerge.*

factor VIII (also **factor eight**) ▶ **noun** [mass noun] Physiology a blood protein (a beta globulin) involved in clotting. A deficiency of this causes one of the main forms of haemophilia.

factorage ▶ **noun** [mass noun] the commission or charges payable to a factor.

factor analysis ▶ **noun** [mass noun] Statistics a process in which the values of observed data are expressed as functions of a number of possible causes in order to find which are the most important.

factor cost ▶ **noun** the cost of an item of goods or a service in terms of the various factors which have played a part in its production or availability, and exclusive of tax costs.

factorial ▶ **noun** Mathematics the product of an integer and all the integers below it; e.g. factorial four (4!) is equal to 24. (Symbol: **!**)
■ the product of a series of factors in an arithmetical progression.
▶ **adjective** chiefly Mathematics relating to a factor or such a product: *a factorial design.*
– DERIVATIVES **factorially** adverb.

factorize (also **-ise**) ▶ **verb** [with obj.] Mathematics express (a number or expression) as a product of factors.
■ [no obj.] (of a number) be capable of resolution into factors: *f factorizes completely into linear factors.*
– DERIVATIVES **factorization** noun.

factory ▶ **noun** (pl. **-ies**) **1** a building or group of buildings where goods are manufactured or assembled chiefly by machine.
■ [with modifier] figurative a person, group, or institution that produces a great quantity of something on a regular basis or in a short space of time: *the group have become a rock-and-roll hit factory.*
2 historical an establishment for traders carrying on business in a foreign country.
– ORIGIN late 16th cent. (in sense 2): via Portuguese *feitoria*; sense 1 based on late Latin *factorium*, literally 'oil press'.

Factory Acts (in the UK) a series of laws regulating the operation of factories, designed to improve the working conditions of employees, especially women and children.

factory farming ▶ **noun** [mass noun] a system of rearing livestock using highly intensive methods, by which poultry, pigs, or cattle are confined indoors under strictly controlled conditions.
– DERIVATIVES **factory farm** noun.

factory floor ▶ **noun** the workers in a company or industry, rather than the management: *the unions had almost no influence on the factory floor.*

factory ship ▶ **noun** a fishing or whaling ship, or a ship accompanying a fishing or whaling fleet, with facilities for immediate processing of the catch.

factory shop (chiefly N. Amer. also **factory outlet**) ▶ **noun** a shop in which goods, especially surplus stock, are sold directly by the manufacturers at a discount.

factotum /fak'təʊtəm/ ▶ **noun** (pl. **factotums**) an employee who does all kinds of work: *he was employed as the general factotum.*
– ORIGIN mid 16th cent. (originally in the phrases *dominum* (or *magister*) *factotum*, translating roughly as 'master of everything', and *Johannes factotem* 'John do-it-all' or 'Jack of all trades'): from medieval Latin, from Latin *fac!* 'do!' (imperative of *facere*) + *totum* 'the whole thing' (neuter of *totus*).

fact sheet ▶ **noun** a paper giving useful information about a particular issue, especially one discussed on a television or radio programme.

factual /'faktʃʊəl, -tjʊəl/ ▶ **adjective** concerned with what is actually the case rather than interpretations of or reactions to it: *a mixture of comment and factual information.*
■ actually occurring: *cases mentioned are factual.*
– DERIVATIVES **factuality** noun, **factually** adverb, **factualness** noun.
– ORIGIN mid 19th cent.: from **FACT**, on the pattern of *actual*.

factum /'faktəm/ ▶ **noun** (pl. **factums** or **facta**) Law, chiefly Canadian a statement of the facts of a case.
– ORIGIN late 18th cent.: from Latin, literally 'something done or made'.

facture /'faktʃə/ ▶ **noun** [mass noun] the quality of the execution of a painting; an artist's characteristic handling of the paint: *Manet's sensuous facture.*
– ORIGIN late Middle English (in the general sense 'construction, workmanship'): via Old French from Latin *factura* 'formation, manufacture', from *facere* 'do, make'. The current sense dates from the late 19th cent.

facula /'fakjʊlə/ ▶ **noun** (pl. **faculae** /-liː/) Astronomy a bright region on the surface of the sun, linked to the subsequent appearance of sunspots in the same area.
■ a bright spot on the surface of a planet.
– DERIVATIVES **facular** adjective.
– ORIGIN early 18th cent.: from Latin, diminutive of *fax, fac-* 'torch'.

facultative /'fak(ə)lˌtətɪv/ ▶ **adjective** occurring optionally in response to circumstances rather than by nature.
■ Biology capable of but not restricted to a particular function or mode of life: *a facultative parasite.* Often contrasted with **OBLIGATE**.
– DERIVATIVES **facultatively** adverb.
– ORIGIN early 19th cent.: from French *facultatif, -ive*, from *faculté* (see **FACULTY**).

faculty ▶ **noun** (pl. **-ies**) **1** an inherent mental or physical power: *her critical faculties.*
■ an aptitude or talent for doing something: *he had the faculty of meeting everyone on the level.*
2 chiefly Brit. a group of university departments concerned with a major division of knowledge: *the Faculty of Arts* | *the law faculty.*
■ [in sing.] the teaching or research staff of such a group of departments, or (N. Amer.) of a university or college, viewed as a body. ■ dated the members of a particular profession, especially medicine, considered collectively.
3 a licence or authorization, especially from a Church authority.
– ORIGIN late Middle English: from Old French *faculte*, from Latin *facultas*, from *facilis* 'easy', from *facere* 'make, do'.

Faculty of Advocates (in the UK) the society constituting the Scottish Bar.

FA Cup the major annual knockout competition for soccer clubs in England, first held in 1872.

FAD Biochemistry ▶ **abbreviation** for flavin adenine dinucleotide, a coenzyme derived from riboflavin and important in various metabolic reactions.

fad ▶ **noun** an intense and widely shared enthusiasm for something, especially one that is short-lived and without basis in the object's qualities; a craze: *the current fad in Hollywood is for TV remakes.*
■ an over-particular insistence on something: *his fads about the type of coffee he must have.*
– DERIVATIVES **faddish** adjective, **faddishly** adverb, **faddishness** noun, **faddism** noun, **faddist** noun.

– ORIGIN mid 19th cent. (originally dialect): probably the second element of *fidfad*, contraction of **FIDDLE-FADDLE**. Compare with **FADDY**.

faddy ▶ **adjective** (**faddier**, **faddiest**) Brit. having many arbitrary and often unusual likes and dislikes about food: *faddy eating*.
– DERIVATIVES **faddily** adverb, **faddiness** noun.

fade ▶ **verb** [no obj.] **1** gradually grow faint and disappear: *the noise **faded away*** | figurative *hopes of peace had faded*.
■ lose or cause to lose colour or brightness: [no obj.] *the fair hair had faded to a dusty grey* | [with obj.] [usu. as adj. **faded**] *faded jeans*. ■ (of a flower) lose freshness and wither. ■ (**fade away**) gradually become thin and weak, especially to the point of death: *fading away in a hospital bed*. ■ (of a racehorse, runner, etc.) lose strength or drop back, especially after a promising start: *she faded near the finish*. ■ (of a radio signal) gradually lose intensity: *the signal faded away*. ■ (of a vehicle brake) become temporarily less efficient as a result of frictional heating.
2 [with adverbial] (with reference to film and television images) come or cause to come gradually into or out of view, or to merge into another shot: [no obj.] *fade into scenes of rooms strewn with festive remains* | [with obj.] *some shots have to be faded in*.
■ (with reference to recorded sound) increase or decrease in volume or merge into another recording: [no obj.] *they let you edit the digital data, making it fade in and out* | [with obj.] *fade up natural sound*.
3 Golf (of the ball) deviate to the right (or, for a left-handed golfer, the left), typically as a result of spin given to the ball.
■ [with obj.] (of a golfer) cause (the ball) to move in such a way: *he had to fade the ball around a light pole*. Compare with **DRAW**.
4 [with obj.] N. Amer. informal (in craps) match the bet of (another player): *Lovejoy faded him for twenty-five cents*.
▶ **noun 1** [mass noun] the process of becoming less bright: *the sun can cause colour fade*.
■ [count noun] an act of causing a film or television picture to darken and disappear gradually: *a fade to black would bring the sequence to a close*. Compare with **FADE-OUT**.
2 Golf a shot causing the ball to deviate to the right (or, for a left-handed golfer, the left), usually purposely.
– PHRASES **do a fade** informal run away.
– DERIVATIVES **fadeless** adjective.
– ORIGIN Middle English (in the sense 'grow weak, waste away'; compare with *fade away*): from Old French *fader*, from *fade* 'dull, insipid', probably based on a blend of Latin *fatuus* 'silly, insipid' and *vapidus* 'vapid'.

fade-in ▶ **noun** a film-making and broadcasting technique whereby an image is made to appear gradually or the volume of sound is gradually increased from zero.

fade-out ▶ **noun** a film-making and broadcasting technique whereby an image is made to disappear gradually or the sound volume is gradually decreased to zero.
■ a gradual and temporary loss of a broadcast signal: *radio fade-outs*.

fader ▶ **noun** a device for varying the volume of sound, the intensity of light, or the gain on a video or audio signal.

fade-up ▶ **noun** an instance of increasing the brightness of an image or the volume of a sound.

fadge /fadʒ/ ▶ **noun** Austral./NZ an unpressed pack of wool containing less than a bale.
– ORIGIN late 16th cent. (originally English dialect): of unknown origin.

fado /ˈfɑːdəʊ/ ▶ **noun** (pl. **-os**) a type of popular Portuguese song, usually with a melancholy theme and accompanied by mandolins or guitars.
■ [mass noun] the music for such a song.
– ORIGIN Portuguese, literally 'fate'.

faeces /ˈfiːsiːz/ (US **feces**) ▶ **plural noun** waste matter remaining after food has been digested, discharged from the bowels; excrement.
– DERIVATIVES **faecal** /ˈfiːk(ə)l/ adjective.
– ORIGIN late Middle English: from Latin, plural of *faex* 'dregs'.

Faenza /fɑːˈɛntsə/ a town in Emilia-Romagna in northern Italy; pop. 54,050 (1990). The town gave its name to the type of pottery known as faience.

faerie /ˈfeɪəri, ˈfɛːri/ (also **faery**) ▶ **noun** [mass noun] archaic or poetic/literary fairyland: *the world of faerie*.
■ [count noun] a fairy. ■ [as modifier] imaginary; mythical: *faerie dragons*.
– ORIGIN late 16th cent. (introduced by Spenser): pseudo-archaic variant of **FAIRY**.

Faeroe Islands (also **the Faeroes**) variant spelling of **FAROE ISLANDS**.

Faeroese ▶ **adjective** & **noun** variant spelling of **FAROESE**.

faff ▶ **verb** [no obj.] Brit. informal bustle ineffectually: *we can't **faff around** forever*.
▶ **noun** [in sing.] a great deal of ineffectual activity: *there was the usual faff of getting back to the plane*.
– ORIGIN late 18th cent. (originally dialect in the sense 'blow in puffs or small gusts', describing the wind): imitative. The current sense may have been influenced by dialect *faffle* 'stammer, stutter', later 'flap in the wind', which came to mean 'fuss, dither' at about the same time as *faff* (late 19th cent.).

fag[1] ▶ **noun** [in sing.] informal, chiefly Brit. a tiring or unwelcome task: *it's too much of a fag to drive all the way there and back again*.
■ Brit. a junior pupil at a public school who works and runs errands for a senior pupil.
▶ **verb** (**fagged**, **fagging**) [no obj.] Brit. informal work hard, especially at a tedious job or task: *he didn't have to **fag away** in a lab to get the right answer*.
■ Brit. (of a public-school pupil) work and run errands for a senior pupil: *the lower boys in each house **fagged for** members of the Library*.
– ORIGIN mid 16th cent. (as a verb in the sense 'grow weary'): of unknown origin. Compare with **FLAG**[4].

fag[2] ▶ **noun** N. Amer. offensive a male homosexual.
– DERIVATIVES **faggy** adjective.
– ORIGIN 1920s: short for **FAGGOT** (in sense 3).

fag[3] ▶ **noun** Brit. informal a cigarette.
– ORIGIN late 19th cent.: elliptically from **FAG END**.

fag end ▶ **noun** informal, chiefly Brit. a cigarette end.
■ an inferior and useless remnant of something: *the fag ends of cereal packets*.
– ORIGIN early 17th cent. (in the sense 'remnant'): from 15th-cent. *fag* 'a flap', of unknown origin. The current sense dates from the early 20th cent.

fagged ▶ **adjective** [predic.] extremely tired; exhausted: *we were all absolutely **fagged out***.

faggot /ˈfaɡət/ ▶ **noun 1** (usu. **faggots**) Brit. a ball or roll of seasoned chopped liver, baked or fried.
2 (US **fagot**) a bundle of sticks or twigs bound together as fuel.
■ a bundle of iron rods bound together for reheating, welding, and hammering into bars.
3 informal, offensive, chiefly N. Amer. a male homosexual.
4 Brit. dated, offensive an unpleasant or contemptible woman.
▶ **verb** (**faggoted**, **faggoting**; US **fagoted**, **fagoting**) [with obj.] archaic bind in or make into faggots.
■ (in embroidery) join by faggoting.
– DERIVATIVES **faggoty** adjective.
– ORIGIN Middle English (in the sense 'bundle of sticks for fuel'): from Old French *fagot*, from Italian *fagotto*, based on Greek *phakelos* 'bundle'.

faggoting (US **fagoting**) ▶ **noun** [mass noun] embroidery in which threads are fastened together in bundles: *a black silk dress with tiers of faggoting*.
■ archaic the joining of materials in such a way.

fag hag ▶ **noun** derogatory, chiefly US a heterosexual woman who spends much of her time with homosexual men.

fah (also **fa**) ▶ **noun** Music (in tonic sol-fa) the fourth note of a major scale.
■ the note F in the fixed-doh system.
– ORIGIN Middle English: representing (as an arbitrary name for the note) the first syllable of *famuli*, taken from a Latin hymn (see **SOLMIZATION**).

fahlerz /ˈfɑːlɛːts/ ▶ **noun** [mass noun] a grey crystalline copper-containing mineral, of which tetrahedrite and tennantite are the typical forms.
– ORIGIN late 18th cent.: from German, from *fahl* 'ash-coloured' + *Erz* 'ore'.

Fahr. ▶ **abbreviation for** Fahrenheit.

Fahrenheit /ˈfar(ə)nhʌɪt, ˈfɑː-/ (abbrev.: **F**) ▶ **adjective** [postpositive when used with a numeral] of or denoting a scale of temperature on which water freezes at 32° and boils at 212° under standard conditions.
▶ **noun** (also **Fahrenheit scale**) this scale of temperature.
– ORIGIN mid 18th cent.: named after Gabriel Daniel *Fahrenheit* (1686–1736), German physicist.

faience /fʌɪˈɒs, feɪ-, -ˈɑːns/ ▶ **noun** [mass noun] glazed ceramic ware, in particular decorated tin-glazed earthenware of the type which includes delftware and maiolica.
– ORIGIN late 17th cent. (originally denoting pottery made at Faenza): from French *faïence*, from *Faïence*, the French name for **FAENZA**.

fail ▶ **verb** [no obj.] **1** be unsuccessful in achieving one's goal: *he **failed in** his attempt to secure election* | [with infinitive] *they failed to be ranked in the top ten*.
■ [with obj.] be unsuccessful in (an examination, test, or interview): *she failed her finals*. ■ [with obj.] (of a person or a commodity) be unable to meet the standards set by (a test of quality or eligibility): *a player has failed a drugs test*. ■ [with obj.] judge (a candidate, especially in an examination) not to have passed.
2 neglect to do something: [with infinitive] *the firm failed to give adequate risk warnings*.
■ [with infinitive] behave in a way contrary to hopes or expectations by not doing something: *commuter chaos has again failed to materialize*. ■ (**cannot fail to be/do something**) used to express a strong belief that something must be the case: *she cannot have failed to be aware of the situation*. ■ (**never fail to do something**) used to indicate that something invariably happens: *such comments never failed to annoy him*. ■ [with obj.] desert or let down (someone): *at the last moment her nerve failed her*.
3 break down; cease to work well: *a lorry whose brakes had failed*.
■ become weaker or of poorer quality; die away: *the light began to fail* | [as adj. **failing**] *his failing health*. ■ (especially of a rain or a crop or supply) be lacking or insufficient when needed or expected. ■ (of a business or a person) be obliged to cease trading because of lack of funds; become bankrupt.
▶ **noun** a mark which is not high enough to pass an examination or test.
– PHRASES **without fail** absolutely predictably; with no exception: *he writes every week without fail*.
– ORIGIN Middle English: from Old French *faillir* (verb), *faille* (noun), based on Latin *fallere* 'deceive'. An earlier sense of the noun was 'failure to do or perform a duty', surviving in the phrase *without fail*.

failed ▶ **adjective** [attrib.] **1** (of an undertaking or a relationship) not achieving its end or not lasting; unsuccessful: *a failed coup attempt*.
■ (of a person) unsuccessful in a particular activity, especially not good enough to make a living by it: *a failed writer*. ■ (of a business) unable to continue owing to financial difficulties.
2 (of a mechanism) not functioning properly; broken-down: *an aircraft with a failed engine*.

failing ▶ **noun** a weakness, especially in character; a shortcoming: *pride is a terrible failing*.
▶ **preposition** in default of; in the absence of: *she longed to be with him and, **failing that**, to be on her own*.

faille /feɪl/ ▶ **noun** [mass noun] a soft, light-woven fabric having a ribbed texture, originally of silk.
– ORIGIN mid 16th cent. (denoting a kind of hood or veil worn by women): from Old French. The current sense dates from the mid 19th cent.

fail-safe ▶ **adjective** causing a piece of machinery to revert to a safe condition in the event of a breakdown or malfunction: *a forklift truck with a fail-safe device*.
■ unlikely or unable to fail: *the computer that runs the place is supposed to be fail-safe*.
▶ **noun** [usu. in sing.] a system or plan that comes into operation in the event of something going wrong or that is there to prevent such an occurrence: *stewards positioned around the track as a fail-safe*.

failure ▶ **noun** [mass noun] **1** lack of success: *an economic policy that is doomed to failure* | [count noun] *the failures of his policies*.
■ [count noun] an unsuccessful person, enterprise, or thing: *bad weather had resulted in crop failures*.
2 the omission of expected or required action: *their failure to comply with the basic rules*.
■ [count noun] a lack or deficiency of a desirable quality: *a failure of imagination*.
3 the action or state of not functioning: *symptoms of heart failure* | [count noun] *a chance engine failure*.
■ [count noun] a sudden cessation of power. ■ [count noun] the collapse of a business.
– ORIGIN mid 17th cent. (originally as *failer*, in the senses 'non-occurrence' and 'cessation of supply'): from Anglo-Norman French *failer* for Old French *faillir* (see **FAIL**).

fain archaic ▶ **adjective** pleased or willing under the circumstances: *the traveller was **fain to** proceed*.
■ compelled by the circumstances; obliged: *he was fain to acknowledge that the agreement was sacrosanct*.

▶**adverb** with pleasure; gladly: *I am weary and would fain get a little rest.*

– ORIGIN Old English *fægen* 'happy, well pleased', of Germanic origin, from a base meaning 'rejoice'; related to **FAWN**².

fainéant /ˈfeɪneɪɒ̃/ ▶**noun** archaic an idle or ineffective person.

– ORIGIN early 17th cent.: from French, from *fait* 'does' + *néant* 'nothing'.

faint ▶**adjective 1** (of a sight, smell, or sound) barely perceptible: *the faint murmur of voices.*
■(of a hope, chance, or possibility) slight; remote: *there is a faint chance that the enemy may flee.*
2 [predic.] weak and dizzy; close to losing consciousness: *the heat made him feel faint.*
■appearing feeble or lacking in strength: *the faint beat of a butterfly's wing.*
▶**verb** [no obj.] lose consciousness for a short time because of a temporarily insufficient supply of oxygen to the brain.
■archaic grow weak or feeble; decline: *the fires were fainting there.*
▶**noun** [in sing.] a sudden loss of consciousness: *she hit the floor in a dead faint.*

– PHRASES **not have the faintest** informal have no idea: *I haven't the faintest what it means.*

– DERIVATIVES **faintly** adverb [as submodifier] *his faintly ridiculous air*, **faintness** noun.

– ORIGIN Middle English (in sense 2; also in the sense 'cowardly', surviving in **FAINT HEART**): from Old French *faint*, past participle of *faindre* (see **FEIGN**). Compare with **FEINT**¹.

faint heart ▶**noun** a person who has a timid or reserved nature.

– PHRASES **faint heart never won fair lady** proverb timidity will prevent you from achieving your objective.

faint-hearted ▶**adjective** lacking courage; timid: *they were feeling faint-hearted at the prospect of war* | [as plural noun **the faint-hearted**] *litigation is not for the faint-hearted.*

– DERIVATIVES **faint-heartedly** adverb, **faint-heartedness** noun.

fair¹ ▶**adjective 1** treating people equally without favouritism or discrimination: *the group has achieved fair and equal representation for all its members.*
■just or appropriate in the circumstances: *to be fair, this subject poses special problems.* ■ archaic (of a means or procedure) gentle; not violent.
2 (of hair or complexion) light; blonde.
■(of a person) having such a complexion or hair.
3 considerable though not outstanding in size or amount: *he did a fair bit of coaching.*
■reasonably good though not outstandingly so: *he believes he has a fair chance of success.* ■ Austral./NZ informal complete; utter: *this cow is a fair swine.*
4 (of weather) fine and dry.
■(of the wind) favourable: *they set sail with a fair wind.*
5 archaic beautiful: attractive: *the fairest of her daughters.*
■(of words, a speech, or a promise) specious despite being initially attractive or pleasing.
▶**adverb 1** without cheating or trying to achieve unjust advantage: *no one could say he played fair.*
2 [as submodifier] dialect to a high degree: *she'll be fair delighted to see you.*
▶**noun** archaic a beautiful woman.
▶**verb** [no obj.] dialect (of the weather) become fine: *looks like it's fairing off some.*

– PHRASES **all's fair in love and war** proverb in certain highly charged situations, any method of achieving your objective is justifiable. **by fair means or foul** using whatever means are necessary: *they were determined to ensure victory for themselves, by fair means or foul.* **fair and square 1** with absolute accuracy: *he got you fair and square in his gun sight.* **2** honestly and straightforwardly: *we won the match fair and square.* **a fair deal** equitable treatment. **fair dinkum** see **DINKUM**. **fair dos** Brit. informal used to request just treatment or accept that it has been given: *Fair dos—you don't believe I've been idle all this time?* **fair enough** informal used to admit that something is reasonable or acceptable: *'I can't come because I'm working late.' 'Fair enough.'* **fair name** dated a good reputation. **the fair sex** (also **the fairer sex**) dated or humorous women. **fair's fair** informal used to request just treatment or assert that an arrangement is just: *Fair's fair—we were here first.* **for fair** US informal completely and finally: *I hope we'll be rid of him for fair.* **in a fair way to do something** having nearly done something, and likely to achieve it: *you are in*

a fair way to have cured yourself. **it's a fair cop** an admission that the speaker has been caught doing wrong and deserves punishment. **no fair** N. Amer. informal unfair (often used in or as a petulant protestation): *no fair—we're the only kids in the whole school who don't get to watch TV on school nights.* **be set fair** Brit. (of the weather) be fine and likely to stay fine for a time.

– DERIVATIVES **fairish** adjective, **fairness** noun.

– ORIGIN Old English *fæger* 'pleasing, attractive', of Germanic origin; related to Old High German *fagar*.

fair² ▶**noun** a gathering of stalls and amusements for public entertainment.
■a periodic gathering for the sale of goods. ■an exhibition, especially to promote particular products: *the European Fine Art Fair.*

– ORIGIN Middle English (in the sense 'periodic gathering for the sale of goods'): from Old French *feire*, from late Latin *feria*, singular of Latin *feriae* 'holy days' (on which such fairs were often held).

fair³ ▶**verb** [with obj.] [usu. as adj. **faired**] streamline (a vehicle, boat, or aircraft) by adding fairings.

– ORIGIN Old English in the senses 'beautify' and 'appear or become clean'. The current sense dates from the mid 19th cent.

Fairbanks the name of two American actors. **Douglas** (Elton) (1883–1939, born *Julius Ullman*) co-founded United Artists in 1919 and became famous for his swashbuckling film roles. His son **Douglas** (1909–2000, known as **Douglas Fairbanks Jr**) played similar roles.

fair copy ▶**noun** written or printed matter transcribed or reproduced after final correction.

Fairfax, Thomas, 3rd Baron Fairfax of Cameron (1612–71), English Parliamentary general. He was appointed commander of the New Model Army in 1645 and won the Battle of Naseby. Fairfax later helped to secure the restoration of Charles II.

fair game ▶**noun** [mass noun] a person or thing that is considered a reasonable target for criticism, exploitation, or attack.

fairground ▶**noun** an outdoor area where a fair is held.

fair-haired ▶**adjective 1** having light-coloured hair.
2 N. Amer. (of a person) favourite; cherished: *the fair-haired boy of American advertising.*

fairies' bonnets ▶**plural noun** a small toadstool with a grooved yellowish-brown thimble-shaped cap, growing in large clusters on rotten wood or in soil.
● *Coprinus disseminatus*, family Coprinaceae, class Hymenomycetes.

fairing¹ ▶**noun** an external metal or plastic structure added to increase streamlining and reduce drag, especially on a high-performance car, motorcycle, boat, or aircraft.

fairing² ▶**noun** Brit. archaic a small present bought at a fair.
■a type of ginger biscuit traditionally sold at fairs in Cornwall and other parts of the West Country.

Fair Isle one of the Shetland Islands, lying about halfway between Orkney and the main Shetland group.
■a shipping forecast area in the NE Atlantic off the north coast of Scotland, including Orkney and Shetland. ■[mass noun] [usu. as modifier] traditional multicoloured geometric designs used in woollen knitwear: *Fair Isle sweaters.*

fairlead /ˈfɛːliːd/ ▶**noun** a ring mounted on a boat to guide a rope, keeping it clear of obstructions and preventing it from cutting or chafing.

fairly ▶**adverb 1** with justice: *he could not fairly be accused of wasting police time.*
2 [usu. as submodifier] to quite a high degree: *I was fairly certain she had nothing to do with the affair.*
■to an acceptable extent: *I get on fairly well with everybody.* ■ actually (used to emphasize something surprising or extreme): *he fairly snarled at her.*

– PHRASES **fairly and squarely** another term for *fair and square* (see **FAIR**¹).

fair-minded ▶**adjective** impartial in judgement; just: *a fair-minded employer.*

– DERIVATIVES **fair-mindedly** adverb, **fair-mindedness** noun.

fair play ▶**noun** [mass noun] respect for the rules or equal treatment of all concerned.

– PHRASES **fair play to someone** Irish used as an expression of approval when someone has done

something praiseworthy or the right thing under the circumstances.

fair-spoken ▶**adjective** archaic (of a person) courteous and pleasant.

fair trade ▶**noun** [mass noun] **1** trade carried on legally.
2 trade in which fair prices are paid to producers in developing countries.

fairwater ▶**noun** a structure that improves the streamlining of a ship to assist its smooth passage through water.

fairway ▶**noun 1** the part of a golf course between a tee and the corresponding green, where the grass is kept short.
2 a navigable channel in a river or harbour.
■a regular course or track followed by ships.

fair-weather friend ▶**noun** a person who stops being a friend in times of difficulty.

fairy ▶**noun** (pl. **-ies**) **1** a small imaginary being of human form that has magical powers, especially a female one.
2 a Central and South American hummingbird with a green back and long tail.
● Genus *Heliothryx*, family Trochilidae: two species.
3 informal, offensive a male homosexual.
▶**adjective** belonging to, resembling, or associated with fairies: *fairy gold.*

– PHRASES **away with the fairies** giving the impression of being mad, distracted, or in a dreamworld.

– DERIVATIVES **fairylike** adjective.

– ORIGIN Middle English (denoting fairyland or fairies collectively): from Old French *faerie*, from *fae*, 'a fairy', from Latin *fata* 'the Fates', plural of *fatum* (see **FATE**). Compare with **FAY**.

fairy armadillo ▶**noun** a very small burrowing armadillo found in southern South America.
● Genus *Clamyphorus*, family Dasypodidae: two species.

fairy bluebird ▶**noun** a South Asian forest songbird related to the orioles, the male of which has bright blue and black plumage.
● Genus *Irena*, family Irenidae (or Oriolidae): two species, in particular the widespread *I. puella.*

fairy cake ▶**noun** Brit. a small individual sponge cake, usually with icing or other decoration.

fairy floss ▶**noun** Australian term for **CANDYFLOSS**.

fairy fly ▶**noun** a minute parasitic wasp which lays its eggs in the eggs of other insects.
● Family Mymaridae, order Hymenoptera: numerous genera.

fairy godmother ▶**noun** a female character in some fairy stories who has magical powers and brings unexpected good fortune to the hero or heroine.

fairyland ▶**noun** the imaginary home of fairies.
■a beautiful or seemingly enchanted place: [as modifier] *a fairyland castle.* ■ an imagined ideal place; a utopia.

fairy lights ▶**plural noun** chiefly Brit. small coloured electric lights used for decoration, especially at festivals such as Christmas.

fairy ring ▶**noun** a circular area of grass that is darker in colour than the surrounding grass due to the growth of certain fungi. They were popularly believed to have been caused by fairies dancing.

fairy ring champignon ▶**noun** see **CHAMPIGNON**.

fairy shrimp ▶**noun** a small transparent crustacean which typically swims on its back, using its legs to filter food particles from the water.
● Order Anostraca, class Branchiopoda: many species, including brine shrimps.

fairy story ▶**noun** a children's tale about magical and imaginary beings and lands.
■an untrue account.

fairy tale ▶**noun** a fairy story.
■[as modifier] denoting something regarded as resembling a fairy story in being magical, idealized, or extremely happy: *a fairy-tale romance.*

fairy tern ▶**noun** a small white tropical tern which lays its single egg on a narrow ledge or on the bare branch of a tree. When flying against a bright sky the wings appear somewhat translucent, allowing the bone structure to be seen.
● *Gygis alba*, family Sternidae.

fairy wren ▶**noun** a small Australian songbird with a long cocked tail, the male of which has partly or mainly blue plumage.
● Genus *Malurus*, family Maluridae: several species, in

particular the common **superb fairy wren** or blue wren (*M. cyaneus*).

Faisal /ˈfʌɪs(ə)l/ the name of two kings of Iraq:
■Faisal I (1885–1933), reigned 1921–33. A British-sponsored ruler, he was also supported by fervent Arab nationalists. Under his rule Iraq achieved full independence in 1932.
■Faisal II (1935–58), grandson of Faisal I, reigned 1939–58. He was assassinated in a military coup, after which a republic was established.

Faisalabad /ˈfʌɪsələˌbad/ an industrial city in Punjab, Pakistan; pop. 1,092,000 (1981). Until 1979 it was known as Lyallpur.

faisandé /ˈfɛzɒ̃deɪ/ ▶ **adjective** poetic/literary affected; artificial.
– ORIGIN French, literally '(of game) hung until high'.

fait accompli /ˌfeɪt əˈkɒmpli, French fɛt akɔ̃pli/ ▶ **noun** [in sing.] a thing that has already happened or been decided before those affected hear about it, leaving them with no option but to accept: *the results were presented to shareholders as a fait accompli.*
– ORIGIN mid 19th cent.: from French, literally 'accomplished fact'.

faith ▶ **noun** [mass noun] **1** complete trust or confidence in someone or something: *this restores one's faith in politicians.*
2 strong belief in the doctrines of a religion, based on spiritual apprehension rather than proof.
■[count noun] a system of religious belief: *the Christian faith.* ■[count noun] a strongly held belief or theory: *the faith that life will expand until it fills the universe.*
– PHRASES **break** (or **keep**) **faith** be disloyal (or loyal): *an attempt to make us* ***break faith with*** *our customers.*
– ORIGIN Middle English: from Old French *feid*, from Latin *fides*.

faithful ▶ **adjective 1** loyal, constant, and steadfast: *he exhorted them to remain* ***faithful to*** *the principles of Reaganism | employees who had notched up decades of faithful service |* [as plural noun **the faithful**] *the struggle to please the party faithful.*
■(of a spouse or partner) never having a sexual relationship with anyone else: *her husband was faithful to her.* ■(of an object) reliable: *my faithful compass.*
2 [usu. as plural noun **the faithful**] having a strong belief in a particular religion, especially Islam.
3 true to the facts or the original: *the rugs they make today remain faithful to their ancestors' methods.*
– DERIVATIVES **faithfulness** noun.

faithfully ▶ **adverb 1** in a loyal manner.
2 in a manner that is true to the facts or the original: *she translated the novel as faithfully as possible.*
– PHRASES **yours faithfully** chiefly Brit. a formula for ending a formal letter to someone whose name you do not know.

faith healing ▶ **noun** [mass noun] healing achieved by religious belief and prayer, rather than by medical treatment.
– DERIVATIVES **faith healer** noun.

faithless ▶ **adjective 1** disloyal, especially to a spouse or partner; untrustworthy: *her faithless lover.*
2 without religious faith.
– DERIVATIVES **faithlessly** adverb, **faithlessness** noun.

fajitas /fəˈhiːtəz, fəˈdʒiːtəz/ ▶ **plural noun** a dish of Mexican origin consisting of strips of spiced beef or chicken, chopped vegetables, and grated cheese, wrapped in a soft tortilla and often served with sour cream.
– ORIGIN Mexican Spanish, literally 'little strips or belts'.

fake[1] ▶ **noun** a thing that is not genuine; a forgery or sham: *fakes of Old Masters.*
■a person who appears or claims to be something that they are not. ■a pretence or trick: *his excuse for coming was a fake.*
▶ **adjective** not genuine; counterfeit: *fake designer clothing | expressing fake emotions.*
■(of a person) claiming to be something that one is not: *a fake doctor.*
▶ **verb** [with obj.] forge or counterfeit (something): *the woman faked her spouse's signature.*
■pretend to feel or suffer from (an emotion or illness): *he had begun to fake a bad stomach ache.* ■make (an event) appear to happen: *he faked his own death.*
– DERIVATIVES **faker** noun, **fakery** noun.
– ORIGIN late 18th cent. (as an adjective; originally slang): origin uncertain; perhaps ultimately related to German *fegen* 'sweep, thrash'. Compare with **FIG**[2].

fake[2] ▶ **noun** & **verb** variant spelling of **FLAKE**[4].
– ORIGIN late Middle English (as a verb): of unknown origin.

fake book ▶ **noun** Music a book of music containing the basic chord sequences of jazz tunes.

fakie /ˈfeɪki/ ▶ **noun** (pl. **-ies**) (in skateboarding or snowboarding) a movement in which the board is ridden backwards.
▶ **adverb** with such a movement: *once you can do it forwards, try it fakie.*

fakir /ˈfeɪkɪə, ˈfa-/ (also **faquir**) ▶ **noun** a Muslim (or, loosely, a Hindu) religious ascetic who lives solely on alms.
– ORIGIN early 17th cent.: via French from Arabic *fakīr* 'needy man'.

Falabella /ˌfaləˈbɛlə/ ▶ **noun** a horse of a miniature breed, the adult of which does not usually exceed 75 cm in height.
– ORIGIN late 20th cent.: named after Julio *Falabella* (died 1981), an Argentinian breeder.

falafel /fəˈlaf(ə)l, -ˈlɑː-/ (also **felafel**) ▶ **noun** [mass noun] a Middle Eastern dish of spiced mashed chickpeas or other pulses formed into balls or fritters and deep-fried, usually eaten with or in pitta bread.
– ORIGIN from colloquial Egyptian Arabic *falāfil*, plural of Arabic *fulful, filfil* 'pepper'.

Falange /fəˈlan(d)ʒ, Spanish faˈlaŋxe/ the Spanish Fascist movement that merged with traditional right-wing elements in 1937 to form the ruling party, the Falange Española Tradicionalista, under General Franco. It was formally abolished in 1977.
– DERIVATIVES **Falangism** noun, **Falangist** noun & adjective.
– ORIGIN Spanish, from Latin *phalanx, phalang-* (see **PHALANX**).

Falasha /fəˈlɑːʃə/ ▶ **noun** (pl. same or **Falashas**) a member of a group of people in Ethiopia who hold the Jewish faith but use Ge'ez rather than Hebrew as a liturgical language. The Falashas were not formally recognized as Jews until 1975, and many of them were airlifted to Israel in 1984–5 and after.
– ORIGIN Amharic, literally 'exile, immigrant'.

falcate /ˈfalkeɪt/ ▶ **adjective** Botany & Zoology curved like a sickle; hooked: *the mandibles are falcate.*
– ORIGIN early 19th cent.: from Latin *falcatus*, from *falx, falc-* 'sickle'.

falcated teal ▶ **noun** a small duck that is native to China and NE Asia.
● *Anas falcata*, family Anatidae.
– ORIGIN early 18th cent.: named from the long sickle-shaped inner secondary feathers of the male.

falchion /ˈfɔːl(t)ʃ(ə)n/ ▶ **noun** historical a broad, slightly curved sword with the cutting edge on the convex side.
– ORIGIN Middle English *fauchon*, from Old French, based on Latin *falx, falc-* 'sickle'. The *-l-* was added in the 16th cent. to conform with the Latin spelling.

falciform /ˈfalsɪfɔːm/ ▶ **adjective** Anatomy & Zoology curved like a sickle; hooked: *the falciform ligament.*
– ORIGIN mid 18th cent.: from Latin *falx, falc-* 'sickle' + **-IFORM**.

falciparum /falˈsɪpərəm/ (also **falciparum malaria**) ▶ **noun** [mass noun] the most severe form of malaria: [as modifier] *the falciparum parasite.*
● This is caused by infection with *Plasmodium falciparum*.
– ORIGIN 1930s: modern Latin, from Latin *falx, falc-* 'sickle' + *-parum* (from *-parus* 'bearing').

falcon /ˈfɔː(l)k(ə)n, ˈfɒlk(ə)n/ ▶ **noun** a diurnal bird of prey with long pointed wings and a notched beak, typically catching prey by diving on it from above. Compare with **HAWK**[1] (in sense 1).
● Family Falconidae, in particular the genus *Falco*: many species, including the peregrine, hobby, merlin, and kestrel.
■one of these birds kept and trained to hunt small game for sport. ■Falconry the female of such a bird, especially a peregrine. Compare with **TERCEL**.
– ORIGIN Middle English *faucon* (originally denoting any diurnal bird of prey used in falconry): from Old French, from late Latin *falco*, from Latin *falx, falc-* 'scythe', or of Germanic origin and related to Dutch *valk* and German *Falke*. The *-l-* was added in the 15th cent. to conform with the Latin spelling.

falconer ▶ **noun** a person who keeps, trains, or hunts with falcons, hawks, or other birds of prey.
– ORIGIN late Middle English: from Old French *fauconier*, from *faucon* (see **FALCON**).

falconet /ˈfɔː(l)k(ə)nɪt/ ▶ **noun 1** historical a light cannon. [ORIGIN: mid 16th cent.: from Italian *falconetto*, diminutive of *falcone* 'falcon', from Latin *falco* (see **FALCON**).]
2 a very small South Asian (or South American) falcon, typically having bold black-and-white plumage. [ORIGIN: mid 19th cent.: from **FALCON** + **-ET**[1].]
● Genus *Microhierax* (and *Spiziapteryx*), family Falconidae: six species.

falconry ▶ **noun** [mass noun] the keeping and training of falcons or other birds of prey; the sport of hunting with such birds.
– ORIGIN late 16th cent.: from French *fauconnerie*, from *faucon* (see **FALCON**).

falderal /ˈfaldəral/ ▶ **noun** variant spelling of **FOLDEROL**.

Faldo /ˈfaldəʊ/, Nick (b.1957), English golfer; full name *Nicholas Alexander Faldo*. He won the British Open championship in 1987 and 1990 and the US Masters Tournament in 1989, 1990, and 1996.

faldstool /ˈfɔːldstuːl/ ▶ **noun 1** a folding chair used by a bishop when not occupying the throne or when officiating in a church other than his own.
2 a small movable folding desk or stool for kneeling at prayer.
– ORIGIN late Old English *fældestōl*, of Germanic origin, from the base of **FOLD**[1] and **STOOL**, influenced by medieval Latin *faldistolium*, from Germanic.

fale /ˈfɑːleɪ/ ▶ **noun** a Samoan house with open sides and a thatched roof.

Falkirk /ˈfɔːlkəːk, ˈfɒl-/ a town in central Scotland, administrative centre of Falkirk region; pop. (1981) 36,880. Edward I defeated the Scots here in 1298.

Falkland Islands /ˈfɔːklənd, ˈfɒlk-/ (also **the Falklands**) a group of islands in the South Atlantic, forming a British Crown Colony; pop. 2,121 (1991); capital, Stanley (on East Falkland).

> The group consists of two main islands and over a hundred smaller ones, about 500 km (300 miles) east of the Strait of Magellan. The Falklands were occupied and colonized by Britain in 1832–3, following the expulsion of an Argentinian garrison. Argentina refused to recognize British sovereignty and continues to refer to the islands by their old Spanish name, the Malvinas.

Falkland Islands Dependencies an overseas territory of the UK in the South Atlantic, consisting of the South Sandwich Islands and South Georgia, which is administered from the Falkland Islands.

Falklands War an armed conflict between Britain and Argentina in 1982.

> On the orders of General Galtieri's military junta, Argentinian forces invaded the Falkland Islands in support of their claim to sovereignty. In response Britain sent a task force of ships and aircraft, which forced the Argentinians to surrender six weeks after its arrival.

fall ▶ **verb** (past **fell**; past participle **fallen**) [no obj., with adverbial] **1** move downwards, typically rapidly and freely without control, from a higher to a lower level: *bombs could be seen* ***falling from*** *the planes |* [as adj. **falling**] *the power lines had been brought down by falling trees.*
■(**fall off**) become detached accidentally and drop to the ground: *my sunglasses fell off and broke on the pavement.* ■hang down: *hair that was allowed to fall to the shoulders.* ■(of land) slope downwards; drop away: *the land* ***fell away*** *in a steep bank.* ■(**fall into**) (of a river) flow or discharge itself into. ■[no obj.] (of someone's eyes or glance) be directed downwards. ■[no obj.] (of someone's face) show dismay or disappointment by appearing to sag or droop: *her face fell as she thought about her life with George.* ■figurative occur, arrive, or become apparent as if by dropping suddenly: *when night fell we managed to crawl back to our lines | the information might* ***fall into*** *the wrong hands.*
2 (of a person) lose one's balance and collapse: *she* ***fell down*** *at school today.*
■throw oneself down, typically in order to worship or implore someone: *they fell on their knees, rendering thanks to God.* ■(of a tree, building, or other structure) collapse to the ground: *the house looked as if it were going to* ***fall down*** *at any moment.* ■(of a building or place) be captured or defeated: *their mountain strongholds* ***fell to*** *enemy attack.* ■die in battle: *an English leader who had fallen at the hands of the Danes.* ■[no obj.] archaic commit sin; yield to temptation: *it is their husbands fault if wives do fall.* ■[no obj.] (of a government or leader) lose office. ■Cricket (of a wicket) be taken by the bowling side. ■(**fall over**) informal (of computer hardware or software) stop working suddenly; crash.

3 decrease in number, amount, intensity, or quality: *in 1987 imports into Britain* **fell by** *12 per cent | we're worried that standards are falling.*
■find a lower level; subside or abate: *the water table in the Rift Valley fell.* ■(of a measuring instrument) show a lower reading: *the barometer had fallen a further ten points.* ■(**fall away**) (in sport) play less well; lose form.
4 pass into a specified state: *many of the buildings* **fell into** *disrepair* | [with complement] *she fell pregnant.*
■(**fall to doing something**) begin to do something: *he fell to musing about how it had happened.* ■be drawn accidentally into: *you must not* **fall into** *this common error.* ■occur at a specified time: *Mother's birthday fell on May Day.* ■be classified or ordered in the way specified: *canals* **fall within** *the Minister's brief.*
▶**noun 1** [usu. in sing.] an act of falling or collapsing; a sudden uncontrollable descent: *his mother had a fall, hurting her leg as she alighted from a train.*
■a controlled act of falling, especially as a stunt or in martial arts. ■Wrestling a move which pins the opponent's shoulders on the ground for a count of three. ■a state of hanging or drooping downwards: **the fall of** *her hair.* ■a downward difference in height between parts of a surface: *at the corner of the massif this fall is interrupted by other heights of considerable stature.* ■a sudden onset or arrival as if by dropping: *the fall of darkness.*
2 a thing which falls or has fallen: *in October came the first thin fall of snow | a rock fall.*
■(usu. **falls**) a waterfall or cascade. ■chiefly poetic/literary a downward turn in a melody: *that strain again, it had a dying fall.* ■(**falls**) the parts or petals of a flower which bend downwards, especially the outer perianth segments of an iris.
3 a decrease in size, number, rate, or level; a decline: *a big* **fall in** *unemployment.*
4 a loss of office: *the fall of the government.*
■the loss of a city or fortified place during battle: *the* **fall of** *Jerusalem.* ■a person's moral descent, typically by succumbing to temptation. ■(**the Fall** or **the Fall of Man**) the lapse of humankind into a state of sin, ascribed in traditional Jewish and Christian theology to the disobedience of Adam and Eve as described in Genesis.
5 (also **Fall**) N. Amer. autumn.
– PHRASES **fall between two stools** see **STOOL**. **fall foul** (or chiefly N. Amer. **afoul**) **of** come into conflict with and be undermined by: *any commitment of resources is likely to fall foul of government cash limitations.* **fall in** (or **into**) **line** conform with others or with accepted behaviour. [ORIGIN: with reference to military formation.] **fall in** (or **out of**) **love** (**with someone**) see **LOVE**. **fall into place** (of a series of events or facts) begin to make sense or cohere: *once he knew what to look for, the theory fell quickly into place.* **fall on stony ground** see **STONY**. **fall over oneself to do something** informal be excessively eager to do something: *critics and audiences fell over themselves to compliment him.* **fall prey to** see **PREY**. **fall short** (**of**) (of a missile) fail to reach its target. ■figurative be deficient or inadequate; fail to reach a required goal: *the total vote fell short of the required two-thirds majority.* **fall to pieces** see *fall apart* below. **fall victim to** see **VICTIM**. **take the fall** N. Amer. informal receive blame or punishment, typically in the place of another person.
– ORIGIN Old English *fallan, feallan*, of Germanic origin; related to Dutch *vallen* and German *fallen*; the noun is partly from the verb, partly from Old Norse *fall* 'downfall, sin'.
▶**fall about** Brit. informal laugh uncontrollably.
fall apart (or **to pieces**) break up, come apart, or disintegrate: *their marriage is likely to fall apart.* ■(of a person) lose one's capacity to cope: *Angie fell to pieces because she had lost everything.*
fall back move or turn back; retreat.
fall back on have recourse to when in difficulty: *they normally fell back on one of three arguments.*
fall behind fail to keep level with one's competitors. ■fail to meet a commitment to make a regular payment: *borrowers* **falling behind with** *their mortgage repayments.*
fall down be shown to be inadequate or false; fail: *the deal fell down partly because there were a lot of unanswered questions.*
fall for informal **1** be captivated by; fall in love with. **2** be deceived by (something): *he should have known better than to expect Duncan to fall for a cheap trick like that.*
fall in 1 take one's place in a military formation: *the soldiers fell in by the side of the road.* **2** (of a structure) collapse inwards.
fall in with 1 meet by chance and become involved with: *he fell in with thieves.* **2** act in accordance with (someone's ideas or suggestions); agree to: *falling in with other people's views.*
fall on (or **upon**) **1** attack fiercely or unexpectedly: *the army fell on the besiegers.* ■seize enthusiastically: *she fell on the sandwiches as though she had not eaten in weeks.* **2** (of someone's eyes or gaze) be directed towards: *her gaze fell on the mud-stained coverlet.* **3** (of a burden or duty) be borne or incurred by: *the cost of tuition should not fall on the student.*
fall out 1 (of the hair, teeth, etc.) become detached and drop out. **2** have an argument: *he had* **fallen out with** *his family.* **3** leave one's place in a military formation, or on parade: *the two policemen at the rear fell out of the formation.* **4** happen; turn out: *matters fell out as Stephen arranged.*
fall through come to nothing; fail: *the project fell through due to lack of money.*
fall to (of a task) become the duty or responsibility of: *it fell to me to write to Shephard.* ■(of property) revert to the ownership of.

Falla /'fʌɪjə/, Manuel de (1876–1946), Spanish composer and pianist. He composed the ballets *Love, the Magician* (1915) and *The Three-Cornered Hat* (1919); the latter was produced by Diaghilev, with designs by Picasso.

fallacy /'faləsi/ ▶**noun** (pl. **-ies**) **1** a mistaken belief, especially one based on unsound argument: *the notion that the camera never lies is a fallacy.*
■Logic a failure in reasoning which renders an argument invalid. ■[mass noun] faulty reasoning; misleading or unsound argument: *the potential for fallacy which lies behind the notion of self-esteem.*
– DERIVATIVES **fallacious** adjective, **fallaciously** adverb, **fallaciousness** /fə'leɪʃəsnɪs/ noun.
– ORIGIN late 15th cent. (in the sense 'deception, guile'; gradually superseding Middle English *fallace*): from Latin *fallacia*, from *fallax, fallac-* 'deceiving', from *fallere* 'deceive'.

fallacy of composition ▶**noun** the error of assuming that what is true of a member of a group is true for the group as a whole.

fallaway ▶**noun** a falling off; a decline: *surges and fallaways of house-buying activity.*

fallback ▶**noun 1** an alternative plan that may be used in an emergency.
2 a reduction.

fallen past participle of **FALL**. ▶**adjective** [attrib.]
1 Theology having sinned: *fallen human nature.*
■dated (of a woman) regarded as having lost her honour through engaging in a sexual relationship outside marriage: *a fallen woman with a chequered past.*
2 (of a soldier) killed in battle: *fallen heroes.*
– DERIVATIVES **fallenness** noun.

fallen angel ▶**noun** (in Christian, Jewish, and Muslim tradition) an angel who rebelled against God and was cast out of heaven.

faller ▶**noun 1** Brit. a person or thing that falls, in particular:
■a horse that falls during a race, especially at a fence in a steeplechase. ■a company whose shares have lost value on the stock market.
2 N. Amer. a person who fells trees for a living.

fallfish ▶**noun** (pl. same or **-fishes**) a North American freshwater fish resembling the chub. Also called **CORPORAL**[1] in North America.
• *Semotilus corporalis*, family Cyprinidae.

fall guy ▶**noun** informal a scapegoat.

fallibilism /'falɪbɪˌlɪz(ə)m/ ▶**noun** [mass noun] Philosophy the principle that propositions concerning empirical knowledge can be accepted even though they cannot be proved with certainty.
– DERIVATIVES **fallibilist** noun & adjective.

fallible /'falɪb(ə)l/ ▶**adjective** capable of making mistakes or being erroneous: *experts can be fallible.*
– DERIVATIVES **fallibility** noun, **fallibly** adverb.
– ORIGIN late Middle English: from medieval Latin *fallibilis*, from Latin *fallere* 'deceive'.

falling-out ▶**noun** [in sing.] a quarrel or disagreement: *the two of them had a falling-out.*

falling sickness ▶**noun** [mass noun] (**the falling sickness**) archaic term for **EPILEPSY**.

falling star ▶**noun** a meteor or shooting star.

fall line ▶**noun 1** (**the fall line**) Skiing the route leading straight down any particular part of a slope.
2 a narrow zone that marks the geological boundary between an upland region and a plain, distinguished by the occurrence of falls and rapids where rivers and streams cross it.
■(**the Fall Line**) (in the US) the zone demarcating the Piedmont from the Atlantic coastal plain.

fall-off ▶**noun** [in sing.] a decrease in something: *a* **fall-off in** *work caused by the recession.*

Fallopian tube /fə'ləʊpɪən/ (also **fallopian**) ▶**noun** Anatomy (in a female mammal) either of a pair of tubes along which eggs travel from the ovaries to the uterus.
– ORIGIN early 18th cent.: from *Fallopius*, Latinized form of the name of Gabriello *Fallopio* (1523–62), the Italian anatomist who first described them.

fallout ▶**noun** [mass noun] radioactive particles that are carried into the atmosphere after a nuclear explosion or accident and gradually fall back as dust or in precipitation.
■figurative the adverse side effects or results of a situation: *almost as dramatic as the financial scale of the mess is the growing political fallout.* ■[usu. with modifier] airborne substances resulting from an industrial process or accident: *acid fallout from power stations.*

fallow[1] ▶**adjective** (of farmland) ploughed and harrowed but left unsown for a period in order to restore its fertility as part of a crop rotation or to avoid surplus production: *incentives for farmers to let land* **lie fallow** *in order to reduce grain surpluses.*
■figurative inactive: *long fallow periods when nothing seems to happen.* ■(of a sow) not pregnant.
▶**noun** a piece of fallow or uncultivated land.
▶**verb** [with obj.] leave (land) fallow for a period after it has been ploughed and harrowed.
– DERIVATIVES **fallowness** noun.
– ORIGIN Old English *fealgian* 'to break up land for sowing', of Germanic origin; related to Low German *falgen*.

fallow[2] ▶**noun** [mass noun] a pale brown or reddish yellow colour.
– ORIGIN Old English *falu, fealu*, of Germanic origin; related to Dutch *vaal* and German *fahl, falb*.

fallow deer ▶**noun** a Eurasian deer with branched palmate antlers, typically having a white-spotted reddish-brown coat in summer.
• *Cervus dama*, family Cervidae.

fall-pipe ▶**noun** a downpipe.

false ▶**adjective 1** not according with truth or fact; incorrect: *remnants of the reagent may give a false reading | the allegations were false.*
■not according with rules or law: *false imprisonment.*
2 appearing to be the thing denoted; deliberately made or meant to deceive: *check to see if the trunk has a false bottom | a false passport.*
■artificial: *false eyelashes.* ■feigned: *a horribly false smile.*
3 illusory; not actually so: *sunscreens give users a false sense of security.*
■[attrib.] used in names of plants, animals, and gems that superficially resemble the thing properly so called, e.g. **false oat**, **false killer whale**.
4 treacherous; unfaithful: *a false lover.*
– PHRASES **false position** a situation in which one is compelled to act in a manner inconsistent with one's true nature or principles. **play someone false** deceive or cheat someone.
– DERIVATIVES **falsely** adverb, **falseness** noun, **falsity** noun.
– ORIGIN Old English *fals* 'fraud, deceit', from Latin *falsum* 'fraud', neuter past participle of *fallere* 'deceive'; reinforced or re-formed in Middle English from Old French *fals, faus* 'false'.

false acacia ▶**noun** a North American tree with compound leaves and dense hanging clusters of fragrant white flowers, widely grown as an ornamental.
• *Robinia pseudoacacia*, family Leguminosae.

false alarm ▶**noun** a warning given about something that fails to happen.

false bedding ▶**noun** Geology another term for **CROSS-BEDDING**.

false card Bridge ▶**noun** a card played in order to give one's opponents a misleading impression of one's strength in the suit led.
▶**verb** (**false-card**) [with obj.] play (a card) in such a way.

false colour ▶**noun** [mass noun] colour added during the processing of a photographic or computer image to aid interpretation of the subject.

false coral snake ▶**noun** a harmless snake that

f

mimics the bright coloration of the venomous coral snakes.
• Several genera in the family Colubridae, in particular *Simophis* and *Pliocercus* of South America.

false cypress ▶ noun a conifer of a genus that includes Lawson's cypress.
• Genus *Chamaecyparis*, family Cupressaceae.

false dawn ▶ noun a transient light which precedes the rising of the sun by about an hour, commonly seen in Eastern countries.
■ figurative a promising sign which comes to nothing.

false economy ▶ noun an apparent financial saving that in fact leads to greater expenditure.

false face ▶ noun a mask, especially as traditionally worn ceremonially by some North American Indian peoples.

false friend ▶ noun a word or expression that has a similar form to one in a person's native language, but a different meaning (for example English *magazine* and French *magasin* 'shop').
– ORIGIN translating French *faux ami*.

false fruit ▶ noun a fruit formed from other parts of the plant as well as the ovary, especially the receptacle, such as the strawberry or fig. Also called **PSEUDOCARP**.

false gharial ▶ noun a rare narrow-snouted crocodile that resembles the gharial, native to Indonesia and Malaysia.
• *Tomistoma schlegelii*, family Crocodylidae.

false helleborine (also **false hellebore**) ▶ noun a herbaceous plant of the lily family which resembles a helleborine, with pleated leaves and a tall dense spike of small flowers, found in north temperate regions.
• Genus *Veratrum*, family Liliaceae: many species.

falsehood ▶ noun [mass noun] the state of being untrue: *the truth or falsehood of the many legends which surround her.*
■ [count noun] a lie. ■ lying: *the right to sue for malicious falsehood.*

false memory ▶ noun Psychology an apparent recollection of an event which did not actually occur, especially one of childhood sexual abuse arising from suggestion during psychoanalysis: [as modifier] *false memory syndrome.*

false move ▶ noun an unwise or careless action that could have dangerous consequences: *one false move would lead to nuclear war.*

false oxlip ▶ noun see **OXLIP**.

false pretences ▶ plural noun behaviour intended to deceive others: *he obtained money by false pretences.*

false rib ▶ noun another term for **FLOATING RIB**.

false scorpion ▶ noun a minute arachnid which has pincers but no long abdomen or sting, occurring abundantly in leaf litter. Also called **PSEUDOSCORPION**.
• Order Pseudoscorpiones.

false start ▶ noun an invalid or disallowed start to a race, usually due to a competitor beginning before the official signal has been given.
■ an unsuccessful attempt to begin something.

false step ▶ noun [usu. in sing.] a slip or stumble: *one false step and we would have fallen in the sea.*
■ a careless or unwise act; a mistake.

false sunbird ▶ noun a small asity of Madagascar that resembles a sunbird.
• Genus *Neodrepanis*, family Philepittidae: two species.

false teeth ▶ plural noun another term for ***dentures*** (see **DENTURE**).

false topaz ▶ noun another term for **CITRINE**.

falsetto /fɔːlˈsɛtəʊ, fɒl-/ ▶ noun (pl. **-os**) Music a method of voice production used by male singers, especially tenors, to sing notes higher than their normal range: *he sang in a piercing falsetto* | [mass noun] *he was singing falsetto in this role.*
■ a singer using this method. ■ a voice or sound that is unusually or unnaturally high.
– ORIGIN late 18th cent.: from Italian, diminutive of *falso* 'false', from Latin *falsus* (see **FALSE**).

false vampire ▶ noun a large carnivorous bat that includes rodents, reptiles, and other small vertebrates among its prey:
• an Old World bat (three species in the family Megadermatidae, including the large Australian ghost bat, *Macroderma gigas*). • a tropical New World bat (*Vampyrum spectrum*, family Phyllostomidae).

falsework ▶ noun [mass noun] temporary framework structures used to support a building during its construction.

falsies ▶ plural noun informal pads of material in women's clothing used to increase the apparent size of the breasts.
■ false eyelashes.

falsify /ˈfɔːlsɪfʌɪ, ˈfɒls-/ ▶ verb (**-ies**, **-ied**) [with obj.] **1** alter (information or evidence) so as to mislead.
■ forge or alter (a document) fraudulently: [as adj. **falsified**] *falsified documents.*
2 prove (a statement or theory) to be false: *the hypothesis is falsified by the evidence.*
■ fail to fulfil (a hope, fear, or expectation); remove the justification for: *changes falsify individual expectations.*
– DERIVATIVES **falsifiability** noun, **falsifiable** adjective, **falsification** noun.
– ORIGIN late Middle English (in sense 2): from French *falsifier* or medieval Latin *falsificare*, from Latin *falsificus* 'making false', from *falsus* 'false'.

Falstaffian /fɔːlˈstɑːfɪən, fɒl-/ ▶ adjective of or resembling Shakespeare's character Sir John Falstaff in being fat, jolly, and debauched: *a Falstaffian gusto for life.*

Falster /ˈfɑːlstə/ a Danish island in the Baltic Sea, south of Zealand.

falter /ˈfɔːltə, ˈfɒl-/ ▶ verb [no obj.] start to lose strength or momentum: *her smile faltered and then faded* | [as adj. **faltering**] *his faltering career.*
■ speak in a hesitant or unsteady voice: [with direct speech] *'A-Adam?' he faltered.* ■ move unsteadily or in a way that shows lack of confidence: *he faltered and finally stopped in midstride.*
– DERIVATIVES **falterer** noun, **falteringly** adverb.
– ORIGIN late Middle English (in the senses 'stammer' and 'stagger'): perhaps from the verb **FOLD**[1] (which was occasionally used of the faltering of the legs or tongue) + *-ter* as in *totter*.

fame ▶ noun [mass noun] the condition of being known or talked about by many people, especially on account of notable achievements: *winning the Olympic title has not just brought her **fame and fortune**.*
– PHRASES **house of ill fame** archaic a brothel. **of —— fame** having a particular famous association; famous for having or being ——: *the village is the birthplace of Mrs Beeton, of cookery fame.*
– ORIGIN Middle English (also in the sense 'reputation', which survives in the phrase *house of ill fame*): via Old French from Latin *fama*.

famed ▶ adjective known about by many people; renowned: *he is **famed for** his eccentricities.*
■ archaic widely reported or rumoured.
– ORIGIN Middle English: past participle of archaic *fame* (verb), from Old French *famer*, from Latin *fama*.

familia /fəˈmɪlɪə/ ▶ noun (pl. **familiae** /-lɪiː/) historical a household or religious community under one head, regarded as a unit.
– ORIGIN Latin.

familial /fəˈmɪljəl/ ▶ adjective of, relating to, or occurring in a family or its members: *the familial Christmas dinner.*
– ORIGIN early 20th cent.: from French, from Latin *familia* 'family'.

familiar ▶ adjective **1** well known from long or close association: *their faces will be **familiar to** many of you* | *a familiar voice.*
■ often encountered or experienced; common: *the situation was all too familiar.* ■ [predic.] (**familiar with**) having a good knowledge of: *ensure that you are familiar with the heating controls.*
2 in close friendship; intimate: *she had not realized they were on such familiar terms.*
■ informal to an inappropriate degree.
▶ noun **1** (also **familiar spirit**) a demon supposedly attending and obeying a witch, often said to assume the form of an animal.
2 (in the Roman Catholic Church) a person rendering certain services in a pope's or bishop's household.
3 a close friend or associate.
– DERIVATIVES **familiarly** adverb.
– ORIGIN Middle English (in the sense 'intimate', 'on a family footing'): from Old French *familier*, from Latin *familiaris*, from *familia* 'household servants, household, family', from *famulus* 'servant'.

familiarity ▶ noun (pl. **-ies**) [mass noun] close acquaintance with or knowledge of something: *increase customer **familiarity with** a product.*
■ the quality of being well known; recognizability based on long or close association: *the reassuring familiarity of his parents' home.* ■ relaxed friendliness or intimacy between people: *familiarity allows us to give each other nicknames.* ■ inappropriate and often offensive informality of behaviour or language: *the unnecessary familiarity made me dislike him at once.*
– PHRASES **familiarity breeds contempt** proverb extensive knowledge of or close association with someone or something leads to a loss of respect for them or it.
– ORIGIN Middle English (in the senses 'close relationship' and 'sexual intimacy'): via Old French from Latin *familiaritas*, from *familiaris* 'familiar, intimate' (see **FAMILIAR**).

familiarize (also **-ise**) ▶ verb [with obj.] give (someone) knowledge or understanding of something: *to **familiarize** pupils **with** the microcomputer and its uses.*
■ make (something) better known or more easily grasped: *exercises which will help to familiarize the terms used.*
– DERIVATIVES **familiarization** noun.

Familist /ˈfamɪlɪst/ ▶ noun a member of the Christian sect of the 16th and 17th centuries called the Family of Love, which asserted the importance of love and the necessity for absolute obedience to any government.

familist /ˈfamɪlɪst/ ▶ adjective of, relating to, or advocating a social framework centred on family relationships.
– DERIVATIVES **familistic** adjective.

famille /faˈmiː/ ▶ noun [mass noun] Chinese enamelled porcelain of particular periods in the 17th and 18th centuries with a predominant colour, **famille jaune** /ʒəʊn/ (yellow), **famille noire** /nwɑː/ (black), **famille rose** /rəʊz/ (red), **famille verte** /vɛːt/ (green).
– ORIGIN French, literally 'family'.

family ▶ noun (pl. **-ies**) **1** [treated as sing. or pl.] a group consisting of two parents and their children living together as a unit.
■ a group of people related to one another by blood or marriage: *friends and family can provide support.* ■ the children of a person or couple being discussed: *she has the sole responsibility for a large family.* ■ [mass noun] a person or people related to one and so to be treated with a special loyalty or intimacy: *I could not turn him away, for he was family.* ■ a group of people united in criminal activity. ■ Biology a principal taxonomic category that ranks above genus and below order, usually ending in *-idae* (in zoology) or *-aceae* (in botany). ■ a group of objects united by a significant shared characteristic. ■ Mathematics a group of curves or surfaces obtained by varying the value of a constant in the equation generating them.
2 all the descendants of a common ancestor: *the house has been owned by the same family for 300 years.*
■ a race or group of peoples from a common stock. ■ all the languages ultimately derived from a particular early language, regarded as a group: *the Austronesian language family.*
▶ adjective [attrib.] designed to be suitable for children as well as adults: *a family newspaper.*
– PHRASES **the** (or **one's**) **family jewels** informal a man's genitals. **in the family way** informal pregnant.
– ORIGIN late Middle English (in sense 2; also denoting the servants of a household or the retinue of a nobleman): from Latin *familia* 'household servants, household, family', from *famulus* 'servant'.

family bible ▶ noun a bible designed to be used at family prayers, typically one with space on its flyleaves for recording important family events.

family credit ▶ noun [mass noun] (in the UK) a regular payment by the state to a family with an income below a certain level.

Family Division (in the UK) the division of the High Court dealing with adoption, divorce, and other family matters.

family man ▶ noun a man who lives with his wife and children, especially one who enjoys home life.

family name ▶ noun a surname.

family planning ▶ noun [mass noun] [often as modifier] the practice of controlling the number of children in a family and the intervals between their births, particularly by means of artificial contraception or voluntary sterilization: *family-planning clinics.*
■ artificial contraception.

family tree ▶ noun a diagram showing the relationship between people in several generations of a family.

family values ▶ plural noun values supposedly learned or reinforced within a traditional, close, family unit, typically those of high moral standards and discipline.

famine /ˈfamɪn/ ▶ **noun** [mass noun] extreme scarcity of food: *drought could result in famine throughout the region* | [count noun] *the famine of 1921–2.*
■ [count noun] a shortage: *the cotton famine of the 1860s.* ■ archaic hunger.
– ORIGIN late Middle English: from Old French, from *faim* 'hunger', from Latin *fames*.

famished /ˈfamɪʃd/ ▶ **adjective** informal extremely hungry.
– ORIGIN late Middle English: past participle of the verb *famish*, from Middle English *fame* 'starve', from Old French *afamer*, based on Latin *fames* 'hunger'.

famous ▶ **adjective 1** known about by many people: *the country is* ***famous for*** *its natural beauty* | *a famous star.*
2 informal excellent; magnificent: *Galway stormed to a* ***famous victory.***
– PHRASES **famous for being famous** having no recognizable or distinct reason for one's fame other than high media exposure. **famous for fifteen minutes** enjoying a brief period of fame before fading back into obscurity. [ORIGIN: coined by Andy Warhol.] **famous last words** said as an ironic comment on or reply to an overconfident assertion that may well be proved wrong by events: *'I'll be perfectly OK on my own.' 'Famous last words,' she thought to herself.*
– DERIVATIVES **famousness** noun.
– ORIGIN late Middle English: from Old French *fameus*, from Latin *famosus* 'famed', from *fama* (see **FAME**).

famously ▶ **adverb 1** informal excellently: *he wasn't difficult at all—we* ***got on famously.***
2 indicating that the fact asserted is widely known: *they have famously reclusive lifestyles.*

famulus /ˈfamjʊləs/ ▶ **noun** (pl. **famuli** /-lʌɪ, -liː/) historical an assistant or servant, especially one working for a magician or scholar.
– ORIGIN mid 19th cent.: from Latin, 'servant'.

Fan /fan/ ▶ **noun & adjective** variant spelling of **FANG**.

fan1 ▶ **noun 1** an apparatus with rotating blades that creates a current of air for cooling or ventilation.
2 a device, typically folding and shaped like a segment of a circle when spread out, that is held in the hand and waved so as to cool the person holding it by causing the air to move.
■ a thing or shape resembling such a device when open. ■ an alluvial or talus deposit spread out in such a shape at the foot of a slope. ■ a small sail for keeping the head of a windmill towards the wind.
▶ **verb** (**fanned**, **fanning**) **1** [with obj.] cool (especially a person or a part of the body) by waving something to create a current of air: *he fanned himself with his hat.*
■ (of breath or a breeze) blow gently on: *his breath fanned her skin as he leant towards her.* ■ [with obj. and adverbial of direction] cause (air or smoke) to move by blowing it: *I lit a cigarette and fanned smoke through my nostrils.* ■ [with obj. and adverbial of direction] brush or drive away with a waving movement: *a veil of smoke which she* ***fanned away*** *with a jewelled hand.* ■ [no obj.] Baseball & Ice Hockey, N. Amer. swing unsuccessfully at the ball or puck. ■ Baseball, N. Amer. strike out (a batter).
2 [with obj.] increase the strength of (a fire) by blowing on it or stirring up the air near it: *fanned by an easterly wind, the fire spread rapidly.*
■ cause (a belief or emotion) to become stronger or more widespread: *a fury fanned by press coverage.*
3 [no obj.] disperse or radiate from a central point to cover a wide area: *the arriving passengers began to* ***fan out*** *through the town in search of lodgings.*
■ (especially of a folded garment or other item made of cloth) spread out or cause to spread out into a semicircular shape: [no obj.] *a dress made of tiny pleats that* ***fanned out*** *as she walked* | [with obj.] *a wind* ***fanned*** *her hair* ***out*** *behind her.*
– DERIVATIVES **fan-like** adjective, **fanner** noun.
– ORIGIN Old English *fann* (as a noun denoting a device for winnowing grain), *fannian* (verb), from Latin *vannus* 'winnowing fan'. Compare with **VANE**.

fan2 ▶ **noun** a person who has a strong interest in or admiration for a particular sport, art form, or famous person: *football fans* | *I'm a fan of this author.*
– DERIVATIVES **fandom** noun.
– ORIGIN late 19th cent. (originally US): abbreviation of **FANATIC**.

Fanakalo /ˌfanagaˈlɒ, ˈfanagalɒ/ (also **Fanagalo**) ▶ **noun** [mass noun] S. African a language developed and used as a lingua franca by the southern African mining companies, composed of elements of the Nguni languages, English, and Afrikaans.
– ORIGIN 1940s: from Nguni *fana ka lo*, from *fana* 'be like' + the possessive suffix *-ka* + *lo* 'this'.

fanatic /fəˈnatɪk/ ▶ **noun** a person filled with excessive and rigidly single-minded zeal or enthusiasm, especially for an extreme religious or political cause.
■ [often with modifier] informal a person with an obsessive interest in and enthusiasm for something, especially an activity: *a fitness fanatic.*
▶ **adjective** [attrib.] filled with or expressing excessive zeal: *his eyes had a fanatic iciness.*
– DERIVATIVES **fanaticism** noun, **fanaticize** (also **-ise**) verb.
– ORIGIN mid 16th cent. (as an adjective): from French *fanatique* or Latin *fanaticus* 'of a temple, inspired by a god', from *fanum* 'temple'. The adjective originally described behaviour or speech that might result from possession by a god or demon, hence the earliest sense of the noun 'a religious maniac' (mid 17th cent.).

fanatical ▶ **adjective** filled with excessive and single-minded zeal: *fanatical revolutionaries.*
■ obsessively concerned with something: *he was* ***fanatical about*** *tidiness.*
– DERIVATIVES **fanatically** adverb.

fan base ▶ **noun** [mass noun] the fans of a sports team, pop group, etc. considered as a distinct social grouping.

fan belt ▶ **noun** (in a motor-vehicle engine) a belt that transmits motion from the driveshaft to the radiator fan and the dynamo or alternator.

fanciable ▶ **adjective** informal sexually attractive.

fancier ▶ **noun** [with modifier] a connoisseur or enthusiast of something, especially someone who has a special interest in or breeds a particular animal: *a pigeon fancier.*

fanciful ▶ **adjective** (of a person or their thoughts and ideas) over-imaginative and unrealistic: *a fanciful story about a pot of gold.*
■ existing only in the imagination or fancy: *the Moon Maiden is one of a number of fanciful lunar inhabitants.* ■ designed to be exotically ornamental rather than practical: *fanciful bonnets.*
– DERIVATIVES **fancifully** adverb, **fancifulness** noun.

fan club ▶ **noun** an organized group of fans of a famous person.

fancy ▶ **verb** (**-ies**, **-ied**) [with obj.] **1** Brit. informal feel a desire or liking for: *do you fancy a drink?*
■ find sexually attractive: *I really fancy him.* ■ (**fancy oneself**) informal have an unduly high opinion of oneself, or of one's ability in a particular area: *he* ***fancied himself as*** *an amateur psychologist.*
2 regard (a horse, team, or player) as a likely winner: [with obj. and infinitive] *I fancy him to win the tournament.*
3 [with clause] imagine; think: *he fancied he could smell the perfume of roses.*
■ [in imperative] used to express one's surprise at something: *fancy meeting all those television actors!*
▶ **adjective** (**fancier**, **fanciest**) **1** elaborate in structure or decoration: *the furniture was very fancy* | *a fancy computerized system.*
■ designed to impress: *converted fishing boats with fancy new names.* ■ chiefly N. Amer. (especially of foodstuffs) of high quality: *fancy molasses.* ■ (of flowers) of two or more colours. ■ (of an animal) bred to develop particular points of appearance: *fancy goldfish.*
2 archaic (of a drawing, painting, or sculpture) created from the imagination rather than from life.
▶ **noun** (pl. **-ies**) **1** a feeling of liking or attraction, typically one that is superficial or transient: *this was no* ***passing fancy,*** *but a feeling he would live by.*
■ a person or thing that one finds attractive: *people jostled to ride alongside their fancy.* ■ a favourite in a race or other sporting contest: *the filly is already a leading fancy for next year's races.* ■ (**the fancy**) dated enthusiasts for a particular sport, especially boxing or racing, considered collectively.
2 [mass noun] the faculty of imagination: *my research assistant is prone to* ***flights of fancy.***
■ [count noun] a thing that one supposes or imagines, typically an unfounded or tentative belief or idea: *I've a fancy they want to be alone.*
3 (also **fancy cake**) a small iced cake or biscuit.
4 (in sixteenth and seventeenth century music) a composition for keyboard or strings in free or variation form.
– PHRASES **as** (or **when** or **where**) **the fancy takes one** according to one's inclination: *you could move about as the fancy took you.* **fancy one's** (or **someone's**) **chances** believe that one (or someone else) is likely to be successful: *we fancy our chances in the replay.* **take** (or **catch**) **someone's fancy** appeal to someone. **take a fancy to** become fond of, especially without an obvious reason.
– DERIVATIVES **fancily** adverb, **fanciness** noun.
– ORIGIN late Middle English: contraction of **FANTASY**.

fancy dress ▶ **noun** [mass noun] an unusual or amusing costume worn to make someone look like a famous person, fictional character, or an animal, especially as part of a theme at a party.

fancy-free ▶ **adjective** not emotionally involved with or committed to anyone: *her recent divorce meant that she was* ***footloose and fancy-free.***

fancy goods ▶ **plural noun** items for sale that are purely or chiefly ornamental.

fancy man ▶ **noun** informal, often derogatory a woman's lover.
■ archaic a pimp.

fancy woman (Brit. also **fancy piece**) ▶ **noun** informal, often derogatory a married man's mistress.

fancy-work ▶ **noun** [mass noun] ornamental needlework, crochet, or knitting, as opposed to plain or purely functional stitches.

fan dance ▶ **noun** a dance in which the female performer is apparently nude and remains partly concealed throughout by large fans.

fandangle /fanˈdaŋg(ə)l/ ▶ **noun** archaic a useless or purely ornamental thing: *a solo with no end of shakes and trills and fandangles.*
– ORIGIN mid 19th cent.: perhaps from **FANDANGO**, influenced by *newfangle*.

fandango /fanˈdaŋgəʊ/ ▶ **noun** (pl. **-oes** or **-os**) **1** a lively Spanish dance for two people, typically accompanied by castanets or tambourine.
2 [mass noun] foolish nonsense: *the Washington inaugural fandango.*
■ [count noun] a useless or purely ornamental thing: *a three story fandango in stone.*
– ORIGIN mid 18th cent.: Spanish, of unknown origin.

fane ▶ **noun** archaic a temple or shrine.
– ORIGIN late Middle English: from Latin *fanum*.

fanfare ▶ **noun** a short ceremonial tune or flourish played on brass instruments,typically to introduce something or someone important.
■ figurative an elaborate welcome or introduction.
– ORIGIN mid 18th cent.: from French, ultimately of imitative origin.

fanfaronade /ˌfanfarəˈneɪd, -ˈnɑːd/ ▶ **noun 1** [mass noun] arrogant or boastful talk.
2 a fanfare.
– ORIGIN mid 17th cent.: from French *fanfaronnade*, from *fanfaron* 'braggart', from *fanfare* (see **FANFARE**).

Fang /faŋ/ (also **Fan**) ▶ **noun** (pl. same or **Fangs**) **1** a member of a people inhabiting parts of Cameroon, Equatorial Guinea, and Gabon.
2 [mass noun] the Bantu language of this people, with over 500,000 speakers.
▶ **adjective** of or relating to this people or their language.
– ORIGIN French, probably from Fang *Pangwe*.

fang ▶ **noun** a large sharp tooth, especially a canine tooth of a dog or wolf.
■ the tooth of a venomous snake, by which poison is injected. ■ the biting mouthpart of a spider. ■ Brit. informal a person's tooth.
– DERIVATIVES **fanged** adjective [also in combination], **fangless** adjective.
– ORIGIN late Old English (denoting booty or spoils), from Old Norse *fang* 'capture, grasp'; compare with **VANG**. A sense 'trap, snare' is recorded from the mid 16th cent.; both this and the original sense survive in Scots. The current sense (also mid 16th cent.) reflects the same notion of 'something that catches and holds'.

Fangio /ˈfandʒɪəʊ/, Juan Manuel (1911–95), Argentinian motor-racing driver. He first won the world championship in 1951 and then held the title from 1954 until 1957.

fango /ˈfaŋgəʊ/ ▶ **noun** [mass noun] [usu. as modifier] mud from thermal springs in Italy, used in curative treatment at spas and health farms: *fango mud baths.*
– ORIGIN early 20th cent.: Italian, literally 'mud'.

fan heater ▶ **noun** an electric heater in which a fan drives air over a hot element and back into the room.

fan-in ▶ **noun** Electronics the number of inputs that can be connected to a circuit.

fan-jet ▶ **noun** another term for **TURBOFAN**.

fankle /ˈfaŋk(ə)l/ ▶ **verb** [with obj.] Scottish entangle: *the tape got fankled in the motorbike's front wheels.*
– ORIGIN late Middle English: from Scots *fank* 'coil of rope' + **-LE**[4].

fanlight ▶ **noun** a small semicircular or rectangular window over a door or another window.
■ another term for **SKYLIGHT**.

fan mail ▶ **noun** [mass noun] letters from fans to a famous person they admire.

Fannie Mae ▶ **noun** US informal the Federal National Mortgage Association, a corporation (now privately owned) which trades in mortgages.
– ORIGIN 1940s: elaboration of the acronym FNMA, suggested by the given names *Fanny* and *Mae*.

fanny ▶ **noun** (pl. **-ies**) **1** Brit. vulgar slang a woman's genitals.
2 informal, chiefly N. Amer. a person's buttocks.
– ORIGIN late 19th cent.: of unknown origin.
▶ **fanny about** (or **around**) Brit. informal mess around and waste time.

Fanny Adams Brit. informal ▶ **noun** **1** (also **sweet Fanny Adams**) nothing at all: *'I know sweet Fanny Adams about mining,' he admits.* [ORIGIN: early 20th cent.: sometimes understood as a euphemism for *fuck all*.]
2 a nautical term for tinned meat or stew. [ORIGIN: late 19th cent.: black humour, from the name of a murder victim *c.*1870.]

fanny pack ▶ **noun** North American term for **BUMBAG**.

fan-out ▶ **noun** Electronics the number of inputs that can be connected to a specified output.

fan palm ▶ **noun** a palm with large lobed fan-shaped leaves.
● *Chamaerops* and other genera, family Palmae: many species, including the **dwarf** (or **European**) **fan palm** (*C. humilis*), which is the only palm native to Europe.

fantabulous /fanˈtabjʊləs/ ▶ **adjective** informal excellent; wonderful: *a fantabulous prize.*
– ORIGIN 1950s: blend of **FANTASTIC** and **FABULOUS**.

fantail ▶ **noun** **1** a fan-shaped tail or end.
■ chiefly US the overhanging part of the stern of a boat, especially a warship. ■ (also **fantail pigeon**) a domestic pigeon of a broad-tailed variety. ■ the fan of a windmill.
2 (also **fantail flycatcher**) a flycatcher with a long tapering tail that is often fanned out, found mainly in SE Asia and Australasia.
● Genus *Rhipidura*, family Monarchidae: numerous species.
– DERIVATIVES **fan-tailed** adjective.

fan-tailed warbler (also **fantail warbler**) ▶ **noun** a small Old World warbler with streaked plumage and a stubby boldly marked tail.
● Genus *Cisticola*, family Sylviidae: several species, in particular *C. juncidis*, found from western Europe to Australia. See also **CISTICOLA**.

fan-tan /ˈfantan/ ▶ **noun** [mass noun] **1** a Chinese gambling game in which players try to guess the remainder after the banker has divided a number of hidden objects into four groups.
2 a card game in which players build on sequences of sevens.
– ORIGIN late 19th cent.: from Chinese *fān tān*, literally 'repeated divisions'.

fantasia /fanˈteɪzɪə, ˌfantəˈziːə/ ▶ **noun** a musical composition with a free form and often an improvisatory style.
■ a musical composition which is based on several familiar tunes. ■ a thing that is composed of a mixture of different forms or styles: *the theatre is a kind of Moorish and Egyptian fantasia.*
– ORIGIN early 18th cent.: from Italian, 'fantasy', from Latin *phantasia* (see **FANTASY**).

fantasize (also **-ise**) ▶ **verb** [no obj.] indulge in daydreaming about something desired: *he sometimes fantasized about emigrating.*
■ [with obj.] imagine (something that one wants to happen): *one might fantasize the death of someone seen as a threat.*
– DERIVATIVES **fantasist** noun.

fantast /ˈfantast/ (also **phantast**) ▶ **noun** archaic or N. Amer. an impractical, impulsive person; a dreamer.
– ORIGIN late 16th cent. (formerly also as *phantast*): originally via medieval Latin from Greek *phantastēs* 'boaster', from *phantazein* or *phantazesthai* (see **FANTASTIC**); in modern use from German *Phantast*.

fantastic ▶ **adjective** **1** imaginative or fanciful; remote from reality: *novels are capable of mixing fantastic and realistic elements.*
■ of an incredible size or degree: *the prices were fantastic, far higher than elsewhere.* ■ (of a shape or design) bizarre or exotic; seeming more appropriate to a fairy tale than to reality or practical use: *visions of a fantastic, maze-like building.*
2 informal incredibly or extraordinarily good or attractive: *your support has been fantastic.*
– DERIVATIVES **fantastical** adjective (only in sense 1), **fantasticality** noun (only in sense 1), **fantastically** adverb.
– ORIGIN late Middle English (in the sense 'existing only in the imagination, unreal'): from Old French *fantastique*, via medieval Latin from Greek *phantastikos*, from *phantazein* 'make visible', *phantazesthai* 'have visions, imagine', from *phantos* 'visible' (related to *phainein* 'to show'). From the 16th to the 19th cents the Latinized spelling *phantastic* was also used.

fantasticate ▶ **verb** [with obj.] rare make (something) seem fanciful or fantastic: *I do not think I have fantasticated these accounts.*
– DERIVATIVES **fantastication** noun.

fantasy ▶ **noun** (pl. **-ies**) **1** [mass noun] the faculty or activity of imagining things, especially things which are impossible or improbable: *his researches had moved into the* ***realms of fantasy****.*
■ the product of this faculty or activity: *the scene is clearly fantasy.* ■ [count noun] a fanciful mental image, typically one on which a person dwells at length or repeatedly and which reflects their conscious or unconscious wishes: *the notion of being independent is a child's ultimate fantasy.* ■ [count noun] an idea with no basis in reality: *it is a misleading fantasy to suggest that the bill can be implemented.* ■ a genre of imaginative fiction involving magic and adventure, especially in a setting other than the real world.
2 a musical composition, free in form, typically involving variation on an existing work or the imaginative representation of a situation or story; a fantasia.
▶ **verb** (**-ies**, **-ied**) [with obj.] poetic/literary imagine the occurrence of; fantasize about.
– ORIGIN late Middle English: from Old French *fantasie*, from Latin *phantasia*, from Greek 'imagination, appearance', later 'phantom', from *phantazein* 'make visible'. From the 16th to the 19th cents the Latinized spelling *phantasy* was also used.

fantasy football ▶ **noun** [mass noun] a competition in which participants select imaginary teams from among the players in a league and score points according to the actual performance of their players.

Fante /ˈfanti/ (also **Fanti**) ▶ **noun** (pl. same or **Fantis**)
1 a member of a people of southern Ghana.
2 [mass noun] the dialect of Akan spoken by this people.
▶ **adjective** of or relating to this people or their language.
– ORIGIN the name in Akan.

fantod /ˈfantɒd/ ▶ **noun** N. Amer. informal a state or attack of uneasiness or unreasonableness: *people calling me Ray just gives me* ***the fantods****.*
– ORIGIN mid 19th cent.: of unknown origin.

fan worm ▶ **noun** a tube-dwelling marine bristle worm which bears a fan-like crown of filaments that are typically brightly coloured and project from the top of the tube, filtering the water for food particles.
● Families Sabellidae and Serpulidae, class Polychaeta: numerous species, including the peacock worm.

fanzine /ˈfanziːn/ ▶ **noun** a magazine, usually produced by amateurs, for fans of a particular performer, group, or form of entertainment.
– ORIGIN 1940s (originally US): blend of **FAN**[2] and **MAGAZINE**.

FAO ▶ **abbreviation** for Food and Agriculture Organization.

FAQ ▶ **noun** Computing a text file containing a list of questions and answers relating to a particular subject, especially one giving basic information for users of an Internet newsgroup.
– ORIGIN 1990s: acronym from *frequently asked questions*.

faquir ▶ **noun** variant spelling of **FAKIR**.

far ▶ **adverb** (**further**, **furthest** or **farther**, **farthest**)
1 [often with adverbial] at, to, or by a great distance (used to indicate the extent to which one thing is distant from another): *it was not too* ***far away*** | *the mountains far in the distance glowed in the sun.*
2 over a large expanse of space or time: *he had not travelled far* | figurative *that's the reason why we have come so far and done as well as we have.*
3 by a great deal: *he is able to function far better than usual* | *the reality has fallen* ***far short of*** *early expectations.*
▶ **adjective** [attrib.] situated at a great distance in space or time: *the far reaches of the universe.*
■ more distant than another object of the same kind: *he was standing in the far corner.* ■ distant from a point seen as central; extreme: *she was brought up in the far north of Scotland* | *the largest electoral success for the far Right since the war.*
– PHRASES **as far as** for as great a distance as: *the river stretched away as far as he could see.* ■ for a great enough distance to reach: *I decided to walk as far as the village.* ■ to the extent that: *as far as I am concerned it is no big deal.* **be a far cry from** be very different to: *the hotel's royal suite is a far cry from the poverty of his home country.* **by far** by a great amount: *this was by far the largest city in the area.* **far and away** by a very large amount: *he is far and away the most accomplished player.* **far and near** everywhere: *people came from far and near to the party.* **far and wide** over a large area: *expanding industry sucked in labour from far and wide.* **far be it from** (or **for**) **me to** used to express reluctance, especially to do something which one thinks may be resented: *far be it from me to speculate on his reasons.* **far from** very different from being; tending to the opposite of: *conditions were far from satisfactory.* **far gone** in a bad or worsening state, especially so as to be beyond recovery: *a few frames from the original film were too far gone to salvage.* ■ advanced in time: *the legislative session is too far gone for the lengthy hearings needed to pass the bill.* **go far** **1** achieve a great deal: *he was the bright one and everyone was sure he would go far.* **2** contribute greatly: *extension of this practice would* ***go far towards*** *resolving unnecessary antagonisms.* **3** be worth or amount to much: *the money would not go far at this year's prices.* **go so far as to do something** do something regarded as extreme: *surely they wouldn't go so far as to break in?* **go too far** exceed the limits of what is reasonable or acceptable. **how far** **1** used to ask how great a distance is: *they wanted to know how far he could travel.* **2** to what extent: *he was not sure how far she was committed.* **so far** **1** to a certain limited extent: *jabs and pills can protect you only so far.* **2** (of a trend that seems likely to continue) up to this time: *diplomatic activity so far has failed.* (**in**) **so far as** (or **that**) to the extent that: *the existing business had priority so far as further investment was concerned.* **so far so good** progress has been satisfactory up to now: *'How's the job going?' 'So far so good.'* **too far** in excess of what is safe, sensible, or desirable: *the statement appears to be a claim too far.*
– ORIGIN Old English *feorr*, of Germanic origin; related to Dutch *ver*, from an Indo-European root shared by Sanskrit *para* and Greek *pera* 'further'.

farad /ˈfarad/ (abbrev.: **F**) ▶ **noun** the SI unit of electrical capacitance, equal to the capacitance of a capacitor in which one coulomb of charge causes a potential difference of one volt.
– ORIGIN mid 19th cent.: shortening of **FARADAY**. The term was originally proposed as a unit of electrical charge.

faradaic /ˌfarəˈdeɪɪk/ (also **faradic**) ▶ **adjective** produced by or associated with electrical induction.
– ORIGIN late 19th cent.: from the name of M. **FARADAY** + **-IC**.

Faraday /ˈfarədeɪ/, Michael (1791–1867), English physicist and chemist. He contributed significantly to the field of electromagnetism, discovering electromagnetic induction and demonstrating electromagnetic rotation (the key to the electric dynamo and motor). Faraday also discovered the laws of electrolysis and set the foundations for the classical field theory of electromagnetic behaviour.

faraday /ˈfarədeɪ/ (abbrev.: **F**) ▶ **noun** Chemistry a unit of electric charge equal to Faraday's constant.
– ORIGIN early 20th cent.: coined in German from the name of M. **FARADAY**.

Faraday cage ▶ **noun** Physics an earthed metal

screen surrounding a piece of equipment in order to exclude electrostatic influences.

Faraday effect ▶**noun** [mass noun] Physics the rotation of the plane of polarization of electromagnetic waves in certain substances in a magnetic field.

Faraday's constant Chemistry the quantity of electric charge carried by one mole of electrons (roughly 96,490 coulombs). Compare with **FARADAY**.

Faraday's law **1** Physics a law stating that when the magnetic flux linking a circuit changes, an electromotive force is induced in the circuit proportional to the rate of change of the flux linkage.
2 Chemistry a law stating that the amount of any substance deposited or liberated during electrolysis is proportional to the quantity of electric charge passed and to the equivalent weight of the substance.

faradic /fəˈradɪk/ ▶**adjective** another term for **FARADAIC**.

farandole /ˌfar(ə)nˈdəʊl, ˈfar(ə)ndəʊl/ ▶**noun** historical a lively Provençal dance in the which the dancers join hands and wind in and out in a chain.
– ORIGIN mid 19th cent.: French, from modern Provençal *farandoulo*.

farang /faˈraŋ/ ▶**noun** (among Thais) a European or other foreigner.
– ORIGIN Thai, from **FRANK**[2].

faraway ▶**adjective** distant in space or time: *exotic and faraway locations.*
■seeming remote from the immediate surroundings; dreamy: *she had a strange faraway look in her eyes.*

farce ▶**noun** a comic dramatic work using buffoonery and horseplay and typically including crude characterization and ludicrously improbable situations.
■[mass noun] the genre of such works. ■ an absurd event: *the debate turned into a drunken farce.*
– ORIGIN early 16th cent.: from French, literally 'stuffing', from *farcir* 'to stuff', from Latin *farcire*. An earlier sense of 'forcemeat stuffing' became used metaphorically for comic interludes 'stuffed' into the texts of religious plays, whence current usage.

farceur /fɑːˈsəː/ ▶**noun** a writer of or performer in farces.
■a joker or comedian.
– ORIGIN late 17th cent.: French, from obsolete *farcer* 'act farces'.

farcical ▶**adjective** of or resembling farce, especially because of absurd or ridiculous aspects: *he considered the whole idea farcical | a farcical situation.*
– DERIVATIVES **farcicality** noun, **farcically** adverb.

farcy /ˈfɑːsi/ ▶**noun** [mass noun] glanders in horses (or a similar disease in cattle) in which there is inflammation of the lymph vessels, causing nodules (**farcy buds** or **buttons**).
– ORIGIN late Middle English: from Old French *farcin*, from late Latin *farciminum*, from *farcire* 'to stuff' (because of the appearance of the swollen nodules).

fardel /ˈfɑːd(ə)l/ ▶**noun** archaic a bundle: *a* **fardel** *of stories, personages, emotions.*
– ORIGIN Middle English: from Old French.

fare ▶**noun** **1** the money a passenger on public transport has to pay.
■a passenger paying to travel in a vehicle, especially a taxi.
2 [mass noun] a range of food, especially of a particular type: *traditional Scottish fare.*
▶**verb** [no obj.] **1** [with adverbial] perform in a specified way in a particular situation or over a particular period of time: *the party fared badly in the spring elections.*
■archaic happen; turn out: *beware that* **it fare** *not with you as with your predecessor.*
2 [with adverbial of direction] archaic travel: *a young knight fares forth.*
– ORIGIN Old English *fær, faru* 'travelling, a journey or expedition', *faran* 'to travel', also 'get on (well or badly)', of Germanic origin; related to Dutch *varen* and German *fahren* 'to travel', Old Norse *ferja* 'ferry boat', also to **FORD**. Sense 1 of the noun stems from an earlier meaning 'a journey for which a price is paid'. Noun sense 2 was originally used with reference to the quality or quantity of food provided, probably from the idea of faring well or badly.

Far East China, Japan, and other countries of east Asia.
– DERIVATIVES **Far Eastern** adjective.

fare stage ▶**noun** Brit. a section of a bus or tram route for which a fixed price is charged.
■a stop marking the end of such a section.

fare-thee-well (also **fare-you-well**) ▶**noun** (in phrase **to a fare-thee-well**) US to perfection; thoroughly: *coated in aspic and decorated to a fare-thee-well.*

farewell ▶**exclamation** used to express good wishes on parting: *Farewell Albert!*
▶**noun** an act of parting or of marking someone's departure: *the dinner had been arranged as a farewell.*
■[mass noun] parting good wishes: *he had come on the pretext of* **bidding** *her* **farewell** | [count noun] *I bade him a fond farewell.*
– ORIGIN late Middle English: from the imperative of **FARE** + the adverb **WELL**[1].

Farewell, Cape **1** the southernmost point of Greenland. Danish name **KAP FARVEL**.
2 the northernmost point of South Island, New Zealand. The cape was named by Captain James Cook as the last land sighted before he left for Australia in March 1770.

farfalle /fɑːˈfaleɪ, -li/ ▶**plural noun** small pieces of pasta shaped like bows or butterflies' wings.
– ORIGIN Italian, plural of *farfalla* 'butterfly'.

far-fetched ▶**adjective** (of an explanation or theory) contrived and unconvincing; unlikely.
■(of a story or idea) implausible, silly, or exaggerated.

far-flung ▶**adjective** distant or remote: *the far-flung corners of the world.*
■widely distributed: *newsletters provided an important link to a far-flung membership.*

Fargo, William, see **WELLS, FARGO, & CO.**

Faridabad /fəˈriːdəbad/ an industrial city in northern India, south of Delhi, in the state of Haryana; pop. 614,000 (1991).

farina /fəˈrʌɪnə, fəˈriːnə/ ▶**noun** [mass noun] flour or meal made of cereal grains, nuts, or starchy roots.
■[count noun] archaic a powdery substance, or a substance in powdered form. ■ archaic starch.
– DERIVATIVES **farinaceous** /ˌfarɪˈneɪʃəs/ adjective.
– ORIGIN late Middle English: from Latin, from *far* 'corn'.

farkleberry /ˈfɑːk(ə)lˌb(ə)ri, -ˌbɛri/ ▶**noun** a shrub or small tree with thickly leathery leaves and inedible black berries, native to the south-eastern US.
• *Vaccinium arboreum*, family Ericaceae.
– ORIGIN mid 18th cent.: probably an alteration of **WHORTLEBERRY**.

farl /fɑːl/ ▶**noun** a thin cake of Scottish origin made of oatmeal or flour, typically triangular in shape.
– ORIGIN late 17th cent.: from obsolete *fardel* 'quarter', contraction of *fourth deal* (i.e. **DEAL**[1] in the earlier sense 'portion, share').

farm ▶**noun** an area of land and its buildings used for growing crops and rearing animals, typically under the control of one owner or manager.
■the main dwelling place on such a site; a farmhouse: *a half-timbered farm.* ■ [with modifier] a place for breeding a particular type of animal or producing a specified crop: *a fish farm.* ■ [with modifier] an establishment at which something is produced or processed: *an energy farm.*
▶**verb** **1** [no obj.] make one's living by growing crops or keeping livestock: *he has farmed organically for five years.*
■[with obj.] use (land) for growing crops and rearing animals, especially commercially. ■ [with obj.] breed or grow commercially (a type of livestock or crop, especially one not normally domesticated or cultivated).
2 [with obj.] (**farm someone/thing out**) send out or subcontract work to others: *it saves time and money to farm out some writing work to specialized companies.*
■arrange for a child to be looked after by someone, usually for payment. ■ dated send a sports player temporarily to another team in return for a fee.
3 [with obj.] historical allow someone to collect and keep the revenues from (a tax) on payment of a fee: *the customs had been farmed to the collector for a fixed sum.*
– DERIVATIVES **farmable** adjective.
– ORIGIN Middle English: from Old French *ferme*, from medieval Latin *firma* 'fixed payment', from Latin *firmare* 'fix, settle' (in medieval Latin 'contract for'), from *firmus* 'constant, firm'; compare with **FIRM**[2]. The noun originally denoted a fixed annual amount payable as rent or tax; this is reflected in sense 3 of the verb, which later gave rise to 'to subcontract' (sense 2). The noun came to denote a lease, and, in the early 16th cent., land leased specifically for farming. The verb sense 'grow crops or keep livestock' dates from the early 19th cent.

farman ▶**noun** another term for **FIRMAN**.

farmer ▶**noun** **1** a person who owns or manages a farm.
2 [with modifier] historical a person to whom the collection of taxes was contracted for a fee.
– ORIGIN late Middle English: from Old French *fermier*, from medieval Latin *firmarius, firmator*, from *firma* (see **FARM**). Sense 1 originally denoted a bailiff or steward who farmed land on the owner's behalf, or a tenant farmer.

farmer's lung ▶**noun** informal term for **ASPERGILLOSIS**.

farm gate ▶**noun** the gateway to a farm, especially as representing the location for direct purchase of farm produce: [as modifier] *farm-gate prices.*

farmhand ▶**noun** a worker on a farm.

farmhouse ▶**noun** a house attached to a farm, especially the main house in which the farmer lives.

farmhouse loaf ▶**noun** a loaf of white bread, oval or rectangular in shape, with a rounded top.

farming ▶**noun** [mass noun] the activity or business of growing crops and raising livestock.

farmland ▶**noun** [mass noun] (also **farmlands**) land used for farming.

farm school ▶**noun** (in South Africa) a rural school providing primary education for the children of a district, typically one situated on a farm.

farmstead ▶**noun** a farm and its buildings.

farmyard ▶**noun** a yard or enclosure attached to a farmhouse.
▶**adjective** [attrib.] (especially of manners or language) coarse: *he insulted them in farmyard language.*

Farnborough /ˈfɑːnbərə/ a town in southern England, in Hampshire; pop. 48,300 (1990). Noted as a centre of aviation, it is the site of an air show held every other year.

Farne Islands /fɑːn/ a group of seventeen small islands off the coast of Northumberland, noted for their wildlife.

Farnese[1] /fɑːˈneɪzeɪ, -zi, Italian farˈnese/, Alessandro, see **PAUL III**.

Farnese[2] /fɑːˈneɪzeɪ, -zi/, Alessandro, Duke of Parma (1545–92), Italian general and statesman. While in the service of Philip II of Spain he acted as Governor General of the Netherlands (1578–92). He captured Antwerp in 1585, securing the southern Netherlands for Spain.

Faro /ˈfɑːruː/ a seaport on the south coast of Portugal, capital of the Algarve; pop. 31,970 (1990).

faro /ˈfɛːrəʊ/ ▶**noun** [mass noun] a gambling card game in which players bet on the order in which the cards will appear.
– ORIGIN early 18th cent. (originally as *pharaoh* or *pharo*): from French *pharaon* (see **PHARAOH**), said to have been the name of the king of hearts.

Faroe Islands /ˈfɛːrəʊ/ (also **Faeroe Islands** or **the Faroes**) a group of islands in the North Atlantic between Iceland and the Shetland Islands, belonging to Denmark but partly autonomous; pop. 43,700 (1994); languages, Faroese (official), Danish; capital, Tórshavn. The shipping forecast area **Faroes** covers this area of the Atlantic.

Faroese /ˌfɛːrəʊˈiːz/ (also **Faeroese**) ▶**adjective** of or relating to the Faroe Islands or their people or language.
▶**noun** (pl. same) **1** a native or national of the Faroes, or a person of Faroese descent.
2 [mass noun] the official language of the Faroes, a Scandinavian language closely related to Icelandic.

far-off ▶**adjective** remote in time or space: *a far-off country.*

farouche /fəˈruːʃ/ ▶**adjective** sullen or shy in company.
– ORIGIN mid 18th cent.: from French, alteration of Old French *forache*, based on Latin *foras* 'out of doors'.

Farouk /faˈruːk/ (1920–65), king of Egypt, reigned 1936–52. Farouk's defeat in the Arab-Israeli conflict of 1948, together with the general corruption of his reign, led to a military coup in 1952, masterminded by Nasser. Farouk was forced to abdicate in favour of his infant son, Fuad.

far out ▶ **adjective** unconventional or avant-garde: *far out radicals.*
■[often as exclamation] informal excellent: *it's really far out!*

Farquhar /ˈfɑːkə/, George (1678–1707), Irish dramatist. He was a principal figure in Restoration comedy. Notable works: *The Recruiting Officer* (1706) and *The Beaux' Stratagem* (1707).

farrago /fəˈrɑːɡəʊ, fəˈreɪɡəʊ/ ▶ **noun** (pl. **-os** or US **-oes**) a confused mixture: *a farrago of fact and myth about Abraham Lincoln.*
– DERIVATIVES **farraginous** /fəˈrɑːdʒɪnəs, -ˈreɪdʒ-/ adjective.
– ORIGIN mid 17th cent.: from Latin, literally 'mixed fodder', from *far* 'corn'.

far-reaching ▶ **adjective** having important and widely applicable effects or implications: *a series of far-reaching political reforms.*

f

Farrell[1] /ˈfarəl/, J. G. (1935–79), English novelist; full name *James Gordon Farrell*. Notable works: *The Siege of Krishnapur* (1973) and *The Singapore Grip* (1978).

Farrell[2] /ˈfarəl/, J. T. (1904–79), American novelist; full name *James Thomas Farrell*. He achieved fame with his trilogy about Studs Lonigan, a young Chicago Catholic of Irish descent, which began with *Young Lonigan* (1932).

farrier /ˈfarɪə/ ▶ **noun** a smith who shoes horses.
– DERIVATIVES **farriery** noun.
– ORIGIN mid 16th cent.: from Old French *ferrier*, from Latin *ferrarius*, from *ferrum* 'iron, horseshoe'.

farrow ▶ **noun** a litter of pigs.
■an act of giving birth to a litter of pigs.
▶ **verb** [with obj.] (of a sow) give birth to (piglets): *the pig is one of a litter of nine farrowed in July.*
– ORIGIN Old English *fearh, færh* 'young pig', of West Germanic origin, from an Indo-European root shared by Greek *porkos* and Latin *porcus* 'pig'.

farruca /fəˈruːkə/ ▶ **noun** a type of flamenco dance.
– ORIGIN 1930s: Spanish, feminine of *farruco* 'Galician or Asturian', from *Farruco*, pet form of the given name *Francisco*.

farse ▶ **adjective** W. Indian another term for **FAST**[1] (in sense 5).

far-seeing ▶ **adjective** having shrewd judgement and an ability to predict and plan for future eventualities.

Farsi /ˈfɑːsiː/ ▶ **noun** [mass noun] the modern Persian language, the official language of Iran, with over 20 million speakers.
– ORIGIN from Arabic *fārsī*, from *Fārs*, from Persian *Pārs* 'Persia'. Compare with **PARSEE**.

far-sighted ▶ **adjective 1** showing a prudent awareness of future possibilities: *he was clever and far-sighted in business.*
2 North American term for **LONG-SIGHTED**.
– DERIVATIVES **far-sightedly** adverb, **far-sightedness** noun.

fart informal ▶ **verb** [no obj.] emit wind from the anus.
■(**fart about/around**) waste time on silly or trivial things.
▶ **noun** an emission of wind from the anus.
■a boring or contemptible person: *he was such an old fart.*
– ORIGIN Old English (recorded in the verbal noun *feorting* 'farting') of Germanic origin; related to German *farzen, furzen*.

farther ▶ **adverb** & **adjective** variant form of **FURTHER**.

USAGE On the difference in use of **farther** and **further**, see usage at **FURTHER**.

farthermost ▶ **adjective** variant form of **FURTHERMOST**.

farthest ▶ **adjective** & **adverb** variant form of **FURTHEST**.

farthing ▶ **noun** a former monetary unit and coin of the UK, withdrawn in 1961, equal to a quarter of an old penny.
■[usu. with negative] the least possible amount: *she didn't care a farthing for the woman.*
– ORIGIN Old English *fēorthing*, from *fēortha* 'fourth', perhaps on the pattern of Old Norse *fjórthungr* 'quarter'.

farthingale /ˈfɑːðɪŋɡeɪl/ ▶ **noun** historical a hooped petticoat or circular pad of fabric around the hips, formerly worn under women's skirts to extend and shape them.
– ORIGIN early 16th cent. (formerly also as *vardingale*): from French *verdugale*, alteration of Spanish *verdugado*, from *verdugo* 'rod, stick', from *verde* 'green'.

fartlek /ˈfɑːtlɛk/ ▶ **noun** [mass noun] Athletics a system of training for distance runners in which the terrain and pace are continually varied to eliminate boredom and enhance psychological aspects of conditioning.
– ORIGIN 1940s: from Swedish, from *fart* 'speed' + *lek* 'play'.

Far West the regions of North America in the Rocky Mountains and along the Pacific coast.
■former term for **MIDWEST**.

FAS ▶ **abbreviation for** fetal alcohol syndrome.

fasces /ˈfasiːz/ ▶ **plural noun** historical (in ancient Rome) a bundle of rods with a projecting axe blade, carried by a lictor as a symbol of a magistrate's power.
■(in Fascist Italy) such items used as emblems of authority.
– ORIGIN Latin, plural of *fascis* 'bundle'.

fascia ▶ **noun 1** /ˈfeɪʃɪə, -ʃə/ (chiefly Brit. also **facia**) a wooden board or other flat piece of material covering the ends of rafters or other fittings.
■chiefly Brit. the dashboard of a motor vehicle. ■ a board or panel of controls on any piece of equipment. ■ a board or sign on the upper part of a shopfront showing the name of the shop. ■(in classical architecture) a long flat surface between mouldings on an architrave.
2 /ˈfaʃə/ (pl. **fasciae** /-ʃiː/) Anatomy a thin sheath of fibrous tissue enclosing a muscle or other organ.
– DERIVATIVES **fascial** adjective (only in sense 2).
– ORIGIN mid 16th cent.: from Latin, 'band, door frame', related to **FASCES**. Compare with **FESS**[1].

fasciated /ˈfaʃɪeɪtɪd, -ɪətɪd/ ▶ **adjective** Botany showing abnormal fusion of parts or organs, resulting in a flattened ribbon-like structure.
– DERIVATIVES **fasciation** noun.
– ORIGIN mid 18th cent. (in the sense 'striped, banded'): from Latin *fasciatus* (past participle of *fasciare* 'swathe', from *fascia* 'band') + **-ED**[1].

fascicle /ˈfasɪk(ə)l/ ▶ **noun 1** (also **fascicule** /-kjuːl/) a separately published instalment of a book or other printed work.
2 (also **fasciculus** /faˈsɪkjʊləs/) Anatomy & Biology a bundle of structures, such as nerve or muscle fibres or conducting vessels in plants.
– DERIVATIVES **fascicled** adjective, **fascicular** adjective, **fasciculate** /-ˈsɪkjʊlət/ adjective.
– ORIGIN late 15th cent. (in sense 2): from Latin *fasciculus*, diminutive of *fascis* 'bundle'.

fasciculation /faˌsɪkjʊˈleɪʃ(ə)n/ ▶ **noun 1** Medicine a brief spontaneous contraction affecting a small number of muscle fibres, often causing a flicker of movement under the skin. It can be a symptom of disease of the motor neurons.
2 [mass noun] chiefly Biology arrangement in bundles.

fasciitis /ˌfasɪˈʌɪtɪs, ˌfaʃɪ-/ ▶ **noun** [mass noun] Medicine inflammation of the fascia of a muscle or organ.

fascinate ▶ **verb** [with obj.] (usu. **be fascinated**) draw irresistibly the attention and interest of (someone): *I've always been fascinated by other cultures* | [with obj. and infinitive] *she was fascinated to learn about this strange land.*
■archaic (especially of a snake) deprive (a person or animal) of the ability to resist or escape by the power of a look or gaze: *the serpent fascinates its prey.*
– DERIVATIVES **fascination** noun, **fascinator** noun.
– ORIGIN late 16th cent. (in the sense 'bewitch, put under a spell'): from Latin *fascinat-* 'bewitched', from the verb *fascinare*, from *fascinum* 'spell, witchcraft'.

fascinating ▶ **adjective** extremely interesting: *fascinating facts.*
– DERIVATIVES **fascinatingly** adverb.

fascine /faˈsiːn/ ▶ **noun** a bundle of rods, sticks, or plastic pipes bound together, used in construction or military operations for filling in marshy ground or other obstacles and for strengthening the sides of embankments, ditches, or trenches.
– ORIGIN late 17th cent.: via French from Latin *fascina*, from *fascis* 'bundle'.

fascioliasis /ˌfasɪəˈlʌɪəsɪs/ ▶ **noun** [mass noun] Medicine infestation of a human or an animal with the liver fluke.
– ORIGIN late 19th cent.: from modern Latin *Fasciola hepatica*, the name of the liver fluke (from Latin *fasciola* 'small bandage') + **-IASIS**.

fascism /ˈfaʃɪz(ə)m, -sɪz(ə)m/ ▶ **noun** [mass noun] an authoritarian and nationalistic right-wing system of government and social organization.
■(in general use) extreme right-wing, authoritarian, or intolerant views or practice.

The term Fascism was first used of the totalitarian right-wing nationalist regime of Mussolini in Italy (1922–43), and the regimes of the Nazis in Germany and Franco in Spain were also Fascist. Fascism tends to include a belief in the supremacy of one national or ethnic group, a contempt for democracy, an insistence on obedience to a powerful leader, and a strong demagogic approach.

– DERIVATIVES **fascist** noun & adjective, **fascistic** adjective.
– ORIGIN from Italian *fascismo*, from *fascio* 'bundle, political group', from Latin *fascis* (see **FASCES**).

fash ▶ **verb** (**fash oneself**) Scottish feel upset or worried: *she'll be coming soon, don't fash yourself.*
– ORIGIN mid 16th cent.: from early modern French *fascher*, based on Latin *fastus* 'disdain, scornful contempt'.

fashion ▶ **noun 1** a popular trend, especially in styles of dress and ornament or manners of behaviour: *they are slaves to the fashion for Americana.*
■[mass noun] the production and marketing of new styles of goods, especially clothing and cosmetics: [as modifier] *a fashion magazine.*
2 a manner of doing something: *the work is done in a rather casual fashion.*
▶ **verb** [with obj.] (often **be fashioned**) make into a particular or the required form: *the bottles were **fashioned from** green glass.*
■(**fashion something into**) use materials to make into: *the skins were fashioned into boots and shoes.*
– PHRASES **after a fashion** to a certain extent but not perfectly or satisfactorily: *he could read after a fashion.* **after** (or **in**) **the fashion of** in a manner similar to: *she took servants for granted after the fashion of wealthy and pampered girls.* **in** (or **out of**) **fashion** popular (or unpopular) and considered (or not considered) to be smart at the time in question.
– DERIVATIVES **fashioner** noun.
– ORIGIN Middle English (in the sense 'make, shape, appearance', also 'a particular make or style'): from Old French *façon*, from Latin *factio(n-)*, from *facere* 'do, make'.

-fashion ▶ **combining form** in the manner of something specified: *dog-fashion* | *castanet-fashion.*
■in the style associated with a specified place or people: *American-fashion* | *Bristol-fashion.*

fashionable ▶ **adjective** characteristic of, influenced by, or representing a current popular trend or style: *fashionable clothes.*
■(of a person) dressing or behaving according to the current trend.
– DERIVATIVES **fashionability** noun, **fashionableness** noun, **fashionably** adverb.

fashion plate ▶ **noun** a picture showing a fashion, especially in dress.
■figurative a person who dresses very fashionably.

fashion victim ▶ **noun** a person who follows popular trends in dress and behaviour slavishly.

Fassbinder /ˈfasbɪndə, German ˈfasbɪndɐ/, Rainer Werner (1946–82), German film director. His films dealt largely with Germany during the Second World War and post-war West German society. Notable films: *The Bitter Tears of Petra von Kant* (1972).

fast[1] ▶ **adjective 1** moving or capable of moving at high speed: *a fast and powerful car.*
■performed or taking place at high speed; taking only a short time: *the journey was fast and enjoyable.* ■ [attrib.] allowing people or things to move at high speed: *a wide, fast road.* ■performing or able to perform a particular type of action quickly: *a fast reader.* ■ (of a sports field or ground) likely to make the ball bounce or run quickly or to allow competitors to reach a high speed. ■ (of a person or their lifestyle) engaging in or involving exciting and daring or shocking activities: *the fast life she led in London.*
2 [predic. or as complement] (of a clock or watch) showing a time ahead of the correct time: *I keep my watch fifteen minutes fast.*
3 firmly fixed or attached: *he **made** a rope **fast** to each corner.*
■(of friends) close and loyal. ■ (of a dye) not fading in light or when washed.
4 Photography (of a film) needing only a short exposure.
■(of a lens) having a large aperture and therefore suitable for use with short exposure times.
5 (also **farse**) W. Indian (of a person) prone to act in an unacceptably familiar way, typically by being

inquisitive or gossipy: *Mammy said, 'Stop asking questions, you too damn farse.'*
▶ **adverb 1** at high speed: *he was driving too fast.*
■ within a short time: *we're going to have to get to the bottom of this fast.*
2 so as to be hard to move; firmly or securely: *the ship was held fast by the anchor chain.*
■ (of sleeping) so as to be hard to wake: *they were too fast asleep to reply.*
– PHRASES **pull a fast one** informal try to gain an unfair advantage: *he had been trying to **pull a fast one** on his co-producer.*
– ORIGIN Old English *fæst* 'firmly fixed, steadfast' and *fæste* 'firmly, securely', of Germanic origin; related to Dutch *vast* and German *fest* 'firm, solid' and *fast* 'almost'. In Middle English the adverb developed the senses 'strongly, vigorously' (compare with *run hard*), and 'close, immediate' (just surviving in the archaic and poetic *fast by*; compare with *hard by*), hence 'closely, immediately' and 'quickly'; the idea of rapid movement was then reflected in adjectival use.

fast[2] ▶ **verb** [no obj.] abstain from all or some kinds of food or drink, especially as a religious observance.
■ (**be fasted**) technical be deprived of all or some kinds of food, especially for medical or experimental reasons: *all patients were fasted before surgery.*
▶ **noun** an act or period of fasting: *a five-day fast.*
– ORIGIN Old English *fæstan* (verb), of Germanic origin; related to Dutch *vasten* and German *fasten*, also to Old Norse *fasta*, the source of the noun.

fast and furious ▶ **adverb** very rapidly: *my heart was beating fast and furious.*
▶ **adjective** full of rapid action; lively and exciting: *he won a fast and furious final.*

fastback ▶ **noun** a car with a rear that slopes continuously down to the bumper.

fastball ▶ **noun** a baseball pitch thrown at or near a pitcher's maximum speed.
■ another term for **FAST-PITCH SOFTBALL**.

fast breeder (also **fast breeder reactor**) ▶ **noun** a breeder reactor in which the neutrons causing fission are not slowed by any moderator.

fast buck ▶ **noun** see **BUCK**[2].

fasten ▶ **verb** [with obj.] close or do up securely: *the tunic was fastened with a row of gilt buttons.*
■ [no obj., with adverbial] be closed or done up in a particular place or part or in a particular way: *a blue nightie that fastens down the back.* ■ [with obj. and adverbial] fix or hold in place: *she fastened her locket round her neck.* ■ (**fasten something on/upon**) direct one's eyes, thoughts, feelings, etc. intently at: *his gaze was fastened on his daughter* | [no obj.] *his eyes seemed to fasten on her.* ■ (**fasten something on/upon**) ascribe responsibility to: *blame hadn't been fastened on anyone.* ■ [no obj.] (**fasten on/upon**) single out (someone or something) and concentrate on them or it obsessively: *the critics fastened upon two sections of the report.* ■ (**fasten something off**) secure the end of a piece of thread with stitches or a knot.
– DERIVATIVES **fastener** noun.
– ORIGIN Old English *fæstnian* 'make sure, confirm', also 'immobilize', of West Germanic origin; related to **FAST**[1].

fastening ▶ **noun** a device that closes or secures something: *a fly-front fastening.*

Fastext /ˈfɑːstɛkst/ ▶ **noun** [mass noun] a facility in certain televisions to store some teletext pages in advance, displaying them instantly when requested by the user.
– ORIGIN late 20th cent.: contraction of *fast teletext*.

fast food ▶ **noun** [mass noun] food that can be prepared quickly and easily and is sold in snack bars and restaurants as a quick meal or to be taken away: [as modifier] *a fast-food restaurant.*

fast forward ▶ **noun** a control on a tape or video player for advancing the tape rapidly: [as modifier] *the fast-forward button.*
■ a facility for cueing audio equipment by allowing the tape to be played at high speed during fast-forward wind and stopped when the desired place is reached.
▶ **verb** (**fast-forward**) [with obj.] advance (a tape) rapidly, sometimes while simultaneously playing it at high speed.
■ [no obj.] figurative move speedily forward in time when considering or dealing with something over a period: *the text fast-forwards to 1990.*

fast ice ▶ **noun** [mass noun] ice that covers seawater but is attached to land.

fastidious /faˈstɪdɪəs/ ▶ **adjective** very attentive to and concerned about accuracy and detail: *his speech is fastidious.*
■ very concerned about matters of cleanliness: *the child seemed fastidious about getting her fingers sticky or dirty.*
– DERIVATIVES **fastidiously** adverb, **fastidiousness** noun.
– ORIGIN late Middle English: from Latin *fastidiosus*, from *fastidium* 'loathing'. The word originally meant 'disagreeable, distasteful', later 'disgusted'. Current senses date from the 17th cent.

fastigiate /faˈstɪdʒɪət, -ɪeɪt/ ▶ **adjective** Botany (of a tree or shrub) having the branches more or less parallel to the main stem.
– ORIGIN mid 17th cent.: from Latin *fastigium* 'tapering point, gable' + **-ATE**[2].

fast lane ▶ **noun** [usu. in sing.] a lane of a motorway or dual carriageway for use by traffic that is overtaking or moving more quickly than the rest.
■ a hectic or highly pressured lifestyle: *his face showed the strain of a life lived **in the fast lane**.*

fastness ▶ **noun 1** a secure refuge, especially a place well protected by natural features: *a remote Himalayan mountain fastness.*
2 [mass noun] the ability of a material or dye to maintain its colour without fading or washing away: *the dyes differ in their fastness to light.*
– ORIGIN Old English *fæstnes* (see **FAST**[1], **-NESS**).

Fastnet /ˈfɑːs(t)nɛt/ a rocky islet off the SW coast of Ireland.
■ a shipping forecast area covering the Celtic Sea off the south coast of Ireland as far as the latitude of the Scilly Isles.

fast neutron ▶ **noun** a neutron with high kinetic energy, especially one released by nuclear fission and not slowed by any moderator.

fast-pitch softball (also **fast-pitch**) ▶ **noun** [mass noun] a variety of the game of softball, featuring fast underhand pitching.

fast reactor ▶ **noun** a nuclear reactor in which fission is caused mainly by fast neutrons.

fast-talk ▶ **verb** [with obj.] informal, chiefly N. Amer. pressurize (someone) into doing something using rapid or misleading speech: *heroin dealers tried to **fast-talk** him **into** a quick sale* | [as adj. **fast-talking**] *a fast-talking confidence trickster.*

fast track ▶ **noun** [in sing.] a route, course, or method which provides for more rapid results than usual: *a career in the fast track of the Civil Service.*
▶ **verb** (**fast-track**) [with obj.] accelerate the development or progress of (a person or project): *the old boys network fast-tracks men to the top of the corporate ladder.*

fast-twitch ▶ **adjective** [attrib.] Physiology (of a muscle fibre) contracting rapidly, thus providing strength rather than endurance.

fast-wind ▶ **verb** [with obj.] wind (magnetic tape) rapidly backwards or forwards.

fast worker ▶ **noun** [usu. in sing.] informal a person who makes rapid progress or achieves results quickly, especially in love affairs.

fat ▶ **noun** [mass noun] a natural oily or greasy substance occurring in animal bodies, especially when deposited as a layer under the skin or around certain organs.
■ a substance of this type, or a similar one made from plant products, used in cooking. ■ the presence of an excessive amount of such a substance in a person or animal, causing them to appear corpulent: *he was a tall man, **running to fat**.* ■ [count noun] Chemistry any of a group of natural esters of glycerol and various fatty acids, which are solid at room temperature and are the main constituents of animal and vegetable fat. Compare with **OIL**.
▶ **adjective** (**fatter**, **fattest**) (of a person or animal) having a large amount of excess flesh: *the driver was a fat wheezing man.*
■ (of an animal bred for food) made plump for slaughter. ■ containing much fat: *fat bacon.* ■ large in bulk or circumference: *a fat cigarette.* ■ informal (of an asset or opportunity) substantial: *a fat profit.* ■ informal used ironically to express the belief that there is none or very little of something: ***fat chance** she had of influencing him.* ■ (of coal) containing a high proportion of volatile oils.
▶ **verb** (**fatted**, **fatting**) archaic make or become fat: [with obj.] *numbers of black cattle are fatted here* | [no obj.] *the hogs have been fatting* | [as adj. **fatted**] *a fatted duck.*
– PHRASES **the fat is in the fire** trouble has been caused and is beginning. **kill the fatted calf** produce one's best food to celebrate, especially at a prodigal's return: [ORIGIN: with biblical allusion to Luke 15.] **live off** (or **on**) **the fat of the land** have the best of everything.
– DERIVATIVES **fatless** adjective, **fatly** adverb, **fatness** noun, **fattish** adjective.
– ORIGIN Old English *fætt* 'well fed, plump', also 'fatty, oily', of West Germanic origin; related to Dutch *vet* and German *feist*.

Fatah, Al /ˈfatə, al/ a Palestinian political and military organization founded in 1958 by Yasser Arafat and others to bring about the establishment of a Palestinian state. It has dominated the Palestine Liberation Organization since the 1960s, despite challenges from more extreme groups.
– ORIGIN Arabic, literally 'victory'.

fatal /ˈfeɪt(ə)l/ ▶ **adjective** causing death: *a fatal accident.*
■ leading to failure or disaster: *there were three fatal flaws in the strategy.*
– DERIVATIVES **fatally** adverb.
– ORIGIN late Middle English (in the senses 'destined by fate' and 'ominous'): from Old French, or from Latin *fatalis*, from *fatum* (see **FATE**).

fatalism ▶ **noun** [mass noun] the belief that all events are predetermined and therefore inevitable.
■ a submissive attitude to events, resulting from such a belief.
– DERIVATIVES **fatalist** noun, **fatalistic** adjective, **fatalistically** adverb.

fatality /fəˈtalɪti, feɪ-/ ▶ **noun** (pl. **-ies**) **1** an occurrence of death by accident, in war, or from disease: *shooting was heard and there were fatalities.*
■ a person killed in this way.
2 [mass noun] helplessness in the face of fate: *the plot needs a darker sense of fatality to cover its absurdities.*
– ORIGIN late 15th cent. (denoting the quality of causing death or disaster): from French *fatalité* or late Latin *fatalitas*, from Latin *fatalis* 'decreed by fate', from *fatum* (see **FATE**). Sense 1 dates from the mid 19th cent.

Fata Morgana /ˌfɑːtə mɔːˈɡɑːnə/ ▶ **noun** a mirage.
– ORIGIN Italian, literally 'fairy Morgan'; originally referring to a mirage seen in the Strait of Messina between Italy and Sicily and attributed to **MORGAN LE FAY**, whose legend and reputation were carried to Sicily by Norman settlers.

fatback ▶ **noun 1** [mass noun] N. Amer. fat from the upper part of a side of pork, especially when dried and salted in strips.
2 US informal term for **MENHADEN**.

fat body ▶ **noun** Zoology each of a number of small white structures in the body of an animal, especially an insect, which act as a store of fats and glycogen.

fat cat ▶ **noun** derogatory a wealthy and powerful person, especially a businessman or politician: [as modifier] *a fat-cat developer.*

fat dormouse ▶ **noun** a squirrel-like burrowing dormouse found in Europe and Asia Minor, sometimes farmed or hunted for food. Also called **EDIBLE DORMOUSE**.
• *Glis glis*, family Gliridae.

fate ▶ **noun 1** [mass noun] the development of events outside a person's control, regarded as predetermined by a supernatural power: *fate decided his course for him* | *his injury is a cruel **twist of fate**.*
■ [count noun] the course of someone's life, or the outcome of a particular situation for someone or something, seen as outside their control: *he suffered the same fate as his companion.* ■ [in sing.] the inescapable death of a person: *the guards led her to her fate.*
2 (**the Fates**) Greek & Roman Mythology the three goddesses who preside over the birth and life of humans. Each person was thought of as a spindle, around which the three Fates (Clotho, Lachesis, and Atropos) would spin the thread of human destiny. Also called the **MOIRAI** and the **PARCAE**.
■ (**Fates**) another term for **NORNS**.
▶ **verb** (**be fated**) be destined to happen, turn out, or act in a particular way: [with infinitive] *the regime was fated to end badly.*
– PHRASES **a fate worse than death** see **DEATH**. **seal someone's fate** make it inevitable that something unpleasant will happen to someone.
– ORIGIN late Middle English: from Italian *fato* or (later) from its source, Latin *fatum* 'that which has been spoken', from *fari* 'speak'.

fateful ▶ **adjective** having far-reaching and typically disastrous consequences or implications: *a fateful oversight.*
– DERIVATIVES **fatefully** adverb, **fatefulness** noun.

fat farm ▶ **noun** informal, chiefly N. Amer. a health farm for people who are overweight.

fat-free ▶ **adjective** (of a food) not containing animal or vegetable fats: *virtually fat-free yogurt.*

fathead ▶ **noun** informal a stupid person.
– DERIVATIVES **fat-headed** adjective, **fat-headedness** noun.

fat hen ▶ **noun** [mass noun] a herbaceous plant with mealy edible leaves, often considered to be a weed. Called **LAMB'S QUARTER** or **PIGWEED** in North America.
• *Chenopodium alba*, family Chenopodiaceae.
– ORIGIN late 18th cent.: said to be so named because the seeds were eaten by poultry.

father ▶ **noun 1** a man in relation to his natural child or children.
■ a man who has continuous care of a child, especially by adoption. ■ a male animal in relation to its offspring. ■ (usu. **fathers**) poetic/literary an ancestor. ■ an important figure in the origin and early history of something: *he is usually regarded as* **the father of** *the factory system.* ■ a man who gives care and protection to someone or something: *the prince is widely regarded as* **the father of** *the nation.* ■ the oldest member or doyen of a society or other body. ■ (**the Father**) (in Christian belief) the first person of the Trinity; God. ■ (**Father**) used in proper names, especially of personifications, to suggest an old and venerable character: *Father Thames.*
2 (also **Father**) (often as a title or form of address) a priest: *pray for me, father.*
3 (**Fathers** or **Fathers of the Church**) early Christian theologians (in particular of the first five centuries) whose writings are regarded as especially authoritative.
▶ **verb** [with obj.] be the father of: *he fathered three children.*
■ [usu. as noun **fathering**] treat with the protective care usually associated with a father: *the two males share the fathering of the cubs.* ■ be the source or originator of: *a culture which has fathered half the popular music in the world.* ■ (**father someone/thing on**) assign the paternity of a child or responsibility for a book, idea, or action to: *a collection of Irish stories was fathered on him.* ■ archaic appear as or admit that one is the father or originator of: *a singular letter from a lady, requesting I would father a novel of hers.*
– PHRASES **how's your father** Brit. informal used euphemistically to refer to sexual intercourse. ■ used euphemistically to refer to a penis. **like father, like son** proverb a son's character or behaviour can be expected to resemble that of his father.
– DERIVATIVES **fatherhood** noun, **fatherless** adjective, **fatherlessness** noun, **fatherlike** adjective & adverb.
– ORIGIN Old English *fæder*, of Germanic origin; related to Dutch *vader* and German *Vater*, from an Indo-European root shared by Latin *pater* and Greek *patēr*.

Father Christmas an imaginary figure said to bring presents for children on the night before Christmas Day. He is conventionally pictured as a jolly old man from the far north, with a long white beard and red garments trimmed with white fur. Also called **SANTA CLAUS**.

father figure ▶ **noun** an older man who is respected for his paternal qualities and may be an emotional substitute for a father.

father-in-law ▶ **noun** (pl. **fathers-in-law**) the father of one's husband or wife.

fatherland ▶ **noun** (often **the Fatherland**) a person's native country, especially when referred to in patriotic terms.
■ chiefly historical Germany, especially during the period of Hitler's control.

fatherly ▶ **adjective** of, resembling, or characteristic of a father, especially in being protective and affectionate: *he gave me such a kind and fatherly look.*
– DERIVATIVES **fatherliness** noun.

father of chapel ▶ **noun** Brit. the shop steward of a printers' trade union.

Father of the House ▶ **noun** (in the UK) the member of the House of Commons with the longest continuous service.

Father's Day ▶ **noun** a day of the year on which fathers are particularly honoured by their children, especially with gifts and greetings cards. It was first observed in the state of Washington in 1910; in the US and Britain, it is usually the third Sunday in June, in Australia, the first Sunday in September.

Father Time ▶ **noun** see **TIME** (sense 1).

fathom ▶ **noun** a unit of length equal to six feet (1.8 metres), chiefly used in reference to the depth of water: *sonar says that we're* **in** *eighteen* **fathoms**.
▶ **verb** [with obj.] **1** [usu. with negative] understand (a difficult problem or an enigmatic person) after much thought: *the locals could not* **fathom out** *the reason behind his new-found prosperity* | [with clause] *he couldn't fathom why she was being so anxious.*
2 measure the depth of (water): *an attempt to fathom the ocean.*
– DERIVATIVES **fathomable** adjective, **fathomless** adjective.
– ORIGIN Old English *fæthm*, of Germanic origin; related to Dutch *vadem*, *vaam* and German *Faden* 'six feet'. The original sense was 'something which embraces', (plural) 'the outstretched arms'; hence, a unit of measurement based on the span of the outstretched arms, later standardized to six feet.

Fathometer /fa'ðɒmɪtə/ ▶ **noun** US trademark a type of echo sounder.

fatigue ▶ **noun 1** [mass noun] extreme tiredness, typically resulting from mental or physical exertion or illness: *he was nearly dead with fatigue.*
■ a reduction in the efficiency of a muscle or organ after prolonged activity. ■ weakness in materials, especially metal, caused by repeated variations of stress: *metal fatigue.* ■ [with modifier] a lessening in one's response to or enthusiasm for something, typically as a result of overexposure to it: *museum fatigue.*
2 (**fatigues**) a menial task of a non-military nature performed by a soldier, sometimes as a punishment: *we're* **on** *cookhouse* **fatigues**, *sir.*
■ (also **fatigue party**) [count noun] a group of soldiers ordered to do such a duty. ■ (**fatigues**) loose-fitting clothing, typically khaki, olive drab, or camouflaged, of a sort worn by soldiers when performing such menial tasks or on active duty: *battle fatigues.*
▶ **verb** (**fatigues**, **fatigued**, **fatiguing**) [with obj.] (often **be fatigued**) cause (someone) to feel tired or exhausted: *they were fatigued by their journey.*
■ reduce the efficiency of (a muscle or organ) by prolonged activity. ■ weaken (a material, especially metal) by repeated variations of stress.
– DERIVATIVES **fatiguability** (also **fatigability**) noun, **fatiguable** (also **fatigable**) adjective.
– ORIGIN mid 17th cent. (in the sense 'task or duty that causes weariness'): from French *fatigue* (noun), *fatiguer* (verb), from Latin *fatigare* 'tire out', from *ad fatim*, *affatim* 'to satiety or surfeit, to bursting'.

Fatiha /'fɑːtɪə, 'fat-/ (also **Fatihah**) ▶ **noun** the short first sura of the Koran, used by Muslims as an essential element of ritual prayer.
– ORIGIN from Arabic *al-Fātiḥah* 'the opening (sura)', from *fātiḥa* 'opening', from *fataḥa* 'to open'.

Fatima /'fatɪmə/ (*c.*606–32 AD), youngest daughter of the prophet Muhammad and wife of the fourth caliph, Ali. The descendants of Muhammad trace their lineage through her; she is revered especially by Shiite Muslims as the mother of the imams Hasan and Husayn.

Fátima /'fatɪmə/ a village in west central Portugal, north-east of Lisbon; pop. 5,445 (1991). It became a centre of Roman Catholic pilgrimage after the reported sighting in the village in 1917 of the Virgin Mary.

Fatimid /'fatɪmɪd/ ▶ **noun** a member of a dynasty which ruled in parts of northern Africa, Egypt, and Syria from 909 to 1171, and founded Cairo as its capital in 969.
▶ **adjective** of or relating to the Fatimids.
– DERIVATIVES **Fatimite** noun & adjective.
– ORIGIN from Arabic *Fāṭima* (see **FATIMA**, from whom the dynasty is said to descend) + **-ID**[3].

fatling ▶ **noun** a young animal that has been fattened in readiness for slaughter.

fatso ▶ **noun** (pl. **-oes**) informal, offensive a fat person.

fatstock ▶ **noun** [mass noun] Brit. livestock that has been fattened for slaughter.

fatten ▶ **verb** [with obj.] make (a person or animal) fat or fatter: *he could do with some good food to* **fatten** *him* **up** | figurative *this may fatten their profits.*
■ [no obj.] become fat or fatter.

fattening ▶ **adjective** (of a foodstuff) causing an increase in the weight of someone who eats it.

fattism ▶ **noun** [mass noun] prejudice or discrimination against people who are fat.
– DERIVATIVES **fattist** noun & adjective.

fatty ▶ **adjective** (**fattier**, **fattiest**) containing a large amount of fat: *go easy on fatty foods* | *fatty tissue.*
■ Medicine (of a disease or lesion) marked by abnormal deposition of fat in cells: *fatty degeneration of the liver.*
▶ **noun** (pl. **-ies**) informal a fat person (especially as a nickname).
– DERIVATIVES **fattiness** noun.

fatty acid ▶ **noun** Chemistry a carboxylic acid consisting of a hydrocarbon chain and a terminal carboxyl group, especially any of those occurring as esters in fats and oils.

fatty oil ▶ **noun** another term for **FIXED OIL**.

fatuous /'fatjʊəs/ ▶ **adjective** silly and pointless: *a fatuous comment.*
– DERIVATIVES **fatuity** noun (pl. **-ies**), **fatuously** adverb, **fatuousness** noun.
– ORIGIN early 17th cent.: from Latin *fatuus* 'foolish' + **-OUS**.

fatwa /'fatwɑː/ ▶ **noun** a ruling on a point of Islamic law given by a recognized authority.
– ORIGIN early 17th cent.: from Arabic *fatwā*, from *'aftā* 'decide a point of law'. Compare with **MUFTI**[1].

faubourg /'fəʊbʊəg, French fobuʀ/ ▶ **noun** [usu. in place names] a suburb, especially one in Paris: *the Faubourg Saint-Germain.*
– ORIGIN French (earlier *faux-bourg* 'false borough'), perhaps an alteration of *forsborc*, literally 'outside the town', but perhaps based on Middle High German *phâlburgere* 'burghers of the pale', i.e. people living outside the city wall but still inside the palisade.

fauces /'fɔːsiːz/ ▶ **plural noun** Anatomy the arched opening at the back of the mouth leading to the pharynx.
– DERIVATIVES **faucial** /'fɔːʃ(ə)l/ adjective.
– ORIGIN late Middle English: from Latin, 'throat'.

faucet /'fɔːsɪt/ ▶ **noun** chiefly N. Amer. a tap.
– ORIGIN late Middle English (denoting a bung for the vent-hole of a cask, or a tap for drawing liquor from a container): from Old French *fausset*, from Provençal *falset*, from *falsar* 'to bore'. The current sense dates from the mid 19th cent.

faugh /fɔː/ ▶ **exclamation** expressing disgust: *'Faugh! This place stinks!'*
– ORIGIN natural exclamation: first recorded in English in the mid 16th cent.

Faulkner /'fɔːknə/, William (1897–1962), American novelist. His works deal with the history and legends of the American South and have a strong sense of a society in decline. Notable works: *The Sound and the Fury* (1929), *As I Lay Dying* (1930), and *Absalom! Absalom!* (1936). Nobel Prize for Literature (1949).

fault /fɔːlt, fɒlt/ ▶ **noun 1** an unattractive or unsatisfactory feature, especially in a piece of work or in a person's character: *my worst fault is impatience.*
■ a break or other defect in an electric circuit or piece of machinery: *a fire caused by an electrical fault.* ■ a misguided or dangerous action or habit: *the fault of the keen therapist is to start to intervene during the assessment phase.* ■ (in tennis and similar games) a service of the ball not in accordance with the rules. ■ (usu. **faults**) (in showjumping) a penalty point imposed for an error.
2 [mass noun] responsibility for an accident or misfortune: *many people who get into debt do so* **through no fault of their own** | *it was his fault she had died.*
3 Geology an extended break in a rock formation, marked by the relative displacement and discontinuity of strata on either side of a particular plane.
▶ **verb** [with obj.] **1** criticize for inadequacy or mistakes: *her colleagues and superiors could not fault her dedication to the job* | *you cannot* **fault him for** *the professionalism of his approach.*
■ [no obj.] archaic do wrong: *the people of Caesarea faulted greatly when they called King Herod a god.*
2 (**be faulted**) Geology (of a rock formation) be broken by a fault or faults: *rift valleys where the crust has been stretched and faulted* | [as noun **faulting**] *a complex pattern of faulting.*
– PHRASES **at fault 1** responsible for an undesirable situation or event; in the wrong: *we recover compensation from the person at fault.* **2** mistaken or defective: *he suspected that his calculator was at fault.*

find fault make an adverse criticism or objection, sometimes unfairly or destructively: *he finds fault with everything I do.* —— **to a fault** (of someone who displays a particular commendable quality) to an extent verging on excess: *you're kind, caring and generous to a fault.*
– ORIGIN Middle English *faut(e)* 'lack, failing', from Old French, based on Latin *fallere* 'deceive'. The *-l-* was added (in French and English) in the 15th cent. to conform with the Latin word, but did not become standard in English until the 17th cent., remaining silent in pronunciation until well into the 18th.

fault-finding ▶ **noun** [mass noun] **1** continual criticism, typically concerning trivial things.
2 the investigation of the cause of malfunction in machinery, especially electronic equipment.
– DERIVATIVES **fault-finder** noun.

faultless ▶ **adjective** free from defect or error: *your logic is faultless.*
– DERIVATIVES **faultlessly** adverb, **faultlessness** noun.

faulty ▶ **adjective** (**faultier**, **faultiest**) working badly or unreliably because of imperfections: *a faulty brake.*
■(of reasoning and other mental processes) mistaken or misleading because of flaws: *faulty logic.* ■ having or displaying weaknesses: *her character was faulty.*
– DERIVATIVES **faultily** adverb, **faultiness** noun.

faun /fɔːn/ ▶ **noun** Roman Mythology one of a class of lustful rural gods, represented as a man with a goat's horns, ears, legs, and tail.
– ORIGIN late Middle English: from the name of the pastoral god **FAUNUS**.

fauna /ˈfɔːnə/ ▶ **noun** [mass noun] the animals of a particular region, habitat, or geological period: *the **flora and fauna** of Siberia* | [count noun] *the local Mesozoic rocks and their faunas.* Compare with **FLORA**.
■[count noun] a book or other work describing or listing the animal life of a region.
– DERIVATIVES **faunal** adjective, **faunistic** /-ˈnɪstɪk/ adjective.
– ORIGIN late 18th cent.: modern Latin application of *Fauna*, the name of a rural goddess, sister of **FAUNUS**.

faunal region ▶ **noun** another term for **ZOOGEOGRAPHICAL REGION**.

Fauntleroy /ˈfɔːntlərɔɪ/ (also **Little Lord Fauntleroy**) ▶ **noun** an excessively good-mannered or elaborately dressed young boy.
– ORIGIN from the name of the boy hero of Frances Hodgson Burnett's novel *Little Lord Fauntleroy* (1886).

Faunus /ˈfɔːnəs/ Roman Mythology an ancient Italian pastoral god, grandson of Saturn, associated with wooded places.

Fauré /ˈfɔːreɪ, French fɔʀe/, Gabriel (Urbain) (1845–1924), French composer and organist. His best-known work is the *Requiem* (1887) for solo voices, choir, and orchestra; he also wrote songs, piano pieces, chamber music, and incidental music for the theatre.

Faust /faʊst/ (also **Faustus** /-təs/) (died *c.*1540), German astronomer and necromancer. Reputed to have sold his soul to the Devil, he became the subject of a drama by Goethe, an opera by Gounod, and a novel by Thomas Mann.
– DERIVATIVES **Faustian** adjective.

faute de mieux /fəʊt də ˈmjəː, French fot də mjø/ ▶ **adverb** for want of a better alternative.
– ORIGIN French.

fauteuil /fəʊˈtəːi/ ▶ **noun** a wooden seat in the form of an armchair with open sides and upholstered arms.
– ORIGIN French, from Old French *faudestuel*, from medieval Latin *faldistolium* (see **FALDSTOOL**).

Fauve /fəʊv, French fov/ ▶ **noun** a member of a group of French painters who favoured fauvism: [as modifier] *a Fauve canvas by Matisse.*

fauvism /ˈfəʊvɪz(ə)m/ ▶ **noun** [mass noun] a style of painting with vivid expressionistic and non-naturalistic use of colour that flourished in Paris from 1905 and, although short-lived, had an important influence on subsequent artists, especially the German expressionists. Matisse was regarded as the movement's leading figure.
– DERIVATIVES **fauvist** noun & adjective.
– ORIGIN from French *fauvisme*, from *fauve* 'wild beast'. The name originated from a remark of the French art critic Louis Vauxcelles at the Salon of 1905; coming across a quattrocento-style statue in the midst of works by Matisse and his associates, he is reputed to have said, 'Donatello au milieu des fauves!' ('Donatello among the wild beasts').

faux /fəʊ/ ▶ **adjective** [attrib.] artificial or imitation; false: *a rope of faux pearls.*
– ORIGIN French, 'false'.

faux naif /ˌfəʊ nʌɪˈiːf, French fonaif/ ▶ **adjective** (of a work of art or a person) artificially or affectedly simple or naive: *faux-naif pastoralism.*
▶ **noun** a person who pretends to be ingenuous.
– ORIGIN from French *faux* 'false' + *naïf* 'naive'.

faux pas /fəʊ ˈpɑː, French fo pa/ ▶ **noun** (pl. same) an embarrassing or tactless act or remark in a social situation.
– ORIGIN French, literally 'false step'.

fava bean /ˈfɑːvə/ (also **faba bean**) ▶ **noun** North American term for **BROAD BEAN**.
– ORIGIN Italian *fava*, from Latin *faba* 'bean'.

fave ▶ **noun** & **adjective** informal short for **FAVOURITE**.

favela /faˈvɛlə/ ▶ **noun** a Brazilian shack or shanty town; a slum.
– ORIGIN Portuguese.

favour (US **favor**) ▶ **noun 1** [mass noun] an attitude of approval or liking: *training is looked upon with favour by many employers.*
■support or advancement given as a sign of approval: *a struggle between competing ministers for royal favour.* ■ overgenerous preferential treatment: *they accused you of showing favour to one of the players.* ■ [count noun] archaic a thing such as a badge or knot of ribbons that is given or worn as a mark of liking or support.
2 an act of kindness beyond what is due or usual: *I've come to ask you a favour.*
■(**one's favours**) dated used with reference to a woman allowing a man to have sexual intercourse with her: *she had granted her favours to him.*
▶ **verb** [with obj.] **1** feel or show approval or preference for: *slashing public spending is a policy that few politicians favour.*
■give unfairly preferential treatment to: *critics argued that the policy favoured the private sector.* ■ work to the advantage of: *natural selection has favoured bats.*
2 (**favour someone with**) (often used in polite requests) give someone (something that they want): *please favour me with an answer.*
3 informal resemble (a parent or relative) in facial features: *she's pretty, and she favours you.*
4 treat (an injured limb) gently, not putting one's full weight on it: *he favours his sore leg.*
– PHRASES **do someone a favour** do something for someone as an act of kindness. ■ [in imperative] Brit. informal used as a way of expressing brusque dismissal or rejection of a remark or suggestion: *'Are you some kind of social worker?' 'Do me a favour!'* **in favour 1** meeting with approval: *they were not in favour with the party.* **2** having or showing approval: *a 2–1 vote **in favour of** industrial action.* **in one's favour** to one's advantage: *events were moving in his favour.* **in favour of 1** to be replaced by: *he stepped down as leader in favour of his rival.* **2** to the advantage of: *the judge decided in favour of the defendant.* **out of favour** lacking or having lost approval or popularity: *proper dancing has gone out of favour.*
– DERIVATIVES **favourer** noun.
– ORIGIN Middle English (in the noun sense 'liking, preference'): via Old French from Latin *favor*, from *favere* 'show kindness to' (related to *fovere* 'cherish').

favourable (US **favorable**) ▶ **adjective 1** expressing approval: *the exhibitions received favourable criticism.*
■giving consent: *their demands rarely received a favourable response.*
2 to the advantage of someone or something: *they made a settlement **favourable to** the unions.*
■(of a wind) blowing in the direction of travel. ■ (of weather, or a period of time judged in terms of its weather) fine. ■ suggesting a good outcome: *a favourable prognosis.*
– DERIVATIVES **favourableness** noun, **favourably** adverb.
– ORIGIN Middle English: via Old French from Latin *favorabilis*, from *favor* (see **FAVOUR**).

favourite (US **favorite**) ▶ **adjective** [attrib.] preferred to all others of the same kind: *their favourite Italian restaurant.*
▶ **noun** a person or thing that is especially popular or particularly well liked by someone: *the song is still a favourite after 20 years.*
■the competitor thought most likely to win a game or contest, especially by people betting on the outcome: *the team are strong favourites.*
– PHRASES **favourite son** a famous man who is particularly popular and praised for his achievements in his native area: *Essex's favourite son will open at Lord's to launch the cricket season.* ■ US a person supported as a presidential candidate by delegates from the candidate's home state.
– ORIGIN late 16th cent. (as a noun): from obsolete French *favorit*, from Italian *favorito*, past participle of *favorire* 'to favour', from Latin *favor* (see **FAVOUR**).

favouritism (US **favoritism**) ▶ **noun** [mass noun] the practice of giving unfair preferential treatment to one person or group at the expense of another.
■the state or condition of being a favourite, especially of being the competitor thought most likely to win a sporting contest: *the horse shares favouritism with her French-trained rival at 6–1.*

favrile glass /fəˈvriːl/ ▶ **noun** [mass noun] a richly coloured iridescent glass, developed by L. C. Tiffany.
– ORIGIN late 19th cent.: formed as a trademark from the obsolete adjective *fabrile* 'of a craftsman'.

Fawkes /fɔːks/, Guy (1570–1606), English conspirator. He was hanged for his part in the Gunpowder Plot of 5 November 1605. The occasion is commemorated annually on Bonfire Night with fireworks, bonfires, and the burning of a guy.

fawn[1] ▶ **noun 1** a young deer in its first year.
2 [mass noun] a light yellowish-brown colour.
▶ **verb** [no obj.] (of a deer) produce young.
– PHRASES **in fawn** (of a deer) pregnant.
– ORIGIN late Middle English: from Old French *faon*, based on Latin *fetus* 'offspring'; compare with **FETUS**.

fawn[2] ▶ **verb** [no obj.] (of a person) give a servile display of exaggerated flattery or affection, typically in order to gain favour or advantage: *congressmen **fawn over** the President.*
■(of an animal, especially a dog) show slavish devotion, especially by crawling and rubbing against someone: *the dogs started **fawning on** me.*
– DERIVATIVES **fawningly** adverb.
– ORIGIN Old English *fagnian* 'make or be glad', of Germanic origin; related to **FAIN**.

fax[1] ▶ **noun** an exact copy of a document made by electronic scanning and transmitted as data by telecommunications links.
■[mass noun] the production or transmission of documents in this way: *he received the report by fax.* ■ (also **fax machine**) a machine for transmitting and receiving such documents.
▶ **verb** [with obj.] send (a document) by such means.
■contact (someone) by such means: *to obtain a brochure fax the agent* | [no obj.] *the best way to order goods was to fax.*
– ORIGIN 1940s.: abbreviation of **FACSIMILE**.

fax[2] ▶ **plural noun** non-standard spelling of 'facts', chiefly in informal headings: *food fax.*

fay ▶ **noun** poetic/literary a fairy.
– ORIGIN late Middle English: from Old French *fae, faie*, from Latin *fata* 'the Fates', plural of *fatum* (see **FATE**). Compare with **FAIRY**.

fayalite /ˈfeɪəlʌɪt/ ▶ **noun** [mass noun] a black or brown mineral which is an iron-rich form of olivine and occurs in many igneous rocks.
– ORIGIN mid 19th cent.: from *Fayal* (the name of an island in the Azores) + **-ITE**[1].

fayre ▶ **noun** pseudo-archaic spelling of **FAIR**[2].

faze ▶ **verb** [with obj.] [usu. with negative] (often **be fazed**) informal disturb or disconcert (someone): *she was not fazed by his show of anger.*
– ORIGIN mid 19th cent. (originally US): variant of dialect *feeze* 'drive or frighten off', from Old English *fēsian*, of unknown origin.

fazenda /fəˈzɛndə/ ▶ **noun** an estate or large farm in Portugal, Brazil, and other Portuguese-speaking countries.
– ORIGIN Portuguese; compare with Spanish *hacienda*.

fazendeiro /ˌfazɛnˈdɛːrəʊ/ ▶ **noun** (pl. **-os**) a person who owns or occupies a fazenda.
– ORIGIN Portuguese.

FBA ▶ **abbreviation for** Fellow of the British Academy.

FBI ▶ **abbreviation for** (in the US) Federal Bureau of Investigation.

FC ▶ **abbreviation for** ■ Football Club: *Liverpool FC.* ■ (in the UK) Forestry Commission.

FCC ▶ **abbreviation for** (in the US) Federal Communications Commission.

FCO ▶ **abbreviation for** (in the UK) Foreign and Commonwealth Office.

FD ▶ **abbreviation for** Defender of the Faith.
– ORIGIN from Latin *Fidei Defensor.*

FDA ▶ **abbreviation for** (in the US) Food and Drug Administration.

FDC ▶ **abbreviation for** first day cover.

FDDI ▶ **abbreviation for** fibre distributed data interface, a communications, cabling, and hardware standard for high-speed optical-fibre networks.

FDIC ▶ **abbreviation for** Federal Deposit Insurance Corporation, a body which underwrites most private bank deposits in the US.

FDR the nickname of President Franklin Delano Roosevelt (see **ROOSEVELT**[2]).

FE ▶ **abbreviation for** (in the UK) further education.

Fe ▶ **symbol for** the chemical element iron.
– ORIGIN from Latin *ferrum.*

fealty /ˈfiːəlti/ ▶ **noun** [mass noun] historical a feudal tenant's or vassal's sworn loyalty to a lord: *they owed* ***fealty to*** *the Earl rather than the King.*
■ formal acknowledgement of this: *a property for which she* ***did fealty.***
– ORIGIN Middle English: from Old French *feau(l)te, fealte,* from Latin *fidelitas* (see **FIDELITY**).

fear ▶ **noun** [mass noun] an unpleasant emotion caused by the belief that someone or something is dangerous, likely to cause pain, or a threat: *drivers are threatening to quit their jobs in fear after a cabby's murder | fear of increasing unemployment |* [count noun] *he is prey to irrational fears.*
■ archaic a mixed feeling of dread and reverence: *the love and fear of God.* ■ [count noun] (**fear for**) a feeling of anxiety concerning the outcome of something or the safety and well-being of someone: *police launched a hunt for the family amid fears for their safety.* ■ the likelihood of something unwelcome happening: *she could observe the other guests without too much fear of attracting attention.*
▶ **verb** [with obj.] be afraid of (someone or something) as likely to be dangerous, painful, or threatening: *I hated him but didn't fear him any more |* [with clause] *farmers fear that they will lose business.*
■ [no obj.] (**fear for**) feel anxiety or apprehension on behalf of: *I fear for the city with this madman let loose in it.* ■ [with infinitive] avoid or put off doing something because one is afraid: *they aim to make war so horrific that potential aggressors will fear to resort to it.* ■ used to express regret or apology: *I shall buy her book, though not, I fear, the hardback version.* ■ archaic regard (God) with reverence and awe.
– PHRASES **for fear of** (or **that**) to avoid the risk of (or that): *no one dared refuse the order for fear of losing their job.* **never fear** used to reassure someone: *we shall meet again, never fear.* **no fear** Brit. informal used as an emphatic expression of denial or refusal: *'Are you coming with me?' 'No fear—it's too exciting here.'* **put the fear of God in** (or **into**) **someone** cause someone to be very frightened. **without fear or favour** impartially: *take all your decisions without fear or favour.*
– ORIGIN Old English *fǣr* 'calamity, danger', *fǣran* 'frighten', also 'revere', of Germanic origin; related to Dutch *gevaar* and German *Gefahr* 'danger'.

fearful ▶ **adjective 1** feeling afraid; showing fear or anxiety: *they are fearful of the threat of nuclear forces |* [with clause] *the mothers were fearful that their daughters would marry and move abroad.*
■ causing or likely to cause people to be afraid; horrifying: *a fearful accident.*
2 informal very great: *he has to get back in a fearful hurry.*
– DERIVATIVES **fearfully** adverb, **fearfulness** noun.

fearless ▶ **adjective** showing a lack of fear: *they leapt with fearless agility to the jetty.*
– DERIVATIVES **fearlessly** adverb, **fearlessness** noun.

fearsome ▶ **adjective** frightening, especially in appearance: *the cat mewed, displaying a fearsome set of teeth.*
– DERIVATIVES **fearsomely** adverb, **fearsomeness** noun.

feart /ˈfɪət/ (also **feared**) ▶ **adjective** Scottish afraid: *ye're feart to stand out from the crowd.*

feasibility ▶ **noun** [mass noun] the state or degree of being easily or conveniently done: *the feasibility of screening athletes for cardiac disease.*

feasibility study ▶ **noun** an assessment of the practicality of a proposed plan or method.

feasible /ˈfiːzɪb(ə)l/ ▶ **adjective** possible to do easily or conveniently: *it is not feasible to put most finds from excavations on public display.*
■ informal likely; probable: *the most feasible explanation.*
– DERIVATIVES **feasibly** adverb.
– ORIGIN late Middle English: from Old French *faisible,* from *fais-,* stem of *faire* 'do, make', from Latin *facere.*

> **USAGE** The use of **feasible** to mean 'likely' or 'probable', as in *the most* ***feasible*** *explanation*, has been in the language for centuries. It was first recorded in the mid 17th century and is supported by 'considerable literary authority', according to the *Oxford English Dictionary.* However, traditionalists object to the use, regarding it as not justifiable on etymological grounds, and it is therefore advisable to avoid it in formal contexts.

feast ▶ **noun** a large meal, typically one in celebration of something: *a wedding feast.*
■ a plentiful supply of something enjoyable, especially for the mind or senses: *the concert season offers a feast of classical music.* ■ an annual religious celebration. ■ a day dedicated to a particular saint: *the feast of St. John.* ■ Brit. an annual village festival.
▶ **verb** [no obj.] eat and drink sumptuously: *the men would congregate and feast after hunting.*
■ (**feast on**) eat large quantities of: *we sat feasting on barbecued chicken and beer.* ■ [with obj.] give (someone) a plentiful and delicious meal: *they feasted the deputation.*
– PHRASES **ghost at the feast** a person or thing that brings gloom or sadness to an otherwise pleasant or celebratory occasion. **feast one's eyes on** gaze at with pleasure. **feast or famine** either too much of something or too little.
– DERIVATIVES **feaster** noun.
– ORIGIN Middle English: from Old French *feste* (noun), *fester* (verb), from Latin *festa,* neuter plural of *festus* 'joyous'. Compare with **FÊTE** and **FIESTA**.

feast day ▶ **noun** a day on which a celebration, especially an annual Christian one, is held.

Feast of Dedication ▶ **noun** another name for **HANUKKAH**.

Feast of Tabernacles ▶ **noun** another name for **SUCCOTH**.

Feast of Weeks ▶ **noun** another name for **SHAVUOTH**.

feat ▶ **noun** an achievement that requires great courage, skill, or strength: *the new printing presses were considerable feats of engineering.*
– ORIGIN late Middle English (in the general sense 'action or deed'): from Old French *fait,* from Latin *factum* (see **FACT**).

feather ▶ **noun** any of the flat appendages growing from a bird's skin and forming its plumage, consisting of a partly hollow horny shaft fringed with vanes of barbs.
■ (**feathers**) a fringe of long hair on the legs of a dog, horse, or other animal. ■ a small side branch on a tree.
▶ **verb 1** [with obj.] rotate the blades of (a propeller) about their own axes in such a way as to lessen the air or water resistance.
■ vary the angle of attack of (rotor blades). ■ Rowing turn (an oar) so that it passes through the air edgeways: *he turned, feathering one oar slowly.*
2 [no obj., with adverbial] float, move, or wave like a feather: *the green fronds feathered against a blue sky.*
■ [with obj. and adverbial] touch (someone or something) very lightly.
3 short for **FEATHER-CUT**.
– PHRASES **a feather in one's cap** an achievement to be proud of. **feather one's** (**own**) **nest** make money illicitly and at someone else's expense. (**as**) **light as a feather** extremely light and insubstantial.
– DERIVATIVES **featheriness** noun, **featherless** adjective, **feathery** adjective.
– ORIGIN Old English *fether,* of Germanic origin; related to Dutch *veer* and German *Feder,* from an Indo-European root shared by Sanskrit *patra* 'wing', Latin *penna* 'feather', and Greek *pteron, pterux* 'wing'.

featherback ▶ **noun** a tropical freshwater fish native to South Asia and Africa, with a strongly humped back, a small feather-like dorsal fin, and a long anal fin that runs from the belly to the tail. Also called **KNIFEFISH**.
● Family Notopteridae: four genera and several species, in particular the large edible *Notopterus chitala* of Asia.

feather bed ▶ **noun** a bed that has a mattress stuffed with feathers.
▶ **verb** (**feather-bed**) [with obj.] provide (someone) with advantageous economic or working conditions.
■ [usu. as noun **feather-bedding**] deliberately limit production or retain excess staff in (a business) in order to create jobs or prevent unemployment, typically as a result of a union contract.

feather-brain (also **feather-head**) ▶ **noun** a silly or absent-minded person.
– DERIVATIVES **feather-brained** (also **feather-headed**) adjective.

feather-cut ▶ **verb** [with obj.] cut (hair) into wispy feather-like points: [as adj.] *black feather-cut hair.*
▶ **noun** (**feathercut**) a hairstyle produced by such cutting.

feather duster ▶ **noun** a long-handled brush with a head made of feathers, used for dusting.
■ (also **feather duster worm**) US another term for **FAN WORM**.

feathered ▶ **adjective** (of a bird) covered with feathers: [in combination] *black-feathered ostriches.*
■ decorated with feathers: *a feathered hat.*

feathered friend ▶ **noun** informal or humorous (usu. **feathered friends**) a bird.

feather edge ▶ **noun** a fine edge produced by tapering a board, plank, or other object.

feathering ▶ **noun** [mass noun] **1** the plumage of a bird or part of a bird.
■ feather-like markings or structure: *traditional finishes such as marbling and feathering.* ■ the feathers of an arrow. ■ fringes of hairs on the appendages or body of a dog. ■ Architecture cusping in tracery.
2 the action of varying the angle of propellers, rotor blades, or oars so as to reduce air or water resistance.

feather-light ▶ **adjective** extremely light: *a feather-light touch.*

feather star ▶ **noun** an echinoderm with a small disc-like body, long feathery arms for feeding and movement, and short appendages for grasping the surface.
● Order Comatulida, class Crinoidea.

feather stitch ▶ **noun** [mass noun] ornamental zigzag sewing.
▶ **verb** (feather-stitch) [with obj.] [usu. as noun **feather-stitching**] sew (something) with such a stitch.

feathertail glider ▶ **noun** an Australian pygmy possum with a flap of skin between the fore- and hindlimbs for gliding, and a feathery tail.
● *Acrobates pygmaeus,* family Burramyidae. Alternative name: **flying mouse**.

featherweight ▶ **noun** [mass noun] a weight in boxing and other sports intermediate between bantamweight and lightweight. In the amateur boxing scale it ranges from 54 to 57 kg.
■ [count noun] a boxer or other competitor of this weight. ■ [count noun] a very light person or thing. ■ [count noun] a person or thing not worth serious consideration: *he is an intellectual featherweight.*

feature ▶ **noun 1** a distinctive attribute or aspect of something: *everyone seemed impressed with the size of the plant and its safety features.*
■ (usu. **features**) a part of the face, such as the mouth or eyes, making a significant contribution to its overall appearance. ■ Linguistics a distinctive characteristic of a linguistic unit, especially a speech sound or vocabulary item, that serves to distinguish it from others of the same type.
2 a newspaper or magazine article or a broadcast programme devoted to the treatment of a particular topic, typically at length: *a special feature on children's reference books.*
■ (also **feature film**) a full-length film intended as the main item in a cinema programme.
▶ **verb** [with obj.] have as a prominent attribute or aspect: *the hotel features a large lounge, a sauna, and a coin-operated solarium.*
■ have as an important actor or participant: *the film featured Glenn Miller and his Orchestra.* ■ [no obj.] be a significant characteristic of or take an important part in: *the latest movies from British directors feature in the current film season.* ■ [no obj.] be apparent: *women rarely feature in writing on land settlement.*
– DERIVATIVES **featured** adjective [in combination] *fine-featured women,* **featureless** adjective.
– ORIGIN late Middle English (originally denoting the form or proportions of the body, or a physical feature): from Old French *faiture* 'form', from Latin *factura* (see **FACTURE**).

feature-length ▶ **adjective** of the length of a typical feature film or programme: *a feature-length documentary.*

Feb. ▶ **abbreviation for** February.

febrifuge /ˈfɛbrɪfjuːdʒ/ ▶ **noun** a medicine used to reduce fever.
– DERIVATIVES **febrifugal** /fɪˈbrɪfjʊɡ(ə)l, ˌfɛbrɪˈfjuːɡ(ə)l/ adjective.
– ORIGIN late 17th cent.: from French *fébrifuge*, from Latin *febris* 'fever' + *fugare* 'drive away'. Compare with **FEVERFEW**.

febrile /ˈfiːbrʌɪl/ ▶ **adjective** having or showing the symptoms of a fever: *a febrile illness.*
■ having or showing a great deal of nervous excitement or energy: *a febrile imagination.*
– DERIVATIVES **febrility** noun.
– ORIGIN mid 17th cent.: from French *fébrile* or medieval Latin *febrilis*, from Latin *febris* 'fever'.

February /ˈfɛbrʊəri, ˈfɛbjʊəri/ ▶ **noun** (pl. **-ies**) the second month of the year, in the northern hemisphere usually considered the last month of winter: *even in February the place is busy* | *the coldest February in 40 years.*
– ORIGIN Middle English *feverer*, from Old French *feverier*, based on Latin *februarius*, from *februa*, the name of a purification feast held in this month. The spelling change in the 15th cent. was due to association with the Latin word.

USAGE To pronounce **February** in the way that some people regard as correct is not easy. It requires the explicit pronunciation of both the **r** following the **Feb-** and the **r** in **-ary**, with an unstressed vowel in between. By a process called *dissimilation*, in which one sound identical or very similar to an adjacent sound is replaced by a different sound, the **r** following **Feb-** has been replaced by a **y** sound: **Feb-yoo-** rather than **Feb-roo-**. This is now the norm, especially in spontaneous speech, and is fast becoming the accepted standard.

February Revolution see **RUSSIAN REVOLUTION**.

feces ▶ **noun** US spelling of **FAECES**.

Fechner /ˈfɛxnə, German ˈfɛçnɐ/, Gustav Theodor (1801–87), German physicist and psychologist. Fechner hoped to make psychology a truly objective science and coined the termed *psychophysics* to define his study of the quantitative relationship between degrees of physical stimulation and the resulting sensations.

feckless ▶ **adjective** (of a person) lacking in efficiency or vitality: *a feckless lot of layabouts.*
■ unthinking and irresponsible: *the feckless exploitation of the world's natural resources.*
– DERIVATIVES **fecklessly** adverb, **fecklessness** noun.
– ORIGIN late 16th cent.: from Scots and northern English dialect *feck* (from *effeck*, variant of **EFFECT**) + **-LESS**.

feculent /ˈfɛkjʊl(ə)nt/ ▶ **adjective** of or containing dirt, sediment, or waste matter: *their feet were forever slipping on feculent bog.*
– DERIVATIVES **feculence** noun.
– ORIGIN late 15th cent.: from French *féculent* or Latin *faeculentus*, from *faex*, *faec-* 'dregs'.

fecund /ˈfɛk(ə)nd, ˈfiːk-/ ▶ **adjective** producing or capable of producing an abundance of offspring or new growth; fertile: *a lush and fecund garden* | figurative *her fecund imagination.*
■ technical (of a woman or women) capable of becoming pregnant and giving birth.
– DERIVATIVES **fecundity** /fɪˈkʌndɪti/ noun.
– ORIGIN late Middle English: from French *fécond* or Latin *fecundus*.

fecundability /fɪˌkʌndəˈbɪlɪti/ ▶ **noun** [mass noun] Medicine & Zoology the probability of a woman or female animal conceiving within a given period of time, especially during a specific month or menstrual cycle.

fecundate /ˈfɛk(ə)ndeɪt, ˈfiːk-/ ▶ **verb** [with obj.] archaic fertilize: *there were no insects to fecundate flowering plants.*
■ poetic/literary make fruitful: *he actuates and fecundates our souls.*
– DERIVATIVES **fecundation** noun.
– ORIGIN mid 17th cent.: from Latin *fecundat-* 'made fruitful', from the verb *fecundare*, from *fecundus* 'fruitful'.

Fed ▶ **noun** US informal **1** a federal agent or official, especially a member of the FBI: *I don't think he has any friends since he grassed to the Feds.*
2 (usu. **the Fed**) short for **FEDERAL RESERVE**.
– ORIGIN early 20th cent.: abbreviation of **FEDERAL**. The abbreviation *fed* had previously been used in the late 18th cent. to denote a member of the Federalist party, who advocated a union of American colonies after the War of Independence.

fed past and past participle of **FEED**.

fedayeen /ˌfɛdɑːˈjiːn, fəˈdɑːjiːn/ ▶ **plural noun** Arab guerrillas operating especially against Israel.
– ORIGIN 1950s: from colloquial Arabic *fidā'iyīn*, plural of classical Arabic *fidā'ī* 'one who gives his life for another or for a cause', from *fadā* 'to ransom someone'. The singular *fedai* (from Arabic and Persian *fidā'ī*) had previously been used (late 19th cent.) to denote an Ismaili Muslim assassin.

federal ▶ **adjective** having or relating to a system of government in which several states form a unity but remain independent in internal affairs: *a federal Europe.*
■ of, relating to, or denoting the central government as distinguished from the separate units constituting a federation: *the health ministry has sole federal responsibility for health care.* ■ (**Federal**) US historical of the Northern States in the Civil War.
– DERIVATIVES **federalization** noun, **federalize** (also **-ise**) verb, **federally** adverb.
– ORIGIN mid 17th cent.: from Latin *foedus*, *foeder-* 'league, covenant' + **-AL**.

Federal Bureau of Investigation (abbrev.: **FBI**) an agency of the US federal government that deals principally with internal security and counter-intelligence and that also conducts investigations in federal law enforcement. It was established in 1908 as a branch of the Department of Justice, but was substantially reorganized under the controversial directorship (1924–72) of J. Edgar Hoover.

federalism ▶ **noun** [mass noun] the federal principle or system of government.
– DERIVATIVES **federalist** noun & adjective.

Federalist Party an early political party in the US, joined by George Washington during his presidency (1789–97) and in power until 1801. The party's emphasis on strong central government was extremely important in the early years after independence, but by the 1820s it had been superseded by the Democratic Republican Party.

Federal Republic of Germany former name for West Germany.

Federal Reserve (in the US) the banking authority that performs the functions of a central bank and is used to implement the country's monetary policy, providing a national system of reserve cash available to banks.

Federal Union see **UNION** (sense 3).

federate ▶ **verb** /ˈfɛdəreɪt/ [no obj.] (of a number of states or organizations) form a single centralized unit, within which each keeps some internal autonomy.
■ [with obj.] [usu. as adj. **federated**] form (states or organizations) into such a centralized unit: *a federated state consisting of 15 union republics.*
▶ **adjective** /ˈfɛd(ə)rət/ of or relating to such an arrangement: *federate armies.*
– DERIVATIVES **federative** adjective.
– ORIGIN early 18th cent. (as an adjective): from late Latin *foederatus*, based on *foedus*, *foeder-* 'league, covenant'.

Federated States of Micronesia full name for **MICRONESIA** (in sense 2).

federation ▶ **noun** a group of states with a central government but independence in internal affairs: [in names] *the Yugoslavian Federation.*
■ an organization or group within which smaller divisions have some degree of internal autonomy: [in names] *the Federation of Housing Associations.* ■ [mass noun] the action of forming states or organizations into a single group with centralized control: *a first step in the federation of Europe.*
– DERIVATIVES **federationist** noun.
– ORIGIN early 18th cent.: from French *fédération*, from late Latin *foederatio(n-)*, from the verb *foederare* 'to ally', from *foedus* 'league'.

fedora /fɪˈdɔːrə/ ▶ **noun** a low, soft felt hat with a curled brim and the crown creased lengthways.
– ORIGIN late 19th cent. (originally US): from *Fédora*, the title of a drama (1882) written by the French dramatist Victorien Sardou (1831–1908).

fed up ▶ **adjective** [predic.] annoyed or upset at a situation or treatment: *I am* **fed up with** *being put down and made to feel stupid.*
– PHRASES **fed up to the teeth** (or **back teeth**) extremely annoyed: *I'm* **fed up to the teeth with** *the mess he's landed us in.*

fee ▶ **noun 1** a payment made to a professional person or to a professional or public body in exchange for advice or services.
■ money paid as part of a special transaction, for example for a privilege or for admission to something: *the gallery charges an admission fee.* ■ (usu. **fees**) money regularly paid (especially to a school or similar institution) for continuing services: *tuition fees have now reached $9000 a year.*
2 Law, historical an estate of land, especially one held on condition of feudal service.
▶ **verb** (**fees**, **fee'd** or **feed**, **feeing**) [with obj.] rare make a payment to (someone) in return for services.
– PHRASES **hold something in fee** Law, historical hold an estate in return for feudal service to a superior.
– ORIGIN Middle English: from an Anglo-Norman French variant of Old French *feu*, *fief*, from medieval Latin *feodum*, *feudum*, ultimately of Germanic origin. Compare with **FEU**, **FEUD**[2], and **FIEF**.

feeb ▶ **noun** N. Amer. informal a feeble-minded person.
– ORIGIN early 20th cent.: abbreviation of **FEEBLE**.

feeble ▶ **adjective** (**feebler**, **feeblest**) lacking physical strength, especially as a result of age or illness: *my legs are very feeble after the flu.*
■ (of a sound) faint: *his voice sounded feeble and far away.* ■ lacking strength of character: *she overreacted in such a feeble, juvenile way.* ■ failing to convince or impress: *a feeble excuse.*
– DERIVATIVES **feebleness** noun, **feebly** adverb.
– ORIGIN Middle English: from Old French *fieble*, earlier *fleible*, from Latin *flebilis* 'lamentable', from *flere* 'weep'.

feeble-minded ▶ **adjective** (of a person) unable to make intelligent decisions or judgements.
■ (of an idea or proposal) lacking in sense or clear direction: *a feeble-minded policy.* ■ dated (of a person) having less than average intelligence.
– DERIVATIVES **feeble-mindedly** adverb, **feeble-mindedness** noun.

feed ▶ **verb** (past and past participle **fed** /fɛd/) [with obj.] **1** give food to: *the raiders fed the guard dog to keep it quiet* | [with two objs] *she fed him bits of biscuit.*
■ [no obj.] (especially of an animal or baby) take food; eat something: *the baby will feed according to her needs.* ■ (**feed someone/thing up**) give a person or animal large amounts of food. ■ provide an adequate supply of food for: *the island's simple agriculture could hardly feed its inhabitants.* ■ [no obj.] (**feed on/off**) derive regular nourishment from (a particular substance): *the bird feeds on cliff-top vegetation* | figurative *his powerful mind fed off political discussion.* ■ encourage the growth of: *I could feed my melancholy by reading Romantic poetry.* ■ give fertilizer to (a plant). ■ put fuel on (a fire).
2 supply (a machine) with material or power: *the programs are* **fed into** *the computer.*
■ [with two objs] supply (someone) with (information, ideas, etc.): *I think he is feeding his old employer commercial secrets.* ■ supply water to (a body of water): *the pond is fed by a small stream* | [no obj.] *water* **feeds into** *the lower pool.* ■ insert further coins into (a meter) to extend the time for which it operates. ■ [with two objs] prompt (an actor) with (a line): *you were still in the wings feeding Micky his lines.* ■ (in ball games) pass the ball to (a player): *he took the ball and fed Salley.*
3 [with obj. and adverbial of direction] cause to move gradually and steadily, typically through a confined space: *make holes through which to feed the cables.*
■ [no obj.] (**feed through**) (of a new factor or development) begin to be influential: *the impact of the cut in interest rates has yet to feed through.*
▶ **noun 1** an act of giving food, especially to animals or a baby, or of having food given to one: *you'll see the baby in the morning for her first feed.*
■ informal a meal: *there were games and a lovely feed.* ■ [mass noun] food for domestic animals: *cow feed.*
2 a device or pipe for supplying material to a machine: *the plotter has a continuous paper feed.*
■ the supply of raw material to a machine or device: [as modifier] *a feed pipe.*
3 a line or prompt given to an actor on stage.
■ an actor who provides such a line or prompt.
– PHRASES **off one's feed** informal having no appetite.

– ORIGIN Old English *fēdan* (verb), of Germanic origin; related to Dutch *voeden* and **FOOD**.

▶**feed back 1** (of a response) influence the development of the thing that has provoked it: *what the audience tells me feeds back into my work.* **2** (of an electrical or other system) produce feedback.

feedback ▶**noun** [mass noun] **1** information about reactions to a product, a person's performance of a task, etc. which is used as a basis for improvement. **2** the modification or control of a process or system by its results or effects, for example in a biochemical pathway or behavioural response. See also **NEGATIVE FEEDBACK, POSITIVE FEEDBACK.**
■the return of a fraction of the output signal from an amplifier, microphone, or other device to the input of the same device; sound distortion produced by this.

feeder ▶**noun 1** a person or animal that eats a particular food or in a particular manner: *a plankton feeder.*
2 a container filled with food for birds or mammals.
■Brit. a child's feeding bottle. ■ Brit. a bib for an infant. ■ Fishing short for **SWIMFEEDER.**
3 a person or thing that supplies something, in particular:
■a device supplying material to a machine: *the automatic sheet feeder holds up to 10 sheets of paper.* ■ a tributary stream. ■ [usu. as modifier] a branch road or railway line linking outlying districts with a main communication system. ■ a main carrying electricity to a distribution point. ■ [usu. as modifier] a school, sports team, etc. from which members move on to one more advanced: *a sixth-form college and its feeder schools.*

feedforward ▶**noun** [mass noun] the modification or control of a process using its anticipated results or effects.

feeding bottle ▶**noun** Brit. a bottle fitted with a teat for giving milk or other drinks to babies and very young children.

feeding frenzy ▶**noun** an aggressive and competitive group attack on prey by a number of sharks or piranhas.
■figurative an episode of frantic competition or rivalry for something: *the remark caused a media feeding frenzy.*

feedlot ▶**noun** an area or building where livestock are fed or fattened up.

feedstock ▶**noun** [mass noun] raw material to supply or fuel a machine or industrial process.

feedstuff ▶**noun** (usu. **feedstuffs**) a food provided for cattle and other livestock.

feedthrough ▶**noun** [mass noun] the passage of something or transfer of an influence through or beyond a specified point or stage: *the feedthrough to further education.*
■[count noun] an electrical connector used to join two parts of a circuit on opposite sides of something, such as a circuit board or an earthing screen.

fee farm ▶**noun** Law, chiefly historical an estate or land held in fee simple subject to a perpetual fixed rent.
■[mass noun] the tenure of land by such means. ■ [mass noun] the rent paid for such land.

feel ▶**verb** (past and past participle **felt**) [with obj.] **1** be aware of (a person or object) through touching or being touched: *she felt someone touch her shoulder.*
■be aware of (something happening) through physical sensation: *she felt the ground give way beneath her.* ■ examine or search by touch: *he touched her head and felt her hair* | [no obj.] *he **felt around** for the matches.* ■ [no obj.] be capable of sensation: *the dead cannot feel.* ■ [no obj., with complement] give a sensation of a particular physical quality when touched: *the wool feels soft.* ■ (**feel one's way**) find one's way by touch rather than sight. ■ (**feel one's way**) figurative act cautiously, especially in an area with which one is unfamiliar: *she was new in the job, still feeling her way.* ■ (**feel something out**) informal investigate something cautiously: *they want to feel out the situation.* ■ (**feel someone up**) informal fondle someone surreptitiously and without their consent, for one's own sexual stimulation.
2 experience (an emotion or sensation): *I felt a sense of excitement* | [no obj., with complement] *I felt angry and humiliated.*
■[no obj., with complement] consider oneself to be in a particular state or exhibiting particular qualities: *he doesn't feel obliged to visit every weekend.* ■ (**feel up to**) have the strength and energy to do or deal with: *after the accident she didn't feel up to driving.* ■ [usu. with negative] (**feel oneself**) be healthy and well: *Ruth was not quite feeling herself.* ■ be emotionally affected by: *he didn't feel the loss of his mother so keenly.* ■ [no obj., with adverbial] have a specified reaction or attitude, especially an emotional one, towards something: *we feel very strongly **about** freedom of expression.* ■ (**feel for**) have compassion for: *poor woman—I do feel for her.*
3 [with clause] have a belief or impression, especially without an identifiable reason: *she felt that the woman positively disliked her.*
■hold an opinion: *I felt I could make a useful contribution.*
▶**noun** [usu. in sing.] **1** an act of touching something to examine it.
■[mass noun] the sense of touch: *he worked by feel rather than using his eyes.*
2 a sensation given by an object or material when touched: *nylon cloth with a cotton feel.*
■the impression given by something: *the restaurant has a modern bistro feel.*
– PHRASES **feel one's age** become aware that one is growing older and less energetic. **feel free (to do something)** have no hesitation or shyness (often used as an invitation or for reassurance): *feel free to say what you like.* **feel like (doing) something** be inclined to have or do: *I feel like celebrating.* **feel one's oats** see **OAT. feel the pinch** see **PINCH. feel the pulse of** see **PULSE**[1]. **feel small** see **SMALL. feel strange** see **STRANGE. get a** (or **the**) **feel for** (or **of**) become accustomed to: *you can explore to get a feel of the place.* **have a feel for** have a sensitive appreciation or an intuitive understanding of: *you have to have a feel for animals.* **make oneself** (or **one's presence**) **felt** make people keenly aware of one; have a noticeable effect: *the economic crisis began to make itself felt.*
– ORIGIN Old English *fēlan*, of West Germanic origin; related to Dutch *voelen* and German *fühlen*.

feeler ▶**noun** an animal organ such as an antenna or palp that is used for testing things by touch or for searching for food.
■figurative a tentative proposal intended to ascertain someone's attitude or opinion: *they were sufficiently depressed to **put out** peace **feelers**.*

feeler gauge ▶**noun** a gauge consisting of a number of thin blades for measuring narrow gaps or clearances.

feel-good ▶**adjective** [attrib.] causing a feeling of happiness and well-being: *a feel-good movie.*
– DERIVATIVES **feel-goodism** noun.

feeling ▶**noun 1** an emotional state or reaction: *a feeling of joy.*
■(**feelings**) the emotional side of someone's character; emotional responses or tendencies to respond: *I don't want to hurt her feelings.* ■ [mass noun] strong emotion: *'God bless you!' she said with feeling.*
2 a belief, especially a vague or irrational one: [with clause] *he had the feeling that he was being watched.*
■an opinion, typically one shared by several people: *a feeling grew that justice had not been done.*
3 [mass noun] the capacity to experience the sense of touch: *a loss of feeling in the hands.*
■the sensation of touching or being touched by a particular thing: *the feeling of the water against your skin.*
4 (**feeling for**) a sensitivity to or intuitive understanding of: *she says I have a feeling for medicine.*
▶**adjective** showing emotion or sensitivity: *she was a feeling child, sensitive and emotional.*
– DERIVATIVES **feelingless** adjective.

feelingly ▶**adverb** (of the expression of a feeling or opinion) in a heartfelt way: *'Thank goodness,' she said feelingly.*

fee simple ▶**noun** (pl. **fees simple**) Law a permanent and absolute tenure of an estate in land with freedom to dispose of it at will, especially (in full **fee simple absolute in possession**) a freehold tenure, which is the main type of land ownership.

feet plural form of **FOOT**.

fee tail ▶**noun** (pl. **fees tail**) Law, historical a former type of tenure of an estate in land with restrictions or entailment regarding the line of heirs to whom it may be willed.
– ORIGIN late Middle English: from Anglo-Norman French *fee tailé* (see **FEE, TAIL**[2]).

Fehling's solution /ˈfeɪlɪŋz/ (also **Fehling's reagent**) ▶**noun** [mass noun] an alkaline solution of copper(II) sulphate and a tartrate, used in a laboratory test for sugars.

feign ▶**verb** [with obj.] pretend to be affected by (a feeling, state, or injury): *she feigned nervousness.*
■archaic invent (a story or excuse). ■ [no obj.] archaic indulge in pretence.
– ORIGIN Middle English: from Old French *feign-*, stem of *feindre*, from Latin *fingere* 'mould, contrive'. Senses in Middle English (taken from Latin) included 'make something', 'invent a story, excuse, or allegation', hence 'make a pretence of a feeling or response'. Compare with **FICTION** and **FIGMENT**.

feijoa /feɪˈ(d)ʒəʊə, fɛ-, fiː-, -ˈjəʊə/ ▶**noun** an evergreen shrub or small tree that bears edible green fruit resembling guavas. It is native to tropical South America and cultivated in New Zealand for its fruit.
● Genus *Feijoa*, family Myrtaceae: two species.
■the fruit of this plant.
– ORIGIN late 19th cent.: modern Latin, named after J. da Silva *Feijó* (1760–1824), Brazilian naturalist.

feijoada /feɪˈ(d)ʒwɑːdə, -də/ ▶**noun** [mass noun] a Brazilian or Portuguese stew of black beans with pork or other meat and vegetables, served with rice.
– ORIGIN Portuguese, from *feijão*, from Latin *phaseolus* 'bean'.

feint[1] /feɪnt/ ▶**noun** a deceptive or pretended blow, thrust, or other movement, especially in boxing or fencing: *a brief feint at the opponent's face.*
■a mock attack or movement in warfare, made in order to distract or deceive an enemy.
▶**verb** [no obj., with adverbial of direction] make a deceptive or distracting movement, especially during a fight: *he feinted left, drawing a punch and slipping it.*
■[with obj. and adverbial of direction] pretend to throw a (punch or blow) in order to deceive or distract an opponent: *'You would, would you?' said Bob, feinting punches back at them.*
– ORIGIN late 17th cent.: from French *feinte*, past participle (used as a noun) of *feindre* 'feign'.

feint[2] /feɪnt/ ▶**adjective** denoting paper printed with faint lines as a guide for handwriting; denoting the lines so printed.
– ORIGIN mid 19th cent.: variant of **FAINT**.

feisty /ˈfʌɪsti/ ▶**adjective** (**feistier, feistiest**) informal having or showing exuberance and strong determination: *Hollywood doesn't have a lot of good feisty roles for girls my age.*
■touchy and aggressive: *he got a bit feisty by trying to hit me back.*
– DERIVATIVES **feistily** adverb, **feistiness** noun.
– ORIGIN late 19th cent.: from earlier *feist, fist* 'small dog', from *fisting cur* or *hound*, a derogatory term for a lapdog, from Middle English *fist* 'break wind', of West Germanic origin. Compare with **FIZZLE**.

felafel /fəˈlaf(ə)l, -ˈlɑː-/ ▶**noun** variant spelling of **FALAFEL**.

Feldenkrais method /ˈfɛld(ə)nkrʌɪs/ ▶**noun** a system designed to promote bodily and mental efficiency and well-being by conscious analysis of neuromuscular activity via exercises which improve flexibility and coordination and increase ease and range of motion.
– ORIGIN 1930s: named after Moshe *Feldenkrais* (1904–84), Russian-born physicist and mechanical engineer.

feldspar /ˈfɛldspɑː/ (also **felspar**) ▶**noun** [mass noun] an abundant rock-forming mineral typically occurring as colourless or pale-coloured crystals and consisting of aluminosilicates of potassium, sodium, and calcium.
– ORIGIN mid 18th cent.: alteration of German *Feldspat, Feldspath*, from *Feld* 'field' + *Spat, Spath* 'spar' (see **SPAR**[3]). The form *felspar* is by mistaken association with German *Fels* 'rock'.

feldspathic /fɛldˈspaθɪk/ ▶**adjective** Geology (of a mineral or rock) of the nature of or containing feldspar.

feldspathoid /ˈfɛl(d)spəˌθɔɪd/ ▶**noun** Geology any of a group of minerals chemically similar to feldspar but containing less silica, such as nepheline and leucite.
– DERIVATIVES **feldspathoidal** /-ˈθɔɪd(ə)l/ adjective.

felicific /ˌfiːlɪˈsɪfɪk/ ▶**adjective** Ethics relating to or promoting increased happiness: *the institution of a rule against murder is in general felicific.*
– ORIGIN mid 19th cent.: from Latin *felicificus*, from *felix, felic-* 'happy'.

felicitate /fɪˈlɪsɪteɪt/ ▶**verb** [with obj.] congratulate: *the award winner was felicitated by the cultural association.*
– ORIGIN early 17th cent. (in the sense 'regard as or

pronounce happy or fortunate'): from late Latin *felicitat-* 'made happy', from the verb *felicitare*, from Latin *felix*, *felic-* 'happy'.

felicitations ▶ plural noun words expressing praise for an achievement or good wishes on a special occasion.

felicitous /fɪˈlɪsɪtəs/ ▶ adjective well chosen or suited to the circumstances: *a felicitous phrase.*
■ pleasing and fortunate: *the view was the room's only felicitous feature.*
– DERIVATIVES **felicitously** adverb, **felicitousness** noun.

felicity ▶ noun (pl. **-ies**) [mass noun] **1** intense happiness: *domestic felicity.*
2 the ability to find appropriate expression for one's thoughts: *he exposed the kernel of the matter with his customary elegance and felicity.*
■ [count noun] a particularly effective feature of a work of literature or art: *a book full of minor felicities.*
– ORIGIN late Middle English: from Old French *felicite*, from Latin *felicitas*, from *felix*, *felic-* 'happy'.

felid /ˈfiːlɪd/ ▶ noun Zoology a mammal of the cat family (Felidae); a wild cat.
– ORIGIN late 19th cent.: from modern Latin *Felidae* (plural), from Latin *feles* 'cat'.

feline /ˈfiːlʌɪn/ ▶ adjective of, relating to, or affecting cats or other members of the cat family: *feline leukaemia.*
■ catlike, especially in beauty or slyness: *her face was feline in shape.*
▶ noun a cat or other member of the cat family.
– DERIVATIVES **felinity** noun.
– ORIGIN late 17th cent.: from Latin *felinus*, from *feles* 'cat'.

felix culpa /ˌfiːlɪks ˈkʌlpə, ˌfeɪlɪks ˈkʊlpə/ ▶ noun Christian Theology the sin of Adam viewed as fortunate, because it brought about the blessedness of the Redemption.
■ an apparent error or disaster with happy consequences: *he presents the revolt of the Noldor as a felix culpa.*
– ORIGIN Latin, literally 'happy fault'.

Felixstowe /ˈfiːlɪkstəʊ/ a port on the east coast of England, in Suffolk; pop. 24,460 (1981).

fell[1] past of FALL.

fell[2] ▶ verb [with obj.] **1** (usu. **be felled**) cut down (a tree).
■ knock down: *she felt an urge to fell him to the floor* | figurative *to have his daughter return nearly felled him.*
2 (also **flat-fell**) stitch down (the edge of a seam) to lie flat: [as adj. **flat-felled**] *a flat-felled seam.*
▶ noun an amount of timber cut.
– ORIGIN Old English *fellan*, of Germanic origin; related to Dutch *vellen* and German *fällen*, also to FALL.

fell[3] ▶ noun a hill or stretch of high moorland, especially in northern England: [in place names] *Cross Fell* | [mass noun] *an area of fell and moor.*
– ORIGIN Middle English: from Old Norse *fjall*, *fell* 'hill'; probably related to German *Fels* 'rock'.

fell[4] ▶ adjective poetic/literary of terrible evil or ferocity; deadly: *sorcerers use spells to achieve their fell ends.*
– PHRASES **in** (or **at**) **one fell swoop** in one go: *in one fell swoop they exceeded the total number of tries scored last year.* [ORIGIN: from Shakespeare's *Macbeth* (IV. iii. 219).]
– ORIGIN Middle English: from Old French *fel*, nominative of *felon* 'wicked (person)' (see FELON[1]).

fell[5] ▶ noun archaic an animal's hide or skin with its hair.
– ORIGIN Old English *fel*, *fell*, of Germanic origin; related to Dutch *vel* and German *Fell*, from an Indo-European root shared by Latin *pellis* and Greek *pella* 'skin'.

fella (also **fellah**) ▶ noun non-standard spelling of FELLOW, used in representing speech in various dialects: *you can't blame the wee fella.*

fellah /ˈfɛlə/ ▶ noun (pl. **fellahin** /-ˈhiːn/) an Egyptian peasant.
– ORIGIN from Arabic *fallāḥ* 'tiller of the soil', from *falaḥa* 'till the soil'.

fellate /fɛˈleɪt/ ▶ verb [with obj.] perform fellatio on (a man).
– ORIGIN late 19th cent.: from Latin *fellat-* 'sucked', from the verb *fellare*.

fellatio /fɛˈleɪʃɪəʊ, -ˈlɑːt-/ ▶ noun [mass noun] oral stimulation of a man's penis.
– DERIVATIVES **fellator** /fɛˈleɪtə/ noun.

– ORIGIN late 19th cent.: modern Latin, from Latin *fellare* 'to suck'.

feller[1] ▶ noun non-standard spelling of FELLOW, used in representing speech in various dialects.

feller[2] ▶ noun a person who cuts down trees.

Fellini /fəˈliːni/, Federico (1920–93), Italian film director. He rose to international fame with *La Strada* (1954), which won an Oscar for best foreign film. Other major films include *La Dolce vita* (1960), a satire on Rome's high society and winner of the Grand Prix at Cannes.

felloes /ˈfɛləʊz/ (also **fellies** /ˈfɛliz/) ▶ plural noun the outer rim of a wheel, to which the spokes are fixed.
– ORIGIN Old English *felg* (singular); related to Dutch *velg* and German *Felge*; of unknown ultimate origin.

fellow ▶ noun **1** informal a man or boy: *he was an extremely obliging fellow.*
■ a boyfriend or lover: *has she got a fellow?*
2 (usu. **fellows**) a person in the same position, involved in the same activity, or otherwise associated with another: *he was learning with a rapidity unique among his fellows.*
■ a thing of the same kind as or otherwise associated with another: *the page has been torn away from its fellows.*
3 a member of a learned society.
■ Brit. an incorporated senior member of a college: *a tutorial fellow.* ■ (also **research fellow**) an elected graduate receiving a stipend for a period of research. ■ a member of the governing body in some universities.
▶ adjective [attrib.] sharing a particular activity, quality, or condition with someone or something: *they urged the troops not to fire on their fellow citizens.*
– ORIGIN late Old English *feolaga* 'a partner or colleague' (literally 'one who lays down money in a joint enterprise'), from Old Norse *félagi*, from *fé* 'cattle, property, money' + the Germanic base of LAY[1].

fellow feeling ▶ noun [mass noun] sympathy and fellowship existing between people based on shared experiences or feelings.

fellowship ▶ noun **1** [mass noun] friendly association, especially with people who share one's interests: *they valued fun and good fellowship as the cement of the community.*
■ [count noun] a group of people meeting to pursue a shared interest or aim. ■ [count noun] a guild or corporation.
2 the status of a fellow of a college or society: *a fellowship in mathematics.*

fellow-traveller ▶ noun a person who travels with another.
■ a person who is not a member of a particular group or political party (especially the Communist Party), but who sympathizes with the group's aims and policies.
– DERIVATIVES **fellow-travelling** adjective.

Fell pony ▶ noun a large pony, typically black, of a breed with a long wavy mane and tail.

fell-walking ▶ noun [mass noun] the activity of walking or rambling on the fells.
– DERIVATIVES **fell-walker** noun.

felo de se /ˌfiːləʊ deɪ ˈseɪ, ˌfɛ-/ ▶ noun (pl. **felos de se**) [mass noun] suicide.
– ORIGIN from Anglo-Latin, literally 'felon of himself'; formerly a criminal act in the UK.

felon[1] /ˈfɛlən/ ▶ noun a person who has committed a felony.
▶ adjective [attrib.] archaic cruel; wicked: *the felon undermining hand of dark corruption.*
– ORIGIN Middle English: from Old French, literally 'wicked, a wicked person' (oblique case of *fel* 'evil'), from medieval Latin *fello*, *fellon-*, of unknown origin. Compare with FELON[2].

felon[2] /ˈfɛlən/ ▶ noun archaic term for WHITLOW.
– ORIGIN Middle English: perhaps a specific use of FELON[1]; medieval Latin *fello*, *fellon-* had the same sense.

felonious /fɛˈləʊnɪəs, fɪ-/ ▶ adjective of, relating to, or involved in crime: *they turned their felonious talents to the smuggling trade.*
■ Law relating to or of the nature of felony: *his conduct was felonious.*
– DERIVATIVES **feloniously** adverb.

felony ▶ noun (pl. **-ies**) a crime, typically one involving violence, regarded in the US and many other judicial systems as more serious than a

misdemeanour: *he pleaded guilty to six felonies* | [mass noun] *an accusation of felony.*

In the US the distinction between felonies and misdemeanours usually depends on the penalties or consequences attaching to the crime. In English law felony originally comprised those offences (murder, wounding, arson, rape, and robbery) for which the penalty included forfeiture of land and goods. Forfeiture was abolished in 1870, and in 1967 felonies and misdemeanours were replaced by indictable and non-indictable offences.

– ORIGIN Middle English: from Old French *felonie*, from *felon* (see FELON[1]).

felsic /ˈfɛlsɪk/ ▶ adjective Geology of, relating to, or denoting a group of light-coloured minerals including feldspar, feldspathoids, quartz, and muscovite. Often contrasted with MAFIC.
– ORIGIN early 20th cent.: from FELDSPAR + a contraction of SILICA.

felspar /ˈfɛlspɑː/ ▶ noun variant spelling of FELDSPAR.

felt[1] ▶ noun [mass noun] a kind of cloth made by rolling and pressing wool or another suitable textile accompanied by the application of moisture or heat, which causes the constituent fibres to mat together to create a smooth surface.
▶ verb [with obj.] make into felt; mat together: *the wood fibres are shredded and felted together.*
■ cover with felt: [as adj. **felted**] *a felted roof.* ■ [no obj.] become matted: *care must be taken in washing, or the wool will shrink and felt.*
– DERIVATIVES **felty** adjective.
– ORIGIN Old English, of West Germanic origin; related to Dutch *vilt*, also to FILTER.

felt[2] past and past participle of FEEL.

felt-tip pen (also **felt-tipped pen** or **felt tip**) ▶ noun a pen with a writing point made of felt or tightly packed fibres, typically containing a brightly coloured ink and used for colouring pictures.

felucca /fɛˈlʌkə/ ▶ noun a small boat propelled by oars or lateen sails or both, used on the Nile and formerly more widely in the Mediterranean region.
– ORIGIN early 17th cent.: from Italian *feluc(c)a*, probably from obsolete Spanish *faluca*, of Arabic origin.

felwort /ˈfɛlwəːt/ ▶ noun a European gentian of dry grassland, which produces mauve flowers in the autumn.
● *Gentianella amarella*, family Gentianaceae.
– ORIGIN Old English *feldwyrt* (see FIELD, WORT).

fem ▶ noun variant spelling of FEMME.

FEMA US ▶ abbreviation for Federal Emergency Management Agency.

female ▶ adjective **1** of or denoting the sex that can bear offspring or produce eggs, distinguished biologically by the production of gametes (ova) which can be fertilized by male gametes: *a herd of female deer.*
■ relating to or characteristic of women or female animals: *a female audience* | *a female name.* ■ (of a plant or flower) having a pistil but no stamens. ■ (of parts of machinery, fittings, etc.) manufactured hollow so that a corresponding male part can be inserted.
▶ noun a female person, animal, or plant.
– DERIVATIVES **femaleness** noun.
– ORIGIN Middle English: from Old French *femelle*, from Latin *femella*, diminutive of *femina* 'a woman'. The change in the ending was due to association with MALE, but the words *male* and *female* are not linked etymologically.

female circumcision ▶ noun [mass noun] (among some peoples) the action or traditional practice of cutting off the clitoris and sometimes the labia of girls or young women.

female condom ▶ noun a contraceptive device made of thin rubber, inserted into a woman's vagina before sexual intercourse.

feme covert /fiːm ˈkʌvət/ ▶ noun Law, historical a married woman.
– ORIGIN early 16th cent.: from Anglo-Norman French, literally 'a woman covered (i.e. protected by marriage)'.

feme sole /fiːm ˈsəʊl/ (also **femme sole**) ▶ noun Law, historical a woman without a husband, especially one that is divorced.
– ORIGIN early 16th cent.: from Anglo-Norman French *feme soule* 'a woman alone'.

feminal /ˈfɛmɪn(ə)l/ ▶ **adjective** archaic of or relating to a woman.
– DERIVATIVES **feminality** noun.
– ORIGIN late Middle English: from medieval Latin *feminalis*, from Latin *femina* 'woman'.

femineity /ˌfɛmɪˈniːɪti, -ˈneɪɪti/ ▶ **noun** [mass noun] archaic the quality of being feminine.
– ORIGIN early 19th cent.: from Latin *femineus* 'womanish' (from *femina* 'woman') + **-ITY**.

feminine ▶ **adjective 1** having qualities or an appearance traditionally associated with women, especially delicacy and prettiness: *a feminine frilled blouse.*
■ of or relating to women; female: *he enjoys feminine company.*
2 Grammar of or denoting a gender of nouns and adjectives, conventionally regarded as female.
▶ **noun** (**the feminine**) the female sex or gender: *the association of the arts with the feminine.*
■ Grammar a feminine word or form.
– DERIVATIVES **femininely** adverb, **feminineness** noun, **femininity** noun.
– ORIGIN late Middle English: from Latin *femininus*, from *femina* 'woman'.

feminine rhyme ▶ **noun** Prosody a rhyme between stressed syllables followed by one or more unstressed syllables (e.g. *stocking/shocking*, *glamorous/amorous*). Compare with **MASCULINE RHYME**.

feminism ▶ **noun** [mass noun] the advocacy of women's rights on the ground of the equality of the sexes.

The issue of rights for women first became prominent during the French and American revolutions in the late 18th century. In Britain it was not until the emergence of the suffragette movement in the late 19th century that there was significant political change. A 'second wave' of feminism arose in the 1960s, with an emphasis on unity and sisterhood; seminal figures included Betty Friedan and Germaine Greer.

– ORIGIN late 19th cent.: from French *féminisme*.

feminist ▶ **noun** a person who supports feminism.
▶ **adjective** of, relating to, or supporting feminism: *feminist literature.*
– ORIGIN late 19th cent.: from French *féministe*, from Latin *femina* 'woman'.

feminity ▶ **noun** rare term for **FEMININITY** (see **FEMININE**).
– ORIGIN late Middle English: from Old French *feminite*, from medieval Latin *feminitas*, from Latin *femina* 'woman'.

feminize (also **-ise**) ▶ **verb** [with obj.] make (something) more characteristic of or associated with women: *as office roles changed, clerical work was increasingly feminized.*
– DERIVATIVES **feminization** noun.

femme /fɛm/ (also **fem**) ▶ **noun** informal a lesbian who takes a traditionally feminine sexual role.
– ORIGIN 1960s: French, 'woman'.

femme fatale /ˌfam fəˈtɑːl/ ▶ **noun** (pl. **femmes fatales** pronunc. same) an attractive and seductive woman, especially one who will ultimately cause distress to a man who becomes involved with her.
– ORIGIN early 20th cent.: French, literally 'disastrous woman'.

femme sole ▶ **noun** variant spelling of **FEME SOLE**.

femto- /ˈfɛmtəʊ/ ▶ **combining form** (used in units of measurement) denoting a factor of 10^{-15}: *femtosecond.*
– ORIGIN from Danish or Norwegian *femten* 'fifteen'.

femur /ˈfiːmə/ ▶ **noun** (pl. **femurs** or **femora** /ˈfɛm(ə)rə/) Anatomy the bone of the thigh or upper hindlimb, articulating at the hip and the knee.
■ Zoology the third segment of the leg in insects and some other arthropods, typically the longest and thickest segment.
– DERIVATIVES **femoral** /ˈfɛm(ə)r(ə)l/ adjective.
– ORIGIN late 15th cent.: from Latin *femur*, *femor-* 'thigh'.

fen[1] ▶ **noun** a low and marshy or frequently flooded area of land: *a flooded fen* | [mass noun] *55 acres of fen.*
■ (**the Fens**) the flat low-lying areas of eastern England, mainly in Lincolnshire, Cambridgeshire, and Norfolk, formerly marshland but largely drained for agriculture since the 17th century. ■ [mass noun] Ecology wetland with alkaline, neutral, or only slightly acid peaty soil. Compare with **BOG**.
– DERIVATIVES **fenny** adjective.
– ORIGIN Old English *fen(n)*, of Germanic origin; related to Dutch *veen* and German *Fenn*.

fen[2] ▶ **noun** (pl. same) a monetary unit of China, equal to one hundredth of a yuan.
– ORIGIN from Chinese *fēn* 'a hundredth part'.

fenberry ▶ **noun** (pl. **-ies**) another term for **CRANBERRY**.

fence ▶ **noun 1** a barrier, railing, or other upright structure, typically of wood or wire, enclosing an area of ground to prevent or control access or escape.
■ a large upright obstacle in steeplechasing, showjumping, or cross-country. ■ a guard or guide on a plane, saw, or other tool.
2 informal a person who deals in stolen goods.
▶ **verb 1** [with obj.] surround or protect with a fence: *our garden was not fully fenced.*
■ (**fence something in/off**) enclose or separate with a fence for protection or to prevent escape: *everything is fenced in to keep out the wolves.* ■ (**fence someone/thing out**) use a barrier to exclude someone or something: *walkers may find themselves fenced out of the moor.*
2 [with obj.] informal deal in (stolen goods): *after stealing your ring, he didn't even know how to fence it.*
3 [no obj.] fight with swords, especially as a sport. See also **FENCING**[1].
■ figurative conduct a discussion or argument in such a way as to avoid the direct mention of something.
– PHRASES **mend (one's) fences** see **MEND**. **over the fence** Austral./NZ informal unreasonable or unacceptable: *it's over the fence, the way you've been carrying on.* **side of the fence** used to refer to either of the opposing or conflicting positions or interests involved in a particular debate or situation: *whatever side of the fence you are on, the issue is here to stay.* **sit on the fence** avoid making a decision or choice.
– DERIVATIVES **fenceless** adjective, **fencer** noun.
– ORIGIN Middle English (in the sense 'defending, defence'): shortening of **DEFENCE**. Compare with **FENCIBLE** and **FEND**.

fence lizard ▶ **noun** a small grey-brown North American spiny lizard that typically has bright markings and often basks on rail fences, logs, and tree stumps.
● *Sceloporus undulatus*, family Iguanidae.

fence post ▶ **noun** a timber or metal post set in the ground as a supporting part of a fence.

fencerow /ˈfɛnsrəʊ/ ▶ **noun** N. Amer. an uncultivated strip of land on each side of and below a fence.

fencible /ˈfɛnsɪb(ə)l/ ▶ **noun** (usu. **fencibles**) historical a soldier belonging to a British militia which could be called up only for service on home soil.
– ORIGIN Middle English (in the sense 'fit or suitable for defence'): shortening of **DEFENSIBLE**. Compare with **FENCE**, **FEND**.

fencing ▶ **noun** [mass noun] **1** the sport of fighting with swords, especially foils, épées, or sabres, according to a set of rules, in order to score points against an opponent: [as modifier] *a fencing foil.*
■ figurative the action of conducting a discussion or argument so as to avoid the direct mention of something.
2 a series of fences: *security fencing.*
■ material used for the construction of fences: *chestnut is still in demand for fencing.* ■ the erection of fences. ■ the jumping of fences by a racehorse: [as modifier] *the horse makes his fencing debut today.*

fend ▶ **verb 1** [no obj.] (**fend for oneself**) look after and provide for oneself, without any help from others: *how could any mother leave a child to fend for itself?*
2 [with obj.] (**fend someone/thing off**) defend oneself from a blow, attack, or attacker.
■ evade someone or something in order to protect oneself: *he fended off the awkward questions.*
– ORIGIN Middle English (in the sense 'defend'): shortening of **DEFEND**. Compare with **FENCE** and **FENCIBLE**.

Fender /ˈfɛndə/, Leo (1907–91), American guitar-maker. He pioneered the production of electric guitars, designing the first solid-body electric guitar to be widely available and founding the Fender company.

fender ▶ **noun 1** a low frame bordering a fireplace to keep in falling coals.
2 a thing used to keep something off or prevent a collision, in particular:
■ a plastic cylinder, tyre, piece of old rope or matting, etc., hung over a ship's side to protect it against impact. ■ N. Amer. the mudguard or area around the wheel well of a vehicle.

fender bender ▶ **noun** N. Amer. informal a minor collision between motor vehicles.

fenestella /ˌfɛnɪˈstɛlə/ ▶ **noun** Architecture a niche in a wall south of a church's altar, holding the piscina and often the credence.
– ORIGIN late Middle English: from Latin, diminutive of *fenestra* 'window'.

fenestra /fɪˈnɛstrə/ ▶ **noun** (pl. **fenestrae** /-triː/) **1** Anatomy & Zoology a small natural hole or opening, especially in a bone. The mammalian middle ear is linked by the **fenestra ovalis** to the vestibule of the inner ear, and by the **fenestra rotunda** to the cochlea.
2 Medicine an artificial opening.
■ an opening in a bandage or cast. ■ a perforation in a forceps blade. ■ a hole made by surgical fenestration.
– ORIGIN early 19th cent. (as a botanical term denoting a small scar left by the separation of the seed from the ovary): from Latin, literally 'window'.

fenestrate /ˈfɛnəstrət, fɪˈnɛstrət/ ▶ **adjective** Botany & Zoology having small window-like perforations or transparent areas.
– ORIGIN mid 19th cent.: from Latin *fenestratus* 'provided with openings', from the verb *fenestrare*.

fenestrated /ˈfɛnəˌstreɪtɪd, fɪˈnɛstreɪtɪd/ ▶ **adjective** provided with a window or windows: *the fenestrated heights of nearby buildings.*
■ chiefly Anatomy having perforations, apertures, or transparent areas: *the capillaries have a fenestrated epithelium.*
– ORIGIN early 19th cent.: from Latin *fenestrare* (see **FENESTRATE**) + **-ED**[1].

fenestration /ˌfɛnɪˈstreɪʃ(ə)n/ ▶ **noun** [mass noun] Architecture the arrangement of windows in a building.
■ Botany & Zoology the condition of being fenestrate. ■ Medicine a surgical operation in which a new opening is formed, especially in the bony labyrinth of the inner ear to treat certain types of deafness.

fen-fire ▶ **noun** a will-o'-the-wisp.

feng shui /ˌfɛŋ ˈʃuːi, ˌfʌŋ ˈʃweɪ/ ▶ **noun** [mass noun] (in Chinese thought) a system of laws considered to govern spatial arrangement and orientation in relation to the flow of energy (chi), and whose favourable or unfavourable effects are taken into account when siting and designing buildings.
– ORIGIN Chinese, from *fēng* 'wind' and *shuǐ* 'water'.

Fenian /ˈfiːnɪən/ ▶ **noun** a member of the Irish Republican Brotherhood, a 19th-century revolutionary nationalist organization among the Irish in the US and Ireland. The Fenians staged an unsuccessful revolt in Ireland in 1867 and were responsible for isolated revolutionary acts against the British until the early 20th century, when they were gradually eclipsed by the IRA.
■ informal, offensive (chiefly in Northern Ireland) a Protestant name for a Catholic.
– DERIVATIVES **Fenianism** noun.
– ORIGIN from Old Irish *féne*, the name of an ancient Irish people, confused with *fiann*, *fianna* (see **FIANNA FÁIL**).

fenland ▶ **noun** [mass noun] (also **fenlands**) land consisting of fens: *thousands of acres of fenland.*
■ (usu. **the Fenland**) the Fens of eastern England.

fennec /ˈfɛnɛk/ (also **fennec fox**) ▶ **noun** a small pale fox with large pointed ears, native to the deserts of North Africa and Arabia.
● *Vulpes zerda*, family Canidae.
– ORIGIN late 18th cent.: via Arabic from Persian *fanak*, *fanaj*.

fennel /ˈfɛn(ə)l/ ▶ **noun** [mass noun] an aromatic yellow-flowered European plant of the parsley family, with feathery leaves.
● *Foeniculum vulgare*, family Umbelliferae: two subspecies, a hardy perennial (subsp. *dulce*), the seeds and leaves of which are used as culinary herbs, and the annual **Florence** (or **sweet**) **fennel** (subsp. *azoricum*), with swollen leaf-bases which are eaten as a vegetable.
– ORIGIN Old English *finule*, *fenol*, from Latin *faeniculum*, diminutive of *faenum* 'hay'.

Fennoscandia /ˌfɛnəʊˈskandɪə/ a land mass in NW Europe comprising Scandinavia, Finland, and the adjacent area of NE Russia.

fenugreek /ˈfɛnjʊɡriːk/ ▶ **noun** [mass noun] a white-flowered herbaceous plant of the pea family, with aromatic seeds that are used for flavouring, especially ground and used in curry powder.
● *Trigonella foenum-graecum*, family Leguminosae.

– ORIGIN Old English *fenogrecum* (superseded in Middle English by forms from Old French *fenugrec*), from Latin *faenugraecum*, from *faenum graecum* 'Greek hay' (the Romans used the dried plant as fodder).

feodary /ˈfjuːdəri/ ▶ **noun** (pl. **-ies**) historical a feudal tenant.

feoffee /fɛˈfiː, fiː-/ ▶ **noun** a trustee invested with a freehold estate to hold in possession for a purpose, typically a charitable one.
■ historical (in feudal law) a person to whom a grant of freehold property is made.
– ORIGIN late Middle English: from Anglo-Norman French *feoffe* 'enfeoffed', past participle of *feoffer*, variant of Old French *fieffer* (see **FEOFFMENT**).

feoffment /ˈfiːfm(ə)nt, ˈfɛf-/ ▶ **noun** historical (in feudal law) a grant of ownership of freehold property to someone.
– DERIVATIVES **feoffor** /ˈfɛfə/ noun.
– ORIGIN Middle English: from an Anglo-Norman French variant of Old French *fieffer* 'put in legal possession', from *fief* (see **FEE** and **FIEF**).

feral /ˈfɛr(ə)l, ˈfɪə-/ ▶ **adjective** (especially of an animal) in a wild state, especially after escape from captivity or domestication: *a feral cat.*
■ resembling a wild animal: *a feral snarl.*
– ORIGIN early 17th cent.: from Latin *fera* 'wild animal' (from *ferus* 'wild') + **-AL**.

feral pigeon ▶ **noun** see **PIGEON**[1] (sense 1).

ferberite /ˈfəːbərʌɪt/ ▶ **noun** [mass noun] a black mineral consisting of ferrous tungstate, typically occurring as elongated prisms.
– ORIGIN early 19th cent.: named after Rudolph *Ferber* (1743–90), Swedish mineralogist, + **-ITE**[1].

fer de lance /ˌfɛː də ˈlɑːns/ ▶ **noun** (pl. **fers de lance** pronunc. same or **fer de lances**) a large and dangerous pit viper native to Central and South America.
● Genus *Bothrops*, family Viperidae: several species, in particular *B. atrox*.
– ORIGIN late 19th cent.: from French, literally 'iron (head) of a lance'.

Ferdinand /ˈfəːdɪnand/ of Aragon (1452–1516), king of Castile 1474–1516 and of Aragon 1479–1516; known as **Ferdinand the Catholic**. His marriage to Isabella of Castile in 1469 ensured his accession (as Ferdinand V) to the throne of Castile with her. Ferdinand subsequently succeeded to the throne of Aragon (as Ferdinand II) and was joined as monarch by Isabella. They instituted the Spanish Inquisition in 1478 and supported Columbus's expedition in 1492. Their capture of Granada from the Moors in the same year effectively united Spain as one country.

Ferguson /ˈfəːgəs(ə)n/, Alex (b.1941), Scottish football manager and footballer; full name *Alexander Chapman Ferguson*. He became manager of Manchester United in 1986, taking them to three Premier League championships and three FA Cup wins in ten years.

feria /ˈfɛrɪə/ ▶ **noun** (in Spain and Spanish-speaking America) a fair.
– ORIGIN Spanish, from Latin, literally 'holiday'.

ferial /ˈfɪərɪəl, ˈfɛ-/ ▶ **adjective** Christian Church denoting an ordinary weekday, as opposed to one appointed for a festival or fast.
– ORIGIN late Middle English: from medieval Latin *ferialis*, from Latin *feria* 'holiday'. In late Latin *feria* was used with a prefixed ordinal number to mean 'day of the week' (e.g. *secunda feria* 'second day, Monday'), but Sunday (Dominicus) and Saturday (Sabbatum) were usually referred to by their names; hence *feria* came to mean 'ordinary weekday'.

feringhee /fəˈrɪŋgi/ (also **feringhi**) ▶ **noun** **1** chiefly derogatory (in India and parts of the Middle and Far East) a foreigner, especially one with white skin.
2 archaic a person of Indian–Portuguese parentage.
– ORIGIN via Urdu from Persian *firangī*, from the base of **FRANK**[2].

Ferlinghetti /ˌfəːlɪŋˈgɛti/, Lawrence (Monsanto) (b.1919), American poet and publisher; born *Lawrence Ferling*. Identified with San Francisco's beat movement, he founded the publishing house City Lights, which produced works such as Allen Ginsberg's *Howl* (1957). Notable works: *A Coney Island of the Mind* (1958).

Ferm. abbreviation for Fermanagh.

Fermanagh /fəˈmanə/ one of the Six Counties of Northern Ireland, formerly an administrative area; chief town, Enniskillen.

Fermat /ˈfəːmɑː, French fɛrma/, Pierre de (1601–65), French mathematician. His work on curves led directly to the general methods of calculus introduced by Newton and Leibniz. He is also recognized as the founder of the theory of numbers.

fermata /fəːˈmɑːtə/ ▶ **noun** Music a pause of unspecified length on a note or rest.
■ a sign indicating a prolonged note or rest.
– ORIGIN Italian, from *fermare* 'to stop'.

Fermat's last theorem Mathematics a conjecture by Fermat that if n is an integer greater than 2, the equation $x^n + y^n = z^n$ has no positive integral solutions. Fermat noted that he had 'a truly wonderful proof' of the conjecture, but never wrote it down. In 1995 a general proof was published by the Princeton-based British mathematician Andrew Wiles.

ferment ▶ **verb** /fəˈmɛnt/ **1** [no obj.] (of a substance) undergo fermentation: *the drink had fermented, turning some of the juice into alcohol.*
■ [with obj.] cause the fermentation of (a substance).
2 [with obj.] incite or stir up (trouble or disorder): *the politicians and warlords who are fermenting this chaos.*
▶ **noun** /ˈfəːmɛnt/ **1** [mass noun] agitation and excitement among a group of people, typically concerning major change and leading to trouble or violence: *Germany at this time was in a state of religious ferment* | [in sing.] *a ferment of revolutionary upheaval.*
2 archaic a fermenting agent or enzyme.
– DERIVATIVES **fermentable** adjective.
– ORIGIN late Middle English: from Old French *ferment* (noun), *fermenter* (verb), based on Latin *fermentum* 'yeast', from *fervere* 'to boil'.

fermentation ▶ **noun** [mass noun] the chemical breakdown of a substance by bacteria, yeasts, or other micro-organisms, typically involving effervescence and the giving off of heat.
■ the process of this kind involved in the making of beers, wines, and spirits, in which sugars are converted to ethyl alcohol. ■ archaic agitation; excitement: *I had found Paris in high fermentation.*
– DERIVATIVES **fermentative** adjective.
– ORIGIN late Middle English: from late Latin *fermentatio(n-)*, from Latin *fermentare* 'to ferment' (see **FERMENT**).

fermenter (US also **fermentor**) ▶ **noun** a container in which fermentation takes place.
■ an organism which causes fermentation.

Fermi /ˈfəːmi, ˈfɛːmi, Italian ˈfermi/, Enrico (1901–54), Italian-born American atomic physicist, who directed the first controlled nuclear chain reaction in 1942. Nobel Prize for Physics (1938).

fermi /ˈfəːmi/ ▶ **noun** (pl. same) a unit of length equal to 10^{-15} metre (one femtometre), used in nuclear physics. It is similar to the diameter of a proton.
– ORIGIN early 20th cent.: named after E. **FERMI**.

Fermi-Dirac statistics ▶ **plural noun** [treated as sing.] Physics a type of quantum statistics used to describe systems of fermions.
– ORIGIN 1920s: named after E. **FERMI** and P. A. M. **DIRAC**.

fermion /ˈfəːmɪɒn/ ▶ **noun** Physics a subatomic particle, such as a nucleon, which has half-integral spin and follows the statistical description given by Fermi and Dirac.
– ORIGIN 1940s: from the name of E. **FERMI** + **-ON**.

fermium /ˈfəːmɪəm/ ▶ **noun** [mass noun] the chemical element of atomic number 100, a radioactive metal of the actinide series. Fermium does not occur naturally and was discovered in 1953 in the debris of the first hydrogen bomb explosion. (Symbol: **Fm**)
– ORIGIN 1950s: from the name of E. **FERMI** + **-IUM**.

fern ▶ **noun** (pl. same or **ferns**) a flowerless plant which has feathery or leafy fronds and reproduces by spores released from the undersides of the fronds. Ferns have a vascular system for the transport of water and nutrients.
● Class Filicopsida, division Pteridophyta.
– DERIVATIVES **fernery** noun (pl. **-ies**), **ferny** adjective.
– ORIGIN Old English *fearn*, of West Germanic origin; related to Dutch *varen* and German *Farn*.

Fernando Póo /fəˌnandəʊ ˈpəʊ/ former name (until 1973) for **BIOKO**.

fernbird ▶ **noun** a secretive warbler found only in New Zealand, with dark streaked plumage.
● *Megalurus punctatus*, family Sylviidae.

fernbrake ▶ **noun** a bed or thicket of ferns.
– ORIGIN early 17th cent.: from **FERN** + **BRAKE**[4].

ferocious ▶ **adjective** savagely fierce, cruel, or violent: *a ferocious beast.*
■ (of a conflict) characterized by or involving aggression, bitterness, and determination: *a ferocious argument.* ■ extreme and unpleasant: *a ferocious headache.*
– DERIVATIVES **ferociously** adverb, **ferociousness** noun.
– ORIGIN mid 17th cent.: from Latin *ferox, feroc-* 'fierce' + **-IOUS**.

ferocity ▶ **noun** (pl. **-ies**) [mass noun] the state or quality of being ferocious: *the ferocity of the storm caught them by surprise* | [count noun] *she hated him with a ferocity that astonished her.*
– ORIGIN mid 16th cent.: from French, or from Latin *ferocitas*, from *ferox, feroc-* 'fierce'.

-ferous (usu. **-iferous**) ▶ **combining form** having, bearing, or containing (a specified thing): *Carboniferous* | *pestiferous.*
– DERIVATIVES **-ferously** combining form in corresponding adverbs, **-ferousness** combining form in corresponding nouns.
– ORIGIN from French *-fère* or Latin *-fer* 'producing', from *ferre* 'to bear'.

ferox /ˈfɛrɒks/ (also **ferox trout**) ▶ **noun** a brown trout of a very large variety, occurring in large deep lakes in NW Europe.
– ORIGIN mid 19th cent.: from modern Latin *Salmo ferox*, literally 'fierce salmon', former name of the variety.

Ferranti /fəˈranti/, Sebastian Ziani de (1864–1930), English electrical engineer. He was one of the pioneers of electricity generation and distribution in Britain, his chief contribution being the use of high voltages for economical transmission over a distance.

Ferrara /fəˈrɑːrə, Italian ferˈrara/ a city in northern Italy, capital of a province of the same name; pop. 140,600 (1990). Ferrara grew to prominence in the 13th century under the rule of the powerful Este family.

Ferrari /fəˈrɑːri, Italian ferˈrari/, Enzo (1898–1988), Italian car designer and manufacturer. In 1929 he founded the company named after him, producing a range of high-quality sports and racing cars. Since the early 1950s Ferraris have won the greatest number of world championship Grands Prix of any car.

ferrate /ˈfɛreɪt/ ▶ **noun** Chemistry a salt in which the anion contains both iron (typically ferric iron) and oxygen.
– ORIGIN mid 19th cent.: from Latin *ferrum* 'iron' + **-ATE**[1].

ferrel /ˈfɛr(ə)l/ ▶ **noun** variant spelling of **FERRULE**.

Ferrel's law /ˈfɛrəlz/ Meteorology a law stating that Coriolis forces deflect winds and freely moving objects to the right in the northern hemisphere and to the left in the southern hemisphere.
– ORIGIN early 20th cent.: named after William Ferrel (1817–91), American meteorologist.

ferret /ˈfɛrɪt/ ▶ **noun** **1** a domesticated polecat used chiefly for catching rabbits. It is typically albino in coloration, but sometimes brown. See **POLECAT-FERRET**.
● *Mustela furo*, family Mustelidae; descended mainly from the European polecat.
2 a search for something, typically in a small or enclosed space: *he had a quick ferret around.*
■ a person who searches assiduously and tenaciously: *the cops rarely liaised with the income tax ferrets.*
▶ **verb** (**ferreted**, **ferreting**) [no obj.] (of a person) hunt with ferrets, typically for rabbits: [as noun **ferreting**] *ferreting is increasing in popularity.*
■ clear (a hole or area of ground) of rabbits with ferrets. ■ [with adverbial of place] rummage about in a place or container in search of something: *he shambled over to the desk and ferreted around.* ■ [with obj.] (**ferret something out**) search tenaciously for something: *she had the ability to ferret out the facts.*
– DERIVATIVES **ferreter** noun, **ferrety** adjective.
– ORIGIN late Middle English: from Old French *fuiret*, alteration of *fuiron*, based on late Latin *furo* 'thief, ferret', from Latin *fur* 'thief'.

ferret-badger ▶ **noun** a small tree-climbing badger found in SE Asia, having a long tail and a brownish coat with conspicuous facial markings.
● Genus *Melogale*, family Mustelidae: three species.

ferri- /ˈfɛri/ ▶ **combining form** Chemistry of iron with a valency of three; ferric. Compare with **FERRO-**.
– ORIGIN from Latin *ferrum* 'iron'.

ferriage /ˈfɛrɪɪdʒ/ ▶ **noun** [mass noun] archaic the action of transporting someone or something by ferry.
▪ the fare paid for a journey by ferry.

ferric /ˈfɛrɪk/ ▶ **adjective** of or relating to iron.
▪ Chemistry of iron with a valency of three; of iron(III). Compare with **FERROUS**.
– ORIGIN late 18th cent.: from Latin *ferrum* 'iron' + **-IC**.

ferricyanide ▶ **noun** Chemistry a salt containing the anion $Fe(CN)_6^{3-}$.

Ferrier /ˈfɛrɪə/, Kathleen (1912–53), English contralto. She is particularly famous for her performance in 1947 of Mahler's song cycle *Das Lied von der Erde*.

ferrimagnetic ▶ **adjective** Physics (of a substance) displaying a weak form of ferromagnetism associated with parallel but opposite alignment of neighbouring atoms. In contrast with antiferromagnetic materials, these alignments do not cancel out and there is a net magnetic moment.
– DERIVATIVES **ferrimagnetism** noun.

Ferris wheel /ˈfɛrɪs/ ▶ **noun** a fairground ride consisting of a giant vertical revolving wheel with passenger cars suspended on its outer edge.
– ORIGIN late 19th cent.: named after George W. G. *Ferris* (1859–96), the American engineer who invented it.

ferrite /ˈfɛrʌɪt/ ▶ **noun** [mass noun] **1** a ceramic compound consisting of a mixed oxide of iron and one or more other metals which has ferrimagnetic properties and is used in high-frequency electrical components such as aerials.
2 Metallurgy a form of pure iron with a body-centred cubic crystal structure, occurring in low-carbon steel.
– DERIVATIVES **ferritic** /fɛˈrɪtɪk/ adjective (only in sense 2).
– ORIGIN mid 19th cent.: from Latin *ferrum* 'iron' + **-ITE**[1].

ferritin /ˈfɛrɪtɪn/ ▶ **noun** [mass noun] Biochemistry a protein produced in mammalian metabolism which serves to store iron in the tissues.
– ORIGIN 1930s: from **FERRI-** + *-t-* (for ease of pronunciation) + **-IN**[1].

ferro- /ˈfɛrəʊ/ ▶ **combining form** containing iron: *ferroconcrete*.
▪ Chemistry of iron with a valency of two; ferrous. Compare with **FERRI-**.
– ORIGIN from Latin *ferrum* 'iron'.

ferrocene /ˈfɛrəsiːn/ ▶ **noun** Chemistry an orange crystalline compound whose molecule has a sandwich structure in which two planar cyclopentadiene ligands enclose an iron atom.
• Chem. formula: $Fe(C_5H_5)_2$.
– ORIGIN 1950s: from **FERRO-** 'containing iron' + *-cene* from *c(yclopentadi)ene*.

ferroconcrete ▶ **noun** [mass noun] [often as modifier] concrete reinforced with steel: *a ferroconcrete storage tank*.

ferrocyanide ▶ **noun** Chemistry a salt containing the anion $Fe(CN)_6^{4-}$.

ferroelectric Physics ▶ **adjective** (of a substance) exhibiting permanent electric polarization which varies in strength with the applied electric field.
▶ **noun** a ferroelectric substance.
– DERIVATIVES **ferroelectricity** noun.

ferrofluid ▶ **noun** [often as modifier] a fluid containing a magnetic suspension: *ferrofluid cooling*.

ferromagnesian /ˌfɛrə(ʊ)magˈniːʒ(ə)n, -zɪən/ ▶ **adjective** Geology (of a rock or mineral) containing iron and magnesium as major components.

ferromagnetic ▶ **adjective** Physics (of a body or substance) having a high susceptibility to magnetization, the strength of which depends on that of the applied magnetizing field, and which may persist after removal of the applied field. This is the kind of magnetism displayed by iron, and is associated with parallel magnetic alignment of neighbouring atoms.
– DERIVATIVES **ferromagnetism** noun.

ferrous /ˈfɛrəs/ ▶ **adjective** (chiefly of metals) containing or consisting of iron.
▪ Chemistry of iron with a valency of two; of iron(II). Compare with **FERRIC**.
– ORIGIN mid 19th cent.: from Latin *ferrum* 'iron' + **-OUS**.

ferrous sulphate ▶ **noun** [mass noun] a pale green iron salt used in inks, tanning, water purification, and treating anaemia.
• Alternative name: **iron(II) sulphate**; chem. formula (crystals): $FeSO_4.7H_2O$.

ferruginous /fɛˈruːdʒɪnəs/ ▶ **adjective** containing iron oxides or rust: *a band of ferruginous limestone*.
▪ reddish brown; rust-coloured: *the ferruginous earth of southern Brazil*.
– ORIGIN mid 17th cent.: from Latin *ferrugo, ferrugin-* 'rust, dark red' (from *ferrum* 'iron') + **-OUS**.

ferruginous duck ▶ **noun** a Eurasian diving duck related to the pochard, the male of which has mainly dark red-brown breeding plumage.
• *Aythya nyroca*, family Anatidae.

ferrule /ˈfɛruːl, ˈfɛr(ə)l/ (also **ferrel**) ▶ **noun** a ring or cap, typically a metal one, which strengthens the end of a handle, stick, or tube and prevents it from splitting or wearing.
▪ a metal band strengthening or forming a joint.
– ORIGIN early 17th cent.: alteration (probably by association with Latin *ferrum* 'iron') of obsolete *verrel*, from Old French *virelle*, from Latin *viriola*, diminutive of *viriae* 'bracelets'.

ferry ▶ **noun** (pl. **-ies**) (also **ferry boat**) a boat or ship for conveying passengers and goods, especially over a relatively short distance and as a regular service.
▪ a service for conveying passengers or goods in this way. ▪ the place where such a service operates from. ▪ a similar service using another mode of transport, especially aircraft.
▶ **verb** (**-ies, -ied**) [with obj. and adverbial of direction] convey in a boat,especially across a short stretch of water: *the British Expeditionary Force was safely ferried across the Channel*.
▪ transport (someone or something) from one place to another, especially as a regular service: *all supplies were ferried in by regular helicopter deliveries*.
– DERIVATIVES **ferryman** (pl. **-men**) noun.
– ORIGIN Middle English: from Old Norse *ferja* 'ferry boat', of Germanic origin and related to **FARE**.

fertile /ˈfəːtʌɪl/ ▶ **adjective** (of soil or land) producing or capable of producing abundant vegetation or crops: *areas of fertile, sandy ground*.
▪ (of a seed or egg) capable of becoming a new individual. ▪ (of a person, animal, or plant) able to conceive young or produce seed: *Karen carefully calculated the period when she was most fertile*. ▪ (of a person's mind or imagination) producing many new and inventive ideas with ease. ▪ (of a situation or subject) being fruitful and productive in generating new ideas: *a series of fertile debates within the social sciences*. ▪ Physics (of nuclear material) able to become fissile by the capture of neutrons.
– DERIVATIVES **fertility** noun.
– ORIGIN late Middle English: via French from Latin *fertilis*, from *ferre* 'to bear'.

Fertile Crescent a crescent-shaped area of fertile land in the Middle East extending from the eastern Mediterranean coast through the valley of the Tigris and Euphrates Rivers to the Persian Gulf. It was the centre of the Neolithic development of agriculture (from 7000 BC), and the cradle of the Assyrian, Sumerian, and Babylonian civilizations.

fertility cult ▶ **noun** a pagan religious system of some agricultural societies in which seasonal rites are performed with the aim of ensuring good harvests and the future well-being of the community.

fertilization (also **-isation**) ▶ **noun** [mass noun] Biology the action or process of fertilizing an egg or a female animal or plant, involving the fusion of male and female gametes to form a zygote.
▪ the action or process of applying a fertilizer to soil or land.

fertilize (also **-ise**) ▶ **verb** [with obj.] cause (an egg, female animal, or plant) to develop a new individual by introducing male reproductive material.
▪ make (soil or land) more fertile or productive by adding suitable substances to it.
– DERIVATIVES **fertilizable** adjective.

fertilizer (also **-iser**) ▶ **noun** a chemical or natural substance added to soil or land to increase its fertility: *a nitrogenous fertilizer* | [mass noun] *these varieties need pesticides and more fertilizer*.

Fertö Tó /ˌfɛrtø ˈtoː/ Hungarian name for **NEUSIEDLER SEE**.

ferula /ˈfɛrjʊlə/ ▶ **noun 1** a tall large-leaved Eurasian plant of a genus that includes asafoetida and its relatives.
• Genus *Ferula*, family Umbelliferae.
2 rare term for **FERULE**.
– ORIGIN late Middle English: from Latin, 'giant fennel, rod'.

ferule /ˈfɛruːl/ ▶ **noun** historical a flat ruler with a widened end, formerly used for beating children.
– ORIGIN late Middle English (denoting the giant fennel): from Latin *ferula* (see **FERULA**).

fervent /ˈfəːv(ə)nt/ ▶ **adjective** having or displaying a passionate intensity: *40,000 fervent admirers of the Great Leader*.
▪ archaic hot, burning, or glowing.
– DERIVATIVES **fervency** noun, **fervently** adverb.
– ORIGIN Middle English: via Old French from Latin *fervent-* 'boiling', from the verb *fervere*. Compare with **FERVID** and **FERVOUR**.

fervid /ˈfəːvɪd/ ▶ **adjective** intensely enthusiastic or passionate, especially to an excessive degree: *she had a fervid interest in sex*.
▪ poetic/literary burning, hot, or glowing.
– DERIVATIVES **fervidly** adverb.
– ORIGIN late 16th cent. (in the sense 'glowing, hot'): from Latin *fervidus*, from *fervere* 'to boil'. Compare with **FERVENT** and **FERVOUR**.

fervour /ˈfəːvə/ (US **fervor**) ▶ **noun** [mass noun] intense and passionate feeling: *he talked with all the fervour of a new convert*.
▪ archaic intense heat.
– ORIGIN Middle English: via Old French from Latin *fervor*, from *fervere* 'to boil'. Compare with **FERVENT** and **FERVID**.

Fès variant spelling of **FEZ**.

fescue /ˈfɛskjuː/ ▶ **noun** any of a number of narrow-leaved grasses:
• a perennial grass that is a valuable pasture and fodder species (genus *Festuca*, family Gramineae). • an annual grass that typically occurs on drier soils such as on dunes and heathland (genus *Vulpia*, family Gramineae).
– ORIGIN Middle English *festu, festue* 'straw, twig', from Old French *festu*, based on Latin *festuca* 'stalk, straw'. The change of *-t-* to *-c-* occurred in the 16th cent.; the current sense dates from the mid 18th cent.

fess[1] /fɛs/ (also **fesse**) ▶ **noun** Heraldry an ordinary in the form of a broad horizontal stripe across the middle of the shield.
– PHRASES **in fess** across the middle third of the field.
– ORIGIN late 15th cent.: from Old French *fesse*, alteration of *faisse*, from Latin *fascia* 'band'. Compare with **FASCIA**.

fess[2] /fɛs/ ▶ **verb** [no obj.] (**fess up**) informal confess; own up: *'Fess up', she demanded. 'What were you doing in Peter's private office?'*
– ORIGIN early 19th cent.: shortening of **CONFESS**.

Fessenden /ˈfɛs(ə)nd(ə)n/, Reginald Aubrey (1866–1932), Canadian-born American pioneer of radiotelephony, who invented the heterodyne receiver.

fess point ▶ **noun** Heraldry a point at the centre of a shield.

-fest ▶ **combining form** in nouns denoting a festival or large gathering of a specified kind: *a media-fest* | *a jazz-fest*.
– ORIGIN from German *Fest* 'festival'.

festa /ˈfɛstə/ ▶ **noun** (in Italy and other Mediterranean countries) a religious or other festival.
– ORIGIN early 19th cent.: from Italian, 'festival', from Latin.

festal ▶ **adjective** chiefly archaic of, like, or relating to a celebration or festival: *plum pudding was originally served on festal days as a main course*.
– DERIVATIVES **festally** adverb.
– ORIGIN late 15th cent.: via Old French from late Latin *festalis*, from Latin *festum*, (plural) *festa* 'feast'.

fester ▶ **verb** [no obj.] [often as adj. **festering**] (of a wound or sore) become septic; suppurate: *a festering abscess*.
▪ (of food or rubbish) become rotten and offensive to the senses: *sandwiches curled open to show festering meats*. ▪ (of a negative feeling or a problem) become worse or more intense, especially through long-term neglect or indifference: *a festering controversy*. ▪ (of a person) undergo physical and mental deterioration in isolated inactivity: *I might be festering in jail now*.
– ORIGIN late Middle English: from the rare word

fester 'fistula', later 'festering sore', or Old French *festrir* (verb), both from Old French *festre* (noun), from Latin *fistula* 'pipe, reed, fistula'.

festival ▶ **noun** a day or period of celebration, typically for religious reasons: *a Jewish festival* | [as modifier] *a festival atmosphere.*
▪an organized series of concerts, plays, or films, typically one held annually in the same place: *a major international festival of song.*
– ORIGIN Middle English (as an adjective): via Old French from medieval Latin *festivalis*, from Latin *festivus*, from *festum*, (plural) *festa* 'feast'.

Festival of Britain a festival celebrated with lavish exhibitions and shows throughout Britain in May 1951 to mark the centenary of the Great Exhibition of 1851.

festival of lights ▶ **noun 1** another term for **HANUKKAH**.
2 another term for **DIWALI**.

Festival of the Dead ▶ **noun** another term for **BON**.

festive ▶ **adjective** of or relating to a festival, especially Christmas: *the* ***festive season.***
▪cheerful and jovially celebratory: *the sombre atmosphere has given way to a festive mood.*
– DERIVATIVES **festively** adverb, **festiveness** noun.
– ORIGIN mid 17th cent.: from Latin *festivus*, from *festum*, (plural) *festa* 'feast'.

festivity ▶ **noun** (pl. **-ies**) [mass noun] the celebration of something in a joyful and exuberant way: *the jolly festivity of the Last Night of the Proms.*
▪(**festivities**) activities or events celebrating a special occasion.
– ORIGIN late Middle English: from Old French *festivite* or Latin *festivitas*, from *festivus* 'festive', from *festum*, (plural) *festa* 'feast'.

festoon /fɛˈstuːn/ ▶ **noun 1** a chain or garland of flowers, leaves, or ribbons, hung in a curve as a decoration.
▪a carved or moulded ornament representing such a garland.
2 a Eurasian butterfly or moth patterned with dark arcs on a lighter background:
• a large yellowish butterfly with black and red markings (*Zerynthia* and other genera, family Papilionidae). • a small brown moth (*Apoda avellana*, family Limacodidae).
▶ **verb** [with obj.] (often **be festooned with**) adorn (a place) with chains, garlands, or other decorations: *the staffroom was festooned with balloons and streamers.*
– ORIGIN mid 17th cent.: from French *feston*, from Italian *festone* 'festal ornament', from *festum*, (plural) *festa* 'feast'.

festoon blind ▶ **noun** a window blind consisting of vertical rows of horizontally gathered fabric that may be drawn up into a series of ruches.

Festschrift /ˈfɛstˌʃrɪft/ ▶ **noun** (pl. **Festschriften** or **Festschrifts**) a collection of writings published in honour of a scholar.
– ORIGIN late 19th cent.: from German, from *Fest* 'celebration' + *Schrift* 'writing'.

FET ▶ **abbreviation for** field-effect transistor.

feta /ˈfɛtə/ (also **feta cheese** or **fetta**) ▶ **noun** [mass noun] a white salty Greek cheese made from the milk of ewes or goats.
– ORIGIN from modern Greek *pheta*.

fetal /ˈfiːt(ə)l/ ▶ **adjective** of or relating to a fetus: *nutrients essential for normal fetal growth.*
▪denoting a posture characteristic of a fetus, with the back curved forwards and the limbs folded in front of the body.

fetal alcohol syndrome (abbrev.: **FAS**) ▶ **noun** [mass noun] Medicine a congenital syndrome associated with excessive consumption of alcohol by the mother during pregnancy, and characterized by retardation of mental development and of physical growth, particularly of the skull and face.

fetch¹ ▶ **verb** [with obj.] **1** go for and then bring back (someone or something) for someone: *he ran to fetch help* | [with two objs] *she fetched me a cup of tea.*
▪(of a person, action, or thing) be the reason for (someone) to come to a place: *it was not horse-trading that fetched Harper to Belgium, but Sharpe.* ▪ archaic bring forth (blood or tears): *kind offers fetched tears from me.* ▪ archaic draw or take a (breath); heave (a sigh).
2 achieve (a particular price) when sold: *the land could fetch over a million pounds.*
3 [with two objs] informal inflict (a blow or slap) on (someone): *he always used to slam the gate and try and fetch her shins a wallop.*
4 informal, dated cause great interest or delight in (someone): *to say that the child has got the father's nose fetches the parents.*
▶ **noun 1** the distance travelled by wind or waves across open water.
▪the distance a vessel must sail to reach open water.
2 [in sing.] an act of going for something and then bringing it back: *he thought the best part of the fetch was wrestling over the stick.*
3 archaic a contrivance, dodge, or trick: *it is no ingenious fetches of argument that we want.*
– PHRASES **fetch and carry** run backwards and forwards bringing things to someone in a servile fashion.
– DERIVATIVES **fetcher** noun.
– ORIGIN Old English *fecc(e)an*, variant of *fetian*, probably related to *fatian* 'grasp', of Germanic origin and related to German *fassen*.
▶**fetch up** informal arrive or come to rest somewhere, typically by accident or unintentionally.

fetch² ▶ **noun** Brit., chiefly archaic the apparition or double of a living person, formerly believed to be a warning of that person's impending death.
– ORIGIN late 17th cent.: of unknown origin.

fetching ▶ **adjective** attractive: *a fetching little garment of pink satin.*
– DERIVATIVES **fetchingly** adverb.

fête /feɪt/ ▶ **noun** Brit. a public function, typically held outdoors and organized to raise funds for charity, including entertainment and the sale of goods and refreshments: *a church fête.*
▪chiefly N. Amer. a celebration or festival.
▶ **verb** [with obj.] (usu. **be fêted**) honour or entertain (someone) lavishly: *she was an instant celebrity, fêted by the media.*
– ORIGIN late Middle English (in the sense 'festival, fair'): from French, from Old French *feste* (see **FEAST**).

fête champêtre /ˌfɛt ʃɒ̃ˈpɛtr(ə), French fɛt ʃɑ̃pɛtʀ/ ▶ **noun** (pl. **fêtes champêtres** pronunc. same) an outdoor entertainment; a rural festival.
– ORIGIN French, literally 'rural festival'.

fête galante /ˌfɛt gaˈlɒ̃t, French fɛt galɑ̃t/ ▶ **noun** (pl. **fêtes galantes** pronunc. same) an outdoor entertainment or rural festival, especially as depicted in 18th-century French painting.
▪a painting in this genre.
– ORIGIN French, literally 'elegant festival'.

fetich ▶ **noun** archaic spelling of **FETISH**.

feticide /ˈfiːtɪsʌɪd/ ▶ **noun** [mass noun] destruction or abortion of a fetus.

fetid /ˈfɛtɪd, ˈfiːt-/ (also **foetid**) ▶ **adjective** smelling extremely unpleasant: *the fetid water of the marsh.*
– DERIVATIVES **fetidly** adverb, **fetidness** noun.
– ORIGIN late Middle English: from Latin *fetidus* (often erroneously spelled *foetidus*), from *fetere* 'to stink'. Compare with **FETOR**.

fetish /ˈfɛtɪʃ/ ▶ **noun** an inanimate object worshipped for its supposed magical powers or because it is considered to be inhabited by a spirit.
▪a course of action to which one has an excessive and irrational commitment: *he* ***had a fetish for*** *writing more opinions each year than any other justice.* ▪ a form of sexual desire in which gratification is linked to an abnormal degree to a particular object, item of clothing, part of the body, etc.: *Victorian men developed fetishes focusing on feet, shoes, and boots.*
– DERIVATIVES **fetishism** noun, **fetishist** noun, **fetishistic** adjective.
– ORIGIN early 17th cent. (originally denoting an object used by the peoples of West Africa as an amulet or charm): from French *fétiche*, from Portuguese *feitiço* 'charm, sorcery' (originally an adjective meaning 'made by art'), from Latin *facticius* (see **FACTITIOUS**).

fetishize (also **-ise**) ▶ **verb** [with obj.] have an excessive and irrational commitment to (something): *an author who fetishizes privacy.*
▪make (something) the object of a sexual fetish: *women's bodies are so intensely fetishized.*
– DERIVATIVES **fetishization** noun.

fetlock /ˈfɛtlɒk/ (also **fetlock joint**) ▶ **noun** the joint of a horse's or other quadruped's leg between the cannon bone and the pastern.
– ORIGIN Middle English: ultimately of Germanic origin; related to German *Fessel* 'fetlock', also to **FOOT**.

feto- ▶ **combining form** representing **FETUS**.

fetor /ˈfiːtə/ ▶ **noun** a strong, foul smell: *the fetor of decay.*
– ORIGIN late 15th cent.: from Latin, from *fetere* 'to stink'. Compare with **FETID**.

fetta ▶ **noun** variant spelling of **FETA**.

fetter ▶ **noun** (usu. **fetters**) a chain or manacle used to restrain a prisoner, typically placed around the ankles: *he lay bound with fetters of iron.*
▪a restraint or check on someone's freedom to do something, typically one considered unfair or overly restrictive: *the fetters of discipline and caution.*
▶ **verb** [with obj.] restrain with chains or manacles, typically around the ankles: [as adj. **fettered**] *a ragged and fettered prisoner.*
▪(often **be fettered**) restrict or restrain (someone) in an unfair or undesirable fashion: *he was not fettered by tradition.*
– ORIGIN Old English *feter*, of Germanic origin; related to Dutch *veter* 'a lace', from an Indo-European root shared by **FOOT**.

fetterlock ▶ **noun** a D-shaped fetter for tethering a horse by the leg, now only as represented as a heraldic charge.

fettle ▶ **noun** [mass noun] condition: *the aircraft remains* ***in fine fettle.***
▶ **verb** [with obj.] trim or clean the rough edges of (a metal casting or a piece of pottery) before firing.
▪N. English make or repair (something): [with two objs] *I paid a smith to fettle me an iron vest.*
– ORIGIN late Middle English (as a verb in the general sense 'get ready, prepare', specifically 'prepare oneself for battle, gird up'): from dialect *fettle* 'strip of material, girdle', from Old English *fetel*, of Germanic origin; related to German *Fessel* 'chain, band'.

fettler ▶ **noun 1** Brit. & Austral. a person who does repair or maintenance work on a railway.
2 a person who fettles metal castings or pottery.

fettuccine /ˌfɛtʊˈtʃiːneɪ, -ni/ (also **fettuccini**) ▶ **plural noun** pasta made in ribbons.
– ORIGIN from Italian, plural of *fettuccina*, diminutive of *fetta* 'slice, ribbon'.

fetus /ˈfiːtəs/ (Brit. (in non-technical use) also **foetus**) ▶ **noun** (pl. **fetuses**) an unborn or unhatched offspring of a mammal, in particular, an unborn human more than eight weeks after conception.
– ORIGIN late Middle English: from Latin *fetus* 'pregnancy, childbirth, offspring'.

USAGE The spelling **foetus** has no etymological basis but is recorded from the 16th century and until recently was the standard British spelling in both technical and non-technical use. In technical usage **fetus** is now the standard spelling throughout the English-speaking world, but **foetus** is still found in British English outside technical contexts.

feu /fjuː/ Scots Law ▶ **noun** a perpetual lease at a fixed rent.
▪a piece of land held by such a lease.
▶ **verb** (**feus**, **feued**, **feuing**) [with obj.] grant (land) on such a lease.
– ORIGIN late 15th cent. (originally denoting a feudal tenure in which an annual payment was made in lieu of military service): from Old French (see **FEE**).

feud ▶ **noun** a prolonged and bitter quarrel or dispute: *his complex arguments and bitter feuds with the Holy See.*
▪a state of prolonged mutual hostility, typically between two families or communities, characterized by murderous assaults in revenge for a previous injuries: *a savage feud over drugs money.*
▶ **verb** [no obj.] take part in such a quarrel or violent conflict: *Hoover* ***feuded with*** *the CIA for decades.*
– ORIGIN Middle English *fede* 'hostility, ill will', from Old French *feide*, from Middle Dutch, Middle Low German *vēde*, of Germanic origin; related to **FOE**.

feudal /ˈfjuːd(ə)l/ ▶ **adjective** according to, resembling, or denoting the system of feudalism: *the feudal system.*
▪absurdly outdated or old-fashioned: *his view of patriotism was more than old-fashioned—it was positively feudal.*
– DERIVATIVES **feudalization** /-ˈzeɪʃ(ə)n/ noun, **feudalize** (also **-ise**) verb, **feudally** adverb.
– ORIGIN early 17th cent.: from medieval Latin *feudalis*, from *feudum* (see **FEE**).

feudalism ▶ **noun** [mass noun] historical the dominant social system in medieval Europe, in which the nobility held lands from the Crown in exchange for military service, and vassals were in turn tenants of

the nobles, while the peasants (villeins or serfs) were obliged to live on their lord's land and give him homage, labour, and a share of the produce, notionally in exchange for military protection.
– DERIVATIVES **feudalist** noun, **feudalistic** adjective.

feudality ▶ noun [mass noun] archaic the principles and practice of the feudal system.
– ORIGIN late 18th cent.: from French *féodalité*, from *féodal*, from medieval Latin *feudalis* 'feudal', from *feudum* (see **FEE**).

feudatory /ˈfjuːdət(ə)ri/ historical ▶ adjective owing feudal allegiance to: *they had for a long period been **feudatory to** the Norwegian Crown.*
▶ noun (pl. **-ies**) a person who holds land under the conditions of the feudal system.
– ORIGIN late 16th cent.: from medieval Latin *feudatorius*, from *feudare* 'enfeoff', from *feudum* (see **FEE**).

feu de joie /ˌfəː də ˈʒwɑː/ ▶ noun (pl. **feux de joie** pronunc. same) a rifle salute fired by soldiers on a ceremonial occasion, each soldier firing in succession along the ranks to make a continuous sound.
– ORIGIN French, literally 'fire of joy'.

feudist ▶ noun US a person taking part in a feud.

Feuerbach /ˈfɔɪəˌbɑːx, German ˈfɔyɐˌbax/, Ludwig (Andreas) (1804–72), German materialist philosopher. In his best-known work, *The Essence of Christianity* (1841), he argued that the dogmas and beliefs of Christianity are figments of human imagination, fulfilling a need inherent in human nature.

feuilleton /ˈfəːɪtɒ̃/ ▶ noun a part of a newspaper or magazine devoted to fiction, criticism, or light literature; an article printed in such a part.
– ORIGIN mid 19th cent.: French, from *feuillet*, diminutive of *feuille* 'leaf'.

fever ▶ noun an abnormally high body temperature, usually accompanied by shivering, headache, and in severe instances, delirium: *her mother died of a fever* | [mass noun] *African equine fever.*
■ a state of nervous excitement or agitation: *I was mystified, and in a fever of expectation.* ■ [mass noun] [with modifier] the excitement felt by a group of people about a particular public event: *election fever reaches its climax tomorrow.*
▶ verb [with obj.] archaic bring about a high body temperature or a state of nervous excitement in (someone): *a heart which sin has fevered.*
– ORIGIN Old English *fēfor*, from Latin *febris*; reinforced in Middle English by Old French *fievre*, also from *febris*.

fevered ▶ adjective having or showing the symptoms associated with a dangerously high temperature: *her fevered eyes.*
■ feeling or displaying an excessive degree of nervous excitement, agitation, or energy: *my fevered adolescent imagination.*

feverfew /ˈfiːvəfjuː/ ▶ noun a small bushy aromatic Eurasian plant of the daisy family, with feathery leaves and daisy-like flowers. It is used in herbal medicine to treat headaches.
• *Tanacetum parthenium*, family Compositae.
– ORIGIN Old English *feferfuge*, from Latin *febrifuga*, from *febris* 'fever' + *fugare* 'drive away'. Compare with **FEBRIFUGE**.

fever grass ▶ noun West Indian term for **LEMON GRASS**.

feverish ▶ adjective having or showing the symptoms of a fever: *he suffered from feverish colds.*
■ displaying a frenetic excitement or energy: *the next couple of weeks were spent in a whirl of feverish activity.*
– DERIVATIVES **feverishly** adverb, **feverishness** noun.

feverous ▶ adjective archaic apt to cause fever.
■ feverish.

fever pitch ▶ noun [mass noun] a state of extreme excitement: *the football crowd was **at fever pitch*** | [in sing.] *a fever pitch of nervous excitement.*

fever tree ▶ noun any of a number of trees which are believed to either cause or cure fever, in particular:
• a North American tree used in the treatment of malaria during the civil war (*Pinckneya pubens*, family Rubiaceae). • a southern African tree which was formerly believed to cause malaria (*Acacia xanthophloea*, family Leguminosae).

few ▶ determiner, pronoun, & adjective **1** (**a few**) a small number of: [as determiner] *may I ask a few questions?* | [as pronoun] *I will recount **a few of** the stories told me* | *many believe it but only a few are prepared to say.*
2 used to emphasize how small a number of people or things is: [as determiner] *he had few friends* | [as pronoun] *few thought to challenge these assumptions* | *very **few of** the titles have any literary merit* | *a club with **as few as** 20 members* | [comparative] *a population of fewer than two million* | [as adj.] *sewing was one of her few pleasures* | *comforts here are few* | [superlative] *ask which products have the fewest complaints.*
▶ noun [as plural noun **the few**] the minority of people; the elect: *a world that increasingly belongs to the few.*
■ (**the Few**) Brit. the RAF pilots who took part in the Battle of Britain. [ORIGIN: alluding to a speech of Sir Winston Churchill (20 August, 1940).]
– PHRASES **every few** once in every small group of (typically units of time): *she visits every few weeks.* **few and far between** scarce; infrequent: *my inspired moments are few and far between.* **a good few** Brit. a fairly large number of: *it had been around for a good few years.* **have a few** informal drink enough alcohol to be slightly drunk. **no fewer than** used to emphasize a surprisingly large number: *there are no fewer than seventy different brand names.* **not a few** a considerable number: *his fiction has caused not a few readers to see red.* **quite a few** a fairly large number: *quite a few people can do it.* **some few** some but not many.
– ORIGIN Old English *fēawe*, *fēawa*, of Germanic origin; related to Old High German *fao*, from an Indo-European root shared by Latin *paucus* and Greek *pauros* 'small'.

USAGE **Fewer** versus **less**: strictly speaking, the rule is that **fewer**, the comparative form of **few**, is used with words denoting people or countable things (***fewer** members*; ***fewer** books*; ***fewer** than ten contestants*). **Less**, on the other hand, is used with mass nouns, denoting things which cannot be counted (***less** money*; ***less** music*). In addition, **less** is normally used with numbers (***less** than 10,000*) and with expressions of measurement or time (***less** than two weeks*; ***less** than four miles away*). But to use **less** with count nouns, as in ***less** people* or ***less** words*, is incorrect in standard English. It is perhaps one of the most frequent errors made by native speakers of English, although in written sources the error is found less frequently (around 8 per cent in the British National Corpus).

fey /feɪ/ ▶ adjective giving an impression of vague unworldliness: *his mother was a strange, fey woman.*
■ having supernatural powers of clairvoyance. ■ chiefly Scottish fated to die or at the point of death: *now he is fey, he sees his own death, and I see it too.*
– DERIVATIVES **feyly** adverb, **feyness** noun.
– ORIGIN Old English *fǣge* (in the sense 'fated to die soon'), of Germanic origin; related to Dutch *veeg* and to German *feige* 'cowardly'.

Feydeau /ˈfeɪdəʊ, French fɛdo/, Georges (1862–1921), French dramatist. His name has become a byword for French bedroom farce. He wrote some forty plays, including *Hotel Paradiso* (1894) and *Le Dindon* (1896).

Feynman /ˈfʌɪnmən/, Richard Phillips (1918–88), American theoretical physicist, noted for his work on quantum electrodynamics. Nobel Prize for Physics (1965).

Feynman diagram ▶ noun Physics a diagram showing electromagnetic interactions between subatomic particles.

Fez /fɛz/ (also **Fès**) a city in northern Morocco, founded in 808; pop. 564,000 (1993).

fez /fɛz/ ▶ noun (pl. **fezzes**) a flat-topped conical red hat with a black tassel on top, worn by men in some Muslim countries (formerly the Turkish national headdress).
– DERIVATIVES **fezzed** adjective.
– ORIGIN early 19th cent.: from Turkish *fes* (perhaps via French *fez*), named after **FEZ**, once the chief place of manufacture.

ff Music ▶ abbreviation for fortissimo.

ff. ▶ abbreviation for ■ folios. ■ following pages.

Fg Off ▶ abbreviation for (in the UK) Flying Officer.

f-hole ▶ noun either of a pair of soundholes resembling an ʃ and a reversed ʃ in shape, cut in the front of musical instruments of the violin family, and some other stringed instruments such as semi-acoustic electric guitars or mandolins.

FHSA Brit. ▶ abbreviation for Family Health Services Authority, a body responsible for running general health services, such as those provided by general practitioners, dentists, and opticians, for a particular area.

fiacre /fɪˈɑːkrə, -kə/ ▶ noun historical a small four-wheeled carriage for public hire.
– ORIGIN late 17th cent.: from French, named after the Hôtel de St Fiacre in Paris, where such vehicles were first hired out.

fiancé /fɪˈɒnseɪ, -ˈɑːns-, -ˈɒ̃s-/ ▶ noun a man to whom a woman is engaged to be married.
– ORIGIN mid 19th cent.: from French, past participle of *fiancer* 'betroth', from Old French *fiance* 'a promise', based on Latin *fidere* 'to trust'.

fiancée /fɪˈɒnseɪ, -ˈɑːns-, -ˈɒ̃s-/ ▶ noun a woman to whom a man is engaged to be married.

fianchetto /ˌfɪənˈtʃɛtəʊ, -ˈkɛtəʊ/ Chess ▶ noun (pl. **-oes**) the development of a bishop by moving it one square to a long diagonal of the board.
▶ verb (**-oes**, **-oed**) [with obj.] develop (a bishop) in such a way.
– ORIGIN mid 19th cent.: from Italian, diminutive of *fianco* 'flank', ultimately of Germanic origin.

Fianna Fáil /fɪˌanə ˈfɔɪl, Irish ˌfʲiənə ˈfaːlʲ/ one of the two main political parties of the Republic of Ireland. Larger and traditionally more republican than its rival Fine Gael, it was formed in 1926 in opposition to the Anglo-Irish Treaty of 1921 by Eamon de Valera together with some of the moderate members of Sinn Fein.
– ORIGIN Irish, from *fianna* 'band of warriors' (applied to the soldiers of Finn MacCool; compare with **FENIAN**) and *Fáil*, genitive of *Fál*, an ancient name for Ireland. The phrase *Fianna Fáil* was used in 15th-cent. poetry in the neutral sense 'people of Ireland', but the founders of the political party interpreted it to mean 'soldiers of destiny'.

fiasco /fɪˈaskəʊ/ ▶ noun (pl. **-os**) a thing that is a complete failure, especially in a ludicrous or humiliating way: *his plans turned into a fiasco.*
– ORIGIN mid 19th cent.: from Italian, literally 'bottle, flask', in the phrase *far fiasco*, literally 'make a bottle', figuratively 'fail in a performance': the reason for the figurative sense is unexplained.

fiat /ˈfʌɪat/ ▶ noun a formal authorization or proposition; a decree: *the reforms left most prices fixed by government fiat.*
– ORIGIN late Middle English: from Latin, 'let it be done', from *fieri* 'be done or made'.

fiat money ▶ noun [mass noun] inconvertible paper money made legal tender by a government decree.

fib ▶ noun a lie, typically an unimportant one: *why did you tell him such a dreadful fib?*
▶ verb (**fibbed**, **fibbing**) [no obj.] [often as noun **fibbing**] tell such a lie.
– DERIVATIVES **fibber** noun.
– ORIGIN mid 16th cent.: perhaps a shortening of obsolete *fible-fable* 'nonsense', reduplication of **FABLE**.

fiber etc. ▶ noun US spelling of **FIBRE** etc.

Fibonacci /ˌfɪbəˈnɑːtʃi/, Leonardo (c.1170–c.1250), Italian mathematician; known as **Fibonacci of Pisa**. Fibonacci popularized the use of the 'new' Arabic numerals in Europe. He made many original contributions in complex calculations, algebra, and geometry, and pioneered number theory and indeterminate analysis, discovering the Fibonacci series.

Fibonacci series ▶ noun Mathematics a series of numbers in which each number (**Fibonacci number**) is the sum of the two preceding numbers. The simplest is the series 1, 1, 2, 3, 5, 8, etc.

fibre (US **fiber**) ▶ noun **1** a thread or filament from which a vegetable tissue, mineral substance, or textile is formed: *the basket comes lined with natural coco fibres.*
■ a substance formed of such threads or filaments: *ordinary synthetics don't breathe as well as natural fibres* | [mass noun] *high strength carbon fibre.* ■ a thread-like structure forming part of the muscular, nervous, connective, or other tissue in the human or animal body: *there were degenerative changes in muscle fibres* | figurative *she wanted him with every fibre of her being.* ■ [mass noun] figurative strength of character: *a weak person with no moral fibre.*
2 [mass noun] dietary material containing substances such as cellulose, lignin, and pectin, that are resistant to the action of digestive enzymes.
– DERIVATIVES **fibred** adjective [in combination] *long-fibred wools*, **fibreless** adjective.
– ORIGIN late Middle English (in the sense 'lobe of the liver', (plural) 'entrails'): via French from Latin *fibra* 'fibre, filament, entrails'.

fibreboard (US **fiberboard**) ▶ **noun** [mass noun] a building material made of wood or other plant fibres compressed into boards.

fibrefill ▶ **noun** [mass noun] synthetic material used for padding and insulation in garments and soft furnishings such as cushions and duvets.

fibreglass (US **fiberglass**) ▶ **noun** [mass noun] **1** a reinforced plastic material composed of glass fibres embedded in a resin matrix.
2 a textile fabric made from woven glass filaments.

fibre optics ▶ **plural noun** [treated as sing.] the use of thin flexible fibres of glass or other transparent solids to transmit light signals, chiefly for telecommunications or for internal inspection of the body.
■ [treated as pl.] the fibres and associated devices so used.
– DERIVATIVES **fibre-optic** adjective.

fibrescope (US **fiberscope**) ▶ **noun** a fibre-optic device for viewing inaccessible internal structures, especially in the human body.

fibre tip ▶ **noun** a pen with a writing point made of tightly packed fibres which hold the ink.
■ [usu. as modifier] a tip of such a kind: *a fibre-tip pen.*

fibril /ˈfʌɪbrɪl/ ▶ **noun** technical a small or slender fibre: *each muscle fibre is subdivided into smaller fibrils.*
– DERIVATIVES **fibrillar** adjective, **fibrillary** adjective.
– ORIGIN mid 17th cent.: from modern Latin *fibrilla*, diminutive of Latin *fibra* (see **FIBRE**).

fibrillate /ˈfʌɪbrɪleɪt, ˈfɪb-/ ▶ **verb** [no obj.] **1** (of a muscle, especially in the heart) make a quivering movement due to uncoordinated contraction of the individual fibrils: *the atria ceased to fibrillate when the temperature was reduced.*
2 (of a fibre) split up into fibrils.
■ [with obj.] break (a fibre) into fibrils.
– DERIVATIVES **fibrillation** noun.

fibrin /ˈfʌɪbrɪn, ˈfɪb-/ ▶ **noun** [mass noun] Biochemistry an insoluble protein formed from fibrinogen during the clotting of blood. It forms a fibrous mesh that impedes the flow of blood.
– DERIVATIVES **fibrinoid** adjective, **fibrinous** adjective.
– ORIGIN early 19th cent.: from **FIBRE** + **-IN**[1].

fibrinogen /fʌɪˈbrɪnədʒ(ə)n, fɪ-/ ▶ **noun** [mass noun] Biochemistry a soluble protein present in blood plasma, from which fibrin is produced by the action of the enzyme thrombin.

fibrinolysis /ˌfʌɪbrɪˈnɒlɪsɪs, ˌfɪb-/ ▶ **noun** [mass noun] Physiology the enzymatic breakdown of the fibrin in blood clots.
– DERIVATIVES **fibrinolytic** adjective.

fibro /ˈfʌɪbrəʊ/ ▶ **noun** (pl. **-os**) [mass noun] Austral./NZ a mixture of asbestos and cement, used in sheets for building.
■ [count noun] a house constructed mainly of such sheets.
– ORIGIN 1950s: abbreviation of *fibro-cement.*

fibro- /ˈfʌɪbrəʊ/ ▶ **combining form** of, relating to, or characterized by fibres: *fibroblast | fibroma.*
– ORIGIN from Latin *fibra* 'fibre'.

fibroadenoma /ˌfʌɪbrəʊadɪˈnəʊmə/ ▶ **noun** (pl. **fibroadenomas** or **fibroadenomata** /-mətə/) Medicine a tumour formed of mixed fibrous and glandular tissue, typically occurring as a benign growth in the breast.

fibroblast /ˈfʌɪbrə(ʊ)blast/ ▶ **noun** Physiology a cell in connective tissue which produces collagen and other fibres.

fibrocystic /ˌfʌɪbrə(ʊ)ˈsɪstɪk/ ▶ **adjective** [attrib.] Medicine (of a disease) characterized by the development of fibrous tissue and cystic spaces, typically in the pancreas or the breast.

fibroid /ˈfʌɪbrɔɪd/ ▶ **adjective** of or characterized by fibres or fibrous tissue.
▶ **noun** Medicine a benign tumour of muscular and fibrous tissues, typically developing in the wall of the womb.

fibroin /ˈfʌɪbrəʊɪn/ ▶ **noun** [mass noun] a protein which is the chief constituent of silk.
– ORIGIN mid 19th cent.: from **FIBRO-** + **-IN**[1].

fibrolite /ˈfʌɪbrə(ʊ)lʌɪt/ ▶ **noun** another term for **SILLIMANITE**.

fibroma /fʌɪˈbrəʊmə/ ▶ **noun** (pl. **fibromas** or **fibromata** /-mətə/) Medicine a benign fibrous tumour of connective tissue.
– ORIGIN mid 19th cent.: from Latin *fibra* (see **FIBRE**) + **-OMA**.

fibrosarcoma /ˌfʌɪbrəʊsɑːˈkəʊmə/ ▶ **noun** (pl. **fibrosarcomas** or **fibrosarcomata** /-mətə/) Medicine a sarcoma in which the predominant cell type is a malignant fibroblast.
– DERIVATIVES **fibrosarcomatous** adjective.

fibrosis /fʌɪˈbrəʊsɪs/ ▶ **noun** [mass noun] Medicine the thickening and scarring of connective tissue, usually as a result of injury.
– DERIVATIVES **fibrotic** adjective.
– ORIGIN late 19th cent.: from Latin *fibra* (see **FIBRE**) + **-OSIS**.

fibrositis /ˌfʌɪbrəˈsʌɪtɪs/ ▶ **noun** [mass noun] Medicine inflammation of fibrous connective tissue, typically affecting the back and causing stiffness and pain.
– DERIVATIVES **fibrositic** adjective.
– ORIGIN early 20th cent.: from Latin *fibrosus* 'fibrous' (from *fibra* 'fibre') + **-ITIS**.

fibrous ▶ **adjective** consisting of or characterized by fibres: *a good fibrous root system.*
– DERIVATIVES **fibrously** adverb, **fibrousness** noun.

fibula /ˈfɪbjʊlə/ ▶ **noun** (pl. **fibulae** /-liː/ or **fibulas**) **1** Anatomy the outer and usually smaller of the two bones between the knee and the ankle (or the equivalent joints in other terrestrial vertebrates), parallel with the tibia.
2 Archaeology a brooch or clasp.
– DERIVATIVES **fibular** adjective.
– ORIGIN late 16th cent.: from Latin, 'brooch', perhaps related to *figere* 'to fix'. The bone is so named because the shape it makes with the tibia resembles a clasp, the fibula being the tongue.

-fic (usu. as **-ific**) ▶ **suffix** (forming adjectives) producing; making: *prolific | soporific.*
– DERIVATIVES **-fically** suffix forming corresponding adverbs.
– ORIGIN from French *-fique* or Latin *-ficus* from *facere* 'do, make'.

-fication (usu. as **-ification**) ▶ **suffix** forming nouns of action from verbs ending in *-fy* (such as *simplification* from *simplify*).
– ORIGIN from French, or from Latin *-fication-* (from verbs ending in *-ficare*).

fiche ▶ **noun** short for **MICROFICHE**.

Fichte /ˈfɪxtə, German ˈfɪçtə/, Johann Gottlieb (1762–1814), German philosopher. A pupil of Kant, he postulated that the ego is the basic reality; the world is posited by the ego in defining and delimiting itself. His political addresses had some influence on the development of German nationalism and the overthrow of Napoleon.

fichu /ˈfiːʃuː/ ▶ **noun** a small triangular shawl, worn round a woman's shoulders and neck.
– ORIGIN mid 18th cent.: from French, from *ficher* 'to fix, pin'.

fickle ▶ **adjective** changing frequently, especially as regards one's loyalties or interests: *his supporters are so fickle.*
– DERIVATIVES **fickleness** noun, **fickly** adverb.
– ORIGIN Old English *ficol* 'deceitful', of Germanic origin.

fictile /ˈfɪktʌɪl, -tɪl/ ▶ **adjective** made of earth or clay by a potter.
■ of or relating to pottery or its manufacture.
– ORIGIN early 17th cent.: from Latin *fictilis*, from *fict-* 'formed, contrived', from the verb *fingere*.

fiction ▶ **noun** [mass noun] literature in the form of prose, especially novels, that describes imaginary events and people.
■ invention or fabrication as opposed to fact: *the president dismissed the allegation as absolute fiction.* ■ [in sing.] a belief or statement which is false, but is often held to be true because it is expedient to do so: *the notion of the country being a democracy is* ***a polite fiction.***
– DERIVATIVES **fictionist** noun.
– ORIGIN late Middle English (in the sense 'invented statement'): via Old French from Latin *fictio(n-)*, from *fingere* 'form, contrive'. Compare with **FEIGN** and **FIGMENT**.

fictional ▶ **adjective** of or relating to fiction; invented for the purposes of fiction: *fictional texts | a fictional character.*
– DERIVATIVES **fictionality** noun, **fictionalization** noun, **fictionalize** (also **-ise**) verb, **fictionally** adverb.

fictitious /fɪkˈtɪʃəs/ ▶ **adjective** not real or true, being imaginary or having been fabricated: *reports of a deal were dismissed as fictitious by the Minister.*
■ of, relating to, or denoting the imaginary characters and events found in fiction.
– DERIVATIVES **fictitiously** adverb, **fictitiousness** noun.
– ORIGIN early 17th cent.: from Latin *ficticius* (from *fingere* 'contrive, form') + **-OUS** (see also **-ITIOUS**[2]).

fictive ▶ **adjective** creating or created by imagination: *the novel's fictive universe.*
– DERIVATIVES **fictiveness** noun.
– ORIGIN early 17th cent. (but rare before the 19th cent.): from French *fictif, -ive* or medieval Latin *fictivus*, from Latin *fingere* 'contrive, form'.

ficus /ˈfiːkəs, ˈfʌɪkəs/ ▶ **noun** (pl. same) a tree, shrub, or climber of a large genus that includes the figs and the rubber plant. They grow in tropical and warm climates and several species are of commercial importance.
● Genus *Ficus*, family Moraceae.
– ORIGIN mid 19th cent.: from Latin, 'fig, fig tree'.

fid ▶ **noun** chiefly Brit. or Nautical a thick peg, wedge, or supporting pin, in particular:
■ a square wooden or iron bar which takes the weight of a topmast stepped to a lower mast by being passed through holes in both masts. ■ a conical pin or spike used in splicing rope.
– ORIGIN early 17th cent.: of unknown origin.

Fid. Def. ▶ **abbreviation** for Fidei Defensor. See **DEFENDER OF THE FAITH**.

fiddle ▶ **noun 1** informal a violin.
2 informal, chiefly Brit. an act of defrauding, cheating, or falsifying: *a major mortgage fiddle.*
3 informal a small task that seems awkward and unnecessarily complex: *inserting a tape is a bit of a fiddle.*
4 Nautical a contrivance, such as a raised rim, that prevents things from rolling or sliding off a table in bad weather.
▶ **verb** informal **1** [no obj.] touch or fidget with something in a restless or nervous way: *Lena* ***fiddled with*** *her cup.*
■ tinker with something in an attempt to make minor adjustments or improvements: *he sat in the car and played the radio,* ***fiddling with*** *the knobs.* ■ (**fiddle around**) pass time aimlessly, without doing or achieving anything of substance.
2 [with obj.] chiefly Brit. falsify (figures, data, or records), typically in order to gain money: *everyone is fiddling their expenses.*
3 [no obj.] archaic play the violin.
– PHRASES **fiddle while Rome burns** be concerned with relatively trivial matters while ignoring the serious or disastrous events going on around one. **(as) fit as a fiddle** in very good health. **on the fiddle** informal engaged in cheating or swindling. **play second fiddle to** take a less important and subordinate role to someone or something in a way often considered demeaning: *she had play second fiddle to the interests of her husband.*
– ORIGIN Old English *fithele*, denoting a violin or similar instrument (originally not an informal or depreciatory term), related to Dutch *vedel* and German *Fiedel*, based on Latin *vitulari* 'celebrate a festival, be joyful', perhaps from *Vitula*, the name of a Roman goddess of joy and victory. Compare with **VIOL**.

fiddle-back ▶ **noun 1** [usu. as modifier] a thing shaped like the back of a violin, with the sides deeply curved inwards, in particular:
■ the back of a chair. ■ the front of a chasuble.
2 (**fiddleback**) [mass noun] a rippled effect in the grain of fine wood, often exploited when making the backs of violins: [as modifier] *fiddleback mahogany.*

fiddle-de-dee ▶ **noun** [mass noun] [often as exclamation] dated nonsense.
– ORIGIN late 18th cent.: from **FIDDLE** + a reduplication without meaning.

fiddle-faddle ▶ **noun** [mass noun] trivial matters: nonsense: *he's concerned with petty fiddle-faddle about his personal arrangements |* [as exclamation] *Are you as fit as you say you are? Fiddle-faddle!*
▶ **verb** [no obj.] mess about; fuss: *you haven't time to* ***fiddle-faddle about*** *like that.*
– ORIGIN late 16th cent.: reduplication of **FIDDLE**.

fiddlehead ▶ **noun 1** (also **fiddlehead fern** or **fiddlehead green**) N. Amer. the young, curled, edible frond of certain ferns.
2 a scroll-like carving at a ship's bows.

fiddle pattern ▶ **noun** [mass noun] a style of spoons and forks, with handles shaped like the body of a violin.

fiddler ▶ **noun 1** informal a person who plays the violin, especially one who plays folk music.

2 Brit. informal a person who cheats or swindles, especially one indulging in petty theft.
– ORIGIN Old English *fithelere*, from *fithele* (see **FIDDLE**).

fiddler crab ▶ **noun** a small amphibious crab, the males of which have one greatly enlarged claw which they wave in territorial display and courtship.
• Genus *Uca*, family Ocypodidae.

Fiddler's Green the sailor's Elysium, traditionally a place of wine, women, and song.

fiddlestick ▶ **exclamation** (**fiddlesticks**) nonsense.
▶ **noun** informal a violin bow.

fiddling ▶ **adjective** **1** annoyingly trivial or petty: *fiddling little details.*
2 [attrib.] informal (of a person) involved with a swindle or embezzlement: *a fiddling financier.*

fiddly ▶ **adjective** (**fiddlier**, **fiddliest**) Brit. informal complicated or detailed and awkward to do or use: *replacing the battery is fiddly.*

Fidei Defensor /ˌfʌɪdɪʌɪ dɪˈfɛnsɔː, ˌfiːdeɪiː/ ▶ **noun** Latin term for **DEFENDER OF THE FAITH**.
– ORIGIN Latin.

fideism /ˈfʌɪdɪɪz(ə)m/ ▶ **noun** [mass noun] the doctrine that knowledge depends on faith or revelation.
– DERIVATIVES **fideist** noun, **fideistic** adjective.
– ORIGIN late 19th cent.: from Latin *fides* 'faith' + **-ISM**.

fidelity /fɪˈdɛlɪti/ ▶ **noun** [mass noun] faithfulness to a person, cause, or belief, demonstrated by continuing loyalty and support: *he sought only the strictest fidelity to justice.*
■ sexual faithfulness to a spouse or partner. ■ the degree of exactness with which something is copied or reproduced: *the 1949 recording provides reasonable fidelity.*
– ORIGIN late Middle English: from Old French *fidelite* or Latin *fidelitas*, from *fidelis* 'faithful', from *fides* 'faith'. Compare with **FEALTY**.

fidelity insurance ▶ **noun** [mass noun] insurance taken out by an employer against losses incurred through dishonesty by employees.

fidget /ˈfɪdʒɪt/ ▶ **verb** (**fidgeted**, **fidgeting**) [no obj.] make small movements, especially of the hands and feet, through nervousness or impatience: *the audience had begun to fidget on their chairs.*
■ be impatient or uneasy: [with infinitive] *he was fidgeting to get back to his shop.* ■ [with obj.] make (someone) uneasy or uncomfortable: *she fidgets me with her never-ending spit and polish.*
▶ **noun** a quick, small movement, typically a repeated one, caused by nervousness or impatience: *he disturbed other people with convulsive fidgets.*
■ a person given to such movements, especially one whom other people find irritating. ■ (usu. **fidgets**) a state of mental or physical restlessness or uneasiness: *a marketing person full of nervous energy and fidgets.*
– DERIVATIVES **fidgeter** noun, **fidgetiness** noun, **fidgety** adjective.
– ORIGIN late 17th cent.: from obsolete or dialect *fidge* 'to twitch'; perhaps related to Old Norse *fikja* 'move briskly, be restless or eager'.

fidget pie ▶ **noun** Brit. a savoury pie containing onions, apples, bacon, and sometimes potatoes.
– ORIGIN late 18th cent. (as *fitchet-pie*): perhaps from *fitchet*, a dialect word for 'polecat', because of the strong, unpleasant odour of the pie during cooking. The change in spelling of the first word was due to association with **FIDGET**.

Fido /ˈfʌɪdəʊ/ historical a system for dispersing fog using petrol-burners on the ground to enable aircraft to land. It was developed by the Allies during the Second World War.
– ORIGIN acronym from *Fog Intensive Dispersal Operation.*

fiducial /fɪˈdjuːʃ(ə)l/ ▶ **adjective** technical (especially of a point or line) assumed as a fixed basis of comparison.
– ORIGIN late 16th cent.: from late Latin *fiducialis*, from *fiducia* 'trust', from *fidere* 'to trust'.

fiduciary /fɪˈdjuːʃ(ə)ri/ ▶ **adjective** Law involving trust, especially with regard to the relationship between a trustee and a beneficiary: *the company has a fiduciary duty to shareholders.*
■ archaic held or given in trust: *fiduciary estates.* ■ Finance (of a paper currency) depending for its value on securities (as opposed to gold) or the reputation of the issuer.
▶ **noun** (pl. **-ies**) a trustee.
– ORIGIN late 16th cent. (in the sense 'something inspiring trust; credentials'): from Latin *fiduciarius*, from *fiducia* 'trust', from *fidere* 'to trust'.

fidus Achates /ˌfʌɪdəs əˈkeɪtiːz/ ▶ **noun** a faithful friend or devoted follower.
– ORIGIN Latin, literally 'faithful Achates' (see **ACHATES**).

fie /fʌɪ/ ▶ **exclamation** archaic or humorous used to express disgust or outrage.
– ORIGIN Middle English: via Old French from Latin *fi*, an exclamation of disgust at a stench.

fief /fiːf/ ▶ **noun** **1** historical another term for **FEE** (in sense 2).
2 a person's sphere of operation or control.
– ORIGIN early 17th cent.: from French (see **FEE**).

fiefdom ▶ **noun** a fief.

Field, John (1782–1837), Irish composer and pianist. He is noted for the invention of the nocturne and for his twenty compositions in this form.

field ▶ **noun** **1** an area of open land, especially one planted with crops or pasture, typically bounded by hedges or fences: *a wheat field | a field of corn.*
■ a piece of land used for a particular purpose, especially an area marked out for a game or sport: *a football field.* ■ a large area of land or water completely covered in a particular substance, especially snow or ice: *an ice field.* ■ an area rich in a natural product, typically oil or gas: *a gas field.* ■ an area on which a battle is fought: *a field of battle.* ■ archaic a battle: *many a bloody field was to be fought.* ■ a place where a subject of scientific study or of artistic representation can be observed in its natural location or context.
2 a particular branch of study or sphere of activity or interest: *we talked to professionals in various fields.*
■ Computing a part of a record, representing an item of data. ■ Linguistics & Psychology a general area of meaning within which individual words make particular distinctions. ■ a space or range within which objects are visible from a particular viewpoint or through a piece of apparatus. See also **FIELD OF VISION**. ■ Heraldry the surface of an escutcheon or of one of its divisions.
3 (usu. **the field**) all the participants in a contest or sport: *he destroyed the rest of the field with a devastating injection of speed.*
■ Cricket fielders collectively, or the manner in which they are spread over the pitch: *he sees the ball early and strokes it through the gap in the field.* ■ a fielder.
4 Physics the region in which a particular condition prevails, especially one in which a force or influence is effective regardless of the presence or absence of a material medium.
■ the force exerted or potentially exerted in such an area: *the variation in the strength of the field.* ■ Mathematics a system subject to two binary operations analogous to those for the multiplication and addition of real numbers, and having similar commutative and distributive laws.
▶ **verb** **1** [no obj.] chiefly Cricket & Baseball attempt to catch or stop the ball and return it after it has been hit by the batsman or batter, thereby preventing runs being scored or base-runners advancing.
■ [with obj.] catch or stop (the ball) and return it: *his swinging bunt was fielded by the Chicago catcher.*
2 [with obj.] send out (a team or individual) to play in a game: *Leeds fielded a team of youngsters.*
■ (of a political party) put up (a candidate) to stand in an election: *the Ecology party fielded 109 candidates.* ■ deploy (an army): *Russia was committed to fielding 800,000 men.*
3 [with obj.] deal with (a difficult question, telephone call, etc.).
▶ **adjective** [attrib.] carried out or working in the natural environment, rather than in a laboratory or office: *field observations and interviews.*
■ (of military equipment) light and mobile for use on campaign: *field artillery.* ■ used in names of animals or plants found in the open country, rather than among buildings or as cultivated varieties, e.g.: **field mouse**. ■ denoting a game played outdoors on a marked field.
– PHRASES **hold the field** remain the most important: *the principles of quantum theory hold the field as the convincing account of the physics of the microworld.* **in the field** on campaign; (while) engaged in combat or manoeuvres: *troops in the field.* ■ away from the laboratory, office, or studio; engaged in practical work in a natural environment. **keep the field** archaic continue a military campaign. **lead the field** be the leader in a race. ■ be the best or most popular: *the brand leads the field in vegetarian ready meals.* **play the field** informal indulge in a series of sexual relationships without committing oneself to anyone. **take the field** (of a sports team) go on to a field to begin a game. ■ start a military campaign.
– ORIGIN Old English *feld* (also denoting a large tract of open country; compare with **VELD**), of West Germanic origin; related to Dutch *veld* and German *Feld*.

field bean ▶ **noun** a bean plant closely related to the broad bean but with smaller seeds, grown to improve soil fertility and for stockfeeding.
• *Vicia faba*, family Leguminosae.

field book ▶ **noun** a book in which a surveyor writes down measurements and other technical notes taken in the field.

field boot ▶ **noun** a close-fitting, knee-length military boot.

field cornet ▶ **noun** S. African historical **1** a civilian official invested with the rank and responsibilities of a military officer and with judicial powers enabling him to act as a local administrator and magistrate.
2 a rank in the army equivalent to that of lieutenant.
– ORIGIN translating South African Dutch *veld kornet*, from *veld* 'field' + *kornet*, specifying a military rank.

fieldcraft ▶ **noun** [mass noun] the techniques involved in living, travelling, or making military or scientific observations in the field, especially while remaining undetected.

field cricket ▶ **noun** a European cricket that lives in a burrow in grassland and has a musical birdlike chirp.
• *Gryllus campestris*, family Gryllidae.

field day ▶ **noun** **1** [in sing.] an opportunity for action, success, or excitement, especially at the expense of others: *shoplifters are **having a field day** in the store.*
2 Military a review or an exercise, especially in manoeuvring.
3 chiefly N. Amer. a day devoted to athletics or other sporting events and contests.
4 Austral./NZ a day set aside for the display of agricultural machinery.

field-effect transistor (abbrev.: **FET**) ▶ **noun** Electronics a transistor in which most current is carried along a channel whose effective resistance can be controlled by a transverse electric field.

field emission ▶ **noun** [mass noun] Physics the emission of electrons from the surface of a conductor under the influence of a strong electrostatic field, as a result of the tunnel effect.

fielder ▶ **noun** chiefly Cricket & Baseball a player on the fielding team, especially one other than the bowler or pitcher.

field events ▶ **plural noun** athletic sports other than races, such as throwing and jumping events. Compare with **TRACK EVENTS**.

fieldfare ▶ **noun** a large migratory thrush with a grey head, breeding in northern Eurasia.
• *Turdus pilaris*, family Turdidae.
– ORIGIN late Old English *feldefare*, perhaps from *feld* 'field' + the base of *faran* 'to travel' (see **FARE**).

field glasses ▶ **plural noun** binoculars for outdoor use.

field goal ▶ **noun** **1** American Football a goal scored by a place kick, scoring three points.
2 Basketball a goal scored while the clock is running and the ball is in play.

field grey ▶ **noun** [mass noun] a dark shade of grey, the regulation colour of the uniform of a German infantryman.

field guide ▶ **noun** a book for the identification of birds, flowers, minerals, or other things in their natural environment.

field hand ▶ **noun** chiefly historical a person, especially a US slave, employed as a farm labourer.

field hockey ▶ **noun** see **HOCKEY**.

field holler ▶ **noun** see **HOLLER**.

field hospital ▶ **noun** a temporary hospital set up near a battlefield to provide emergency care for the wounded.

Fielding, Henry (1707–54), English novelist. He provoked the introduction of censorship in theatres with his political satire *The Historical Register for 1736.* He then turned to writing picaresque novels, notably *Joseph Andrews* (1742) and *Tom Jones* (1749). Fielding was also responsible for the formation of the Bow Street Runners in 1749.

field mark ▶ **noun** a visible mark or characteristic that can be used in identifying a bird or other animal in the field.

field marshal ▶ **noun** the highest rank of officer in the British army.

field mouse (also **long-tailed field mouse**) ▶ **noun** another term for **WOOD MOUSE**.

field mushroom ▶ **noun** the common edible mushroom, which is widely grown commercially.
● *Agaricus campestris*, family Agaricaceae, class Hymenomycetes.

field mustard ▶ **noun** another term for **CHARLOCK**.

field notes ▶ **plural noun** notes made by someone who is engaged in fieldwork.

field officer ▶ **noun** a person in an organization with a position of responsibility involving practical activities in a particular area or region.
■ Military a major, lieutenant colonel, or colonel.

field of honour ▶ **noun** the place where a duel or battle is fought.

Field of the Cloth of Gold the scene of a meeting between Henry VIII of England and Francis I of France near Calais in 1520, for which both monarchs erected elaborate temporary palaces, including a sumptuous display of golden cloth. Little of importance was achieved, although the meeting symbolized Henry's determination to play a full part in European dynastic politics.

field of vision ▶ **noun** the entire area that a person or animal is able to see when their eyes are fixed in one position.

field pea ▶ **noun** a pea plant of a variety grown chiefly for stockfeeding or as green manure.
– ORIGIN early 18th cent.: said to be so named because they were once the only agricultural peas cultivated in the UK.

field rank ▶ **noun** [mass noun] the rank attained by a military field officer.

Fields[1], Dame Gracie (1898–1979), English singer and comedienne; born *Grace Stansfield*. During the 1930s she enjoyed great success with English music-hall audiences, and went on to star in a series of popular films.

Fields[2], W. C. (1880–1946), American comedian; born *William Claude Dukenfield*. Having made his name as a comedy juggler he became a vaudeville star, appearing in the *Ziegfeld Follies* revues between 1915 and 1921. Notable films: *The Bank Dick* (1940).

fieldsman ▶ **noun** (pl. **-men**) **1** Cricket a fielder.
2 an agent or salesman working for a company.

field sports ▶ **plural noun** outdoor sports, especially hunting, shooting, and fishing.

fieldstone ▶ **noun** [mass noun] [often as modifier] stone used in its natural form: *a fieldstone fireplace.*

field telegraph ▶ **noun** historical a movable telegraph for use on campaign.

field test ▶ **noun** a test carried out in the environment in which a product or device is to be used.
▶ **verb** (**field-test**) [with obj.] test (something) in the environment in such a way.

field theory ▶ **noun** Physics a theory that explains physical phenomena in terms of a field and the manner in which it interacts with matter or with other fields.

field trial ▶ **noun** **1** a field test.
2 a competition for gun dogs to test their levels of skill and training in retrieving or pointing.

field trip ▶ **noun** a trip made by students or research workers to study something at first hand.

field vole ▶ **noun** a vole with a dark shaggy coat and short tail, found abundantly in the grasslands of northern Eurasia. Also called **SHORT-TAILED VOLE**.
● *Microtus arvalis*, family Muridae.

field walking ▶ **noun** [mass noun] a technique for finding or studying archaeological sites by walking systematically across a ploughed field collecting artefacts on the surface.

fieldwork ▶ **noun** **1** [mass noun] practical work conducted by a researcher in the natural environment, rather than in a laboratory or office.
2 rare a temporary fortification.
– DERIVATIVES **fieldworker** noun.

fiend /fiːnd/ ▶ **noun** an evil spirit or demon.
■ (**the fiend**) archaic the Devil. ■ a very wicked or cruel person: *a fiend thirsty for blood and revenge.* ■ a person causing mischief or annoyance: *you little fiend!* ■ informal a person who is extremely keen on or addicted to something: *the restaurant's owner is a wine fiend.*
– DERIVATIVES **fiendlike** adjective.
– ORIGIN Old English *fēond* 'an enemy, the devil, a demon', of Germanic origin; related to Dutch *vijand* and German *Feind* 'enemy'.

fiendish ▶ **adjective** extremely cruel or unpleasant: *shrieks of fiendish laughter.*
■ extremely awkward or complex: *a fiendish problem.*
– DERIVATIVES **fiendishly** adverb, **fiendishness** noun.

fierce ▶ **adjective** (**fiercer**, **fiercest**) having or displaying an intense or ferocious aggressiveness: *the fierce air battles that ensued over the Pacific.*
■ (of a feeling, emotion, or action) showing a heartfelt and powerful intensity: *he kissed her with a fierce, demanding passion.* ■ (of the weather or temperature) powerful and destructive in extent or intensity: *fierce storms lashed the country.* ■ (of a mechanism) having a jolting and powerful abruptness of action: *the fire door had a fierce pneumatic return.*
– PHRASES **something fierce** informal, chiefly N. Amer. to a great and almost overwhelming extent: *he said he missed me something fierce.*
– DERIVATIVES **fiercely** adverb, **fierceness** noun.
– ORIGIN Middle English: from Old French *fiers* 'fierce, brave, proud', from Latin *ferus* 'untamed'.

fieri facias /ˌfʌɪərʌɪ ˈfeɪʃɪas/ ▶ **noun** [mass noun] Law a writ to a sheriff for executing a judgement.
– ORIGIN Latin, 'cause to be made or done'.

fiery ▶ **adjective** (**fierier**, **fieriest**) consisting of fire or burning strongly and brightly: *the sun was a fiery ball low on the hills* | [as submodifier] figurative *a fiery hot chilli sauce.*
■ having the bright colour of fire: *the car was painted a fiery red.* ■ (of a person) having a passionate, quick-tempered nature: *a fiery, imaginative Aries.* ■ (of behaviour or words) passionately angry and deeply felt: *a fiery speech.*
– DERIVATIVES **fierily** adverb, **fieriness** noun.

fiery cross ▶ **noun** a burning wooden cross carried as a symbol by the Ku Klux Klan.
■ historical a wooden cross, charred and dipped in blood, used among Scottish clans to summon men to battle.

fiesta /fɪˈɛstə/ ▶ **noun** (in Spanish-speaking countries) a religious festival: *the yearly fiesta of San Juan.*
■ an event marked by festivities or celebration: *the World Cup fiesta.*
– ORIGIN Spanish, from Latin *festum*, (plural) *festa* (see **FEAST**).

FIFA /ˈfiːfə/ the international governing body of soccer, formed in 1904 and based in Zurich, Switzerland.
– ORIGIN acronym from French *Fédération internationale de football association.*

fi. fa. ▶ **abbreviation for** fieri facias.

Fife an administrative region and former county of east central Scotland; administrative centre, Glenrothes.

fife ▶ **noun** a kind of small shrill flute used with the drum in military bands.
▶ **verb** [no obj.] archaic play the fife.
– DERIVATIVES **fifer** noun.
– ORIGIN mid 16th cent.: from German *Pfeife* 'pipe', or from French *fifre* from Swiss German *Pfifer* 'piper'.

fife rail ▶ **noun** chiefly historical a rail round the mainmast of a sailing ship, holding belaying pins.
■ the rail on top of the bulwark at the edge of a sailing ship's poop or forecastle.
– ORIGIN early 18th cent.: of unknown origin.

FIFO /ˈfʌɪfəʊ/ ▶ **abbreviation for** first in, first out (chiefly with reference to methods of stock valuation and data storage). Compare with **LIFO**.

fifteen ▶ **cardinal number** equivalent to the product of three and five; one more than fourteen, or five more than ten; 15: *all fifteen bedrooms have private facilities* | *fifteen feet high* | *fifteen of Howard's troops were killed.* (Roman numeral: **xv** or **XV**.)
■ a size of garment or other merchandise denoted by fifteen. ■ fifteen years old: *she must be fifteen by now.* ■ a team of fifteen players, especially in rugby. ■ (**15**) Brit. (of a film) classified as suitable for people of 15 years and over. ■ (**the Fifteen**) historical the Jacobite rebellion of 1715.
– PHRASES **fifteen minutes of fame** a brief period of fame enjoyed by an ordinary person.
– ORIGIN Old English *fīftēne*, *fīftiene* (see **FIVE**, **-TEEN**).

fifteenth ▶ **ordinal number** constituting number fifteen in a sequence; 15th: *August the fifteenth* | *the fifteenth century* | *on the fifteenth floor.*
■ (**a fifteenth/one fifteenth**) each of fifteen equal parts into which something is or may be divided. ■ an organ stop sounding a register of pipes two octaves (fifteen notes) above the diapason.

fifth ▶ **ordinal number** constituting number five in a sequence; 5th: *the fifth century* BC | *her mother had just given birth to another child, her fifth* | *the world's fifth-largest oil exporter* | *the fifth of November.*
■ (**a fifth/one fifth**) each of five equal parts into which something is or may be divided. ■ the fifth finisher or position in a race or competition: *he finished fifth.* ■ (in some vehicles) the fifth (and typically highest) in a sequence of gears: *in my panic I changed from third to fifth.* ■ chiefly Brit. the fifth form of a school or college. ■ fifthly (used to introduce a fifth point or reason): *fourth, it can aid the process of life review, and fifth, it is an enjoyable and stimulating experience.* ■ Music an interval spanning five consecutive notes in a diatonic scale, in particular (also **perfect fifth**) an interval of three tones and a semitone (e.g. C to G): *strings tuned a fifth apart.* ■ Music the note which is higher by such an interval than the root of a diatonic scale. ■ (**a fifth of**) US informal a fifth of a gallon, as a measure of alcoholic liquor, or a bottle of this capacity: *a fifth of whisky.*
– PHRASES **take the fifth** (in the US) exercise the right guaranteed by the Fifth Amendment to the Constitution of refusing to answer questions in order to avoid incriminating oneself.
– DERIVATIVES **fifthly** adverb.

fifth column ▶ **noun** a group within a country at war who are sympathetic to or working for its enemies.
– DERIVATIVES **fifth columnist** noun.
– ORIGIN The term dates from the Spanish Civil War, when General Mola, leading four columns of troops towards Madrid, declared that he had a fifth column inside the city.

fifth-generation ▶ **adjective** denoting a proposed new class of computer or programming language employing artificial intelligence.

Fifth-monarchy-man ▶ **noun** historical a member of a 17th-century sect expecting the immediate second coming of Christ and repudiating all other government.
– ORIGIN from *Fifth Monarchy*, denoting the last of the five great empires prophesied by Daniel (Dan. 2:44).

fifth position ▶ **noun** **1** Ballet a posture in which the feet are placed turned outwards, one immediately in front of but touching the other so that the toe of the back foot just protrudes beyond the heel of the front foot.
■ a position of the arms in which they are held curved in front of the body, at hip level, waist level, or above the head, with the palms facing the body.
2 Music a position of the left hand on the fingerboard of a stringed instrument nearer to the bridge than the fourth position, enabling a higher set of notes to be played.

Fifth Republic the republican regime established in France with de Gaulle's introduction of a new constitution in 1958.

fifth wheel ▶ **noun** chiefly N. Amer. **1** an extra wheel for a four-wheeled vehicle.
■ informal a superfluous person or thing.
2 a coupling between a vehicle used for towing and a trailer.
■ (also **fifth-wheel trailer**) a trailer with accommodation for camping out. ■ historical a horizontal turntable over the front axle of a carriage as an extra support to prevent its tipping.

fifty ▶ **cardinal number** (pl. **-ies**) the number equivalent to the product of five and ten; half of one hundred; 50: *only fifty per cent of the aircraft were serviceable* | *about fifty of us filed in* | *a fifty-pound salmon.* (Roman numeral: **l** or **L**.)
■ (**fifties**) the numbers from 50 to 59, especially the years of a century or of a person's life: *Elvis is the icon of the Fifties.* ■ fifty years old: *she looked about fifty.* ■ fifty miles an hour: *doing about fifty.* ■ a size of garment or other merchandise denoted by fifty. ■ a fifty-pound note or fifty-dollar bill.

– DERIVATIVES **fiftieth** ordinal number, **fiftyfold** adjective & adverb.
– ORIGIN Old English *fīftig* (see **FIVE**, **-TY**[2]).

fifty-fifty ▶ **adjective** the same in share or proportion; equal: *fifty-fifty partners.*
■ used to refer to one of two possibilities that are equally likely to happen: *he has a fifty-fifty chance of surviving the operation.*
▶ **adverb** in two amounts or parts that are the same in size; equally: *they divided the spoil fifty-fifty.*

fifty-year rule ▶ **noun** Brit. historical a rule that public records may be open to inspection after a lapse of fifty years. Superseded in the UK in 1968 by the thirty-year rule.

fig[1] ▶ **noun** **1** a soft pear-shaped fruit with sweet dark flesh and many small seeds, eaten fresh or dried.
2 (also **fig tree**) the deciduous Old World tree or shrub which bears this fruit.
• *Ficus carica*, family Moraceae.
■ used in names of other plants of this genus, e.g. **strangling fig**, **weeping fig**.
– PHRASES **not give** (or **care**) **a fig** not have the slightest concern about: *Elaine didn't give a fig for Joe's comfort or his state of mind.*
– ORIGIN Middle English: from Old French *figue*, from Provençal *fig(u)a*, based on Latin *ficus*.

fig[2] informal ▶ **noun** (in phrase **full fig**) smart clothes, especially those appropriate to a particular occasion or profession: *a soldier walking up the street* ***in full fig.***
▶ **verb** (**figged**, **figging**) [with obj.] archaic dress up (someone) to look smart: *landsmen are* ***figged out*** *as fine as Lord Harry.*
– ORIGIN late 17th cent. (as a verb): variant of obsolete *feague* 'liven up' (earlier 'whip'); perhaps related to German *fegen* 'sweep, thrash'; compare with **FAKE**[1]. An early sense of the verb was 'fill the head with nonsense'; later (early 19th cent.) 'cause (a horse) to be lively and carry its tail well (by applying ginger to its anus)'; hence 'smarten up'.

fig. ▶ **abbreviation for** figure: *see fig.34.*

figbird ▶ **noun** a gregarious fruit-eating Australasian bird of the oriole family, the male of which has a green back and a yellow or green breast.
• *Sphecotheres viridis*, family Oriolidae; formerly treated as several species.

fight ▶ **verb** (past and past participle **fought**) [no obj.] take part in a violent struggle involving the exchange of physical blows or the use of weapons: *the men were fighting | they fight with other children.*
■ [with obj.] engage in (a war or battle): *there was another war to fight* | [no obj.] *those who had fought for King and country.* ■ [with obj.] archaic command, manage, or manoeuvre (troops, a ship, or military equipment) in battle: *General Hill fights his troops well.* ■ quarrel or argue: *she didn't want to fight with her mother all the time.* ■ [with obj.] struggle to put out (a fire, especially a large one): *two appliances raced to the scene to fight the blaze.* ■ [with obj.] endeavour vigorously to win (an election or other contest). ■ campaign determinedly for or against something, especially to put right what one considers unfair or unjust: *I will* ***fight for*** *a fairer society.* ■ [with obj.] struggle or campaign against (something): *a churchman who has dedicated his life to fighting racism.* ■ [with obj.] attempt to repress (a feeling or an expression of a feeling): *she had to* ***fight back*** *tears of frustration.* ■ (of two or more parties) quarrel or disagree: *they were* ***fighting over*** *who pays the bill.* ■ [with obj.] take part in a boxing match against (an opponent): *McCracken will fight Sheffield's Martin Smith* | [no obj.] *I've earned the right to fight for the world title.* ■ (**fight one's way**) move forward with difficulty, especially by pushing through a crowd or overcoming physical obstacles: *she watched him fight his way across the room.*
▶ **noun** a violent confrontation or struggle: *I had a fight with my brother.*
■ a boxing match. ■ a battle or war: *Britain might have given up her fight against Germany.* ■ a vigorous struggle or campaign for or against something: *a long fight against cancer.* ■ an argument or quarrel. ■ [mass noun] the inclination or ability to fight or struggle: *Ginny felt the fight trickle out of her.*
– PHRASES **fight fire with fire** use the weapons or tactics of one's enemy or opponent, even if one finds them distasteful. **fight a losing battle** be fated to fail in one's efforts: *he was fighting a losing battle to stem the tears.* **fight shy of** be unwilling to undertake or become involved with: *many women fight shy of motherhood for one reason or another.* **make a fight of it** put up a spirited show of resistance in a fight or contest: *United certainly made a fight of it in the second half.* **fight or flight** the instinctive physiological response to a threatening situation, which readies one either to resist forcibly or to run away. **put up a fight** offer resistance to an attack.
– ORIGIN Old English *feohtan* (verb), *feoht(e)*, *gefeoht* (noun), of West Germanic origin; related to Dutch *vechten*, *gevecht* and German *fechten*, *Gefecht*.
▶ **fight back** counter-attack or retaliate in a fight, struggle, or contest.
fight it out settle a dispute by fighting or competing aggressively: *they fought it out with a tug-of-war.*
fight someone/thing off defend oneself against an attack by someone or something: *well-fed people are better able to fight off infectious disease.*

fightback ▶ **noun** Brit. a great effort to gain a position of strength made by a person or group who seem likely to lose a contest: *a storming second-half fightback from Chelsea.*

fighter ▶ **noun** **1** a person or animal that fights, especially as a soldier or in sport.
■ a person who does not easily admit defeat in spite of difficulties or opposition: *there'll be months of physiotherapy but medical staff say she's a fighter.*
2 a fast military aircraft designed for attacking other aircraft: [as modifier] *fighter pilots.*

fighting chair ▶ **noun** N. Amer. a fixed chair on a boat used by a person trying to catch large fish.

fighting chance ▶ **noun** a possibility of success if great effort is made: *they still have a fighting chance of clinching the title.*

fighting fish (also **Siamese fighting fish**) ▶ **noun** a small labyrinth fish native to Thailand, the males of which fight vigorously. It has been bred in a variety of colours for fighting and for aquaria.
• *Betta splendens*, family Belontiidae.

fighting fit ▶ **adjective** in excellent health: *Mary had responded to treatment and seemed fighting fit.*

fighting fund ▶ **noun** Brit. money raised to finance a campaign, especially one supporting a political or social cause.

fighting top ▶ **noun** historical a platform high on a warship's mast on which guns or marksmen can be stationed.

fighting words ▶ **plural noun** (also **fighting talk**) informal words indicating a willingness to fight or challenge a person or thing.
■ US words expressing an insult, especially of an ethnic, racial, or sexist nature, which are considered unacceptable or illegal by certain institutions.

fig leaf ▶ **noun** a leaf of a fig tree, often used for concealing the genitals in paintings and sculpture.
■ figurative a thing designed to conceal a difficulty or embarrassment: *the amendment was just a fig leaf designed to cover the cracks in the party.*
– ORIGIN early 16th cent.: with reference to the story of Adam and Eve (Gen. 3:7).

figment /ˈfɪgm(ə)nt/ ▶ **noun** a thing that someone believes to be real but that exists only in their imagination: *it really was Ross and not* ***a figment of her*** *overheated* ***imagination.***
– ORIGIN late Middle English (denoting an invented statement or story): from Latin *figmentum*, related to *fingere* 'form, contrive'. Compare with **FEIGN** and **FICTION**. The current sense dates from the early 17th cent.

fig parrot ▶ **noun** a very small short-tailed Australasian parrot, with mainly green plumage and a coloured head, feeding on soft fruit. Also called **LORILET**.
• Genera *Opopsitta* and *Psittaculirostris*, family Psittacidae: five species.

figura /fɪˈgjʊərə/ ▶ **noun** (pl. **figurae** /-riː/) (in literary theory) a person or thing representing or symbolizing a fact or ideal.
– ORIGIN Latin, literally 'figure' (representing an early use of *figure* to denote an emblem or type).

figural /ˈfɪgjʊr(ə)l/ ▶ **adjective** **1** another term for **FIGURATIVE** (in sense 1).
■ (in postmodernist writing) relating to or denoting a form of signification which relies on imagery and association rather than on rational and linguistic concepts.
2 Art another term for **FIGURATIVE** (in sense 2).
– ORIGIN late Middle English: from Old French, or from late Latin *figuralis*, from *figura* 'form, shape' (see **FIGURE**).

figurant /ˈfɪgjʊr(ə)nt/ ▶ **noun** a supernumerary actor who has little or nothing to say.
– ORIGIN French, present participle of *figurer* 'to figure'.

figurante /ˌfɪgjʊˈrɒt/ ▶ **noun** a female figurant.

figuration /ˌfɪgəˈreɪʃ(ə)n, -gjʊ-/ ▶ **noun** [mass noun] **1** ornamentation by means of figures or designs.
■ Music use of florid counterpoint: *the figuration of the accompaniment comes out too strongly* | [count noun] *in modern music we have small ostinato figurations.*
2 allegorical representation: *the figuration of 'The Possessed' is much more complex* | [count noun] *the opening parable may be read as a figuration of the main idea behind the novel.*
– ORIGIN Middle English (in the senses 'outline' and 'making of arithmetical figures'): from Latin *figuratio(n-)*, from *figurare* 'to form or fashion', from *figura* (see **FIGURE**).

figurative ▶ **adjective** **1** departing from a literal use of words; metaphorical: *there are no such things as natural rights, the expression is merely figurative.*
2 (of an artist or work of art) representing forms that are recognizably derived from life.
– DERIVATIVES **figuratively** adverb, **figurativeness** noun.
– ORIGIN Middle English: from late Latin *figurativus*, from *figurare* 'to form or fashion', from *figura* (see **FIGURE**).

figure /ˈfɪgə/ ▶ **noun** **1** a number, especially one which forms part of official statistics or relates to the financial performance of a company: *the trade figures | a figure of 30,000 deaths annually from snakebite.*
■ a numerical symbol, especially any of the ten in Arabic notation: *the figure 7.* ■ one of a specified number of digits making up a larger number, used to give a rough idea of the order of magnitude: *he reached three figures against England in only 130 minutes* | [in combination] *a six-figure sum of money.* ■ an amount of money: *a figure of two thousand pounds.* ■ (**figures**) arithmetical calculations: *she has no* ***head for figures.***
2 a person's bodily shape, especially that of a woman and when considered to be attractive: *she had always been so proud of her figure.*
■ a person seen indistinctly, especially at a distance: *a backpacked figure appeared in the distance.* ■ a person of a particular kind, especially one who is important or distinctive in some way: *Williams became something of a cult figure.* ■ a representation of a human or animal form in drawing or sculpture: *starkly painted figures.*
3 a shape which is defined by one or more lines in two dimensions (such as a circle or a triangle), or one or more surfaces in three dimensions (such as a sphere or a cuboid), either considered mathematically in geometry or used as a decorative design: *a red ground with white and blue geometrical figures.*
■ a diagram or illustrative drawing, especially in a book or magazine: *figure 1 shows an ignition circuit.* ■ (in skating) a movement or series of movements following a prescribed pattern and often beginning and ending at the same point. ■ a pattern formed by the movements of a group of people, for example in country dancing or synchronized swimming, as part of a longer dance or display. ■ archaic the external form or shape of a thing.
4 Music a short succession of notes producing a single impression; a brief melodic or rhythmic formula out of which longer passages are developed.
5 Logic the form of a syllogism, classified according to the position of the middle term.
▶ **verb** [no obj.] **1** be a significant and noticeable part of something: *the issue of nuclear policy* ***figured*** *prominently* ***in*** *the talks.*
■ (of a person) play a significant role in a situation or event: *he* ***figured*** *largely* ***in*** *opposition to the Bill.* ■ (of a fictional character) play a part in a novel, play, or film: *the four characters who* ***figure in*** *Ridley's play.*
2 [with obj.] calculate or work out (an amount or value) arithmetically.
3 [with clause] informal, chiefly N. Amer. think, consider, or expect to be the case: *I* ***figure that*** *wearing a suit makes you look like a bank clerk* | [with obj.] *for years, teachers had figured him for a dullard.*
■ (of a recent event or newly discovered fact) be perfectly understandable and only to be expected: *well, she supposed* ***that figured.***
4 [with obj.] represent (something) in a diagram or picture: *varieties of this Cape genus are figured from drawings made there.*
■ [usu. as adj. **figured**] embellish (something) with a pattern: *the floors were covered with figured linoleum.*
– PHRASES **figure of fun** a person who is considered

ridiculous. **figure of speech** a word or phrase used in a non-literal sense to add rhetorical force or interest to a spoken or written passage. **lose** (or **keep**) **one's figure** lose (or retain) a slim and attractive bodily shape. **put a figure on something** give a price or exact number for.
– DERIVATIVES **figureless** adjective.
– ORIGIN Middle English (in the senses 'distinctive shape of a person or thing', 'representation of something material or immaterial', and 'numerical symbol', among others): from Old French *figure* (noun), *figurer* (verb), from Latin *figura* 'shape, figure, form'; related to *fingere* 'form, contrive'.
▶**figure on** N. Amer. informal count or rely on something happening or being the case in the future: *anyone thinking of salmon fishing should figure on paying $200 a day.*
figure something out informal solve or discover the cause of a problem: *he was trying to figure out why the camera wasn't working.*
figure someone out reach an understanding of a person's actions, motives, or personality.

figured bass ▶**noun** Music a bass line with the intended harmonies indicated by figures rather than written out as chords, typical of continuo parts in baroque music.

figure-ground ▶**adjective** [attrib.] Psychology & Art relating to or denoting the perception of images by the distinction of objects from a background from which they appear to stand out, especially in contexts where this distinction is ambiguous.

figurehead ▶**noun 1** a nominal leader or head without real power.
2 a carving, typically a bust or a full-length figure, set at the prow of an old-fashioned sailing ship.

figure of eight (US **figure eight**) ▶**noun** an object or movement having the shape of the number eight.

figure of merit ▶**noun** a numerical expression taken as representing the performance or efficiency of a given device, material, or procedure.

figure-skating ▶**noun** [mass noun] the sport of skating in prescribed patterns from a stationary position.
– DERIVATIVES **figure-skater** noun.

figurine /ˈfɪɡəriːn, -ɡjʊ-/ ▶**noun** a statuette, especially one of a human form.
– ORIGIN mid 19th cent.: from French, from Italian *figurina*, diminutive of *figura*, from Latin *figura* (see **FIGURE**).

fig wasp ▶**noun** a minute Old World wasp which lays its eggs inside the flower of the wild fig. It was introduced into the New World to effect cross-fertilization of the cultivated fig.
• *Blastophaga psenes*, family Agaonidae, superfamily Chalcidoidea.

figwort ▶**noun** a widely distributed herbaceous plant with purplish-brown two-lobed flowers. It was formerly considered to be effective in the treatment of scrofula.
• Genus *Scrophularia*, family Scrophulariaceae (the **figwort family**): several species. Plants of this family have distinctive two-lobed flowers and include the snapdragons, toadflaxes, foxgloves, mulleins, monkey flowers, and speedwells.
– ORIGIN mid 16th cent.: from obsolete *fig* 'piles' + **WORT**. The word originally denoted the pilewort or lesser celandine, which was used as a treatment for piles; the current sense dates from the late 16th cent.

Fiji /ˈfiːdʒi/ a country in the South Pacific consisting of a group of some 840 islands, of which about a hundred are inhabited; pop. 800,000 (est. 1990); languages, English (official), Fijian, Hindi; capital, Suva.

First visited by Abel Tasman in 1643, the Fiji Islands became a British Crown Colony in 1874 and an independent Commonwealth state in 1970. In 1987, following a coup, Fiji became a republic and withdrew from the Commonwealth.

Fijian /fiːˈdʒiːən/ ▶**adjective** of or relating to Fiji, its people, or language.
▶**noun 1** a native or national of Fiji, or a person of Fijian descent.
2 [mass noun] the Austronesian language of the indigenous people of Fiji.

filabeg /ˈfɪləbɛɡ/ ▶**noun** variant spelling of **FILIBEG**.

filagree /ˈfɪləɡriː/ ▶**noun** variant spelling of **FILIGREE**.

filagreed ▶**adjective** variant spelling of **FILIGREED**.

filament /ˈfɪləm(ə)nt/ ▶**noun** a slender thread-like object or fibre, especially one found in animal or plant structures: *each myosin filament is usually surrounded by 12 actin filaments.*
■a conducting wire or thread with a high melting point, forming part of an electric bulb or thermionic valve and heated or made incandescent by an electric current. ■Botany the slender part of a stamen that supports the anther. ■Astronomy a narrow streamer from the sun's chromosphere or in its corona.
– DERIVATIVES **filamentary** adjective, **filamented** adjective, **filamentous** adjective.
– ORIGIN late 16th cent.: from French, or from modern Latin *filamentum*, from late Latin *filare* 'to spin', from Latin *filum* 'thread'.

filaria /fɪˈlɛːrɪə/ ▶**noun** (pl. **filariae** /-rɪiː/) a thread-like parasitic nematode worm which is transmitted by biting flies and mosquitoes, causing filariasis and related diseases.
• Superfamily Filarioidea, class Phasmida.
– DERIVATIVES **filarial** adjective.
– ORIGIN mid 19th cent.: from modern Latin *Filaria* (former genus name), from Latin *filum* 'thread'.

filariasis /fɪˌlɛːrɪˈeɪsɪs, ˌfɪləˈrʌɪəsɪs/ ▶**noun** [mass noun] Medicine a tropical disease caused by the presence of filarial worms, especially in the lymph vessels where heavy infestation can result in elephantiasis.

filature /ˈfɪlətʃə, -tjə/ ▶**noun** [mass noun] the process of obtaining silk thread from silkworm cocoons.
■[count noun] an establishment where such activity takes place.
– ORIGIN mid 18th cent.: from French, from Italian *filatura*, from *filare* 'to spin'.

filbert ▶**noun 1** a cultivated hazel tree that bears edible oval nuts.
• Genus *Corylus*, family Betulaceae: several species, in particular the Kentish cob (*Corylus maxima*).
■the nut of this tree. Also called **COB**[1].
2 (also **filbert brush**) a brush with bristles forming a flattened oval head, used in oil painting.
– ORIGIN Middle English *fylberd*, from Anglo-Norman French *philbert*, dialect French *noix de filbert* (so named because it is ripe about 20 August, the feast day of *St Philibert*).

filch /fɪltʃ/ ▶**verb** [with obj.] informal pilfer or steal (something, especially a thing of small value) in a casual way: *they filched milk off morning doorsteps.*
– DERIVATIVES **filcher** noun.
– ORIGIN Middle English: of unknown origin.

file[1] ▶**noun** a folder or box for holding loose papers that are typically arranged in a particular order for easy reference: *a file of correspondence.*
■the contents of such a folder or box. ■Computing a collection of data, programs, etc. stored in a computer's memory or on a storage device under a single identifying name: [as modifier] *a file name.* ■Canadian a number of issues and responsibilities relating to a particular policy area: *what progress has the Prime Minister made on the unity file?*
▶**verb** [with obj.] place (a document) in a cabinet, box, or folder in a particular order for preservation and easy reference: *the contract, when signed, is filed* | figurative *he still had the moment* ***filed away*** *in his memory.*
■submit (a legal document, application, or charge) to be placed on record by the appropriate authority: *criminal charges were* ***filed against*** *the firm* | [no obj.] *the company had* ***filed for*** *bankruptcy.* ■(of a reporter) send (a story) to a newspaper or news organization.
– PHRASES **on file** in a file or filing system.
– DERIVATIVES **filer** noun.
– ORIGIN late Middle English (as a verb meaning 'string documents on a thread or wire to keep them in order'): from French *filer* 'to string', *fil* 'a thread', both from Latin *filum* 'a thread'. Compare with **FILE**[2].

file[2] ▶**noun** a line of people or things one behind another: ***a file of*** *Christians trudged through the mud.*
■Military a small detachment of men: *a file of English soldiers had ridden out from Perth.* ■Chess each of the eight rows of eight squares on a chessboard running away from the player towards the opponent. Compare with **RANK**[1] (in sense 2).
▶**verb** [no obj., with adverbial of direction] (of a group of people) walk one behind the other, typically in an orderly and solemn manner: *the mourners filed into the church.*
– ORIGIN late 16th cent.: from French *file*, from *filer* 'to string'.

file[3] ▶**noun** a tool with a roughened surface or surfaces, typically of steel, used for smoothing or shaping a hard material.
▶**verb** [with obj.] smooth or shape (something) with such a tool.
■(**file something away/off**) remove something by grinding it off with a file: *the engine numbers were filed away.*
– DERIVATIVES **filer** noun.
– ORIGIN Old English *fīl*, of West Germanic origin; related to Dutch *vijl* and German *Feile*.

filé /ˈfiːleɪ/ ▶**noun** [mass noun] N. Amer. pounded or powdered sassafras leaves used to flavour and thicken soup, especially gumbo.
– ORIGIN mid 19th cent.: from French, past participle of *filer* 'to twist'.

file cabinet ▶**noun** N. Amer. another term for **FILING CABINET**.

file extension ▶**noun** Computing a group of letters occurring after a full stop in a file name, indicating the purpose or contents of the file.

filefish ▶**noun** (pl. same or **-fishes**) a fish with a dorsal spine and rough scales, related to the triggerfishes and occurring in tropical and sometimes temperate seas.
• Numerous genera and species, family Balistidae (or Monacanthidae).
– ORIGIN late 18th cent.: from **FILE**[3] (because of its rough skin, suggesting the surface of a file).

file server ▶**noun** Computing a device which controls access to separately stored files, as part of a multi-user system.

file shell ▶**noun** a free-swimming bivalve mollusc, the shell of which is typically white and has a rough, ribbed external surface.
• Family Limidae.

file snake ▶**noun 1** a widespread but rarely seen nocturnal African constricting snake which is triangular in cross section with rough scales, giving it the appearance of a three-cornered file.
• Genus *Mehelya*, family Colubridae; several species.
2 another term for **WART SNAKE**.

filet /ˈfiːleɪ, ˈfɪlɪt/ ▶**noun 1** French spelling of **FILLET**, used especially in the names of French or French-sounding dishes: *filet de boeuf.*
2 [mass noun] a kind of net or lace with a square mesh. [ORIGIN: late 19th cent.: from French, 'net'.]

filet mignon /ˌfiːleɪ ˈmiːnjɒ̃/ ▶**noun** [mass noun] a small tender piece of beef from the end of the undercut.
– ORIGIN French, literally 'dainty fillet'.

filial /ˈfɪlɪəl/ ▶**adjective** of, relating to, or due from a son or daughter: *a display of filial affection.*
■Biology denoting the offspring of a cross. See also F_1.
– DERIVATIVES **filially** adverb.
– ORIGIN late Middle English: from Old French, or from ecclesiastical Latin *filialis*, from *filius* 'son', *filia* 'daughter'.

filiation /ˌfɪlɪˈeɪʃ(ə)n/ ▶**noun** [mass noun] the fact of being or of being designated the child of a particular parent or parents: *relationships based on ties of filiation as opposed to marriage.*
■the manner in which a thing is related to another from which it is derived or descended in some respect: *the filiation of Old Norse manuscripts.* ■[count noun] a branch of a society or language.
– ORIGIN late Middle English: from French, from ecclesiastical and medieval Latin *filiatio(n-)*, from Latin *filius* 'son', *filia* 'daughter'.

filibeg /ˈfɪlɪbɛɡ/ (also **philibeg**, **filabeg**) ▶**noun** Scottish, chiefly historical a kilt.
– ORIGIN mid 18th cent.: from Scottish Gaelic *feileadh-beag* 'little kilt', from *feileadh* 'plaid' and *beag* 'little'.

filibuster /ˈfɪlɪbʌstə/ ▶**noun 1** an action such as prolonged speaking which obstructs progress in a legislative assembly in a way that does not technically contravene the required procedures: *the Liberals began a filibuster* | [mass noun] *many hours in Committee characterized by filibuster and slow progress.*
2 historical a person engaging in unauthorized warfare against a foreign state.
▶**verb** [no obj.] [often as noun **filibustering**] act in an obstructive manner in a parliament, especially by speaking at inordinate length: *several measures were killed by Republican filibustering.*
■[with obj.] obstruct (a measure) in such a way.
– ORIGIN late 18th cent.: from French *flibustier*, first applied to pirates who pillaged the Spanish colonies in the West Indies. In the mid 19th cent. (via Spanish *filibustero*), the term denoted American adventurers who incited revolution in several Latin

American states, whence sense 2. The verb was used to describe tactics intended to sabotage US congressional proceedings, whence sense 1.

filicide /ˈfɪlɪsʌɪd/ ▶ **noun** [mass noun] the killing of one's son or daughter: *maternal filicide*.
■ [count noun] a person who kills their son or daughter.
– ORIGIN mid 17th cent. from Latin *filius* 'son', *filia* 'daughter' + **-CIDE**.

Filicopsida /ˌfɪlɪˈkɒpsɪdə/ Botany a class of pteridophyte plants that comprises the ferns.
– ORIGIN modern Latin (plural), from Latin *filix*, *filic-* 'fern' + *opsis* 'appearance'.

filiform /ˈfʌɪlɪfɔːm/ ▶ **adjective** Biology thread-like: *the antennae are filiform*.
– ORIGIN mid 18th cent.: from Latin *filum* 'thread' + **-IFORM**.

filigree /ˈfɪlɪɡriː/ (also **filagree**) ▶ **noun** [mass noun] ornamental work of fine (typically gold or silver) wire formed into delicate tracery: [as modifier] *filigree silverwork* | [count noun] *intricate gold filigrees*.
■ a thing resembling such fine ornamental work: [as modifier] *silver filigree foliage*.
– ORIGIN late 17th cent. (earlier as *filigreen*, *filigrane*): from French *filigrane*, from Italian *filigrana* (from Latin *filum* 'thread' + *granum* 'seed').

filigreed (also **filagreed**) ▶ **adjective** ornamented with or resembling filigree work: *white filigreed stockings*.

filing ▶ **noun** (usu. **filings**) a small particle rubbed off by a file when smoothing or shaping something: *iron filings*.

filing cabinet ▶ **noun** a large piece of office furniture, typically made of metal, with deep drawers for storing documents.

Filioque /ˌfiːlɪˈəʊkwiː/ the word inserted in the Western version of the Nicene Creed to assert the doctrine of the procession of the Holy Ghost from the Son as well as from the Father, which is not admitted by the Eastern Church. It was one of the central issues in the Great Schism of 1054.
– ORIGIN Latin, literally 'and from the Son'.

Filipina /ˌfɪlɪˈpiːnə/ ▶ **noun** a female Filipino.
– ORIGIN Spanish.

Filipino /ˌfɪlɪˈpiːnəʊ/ (also **Pilipino**) ▶ **adjective** of or relating to the Philippines, the Filipinos, or their language.
▶ **noun** (pl. **-os**) **1** a native or national of the Philippines, or a person of Filipino descent.
2 [mass noun] the national language of the Philippines, a standardized form of Tagalog.
– ORIGIN Spanish, from *las Islas Filipinas* 'the Philippine Islands'.

Fílippoi /ˈfilipi/ Greek name for **PHILIPPI**.

fill ▶ **verb** [with obj.] put someone or something into (a space or container) so that it is completely or almost completely full: *I* ***filled up*** *the bottle with water* | *the office was* ***filled with*** *reporters*.
■ block up (a cavity in a tooth) with cement, amalgam, or gold. ■ [no obj.] (**fill with**) become full of: *Elinor's eyes filled with tears*. ■ become an overwhelming presence in: *a pungent smell of garlic filled the air*. ■ cause (someone) to have an intense experience of an emotion or feeling: *his presence* ***filled*** *us* ***with*** *foreboding*. ■ [no obj.] (of a sail) curve out tautly from its supports as the wind blows into it. ■ [with obj.] (of the wind) blow into (a sail), causing it to curve outwards. ■ Poker complete (a good hand) by drawing the necessary cards. ■ appoint a person to hold (a vacant post). ■ hold and perform the expected duties of (a position or role): *she fills the role of the 'good' child*. ■ occupy or take up (a period of time): *the next few days were* ***filled with*** *meetings*. ■ chiefly N. Amer. be supplied with the items described in (a prescription or order).
▶ **noun** (**one's fill**) an amount of something which is as much as one wants or can bear: *we have eaten our fill* | *I've* ***had my fill*** *of surprises for one day*.
■ an amount of something which will occupy all the space in a container: *a* ***fill of*** *tobacco*. ■ [mass noun] material, typically loose or compacted, which fills a space, especially in building or engineering work: *loose polystyrene fill*. ■ [mass noun] the action of filling something, especially of shading in a region of a computer graphics display. ■ (in popular music) a short interjected phrase on a particular instrument.
– PHRASES **fill the bill** see **BILL**[1]. **fill someone's shoes** (or **boots**) informal take over someone's function or duties and fulfil them satisfactorily.
– ORIGIN Old English *fyllan* (verb), *fyllu* (noun) of Germanic origin; related to Dutch *vullen* and German *füllen* (verbs), *Fülle* (noun), also to **FULL**[1].
▶ **fill in** act as a substitute for someone when they are unable to do their job: *my producer will have to have someone standing by to* ***fill in for*** *me*.
fill someone in 1 inform someone more fully of a matter, giving all the details: *I patiently* ***filled*** *him* ***in on*** *the British tradition of sherry tippling*. **2** Brit. informal, dated hit or punch someone: *I filled in a chap and took his money*.
fill something in put material into a hole, trench, or space so that it is completely full: *the canal is now disused and partly filled in*. ■ complete a drawing by adding colour or shade to the spaces within an outline: *incised letters, filled in with gold*. ■ Brit. add information to complete a form or other official document. ■ use one's spare time between other more important activities: *we spent an uneasy few days filling in time*.
fill out (of a person) put on weight to a noticeable extent.
fill something out chiefly N. Amer. add information to complete an official form or document. ■ give more details to add to someone's understanding of something: *he filled out the background by going into historical questions*.
fill up become completely full: *the dining car filled up*.
■ fill the fuel tank of a car.

fille de joie /ˌfiː də ˈʒwɑː/ ▶ **noun** used euphemistically to refer to a prostitute.
– ORIGIN French, literally 'girl of pleasure'.

filler[1] /ˈfɪlə/ ▶ **noun 1** [usu. in combination] a thing put in a space or container to fill it: *these plants are attractive gap-fillers or ground cover*.
■ [mass noun] a substance used for filling cracks or holes in a surface, especially before painting it: *rapid-hardening wood filler*. ■ [mass noun] material used to fill a cavity or increase bulk: *foam filler*. ■ an item serving only to fill space or time, especially in a newspaper, broadcast, or recording. ■ a word or sound filling a pause in an utterance or conversation (e.g. *er*, *well*, *you know*). ■ a linguistic unit that fills a particular slot in syntactic structure. ■ [mass noun] US the tobacco used in a cigar.
2 [in combination] a person or thing that fills a space or container: *supermarket shelf-fillers*.

filler[2] /ˈfɪlɑː/ ▶ **noun** (pl. same) a monetary unit of Hungary, equal to one hundredth of a forint.
– ORIGIN from Hungarian *fillér*.

filler cap ▶ **noun** a cap closing the pipe leading to the petrol tank of a motor vehicle.

fillet ▶ **noun 1** a fleshy boneless piece of meat from near the loins or the ribs of an animal: *a chicken breast fillet* | [mass noun] *roast* ***fillet of*** *lamb*.
■ (also **fillet steak**) a beef steak cut from the lower part of a sirloin. ■ a boned side of a fish.
2 a band or ribbon worn round the head, especially for binding the hair.
■ Architecture a narrow flat band separating two mouldings. ■ Architecture a small band between the flutes of a column. ■ a plain line impressed on the cover of a book. ■ a roller used to impress such a line.
3 a roughly triangular strip of material which rounds off an interior angle between two surfaces: *a splayed mortar fillet at the junction of the roof with the chimney stack* | [as modifier] *a fillet weld*.
▶ **verb** (**filleted**, **filleting**) [with obj.] remove the bones from (a fish).
■ cut (fish or meat) into boneless strips.
– DERIVATIVES **filleter** noun.
– ORIGIN Middle English (denoting a band worn round the head): from Old French *filet* 'thread', based on Latin *filum* 'thread'.

filling ▶ **noun** a quantity of material that fills or is used to fill something: *duvets with synthetic fillings*.
■ a piece of material used to fill a cavity in a tooth: *a gold filling*. ■ an edible substance placed between the layers of a sandwich, cake, or other foodstuff: *a Swiss roll with a chocolate filling*. ■ N. Amer. another term for **WEFT**[1].
▶ **adjective** (of food) leaving one with a pleasantly satiated feeling: *a filling spicy bean soup*.

filling station ▶ **noun** a petrol station.

fillip /ˈfɪlɪp/ ▶ **noun 1** something which acts as a stimulus or boost to an activity: *the halving of car tax would provide* ***a fillip to*** *sales*.
2 archaic a movement made by bending the last joint of the finger against the thumb and suddenly releasing it; a flick of the finger: *the Prince, by a fillip, made some of the wine fly in Oglethorpe's face*.
■ a slight smart stroke or tap given in such a way.
▶ **verb** (**filliped**, **filliping**) [with obj.] archaic propel (a small object) with a flick of the fingers: *our aforesaid merchant filliped a nut sharply against his bullying giant*.
■ strike (someone or something) slightly and smartly: *he filliped him over the nose*. ■ stimulate or urge (someone or something): *pour, that the draught may fillip my remembrance*.
– ORIGIN late Middle English (in the sense 'make a fillip with the fingers'): symbolic; compare with **FLICK**, **FLIP**[1].

fillis /ˈfɪlɪs/ ▶ **noun** [mass noun] Brit. loosely twisted string, used especially for tying up plants.
– ORIGIN early 20th cent.: from French *filasse* 'tow'.

fill light ▶ **noun** a supplementary light used in photography or filming that does not change the character of the main light and is used chiefly to lighten shadows.

Fillmore, Millard (1800–74), American Whig statesman, 13th President of the US 1850–3. He was an advocate of compromise on the slavery issue, but his unpopular enforcement of the 1850 Fugitive Slave Act hastened the end of the Whig Party.

fill-up ▶ **noun** an instance of making something, especially the fuel tank of a car, completely full: *drivers are never far from a fill-up*.
■ a piece of music used to extend the playing time of a cassette or CD to an acceptable length.

filly ▶ **noun** (pl. **-ies**) a young female horse, especially one less than four years old.
■ dated a lively girl or young woman.
– ORIGIN late Middle English: from Old Norse *fylja*, of Germanic origin; related to **FOAL**.

film ▶ **noun 1** [mass noun] a thin flexible strip of plastic or other material coated with light-sensitive emulsion for exposure in a camera, used to produce photographs or motion pictures: *he had already shot a whole roll of film* | [count noun] *a new range of films and cameras*.
■ material in the form of a very thin flexible sheet: *clear plastic film between the layers of glass*. ■ [count noun] a thin layer covering a surface: *she quickly wiped away the light film of sweat*. ■ archaic a fine thread or filament: *films of silk*.
2 a story or event recorded by a camera as a set of moving images and shown in a cinema or on television: *a horror film* | [as modifier] *a film director*.
■ [mass noun] cinema considered as an art or industry: *a critical overview of feminist writing on film*.
▶ **verb 1** [with obj.] capture on film as part of a series of moving images; make a film of (a story or event): *she glowered at the television crew who were filming them*.
■ make a cinema or television film of (a book). ■ [no obj.] (**film well/badly**) be well or badly suited to portrayal in a film: *an adventure story which would film well*.
2 [no obj.] become or appear to become covered with a thin layer of something: *his eyes had* ***filmed over***.
– ORIGIN Old English *filmen* 'membrane', of West Germanic origin; related to **FELL**[5].

film badge ▶ **noun** a device containing photographic film which registers the wearer's exposure to radiation.

filmi /ˈfɪlmi/ Indian ▶ **adjective** related to or characteristic of the Bombay film industry: *a filmi magazine*.
▶ **noun** a well-known actor in the Bombay film industry.

filmic ▶ **adjective** of or relating to films or cinematography: *he has reconceived the stage production in filmic terms*.

film-maker ▶ **noun** a person who directs or produces films for the cinema or television.
– DERIVATIVES **film-making** noun.

film noir /fɪlm ˈnwɑː, French film nwaʀ/ ▶ **noun** [mass noun] a style or genre of cinematographic film marked by a mood of pessimism, fatalism, and menace. The term was originally applied (by a group of French critics) to American thriller or detective films made in the period 1944–54 and to the work of directors such as Orson Welles, Fritz Lang, and Billy Wilder.
■ [count noun] a film of this genre.
– ORIGIN French, literally 'black film'.

filmography ▶ **noun** (pl. **-ies**) a list of films by one director or actor, or on one subject.
– ORIGIN 1960s: from **FILM** + **-GRAPHY**, on the pattern of *bibliography*.

filmsetting ▶ **noun** [mass noun] Printing the setting of material to be printed by projecting it on to photographic film from which the printing surface is prepared.

– DERIVATIVES **filmset** verb, **filmsetter** noun.

film star ▶ noun a well-known actor or actress in films.

film stock ▶ noun see **STOCK** (sense 1).

filmstrip ▶ noun a series of transparencies in a strip for projection, used especially as a teaching aid.

filmy ▶ adjective (**filmier**, **filmiest**) (especially of fabric) thin and translucent: *filmy white voile.*
■ covered with or forming a thin layer of something: *her eyes were dull and filmy.*
– DERIVATIVES **filmily** adverb, **filminess** noun.

filmy fern ▶ noun a small fern of damp shady places, with wiry creeping stems and delicate forked fronds which are only one cell thick. They occur chiefly in tropical and subtropical regions.
• Family Hymenophyllaceae: *Hymenophyllum* and other genera.

filo /ˈfiːləʊ/ (also **phyllo**) ▶ noun [mass noun] a kind of dough that can be stretched into very thin sheets, used in layers to make both sweet and savoury pastries, especially in eastern Mediterranean cookery: [as modifier] *filo pastry.*
– ORIGIN 1950s: from modern Greek *phullo* 'leaf'.

Filofax /ˈfʌɪlə(ʊ)faks/ ▶ noun trademark a loose-leaf notebook for recording appointments, addresses, and notes.
– ORIGIN 1930s: representing a colloquial pronunciation of *file of facts.*

filopodium /ˌfʌɪlə(ʊ)ˈpəʊdɪəm/ ▶ noun (pl. **filopodia**) Biology a long, slender, tapering pseudopodium, as found in some protozoans and in embryonic cells.
– DERIVATIVES **filopodial** adjective.
– ORIGIN early 20th cent.: from Latin *filium* 'thread' + **PODIUM**.

filoselle /ˈfɪlə(ʊ)sɛl/ ▶ noun [mass noun] floss silk, or silk thread resembling this, used in embroidery.
– ORIGIN mid 16th cent.: from French, from Italian *filosello*, of uncertain ultimate origin.

filovirus /ˈfiːləʊˌvʌɪrəs/ ▶ noun a filamentous RNA virus of a genus which causes severe haemorrhagic fevers in humans and primates, and which includes the Ebola and Marburg viruses.

fils¹ /fɪls/ ▶ noun (pl. same) a monetary unit of Iraq, Bahrain, Jordan, Kuwait, and Yemen, equal to one hundredth of a riyal in Yemen and one thousandth of a dinar elsewhere.
– ORIGIN from a colloquial pronunciation of Arabic *fals*, denoting a small copper coin.

fils² /fiːs, French fis/ ▶ noun used after a surname to distinguish a son from a father of the same name: *Alexandre Dumas fils.* Compare with **PÈRE**.
– ORIGIN French, 'son'.

filter ▶ noun a porous device for removing impurities or solid particles from a liquid or gas passed through it: *an oil filter.*
■ short for **FILTER TIP**: [as modifier] *a cheap filter cigarette.* ■ a screen, plate, or layer of a substance which absorbs light or other radiation or selectively absorbs some of its components: *filters can be used in photography to reduce haze.* ■ a device for suppressing electrical or sound waves of frequencies not required. ■ Brit. an arrangement whereby vehicles may turn left (or right) while other traffic waiting to go straight ahead or turn right (or left) is stopped by a red light: [as modifier] *a filter lane.* ■ a traffic light signalling such an arrangement, typically one partly blacked out to form an arrow. ■ Computing a piece of software that processes text, for example to remove unwanted spaces or to format it for use in another application.
▶ verb [with obj.] (often **be filtered**) pass (a liquid, gas, light, or sound) through a device to remove unwanted material: *the eye **filters out** ultraviolet radiation* | figurative *you'll be put through to a secretary whose job it is to filter calls.*
■ [no obj., with adverbial of direction] move slowly or in small quantities or numbers through something or in a specified direction: *people filtered out of the concert during the last set.* ■ [no obj., with adverbial] (of information) gradually become known: *the news began to filter in from the hospital.* ■ [no obj., with adverbial of direction] Brit. (of traffic) be allowed to pass to the left or right at a junction while traffic going straight ahead is halted.
– ORIGIN late Middle English (denoting a piece of felt): from French *filtre*, from medieval Latin *filtrum* 'felt used as a filter', of West Germanic origin and related to **FELT¹**.

filterable (also **filtrable**) ▶ adjective **1** capable of passing through a filter.
2 capable of being separated out by a filter: *filterable solids.*

filter bed ▶ noun a tank or pond containing a layer of sand or gravel, used for filtering large quantities of liquid.

filter cake ▶ noun a deposit of insoluble material left on a filter.

filter-feeding ▶ adjective Zoology (of an aquatic animal) feeding by filtering out plankton or nutrients suspended in the water.
– DERIVATIVES **filter-feeder** noun.

filter paper ▶ noun a piece of porous paper for filtering liquids, used especially in chemical processes and coffee-making.

filter press ▶ noun a device consisting of a series of cloth filters fixed to frames, used for the large-scale filtration of liquid under pressure.

filter tip ▶ noun a filter attached to a cigarette for removing impurities from the inhaled smoke.
■ a cigarette with such a filter.
– DERIVATIVES **filter-tipped** adjective.

filth ▶ noun [mass noun] disgusting dirt: *stagnant pools of filth.*
■ obscene and offensive language or printed material. ■ corrupt behaviour; decadence. ■ used as a term of abuse for a person or people one greatly despises: *Nazi filth.* ■ [as plural noun **the filth**] Brit. informal, derogatory the police.
– ORIGIN Old English *fȳlth* 'rotting matter, rottenness', also 'corruption, obscenity', of Germanic origin; related to Dutch *vuilte*, also to **FOUL**.

filthy ▶ adjective (**filthier**, **filthiest**) disgustingly dirty: *a filthy hospital with no sanitation.*
■ Brit. informal (of weather) very unpleasant: *it looked like being a filthy night.* ■ obscene and offensive: *filthy language.* ■ informal used to express one's anger and disgust: *you filthy beast.* ■ (of a mood) bad-tempered and aggressive: *he arrived at the meeting half an hour late in a filthy temper.*
▶ adverb [as submodifier] informal to an extreme and often disgusting extent: *he has become filthy rich.*
– DERIVATIVES **filthily** adverb, **filthiness** noun.

filtrable ▶ adjective variant spelling of **FILTERABLE**.

filtrate /ˈfɪltreɪt/ ▶ noun a liquid which has passed through a filter: *filtrates of bacterial cultures* | [mass noun] *a few drops of clear filtrate.*
▶ verb [with obj.] rare filter: *the remaining alkali is filtrated.*
– ORIGIN early 17th cent.: from modern Latin *filtrat-* 'filtered', from the verb *filtrare*, from medieval Latin *filtrum* (see **FILTER**).

filtration ▶ noun [mass noun] the action or process of filtering something: *small particles are difficult to remove without filtration.*

fimbria /ˈfɪmbrɪə/ ▶ noun (pl. **fimbriae** /-iiː/) chiefly Anatomy a series of threads or other projections resembling a fringe.
■ (usu. **fimbriae**) an individual thread in such a structure, especially a finger-like projection at the end of the Fallopian tube near the ovary.
– DERIVATIVES **fimbrial** adjective.
– ORIGIN mid 18th cent.: from late Latin, 'border, fringe'.

fimbriated /ˈfɪmbrɪeɪtɪd/ (also **fimbriate**) ▶ adjective **1** Biology having a fringe or border of hair-like or finger-like projections.
2 Heraldry having a narrow border, typically of a specified tincture.
– ORIGIN late 15th cent. (in sense 2): from Latin *fimbriatus* (from *fimbria* 'fringe') + **-ED¹**.

fin ▶ noun a flattened appendage on various parts of the body of many aquatic vertebrates, including fish and cetaceans, and some invertebrates, used for propelling, steering, and balancing.
■ an underwater swimmer's flipper. ■ a small flattened projecting surface or attachment on an aircraft, rocket, or motor car, for providing aerodynamic stability. ■ a flattened projection on a device, used for increasing heat transfer.
▶ verb (**finned**, **finning**) [no obj., with adverbial of direction] swim under water by means of flippers: *I finned madly for the surface.*
– DERIVATIVES **finless** adjective, **finned** adjective [in combination] *primitive ray-finned fishes.*
– ORIGIN Old English *finn*, *fin*, of Germanic origin; related to Dutch *vin* and probably ultimately to Latin *pinna* 'feather, wing'.

finagle /fɪˈneɪɡ(ə)l/ ▶ verb [with obj.] informal obtain (something) by dishonest or devious means: *Ted attended all the football games he could finagle tickets for.*
■ [no obj.] act in a dishonest or devious manner: *they wrangled and finagled over the fine points.*
– DERIVATIVES **finagler** noun.
– ORIGIN 1920s (originally US): from dialect *fainaigue* 'cheat'; perhaps from Old French *fornier* 'deny'.

final ▶ adjective coming at the end of a series: *the final version of the report was presented.*
■ reached or designed to be reached as the outcome of a process or a series of actions and events: *the final cost will easily run into six figures.* ■ allowing no further doubt or dispute: *the decision of the judging panel is final.*
▶ noun **1** the last game in a sports tournament or other competition, which will decide the winner of the tournament.
■ (**finals**) a series of games constituting the final stage of a competition: *the World Cup finals.*
2 (**finals**) Brit. a series of examinations at the end of a degree course: *she was doing her history finals.*
■ (**final**) N. Amer. an examination at the end of a term, school year, or particular class.
3 Music the principal note in a mode.
4 (**finals**) the final approach of an aircraft to the runway it will be landing on: *the plane piloted by Richards was on finals.*
– PHRASES **the final straw** see **STRAW**.
– ORIGIN Middle English (in the adjectival sense 'conclusive'): from Old French, or from Latin *finalis*, from *finis* 'end'. Compare with **FINISH**.

final cause ▶ noun Philosophy the purpose or aim of an action or the end towards which a thing naturally develops.

final clause ▶ noun Grammar a clause expressing purpose or intention (e.g. one introduced by *in order that* or *lest*).

final demand ▶ noun a creditor's last request for payment of money owed, before taking punitive measures.

final drive ▶ noun the last part of the transmission system in a motor vehicle.

finale /fɪˈnɑːli, -leɪ/ ▶ noun the last part of a piece of music, an entertainment, or a public event, especially when particularly dramatic or exciting: *the festival ends with a grand finale.*
– ORIGIN mid 18th cent.: from Italian, from Latin *finalis* (see **FINAL**).

finalism ▶ noun [mass noun] the doctrine that natural processes, for example evolution, are directed towards some goal.
– DERIVATIVES **finalistic** adjective.

finalist ▶ noun a competitor or team in the final or finals of a competition.
■ a student taking finals.

finality /fʌɪˈnalɪti/ ▶ noun (pl. **-ies**) [mass noun] the fact or impression of being an irreversible ending: *the abrupt finality of death* | [in sing.] *there's a dreadful finality about cutting down a tree.*
■ a tone or manner which indicates that no further comment or argument is possible: *'No,' she said with finality.* ■ the quality of being complete or conclusive: *the desire for justice rather than finality fuels challenges to decisions.* ■ [count noun] an action or event that ends something irreversibly: *death is the ultimate finality.*
– ORIGIN mid 19th cent.: from French *finalité*, from late Latin *finalitas*, from Latin *finalis* (see **FINAL**).

finalize (also **-ise**) ▶ verb [with obj.] complete (a transaction, especially in commerce or diplomacy) after discussion of the terms.
■ produce or agree on a finished and definitive version of: *efforts intensified to finalize plans for post-war reconstruction.*
– DERIVATIVES **finalization** noun.

finally ▶ adverb after a long time, typically involving difficulty or delay: *he finally arrived to join us.*
■ as the last in a series of related events or objects: *a referendum followed by local, legislative and, finally, presidential elections.* ■ [sentence adverb] used to introduce a final point or reason: *finally, it is common knowledge that travel broadens the horizons.* ■ in such a way as to put an end to doubt and dispute: *to dispel finally the belief that auditors were clients of the company.*

final solution ▶ noun the Nazi policy of exterminating European Jews. Introduced by Heinrich Himmler and administered by Adolf Eichmann, the policy resulted in the murder of 6 million Jews in concentration camps between 1941 and 1945.
– ORIGIN translation of German *Endlösung*.

finance /fʌɪˈnans, fɪ-, ˈfʌɪnans/ ▶ noun [mass noun] the

management of large amounts of money, especially by governments or large companies.
■monetary support for an enterprise: *the clearing banks are important sources of finance.* ■ (**finances**) the monetary resources and affairs of a state, organization, or person.
▶**verb** [with obj.] provide funding for (a person or enterprise): *the health service is financed almost entirely by the taxpayer.*
– ORIGIN late Middle English: from Old French, from *finer* 'make an end, settle a debt', from *fin* 'end' (see **FINE**[2]). The original sense was 'payment of a debt, compensation, or ransom'; later 'taxation, revenue'. Current senses date from the 18th cent., and reflect sense development in French.

finance company (also **finance house**) ▶**noun** a company concerned primarily with providing money, e.g. for hire-purchase transactions.

f

financial /fʌɪˈnanʃ(ə)l, fɪ-/ ▶**adjective** of or relating to finance: *an independent financial adviser.*
■Austral./NZ informal possessing money. ■ W. Indian (of a member of a club or society) paid-up.
– DERIVATIVES **financially** adverb.

financial intermediary ▶**noun** an institution, such as a bank, building society, or unit-trust company, that holds funds from lenders in order to make loans to borrowers.

Financial Times index another term for **FTSE INDEX**.

financial year ▶**noun** a year as reckoned for taxing or accounting purposes, for example the British tax year, reckoned from 6 April.

financier ▶**noun** /fʌɪˈnansɪə, fɪ-/ a person concerned in the management of large amounts of money on behalf of governments or other large organizations.
– ORIGIN early 17th cent.: from French, from *finance* (see **FINANCE**).

finback (also **finback whale**) ▶**noun** another term for **FIN WHALE**.

finca /ˈfɪŋkə/ ▶**noun** (in Spain and Spanish-speaking countries) a country estate; a ranch.

finch ▶**noun** a seed-eating songbird that typically has a stout bill and colourful plumage.
• The true finches belong to the family Fringillidae (the **finch family**), which includes chaffinches, canaries, linnets, crossbills, etc. Many other finches belong to the bunting, waxbill, or sparrow families.
– ORIGIN Old English *finc*, of West Germanic origin; related to Dutch *vink* and German *Fink*.

find ▶**verb** (past and past participle **found**) [with obj.] **1** discover or perceive by chance or unexpectedly: *Lindsey looked up to find Niall watching her | the remains of a headless body had been found.*
■discover (someone or something) after a deliberate search: *in this climate it could be hard to find a buyer.* ■ (**find oneself**) discover oneself to be in a surprising or unexpected situation: *phobia sufferers often find themselves virtual prisoners in their own home.* ■ succeed in obtaining (something): *she also found the time to raise five children.* ■ summon up (a quality, especially courage) with an effort: *I found the courage to speak.* ■ [no obj.] (of hunters or hounds) discover game, especially a fox: *Lady Montego heard the new halloo—they had found.*
2 (often **be found**) recognize or discover (something) to be present: *vitamin B12 is found in dairy products.*
■become aware of; discover to be the case: [with obj. and infinitive] *the majority of staff find the magazine to be informative and useful* | [with clause] *she found that none of the local nursery schools had an available slot.* ■ ascertain (something) by study, calculation, or inquiry: *the class are encouraged to find their own solutions to problems.* ■ (**find oneself**) discover the fundamental truths about one's own character and identity. ■ Law (of a court) officially declare to be the case: [with obj. and complement] *he was found guilty of speeding* | [with clause] *the court found that a police lab expert had fabricated evidence.* ■ [with obj. and complement] perceive or experience (something) to be the case: *both men found it difficult to put ideas into words.*
3 (of a thing) reach or arrive at, either of its own accord or without the human agent being known: *water finds its own level.*
■(**find one's way**) reach one's destination by one's own efforts, without knowing or having been told in advance how to get there: *he **found his way to** the front door.* ■ (**find one's way**) come to be in a certain situation: *each and every boy **found his way into** a suitable occupation.* ■ (of a letter) reach (someone). ■ archaic reach the understanding or conscience of (someone): *whatever finds me, bears witness for itself that it has proceeded from a Holy Spirit.*
▶**noun** a discovery of something valuable, typically something of archaeological interest: *he made his most spectacular finds in the Valley of the Kings.*
■a person who is discovered to be useful or interesting in some way: *Paul had been a real find—he could design the whole hotel complex.* ■ Hunting the finding of a fox.
– PHRASES **all found** Brit. dated (of an employee's wages) with board and lodging provided free: *your wages would be five shillings all found.* **find fault** see **FAULT**. **find favour** be liked or prove acceptable: *the ballets did not **find favour with** the public.* **find one's feet** stand up and become able to walk. ■ establish oneself in a particular field: *he never really found his feet in the House of Lords.* **find God** experience a religious conversion or awakening. **find in favour of** see *find for* below. **find it in one's heart to do something** allow or force oneself to do something: *Seb could not find it in his heart to dislike Plunkett.*
– DERIVATIVES **findable** adjective.
– ORIGIN Old English *findan*, of Germanic origin; related to Dutch *vinden* and German *finden*.
▶**find against** Law (of a court) make a decision against or judge to be guilty.
find for (or **find in favour of**) Law (of a court) make a decision in favour of, or judge to be innocent: *the Court of Exchequer found for the plaintiffs.*
find someone out detect a person's immoral or offensive actions: *she would always find him out if he tried to lie.*
find something out (or **find out about something**) discover a fact: *he hadn't time to find out what was bothering her.*

finder ▶**noun** a person that finds someone or something.
■a small telescope attached to a large one to locate an object for observation. ■ the viewfinder of a camera.
– PHRASES **finders keepers** (**losers weepers**) informal used, often humorously, to assert that whoever finds something by chance is entitled to keep it.

fin de siècle /ˌfã də ˈsjɛkl(ə)/ ▶**adjective** relating to or characteristic of the end of a century, especially the 19th century: *fin-de-siècle art.*
■decadent: *there was a fin-de-siècle air in London's clubland last night.*
▶**noun** the end of a century, especially the 19th century.
– ORIGIN French, 'end of century'.

finding ▶**noun** **1** [mass noun] the action of finding someone or something: *a local doctor reported the finding of numerous dead rats.*
■[count noun] (often **findings**) a conclusion reached as a result of an inquiry, investigation, or trial: *experimental findings.*
2 (**findings**) N. Amer. small articles or tools used in making garments, shoes, or jewellery.

find-spot ▶**noun** Archaeology the place where an object is found.

fine[1] /fʌɪn/ ▶**adjective** **1** of very high quality: *this was a fine piece of film-making | fine wines.*
■(of a person) worthy of or eliciting admiration: *what a fine human being he is.* ■ good; satisfactory: *relations in the group were fine.* ■ used to express one's agreement with or acquiescence to something: *anything you want is **fine by me**, Linda | he said such a solution would be fine.* ■ in good health and feeling well: *'I'm fine, just fine. And you?'* ■ (of the weather) bright and clear: *it was another fine winter day.* ■ of imposing and dignified appearance or size: *a very fine Elizabethan mansion.* ■ (of speech or writing) sounding impressive and grand but ultimately insincere: *fine words seemed to produce few practical benefits.* ■ denoting or displaying a state of good, though not excellent, preservation in stamps, books, coins, etc. ■ (of gold or silver) containing a specified high proportion of pure metal: *the coin is struck in .986 fine gold.*
2 (of a thread, filament, or person's hair) thin: *I have always had fine and dry hair.*
■(of a point) sharp: *I sharpened the leads to a fine point.* ■ consisting of small particles: *the soils were all fine silt.* ■ having or requiring an intricate delicacy of touch: *exquisitely fine work.* ■ (of something abstract) subtle and therefore perceived only with difficulty and care: *the fine distinctions between the new and old definitions of refugee.* ■ (of feelings) refined; elevated: *you might appeal to their finer feelings.*
3 Cricket directed or stationed behind the wicket and close to the line of flight of the ball when it is bowled.
▶**noun** (**fines**) very small particles found in mining, milling, etc.
▶**adverb** **1** informal in a satisfactory or pleasing manner; very well: *'And how's the job-hunting going?' 'Oh, fine.'*
2 Cricket behind the wicket and close to the line of flight of the ball when it is bowled.
▶**verb** **1** [with obj.] clarify (beer or wine) by causing the precipitation of sediment during production.
■[no obj.] (of liquid) become clear: *the ale hadn't had quite time to fine down.*
2 make or become thinner: [with obj.] *it can be **fined right down** to the finished shape* | [no obj.] *she'd certainly **fined down**—her face was thinner.*
3 [no obj.] (**fine up**) N. English & Austral./NZ informal (of the weather) become bright and clear.
– PHRASES **cut it** (or **things**) **fine** allow a very small margin of something, especially time: *boys who have cut it rather fine are scuttling into chapel.* **do fine** be entirely satisfactory: *an omelette will do fine.* ■ be healthy or well: *the baby's doing fine.* ■ do something in a satisfactory manner: *he was doing fine acquiring all the necessary disciplines in finance.* **do someone fine** suit or be enough for someone. **fine feathers make fine birds** proverb beautiful clothes or an eye-catching appearance make a person appear similarly beautiful or impressive. **the finer points of** the more complex or detailed aspects of: *he went on to discuss the finer points of his work.* **——'s finest** N. Amer. informal the police of a particular city: *Moscow's finest.* **one's finest hour** the time of one's greatest success. **fine words butter no parsnips** proverb nothing is achieved by empty promises or flattery. **not to put too fine a point on it** to speak bluntly: *not to put too fine a point on it, your Emily is a liar.* [ORIGIN: figuratively, with reference to the sharpening of a weapon, tool, etc.] **one fine day** at some unspecified or unknown time: *you want to be the Chancellor one fine day.*
– DERIVATIVES **finely** adverb, **fineness** noun.
– ORIGIN Middle English: from Old French *fin*, based on Latin *finire* 'to finish' (see **FINISH**).

fine[2] /fʌɪn/ ▶**noun** a sum of money exacted as a penalty by a court of law or other body or person in authority: *a parking fine.*
▶**verb** [with obj.] (often **be fined**) punish (someone), typically for breaking the law, by making them pay a sum of money: *she was **fined** £1500 **for** driving offences.*
– DERIVATIVES **fineable** adjective.
– ORIGIN Middle English: from Old French *fin* 'end, payment', from Latin *finis* 'end' (in medieval Latin denoting a sum paid on settling a lawsuit). The original sense was 'conclusion' (surviving in the phrase **IN FINE**); also used in the medieval Latin sense, the word came to denote a penalty of any kind, later specifically a monetary penalty.

fine[3] /fiːn/ ▶**noun** [mass noun] French brandy of high quality made from distilled wine rather than from pomace.
■short for **FINE CHAMPAGNE**.

fine[4] /ˈfiːneɪ/ ▶**noun** (in musical directions) the place where a piece of music finishes (when this is not at the end of the score but at the end of an earlier section which is repeated at the end of the piece).
– ORIGIN Italian, from Latin *finis* 'end'.

fine art ▶**noun** **1** [mass noun] (also **fine arts**) creative art, especially visual art whose products are to be appreciated primarily or solely for their imaginative, aesthetic, or intellectual content: *the convergence of popular culture and fine art.*
2 an activity requiring great skill or accomplishment: ***the fine art of** drinking tequila.*
– PHRASES **have** (or **get**) **something down to a fine art** achieve a high level of skill, facility, or accomplishment in some activity through experience: *Mike had got the breakfast routine down to a fine art.*

fine champagne /ˌfiːn ʃɒ̃ˈpɑːnj(ə)/ ▶**noun** [mass noun] brandy from the Champagne district of the Cognac region of which half or more of the content comes from the central Grande Champagne.
– ORIGIN French, 'fine (brandy from) Champagne'.

fine chemicals ▶**plural noun** chemical substances prepared to a very high degree of purity for use in research and industry.

fine-draw ▶**verb** [with obj.] sew together (two pieces of cloth or edges of a tear) so that the join is imperceptible: *a table cover composed of cloth fine-drawn together.*

Fine Gael /ˌfiːnə ˈɡeɪl, Irish ˌfʲinʲə ˈɡeːl/ one of the two major political parties of the Republic of Ireland (the other being Fianna Fáil). Founded in

1923 as Cumann na nGaedheal, it changed its name in 1933. It has advocated the concept of a united Ireland achieved by peaceful means.
– ORIGIN Irish, literally 'tribe of Gaels'.

fine-grained ▶ **adjective** (chiefly of wood) having a fine or delicate arrangement of fibres.
■(chiefly of rock) consisting of small particles. ■ involving great attention to detail: *fine-grained analysis.*

fine leg ▶ **noun** Cricket a fielding position behind the batsman on the leg side, between long leg and square leg.
■a fielder at this position.

fine print ▶ **noun** another term for **SMALL PRINT**.

finery[1] /ˈfʌɪn(ə)ri/ ▶ **noun** [mass noun] expensive or ostentatious clothes or decoration: *officers in their blue, gold, and scarlet finery.*
– ORIGIN late 17th cent.: from **FINE**[1], on the pattern of *bravery*.

finery[2] /ˈfʌɪnəri/ ▶ **noun** (pl. **-ies**) historical a hearth where pig iron was converted into wrought iron.
– ORIGIN late 16th cent.: from French *finerie*, from Old French *finer* 'refine'.

fines herbes /fiːnz ˈɛːb/ ▶ **plural noun** mixed herbs used in cooking, especially fresh herbs chopped as a flavouring for omelettes.
– ORIGIN French, literally 'fine herbs'.

fine-spun ▶ **adjective** (especially of fabric) fine or delicate in texture.

finesse ▶ **noun** [mass noun] intricate and refined delicacy: *orchestral playing of great finesse.*
■artful subtlety, typically that needed for tactful handling of a difficulty: *clients want advice and action that calls for considerable finesse.* ■ subtle or delicate manipulation: *a certain amount of finesse is required to fine-tune the heat output.* ■ [count noun] (in bridge and whist) an attempt to win a trick with a card that is not a certain winner, typically by playing it as the third card in a trick in the hope that any card that could beat it is in the hand of the opponent who has already played.
▶ **verb** [with obj.] **1** do (something) in a subtle and delicate manner: *his third shot, which he attempted to finesse, failed by a fraction.*
■slyly attempt to avoid blame or censure when dealing with (a situation or action): *the administration's attempts to finesse its mishaps.*
2 (in bridge and whist) play (a card) in the hope of winning a trick with it because any card that could beat it is in the hand of the opponent who has already played: *the declarer finesses ♦J* | [no obj.] *he knew I would finesse fatally in trumps.*
– ORIGIN late Middle English (in the sense 'purity, delicacy': from French, related to **FINE**[1].

fine structure ▶ **noun** [mass noun] the composition of an object, substance, or energy phenomenon as viewed on a small scale and in considerable detail.
■Physics the presence of groups of closely spaced lines in spectra corresponding to slightly different energy levels.

fine-structure constant ▶ **noun** Physics a fundamental and dimensionless physical constant, equal to approximately $\frac{1}{137}$, which occurs in expressions describing the fine structure of atomic spectra.

fine-tooth comb (also **fine-toothed comb**) ▶ **noun** a comb with narrow teeth that are close together.
■[in sing.] used with reference to a very thorough search or analysis of something: *you should check the small print with a fine-tooth comb.* See also **TOOTHCOMB**.

fine-tune ▶ **verb** [with obj.] make small adjustments to (something) in order to achieve the best or a desired performance: *they can fine-tune the computer programs to focus on a small region of space.*

finfoot ▶ **noun** (pl. **finfoots**) a grebe-like waterbird with a long bill, neck, and tail, and lobed feet.
● Family Heliornithidae: three genera and species, one each in Africa, Asia, and America. See also **SUNGREBE**.

Fingal /ˈfɪŋg(ə)l/ a character in an epic poem by the Scottish poet James Macpherson (1736–96), based on the legendary Irish hero Finn MacCool but fictionally transformed and depicted as fighting both the Norse invaders and the Romans from an invented kingdom in NW Scotland.

Fingal's Cave a cave on the island of Staffa in the Inner Hebrides, noted for the clustered basaltic pillars that form its cliffs. It is said to have been the inspiration of Mendelssohn's overture *The Hebrides* (also known as *Fingal's Cave*).

finger ▶ **noun** each of the four slender jointed parts attached to either hand (or five, if the thumb is included): *she raked her hair back with her fingers.*
■a part of a glove intended to cover a finger. ■ a measure of liquor in a glass, based on the breadth of a finger: *Wickham poured three fingers of vodka into a glass.* ■ an object that has roughly the long, narrow shape of a finger: *a shortbread finger.*
▶ **verb** [with obj.] **1** touch or feel (something) with the fingers: *the thin man fingered his moustache.*
■play (a musical instrument) with the fingers, especially in a tentative or casual manner: *a woman fingered a lute.*
2 informal, chiefly N. Amer. inform on (someone) to the police: *you **fingered** me **for** those burglaries.*
■(**finger someone for**) chiefly N. Amer. identify or choose someone for (a particular purpose): *a research biologist with impeccable credentials was fingered for team leader.*
3 Music play (a passage) with a particular sequence of positions of the fingers. See also **FINGERING**[1].
■mark (music) with signs showing which fingers are to be used.
– PHRASES **be all fingers and thumbs** Brit. informal be clumsy or awkward in one's actions. **get** (or **pull**) **one's finger out** Brit. informal cease prevaricating and start to act. **get one's fingers burned/burnt** (or **burn one's fingers**) (especially in a financial context) suffer unpleasant consequences as a result of one's actions, discouraging one from trying a similar action again. **give someone the finger** N. Amer. informal make a gesture with the middle finger raised as an obscene sign of contempt. **have a finger in every pie** be involved in a large and varied number of activities or enterprises. **have a finger in the pie** be involved in a matter, especially in an annoyingly interfering way. **have** (or **keep**) **one's finger on the pulse** be aware of all the latest news or developments: *he keeps his finger on the pulse of world music.* **lay a finger on someone** touch someone, especially with the intention of harming them. **put the finger on** informal inform against someone to the authorities. **put one's finger on something** identify something exactly: *he cannot put his finger on what has gone wrong.* **snap** (or **click**) **one's fingers** make a sharp clicking sound by bending the last joint of the middle finger against the thumb and suddenly releasing it, typically in order to attract attention in a peremptory way or to accompany the beat of music. **twist** (or **wind** or **wrap**) **someone around one's little finger** see **LITTLE FINGER**. **work one's fingers to the bone** see **BONE**.
– DERIVATIVES **fingered** adjective [in combination] *a two-fingered whistle*, **fingerless** adjective.
– ORIGIN Old English, of Germanic origin; related to Dutch *vinger* and German *Finger*.

finger alphabet ▶ **noun** a form of sign language using the fingers to spell out words.

fingerboard ▶ **noun** a flat or roughly flat strip on the neck of a stringed instrument, against which the strings are pressed to shorten the vibrating length and produce notes of higher pitches.

finger bowl ▶ **noun** a small bowl holding water for rinsing the fingers during or after a meal.

finger chip ▶ **noun** Indian term for **CHIP** (in sense 2).

finger-dry ▶ **verb** [with obj.] dry and style (hair) by repeatedly running one's fingers through it.

fingerfish ▶ **noun** (pl. same or **-fishes**) a small silvery fish with a deep laterally compressed body, occurring in warm inshore and estuarine waters. Also called **MOONFISH**.
● Family Monodactylidae and genus *Monodactylus*: several species, in particular *M. argenteus*.
– ORIGIN late 18th cent.: from the genus name *monodactylus*, literally 'single finger'.

finger food ▶ **noun** [mass noun] food served in such a form and style that it can conveniently be eaten with the fingers.

finger glass ▶ **noun** old-fashioned term for **FINGER BOWL**.

fingering[1] ▶ **noun** [mass noun] a manner or technique of using the fingers, especially to play a musical instrument: *he once studied keyboard fingering* | [count noun] *the tuning makes some chord fingerings awkward.*
■[count noun] an indication of this in a musical score.

fingering[2] ▶ **noun** [mass noun] dated fine wool for hand knitting.
– ORIGIN early 17th cent. (as *fingram*): perhaps from French *fin grain* 'fine grain'. Compare with **GROGRAM** and **GROSGRAIN**.

finger jam (also **finger lock**) ▶ **noun** Climbing a handhold formed by wedging a finger in a crack in the rock.

finger language ▶ **noun** [mass noun] language expressed by means of the finger alphabet.

finger-licking chiefly N. Amer. ▶ **adjective** tasty; delicious: *a finger-licking meal* | [as submodifier] *finger-licking good.*

fingerling ▶ **noun** a salmon parr.
– ORIGIN early 18th cent.: from **FINGER** (with reference to its transverse dusky bars) + **-LING**.

fingermark ▶ **noun** a mark left on a surface by a dirty or greasy finger.
■a mark left on a person's skin by a finger as a result of an act of violence.

fingernail ▶ **noun** the flattish horny part on the upper surface of the tip of each finger.

finger of God (also **finger of fate**) ▶ **noun** Astrology an aspect between three planets where one is quincunx to each of the other two, which are sextile to each other.
– ORIGIN so named because of the resemblance of the aspect to a pointed finger.

finger-paint ▶ **noun** [mass noun] thick paint designed to be applied with the fingers, used especially by young children.
▶ **verb** [no obj.] (especially of children) apply paint with the fingers.

fingerpick ▶ **verb** [with obj.] play (a guitar or similar instrument) using the fingernails or small plectrums worn on the fingertips to pluck the strings: *black southern guitarists were fingerpicking guitars long before white musicians* | [no obj.] *he fingerpicked with facility.*
▶ **noun** a plectrum worn on a fingertip.
– DERIVATIVES **fingerpicker** noun.

fingerplate ▶ **noun** a piece of metal or porcelain fixed to a door above the handle to prevent fingermarks on the surface of the door itself.

fingerpost ▶ **noun** a post at a road junction from which signs project in the direction of the place or route indicated.

fingerprint ▶ **noun** an impression or mark made on a surface by a person's fingertip, especially as used for identifying individuals from the unique pattern of whorls and lines.
■figurative a distinctive identifying characteristic: *the faint chemical fingerprint of plastic explosives.*
▶ **verb** [with obj.] record the fingerprints of (someone): *I was booked, fingerprinted, and locked up for the night.*

fingerstall ▶ **noun** a cover to protect a finger, used in some handicrafts or when a finger is injured.

fingertip ▶ **noun** the tip of a finger.
▶ **adjective** [attrib.] using or operated by the fingers: *police made a fingertip search of the area.*
– PHRASES **at one's fingertips** (especially of information) readily available; accessible: *until we have more facts at our fingertips, there is no use in speculating.* **by one's fingertips** only with difficulty: *the prime minister clung on by his fingertips.* **to one's fingertips** completely: *he is a professional to his fingertips.*

finger wave ▶ **noun** a wave set in wet hair using the fingers.

fingle ▶ **verb** [with obj.] W. Indian handle or finger (something); touch all over.
– ORIGIN blend of obsolete *fangle* 'to trifle' and the verb **FINGER**.

finial /ˈfɪnɪəl, ˈfʌɪn-/ ▶ **noun** a distinctive section or ornament at the apex of a roof, pinnacle, canopy, or similar structure in a building.
■an ornament at the top, end, or corner of an object: *ornate curtain poles with decorative finials.*
– ORIGIN late Middle English: from Old French *fin* or Latin *finis* 'end'.

finical /ˈfɪnɪk(ə)l/ ▶ **adjective** another term for **FINICKY**.
– DERIVATIVES **finicality** noun, **finically** adverb, **finicalness** noun.
– ORIGIN late 16th cent. (probably originally university slang): probably from **FINE**[1] + **-ICAL**, perhaps suggested by Middle Dutch *fijnkens* 'accurately, neatly, prettily'.

finicking ▶ **adjective** another term for **FINICKY**.
– ORIGIN mid 17th cent.: from **FINICAL** + **-ING**[2].

finicky ▶ **adjective** (of a person) fussy about their needs or requirements: *a finicky eater.*
■ showing or requiring great attention to detail; fiddly: *his finicky copperplate hand.*
– DERIVATIVES **finickiness** noun.

fining ▶ **noun** (usu. **finings**) a substance used for clarifying liquid, especially beer or wine.
■ [mass noun] the process of clarifying wine or beer: [as modifier] *a fining agent.*

finis /ˈfiːnɪs, ˈfɪnɪs, ˈfʌɪnɪs/ ▶ **noun** the end (printed at the end of a book or shown at the end of a film).
– ORIGIN late Middle English: from Latin.

finish ▶ **verb** [with obj.] **1** bring (a task or activity) to an end; complete: *they were straining to finish the job* | [with present participle] *we finished eating our meal* | [no obj.] *the musician finished to thunderous applause.*
■ consume or get through the final amount or portion of (something, especially food or drink): *Seagram* ***finished off*** *a margarita as he waited.* ■ [no obj.] (of an activity) come to an end: *the war has finished but nothing has changed.* ■ [no obj.] (**finish with**) have no more need for or nothing more to do with: *'I've finished with Tom,' Gloria said.* ■ reach the end of a race or other sporting competition, typically in a particular position: [with complement] *Falkirk finished fifth in the Scottish Premier League.*
2 (usu. **be finished**) complete the manufacture or decoration of (a material, object, or place) by giving it an attractive surface appearance: *the interior was finished with V-jointed American oak.*
■ complete the fattening of (livestock) before slaughter. ■ dated prepare (a girl) for entry into fashionable society.
▶ **noun 1** [usu. in sing.] an end or final part or stage of something: *a bowl of raspberries was the perfect finish to the meal* | *I really enjoyed the film* ***from start to finish.***
■ a point or place at which a race or competition ends: *he surged into a winning lead 200 metres from the finish.*
2 [mass noun] the manner in which the manufacture of an article is completed in detail: *wide variation in specification and finish.*
■ [count noun] the surface appearance of a manufactured material or object, or the material used to produce this: *lightweight nylon with a shiny finish.* ■ the final taste impression of a wine or beer: *the wine has a lemony tang on the finish.*
– PHRASES **a fight to the finish** a fight, contest, or match which only ends with the complete defeat of one of the parties involved.
– ORIGIN Middle English: from Old French *feniss-*, lengthened stem of *fenir*, from Latin *finire*, from *finis* 'end'.
▶ **finish someone off** kill, destroy, or comprehensively defeat someone.
finish up chiefly Brit. end a period of time or course of action by doing something or being in a particular position: *he finished up as one of Britain's greatest architects.*

finished ▶ **adjective** (of an action, activity, or piece of work) having been completed or ended: *a preparatory drawing for the finished painting.*
■ [predic.] (of a person) having completed or ended an action or activity: *they'll be finished here in an hour.* ■ [predic.] having lost effectiveness, power, or prestige: *he was told he was finished at the club.* ■ (of an object or room) having been given a particular decorative surface as the final stage in its manufacture or decoration: [in combination] *plastic-finished lining paper.* ■ [attrib.] (of livestock) having completed fattening before slaughter: *a reduction in prices for finished cattle.*

finisher ▶ **noun 1** a person or thing that finishes something, in particular:
■ a person who reaches the end of a race or other sporting competition. ■ a worker or machine performing the last operation in a manufacturing process.
2 an animal that has been fattened ready for slaughter: [as modifier] *finisher pigs.*

finishing line (also **finish line**) ▶ **noun** a line marking the end of a race.

finishing school ▶ **noun** a private college where girls are prepared for entry into fashionable society.

finishing touch (also **finishing stroke**) ▶ **noun** (usu. **finishing touches**) a final detail or action completing and enhancing a piece of work: *now they're* ***putting the finishing touches to*** *a new album.*

Finisterre, Cape /ˌfɪnɪˈstɛː/ a promontory of NW Spain, forming the westernmost point of the mainland. The shipping forecast area **Finisterre** covers part of the Atlantic off NW Spain, west of the Bay of Biscay.

finite /ˈfʌɪnʌɪt/ ▶ **adjective 1** having limits or bounds: *every computer has a finite amount of memory.*
■ not infinitely small: *one's chance of winning may be small but it is finite.*
2 Grammar (of a verb form) having a specific tense, number, and person. Contrasted with **NON-FINITE**.
– DERIVATIVES **finitely** adverb, **finiteness** noun.
– ORIGIN late Middle English: from Latin *finitus* 'finished', past participle of *finire* (see **FINISH**).

finite state grammar ▶ **noun** [mass noun] Linguistics a deliberately oversimplified form of generative grammar, which generates sentences by working through word by word in a strictly linear fashion. It was used by Chomsky to illustrate the need for more complex features, such as transformations, to account adequately for real language.

finitism /ˈfʌɪnʌɪtɪz(ə)m/ ▶ **noun** [mass noun] Philosophy & Mathematics rejection of the belief that anything can actually be infinite.
– DERIVATIVES **finitist** noun.

finito /fɪˈniːtəʊ/ ▶ **adjective** [predic.] informal finished: *it's all done—finito.*
– ORIGIN Italian.

finitude /ˈfɪnɪtjuːd/ ▶ **noun** [mass noun] formal the state of having limits or bounds: *one quickly senses the finitude of his patience.*

fink[1] N. Amer. informal ▶ **noun** an unpleasant or contemptible person, in particular:
■ a person who informs on people to the authorities: *he was assumed by some to be the management's fink.* ■ dated a strike-breaker.
▶ **verb** [no obj.] **1** (**fink on**) inform on to the authorities: *there was no shortage of people willing to fink on their neighbours.*
2 (**fink out**) fail to do something promised or expected because of a lack of courage or commitment: *administration officials had finked out.*
■ cease to function: *your immune system begins finking out and you get sick.*
– ORIGIN late 19th cent.: of unknown origin; perhaps from German, literally 'finch', but also a pejorative term. Students started to refer to non-members of fraternities as *finks*, probably by association with the freedom of wild birds as opposed to caged ones. The term was later generalized to denote those not belonging to organizations such as trade unions.

fink[2] ▶ **noun** S. African a weaver bird.
– ORIGIN early 19th cent.: Anglicized form of South African Dutch *vink* 'finch'.

fin keel ▶ **noun** a boat's keel shaped like an inverted dorsal fin.

Finland /ˈfɪnlənd/ a country on the Baltic Sea, between Sweden and Russia; pop. 4,998,500 (1990); official languages, Finnish and Swedish; capital, Helsinki. Finnish name **SUOMI**.

> The northern third of the country lies within the Arctic Circle. Long an area of Swedish–Russian rivalry, Finland was ceded to Russia in 1809, becoming an independent republic after the Russian Revolution. Wars with the USSR were fought in 1939–40. Finland joined the European Union in 1995.

Finland, Gulf of an arm of the Baltic Sea between Finland and Estonia, extending eastwards to St Petersburg in Russia.

Finlandization /ˌfɪnləndʌɪˈzeɪʃ(ə)n/ (also **-isation**) ▶ **noun** [mass noun] historical the process or result of being obliged for economic reasons to favour, or at least not oppose, the interests of the former Soviet Union despite not being politically allied to it.
– DERIVATIVES **Finlandize** (also **-ise**) verb.
– ORIGIN 1960s: translation of German *Finnlandisierung*, referring to the case of Finland after 1944.

Finn ▶ **noun** a native or national of Finland or a person of Finnish descent.
– ORIGIN Old English *Finnas* (plural), originally applied more widely to denote a people of Scandinavia and NE Europe speaking a Finno-Ugric language.

finnan /ˈfɪnən/ (also **finnan haddock**) ▶ **noun** [mass noun] haddock cured with the smoke of green wood, turf, or peat.
– ORIGIN early 18th cent.: alteration of *Findon*, the name of a fishing village near Aberdeen in Scotland, but sometimes confused with the Scottish river and village of *Findhorn*.

finnesko /ˈfɪnəskəʊ/ ▶ **noun** (pl. same) a boot of tanned reindeer skin with the hair on the outside.
– ORIGIN late 19th cent.: from Norwegian *finnsko*, from *Finn* (see **FINN**) + *sko* (see **SHOE**).

Finney /ˈfɪni/, Sir Tom (b.1929), English footballer; full name *Thomas Finney*. He played for Preston North End as a winger and won 76 caps for England between 1946 and 1958.

Finnic ▶ **adjective 1** of, relating to, or denoting a group of Finno-Ugric languages including Finnish and Estonian.
2 of, relating to, or denoting the group of peoples which includes the Finns.

Finnish ▶ **adjective** of or relating to the Finns or their language.
▶ **noun** [mass noun] the language of the Finns, spoken by about 4.6 million people in Finland, and also in parts of Russia and Sweden. It is a Finno-Ugric language related to Estonian, and more distantly to Hungarian, and is noted for its morphological complexity.

Finn MacCool /ˌfɪn məˈkuːl/ (also **Finn Mac Cumhaill**) Irish Mythology the warrior hero of a cycle of legends about a band of warriors defending Ireland. Father of the legendary Irish warrior and bard Ossian, he is supposed to have lived in the 3rd century AD. See also **FINGAL**.

Finno-Ugric /ˌfɪnəʊˈuːgrɪk, -ˈjuːgrɪk/ (also **Finno-Ugrian** /-ˈuːgrɪən, -ˈjuːgrɪən/) ▶ **adjective** of or relating to the major group of Uralic languages, which includes Finnish, Estonian, Hungarian (Magyar), and several north central Asian languages.
▶ **noun** [mass noun] this group of languages.

finny ▶ **adjective** poetic/literary of, relating to, or resembling a fish: *it transfixes its finny prey.*

fino /ˈfiːnəʊ/ ▶ **noun** (pl. **-os**) [mass noun] a light-coloured dry sherry.
■ sherry on which a covering of flor (yeast) is developed during production, used to make commercial fino and manzanilla sherries. Compare with **OLOROSO**.
– ORIGIN Spanish, literally 'fine', based on Latin *finire* 'to finish' (see **FINISH**).

finocchio /fɪˈnɒkɪəʊ/ ▶ **noun** another term for ***Florence fennel*** (see **FENNEL**).
– ORIGIN early 18th cent.: from Italian, from a popular Latin variant of Latin *faeniculum* (see **FENNEL**).

fin ray ▶ **noun** see **RAY**[1] (sense 2).

fin whale ▶ **noun** a large rorqual with a small dorsal fin, a dark grey back, and white underparts. Also called **FINBACK**, ***common rorqual***.
• *Balaenoptera physalus*, family Balaenopteridae.

fiord ▶ **noun** variant spelling of **FJORD**.

fioritura /fɪˌɔːrɪˈt(j)ʊərə/ ▶ **noun** (pl. **fioriture** /fɪˌɔːrɪˈt(j)ʊəri, -reɪ/) Music an embellishment of a melody, especially as improvised by an operatic singer.
– ORIGIN Italian, literally 'flowering', from *fiorire* 'to flower'.

fipple /ˈfɪp(ə)l/ ▶ **noun** the mouthpiece of a recorder or similar wind instrument which is blown endwise, in which a thin channel cut through a block directs a stream of air against a sharp edge. The term has been applied to various parts of this, including the block and the channel.
– ORIGIN early 17th cent.: perhaps related to Icelandic *flipi* 'horse's lip'.

fipple flute ▶ **noun** a flute, such as a recorder, played by blowing endwise.

fir ▶ **noun** (also **fir tree**) an evergreen coniferous tree with upright cones and flat needle-shaped leaves, typically arranged in two rows. Firs are an important source of timber and resins. Compare with **PINE**[1] (in sense 1).
• Genus *Abies*, family Pinaceae: many species.
– DERIVATIVES **firry** adjective.
– ORIGIN late Middle English: probably from Old Norse *fyri-* (recorded in *fyriskógr* 'fir-wood').

fir cone ▶ **noun** chiefly Brit. the dry fruit of a fir tree or other conifer.

fire ▶ **noun** [mass noun] **1** combustion or burning, in which substances combine chemically with oxygen from the air and typically give out bright light, heat, and smoke: *his house was destroyed by fire.*
■ one of the four elements in ancient and medieval philosophy and in astrology (considered essential to the nature of the signs Aries, Leo, and Sagittarius): [as modifier] *a fire sign.* ■ [count noun] a destructive burning of something: *a fire at a hotel.* ■ [count noun] a

collection of fuel, especially coal or wood, burnt in a controlled way to provide heat or a means for cooking: *we had a bath in a tin tub by the fire.* ■ [count noun] Brit. short for **ELECTRIC FIRE** or **GAS FIRE**. ■ [count noun] a burning sensation in the body: *the whisky lit a fire in the back of his throat.* ■ fervent or passionate emotion or enthusiasm: *the fire of their religious conviction.* ■ poetic/literary luminosity; glow: *their soft smiles light the air like a star's fire.*
2 the shooting of projectiles from weapons, especially bullets from guns: *a burst of machine-gun fire.*
■ strong criticism or antagonism: *he directed his fire against policies promoting American capital flight.*
▶ **verb** [with obj.] **1** discharge a gun or other weapon in order to explosively propel (a bullet or projectile): *he fired a shot at the retreating prisoners | they **fired off** a few rounds.*
■ discharge (a gun or other weapon): *another gang fired a pistol through the window of a hostel* | [no obj.] *troops **fired on** crowds.* ■ [no obj.] (of a gun) be discharged. ■ direct (questions or statements, especially unwelcome ones) towards someone in rapid succession: *they **fired** questions **at** me for what seemed like ages.* ■ (**fire something off**) send a message aggressively, especially as one of a series: *he fired off a letter informing her that he regarded the matter with the utmost seriousness.*
2 informal dismiss (an employee) from a job: *having to fire men who've been with me for years | you're fired!*
3 supply (a furnace, engine, boiler, or power station) with fuel.
■ [no obj.] (of an internal-combustion engine, or a cylinder in one) undergo ignition of its fuel when started: *the engine fired and she pushed her foot down on the accelerator.* ■ archaic set fire to: *I fired the straw.*
4 stimulate or excite (the imagination or an emotion): *India fired my imagination.*
■ fill (someone) with enthusiasm: *he was **fired up** for last season's FA Cup final.* ■ [no obj.] (**fire up**) archaic show sudden anger: *If I were to hear anyone speak slightingly of you, I should fire up in a moment.*
5 bake or dry (pottery, bricks, etc.) in a kiln.
– PHRASES **breathe fire** be extremely angry: *I don't want an indignant boyfriend on my doorstep breathing fire.* **catch fire** begin to burn. ■ figurative become interesting or exciting: *the show never caught fire.* **fire and brimstone** the supposed torments of hell: *his father was preaching fire and brimstone sermons.* **fire away** informal used to give someone permission to begin speaking, typically to ask questions: *'I want to clear up some questions which have been puzzling me.' 'Fire away.'* **fire in the** (or **one's**) **belly** a powerful sense of ambition or determination. **firing on all** (**four**) **cylinders** working or functioning at a peak level. **go on fire** Scottish & Irish begin to burn; catch fire. **go through fire** (**and water**) face any peril. **light a fire under someone** N. Amer. stimulate someone to work or act more quickly or enthusiastically. **on fire** in flames; burning. ■ in a state of excitement: *Wright is now **on fire** with confidence.* **set fire to** (or **set something on fire**) cause to burn; ignite. **set the world** (or Brit. **Thames**) **on fire** do something remarkable or sensational: *the film hasn't exactly set the world on fire.* **take fire** start to burn. **under fire** being shot at: *observers sent to look for the men came under heavy fire.* ■ being rigorously criticized: *the president was under fire from all sides.* **where's the fire?** informal used to ask someone why they are in such a hurry or state of excitement.
– DERIVATIVES **fireless** adjective, **firer** noun.
– ORIGIN Old English *fȳr* (noun), *fȳrian* 'supply with material for a fire', of West Germanic origin; related to Dutch *vuur* and German *Feuer*.

fire alarm ▶ **noun** a device making a loud noise that gives warning of a fire.

fire-and-forget ▶ **adjective** [attrib.] (of a missile) able to guide itself to its target once fired.

fire ant ▶ **noun** a tropical American ant that has a painful and sometimes dangerous sting.
● Genus *Solenopsis*, family Formicidae: several species, in particular the South American *S. invicta*, which has become a serious pest in the south-eastern US.

firearm ▶ **noun** a rifle, pistol, or other portable gun.

fireback ▶ **noun 1** the back wall of a fireplace.
■ a metal plate covering such a wall.
2 (also **fireback pheasant**) a SE Asian pheasant, the male of which has mainly grey or blue plumage with a reddish rump.
● Genus *Lophura*, family Phasianidae: three species.

fireball ▶ **noun** a ball of flame or fire: *a crashed petrol tanker exploded in a fireball.*
■ an extremely hot, luminous ball of gas generated by a nuclear explosion. ■ a large bright meteor. ■ historical a ball filled with combustibles or explosives, fired at an enemy or enemy fortifications. ■ figurative a person with a fiery temper or a great deal of energy.

fireballer ▶ **noun** Baseball a pitcher who throws a very good fastball.
– DERIVATIVES **fireballing** adjective.

fire-balloon ▶ **noun** a balloon made buoyant by the heat of a fire burning at its mouth.

fire-bellied toad ▶ **noun** a warty European aquatic toad, the underside of which is vividly marked in red, orange, yellow, black, and white.
● Genus *Bombina*, family Discoglossidae: in particular *B. bombina*.

fire blanket ▶ **noun** a sheet of flexible material, typically woven fibreglass, used to smother a fire in an emergency.

fireblight ▶ **noun** [mass noun] a serious bacterial disease of plants of the rose family, especially fruit trees, giving the leaves a scorched appearance.
● The bacterium is the Gram-nagative *Erwinia amylovora*.

firebomb ▶ **noun** a bomb designed to cause a fire.
▶ **verb** [with obj.] attack or destroy (something) with such a bomb: *two bookshops and a newspaper office have been firebombed.*

firebox ▶ **noun** the chamber of a steam engine or boiler in which the fuel is burnt.

firebrand ▶ **noun 1** a person who is very passionate about a particular cause, typically inciting change and taking radical action: *a political firebrand.*
2 a piece of burning wood.

firebrat ▶ **noun** a fast-moving brownish bristletail that frequents warm places indoors.
● *Thermobia domestica*, family Lepismatidae, order Thysanura.

firebreak ▶ **noun** an obstacle to the spread of fire: *a fire-resistant door designed to be a firebreak* | figurative *a firebreak against the spread of revolution from Russia.*
■ a strip of open space in a forest or other area of dense vegetation.

firebrick ▶ **noun** a brick capable of withstanding intense heat, used especially to line furnaces and fireplaces.

fire brigade ▶ **noun** chiefly Brit. an organized body of people trained and employed to extinguish fires.

firebug ▶ **noun** informal an arsonist.

fire certificate ▶ **noun** a certificate confirming that statutory fire regulations have been complied with in a building.

fireclay ▶ **noun** [mass noun] clay capable of withstanding high temperatures, chiefly used for making firebricks.

fire company ▶ **noun** US term for **FIRE BRIGADE**.

fire control ▶ **noun** [mass noun] **1** the process of targeting and firing heavy weapons.
2 the prevention and monitoring of forest fires and grass fires.
■ the containment and extinguishing of fires in buildings, ships, etc.

fire coral ▶ **noun** a colonial coral-like hydrozoan, the heavy external skeleton of which forms reefs. The polyps bear nematocysts which can inflict painful stings.
● Genus *Millepora*, order Hydroida (or Milleporina), class Hydrozoa.

firecracker ▶ **noun** chiefly N. Amer. a loud, explosive firework; a banger.

firecrest ▶ **noun** a very small warbler related to the goldcrest, having a red and orange crest and occurring mainly in Europe.
● *Regulus ignicapillus*, family Sylviidae.

firedamp ▶ **noun** [mass noun] methane, especially as forming an explosive mixture with air in coal mines.

fire department ▶ **noun** N. Amer. the department of a local or municipal authority in charge of preventing and fighting fires.

firedog ▶ **noun** one of a pair of decorative metal supports for wood burning in a fireplace.

fire door ▶ **noun** a fire-resistant door to prevent the spread of fire.
■ a door to the outside of a building used only as an emergency exit.

firedrake ▶ **noun** Germanic Mythology a dragon.
– ORIGIN Old English *fȳr-draca*, from *fȳr* (see **FIRE**) + *draca* 'dragon', from Latin *draco*.

fire drill ▶ **noun 1** a practice of the emergency procedures to be used in case of fire.
2 a primitive device for kindling fire, consisting of a pointed stick which is twirled in a hole in a flat piece of soft wood.

fire-eater ▶ **noun 1** an entertainer who appears to eat fire.
2 dated a person prone to quarrelling or fighting.

fire engine ▶ **noun** a vehicle carrying firefighters and equipment for fighting large fires.

fire escape ▶ **noun** a staircase or other apparatus used for escaping from a building on fire.

fire extinguisher ▶ **noun** a portable device that discharges a jet of water, foam, gas, or other material to extinguish a fire.

firefight ▶ **noun** Military a battle using guns rather than bombs or other weapons.

firefighter ▶ **noun** a person whose job is to extinguish fires.
– DERIVATIVES **firefighting** noun.

firefinch ▶ **noun** a small African songbird of the waxbill family, the male of which has mainly pink or reddish plumage.
● Genus *Lagonosticta*, family Estrildidae: several species.

firefish ▶ **noun** (pl. same or **-fishes**) **1** a scorpionfish with venomous spines.
● Genera *Pterois* and *Dendrochirus*, family Scorpaenidae.
2 a pink- or red-coloured fish related to the wormfishes.
● Subfamily Ptereleotrinae, family Microdesmidae.

firefly ▶ **noun** (pl. **-flies**) a soft-bodied beetle related to the glow-worm, the winged male and flightless female of which both have luminescent organs. The light is chiefly produced, especially in flashes, as a signal between the sexes.
● Family Lampyridae: many species, especially in the tropics, and including the European *Luciola lusitanica*.

fireguard ▶ **noun 1** a protective screen or grid placed in front of an open fire.
2 N. Amer. a firebreak in a forest.

firehall ▶ **noun** N. Amer. a fire station.

fire hose ▶ **noun** a broad hosepipe used in extinguishing fires.

firehouse ▶ **noun** N. Amer. a fire station.

fire irons ▶ **plural noun** implements for tending a domestic fire, typically tongs, a poker, and a shovel.

fireless cooker ▶ **noun** an insulated container capable of maintaining a temperature at which food can be cooked; a haybox.

firelight ▶ **noun** [mass noun] light from a fire in a fireplace.
– ORIGIN Old English *fȳr-lēoht* (see **FIRE**, **LIGHT**[1]).

firelighter ▶ **noun** Brit. a piece of flammable material used to help start a fire.

fire line ▶ **noun** N. Amer. a firebreak in a forest.

firelock ▶ **noun** historical a musket in which the priming is ignited by sparks.

fireman ▶ **noun** (pl. **-men**) **1** a male firefighter.
2 a person who tends a furnace or the fire of a steam engine or steamship.

firemaster ▶ **noun** Scottish the chief officer of a fire brigade.

Firenze /fiˈrɛntse/ Italian name for **FLORENCE**.

Fire of London the huge and devastating fire which destroyed some 13,000 houses over 400 acres of London between 2 and 6 September 1666, having started in a bakery in Pudding Lane. Also called **GREAT FIRE**.

fire opal ▶ **noun** another term for **GIRASOL** (in sense 1).

fireplace ▶ **noun** a place for a domestic fire, especially a grate or hearth at the base of a chimney.
■ a structure surrounding such a place.

fireplug ▶ **noun** US a hydrant for a fire hose.
■ N. Amer. informal a short, stocky person, especially an athlete.

firepower ▶ **noun** [mass noun] the destructive capacity of guns, missiles, or a military force (used with reference to the number and size of guns available): *the enormous disparity in firepower between the two sides* | figurative *I left three strikers up front to add more firepower.*

fire practice ▶ **noun** Brit. a fire drill.

f

fireproof ▶ **adjective** able to withstand fire or great heat: *a fireproof dish.*
▶ **verb** [with obj.] make (something) fireproof: *nearby museum buildings will be fireproofed.*

fire-raiser ▶ **noun** Brit. an arsonist.
– DERIVATIVES **fire-raising** noun.

fire salamander ▶ **noun** a robust short-tailed nocturnal salamander that has black skin with bright red, orange, and yellow markings, native to upland forests of Europe, NW Africa, and SW Asia.
• *Salamandra salamandra*, family Salamandridae.

fire sale ▶ **noun** a sale of goods remaining after the destruction of commercial premises by fire.
■ a sale of goods or assets at a very low price, typically when the seller is facing bankruptcy.

fire screen ▶ **noun** a fireguard placed in front of an open fire to deflect the direct heat or protect against sparks.
■ an ornamental screen placed in front of a fireplace when the fire is unlit.

fire service ▶ **noun** Brit. an organization in charge of preventing and fighting fires.

fireship ▶ **noun** historical a ship loaded with burning material and explosives and set adrift to ignite and blow up an enemy's ships.

fireside ▶ **noun** the area round a fireplace (used especially with reference to a person's home or family life).

fireside chat ▶ **noun** an informal conversation.

fire starter ▶ **noun** North American term for **FIRELIGHTER**.

fire station ▶ **noun** the headquarters of a fire brigade, where fire engines and other equipment are housed.

fire step ▶ **noun** a step or ledge on which soldiers in a trench stand to fire.

fire stone ▶ **noun** [mass noun] stone that can withstand fire and great heat, used especially for lining furnaces and ovens.

firestorm ▶ **noun** a very intense and destructive fire (typically one caused by bombing) in which strong currents of air are drawn into the blaze from the surrounding area making it burn more fiercely: *firestorms after a nuclear exchange* | figurative *the incident ignited a firestorm of controversy.*

firethorn ▶ **noun** another term for **PYRACANTHA**.

fire trail ▶ **noun** N. Amer. & Austral. a track through forest or bush for use in fighting fires.

fire trap ▶ **noun** a building which would be extremely dangerous if a fire should start due to a lack of precautions such as fire exits.

fire tree ▶ **noun** NZ another term for **POHUTUKAWA**.

fire truck ▶ **noun** US term for **FIRE ENGINE**.

fire-walking ▶ **noun** [mass noun] the practice of walking barefoot over something such as hot stones or wood ashes, often as part of a traditional ceremony.
– DERIVATIVES **fire-walker** noun.

firewall ▶ **noun** a wall or partition designed to inhibit or prevent the spread of fire.
■ Computing a part of a computer system or network which is designed to block unauthorized access while permitting outward communication. ■ another term for **CHINESE WALL**.

fire warden ▶ **noun** N. Amer. a person employed to prevent or extinguish fires, especially in a town, camp, or forest.

fire-watcher ▶ **noun** a person keeping watch for fires, especially forest fires or those caused by bombs.
– DERIVATIVES **fire-watching** noun.

firewater ▶ **noun** [mass noun] informal strong alcoholic liquor.

fireweed ▶ **noun** [mass noun] a plant that springs up on burnt land, especially the rosebay willowherb.

firewood ▶ **noun** [mass noun] wood that is burnt as fuel.

firework ▶ **noun** a device containing gunpowder and other combustible chemicals which causes spectacular effects and explosions when ignited, used typically for display or in celebrations: [as modifier] *a firework display.*
■ (**fireworks**) figurative an outburst of anger or other emotion, or a display of brilliance or energy: *when you put these men together you're bound to get fireworks.*

firing ▶ **noun** [mass noun] the action of setting fire to something: *the deliberate firing of 600 oil wells.*
■ the discharging of a gun or other weapon: *the prolonged firing caused heavy losses* | [count noun] *no missile firings were planned.* ■ the dismissal of an employee from a job: *the recent firing of the head of the department* | [count noun] *a series of firings and resignations.* ■ the baking or drying of pottery or bricks in a kiln.

firing line ▶ **noun** the front line of troops in a battle.
■ (**the firing line**) a position where one is subject to criticism or blame because of one's responsibilities or position: *the referee* ***in the firing line*** *is an experienced official.*

firing party ▶ **noun 1** a group of soldiers detailed to fire the salute at a military funeral.
2 another term for **FIRING SQUAD**.

firing squad ▶ **noun** a group of soldiers detailed to shoot a condemned person.

firing step ▶ **noun** another term for **FIRE STEP**.

firkin /ˈfəːkɪn/ ▶ **noun** chiefly historical a small cask used chiefly for liquids, butter, or fish.
■ a unit of liquid volume equal to half a kilderkin (usually 9 imperial gallons or about 41 litres).
– ORIGIN Middle English *ferdekyn*, probably from the Middle Dutch diminutive of *vierde* 'fourth' (a firkin originally contained a quarter of a barrel).

firm[1] ▶ **adjective 1** having a solid, almost unyielding surface or structure: *the bed should be reasonably firm, but not too hard.*
■ solidly in place and stable: *no building can stand without firm foundations* | figurative *he was unable to establish the shop on a firm financial footing.* ■ having steady but not excessive power or strength: *you need a firm grip on the steering.* ■ (of a person, action, or attitude) showing resolute determination and strength of character: *he didn't like being* ***firm with*** *Lennie, but he had to.*
2 strongly felt and unlikely to change: *he retains a firm belief in the efficacy of prayer.*
■ (of a person) steadfast and constant: *we became firm friends.* ■ decided upon and fixed or definite: *she had no firm plans for the next day.* ■ (of a currency, a commodity, or shares) having a steady value or price which is more likely to rise than fall: *the pound was* ***firm against*** *the dollar.*
▶ **verb** [with obj.] make (something) physically solid or resilient: *how can I* ***firm up*** *a sagging bustline?*
■ fix (a plant) securely in the soil. ■ [no obj.] (of a price) rise slightly to reach a level considered secure: *he believed house prices would firm by the end of the year* | [with complement] *the shares firmed 15p to 620p.* ■ make (an agreement or plan) explicit and definite: *the agreements still have to be* ***firmed up.***
▶ **adverb** in a resolute and determined manner: *the Chancellor has* ***held firm*** *to tough economic policies* | *she will* ***stand firm*** *against the government's proposal.*
– PHRASES **be on firm ground** be sure of one's facts or secure in one's position, especially in a discussion. **a firm hand** strict discipline or control.
– DERIVATIVES **firmly** adverb, **firmness** noun.
– ORIGIN Middle English: from Old French *ferme*, from Latin *firmus*.

firm[2] ▶ **noun** a business concern, especially one involving a partnership of two or more people: *a* ***firm of*** *estate agents.*
■ a group of hospital doctors working as a team, headed by a consultant.
– ORIGIN late 16th cent.: from Spanish and Italian *firma*, from medieval Latin, from Latin *firmare* 'fix, settle' (in late Latin 'confirm by signature'), from *firmus* 'firm'; compare with **FARM**. The word originally denoted one's autograph or signature; later (mid 18th cent.) the name under which the business of a firm was transacted, hence the firm itself (late 18th cent.).

firmament /ˈfəːməm(ə)nt/ ▶ **noun** poetic/literary the heavens or the sky, especially when regarded as a tangible thing.
■ figurative a sphere or world viewed as a collection of people: *one of the great* ***stars in the*** *American golfing* ***firmament.***
– DERIVATIVES **firmamental** adjective.
– ORIGIN Middle English: via Old French from Latin *firmamentum*, from *firmare* 'fix, settle'.

firman /ˈfəːmən, fəːˈmɑːn/ (also **farman**) ▶ **noun** (pl. **-mans**) **1** an oriental sovereign's edict.
2 a grant or permit.
– ORIGIN early 17th cent.: from Persian *firmān*, Sanskrit *pramāṇa* 'right measure, standard, authority'.

firmware ▶ **noun** [mass noun] Computing permanent software programmed into a read-only memory.

firn /fɪən/ ▶ **noun** [mass noun] crystalline or granular snow, especially on the upper part of a glacier, where it has not yet been compressed into ice.
– ORIGIN mid 19th cent.: from German, from Old High German *firni* 'old'; related to Swedish *forn* 'former'.

firni /ˈfɪəni/ ▶ **noun** [mass noun] a sweet Indian dish of milk, nuts, raisins, and vermicelli or rice.
– ORIGIN from Hindi *firnī*, from Persian.

first ▶ **ordinal number 1** coming before all others in time or order; earliest; 1st: *his first wife* | *the first of five daughters* | *many valuable drugs have been recognized first as poisons.*
■ never previously done or occurring: *her first day at school.* ■ coming next after a specified or implied time or occurrence: *I didn't take the first bus.* ■ met with or encountered before any others: *the first house I came to.* ■ before doing something else specified or implied: *Do you mind if I take a shower first?* ■ for the first time: *she first picked up a guitar out of sheer boredom.* ■ firstly; in the first place (used to introduce a first point or reason): *first, it is wrong that the victims should have no remedy.* ■ in preference; rather (used when strongly rejecting a suggestion or possibility): *she longed to go abroad, but not at this man's expense—she'd die first!* ■ with a specified part or person in a leading position: *it plunged nose first into the river.* ■ informal the first occurrence of something notable: *we travelled by air, a first for both of us.* ■ the first in a sequence of a vehicle's gears: *he stuck the car in first and revved.* ■ Baseball first base: *he made it all the way home from first.* ■ chiefly Brit. the first form of a school or college. ■ a first edition of a book.
2 foremost in position, rank, or importance: *the doctor's first duty is to respect this right* | *career women who* ***put*** *work* ***first*** | *football must* ***come first.***
■ [often with infinitive] the most likely, pressing, or suitable: *his first problem is where to live* | *he is the first to admit he was not the best of patients.* ■ the first finisher or position in a race or competition. ■ [in titles] having precedence over all others of a similar kind: *First Lord of the Admiralty.* ■ Music performing the highest or chief of two or more parts for the same instrument or voice: *the first violins.* ■ Brit. a place in the top grade in an examination, especially that for a degree: *chaps with firsts from Oxbridge.* ■ Brit. a person having achieved such a degree. ■ (**the firsts**) the best or main team of a sports club. ■ (**firsts**) goods of the best quality: *factory firsts, seconds, and discontinued styles.*
– PHRASES **at first** at the beginning; in the initial stage or stages: *at first Hugo tried to be patient.* **at first glance** see **GLANCE**[1]. **at first hand** see **FIRST-HAND**. **at first instance** see **INSTANCE**. **at first sight** see **SIGHT**. **(the) first among equals** see **EQUAL**. **first blood** see **BLOOD**. **first come, first served** used to indicate that people will be dealt with strictly in the order in which they arrive or apply: *tickets are available on a first come, first served basis.* **first and foremost** most importantly; more than anything else: *Delhi was first and foremost a barracks town.* **first and last** fundamentally; on the whole: *museums are first and last about curatorship.* **first of all** before doing anything else; at the beginning: *first of all, let me ask you something.* ■ most importantly: *German unity depends first of all on the German people.* **first off** informal, chiefly N. Amer. as a first point; first of all: *first off, I owe you a heck of an apology.* **first past the post** (of a contestant, especially a horse, in a race) winning a race by being the first to reach the finishing line. ■ [attrib.] Brit. denoting an electoral system in which a candidate or party is selected by achievement of a simple majority: *our first-past-the-post electoral system.* **first thing** early in the morning; before anything else: *I have to meet Josh first thing tomorrow.* **first things first** used to assert that important matters should be dealt with before other things. **first up** first of all. ■ Austral./NZ at the first attempt. **from the (very) first** from the beginning or the early stages: *he should have realized it from the first.* **from first to last** from beginning to end; throughout: *it's a fine performance that commands attention from first to last.* **get to first base** see **BASE**[1]. **in the first place** as the first consideration or point: *political reality was not quite that simple—in the first place, divisions existed within the parties.* ■ at the beginning; to begin with (especially in reference to the time when an action was being planned or discussed): *I should have told you in the first place.* **of the first order** (or **magnitude**) used to denote something that is excellent or considerable

of its kind: *it is a media event of the first order.* **of the first water** see **WATER**.
– ORIGIN Old English *fyr(e)st*; of Germanic origin, related to Old Norse *fyrstr* and German *Fürst* 'prince', from an Indo-European root shared by Sanskrit *prathama*, Latin *primus*, and Greek *prōtos*.

First Adar see **ADAR**.

first aid ▶ **noun** [mass noun] help given to a sick or injured person until full medical treatment is available: [as modifier] *a first-aid kit.*
– DERIVATIVES **first aider** noun.

First Boer War see **BOER WARS**.

firstborn ▶ **adjective** (of a person's child) the first to be born: *the firstborn child of the queen.*
▶ **noun** a person's first child: *their firstborn arrived.*

First Cause ▶ **noun** Philosophy a supposed ultimate cause of all events, which does not itself have a cause, identified with God.

first class ▶ **noun** [in sing.] a set of people or things grouped together as the best: *the first class of the orders of chivalry.*
■ [mass noun] the best accommodation in a plane, train, or ship: *a seat in first class.* ■ Brit. the highest division in the results of the examinations for a university degree.
▶ **adjective** & **adverb** of the best quality or in the highest division: [as adj.] *the hotel offers first-class accommodation.*
■ of or relating to the best accommodation in a train, ship, or plane: [as adj.] *a first-class carriage* | [as adv.] *you can travel first class on any train.* ■ of or relating to a class of mail given priority: [as adj.] *first-class mail* | [as adv.] *send it first class.* ■ [as adj.] Brit. of or relating to the highest division in a university examination: *a first-class honours degree.* ■ (of cricket) played between sides of recognized stature and with matches of two innings per side.

First Consul the title held by Napoleon Bonaparte from 1799 to 1804, when he became Emperor of France.

first cost ▶ **noun** another term for **PRIME COST**.

first cousin ▶ **noun** see **COUSIN**.

first-day cover ▶ **noun** an envelope bearing a stamp or set of stamps postmarked on their day of issue.

first-degree ▶ **adjective** [attrib.] **1** Medicine denoting burns that affect only the surface of the skin and cause reddening.
2 Law, chiefly N. Amer. denoting the most serious category of a crime, especially murder.
– PHRASES **first-degree relative** a person's parent, sibling, or child.

first down ▶ **noun** American Football the score achieved by a team who have kept possession of the ball by advancing at least ten yards in a series of four downs.

First Empire the period of the reign of Napoleon I as emperor of the French (1804–15).

first finger ▶ **noun** the finger next to the thumb; the forefinger; the index finger.

first-foot ▶ **verb** [with obj.] be the first person to cross the threshold of the house of (someone) in the New Year, in accordance with a Scottish custom.
▶ **noun** the first person to cross a threshold in the New Year.
– DERIVATIVES **first-footer** noun.

first fruits ▶ **plural noun** the first agricultural produce of a season, especially when given as an offering to God.
■ the initial results of an enterprise or endeavour: *the first fruits of the companies' collaboration.* ■ historical a payment to a superior by the new holder of an office.

first-hand ▶ **adjective** & **adverb** (of information or experience) from the original source or personal experience; direct: [as adj.] *first-hand accounts of activities behind the enemy lines* | [as adv.] *data which is obtained first-hand from customers.*
– PHRASES **at first hand** directly or from personal experience: *scientists observed the process at first hand.*

first intention ▶ **noun** [mass noun] Medicine the healing of a wound by natural contact of the parts involved: *healing* ***by first intention.*** Compare with **SECOND INTENTION**.

First International see **INTERNATIONAL** (sense 2).

first lady ▶ **noun** the wife of the President of the US or other head of state.
■ the leading woman in a particular activity or profession: *the first lady of rock.*

first language ▶ **noun** a person's native language.

first lieutenant ▶ **noun** a naval officer with executive responsibility for a ship or other command.
■ a rank of officer in the US army or air force, above second lieutenant and below captain. ■ informal a second in command.

first light ▶ **noun** the time when light first appears in the morning; dawn: *you are to set off at first light.*

firstling ▶ **noun** (usu. **firstlings**) archaic the first agricultural produce or animal offspring of a season.

firstly ▶ **adverb** used to introduce a first point or reason: *firstly it is wrong and secondly it is extremely difficult to implement.*

first mate ▶ **noun** the officer second in command to the master of a merchant ship.

first name ▶ **noun** a personal name given to someone at birth or baptism and used before a family name.
– PHRASES **on first-name terms** having a friendly and informal relationship: *staff and pupils were on first-name terms.*

first night ▶ **noun** the first public performance of a play or show: [as modifier] *first-night nerves.*

first-nighter ▶ **noun** a person who attends a first night.

first offender ▶ **noun** a person who is convicted of a criminal offence for the first time.

first officer ▶ **noun** the first mate on a merchant ship.
■ the second in command to the captain on an aircraft.

first-order ▶ **adjective** of or relating to the simplest or most fundamental level of organization, experience, or analysis; primary or immediate: *for a teacher, of course, drama must be a first-order experience.*
■ technical having an order of one, especially denoting mathematical equations involving only the first power of the independent variable or only the first derivative of a function.

first person ▶ **noun** see **PERSON** (sense 2).

first position ▶ **noun 1** Ballet a posture in which the feet are placed turned outwards with the heels touching.
■ a position of the arms in which both are held curved in front of the body at waist level, with the palms facing the body.
2 Music the position of the hand on the fingerboard of a stringed instrument furthest from the bridge.

first post ▶ **noun** (in the British armed forces) the first of two bugle calls giving notice of the hour of retiring at night.

first principles ▶ **plural noun** the fundamental concepts or assumptions on which a theory, system, or method is based: *I think we have to start again and go right back to first principles.*

first-rate ▶ **adjective** of the best class or quality; excellent: *first-rate musicians.*
■ in good health or condition; very well: *I think you look first-rate.*

first reading ▶ **noun** the first presentation of a bill to a legislative assembly, to permit its introduction.

first refusal ▶ **noun** [mass noun] the privilege of deciding whether to accept or reject something before it is offered to others: *tenants have a* ***right of first refusal*** *if the landlord proposes to sell the property* | *group employees* ***have first refusal on*** *the tickets.*

First Reich see **REICH**[1].

First Republic the republican regime in France from the abolition of the monarchy in 1792 until Napoleon's accession as emperor in 1804.

first school ▶ **noun** Brit. a school for children from 5 to 9 years old.

first sergeant ▶ **noun** (in the US army) the highest-ranking non-commissioned officer in a company or equivalent unit.

First State informal name for **DELAWARE**[1].

first strike ▶ **noun** an attack with nuclear weapons designed to destroy the enemy's nuclear weapons before use.

First World ▶ **noun** the industrialized capitalist countries of western Europe, North America, Japan, Australia, and New Zealand. Compare with **SECOND WORLD** and **THIRD WORLD**.

First World War a war (1914–18) in which the Central Powers (Germany and Austria-Hungary, joined later by Turkey and Bulgaria) were defeated by an alliance of Britain and its dominions, France, Russia, and others, joined later by Italy and the US.

Political tensions over the rise of the German Empire were the war's principal cause, although it was set off by the assassination of Archduke Franz Ferdinand of Austria by a Bosnian Serb nationalist in Sarajevo, an event used as a pretext by Austria for declaring war on Serbia. Most of the fighting took place on land in Europe and was generally characterized by long periods of bloody stalemate; the balance eventually shifted in the Allies' favour in 1917 when the US joined the war. Total casualties of the war are estimated at 10 million killed. One of the consequences of the war was the collapse of the German, Austro-Hungarian, Russian, and Ottoman empires.

Firth, J. R. (1890–1960), English linguist; full name *John Rupert Firth*. Firth was noted for his contributions to linguistic semantics and prosodic phonology and for his insistence on studying both speech sounds and words in context. He was a major influence on the development of systemic grammar.

firth ▶ **noun** a narrow inlet of the sea; an estuary: [in place names] *the Moray Firth.*
– ORIGIN Middle English (originally Scots), from Old Norse *fjǫrthr* (see **FJORD**).

fir tree ▶ **noun** see **FIR**.

fisc /fɪsk/ ▶ **noun** Roman History the public treasury of Rome or the emperor's privy purse.
■ archaic & N. Amer. a public treasury or exchequer. ■ (also **fisk**) Scottish archaic the public treasury to which estates lapse by escheat.
– ORIGIN late 16th cent.: from French, or from Latin *fiscus* 'rush basket, purse, treasury'.

fiscal /ˈfɪsk(ə)l/ ▶ **adjective** of or relating to government revenue, especially taxes: *monetary and fiscal policy.*
■ chiefly N. Amer. of or relating to financial matters: *the domestic fiscal crisis.* ■ N. Amer. used to denote a financial year: *the budget deficit for fiscal 1996.*
▶ **noun 1** archaic a legal or treasury official in some countries.
■ Scottish archaic short for **PROCURATOR FISCAL**.
2 (also **fiscal shrike**) an African shrike with black-and-white plumage.
• Genus *Lanius*, family Laniidae: several species, in particular the widespread *L. collaris*.
– DERIVATIVES **fiscally** adverb.
– ORIGIN mid 16th cent.: from French, or from Latin *fiscalis*, from *fiscus* 'purse, treasury' (see **FISC**).

fiscal drag ▶ **noun** [mass noun] Economics the deflationary effect of a progressive taxation system on a country's economy. As wages rise, a higher proportion of income is paid in tax.

fiscal year ▶ **noun** North American term for **FINANCIAL YEAR**.

Fischer[1] /ˈfɪʃə/, Bobby (b.1943), American chess player; full name *Robert James Fischer*. He defeated Boris Spassky in 1972 to take the world championship, which he held until 1975.

Fischer[2] /ˈfɪʃə/, Emil Hermann (1852–1919), German organic chemist. He studied the structure of sugars, other carbohydrates, and purines, and synthesized many of them. He also confirmed that peptides and proteins consist of chains of amino acids. Nobel Prize for Chemistry (1902).

Fischer[3] /ˈfɪʃə, German ˈfɪʃɐ/, Hans (1881–1945), German organic chemist. He determined the structure of the porphyrin group of many natural pigments, including the red oxygen-carrying part of haemoglobin, the green chlorophyll pigments found in plants, and the orange bile pigment bilirubin. Nobel Prize for Chemistry (1930).

Fischer-Dieskau /ˌfɪʃəˈdiːskaʊ/, Dietrich (b.1925), German baritone. He is noted for his interpretations of German lieder, in particular Schubert's song cycles.

fish[1] ▶ **noun** (pl. same or **fishes**) a limbless cold-blooded vertebrate animal with gills and fins living wholly in water: *the huge lakes are now devoid of fish.*
■ [mass noun] the flesh of such animals as food. ■ (**the Fish** or **Fishes**) the zodiacal sign or constellation Pisces. ■ used in names of invertebrate animals living wholly in water, e.g. **cuttlefish**, **shellfish**, **jellyfish**. ■ [with adj.] informal a person who is strange in a specified way: *he is generally thought to be a bit of a cold fish.* ■ informal a torpedo.
▶ **verb** [no obj.] catch or try to catch fish, typically by

using a net or hook and line: *he was fishing for bluefish* | *I've told the girls we've gone fishing.*

■[with obj.] catch or try to catch fish in (a particular body of water): *many of the lochs we used to fish are now affected by forestry.* ■ search, typically by groping or feeling for something concealed: *he fished for his registration certificate and held it up to the policeman's torch.* ■ try subtly or deviously to elicit a response or some information from someone: *I was not fishing for compliments.* ■ [with obj.] (**fish something out**) pull or take something out of water or a container or receptacle: *the body of a woman had been fished out of the river.*

− PHRASES **all's fish that comes to the net** proverb you can or should take advantage of anything that comes your way. **a big fish** an important or influential person: *he became a big fish in the world of politics.* **a big fish in a small** (or **little**) **pond** a person seen as important and influential only within the limited scope of a small organization or group. **drink like a fish** drink excessive amounts of alcohol. **a fish out of water** a person in a completely unsuitable environment or situation. **have other** (or **bigger**) **fish to fry** have other (or more important) matters to attend to. **like shooting fish in a barrel** used to convey the extreme ease with which something can or has been accomplished: *picking cultivated berries is like shooting fish in a barrel.* **neither fish nor fowl** (**nor good red herring**) of indefinite character and difficult to identify or classify. **there are plenty more fish in the sea** used to console someone whose romantic relationship has ended by pointing out that there are many other people with whom they may have a successful relationship in the future.

− DERIVATIVES **fishlike** adjective.

− ORIGIN Old English *fisc* (as a noun denoting any animal living exclusively in water), *fiscian* (verb), of Germanic origin; related to Dutch *vis, vissen* and German *Fisch, fischen.*

USAGE The normal plural of **fish** is **fish** (*a shoal of fish; he caught two huge fish*). The older form **fishes** is still used, when referring to different kinds of fish (*freshwater fishes of the British Isles*).

fish² ▶ noun a flat plate of metal, wood, or another material that is fixed on a beam or across a joint in order to give additional strength.

■a long, slightly curved piece of wood that is lashed to a ship's damaged mast or spar as a temporary repair.
▶ verb [with obj.] mend or strengthen (a beam, joint, mast, etc.) with a fish.
■join (rails in a railway track) with a fishplate.

− ORIGIN early 16th cent.: probably from French *fiche,* from *ficher* 'to fix', based on Latin *figere.*

fishbowl ▶ noun a round glass bowl for keeping pet fish in.

fish cake ▶ noun a patty of shredded fish and mashed potato, typically coated in batter or breadcrumbs and fried.

fish eagle ▶ noun an eagle that catches and feeds on fish.
● Genus *Haliaeetus,* family Accipitridae: two or three species, in particular the white-headed **African fish eagle** (*H. vocifer*).

Fisher¹ a shipping forecast area in the North Sea off northern Jutland and the mouth of the Skagerrak.

Fisher², Sir Ronald Aylmer (1890–1962), English statistician and geneticist. Fisher made major contributions to the development of statistics, publishing influential books on statistical theory, the design of experiments, statistical methods for research workers, and the relationship between Mendelian genetics and evolutionary theory.

fisher ▶ noun a large brown marten valued for its fur, found in North American woodland where it frequently preys on porcupines. Also called **PEKAN** in North America.
● *Martes pennanti,* family Mustelidae.

− ORIGIN Old English *fiscere* 'fisherman', of Germanic origin; related to Dutch *visser* and German *Fischer,* also to **FISH¹**.

Fisher, St John (1469–1535), English churchman. In 1504 he became bishop of Rochester and earned the disfavour of Henry VIII by opposing his divorce from Catherine of Aragon. When he refused to accept the king as supreme head of the Church, he was condemned to death. Feast day, 22 June.

fisherfolk ▶ plural noun people who catch fish for a living.

fisherman ▶ noun (pl. **-men**) a person who catches fish for a living or for sport.

fisherman bat ▶ noun another term for **BULLDOG BAT.**

fisherman's bend ▶ noun a knot tied by making a full turn round something (typically the ring of an anchor), a half hitch through the turn, and a half hitch round the standing part of the rope.

fisherman's knot ▶ noun a knot used to join two small ropes by tying an overhand knot in the end of each around the opposite standing part.

fisherman's rib (also **fisherman knit**) ▶ noun [mass noun] a type of thick ribbed knitting.

fisherwoman ▶ noun (pl. **-women**) a woman who catches fish, especially for a living.

fishery ▶ noun (pl. **-ies**) a place where fish are reared for commercial purposes.
■a fishing ground or area where fish are caught. ■ [mass noun] the occupation or industry of catching or rearing fish.

fisheye ▶ noun **1** (also **fisheye lens**) a very wide-angle lens with a field of vision covering up to 180°, the scale being reduced towards the edges.
2 US informal a suspicious or unfriendly look: *Wally gave him the fisheye.*
3 a defect in metal causing a spot to stand out brightly against its surroundings.

fish farm ▶ noun a place where fish are artificially bred or cultivated, e.g. for food, to restock lakes for angling, or to supply aquaria.
− DERIVATIVES **fish farmer** noun, **fish farming** noun.

fish finger ▶ noun Brit. a small oblong piece of flaked or minced fish coated in batter or breadcrumbs and fried or grilled.

fish hawk ▶ noun another term for **OSPREY.**

fish-hook ▶ noun see **HOOK** (sense 1).

fishing ▶ noun [mass noun] the activity of catching fish, either for food or as a sport.
− PHRASES **fishing expedition** a search or investigation undertaken with the hope, though not the stated purpose, of discovering information: *they worried about an FBI fishing expedition.*

fishing cat ▶ noun a small wild cat found in wetland habitats in India and SE Asia, having a light brown coat with dark spots, a ringed tail, and slightly webbed paws.
● *Felis viverrina,* family Felidae.

fishing fly ▶ noun a natural or artificial flying insect used as bait in fishing.

fishing line ▶ noun a long thread of silk or nylon attached to a baited hook, with a sinker or float, and used for catching fish.

fishing pole ▶ noun N. Amer. a fishing rod, especially a simple one with no reel.

fishing rod ▶ noun a long, tapering rod to which a fishing line is attached, typically on a reel.

fish kettle ▶ noun an oval pan for boiling fish.

fish knife ▶ noun a blunt knife with a broad blade for eating or serving fish.

fish ladder ▶ noun a series of pools built like steps to enable fish to ascend a dam or waterfall.

fish louse ▶ noun an aquatic crustacean which is a parasite of fish, typically attached to the skin or gills:
● a free-swimming crustacean with a shield-like carapace and a pair of suckers (class Branchiura: several genera, in particular *Argulus*). ● an elongated crustacean that becomes permanently attached to the host and typically highly modified (class Copepoda: several orders and numerous species).

fishmeal ▶ noun [mass noun] ground dried fish used as fertilizer or animal feed.

fishmonger ▶ noun a person or shop that sells fish for food.

fishnet ▶ noun [mass noun] a fabric with an open mesh resembling a fishing net: [as modifier] *black fishnet stockings.*

fishplate ▶ noun a flat piece of metal used to connect adjacent rails in a railway track.
■a flat piece of metal with ends like a fish's tail, used to position masonry.

fish pond ▶ noun a pond in which live fish are kept.
■N. Amer. an attraction at a fair where contestants use a rod and line to attempt to extract a prize, or a token representing a prize, from a pool or other enclosure.

fish slice ▶ noun Brit. a kitchen utensil with a broad flat blade for lifting fish and fried foods.

fishtail ▶ noun [usu. as modifier] an object which is forked like a fish's tail: *fishtail battlements.*
■an uncontrolled sideways movement of the back of a motor vehicle: *he hit the brake, sending the car into a fishtail that carried him across the street.*
▶ verb [no obj.] [usu. with adverbial of direction] (of a vehicle) make such a movement: *the vehicle fishtailed from one side of the road to the other.*
■[with obj.] cause (a vehicle) to make such a movement.

fishway ▶ noun another term for **FISH LADDER.**

fishwife ▶ noun (pl. **-wives**) **1** a coarse-mannered woman who is prone to shouting.
2 archaic a woman who sells fish.

fishy ▶ adjective (**fishier, fishiest**) **1** of, relating to, or resembling fish or a fish: *a fishy smell.*
2 informal arousing feelings of doubt or suspicion: *I'm convinced there is something fishy going on.*
− DERIVATIVES **fishily** adverb, **fishiness** noun.

fisk ▶ noun Scottish archaic variant spelling of **FISC.**

fissile /ˈfɪsʌɪl/ ▶ adjective (of an atom or element) able to undergo nuclear fission: *a fissile isotope.*
■(chiefly of rock) easily split: *flat-bedded and very highly fissile shale.*
− DERIVATIVES **fissility** /-ˈsɪlɪti/ noun.
− ORIGIN mid 17th cent. (in the sense 'easily split'): from Latin *fissilis,* from *fiss-* 'split, cracked', from the verb *findere.*

fission /ˈfɪʃ(ə)n/ ▶ noun [mass noun] the action of dividing or splitting something into two or more parts: *the party dissolved into fission and acrimony.*
■short for **NUCLEAR FISSION.** ■ Biology reproduction by means of a cell or organism dividing into two or more new cells or organisms: *bacteria divide by transverse binary fission.*
▶ verb [no obj.] (chiefly of atoms) undergo fission: *these heavy nuclei can also fission.*
− ORIGIN early 17th cent.: from Latin *fissio(n-),* from *findere* 'to split'.

fissionable ▶ adjective another term for **FISSILE.**

fission bomb ▶ noun another term for **ATOM BOMB.**

fission-track dating ▶ noun [mass noun] Geology a technique for establishing the age of a mineral sample from its uranium content. It involves microscopically counting tracks produced by uranium fission fragments and then establishing the existing concentration of uranium by counting again after irradiating the sample with neutrons.

fissiparous /fɪˈsɪp(ə)rəs/ ▶ adjective inclined to cause or undergo division into separate parts or groups.
■Biology (of an organism) reproducing by fission: *small fissiparous worms.*
− DERIVATIVES **fissiparity** noun, **fissiparousness** noun.
− ORIGIN mid 19th cent.: from Latin *fissus,* past participle of *findere* 'split', on the pattern of *viviparous.*

fissure /ˈfɪʃə/ ▶ noun a long, narrow opening or line of breakage made by cracking or splitting, especially in rock or earth.
■chiefly Anatomy a long narrow opening in the form of a crack or groove, e.g. any of the spaces separating convolutions of the brain. ■ a state of incompatibility or disagreement: *the fissure between private sector business and the newly expanding public sector.*
▶ verb [with obj.] [usu. as adj. **fissured**] split or crack (something) to form a long narrow opening: *low cliffs of fissured Silurian rock.*
− ORIGIN late Middle English: from Old French, or from Latin *fissura,* from *findere* 'to split'.

fissure of Sylvius /ˈsɪlvɪəs/ ▶ noun another term for **SYLVIAN FISSURE.**

fist ▶ noun a person's hand when the fingers are bent in towards the palm and held there tightly, typically in order to strike a blow or grasp something.
▶ verb **1** [with obj. and adverbial of direction] (of a goalkeeper) strike (a ball or shot) with the fist: *he fisted a goal-bound shot over the bar.*
2 (also **fist-fuck**) [with obj.] vulgar slang penetrate (a person's anus or vagina) with one's fist.
− PHRASES **make a —— fist of** (or **at**) informal do something to the specified degree of success: *they're all solid citizens, all capable of making a good fist of being an MP.*
− DERIVATIVES **fisted** adjective [in combination], **fistful** noun.

– ORIGIN Old English *fȳst*, of West Germanic origin; related to Dutch *vuist* and German *Faust*.

fist fight ▶ noun a fight with the fists.

fist fighting ▶ noun [mass noun] fighting with the fists.

fisticuffs ▶ plural noun fighting with the fists.
– ORIGIN early 17th cent.: probably from obsolete *fisty* 'relating to the fists or to fist fighting' + CUFF².

fistula /ˈfɪstjʊlə/ ▶ noun (pl. **fistulas** or **fistulae** /-liː/) Medicine an abnormal or surgically made passage between a hollow or tubular organ and the body surface, or between two hollow or tubular organs.
– DERIVATIVES **fistular** adjective, **fistulous** adjective.
– ORIGIN late Middle English: from Latin, 'pipe, flute, fistula'. Compare with FESTER.

fit¹ ▶ adjective (**fitter**, **fittest**) **1** [predic.] (of a thing) of a suitable quality, standard, or type to meet the required purpose: *the meat is **fit for** human consumption* | [with infinitive] *is the water clean and fit to drink?*
■ (of a person) having the requisite qualities or skills to undertake something competently: *they say all girls are **fit for** is menial work* | [with infinitive] *the party was fit to govern.* ■ suitable and correct according to accepted social standards: *a fit subject on which to correspond.* ■ [with infinitive] informal (of a person or thing) having reached such an extreme condition as to be on the point of doing the thing specified: *he baited even his close companions until they were fit to kill him.* ■ informal ready: *well, are you fit?*
2 in good health, especially because of regular physical exercise: *my family keep fit by walking* | figurative *the measures would ensure a leaner, fitter company.*
■ Brit. informal sexually attractive; good-looking.
▶ verb (**fitted** (US also **fit**), **fitting**) [with obj.] **1** be of the right shape and size for: *those jeans still fit me* | [no obj.] *the shoes fitted better after being stretched.*
■ (usu. **be fitted for**) try clothing on (someone) in order to make or alter it to the correct size: *she was about to be fitted for her costume.* ■ [no obj., with adverbial of place] be of the right size, shape, or number to occupy a particular position or place: *Fiona says we can all fit in her car.*
2 fix or put (something) into place: *they fitted smoke alarms to their home.*
■ (often **be fitted with**) provide (something) with a particular component or article: *most tools can be fitted with a new handle.* ■ join or cause to join together to form a whole: [no obj.] *it took a while to figure out how the confounded things **fit together*** | [with obj.] *many physicists tried to **fit together** the various pieces of the puzzle.*
3 be in agreement or harmony with; match: *the punishment should fit the crime.*
■ (of an attribute, qualification, or skill) make (someone) suitable to fulfil a particular role or undertake a particular task: *an MSc **fits** the student **for** a professional career.*
▶ noun the particular way in which something, especially a garment or component, fits round or into something: *the dress was a perfect fit* | [mass noun] *the angle of fit.*
■ the particular way in which a thing matches something: *a close fit between teachers' qualifications and their teaching responsibilities.* ■ Statistics the correspondence between observed data and the values expected by theory.
– PHRASES (**as**) **fit as a fiddle** see FIDDLE. **fit the bill** see BILL¹. **fit like a glove** see GLOVE. **fit to be tied** informal very angry: *Daddy was fit to be tied when I separated from Hugh.* **fit to bust** with great energy: *they laughed fit to bust.* **if the cap fits** (**wear it**) see CAP. **see** (or **think**) **fit** consider it correct or acceptable to do something: *why did the company see fit to give you the job?*
– DERIVATIVES **fitly** adverb.
– ORIGIN late Middle English: of unknown origin.
▶ **fit in** (of a person) be socially compatible with other members of a group: *he feels he should become tough to **fit in with** his friends.* ■ (of a thing) be in harmony with other things within a larger structure: *produce ideas that **fit in with** an established approach.* ■ (also **fit into**) (of a person or thing) constitute part of a particular situation or larger structure: *where do your sisters fit in?*
fit someone/thing in (or **into**) find room or have sufficient space for someone or something: *can you fit any more water into the jug?* ■ succeed in finding time in a busy schedule to see someone or do something: *you're never too busy to fit exercise into your life.*
fit someone/thing out (or **up**) provide with the necessary equipment, supplies, clothes, or other items for a particular situation: *the cabin had been fitted out to a high standard.*
fit someone up Brit. informal incriminate someone by falsifying evidence against them.

fit² ▶ noun a sudden uncontrollable outbreak of intense emotion, laughter, hysterics, coughing, or other action or activity: *in **a fit of** temper* | *he got coughing fits.*
■ a sudden attack of convulsions and/or loss of consciousness, typical of epilepsy and some other medical conditions: *he thought she was **having a fit**.*
– PHRASES **give someone a fit** informal greatly shock or anger someone. **have** (or **throw**) **a fit** informal be very surprised or angry. **in fits** (**of laughter**) informal highly amused: *he had us all in fits.* **in** (or **by**) **fits and starts** with irregular bursts of activity: *the machine tends to go forward in fits and starts.*
– ORIGIN Old English *fitt* 'conflict', in Middle English 'position of danger or excitement', also 'short period'; the sense 'sudden attack of illness' dates from the mid 16th cent.

fit³ (also **fytte**) ▶ noun archaic a section of a poem.
– ORIGIN Old English *fitt*, perhaps the same word as FIT², or related to German *Fitze* 'skein of yarn', in the obsolete sense 'thread with which weavers mark off a day's work'.

fitch ▶ noun old-fashioned term for POLECAT.
■ (also **fitch fur**) [mass noun] the fur of a polecat.
– ORIGIN late Middle English (denoting the fur of a polecat): from Middle Dutch *visse* 'polecat'. Compare with FITCHEW.

fitché /ˈfɪtʃeɪ/ (also **fitchy** or **fitched**) ▶ adjective Heraldry (of a cross) having the foot extended into a point.
– ORIGIN late 16th cent.: from French *fiché*, past participle of *ficher* 'to fix'.

fitchew /ˈfɪtʃuː/ ▶ noun archaic term for POLECAT.
– ORIGIN late Middle English: from Old French *ficheau*, *fissel*, diminutive related to Middle Dutch *visse*. Compare with FITCH.

fitful ▶ adjective active or occurring spasmodically or intermittently; not regular or steady: *a few hours' fitful sleep* | *business was fitful.*
– DERIVATIVES **fitfully** adverb, **fitfulness** noun.

fitment ▶ noun (usu. **fitments**) chiefly Brit. a fixed item of furniture or piece of equipment, especially in a house.

fitness ▶ noun [mass noun] the condition of being physically fit and healthy: *disease and lack of fitness are closely related* | [as modifier] *a fitness test.*
■ (**fitness for/to do**) the quality of being suitable to fulfil a particular role or task: *he had a year in which to establish his fitness for the office.* ■ Biology an organism's ability to survive and reproduce in a particular environment: *if sharp teeth increase fitness, then genes causing teeth to be sharp will increase in frequency.*

fit-out ▶ noun an act of providing the necessary equipment for a house or flat, especially the final decoration and fitments.

fitted ▶ adjective **1** made or shaped to fill a space or to cover something closely or exactly: *the blouse has a fitted bodice* | *navy-blue fitted sheets.*
■ chiefly Brit. (of a carpet) cut and laid to cover a floor completely. ■ chiefly Brit. (of furniture) built to be fixed into a particular space: *a fitted wardrobe.* ■ chiefly Brit. (of a room) equipped with matching units of such furniture: *a fitted kitchen.*
2 attached to or provided with a particular component or article: *a piping bag **fitted with** a large star nozzle.*
3 [predic.] (**fitted for/to do**) having the appropriate qualities or skills to do something: *physicists may not be fitted for involvement in industrial processes.*

fitter ▶ noun **1** a person who puts together or installs machinery, engine parts, or other equipment: *a qualified gas fitter* | *kitchen fitters.*
2 a person who supervises the cutting, fitting, or alteration of garments or shoes.

fitting ▶ noun **1** (often **fittings**) a small part on or attached to a piece of furniture or equipment: *the wooden fittings were made of walnut.*
■ (**fittings**) items, such as a cooker or shelves, which are fixed in a building but can be removed when the owner moves: *little remains of the house's Victorian fittings.* Compare with FIXTURE (in sense 1).
2 [mass noun] the action of fitting something, in particular:
■ the installing, assembling, and adjusting of machine parts: *the fitting of new engines by the shipyard.* ■ [count noun] an occasion when one tries on a garment that is being made or altered for one: *she's coming tomorrow for a fitting.*
▶ adjective **1** suitable or appropriate under the circumstances; right or proper: *a fitting reward* | [with clause] ***it was fitting that** his last innings for Middlesex should bring him his highest first-class score.*
2 [in combination] fitted around or to something or someone in a specified way: *loose-fitting trousers.*
– DERIVATIVES **fittingly** adverb, **fittingness** noun.

fitting room ▶ noun a room in a shop in which one can try on clothes before deciding whether to purchase them.

fitting shop ▶ noun a part of a factory where machine parts are put together.

Fittipaldi /ˌfɪtɪˈpaldi/, Emerson (b.1946), Brazilian motor-racing driver. He was the Formula One world champion in 1972 and 1974, and won the Indianapolis 500 in 1989.

fit-up ▶ noun Brit. informal **1** an instance of incriminating someone by falsifying evidence against them.
2 dated a temporary stage or other piece of theatrical equipment: [as modifier] *a fit-up company.*

FitzGerald¹ /fɪtsˈdʒɛr(ə)ld/, Edward (1809–83), English scholar and poet. Notable works: *The Rubáiyát of Omar Khayyám* (translation, 1859).

FitzGerald² /fɪtsˈdʒɛr(ə)ld/, Ella (1917–96), American jazz singer, known for her distinctive style of scat singing.

FitzGerald³ /fɪtsˈdʒɛr(ə)ld/, F. Scott (1896–1940), American novelist; full name *Francis Scott Key FitzGerald*. His novels, in particular *The Great Gatsby* (1925), provide a vivid portrait of the US during the jazz era of the 1920s.

FitzGerald contraction (also **FitzGerald–Lorentz contraction**) ▶ noun Physics the shortening of a moving body in the direction of its motion, especially at speeds close to that of light.
– ORIGIN named after George. F. *Fitzgerald* (1851–1901), Irish physicist, and H. A. LORENTZ, who independently postulated the theory in 1892.

Fiume /ˈfjume/ Italian name for RIJEKA.

five ▶ cardinal number equivalent to the sum of two and three; one more than four, or half of ten; 5: *a circlet of five petals* | *five of Sweden's top financial experts.* (Roman numeral: **v, V.**)
■ a group or unit of five people or things: *the bulbs are planted in threes or fives.* ■ five years old: *Vic moved to Darlington when he was five.* ■ five o'clock: *at half past five.* ■ a size of garment or other merchandise denoted by five. ■ a playing card or domino with five pips.
– ORIGIN Old English *fīf*, of Germanic origin; related to Dutch *vijf* and German *fünf*, from an Indo-European root shared by Latin *quinque* and Greek *pente*.

five-alarm ▶ adjective [attrib.] US informal (of a fire) very large or fierce.
■ (of food, such as chillies) extremely pungent.

five-and-dime (also **five-and-dime store** or **five-and-ten**) ▶ noun N. Amer. a shop selling a wide variety of inexpensive household and personal goods.
■ historical a shop where all the articles were priced at five or ten cents.

five-a-side ▶ noun [mass noun] a form of soccer with five players in each team, typically played on an indoor pitch: [as modifier] *a five-a-side tournament.*

five-corner (also **five-corners**) ▶ noun an Australian shrub that has stiff pointed leaves, tubular flowers, and five-cornered fruit.
● Genus *Styphelia*, family Epacridaceae: several species.
■ the pentagonal fruit of this plant.

five-eighth ▶ noun Rugby, chiefly Austral./NZ a player positioned between the scrum half and the three-quarters.

five finger (also **five fingers**) ▶ noun any of a number of plants with leaves that are divided into five leaflets or with flowers that have five petals, such as cinquefoil.

five-finger discount ▶ noun N. Amer. informal an act of shoplifting.

five-finger exercise ▶ noun an exercise on the piano for all the fingers on both hands.
■ an easy task.

fivefold ▶ adjective five times as great or as numerous: *a fivefold increase in funding.*

■having five parts or elements: *fivefold rotational symmetry.*
▶ **adverb** by five times; to five times the number or amount: *the unemployment rate rose almost fivefold.*

five hundred ▶ **noun** [mass noun] a form of euchre in which making 500 points wins a game.

five Ks ▶ **plural noun** (**the five Ks**) See KHALSA.

Five Nations ▶ **plural noun 1** [treated as sing.] [often as modifier] Brit. an annual international rugby union championship involving England, France, Ireland, Scotland, and Wales.
2 N. Amer. historical the Iroquois confederacy as originally formed, including the Mohawk, Oneida, Seneca, Onondaga, and Cayuga peoples. Compare with SIX NATIONS.

five o'clock shadow ▶ **noun** a dark appearance on a man's chin and face caused by the slight growth of beard that has occurred since he shaved in the morning.

Five Pillars of Islam the five duties expected of every Muslim – profession of the faith in a prescribed form, observance of ritual prayer, giving alms to the poor, fasting during the month of Ramadan, and performing a pilgrimage to Mecca.

fiver ▶ **noun** Brit. informal a five-pound note.
■N. Amer. a five-dollar bill.

fives ▶ **plural noun** [treated as sing.] a game, played especially in the UK, in which a ball is hit with a gloved hand or a bat against the walls of a court with three walls (**Eton fives**) or four walls (**Rugby fives**).
– ORIGIN mid 17th cent.: plural of FIVE used as a singular noun; the significance is unknown.

five senses ▶ **plural noun** (**the five senses**) the faculties of sight, smell, hearing, taste, and touch.

five-spice (also **five-spice powder**) ▶ **noun** [mass noun] a blend of five powdered spices, typically fennel seeds, cinnamon, cloves, star anise, and peppercorns, used in Chinese cuisine.

five-star ▶ **adjective** (especially of accommodation or service) of the highest class or quality: *a luxury five-star hotel.* [ORIGIN: early 20th cent.: from a system used to grade hotels, the highest grade being indicated by five asterisks or stars.]
■having or denoting the highest military rank, distinguished in the US armed forces by five stars on the uniform: *a five-star general.*

fivestones ▶ **noun** Brit. a game of jacks played with five pieces of metal or stone and usually no ball.

fix ▶ **verb** [with obj.] **1** [with obj. and adverbial of place] fasten (something) securely in a particular place or position: *they had candles fixed to their helmets | fix the clamp on a rail.*
■figurative lodge or implant (an idea, image, or memory) firmly in a person's mind: *he turned back to fix the scene in his mind.*
2 (**fix something on/upon**) direct one's eyes, mind, or attention steadily or unwaveringly toward: *I fixed my attention on the tower.*
■[no obj.] (**fix on/upon**) (of a person's eyes, attention, or mind) be directed steadily or unwaveringly toward: *her gaze fixed on Jess.* ■attract and hold (a person's attention or gaze): *the men's taut relationship fixes your attention.* ■(**fix someone with**) look at someone unwaveringly: *she fixed her nephew with an unwavering stare.*
3 mend; repair: *you've forgotten to fix that shelf.*
■(**fix something up**) do the necessary work to improve or adapt something: *we were trying to fix up the house so that it became vaguely comfortable.* ■make arrangements for (something); organize: *he's sent her on ahead to fix things up* | [no obj.] *I've fixed for you to see him on Thursday.* ■informal restore order or tidiness to (something, especially one's hair, clothes, or make-up): *Laura was fixing her hair.* ■informal prepare or arrange for the provision of (food or drink): [with two objs] *they were fixing him breakfast | Ruth fixed herself a cold drink.* ■(**fix someone up**) informal arrange for someone to have something; provide someone with something: *I'll fix you up with a room.* ■(**fix someone up**) informal arrange for someone to meet or go out with someone in order to help them establish a romantic relationship. ■(**be fixing to do something**) N. Amer. informal be intending or planning to do something: *you're fixing to get into trouble.*
4 decide or settle on (a specific price, date, course of action, etc.): *no date has yet been fixed for a hearing | the rent will be fixed at £300 a month* | [no obj.] *the government has fixed on a policy.*
■discover the exact location of (something) by using radar or visual bearings or astronomical observation:

he fixed his position. ■ settle the form of (a language). ■ assign or determine (a person's liability or responsibility) for legal purposes: *there are no facts which fix the defendant with liability.*
5 make (something) permanent or static in nature: *the rate of interest is fixed for the life of the loan.*
■make (a dye, photographic image, or drawing) permanent. ■ Biology preserve or stabilize (a specimen) with a chemical substance prior to microscopy or other examination: *specimens were fixed in buffered formalin.* ■(of a plant or micro-organism) assimilate (nitrogen or carbon dioxide) by forming a non-gaseous compound: *lupins fix gaseous nitrogen in their root nodules.*
6 informal influence the outcome of (something, especially a race, match, or election) by illegal or underhand means: *the club attempted to fix last Thursday's league match.*
■put (an enemy or rival) out of action, especially by killing them: *don't you tell nobody, or I'll fix you good!*
7 informal [no obj.] take an injection of a narcotic drug.
8 castrate or spay (an animal).
▶ **noun 1** [in sing.] informal a difficult or awkward situation from which it is hard to extricate oneself; a predicament: *how on earth did you get into such a fix?*
2 informal a dose of a narcotic drug to which one is addicted: *he hadn't had his fix.*
■figurative a thing or activity that gives a person a feeling of euphoria or pleasure and that it is difficult to do without: *that rush of adrenalin which is the fix of the professional newsman.*
3 informal a solution to a problem, especially one that is hastily devised or makeshift: *representatives trying to find cheap fixes to meet their obligations.* See also QUICK FIX.
4 a position determined by visual or radio bearings or astronomical observations.
5 [in sing.] informal a dishonest or underhand arrangement: *obviously, his appointment was a fix.*
– PHRASES **get a fix on** determine the position of (something) by visual or radio bearings or astronomical observation. ■ informal assess or determine the nature or facts of: obtain a clear understanding of: *it is hard to get a fix on their ages.*
– DERIVATIVES **fixable** adjective.
– ORIGIN late Middle English: partly from Old French *fix* 'fixed', partly from medieval Latin *fixare* 'to fix', both from Latin *fixus*, past participle of *figere* 'fix, fasten'. The noun dates from the early 19th cent.

fixate /fɪkˈseɪt/ ▶ **verb** [with obj.] **1** (usu. **be fixated on/upon**) cause (someone) to acquire an obsessive attachment to someone or something: *she has for some time been fixated on photography.*
■[no obj.] (**fixate on/upon**) acquire such an obsessive attachment to: *it is important not to fixate on animosity.* ■(in Freudian theory) arrest (a person or their libidinal energy) at an immature stage, causing an obsessive attachment.
2 technical direct one's eyes towards: *subjects fixated a central point* | [no obj.] *there is tendency to fixate near the beginning of the line of print.*
– ORIGIN late 19th cent.: from Latin *fixus*, past participle of *figere* (see FIX) + -ATE[3].

fixation ▶ **noun** [mass noun] **1** an obsessive interest in or feeling about someone or something: *his fixation on the details of other people's erotic lives* | *our fixation with diet and fitness.*
■Psychoanalysis the arresting of part of the libido at an immature stage, causing an obsessive attachment: *fixation at the oral phase might result in dependence on others* | [count noun] *such mothers may have created an oral-maternal fixation in their children.*
2 the action of making something firm or stable: *sand-dune fixation.*
■the process by which some plants and micro-organisms combine chemically with gaseous nitrogen or carbon dioxide to form non-gaseous compounds: *his work on nitrogen fixation in plants.* ■Biology the process of preserving or stabilizing (a specimen) with a chemical substance prior to microscopy or other examination: *biopsy specimens were placed in cassettes before fixation in formalin.*
3 technical the action of concentrating the eyes directly on something: *the dissociation between fixation and recall* | [count noun] *experimenters recorded the driver's visual fixations.*
– ORIGIN late Middle English (originally as an alchemical term denoting the process of reducing a volatile spirit or essence to a permanent bodily form): from medieval Latin *fixatio(n-)*, from *fixare* (see FIX).

fixative /ˈfɪksətɪv/ ▶ **noun 1** a chemical substance

used to preserve or stabilize biological material prior to microscopy or other examination: *an alcoholic fixative* | [mass noun] *ten double drops of fixative.*
■a substance used to stabilize the volatile components of perfume. ■a liquid sprayed on to a pastel or charcoal drawing to fix colours or prevent smudging.
2 a substance used to keep things in position or stick them together: *the swift glues these thin twigs to a wall using its own saliva as a fixative.*
▶ **adjective** (of a substance) used to fix or stabilize something.

fixed ▶ **adjective 1** fastened securely in position: *a fixed iron ladder down the port side.*
■(especially of a price, rate, or time) predetermined and not subject to or able to be changed: *loans are provided for fixed period.* ■(of a person's expression) held for a long time without changing, especially to conceal other feelings: *a fixed smile.* ■(of a view or idea) held inflexibly: *the fixed assumptions of the cold war.*
2 [predic.] (**fixed for**) informal situated with regard to: *how's the club fixed for money now?*
– DERIVATIVES **fixedly** adverb, **fixedness** noun.

fixed assets ▶ **plural noun** assets which are purchased for long-term use and are not likely to be converted quickly into cash, such as land, buildings, and equipment. Compare with CURRENT ASSETS.

fixed capital ▶ **noun** [mass noun] capital invested in fixed assets.

fixed charge ▶ **noun** a liability to a creditor which relates to specific assets of a company. Compare with FLOATING CHARGE.

fixed costs ▶ **plural noun** business costs, such as rent, that are constant whatever the amount of goods produced.

fixed-doh (also **fixed-do**) ▶ **adjective** [attrib.] denoting a system of solmization in which C is called 'doh', D is called 'ray', etc., irrespective of the key in which they occur. Compare with MOVABLE-DOH.

fixed focus ▶ **noun** a camera focus that cannot be adjusted, typically used with a small-aperture lens having a large depth of field.

fixed idea ▶ **noun** another term for IDÉE FIXE.

fixed income ▶ **noun** an income from a pension or investment that is set at a particular figure and does not vary like a dividend or rise with the rate of inflation.

fixed odds ▶ **plural noun** odds in betting (especially on soccer results) that are predetermined, as opposed to a pool system or a starting price.

fixed oil ▶ **noun** a non-volatile oil of animal or plant origin.

fixed point ▶ **noun 1** Physics a well-defined reproducible temperature which can be used as a reference point, e.g. one defined by a change of phase.
2 [as modifier] Computing denoting a mode of representing a number by a single sequence of digits whose values depend on their location relative to a predetermined radix point. Often contrasted with FLOATING-POINT.

fixed star ▶ **noun** see STAR (sense 1).

fixed-wing ▶ **adjective** [attrib.] denoting aircraft of the conventional type as opposed to those with rotating wings, such as helicopters.

fixer ▶ **noun 1** a person who makes arrangements for other people, especially of an illicit or devious kind.
2 [mass noun] a substance used for fixing a photographic image.

fixer-upper ▶ **noun** N. Amer. informal a house in need of repairs (used chiefly in connection with the purchase of such a house).

fixing ▶ **noun 1** [mass noun] the action of fixing something: *artificial price fixing.*
2 (**fixings**) Brit. screws, bolts, or other items used to fix or assemble building material, furniture, or equipment.
■N. Amer. the ingredients necessary to make a dish or meal: *have all the fixings ready before starting.* ■N. Amer. apparatus or equipment for a particular purpose: *picnic fixings.*

fixit ▶ **noun** [usu. as modifier] informal, chiefly N. Amer. an act of repairing or putting something right: *Francis was working as a fixit man.*

▪a person known for repairing things or putting things in order: *he pictured himself as a Mr Fixit.*
– ORIGIN early 20th cent.: from *Little Miss Fixit*, the title of a musical show.

fixity ▶**noun** [mass noun] the state of being unchanging or permanent: *the fixity of his stare.*
– ORIGIN mid 17th cent. (denoting the property of a substance of not evaporating or losing weight when heated): partly from obsolete *fix* 'fixed', partly from French *fixité*.

fixture /ˈfɪkstʃə, -tjə/ ▶**noun 1** a piece of equipment or furniture which is fixed in position in a building or vehicle: *she saw his eyes go to the coat fixture.*
▪(**fixtures**) articles attached to a house or land and considered legally part of it so that they normally remain in place when an owner moves: *the hotel retains many original* ***fixtures and fittings****.* Compare with **FITTING** (in sense 1). ▪ informal a person or thing that is established in a particular place or situation: *the midfielder is set to become* ***a permanent fixture in*** *the England line-up.*
2 Brit. a sporting event, especially a match or race, which takes place on a particular date: *there is no under-21 fixture against the English this season.*
– ORIGIN late 16th cent. (in the sense 'fixing, becoming fixed'): alteration (first found in Shakespeare) of obsolete *fixure* (from late Latin *fixura*, from Latin *figere* 'to fix'), with *t* inserted on the pattern of *mixture*.

fizgig /ˈfɪzgɪg/ ▶**noun 1** Austral. informal a police informer.
2 archaic a silly or flirtatious young woman.
– ORIGIN early 16th cent.: probably from **FIZZ** + obsolete *gig* 'flighty girl'. Compare with **GIG**[1] and **WHIRLIGIG**.

fizz ▶**verb** [no obj.] (of a liquid) produce bubbles of gas and make a hissing sound: *the mixture fizzed like mad.*
▪make a buzzing or crackling sound: *lightning starts to crackle and fizz.* ▪ [with adverbial] figurative move with or display excitement, exuberance, or liveliness: *anticipation began to fizz through his veins.*
▶**noun** [mass noun] effervescence: *the champagne had lost its fizz.*
▪informal an effervescent drink, especially sparkling wine: *a glass of your favourite fizz.* ▪ figurative exuberance; liveliness: *she saw I had lost some of my fizz.* ▪a buzzing or crackling sound: *the fizz of 300 sparklers.*
– ORIGIN mid 17th cent.: imitative.

fizzer ▶**noun** informal **1** Brit. an outstandingly lively, energetic, or excellent thing: *that fizzer of a letter.*
2 Austral./NZ a failure or fiasco: *the party was a fizzer.*

fizzle ▶**verb** [no obj.] make a feeble hissing or spluttering sound: *the strobe lights fizzled and flickered.*
▪end or fail in a weak or disappointing way: *their threatened revolt* ***fizzled out*** *at yesterday's meeting.*
▶**noun** a feeble hissing or spluttering sound: *the electric fizzle of the waves.*
▪a failure: *in the end the fireworks were a fizzle.*
– ORIGIN late Middle English (in the sense 'break wind quietly'): probably imitative (compare with **FIZZ**), but perhaps related to Middle English *fist* (see **FEISTY**). Current senses date from the 19th cent.

fizzog ▶**noun** variant spelling of **PHIZ**.

fizzy ▶**adjective** (**fizzier**, **fizziest**) (of a drink) containing bubbles of gas; effervescent: *fizzy mineral water.*
– DERIVATIVES **fizzily** adverb, **fizziness** noun.

fjord /fjɔːd/ (also **fiord**) ▶**noun** a long, narrow, deep inlet of the sea between high cliffs, as in Norway, typically formed by submergence of a glaciated valley.
– ORIGIN late 17th cent.: Norwegian, from Old Norse *fjǫrthr*. Compare with **FIRTH**.

FL ▶**abbreviation for** ▪ Florida (in official postal use). ▪ Liechtenstein (international vehicle registration). [ORIGIN: from German *Fürstentum Liechtenstein* 'Principality of Liechtenstein'.]

fl. ▶**abbreviation for** ▪ floor. ▪ floruit. ▪ fluid.

Fla ▶**abbreviation for** Florida.

flab ▶**noun** [mass noun] informal soft loose flesh on a person's body; fat.
– ORIGIN 1950s: back-formation from **FLABBY**.

flabbergast /ˈflabəgɑːst/ ▶**verb** [with obj.] [usu. as adj. **flabbergasted**] informal surprise (someone) greatly; astonish: *this news has left me totally flabbergasted.*
– ORIGIN late 18th cent.: of unknown origin.

flabby ▶**adjective** (**flabbier**, **flabbiest**) (of a part of a person's body) soft, loose, and fleshy: *this exercise helps to flatten a flabby stomach.*
▪(of a person) having soft loose flesh. ▪ figurative not tightly controlled, powerful, or effective: *the quartet playing was uncommitted and flabby.* ▪ figurative (of a business) poorly managed and inefficient: *tough private bosses take over flabby state-run factories.*
– DERIVATIVES **flabbily** adverb, **flabbiness** noun.
– ORIGIN late 17th cent.: alteration of earlier *flappy*.

flaccid /ˈflasɪd, ˈflaksɪd/ ▶**adjective** (of part of the body) soft and hanging loosely or limply, especially so as to look or feel unpleasant: *she took his flaccid hand in hers.*
▪(of plant tissue) drooping or inelastic through lack of water. ▪ figurative lacking force or effectiveness: *the flaccid leadership campaign was causing concern.*
– DERIVATIVES **flaccidity** /flək'sɪdɪti, flə'sɪd-/ noun, **flaccidly** adverb.
– ORIGIN early 17th cent.: from French *flaccide* or Latin *flaccidus*, from *flaccus* 'flabby'.

flack[1] N. Amer. informal ▶**noun** a publicity agent.
▶**verb** [with obj.] publicize or promote (something or someone): *a crass ambulance-chaser who* ***flacks himself*** *in TV ads* | [no obj.] *the local news media shamelessly* ***flack for*** *the organizing committee.*
– DERIVATIVES **flackery** noun.
– ORIGIN 1940s: of unknown origin.

flack[2] ▶**noun** variant spelling of **FLAK**.

flacon /flakɔ̃/ ▶**noun** (pl. pronounced same) a small stoppered bottle, especially one for perfume.
– ORIGIN early 19th cent.: French, 'flask'.

flag[1] ▶**noun 1** a piece of cloth or similar material, typically oblong or square, attachable by one edge to a pole or rope and used as the symbol or emblem of a country or institution or as a decoration during public festivities: *the American flag.*
▪used in reference to the country to which a person has allegiance: *Black had to be made to serve as an example for every soldier under the flag.* ▪ a small piece of cloth attached at one edge to a pole and used as a marker or signal in various sports: *the flag's up.* ▪ a small paper badge given to people who donate to a charity appeal in the street. ▪ the ensign carried by a flagship as an emblem of an admiral's rank: *Hawke first hoisted his flag at Spithead.*
2 a device, symbol, or drawing typically resembling a flag, used as a marker: *golf courses are indicated by a numbered flag on the map.*
▪a mechanism that is raised to indicate that a taxi is for hire. ▪ Computing a variable used to indicate a particular property of the data in a record.
▶**verb** (**flagged**, **flagging**) [with obj.] **1** (often **be flagged**) mark (an item) for attention or treatment in a specified way: *'greatfully' would be flagged as a misspelling of 'gratefully'.*
▪figurative draw attention to: *problems often flag the need for organizational change.*
2 [with obj. and adverbial] direct (someone) to go in the specified direction by waving a flag or using hand signals: *have him flagged off the course.*
▪(**flag someone/thing down**) signal to a vehicle or driver to stop, especially by waving one's arm. ▪ (**flag someone/thing off**) wave a flag at someone or something as a starting signal: *the vintage car fiesta will be flagged off by the minister for tourism.* ▪ [no obj.] (of an official) raise a flag to draw the referee's attention to a breach of the rules in soccer, rugby, and other sports: *the goalkeeper brought down Hendrie and a linesman immediately flagged.*
3 [usu. as noun **flagging**] provide with a flag or flags: *local reports from Bavaria mentioned very sparse flagging on Hitler's birthday.*
▪register (a vessel) in a specific country, under whose flag it then sails: *the* ***flagging out*** *of much of the fleet to flags of convenience.*
– PHRASES **fly the flag** (of a ship) be registered in a particular country and sail under its flag. ▪ (also **show** or **carry** or **wave the flag**) represent or demonstrate support for one's country, political party, or organization, especially when one is abroad: *he will* ***fly the flag for*** *North Wales golf in Europe next month.* **keep the flag flying** represent one's country or organization, especially when abroad: *British products are keeping the flag flying for the home country.* **put the flags** (or **flag**) **out** celebrate: *temperatures are increasing again—that's why we're putting out the flags.* **show the flag** (of a naval vessel) make an official visit to a foreign port, especially as a show of strength. **wrap oneself in the flag** chiefly N. Amer. make an excessive show of one's patriotism, especially for political ends.
– DERIVATIVES **flagger** noun.
– ORIGIN mid 16th cent.: perhaps from obsolete *flag* 'drooping', of unknown ultimate origin.

flag[2] ▶**noun** a flat stone slab, typically rectangular or square, used for paving.
– DERIVATIVES **flagged** adjective [often in combination] *stone-flagged steps.*
– ORIGIN late Middle English (also in the sense 'turf, sod'): probably of Scandinavian origin and related to Icelandic *flag* 'spot from which a sod has been cut' and Old Norse *flaga* 'slab of stone'.

flag[3] ▶**noun** a plant with sword-shaped leaves that grow from a rhizome:
• a plant of the iris family (genus *Iris*, family Iridaceae). See **YELLOW FLAG** (sense 2). • see **SWEET FLAG**.
▪the long slender leaf of such a plant.
– ORIGIN late Middle English: related to Middle Dutch *flag* and Danish *flæg*; of unknown ultimate origin.

flag[4] ▶**verb** (**flagged**, **flagging**) [no obj.] (of a person) become tired, weaker, or less enthusiastic: *if you begin to flag, there is an excellent cafe to revive you.*
▪[often as adj. **flagging**] (especially of an activity or quality) become weaker or less dynamic: *she should make another similar film to revive her flagging career.*
– ORIGIN mid 16th cent. (in the sense 'flap about loosely, hang down'): related to obsolete *flag* 'hanging down'.

flag boat ▶**noun** a boat serving as a mark in sailing matches.

flag captain ▶**noun** the captain of a flagship.

Flag Day ▶**noun** (in the US) 14 June, the anniversary of the adoption of the Stars and Stripes in 1777.

flag day ▶**noun** Brit. a day on which money is collected for a charity in the street and donors are given small paper badges to show they have contributed.

flagellant /ˈfladʒ(ə)l(ə)nt, flə'dʒɛl(ə)nt/ ▶**noun** a person who subjects themselves or others to flogging, either as a religious discipline or for sexual gratification.
– ORIGIN late 16th cent.: from Latin *flagellant-* 'whipping', from the verb *flagellare*, from *flagellum* 'whip' (see **FLAGELLUM**).

flagellate[1] /ˈfladʒ(ə)leɪt/ ▶**verb** [with obj.] flog (someone), either as a religious discipline or for sexual gratification: *he* ***flagellated himself*** *with branches.*
– DERIVATIVES **flagellation** noun, **flagellator** noun, **flagellatory** /-lət(ə)ri/ adjective.
– ORIGIN early 17th cent.: from Latin *flagellat-* 'whipped', from *flagellare*.

flagellate[2] /ˈfladʒ(ə)lət, -eɪt/ Zoology ▶**noun** a protozoan that has one or more flagella used for swimming.
• Several phyla in the kingdom Protista (formerly subphylum Mastigophora, phylum Protozoa), including forms such as euglena that are sometimes regarded as algae.
▶**adjective** (of a cell or single-celled organism) bearing one or more flagella: *motile flagellate cells.*
– ORIGIN mid 19th cent.: from **FLAGELLUM** + **-ATE**[2].

flagellum /flə'dʒɛləm/ ▶**noun** (pl. **flagella**) Biology a slender thread-like structure, especially a microscopic whip-like appendage which enables many protozoa, bacteria, spermatozoa, etc. to swim.
– DERIVATIVES **flagellar** adjective.
– ORIGIN early 19th cent. (denoting a whip or scourge): from Latin, diminutive of *flagrum* 'scourge'.

flageolet[1] /ˌfladʒə'lɛt, ˈfladʒəlɪt, ˈfla(d)ʒəleɪ/ (also **French flageolet**) ▶**noun** a very small flute-like instrument resembling a recorder but with four finger holes on top and two thumb holes below.
▪another term for **TIN WHISTLE**.
– ORIGIN mid 17th cent.: from French, diminutive of Old French *flageol*, from Provençal *flaujol*, of unknown origin.

flageolet[2] /ˈfla(d)ʒəleɪ, ˌfladʒə'lɛt/ ▶**noun** a French kidney bean of a small variety used in cooking.
– ORIGIN late 19th cent.: from French, based on Latin *phaseolus* 'bean'.

flagfish ▶**noun** (pl. same or **-fishes**) any of a number of small fish with prominent or boldly marked fins, in particular:
• a colourful freshwater fish with spots and iridescent scales, native to Florida (*Jordanella floridae*, family Cyprinodontidae).
• a marine fish with a dark-barred tail, of shallow Indo-Pacific waters (*Kuhlia taeniurus*, family Kuhliidae).

flag-flying ▶ **noun** [mass noun] the action of making a public display to promote the interests of one's country, or of another organization or group.

flagitious /flə'dʒɪʃəs/ ▶ **adjective** (of a person or their actions) criminal; villainous.
– DERIVATIVES **flagitiously** adverb, **flagitiousness** noun.
– ORIGIN late Middle English: from Latin *flagitiosus*, from *flagitium* 'importunity, shameful crime', from *flagitare* 'demand earnestly'.

flag lieutenant ▶ **noun** a lieutenant acting as an admiral's aide-de-camp.

flagman ▶ **noun** (pl. **-men**) a person who gives signals with a flag, especially at horse races or on railway lines.

flag of convenience ▶ **noun** a flag of a country under which a ship is registered in order to avoid financial charges or restrictive regulations in the owner's country.

flag officer ▶ **noun** an admiral, vice admiral, or rear admiral, or the commodore of a yacht club.

flag of truce ▶ **noun** a white flag indicating a desire for a truce.

flagon /'flag(ə)n/ ▶ **noun** a large container in which drink is served, typically with a handle and spout: *there was a flagon of beer in his vast fist.*
■ the amount of liquid held in such a container: *he had at least three **flagons of** wine down him already.* ■ a similar container used to hold the wine for the Eucharist. ■ a large bottle in which wine or cider is sold, typically holding 1.13 litres (about 2 pints).
– ORIGIN late Middle English: from Old French *flacon*, based on late Latin *flasco*, *flascon-*, of unknown origin. Compare with **FLASK**.

flagpole ▶ **noun** a pole used for flying a flag.
– PHRASES **run something up the flagpole (to see who salutes)** test the popularity of a new idea or proposal: *the idea was first run up the flagpole in 1997.*

flag rank ▶ **noun** [mass noun] the rank attained by flag officers.

flagrant /'fleɪgr(ə)nt/ ▶ **adjective** (of an action considered wrong or immoral) conspicuously or obviously offensive: *a flagrant violation of the law.*
– DERIVATIVES **flagrancy** noun, **flagrantly** adverb.
– ORIGIN late 15th cent. (in the sense 'blazing, resplendent'): from French, or from Latin *flagrant-* 'blazing', from the verb *flagrare*.

flagship ▶ **noun** the ship in a fleet which carries the admiral commanding.
■ the best or most important thing owned or produced by a particular organization: *this bill is the flagship of the government's legislative programme* | [as modifier] *their flagship product.*

flagstaff /'flagstɑːf/ ▶ **noun** another term for **FLAGPOLE**.

flagstone ▶ **noun** a flat stone slab, typically rectangular or square, used for paving.
– DERIVATIVES **flagstoned** adjective.

flag-waving ▶ **noun** [mass noun] the expression of patriotism in a populist and emotional way: [as modifier] *flag-waving conservatism.*
– DERIVATIVES **flag-waver** noun.

flail /fleɪl/ ▶ **noun** a threshing tool consisting of a wooden staff with a short heavy stick swinging from it.
■ a similar device used as a weapon or for flogging. ■ a machine for threshing or slashing, with a similar action: [as modifier] *a flail hedge trimmer.*
▶ **verb 1** wave or swing or cause to wave or swing wildly: [no obj.] *his arms were flailing helplessly* | [with obj.] *he flailed his arms and drove her away.*
■ [no obj.] flounder; struggle uselessly: *I was **flailing about** in the water* | *he **flailed around** on the snow.*
2 [with obj.] beat; flog: *he escorted them, flailing their shoulders with his cane.*
– ORIGIN Old English, of West Germanic origin, based on Latin *flagellum* 'whip' (see **FLAGELLUM**); probably influenced in Middle English by Old French *flaiel* or Dutch *vlegel*.

flair ▶ **noun 1** [in sing.] a special or instinctive aptitude or ability for doing something well: *she had a flair for languages* | [mass noun] *none of us had much artistic flair.*
2 [mass noun] stylishness and originality: *she dressed with flair.*
– ORIGIN late 19th cent.: from French, from *flairer* 'to smell', based on Latin *fragrare* 'smell sweet'. Compare with **FRAGRANT**.

flak (also **flack**) ▶ **noun** [mass noun] anti-aircraft fire.
■ strong criticism: *you must be strong enough to **take the flak** if things go wrong.*
– ORIGIN 1930s: from German, abbreviation of *Fliegerabwehrkanone*, literally 'aviator-defence gun'.

flake[1] ▶ **noun 1** a small, flat, very thin piece of something, typically one which has broken away or been peeled off from a larger piece: *paint peeling off the walls in unsightly flakes* | *flakes of pastry.*
■ a snowflake. ■ Archaeology a piece of hard stone chipped off for use as a tool by prehistoric humans: [as modifier] *flake tools.* ■ [mass noun] thin pieces of crushed dried food or bait for fish.
2 N. Amer. informal a crazy or eccentric person.
▶ **verb 1** [no obj.] come or fall away from a surface in thin pieces: *the paint had been **flaking off** for years.*
■ lose small fragments from the surface: *my nails have started to flake at the ends.*
2 [with obj.] break or divide (food) into thin pieces: *flake the fish* | [as adj. **flaked**] *flaked almonds.*
■ [no obj.] (of food) come apart in thin pieces.
– ORIGIN Middle English: the immediate source is unknown, the senses perhaps deriving from different words; probably of Germanic origin and related to **FLAG**[2] and **FLAW**[1].

flake[2] ▶ **noun** a rack or shelf for storing or drying food such as fish.
– ORIGIN Middle English (denoting a wicker hurdle): perhaps of Scandinavian origin and related to Old Norse *flaki*, *fleki* 'wicker shield' and Danish *flage* 'hurdle'.

flake[3] ▶ **verb** [no obj.] (**flake out**) informal fall asleep; drop from exhaustion.
– ORIGIN late 15th cent. (in the senses 'become languid' and (of a garment) 'fall in folds'): variant of obsolete *flack* and the verb **FLAG**[4]. The current sense dates from the 1940s.

flake[4] (also **fake**) Nautical ▶ **noun** a single turn of a coiled rope or hawser.
▶ **verb** [with obj.] lay (a rope) in loose coils in order to prevent it tangling: *a cable had to be **flaked out**.*
■ lay (a sail) down in folds either side of the boom.
– ORIGIN early 17th cent. (as a noun): of unknown origin; compare with German *Flechte* in the same sense.

flake white ▶ **noun** [mass noun] a pure white pigment made from flakes of white lead.

flak jacket ▶ **noun** a sleeveless jacket made of heavy fabric reinforced with metal, worn as protection against bullets and shrapnel.

flaky ▶ **adjective** (**flakier**, **flakiest**) **1** breaking or separating easily into small thin pieces: *she ate flaky rolls spread with cherry jam.*
■ (especially of skin or paint) tending to crack and come away from a surface in small pieces: *the skin on the shins is often very flaky and dry.*
2 informal, chiefly N. Amer. crazy or eccentric: *flaky ideas about taxes.*
■ informal (of a device or software) prone to break down; unreliable.
– DERIVATIVES **flakiness** noun, **flakily** adverb.

flaky pastry ▶ **noun** [mass noun] pastry consisting of thin light layers when baked.

flam ▶ **noun** Music one of the basic patterns (rudiments) of drumming, consisting of a stroke preceded by a grace note.
– ORIGIN late 18th cent.: probably imitative.

flambé /'flɒmbeɪ/ ▶ **adjective 1** [postpositive] (of food) covered with spirits and set alight briefly: *crêpes flambé.*
2 denoting or characterized by a lustrous red copper-based porcelain glaze with purple streaks.
▶ **verb** (**flambés**, **flambéed**, **flambéing**) [with obj.] cover (food) with spirits and set it alight briefly.
– ORIGIN late 19th cent.: French, literally 'singed', past participle of *flamber*, from *flambe* 'a flame'.

flambeau /'flambəʊ/ ▶ **noun** (pl. **flambeaus** or **flambeaux** /-əʊz/) historical a flaming torch, especially one made of several thick wicks dipped in wax.
■ a large candlestick with several branches.
– ORIGIN mid 17th cent.: from French, from *flambe* 'a flame'.

Flamborough Head /'flamb(ə)rə/ a rocky promontory on the east coast of England, in the East Riding of Yorkshire.

flamboyant[1] /flam'bɔɪənt/ ▶ **adjective 1** (of a person or their behaviour) tending to attract attention because of their exuberance, confidence, and stylishness: *a flamboyant display of aerobatics.*
■ (especially of clothing) noticeable because brightly coloured, highly patterned, or unusual in style.
2 Architecture of or denoting a style of French Gothic architecture marked by wavy flamelike tracery and ornate decoration. Compare with **RAYONNANT**.
– DERIVATIVES **flamboyance** noun, **flamboyancy** noun, **flamboyantly** adverb.
– ORIGIN mid 19th cent.: from French, literally 'flaming, blazing', present participle of *flamboyer*, from *flambe* 'a flame'.

flamboyant[2] /flam'bɔɪənt/ ▶ **noun** a Madagascan tree with bright red flowers and leaves composed of numerous leaflets, planted as a street tree in the tropics.
• *Delonix regia*, family Leguminosae.
– ORIGIN late 19th cent.: probably a noun use of the French adjective *flamboyant* 'blazing' (see **FLAMBOYANT**[1]).

flame ▶ **noun 1** a hot glowing body of ignited gas that is generated by something on fire: *the flame of a candle* | [mass noun] *a sheet of flame blocked my escape.*
2 figurative used in similes and metaphors to refer to something resembling a flame in various respects, in particular:
■ a thing resembling a flame in heat, shape, or brilliance: *redstarts darted, like orange flames.* ■ [mass noun] a brilliant orange-red colour: [in combination] *a **flame-red** trench coat.* ■ a thing compared to a flame's ability to burn fiercely or be extinguished: *the flame of hope burns brightly here.* ■ a very intense emotion: *the sound of his laughter fanned the flame of anger to new heights.* ■ a cause which generates passionate feelings: ***a keeper of the** Thatcherite **flame**.* ■ Computing a vitriolic or abusive message sent via electronic mail, typically in quick response to another message: *flames about inexperienced users posting stupid messages.*
▶ **verb** [no obj.] burn and give off flames: *a great fire flamed in an open fireplace.*
■ [with obj.] set (something) alight: *warm the whisky slightly, pour over the lobster, and flame it.* ■ figurative shine or glow like a flame: *her thick hair flamed against the light.* ■ figurative (of an intense emotion) appear suddenly and fiercely: *hope flamed in her.* ■ (of a person's face) suddenly become red with intense emotion, especially anger or embarrassment: *Jess's cheeks flamed.* ■ [with obj.] Computing send (someone) abusive or vitriolic electronic mail messages, typically in a quick exchange.
– PHRASES **burst into flame** (or **flames**) suddenly begin to burn fiercely: *the grass looked ready to burst into flame.* **go up in flames** be destroyed by fire: *last night two factories went up in flames.* **in flames** on fire; burning fiercely: *the plane plunged to the ground in flames.* **old flame** informal a former lover.
– DERIVATIVES **flameless** adjective, **flame-like** adjective, **flamer** noun (Computing), **flamy** adjective.
– ORIGIN Middle English: from Old French *flame* (noun), *flamer* (verb), from Latin *flamma* 'a flame'.
▶ **flame out** (of a jet engine) lose power through the extinction of the flame in the combustion chamber. ■ informal, chiefly N. Amer. fail, especially conspicuously: *journalists had seared him for flaming out in the second round of the Olympics.*

flame gun ▶ **noun** a device for producing a jet of flame, used especially for destroying weeds.

flamen /'fleɪmɛn, 'flɑː-/ ▶ **noun** (pl. **flamens** or **flamines**) Roman History a priest serving a particular deity.
– ORIGIN Latin.

flamenco /flə'mɛŋkəʊ/ ▶ **noun** [mass noun] a style of Spanish music, played especially on the guitar and accompanied by singing and dancing.
■ a style of spirited, rhythmical dance performed to such music, often with castanets.
– ORIGIN late 19th cent.: Spanish, 'like a gypsy', literally 'Fleming', from Middle Dutch *Vlaminc*.

flame of the forest ▶ **noun** a tropical tree which bears showy bright red flowers, in particular:
• an Asian tree of the pea family (*Butea monosperma*, family Leguminosae). • another term for **FLAMBOYANT**[2].

flameout ▶ **noun** an instance of the flame in the combustion chamber of a jet engine being extinguished, with a resultant loss of power.
■ informal, chiefly N. Amer. a complete or conspicuous failure: *his first-round flameout at the US Open.*

flameproof ▶ **adjective** (especially of a fabric) treated so as to be non-flammable.
■ (of cookware) able to be used either in an oven or on a hob: *a flameproof casserole.*
▶ **verb** [with obj.] make (something) flameproof.

flame-thrower ▶ **noun** a weapon that sprays out burning fuel.

flame tree ▶ **noun** any of a number of trees with brilliant red flowers, in particular:
• an Australian bottle tree (*Brachychiton acerifolius*, family Sterculiaceae). • another term for **FLAMBOYANT**[2].

flaming ▶ **adjective** [attrib.] **1** burning fiercely and emitting flames: *they dragged her away from the flaming car.*
■ very hot: *flaming June.* ■ glowing with a bright orange or red colour: *the flaming autumn maples of the St Lawrence Valley.* ■ (of red or orange) brilliant or intense: *flaming red hair.* ■ (especially of an argument) passionate: *a flaming row.*
2 informal used for emphasis to express annoyance: *what d'you want a flaming book for?*

flamingo /flə'mɪŋɡəʊ/ ▶ **noun** (pl. **-os** or **-oes**) a tall wading bird with mainly pink or scarlet plumage and long legs and neck. It has a heavy bent bill that is held upside down in the water in order to filter-feed on small organisms.
• Family Phoenicopteridae: three genera and four species, in particular the **greater flamingo** (*Phoenicopterus ruber*).
– ORIGIN mid 16th cent.: from Spanish *flamengo*, earlier form of *flamenco* (see **FLAMENCO**); associated, because of its colour, with Latin *flamma* 'a flame'.

flammable /'flaməb(ə)l/ ▶ **adjective** easily set on fire: *the use of highly flammable materials.*
– DERIVATIVES **flammability** noun.
– ORIGIN early 19th cent.: from Latin *flammare*, from *flamma* 'a flame'.

USAGE The words **flammable** and **inflammable** actually mean the same thing: see **usage** at **INFLAMMABLE**.

flammulated owl /'flamjʊleɪtɪd/ ▶ **noun** a small reddish-grey migratory American owl which sometimes occurs in loose colonies.
• *Otus flammeolus*, family Strigidae.

Flamsteed /'flamsti:d/, John (1646–1719), English astronomer. He was the first Astronomer Royal at the Royal Greenwich Observatory and produced the first star catalogue (for use in navigation).

flan ▶ **noun** **1** a baked dish consisting of an open-topped pastry case with a savoury or sweet filling.
■ a sponge base with a sweet topping.
2 a disc of metal such as one from which a coin is made.
– ORIGIN mid 19th cent.: from French (originally denoting a round cake) from Old French *flaon*, from medieval Latin *flado, fladon-*, of West Germanic origin; related to Dutch *vlade* 'custard'.

Flanders /'flɑ:ndəz/ a region in the south-western part of the Low Countries, now divided between Belgium (where it forms the provinces of East and West Flanders), France, and the Netherlands. It was a powerful medieval principality and the scene of prolonged fighting during the First World War.

Flanders poppy ▶ **noun** a red poppy.

Flandrian /'flɑ:ndrɪən/ ▶ **adjective** Geology of, relating to, or denoting the current (Holocene or Recent) stage in northern Europe, especially when treated as an interglacial period.
■ [as noun **the Flandrian**] the Flandrian interglacial or the system of deposits laid down during it.
– ORIGIN mid 17th cent.: from **FLANDERS** + **-IAN**.

flânerie /flan'ri:, French flanʀi/ ▶ **noun** [mass noun] aimless idle behaviour.
– ORIGIN French, from *flâner* 'saunter, lounge'.

flâneur /fla'nə:, French flanœʀ/ ▶ **noun** (pl. **flâneurs** pronunc. same) an idler or lounger.
– ORIGIN French, from *flâner* 'saunter, lounge'.

flange /flan(d)ʒ/ ▶ **noun** a projecting flat rim, collar, or rib on an object, serving for strengthening or attachment or (on a wheel) for maintaining position on a rail.
– DERIVATIVES **flanged** adjective, **flangeless** adjective.
– ORIGIN late 17th cent.: perhaps based on Old French *flanchir* 'to bend'.

flanger /'flan(d)ʒə/ ▶ **noun** an electronic device which alters a sound signal by introducing a cyclically varying phase shift into one of two identical copies of the signal and recombining them, used especially in popular music to alter the sound of an instrument.

flanging /'flandʒɪŋ/ ▶ **noun** [mass noun] **1** the provision of a flange or flanges on an object: *the rim displays the same flanging.*
2 the alteration of sound using a flanger.

flank ▶ **noun** **1** the side of a person's or animal's body between the ribs and the hip: *leaning against his horse's flanks.*
■ a cut of meat from such a part of an animal: *a thick flank of beef on a spit* | [mass noun] *you need 2 lb of flank.* ■ the side of something large, such as a mountain, building, or ship: *the northern flank of the volcano.*
2 the right or left side of a body of people such as an army, a naval force, or a soccer team: *the left flank of the Russian Third Army.*
■ the right or left side of a gaming area such as a chessboard. ■ (also **flank forward**) Rugby another term for **WING FORWARD**.
▶ **verb** [with obj.] (often **be flanked**) be situated on each side of or on one side of (someone or something): *the hall was flanked by two towers.*
■ [usu. as adj. **flanking**] guard or strengthen (a military force or position) from the side: *massive walls, defended by four flanking towers.* ■ [usu. as adj. **flanking**] attack down or from the sides, or rake with gunfire from the sides: *a flanking attack from the north-east.*
– PHRASES **in flank** Military at the side: *they were to hit the tail of the column in flank.*
– ORIGIN late Old English, from Old French *flanc*, of Germanic origin.

flanker ▶ **noun** **1** a person or thing situated on the flank of something, in particular:
■ Rugby another term for **WING FORWARD**. ■ American Football an offensive back who is positioned to the outside of an end. ■ Military a fortification guarding or menacing the side of a force or position.
2 Brit. informal, dated a trick; a swindle: *he's certainly* ***pulled a flanker on*** *the army.*

flannel ▶ **noun** **1** [mass noun] a kind of soft-woven fabric, typically made of wool or cotton and slightly milled and raised: [as modifier] *a check flannel shirt.*
■ (**flannels**) men's trousers made of such material. ■ short for **FLANNELETTE**.
2 Brit. a small piece of towelling used for washing oneself.
3 [mass noun] Brit. informal bland fluent talk indulged in to avoid addressing a difficult subject or situation directly: *a simple admittance of ignorance was much to be preferred to any amount of flannel.*
▶ **verb** (**flannelled**, **flannelling**; US also **flanneled**, **flanneling**) [no obj.] [often as noun **flannelling**] informal, chiefly Brit. use bland fluent talk so as to avoid addressing a difficult subject or situation directly.
– ORIGIN Middle English: probably from Welsh *gwlanen* 'woollen article', from *gwlân* 'wool'.

flannelboard ▶ **noun** a board covered with flannel to which paper or cloth cut-outs will stick, used as a toy or a teaching aid.

flannelette /ˌflanə'lɛt/ ▶ **noun** [mass noun] a napped cotton fabric resembling flannel: [as modifier] *a flannelette nightdress.*

flannelgraph ▶ **noun** another term for **FLANNELBOARD**.

flannelled (US also **flanneled**) ▶ **adjective** [usu. in combination] wearing flannel trousers: *a rather stout boy, grey-flannelled, pulling off a school cap.*

flannelmouth ▶ **noun** N. Amer. informal a person who talks too much, especially in a boastful or deceitful way.

flap ▶ **verb** (**flapped**, **flapping**) **1** [with obj.] (of a bird) move (its wings) up and down when flying or preparing to fly: *a pheasant flapped its wings* | [no obj.] *gulls* ***flapped around*** *uttering their strange cries.*
■ [no obj.] (of something attached at one point or loosely fastened) flutter or wave around: *the sides of the tent had a tendency to* ***flap about.*** ■ move (one's arms or hands) up and down or to and fro. ■ gesture at someone with (one's hand), especially in a dismissive way: *Bernice flapped a hand at him in dismissal.* ■ [with obj. and adverbial of direction] strike or attempt to strike (something) loosely with one's hand, a cloth, or a broad implement, especially to drive it away: *they flap away the flies with peacock tails.* ■ wave (something, especially a cloth) around or at something or someone: *she flapped the duster angrily.*
2 [no obj.] informal be agitated or panicky: *it's all right, Mother, don't flap.*
▶ **noun** **1** a piece of something thin, such as cloth, paper, or metal hinged or attached on one side only, that covers an opening or hangs down from something: *the flap of the envelope* | *he pushed through the tent flap.*
■ a hinged or sliding section of an aircraft wing used to control lift: *flaps are normally moved by the hydraulics* | [mass noun] *a final approach at sixty knots with 45° of flap.* ■ a large broad mushroom. ■ Phonetics a type of consonant produced by allowing the tip of the tongue to strike the palate very briefly.
2 a movement of a wing or an arm from side to side or up and down: *the surviving bird made a few final despairing flaps.*
■ [in sing.] the sound of something making such a movement: *hear the coo of the dove, the flap of its wings.*
3 [in sing.] informal a state of agitation; a panic: *they're* ***in a flap*** *over who's going to take Hugh's lectures .*
– PHRASES **someone's ears are flapping** informal someone is listening intently and in a nosy and intrusive way: *your ears are flapping, Mr O'Brien!*
– DERIVATIVES **flappy** adjective.
– ORIGIN Middle English: probably imitative.

flapdoodle ▶ **noun** [mass noun] informal, chiefly US nonsense: *people who are prey to dogmatic flapdoodle.*
■ [count noun] a fool.
– ORIGIN mid 19th cent.: an arbitrary formation.

flapjack ▶ **noun** **1** Brit. a sweet dense cake made from oats, golden syrup and melted butter, served in rectangles. [ORIGIN: probably a regional coinage.]
2 N. Amer. a pancake. [ORIGIN: from **FLAP** (in the dialect sense 'toss a pancake') + **JACK**[1].]

flapper ▶ **noun** informal (in the 1920s) a fashionable young woman intent on enjoying herself and flouting conventional standards of behaviour.

flapshell (also **flap-shelled turtle**) ▶ **noun** a soft-shelled turtle, native to India and Africa, with flaps of skin on the lower shell that fold to protect the hindlimbs and tail, and flexible margins to the upper shell that protect the head and limbs.
• Genera *Lissemys* and other genera, family Trionychidae: several species, in particular the **Indian flapshell** (*L. punctata*).

flap valve (also **flapper valve**) ▶ **noun** a valve opened and closed by a plate hinged at one side.

flare ▶ **noun** **1** a sudden brief burst of bright flame or light: *the flare of the match lit up his face.*
■ a device producing a very bright flame, used especially as a signal or marker: *a distress flare* | [as modifier] *a flare gun.* ■ [in sing.] a sudden burst of intense emotion: *she felt a flare of anger within her.* ■ a sudden recurrence of an inflammation or other medical condition: *treatment for colitis flares.* ■ Astronomy a sudden explosion in the chromosphere and corona of the sun or another star, resulting in an intense burst of radiation. See also **SOLAR FLARE**. ■ [mass noun] Photography extraneous illumination on film caused by internal reflection in the camera.
2 [in sing.] a gradual widening, especially of a skirt or trousers: *as you knit, add a flare or curve a hem.*
■ (**flares**) trousers of which the legs get progressively wider from the knees down. ■ [mass noun] an upward and outward curve of a ship's bows, designed to throw the water outwards when in motion.
▶ **verb** [no obj.] **1** burn with a sudden intensity: *the blaze across the water flared* | *the bonfire crackled and* ***flared up.***
■ (of a light or a person's eyes) glow with a sudden intensity: *her eyes flared at the stinging insult.* ■ (of an emotion) suddenly become manifest in someone or their expression: *alarm flared in her eyes* | *tempers flared.* ■ (**flare up**) (of an illness or chronic medical complaint) recur unexpectedly and cause further discomfort. ■ (especially of an argument, conflict, or trouble) suddenly become more violent or intense: *in 1943 the Middle East crisis* ***flared up*** *again.* ■ (**flare up**) (of a person) suddenly become angry: *she flared up, shouting at Geoffrey.*
2 [often as adj. **flared**] gradually become wider at one end: *a flared skirt* | *the dress flared out into a huge train.*
■ (of a person's nostrils) dilate. ■ [with obj.] (of a person) cause (the nostrils) to dilate.
– ORIGIN mid 16th cent. (in the sense 'spread out (one's hair)'): of unknown origin. Current senses date from the 17th cent.

flarepath ▶ **noun** an area illuminated to enable an aircraft to land or take off.

flare star ▶ **noun** Astronomy a dwarf star which displays spasmodic outbursts of radiation, believed to be due to extremely intense flares.

flare-up ▶ **noun** a sudden outburst of something, especially violence: *a flare-up between the two countries.*

flash[1] ▶ **verb** **1** [no obj.] (of a light or something which reflects light) shine in a bright but brief, sudden, or intermittent way: *the lights started flashing* | [as adj. **flashing**] *a police car with a flashing light.*
■ [with obj.] cause to shine briefly or suddenly: *the oncoming car flashed its lights.* ■ [with obj.] shine or show a light to send (a signal): *red lights started to flash a*

warning. ■ [with obj.] give (a swift or sudden look): *Carrie flashed a glance in his direction* | [with two objs] *she flashed him a withering look.* ■ express a sudden burst of emotion, especially anger, with such a look: *she glared at him, her eyes flashing.*
2 [with obj.] display (an image, words, or information) suddenly on a television or computer screen or electronic sign, typically briefly or repeatedly: *the screen* ***flashed up*** *a menu.*
■ [no obj.] (of an image or message) be displayed in such a way: *the election results flashed on the screen.* ■ informal hold up or show (something, often proof of one's identity) quickly before replacing it: *she opened her purse and flashed her ID card.* ■ informal make a conspicuous display of (something) so as to impress or attract attention: *they all wear those macs and flash their money about.* ■ [no obj.] [often as noun **flashing**] informal (especially of a man) show one's genitals briefly in public.
3 [no obj., with adverbial of direction] move or pass very quickly: *a look of terror flashed across Kirov's face* | *the scenery flashed by.*
■ (of a thought or memory) suddenly come into or pass through the mind: *another stray thought* ***flashed through*** *her mind.* ■ [with obj. and adverbial of direction] send (news or information) swiftly by means of telegraphy or telecommunications: *the story* ***was flashed around*** *the world.*
▶ **noun 1** a sudden brief burst of bright light or a sudden glint from a reflective surface: *the grenade exploded with a yellow flash of light* | *a lightning flash.*
■ a bright patch of colour, often one used for decoration or identification: *orange flashes adorn the aircraft.* ■ a coloured band or highlighting field on the packaging of a product used to catch the consumer's eye: *on-pack flashes offer a free 'Taste of the Caribbean'.* ■ Brit. a coloured patch of cloth on a uniform, worn especially on the upper arm or shoulder, used as the distinguishing emblem of a regiment, formation, or country: *a short man with the black flashes of the tank units.*
2 a thing that occurs suddenly and within a brief period of time, in particular:
■ a sudden instance or manifestation of a quality, understanding, or humour: *she had a* ***flash*** *of inspiration.* ■ a fleeting glimpse of something, especially something vivid or eye-catching: *the blue flash of a kingfisher.* ■ a newsflash.
3 a camera attachment that produces a brief very bright light, used for taking photographs in poor light: *an electronic flash* | [mass noun] *if in any doubt, use flash* | [as modifier] *flash photography.*
4 [mass noun] excess plastic or metal forced between facing surfaces as two halves of a mould close up, forming a thin projection on the finished object.
5 a rush of water, especially down a weir to take a boat over shallows.
■ a device for producing such a rush of water.
▶ **adjective** informal **1** (of a thing) ostentatiously expensive, elaborate, or up to date: *a flash new car.*
■ (of a person) superficially attractive because stylish and full of brash charm: *he was carrying this money around and trying to be flash.*
2 archaic of or relating to thieves, prostitutes, or the underworld, especially their language.
– PHRASES **flash in the pan** a thing or person whose sudden but brief success is not repeated or repeatable: *our start to the season was just a flash in the pan.* [ORIGIN: with allusion to priming of a firearm, the flash arising from an explosion of gunpowder within the lock.] **in** (or **like**) **a flash** very quickly; immediately: *she was out of the back door in a flash.* **(as) quick as a flash** (especially of a person's response or reaction) very quickly: *quick as a flash he was at her side.*
– ORIGIN Middle English (in the sense 'splash water about'): probably imitative; compare with **FLUSH**[1] and **SPLASH**.
▶ **flash back** (of a person's thoughts or mind) briefly and suddenly recall a previous time or incident: *her thoughts immediately flashed back to last night.*
flash over make an electric circuit by sparking across a gap. ■ (of a fire) spread instantly across a gap because of intense heat.

flash[2] ▶ **noun** Brit. a water-filled hollow formed by subsidence, especially any of those due to rock salt extraction in or near Cheshire.
– ORIGIN Middle English (in the sense 'a marshy place'): from Old French *flache*, variant of Picard and Norman dialect *flaque*, from Middle Dutch *vlacke*. The current sense dates from the late 19th cent.

flashback ▶ **noun 1** a scene in a film, novel, etc. set in a time earlier than the main story: *in a series of flashbacks, we follow the pair through their teenage years* | [mass noun] *the movie tells the story* ***in flashback.***
■ a disturbing sudden vivid memory of an event in the past, typically as the result of psychological trauma or taking LSD.
2 a flame moving rapidly back through a combustible vapour: *cooling the area prevented a flashback.*

flashboard ▶ **noun** a board used for sending more water from a mill dam into a mill race.

flashbulb ▶ **noun** a bulb for a flashgun, of a type that is used only once.

flash burn ▶ **noun** a burn caused by sudden intense heat, e.g. from a nuclear explosion.

flashcard ▶ **noun** a card containing a small amount of information, held up for pupils to see, as an aid to learning.

flashcube ▶ **noun** chiefly historical a set of four flashbulbs arranged in a cube and operated in turn.

flasher ▶ **noun 1** an automatic device causing a light to flash on and off rapidly.
■ a signal using such a device, for example a car's indicator.
2 informal a man who exposes his genitals in public.

flash flood ▶ **noun** a sudden local flood, typically due to heavy rain.

flash-freeze ▶ **verb** [with obj.] freeze (food or other material) very rapidly so as to prevent the formation of ice crystals: *the steaks were flash-frozen.*
– DERIVATIVES **flash-freezer** noun.

flashgun ▶ **noun** a device which gives a brief flash of intense light, used for taking photographs indoors or in poor light.

flashing ▶ **noun** a strip of metal used to stop water penetrating the junction of a roof with another surface: *flashings around chimneys* | [mass noun] *the lead flashing on the roof.*
– ORIGIN late 18th cent.: from the earlier synonym *flash* (of unknown origin) + **-ING**[1].

flash lamp ▶ **noun** a portable flashing electric lamp such as a flashgun.

flashlight ▶ **noun 1** chiefly N. Amer. an electric torch.
2 a flashing light used for signals and in lighthouses.
3 another term for **FLASHGUN**.

flash memory ▶ **noun** [mass noun] Computing memory that retains data in the absence of a power supply: *the diagnostics are kept in flash memory.*

flashover ▶ **noun 1** a high-voltage electric short circuit made through the air between exposed conductors.
2 an instance of a fire spreading very rapidly through the air because of intense heat.

flash photolysis ▶ **noun** [mass noun] Chemistry the use of a very intense flash of light to bring about decomposition or dissociation in a heated gas, usually as a means of generating and studying short-lived molecules.

flashpoint ▶ **noun 1** a place, event, or time at which trouble, such as violence or anger, flares up: *the port is a flashpoint between gangs.*
2 Chemistry the temperature at which a particular organic compound gives off sufficient vapour to ignite in air.

flash suit ▶ **noun** a set of heatproof protective clothing.

flash tube ▶ **noun** a gas-discharge tube used, especially in photography, to provide an electronic flash when a current is suddenly passed through it.

flashy ▶ **adjective** (**flashier**, **flashiest**) ostentatiously attractive or impressive: *he always had a flashy car.*
– DERIVATIVES **flashily** adverb, **flashiness** noun.

flask ▶ **noun** a container or bottle, in particular:
■ a narrow-necked glass container, typically conical or spherical, used in a laboratory to hold reagents or samples. ■ a narrow-necked bulbous glass container, typically with a covering of wickerwork, for storing wine or oil. ■ a small glass bottle for perfume. ■ Brit. a vacuum flask. ■ a hip flask. ■ (also **nuclear flask**) an extremely strong lead-lined container for transporting or storing radioactive nuclear waste. ■ the contents of any of these containers: *a flask of coffee.* ■ historical short for **POWDER FLASK**.
– ORIGIN Middle English (in the sense 'cask'): from medieval Latin *flasca*. From the mid 16th cent. the word denoted a case of horn, leather, or metal for carrying gunpowder. The sense 'glass container' (late 17th cent.) was influenced by Italian *fiasco*, from medieval Latin *flasco*. Compare with **FLAGON**.

flat[1] ▶ **adjective** (**flatter**, **flattest**) **1** smooth and even; without marked lumps or indentations: *a flat wall* | *trim the surface of the cake to make it completely flat.*
■ (of land) without hills: *thirty-five acres of flat countryside.* ■ (of an expanse of water) calm and without waves. ■ not sloping: *the flat roof of a garage.* ■ having a broad level surface but little height or depth; shallow: *a flat rectangular box* | *a flat cap.* ■ (of shoes) without heels or with very low heels.
2 lacking interest or emotion; dull and lifeless: *'I'm sorry,' he said, in a flat voice* | *her drawings were flat and unimaginative.*
■ (of a person) without energy; dispirited: *his sense of intoxication wore off until he felt flat and weary.* ■ (of a market, prices, etc.) not showing much activity; sluggish: *turnover was flat at £3.2 m* | *flat sales in the drinks industry.* ■ (of a sparkling drink) having lost its effervescence. ■ Brit. (of a battery) having exhausted its charge. ■ (of something kept inflated, especially a tyre) having lost some or all of its air, typically because of a puncture: *you've got a flat tyre.* ■ (of a colour) uniform: *the dress was a deadly, flat shade of grey.* ■ (of a photographic print or negative) lacking contrast.
3 [attrib.] (of a fee, wage, or price) the same in all cases, not varying with changed conditions or in particular cases: *a 10p flat fare.* See also **FLAT RATE**.
■ (of a denial, contradiction, or refusal) completely definite and firm; absolute: *his statement was a flat denial that he had misbehaved.*
4 (of musical sound) below true or normal pitch.
■ [postpositive] (of a key) having a flat or flats in the signature. ■ [postpositive] (of a note) a semitone lower than a specified note: *E flat.*
5 (**Flat**) of or relating to flat racing: *the Flat season.*
▶ **adverb 1** in or to a horizontal position: *he was lying flat on his back* | *she had been knocked flat by the blast.*
■ lying in close juxtaposition, especially against another surface: *his black curly hair was blown flat across his skull.* ■ so as to become smooth and even: *I hammered the metal flat.*
2 informal completely; absolutely: *I'm turning you down flat* | [as submodifier] *she was going to be flat broke in a couple of days.*
■ after a phrase expressing a period of time to emphasize how quickly something can be done or has been done: *you can prepare a healthy meal* ***in ten minutes flat.***
3 below the true or normal pitch of musical sound: *it wasn't a question of singing flat, but of simply singing the wrong notes.*
▶ **noun 1** [in sing.] the flat part of something: *she placed the flat of her hand over her glass.*
2 a flat object, in particular:
■ (often **flats**) an upright section of stage scenery mounted on a movable frame. ■ informal a flat tyre. ■ N. Amer. a shallow container in which seedlings are grown and sold. ■ (often **flats**) chiefly US a shoe with a very low heel or no heel. ■ a railway wagon with a flat floor and no sides or roof; a flatcar.
3 (usu. **flats**) an area of low level ground, especially near water: *the shingle flats of the lake.* See also **MUDFLAT**.
4 (**the Flat**) Brit. flat racing.
5 a musical note lowered a semitone below natural pitch.
■ the sign (♭) indicating this.
▶ **verb** (**flatted**, **flatting**) [with obj.] **1** [usu. as adj. **flatted**] Music, N. Amer. lower (a note) by a semitone: *'blue' harmony emphasizing the flatted third and seventh.*
2 archaic make flat; flatten: *flat the loaves down.*
– PHRASES **fall flat** fail completely to produce the intended or expected effect: *his jokes fell flat.* **fall flat on one's face** fall over forwards. ■ figurative fail in an embarrassingly obvious way: *the president could fall flat on his face if the economy doesn't start improving soon.* **(as) flat as a pancake** see **PANCAKE**. **flat out 1** as fast or as hard as possible: *the whole team is working flat out to satisfy demand* | [as adj. **flat-out**] *the album lacks the flat-out urgency of its predecessor.* **2** informal, chiefly N. Amer. without hesitation or reservation; unequivocally: *in those early days I'd just flat out vote against foreign aid* | [as adj. **flat-out**] *flat-out perjury.* **3** lying completely stretched out, especially asleep or exhausted: *she was lying flat out on her pink bath towel.* **on the flat** on level ground as opposed to uphill: *the car wouldn't go uphill or overtake on the flat.* ■ (**on the Flat**) (of a horse race) on an open course as opposed to one with jumps. **that's flat** informal used to indicate that one has reached a decision and will not be persuaded to

change one's mind: *he won't go into a home and that's flat.*
– DERIVATIVES **flatness** noun, **flattish** adjective.
– ORIGIN Middle English: from Old Norse *flatr*.

flat[2] ▶ **noun** chiefly Brit. a set of rooms for living in, typically on one floor of a large building and including a kitchen and bathroom: *a block of flats.*
▶ **verb** (**flatted**, **flatting**) [no obj., with adverbial of place] Austral./NZ live in or share a flat: *my sister Zoë flats in Auckland.*
– PHRASES **go flatting** Austral./NZ leave one's family home to live in a flat: *in my third year I left home and went flatting with David.*
– DERIVATIVES **flatlet** noun.
– ORIGIN early 19th cent. (denoting a floor or storey): alteration of obsolete *flet* 'floor, dwelling', of Germanic origin and related to **FLAT**[1].

flatbed ▶ **noun** a long flat area or structure: *the flatbed of a truck.*
■ a vehicle with a flat load-carrying area: [as modifier] *a flatbed truck.* ■ [as modifier] denoting a letterpress printing machine in which the forme is carried on a horizontal surface: *a flatbed press.* ■ Computing a scanner, plotter, or other device which keeps paper flat during use.

flatbill ▶ **noun** a tropical American bird of the tyrant flycatcher family, with a wide flat bill and mainly olive-green plumage.
• Genera *Ramphotrigon* and *Rhynchocyclus*, family Tyrannidae: several species.

flatbill flycatcher ▶ **noun** another term for **BOATBILL** (in sense 2).

flatboat ▶ **noun** a boat with a flat bottom for transport in shallow water.

flatbread ▶ **noun** [mass noun] N. Amer. flat, thin, often unleavened bread.

flatbug ▶ **noun** a broad, very flat bug that typically lives on or under loose bark.
• Family Aradidae, suborder Heteroptera: several species.

flatcar ▶ **noun** chiefly N. Amer. a railway freight wagon without a roof or sides.

flat-chested ▶ **adjective** (of a woman) having small breasts.

flat-fell ▶ **verb** see **FELL**[2] (sense 2).

flat file ▶ **noun** Computing a file having no internal hierarchy.

flatfish ▶ **noun** (pl. same or **-fishes**) a flattened marine fish that swims on its side with both eyes on the upper side. They live typically on the seabed and are coloured to resemble it.
• Order Pleuronectiformes: several families, in particular Bothidae (left-eye flounders), Pleuronectidae (right-eye flounders), and Soleidae (soles).

flatfoot ▶ **noun** (pl. **flatfoots** or **flatfeet**) informal, dated a police officer.

flat foot ▶ **noun** a foot with an arch that is lower than usual. Also called **PES PLANUS**.

flat-footed ▶ **adjective 1** having flat feet: *a flat-footed, overweight colonel.*
2 having one's feet flat on the ground: *he landed with a flat-footed thud* | [as adv.] *he went upstairs very slowly, walking flat-footed.*
■ informal unable to move quickly and smoothly; clumsy: *we did look flat-footed in that game.* ■ informal not clever or imaginative; uninspired: *he has little space for anecdote, but the text is no flat-footed catalogue.*
– DERIVATIVES **flat-footedly** adverb, **flat-footedness** noun.

flat-four ▶ **adjective** (of an engine) having four horizontal cylinders, two on each side of the crankshaft.
▶ **noun** an engine of this type.

flathead ▶ **noun 1** an edible tropical marine fish that has a pointed flattened head with the eyes positioned on the top, typically burrowing in the seabed with just the eyes showing.
• Family Platycephalidae: several genera and species.
2 [often as modifier] (**Flathead**) a member of certain North American Indian peoples such as Chinook, Choctaw, and Salish, named from their supposed practice of flattening their children's heads artificially: *the Flathead Indians.*
3 [as modifier] US (of an engine) having the valves and spark plugs in the cylinder block rather than the cylinder head, which is essentially a flat plate.
■ (of a vehicle) having such an engine.
4 [as modifier] US (of a screw) countersunk.

flat iron ▶ **noun** historical an iron used for pressing clothes which was heated externally.

flatland ▶ **noun 1** [mass noun] (also **flatlands**) land with no hills, valleys, or mountains: *another 100 miles of flatland* | [count noun] *a sandy flatland dotted with marshes.*
2 [as place name] an imagined land existing in only two dimensions. [ORIGIN: from the title of a book by E. A. Abbot (1884).]

flat-leaved parsley (also **flat** or **flat-leaf parsley**) ▶ **noun** [mass noun] parsley of a variety with large flat leaves, popular in southern Europe. Also called **ITALIAN PARSLEY**.

flatline ▶ **verb** [no obj.] informal (of a person) die.
– DERIVATIVES **flatliner** noun.
– ORIGIN 1980s: from **FLAT**[1] + **LINE**[1] (with reference to the continuous straight line displayed on a heart monitor, indicating death).

flatly ▶ **adverb 1** showing little interest or emotion: *'You'd better go' she said flatly.*
2 in a firm and unequivocal manner; absolutely: *they flatly refused to play* | [as submodifier] *his view seems to me flatly contrary to our evidence.*
3 in a smooth and even way: *I applied the paint flatly.*
■ Photography without marked contrast of light and dark: *the photographs were lit very flatly.*

flatmate ▶ **noun** Brit. a person who shares a flat with others: *my flatmate moved out a month ago.*

flat-pack ▶ **noun 1** [often as modifier] a piece of furniture or other equipment that is sold in pieces packed flat in a box for easy transport and is assembled by the buyer: *a flat-pack bookcase.*
2 Electronics a package for an integrated circuit consisting of a rectangular sealed unit with a number of horizontal metal pins protruding from its sides.
▶ **verb** [with obj.] [usu. as adj. **flat-packed**] pack (a self-assembly item) flat in a box: *this workstation is provided flat-packed.*

flat parsley ▶ **noun** another term for **FLAT-LEAVED PARSLEY**.

flat race ▶ **noun** a horse race over a course with no jumps, as opposed to a steeplechase or hurdles.
– DERIVATIVES **flat racing** noun.

flat rate ▶ **noun** a charge that is the same in all cases, not varying in proportion with something: *clients are charged a flat rate of £250 annually* | [as modifier] *the flat-rate state pension.*
■ a rate of taxation that is not progressive, but remains at the same proportion on all amounts.

flat spin ▶ **noun** Aeronautics a spin in which an aircraft descends in tight circles while remaining almost horizontal.
■ [in sing.] Brit. informal a state of agitation or panic: *a scandal has put the university **into a flat spin**.*

flatten ▶ **verb 1** make or become flat or flatter: [with obj.] *Martin **flattened** a book **out** in front of him* | [no obj.] *after Kendal, the countryside begins to **flatten out*** | [as adj. **flattened**] *they were dancing on the flattened grass.*
■ [with obj. and adverbial of place] press (oneself or one's body) against a surface, typically to get away from something or someone or to let someone pass: *they **flattened themselves** on the pavement as a bomb came whistling down.* ■ [with obj.] Music lower (a note) in pitch by a semitone.
2 [with obj.] raze (a building or settlement) to the ground: *the hurricane flattened thousands of homes.*
■ informal strike (someone) so as to make them fall down: *Flynn flattened him with a single punch.* ■ informal defeat (someone) completely, especially in a sporting contest. ■ figurative humiliate or depress (someone): *the controversy has flattened everybody here, including the players.*
– DERIVATIVES **flattener** noun.
▶ **flatten out 1** (of an increasing quantity or rate) show a less marked rise; slow down. **2** make an aircraft fly horizontally after a dive or climb: *he flattened out and made a fine three-point landing.*

flatter ▶ **verb** [with obj.] lavish insincere praise and compliments upon (someone), especially to further one's own interests: *she was flattering him in order to avoid doing what he wanted.*
■ give an unrealistically favourable impression of: *the portraitist flatters his sitter to the detriment of his art.* ■ (usu. **be flattered**) make (someone) feel honoured and pleased: [with obj. and infinitive] *I was very flattered to be given the commission* | [with obj. and clause] *at least I am flattered that you don't find me boring.* ■ (**flatter oneself**) make oneself feel pleased by believing something favourable about oneself, typically something that is unfounded: [with clause] *I flatter myself I'm the best dressed man here.* ■ (of a colour or a style of clothing) make (someone) appear more attractive or to the best advantage: *the muted fuchsia shade flattered her pale skin.* ■ archaic please (the ear or eye): *the beauty of the stone flattered the young clergyman's eyes.*
– DERIVATIVES **flatterer** noun.
– ORIGIN Middle English: perhaps a back-formation from **FLATTERY**.

flattering ▶ **adjective** (of a person or their remarks) full of insincere praise and compliments: *the article began with some flattering words about us.*
■ pleasing; gratifying: [with infinitive] *it was flattering to have a pretty girl like Fiona so obviously fond of him.* ■ (especially of a garment or colour) enhancing someone's appearance: *I don't think anything sleeveless is very flattering.* ■ (of a picture or portrait) giving an unrealistically favourable impression of someone or something: *that's a rather flattering picture of him.*
– DERIVATIVES **flatteringly** adverb.

flattery ▶ **noun** (pl. **-ies**) [mass noun] excessive and insincere praise, especially that given to further one's own interests: *she allowed no hint of flattery to enter her voice* | [count noun] *the honours and flatteries which governments poured on to the maverick ruler.*
■ unrealistically favourable representation of someone in a picture.
– ORIGIN Middle English: from Old French *flaterie*, from *flater* 'stroke, flatter', probably of Germanic origin and related to **FLAT**[1].

flattie (also **flatty**) informal ▶ **noun** (pl. **-ies**) **1** a flat-heeled shoe.
2 a flatfish.
3 a flatboat.
4 dated a police officer. [ORIGIN: late 19th cent.: informal abbreviation of **FLATFOOT**.]

flat-top ▶ **noun 1** US informal an aircraft carrier.
2 [often as modifier] a man's hairstyle in which the hair is cropped short so that it bristles up into a flat surface: *a flat-top hairstyle.*
3 an acoustic guitar that has a flat rather than a curved front.

flatulent /ˈflatjʊl(ə)nt/ ▶ **adjective** suffering from or marked by an accumulation of gas in the alimentary canal: *treat flatulent cows with caustic soda.*
■ related to or causing this condition: *the flatulent effect of beans.* ■ figurative inflated or pretentious in speech or writing: *I had expected an American senator to be as pompous and flatulent as a British MP.*
– DERIVATIVES **flatulence** noun, **flatulency** noun, **flatulently** adverb.
– ORIGIN late 16th cent.: via French from modern Latin *flatulentus*, from Latin *flatus* 'blowing' (see **FLATUS**).

flatus /ˈfleɪtəs/ ▶ **noun** [mass noun] formal gas in or from the stomach or intestines, produced by swallowing air or by bacterial fermentation.
– ORIGIN mid 17th cent.: from Latin, literally 'blowing', from *flare* 'to blow'.

flatware ▶ **noun** [mass noun] relatively flat items of crockery such as plates and saucers.
■ N. Amer. domestic cutlery.

flatworm ▶ **noun** a worm of a phylum which includes the planarians together with the parasitic flukes and tapeworms. They are distinguished by having a simple flattened body which lacks blood vessels, and a digestive tract which, if present, has a single opening.
• Phylum Platyhelminthes: several classes.

flat-woven ▶ **adjective** (of a carpet or rug) woven so as not to form a projecting pile.
– DERIVATIVES **flat-weave** noun.

Flaubert /ˈfləʊbɛː, French flobɛʀ/, Gustave (1821–80), French novelist and short-story writer. A dominant figure in the French realist school, he achieved fame with his first published novel, *Madame Bovary* (1857). Its portrayal of the adulteries and suicide of a provincial doctor's wife caused Flaubert to be tried for immorality (and acquitted).

flaunching /ˈflɔːntʃɪŋ/ ▶ **noun** [mass noun] the sloping fillet of cement or mortar embedding the base of a chimney pot.

flaunt ▶ **verb** [with obj.] display (something) ostentatiously, especially in order to provoke envy or admiration or to show defiance: *newly rich consumers eager to flaunt their prosperity.*
■ (**flaunt oneself**) dress or behave in a sexually provocative way.
– PHRASES **if you've got it, flaunt it** informal one should make a conspicuous and confident show of one's wealth or attributes rather than be modest about them.

– DERIVATIVES **flaunter** noun, **flaunty** adjective.
– ORIGIN mid 16th cent.: of unknown origin.

USAGE Flaunt and flout may sound similar but they have different meanings. **Flaunt** means 'display ostentatiously', as in *visitors who liked to **flaunt** their wealth*, while **flout** means 'openly disregard (a rule or convention)', as in *new recruits growing their hair and **flouting** convention*. It is a common error, recorded since around the 1940s, to use **flaunt** when **flout** is intended, as in *the young woman had been **flaunting** the rules and regulations*. Around 20 per cent of the uses of **flaunt** in the British National Corpus are incorrect in this respect.

flautist /ˈflɔːtɪst/ ▶ **noun** a flute player.
– ORIGIN mid 19th cent. (superseding 17th-cent. *flutist* in British English use): from Italian *flautista*, from *flauto* 'flute'.

flavescent /fləˈvɛs(ə)nt/ ▶ **adjective** yellowish or turning yellow.
– ORIGIN mid 19th cent.: from Latin *flavescent-* 'turning yellow', from the verb *flavescere*, from *flavus* 'yellow'.

Flavian /ˈfleɪvɪən/ ▶ **adjective** of or relating to a dynasty (AD 69–96) of Roman emperors including Vespasian and his sons Titus and Domitian.
▶ **noun** a member of this dynasty.
– ORIGIN from Latin *Flavianus*, from *Flavius*, a given name used by this dynasty.

flavin /ˈfleɪvɪn/ ▶ **noun** Biochemistry any of a group of naturally occurring pigments including riboflavin. They have a tricyclic aromatic molecular structure.
– ORIGIN mid 19th cent.: from Latin *flavus* 'yellow' + **-IN**[1].

flavone /ˈfleɪvəʊn/ ▶ **noun** [mass noun] Chemistry a colourless crystalline compound which is the basis of a number of white or yellow plant pigments.
● A tricyclic aromatic compound; chem. formula: $C_{15}H_{10}O_2$.
■ [count noun] any of these pigments.
– ORIGIN late 19th cent.: from Latin *flavus* 'yellow' + **-ONE**.

flavonoid /ˈfleɪvənɔɪd/ ▶ **noun** Chemistry any of a large class of plant pigments having a structure based on or similar to that of flavone.

flavoprotein /ˌfleɪvə(ʊ)ˈprəʊtiːn/ ▶ **noun** Biochemistry any of a class of conjugated proteins that contain flavins and are involved in oxidation reactions in cells.
– ORIGIN 1930s: blend of **FLAVIN** and **PROTEIN**.

flavorous ▶ **adjective** dated having a pleasant or pungent flavour.

flavour (US **flavor**) ▶ **noun 1** the distinctive quality of a particular food or drink as perceived by the taste buds: *the crisps come in pizza and barbecue flavours* | [mass noun] *mozzarella cheese adds flavour to any salad.*
■ [in sing.] figurative a distinctive quality of something, especially one reminiscent of something else: *this year's seminars have a European flavour.* ■ [in sing.] figurative an indication of the essential character of something: *the extracts give **a flavour of** the content and tone of the conversation.* ■ chiefly US a substance used to alter or enhance the taste of food or drink; a flavouring.
2 Physics a quantized property of quarks which differentiates them into at least six varieties (up, down, charmed, strange, top, bottom). Compare with **COLOUR**.
▶ **verb** [with obj.] alter or enhance the taste of (food or drink) by adding a particular ingredient: *they use a wide range of spices to flavour their foods* | *chunks of chicken flavoured with herbs.*
■ figurative give a distinctive quality to: *the faint exasperation that had flavoured her tone.*
– PHRASES **flavour of the month** a person or thing that enjoys a short period of great popularity: *don't opt for a system that's flavour of the month.*
– DERIVATIVES **flavourful** adjective, **flavourless** adjective, **flavoursome** adjective.
– ORIGIN late Middle English (in the sense 'fragrance, aroma'): from Old French *flaor*, perhaps based on a blend of Latin *flatus* 'blowing' and *foetor* 'stench'; the *-v-* appears to have been introduced in Middle English by association with **SAVOUR**. Sense 1 dates from the late 17th cent.

flavoured (US **flavored**) ▶ **adjective** (of food or drink) having a particular type of taste: [in combination] *the peanut oil is light but fairly full-flavoured.*
■ (of food or drink) having been given a particular taste by the addition of a flavouring: *a flavoured drink* | [in combination] *chicken breasts pre-poached in lemon-flavoured stock.* ■ [in combination] figurative having a particular distinctive quality: *the band knocked out some fine rock 'n' roll-flavoured singles.*

flavour enhancer ▶ **noun** a chemical additive, e.g. monosodium glutamate, used to intensify the flavour of food.

flavouring (US **flavoring**) ▶ **noun** [mass noun] a substance used to give a different, stronger, or more agreeable taste to food or drink: *vanilla flavouring* | [count noun] *mustard has been used as a flavouring for thousands of years.*

flaw[1] ▶ **noun** a mark, fault, or other imperfection which mars a substance or object: *flaws in paint and plaster.*
■ a fault or weakness in a person's character: *he had his flaws, but he was still a great teacher.* ■ a mistake or shortcoming in a plan, theory, or legal document which causes it to fail or reduces its effectiveness: *there were fundamental **flaws in** the case for reforming local government.*
▶ **verb** [with obj.] (usu. **be flawed**) (of an imperfection) mar, weaken, or invalidate (something): *the computer game was flawed by poor programming.*
– ORIGIN Middle English: perhaps from Old Norse *flaga* 'slab'. The original sense was 'a flake of snow', later, 'a fragment or splinter', hence 'a defect or imperfection'(late 15th cent.).

flaw[2] ▶ **noun** poetic/literary a squall of wind; a short storm.
– ORIGIN early 16th cent.: probably from Middle Dutch *vlāghe*, Middle Low German *vlāge*.

flawed ▶ **adjective** (of a substance or object) blemished, damaged, or imperfect in some way: *flawed crystals.*
■ (of something abstract) containing a mistake, weakness, or fault: *a flawed strategy.* ■ (of a person) having a weakness in their character: *a flawed hero.*

flawless ▶ **adjective** without any blemishes or imperfections; perfect: *his brown flawless skin.*
■ without any mistakes or shortcomings: *he greeted her in almost flawless English.* ■ (of a person) lacking any faults or weaknesses of character.
– DERIVATIVES **flawlessly** adverb, **flawlessness** noun.

flax ▶ **noun** [mass noun] a blue-flowered herbaceous plant that is cultivated for its seed (linseed) and for textile fibre made from its stalks.
● *Linum usitatissimum*, family Linaceae.
■ textile fibre obtained from this plant: *a mill for the preparation and spinning of flax.* ■ used in names of other plants of the flax family (e.g. **purging flax**) or plants that yield similar fibre (e.g. **false flax**). ■ (also **New Zealand flax**) another term for **FLAX-LILY**.
– ORIGIN Old English *flæx*, of West Germanic origin; related to Dutch *vlas* and German *Flachs*, from an Indo-European root shared by Latin *plectere* and Greek *plekein* 'to plait, twist'.

flaxen ▶ **adjective** of flax.
■ poetic/literary (especially of hair) of the pale yellow colour of dressed flax: *her long flaxen hair.*

flax-lily ▶ **noun** a New Zealand plant that yields valuable fibre and is also grown as an ornamental. Also called **NEW ZEALAND FLAX**.
● *Phormium tenax*, family Agavaceae.

Flaxman /ˈflaksmən/, John (1755–1826), English sculptor and draughtsman, noted for his church monuments and his engraved illustrations to Homer (1793).

flaxseed ▶ **noun** another term for **LINSEED**.

flay ▶ **verb** [with obj.] peel the skin off (a corpse or carcass): *one shoulder had been flayed to reveal the muscles* | *the captured general was **flayed alive**.*
■ peel (the skin) off a corpse or carcass: *she flayed the white skin from the flesh.* ■ whip or beat (someone) so harshly as to remove their skin: *Matthew flayed them viciously with a branch.* ■ figurative criticize severely and brutally: *he flayed the government for not moving fast enough on economic reform.* ■ figurative extort or exact money or belongings from (someone): *plundering cities and temples and flaying the people with requisitions.*
– DERIVATIVES **flayer** noun.
– ORIGIN Old English *flēan*, of Germanic origin; related to Middle Dutch *vlaen*.

F-layer ▶ **noun** the highest and most strongly ionized region of the ionosphere.
– ORIGIN 1920s: arbitrary use of *F* + **LAYER**.

flea ▶ **noun** a small wingless jumping insect which feeds on the blood of mammals and birds. It sometimes transmits diseases through its bite, including plague and myxomatosis.
● Order Siphonaptera: several families and many species, including the **human flea** (*Pulex irritans*).
■ short for **FLEA BEETLE**. ■ see also **WATER FLEA**.
– PHRASES **(as) fit as a flea** in very good health. **a flea in one's ear** a sharp reproof: *she expected to be sent away with a flea in her ear.*
– ORIGIN Old English *flēa*, *flēah*, of Germanic origin; related to Dutch *vlo* and German *Floh*.

fleabag ▶ **noun** informal a shabby unpleasant person or thing.
■ N. Amer. a seedy run-down hotel or lodging house.

fleabane ▶ **noun** a herbaceous plant of the daisy family, reputed to drive away fleas.
● *Pulicaria*, *Erigeron*, and other genera, family Compositae: in particular the yellow-flowered **common fleabane** (*P. dysenterica*).

flea beetle ▶ **noun** a small jumping leaf beetle that can be a pest of plants such as crucifers.
● *Phyllotreta* and other genera, family Chrysomelidae.

flea bite ▶ **noun** a small red mark caused by the bite of a flea.
■ figurative a trivial injury or cost: *the proposed energy tax amounted to little more than a flea bite.*

flea-bitten ▶ **adjective** sordid, dilapidated, or disreputable: *a crowd of flea-bitten louts.*

flea circus ▶ **noun** a novelty show of performing fleas.

flea collar ▶ **noun** a collar for a cat or dog that is impregnated with insecticide in order to keep the pet free of fleas.

fleadh /ˈflɑː/ ▶ **noun** a festival of Irish or Celtic music, dancing, and culture.
– ORIGIN from Irish *fleadh ceoil* 'music festival'.

flea market ▶ **noun** a street market selling second-hand goods.

fleapit ▶ **noun** chiefly Brit. a dingy dirty place, especially a run-down cinema.

fleawort ▶ **noun** a Eurasian plant related to ragwort, reputed to drive away fleas.
● Genus *Senecio*, family Compositae: several species, in particular *S. integrifolius*.

flèche /fleɪʃ, flɛʃ/ ▶ **noun** a slender spire, typically over the intersection of the nave and the transept of a church.
– ORIGIN mid 19th cent.: French, literally 'arrow'.

flechette /fleɪˈʃɛt, flɛ-/ ▶ **noun** a type of ammunition resembling a small dart, shot from a gun.
– ORIGIN early 20th cent.: from French *fléchette*, diminutive of *flèche* 'arrow'.

fleck ▶ **noun** a very small patch of colour or light: *his blue eyes had grey flecks in them* | ***flecks of** sunshine.*
■ a small particle or speck of something: *brushing a few flecks of dandruff from his suit.*
▶ **verb** [with obj.] (often **be flecked**) mark or dot with small patches of colour or particles of something: *the minarets are flecked with gold leaf.*
– ORIGIN late Middle English (as a verb): perhaps from Old Norse *flekkr* (noun), *flekka* (verb), or from Middle Low German, Middle Dutch *vlecke*.

Flecker, James (Herman) Elroy (1884–1915), English poet. Notable works: *The Golden Journey to Samarkand* (collection, 1913) and *Hassan* (play, 1922).

fled past and past participle of **FLEE**.

fledge /flɛdʒ/ ▶ **verb** [no obj.] (of a young bird) develop wing feathers that are large enough for flight.
■ [with obj.] bring up (a young bird) until its wing feathers are developed enough for flight.
– ORIGIN mid 16th cent.: from the obsolete adjective *fledge* 'ready to fly', from Old English, of Germanic origin; related to Dutch *vlug* 'quick, agile', also to **FLY**[1].

fledged ▶ **adjective** (of a young bird) having wing feathers that are large enough for flight; able to fly. See also **FULLY-FLEDGED**.
■ [in combination] (of a person or thing) having just taken on the role specified: *a newly-fledged Detective Inspector.* ■ (of an arrow) provided with feathers.

fledgling (also **fledgeling**) ▶ **noun** a young bird that has just fledged.
■ [usu. as modifier] a person or organization that is immature, inexperienced, or underdeveloped: *the fledgling democracies of eastern Europe.*
– ORIGIN mid 19th cent.: from the obsolete adjective *fledge* (see **FLEDGE**), on the pattern of *nestling*.

flee ▶ **verb** (**flees**, **fleeing**; past and past participle **fled**) [no obj.] run away from a place or situation of danger: *a man was shot twice as he **fled from** five masked youths.*
■ [with obj.] run away from (someone or something): *he*

was forced to ***flee the country*** | figurative *all the rules of the racing school fled my mind.*
– ORIGIN Old English *flēon*, of Germanic origin; related to Dutch *vlieden* and German *fliehen*.

fleece ▶ **noun 1** the woolly covering of a sheep or goat: *as the sheep came on board, we grabbed their long shaggy fleeces* | [mass noun] *he clutched the ram by two handfuls of thick fleece.*
■ the amount of wool shorn from a sheep in a single piece at one time.
2 a thing resembling a sheep's woolly covering, in particular:
■ [mass noun] a soft warm fabric with a texture similar to sheep's wool, used as a lining material. ■ a jacket or other garment made from such a fabric. ■ Heraldry a representation of a fleece suspended from a ring.
▶ **verb** [with obj.] **1** informal obtain a great deal of money from (someone), typically by overcharging or swindling them: *we were fleeced by a tout for tickets.*
2 figurative cover as if with a fleece: *the sky was half blue, half fleeced with white clouds.*
– DERIVATIVES **fleeced** adjective.
– ORIGIN Old English *flēos, flēs*, of West Germanic origin; related to Dutch *vlies* and German *Vlies*.

fleecy ▶ **adjective** (**fleecier**, **fleeciest**) **1** (especially of a towel or garment) made of or lined with a soft, warm fabric: *a fleecy sweatshirt.*
2 (especially of a cloud) white and fluffy.
– DERIVATIVES **fleecily** adverb, **fleeciness** noun.

fleer /flɪə/ ▶ **verb** [no obj.] poetic/literary laugh impudently or jeeringly: *he fleered at us.*
▶ **noun** archaic an impudent or jeering look or speech.
– ORIGIN late Middle English: probably of Scandinavian origin and related to Norwegian and Swedish dialect *flira* 'to grin'.

fleet[1] ▶ **noun** a group of ships sailing together, engaged in the same activity, or under the same ownership: *the small port supports a fishing fleet* | *a* ***fleet of*** *battleships.*
■ (**the fleet**) a country's navy: *the US fleet.* ■ a number of vehicles or aircraft operating together or under the same ownership: *a* ***fleet of*** *ambulances took the injured to hospital.*
– ORIGIN Old English *flēot* 'ship, shipping', from *flēotan* 'float, swim' (see **FLEET**[5]).

fleet[2] ▶ **adjective** chiefly poetic/literary fast and nimble in movement: *a man of advancing years, but* ***fleet of foot.***
– DERIVATIVES **fleetly** adverb, **fleetness** noun.
– ORIGIN early 16th cent.: probably from Old Norse *fljótr*, of Germanic origin and related to **FLEET**[5].

fleet[3] ▶ **noun** dialect a marshland creek, channel, or ditch.
– ORIGIN Old English *flēot*, of Germanic origin; related to Dutch *vliet*, also to **FLEET**[5].

fleet[4] dialect ▶ **adjective** (of water) shallow.
▶ **adverb** at or to a small depth.
– ORIGIN early 17th cent.: perhaps based on an Old English cognate of Dutch *vloot* 'shallow' and related to **FLEET**[5].

fleet[5] ▶ **verb** [no obj.] poetic/literary move or pass quickly: *a variety of expressions fleeted across his face* | *time may fleet and youth may fade.*
■ [with obj.] pass (time) rapidly. ■ fade away; be transitory: *the cares of boyhood* ***fleet away.***
– ORIGIN Old English *flēotan* 'float, swim', of Germanic origin; related to Dutch *vlieten* and German *fliessen*, also to **FLIT** and **FLOAT**.

Fleet Admiral ▶ **noun** the highest rank of admiral in the US navy.

Fleet Air Arm historical the aviation service of the Royal Navy.

fleet-footed ▶ **adjective** nimble and fast on one's feet: *the fleet-footed sprinter ran full out.*

fleeting ▶ **adjective** lasting for a very short time: *for a fleeting moment I saw the face of a boy.*
– DERIVATIVES **fleetingly** adverb.

Fleet Street a street in central London in which the offices of national newspapers were located until the mid 1980s (often used to refer to the British Press): *the hottest story in Fleet Street.*

Fleming[1] /ˈflɛmɪŋ/, Sir Alexander (1881–1955), Scottish bacteriologist. In 1928, Fleming discovered the effect of penicillin on bacteria. Twelve years later Howard Florey and Ernst Chain established its therapeutic use as an antibiotic. Nobel Prize for Physiology or Medicine (1945, shared with Florey and Chain).

Fleming[2] /ˈflɛmɪŋ/, Ian (Lancaster) (1908–64), English novelist. He is known for his spy novels whose hero is the secret agent James Bond.

Fleming[3] /ˈflɛmɪŋ/, Sir John Ambrose (1849–1945), English electrical engineer, chiefly remembered for his invention of the thermionic valve (1900).

Fleming[4] /ˈflɛmɪŋ/ ▶ **noun 1** a native of Flanders.
2 a member of the Flemish-speaking people inhabiting northern and western Belgium. Compare with **WALLOON**.
– ORIGIN late Old English *Flǣmingi*, from Old Norse, reinforced by Middle Dutch *Vlāming*, related to *Vlaanderen* 'Flanders'.

Fleming's left-hand rule Physics a mnemonic concerning the behaviour of a current-carrying conductor in a magnetic field, according to which the directions of the magnetic field, the current, and the force exerted on the conductor are indicated respectively by the first finger, second finger, and thumb of the left hand when these are held out perpendicular to each other.
– ORIGIN 1920s: proposed by J. A. Fleming (see **FLEMING**[3]).

Fleming's right-hand rule Physics a mnemonic concerning the behaviour of a conductor moving in a magnetic field, according to which the directions of the magnetic field, the induced current, and the motion of the conductor are indicated respectively by the first finger, second finger, and thumb of the right hand when these are held out perpendicular to each other.

Flemish /ˈflɛmɪʃ/ ▶ **adjective** of or relating to Flanders, its people, or their language.
▶ **noun 1** [mass noun] the Dutch language as spoken in Flanders. It is one of the two official languages of Belgium.
2 (**the Flemish**) [as plural noun] the people of Flanders.
– ORIGIN Middle English: from Middle Dutch *Vlāmisch*, related to *Vlaanderen* 'Flanders'.

Flemish bond ▶ **noun** Building a pattern of bricks in a wall in which each course consists of alternate headers and stretchers.

flense /flɛns/ (also **flench** /flɛn(t)ʃ/, **flinch**) ▶ **verb** [with obj.] slice the skin or fat from (a carcass, especially that of a whale).
■ strip (skin or fat) from a carcass: *the skin had been* ***flensed off.***
– DERIVATIVES **flenser** noun.
– ORIGIN early 19th cent.: from Danish *flensa*.

flesh ▶ **noun** [mass noun] the soft substance consisting of muscle and fat that is found between the skin and bones of an animal or a human: *she grabbed Anna's arm, her fingers sinking into the flesh.*
■ this substance in an animal or fish, regarded as food: *boned lamb flesh* | [in combination] *a flesh-eater.* ■ the pulpy substance of a fruit or vegetable, especially the part that is eaten: *halve the avocados and scrape out the flesh.* ■ fat: *he carries no spare flesh.* ■ the skin or surface of the human body with reference to its colour, appearance, or sensual properties: *she gasped as the cold water hit her flesh.* ■ (**the flesh**) the human body and its physical needs and desires, especially as contrasted with the mind or the soul: *I have never been one to deny the* ***pleasures of the flesh.*** ■ flesh colour.
▶ **verb 1** [no obj.] (**flesh out**) put weight on: *he had fleshed out to a solid 220 pounds.*
■ [with obj.] (**flesh something out**) add more details to something which only exists in a draft or outline form: *the arguments were fleshed out by the minister.*
2 [with obj.] give (a hound or hawk) a piece of the flesh of game that has been killed in order to incite it.
■ poetic/literary initiate (someone) in bloodshed or warfare: *he fleshed his troops by indulging them with enterprises against the enemy's posts.*
3 [with obj.] [often as noun **fleshing**] remove the flesh adhering to (a skin or hide).
– PHRASES **all flesh** all human and animal life. **go the way of all flesh** die or come to an end: *the film has gone the way of all flesh after being slated by the critics.* **in the flesh** in person rather than via a telephone, film, the written word, or other means: *they decided that they should meet Alexander in the flesh.* **lose flesh** archaic become thinner. **make someone's flesh creep** (or **crawl**) cause someone to feel fear, horror, or disgust: *his story will make your flesh creep.* **one flesh** used to refer to the spiritual and physical union of two people in a relationship, especially marriage: *my body is his, his is mine: one flesh.* [ORIGIN: with biblical allusion to Gen. 2:24.] **put flesh on** (**the bones of**) **something** add more details to something which only exists in a draft or outline form: *he has yet to put flesh on his 'big idea'.* **put on flesh** put on weight. **sins of the flesh** archaic or humorous sins related to physical indulgence, especially sexual gratification.
– DERIVATIVES **fleshed** adjective [usu. in combination] *a white-fleshed fish*, **fleshless** adjective.
– ORIGIN Old English *flǣsc*, of Germanic origin; related to Dutch *vlees* and German *Fleisch*.

flesh and blood ▶ **noun** used to emphasize that a person is a physical, living being with human emotions or frailties, often in contrast to something abstract, spiritual, or mechanical: *the customer is flesh and blood, not just a sales statistic* | [as modifier] *he seemed more like a creature from a dream than a flesh-and-blood father.*
– PHRASES **one's (own) flesh and blood** a near relative or one's close family: *he felt as much for that girl as if she had been his own flesh and blood.*

flesh colour ▶ **noun** [mass noun] a light brownish pink.
– DERIVATIVES **flesh-coloured** adjective.

flesher ▶ **noun 1** chiefly Scottish a butcher.
2 N. Amer. a knife for fleshing hides.

flesh fly ▶ **noun** a fly that breeds in carrion, typically producing live young which are deposited on a carcass.
• Family Sarcophagidae: *Sarcophaga* and other genera.

fleshings ▶ **plural noun** flesh-coloured tights worn by actors.

fleshly ▶ **adjective** (**fleshlier**, **fleshliest**) **1** of or relating to human desire or bodily appetites; sensual: *fleshly pleasures.*
2 having an actual physical presence.
– ORIGIN Old English *flǣsclic* (see **FLESH**, **-LY**[1]).

fleshpots ▶ **plural noun** places providing luxurious or hedonistic living: *he had lived the life of a roué in the fleshpots of London and Paris.*
– ORIGIN early 16th cent.: with biblical allusion to the *fleshpots of Egypt* (Exod. 16:3).

flesh side ▶ **noun** the side of a hide that adjoined the flesh.

flesh tints ▶ **plural noun** flesh colours as rendered by a painter.

flesh wound ▶ **noun** a wound that breaks the skin but does not damage bones or vital organs.

fleshy ▶ **adjective** (**fleshier**, **fleshiest**) **1** (of a person or part of the body) having a substantial amount of flesh; plump: *her torso was full, fleshy, and heavy.*
■ (of plant or fruit tissue) soft and thick: *fleshy, greeny-grey leaves.* ■ (of a wine) full-bodied.
2 resembling flesh in appearance or texture: *colour some fondant fleshy pink.*
– DERIVATIVES **fleshiness** noun.

fletch /flɛtʃ/ ▶ **verb** [with obj.] provide (an arrow) with feathers for flight: *most arrows are fletched with 3 to 5-inch feathers.*
▶ **noun** each of the feathered vanes of an arrow: [in combination] *a four-fletch arrow.*
– ORIGIN mid 17th cent.: alteration of **FLEDGE**, probably influenced by *fletcher*.

Fletcher, John (1579–1625), English dramatist. A writer of Jacobean tragicomedies, he wrote some fifteen plays with Francis Beaumont, including *The Maid's Tragedy* (1610–11).

fletcher ▶ **noun** chiefly historical a person who makes and sells arrows.
– ORIGIN Middle English: from Old French *flechier*, from *fleche* 'arrow'.

fletching ▶ **noun** [mass noun] the feathers of an arrow: *it has good-sized fletching* | [count noun] *he repairs damaged fletchings.*

fleur-de-lis /ˌflәːdәˈliː/ (also **fleur-de-lys**) ▶ **noun** (pl. **fleurs-de-lis** pronunc. same) **1** Art & Heraldry a stylized lily composed of three petals bound together near their bases. It is especially known from the former royal arms of France, in which it appears in gold on a blue field.
2 a European iris.
• Genus *Iris*, family Iridaceae, in particular *I.* × *germanica* 'Florentina' (with bluish-white flowers) or *I. pseudacorus* (the yellow flag).
– ORIGIN Middle English: from Old French *flour de lys* 'flower of the lily'.

fleuron /ˈflʊәrɒn, ˈflәː-/ ▶ **noun** a flower-shaped ornament, used especially on buildings, coins, and books.
■ a small pastry puff used for garnishing.

– ORIGIN late Middle English: from Old French *floron*, from *flour* 'flower'.

fleury /ˈflʊəri/ ▶ **adjective** variant spelling of **FLORY**.

Flevoland /ˈfleɪvəʊland/ a province of the Netherlands, created in 1986 and reclaimed from the Zuider Zee during the 1950s and 1960s.

flew past of **FLY**[1].

flews /fluːz/ ▶ **plural noun** the thick hanging lips of a bloodhound or similar dog.
– ORIGIN late 16th cent.: of unknown origin.

flex[1] ▶ **verb** [with obj.] bend (a limb or joint): *she saw him flex his ankle and wince.*
■ [no obj.] (of a limb or joint) become bent: *prevent the damaged wrist from flexing.* ■ cause (a muscle) to stand out by contracting or tensing it: *bodybuilders flexing their muscles.* ■ [no obj.] (of a muscle) contract or be tensed: *a muscle flexed in his jaw.* ■ [no obj.] (of a material) be capable of warping or bending and then reverting to shape: *set windows in rubber so they flex during an earthquake.* ■ [usu. as adj. **flexed**] Archaeology place (a corpse) with the legs drawn up under the chin: *a flexed burial.*
– PHRASES **flex one's muscles** see **MUSCLE**.
– ORIGIN early 16th cent.: from Latin *flex-* 'bent', from the verb *flectere*.

flex[2] ▶ **noun** chiefly Brit. a flexible insulated cable used for carrying electric current to an appliance.
– ORIGIN early 20th cent.: abbreviation of **FLEXIBLE**.

flexible ▶ **adjective** capable of bending easily without breaking: *flexible rubber seals.*
■ able to be easily modified to respond to altered circumstances or conditions: *flexible forms of retirement.* ■ (of a person) ready and able to change so as to adapt to different circumstances: *you can save money if you're flexible about where your room is located.*
– DERIVATIVES **flexibility** noun, **flexibly** adverb.
– ORIGIN late Middle English: from Old French, or from Latin *flexibilis*, from *flectere* 'to bend'.

flexile /ˈflɛksʌɪl/ ▶ **adjective** archaic pliant and flexible: *the serpent's flexile body.*
– DERIVATIVES **flexility** noun.
– ORIGIN mid 17th cent.: from Latin *flexilis*, from *flectere* 'to bend'.

flexion /ˈflɛkʃ(ə)n/ (also **flection**) ▶ **noun** [mass noun] the action of bending or the condition of being bent, especially the bending of a limb or joint: *flexion of the fingers* | [count noun] *these protozoans can move by body flexions.*
– ORIGIN early 17th cent.: from Latin *flexio(n-)*, from *flectere* 'to bend'.

flexitime (N. Amer. also **flextime**) ▶ **noun** [mass noun] a system of working a set number of hours with the starting and finishing times chosen within agreed limits by the employee: *a 35-hour week with flexitime.*
– ORIGIN 1970s: blend of **FLEXIBLE** and **TIME**.

flexo ▶ **noun** short for **FLEXOGRAPHY**.
▶ **adjective** short for *flexographic* (see **FLEXOGRAPHY**).

flexography /flɛkˈsɒɡrəfi/ ▶ **noun** [mass noun] a rotary relief printing method using rubber or plastic plates and fluid inks or dyes for printing on fabrics and impervious materials such as plastics, as well as on paper.
– DERIVATIVES **flexographic** adjective.
– ORIGIN 1950s: from Latin *flexus* 'a bending' (from the verb *flectere*) + **-GRAPHY**.

flexor /ˈflɛksə/ (also **flexor muscle**) ▶ **noun** Anatomy a muscle whose contraction bends a limb or other part of the body. Often contrasted with **EXTENSOR**.
■ any of a number of specific muscles in the arm, hand, leg, or foot.

flexuous /ˈflɛksjʊəs/ ▶ **adjective** full of bends and curves.
– DERIVATIVES **flexuosity** noun, **flexuously** adverb.
– ORIGIN early 17th cent.: from Latin *flexuosus*, from *flexus* 'a bending', from the verb *flectere*.

flexure /ˈflɛkʃə/ ▶ **noun** [mass noun] technical, chiefly Anatomy & Geology the action of bending or curving, or the condition of being bent or curved.
■ [count noun] a bent or curved part: *these lesser hills were flexures of the San Andreas system.*
– DERIVATIVES **flexural** adjective.
– ORIGIN late 16th cent.: from Latin *flexura*, from *flectere* 'to bend'.

flexwing ▶ **noun** a collapsible fabric delta wing, as used in hang-gliders: [as modifier] *a flexwing microlight.*

flibbertigibbet /ˌflɪbətɪˈdʒɪbɪt/ ▶ **noun** a frivolous, flighty, or excessively talkative person.
– ORIGIN late Middle English: probably imitative of idle chatter.

flic ▶ **noun 1** Computing a data file containing computer animations. [ORIGIN: usage of the cinematographic sense of **FLICK**.]
2 informal a French policeman. [ORIGIN: French.]

flick ▶ **noun 1** a sudden smart movement: *the flick of a switch* | *a flick of the wrist* | *a back-heeled flick.*
■ the sudden release of a bent finger or thumb, especially to propel a small object: *he sent his cigarette spinning away with a flick of his fingers.* ■ a light, sharp, quickly retracted blow, especially with a whip. ■ (**a flick through**) a quick look or search through (a volume or a collection of papers): *have a flick through any gun magazine.*
2 informal a cinema film: *a Hollywood action flick.*
■ (**the flicks**) the cinema: *fancy a night at the flicks?*
▶ **verb** [with obj. and adverbial of direction] propel (something) with a sudden sharp movement, especially of the fingers: *Ursula **flicked** some ash **off** her sleeve.*
■ (**flick something on/off**) turn something electrical on or off by means of a switch: *he flicked on the air conditioning.* ■ [no obj., with adverbial of direction] make a sudden sharp movement: *the finch's tail flicks up and down.* ■ [with obj.] move (a whip) so as to strike.
– PHRASES **give someone the flick** (or **get the flick**) informal, chiefly Austral. reject (or be rejected) in a casual or offhand way.
– ORIGIN late Middle English: symbolic, *fl-* frequently beginning words denoting sudden movement.
▶ **flick through** look or search quickly through (a volume or a collection of papers): *flick through the phone book and pick a company.*

flicker[1] ▶ **verb** [no obj.] **1** (of light or a source of light) shine unsteadily; vary rapidly in brightness: *the interior lights flickered, and came on.*
■ (of a flame) burn fitfully, alternately flaring up and dying down: *the candle flickered again* | [as adj. **flickering**] *the flickering flames of the fire.* ■ [with adverbial of place] figurative (of a feeling or emotion) be experienced or show itself briefly and faintly, especially in someone's eyes: *amusement flickered briefly in his eyes.*
2 make small, quick movements; flutter rapidly: *her eyelids flickered* | [with complement] *the injured killer's eyes flickered open.*
■ [with adverbial of direction] (of someone's eyes) move quickly in a particular direction in order to look at something: *her alert hazel eyes flickered around the room.* ■ [with adverbial] (of a facial expression) appear briefly: *a look of horror flickered across his face.*
▶ **noun 1** an unsteady movement of a flame or light which causes rapid variations in brightness: *the flicker of a candle flame caught our eyes.*
■ [mass noun] fluctuations in the brightness of a film or television image such as occur when the number of frames per second is too small for persistence of vision.
2 a tiny movement: *then a flicker of movement caught his eye.*
■ a faint indication of a facial expression: *a flicker of a smile passed across her face.* ■ figurative a very brief and faint experience of an emotion or feeling: *she felt a small flicker of alarm.*
– ORIGIN Old English *flicorian*, *flycerian* 'to flutter', probably of Germanic origin and related to Low German *flickern* and Dutch *flikkeren*.
▶ **flicker out** (of a flame or light) die away and go out after a series of flickers. ■ figurative (of a feeling) die away and finally disappear: *the swift burst of curiosity and eagerness flickered out.*

flicker[2] ▶ **noun** an American woodpecker that often feeds on ants on the ground.
• Genus *Colaptes*, family Picidae: several species, in particular the **common** (or **northern**) **flicker** (*C. auratus*).
– ORIGIN early 19th cent.: imitative of its call.

flick knife ▶ **noun** Brit. a knife with a blade that springs out from the handle when a button is pressed.

flick roll ▶ **noun** another term for **SNAP ROLL**.

flier ▶ **noun** variant spelling of **FLYER**.

flight ▶ **noun 1** [mass noun] the action or process of flying through the air: *an eagle in flight* | *the history of space flight* | [as modifier] *insect flight muscles.*
■ [count noun] an act of flying; a journey made through the air or in space, especially a timetabled journey made by an airline: *I got the first flight.* ■ the movement or trajectory of a projectile or ball through the air. ■ [as modifier] relating to or denoting archery in which the main concern is shooting long distances: *short, light flight arrows.* ■ poetic/literary swift passage of time: *the never-ending flight of future days.*
2 a group of creatures or objects flying together, in particular:
■ a flock or large body of birds or insects in the air, especially when migrating: *flights of whooper swans.* ■ a group of aircraft operating together, especially an RAF or USAF unit of about six aircraft: *he dispatched the Hurricanes in three flights.*
3 [mass noun] the action of fleeing or attempting to escape: *the enemy were now in flight* | [count noun] *a flight from shortages and cold to liberation.*
■ the selling of currency or shares by many investors: *lack of confidence triggered a **flight out of** the currency.*
4 a series of steps between floors or levels: *she has to come up four flights of stairs to her flat.*
■ a series of hurdles across a racetrack. ■ a sequence of locks by which a canal ascends an incline.
5 an extravagant or far-fetched idea or account: *ignoring such ridiculous **flights of fancy**.*
6 the tail of a dart.
▶ **verb** [with obj.] **1** Brit. (in soccer, cricket, etc.) deliver (a ball) with well-judged trajectory and pace: *he flighted a free kick into the box.*
2 provide (an arrow or dart) with feathers or vanes; fletch: *shafts of wood flighted with a handful of feathers.*
3 shoot (wildfowl) in flight: [as noun **flighting**] *duck and geese flighting.*
– PHRASES **in full flight** escaping as fast as possible. ■ having gained momentum in a run or activity: *Yorke was brought down in full flight.* **put someone/thing to flight** cause someone or something to flee: *the hussars would have been put to flight.* **take flight 1** (of a bird) take off and fly. **2** (also **take to flight**) flee: *they took flight into exile on Eadwine's accession.*
– ORIGIN Old English *flyht* 'action or manner of flying', of Germanic origin; related to Dutch *vlucht* and **FLY**[1]. This was probably merged in Middle English with an unrecorded Old English word related to German *Flucht* and to **FLEE**, which is represented by sense 3 of the noun.

flight attendant ▶ **noun** a steward or stewardess on an aircraft.

flight bag ▶ **noun** a small zipped shoulder bag carried by air travellers.

flight capital ▶ **noun** [mass noun] money transferred abroad to avoid taxes or inflation or provide for possible emigration.

flight case ▶ **noun** a sturdy case used for transporting equipment.

flight control ▶ **noun** [mass noun] the activity of directing the movement of aircraft.
■ [count noun] a control surface on an aircraft.

flight crew ▶ **noun** [treated as sing. or pl.] the personnel who are responsible for the operation of an aircraft during flight.

flight deck ▶ **noun 1** the cockpit of a large aircraft from which the pilot and crew fly it.
2 the deck of an aircraft carrier, used for take-off and landing.

flight engineer ▶ **noun** a member of a flight crew responsible for the aircraft's engines and other systems during flight.

flight envelope ▶ **noun** the range of combinations of speed, altitude, angle of attack, etc., within which a flying object is aerodynamically stable.

flight feather ▶ **noun** any of the large primary or secondary feathers in a bird's wing, supporting it in flight. Also called **REMEX**.

flightless ▶ **adjective** (of a bird or an insect) naturally unable to fly.
– DERIVATIVES **flightlessness** noun.

flight lieutenant ▶ **noun** a rank of officer in the RAF, above flying officer and below squadron leader.

flightline ▶ **noun 1** the part of an airport around the hangars where aircraft can be parked and serviced.
2 a line of flight: *the birds move in well-defined flightlines to the feeding grounds.*

flight path ▶ **noun** the actual or planned course of an aircraft or spacecraft.

flight plan ▶ **noun** Aeronautics a written account of the details of a particular proposed flight.

flight recorder ▶ **noun** a device in an aircraft to record technical details during a flight, used in the event of an accident to discover its cause.

flight sergeant ▶ **noun** a rank of non-commissioned officer in the RAF, above sergeant and below warrant officer.

flight simulator ▶ **noun** a machine designed to resemble the cockpit of an aircraft, with computer-generated images that mimic the pilot's view, typically with mechanisms which move the entire structure in corresponding imitation of an aircraft's motion, used for training pilots.

flight test ▶ noun a flight of an aircraft, rocket, or equipment to see how well it functions.
▶ verb (**flight-test**) [with obj.] test (an aircraft or rocket) by flying it: [as noun **flight-testing**] *it was undergoing cold-weather flight-testing.*

flighty ▶ adjective (**flightier**, **flightiest**) fickle and irresponsible: *her mother was a flighty Southern belle.*
– DERIVATIVES **flightily** adverb, **flightiness** noun.
– ORIGIN mid 16th cent.: from **FLIGHT** + **-Y**[1].

flimflam informal ▶ noun [mass noun] nonsensical or insincere talk: *I suppose that you suspect me of pseudo-intellectual flimflam.*
■ [count noun] a confidence trick: *flimflams perpetrated against us by our elected officials.*
▶ verb (**flimflammed**, **flimflamming**) [with obj.] swindle (someone) with a confidence trick: *the tribe was flimflammed out of its land.*
– DERIVATIVES **flimflammer** noun, **flimflammery** noun.
– ORIGIN mid 16th cent.: symbolic reduplication.

flimsy ▶ adjective (**flimsier**, **flimsiest**) comparatively light and insubstantial; easily damaged: *a flimsy barrier.*
■ (of clothing) light and thin: *the flimsy garment fell from her.* ■ (of a pretext or account) weak and unconvincing: *a pretty flimsy excuse.*
▶ noun (pl. **-ies**) Brit. a document, especially a copy, made on very thin paper: *credit-card flimsies.*
■ [mass noun] very thin paper: *sheets of yellow flimsy.*
– DERIVATIVES **flimsily** adverb, **flimsiness** noun.
– ORIGIN early 18th cent.: probably from **FLIMFLAM**.

flinch[1] ▶ verb [no obj.] make a quick, nervous movement of the face or body as an instinctive reaction to fear or pain: *she **flinched at** the acidity in his voice | he had faced death **without flinching**.*
■ (**flinch from**) figurative avoid doing or becoming involved in (something) through fear or anxiety: *I rarely flinch from a fight when I'm sure of myself.*
▶ noun [in sing.] an act of flinching: *'Don't call me that,' he said with a flinch.*
– DERIVATIVES **flincher** noun, **flinchingly** adverb.
– ORIGIN mid 16th cent. (in the sense 'slink or sneak off'): from Old French *flenchir* 'turn aside', of West Germanic origin and related to German *lenken* 'to guide, steer'.

flinch[2] /flɪn(t)ʃ/ ▶ verb variant spelling of **FLENSE**.

Flinders, Matthew (1774–1814), English explorer. He explored the coast of New South Wales (1795–1800) and circumnavigated Australia (1801–3) for the Royal Navy, charting much of the west coast of the continent for the first time.

flinders ▶ plural noun small fragments or splinters: *the panel has been smashed to flinders.*
– ORIGIN late Middle English: probably of Scandinavian origin and related to Norwegian *flindra* 'chip, splinter'.

Flinders bar ▶ noun a bar of soft iron placed vertically in or near the housing of a ship's compass to correct deviation caused by the local magnetic field of the ship.
– ORIGIN late 19th cent.: name after Captain M. **FLINDERS**.

Flinders Island the largest island in the Furneaux group, situated in the Bass Strait between Tasmania and mainland Australia. It is named after Matthew Flinders.

fling ▶ verb (past and past participle **flung**) [with obj. and adverbial of direction] throw or hurl forcefully: *he picked up the debris and flung it away | figurative I was flung into jail.*
■ move or push (something) suddenly or violently: *he flung back the bedclothes | [with obj. and complement] Jennifer flung open a door.* ■ (**fling oneself**) throw oneself headlong: *she flung herself down on his bed.* ■ (**fling oneself into**) wholeheartedly engage in or begin on (an enterprise): *he flung himself into his athletics.* ■ (**fling something on/off**) put on or take off clothes carelessly or rapidly. ■ utter (words) forcefully: *the words were flung at her like an accusation.* ■ [with two objs] give (someone) (a look) in an animated or emotional way: *Meredith flung him an eager glance.* ■ [no obj., with adverbial of direction] go angrily or violently; rush: *he flung away to his study, slamming the door behind him.*
▶ noun **1** a short period of enjoyment or wild behaviour: *one final fling before a tranquil retirement.*
■ a short, spontaneous sexual relationship: *I had a fling with someone when I was at college.*
2 short for **HIGHLAND FLING**.
– DERIVATIVES **flinger** noun.
– ORIGIN Middle English (in the sense 'go violently'): perhaps related to Old Norse *flengja* 'flog'. Sense 1 is based on an earlier sense 'reckless movement of the body' and dates from the early 19th cent.

flint ▶ noun [mass noun] a hard grey rock consisting of nearly pure silica (chert), occurring chiefly as nodules in chalk.
■ [count noun] a piece of this stone, especially as flaked or ground in ancient times to form a tool or weapon. ■ [count noun] a piece of flint used with steel to produce an igniting spark, e.g. in a flintlock gun, or (in modern use) a piece of an alloy used similarly, especially in a cigarette lighter. ■ used in expressing how hard and unyielding something or someone is: *mean faces with eyes like flints.*
– ORIGIN Old English; related to Middle Dutch *vlint* and Old High German *flins*.

flint corn ▶ noun [mass noun] maize of a variety that has hard slightly translucent grains.

flint glass ▶ noun [mass noun] a pure lustrous kind of glass originally made with flint.

flintlock ▶ noun an old-fashioned type of gun fired by a spark from a flint.
■ [usu. as modifier] the lock on such a gun: *an antique flintlock pistol.*

Flintshire /ˈflɪntʃɪə, -ʃə/ a county of NE Wales; administrative centre, Mold. It was part of Clwyd from 1974 to 1996.

flinty ▶ adjective (**flintier**, **flintiest**) of, containing, or reminiscent of flint: *flinty soil | a flinty wine.*
■ (of a person or their expression) very hard and unyielding: *a flinty stare.*
– DERIVATIVES **flintily** adverb, **flintiness** noun.

flip[1] ▶ verb (**flipped**, **flipping**) **1** turn over or cause to turn over with a sudden sharp movement: [with obj.] *the yacht was flipped by a huge wave* | [no obj.] *the plane **flipped over** and then exploded.*
2 [with obj. and adverbial] move, push, or throw (something) with a sudden sharp movement: *she flipped off her dark glasses | she flipped a few coins on to the bar.*
■ [with obj.] turn (an electrical appliance or switch) on or off: *he flipped a switch and the front door opened.* ■ [with obj.] toss (a coin) to decide an issue: *given those odds one might as well flip a coin* | [no obj.] *you want to flip for it?*
3 [no obj.] informal suddenly become deranged or very angry: *he had clearly flipped under the pressure.*
■ suddenly become very enthusiastic: *I walked into a store, saw it on the wall, and just flipped.*
▶ noun **1** a sudden sharp movement: *the fish made little leaps and flips.*
■ (**a flip through**) a quick look or search through a volume or a collection of papers: *a quick flip through my cookery books.*
2 Brit. informal a quick tour or pleasure trip: *I did a flip round the post-show party.* [ORIGIN: derived from an earlier sense 'short flight in an aircraft'.]
▶ adjective glib; flippant: *he couldn't get away with flip, funny conversation.*
▶ exclamation used to express mild annoyance.
– PHRASES **flip one's lid** (or chiefly US **one's wig**) informal suddenly become deranged or lose one's self-control.
– ORIGIN mid 16th cent. (as a verb in the sense 'make a flick with the finger and thumb'): probably a contraction of **FILLIP**.
▶ **flip through** another way of saying ***flick through*** (see **FLICK**).

flip[2] ▶ noun [mass noun] another term for **EGG-NOG**.
– ORIGIN late 17th cent.: perhaps from **FLIP**[1] in the sense 'whip up'.

flip chart ▶ noun a large pad of paper bound so that each page can be turned over at the top to reveal the next, used on a stand at presentations.

flip-flop ▶ noun **1** a light sandal, typically of plastic or rubber, with a thong between the big and second toe.
2 N. Amer. a backward somersault or handspring.
■ informal an abrupt reversal of policy: *his **flip-flop** on taxes.*
3 Electronics a switching circuit which works by changing from one stable state to another, or through an unstable state back to its stable state, in response to a triggering pulse.
▶ verb [no obj.] **1** [with adverbial of direction] move with a flapping sound or motion: *she flip-flopped off the porch in battered trainers.*
2 N. Amer. informal make an abrupt reversal of policy: *the candidate **flip-flopped on** a number of issues.*
– ORIGIN mid 17th cent. (in the general sense 'something that flaps or flops'): imitative reduplication of **FLOP**.

flippant ▶ adjective not showing a serious or respectful attitude: *a flippant remark.*
– DERIVATIVES **flippancy** noun, **flippantly** adverb.
– ORIGIN early 17th cent.: from **FLIP**[1] + **-ANT**, perhaps on the pattern of heraldic terms such as *couchant* and *rampant*. Early senses included 'nimble' and 'talkative', hence 'playful', giving rise to the current use 'lacking seriousness'.

flipper ▶ noun a broad flat limb without fingers, used for swimming by various sea animals such as seals, whales, and turtles.
■ a flat rubber attachment worn on the foot for underwater swimming. ■ a pivoted arm in a pinball machine, controlled by the player and used for sending the ball back up the table.

flipping ▶ adjective [attrib.] informal, chiefly Brit. used for emphasis or to express mild annoyance: *are you out of your flipping mind?* | [as submodifier] *it's flipping cold today.*
– ORIGIN early 20th cent.: from **FLIP**[1] + **-ING**[2].

flip side ▶ noun informal the less important side of a pop single; the B-side.
■ another aspect or version of something, especially its reverse or its unwanted concomitant: *virtues are the flip side of vices.*

flip-top ▶ adjective [attrib.] denoting or having a lid or cover that can be easily opened by lightly pulling, pushing, or flicking it with the fingers: *a large flip-top rubbish bin.*
▶ noun a lid or cover of this kind.

flirt ▶ verb **1** [no obj.] behave as though attracted to or trying to attract someone, but for amusement rather than with serious intentions: *it amused him to **flirt with** her*
■ (**flirt with**) experiment with or show a superficial interest in (an idea, activity, or movement) without committing oneself to it seriously: *a painter who had flirted briefly with Cubism.* ■ (**flirt with**) deliberately expose oneself to (danger or difficulty): *the need of some individuals to flirt with death.*
2 [with obj.] (of a bird) wave or open and shut (its wings or tail) with a quick flicking motion.
■ [no obj., with adverbial of direction] move to and fro with a flicking or fluttering motion: *the lark was flirting around the site.*
▶ noun a person who habitually flirts.
– DERIVATIVES **flirtation** noun, **flirtatious** adjective, **flirtatiously** adverb, **flirtatiousness** noun, **flirty** adjective (**flirtier**, **flirtiest**).
– ORIGIN mid 16th cent.: apparently symbolic, the elements *fl-* and *-irt* both suggesting sudden movement; compare with **FLICK** and **SPURT**. The original verb senses were 'give someone a sharp blow' and 'sneer at'; the earliest noun senses were 'joke, gibe' and 'flighty girl' (defined by Dr Johnson as 'a pert young hussey'), with a notion originally of cheeky behaviour, later of playfully amorous behaviour.

flit ▶ verb (**flitted**, **flitting**) [no obj., with adverbial of direction] move swiftly and lightly: *small birds flitted about in the branches | figurative the idea had flitted through his mind.*
■ [no obj.] chiefly Scottish & N. English move house or leave one's home, typically secretly so as to escape creditors or obligations.
▶ noun Brit. informal an act of moving house or leaving one's home, typically secretly so as to escape creditors or obligations: ***moonlight flits** from one insalubrious dwelling to another.*
– ORIGIN Middle English (in the Scots and northern English sense): from Old Norse *flytja*; related to **FLEET**[5].

flitch /flɪtʃ/ ▶ noun **1** a slab of timber cut from a tree trunk, usually from the outside.
2 (also **flitch plate**) the strengthening plate in a flitch beam.
3 chiefly dialect a side of bacon.
– ORIGIN Old English *flicce*, originally denoting the salted and cured side of any meat, of Germanic origin; related to Middle Low German *vlicke*.

flitch beam ▶ noun a compound beam made of an iron plate between two slabs of wood.

flitter ▶ verb [no obj., with adverbial of direction] move quickly in an apparently random or purposeless manner: *if only you would settle down instead of flittering around the countryside.*

▶ noun a fluttering movement: *the flash and flitter of coloured wings.*

■ (in science fiction) a small personal aircraft.

– ORIGIN late Middle English: frequentative of **FLIT**.

flittermouse ▶ noun (pl. **-mice**) old-fashioned term for **BAT**[2] (in sense 1).

– ORIGIN mid 16th cent.: on the pattern of Dutch *vledermuis* or German *Fledermaus*.

flivver /ˈflɪvə/ ▶ noun N. Amer. informal, dated a cheap car or aircraft, especially one in bad condition.

– ORIGIN early 20th cent.: of unknown origin.

flixweed /ˈflɪkswiːd/ ▶ noun [mass noun] a Eurasian plant with small yellow flowers and finely divided leaves, which was formerly thought to cure dysentery.

● *Descurainia sophia*, family Cruciferae.

– ORIGIN late 16th cent.: from obsolete *flix* (variant of **FLUX**) + **WEED**.

FLN ▶ abbreviation for Front de Libération Nationale.

float ▶ verb [no obj.] **1** rest or move on or near the surface of a liquid without sinking: *she relaxed, floating gently in the water.*

■ [with obj. and adverbial] cause (a buoyant object) to rest or move in such a way: *trees were felled and floated downstream.* ■ be suspended freely in a liquid or gas: *fragments of chipped cartilage floated in the joint.* **2** [with adverbial of direction] move or hover slowly and lightly in a liquid or the air; drift: *clouds floated across a brilliant blue sky* | figurative *through the open window floated the sound of traffic.*

■ (**float about/around**) (of a rumour, idea, or substance) circulate: *the notion was floating around Capitol Hill.* ■ (of a sight or idea) come before the eyes or mind: *the advice his father had given him floated into his mind.* ■ [with obj. and adverbial of direction] (in sport) make (the ball) travel lightly and effortlessly through the air: *he floated the kick into the net.* **3** [with obj.] put forward (an idea) as a suggestion or test of reactions.

■ [with obj.] offer the shares of (a company) for sale on the stock market for the first time. **4** (of a currency) fluctuate freely in value in accordance with supply and demand in the financial markets: *a policy of letting the pound float.*

■ [with obj.] allow (a currency) to fluctuate in such a way.

▶ noun **1** a thing that is buoyant in water, in particular:

■ a small object attached to a fishing line to indicate by moving when a fish bites. ■ a cork or buoy supporting the edge of a fishing net. ■ a hollow or inflated organ enabling an organism (such as the Portuguese man-of-war) to float in the water. ■ a hollow structure fixed underneath an aircraft enabling it to take off and land on water. ■ a floating device on the surface of a liquid which forms part of a valve apparatus controlling flow in and out of the enclosing container, e.g. in a water cistern or a carburettor. **2** Brit. a small vehicle or cart, especially one powered by electricity. See also **MILK FLOAT**.

■ a platform mounted on a lorry and carrying a display in a procession: *a carnival float.* **3** Brit. a sum of money used for change at the beginning of a period of selling in a shop or stall.

■ a small sum of money kept available for minor expenditure or petty cash. **4** a hand tool with a rectangular blade used for smoothing plaster. **5** a soft drink with a scoop of ice cream floating in it: *ice-cream floats.* **6** (in critical path analysis) the period of time by which the duration of an activity may be extended without affecting the overall time for the process.

– PHRASES **float someone's boat** informal appeal to or excite someone, especially sexually: *Kevin doesn't exactly float her boat.*

– ORIGIN Old English *flotian* (verb), of Germanic origin and related to **FLEET**[5], reinforced in Middle English by Old French *floter*, also from Germanic.

floatable ▶ adjective capable of floating.

■ chiefly US (of water) able to support floating objects; deep enough to float in.

float arm ▶ noun the hinged arm attached to the ball float in the ballcock of a water cistern.

floatation ▶ noun variant spelling of **FLOTATION**.

float chamber ▶ noun the cavity in a carburettor containing a device which floats on the surface of the fuel and seals off the flow as the level rises.

floatel /fləʊˈtɛl/ (also **flotel**) ▶ noun a floating hotel, especially a boat used as a hotel.

■ an accommodation vessel for workers on an offshore oil rig.

– ORIGIN 1950s: blend of **FLOAT** and **HOTEL**; compare with **BOTEL**.

floater ▶ noun **1** a person or thing that floats, in particular:

■ short for **FLOATING VOTER**. ■ informal, chiefly N. Amer. a person who frequently changes occupation or residence. ■ N. Amer. a worker who is required to do a variety of tasks as the need for each arises. ■ a fishing float. ■ a loose particle within the eyeball which is apparent in one's field of vision. **2** Brit. informal, dated a mistake; a gaffe. **3** US an insurance policy covering loss of articles without specifying a location.

float glass ▶ noun [mass noun] glass made by allowing it to solidify on molten metal.

floating ▶ adjective [attrib.] **1** buoyant or suspended in water or air: *a massive floating platform.* **2** not settled in a definite place; fluctuating or variable: *the floating population that is migrating to the cities.*

floating bridge ▶ noun a temporary bridge supported by pontoons or other floating vessels.

floating charge ▶ noun a liability to a creditor which relates to the company's assets as a whole and may become fixed in particular circumstances (such as liquidation). Compare with **FIXED CHARGE**.

floating cloche ▶ noun a lightweight material (such as polypropylene film) placed over growing plants to protect them, unsupported except by the plants themselves.

floating debt ▶ noun [mass noun] a debt which is repayable in the short term. Compare with **FUNDED DEBT**.

floating dock ▶ noun a floating structure used as a dry dock.

floating kidney ▶ noun [mass noun] a condition in which the kidneys are abnormally movable.

■ [count noun] such a kidney.

floating light ▶ noun a lightship.

floating-point ▶ noun [as modifier] Computing denoting a mode of representing numbers as two sequences of bits, one representing the digits in the number and the other an exponent which determines the position of the radix point. Often contrasted with **FIXED POINT** (in sense 2).

floating rib ▶ noun any of the lower ribs which are not attached directly to the breastbone. Also called **FALSE RIB**.

floating voter ▶ noun a person who has not decided which way to vote in an election, or one who does not consistently vote for the same political party.

floatplane ▶ noun an aircraft equipped with floats for landing on water; a seaplane.

float process ▶ noun (usu. **the float process**) the process used to make float glass.

float stone ▶ noun [mass noun] light, porous stone that floats, e.g. pumice.

float valve ▶ noun a ball valve.

floaty ▶ adjective chiefly Brit. (especially of a woman's garment or a fabric) light and flimsy: *elegant floaty dresses.*

floc /flɒk/ ▶ noun technical a loosely clumped mass of fine particles.

– ORIGIN 1920s: abbreviation of **FLOCCULUS**.

floccinaucinihilipilification /ˌflɒksɪˌnɔːsɪˌnɪhɪlɪˌpɪlɪfɪˈkeɪʃ(ə)n/ ▶ noun [mass noun] the action or habit of estimating something as worthless. (The word is used chiefly as a curiosity.)

– ORIGIN mid 18th cent.: from Latin *flocci, nauci, nihili, pili* (words meaning 'at little value') + **-FICATION**. The Latin elements were listed in a well-known rule of the Eton Latin Grammar.

floccose /ˈflɒkəʊs/ ▶ adjective chiefly Botany covered with or consisting of woolly tufts.

– ORIGIN mid 18th cent.: from late Latin *floccosus*, from Latin *floccus* 'flock'.

flocculant /ˈflɒkjʊl(ə)nt/ ▶ noun a substance which promotes the clumping of particles, especially one used in treating waste water.

flocculate /ˈflɒkjʊleɪt/ ▶ verb technical form or cause to form into small clumps or masses: [no obj.] *it tends to flocculate in high salinities* | [with obj.] *its ability to flocculate suspended silt.*

– DERIVATIVES **flocculation** noun.

– ORIGIN late 19th cent.: from modern Latin *flocculus* 'floccule' + **-ATE**[3].

floccule /ˈflɒkjuːl/ ▶ noun a small clump of material that resembles a tuft of wool.

– ORIGIN mid 19th cent.: from modern Latin *flocculus*, diminutive of *floccus* 'flock'.

flocculent /ˈflɒkjʊl(ə)nt/ ▶ adjective having or resembling tufts of wool: *the first snows of winter lay thick and flocculent.*

■ having a loosely clumped texture: *a brown flocculent precipitate.*

– DERIVATIVES **flocculence** noun.

– ORIGIN early 19th cent.: from Latin *floccus* 'tuft of wool' + **-ULENT**.

flocculus /ˈflɒkjʊləs/ ▶ noun (pl. **flocculi** /-lʌɪ, -liː/)
1 Anatomy a small egg-shaped lobe on the undersurface of the cerebellum.
2 Astronomy a small cloudy wisp on the surface of the sun.
3 a floccule.

– ORIGIN late 18th cent.: modern Latin, diminutive of Latin *floccus* (see **FLOCCUS**).

floccus /ˈflɒkəs/ ▶ noun (pl. **flocci** /ˈflɒksʌɪ/) a tuft of wool or similar clump of fibres or filaments.

– ORIGIN mid 19th cent.: from Latin, 'lock or tuft of wool'. Compare with **FLOCK**[2].

flock[1] ▶ noun a number of birds of one kind feeding, resting, or travelling together: *a flock of gulls.*

■ a number of domestic animals, especially sheep, goats, or geese, that are kept together: *a flock of sheep.* ■ (**flocks**) large crowds of people: *flocks of young people hung around at twilight.* ■ a group of children or pupils in someone's charge. ■ a Christian congregation or body of believers, especially one under the charge of a particular minister: *Thomas addressed his flock.* [ORIGIN: alluding to the metaphor of Christ or a Christian pastor as a shepherd.]

▶ verb [no obj., with adverbial] congregate or mass in a flock or large group: *young men flocked about her.*

■ go together in a crowd: *tourists flock to Oxford in their thousands* | [with infinitive] *millions flocked to watch.*

– ORIGIN Old English *flocc*, of unknown origin. The original sense was 'a band or body of people': this became obsolete, but has been reintroduced as a transferred use of the sense 'a number of animals kept together'.

flock[2] ▶ noun [mass noun] [often as modifier] a soft material for stuffing cushions, quilts, and other soft furnishings, made of wool refuse or torn-up cloth: *flock mattresses.*

■ powdered wool or cloth, used in making flock wallpaper. ■ [count noun] a lock or tuft of wool or cotton.

– DERIVATIVES **flocky** adjective.

– ORIGIN Middle English: from Old French *floc*, from Latin *floccus* (see **FLOCCUS**).

flockmaster ▶ noun a sheep farmer.

flock wallpaper ▶ noun [mass noun] wallpaper sized and sprinkled with powdered wool to make a raised pattern.

Flodden, Battle of /ˈflɒd(ə)n/ (also **Flodden Field**) a decisive battle of the Anglo-Scottish war of 1513, at Flodden, a hill near the Northumbrian village of Branxton. A Scottish army under James IV was defeated by a smaller but better-led English force and suffered heavy losses, including the king and most of his nobles.

floe /fləʊ/ (also **ice floe**) ▶ noun a sheet of floating ice.

– ORIGIN early 19th cent. (superseding **FLAKE**[1] in this sense): probably from Norwegian *flo*, from Old Norse *fló* 'layer'.

flog ▶ verb (**flogged**, **flogging**) [with obj.] **1** beat (someone) with a whip or stick to punish or torture them: *the executioner flogged the woman* | [as noun **flogging**] *public floggings.*

■ informal promote or talk about (something) repetitively or at excessive length: *rather than flogging one idea to death, they should be a light-hearted pop group.* **2** Brit. informal sell or offer for sale: *he made a fortune flogging beads to hippies.* **3** [no obj., with adverbial of direction] Brit. informal make one's way with strenuous effort: *I was pleasantly warm flogging up to the bottom of the crag.*

▶ noun (in sing.) Brit. informal an arduous climb or struggle: *a long flog up the mountainside.*

– PHRASES **flog a dead horse** waste energy on a lost cause or unalterable situation.

– ORIGIN late 17th cent. (originally slang): perhaps imitative, or from Latin *flagellare* 'to whip', from *flagellum* 'whip'.

flogger ▶ noun **1** a person who is in favour of flogging as a punishment.
2 a brush used in interior decorating to give a marbled or woodgrain effect.

flogging brush ▶ noun another term for **FLOGGER** (in sense 2).

flokati /flɒˈkɑːti/ (also **flokati rug**) ▶ noun (pl. **flokatis**) a Greek woven woollen rug with a thick loose pile.
– ORIGIN mid 20th cent.: from modern Greek *phlokatē* 'peasant's blanket'.

flood ▶ noun **1** an overflowing of a large amount of water beyond its normal confines, especially over what is normally dry land: *the flood caused tremendous havoc* | [mass noun] *people uprooted by drought or flood* | [as modifier] *a flood barrier.*
■(**the Flood**) the biblical flood brought by God upon the earth because of the wickedness of the human race (Gen. 6 ff.). ■ the inflow of the tide. ■ poetic/literary a river, stream, or sea.
2 an outpouring of tears or emotion: *she burst into **floods of** tears.*
■a very large quantity of things or people that appear or need to be dealt with: *a constant **flood of** callers.*
3 short for **FLOODLIGHT**.
▶verb **1** [with obj.] cover or submerge (a place or area) with water in a flood: *the dam burst, flooding a small town* | [as noun **flooding**] *a serious risk of flooding.*
■[no obj.] become covered or submerged in this way: *part of the vessel flooded* | figurative *Sarah's eyes **flooded with** tears.* ■ (usu. **be flooded out**) drive someone out of their home or business with a flood. ■ (of a river or sea) become swollen and overflow (its banks): *the river flooded its banks* | [no obj.] *the river will flood if it gets much worse.* ■ overfill the carburettor of (an engine) with petrol, causing the engine to fail to start. ■ [no obj.] (of a woman) experience a uterine haemorrhage.
2 [no obj., with adverbial of direction] arrive in overwhelming amounts or quantities: *congratulatory messages flooded in* | *his old fears came flooding back*
■[with obj.] overwhelm or swamp with large amounts or quantities: *our switchboard was **flooded with** calls.* ■ [with obj.] fill or suffuse completely: *she flooded the room with light.*
– PHRASES **be in** (**full**) **flood** (of a river) be swollen and overflowing its banks. ■(**be in full flood**) figurative (of a person or action) have gained momentum; be at the height of activity: *discussion was already in full flood and refused to be dammed.*
– ORIGIN Old English *flōd*, of Germanic origin; related to Dutch *vloed* and German *Flut*, also to **FLOW**.

floodgate ▶ noun a gate that can be opened or closed to admit or exclude water, especially the lower gate of a lock.
■figurative (usu. **the floodgates**) a last restraint holding back an outpouring of something powerful or substantial: *his lawsuit could **open the floodgates** for thousands of similar claims.*

floodlight ▶ noun a large, powerful light, typically one of several used to illuminate a sports ground, a stage, or the exterior of a building.
■[mass noun] the illumination provided by such a light: *a tennis court where you can play by floodlight.*
▶verb (past and past participle **-lit**) [with obj.] [usu. as adj. **floodlit**] illuminate (a building or outdoor area) with such lights: *floodlit football pitches.*

flood plain ▶ noun an area of low-lying ground adjacent to a river, formed mainly of river sediments and subject to flooding.

flood tide ▶ noun an incoming tide.
■a powerful surge or flow of something: *the trickle of tourists has become a flood tide.*

floor ▶ noun **1** the lower surface of a room, on which one may walk: *he dropped the cup and it fell to **the floor*** | *the kitchen floor.*
■all the rooms or areas on the same level of a building; a storey: [as modifier, in combination] *a third-floor flat.* ■ a level area or space used or designed for a particular activity. ■ figurative the minimum level of prices or wages: *sterling's floor against the D-mark.* ■ informal the ground: *the best way to play is to pass the ball on the floor.* ■ the bottom of the sea, a cave, or an area of land: *the ocean floor.*
2 (**the floor**) (in a legislative assembly) the part of the house in which members sit and from which they speak.
■the right or opportunity to speak next in debate: *other speakers **have the floor**.*
▶verb [with obj.] **1** (often **be floored**) provide (a room or area) with a floor: *a hall floored in gleaming yellow wood* | [as adj., in combination **-floored**] *a stone-floored building.*
2 informal knock (someone) to the ground, especially with a punch.
■baffle or confound (someone) completely: *that question floored him.*
– PHRASES **cross the floor** see **CROSS**. **from the floor** (of a speech or question) delivered by an individual member at a meeting, not by a representative on the platform: *questions from the floor will be invited.* **take the floor 1** begin to dance on a dance floor. **2** speak in a debate or assembly.
– ORIGIN Old English *flōr*, of Germanic origin; related to Dutch *vloer* and German *Flur*.

floorboard ▶ noun a long plank making up part of a wooden floor in a building.

floorcloth ▶ noun **1** Brit. a cloth used for washing a floor.
2 N. Amer. a thin canvas rug or similar light floor covering.

floor exercise ▶ noun (usu. **floor exercises**) a routine of gymnastic exercises performed without the use of apparatus.

flooring ▶ noun [mass noun] the boards or other material of which a floor is made.

floor lamp ▶ noun chiefly N. Amer. a standard lamp.

floor leader ▶ noun US the leader of a party in a legislative assembly.

floor manager ▶ noun **1** the stage manager of a television production.
2 a member of staff in a large store who supervises other shop assistants.

floorpan ▶ noun the lower part of the body of a motor vehicle, that forms the floor of the passenger compartment.

floor plan ▶ noun a scale diagram of the arrangement of rooms in one storey of a building.

floor show ▶ noun an entertainment presented on the floor (as opposed to the stage) of a nightclub, restaurant, or similar venue.

floorwalker ▶ noun N. Amer. a shopwalker.

floozie (also **floosie**, **floozy**) ▶ noun (pl. **-ies**) informal a girl or a woman who has a reputation for promiscuity.
– ORIGIN early 20th cent.: perhaps related to **FLOSSY** or to dialect *floosy* 'fluffy'.

flop ▶ verb (**flopped**, **flopping**) [no obj.] **1** [with adverbial] fall, move, or hang in a heavy, loose, and ungainly way: *black hair flopped across his forehead.*
■sit or lie down heavily and awkwardly or suddenly in a specified place, especially when very tired: *Liz flopped down into the armchair.* ■ informal rest or sleep in a specified place: *I'm going to flop here for the night.*
2 informal (of a performer or show) be completely unsuccessful; fail totally: *the show flopped in London.*
▶noun **1** a heavy, loose, and ungainly movement, or a sound made by it: *they hit the ground with a flop.*
■informal, chiefly US a cheap place to sleep.
2 informal a total failure: *the play had been a flop.*
– ORIGIN early 17th cent.: variant of **FLAP**.

-flop ▶ combining form Computing floating-point operations per second (used as a measure of computing power): *a gigaflop computer.*
– ORIGIN acronym; originally spelled *-flops* (*s* = second) but shortened to avoid misinterpretation as plural.

flophouse ▶ noun informal, chiefly US a dosshouse.

flopperoo ▶ noun informal a complete failure, especially with theatre, cinema, or TV audiences or critics.
– ORIGIN 1930s: from the verb **FLOP** + *-eroo*, suffix in the sense 'large, unexpected'.

floppy ▶ adjective (**floppier**, **floppiest**) tending to hang or move in a limp, loose, and ungainly way: *the dog had floppy ears* | *floppy hats.*
▶noun (pl. **-ies**) (also **floppy disk**) Computing a flexible removable magnetic disk (typically encased in a hard plastic shell) used for storing data.
– DERIVATIVES **floppily** adverb, **floppiness** noun.

floptical /ˈflɒptɪk(ə)l/ ▶ adjective Computing, trademark denoting or relating to a type of floppy-disk drive using a laser to position the read-write head.
▶noun a floppy-disk drive of this type.
– ORIGIN 1980s: blend of **FLOPPY** and **OPTICAL**.

flor ▶ noun [mass noun] yeast allowed to develop in a whitish film on the surface of dry (fino) sherries and similar wines during fermentation.
– ORIGIN late 19th cent.: from Spanish, literally 'flower'.

flor. ▶ abbreviation for floruit.

Flora Roman Mythology the goddess of flowering plants.

flora ▶ noun (pl. **floras** or **florae** /-riː/) [mass noun] the plants of a particular region, habitat, or geological period: *Britain's native flora* | [count noun] *the island has acquired a flora.* Compare with **FAUNA**.
■[count noun] a treatise on or list of such plant life.
– ORIGIN late 18th cent.: from Latin *flos*, *flor-* 'flower'.

floral /ˈflɔːr(ə)l, ˈflɒ-/ ▶ adjective of flowers: *floral tributes.*
■decorated with or depicting flowers: *a floral pattern.* ■ Botany of flora or floras: *faunal and floral evolution.*
▶noun a fabric with a floral design.
– DERIVATIVES **florally** adverb.
– ORIGIN mid 18th cent.: from Latin *flos*, *flor-* 'flower' + **-AL**.

floral kingdom ▶ noun another term for **PHYTOGEOGRAPHICAL KINGDOM**.

Floréal /ˈflɔːrɪəl/ (/French flɔreal/) ▶ noun the eighth month of the French Republican calendar (1793–1805), originally running from 20 April to 19 May.
– ORIGIN French, from Latin *floreus* 'flowery', from *flos*, *flor-* 'flower'.

floreat /ˈflɒrɪat/ ▶ exclamation used before a name to express one's desire that the specified institution or person will flourish.
– ORIGIN Latin, 'let flourish ...', originally used in *floreat Etona*, the motto of Eton College.

Florence a city in west central Italy, the capital of Tuscany, on the River Arno; pop. 408,400 (1990). Florence was a leading centre of the Italian Renaissance from the 14th to the 16th century, especially under the rule of the Medici family during the 15th century. Italian name **FIRENZE**.

Florence fennel ▶ noun see **FENNEL**.

Florentine /ˈflɒr(ə)ntʌɪn/ ▶ adjective **1** of or relating to Florence.
2 (**florentine** /-tiːn/) [postpositive] (of a dish) served on a bed of spinach: *eggs florentine.*
▶noun **1** a native or citizen of Florence.
2 a biscuit consisting mainly of nuts and preserved fruit, coated on one side with chocolate.
– ORIGIN Middle English (as a noun): from French *Florentin(e)* or Latin *Florentinus*, from *Florentia* 'Florence'.

flore pleno /ˌflɔːreɪ ˈpleɪnəʊ, ˌflɔːri/ ▶ adjective (of a plant variety) double-flowered.
– ORIGIN Latin, literally 'with a full flower'.

Flores /ˈflɔːrɛs/ the largest of the Lesser Sunda Islands in Indonesia.

florescence /flɔːˈrɛs(ə)ns, flə-/ ▶ noun [mass noun] the process of flowering: *the Hieracia are erect throughout the process of florescence* | [count noun] figurative *a spectacular cultural florescence.*
– ORIGIN late 18th cent.: from modern Latin *florescentia*, from Latin *florescere* 'begin to flower', based on *flos*, *flor-* 'flower'.

floret /ˈflɒrɪt, ˈflɔː-/ ▶ noun Botany one of the small flowers making up a composite flower head.
■one of the flowering stems making up a head of cauliflower or broccoli. ■ a small flower.
– ORIGIN late 17th cent.: from Latin *flos*, *flor-* 'flower' + **-ET**[1].

Florey /ˈflɔːri/, Howard Walter, Baron (1898–1968), Australian pathologist. With Ernst Chain he isolated and purified penicillin; in 1945 they shared a Nobel Prize with Alexander Fleming.

Florianópolis /ˌflɔːrɪəˈnɒpəlɪs/ a city in southern Brazil, on the Atlantic coast, capital of the state of Santa Catarina; pop. 293,300 (1990).

floriated /ˈflɔːrɪeɪtɪd/ ▶ adjective decorated with floral designs.

floribunda /ˌflɒrɪˈbʌndə, ˌflɔː-/ ▶ noun a plant, especially a rose, which bears dense clusters of flowers.
– ORIGIN late 19th cent.: modern Latin, feminine (used as a noun) of *floribundus* 'freely flowering', from Latin *flos*, *flor-* 'flower', influenced by Latin *abundus* 'copious'.

florican /ˈflɔːrɪkan/ ▶ noun a small South Asian bustard, the male of which has mainly black plumage with white wings.

● Family Otidae: the **Bengal florican** (*Houbaropsis begalensis*) and the **lesser florican** (*Sypheotides indica*).

– ORIGIN late 18th cent.: of unknown origin.

floriculture /ˈflɒrɪˌkʌltʃə, ˈflɔː-/ ▶ noun [mass noun] the cultivation of flowers.

– DERIVATIVES **floricultural** adjective, **floriculturist** noun.

– ORIGIN early 19th cent.: from Latin *flos, flor-* 'flower' + **CULTURE**, on the pattern of *horticulture*.

florid /ˈflɒrɪd/ ▶ adjective **1** having a red or flushed complexion: *a stout man with a florid face.* **2** elaborately or excessively intricate or complicated: *florid operatic-style music was out.* ■ (of language) using unusual words or complicated rhetorical constructions: *the florid prose of the nineteenth century.* **3** Medicine (of a disease or its manifestations) occurring in a fully developed form: *florid symptoms of psychiatric disorder.*

– DERIVATIVES **floridity** noun, **floridly** adverb, **floridness** noun.

– ORIGIN mid 17th cent.: from Latin *floridus*, from *flos, flor-* 'flower'.

Florida /ˈflɒrɪdə/ a state forming a peninsula of the south-eastern US; pop. 12,937,900 (1990); capital, Tallahassee. Explored by Ponce de León in 1513, it was purchased from Spain by the US in 1819; it became the 27th state of the Union in 1845.

– DERIVATIVES **Floridian** adjective & noun.

Florida Keys a chain of small islands off the tip of the Florida peninsula. Linked to each other and to the mainland by a series of causeways and bridges forming the Overseas Highway, the islands extend south-westwards over a distance of 160 km (100 miles).

Florida room ▶ noun N. Amer. a room built at the back of a house and partly or wholly glazed, typically with a brick or tile floor and a drinks bar.

floriferous /flɒˈrɪf(ə)rəs, flɔː-/ ▶ adjective (of a plant) producing many flowers.

– ORIGIN mid 17th cent.: from Latin *florifer* (from *flos, flor-* 'flower', + *-fer* 'producing') + **-OUS**.

florilegium /ˌflɒrɪˈliːdʒɪəm, flɔː-/ ▶ noun (pl. **florilegia** /-ˈliːdʒɪə/ or **florilegiums**) a collection of literary extracts; an anthology.

– ORIGIN early 17th cent.: modern Latin, literally 'bouquet' (from Latin *flos, flor-* 'flower' + *legere* 'gather'), translation of Greek *anthologion* (see **ANTHOLOGY**).

florin /ˈflɒrɪn/ ▶ noun **1** a former British coin and monetary unit worth two shillings. ■ an English gold coin of the 14th c., worth six shillings and eight old pence. **2** a foreign coin of gold or silver, especially a Dutch guilder. **3** the basic monetary unit of Aruba, equal to 100 cents.

– ORIGIN via Old French from Italian *fiorino*, diminutive of *fiore* 'flower', from Latin *flos, flor-*. The word originally denoted a gold coin issued in Florence, bearing a fleur-de-lis (the city's emblem) on the reverse.

Florio /ˈflɔːrɪəʊ/, John (c.1553–1625), English lexicographer, of Italian descent. He produced an Italian–English dictionary entitled *A Worlde of Wordes* (1598) and translated Montaigne's essays into English (1603).

florist ▶ noun a person who sells and arranges cut flowers.

– DERIVATIVES **floristry** noun.

– ORIGIN early 17th cent.: from Latin *flos, flor-* 'flower', on the pattern of French *fleuriste* or Italian *florista*.

floristic /flɒˈrɪstɪk/ ▶ adjective Botany relating to the study of the distribution of plants.

– DERIVATIVES **floristically** adverb.

floristics ▶ plural noun [treated as sing.] Botany the branch of phytogeography concerned with the study of plant species present in an area.

floruit /ˈflɒrʊɪt, ˈflɔː-/ (abbrev. **fl.** or **flor.**) ▶ verb used in conjunction with a specified period or set of dates to indicate when a particular historical figure lived, worked, or was most active. ▶ noun such a period: *they place Nicander's floruit in the middle of the 2nd century BC.*

– ORIGIN Latin, literally 'he or she flourished', from *florere* 'to flourish'.

flory /ˈflɔːri/ (also **fleury**) ▶ adjective [predic. or postpositive] Heraldry decorated with fleurs-de-lis.

■ (of a cross) having the end of each limb splayed out into three pointed lobes.

– PHRASES **flory counter-flory** decorated with fleurs-de-lis set in alternating directions.

– ORIGIN late Middle English: from Old French *floure*, from *flour* 'flower'.

floss ▶ noun [mass noun] the rough silk enveloping a silkworm's cocoon. ■ (also **floss silk**) untwisted silk fibres used in embroidery. ■ the silky down in maize and other plants: *milkweed floss.* ■ short for **DENTAL FLOSS**. ▶ verb [with obj.] clean between (one's teeth) with dental floss: *I flossed my teeth* | [no obj.] *you must floss well.*

– ORIGIN mid 18th cent.: from French (*soie*) *floche* 'floss (silk)', from Old French *flosche* 'down, nap of velvet', of unknown origin.

flossy ▶ adjective (**flossier, flossiest**) **1** of or like floss: *short flossy curls.* **2** N. Amer. informal excessively showy: *the flossy gleam of a cheap suit* | *she cultivated flossy friends.*

flotation /fləʊˈteɪʃ(ə)n/ (also **floatation**) ▶ noun [mass noun] the action of floating in a liquid or gas: *the body form is modified to assist in flotation.* ■ the process of offering a company's shares for sale on the stock market for the first time. ■ the separation of small particles of a solid by their different capacities to float. ■ the capacity to float; buoyancy.

– ORIGIN early 19th cent.: alteration of *floatation* (from **FLOAT**) on the pattern of French *flottaison*. The spelling *flot-* was influenced by **FLOTILLA**.

flotation tank ▶ noun a lightproof, soundproof tank of salt water in which a person floats as a form of deep relaxation.

flotel ▶ noun variant spelling of **FLOATEL**.

flotilla /fləˈtɪlə/ ▶ noun a small fleet of ships or boats: *a flotilla of cargo boats.*

– ORIGIN early 18th cent.: from Spanish, diminutive of *flota* 'fleet'.

flotsam /ˈflɒts(ə)m/ ▶ noun [mass noun] the wreckage of a ship or its cargo found floating on or washed up by the sea. Compare with **JETSAM**. ■ figurative people or things that have been rejected and are regarded as worthless: *the room was cleared of boxes and other flotsam.*

– PHRASES **flotsam and jetsam** useless or discarded objects.

– ORIGIN early 17th cent.: from Anglo-Norman French *floteson*, from *floter* 'to float'.

flounce[1] ▶ verb [no obj., with adverbial of direction] go or move in an exaggeratedly impatient or angry manner: *he stood up in a fury and flounced out.* ▶ noun [in sing.] an exaggerated action intended to express one's annoyance or impatience: *she left the room with a flounce.*

– ORIGIN mid 16th cent.: perhaps of Scandinavian origin and related to Norwegian *flunsa* 'hurry', or perhaps symbolic, like *bounce* or *pounce*.

flounce[2] ▶ noun a wide ornamental strip of material gathered and sewn to a skirt or dress; a frill. ▶ verb [as adj. **flounced**] trimmed with a flounce or flounces: *a flounced skirt.*

– DERIVATIVES **flouncy** adjective.

– ORIGIN early 18th cent.: from an alteration of obsolete *frounce* 'a fold or pleat', from Old French *fronce*, of Germanic origin; related to **RUCK**[2].

flounder[1] ▶ verb [no obj.] struggle or stagger helplessly or clumsily in mud or water: *he was floundering about in the shallow offshore waters.* ■ figurative struggle mentally; show or feel great confusion: *she floundered, not knowing quite what to say.* ■ figurative be in serious difficulty: *many firms are floundering.*

– DERIVATIVES **flounderer** noun.

– ORIGIN late 16th cent.: perhaps a blend of **FOUNDER**[3] and **BLUNDER**, or perhaps symbolic, *fl-* frequently beginning words connected with swift or sudden movement.

flounder[2] ▶ noun a small flatfish that typically occurs in shallow coastal water.

● Families Pleuronectidae and Bothidae: several species, in particular the edible *Platichthys flesus* of European waters.

■ (flounders) a collective term for flatfishes other than soles. See **FLATFISH**.

– ORIGIN Middle English: from Old French *flondre*, probably of Scandinavian origin and related to Danish *flynder*.

flour ▶ noun [mass noun] a powder obtained by grinding grain, typically wheat, and used to make bread, cakes, and pastry.

■ fine soft powder obtained by grinding the seeds or roots of starchy vegetables: *manioc flour.* ▶ verb [with obj.] sprinkle (something, especially a work surface or cooking utensil) with a thin layer of flour. ■ US grind (grain) into flour.

– ORIGIN Middle English: a specific use of **FLOWER** in the sense 'the best part', used originally to mean 'the finest quality of ground wheat'. The spelling *flower* remained in use alongside *flour* until the early 19th cent.

flour beetle ▶ noun a small brown darkling beetle that is a widespread pest of flour and other cereal products.

● Genera *Tribolium, Gnathocerus*, and others, family Tenebrionidae: several species.

flourish ▶ verb **1** [no obj.] (of a person, animal, or other living organism) grow or develop in a healthy or vigorous way, especially as the result of a particularly congenial environment: *wild plants flourish on the banks of the lake.* ■ develop rapidly and successfully: *the organization has continued to flourish.* ■ [with adverbial] (of a person) be working or at the height of one's career during a specified period: *the caricaturist and wit who flourished in the early years of this century.* **2** [with obj.] (of a person) wave (something) about to attract the attention of others: *'Happy New Year!' he yelled, flourishing a bottle of whisky.* ▶ noun **1** a bold or extravagant gesture or action, made especially to attract the attention of others: *with a flourish, she ushered them inside.* ■ an instance of suddenly performing or developing in an impressively successful way: *Wigan produced a late second-half flourish.* ■ an elaborate rhetorical or literary expression. ■ an ornamental flowing curve in handwriting or scrollwork: *spiky gothic letters with an emphatic flourish beneath them.* **2** Music a fanfare played by brass instruments: *a flourish of trumpets.* ■ an ornate musical passage. ■ an extemporized addition played especially at the beginning or end of a composition.

– DERIVATIVES **flourisher** noun.

– ORIGIN Middle English: from Old French *floriss-*, lengthened stem of *florir*, based on Latin *florere*, from *flos, flor-* 'a flower'. The noun senses 'ornamental curve' and 'florid expression' come from an obsolete sense of the verb, 'adorn' (originally with flowers).

flour moth ▶ noun a greyish-buff moth, the caterpillar of which is a pest of flour and cereal products.

● *Ephestia keuhniella*, family Pyralidae.

floury ▶ adjective covered with flour: *Maggie wiped her floury hands on her apron.* ■ of or resembling flour: *floury white make-up.* ■ (of a potato) having a soft, fluffy texture when cooked.

– DERIVATIVES **flouriness** noun.

flout /flaʊt/ ▶ verb [with obj.] openly disregard (a rule, law or convention): *the advertising code is being flouted.* ■ [no obj.] archaic mock; scoff: *the women pointed and flouted at her.*

– ORIGIN mid 16th cent.: perhaps from Dutch *fluiten* 'whistle, play the flute, hiss (in derision)'; German dialect *pfeifen auf*, literally 'pipe at', has a similar extended meaning.

USAGE Flout and flaunt do not have the same meaning: see usage at **FLAUNT**.

flow ▶ verb [no obj.] (especially of a liquid) move along or out steadily and continuously in a current or stream: *from here the river flows north* | *a cross-current of electricity seemed to flow between them.* ■ (of the sea or a tidal river) move towards the land; rise. Compare with **EBB**. ■ [with adverbial of direction] (of clothing or hair) hang loosely in an easy and graceful manner: *her red hair flowed over her shoulders.* ■ [with adverbial of direction] (of people or things) go from one place to another in a steady stream, typically in large numbers: *the firm is hoping the orders will keep flowing in.* ■ proceed or be produced smoothly, continuously, and effortlessly: *talk flowed freely around the table.* ■ (**flow from**) result from; be caused by: *there are certain advantages that may flow from that decision.* ■ be available in copious quantities: *their talk and laughter grew louder as the excellent brandy flowed.* ■ (of a solid) undergo a permanent change of shape under stress, without melting. ▶ noun **1** [in sing.] the action or fact of moving along in a steady, continuous stream: *the flow of water into the pond.*

---

b **b**ut | d **d**og | f **f**ew | g **g**et | h **h**e | j **y**es | k **c**at | l **l**eg | m **m**an | n **n**o | p **p**en | r **r**ed | s **s**it | t **t**op | v **v**oice | w **w**e | z **z**oo | ʃ **sh**e | ʒ deci**s**ion | θ **th**in | ð **th**is | ŋ ri**ng** | x lo**ch** | tʃ **ch**ip | dʒ **j**ar

■the rate or speed at which such a stream moves: *under the ford the river backs up, giving a deep sluggish flow.* ■ the rise of a tide or a river. Compare with **EBB**. ■ a steady, continuous stream of something: *she eased the car into **the flow of** traffic.* ■ the gradual permanent deformation of a solid under stress, without melting.

2 Scottish a watery swamp; a morass: [as modifier] *the flow country of Caithness and Sutherland.*

– PHRASES **go with the flow** informal be relaxed and accept a situation, rather than trying to alter or control it. **in full flow** talking fluently and easily and showing no sign of stopping. ■ performing vigorously and enthusiastically: *Richardson was run out when he was in full flow.*

– ORIGIN Old English *flōwan*, of Germanic origin; related to Dutch *vloeien*, also to **FLOOD**.

flow chart (also **flow diagram**) ▶ **noun** a diagram of the sequence of movements or actions of people or things involved in a complex system or activity.

■a graphical representation of a computer program in relation to its sequence of functions (as distinct from the data it processes).

flower ▶ **noun** Botany the seed-bearing part of a plant, consisting of reproductive organs (stamens and carpels) that are typically surrounded by a brightly coloured corolla (petals) and a green calyx (sepals).

■a brightly coloured and conspicuous example of such a part of a plant together with its stalk, typically used with others as a decoration or gift. ■ [mass noun] the state or period in which a plant's flowers have developed and opened: *the roses were just coming **into flower**.* ■ Brit. informal used as a friendly form of address, especially to a young girl or woman: *'course you have, flower.'*

▶ **verb** [no obj.] (of a plant) produce flowers; bloom: *Michaelmas daisies can flower as late as October.*

■figurative be in or reach an optimum stage of development; develop fully and richly: *she **flowered into** as striking a beauty as her mother* | [as noun **flowering**] *the flowering of Viennese intellectual life.* ■ [with obj.] induce (a plant) to produce flowers.

– PHRASES **the flower of** the finest individuals out of a number of people or things: *he wasted the flower of French youth on his dreams of empire.*

– DERIVATIVES **flowerless** adjective, **flower-like** adjective.

– ORIGIN Middle English *flour*, from Old French *flour*, *flor*, from Latin *flos*, *flor-*. The original spelling was no longer in use by the late 17th cent. except in its specialized sense 'ground grain' (see **FLOUR**).

flower bed ▶ **noun** a garden plot in which flowers are grown.

flower beetle ▶ **noun** any of a number of beetles that frequent flowers, in particular:

● an elongated beetle with soft wing cases (chiefly of the family Melyridae). ● a day-flying chafer (family Scarabaeidae). ● a small dark beetle that frequently occurs in large numbers (family Nitidulidae).

flowered ▶ **adjective** **1** (especially of fabric or a garment) having a floral design: *flowered curtains.*

2 [in combination] (of a plant) bearing flowers of a specified kind or number: *yellow-flowered japonica.*

flowerer ▶ **noun** a plant that flowers at a specified time or in a specified manner: *bedding plants and other summer flowerers.*

floweret /ˈflaʊərɪt/ ▶ **noun** a floret, especially of cauliflower or broccoli.

flower girl ▶ **noun** **1** Brit. dated a woman or girl who sells flowers, especially in the street.

2 a young girl who carries flowers or scatters them in front of the bride at a wedding; a child bridesmaid.

flower head ▶ **noun** a compact mass of flowers at the top of a stem, especially a capitulum.

flowering ▶ **adjective** (of a plant) in bloom: *a basket of flowering plants.*

■capable of producing flowers, especially in contrast to a similar plant with the flowers inconspicuous or absent: *flowering dogwood.* ■ [in combination] producing flowers at a specified time or of a specified type: *winter-flowering heathers.*

flowering cherry ▶ **noun** an ornamental tree grown for its spring blossom, the fruit not being considered edible.

● Genus *Prunus*, family Rosaceae: several species, in particular *P. serrulata* and its hybrids.

flowering currant ▶ **noun** an ornamental shrub grown for its clusters of small pinkish-red flowers.

● Genus *Ribes*, family Grossulariaceae: several species, in particular *R. sanguineum*.

flowering plant ▶ **noun** a plant that produces flowers; an angiosperm.

flowering rush ▶ **noun** a tall rush-like plant with long narrow leaves and pinkish flowers, living in shallow slow-moving water and native to Eurasia.

● *Butomus umbellatus*, the only member of the family Butomaceae.

flowerpecker ▶ **noun** a very small songbird with a short bill and tail, feeding chiefly on insects in flowers and found in Australasia and SE Asia.

● Family Dicaeidae (the **flowerpecker family**): two genera, especially *Dicaeum*. The flowerpecker family also includes the pardalotes and the mistletoe bird.

flower people ▶ **plural noun** historical hippies who wore flowers as symbols of peace and love.

flowerpot ▶ **noun** a small container, typically with sloping sides and made from plastic or earthenware, used for growing a plant in.

flowerpot snake ▶ **noun** a small slender grey-brown blind snake which occurs widely in the warmer parts of the Old World. It is often accidentally distributed by nurseries due to its habit of burrowing in plant pots.

● *Ramphlotyphlops braminus*, family Typhlopidae.

flower power ▶ **noun** [mass noun] historical the ideas of the flower people, especially the promotion of peace and love as means of changing the world.

flowers of sulphur ▶ **plural noun** [treated as sing.] Chemistry a fine yellow powdered form of sulphur produced by sublimation.

flowers of zinc ▶ **plural noun** [treated as sing.] finely powdered zinc oxide.

flowery ▶ **adjective** full of, resembling, or smelling of flowers: *a flowery meadow* | *flowery wallpaper.*

■(of a style of speech or writing) full of elaborate or literary words and phrases: *flowery language.*

– DERIVATIVES **floweriness** noun.

flowing ▶ **adjective** (especially of long hair or clothing) hanging or draping loosely and gracefully: *a long flowing gown of lavender silk.*

■(of a line or contour) smoothly continuous: *the flowing curves of the lawn.* ■ (of language, movement, or style) graceful and fluent: *a flowing prose style.*

– DERIVATIVES **flowingly** adverb.

flowing sheet ▶ **noun** Sailing a sheet that has been eased to allow free movement in the wind.

flow line ▶ **noun** a route followed by a product through successive stages of manufacture or treatment: [as modifier] *flow-line production.*

flowmeter ▶ **noun** an instrument for measuring the rate of flow of water, gas, or fuel, especially through a pipe.

flown past participle of **FLY**[1].

flow-on ▶ **noun** Austral./NZ a wage adjustment or an improvement in working conditions made as a consequence of one already made in a similar or related occupation.

flowsheet ▶ **noun** another term for **FLOW CHART**.

flowstone ▶ **noun** [mass noun] Geology rock deposited as a thin sheet by precipitation from flowing water.

FLQ ▶ **abbreviation for** (in Canada) Front de Libération du Québec, a Quebec separatist terrorist organization, especially active in the 1960s and early 1970s.

– ORIGIN French.

Flt Lt ▶ **abbreviation for** Flight Lieutenant.

Flt Sgt ▶ **abbreviation for** Flight Sergeant.

flu ▶ **noun** [mass noun] influenza: *she was in bed with flu.*

– ORIGIN mid 19th cent.: abbreviation.

flub N. Amer. informal ▶ **verb** (**flubbed**, **flubbing**) [with obj.] botch or bungle (something): *she glanced at her notes and flubbed her lines* | [no obj.] *don't flub again.*

▶ **noun** a thing badly or clumsily done; a blunder: *the textbooks are littered with flubs.*

– ORIGIN 1920s: of unknown origin.

fluctuant ▶ **adjective** poetic/literary fluctuating; unstable.

– ORIGIN mid 16th cent.: from Old French 'undulating', from Latin *fluctuare* 'undulate'.

fluctuate /ˈflʌktʃʊeɪt, -tjʊ-/ ▶ **verb** [no obj.] rise and fall irregularly in number or amount: *trade with other countries tends to fluctuate from year to year* | [as adj. **fluctuating**] *a fluctuating level of demand.*

– DERIVATIVES **fluctuation** noun.

– ORIGIN mid 17th cent.: from Latin *fluctuat-* 'undulated', from the verb *fluctuare*, from *fluctus* 'flow, current, wave', from *fluere* 'to flow'.

flue /fluː/ ▶ **noun** a duct for smoke and waste gases produced by a fire, a gas heater, a power station, or other fuel-burning installation: [as modifier] *flue gases.*

■a channel for conveying heat.

– ORIGIN late Middle English (denoting the mouthpiece of a hunting horn): of unknown origin. Current senses date from the late 16th cent.

flue-cure ▶ **verb** [with obj.] [often as adj. **flue-cured**] cure (tobacco) using heat from pipes or flues connected to a furnace.

fluellen /flʊˈɛlɪn/ ▶ **noun** a small creeping Eurasian plant with yellow and purple flowers, widely occurring in cornfields.

● Genus *Kickxia*, family Scrophulariaceae: two species.

– ORIGIN mid 16th cent.: alteration of Welsh *llysiau Llywelyn* 'Llewelyn's herbs'; compare with *Fluellen*, used by Shakespeare to represent the Welsh name *Llywelyn*.

fluence[1] /ˈfluːəns/ ▶ **noun** [mass noun] Brit. informal mysterious, magical, or hypnotic power: *you've **put the fluence on** me, haven't you?*

– ORIGIN early 20th cent.: shortening of **INFLUENCE**.

fluence[2] /ˈfluːəns/ ▶ **noun** Physics a stream of particles crossing a unit area, usually expressed as the number of particles per second.

– ORIGIN early 17th cent. (in the sense 'a flowing, a stream'): from French, from Latin *fluentia*, from *fluere* 'to flow'.

fluency ▶ **noun** [mass noun] the quality or condition of being fluent, in particular:

■the ability to speak or write a particular foreign language easily and accurately: *fluency in Spanish is essential.* ■ the ability to express oneself easily and articulately. ■ gracefulness and ease of movement or style: *the horse was jumping with breathtaking fluency.*

– ORIGIN early 17th cent.: from Latin *fluentia*, from *fluere* 'to flow'.

fluent /ˈfluːənt/ ▶ **adjective** (of a person) able to express oneself easily and articulately: *a fluent speaker and writer on technical subjects.*

■(of a person) able to speak or write a particular foreign language easily and accurately: *she became **fluent in** French and German.* ■ (of a foreign language) spoken accurately and with facility: *he spoke fluent Spanish.* ■ (of speech, language, movement, or style) smoothly graceful and easy: *his style of play was fast and fluent.* ■ able to flow freely; fluid: *a fluent discharge from the nose.*

– DERIVATIVES **fluently** adverb.

– ORIGIN late 16th cent. (also in the literal sense 'flowing freely or abundantly'): from Latin *fluent-* 'flowing', from the verb *fluere*.

flue pipe ▶ **noun** **1** a pipe acting as a flue.

2 an organ pipe into which the air enters directly without striking a reed.

fluff ▶ **noun** **1** [mass noun] soft fibres from fabrics such as wool or cotton which accumulate in small light clumps: *he brushed his sleeve to remove the fluff.*

■any soft downy substance, especially the fur or feathers of a young mammal or bird. ■ figurative entertainment or writing perceived as trivial or superficial: *the film is a piece of typical Hollywood fluff.*

2 informal a mistake made in speaking or playing music, or by an actor in delivering their lines.

▶ **verb** [with obj.] **1** make (something) appear fuller and softer, typically by shaking or brushing it: *I **fluffed up** the pillows.*

2 informal fail to perform or accomplish (something) successfully or well (used especially in a sporting or acting context): *the extra fluffed his only line.*

– ORIGIN late 18th cent.: probably a dialect alteration of 16th-cent. *flue* 'down, nap, fluff', apparently from Flemish *vluwe*.

flufftail ▶ **noun** a small secretive African crake with a cocked tail and dark plumage, the male of which typically has a reddish-brown head.

● Genus *Coturnicops* (or *Sarothura*), family Rallidae: several species.

fluffy ▶ **adjective** (**fluffier**, **fluffiest**) **1** of, like, or covered with fluff: *fluffy white clouds* | *a fluffy towel.*

■(of food) light in texture and containing air: *cream the butter and sugar until pale and fluffy.*

2 informal (of a person, especially a woman) frivolous, silly, or vague: *a fluffy gangster's moll.*

■chiefly N. Amer. lacking substance, depth, or seriousness: *the commercial wallows in soft, fluffy, feel-good territory.*

– DERIVATIVES **fluffily** adverb, **fluffiness** noun.

flugelhorn /ˈfluːg(ə)lhɔːn/ ▶ **noun** a valved brass musical instrument like a cornet but with a broader tone.

f

– ORIGIN mid 19th cent.: from German *Flügelhorn*, from *Flügel* 'wing' + *Horn* 'horn'.

fluid ▶ noun [mass noun] a substance that has no fixed shape and yields easily to external pressure; a gas or (especially) a liquid: *drink a litre of fluid a day* | [count noun] *a cleaning fluid.*
▶ adjective (of a substance) able to flow easily: *the paint is more fluid than tube watercolours* | *a fluid medium.*
■ not settled or stable; likely or able to change: *our plans are still fluid* | *the fluid political situation of the 1930s.* ■ smoothly elegant or graceful: *her movements were fluid and beautiful to watch.* ■ (of a clutch or coupling) using a liquid to transmit power.
– DERIVATIVES **fluidity** noun, **fluidly** adverb.
– ORIGIN late Middle English (as an adjective): from French *fluide* or Latin *fluidus*, from *fluere* 'to flow'.

fluid drachm ▶ noun see **DRACHM**.

fluidics /fluːˈɪdɪks/ ▶ plural noun [often treated as sing.] the study and technique of using small interacting flows and fluid jets for functions usually performed by electronic devices.
– DERIVATIVES **fluidic** adjective.

fluidize /ˈfluːɪdʌɪz/ (also **-ise**) ▶ verb [with obj.] technical cause (a finely divided solid) to acquire the characteristics of a fluid by passing a gas upwards through it.
– DERIVATIVES **fluidization** noun.

fluidized bed ▶ noun a layer of a fluidized solid, used in chemical processes and in the efficient burning of coal for power generation.

fluid mechanics ▶ plural noun [treated as sing.] the study of forces and flow within fluids.

fluid ounce ▶ noun **1** Brit. a unit of capacity equal to one twentieth of a pint (approximately 0.028 litre).
2 (also **fluidounce**) US a unit of capacity equal to one sixteenth of a US pint (approximately 0.03 litre).

fluidram /ˈfluːɪdram/ ▶ noun US a fluid drachm. See **DRACHM**.

fluke[1] ▶ noun an unlikely chance occurrence, especially a surprising piece of luck: *their triumph was no fluke.*
▶ verb [with obj.] achieve (something) by luck rather than skill: *he fluked the pink to win the frame.*
– ORIGIN mid 19th cent. (originally a term in games such as billiards denoting a lucky stroke): perhaps a dialect word.

fluke[2] ▶ noun **1** a parasitic flatworm which typically has suckers and hooks for attachment to the host. Some species are of veterinary or medical importance.
• Classes Trematoda and Monogenea, phylum Platyhelminthes. See **DIGENEAN** and **MONOGENEAN**.
2 chiefly dialect or N. Amer. a flatfish, especially a flounder.
– ORIGIN Old English *flōc* (in sense 2), of Germanic origin; related to German *flach* 'flat'.

fluke[3] ▶ noun a broad triangular plate on the arm of an anchor.
■ either of the lobes of a whale's tail.
– ORIGIN mid 16th cent.: perhaps from **FLUKE**[2] (because of the shape).

fluky (also **flukey**) ▶ adjective (**flukier**, **flukiest**) obtained or achieved more by chance than skill: *a fluky goal.*
– DERIVATIVES **flukily** adverb, **flukiness** noun.

flume /fluːm/ ▶ noun an artificial channel conveying water, typically used for transporting logs or timber.
■ a winding tubular water slide at a swimming pool. ■ a water chute ride at an amusement park.
– ORIGIN Middle English (denoting a river or stream): from Old French *flum*, from Latin *flumen* 'river', from *fluere* 'to flow'. The sense 'artificial channel' dates from the mid 18th cent.; 'water chute for amusement' is a late 20th-cent. usage.

flummery /ˈflʌm(ə)ri/ ▶ noun (pl. **-ies**) [mass noun] **1** empty compliments; nonsense: *she hated the flummery of public relations.*
2 a sweet dish made with beaten eggs, sugar, and flavourings.
– ORIGIN early 17th cent. (denoting a dish made with oatmeal or wheatmeal boiled to a jelly): from Welsh *llymru*; perhaps related to *llymrig* 'soft, slippery'.

flummox /ˈflʌməks/ ▶ verb [with obj.] (usu. **be flummoxed**) informal perplex (someone) greatly; bewilder.
– ORIGIN mid 19th cent.: probably of dialect origin; *flummock* 'to make untidy, confuse' is recorded in western counties and the north Midlands.

flump ▶ verb [no obj., with adverbial of direction] fall or sit down heavily: *he took himself off to flump into a chair.*
■ [with obj. and adverbial of direction] set or throw (something) down heavily: *Ellie flumped her hands down on her sewing.*
▶ noun [in sing.] the action or sound of such a heavy fall: *the rocks hit the ground with a flump.*
– ORIGIN early 17th cent.: imitative.

flung past and past participle of **FLING**.

flunk informal, chiefly N. Amer. ▶ verb [with obj.] fail to reach the required standard in (an examination, test, or course of study): *I flunked biology in the tenth grade* | [no obj.] *I didn't flunk but I didn't do too well.*
■ judge (an examination candidate) to have failed to reach the required standard. ■ [no obj.] (**flunk out**) (of a student) leave or be dismissed from school or college as a result of failing to reach the required standard: *he had flunked out of college.*
– ORIGIN early 19th cent. (in the general sense 'back down, fail utterly'; originally US): perhaps related to **FUNK**[1] or to US *flink* 'be a coward', perhaps a variant of **FLINCH**[1].

flunkey (also **flunky**) ▶ noun (pl. **-eys** or **-ies**) chiefly derogatory a liveried manservant or footman.
■ a person who performs relatively menial tasks for someone else, especially obsequiously.
– DERIVATIVES **flunkeyism** noun.
– ORIGIN mid 18th cent. (originally Scots): perhaps from **FLANK** in the sense 'a person who stands at one's flank'.

fluoresce /flʊəˈrɛs, flɔː-/ ▶ verb [no obj.] shine or glow brightly due to fluorescence: *the molecules fluoresce when excited by ultraviolet radiation.*
– ORIGIN late 19th cent.: back-formation from **FLUORESCENCE**.

fluorescein /ˈflʊərəsiːn, -sɪn, ˈflɔː-/ ▶ noun [mass noun] Chemistry an orange dye with a yellowish-green fluorescence, used as an indicator and tracer.
• A derivative of resorcinol and phthalic anhydride; chem. formula: $C_{20}H_{12}O_5$.
– ORIGIN late 19th cent.: from **FLUORESCENCE** + **-IN**[1].

fluorescence /flʊəˈrɛs(ə)ns, flɔː-/ ▶ noun [mass noun] the visible or invisible radiation produced from certain substances as a result of incident radiation of a shorter wavelength such as X-rays or ultraviolet light.
■ the property of absorbing light of short wavelength and emitting light of longer wavelength.
– ORIGIN mid 19th cent.: from **FLUORSPAR** (which fluoresces), on the pattern of *opalescence*.

fluorescent ▶ adjective (of a substance) having or showing fluorescence: *a fluorescent dye.*
■ containing a fluorescent tube: *fluorescent lighting.* ■ vividly colourful: *a fluorescent T-shirt.*
▶ noun a fluorescent tube or lamp.

fluorescent screen ▶ noun a transparent screen coated with fluorescent material to show images from X-rays.

fluorescent tube (also **fluorescent bulb**) ▶ noun a glass tube which radiates light when phosphor on its inside surface is made to fluoresce by ultraviolet radiation from mercury vapour.

fluoridate /ˈflʊərɪdeɪt, ˈflɔː-/ ▶ verb [with obj.] add traces of fluorides to (something, especially a water supply): [as adj. **fluoridated**] *fluoridated toothpaste.*
– DERIVATIVES **fluoridation** noun.
– ORIGIN 1940s: back-formation from earlier *fluoridation*.

fluoride /ˈflʊərʌɪd, flɔː-/ ▶ noun [mass noun] Chemistry a compound of fluorine with another element or group, especially salt of the anion F^- or an organic compound with fluorine bonded to an alkyl group.
■ [mass noun] sodium fluoride or another fluorine-containing salt added to water supplies or toothpaste in order to reduce tooth decay.
– ORIGIN early 19th cent.: from **FLUORINE** + **-IDE**.

fluorinate /ˈflʊərɪneɪt, ˈflɔː-/ ▶ verb [with obj.] Chemistry introduce fluorine into (a compound).
■ another term for **FLUORIDATE**.
– DERIVATIVES **fluorination** noun.

fluorine /ˈflʊəriːn, ˈflɔː-/ ▶ noun [mass noun] the chemical element of atomic number 9, a poisonous pale yellow gas of the halogen series. It is the most reactive of all the elements, causing very severe burns on contact with skin. (Symbol: **F**)
– ORIGIN early 19th cent.: from *fluor* (see **FLUORSPAR**) + **-INE**[4].

fluorite /ˈflʊərʌɪt, ˈflɔː-/ ▶ noun [mass noun] a mineral consisting of calcium fluoride which typically occurs as cubic crystals, colourless when pure but often coloured by impurities.
– ORIGIN mid 19th cent.: from *fluor* (see **FLUORSPAR**) + **-ITE**[1].

fluoro- /ˈflʊərəʊ, ˈflɔː-/ ▶ combining form **1** representing **FLUORINE**.
2 representing **FLUORESCENCE**.

fluorocarbon ▶ noun Chemistry a compound formed by replacing one or more of the hydrogen atoms in a hydrocarbon with fluorine atoms.

fluorochrome ▶ noun a chemical that fluoresces, especially one used as a label in biological research.

fluorography /flʊəˈrɒgrəfi, flɔː-/ ▶ noun [mass noun] photography in which the image is formed by fluorescence, used chiefly in biomedical research.
– DERIVATIVES **fluorograph** noun.

fluorometer /flʊəˈrɒmɪtə, flɔː-/ (also **fluorimeter**) ▶ noun an instrument for measuring the intensity of fluorescence, used chiefly in biochemical analysis.
– DERIVATIVES **fluorometric** adjective, **fluorometrically** adverb, **fluorometry** noun.

fluoropolymer /ˈflʊərəʊˌpɒlɪmə, ˈflɔː-/ ▶ noun an organic polymer containing fluorine atoms, such as PTFE.

fluoroscope ▶ noun an instrument with a fluorescent screen used for viewing X-ray images without taking and developing X-ray photographs.
– DERIVATIVES **fluoroscopic** adjective, **fluoroscopy** noun.

fluorosis /flʊəˈrəʊsɪs, flɔː-/ ▶ noun [mass noun] Medicine a chronic condition caused by excessive intake of fluorine compounds, marked by mottling of the teeth and, if severe, calcification of the ligaments.

fluorspar /ˈflʊəspɑː, ˈflɔː-/ ▶ noun another term for **FLUORITE**.
– ORIGIN late 18th cent.: from *fluor* 'a flow, a mineral used as a flux, fluorspar' (from Latin *fluor*, from *fluere* 'to flow') + **SPAR**[3].

fluoxetine /fluːˈɒksətiːn/ ▶ noun [mass noun] Medicine a synthetic compound which inhibits the uptake of serotonin in the brain and is taken to treat depression. Also called **PROZAC** (trademark).
– ORIGIN 1970s: from *fluo(rine)* + *ox(y)* + *-etine* (perhaps from *e* + a blend of **TOLUENE** and **AMINE**).

flurried ▶ adjective (of a person) agitated, nervous, or anxious: *Jack was never flurried.*

flurry ▶ noun (pl. **-ies**) a small swirling mass of something, especially snow or leaves, moved by sudden gusts of wind: *a flurry of snow.*
■ a sudden short period of commotion or excitement: *there was a brief flurry of activity in the hall.* ■ a number of things arriving or happening suddenly and during the same period: *a flurry of editorials hostile to the government.*
▶ verb (**-ies**, **-ied**) [no obj., with adverbial of direction] (especially of snow or leaves) be moved in small swirling masses by sudden gusts of wind: *gusts of snow flurried through the door.*
■ (of a person) move quickly in a busy or agitated way: *the waiter flurried between them.*
– ORIGIN late 17th cent.: from obsolete *flurr* 'fly up, flutter, whirr' (imitative), probably influenced by **HURRY**.

flush[1] ▶ verb **1** [no obj.] (of a person's skin or face) become red and hot, typically as the result of illness or strong emotion: *Rachel flushed angrily* | [as adj. **flushed**] *her flushed cheeks.*
■ [with obj.] cause (a person's skin or face) to become red and hot: *the chill air flushed the parson's cheeks.* ■ glow or cause to glow with warm colour or light: [no obj.] *the ash in the centre of the fire flushed up* | [with obj.] *the sky was flushed with the gold of dawn.* ■ (**be flushed with**) figurative be excited or elated by: *flushed with success, I was getting into my stride.*
2 [with obj.] cleanse (something, especially a toilet) by causing large quantities of water to pass through it: *she flushed the loo* | *the nurse **flushed out** the catheter.*
■ [no obj.] (of a toilet) be cleansed in such a way: *Cally heard the toilet flush.* ■ [with obj. and adverbial of direction] remove or dispose of (an object or substance) in such a way: *I **flushed** the pills **down** the lavatory* | *the kidneys require more water to **flush out** waste products.* ■ [with obj. and adverbial of direction] cause (a liquid) to flow through something: *0.3 ml of saline is gently flushed through the tube.*
3 [with obj. and adverbial of direction] drive (a bird,

especially a game bird, or an animal) from its cover: *the grouse were flushed from the woods*.
■ figurative cause to be revealed; force into the open: *they're trying to flush Nader out of hiding*.
4 [no obj.] (of a plant) send out fresh shoots: *the plant had started to flush by late March*.

▶ noun **1** a reddening of the face or skin that is typically caused by illness or strong emotion: *a flush of embarrassment rose to her cheeks*.
■ an area of warm colour or light: *the bird has a pinkish flush on the breast*. ■ (**hot flush**) a sudden feeling of feverish heat, typically as a symptom of the menopause.
2 [in sing.] a sudden rush of intense emotion: *I was carried away in a **flush** of enthusiasm*.
■ a sudden abundance or spate of something: *the frogs feast on the great **flush** of insects*. ■ figurative a period when something is new or particularly fresh and vigorous: *he is no longer **in the first flush** of youth*. ■ a fresh growth of leaves, flowers, or fruit.
3 an act of cleansing something, especially a toilet, with a sudden flow of water: *an old-fashioned toilet uses six or seven gallons a flush* | *leave the hosepipe running to give the system a good **flush out***.
■ the device used for producing such a flow of water in a toilet: *he pressed the flush absent-mindedly*. ■ [as modifier] denoting a type of toilet that has such a device: *a flush toilet*. ■ a sudden flow: *the melting snow provides a flush of water*.
4 the action of driving a game bird from its cover: *labradors retrieve the birds after the flush*.
– DERIVATIVES **flusher** noun.
– ORIGIN Middle English (in the sense 'move rapidly, spring up', especially of a bird 'fly up suddenly'): symbolic, *fl-* frequently beginning words connected with sudden movement; perhaps influenced by **FLASH**[1] and **BLUSH**.

flush[2] ▶ adjective **1** completely level or even with another surface: *the gates are **flush with** the adjoining fencing*.
■ (of printed text) not indented or protruding: *each line is **flush with** the left-hand margin*. ■ (of a door) having a smooth surface, without indented or protruding panels or mouldings.
2 [predic.] informal having plenty of something, especially money: *the banks are flush with funds*.
■ (of money) plentiful: *the years when cash was flush*.
▶ adverb so as to be level or even: *the screw must fit **flush** with the surface*.
■ so as to be directly centred; squarely: *Hodson caught him flush on the jaw with a straight right*.
▶ verb [with obj.] fill in (a joint) level with a surface.
– DERIVATIVES **flushness** noun.
– ORIGIN mid 16th cent. (in the sense 'perfect, lacking nothing'): probably related to **FLUSH**[1].

flush[3] ▶ noun (in poker or brag) a hand of cards all of the same suit.
– ORIGIN early 16th cent.: from French *flux* (formerly *flus*), from Latin *fluxus* 'a flow' (see **FLUX**: the use in cards can be compared with English *run*).

flush[4] ▶ noun Ecology a piece of wet ground over which water flows without being confined to a definite channel.
– ORIGIN late Middle English (in the sense 'marshy place'): variant of **FLASH**[2].

Flushing /ˈflʌʃɪŋ/ a port in the SW Netherlands; pop. 43,800 (1991). Dutch name **VLISSINGEN**.

fluster ▶ verb [with obj.] [often as adj. **flustered**] make (someone) agitated or confused: *Rosamund seemed rather flustered this morning*.
▶ noun [in sing.] an agitated or confused state: *the main thing is not to get all in a fluster*.
– ORIGIN early 17th cent. (in the sense 'make slightly drunk'): perhaps of Scandinavian origin and related to Icelandic *flaustra* 'hurry, bustle'.

flute ▶ noun **1** a wind instrument made from a tube with holes along it that are stopped by the fingers or keys, held vertically or horizontally (**transverse flute**) so that the player's breath strikes a narrow edge.
■ a modern orchestral instrument of this type, typically of metal, held horizontally, with the mouthpiece near one end, which is closed. ■ an organ stop with wooden or metal flue pipes producing a similar tone.
2 Architecture an ornamental vertical groove in a column.
■ a trumpet-shaped frill on a dress or other garment.
3 a tall, narrow wine glass: *a flute of champagne*.
▶ verb **1** [with direct speech] speak in a melodious way

reminiscent of the sound of a flute: *'What do you do?' she fluted*.
■ [no obj.] poetic/literary play a flute or pipe: *to him who sat upon the rocks, and fluted to the morning sea* | [with obj.] *some swan fluting a wild carol*.
2 [with obj.] [often as adj. **fluted**] make flutes or grooves in: *fluted columns*.
■ make trumpet-shaped frills on (a garment): *a fluted collar*.
– DERIVATIVES **flute-like** adjective.
– ORIGIN Middle English: from Old French *flahute*, probably from Provençal *flaüt*, perhaps a blend of *flaujol* 'flageolet' + *laüt* 'lute'.

fluting ▶ noun **1** [mass noun] sound reminiscent of that of a flute: *the silvery fluting of a blackbird*.
2 a groove or set of grooves forming a surface decoration: *a hollow stem with vertical flutings* | [mass noun] *pieces decorated with fluting*.
▶ adjective reminiscent of the sound of a flute: *the golden, fluting voice filled the room*.

flutist ▶ noun US term for **FLAUTIST**.

flutter ▶ verb [no obj.] (of a bird or other winged creature) fly unsteadily or hover by flapping the wings quickly and lightly: *a couple of butterflies fluttered around the garden*.
■ (with reference to a bird's wings) flap in such a way: [with obj.] *the lark fluttered its wings, hovering* | [no obj.] *their wings flutter and spread*. ■ [with adverbial] move or fall with a light irregular or trembling motion: *the remaining petals fluttered to the ground*. ■ [with adverbial of direction] (of a person) move restlessly or uncertainly: *the hostess fluttered forward to greet her guests*. ■ (of a pulse or heartbeat) beat feebly or irregularly.
▶ noun **1** an act of fluttering: *there was a flutter of wings at the window*.
■ a state or sensation of tremulous excitement: *Shiona felt a flutter in the pit of her stomach* | *her insides were in a flutter*. ■ [mass noun] Aeronautics undesired oscillation in a part of an aircraft under stress. ■ [mass noun] Medicine disturbance of the rhythm of the heart that is less severe than fibrillation: *atrial flutter* | [count noun] *I was diagnosed as having a heart flutter*. ■ [mass noun] Electronics rapid variation in the pitch or amplitude of a signal, especially of recorded sound. Compare with **WOW**[2].
2 Brit. informal a small bet: *a flutter on the horses*.
– PHRASES **flutter the dovecotes** informal cause alarm among normally imperturbable people. **flutter one's eyelashes** open and close one's eyes rapidly in a coyly flirtatious manner.
– DERIVATIVES **flutterer** noun, **flutteringly** adverb, **fluttery** adjective.
– ORIGIN Old English *floterian*, *flotorian*, a frequentative form related to **FLEET**[5].

flutter-tonguing ▶ noun [mass noun] the action of vibrating the tongue (as if rolling an *r*) in playing a wind instrument to produce a whirring effect.

fluty (also **flutey**) ▶ adjective (**-ier**, **-iest**) reminiscent of the sound of a flute: *a drawn-out fluty whistle*.

fluvial /ˈfluːvɪəl/ ▶ adjective chiefly Geology of or found in a river.
– ORIGIN Middle English: from Latin *fluvialis*, from *fluvius* 'river', from *fluere* 'to flow'.

fluviatile /ˈfluːvɪəˌtʌɪl/ ▶ adjective of, found in, or produced by a river: *fluviatile sediments*.
– ORIGIN late 16th cent.: from French, from Latin *fluviatilis*, from *fluviatus* 'moistened', from *fluvius* 'river'.

fluvio- /ˈfluːvɪəʊ/ ▶ combining form river; relating to rivers: *fluvioglacial*.
– ORIGIN from Latin *fluvius* 'river'.

fluvioglacial ▶ adjective Geology relating to or denoting erosion or deposition caused by flowing meltwater from glaciers or ice sheets.

fluviolacustrine /ˌfluːvɪə(ʊ)ləˈkʌstrʌɪn, -trɪn/ ▶ adjective Geology (of sediments) produced by both rivers and lakes.

fluviometer /ˌfluːvɪˈɒmɪtə/ ▶ noun an instrument for measuring the rise and fall of rivers.

fluvoxamine /fluːˈvɒksəmiːn/ ▶ noun [mass noun] Medicine a synthetic antidepressant drug which acts by prolonging the effect of the neurotransmitter serotonin on the brain.

flux /flʌks/ ▶ noun [mass noun] **1** the action or process of flowing or flowing out: *the flux of men and women moving back and forth* | [count noun] *a localized flux of calcium into the cell*.
■ [count noun] Medicine an abnormal discharge of blood or other matter from or within the body. ■ (usu. **the flux**) archaic diarrhoea or dysentery.

2 continuous change: *the whole political system is in a state of flux*.
3 Physics the rate of flow of a fluid, radiant energy, or particles across a given area.
■ the amount of radiation or particles incident on an area in a given time. ■ the total electric or magnetic field passing through a surface.
4 a substance mixed with a solid to lower its melting point, used especially in soldering and brazing metals or to promote vitrification in glass or ceramics.
■ a substance added to a furnace during metal smelting or glass-making which combines with impurities to form slag.
▶ verb [with obj.] treat (a metal object) with a flux to promote melting.
– ORIGIN late Middle English: from Latin *fluxus*, from *fluere* 'to flow'.

flux density ▶ noun the amount of magnetic, electric, or other flux passing through a unit area.

fluxgate ▶ noun a device consisting of one or more soft iron cores each surrounded by primary and secondary windings, used for determining the characteristics of an external magnetic field from the signals produced in the secondary windings.

fluxion /ˈflʌkʃ(ə)n/ ▶ noun Mathematics, dated a function corresponding to the rate of change of a variable quantity; a derivative.
– ORIGIN late 17th cent.: from French, or from Latin *flux-* 'flowed', from the verb *fluere*.

fluxional ▶ adjective **1** subject to flux.
2 Mathematics, dated relating to fluxions.

fly[1] ▶ verb (**flies**; past **flew**; past participle **flown**) [no obj.]
1 (of a bird or other winged creature) move through the air under control: *close the door or the moths will fly in* | *the bird can fly enormous distances*.
■ (of an aircraft or its occupants) travel through the air: *I fly back to London this evening*. ■ [with obj.] control the flight of (an aircraft); pilot. ■ [with obj. and adverbial of direction] transport in an aircraft: *helicopters flew the injured to hospital*. ■ [with obj.] accomplish (a purpose) in an aircraft: *pilots trained to fly combat missions*. ■ [with obj.] release (a bird) to fly, especially a hawk for hunting or a pigeon for racing.
2 move or be hurled quickly through the air: *balls kept flying over her hedge* | *he was **sent flying** by the tackle*.
■ [with adverbial of direction] Baseball hit a ball high into the air: *he flied out to the left field*. ■ [with adverbial of direction] go or move quickly: *she flew along the path*. ■ informal depart hastily: *I must fly!* ■ (of time) pass swiftly: *how time flies!* ■ (of a report) be circulated among many people: *rumours were **flying around** Manchester*. ■ (of accusations or insults) be exchanged swiftly and heatedly: *the accusations flew thick and fast*.
3 [with adverbial] (especially of hair) wave or flutter in the wind: *they were running, hair flying everywhere*.
■ (of a flag) be displayed, especially on a flagpole: *flags were flying at half mast*. ■ [with obj.] display (a flag).
4 archaic flee; run away: *those that fly may fight again*.
■ [with obj.] flee from; escape from in haste: *you must fly the country for a while*.
▶ noun (pl. **flies**) **1** (Brit. often **flies**) an opening at the crotch of a pair of trousers, closed with a zip or buttons and typically covered with a flap.
■ a flap of material covering the opening or fastening of a garment or of a tent: [as modifier, in combination] *a fly-fronted shirt*.
2 (**the flies**) the space over the stage in a theatre.
3 Baseball short for **FLY BALL**.
4 (pl. usu. **flys**) Brit. historical a one-horse hackney carriage.
5 Austral. informal an attempt: *we decided to give it a fly*.
– PHRASES **fly the coop** informal make one's escape. **fly the flag** see **FLAG**[1]. **fly high** be very successful; prosper: *that young man is the sort to fly high*. **fly in the face of** be openly at variance with (what is usual or expected): *a need to fly in the face of convention*. **fly into a rage** (or **temper**) become suddenly or violently angry. **fly a kite** informal, figurative try something out to test public opinion: *I thought that I would fly a kite for a somewhat unfashionable theory*. ■ historical raise money by an accommodation bill. **fly the nest** (of a young bird) leave its nest on becoming able to fly. ■ informal (of a young person) leave their parents' home to set up home elsewhere. **fly off the handle** informal lose one's temper suddenly and unexpectedly. [ORIGIN: figuratively, with reference to the loose head of an axe.] **go fly a kite** [in imperative] N. Amer. informal go away. **on the fly** while in motion or progress: *his deep shot was caught on the fly*. ■ Computing during the running

of a computer program without interrupting the run.
– DERIVATIVES **flyable** adjective.
– ORIGIN Old English *flēogan*, of Germanic origin; related to Dutch *vliegen* and German *fliegen*, also to **FLY**[2].
▶**fly at** attack (someone) verbally or physically: *Robbie flew at him, fists clenched.* ■ (of a hawk) pursue and attack, or habitually pursue (prey). ■ (**fly a hawk at**) send a hawk to pursue and attack (prey).

fly[2] ▶ noun (pl. **flies**) a flying insect of a large order characterized by a single pair of transparent wings and sucking (and often also piercing) mouthparts. Flies are of great importance as vectors of disease. See also **DIPTERA**.
• Order Diptera: numerous families.
■[usu. in combination] used in names of flying insects of other orders, e.g. **butterfly**, **dragonfly**, **firefly**. ■ [mass noun] an infestation of flying insects on a plant or animal: *cattle to be treated for warble fly.* ■ a natural or artificial flying insect used as bait in fishing, especially a mayfly.
– PHRASES **die** (or **drop**) **like flies** die or collapse in large numbers: *people in the area seemed to die like flies in the winter.* **drink with the flies** Austral./NZ drink alone. **a fly in the ointment** a minor irritation that spoils the success or enjoyment of something. **fly on the wall** an unnoticed observer of a particular situation. ■ [as modifier] denoting a film-making technique whereby events are observed realistically with minimum interference rather than acted out under direction: *a fly-on-the-wall documentary.* **like a blue-arsed fly** Brit. vulgar slang in an extremely hectic or frantic way. **there are no flies on ——** used to emphasize a person's quickness and astuteness: *I knew there were no flies on her, but I wondered how she had found out.* **wouldn't hurt** (or **harm**) **a fly** used to emphasize how inoffensive and harmless a person or animal is.
– ORIGIN Old English *flȳge*, *flēoge*, denoting any winged insect, of West Germanic origin; related to Dutch *vlieg* and German *Fliege*, also to **FLY**[1].

fly[3] ▶ adjective (**flyer**, **flyest**) informal **1** Brit. knowing and clever; worldly-wise: *she's fly enough not to get done out of it.*
2 N. Amer. stylish and fashionable: *they were wearin' fly clothes.*
– DERIVATIVES **flyness** noun.
– ORIGIN early 19th cent.: of unknown origin.

fly agaric ▶ noun a poisonous toadstool which has a red cap with fluffy white spots, growing particularly among birch trees. It contains hallucinogenic alkaloids and has long been used by the native peoples of NE Siberia.
• *Amanita muscaria*, family Amanitaceae, class Hymenomycetes.

fly ash ▶ noun [mass noun] ash produced in small dark flecks by the burning of powdered coal or other materials and carried into the air.

flyaway ▶ adjective (of a person's hair) fine and difficult to control.

flyback ▶ noun [mass noun] the return of the scanning spot in a cathode ray tube to the starting point.

fly ball ▶ noun Baseball a ball batted high into the air.

flyblow ▶ noun [mass noun] flies' eggs contaminating food, especially meat.

flyblown ▶ adjective dirty or contaminated, especially through contact with flies and their eggs and larvae: *flyblown meat.*

fly boy ▶ noun N. Amer. informal a pilot, especially one in the air force.

flybridge ▶ noun an open deck above the main bridge of a vessel such as a yacht or cabin cruiser, typically equipped with duplicate controls.

fly-by ▶ noun (pl. **-bys**) a flight past a point, especially the close approach of a spacecraft to a planet or moon for observation.

fly-by-night ▶ adjective [attrib.] unreliable or untrustworthy, especially in business or financial matters: *cheap suits made by fly-by-night operators.*
▶ noun (also **fly-by-nighter**) an unreliable or untrustworthy person.

fly-by-wire ▶ noun [often as modifier] a semi-automatic and typically computer-regulated system for controlling the flight of an aircraft or spacecraft: *sophisticated fly-by-wire technology.*

flycatcher ▶ noun a perching bird that catches flying insects, especially in short flights from a perch.
• Typical Old World flycatchers belong to the family Muscicapidae. Many others belong to the Old World family Monarchidae (**monarch** and **paradise flycatchers**) and the New World family Tyrannidae (**tyrant flycatchers**), while some belong to families Eopsaltridae (Australasia), Platysteiridae (Africa), and Bombycillidae (America).

fly-drive ▶ adjective denoting a package holiday which includes a flight and car rental at the destination.
▶ noun a holiday of this type.

flyer (also **flier**) ▶ noun **1** a person or thing that flies, especially in a particular way: *a nervous flyer.*
■a person who flies something, especially an aircraft. ■ informal a fast-moving person or thing: *his free kick was a real flyer.*
2 a small handbill advertising an event or product.
3 short for **FLYING START**.
4 chiefly N. Amer. a speculative investment.
– PHRASES **take a flyer** chiefly N. Amer. take a chance.

fly-fishing ▶ noun [mass noun] the sport of fishing using a rod and an artificial fly as bait.
– DERIVATIVES **fly-fish** verb.

fly half ▶ noun Rugby another term for **STAND-OFF HALF**.

fly-in ▶ noun a meeting for pilots who arrive by air: *they are holding a helicopter fly-in.*
■an act of transporting people or goods by air: *one or two fly-ins to remote lakes.* ■ [as modifier] denoting a place or activity which is reached using an aircraft: *fly-in canoe trips.*

flying ▶ adjective moving or able to move through the air with wings: *a flying ant.*
■done while hurling oneself through the air: *he took a flying kick at a policeman.* ■ moving rapidly, especially through the air: *one passenger was cut by flying glass.* ■ hasty; brief: *a flying visit.* ■ used in names of animals that can glide by using wing-like membranes or other structures, e.g. **flying squirrel**.
▶ noun [mass noun] flight, especially in an aircraft: *she hates flying* | [as modifier] *a flying accident.*
– PHRASES **with flying colours** with distinction: *Sylvia had passed her exams with flying colours.*

flying boat ▶ noun a large seaplane that lands with its fuselage in the water.

flying bomb ▶ noun a small pilotless aircraft with an explosive warhead, especially a V-1.

flying bridge ▶ noun see **FLYBRIDGE**.

flying buttress ▶ noun Architecture a buttress slanting from a separate column, typically forming an arch with the wall it supports.

flying change ▶ noun a movement in riding in which the leading leg in the canter position is changed without loss of speed while the horse is in the air.

flying doctor ▶ noun (in Australia) a doctor who uses radio communication and travels by aircraft to visit patients in remote areas of the country.

flying dragon ▶ noun see **DRAGON** (sense 2).

Flying Dutchman a legendary spectral ship supposedly seen in the region of the Cape of Good Hope and presaging disaster.
■the captain of this ship.

flying fish ▶ noun a fish of warm seas which leaps out of the water and uses its wing-like pectoral fins to glide over the surface for some distance.
• Family Exocoetidae: several genera and species, in particular *Exocoetus volitans*.

flying fox ▶ noun a large fruit bat with a foxlike face, found in Madagascar, SE Asia, and northern Australia.
• *Pteropus* and two other genera, family Pteropodidae: numerous species.

flying frog ▶ noun a nocturnal arboreal Asian frog which is able to glide between trees using the large webs between its extended toes.
• *Polypedates leucomystax*, family Rhacophoridae.

flying gurnard ▶ noun a bottom-dwelling marine fish that has bony armour on the skull, spines behind the head, and large brightly coloured pectoral fins. It moves through the water with a gliding or flying motion.
• Family Dactylopteridae: two genera and several species.

flying jacket ▶ noun a short jacket similar to a bomber jacket, typically of leather and with a warm lining or collar and several pockets.

flying lemur ▶ noun a nocturnal tree-dwelling lemur-like mammal with a membrane between the fore- and hindlimbs for gliding from tree to tree. It is native to SE Asia. Also called **COLUGO**.
• Family Cynocephalidae and genus *Cynocephalus*, order Dermoptera: two species.

flying lizard ▶ noun an arboreal SE Asian lizard which has expanding membranes along the sides of the body, used for gliding between trees. Also called **DRAGON**.
• Genus *Draco*, family Agamidae: several species.

flying machine ▶ noun an aircraft, especially an early or unconventional one.

flying mouse ▶ noun **1** another term for **FEATHERTAIL GLIDER**.
2 Computing a mouse that can be lifted from the desk and used in three dimensions.

flying officer ▶ noun a rank of commissioned officer in the RAF, above pilot officer and below flight lieutenant.

flying phalanger ▶ noun a small Australasian marsupial with a membrane between the fore- and hindlimbs for gliding. Also called **GLIDER**.
• Genera *Petaurus* and *Petauroides*, family Petauridae: five species.

flying picket ▶ noun Brit. a person who, with others, travels to picket any workplace where there is an industrial dispute.

flying saucer ▶ noun a disc-shaped flying craft supposedly piloted by aliens; a UFO.

flying snake ▶ noun a greenish semi-arboreal SE Asian snake which can glide down from a tree in a stiff horizontal position, with the belly hollowed to slow its descent.
• *Chrysopelea ornata*, family Colubridae.

flying squad ▶ noun Brit. a division of a police force or other organization which is capable of reaching an incident quickly.

flying squirrel ▶ noun a small squirrel that has skin joining the fore- and hindlimbs for gliding from tree to tree.
• Subfamily Pteromyinae, family Sciuridae (many species in SE Asia, northern Eurasia, and North America), and family Anomaluridae (several species in Africa; see also **SCALY-TAILED SQUIRREL**.)

flying start ▶ noun a start of a race or time trial in which the starting point is passed at speed.
■a good beginning, especially one giving an advantage over competitors: *the team* **got off to a flying start** *in last year's rally.*

flying suit ▶ noun a one-piece garment worn by the pilot and crew of a military or light aircraft.

flying trapeze ▶ noun another term for **TRAPEZE** (in sense 1).

flying wing ▶ noun an aircraft with little or no fuselage and no tailplane.

flyleaf ▶ noun (pl. **-leaves**) a blank page at the beginning or end of a book.

flyman ▶ noun (pl. **-men**) Theatre a person positioned in the flies to raise and lower scenery.

Flynn, Errol (1909–59), Australian-born American actor; born *Leslie Thomas Flynn*. His usual role was the swashbuckling hero of romantic costume dramas in films such as *Captain Blood* (1935) and *The Adventures of Robin Hood* (1938).

fly orchid ▶ noun a European woodland orchid with flowers that resemble flies.
• *Ophrys insectifera*, family Orchidaceae.

flyover ▶ noun **1** chiefly Brit. a bridge carrying one railway line or road over another.
2 N. Amer. a low flight by one or more aircraft over a specific location.
■another term for **FLY-PAST**.

flypaper ▶ noun [mass noun] sticky, poison-treated strips of paper that are hung indoors to catch and kill flies.

fly-past ▶ noun Brit. a ceremonial flight of aircraft past a person or a place.

fly-pitcher ▶ noun Brit. informal a street trader.
– DERIVATIVES **fly-pitching** noun.

fly-post ▶ verb [with obj.] Brit. put up (advertising posters) in unauthorized places: *notices appealing for help were fly-posted around Colchester* | [no obj.] *I fly-post every Friday night.*

fly-poster ▶ noun Brit. **1** an advertising poster put up in an unauthorized place.
2 a person who fly-posts.

flysch /flɪʃ/ ▶ noun [mass noun] Geology a sedimentary deposit consisting of thin beds of shale or marl alternating with coarser strata such as sandstone or conglomerate.

– ORIGIN mid 19th cent.: from Swiss German dialect.

flysheet ▶ **noun** **1** Brit. a fabric cover pitched outside and over a tent to give extra protection against bad weather.
2 a tract or circular of two or four pages.

flyspeck ▶ **noun** a tiny stain made by the excrement of an insect.
■ a thing which is contemptibly small or insignificant: *a sleepy flyspeck of a town.*
– DERIVATIVES **flyspecked** adjective.

fly spray ▶ **noun** a substance sprayed from an aerosol that kills flying insects: *an alternative to chemical fly sprays* | [mass noun] *a dose of fly spray.*

fly strike ▶ **noun** [mass noun] infestation of an animal with blowfly maggots.

fly swatter (also **fly swat**) ▶ **noun** an implement used for swatting insects.

fly-through ▶ **noun** a computer-animated simulation of what would be seen by one flying through a particular real or imaginary region.

fly-tip ▶ **verb** [no obj.] Brit. illegally dump waste: *residents have been asked not to fly-tip* | [as noun **fly-tipping**] *some damage is caused by fly-tipping.*
– DERIVATIVES **fly-tipper** noun.

flytrap ▶ **noun** see **VENUS FLYTRAP**.

flyway ▶ **noun** Ornithology a route regularly used by large numbers of migrating birds.

flyweight ▶ **noun** [mass noun] a weight in boxing and other sports intermediate between light flyweight and bantamweight. In the amateur boxing scale it ranges from 48 to 51 kg.
■ [count noun] a boxer or other competitor of this weight.

flywheel ▶ **noun** a heavy revolving wheel in a machine which is used to increase the machine's momentum and thereby provide greater stability or a reserve of available power.

fly whisk ▶ **noun** see **WHISK** (sense 2).

FM ▶ **abbreviation for** ■ Field Marshal. ■ frequency modulation: [as modifier] *an FM radio station.*

Fm ▶ **symbol for** the chemical element fermium.

fm ▶ **abbreviation for** fathom(s).

FMCG ▶ **abbreviation for** fast-moving consumer goods: [as modifier] *the FMCG sector.*

FMV ▶ **abbreviation for** full-motion video.

f-number ▶ **noun** Photography the ratio of the focal length of a camera lens to the diameter of the aperture being used for a particular shot (e.g. *f*8, indicating that the focal length is eight times the diameter).
– ORIGIN early 20th cent.: from *f* (denoting the focal length) and **NUMBER**.

FO ▶ **abbreviation for** ■ Flying Officer. ■ Foreign Office.

Fo /fəʊ/, Dario (b.1926), Italian dramatist. Notable works: *Accidental Death of an Anarchist* (political satire, 1970) and *Open Couple* (farce, 1983). Nobel Prize for Literature (1997).

fo. ▶ **abbreviation for** folio.

foal ▶ **noun** a young horse or related animal.
▶ **verb** [no obj.] (of a mare) give birth to a foal.
■ (**be foaled**) (of a foal) be born.
– PHRASES **in** (or **with**) **foal** (of a mare) pregnant.
– ORIGIN Old English *fola*, of Germanic origin; related to Dutch *veulen* and German *Fohlen*, also to **FILLY**.

foam ▶ **noun** [mass noun] a mass of small bubbles formed on or in liquid, typically by agitation or fermentation: *a beer with a thick head of foam.*
■ a similar mass formed from saliva or sweat. ■ a liquid preparation containing many small bubbles: *shaving foam.* ■ a lightweight form of rubber or plastic made by solidifying such a liquid: [as modifier] *foam rubber.* ■ (**the foam**) poetic/literary the sea: *Venus rising from the foam.*
▶ **verb** [no obj.] form or produce a mass of small bubbles; froth: *the sea foamed beneath them.*
■ figurative, informal be very angry: *staff are foaming at the mouth.*
– DERIVATIVES **foamless** adjective, **foamy** adjective.
– ORIGIN Old English *fām* (noun), *fǣman* (verb), of West Germanic origin; related to Old High German *feim* (noun), *feimen* (verb).

foam board ▶ **noun** [mass noun] a type of thin, pliable polystyrene board used for insulation and in arts and crafts.

fob¹ ▶ **noun** (also **fob chain**) a chain attached to a watch for carrying in a waistcoat or waistband pocket.
■ a small ornament attached to a watch chain. ■ (also **fob pocket**) a small pocket for carrying a watch. ■ a tab on a key ring.
– ORIGIN mid 17th cent. (denoting a fob pocket in a waistband): origin uncertain; probably related to German dialect *Fuppe* 'pocket'.

fob² ▶ **verb** (**fobbed**, **fobbing**) [with obj.] (**fob someone off**) deceitfully attempt to satisfy someone by making excuses or giving them something inferior: *I was **fobbed off with** bland reassurances.*
■ (**fob something off on**) give (someone) something inferior to or different from what they want: *he fobbed off the chairmanship on Clifford.*
– ORIGIN late Middle English (in the sense 'cheat out of'): origin uncertain; perhaps related to German *foppen* 'deceive, cheat, banter', or to **FOP**.

f.o.b. ▶ **abbreviation for** free on board. See **FREE**.

fob watch ▶ **noun** a pocket watch.

focaccia /fəˈkatʃə/ ▶ **noun** [mass noun] a type of flat Italian bread made with yeast and olive oil and flavoured with herbs.
– ORIGIN Italian.

focal /ˈfəʊk(ə)l/ ▶ **adjective** of or relating to the centre or main point of interest: *the focal symbol of sovereignty is the crown.*
■ Optics of or relating to the focus of a lens. ■ (of a disease or medical condition) occurring in one particular site in the body.
– ORIGIN late 17th cent.: from modern Latin *focalis*, from Latin *focus*, or directly from **FOCUS**.

focalize (also **-ise**) ▶ **verb** [with obj.] technical focus (something), in particular:
■ (in literary theory) provide an internal focus for (a text): *the narrative discourse is focalized around the consciousness of the central protagonist.* ■ Medicine confine (a disease or infection) to a particular site in the body.
– DERIVATIVES **focalization** noun.

focal length ▶ **noun** the distance between the centre of a lens or curved mirror and its focus.
■ the equivalent distance in a compound lens or telescope.

focal plane ▶ **noun** the plane through the focus perpendicular to the axis of a mirror or lens.

focal point ▶ **noun** the point at which rays or waves meet after reflection or refraction, or the point from which diverging rays or waves appear to proceed.
■ the centre of interest or activity.

Foch /fɒʃ/, Ferdinand (1851–1929), French general. He supported the use of offensive warfare which resulted in many of his 20th Corps being killed in August 1914. He was later the senior French representative at the Armistice negotiations.

fo'c's'le /ˈfəʊks(ə)l/ ▶ **noun** variant spelling of **FORECASTLE**.

focus ▶ **noun** (pl. **focuses** or **foci** /ˈfəʊsʌɪ/) **1** the centre of interest or activity: *this generation has made the environment a focus of attention.*
■ an act of concentrating interest or activity on something: *our **focus on** the customer's requirements.* ■ Geology the point of origin of an earthquake. Compare with **EPICENTRE**. ■ Medicine the principal site of an infection or other disease. ■ Linguistics another term for **RHEME**.
2 [mass noun] the state or quality of having or producing clear visual definition: *his face is rather **out of focus**.*
■ another term for **FOCAL POINT**. ■ [count noun] the point at which an object must be situated with respect to a lens or mirror for an image of it to be well defined. ■ [count noun] a device on a lens which can be adjusted to produce a clear image.
3 Geometry one of the fixed points from which the distances to any point of a given curve, such as an ellipse or parabola, are connected by a linear relation.
▶ **verb** (**focused**, **focusing** or **focussed**, **focussing**) [no obj.] **1** (of a person or their eyes) adapt to the prevailing level of light and become able to see clearly: *try to **focus on** a stationary object.*
■ [with obj.] bring (one's eyes) into such a state: *trying to **focus** his bleary eyes **on** Corbett.* ■ [with obj.] adjust the focus of (a telescope, camera, or other instrument): *they were **focusing** a telescope **on** a star.* ■ (of rays or waves) meet at a single point. ■ [with obj.] (of a lens) make (rays or waves) meet at a single point. ■ [no obj.] (of light, radio waves, or other energy) become concentrated into a sharp beam of light or energy. ■ [with obj.] (of a lens) concentrate (light, radio waves, or energy) into a sharp beam.
2 (**focus on**) pay particular attention to: *the study will focus on a number of areas in Wales.*
■ [with obj.] concentrate: *the course helps to focus and stimulate your thoughts.* ■ [with obj.] Linguistics place the focus on (a part of a sentence).
– DERIVATIVES **focuser** noun.
– ORIGIN mid 17th cent. (as a term in geometry and physics): from Latin, literally 'domestic hearth'.

focus group ▶ **noun** a demographically diverse group of people assembled to participate in a guided discussion about a particular product before it is launched, or to provide ongoing feedback on a political campaign, television series, etc.

focus puller ▶ **noun** an assistant to a film or television cameraman, who is responsible for keeping the lens focused during filming.

fodder ▶ **noun** [mass noun] food, especially dried hay or straw, for cattle and other livestock.
■ a person or thing regarded only as material for a specific use: *young people ending up as factory fodder.*
▶ **verb** [with obj.] give fodder to (cattle or other livestock): *the animals need foddering.*
– ORIGIN Old English *fōdor*, of Germanic origin; related to Dutch *voeder* and German *Futter*, also to **FOOD**.

fody /ˈfəʊdi/ ▶ **noun** (pl. **-ies**) a songbird of the weaver family occurring in Madagascar and islands in the Indian Ocean, the male of which typically has mainly red plumage.
● Genus *Foudia*, family Ploceidae: several species.
– ORIGIN a local word.

FoE ▶ **abbreviation for** Friends of the Earth.

foe ▶ **noun** poetic/literary or formal an enemy or opponent: *join forces against the common foe.*
– ORIGIN Old English *fāh* 'hostile' and *gefā* 'enemy', of West Germanic origin; related to **FEUD**.

foehn ▶ **noun** variant spelling of **FÖHN**.

foetid ▶ **adjective** variant spelling of **FETID**.

foetus ▶ **noun** variant spelling of **FETUS** (chiefly in British non-technical use).
– DERIVATIVES **foetal** adjective, **foeticide** noun.

fog¹ ▶ **noun** [mass noun] a thick cloud of tiny water droplets suspended in the atmosphere at or near the earth's surface which obscures or restricts visibility (to a greater extent than mist; strictly, reducing visibility to below 1 km): *the collision occurred in thick fog.*
■ [in sing.] an opaque mass of something in the atmosphere: *a whirling **fog of** dust.* ■ [in sing.] figurative something that obscures and confuses a situation or someone's thought processes: *the origins of local government are lost in a fog of detail.* ■ Photography cloudiness which obscures the image on a developed negative or print.
▶ **verb** (**fogged**, **fogging**) [with obj.] **1** cause (a glass surface) to become covered with steam: *hot steam drifted about her, **fogging up** the window.*
■ [no obj.] (of a glass surface) become covered with steam: *the windscreen was starting to **fog up**.* ■ figurative bewilder or puzzle (someone): *she stared at him, confusion fogging her brain.* ■ figurative make (an idea or situation) difficult to understand: *the government has been fogging the issue.* ■ Photography make (a film, negative, or print) obscure or cloudy.
2 treat with something, especially an insecticide, in the form of a spray.
– PHRASES **in a fog** in a state of perplexity; unable to think clearly or understand something.
– ORIGIN mid 16th cent.: perhaps a back-formation from **FOGGY**.

fog² ▶ **noun** [mass noun] the grass which grows in a field after a crop of hay has been taken.
■ long grass left standing in a pasture and used as winter grazing.
– ORIGIN late Middle English: origin uncertain; perhaps related to Norwegian *fogg*.

fog bank ▶ **noun** a dense mass of fog, especially at sea.

fogbound ▶ **adjective** unable to travel or function normally because of thick fog.
■ enveloped or obscured by fog: *a fogbound forest.*

fogbow ▶ **noun** a phenomenon similar to a rainbow, produced by sunlight shining on fog.

fogey /ˈfəʊgi/ (also **fogy**) ▶ **noun** (pl. **-eys** or **-ies**) a person, typically an old one, who is considered to be very old-fashioned or conservative in their attitude or tastes: *a bunch of **old fogeys**.*
– DERIVATIVES **fogeydom** noun, **fogeyish** adjective, **fogeyism** noun.

f

– ORIGIN late 18th cent.: related to earlier slang *fogram*, of unknown origin.

Foggia /ˈfɒdʒə/ a town in SE Italy, in Apulia; pop. 159,540 (1990).

foggy ▶ adjective (**foggier**, **foggiest**) full of or accompanied by fog: *a dark and foggy night.*
■ unable to think clearly; confused: *she was foggy with sleep.* ■ indistinctly expressed or perceived; obscure: *exactly what the company hopes to achieve is still foggy.*
– PHRASES **not have the foggiest** (**idea** or **notion**) informal, chiefly Brit. have no idea at all.
– DERIVATIVES **fogginess** noun.
– ORIGIN late 15th cent.: perhaps from **FOG**[2].

foghorn ▶ noun a device making a loud, deep sound as a warning to ships in fog.

fog lamp (also **fog light**) ▶ noun a bright light on a motor vehicle, used in foggy conditions to improve road visibility or warn other drivers of one's presence.

fogou /ˈfəʊguː, -gəʊ/ ▶ noun (pl. **fogous**) Archaeology a form of artificial underground passage or chamber found in Cornwall.
– ORIGIN from Cornish *fogo, fougo*.

fog signal ▶ noun a small explosive charge which can be placed on a railway line in fog to be set off by the train as a signal to the driver. Also called **DETONATOR**.

fogy ▶ noun variant spelling of **FOGEY**.

föhn /fəːn/ (also **foehn**) ▶ noun (often **the föhn**) a hot southerly wind on the northern slopes of the Alps.
■ (also **föhn wind**) Meteorology a warm dry wind of this type developing in the lee of any mountain range.
– ORIGIN mid 19th cent.: from German, based on Latin (*ventus*) *Favonius* 'mild west wind', *Favonius* being the Roman personification of the west or west wind.

foible /ˈfɔɪb(ə)l/ ▶ noun **1** a minor weakness or eccentricity in someone's character: *they have to tolerate each other's little foibles.*
2 Fencing the part of a sword blade from the middle to the point. Compare with **FORTE**[1].
– ORIGIN late 16th cent. (as an adjective in the sense 'feeble'): from obsolete French, in Old French *fieble* (see **FEEBLE**). Both noun senses also formerly occurred as senses of the word *feeble* and all date from the 17th cent.

foie gras /fwɑː ˈɡrɑː/ ▶ noun short for **PÂTÉ DE FOIE GRAS**.

foil[1] ▶ verb [with obj.] prevent (something considered wrong or undesirable) from succeeding: *a brave policewoman foiled the armed robbery.*
■ frustrate the efforts or plans of: *their rivals were foiled by the weather.* ■ Hunting (of a hunted animal) run over or cross (ground or a scent or track) in such a way as to confuse the hounds.
▶ noun **1** Hunting the track or scent of a hunted animal.
2 archaic a setback in an enterprise; a defeat.
– ORIGIN Middle English (in the sense 'trample down'): perhaps from Old French *fouler* 'to full cloth, trample', based on Latin *fullo* 'fuller'. Compare with **FULL**[2].

foil[2] ▶ noun **1** [mass noun] metal hammered or rolled into a thin flexible sheet, used chiefly for covering or wrapping food.
2 a person or thing that contrasts with and so emphasizes and enhances the qualities of another: *his white cravat was a perfect foil for his bronzed features.*
■ a thin leaf of metal placed under a precious stone to increase its brilliance.
3 Architecture a leaf-shaped curve formed by the cusping of an arch or circle.
– ORIGIN Middle English: via Old French from Latin *folium* 'leaf'.

foil[3] ▶ noun a light, blunt-edged fencing sword with a button on its point.
– DERIVATIVES **foilist** noun.
– ORIGIN late 16th cent.: of unknown origin.

foil[4] ▶ noun each of the structures fitted to a hydrofoil's hull to lift it clear of the water at speed.

foist /fɔɪst/ ▶ verb [with obj.] (**foist someone/thing on**) impose an unwelcome or unnecessary person or thing on: *beers are foisted on a public unaware of their inferior ingredients.*
■ (**foist someone/thing into**) introduce someone or something surreptitiously or unwarrantably into: *he attempted to foist a new minister into the conference.*
– ORIGIN mid 16th cent. (in the sense 'palm a false die, so as to produce it at the right moment'): from Dutch dialect *vuisten* 'take in the hand', from *vuist* (see **FIST**).

Fokine /ˈfəʊkiːn/, Michel (1880–1942), Russian-born American dancer and choreographer; born *Mikhail Mikhailovich Fokin*. He was a reformer of modern ballet: as Diaghilev's chief choreographer he staged the premières of Stravinsky's *The Firebird* (1910) and Ravel's *Daphnis and Chloë* (1912).

Fokker /ˈfɒkə/, Anthony Herman Gerard (1890–1939), Dutch-born American aircraft designer and pilot. Having built his first aircraft in 1908, he designed fighters used by the Germans in the First World War and founded the Fokker company.

fol. ▶ abbreviation for folio.

folacin /ˈfəʊləsɪn/ ▶ noun another term for **FOLIC ACID**.

fold[1] ▶ verb [with obj.] **1** bend (something flexible and relatively flat) over on itself so that one part of it covers another: *I **folded** the clothes **up**.*
■ (**fold something in/into**) mix an ingredient gently with (another ingredient), especially by lifting a mixture with a spoon so as to enclose it without stirring or beating: *fold the egg whites into the chocolate mixture.* ■ [no obj.] (of a piece of furniture or equipment) be able to be bent or rearranged into a flatter or more compact shape, typically in order to make it easier to store or carry: [with complement] *the deckchair folds flat* | [as adj. **folding**] *a folding chair.* ■ bend or rearrange (a piece of furniture or equipment) in such a way: *the small card table was **folded up** and put away.* ■ [no obj.] (**fold out**) be able to be opened out; unfold: *the sofa folds out.* ■ (often **be folded**) Geology cause (rock strata) to undergo bending or curvature: [as noun **folding**] *a more active period of igneous activity caused intense folding.*
2 [with adverbial] cover or wrap something in (a soft or flexible material): *a plastic bag was folded around the book.*
■ hold or clasp (someone) closely in one's arms with passion or deep affection: *Bob folded her in his arms and kissed her.*
3 [no obj.] informal (of an enterprise or organization) cease trading or operating as a result of financial problems or a lack of support: *the club folded earlier this year.*
■ (especially of a sports player or team) suddenly stop performing well or effectively. ■ (of a poker player) drop out of a hand.
▶ noun **1** (usu. **folds**) a form or shape produced by the gentle draping of a loose, full garment or piece of cloth: *the fabric fell in soft folds.*
■ an area of skin that sags or hangs loosely. ■ chiefly Brit. an undulation or gentle curve of the ground; a slight hill or hollow: *the house lay in a fold of the hills.* ■ Geology a bend or curvature of strata.
2 a line or crease produced in paper or cloth as the result of folding it.
■ a piece of paper or cloth that has been folded: *a fold of paper slipped out of the diary.*
– PHRASES **fold one's arms** bring one's arms together and cross them over one's chest. **fold one's hands** bring or hold one's hands together.
– DERIVATIVES **foldable** adjective.
– ORIGIN Old English *falden, fealden*, of Germanic origin; related to Dutch *vouwen* and German *falten*.

fold[2] ▶ noun a pen or enclosure in a field where livestock, especially sheep, can be kept.
■ (**the fold**) a group or community, especially when perceived as the locus of a particular set of aims and values: *government whips tried to persuade the waverers back into the fold.*
▶ verb [with obj.] shut (livestock) in a fold.
– ORIGIN Old English *fald*, of Germanic origin; related to Dutch *vaalt*.

-fold ▶ suffix forming adjectives and adverbs from cardinal numbers: **1** in an amount multiplied by: *threefold.*
2 consisting of so many parts or facets: *twofold.*
– ORIGIN Old English *-fald, -feald*; related to **FOLD**[1].

foldaway ▶ adjective [attrib.] adapted or designed to be folded up for ease of storage or transport: *a foldaway table.*

folder ▶ noun a folding cover or holder, typically made of stiff paper or card, for storing loose papers.
■ an icon on a computer screen which can be used to access a directory containing related files or documents. ■ N. Amer. a folded leaflet or a booklet made of folded sheets of paper.

folderol /ˈfɒldərɒl/ (also **falderal**) ▶ noun [mass noun] trivial or nonsensical fuss: *all the folderol of the athletic contests and the cheerleaders.*
■ archaic used as a meaningless recurring phrase in a song. ■ [count noun] dated a showy but useless item.

folding door ▶ noun a door with vertical jointed sections that can be folded together to one side to allow access to a room or building.

folding money ▶ noun [mass noun] informal money in the form of notes.

fold-out ▶ adjective [attrib.] (of a page in a book or magazine or a piece of furniture) designed to be opened out for use and folded away for convenient storage: *a fold-out map.*
▶ noun a page or piece of furniture designed in such a way.

foley /ˈfəʊli/ ▶ noun [as modifier] chiefly US relating to or concerned with the addition of recorded sound effects after the shooting of a film: *a foley artist.*
– ORIGIN named after the inventor of the editing process.

folia plural form of **FOLIUM**.

foliaceous /ˌfəʊlɪˈeɪʃəs/ ▶ adjective of or resembling a leaf or leaves.
■ chiefly Geology consisting of thin sheets or laminae.
– ORIGIN mid 17th cent.: from Latin *foliaceus* 'leafy' (from *folium* 'leaf') + **-OUS**.

foliage /ˈfəʊlɪɪdʒ/ ▶ noun [mass noun] plant leaves, collectively: *healthy green foliage.*
– ORIGIN late Middle English *foilage* (in the sense 'design resembling leaves'): from Old French *feuillage*, from *feuille* 'leaf', from Latin *folium*. The change in the first syllable was due to association with Latin *folium*.

foliage leaf ▶ noun Botany a normal leaf, as opposed to petals and other modified leaves.

foliar /ˈfəʊlɪə/ ▶ adjective [attrib.] technical of or relating to leaves: *foliar colour and shape.*
– ORIGIN late 19th cent.: from modern Latin *foliaris*, from Latin *folium* 'leaf'.

foliar feed ▶ noun [mass noun] nutrients supplied to the leaves of a plant.
– DERIVATIVES **foliar feeding** noun.

foliate ▶ adjective /ˈfəʊlɪət, -eɪt/ decorated with leaves or leaf-like motifs: *foliate scrolls.*
▶ verb /ˈfəʊlɪeɪt/ [with obj.] **1** decorate with leaves or leaf-like motifs: *the dome is to be foliated.*
2 number the leaves of (a book) rather than the pages.
– ORIGIN mid 17th cent.: from Latin *foliatus* 'leaved', from *folium* 'leaf'.

foliated ▶ adjective decorated with leaves or leaf-like motifs: *foliated capitals.*
■ Architecture decorated with foils. ■ chiefly Geology consisting of thin sheets or laminae.

foliation /ˌfəʊlɪˈeɪʃ(ə)n/ ▶ noun [mass noun] chiefly Geology the process of splitting into thin sheets or laminae.

folic acid /ˈfəʊlɪk, ˈfɒl-/ ▶ noun [mass noun] Biochemistry a vitamin of the B complex found especially in leafy green vegetables, liver, and kidney. A deficiency of folic acid causes megaloblastic anaemia. Also called **PTEROYLGLUTAMIC ACID**, **VITAMIN M**.
– DERIVATIVES **folate** noun.
– ORIGIN 1940s: *folic* from Latin *folium* 'leaf' + **-IC**.

folie à deux /ˌfɒlɪ a ˈdəː/ ▶ noun (pl. **folies à deux**) [mass noun] delusion or mental illness shared by two people in close association.
– ORIGIN French, literally 'shared madness'.

folie de grandeur /ˌfɒlɪ də ɡrɒ̃ˈdəː/ ▶ noun [mass noun] delusions of grandeur.
– ORIGIN French.

Folies-Bergère /ˌfɒlɪbɛːˈʒɛː, French fɔli bɛrʒɛr/ a variety theatre in Paris, opened in 1869, known for its lavish productions featuring nude and semi-nude female performers.

folio /ˈfəʊlɪəʊ/ ▶ noun (pl. **-os**) an individual leaf of paper or parchment, either loose as one of a series or forming part of a bound volume, which is numbered on the recto or front side only.
■ the page number in a printed book. ■ a sheet of paper folded once to form two leaves (four pages) of a book. ■ a size of book made up of such sheets: *imperial folio* | *copies **in folio**.* ■ a book or manuscript made up of sheets of paper folded in such a way; a volume of the largest standard size: *old vellum-bound folios* | [as modifier] *a folio volume.*
– ORIGIN late Middle English: from Latin, ablative of *folium* 'leaf', in medieval Latin used in references to mean 'on leaf so-and-so'. The original sense of *in folio* (from Italian *in foglio*) was 'in the form of a full-

sized sheet or leaf folded once' (designating the largest size of book).

foliose /ˈfəʊlɪəʊs, -z/ ▶ **adjective** Botany (of a lichen) having a lobed, leaf-like shape.
– ORIGIN early 18th cent.: from Latin *foliosus*, from *folium* 'leaf'.

folium /ˈfəʊlɪəm/ ▶ **noun** (pl. **folia**) technical a thin leaf-like structure, e.g. in some rocks or in the cerebellum of the brain.
– ORIGIN mid 18th cent.: from Latin, literally 'leaf'.

folivore /ˈfəʊlɪvɔː/ ▶ **noun** Zoology an animal that feeds on leaves.
– DERIVATIVES **folivorous** adjective, **folivory** noun.

folk /fəʊk/ (also **folks**) ▶ **plural noun 1** informal people in general: *some folk will do anything for money* | *an old folks' home.*
▪ (**folks**) used as a friendly form of address to a group of people: *meanwhile folks, why not relax and enjoy the atmosphere?* ▪ (**one's folks**) the members of one's family, especially one's parents: *I get on all right with your folks.*
2 [mass noun] folk music: *a mixture of folk and reggae.*
▶ **adjective** [attrib.] of or relating to the traditional art or culture of a community or nation: *a revival of interest in folk customs* | *a folk museum.*
▪ relating to or originating from the beliefs and opinions of ordinary people: *a folk hero* | *folk wisdom.*
– ORIGIN Old English *folc*, of Germanic origin; related to Dutch *volk* and German *Volk*.

folk dance ▶ **noun** a popular dance, considered as part of the tradition or custom of a particular people: *well-known folk dances* | [mass noun] *ballet steps complicated by borrowings from folk dance.*
– DERIVATIVES **folk dancer** noun, **folk dancing** noun.

folk devil ▶ **noun** a person or thing held to be a bad influence on society: *the choice of prostitutes as folk devils.*

Folkestone /ˈfəʊkstən/ a seaport and resort in Kent, on the SE coast of England; pop. 44,000 (1981).

folk etymology ▶ **noun** a popular but mistaken account of the origin of a word or phrase.
▪ [mass noun] the process by which the form of an unfamiliar or foreign word is adapted to a more familiar form through popular usage.

folkie ▶ **noun** informal a singer, player, or fan of folk music.

folkish ▶ **adjective** characteristic of ordinary people or traditional culture: *folkish humour.*
▪ relating to or like folk music or folk singers: *the most conventionally folkish number on the album.*

folklife ▶ **noun** [mass noun] the way of life of a rural or traditional community.

folklore ▶ **noun** [mass noun] the traditional beliefs, customs, and stories of a community, passed through the generations by word of mouth.
▪ a body of popular myth and beliefs relating to a particular place, activity, or group of people: *Hollywood folklore.*
– DERIVATIVES **folkloric** adjective, **folklorist** noun, **folkloristic** adjective.

folk memory ▶ **noun** [mass noun] a body of recollections or legends connected with the past that persists among a group of people.

folk music ▶ **noun** [mass noun] music that originates in traditional popular culture or that is written in such a style. Folk music is typically of unknown authorship and is transmitted orally from generation to generation.

folk rock ▶ **noun** [mass noun] popular music resembling or derived from folk music but incorporating the stronger beat of rock music and using electric instruments.

folk song ▶ **noun** a song that originates in traditional popular culture or that is written in such a style.

folksy ▶ **adjective** (**folksier**, **folksiest**) having the characteristics of traditional culture and customs, especially in a contrived or artificial way: *the shop's folksy, small-town image.*
▪ (of a person) informal and unpretentious: *his tireless energy and folksy oratory were much in demand at constituency lunches.*
– DERIVATIVES **folksiness** noun.

folk tale ▶ **noun** a story originating in popular culture, typically passed on by word of mouth.

folkways ▶ **plural noun** the traditional behaviour or way of life of a particular community or group of people: *a study of Cherokee folklore and folkways.*

folkweave ▶ **noun** [mass noun] Brit. a rough, loosely woven fabric.

folky ▶ **adjective** (**folkier**, **folkiest**) another term for **FOLKSY** or **FOLKISH**.
– DERIVATIVES **folkiness** noun.

follicle /ˈfɒlɪk(ə)l/ ▶ **noun 1** Anatomy a small secretory cavity, sac, or gland, in particular:
▪ (also **hair follicle**) the sheath of cells and connective tissue which surrounds the root of a hair. ▪ short for **GRAAFIAN FOLLICLE**.
2 Botany a dry fruit that is derived from a single carpel and opens on one side only to release its seeds.
– DERIVATIVES **follicular** /fɒˈlɪkjʊlə/ adjective, **folliculate** /-lət/ adjective, **folliculated** adjective.
– ORIGIN late Middle English: from Latin *folliculus* 'little bag', diminutive of *follis* 'bellows'.

follicle mite ▶ **noun** a parasitic mite which burrows into the hair follicles, causing demodectic mange.
• Genus *Demodex*, family Demodicidae.

follicle-stimulating hormone (abbrev.: **FSH**) ▶ **noun** Biochemistry a hormone secreted by the anterior pituitary gland which promotes the formation of ova or sperm.

folliculitis /fəˌlɪkjʊˈlʌɪtɪs/ ▶ **noun** [mass noun] Medicine inflammation of the hair follicles.

follis /ˈfɒlɪs/ ▶ **noun** (pl. **folles**) a bronze or copper coin of a type introduced by the Roman emperor Diocletian in AD 296 and also used later in Byzantine currency.
– ORIGIN Latin.

follow ▶ **verb** [with obj.] **1** go or come after (a person or thing proceeding ahead); move or travel behind: *she went back into the house, and Ben followed her* | [no obj.] *he was following behind in his car.*
▪ go after (someone) in order to observe or monitor: *the KGB man followed her everywhere.* ▪ archaic strive after; aim at: *I follow fame.* ▪ go along (a route or path). ▪ (of a route or path) go in the same direction as or parallel to (another): *the road follows the track of the railway line.*
2 come after in time or order: *the six years that followed his restoration* | [no obj.] *the rates are* ***as follows.***
▪ happen after (something else) as a consequence: *raucous laughter followed the ribald remark* | [no obj.] *retribution soon followed.* ▪ [no obj.] be a logical consequence: *it thus* ***follows from*** *this equation that the value must be negative.* ▪ [with obj. and adverbial] (of a person) do something after (something else): *they* ***follow*** *their March show* ***with*** *four UK dates next month.* ▪ (often **be followed by**) have (a dish or course) after another or others in a meal: *turkey was followed by dessert.*
3 act according to (an instruction or precept): *he has difficulty in following written instructions.*
▪ conform to: *the film faithfully follows Shakespeare's plot.* ▪ act according to the lead or example of (someone): *he follows Aristotle in believing this.* ▪ treat as a teacher or guide: *those who seek to follow Jesus Christ.*
4 pay close attention to (something): *I've been following this discussion closely.*
▪ keep track of; trace the movement or direction of: *she followed his gaze, peering into the gloom.* ▪ maintain awareness of the current state or progress of (events in a particular sphere or account): *young Italians follow football like we follow the Royal Family.* ▪ (of a person or account) be concerned with the development of (something): *the book follows the life and career of Henry Clay.* ▪ understand the meaning or tendency of (a speaker or argument): *I still don't follow you.*
5 practise (a trade or profession).
▪ undertake or carry out (a course of action or study): *she followed a strict diet.*
– PHRASES **follow in someone's footsteps** see **FOOTSTEP**. **follow one's nose 1** trust to one's instincts: *you are on the right track so follow your nose.* **2** move along guided by one's sense of smell. **3** go straight ahead. **follow suit** (in bridge, whist, and other card games) play a card of the suit led. ▪ conform to another's actions: *Spain cut its rates by half a per cent but no other country has followed suit.*
– ORIGIN Old English *folgian*, of Germanic origin; related to Dutch *volgen* and German *folgen*.
▶ **follow on** (of a cricket team) be required to bat again immediately after failing in their first innings to reach a score within a set number of runs of the score made by their opponents.
follow on from occur as a consequence or result of: *the announcement followed on from the collapse of the merchant bank.*
follow through (in golf, cricket, and other sports) continue the movement of a stroke after the ball has been struck.
follow something through continue an action or task to its conclusion.
follow something up pursue or investigate something further: *I decided to follow up the letters with phone calls.*

follower ▶ **noun** a person who supports or maintains awareness of a particular person, cause, or activity: *he is a keen follower of football.*
▪ a person who moves or travels behind someone or something.

following ▶ **preposition** coming after or as a result of: *police are hunting for two men following a spate of robberies in the area.*
▶ **noun 1** a body of supporters or admirers.
2 (**the following**) [treated as sing. or pl.] what follows or comes next: *the following are both grammatically correct sentences.*
▶ **adjective** [attrib.] **1** next in time: *the following day there was a ceremony in St Peter's Square.*
▪ about to be mentioned: *you are required to provide us with the following information.*
2 (of a wind) blowing in the same direction as the course of a vehicle or vessel.

follow-on ▶ **noun** [mass noun] the action of following on from something: [as modifier] *follow-on treatment.*
▪ [count noun] a thing which follows on from another: *it will act as the follow-on to the current version of the software.* ▪ [count noun] Cricket a second innings played immediately after their first by a team that failed to reach a score within a set number of runs of that made by their opponents.

follow-the-leader (also **follow-my-leader**) ▶ **noun** [mass noun] a children's game in which the participants must copy the actions and words of a person who has been chosen as leader.

follow-through ▶ **noun** [mass noun] the continuing of an action or task to its conclusion: *the firm assures follow-through on all aspects of the contract.*
▪ [count noun] a continuation of the movement of a bat, racket, or club after a ball has been struck.

follow-up ▶ **noun** a continuation or repetition of something that has already been started or done, in particular:
▪ an activity carried out as part of a study in order to monitor or further develop earlier work: [as modifier] *follow-up interviews.* ▪ [mass noun] further observation or treatment of a patient, especially to monitor earlier treatment: *patients who require proper medical follow-up.* ▪ a piece of work that builds on or exploits the success of earlier work: *she is writing* ***a follow-up to*** *Jane Austen's* Pride and Prejudice.

folly ▶ **noun** (pl. **-ies**) **1** [mass noun] lack of good sense; foolishness: *an act of sheer folly.*
▪ [count noun] a foolish act, idea, or practice: *the follies of youth.*
2 a costly ornamental building with no practical purpose, especially a tower or mock-Gothic ruin built in a large garden or park.
3 (**Follies**) a theatrical revue with glamorous female performers: [in names] *the Ziegfeld Follies.*
– ORIGIN Middle English: from Old French *folie* 'madness', in modern French also 'delight, favourite dwelling' (compare with sense 2), from *fol* 'fool, foolish'.

Folsom /ˈfəʊlsəm/ ▶ **noun** [usu. as modifier] Archaeology a Palaeo-Indian culture of Central and North America, dated to about 10,500–8,000 years ago. The culture is distinguished by fluted stone projectile points or spearheads (**Folsom points**), the discovery of which (in 1926) forced a radical rethinking of the date at which humans first inhabited the New World. Compare with **CLOVIS**[2].
– ORIGIN early 20th cent.: from *Folsom*, NE New Mexico, the area where remains were first found.

Fomalhaut /ˈfəʊm(ə)lˌhɔːt, -məˌləʊt/ Astronomy the brightest star in the constellation Piscis Austrinus.
– ORIGIN Arabic, 'mouth of the fish'.

foment /fə(ʊ)ˈmɛnt/ ▶ **verb** [with obj.] **1** instigate or stir up (an undesirable or violent sentiment or course of action): *they accused him of fomenting political unrest.*
2 archaic bathe (a part of the body) with warm or medicated lotions.
– DERIVATIVES **fomenter** noun.
– ORIGIN late Middle English (in sense 2): from

French *fomenter*, from late Latin *fomentare*, from Latin *fomentum* 'poultice, lotion', from *fovere* 'to heat, cherish'.

fomentation /ˌfəʊmɛnˈteɪʃ(ə)n/ ▶ **noun** **1** [mass noun] the action of instigating or stirring up undesirable sentiment or actions.
2 archaic a poultice.
– ORIGIN late Middle English: from late Latin *fomentatio(n-)*, from the verb *fomentare* (see **FOMENT**).

fomites /ˈfəʊmɪtiːz/ ▶ **plural noun** Medicine objects or materials which are likely to carry infection, such as clothes, utensils, and furniture.
– ORIGIN early 19th cent.: from Latin, plural of *fomes*, literally 'touchwood, tinder'.

Fon /fɒn/ ▶ **noun** (pl. same or **Fons**) **1** a member of a people inhabiting the southern part of Benin.
2 [mass noun] the language of this people, belonging to the Kwa group, with about 1 million speakers.
▶ **adjective** of or relating to this people or their language.
– ORIGIN the name in Fon.

fond ▶ **adjective** [predic.] (**fond of**) having an affection or liking for: *I'm very fond of Mel | he was not too fond of dancing.*
■ [attrib.] affectionate; loving: *I have very fond memories of Oxford.* ■ [attrib.] (of a hope or belief) foolishly optimistic; naive.
– DERIVATIVES **fondly** adverb, **fondness** noun.
– ORIGIN late Middle English (in the sense 'infatuated, foolish'): from obsolete *fon* 'a fool, be foolish', of unknown origin. Compare with **FUN**.

Fonda /ˈfɒndə/ a family of American actors. **Henry Fonda** (1905–82) was noted for his roles in such films as *The Grapes of Wrath* (1939) and *Twelve Angry Men* (1957). He won his only Oscar for his role in his final film, *On Golden Pond* (1981). His daughter **Jane** (b.1937) is known for films including *Klute* (1971), for which she won an Oscar, and *The China Syndrome* (1979); she also acted alongside her father in *On Golden Pond*.

fondant /ˈfɒnd(ə)nt/ ▶ **noun** [mass noun] a thick paste made of sugar and water and often flavoured or coloured, used in the making of sweets and the icing and decoration of cakes.
■ [count noun] a sweet made of such a paste.
– ORIGIN late 19th cent.: from French, literally 'melting', present participle of *fondre*.

fondle ▶ **verb** [with obj.] stroke or caress lovingly or erotically: *he had kissed and fondled her.*
▶ **noun** an act of fondling.
– DERIVATIVES **fondler** noun.
– ORIGIN late 17th cent. (in the sense 'pamper'): back-formation from obsolete *fondling* 'much-loved or petted person', from **FOND** + **-LING**.

fondu /fɒ̃ˈd(j)uː/ ▶ **adjective** [postpositive] Ballet (of a position) involving a lowering of the body by bending the knee of the supporting leg: *an arabesque fondu.*
– ORIGIN French, literally 'melted'.

fondue /ˈfɒnd(j)uː/ ▶ **noun** a dish in which small pieces of food are dipped into a hot sauce or a hot cooking medium such as oil or broth: *a Swiss cheese fondue.*
– ORIGIN French, feminine past participle of *fondre* 'to melt'.

fons et origo /ˌfɒnz ɛt ˈɒrɪɡəʊ, ɒˈrʌɪɡəʊ/ ▶ **noun** the source and origin of something: *they recognized the sixties as the fons et origo of music as they knew it.*
– ORIGIN Latin, originally as *fons et origo mali* 'the source and origin of evil'.

font[1] ▶ **noun** a receptacle in a church for the water used in baptism, typically a free-standing stone structure.
■ a reservoir for oil in an oil lamp.
– DERIVATIVES **fontal** adjective.
– ORIGIN late Old English: from Latin *fons, font-* 'spring, fountain', occurring in the ecclesiastical Latin phrase *fons* or *fontes baptismi* 'baptismal water(s)'.

font[2] (Brit. also **fount**) ▶ **noun** Printing a set of type of one particular face and size.
– ORIGIN late 16th cent. (denoting the action or process of casting or founding): from French *fonte*, from *fondre* 'to melt'.

fontanelle /ˌfɒntəˈnɛl/ (US **fontanel**) ▶ **noun** a space between the bones of the skull in an infant or fetus, where ossification is not complete and the sutures not fully formed. The main one is between the frontal and parietal bones.
– ORIGIN mid 16th cent. (denoting a hollow of the skin between muscles): from French, from modern Latin *fontanella*, from an Old French diminutive of *fontaine* (see **FOUNTAIN**). The current sense dates from the mid 18th cent.

Fonteyn /fɒnˈteɪn/, Dame Margot (1919–91), English ballet dancer; born *Margaret Hookham*. In 1962 she began a celebrated partnership with Rudolf Nureyev, dancing with him in *Giselle* and *Romeo and Juliet*. In 1979 she was named *prima ballerina assoluta*, a title given only three times in the history of ballet.

fontina /fɒnˈtiːnə/ ▶ **noun** [mass noun] a kind of pale yellow Italian cheese.

Foochow /fuːˈtʃaʊ/ variant of **FUZHOU**.

food ▶ **noun** [mass noun] any nutritious substance that people or animals eat or drink or that plants absorb in order to maintain life and growth: *tins of cat food* | [count noun] *baby foods.*
– PHRASES **food for thought** something that warrants serious consideration.
– ORIGIN late Old English *fōda*, of Germanic origin; related to **FODDER**.

Food and Agriculture Organization (abbrev.: **FAO**) an agency of the United Nations established in 1945 to secure improvements in the production and distribution of all food and agricultural products and to raise levels of nutrition. Its headquarters are in Rome.

food body ▶ **noun** Botany a small nutrient-rich structure developed on the leaves, flowers, or petioles of some tropical plants to attract ants.

food chain ▶ **noun** a series of organisms each dependent on the next as a source of food.

food court ▶ **noun** N. Amer. an area in a shopping mall where fast-food outlets, tables, and chairs are located.

food fish ▶ **noun** a species of fish which is used as food by humans, or forms a major part of the diet of a particular predator.

food hall ▶ **noun** Brit. a large section of a department store, where food is sold.

foodie (also **foody**) ▶ **noun** (pl. **-ies**) informal a person with a particular interest in food; a gourmet.

food poisoning ▶ **noun** [mass noun] illness caused by bacteria or other toxins in food, typically with vomiting and diarrhoea.

food processor ▶ **noun** an electric kitchen appliance used for chopping, mixing, or puréeing foods.

food stamp ▶ **noun** (in the US) a voucher issued cheaply by the state to those on low income and exchangeable for food.

foodstuff ▶ **noun** a substance suitable for consumption as food.

food value ▶ **noun** [mass noun] the nutritional value of a foodstuff.

food web ▶ **noun** Ecology a system of interlocking and interdependent food chains.

foody ▶ **noun** (pl. **-ies**) variant spelling of **FOODIE**.

foo-foo ▶ **noun** variant spelling of **FUFU**.

fool[1] ▶ **noun** a person who acts unwisely or imprudently; a silly person: *I felt a bit of a fool.*
■ historical a jester or clown, especially one retained in a great household. ■ archaic a person who is duped or imposed on: *he is the fool of circumstances.*
▶ **verb** [with obj.] trick or deceive (someone); dupe: *she had been **fooling herself** in thinking she could remain indifferent | he **fooled** nightclub managers **into** believing he was a successful businessman.*
■ [no obj.] act in a joking, frivolous, or teasing way: *I shouted at him impatiently to stop **fooling around**.* ■ [no obj.] (**fool around**) N. Amer. engage in casual or extramarital sexual activity.
▶ **adjective** [attrib.] N. Amer. informal foolish or silly: *that damn fool waiter.*
– PHRASES **be no** (or **nobody's**) **fool** be a shrewd or prudent person. **a fool and his money are soon parted** proverb a foolish person spends money carelessly and will soon be penniless. **fools rush in where angels fear to tread** proverb people without good sense or judgement will have no hesitation in tackling a situation that even the wisest would avoid. **make a fool of** trick or deceive (someone) so that they look foolish. ■ (**make a fool of oneself**) behave in an incompetent or inappropriate way that makes one appear foolish. **more fool ——** used as an exclamation indicating that a specified person is unwise to behave in such a way: *if suckers will actually pay to do the work, more fool them.* **play** (or **act**) **the fool** behave in a playful or silly way. **there's no fool like an old fool** proverb the foolish behaviour of an older person seems especially foolish as they are expected to think and act more sensibly than a younger one. **you could have fooled me!** used to express cynicism or doubt about an assertion: *'Fun, was it? Well, you could have fooled me!'*
– ORIGIN Middle English: from Old French *fol* 'fool, foolish', from Latin *follis* 'bellows, windbag', by extension 'empty-headed person'.

fool[2] ▶ **noun** [mass noun] [usu. with modifier] chiefly Brit. a cold dessert made of puréed fruit mixed or served with cream or custard: *raspberry fool with cream.*
– ORIGIN late 16th cent.: perhaps from **FOOL**[1].

foolery ▶ **noun** [mass noun] silly or foolish behaviour.

foolhardy ▶ **adjective** (**foolhardier**, **foolhardiest**) recklessly bold or rash: *it would be foolhardy to go into the scheme without support.*
– DERIVATIVES **foolhardily** adverb, **foolhardiness** noun.
– ORIGIN Middle English: from Old French *folhardi*, from *fol* 'foolish' + *hardi* 'bold' (see **HARDY**).

foolish ▶ **adjective** (of a person or action) lacking good sense or judgement; unwise: *it was foolish of you to enter into correspondence.*
■ [as complement] silly; ridiculous: *he felt that he'd been made to look foolish.*
– DERIVATIVES **foolishly** adverb, **foolishness** noun.

foolproof ▶ **adjective** incapable of going wrong or being misused: *a foolproof security system.*

foolscap /ˈfuːlzkap, ˈfuːls-/ ▶ **noun** [mass noun] Brit. a size of paper, about 330 × 200 (or 400) mm.
■ paper of this size: *several sheets of foolscap.*
– ORIGIN late 17th cent.: said to be named from a former watermark representing a fool's cap.

fool's errand ▶ **noun** a task or activity that has no hope of success.

fool's gold ▶ **noun** [mass noun] a brassy yellow mineral that can be mistaken for gold, especially pyrite.

fool's mate ▶ **noun** see **MATE**[2].

fool's paradise ▶ **noun** [in sing.] a state of happiness based on a person's not knowing about or denying the existence of potential trouble: *they were living in a fool's paradise, refusing to accept that they were in debt.*

fool's parsley ▶ **noun** a poisonous white-flowered plant of the parsley family, with fern-like leaves and an unpleasant smell, native to Eurasia and North Africa.
• *Aethusa cynapium*, family Umbelliferae.

foot ▶ **noun** (pl. **feet** /fiːt/) **1** the lower extremity of the leg below the ankle, on which a person stands or walks.
■ a corresponding part of the leg in vertebrate animals. ■ Zoology a locomotory or adhesive organ of an invertebrate. ■ the part of a sock or stocking that covers the foot. ■ W. Indian a person's body below the torso, including the entire leg and the foot. ■ [mass noun] poetic/literary a person's manner or speed of walking or running: *fleet of foot.* ■ [treated as pl.] Brit. historical or formal infantry; foot soldiers: *a captain of foot.*
2 the lower or lowest part of something standing or perceived as standing vertically; the base or bottom: *the foot of the stairs.*
■ the end of a table that is furthest from where the host sits. ■ the end of a bed, couch, or grave where the occupant's feet normally rest. ■ a device on a sewing machine for holding the material steady as it is sewn. ■ Botany the part by which a petal is attached. ■ the lower edge of a sail.
3 a unit of linear measure equal to 12 inches (30.48 cm): *shallow water no more than a foot deep.*
■ [usu. as modifier] Music a unit used in describing sets of organ pipes or harpsichord strings, in terms of the average or approximate length of the vibrating column of air or the string which produces the sound: *a sixteen-foot stop.*
4 Prosody a group of syllables constituting a metrical unit. In English poetry it consists of stressed and unstressed syllables, while in ancient classical poetry it consists of long and short syllables.
▶ **verb** [with obj.] **1** informal pay (the bill) for something, especially when the bill is considered large or unreasonable.
2 (**foot it**) cover a distance, especially a long one, on

foot: *the rider was left to foot it ten or twelve miles back to camp.*
■archaic dance: *the dance of fairies, footing it to the cricket's song.*

– PHRASES **at someone's feet** as someone's disciple or subject: *you would like to sit at my feet and thus acquire my wisdom.* **be rushed** (or **run**) **off one's feet** be very busy. **feet of clay** a fundamental flaw or weakness in a person otherwise revered. [ORIGIN: with biblical allusion (Dan. 2:33) to the dream of Nebuchadnezzar, in which a magnificent idol has feet 'part of iron and part of clay'; Daniel interprets this to signify a future kingdom that will be 'partly strong, and partly broken', and will eventually fall.] **get one's feet under the table** chiefly Brit. establish oneself securely in a new situation. **get one's feet wet** begin to participate in an activity. **get** (or **start**) **off on the right** (or **wrong**) **foot** make a good (or bad) start at something, especially a task or relationship. **have something at one's feet** have something in one's power or command: *a perfect couple with the world at their feet.* **have** (or **keep**) **one's** (or **both**) **feet on the ground** be (or remain) practical and sensible. **have a foot in both camps** have an interest or stake concurrently in two parties or sides: *I can have a foot in both the creative and business camps.* **have** (or **get**) **a foot in the door** gain or have a first introduction to a profession or organization. **have one foot in the grave** informal, often humorous be near death through old age or illness. **my foot!** informal said to express strong contradiction: *'He's clever at his business,' Matilda said. 'Clever my foot!'* **off one's feet** so as to be no longer standing: *she was blown off her feet by the shock wave from the explosion.* **on one's feet** standing: *she's in the shop on her feet all day.* ■ well enough after an illness or injury to walk about: *we'll have you back on your feet in no time.* **on** (or **by**) **foot** walking rather than travelling by car or using other transport. **put one's best foot forward** embark on an undertaking with as much effort and determination as possible. **put one's feet up** informal take a rest, especially when reclining with one's feet raised and supported. **put foot** S. African informal hurry up; make a prompt start: *we'd better put foot—we've only got a couple of hours.* [ORIGIN: originally in the sense 'press on the accelerator (of a car)'.] **put one's foot down** informal **1** adopt a firm policy when faced with opposition or disobedience. **2** Brit. accelerate a motor vehicle by pressing the accelerator pedal. **put one's foot in it** (or **put one's foot in one's mouth**) informal say or do something tactless or embarrassing; commit a blunder or indiscretion. **put a foot wrong** [usu. with negative] make a mistake in performing an action: *he hardly put a foot wrong in the first round.* **set foot on** (or **in**) [often with negative] enter; go into: *he hasn't set foot in the place since the war.* **set something on foot** archaic set an action or process in motion: *a plan had lately been set on foot for their relief.* **sweep someone off their feet** quickly and overpoweringly charm someone. **think on one's feet** react to events decisively, effectively, and without prior thought or planning. **to one's feet** to a standing position: *he leaped to his feet.* **under one's feet** in one's way: *when you're at home you just get under my feet.* **under foot** on the ground: *it is very wet under foot in places.*

– DERIVATIVES **footed** adjective [in combination] *the black-footed ferret*, **footless** adjective.

– ORIGIN Old English *fōt*, of Germanic origin; related to Dutch *voet* and German *Fuss*, from an Indo-European root shared by Sanskrit *pad*, *pāda*, Greek *pous*, *pod-*, and Latin *pes*, *ped-* 'foot'.

footage ▶ noun [mass noun] **1** a length of film made for cinema or television: *film footage of the riot.*
2 size or length measured in feet: *the square footage of the room.*

foot-and-mouth disease ▶ noun [mass noun] a contagious viral disease of cattle and sheep, causing ulceration of the hoofs and around the mouth.

football ▶ noun **1** [mass noun] any of various forms of team game involving kicking (and in some cases also handling) a ball, in particular (in the UK) soccer or (in the US) American football.
■play in such a game, especially when stylish and entertaining: *his team played some impressive football.*
2 a ball used in such a game, either round (as in soccer) or oval (as in rugby and American football) and typically made of leather or plastic and filled with compressed air.
■figurative a topical issue or problem that is the subject of continued argument or controversy: *the use of education as a **political football**.*

– DERIVATIVES **footballer** noun, **footballing** adjective.

football pool ▶ noun (usu. **the football pools**) a form of gambling on the results of football matches, the winners receiving large sums accumulated from entry money.

footbath ▶ noun an act of washing one's feet.
■a small shallow bowl used for such a purpose.

footbed ▶ noun an insole in a boot or shoe, used for cushioning or to provide a better fit.

footboard ▶ noun **1** an upright panel forming the foot of a bed.
2 a board serving as a step up to a vehicle such as a carriage or train.

footbrake ▶ noun a brake lever in a motor vehicle, which the driver operates by pressing down with their foot.

footbridge ▶ noun a bridge designed to be used by pedestrians.

foot-candle ▶ noun a unit of illumination (now little used) equal to that given by a source of one candela at a distance of one foot (equivalent to one lumen per square foot or 10.764 lux).

foot-dragging ▶ noun [mass noun] reluctance or deliberate delay concerning a decision or action.

– DERIVATIVES **foot-dragger** noun.

footer[1] /ˈfʊtə/ ▶ noun **1** [in combination] a person or thing of a specified number of feet in length or height: *a tall, sturdy six-footer.*
■a kick of a football performed with a specified foot: *he hammered a low left-footer past the keeper.*
2 variant of **FOOTY**.
3 a line or block of text appearing at the foot of each page of a book or document. Compare with **HEADER**.

footer[2] /ˈfuːtə/ ▶ verb [no obj.] Scottish fiddle about: *he nodded and started to **footer with** his watch.*

footfall ▶ noun the sound of a footstep or footsteps: *you will recognize his footfall on the stairs.*

foot fault ▶ noun (in tennis, squash, and similar games) an infringement of the rules made by overstepping the baseline when serving.
▶ verb (**foot-fault**) [no obj.] (of a player) make a foot fault.
■[with obj.] award a foot fault against (a player).

footgear ▶ noun another term for **FOOTWEAR**.

foot guards ▶ noun infantrymen with a specific guarding role.
■(**Foot Guards**) (in the British army) the regiments of the Brigade of Guards: the Grenadier, Coldstream, Scots, Irish, and Welsh Guards.

foothill ▶ noun (usu. **foothills**) a low hill at the base of a mountain or mountain range: *the camp lies in the foothills of the Andes.*

foothold ▶ noun a place where a person's foot can be lodged to support them securely, especially while climbing.
■[usu. in sing.] figurative a secure position from which further progress may be made: *the company is attempting to gain **a foothold in** the Russian market.*

footie ▶ noun variant spelling of **FOOTY**.

footing ▶ noun **1** (**one's footing**) a secure grip with one's feet: *he suddenly lost his footing.*
2 [in sing.] the basis on which something is established or operates: *attempts to establish the shop on a firm financial footing.*
■the position or status of a person in relation to others: *the suppliers are **on an equal footing with** the buyers.*
3 (usu. **footings**) the foundations of a wall, usually with a course of brickwork wider than the base of the wall.

footle /ˈfuːt(ə)l/ ▶ verb [no obj.] chiefly Brit. engage in fruitless activity; mess about: *where's that pesky creature that was **footling about** outside?*

– ORIGIN late 19th cent.: perhaps from dialect *footer* 'idle, potter about', from 16th-cent. *foutre* 'worthless thing', from Old French, literally 'have sexual intercourse with'.

footlights ▶ plural noun (usu. **the footlights**) a row of spotlights along the front of a stage at the level of the actors' feet.

footling /ˈfuːtlɪŋ/ ▶ adjective trivial and irritating: *year after year you come with the same footling complaint.*

footlocker ▶ noun N. Amer. a small trunk or storage chest.

foot log ▶ noun N. Amer. a log used as a simple footbridge.

footloose ▶ adjective able to travel freely and do as one pleases due to a lack of responsibilities or commitments: *I am **footloose and fancy-free**—I can follow my job wherever it takes me.*
■(of a commercial, industrial, or financial operation) unrestricted in its location or field of operations and able to respond to fluctuations in the market: *modern factories are largely footloose.*

footman ▶ noun (pl. **-men**) **1** a liveried servant whose duties include admitting visitors and waiting at table.
2 historical a soldier in the infantry.
3 archaic a trivet to hang on the bars of a grate.
4 a slender moth that is typically of a subdued colour, the caterpillar feeding almost exclusively on lichens.
• Several genera in the family Arctiidae: many species, including the common European *Eilem lurideola*.

footmark ▶ noun a footprint.

footnote ▶ noun an additional piece of information printed at the bottom of a page.
■figurative a thing that is additional or less important: *this incident seemed destined to become a mere footnote in history.*
▶ verb [with obj.] add a footnote or footnotes to (a piece of writing).

foot pace ▶ noun **1** [mass noun] walking speed.
2 a raised piece of flooring.

footpad ▶ noun historical a highwayman operating on foot rather than riding a horse.

foot passenger ▶ noun a person travelling on foot rather than by car, especially one taking a ferry.

footpath ▶ noun a path for people to walk along, especially one in the countryside.
■Brit. a path for pedestrians in a built-up area; a pavement.

footplate ▶ noun chiefly Brit. the platform for the crew in the cab of a locomotive.
■[as modifier] denoting railway staff responsible for operating trains, as opposed to other employees.

foot-pound ▶ noun a unit of energy equal to the amount required to raise 1 lb a distance of 1 foot.

foot-pound-second system ▶ noun a system of measurement with the foot, pound, and second as basic units.

footprint ▶ noun **1** the impression left by a foot or shoe on the ground or a surface.
2 the area covered by something, in particular:
■the area beneath an aircraft or a land vehicle which is affected by its noise or weight. ■ the area in which a broadcast signal from a particular source can be received. ■ the space taken up on a surface by a piece of computer hardware.

footrest ▶ noun a support for the feet or a foot, used when sitting.

foot rope ▶ noun Sailing **1** a rope to which the lower edge of a sail is sewn.
2 a rope below a yard on which a sailor can stand while furling or reefing a sail.

foot rot ▶ noun [mass noun] a bacterial disease of the feet in hoofed animals, especially sheep.
• The bacteria belong to the Gram-negative genera *Bacteroides* and *Fusobacterium*.
■any of a number of fungal diseases of plants in which the base of the stem rots.

Footsie /ˈfʊtsi/ ▶ noun Brit. trademark informal term for **FTSE INDEX**.

– ORIGIN 1980s: fanciful elaboration of **FTSE**, influenced by *footsie*.

footsie /ˈfʊtsi/ ▶ noun [mass noun] informal the action of touching someone's feet lightly with one's own feet,especially under a table, as a playful expression of romantic interest.

– PHRASES **play footsie** touch someone's feet in such a way. ■ work with someone in a close but covert way: *the FBI reported that the delegate was **playing footsie with** the Soviets.*

– ORIGIN 1940s: humorous diminutive of **FOOT**.

footslog ▶ verb (**-slogged**, **-slogging**) [no obj.] (especially of a soldier) walk or march for a long distance, typically wearily or with effort: *they footslogged around the two villages.*
▶ noun a long and exhausting walk or march.

– DERIVATIVES **footslogger** noun.

f

foot soldier ▶ noun a soldier who fights on foot.
■ a person who carries out important work but does not have a role of authority in an organization or field: *programmers are the foot soldiers of the computer revolution.*

footsore ▶ adjective (of a person or animal) having raw and painful feet from much walking.

footstalk ▶ noun the short supporting stalk of a leaf or flower.

footstep ▶ noun a step taken by a person in walking, especially as heard by another person.
– PHRASES **follow** (or **tread**) **in someone's footsteps** do as another person did before, especially in making a journey or following a particular career.

footstool ▶ noun a low stool for resting the feet on when sitting.

footsure ▶ adjective another term for **SURE-FOOTED**.

foot valve ▶ noun a one-way valve at the inlet of a pipe or the base of a suction pump.

footwall ▶ noun Geology the block of rock which lies on the underside of an inclined fault or of a vein of mineral.

footway ▶ noun Brit. a path or track for pedestrians.

footwear ▶ noun [mass noun] outer coverings for the feet, such as shoes, boots, and sandals.

footwell ▶ noun a space for the feet in front of a seat in a vehicle or aircraft.
– ORIGIN 1980s: from **FOOT** + **WELL**[2] (in the sense 'a depression in the floor').

footwork ▶ noun [mass noun] the manner in which one moves one's feet in various sports, especially in dancing, boxing, and football: *a deft piece of footwork.*
■ [usu. with modifier] adroit response to sudden danger or new opportunities: *the company had to do a lot of nimble footwork to stay alive.*

footy (also **footie** or **footer**) ▶ noun Brit. informal term for **FOOTBALL** (in sense 1).

foo yong /fuː ˈjɒŋ/ ▶ noun [mass noun] a Chinese dish or sauce made with egg as a main ingredient.
– ORIGIN from Chinese (Cantonese dialect) *foō yung*, literally 'hibiscus'.

foozle /ˈfuːz(ə)l/ informal ▶ noun a clumsy or botched attempt at something, especially a shot in golf.
▶ verb [with obj.] botch; bungle: [as adj. **foozled**] *sliced approach shots and foozled putts.*
– ORIGIN mid 19th cent.: from German dialect *fuseln* 'work badly'; compare with **FUSEL OIL**.

fop ▶ noun a man who is concerned with his clothes and appearance in an affected and excessive way.
– DERIVATIVES **foppery** noun, **foppish** adjective, **foppishly** adverb, **foppishness** noun.
– ORIGIN late Middle English (in the sense 'fool'): perhaps related to **FOB**[2].

for ▶ preposition **1** in support of or in favour of (a person or policy): *they voted for independence in a referendum.*
2 affecting, with regard to, or in respect of (someone or something): *she is responsible for the efficient running of their department | the demand for money.*
3 on behalf of or to the benefit of (someone or something): *these parents aren't speaking for everyone.*
■ employed by: *she is a tutor for the Open University.*
4 having (the thing mentioned) as a purpose or function: *she is searching for enlightenment | the necessary tools for making a picture frame.*
5 having (the thing mentioned) as a reason or cause: *Aileen is proud of her family for their support | I could dance and sing for joy.*
6 having (the place mentioned) as a destination: *they are leaving for London tomorrow.*
7 representing (the thing mentioned): *the 'F' is for Fascinating.*
8 in place of or in exchange for (something): *swap these two bottles for that one.*
■ charged as (a price): *copies are available for £1.20.*
9 in relation to the expected norm of (something): *warm weather for the time of year.*
10 indicating the length of (a period of time): *he was jailed for 12 years | I haven't seen him for some time.*
11 indicating the extent of (a distance): *he crawled for 300 yards.*
12 indicating an occasion in a series: *the camcorder failed for the third time.*
▶ conjunction poetic/literary because; since: *he felt guilty, for he knew that he bore a share of responsibility for Fanny's death.*
– PHRASES **be for it** Brit. informal be in imminent danger of punishment or other trouble. **for Africa** S. African informal in huge numbers or quantities; galore: *I've got homework for Africa.* **for all** —— see **ALL**. **for ever** see **FOREVER**. **for why** informal for what reason: *you're going to and I'll tell you for why.* **oh for** —— I long for ——: *oh for a strong black coffee!* **there's** (or **that's**) —— **for you** used ironically to indicate a particularly poor example of (a quality mentioned): *there's gratitude for you.*
– ORIGIN Old English, probably a reduction of a Germanic preposition meaning 'before' (in place or time); related to German *für*, also to **FORE**.

for- ▶ prefix **1** denoting prohibition: *forbid.*
2 denoting abstention, neglect, or renunciation: *forgive | forget | forgo.*
3 used as an intensifier: *forlorn.*
– ORIGIN Old English.

f.o.r. ▶ abbreviation for free on rail. See **FREE**.

fora plural form of **FORUM** (in sense 3).

forage /ˈfɒrɪdʒ/ ▶ verb [no obj.] (of a person or animal) search widely for food or provisions: *gulls are equipped by nature to **forage for** food.*
■ [with obj.] obtain (food or provisions): *a girl foraging grass for oxen.* ■ [with obj.] obtain food or provisions from (a place). ■ [with obj.] archaic supply (an animal or person) with food.
▶ noun **1** [mass noun] bulky food such as grass or hay for horses and cattle; fodder.
2 [in sing.] a wide search over an area in order to obtain something, especially food or provisions: *the nightly forage produces things which can be sold.*
– DERIVATIVES **forager** noun.
– ORIGIN Middle English: from Old French *fourrage* (noun), *fourrager* (verb), from *fuerre* 'straw', of Germanic origin and related to **FODDER**.

forage cap ▶ noun a peaked cap forming part of a soldier's uniform.

forage fish ▶ noun a species of fish of interest to humans chiefly as the prey of more valuable game fish.

forage harvester ▶ noun a large agricultural machine for harvesting forage crops.

foramen /fəˈreɪmɛn/ ▶ noun (pl. **foramina** /-ˈramɪnə/) Anatomy an opening, hole, or passage, especially in a bone.
– ORIGIN late 17th cent.: from Latin, from *forare* 'bore a hole'.

foramen magnum /ˈmagnəm/ ▶ noun Anatomy the hole in the base of the skull through which the spinal cord passes.
– ORIGIN Latin, 'large opening'.

foraminifer /ˌfɒrəˈmɪnɪfə/ ▶ noun (pl. **foraminifers** or **foraminifera** /ˌfɒrəmɪˈnɪf(ə)rə/) Zoology a single-celled planktonic animal with a perforated chalky shell through which slender protrusions of protoplasm extend. Most kinds are marine, and when they die thick ocean-floor sediments are formed from their shells. See also **GLOBIGERINA**.
● Order Foraminiferida, phylum Rhizopoda, kingdom Protista.
– DERIVATIVES **foraminiferal** /ˌfɒrəmɪˈnɪf(ə)rəl/ adjective, **foraminiferan** noun & adjective, **foraminiferous** adjective.
– ORIGIN mid 19th cent.: from Latin *foramen*, *foramin-* (see **FORAMEN**) + *-fer* 'bearing' (from *ferre* 'to bear').

for'ard /ˈfɒrəd/ ▶ adjective & adverb non-standard spelling of **FORWARD**, used to represent a nautical pronunciation.

forasmuch as ▶ conjunction archaic because; since: *forasmuch as the tree returned to life, so too could Arthur be returned to her.*
– ORIGIN Middle English *for as much*, translating Old French *por tant que* 'for so much as'.

forastero /ˌfɒrəˈstɛːrəʊ/ (also **forastero tree**) ▶ noun (pl. **-os**) a widely grown cacao tree of a variety which provides the bulk of the world's cocoa beans.
– ORIGIN mid 19th cent.: from Spanish, literally 'foreign', because the tree was a 'foreign' import to Venezuela from the West Indies, as distinct from the **CRIOLLO** or native variety.

foray /ˈfɒreɪ/ ▶ noun a sudden attack or incursion into enemy territory, especially to obtain something; a raid: *the garrison made a foray against Richard's camp.*
■ a brief but spirited attempt to become involved in a new activity or sphere: *my first **foray into** journalism.*
▶ verb [no obj., with adverbial of direction] make or go on a foray: *the place into which they were forbidden to foray.*
– DERIVATIVES **forayer** noun.
– ORIGIN Middle English: back-formation from *forayer* 'a person who forays', from Old French *forrier* 'forager', from *fuerre* 'straw' (see **FORAGE**).

forb /fɔːb/ ▶ noun Botany a herbaceous flowering plant other than a grass.
– ORIGIN 1920s: from Greek *phorbē* 'fodder', from *phorbein* 'to feed'.

forbade (also **forbad**) past of **FORBID**.

forbear[1] /fɔːˈbɛː/ ▶ verb (past **forbore**; past participle **forborne**) [no obj.] poetic/literary or formal politely or patiently restrain an impulse to do something; refrain: *the boy **forbore from** touching anything* | [with infinitive] *he modestly forbears to include his own work.*
■ [with obj.] refrain from doing or using (something): *Theda could not forbear a smile.*
– ORIGIN Old English *forberan* (see **FOR-**, **BEAR**[1]). The original senses were 'endure, bear with', hence 'endure the absence of something, do without', also 'bear up against, control oneself', hence 'refrain from' (Middle English).

forbear[2] /ˈfɔːbɛː/ ▶ noun variant spelling of **FOREBEAR**.

forbearance ▶ noun [mass noun] formal patient self-control; restraint and tolerance: ***forbearance from** taking action.*
■ Law the action of refraining from exercising a legal right, especially enforcing the payment of a debt.

forbearing ▶ adjective (of a person) patient and restrained.

forbid ▶ verb (**forbidding**; past **forbade** /-ˈbad, -ˈbeɪd/ or **forbad**; past participle **forbidden**) [with obj.] refuse to allow (something): *mixed marriages were forbidden.*
■ order (someone) not to do something: *I was **forbidden from** leaving Russia* | [with obj. and infinitive] *my doctor has forbidden me to eat sugar.* ■ refuse (someone or something) entry to a place or area. ■ (of a circumstance or quality) make (something) impossible; prevent: *the cliffs forbid any easy turning movement.*
– PHRASES **the forbidden degrees** the number of steps of descent from the same ancestor that bar two related people from marrying. **forbidden fruit** a thing that is desired all the more because it is not allowed. [ORIGIN: with biblical allusion to Gen. 2:17.] **God** (or **Heaven**) **forbid** used to express a fervent wish that something does not happen: [with clause] *God forbid that this should happen to anyone ever again.*
– ORIGIN Old English *forbēodan* (see **FOR-**, **BID**[2]).

forbidden ▶ adjective not allowed; banned: *a list of forbidden books.*
■ Physics denoting or involving a transition between two quantum-mechanical states that does not conform to some selection rule, especially for electric dipole radiation.

Forbidden City 1 an area of Beijing containing the former imperial palaces, to which entry was forbidden to all except the members of the imperial family and their servants.
2 a name given to Lhasa.

forbidding ▶ adjective unfriendly or threatening in appearance: *a grim and forbidding building.*
– DERIVATIVES **forbiddingly** adverb.

forbore past of **FORBEAR**[1].

forborne past participle of **FORBEAR**[1].

forbye /fəˈbʌɪ, fɔː-/ (also **forby**) ▶ adverb & preposition archaic or Scottish in addition; besides: [as prep.] *no doubt he had many a sin on his soul, forbye murder.*

force[1] ▶ noun [mass noun] **1** strength or energy as an attribute of physical action or movement: *he was thrown backwards by the force of the explosion.*
■ Physics an influence tending to change the motion of a body or produce motion or stress in a stationary body. The magnitude of such an influence is often calculated by multiplying the mass of the body and its acceleration. ■ [count noun] a person or thing regarded as exerting power or influence: *he might still be **a force for** peace and unity.* ■ [in combination] used with a number as a measure of wind strength on the Beaufort scale: *a force-nine gale.*
2 coercion or compulsion, especially with the use or threat of violence: *they ruled by law and not **by force**.*
3 mental or moral strength or power: *the force of popular opinion.*
■ the state of being in effect or valid: *the law came into force in January.* ■ the powerful effect of something: *the force of her writing is undiminished.*
4 [count noun] an organized body of military personnel or police: *a British peacekeeping force.*

■(**forces**) troops and weaponry: *the Iraqi forces* | figurative *a battle between the forces of good and evil.* ■ (**the forces**) Brit. informal the army, navy, and air force of a country. ■ (**the force**) Brit. informal the police. ■ a group of people brought together and organized for a particular activity: *a sales force.*

▶ **verb** [with obj.] **1** make a way through or into by physical strength; break open by force: *the back door of the bank was forced.*
■ [with obj. and adverbial] drive or push into a specified position or state using physical strength or against resistance: *she forced her feet into flat leather sandals* | figurative *Fields was forced out as director.* ■ achieve or bring about (something) by coercion or effort: *Sabine forced a smile* | *they* **forced a way** *through the crowd.* ■ push or strain (something) to the utmost: *she knew if she forced it she would rip it.* ■ artificially hasten the development or maturity of (a plant).
2 make (someone) do something against their will: *she was* **forced into** *early retirement* | [with obj. and infinitive] *the universities were forced to cut staff.*
■ Baseball put out (a runner) by necessitating an advance to the next base when it is not possible to do so safely.

– PHRASES **by force of** by means of: *exercising authority by force of arms.* **force the bidding** (at an auction) make bids to raise the price rapidly. **force someone's hand** make someone do something. **force the issue** compel the making of an immediate decision. **force the pace** adopt a fast pace in a race in order to tire out one's opponents quickly. **in force** in great strength or numbers: *birdwatchers were out in force.*

– DERIVATIVES **forceable** adjective, **forcer** noun.

– ORIGIN Middle English: from Old French *force* (noun), *forcer* (verb), based on Latin *fortis* 'strong'.

▶ **force something down 1** manage to swallow food or drink when one does not want to. **2** compel an aircraft to land.
force oneself on/upon rape (a woman).
force something on/upon impose or press something on (a person or organization): *economic cutbacks were forced on the government.*

force² ▶ **noun** N. English a waterfall.
– ORIGIN late Middle English: from Old Norse *fors.*

forced ▶ **adjective** obtained or imposed by coercion or physical power: *the brutal regime of forced labour.*
■ (of a gesture or expression) produced or maintained with effort; affected or unnatural: *a forced smile.* ■ (of a plant) having its development or maturity artificially hastened.
– PHRASES **forced march** a fast march by soldiers, typically over a long distance.

forced landing ▶ **noun** an act of abruptly bringing an aircraft to the ground or the surface of water in an emergency.
– DERIVATIVES **force-land** verb.

force-feed ▶ **verb** [with obj.] force (a person or animal) to eat food.
■ [with two objs] figurative impose or force (information or ideology) upon (someone): *missionaries force-fed them Christianity.*

force feedback ▶ **noun** [mass noun] Computing the simulating of physical attributes such as weight in virtual reality, allowing the user to interact directly with virtual objects using touch.

force field ▶ **noun** (chiefly in science fiction) an invisible barrier of exerted strength or impetus.

forceful ▶ **adjective** (especially of a person or argument) strong and assertive; vigorous and powerful: *she was a forceful personality.*
– DERIVATIVES **forcefully** adverb, **forcefulness** noun.

force majeure /ˌfɔːs maˈʒəː/ ▶ **noun** [mass noun] **1** unforeseeable circumstances that prevent someone from fulfilling a contract.
2 irresistible compulsion or superior strength.
– ORIGIN French, literally 'superior strength'.

forcemeat ▶ **noun** [mass noun] a mixture of meat or vegetables chopped and seasoned for use as a stuffing or garnish.
– ORIGIN late 17th cent.: from obsolete *force* 'to stuff', alteration (influenced by the verb **FORCE**¹) of *farce*, from French *farcir* (see **FARCE**).

force-out ▶ **noun** Baseball a putting out of a base-runner who is forced to advance to a base at which a fielder is holding the ball.

forceps /ˈfɔːsɛps, -sɪps/ (also **a pair of forceps**) ▶ **plural noun** a pair of pincers or tweezers used in surgery or in a laboratory.
■ a large instrument of such a type with broad blades, used to encircle a baby's head and assist in birth: [as modifier] *a forceps delivery.* ■ Zoology an organ or structure resembling forceps, especially the cerci of an earwig.
– ORIGIN late 16th cent.: from Latin, 'tongs, pincers'.

force pump ▶ **noun** a pump used to move water or other liquid under greater than ambient pressure.

force-ripe ▶ **adjective** W. Indian (of a person) old or mature in certain respects without having developed fully in others.
– ORIGIN by association with a fruit that has ripened by forcing.

forcible ▶ **adjective** done by force: *signs of forcible entry.*
■ vigorous and strong; forceful: *they could only be deterred by forcible appeals.*
– DERIVATIVES **forcibly** adverb.
– ORIGIN late Middle English: from Old French, from *force* (see **FORCE**¹).

forcing ▶ **adjective** Bridge (of a bid) requiring by convention a response from one's partner, no matter how weak their hand may be.

forcing house ▶ **noun** a place in which the growth or development of something (especially plants) is artificially hastened.

Ford¹, Ford Madox (1873–1939), English novelist and editor; born *Ford Hermann Hueffer.* He is chiefly remembered as the author of the novel *The Good Soldier* (1915).

Ford², Gerald (Rudolph) (b.1913), American Republican statesman, 38th President of the US 1974–7. He became President on the resignation of Richard Nixon in the wake of the Watergate affair.

Ford³, Harrison (b.1942), American actor. He became internationally famous with his leading roles in the science-fiction film *Star Wars* (1977) and its two sequels.

Ford⁴, Henry (1863–1947), American motor manufacturer. A pioneer of large-scale mass production, he founded the Ford Motor Company, which in 1909 produced his famous Model T. Control of the company passed to his grandson, Henry Ford II (1917–1987) in 1945.

Ford⁵, John (1586–*c.*1639), English dramatist. His plays, which include *'Tis Pity She's a Whore* (1633) and *The Broken Heart* (1633), explore human delusion, melancholy, and horror.

Ford⁶, John (1895–1973), American film director; born *Sean Aloysius O'Feeney.* He is chiefly known for his westerns of which many, including *Stagecoach* (1939) and *She Wore a Yellow Ribbon* (1949), starred John Wayne.

ford ▶ **noun** a shallow place in a river or stream allowing one to walk or drive across.
▶ **verb** [with obj.] (of a person or vehicle) cross (a river or stream) at a shallow place.
– DERIVATIVES **fordable** adjective, **fordless** adjective.
– ORIGIN Old English, of West Germanic origin; related to Dutch *voorde*, also to **FARE**.

Fordism ▶ **noun** [mass noun] the use in manufacturing industry of the methods pioneered by Henry Ford, typified by large-scale mechanized mass production.
– DERIVATIVES **Fordist** noun & adjective.

fordo /fɔːˈduː/ (also **foredo**) ▶ **verb** (**-does**; past **-did**; past participle **-done**) [with obj.] archaic kill; destroy: *by the sword's edge his life shall be foredone.*
– ORIGIN Old English *fordōn*; related to Dutch *verdoen* and German *vertun*, and ultimately to **FOR** and **DO**¹.

fore ▶ **adjective** [attrib.] situated or placed in front: *the fore and hind pairs of wings.*
▶ **noun** the front part of something, especially a ship.
▶ **exclamation** called out as a warning to people in the path of a golf ball.
▶ **preposition** (also **'fore**) non-standard form of **BEFORE**: *many years will go by fore you have a Europound in your pocket.*
– PHRASES **to the fore** in or to a conspicuous or leading position: *the succession issue* **came to the fore**.
– ORIGIN Old English (as a preposition, also in the sense 'before in time, previously'): of Germanic origin; related to Dutch *voor* and German *vor.* The adjective and noun represent the prefix **FORE-** used independently (late 15th cent.).

fore- ▶ **combining form 1** (added to verbs) in front: *foreshorten.*
■ beforehand; in advance: *forebode* | *foreshadow.*
2 (added to nouns) situated in front of: *forecourt.*
■ the front part of: *forebrain.* ■ of or near the bow of a ship: *forecastle.* ■ preceding; going before: *forefather.*
– ORIGIN Old English (see **FORE**).

fore and aft ▶ **adverb** at the front and rear (often used with reference to a ship or plane): *we're moored fore and aft.*
■ backwards and forwards: *a sperm whale cannot see directly fore and aft.*
▶ **adjective** [attrib.] backwards and forwards: *the fore-and-aft motion of the handles.*
■ historical (of a man's hat) having three corners and a peak at the front and back. ■ (of a sail or rigging) set lengthwise, not on the yards: *a fore-and-aft rigged yacht.* ■ N. Amer. (of a road) constructed of logs laid end to end.
– ORIGIN early 17th cent.: perhaps translating a phrase of Low German origin; compare with Dutch *van voren en van achteren.*

forearm¹ /ˈfɔːrɑːm/ ▶ **noun** the part of a person's arm extending from the elbow to the wrist or the fingertips.

forearm² /fɔːrˈɑːm/ ▶ **verb** [with obj.] (usu. **be forearmed**) prepare (someone) in advance for danger, attack, or another undesirable future event.

forebear (also **forbear**) ▶ **noun** (usu. **one's forebears**) an ancestor.
– ORIGIN late 15th cent.: from **FORE** + *bear*, variant of obsolete *beer* 'someone who exists' (from **BE** + **-ER**¹).

forebode ▶ **verb** [with obj.] archaic or poetic/literary (of a situation or occurrence) act as an advance warning of (something bad): *this lull foreboded some new assault upon him.*
■ have a presentiment of (something bad): *I foreboded mischief the moment I heard.*

foreboding ▶ **noun** [mass noun] fearful apprehension; a feeling that something bad will happen: *with a sense of foreboding she read the note.*
▶ **adjective** implying or seeming to imply that something bad is going to happen: *when the Doctor spoke, his voice was dark and foreboding.*
– DERIVATIVES **forebodingly** adverb.

forebrain ▶ **noun** Anatomy the anterior part of the brain, including the cerebral hemispheres, the thalamus, and the hypothalamus. Also called **PROSENCEPHALON**.

forecabin ▶ **noun** a cabin in the forward part of a vessel.

forecaddie ▶ **noun** (pl. **-ies**) a caddie who goes ahead of golfers to see where the balls fall.

forecast ▶ **verb** (past and past participle **-cast** or **-casted**) [with obj.] predict or estimate (a future event or trend): *rain is forecast for Scotland* | [with obj. and infinitive] *coal consumption in Europe is forecast to increase.*
▶ **noun** a calculation or estimate of future events, especially coming weather or a financial trend.
– DERIVATIVES **forecaster** noun.

forecastle /ˈfəʊks(ə)l/ (also **fo'c's'le**) ▶ **noun** the forward part of a ship below the deck, traditionally used as the crew's living quarters.
■ a raised deck at the front of a ship.

forecheck ▶ **verb** [no obj.] Ice Hockey play an aggressive style of defence, checking opponents before they can organize an attack.
– DERIVATIVES **forechecker** noun.

foreclose ▶ **verb 1** [no obj.] take possession of a mortgaged property as a result of someone's failure to keep up their mortgage payments: *the bank was threatening to* **foreclose on** *his mortgage.*
■ [with obj.] take away someone's power of redeeming (a mortgage) and take possession of the mortgaged property.
2 [with obj.] rule out or prevent (a course of action): *the decision effectively foreclosed any possibility of his early rehabilitation.*
– ORIGIN Middle English: from Old French *forclos*, past participle of *forclore*, from *for-* 'out' (from Latin *foras* 'outside') + *clore* 'to close'. The original sense was 'bar from escaping', in late Middle English 'shut out', and 'bar from doing something' (sense 2), hence specifically 'bar someone from redeeming a mortgage' (sense 1, early 18th cent.).

foreclosure ▶ **noun** [mass noun] the process of taking possession of a mortgaged property as a result of someone's failure to keep up their mortgage repayments.

forecourt ▶ **noun 1** an open area in front of a large building or petrol station.

2 Tennis the part of the court between the service line and the net.

foredawn ▶ noun poetic/literary the time before dawn.

foredeck ▶ noun the deck at the forward part of a ship.

foredo ▶ verb variant spelling of FORDO.

foredoom ▶ verb [with obj.] (usu. **be foredoomed**) condemn beforehand to certain failure or destruction: *the policy is foredoomed to failure.*

foredune ▶ noun Ecology a part of a system of sand dunes on the side nearest to the sea.

fore-edge ▶ noun technical the outer vertical edge of the pages of a book.

forefather ▶ noun (usu. **one's forefathers**) a member of the past generations of one's family or people; an ancestor.
■ a precursor of a particular movement: *the forefathers of modern British socialism.*

forefend ▶ verb variant spelling of FORFEND (in sense 2).

forefinger ▶ noun the finger next to the thumb; the first or index finger.

forefoot ▶ noun (pl. **forefeet**) each of the front feet of a four-footed animal.
■ the very front section of a shoe. ■ the very front section of a ship's keel.

forefront ▶ noun (**the forefront**) the leading or most important position or place: *we are at the forefront of developments.*

foregather (also **forgather**) ▶ verb [no obj.] formal assemble or gather together.
– ORIGIN late 15th cent. (originally Scots as *forgadder*): from Dutch *vergaderen*.

forego¹ ▶ verb variant spelling of FORGO.

forego² ▶ verb (**-goes**; past **-went**; past participle **-gone**) [with obj.] archaic precede in place or time.
– DERIVATIVES **foregoer** noun.

foregoing formal ▶ adjective [attrib.] just mentioned or stated; preceding: *the foregoing discussion has juxtaposed management and owner control.*
▶ noun (**the foregoing**) [treated as sing. or pl.] the things just mentioned or stated.

foregone past participle of FOREGO². ▶ adjective [often postpositive] archaic past: *poets dream of lives foregone in worlds fantastical.*
– PHRASES **a foregone conclusion** a result that can be predicted with certainty.

foreground ▶ noun (**the foreground**) the part of a view that is nearest to the observer, especially in a picture or photograph: *the images show vegetation in the foreground.*
■ the most prominent or important position or situation: *whenever results are chosen for children, meaning should always be in the foreground.*
▶ verb [with obj.] make (something) the most prominent or important feature: *sexual relationships are foregrounded and idealized.*
– ORIGIN late 17th cent.: from FORE- + GROUND¹, on the pattern of Dutch *voorgrond.*

foregut ▶ noun Anatomy & Zoology the anterior part of the gut, towards the mouth.

forehand ▶ noun **1** (in tennis and other racket sports) a stroke played with the palm of the hand facing in the direction of the stroke: [as modifier] *a good forehand drive.*
2 the part of a horse in front of the saddle.

forehanded ▶ adjective US looking to the future; prudent; thrifty.
▶ adverb (in tennis and other racket sports) with a forehand stroke.

forehead /ˈfɒrɪd, ˈfɔːhɛd/ ▶ noun the part of the face above the eyebrows.
– ORIGIN Old English *forhēafod* (see FORE-, HEAD).

forehock /ˈfɔːhɒk/ ▶ noun Brit. a foreleg cut of pork or bacon.

foreign /ˈfɒrɪn/ ▶ adjective **1** of, from, in, or characteristic of a country or language other than one's own: *a foreign language.*
■ dealing with or relating to other countries: *foreign policy.* ■ of or belonging to another district or area: *a visit to a foreign clan.* ■ coming or introduced from outside: *the quotation is a foreign element imported into the work.*
2 strange and unfamiliar: *I suppose this all feels pretty foreign to you.*
■ (**foreign to**) not belonging to or characteristic of:

crime and brutality are foreign to our nature and our country.
– DERIVATIVES **foreignness** /ˈfɒr(ə)nnɪs/ noun.
– ORIGIN Middle English *foren, forein*, from Old French *forein, forain*, based on Latin *foras, foris* 'outside', from *fores* 'door'. The current spelling arose in the 16th cent., by association with SOVEREIGN.

foreign aid ▶ noun [mass noun] money, food, or other resources given or lent by one country to another.

Foreign and Commonwealth Office the British government department dealing with foreign affairs.

foreign body ▶ noun an object or piece of extraneous matter that has entered the body by accident or design.

foreigner ▶ noun a person born in or coming from a country other than one's own.
■ informal a person not belonging to a particular place or group; a stranger or outsider. ■ Brit. informal a piece of work done for private gain without an employer's permission or without declaration to the relevant authorities.

foreign exchange ▶ noun [mass noun] the currency of other countries.
■ [count noun] an institution or system for dealing in such currency.

Foreign Legion a military formation of the French army founded in the 1830s to fight France's colonial wars. Composed, except for the higher ranks, of non-Frenchmen, the Legion was famed for its audacity and endurance. Its most famous campaigns were in French North Africa in the late 19th and early 20th centuries.

foreign minister ▶ noun a government minister in charge of their country's relations with other countries.

Foreign Office short for FOREIGN AND COMMONWEALTH OFFICE.

foreign-returned ▶ adjective Indian (of a person) educated or trained abroad and now living again in India.

Foreign Secretary ▶ noun (in the UK) the government minister who heads the Foreign and Commonwealth Office.

foreign service ▶ noun another term for DIPLOMATIC SERVICE.

foreknow ▶ verb (past **-knew**; past participle **-known**) [with obj.] poetic/literary be aware of (an event) before it happens: *he foreknows his death like a saint.*

foreknowledge ▶ noun [mass noun] awareness of something before it happens or exists.

foreland ▶ noun an area of land bordering on another or lying in front of a particular feature.
■ a cape or promontory. ■ Geology a stable unyielding block of the earth's crust, against which compression produces a folded mountain range.

forelock ▶ noun a lock of hair growing just above the forehead.
■ the part of the mane of a horse or similar animal, which grows from the poll and hangs down over the forehead.
– PHRASES **take time by the forelock** poetic/literary seize an opportunity. **touch** (or **tug**) **one's forelock** raise a hand to one's forehead in deference when meeting a person of higher social rank.

Foreman, George (b.1948), American boxer. He won the world heavyweight title in 1973–4, regaining it in 1994–5 to become the oldest world heavyweight champion.

foreman ▶ noun (pl. **-men**) a male worker who supervises and directs other workers.
■ (in a law court) a person who presides over a jury and speaks on its behalf.
– ORIGIN Middle English: perhaps suggested by Dutch *voorman* (compare with German *Vormann*).

foremast ▶ noun the mast of a ship nearest the bow.

foremost ▶ adjective the most prominent in rank, importance, or position: *one of the foremost art collectors of his day.*
▶ adverb before anything else in rank, importance, or position; in the first place: *it was, foremost, the first unequivocal demonstration of the process.*
– ORIGIN Old English *formest, fyrmest*, from *forma* 'first' (ultimately a superlative formed from the Germanic base of FORE) + -EST¹. Compare with

FIRST and FORMER¹. The current spelling arose by association with FORE and MOST.

foremother ▶ noun (usu. **one's foremothers**) a female ancestor or precursor of something.

forename ▶ noun another term for FIRST NAME.

forenoon ▶ noun [in sing.] N. Amer. or Nautical the morning.

forensic /fəˈrɛnsɪk/ ▶ adjective of, relating to, or denoting the application of scientific methods and techniques to the investigation of crime: *forensic evidence.*
■ of or relating to courts of law.
▶ noun (**forensics**) scientific tests or techniques used in connection with the detection of crime.
■ (also **forensic**) [treated as sing. or pl.] informal a laboratory or department responsible for such tests.
– DERIVATIVES **forensically** adverb.
– ORIGIN mid 17th cent.: from Latin *forensis* 'in open court, public', from *forum* (see FORUM).

forensic medicine ▶ noun [mass noun] the application of medical knowledge to the investigation of crime, particularly in establishing the causes of injury or death.

foreordain /ˌfɔːrɔːˈdeɪn/ ▶ verb [with obj.] (of God or fate) appoint or decree (something) beforehand: *progress is not foreordained.*
– DERIVATIVES **foreordination** noun.

forepeak ▶ noun the front end of the hold in the angle of the bows of a ship.

foreperson ▶ noun a foreman or forewoman (used as a neutral alternative).

foreplay ▶ noun [mass noun] sexual activity that precedes intercourse.

forequarters ▶ plural noun the front legs and adjoining parts of a quadruped.

forerib ▶ noun a cut of beef for roasting, containing the rib from just in front of the sirloin.

forerun ▶ verb (**-running**; past **-ran**; past participle **-run**) [with obj.] poetic/literary go before or indicate the coming of: *the vast inquietude that foreruns the storm.*

forerunner ▶ noun a person or thing that precedes the coming or development of someone or something else: *the ice safe was a forerunner of today's refrigerator.*
■ a sign or warning of something to come: *overcast mornings are the sure forerunners of steady rain.* ■ archaic an advance messenger.

foresail /ˈfɔːseɪl, -s(ə)l/ ▶ noun the principal sail on a foremast.

foresee ▶ verb (**-sees, -seeing;** past **-saw;** past participle **-seen**) [with obj.] be aware of beforehand; predict: *we did not foresee any difficulties* | [with clause] *it is impossible to foresee how life will work out.*
– DERIVATIVES **foreseer** /-ˈsiːə/ noun.
– ORIGIN Old English *foresēon* (see FORE-, SEE¹).

foreseeable ▶ adjective able to be foreseen or predicted: *the situation is unlikely to change in the foreseeable future.*
– DERIVATIVES **foreseeability** noun, **foreseeably** adverb.

foreshadow ▶ verb [with obj.] be a warning or indication of (a future event): *other new measures are foreshadowed in the White Paper.*

foresheet ▶ noun **1** a rope by which the lee corner of a foresail is kept in place.
2 (**foresheets**) the inner part of the bows of a boat.

foreshock ▶ noun a mild tremor preceding the violent shaking movement of an earthquake.

foreshore ▶ noun the part of a shore between high- and low-water marks, or between the water and cultivated or developed land.

foreshorten ▶ verb [with obj.] portray or show (an object or view) as closer than it really is or as having less depth or distance, as an effect of perspective or the angle of vision: *seen from the road, the mountain is greatly foreshortened.*
■ prematurely or dramatically shorten or reduce (something) in time or scale: [as adj. **foreshortened**] *Leicestershire won by 133 runs in a foreshortened contest.*

foreshow ▶ verb (past participle **-shown**) [with obj.] archaic give warning or promise of (something); foretell.

foresight ▶ noun **1** [mass noun] the ability to predict or action of predicting what will happen or be needed in the future: *he had the foresight to check that his escape route was clear.*
2 the front sight of a gun.
3 Surveying a sight taken forwards.

– ORIGIN Middle English: from **FORE-** + **SIGHT**, probably suggested by Old Norse *forsjá, forsjó*.

foresighted ▶ **adjective** having or using foresight.
– DERIVATIVES **foresightedly** adverb, **foresightedness** noun.

foreskin ▶ **noun** the retractable roll of skin covering the end of the penis. Also called **PREPUCE**.

forest ▶ **noun** a large area covered chiefly with trees and undergrowth: *a pine forest* | [mass noun] *much of Britain and Europe was covered with forest*.
■ a large number or dense mass of vertical or tangled objects: *a* ***forest of*** *connecting wires*. ■ [as modifier] [in place names] denoting an area that was formerly a royal forest: *Waltham Forest*. ■ historical an area, typically owned by the sovereign and partly wooded, kept for hunting and having its own laws.
▶ **verb** [with obj.] [usu. as adj. **forested**] cover (land) with forest; plant with trees: *a forested area*.
– DERIVATIVES **forestation** noun.
– ORIGIN Middle English (in the sense 'wooded area kept for hunting', also denoting any uncultivated land): via Old French from late Latin *forestis (silva)*, literally '(wood) outside' from Latin *foris* 'outside' (see **FOREIGN**).

forestall /fɔːˈstɔːl/ ▶ **verb** [with obj.] prevent or obstruct (an anticipated event or action) by taking action ahead of time: *they will present their resignations to forestall a vote of no confidence*.
■ act in advance of (someone) in order to prevent them from doing something: *she made to rise but Erika forestalled her and got the telephone pad*. ■ historical buy up (goods) in order to profit by an enhanced price.
– DERIVATIVES **forestaller** noun, **forestalment** noun.
– ORIGIN Old English *foresteall* 'an ambush' (see **FORE-** and **STALL**). As a verb the earliest sense (Middle English) was 'intercept and buy up (goods) before they reach the market, so as to raise the price' (formerly an offence).

forestay /ˈfɔːsteɪ/ ▶ **noun** a rope to support a ship's foremast, running from its top to the deck at the bow.

Forester, C. S. (1899–1966), English novelist; pseudonym of *Cecil Lewis Troughton Smith*. He is remembered for his seafaring novels set during the Napoleonic Wars, featuring Captain Horatio Hornblower.

forester ▶ **noun 1** a person in charge of a forest or skilled in planting, managing, or caring for trees.
2 chiefly archaic a person or animal living in a forest.
■ Austral. the eastern grey kangaroo. See **GREY KANGAROO**.
3 a small day-flying moth with metallic green forewings and a greenish-bronze body.
• Genus *Adscita*, family Zygaenidae: several species.
4 (**Forester**) Brit. a member of the Ancient Order of Foresters, a friendly society.
– ORIGIN Middle English: from Old French *forestier*, from *forest* (see **FOREST**).

forest fly ▶ **noun** a bloodsucking European louse fly of wooded areas, attacking horses and other animals.
• *Hippobosca equina*, family Hippoboscidae.

forestry ▶ **noun** [mass noun] the science or practice of planting, managing, and caring for forests.
■ country covered by forests.

Forestry Commission the government department responsible for forestry policy in the UK, established in 1919.

forest tree ▶ **noun** a large tree growing in or typical of those growing in a forest.

foretaste ▶ **noun** [in sing.] a sample or suggestion of something that lies ahead: *his behemoth task force is just a foretaste of what is to come*.

foretell ▶ **verb** (past and past participle **-told**) [with obj.] predict (the future or a future event): [with clause] *a seer had foretold that the earl would assume the throne*.
– DERIVATIVES **foreteller** noun.

forethought ▶ **noun** [mass noun] careful consideration of what will be necessary or may happen in the future: *Jim had the forethought to book in advance*.

foretoken ▶ **verb** /fɔːˈtəʊk(ə)n/ [with obj.] poetic/literary be a sign of (something to come): *a shiver in the night air foretokening December*.
▶ **noun** /ˈfɔːtəʊk(ə)n/ a sign of something to come.
– ORIGIN Old English *foretācn* (noun: see **FORE-**, **TOKEN**).

foretold past and past participle of **FORETELL**.

foretop /ˈfɔːtɒp, -təp/ ▶ **noun** a platform around the head of the lower section of a sailing ship's foremast.

fore-topgallant-mast ▶ **noun** the third section of a sailing ship's foremast, above the foretopmast.

fore-topgallant-sail ▶ **noun** the sail above a sailing ship's foretopsail.

foretopmast /fɔːˈtɒpmɑːst, -məst/ ▶ **noun** the second section of a sailing ship's foremast.

foretopsail /fɔːˈtɒps(ə)l, -seɪl/ ▶ **noun** the sail above a sailing ship's foresail.

foretriangle ▶ **noun** the triangular space between the deck, foremast, and forestay of a sailing vessel.
■ the area of sail within this area.

forever ▶ **adverb 1** (also **for ever**) for all future time; for always: *she would love him forever*.
■ a very long time (used hyperbolically): *it took forever to get a passport*. ■ used in slogans of support after the name of something or someone: *Scotland Forever!*
2 continually: *she was forever pushing her hair out of her eyes*.

for evermore (also **forever more** and N. Amer. **forevermore**) ▶ **adverb** Brit. forever (used for rhetorical effect): *time has been and shall be for evermore*.

forewarn ▶ **verb** [with obj.] inform (someone) of a possible future danger or problem: *he had been* ***forewarned of*** *a coup plot*.
– PHRASES **forewarned is forearmed** proverb prior knowledge of possible dangers or problems gives one a tactical advantage.
– DERIVATIVES **forewarner** noun.

forewent past of **FOREGO**[1], **FOREGO**[2].

forewing ▶ **noun** either of the two front wings of a four-winged insect.

forewoman ▶ **noun** (pl. **-women**) a female worker who supervises and directs other workers.
■ chiefly N. Amer. (in law court) a woman who presides over a jury and speaks on its behalf.

foreword ▶ **noun** a short introduction to a book, typically by a person other than the author.
– ORIGIN mid 19th cent.: from **FORE-** + **WORD**, on the pattern of German *Vorwort*.

forex ▶ **abbreviation for** foreign exchange.

foreyard ▶ **noun** the lowest yard on a sailing ship's foremast.

Forfar /ˈfɔːfə/ a town in eastern Scotland, administrative centre of Angus region. It is noted for its castle, the meeting place in 1057 of an early Scottish Parliament and the home of several Scottish kings.

Forfarshire former name (from the 16th century until 1928) for **ANGUS**[1].

forfeit /ˈfɔːfɪt/ ▶ **verb** (**forfeited**, **forfeiting**) [with obj.] lose or be deprived of (property or a right or privilege) as a penalty for wrongdoing: *those unable to meet their taxes were liable to forfeit their estates*.
■ lose or give up (something) as a necessary consequence of something else: *she didn't mind forfeiting an extra hour in bed to get up and muck out the horses*.
▶ **noun** a fine or penalty for wrongdoing or for a breach of the rules in a club or game.
■ Law an item of property or a right or privilege lost as a legal penalty. ■ (**forfeits**) a game in which trivial penalties are exacted. ■ [mass noun] the action of forfeiting something.
▶ **adjective** [predic.] lost or surrendered as a penalty for wrongdoing or neglect: *the lands which he had acquired were automatically forfeit*.
– DERIVATIVES **forfeitable** adjective, **forfeiter** noun, **forfeiture** noun.
– ORIGIN Middle English (originally denoting a crime or transgression, hence a fine or penalty for this): from Old French *forfet, forfait*, past participle of *forfaire* 'transgress', from *for-* 'out' (from Latin *foris* 'outside') + *faire* 'do' (from Latin *facere*).

forfend /fɔːˈfɛnd/ ▶ **verb** [with obj.] **1** archaic avert, keep away, or prevent (something evil or unpleasant).
2 (also **forefend**) US protect (something) by precautionary measures.
– PHRASES **God** (or **Heaven**) **forfend** archaic or humorous used to express dismay or horror at the thought of something happening: *God forfend that we should ever allow the media to tell us how to run our business*.

forgather ▶ **verb** variant spelling of **FOREGATHER**.

forgave past of **FORGIVE**.

forge[1] /fɔːdʒ/ ▶ **verb** [with obj.] **1** make or shape (a metal object) by heating it in a fire or furnace and beating or hammering it.
■ figurative create (a relationship or new conditions): *the two women forged a close bond* | *the country is forging a bright new future*.
2 produce a copy or imitation of (a document, signature, banknote, or work of art) for the purpose of deception.
▶ **noun** a blacksmith's workshop; a smithy.
■ a furnace or hearth for melting or refining metal. ■ a workshop or factory containing such a furnace.
– DERIVATIVES **forgeable** adjective, **forger** noun.
– ORIGIN Middle English (also in the general sense 'make, construct'): from Old French *forger*, from Latin *fabricare* 'fabricate', from *fabrica* 'manufactured object, workshop'. The noun is via Old French from Latin *fabrica*.

forge[2] /fɔːdʒ/ ▶ **verb** [no obj., with adverbial of direction] move forward gradually or steadily: *he forged through the crowded side streets*.
– ORIGIN mid 18th cent. (originally of a ship): perhaps an aberrant pronunciation of **FORCE**[1].
▶ **forge ahead** move forward or take the lead in a race. ■ continue or make progress with a course or undertaking: *the government is* ***forging ahead with*** *reforms*.

forgery ▶ **noun** (pl. **-ies**) [mass noun] the action of forging or producing a copy of a document, signature, banknote, or work of art.
■ [count noun] a forged or copied document, signature, banknote, or work of art.

forget ▶ **verb** (**forgetting**; past **forgot**; past participle **forgotten** or chiefly US **forgot**) [with obj.] fail to remember: *he had forgotten his lines* | [with clause] *she had completely forgotten how tired and hungry she was*.
■ inadvertently neglect to attend to, do, or mention something: [with infinitive] *she forgot to lock her door* | [no obj.] *I'm sorry, I just forgot*. ■ put out of one's mind; cease to think of or consider: *forget all this romantic stuff* | [no obj.] *for years she had struggled to* ***forget about*** *him*. ■ (**forget it**) said when insisting to someone that there is no need for apology or thanks. ■ (**forget it**) said when telling someone that their idea or aspiration is impracticable. ■ (**forget oneself**) stop thinking about one's own problems or feelings: *he must forget himself in his work*. ■ (**forget oneself**) act improperly or unbecomingly.
– PHRASES **not forgetting ——** (at the end of a list) and also ——: *there are wild goats, deer, and sheep, not forgetting the famous Lundy ponies*.
– DERIVATIVES **forgetter** noun.
– ORIGIN Old English *forgietan*, of West Germanic origin; related to Dutch *vergeten* and German *vergessen*, and ultimately to **FOR-** and **GET**.

forgetful ▶ **adjective** apt or likely not to remember: *I'm a bit forgetful these days* | *she was soon* ***forgetful of*** *the time*.
– DERIVATIVES **forgetfully** adverb, **forgetfulness** noun.

forget-me-not ▶ **noun** a low-growing plant of the borage family, which typically has blue flowers and is a popular ornamental.
• *Myosotis* and other genera, family Boraginaceae: several species, in particular the common European *M. scorpioides*, whose bright blue flowers have a yellow centre.
– ORIGIN mid 16th cent.: translating the Old French name *ne m'oubliez mye*; said to have the virtue of ensuring that the wearer of the flower would never be forgotten by a lover.

forgettable ▶ **adjective** easily forgotten, especially through being uninteresting or mediocre.

forgive ▶ **verb** (past **forgave**; past participle **forgiven**) [with obj.] stop feeling angry or resentful towards (someone) for an offence, flaw, or mistake: *I don't think I'll ever* ***forgive*** *David* ***for*** *the way he treated her*.
■ (usu. **be forgiven**) stop feeling angry or resentful towards someone for (an offence, flaw, or mistake): *they are not going to pat my head and say* ***all is forgiven*** | [no obj.] *he was not a man who found it easy to* ***forgive and forget***. ■ used in polite expressions as a request to excuse or regard indulgently one's foibles, ignorance, or impoliteness: *you will have to forgive my suspicious mind*.
– PHRASES **one could** (or **may**) **be forgiven for doing something** it would be understandable if one mistakenly did a particular thing: *with the plaster palm trees, you could be forgiven for thinking you were somewhere on Hollywood Boulevard*.
– DERIVATIVES **forgivable** adjective, **forgivably** adverb, **forgiver** noun.
– ORIGIN Old English *forgiefan*, of Germanic origin,

related to Dutch *vergeven* and German *vergeben*, and ultimately to **FOR-** and **GIVE**.

forgiveness ▶ noun [mass noun] the action or process of forgiving or being forgiven: *she is quick to ask forgiveness when she has overstepped the line.*
– ORIGIN Old English *forgiefenes*, from *forgiefen* (past participle of *forgiefan* 'forgive') + the noun suffix *-nes*.

forgiving ▶ adjective ready and willing to forgive: *Taylor was in a forgiving mood.*
– DERIVATIVES **forgivingly** adverb.

forgo (also **forego**) ▶ verb (**-goes**; past **-went**; past participle **-gone**) [with obj.] omit or decline to take (something pleasant or valuable); go without: *she wanted to forgo the tea and leave while they could.*
■ refrain from: *we forgo any comparison between the two men.*
– ORIGIN Old English *forgān* (see **FOR-**, **GO**¹).

forgone past participle of **FORGO**.

forgot past of **FORGET**.

forgotten past participle of **FORGET**.

forint /ˈfɒrɪnt/ ▶ noun the basic monetary unit of Hungary, equal to 100 filler.
– ORIGIN Hungarian, from Italian *fiorino* (see **FLORIN**).

fork ▶ noun 1 an implement with two or more prongs used for lifting food to the mouth or holding it when cutting.
■ a tool of larger but similar form used for digging or lifting in a garden or farm. ■ [as modifier] denoting a light meal or buffet that may be eaten solely with a fork, while standing.
2 a device, component, or part with two or more prongs, in particular:
■ (usu. **forks**) each of a pair of supports in which a bicycle or motorcycle wheel revolves. ■ a flash of forked lightning.
3 the point where something, especially a road or (N. Amer.) river, divides into two parts.
■ either of two such parts.
4 Chess a simultaneous attack on two or more pieces by one.
▶ verb 1 [no obj.] (especially of a road or other route) divide into two parts: *the place where the road forks.*
■ [no obj., with adverbial of direction] take or constitute one part or the other at the point where a road or other route divides: *we forked north-west for Rannoch.*
2 [with obj.] dig, lift, or manipulate (something) with a fork: *fork in some compost.*
3 [with obj.] Chess attack (two pieces) simultaneously with one.
– DERIVATIVES **forkful** noun (pl. **-fuls**).
– ORIGIN Old English *forca*, *force* (denoting an agricultural implement), based on Latin *furca* 'pitchfork, forked stick'; reinforced in Middle English by Anglo-Norman French *furke* (also from Latin *furca*).
▶ **fork something out/up** (or **fork out/up**) informal pay money for something, especially reluctantly. **fork something over 1** turn over soil or other material with a gardening fork. **2** informal, chiefly N. Amer. another way of saying **fork something out**.

forkball ▶ noun Baseball a pitch released from between the widely spread index finger and middle finger.

Forkbeard, Sweyn, see **SWEYN I**.

forked ▶ adjective having a divided or pronged end or branches; bifurcated: *a deeply forked tail.*
– PHRASES **with forked tongue** humorous untruthfully; deceitfully.

forked lightning ▶ noun [mass noun] lightning that is visible in the form of a zigzag or branching line across the sky.

forklift ▶ noun (also **forklift truck**) a vehicle with a pronged device in front for lifting and carrying heavy loads.
▶ verb [with obj. and adverbial of place] lift and carry (a heavy load) with such a vehicle: *he eyed the blocks of compacted garbage being forklifted on to a trailer.*

forktail ▶ noun an Asian songbird of the thrush family, with a long forked tail and typically with black-and-white plumage.
● Genus *Enicurus*, family Turdidae: several species.

forlorn /fəˈlɔːn/ ▶ adjective 1 pitifully sad and abandoned or lonely: *forlorn figures at bus stops.*
2 (of an aim or endeavour) unlikely to succeed or be fulfilled; hopeless: *a forlorn attempt to escape.*
– PHRASES **forlorn hope** a persistent or desperate hope that is unlikely to be fulfilled. [ORIGIN: mid

16th cent.: from Dutch *verloren hoop* 'lost troop', from *verloren* (past participle of *verliezen* 'lose') and *hoop* 'company' (related to **HEAP**). The phrase originally denoted a band of soldiers picked to begin an attack, many of whom would not survive; the current sense (mid 17th cent.), derives from a misunderstanding of the etymology.]
– DERIVATIVES **forlornly** adverb, **forlornness** noun.
– ORIGIN Old English *forloren* 'depraved, morally abandoned', past participle of *forlēosan* 'lose', of Germanic origin; related to Dutch *verliezen* and German *verlieren*, and ultimately to **FOR-** and **LOSE**. Sense 1 dates from the 16th cent.

form ▶ noun 1 the visible shape or configuration of something: *the form, colour, and texture of the tree.*
■ [mass noun] arrangement of parts; shape: *the entities underlying physical form.* ■ the body or shape of a person or thing: *his eyes scanned her slender form.* ■ [mass noun] arrangement and style in literary or musical composition: *these videos are a triumph of form over content.* ■ Philosophy the essential nature of a species or thing, especially (in Plato's thought) regarded as an abstract ideal which real things imitate or participate in.
2 a particular way in which a thing exists or appears; a manifestation: *her obsession has taken the form of compulsive exercise.*
■ any of the ways in which a word may be spelled, pronounced, or inflected: *an adjectival rather than adverbial form.* ■ [mass noun] the structure of a word, phrase, sentence, or discourse: *every distinction in meaning is associated with a distinction in form.*
3 a type or variety of something: *sponsorship is a form of advertising.*
■ an artistic or literary genre. ■ Botany a taxonomic category that ranks below variety, which contains organisms differing from the typical kind in some trivial, frequently impermanent, character, e.g. a colour variant. Also called **FORMA**. Compare with **SUBSPECIES** and **VARIETY**.
4 [mass noun] the customary or correct method or procedure; what is usually done: *the Englishman knew the form.*
■ [count noun] a set order of words; a formula. ■ [count noun] a formality or item of mere ceremony: *the outward forms of religion.*
5 a printed document with blank spaces for information to be inserted: *an application form.*
6 chiefly Brit. a class or year in a school, usually given a specifying number: *the fifth form.*
7 [mass noun] the state of a sports player or team with regard to their current standard of play: *they are one of the best teams around on current form.*
■ details of previous performances by a racehorse or greyhound: *an interested bystander studying the form.* ■ a person's mood and state of health: *she seemed to be on good form.* ■ Brit. informal a criminal record: *they both had form.*
8 Brit. a long bench without a back.
9 Printing, chiefly US variant spelling of **FORME**.
10 Brit. a hare's lair.
11 another term for **SHUTTERING**.
▶ verb [with obj.] 1 bring together parts or combine to create (something): *the company was formed in 1982.*
■ (**form people/things into**) organize people or things into (a group or body): *peasants and miners were formed into a militia.* ■ go to make up or constitute: *the precepts which form the basis of the book.* ■ [no obj.] gradually appear or develop: *a thick mist was forming all around.* ■ conceive (an idea or plan) in one's mind. ■ enter into or contract (a relationship): *the women would form supportive friendships.* ■ articulate (a word, speech sound, or other linguistic unit). ■ construct (a new word) by derivation or inflection.
2 make or fashion into a certain shape or form: *form the dough into balls.*
■ [no obj.] (**form into**) be made or fashioned into a certain shape or form: *his strong features formed into a smile of pleasure.* ■ (**be formed**) have a specified shape: *her body was slight and flawlessly formed.* ■ influence or shape (something abstract): *the role of the news media in forming public opinion.*
– PHRASES **in** (or chiefly Brit. **on**) **form** (of a sports player or team) playing or performing well. **off** (or chiefly Brit. **out of**) **form** (of a sports player or team) not playing or performing well.
– DERIVATIVES **formability** noun, **formable** adjective.
– ORIGIN Middle English: from Old French *forme* (noun), *fo(u)rmer* (verb, from Latin *formare* 'to form'), both based on Latin *forma* 'a mould or form'.
▶ **form people/things up** (or **form up**) chiefly Military bring or be brought into a certain arrangement or formation: *Mortimer formed up his troops for the march.*

-form (usu. as **-iform**) ▶ combining form 1 having the form of: *cruciform.*
2 having a particular number of: *multiform.*
– ORIGIN from French *-forme*, from Latin *-formis*, from *forma* 'form'.

forma /ˈfɔːmə/ ▶ noun (pl. **formas** or **formae** /-miː/) Botany another term for **FORM** (in sense 3).

formal ▶ adjective 1 done in accordance with rules of convention or etiquette; suitable for or constituting an official or important situation or occasion: *a formal dinner party.*
■ (of a person or their manner) prim or stiff. ■ of or denoting a style of writing or public speaking characterized by more elaborate grammatical structures and more conservative and technical vocabulary. ■ (especially of a house or garden) arranged in a regular, classical, and symmetrical manner.
2 officially sanctioned or recognized: *a formal complaint.*
■ having a conventionally recognized form, structure, or set of rules: *he had little formal education.*
3 of or concerned with outward form or appearance, especially as distinct from content or matter: *I don't know enough about art to appreciate the purely formal qualities.*
■ having the form or appearance without the spirit: *the committee stage would be purely formal.* ■ of or relating to linguistic or logical form as opposed to function or meaning.
▶ noun N. Amer. an evening dress.
■ an occasion on which evening dress is worn.
– ORIGIN late Middle English: from Latin *formalis*, from *forma* 'shape, mould' (see **FORM**).

formal cause ▶ noun Philosophy (in Aristotelian thought) the pattern which determines the form taken by something.

formaldehyde /fɔːˈmaldɪhʌɪd/ ▶ noun [mass noun] Chemistry a colourless pungent gas in solution made by oxidizing methanol.
● Alternative name: **methanal**; chem. formula: CH_2O.
– ORIGIN late 19th cent.: blend of **FORMIC ACID** and **ALDEHYDE**.

formalin /ˈfɔːm(ə)lɪn/ ▶ noun [mass noun] a colourless solution of formaldehyde in water, used chiefly as a preservative for biological specimens.
– ORIGIN late 19th cent.: from **FORMALDEHYDE** + **-IN**¹.

formalism ▶ noun 1 [mass noun] excessive adherence to prescribed forms: *academic dryness and formalism.*
■ the use of forms of worship without regard to inner significance. ■ the basing of ethics on the form of the moral law without regard to intention or consequences. ■ concern or excessive concern with form and technique rather than content in artistic creation. ■ (in the theatre) a symbolic and stylized manner of production. ■ the treatment of mathematics as a manipulation of meaningless symbols.
2 [count noun] a description of something in formal mathematical or logical terms.
– DERIVATIVES **formalist** noun, **formalistic** adjective.

formality ▶ noun (pl. **-ies**) [mass noun] the rigid observance of rules of convention or etiquette: *the formality of life in an English public school.*
■ stiffness of behaviour or style: *with disconcerting formality the brothers shook hands.* ■ [count noun] (usu. **formalities**) a thing that is done simply to comply with requirements of etiquette, regulations, or custom: *legal formalities.* ■ (**a formality**) something that is done as a matter of course and without question; an inevitability: *promotion looks a formality.*
– ORIGIN mid 16th cent. (in the sense 'accordance with legal rules or conventions'): from French *formalité* or medieval Latin *formalitas*, from *formalis* (see **FORMAL**).

formalize (also **-ise**) ▶ verb [with obj.] give (something) legal or formal status.
■ give (something) a definite structure or shape: *we became able to formalize our thoughts.*
– DERIVATIVES **formalization** noun.

formally ▶ adverb 1 in accordance with the rules of convention or etiquette: *he was formally attired.*
2 officially: *the Mayor will formally open the new Railway Centre.*
3 [sentence adverb] in outward form or appearance; in theory: *all Javanese are formally Muslims.*
■ in terms of form or structure: *formally complex types of text.*

Forman /ˈfɔːmən/, Milos (b.1932), Czech-born American film director. He made *One Flew Over the Cuckoo's Nest* (1975), which won five Oscars, and

Amadeus (1983), which won eight Oscars, including that for best director.

formant /ˈfɔːm(ə)nt/ ▶ **noun** Phonetics any of the three characteristic pitch constituents of a vowel. In a high front vowel such as /iː/ the formants are bunched closely together, whereas in a low back vowel such as /ɑː/ they are further apart.
– ORIGIN early 20th cent.: coined in German from Latin *formant-* 'forming', from the verb *formare*.

format ▶ **noun** the way in which something is arranged or set out: *the format of the funeral service.*
▪the shape, size, and presentation of a book or periodical. ▪the medium in which a sound recording is made available: *the album is available as a CD as well as on LP and cassette formats.* ▪Computing a defined structure for the processing, storage, or display of data: *a data file in binary format.*
▶**verb** (**formatted**, **formatting**) [with obj.] (especially in computing) arrange or put into a format.
▪prepare (a storage medium) to receive data.
– ORIGIN mid 19th cent.: via French and German from Latin *formatus* (*liber*) 'shaped (book)', past participle of *formare* 'to form'.

formation ▶ **noun 1** [mass noun] the action of forming or process of being formed: *the formation of the Great Rift Valley.*
2 a structure or arrangement of something: *a cloud formation.*
▪a formal arrangement of aircraft in flight or troops: *a battle formation* | [mass noun] *the helicopters hovered overhead* ***in formation***.
– DERIVATIVES **formational** adjective.
– ORIGIN late Middle English: from Latin *formatio(n-)*, from *formare* 'to form' (see **FORM**).

formation dancing ▶ **noun** [mass noun] a variety of competitive ballroom dancing in which a team of couples dance a prepared routine.

formative ▶ **adjective** serving to form something, especially having a profound and lasting influence on a person's development: *his formative years.*
▪of or relating to a person's development: *a formative assessment.* ▪Linguistics denoting or relating to any of the smallest meaningful units that are used to form words in a language, typically combining forms and inflections.
▶**noun** Linguistics a formative element.
– DERIVATIVES **formatively** adverb.
– ORIGIN late 15th cent.: from Old French *formatif, -ive* or medieval Latin *formativus*, from Latin *formare* 'to form' (see **FORM**).

Formby /ˈfɔːmbi/, George (1904–61), English comedian; born *George Booth*. He became famous for his numerous musical films in the 1930s in which he projected the image of a Lancashire working lad and accompanied his songs on the ukulele.

form class ▶ **noun** Linguistics a class of linguistic forms with grammatical or syntactic features in common; a part of speech or subset of a part of speech.

form criticism ▶ **noun** [mass noun] analysis of the Bible by tracing the history of its content of parables, psalms, and other literary forms.

form drag ▶ **noun** [mass noun] Aeronautics that part of the drag on an aerofoil which arises from its shape. It varies according to the angle of attack and can be decreased by streamlining.

forme /fɔːm/ (also **form**) ▶ **noun** Printing a body of type secured in a chase for printing.
▪a quantity of film arranged for making a plate.
– ORIGIN late 15th cent.: variant of **FORM**.

Formentera /ˌfɔːmənˈtɛːrə/ a small island in the Mediterranean, south of Ibiza. It is the southernmost of the Balearic Islands.

former¹ ▶ **adjective** [attrib.] **1** having previously filled a particular role or been a particular thing: *her former boyfriend.*
▪of or occurring in the past or an earlier period: *in former times.*
2 (**the former**) denoting the first or first mentioned of two people or things: *those who take the former view* | [as noun] *the powers of the former are more comprehensive than those of the latter.*
– ORIGIN Middle English: from Old English *forma* (see **FOREMOST**) + **-ER**².

USAGE Traditionally, **former** and **latter** are used in relation to pairs of items: either the first of two items (**former**) or the second of two items (**latter**). The reason for this is that **former** and **latter** were formed as comparatives, and comparatives are correctly used with reference to just two things, while a superlative is used where there are more than two things. So, for example, strictly speaking one should say *the* ***longest*** *of the* ***three*** *books* but *the* ***longer*** *of the* ***two*** *books*. In practice, **former** and **latter** are now sometimes used just as synonyms for **first** and **last** and are routinely used to refer to a contrast involving more than two items. Such uses, however, are not acceptable in good English style.

former² ▶ **noun 1** a person or thing that forms something: [in combination] *an opinion-former.*
▪a tool, mould, or other device used to form articles or shape materials: *an arch former.* ▪a transverse strengthening part in an aircraft wing or fuselage. ▪a frame or core around which an electrical coil can be wound.
2 [in combination] Brit. a person in a particular school year: *fifth-formers.*

formerly ▶ **adverb** in the past; in earlier times: *Bangladesh, formerly East Pakistan* | [sentence adverb] *the building formerly housed the National Assembly.*

form factor ▶ **noun** a mathematical factor which compensates for irregularity in the shape of an object, usually the ratio between its volume and that of a regular object of the same breadth and height.
▪the physical size and shape of a piece of computer hardware.

form genus ▶ **noun** Palaeontology a classificatory category used for fossils which are similar in appearance but cannot be reliably assigned to an established animal or plant genus, such as fossil parts of organisms and trace fossils.

Formica /fɔːˈmʌɪkə/ ▶ **noun** [mass noun] trademark a hard durable plastic laminate used for worktops, cupboard doors, and other surfaces.
– ORIGIN 1920s (originally US): of unknown origin.

formic acid /ˈfɔːmɪk/ ▶ **noun** [mass noun] Chemistry a colourless irritant volatile acid made catalytically from carbon monoxide and steam. It is present in the fluid emitted by some ants.
● Alternative name: **methanoic acid**; chem. formula: HCOOH.
– DERIVATIVES **formate** noun.
– ORIGIN late 18th cent.: *formic* from Latin *formica* 'ant'.

formicarium /ˌfɔːmɪˈkɛːrɪəm/ ▶ **noun** (pl. **formicaria**) an ant's nest, especially one in an artificial container for purposes of study.
– ORIGIN early 19th cent.: from medieval Latin, from Latin *formica* 'ant'.

formication /ˌfɔːmɪˈkeɪʃ(ə)n/ ▶ **noun** [mass noun] a sensation like insects crawling over the skin.
– ORIGIN early 18th cent.: from Latin *formicatio(n-)*, from *formicare* 'crawl like an ant' (said of the pulse or skin), from *formica* 'ant'.

formidable /ˈfɔːmɪdəb(ə)l, fɔːˈmɪd-/ ▶ **adjective** inspiring fear or respect through being impressively large, powerful, intense, or capable: *a formidable opponent.*
– DERIVATIVES **formidableness** noun, **formidably** adverb.
– ORIGIN late Middle English: from French, or from Latin *formidabilis*, from *formidare* 'to fear'.

USAGE There are two possible pronunciations of **formidable**: one with the stress on the **for-** and the other with the stress on the **-mid-**. The second pronunciation is now common in British English, but the traditional pronunciation places the stress on the first syllable. Both pronunciations are acceptable in modern standard English.

formless ▶ **adjective** without a clear or definite shape or structure: *a dark and formless idea.*
– DERIVATIVES **formlessly** adverb, **formlessness** noun.

form letter ▶ **noun** a standardized letter to deal with frequently occurring matters.

formol /ˈfɔːmɒl/ ▶ **noun** another term for **FORMALIN**.

Formosa /fɔːˈməʊsə/ former name for **TAIWAN**.
– ORIGIN Portuguese, literally 'beautiful'.

formula /ˈfɔːmjʊlə/ ▶ **noun 1** (pl. **formulae** /-liː/) a mathematical relationship or rule expressed in symbols.
▪(also **chemical formula**) a set of chemical symbols showing the elements present in a compound and their relative proportions.
2 (pl. **formulas**) a fixed form of words, especially one used in particular contexts or as a conventional usage: *a legal formula.*
▪a method, statement, or procedure for achieving something, especially reconciling different aims or positions: *the forlorn hope of finding a peace formula.* ▪a rule or style unintelligently or slavishly followed: [as modifier] *one of those formula tunes.* ▪a stock epithet, phrase, or line repeated for various effects in literary composition, especially epic poetry.
3 (pl. **formulas**) a list of ingredients for or constituents of something: *a blend of fifteen whiskies of different ages compiled to a secret formula.*
▪a formulation: *an original coal tar formula that helps prevent dandruff.* ▪[mass noun] an infant's liquid food preparation based on cow's milk or soya protein, given as a substitute for breast milk.
4 (usually followed by a numeral) a classification of racing car, especially by the engine capacity.
– ORIGIN early 17th cent. (in the sense 'fixed form of words (for use on ceremonial or social occasions)'): from Latin, diminutive of *forma* 'shape, mould'.

formulable ▶ **adjective** capable of being formulated.

formulaic /ˌfɔːmjʊˈleɪɪk/ ▶ **adjective** constituting or containing a verbal formula or set form of words: *a formulaic greeting.*
▪produced in accordance with a slavishly followed rule or style; predictable: *much romantic fiction is stylized, formulaic, and unrealistic.*
– DERIVATIVES **formulaically** adverb.

Formula One ▶ **noun** [mass noun] an international form of motor racing, whose races are called Grands Prix.

formularize (also **-ise**) ▶ **verb** [with obj.] make (something) formulaic or predictable: *their stage shows have become a little formularized.*

formulary /ˈfɔːmjʊləri/ ▶ **noun** (pl. **-ies**) **1** a collection of formulas or set forms, especially for use in religious ceremonies.
2 an official list giving details of prescribable medicines.
▶**adjective** relating to or using officially prescribed formulas.
– ORIGIN mid 16th cent.: the noun from French *formulaire* or medieval Latin *formularius* (*liber*) '(book) of formulae', from Latin *formula* (see **FORMULA**); the adjective (early 18th cent.) is directly from **FORMULA**.

formulate /ˈfɔːmjʊleɪt/ ▶ **verb** [with obj.] create or devise methodically (a strategy or a proposal).
▪express (an idea) in a concise or systematic way: *the argument is sufficiently clear that it can be formulated mathematically.*
– DERIVATIVES **formulator** noun.
– ORIGIN mid 19th cent.: from **FORMULA** + **-ATE**³, on the pattern of French *formuler*, from medieval Latin *formulare*.

formulation ▶ **noun 1** [mass noun] the action of devising or creating something: *the formulation of foreign policy.*
▪[count noun] a particular expression of an idea, thought, or theory.
2 a material or mixture prepared according to a particular formula.

formwork ▶ **noun** another term for **SHUTTERING**.

formyl /ˈfɔːmʌɪl, -mɪl/ ▶ **noun** [as modifier] Chemistry of or denoting the acyl radical —CHO, derived from formic acid: *N-formyl methionine.*

Fornax /ˈfɔːnaks/ Astronomy an inconspicuous southern constellation (the Furnace), near Eridanus.
▪[as genitive **Fornacis** /fɔːˈneɪsɪs/] used with preceding letter or numeral to designate a star in this constellation: *the star Beta Fornacis.*
– ORIGIN Latin.

fornent /fɔːˈnɛnt, fə-/ (also **fornenst**) ▶ **preposition** dialect, chiefly Scottish alongside, opposite, or close by.
– ORIGIN late Middle English: blend of the adverb **FORE** and **ANENT**.

fornicate ▶ **verb** [no obj.] formal or humorous have sexual intercourse with someone one is not married to.
– DERIVATIVES **fornication** noun, **fornicator** noun.
– ORIGIN Middle English (as *fornication*): from ecclesiastical Latin *fornicat-* 'arched', from *fornicari*, from Latin *fornix, fornic-* 'vaulted chamber', later 'brothel'.

fornix /ˈfɔːnɪks/ ▶ **noun** (pl. **fornices** /ˈfɔːnɪsiːz/) Anatomy

a vaulted or arched structure in the body, in particular:
■(also **fornix cerebri** /ˈsɛrɪbrʌɪ/) a triangular area of white matter in the mammalian brain between the hippocampus and the hypothalamus.
– ORIGIN late 17th cent.: from Latin, literally 'arch, vaulted chamber'.

for-profit ▶ **adjective** [attrib.] denoting an organization operated to make a profit, especially one (such as a hospital or school) which would more usually be non-profit-making.

forrader /ˈfɒrədə/ ▶ **adjective** & **adverb** non-standard spelling of **FORWARDER**[2], used humorously or to represent dialect pronunciation: [as adv.] *well, that didn't get me much forrader, but it was something.*

forrard /ˈfɒrəd/ ▶ **adjective** & **adverb** non-standard spelling of **FORWARD**, used to represent a nautical or dialect pronunciation.

Forrest, John, 1st Baron (1847–1918), Australian explorer and statesman, first Premier of Western Australia 1890–1901.

forsake ▶ **verb** (past **forsook**; past participle **forsaken**) [with obj.] chiefly poetic/literary abandon (someone or something): *he would never forsake Tara.*
■renounce or give up (something valued or pleasant): *I won't forsake my vegetarian principles.*
– DERIVATIVES **forsakenness** noun, **forsaker** noun.
– ORIGIN Old English *forsacan* 'renounce, refuse', of West Germanic origin; related to Dutch *verzaken*, and ultimately to **FOR-** and **SAKE**[1].

forsooth /fəˈsuːθ/ ▶ **adverb** [sentence adverb] archaic or humorous indeed (often used ironically or to express surprise or indignation): *it's a kind of wine bar for royals, forsooth.*
■used to give an ironic politeness to questions: *and what, forsooth, induced this transformation?*
– ORIGIN Old English *forsōth* (see **FOR**, **SOOTH**).

Forster /ˈfɔːstə/, E. M. (1879–1970), English novelist and literary critic; full name *Edward Morgan Forster*. His novels, several of which have been made into successful films, include *A Room with a View* (1908) and *A Passage to India* (1924).

forsterite /ˈfɔːstərʌɪt/ ▶ **noun** [mass noun] a magnesium-rich variety of olivine, occurring as white, yellow, or green crystals.
– ORIGIN early 19th cent.: from the name of J. R. Forster (1729–98), German naturalist, + **-ITE**[1].

forswear ▶ **verb** (past **forswore**; past participle **forsworn**) [with obj.] formal agree to give up or do without (something): *it is currently fashionable to forswear meat-eating in the interests of animal rights.*
■(**forswear oneself/be forsworn**) swear falsely; commit perjury: *I swore that I would lead us safely home and I do not mean to be forsworn.*
– ORIGIN Old English *forswerian* (see **FOR-**, **SWEAR**).

Forsyth /fɔːˈsʌɪθ/, Frederick (b.1938), English novelist, known for political thrillers such as *The Day of the Jackal* (1971), *The Odessa File* (1972), and *The Fourth Protocol* (1984).

forsythia /fɔːˈsʌɪθɪə, fə-/ ▶ **noun** an ornamental Eurasian shrub whose bright yellow flowers appear in early spring before the leaves.
• Genus *Forsythia*, family Oleaceae: several species.
– ORIGIN modern Latin, named after William *Forsyth* (1737–1804), Scottish botanist and horticulturalist, said to have introduced the shrub into Britain from China.

fort ▶ **noun** a fortified building or strategic position.
■historical a trading station. [ORIGIN: so named because such stations were originally fortified.]
– ORIGIN late Middle English: from Old French *fort* or Italian *forte*, from Latin *fortis* 'strong'.

Fortaleza /ˌfɔːtəˈleɪzə/ a port in NE Brazil, on the Atlantic coast, capital of the state of Ceará; pop. 1,768,640 (1991).

fortalice /ˈfɔːtəlɪs/ ▶ **noun** a small fort, fortified house, or outwork of fortification.
– ORIGIN late Middle English: from medieval Latin *fortalitia, -itium*, from Latin *fortis* 'strong'.

Fort-de-France /ˌfɔːdəˈfrɑːns, French fɔʀ də fʀɑ̃s/ the capital of Martinique; pop. 101,540 (1990).

forte[1] /ˈfɔːteɪ, ˈfɔːti, fɔːt/ ▶ **noun** **1** [in sing.] a thing at which someone excels: *small talk was not his forte.*
2 Fencing the part of a sword blade from the hilt to the middle. Compare with **FOIBLE**.
– ORIGIN mid 17th cent. (in sense 2; originally as *fort*): from French *fort* (masculine), *forte* (feminine) 'strong', from Latin *fortis*.

forte[2] /ˈfɔːteɪ/ Music ▶ **adverb** & **adjective** (especially as a direction) loud or loudly.
▶ **noun** a passage performed or marked to be performed loudly.
– ORIGIN Italian, literally 'strong, loud', from Latin *fortis*.

Fortean /ˈfɔːtɪən/ ▶ **adjective** of, relating to, or denoting paranormal phenomena.
– DERIVATIVES **Forteana** plural noun.
– ORIGIN 1970s: from the name of Charles H. *Fort* (1874–1932), American student of paranormal phenomena.

fortepiano /ˌfɔːteɪˈpjɑːnəʊ, -ˈpjanəʊ/ ▶ **noun** (pl. **-os**) Music a piano, especially of the kind made in the 18th and early 19th centuries.
– ORIGIN mid 18th cent.: from **FORTE**[2] + **PIANO**[2].

forte piano /ˌfɔːteɪ ˈpjɑːnəʊ/ ▶ **adverb** & **adjective** Music (especially as a direction) loud and then immediately soft.
– ORIGIN Italian.

Forth a river of central Scotland, rising on Ben Lomond and flowing eastwards through Stirling into the North Sea.
■a shipping forecast area covering Scottish coastal waters roughly from Berwick in the south to Aberdeen in the north, including the Firth of Forth.

forth ▶ **adverb** chiefly archaic out from a starting point and forwards or into view: *the plants will bush out, putting forth fresh shoots.*
■onwards in time: *from that day forth he gave me endless friendship.*
– PHRASES **and so forth** and so on: *particular services like education, housing, and so forth.*
– ORIGIN Old English, of Germanic origin; related to Dutch *voort* and German *fort*, from an Indo-European root shared by **FORE-**.

Forth, Firth of the estuary of the River Forth, spanned by a cantilever railway bridge (opened 1890) and a road suspension bridge (1964).

forthcoming ▶ **adjective** **1** planned for or about to happen in the near future: *the forthcoming cricket season.*
2 [predic.] [often with negative] (of something required) ready or made available when wanted or needed: *financial support was not forthcoming.*
■(of a person) willing to divulge information: *her daughter had never been forthcoming about her time in the States.*
– DERIVATIVES **forthcomingness** noun.

forthright ▶ **adjective** **1** (of a person or their manner or speech) direct and outspoken; straightforward and honest: *his most forthright attack yet on the reforms.*
2 archaic proceeding directly forwards.
▶ **adverb** archaic directly forwards.
■immediately.
– DERIVATIVES **forthrightly** adverb, **forthrightness** noun.
– ORIGIN Old English *forthriht* 'straight forward, directly' (see **FORTH**, **RIGHT**).

forthwith /fɔːθˈwɪθ, -ð/ ▶ **adverb** (especially in official use) immediately; without delay: *we undertake to pay forthwith the money required.*
– ORIGIN Middle English (in the sense 'along with, at the same time'): partly from earlier *forthwithal*, partly representing *forth with* used alone without a following noun.

fortification /ˌfɔːtɪfɪˈkeɪʃ(ə)n/ ▶ **noun** (often **fortifications**) a defensive wall or other reinforcement built to strengthen a place against attack.
■[mass noun] the action of fortifying or process of being fortified: *the fortification of the frontiers.*
– ORIGIN late Middle English: via French from late Latin *fortificatio(n-)*, from *fortificare* (see **FORTIFY**).

fortify /ˈfɔːtɪfʌɪ/ ▶ **verb** (**-ies**, **-ied**) [with obj.] strengthen (a place) with defensive works so as to protect it against attack: *the whole town was heavily fortified* | [as adj. **fortified**] *a fortified manor house.*
■strengthen or invigorate (someone) mentally or physically: *I was fortified by the knowledge that I was in a sympathetic house.* ■[often as adj. **fortified**] strengthen (a drink) with alcohol: *fortified wine.* ■increase the nutritive value of (food), especially with vitamins.
– DERIVATIVES **fortifiable** adjective, **fortifier** noun.
– ORIGIN late Middle English: from French *fortifier*, from late Latin *fortificare*, from Latin *fortis* 'strong'.

fortis /ˈfɔːtɪs/ ▶ **adjective** Phonetics (of a consonant, in particular a voiceless consonant) strongly articulated, especially more so than another consonant articulated in the same place. The opposite of **LENIS**.
– ORIGIN mid 20th cent.: from Latin, literally 'strong'.

fortissimo /fɔːˈtɪsɪməʊ/ Music ▶ **adverb** & **adjective** (especially as a direction) very loud or loudly.
▶ **noun** (pl. **fortissimos** or **fortissimi** /-mi/) a passage performed or marked to be performed very loudly.
– ORIGIN Italian, from Latin *fortissimus* 'very strong'.

fortitude /ˈfɔːtɪtjuːd/ ▶ **noun** [mass noun] courage in pain or adversity: *she endured her illness with great fortitude.*
– ORIGIN Middle English: via French from Latin *fortitudo*, from *fortis* 'strong'.

Fort Knox /nɒks/ a US military reservation in Kentucky, famous as the site of the depository (built in 1936) which holds the bulk of the nation's gold bullion in its vaults.

Fort Lamy /ˈlɑːmi/ former name (until 1973) for **N'DJAMENA**.

fortnight ▶ **noun** chiefly Brit. a period of two weeks.
■informal used after the name of a day to indicate that something will take place two weeks after that day.
– ORIGIN Old English *fēowertīene niht* 'fourteen nights'.

fortnightly chiefly Brit. ▶ **adjective** happening or produced every two weeks: *a fortnightly bulletin.*
▶ **adverb** every two weeks: *evening classes will run fortnightly.*
▶ **noun** (pl. **-ies**) a magazine or similar publication issued every two weeks.

Fortran /ˈfɔːtran/ ▶ **noun** [mass noun] a high-level computer programming language used especially for scientific calculations.
– ORIGIN 1950s: contraction of *formula translation*.

fortress ▶ **noun** a military stronghold, especially a strongly fortified town fit for a large garrison.
■a heavily protected and impenetrable building. ■figurative a person or thing not susceptible to outside influence or disturbance: *he had proved himself to be a fortress of moral rectitude.*
– ORIGIN Middle English: from Old French *forteresse* 'strong place', based on Latin *fortis* 'strong'.

fortuitous /fɔːˈtjuːɪtəs/ ▶ **adjective** happening by accident or chance rather than design: *the similarity between the paintings may not be simply fortuitous.*
■informal happening by a lucky chance; fortunate: *from a cash standpoint, the company's timing is fortuitous.*
– DERIVATIVES **fortuitously** adverb, **fortuitousness** noun.
– ORIGIN mid 17th cent.: from Latin *fortuitus*, from *forte* 'by chance', from *fors* 'chance, luck'.

> **USAGE** The traditional, etymological meaning of **fortuitous** is 'happening by chance': a ***fortuitous meeting*** is a chance meeting, which might turn out to be either a good thing or a bad thing. In modern uses, however, **fortuitous** tends to be often used to refer only to fortunate outcomes and the word has become more or less a synonym for 'lucky' or 'fortunate'. This use is frowned upon as being not etymologically correct and is best avoided except in informal contexts.

fortuity /fɔːˈtjuːɪti/ ▶ **noun** (pl. **-ies**) a chance occurrence.
■[mass noun] the state of being controlled by chance rather than design.

fortunate ▶ **adjective** favoured by or involving good luck or fortune; lucky: [with infinitive] *she'd been fortunate to escape more serious injury* | ***it was fortunate that*** *the weather was good.*
■auspicious or favourable: *a most fortunate match for our daughter.* ■materially well off; prosperous: *less fortunate children still converged on the soup kitchens.*
– ORIGIN late Middle English: from Latin *fortunatus*, from *fortuna* (see **FORTUNE**).

fortunately ▶ **adverb** [sentence adverb] it is fortunate that: *fortunately, no shots were fired and no one was hurt.*

fortune ▶ **noun** **1** [mass noun] chance or luck as an external, arbitrary force affecting human affairs: *some malicious act of fortune keeps them separate.*
■luck, especially good luck: *this astounding piece of good fortune that has befallen me.* ■(**fortunes**) the success or failure of a person or enterprise over a period of time or in the course of a particular activity: *he is credited with turning round the company's fortunes.*
2 a large amount of money or assets: *he eventually inherited a substantial fortune.*
■(**a fortune**) informal a surprisingly high price or

amount of money: *I spent a fortune on drink and drugs.*
– PHRASES **fortune favours the brave** proverb a successful person is often one who is willing to take risks. **the fortunes of war** the unpredictable, haphazard events of war. **make a** (or **one's**) **fortune** acquire great wealth by one's own efforts. **a small fortune** informal a large amount of money. **tell someone's fortune** make predictions about a person's future by palmistry, using a crystal ball, or similar divining methods.
– ORIGIN Middle English: via Old French from Latin *Fortuna*, the name of a goddess personifying luck or chance.

Fortune 500 ▶ **noun** (trademark in the US) an annual list of the five hundred most profitable US industrial corporations.

fortune cookie ▶ **noun** N. Amer. a small biscuit containing a slip of paper with a prediction or motto written on it, served in Chinese restaurants.

fortune hunter ▶ **noun** a person who seeks to become rich through marrying someone wealthy.

fortune teller ▶ **noun** a person who tells people's fortunes.
– DERIVATIVES **fortune telling** noun.

Fort William a town in western Scotland, on Loch Linnhe near Ben Nevis; pop 10,900 (1991).

Fort Worth a city in northern Texas; pop. 447,600 (1990).

forty ▶ **cardinal number** (pl. **-ies**) **1** the number equivalent to the product of four and ten; ten less than fifty; 40: *Troy was only forty miles away | forty were arrested | there were about thirty or forty of them.* (Roman numeral: **xl** or **XL**)
■ (**forties**) the numbers from forty to forty-nine, especially the years of a century or of a person's life: *Terry was in his early forties.* ■ forty years old: *a tall woman of about forty.* ■ forty miles an hour: *they were doing about forty.* ■ a size of garment or other merchandise denoted by forty.
2 (**the Forties**) the central North Sea between Scotland and southern Norway, so called from its prevailing depth of forty fathoms or more. The area is an important centre of North Sea oil production. See also **ROARING FORTIES**.
■ (**Forties**) a shipping forecast area covering the central North Sea east of Scotland.
– PHRASES **forty winks** informal a short sleep or nap, especially during the day.
– DERIVATIVES **fortieth** ordinal number, **fortyfold** adjective & adverb.
– ORIGIN Old English *fēowertig* (see **FOUR**, **-TY**[2]).

forty-five ▶ **noun** a gramophone record played at 45 rpm; a single.
– PHRASES **the Forty-five** an informal name for the Jacobite rebellion of 1745.

forty-niner ▶ **noun** a seeker for gold in the Californian gold rush of 1849.

forty-ninth parallel the parallel of latitude 49° north of the equator, especially as forming the boundary between Canada and the US west of the Lake of the Woods.

forum /ˈfɔːrəm/ ▶ **noun** (pl. **forums**) **1** a place, meeting, or medium where ideas and views on a particular issue can be exchanged: *we hope these pages act as* ***a forum for*** *debate.*
2 chiefly N. Amer. a court or tribunal.
3 (pl. **fora**) (in an ancient Roman city) a public square or marketplace used for judicial and other business.
– ORIGIN late Middle English (in sense 3): from Latin, literally 'what is out of doors', originally denoting an enclosure surrounding a house; related to *fores* '(outside) door'. Sense 1 dates from the mid 18th cent.

forward ▶ **adverb** (also **forwards**) **1** towards the front; in the direction that one is facing or travelling: *he started up the engine and the car moved forward | Rory leaned forward over the table.*
■ in, near, or towards the bow or nose of a ship or aircraft. ■ (in sport) towards the opponents' goal: *Rangers pressed forward.* ■ in the normal order or sequence: *the number was the same backwards as forwards.*
2 onward so as to make progress; towards a successful conclusion: *there's no way forward for the relationship.*
■ into a position of prominence or notice: *he is pushing forward a political ally.*
3 towards the future; ahead in time: *from that day forward the Assembly was at odds with us.*
■ to an earlier time: *the special issue has been moved forward to November.*
▶ **adjective 1** directed or facing towards the front or the direction that one is facing or travelling: *forward flight | the pilot's forward view.*
■ positioned near the enemy lines: *troops moved to the forward areas.* ■ (in sport) moving towards the opponents' goal: *a forward pass.* ■ in, near, or towards the bow or nose of a ship or aircraft. ■ figurative moving or tending onwards to a successful conclusion: *the decision is a forward step.* ■ Electronics (of a voltage applied to a semiconductor junction) in the direction which allows significant current to flow.
2 [attrib.] relating to or concerned with the future: *forward planning.*
3 (of a person) bold or familiar in manner, especially in a presumptuous way.
4 developing or acting earlier than expected or required; advanced or precocious: *an alarmingly forward yet painfully vulnerable child.*
■ (of a plant) well advanced or early. ■ progressing towards or approaching maturity or completion.
▶ **noun 1** an attacking player in football, hockey, or other sports.
2 (**forwards**) agreements to trade specified assets, typically currency, at a specified price at a certain future date. Compare with **FUTURE** (in sense 2).
▶ **verb** [with obj.] **1** send (a letter) on to a further destination: [as adj. **forwarding**] *a forwarding address.*
■ hand over or send (an official document): *apply by forwarding a CV.* ■ dispatch (goods): [as adj. **forwarding**] *a freight forwarding company.*
2 help to advance (something); promote.
– DERIVATIVES **forwardly** adverb, **forwardness** noun.
– ORIGIN Old English *forweard* (in the sense 'towards the future', as in *from this day forward*), variant of *forthweard* (see **FORTH**, **-WARD**).

forwarder[1] /ˈfɔːwədə/ ▶ **noun** a person or organization that dispatches or delivers goods.

forwarder[2] /ˈfɒrədə/ ▶ **adjective** & **adverb** informal further forward; more advanced: *time was drawing on and we were no forwarder.*

forward-looking ▶ **adjective** favouring innovation and development; progressive.

forwards ▶ **adverb** variant spelling of **FORWARD**.

forward scattering ▶ **noun** [mass noun] Physics the scattering of radiation involving a change of direction of less than 90 degrees, in particular the propagation of high-frequency radio waves beyond the horizon by scattering or reflection from the ionosphere.

forwent past of **FORGO**.

Fosbury /ˈfɒzb(ə)ri/, Richard (b.1947), American high jumper. He originated the now standard style of jumping known as the 'Fosbury flop', in which the jumper clears the bar head first and backwards. In 1968 he won the Olympic gold medal using this technique.

fossa[1] /ˈfɒsə/ ▶ **noun** (pl. **fossae** /-siː/) Anatomy a shallow depression or hollow.
– ORIGIN mid 17th cent.: from Latin, literally 'ditch', feminine past participle of *fodere* 'to dig'.

fossa[2] /ˈfɒsə/ ▶ **noun** a large nocturnal reddish-brown catlike mammal of the civet family, found in the rainforests of Madagascar.
• *Cryptoprocta ferox*, family Viverridae.
– ORIGIN mid 19th cent.: from Malagasy *fosa*.

fosse /fɒs/ ▶ **noun** Archaeology a long narrow trench or excavation, especially in a fortification.
– ORIGIN late Old English, via Old French from Latin *fossa* (see **FOSSA**[1]).

Fosse Way an ancient road in Britain. It ran from Axminster to Lincoln, via Bath and Leicester (about 300 km, 200 miles), and marked the limit of the first stage of the Roman occupation (mid 1st century AD).

fossick /ˈfɒsɪk/ ▶ **verb** [no obj.] informal Austral./NZ rummage; search: *he spent years* ***fossicking through*** *documents.*
■ search for gold in abandoned workings.
– DERIVATIVES **fossicker** noun.
– ORIGIN mid 19th cent. (referring to mining): probably from the English dialect sense 'obtain by asking' (i.e. 'ferret out').

fossil /ˈfɒs(ə)l, -sɪl/ ▶ **noun** the remains or impression of a prehistoric plant or animal preserved in petrified form or as a mould or cast in rock.
■ derogatory or humorous an antiquated or stubbornly unchanging person or thing: *he can be a cantankerous old fossil at times.* ■ a word or phrase that has become obsolete except in set phrases or forms, e.g. *hue* in *hue and cry.*
– ORIGIN mid 16th cent. (denoting a fossilized fish found, and believed to have lived, underground): from French *fossile*, from Latin *fossilis* 'dug up', from *fodere* 'dig'.

fossil fuel ▶ **noun** a natural fuel such as coal or gas, formed in the geological past from the remains of living organisms.

fossiliferous /ˌfɒsɪˈlɪf(ə)rəs/ ▶ **adjective** Geology (of a rock or stratum) containing fossils or organic remains.

fossil ivory ▶ **noun** [mass noun] ivory from the tusks of a mammoth.

fossilize (also **-ise**) ▶ **verb** [with obj.] (usu. **be fossilized**) preserve (an animal or plant) so that it becomes a fossil: *the hard parts of the body are readily fossilized* | [as adj. **fossilized**] *the fossilized remains of a dinosaur.*
■ [no obj.] become a fossil: *flowers do not readily fossilize.*
– DERIVATIVES **fossilization** noun.

fossorial /fɒˈsɔːrɪəl/ ▶ **adjective** Zoology (of an animal) burrowing.
■ (of limbs) adapted for use in burrowing.
– ORIGIN mid 19th cent.: from medieval Latin *fossorius* (from Latin *fossor* 'digger', from *fodere* 'to dig') + **-AL**.

Foster[1], Jodie (b.1962), American film actress; born *Alicia Christian Foster*. She has won Oscars for her performances in *The Accused* (1988) and *Silence of the Lambs* (1991).

Foster[2], Sir Norman (Robert), Baron Foster of Thames Bank (b.1935), English architect. His work is notable for its sophisticated engineering approach and technological style.

Foster[3], Stephen (Collins) (1826–64), American composer. He wrote more than 200 songs and, though a Northerner, was best known for songs which captured the Southern plantation spirit, such as 'Oh! Susannah' (1848) and 'Camptown Races' (1850).

foster ▶ **verb** [with obj.] **1** encourage or promote the development of (something, typically something regarded as good): *the teacher's task is to foster learning.*
■ develop (a feeling or idea) in oneself: *appropriate praise helps a child foster a sense of self-worth.*
2 bring up (a child that is not one's own by birth).
■ Brit. (of a parent or authority) assign (a child) to be brought up by someone other than its parents: *when* ***fostering out*** *a child, placement workers will be looking for a home similar to their own.*
– DERIVATIVES **fosterage** noun, **fosterer** noun.
– ORIGIN Old English *fōstrian* 'feed, nourish', from *fōster* 'food, nourishment', of Germanic origin; related to **FOOD**. The sense 'bring up another's (originally also one's own) child' dates from Middle English. See also **FOSTER-**.

foster- ▶ **combining form** denoting someone that has a specified family connection through fostering rather than birth: *foster-parent | foster-child.*
■ involving or concerned with fostering a child: *foster care | foster home.*
– ORIGIN *foster-father*, *foster-mother*, *foster-child*, and *foster-brother* all date from Old English. *Foster-mother* has also been used to mean a wet nurse, her husband being *foster-father* to the child she fed, and a *foster-brother* or *-sister* one reared at the same breast.

fosterling ▶ **noun** chiefly archaic a child who is fostered or adopted.
– ORIGIN Old English *fōstorling* (see **FOSTER**, **-LING**).

fou /fuː/ ▶ **adjective** Scottish inebriated; drunk.
– ORIGIN mid 16th cent.: variant of **FULL**.

Foucault[1] /ˈfuːkəʊ, French fuko/, Jean Bernard Léon (1819–68), French physicist. He is chiefly remembered for the huge pendulum which he hung from the roof of the Panthéon in Paris in 1851 to demonstrate the rotation of the earth. He also invented the gyroscope and was the first to determine the velocity of light reasonably accurately.

Foucault[2] /ˈfuːkəʊ, French fuko/, Michel (Paul) (1926–84), French philosopher. A student of Louis Althusser, he was mainly concerned with exploring how society defines categories of abnormality such as insanity, sexuality, and criminality, and the manipulation of social attitudes towards such things by those in power.

– DERIVATIVES **Foucauldian** /fuːˈkəʊdɪən/ adjective, **Foucaultian** /-ˈkəʊɪən/ adjective.

fouetté /ˈfwɛteɪ/ ▶ noun Ballet a pirouette performed with a circular whipping movement of the raised leg to the side.
  ■ a quick shift of direction of the upper body, performed with one leg extended.
– ORIGIN French, past participle of *fouetter* 'to whip'.

fought past and past participle of FIGHT.

Fou-hsin variant spelling of FUXIN.

foul ▶ adjective **1** offensive to the senses, especially through having a disgusting smell or taste or being unpleasantly soiled: *a foul odour* | *his foul breath*.
  ■ informal very disagreeable or unpleasant: *the news had put Michelle in a foul mood*. ■ (of the weather) wet and stormy. ■ Sailing (of wind or tide) opposed to one's desired course.
  2 wicked or immoral: *murder most foul*.
  ■ (of language) obscene or profane. ■ done contrary to the rules of a sport: *a foul tackle*.
  3 containing or charged with noxious matter; polluted: *foul, swampy water*.
  ■ [predic.] (**foul with**) clogged or choked with: *the land was foul with weeds*. ■ Nautical (of a rope or anchor) entangled. ■ (of a ship's bottom) overgrown with weed, barnacles, or similar matter.
▶ noun **1** (in sport) an unfair or invalid stroke or piece of play, especially one involving interference with an opponent.
  ■ a collision or entanglement in riding, rowing, or running.
  2 [mass noun] informal, dated a disease in the feet of cattle.
▶ adverb unfairly; contrary to the rules.
▶ verb [with obj.] **1** make foul or dirty; pollute: *factories which fouled the atmosphere*.
  ■ (of an animal) make (something) dirty with excrement: *make sure that your pet never fouls paths*. ■ (**foul oneself**) (of a person) defecate involuntarily.
  2 (in sport) commit a foul against (an opponent).
  3 (of a ship) collide with or interfere with the passage of (another).
  ■ cause (a cable, anchor, or other object) to become entangled or jammed: *watch out for driftwood which might foul up the engine*. ■ [no obj.] become entangled in this way.
– PHRASES **foul one's** (**own**) **nest** do something damaging or harmful to oneself or one's own interests.
– DERIVATIVES **foully** adverb, **foulness** noun.
– ORIGIN Old English *fūl*, of Germanic origin; related to Old Norse *fúll* 'foul', Dutch *vuil* 'dirty', and German *faul* 'rotten, lazy', from an Indo-European root shared by Latin *pus*, Greek *puos* 'pus', and Latin *putere* 'to stink'.
▶ **foul something up** (or **foul up**) make a mistake with or spoil something: *leaders should admit when they completely foul things up*.

Foulah /ˈfuːlə/ ▶ noun (pl. same or **Foulahs**) & adjective variant spelling of FULA.

foulard /ˈfuːlɑː(d)/ ▶ noun [mass noun] a thin, soft material of silk or silk and cotton, typically having a printed pattern.
  ■ [count noun] a tie or handkerchief made of such material.
– ORIGIN mid 19th cent.: from French, of unknown origin.

foul ball ▶ noun Baseball a ball struck so that it falls outside the lines drawn from home plate down to the first and third bases.

foul brood ▶ noun [mass noun] a fatal bacterial disease of larval honeybees.
  ● This disease is caused by the bacteria *Bacillus larvae* or *Melissococcus pluton*.

foul line ▶ noun Baseball either of the straight lines extending from home plate down to the first and third bases and marking the limit of the playing area, within which a hit is deemed to be fair.

foul mouth ▶ noun a tendency to use bad language: *he had a foul mouth and an even fouler disposition*.
– DERIVATIVES **foul-mouthed** adjective.

foul play ▶ noun [mass noun] **1** unfair play in a game or sport.
  2 unlawful or dishonest behaviour, in particular violent crime resulting in another's death.

foul-up ▶ noun a mistake resulting in confusion.

foumart /ˈfuːmət, -mɑːt/ ▶ noun old-fashioned term for POLECAT.
– ORIGIN Middle English: from FOUL + Old English

mearth 'marten'; of Germanic origin and related to MARTEN.

found[1] past and past participle of FIND. ▶ adjective **1** having been discovered by chance or unexpectedly, in particular:
  ■ (of an object or sound) collected in its natural state and presented in a new context as part of a work of art or piece of music: *collages of found photos*. ■ (of art) comprising or making use of such objects. ■ (of poetry) formed by taking a piece of text and reinterpreting its structure metrically.
  2 [with submodifier] (of a ship) equipped; supplied: *the ship was two years old, well found and seaworthy*.

found[2] ▶ verb [with obj.] **1** establish or originate (a continuing institution or organization), especially by providing an endowment: *the monastery was founded in 1665* | [as adj.] **founding**] *the three founding partners*.
  ■ plan and begin the building of (a town or colony).
  2 (usu. **be founded on/upon**) construct or base (a principle or other abstract thing) according to a particular principle or grounds: *a society founded on the highest principles of religion and education*.
  ■ (of a thing) serve as a basis for: *the company's fortunes are founded on its minerals business*.
– ORIGIN Middle English: from Old French *fonder*, from Latin *fundare*, from *fundus* 'bottom, base'.

found[3] ▶ verb [with obj.] melt and mould (metal).
  ■ fuse (materials) to make glass. ■ make (an article) by melting and moulding metal.
– ORIGIN early 16th cent.: from French *fondre*, from Latin *fundere* 'melt, pour'.

foundation ▶ noun **1** (often **foundations**) the lowest load-bearing part of a building, typically below ground level.
  ■ figurative a body or ground on which other parts rest or are overlaid: *he starts playing melody lines on the bass instead of laying the foundation down*. ■ (also **foundation garment**) a woman's supporting undergarment, such as a corset. ■ a cream or powder used as a base to even out facial skin tone before applying other cosmetics.
  2 an underlying basis or principle for something: *specific learning skills as a foundation for other subjects*.
  ■ [mass noun] [often with negative] justification or reason: *distorted and misleading accusations with no foundation*.
  3 [mass noun] the action of establishing an institution or organization on a permanent basis, especially with an endowment.
  ■ [count noun] an institution established with an endowment, for example a college or a body devoted to financing research or charity.
– DERIVATIVES **foundational** adjective.
– ORIGIN late Middle English: from Old French *fondation*, from Latin *fundatio(n-)*, from *fundare* 'to lay a base for' (see FOUND[2]).

foundation course ▶ noun Brit. a course taken at some colleges and universities, either in a wide range of subjects or in one subject at a basic level, preparing students for more advanced study.

foundation stone ▶ noun a stone laid with ceremony to celebrate the founding of a building.
  ■ figurative a basic or essential element of something.

foundation subjects ▶ plural noun Brit. the subjects which form the basis of the National Curriculum, including (or loosely, those other than) the compulsory core subjects.

founder[1] ▶ noun a person who establishes or originates an institution, city, or colony.
  ■ Zoology an animal, especially a fertilized female insect, that founds a new colony.

founder[2] ▶ noun a person who manufactures articles of cast metal; the owner or operator of a foundry: *an iron founder*.
– ORIGIN Middle English: probably from Old French *fondeur*, from *fondre* (see FOUND[3]).

founder[3] ▶ verb [no obj., with adverbial] (of a ship) fill with water and sink: *six drowned when the yacht foundered off the Cornish coast*.
  ■ figurative (of a plan or undertaking) fail or break down, typically as a result of a particular problem or setback: *the talks foundered on the issue of reform*. ■ (of a horse or its rider) stumble or fall from exhaustion, lameness, or because of uneven or boggy ground.
  ■ chiefly N. Amer. (of a hoofed animal, especially a horse or pony) succumb to laminitis.
▶ noun [mass noun] chiefly N. Amer. laminitis in horses, ponies, or other hoofed animals.
– ORIGIN Middle English (in the sense 'knock to the ground'): from Old French *fondrer*, *esfondrer*

'submerge, collapse', based on Latin *fundus* 'bottom, base'.

USAGE It is easy to confuse the words **founder** and **flounder**, not only because they sound similar but also because the contexts in which they are used tend to overlap. **Founder** means, in its general and extended use, 'fail or come to nothing', as in *the scheme foundered because of lack of organizational backing*. **Flounder**, on the other hand, means 'struggle; be in a state of confusion', as in *new recruits floundering about in their first week*.

founder effect ▶ noun Biology the reduced genetic diversity which results when a population is descended from a small number of colonizing ancestors.

founding father ▶ noun a person who starts or helps to start a movement or institution.
  ■ (**Founding Father**) a member of the convention that drew up the constitution of the US in 1787.

foundling ▶ noun an infant that has been abandoned by its parents and is discovered and cared for by others.
– ORIGIN Middle English: from FOUND[1] (past participle) + -LING, perhaps on the pattern of Dutch *vondeling*.

foundress ▶ noun a female founder, especially a fertile female animal that founds a colony.

foundry ▶ noun (pl. -ies) a workshop or factory for casting metal.
– ORIGIN early 17th cent. (earlier as *foundery*): from FOUND[3] + -RY, perhaps suggested by French *fonderie*.

fount[1] ▶ noun a source of a desirable quality or commodity: *our courier was a fount of knowledge*.
  ■ poetic/literary a spring or fountain.
– ORIGIN late 16th cent.: back-formation from FOUNTAIN, on the pattern of the pair *mountain*, *mount*.

fount[2] ▶ noun Brit. variant spelling of FONT[2].

fountain ▶ noun **1** an ornamental structure in a pool or lake from which one or more jets of water are pumped into the air.
  ■ short for DRINKING FOUNTAIN. ■ figurative a thing that spurts or cascades into the air: *little fountains of dust*.
  2 poetic/literary or S. African a natural spring of water.
  ■ a source of a desirable quality: *the government always quote this report as the fountain of truth*.
  3 Heraldry a roundel barry wavy argent and azure (i.e. a circle with wavy horizontal stripes of blue and white).
▶ verb [no obj.] spurt or cascade like a fountain: *she watched the blood fountaining from her wrists*.
– DERIVATIVES **fountained** adjective (poetic/literary).
– ORIGIN Middle English (in sense 2): from Old French *fontaine*, from late Latin *fontana*, feminine of Latin *fontanus*, adjective from *fons*, *font-* 'a spring'.

fountainhead ▶ noun an original source of something.

fountain pen ▶ noun a pen with a reservoir or cartridge from which ink flows continuously to the nib.

four ▶ cardinal number equivalent to the product of two and two; one more than three, or six less than ten; 4: *Francesca's got four brothers* | *it took four of them to lift it* | *a four-bedroom house*. (Roman numeral: **iv** or **IV**, archaic **iiii** or **IIII**.)
  ■ a group or unit of four people or things: *the girls walked in pairs or fours*. ■ Four years old: *I began to teach myself to read at four*. ■ four o'clock: *it's half past four*. ■ Cricket a hit that reaches the boundary after first striking the ground, scoring four runs. Compare with SIX. ■ a size of garment or other merchandise denoted by four. ■ a playing card or domino with four pips. ■ a four-oared rowing boat or its crew: *the British women's coxed four*. See also FOURS.
– PHRASES **the four freedoms** the four essential human freedoms as proclaimed in a speech to Congress by Franklin D. Roosevelt in 1941: freedom of speech and expression, freedom of worship, freedom from want, and freedom from fear. **four noble truths** the four central beliefs containing the essence of Buddhist teaching. See BUDDHISM.
– ORIGIN Old English *fēower*, of Germanic origin; related to Dutch and German *vier*, from an Indo-European root shared by Latin *quattuor* and Greek *tessares*.

Four Cantons, Lake of the another name for Lake Lucerne (see LUCERNE, LAKE).

fourchette /fʊəˈʃɛt/ ▶ noun Anatomy a thin fold of skin at the back of the vulva.

– ORIGIN mid 18th cent.: from French, diminutive of *fourche* 'fork'.

four-dimensional ▶ adjective having four dimensions, typically the three dimensions of space (length, breadth, and depth) plus time.

Fourdrinier machine /fʊəˈdrɪnɪə, -ɪeɪ/ ▶ noun a machine for making paper as a continuous sheet by drainage on a wire mesh belt.
– ORIGIN mid 19th cent.: named after Henry (died 1854) and Sealy (died 1847) *Fourdrinier*, British papermakers and patentees of such a machine.

four-eyed fish ▶ noun a small live-bearing freshwater fish of tropical America. Each eye is divided into two, allowing the fish to see both above and below the water while swimming at the surface.
• Family Anablepidae and genus *Anableps*: several species.

four-eyes ▶ noun informal **1** a person who wears glasses (used as a nickname or taunt).
2 another term for **FOUR-EYED FISH**.

four-flush N. Amer. ▶ noun a poker hand of little value, having four cards of the same suit and one of another.
▶ verb [no obj.] informal keep up a pretence; bluff: *your mother will get wise that you're four-flushing.*
– DERIVATIVES **four-flusher** noun.

fourfold ▶ adjective four times as great or as numerous: *there has been a fourfold increase in break-ins.*
■ having four parts or elements: *fourfold symmetry.*
▶ adverb by four times; to four times the number or amount; *the price of electricity rose fourfold.*

four hundred ▶ noun US the social elite of a community.
– ORIGIN mid 19th cent.: from Ward McAllister's remark 'There are only 400 people in New York that one really knows', later popularized in society reports by the New York *Sun*. The notion 'elite' is said to be from the selection of high society guests by the socialite, Mrs William B. Astor Jr, whose ballroom could hold 400.

Fourier /ˈfʊərɪeɪ, French furje/, Jean Baptiste Joseph (1768–1830), French mathematician. His studies involved him in the solution of partial differential equations by the method of separation of variables and superposition; this led him to analyse the series and integrals that are now known by his name.

Fourier analysis /ˈfʊrɪə, -rɪeɪ/ ▶ noun Mathematics the analysis of a complex waveform expressed as a series of sinusoidal functions, the frequencies of which form a harmonic series.

Fourierism /ˈfʊrɪərɪz(ə)m/ ▶ noun [mass noun] a system for the reorganization of society into self-sufficient cooperatives, in accordance with the principles of the French socialist Charles Fourier (d.1837).
– DERIVATIVES **Fourierist** noun & adjective.

Fourier series ▶ noun Mathematics an infinite series of trigonometric functions which represents an expansion or approximation of a periodic function, used in Fourier analysis.

Fourier transform ▶ noun Mathematics a function derived from a given function and representing it by a series of sinusoidal functions.

four-in-hand ▶ noun **1** a vehicle with four horses driven by one person.
2 N. Amer. historical a necktie tied in a loose knot with two hanging ends, popular in the late 19th and early 20th centuries. [ORIGIN: said to be by association with the sport of driving four-in-hand carriages.]

four-leaf clover (also **four-leaved clover**) ▶ noun a clover leaf with four lobes, thought to bring good luck.

four-letter word ▶ noun any of several short words referring to sexual or excretory functions, regarded as coarse or offensive.

four o'clock (also **four o'clock plant**) ▶ noun another term for **MARVEL OF PERU**.

fourpenny ▶ adjective [attrib.] Brit. costing or worth four pence, especially before decimalization (1971).

fourpenny one ▶ noun Brit. informal a blow: *I hit her such a fourpenny one that I sent her flying.*

four-ply ▶ adjective (of a material) having four strands or layers: *four-ply yarn.*
▶ noun [mass noun] knitting wool made of four strands.

four-poster (also **four-poster bed**) ▶ noun a bed with a post at each corner supporting a canopy.

fours ▶ plural noun **1** a race for four-oared rowing boats.
2 a competition for teams of four players, especially in bowls.

fourscore ▶ cardinal number archaic eighty.

foursome ▶ noun a group of four people.
■ a golf match between two pairs of players, with partners playing the same ball.

four-square ▶ adjective (of a building or structure) having a square shape and solid appearance.
■ (of a person or quality) firm and resolute: *a four-square and formidable hero.* ■ (of a musical performance or composition) interpreting or marking phrasing or rhythm in a heavy and simplistic way.
▶ adverb squarely and solidly: *a castle **standing four-square** and isolated on a peninsula.*
■ firmly or resolutely, especially in support of someone or something: *they **stand four-square behind** integration.*

four-star ▶ adjective (especially of accommodation) given four stars in a grading system, typically one in which this denotes the highest standard or the next standard to the highest.
■ having or denoting the second-highest military rank, distinguished in the US armed forces by four stars on the uniform.
▶ noun [mass noun] petrol with a grading of four stars.

four-stroke ▶ adjective denoting an internal-combustion engine having a cycle of four strokes (intake, compression, combustion, and exhaust).
■ denoting a vehicle having such an engine.
▶ noun an engine or vehicle of this type.

fourteen ▶ cardinal number **1** equivalent to the product of seven and two; one more than thirteen, or six less than twenty; 14: *they had spent fourteen days in solitary confinement | all fourteen of us were seated.* (Roman numeral: **xiv** or **XIV**.)
■ a size of garment or other merchandise denoted by fourteen. ■ fourteen years old: *he left school at fourteen.*
– DERIVATIVES **fourteenth** ordinal number.
– ORIGIN Old English *fēowertīene* (see **FOUR**, **-TEEN**).

fourth ▶ ordinal number constituting number four in a sequence; 4th: *the fourth and fifth centuries | there were three bedrooms, with potential for a fourth.*
■ (**a fourth/one fourth**) chiefly US a quarter: *nearly three fourths of that money is now gone.* ■ the fourth finisher or position in a race or competition: *he could do no better than finish fourth.* ■ the fourth (and often highest) in a sequence of a vehicle's gears: *he took the corner at the end of the road in fourth.* ■ chiefly Brit. the fourth form of a school or college. ■ fourthly (used to introduce a fourth point or reason): *third, visit popular attractions during lunch; fourth, stay late.* ■ Music an interval spanning four consecutive notes in a diatonic scale, in particular (also **perfect fourth**) an interval of two tones and a semitone (e.g. C to F). ■ Music the note which is higher by this interval than the tonic of a diatonic scale or root of a chord.
– PHRASES **the fourth estate** the press; the profession of journalism. [ORIGIN: originally used humorously in various contexts; its first usage with reference to the press has been attributed to Edmund Burke but this remains unconfirmed.]

fourth dimension ▶ noun **1** a postulated spatial dimension additional to those determining length, area, and volume.
2 time regarded as analogous to linear dimensions.

Fourth International see **INTERNATIONAL** (sense 2 of the noun).

fourthly ▶ adverb in the fourth place (used to introduce a fourth point or reason): *fourthly, and last, there are variations in context that influence the process.*

Fourth of July ▶ noun (in the US) a national holiday celebrating the anniversary of the adoption of the Declaration of Independence in 1776. Also called **INDEPENDENCE DAY**.

fourth position ▶ noun **1** Ballet a posture in which the feet are placed turned outwards one in front of the other, separated by the distance of one step.
■ a position of the arms in which one is held curved over the head and the other curved in front of the body at waist level.
2 Music a position of the left hand on the fingerboard of a stringed instrument nearer to the bridge than the third position, enabling a higher set of notes to be played.

Fourth Republic the republican regime in France between the end of the Second World War (1945) and the introduction of a new constitution by Charles de Gaulle in 1958.

Fourth World ▶ noun those countries and communities considered to be the poorest and most underdeveloped of the Third World.

4to ▶ abbreviation for quarto.

4WD ▶ abbreviation for four-wheel drive.

four-wheel drive ▶ noun [mass noun] a transmission system which provides power directly to all four wheels of a vehicle.
■ a vehicle with such a system, typically designed for off-road driving.

fovea /ˈfəʊvɪə/ (also **fovea centralis**) ▶ noun (pl. **foveae** /-vɪiː/) Anatomy a small depression in the retina of the eye where visual acuity is highest. The centre of the field of vision is focused in this region, where retinal cones are particularly concentrated.
– DERIVATIVES **foveal** adjective.
– ORIGIN late 17th cent.: from Latin, literally 'small pit'.

fowl ▶ noun (pl. same or **fowls**) (also **domestic fowl**) a gallinaceous bird kept chiefly for its eggs and flesh; a domestic cock or hen.
• The domestic fowl is derived from the wild **red junglefowl** of SE Asia (see **JUNGLEFOWL**).
■ any other domesticated bird kept for its eggs or flesh, e.g. the turkey, duck, goose, and guineafowl. ■ [mass noun] the flesh of birds, especially of the domestic cock or hen, as food; poultry. ■ in the names of birds that resemble the domestic fowl: *spurfowl | malleefowl.* ■ birds collectively, especially as the quarry of hunters. ■ archaic a bird.
– ORIGIN Old English *fugol*, originally the general term for a bird, of Germanic origin; related to Dutch *vogel* and German *Vogel*, also to **FLY**[1].

fowl cholera ▶ noun another term for **CHICKEN CHOLERA**.

Fowler, H. W. (1858–1933), English lexicographer and grammarian; full name *Henry Watson Fowler*. He compiled the first *Concise Oxford Dictionary* (1911) with his brother F. G. Fowler, and wrote the moderately prescriptive guide to style and idiom, *Modern English Usage*, first published in 1926.

Fowles /faʊlz/, John (Robert) (b.1926), English novelist. His works include the psychological thriller *The Collector* (1963), the magic realist novel *The Magus* (1966), and the semi-historical novel *The French Lieutenant's Woman* (1969).

fowling ▶ noun [mass noun] the hunting, shooting, or trapping of wildfowl.
– DERIVATIVES **fowler** noun.

fowl pest ▶ noun [mass noun] either of two similar viral diseases of poultry:
■ Newcastle disease. ■ fowl plague.

fowl plague ▶ noun [mass noun] an acute and often fatal infectious disease of birds, especially poultry, caused by certain strains of influenza virus.

Fox[1], Charles James (1749–1806), British statesman. He became a Whig MP in 1768, supporting American independence and the French Revolution, and collaborated with Lord North to form a coalition government (1783–4).

Fox[2], George (1624–91), English preacher and founder of the Society of Friends (Quakers).

Fox[3] ▶ noun (pl. same) **1** a member of an American Indian people formerly living in southern Wisconsin, and now mainly in Iowa, Nebraska, and Kansas.
2 [mass noun] the Algonquian language of this people, now almost extinct.
▶ adjective of or relating to this people or their language.

fox ▶ noun **1** a carnivorous mammal of the dog family with a pointed muzzle and bushy tail, proverbial for its cunning.
• *Vulpes* and three other genera, family Canidae: several species, including the red fox and the arctic fox.
■ [mass noun] the fur of a fox.
2 informal a cunning or sly person: *a wily old fox.*
■ N. Amer. a sexually attractive woman.
▶ verb [with obj.] informal baffle or deceive (someone): *the bad light and dark shadows foxed him.*
■ [no obj.] dated behave in a cunning or sly way.
– DERIVATIVES **foxlike** adjective.
– ORIGIN Old English, of Germanic origin; related to Dutch *vos* and German *Fuchs*.

a cat | ɑː arm | ɛ bed | ɛː hair | ə ago | əː her | ɪ sit | i cosy | iː see | ɒ hot | ɔː saw | ʌ run | ʊ put | uː too | ʌɪ my | aʊ how | eɪ day | əʊ no | ɪə near | ɔɪ boy | ʊə poor | ʌɪə fire | aʊə sour

Foxe, John (1516–87), English religious writer. He is famous for his *Actes and Monuments*, popularly known as *The Book of Martyrs*, which appeared in England in 1563. This passionate account of the persecution of English Protestants fuelled hostility to Catholicism for generations.

foxed ▶ **adjective 1** (of the paper of old books or prints) discoloured with brown spots.
2 archaic, informal drunk.
– DERIVATIVES **foxing** noun (only in sense 1).

foxfire ▶ **noun** [mass noun] N. Amer. the phosphorescent light emitted by certain fungi on decaying timber.

foxglove ▶ **noun** a tall Eurasian plant with erect spikes of pinkish-purple (or white) flowers shaped like the fingers of gloves. It is a source of the drug digitalis.
• Genus *Digitalis*, family Scrophulariaceae: many species, in particular *D. purpurea*.

foxhole ▶ **noun** a hole in the ground used by troops as a shelter against enemy fire or as a firing point.
■ a place of refuge or concealment.

foxhound ▶ **noun** a dog of a smooth-haired breed with drooping ears, often trained to hunt foxes in packs over long distances.

fox-hunting ▶ **noun** [mass noun] the sport of hunting a fox across country with a pack of hounds by a group of people on foot and horseback, a traditional sport of the English landed gentry.
– DERIVATIVES **fox-hunter** noun.

foxie ▶ **noun** (pl. **-ies**) Austral./NZ a fox terrier.
– ORIGIN early 20th cent.: abbreviation.

fox moth ▶ **noun** a reddish-brown moth with a velvety black and orange caterpillar.
• *Macrothylacia rubi*, family Lasiocampidae.

foxtail ▶ **noun** a common meadow grass that has soft brush-like flowering spikes.
• Genus *Alopecurus*, family Gramineae: several species, in particular *A. pratensis*.

Fox Talbot, William Henry, see **TALBOT**.

fox terrier ▶ **noun** a terrier of a short-haired or wire-haired breed originally used for unearthing foxes.

foxtrot ▶ **noun 1** a ballroom dance having an uneven rhythm with alternation of slow and quick steps.
■ a piece of music written for such a dance.
2 a code word representing the letter F, used in radio communication.
▶ **verb** (**-trotted**, **-trotting**) [no obj.] perform such a ballroom dance.

foxy ▶ **adjective** (**foxier**, **foxiest**) resembling or likened to a fox: *a terrier with prick ears and a foxy expression.*
■ informal cunning or sly in character. ■ N. Amer. informal (of a woman) sexually attractive. ■ reddish brown in colour. ■ (of wine) having a musky flavour. ■ (of paper or other material) marked with spots; foxed.
– DERIVATIVES **foxily** adverb, **foxiness** noun.

foyer /ˈfɔɪeɪ/ ▶ **noun** an entrance hall or other open area in a building used by the public, especially a hotel or theatre.
– ORIGIN late 18th cent. (denoting the centre of attention or activity): from French, 'hearth, home', based on Latin *focus* 'domestic hearth'.

FP ▶ **abbreviation for** former pupils (especially in the name of some rugby teams).

fp ▶ **abbreviation for** ■ forte piano. ■ (**f.p.**) freezing point.

FPA ▶ **abbreviation for** (in the UK) Family Planning Association.

FPS ▶ **abbreviation for** Fellow of the Pharmaceutical Society of Great Britain.

fps (also **f.p.s.**) ▶ **abbreviation for** ■ feet per second. ■ foot-pound-second. ■ frames per second.

FPU ▶ **abbreviation for** Computing floating-point unit, a processor that performs arithmetic operations.

Fr ▶ **abbreviation for** Father (as a courtesy title of priests): *Fr. Buckley*. [ORIGIN: from French *frère*, literally 'brother'.]
▶ **symbol for** the chemical element francium.

fr. ▶ **abbreviation for** franc(s).

Fra /frɑː/ ▶ **noun** a prefixed title given to an Italian monk or friar: *Fra Angelico*.
– ORIGIN Italian, abbreviation of *frate* 'brother', from Latin *frater*.

frabjous /ˈfrabdʒəs/ ▶ **adjective** humorous delightful; joyous: *'Oh frabjous day!' she giggled.*
– DERIVATIVES **frabjously** adverb.
– ORIGIN 1871: coined by Lewis Carroll in *Through the Looking Glass*, apparently to suggest *fair* and *joyous*.

fracas /ˈfrakɑː/ ▶ **noun** (pl. same /-kɑːz/ or US **fracases**) a noisy disturbance or quarrel.
– ORIGIN early 18th cent.: French, from *fracasser*, from Italian *fracassare* 'make an uproar'.

fractal /ˈfrakt(ə)l/ Mathematics ▶ **noun** a curve or geometrical figure, each part of which has the same statistical character as the whole. They are useful in modelling structures (such as eroded coastlines or snowflakes) in which similar patterns recur at progressively smaller scales, and in describing partly random or chaotic phenomena such as crystal growth, fluid turbulence, and galaxy formation.
▶ **adjective** relating to or of the nature of a fractal or fractals: *fractal geometry.*
– ORIGIN 1970s: from French, from Latin *fract-* 'broken', from the verb *frangere*.

fraction /ˈfrakʃ(ə)n/ ▶ **noun 1** a numerical quantity that is not a whole number (e.g. ½, 0.5).
■ a small or tiny part, amount, or proportion of something: *he hesitated for **a fraction of** a second | her eyes widened a fraction.* ■ a dissenting group within a larger one. ■ each of the portions into which a mixture may be separated by a process in which the individual components behave differently according to their physical properties.
2 (usu. **the Fraction**) (in the Christian Church) the breaking of the Eucharistic bread.
– ORIGIN late Middle English: via Old French from ecclesiastical Latin *fractio(n-)* 'breaking (bread)', from Latin *frangere* 'to break'.

fractional ▶ **adjective** of, relating to, or expressed as a numerical value which is not a whole number, especially a fraction less than one.
■ small or tiny in amount: *there was a fractional hesitation before he said yes.* ■ Chemistry relating to or denoting the separation of components of a mixture by making use of their differing physical properties: *fractional crystallization.*
– DERIVATIVES **fractionally** adverb.

fractional distillation ▶ **noun** [mass noun] Chemistry separation of a liquid mixture into fractions differing in boiling point (and hence chemical composition) by means of distillation, typically using a fractionating column.

fractionalize (also **-ise**) ▶ **verb** [with obj.] [usu. as adj. **fractionalized**] divide (someone or something) into separate groups or parts: *fractionalized consumer markets.*
– DERIVATIVES **fractionalization** noun.

fractionate /ˈfrakʃ(ə)neɪt/ ▶ **verb** [with obj.] chiefly technical divide into fractions or components.
■ separate (a mixture) by fractional distillation.
– DERIVATIVES **fractionation** noun.

fractionating column ▶ **noun** Chemistry a tall, horizontally subdivided container for fractional distillation in which vapour passes upwards and condensing liquid flows downwards. The vapour becomes progressively enriched in more volatile components as it ascends, and the less volatile components become concentrated in the descending liquid, which can be drawn off.

fractious /ˈfrakʃəs/ ▶ **adjective** easily irritated; bad-tempered: *they fight and squabble like fractious children.*
■ (of an organization) difficult to control; unruly: *King Malcolm struggled to unite his fractious kingdom.*
– DERIVATIVES **fractiously** adverb, **fractiousness** noun.
– ORIGIN late 17th cent.: from **FRACTION**, probably on the pattern of the pair *faction*, *factious*.

fracture ▶ **noun** [mass noun] **1** the cracking or breaking of a hard object or material: *ground movements could cause fracture of the pipe.*
■ [count noun] a crack or break in a hard object or material, typically a bone or a rock stratum: *a fracture of the left leg.* ■ the physical appearance of a freshly broken rock or mineral, especially as regards the shape of the surface formed.
2 Phonetics the replacement of a simple vowel by a diphthong owing to the influence of a following sound, typically a consonant.
■ [count noun] a diphthong substituted in this way.
▶ **verb** break or cause to break: [no obj.] *the stone has fractured* | [with obj.] *ancient magmas fractured by the forces of wind and ice.*
■ [with obj.] sustain a fracture of (a bone): [as adj. **fractured**] *she suffered a fractured skull.* ■ figurative (with reference to an organization or other abstract thing) split or fragment so as to no longer function or exist: [no obj.] *the movement had fractured without his leadership.* ■ [as adj. **fractured**] (of speech or a language) broken.
– ORIGIN late Middle English: from French, or from Latin *fractura*, from *frangere* 'to break'.

frae /freɪ/ ▶ **preposition** Scottish from: *you better collect the tab frae the office.*

fraenulum ▶ **noun** variant spelling of **FRENULUM**.

fraenum ▶ **noun** variant spelling of **FRENUM**.

frag N. Amer. military slang ▶ **noun** a hand grenade.
▶ **verb** (**fragged**, **fragging**) [with obj.] deliberately kill (an unpopular senior officer) with a hand grenade.
– ORIGIN late 20th cent.: from *fragmentation grenade.*

fragile /ˈfradʒʌɪl/ ▶ **adjective** (of an object) easily broken or damaged.
■ easily destroyed or threatened: *you have a fragile grip on reality.* ■ (of a person) not strong or sturdy; delicate and vulnerable.
– DERIVATIVES **fragilely** adverb, **fragility** noun.
– ORIGIN late 15th cent. (in the sense 'morally weak'): from Latin *fragilis*, from *frangere* 'to break'. The sense 'liable to break' dates from the mid 16th cent.

fragile X syndrome ▶ **noun** [mass noun] Medicine an inherited condition characterized by an X chromosome that is abnormally susceptible to damage, especially by folic acid deficiency. Affected individuals tend to be mentally handicapped.

fragment ▶ **noun** /ˈfragm(ə)nt/ a small part broken or separated off something: *small **fragments of** pottery, glass, and tiles.*
■ an isolated or incomplete part of something: *Nathan remembered fragments of that conversation.*
▶ **verb** /fragˈmɛnt/ break or cause to break into fragments: [no obj.] *Lough Erne **fragmented into** a series of lakes.*
– DERIVATIVES **fragmental** adjective (chiefly Geology).
– ORIGIN late Middle English: from French, or from Latin *fragmentum*, from *frangere* 'to break'.

fragmentary ▶ **adjective** consisting of small parts that are disconnected or incomplete: *excavations have revealed fragmentary remains of masonry.*
– DERIVATIVES **fragmentarily** adverb.

fragmentation ▶ **noun** [mass noun] the process or state of breaking or being broken into small or separate parts: *the **fragmentation** of society **into** a collection of interest groups.*
■ Computing the storing of a file in several separate areas of memory scattered throughout a hard disk.

fragmentation bomb ▶ **noun** a bomb designed to break into small fragments as it explodes.

Fragonard /ˈfragənɑː/, French /fʀagɔnaʀ/, Jean-Honoré (1732–1806), French painter in the rococo style. He is famous for landscapes and for erotic canvases such as *The Progress of Love* (1771).

fragrance /ˈfreɪgr(ə)ns/ ▶ **noun** a pleasant, sweet smell: *the fragrance of fresh-ground coffee* | [mass noun] *the bushes fill the air with fragrance.*
■ a perfume or aftershave.
– DERIVATIVES **fragranced** adjective.
– ORIGIN mid 17th cent.: from French, or from Latin *fragrantia*, from *fragrare* 'smell sweet'.

fragrancy ▶ **noun** (pl. **-ies**) dated fragrance.

fragrant ▶ **adjective** having a pleasant or sweet smell.
– DERIVATIVES **fragrantly** adverb.
– ORIGIN late Middle English: from French, or from Latin *fragrant-* 'smelling sweet', from the verb *fragrare*.

'fraid ▶ **verb** informal non-standard contraction of 'afraid' or 'I'm afraid', expressing regret: *'fraid not, doll.*
■ W. Indian non-standard contraction of 'be afraid' or 'be afraid of': *the kind of person who never 'fraid nobody.*

frail ▶ **adjective** (of a person) weak and delicate: *a frail voice | she looked frail and vulnerable.*
■ easily damaged or broken; fragile or insubstantial: *the balcony is frail | the frail Russian economy.* ■ weak in character or morals.
▶ **noun** US informal, dated a woman.
– DERIVATIVES **frailly** adverb, **frailness** noun.
– ORIGIN Middle English: from Old French *fraile*, from Latin *fragilis* (see **FRAGILE**).

frailty ▶ **noun** (pl. **-ies**) [mass noun] the condition of being weak and delicate: *the increasing frailty of old age.*
■ weakness in character or morals: *all drama begins with*

human frailty | [count noun] *you're too self-righteous to see your own frailties.*
– ORIGIN Middle English (in the sense 'weakness in morals'): from Old French *frailete*, from Latin *fragilitas*, from *fragilis* (see **FRAGILE**).

fraise /frɛz, freɪz/ ▶ **noun** (pl. pronounced same) (in cookery) a strawberry.
▪[mass noun] a white brandy distilled from strawberries.
– ORIGIN French.

Fraktur /ˈfraktʊə, German frakˈtuːɐ/ ▶ **noun** [mass noun] a German style of black-letter type.
– ORIGIN late 19th cent.: German, from Latin *fractura* 'fracture' (because of its angularity).

framboesia /framˈbiːzɪə/ (US **frambesia**) ▶ **noun** another term for **YAWS**.
– ORIGIN early 19th cent.: modern Latin, from French *framboise* 'raspberry', so named because of the red swellings caused by the disease, likened to raspberries.

framboise /frɒmˈbwɑːz/ ▶ **noun** (in cookery) a raspberry.
▪[mass noun] a white brandy distilled from raspberries.
– ORIGIN French, 'raspberry', from a conflation of Latin *fraga ambrosia* 'ambrosial strawberry'.

Frame, Janet (Paterson) (b.1924), New Zealand novelist. Her novels draw on her experiences of psychiatric hospitals after she suffered a severe mental breakdown. Her three-volume autobiography (1982–5) was made into the film *An Angel at my Table* (1990).

frame ▶ **noun 1** a rigid structure that surrounds or encloses a picture, door, windowpane, or similar.
▪(**frames**) a metal or plastic structure holding the lenses of a pair of glasses. ▪the rigid supporting structure of an object such as a vehicle, building, or piece of furniture. ▪a person's body with reference to its size or build: *a shiver shook her slim frame.* ▪a box-like structure of glass or plastic in which seeds or young plants are grown. ▪an apparatus with a surrounding structure, especially one used in weaving, knitting, or embroidery. ▪[in sing.] archaic the universe, or part of it, regarded as an embracing structure. ▪[in sing.] archaic the structure, constitution, or nature of someone or something: *we have in our inward frame various affections.*
2 [usu. in sing.] a basic structure that underlies or supports a system, concept, or text: *the establishment of conditions provides a frame for interpretation.*
▪technical short for **FRAME OF REFERENCE**.
3 Linguistics a structural environment within which a class of words or other linguistic units can be correctly used. For example *I — him* is a frame for a large class of transitive verbs.
▪a feature which marks a transition from one section of discourse to another: *frames are realized by linguistic items such as 'well', 'right', and 'OK'.* ▪a section of a discourse separated in such a way. ▪(in semantics) an underlying conceptual structure into which the meanings of a number of related words fit: *the frame of verbs of perception.* ▪a social context determining the interpretation of an utterance: *an utterance may mean the opposite of what it says if used within a frame of teasing.*
4 a single complete picture in a series forming a cinema, television, or video film.
▪a single picture in a comic strip.
5 the triangular structure for positioning the red balls in snooker. Compare with **RACK**[1] (in sense 4).
▪a single game of snooker.
6 N. Amer. short for **FRAME-UP**.
▶ **verb** [with obj.] **1** place (a picture or photograph) in a frame: *he had had the photo framed.*
▪surround so as to create a sharp or attractive image: *a short, strong style cut to frame the face.*
2 create or formulate (a concept, plan, or system): *staff have proved invaluable in framing the proposals.*
▪form or articulate (words): *he walked out before she could frame a reply.* ▪archaic make or construct (something) by fitting parts together or in accordance with a plan: *what immortal hand or eye could frame thy fearful symmetry?*
3 informal produce false evidence against (an innocent person) so that they appear guilty: *he claims he was framed.*
– PHRASES **be in** (or **out of**) **the frame** be (or not be) eligible or the centre of attention. ▪be under suspicion or wanted (or not) by the police: *he was always in the frame for the killing.* **frame of mind** a particular mood that influences one's attitude or behaviour.
– DERIVATIVES **framable** adjective, **frameless** adjective, **framer** noun.
– ORIGIN Old English *framian* 'be useful', of Germanic origin and related to **FROM**. The general sense in Middle English, 'make ready for use', probably led to sense 2 of the verb; it also gave rise to the specific meaning 'prepare timber for use in building', later 'make the wooden parts of a building', essentially the framework, hence the noun sense 'structure' (late Middle English).

framed ▶ **adjective 1** (of a picture or similar) held in a frame: *a framed photograph of her father.*
2 [in combination] (of a building) having a frame of a specified material: *a traditional* ***oak-framed*** *house.*

frame house ▶ **noun** chiefly N. Amer. a house constructed from a wooden skeleton, typically covered with timber boards.

frame of reference ▶ **noun** a set of criteria or stated values in relation to which measurements or judgements can be made: *the observer interprets what he sees in terms of his own cultural frame of reference.*
▪(also **reference frame**) a system of geometrical axes in relation to which measurements of size, position, or motion can be made.

frame saw ▶ **noun** a saw with a thin blade kept rigid by being stretched in a frame.

frameset ▶ **noun** the frame and front fork of a bicycle.

frame tent ▶ **noun** chiefly Brit. a tent supported by a tall frame, giving it nearly perpendicular sides and standing headroom throughout.

frame-up ▶ **noun** [in sing.] informal a conspiracy to falsely incriminate someone.

framework ▶ **noun** an essential supporting structure of a building, vehicle, or object: *a conservatory in a delicate framework of iron.*
▪a basic structure underlying a system, concept, or text: *the theoretical framework of political sociology.*

framing ▶ **noun** [mass noun] the action of framing something.
▪frames collectively.

franc /fraŋk/ ▶ **noun** the basic monetary unit of France, Belgium, Switzerland, Luxembourg, and several other countries, equal to 100 centimes (replaced in France, Belgium, and Luxembourg by the euro in 2002).
– ORIGIN from Old French, from Latin *Francorum Rex* 'king of the Franks', the legend on gold coins struck in the 14th cent. in the reign of Jean le Bon.

France[1] /frɑːns/ a country in western Europe; pop. 56,556,000 (1990); official language, French; capital, Paris.

France became a major power under the Valois and Bourbon dynasties in the 16th–18th centuries, and, after the overthrow of the monarchy in the French Revolution (1789), briefly dominated Europe under Napoleon. Defeated in the Franco-Prussian war (1870–1), the country suffered much destruction and loss of life in the First World War and during the Second World War was occupied by the Germans. France was a founder member of the EEC in 1957.

France[2] /frɑːns, French frɑ̃s/, Anatole (1844–1924), French writer; pseudonym of *Jacques-Anatole-François Thibault*. Works include the novel *Le Crime de Sylvestre Bonnard* (1881) and his ironic version of the Dreyfus case, *L'Île des pingouins* (1908). Nobel Prize for Literature (1921).

Franche-Comté /ˌfrɒ̃ʃkɒ̃ˈteɪ, French frɑ̃ʃkɔ̃te/ a region of eastern France, in the northern foothills of the Jura mountains.

franchise /ˈfran(t)ʃʌɪz/ ▶ **noun 1** an authorization granted by a government or company to an individual or group enabling them to carry out specified commercial activities, for example providing a broadcasting service or acting as an agent for a company's products.
▪a business or service given such authorization to operate. ▪N. Amer. an authorization given by a league to own a sports team. ▪N. Amer. informal a professional sports team. ▪(also **franchise player**) N. Amer. informal a star player in a team.
2 (usu. **the franchise**) the right to vote in public elections, especially for members of parliament.
▪the rights of citizenship.
▶ **verb** [with obj.] grant a franchise to (an individual or group).
▪grant a franchise for the sale of (goods) or the operation of (a service): *the catering was* ***franchised out.***
– DERIVATIVES **franchisee** noun, **franchiser** (also **franchisor**) noun.
– ORIGIN Middle English (denoting a grant of legal immunity): from Old French, based on *franc, franche* 'free' (see **FRANK**[1]). Sense 2 dates from the late 18th cent. and sense 1 from the 20th cent.

Francis, Dick (b.1920), English jockey and writer; full name *Richard Stanley Francis*. He was champion jockey 1953–4. After his retirement in 1957 he began writing thrillers, mostly set in the world of horse racing.

Francis I (1494–1547), king of France 1515–47. Much of his reign (1521–44) was spent at war with Charles V of Spain. He supported the arts and commissioned new buildings, including the Louvre.

Franciscan /franˈsɪsk(ə)n/ ▶ **noun** a friar, sister, or lay member of a Christian religious order founded in 1209 by St Francis of Assisi or based on its rule, and noted for its preachers and missionaries.

Divergences of practice led to the separation of the Friars Minor of the Observance (the Observants) and the Friars Minor Conventual (the Conventuals) in 1517, and to the foundation of the stricter Friars Minor Capuchin (the Capuchins) in 1529. The order of Franciscan nuns was founded by St Clare (*c.*1212) under the direction of St Francis; they are known as 'Poor Clares'.

▶ **adjective** of, relating to, or denoting St Francis or the Franciscans.
– ORIGIN from French *franciscain*, from modern Latin *Franciscanus*, from *Franciscus* 'Francis'.

Francis of Assisi, St (*c.*1181–1226), Italian monk, founder of the Franciscan order; born *Giovanni di Bernardone*. He founded the Franciscan order in 1209 and drew up its original rule (based on complete poverty). He is revered for his generosity, simple faith, humility, and love of nature. Feast day, 4 October.

Francis of Sales, St /sɑːl/ (1567–1622), French bishop. One of the leaders of the Counter-Reformation, he was bishop of Geneva 1602–22. The Salesian order (founded in 1859) is named after him. Feast day, 24 January.

Francis Xavier, St, see **XAVIER, ST FRANCIS**.

francium /ˈfransɪəm/ ▶ **noun** [mass noun] the chemical element of atomic number 87, a radioactive member of the alkali metal group. Francium occurs naturally as a decay product in uranium and thorium ores. (Symbol: **Fr**)
– ORIGIN 1940s: from **FRANCE**[1] (the discoverer's native country) + **-IUM**.

francize /ˈfransʌɪz/ (also **-ise**) ▶ **verb** [with obj.] Canadian (in Quebec) cause (a person or business) to adopt French as an official or working language.
– DERIVATIVES **francization** noun.

Franck[1] /fraŋk, French frɑ̃k/, César (Auguste) (1822–90), Belgian-born French composer and organist. His reputation as a composer rests on the *Symphonic Variations* for piano and orchestra (1885), the D minor Symphony (1886–8), and the *String Quartet* (1889).

Franck[2] /fraŋk/, James (1882–1964), German-born American physicist. He worked on the bombardment of atoms by electrons and became involved in the US atom bomb project; he advocated the explosion of the bomb in an uninhabited area to demonstrate its power to Japan.

Franco, Francisco (1892–1975), Spanish general and statesman, head of state 1939–75. Leader of the Nationalists in the Civil War, in 1937 Franco became head of the Falange Party and proclaimed himself *Caudillo* ('leader') of Spain. With the defeat of the republic in 1939, he took control of the government and established a dictatorship that ruled Spain until his death.
– DERIVATIVES **Francoist** noun & adjective.

Franco- (also **franco-**) ▶ **combining form** French; French and ...: *francophone* | *Franco-German.*
▪relating to France.
– ORIGIN from medieval Latin *Francus* 'Frank'.

francolin /ˈfraŋkəlɪn/ ▶ **noun** a large game bird resembling a partridge, with bare skin on the head or neck, found in Africa and South Asia.
• Genus *Francolinus*, family Phasianidae: many species.
– ORIGIN mid 17th cent.: from French, from Italian *francolino*, of unknown origin.

Franconia /fraŋˈkəʊnɪə/ a medieval duchy of southern Germany, inhabited by the Franks.

Franconian ▶ **adjective** of or relating to Franconia or its inhabitants.
▶ **noun 1** a native or inhabitant of Franconia.
2 [mass noun] a group of medieval West Germanic

dialects, combining features of Low and High German.

■the group of modern German dialects of Franconia.

Francophile ▶ noun a person who is fond of or greatly admires France or the French.

francophone /ˈfraŋkə(ʊ)fəʊn/ ▶ adjective French-speaking: *a summit of francophone countries.*
▶ noun a person who speaks French.
– ORIGIN early 20th cent.: from **FRANCO-** 'French' + Greek *phōnē* 'voice'.

Franco-Prussian War the war of 1870–1 between France (under Napoleon III) and Prussia, in which Prussian troops advanced into France and decisively defeated the French at Sedan. The defeat marked the end of the French Second Empire. For Prussia, the proclamation of the new German Empire at Versailles was the climax of Bismarck's ambitions to unite Germany.

frangible /ˈfran(d)ʒɪb(ə)l/ ▶ adjective formal fragile; brittle.
– ORIGIN late Middle English: from Old French, or from medieval Latin *frangibilis*, from Latin *frangere* 'to break'.

frangipane /ˈfran(d)ʒɪpeɪn/ ▶ noun [mass noun] an almond-flavoured cream or paste.
– ORIGIN late 17th cent.: from French, named after the Marquis Muzio *Frangipani* (see **FRANGIPANI**). The term originally denoted the frangipani shrub or tree, the perfume of which is said to have been used to flavour the almond cream.

frangipani /ˌfran(d)ʒɪˈpani, -ˈpɑːni/ ▶ noun (pl. **frangipanis**) a tropical American tree or shrub with clusters of fragrant white, pink, or yellow flowers.
● Genus *Plumeria*, family Apocynaceae: several species, in particular *P. rubra.*
■[mass noun] perfume obtained from this plant.
– ORIGIN mid 19th cent.: named after the Marquis Muzio *Frangipani*, a 16th-cent. Italian nobleman who invented a perfume for scenting gloves.

franglais /ˈfrɒ̃gleɪ/ ▶ noun [mass noun] a blend of French and English, either French speech that makes excessive use of English expressions, or unidiomatic French spoken by an English person.
– ORIGIN 1960s: coined in French, from a blend of *français* 'French' and *anglais* 'English'.

Frank[1], Anne (1929–45), German Jewish girl known for her diary, which records the experiences of her family living for two years in hiding from the Nazis in occupied Amsterdam. They were eventually betrayed and sent to concentration camps; Anne died in Belsen.

Frank[2] ▶ noun a member of a Germanic people that conquered Gaul in the 6th century and controlled much of western Europe for several centuries afterwards.
■(in the eastern Mediterranean region) a person of western European nationality or descent.
– ORIGIN Old English *Franca*, of Germanic origin; perhaps from the name of a weapon and related to Old English *franca* 'javelin' (compare with **SAXON**); reinforced in Middle English by medieval Latin *Francus* and Old French *Franc*, of the same origin and related to **FRENCH**.

frank[1] ▶ adjective open, honest, and direct in speech or writing, especially when dealing with unpalatable matters: *a long and frank discussion | to be perfectly frank, I don't know.*
■open, sincere, or undisguised in manner or appearance: *Katherine saw her look at Sam with frank admiration.* ■Medicine unmistakable; obvious: *frank ulceration.*
– DERIVATIVES **frankness** noun.
– ORIGIN Middle English (in the sense 'free'): from Old French *franc*, from medieval Latin *francus* 'free', from *Francus* (see **FRANK**[2]: only Franks had full freedom in Frankish Gaul). Another Middle English sense was 'generous', which led to the current sense.

frank[2] ▶ verb [with obj.] **1** (often **be franked**) stamp an official mark on (a letter or parcel), especially to indicate that postage has been paid or does not need to be paid.
■historical sign (a letter or parcel) to ensure delivery free of charge. ■[as adj. **franked**] Brit. denoting dividends and other payments carrying a tax credit which can be offset against advance corporation tax by the company which receives them. ■archaic facilitate or pay the passage of (someone): *English will frank the traveller through most of North America.*

2 (of a runner-up in a horse race) respond to (a winning performance) by another jockey with a similar performance of one's own.
▶ noun an official mark or signature on a letter or parcel, especially to indicate that postage has been paid or does not need to be paid. [ORIGIN: formerly as a superscribed signature of an eminent person entitled to send letters free of charge.]
– DERIVATIVES **franker** noun.
– ORIGIN early 18th cent.: from **FRANK**[1], an early sense being 'free of obligation'.

frank[3] ▶ noun N. Amer. short for **FRANKFURTER**.

franked investment income ▶ noun [mass noun] (in the UK) income in the form of dividends paid to a company from earnings on which corporation tax has already been paid by the originating company.

Frankenstein /ˈfraŋk(ə)nstʌɪn/ a character in the novel *Frankenstein, or the Modern Prometheus* (1818) by Mary Shelley. Baron Frankenstein is a scientist who creates and brings to life a manlike monster which eventually turns on him and destroys him; Frankenstein is not the name of the monster itself, as is often assumed.
■(also **Frankenstein's monster**) [as noun] a thing that becomes terrifying or destructive to its maker.

Frankfort /ˈfraŋkfət/ the state capital of Kentucky; pop. 26,000 (1990).

Frankfurt /ˈfraŋkfɔːt, German ˈfraŋkfʊrt/ a commercial city in western Germany, in Hesse; pop. 654,080 (1991). The headquarters of the Bundesbank are located there. Full name **FRANKFURT AM MAIN** /am ˈmʌɪn/.

frankfurter ▶ noun a seasoned smoked sausage made of beef and pork.
– ORIGIN from German *Frankfurter Wurst* 'Frankfurt sausage'.

Frankfurt School a school of philosophy of the 1920s whose adherents were involved in a reappraisal of Marxism, particularly in terms of the cultural and aesthetic dimension of modern industrial society. Principal figures include Theodor Adorno, Max Horkheimer, and Herbert Marcuse.

frankincense /ˈfraŋkɪnsɛns/ ▶ noun [mass noun] an aromatic gum resin obtained from an African tree and burnt as incense. Also called **OLIBANUM**, **GUM OLIBANUM**.
● This resin is obtained from the tree *Boswellia sacra*, family Burseraceae, native to Somalia.
– ORIGIN late Middle English: from Old French *franc encens*, literally 'high-quality incense', from *franc* (see **FRANK**[1]) in an obsolete sense 'superior, of high quality' (which also existed in English) + *encens* 'incense'.

franking ▶ noun [mass noun] the action of franking a letter or parcel: [as modifier] *a franking machine.*
■[count noun] an official mark or signature on a letter or parcel to indicate that postage has been paid or does not need to be paid.

Frankish ▶ adjective of or relating to the ancient Franks or their language.
▶ noun [mass noun] the Germanic language of the ancient Franks.

Franklin[1], Aretha (b.1942), American soul and gospel singer. Her best-known songs include 'I Say a Little Prayer' (1967).

Franklin[2], Benjamin (1706–90), American statesman, inventor, and scientist. He was one of the signatories to the peace between the US and Great Britain after the War of American Independence. His main scientific achievements were the formulation of a theory of electricity, which introduced positive and negative electricity, and a demonstration of the electrical nature of lightning, which led to the invention of the lightning conductor.

Franklin[3], (Stella Maria Sarah) Miles (1879–1954), Australian novelist. She wrote the first true Australian novel, *My Brilliant Career* (1901). She also produced a series of chronicle novels under her pseudonym 'Brent of Bin Bin' (1928–56).

Franklin[4], Rosalind Elsie (1920–58), English physical chemist and molecular biologist. Together with Maurice Wilkins she investigated the structure of DNA by means of X-ray crystallography, and contributed to the discovery of its helical structure.

franklin ▶ noun a landowner of free but not noble birth in the 14th and 15th centuries in England.

– ORIGIN Middle English: from Anglo-Latin *francalanus*, from *francalis* 'held without dues', from *francus* 'free' (see **FRANK**[1]).

Franklin stove ▶ noun N. Amer. a large cast-iron stove for heating a room, resembling an open fireplace in shape.
– ORIGIN late 18th cent.: named after B. *Franklin* (see **FRANKLIN**[2]).

frankly ▶ adverb in an open, honest, and direct manner: *she talks very frankly about herself.*
■[sentence adverb] used to emphasize the truth of a statement, however unpalatable or shocking this may be: *frankly, I was pleased to leave.*

frantic ▶ adjective wild or distraught with fear, anxiety, or other emotion: *she was frantic with worry.*
■conducted in a hurried, excited, and chaotic way, typically because of the need to act quickly: *frantic attempts to resuscitate the girl.*
– DERIVATIVES **frantically** adverb, **franticness** noun.
– ORIGIN late Middle English *frentik*, 'insane, violently mad', from Old French *frenetique* (see **FRENETIC**).

Franz Josef /ˌfrants ˈjəʊzɛf/ (1830–1916), emperor of Austria 1848–1916 and king of Hungary 1867–1916. He gave Hungary equal status with Austria in 1867. His annexation of Bosnia–Herzegovina (1908) contributed to European political tensions, and the assassination in Sarajevo of his heir apparent, Archduke Franz Ferdinand, precipitated the First World War.

Franz Josef Land a group of islands in the Arctic Ocean, discovered in 1873 by an Austrian expedition and annexed by the USSR in 1928.

frap ▶ verb (**frapped**, **frapping**) [with obj.] Nautical bind (something) tightly.
– ORIGIN Middle English (in the sense 'strike, beat', now rare): from Old French *fraper* 'to bind, strike', of unknown origin. The current sense dates from the mid 16th cent.

frappé[1] /ˈfrapeɪ/ ▶ adjective [postpositive] (of a drink) iced or chilled: *a crème de menthe frappé.*
▶ noun a drink served with ice or frozen to a slushy consistency.
– ORIGIN French.

frappé[2] /ˈfrapeɪ/ ▶ adjective [postpositive] Ballet (of a position) involving a beating action of the toe of one foot against the ankle of the supporting leg: *a battement frappé.*
– ORIGIN French, literally 'struck'.

Frascati /frəˈskɑːti/ ▶ noun [mass noun] a wine, typically white, produced in the region of Frascati, Italy.

Fraser[1] /ˈfreɪzə/ a river of British Columbia. It rises in the Rocky Mountains and flows in a wide curve 1,360 km (850 miles) into the Strait of Georgia, just south of Vancouver.

Fraser[2] /ˈfreɪzə/, Dawn (b.1937), Australian swimmer. She won the Olympic gold medal for the 100-metres freestyle in 1956, 1960, and 1964, the first competitor to win the same title at three successive Olympics.

Fraser[3] /ˈfreɪzə/, (John) Malcolm (b.1930), Australian Liberal statesman, Prime Minister 1975–83. He was the youngest-ever Australian MP when elected in 1955.

frass /fras/ ▶ noun [mass noun] fine powdery refuse or fragile perforated wood produced by the activity of boring insects.
■the excrement of insect larvae.
– ORIGIN mid 19th cent.: from German *Frass*, from *fressen* 'devour'.

frat ▶ noun [usu. as modifier] N. Amer. informal a students' fraternity: *a frat party.*
– ORIGIN late 19th cent.: abbreviation.

frater /ˈfreɪtə/ ▶ noun historical the dining room or refectory of a monastery.
– ORIGIN Middle English: from Old French *fraitur*, shortening of *refreitor*, from late Latin *refectorium* 'refectory'.

fraternal /frəˈtəːn(ə)l/ ▶ adjective **1** of or like a brother or brothers: *his lack of fraternal feeling shocked me.*
■of or denoting an organization or order for people, especially men, that have common interests or beliefs.
2 (of twins) developed from separate ova and therefore genetically distinct and not necessarily of

the same sex or more similar than other siblings. Compare with **IDENTICAL** (in sense 1).
– DERIVATIVES **fraternalism** noun, **fraternally** adverb.
– ORIGIN late Middle English: from medieval Latin *fraternalis*, from Latin *fraternus*, from *frater* 'brother'.

fraternity /frəˈtəːnɪti/ ▶ **noun** (pl. **-ies**) **1** [treated as sing. or pl.] a group of people sharing a common profession or interests: *members of the hunting fraternity.*
■N. Amer. a male students' society in a university or college. ■ a religious or masonic society or guild.
2 [mass noun] the state or feeling of friendship and mutual support within a group: *the ideals of liberty, equality, and fraternity.*
– ORIGIN Middle English: from Old French *fraternite*, from Latin *fraternitas*, from *fraternus* (see **FRATERNAL**).

fraternize /ˈfratənʌɪz/ (also **-ise**) ▶ **verb** [no obj.] associate or form a friendship with someone, especially when one is not supposed to: *she ignored Elisabeth's warning glare against* ***fraternizing with*** *the enemy.*
– DERIVATIVES **fraternization** noun.
– ORIGIN early 17th cent.: from French *fraterniser*, from medieval Latin *fraternizare*, from Latin *fraternus* 'brotherly' (see **FRATERNAL**).

fratricidal /ˌfratrɪˈsʌɪd(ə)l/ ▶ **adjective** relating to or denoting conflict within a single family or organization: *the fratricidal strife within the Party.*

fratricide /ˈfratrɪsʌɪd/ ▶ **noun** [mass noun] the killing of one's brother or sister.
■[count noun] a person who kills their brother or sister. ■ [mass noun] the accidental killing of one's own forces in war.
– ORIGIN late 15th cent. (denoting a person who kills their brother or sister, derived from Latin *fratricida*): the primary current sense comes via French from late Latin *fratricidium*, from *frater* 'brother' + *-cidium* (see **-CIDE**).

Frau /fraʊ/ ▶ **noun** (pl. **Frauen** /ˈfraʊən/) a title or form of address for a married or widowed German-speaking woman: *Frau Nordern.*
– ORIGIN German.

fraud /frɔːd/ ▶ **noun** [mass noun] wrongful or criminal deception intended to result in financial or personal gain: *he was convicted of fraud* | [count noun] *prosecutions for social security frauds.*
■[count noun] a person or thing intended to deceive others, typically by unjustifiably claiming or being credited with accomplishments or qualities: *mediums exposed as tricksters and frauds.*
– ORIGIN Middle English: from Old French *fraude*, from Latin *fraus*, *fraud-* 'deceit, injury'.

fraud squad ▶ **noun** [treated as sing. or pl.] Brit. a division of a police force appointed to investigate fraud.

fraudster ▶ **noun** a person who commits fraud, especially in business dealings.

fraudulent /ˈfrɔːdjʊl(ə)nt/ ▶ **adjective** obtained, done by, or involving deception, especially criminal deception: *fraudulent share dealing.*
■unjustifiably claiming or being credited with particular accomplishments or qualities: *the fraudulent illusion of choice prepared by the hospitality industry.*
– DERIVATIVES **fraudulence** noun, **fraudulently** adverb.
– ORIGIN late Middle English: from Old French, or from Latin *fraudulentus*, from *fraus*, *fraud-* 'deceit, injury'.

fraught /frɔːt/ ▶ **adjective 1** [predic.] (**fraught with**) (of a situation or course of action) filled with or destined to result in (something undesirable): *marketing any new product is fraught with danger.*
2 causing or affected by great anxiety or stress: *there was a fraught silence* | *she sounded a bit fraught.*
– ORIGIN late Middle English, 'laden, provided, equipped', past participle of obsolete *fraught* 'load with cargo', from Middle Dutch *vrachten*, from *vracht* 'ship's cargo'. Compare with **FREIGHT**.

Fräulein /ˈfrɔɪlʌɪn, German ˈfrɔylaɪn/ ▶ **noun** a title or form of address for an unmarried German-speaking woman, especially a young woman: *Fräulein Winkelmann.*
– ORIGIN German, diminutive of **FRAU**.

Fraunhofer /ˈfraʊnˌhəʊfə, German ˈfraʊnˌhoːfɐ/, Joseph von (1787–1826), German optician and pioneer in spectroscopy. He observed and mapped the dark lines in the solar spectrum (**Fraunhofer lines**) which result from the absorption of particular frequencies of light by elements present in the outer layers; these are now used to determine the chemical composition of the sun and stars.

fraxinella /ˌfraksɪˈnɛlə/ ▶ **noun** another term for **GAS PLANT**.
– ORIGIN mid 17th cent.: modern Latin (former specific epithet), diminutive of Latin *fraxinus* 'ash tree' (because of its leaves, thought to resemble those of the ash).

fray[1] ▶ **verb** [no obj.] (of a fabric, rope, or cord) unravel or become worn at the edge, typically through constant rubbing: *cheap fabric soon frays* | [as adj. **frayed**] *the frayed collar of her old coat.*
■figurative (of a person's nerves or temper) show the effects of strain. ■ [with obj.] (of a male deer) rub (a bush or small tree) with the head in order to remove the velvet from newly formed antlers, or to mark territory during the rut.
– ORIGIN late Middle English: from Old French *freiier*, from Latin *fricare* 'to rub'.

fray[2] ▶ **noun** (**the fray**) a situation of intense activity, typically one incorporating an element of aggression or competition: *nineteen companies intend to bid for the contract, with three more expected to* ***enter the fray.***
■a battle or fight.
– ORIGIN late Middle English: from archaic *fray* 'to quarrel', from *affray* 'startle', from Anglo-Norman French *afrayer* (see **AFFRAY**).

Fray Bentos /ˌfreɪ ˈbɛntɒs/ a port and meat-packing centre in western Uruguay; pop. 20,000 (1985).

Frazer, Sir James George (1854–1941), Scottish anthropologist. In *The Golden Bough* (1890–1915) he proposed an evolutionary theory of the development of human thought, from the magical and religious to the scientific.

Frazier /ˈfreɪzɪə/, Joe (b.1944), American boxer; full name *Joseph Frazier*. He first won the world title in 1968, lost it to George Foreman in 1973, and subsequently lost to Muhammad Ali twice before retiring in 1976.

frazil /ˈfreɪz(ə)l, frəˈzɪl/ (also **frazil ice**) ▶ **noun** [mass noun] N. Amer. soft or amorphous ice formed by the accumulation of ice crystals in water that is too turbulent to freeze solid.
– ORIGIN late 19th cent.: from Canadian French *frasil* 'snow floating in the water', from French *fraisil* 'cinders'.

frazzle informal ▶ **verb** [with obj.] **1** [usu. as adj. **frazzled**] cause to feel completely exhausted; wear out: *a frazzled parent.*
2 cause to shrivel up with burning: *we frazzle our hair with heated appliances.*
▶ **noun** (**a frazzle**) **1** the state of being completely exhausted or worn out: *I'm tired,* ***worn to a frazzle.***
2 the state of being completely burnt: *you need to understand how much sun your skin can tolerate before it* ***burns to a frazzle.***
– ORIGIN early 19th cent.: perhaps a blend of **FRAY**[1] and obsolete *fazle* 'ravel out', of Germanic origin. The word was originally East Anglian dialect; it came into standard British English via the US.

freak ▶ **noun 1** a very unusual and unexpected event or situation: *the teacher says the accident was a total freak* | [as modifier] *a freak storm.*
■(also **freak of nature**) a person, animal, or plant with an unusual physical abnormality. ■ informal a person regarded as strange because of their unusual appearance or behaviour. ■ [with modifier] informal a person who is obsessed with or unusually enthusiastic about a specified interest: *a fitness freak.* ■ [usu. with modifier] informal a person addicted to a drug of a particular kind: *the twins were cocaine freaks.*
2 archaic a sudden arbitrary change of mind; a whim: *follow this way or that, as the freak takes you.*
▶ **verb 1** [no obj.] informal react or behave in a wild and irrational way, typically because of the effects of extreme emotion, mental illness, or drugs: *I could have* ***freaked out*** *and started smashing the place up.*
■[with obj.] cause to act in such a way: *it really freaks me to think that people have travelled from all over Britain to see this.*
2 [with obj.] archaic fleck or streak randomly: *the white pink and the pansy freaked with jet.*

freaking ▶ **adjective** US informal used as a euphemism for 'fucking': *I'm going out of my freaking mind!*

freakish ▶ **adjective** very unusual, strange, or unexpected: *freakish weather.*
– DERIVATIVES **freakishly** adverb, **freakishness** noun.

freak-out ▶ **noun** informal a wildly irrational reaction or spell of behaviour.

freak show ▶ **noun** a sideshow at a fair, featuring abnormally developed people or animals.
■an unusual or grotesque event viewed for pleasure, especially when in bad taste.

freaky ▶ **adjective** (**freakier**, **freakiest**) informal very odd, strange, or eccentric.
– DERIVATIVES **freakily** adverb, **freakiness** noun.

freckle ▶ **noun** a small patch of light brown colour on the skin, often becoming more pronounced through exposure to the sun.
▶ **verb** cover or become covered with freckles: [no obj.] *skin which freckles easily* | [as adj. **freckled**] *a freckled face.*
– DERIVATIVES **freckly** adjective.
– ORIGIN late Middle English: alteration of dialect *frecken*, from Old Norse *freknur* (plural).

freckle-faced ▶ **adjective** having freckles on the face.

Frederick I (*c.*1123–90), king of Germany and Holy Roman emperor 1152–90; known as **Frederick Barbarossa** ('Redbeard'). He made a sustained attempt to subdue Italy and the papacy, but was eventually defeated at the battle of Legnano in 1176.

Frederick II (1712–86), king of Prussia 1740–86; known as **Frederick the Great**. His campaigns in the War of the Austrian Succession (1740–8) and the Seven Years War (1756–63) succeeded in considerably strengthening Prussia's position; by the end of his reign he had doubled the area of his country.

Frederick William (1620–88), Elector of Brandenburg 1640–88; known as **the Great Elector**. His programme of reconstruction and reorganization following the Thirty Years War brought stability to his country and laid the basis for the expansion of Prussian power in the 18th century.

Fredericton /ˈfrɛdrɪktən/ the capital of New Brunswick, Canada; pop. 45,360 (1991).
– ORIGIN named after *Frederick* Augustus, second son of George III.

free ▶ **adjective** (**freer**, **freest**) **1** not under the control or in the power of another; able to act or be done as one wishes: *I have no ambitions other than to have a happy life and be free* | *a free choice.*
■(of a state or its citizens or institutions) subject neither to foreign domination nor to despotic government: *a free press.* ■ [often as complement] not or no longer confined or imprisoned: *the researchers set the birds free.* ■ historical not a slave. ■ [with infinitive] able or permitted to take a specified action: *you are free to leave.* ■ [in names] denoting an ethnic or political group actively opposing an occupying or invading force, in particular the groups that continued resisting the Germans in the Second World War after the fall of their countries. See also **FREE FRENCH**.
2 [often as complement] not physically restrained, obstructed, or fixed; unimpeded: *she lifted the cat free.*
■Physics (of power or energy) disengaged or available. See also **FREE ENERGY**. ■ Physics & Chemistry not bound in an atom, a molecule, or a compound: *the atmosphere of that time contained virtually no free oxygen.* See also **FREE RADICAL**. ■ Linguistics denoting a linguistic form that can be used in isolation.
3 not subject to or constrained by engagements or obligations: *she spent her free time shopping.*
■(of a facility or piece of equipment) not occupied or in use: *the bathroom was free.*
4 [predic.] (**free of/from**) not subject to or affected by (a specified thing, typically an undesirable one): *membership is free of charge.*
5 given or available without charge: *free health care.*
6 using or expending something without restraint; lavish: *she was always* ***free with*** *her money.*
■frank or unrestrained in speech, expression, or action: *he was free in his talk of revolution.* ■ archaic overfamiliar or forward in manner.
7 (of a literary style) not observing the strict laws of form.
■(of a translation) conveying only the broad sense; not literal.
8 Sailing (of the wind) blowing from a favourable direction to the side or aft of a vessel.
▶ **adverb 1** without cost or payment: *ladies were admitted free.*

a **cat** | ɑː **arm** | ɛ **bed** | ɛː **hair** | ə **ago** | əː **her** | ɪ **sit** | i **cosy** | iː **see** | ɒ **hot** | ɔː **saw** | ʌ **run** | ʊ **put** | uː **too** | ʌɪ **my** | aʊ **how** | eɪ **day** | əʊ **no** | ɪə **near** | ɔɪ **boy** | ʊə **poor** | ʌɪə **fire** | aʊə **sour**

2 Sailing with the sheets eased.

▶ verb (**frees**, **freed**, **freeing**) [with obj.] make free, in particular:

■from captivity, confinement, or slavery: *they were freed from jail.* ■ from physical obstruction, restraint, or entanglement: *I had to tug hard and at last freed him.* ■ from restriction or excessive regulation: *his inheritance freed him from financial constraints.* ■ from something undesirable: *free your mind and body of excess tension.* ■ so as to become available for a particular purpose: *we are freeing management time for alternative work.*

– PHRASES **for free** informal without cost or payment: *these professionals were giving their time for free.* **free and easy** informal and relaxed. **free, gratis, and for nothing** humorous without charge. **a free hand** freedom to act at one's own discretion. **free on board** (or **rail**) (abbrev.: **f.o.b.** or **f.o.r.**) including or assuming delivery without charge to a ship or railway wagon. **(a) free rein** see REIN. **a free ride** used in reference to a situation in which someone benefits without having to make a fair contribution: *people have been having a free ride, paying so little rent that there is no money for maintenance.* **the free world** the non-communist countries of the world, as formerly opposed to the Soviet bloc. **it's a free country** said when asserting that a course of action is not illegal or forbidden, often in justification of it. **make free with** treat without ceremony or proper respect: *he'll have something to say about your making free with his belongings.*

– DERIVATIVES **freeness** noun.

– ORIGIN Old English *frēo* (adjective), *frēon* (verb), of Germanic origin; related to Dutch *vrij* and German *frei*, from an Indo-European root meaning 'to love', shared by FRIEND.

-free ▶ combining form free of or from: *smoke-free* | *tax-free.*

– ORIGIN from FREE.

free agent ▶ noun a person who does not have any commitments that restrict their actions.

■a sports player who is not bound by a contract and so is eligible to join any team.

free association ▶ noun [mass noun] **1** Psychology the mental process by which one word or image may spontaneously suggest another without any necessary logical connection.

■a psychoanalytic technique for investigation of the unconscious mind, in which a relaxed subject reports all passing thoughts without reservation. **2** the forming of a group, political alliance, or other organization without any constraint or external restriction.

free ball ▶ noun Snooker the option to nominate any ball as the object ball when snookered as a result of a foul stroke.

freebase (also **freebase cocaine**) ▶ noun [mass noun] cocaine that has been purified by heating with ether, taken by inhaling the fumes or smoking the residue.

▶ verb [with obj.] take (cocaine) in such a way.

freebie ▶ noun informal a thing given free of charge.

– ORIGIN 1940s (originally US): an arbitrary formation from FREE.

freeboard ▶ noun the height of a ship's side between the waterline and the deck.

freebooter ▶ noun a pirate or lawless adventurer.

– DERIVATIVES **freeboot** verb.

– ORIGIN late 16th cent.: from Dutch *vrijbuiter*, from *vrij* 'free' + *buit* 'booty', + the noun suffix *-er*. Compare with FILIBUSTER.

freeborn ▶ adjective not born in slavery.

Free Church ▶ noun a Christian Church which has dissented or seceded from an established Church.

Free Church of Scotland a strict Presbyterian Church organized by dissenting members of the established Church of Scotland in 1843. In 1900 its majority amalgamated with the United Presbyterian Church to form the United Free Church; its name was retained by the minority group, nicknamed the **Wee Free Kirk** (see WEE FREE).

free climbing ▶ noun [mass noun] rock climbing without the assistance of devices such as pegs placed in the rock, but occasionally using ropes and belays. Compare with AID CLIMBING.

– DERIVATIVES **free climb** noun & verb.

freedman ▶ noun (pl. **-men**) historical an emancipated slave.

freedom ▶ noun [mass noun] the power or right to act, speak, or think as one wants without hindrance or restraint: *we do have some freedom of choice* | [count noun] *he talks of revoking some of the freedoms.*

■absence of subjection to foreign domination or despotic government: *he was a champion of Irish freedom.* ■ the state of not being imprisoned or enslaved: *the shark thrashed its way to freedom.* ■ the state of being physically unrestricted and able to move easily: *the shorts have a side split for freedom of movement.* ■ **(freedom from)** the state of not being subject to or affected by (a particular undesirable thing): *government policies to achieve freedom from want.* ■ the power of self-determination attributed to the will; the quality of being independent of fate or necessity. ■ **(the freedom of —)** a special right or privilege given to someone, especially as an honour to a distinguished public figure, allowing them full citizenship of a particular city: *he accepted the freedom of the City of Glasgow.* ■ unrestricted use of something: *the dog is happy having the freedom of the house when we are out.* ■ archaic familiarity or openness in speech or behaviour.

– ORIGIN Old English *frēodōm* (see FREE, -DOM).

freedom fighter ▶ noun a person who takes part in a violent struggle to achieve a political goal, especially in order to overthrow their government.

freedom of conscience ▶ noun [mass noun] the right to follow one's own beliefs in matters of religion and morality.

freedom of religion ▶ noun [mass noun] the right to practise whatever religion one chooses.

freedom song ▶ noun (in South Africa) a song or chant sung at protest gatherings and demonstrations, strongly political in content and typically in a formulaic call-and-response style.

free energy ▶ noun [mass noun] Physics a thermodynamic quantity equivalent to the capacity of a system to do work. See also GIBBS FREE ENERGY.

free enterprise ▶ noun [mass noun] an economic system in which private business operates in competition and largely free of state control.

free fall ▶ noun [mass noun] downward movement under the force of gravity only: *the path of a body in free fall.*

■the movement of a spacecraft in space without thrust from the engines.

▶ verb (**free-fall**) [no obj.] move under the force of gravity only; fall rapidly.

free fight ▶ noun a general fight involving all of those present.

free flight ▶ noun [mass noun] the flight of a spacecraft, rocket, or missile when the engine is not producing thrust.

free-floating ▶ adjective not attached to anything and able to move freely: *free-floating aquatic plants.*

■figurative not assigned to a fixed or particular position, category, or level: *free-floating exchange rates.* ■ (of a person) not committed to a particular cause or political party. ■ Psychiatry (of anxiety) chronic and generalized, without an obvious cause.

– DERIVATIVES **free-float** verb, **free-floater** noun.

Freefone ▶ noun variant spelling of FREEPHONE.

free-for-all ▶ noun a disorganized or unrestricted situation or event in which everyone may take part, especially a fight, discussion, or trading market.

free-form ▶ adjective not conforming to a regular or formal structure or shape: *a free-form jazz improvisation.*

Free French ▶ plural noun an organization of French troops and volunteers in exile formed under General de Gaulle in 1940. Based in London, the movement organized forces that opposed the Axis powers in French Equatorial Africa, Lebanon, and elsewhere, and cooperated with the French Resistance.

freehand ▶ adjective & adverb (especially with reference to drawing) done manually without the aid of instruments such as rulers: [as adj.] *a freehand sketch* | [as adv.] *the pictures should be drawn freehand.*

free-handed ▶ adjective generous, especially with money.

– DERIVATIVES **free-handedly** adverb, **free-handedness** noun.

freehold ▶ noun [mass noun] permanent and absolute tenure of land or property with freedom to dispose of it at will. Often contrasted with LEASEHOLD.

■**(the freehold)** the ownership of a piece of land or property by such tenure. ■ [count noun] chiefly Brit. a piece of land or property held by such tenure.

▶ adjective held by or having the status of freehold.

– DERIVATIVES **freeholder** noun.

free house ▶ noun Brit. a public house not controlled by a brewery and therefore not restricted to selling particular brands of beer or liquor.

free jazz ▶ noun [mass noun] an improvised style of jazz characterized by the absence of set chord patterns or time patterns.

free kick ▶ noun (in soccer and rugby) an unimpeded kick of the stationary ball awarded to one side as a penalty for a foul or infringement by the other side.

free labour ▶ noun [mass noun] chiefly Brit. the labour of workers not in a trade union.

freelance /ˈfriːlɑːns/ ▶ adjective working for different companies at different times rather than being permanently employed by one company: *a freelance journalist.*

■independent or uncommitted in politics or personal life.

▶ adverb earning one's living in such a way: *I work freelance from home.*

▶ noun **1** a person who earns their living in such a way.

2 historical a medieval mercenary.

▶ verb [no obj.] earn one's living as a freelance.

– ORIGIN early 19th cent. (denoting a mercenary): originally as two words.

freelancer ▶ noun a person who works freelance.

free-living ▶ adjective Biology living freely and independently, not as a parasite or attached to a substrate.

freeloader ▶ noun informal a person who takes advantage of others' generosity without giving anything in return.

– DERIVATIVES **freeload** verb.

free love ▶ noun [mass noun] the idea or practice of having sexual relations according to choice, without being restricted by marriage or long-term relationships.

freely ▶ adverb not under the control of another; as one wishes: *I roamed freely.*

■without restriction or interference: *air can freely circulate.* ■ in copious or generous amounts: *she drank freely to keep up her courage.* ■ openly and honestly: *you may speak freely.* ■ willingly and readily; without compulsion: *I freely confess to this failing.*

freeman ▶ noun (pl. **-men**) **1** a person who has been given the freedom of a city or borough. **2** historical a person who is not a slave or serf.

free market ▶ noun an economic system in which prices are determined by unrestricted competition between privately owned businesses.

– DERIVATIVES **free marketeer** noun.

freemartin /ˈfriːmɑːtɪn/ ▶ noun a hermaphrodite or imperfect sterile female calf which is the twin of a male calf whose hormones affected its development.

– ORIGIN late 17th cent.: of unknown origin.

Freemason ▶ noun a member of an international order established for mutual help and fellowship, which holds elaborate secret ceremonies.

> The original **free masons** were itinerant skilled stonemasons of the 14th century, who are said to have recognized fellow craftsmen by secret signs. Modern freemasonry is usually traced to the formation of the Grand Lodge in London in 1717; members are typically professionals and businessmen.

freemasonry ▶ noun [mass noun] **1** the system and institutions of the Freemasons. **2** instinctive sympathy or fellow feeling between people with something in common: *the unshakeable freemasonry of actors in a crisis.*

free pardon ▶ noun an unconditional remission of the legal consequences of an offence or conviction.

Freephone (also trademark **Freefone**) ▶ noun a telephone service whereby a subscribing organization can pay for incoming calls made by its clients or customers.

free port ▶ noun a port open to all traders.

■a port area where goods in transit are exempt from customs duty.

Freepost ▶ noun [mass noun] Brit. (chiefly as an

element of an address) a postal service whereby the cost of postage is paid by the business that receives the letter.

free radical ▶ noun Chemistry an uncharged molecule (typically highly reactive and short-lived) having an unpaired valency electron.

free-range ▶ adjective (of livestock, especially poultry) kept in natural conditions, with freedom of movement.
■(of eggs) produced by birds reared under such conditions.

freeride ▶ noun (also **freeride board**) a type of snowboard designed for all-round use on and off piste.
▶ verb [no obj.] ride such a snowboard, especially when not competing in races or performing tricks.

free safety ▶ noun American Football a defensive back who is usually free from an assignment to cover a particular player on the opposing team.

free school ▶ noun historical a school for which no fees are charged, typically run at public expense.

free sheet ▶ noun a free newspaper.

freesia /ˈfriːzɪə/ ▶ noun a small southern African plant with fragrant, colourful, tubular flowers, many varieties of which are cultivated for the cut-flower trade.
● Genus *Freesia*, family Iridaceae.
– ORIGIN modern Latin, named after Friedrich H. T. *Freese* (died 1876), German physician.

free skating ▶ noun [mass noun] the sport of performing variable skating figures to music.

free space ▶ noun [mass noun] Physics space unoccupied by matter or, more particularly, containing no electromagnetic or gravitational field and used as a reference.

free speech ▶ noun [mass noun] the right to express any opinions without censorship or restraint.

free spirit ▶ noun an independent or uninhibited person.

free-spoken ▶ adjective archaic speaking candidly and openly.

free-standing ▶ adjective not supported by another structure.
■not relying on or linked to anything else; independent: *if extracts rather than complete texts are used, they should be free-standing and coherent.*

free state ▶ noun **1** US historical a state of the US in which slavery did not exist.
■(the Free State) informal name for MARYLAND.
2 (Free State) a province in central South Africa, situated to the north of the Orange River; capital, Bloemfontein. Formerly called (until 1995) ORANGE FREE STATE.

Free Stater ▶ noun historical a member of the Irish Free State army.

freestone ▶ noun **1** [mass noun] a fine-grained stone which can be cut easily in any direction, in particular a type of sandstone or limestone.
2 a stone fruit in which the stone is easily separated from the flesh when the fruit is ripe: [as modifier] *freestone peaches.* Contrasted with CLINGSTONE.

freestyle ▶ adjective denoting a contest or version of a sport in which there are few restrictions on the moves or techniques that competitors employ: *freestyle wrestling.*
▶ noun a contest of such a kind, in particular a swimming race in which competitors may use any stroke.
– DERIVATIVES **freestyler** noun.

free-tailed bat ▶ noun a streamlined fast-flying insectivorous bat with a projecting tail, found in tropical and subtropical countries.
● Family Molossidae: several genera and numerous species, including the mastiff bats and hairless bats.

freethinker ▶ noun a person who rejects accepted opinions, especially those concerning religious belief.
– DERIVATIVES **freethinking** noun & adjective.

free throw ▶ noun Basketball an unimpeded attempt at a goal awarded to a player following a foul or other infringement.

Freetown the capital and chief port of Sierra Leone; pop. 505,080 (1992).

free trade ▶ noun [mass noun] international trade left to its natural course without tariffs, quotas, or other restrictions.

free vector ▶ noun Mathematics a vector of which only the magnitude and direction are specified, not the position or line of action.

free verse ▶ noun [mass noun] poetry that does not rhyme or have a regular rhythm. Also called VERS LIBRE.

free vote ▶ noun chiefly Brit. a parliamentary division in which members vote according to their own beliefs rather than following a party policy.

freeware ▶ noun [mass noun] software that is available free of charge.

freeway ▶ noun N. Amer. a dual-carriageway main road, especially one with controlled access.
■a toll-free highway.

freewheel ▶ verb [no obj.] ride a bicycle with the pedals at rest, especially downhill: *the postman had come freewheeling down the track.*
■[usu. as adj. **freewheeling**] act without concern for rules, conventions, or the consequences of one's actions: *the freewheeling drug scene of the sixties.*

free wheel ▶ noun a bicycle wheel which is able to revolve freely when no power is being applied to it.

free will ▶ noun [mass noun] the power of acting without the constraint of necessity or fate; the ability to act at one's own discretion.
▶ adjective [attrib.] (especially of a donation) given readily; voluntary: *free-will offerings.*

freeze ▶ verb (past **froze**; past participle **frozen**) **1** [no obj.] (of a liquid) be turned into ice or another solid as a result of extreme cold: *in the winter the milk froze.*
■[with obj.] turn (a liquid) into ice or another solid in such a way. ■(of something wet or containing liquid) become blocked, covered, or rigid with ice: *the pipes had frozen.* ■[with obj.] cause (something wet or containing liquid) to become blocked, covered, or rigid with ice: [with complement] *the ground was frozen hard.* ■be or feel so cold that one is near death (often used hyperbolically): *you'll freeze to death standing there.* ■[with obj.] (of the weather) cause (someone) to feel so cold that they are near death. ■(of the weather) be at or below freezing: *at night it froze again.* ■[with obj.] deprive (a part of the body) of feeling, especially by the application of a chilled anaesthetic substance. ■[with obj.] treat (someone) with a cold manner; stare coldly at (someone): *she would freeze him with a look when he tried to talk to her.*
2 [with obj.] store (something) at a very low temperature in order to preserve it: *the cake can be frozen.*
■[no obj., with complement] (of food) be able to be preserved in such a way: *this soup freezes well.*
3 [no obj.] become suddenly motionless or paralysed with fear or shock: *she froze in horror* | *some people freeze up and look completely false.*
■stop moving when ordered or directed.
4 [with obj.] hold (something) at a fixed level or in a fixed state for a period of time: *new spending on defence was to be frozen.*
■prevent (assets) from being used for a period of time: *the charity's bank account has been frozen.* ■stop (a moving image) at a particular frame when filming or viewing: *the camera will set fast shutter speeds to freeze the action.* ■[no obj.] (of a computer screen) become temporarily locked because of system problems.
▶ noun **1** an act of holding or being held at a fixed level or in a fixed state: *workers faced a pay freeze.*
■short for FREEZE-FRAME.
2 informal a period of frost or very cold weather: *the big freeze surprised the weathermen.*
– PHRASES **freeze one's blood** (or **one's blood freezes**) fill (or be filled) with a sudden feeling of great fear or horror.
– DERIVATIVES **freezable** adjective, **frozenly** adverb.
– ORIGIN Old English *frēosan* (in the phrase *hit frēoseth* 'it is freezing, it is so cold that water turns to ice'), of Germanic origin; related to Dutch *vriezen* and German *frieren*, from an Indo-European root shared by Latin *pruina* 'hoar frost' and FROST.
▶**freeze someone out** informal behave in a hostile or obstructive way so as to exclude someone from something.
freeze on to informal, dated hold on tightly or be very attentive to: *we'll freeze on to those facts.*

freeze-dry ▶ verb [with obj.] [usu. as adj. **freeze-dried**] preserve (something) by rapidly freezing it and then subjecting it to a high vacuum which removes ice by sublimation: *freeze-dried beef stew.*

freeze-frame ▶ noun [mass noun] the facility of stopping a film or videotape in order to view a motionless image.

■[count noun] a motionless image obtained with such a facility.
▶ verb [with obj.] use such a facility on (an image or a recording).

freeze-out ▶ noun informal an exclusion of a person or organization from something, by boycotting or ignoring them.

freezer ▶ noun a refrigerated cabinet or room for preserving food at very low temperatures.

freeze-up ▶ noun a period of extreme cold.

freezing ▶ adjective below 0°C: *strong winds and freezing temperatures.*
■(used hyperbolically) very cold: *he was freezing and miserable* | [as submodifier] *it was freezing cold outside.* ■(of fog or rain) consisting of droplets which freeze rapidly on contact with a surface to form ice crystals.
▶ noun the freezing point of water: *the temperature was well above freezing.*

freezing mixture ▶ noun a mixture of two or more substances (e.g. ice water and salt, or dry ice and alcohol) which can be used to produce temperatures below the freezing point of water.

freezing point ▶ noun the temperature at which a liquid turns into a solid when cooled.

freezing works ▶ plural noun [treated as sing.] Austral./NZ a place where animals are slaughtered and carcasses frozen for export.

Frege /ˈfreɪɡə/, Gottlob (1848–1925), German philosopher and mathematician, founder of modern logic. He developed a logical system for the expression of mathematics. He also worked on general questions of philosophical logic and semantics and devised his influential theory of meaning, based on his use of a distinction between what a linguistic term refers to and what it expresses.

Freiburg /ˈfraɪbɜːɡ, German ˈfraɪbʊrk/ an industrial city in SW Germany, in Baden-Württemberg, on the edge of the Black Forest; pop. 193,775 (1991). Full name **FREIBURG IM BREISGAU** /ɪm ˈbraɪsɡaʊ/, German ɪm ˈbraɪsɡaʊ/.

freight /freɪt/ ▶ noun [mass noun] goods transported in bulk by truck, train, ship, or aircraft.
■a charge for such transport.
▶ verb [with obj.] transport (goods) in bulk by truck, train, ship, or aircraft: *the metals had been freighted from the city* | [no obj.] *collieries selling produce to ships freighting to Dublin.*
■(be freighted with) figurative be laden or burdened with: *each word was freighted with anger.*
– ORIGIN late Middle English (in the sense 'hire of a ship for transporting goods'): from Middle Dutch, Middle Low German *vrecht*, variant of *vracht* 'ship's cargo'. Compare with FRAUGHT.

freightage ▶ noun [mass noun] the carrying of goods in bulk.
■goods carried in bulk; freight.

freighter ▶ noun a large ship or aircraft designed to carry goods in bulk.
■a person who loads, receives, or forwards goods for transport.

freighting ▶ noun [mass noun] the action of transporting goods in bulk by truck, train, ship, or aircraft.

Freightliner ▶ noun Brit. trademark a train carrying freight in containers.

freight ton ▶ noun see TON¹ (sense 1).

Frelimo /frɛˈliːməʊ/ the nationalist liberation party of Mozambique, founded in 1962. After independence in 1975, Frelimo governed Mozambique as a one-party state until 1990, when a multiparty system was introduced.
– ORIGIN Portuguese, contraction of *Frente de Libertação de Moçambique*, the name of the party.

Fremantle /ˈfriːmant(ə)l/ the principal port of Western Australia, part of the Perth metropolitan area; pop. 24,000 (est. 1987).

Frémont /ˈfriːmɒnt/, John Charles (1813–90), American explorer and politician. He was responsible for exploring several viable routes to the Pacific across the Rockies in the 1840s.

French ▶ adjective of or relating to France or its people or language.
▶ noun **1** [mass noun] the language of France, also used in parts of Belgium, Switzerland, and Canada, in several countries of northern and western Africa and the Caribbean, and elsewhere.

2 short for **FRENCH VERMOUTH**.
3 [as plural noun **the French**] the people of France collectively.

French is the first or official language of over 200 million people and is widely used as a second language. It is a Romance language which developed from the Latin spoken in Gaul; it had a very great influence on English as the language of the Norman ruling class.

– PHRASES (**if you'll**) **excuse** (or **pardon**) **my French** informal used to apologize for swearing.
– DERIVATIVES **Frenchness** noun.
– ORIGIN Old English *Frencisc*, of Germanic origin, from the base of **FRANK**[2].

French bean ▶ noun Brit. a tropical American bean plant of which many varieties are commercially cultivated.
 ● *Phaseolus vulgaris*, family Leguminosae: many varieties, including the haricot bean and the kidney bean.
 ■ the seed of this plant used as food.

French bread ▶ noun [mass noun] white bread in a long, crisp loaf.

French Canadian ▶ noun a Canadian whose principal language is French.
▶ adjective of or relating to French-speaking Canadians or their language.

French chalk ▶ noun [mass noun] a kind of steatite used for marking cloth and removing grease and, in powder form, as a dry lubricant.

French Congo former name (until 1910) for **FRENCH EQUATORIAL AFRICA**.

French cricket ▶ noun [mass noun] an informal game resembling cricket but played with a soft ball which is bowled at the batter's legs.

French cuff ▶ noun a shirt cuff that is folded back before fastening, creating a double-layered cuff.

French curve ▶ noun a template used for drawing curved lines.

French door ▶ noun chiefly N. Amer. a French window.

French dressing ▶ noun [mass noun] a salad dressing of vinegar, oil, and seasonings.
 ■ N. Amer. a sweet, creamy salad dressing commercially prepared from oil, tomato purée, and spices.

French Equatorial Africa a former federation of French territories in west central Africa (1910–58). Previously called French Congo, its constituent territories were Chad, Ubanghi Shari (now the Central African Republic), Gabon, and Middle Congo (now Congo).

French flageolet ▶ noun see **FLAGEOLET**[1].

French fries (chiefly Brit. also **French fried potatoes**) ▶ plural noun chiefly N. Amer. potatoes deep-fried in thin strips; chips.

French Guiana an overseas department of France, in northern South America; pop. 96,000 (est. 1991); capital, Cayenne.

French horn ▶ noun a brass instrument with a coiled tube, valves, and a wide bell, developed from the simple hunting horn in the 17th century. It is played with the right hand in the bell to soften the tone and increase the range of available harmonics.

Frenchie ▶ noun (pl. **-ies**) variant spelling of **FRENCHY**.

Frenchify ▶ verb (**-ies**, **-ied**) [with obj.] [usu. as adj. **Frenchified**] often derogatory make French in form, character, or manners: *Frenchified academicians*.

French kiss ▶ noun a kiss with contact between tongues.
– DERIVATIVES **French kissing** noun.

French knickers ▶ plural noun loose-fitting, wide-legged knickers, typically of silk or satin.

French knot ▶ noun (in embroidery) a stitch in which the thread is wound around the needle, which is then passed back through the fabric at almost the same point to form a small dot.

French leave ▶ noun [mass noun] informal, dated absence from work or duty without permission.
– ORIGIN mid 18th cent.: said to derive from the French custom of leaving a dinner or ball without saying goodbye to the host or hostess. The phrase was first recorded shortly after the Seven Years War; the equivalent French expression is *filer à l'Anglaise*, literally 'to escape in the style of the English'.

French letter ▶ noun Brit. informal, dated a condom.

French loaf ▶ noun a loaf of French bread.

Frenchman ▶ noun (pl. **-men**) **1** a man who is French by birth or descent.

2 a knife with a right-angled bend in its blade, used in bricklaying.

French mustard ▶ noun [mass noun] Brit. mild mustard mixed with vinegar.

French plait ▶ noun a woman's hairstyle in which all the hair is gathered into one large plait down the back of the head, starting from the forehead.

French pleat ▶ noun **1** a French roll.
2 a pleat at the top of a curtain consisting of three smaller pleats.

French polish ▶ noun [mass noun] shellac polish that produces a high gloss on wood.
▶ verb (**french-polish**) [with obj.] treat (wood) with such a polish.

French Polynesia an overseas territory of France in the South Pacific; pop. 200,000 (est. 1991); capital, Papeete (on Tahiti). French Polynesia comprises the Society Islands, the Gambier Islands, the Tuamotu Archipelago, the Tubuai Islands, and the Marquesas. It became an overseas territory of France in 1946, and was granted partial autonomy in 1977.

French Republican calendar ▶ noun a reformed calendar officially introduced by the French Republican government on 5 October 1793, having twelve months of thirty days each, with five days of festivals at the year's end (six in leap years). It was abandoned under the Napoleonic regime and the Gregorian calendar was formally reinstated on 1 January 1806.

French Revolution the overthrow of the Bourbon monarchy in France (1789–99).

The Revolution began with the meeting of the legislative assembly (the States General) in May 1789, when the French government was already in crisis; the Bastille was stormed in July of the same year. The Revolution became steadily more radical and ruthless with power increasingly in the hands of the Jacobins and Robespierre; Louis XVI's execution in January 1793 was followed by Robespierre's Reign of Terror. The Revolution failed to produce a stable form of republican government and after several different forms of administration the last, the Directory, was overthrown by Napoleon in 1799.

French roll ▶ noun a hairstyle in which the hair is tucked into a vertical roll down the back of the head.

French roof ▶ noun a mansard roof.

French seam ▶ noun a seam with the raw edges enclosed.

French Somaliland /səˈmɑːlɪˌland/ former name (until 1967) for **DJIBOUTI**.

French Southern and Antarctic Territories an overseas territory of France, comprising Adélie Land in Antarctica, and the Kerguelen and Crozet archipelagos and the islands of Amsterdam and St Paul in the southern Indian Ocean.

French stick ▶ noun a French loaf.

French Sudan former name for **MALI**.

French tickler ▶ noun informal a condom with ribbed protrusions.

French toast ▶ noun [mass noun] bread coated in egg and milk and fried.
 ■ Brit. bread buttered on one side and toasted on the other.

French vermouth ▶ noun [mass noun] Brit. dry vermouth.

French Wars of Religion a series of religious and political conflicts in France (1562–98) involving the Protestant Huguenots on one side and Catholic groups on the other. The wars were complicated by interventions from Spain, Rome, England, the Netherlands, and elsewhere, and were not brought to an end until the settlement of the Edict of Nantes.

French West Africa a former federation of French territories in NW Africa (1895–1959). Its constituent territories were Senegal, Mauritania, French Sudan (now Mali), Upper Volta (now Burkina), Niger, French Guinea (now Guinea), the Ivory Coast, and Dahomey (now Benin).

French window ▶ noun (usu. **French windows**) each of a pair of glazed doors in an outside wall, serving as a window and door, typically opening on to a garden or balcony.

Frenchwoman ▶ noun (pl. **-women**) a female native or national of France, or a woman of French descent.

Frenchy (also **Frenchie**) ▶ adjective informal, chiefly derogatory perceived as characteristically French: *a perfect example of that kind of progressive Frenchy art*.
▶ noun (pl. **-ies**) **1** informal, chiefly derogatory a French person.
 ■ Canadian a French Canadian.
 2 Brit. informal, dated short for **FRENCH LETTER**.

frenetic /frəˈnɛtɪk/ ▶ adjective fast and energetic in a rather wild and uncontrolled way: *a frenetic pace of activity*.
– DERIVATIVES **frenetically** adverb, **freneticism** noun.
– ORIGIN late Middle English (in the sense 'insane'): from Old French *frenetique*, via Latin fróm Greek *phrenitikos*, from *phrenitis* 'delirium', from *phrēn* 'mind'. Compare with **FRANTIC**.

frenulum /ˈfriːnjʊləm/ (also **fraenulum**) ▶ noun Anatomy a small fold or ridge of tissue which supports or checks the motion of the part to which it is attached, in particular a fold of skin beneath the tongue, or between the lip and the gum.
 ■ Entomology (in some moths and butterflies) a bristle or row of bristles on the edge of the hindwing which keeps it in contact with the forewing.
– ORIGIN early 18th cent.: modern Latin, diminutive of Latin *frenum* 'bridle'.

frenum /ˈfriːnəm/ (also **fraenum**) ▶ noun another term for **FRENULUM**.
– ORIGIN mid 18th cent.: from Latin, literally 'bridle'.

frenzied ▶ adjective wildly excited or uncontrolled: *a frenzied attack*.
– DERIVATIVES **frenziedly** adverb.

frenzy ▶ noun (pl. **-ies**) [usu. in sing.] a state or period of uncontrolled excitement or wild behaviour: *Doreen worked herself into a frenzy of rage*.
– ORIGIN Middle English: from Old French *frenesie*, from medieval Latin *phrenesia*, from Latin *phrenesis*, from Greek *phrēn* 'mind'.

freon /ˈfriːɒn/ (also **Freon**) ▶ noun [mass noun] trademark an aerosol propellant, refrigerant, or organic solvent consisting of one or more of a group of chlorofluorocarbons and related compounds.
– ORIGIN 1930s: of unknown origin.

frequency ▶ noun (pl. **-ies**) **1** [mass noun] the rate at which something occurs or is repeated over a particular period of time or in a given sample: *shops have closed with increasing frequency during the period*.
 ■ the fact of being frequent or happening often.
 2 the rate at which a vibration occurs which constitutes a wave, either in a material (as in sound waves), or in an electromagnetic field (as in radio waves and light), usually measured per second. (Symbol: **f** or **ν**)
 ■ the particular waveband at which a radio station or other system broadcasts or transmits signals.
– ORIGIN mid 16th cent. (gradually superseding late Middle English *frequence*; originally denoting a gathering of people): from Latin *frequentia*, from *frequens*, *frequent-* 'crowded, frequent'.

frequency distribution ▶ noun Statistics a mathematical function showing the number of instances in which a variable takes each of its possible values.

frequency division multiplex ▶ noun [mass noun] Telecommunications a technique for sending two or more signals over the same telephone line, radio channel, or other medium. Each signal is transmitted as a unique range of frequencies within the bandwidth of the channel as a whole, enabling several signals to be transmitted simultaneously. Compare with **TIME DIVISION MULTIPLEX**.

frequency modulation (abbrev.: **FM**) ▶ noun [mass noun] the modulation of a radio or other wave by variation of its frequency, especially to carry an audio signal. Often contrasted with **AMPLITUDE MODULATION**.

frequency response ▶ noun [mass noun] Electronics the dependence on signal frequency of the output–input ratio of an amplifier or other device.

frequent ▶ adjective /ˈfriːkw(ə)nt/ occurring or done on many occasions, in many cases, or in quick succession: *frequent changes in policy* | *the showers will become heavier and more frequent*.
 ■ [attrib.] (of a person) doing something often; habitual: *a frequent visitor to Scotland*. ■ archaic found at short distances apart: *walls flanked by frequent square towers*. ■ Medicine, dated (of the pulse) rapid.
▶ verb /frɪˈkwɛnt/ [with obj.] visit (a place) often or habitually: *pubs frequented by soldiers* | [as adj., with

submodifier] (**frequented**) *one of the most frequented sites.*
– DERIVATIVES **frequentation** noun, **frequenter** noun, **frequently** adverb.
– ORIGIN late Middle English (in the sense 'profuse, ample'): from French, or from Latin *frequens, frequent-* 'crowded, frequent', of unknown ultimate origin.

frequentative /frɪˈkwɛntətɪv/ Grammar ▶ **adjective** (of a verb or verbal form) expressing frequent repetition or intensity of action.
▶ **noun** a verb or verbal form of this type (for example *chatter* in English).
– ORIGIN mid 16th cent.: from French *fréquentatif, -ive* or Latin *frequentativus*, from *frequens, frequent-* 'crowded, frequent'.

fresco /ˈfrɛskəʊ/ ▶ **noun** (pl. **-oes** or **-os**) a painting done rapidly in watercolour on wet plaster on a wall or ceiling, so that the colours penetrate the plaster and become fixed as it dries.
■ [mass noun] this method of painting, used in Roman times and by the great masters of the Italian Renaissance including Giotto, Masaccio, and Michelangelo.
– DERIVATIVES **frescoed** adjective.
– ORIGIN late 16th cent.: Italian, literally 'cool, fresh'. The word was first recorded in the phrase *in fresco*, representing Italian *affresco, al fresco* 'on the fresh (plaster)'.

fresco secco ▶ **noun** see **SECCO**.

fresh ▶ **adjective** **1** not previously known or used; new or different: *the court had heard fresh evidence.*
2 recently created or experienced and not faded or impaired: *the memory was still fresh in their minds.*
■ (of food) recently made or obtained; not tinned, frozen, or otherwise preserved. ■ [predic.] (of a person) full of energy and vigour: *they are feeling fresh after a good night's sleep.* ■ (of a colour or a person's complexion) bright or healthy in appearance. ■ (of a person) attractively youthful and inexperienced. ■ [predic.] (**fresh from/out of**) (of a person) having just had (a particular experience) or come from (a particular place): *we were fresh out of art school.*
3 (of water) not salty.
■ pleasantly clean, pure, and cool: *a bit of fresh air does her good.*
4 (of the wind) cool and fairly strong:
■ Brit. informal (of the weather) rather cold and windy.
5 informal presumptuous or impudent towards someone, especially in a sexual way: *some of the men tried to* ***get fresh with*** *the girls.*
6 W. Indian having an unpleasant, slightly rotten smell: *this place was covered in water and smelled fresh like hell.*
▶ **adverb** [usu. in combination] newly; recently: *fresh-baked bread | fresh-cut grass.*
– PHRASES **be fresh out of** informal have just sold or run out of a supply of (something). (**as**) **fresh as a daisy** see **DAISY**. **fresh blood** see **BLOOD**.
– DERIVATIVES **freshness** noun.
– ORIGIN Old English *fersc* 'not salt, fit for drinking', superseded in Middle English by forms from Old French *freis, fresche*; both ultimately of Germanic origin and related to Dutch *vers* and German *frisch*.

fresh breeze ▶ **noun** a wind of force 5 on the Beaufort scale (22–27 knots or 40–50 kph).

freshen ▶ **verb** **1** [with obj.] make (something) newer, cleaner, or more attractive: *it didn't take long to freshen her make-up.*
■ chiefly N. Amer. add more liquid to (a drink); top up.
2 [no obj.] (of wind) become stronger and colder.
3 [no obj.] N. Amer. (of a cow) give birth and come into milk.
▶ **freshen up** revive oneself by washing oneself or changing into clean clothes: *he went off to freshen up in the local baths.* ■ (**freshen something up**) make something look newer or more attractive.

fresher ▶ **noun** Brit. informal term for **FRESHMAN**.

freshet /ˈfrɛʃɪt/ ▶ **noun** the flood of a river from heavy rain or melted snow.
■ a rush of fresh water flowing into the sea.
– ORIGIN late 16th cent.: probably from Old French *freschete*, diminutive of *freis* 'fresh'.

fresh-faced ▶ **adjective** having a clear and young-looking complexion.

fresh gale ▶ **noun** see **GALE**.

freshie (also **freshy**) ▶ **noun** Austral. a freshwater crocodile native to northern Australia.
• *Crocodylus johnstoni*, family Crocodylidae.

freshly ▶ **adverb** [usu. as submodifier] newly; recently: *freshly ground black pepper.*

freshman ▶ **noun** (pl. **-men**) a first-year student at university.
■ N. Amer. a first-year student at high school.

fresh-run ▶ **adjective** (of a migratory fish, especially a salmon) newly arrived in fresh water from the sea in order to spawn.

freshwater ▶ **adjective** **1** of or found in fresh water; not of the sea: *freshwater and marine fish.*
2 US informal (especially of a school or college) situated in a remote or obscure area; provincial.

freshwater flea ▶ **noun** another term for **DAPHNIA**.

freshwoman ▶ **noun** (pl. **-women**) a female first-year student.

freshy ▶ **noun** variant spelling of **FRESHIE**.

Fresnel /ˈfreɪn(ə)l, French frɛnɛl/, Augustin Jean (1788–1827), French physicist and civil engineer. He correctly postulated that light moves in a wave-like motion transverse to the direction of propagation, contrary to the longitudinal direction suggested by Christiaan Huygens and Thomas Young.

fresnel /freɪˈnɛl/ (also **fresnel lens**) ▶ **noun** Photography a flat lens made of a number of concentric rings, to reduce spherical aberration.
– ORIGIN mid 19th cent.: named after A. J. **FRESNEL**.

Fresno /ˈfrɛznəʊ/ a city in central California, in the San Joaquin valley; pop. 354,200 (1990).

fret[1] ▶ **verb** (**fretted, fretting**) **1** [no obj.] be constantly or visibly worried or anxious: *she fretted about the cost of groceries* | [with clause] *I fretted that my fingers were so skinny.*
■ [with obj.] cause (someone) worry or distress.
2 [with obj.] gradually wear away (something) by rubbing or gnawing: *the bay's black waves fret the seafront.*
■ form (a channel or passage) by rubbing or wearing away. ■ [no obj.] flow or move in small waves: *squelchy clay that fretted between his toes.*
▶ **noun** [in sing.] chiefly Brit. a state of anxiety or worry.
– ORIGIN Old English *fretan* 'devour, consume', of Germanic origin; related to Dutch *vreten* and German *fressen*, and ultimately to **FOR-** and **EAT**.

fret[2] ▶ **noun** **1** Art & Architecture a repeating ornamental design of vertical and horizontal lines, such as the Greek key pattern.
2 Heraldry a device of narrow diagonal bands interlaced through a diamond.
▶ **verb** (**fretted, fretting**) [with obj.] [usu. as adj. **fretted**] decorate with fretwork: *intricately carved and fretted balustrades.*
– ORIGIN late Middle English: from Old French *frete* 'trelliswork' and *freter* (verb), of unknown origin.

fret[3] ▶ **noun** each of a sequence of bars or ridges on the fingerboard of some stringed musical instruments (such as the guitar), used for fixing the positions of the fingers to produce the desired notes.
▶ **verb** (**fretted, fretting**) [with obj.] [often as adj. **fretted**] **1** provide (a stringed instrument) with frets.
2 play (a note) while pressing the string down against a fret: *fretted notes.*
– DERIVATIVES **fretless** adjective.
– ORIGIN early 16th cent.: of unknown origin.

fret[4] (also **sea fret**) ▶ **noun** N. English a mist coming in off the sea; a sea fog.
– ORIGIN mid 19th cent.: of unknown origin.

fretboard ▶ **noun** a fretted fingerboard on a guitar or other musical instrument.

fretful ▶ **adjective** feeling or expressing distress or irritation: *the baby was crying with a fretful whimper.*
– DERIVATIVES **fretfully** adverb, **fretfulness** noun.

fretsaw ▶ **noun** a saw with a narrow blade stretched vertically on a frame, for cutting thin wood in patterns.

fretwork ▶ **noun** [mass noun] ornamental design in wood, typically openwork, done with a fretsaw.

Freud[1] /frɔɪd/, Anna (1895–1982), Austrian-born British psychoanalyst, the youngest child of Sigmund Freud. She introduced important innovations in method and theory to her father's work, notably with regard to disturbed children, and set up a child therapy course and clinic in London.

Freud[2] /frɔɪd/, Lucian (b.1922), German-born British painter, grandson of Sigmund Freud. His subjects, typically portraits and nudes, are painted in a powerful naturalistic style.

Freud[3] /frɔɪd/, Sigmund (1856–1939), Austrian neurologist and psychotherapist.

> He was the first to emphasize the significance of unconscious processes in normal and neurotic behaviour, and was the founder of psychoanalysis as both a theory of personality and a therapeutic practice. He proposed the existence of an unconscious element in the mind which influences consciousness, and of conflicts in it between various sets of forces. Freud also stated the importance of a child's semi-consciousness of sex as a factor in mental development; his theory of the sexual origin of neuroses aroused great controversy.

Freudian Psychology ▶ **adjective** relating to or influenced by Sigmund Freud and his methods of psychoanalysis, especially with reference to the importance of sexuality in human behaviour.
■ susceptible to analysis in terms of unconscious desires: *he wasn't sure whether his passion for water power had some deep Freudian significance.*
▶ **noun** a follower of Freud or his methods.
– DERIVATIVES **Freudianism** noun.

Freudian slip ▶ **noun** an unintentional error regarded as revealing subconscious feelings.

Frey /freɪ/ (also **Freyr** /ˈfreɪə/) Scandinavian Mythology the god of fertility and dispenser of rain and sunshine.

Freya /ˈfreɪə/ Scandinavian Mythology the goddess of love and of the night, sister of Frey. She is often identified with Frigga.

Fri. ▶ **abbreviation for** Friday.

friable /ˈfrʌɪəb(ə)l/ ▶ **adjective** easily crumbled: *the soil was friable between her fingers.*
– DERIVATIVES **friability** noun, **friableness** noun.
– ORIGIN mid 16th cent.: from French, or from Latin *friabilis*, from *friare* 'to crumble'.

friar ▶ **noun** a member of any of certain religious orders of men, especially the four mendicant orders (Augustinians, Carmelites, Dominicans, and Franciscans).
– ORIGIN Middle English: from Old French *frere*, from Latin *frater* 'brother'.

friarbird ▶ **noun** a large Australasian honeyeater with a dark, partly naked head and a long curved bill.
• Genus *Philemon*, family Meliphagidae: many species.

Friar Minor ▶ **noun** a Franciscan friar.
– ORIGIN so named because the Franciscans regarded themselves of humbler rank than members of other orders.

friar's balsam (also **friars' balsam**) ▶ **noun** [mass noun] a solution containing benzoin in alcohol, used chiefly as an inhalant.

friary ▶ **noun** (pl. **-ies**) a building or community occupied by or consisting of friars.

fribble ▶ **noun** informal a frivolous or foolish person.
■ a thing of no great importance.
– ORIGIN mid 17th cent.: symbolic, from the earlier (now obsolete) verb meaning 'stammer', also 'act aimlessly or frivolously'.

fricandeau /ˈfrɪkandəʊ/ ▶ **noun** (pl. **fricandeaux** /-dəʊz/) a slice of meat, especially veal, cut from the leg.
■ a dish made from such meat, usually fried or stewed and served with a sauce.
– ORIGIN French, probably related to *fricassée* 'stew', from the verb *fricasser* (see **FRICASSEE**).

fricassee /ˈfrɪkəsiː, ˌfrɪkəˈsiː/ ▶ **noun** a dish of stewed or fried pieces of meat served in a thick white sauce.
▶ **verb** (**fricassees, fricasseed, fricasseeing**) [with obj.] make a fricassee of (something).
– ORIGIN from French *fricassée*, feminine past participle of *fricasser* 'cut up and cook in sauce' (probably a blend of *frire* 'to fry' and *casser* 'to break').

fricative /ˈfrɪkətɪv/ Phonetics ▶ **adjective** denoting a type of consonant made by the friction of breath in a narrow opening, producing a turbulent air flow.
▶ **noun** a consonant made in this way, e.g. *f* and *th*.
– ORIGIN mid 19th cent.: from modern Latin *fricativus*, from Latin *fricare* 'to rub'.

friction ▶ **noun** [mass noun] the resistance that one surface or object encounters when moving over another: *a lubrication system which reduces friction.*
■ the action of one surface or object rubbing against another: *the friction of braking.* ■ conflict or animosity caused by a clash of wills, temperaments, or

opinions: *a considerable amount of **friction** between father and son.*
– DERIVATIVES **frictionless** adjective.
– ORIGIN mid 16th cent. (denoting chafing or rubbing of the body or limbs, formerly much used in medical treatment): via French from Latin *frictio(n-)*, from *fricare* 'to rub'.

frictional ▶ **adjective** of or produced by the action of one surface or object rubbing against or moving over another: *frictional drag.*

frictional unemployment ▶ **noun** [mass noun] Economics the unemployment which exists in any economy due to people being in the process of moving from one job to another.

friction tape ▶ **noun** another term for **INSULATING TAPE**.

friction welding ▶ **noun** [mass noun] welding in which the heat is produced by rotating one component against the other under compression.

Friday ▶ **noun** the day of the week before Saturday and following Thursday: *he was arrested **on Friday** | the cleaning woman came on Fridays |* [as modifier] *Friday evening.*
▶ **adverb** on Friday: *we'll try again Friday.*
■ (**Fridays**) on Fridays; each Friday: *he goes there Fridays.*
– ORIGIN Old English *Frīgedæg*, named after the Germanic goddess **FRIGGA**; translation of late Latin *Veneris dies* 'day of the planet Venus'; compare with Dutch *vrijdag* and German *Freitag*.

fridge ▶ **noun** informal a refrigerator.
– ORIGIN 1920s: abbreviation, probably influenced by the proprietary name *Frigidaire*.

fridge-freezer ▶ **noun** chiefly Brit. an upright unit comprising a refrigerator and a freezer, each self-contained.

fried past and past participle of **FRY**[1]. ▶ **adjective** **1** (of food) cooked in hot fat or oil: *a breakfast of fried eggs and bacon.*
2 [predic.] N. Amer. informal exhausted or worn out: *I had just come from doing a shoot and I was really fried.*

Friedan /'friːd(ə)n/, Betty (b.1921), American feminist and writer, known for *The Feminine Mystique* (1963), which presented femininity as an artificial construct and traced the ways in which American women are socialized to become mothers and housewives.

Friedman /'friːdmən/, Milton (b.1912), American economist. A principal exponent of monetarism, he acted as a policy adviser to President Reagan from 1981 to 1989. Nobel Prize for Economics (1976).

Friedrich /'friːdrɪx, German 'friːdrɪç/, Caspar David (1774–1840), German painter, noted for his romantic landscapes. He caused controversy with his altarpiece *The Cross in the Mountains* (1808), which lacked a specifically religious subject.

friend ▶ **noun** a person whom one knows and with whom one has a bond of mutual affection, typically exclusive of sexual or family relations.
■ a person who acts as a supporter of a cause, organization, or country by giving financial or other help: *the Friends of the Welsh National Opera.* ■ a person who is not an enemy or who is on the same side: *she was unsure whether he was **friend or foe**.* ■ (**one's friends**) archaic one's close relatives. ■ a familiar or helpful thing: *he settled for that old friend the compensation grant.* ■ (often as a polite form of address or in ironic reference) an acquaintance or a stranger one comes across: *my friends, let me introduce myself.* ■ (**Friend**) a member of the Religious Society of Friends; a Quaker.
▶ **verb** [with obj.] archaic or poetic/literary befriend (someone).
■ [no obj.] (**friend with**) black English have a sexual relationship with: *the woman got married and you still used to friend with she?*
– PHRASES **be** (or **make**) **friends with** be (or become) on good or affectionate terms with (someone). **a friend at court** a person in a position to use their influence on one's behalf. **a friend in need is a friend indeed** proverb a person who helps at a difficult time is a person who you can really rely on. **friends in high places** people in senior positions who are able and willing to use their influence on one's behalf. **my honourable friend** Brit. used to address or refer to another member of one's own party in the House of Commons. **my learned friend** used by a barrister or lawyer in court to address or refer to another barrister or lawyer. **my noble friend** Brit. used to address or refer to another member of one's own party in the House of Lords. **my Right Honourable friend** Brit. used to address or refer to another member of one's own party in the House of Commons who is also a privy counsellor.
– DERIVATIVES **friendless** adjective.
– ORIGIN Old English *frēond*, of Germanic origin; related to Dutch *vriend* and German *Freund*, from an Indo-European root meaning 'to love', shared by **FREE**.

friendly ▶ **adjective** (**friendlier**, **friendliest**) kind and pleasant: *they were **friendly to** me | she gave me a friendly smile.*
■ [predic.] (of a person) on good or affectionate terms: *I was **friendly with** one of the local farmers.* ■ (of a contest) not seriously or unpleasantly competitive or divisive: *friendly rivalry between the two schools.* ■ Brit. (of a game or match) not forming part of a serious competition. ■ [in combination] denoting something that is adapted for or is not harmful to a specified thing: *an environment-friendly agronomic practice.* ■ favourable or serviceable: *trees providing a friendly stage on which seedlings begin to grow.* ■ Military (of troops or equipment) of, belonging to, or in alliance with one's own forces.
▶ **noun** (pl. **-ies**) Brit. a game or match that does not form part of a serious competition.
– DERIVATIVES **friendlily** adverb, **friendliness** noun.

friendly fire ▶ **noun** [mass noun] Military weapon fire coming from one's own side that causes accidental injury or death to one's own forces.

Friendly Islands another name for **TONGA**[1].

friendly society ▶ **noun** (in the UK) a mutual association providing sickness benefits, life assurance, and pensions.
– ORIGIN originally the name of a particular fire-insurance company operating *c.*1700.

friendship ▶ **noun** [mass noun] the emotions or conduct of friends; the state of being friends.
■ [count noun] a relationship between friends: *she formed close friendships with women.* ■ a state of mutual trust and support between allied nations.
– ORIGIN Old English *frēondscipe* (see **FRIEND**, **-SHIP**).

Friends of the Earth (abbrev.: **FoE**) an international pressure group established in 1971 to campaign for a better awareness of and response to environmental problems.

frier ▶ **noun** variant spelling of **FRYER**.

Friesian /'friːʒ(ə)n/ ▶ **noun** Brit. an animal of a black-and-white breed of chiefly dairy cattle originally from Friesland.
– ORIGIN 1920s: alteration of **FRISIAN**.

Friesland[1] /'friːzlənd/ the western part of the ancient region of Frisia.
■ a northern province of the Netherlands, bounded to the west and north by the IJsselmeer and the North Sea; capital, Leeuwarden.

Friesland[2] /friːzlənd/ ▶ **noun** South African term for **FRIESIAN**.

frieze[1] /friːz/ ▶ **noun** a broad horizontal band of sculpted or painted decoration, especially on a wall near the ceiling.
■ a horizontal paper strip mounted on a wall to give a similar effect. ■ Architecture the part of an entablature between the architrave and the cornice.
– ORIGIN mid 16th cent.: from French *frise*, from medieval Latin *frisium*, variant of *frigium*, from Latin *Phrygium (opus)* '(work) of Phrygia'.

frieze[2] /friːz/ ▶ **noun** [mass noun] heavy, coarse woollen cloth with a nap, usually on one side only.
– ORIGIN late Middle English: from French *frise*, from medieval Latin *frisia*, 'Frisian wool'.

frig[1] vulgar slang ▶ **verb** (**frigged**, **frigging**) [with obj.] have sexual intercourse with (someone).
■ masturbate.
▶ **noun** **1** an act of sexual intercourse or masturbation.
2 used in various phrases for emphasis, especially to express anger, annoyance, or surprise.
▶ **exclamation** expressing extreme anger, annoyance, or contempt.
– ORIGIN late Middle English: of unknown origin. The original sense was 'move restlessly, wriggle', later 'rub, chafe', hence 'masturbate' (late 17th cent.).
▶ **frig about** (or **around**) spend time doing unimportant or trivial things.

frig[2] ▶ **noun** informal, chiefly Brit. old-fashioned spelling of **FRIDGE**.

frigate /'frɪgət/ ▶ **noun** a warship with a mixed armament, generally lighter than a destroyer (in the US navy, heavier) and of a kind originally introduced for convoy escort work.
■ historical a sailing warship of a size and armament just below that of a ship of the line.
– ORIGIN late 16th cent. (denoting a light, fast boat which was rowed or sailed): from French *frégate*, from Italian *fregata*, of unknown origin.

frigate bird ▶ **noun** a predatory tropical seabird with dark plumage, long narrow wings, a deeply forked tail, and a long hooked bill. Also called ***man-o'-war bird***.
• Family Fregatidae and genus *Fregata*: five species.

Frigga /'frɪgə/ Scandinavian Mythology the wife of Odin and goddess of married love and of the hearth, often identified with Freya. Friday is named after her.

frigging ▶ **adjective** & **adverb** vulgar slang used for emphasis, especially to express anger, annoyance, contempt, or surprise.

fright ▶ **noun** [mass noun] a sudden intense feeling of fear: *I jumped up in fright.*
■ [count noun] an experience that causes one to feel sudden intense fear: *she's had a nasty fright | I got **the fright of my life** seeing that woman in the hotel.*
▶ **verb** [with obj.] archaic frighten: *come, be comforted, he shan't fright you.*
– PHRASES **look a fright** informal have a dishevelled or grotesque appearance. **take fright** suddenly become frightened or panicked.
– ORIGIN Old English *fryhto*, *fyrhto* (noun), of Germanic origin; related to Dutch *furcht* and German *furcht*.

frighten ▶ **verb** [with obj.] make (someone) afraid or anxious: *the savagery of his thoughts frightened him | people were no longer easily **frightened into** docility.*
■ (**frighten someone/thing off**) deter someone or something from involvement or action by making them afraid. ■ [no obj.] (of a person) become afraid or anxious: *at his age, I guess he doesn't frighten any more.*
– DERIVATIVES **frighteningly** adverb.

frightened ▶ **adjective** afraid or anxious: *a frightened child.*

frightener ▶ **noun** a person or thing that frightens someone.
■ Brit. informal a member of a criminal gang who intimidates its victims.
– PHRASES **put the frighteners on** Brit. informal threaten or intimidate (someone).

frightful ▶ **adjective** very unpleasant, serious, or shocking: *there's been a most frightful accident.*
■ informal used for emphasis, especially of something bad: *her hair was a frightful mess.*
– DERIVATIVES **frightfulness** noun.

frightfully ▶ **adverb** [as submodifier] dated very (used for emphasis): *it was frightfully hot | I'm frightfully sorry.*

fright wig ▶ **noun** a wig with the hair arranged standing up or sticking out, as worn by a clown or similar performer.

frigid /'frɪdʒɪd/ ▶ **adjective** very cold in temperature: *frigid water.*
■ (of a woman) unable to be sexually aroused and responsive. ■ showing no friendliness or enthusiasm; stiff or formal in behaviour or style: *Henrietta looked back with a frigid calm.*
– DERIVATIVES **frigidity** noun, **frigidly** adverb, **frigidness** noun.
– ORIGIN late Middle English: from Latin *frigidus*, from *frigere* 'be cold', from *frigus* (noun) 'cold'.

frigidarium /ˌfrɪdʒɪ'dɛːrɪəm/ ▶ **noun** (pl. **frigidaria** /-rɪə/) historical a cold room in an ancient Roman bath.
– ORIGIN Latin.

frigid zone ▶ **noun** each of the two areas of the earth respectively north of the Arctic Circle and south of the Antarctic Circle.

frijoles /frɪ'həʊlɛs/ ▶ **plural noun** (in Mexican cookery) beans.
– ORIGIN Spanish, plural of *frijol* 'bean'.

frikkadel /ˌfrɪkə'dɛl/ ▶ **noun** (pl. **frikkadels** or **frikkadelle**) S. African a fried or baked meatball; a rissole.
– ORIGIN Afrikaans, from French *fricadelle*.

frill ▶ **noun** a strip of gathered or pleated material sewn by one side on to a garment or larger piece of material as a decorative edging or ornament.
■ a thing resembling such a strip in appearance or function: *a frill of silver hair surrounded a shining bald pate.* ■ a natural fringe of feathers or hair on a bird or other animal. ■ Palaeontology an upward-curving

bony plate extending behind the skull of many ceratopsian dinosaurs. ▪(usu. **frills**) figurative an unnecessary extra feature or embellishment: *it was just a comfortable flat with no frills.*
– DERIVATIVES **frilled** adjective, **frillery** noun.
– ORIGIN late 16th cent.: from or related to Flemish *frul*.

frilled lizard (also **frill-necked lizard**) ▶**noun** a large north Australian lizard with a membrane round the neck which can be erected to form a ruff for defensive display. When disturbed it runs away on its hind legs.
• *Chlamydosaurus kingii*, family Agamidae.

frilled shark ▶**noun** an elongated deep-sea shark of snake-like appearance, with prominent gill covers that give the appearance of a frill around the neck.
• *Chlamydoselachus anguineus*, the only member of the family Clamydoselachidae.

frilling ▶**noun** [mass noun] material for frills; frills collectively.

frilly ▶**adjective** (**frillier**, **frilliest**) decorated with frills or similar ornamentation: *a frilly apron.*
▪over-elaborate or showy in character or style: *seafood dishes that avoid being too frilly or rich.*
▶**plural noun** (**frillies**) informal an item of women's underwear.
– DERIVATIVES **frilliness** noun.

Frimaire /frɪˈmɛː, French frimɛr/ ▶**noun** the third month of the French Republican calendar (1793–1805), originally running from 21 November to 20 December.
– ORIGIN French, from *frimas* 'hoar frost'.

fringe ▶**noun 1** an ornamental border of threads left loose or formed into tassels or twists, used to edge clothing or material.
2 chiefly Brit. the front part of someone's hair, cut so as to hang over the forehead.
▪a natural border of hair or fibres in an animal or plant.
3 (often **the fringes**) the outer, marginal, or extreme part of an area, group, or sphere of activity: *his uncles were on the fringes of crooked activity.*
▪(**the Fringe**) a secondary festival on the periphery of the Edinburgh Festival.
4 a band of contrasting brightness or darkness produced by diffraction or interference of light.
▪a strip of false colour in an optical image.
5 N. Amer. short for **FRINGE BENEFIT**.
▶**adjective** [attrib.] not part of the mainstream; unconventional, peripheral, or extreme: *fringe theatre.*
▶**verb** [with obj.] decorate (clothing or material) with a fringe: *a rich robe of gold, fringed with black velvet.*
▪(often **be fringed**) form a border around (something): *the sea is fringed by palm trees.* ▪[as adj. **fringed**] (of a plant or animal) having a natural border of hair or fibre.
– DERIVATIVES **fringeless** adjective, **fringy** adjective.
– ORIGIN Middle English: from Old French *frenge*, based on late Latin *fimbria*, earlier a plural noun meaning 'fibres, shreds'.

fringe benefit ▶**noun** an extra benefit supplementing an employee's money wage or salary, for example a company car, subsidized meals, private health care, etc.

fringed orchid ▶**noun** a North American orchid with a flower that has a fringed lip.
• Genus *Habenaria*, family Orchidaceae: many species.

fringe medicine ▶**noun** another term for **ALTERNATIVE MEDICINE**.

fringing ▶**noun** [mass noun] material used to make a fringe.

fringing reef ▶**noun** a coral reef that lies close to the shore.

Frink /frɪŋk/, Dame Elisabeth (1930–93), English sculptor and graphic artist. She made her name with angular bronzes, often of birds. During the 1960s her figures—typically male nudes, horses, and riders—became smoother, although she retained a feeling for the bizarre.

frippery /ˈfrɪp(ə)ri/ ▶**noun** (pl. **-ies**) [mass noun] showy or unnecessary ornament in architecture, dress, or language.
▪[count noun] a tawdry or frivolous thing.
▶**adjective** archaic frivolous and tawdry.
– ORIGIN mid 16th cent. (denoting old or second-hand clothes): from French *friperie*, from Old French *freperie*, from *frepe* 'rag', of unknown ultimate origin.

frippet /ˈfrɪpɪt/ ▶**noun** Brit. informal, dated a frivolous or showy young woman.
– ORIGIN early 20th cent.: of unknown origin.

frisbee /ˈfrɪzbi/ ▶**noun** trademark a concave plastic disc designed for skimming through the air as an outdoor game or amusement.
▪[mass noun] the game or amusement of skimming such a disc.
– ORIGIN 1950s: said to be named after the *Frisbie* bakery (Bridgeport, Connecticut), whose pie tins could be used similarly.

Frisch[1] /frɪʃ/, Karl von (1886–1982), Austrian zoologist. He worked mainly on honeybees, studying particularly their vision, navigation, and communication. He showed that they perform an elaborate dance in the hive to indicate the direction and distance of food.

Frisch[2] /frɪʃ/, Otto Robert (1904–79), Austrian-born British physicist. With his aunt, Lise Meitner, he recognized that Otto Hahn's experiments with uranium had produced a new type of nuclear reaction. Frisch named it nuclear fission, and indicated the explosive potential of its chain reaction.

Frisch[3] /frɪʃ/, Ragnar (Anton Kittil) (1895–1973), Norwegian economist. A pioneer of econometrics, he shared the first Nobel Prize for Economics with Jan Tinbergen (1969).

frisée /ˈfriːzeɪ/ ▶**noun** [mass noun] the curly endive (see **ENDIVE** sense 1).
– ORIGIN French, from *chicorée frisée* 'curly endive'.

Frisia /ˈfrɪzɪə, ˈfriːʒə/ an ancient region of NW Europe. It consisted of the Frisian Islands and parts of the mainland corresponding to the modern provinces of Friesland and Groningen in the Netherlands and the regions of Ostfriesland and Nordfriesland in NW Germany.

Frisian /ˈfriːzɪən, ˈfriːʒ(ə)n, ˈfrɪ-/ ▶**adjective** of or relating to Frisia or Friesland, its people, or language.
▶**noun 1** a native or inhabitant of Frisia or Friesland.
2 [mass noun] the Germanic language of Frisia or Friesland, most closely related to English and Dutch, now with fewer than 400,000 speakers.
– ORIGIN late 16th cent.: from Latin *Frisii* 'Frisians' (from Old Frisian *Frīsa*, *Frēsa*) + **-IAN**.

Frisian Islands a chain of islands lying off the coast of NW Europe, extending from the IJsselmeer in the Netherlands to Jutland. The islands consist of three groups: the **West Frisian Islands** form part of the Netherlands, the **East Frisian Islands** form part of Germany, and the **North Frisian Islands** are divided between Germany and Denmark.

frisk ▶**verb 1** [with obj.] (of a police officer or other official) pass the hands over (someone) in a search for hidden weapons, drugs, or other items.
2 [no obj., with adverbial of direction] (of an animal or person) skip or leap playfully; frolic: *spaniels frisked around me.*
▪[with obj.] (of an animal) move or wave (its tail or legs) playfully: *a horse was frisking his back legs like a colt.*
▶**noun 1** [in sing.] an act of frisking someone.
2 a playful skip or leap.
– DERIVATIVES **frisker** noun.
– ORIGIN early 16th cent. (in sense 2): from obsolete *frisk* 'lively, frisky', from Old French *frisque* 'alert, lively, merry', perhaps of Germanic origin. Sense 1, originally a slang term, dates from the late 18th cent.

frisket /ˈfrɪskɪt/ ▶**noun** Printing a thin metal frame keeping the paper in position during printing on a hand press.
▪[mass noun] US fluid or adhesive paper used in painting or crafts to cover areas of a surface on which paint is not wanted.
– ORIGIN late 17th cent.: from French *frisquette*, from Provençal *frisqueto*, from Spanish *frasqueta*.

frisky ▶**adjective** (**friskier**, **friskiest**) playful and full of energy: *he bounds about like a frisky pup.*
– DERIVATIVES **friskily** adverb, **friskiness** noun.

frisson /ˈfriːsɔ̃, ˈfrɪsɒn/ ▶**noun** a sudden strong feeling of excitement or fear; a thrill: *a frisson of excitement.*
– ORIGIN late 18th cent.: French, 'a shiver or thrill'.

frit[1] ▶**noun** [mass noun] the mixture of silica and fluxes which is fused at high temperature to make glass.
▪a similar calcined and pulverized mixture used to make soft-paste porcelain or ceramic glazes.
▶**verb** (**fritted**, **fritting**) [with obj.] make into frit.
– ORIGIN mid 17th cent.: from Italian *fritta*, feminine past participle of *friggere* 'to fry'.

frit[2] ▶**adjective** [predic.] dialect frightened.
– ORIGIN early 19th cent.: dialect past participle of **FRIGHT**.

frites /friːt(s)/ ▶**plural noun** short for **POMMES FRITES**.

frit fly ▶**noun** a very small black fly whose larvae are a serious pest of cereal crops and maize.
• *Oscinella frit*, family Chloropidae.
– ORIGIN late 19th cent.: from Latin *frit* 'particle on an ear of corn'.

Frith, William Powell (1819–1909), English painter. He is remembered for his panoramic paintings of Victorian life, including *Derby Day* (1858) and *The Railway Station* (1862).

frith ▶**noun** archaic spelling of **FIRTH**.

fritillary /frɪˈtɪləri/ ▶**noun 1** a Eurasian plant of the lily family, with hanging bell-like flowers.
• Genus *Fritillaria*, family Liliaceae: numerous species, in particular the snake's head.
2 a butterfly with orange-brown wings that are chequered with black.
• Subfamilies Argynninae and Melitaeinae, family Nymphalidae: *Argynnis* and other genera, and numerous species.
– ORIGIN mid 17th cent.: from modern Latin *fritillaria*, from Latin *fritillus* 'dice-box' (probably with reference to the chequered corolla of the snake's head fritillary).

frittata /frɪˈtɑːtə/ ▶**noun** an Italian dish made with fried beaten eggs, resembling a Spanish omelette.
– ORIGIN Italian, from *fritto*, past participle of *friggere* 'to fry'. Compare with **FRITTER**[2].

fritter[1] ▶**verb** [with obj.] **1** (**fritter something away**) waste time, money, or energy on trifling matters: *I wish we hadn't frittered the money away so easily.*
2 archaic divide (something) into small pieces: *they become frittered into minute tatters.*
– ORIGIN early 18th cent.: based on obsolete *fitter* 'break into fragments, shred'; perhaps related to German *Fetzen* 'rag, scrap'.

fritter[2] ▶**noun** a piece of fruit, vegetable, or meat that is coated in batter and deep-fried.
– ORIGIN late Middle English: from Old French *friture*, based on Latin *frigere* (see **FRY**[1]). Compare with **FRITTATA**.

fritto misto /ˌfrɪtəʊ ˈmɪstəʊ/ ▶**noun** [mass noun] a dish of various foods, typically seafood, deep-fried in batter.
– ORIGIN Italian, 'mixed fry'.

Fritz ▶**noun** Brit. informal, dated a German, especially a soldier in the First World War (often used as a nickname).
▪[in sing.] the Germans collectively.
– ORIGIN abbreviation of the German given name *Friedrich*.

fritz ▶**noun** (in phrase **go** or **be on the fritz**) N. Amer. informal (of a machine) stop working properly.
– ORIGIN early 20th cent.: said to be a use of **FRITZ**, with allusion to cheap German imports into the US before the First World War.

Friuli /friːˈuːli/ a historic region of SE Europe now divided between Slovenia and the Italian region of Friuli-Venezia Giulia. A Rhaeto-Romance dialect is spoken locally in the region.
– DERIVATIVES **Friulian** adjective & noun.

Friuli-Venezia Giulia /frɪˌuːlɪvɛˌnɛtsɪə ˈdʒuːlɪə/ a region in NE Italy, on the border with Slovenia and Austria; capital, Trieste.

frivol /ˈfrɪv(ə)l/ ▶**verb** (**frivolled**, **frivolling**; US **frivoled**, **frivoling**) [no obj.] behave in a frivolous way.
– ORIGIN mid 19th cent.: back-formation from **FRIVOLOUS**.

frivolous ▶**adjective** not having any serious purpose or value: *rules to stop frivolous lawsuits.*
▪(of a person) carefree and not serious.
– DERIVATIVES **frivolity** noun, **frivolously** adverb, **frivolousness** noun.
– ORIGIN late Middle English: from Latin *frivolus* 'silly, trifling' + **-OUS**.

frizz /frɪz/ ▶**verb** [with obj.] **1** form (hair) into a mass of small, tight curls: *her hair was frizzed up in a style that seemed matronly.*
▪[no obj.] (of hair) form itself into such a mass: *his hair had frizzed out symmetrically.*
2 dress (wash leather) with pumice or a scraping knife.
▶**noun** [mass noun] the state of being formed into such a

mass of curls: *a perm system designed to add curl without frizz.*
– ORIGIN late Middle English (in sense 2): from French *friser*. Sense 1 dates from the late 16th cent.

frizzante /frɪˈzanteɪ, -ti/ ▶ adjective (of wine) semi-sparkling.
– ORIGIN Italian.

frizzle[1] ▶ verb [no obj.] fry or grill with a sizzling noise: *Elsie had the fat frizzling in the chip pan.*
■ [with obj.] fry until crisp, shrivelled, or burnt: [as adj. **frizzled**] *add diced frizzled salt pork to taste.*
▶ noun [in sing.] the sound or act of frying: *the frizzle of the pan.*
– ORIGIN mid 18th cent.: from **FRY**[1], probably influenced by **SIZZLE**.

frizzle[2] ▶ verb [with obj.] form (hair) into tight curls.
▶ noun a tight curl in hair.
– DERIVATIVES **frizzly** adjective.
– ORIGIN mid 16th cent.: from **FRIZZ** + **-LE**[4].

frizzy ▶ adjective (**frizzier**, **frizziest**) formed of a mass of small, tight curls: *frizzy red hair.*
– DERIVATIVES **frizziness** noun.

Frl. ▶ abbreviation for Fräulein.

fro ▶ adverb see **TO AND FRO**.
– ORIGIN Middle English: from Old Norse *frá* (see **FROM**).

Frobisher /ˈfrəʊbɪʃə/, Sir Martin (c.1535–94), English explorer. In 1576 he led an unsuccessful expedition in search of the North-West Passage. Frobisher served in Sir Francis Drake's Caribbean expedition of 1585–6 and played a prominent part in the defeat of the Spanish Armada.

frock ▶ noun **1** a woman's or girl's dress.
2 a loose outer garment, in particular:
■ a long gown with flowing sleeves worn by monks, priests, or clergy. ■ historical a field labourer's smock-frock. ■ short for **FROCK COAT**. ■ archaic a woollen jersey worn by sailors.
3 [in sing.] archaic priestly office: *such words as these cost the preacher his frock.*
– DERIVATIVES **frocked** adjective [in combination] *a black-frocked Englishman.*
– ORIGIN late Middle English: from Old French *froc*, of Germanic origin. The sense 'priest's or monk's gown' is preserved in *defrock*.

frock coat ▶ noun a man's double-breasted, long-skirted coat, now worn chiefly on formal occasions.

froe /frəʊ/ ▶ noun a cleaving tool with a handle at right angles to the blade.
– ORIGIN late 16th cent.: abbreviation of obsolete *frower*, from **FROWARD** in the sense 'turned away'.

Froebel /ˈfrəʊb(ə)l, ˈfrəːb-, German ˈfrøːbl/, Friedrich (Wilhelm August) (1782–1852), German educationist and founder of the kindergarten system. Believing that play materials, practical occupations, and songs are needed to develop a child's real nature, he opened a school for young children in 1837.
– DERIVATIVES **Froebelian** /frəʊˈbiːlɪən, frəːˈbiː-/ adjective, **Froebelism** noun.

frog[1] ▶ noun **1** a tailless amphibian with a short squat body, moist smooth skin, and very long hind legs for leaping.
● Frogs are found in most families of the order Anura, but the 'true frogs' are confined to the large family Ranidae, which includes the **European common frog** (*Rana temporaria*).
■ informal a person regarded as repulsive in character or appearance.
2 (**Frog**) derogatory a French person.
– PHRASES **have a frog in one's throat** informal lose one's voice or find it hard to speak because of hoarseness.
– ORIGIN Old English *frogga*, of Germanic origin; related to Dutch *vors* and German *Frosch*. Used as a general term of abuse in Middle English, the term was applied specifically to the Dutch in the 17th cent.; its application to the French (late 18th cent.) is partly alliterative, partly from the reputation of the French for eating frogs' legs.

frog[2] ▶ noun a thing used to hold or fasten something, in particular:
■ an ornamental coat fastener or braid consisting of a spindle-shaped button and a loop through which it passes. ■ an attachment to a belt for holding a sword, bayonet, or similar weapon. ■ a perforated or spiked device for holding the stems of flowers in an arrangement. ■ the piece into which the hair is fitted at the lower end of the bow of a stringed instrument. ■ a grooved metal plate for guiding the wheels of a railway vehicle at an intersection.
– DERIVATIVES **frogging** noun.
– ORIGIN early 18th cent.: perhaps a use of **FROG**[1], influenced by synonymous Italian *forchetta* or French *fourchette* 'small fork', because of the shape.

frog[3] ▶ noun an elastic horny pad growing in the sole of a horse's hoof, helping to absorb the shock when the hoof hits the ground.
■ a raised or swollen area on a surface.
– ORIGIN early 17th cent.: perhaps from **FROG**[2].

frogbit ▶ noun a floating freshwater plant with creeping stems which bear clusters of small rounded leaves.
● Two species in the family Hydrocharitaceae: **Eurasian frogbit** (*Hydrocharis morsus-ranae*) and **American frogbit** (*Hydromystria laevigatum*).

frogfish ▶ noun (pl. same or **-fishes**) an anglerfish that typically lives on the seabed, where its warty skin and colour provide camouflage.
● Families Antennariidae (numerous species, including *Antennaria hispidus* of the Indo-Pacific), and Brachionichthyidae (four Australian species).

frogged ▶ adjective (of a coat) having an ornamental braid or fastening consisting of a spindle-shaped button and a loop.

froggy ▶ adjective **1** of or like a frog or frogs.
2 derogatory French.
▶ noun (**Froggy**) (pl. **-ies**) derogatory a French person.

froghopper ▶ noun a jumping, plant-sucking bug, the larva of which produces cuckoo spit. Also called **SPITTLEBUG**.
● Family Cercopidae, suborder Homoptera: several genera.

frog kick ▶ noun a movement used in swimming, especially in the breast stroke, in which the legs are brought towards the body with the knees bent and the feet together and then kicked outwards before being brought together again, all in one continuous movement.

froglet ▶ noun **1** a small kind of frog.
● Several genera, including *Crinia* of Australia (family Myobatrachidae), and *Philautus* of Malaysia (family Rhacophoridae).
2 a tiny frog that has recently developed from a tadpole.

frogman ▶ noun (pl. **-men**) a person who swims under water wearing a rubber suit, flippers, and an oxygen supply.

frogmarch ▶ verb [with obj. and adverbial of direction] force (someone) to walk forward by holding and pinning their arms from behind: *the cop frogmarched him down the steep stairs.*

frogmouth ▶ noun a nocturnal bird resembling a nightjar, occurring in SE Asia and Australasia.
● Family Podargidae: two genera and several species, in particular the **tawny frogmouth** (*Podargus strigoides*) of Australia.

frog orchid ▶ noun a small orchid with inconspicuous green flowers, growing chiefly on calcareous grassland in north temperate regions.
● *Coeloglossum viride*, family Orchidaceae.

frogspawn ▶ noun [mass noun] the eggs of a frog, which are surrounded by transparent jelly.

froideur /frwʌˈdəː, French frwadœr/ ▶ noun [mass noun] coolness or reserve between people.
– ORIGIN French, from *froid* 'cold'.

frolic ▶ verb (**frolicked**, **frolicking**) [no obj., with adverbial of place] (of an animal or person) play and move about cheerfully, excitedly, or energetically: *Edward frolicked on the sand.*
■ play about with someone in a flirtatious or sexual way: *he frolicked with a bikini-clad beauty.*
▶ noun (often **frolics**) a playful action or movement: *his injuries were inflicted by the frolics of a young filly* | [mass noun] *the days of fun and frolic were gone for good.*
■ flirtatious or sexual activity or actions: *her poolside frolics.*
▶ adjective archaic cheerful, merry, or playful: *a thousand forms of frolic life.*
– DERIVATIVES **frolicker** noun.
– ORIGIN early 16th cent. (as an adjective): from Dutch *vrolijk* 'merry, cheerful'.

frolicsome ▶ adjective lively and playful.
– DERIVATIVES **frolicsomely** adverb, **frolicsomeness** noun.

from ▶ preposition **1** indicating the point in space at which a journey, motion, or action starts: *she began to walk away from him* | *I leapt from my bed* | figurative *he was turning the Chamberlain government away from appeasement.*
■ indicating the distance between a particular place and another place used as a point of reference: *the ambush occurred 50 metres from a checkpoint.*
2 indicating the point in time at which a particular process, event, or activity starts: *the show will run from 10am to 2pm.*
3 indicating the source or provenance of someone or something: *I'm from Hackney* | *she rang him from the hotel* | *she demanded the keys from her husband.*
■ indicating the date at which something was created: *a document dating from the thirteenth century.*
4 indicating the starting point of a specified range on a scale: *men who ranged in age* ***from*** *seventeen* ***to*** *eighty-four.*
■ indicating one extreme in a range of conceptual variations: *anything* ***from*** *geography* ***to*** *literature.*
5 indicating the point at which an observer is placed: *you can see the island from here* | figurative *the ability to see things from another's point of view.*
6 indicating the raw material out of which something is manufactured: *a varnish made from copal.*
7 indicating separation or removal: *the party was ousted from power after sixteen years.*
8 indicating prevention: *the story of how he was saved from death.*
9 indicating a cause: *a child suffering from asthma.*
10 indicating a source of knowledge or the basis for one's judgement: *information obtained from papers, books, and presentations.*
11 indicating a distinction: *the courts view him in a different light from that of a manual worker.*
– PHRASES **as from** see **AS**[1]. **from day to day** (or **hour to hour** etc.) daily (or hourly etc.); as the days (or hours etc.) pass. **from now** (or **then** etc.) **on** now (or then etc.) and in the future: *they were friends from that day on.* **from time to time** occasionally.
– ORIGIN Old English *fram*, *from*, of Germanic origin; related to Old Norse *frá* (see **FRO**).

fromage blanc /ˌfrɒmɑːʒ ˈblɒ̃/ ▶ noun [mass noun] a type of soft French cheese made from cow's milk and having a creamy sour taste.
– ORIGIN French, literally 'white cheese'.

fromage frais /ˈfreɪ/ ▶ noun [mass noun] a type of smooth soft fresh cheese, with the consistency of thick yogurt.
– ORIGIN French, literally 'fresh cheese'.

Fromm /frɒm/, Erich (1900–80), German-born American psychoanalyst and social philosopher. His works, which include *Escape from Freedom* (1941), *Man for Himself* (1947), and *The Sane Society* (1955), emphasize the role of culture in neurosis and strongly criticize materialist values.

frond ▶ noun the leaf or leaf-like part of a palm, fern, or similar plant: *fronds of bracken* | figurative *her hair escaped in wayward fronds.*
– DERIVATIVES **frondage** noun, **fronded** adjective, **frondose** adjective.
– ORIGIN late 18th cent.: from Latin *frons*, *frond-* 'leaf'.

Fronde /frɒnd, French frɔ̃d/ a series of civil wars in France 1648–53, in which the nobles rose in rebellion against Mazarin and the court during the minority of Louis XIV. Although some concessions were obtained, the nobles were not successful in curbing the power of the monarchy.
– ORIGIN French, from the name for a type of sling used in a children's game played in the streets of Paris at this time.

frondeur /frɒnˈdəː, French frɔ̃dœr/ ▶ noun rare a political rebel.
– ORIGIN French, literally 'slinger', used to denote a member of the **FRONDE**.

frons /frɒnz/ ▶ noun (pl. **frontes**) Zoology the forehead or equivalent part of an animal, especially the middle part of an insect's face between the eyes and above the clypeus.
– ORIGIN mid 19th cent.: from Latin, 'front, forehead'.

front ▶ noun **1** the side or part of an object that presents itself to view or that is normally seen or used first; the most forward part of something: *a page at the front of the book had been torn out* | *he sealed the envelope and wrote on the front.*
■ [in sing.] the position directly ahead of someone or something; the most forward position or place: *she quickly turned her head to face the front.* ■ the forward-facing part of a person's body, on the opposite side to their back. ■ the part of a garment covering this: *porridge slopped from the tray on to his shirt front.* ■ informal a woman's bust or cleavage. ■ any face of a

building, especially that of the main entrance: *the west front of the Cathedral.* ■ chiefly Brit. short for **SEAFRONT** or **WATERFRONT**.
2 the foremost line or part of an armed force; the furthest position that an army has reached and where the enemy is or may be engaged: *his regiment was immediately sent to the front.*
■ the direction towards which a line of troops faces when formed. ■ a particular formation of troops for battle. ■ a particular situation or sphere of operation: *there was some good news on the jobs front.* ■ [often in names] an organized political group: *the National Progressive Patriotic Front.* ■ Meteorology the forward edge of an advancing mass of air. See **COLD FRONT**, **WARM FRONT**.
3 [in sing.] an appearance or form of behaviour assumed by a person to conceal their genuine feelings: *she put on a brave front.*
■ a person or organization serving as a cover for subversive or illegal activities: *the CIA identified the company as **a front for** a terrorist group.*
4 [mass noun] boldness and confidence of manner: *he's got a bit of talent and a lot of front.*
5 archaic a person's face or forehead.
▶ **adjective** [attrib.] **1** of or at the front: *the front cover of the magazine | she was in the front garden.*
2 Phonetics (of a vowel sound) formed by raising the tongue, excluding the blade and tip, towards the hard palate.
▶ **verb** [with obj.] **1** (of a building or piece of land) have the front facing or directed towards: *the flats which fronted Crow Road* | [no obj.] *both properties **fronted on to** the same beach.*
■ be or stand in front of: *they reached the hedge fronting the garden.* ■ archaic stand face to face with; confront: *Tom fronted him with unwavering eyes.*
2 (usu. **be fronted**) provide (something) with a front or facing of a particular type or material: *a metal box fronted by an alloy panel* | [as adj., in combination **-fronted**] *a glass-fronted bookcase.*
3 lead or be the most prominent member in (an organization, activity, or group of musicians): *the group is fronted by two girl singers.*
■ present or host (a television or radio programme). ■ [no obj.] act as a front or cover for someone or something acting illegally or wishing to conceal something: *he **fronted for** them in illegal property deals.*
4 Phonetics articulate (a vowel sound) with the tongue further forward: [as adj. **fronted**] *all speakers use raised and fronted variants more in spontaneous speech.*
5 Linguistics place (a sentence element) at the beginning of a sentence instead of in its usual position, typically for emphasis or as feature of some dialects, as in *horrible it was.*
– PHRASES **front of house** the parts of a theatre in front of the proscenium arch. ■ the business of a theatre that concerns the audience, such as ticket sales. **in front 1** in a position just ahead of or further forward than someone or something else: *the car in front stopped suddenly.* ■ in the lead in a game or contest: *United went back in front thanks to a penalty.* **2** on the part or side that normally first presents itself to view: *a house with a wide porch in front.* **in front of 1** in a position just ahead or at the front part of someone or something else: *the lawn in front of the house.* ■ in a position facing someone or something: *she sat in front of the mirror.* **2** in the presence of: *the teacher didn't want his authority challenged in front of the class.* **out front** chiefly N. Amer. at or to the front; in front: *two station wagons stopped out front.* ■ in the auditorium of a theatre.
– DERIVATIVES **frontless** adjective, **frontward** adjective & adverb, **frontwards** adverb.
– ORIGIN Middle English (denoting the forehead): from Old French *front* (noun), *fronter* (verb), from Latin *frons, front-* 'forehead, front'.

frontage ▶ **noun** the facade of a building.
■ a strip or extent of land abutting on a street or water: *the houses have a narrow **frontage** to the street* | [mass noun] *the house is set in parkland with river frontage.*

frontager /ˈfrɒntɪdʒə/ ▶ **noun** an owner of land or property adjoining a street or water.

frontage road ▶ **noun** N. Amer. a service road.

frontal[1] ▶ **adjective** of or at the front: *the frontal view misses the octagonal tower.*
■ (of an attack) delivered directly on the front, not the side or back. ■ of or relating to the forehead or front part of the skull: *the frontal sinuses.*
– DERIVATIVES **frontally** adverb.
– ORIGIN mid 17th cent. (in the sense 'relating to the forehead'): from modern Latin *frontalis*, from Latin *frons, front-* 'front, forehead'.

frontal[2] ▶ **noun** a decorative cloth for covering the front of an altar.
– ORIGIN Middle English (denoting a band or ornament worn on the forehead): from Old French *frontel*, from Latin *frontale*, from *frons, front-* 'front, forehead'.

frontal bone ▶ **noun** the bone which forms the front part of the skull and the upper part of the eye sockets.
■ either of the pair of bones from which this is formed by fusion in infancy.

frontal lobe ▶ **noun** each of the paired lobes of the brain lying immediately behind the forehead, including areas concerned with behaviour, learning, personality, and voluntary movement.

front bench ▶ **noun** (in the UK) the foremost seats in the House of Commons, occupied by the members of the cabinet and shadow cabinet.
– DERIVATIVES **frontbencher** noun.

Front de Libération Nationale /ˌfrɔ̃ də ˌlɪbəˌrasjɔ̃ ˌnasjəˈnɑːl, French frɔ̃ də liberasjɔ̃ nasjɔnal/ (abbrev.: **FLN**) a revolutionary political party in Algeria that supported the war of independence against France 1954–62.
– ORIGIN French, 'National Liberation Front'.

front-end ▶ **adjective** [attrib.] of or relating to the front of a car or other vehicle: *front-end styling.*
■ informal (of money) paid or charged at the beginning of a transaction: *a front-end fee.* ■ Computing (of a device or program) directly accessed by the user and allowing access to further devices or programs.
▶ **noun** Computing a part of a computer or program that allows access to other parts.

front-end loader ▶ **noun** a machine with a scoop or bucket on an articulated arm at the front for digging and loading earth.
■ a hydraulic bucket or scoop that fits on to the front of a tractor.

front-fanged ▶ **adjective** (of a snake such as a cobra or viper) having the front pair of teeth modified as fangs, with grooves or canals to conduct the venom. Compare with **BACK-FANGED**.

frontier /ˈfrʌntɪə, frʌnˈtɪə/ ▶ **noun** a line or border separating two countries.
■ the district near such a line. ■ the extreme limit of settled land beyond which lies wilderness, especially referring to the western US before Pacific settlement: *his novel of the American frontier.* ■ the extreme limit of understanding or achievement in a particular area: *the success of science in extending the frontiers of knowledge.*
– DERIVATIVES **frontierless** adjective.
– ORIGIN late Middle English: from Old French *frontiere*, based on Latin *frons, front-* 'front'.

frontiersman ▶ **noun** (pl. **-men**) a man living in the region of a frontier, especially that between settled and unsettled country.

frontierswoman ▶ **noun** (pl. **-women**) a woman living in the region of a frontier, especially that between settled and unsettled country.

frontispiece /ˈfrʌntɪspiːs/ ▶ **noun 1** an illustration facing the title page of a book.
2 Architecture the principal face of a building.
■ a decorated entrance. ■ a pediment over a door or window.
– ORIGIN late 16th cent. (in sense 2): from French *frontispice* or late Latin *frontispicium* 'facade', from Latin *frons, front-* 'front' + *specere* 'to look'. The change in the ending (early in the word's history) was by association with **PIECE**.

frontlet ▶ **noun 1** an ornamental piece of cloth hanging over the upper part of an altar frontal.
2 dated a decorative band or ornament worn on the forehead.
■ another term for **PHYLACTERY**. ■ a piece of armour or harness for an animal's forehead.
– ORIGIN late 15th cent. (in sense 2): from Old French *frontelet*, diminutive of *frontel* (see **FRONTAL[2]**).

front line ▶ **noun** (usu. **the front line**) the military line or part of an army that is closest to the enemy: [as modifier] *the front-line troops.*
■ the most important or influential position in a debate or movement: *it is doctors who are on the front line of the euthanasia debate.*

front-line states ▶ **plural noun** those countries bordering on an area troubled by a war or other crisis (used particularly of the countries bordering on South Africa and opposed to its policy of apartheid while this was in operation).

frontman ▶ **noun** (pl. **-men**) a person who leads or represents a group or organization, in particular:
■ the leader of a group of musicians, especially the lead singer of a pop group. ■ a presenter of a television programme. ■ a person who represents an illegal or disreputable organization to give it an air of legitimacy.

front matter ▶ **noun** [mass noun] the pages of a book, such as the title page and preface, that precede the main text.

front office ▶ **noun** chiefly N. Amer. the main administrative office of a business or other organization.

fronton /ˈfrʌnt(ə)n/ ▶ **noun 1** a building where pelota or jai alai is played.
2 another term for **PEDIMENT**.
– ORIGIN late 17th cent.: from French, from Italian *frontone*, from *fronte* 'forehead', from Latin *frons, front-* 'front, forehead'.

front page ▶ **noun** the first page of a newspaper, containing the most important or remarkable news of the day: [as modifier] *a front-page story.*

front row ▶ **noun** Rugby the forwards who make up the first row in a scrum.

front runner ▶ **noun** the contestant that is leading in a race or other competition.
■ an athlete or horse that runs best when in the front of the field.

front-running ▶ **adjective** ahead in a race or other competition.
■ (of an athlete or horse) running best when in front of the field.
▶ **noun** [mass noun] **1** Stock Exchange the practice by market-makers of dealing on advance information provided by their brokers and investment analysts, before their clients have been given the information.
2 US the practice of giving one's support to a competitor because they are in front.

frontside ▶ **adjective** [attrib.] denoting a manoeuvre in surfing and other board sports which is done anticlockwise for a regular rider and clockwise for a goofy rider.

front-wheel drive ▶ **noun** [mass noun] a transmission system that provides power to the front wheels of a motor vehicle.

frore /frɔː/ ▶ **adjective** poetic/literary frozen; frosty.
– ORIGIN Middle English: archaic past participle of **FREEZE**.

Frost, Robert (Lee) (1874–1963), American poet, noted for his ironic tone and simple language. Much of his poetry reflects his affinity with New England, including the collections *North of Boston* (1914) and *New Hampshire* (1923). He won the Pulitzer Prize on three occasions (1924; 1931; 1937).

frost ▶ **noun** [mass noun] a deposit of small white ice crystals formed on the ground or other surfaces when the temperature falls below freezing.
■ [count noun] a period of cold weather when such deposits form: *there have been several sharp frosts recently.* ■ [count noun] figurative a chilling or dispiriting quality, especially one conveyed by a cold manner: *there was a light frost of anger in Jackson's tone.* ■ [in sing.] Brit. informal, dated a failure.
▶ **verb** [with obj.] cover (something) with or as if with small ice crystals; freeze: *shop windows were still frosted over.*
■ [no obj.] become covered with small ice crystals: *no one has managed to stop outdoor heat exchangers **frosting up** during winter.* ■ chiefly US decorate (a cake or biscuit) with icing. ■ injure (a plant) by freezing weather.
– PHRASES **degrees of frost** Brit. degrees below freezing point.
– DERIVATIVES **frostless** adjective.
– ORIGIN Old English *frost, forst*, of Germanic origin; related to Dutch *vorst* and German *Frost*, also to **FREEZE**.

frostbite ▶ **noun** [mass noun] injury to body tissues caused by exposure to extreme cold, typically affecting the nose, fingers, or toes and often resulting in gangrene.

frosted ▶ **adjective** covered with or as if with frost: *I stood looking out on the frosted garden.*
■ (of glass or a window) having a translucent textured surface so that it is difficult to see through. ■ (of food) decorated or dusted with icing or sugar.

frost heave ▶ **noun** [mass noun] the uplift of soil or

f

other surface deposits due to expansion of groundwater on freezing.
■[count noun] a mound formed in this way.
– DERIVATIVES **frost heaving** noun.

frost hollow ▶ **noun** a valley bottom or other hollow which is prone to frost.

frosting ▶ **noun** [mass noun] **1** N. Amer. icing.
2 a roughened matt finish on otherwise shiny material such as glass or steel.

frost line ▶ **noun** [in sing.] N. Amer. the maximum depth of ground below which the soil does not freeze in winter.

frost stat ▶ **noun** a thermostat used to turn on a heating system automatically when the ambient temperature drops below a set threshold.

frost work ▶ **noun** [mass noun] attractive patterns made by frost on a window or other surface.

frosty ▶ **adjective** (**frostier**, **frostiest**) **1** (of the weather) very cold with frost forming on surfaces: *a cold and frosty morning.*
■covered with or as if with frost: *the dog crouched in the frosty grass.*
2 cold and unfriendly in manner: *Sebastian gave her a frosty look.*
– DERIVATIVES **frostily** adverb, **frostiness** noun.

froth ▶ **noun** [mass noun] a mass of small bubbles in liquid caused by agitation, fermentation, or salivating: *leave the yeast until there is a good head of froth.*
■[mass noun] impure matter that rises to the surface of liquid: *skim off any surface froth.* ■ figurative a thing that rises or overflows in a soft, light mass: *her skirt swirled in a froth of black lace.* ■ worthless or insubstantial talk, ideas, or activities: *the froth of party politics.*
▶ **verb** [no obj.] form or contain a rising or overflowing mass of small bubbles: *the red blood frothed at his lips* | [as adj. **frothing**] *frothing tankards of ale.*
■figurative rise or overflow in a soft, light mass: *she wore an ivory silk blouse, frothing at neck and cuffs.* ■ [with obj.] agitate (a liquid) so as to produce a mass of small bubbles. ■ (of a person) behave or talk angrily: *the cinema lobby frothed with indignation.*
– PHRASES **froth at the mouth** emit a large amount of saliva from the mouth in a bodily seizure. ■ figurative be very angry.
– ORIGIN late Middle English: from Old Norse *frotha, frauth.*

frothy ▶ **adjective** (**frothier**, **frothiest**) full of or covered with a mass of small bubbles: *steaming mugs of frothy coffee.*
■light and entertaining but of little substance: *lots of frothy interviews.*
– DERIVATIVES **frothily** adverb, **frothiness** noun.

frottage /ˈfrɒtɑːʒ/ ▶ **noun** [mass noun] **1** Art the technique or process of taking a rubbing from an uneven surface to form the basis of a work of art.
■[count noun] a work of art produced in this way.
2 the practice of touching or rubbing against the clothed body of another person in a crowd as a means of obtaining sexual gratification.
– DERIVATIVES **frotteur** noun (pl. same) (only in sense 2), **frotteurism** noun (only in sense 2).
– ORIGIN 1930s: French, 'rubbing, friction', from *frotter* 'to rub', of unknown origin.

frottola /ˈfrɒtələ/ ▶ **noun** (pl. **frottole** /-leɪ/) Music a form of Italian comic or amorous song, especially from the 15th and 16th centuries.
– ORIGIN Italian, literally 'fib, tall story'.

Froude number /ˈfruːd/ ▶ **noun** a dimensionless number used in hydrodynamics to indicate how well a particular model works in relation to a real system.
– ORIGIN mid 19th cent.: named after William *Froude* (1810–79), English civil engineer.

frou-frou /ˈfruːfruː/ ▶ **noun** a rustling noise made by someone walking in a dress.
■[mass noun] frills or other ornamentation, particularly of women's clothes: [as modifier] *a little frou-frou skirt.*
– ORIGIN late 19th cent.: from French, imitative.

frounce /fraʊns/ ▶ **noun** [mass noun] Falconry a form of trichomoniasis affecting hawks, resulting in a sore with a cheesy secretion in the mouth or throat.
– ORIGIN late Middle English: of unknown origin.

frow /fraʊ/ ▶ **noun** Brit. archaic a Dutchwoman.
– ORIGIN late Middle English: from Dutch *vrouw* 'woman'.

froward /ˈfrəʊəd/ ▶ **adjective** archaic (of a person) difficult to deal with; contrary.
– DERIVATIVES **frowardly** adverb, **frowardness** noun.
– ORIGIN late Old English *frāward* 'leading away from, away', based on Old Norse *frá* (see **FRO, FROM**).

frown ▶ **verb** [no obj.] furrow one's brows in an expression indicating disapproval, displeasure, or concentration: *he frowned as he reread the letter.*
■(**frown on/upon**) disapprove of: *promiscuity was frowned upon.*
▶ **noun** a facial expression or look characterized by such a furrowing of one's brows: *a frown of disapproval.*
– DERIVATIVES **frowner** noun, **frowningly** adverb.
– ORIGIN late Middle English: from Old French *froignier*, from *froigne* 'surly look', of Celtic origin.

frowst /fraʊst/ informal, chiefly Brit. ▶ **noun** [in sing.] a warm stuffy atmosphere in a room.
▶ **verb** [no obj.] lounge about in such an atmosphere: *don't frowst by the fire all day.*
– DERIVATIVES **frowster** noun.
– ORIGIN late 19th cent.: back-formation from **FROWSTY**.

frowsty ▶ **adjective** (**frowstier**, **frowstiest**) Brit. having a stale, warm, and stuffy atmosphere: *a small, frowsty office.*
– DERIVATIVES **frowstiness** noun.
– ORIGIN mid 19th cent. (originally dialect): variant of **FROWZY**.

frowzy /ˈfraʊzi/ (also **frowsy**) ▶ **adjective** (**frowzier**, **frowziest**) scruffy and neglected in appearance.
■dingy and stuffy: *a frowzy drinking-club.*
– DERIVATIVES **frowziness** noun.
– ORIGIN late 17th cent. (originally dialect): of unknown origin.

froze past of **FREEZE**.

frozen past participle of **FREEZE**.

frozen shoulder ▶ **noun** [mass noun] Medicine chronic painful stiffness of the shoulder joint.

FRS ▶ **abbreviation for** ■(in the UK) Fellow of the Royal Society. ■(in the UK) Financial Reporting Standard.

FRSE ▶ **abbreviation for** Fellow of the Royal Society of Edinburgh.

Fructidor /ˈfrʊktɪdɔː, French fʀyktidɔʀ/ ▶ **noun** the twelfth month of the French Republican calendar (1793–1805), originally running from 18 August to 16 September.
– ORIGIN French, from Latin *fructus* 'fruit' + Greek *dōron* 'gift'.

fructification /ˌfrʌktɪfɪˈkeɪʃ(ə)n/ ▶ **noun** [mass noun] the process of fructifying.
■[count noun] Botany a spore-bearing or fruiting structure, especially in a fungus.
– ORIGIN late 15th cent.: from late Latin *fructificatio(n-)*, from Latin *fructificare* 'fructify', from *fructus* 'fruit'.

fructify /ˈfrʌktɪfʌɪ/ ▶ **verb** (**-ies**, **-ied**) [with obj.] formal make (something) fruitful or productive: *they were sacrificed in order that their blood might fructify the crops.*
■[no obj.] bear fruit or become productive.
– ORIGIN Middle English: from Old French *fructifier*, from Latin *fructificare*, from *fructus* 'fruit'.

fructose /ˈfrʌktəʊz, -s/ ▶ **noun** [mass noun] Chemistry a sugar of the hexose class found especially in honey and fruit.
– ORIGIN mid 19th cent.: from Latin *fructus* 'fruit' + **-OSE**[2].

fructuous /ˈfrʌktjʊəs/ ▶ **adjective** formal full of or producing a great deal of fruit.
– ORIGIN late Middle English: from Latin *fructuosus*, from *fructus* 'fruit'.

frug ▶ **noun** a vigorous dance to pop music, popular in the mid 1960s.
▶ **verb** (**frugged**, **frugging**) [no obj.] perform such a dance.
– ORIGIN of unknown origin.

frugal /ˈfruːg(ə)l/ ▶ **adjective** sparing or economical as regards money or food: *he led a remarkably frugal existence.*
■simple and plain and costing little: *a frugal meal.*
– DERIVATIVES **frugality** noun, **frugally** adverb, **frugalness** noun.
– ORIGIN mid 16th cent.: from Latin *frugalis*, from *frugi* 'economical, thrifty', from *frux, frug-* 'fruit'.

frugivore /ˈfruːdʒɪvɔː/ ▶ **noun** Zoology an animal that feeds on fruit.
– DERIVATIVES **frugivorous** adjective.
– ORIGIN mid 20th cent.: from Latin *frux, frug-* 'fruit' + *-vore* (see **-VOROUS**).

fruit ▶ **noun 1** the sweet and fleshy product of a tree or other plant that contains seed and can be eaten as food: *tropical fruits such as mangoes and papaya* | [mass noun] *eat plenty of fresh fruit and vegetables.*
■Botany the seed-bearing structure of a plant, e.g. an acorn. ■ archaic or poetic/literary natural produce that can be used for food: *we give thanks for the fruits of the earth.* ■ the result or reward of work or activity: *the pupils began to appreciate the fruits of their labours.* ■ archaic offspring: *she couldn't bear not to see the fruit of her womb.*
2 derogatory, chiefly US a male homosexual.
▶ **verb** [no obj.] (of a tree or other plant) produce fruit, typically at a specified time: *the trees fruit very early* | [as noun **fruiting**] *cover strawberries with cloches to encourage early fruiting.*
– PHRASES **bear fruit** have good results: *his government's monetarism was beginning to bear fruit.* **in fruit** (of a tree or plant) at the stage of producing fruit. **old fruit** informal, dated a friendly form of address used by one man to another.
– ORIGIN Middle English: from Old French, from Latin *fructus* 'enjoyment of produce, harvest', from *frui* 'enjoy', related to *fruges* 'fruits of the earth', plural (and most common form) of *frux, frug-* 'fruit'.

fruitage ▶ **noun** [mass noun] archaic or poetic/literary fruit collectively.

fruitarian ▶ **noun** a person who eats only fruit.
– DERIVATIVES **fruitarianism** noun.
– ORIGIN late 19th cent.: from **FRUIT**, on the pattern of *vegetarian.*

fruit bat ▶ **noun** a bat with a long snout and large eyes, feeding chiefly on fruit or nectar and found mainly in the Old World tropics.
• Family Pteropodidae: many genera and numerous species. See also **FLYING FOX**.

fruit body ▶ **noun** another term for **FRUITING BODY**.

fruit cake ▶ **noun** a cake containing dried fruit and nuts.
■(**fruitcake**) informal an eccentric or mad person. [ORIGIN: compare with *nutty as a fruitcake* (see **NUTTY**).]

fruit cocktail ▶ **noun** [mass noun] a finely chopped fruit salad, often commercially produced in tins.

fruitcrow ▶ **noun** a large tropical American cotinga with mainly black or red and black plumage.
• Family Cotingidae: four genera and species.

fruit cup ▶ **noun 1** Brit. a drink consisting of a mixture of fruit juices, typically with pieces of fruit in it.
2 N. Amer. a fruit salad.

fruit dove ▶ **noun** a tropical fruit-eating dove that typically has brightly coloured plumage, usually with a green back, and occurs mainly in Indonesia and Australasia. Compare with **FRUIT PIGEON**.
• Genus *Ptilonopus* (and *Phapitreron*), family Columbidae: many species.

fruit drop ▶ **noun** [mass noun] the shedding of unripe fruit from a tree.

fruited ▶ **adjective** [usu. in combination] (of a tree or plant) producing fruit, especially of a specified kind: *heavy-fruited plants like tomatoes.*

fruiter ▶ **noun** a tree producing fruit at a specified time or in a specified manner: *the wet-season fruiters.*
– ORIGIN Middle English (in the sense 'fruit grower'): from Old French *fruitier*, from *fruit* 'fruit'; in later use from **FRUIT** + **-ER**[1]. Current senses date from the 19th cent.

fruiterer ▶ **noun** chiefly Brit. a retailer of fruit.
– ORIGIN late Middle English: from **FRUITER** + **-ER**[1]; the reason for the addition of the suffix is unclear.

fruit fly ▶ **noun** a small fly which feeds on fruit in both its adult and larval stages.
• Families Drosophilidae and Tephritidae: many genera. See also **DROSOPHILA**.

fruitful ▶ **adjective** (of a tree, plant, or land) producing much fruit; fertile.
■producing good or helpful results; productive: *memoirs can be a fruitful source of information.* ■ (of a person) producing many offspring.
– DERIVATIVES **fruitfully** adverb, **fruitfulness** noun.

fruiting body ▶ **noun** Botany the spore-producing organ of a fungus, often seen as a toadstool.

fruition /frʊˈɪʃ(ə)n/ ▶ **noun** [mass noun] **1** the point at which a plan or project is realized: *the plans have come to fruition rather sooner than expected.*
■[in sing.] the realization of a plan or project: *new methods will come with the fruition of that research.*
2 poetic/literary the state or action of producing fruit.

– ORIGIN late Middle English (in the sense 'enjoyment'): via Old French from late Latin *fruitio(n-)*, from *frui* 'enjoy' (see FRUIT); the current senses (dating from the late 19th cent.) arose by association with FRUIT.

fruitless ▶ adjective **1** failing to achieve the desired results; unproductive or useless: *his fruitless attempts to publish poetry.*
2 (of a tree or plant) not producing fruit.
– DERIVATIVES **fruitlessly** adverb, **fruitlessness** noun.

fruitlet ▶ noun an immature or small fruit.
■Botany another term for DRUPEL.

fruit machine ▶ noun Brit. a coin-operated gaming machine that generates random combinations of symbols (typically representing fruit) on a dial, certain combinations winning varying amounts of money for the player.

fruit pigeon ▶ noun a fruit-eating pigeon occurring in the Old World tropics. Compare with FRUIT DOVE.
● a relative of the imperial pigeons occurring in New Guinea (genus *Ducula*, family Columbidae). ● a green pigeon occurring in Africa (genus *Treron*, family Columbidae).

fruit salad ▶ noun [mass noun] a mixture of different types of chopped fruit served in syrup or juice.
■military slang a display of medals and other decorations.

fruit sugar ▶ noun [mass noun] **1** another term for FRUCTOSE.
2 Canadian a very fine type of granulated sugar suitable for sprinkling on fruit.

fruit tree ▶ noun a tree grown for its edible fruit.

fruitwood ▶ noun [mass noun] [usu. as modifier] the wood of a fruit tree, especially when used in furniture: *a fruitwood dressing table.*

fruity ▶ adjective (**fruitier**, **fruitiest**) **1** (especially of food or drink) of, resembling, or containing fruit: *a light and fruity Beaujolais.*
2 (of a voice or sound) mellow, deep, and rich: *Jeffery had a wonderfully fruity voice.*
■Brit. informal sexually suggestive in content or style.
3 derogatory, chiefly US relating to or associated with homosexuals.
4 informal, chiefly US eccentric or crazy: *a kind of fruity professor.*
– DERIVATIVES **fruitily** adverb, **fruitiness** noun.

frumenty /ˈfruːm(ə)nti/ (also **furmety**) ▶ noun [mass noun] Brit. an old-fashioned dish consisting of hulled wheat boiled in milk and seasoned with cinnamon and sugar.
– ORIGIN late Middle English: from Old French *frumentee*, from *frument*, from Latin *frumentum* 'corn'.

frump ▶ noun an unattractive woman who wears dowdy old-fashioned clothes.
– DERIVATIVES **frumpily** adverb, **frumpiness** noun, **frumpish** adjective, **frumpishly** adverb, **frumpy** adjective.
– ORIGIN mid 16th cent.: probably a contraction of late Middle English *frumple* 'wrinkle', from Middle Dutch *verrompelen*. The word originally denoted a mocking speech or action; later (in the plural) ill humour, the sulks; hence a bad-tempered, (later) dowdy woman (early 19th cent.).

Frunze /ˈfruːnzi/ former name (1926–91) for BISHKEK.

frusemide /ˈfruːsəmʌɪd/ (chiefly US also **furosemide**) ▶ noun [mass noun] Medicine a synthetic compound with a strong diuretic action, used especially in the treatment of oedema.
● Chem. formula: $C_{12}H_{11}ClN_2O_5S$.
– ORIGIN 1960s: from *fru–* (alteration of *fur(yl)*, denoting a radical derived from furan) + *sem–* (of unknown origin) + -IDE.

frustrate ▶ verb [with obj.] prevent (a plan or attempted action) from progressing, succeeding, or being fulfilled: *Alfonso tried to frustrate his plans.*
■prevent (someone) from doing or achieving something that they plan or want to do: *in numerous policy areas, central government has been frustrated by local authorities.* ■ cause (someone) to feel upset or annoyed, typically as a result of being unable to change or achieve something: [as adj. **frustrating**] *it can be very frustrating to find that the size you want isn't there.*
▶ adjective archaic frustrated.
– DERIVATIVES **frustrater** noun, **frustratingly** adverb [as submodifier] *progress turned out to be frustratingly slow.*
– ORIGIN late Middle English: from Latin *frustrat-*

'disappointed', from the verb *frustrare*, from *frustra* 'in vain'.

frustrated ▶ adjective feeling or expressing distress and annoyance, especially because of inability to change or achieve something: *young people get frustrated with the system.*
■[attrib.] (of a person) unable to follow or be successful in a particular career: *a frustrated actor.* ■ [attrib.] prevented from progressing, succeeding, or being fulfilled: *our parents may want us to fulfil their own frustrated dreams.* ■(of a person or sexual desire) unfulfilled sexually: *jealousies and frustrated passions.*
– DERIVATIVES **frustratedly** adverb.

frustration ▶ noun [mass noun] the feeling of being upset or annoyed, especially because of inability to change or achieve something: *I sometimes feel like screaming with frustration.*
■[count noun] an event or circumstance that causes one to have such a feeling: *the inherent frustrations of assembly line work.* ■ the prevention of the progress, success, or fulfilment of something: *the frustration of their wishes.*
– ORIGIN mid 16th cent.: from Latin *frustratio(n-)*, from *frustrare* 'disappoint' (see FRUSTRATE).

frustule /ˈfrʌstjuːl/ ▶ noun Botany the silicified cell wall of a diatom, consisting of two valves or overlapping halves.
– ORIGIN mid 19th cent.: from Latin *frustulum*, diminutive of *frustum* (see FRUSTUM).

frustum /ˈfrʌstəm/ ▶ noun (pl. **frusta** /-tə/ or **frustums**) Geometry the portion of a cone or pyramid which remains after its upper part has been cut off by a plane parallel to its base, or which is intercepted between two such planes.
– ORIGIN mid 17th cent.: from Latin, 'piece cut off'.

fruticose /ˈfruːtɪkəʊz, -s/ ▶ adjective Botany (of a lichen) having upright or pendulous branches.
– ORIGIN mid 17th cent.: from Latin *fruticosus*, from *frutex, frutic-* 'bush, shrub'.

Fry[1], Christopher (Harris) (b.1907), English dramatist. He is known chiefly for his comic verse dramas, especially *The Lady's not for Burning* (1948) and *Venus Observed* (1950).

Fry[2], Elizabeth (1780–1845), English Quaker prison reformer, a leading figure in the early 19th-century campaign for penal reform.

Fry[3], Roger (Eliot) (1866–1934), English art critic and painter. He argued for an aesthetics of pure form, regarding content as incidental.

fry[1] ▶ verb (**-ies, -ied**) [with obj.] cook (food) in hot fat or oil, typically in a shallow pan.
■[no obj.] (of food) be cooked in such a way: *put half a dozen steaks to fry in a pan.* ■ [no obj.] informal (of a person) burn or overheat: *with the sea and sun and wind you'll fry if you don't take care.* ■ N. Amer. informal execute or be executed by electrocution.
▶ noun (pl. **-ies**) [in sing.] a meal of meat or other food cooked in such a way: *would you like a fry in the morning?*
■[mass noun] Brit. any of various types of offal, usually eaten fried. ■ (**fries**) N. Amer. another term for FRENCH FRIES. ■ N. Amer. a social gathering where fried food is served: *you'll explore islands and stop for a fish fry.*
– ORIGIN Middle English: from Old French *frire*, from Latin *frigere*.

fry[2] ▶ plural noun young fish, especially when newly hatched.
■the young of other animals produced in large numbers, such as frogs.
– ORIGIN Middle English: from Old Norse *frjó*.

Frye, (Herman) Northrop (1912–91), Canadian literary critic. His work explores the use of myth and symbolism. Notable works: *Fearful Symmetry* (1947) and *The Great Code: The Bible and Literature* (1982).

fryer (also **frier**) ▶ noun **1** a large, deep container for frying food.
2 N. Amer. a small young chicken suitable for frying.

frying pan (N. Amer. also **frypan**) ▶ noun a shallow pan with a long handle, used for cooking food in hot fat or oil.
– PHRASES **out of the frying pan into the fire** from a bad situation to one that is worse.

fry-up ▶ noun Brit. informal a dish of various types of fried food.

FS ▶ abbreviation for (in the UK) Flight Sergeant.

FSA ▶ abbreviation for (in the UK) Fellow of the Society of Antiquaries.

FSH ▶ abbreviation for follicle-stimulating hormone.

FST ▶ abbreviation for flat screen television.

f-stop ▶ noun Photography a camera setting corresponding to a particular f-number.

FT ▶ abbreviation for (in the UK) Financial Times.

Ft ▶ abbreviation for Fort: *Ft Lauderdale.*

ft ▶ abbreviation for foot; feet.

FTA N. Amer. ▶ abbreviation for Free Trade Agreement, used to refer to that signed in 1988 between the US and Canada.

FTC ▶ abbreviation for (in the US) Federal Trade Commission.

FT index another term for FTSE INDEX.

FTP Computing ▶ abbreviation for file transfer protocol, a standard for the exchange of program and data files across a network.
▶ verb (**FTP'd** or **FTPed**, **FTPing**) [with obj.] informal transfer (a file) from one computer or system to another, especially on the Internet.

FTSE index a figure (published by the *Financial Times*) indicating the relative prices of shares on the London Stock Exchange, especially (also **FTSE 100 index**) one calculated on the basis of Britain's one hundred largest public companies.
– ORIGIN *FTSE*, abbreviation of *Financial Times Stock Exchange*.

Fuad /ˈfuːad/ the name of two kings of Egypt:
■Fuad I (1868–1936), reigned 1922–36. Formerly sultan of Egypt (1917–1922), he became Egypt's first king after independence.
■Fuad II (b.1952), grandson of Fuad I, reigned 1952–3. Named king as an infant on the forced abdication of his father, Farouk, he was deposed when Egypt became a republic.

fubsy /ˈfʌbzi/ ▶ adjective (**fubsier**, **fubsiest**) Brit. informal fat and squat.
– ORIGIN late 18th cent.: from dialect *fubs* 'small fat person', perhaps a blend of FAT and CHUB.

Fuchs[1] /fʊks/, (Emil) Klaus (Julius) (1911–88), German-born British physicist. He was a communist who fled Nazi persecution. During the 1940s he passed to the USSR secret information acquired while working on the development of the atom bomb in the US, and while engaged in research in Britain.

Fuchs[2] /fʊks/, Sir Vivian (Ernest) (1908–99), English geologist and explorer. He led the Commonwealth Trans-Antarctic Expedition (1955–8), making the first overland crossing of the Antarctic.

fuchsia /ˈfjuːʃə/ ▶ noun a shrub with pendulous tubular flowers that are typically of two contrasting colours. They are native to America and New Zealand and are commonly grown as ornamentals.
● Genus *Fuchsia*, family Onagraceae: many cultivars.
■Austral. used in names of plants of other families with similar flowers, e.g. **native fuchsia**. ■ [mass noun] a vivid purplish-red colour like that of the sepals of a typical fuchsia flower.
– ORIGIN modern Latin, named in honour of Leonhard *Fuchs* (1501–66), German botanist.

fuchsin /ˈfuːksiːn/ (also **fuchsine**) ▶ noun [mass noun] a deep red synthetic dye used as a biological stain and disinfectant.
● A chloride of rosaniline; chem. formula: $C_{20}H_{20}N_3Cl$.
– ORIGIN mid 19th cent.: from German *Fuchs* 'fox', translating French *Renard* (the name of the chemical company which first produced fuchsin commercially) + -IN[1].

fuck vulgar slang ▶ verb [with obj.] **1** have sexual intercourse with (someone).
■[no obj.] (of two people) have sexual intercourse.
2 damage or ruin (something).
▶ noun an act of sexual intercourse.
■[with adj.] a sexual partner of a specified ability.
▶ exclamation used alone or as a noun (**the fuck**) or a verb in various phrases to express anger, annoyance, contempt, impatience, or surprise, or simply for emphasis.
– PHRASES **fuck all** Brit. absolutely nothing.
– DERIVATIVES **fuckable** adjective.
– ORIGIN early 16th cent.: of Germanic origin (compare Swedish dialect *focka* and Dutch dialect *fokkelen*); possibly from an Indo-European root meaning 'strike', shared by Latin *pugnus* 'fist'.

USAGE Despite the wideness and proliferation of its use in many sections of society, the word **fuck** remains (and has been for centuries) one of the most taboo words in English. Until relatively recently it rarely appeared in print; even today, there are a number of euphemistic ways of referring to it in speech and writing, e.g. **the F-word**, **f*****, or **f—k**.

▶**fuck about** (or **around**) spend time doing unimportant or trivial things.
fuck someone around (or **about**) waste someone's time.
fuck off 1 [usu. in imperative] (of a person) go away. **2** chiefly US another way of saying **fuck about**.
fuck someone off make someone angry.
fuck someone over US treat someone in an unfair or humiliating way.
fuck someone up damage or confuse someone emotionally.
fuck something up (or **fuck up**) do something badly or ineptly.

fucker ▶ noun vulgar slang a contemptible or stupid person (often used as a general term of abuse).

fuckhead ▶ noun vulgar slang a stupid or contemptible person (often used as a general term of abuse).

fucking ▶ adjective [attrib.] & adverb [as submodifier] vulgar slang used for emphasis or to express anger, annoyance, contempt, or surprise.

fuck-me ▶ adjective vulgar slang (of clothing, especially shoes) inviting or perceived as inviting sexual interest.

fuck-up ▶ noun vulgar slang a mess or muddle.
■a person who has a tendency to make a mess of things.

fuckwit ▶ noun vulgar slang a stupid or contemptible person (often used as a general term of abuse).

fucoid /ˈfjuːkɔɪd/ Botany ▶ noun a brown seaweed or fossil plant of a group to which bladderwrack belongs.
● Order Fucales, class Phaeophyceae, including genus *Fucus*.
▶ adjective of, relating to, or resembling a brown seaweed, especially a fucoid.
– ORIGIN mid 19th cent.: from **FUCUS** + **-OID**.

fucoxanthin /ˌfjuːkəˈzanθɪn/ ▶ noun [mass noun] Chemistry a brown carotenoid pigment occurring in and generally characteristic of the brown algae.
– ORIGIN late 19th cent.: from **FUCUS** + *xanthin*, variant of **XANTHINE**.

fucus /ˈfjuːkəs/ ▶ noun (pl. **fuci** /ˈfjuːsʌɪ/) a seaweed of a large genus of brown algae having flat leathery fronds.
● Genus *Fucus*, class Phaeophyceae.
– DERIVATIVES **fucoid** adjective.
– ORIGIN early 17th cent. (denoting a cosmetic): from Latin, 'rock lichen, red dye, rouge', from Greek *phukos* 'seaweed', of Semitic origin.

fuddle /ˈfʌd(ə)l/ ▶ verb [with obj.] [usu. as adj. **fuddled**] confuse or stupefy (someone), especially with alcohol.
■[no obj.] archaic go on a drinking bout.
▶ noun [in sing.] a state of confusion or intoxication: *through the fuddle of wine he heard some of the conversation.*
■archaic a drinking bout.
– ORIGIN late 16th cent. (in the sense 'go on a drinking bout'): of unknown origin.

fuddled ▶ adjective confused or stupefied, especially as a result of drinking alcohol: [in combination] *Benjamin was trying to clear his drink-fuddled brain.*

fuddy-duddy ▶ noun (pl. **-ies**) informal a person who is very old-fashioned and pompous: *he probably thinks I'm an old fuddy-duddy.*
– ORIGIN early 20th cent. (originally dialect): of unknown origin.

fudge ▶ noun **1** [mass noun] a soft crumbly or chewy sweet made from sugar, butter, and milk or cream.
■[as modifier] chiefly N. Amer. rich chocolate, used especially as a filling for cakes or a sauce on ice cream.
2 an effort to address an issue that fails to resolve it properly and seeks to disguise this inadequacy: *the new settlement is a fudge rushed out to win cheers at conference* | [mass noun] *the report's final wording is a classic piece of fudge.*
■[mass noun] archaic nonsense.
3 a piece of late news inserted in a newspaper page.
▶ verb [with obj.] present or deal with (something) in a vague, non-committal, or inadequate way,

especially so as to conceal the truth or mislead: *the minister tried to fudge the issue by saying he did not want to specify periods.*
■adjust or manipulate (facts or figures) so as to present a desired picture.
▶ exclamation dated nonsense (expressing disbelief or annoyance).
– ORIGIN early 17th cent.: probably an alteration of obsolete *fadge* 'to fit'. Early usage was as a verb in the sense 'turn out as expected', also 'merge together': this probably gave rise to its use in confectionery. In the late 17th cent. the verb came to mean 'fit together in a clumsy or underhand manner', which included facts or figures being cobbled together in a superficially convincing way: this led to the exclamation 'fudge!' and to noun sense 3.

fudge factor ▶ noun informal a figure included in a calculation to account for some unquantified but significant phenomenon or to ensure a desired result.

fuehrer ▶ noun variant spelling of **FÜHRER**.

fuel ▶ noun [mass noun] material such as coal, gas, or oil that is burned to produce heat or power.
■short for **NUCLEAR FUEL**. ■ food, drink, or drugs as a source of energy: *any protein intake can also be used as fuel.* ■ a thing that sustains or inflames passion, argument, or other intense emotion or activity: *the remuneration packages will add fuel to the debate about top-level rewards.*
▶ verb (**fuelled**, **fuelling**; US **fueled**, **fueling**) [with obj.] **1** supply or power (an industrial plant, vehicle, or machine) with fuel: *the plan includes a hydroelectric plant to fuel a paper factory* | figurative *most mindless hooligans are fuelled by alcohol.*
■fill up (a vehicle, aircraft, or ship) with oil or petrol. ■ [no obj.] (**fuel up**) (of a vehicle, aircraft, or ship) be filled up with oil or petrol.
2 cause (a fire) to burn more intensely.
■sustain or inflame (intense feeling or activity): *his resignation fuelled speculation of an imminent cabinet reshuffle.*
– PHRASES **add fuel to the fire** (or **flames**) figurative cause a situation or conflict to become more intense, especially by provocative comments.
– ORIGIN Middle English: from Old French *fouaille*, based on Latin *focus* 'hearth' (in late Latin 'fire').

fuel cell ▶ noun a cell producing an electric current direct from a chemical reaction.

fuel element ▶ noun an element consisting of nuclear fuel and other materials for use in a reactor.

fuel injection ▶ noun [mass noun] the direct introduction of fuel under pressure into the combustion units of an internal-combustion engine.
– DERIVATIVES **fuel-injected** adjective.

fuel oil ▶ noun [mass noun] oil used as fuel in an engine or furnace.

fuel rod ▶ noun a rod-shaped fuel element in a nuclear reactor.

fuelwood ▶ noun [mass noun] wood used as fuel.

Fuentes /ˈfwɛntɛz/, Carlos (b.1928), Mexican novelist and writer. Notable works: *Where the Air is Clear* (1958), *Terra nostra* (1975), and *The Old Gringo* (1984).

fufu /ˈfuːfuː/ (also **foo-foo**) ▶ noun [mass noun] dough made from boiled and ground plantain or cassava, used as a staple food in parts of West and central Africa.
– ORIGIN mid 18th cent.: from Twi *fufuu*.

fug ▶ noun [in sing.] Brit. informal a warm stuffy or smoky atmosphere in a room: *the cosy fug of the music halls.*
– DERIVATIVES **fuggy** adjective.
– ORIGIN late 19th cent. (originally dialect and schoolchildren's slang): of unknown origin.

fugacious /fjʊˈɡeɪʃəs/ ▶ adjective poetic/literary tending to disappear; fleeting: *she was acutely conscious of her fugacious youth.*
– DERIVATIVES **fugaciously** adverb, **fugaciousness** noun.
– ORIGIN mid 17th cent.: from Latin *fugax, fugac-* (from *fugere* 'flee') + **-IOUS**.

fugacity /fjʊˈɡasɪti/ ▶ noun [mass noun] **1** poetic/literary the quality of being fleeting or evanescent.
2 Chemistry a thermodynamic property of a real gas which if substituted for the pressure or partial pressure in the equations for an ideal gas gives equations applicable to the real gas.

fugal /ˈfjuːɡ(ə)l/ ▶ adjective of the nature of a fugue: *the virtuosity of the fugal finale.*
– DERIVATIVES **fugally** adverb.

Fugard /ˈfuːɡɑːd/, Athol (b.1932), South African dramatist. His plays, including *Blood Knot* (1963) and *The Road to Mecca* (1985), are mostly set in contemporary South Africa and deal with social deprivation and other aspects of life under apartheid.

fugato /fjuːˈɡɑːtəʊ, fu:-/ Music ▶ adjective & adverb in the style of a fugue, but not in strict or complete fugal form.
▶ noun (pl. **-os**) a passage in this style.
– ORIGIN Italian.

-fuge ▶ combining form expelling or dispelling either a specified thing or in a specified way: *vermifuge* | *centrifuge.*
– ORIGIN from modern Latin *-fugus*, from Latin *fugare* 'cause to flee'.

Fuggle ▶ noun (usu. **Fuggles**) hops of a variety used in beer-making.
– ORIGIN late 19th cent.: of unknown origin.

fugitive ▶ noun a person who has escaped from a place or is in hiding, especially to avoid arrest or persecution: *fugitives from justice* | [as modifier] *fugitive criminals.*
■[as modifier] figurative quick to disappear; fleeting: *he entertained a fugitive idea that Bella needed him.*
– ORIGIN late Middle English: from Old French *fugitif, -ive*, from Latin *fugitivus*, from *fugere* 'flee'.

fugleman /ˈfjuːɡ(ə)lmən/ ▶ noun (pl. **-men**) historical a soldier placed in front of a regiment or company while drilling to demonstrate the motions and time.
■figurative a leader, organizer, or spokesman: *fuglemen of the ideological right.*
– ORIGIN early 19th cent.: from German *Flügelmann* 'leader of the file', from *Flügel* 'wing' + *Mann* 'man'.

fugu /ˈfuːɡuː/ ▶ noun [mass noun] a pufferfish that is eaten as a Japanese delicacy, after some highly poisonous parts have been removed.
– ORIGIN mid 20th cent.: from Japanese.

fugue /fjuːɡ/ ▶ noun **1** Music a contrapuntal composition in which a short melody or phrase (the subject) is introduced by one part and successively taken up by others and developed by interweaving the parts.
2 Psychiatry a state or period of loss of awareness of one's identity, often coupled with flight from one's usual environment, associated with certain forms of hysteria and epilepsy.
– DERIVATIVES **fuguist** noun.
– ORIGIN late 16th cent.: from French, or from Italian *fuga*, from Latin *fuga* 'flight', related to *fugere* 'flee'.

führer /ˈfjʊərə/ (also **fuehrer**) ▶ noun a tyrannical leader.
– ORIGIN from German *Führer* 'leader', part of the title *Führer und Reichskanzler* 'Leader and Chancellor of the Empire' assumed in 1934 by Adolf **HITLER**.

Fujairah /fuːˈdʒʌɪərə/ (also **Al Fujayrah**) one of the seven member states of the United Arab Emirates; pop. 76,200 (1995).

Fuji /ˈfuːdʒi/ ▶ noun a Japanese dessert apple of a variety with crisp sweet flesh and an orange flush to the skin.

Fuji, Mount /ˈfuːdʒi/ a dormant volcano in the Chubu region of Japan. Rising to 3,776 m (12,385 ft), it is Japan's highest mountain and is regarded by the Japanese as sacred. Also called **FUJIYAMA** /ˌfuːdʒɪˈjɑːmə/.

Fujian /ˌfuːdʒiˈan/ (also **Fukien** /fuːˈkjɛn/) a province of SE China, on the China Sea; capital, Fuzhou.

Fukuoka /ˌfuːkuːˈəʊkə/ an industrial city and port in southern Japan, capital of Kyushu island; pop. 1,237,100 (1990).

-ful ▶ suffix **1** (forming adjectives from nouns) full of: *sorrowful.*
■having the qualities of: *masterful.*
2 forming adjectives from adjectives or from Latin stems with little change of sense: *grateful.*
3 (forming adjectives from verbs) apt to; able to; accustomed to: *forgetful* | *watchful.*
4 (pl. **-fuls**) forming nouns denoting the amount needed to fill the specified container, holder, etc.: *bucketful* | *handful.*
– ORIGIN from **FULL**.

Fula /ˈfuːlə/ (also **Foulah**) ▶ noun [mass noun] the

language of the Fulani people, spoken as a first language by about 10 million people and widely used in West Africa as a lingua franca. It belongs to the Benue-Congo language family. Also called **FUL**, **FULANI**, **FULFULDE**.

Fulani /fuːˈlɑːni/ ▶ **noun** (pl. same) **1** a member of a people living in a region of West Africa from Senegal to northern Nigeria and Cameroon. They are traditionally nomadic cattle herders of Muslim faith.
2 another term for **FULA**.
▶ **adjective** of or relating to this people or their language.
– ORIGIN the name in Hausa.

Fulbe /ˈfʊlbeɪ/ ▶ **plural noun** (**the Fulbe**) another term for the **FULANI** people.

Fulbright, (James) William (1905–95), American senator. His name designates grants awarded under the Fulbright Act of 1946, which authorized funds from the sale of surplus war materials overseas to be used to finance exchange programmes of students and teachers between the US and other countries. The scheme was later supported by grants from the US government.

fulcrum /ˈfʊlkrəm, ˈfʌl-/ ▶ **noun** (pl. **fulcra** /-rə/ or **fulcrums**) the point against which a lever is placed to get a purchase, or on which it turns or is supported.
■ a thing that plays a central or essential role in an activity, event, or situation: *research is the fulcrum of the academic community.*
– ORIGIN late 17th cent. (originally in the general sense 'a prop or support'): from Latin, literally 'post of a couch', from *fulcire* 'to prop up'.

fulfil (US **fulfill**) ▶ **verb** (**fulfilled**, **fulfilling**) **1** bring to completion or reality; achieve or realize (something desired, promised, or predicted): *he wouldn't be able to fulfil his ambition to visit Naples.*
■ (**fulfil oneself**) gain happiness or satisfaction by fully developing one's abilities or character. ■ archaic complete (a period of time or piece of work).
2 carry out (a task, duty, or role) as required, pledged, or expected.
■ satisfy or meet (a requirement, condition, or need): *goods must fulfil three basic conditions.*
– DERIVATIVES **fulfillable** adjective, **fulfiller** noun.
– ORIGIN late Old English *fullfyllan* 'fill up, make full' (see **FULL**[1], **FILL**).

fulfilled ▶ **adjective** satisfied or happy because of fully developing one's abilities or character.

fulfilling ▶ **adjective** making someone satisfied or happy because of having fully developed their character or abilities: *a fulfilling and rewarding career.*

fulfilment (US **fulfillment**) ▶ **noun** [mass noun] **1** satisfaction or happiness as a result of fully developing one's abilities or character: *she did not believe that marriage was the key to happiness and fulfilment.*
2 the achievement of something desired, promised, or predicted: *winning the championship was the fulfilment of a childhood dream.*
■ the meeting of a requirement, condition, or need: *the fulfilment of statutory requirements.* ■ the performance of a task, duty, or role as required, pledged, or expected.

Fulfulde /fʊlˈfʊldeɪ/ ▶ **noun** another term for **FULA**.

fulgent /ˈfʌldʒ(ə)nt/ ▶ **adjective** poetic/literary shining brightly.
– ORIGIN late Middle English: from Latin *fulgent-* 'shining', from the verb *fulgere.*

fulguration /ˌfʌlgjʊˈreɪʃ(ə)n/ ▶ **noun 1** [mass noun] Medicine the destruction of small growths or areas of tissue using diathermy.
2 poetic/literary a flash like that of lightning.
– DERIVATIVES **fulgurant** adjective (only in sense 2), **fulgurate** verb (only in sense 2), **fulgurous** adjective (only in sense 2).
– ORIGIN mid 17th cent. (usually plural in the sense 'flashes of lightning'): from Latin *fulguratio(n-)* 'sheet lightning', from *fulgur* 'lightning'. Sense 1 dates from the early 20th cent.

fulgurite /ˈfʌlgjʊrʌɪt/ ▶ **noun** [mass noun] Geology vitreous material formed of sand or other sediment fused by lightning.
■ [count noun] a piece of such material.
– ORIGIN mid 19th cent.: from Latin *fulgur* 'lightning' + **-ITE**[1].

fuliginous /fjuːˈlɪdʒɪnəs/ ▶ **adjective** poetic/literary sooty; dusky.
– ORIGIN late 16th cent. (originally describing a vapour as 'thick and noxious'): from late Latin *fuliginosus*, from *fuligo, fuligin-* 'soot'.

full[1] ▶ **adjective 1** containing or holding as much or as many as possible; having no empty space: *waste bins full of rubbish | she could only nod, for her mouth was full.*
■ having eaten or drunk to one's limits or satisfaction. See also ***full up*** below. ■ [predic.] (**full of**) containing or holding much or many; having a large number of: *his diary is full of entries about her.* ■ [predic.] (**full of**) having a lot of (a particular quality): *she was full of confidence.* ■ [predic.] (**full of**) completely engrossed with; unable to stop talking or thinking about: *Anna had been full of her day, saying how Mitch had described England to her.* ■ filled with intense emotion: *she picked at her food, her heart too full to eat.* ■ involving a lot of activities: *he lived a full life.* ■ informal, chiefly Austral. & Scottish drunk.
2 [attrib.] not lacking or omitting anything; complete: *fill in your full name below | full details on request.*
■ (often used for emphasis) reaching the utmost limit; maximum: *he reached for the engine control and turned it up to full power | John made full use of all the tuition provided.* ■ having all the privileges and status attached to a particular position: *the country applied for full membership of the European Community.* ■ (of a report or account) containing as much detail or information as possible. ■ used to emphasize an amount or quantity: *he kept his fast pace going for the full 14-mile distance.* ■ [attrib.] (of a covering material in bookbinding) used for the entire cover: *bound in full cloth.*
3 (of a person or part of their body) plump or rounded: *she had full lips | the fuller figure.*
■ (of the hair) having body. ■ (of a garment) made using much material arranged in folds or gathers, or generously cut so as to fit loosely: *the dress has a square neck and a full skirt.* ■ (of a sound) strong and resonant. ■ (of a flavour or colour) rich or intense.
▶ **adverb 1** straight; directly: *she turned her head and looked full into his face.*
2 very: *he **knew full well** she was too polite to barge in.*
■ archaic entirely (used to emphasize an amount or quantity): *they talked for full half an hour.*
▶ **noun** (**the full**) archaic the period, point, or state of the greatest fullness or strength; the height of a period of time.
■ the state or time of full moon. ■ archaic or Irish the whole.
▶ **verb 1** [with obj.] black English make (something) full; fill up: *he **full up** the house with bawling.*
2 [with obj.] gather or pleat (fabric) so as to make a garment full.
3 [no obj.] dialect or US (of the moon or tide) become full.
– PHRASES (**as**) **full as a goog** see **GOOG**. **full and by** Sailing close-hauled but with sails filling. **full of beans** see **BEAN**. **full of oneself** very self-satisfied and with an exaggerated sense of self-worth. **full of years** archaic having lived to a considerable age. **full on 1** running at or providing maximum power or capacity: *he had the heater full on.* **2** so as to make a direct or significant impact: *the recession has hit us full on.* ■ (**full-on**) informal (of an activity or thing) not diluted in nature or effect: *this is full-on ballroom boogie.* ■ (**full-on**) informal (of a person) entirely and unrestrainedly of a specified type: *at school he'd been this full-on aggro animal.* **full out 1** as much or as far as possible; with maximum effort or power: *he held his foot to the floor until the car raced full out.* **2** Printing flush with the margin. **full steam** (or **speed**) **ahead** used to indicate that one should proceed with as much speed or energy as possible. **full to the brim** see **BRIM**. **full up** filled to capacity. ■ having eaten or drunk so much that one is replete. **in full** with nothing omitted: *I shall expect your life story in full.* ■ to the full amount due: *their relocation costs would be paid in full.* ■ to the utmost; completely: *the textbooks have failed to exploit in full the opportunities offered.* **to the full** to the greatest possible extent: *enjoy your free trip to Europe to the full.*
– ORIGIN Old English, of Germanic origin; related to Dutch *vol* and German *voll.*

full[2] ▶ **verb** [with obj.] [often as noun **fulling**] clean, shrink, and felt (cloth) by heat, pressure, and moisture.
– ORIGIN Middle English: probably a back-formation from *fuller*, influenced by Old French *fouler* 'press hard upon' or medieval Latin *fullare*, based on Latin *fullo* 'fuller'.

full age ▶ **noun** [mass noun] Brit. adult status (especially with reference to legal rights and duties).

fullback ▶ **noun** a player in a defensive position near the goal in a ball game such as soccer, rugby, or field hockey.

full beam ▶ **noun** [mass noun] the brightest setting of a vehicle's headlights.

full-blooded ▶ **adjective 1** [attrib.] of unmixed race: *a full-blooded Cherokee.*
2 vigorous, enthusiastic, and without compromise: *his belief in full-blooded socialism.*
– DERIVATIVES **full-blood** noun (only in sense 1), **full-bloodedly** adverb, **full-bloodedness** noun.

full-blown ▶ **adjective** fully developed: *the onset of full-blown Aids in persons infected with HIV.*
■ (of a flower) in full bloom.

full board ▶ **noun 1** [mass noun] Brit. provision of accommodation and all meals at a hotel or guest house.
2 Austral./NZ a full complement of shearers. [ORIGIN: *board*, denoting part of the floor of a shearing shed (see **BOARD**).]

full-bodied ▶ **adjective** rich and satisfying in flavour or sound: *a spicy, full-bodied white wine.*

full bore chiefly N. Amer. ▶ **adverb** at full speed or maximum capacity: *the boat came full bore towards us.*
▶ **adjective** [attrib.] denoting firearms of relatively large calibre: *full-bore hand guns.*
■ figurative complete; thoroughgoing: *a full-bore leftist.*

full-bottomed ▶ **adjective** (of a wig) long at the back.

full brother ▶ **noun** a brother born of the same mother and father.

full-court press ▶ **noun** Basketball an aggressive tactic in which members of a team cover their opponents throughout the court and not just in the region near their own basket.

full-cream ▶ **adjective** Brit. (of milk) unskimmed.

full dress ▶ **noun** [mass noun] clothes worn on ceremonial or very formal occasions.
▶ **adjective** [attrib.] denoting an event, activity, or process which is treated with complete seriousness or which possesses all the characteristics of a genuine example of the type: *shuttle diplomacy might be better than a full-dress conference.*

full dress uniform ▶ **noun** [mass noun] military uniform worn on ceremonial occasions.

Fuller[1], R. Buckminster (1895–1983), American designer and architect; full name *Richard Buckminster Fuller.* He is best known for his invention of the geodesic dome and for his ideals of using the world's resources with maximum purpose and least waste.

Fuller[2], Thomas (1608–61), English cleric and historian. He is chiefly remembered for *The History of the Worthies of England* (1662), a description of the counties with short biographies of local personages.

fuller[1] ▶ **noun** a person whose occupation is fulling cloth.

fuller[2] ▶ **noun** a grooved or rounded tool on which iron is shaped.
■ a groove made by this, especially in a horseshoe.
▶ **verb** [with obj.] stamp (iron) with a such a tool.
– ORIGIN early 19th cent. (as a verb): of unknown origin.

fullerene /ˈfʊləriːn/ ▶ **noun** Chemistry a form of carbon having a large spheroidal molecule consisting of a hollow cage of sixty or more atoms, of which buckminsterfullerene was the first known example. Fullerenes are produced chiefly by the action of an arc discharge between carbon electrodes in an inert atmosphere.
– ORIGIN late 20th cent.: contraction of **BUCKMINSTERFULLERENE**.

fuller's earth ▶ **noun** [mass noun] a type of clay used in fulling cloth and as an adsorbent.

fuller's teasel ▶ **noun** a teasel with stiff bracts which curve backwards from the prickly flower head.
• *Dipsacus sativus*, family Dipsacaceae.
– ORIGIN so named because it was formerly dried and used for raising the nap on woven cloth.

full face ▶ **adverb** (also **in full face**) with all the face visible; facing directly at someone or something: *she looked full face at the mirror.*
▶ **adjective** [attrib.] **1** showing all of the face: *a full-face mugshot.*
2 covering all of the face: *a full-face motorcycle helmet.*

full-fledged ▶ **adjective** North American term for **FULLY-FLEDGED**.

full flood ▶ **noun** [mass noun] the tide at its highest.
■(**in full flood**) speaking enthusiastically and volubly: *she was in full flood about the glories of bicycling.*

full forward ▶ **noun** Australian Rules the centrally positioned player in front of the goal on the forward line of the attacking team.

full-frontal ▶ **adjective** (of nudity or a nude figure) with full exposure of the front of the body.
■with nothing concealed or held back: *they put a full-frontal guitar assault to clever lyrics.*

full-grown ▶ **adjective** having reached maturity.

full growth ▶ **noun** [mass noun] the greatest size that a plant or animal naturally attains; maturity.

full-hearted ▶ **adjective** with great enthusiasm and commitment; full of sincere feeling: *a full-hearted commitment to proportional representation.*
– DERIVATIVES **full-heartedly** adverb, **full-heartedness** noun.

full house ▶ **noun** [in sing.] **1** an audience, or group of people attending a meeting, that fills the venue for the event to capacity.
2 a poker hand with three of a kind and a pair, which beats a flush and loses to four of a kind.
■a winning card at bingo in which all the numbers have been successfully marked off.

full-length ▶ **adjective** of the standard length: *a full-length Disney cartoon.*
■(of a garment or curtain) extending to, or almost to, the ground. ■ (of a mirror or portrait) showing the whole human figure.
▶ **adverb** (usu. **full length**) (of a person) with the body lying stretched out and flat: *Lucy flung herself full length on the floor.*

full lock ▶ **noun** see **LOCK**[1] (sense 3).

full marks ▶ **plural noun** the maximum award in an examination or assessment.
■showing praise for someone's intelligence, hard work, or other quality: *she had to give him full marks for originality.*

full measure ▶ **noun** [mass noun] the total amount or extent: *the full measure of their worth.*
■[count noun] an amount not less than that professed: *only one out of 208 pints served came up to a full measure.*

full moon ▶ **noun** the phase of the moon in which its whole disc is illuminated.
■the time when this occurs: *it was several days after full moon.*

full-motion video (abbrev.: **FMV**) ▶ **noun** [mass noun] digital video data that is transmitted or stored on video discs for real-time reproduction on a computer (or other multimedia system) at a rate of not less than 25 frames per second.

full-mouthed ▶ **adjective 1** (of cattle, sheep, etc.) having a full set of adult teeth.
2 spoken loudly or vigorously.

full nelson ▶ **noun** see **NELSON**.

fullness (also **fulness**) ▶ **noun** [mass noun] **1** the state of being filled to capacity: *scores of tins in different states of fullness.*
■the state of having eaten enough or more than enough and feeling full up. ■ the state of being complete or whole: *the honesty and fullness of the information they provide.* ■ (in or alluding to biblical use) all that is contained in the world: *God's green earth in all its fullness is for the people.*
2 (of a person's body or part of it) the state of being filled out so as to produce a rounded shape: *the childish fullness of his cheeks.*
■(of a garment or the hair) the condition of having been cut or designed to give a full shape. ■ richness or intensity of flavour, sound, or colour: *the champagne is a fine example of mature fullness and ripeness.*
– PHRASES **the fullness of one's** (or **the**) **heart** poetic/literary overwhelming emotion. **in the fullness of time** after a due length of time has elapsed; eventually: *he'll tell us in the fullness of time.*

full page ▶ **noun** [usu. as modifier] an entire page of a newspaper or magazine: *full-page advertisements.*

full point ▶ **noun** another term for **FULL STOP** (as a punctuation mark).

full professor ▶ **noun** chiefly N. Amer. a professor of the highest grade in a university.
– DERIVATIVES **full professorship** noun.

full-rigged ▶ **adjective** (of a sailing ship) having three or more masts that all carry square sails.

full-scale ▶ **adjective** of the same size as the thing represented: *a full-scale model of the Golden Hind.*
■unrestricted in size, extent, or intensity; complete and thorough: *a full-scale invasion of the mainland.*

full score ▶ **noun** a score of a musical composition giving the parts for all performers on separate staves.

full sister ▶ **noun** a sister born of the same mother and father.

full stop ▶ **noun** a punctuation mark (.) used at the end of a sentence or an abbreviation.
■[as exclamation] used to suggest that there is nothing more to say on a topic: *women are just generally better people full stop.*

full term ▶ **noun 1** see **TERM** (sense 2).
2 (at Oxford and Cambridge) the main part of the university term, during which lectures are given.

full tilt ▶ **adverb** see **TILT**.

full-time ▶ **adjective** occupying or using the whole of someone's available working time: *a full-time job.*
▶ **adverb** on a full-time basis: *both parents were employed full-time.*
▶ **noun** (**full time**) the end of a game, especially a football match.

full-timer ▶ **noun** a person who does a full-time job.

full toss Cricket ▶ **noun** a ball pitched right up to the batsman.
▶ **adverb** without the ball having touched the ground.

fully ▶ **adverb 1** completely or entirely; to the furthest extent: *I fully understand the fears of the workers.*
■without lacking or omitting anything: *this issue is discussed more fully in chapter seven* | [as submodifier] *a fully equipped gymnasium.*
2 no less or fewer than (used to emphasize an amount): *fully 65 per cent of all funerals are by cremation.*
– ORIGIN Old English *fullīce* (see **FULL**[1], **-LY**[2]).

-fully ▶ **suffix** forming adverbs corresponding to adjectives ending in *-ful* (such as *sorrowfully* corresponding to *sorrowful*).

fully-fashioned ▶ **adjective** (of women's clothing, especially hosiery) shaped and seamed to fit the body.
■(of a knitted garment) shaped by increasing or decreasing the number of loops made along the fabric length without alteration of the stitch.

fully-fledged ▶ **adjective** Brit. completely developed or established; of full status: *David had become a fully-fledged pilot.*
■(of a bird) having grown all its feathers and able to fly.

fulmar /ˈfʊlmə/ ▶ **noun** a gull-sized grey and white seabird of the petrel family, with a stocky body and tubular nostrils.
• Genus *Fulmarus*, family Procellariidae: two species, in particular the **northern fulmar** (*F. glacialis*) of the arctic area and British Isles.
– ORIGIN late 17th cent.: from Hebridean Norn dialect, from Old Norse *fúll* 'stinking, foul' (because of its habit of regurgitating its stomach contents when disturbed) + *már* 'gull'.

fulminant /ˈfʊlmɪnənt, ˈfʌl-/ ▶ **adjective** Medicine (of a disease or symptom) severe and sudden in onset.
– ORIGIN early 17th cent.: from French, or from Latin *fulminant-* 'striking with lightning', from the verb *fulminare* (see **FULMINATE**).

fulminate /ˈfʊlmɪneɪt, ˈfʌl-/ ▶ **verb** [no obj.] express vehement protest: *all* ***fulminated against*** *the new curriculum.*
■poetic/literary explode violently or flash like lightning: *thunder fulminated around the house.* ■ [usu. as adj.] Medicine (**fulminating**) (of a disease or symptom) develop suddenly and severely: *fulminating appendicitis.*
▶ **noun** Chemistry a salt or ester of fulminic acid.
– ORIGIN late Middle English: from Latin *fulminat-* 'struck by lightning', from *fulmen, fulmin-* 'lightning'. The earliest sense (derived from medieval Latin *fulminare*) was 'denounce formally', later 'issue formal censures' (originally said of the Pope). A sense 'emit thunder and lightning', based on the original Latin meaning, arose in the early 17th cent., and hence 'explode violently' (late 17th cent.).

fulmination ▶ **noun** (usu. **fulminations**) an expression of vehement protest: *the fulminations of media moralists.*
■a violent explosion or a flash like lightning.

fulminic acid /fʌlˈmɪnɪk, fʊl-/ ▶ **noun** [mass noun] Chemistry a very unstable acid isomeric with cyanic acid.
• Chem. formula: HONC.
– ORIGIN early 19th cent.: *fulminic* from Latin *fulmen, fulmin-* 'lightning' + **-IC**.

fulness ▶ **noun** variant spelling of **FULLNESS**.

fulsome ▶ **adjective 1** complimentary or flattering to an excessive degree: *the press are embarrassingly fulsome in their appreciation.*
2 of large size or quantity; generous or abundant: *the fulsome details of the later legend.*
– DERIVATIVES **fulsomely** adverb, **fulsomeness** noun.
– ORIGIN Middle English (in the sense 'abundant'): from **FULL**[1] + **-SOME**[1].

USAGE Although the earliest use of **fulsome** (first recorded in the 13th century) was 'abundant', this meaning in modern use is held by many people to be wrong. The correct meaning today is 'excessively flattering', although the word is still sometimes used to mean simply 'abundant'. This gives rise to ambiguity: the possibility that while for one speaker **fulsome praise** will be a genuine compliment, for others it will be interpreted as an insult. For this reason alone, it is best to avoid the word altogether if the context is likely to be sensitive.

Fulton, Robert (1765–1815), American pioneer of the steamship. He constructed a steam-propelled 'diving-boat' in 1800, which submerged to a depth of 7.6 m (25 ft), and in 1806 he built the first successful paddle steamer, the *Clermont*.

fulvous /ˈfʌlvəs, ˈfʊl-/ ▶ **adjective** reddish yellow; tawny.
– ORIGIN mid 17th cent.: from Latin *fulvus* + **-OUS**.

fumaric acid /fjuːˈmarɪk/ ▶ **noun** [mass noun] Chemistry a crystalline acid, isomeric with maleic acid, present in fumitory and many other plants.
• Alternative name: *trans*-**butenedioic acid**; chem. formula: HOOCCH=CHCOOH.
– DERIVATIVES **fumarate** noun.
– ORIGIN mid 19th cent.: *fumaric* from modern Latin *Fumaria* 'fumitory' + **-IC**.

fumarole /ˈfjuːmərəʊl/ ▶ **noun** an opening in or near a volcano, through which hot sulphurous gases emerge.
– DERIVATIVES **fumarolic** adjective.
– ORIGIN early 19th cent.: from obsolete Italian *fumaruolo*, from late Latin *fumariolum* 'vent, hole for smoke', a diminutive based on Latin *fumus* 'smoke'.

fumble ▶ **verb** [no obj., with adverbial] use the hands clumsily while doing or handling something: *she fumbled with the lock.*
■(of the hands) do or handle something clumsily: *her hands fumbled with the waistband of his trousers.* ■ (**fumble about/around**) move clumsily in various directions using the hands to find one's way: *he fumbled about in the dark but could not find her.* ■ [with obj. and adverbial] use the hands clumsily to move (something) as specified: *she fumbled a cigarette from her bag.* ■ [with obj.] (in ball games) fail to catch or field (the ball, a pass, a shot, etc.) cleanly. ■ express oneself or deal with something clumsily or nervously: *asked for explanations, Michael had fumbled for words.*
▶ **noun** [usu. in sing.] an act of using the hands clumsily while doing or handling something: *just one fumble during a tyre change could separate the winners from the losers.*
■informal an act of fondling someone for sexual pleasure. ■ (in ball games) an act of failing to catch or field the ball cleanly. ■ an act of managing or dealing with something clumsily: *we are not talking about subtle errors of judgement, but major fumbles.*
– DERIVATIVES **fumbler** noun, **fumblingly** adverb.
– ORIGIN late Middle English: from Low German *fommeln* or Dutch *fommelen*.

fume ▶ **noun** (usu. **fumes**) gas, smoke, or vapour that smells strongly or is dangerous to inhale: *clouds of exhaust fumes spewed by cars.*
■a pungent odour of a particular thing or substance: *he breathed* ***fumes of*** *wine into her face.* ■ poetic/literary a watery vapour, steam, or mist rising from the earth or sea.
▶ **verb** [no obj.] **1** emit gas, smoke, or vapour: *fragments of lava hit the ground, fuming and sizzling.*
■[with obj.] [usu. as adj. **fumed**] expose (especially wood) to ammonia fumes in order to produce dark tints.
2 feel, show, or express great anger: *he is fuming over the interference in his work.*
– DERIVATIVES **fumingly** adverb, **fumy** adjective.

– ORIGIN late Middle English: from Old French *fumer* (verb), from Latin *fumare* 'to smoke'.

fume cupboard ▶ noun Brit. a ventilated enclosure in a chemistry laboratory, in which harmful volatile chemicals can be used or kept.

fume hood ▶ noun US a fume cupboard.

fumet[1] /fju:ˈmɛt/ ▶ noun [mass noun] a concentrated stock, especially of game or fish, used as flavouring.
– ORIGIN early 18th cent. (in the senses 'smell of game' and 'game flavour'): from French, from *fumer* 'to smoke'. The current sense dates from the early 20th cent.

fumet[2] /ˈfju:mɛt/ ▶ noun (usu. **fumets**) archaic the excrement of a deer.
– ORIGIN late Middle English: from an Anglo-Norman French variant of Old French *fumees* 'droppings'.

fumigate ▶ verb [with obj.] disinfect or purify (an area) with the fumes of certain chemicals.
– DERIVATIVES **fumigant** noun, **fumigation** noun, **fumigator** noun.
– ORIGIN mid 16th cent. (in the sense 'to perfume'): from Latin *fumigat-* 'fumigated', from the verb *fumigare*, from *fumus* 'smoke'.

fumitory /ˈfju:mɪt(ə)ri/ ▶ noun an Old World plant with spikes of small tubular pink or white flowers and finely divided greyish leaves, often considered a weed.
• Genus *Fumaria*, family Fumariaceae.
– ORIGIN late Middle English: from Old French *fumeterre*, from medieval Latin *fumus terrae* 'smoke of the earth' (because of its greyish leaves).

fun ▶ noun [mass noun] enjoyment, amusement, or light-hearted pleasure. *the children were having fun in the play area*
▪ a source of this: *people-watching is great fun.* ▪ playful behaviour or good humour: *she's full of fun.* ▪ behaviour or an activity that is intended purely for amusement and should not be interpreted as having serious or malicious purposes: *the column's* ***just a bit of fun.***
▶ adjective informal amusing, entertaining, or enjoyable: *it was a fun evening.*
▪ [attrib.] (of a place or event) providing entertainment or leisure activities for children: *a school fun day.*
▶ verb informal, chiefly N. Amer. joke or tease: [no obj.] *no need to get sore—I was only funning* | [with obj.] *they are just funning you.*
– PHRASES **for fun** (or **for the fun of it**) in order to amuse oneself and not for any more serious purpose. **fun and games** amusing and enjoyable activities: *teaching isn't all fun and games.* **someone's idea of fun** used to emphasize one's dislike for an activity or to mock someone else's liking for it: *being stuck behind a desk all day* ***isn't my idea of fun.*** **in fun** not intended seriously; as a joke: *remember when you meet the press to say that your speech was all in fun.* **like fun 1** dated, chiefly N. Amer. an ironic exclamation of contradiction or disbelief in response to a statement. **2** Brit. archaic vigorously or quickly: *the mill is blazing away like fun.* **make fun of** tease, laugh at, or joke about (someone) in a mocking or unkind way. **not much** (or **a lot of**) **fun** used to indicate that something strikes one as extremely unpleasant and depressing: *it can't be much fun living next door to him.* **what fun!** used to convey that an activity or situation sounds amusing or enjoyable.
– ORIGIN late 17th cent. (denoting a trick or hoax): from obsolete *fun* 'to cheat or hoax', dialect variant of late Middle English *fon* 'make a fool of, be a fool', related to *fon* 'a fool', of unknown origin. Compare with **FOND**.

> **USAGE** The use of **fun** as an adjective meaning 'enjoyable', as in *we had a* **fun** *evening* is not fully accepted in standard English and should only be used in informal contexts. There are signs that this situation is changing, though, given the recent appearance in US English of comparative and superlative forms **funner** and **funnest**, formed as if **fun** were a normal adjective.

Funafuti /ˌfu:nəˈfu:ti/ the capital of Tuvalu, situated on an island of the same name; pop. 2,500 (est. 1981).

funambulist /fju:ˈnambjʊlɪst/ ▶ noun a tightrope walker.
– ORIGIN late 18th cent.: from French *funambule* or Latin *funambulus* (from *funis* 'rope' + *ambulare* 'to walk') + **-IST**.

funboard ▶ noun a type of windsurfing board that is less stable but faster than a standard board.

Funchal /fʊnˈʃɑ:l/ the capital and chief port of Madeira, on the south coast of the island; pop. 109,960 (1991).

function ▶ noun **1** an activity or purpose natural to or intended for a person or thing: *bridges perform the function of providing access across water* | *I was losing control of my bodily functions* | [mass noun] *Vitamin A is required for good eye function.*
▪ [mass noun] practical use or purpose in design: *building designs that prioritize style over function.* ▪ a basic task of a computer, especially one that corresponds to a single instruction from the user.
2 Mathematics a relation or expression involving one or more variables: *the function (bx + c).*
▪ a variable quantity regarded in relation to one or more other variables in terms of which it may be expressed or on which its value depends. ▪ figurative a thing dependent on another factor or factors: *class shame is a function of social power.* ▪ Chemistry a functional group.
3 a large or formal social event or ceremony.
▶ verb [no obj.] work or operate in a proper or particular way: *her liver is functioning normally.*
▪ (**function as**) fulfil the purpose or task of (a specified thing): *the museum intends to function as an educational and study centre.*
– DERIVATIVES **functionless** adjective.
– ORIGIN mid 16th cent.: from French *fonction*, from Latin *functio(n-)*, from *fungi* 'perform'.

functional ▶ adjective **1** of or having a special activity, purpose, or task; relating to the way in which something works or operates: *there are important functional differences between left and right brain.*
▪ designed to be practical and useful, rather than attractive: *she had assumed the flat would be functional and simple.* ▪ working or operating: *the museum will be fully functional from the opening of the festival.* ▪ (of a disease) affecting the operation, rather than the structure, of an organ: *functional diarrhoea.* ▪ (of a mental illness) having no discernible organic cause: *functional psychosis.*
2 Mathematics of or relating to a variable quantity whose value depends upon one or more other variables.
– DERIVATIVES **functionally** adverb [sentence adverb] *functionally, the role of the library service is clearly educational.*

functional food ▶ noun a food containing health-giving additives.

functional grammar ▶ noun [mass noun] a theory of grammar concerned with the social and pragmatic functions of language, relating these to both formal syntactic properties and prosodic properties.

functional group ▶ noun Chemistry a group of atoms responsible for the characteristic reactions of a particular compound.

functionalism ▶ noun [mass noun] belief in or stress on the practical application of a thing, in particular:
▪ (in the arts) the doctrine that the design of an object should be determined solely by its function, rather than by aesthetic considerations, and that anything practically designed will be inherently beautiful. ▪ (in the social sciences) the theory that all aspects of a society serve a function and are necessary for the survival of that society. ▪ (in the philosophy of mind) the theory that mental states can be sufficiently defined by their cause, their effect on other mental states, and their effect on behaviour.
– DERIVATIVES **functionalist** noun & adjective.

functionality ▶ noun [mass noun] **1** the quality of being suited to serve a purpose well; practicality: *I like the feel and functionality of this bakeware.*
▪ the purpose that something is designed or expected to fulfil: *manufacturing processes may be affected by the functionality of the product.*
2 the range of operations that can be run on a computer or other electronic system: *new software with additional functionality.*

functionary /ˈfʌŋ(k)ʃ(ə)n(ə)ri/ ▶ noun (pl. **-ies**) a person who has to perform official functions or duties; an official.

function key ▶ noun Computing a button on a computer keyboard, distinct from the main alphanumeric keys, to which software can assign a particular function.

function word ▶ noun Linguistics a word whose purpose is to contribute to the syntax rather than the meaning of a sentence, for example *do* in *we do not live here.*

functor /ˈfʌŋktə/ ▶ noun Logic & Mathematics a function; an operator. [ORIGIN: 1930s: from **FUNCTION**, on the pattern of words such as *factor*.]
▪ Linguistics another term for **FUNCTION WORD**.

fund ▶ noun a sum of money saved or made available for a particular purpose: *he had set up a fund to coordinate economic investment.*
▪ (**funds**) financial resources: *the misuse of public funds.* ▪ a large stock or supply of something: *a vast* ***fund of*** *information.*
▶ verb [with obj.] provide with money for a particular purpose: *the World Bank refused to fund the project* | [in combination] *government-funded research.*
– PHRASES **in funds** Brit. having money to spend.
– ORIGIN mid 17th cent.: from Latin *fundus* 'bottom, piece of landed property'. The earliest sense was 'the bottom or lowest part', later 'foundation or basis'; the association with money has perhaps arisen from the idea of landed property being a source of wealth.

fundal /ˈfʌnd(ə)l/ ▶ adjective Medicine of or relating to the fundus of an organ, especially of the stomach, uterus, or eyeball.

fundament /ˈfʌndəm(ə)nt/ ▶ noun **1** the foundation or basis of something.
2 formal or humorous a person's buttocks or anus.
– ORIGIN Middle English (also denoting the base of a building, or the founding of a building or institution): from Old French *fondement*, from Latin *fundamentum*, from *fundare* 'to found'.

fundamental /fʌndəˈmɛnt(ə)l/ ▶ adjective forming a necessary base or core; of central importance: *the protection of fundamental human rights* | *interpretation of evidence is* ***fundamental to*** *the historian's craft.*
▪ affecting or relating to the essential nature of something or the crucial point about an issue: *the fundamental problem remains that of the housing shortage.* ▪ so basic as to be hard to alter, resolve, or overcome: *the theories are based on a fundamental error.*
▶ noun (usu. **fundamentals**) a central or primary rule or principle on which something is based: *two courses cover the fundamentals of microbiology.*
▪ a fundamental note, tone, or frequency.
– DERIVATIVES **fundamentality** noun.
– ORIGIN late Middle English: from French *fondamental*, or late Latin *fundamentalis*, from Latin *fundamentum*, from *fundare* 'to found'.

fundamental frequency ▶ noun Physics the lowest frequency which is produced by the oscillation of the whole of an object, as distinct from the harmonics of higher frequency.

fundamentalism ▶ noun [mass noun] a form of Protestant Christianity which upholds belief in the strict and literal interpretation of the Bible, including its narratives, doctrines, prophecies, and moral laws.
▪ strict maintenance of ancient or fundamental doctrines of any religion or ideology, notably Islam.

> Modern Christian fundamentalism arose from American millenarian sects of the 19th century, and has become associated with reaction against social and political liberalism and rejection of the theory of evolution. Islamic fundamentalism appeared in the 18th and 19th centuries as a reaction to the disintegration of Islamic political and economic power, asserting that Islam is central to both state and society and advocating strict adherence to the Koran (*Qur'an*) and to Islamic law (*sharia*), supported if need be by jihad or holy war.

– DERIVATIVES **fundamentalist** noun & adjective.

fundamentally ▶ adverb [often as submodifier] in central or primary respects: *two fundamentally different concepts of democracy.*
▪ [sentence adverb] used to make an emphatic statement about the basic truth of something: *fundamentally, this is a matter for doctors.*

fundamental note ▶ noun Music the lowest note of a chord in its original (uninverted) form.

fundamental particle ▶ noun another term for **ELEMENTARY PARTICLE**.

fundamental tone ▶ noun Music the tone which represents the fundamental frequency of a vibrating object such as a string or bell.

fundamental unit ▶ noun one of a set of unrelated units of measurement, which are arbitrarily defined and from which other units are derived. For example, in the SI system the fundamental units are the metre, kilogram, and second.
▪ a thing which is or is perceived as being the smallest

part into which a complex whole can be analysed: *the house is the fundamental unit of Basque society.*

funded debt ▶ **noun** [mass noun] debt in the form of securities with long-term or indefinite redemption. Compare with **FLOATING DEBT**.

fundholder ▶ **noun** (in the UK) a general practitioner who is provided with and controls their own budget.

fundholding ▶ **noun** [mass noun] (in the UK) a system of state funding for general practitioners, in which a GP is allocated a budget with which they can buy a limited range of hospital services.

fundi¹ plural form of **FUNDUS**.

fundi² /ˈfʌndi/ ▶ **noun** (pl. **fundis**) variant spelling of **FUNDIE**.

fundi³ /ˈfʊndi/ ▶ **noun** (pl. **fundis**) S. African informal an expert in a particular area: *a turtle fundi.*
▪ an enthusiast for a subject or activity: *she provides classes for the fitness fundis.*
– ORIGIN perhaps originally Rhodesian (Zimbabwean) English, from Ndebele *umfundi* 'disciple, learner', or from Xhosa and Zulu words.

fundie /ˈfʌndi/ ▶ **noun** (pl. **-ies**) informal a fundamentalist, especially a Christian fundamentalist.
▪ (also **fundi**) (pl. also **fundis**) a member of the radical, as opposed to the pragmatic, wing of the Green movement. Often contrasted with **REALO**.
– ORIGIN 1980s: from German, abbreviation of *Fundamentalist* 'fundamentalist'.

funding ▶ **noun** [mass noun] money provided, especially by an organization or government, for a particular purpose.
▪ the action or practice of providing such money.

fund manager ▶ **noun** an employee of a large institution (such as a pension fund or an insurance company) who manages the investment of money on its behalf.

fund-raiser ▶ **noun** a person whose job or task is to seek financial support for a charity, cause, or other enterprise.
▪ an event held to generate financial support for such an enterprise.
– DERIVATIVES **fund-raising** noun.

fundus /ˈfʌndəs/ ▶ **noun** (pl. **fundi** /-dʌɪ/) Anatomy the part of a hollow organ (such as the uterus or the gall bladder) that is furthest from the opening.
▪ the upper part of the stomach, which forms a bulge above level of the opening of the oesophagus (furthest from the pylorus). ▪ the part of the eyeball opposite the pupil.
– ORIGIN mid 18th cent.: from Latin, literally 'bottom'.

Fundy, Bay of /ˈfʌndi/ an arm of the Atlantic Ocean extending between the Canadian provinces of New Brunswick and Nova Scotia. It is subject to fast-running tides, the highest in the world, which reach 12–15 m (50–80 ft) and are now used to generate electricity.

funeral ▶ **noun** a ceremony in which a dead person is buried or cremated.
▪ US rare a sermon delivered at such a ceremony. ▪ archaic or poetic/literary a procession of mourners at a burial.
– PHRASES **it's** (or **that's**) **someone's funeral** informal used to warn someone that an unwise act or decision is their responsibility: *'I won't discuss it.' 'Don't then—**it's your funeral**.'*
– ORIGIN late Middle English: from Old French *funeraille*, from medieval Latin *funeralia*, neuter plural of late Latin *funeralis*, from Latin *funus, funer-* 'funeral, death, corpse'.

funeral director ▶ **noun** an undertaker.

funeral parlour (also **funeral home**, **funeral chapel**) ▶ **noun** an establishment where the dead are prepared for burial or cremation.

funeral pyre (also **funeral pile**) ▶ **noun** a pile of wood on which a corpse is burnt as part of a funeral ceremony.

funeral urn ▶ **noun** an urn holding the ashes of a cremated body.

funerary /ˈfjuːn(ə)(rə)ri/ ▶ **adjective** relating to a funeral or the commemoration of the dead: *funerary ceremonies.*
– ORIGIN late 17th cent.: from late Latin *funerarius*, from *funus, funer-* 'funeral'.

funereal /fjuːˈnɪərɪəl/ ▶ **adjective** having the mournful, sombre character appropriate to a funeral: *Erika was moving at a funereal pace.*
– DERIVATIVES **funereally** adverb.
– ORIGIN early 18th cent.: from Latin *funereus* (from *funus, funer-* 'funeral') + **-AL**.

funfair ▶ **noun** chiefly Brit. a fair consisting of rides, sideshows, and other amusements.

fun fur ▶ **noun** [mass noun] an artificial fabric with a texture resembling fur, typically in bright colours.

fungal /ˈfʌŋg(ə)l/ ▶ **adjective** of or caused by a fungus or fungi: *fungal diseases such as mildew.*

fungi plural form of **FUNGUS**.

fungible /ˈfʌn(d)ʒɪb(ə)l/ ▶ **adjective** Law (of goods contracted for without an individual specimen being specified) able to replace or be replaced by another identical item; mutually interchangeable.
– DERIVATIVES **fungibility** noun.
– ORIGIN late 17th cent.: from medieval Latin *fungibilis*, from *fungi* 'perform, enjoy', with the same sense as *fungi vice* 'serve in place of'.

fungicide /ˈfʌn(d)ʒɪsʌɪd, ˈfʌŋgɪ-/ ▶ **noun** a chemical that destroys fungus.
– DERIVATIVES **fungicidal** adjective.

fungiform /ˈfʌŋ(d)ʒɪfɔːm/ ▶ **adjective** having the shape of or resembling a fungus or mushroom.

fungistatic /ˌfʌn(d)ʒɪˈstatɪk/ ▶ **adjective** inhibiting the growth of fungi.
– DERIVATIVES **fungistatically** adverb.

fungivorous /fʌŋˈdʒɪv(ə)rəs/ ▶ **adjective** feeding on fungi or mushrooms.

fungo /ˈfʌŋgəʊ/ ▶ **noun** (also **fungo fly**) (pl. **-oes** or **-os**) Baseball a fly ball hit for practice.
▪ (also **fungo bat** or **stick**) a long lightweight bat for hitting practice balls to fielders.
– ORIGIN mid 19th cent.: of unknown origin.

fungoid /ˈfʌŋgɔɪd/ ▶ **adjective** of or caused by a fungus or fungi: *she suffered from a fungoid disease of her feet.*
▪ resembling a fungus in shape, texture, or speed of growth: *his skin looked moist and fungoid.*
▶ **noun** a fungoid plant.

fungous /ˈfʌŋgəs/ ▶ **adjective** resembling, caused by, or having the nature of a fungus.
– ORIGIN late Middle English: from Latin *fungosus*, from *fungus* (see **FUNGUS**).

fungus /ˈfʌŋgəs/ ▶ **noun** (pl. **fungi** /-gʌɪ, -(d)ʒʌɪ/ or **funguses**) any of a group of unicellular, multicellular, or syncytial spore-producing organisms feeding on organic matter, including moulds, yeast, mushrooms, and toadstools.
▪ [mass noun] fungal infection (especially on fish). ▪ [in sing.] used to describe something that has appeared or grown rapidly and is considered unpleasant or unattractive: *there was a fungus of outbuildings behind the house.*

> Fungi lack chlorophyll and are therefore incapable of photosynthesis. Many play an ecologically vital role in breaking down dead organic matter, some are an important source of antibiotics or are used in fermentation, and others cause disease. The familiar mushrooms and toadstools are merely the fruiting bodies of organisms that exist mainly as a thread-like mycelium in the soil. Some fungi form associations with other plants, growing with algae to form lichens, or in the roots of higher plants to form mycorrhizas. Fungi are now often classified as a separate kingdom distinct from the green plants.

– ORIGIN late Middle English: from Latin, perhaps from Greek *spongos* (see **SPONGE**).

fungus beetle ▶ **noun** a small beetle that feeds chiefly on fungi and is typically black with red or yellow markings.
• Families Mycetophagidae, Erotylidae, and others: several genera.

fungus garden ▶ **noun** Entomology a growth of fungus cultivated by certain ants or termites as a source of food.

fungus gnat ▶ **noun** a small slender delicate fly whose larvae feed chiefly on fungi.
• Family Mycetophilidae: numerous species.

funhouse ▶ **noun** chiefly N. Amer. (in an amusement park) a building equipped with trick mirrors, shifting floors, and other devices designed to scare or amuse people as they walk through.

funicle /ˈfjuːnɪk(ə)l/ ▶ **noun** Botany a filamentous stalk attaching a seed or ovule to the placenta. Also called **FUNICULUS**.
▪ Entomology a filamentous section of an insect's antenna, supporting the club.
– ORIGIN mid 17th cent.: Anglicized form of Latin *funiculus* (see **FUNICULUS**).

funicular /fjʊˈnɪkjʊlə, fəˈnɪk-/ ▶ **adjective** **1** (of a railway, especially one on a mountainside) operating by cable with ascending and descending cars counterbalanced.
2 of or relating to a rope or its tension.
▶ **noun** a railway operating in such a way.
– ORIGIN mid 17th cent. (in the sense 'of or like a cord or thread'): from Latin *funiculus* (diminutive of *funis* 'rope') + **-AR¹**.

funiculus /fjʊˈnɪkjʊləs/ ▶ **noun** (pl. **funiculi** /-lʌɪ, -liː/) Anatomy a bundle of nerve fibres enclosed in a sheath of connective tissue, or forming one of the main tracts of white matter in the spinal cord.
▪ another term for **FUNICLE**.
– ORIGIN mid 17th cent.: from Latin, diminutive of *funis* 'rope'.

Funk /fʌŋk/, Casimir (1884–1967), Polish-born American biochemist. He showed that a number of diseases, including scurvy, rickets, beriberi, and pellagra, were each caused by the deficiency of a particular dietary component, and coined the term *vitamins* for the chemicals concerned.

funk¹ informal ▶ **noun** **1** (also **blue funk**) [in sing.] chiefly Brit. a state of great fear or panic: *are you in a blue funk about running out of things to say?*
▪ chiefly N. Amer. a state of depression: *I sat absorbed in my own blue funk.*
2 dated, chiefly Brit. a coward.
▶ **verb** [with obj.] chiefly Brit. avoid (a task or thing) out of fear: *I could have seen him this morning but I **funked** it.*
– ORIGIN mid 18th cent. (first recorded as Oxford University slang): perhaps from **FUNK²** in the slang sense 'tobacco-smoke', or from obsolete Flemish *fonck* 'disturbance, agitation'.

funk² ▶ **noun** **1** [mass noun] a style of popular dance music of US black origin, based on elements of blues and soul and having a strong rhythm that typically accentuates the first beat in the bar.
2 [in sing.] N. Amer. informal, dated a strong musty smell of sweat or tobacco.
– ORIGIN early 17th cent. (in the sense 'musty smell'): perhaps from French dialect *funkier* 'blow smoke on', based on Latin *fumus* 'smoke'.
▶ **funk something up** give music elements of such a style.

funkia /ˈfʌŋkɪə/ ▶ **noun** another term for **HOSTA**.
– ORIGIN mid 19th cent.: modern Latin (former genus name), named after Heinrich Christian *Funck* (1771–1839), Prussian botanist.

funkster ▶ **noun** informal a performer or fan of funky music.

funky¹ ▶ **adjective** (**funkier**, **funkiest**) informal **1** (of music) having or using a strong dance rhythm, in particular that of funk: *some excellent funky beats.*
▪ modern and stylish in an unconventional or striking way: *she likes wearing funky clothes.*
2 N. Amer. strongly musty: *cooked greens make the kitchen smell really funky.*
– DERIVATIVES **funkily** adverb, **funkiness** noun.
– ORIGIN late 18th cent. (in the sense 'smelling strong or bad'): from **FUNK²**.

funky² ▶ **adjective** (**funkier**, **funkiest**) Brit. archaic, informal frightened, panicky, or cowardly.
– ORIGIN mid 19th cent.: from **FUNK¹**.

funnel ▶ **noun** a tube or pipe that is wide at the top and narrow at the bottom, used for guiding liquid or powder into a small opening.
▪ a thing resembling such a tube or pipe in shape or function: *a funnel of light fell from a circular ceiling.* ▪ a metal chimney on a ship or steam engine.
▶ **verb** (**funnelled**, **funnelling**; US **funneled**, **funneling**) [with obj. and adverbial of direction] guide or channel (something) through or as if through a funnel: *some $12.8 billion was **funnelled through** the Marshall Plan.*
▪ [no obj., with adverbial of direction] move or be guided through or as if through a funnel: *the wind **funnelled down** through the valley.* ▪ [no obj.] assume the shape of a funnel by widening or narrowing at the end: *the crevice **funnelled out**.*
– DERIVATIVES **funnel-like** adjective.
– ORIGIN late Middle English: apparently via Old French from Provençal *fonilh*, from late Latin *fundibulum*, from Latin *infundibulum*, from *infundere*, from *in-* 'into' + *fundere* 'pour'.

funnel cake ▶ **noun** US a cake made of batter that is poured through a funnel into hot fat or oil, deep-fried until crisp, and served sprinkled with sugar.

funnel cap ▶ **noun** a common edible European mushroom with a cream-coloured funnel-shaped

cap, growing in open grassy places and woodland clearings.
• *Clitocybe infundibuliformis*, family Tricholomataceae, class Hymenomycetes.

funnel cloud ▶ **noun** a rotating funnel-shaped cloud forming the core of a tornado or waterspout.

funnel-web spider ▶ **noun** any of a number of spiders that build a funnel-shaped web, in particular:
• a large and dangerously venomous Australian spider (genera *Atrax* and *Hadronyche*, family Dipluridae, suborder Mygalomorphae). Also called **TRAPDOOR SPIDER** in Australia. • US a spider of the family Agelenidae.

funnily ▶ **adverb** in a strange or amusing way: *you do talk funnily.*
■ [sentence adverb] (**funnily enough**) used to admit that a situation or fact is surprising or curious: *funnily enough, I was starting to like the idea.*

funniosity /ˌfʌnɪˈɒsɪti/ ▶ **noun** (pl. **-ies**) Brit. humorous a comical person, object, act, or remark: *Grandma looked a bit of a funniosity.*

funny ▶ **adjective** (**funnier**, **funniest**) **1** causing laughter or amusement; humorous: *a funny story | the play is hilariously funny.*
■ [predic.] [with negative] informal used to emphasize that something is unpleasant or wrong and should be regarded seriously or avoided: *stealing other people's work isn't funny.*
2 difficult to explain or understand; strange or curious: *I had a funny feeling you'd be around | it's a funny old world.*
■ unusual, especially in such a way as to arouse suspicion: *there was something funny going on.* ■ used to draw attention to or express surprise at a curious or interesting fact or occurrence: ***that's funny!***—*that vase of flowers has been moved |* ***the funny thing is*** *I can't remember much about it.* ■ informal (of a person or part of the body) not in wholly good health or order; slightly ill: *when he heard this, Nigel felt rather funny.* ■ informal used euphemistically to refer to someone whom one considers to be slightly deranged or eccentric: *I heard she'd gone a bit funny.*
▶ **noun** (pl. **-ies**) (**funnies**) informal amusing jokes.
■ N. Amer. the comic strips in newspapers. ■ strange or peculiar people.
– PHRASES **I'm not being funny, but ——** informal used before a statement or suggestion to point out that it is serious, however facetious or strange it may seem: *I'm not being funny but I haven't got all day.* **see the funny side** (**of something**) appreciate the humorous aspect of a situation or experience. (**oh**) **very funny!** informal used ironically to indicate that a speaker does not share another's joke or amusement: *'D'yeh want a celery choc ice?' 'Very funny, I don't think.'*
– DERIVATIVES **funniness** noun.

funny bone ▶ **noun** informal the part of the elbow over which passes the ulnar nerve, which may cause numbness and pain along the forearm and hand if knocked.
■ a person's sense of humour, as located in an imaginary physical organ: *photographs to jostle the mind and the funny bone.*

funny business ▶ **noun** [mass noun] deceptive, disobedient, or lecherous behaviour: *they sent a big strong farmer's lad to make sure there was no funny business.*

funny-face ▶ **noun** informal, dated an affectionate form of address.

funny farm ▶ **noun** (often **the funny farm**) informal, offensive a psychiatric hospital.

funny ha-ha ▶ **adjective** informal amusing (as opposed to 'funny peculiar'; used to distinguish the two main senses of 'funny').
– ORIGIN coined by Ian Hay in his novel *Housemaster* (1936).

funny man ▶ **noun** a professional clown or comedian.

funny money ▶ **noun** [mass noun] informal currency that is forged or otherwise worthless.

funny paper ▶ **noun** N. Amer. a section of a newspaper containing cartoons and humorous matter.

funny peculiar ▶ **adjective** informal strange (as opposed to 'funny ha-ha'; used to distinguish the two main senses of 'funny').
– ORIGIN coined by Ian Hay in his novel *Housemaster* (1936).

fun run ▶ **noun** informal an uncompetitive run, especially for sponsored runners in support of a charity.

funster ▶ **noun** informal a person who makes fun; a joker.

Fur /fʊə, fəː/ ▶ **noun** (pl. same) **1** a member of a Muslim people of the mountainous and desert regions of SW Sudan.
2 [mass noun] the language of this people, an isolated member of the Nilo-Saharan family, with about 500,000 speakers.
▶ **adjective** of or relating to this people or their language.

fur ▶ **noun 1** [mass noun] the short, fine, soft hair of certain animals: *a long, lean, muscular cat with sleek fur.*
■ [count noun] the skin of an animal with such hair on it. ■ skins of this type, or fabrics resembling these, used as material for making, trimming, or lining clothes: *a Parka with nylon fur round the hood |* [as modifier] *a fur coat.* ■ [count noun] a garment made of, trimmed, or lined with fur. ■ Heraldry any of several heraldic tinctures representing animal skins in stylized form (e.g. ermine, vair).
2 Brit. a coating formed by hard water on the inside surface of a pipe, kettle, or other container.
■ a coating formed on the tongue as a symptom of sickness.
▶ **verb** (**furred**, **furring**) [with obj.] **1** Brit. coat or clog with a deposit: *the stuff that* ***furs up*** *coronary arteries.*
2 [as adj., often in combination] (**furred**) covered with or made from a particular type of fur: *a tatty-furred lion.*
3 level (floor or wall timbers) by inserting strips of wood.
– PHRASES **fur and feather** game mammals and birds. **the fur will fly** informal there will be serious, perhaps violent, trouble.
– DERIVATIVES **furless** adjective.
– ORIGIN Middle English (as a verb): from Old French *forrer* 'to line, sheathe', from *forre* 'sheath', of Germanic origin.

fur. ▶ **abbreviation for** furlong(s).

furan /ˈfjʊəran/ ▶ **noun** [mass noun] Chemistry a colourless volatile liquid with a planar unsaturated five-membered ring in its molecule.
• Chem. formula: C_4H_4O.
■ [count noun] any substituted derivative of this.
– ORIGIN late 19th cent.: from synonymous *furfuran*.

furbelow /ˈfəːbɪləʊ/ ▶ **noun** a gathered strip or pleated border of a skirt or petticoat.
■ (**furbelows**) showy ornaments or trimmings: ***frills and furbelows*** *just made her look stupid.*
▶ **verb** [with obj.] [usu. as adj. **furbelowed**] poetic/literary adorn with trimmings.
– ORIGIN late 17th cent.: from French *falbala* 'trimming, flounce', of unknown ultimate origin.

furbish /ˈfəːbɪʃ/ ▶ **verb** [with obj.] [usu. as adj. **furbished**] give a fresh look to (something old or shabby); renovate: *the newly furbished church.*
■ archaic brighten up (a weapon) by polishing it.
– DERIVATIVES **furbisher** noun.
– ORIGIN late Middle English: from Old French *forbiss-*, lengthened stem of *forbir*, of Germanic origin.

fur brigade ▶ **noun** Canadian historical a convoy that transported furs to and from trading posts by land and river.

furca /ˈfəːkə/ ▶ **noun** (pl. **furcae** /-siː, -kiː/) Zoology a forked appendage or projection in an arthropod, in particular:
■ an ingrowth of the thorax of many insects. ■ the furcula of a springtail.
– DERIVATIVES **furcal** adjective.
– ORIGIN early 17th cent.: from Latin, literally 'fork'.

furcate technical ▶ **verb** /ˈfəːkeɪt, fəːˈkeɪt/ [no obj.] divide into two or more branches; fork: *lines of descent furcating from a common source.*
▶ **adjective** /ˈfəːkeɪt, -kət/ divided into two or more branches; forked.
– DERIVATIVES **furcation** noun.
– ORIGIN early 19th cent.: from late Latin *furcatus* 'cloven', from Latin *furca* 'fork'.

furcula /ˈfəːkjʊlə/ ▶ **noun** (pl. **furculae** /-liː/) Zoology a forked organ or structure, in particular:
■ the wishbone of a bird. ■ the forked appendage at the end of the abdomen in a springtail, by which the insect jumps.
– DERIVATIVES **furcular** adjective.
– ORIGIN mid 19th cent.: from Latin, diminutive of *furca* 'fork'.

furfuraceous /ˌfəːf(j)əˈreɪʃəs/ ▶ **adjective** Botany & Medicine covered with or characterized by bran-like scales.
– ORIGIN mid 17th cent.: from late Latin *furfuraceus* (from Latin *furfur* 'bran') + **-OUS**.

furfural /ˈfəːf(j)əral/ ▶ **noun** [mass noun] Chemistry a colourless liquid used in synthetic resin manufacture, originally obtained by distilling bran.
• An aldehyde derived from furan; chem. formula: C_4H_3OCHO.
– ORIGIN late 19th cent.: from obsolete *furfurol* (in the same sense) + **-AL**.

furfuraldehyde /ˌfəːf(j)əˈraldɪhʌɪd/ ▶ **noun** Chemistry another term for **FURFURAL**.

furioso /ˌfjʊərɪˈəʊzəʊ, -səʊ/ ▶ **adverb** & **adjective** Music (especially as a direction) furiously and wildly.
– ORIGIN Italian.

furious ▶ **adjective** extremely angry: *she was* ***furious at*** *this attempt to manipulate her.*
■ full of anger or energy; violent or intense: *he drove at a furious speed.*
– DERIVATIVES **furiously** adverb, **furiousness** noun.
– ORIGIN late Middle English: from Old French *furieus*, from Latin *furiosus*, from *furia* 'fury'.

furl ▶ **verb** [with obj.] roll or fold up and secure neatly (a flag, sail, umbrella, or other piece of fabric): *the flag was tightly furled |* [as adj. **furled**] *a furled umbrella.*
■ [no obj.] poetic/literary become rolled up; curl: [as adj. **furled**] *the plant sends up cones of furled leaves.*
– DERIVATIVES **furlable** adjective.
– ORIGIN late 16th cent.: from French *ferler*, from Old French *fer, ferm* 'firm' + *lier* 'bind' (from Latin *ligare*).

furling ▶ **noun** [mass noun] equipment for rolling up sails securely and neatly around their yards or booms.

furlong ▶ **noun** an eighth of a mile, 220 yards.
– ORIGIN Old English *furlang*, from *furh* 'furrow' + *lang* 'long'. The word originally denoted the length of a furrow in a common field (formally regarded as a square of ten acres). It was also used as the equivalent of the Roman *stadium*, one eighth of a Roman mile, whence the current sense. Compare with **STADIUM**.

furlough /ˈfəːləʊ/ ▶ **noun** [mass noun] leave of absence, especially that granted to a member of the services or a missionary: *a civil servant home on furlough |* [count noun] *a six-week furlough in Australia.*
▶ **verb** [with obj.] [usu. as adj. **furloughed**] US grant such leave of absence to: *furloughed workers.*
– ORIGIN early 17th cent.: from Dutch *verlof*, modelled on German *Verlaub*, of West Germanic origin and related to **LEAVE**[2].

furmety /ˈfəːmɪti/ ▶ **noun** variant of **FRUMENTY**.

furnace ▶ **noun** an enclosed structure in which material can be heated to very high temperatures, e.g. for smelting metals.
■ an appliance fired by gas or oil in which air or water is heated to be circulated throughout a building in a heating system. ■ used to describe a very hot place: *her car was a furnace.*
– ORIGIN Middle English: from Old French *fornais(e)*, from Latin *fornax, fornac-*, from *fornus* 'oven'.

Furneaux Islands /ˈfəːnəʊ/ a group of islands off the coast of NE Tasmania, in the Bass Strait. The largest island is Flinders Island.

furnish ▶ **verb** [with obj.] provide (a house or room) with furniture and fittings: *the proprietor has furnished the bedrooms in a variety of styles.*
■ (**furnish someone with**) supply someone with (something); give (something) to someone: *she was able to furnish me with details of the incident.* ■ be a source of; provide: *fish furnish an important source of protein.*
– ORIGIN late Middle English (in the general sense 'provide or equip with what is necessary or desirable'): from Old French *furniss-*, lengthened stem of *furnir*, ultimately of West Germanic origin.

furnished ▶ **adjective** (of accommodation) available to be rented with furniture.

furnisher ▶ **noun** a person who supplies furniture.

furnishing ▶ **noun 1** (usu. **furnishings**) furniture, fittings, and other decorative accessories such as curtains and carpets, for a house or room.
2 [mass noun] the action of decorating a house or room and providing it with furniture and fittings.
■ [usu. as modifier] the action of making curtains or covers for chairs and cushions: *furnishing fabrics.*

furniture ▶ **noun** [mass noun] **1** large movable equipment, such as tables and chairs, that are used

to make a house, office, or other space suitable for living or working.
■ figurative a person's habitual attitude, outlook, and way of thinking: *the mental furniture of the European.*
2 [usu. with adj. or noun modifier] small accessories or fittings for a particular use or piece of equipment: *the more sophisticated Mac furniture—number wheels, colour pickers, and so on.*
■ the mountings of a rifle. ■ Printing pieces of wood or metal placed round or between metal type to make blank spaces and fasten the matter in the chase.
– PHRASES **part of the furniture** informal a person or thing that has been somewhere so long as to seem a permanent, unquestioned, or invisible feature of the landscape.
– ORIGIN early 16th cent. (denoting the action of furnishing): from French *fourniture*, from *fournir*, from Old French *furnir* 'to furnish'.

furniture beetle ▶ **noun** a small brown beetle, the larva of which (the woodworm) bores holes in dead wood and causes considerable damage to old furniture and building timbers.
● *Anobium punctatum*, family Anobiidae.

furore /ˌfjʊ(ə)ˈrɔːri, ˌfjʊ(ə)ˈrɔː/ (US **furor** /ˈfjʊərɔː/) ▶ **noun** [in sing.] an outbreak of public anger or excitement: *the verdict raised a furore over the role of courtroom psychiatry.*
■ archaic a wave of enthusiastic admiration; a craze.
– ORIGIN late 18th cent.: from Italian, from Latin *furor*, from *furere* 'be mad, rage'.

furosemide /ˌfjʊəˈrɒsəmʌɪd/ ▶ **noun** variant spelling of **FRUSEMIDE**.

furphy /ˈfəːfi/ ▶ **noun** (pl. **-ies**) Austral./NZ informal a rumour or story, especially one that is untrue or absurd.
– ORIGIN First World War: from the name painted on water and sanitary carts manufactured by the Furphy family of Shepparton, Victoria.

furrier /ˈfʌrɪə/ ▶ **noun** a person who prepares or deals in furs.
– ORIGIN Middle English: from Old French *forreor*, from *forrer* 'to line, sheathe' (see **FUR**). The change in the ending in the 16th cent. was due to association with **-IER**.

furriery /ˈfʌrɪəri/ ▶ **noun** [mass noun] the art or trade of dressing and preparing furs.

furring strip ▶ **noun** a length of wood tapering to nothing, used in roofing and other construction work.

furrow ▶ **noun** a long narrow trench made in the ground by a plough, especially for planting seeds or irrigation.
■ a rut, groove, or trail in the ground or another surface: *lorry wheels had dug furrows in the sand.* ■ a line or wrinkle on a person's face: *there were deep furrows in his brow.*
▶ **verb** [with obj.] make a rut, groove, or trail in (the ground or the surface of something): *gorges furrowing the deep-sea floor* | *John's face was* **furrowed** *with tears.*
■ (with reference to the forehead or face) mark or be marked with lines or wrinkles caused by frowning, anxiety, or concentration: [with obj.] *a look of concern furrowed his brow* | [no obj.] *her brow furrowed* | [as adj. **furrowed**] *he stroked his furrowed brow.* ■ (with reference to the eyebrows) tighten or be tightened and lowered in anxiety, concentration, or disapproval, so wrinkling the forehead: [no obj.] *his brows furrowed in concentration* | [with obj.] *she furrowed her brows, thinking hard.* ■ [usu. as adj. **furrowed**] use a plough to make a long narrow trench in (land or earth): *furrowed fields.*
– DERIVATIVES **furrowy** adjective.
– ORIGIN Old English *furh*, of Germanic origin; related to Dutch *voor* and German *Furche*, from an Indo-European root shared by Latin *porca* 'ridge between furrows'.

furrow slice ▶ **noun** a slice of earth turned up by the mould-board of a plough.

furry ▶ **adjective** (**furrier**, **furriest**) covered with fur: *furry creatures in fields.*
■ having a soft surface like fur: *a layer of furry soot.*
– DERIVATIVES **furriness** noun.

fur seal ▶ **noun** a gregarious eared seal that frequents the coasts of the Pacific and southern oceans, the male of which is substantially larger than the female. The thick fur on the underside is used commercially as sealskin.
● Two genera in the family Otariidae: the **northern fur seal** (*Callorhinus ursinus*) and the **southern fur seal** (genus *Arctocephalus*).

further used as comparative of **FAR**. ▶ **adverb** (also **farther**) **1** at, to, or by a greater distance (used to indicate the extent to which one thing or person is or becomes distant from another): *for some time I had wanted to move further from London* | figurative *the EC seems to have moved further away from the original aims.*
■ [with negative] used to emphasize the difference between a supposed or suggested fact or state of mind and the truth: *as for her being a liar, nothing could be further from the truth* | *nothing could be further from his mind than marrying.*
2 over a greater expanse of space or time; for a longer way: *we had walked further than I realized* | figurative *wages have been driven down even further.*
■ beyond the point already reached or the distance already covered: *Amelie decided to drive further up the coast* | *before going any further we need to define our terms.* ■ beyond or in addition to what has already been done: *we are investigating ways to further increase customer satisfaction.* ■ [sentence adverb] used to introduce a new point relating to or reinforcing a previous statement: *Ethnic minorities are more prone to unemployment. Further, this disadvantage extends to other areas of life.* ■ at or to a more advanced, successful, or desirable stage: *determination could not get her any further* | *at the end of three years they were no further on.*
▶ **adjective 1** (also **farther**) more distant in space than another item of the same kind: *two men were standing at the further end of the clearing.*
■ more remote from a central point: *the museum is in the further reaches of the town.*
2 additional to what already exists or has already taken place, been done, or been accounted for: *cook for a further ten minutes.*
▶ **verb** [with obj.] help the progress or development of (something); promote: *he had depended on using them to further his own career.*
– PHRASES **further to your** (or **our**) —— formal used at the beginning of a letter or in speech as a way of raising a matter discussed in an earlier letter, article, or conversation: **further to your letter** *of 10.10.96, I enclose some correspondence from my previous addresses.* **not go any further** (of a secret) not be told to anyone else. **until further notice** used to indicate that a situation will not change until another announcement is made: *the museum is closed to the public until further notice.* **until further orders** used to indicate that a situation is only to change when another command is received: *they were to be kept in prison until further orders.*
– DERIVATIVES **furtherer** noun.
– ORIGIN Old English *furthor* (adverb), *furthra* (adjective), *fyrthrian* (verb), of Germanic origin; related to **FORTH**.

USAGE Is there any difference between **further** and **farther** in *she moved* **further** *down the train* and *she moved* **farther** *down the train*? Both words share the same roots: in the sentences given above, where the sense is 'at, to, or by a greater distance', there is no difference in meaning, and both are equally correct. **Further** is a much commoner word, though, and is in addition used in various abstract and metaphorical contexts, for example referring to time, in which it would be unusual to substitute **farther**, e.g. *without* **further** *delay; have you anything* **further** *to say?; we intend to stay a* **further** *two weeks.* The same distinction is made between **farthest** and **furthest**: *the* **farthest** *point from the sun* versus *this first team has gone* **furthest** *in its analysis.*

furtherance ▶ **noun** [mass noun] the advancement of a scheme or interest: *acts* **in furtherance of** *an industrial dispute.*

further education ▶ **noun** [mass noun] Brit. education below degree level for people above school age.

furthermore ▶ **adverb** [sentence adverb] in addition; besides (used to introduce a fresh consideration in an argument): *It was also a highly desirable political end. Furthermore, it gave the English a door into France.*

furthermost (also **farthermost**) ▶ **adjective** (of an edge or extreme) at the greatest distance from a central point or implicit standpoint: *the furthermost end of the street.*

furthest (also **farthest**) used as superlative of **FAR**.
▶ **adjective** [attrib.] situated at the greatest distance from a specified or understood point: *the furthest door led to a kitchen* | figurative *it was the furthest thing from my mind.*
■ covering the greatest area or distance: *his record for the farthest flight.* ■ extremely remote: *the furthest ends of the earth.*
▶ **adverb 1** at or by the greatest distance (used to indicate how far one thing or person is or becomes distant from another): *the bed furthest from the window* | figurative *the people who are furthest removed from the political process.*
2 over the greatest distance or area: *his group probably had furthest to ride* | figurative *the areas where prices have fallen furthest.*
■ used to indicate the most distant point reached in a specified direction: *it was the furthest north I had ever travelled.* ■ to the most extreme or advanced point: *countries where industrialization had gone furthest* | **the farthest** *he'll go is to admit a sort of resentment.*
– PHRASES **at the furthest** at the greatest distance; at most: *the Allied line had been pushed forward, at the furthest, about 1.6 km.*
– ORIGIN late Middle English: formed as a superlative of **FURTHER**.

USAGE For a discussion of the differences between **farther** and **further**, **farthest** and **furthest**, see **usage** at **FURTHER**.

furtive /ˈfəːtɪv/ ▶ **adjective** attempting to avoid notice or attention, typically because of guilt or a belief that discovery would lead to trouble; secretive: *they spent a furtive day together* | *he stole a furtive glance at her.*
■ suggestive of guilty nervousness: *the look in his eyes became furtive.*
– DERIVATIVES **furtively** adverb, **furtiveness** noun.
– ORIGIN early 17th cent.: from French *furtif*, *-ive* or Latin *furtivus*, from *furtum* 'theft'.

Furtwängler /ˈfʊətˌvɛŋlə, German ˈfʊrtˌvɛŋlɐ/, Wilhelm (1886–1954), German conductor, chief conductor of the Berlin Philharmonic Orchestra from 1922. He is noted particularly for his interpretations of Beethoven and Wagner.

furuncle /ˈfjʊərʌŋk(ə)l/ ▶ **noun** technical term for **BOIL**[2].
– DERIVATIVES **furuncular** adjective, **furunculous** adjective.
– ORIGIN late Middle English: from Latin *furunculus*, literally 'petty thief', also 'knob on a vine' (regarded as stealing the sap), from *fur* 'thief'.

furunculosis /fjʊˌrʌŋkjʊˈləʊsɪs/ ▶ **noun** [mass noun] **1** Medicine the simultaneous or repeated occurrence of boils on the skin.
2 a bacterial disease of salmon and trout.
– ORIGIN late 19th cent.: from **FURUNCLE** + **-OSIS**.

fury ▶ **noun** (pl. **-ies**) **1** [mass noun] wild or violent anger: *tears of fury and frustration* | *Rachel shouted, beside herself with fury.*
■ (**a fury**) a surge of violent anger or other feeling: *in a fury, he lashed the horse on.* ■ [in sing.] violence or energy displayed in natural phenomena or in someone's actions: *the fury of a gathering storm* | *she was paddling with a new fury.*
2 (**Fury**) Greek Mythology a spirit of punishment, often represented as one of three goddesses who executed the curses pronounced upon criminals, tortured the guilty with stings of conscience, and inflicted famines and pestilences. The Furies were identified at an early date with the Eumenides.
■ used to convey a woman's anger or aggression by comparing her to such a spirit: *she rounded on him like a vengeful fury.*
– PHRASES **like fury** informal with great energy or effort: *she fought like fury in his arms.*
– ORIGIN late Middle English: from Old French *furie*, from Latin *furia*, from *furiosus* 'furious', from *furere* 'be mad, rage'.

furze /fəːz/ ▶ **noun** another term for **GORSE**.
– DERIVATIVES **furzy** adjective.
– ORIGIN Old English *fyrs*, of unknown origin.

fusain /ˈfjuːzeɪn/ ▶ **noun** [mass noun] Geology a lustreless, crumbly, porous type of coal resembling wood charcoal.
– ORIGIN late 19th cent.: from French, literally 'spindle tree', also 'fine charcoal' (made from the spindle tree).

fusarium /fjʊˈzɛːrɪəm/ ▶ **noun** a mould of a large genus which includes a number that cause plant diseases, especially wilting.
● Genus *Fusarium*, subdivision Deuteromycotina.
■ [mass noun] infestation with any of these or related moulds.
– ORIGIN early 20th cent.: modern Latin, from Latin *fusus* 'spindle'.

fuscous /ˈfʌskəs/ ▶ **adjective** technical or poetic/literary dark and sombre in colour.

– ORIGIN mid 17th cent.: from Latin *fuscus* 'dusky' + **-OUS**.

fuse[1] ▶ **verb 1** [with obj.] join or blend to form a single entity: *intermarriage had fused the families into a large unit.*
■ [no obj.] (of groups of atoms or cellular structures) join or coalesce: *the two nuclei move together and* **fuse into** *one nucleus.* ■ melt (a material or object) with intense heat, especially so as to join it with something else: *powdered glass was* **fused to** *a metal base.* | [no obj.] *when fired in a special kiln, the metals* **fused on to** *the pot.*
2 [no obj.] Brit. (of an electrical appliance) stop working when a fuse melts: *the crew were left in darkness after the lights fused.*
■ [with obj.] cause (an electrical appliance) to stop working in such a way.
3 [with obj.] provide (a circuit or electrical appliance) with a fuse: [as adj. **fused**] *a fused plug.*
▶ **noun** a safety device consisting of a strip of wire that melts and breaks an electric circuit if the current exceeds a safe level.
– ORIGIN late 16th cent.: from Latin *fus-* 'poured, melted', from the verb *fundere*.

fuse[2] (also **fuze**) ▶ **noun** a length of material along which a small flame moves to explode a bomb or firework, meanwhile allowing time for those who light it to move to a safe distance.
■ a device in a bomb, shell, or mine that makes it explode on impact, after an interval, at set distance from the target, or when subjected to magnetic or vibratory stimulation.
▶ **verb** [with obj.] fit a fuse to (a bomb, shell or mine): *the bomb was fused to go off during a charity performance.*
– PHRASES **light the** (or **a**) **fuse** do something that creates a tense or exciting situation: *his goal midway through the first half lit the fuse.* **a** (or **on a**) **short fuse** used to indicate that someone has a tendency to lose their temper quickly.
– DERIVATIVES **fuseless** adjective.
– ORIGIN mid 17th cent.: from Italian *fuso*, from Latin *fusus* 'spindle'.

fuse board ▶ **noun** another term for **FUSE BOX**.

fuse box ▶ **noun** a box housing the fuses for circuits in a building.

fusee /fjuːˈziː/ (US **fuzee**) ▶ **noun 1** a conical pulley or wheel, especially in a watch or clock.
2 a large-headed match capable of staying alight in strong wind.
3 N. Amer. a railway signal flare.
– ORIGIN late 16th cent. (denoting a spindle-shaped figure): from French *fusée* 'spindleful', based on Latin *fusus* 'spindle'.

fuselage /ˈfjuːzəlɑːʒ, -lɪdʒ/ ▶ **noun** the main body of an aircraft.
– ORIGIN early 20th cent.: from French, from *fuseler* 'shape into a spindle', from *fuseau* 'spindle'.

Fuseli /ˈfjuːz(ə)li, fjuːˈzɛli/, Henry (1741–1825), Swiss-born British painter and art critic; born *Johann Heinrich Füssli*. A prominent figure of the romantic movement, he tended towards the horrifying and the fantastic, as in *The Nightmare* (1781).

fusel oil /ˈfjuːz(ə)l/ ▶ **noun** [mass noun] a mixture of several alcohols (chiefly amyl alcohol) produced as a by-product of alcoholic fermentation.
– ORIGIN mid 19th cent.: from German *Fusel* 'bad liquor', probably related to *fuseln* 'to bungle'.

fuseway ▶ **noun** a fused connection point in a fuse box.

fuse wire ▶ **noun** [mass noun] thin wire used in an electric fuse.

Fushun /fuːˈʃʊn/ a coal-mining city in NE China, in the province of Liaoning; pop. 1,330,000 (1990).

fusible /ˈfjuːzɪb(ə)l/ ▶ **adjective** able to be fused or melted easily.
– DERIVATIVES **fusibility** noun.
– ORIGIN late Middle English: from Old French, or from medieval Latin *fusibilis*, from *fundere* 'pour, melt'.

fusiform /ˈfjuːzɪfɔːm/ ▶ **adjective** Botany & Zoology tapering at both ends; spindle-shaped.
– ORIGIN mid 18th cent.: from Latin *fusus* 'spindle' + **-IFORM**.

fusil[1] /ˈfjuːzɪl/ ▶ **noun** historical a light musket.
– ORIGIN late 16th cent. (denoting a flint in a tinderbox): from French, based on Latin *focus* 'hearth, fire'.

fusil[2] /ˈfjuːzɪl/ ▶ **noun** Heraldry an elongated lozenge.
– ORIGIN late Middle English: from Old French *fusel*, from a diminutive of Latin *fusus* 'spindle'.

fusilier /ˌfjuːzɪˈlɪə/ (N. Amer. also **fusileer**) ▶ **noun** (usu. **Fusiliers**) a member of any of several British regiments formerly armed with fusils: *the Royal Scots Fusiliers.*
■ historical a soldier armed with a fusil.
– ORIGIN late 17th cent.: from French, from *fusil* (see **FUSIL**[1]).

fusillade /ˌfjuːzɪˈleɪd, -ˈlɑːd/ ▶ **noun** a series of shots fired or missiles thrown all at the same time or in quick succession: *marchers had to dodge a fusillade of missiles* | figurative *a fusillade of accusations.*
▶ **verb** [with obj.] archaic attack (a place) or shoot down (someone) by a series of shots fired at the same time or in quick succession.
– ORIGIN early 19th cent.: from French, from *fusiller* 'to shoot', from *fusil* (see **FUSIL**[1]).

fusilli /f(j)ʊˈziːli/ ▶ **plural noun** pasta pieces in the form of short spirals.
– ORIGIN Italian, literally 'little spindles', diminutive of *fuso*.

fusimotor /ˈfjuːzɪməʊtə/ ▶ **adjective** Anatomy relating to or denoting the motor neurons with slender fibres which innervate muscle spindles.

fusion ▶ **noun** [mass noun] the process or result of joining two or more things together to form a single entity: *the election results produced pressure for fusion of the parties* | [in sing.] *the film showed a perfect fusion of image and sound.*
■ Physics short for **NUCLEAR FUSION**. ■ the process of causing a material or object to melt with intense heat, especially so as to join with another: *the fusion of resin and glass fibre in the moulding process.* ■ music that is a mixture of different styles, especially jazz and rock.
– DERIVATIVES **fusional** adjective.
– ORIGIN mid 16th cent.: from Latin *fusio(n-)*, from *fundere* 'pour, melt'.

fusion bomb ▶ **noun** a bomb deriving its energy from nuclear fusion, especially a hydrogen bomb.

fusionist ▶ **noun 1** a person who strives for coalition between political parties or factions.
2 a player or fan of music that is mixture of two modern styles.
– DERIVATIVES **fusionism** noun.

fuss ▶ **noun** [in sing.] a display of unnecessary or excessive excitement, activity, or interest: *I don't know what all the fuss is about.*
■ a protest or dispute of a specified degree or kind: *he didn't put up too much of a fuss.* ■ [mass noun] elaborate or complex procedures; trouble or difficulty: *they settled in with very little fuss.*
▶ **verb** [no obj.] show unnecessary or excessive concern about something: *she's always fussing about her food.*
■ move about or busy oneself restlessly: *beside him Kegan was fussing with sheets of paper.* ■ [with obj.] Brit. disturb or bother (someone): *when she cries in her sleep, try not to fuss her.* ■ [with obj.] treat (someone) with excessive attention or affection: *she flattered and fussed her.*
– PHRASES **make a fuss** become angry and complain. **make a fuss over** (or Brit. **of**) treat (a person or animal) with excessive attention or affection.
– DERIVATIVES **fusser** noun.
– ORIGIN early 18th cent.: perhaps Anglo-Irish.

fussed ▶ **adjective** [predic.] Brit. informal (of a person) feeling concern, distress, or annoyance; having strong feelings about something: *it'd be great to be there but* **I'm not that fussed.**

fusspot ▶ **noun** informal a fussy person.

fussy ▶ **adjective** (**fussier**, **fussiest**) (of a person) fastidious about one's needs or requirements; hard to please: *he is very fussy about what he eats.*
■ showing excessive or anxious concern about detail: *Eleanor patted her hair with quick, fussy movements.* ■ full of unnecessary detail or decoration: *I hate fussy clothes.*
– PHRASES **not be fussy** informal used to indicate that one does not mind about something, especially a decision that is to be made: *'How long are you staying?' 'I'm not fussy.'*
– DERIVATIVES **fussily** adverb, **fussiness** noun.

fustanella /ˌfʌstəˈnɛlə/ ▶ **noun** a stiff white kilt, worn by men in Albania and Greece.
– ORIGIN mid 19th cent.: from Italian, from modern Greek *phoustani*, *phoustanela*, probably from Italian *fustagno*, from medieval Latin *fustaneum* (see **FUSTIAN**).

fustian /ˈfʌstɪən/ ▶ **noun** [mass noun] **1** thick, hard-wearing twilled cloth with a short nap, usually dyed in dark colours.
2 pompous or pretentious speech or writing: *a smokescreen of fustian and fantasy.*
– ORIGIN Middle English: from Old French *fustaigne*, from medieval Latin *fustaneum*, from (*pannus*) *fustaneus* 'cloth from *Fostat*', a suburb of Cairo; sense 2 perhaps from the fact that fustian was sometimes used to cover pillows and cushions, implying that the language was 'padded'; compare with **BOMBAST**.

fustic /ˈfʌstɪk/ ▶ **noun 1** [mass noun] archaic a yellow dye obtained from either of two kinds of timber, especially that of old fustic.
2 (also **old fustic**) a tropical American tree with heartwood that yields dyes and other products. See also **YOUNG FUSTIC**.
• *Maclura* (or *Chlorophora*) *tinctoria*, family Moraceae.
– ORIGIN late Middle English: via French from Spanish *fustoc*, from Arabic *fustuḳ*, from Greek *pistakē* 'pistachio tree'.

fusty ▶ **adjective** (**fustier**, **fustiest**) smelling stale, damp, or stuffy: *the fusty odour of decay.*
■ old-fashioned in attitude or style: *grammar in the classroom became a fusty notion.*
– DERIVATIVES **fustily** adverb, **fustiness** noun.
– ORIGIN late 15th cent.: from Old French *fuste* 'smelling of the cask', from *fust* 'cask, tree trunk', from Latin *fustis* 'cudgel'.

futhark /ˈfuːθɑːk/ (also **futhorc** /ˈfuːθɔːk/, **futhork**) ▶ **noun** the runic alphabet.
– ORIGIN mid 19th cent.: from its first six letters: *f*, *u*, *th*, *a* (or *o*), *r*, *k*.

futile ▶ **adjective** incapable of producing any useful result; pointless: *a futile attempt to keep fans from mounting the stage* | *it is futile to allocate blame for this.*
– DERIVATIVES **futilely** adverb, **futility** noun.
– ORIGIN mid 16th cent.: from Latin *futilis* 'leaky, futile', apparently from *fundere* 'pour'.

futilitarian /fjuːˌtɪlɪˈtɛːrɪən/ ▶ **adjective** devoted to futile pursuits.
▶ **noun** a person devoted to futile pursuits.

futon /ˈfuːtɒn/ ▶ **noun** a Japanese quilted mattress rolled out on the floor for use as a bed.
■ a type of low wooden sofa bed having such a mattress.
– ORIGIN late 19th cent.: Japanese.

futtock /ˈfʌtək/ ▶ **noun** each of the middle timbers of a ship's frame, between the floor and the top timbers.
– ORIGIN Middle English: perhaps from Middle Low German, or from **FOOT** + **HOOK**.

future ▶ **noun 1** (usu. **the future**) the time or a period of time following the moment of speaking or writing; time regarded as still to come: *we plan on getting married in the near future* | *work on the building will be shelved for the foreseeable future.*
■ events that will or are likely to happen in time to come: *nobody can predict the future.* ■ used to refer to what will happen to someone or something in time to come: *MPs will debate the future of the railways.* ■ a prospect of success or happiness: *he'd decided that there was no future in the gang* | *I began to believe I might have a future as an artist.* ■ Grammar a tense of verbs expressing events that have not yet happened.
2 (**futures**) contracts for assets (especially commodities or shares) bought at agreed prices but delivered and paid for later. Compare with **FORWARD** (in sense 2).
▶ **adjective** [attrib.] at a later time; going or likely to happen or exist: *the needs of future generations.*
■ (of a person) planned or destined to hold a specified position: *his future wife.* ■ existing after death: *heaven and the future life with Christ.* ■ Grammar (of a tense) expressing an event yet to happen.
– PHRASES **for future reference** see **REFERENCE**. **in future** from now onwards: *she would be more careful in future.*
– DERIVATIVES **futureless** adjective.
– ORIGIN late Middle English: via Old French from Latin *futurus*, future participle of *esse* 'be' (from the stem *fu-*, ultimately from a base meaning 'grow, become').

future history ▶ **noun** (in science fiction) a narration of imagined future events.

future perfect ▶ **noun** Grammar a tense of verbs expressing expected completion in the future, in English exemplified by *will have done.*

future-proof ▶ **adjective** (of a product) unlikely to become obsolete.

– DERIVATIVES **future-proofed** adjective, **future-proofing** noun.

future shock ▶ noun [mass noun] a state of distress or disorientation due to rapid social or technological change.

futurism ▶ noun [mass noun] concern with events and trends of the future, or which anticipate the future.
■ (**Futurism**) an artistic movement begun in Italy in 1909, which violently rejected traditional forms so as to celebrate and incorporate into art the energy and dynamism of modern technology. Launched by Filippo Marinetti, it had effectively ended by 1918 but was widely influential, particularly in Russia on figures such as Malevich and Mayakovsky.
– ORIGIN from **FUTURE** + **-ISM**, translating Italian *futurismo*, French *futurisme*.

futurist ▶ noun **1** (**Futurist**) an adherent of futurism.
2 a person who studies the future and makes predictions about it based on current trends.
3 Theology a person who believes that eschatological prophecies are still to be fulfilled.
▶ adjective **1** (often **Futurist**) of or relating to futurism or the Futurists.
2 relating to a vision of the future, especially one involving the development of technology: *the grim urban setting of the novel would have been a futurist nightmare.*

futuristic ▶ adjective having or involving very modern technology or design: *a swimming pool and futuristic dome.*
■ (of a film or book) set in the future, typically in a world of advanced or menacing technology. ■ dated of or characteristic of Futurism.
– DERIVATIVES **futuristically** adverb.

futurity /fju:ˈtjʊərɪti, -tʃ-/ ▶ noun (pl. **-ies**) [mass noun] the future time: *the tremendous shadows which futurity casts upon the present.*
■ [count noun] a future event. ■ renewed or continuing existence: *the snowdrops were a promise of futurity.* ■ US short for **FUTURITY RACE**.

futurity race (also **futurity stakes**) ▶ noun US a horse race for young horses for which entries are made long in advance, sometimes before the horses are born.

futurology /ˌfju:tʃəˈrɒlədʒi/ ▶ noun [mass noun] systematic forecasting of the future, especially from present trends in society.
– DERIVATIVES **futurological** adjective, **futurologist** noun.

futz /fʌts/ ▶ verb [no obj.] N. Amer. informal waste time; idle or busy oneself aimlessly: *mother futzed around in the kitchen.*
– ORIGIN 1930s: perhaps an alteration of Yiddish *arumfartzen* 'fart about'.

FUW ▶ abbreviation for Farmers' Union of Wales.

Fuxin /fuːˈʃɪn/ (also **Fou-hsin**) an industrial city in NE China, in Liaoning province; pop. 743,100 (1990).

fuze ▶ noun variant spelling of **FUSE**².

fuzee ▶ noun US spelling of **FUSEE**.

Fuzhou /fuːˈdʒəʊ/ (also **Foochow**) a port in SE China, capital of Fujian province; pop. 1,270,000 (1990).

fuzz¹ ▶ noun a fluffy or frizzy mass of hair or fibre: *a fuzz of black hair* | [mass noun] *his face was covered with white fuzz.*
■ a blurred image or area: *she saw Jess surrounded by a fuzz of sunlight.* ■ a buzzing or distorted sound, especially one deliberately produced as an effect on an electric guitar: *the fuzz of the radio.*
▶ verb **1** make or become blurred or indistinct: [with obj.] *snow fuzzes the outlines of the signs* | [no obj.] *tiny detail can be enlarged to poster size without fuzzing out.*
2 [no obj.] (of hair) become fluffy or frizzy: *her hair fuzzed out uncontrollably in the heat.*
– ORIGIN late 16th cent.: probably of Low German or Dutch origin; compare with Dutch *voos*, Low German *fussig* 'spongy'.

fuzz² ▶ noun (**the fuzz**) informal the police.
– ORIGIN 1920s (originally US): of unknown origin.

fuzzbox ▶ noun a device which adds a distorted buzzing quality to the sound of an electric guitar or other instrument.

fuzzed ▶ adjective (of popular music or electric instruments) having or producing a distorted buzzing tone: *fuzzed guitars.*

fuzzy ▶ adjective (**fuzzier**, **fuzziest**) **1** having a frizzy, fluffy, or frayed texture or appearance: *a girl with fuzzy dark hair.*
2 difficult to perceive clearly or understand and explain precisely; indistinct or vague: *the picture is very fuzzy* | *that fuzzy line between right and wrong.*
■ (of a person or the mind) unable to think clearly; confused: *my mind felt fuzzy.* ■ another term for **FUZZED**.
3 Computing & Logic of or relating to a form of set theory and logic in which predicates may have degrees of applicability, rather than simply being true or false. It has important uses in artificial intelligence and the design of control systems.
– PHRASES **warm fuzzy** (or **warm and fuzzy**) informal used to refer to a sentimentally emotional response

or something designed to evoke such a response: *babies require a lot of attention, not just momentary warm fuzzies.*
– DERIVATIVES **fuzzily** adverb, **fuzziness** noun.

fuzzy-wuzzy ▶ noun (pl. **-ies**) Brit. informal, offensive a black person, especially one with tightly curled hair.
■ historical a Sudanese soldier.
– ORIGIN late 19th cent.: reduplication of **FUZZY**.

fwd ▶ abbreviation for forward.

f.w.d. ▶ abbreviation for ■ four-wheel drive. ■ front-wheel drive.

F-word ▶ noun informal used instead of or in reference to the word 'fuck' because of its taboo nature.

FX ▶ abbreviation for (visual or sound) effects: *films which require actors rather than special FX.*
– ORIGIN from the pronunciation of the two letters forming the two syllables of *effects*.

FY ▶ abbreviation for ■ Brit. financial year. ■ N. Amer. fiscal year.

-fy ▶ suffix **1** (added to nouns) forming verbs denoting making or producing: *speechify.*
■ denoting transformation or the process of making into: *deify* | *petrify.*
2 forming verbs denoting the making of a state defined by an adjective: *amplify* | *falsify.*
3 forming verbs expressing a causative sense: *horrify.*
– ORIGIN from French *-fier*, from Latin *-ficare*, *-facere*, from *facere* 'do, make'.

FYI N. Amer. ▶ abbreviation for for your information.

fyke /fʌɪk/ (also **fyke net**) ▶ noun chiefly US a bag net for catching fish.
– ORIGIN mid 19th cent.: from Dutch *fuik* 'fish trap'.

fylfot /ˈfɪlfɒt/ ▶ noun a swastika.
– ORIGIN late 15th cent.: perhaps from *fill-foot* 'pattern filling the foot of a painted window'.

fynbos /ˈfeɪnbɒs/ ▶ noun [mass noun] a distinctive type of vegetation found only on the southern tip of Africa. It includes a very wide range of plant species, particularly small heather-like trees and shrubs.
– ORIGIN Afrikaans, literally 'fine bush'.

fyrd /fəːd, fɪəd/ ▶ noun the English militia before 1066.
– ORIGIN Old English, of Germanic origin; related to German *Fahrt*, also to **FARE**.

fytte ▶ noun variant spelling of **FIT**³.

Gg

G¹ (also **g**) ▶ noun (pl. **Gs** or **G's**) **1** the seventh letter of the alphabet.
■denoting the next after F in a set of items, categories, etc. ■ (**g**) Chess denoting the seventh file from the left, as viewed from White's side of the board.
2 Music the fifth note in the diatonic scale of C major.
■a key based on a scale with G as its keynote.

G² ▶ abbreviation for ■ Physics gauss. ■ [in combination] (in units of measurement) giga- (10⁹). ■ N. Amer. informal grand (a thousand dollars). ■ a unit of gravitational force equal to that exerted by the earth's gravitational field.
▶ symbol for ■ Chemistry Gibbs free energy. ■ Physics the gravitational constant, equal to 6.67×10^{-11} N m² kg⁻².

g ▶ abbreviation for ■ Chemistry gas. ■ gelding. ■ gram(s). ■ Physics denoting quantum states or wave functions which do not change sign on inversion through the origin. The opposite of **u**. [ORIGIN: from German *gerade* 'even'.]
▶ symbol for Physics the acceleration due to gravity, equal to 9.81 m s⁻².

G8 ▶ abbreviation for Group of Eight.

GA ▶ abbreviation for ■ general aviation. ■ Georgia (in official postal use).

Ga ▶ symbol for the chemical element gallium.

Ga. ▶ abbreviation for Georgia (US).

gab informal ▶ verb (**gabbed**, **gabbing**) [no obj.] talk, typically at length about trivial matters: *Franny walked right past a woman gabbing on the phone.*
▶ noun [mass noun] talk; chatter.
– PHRASES **the gift of the gab** the ability to speak with eloquence and fluency.
– ORIGIN early 18th cent.: variant of **GOB¹**.

GABA ▶ abbreviation for gamma-aminobutyric acid.

gabardine ▶ noun variant spelling of **GABERDINE**.

gabba /ˈxabə/ ▶ noun S. African informal a friend.
– ORIGIN via Yiddish from Hebrew *ḥāḇēr* 'friend'.

gabble ▶ verb [no obj.] talk rapidly and unintelligibly: *he gabbled on in a panicky way until he was dismissed.*
▶ noun [mass noun] rapid unintelligible talk.
– DERIVATIVES **gabbler** noun.
– ORIGIN late 16th cent.: from Dutch *gabbelen*, of imitative origin.

gabbro /ˈgabrəʊ/ ▶ noun (pl. **-os**) [mass noun] Geology a dark, coarse-grained plutonic rock of crystalline texture, consisting mainly of pyroxene, plagioclase feldspar, and often olivine.
– DERIVATIVES **gabbroic** adjective, **gabbroid** adjective.
– ORIGIN mid 19th cent.: from Italian, from Latin *glaber*, *glabr-* 'smooth'.

gabby ▶ adjective (**gabbier**, **gabbiest**) informal excessively or annoyingly talkative.

gaberdine /ˌgabəˈdiːn, ˈgabədiːn/ (also **gabardine**) ▶ noun [mass noun] a smooth, durable twill-woven cloth, typically of worsted or cotton.
■ [count noun] Brit. a raincoat made of such cloth. ■ historical a loose long upper garment, associated particularly with Jews and beggars.
– ORIGIN early 16th cent.: from Old French *gauvardine*, earlier *gallevardine*, perhaps from Middle High German *wallevart* 'pilgrimage' and originally 'a garment worn by a pilgrim'. The textile sense is first recorded in the early 20th cent.

Gabès /ˈgaːbɪs/ (also **Qabis**) an industrial seaport in eastern Tunisia; pop. 98,900 (1994).

gabfest ▶ noun informal, chiefly N. Amer. a prolonged conference or other gathering with much talking.

gabion /ˈgeɪbɪən/ ▶ noun a cylindrical basket filled with earth, stones, or other material and used as a component of civil engineering works or (formerly) fortifications.
– DERIVATIVES **gabionage** noun.
– ORIGIN mid 16th cent.: via French from Italian *gabbione*, from *gabbia* 'cage', from Latin *cavea*.

Gable, (William) Clark (1901–60), American actor, famous for films such as *It Happened One Night* (1934), for which he won an Oscar, and *Gone with the Wind* (1939).

gable ▶ noun the triangular upper part of a wall at the end of a ridged roof.
■(also **gable end**) a wall topped with a gable. ■ a gable-shaped canopy over a window or door.
– DERIVATIVES **gabled** adjective.
– ORIGIN Middle English: via Old French from Old Norse *gafl*, of Germanic origin; related to Dutch *gaffel* and German *Gabel* 'fork' (the point of the gable originally being the fork of two crossed timbers supporting the end of the roof-tree).

Gabo /ˈgɑːbəʊ/, Naum (1890–1977), Russian-born American sculptor, brother of Antoine Pevsner; born *Naum Neemia Pevsner*. A founder of Russian constructivism, Gabo experimented with kinetic art and transparent materials.

Gabon /ɡəˈbɒn/ an equatorial country in West Africa, on the Atlantic coast; pop. 1,200,000 (est. 1991); languages, French (official), West African languages; capital, Libreville. Gabon became a French territory in 1888. Part of French Equatorial Africa from 1910 to 1958, it became an independent republic in 1960.
– DERIVATIVES **Gabonese** /ˌgabəˈniːz/ adjective & noun.

gaboon /ɡəˈbuːn/ (also **gaboon mahogany**) ▶ noun a tropical West African hardwood tree which is valued for its timber.
● *Aucoumea klaineana*, family Burseraceae.
– ORIGIN early 20th cent.: from *Gaboon* (now **GABON**).

Gaboon viper /ɡəˈbuːn/ ▶ noun a large, thick-bodied venomous African snake with a pair of horn-like scales on the snout, and the scales richly patterned with brown, purple, and cream.
● *Bitis gabonica*, family Viperidae.
– ORIGIN early 20th cent.: named after *Gaboon* (now **GABON**).

Gabor /ˈgɑːbɔː, gəˈbɔː/, Dennis (1900–79), Hungarian-born British electrical engineer, who conceived the idea of holography. Nobel Prize for Physics (1971).

Gaborone /ˌgabəˈrəʊni/ the capital of Botswana, in the south of the country near the border with South Africa; pop. 133,470 (1991).

Gabriel /ˈgeɪbrɪəl/ (in the Bible) the archangel who foretold the birth of Jesus to the Virgin Mary (Luke 1:26–38), and who also appeared to Zacharias, father of John the Baptist, and to Daniel; (in Islam) the archangel who revealed the Koran to the Prophet Muhammad.

Gabrieli /ˌgabrɪˈɛli, -ˈeɪli/, Giovanni (c.1556–1612), Italian composer and organist. He was a leading Venetian musician who wrote a large number of motets with instrumental accompaniments for St Mark's Cathedral.

Gad /gad/ (in the Bible) a Hebrew patriarch, son of Jacob and Zilpah.
■the tribe of Israel traditionally descended from him.

gad¹ ▶ verb (**gadded**, **gadding**) [no obj.] informal go around from one place to another, in the pursuit of pleasure or entertainment: *he had heard gossip that I was gadding about with an airline stewardess.*
– PHRASES **on** (or **upon**) **the gad** archaic on the move.
– ORIGIN late Middle English: back-formation from obsolete *gadling* 'wanderer, vagabond', (earlier) 'companion', of Germanic origin.

gad² (also **by gad**) ▶ exclamation archaic an expression of surprise or emphatic assertion.
– ORIGIN late 15th cent.: euphemistic alteration of **GOD**.

gadabout ▶ noun a habitual pleasure-seeker.

Gadarene /ˈgadəriːn/ ▶ adjective involving or engaged in a headlong or potentially disastrous rush to do something.
– ORIGIN early 19th cent. (in the current sense): from New Testament Greek *Gadarēnos* 'inhabitant of *Gadara*' (see Matt. 8:28–32).

Gaddafi /ɡəˈdɑːfi/ (also **Qaddafi**), Mu'ammer Muhammad al (b.1942), Libyan colonel, head of state since 1970. After leading the coup which overthrew King Idris in 1969, he established the Libyan Arab Republic and has since pursued an anti-colonial policy at home; he has also been accused of supporting international terrorism.

gadfly ▶ noun (pl. **-flies**) a fly that bites livestock, especially a horsefly, warble fly, or botfly.
■figurative an annoying person, especially one who provokes others into action by criticism.
– ORIGIN late 16th cent.: from **GAD¹**, or obsolete *gad* 'goad, spike', from Old Norse *gaddr*, of Germanic origin; related to **YARD¹**.

gadget ▶ noun a small mechanical device or tool, especially an ingenious or novel one.
– DERIVATIVES **gadgeteer** noun, **gadgetry** noun, **gadgety** adjective.
– ORIGIN late 19th cent. (originally in nautical use): probably from French *gâchette* 'lock mechanism' or from the French dialect word *gagée* 'tool'.

gadid /ˈgeɪdɪd/ ▶ noun Zoology a fish of the cod family (Gadidae).
– ORIGIN late 19th cent.: from modern Latin *Gadidae* (plural), from *gadus* 'cod'.

gadoid /ˈgeɪdɔɪd, ˈga-/ ▶ noun Zoology a bony fish of an order (Gadiformes) that comprises the cods, hakes, and their relatives.
– ORIGIN mid 19th cent.: from modern Latin *gadus* (from Greek *gados* 'cod') + **-OID**.

gadolinite /ˈgad(ə)lɪnʌɪt, gəˈdɒlɪnʌɪt/ ▶ noun [mass noun] a rare dark brown or black mineral, consisting of a silicate of iron, beryllium, and rare earths.
– ORIGIN early 19th cent.: named after Johan *Gadolin* (1760–1852), the Finnish mineralogist who first identified it.

gadolinium /ˌgadəˈlɪnɪəm/ ▶ noun [mass noun] the chemical element of atomic number 64, a soft silvery-white metal of the lanthanide series. (Symbol: **Gd**)

– ORIGIN late 19th cent.: from **GADOLINITE**.

gadroon /ɡəˈdruːn/ ▶ **noun** a decorative edging on metal or wood formed by parallel rounded strips (reeding) like inverted fluting.
– DERIVATIVES **gadrooned** adjective, **gadrooning** noun.
– ORIGIN late 17th cent.: from French *godron*, probably related to *goder* 'to pucker', also to **GODET**.

gadwall /ˈɡadwɔːl/ ▶ **noun** (pl. same or **gadwalls**) a brownish-grey freshwater duck found across Eurasia and North America.
• *Anas strepera*, family Anatidae.
– ORIGIN mid 17th cent.: of unknown origin.

gadzooks /ɡadˈzuːks/ ▶ **exclamation** archaic an exclamation of surprise or annoyance.
– ORIGIN late 17th cent.: alteration of *God's hooks*, i.e. the nails by which Christ was fastened to the cross; see **GAD**[2].

Gaea /ˈdʒiːə/ variant spelling of **GAIA** (in sense 1).

Gael /ɡeɪl/ ▶ **noun** a Gaelic-speaking person.
■ a person whose ancestors spoke Gaelic.
– DERIVATIVES **Gaeldom** noun.
– ORIGIN from Scottish Gaelic *Gaidheal*.

Gaelic /ˈɡeɪlɪk, ˈɡalɪk/ ▶ **adjective** of or relating to the Goidelic group of Celtic languages, particularly the Celtic language of Scotland, and the culture associated with speakers of these languages and their descendants.
▶ **noun** (also **Scottish Gaelic**) [mass noun] a Celtic language spoken in the highlands and islands of western Scotland. It was brought from Ireland in the 5th and 6th centuries AD and is now spoken by about 40,000 people.
■ (also **Irish Gaelic**) another term for **IRISH** (the language).

Gaelic coffee ▶ **noun** [mass noun] coffee served with cream and whisky.

Gaelic football ▶ **noun** [mass noun] a type of football played mainly in Ireland between teams of fifteen players, with a goal resembling that used in rugby but having a net attached. The object is to kick or punch the round ball into the net (scoring three points) or over the crossbar (one point).

Gaelic League a movement founded in 1893 to revive Irish language and culture.

Gaeltacht /ˈɡeɪltəxt, Irish ˈɡeːltəxt/ (**the Gaeltacht**) a region of Ireland in which the vernacular language is Irish.
– ORIGIN Irish, earlier *Gaedhealtacht*, from *Gaedheal* 'Gael' + *tacht* 'talk, speech'.

gaff[1] ▶ **noun 1** a stick with a hook, or a barbed spear, for landing large fish.
2 Sailing a spar to which the head of a fore-and-aft sail is bent.
▶ **verb** [with obj.] seize or impale with a gaff.
– ORIGIN Middle English: from Provençal *gaf* 'hook'; related to **GAFFE**.

gaff[2] ▶ **noun** (in phrase **blow the gaff**) Brit. informal reveal a plot or secret.
– ORIGIN early 19th cent.: of unknown origin.

gaff[3] ▶ **noun** Brit. informal a house, flat, or other building, especially as being a person's home: *Gav's new gaff is in McDonald Road.*
– ORIGIN 1930s: of unknown origin.

gaffe /ɡaf/ ▶ **noun** an unintentional act or remark causing embarrassment to its originator; a blunder.
– ORIGIN early 20th cent.: from French, literally 'boathook' (from Provençal *gaf*: see **GAFF**[1]), used colloquially to mean 'blunder'.

gaffer ▶ **noun 1** Brit. informal a person in charge of others; a boss.
■ the chief electrician in a film or television production unit.
2 informal an old man.
– ORIGIN late 16th cent.: probably a contraction of **GODFATHER**; compare with **GAMMER**.

gaffer tape ▶ **noun** [mass noun] strong cloth-backed waterproof adhesive tape.

gag[1] ▶ **noun** a thing, typically a piece of cloth, put in or over a person's mouth to prevent them from speaking or crying out.
■ figurative a restriction on freedom of speech or dissemination of information: *every contract contains a self-signed gag.* ■ a device for keeping the patient's mouth open during a dental or surgical operation.
▶ **verb** (**gagged**, **gagging**) **1** [with obj.] (often **be gagged**) put a gag on (someone): *she was bound and gagged by robbers in her home.*
■ figurative (of a person or body with authority) prevent (someone) from speaking freely or disseminating information: *the government is trying to gag its critics* | [as adj. **gagging**] *the minister refused to sign a gagging order.*
2 [no obj.] choke or retch: *he **gagged on** the sourness of the wine.*
– ORIGIN Middle English: perhaps related to Old Norse *gagháls* 'with the neck thrown back', or imitative of a person choking.

gag[2] ▶ **noun** a joke or an amusing story or scene, especially one forming part of a comedian's act or in a film or play.
▶ **verb** [no obj.] tell jokes.
– ORIGIN mid 19th cent. (originally theatrical slang): of unknown origin.

gaga /ˈɡɑːɡɑː, ˈɡaɡə/ ▶ **adjective** informal slightly mad, typically as a result of old age, infatuation, or excessive enthusiasm.
– ORIGIN early 20th cent.: from French, 'senile, a senile person', reduplication based on *gâteux*, variant of *gâteur*, hospital slang in the sense 'bed-wetter'.

Gagarin /ɡəˈɡɑːrɪn/, Yuri (Alekseevich) (1934–68), Russian cosmonaut. In 1961 he made the first manned space flight, completing a single orbit of the earth in 108 minutes.

Gagauz /ɡəˈɡaʊz/ ▶ **noun** (pl. same) **1** a member of a people living mainly in southern Moldova and speaking a Turkic language.
2 [mass noun] the language of this people, closely related to Turkish and having about 150,000 speakers.
▶ **adjective** of or relating to this people or their language.

gag bit ▶ **noun** a powerful bit which is sometimes used on difficult horses.

gage[1] /ɡeɪdʒ/ archaic ▶ **noun** a valued object deposited as a guarantee of good faith.
■ a pledge, especially a glove, thrown down as a symbol of a challenge to fight.
▶ **verb** [with obj.] offer (a thing or one's life) as a guarantee of good faith.
– ORIGIN Middle English: from Old French *gage* (noun), *gager* (verb), of Germanic origin; related to **WAGE** and **WED**.

gage[2] ▶ **noun** & **verb** variant spelling of **GAUGE**.

gage[3] /ɡeɪdʒ/ ▶ **noun** another term for **GREENGAGE**.
– ORIGIN mid 19th cent.: from the name of Sir William *Gage* (1657–1727), the English botanist who introduced it to England.

gaggle ▶ **noun** a flock of geese.
■ informal a disorderly or noisy group of people: *the **gaggle of** reporters and photographers that dogged his every step.*
– ORIGIN Middle English (as a verb): imitative of the noise that a goose makes; compare with Dutch *gaggelen* and German *gackern*.

gagster ▶ **noun** a writer or performer of gags.

Gaia /ˈɡʌɪə/ **1** (also **Gaea, Ge**) Greek Mythology the Earth personified as a goddess, daughter of Chaos. She was the mother and wife of Uranus (Heaven); their offspring included the Titans and the Cyclops. [ORIGIN: Greek, 'Earth'.]
2 the earth viewed as a vast self-regulating organism. [ORIGIN: 1970s: coined by James Lovelock, at the suggestion of the writer William Golding, from the name of the goddess *Gaia*.]
– DERIVATIVES **Gaian** noun & adjective.

Gaia hypothesis the theory, put forward by James Lovelock, that living matter on the earth collectively defines and regulates the material conditions necessary for the continuance of life. The planet, or rather the biosphere, is thus likened to a vast self-regulating organism.

gaiety (US also **gayety**) ▶ **noun** (pl. **-ies**) [mass noun] the state or quality of being light-hearted or cheerful: *the sudden gaiety of children's laughter.*
■ merrymaking or festivity: *he seemed to be a part of the gaiety, having a wonderful time.* ■ (**gaieties**) dated entertainments or amusements.
– ORIGIN mid 17th cent.: from French *gaieté*, from *gai* (see **GAY**).

gaijin /ɡʌɪˈdʒɪn/ ▶ **noun** (pl. same) (in Japan) a foreigner.
– ORIGIN Japanese, contraction of *gaikoku-jin*, from *gaikoku* 'foreign country' + *jin* 'person'.

gaillardia /ɡeɪˈlɑːdɪə/ ▶ **noun** an American plant of the daisy family, which is cultivated for its bright red and yellow flowers.
• Genus *Gaillardia*, family Compositae.
– ORIGIN modern Latin, named in memory of *Gaillard* de Marentonneau, 18th-cent. French amateur botanist.

gaily ▶ **adverb** in a cheerful or light-hearted way: *he waved gaily to the little crowd.*
■ without thinking of the consequences: *she plunged gaily into speculation on the stock market.* ■ [as submodifier] with a bright or cheerful appearance: *gaily coloured sailing boats dot the lake.*

gain ▶ **verb** [with obj.] **1** obtain or secure (something desired, favourable, or profitable): *victory was gained for the loss of just two wickets* | [with two objs] *their blend of acoustic folk pop gained them several chart hits.*
■ reach or arrive at (a desired destination): *we gained the ridge.* ■ [no obj.] (**gain on**) come closer to (a person or thing pursued): *a huge bear gaining on him with every stride.* ■ archaic bring over to one's interest or views; win over: *to gratify the queen, and gain the court.*
2 increase the amount or rate of (something, typically weight or speed): *she had gradually gained weight since her wedding.*
■ [no obj.] increase in value: *shares also gained for the third day in a row.* ■ [no obj.] (**gain in**) improve or advance in some respect: *canoeing is gaining in popularity.* ■ (of a clock or watch) become fast by (a specific amount of time): *this atomic clock will neither gain nor lose a second in the next 1 million years.*
▶ **noun** [mass noun] an increase in wealth or resources: *the mayor was accused of using municipal funds for personal gain* | [count noun] *water shares were showing gains of up to 21 per cent.*
■ a thing that is achieved or acquired: *the potential gain from rail privatization would be a more commercial railway.* ■ [mass noun] the factor by which power or voltage is increased in an amplifier or other electronic device, usually expressed as a logarithm.
– DERIVATIVES **gainable** adjective, **gainer** noun.
– ORIGIN late 15th cent. (as a noun, originally in the sense 'booty'): from Old French *gaigne* (noun), *gaignier* (verb), of Germanic origin.

gainful ▶ **adjective** [attrib.] serving to increase wealth or resources: *he soon found gainful employment.*
– DERIVATIVES **gainfully** adverb, **gainfulness** noun.

gainsay /ɡeɪnˈseɪ/ ▶ **verb** (past and past participle **-said**) [with obj.] [with negative] formal deny or contradict (a fact or statement): *the impact of the railways cannot be gainsaid.*
■ speak against or oppose (someone).
– DERIVATIVES **gainsayer** noun.
– ORIGIN Middle English: from obsolete *gain-* 'against' + **SAY**.

Gainsborough /ˈɡeɪnzbərə/, Thomas (1727–88), English painter. He was famous for his society portraits, including *Mr and Mrs Andrews* (1748) and *The Blue Boy* (c.1770), and for landscapes such as *The Watering Place* (1777).

'gainst ▶ **preposition** poetic/literary short for **AGAINST**.

gain-up ▶ **noun** a control on a video camera used to increase the gain when filming in dark conditions.

gait /ɡeɪt/ ▶ **noun** a person's manner of walking: *the easy gait of an athlete.*
■ the paces of an animal, especially a horse or dog.
– ORIGIN late Middle English (originally Scots): variant of **GATE**[2].

gaita /ˈɡʌɪtə/ ▶ **noun** a kind of bagpipe played in northern Spain and Portugal.
– ORIGIN Spanish and Portuguese.

gaiter ▶ **noun** (usu. **gaiters**) a garment similar to leggings, worn to cover or protect the ankle and lower leg.
■ chiefly US a shoe or overshoe extending to the ankle or above. ■ a garment of this kind worn as part of the traditional costume of an Anglican bishop. ■ a flexible covering for the base of a gear lever or other mechanical part.
– DERIVATIVES **gaitered** adjective.
– ORIGIN early 18th cent.: from French *guêtre*, probably of Germanic origin and related to **WRIST**.

Gaitskell /ˈɡeɪtskɪl/, Hugh (Todd Naylor) (1906–63), British Labour statesman, Chancellor of the Exchequer 1950–1 and leader of the Labour Party 1955–63. He opposed the government over the Suez crisis and resisted calls within his own party for unilateral disarmament.

Gal. ▶ **abbreviation for** Epistle to the Galatians (in biblical references).

b **b**ut | d **d**og | f **f**ew | g **g**et | h **h**e | j **y**es | k **c**at | l **l**eg | m **m**an | n **n**o | p **p**en | r **r**ed | s **s**it | t **t**op | v **v**oice | w **w**e | z **z**oo | ʃ **sh**e | ʒ deci**s**ion | θ **th**in | ð **th**is | ŋ ri**ng** | x lo**ch** | tʃ **ch**ip | dʒ **j**ar

gal¹ ▶ noun informal, chiefly N. Amer. a girl or young woman.
– ORIGIN late 18th cent.: representing a pronunciation.

gal² ▶ noun Physics a unit of gravitational acceleration equal to one centimetre per second per second.
– ORIGIN early 20th cent.: named after **GALILEO GALILEI**.

gal. ▶ abbreviation for gallon(s).

gala¹ /'gɑːlə, 'geɪlə/ ▶ noun a social occasion with special entertainments or performances: [as modifier] *a gala performance by the Royal Ballet.*
■ Brit. a special sports meeting, especially a swimming competition.
– ORIGIN early 17th cent. (in the sense 'showy dress'): via Italian and Spanish from Old French *gale* 'rejoicing'.

gala² ▶ verb variant spelling of **GALLA**.

galactagogue /gə'laktəgɒg/ ▶ noun Medicine a food or drug that promotes or increases the flow of a mother's milk.
– ORIGIN mid 19th cent.: from Greek *gala, galakt-* 'milk' + *agōgos* 'leading'.

galactic /gə'laktɪk/ ▶ adjective of or relating to a galaxy or galaxies, especially the galaxy containing the solar system.
■ Astronomy measured relative to the galactic equator.
– ORIGIN mid 19th cent.: from Greek *galaktias* (variant of *galaxias* 'galaxy') + -IC.

galactic equator ▶ noun Astronomy the great circle or the celestial sphere passing as closely as possible through the densest parts of the Milky Way.

galactorrhoea /gə,laktə'rɪːə/ ▶ noun [mass noun] Medicine excessive or inappropriate production of milk.
– ORIGIN mid 19th cent.: from Greek *gala, galakt-* 'milk' + *rhoia* 'flux, flow'.

galactose /gə'laktəʊz, -s/ ▶ noun [mass noun] Chemistry a sugar of the hexose class which is a constituent of lactose and many polysaccharides.
– ORIGIN mid 19th cent.: from Greek *gala, galaktos* 'milk' + -OSE².

galago /gə'leɪgəʊ/ ▶ noun (pl. -os) another term for **BUSHBABY**.
– ORIGIN modern Latin (genus name).

galah /gə'lɑː/ ▶ noun 1 a small Australian cockatoo with a grey back and rosy pink head and underparts, abundant and regarded as a pest.
● *Eulophus roseicapillus*, family Cacatuidae (or Psittacidae).
2 Austral. informal a stupid person.
– ORIGIN mid 19th cent.: from Yuwaalaraay (an Aboriginal language of New South Wales).

Galahad /'galəhad/ (also **Sir Galahad**) the noblest of King Arthur's knights, renowned for immaculate purity and destined to find the Holy Grail.
■ [as noun **a (Sir) Galahad**] a person characterized by nobility, integrity, or courtesy.

galangal /'gal(ə)ngal/ (also **galingale**) ▶ noun [mass noun] an Asian plant of the ginger family, the aromatic rhizome of which is widely used in cookery and herbal medicine.
● Genera *Alpinia* and *Kaempferia*, family Zingiberaceae.
– ORIGIN Middle English *galingale*, via Old French from Arabic *kalanjān*, perhaps from Chinese *gāoliángjiāng*, from *gāoliáng* (the name of a district in Guangdong Province, China) + *jiāng* 'ginger'.

galant /ɡa'lant, ɡa'lõ/ ▶ adjective of, relating to, or denoting a light and elegant style of 18th-century music.
– ORIGIN French and German (see **GALLANT**).

galantine /'gal(ə)ntiːn/ ▶ noun [mass noun] a dish of white meat or fish boned, cooked, pressed, and served cold in aspic.
– ORIGIN Middle English (in the sense 'sauce for fish'): from Old French, alteration of *galatine*, from medieval Latin *galatina*; the current sense dates from the early 18th cent.

galanty show /ɡə'lanti/ ▶ noun historical a performance of shadow theatre.
– ORIGIN early 19th cent.: *galanty* perhaps from Italian *galanti*, plural of *galante* 'a gallant'.

Galapagos finches ▶ plural noun another term for **DARWIN'S FINCHES**.

Galapagos Islands /ɡə'lapəgɒs/ a Pacific archipelago on the equator, about 1,045 km (650 miles) west of Ecuador, to which it belongs; pop. 9,750 (1990). Spanish name **ARCHIPIÉLAGO DE COLÓN**.

The islands are noted for their abundant wildlife, including giant tortoises and many other endemic species. They were the site of Charles Darwin's observations of 1835, which helped him to form his theory of natural selection.

Galatea /,ɡalə'tɪə/ 1 Greek Mythology a sea nymph courted by the Cyclops Polyphemus, who in jealousy killed his rival Acis.
2 the name given to the statue fashioned by Pygmalion and brought to life.

Galaţi /ɡa'lats/ an industrial city in eastern Romania, a river port on the lower Danube; pop. 324,200 (1993).

Galatia /ɡə'leɪʃə/ an ancient region in central Asia Minor, settled by invading Gauls (the Galatians) in the 3rd century BC. It later became a province of the Roman Empire.
– DERIVATIVES **Galatian** adjective & noun.

Galatians, Epistle to the /ɡə'leɪʃ(ə)nz/ a book of the New Testament, an epistle of St Paul to the Church in Galatia.

galaxy ▶ noun (pl. -ies) a system of millions or billions of stars, together with gas and dust, held together by gravitational attraction.
■ (**the Galaxy**) the galaxy of which the solar system is a part; the Milky Way. ■ figurative a large or impressive group of people or things: *a galaxy of boundless young talent.*

The Galaxy in which the earth is located is a disc-shaped spiral galaxy with approximately 100,000 million stars. The sun is located about two thirds of the way out from the centre.

– ORIGIN late Middle English (originally referring to the Milky Way): via Old French from medieval Latin *galaxia*, from Greek *galaxias* (*kuklos*) 'milky (vault)', from *gala, galakt-* 'milk'.

Galba /'ɡalbə/ (*c*.3 BC–AD 69), Roman emperor AD 68–9; full name *Servius Sulpicius Galba*. The successor to Nero, he aroused hostility by his severity and parsimony and was murdered in a conspiracy organized by Otho.

galbanum /'ɡalbənəm/ ▶ noun [mass noun] a bitter aromatic resin produced from kinds of ferula.
– ORIGIN Middle English: via Latin from Greek *khalbanē*, probably of Semitic origin.

Galbraith /ɡal'breɪθ/, John Kenneth (b.1908), Canadian-born American economist. He is well known for his criticism of consumerism and of the power of large multinational corporations.

gale ▶ noun a very strong wind: *it was almost blowing a gale* | [as modifier] *gale-force winds.*
■ (also **fresh gale**) (on the Beaufort scale) a wind of force 8 (34–40 knots or 63–74 kph). ■ a storm at sea. ■ (**a gale of/gales of**) figurative a burst of sound, especially of laughter: *she collapsed into gales of laughter.*
– ORIGIN mid 16th cent.: perhaps related to Old Norse *galinn* 'mad, frantic'.

galea /'ɡeɪlɪə/ ▶ noun (pl. **galeae** /-liː/ or **galeas**) Botany & Zoology a structure shaped like a helmet.
– ORIGIN mid 19th cent.: from Latin, literally 'helmet'.

Galen /'ɡeɪlən/ (129–99), Greek physician; full name *Claudius Galenos*; Latin name *Claudius Galenus*. He attempted to systematize the whole of medicine, making important discoveries in anatomy and physiology. His works became influential in Europe when retranslated from Arabic in the 12th century.

galena /ɡə'liːnə/ ▶ noun [mass noun] a bluish, grey, or black mineral of metallic appearance, consisting of lead sulphide. It is the chief ore of lead.
– ORIGIN late 17th cent.: from Latin, 'lead ore' (in a partly purified state).

galenic /ɡə'lɛnɪk/ ▶ adjective (also **Galenic**) Medicine of or relating to Galen or his methods.
■ (of a medicine) galenical.

galenical Medicine ▶ adjective (of a medicine) made of natural rather than synthetic components.
■ of or relating to Galen.
▶ noun a medicine of this type.

galère /ɡa'lɛː, French ɡalɛʀ/ ▶ noun an undesirable group or coterie: *the repulsive galère of Lolita's admirers.*
– ORIGIN French, literally 'galley'. The term was used in Molière's play *Scapin* meaning 'coterie'.

galette /ɡə'lɛt/ ▶ noun a savoury pancake made from grated potatoes or a buckwheat batter.
– ORIGIN French.

gali /'ɡʌli/ ▶ noun (pl. **galis**) Indian variant spelling of **GULLY** (in sense 2).

galia melon /'ɡɑːlɪə/ ▶ noun a small rounded melon of a variety with rough skin and fragrant orange flesh.

Galibi /ɡə'liːbi/ ▶ noun another term for **CARIB** (in sense 2).
– ORIGIN Carib, literally 'strong man'.

Galicia /ɡə'lɪsɪə, -'lɪʃə, Spanish ɡa'liθja, -sja/ 1 an autonomous region and former kingdom of NW Spain; capital Santiago de Compostela.
2 a region of east central Europe, north of the Carpathian Mountains. A former province of Austria, it now forms part of SE Poland and western Ukraine.

Galician ▶ adjective 1 of or relating to Galicia in NW Spain, its people, or their language.
2 of or relating to Galicia in east central Europe.
▶ noun 1 a native or inhabitant of Galicia in NW Spain.
2 [mass noun] the language of Galicia in NW Spain, a Romance language closely related to Portuguese. It is spoken by about 3 million people, most of whom also speak Spanish.
3 a native or inhabitant of Galicia in east central Europe.

Galilean¹ /,ɡalɪ'liːən/ ▶ adjective of or relating to Galileo or his methods.

Galilean² /,ɡalɪ'liːən/ ▶ adjective of or relating to Galilee.
■ archaic, derogatory Christian.
▶ noun a native of Galilee.
■ archaic, derogatory a Christian.

Galilean moons Astronomy the four largest satellites of Jupiter (Callisto, Europa, Ganymede, and Io), discovered by Galileo in 1610 and independently by the German astronomer Simon Marius (1573–1624).

Galilean telescope ▶ noun an astronomical telescope of the earliest type, with a biconvex objective and biconcave eyepiece.

Galilee /'ɡalɪli/ a northern region of ancient Palestine, west of the River Jordan, associated with the ministry of Jesus. It is now part of Israel.

galilee /'ɡalɪliː/ ▶ noun a chapel or porch at the entrance of a church.
– ORIGIN Middle English: from Old French, from medieval Latin *galilea* 'Galilee'. Compare with **GALLERY**.

Galilee, Sea of a lake in northern Israel. The River Jordan flows through it from north to south. Also called **LAKE TIBERIAS**, **LAKE KINNERET**.

Galileo /,ɡalɪ'leɪəʊ/ an American space probe to Jupiter, launched in 1989. It reached the vicinity of Jupiter in 1995 and released a probe which descended into Jupiter's atmosphere.

Galileo Galilei /,ɡalɪ'leɪəʊ ,ɡalɪ'leɪi/ (1564–1642), Italian astronomer and physicist. He discovered the constancy of a pendulum's swing, formulated the law of uniform acceleration of falling bodies, and described the parabolic trajectory of projectiles. He applied the telescope to astronomy and observed craters on the moon, sunspots, Jupiter's moons, and the phases of Venus.

galingale /'ɡalɪŋ,ɡeɪl/ ▶ noun 1 (also **English** or **sweet galingale**) a Eurasian sedge with an aromatic rhizome, formerly used in perfumes. [ORIGIN: late 16th cent.: variant of **GALANGAL**.]
● *Cyperus longus*, family Cyperaceae.
2 variant spelling of **GALANGAL**.

galipot /'ɡalɪpɒt/ ▶ noun [mass noun] hardened resin deposits formed on the stem of the maritime pine.
– ORIGIN late 18th cent.: from French, of unknown origin.

galjoen /xal'jʊn/ ▶ noun (pl. same) a deep-bodied marine fish with a spiny dorsal fin, occurring in shallow waters around South Africa. Also called **BLACKFISH**.
● *Coracinus capensis*, family Coracinidae.
– ORIGIN mid 19th cent.: from Afrikaans and Dutch, literally 'galleon'.

gall¹ /ɡɔːl/ ▶ noun [mass noun] 1 bold, impudent behaviour: *the bank had the gall to demand a fee.*
2 the contents of the gall bladder; bile (proverbial for its bitterness).
■ [count noun] an animal's gall bladder. ■ used to refer to something bitter or cruel: *accept life's gall without blaming somebody else.*
– ORIGIN Old English *gealla* (denoting bile), of Germanic origin; related to Dutch *gal*, German

Galle 'gall', from an Indo-European root shared by Greek *kholē* and Latin *fel* 'bile'.

gall² /gɔːl/ ▶ **noun 1** [mass noun] annoyance; irritation: *he imagined Linda's gall as she found herself still married and not rich.*
2 a sore on the skin made by chafing.
▶ **verb** [with obj.] **1** make (someone) feel annoyed: *the duke knew he was losing, and it galled him.*
2 make sore by rubbing: *the straps that galled their shoulders.*
– ORIGIN Old English *gealle* 'sore on a horse', perhaps related to GALL¹; superseded in Middle English by forms from Middle Low German or Middle Dutch.

gall³ /gɔːl/ ▶ **noun** an abnormal growth formed in response to the presence of insect larvae, mites, or fungi on plants and trees, especially oaks.
■ [as modifier] denoting insects or mites that produce such growths: *gall flies.*
– ORIGIN Middle English: via Old French from Latin *galla.*

gall. ▶ abbreviation for gallon(s).

Galla /ˈgalə/ ▶ **noun** & **adjective** another term for OROMO.
– ORIGIN of unknown origin.

galla /ˈxala/ (also **gallah** or **gala**) ▶ **verb** [no obj.] S. African informal feel a strong desire; look longingly: *I can't eat the chocolate if you sit and galla for a piece.*
– ORIGIN Afrikaans, from Xhosa *rhala* 'crave'.

gallant ▶ **adjective 1** /ˈgal(ə)nt/ (of a person or their behaviour) brave; heroic: *she had made gallant efforts to pull herself together.*
■ archaic grand; fine: *they made a gallant array next morning as they marched off.*
2 /ˈgal)nt, gəˈlant/ (of a man or his behaviour) giving special attention and respect to women; chivalrous.
▶ **noun** /ˈgal(ə)nt, gəˈlant/ archaic a man who pays special attention to women.
■ a dashing man of fashion; a fine gentleman.
▶ **verb** /gəˈlant, ˈgal(ə)nt/ [with obj.] archaic (of a man) flirt with (a woman).
– DERIVATIVES **gallantly** adverb.
– ORIGIN Middle English (in the sense 'finely dressed'): from Old French *galant*, from *galer* 'have fun, make a show', from *gale* 'pleasure, rejoicing'.

gallantry ▶ **noun** (pl. **-ies**) [mass noun] **1** courageous behaviour, especially in battle: *a medal awarded for outstanding gallantry during the raid.*
2 polite attention or respect given by men to women.
■ (**gallantries**) actions or words used when paying such attention. ■ archaic sexual intrigue.
– ORIGIN late 16th cent. (in the sense 'splendour, ornamentation'): from French *galanterie*, from *galant* (see GALLANT).

gallberry /ˈgɔːlb(ə)ri, -bɛri/ ▶ **noun** (pl. **-ies**) another term for INKBERRY.

gall bladder ▶ **noun** the small sac-shaped organ beneath the liver, in which bile is stored after secretion by the liver and before release into the intestine.

Galle /ˈgɑːlə/ a seaport on the SW coast of Sri Lanka; pop. 76,800 (1981).

galleon ▶ **noun** a sailing ship in use (especially by Spain) from the 15th to the 18th centuries, originally as a warship, later for trade. Galleons were mainly square-rigged and usually had three or more decks and masts.
– ORIGIN early 16th cent.: either via Middle Dutch from French *galion*, from *galie* 'galley', or from Spanish *galeón.*

galleria /ˌgaləˈriːə/ ▶ **noun** a collection of small shops under a single roof; an arcade.
– ORIGIN Italian (see GALLERY).

gallery ▶ **noun** (pl. **-ies**) **1** a room or building for the display or sale of works of art.
■ a collection of pictures.
2 a balcony, especially a platform or upper floor, projecting from the back or side wall inside a church or hall, providing space for an audience or musicians.
■ (**the gallery**) the highest of such balconies in a theatre, containing the cheapest seats. ■ a group of spectators, especially those at a golf tournament.
3 a long room or passage, typically one that is partly open at the side to form a portico or colonnade.
■ a horizontal underground passage, especially in a mine.

– PHRASES **play to the gallery** act in an exaggerated or histrionic manner, especially in order to appeal to popular taste.
– DERIVATIVES **galleried** adjective.
– ORIGIN late Middle English (in sense 3): via Old French from Italian *galleria* 'gallery', formerly also 'church porch', from medieval Latin *galeria*, perhaps an alteration of *galilea* (see GALILEE).

gallery forest ▶ **noun** a forest restricted to the banks of a river or stream.

gallery grave ▶ **noun** Archaeology an underground megalithic burial chamber which may be divided into sections but has no separate entrance passage.

gallet /ˈgalɪt/ ▶ **noun** a chip or splinter of stone inserted into wet mortar.
– ORIGIN early 18th cent.: from French *galet* 'rounded beach pebble', from Old French *gal* 'pebble, stone'.

galley ▶ **noun** (pl. **-eys**) **1** historical a low, flat ship with one or more sails and up to three banks of oars, chiefly used for warfare or piracy and often manned by slaves or criminals.
■ a large open rowing boat kept on a warship especially for use by the captain.
2 the kitchen in a ship or aircraft.
3 (also **galley proof**) a printer's proof in the form of long single-column strips, not in sheets or pages. [ORIGIN: *galley* from French *galée* denoting an oblong tray for holding set-up type.]
– ORIGIN Middle English: via Old French from medieval Latin *galea*, from medieval Greek *galaia*, of unknown origin.

galley slave ▶ **noun** historical a person condemned to row in a galley.

galliambic /ˌgalɪˈambɪk/ Prosody ▶ **adjective** relating to or written in a metre consisting of two catalectic iambic dimeters.
▶ **noun** (usu. **galliambics**) galliambic verse.
– ORIGIN mid 19th cent.: from Latin *galliambus*, a song of the *Galli* (name given to priests of Cybele) + -IC.

Gallia Narbonensis /ˌgalɪə ˌnɑːbəˈnɛnsɪs/ the southern province of Transalpine Gaul.

Galliano /ˌgalɪˈɑːnəʊ/ ▶ **noun** [mass noun] a golden-yellow Italian liqueur flavoured with herbs.
– ORIGIN named after Major Giuseppe *Galliáno*, noted for halting Ethiopian forces in the war of 1895–6.

galliard /ˈgalɪɑːd, -ɪəd/ ▶ **noun** historical a lively dance in triple time for two people, including complicated turns and steps.
– ORIGIN late Middle English (as an adjective meaning 'valiant, sturdy' and 'lively, brisk'): from Old French *gaillard* 'valiant', of Celtic origin. The current sense dates from the mid 16th cent.

galliass /ˈgalɪas/ ▶ **noun** a large type of galley, chiefly used as a warship during the 16th and 17th centuries.
– ORIGIN mid 16th cent.: from Old French *galleasse*, from Italian *galeaza* 'large galley', from *galea* (see GALLEY).

Gallic /ˈgalɪk/ ▶ **adjective 1** French or typically French: *a Gallic shrug.*
2 of or relating to the Gauls.
– DERIVATIVES **Gallicize** (also **-ise**) verb.
– ORIGIN late 17th cent.: from Latin *Gallicus*, from *Gallus* 'a Gaul'.

gallic acid ▶ **noun** [mass noun] Chemistry an acid extracted from oak galls and other vegetable products, formerly used in making ink.
● Alternative name: **3, 4, 5-trihydroxybenzoic acid**; chem. formula: $C_6H_2(OH)_3COOH$.
– DERIVATIVES **gallate** noun.
– ORIGIN late 18th cent.: *gallic* from Latin *galla* 'oak gall' (see GALL³) + -IC.

Gallican /ˈgalɪk(ə)n/ ▶ **adjective 1** of or relating to the ancient Church of Gaul or France.
2 of or holding a doctrine (reaching its peak in the 17th century) which asserted the freedom of the Roman Catholic Church in France and elsewhere from the ecclesiastical authority of the papacy. Compare with ULTRAMONTANE.
▶ **noun** an adherent of the Gallican doctrine.
– DERIVATIVES **Gallicanism** noun.
– ORIGIN late Middle English: from Old French *gallican*, or from Latin *Gallicanus*, from *Gallicus* (see GALLIC).

gallice /ˈgalɪsi/ ▶ **adverb** archaic in French.
– ORIGIN Latin, 'in Gaulish'.

Gallicism /ˈgalɪˌsɪz(ə)m/ ▶ **noun** a French idiom, especially one adopted by speakers of another language.
– ORIGIN mid 17th cent.: from French *gallicisme*, from Latin *Gallicus* (see GALLIC).

Gallic Wars Julius Caesar's campaigns 58–51 BC, which established Roman control over Gaul north of the Alps and west of the River Rhine (Transalpine Gaul). During this period Caesar twice invaded Britain (55 and 54 BC).

galligaskins /ˌgalɪˈgaskɪnz/ ▶ **plural noun** Brit. historical breeches, trousers, or gaiters.
– ORIGIN late 16th cent.: perhaps an alteration (influenced by *galley* and *Gascon*) of obsolete French *gargesque*, from Italian *grechesca*, feminine of *grechesco* 'Greek'.

gallimaufry /ˌgalɪˈmɔːfri/ ▶ **noun** [in sing.] a confused jumble or medley of things.
– ORIGIN mid 16th cent.: from archaic French *galimafrée* 'unappetizing dish', perhaps from Old French *galer* 'have fun' + Picard *mafrer* 'eat copious quantities'.

gallimimus /ˌgalɪˈmʌɪməs/ ▶ **noun** an ostrich dinosaur of the late Cretaceous period.
● Genus *Gallimimus*, infraorder Ornithomimosauria, suborder Theropoda.
– ORIGIN modern Latin, from Latin *galli* 'of a cockerel' (genitive of *gallus*) + *mimus* 'mime, pretence'.

gallinaceous /ˌgalɪˈneɪʃəs/ ▶ **adjective** dated of or relating to birds of an order (Galliformes) which includes domestic poultry and game birds.
– ORIGIN late 18th cent.: from Latin *gallinaceus* (from *gallina* 'hen', from *gallus* 'cock') + -OUS.

galling /ˈgɔːlɪŋ/ ▶ **adjective** annoying; humiliating.
– DERIVATIVES **gallingly** adverb.

gallinule /ˈgalɪnjuːl/ ▶ **noun** a marshbird of the rail family, with mainly black, purplish-blue, or dark green plumage, and a red bill.
● Genera *Porphyrio* and *Porphyrula* (or *Gallinula*), family Rallidae: several species, e.g. the **American purple gallinule** (*Porphyrula martinica*).
– ORIGIN late 18th cent.: from modern Latin *Gallinula* (genus term), diminutive of Latin *gallina* 'hen', from *gallus* 'cock'.

galliot /ˈgalɪət/ ▶ **noun** historical a single-masted Dutch cargo boat or fishing vessel.
■ a small fast galley, especially in the Mediterranean.
– ORIGIN Middle English: from Old French *galiote* or Dutch *galjoot*, from a diminutive of medieval Latin *galea* 'galley'.

Gallipoli /gəˈlɪpəli/ a major campaign of the First World War which took place on the Gallipoli peninsula, on the European side of the Dardanelles, in 1915–16. The Allies (with heavy involvement of troops from Australia and New Zealand) hoped to gain control of the strait, but the campaign reached stalemate after each side suffered heavy casualties.

gallipot /ˈgalɪpɒt/ ▶ **noun** historical a small pot made from glazed earthenware or metal, used by pharmacists to hold medicines or ointments.
– ORIGIN late Middle English: probably from GALLEY + POT¹ (because gallipots were brought from the Mediterranean in galleys).

gallium /ˈgalɪəm/ ▶ **noun** [mass noun] the chemical element of atomic number 31, a soft, silvery-white metal which melts at about 30°C, just above room temperature. (Symbol: **Ga**)
– ORIGIN late 19th cent.: modern Latin, from Latin *Gallia* 'France' or *gallus* 'cock'; named (either patriotically or as a translation of his own name) by Paul-Émile *Lecoq de Boisbaudran* (1838–1912), the French chemist who discovered it in 1875.

gallivant /ˈgalɪvant, ˌgalɪˈvant/ ▶ **verb** [no obj., with adverbial] informal go around from one place to another in the pursuit of pleasure or entertainment: *she quit her job to go gallivanting around the globe.*
– ORIGIN early 19th cent.: perhaps an alteration of GALLANT.

galliwasp /ˈgalɪwɒsp/ ▶ **noun** a marsh lizard found in Central America and the Caribbean.
● Genus *Diploglossus*, family Anguidae: many species, in particular *D. monotropis* of the West Indies.
– ORIGIN late 17th cent.: of unknown origin.

gall midge ▶ **noun** a small, delicate fly which induces gall formation in plants or may cause other damage to crops.
● Family Cecidomyiidae: numerous genera and species,

including the **saddle gall midge** (*Haplodiplosis marginata*), which is a pest of cereals.

gall mite ▶ **noun** a minute mite which is parasitic on plants, typically living inside buds and causing them to form hard galls.
• Family Eriophyidae, order Prostigmata: numerous species, in particular *Cecidophyopsis ribis*, which affects blackcurrant bushes, causing big bud and transmitting the reversion virus.

Gallo- /ˈgaləʊ/ ▶ **combining form** French; French and ...: *Gallo-German*.
■ relating to France.
– ORIGIN from Latin *Gallus* 'a Gaul'.

gallon /ˈgalən/ ▶ **noun 1** a unit of volume for liquid measure equal to eight pints, in particular:
■ (also **imperial gallon**) Brit. (also used for dry measure) equivalent to 4.55 litres. ■ US equivalent to 3.79 litres.
2 (**gallons of**) informal a large volume: *gallons of fake blood*.
– DERIVATIVES **gallonage** noun.
– ORIGIN Middle English: from Anglo-Norman French *galon*, from the base of medieval Latin *galleta*, *galletum* 'pail, liquid measure', perhaps of Celtic origin.

galloon /gəˈluːn/ ▶ **noun** a narrow ornamental strip of fabric, typically a silk braid or piece of lace, used to trim clothing or finish upholstery.
– ORIGIN early 17th cent.: from French *galon*, from *galonner* 'to trim with braid', of unknown ultimate origin.

gallop ▶ **noun** [in sing.] the fastest pace of a horse or other quadruped, with all the feet off the ground together in each stride: *the horse broke into a furious gallop* | [mass noun] *a mounted police charge at full gallop*.
■ a ride on a horse at this pace: *Wilfred went for a gallop on the sands*. ■ a very fast pace of running by a person. ■ Brit. a track or ground where horses are exercised at a gallop.
▶ **verb** (**galloped**, **galloping**) [no obj., with adverbial of direction] (of a horse) go at the pace of a gallop.
■ [with obj. and adverbial of direction] make (a horse) gallop: *Fred galloped the horse off to the start*. ■ (of a person) run fast and rather boisterously. ■ (**gallop through**) figurative win (something) at great speed or without effort: *Poole galloped through all his heats*. ■ figurative (of a process or time) progress rapidly in a seemingly uncontrollable manner: *panic about the deadline galloping towards them* | [as adj. **galloping**] *galloping inflation*.
– DERIVATIVES **galloper** noun.
– ORIGIN early 16th cent.: from Old French *galop* (noun), *galoper*, variants of Old Northern French *walop*, *waloper* (see **WALLOP**).

galloping consumption ▶ **noun** [mass noun] dated consumption that progresses at a rapid rate.

gallous ▶ **adjective** variant spelling of **GALLUS**.

Galloway /ˈgaləweɪ/ an area of SW Scotland consisting of the two former counties of Kirkcudbrightshire and Wigtownshire, and now part of Dumfries and Galloway region.

galloway /ˈgaləweɪ/ ▶ **noun** an animal of a breed of cattle which originated in Galloway. They are hornless and black and are kept for beef.
■ (also **belted galloway**) a variety of such cattle marked with a broad white band.

gallows ▶ **plural noun** [usu. treated as sing.] a structure, typically of two uprights and a crosspiece, for the hanging of criminals.
■ (**the gallows**) execution by hanging: *he was saved from the gallows by a last-minute reprieve*.
– ORIGIN Old English *galga*, *gealga*, of Germanic origin; related to Dutch *galg* and German *Galgen*; reinforced in Middle English by Old Norse *gálgi*.

gallows humour ▶ **noun** [mass noun] grim and ironical humour in a desperate or hopeless situation.

gallows tree ▶ **noun** another term for **GALLOWS**.

gallstone /ˈgɔːlstəʊn/ ▶ **noun** a small, hard crystalline mass formed abnormally in the gall bladder or bile ducts from bile pigments, cholesterol, and calcium salts. Gallstones can cause severe pain and blockage of the bile duct.

Gallup poll /ˈgaləp/ ▶ **noun** trademark an assessment of public opinion by the questioning of a representative sample, typically as a basis for forecasting votes in an election.
– ORIGIN 1940s: named after George H. Gallup (1901–84), the American statistician who devised the method.

gallus /ˈgaləs/ (also **gallous**) ▶ **adjective** chiefly Scottish dashing; mischievous.
– ORIGIN late Middle English (in the sense 'fit to be hanged'): variant of **GALLOWS** used attributively.

galluses /ˈgaləsɪz/ ▶ **plural noun** chiefly Scottish & US braces for a person's trousers.
– ORIGIN mid 19th cent.: plural of *gallus*, variant of **GALLOWS**.

gall wasp ▶ **noun** a small winged insect of ant-like appearance. The female lays its egg in the food plant and when the larva hatches the surrounding plant tissue swells up around it to form a gall.
• Superfamily Cynipoidea, order Hymenoptera: several genera.

Galois /ˈgalwʌ, French galwa/, Évariste (1811–32), French mathematician. His memoir on the conditions for solubility of polynomial equations was highly innovative but was not published until 1846, after his death.

Galois theory Mathematics a method of applying group theory to the solution of algebraic equations.

galoot /gəˈluːt/ ▶ **noun** N. Amer. & Scottish informal a clumsy or stupid person (often as a term of abuse).
– ORIGIN early 19th cent. (originally in nautical use meaning 'an experienced marine'): of unknown origin.

galop /ˈgaləp, gəˈlɒp/ ▶ **noun** a lively ballroom dance in duple time, popular in the late 18th century.
– ORIGIN mid 19th cent.: French, literally 'gallop'.

galore ▶ **adjective** [postpositive] in abundance: *there were prizes galore for everything*.
– ORIGIN early 17th cent.: from Irish *go leor*, literally 'to sufficiency'.

galosh /gəˈlɒʃ/ ▶ **noun** (usu. **galoshes**) a waterproof overshoe, typically made of rubber.
– ORIGIN Middle English (denoting a type of clog): via Old French from late Latin *gallicula*, diminutive of Latin *gallica* (*solea*) 'Gallic (shoe)'. The current sense dates from the mid 19th cent.

Galsworthy /ˈgɔːlzwəːði/, John (1867–1933), English novelist and dramatist. He is remembered chiefly for *The Forsyte Saga* (1906–28), a series of novels which was adapted for television in 1967. Nobel Prize for Literature (1932).

Galtieri /ˌgaltɪˈɛːri/, Leopoldo Fortunato (b.1926), Argentinian general and statesman, President 1981–2. Galtieri's military junta ordered the invasion of the Falkland Islands in 1982, precipitating the Falklands War.

Galton /ˈgɔːlt(ə)n/, Sir Francis (1822–1911), English scientist. He founded eugenics and introduced methods of measuring human mental and physical abilities. He also pioneered the use of fingerprints as a means of identification.

galumph /gəˈlʌmf/ ▶ **verb** [no obj., with adverbial of direction] informal move in a clumsy, ponderous, or noisy manner: *she galumphed along beside him* | [as adj. **galumphing**] *a galumphing giant*.
– ORIGIN 1871 (in the sense 'prance in triumph'): coined by Lewis Carroll in *Through the Looking Glass*; perhaps a blend of **GALLOP** and **TRIUMPH**.

Galvani /galˈvɑːni/, Luigi (1737–98), Italian anatomist. He studied the structure of organs and the physiology of tissues, but he is best known for his discovery of the twitching of frogs' legs in an electric field.

galvanic /galˈvanɪk/ ▶ **adjective 1** relating to or involving electric currents produced by chemical action.
2 sudden and dramatic: *the effect on Deitz was galvanic*.
– DERIVATIVES **galvanically** adverb.
– ORIGIN late 18th cent.: from French *galvanique*, from **GALVANI**.

galvanic skin response (also **galvanic skin reflex**) (abbrev.: **GSR**) ▶ **noun** a change in the electrical resistance of the skin caused by emotional stress, measurable with a sensitive galvanometer, e.g. in lie-detector tests.

galvanism ▶ **noun** [mass noun] historical **1** electricity produced by chemical action.
2 the therapeutic use of electric currents.
– ORIGIN late 18th cent.: from French *galvanisme*, from **GALVANI**.

galvanize /ˈgalvənʌɪz/ (also **-ise**) ▶ **verb** [with obj.] **1** shock or excite (someone), typically into taking action: *the urgency of his voice galvanized them into action*.
2 [often as adj. **galvanized**] coat (iron or steel or an object made of iron or steel) with a protective layer of zinc: *an old galvanized bucket*.
▶ **noun** [mass noun] W. Indian galvanized tin sheeting, typically as used for roofing or fencing: *the rain was beating hard against Miss Orilie's galvanize*.
– DERIVATIVES **galvanization** noun, **galvanizer** noun.
– ORIGIN early 19th cent. (in the sense 'stimulate by electricity'): from French *galvaniser* (see **GALVANI**).

galvanometer /ˌgalvəˈnɒmɪtə/ ▶ **noun** an instrument for detecting and measuring small electric currents.
– DERIVATIVES **galvanometric** adjective.

galvanoscope /ˈgalv(ə)nəˌskəʊp/ ▶ **noun** a galvanometer that works by measuring the deflection of a needle in the magnetic field induced by the electric current.
– DERIVATIVES **galvanoscopic** adjective.

Galveston /ˈgalvɪst(ə)n/ a port in Texas, south-east of Houston; pop. 59,100 (1990). It is situated on Galveston Bay, an inlet of the Gulf of Mexico.

galvo /ˈgalvəʊ/ ▶ **noun** [mass noun] Austral. informal galvanized iron.

g

Galway /ˈgɔːlweɪ/ a county of the Republic of Ireland, on the west coast in the province of Connacht.
■ its county town, a seaport at the head of Galway Bay; pop. 50,800 (1991).

Galway Bay an inlet of the Atlantic Ocean on the west coast of Ireland.

gam ▶ **noun** informal a leg, especially a woman's.
– ORIGIN late 18th cent.: probably a variant of the heraldic term *gamb*, which denotes a charge representing an animal's leg, from Old Northern French *gambe* 'leg'.

gamadoelas ▶ **plural noun** variant of **GRAMADOELAS**.

Gama, Vasco da see **DA GAMA**.

Gamay /ˈgameɪ/ ▶ **noun** [mass noun] a variety of black wine grape native to the Beaujolais district of France.
■ a fruity red wine made from this grape. ■ (also **Gamay-Beaujolais**) US a red wine with a similar flavour.
– ORIGIN from the name of a hamlet in Burgundy, eastern France.

gamba /ˈgambə/ ▶ **noun** short for **VIOLA DA GAMBA**.

gambado[1] /gamˈbeɪdəʊ, -ˈbɑːdəʊ/ (also **gambade** /-ˈbeɪd, -ˈbɑːd/) ▶ **noun** (pl. **-os** or **-oes**) a leap or bound, especially an exaggerated one.
– ORIGIN early 19th cent.: from Spanish *gambada*, from *gamba* 'leg'.

gambado[2] /gamˈbeɪdəʊ/ ▶ **noun** (pl. **-os** or **-oes**) a gaiter, typically one attached to a saddle to protect a rider's leg from the weather.
– ORIGIN mid 17th cent.: from Italian *gamba* 'leg' + **-ADO**.

Gambia /ˈgambɪə/ **1** (also **the Gambia**) a country on the coast of West Africa; pop. 900,000 (est. 1991); languages, English (official), Malinke and other indigenous languages, Creole; capital, Banjul.

Gambia consists of a narrow strip of territory on either side of the Gambia River that forms an enclave in Senegal. It was created a British colony in 1843, becoming an independent member of the Commonwealth in 1965 and a republic in 1970.

2 a river of West Africa, which rises near Labé in Guinea and flows 800 km (500 miles) through Senegal and Gambia to meet the Atlantic at Banjul.
– DERIVATIVES **Gambian** adjective & noun.

gambier /ˈgambɪə/ ▶ **noun** [mass noun] an astringent extract of a tropical Asiatic plant, used in tanning. Also called **CATECHU**.
• The chief source of gambier is the climber *Uncaria gambier*, family Rubiaceae.
– ORIGIN early 19th cent.: from Malay *gambir*, the name of the plant.

Gambier Islands /ˈgambɪə/ a group of coral islands in the South Pacific, forming part of French Polynesia; pop. 582 (1986).

gambit ▶ **noun** (in chess) an opening in which a player makes a sacrifice, typically of a pawn, for the sake of some compensating advantage.
■ a device, action, or opening remark, typically one entailing a degree of risk, that is calculated to gain an advantage: *his resignation was a tactical gambit*.
– ORIGIN mid 17th cent.: originally *gambett*, from Italian *gambetto*, literally 'tripping up', from *gamba* 'leg'.

gamble ▶ verb [no obj.] play games of chance for money; bet: *she was fond of* **gambling on** *cards and horses.*
■ [with obj.] bet (a sum of money) in such a way: *he was gambling every penny he had on the spin of a wheel.* ■ figurative take risky action in the hope of a desired result: [with clause] *the British could only gamble that something would turn up.*
▶ noun [usu. in sing.] an act of gambling; an enterprise undertaken or attempted with a risk of loss and a chance of profit or success.
– DERIVATIVES **gambler** noun.
– ORIGIN early 18th cent.: from obsolete *gamel* 'play games', or from the verb **GAME**[1].

gamboge /gam'bəʊʒ, -'buːʒ/ ▶ noun [mass noun] a gum resin produced by various East Asian trees, used as a yellow pigment and in medicine as a purgative.
– ORIGIN early 18th cent. (earlier in the Latin form): from modern Latin *gambaugium*, from **CAMBODIA**.

gambol ▶ verb (**gambolled**, **gambolling**; US **gamboled**, **gamboling**) [no obj., usu. with adverbial] run or jump about playfully: *the mare gambolled towards Constance.*
▶ noun [usu. in sing.] an act of running or jumping about playfully.
– ORIGIN early 16th cent.: alteration of obsolete *gambade*, via French from Italian *gambata* 'trip up', from *gamba* 'leg'.

gambrel /'gambr(ə)l/ (also **gambrel roof**) ▶ noun a roof with two sides, each of which has a shallower slope above a steeper one.
■ Brit. a hip roof with a small gable forming the upper part of each end.
– ORIGIN mid 16th cent. (in the sense 'bent piece of wood or iron used by butchers to hang carcasses on'): from Old Northern French *gamberel*, from *gambier* 'forked stick', from *gambe* 'leg'. The sense 'hip roof' (mid 19th cent.) is based on an earlier meaning 'joint in the upper part of a horse's hind leg', the shape of which the roof resembles.

gambusia /gam'b(j)uːsɪə/ ▶ noun a small live-bearing fish found in mangrove creeks and brackish waters of the southern US and northern Mexico.
• Genus *Gambusia*, family Poeciliidae: several species, in particular *G. affinis*, widely introduced for mosquito control (also called **MOSQUITO FISH**).
– ORIGIN modern Latin, alteration of American Spanish *gambusino*.

game[1] ▶ noun **1** a form of play or sport, especially a competitive one played according to rules and decided by skill, strength, or luck.
■ a complete episode or period of play, typically ending in a definite result: *a baseball game.* ■ a single portion of play forming a scoring unit in a match, especially in tennis. ■ Bridge a score of 100 points for tricks bid and made (the best of three games constituting a rubber). ■ a person's performance in a game; a person's standard or method of play: *Rooks will attempt to raise his game to another level.* ■ (**games**) a meeting for sporting contests, especially athletics: *the Olympic Games.* ■ (**games**) Brit. athletics or sports as organized in a school. ■ the equipment for a game, especially a board game or a computer game.
2 a type of activity or business, especially when regarded as a game: *this was a game of shuttle diplomacy at which I had become adept.*
■ a secret and clever plan or trick: *I was on to his little game, but I didn't want him to know.* ■ [often with negative] a thing that is frivolous or amusing: *a Tarot reading is not a game or a stunt.*
3 [mass noun] wild mammals or birds hunted for sport or food.
■ the flesh of these mammals or birds, used as food: [as modifier] *a game pie.*
▶ adjective eager and willing to do something new or challenging: *they were* **game for** *anything after the traumas of Monday.*
▶ verb [no obj.] [often as noun modifier] (**gaming**) play at games of chance for money: *a gaming machine.*
■ play video or computer games.
– PHRASES **ahead of the game** ahead of one's competitors or peers in the same sphere of activity. **beat someone at their own game** use someone's own methods to outdo them in their chosen activity. **the game is up** the deception or crime is revealed or foiled. **game over** informal, chiefly N. Amer. said when a situation is regarded as hopeless or irreversible. **make (a) game of** archaic mock; taunt. **off** (or **on**) **one's game** playing badly (or well). **on the game** Brit. informal working as a prostitute. **the only game in town** informal the best or most important of its kind; the only thing worth concerning oneself with. **play someone's game** advance another's plans, whether intentionally or not: *to what extent are they playing the government's game?* **play the game** behave in a fair or honourable way; abide by the rules or conventions. **play games** deal with someone or something in a way that lacks due seriousness or respect: *Don't* **play games with** *me!* **what's your** (or **the**) **game?** informal what's going on?; what are you up to?
– DERIVATIVES **gamely** adverb, **gameness** noun, **gamester** noun.
– ORIGIN Old English *gamen* 'amusement, fun', *gamenian* 'play, amuse oneself', of Germanic origin.

game[2] ▶ adjective dated (of a person's leg) permanently injured; lame.
– ORIGIN late 18th cent.: originally dialect, of unknown origin.

game bird ▶ noun **1** a bird shot for sport or food. **2** a bird of a large group that includes pheasants, grouse, quails, guineafowl, guans, etc.
• Order Galliformes: several families.

gamecock (also **gamefowl**) ▶ noun a cock bred and trained for cockfighting.

game fish ▶ noun (pl. same) a fish caught by anglers for sport, especially (in fresh water) salmon and trout and (in the sea) billfishes, sharks, bass, and many members of the mackerel family. Compare with **COARSE FISH**.

gamekeeper ▶ noun a person employed to breed and protect game, typically for a large estate.
– DERIVATIVES **gamekeeping** noun.

gamelan /'gaməlan/ ▶ noun a traditional instrumental ensemble in Java and Bali, including many bronze percussion instruments.
– ORIGIN early 19th cent.: from Javanese.

game misconduct ▶ noun Ice Hockey a punitive suspension of a player for the remainder of a game, with a substitution permitted.

game plan ▶ noun a strategy worked out in advance, especially in sport, politics, or business.

gameplay ▶ noun [mass noun] the features of a computer game, such as its plot and the way it is played, as distinct from the graphics and sound effects.

game point ▶ noun (in tennis and other sports) a point which if won by one of the players or sides will also win them a game.

gamer ▶ noun a person who plays a game or games, typically a participant in a computer or role-playing game.
■ N. Amer. (especially in sporting contexts) a person known for consistently making a strong effort.

game show ▶ noun a light entertainment programme on television, in which people compete to win prizes.

gamesmanship ▶ noun [mass noun] the art of winning games by using various ploys and tactics to gain a psychological advantage.
– DERIVATIVES **gamesman** noun (pl. **-men**).

gamesome ▶ adjective playful and merry.
– DERIVATIVES **gamesomely** adverb, **gamesomeness** noun.

gametangium /ˌgamɪ'tan(d)ʒɪəm/ ▶ noun (pl. **gametangia**) Botany a specialized organ or cell in which gametes are formed in algae, ferns, and some other plants.
– ORIGIN late 19th cent.: from modern Latin *gameta* (see **GAMETE**) + Greek *angeion* 'vessel' + **-IUM**.

gamete /'gamiːt/ ▶ noun Biology a mature haploid male or female germ cell which is able to unite with another of the opposite sex in sexual reproduction to form a zygote.
– DERIVATIVES **gametic** /gə'mɛtɪk/ adjective.
– ORIGIN late 19th cent.: from modern Latin *gameta*, from Greek *gametē* 'wife', *gametēs* 'husband', from *gamos* 'marriage'.

game theory (also **games theory**) ▶ noun [mass noun] the branch of mathematics concerned with the analysis of strategies for dealing with competitive situations where the outcome of a participant's choice of action depends critically on the actions of other participants. Game theory has been applied to contexts in war, business, and biology. Compare with **DECISION THEORY**.

gameto- /gə'miːtəʊ/ ▶ combining form Biology representing **GAMETE**.

gametocyte /gə'miːtə(ʊ)sʌɪt/ ▶ noun Biology a cell that divides (by meiosis) to form gametes.

gametogenesis /gəˌmiːtə(ʊ)'dʒɛnɪsɪs/ ▶ noun [mass noun] Biology the process in which cells undergo meiosis to form gametes.
– DERIVATIVES **gametogenic** adjective, **gametogeny** noun.

gametophyte /gə'miːtə(ʊ)fʌɪt/ ▶ noun Botany (in the life cycle of plants with alternating generations) the gamete-producing and usually haploid phase, producing the zygote from which the sporophyte arises. It is the dominant form in bryophytes.
– DERIVATIVES **gametophytic** adjective.

game warden ▶ noun a person who is employed to supervise game and hunting in a particular area.

gamey ▶ adjective variant spelling of **GAMY**.

gamgee /'gamdʒi/ ▶ noun [mass noun] surgical dressing consisting of a thickness of cotton wool between two layers of gauze.
– ORIGIN late 19th cent.: named after Joseph S. *Gamgee* (1828–86), English surgeon.

gamin /'gamɪn, -mã/ ▶ noun dated a street urchin.
– ORIGIN mid 19th cent.: French, originally an eastern dialect word, of unknown origin.

gamine /ga'miːn/ ▶ noun a girl with mischievous or boyish charm.
■ dated a female street urchin.
▶ adjective characteristic of or relating to such a girl.
– ORIGIN late 19th cent.: French, feminine of *gamin* (see **GAMIN**).

gamma /'gamə/ ▶ noun the third letter of the Greek alphabet (**Γ**, **γ**), transliterated as 'g'.
• The combinations γγ, γκ, and γχ are usually transliterated as 'ng', 'nk', and 'nkh' or 'nch'.
■ [as modifier] denoting the third in a series of items, categories, etc. ■ Brit. a third-class mark given for an essay, examination paper, or other piece of work. ■ (**Gamma**) [followed by Latin genitive] Astronomy the third (usually third-brightest) star in a constellation: *Gamma Orionis.* ■ [as modifier] relating to gamma rays: *gamma detector.* ■ Physics (pl. same) a unit of magnetic field strength equal to 10^{-5} oersted.
– ORIGIN via Latin from Greek.

gamma-aminobutyric acid /ˌgaməəˌmiːnəʊbjuː'tɪrɪk, -əˌmʌɪnəʊ-, -'amɪnəʊ-/ ▶ noun [mass noun] Biochemistry an amino acid which acts to inhibit the transmission of nerve impulses in the central nervous system.
• Chem. formula: $H_2NCH_2CH_2CH_2COOH$.
– ORIGIN early 20th cent.: *gamma* indicating the relative position of amino on the third carbon away from the acid group.

gamma globulin ▶ noun [mass noun] Biochemistry a mixture of blood plasma proteins, mainly immunoglobulins, which have relatively low electrophoretic mobility.

gamma-HCH ▶ noun another term for **LINDANE**.
– ORIGIN *HCH* from *hexachlorocyclohexane*.

gamma radiation ▶ noun [mass noun] gamma rays.

gamma rays ▶ plural noun penetrating electromagnetic radiation of shorter wavelength than X-rays.

gammer ▶ noun archaic an old countrywoman.
– ORIGIN late 16th cent.: probably a contraction of **GODMOTHER**; see also **GAFFER**.

gammon[1] ▶ noun [mass noun] ham which has been cured or smoked like bacon.
■ [count noun] the bottom piece of a side of bacon, including a hind leg.
– ORIGIN late 15th cent. (denoting the haunch of a pig): from Old Northern French *gambon*, from *gambe* 'leg'.

gammon[2] ▶ noun a victory in backgammon (carrying a double score) in which the winner removes all his or her pieces before the loser has removed any.
▶ verb [with obj.] defeat (a backgammon opponent) in such a way.
– ORIGIN mid 18th cent.: apparently from Old English *gamen* or *gamenian* (see **GAME**[1]), with survival of the *-n* ending.

gammon[3] informal, dated chiefly Brit. ▶ noun nonsense; rubbish.
▶ verb [with obj.] hoax or deceive (someone).
– ORIGIN early 18th cent.: origin uncertain; the term was first used as criminals' slang in *give gammon to* 'give cover to (a pickpocket)' and *keep in gammon* 'distract (a victim) for a pickpocket'.

gammy ▶ **adjective** Brit. informal (of part of a person's body, especially the leg) unable to function normally because of injury or chronic pain.
– ORIGIN mid 19th cent. (in the sense 'bad, false'): dialect form of **GAME**[2].

Gamow /ˈɡeɪməʊ/, George (1904–68), Russian-born American physicist. He was a proponent of the big bang theory and also suggested the triplet code of bases in DNA, which governs the synthesis of amino acids.

gamp ▶ **noun** Brit. dated an umbrella, especially a large unwieldy one.
– ORIGIN mid 19th cent.: named after Mrs *Gamp* in Charles Dickens's *Martin Chuzzlewit*, who carried such an umbrella.

gamut /ˈɡamət/ ▶ **noun** (**the gamut**) **1** the complete range or scope of something: *the whole gamut of human emotion.*
2 Music a complete scale of musical notes; the compass or range of a voice or instrument.
■historical a scale consisting of seven overlapping hexachords, containing all the recognized notes used in medieval music, covering almost three octaves from bass G to treble E. ■ historical the lowest note in this scale.
– PHRASES **run the gamut** experience, display, or perform the complete range of something: *Rhine Riesling runs the gamut from dry to sweet.*
– ORIGIN late Middle English: from medieval Latin *gamma ut*, originally the name of the lowest note in the medieval scale (bass G an octave and a half below middle C), then applied to the whole range of notes used in medieval music. The Greek letter Γ (gamma) was used for bass G, with *ut* indicating that it was the first note in the lowest of the hexachords or six-note scales (see **SOLMIZATION**).

gamy (also **gamey**) ▶ **adjective** (**gamier**, **gamiest**) (of meat) having the strong flavour or smell of game, especially when it is high.
■chiefly N. Amer. racy; disreputable: *gamy language.*
– DERIVATIVES **gamily** adverb, **gaminess** noun.

Gan /ɡan/ ▶ **noun** [mass noun] a dialect of Chinese spoken by about 20 million people, mainly in Jiangxi province.

ganache /ɡəˈnaʃ/ ▶ **noun** [mass noun] a whipped filling of chocolate and cream, used in confectioneries such as cakes and truffles.
– ORIGIN French.

Ganapati /ˌɡʌnəˈpʌti/ Hinduism another name for **GANESH**.

Gäncä /ˈɡəndʒə/ an industrial city in Azerbaijan; pop. 281,000 (1990). The city was formerly called Elizavetpol (1804–1918) and Kirovabad (1935–89). Russian name **GYANDZHE**.

Gance /ɡɒ̃s/, Abel (1889–1991), French film director. He was an early pioneer of technical experimentation in film. Notable films: *La Roue* (1921) and *Napoléon* (1926).

Gand /ɡɒ̃/ French name for **GHENT**.

Ganda ▶ **noun** & **adjective** see **LUGANDA**.

Gander /ˈɡandə/ a town on the island of Newfoundland, on Lake Gander; pop. 10,100 (1991). Its airport served the first regular transatlantic flights during the Second World War.

gander /ˈɡandə/ ▶ **noun** **1** a male goose.
2 [in sing.] informal a look or glance. [ORIGIN: from criminals' slang.]
– ORIGIN Old English *gandra*, of Germanic origin; related to Dutch *gander*, also to **GANNET**.

Gandhi[1] /ˈɡandi, ˈɡɑːndi/, Mrs Indira (1917–84), Indian stateswoman, Prime Minister 1966–77 and 1980–4. The daughter of Jawaharlal Nehru, she sought to establish a secular state and to lead India out of poverty. She was assassinated by her own Sikh bodyguards following prolonged religious disturbance.

Gandhi[2] /ˈɡandi, ˈɡɑːndi/, Mahatma (1869–1948), Indian nationalist and spiritual leader; full name *Mohandas Karamchand Gandhi*. He became prominent in the opposition to British rule in India, pursuing a policy of non-violent civil disobedience. He never held government office, but was regarded as the country's supreme political and spiritual leader; he was assassinated by a Hindu following his agreement to the creation of the state of Pakistan.

Gandhi[3] /ˈɡandi, ˈɡɑːndi/, Rajiv (1944–91), Indian statesman, Prime Minister 1984–9. The eldest son of Indira Gandhi, he became Prime Minister after his mother's assassination. His premiership was marked by continuing unrest and he was assassinated during an election campaign.

Gandhinagar /ˌɡandɪˈnʌɡə/ a city in western India, capital of the state of Gujarat; pop. 121,750 (1991).

gandy dancer ▶ **noun** N. Amer. informal a track maintenance worker on a railway.
– ORIGIN early 20th cent.: of unknown origin.

Ganesh /ɡəˈneɪʃ/ (also **Ganesha** /ɡəˈneɪʃə/) Hinduism an elephant-headed deity, son of Shiva and Parvati. He is usually depicted coloured red, with a pot belly and one broken tusk, riding a rat. Also called **GANAPATI**.
– ORIGIN from Sanskrit *Gaṇeśa* 'lord of the ganas' (Shiva's attendants).

gang[1] ▶ **noun** **1** an organized group of criminals.
■a group of young people involved in petty crime or violence. ■ informal a group of people, especially young people, who regularly associate together. ■ an organized group of people doing manual work: *a government road gang.*
2 a set of switches, sockets, or other electrical or mechanical devices grouped together.
▶ **verb** **1** [no obj.] (**gang together**) (of a number of people) form a group or gang: *the smaller supermarket chains are ganging together to beat the big boys.*
■(**gang up**) (of a number of people) join together, typically in order to intimidate someone: *they ganged up on me and nicked my pocket money.*
2 [with obj.] (often **be ganged**) arrange (electrical devices or machines) together to work in coordination.
– ORIGIN Old English, from Old Norse *gangr*, *ganga* 'gait, course, going', of Germanic origin; related to **GANG**[2]. The original meaning was 'going, a journey', later in Middle English 'a way, passage', also 'set of things or people which go together'.

gang[2] ▶ **verb** [no obj.] Scottish go; proceed: *gang to your bed, lass.*
▶ **gang agley** (of a plan) go wrong: *even the best laid plans gang aft agley.* [ORIGIN: 1786: from Robert Burns's 'The best laid schemes o' Mice an' Men, Gang aft agley' (*Poems and Songs*).]
– ORIGIN Old English *gangan*, of Germanic origin; related to **GO**[1].

Ganga /ˈɡʌŋɡə/ Hindi name for **GANGES**.

gang bang ▶ **noun** informal **1** the successive rape of one person by a group of other people.
■a sexual orgy involving changes of partner.
2 chiefly N. Amer. an instance of violence involving members of a criminal gang.
– DERIVATIVES **gang-bang** verb, **gang banger** noun.

gangboard ▶ **noun** another term for **GANGPLANK**.

gangbuster ▶ **noun** informal a police officer or other person who takes part in breaking up criminal gangs.
■[as modifier] N. Amer. very successful, especially commercially: *the restaurant did gangbuster business.*
– PHRASES **go** (or **like**) **gangbusters** N. Amer. used to refer to great vigour, speed, or success: *the real estate market was going gangbusters.*

ganger ▶ **noun** Brit. the foreman of a gang of labourers.

Ganges /ˈɡandʒiːz/ a river of northern India and Bangladesh, which rises in the Himalayas and flows some 2,700 km (1,678 miles) south-east to the Bay of Bengal, where it forms the world's largest delta. The river is regarded by Hindus as sacred. Hindi name **GANGA**.
– DERIVATIVES **Gangetic** adjective.

gangland ▶ **noun** the world of criminal gangs: [as modifier] *he was the victim of a gangland killing.*

gangling ▶ **adjective** (of a person) tall, thin, and awkward in movements or bearing.
– ORIGIN early 19th cent.: from the verb **GANG**[2] + **-LE**[4] + **-ING**[2].

ganglion /ˈɡaŋɡlɪən/ ▶ **noun** (pl. **ganglia** or **ganglions**) **1** Anatomy a structure containing a number of nerve cell bodies, typically linked by synapses, and often forming a swelling on a nerve fibre.
■a network of cells forming a nerve centre in the nervous system of an invertebrate. ■ a well-defined mass of grey matter within the central nervous system. See also **BASAL GANGLIA**.
2 Medicine an abnormal benign swelling on a tendon sheath.
– DERIVATIVES **ganglionic** adjective.
– ORIGIN late 17th cent.: from Greek *ganglion* 'tumour on or near sinews or tendons', used by Galen to denote the complex nerve centres.

ganglioside /ˈɡaŋɡlɪə(ʊ)sʌɪd/ ▶ **noun** Biochemistry any of a group of complex lipids which are present in the grey matter of the human brain.
– ORIGIN 1940s: from **GANGLION** + *-oside* (see **-OSE**[2], **-IDE**).

gangly ▶ **adjective** (**ganglier**, **gangliest**) another term for **GANGLING**.

Gang of Four (in China) a group of four associates, including Mao Zedong's wife, involved in implementing the Cultural Revolution. They were among the groups competing for power on Mao's death in 1976, but were arrested and imprisoned.

gangplank ▶ **noun** a movable plank, typically with cleats nailed on it, used by passengers to board or disembark from a ship or boat.

gang rape ▶ **noun** the rape of one person by a group of other people.
– DERIVATIVES **gang-rape** verb.

gangrene /ˈɡaŋɡriːn/ ▶ **noun** [mass noun] Medicine localized death and decomposition of body tissue, resulting from either obstructed circulation or bacterial infection.
▶ **verb** [no obj.] become affected with gangrene.
– DERIVATIVES **gangrenous** /ˈɡaŋɡrɪnəs/ adjective.
– ORIGIN mid 16th cent.: via French from Latin *gangraena*, from Greek *gangraina*.

gangsta ▶ **noun** **1** US black slang a gang member.
2 (also **gangsta rap**) [mass noun] a type of rap music featuring aggressive macho lyrics, often with reference to gang warfare and gun battles.
– ORIGIN 1980s: alteration of **GANGSTER**.

gangster ▶ **noun** a member of a gang of violent criminals.
– DERIVATIVES **gangsterism** noun.

Gangtok /ɡaŋˈtɒk/ a city in northern India, in the foothills of the Kanchenjunga mountain range, capital of the state of Sikkim; pop. 24,970 (1991).

gangue /ɡaŋ/ ▶ **noun** [mass noun] the commercially valueless material in which ore is found.
– ORIGIN early 19th cent.: from French, from German *Gang* 'course, lode'; related to **GANG**[1].

gangway ▶ **noun** a raised platform or walkway providing a passage.
■Brit. a passage between rows of seats, especially in a theatre or aircraft. ■ a movable bridge linking a ship to the shore. ■ an opening in the bulwarks by which a ship is entered or left. ■ a temporary arrangement of planks for crossing muddy or difficult ground on a building site.
▶ **exclamation** make way!

ganister /ˈɡanɪstə/ ▶ **noun** [mass noun] a close-grained, hard siliceous rock found in the coal measures of northern England, and used for furnace-linings.
– ORIGIN early 19th cent.: of unknown origin.

ganja /ˈɡan(d)ʒə, ˈɡɑː-/ ▶ **noun** [mass noun] cannabis.
– ORIGIN early 19th cent.: from Hindi *gā̃jā*.

gannet /ˈɡanɪt/ ▶ **noun** **1** a large seabird with mainly white plumage, catching fish by plunge-diving.
• Genus *Morus* (or *Sula*), family Sulidae: three species, in particular the **northern gannet** (*M. bassanus*) of the North Atlantic (also called ***solan goose***.)
2 Brit. informal a greedy person.
– ORIGIN Old English *ganot*, of Germanic origin; related to Dutch *gent* 'gander', also to **GANDER**.

gannetry ▶ **noun** (pl. **-ies**) a breeding colony of gannets, usually on an isolated rock.

ganoid /ˈɡanɔɪd/ Zoology ▶ **adjective** (of fish scales) hard and bony with a shiny enamelled surface. Compare with **CTENOID** and **PLACOID**.
■(of a fish) having ganoid scales.
▶ **noun** a primitive fish that has ganoid scales, e.g. a bichir, sturgeon, or freshwater garfish.
– ORIGIN mid 19th cent.: from French *ganoïde*, from Greek *ganos* 'brightness'.

Gansu /ɡanˈsuː/ (also **Kansu**) a province of NW central China, between Mongolia and Tibet; capital, Lanzhou. This narrow, mountainous province forms a corridor through which the Silk Road passed.

gantlet /ˈɡantlɪt/ ▶ **noun** US spelling of **GAUNTLET**[2].

gantline /ˈɡantlʌɪn/ ▶ **noun** Sailing a line passed through a block near the masthead and used to hoist sails or rigging.

– ORIGIN mid 18th cent. (originally *girtline*): of unknown origin.

gantry ▶ noun (pl. **-ies**) a bridge-like overhead structure with a platform supporting equipment such as a crane, signals, lights, or cameras.
■ a tall framework supporting a space rocket prior to launching. ■ (in a bar) a collection of inverted bottles with optics for serving measures.
– ORIGIN late Middle English (denoting a wooden stand for barrels): probably from dialect *gawn* (contraction of **GALLON**) + **TREE**.

Gantt chart /gant/ ▶ noun a chart in which a series of horizontal lines shows the amount of work done or production completed in certain periods of time in relation to the amount planned for those periods.
– ORIGIN early 20th cent.: named after Henry L. *Gantt* (1861–1919), American management consultant.

Ganymede /ˈɡanɪmiːd/ **1** Greek Mythology a Trojan youth who was so beautiful that he was carried off to be Zeus' cup-bearer.
2 Astronomy one of the Galilean moons of Jupiter, the seventh closest satellite to the planet and the largest satellite in the solar system (diameter 5,262 km).

ganzfeld /ˈɡanzfɛld/ ▶ noun a technique of controlled sensory input used in parapsychology with the aim of improving results in tests of telepathy and other paranormal phenomena.
– ORIGIN late 20th cent.: from German, literally 'whole field'.

GAO ▶ abbreviation for General Accounting Office, a body that undertakes investigations for the US Congress.

gaol ▶ noun Brit. variant spelling of **JAIL**.

gaoler ▶ noun Brit. variant spelling of **JAILER**.

gap ▶ noun **1** a break or hole in an object or between two objects: *he peeped through the gap in the curtains.*
■ a pass or way through a range of hills.
2 an unfilled space or interval; a break in continuity: *there are many gaps in our understanding of what happened.*
■ a difference, especially an undesirable one, between two views or situations: *the media were **bridging the gap** between government and people.*
– DERIVATIVES **gapped** adjective, **gappy** adjective.
– ORIGIN Middle English: from Old Norse, 'chasm'; related to **GAPE**.

gape ▶ verb [no obj.] stare with one's mouth open wide, typically in amazement or wonder: *they gaped at her as if she was an alien.*
■ be or become wide open: [with complement] *a large carpet bag gaped open by her feet* | [as adj. **gaping**] *there was a gaping hole in the wall.*
▶ noun a wide opening or rent: *a wide gape of the jaws.*
■ an open-mouthed stare: *she climbed into her sports car to the gapes of passers-by.* ■ a widely open mouth or beak: *juvenile birds with yellow gapes.* ■ (**the gapes**) a disease of birds with gaping of the mouth as a symptom, caused by infestation with gapeworm.
– DERIVATIVES **gapingly** adverb.
– ORIGIN Middle English: from Old Norse *gapa*; related to **GAP**.

gaper ▶ noun **1** a burrowing bivalve mollusc, the shell valves of which have an opening at one or both ends.
● Genus *Mya*, family Myidae.
2 another term for **COMBER**[2].
3 a deep-sea anglerfish that is able to inflate itself with water.
● Family Chaunacidae and genus *Chaunax*.
4 a person who stares, typically in amazement or wonder.

gapeworm ▶ noun a parasitic nematode worm that infests the trachea and bronchi of birds, causing the gapes.
● *Syngamus trachea*, class Phasmida.

gapping ▶ noun [mass noun] Grammar the omission of a verb in the second of two coordinated clauses, as in *I went by bus and Mary by car.*

gap-toothed ▶ adjective having or showing gaps between the teeth.

gar ▶ noun the freshwater garfish of North America.
– ORIGIN mid 19th cent.: abbreviation.

garage /ˈɡaraː(d)ʒ, -ɑːʒ, ɡəˈrɑːʒ/ ▶ noun **1** a building or shed for housing a motor vehicle or vehicles.
■ an establishment which sells petrol, oil, and diesel or which repairs and sells motor vehicles.

2 (also **garage rock**) [mass noun] a style of unpolished energetic rock music associated with suburban amateur bands.
■ [mass noun] a variety of house music influenced by soul music. [ORIGIN: from *Paradise Garage*, the name of a Manhattan dance club.]
▶ verb [with obj.] put or keep (a motor vehicle) in a garage.
– ORIGIN early 20th cent.: from French, from *garer* 'to shelter'.

garage sale ▶ noun chiefly N. Amer. a sale of unwanted household goods held in the garage or front garden of someone's house.

garam masala /ˌɡʌrəm məˈsɑːlə/ ▶ noun [mass noun] a spice mixture used in Indian cookery.
– ORIGIN from Urdu *garam maṣālaḥ*, from *garam* 'hot, pungent' + *maṣālaḥ* 'spice'.

Garamond /ˈɡarəmɒnd/ ▶ noun [mass noun] a typeface much used in books.
– ORIGIN mid 19th cent.: named after Claude *Garamond* (1499–1561), French type founder.

garb[1] ▶ noun [mass noun] clothing or dress, especially of a distinctive or special kind: *the black and brown garb of a Franciscan friar.*
▶ verb [with obj.] (usu. **be garbed**) be dressed in distinctive clothes: *she was **garbed in** Indian shawls.*
– ORIGIN late 16th cent.: via French from Italian *garbo* 'elegance', of Germanic origin; related to **GEAR**.

garb[2] ▶ noun Heraldry a sheaf of wheat.
– ORIGIN early 16th cent.: from Old Northern French *garbe*; compare with French *gerbe*.

garbage ▶ noun [mass noun] rubbish or waste, especially domestic refuse.
■ a thing that is considered worthless or meaningless: *a store full of overpriced garbage.*
– PHRASES **garbage in, garbage out** (abbrev.: **GIGO**) used to express the idea that in computing and other spheres, incorrect or poor quality input will always produce faulty output.
– ORIGIN late Middle English (in the sense 'offal'): from Anglo-Norman French, of unknown ultimate origin.

garbage collector ▶ noun **1** a dustman.
2 Computing a program that automatically removes unwanted data held temporarily in memory during processing.

garbanzo /ɡɑːˈbanzəʊ/ (also **garbanzo bean**) ▶ noun (pl. **-os**) N. Amer. a chickpea.
– ORIGIN mid 18th cent.: from Spanish.

garble ▶ verb [with obj.] reproduce (a message, sound, or transmission) in a confused and distorted way: *the connection was awful and kept garbling his voice* | [as adj. **garbled**] *I got a garbled set of directions.*
▶ noun a garbled account or transmission.
– DERIVATIVES **garbler** noun.
– ORIGIN late Middle English (in the sense 'sift out, cleanse'): from Anglo-Latin and Italian *garbellare*, from Arabic *ḡarbala* 'sift', perhaps from late Latin *cribellare* 'to sieve', from Latin *cribrum* 'sieve'.

Garbo, Greta (1905–90), Swedish-born American actress; born *Greta Gustafsson*. Notable films: *Anna Christie* (1930), *Mata Hari* (1931) and *Anna Karenina* (1935). After her retirement in 1941 she lived as a recluse.

garbo ▶ noun (pl. **-os**) Austral. informal a garbage collector.
– ORIGIN 1950s: abbreviation.

garboard /ˈɡɑːbɔːd/ (also **garboard strake**) ▶ noun the first range of planks or plates laid on a ship's bottom next to the keel.
– ORIGIN early 17th cent.: from Dutch *gaarboord*, perhaps from *garen* 'gather' + *boord* 'board'.

garbology /ɡɑːˈbɒlədʒi/ ▶ noun [mass noun] the study of a community or culture by analysing its waste.
– DERIVATIVES **garbologist** noun.
– ORIGIN 1960s: from **GARBAGE** + **-LOGY**.

García Lorca see **LORCA**.

García Márquez /ɡɑːˌsiːə ˈmɑːkɛz, mɑːˈkɛz, Spanish ɡarˌθia marˈkeθ, -ˈsia, -ˈkes/, Gabriel (b.1928), Colombian novelist. His works include *One Hundred Years of Solitude* (1967), a classic example of magic realism, and *Chronicle of a Death Foretold* (1981). Nobel Prize for Literature (1982).

garçon /ˈɡɑːsɒn, ˈɡɑːsɔ̃, French ɡaʁsɔ̃/ ▶ noun a waiter in a French restaurant or hotel.
– ORIGIN French, literally 'boy'.

garçonnière /ˌɡɑːsɒnˈjɛː/ ▶ noun a bachelor's flat or set of rooms.
– ORIGIN French, from *garçon* 'boy'.

Garda /ˈɡɑːdə, Irish ˈɡaːrdə/ ▶ noun [treated as sing. or pl.] the state police force of the Irish Republic.
■ (pl. **Gardai** /-diː, Irish ɡaːrˈdiː/) a member of the Irish police force.
– ORIGIN from Irish *Garda Síochána* 'Civic Guard'.

Garda, Lake /ˈɡɑːdə, Italian ˈɡarda/ a lake in NE Italy, lying between Lombardy and Venetia.

garden ▶ noun **1** a piece of ground adjoining a house, used for growing flowers, fruit, or vegetables.
■ (**gardens**) ornamental grounds laid out for public enjoyment and recreation: *botanical gardens.* ■ Brit. used as part of the name of a street or square: *Burlington Gardens.*
2 [in names] N. Amer. a large public hall: *Madison Square Garden.*
▶ verb [no obj.] cultivate or work in a garden.
– PHRASES **the garden of England** a very fertile region of England, in particular Kent or the Vale of Evesham.
– DERIVATIVES **gardener** noun.
– ORIGIN Middle English: from Old Northern French *gardin*, variant of Old French *jardin*, of Germanic origin; related to **YARD**[2].

garden centre ▶ noun an establishment where plants and gardening equipment are sold.

garden chafer ▶ noun a small brown and metallic-green chafer which sometimes swarms in sunshine and may damage pasture and fruit crops. Also called **JUNE BUG**.
● *Phyllopertha horticola*, family Scarabaeidae.

garden city ▶ noun a new town designed as a whole with much open space and greenery.

garden cress ▶ noun [mass noun] a type of cress that is usually grown as a sprouting vegetable, often mixed with sprouting mustard, and used in salads.
● *Lepidium sativum*, family Cruciferae.

garden eel ▶ noun an eel of warm seas which lives in a community or 'garden'. Each individual occupies a burrow from which its head and foreparts protrude, enabling it to catch passing food.
● Several genera and species, family Congridae.

gardener bowerbird ▶ noun a drab New Guinea bowerbird that builds its bower over a mat of moss decorated with colourful flowers and fruits.
● Genus *Amblyornis*, family Ptilonorhynchidae: four species.

garden gnome ▶ noun a figure of a gnome used as a garden ornament.

gardenia /ɡɑːˈdiːnɪə/ ▶ noun a tree or shrub of warm climates, with large fragrant white or yellow flowers.
● Genus *Gardenia*, family Rubiaceae: several species, in particular the Cape jasmine.
– ORIGIN modern Latin, named in honour of Dr Alexander *Garden* (1730–91), Scottish naturalist.

gardening ▶ noun [mass noun] the activity of tending and cultivating a garden, especially as a pastime.

gardening leave ▶ noun [mass noun] Brit. used euphemistically to refer to an employee's suspension from work on full pay, typically to prevent them from seeking work with a competitor before the end of their contractual notice period.

Garden of Eden see **EDEN**[2].

Garden of Gethsemane see **GETHSEMANE, GARDEN OF**.

garden party ▶ noun a social event held on a lawn in a garden.

garden pea ▶ noun a variety of pea grown for food.
■ a pea canned or frozen when freshly picked.

garden snail ▶ noun a large European snail with a brownish shell, often abundant in gardens.
● *Helix aspersa*, family Helicidae.
■ (also **English garden snail**) North American term for **BANDED SNAIL**.

garden spider ▶ noun a common European orb-web spider with pale markings on the large rounded abdomen.
● *Araneus diadematus*, family Araneidae.

Garden State informal name for **NEW JERSEY**.

garden suburb ▶ noun Brit. a suburb set in rural surroundings or incorporating much landscaping.

garden tiger ▶ noun a large European tiger moth

with boldly marked chiefly brown and white forewings and orange and black hindwings.
● *Arctia caja*, family Arctiidae.

garden-variety ▶ adjective [attrib.] N. Amer. of the usual or ordinary type; commonplace.

garden warbler ▶ noun a migratory Eurasian songbird with drab plumage, frequenting woodland.
● *Sylvia borin*, family Sylviidae.

garderobe /ˈgɑːdrəʊb/ ▶ noun a toilet in a medieval building.
■ a wardrobe or small storeroom in a medieval building.
– ORIGIN late Middle English: French, from *garder* 'to keep' + *robe* 'robe, dress'; compare with **WARDROBE**.

Gardner[1], Ava (Lavinia) (1922–90), American actress. Notable films: *The Killers* (1946), *Bhowani Junction* (1956), and *The Night of the Iguana* (1964).

Gardner[2], Erle Stanley (1899–1970), American novelist and short-story writer. He practised as a defence lawyer before writing his novels featuring the lawyer-detective Perry Mason.

Garfield, James Abram (1831–81), American Republican statesman, 20th President of the US March–September 1881. He was assassinated within months of becoming President.

garfish ▶ noun (pl. same or **-fishes**) any of a number of long, slender fish with elongated beak-like jaws containing sharply pointed teeth:
● a marine fish (family Belonidae, in particular the common European *Belone belone*). Also called **GARPIKE** or (in North America) **NEEDLEFISH**. ● N. Amer. a freshwater fish (family Lepisosteidae and genus *Lepisosteus*). Also called **GAR** or **GARPIKE**. ● Australian and New Zealand term for **HALFBEAK**.
– ORIGIN Middle English: apparently from Old English *gār* 'spear' + **FISH**[1].

garganey /ˈgɑːɡ(ə)ni/ ▶ noun (pl. same or **-eys**) a small Eurasian duck, the male of which has a dark brown head with a white stripe from the eye to the neck.
● *Anas querquedula*, family Anatidae.
– ORIGIN mid 17th cent.: from Italian dialect *garganei*, of imitative origin.

gargantuan /gɑːˈgantjʊən/ ▶ adjective enormous: *a gargantuan appetite*.
– ORIGIN late 16th cent.: from *Gargantua*, the name of a voracious giant in Rabelais' book of the same name (1534), + **-AN**.

garget /ˈgɑːgɪt/ ▶ noun [mass noun] inflammation of a cow's or ewe's udder.
– ORIGIN early 18th cent.: perhaps a special use of Old French *gargate* 'throat'; related to **GARGOYLE**. The term was used earlier to denote inflammation of the throat in cattle.

gargle ▶ verb [no obj.] wash one's mouth and throat with a liquid kept in motion by breathing through it: *he had gargled with alcohol for toothache*.
▶ noun an act or instance or the sound of gargling: *a swig and gargle of mouthwash*.
■ [usu. in sing.] a liquid used for gargling. ■ Brit. informal an alcoholic drink.
– ORIGIN early 16th cent.: from French *gargouiller* 'gurgle, bubble', from *gargouille* 'throat' (see **GARGOYLE**).

gargoyle /ˈgɑːɡɔɪl/ ▶ noun a grotesque carved human or animal face or figure projecting from the gutter of a building, typically acting as a spout to carry water clear of a wall.
– ORIGIN Middle English: from Old French *gargouille* 'throat', also 'gargoyle' (because of the water passing through the throat and mouth of the figure); related to Greek *gargarizein* 'to gargle' (imitating the sounds made in the throat).

gargoylism ▶ noun another term for **HURLER'S SYNDROME**.
– ORIGIN early 20th cent.: from **GARGOYLE** (because the deformities which characterize the syndrome were thought to resemble Gothic gargoyles) + **-ISM**.

Garibaldi /ˌɡarɪˈbɔːldi, Italian garɪˈbaldi/, Giuseppe (1807–82), Italian patriot and military leader of the Risorgimento. With his volunteer force of 'Red Shirts' he captured Sicily and southern Italy from the Austrians in 1860–1, thereby playing a key role in the establishment of a united kingdom of Italy.

garibaldi /ˌɡarɪˈbɔːldi, -ˈbaldi/ ▶ noun (pl. **garibaldis**)
1 Brit. a biscuit containing a layer of currants.
2 a small bright orange marine fish found off California.
● *Hypsypops rubicundus*, family Pomacentridae.

3 historical a woman's or children's loose blouse, originally bright red in imitation of the shirts worn by Garibaldi and his followers.
– ORIGIN mid 19th cent.: named after G. **GARIBALDI**.

garish /ˈɡɛːrɪʃ/ ▶ adjective derogatory obtrusively bright and showy; lurid: *garish shirts in all sorts of colours*.
– DERIVATIVES **garishly** adverb, **garishness** noun.
– ORIGIN mid 16th cent.: of unknown origin.

Garland, Judy (1922–69), American singer and actress; born *Frances Gumm*. Her most famous early film role was in *The Wizard of Oz* (1939), in which she played Dorothy and sang 'Over the Rainbow'. Other notable films: *Meet Me in St Louis* (1944) and *A Star is Born* (1954).

garland ▶ noun a wreath of flowers and leaves, worn on the head or hung as a decoration.
■ dated a prize or distinction. ■ archaic a literary anthology or miscellany.
▶ verb [with obj.] adorn or crown with a garland: *they were garlanded with flowers*.
– ORIGIN Middle English: from Old French *garlande*, of unknown origin.

garlic ▶ noun [mass noun] **1** a strong-smelling pungent-tasting bulb, used as a flavouring in cookery and in herbal medicine.
2 the central Asian plant, closely related to the onion, which produces this bulb.
● *Allium sativum*, family Liliaceae (or Alliaceae).
■ used in names of plants with a similar smell or flavour, e.g. **hedge garlic**, **wild garlic**.
– DERIVATIVES **garlicky** adjective.
– ORIGIN Old English *gārlēac*, from *gār* 'spear' (because the shape of a clove resembles the head of a spear) + *lēac* 'leek'.

garment ▶ noun an item of clothing.
– ORIGIN Middle English: from Old French *garnement* 'equipment', from *garnir* 'equip' (see **GARNISH**).

Garmo, Mount /ˈɡɑːməʊ/ former name (until 1933) for **COMMUNISM PEAK**.

garner ▶ verb [with obj.] gather or collect (something, especially information or approval): *the police struggled to garner sufficient evidence*.
■ archaic store; deposit: *the crop was ready to be reaped and garnered*.
▶ noun archaic a storehouse; a granary.
– ORIGIN Middle English (originally as a noun meaning 'granary'): from Old French *gernier*, from Latin *granarium* 'granary', from *granum* 'grain'.

garnet /ˈɡɑːnɪt/ ▶ noun a precious stone consisting of a deep red vitreous silicate mineral.
■ Mineralogy any of a class of silicate minerals including this, which belong to the cubic system and have the general chemical formula $A_3B_2(SiO_4)_3$ (A and B being respectively divalent and trivalent metals).
– ORIGIN Middle English: probably via Middle Dutch from Old French *grenat*, from medieval Latin *granatus*, perhaps from *granatum* (see **POMEGRANATE**), because the garnet is similar in colour to the pulp of the fruit.

garnierite /ˈɡɑːnɪərʌɪt, ˌɡɑːˈnɪərʌɪt/ ▶ noun [mass noun] a bright green amorphous mineral consisting of a hydrated silicate of nickel and magnesium.
– ORIGIN 1875: named after Jules *Garnier* (1839–1904), French geologist.

garnish ▶ verb [with obj.] **1** decorate or embellish (something, especially food): *capers are often used to garnish cocktail savouries*.
2 Law serve notice on (a third party) for the purpose of legally seizing money belonging to a debtor or defendant.
■ seize (money, especially part of a person's salary) to settle a debt or claim: *the IRS garnished his earnings*.
▶ noun a decoration or embellishment for something, especially food.
– DERIVATIVES **garnishment** noun.
– ORIGIN Middle English (in the sense 'equip, arm'): from Old French *garnir*, probably of Germanic origin and related to **WARN**. Sense 1 dates from the late 17th cent.

garnishee /ˌɡɑːnɪˈʃiː/ Law ▶ noun a third party who is served notice by a court to surrender money in settlement of a debt or claim: [as modifier] *a garnishee order*.
▶ verb (**garnishees**, **garnisheed**) another term for **GARNISH** (in sense 2).

garniture /ˈɡɑːnɪtʃə/ ▶ noun a set of decorative vases.
– ORIGIN late 15th cent.: from French, from *garnir* 'to garnish'.

Garonne /ɡaˈrɒn, French garɔn/ a river of SW France, which rises in the Pyrenees and flows 645 km (400 miles) north-west through Toulouse and Bordeaux to join the Dordogne at the Gironde estuary.

garotte ▶ verb & noun variant spelling of **GARROTTE**.

Garoua /ɡaˈruːə/ a river port in northern Cameroon, on the River Bénoué; pop. 77,850 (1981).

garpike ▶ noun another term for **GARFISH**.
– ORIGIN late 18th cent.: from **GAR** + **PIKE**[1].

garret ▶ noun a top-floor or attic room, especially a small dismal one (traditionally inhabited by an artist).
– ORIGIN Middle English (in the sense 'watchtower'): from Old French *garite*, from *garir* (see **GARRISON**).

Garrick, David (1717–79), English actor and dramatist. He was a notably versatile actor and the manager of the Drury Lane Theatre.

garrick ▶ noun South African term for **LEERVIS**.
– ORIGIN of unknown origin.

garrison ▶ noun the troops stationed in a fortress or town to defend it.
■ the building occupied by such troops.
▶ verb [with obj.] provide (a place) with a body of troops: *a king needed to garrison a number of castles and towns to control his subjects*.
■ [with obj. and adverbial of place] station (troops) in a particular place: *Soviet forces were garrisoned in Lithuania*.
– ORIGIN Middle English (in the sense 'safety, means of protection'): from Old French *garison*, from *garir* 'defend, provide', of Germanic origin.

garrison cap ▶ noun US a peakless cap, especially one worn as part of a military uniform.

garrison town ▶ noun a town that has troops permanently stationed in it.

garron /ˈɡarən/ ▶ noun a small, sturdy workhorse of a breed originating in Ireland and Scotland.
– ORIGIN mid 16th cent.: from Scottish Gaelic *gearran*, Irish *gearrán*.

garrotte /ɡəˈrɒt/ (also **garotte**; US **garrote**) ▶ verb [with obj.] kill (someone) by strangulation, typically with an iron collar or a length of wire or cord: *he had been garrotted with piano wire*.
▶ noun a wire, cord, or apparatus used for such a killing.
– ORIGIN early 17th cent.: via French from Spanish *garrote* 'a cudgel, a garrotte', perhaps of Celtic origin.

garrulous /ˈɡar(j)ʊləs/ ▶ adjective excessively talkative, especially on trivial matters: *Polonius is portrayed as a foolish, garrulous old man*.
– DERIVATIVES **garrulity** /ɡaˈruːlɪti/ noun, **garrulously** adverb, **garrulousness** noun.
– ORIGIN early 17th cent.: from Latin *garrulus* (from *garrire* 'to chatter, prattle') + **-OUS**.

garryowen /ˌɡarɪˈəʊɪn/ ▶ noun Rugby an up-and-under.
– ORIGIN 1960s: named after a rugby club in Limerick, Republic of Ireland.

garter ▶ noun **1** a band worn around the leg to keep up a stocking or sock.
■ a band worn on the arm to keep a shirtsleeve up. ■ N. Amer. a suspender for a sock or stocking.
2 (**the Garter**) short for **ORDER OF THE GARTER**.
■ the badge or membership of this order.
– PHRASES **have someone's guts for garters** humorous punish someone severely (used in a threat or warning of potential future punishment).
– DERIVATIVES **gartered** adjective.
– ORIGIN Middle English: from Old French *gartier*, from *garet* 'bend of the knee, calf of the leg', probably of Celtic origin.

garter belt ▶ noun N. Amer. a suspender belt.

Garter King of Arms ▶ noun Heraldry (in the UK) the principal King of Arms of the English College of Arms.

garter snake ▶ noun **1** a common, harmless North American snake that typically has well-defined longitudinal stripes and favours damp habitats. It is occasionally kept as a pet.
● Genus *Thamnophis*, family Colubridae: several species, in particular *T. sirtalis*.
2 a venomous burrowing African snake that is typically dark with lighter bands.
● Genus *Elapsoidea*, family Elapidae: several species.

garter stitch ▶ noun [mass noun] knitting in which

all of the rows are knitted in plain stitch, rather than alternating with purl rows.

garth ▶ noun Brit. an open space surrounded by cloisters.
■ archaic a yard or garden.
– ORIGIN Middle English (also, in early use, denoting a hollow): from Old Norse *garthr*; related to **YARD**².

Garuda /ˈɡarʊdə/ Hinduism an eagle-like being that serves as the mount of Vishnu.
– ORIGIN from Sanskrit *garuḍa*.

Garvey /ˈɡɑːvi/, Marcus (Mosiah) (1887–1940), Jamaican political activist and black nationalist leader. He advocated the establishment of an African homeland for black Americans and his thinking was later an important influence on Rastafarianism.

Gary /ˈɡari/ an industrial city in NW Indiana, on Lake Michigan south-east of Chicago; pop. 116,600 (1991).

gas ▶ noun (pl. **gases** or chiefly US **gasses**) [mass noun] **1** an air-like fluid substance which expands freely to fill any space available, irrespective of its quantity: *hot balls of gas that become stars* | [count noun] *poisonous gases*.
■ Physics a substance of this type that cannot be liquefied by the application of pressure alone. Compare with **VAPOUR**. ■ a flammable substance of this type used as a fuel. ■ a gaseous anaesthetic such as nitrous oxide, used in dentistry. ■ gas or vapour used as a poisonous agent to kill or disable an enemy in warfare. ■ chiefly N. Amer. gas generated in the alimentary canal; flatulence. ■ Mining an explosive mixture of firedamp with air.
2 N. Amer. informal short for **GASOLINE**.
3 (**a gas**) informal a person or thing that is entertaining or amusing: *the party would be a gas*.
▶ verb (**gases**, **gassed**, **gassing**) [with obj.] **1** attack with or expose to gas: *my son was gassed at Verdun*.
■ kill by exposure to gas: *a mother and her children were found gassed in their car*. ■ [no obj.] (of a storage battery or dry cell) give off gas.
2 N. Amer. informal fill the tank of (a motor vehicle) with petrol: *after gassing up the car, he went into the restaurant*.
3 [no obj.] informal talk, especially excessively, idly, or boastfully: *I thought you'd never stop gassing*.
– PHRASES **run out of gas** N. Amer. informal run out of energy; lose momentum. **step on the gas** N. Amer. informal press on the accelerator to make a car go faster.
– ORIGIN mid 17th cent.: invented by J. B. van Helmont (1577–1644), Belgian chemist, to denote an occult principle which he believed to exist in all matter; suggested by Greek *khaos* 'chaos', with Dutch *g* representing Greek *kh*.

gasbag ▶ noun informal **1** a person who talks too much, typically about unimportant things.
2 the container holding the gas in a balloon or airship.

gas chamber ▶ noun an airtight room that can be filled with poisonous gas to kill people or animals.

gas chromatography ▶ noun [mass noun] chromatography employing a gas as the moving carrier medium. Compare with **GAS–LIQUID CHROMATOGRAPHY**.

Gascogne /ɡasˈkɔn/ French name for **GASCONY**.

Gascoigne /ˈɡaskɔɪn/, Paul (John) (b.1967), English footballer; known as **Gazza**. A gifted though controversial attacking midfielder, he played for clubs including Tottenham Hotspur, Lazio, Glasgow Rangers, and Everton.

Gascon /ˈɡask(ə)n/ ▶ noun **1** a native or inhabitant of Gascony.
2 (**gascon**) archaic a person who boasts about their achievements or possessions. [ORIGIN: with allusion to the perceived character of natives of Gascony.]
▶ adjective of or relating to Gascony or its people.
– ORIGIN via Old French from Latin *Vasco, Vascon-*; related to **BASQUE**.

gasconade /ˌɡaskəˈneɪd/ ▶ noun [mass noun] poetic/literary extravagant boasting.
– ORIGIN mid 17th cent.: from French *gasconnade*, from *gasconner* 'talk like a Gascon, brag'.

gas constant (Symbol: **R**) ▶ noun Chemistry the constant of proportionality in the gas equation. It is equal to 8.314 joule kelvin⁻¹ mole⁻¹.

Gascony /ˈɡaskəni/ a region and former province of SW France, in the northern foothills of the Pyrenees. It was held by England between 1154 and 1453. French name **GASCOGNE**.

gaseous /ˈɡasɪəs, ˈɡeɪsɪəs/ ▶ adjective of, relating to, or having the characteristics of a gas: *gaseous emissions from motor vehicles* | *gaseous oxygen*.
– DERIVATIVES **gaseousness** noun.

gas equation ▶ noun Chemistry the equation of state of an ideal gas, $PV = nRT$, where P = pressure, V = volume, T = absolute temperature, R = the gas constant, and n = the number of moles of gas.

gas fire ▶ noun a domestic heating appliance which uses gas as its fuel.

gas-fired ▶ adjective using gas as its fuel: *gas-fired central heating*.

gas gangrene ▶ noun [mass noun] rapidly spreading gangrene affecting injured tissue infected by a soil bacterium and accompanied by the evolution of foul-smelling gas.
● This disease is usually caused by anaerobic bacteria of the genus *Clostridium*.

gas giant ▶ noun Astronomy a large planet of relatively low density consisting predominantly of hydrogen and helium, such as Jupiter, Saturn, Uranus, or Neptune.

gas guzzler ▶ noun informal, chiefly N. Amer. a large motor car with a high fuel consumption.

gash¹ ▶ noun **1** a long deep slash, cut, or wound: *a bad gash in one leg became infected*.
■ a cleft made as if by a slashing cut: *the blast ripped a 25-foot gash in the hull*.
2 vulgar slang a woman's vulva.
■ [mass noun] offensive women collectively regarded in sexual terms.
▶ verb [with obj.] make a gash in; cut deeply: *the jagged edges gashed their fingers*.
– ORIGIN Middle English *garse*, from Old French *garcer* 'to chap, crack', perhaps based on Greek *kharassein* 'sharpen, scratch, engrave'. The current spelling is recorded from the mid 16th cent.

gash² ▶ noun [mass noun] Brit. informal rubbish or waste: [as modifier] *the gash bucket*.
– ORIGIN early 20th cent. (originally in nautical use): of unknown origin.

gasholder ▶ noun another term for **GASOMETER**.

gasify /ˈɡasɪfʌɪ/ ▶ verb (**-ies**, **-ied**) [with obj.] (often be **gasified**) convert (a solid or liquid, especially coal) into gas: *5 million tonnes of coal have been gasified*.
■ [no obj.] become a gas: *if PVC is overheated it will gasify*.
– DERIVATIVES **gasification** noun.

Gaskell /ˈɡask(ə)l/, Mrs Elizabeth (Cleghorn) (1810–65), English novelist. Notable works: *Mary Barton* (1848), *Cranford* (1853), and *North and South* (1855). She also wrote a biography (1857) of her friend Charlotte Brontë.

gasket /ˈɡaskɪt/ ▶ noun **1** a shaped sheet or ring of rubber or other material sealing the junction between two surfaces in an engine or other device.
2 archaic a cord securing a furled sail to the yard of a sailing ship.
– PHRASES **blow a gasket 1** suffer a leak in a gasket of an engine. **2** informal lose one's temper.
– ORIGIN early 17th cent. (in sense 2): perhaps from French *garcette* 'thin rope' (originally 'little girl'), diminutive of *garce*, feminine of *gars* 'boy'.

gaskin /ˈɡaskɪn/ ▶ noun the muscular part of the hind leg of a horse between the stifle and the hock.
– ORIGIN late 16th cent.: perhaps from **GALLIGASKINS** (the original sense).

gas laws ▶ plural noun Chemistry the physical laws that describe the properties of gases, including Boyle's and Charles's laws.

gaslight ▶ noun a type of lamp in which an incandescent mantle is heated by a jet of burning gas.
■ [mass noun] the light produced by such a lamp: *in the gaslight she looked paler than ever*.
– DERIVATIVES **gaslit** adjective.

gas–liquid chromatography ▶ noun [mass noun] chromatography employing a gas as the moving carrier medium and a liquid as the stationary medium.

gasman ▶ noun (pl. **-men**) a man who installs or services gas appliances or reads gas meters.

gas mantle ▶ noun see **MANTLE**¹ (sense 1).

gas mask ▶ noun a protective mask used to cover a person's face as a defence against poison gas.

gasohol /ˈɡasəhɒl/ ▶ noun [mass noun] a mixture of petrol and ethanol used as fuel in internal-combustion engines.
– ORIGIN 1970s: blend of **GAS** and **ALCOHOL**.

gas oil ▶ noun [mass noun] a type of fuel oil distilled from petroleum and heavier than paraffin oil.

gasoline (also **gasolene**) ▶ noun North American term for **PETROL**.
– ORIGIN mid 19th cent.: from **GAS** + **-OL** + **-INE**⁴ (or **-ENE**).

gasometer ▶ noun a large metal tank, typically cylindrical, in which gas for use as fuel is stored before being distributed through pipes to consumers.
– ORIGIN late 18th cent. (in the sense 'container for holding or measuring a gas'): from French *gazomètre*, from *gaz* 'gas' + *-mètre* '(instrument) measuring'.

gasp ▶ verb [no obj.] catch one's breath with an open mouth, owing to pain or astonishment: *a woman gasped in horror at the sight of him*.
■ [with obj.] say (something) while catching one's breath, especially as a result of strong emotion: *Jeremy gasped out an apology* | [with direct speech] *'It's beautiful!,' she gasped, much impressed*. ■ (**gasp for**) strain to obtain (air or breath) by gasping: *she surfaced and gasped for air*. ■ (**be gasping for**) figurative, informal be desperate to obtain or consume; crave: *I'm gasping for a drink!*
▶ noun a convulsive catching of breath: *his breath was coming in gasps*.
– PHRASES **one's** (or **the**) **last gasp** the point of exhaustion, death, or completion: *the last gasp of the cold war*.
– ORIGIN late Middle English: from Old Norse *geispa* 'to yawn'.

gasper ▶ noun Brit. informal, dated a cigarette.

gas-permeable ▶ adjective (of a contact lens) allowing the diffusion of gases into and out of the cornea.

gas plant ▶ noun an aromatic Eurasian plant of the rue family, with showy white flowers and fragrant leaves that emit a flammable vapour. This can sometimes be ignited without harming the plant. Also called **BURNING BUSH, DITTANY, FRAXINELLA**.
● *Dictamnus* (formerly *Fraxinella*) *albus*, family Rutaceae.

gas ring ▶ noun a hollow, perforated metal ring through which gas is piped and lit to provide heat for cooking.

Gassendi /ɡaˈsɛndi, French ɡasɑ̃di/, Pierre (1592–1655), French astronomer and philosopher. He is best known for his atomic theory of matter, which was based on his interpretation of the works of Epicurus.

Gasser, Herbert Spencer (1888–1963), American physiologist. Collaborating with Joseph Erlanger, he used an oscilloscope to show that the velocity of a nerve impulse is proportional to the diameter of the fibre. Nobel Prize for Physiology or Medicine (1944, shared with Erlanger).

gasser ▶ noun informal **1** an idle talker; a chatterer.
2 a very attractive or impressive person or thing: *that story you wrote for me is a gasser!*

gas station ▶ noun N. Amer. a petrol station.

gassy ▶ adjective (**gassier, gassiest**) **1** of, like, or full of gas: *the beer was served too gassy and too cold* | *gassy planets like Jupiter*.
2 informal (of people or language) inclined to be verbose: *a long and gassy book*.
– DERIVATIVES **gassiness** noun.

Gastarbeiter /ˈɡastˌɑːbʌɪtə, German ˈɡastˌarbaɪtɐ/ ▶ noun (pl. same or **Gastarbeiters**) a person with temporary permission to work in another country, especially in Germany.
– ORIGIN German, from *Gast* 'guest' + *Arbeiter* 'worker'.

gasteropod ▶ noun old-fashioned spelling of *gastropod* (see **GASTROPODA**).

Gasthaus /ˈɡasthaʊs/ ▶ noun (pl. **Gasthäuser** /-ˌhɔɪzə/) a small inn or hotel in a German-speaking country.
– ORIGIN from German, from *Gast* 'guest' + *Haus* 'house'.

Gasthof /ˈɡasthɒf, German ˈɡasthoːf/ ▶ noun (pl. **Gasthöfe** or **Gasthofs** /-ˌhɔːfə, German -ˌhøːfə/) a hotel in a German-speaking country, typically larger than a gasthaus.
– ORIGIN from German, from *Gast* 'guest' + *Hof* 'hotel, large house'.

gas-tight ▶ adjective sealed so as to prevent the leakage of gas.

gastr- ▶ combining form variant spelling of **GASTRO-** shortened before a vowel (as in *gastrectomy*).

gastrectomy /gaˈstrɛktəmi/ ▶ noun (pl. **-ies**) [mass noun] surgical removal of a part or the whole of the stomach.

gastric ▶ adjective of the stomach.
– ORIGIN mid 17th cent.: from modern Latin *gastricus*, from Greek *gastēr*, *gastr-* 'stomach'.

gastric flu ▶ noun [mass noun] a short-lived stomach disorder of unknown cause, popularly attributed to a virus.

gastric juice ▶ noun [mass noun] a thin, clear, virtually colourless acid fluid secreted by the stomach glands and active in promoting digestion.

gastrin ▶ noun [mass noun] Biochemistry a hormone which stimulates secretion of gastric juice, and is secreted into the bloodstream by the stomach wall in response to the presence of food.
– ORIGIN early 20th cent.: from **GASTRIC** + **-IN**[1].

gastritis /gaˈstrʌɪtɪs/ ▶ noun [mass noun] Medicine inflammation of the lining of the stomach.

gastro- /ˈgastrəʊ/ (also **gastr-** before a vowel) ▶ combining form of or relating to the stomach: *gastrectomy | gastro-enteritis*.
– ORIGIN from Greek *gastēr*, *gastr-* 'stomach'.

gastrocnemius /ˌgastrə(ʊ)ˈkniːmɪəs/ (also **gastrocnemius muscle**) ▶ noun (pl. **gastrocnemii** /-mɪʌɪ/) Anatomy the chief muscle of the calf of the leg, which flexes the knee and foot. It runs to the Achilles tendon from two heads attached to the femur.
– ORIGIN late 17th cent.: modern Latin, from Greek *gastroknēmia* 'calf of the leg', from *gaster*, *gastr-* 'stomach' + *knēmē* 'leg' (from the bulging shape of the calf).

gastrocolic /ˌgastrə(ʊ)ˈkɒlɪk/ ▶ adjective [attrib.] of or relating to the stomach and the colon.

gastro-enteric ▶ adjective [attrib.] Medicine & Physiology of or relating to the stomach and intestines.

gastro-enteritis ▶ noun [mass noun] inflammation of the stomach and intestines, typically resulting from bacterial toxins or viral infection and causing vomiting and diarrhoea.

gastroenterology /ˌgastrəʊɛntəˈrɒlədʒi/ ▶ noun [mass noun] the branch of medicine which deals with disorders of the stomach and intestines.
– DERIVATIVES **gastroenterological** adjective, **gastroenterologist** noun.

gastrointestinal /ˌgastrəʊɪnˈtɛstɪn(ə)l, ˌgastrəʊ-ɪnˌtɛsˈtʌɪn(ə)l/ ▶ adjective of or relating to the stomach and the intestines.

gastrolith /ˈgastrə(ʊ)lɪθ/ ▶ noun 1 Zoology a small stone swallowed by a bird, reptile, or fish, to aid digestion in the gizzard.
2 Medicine a hard concretion in the stomach.

gastronome /ˈgastrənəʊm/ ▶ noun a gourmet.
– ORIGIN early 19th cent.: from French, from *gastronomie* (see **GASTRONOMY**).

gastronomy /gaˈstrɒnəmi/ ▶ noun [mass noun] the practice or art of choosing, cooking, and eating good food.
■ the cookery of a particular area: *traditional American gastronomy.*
– DERIVATIVES **gastronomic** adjective, **gastronomical** adjective, **gastronomically** adverb.
– ORIGIN early 19th cent.: from French *gastronomie*, from Greek *gastronomia*, alteration of *gastrologia* (see **GASTRO-**, **-LOGY**).

Gastropoda /ˌgastrəˈpəʊdə, gaˈstrɒpədə/ Zoology a large class of molluscs which includes snails, slugs, whelks, and all terrestrial kinds. They have a large muscular foot for movement and (in many kinds) a single asymmetrical spiral shell.
– DERIVATIVES **gastropod** noun.
– ORIGIN modern Latin (plural), from Greek *gastēr*, *gastr-* 'stomach' + *pous*, *pod-* 'foot'.

gastroscope ▶ noun an optical instrument used for inspecting the interior of the stomach.
– DERIVATIVES **gastroscopic** adjective, **gastroscopy** noun.

gastrostomy /gaˈstrɒstəmi/ ▶ noun (pl. **-ies**) an opening into the stomach from the abdominal wall, made surgically for the introduction of food.
■ a surgical operation for making such an opening.

Gastrotricha /ˌgastrəˈtrʌɪkə/ Zoology a small phylum of minute aquatic worm-like animals which bear bristles and cilia. They are thought to be related to the nematode worms and rotifers.
– DERIVATIVES **gastrotrich** /ˈgastrətrɪk/ noun.
– ORIGIN modern Latin (plural), from Greek *gastēr*, *gastr-* 'stomach' + *thrix*, *trikh-* 'hair'.

gastrula /ˈgastrʊlə/ ▶ noun (pl. **gastrulae** /-liː/) Embryology an embryo at the stage following the blastula, when it is a hollow cup-shaped structure having three layers of cells.
– DERIVATIVES **gastrulation** noun.
– ORIGIN late 19th cent.: modern Latin, from Greek *gastēr*, *gastr-* 'stomach' + the Latin diminutive ending *-ula*.

gas turbine ▶ noun a turbine driven by expanding hot gases produced by burning fuel, as in a jet engine.

gasworks ▶ plural noun [treated as sing.] a place where gas is manufactured and processed.

gat[1] ▶ noun informal a revolver or pistol.
– ORIGIN early 20th cent.: abbreviation of **GATLING GUN**.

gat[2] archaic past of **GET**.

gate[1] ▶ noun 1 a hinged barrier used to close an opening in a wall, fence, or hedge.
■ a gateway: *she went out through the gate.* ■ figurative a means of entrance or exit: *they were opening the gates of their country wide to the enemy.* ■ an exit from an airport building to an aircraft: *a departure gate.* ■ [in names] a mountain pass or other natural passage: *the Golden Gate.*
2 the number of people who pay to enter a sports ground for any one event: [as modifier] *gate receipts.*
■ the money taken for admission.
3 a device resembling a gate in structure or function, in particular:
■ a hinged or sliding barrier for controlling the flow of water: *a sluice gate.* ■ an arrangement of slots into which the gear lever of a motor vehicle moves to engage each gear. ■ a device for holding each frame of a movie film in position behind the lens of a camera or projector.
4 an electric circuit with an output which depends on the combination of several inputs: *a logic gate.*
■ the part of a field-effect transistor to which a signal is applied to control the resistance of the conductive channel of the device.
▶ verb Brit. [with obj.] (usu. **be gated**) confine (a pupil or student) to school or college: *he was gated for the rest of term.*
– PHRASES **get** (or **be given**) **the gate** N. Amer. informal be dismissed from a job.
– ORIGIN Old English *gæt*, *geat*, plural *gatu*, of Germanic origin; related to Dutch *gat* 'gap, hole, breach'.

gate[2] ▶ noun Brit. (in place names) a street: *Kirkgate.*
– ORIGIN Middle English (also meaning 'way' in general): from Old Norse *gata*; related to German *Gasse* 'street, lane'.

-gate ▶ combining form in nouns denoting an actual or alleged scandal, especially one involving a cover-up: *Irangate.*
– ORIGIN early 1970s: suggested by the *Watergate* scandal in the US, 1972.

gate array ▶ noun Computing a regular arrangement of logic gates.
■ an electronic chip consisting of such an arrangement.

gateau /ˈgatəʊ/ ▶ noun (pl. **gateaus** or **gateaux** /-əʊz/) chiefly Brit. a rich cake, typically one containing layers of cream or fruit.
– ORIGIN mid 19th cent.: from French *gâteau* 'cake'.

gatecrash ▶ verb [with obj.] enter (a party or other gathering) without an invitation or ticket.
– DERIVATIVES **gatecrasher** noun.

gated ▶ adjective having a gate or gates, in particular:
■ having gates to control the movement of traffic, people, or animals: *a gated community near Los Angeles.* ■ technical denoting a channel or pathway through a system that can be opened and closed depending on set conditions.

gatefold ▶ noun an oversized page in a book or magazine folded to the same size as the other pages but intended to be opened out for reading.

gatehouse ▶ noun 1 a house standing by a gateway, especially on a country estate.
2 historical a room over a city or palace gate, often used as a prison.

gatekeeper ▶ noun 1 an attendant at a gate who is employed to control who goes through it.
■ figurative a person or thing that controls access to something: *GPs can act as gatekeepers, filtering demands made on hospital services.*
2 an orange and brown European butterfly with small eyespots on the wings, frequenting hedgerows and meadows. Also called **HEDGE BROWN**.
● *Pyronia tithonus*, subfamily Satyrinae, family Nymphalidae.

gateleg table ▶ noun a table with hinged legs that are swung out from the centre to support folding leaves and make the table larger.
– DERIVATIVES **gatelegged** adjective.

gatepost ▶ noun a post on which a gate is hinged, or against which it shuts.
– PHRASES **between you and me and the gatepost** see **BEDPOST**.

Gates, Bill (b.1955), American computer entrepreneur; full name *William Henry Gates*. He co-founded the computer software company Microsoft and became the youngest multi-billionaire in American history.

Gateshead an industrial town in NE England, on the south bank of the River Tyne opposite Newcastle; pop. 196,500 (1991).

gate valve ▶ noun a valve with a sliding part that controls the extent of the aperture.

gateway ▶ noun an opening that can be closed by a gate: *we turned into a gateway leading to a small cottage.*
■ a frame or arch built around or over a gate: *a big house with a wrought-iron gateway.* ■ a means of access or entry to a place: *Mombasa, the gateway to East Africa.* ■ a means of achieving a state or condition: *the Christian symbolism of death as the gateway to life.* ■ Computing a device used to connect two different networks, especially a connection to the Internet.

Gatha /ˈgɑːθɑː/ ▶ noun any of seventeen poems attributed to Zoroaster which are the most ancient texts of the Avesta.
– ORIGIN from Avestan *gāthā.*

gather ▶ verb 1 [no obj.] come together; assemble or accumulate: *as soon as a crowd gathered, the police came.*
2 [with obj.] bring together and take in from scattered places or sources: *information that we have gathered about people.*
■ (**gather something up**) pick up from the ground or a surface: *I gather up the prescription and follow him to the door.* ■ (**gather something in**) collect grain or other crops as a harvest. ■ [no obj.] collect plants, fruits, etc., for food: *the Bushmen live by hunting and gathering.* ■ draw together or towards oneself: *she gathered the child in her strong young arms and held him close.* ■ draw and hold together (fabric or a part of a garment) by running thread through it: *the front is gathered at the waist.*
3 [with obj.] infer; understand: *you're still with Anthea, I gather.*
4 [with obj.] develop a higher degree of: *the green movement is gathering pace | 100,000 of the machines are gathering dust in stockrooms.*
5 [with obj.] summon up (a mental or physical attribute such as one's thoughts or strength) for a purpose: *he lay gathering his thoughts together | he gathered himself for a tremendous leap.*
■ gain or recover (one's breath).
▶ noun (**gathers**) a part of a garment that is gathered or drawn in.
– PHRASES **gather way** (of a ship) begin to move.
– DERIVATIVES **gatherer** noun.
– ORIGIN Old English *gaderian*, of West Germanic origin; related to Dutch *gaderen*, also to **TOGETHER**.

gathering ▶ noun 1 an assembly or meeting, especially a social or festive one or one held for a specific purpose: *a family gathering.*
2 a group of leaves taken together, one inside another, in binding a book.

Gatling gun (also **Gatling**) ▶ noun a rapid-fire, crank-driven gun with clustered barrels. The first practical machine gun, it was officially adopted by the US army in 1866.
– ORIGIN named after Richard J. *Gatling* (1818–1903), its American inventor.

gator ▶ noun informal, chiefly US an alligator.
– ORIGIN mid 19th cent.: shortened form.

GATT General Agreement on Tariffs and Trade, an international treaty (1948–94) to promote trade and economic development by reducing tariffs and other restrictions. It was superseded by the establishment of the World Trade Organization in 1995.

Gatwick an international airport in SE England, to the south of London.

gauche /ɡəʊʃ/ ▶ **adjective** lacking ease or grace; unsophisticated and socially awkward.
– DERIVATIVES **gauchely** adverb, **gaucheness** noun.
– ORIGIN mid 18th cent.: French, literally 'left'.

gaucherie /ˈɡəʊʃ(ə)ri/ ▶ **noun** [mass noun] awkward or unsophisticated ways: *I was ridiculed for my sartorial gaucherie* | [count noun] *she had long since got over gaucheries such as blushing.*
– ORIGIN late 18th cent.: French, from *gauche* (see **GAUCHE**).

Gaucher's disease /ˈɡəʊʃeɪz, ɡəʊˈʃeɪz/ ▶ **noun** [mass noun] a hereditary disease in which the metabolism and storage of fats is abnormal. It results in bone fragility, neurological disturbance, anaemia, and enlargement of the liver and spleen.
– ORIGIN mid 20th cent.: named after Phillippe C. E. *Gaucher* (1854–1918), French physician.

gaucho /ˈɡaʊtʃəʊ, ˈɡɔː-/ ▶ **noun** (pl. **-os**) a cowboy from the South American pampas.
– ORIGIN Latin American Spanish, probably from Araucanian *kauču* 'friend'.

gaud /ɡɔːd/ ▶ **noun** archaic a showy and purely ornamental thing: *displays of overpriced gauds.*
– ORIGIN Middle English (denoting a trick or pretence): perhaps via Anglo-Norman French from Old French *gaudir* 'rejoice', from Latin *gaudere*. Current senses may have been influenced by obsolete *gaud* 'a large ornamental bead in a rosary'.

Gaudí /ɡaʊˈdiː/, Antonio (1853–1926), Spanish architect; full name *Antonio Gaudí y Cornet*. He was a leading but idiosyncratic exponent of art nouveau, known mainly for his ornate and extravagant church of the Sagrada Familia in Barcelona (begun 1884).

Gaudier-Brzeska /ˌɡəʊdɪeɪˈbʒɛskə/, Henri (1891–1915), French sculptor, a leading member of the vorticist movement. Notable works: the faceted bust of Horace Brodzky (1912) and *Bird Swallowing a Fish* (1913).

gaudy[1] ▶ **adjective** (**gaudier**, **gaudiest**) extravagantly bright or showy, typically so as to be tasteless: *silver bows and gaudy ribbons.*
– DERIVATIVES **gaudily** adverb, **gaudiness** noun.
– ORIGIN late 15th cent.: probably from **GAUD** + **-Y**[1].

gaudy[2] ▶ **noun** (pl. **-ies**) Brit. a celebratory dinner or entertainment held by a college for old members.
– ORIGIN mid 16th cent. (in the sense 'rejoicing, a celebration'): from Latin *gaudium* 'joy', or from *gaude* 'rejoice!', imperative of *gaudere*.

gauge /ɡeɪdʒ/ (chiefly US also **gage**) ▶ **noun 1** an instrument or device for measuring the magnitude, amount, or contents of something, typically with a visual display of such information.
■ a tool for checking whether something conforms to a desired dimension. ■ figurative a means of estimating something; a criterion or test: *emigration is perhaps the best gauge of public unease.*
2 the thickness, size, or capacity of something, especially as a standard measure, in particular:
■ the diameter of a string, fibre, tube, etc.: [as modifier] *a fine 0.018-inch gauge wire.* ■ [in combination] a measure of the diameter of a gun barrel, or of its ammunition, expressed as the number of spherical pieces of shot of the same diameter as the barrel that can be made from 1 lb (454 g) of lead: [as modifier] *a 12-gauge shotgun.* ■ [in combination] the thickness of sheet metal or plastic: [as modifier] *500-gauge polythene.* ■ the distance between the rails of a line of railway track: *the line was laid to a gauge of 2 ft 9 ins.* See also **LOADING GAUGE**.
3 (usu. **the gage**) Nautical, historical the position of a sailing vessel to windward (**weather gage**) or leeward (**lee gage**) of another.
▶ **verb** [with obj.] **1** estimate or determine the magnitude, amount, or volume of: *astronomers can gauge the star's intrinsic brightness.*
■ form a judgement or estimate of (a situation, mood, etc.): *she is unable to gauge his mood.*
2 measure the dimensions of (an object) with a gauge: *when dry the assemblies can be gauged exactly and planed to width.*
■ [as adj. **gauged**] made in standard dimensions: *gauged sets of strings.*
– DERIVATIVES **gaugeable** adjective, **gauger** noun.
– ORIGIN Middle English (denoting a standard measure): from Old French *gauge* (noun), *gauger* (verb), variant of Old Northern French *jauge* (noun), *jauger* (verb), of unknown origin.

gauge pressure ▶ **noun** Engineering the amount by which the pressure measured in a fluid exceeds that of the atmosphere.

gauge theory ▶ **noun** Physics a quantum theory using mathematical functions to describe subatomic interactions in terms of particles that are not directly detectable.

Gauguin /ˈɡəʊɡã, French ɡoɡɛ̃/, (Eugène Henri) Paul (1848–1903), French painter. From 1891 on he lived mainly in Tahiti, painting in a post-Impressionist style that was influenced by primitive art. Notable works: *The Vision after the Sermon* (1888) and *Faa Iheihe* (1898).

Gauhati /ɡaʊˈhɑːti/ an industrial city in NE India, in Assam, a river port on the Brahmaputra; pop. 578,000 (1991).

Gaul[1] /ɡɔːl/ an ancient region of Europe, corresponding to modern France, Belgium, the south Netherlands, SW Germany, and northern Italy. The area south of the Alps was conquered in 222 BC by the Romans, who called it **Cisalpine Gaul**. The area north of the Alps, known as **Transalpine Gaul**, was taken by Julius Caesar between 58 and 51 BC.

Gaul[2] /ɡɔːl/ ▶ **noun** a native or inhabitant of ancient Gaul.
– ORIGIN from Latin *Gallus*, probably of Celtic origin.

Gauleiter /ˈɡaʊlʌɪtə, German ˈɡaʊlaɪtɐ/ ▶ **noun 1** historical a political official governing a district under Nazi rule.
2 an overbearing official.
– ORIGIN 1930s: German, from *Gau* 'administrative district' + *Leiter* 'leader'.

Gaulish ▶ **adjective** of, relating to, or denoting the ancient Gauls.
▶ **noun** [mass noun] the Celtic language of the ancient Gauls.

Gaulle, Charles de, see **DE GAULLE**.

Gaullism /ˈɡəʊlɪz(ə)m/ ▶ **noun** [mass noun] the principles and policies of Charles de Gaulle, characterized by their conservatism, nationalism, and advocacy of centralized government.
– DERIVATIVES **Gaullist** noun & adjective.
– ORIGIN 1940s: from French *Gaullisme*.

gault /ɡɔːlt/ ▶ **noun** (also **gault clay**) [mass noun] a thick, heavy clay.
■ (usu. **Gault**) Geology a series of Cretaceous clays and marls forming strata in southern England.
– ORIGIN late 16th cent.: possibly related to Old Swedish *galt*, neuter of *galder* 'barren'.

Gaunt[1] former name for **GHENT**.

Gaunt[2], John of, see **JOHN OF GAUNT**.

gaunt ▶ **adjective** (of a person) lean and haggard, especially because of suffering, hunger, or age.
■ (of a building or place) grim or desolate in appearance.
– DERIVATIVES **gauntly** adverb, **gauntness** noun.
– ORIGIN late Middle English: of unknown origin.

gauntlet[1] ▶ **noun** a stout glove with a long loose wrist.
■ historical an armoured glove. ■ the part of a glove covering the wrist.
– PHRASES **take up** (or **throw down**) **the gauntlet** accept (or issue) a challenge. [ORIGIN: from the medieval custom of issuing a challenge by throwing one's gauntlet to the ground; whoever picked it up was deemed to have accepted the challenge.]
– ORIGIN late Middle English: from Old French *gantelet*, diminutive of *gant* 'glove', of Germanic origin.

gauntlet[2] (US also **gantlet**) ▶ **noun** (in phrase **run the gauntlet**) **1** go through an intimidating or dangerous crowd, place, or experience in order to reach a goal: *they had to run the gauntlet of television cameras.*
2 historical undergo the military punishment of receiving blows while running between two rows of men with sticks.
– ORIGIN mid 17th cent.: alteration of *gantlope* (from Swedish *gatlopp*, from *gata* 'lane' + *lopp* 'course') by association with **GAUNTLET**[1].

gaur /ˈɡaʊə/ ▶ **noun** a wild ox with a large head, a dark brown or black coat with white stockings, and a hump, native to India and Malaysia. Also called **INDIAN BISON**, **SELADANG**.
• *Bos gaurus*, family Bovidae; it is the ancestor of the domestic gayal.
– ORIGIN early 19th cent.: from Sanskrit *gaura*; related to **COW**.

Gauss /ɡaʊs/, Karl Friedrich (1777–1855), German mathematician, astronomer, and physicist. Gauss laid the foundations of number theory, and applied rigorous mathematical analysis to geometry, geodesy, electrostatics, and electromagnetism.

gauss /ɡaʊs/ (abbrev.: **G**) ▶ **noun** (pl. same or **gausses**) a unit of magnetic induction, equal to one ten-thousandth of a tesla.
– ORIGIN late 19th cent.: named after K. **GAUSS**.

Gaussian distribution /ˈɡaʊsɪən/ ▶ **noun** Statistics another term for **NORMAL DISTRIBUTION**.
– ORIGIN early 20th cent.: named after K. **GAUSS**, who described it.

Gautama /ˈɡaʊtəmə/, Siddhartha, see **BUDDHA**.

Gauteng /xaʊˈtɛŋ, xaʊəˈtɛŋ/ a province of north-eastern South Africa, formerly part of Transvaal; capital, Johannesburg. Former name (until 1995) **PRETORIA-WITWATERSRAND-VEREENIGING**.

gauze /ɡɔːz/ ▶ **noun** [mass noun] a thin transparent fabric of silk, linen, or cotton.
■ (also **wire gauze**) a very fine wire mesh. ■ Medicine thin, loosely woven cloth used for dressing and swabs. ■ [in sing.] figurative a transparent haze or film: *they saw the grasslands through a gauze of golden dust.*
– ORIGIN mid 16th cent.: from French *gaze*, perhaps from *Gaza*, the name of a town in Palestine.

gauzy ▶ **adjective** (**gauzier**, **gauziest**) resembling gauze; thin and translucent: *a gauzy dress.*
– DERIVATIVES **gauzily** adverb, **gauziness** noun.

gavage /ɡaˈvɑːʒ/ ▶ **noun** [mass noun] the administration of food or drugs by force, especially to an animal, typically through a tube leading down the throat to the stomach.
– ORIGIN late 19th cent.: French, from *gaver* 'force-feed', from a base meaning 'throat'.

Gavaskar /ˈɡavəskə, -kɑː/, Sunil Manohar (b.1949), Indian cricketer. He made his Test debut in the West Indies in 1970, later captained India, and in 1987 became the first batsman to score 10,000 runs in Test cricket.

gave past of **GIVE**.

gavel /ˈɡav(ə)l/ ▶ **noun** a small hammer with which an auctioneer, a judge, or the chair of a meeting hits a surface to call for attention or order.
▶ **verb** (**gavelled**, **gavelling**; US **gaveled**, **gaveling**) [with obj. and adverbial] bring (a hearing or person) to order by use of such a hammer: *he gavelled the convention to order.*
– ORIGIN early 19th cent. (originally US in the sense 'stonemason's mallet'): of unknown origin.

gavelkind /ˈɡav(ə)lkʌɪnd/ ▶ **noun** [mass noun] historical a system of inheritance in which a deceased person's land is divided equally among all male heirs.
– ORIGIN Middle English: from obsolete *gavel* 'payment, rent' + **KIND**[1].

gavial /ˈɡeɪvɪəl/ ▶ **noun** variant spelling of **GHARIAL**.
– ORIGIN from French, the *-v-* probably being substituted for *-r-* by scribal error.

gavotte /ɡəˈvɒt/ ▶ **noun** a medium-paced French dance, popular in the 18th century.
■ a piece of music accompanying or in the rhythm of such a dance, composed in common time beginning on the third beat of the bar.
– ORIGIN French, from Provençal *gavoto* 'dance of the mountain people', from *Gavot* 'a native of the Alps'.

Gawain /ˈɡɑːweɪn, ɡəˈweɪn/ (in Arthurian legend) one of the knights of the Round Table who quested after the Holy Grail. He is the hero of the medieval poem *Sir Gawain and the Green Knight*.

gawk ▶ **verb** [no obj.] stare openly and stupidly: *they were gawking at some pin-up.*
▶ **noun** an awkward or shy person.
– DERIVATIVES **gawker** noun, **gawkish** adjective.
– ORIGIN late 17th cent. (as a noun): perhaps related to obsolete *gaw* 'to gaze', from Old Norse *gá* 'heed'.

gawky ▶ **adjective** (**gawkier**, **gawkiest**) nervously awkward and ungainly: *a gawky teenager.*
– DERIVATIVES **gawkily** adverb, **gawkiness** noun.

gawp ▶ **verb** [no obj.] Brit. informal stare openly in a stupid or rude manner: *what are you gawping at?*
– DERIVATIVES **gawper** noun.
– ORIGIN late 17th cent.: perhaps an alteration of **GAPE**.

Gay, John (1685–1732), English poet and dramatist.

He is chiefly known for *The Beggar's Opera* (1728), a low-life ballad opera combining burlesque and political satire.

gay ▶ **adjective** (**gayer**, **gayest**) **1** (of a person, especially a man) homosexual.
■relating to or used by homosexuals: *feminist, black, and gay perspectives.*
2 dated light-hearted and carefree: *Nan had a gay disposition and a very pretty face.*
■brightly coloured; showy; brilliant: *a gay profusion of purple and pink sweet peas.*
▶**noun** a homosexual, especially a man.
– DERIVATIVES **gayness** noun.
– ORIGIN Middle English (in sense 2): from Old French *gai*, of unknown origin.

USAGE Gay meaning 'homosexual' became established in the 1960s as the term preferred by homosexual men to describe themselves. It is now the standard accepted term throughout the English-speaking world. As a result, the centuries-old other senses of **gay** meaning either 'carefree' or 'bright and showy' have more or less dropped out of natural use. The word **gay** cannot be readily used unselfconsciously today in these older senses without arousing a sense of double entendre, despite concerted attempts by some to keep them alive.
Gay in its modern sense typically refers to men (**lesbian** being the standard term for homosexual women) but in some contexts it can be used of both men and women.

Gaya /ˈɡɑːjə/ a city in NE India, in the state of Bihar south of Patna; pop. 291,000 (1991). It is a place of Hindu pilgrimage.

gayal /ɡʌɪˈjɑːl, -ˈjal/ ▶ **noun** a domesticated ox used in the Indian subcontinent.
• *Bos frontalis*, family Bovidae, descended from the wild gaur.
– ORIGIN late 18th cent.: from Bengali.

Gaye, Marvin (1939–84), American soul singer, composer, and musician. Best known for 'I Heard It Through the Grapevine' (1968), he later recorded the albums *Let's Get It On* (1973) and *Midnight Love* (1982). He was shot dead by his father in a quarrel.

gayelle /ˈɡajɛl, ˈɡajal/ ▶ **noun** W. Indian an arena or ring for cockfighting or stick-fighting.

gayety ▶ **noun** US variant spelling of **GAIETY**.

gay liberation ▶ **noun** [mass noun] the freeing of homosexuals from social and legal discrimination.

Gay-Lussac's law /ɡeɪˈluːsaks/ Chemistry a law stating that the volumes of gases undergoing a reaction at constant pressure and temperature are in a simple ratio to each other and to that of the product.
– ORIGIN early 19th cent.: named after Joseph L. Gay-Lussac (1778–1850), French chemist and physicist.

gay pride ▶ **noun** [mass noun] a sense of strong self-esteem associated with a person's public acknowledgement of their homosexuality.

gay rights ▶ **plural noun** equal legal and social rights for homosexuals compared with heterosexuals.

gazania /ɡəˈzeɪnɪə/ ▶ **noun** a tropical herbaceous plant of the daisy family, with showy flowers that are typically orange or yellow.
• Genus *Gazania*, family Compositae.
– ORIGIN modern Latin, named after Theodore of Gaza (1398–1478), Greek scholar.

Gazankulu /ˌɡazəŋˈkuːluː/ a former homeland established in South Africa for the Tsonga people, now part of the provinces of Northern Province and Mpumalanga.

Gaza Strip /ˈɡɑːzə/ a strip of territory in Palestine, on the SE Mediterranean coast, including the town of Gaza; pop. 748,400 (1993). Administered by Egypt from 1949, and occupied by Israel from 1967, it became a self-governing enclave under the PLO–Israeli accord of 1994 and elected its own legislative council in 1996.

gaze ▶ **verb** [no obj., with adverbial of direction] look steadily and intently, especially in admiration, surprise, or thought: *he could only gaze at her in astonishment.*
▶**noun** a steady intent look: *he turned, following her gaze | offices screened from the public gaze.*
■[in sing.] (in literary theory) a particular perspective taken to embody certain aspects of the relationship between observer and observed: *the male gaze.*
– DERIVATIVES **gazer** noun.
– ORIGIN late Middle English: perhaps related to obsolete *gaw* (see **GAWK**).

gazebo /ɡəˈziːbəʊ/ ▶ **noun** (pl. **-os** or **-oes**) a small building, especially one in the garden of a house, that gives a wide view of the surrounding area.
– ORIGIN mid 18th cent.: perhaps humorously from **GAZE**, in imitation of Latin future tenses ending in *-ebo*: compare with **LAVABO**.

gazelle ▶ **noun** a small slender antelope that typically has curved horns and a fawn-coloured coat with white underparts, found in open country in Africa and Asia.
• *Gazella* and other genera, family Bovidae: several species.
– ORIGIN early 17th cent.: from French, probably via Spanish from Arabic *ghazāl*.

gazette ▶ **noun** a journal or newspaper, especially the official one of an organization or institution.
■historical a news-sheet.
▶**verb** Brit. [with obj.] announce or publish in an official gazette: *we will need to gazette the bill if a decision cannot be reached imminently* | [as adj. **gazetted**] *a gazetted holiday.*
■[with obj. and adverbial] publish the fact of the appointment of (someone) to a military or other official post: *Lewis was gazetted to the Somerset Light Infantry.*
– ORIGIN early 17th cent.: via French from Italian *gazzetta*, originally Venetian *gazeta de la novità* 'a halfpennyworth of news' (because the news-sheet sold for a *gazeta*, a Venetian coin of small value).

gazetteer /ˌɡazəˈtɪə/ ▶ **noun** a geographical index or dictionary.
– ORIGIN early 17th cent. (in the sense 'journalist'): via French from Italian *gazzettiere*, from *gazzetta* (see **GAZETTE**). The current sense comes from a late 17th-cent. gazetteer called *The Gazetteer's: or, Newsman's Interpreter: Being a Geographical Index.*

Gaziantep /ˌɡazɪənˈtɛp/ a city in southern Turkey, near the border with Syria; pop. 603,400 (1990). Former name (until 1921): **AINTAB**.

gazillion /ɡəˈzɪljən/ (also **kazillion**) ▶ **cardinal number** N. Amer. informal a very large number or quantity (used for emphasis): ***gazillions of** books.*
– ORIGIN late 20th cent.: fanciful formation on the pattern of *billion* and *million*.

gazpacho /ɡəsˈpatʃəʊ/ ▶ **noun** (pl. **-os**) [mass noun] a cold Spanish soup made from tomatoes, peppers, and other salad vegetables.
– ORIGIN Spanish.

gazump /ɡəˈzʌmp/ ▶ **verb** [with obj.] Brit. **1** (usu. **be gazumped**) make an offer for a house that is higher than that made by (someone whose offer has already been accepted by the seller) and thus succeed in acquiring the property.
2 archaic swindle (someone): *I gazumped a friend of mine with complete success last night.*
– DERIVATIVES **gazumper** noun.
– ORIGIN 1920s (in sense 2): from Yiddish *gezumph* 'overcharge'. Sense 1 dates from the 1970s.

GB ▶ **abbreviation for** ■ Computing (also **Gb**) gigabyte(s). ■ Great Britain.

GBA ▶ **abbreviation for** Alderney (international vehicle registration).

GBE ▶ **abbreviation for** (in the UK) Knight or Dame Grand Cross of the Order of the British Empire.

GBG ▶ **abbreviation for** Guernsey (international vehicle registration).

GBH Brit. ▶ **abbreviation for** grievous bodily harm.

GBJ ▶ **abbreviation for** Jersey (international vehicle registration)

GBM ▶ **abbreviation for** Isle of Man (international vehicle registration).

Gbyte ▶ **abbreviation for** gigabyte(s).

GBZ ▶ **abbreviation for** Gibraltar (international vehicle registration).

GC ▶ **abbreviation for** (in the UK and Commonwealth countries) George Cross.

GCA ▶ **abbreviation for** Guatemala (international vehicle registration).

GCB ▶ **abbreviation for** (in the UK) Knight or Dame Grand Cross of the Order of the Bath.

GCE ▶ **abbreviation for** (in the UK) General Certificate of Education.

GCHQ ▶ **abbreviation for** (in the UK) Government Communications Headquarters.

GCMG ▶ **abbreviation for** (in the UK) Knight or Dame Grand Cross of the Order of St Michael and St George.

GCSE ▶ **abbreviation for** General Certificate of Secondary Education: *grade A in GCSE English.*

GCVO ▶ **abbreviation for** (in the UK) Knight or Dame Grand Cross of the Royal Victorian Order.

Gd ▶ **symbol for** the chemical element gadolinium.

Gdańsk /ɡ(ə)ˈdansk/ an industrial port and shipbuilding centre in northern Poland, on an inlet of the Baltic Sea; pop. 465,100 (1990). Disputed between Prussia and Poland during the 19th century, it was a free city under a League of Nations mandate from 1919 until 1939, when it was annexed by Nazi Germany, precipitating hostilities with Poland and the outbreak of the Second World War. German name **DANZIG**.

g'day ▶ **exclamation** Austral./NZ good day.

Gdns ▶ **abbreviation for** Gardens, especially as part of an address: *Milbrook Gdns.*

GDP ▶ **abbreviation for** gross domestic product.

GDR historical ▶ **abbreviation for** German Democratic Republic. See **GERMANY**.

Gdynia /ˈɡdɪnjə/ a port and naval base in northern Poland, on the Baltic Sea north-west of Gdańsk; pop. 251,500 (1990).

Ge[1] ▶ **symbol for** the chemical element germanium.

Ge[2] /ɡeɪ/ Greek Mythology another name for **GAIA**.

gean /ɡiːn/ ▶ **noun** the wild or sweet cherry, which is native to both Eurasia and North America.
• *Prunus avium*, family Rosaceae.
– ORIGIN mid 16th cent.: from Old French *guine*, of unknown origin.

geanticline /dʒiːˈantɪklʌɪn/ ▶ **noun** Geology a large-scale upwardly flexed structure in the earth's crust.
– ORIGIN late 19th cent.: from Greek *gē* 'earth' + **ANTICLINE**.

gear ▶ **noun 1** (often **gears**) a set of toothed wheels that work together to alter the relation between the speed of a driving mechanism (such as the engine of a vehicle or the pedals of a bicycle) and the speed of the driven parts (the wheels).
■a particular function or state of adjustment of engaged gears: *he was belting along in fifth gear.*
2 [mass noun] informal equipment that is used for a particular purpose.
■a person's personal possessions and clothes. ■clothing, especially of a specified kind: *designer gear.* ■ illegal drugs.
▶**verb** [with obj.] design or adjust the gears in a machine to give a specified speed or power output: *it's geared too high for serious off-road use.*
– PHRASES **in gear** with a gear engaged: *the captain revved the engines and put them in gear* | figurative *I've got to get my act in gear.* **move up a gear** change to a higher gear. ■ figurative put more energy or effort into an activity: *now the champions moved up a gear.* **out of gear** with no gear engaged: *she took the engine out of gear* | figurative *sometimes his brain seems to slip out of gear.*
– ORIGIN Middle English: of Scandinavian origin; compare with Old Norse *gervi*. Early senses expressed the general meaning 'equipment or apparatus', later 'mechanism': hence sense 1 (early 19th cent.).
▶**gear down** (or **up**) change to a lower (or higher) gear.
gear someone for make ready or prepared: *a nation geared for war.*
gear something to/towards adjust or adapt something to make it suitable for (someone or something).
gear up equip or prepare oneself: *the region started to gear up for the tourist season.* ■(of a company) increase its borrowings.
gear someone/thing up equip someone or something for a particular purpose: *a city not **geared up to** an outdoor lifestyle.*

gearbox ▶ **noun** a set of gears with its casing, especially in a motor vehicle; the transmission.

gear change ▶ **noun** an act of engaging a different gear while driving a vehicle.
■a mechanism which changes gear on a motor vehicle.

geared ▶ **adjective 1** fitted with gears: *a geared engine* | [in combination] *a multi-geared cycle.*
2 [with adv.] (of a company) having a specified ratio of loan capital (debt) to the value of its ordinary shares (equity): *some of the most highly geared US companies.*

gearing ▶ **noun** [mass noun] **1** the set or arrangement of gears in a machine: *the mill's internal waterwheel and gearing survive.*

2 the ratio of a company's loan capital (debt) to the value of its ordinary shares (equity).

gear lever (also **gearstick**) ▶ noun Brit. a lever used to engage or change gear in a motor vehicle.

gear shift ▶ noun chiefly N. Amer. a gear lever.

gear train ▶ noun a system of gears which transmits motion from one shaft to another.

gearwheel ▶ noun a toothed wheel in a set of gears.
  ■ (on a bicycle) a cogwheel driven directly by the chain.

Geber /'dʒiːbə/ (c.721–c.815), Arab chemist; Latinized name of *Jabir ibn Hayyan*. Many works are attributed to him, but his name was used by later writers. He was familiar with many chemicals and laboratory techniques, including distillation and sublimation.

gecko /'gɛkəʊ/ ▶ noun (pl. **-os** or **-oes**) a nocturnal and often highly vocal lizard which has adhesive pads on the feet to assist in climbing on smooth surfaces. It is widespread in warm regions.
  ● Gekkonidae and related families: numerous genera and species.
  – ORIGIN late 18th cent.: from Malay dialect *geko, gekok*, imitative of its cry.

GED N. Amer. ▶ abbreviation for General Educational Development, a certificate attesting that the holder has passed examinations considered by the Department of Education as equivalent to completion of high school.

Gedankenexperiment /gə'daŋk(ə)nɛks,pɛrɪm(ə)nt/ ▶ noun another term for THOUGHT EXPERIMENT.
  – ORIGIN German.

gee[1] (also **gee whiz**) ▶ exclamation informal, chiefly N. Amer. a mild expression, typically of surprise, enthusiasm, or sympathy: *Gee, Linda looks great at fifty!*
  – ORIGIN mid 19th cent.: perhaps an abbreviation of JESUS.

gee[2] ▶ exclamation (**gee up**) a command to a horse to go faster.
  ▶ verb (**gees, geed, geeing**) [with obj.] command (a horse) to go faster.
  ■ encourage (someone) to work more quickly: *I was running around geeing people up.*
  – ORIGIN early 17th cent.: of unknown origin.

gee[3] ▶ noun US informal a thousand dollars.
  – ORIGIN 1930s: representing the initial letter of GRAND.

geebung /'dʒiːbʌŋ/ ▶ noun an Australian shrub or small tree which bears creamy-yellow flowers and small green fruit.
  ● Genus *Persoonia*, family Proteaceae.
  – ORIGIN early 19th cent.: from Dharuk.

Geechee /'giːtʃiː/ ▶ noun **1** [mass noun] an English creole spoken by blacks in parts of South Carolina and Georgia. Compare with GULLAH. **2** a speaker of this creole.
  – ORIGIN from the name of the *Ogeechee* River, in Georgia, US.

gee-gee ▶ noun Brit. informal (in children's use or in racehorse betting) a horse.
  – ORIGIN mid 19th cent. (originally a child's word): reduplication of GEE[2].

geek[1] /giːk/ ▶ noun informal, chiefly US an unfashionable or socially inept person.
  ■ [usu. with modifier] a knowledgeable and obsessive enthusiast: *a computer geek.*
  – DERIVATIVES **geeky** adjective.
  – ORIGIN late 19th cent.: from the related English dialect *geck* 'fool', of Germanic origin; related to Dutch *gek* 'mad, silly'.

geek[2] /giːk/ ▶ noun Austral. informal a look: *there was a lot I wanted to have a geek at.*
  – ORIGIN early 20th cent.: from Scots and northern English dialect *geck* 'toss the head scornfully'.

Geelong /dʒiː'lɒŋ/ a port and oil-refining centre on the south coast of Australia, in the state of Victoria; pop. 126,300 (1991).

geese plural form of GOOSE.

gee-string ▶ noun variant spelling of G-STRING.

gee whiz informal, chiefly N. Amer. ▶ exclamation another term for GEE[1].
  ▶ adjective (**gee-whiz**) [attrib.] characterized by or causing naive astonishment or wonder, in particular at new technology: *this era of gee-whiz gadgetry.*

Geez ▶ exclamation variant spelling of JEEZ.

Ge'ez /'giːɛz/ ▶ noun [mass noun] an ancient Semitic language of Ethiopia, which survives as the liturgical language of the Ethiopian Orthodox Church. It is the ancestor of the modern Ethiopian languages such as Amharic. Also called ETHIOPIC.
  – ORIGIN of Ethiopic origin.

geezer /'giːzə/ ▶ noun informal a man: *he put up an amazing fight for an old geezer.*
  – ORIGIN late 19th cent.: representing a dialect pronunciation of earlier *guiser* 'mummer'.

GEF ▶ abbreviation for Global Environment Facility.

gefilte fish /gə'fɪltə/ ▶ noun [mass noun] a dish of stewed or baked stuffed fish, or of fish cakes boiled in a fish or vegetable broth.
  – ORIGIN Yiddish, 'stuffed fish', from *filn* 'to fill' + FISH[1].

gegenschein /'geɪgən,ʃʌɪn/ ▶ noun [mass noun] Astronomy a patch of very faint nebulous light sometimes seen in the night sky opposite the position of the sun. It is thought to be the image of the sun reflected from gas and dust outside the atmosphere.
  – ORIGIN late 19th cent.: German *Gegenschein*, from *gegen* 'opposite' + *Schein* 'glow, shine'.

Gehenna /gə'hɛnə/ (in Judaism and the New Testament) hell.
  – ORIGIN via ecclesiastical Latin from Greek *geenna*, from Hebrew *gē' hinnōm* 'hell', literally 'valley of Hinnom', a place near Jerusalem where children were sacrificed to Baal (Jer. 19:5,6).

Gehrig /'gɛrɪg/, Lou (1903–41), American baseball player; full name *Henry Louis Gehrig*; known as **the Iron Horse**. He played a record 2,130 major-league games for the New York Yankees from 1925 to 1939. He died from a form of motor neuron disease now often called Lou Gehrig's disease.

Geiger /'gʌɪgə/, Hans (Johann) Wilhelm (1882–1945), German nuclear physicist. In 1908 he developed his prototype radiation counter for detecting alpha particles, later improved in collaboration with Walther Müller.

Geiger counter (also **Geiger-Müller counter**) ▶ noun a device for measuring radioactivity by detecting and counting ionizing particles.

Geikie /'giːki/, Sir Archibald (1835–1924), Scottish geologist. He specialized in Pleistocene geology, especially the geomorphological effects of glaciations and the resulting deposits.

geisha /'geɪʃə/ (also **geisha girl**) ▶ noun (pl. same or **geishas**) a Japanese hostess trained to entertain men with conversation, dance, and song.
  – ORIGIN Japanese, 'entertainer', from *gei* 'performing arts' + *sha* 'person'.

Geissler tube /'gʌɪslə/ ▶ noun a sealed tube of glass or quartz with a central constriction, filled with vapour for the production of a luminous electrical discharge.
  – ORIGIN mid 19th cent.: named after Heinrich *Geissler* (1814–79), the German mechanic and glass-blower who invented it.

Geist /gʌɪst/ ▶ noun [in sing.] the spirit of an individual or group.
  – ORIGIN German; related to GHOST.

geitonogamy /,gʌɪtə'nɒgəmi/ ▶ noun [mass noun] Botany the fertilization of a flower by pollen from another flower on the same (or a genetically identical) plant. Compare with XENOGAMY.
  – DERIVATIVES **geitonogamous** adjective.
  – ORIGIN late 19th cent.: from Greek *geitōn, geitono-* 'neighbour' + *-gamos* 'marrying'.

Gejiu /gɛ'dʒuː/ (also **Geju**) a tin-mining city in southern China, near the border with Vietnam; pop. 384,500 (1990).

gel[1] /dʒɛl/ ▶ noun [mass noun] a jelly-like substance containing a cosmetic, medicinal, or other preparation: *try rubbing some teething gel onto sore gums.*
  ■ a substance of this type used for setting the hair. ■ Chemistry a semi-solid colloidal suspension of a solid dispersed in a liquid. ■ Biochemistry a semi-rigid slab or cylinder of an organic polymer used as a medium for the separation of macromolecules.
  ▶ verb (**gelled, gelling**) [no obj.] Chemistry form into a gel: *the mixture gelled at 7 degrees Celsius.*
  ■ [with obj.] treat (the hair) with gel.
  – ORIGIN late 19th cent.: abbreviation of GELATIN.

gel[2] /dʒɛl/ (also **jell**) ▶ verb (**gelled, gelling**) [no obj.] (of jelly or a similar substance) set or become firmer: *the stew is gelling.*
  ■ (of a project or idea) take a definite shape; begin to work well: *everything seemed to gel for the magazine.* ■ (of people) relate well to one another: *it's gratifying seeing everybody gelling.*
  – ORIGIN late 19th cent.: *gel* from GEL[1]; the variant *jell* is a back-formation from JELLY.

gelada /dʒə'lɑːdə/ (also **gelada baboon**) ▶ noun (pl. same or **geladas**) a brownish baboon with a long mane and naked red rump, native to Ethiopia.
  ● *Theropithecus gelada*, family Cercopithecidae.
  – ORIGIN mid 19th cent.: from Amharic *č'ällada*.

gelati plural form of GELATO.

gelatin /'dʒɛlətɪn/ (also **gelatine** /-tiːn/) ▶ noun [mass noun] a virtually colourless and tasteless water-soluble protein prepared from collagen and used in food preparation as the basis of jellies, in photographic processes, and in glue.
  ■ (usu. **blasting gelatin**) a high explosive consisting chiefly of a gel of nitroglycerine with added cellulose nitrate.
  – ORIGIN early 19th cent.: from French *gélatine*, from Italian *gelatina*, from *gelata*, from Latin (see JELLY).

gelatinize /dʒɪ'latɪnʌɪz/ (also **-ise**) ▶ verb make or become gelatinous or jelly-like.
  ■ [with obj.] [usu. as adj. **gelatinized**] coat with gelatin: *gelatinized glass microscope slides.*
  – DERIVATIVES **gelatinization** noun.

gelatinous ▶ adjective having a jelly-like consistency: *a sweet, gelatinous drink.*
  ■ of or like the protein gelatin: *tooth enamel is coated with a gelatinous layer of protein.*
  – DERIVATIVES **gelatinously** adverb.

gelatin paper ▶ noun [mass noun] Brit. paper coated with sensitized gelatin for photographic use.

gelation[1] ▶ noun [mass noun] technical solidification by freezing.
  – ORIGIN mid 19th cent.: from Latin *gelatio(n-)*, from *gelare* 'freeze'.

gelation[2] ▶ noun [mass noun] Chemistry the process of forming a gel.

gelato /dʒə'lɑːtəʊ/ ▶ noun (pl. **gelati** /dʒə'lɑːti/) an Italian or Italian-style ice cream.
  – ORIGIN Italian.

gelcoat /'dʒɛlkəʊt/ ▶ noun the smooth, hard polyester resin surface coating of a fibreglass structure.

geld ▶ verb [with obj.] castrate (a male animal).
  ■ figurative deprive of vitality or vigour: *the English version of the book has been gelded.*
  – ORIGIN Middle English: from Old Norse *gelda*, from *geldr* 'barren'.

Gelderland /'gɛldəland/ a province of the Netherlands, on the border with Germany; capital, Arnhem. Formerly a duchy, the province was variously occupied by the Spanish, the French, and the Prussians until 1815.

gelding ▶ noun a castrated animal, especially a male horse.
  – ORIGIN late Middle English: from Old Norse *geldingr*, from *geldr* 'barren'.

gelid /'dʒɛlɪd/ ▶ adjective icy; extremely cold: *the gelid pond* | figurative *she gave a gelid reply.*
  – ORIGIN early 17th cent.: from Latin *gelidus*, from *gelu* 'frost, intense cold'.

gelignite /'dʒɛlɪgnʌɪt/ ▶ noun [mass noun] a high explosive made from a gel of nitroglycerine and nitrocellulose in a base of wood pulp and sodium or potassium nitrate, used particularly for rock-blasting.
  – ORIGIN late 19th cent.: probably from GELATIN + Latin (l)*ignis* 'wood' + -ITE[1].

Gell-Mann /gɛl'man/, Murray (b.1929), American theoretical physicist. He coined the word *quark* and proposed the concept of strangeness in quarks. Nobel Prize for Physics (1969).

gelly ▶ noun [mass noun] Brit. informal gelignite.
  – ORIGIN mid 20th cent.: abbreviation.

gelsemium /dʒɛl'siːmɪəm/ ▶ noun **1** [mass noun] a preparation of the rhizome of yellow jasmine, used in homeopathy to treat flu-like symptoms. **2** a plant of a genus that includes the yellow jasmine.
  ● Genus *Gelsemium*, family Loganiaceae.
  – ORIGIN late 19th cent.: modern Latin, from Italian *gelsomino* 'jasmine'.

Gelsenkirchen /'gɛlz(ə)n,kɪəx(ə)n, German

ˌgɛlzn'kɪrçn/ an industrial city in western Germany, in North Rhine-Westphalia north-east of Essen; pop. 293,840 (1991).

gelt /gɛlt/ ▶ noun [mass noun] informal money.
– ORIGIN early 16th cent. (originally often used to refer to the pay of a German army): from German *Geld* 'money'.

gem ▶ noun a precious or semi-precious stone, especially when cut and polished or engraved.
■ a person or thing considered to be outstandingly good or special in some respect: *this architectural gem of a palace.* ■ used in names of some brilliantly coloured hummingbirds, e.g. **mountain gem.**
▶ verb (**gemmed, gemming**) [with obj.] [usu. as adj. **gemmed**] rare decorate with or as with gems.
– DERIVATIVES **gem-like** adjective.
– ORIGIN Old English *gim*, from Latin *gemma* 'bud, jewel'; influenced in Middle English by Old French *gemme.*

Gemara /gə'mɑːrə/ ▶ noun (**the Gemara**) a rabbinical commentary on the Mishnah, forming the second part of the Talmud.
– ORIGIN from Aramaic *gĕmārā* 'completion'.

gematria /gɪ'meɪtrɪə/ ▶ noun [mass noun] a Kabbalistic method of interpreting the Hebrew scriptures by computing the numerical value of words, based on those of their constituent letters.
– ORIGIN mid 17th cent.: from Aramaic *gīmaṭrĕyā*, from Greek *gēometria* (see GEOMETRY).

Gemayel /dʒə'mʌɪɛl/, Pierre (1905–84), Lebanese political leader. A Maronite Christian, he founded the right-wing Phalange Party in 1936 and served as a Member of Parliament 1960–84. His youngest son, **Bashir** (1947–82), was assassinated while President-elect; his eldest son, **Amin** (b.1942), served as President 1982–8.

Gemeinschaft /gə'mʌɪnʃaft/ ▶ noun [mass noun] social relations between individuals, based on close personal and family ties; community. Contrasted with GESELLSCHAFT.
– ORIGIN German, from *gemein* 'common' + *-schaft* (see -SHIP).

geminal /'dʒɛmɪn(ə)l/ ▶ adjective Chemistry denoting substituent atoms or groups, especially protons, attached to the same atom in a molecule.
– DERIVATIVES **geminally** adverb.
– ORIGIN late 20th cent.: from Latin *geminus* 'twin' + -AL.

geminate Phonetics ▶ adjective /'dʒɛmɪneɪt, -nət/ consisting of identical adjacent speech sounds; doubled: *consonants motivating a short vowel were all originally geminate.*
▶ verb /'dʒɛmɪneɪt/ [with obj.] double or repeat (a speech sound).
– DERIVATIVES **gemination** noun.
– ORIGIN late Middle English: from Latin *geminatus*, past participle of *geminare* 'double, pair with', from *geminus* 'twin'.

Gemini 1 Astronomy a northern constellation (the Twins), said to represent the twins Castor and Pollux, whose names are given to its two brightest stars. See DIOSCURI.
■ [as genitive **Geminorum** /ˌdʒɛmɪ'nɔːrəm/] used with preceding letter or numeral to designate a star in this constellation: *the star Eta Geminorum.*
2 Astrology the third sign of the zodiac, which the sun enters about 21 May.
■ (**a Gemini**) (pl. **Geminis**) a person born when the sun is in this sign.
3 a series of twelve manned American orbiting spacecraft, launched in the 1960s in preparation for the Apollo programme.
– DERIVATIVES **Geminian** /dʒɛmɪ'nɪːən/ noun & adjective (only in sense 2).
– ORIGIN Latin, plural of *geminus* 'twin'.

Geminids Astronomy an annual meteor shower with a radiant in the constellation Gemini, reaching a peak about 13 December.

gemma /'dʒɛmə/ ▶ noun (pl. **gemmae** /-miː/) Biology a small cellular body or bud that can separate to form a new organism.
■ another term for CHLAMYDOSPORE.
– ORIGIN late 18th cent. (denoting a leaf bud, as distinct from a flower bud): from Latin, literally 'bud, jewel'.

gemmation /dʒɛ'meɪʃ(ə)n/ ▶ noun [mass noun] Biology asexual reproduction by the production of gemmae; budding.

– ORIGIN mid 18th cent.: from French, from *gemmer* 'to bud', from *gemme* 'bud', from Latin *gemma.*

gemmiparous /dʒɛ'mɪp(ə)rəs/ ▶ adjective Biology (of a plant or animal) reproducing by gemmation.
– ORIGIN late 18th cent.: from modern Latin *gemmiparus*, from Latin *gemma* 'bud, jewel' + *parere* 'produce, give birth to'.

gemmology (also **gemology**) ▶ noun [mass noun] the study of precious stones.
– DERIVATIVES **gemmological** adjective, **gemmologist** noun.
– ORIGIN early 19th cent.: from Latin *gemma* 'bud, jewel' + -LOGY.

gemmule /'dʒɛmjuːl/ ▶ noun Zoology a tough-coated dormant cluster of embryonic cells produced by a freshwater sponge for development in more favourable conditions.
– DERIVATIVES **gemmulation** noun.
– ORIGIN mid 19th cent.: from French, from Latin *gemmula*, diminutive of *gemma* 'bud, jewel'.

gemsbok /'xɛmzbɒk, 'xɛms-/ ▶ noun a large antelope that has a grey coat, distinctive black-and-white head markings, and long straight horns, native to SW and East Africa.
● *Oryx gazella*, family Bovidae. See also BEISA.
– ORIGIN late 18th cent.: via Afrikaans from Dutch, literally 'chamois', from *gems* 'chamois' + *bok* 'buck'.

Gem State informal name for IDAHO.

gemstone ▶ noun a precious or semi-precious stone, especially one cut, polished, and used in a piece of jewellery.

gemütlich /gə'muːtlɪx, German gə'myːtlɪç/ ▶ adjective pleasant and cheerful.
– ORIGIN German.

Gemütlichkeit /gə'muːtlɪxkʌɪt, German gə'myːtlɪçkaɪt/ ▶ noun [mass noun] geniality; friendliness.
– ORIGIN German.

Gen. ▶ abbreviation for ■ General: *Gen. Eisenhower.* ■ Genesis (in biblical references).

gen /dʒɛn/ Brit. informal ▶ noun [mass noun] information: *it gives me really authoritative gen on printing.*
▶ verb (**genned, genning**) [with obj.] (**gen someone up**) provide (someone) with information.
■ [no obj.] (**gen up on**) find out about; learn about: *I gen up on any developments with my manageress.*
– ORIGIN Second World War (originally used in the armed services): perhaps from the first syllable of *general information.*

-gen ▶ combining form **1** Chemistry denoting a substance that produces something: *oxygen* | *allergen.*
2 Botany denoting a substance or plant that is produced: *cultigen.*
– ORIGIN via French *-gène* from Greek *genēs* '-born, of a specified kind', from *gen-* (root of *gignomai* 'be born, become', *genos* 'a kind').

gena /'dʒiːnə/ ▶ noun (pl. **genae** /'dʒiːniː/) Zoology the lateral part of the head of an insect or other arthropod below the level of the eyes.
– DERIVATIVES **genal** adjective.
– ORIGIN early 19th cent.: Latin, literally 'cheek'.

gendarme /'ʒɒndɑːm, French ʒɑ̃darm/ ▶ noun **1** a paramilitary police officer in France and other French-speaking countries.
2 a rock pinnacle on a mountain, occupying and blocking an arête.
– ORIGIN mid 16th cent. (originally denoting a mounted officer in the French army): French, from *gens d'armes* 'men of arms'. Sense 1 dates from the late 18th cent.

gendarmerie /ʒɒn'dɑːməri, French ʒɑ̃darm(ə)ri/ ▶ noun a force of gendarmes.
■ the headquarters of such a force.
– ORIGIN mid 16th cent.: French (see GENDARME).

gender ▶ noun **1** Grammar (in languages such as Latin, French, and German) each of the classes (typically masculine, feminine, common, neuter) of nouns and pronouns distinguished by the different inflections which they have and which they require in words syntactically associated with them. Grammatical gender is only very loosely associated with natural distinctions of sex.
■ [mass noun] the property (in nouns and related words) of belonging to such a class: *determiners and adjectives usually agree with the noun in gender and number.*
2 [mass noun] the state of being male or female

(typically used with reference to social and cultural differences rather than biological ones): *traditional concepts of gender* | [as modifier] *gender roles.*
■ [count noun] the members of one or other sex: *differences between the genders are encouraged from an early age.*
– ORIGIN late Middle English: from Old French *gendre* (modern *genre*), based on Latin *genus* 'birth, family, nation'. The earliest meanings were 'kind, sort, genus' and 'type or class of noun, etc.' (which was also a sense of Latin *genus*).

USAGE The word **gender** has been used since the 14th century primarily as a grammatical term, referring to the classes of noun in Latin, Greek, German, and other languages designated as *masculine, feminine,* or *neuter.* It has also been used since the 14th century in the sense 'the state of being male or female', but this did not become a common standard use until the mid 20th century. Although the words **gender** and **sex** both have the sense 'the state of being male or female', they are typically used in slightly different ways: **sex** tends to refer to biological differences, while **gender** tends to refer to cultural or social ones.

gender bender ▶ noun informal a person who dresses and behaves in a way characteristic of the opposite sex.

gender changer ▶ noun an electrical adaptor which allows two male or two female connectors to be connected to each other.

gender dysphoria ▶ noun [mass noun] Medicine the condition of feeling one's emotional and psychological identity as male or female to be opposite to one's biological sex.
– DERIVATIVES **gender dysphoric** adjective & noun.

gendered ▶ adjective of, specific to, or biased towards the male or female sex: *gendered occupations.*

gene /dʒiːn/ ▶ noun Biology (in informal use) a unit of heredity which is transferred from a parent to offspring and is held to determine some characteristic of the offspring: *divorce is determined by your genes.*
■ (in technical use) a distinct sequence of nucleotides forming part of a chromosome, the order of which determines the order of monomers in a polypeptide or nucleic acid molecule which a cell (or virus) may synthesize.
– ORIGIN early 20th cent.: from German *Gen*, from *Pangen*, a supposed ultimate unit of heredity (from Greek *pan-* 'all' + *genos* 'race, kind, offspring').

genealogical /ˌdʒiːnɪə'lɒdʒɪk(ə)l, ˌdʒɛn-/ ▶ adjective of or relating to the study or tracing of lines of family descent: *genealogical research.*
– DERIVATIVES **genealogically** adverb.
– ORIGIN late 16th cent.: from French *généalogique*, via medieval Latin from Greek *genealogikos*, from *genealogia* (see GENEALOGY).

genealogical tree ▶ noun a chart like an inverted branching tree showing the lines of descent of a family or of an animal species.

genealogy /dʒiːnɪ'alədʒi, dʒɛn-/ ▶ noun (pl. **-ies**) a line of descent traced continuously from an ancestor: *the genealogies of the kings of Mercia.*
■ [mass noun] the study and tracing of lines of descent. ■ a plant's or animal's line of evolutionary development from earlier forms.
– DERIVATIVES **genealogist** noun, **genealogize** (also **-ise**) verb.
– ORIGIN Middle English: via Old French and late Latin from Greek *genealogia*, from *genea* 'race, generation' + *-logia* (see -LOGY).

gene expression ▶ noun see EXPRESSION (sense 1).

gene pool ▶ noun the stock of different genes in an interbreeding population.

genera plural form of GENUS.

general ▶ adjective **1** affecting or concerning all or most people, places, or things; widespread: *books of general interest.*
■ not specialized or limited in range of subject, application, activity, etc.: *brush up on your general knowledge.* ■ (of a rule, principle, etc.) true for all or most cases. ■ normal or usual: *it is not general practice to confirm or deny such reports.*
2 considering or including the main features or elements of something, and disregarding exceptions; overall: *they fired in the general direction of the enemy* | *a general introduction to the subject.*
3 [often in titles] chief or principal: *the Director General of the BBC* | *a general manager.*

▶ noun 1 a commander of an army, or an army officer of very high rank.
■ a high rank of officer in the army and in the US air force, above lieutenant general and below field marshal, general of the army, or general of the air force. ■ informal short for **LIEUTENANT GENERAL** or **MAJOR GENERAL**. ■ the head of a religious order organized on quasi-military lines, e.g. the Jesuits, the Dominicans, or the Salvation Army.
2 archaic (**the general**) the general public.
– PHRASES **as a general rule** in most cases. **in general 1** usually; mainly: *in general, Alexander was a peaceful, loving man.* **2** as a whole: *our understanding of culture in general and of literature in particular.*
– ORIGIN Middle English: via Old French from Latin *generalis*, from *genus, gener-* 'class, race, kind'. The noun primarily denotes a person having overall authority: the sense 'army commander' is an abbreviation of *captain general*, from French *capitaine général* 'commander-in-chief'.

General American ▶ noun [mass noun] the accent of English with which people speak in the greater part of the US, excluding New England, New York, and the South.

general anaesthetic ▶ noun [mass noun] an anaesthetic that affects the whole body and usually causes a loss of consciousness: *he had the operation under general anaesthetic.* Compare with **LOCAL ANAESTHETIC**.

general average ▶ noun [mass noun] (in maritime law) the apportionment of financial liability for the loss arising from the jettisoning of cargo among all those whose property (ship or cargo) has been preserved by the action.

general aviation ▶ noun [mass noun] civil aviation other than large-scale passenger or freight operations.

General Certificate of Education (abbrev.: **GCE**) ▶ noun an examination set especially for secondary-school pupils in England, Wales, and Northern Ireland at Advanced level (at about age 18) and, formerly, at Ordinary level (at about age 16).

General Certificate of Secondary Education (abbrev.: **GCSE**) ▶ noun an examination set especially for secondary-school pupils of about age 16 in England, Wales, and Northern Ireland.

general dealer ▶ noun (in South Africa) the keeper of a rural or township store.

general delivery ▶ noun North American term for **POSTE RESTANTE**.

general election ▶ noun the election of representatives to a legislature (in the UK, to the House of Commons) from constituencies throughout the country.

general headquarters ▶ noun [treated as sing. or pl.] the headquarters of a military commander.

generalissimo /ˌdʒɛn(ə)rəˈlɪsɪməʊ/ ▶ noun (pl. **-os**) the commander of a combined military force consisting of army, navy, and air force units.
– ORIGIN early 17th cent.: Italian, 'having greatest authority', superlative of *generale* (see **GENERAL**).

generalist ▶ noun a person competent in several different fields or activities.
▶ adjective able to carry out a range of activities, or adapt to different situations: *a generalist doctor.*

generality ▶ noun (pl. **-ies**) **1** a statement or principle having general rather than specific validity or force: *he confined his remarks to generalities.*
■ [mass noun] the quality or state of being general: *policy should be formulated at an appropriate level of generality.*
2 (**the generality**) the majority: *his service was better than that offered by the generality of doctors.*
– ORIGIN late Middle English: from Old French *generalite*, from late Latin *generalitas*, from *generalis* (see **GENERAL**).

generalization (also **-isation**) ▶ noun a general statement or concept obtained by inference from specific cases: *he was making sweeping generalizations.*
■ [mass noun] the action of generalizing: *such anecdotes cannot be a basis for generalization.*

generalize (also **-ise**) ▶ verb **1** [no obj.] make general or broad statements: *it is not easy to generalize about the poor.*
■ make or become more widely or generally applicable: [with obj.] *most of what we have observed in this field can be generalized to other fields* | [no obj.] *many of the results generalize to multibody structures.*
2 [with obj.] make (something) more widespread or common: *attempts to generalize an elite education.*
■ make for general use: [as adj. **generalized**] *a generalized payroll package.* ■ [as adj. **generalized**] Medicine (of a disease) affecting much or all of the body; not localized: *generalized myalgia.*
– DERIVATIVES **generalizability** noun, **generalizable** adjective, **generalizer** noun.
– ORIGIN Middle English (in the sense 'reduce to a general statement'): from **GENERAL** + **-IZE**.

generally ▶ adverb **1** [sentence adverb] in most cases; usually: *the term of a lease is generally 99 years.*
2 in general terms; without regard to particulars or exceptions: *a decade when France was moving generally to the left.*
3 widely: *the best scheme is generally reckoned to be the Canadian one.*

general meeting ▶ noun a meeting open to all members of an organization.

general of the air force ▶ noun the highest rank of officer in the US air force, above general.

general of the army ▶ noun the highest rank of officer in the US army, above general.

general paralysis of the insane ▶ noun see **GPI**.

general practitioner (abbrev.: **GP**) ▶ noun a doctor based in the community who treats patients with minor or chronic illnesses and refers those with serious conditions to a hospital.
– DERIVATIVES **general practice** noun.

general purpose ▶ adjective having a range of potential uses or functions; not specialized in design: *a general purpose detergent.*

generalship ▶ noun [mass noun] the skill or practice of exercising military command.

general staff ▶ noun [treated as sing. or pl.] the staff assisting a military commander in planning and executing operations.

general strike ▶ noun a strike of workers in all or most industries.
■ (**General Strike**) the strike of May 1926 in the UK, called by the Trades Union Congress in support of the mineworkers.

General Synod ▶ noun the highest governing body of the Church of England, an elected assembly of three houses (bishops, clergy, and laity).

General Thanksgiving ▶ noun a form of thanksgiving in the Book of Common Prayer or the Alternative Service Book.

general theory of relativity ▶ noun see **RELATIVITY** (sense 2).

generate ▶ verb [with obj.] cause (something, especially an emotion or situation) to arise or come about: *changes which are likely to generate controversy* | *the income generated by the sale of council houses.*
■ produce (energy, especially electricity). ■ produce (a set or sequence of items) by performing specified mathematical or logical operations on an initial set. ■ Linguistics produce (a sentence or other unit, especially a well-formed one) by the application of a finite set of rules to lexical or other linguistic input. ■ Mathematics form (a line, surface, or solid) by notionally moving a point, line, or surface.
– DERIVATIVES **generable** adjective.
– ORIGIN early 16th cent. (in the sense 'beget, procreate'): from Latin *generat-* 'created', from the verb *generare*, from *genus, gener-* 'stock, race'.

generation ▶ noun **1** all of the people born and living at about the same time, regarded collectively: *one of his generation's finest songwriters.*
■ the average period, generally considered to be about thirty years, in which children grow up, become adults, and have children of their own: *the books are printed on acid-neutral paper to last for generations.* ■ a set of members of a family regarded as a single step or stage in descent: [as modifier, in combination] *a third-generation Canadian.* ■ a single stage in the development of a type of product: *a new generation of rear-engined sports cars.*
2 [mass noun] the production of something: *methods of electricity generation* | *the generation of wealth.*
■ the propagation of living organisms; procreation.
– DERIVATIVES **generational** adjective.
– ORIGIN Middle English: via Old French from Latin *generatio(n-)*, from the verb *generare* (see **GENERATE**).

generation gap ▶ noun (usu. **the generation gap**) differences of outlook or opinion between people of different generations.

Generation X ▶ noun the generation born after that of the baby boomers (roughly from the early 1960s to mid 1970s), typically perceived to be disaffected and directionless.
– DERIVATIVES **Generation Xer** noun.

generative /ˈdʒɛn(ə)rətɪv/ ▶ adjective of or relating to reproduction.
■ able to produce: *the generative power of the life force.* ■ denoting an approach to any field of linguistics that involves applying a finite set of rules to linguistic input in order to produce all and only the well-formed items of a language: *generative phonology.*
– ORIGIN late Middle English: from late Latin *generativus*, from *generare* 'beget' (see **GENERATE**).

generative grammar ▶ noun [mass noun] a type of grammar which describes a language in terms of a set of logical rules formulated so as to be capable of generating the infinite number of possible sentences of that language and providing them with the correct structural description.
■ [count noun] a set of rules of this kind.

generator ▶ noun a thing that generates something, in particular:
■ an apparatus for producing gas, steam, or another product. ■ a dynamo or similar machine for converting mechanical energy into electricity. ■ a company or organization which generates electricity for public use. ■ [with modifier] Computing a routine that constructs other routines or subroutines using given parameters, for specific applications: *a report generator.* ■ Mathematics a point, line, or surface regarded as moving and so notionally forming a line, surface, or solid.

generatrix /ˌdʒɛnəˈreɪtrɪks/ ▶ noun (pl. **generatrices** /-trɪsiːz/) Mathematics another term for **GENERATOR**.
– ORIGIN mid 19th cent.: from Latin (feminine).

generic /dʒɪˈnɛrɪk/ ▶ adjective **1** characteristic of or relating to a class or group of things; not specific: *chèvre is a generic term for all goats' milk cheese.*
■ (of goods, especially medicinal drugs) having no brand name; not protected by a registered trade mark.
2 Biology of or relating to a genus.
– DERIVATIVES **generically** adverb.
– ORIGIN late 17th cent.: from French *générique*, from Latin *genus, gener-* 'stock, race'.

generosity ▶ noun [mass noun] the quality of being kind and generous: *I was overwhelmed by the generosity of friends and neighbours.*
■ the quality or fact of being plentiful or large: *diners certainly cannot complain about the generosity of portions.*
– ORIGIN late Middle English (denoting nobility of birth): from Latin *generositas*, from *generosus* 'magnanimous' (see **GENEROUS**). Current senses date from the 17th cent.

generous ▶ adjective (of a person) showing a readiness to give more of something, especially money, than is strictly necessary or expected: *she was generous with her money.*
■ showing kindness towards others: *it was generous of them to ask her along.* ■ (of a thing) larger or more plentiful than is usual or necessary: *a generous sprinkle of pepper.*
– DERIVATIVES **generously** adverb, **generousness** noun.
– ORIGIN late 16th cent.: via Old French from Latin *generosus* 'noble, magnanimous', from *genus, gener-* 'stock, race'. The original sense was 'of noble birth', hence 'characteristic of noble birth, courageous, magnanimous, not mean' (a sense already present in Latin).

Genesis /ˈdʒɛnɪsɪs/ the first book of the Bible, which includes the stories of the creation of the world, Noah's Ark, the Tower of Babel, and the patriarchs Abraham, Isaac, Jacob, and Joseph.
– ORIGIN late Old English, via Latin from Greek, 'generation, creation, nativity, horoscope', from the base of *gignesthai* 'be born or produced'. The name was given to the first book of the Old Testament in the Greek translation (the Septuagint), hence in the Latin translation (the Vulgate).

genesis /ˈdʒɛnɪsɪs/ ▶ noun [in sing.] the origin or mode of formation of something: *this tale had its genesis in fireside stories.*
– ORIGIN early 17th cent.: from Greek (see **GENESIS**).

Genet /ʒəˈneɪ, French ʒənɛ/, Jean (1910–86), French novelist, poet, and dramatist. Much of his work portrayed life in the criminal and homosexual underworlds, of which he was a part. Notable works: *Our Lady of the Flowers* (novel, 1944), *The Thief's*

Journal (autobiography, 1949), and *The Maids* (play, 1947).

genet /ˈdʒɛnɪt/ ▶ noun a nocturnal, catlike mammal of the civet family with short legs, spotted fur, and a long bushy ringed tail, found in Africa, SW Europe, and Arabia.
● Genus *Genetta*, family Viverridae: several species, in particular the **common** (or **small-spotted**) **genet** (*G. genetta*).
■[mass noun] the fur of the genet.
– ORIGIN Middle English (used in the plural meaning 'genet-skins'): from Old French *genete*, probably via Catalan, Portuguese, or Spanish from Arabic *jarnaiṭ*.

gene therapy ▶ noun [mass noun] the introduction of normal genes into cells in place of missing or defective ones in order to correct genetic disorders. The technique is still experimental.

genetic /dʒɪˈnɛtɪk/ ▶ adjective **1** of or relating to genes or heredity: *all the cells in the body contain the same genetic information.*
■of or relating to genetics: *an attempt to control mosquitoes by genetic techniques.*
2 of or relating to origin; arising from a common origin: *the genetic relations between languages.*
– DERIVATIVES **genetical** adjective, **genetically** adverb.
– ORIGIN mid 19th cent. (in sense 2): from **GENESIS**, on the pattern of pairs such as *antithesis, antithetic.*

genetic code ▶ noun [mass noun] the means by which DNA and RNA molecules carry genetic information in living cells. See **TRIPLET CODE**.

genetic counselling ▶ noun [mass noun] the giving of advice to prospective parents concerning the chances of genetic disorders in a future child.

genetic drift ▶ noun [mass noun] Biology variation in the relative frequency of different genotypes in a small population, owing to the chance disappearance of particular genes as individuals die or do not reproduce.

genetic engineering ▶ noun [mass noun] the deliberate modification of the characteristics of an organism by manipulating its genetic material.

genetic fingerprinting (also **genetic profiling**) ▶ noun [mass noun] the analysis of DNA from samples of body tissues or fluids in order to identify individuals.

genetic load ▶ noun [mass noun] Biology the presence of unfavourable genetic material in the genes of a population.

genetics ▶ plural noun [treated as sing.] the study of heredity and the variation of inherited characteristics.
■[treated as sing. or pl.] the genetic properties or features of an organism, characteristic, etc.: *the effects of family genetics on the choice of career.*
– DERIVATIVES **geneticist** noun.

Geneva /dʒɪˈniːvə/ a city in SW Switzerland, on Lake Geneva; pop. 167,200 (1990). It is the headquarters of international bodies such as the Red Cross, various organizations of the United Nations, and the World Health Organization. French name **GENÈVE**.

Geneva, Lake a lake in SW central Europe, between the Jura mountains and the Alps. Its southern shore forms part of the border between France and Switzerland. French name **LAC LÉMAN**.

Geneva bands ▶ plural noun two white cloth strips attached to the collar of some Protestants' clerical dress.
– ORIGIN late 19th cent.: from the place name **GENEVA**, where they were originally worn by Calvinists.

Geneva Bible ▶ noun an English translation of the Bible published in 1560 by Protestant scholars working in Europe.

Geneva Convention an international agreement first made at Geneva in 1864 and later revised, governing the status and treatment of captured and wounded military personnel and civilians in wartime.

Geneva Protocol any of various protocols drawn up in Geneva, especially that of 1925 limiting chemical and bacteriological warfare.

Genève /ʒənɛv/ French name for **GENEVA**.

genever /dʒɪˈniːvə/ (also poetic/literary **geneva**) ▶ noun [mass noun] Dutch gin.
– ORIGIN early 18th cent.: from Dutch, from Old

French *genevre*, from an alteration of Latin *juniperus* (gin being flavoured with juniper berries). The variant spelling is due to association with **GENEVA**.

Genghis Khan /ˌɡɛŋɡɪs ˈkɑːn, ˌdʒɛŋ-/ (1162–1227), founder of the Mongol empire; born *Temujin*. He took the name Genghis Khan ('ruler of all') in 1206 after uniting the nomadic Mongol tribes, and by the time of his death his empire extended from China to the Black Sea.

genial[1] /ˈdʒiːnɪəl/ ▶ adjective friendly and cheerful: *a big, genial man of 45* | *the meeting proved surprisingly genial.*
■(especially of air or climate) pleasantly mild and warm.
– DERIVATIVES **geniality** noun, **genially** adverb.
– ORIGIN mid 16th cent.: from Latin *genialis* 'nuptial, productive', from *genius* (see **GENIUS**). The Latin sense was adopted into English; hence the senses 'mild and conducive to growth' (mid 17th cent.), later 'cheerful, kindly' (mid 18th cent.).

genial[2] /dʒɪˈniːəl/ ▶ adjective Anatomy rare, of or relating to the chin.
– ORIGIN mid 19th cent.: from Greek *geneion* 'chin' (from *genus* 'jaw') + **-AL**.

genic /ˈdʒiːnɪk, ˈdʒɛn-/ ▶ adjective [attrib.] Biology of or relating to genes: *a genic mutation.*

-genic ▶ combining form **1** producing: *carcinogenic.*
■produced by: *iatrogenic.*
2 well suited to: *mediagenic.* [ORIGIN: on the pattern of words such as (*photo*)*genic.*]
– DERIVATIVES **-genically** suffix forming corresponding adverbs.
– ORIGIN from **-GEN** + **-IC**.

geniculate /dʒɪˈnɪkjʊlət/ ▶ adjective Anatomy bent at a sharp angle.
– ORIGIN mid 17th cent.: from Latin *geniculatus*, from *geniculum* 'small knee, joint (of a plant)'.

geniculate body (also **geniculate nucleus**) ▶ noun Anatomy either of two protuberances on the inferior surface of the thalamus which relay auditory and visual impulses respectively to the cerebral cortex.

genie ▶ noun (pl. **genii** /ˈdʒiːnɪʌɪ/) a spirit of Arabian folklore, as traditionally depicted imprisoned within a bottle or oil lamp, and capable of granting wishes when summoned. Compare with **JINN**.
– ORIGIN mid 17th cent. (denoting a guardian or protective spirit): from French *génie*, from Latin *genius* (see **GENIUS**). *Génie* was adopted in the current sense by the 18th-cent. French translators of *The Arabian Nights' Entertainments*, because of its resemblance in form and sense to Arabic *jinnī* 'jinnee'.

genii plural form of **GENIE, GENIUS**.

genip /ɡɛˈnɪp/ ▶ noun **1** the edible fruit of a tropical American tree.
2 (also **genipap tree**) either of two tropical American trees which yield this fruit:
● (also **guinep**) a large spreading tree (*Melicoccus bijugatus*, family Sapindaceae). ● another term for **GENIPAPO**.
– ORIGIN mid 18th cent.: from American Spanish *quenepo* 'guinep tree', *quenepa*, denoting the fruit.

genipapo /ˌdʒɛnɪˈpapəʊ/ (also **genipap** /ˈdʒɛnɪpap/) ▶ noun a tropical American tree which yields useful timber. Its fruit has a jelly-like pulp which is used for flavouring drinks and to make a black dye. Also called **GENIP**.
● *Genipa americana*, family Rubiaceae.
■[mass noun] a drink, flavouring, or dye made from this fruit.
– ORIGIN early 17th cent.: from Portuguese *jenipapo*, from Tupi.

genista /dʒɪˈnɪstə, dʒɛ-/ ▶ noun an almost leafless Eurasian shrub of the pea family, which bears a profusion of yellow flowers.
● Genus *Genista*, family Leguminosae: many species, including dyer's greenweed and several kinds of broom.
– ORIGIN modern Latin, from Latin, 'broom plant'.

genital ▶ adjective of or relating to the human or animal reproductive organs: *the genital area.*
■Psychoanalysis (in Freudian theory) relating to or denoting the final stage of psychosexual development reached in adulthood.
▶ noun (**genitals**) a person or animal's external organs of reproduction.
– ORIGIN late Middle English: from Old French, or from Latin *genitalis*, from *genitus*, past participle of *gignere* 'beget'.

genitalia /ˌdʒɛnɪˈteɪlɪə/ ▶ plural noun formal or technical the genitals.
– ORIGIN late 19th cent.: from Latin, neuter plural of *genitalis* (see **GENITAL**).

genitive /ˈdʒɛnɪtɪv/ Grammar ▶ adjective relating to or denoting a case of nouns and pronouns (and words in grammatical agreement with them) indicating possession or close association.
▶ noun a word in the genitive case.
■(the genitive) the genitive case.
– DERIVATIVES **genitival** /-ˈtʌɪv(ə)l/ adjective, **genitivally** adverb.
– ORIGIN late Middle English: from Old French *genitif, -ive* or Latin *genitivus (casus)* '(case) of production or origin', from *gignere* 'beget'.

genitor /ˈdʒɛnɪtə/ ▶ noun Anthropology a person's biological father. Often contrasted with **PATER**.
– ORIGIN late Middle English (in the sense 'father'): from Old French *geniteur* or Latin *genitor*, from the root of *gignere* 'beget'. The current sense dates from the mid 20th cent.

genito-urinary /ˌdʒɛnɪtəʊˈjʊərɪn(ə)ri/ ▶ adjective [attrib.] chiefly Medicine of or relating to the genital and urinary organs.

geniture /ˈdʒɛnɪtʃə/ ▶ noun archaic a person's birth or parentage.
– ORIGIN late Middle English: from Old French *geniture* or Latin *genitura*, from the root of *gignere* 'beget'.

genius ▶ noun (pl. **geniuses**) **1** [mass noun] exceptional intellectual or creative power or other natural ability: *she was a teacher of genius* | [in sing.] *Gardner had a real genius for tapping wealth.*
2 a person who is exceptionally intelligent or able in some respect.
3 (pl. **genii** /-nʌɪ/) (in some mythologies) a tutelary spirit associated with a person, place, or institution.
■a person regarded as exerting a powerful influence over another for good or evil: *he sees Adams as the man's evil genius.*
4 [mass noun] the prevalent character or spirit of something such as a nation or age: *Boucher's paintings did not suit the austere genius of neoclassicism.*
– ORIGIN late Middle English: from Latin, 'attendant spirit present from one's birth, innate ability or inclination', from the root of *gignere* 'beget'. The original sense 'tutelary spirit attendant on a person' gave rise to a sense 'a person's characteristic disposition' (late 16th cent.), which led to a sense 'a person's natural ability', and finally 'exceptional natural ability' (mid 17th cent.).

genius loci /ˈləʊsʌɪ, ˈlɒkiː/ ▶ noun [in sing.] the prevailing character or atmosphere of a place.
■the presiding god or spirit of a place.
– ORIGIN Latin, literally 'spirit of the place'.

Genizah /ɡɛˈniːzə/ ▶ noun a room attached to an ancient synagogue in Cairo, where vast quantities of fragments of biblical and other Jewish manuscripts were discovered in 1896–8.
– ORIGIN from Hebrew *gĕnīzāh*, literally 'hiding place', from *gānaz* 'hide, set aside'.

genlock /ˈdʒɛnlɒk/ ▶ noun a device for maintaining synchronization between two different video signals, or between a video signal and a computer or audio signal, enabling video images and computer graphics to be mixed.
▶ verb [no obj.] maintain synchronization between two signals using the genlock technique.
– ORIGIN 1960s: from **GENERATOR** + the verb **LOCK**[1].

Genoa /ˈdʒɛnəʊə/ a seaport on the NW coast of Italy, capital of Liguria region; pop. 701,000 (1990). It was the birthplace of Christopher Columbus. Italian name **GENOVA**.
– DERIVATIVES **Genoese** /ˌdʒɛnəʊˈiːz/ adjective & noun.

genoa /ˈdʒɛnəʊə, dʒɛˈnəʊə/ ▶ noun **1** (also **genoa jib**) Sailing a large jib or foresail whose foot extends aft of the mast, used especially on racing yachts.
2 (also **Genoa cake**) a rich fruit cake with almonds on top.
– ORIGIN late 19th cent.: so named because of association with the city of **GENOA**.

genocide /ˈdʒɛnəsʌɪd/ ▶ noun [mass noun] the deliberate killing of a large group of people, especially those of a particular race or nation.
– DERIVATIVES **genocidal** adjective.
– ORIGIN 1940s: from Greek *genos* 'race' + **-CIDE**.

genome /ˈdʒiːnəʊm/ ▶ noun [mass noun] Biology the haploid set of chromosomes in a gamete or micro-

organism, or in each cell of a multicellular organism.
■the complete set of genes or genetic material present in a cell or organism.
– DERIVATIVES **genomic** adjective.
– ORIGIN 1930s: blend of **GENE** and **CHROMOSOME**.

genotype /ˈdʒɛnətʌɪp, ˈdʒiːn-/ ▶ **noun** Biology the genetic constitution of an individual organism. Often contrasted with **PHENOTYPE**.
– DERIVATIVES **genotypic** /-ˈtɪpɪk/ adjective.
– ORIGIN early 20th cent.: from German *Genotypus*, from Greek *genos* 'race, offspring' + *-tupos* 'type'.

-genous ▶ **combining form 1** producing; inducing: *erogenous*.
2 originating in: *endogenous*.
– ORIGIN from **-GEN** + **-OUS**.

Genova /ˈdʒɛnova/ Italian name for **GENOA**.

genre /ˈʒɒ̃rə, ˈ(d)ʒɒnrə/ ▶ **noun** a category of artistic composition, as in music or literature, characterized by similarities in form, style, or subject matter.
– ORIGIN early 19th cent.: French, literally 'a kind' (see **GENDER**).

genre painting ▶ **noun** [mass noun] a style of painting depicting scenes from ordinary life, especially domestic situations. Genre painting is associated particularly with 17th-century Dutch and Flemish artists.
– DERIVATIVES **genre painter** noun.

gens /dʒɛnz/ ▶ **noun** (pl. **gentes** /-tiːz, -teɪz/) **1** a group of families in ancient Rome who shared a name and claimed a common origin.
2 Anthropology a group of people who are related through their male ancestors.
– ORIGIN Latin, from the root of *gignere* 'beget'.

Gent /xɛnt/ Flemish name for **GHENT**.

gent ▶ **noun** informal a gentleman.
■(**gents**) Brit. (in shop titles) men's: *a gents hairdressing shop*. ■ (**the Gents**) Brit. a men's public toilet.
– ORIGIN mid 16th cent.: originally a standard written abbreviation; a colloquial usage since the early 19th cent.

gentamicin /ˌdʒɛntəˈmʌɪsɪn/ ▶ **noun** [mass noun] a broad-spectrum antibiotic used chiefly for severe systemic infections.
● This antibiotic is derived from bacteria of the genus *Micromonospora*.
– ORIGIN mid 20th cent.: from *genta-* (of unknown origin) + *-micin* (alteration of **-MYCIN**).

genteel ▶ **adjective** polite, refined, or respectable, especially in an affected or ostentatious way so as to appear upper class.
– DERIVATIVES **genteelly** adverb, **genteelness** noun.
– ORIGIN late 16th cent. (in the sense 'fashionable, stylish'): from French *gentil* 'well-born'. From the 17th cent. to the 19th cent. the word was used in such senses as 'of good social position', 'having the manners of a well-born person', 'well bred'. The ironic or derogatory implication dates from the 19th cent.

genteelism ▶ **noun** a word or expression used because it is thought to be socially more acceptable than the everyday word: *in German usage 'sister' was the accepted genteelism for 'mistress'*.

gentes plural form of **GENS**.

gentian /ˈdʒɛnʃ(ə)n/ ▶ **noun** a plant of temperate and mountainous regions, which typically has violet or vivid blue trumpet-shaped flowers. Many kinds are cultivated as ornamentals, especially as arctic-alpines, and some are of medicinal use.
● Family Gentianaceae: genera *Gentiana* and *Gentianella*.
■[mass noun] a tonic liquor formerly extracted from the root of the gentian.
– ORIGIN late Middle English: from Latin *gentiana*, according to Pliny named after *Gentius*, king of Illyria, who is said to have discovered the medicinal properties of a common species.

gentian violet ▶ **noun** [mass noun] a synthetic violet dye derived from rosaniline, used as an antiseptic.

gentile /ˈdʒɛntʌɪl/ ▶ **adjective 1** (**Gentile**) not Jewish: *Christianity spread from Jewish into Gentile cultures*.
■(of a person) not belonging to one's own religious community. ■ historical non-Mormon.
2 chiefly Anthropology of, relating to, or indicating a nation or clan, especially a gens.
▶ **noun** (**Gentile**) a person who is not Jewish.
– ORIGIN late Middle English: from Latin *gentilis* 'of a family or nation, of the same clan' (used in the Vulgate to refer to non-Jews), from *gens, gent-* 'family, race', from the root of *gignere* 'beget'.

Gentile da Fabriano /dʒɛnˌtiːleɪ da ˌfabrɪˈɑːnəʊ/ (*c.*1370–1427), Italian painter. His major surviving work is the altarpiece *The Adoration of the Magi* (1423), most others having been destroyed.

gentility /dʒɛnˈtɪlɪti/ ▶ **noun** [mass noun] social superiority as demonstrated by genteel manners, behaviour, or appearances: *her grandmother's pretensions to gentility*.
■genteel manners, behaviour, or appearances.
– ORIGIN Middle English (in the sense 'honourable birth'): from Old French *gentilite*, from *gentil* (see **GENTLE**[1]).

gentle[1] ▶ **adjective** (**gentler**, **gentlest**) **1** (of a person) mild in temperament or behaviour; kind or tender: *he was a gentle, sensitive man*.
■archaic (of a person) noble or having the qualities attributed to noble birth; courteous; chivalrous.
2 moderate in action, effect, or degree; not harsh or severe: *a little gentle persuasion | a gentle breeze*.
■(of a slope) gradual: *a gentle embankment*.
▶ **verb** make or become gentle; calm or pacify: [no obj.] *Cobb's tone gentled a little*.
■[with obj.] touch gently: *her lips were gentling his cheek*. ■ [with obj.] make (an animal) docile by gentle handling: *a bird that has been gentled enough to sit on the hand*.
– DERIVATIVES **gentleness** noun, **gently** adverb.
– ORIGIN Middle English: from Old French *gentil* 'high-born, noble', from Latin *gentilis* 'of the same clan' (see **GENTILE**). The original sense was 'nobly born', hence 'courteous, chivalrous', later 'mild, moderate in action or disposition' (mid 16th cent.).

gentle[2] ▶ **noun** Fishing a maggot, especially the larva of a blowfly, used as bait.
– ORIGIN late 16th cent. : probably from an obsolete sense of the adjective, 'soft, pliant'.

gentle breeze ▶ **noun** a light wind of force 3 on the Beaufort scale (7–10 knots or 13–19 kph).

gentlefolk ▶ **plural noun** archaic people of noble birth or good social position.

gentleman ▶ **noun** (pl. **-men**) **1** a chivalrous, courteous, or honourable man: *he behaved throughout like a perfect gentleman*.
■a man of good social position, especially one of wealth and leisure. ■ a man of noble birth attached to a royal household: *a Gentleman of the Bedchamber*.
2 a polite or formal way of referring to a man: *opposite her an old gentleman sat reading*.
■(**gentlemen**) used as a polite form of address to a group of men: *'Can I help you, gentlemen?'* ■ used as a courteous designation for a male fellow member of the House of Commons or the House of Representatives: *the Right Honourable Gentleman opposite*.
– ORIGIN Middle English (in the sense 'man of noble birth'): from **GENTLE**[1] + **MAN**, translating Old French *gentilz hom*. In later use the term denoted a man of a good family (especially one entitled to a coat of arms) but not of the nobility.

gentleman-at-arms ▶ **noun** one of the bodyguards of the British monarch on ceremonial occasions.

gentleman farmer ▶ **noun** (pl. **gentlemen farmers**) a country gentleman who has a farm as part of his estate.

gentlemanly ▶ **adjective** (of a man) chivalrous, courteous, or honourable: *gentlemanly conduct*.
■befitting a gentleman: *literature has never been a gentlemanly profession*.
– DERIVATIVES **gentlemanliness** noun.

gentleman's agreement (also **gentlemen's agreement**) ▶ **noun** an arrangement or understanding which is based upon the trust of both or all parties, rather than being legally binding.

gentleman's gentleman ▶ **noun** a valet.

Gentleman's Relish ▶ **noun** [mass noun] Brit. trademark a highly seasoned anchovy paste.

Gentleman Usher of the Black Rod ▶ **noun** see **BLACK ROD**.

gentlewoman ▶ **noun** (pl. **-women**) archaic a woman of noble birth or good social standing.

gentoo /dʒɛnˈtuː/ (also **gentoo penguin**) ▶ **noun** a tall penguin with a white triangular patch above the eye, breeding on subantarctic islands.
● *Pygoscelis papua*, family Spheniscidae.
– ORIGIN mid 19th cent.: perhaps from Anglo-Indian *Gentoo* 'a Hindu', from Portuguese *gentio* 'gentile'.

gentrify ▶ **verb** (**-ies**, **-ied**) [with obj.] renovate and improve (a house or district) so that it conforms to middle-class taste.
■[usu. as adj. **gentrified**] make (someone or their way of life) more genteel: *a gentrified Irish American*.
– DERIVATIVES **gentrification** noun, **gentrifier** noun.

gentry /ˈdʒɛntri/ ▶ **noun** [mass noun] (often **the gentry**) people of good social position, specifically the class of people next below the nobility in position and birth: *a member of the landed gentry*.
■[with adj.] derogatory or humorous people of a specified kind: *radar devices beyond the comprehension of all but the bespectacled gentry who invented them*.
– ORIGIN late Middle English (in the sense 'superiority of birth or rank'): from Anglo-Norman French *genterie*, based on *gentil* (see **GENTLE**[1]).

genu /ˈdʒɛnjuː/ ▶ **noun** (pl. **genua**) Anatomy the knee.
■Anatomy & Biology a part of certain structures resembling a knee, in particular a bend in the corpus callosum of mammals.
– ORIGIN mid 19th cent.: from Latin.

genuflect /ˈdʒɛnjʊflɛkt/ ▶ **verb** [no obj.] lower one's body briefly by bending one knee to the ground, typically in worship or as a sign of respect: *she genuflected and crossed herself*.
■[with adverbial] figurative show deference or servility: *politicians had to genuflect to the far left to advance their careers*.
– DERIVATIVES **genuflection** (also **genuflexion**) noun, **genuflector** noun.
– ORIGIN mid 17th cent. (in the sense 'bend (the knee)'): from ecclesiastical Latin *genuflectere*, from Latin *genu* 'knee' + *flectere* 'to bend'.

genuine ▶ **adjective** truly what something is said to be; authentic: *each book is bound in genuine leather*.
■(of a person, emotion, or action) sincere: *she had no doubts as to whether Tom was genuine | a genuine attempt to delegate authority*.
– DERIVATIVES **genuinely** adverb, **genuineness** noun.
– ORIGIN late 16th cent. (in the sense 'natural or proper'): from Latin *genuinus*, from *genu* 'knee' (with reference to the Roman custom of a father acknowledging paternity of a newborn child by placing it on his knee); later associated with *genus* 'birth, race, stock'.

genus /ˈdʒiːnəs, ˈdʒɛnəs/ ▶ **noun** (pl. **genera** /ˈdʒɛn(ə)rə/) Biology a grouping of organisms having common characteristics distinct from those of other such groupings. The genus is a principal taxonomic category that ranks above species and below family, and is denoted by a capitalized Latin name, e.g. *Leo*.
■(in philosophical and general use) a class of things which have common characteristics and which can be divided into subordinate kinds.
– ORIGIN mid 16th cent.: from Latin, 'birth, race, stock'.

-geny ▶ **combining form** denoting the mode by which something develops or is produced: *orogeny | organogeny*.
– ORIGIN related to French *-génie*; both forms derive from Greek *-geneia*, from *gen-* (root of *gignomai* 'be born, become' and *genos* 'a kind').

Geo. dated ▶ **abbreviation for** George.

geo /gjəʊ, ˈdʒiːəʊ/ ▶ **noun** a long, narrow, steep-sided cleft formed by erosion in coastal cliffs.
– ORIGIN early 17th cent. (originally Orkney and Shetland dialect): from Old Norse *gjá*.

geo- /ˈdʒiːəʊ/ ▶ **combining form** of or relating to the earth: *geocentric | geochemistry*.
– ORIGIN from Greek *gē* 'earth'.

geobotany ▶ **noun** another term for **PHYTOGEOGRAPHY**.
– DERIVATIVES **geobotanical** adjective, **geobotanist** noun.

geocentric ▶ **adjective** having or representing the earth as the centre, as in former astronomical systems. Compare with **HELIOCENTRIC**.
■Astronomy measured from or considered in relation to the centre of the earth.
– DERIVATIVES **geocentrically** adverb, **geocentrism** noun.

geocentric latitude ▶ **noun** the latitude at which a planet would appear if viewed from the centre of the earth.

geochemistry ▶ **noun** [mass noun] the study of the

chemical composition of the earth and its rocks and minerals.
– DERIVATIVES **geochemical** adjective, **geochemist** noun.

geochronology ▶ noun [mass noun] the branch of geology concerned with the dating of rock formations and geological events.
– DERIVATIVES **geochronological** adjective, **geochronologist** noun.

geochronometric /ˌdʒiːə(ʊ)ˌkrɒnəˈmɛtrɪk/ ▶ adjective of or relating to geochronological measurement.
– DERIVATIVES **geochronometry** noun.

geode /ˈdʒiːəʊd/ ▶ noun a small cavity in rock lined with crystals or other mineral matter.
■ a rock containing such a cavity.
– DERIVATIVES **geodic** /dʒiːˈɒdɪk/ adjective.
– ORIGIN late 17th cent.: via Latin from Greek geōdēs 'earthy', from gē 'earth'.

geodesic /ˌdʒiːə(ʊ)ˈdɛsɪk, -ˈdiːsɪk/ ▶ adjective **1** of, relating to, or denoting the shortest possible line between two points on a sphere or other curved surface.
■ (of a dome or other structure) constructed from struts which follow geodesic lines and typically form an open framework of triangles and polygons.
2 another term for **GEODETIC**.
▶ noun a geodesic line or structure.

geodesy /dʒiːˈɒdɪsi/ ▶ noun [mass noun] the branch of mathematics dealing with the shape and area of the earth or large portions of it.
– DERIVATIVES **geodesist** noun.
– ORIGIN late 16th cent.: from modern Latin geodaesia, from Greek geōdaisia, from gē 'earth' + daiein 'to divide'.

geodetic /ˌdʒiːə(ʊ)ˈdɛtɪk/ ▶ adjective of or relating to geodesy, especially as applied to land surveying.
– ORIGIN late 17th cent.: from Greek geōdaitēs 'land surveyor', from geōdaisia (see **GEODESY**).

geoduck /ˈdʒiːəʊdʌk/ ▶ noun a giant mud-burrowing bivalve mollusc occurring on the west coast of North America, where it is collected for food. Its shell valves are not large enough to enclose its body and very long siphon.
● *Panopea generosa*, family Hyatellidae.
– ORIGIN late 19th cent.: from Chinook Jargon.

Geoffrey of Monmouth (c.1100–c.1154), Welsh chronicler. His *Historia Regum Britanniae* (c.1139; first printed in 1508), an account of the kings of Britain, was a major source for English literature but is now thought to contain little historical fact.

geographical ▶ adjective of or relating to geography.
– DERIVATIVES **geographic** adjective, **geographically** adverb.
– ORIGIN mid 16th cent.: from French géographique or late Latin geographicus, from Greek geōgraphikos, from geōgraphos 'geographer', from gē 'earth' + graphein 'write, draw').

geographical latitude ▶ noun the angle made with the plane of the equator by a perpendicular to the earth's surface at any point.

geographical mile ▶ noun a distance equal to one minute of longitude or latitude at the equator (about 1,850 metres).

geography ▶ noun [mass noun] the study of the physical features of the earth and its atmosphere, and of human activity as it affects and is affected by these, including the distribution of populations and resources and political and economic activities.
■ [usu. in sing.] the nature and relative arrangement of places and physical features: *the geography of your college.*
– DERIVATIVES **geographer** noun.
– ORIGIN late 15th cent.: from French géographie or Latin geographia, from Greek geōgraphia, from gē 'earth' + -graphia 'writing'.

geoid /ˈdʒiːɔɪd/ ▶ noun (the **geoid**) the shape of the earth taken as mean sea level and its imagined extension under (or over) land areas.
– ORIGIN late 19th cent.: from Greek geoeidēs, from gē 'earth' + -oeidēs (see **-OID**).

geology ▶ noun [mass noun] the science which deals with the physical structure and substance of the earth, their history, and the processes which act on them.
■ the geological features of a district: *the geology of the*

Outer Hebrides. ■ the geological features of a planetary body: *an article on the Moon's geology.*
– DERIVATIVES **geologic** adjective, **geological** adjective, **geologically** adverb, **geologist** noun, **geologize** (also **-ise**) verb.
– ORIGIN late 18th cent.: from modern Latin geologia, from Greek gē 'earth' + -logia (see **-LOGY**).

geomagnetism ▶ noun [mass noun] the branch of geology concerned with the magnetic properties of the earth.
– DERIVATIVES **geomagnetic** adjective, **geomagnetically** adverb.

geomancy /ˈdʒiːə(ʊ)mansi/ ▶ noun [mass noun] **1** the art of placing or arranging buildings or other sites auspiciously.
2 divination from the configuration of a handful of earth or random dots.
– DERIVATIVES **geomantic** adjective.

geometer /dʒɪˈɒmɪtə/ ▶ noun **1** a person skilled in geometry.
2 (also **geometer moth**) Entomology a geometrid moth or its caterpillar.
– ORIGIN late Middle English: from late Latin geometra, based on Greek geōmetrēs, from gē 'earth' + metrēs 'measurer'.

geometric /ˌdʒiːəˈmɛtrɪk/ ▶ adjective **1** of or relating to geometry, or according to its methods.
2 (of a design) characterized by or decorated with regular lines and shapes: *the predominantly geometric mosaics at Silchester.*
■ (**Geometric**) Archaeology of or denoting a period of Greek culture (around 900–700 BC) characterized by geometrically decorated pottery. ■ (**Geometric**) Architecture relating to or denoting a style of early English Decorated tracery based on the geometry of circles.
– DERIVATIVES **geometrical** adjective, **geometrically** adverb.
– ORIGIN mid 17th cent.: via French from Latin geometricus, from Greek geōmetrikos, from geōmetrēs (see **GEOMETER**).

geometric isomer (also **geometric isomer**) ▶ noun Chemistry each of two or more compounds which differ from each other in the arrangement of groups with respect to a double bond, ring, or other rigid structure.
– DERIVATIVES **geometrical isomerism** noun.

geometrical series ▶ noun a series of numbers or quantities in geometric progression.

geometric mean ▶ noun the central number in a geometric progression (e.g. 9 in 3, 9, 27), also calculable as the nth root of a product of n numbers.

geometric progression ▶ noun a progression of numbers with a constant ratio between each number and the one before (e.g. 1, 3, 9, 27, 81).

geometrid /dʒɪˈɒmɪtrɪd/ ▶ noun Entomology a moth of a large family (Geometridae), distinguished by having twig-like caterpillars that move by looping and straightening the body. Also called **GEOMETER**. Compare with **LOOPER**.
– ORIGIN late 19th cent.: from modern Latin Geometridae (plural), from the genus name *Geometra*, from Latin *geometres* (see **GEOMETER**).

geometry /dʒɪˈɒmɪtri/ ▶ noun [mass noun] the branch of mathematics concerned with the properties and relations of points, lines, surfaces, solids, and higher dimensional analogues.
■ [count noun] (pl. **-ies**) a particular mathematical system describing such properties: *non-Euclidean geometries.* ■ [in sing.] the shape and relative arrangement of the parts of something: *the geometry of spiders' webs.*
– DERIVATIVES **geometrician** /dʒɪˌɒmɪˈtrɪʃ(ə)n/ noun.
– ORIGIN Middle English: via Old French from Latin geometria, from Greek, from gē 'earth' + metria (see **-METRY**).

geomorphic /ˌdʒiːə(ʊ)ˈmɔːfɪk/ ▶ adjective of or relating to the form of the landscape and other natural features of the earth's surface; geomorphological.

geomorphology /ˌdʒiːə(ʊ)mɔːˈfɒlədʒi/ ▶ noun [mass noun] the study of the physical features of the surface of the earth and their relation to its geological structures.
– DERIVATIVES **geomorphological** adjective, **geomorphologist** noun.

geophagy /dʒɪˈɒfədʒi/ ▶ noun [mass noun] the practice in some tribal societies of eating earth.

– ORIGIN mid 19th cent.: from **GEO-** 'earth' + Greek *phagia* 'eating, feeding' (from *phagein* 'eat').

geophysics ▶ plural noun [treated as sing.] the physics of the earth.
– DERIVATIVES **geophysical** adjective, **geophysicist** noun.

geopolitics ▶ plural noun [treated as sing. or pl.] politics, especially international relations, as influenced by geographical factors.
■ [treated as sing.] the study of politics of this type.
– DERIVATIVES **geopolitical** adjective, **geopolitically** adverb, **geopolitician** noun.

Geordie Brit. informal ▶ noun a person from Tyneside.
■ [mass noun] the English dialect or accent typical of people from Tyneside.
▶ adjective of or relating to Tyneside, its people, or their accent or dialect: *Geordie humour.*
– ORIGIN mid 19th cent.: diminutive of the given name *George*.

George the name of four kings of Great Britain and Ireland, one of Great Britain and Ireland (from 1920 of the United Kingdom), and one of the United Kingdom:
■ George I (1660–1727), great-grandson of James I, reigned 1714–27, Elector of Hanover 1698–1727. He succeeded to the British throne as a result of the Act of Settlement (1701). Unpopular in England as a foreigner who never learned English, he left administration to his ministers.
■ George II (1683–1760), son of George I, reigned 1727–60, Elector of Hanover 1727–60. He depended heavily on his ministers, although he took an active part in the War of the Austrian Succession (1740–8). His later withdrawal from active politics allowed the development of constitutional monarchy.
■ George III (1738–1820), grandson of George II, reigned 1760–1820, Elector of Hanover 1760–1815 and king of Hanover 1815–20. He exercised considerable political influence, but it declined from 1788 after bouts of mental illness, as a result of which his son was made regent in 1811.
■ George IV (1762–1830), son of George III, reigned 1820–30. Known as a patron of the arts and *bon viveur*, he gained a bad reputation which was further damaged by his attempt to divorce his estranged wife Caroline of Brunswick just after coming to the throne.
■ George V (1865–1936), son of Edward VII, reigned 1910–36. He exercised restrained but important influence over British politics, playing an especially significant role in the formation of the government in 1931.
■ George VI (1894–1952), son of George V, reigned 1936–52. He came to the throne on the abdication of his elder brother Edward VIII. Despite a retiring disposition he became a popular monarch, gaining respect for the staunch example he and his family set during the London Blitz.

George, St, patron saint of England. He is reputed in legend to have slain a dragon, and may have been martyred near Lydda in Palestine some time before the reign of Constantine. His cult did not become popular until the 6th century, and he probably became patron saint of England in the 14th century. Feast day, 23 April.

George Cross (abbrev.: **GC**) ▶ noun (in the UK and Commonwealth countries) a decoration for bravery awarded especially to civilians, instituted in 1940 by King George VI and taking precedence over all other medals and decorations except the Victoria Cross.

George Medal (abbrev.: **GM**) ▶ noun (in the UK and Commonwealth countries) a medal for bravery awarded especially to civilians, instituted with the George Cross in 1940 .

Georgetown the capital of Guyana, a port at the mouth of the Demerara River; pop. 188,000 (est. 1983).

George Town 1 the capital of the Cayman Islands, on the island of Grand Cayman; pop. 12,000 (est. 1988).
2 the chief port of Malaysia and capital of the state of Penang, on Penang island; pop. 219,380 (1991). It was founded in 1786 by the British East India Company. Also called **PENANG**.

georgette /dʒɔːˈdʒɛt/ ▶ noun [mass noun] a thin silk or crêpe dress material.
– ORIGIN early 20th cent.: named after *Georgette* de la Plante (c.1900), French dressmaker.

Georgia 1 a country of SE Europe, on the eastern shore of the Black Sea; pop. 5,500,000 (1994);

languages, Georgian (official), Russian, and Armenian; capital, Tbilisi.

An independent kingdom in medieval times, Georgia became part of the Russian empire in the 19th century and then was absorbed into the Soviet Union. On the break-up of the USSR in 1991, Georgia became an independent republic outside the Commonwealth of Independent States.

2 a state of the south-eastern US, on the Atlantic coast; pop. 5,463,100 (1990); capital, Atlanta. Founded as an English colony in 1732 and named after George II, it became one of the original thirteen states of the Union (1788).

Georgian¹ ▶ adjective **1** of or characteristic of the reigns of the British Kings George I–IV (1714–1830).
■of or relating to British architecture of this period which was characterized especially by restrained elegance and the use of neoclassical styles.
2 of or characteristic of the reigns of the British Kings George V and VI (1910–52).
■of or relating to British literature of 1910–20, in particular pastoral poetry of a type strongly attacked by the early modernists.

Georgian² ▶ adjective of or relating to the country of Georgia, its people, or their language.
▶ noun **1** a native or national of Georgia, or a person of Georgian descent.
2 [mass noun] the official language of Georgia, spoken by around 4 million people. It is the main member of the small South Caucasian (or Kartvelian) language family, and has its own alphabet.

Georgian³ ▶ adjective of or relating to the state of Georgia in the US.
▶ noun a native of Georgia.

georgic /ˈdʒɔːdʒɪk/ ▶ noun a poem or book dealing with agriculture or rural topics.
■(**Georgics**) the title of a poetic treatise by Virgil.
▶ adjective poetic/literary rustic; pastoral.
– ORIGIN early 16th cent.: via Latin from Greek geōrgikos, from geōrgos 'farmer'.

geoscience ▶ noun [mass noun] (also **geosciences**) earth sciences, especially geology.
– DERIVATIVES **geoscientist** noun.

geostationary ▶ adjective (of an artificial satellite of the earth) moving in a circular geosynchronous orbit in the plane of the equator, so that it appears to be stationary in the sky above a fixed point on the surface.

geostrophic /ˌdʒiːəˈstrɒfɪk, -ˈstrəʊf-/ ▶ adjective Meteorology & Oceanography relating to or denoting the component of a wind or current that arises from a balance between pressure gradients and coriolis forces.
– ORIGIN early 20th cent.: from GEO- 'of the earth' + Greek strophē 'a turning' (from strephein 'to turn').

geosynchronous /ˌdʒiːəˈsɪŋkrənəs/ ▶ adjective another term for SYNCHRONOUS (in sense 2). Compare with GEOSTATIONARY.

geosyncline /ˌdʒiːəˈsɪŋklaɪn/ ▶ noun Geology a large-scale depression in the earth's crust containing very thick deposits.

geotaxis /ˌdʒiːəˈtaksɪs/ ▶ noun [mass noun] Biology the motion of a motile organism or cell in response to the force of gravity.
– DERIVATIVES **geotactic** adjective.

geotechnics ▶ plural noun [treated as sing.] the branch of civil engineering concerned with the study and modification of soil and rocks.
– DERIVATIVES **geotechnic** adjective, **geotechnical** adjective.

geothermal ▶ adjective of, relating to, or produced by the internal heat of the earth: *some 70% of Iceland's energy needs are met from geothermal sources.*

geotropism /ˌdʒiːəˈtrəʊpɪz(ə)m/ ▶ noun [mass noun] Botany the growth of the parts of plants in response to the force of gravity. The upward growth of plant shoots is an instance of **negative geotropism**; the downward growth of roots is **positive geotropism**.
– DERIVATIVES **geotropic** adjective.
– ORIGIN late 19th cent.: from GEO- 'earth' + Greek tropē 'turning' + -ISM.

Gera /ˈɡɛːrə/ an industrial city in east central Germany, in Thuringia; pop. 126,520 (1991).

Geraldton /ˈdʒɛrəldt(ə)n/ a seaport and resort on the west coast of Australia, to the north of Perth; pop. 24,360 (1991).

geranial /dʒɪˈreɪnɪəl/ ▶ noun [mass noun] Chemistry a fragrant oil present in lemon grass oil and used in perfumery.

● an isomer of citral; chem. formula: $C_{10}H_{16}O$.
– ORIGIN late 19th cent.: from German, contraction of *Geraniumaldehyde.*

geraniol /dʒɪˈreɪnɪɒl/ ▶ noun [mass noun] Chemistry a fragrant liquid present in some floral oils and used in perfumery.
● A terpenoid alcohol; chem. formula: $C_{10}H_{18}O$.
– ORIGIN late 19th cent.: from German, from GERANIUM + -OL.

geranium /dʒɪˈreɪnɪəm/ ▶ noun a herbaceous plant or small shrub of a genus that comprises the cranesbills and their relatives. Geraniums bear a long narrow fruit that is said to be shaped like the bill of a crane.
● Genus Geranium, family Geraniaceae.
■(in general or informal use) a cultivated pelargonium. ■ [mass noun] the scarlet colour of many cultivated pelargoniums.
– ORIGIN modern Latin, from Greek geranion, from geranos 'crane'.

Gerard /ˈdʒɛrɑːd/, John (1545–1612), English herbalist. He was curator of the physic garden of the College of Surgeons and published his *Herball*, containing over 1,800 woodcuts, in 1597.

gerbera /ˈdʒɜːb(ə)rə, ˈɡɜː-/ ▶ noun a tropical Old World plant of the daisy family, with large brightly coloured flowers, cultivated under glass in cooler regions.
● Genus Gerbera, family Compositae: many species, in particular the Transvaal daisy.
– ORIGIN modern Latin, named after Traugott Gerber (died 1743), German naturalist.

gerbil /ˈdʒɜːbɪl/ ▶ noun a burrowing mouse-like rodent that is specially adapted to living in arid conditions, found in Africa and Asia.
● Subfamily Gerbillinae, family Muridae: several genera, in particular Gerbillus; the **Mongolian gerbil** (Meriones unguiculatus) is popular as a pet.
– ORIGIN mid 19th cent.: from French gerbille, from modern Latin gerbillus, diminutive of gerboa (see JERBOA).

gerenuk /ˈɡɛrənʊk/ ▶ noun a slender East African antelope with a long neck, often browsing on tall bushes by standing on its hind legs.
● Litocranius walleri, family Bovidae.
– ORIGIN late 19th cent.: from Somali.

geriatric /ˌdʒɛrɪˈatrɪk/ ▶ adjective [attrib.] of or relating to old people, especially with regard to their health care: *a geriatric hospital.*
■informal decrepit; out of date: *replacements for a geriatric locomotive fleet.*
▶ noun an old person, especially one receiving special care: *a rest home for geriatrics.*
– ORIGIN 1920s: from Greek gēras 'old age' + iatros 'doctor', on the pattern of paediatric.

USAGE **Geriatric** is the normal, semi-official term used in Britain and the US when referring to the health care of old people (*a geriatric ward*; *geriatric patients*). When used outside such contexts, it typically carries overtones of being worn out and decrepit and can therefore be offensive if used with reference to people.

geriatrics ▶ plural noun [treated as sing. or pl.] the branch of medicine or social science dealing with the health and care of old people.
– DERIVATIVES **geriatrician** noun.

Géricault /ˈʒɛrɪkəʊ, French ʒeriko/, (Jean Louis André) Théodore (1791–1824), French painter, criticized for his rejection of classicism in favour of a more realistic style. His most famous work, *The Raft of the Medusa* (1819), depicts the survivors of a famous shipwreck of 1816.

germ ▶ noun **1** a micro-organism, especially one which causes disease.
2 a portion of an organism capable of developing into a new one or part of one. Compare with GERM CELL.
■the embryo in a cereal grain or other plant seed. Compare with WHEATGERM. ■ an initial stage from which something may develop: *the germ of a brilliant idea.*
– DERIVATIVES **germy** adjective (informal, only in sense 1).
– ORIGIN late Middle English (in sense 2): via Old French from Latin germen 'seed, sprout'. Sense 1 dates from the late 19th cent.

German ▶ noun **1** a native or national of Germany.
■a person of German descent: *Sudeten Germans.*
2 [mass noun] a West Germanic language used in Germany, Austria, and parts of Switzerland, and by communities in the US and elsewhere. It is spoken

by some 100 million people. See also HIGH GERMAN, LOW GERMAN.
▶ adjective of or relating to Germany, its people, or their language.
– ORIGIN from Latin Germanus, used to designate related peoples of central and northern Europe, a name perhaps given by Celts to their neighbours; compare with Old Irish gair 'neighbour'.

german ▶ adjective archaic closely akin. See also BROTHER-GERMAN, COUSIN-GERMAN, SISTER-GERMAN.
– ORIGIN Middle English: from Old French germain, from Latin germanus 'genuine, of the same parents'.

German Bight a shipping forecast area covering the eastern North Sea off the northern Netherlands, Germany, and southern Denmark.

German Democratic Republic (abbrev.: **GDR, DDR**) official name for the former state of East Germany.

germander /dʒəˈmandə/ ▶ noun a widely distributed plant of the mint family. Some kinds are cultivated as ornamentals and some are used in herbal medicine.
● Genus Teucrium, family Labiatae: many species, including the European **wall germander** (T. chamaedrys).
– ORIGIN late Middle English: from medieval Latin germandra, based on Greek khamaidrus, literally 'ground oak', from khamai 'on the ground' + drus 'oak' (because the leaves of some species were thought to resemble those of the oak).

germander speedwell ▶ noun a speedwell with bright blue flowers and leaves resembling those of the germander, native to Eurasia.
● Veronica chamaedrys, family Scrophulariaceae.

germane /dʒəˈmeɪn/ ▶ adjective relevant to a subject under consideration: *that is not germane to our theme.*
– DERIVATIVES **germanely** adverb, **germaneness** noun.
– ORIGIN early 17th cent.: variant of GERMAN, with which it was synonymous from Middle English. The current sense has arisen from a usage in Shakespeare's *Hamlet*.

German East Africa a former German protectorate in East Africa (1891–1918), corresponding to present-day Tanzania, Rwanda, and Burundi.

German Empire an empire in German-speaking central Europe, created by Bismarck in 1871 after the Franco-Prussian War by the union of twenty-five German states under the Hohenzollern king of Prussia. Also called SECOND REICH.

Forming an alliance with Austria–Hungary, the German Empire became the greatest industrial power in Europe and engaged in colonial expansion in Africa, China, and the Far East. Tensions arising with other colonial powers led to the First World War, after which the German Empire collapsed and the Weimar Republic was created.

Germanic ▶ adjective **1** of, relating to, or denoting the branch of the Indo-European language family that includes English, German, Dutch, Frisian, and the Scandinavian languages.
■of, relating to, or denoting the peoples of ancient northern and western Europe speaking such languages.
2 having characteristics of or attributed to Germans or Germany: *she had an almost Germanic regard for order.*
▶ noun [mass noun] the Germanic languages collectively. See also EAST GERMANIC, NORTH GERMANIC, WEST GERMANIC.
■the unrecorded ancient language from which these developed, thought to have been spoken on the shores of the Baltic Sea in the 3rd millennium BC. Also called PROTO-GERMANIC.
– ORIGIN mid 17th cent.: from Latin Germanicus, from Germanus (see GERMAN).

Germanist ▶ noun an expert in or student of the language, literature, and civilization of Germany, or of Germanic languages.

germanium /dʒəˈmeɪnɪəm/ ▶ noun [mass noun] the chemical element of atomic number 32, a shiny grey semimetal. Germanium was important in the making of transistors and other semiconductor devices, but has been largely replaced by silicon. (Symbol: **Ge**)
– ORIGIN late 19th cent.: modern Latin, from Latin Germanus (see GERMAN).

Germanize (also **-ise**) ▶ verb [with obj.] make German; cause to adopt German language and

customs: *the Poles had Germanized their family names.*
– DERIVATIVES **Germanization** noun, **Germanizer** noun.

German measles ▶ **plural noun** [usu. treated as sing.] a contagious viral disease, with symptoms like mild measles. It can cause fetal malformation if caught in early pregnancy. Also called **RUBELLA**.

Germano- /dʒəːˈmanəʊ, ˈdʒəːmənəʊ/ ▶ **combining form** German; German and …: *Germanophile.*
■relating to Germany: *Germanocentric.*

German shepherd ▶ **noun** an Alsatian.

German silver ▶ **noun** [mass noun] a white alloy of nickel, zinc, and copper.

German South West Africa a former German protectorate in SW Africa (1884–1918), corresponding to present-day Namibia.

Germany a country in central Europe; pop. 78,700,000 (1991); official language, German; capital, Berlin; seat of government, Bonn. German name **DEUTSCHLAND**.

The multiplicity of small German states achieved real unity only with the rise of Prussia and the formation of the German Empire in the mid 19th century. After being defeated in the First World War, Germany was taken over in the 1930s by the Nazi dictatorship which led to a policy of expansionism and eventually to complete defeat in the Second World War. Germany was occupied for a time by the victorious Allies and was partitioned. The western part (including West Berlin), which was occupied by the US, Britain, and France, became the Federal Republic of Germany or **West Germany**, with its capital at Bonn. The eastern part, occupied by the Soviet Union, became the German Democratic Republic or **East Germany**, with its capital in East Berlin. West Germany emerged as a major European industrial power and was a founder member of the EEC while the East remained under Soviet domination. After the general collapse of communism in eastern Europe, East and West Germany reunited on 3 October 1990.

germ cell ▶ **noun** Biology a cell containing half the number of chromosomes of a somatic cell and able to unite with one from the opposite sex to form a new individual; a gamete.
■an embryonic cell with the potential of developing into a gamete.

germicide ▶ **noun** [mass noun] a substance or other agent which destroys harmful micro-organisms.
– DERIVATIVES **germicidal** adjective.

Germinal /ˈdʒəːmɪn(ə)l, French ʒɛrminal/ ▶ **noun** the seventh month of the French Republican calendar (1793–1805), originally running from 21 March to 19 April.

germinal ▶ **adjective** [attrib.] relating to or of the nature of a germ cell or embryo.
■in the earliest stage of development. ■providing material for future development: *the subject was revived in a germinal article by Charles Ferguson.*
– DERIVATIVES **germinally** adverb.
– ORIGIN early 19th cent.: from Latin *germen, germin-* 'sprout, seed' + **-AL**.

germinate /ˈdʒəːmɪneɪt/ ▶ **verb** [no obj.] (of a seed or spore) begin to grow and put out shoots after a period of dormancy.
■[with obj.] cause (a seed or spore) to sprout in such a way. ■figurative come into existence and develop: *the idea germinated and slowly grew into an obsession.*
– DERIVATIVES **germination** noun, **germinative** adjective, **germinator** noun.
– ORIGIN late 16th cent.: from Latin *germinat-* 'sprouted forth, budded', from the verb *germinare*, from *germen, germin-* 'sprout, seed'.

Germiston /ˈdʒəːmɪst(ə)n/ a city in South Africa, in the province of Gauteng, south-east of Johannesburg; pop. 134,000 (1991). It is the site of a large gold refinery, which serves the Witwatersrand gold-mining region.

germ layer ▶ **noun** Embryology each of the three layers of cells (ectoderm, mesoderm, and endoderm) that are formed in the early embryo.

germ line ▶ **noun** Biology a series of germ cells each descended or developed from earlier cells in the series, regarded as continuing through successive generations of an organism.

germ plasm ▶ **noun** [mass noun] Biology germ cells, collectively.
■the genetic material of such cells.

germ warfare ▶ **noun** [mass noun] the use of harmful, disease-spreading micro-organisms as a military weapon.

Geronimo[1] /dʒəˈrɒnɪməʊ/ (*c.*1829–1909), Apache chief. He led his people in raids on settlers and US troops before surrendering in 1886.

Geronimo[2] /dʒəˈrɒnɪməʊ/ ▶ **exclamation** used to express exhilaration, especially when leaping from a great height or moving at speed.
– ORIGIN Second World War: by association with **GERONIMO**[1], adopted as a slogan by American paratroopers.

gerontic /dʒɛˈrɒntɪk/ ▶ **adjective** of or relating to old age, elderly people, or senescent animals or plants.
– ORIGIN late 19th cent.: from Greek *gerōn, geront-* 'old man' + **-IC**.

gerontocracy /ˌdʒɛrənˈtɒkrəsi/ ▶ **noun** a state, society, or group governed by old people.
■[mass noun] government based on rule by old people.
– DERIVATIVES **gerontocrat** noun, **gerontocratic** adjective.
– ORIGIN mid 19th cent.: from Greek *gerōn, geront-* 'old man' + **-CRACY**.

gerontology /ˌdʒɛrənˈtɒlədʒi/ ▶ **noun** [mass noun] the scientific study of old age, the process of ageing, and the particular problems of old people.
– DERIVATIVES **gerontological** adjective, **gerontologist** noun.
– ORIGIN early 20th cent.: from Greek *gerōn, geront-* 'old man' + **-LOGY**.

-gerous ▶ **combining form** bearing (a specified thing): *armigerous.*
– ORIGIN from Latin *-ger* 'bearing' (from the root of *gerere* 'to bear, carry') + **-OUS**.

gerrymander /ˈdʒɛrɪˌmandə/ (Brit. also **jerrymander**) ▶ **verb** [with obj.] [often as noun **gerrymandering**] manipulate the boundaries of (an electoral constituency) so as to favour one party or class.
■achieve (a result) by such manipulation: *a total freedom to gerrymander the results they want.*
▶ **noun** an instance of such a practice.
– DERIVATIVES **gerrymanderer** noun.
– ORIGIN early 19th cent.: from the name of Governor Elbridge *Gerry* of Massachusetts + **SALAMANDER**, from the supposed similarity between a salamander and the shape of a new voting district on a map drawn when he was in office (1812), the creation of which was felt to favour his party: the map (with claws, wings, and fangs added), was published in the Boston *Weekly Messenger*, with the title *The Gerry-Mander.*

Gershwin, George (1898–1937), American composer and pianist, of Russian-Jewish descent; born *Jacob Gershovitz*. He composed many successful songs and musicals, the orchestral work *Rhapsody in Blue* (1924), and the opera *Porgy and Bess* (1935). The lyrics for many of these were written by his brother Ira Gershwin (1896–1983).

gerund /ˈdʒɛrʌnd/ ▶ **noun** Grammar a verb form which functions as a noun, in Latin ending in *-ndum* (declinable), in English ending in *-ing* (e.g. *asking* in *do you mind my asking you?*).
– ORIGIN early 16th cent.: from late Latin *gerundium*, from *gerundum*, variant of *gerendum*, the gerund of Latin *gerere* 'do'.

gerundive /dʒəˈrʌndɪv/ ▶ **noun** Grammar a form of a Latin verb, ending in *-ndus* (declinable) and functioning as an adjective meaning 'that should or must be done'.
– ORIGIN Middle English (in the sense 'gerund'): from late Latin *gerundivus* (*modus*) 'gerundive (mood)', from *gerundium* (see **GERUND**).

Gesellschaft /gəˈzɛlʃaft/ ▶ **noun** [mass noun] social relations based on impersonal ties, as duty to a society or organization. Contrasted with **GEMEINSCHAFT**.
– ORIGIN German, from *Gesell(e)* 'companion' + *-schaft* (see **-SHIP**).

gesneriad /gɛsˈnɪərɪad, dʒɛs-/ ▶ **noun** a tropical plant of a family that includes African violets, gloxinias, and their relatives.
• Family Gesneriaceae.
– ORIGIN mid 19th cent.: from modern Latin *Gesneria* (genus name), from the name of Conrad von Gesner (1516–65), Swiss naturalist, + **-AD**[1].

gesso /ˈdʒɛsəʊ/ ▶ **noun** (pl. **-oes**) [mass noun] a hard compound of plaster of Paris or whiting in glue, used in sculpture or as a base for gilding or painting on wood.
– ORIGIN late 16th cent.: Italian, from Latin *gypsum* (see **GYPSUM**).

gestalt /gəˈʃtaːlt, -ˈʃtalt/ ▶ **noun** Psychology an organized whole that is perceived as more than the sum of its parts.
– DERIVATIVES **gestaltism** noun, **gestaltist** noun.
– ORIGIN 1920s: from German *Gestalt*, literally 'form, shape'.

gestalt psychology ▶ **noun** [mass noun] a movement in psychology founded in Germany in 1912, seeking to explain perceptions in terms of gestalts rather than by analysing their constituents.

gestalt therapy ▶ **noun** [mass noun] a psychotherapeutic approach developed by Fritz Perls (1893–1970). It focuses on insight into gestalts in patients and their relations to the world, and often uses role playing to aid the resolution of past conflicts.

Gestapo /gəˈstaːpəʊ/ the German secret police under Nazi rule. It ruthlessly suppressed opposition to the Nazis in Germany and occupied Europe and sent Jews and others to concentration camps. From 1936 it was headed by Heinrich Himmler.
– ORIGIN German, from *Geheime Staatspolizei* 'secret state police'.

gestate /dʒɛˈsteɪt/ ▶ **verb** [with obj.] carry (a fetus) in the womb from conception to birth: *these individuals gestate male-based litters* | [no obj.] *rabbits gestate for approximately twenty-eight days.*
■[no obj.] (of a fetus) undergo gestation. ■[with obj.] figurative develop in the mind over a long period: [with obj.] *a research trip he made while gestating his new book.*
– ORIGIN mid 19th cent.: from Latin *gestat-* 'carried in the womb', from the verb *gestare*.

gestation ▶ **noun** [mass noun] the process of carrying or being carried in the womb between conception and birth.
■the duration of such a process. ■figurative the development of something over a period of time: *various ideas are in the process of gestation.*
– ORIGIN mid 16th cent. (denoting an excursion on horseback, in a carriage, etc., considered as exercise): from Latin *gestatio(n-)*, from *gestare* 'carry, carry in the womb', frequentative of *gerere* 'carry'.

gesticulate /dʒɛˈstɪkjʊleɪt/ ▶ **verb** [no obj.] use gestures, especially dramatic ones, instead of speaking or to emphasize one's words: *they were shouting and gesticulating frantically at drivers who did not slow down.*
– DERIVATIVES **gesticulation** noun, **gesticulative** adjective, **gesticulator** noun, **gesticulatory** adjective.
– ORIGIN early 17th cent.: from Latin *gesticulat-* 'gesticulated', from the verb *gesticulari*, from *gesticulus*, diminutive of *gestus* 'action'.

gesture ▶ **noun** a movement of part of the body, especially a hand or the head, to express an idea or meaning: *Alex made a gesture of apology* | [mass noun] *so much is conveyed by gesture.*
■an action performed to convey one's feelings or intentions: *Maggie was touched by the kind gesture.* ■an action performed for show in the knowledge that it will have no effect: *I hope the amendment will not be just a gesture.*
▶ **verb** [no obj.] make a gesture: *she gestured meaningfully with the pistol.*
■[with obj.] express (something) with a gesture or gestures: *he gestured his dissent at this.* ■[with obj. and adverbial or infinitive] direct or invite (someone) to move somewhere specified: *he gestured her to a chair.*
– DERIVATIVES **gestural** adjective.
– ORIGIN late Middle English: from medieval Latin *gestura*, from Latin *gerere* 'bear, wield, perform'. The original sense was 'bearing, deportment', hence 'the use of posture and bodily movements for effect in oratory'.

gesundheit /gɛˈzʊndhʌɪt, German gɛˈzʊnthaɪt/ ▶ **exclamation** used to wish good health to a person who has just sneezed.
– ORIGIN from German *Gesundheit* 'health'.

get ▶ **verb** (**getting**; past **got**; past participle **got**, N. Amer. or archaic **gotten**) **1** [with obj.] come to have or hold (something); receive: *I got the impression that she wasn't happy.*
■experience, suffer, or be afflicted with (something bad): *I got a sudden pain in my left eye.* ■receive as a punishment or penalty: *I'll get the sack if things go wrong.* ■contract (a disease or ailment): *I might be getting the flu.* ■receive (a communication): *I got a letter from my fiancé.*
2 [with obj.] succeed in attaining, achieving, or experiencing; obtain: *I need all the sleep I can get.*
■move in order to pick up or bring (something); fetch:

get another chair | [with two objs] *I'll get you a drink.* ■ [with obj. and adverbial] tend to meet with or find in a specified place or situation: *for someone used to the tiny creatures we get in England it was something of a shock.* ■ travel by or catch (a bus, train, or other form of transport): *I got a taxi across to Baker Street.* ■ obtain (a figure or answer) as a result of calculation. ■ respond to a ring of (a telephone or doorbell): *I'll get the door!* ■ [in imperative] informal said as an invitation to notice or look at someone, especially to criticize or ridicule them: *get her!*

3 [no obj., with complement] enter or reach a specified state or condition; become: *he got very worried* | *it's getting late* | [with past participle] *you'll get used to it.*
■ [as auxiliary verb] used with past participle to form the passive mood: *the cat got drowned.* ■ [with obj. and past participle] cause to be treated in a specified way: *get the form signed by a doctor.* ■ [with obj. and infinitive] induce or prevail upon (someone) to do something: *Sophie got a housemaid to make a fire.* ■ [no obj., with infinitive] have the opportunity to do: *he got to try out a few of these nice new cars.* ■ [no obj., with present participle or infinitive] begin to be or do something, especially gradually or by chance: *we got talking one evening.*

4 [no obj., with adverbial of direction] come, go, or make progress eventually or with some difficulty: *I got to the airport* | *they weren't going to get anywhere.*
■ [no obj., with adverbial] move or come into a specified position, situation, or state: *she got into the car.* ■ [with obj. and adverbial] succeed in making (someone or something) come, go, or make progress: *my honesty often gets me into trouble.* ■ [no obj., with clause] informal, chiefly N. Amer. reach a specified point or stage: ***it's getting so** I can't even think.* ■ [usu. in imperative] informal go away.

5 (**have got**) see **HAVE**.

6 [with obj.] catch or apprehend (someone): *the police have got him.*
■ strike or wound (someone) with a blow or missile: *you got me in the eye!* ■ informal punish, injure, or kill (someone), especially as retribution: *I'll get you for this!* ■ (**get it**) informal be punished, injured, or killed: *wait until dad comes home, then you'll get it!* ■ (**get mine, his,** etc.) informal be killed or appropriately punished or rewarded: *I'll get mine, you get yours, we'll all get wealthy.* ■ informal annoy or amuse (someone) greatly: *cleaning the same things all the time, that's what gets me.* ■ baffle (someone): *she had got me there: I could not answer.*

7 [with obj.] informal understand (an argument or the person making it): *What do you mean? I don't get it.*

8 [with obj.] archaic acquire (knowledge) by study; learn: *that knowledge which is gotten at school.*

▶ **noun 1** dated an animal's offspring: *he passes this on to his get.*

2 Brit. informal or dialect a person whom the speaker dislikes or despises.

– PHRASES **get in there** informal take positive action to achieve one's aim (often said as an exhortation): *you get in there son, and you work.* **get it on** informal embark on an activity; get going. ■ informal, chiefly N. Amer. have sexual intercourse: *he'd been **getting it on with** a girl.* **get it up** vulgar slang (of a man) achieve an erection. **get one's own back** Brit. informal have one's revenge; retaliate. **get-rich-quick** derogatory designed or concerned to make a lot of money fast. **getting on for** chiefly Brit. approaching (a specified time, age, or amount); almost: *there are getting on for 700 staff.* **get-up-and-go** informal energy, enthusiasm, and initiative. **get someone with child** archaic make a woman pregnant.

– DERIVATIVES **gettable** adjective.

– ORIGIN Middle English: from Old Norse *geta* 'obtain, beget, guess'; related to Old English *gietan* (in *begietan* 'beget', *forgietan* 'forget'), from an Indo-European root shared by Latin *praeda* 'booty, prey', *praehendere* 'get hold of, seize', and Greek *khandanein* 'hold, contain, be able'.

USAGE The verb **get** is in the top five of the most common verbs in the English language, with nearly 125,000 citations (out of 100 million) in the British National Corpus. Nevertheless, despite the high frequency, there is still a feeling that almost any use containing **get** is somewhat informal. No general informal label has been applied to this dictionary entry, but in formal writing it is worth bearing this reservation in mind.

▶ **get something across** manage to communicate an idea clearly.

get ahead become successful in one's life or career: *how to get ahead in advertising.*

get along 1 chiefly N. Amer. another way of saying ***get on*** (in sense 2). **2** manage to live or survive: *don't worry, we'll get along without you.* ■ [in imperative] Brit. informal used to express scepticism or disbelief or to tell someone to go away: *oh, get along with you!*

get around see ***get round***.

get at 1 reach or gain access to (something): *it's difficult to get at the screws.* ■ bribe or unfairly influence (someone): *he had been got at by government officials.* **2** informal imply (something): *I can see what you're getting at.* **3** Brit. informal criticize (someone) subtly and repeatedly: *I hope you didn't think I was getting at you.*

get away 1 escape: *he was very lucky to **get away with** his life.* **2** [in imperative] informal said to express disbelief or scepticism.

get away with escape blame, punishment, or undesirable consequences for (an act that is wrong or mistaken): *you'll never get away with this.*

get back at take revenge on (someone): *I wanted to get back at them for what they did.*

get back to contact (someone) later to give a reply or return a message: *I'll find out and get back to you.*

get by manage with difficulty to live or accomplish something: *he had just enough money to get by.*

get down N. Amer. informal dance energetically: *get down and party!*

get someone down depress or demoralize someone.

get something down 1 write something down. **2** swallow food or drink, especially with difficulty.

get down to begin to do or give serious attention to: *let's get down to business.*

get in 1 (of a train, aircraft, or other transport) arrive at its destination. **2** (of a political party or candidate) be elected.

get in on become involved in (a profitable or exciting activity).

get into (of a feeling) affect, influence, or take control of (someone): *I don't know what's got into him.*

get in with become friendly with (someone), especially in order to gain an advantage: *I hope he doesn't get in with the wrong crowd.*

get off 1 informal escape a punishment; be acquitted: *she got off lightly* | *you'll **get off with** a caution.* **2** go to sleep, especially after some difficulty. **3** Brit. informal have a sexual encounter: *he accused her of trying to **get off with** that drummer.*

get off on informal, chiefly N. Amer. be excited or aroused by (something): *he was obviously getting off on the adrenalin of performing before the crowd.*

get on 1 perform or make progress in a specified way: *how are you getting on?* ■ continue doing something, especially after an interruption: *I've got to **get on with** this job.* ■ chiefly Brit. be successful in one's life or career. **2** chiefly Brit. have a harmonious or friendly relationship: *they seem to get on pretty well.* **3** (**be getting on**) informal be old or comparatively old: *we are both getting on a bit.*

get on to chiefly Brit. make contact with (someone) about a particular topic.

get out 1 (of something previously secret) become known: *news got out that we were coming.* **2** (also **get out of here**) [in imperative] informal, chiefly N. Amer. used to express disbelief: *get out, you're a liar.*

get something out 1 succeed in uttering, publishing, or releasing something: *we're keen to get a record out.* **2** Brit. succeed in solving or finishing a puzzle or mathematical problem.

get out of contrive to avoid or escape (a duty or responsibility): *they wanted to get out of paying.*

get something out of achieve benefit from (an undertaking or stressful exercise): *these institutions think they're going to get something out of it that will enhance their image.*

get outside (of) Brit. informal eat or drink (something) heartily: *we'll get outside of some bacon and eggs.*

get over 1 recover from (an ailment or an upsetting or startling experience): *the trip will help him get over Sal's death.* **2** overcome (a difficulty).

get something over 1 manage to communicate an idea or theory: *the company is keen to get the idea over.* **2** complete an unpleasant or tedious but necessary task promptly: *Come on, let's **get it over with**.*

get round (or N. Amer. **around**) chiefly Brit. **1** coax or persuade (someone) to do or allow something that they initially do not want to. **2** deal successfully with (a problem). ■ evade (a regulation or restriction) without contravening it: *the company changed its name to get round the law.*

get round to (or N. Amer. **around to**) chiefly Brit. deal with (a task) in due course: *I didn't get round to putting all the photos in frames.*

get through 1 (also **get someone through**) pass or assist someone in passing (a difficult or testing experience or period): *I need these lessons to get me through my exam.* ■ (**get something through**) (with reference to a piece of legislation) make or become law. **2** chiefly Brit. finish or use up (a large amount or number of something), especially within a short time: *we got through four whole jars of mustard.* **3** make contact by telephone. ■ succeed in communicating with someone in a meaningful way: *I just don't think anyone can **get through to** these kids.*

get to 1 informal annoy or upset (someone) by persistent action: *he started crying—we were getting to him.* **2** another way of saying ***get round to***.

get together gather or assemble socially or to cooperate.

get up 1 (also **get someone up**) rise or cause to rise from bed after sleeping. **2** (of wind or the sea) become strong or agitated.

get someone up (usu. **be got up**) dress someone in a specified smart, elaborate, or unusual way: *he was got up in striped trousers and a dinner jacket.*

get something up 1 prepare or organize a project or piece of work: *we used to get up little plays.* **2** enhance or refine one's knowledge of a subject.

get up to Brit. informal be involved in (typically something illicit or surprising): *what did you get up to last weekend?*

get-at-able ▶ **adjective** informal accessible.

getaway ▶ **noun 1** an escape or quick departure, especially after committing a crime: *the thugs made their getaway* | [as modifier] *a getaway car.*
■ a fast start by a racing car: *the Frenchman on pole position made a poor getaway.*
2 informal a holiday: *a perfect family getaway.*
■ the destination or accommodation for a holiday: *the popular island getaway of Penang.*

Gethsemane, Garden of /gɛθˈsɛməni/ a garden between Jerusalem and the Mount of Olives, where Jesus went with his disciples after the Last Supper and was betrayed (Matt. 26:36–46).

– ORIGIN from Hebrew *gath-shemen* 'oil-press'.

get-out ▶ **noun** Brit. a means of avoiding something; an excuse: [as modifier] *a get-out clause.*

– PHRASES **as —— as all get-out** N. Amer. informal as —— as is possible; to the highest degree: *the rituals of the racing world are as macho as all get-out.*

getter ▶ **noun 1** [usu. in combination] a person or thing that gets a specified desirable thing: *an attention-getter* | *a vote-getter.*
2 Electronics & Physics a substance used to remove residual gas from a vacuum tube, or impurities or defects from a semiconductor crystal.

gettering ▶ **noun** [mass noun] Electronics & Physics the removal of impurities or defects by the use of a getter.

get-together ▶ **noun** an informal gathering.

Getty /ˈgɛti/, Jean Paul (1892–1976), American industrialist. He made a large fortune in the oil industry and was also a noted art collector. He founded the J. Paul Getty Museum in Los Angeles.

Gettysburg, Battle of /ˈgɛtɪzbəːg/ a decisive battle of the American Civil War, fought near the town of Gettysburg in Pennsylvania in July 1863. A Union army under General Meade repulsed the Confederate army of General Lee and forced him to abandon his invasion of the north.

Gettysburg address a speech delivered on 18 November 1863 by President Abraham Lincoln at the dedication of the national cemetery on the site of the Battle of Gettysburg.

get-up ▶ **noun** informal a style or arrangement of dress, especially an elaborate or unusual one: *her ridiculous Cossack's get-up.*

Getz, Stan (1927–91), American jazz saxophonist; born *Stanley Gayetsky*. He was a leader of the 'cool' school of jazz; his recordings include 'Early Autumn' (1948) and 'The Girl from Ipanema' (1963).

geum /ˈdʒiːəm/ ▶ **noun** a plant of a genus which comprises the avens.
• Genus *Geum*, family Rosaceae.

– ORIGIN modern Latin, variant of Latin *gaeum*.

GeV ▶ **abbreviation for** gigaelectronvolt, equivalent to 10^9 electronvolts.

gewgaw /ˈgjuːgɔː/ ▶ **noun** (usu. **gewgaws**) a showy thing, especially one that is useless or worthless.

– ORIGIN Middle English: of unknown origin.

Gewürztraminer /gəˈvʊətstrə,miːnə, German gəˈvyrtstra,miːnɐ/ ▶ **noun** [mass noun] a variety of white grape grown mainly in the Alsace, Austria, and the Rhine valley.
■ a wine made from this grape.
– ORIGIN German, from *Gewürz* 'spice' + **TRAMINER**.

geyser /ˈɡiːzə, ˈɡʌɪ-/ ▶ **noun** **1** a hot spring in which water intermittently boils, sending a tall column of water and steam into the air.
■ a jet or stream of liquid: *the pipe sent up* ***a geyser of*** *sewer water into the street.*
2 /ˈɡiːzə/ Brit. a gas-fired water heater through which water flows as it is rapidly heated.
■ S. African a hot-water storage tank with an electric heating element.
▶ **verb** [no obj., with adverbial of direction] (especially of water or steam) gush or burst out with great force: *a fissure opened and yellow smoke geysered upward.*
– ORIGIN late 18th cent.: from Icelandic *Geysir*, the name of a particular spring in Iceland; related to *geysa* 'to gush'.

geyserite ▶ **noun** [mass noun] a hard opaline siliceous deposit occurring around geysers and hot springs.
– ORIGIN early 19th cent.: from **GEYSER** + **-ITE**[1].

GG Brit. ▶ **abbreviation for** Governor General.

GH ▶ **abbreviation for** Ghana (international vehicle registration).

Ghana /ˈɡɑːnə/ a country of West Africa, with its southern coastline bordering on the Atlantic Ocean; pop. 16,500,000 (est. 1991); languages, English (official), West African languages; capital, Accra. Former name (until 1957) **GOLD COAST**.

> Formerly a centre of the slave trade, the area became the British colony of Gold Coast in 1874. In 1957 it gained independence as a member of the Commonwealth, under the leadership of Kwame Nkrumah. It was the first British colony to become independent.

– DERIVATIVES **Ghanaian** /ɡɑːˈneɪən/ adjective & noun.

gharana /ɡʌˈrɑːnə/ ▶ **noun** (in the Indian subcontinent) one of the various specialist schools or methods of classical music or dance.
– ORIGIN from Hindi *gharānā* 'family'.

gharara /ɡʌˈrɑːrə/ ▶ **noun** a pair of loose trousers with pleats below the knee, worn by women from the Indian subcontinent, typically with a kameez.

gharial /ˈɡarɪɑːl, ˌɡʌrɪˈɑːl, ˈɡɛːrɪəl/ (also **gavial**) ▶ **noun** a large fish-eating crocodile with a long narrow snout that widens at the nostrils, native to the Indian subcontinent. See also **FALSE GHARIAL**.
● *Gavialis gangeticus*, the only member of the family Gavialidae.
– ORIGIN early 19th cent.: from Hindi *ghariyāl*. The spelling *gavial* (from French) is an alteration probably due to scribal error.

gharry /ˈɡari/ ▶ **noun** (pl. **-ies**) (in the Indian subcontinent) a horse-drawn carriage available for hire.
– ORIGIN from Hindi *gāṛī*.

ghastly ▶ **adjective** (**ghastlier**, **ghastliest**) **1** causing great horror or fear; frightful or macabre: *she was overcome with horror at the ghastly spectacle.*
■ informal objectionable; unpleasant: *we had to wear ghastly old-fashioned dresses.*
2 extremely unwell: *he always felt ghastly on getting out of bed.*
■ deathly white or pallid: *a ghastly pallor* | [as submodifier] *he turned ghastly pale and rushed to the bathroom.*
– DERIVATIVES **ghastliness** noun.
– ORIGIN Middle English: from obsolete *gast* 'terrify', from Old English *gǣstan*, of Germanic origin; related to **GHOST**. The *gh* spelling is by association with **GHOST**. The sense 'objectionable' dates from the mid 19th cent.

ghat /ɡɑːt/ ▶ **noun** **1** (in the Indian subcontinent) a flight of steps leading down to a river.
■ (also **burning-ghat**) a level place on the edge of a river where Hindus cremate their dead.
2 (in the Indian subcontinent) a mountain pass.
– ORIGIN from Hindi *ghāṭ*.

Ghats /ɡɑːts/ two mountain ranges in central and southern India. Known as **the Eastern Ghats** and **the Western Ghats**, they run parallel to the coast on either side of the Deccan plateau.

ghazal /ˈɡʌʒʌl/ ▶ **noun** (in Middle Eastern and Indian literature and music) a lyric poem with a fixed number of verses and a repeated rhyme, typically on the theme of love, and normally set to music.
– ORIGIN via Persian from Arabic *ġazal*.

Ghazi /ˈɡɑːzi/ ▶ **noun** (pl. **Ghazis**) (often as an honorific title) a Muslim fighter against non-Muslims.
– ORIGIN from Arabic *al-ġāzī*, participle of *ġazā* 'invade, raid'.

Ghaziabad /ˈɡɑːzɪəbad/ a city in northern India, in Uttar Pradesh east of Delhi; pop. 461,000 (1991).

Ghaznavid /ɡazˈnɑːvɪd/ ▶ **noun** a member of a Turkish Muslim dynasty founded in Ghazna, Afghanistan, in AD 977. The dynasty extended its power into Persia and the Punjab and lasted until 1186.
▶ **adjective** of or relating to this dynasty.

GHB ▶ **abbreviation for** (sodium) gamma-hydroxybutyrate, a designer drug with anaesthetic properties.
● Chem. formula: $CH_2OH(CH_2)_2COONa$.

ghee /ɡiː/ ▶ **noun** [mass noun] clarified butter made from the milk of a buffalo or cow, used in Indian cooking.
– ORIGIN from Hindi *ghī*, from Sanskrit *ghṛtá* 'sprinkled'.

Gheg /ɡɛɡ/ ▶ **noun** (pl. same or **Ghegs**) **1** a member of one of the two main ethnic groups of Albania, living mainly in the north of the country.
2 [mass noun] the dialect of Albanian spoken by this people, with about 2 million speakers. Compare with **TOSK**.
▶ **adjective** of or relating to the Ghegs or their dialect.
– ORIGIN from Albanian *Geg*.

Ghent /ɡɛnt/ a city in Belgium, capital of the province of East Flanders; pop. 230,200 (1991). Founded in the 10th century, it became the capital of the medieval principality of Flanders. It was formerly known in English as Gaunt (surviving in names, e.g. John of Gaunt). Flemish name **GENT**, French name **GAND**.

gherao /ɡɛˈraʊ/ ▶ **noun** (pl. **-os**) Indian a protest in which workers prevent employers leaving a place of work until certain demands are met.
– ORIGIN from Hindi *gherāo* 'surround, besiege'.

gherkin /ˈɡəːkɪn/ ▶ **noun** a small variety of cucumber, or a young green cucumber used for pickling.
– ORIGIN early 17th cent.: from Dutch *augurkje*, *gurkje*, diminutive of *augurk*, *gurk*, from Slavic, based on medieval Greek *angourion* 'cucumber'.

ghetto /ˈɡɛtəʊ/ ▶ **noun** (pl. **-os** or **-oes**) a part of a city, especially a slum area, occupied by a minority group or groups.
■ historical the Jewish quarter in a city: *the Warsaw Ghetto.* ■ an isolated or segregated group or area: *the relative security of the gay ghetto.*
▶ **verb** (**-oes**, **-oed**) [with obj.] put in or restrict to an isolated or segregated area or group: *we're unhappy to see our guides ghettoed in the shelves of transport books.*
– ORIGIN early 17th cent.: perhaps from Italian *getto* 'foundry' (because the first ghetto was established in 1516 on the site of a foundry in Venice), or from Italian *borghetto*, diminutive of *borgo* 'borough'.

ghetto blaster ▶ **noun** informal a large portable radio and cassette or CD player.

ghettoize (also **-ise**) ▶ **verb** [with obj.] put in or restrict to an isolated or segregated place, group, or situation: *the Arabs are ghettoized and have few rights.*
– DERIVATIVES **ghettoization** noun.

Ghibelline /ˈɡɪbɪlʌɪn/ ▶ **noun** a member of one of the two great political factions in Italian medieval politics, traditionally supporting the Holy Roman emperor against the Pope and his supporters, the Guelphs.
– ORIGIN from Italian *Ghibellino*, perhaps from German *Waiblingen*, an estate belonging to Hohenstaufen emperors.

Ghiberti /ɡɪˈbɛːti, Italian ɡiˈbɛrti/, Lorenzo (1378–1455), Italian sculptor and goldsmith. His career was dominated by his work on two successive pairs of bronze doors for the baptistery in Florence.

ghibli /ˈɡɪbli/ ▶ **noun** [mass noun] a hot dry southerly wind of North Africa.
– ORIGIN early 19th cent.: from Arabic *ḳiblī* 'southern'.

ghillie ▶ **noun** variant spelling of **GILLIE**.

Ghirlandaio /ˌɡɪəlanˈdʌɪəʊ, Italian ɡirlanˈdajo/ (*c.*1448–94), Italian painter; born *Domenico di Tommaso Bigordi*. He is noted for his religious frescoes, particularly *Christ Calling Peter and Andrew* (1482–4) in the Sistine Chapel, Rome.

ghost ▶ **noun** an apparition of a dead person which is believed to appear or become manifest to the living, typically as a nebulous image: *the building is haunted by the ghost of a monk* | figurative *the ghosts of communism returned to haunt the living.*
■ [as modifier] appearing or manifesting but not actually existing: *the Flying Dutchman is the most famous ghost ship.* ■ a faint trace of something: *she gave the* ***ghost of*** *a smile.* ■ archaic a spirit or soul. ■ a faint secondary image produced by a fault in an optical system or on a cathode ray screen, e.g. by faulty television reception or internal reflection in a mirror or camera.
▶ **verb** **1** [with obj.] act as ghost writer of (a work): *his memoirs were smoothly ghosted by a journalist.*
2 [no obj., with adverbial of direction] glide smoothly and effortlessly: *they ghosted up the river.*
– PHRASES **the ghost in the machine** Philosophy the mind viewed as distinct from the body (usually used in a derogatory fashion by critics of dualism). [ORIGIN: coined by the philosopher Gilbert Ryle (1949).] **give up the ghost** die. ■ (of a machine) stop working. **look as if you have seen a ghost** look very pale and shocked. **not stand the ghost of a chance** have no chance at all.
– DERIVATIVES **ghostlike** adjective.
– ORIGIN Old English *gāst* (in the sense 'spirit, soul'), of Germanic origin; related to Dutch *geest* and German *Geist*. The *gh-* spelling occurs first in Caxton, probably influenced by Flemish *gheest*.

ghost bat ▶ **noun** any of a number of bats with mainly white or grey fur, in particular:
■ N. Amer. see **WHITE BAT**. ■ Austral. another term for **FALSE VAMPIRE**.

ghostbuster ▶ **noun** informal a person who claims to be able to banish ghosts and poltergeists.

ghost crab ▶ **noun** a pale yellowish crab that lives in a burrow in the sand above the high-water mark and goes down to the sea at night to feed.
● Genus *Ocypode*, family Ocypodidae.

Ghost Dance an American Indian religious cult of the second half of the 19th century, based on the performance of a ritual dance, which, it was believed, would drive away white people and restore the traditional lands and way of life.

ghosting ▶ **noun** [mass noun] the appearance of a ghost or secondary image on a television or other display screen.

ghostly ▶ **adjective** (**ghostlier**, **ghostliest**) of or like a ghost in appearance or sound; eerie and unnatural: *a frightening, ghostly figure with a hood.*
– DERIVATIVES **ghostliness** noun.
– ORIGIN Old English *gāstlic*, from *gāst* 'ghost'.

ghost moth (also **ghost swift**) ▶ **noun** a large European swift moth, the male of which has white wings.
● *Hepialus humuli*, family Hepialidae. See **SWIFT** (sense 2).

ghost story ▶ **noun** a story about ghosts, intended to be scary.

ghost town ▶ **noun** a deserted town with few or no remaining inhabitants.

ghost train ▶ **noun** a miniature train at a funfair designed to scare its passengers with mock-horror ghoulish sights and sounds.

ghost word ▶ **noun** a word recorded in a dictionary or other reference work which is not actually used.

ghostwriter ▶ **noun** a person whose job it is to write material for someone else who is the named author.
– DERIVATIVES **ghostwrite** verb.

ghoul /ɡuːl/ ▶ **noun** an evil spirit or phantom, especially one supposed to rob graves and feed on dead bodies.
■ a person morbidly interested in death or disaster.
– DERIVATIVES **ghoulish** adjective, **ghoulishly** adverb, **ghoulishness** noun.
– ORIGIN late 18th cent.: from Arabic *ġūl*, a desert demon believed to rob graves and devour corpses.

GHQ ▶ **abbreviation for** General Headquarters.

Ghulghuleh /ɡʊlˈɡʊlə/ a ruined ancient city near Bamian in central Afghanistan. It was destroyed by Genghis Khan *c.*1221.

ghyll ▶ **noun** variant spelling of **GILL**[3].

GI ▶ **noun** (pl. **GIs**) a private soldier in the US army.
– ORIGIN 1930s (originally denoting equipment

g

supplied to US forces): abbreviation of *government* (or *general*) *issue*.

gi /giː/ ▶ **noun** the loose white jacket worn in judo.
– ORIGIN Japanese.

Giacometti /ˌdʒakəˈmɛti/, Alberto (1901–66), Swiss sculptor and painter. His most typical works are emaciated and extremely elongated human forms, such as *Pointing Man* (1947).

giant ▶ **noun 1** an imaginary or mythical being of human form but superhuman size.
■(in Greek mythology) any of the beings of this kind who rebelled unsuccessfully against the gods of Olympus. ■ an abnormally tall or large person, animal, or plant. ■ a very large company or organization. ■ a person of exceptional talent or qualities: *a giant among sportsmen*.
2 Astronomy a star of relatively great size and luminosity compared to ordinary stars of the main sequence, and 10–100 times the diameter of the sun.
▶ **adjective** [attrib.] of very great size or force; gigantic: *giant multinational corporations | a giant transport plane | a giant meteorite*.
■used in names of very large animals and plants, e.g. **giant hogweed**, **giant tortoise**.
– DERIVATIVES **giantlike** adjective.
– ORIGIN Middle English *geant* (with the first syllable later influenced by Latin *gigant-*), from Old French, via Latin from Greek *gigas, gigant-*.

g

giant anteater ▶ **noun** a large insectivorous mammal with long coarse fur, large claws, an elongated snout, and a long tongue for catching ants. It is native to Central and South America.
● *Myrmecophaga tridactyla*, family Myrmecophagidae, order Xenartha (or Edentata).

giant clam ▶ **noun** a very large bivalve mollusc that occurs in the tropical Indo-Pacific.
● Family Tridacnidae: several species, including *Tridacna gigas*, which is the largest living shelled mollusc.

giant deer ▶ **noun** another term for **IRISH ELK**.

giantess ▶ **noun** a female giant.

giant gourami ▶ **noun** a large edible freshwater fish that is native to Asia. It is widely farmed there and has been introduced elsewhere.
● Family Osphronemidae and genus *Osphronemus*, in particular *O. goramy*.

giant groundsel ▶ **noun** a large tree-like plant of the daisy family, having a thick stem and a few short branches tipped with broad leaves, growing chiefly on high mountains in central and eastern Africa.
● Genus *Senecio* (or *Dendrosenecio*), family Compositae.

giantism ▶ **noun** [mass noun] a tendency towards abnormally large size; gigantism.

giant-killer ▶ **noun** a person or team that defeats a seemingly much more powerful opponent.
– DERIVATIVES **giant-killing** noun.

giant panda ▶ **noun** see **PANDA**[1].

giant petrel ▶ **noun** the largest petrel, which is found around southern oceans, has a massive bill, and scavenges from carcasses.
● Genus *Macronectes*, family Procellariidae: two species.

giant puffball ▶ **noun** a European fungus which produces a spherical white fruiting body with a diameter of up to 80 cm, edible when young.
● *Langermannia gigantea*, family Lycoperdaceae, class Gasteromycetes.

giant salamander ▶ **noun** a very large salamander that is native to North America and east Asia, in particular:
● a permanently aquatic salamander (three species in the family Cryptobranchidae), e.g. the American hellbender. ● a terrestrial salamander (three species in the family Dicamptodontidae), of western North America.

Giant's Causeway a geological formation of basalt columns, dating from the Tertiary period, on the north coast of Northern Ireland. It was once believed to be the end of a road made by a legendary giant to Staffa in the Inner Hebrides, where there is a similar formation.

giant sequoia ▶ **noun** the giant redwood. See **REDWOOD**.

giant silk moth ▶ **noun** see **SILK MOTH**.

giant slalom ▶ **noun** a long-distance slalom with fast, wide turns.

giant squid ▶ **noun** a deep-sea squid which is the largest known invertebrate, reaching a length of 18 m (59 ft) or more.
● Genus *Architeuthis*, order Teuthoidea.

giant toad ▶ **noun** another term for **CANE TOAD**.

giant tortoise ▶ **noun** a very large tortoise with a long lifespan, occurring on several tropical oceanic islands.
● Genus *Geochelone*, family Testudinidae: *G. nigra* (Galapagos Islands) and *G. gigantea* (Aldabra and the Seychelles).

giant zonure ▶ **noun** another term for **SUNGAZER**.

giaour /ˈdʒaʊə/ ▶ **noun** archaic, derogatory a non-Muslim, especially a Christian.
– ORIGIN from Turkish *gâvur*, from Persian *gaur*, probably from Arabic *kāfir* (see **KAFFIR**).

giardiasis /ˌdʒɪɑːˈdʌɪəsɪs/ ▶ **noun** [mass noun] infection of the intestine with a flagellate protozoan, which causes diarrhoea and other symptoms.
● The protozoan is *Giardia lamblia*, phylum Metamonada, kingdom Protista.
– ORIGIN early 20th cent.: from modern Latin *Giardia* (from the name of Alfred M. *Giard* (1846–1908), French biologist + **-ASIS**.

Gib ▶ **noun** Brit. short for **GIBRALTAR**.

gibber[1] /ˈdʒɪbə, ˈgɪbə/ ▶ **verb** [no obj.] speak rapidly and unintelligibly, typically through fear or shock: *they shrieked and gibbered as flames surrounded them* | [as adj. **gibbering**] *a gibbering idiot*.
– ORIGIN early 17th cent.: imitative.

gibber[2] /ˈgɪbə/ (also **gibber stone**) ▶ **noun** Austral. a stone or boulder forming part of a boulder plain.
■any small stone.
– ORIGIN from Dharuk *giba* 'stone'.

gibberbird /ˈgɪbəbəːd/ ▶ **noun** Austral. the desert chat, which has a sandy-grey back and yellowish underparts, inhabiting the arid stony plains of central Australia.
● *Ashbyia lovensis*, family Ephthianuridae.
– ORIGIN *gibber* from **GIBBER**[2].

gibberellic acid /ˌdʒɪbəˈrɛlɪk/ ▶ **noun** [mass noun] a gibberellin which is used commercially, notably in germinating barley for malt.
– ORIGIN 1950s: *gibberellic* from modern Latin *Gibberella* (see **GIBBERELLIN**) + **-IC**.

gibberellin /ˌdʒɪbəˈrɛlɪn/ ▶ **noun** any of a group of plant hormones that stimulate stem elongation, germination, and flowering.
– ORIGIN 1930s: from modern Latin *Gibberella* (from *Gibberella fujikuroi*, the fungus from which one of the gibberellins was first extracted), diminutive of the genus name *Gibbera*, from Latin *gibber* 'hump', + **-IN**[1].

gibberish /ˈdʒɪb(ə)rɪʃ, ˈgɪb-/ ▶ **noun** [mass noun] unintelligible or meaningless speech or writing; nonsense: *he talks gibberish*.
– ORIGIN early 16th cent.: perhaps from **GIBBER**[1] (but recorded earlier) + the suffix **-ISH**[1] (denoting a language as in *Spanish, Swedish*, etc.).

gibbet historical ▶ **noun** a gallows.
■an upright post with an arm on which the bodies of executed criminals were left hanging as a warning or deterrent to others. ■ (**the gibbet**) execution by hanging: *the four ringleaders were sentenced to the gibbet*.
▶ **verb** (**gibbeted, gibbeting**) [with obj.] hang up (a body) on a gibbet.
■execute (someone) by hanging. ■ archaic, figurative hold up to contempt: *poor Melbourne is gibbeted in the Times*.
– ORIGIN Middle English: from Old French *gibet* 'staff, cudgel, gallows', diminutive of *gibe* 'club, staff', probably of Germanic origin.

Gibbon[1], Edward (1737–94), English historian. He is best known for his multi-volume work *The History of the Decline and Fall of the Roman Empire* (1776–88), chapters of which aroused controversy for their critical account of the spread of Christianity.

Gibbon[2], Lewis Grassic (1901–35), Scottish writer; pseudonym of *James Leslie Mitchell*. From 1927 his short stories were regularly published in the *Cornhill Magazine*, and his novels include the trilogy *A Scots Quair* (1932–4).

gibbon ▶ **noun** a small, slender tree-dwelling ape with long powerful arms and loud hooting calls, native to the forests of SE Asia.
● Family Hylobatidae and genus *Hylobates*: several species.
– ORIGIN late 18th cent.: from French, from an Indian dialect word.

Gibbons[1], Grinling (1648–1721), Dutch-born English sculptor. He is famous for his decorative carvings, chiefly in wood, as in the choir stalls of St Paul's Cathedral, London.

Gibbons[2], Orlando (1583–1625), English composer and musician. He was the organist of Westminster Abbey from 1623 and composed mainly sacred music, although he is also known for madrigals such as *The Silver Swan* (1612).

gibbous /ˈgɪbəs/ ▶ **adjective** (of the moon) having the illuminated part greater than a semicircle and less than a circle.
■convex or protuberant: *gibbous eyes*.
– DERIVATIVES **gibbosity** /-ˈbɒsɪti/ noun, **gibbously** adverb, **gibbousness** noun.
– ORIGIN late Middle English: from late Latin *gibbosus*, from Latin *gibbus* 'hump'.

Gibbs[1], James (1682–1754), Scottish architect. He developed Wren's ideas for London's city churches, especially in his masterpiece, St Martin's-in-the-Fields (1722–6).

Gibbs[2], Josiah Willard (1839–1903), American physical chemist. He pioneered chemical thermodynamics and statistical mechanics, though his theoretical work was not generally appreciated until after his death.

Gibbs free energy ▶ **noun** Chemistry a thermodynamic quantity equal to the enthalpy (of a system or process) minus the product of the entropy and the absolute temperature. (Symbol: **G**)
– ORIGIN named after J. W. *Gibbs* (see **GIBBS**[2]).

gibbsite /ˈgɪbzʌɪt/ ▶ **noun** [mass noun] a colourless mineral consisting of hydrated aluminium hydroxide, occurring chiefly as a constituent of bauxite or in encrustations.
– ORIGIN early 19th cent.: named after George *Gibbs* (1776–1833), American mineralogist, + **-ITE**[1].

gibe /dʒʌɪb/ ▶ **noun** & **verb** variant spelling of **JIBE**[1].

giblets /ˈdʒɪblɪts/ ▶ **plural noun** the liver, heart, gizzard, and neck of a chicken or other fowl, usually removed before the bird is cooked, and often used to make gravy, stuffing, or soup.
– ORIGIN Middle English (in the sense 'an inessential appendage', later 'garbage, offal'): from Old French *gibelet* 'game bird stew', probably from *gibier* 'birds or mammals hunted for sport'.

Gibraltar /dʒɪˈbrɔːltə/ a British dependency near the southern tip of the Iberian peninsula, at the eastern end of the Strait of Gibraltar; pop. 28,075 (1991); languages, English (official), Spanish.

> Occupying a site of great strategic importance, Gibraltar consists of a fortified town and military base at the foot of a rocky headland, the **Rock of Gibraltar**. Britain captured it during the War of the Spanish Succession in 1704 and is responsible for its defence, external affairs, and internal security.

– DERIVATIVES **Gibraltarian** /ˌdʒɪbrɔːlˈtɛːrɪən/ adjective & noun.

Gibraltar, Strait of a channel between the southern tip of the Iberian peninsula and North Africa, forming the only outlet of the Mediterranean Sea to the Atlantic. It is some 60 km (38 miles) long and varies in width from 24 km (15 miles) to 40 km (25 miles) at its western extremity.

Gibran /dʒɪˈbrɑːn/ (also **Jubran**), Khalil (1883–1931), Lebanese-born American writer and artist. His writings in both Arabic and English are deeply romantic, displaying his religious and mystical nature.

Gibson[1], Althea (b.1927), American tennis player. She was the first black player to succeed at the highest level of tennis, winning all the major world women's singles titles in the late 1950s.

Gibson[2], Mel (Columcille Gerard) (b.1956), American-born Australian actor and director. Notable film appearances: *Mad Max* (1979), the *Lethal Weapon* series (1987, 1989, 1992, 1998), and *Braveheart* (1995), which he also directed and which won five Oscars.

Gibson Desert a desert region in Western Australia, to the south-east of the Great Sandy Desert. The first European to cross it (1876) was Ernest Giles, who named it after his companion Alfred Gibson, who went missing on an earlier expedition.

Gibson girl ▶ **noun** a girl typifying the fashionable ideal of the late 19th and early 20th centuries.
– ORIGIN represented in the work of Charles D. *Gibson* (1867–1944), American artist and illustrator.

gibus /ˈdʒʌɪbəs/ (also **gibus hat**) ▶ **noun** a kind of collapsible top hat.
– ORIGIN mid 19th cent.: named after *Gibus*, the French inventor of this type of hat.

gid /gɪd/ ▶ **noun** [mass noun] (often **the gid**) a fatal

disease of sheep and goats, marked by loss of balance. It is caused by larvae of the dog tapeworm encysted in the brain.
– ORIGIN early 17th cent.: back-formation from GIDDY.

giddap /ˈɡɪdap, ɡɪˈdap/ ▶ exclamation N. Amer. another term for GIDDY-UP.

giddy ▶ adjective (**giddier**, **giddiest**) having a sensation of whirling and a tendency to fall or stagger; dizzy: *I felt giddy and had to steady myself | Luke felt almost giddy with relief.*
■ disorientating and alarming, but exciting: *he has risen to the giddy heights of master.* ■ excitable and frivolous: *Isobel's giddy young sister-in-law.*
▶ verb (**-ies**, **-ied**) [with obj.] make (someone) feel excited to the point of disorientation.
– PHRASES **my giddy aunt!** dated used to express astonishment. **play the giddy goat** dated act irresponsibly; fool around.
– DERIVATIVES **giddily** adverb, **giddiness** noun.
– ORIGIN Old English *gidig* 'insane', literally 'possessed by a god', from the base of GOD. Current senses date from late Middle English.

giddy-up ▶ exclamation used to get a horse to start moving or go faster.
– ORIGIN 1920s (originally US as *giddap*): reproducing a pronunciation of *get up.*

Gide /ʒiːd/, André (Paul Guillaume) (1869–1951), French novelist, essayist, and critic, regarded as the father of modern French literature. Notable works: *The Immoralist* (1902), *La Porte étroite* (1909, *Strait is the Gate*), *The Counterfeiters* (1927), and his *Journal* (1939–50). Nobel Prize for Literature (1947).

Gideon /ˈɡɪdɪən/ **1** (in the Bible) an Israelite leader, described in Judges 6:11 ff.
2 a member of Gideons International.

Gideons International an international Christian organization of business and professional people, founded in 1899 in the US with the aim of spreading the Christian faith by placing bibles in hotel rooms and hospital wards.

gidgee /ˈɡɪdʒiː/ ▶ noun Austral. any of a number of acacia trees of inland Australia.
● Genus *Acacia*, family Labiatae: several species, in particular *A. cambagei*, whose foliage emits an unpleasant odour at times .
– ORIGIN mid 19th cent.: from Wiradhuri *gijir.*

gie /ɡiː/ ▶ verb Scottish form of GIVE.

Gielgud /ˈɡiːlɡʊd/, Sir (Arthur) John (1904–2000), English actor and director. A notable Shakespearean actor, particularly remembered for his interpretation of the role of Hamlet, he also appeared in contemporary plays and films and won an Oscar for his role as a butler in *Arthur* (1980).

GIF ▶ noun [mass noun] Computing a popular format for image files, with built-in data compression.
■ (also **gifs**) [count noun] a file in this format.
– ORIGIN late 20th cent.: acronym from *graphic interchange format.*

GIFT ▶ noun [mass noun] Medicine gamete intrafallopian transfer, a technique for assisting conception by introducing mixed ova and sperm into a Fallopian tube.
– ORIGIN 1980s: acronym.

gift ▶ noun **1** a thing given willingly to someone without payment; a present: *a Christmas gift | [as modifier] a gift shop.*
■ an act of giving something as a present: *his mother's gift of a pen.* ■ informal a very easy task or unmissable opportunity: *that goal was an absolute gift.*
2 a natural ability or talent: *he has a gift for comedy.*
▶ verb [with obj.] give (something) as a gift, especially formally or as a donation or bequest: *the company gifted 2,999 shares to a charity.*
■ present (someone) with a gift or gifts: *the queen gifted him with a heart-shaped brooch.* ■ informal inadvertently allow (an opponent) to have something: [with two objs] *the goalkeeper gifted Liverpool their last-minute winner.* ■ (**gift someone with**) endow with (something): *man is gifted with a moral sense.*
– PHRASES **the gift of the gab** see GAB. **the gift of tongues** see TONGUE. **in the gift of** (of a church living or official appointment) in the power of someone to award: *nine seats in parliament were now in his gift.* **don't look a gift horse in the mouth** proverb don't find fault with something that you have discovered or been given. [ORIGIN: earlier as *look a given horse in the mouth.*]
– ORIGIN Middle English: from Old Norse *gipt*; related to GIVE.

gift certificate ▶ noun N. Amer. a gift token.

gifted ▶ adjective having exceptional talent or natural ability: *a gifted amateur musician.*
– DERIVATIVES **giftedness** noun.

gift token (also **gift voucher**) ▶ noun Brit. a voucher given as a present which is exchangeable for goods, usually in a particular shop.

giftware ▶ noun [mass noun] goods sold as being suitable as gifts.

gift wrap ▶ noun [mass noun] decorative paper for wrapping presents.
▶ verb (**gift-wrap**) [with obj.] [usu. as adj. **gift-wrapped**] wrap (a present) in decorative paper.
■ figurative hand over (something) as if a gift: *the first England goal came gift-wrapped.*

Gifu /ˈɡiːfuː/ a city in central Japan, on the island of Honshu; pop. 410,300 (1990).

gig[1] /ɡɪɡ/ ▶ noun **1** chiefly historical a light two-wheeled carriage pulled by one horse.
2 a light, fast, narrow boat adapted for rowing or sailing.
– ORIGIN late 18th cent.: apparently a transferred sense of obsolete *gig* 'a flighty girl', which was also applied to various objects or devices that whirled.

gig[2] /ɡɪɡ/ informal ▶ noun a live performance by or engagement for a musician or group playing popular or jazz music.
▶ verb (**gigged, gigging**) [no obj.] perform a gig or gigs.
■ [with obj.] use (a piece of musical equipment) at a gig.
– ORIGIN 1920s: of unknown origin.

gig[3] /ɡɪɡ/ ▶ noun a harpoon-like weapon used for catching fish.
▶ verb (**gigged, gigging**) [no obj.] fish using such a weapon.
– ORIGIN early 18th cent.: shortening of earlier (rarely used) *fizgig*, probably from Spanish *fisga* 'harpoon'.

gig[4] /ɡɪɡ, dʒɪɡ/ ▶ noun Computing, informal short for GIGABYTE.

giga- /ˈɡɪɡə, ˈdʒɪɡə/ ▶ combining form used in units of measurement: **1** denoting a factor of 10^9: *gigahertz.*
2 Computing denoting a factor of 2^{30}.
– ORIGIN from Greek *gigas* 'giant'.

gigabyte /ˈɡɪɡəbʌɪt, ˈdʒ-/ (abbrev.: **GB**) ▶ noun Computing a unit of information equal to one thousand million (10^9) or strictly, 2^{30} bytes.

gigaflop /ˈɡɪɡəflɒp, ˈdʒ-/ ▶ noun Computing a unit of computing speed equal to one thousand million floating-point operations per second.
– ORIGIN 1970s: back-formation from *gigaflops* (see GIGA-, -FLOP).

gigantic ▶ adjective of very great size or extent; huge or enormous: *a gigantic concrete tower.*
– DERIVATIVES **gigantically** adverb.
– ORIGIN early 17th cent. (in the sense 'like or suited to a giant'): from Latin *gigas, gigant-* (see GIANT) + -IC.

gigantism /ˈdʒʌɪɡantɪz(ə)m, dʒʌɪˈɡantɪz(ə)m/ ▶ noun [mass noun] chiefly Biology unusual or abnormal largeness.
■ Medicine excessive growth due to hormonal imbalance. ■ Botany excessive size in plants due to polyploidy.

gigantomachy /ˌdʒʌɪɡanˈtɒməki/ ▶ noun (in Greek mythology) the struggle between the gods and the giants.
– ORIGIN late 16th cent.: from Greek *gigantomakhia*, from *gigas, gigant-* (see GIANT) + *-makhia* 'fighting'.

Gigantopithecus /dʒʌɪˌɡantəˈpɪθɪkəs/ ▶ noun a very large fossil Asian ape of the Upper Miocene to Lower Pleistocene epochs.
● Genus *Gigantopithecus*, family Pongidae.
– ORIGIN modern Latin, from Greek *gigas, gigant-* (see GIANT) + *pithēkos* 'ape'.

giggle ▶ verb [no obj.] laugh lightly in a nervous, affected, or silly manner: *they giggled at some private joke | [as adj. **giggling**] three young, giggling girls.*
▶ noun a laugh of such a kind.
■ (**the giggles**) continuous uncontrollable giggling: *I got a fit of the giggles.* ■ informal an amusing person or thing; a joke: *it should be a right giggle.*
– DERIVATIVES **giggler** noun, **giggly** adjective (**gigglier, giggliest**).
– ORIGIN early 16th cent.: imitative.

Gigli /ˈdʒiːli, Italian ˈdʒiʎʎi/, Beniamino (1890–1957), Italian operatic tenor. He made his Milan debut with the conductor Toscanini in 1918, and retained his singing talents to a considerable age.

GIGO /ˈɡʌɪɡəʊ/ chiefly Computing ▶ abbreviation for garbage in, garbage out.

gigolo /ˈ(d)ʒɪɡələʊ/ ▶ noun (pl. **-os**) often derogatory a young man paid or financially supported by an older woman to be her escort or lover.
■ a professional male dancing partner or escort.
– ORIGIN 1920s (in the sense 'dancing partner'): from French, formed as the masculine of *gigole* 'dance hall woman', from colloquial *gigue* 'leg'.

gigot /ˈdʒɪɡət/ ▶ noun a leg of mutton or lamb.
– ORIGIN French, diminutive of colloquial *gigue* 'leg', from *giguer* 'to hop, jump', of unknown origin.

gigot sleeve ▶ noun a leg-of-mutton sleeve.

gigue /ʒiːɡ/ ▶ noun Music a lively piece of music in the style of a dance, typically of the Renaissance or baroque period, and usually in compound time.
– ORIGIN late 17th cent.: French, literally 'jig'.

Gijón /ɡɪˈhɒn, Spanish xiˈxon/ a port and industrial city in northern Spain, on the Bay of Biscay; pop. 260,250 (1991).

Gila monster /ˈhiːlə/ ▶ noun a venomous beaded lizard native to the south-western US and Mexico.
● Heloderma suspectum, family Helodermatidae.
– ORIGIN late 19th cent.: named after *Gila*, a river in New Mexico and Arizona.

Gilbert[1], Sir Humphrey (c.1539–83), English explorer. He claimed Newfoundland for Elizabeth I in 1583, but was lost when his ship foundered in a storm on the way home.

Gilbert[2], William (1544–1603), English physician and physicist. He discovered how to make magnets, and coined the term *magnetic pole*. His book *De Magnete* (1600) is an important early work on physics.

Gilbert[3], Sir W. S. (1836–1911), English dramatist; full name *William Schwenck Gilbert*. He is best known as a librettist who collaborated on light operas with the composer Sir Arthur Sullivan. Notable works: *HMS Pinafore* (1878), *The Pirates of Penzance* (1879), and *The Mikado* (1885).
– DERIVATIVES **Gilbertian** adjective.

Gilbert and Ellice Islands a former British colony (1915–75) in the central Pacific, consisting of two groups of islands: the Gilbert Islands, now a part of Kiribati, and the Ellice Islands, now Tuvalu.

Gilbertese ▶ adjective of or relating to the Gilbert Islands.
▶ noun a native or inhabitant of the Gilbert Islands.
■ [mass noun] the Micronesian language spoken there (see KIRIBATI).

Gilbert Islands a group of islands in the central Pacific, forming part of Kiribati. The islands straddle the equator and lie immediately west of the International Date Line. They were formerly part of the British colony of the Gilbert and Ellice Islands.
– ORIGIN named by the British after Thomas *Gilbert*, an English adventurer who arrived there in 1788.

gild[1] ▶ verb [with obj.] cover thinly with gold.
■ give a specious or false brilliance to: *the useless martyrs' deaths of the pilots gilded the operation.*
– PHRASES **gild the lily** try to improve what is already beautiful or excellent. [ORIGIN: misquotation, from 'To gild refined gold, to paint the lily; to throw perfume on the violet, … is wasteful, and ridiculous excess' (Shakespeare's *King John* VI. ii. 11).]
– DERIVATIVES **gilder** noun.
– ORIGIN Old English *gyldan*, of Germanic origin; related to GOLD.

gild[2] ▶ noun archaic spelling of GUILD.

gilded /ˈɡɪldɪd/ ▶ adjective covered thinly with gold leaf or gold paint: *an elegant gilded birdcage.*
■ wealthy and privileged; upper class: *the gilded fools who surrounded the Prince.*

gilded cage ▶ noun a luxurious but restrictive environment.

gilded youth ▶ noun [treated as sing. or pl.] young people of wealth, fashion, and flair.
– ORIGIN late 19th cent.: translating JEUNESSE DORÉE.

gilding ▶ noun [mass noun] the material used in or the surface produced by gilding.

gilet /ˈʒɪleɪ, ˈʒiːleɪ/ ▶ noun (pl. **gilets** pronunc. same) a light sleeveless padded jacket.
– ORIGIN late 19th cent.: French, 'waistcoat', from Spanish *jileco*, from Turkish *yelek*.

gilgai /ˈɡɪlɡʌɪ/ (also **gilgai hole**) ▶ noun Austral. a hollow where rainwater collects; a waterhole.
– ORIGIN from Wiradhuri and Kamilaroi *gilgaay*.

Gilgamesh /ˈɡɪlɡəmɛʃ/ a legendary king of the Sumerian city state of Uruk who is supposed to have ruled sometime during the first half of the 3rd millennium BC. He is the hero of the Babylonian epic of Gilgamesh, which recounts his exploits in an ultimately unsuccessful quest for immortality.

Gill /ɡɪl/, (Arthur) Eric (Rowton) (1882–1940), English sculptor, engraver, and typographer. His best-known sculptures are the relief carvings *Stations of the Cross* (1914–18) at Westminster Cathedral and *Prospero and Ariel* (1931) on Broadcasting House in London. He designed the first sans serif typeface, Gill Sans.

gill[1] /ɡɪl/ ▶ noun (often **gills**) **1** the paired respiratory organ of fishes and some amphibians, by which oxygen is extracted from water flowing over surfaces within or attached to the walls of the pharynx.
■ an organ of similar function in an invertebrate animal. **2** the vertical plates arranged radially on the underside of mushrooms and many toadstools. **3** the wattles or dewlap of a fowl. ■ (**gills**) the flesh below a person's jaws and ears: *we stuffed ourselves* **to the gills** *with scrambled eggs on toast.* ▶ verb [with obj.] **1** gut or clean (a fish). **2** catch (a fish) in a gill net.
– PHRASES **green about** (or **around** or **at**) **the gills** (of a person) sickly-looking.
– DERIVATIVES **gilled** adjective [in combination] *a six-gilled shark.*
– ORIGIN Middle English: from Old Norse.

gill[2] /dʒɪl/ ▶ noun a unit of liquid measure, equal to a quarter of a pint.
– ORIGIN Middle English: from Old French *gille* 'measure or container for wine', from late Latin *gillo* 'water pot'.

gill[3] /ɡɪl/ (also **ghyll**) ▶ noun a deep ravine, especially a wooded one.
■ a narrow mountain stream.
– ORIGIN Middle English: from Old Norse *gil* 'deep glen'. The spelling *ghyll* was introduced by Wordsworth.

gill[4] /dʒɪl/ (also **jill**) ▶ noun **1** derogatory a young woman. **2** a female ferret. Compare with HOB[2] (in sense 1).
– ORIGIN late Middle English: abbreviation of the given name *Gillian*.

gill cover ▶ noun a flap of skin protecting a fish's gills, typically stiffened by bony plates. Also called OPERCULUM.

Gillespie /ɡɪˈlɛspi/, Dizzy (1917–93), American jazz trumpet player and bandleader; born *John Birks Gillespie*. He was a virtuoso trumpet player and a leading exponent of the bebop style.

gillie /ˈɡɪli/ (also **ghillie**) ▶ noun **1** (in Scotland) a man or boy who attends someone on a hunting or fishing expedition.
■ historical a Highland chief's attendant. **2** (usu. **ghillie**) a type of shoe with laces along the instep and no tongue, especially those used for Scottish country dancing.
– ORIGIN late 16th cent.: from Scottish Gaelic *gille* 'lad, servant'. The word was also found in the term *gilliewetfoot*, denoting a servant who carried the chief over a stream, used as a contemptuous name by Lowlanders for the follower of a Highland chief. Sense 2 dates from the 1930s.

Gillingham /ˈdʒɪlɪŋəm/ a town on the Medway estuary south-east of London; pop. 93,700 (1981).

gill net ▶ noun a fishing net which is hung vertically so that fish get trapped in it by their gills.
– DERIVATIVES **gill-netter** noun.

gillyflower /ˈdʒɪliˌflaʊə/ (also **gilliflower**) ▶ noun any of a number of fragrant flowers, such as the wallflower or white stock.
■ (also **clove gillyflower**) archaic a clove-scented pink or carnation. See CLOVE (sense 3).
– ORIGIN Middle English *gilofre* (in the sense 'clove'), from Old French *gilofre*, *girofle*, via medieval Latin from Greek *karuophullon* (from *karuon* 'nut' + *phullon* 'leaf'). The ending was altered by association with FLOWER, but *gilliver* survived in dialect.

Gilsonite /ˈɡɪlsənʌɪt/ ▶ noun [mass noun] trademark a very

pure, shiny black, brittle form of asphalt, used in making inks, paints, and varnishes.
– ORIGIN late 19th cent.: named after Samuel H. Gilson, 19th-cent. American mineralogist, + -ITE[1].

gilt[1] ▶ adjective covered thinly with gold leaf or gold paint.
▶ noun **1** [mass noun] gold leaf or gold paint applied in a thin layer to a surface. **2** (**gilts**) fixed-interest loan securities issued by the UK government.
– PHRASES **take the gilt off the gingerbread** see GINGERBREAD.
– ORIGIN Middle English: archaic past participle of GILD[1].

gilt[2] ▶ noun a young sow.
– ORIGIN Middle English: from Old Norse *gyltr*.

gilt-edged ▶ adjective (especially of paper or a book) having a gilded edge or edges.
■ relating to or denoting stocks or securities (such as gilts) that are regarded as extremely reliable investments. ■ of very high quality: *the striker failed to convert three gilt-edged chances.*

gimbal /ˈdʒɪmb(ə)l/ (also **gimbals**) ▶ noun a contrivance, typically consisting of rings pivoted at right angles, for keeping an instrument such as a compass or chronometer horizontal in a moving vessel or aircraft.
– DERIVATIVES **gimballed** adjective.
– ORIGIN late 16th cent. (used in the plural denoting connecting parts in machinery): variant of earlier *gimmal*, itself a variant of late Middle English *gemel* 'twin, hinge, finger ring which can be divided into two rings', from Old French *gemel* 'twin', from Latin *gemellus*, diminutive of *geminus*.

gimcrack /ˈdʒɪmkrak/ ▶ adjective flimsy or poorly made but deceptively attractive: *plastic gimcrack cookware.*
▶ noun a cheap and showy ornament; a knick-knack.
– DERIVATIVES **gimcrackery** noun.
– ORIGIN Middle English *gibecrake*, of unknown origin. Originally a noun, the term denoted some kind of inlaid work in wood, later a fanciful notion or mechanical contrivance, hence a knick-knack.

gimlet /ˈɡɪmlɪt/ ▶ noun **1** a small T-shaped tool with a screw-tip for boring holes. **2** a cocktail of gin (or sometimes vodka) and lime juice.
– ORIGIN Middle English: from Old French *guimbelet*, diminutive of *guimble* 'drill', ultimately of Germanic origin.

gimlet eye ▶ noun an eye with a piercing stare.
– DERIVATIVES **gimlet-eyed** adjective.

gimme informal ▶ contraction of give me (not acceptable in standard use): *just gimme the damn thing.*
▶ noun chiefly N. Amer. a thing that is very easy to perform or obtain, especially in a game or sport: *the kick would hardly be a gimme in that wind.*

gimme cap (also **gimme hat**) ▶ noun N. Amer. informal a baseball cap bearing a company name or slogan which is given away for publicity purposes.

gimmick ▶ noun a trick or device intended to attract attention, publicity, or trade.
– DERIVATIVES **gimmicky** adjective.
– ORIGIN 1920s (originally US): of unknown origin but possibly an approximate anagram of *magic*, the original sense being 'a piece of magicians' apparatus'.

gimmickry ▶ noun [mass noun] gimmicks collectively; the use of gimmicks: *it does what it says it does, with no design gimmickry.*

gimp[1] /ɡɪmp/ (also **guimp** or **gymp**) ▶ noun **1** [mass noun] twisted silk, worsted, or cotton with cord or wire running through it, used chiefly as upholstery trimming.
■ (in lacemaking) coarser thread which forms the outline of the design in some techniques. **2** fishing line made of silk bound with wire.
– ORIGIN mid 17th cent.: from Dutch, of unknown ultimate origin.

gimp[2] /ɡɪmp/ N. Amer. informal, derogatory ▶ noun a physically handicapped or lame person.
■ a limp. ■ a feeble or contemptible person.
▶ verb [no obj., with adverbial of direction] limp; hobble: *she gimped around thereafter on an artificial leg.*
– DERIVATIVES **gimpy** adjective.
– ORIGIN 1920s (originally US): of unknown origin.

gin[1] ▶ noun **1** [mass noun] a clear alcoholic spirit

distilled from grain or malt and flavoured with juniper berries. **2** (also **gin rummy**) a form of the card game rummy in which a player holding unmelded cards totalling ten or less may terminate play.
– ORIGIN early 18th cent.: abbreviation of GENEVER.

gin[2] ▶ noun **1** a machine for separating cotton from its seeds. **2** a machine for raising and moving heavy weights.
▶ verb (**ginned**, **ginning**) [with obj.] treat (cotton) in a gin.
– DERIVATIVES **ginner** noun, **ginnery** noun.
– ORIGIN Middle English (in the sense 'a tool or device, a trick'): from Old French *engin* (see ENGINE).

gin[3] ▶ noun Austral. derogatory an Aboriginal woman.
– ORIGIN from Dharuk *diyin* 'woman, wife'.

ginger ▶ noun [mass noun] **1** a hot fragrant spice made from the rhizome of a plant. It is chopped or powdered for cooking, preserved in syrup, or candied.
■ spirit; mettle: *he puts some ginger in the poet.* **2** a SE Asian plant, which resembles bamboo in appearance, from which this rhizome is taken. ● *Zingiber officinale*, family Zingiberaceae. **3** a light reddish-yellow colour.
▶ adjective (chiefly of hair or fur) of a light reddish-yellow colour.
■ (of a person or animal) having ginger hair or fur.
▶ verb [with obj.] **1** [usu. as adj. **gingered**] flavour with ginger: *spring rolls on chinese leaf with gingered sauce.* **2** (**ginger someone/thing up**) stimulate; enliven: *she slapped his hand lightly to ginger him up.*
– DERIVATIVES **gingery** adjective.
– ORIGIN late Old English *gingifer*, conflated in Middle English with Old French *gingimbre*, from medieval Latin *gingiber*, from Greek *zingiberis*, from Pali *singivera*, of Dravidian origin.

ginger ale ▶ noun [mass noun] a clear, effervescent non-alcoholic drink flavoured with ginger extract.

ginger beer ▶ noun [mass noun] a cloudy, effervescent mildly alcoholic drink, made by fermenting a mixture of ginger and syrup.
■ a non-alcoholic commercial variety of this.

gingerbread ▶ noun [mass noun] cake made with treacle or syrup and flavoured with ginger.
■ fancy decoration, especially on a building: [as modifier] *a high-gabled gingerbread house.*
– PHRASES **take the gilt off the gingerbread** make something no longer attractive or desirable.
– ORIGIN Middle English (originally denoting preserved ginger), from Old French *gingembrat*, from medieval Latin *gingibratum*, from *gingiber* (see GINGER). The change in the ending in the 15th cent. was due to association with BREAD.

gingerbread man ▶ noun a flat ginger biscuit shaped like a person.

ginger group ▶ noun chiefly Brit. a highly active faction within a party or movement that presses for stronger action on a particular issue.

ginger jar ▶ noun a small ceramic jar with a high rim over which a lid fits.

gingerly ▶ adverb in a careful or cautious manner: *Jackson sat down very gingerly.*
▶ adjective showing great care or caution: *with strangers the preliminaries are taken at a gingerly pace.*
– DERIVATIVES **gingerliness** noun.
– ORIGIN early 16th cent. (in the sense 'daintily, mincingly'): perhaps from Old French *gensor* 'delicate', comparative of *gent* 'graceful', from Latin *genitus* '(well-) born'.

ginger nut ▶ noun (chiefly in the UK) a hard ginger-flavoured biscuit.

ginger snap ▶ noun (chiefly in North America) a thin brittle biscuit flavoured with ginger.

ginger wine ▶ noun [mass noun] an alcoholic drink made from fermented sugar, water, and bruised ginger.

gingham /ˈɡɪŋəm/ ▶ noun [mass noun] lightweight plain-woven cotton cloth, typically checked in white and a bold colour: [as modifier] *gingham curtains.*
– ORIGIN early 17th cent.: from Dutch *gingang*, from Malay *genggang* (originally an adjective meaning 'striped').

gingili /ˈdʒɪndʒɪli/ ▶ noun [mass noun] (especially in Indian cookery) sesame.
– ORIGIN from Hindi and Marathi *jiñjali*, from Arabic dialect *jonjolin*, from Arabic *juljulān*.

gingival /dʒɪn'dʒaɪv(ə)l/ ▶ adjective Medicine concerned with the gums: *the gingival tissues.*
– ORIGIN mid 17th cent.: from Latin *gingiva* 'gum' + **-AL**.

gingivitis /ˌdʒɪndʒɪ'vaɪtɪs/ ▶ noun [mass noun] Medicine inflammation of the gums.

ginglymus /'gɪŋglɪməs/ ▶ noun (pl. **ginglymi** /-maɪ/) Anatomy a hinge-like joint such as the elbow or knee, which allows movement in only one plane.
– ORIGIN late 16th cent.: modern Latin, from Greek *ginglumos* 'hinge'.

gink /gɪŋk/ ▶ noun informal, chiefly N. Amer. a foolish or contemptible person.
– ORIGIN early 20th cent. (originally US): of unknown origin.

ginkgo /'gɪŋkgəʊ, 'gɪŋkəʊ/ (also **ginko**) ▶ noun (pl. **-os** or **-oes**) a deciduous Chinese tree related to the conifers, with fan-shaped leaves and yellow flowers. It has a number of primitive features and is similar to some Jurassic fossils. Also called **MAIDENHAIR TREE**.
● *Ginkgo biloba*, the only living member of the family Ginkgoaceae and order Ginkgoales, class Coniferopsida.
– ORIGIN late 18th cent.: from Japanese *ginkyō*, from Chinese *yinxing*.

gin mill ▶ noun N. Amer. informal a run-down or seedy nightclub or bar.

ginnel /'gɪn(ə)l/ ▶ noun N. English a narrow passage between buildings; an alley.
– ORIGIN early 17th cent.: perhaps from French *chenel* 'channel'.

ginormous ▶ adjective Brit. informal extremely large.
– ORIGIN 1940s (originally military slang): blend of **GIANT** and **ENORMOUS**.

gin rummy ▶ noun see **GIN**¹.

Ginsberg /'gɪnzbə:g/, Allen (1926–97), American poet. A leading poet of the beat generation, and later influential in the hippy movement of the 1960s, he is notable for *Howl and Other Poems* (1956), in which he attacked American society for its materialism and complacency.

ginseng /'dʒɪnsɛŋ/ ▶ noun 1 [mass noun] a plant tuber credited with various tonic and medicinal properties, especially in the Far East.
2 the plant from which this tuber is obtained, native to east Asia and North America.
● Genus *Panax*, family Araliaceae: several species, in particular the Asian *P. pseudoginseng* and the North American *P. quinquefolius*.
– ORIGIN mid 17th cent.: from Chinese *rénshēn*, from *rén* 'man' + *shēn*, a kind of herb (because of the supposed resemblance of the forked root to a person).

gin sling ▶ noun a drink of gin and water, sweetened and flavoured with lemon or lime juice.

gin trap ▶ noun a mechanical trap for catching small game.

ginzo /'gɪnzəʊ/ US informal, derogatory ▶ noun an Italian; a person of Italian descent.
▶ adjective Italian.
– ORIGIN mid 20th cent.: perhaps from US slang *Guinea*, denoting an Italian or Spanish immigrant.

Giorgione /ˌdʒɔ:'dʒɪ'əʊneɪ, -ni, Italian dʒor'dʒone/ (c.1478–1510), Italian painter; also called **Giorgio Barbarelli** or **Giorgio da Castelfranco**. An influential figure in Renaissance art, he introduced the small easel picture in oils intended for private collectors. Notable works: *The Tempest* (c.1505) and *Sleeping Venus* (c.1510).

Giotto¹ /'dʒɒtəʊ/ (c.1267–1337), Italian painter; full name *Giotto di Bondone*. He introduced a naturalistic style showing human expression. Notable works include the frescoes in the Arena Chapel, Padua (1305–8) and the church of Santa Croce in Florence (c.1320).

Giotto² /'dʒɒtəʊ/ a European space probe which photographed the nucleus of Halley's Comet in March 1986.

Giovanni de' Medici the name of the Pope Leo X (see **LEO**¹).

gip ▶ noun variant spelling of **GYP**¹.

gippo ▶ noun variant spelling of **GYPPO**.

gippy tummy /'dʒɪpi/ (also **gyppy tummy**) ▶ noun [in sing.] Brit. informal diarrhoea affecting visitors to hot countries.
– ORIGIN 1940s: *gippy*, abbreviation of **EGYPTIAN**.

gipsy ▶ noun variant spelling of **GYPSY**.

gipsywort ▶ noun variant spelling of **GYPSYWORT**.

giraffe ▶ noun (pl. same or **giraffes**) a large African mammal with a very long neck and forelegs, having a coat patterned with brown patches separated by lighter lines. It is the tallest living animal.
● *Giraffa camelopardalis*, family Giraffidae.
– ORIGIN late 16th cent.: from French *girafe*, Italian *giraffa*, or Spanish and Portuguese *girafa*, based on Arabic *zarāfa*. The animal was known in Europe in the medieval period, and isolated instances of names for it based on the Arabic are recorded in Middle English, when it was commonly called the **CAMELOPARD**.

girandole /'dʒɪr(ə)ndəʊl/ ▶ noun a branched support for candles or other lights, which either stands on a surface or projects from a wall.
– ORIGIN mid 17th cent. (denoting a revolving cluster of fireworks): from French, from Italian *girandola*, from *girare* 'gyrate, turn', from Latin *gyrare* (see **GYRATE**).

girasol /'dʒɪrəsɒl, -səʊl/ (also **girasole** /-səʊl/) ▶ noun
1 a kind of opal reflecting a reddish glow.
2 North American term for **JERUSALEM ARTICHOKE**.
– ORIGIN late 16th cent. (in the sense 'sunflower'): from French, or from Italian *girasole*, from *girare* 'to turn' + *sole* 'sun' (because the sunflower turns to follow the path of the sun).

gird¹ ▶ verb (past and past participle **girded** or **girt**) [with obj.] poetic/literary encircle (a person or part of the body) with a belt or band: *a young man was to be girded with the belt of knighthood.*
■secure (a garment or sword) on the body with a belt or band: *a white robe girded with a magenta sash.* ■ surround; encircle: *the mountains girding Kabul.*
– PHRASES **gird (up) one's loins** prepare and strengthen oneself for what is to come.
– ORIGIN Old English *gyrdan*, of Germanic origin; related to Dutch *gorden* and German *gürten*, also to **GIRDLE**¹ and **GIRTH**.
▶ **gird oneself for** prepare oneself for (dangerous or difficult future actions).

gird² archaic ▶ verb [no obj.] make cutting or critical remarks: *the clubmen girded at the Committee.*
▶ noun a cutting or critical remark; a taunt.
– ORIGIN Middle English (in the sense 'strike, stab'): of unknown origin.

girder ▶ noun a large iron or steel beam or compound structure used for building bridges and the framework of large buildings.
– ORIGIN early 17th cent.: from **GIRD**¹ in the archaic sense 'brace, strengthen'.

girdle¹ ▶ noun a belt or cord worn round the waist.
■a woman's elasticated corset extending from waist to thigh. ■ a thing that surrounds something like a belt or girdle: *a communications girdle around the world.* ■ Anatomy either of two sets of bones encircling the body, to which the limbs are attached. See **PECTORAL GIRDLE**, **PELVIC GIRDLE**. ■ the part of a cut gem dividing the crown from the base and embraced by the setting. ■ a ring round a tree made by removing bark.
▶ verb [with obj.] 1 encircle (the body) with or as with a girdle or belt: *the Friar loosened the rope that girdled his waist.*
■surround; encircle: *the chain of volcanoes which girdles the Pacific.*
2 cut through the bark all the way round (a tree or branch), typically in order to kill it or to kill a branch to make the tree more fruitful.
– ORIGIN Old English *gyrdel*, of Germanic origin; related to Dutch *gordel* and German *Gürtel*, also to **GIRD**¹ and **GIRTH**.

girdle² ▶ noun Scottish and northern English term for **GRIDDLE** (in sense 1).
– ORIGIN late Middle English: variant of **GRIDDLE**.

girdled lizard (also **girdle-tailed lizard**) ▶ noun an African lizard with rough or spiny scales which give a banded appearance to the body and tail. Also called **ZONURE**.
● Genus *Cordylus*, family Cordylidae: several species, in particular the **common** (or **Cape**) **girdled lizard** (*C. cordylus*).

girdler ▶ noun 1 archaic a maker of girdles.
2 an insect which removes rings of bark from trees: [in combination] *a twig-girdler.*

girl ▶ noun 1 a female child.
■a person's daughter, especially a young one: *he was devoted to his little girl.*
2 a young or relatively young woman.
■[with modifier] a young woman of a specified kind or having a specified job: *a career girl* | *a chorus girl.* ■ (girls) informal women who mix socially or belong to a particular group, team, or profession: *I look forward to having a blather with the girls.* ■ a person's girlfriend: *his girl eloped with an accountant.* ■ dated a female servant.
– ORIGIN Middle English (denoting a child or young person of either sex): perhaps related to Low German *gör* 'child'.

girlfriend ▶ noun a person's regular female companion with whom they have a romantic or sexual relationship.
■a woman's female friend.

Girl Guide ▶ noun a member of the Guides Association.

Girl Guides Association former name for **GUIDES ASSOCIATION**.

girlhood ▶ noun [mass noun] the state or time of being a girl: *they had been friends since girlhood.*

girlie ▶ noun (also **girly**) (pl. **-ies**) informal a girl or young woman (often used as a term of address).
▶ adjective 1 (usu. **girly**) often derogatory like, characteristic of, or appropriate to a girl or young woman: *men aren't afraid to be soft, girly, and foppish.*
2 [attrib.] depicting or featuring nude or partially nude young women in erotic poses: *girlie magazines.*

girlish ▶ adjective of, like, or characteristic of a girl: *girlish giggles.*
– DERIVATIVES **girlishly** adverb, **girlishness** noun.

Girl Scout ▶ noun a girl belonging to the Scout Association.

girn ▶ verb variant spelling of **GURN**.

giro /'dʒaɪrəʊ/ ▶ noun (pl. **-os**) [mass noun] a system of electronic credit transfer used in Europe and Japan, largely involving banks, post offices, and public utilities.
■[count noun] [often as modifier] a cheque or payment by such a system, especially a social security payment: *a giro cheque.*
– ORIGIN late 19th cent.: via German from Italian, 'circulation (of money)'.

Gironde /ʒɪ'rɒnd, French ʒirɔ̃d/ a river estuary in SW France, formed at the junction of the Garonne and Dordogne Rivers, north of Bordeaux, and flowing north-west for 72 km (45 miles) into the Bay of Biscay.
■a department in Aquitaine, SW France.

Girondist /dʒɪ'rɒndɪst/ (also **Girondin** /dʒɪ'rɒndɪn, French ʒirɔ̃dɛ̃/) ▶ noun a member of the French moderate republican Party in power during the Revolution 1791–3, so called because the party leaders were the deputies from the department of the Gironde.
– ORIGIN from archaic French *Girondiste* (now *Girondin*).

girt¹ past participle of **GIRD**¹.

girt² ▶ noun old-fashioned term for **GIRTH**.

girth ▶ noun 1 [mass noun] the measurement around the middle of something, especially a person's waist.
■a person's middle or stomach, especially when large.
2 a band attached to a saddle, used to secure it on a horse by being fastened around its belly.
▶ verb [with obj.] archaic surround; encircle: *the four seas that girth Britain.*
– ORIGIN Middle English (in sense 2): from Old Norse *gjorth*.

GIS ▶ abbreviation for geographic information system, a system for storing and manipulating geographical information on computer.

Gisborne /'gɪzbən/ a port and resort on the east coast of North Island, New Zealand; pop. 31,480 (1991).

Giscard d'Estaing /ˌʒiː'skɑː dɛ'stã, French ʒiskar dɛstɛ̃/, Valéry (b.1926), French statesman, President 1974–81. He was a member of the European Parliament (1989–93) and has been leader of the centre-right *Union pour la démocratie française* since 1988.

Gish /gɪʃ/, Lillian (1896–1993), American actress. She and her sister **Dorothy** (1898–1968) appeared in a number of D. W. Griffith's films, including *Hearts of the World* (1918) and *Orphans of the Storm* (1922).

gismo ▶ noun variant spelling of **GIZMO**.

Gissing /'gɪsɪŋ/, George (Robert) (1857–1903), English novelist. Notable works: *New Grub Street*

(1891), *Born in Exile* (1892), and *The Private Papers of Henry Ryecroft* (1903).

gist /dʒɪst/ ▶ **noun** [in sing.] **1** the substance or essence of a speech or text: *she noted the gist of each message.* **2** Law the real point of an action: *damage is the gist of the action and without it the plaintiff must fail.*
– ORIGIN early 18th cent.: from Old French, third person singular present tense of *gesir* 'to lie', from Latin *jacere*. The Anglo-French legal phrase *cest action gist* 'this action lies' denoted that there were sufficient grounds to proceed; *gist* was adopted into English denoting the grounds themselves (sense 2).

git ▶ **noun** Brit. informal an unpleasant or contemptible person.
– ORIGIN 1940s: variant of the noun **GET** (see sense 2).

Gita /ˈgiːtə/ ▶ **noun** short for **BHAGAVADGITA**.

gîte /ʒiːt, French ʒit/ ▶ **noun** a small furnished holiday house in France, typically in a rural district.
– ORIGIN French, from Old French *giste*; related to *gésir* 'to lie'.

g

gittern /ˈgɪtəːn/ ▶ **noun** historical a lute-like medieval stringed instrument, forerunner of the guitar.
– ORIGIN late Middle English: from Old French *guiterne*; perhaps related to **CITTERN** and **GUITAR**.

give ▶ **verb** (past **gave**; past participle **given**) **1** [with two objs] freely transfer the possession of (something) to (someone); hand over to: *they gave her water to drink* | *the cheque **given to** the jeweller proved worthless* | [with obj.] *he **gave** the papers **back**.*
■ bestow (love, affection, or other emotional support): *his parents gave him the encouragement he needed to succeed* | [as adj. **giving**] *he was very giving and supportive.* ■ administer (medicine): *she was given antibiotics.* ■ hand over (an amount) in exchange or payment; pay: *how much did you **give for** that?* ■ (**give something for**) place a specified value on (something): *he never **gave** anything **for** French painting or for abstraction.* ■ [with obj.] used hyperbolically to express how greatly one wants to have or do something: *I'd **give** anything **for** a cup of tea* | ***I'd give my right arm** to be in* Othello. ■ communicate or impart (a message) to (someone): *give my love to all the girls.* ■ [with obj.] commit, consign, or entrust: *a baby **given into** their care by the accident of her birth.* ■ freely devote, set aside, or sacrifice for a purpose: *all who have **given** thought **to** the matter agree* | [no obj.] *group committees who **give** so generously **of** their time and effort.* ■ [with obj.] (of a man) sanction the marriage of (his daughter) to someone: *he **gave her in marriage** to an English noble.* ■ (**give oneself to**) dated (of a woman) consent to have sexual intercourse with (a man). ■ pass on (an illness or infection) to (someone): *I hope I don't give you my cold.* ■ [usu. in imperative] make a connection to allow (someone) to speak to (someone else) on the telephone: *give me the police.* ■ cite or present when making a toast or introducing a speaker or entertainer: *for your entertainment this evening I give you … Mister Albert DeNero!*
2 [with two objs] cause or allow (someone or something) to have (something, especially something abstract); provide or supply with: *you gave me such a fright* | [with obj.] *this leaflet gives our opening times.*
■ allot or assign (a score) to: *I gave it five out of ten.* ■ [with obj. and complement] (of an umpire or referee) declare whether or not (a player) is out or offside: *Gooch was given out, caught behind.* ■ [with obj.] adjudicate that (a goal) has been legitimately scored. ■ sentence (someone) to (a specified penalty): *for the first offence I was given a fine.* ■ concede or yield (something) as valid or deserved in respect of (someone): *give him his due.* ■ informal predict that (an activity, undertaking, or relationship) will last no longer than (a specified time): *this is a place that will not improve with time—I give it three weeks.* ■ [with obj.] yield as a product or result: *milk is sometimes added to give a richer cheese.* ■ [with obj.] (**give something off/out/forth**) emit odour, vapour, or similar substances: *it can be burnt without giving off toxic fumes.*
3 [with obj.] carry out or perform (a specified action): *I gave a bow* | [with two objs] *he gave the counter a polish.*
■ utter or produce (a sound): *he gave a gasp.* ■ provide (a party or social meal) as host or hostess: *a dinner given in honour of an American diplomat* | [with two objs] *Korda gave him a leaving party.*
4 [with obj.] state or put forward (information or argument): *he did not give his name.*
■ pledge or assign as a guarantee: [with two objs] *I give you my word.* ■ [with two objs, usu. with negative] say to (someone) as an excuse or inappropriate answer: *don't give me any of your backchat.* ■ deliver (a judgement) authoritatively: *I gave my verdict.* ■ present (an appearance or impression): *he gave no sign of life.* ■ [no obj.] informal tell what one knows: *okay, give—what's that all about?*
5 [no obj.] alter in shape under pressure rather than resist or break: *that chair doesn't give.*
■ yield or give way to pressure: *the heavy door didn't give until the fifth push* | figurative *when two people who don't get on are thrust together, something's got to give.* ■ [no obj.] N. Amer. informal concede defeat; surrender: *I give!*
▶ **noun** [mass noun] capacity to bend or alter in shape under pressure; elasticity: *plastic pots that have enough give to accommodate the vigorous roots.*
■ figurative ability to adapt or comply; flexibility: *there is no give at all in the British position.*
– PHRASES **give oneself airs** act pretentiously or snobbishly. **give and take** mutual concessions and compromises. ■ [as verb] make concessions and compromises. **give as good as one gets** respond with equal force or vehemence when attacked. **give the game** (or **show**) **away** inadvertently reveal something secret or concealed. **give it to someone** informal scold or punish someone. **give me ——** I prefer or admire ——: *give me the mainland any day!* **give me a break** informal used to express exasperation, protest, or disbelief. **give someone one** Brit. vulgar slang (of a man) have sexual intercourse with a woman. **give or take ——** informal to within —— (used to express the degree or accuracy of a figure): *three hundred and fifty years ago, give or take a few.* ■ apart from: *give or take the odd aircraft bit, there are few new products.* **give rise to** cause or induce to happen: *decisions which give rise to arguments.* **give someone to understand** (or **believe** or **know**) inform someone in a formal and rather indirect way: *I was given to understand that I had been invited.* **give up the ghost** see **GHOST**. **give someone what for** informal, chiefly Brit. punish or scold someone severely. **not give a damn** (or **hoot** etc.) informal not care at all: *people who don't give a damn about the environment.* **what gives?** informal what's the news?; what's happening? (frequently used as a friendly greeting).
– DERIVATIVES **giver** noun.
– ORIGIN Old English *giefan, gefan*, of Germanic origin; related to Dutch *geven* and German *geben*.
▶ **give someone away 1** reveal the true identity of someone: *his strangely shaped feet gave him away.* ■ reveal information which incriminates someone. **2** hand over a bride ceremonially to her bridegroom as part of a wedding ceremony.
give something away 1 reveal something secret or concealed. **2** (in sport) concede a goal or advantage to the opposition, especially through careless play. **3** Austral./NZ stop doing something: *he'd given away some of the things he got up to.*
give in cease fighting or arguing; yield; surrender: *he reluctantly **gave in to** the pressure.*
give something in Brit. hand in a completed document to an official or a piece of work to a supervisor.
give on to (or **into**) Brit. (of a window, door, corridor, etc.) overlook or lead into: *a plate glass window gave on to the roof.*
give out 1 be completely used up: *her energy was on the verge of giving out.* ■ stop functioning; break down: *he curses and swears till his voice gives out.* **2** Irish speak in an angry or scolding way: *the woman began **giving out to** poor Paddy.*
give something out distribute or broadcast something: *I've been giving out leaflets* | (**give out**) *I've told the girls to give out that we've gone fishing.*
give over [often in imperative] Brit. informal stop doing something. ■ used to express vehement disagreement or denial: *I suggested her salary might be £100,000. 'Give over!'*
give up cease making an effort; resign oneself to failure.
give it up [usu. in imperative] US informal applaud a performer or entertainer.
give oneself up (or **over**) **to** allow oneself to be taken over by (an emotion or addiction): *he gave himself up to pleasure.*
give someone up 1 deliver a wanted person to authority: *a voice told him to come out and **give himself up**.* **2** stop hoping that someone is still going to arrive: *oh, it's you—we'd almost given you up.* ■ pronounce a sick person incurable.
give something up part with something that one would prefer to keep: *she would have given up everything for love.* ■ stop the habitual doing or consuming of something: *I've decided to give up drinking.*
give up on stop having faith or belief in: *they weren't about to give up on their heroes so easily.*

giveaway informal ▶ **noun 1** a thing that is given free, especially for promotional purposes: *a pre-election tax giveaway.*
2 a thing that makes an inadvertent revelation: *the shape of the parcel was a dead giveaway.*
▶ **adjective** [attrib.] **1** free of charge: *giveaway goodies.*
■ (of prices) very low.
2 revealing: *small giveaway mannerisms.*

giveback ▶ **noun** N. Amer. an agreement by workers to surrender benefits and conditions previously agreed in return for new concessions or awards.

given past participle of **GIVE**. ▶ **adjective 1** specified or stated: *lines telling each player where they should be for any given moment.*
2 [predic.] (**given to**) inclined or disposed to: *she was not often given to anger.*
3 Law, archaic (of a document) signed and dated: *given under my hand this eleventh day of April.*
▶ **preposition** taking into account: *given the complexity of the task, they were able to do a good job.*
▶ **noun** a known or established fact or situation: *at a couture house, attentive service is a given.*

given name ▶ **noun** another term for **FIRST NAME**.

Giza /ˈgiːzə/ a city south-west of Cairo in northern Egypt, on the west bank of the Nile, site of the Pyramids and the Sphinx; pop. 2,156,000 (est. 1990). Also called **EL GIZA**; Arabic name **AL JIZAH**.

gizmo /ˈgɪzməʊ/ (also **gismo**) ▶ **noun** (pl. **-os**) informal a gadget, especially one whose name the speaker does not know or cannot recall: *the latest multimedia gizmo.*
– ORIGIN 1940s (originally US): of unknown origin.

gizzard /ˈgɪzəd/ ▶ **noun** a muscular, thick-walled part of a bird's stomach for grinding food, typically with grit.
■ a muscular stomach of some fish, insects, molluscs, and other invertebrates. ■ informal a person's stomach or throat: *the fans wanted to see him rip the gizzards out of bad guys.*
– ORIGIN late Middle English *giser*: from Old French, based on Latin *gigeria* 'cooked entrails of fowl'. The final *-d* was added in the 16th cent.

Gjetost /ˈjɛtɒst/ ▶ **noun** [mass noun] a very sweet, firm, golden-brown Norwegian cheese, traditionally made with goat's milk.
– ORIGIN Norwegian, from *gjet, geit* 'goat' + *ost* 'cheese'.

GLA ▶ **abbreviation for** gamma linolenic acid.

glabella /gləˈbɛlə/ ▶ **noun** (pl. **glabellae** /-liː/) Anatomy the smooth part of the forehead above and between the eyebrows.
– DERIVATIVES **glabellar** adjective.
– ORIGIN early 19th cent.: modern Latin, from Latin *glabellus* (adjective), diminutive of *glaber* 'smooth'.

glabrous /ˈgleɪbrəs/ ▶ **adjective** technical (chiefly of the skin or a leaf) free from hair or down; smooth.
– ORIGIN mid 17th cent.: from Latin *glaber, glabr-* 'hairless, smooth' + **-OUS**.

glacé /ˈglaseɪ/ ▶ **adjective** [attrib.] **1** (of fruit) having a glossy surface due to preservation in sugar: *a glacé cherry.*
2 (of cloth or leather) smooth and highly polished.
– ORIGIN mid 19th cent.: French, literally 'iced', past participle of *glacer*, from *glace* 'ice'.

glacé icing ▶ **noun** [mass noun] icing made with icing sugar and water.

glacial /ˈgleɪʃ(ə)l, -sɪəl/ ▶ **adjective** relating to, resulting from, or denoting the presence or agency of ice, especially in the form of glaciers: *thick glacial deposits* | *a glacial lake.*
■ of or resembling ice; icy: *glacial temperatures* | *glacial blue eyes.* ■ Chemistry denoting pure organic acids (especially acetic acid) which form ice-like crystals on freezing. ■ extremely slow (like the movement of a glacier): *an official described progress in the talks as glacial.*
▶ **noun** Geology a glacial period.
– DERIVATIVES **glacially** adverb.
– ORIGIN mid 17th cent.: from French, or from Latin *glacialis* 'icy', from *glacies* 'ice'.

glacial period ▶ **noun** a period in the earth's history when polar and mountain ice sheets were unusually extensive across the earth's surface.

glaciated /ˈgleɪsɪeɪtɪd, ˈglas-/ ▶ **adjective** covered or

having been covered by glaciers or ice sheets: *a glaciated valley.*
– ORIGIN mid 19th cent.: past participle of obsolete *glaciate*, from Latin *glaciare* 'freeze', from *glacies* 'ice'.

glaciation /ˌɡleɪsɪˈeɪʃ(ə)n/ ▶ **noun** [mass noun] Geology the process, condition, or result of being covered by glaciers or ice sheets.
▪[count noun] a glacial period.

glacier /ˈɡlasɪə, ˈɡleɪs-/ ▶ **noun** a slowly moving mass or river of ice formed by the accumulation and compaction of snow on mountains or near the poles.
– ORIGIN mid 18th cent.: from French, from *glace* 'ice', based on Latin *glacies*.

Glacier Bay National Park a national park in SE Alaska, on the Pacific coast. Extending over an area of 12,880 sq. km (4,975 sq. miles), it contains the terminus of the Grand Pacific Glacier.

glaciology /ˌɡleɪsɪˈɒlədʒi/ ▶ **noun** [mass noun] the study of the internal dynamics and effects of glaciers.
– DERIVATIVES **glaciological** adjective, **glaciologist** noun.
– ORIGIN late 19th cent.: from Latin *glacies* 'ice' + **-LOGY**.

glacis /ˈɡlasɪs, -si/ ▶ **noun** (pl. same /-sɪz, -siːz/) a bank sloping down from a fort which exposes attackers to the defenders' missiles.
▪(also **glacis plate**) a sloping piece of armour plate protecting part of a vehicle.
– ORIGIN late 17th cent.: from French, from Old French *glacier* 'to slip', from *glace* 'ice', based on Latin *glacies*.

glad[1] ▶ **adjective** (**gladder, gladdest**) [predic.] pleased; delighted: *she was alive, which was something to be glad about* | [with infinitive] *I'm really glad to hear that.*
▪happy for someone's good fortune: *I'm so* **glad for** *you.* ▪ [attrib.] causing happiness: *glad tidings.* ▪ grateful: *he was* **glad for** *the excuse to put it off.*
▶ **verb** (**gladded, gladding**) [with obj.] poetic/literary make happy; please: *Albion's lessening shore could grieve or glad mine eye.*
– DERIVATIVES **gladly** adverb, **gladness** noun, **gladsome** adjective (poetic/literary).
– ORIGIN Old English *glæd* (originally in the sense 'bright, shining'), of Germanic origin; related to Old Norse *glathr* 'bright, joyous' and German *glatt* 'smooth', also to Latin *glaber* 'smooth, hairless'.

glad[2] (also **gladdie**) ▶ **noun** informal a gladiolus.
– ORIGIN 1920s: abbreviation.

gladden ▶ **verb** [with obj.] make glad: *the high, childish laugh was a sound that gladdened her heart.*

gladdon /ˈɡlad(ə)n/ ▶ **noun** a purple-flowered iris native to Eurasia and North Africa, which produces an unpleasant odour, especially when bruised. Also called **STINKING IRIS**.
• *Iris foetidissima*, family Iridaceae.
– ORIGIN Old English *glædene*, based on Latin *gladiolus* (see **GLADIOLUS**).

glade ▶ **noun** an open space in a wood or forest.
– ORIGIN late Middle English: of unknown origin; perhaps related to **GLAD**[1] or **GLEAM**, with reference to the comparative brightness of a clearing (obsolete senses of *glade* include 'a gleam of light' and 'a bright space between clouds').

glad eye ▶ **noun** informal a glance that is intended to be sexually alluring: *smile at them,* **give them the glad eye.**

glad-hand chiefly US ▶ **verb** [with obj.] (especially of a politician) greet or welcome warmly or with the appearance of warmth: *they had been taking every free minute to glad-hand loyal supporters.*
▶ **noun** (**glad hand**) [in sing.] a warm and hearty, but often insincere, greeting or welcome.
– DERIVATIVES **glad-hander** noun.

gladiator /ˈɡladɪeɪtə/ ▶ **noun** (in ancient Rome) a man trained to fight with weapons against other men or wild animals in an arena.
– DERIVATIVES **gladiatorial** adjective.
– ORIGIN late Middle English: from Latin, from *gladius* 'sword'.

gladiolus /ˌɡladɪˈəʊləs/ ▶ **noun** (pl. **gladioli** /-lʌɪ/ or **gladioluses**) an Old World plant of the iris family, with sword-shaped leaves and spikes of brightly coloured flowers, popular in gardens and as a cut flower.
• Genus *Gladiolus*, family Iridaceae: many species.
– ORIGIN Old English (originally denoting the gladdon), from Latin, diminutive of *gladius* 'sword' (used as a plant name by Pliny).

glad rags ▶ **plural noun** informal clothes for a special occasion; one's best clothes.

Gladstone, William Ewart (1809–98), British Liberal statesman, Prime Minister 1868–74, 1880–5, 1886, and 1892–4. At first a Conservative minister, he later joined the Liberal Party, becoming its leader in 1867. His ministries saw the introduction of elementary education, the passing of the Irish Land Acts and the third Reform Act, and his campaign in favour of Home Rule for Ireland.
– DERIVATIVES **Gladstonian** adjective.

Gladstone bag ▶ **noun** a bag like a briefcase having two equal compartments joined by a hinge.
– ORIGIN late 19th cent.: named after W. E. **GLADSTONE**, who was noted for the amount of travelling he undertook when electioneering.

Glagolitic /ˌɡlaɡəˈlɪtɪk/ ▶ **adjective** denoting or relating to an alphabet based on Greek minuscules, formerly used in writing some Slavic languages.
▶ **noun** [mass noun] this alphabet.

The alphabet is of uncertain origin, and was introduced in the 9th century, at about the same time as the Cyrillic alphabet, which has superseded it except in some Orthodox Church liturgies.

– ORIGIN from modern Latin *glagoliticus*, from *glagòljica*, the name in Serbo-Croat of the Glagolitic alphabet, from Old Church Slavonic *glagolŭ* 'word'.

glaikit /ˈɡleɪkɪt/ ▶ **adjective** Scottish & N. English stupid, foolish, or thoughtless.
– ORIGIN late Middle English: related to Scots *glaiks* 'tricks, pranks'.

glair /ˈɡlɛː/ ▶ **noun** [mass noun] a preparation made from egg white, especially as an adhesive for bookbinding and gilding.
▪dated egg white.
– DERIVATIVES **glairy** adjective.
– ORIGIN Middle English: from Old French *glaire*, based on Latin *clara*, feminine of *clarus* 'clear'.

glaive /ɡleɪv/ ▶ **noun** poetic/literary a sword.
– ORIGIN Middle English (denoting a lance or halberd): from Old French, apparently from Latin *gladius* 'sword'.

Glam. ▶ **abbreviation for** Glamorgan.

glam informal ▶ **adjective** glamorous: *a dapper magician and his glam assistant.*
▪relating to or denoting glam rock.
▶ **noun** [mass noun] glamour: *Nigel, for all his glam, was Karen's sort.*
▪glam rock.
▶ **verb** (**glammed, glamming**) [no obj.] (**glam up**) make oneself look glamorous.
– ORIGIN 1930s: abbreviation.

Glamorgan /ɡləˈmɔːɡ(ə)n/ a former county of South Wales.

glamorize (also **glamourize** or **-ise**) ▶ **verb** [with obj.] make (something) seem glamorous or desirable, especially spuriously so: *the lyrics glamorize drugs.*
– DERIVATIVES **glamorization** noun.

glamorous ▶ **adjective** having glamour: *one of the world's most glamorous women.*
– DERIVATIVES **glamorously** adverb.

glamour (US also **glamor**) ▶ **noun** [mass noun] the attractive or exciting quality that makes certain people or things seem appealing or special: *the glamour of Monte Carlo.*
▪beauty or charm that is sexually attractive: *George had none of his brother's glamour.* ▪ archaic enchantment; magic: *that maiden, made by glamour out of flowers.*
– ORIGIN early 18th cent. (originally Scots in the sense 'enchantment, magic'): alteration of **GRAMMAR**. Although *grammar* itself was not used in this sense, the Latin word *grammatica* (from which it derives) was often used in the Middle Ages to mean 'scholarship, learning', including the occult practices popularly associated with learning.

glamour girl ▶ **noun** a fashionable, attractive young woman, especially a model or film star.

glamour puss ▶ **noun** informal a glamorous woman.

glam rock ▶ **noun** [mass noun] a style of rock music first popular in the early 1970s, characterized by male performers wearing exaggeratedly flamboyant clothes and make-up.

glance[1] ▶ **verb** [no obj., with adverbial of direction] **1** take a brief or hurried look: *Ginny glanced at her watch.*
▪(**glance at/through**) read quickly or cursorily: *I glanced through your personnel file last night.*
2 hit something at an angle and bounce off obliquely: *he saw a stone* **glance off** *a crag and hit Tom on the head.*
▪(especially of light) reflect off (something) with a brief flash: *sunlight* **glanced off** *the curved body of a dolphin.* ▪ [with obj. and adverbial of direction] (in ball games) deflect (the ball) slightly with a delicate contact: *he glanced the ball into the right corner of the net.* ▪ [with obj.] Cricket deflect (the ball) with the bat held slantwise; play such a stroke against (the bowler).
▶ **noun 1** a brief or hurried look: *Sean and Michael exchanged glances.*
2 poetic/literary a flash or gleam of light.
3 Cricket a stroke with the bat's face turned slantwise to deflect the ball slightly.
– PHRASES **at a glance** immediately upon looking: *she saw at a glance what had happened.* **at first glance** when seen or considered for the first time, especially briefly: *good news, at first glance, for frequent travellers.* **glance one's eye** archaic look briefly: *glancing his severe eye around the group.*
– DERIVATIVES **glancingly** adverb.
– ORIGIN late Middle English (in the sense 'rebound obliquely'): probably a nasalized form of obsolete *glace* in the same sense, from Old French *glacier* 'to slip', from *glace* 'ice', based on Latin *glacies*.

glance[2] ▶ **noun** [mass noun] a shiny black or grey sulphide ore of lead, copper, or other metal.
– ORIGIN late Middle English: from German *Glanz* 'brightness, lustre'; compare with Dutch *glanserts* 'glance ore'.

glancing ▶ **adjective** [attrib.] striking someone or something at an angle rather than directly and with full force: *he was struck a glancing blow.*

gland[1] ▶ **noun** an organ in the human or animal body which secretes particular chemical substances for use in the body or for discharge into the surroundings.
▪a structure resembling this, especially a lymph node. ▪ Botany a secreting cell or group of cells on or within a plant structure.
– ORIGIN late 17th cent.: from French *glande*, alteration of Old French *glandre*, from Latin *glandulae* 'throat glands'.

gland[2] ▶ **noun** a sleeve used to produce a seal round a piston rod or other shaft.
– ORIGIN early 19th cent.: probably a variant of Scots *glam* 'a vice or clamp'; related to **CLAMP**[1].

glanders /ˈɡlandəz/ ▶ **plural noun** [usu. treated as sing.] a rare contagious disease that mainly affects horses, characterized by swellings below the jaw and mucous discharge from the nostrils.
• This disease is caused by the bacterium *Pseudomonas mallei*.
– ORIGIN late 15th cent.: from Old French *glandre* (see **GLAND**[1]).

glandular /ˈɡlandjʊlə, ˈɡlan(d)ʒʊlə/ ▶ **adjective** of, relating to, or affecting a gland or glands.
– ORIGIN mid 18th cent.: from French *glandulaire*, from *glandule* 'gland', from Latin *glandulae* (see **GLAND**[1]).

glandular fever ▶ **noun** [mass noun] an infectious viral disease characterized by swelling of the lymph glands and prolonged lassitude. Also called **infectious mononucleosis.**

glans /ɡlanz/ ▶ **noun** (pl. **glandes** /ˈɡlandiːz/) Anatomy the rounded part forming the end of the penis or clitoris.
– ORIGIN mid 17th cent.: from Latin, literally 'acorn'.

glare ▶ **verb** [no obj.] **1** stare in an angry or fierce way: *she* **glared at** *him, her cheeks flushing.*
▪[with obj.] express (a feeling, especially defiance) by staring in such a way: *he glared defiance at the pistols pointing down at him.*
2 [with adverbial] (of the sun or an electric light) shine with a strong or dazzling light: *the sun glared out of a clear blue sky.*
▶ **noun 1** a fierce or angry stare.
2 [mass noun] strong and dazzling light: *Murray narrowed his eyes against the glare of the sun.*
▪figurative oppressive public attention or scrutiny: *he carried on his life in the full* **glare of publicity.** ▪ archaic dazzling or showy appearance; tawdry brilliance: *the pomp and glare of rhetoric.*
– DERIVATIVES **glary** adjective.
– ORIGIN Middle English (in the sense 'shine brilliantly or dazzlingly'): from Middle Dutch and Middle Low German *glaren* 'to gleam, glare': perhaps related to **GLASS**. The sense 'stare' occurred first in the adjective *glaring* (late Middle English).

g

glare ice ▶ noun [mass noun] N. Amer. smooth, glassy ice.
– ORIGIN mid 19th cent.: probably from obsolete *glare* 'frost'; perhaps related to **GLARE**.

glareshield ▶ noun a screen attached to the cockpit canopy of an aircraft designed to reduce the effects of glare.

glaring ▶ adjective **1** [attrib.] giving out or reflecting a strong or dazzling light: *the glaring sun*.
■staring fiercely or fixedly: *their glaring eyes*.
2 highly obvious or conspicuous: *there is a glaring omission in the above data*.
– DERIVATIVES **glaringly** adverb.

Glasgow a city in Scotland on the River Clyde; pop. 654,500 (1991). It was formerly a major shipbuilding centre, is still an important commercial and cultural centre, and is the largest city in Scotland.

Glashow /ˈglaʃaʊ/, Sheldon Lee (b.1932), American theoretical physicist. He independently developed a unified theory to explain electromagnetic interactions and the weak nuclear force, and extended the quark theory of Murray Gell-Mann. Nobel Prize for Physics (1979).

g

glasnost /ˈglaznɒst, ˈglɑːs-/ ▶ noun [mass noun] (in the former Soviet Union) the policy or practice of more open consultative government and wider dissemination of information, initiated by leader Mikhail Gorbachev from 1985.
– ORIGIN from Russian *glasnost'*, literally 'the fact of being public', from *glasnyy* 'public, open' + *-nost'* '-ness'.

Glass, Philip (b.1937), American composer, a leading minimalist. Notable works: *Einstein on the Beach* (opera 1976), *Glass Pieces* (ballet 1982), and *Low Symphony* (1993).

glass ▶ noun **1** [mass noun] a hard, brittle substance, typically transparent or translucent, made by fusing sand with soda, lime, and sometimes other ingredients and cooling rapidly. It is used to make windows, drinking containers, and other articles.
■any similar substance which has solidified from a molten state without crystallizing.
2 a thing made from, or partly from, glass, in particular:
■a container to drink from: *a beer glass*. ■ [mass noun] glassware. ■ [mass noun] greenhouses or cold frames considered collectively. ■ chiefly Brit. a mirror. ■ dated short for **WEATHER GLASS**. ■ archaic an hourglass.
3 a lens, or an optical instrument containing a lens or lenses, in particular a monocle or a magnifying lens.
▶ verb [with obj.] **1** cover or enclose with glass: *the inn has a long gallery, now* ***glassed in***.
2 (especially in hunting) scan (one's surroundings) with binoculars: *the first day was spent glassing the rolling hills*.
3 poetic/literary reflect in or as if in a mirror: *the opposite slopes* ***glassed themselves*** *in the deep dark water*.
4 Brit. informal hit (someone) in the face with a beer glass.
– PHRASES **people (who live) in glass houses shouldn't throw stones** proverb you shouldn't criticize others when you have similar faults of your own. **under glass** (of plants) grown in a greenhouse or cold frame.
– DERIVATIVES **glassful** noun (pl. **-fuls**), **glassless** adjective, **glass-like** adjective.
– ORIGIN Old English *glæs*, of Germanic origin; related to Dutch *glas* and German *Glas*.

glass-blowing ▶ noun [mass noun] the craft of making glassware by blowing semi-molten glass through a long tube.
– DERIVATIVES **glass-blower** noun.

glass case ▶ noun an exhibition display case made mostly from glass.

glass ceiling ▶ noun [usu. in sing.] an unacknowledged barrier to advancement in a profession, especially affecting women and members of minorities.

glass cloth ▶ noun **1** Brit. a cloth covered with powdered glass or other abrasive, used for smoothing and polishing.
2 [mass noun] woven fabric of fine-spun glass thread.

glass cutter ▶ noun a tool which scores a line on a piece of glass, allowing the glass to be snapped along the line.

glassed-in ▶ adjective (of a building or part of a building) covered or enclosed with glass.

glass eel ▶ noun an elver at the time that it first enters brackish or fresh water, when it is translucent.

glasses ▶ plural noun a pair of lenses set in a frame resting on the nose and ears, used to correct or assist defective eyesight or protect the eyes.
■a pair of binoculars.

glass eye ▶ noun a false eye made from glass.

glass fibre ▶ noun [mass noun] chiefly Brit. a strong plastic, textile, or other material containing embedded glass filaments for reinforcement.
■[count noun] a filament of glass.

glassfish ▶ noun (pl. same or **-fishes**) a small fish with an almost transparent body, in particular:
• a marine or freshwater fish which is popular in aquaria (genus *Chanda*, family Centropomidae), including the **Indian glassfish** (*C. ranga*). • an elongated marine fish of the West Pacific (*Salangichthys microdon*, family Salangidae), eaten as a delicacy in Japan.

glass harmonica ▶ noun a musical instrument in which the sound is made by a row of rotating, concentric glass bowls, kept moist and pressed with the fingers or with keys. It was invented in 1761 by Benjamin Franklin and was popular until about 1830.

glasshouse ▶ noun **1** Brit. a greenhouse.
2 Brit. military slang a place of detention.
3 the glass enclosing a car's passenger cabin, considered from a design point of view.

glassine /ˈglɑːsiːn/ ▶ noun [mass noun] [usu. as modifier] a glossy transparent paper.
– ORIGIN early 20th cent.: from **GLASS** + **-INE**[4].

glass lizard ▶ noun a legless burrowing lizard of snake-like appearance, with smooth shiny skin and an easily detached tail, native to Eurasia, Africa, and America. Also called **GLASS SNAKE**.
• Genus *Ophisaurus*, family Anguidae: several species.

glass-making ▶ noun [mass noun] the manufacture of glass.
– DERIVATIVES **glass-maker** noun.

glasspaper ▶ noun [mass noun] paper covered with powdered glass, used for smoothing and polishing.

glass snake ▶ noun another term for **GLASS LIZARD**.

glass sponge ▶ noun a deep-water sponge which has a skeleton of intricately shaped spines of silica that may fuse to form a filmy lattice with a glass-like appearance. See also **VENUS'S FLOWER BASKET**.
• Class Hexactinellida.

glassware ▶ noun [mass noun] ornaments and articles made from glass.

glass wool ▶ noun [mass noun] glass in the form of fine fibres used for packing and insulation.

glasswort ▶ noun a widely distributed salt-marsh plant with fleshy scale-like leaves. The ashes of the burnt plant were formerly used in glass-making.
• Genus *Salicornia*, family Chenopodiaceae: several species.

glassy ▶ adjective (**glassier**, **glassiest**) **1** of or resembling glass in some way, in particular:
■having the physical properties of glass; vitreous: *glassy lavas*. ■ (of water) having a smooth surface. ■ (of sound) resembling the sharp or ringing noise made when glass is struck: *a glassy clink*. ■ (of a building) having glass walls.
2 (of a person's eyes or expression) showing no interest or animation; dull and glazed.
▶ noun (also **glassie**) dialect a glass marble.
– PHRASES **(just) the glassy** Austral. informal the most excellent person or thing. [ORIGIN: *glassy*, figurative use of the sense '(highly prized) marble'.]
– DERIVATIVES **glassily** adverb, **glassiness** noun.

Glastonbury /ˈglastənb(ə)ri/ a town in Somerset; pop. 6,770 (1981). It is the legendary burial place of King Arthur and Queen Guinevere and the site of a ruined abbey held by legend to have been founded by Joseph of Arimathea.

Glaswegian /glazˈwiːdʒ(ə)n, glas-, glɑːz-, glɑːs-/ ▶ adjective of or relating to Glasgow.
▶ noun a native of Glasgow.
■[mass noun] the dialect or accent of people from Glasgow.
– ORIGIN from **GLASGOW**, on the pattern of words such as *Norwegian*.

Glatzer Neisse /ˈglatsɐ ˌnaɪsə/ German name for **NEISSE** (in sense 2).

Glauber's salt /ˈglaʊbəz, ˈglɔː-/ ▶ noun (also **Glauber's salts**) a crystalline hydrated form of sodium sulphate, used chiefly as a laxative.
– ORIGIN mid 18th cent.: named after Johann R. *Glauber* (1604–1668), the German chemist who first produced the substance artificially.

glaucoma /glɔːˈkəʊmə/ ▶ noun [mass noun] Medicine a condition of increased pressure within the eyeball, causing gradual loss of sight.
– DERIVATIVES **glaucomatous** adjective.
– ORIGIN mid 17th cent.: via Latin from Greek *glaukōma*, based on *glaukos* 'bluish-green, bluish-grey' (because of the grey-green haze in the pupil).

glauconite /ˈglɔːkənʌɪt/ ▶ noun [mass noun] a greenish clay mineral of the illite group, found chiefly in marine sands.
– ORIGIN mid 19th cent.: from German *Glaukonit*, from Greek *glaukon* (neuter of *glaukos* 'bluish-green') + **-ITE**[1].

glaucophane /ˈglɔːkəfeɪn/ ▶ noun [mass noun] a bluish sodium-containing mineral of the amphibole group, found chiefly in schists and other metamorphic rocks.
– ORIGIN mid 19th cent.: from German *Glaukophan*, from Greek *glaukos* 'bluish-green' + *-phanēs* 'shining'.

glaucous /ˈglɔːkəs/ ▶ adjective technical or poetic/literary
1 of a dull greyish-green or blue colour.
2 covered with a powdery bloom like that on grapes.
– ORIGIN late 17th cent.: via Latin from Greek *glaukos* + **-OUS**.

glaucous gull ▶ noun a large white and pale grey gull breeding on Arctic coasts.
• *Larus hyperboreus*, family Laridae.

glaze ▶ verb [with obj.] **1** fit panes of glass into (a window or door frame or similar structure): *windows can be glazed using laminated glass*.
■enclose or cover with glass: *the verandas were* ***glazed in***.
2 (often **be glazed**) cover with a glaze or similar finish: *new potatoes which had been glazed in mint-flavoured butter*.
3 [no obj.] lose brightness and animation: *the prospect makes my eyes* ***glaze over*** *with boredom* | [as adj. **glazed**] *she had that glazed look in her eyes again*.
▶ noun [usu. in sing.] **1** a substance used to give a smooth, shiny surface to something, in particular:
■a vitreous substance fused on to the surface of pottery to form a hard, impervious decorative coating. ■ a liquid such as milk or beaten egg, used to form a smooth shiny coating on food. ■ chiefly Art a thin topcoat of transparent paint used to modify the tone of an underlying colour.
2 a smooth, shiny surface formed especially by glazing: *the glaze of the white cups*.
■N. Amer. a thin, glassy coating of ice on the ground or the surface of water.
– DERIVATIVES **glazer** noun.
– ORIGIN late Middle English *glase*, from **GLASS**.

glazed frost ▶ noun [mass noun] a glassy coating of ice, typically caused by rain freezing on impact.

glazier /ˈgleɪzɪə/ ▶ noun a person whose trade is fitting glass into windows and doors.

glazing ▶ noun [mass noun] the action of installing windows.
■glass windows: *sealed protective glazing*. ■ [count noun] a material used to produce a glaze.

glazing bar ▶ noun a bar or rigid supporting strip between adjacent panes of glass.

Glazunov /ˈglazʊnɒf/, Aleksandr (Konstantinovich) (1865–1936), Russian composer, a pupil of Rimsky-Korsakov. Notable work: *The Seasons* (ballet, 1901).

GLC ▶ abbreviation for ■ Chemistry gas–liquid chromatography. ■ (in the UK) Greater London Council, abolished in 1986.

gleam ▶ verb [no obj.] shine brightly, especially with reflected light: *light gleamed on the china cats* | *her eyes gleamed with satisfaction*.
■(of a smooth surface or object) reflect light because well polished: *Victor buffed the glass until it gleamed* | [as adj. **gleaming**] *sleek and gleaming black limousines*. ■ (of an emotion or quality) appear or be expressed through the brightness of someone's eyes or expression: *a hint of mischief gleaming in her eyes*.
▶ noun [usu. in sing.] a faint or brief light, especially one reflected from something: *the gleam of a silver tray*.
■a brief or faint instance of a quality or emotion, especially a desirable one: *the* ***gleam of*** *hope vanished*. ■ a brightness in a person's eyes taken as a sign of a

particular emotion: *she saw an unmistakable gleam of triumph in his eyes.*

– PHRASES **a gleam in someone's eye** see **EYE**.

– DERIVATIVES **gleamingly** adverb, **gleamy** adjective (archaic).

– ORIGIN Old English *glǣm* 'brilliant light', of Germanic origin.

glean /gliːn/ ▶ **verb** [with obj.] **1** extract (information) from various sources: *the information is gleaned from press cuttings.*
▪collect gradually and bit by bit: *objects gleaned from local markets.*
2 historical gather (leftover grain) after a harvest: [as noun **gleaning**] *the conditions of farm workers in the 1890s made gleaning essential.*
– DERIVATIVES **gleaner** noun.
– ORIGIN late Middle English: from Old French *glener*, from late Latin *glennare*, probably of Celtic origin.

gleanings ▶ **plural noun** things, especially facts, that are gathered or collected from various sources rather than acquired as a whole.

glebe /gliːb/ ▶ **noun** historical a piece of land serving as part of a clergyman's benefice and providing income.
▪[mass noun] archaic land; fields.
– ORIGIN late Middle English: from Latin *gleba*, *glaeba* 'clod, land, soil'.

glee ▶ **noun 1** [mass noun] great delight: *his face lit up with impish glee.*
2 a song for men's voices in three or more parts, usually unaccompanied, of a type popular especially *c.*1750–1830.
– ORIGIN Old English *glēo* 'entertainment, music, fun', of Germanic origin. Sense 2 dates from the mid 17th cent.

glee club ▶ **noun** a society for singing part-songs.

gleeful ▶ **adjective** exuberantly or triumphantly joyful: *she gave a gleeful chuckle.*
– DERIVATIVES **gleefully** adverb, **gleefulness** noun.

gleeman ▶ **noun** (pl. **-men**) historical a professional entertainer, especially a singer.

gleesome ▶ **adjective** archaic gleeful.

gleet /gliːt/ ▶ **noun** [mass noun] Medicine a watery discharge from the urethra caused by gonorrhoeal infection.
– DERIVATIVES **gleety** adjective.
– ORIGIN Middle English (denoting mucus formed in the stomach): from Old French *glette* 'slime, secretion', of unknown origin.

Gleichschaltung /ˈglʌɪxˌʃaltʊŋ, German ˈglaɪçˌʃaltʊŋ/ ▶ **noun** [mass noun] the standardization of political, economic, and social institutions as carried out in authoritarian states.
– ORIGIN German, from *gleich* 'same' + *schalten* 'force or bring into line'.

glen ▶ **noun** a narrow valley, especially in Scotland or Ireland.
– ORIGIN late Middle English: from Scottish Gaelic and Irish *gleann* (earlier *glenn*).

Glencoe, Massacre of /glɛnˈkəʊ/ a massacre in 1692 of members of the Jacobite MacDonald clan by Campbell soldiers, which took place near Glencoe in the Scottish Highlands.

Glendower /glɛnˈdaʊə/ (also **Glyndwr**), Owen (*c.*1354–*c.*1417), Welsh chief. He proclaimed himself Prince of Wales and led a national uprising against Henry IV.

Gleneagles /glɛnˈiːg(ə)lz/ a valley in eastern Scotland, south-west of Perth, site of a noted hotel and golfing centre.

glengarry ▶ **noun** (pl. **-ies**) a brimless boat-shaped hat with a cleft down the centre, typically having two ribbons hanging at the back, worn as part of Highland dress.
– ORIGIN mid 19th cent.: from *Glengarry*, the name of a valley in the Highlands of Scotland.

Glen More another name for **GREAT GLEN**.

glenoid cavity /ˈgliːnɔɪd/ (also **glenoid fossa**) ▶ **noun** Anatomy a shallow depression on a bone into which another bone fits to form a joint, especially that on the scapula into which the head of the humerus fits.
– ORIGIN early 18th cent.: *glenoid* from French *glénoïde*, from Greek *glēnoeidēs*, from *glēnē* 'socket'.

Glenrothes /glɛnˈrɒθɪs/ a town in eastern Scotland, administrative centre of Fife region; pop. 39,400 (1993).

gley /gleɪ/ ▶ **noun** Soil Science a sticky waterlogged soil lacking in oxygen, typically grey to blue in colour.
– ORIGIN 1920s: from Ukrainian, 'sticky blue clay'; related to **CLAY**.

glia /ˈglʌɪə, ˈgliːə/ ▶ **noun** [mass noun] Anatomy the connective tissue of the nervous system, consisting of several different types of cell associated with neurons. Also called **NEUROGLIA**.
– DERIVATIVES **glial** adjective.
– ORIGIN late 19th cent.: from Greek, literally 'glue'.

glib ▶ **adjective** (**glibber**, **glibbest**) derogatory (of words or the person speaking them) fluent and voluble but insincere and shallow: *she was careful not to let the answer sound too glib.*
– DERIVATIVES **glibly** adverb, **glibness** noun.
– ORIGIN late 16th cent. (also in the sense 'smooth, unimpeded'): ultimately of Germanic origin; related to Dutch 'slippery' and German *glibberig* 'slimy'.

glide ▶ **verb 1** [no obj., with adverbial of direction] move with a smooth continuous motion, typically with little noise: *a few gondolas glided past.*
▪[with obj. and adverbial of direction] cause to move with a smooth continuous motion.
2 [no obj.] make an unpowered flight, either in a glider or in an aircraft with engine failure.
▪(of a bird) fly through the air with very little movement of the wings.
▶ **noun** [in sing.] **1** a smooth continuous movement.
▪an unpowered manoeuvre in an aircraft. ▪a flight in a glider or unpowered aircraft. ▪Cricket a glancing stroke which slightly deflects the ball, especially towards the leg side. ▪a smooth continuous step in ballroom dancing.
2 Phonetics a sound produced as the vocal organs move towards or away from articulation of a vowel or consonant, for example /j/ in *duke* /djuːk/.
– ORIGIN Old English *glīdan*, of Germanic origin; related to Dutch *glijden* and German *gleiten*.

glide path ▶ **noun** an aircraft's line of descent to land, especially as indicated by ground radar.

glider ▶ **noun 1** a light aircraft that is designed to fly for long periods without using an engine.
2 a person or thing that glides: *the flying lemur is an efficient glider as well as climber.*
3 another term for **FLYING PHALANGER**.
4 US a long swinging seat suspended from a frame in a porch.

glide reflection ▶ **noun** Mathematics a transformation consisting of a translation combined with a reflection about a plane parallel to the direction of the translation.

gliding ▶ **noun** [mass noun] the sport of flying in a glider.

glim ▶ **noun** archaic, informal a candle or lantern.
– ORIGIN late Middle English (denoting brightness): perhaps an abbreviation of **GLIMMER**. The current sense dates from the late 17th cent.

glimmer ▶ **verb** [no obj.] shine faintly with a wavering light: [as adj. **glimmering**] *pools of glimmering light.*
▶ **noun** a faint or wavering light.
▪a faint sign of a feeling or quality, especially a desirable one: *there is one glimmer of hope for Becky.*
– DERIVATIVES **glimmeringly** adverb.
– ORIGIN late Middle English: probably of Scandinavian origin; related to Swedish *glimra* and Danish *glimre*.

glimmering ▶ **noun** a glimmer.

glimpse ▶ **noun** a momentary or partial view: *she caught a glimpse of the ocean* | *a glimpse into the world of the well heeled.*
▶ **verb** [with obj.] see or perceive briefly or partially: *he glimpsed a figure standing in the shade.*
▪[no obj.] archaic shine or appear faintly or intermittently: *glow-worms glimpsing in the dark.*
– ORIGIN Middle English (in the sense 'shine faintly'): probably of Germanic origin; related to Middle High German *glimsen*, also to **GLIMMER**.

Glinka /ˈglɪŋkə/, Mikhail (Ivanovich) (1804–57), Russian composer. Regarded as the father of the Russian national school of music, he is best known for his operas *A Life for the Tsar* (1836) and *Russlan and Ludmilla* (1842).

glint ▶ **verb** [no obj.] give out or reflect small flashes of light: *her glasses were glinting in the firelight.*
▪(of a person's eyes) shine with a particular emotion: *his eyes glinted angrily.*
▶ **noun** a small flash of light, especially as reflected from a shiny surface: *the glint of gold in his teeth.*
▪[in sing.] a brightness in someone's eyes seen as a sign of enthusiasm or a particular emotion: *she saw the glint of excitement in his eyes.*
– ORIGIN Middle English (in the sense 'move quickly or obliquely'): variant of dialect *glent*, probably of Scandinavian origin and related to Swedish dialect *glänta*, *glinta* 'to slip, slide, gleam'.

glioblastoma /ˌglʌɪə(ʊ)blaˈstəʊmə/ ▶ **noun** (pl. **glioblastomas** or **glioblastomata** /-mətə/) Medicine a highly invasive glioma in the brain.

glioma /glʌɪˈəʊmə/ ▶ **noun** (pl. **gliomas** or **gliomata** /-mətə/) Medicine a malignant tumour of the glial tissue of the nervous system.
– ORIGIN late 19th cent.: from Greek *glia* 'glue' + **-OMA**.

glissade /glɪˈsɑːd, -ˈseɪd/ ▶ **noun 1** a way of sliding down a steep slope of snow or ice, typically on the feet with the support of an ice axe.
2 Ballet a movement, typically used as a joining step, in which one leg is brushed outwards from the body, which then takes the weight while the second leg is brushed in to meet it.
▶ **verb** [no obj.] slide down a steep slope of snow or ice with the support of an ice axe.
– ORIGIN mid 19th cent.: French, from *glisser* 'to slip, slide'.

glissando /glɪˈsandəʊ/ ▶ **noun** (pl. **glissandi** /-di/ or **glissandos**) Music a continuous slide upwards or downwards between two notes.
– ORIGIN Italian, from French *glissant*, present participle of *glisser* 'to slip, slide'.

glissé /gliːˈseɪ/ ▶ **noun** (pl. pronounced same) Ballet a movement in which weight is transferred from one foot, which is slid outward from the body and briefly extended off the ground, to the other, which is then brought to meet it.
– ORIGIN French, literally 'slipped, glided', past participle of *glisser*.

glisten ▶ **verb** [no obj.] (of something wet or greasy) shine; glitter: *his cheeks glistened with tears* | [as adj. **glistening**] *the glistening pavements.*
▶ **noun** [in sing.] a sparkling light reflected from something wet: *there was a glisten of perspiration across her top lip.*
– ORIGIN Old English *glisnian*, of Germanic origin; related to Middle Low German *glisen*. The noun dates from the mid 19th cent.

glister /ˈglɪstə/ poetic/literary ▶ **verb** [no obj.] sparkle; glitter.
▶ **noun** a sparkle.
– ORIGIN late Middle English: probably from Middle Low German *glistern* or Middle Dutch *glisteren*.

glitch informal ▶ **noun** a sudden, usually temporary malfunction or irregularity of equipment: *a draft version was lost in a computer glitch.*
▪an unexpected setback in a plan: *this has been the first real glitch they've encountered in a three months' tour.* ▪Astronomy a brief irregularity in the rotation of a pulsar.
▶ **verb** [no obj.] chiefly US suffer a sudden malfunction or irregularity: *her job involves troubleshooting when systems glitch.*
– ORIGIN 1960s (originally US): of unknown origin. The original sense was 'a sudden surge of current', hence 'malfunction, hitch' in astronautical slang.

glitchy ▶ **adjective** informal prone to glitches.

glitter ▶ **verb** [no obj.] shine with a bright, shimmering, reflected light: *trees and grass glittered with dew.*
▪shine as a result of strong feeling: *her eyes were glittering with excitement.*
▶ **noun** [in sing.] bright, shimmering, reflected light: *the blue glitter of the sea.*
▪[mass noun] tiny pieces of sparkling material used for decoration: *sneakers trimmed with sequins and glitter.* ▪figurative an attractive, exciting, often superficial, quality: *he avoids the glitter of show business.* ▪a glint in a person's eye indicating a particular emotion: *the scathing glitter in his eyes.*
– PHRASES **all that glitters is not gold** proverb the attractive external appearance of something is not a reliable indication of its true nature.
– DERIVATIVES **glittery** adjective.
– ORIGIN late Middle English: from Old Norse *glitra*.

glitterati /ˌglɪtəˈrɑːti/ ▶ **plural noun** informal the fashionable set of people engaged in show business or some other glamorous activity.

a **cat** | ɑː **arm** | ɛ **bed** | ɛː **hair** | ə **ago** | əː **her** | ɪ **sit** | i **cosy** | iː **see** | ɒ **hot** | ɔː **saw** | ʌ **run** | ʊ **put** | uː **too** | ʌɪ **my** | aʊ **how** | eɪ **day** | əʊ **no** | ɪə **near** | ɔɪ **boy** | ʊə **poor** | ʌɪə **fire** | aʊə **sour**

– ORIGIN 1950s (originally US): blend of **GLITTER** and **LITERATI**.

glittering ▶ adjective [attrib.] shining with a shimmering or sparkling light: *glittering chandeliers.*
■ figurative impressively successful or elaborate: *a glittering military career.*
– DERIVATIVES **glitteringly** adverb.

Glittertind /ˈglɪtətɪn/ a mountain in Norway, in the Jotunheim range. Rising to 2,470 m (8,104 ft), it is the highest mountain in the country.

glitz informal ▶ noun [mass noun] extravagant but superficial display: *the glitz and sophisticated night life of Ibiza.*
▶ verb [with obj.] N. Amer. make (something) glamorous or showy.
– ORIGIN 1970s (originally a North American usage): back-formation from **GLITZY**.

glitzy ▶ adjective (**glitzier**, **glitziest**) informal ostentatiously attractive (often used to suggest superficial glamour): *I wanted something glitzy to wear to the launch party.*
– DERIVATIVES **glitzily** adverb, **glitziness** noun.
– ORIGIN 1960s (originally a North American usage): from **GLITTER**, suggested by **RITZY**, and perhaps also by German *glitzerig* 'glittering'.

Gliwice /gliːˈviːtsə/ a mining and industrial city in southern Poland, near the border with the Czech Republic; pop. 214,200 (1990).

gloaming ▶ noun (**the gloaming**) poetic/literary twilight; dusk.
– ORIGIN Old English *glōmung*, from *glōm* 'twilight', of Germanic origin; related to **GLOW**.

gloat ▶ verb [no obj.] contemplate or dwell on one's own success or another's misfortune with smugness or malignant pleasure: *his enemies* ***gloated over*** *his death.*
▶ noun [in sing.] informal an act of gloating.
– DERIVATIVES **gloater** noun, **gloatingly** adverb.
– ORIGIN late 16th cent.: of unknown origin; perhaps related to Old Norse *glotta* 'to grin' and Middle High German *glotzen* 'to stare'. The original sense was 'give a sideways or furtive look', hence 'cast amorous or admiring glances'; the current sense dates from the mid 18th cent.

glob ▶ noun informal a lump of a semi-liquid substance: *thick* ***globs of*** *mozzarella cheese.*
– ORIGIN early 20th cent.: perhaps a blend of **BLOB** and **GOB**[2].

global /ˈgləʊb(ə)l/ ▶ adjective of or relating to the whole world; worldwide: *the downturn in the global economy.*
■ of or relating to the entire earth as a planet: *global environmental change.* ■ relating to or embracing the whole of something, or of a group of things: *some students may prefer to be given a global picture of what is involved in the task.* ■ Computing operating or applying through the whole of a file, program, etc.: *global searches.*
– DERIVATIVES **globally** adverb.

globalist ▶ noun a person who advocates the interpretation or planning of economic and foreign policy in relation to events and developments throughout the world.
■ a person or organization advocating or practising operations across national divisions.

globalize (also **-ise**) ▶ verb develop or be developed so as to make possible international influence or operation: [with obj.] *communication globalizes capital markets* | [no obj.] *building facilities overseas is part of the strategy of every company that aims to globalize.*
– DERIVATIVES **globalization** (also **-isation**) noun.

Global Surveyor (in full **Mars Global Surveyor**) an unmanned American spacecraft which went into orbit around Mars in 1997 to begin detailed photography and mapping of the surface.

global village ▶ noun the world considered as a single community linked by telecommunications.

global warming ▶ noun [mass noun] the gradual increase in the overall temperature of the earth's atmosphere due to the greenhouse effect caused by increased levels of carbon dioxide, CFCs, and other pollutants.

globe ▶ noun **1** (**the globe**) the earth: *collecting goodies from all over the globe.*
■ a spherical representation of the earth or of the constellations with a map on the surface.
2 a spherical or rounded object: *orange trees clipped into giant globes.*
■ a glass sphere protecting a light. ■ a drinking glass shaped approximately like a sphere: *a brandy globe.*
■ a golden orb as an emblem of sovereignty.
▶ verb [with obj.] poetic/literary form (something) into a globe.
– DERIVATIVES **globe-like** adjective, **globoid** adjective & noun, **globose** adjective.
– ORIGIN late Middle English (in the sense 'spherical object'): from Old French, or from Latin *globus*.

globe artichoke ▶ noun see **ARTICHOKE** (sense 1).

globefish ▶ noun (pl. same or **-fishes**) a pufferfish or a porcupine fish.

globeflower ▶ noun a plant of the buttercup family with globular yellow or orange flowers, native to north temperate regions.
• Genus *Trollius*, family Ranunculaceae.

Globe Theatre a theatre in Southwark, London, erected in 1599, where many of Shakespeare's plays were first publicly performed. The theatre's site was rediscovered in 1989 and a reconstruction of the original theatre was opened in 1997.

globe thistle ▶ noun an Old World thistle with globe-shaped heads of metallic blue-grey flowers.
• Genus *Echinops*, family Compositae.

globetrotter ▶ noun informal a person who travels widely.
– DERIVATIVES **globetrot** verb, **globetrotting** noun & adjective.

globigerina /ˌgləʊbɪdʒəˈrʌɪnə/ ▶ noun (pl. **globigerinas** or **globigerinae** /-niː/) a planktonic marine protozoan with a calcareous shell. The shells collect as a deposit (**globigerina ooze**) over much of the ocean floor.
• Genus *Globigerina*, order Foraminiferida, kingdom Protista.
– ORIGIN modern Latin, from Latin *globus* 'spherical object, globe' (because of the globular chambers in its shell) + *-ger* 'carrying' + **-INA**.

globular /ˈglɒbjʊlə/ ▶ adjective **1** globe-shaped; spherical.
2 composed of globules.
▶ noun Astronomy short for **GLOBULAR CLUSTER**.
– DERIVATIVES **globularity** noun.

globular cluster ▶ noun Astronomy a large compact spherical star cluster, typically of old stars in the outer regions of a galaxy.

globule /ˈglɒbjuːl/ ▶ noun a small round particle of a substance; a drop: *globules of fat.*
■ Astronomy a small dark cloud of gas and dust seen against a brighter background such as a luminous nebula.
– DERIVATIVES **globulous** adjective.
– ORIGIN mid 17th cent.: from French, or from Latin *globulus*, diminutive of *globus* 'spherical object, globe'.

globulin /ˈglɒbjʊlɪn/ ▶ noun Biochemistry any of a group of simple proteins soluble in salt solutions and forming a large fraction of blood serum protein.
– ORIGIN mid 19th cent.: from **GLOBULE** (in the archaic sense 'blood corpuscle') + **-IN**[1].

globus hystericus /ˌgləʊbəs hɪˈstɛrɪkəs/ ▶ noun [mass noun] Medicine the sensation of a lump in the throat, as a symptom of anxiety or hysteria.
– ORIGIN late 18th cent.: from Latin.

globus pallidus /ˈpalɪdəs/ ▶ noun Anatomy the median part of the lentiform nucleus in the brain.
– ORIGIN late 18th cent.: from Latin, 'pale globus'.

glochid /ˈgləʊkɪd/ ▶ noun Botany a barbed bristle on the areole of some cacti.
– ORIGIN late 19th cent.: from Greek *glōkhis*, *glōkhid-* 'arrowhead'.

glochidium /gləʊˈkɪdɪəm/ ▶ noun (pl. **glochidia**) Zoology a parasitic larva of certain freshwater bivalve molluscs, which attaches itself by hooks and suckers to the fins or gills of fish.
– ORIGIN late 19th cent.: modern Latin, based on Greek *glōkhis* 'arrowhead'.

glockenspiel /ˈglɒk(ə)nspiːl, -ʃpiːl/ ▶ noun a musical percussion instrument having a set of tuned metal pieces mounted in a frame and struck with small hammers.
– ORIGIN early 19th cent. (denoting an organ stop imitating the sound of bells): from German *Glockenspiel*, literally 'bell-play'.

glom /glɒm/ ▶ verb (**glommed**, **glomming**) US informal [with obj.] steal: *I thought he was about to glom my wallet.*
■ [no obj.] (**glom on to**) become stuck or attached to.
– ORIGIN early 20th cent.: variant of Scots *glaum*, of unknown origin.

glomerulonephritis /glɒˌmɛrjʊləʊnɪˈfrʌɪtɪs/ ▶ noun [mass noun] Medicine acute inflammation of the kidney, typically caused by an immune response.

glomerulus /glɒˈmɛr(j)ʊləs/ ▶ noun (pl. **glomeruli** /-lʌɪ, -liː/) Anatomy & Biology a cluster of nerve endings, spores, or small blood vessels, in particular:
■ a cluster of capillaries around the end of a kidney tubule, where waste products are filtered from the blood.
– DERIVATIVES **glomerular** adjective.
– ORIGIN mid 19th cent.: modern Latin, diminutive of Latin *glomus*, *glomer-* 'ball of thread'.

gloom ▶ noun [mass noun] **1** partial or total darkness: *he strained his eyes peering into the gloom.*
■ [count noun] poetic/literary a dark or shady place.
2 a state of depression or despondency: *a year of economic gloom for the car industry* | *his gloom deepened.*
▶ verb [no obj.] **1** poetic/literary have a dark or sombre appearance: *the black gibbet glooms beside the way.*
■ [with obj.] cover with gloom; make dark or dismal: *a black yew gloom'd the stagnant air.*
2 be or look depressed or despondent: *Charles was always glooming about money*
– PHRASES **gloom and doom** see **DOOM**.
– ORIGIN late Middle English (as a verb): of unknown origin.

gloomy ▶ adjective (**gloomier**, **gloomiest**) dark or poorly lit, especially so as to appear depressing or frightening: *a gloomy corridor badly lit by oil lamps.*
■ feeling distressed or pessimistic: *I am by no means gloomy about the prospects for British industry.* ■ causing distress or depression: *a gloomy atmosphere.*
– DERIVATIVES **gloomily** adverb, **gloominess** noun.

gloop ▶ noun [mass noun] informal sloppy or sticky semi-fluid matter, typically something unpleasant.
– DERIVATIVES **gloopy** adjective.
– ORIGIN late 20th cent.: the letters *gl*, *o*, and *p* are said to be symbolic of semi-liquid matter (compare with **GLOP**).

glop ▶ noun [mass noun] informal, chiefly N. Amer. a sticky and amorphous substance, typically something unpleasant: *the snow was sun-softened glop.*
■ [count noun] a soft, shapeless lump of something: *a* ***glop of*** *creamy dressing.*
– DERIVATIVES **gloppy** adjective (**gloppier**, **gloppiest**).
– ORIGIN 1940s: symbolic (see **GLOOP**).

Gloria ▶ noun a Christian liturgical hymn or formula beginning (in the Latin text) with *Gloria*, in particular:
■ the hymn beginning *Gloria in excelsis Deo* (Glory be to God in the highest), forming a set part of the Mass. ■ a musical setting of this: *Vivaldi's Gloria.* ■ the doxology beginning *Gloria Patris* (Glory be to the Father), used after psalms and in formal prayer (e.g. in the rosary).
– ORIGIN Latin, 'glory'.

Gloriana /ˌglɔːrɪˈɑːnə/ the nickname of Queen Elizabeth I.

glorified ▶ adjective **1** [attrib.] (especially of something or someone ordinary or unexceptional) represented in such a way as to appear more elevated or special: *all Peter will be is a sort of glorified secretary.*
2 (in religious contexts) made glorious: *the transformed and glorified Jesus.*

glorify ▶ verb (**-ies**, **-ied**) [with obj.] **1** reveal or make clearer the glory of (God) by one's actions: *God can be glorified through a life of scholarship.*
■ give praise to (God).
2 describe or represent as admirable, especially unjustifiably or undeservedly: *a football video glorifying violence.*
– DERIVATIVES **glorification** noun, **glorifier** noun.
– ORIGIN Middle English: from Old French *glorifier*, from ecclesiastical Latin *glorificare*, from late Latin *glorificus*, from Latin *gloria* 'glory'.

glorious ▶ adjective **1** having, worthy of, or bringing fame or admiration: *the most glorious victory of all time.*
2 having a striking beauty or splendour that evokes feelings of delighted admiration: *a glorious autumn day.*
– DERIVATIVES **gloriously** adverb, **gloriousness** noun.
– ORIGIN Middle English: from Old French *glorieus*, from Latin *gloriosus*, from *gloria* 'glory'.

Glorious Revolution the events (1688–9) that led to the replacement, in 1689, of James II by his daughter Mary II and her husband William of Orange (who became William III) as joint monarchs. The bloodless 'revolution' greatly enhanced the constitutional powers of Parliament, with William and Mary's acceptance of the conditions laid down in the Bill of Rights.

glory ▶ noun (pl. **-ies**) **1** [mass noun] high renown or honour won by notable achievements: *to fight and die for the glory of one's nation.*
■ praise, worship, and thanksgiving offered to God.
2 [mass noun] magnificence; great beauty: *the train has been restored to all its former glory.*
■ [count noun] (often **glories**) a thing that is beautiful or distinctive; a special cause for pride, respect, or delight: *the glories of Paris.* ■ the splendour and bliss of heaven: *with the saints in glory.*
3 a luminous ring or halo, especially as depicted around the head of Christ or a saint.
▶ verb [no obj.] (**glory in**) take great pride or pleasure in: *they were individuals who gloried in their independence.*
■ exult in unpleasantly or boastfully: *readers tended to defend their paper or even to glory in its bias.*
– PHRASES **glory be!** expressing enthusiastic piety. ■ informal used as an exclamation of surprise or delight. ■ (**Glory Be**) [as noun] (especially in Roman Catholic use) the doxology beginning 'Glory be to the Father'. **go to glory** die; be destroyed. **in one's glory** informal in a state of extreme joy or exaltation.
– ORIGIN Middle English: from Old French *glorie*, from Latin *gloria*.

glory box ▶ noun Austral./NZ a box for a woman's clothes and household items, stored in preparation for marriage.

glory days ▶ plural noun a time in the past regarded as being better than the present: *the glory days of 90 per cent viewership.*

glory hole ▶ noun **1** informal an untidy storage place, especially a room or cupboard.
2 N. Amer. an open quarry.
3 a small furnace used to keep glass malleable for handworking.
4 US informal a hole in a wall through which fellatio or masturbation is conducted incognito between male homosexuals.
– ORIGIN early 19th cent.: of unknown origin.

glory-of-the-snow ▶ noun another term for **CHIONODOXA**.

glory pea ▶ noun another term for **CLIANTHUS**.

Glos. ▶ abbreviation for Gloucestershire.

gloss[1] ▶ noun [mass noun] shine or lustre on a smooth surface: *hair with a healthy gloss.*
■ see **LIPGLOSS**. ■ (also **gloss paint**) a type of paint which dries to a bright shiny surface. ■ [in sing.] a superficially attractive appearance or impression: *beneath the gloss of success was a tragic private life.*
▶ verb [with obj.] apply a cosmetic gloss to.
■ apply gloss paint to. ■ (**gloss over**) try to conceal or disguise (something embarrassing or unfavourable) by treating it briefly or representing it misleadingly: *the social costs of this growth are glossed over.*
– DERIVATIVES **glosser** noun.
– ORIGIN mid 16th cent.: of unknown origin.

gloss[2] ▶ noun a translation or explanation of a word or phrase.
■ an explanation, interpretation, or paraphrase: *the chapter acts as a helpful* **gloss on** *Pynchon's general method.*
▶ verb [with obj.] (usu. **be glossed**) provide an explanation, interpretation, or paraphrase for (a text, word, etc.).
■ [no obj.] (**gloss on/upon**) archaic write or make comments, especially unfavourable ones, about (something): *those laws, which they assumed the liberty of interpreting and glossing upon.*
– ORIGIN mid 16th cent.: alteration of the noun *gloze*, from Old French *glose* (see **GLOZE**), suggested by medieval Latin *glossa* 'explanation of a difficult word', from Greek *glōssa* 'word needing explanation, language, tongue'.

glossal /ˈglɒs(ə)l/ ▶ adjective Anatomy, rare of the tongue; lingual.
– ORIGIN early 19th cent.: from Greek *glōssa* 'tongue' + **-AL**.

glossary ▶ noun (pl. **-ies**) an alphabetical list of terms or words found in or relating to a specific subject, text, or dialect, with explanations; a brief dictionary.
– DERIVATIVES **glossarial** adjective, **glossarist** noun.
– ORIGIN late Middle English: from Latin *glossarium*, from *glossa* (see **GLOSS**[2]).

glossator /glɒˈseɪtə/ ▶ noun chiefly historical a person who writes glosses, especially a scholarly commentator on the texts of classical, civil, or canon law.
– ORIGIN late Middle English: from medieval Latin, from *glossare*, from Latin *glossa* (see **GLOSS**[2]).

glossitis /glɒˈsʌɪtɪs/ ▶ noun [mass noun] Medicine inflammation of the tongue.
– ORIGIN early 19th cent.: from Greek *glōssa* 'tongue' + **-ITIS**.

glossographer /glɒˈsɒgrəfə/ ▶ noun a writer of glosses or commentaries.

glossolalia /ˌglɒsəˈleɪlɪə/ ▶ noun [mass noun] the phenomenon of (apparently) speaking in an unknown language, especially in religious worship. It is practised especially by Pentecostal and charismatic Christians.
– DERIVATIVES **glossolalic** adjective.
– ORIGIN late 19th cent.: from Greek *glōssa* 'language, tongue' + *lalia* 'speech'.

glossopharyngeal nerve /ˌglɒsə(ʊ)fəˈrɪn(d)ʒɪəl, -ˌfar(ə)nˈdʒiːəl/ ▶ noun Anatomy each of the ninth pair of cranial nerves, supplying the tongue and pharynx.

glossy ▶ adjective (**glossier**, **glossiest**) shiny and smooth: *thick, glossy, manageable hair.*
■ (of a magazine or photograph) printed on high-quality smooth shiny paper. ■ superficially attractive and stylish, and suggesting wealth or expense: *glossy TV miniseries and soaps.*
▶ noun (pl. **-ies**) informal a magazine printed on glossy paper, expensively produced with many colour photographs.
■ a photograph printed on glossy paper.
– DERIVATIVES **glossily** adverb, **glossiness** noun.

glossy starling ▶ noun an African starling with dark glossy plumage that has metallic blue, green, and purple reflections.
● Genus *Lamprotornis*, family Sturnidae: several species.

glost ▶ noun the second firing of ceramic ware, in which the glaze is fused: [as modifier] *glost kiln.*

glottal ▶ adjective [attrib.] of or produced by the glottis.

glottal stop ▶ noun a consonant formed by the audible release of the airstream after complete closure of the glottis. It is widespread in some non-standard English accents and in some other languages, such as Arabic, it is a standard consonant.

glottis /ˈglɒtɪs/ ▶ noun the part of the larynx consisting of the vocal cords and the slit-like opening between them. It affects voice modulation through expansion or contraction.
– DERIVATIVES **glottic** adjective.
– ORIGIN late 16th cent.: modern Latin, from Greek *glōttis*, from *glōtta*, variant of *glōssa* 'tongue'.

glottochronology /ˌglɒtəʊkrəˈnɒlədʒi/ ▶ noun [mass noun] the use of statistical data to date the divergence of languages from their common sources.
– DERIVATIVES **glottochronological** adjective.

Gloucester /ˈglɒstə/ a city in SW England, the county town of Gloucestershire; pop. 91,800 (1991). It was founded by the Romans, who called it Glevum, in AD 96.

Gloucester Old Spot ▶ noun a pig of a white breed with black spots, now rarely kept commercially.

Gloucestershire a county of SW England; county town, Gloucester.

glove ▶ noun a covering for the hand worn for protection against cold or dirt and typically having separate parts for each finger and the thumb.
■ a padded protective covering for the hand used in boxing, cricket, baseball, and other sports.
▶ verb [with obj.] informal (of a wicketkeeper, baseball catcher, etc.) catch, deflect, or touch (the ball) with one's glove.
– PHRASES **fit like a glove** (of clothes) fit exactly. **the gloves are off** (or **with the gloves off** or **take the gloves off**) used to express the notion that something will be done in an uncompromising or brutal way, without compunction or hesitation: *for the banks chasing this growing business, the gloves are now definitely off.*
– DERIVATIVES **gloved** adjective, **gloveless** adjective.
– ORIGIN Old English *glōf*, of Germanic origin.

glovebox ▶ noun **1** a glove compartment in a vehicle.
2 a closed chamber with sealed-in gloves for handling radioactive or other hazardous material.

glove compartment ▶ noun a recess with a flap in the dashboard of a motor vehicle, used for storing small items.

glove puppet ▶ noun chiefly Brit. a cloth puppet fitted on the hand and worked by the fingers.

glover ▶ noun a maker of gloves.

glow ▶ verb [no obj.] give out steady light without flame: *the tips of their cigarettes glowed in the dark.*
■ have an intense colour and a slight shine: [with complement] *faces that glowed red with the cold.* ■ have a heightened colour or a bloom on the skin as a result of warmth or health: *he was glowing with health.* ■ feel deep pleasure or satisfaction and convey it through one's expression and bearing: *Katy always glowed when he praised her.*
▶ noun [in sing.] a steady radiance of light or heat. *the setting sun cast a deep red glow over the city.*
■ a feeling of warmth in the face or body; the visible effects of this as a redness of the cheeks: *he could feel the brandy filling him with a warm glow.* ■ a strong feeling of pleasure or well-being: *with a* **glow of** *pride, Mildred walked away.*
– ORIGIN Old English *glōwan*, of Germanic origin; related to Dutch *gloeien* and German *glühen*.

glow discharge ▶ noun a luminous sparkless electrical discharge from a pointed conductor in a gas at low pressure.

glower /ˈglaʊə/ ▶ verb [no obj.] have an angry or sullen look on one's face; scowl: *she* **glowered at** *him suspiciously.*
▶ noun [in sing.] an angry or sullen look.
– DERIVATIVES **gloweringly** adverb.
– ORIGIN late 15th cent.: perhaps a Scots variant of synonymous dialect *glore*, or from obsolete *glow* 'to stare', both possibly of Scandinavian origin.

glowing ▶ adjective [attrib.] expressing great praise: *he received a glowing report from his teachers.*
– DERIVATIVES **glowingly** adverb.

glow-worm ▶ noun a soft-bodied beetle with luminescent organs in the abdomen, especially the larvalike wingless female which emits light to attract the flying male.
● Families Lampyridae (in particular the European *Lampyris noctiluca*) and Phengodidae (in particular the American *Zarhipis integripennis*).

gloxinia /glɒkˈsɪnɪə/ ▶ noun a tropical American plant with large, velvety, bell-shaped flowers.
● Genera *Gloxinia* and *Sinningia*, family Gesneriaceae: several species, in particular the florists' gloxinia (*S. speciosa*), which is a popular house plant.
– ORIGIN modern Latin, named after Benjamin P. *Gloxin*, the 18th-cent. German botanist who first described it.

gloze /gləʊz/ ▶ verb [with obj.] rare make excuses for: *the demeanour of Mathews is rather* **glozed over**.
■ [no obj.] archaic use ingratiating or fawning language. ■ [no obj.] archaic make a comment or comments.
– ORIGIN Middle English: from Old French *gloser*, from *glose* 'a gloss, comment', based on Latin *glossa* (see **GLOSS**[2]).

glucagon /ˈgluːkəg(ə)n, -gɒn/ ▶ noun [mass noun] Biochemistry a hormone formed in the pancreas which promotes the breakdown of glycogen to glucose in the liver.
– ORIGIN 1920s: from Greek *glukus* 'sweet' + *agōn* 'leading, bringing'.

glucan /ˈgluːkan/ ▶ noun Biochemistry a polysaccharide consisting of glucose units.
– ORIGIN 1940s: from **GLUCOSE** + **-AN**.

Gluck /glʊk/, Christoph Willibald von (1714–87), German composer, notable for operas in which he sought a balance of music and drama and reduced the emphasis on the star singer. Notable operas: *Orfeo ed Euridice* (1762) and *Iphigénie en Aulide* (1774).

glucocorticoid /ˌgluːkə(ʊ)ˈkɔːtɪkɔɪd/ ▶ noun Biochemistry any of a group of corticosteroids (e.g. hydrocortisone) which are involved in the metabolism of carbohydrates, proteins, and fats and have anti-inflammatory activity.

glucose /ˈgluːkəʊs, -z/ ▶ noun [mass noun] a simple sugar which is an important energy source in living organisms and is a component of many carbohydrates.
● A hexose; chem. formula: $C_6H_{12}O_6$.
■ a syrup containing glucose and other sugars, made by hydrolysis of starch and used in the food industry.
– ORIGIN mid 19th cent.: from French, from Greek *gleukos* 'sweet wine', related to *glukus* 'sweet'.

glucoside /ˈgluːkəsʌɪd/ ▶ noun Biochemistry a glycoside derived from glucose.

– DERIVATIVES **glucosidic** adjective.

glucuronic acid /ˌgluːkjʊˈrɒnɪk/ ▶ **noun** [mass noun] Biochemistry an acid derived from glucose which occurs naturally as a constituent of hyaluronic acid and other mucopolysaccharides.
● A uronic acid; chem. formula: $HOOC(CHOH)_4CHO$.

– DERIVATIVES **glucuronate** noun.

glue ▶ **noun** [mass noun] an adhesive substance used for sticking objects or materials together.
▶ **verb** (**glues**, **glued**, **gluing** or **glueing**) [with obj. and adverbial] fasten or join with or as if with glue: *the wood is cut up into small pieces which are then glued together.*
■ (**be glued to**) informal be paying very close attention to (something, especially a television or computer screen): *I was glued to the telly when the Olympics were on.*

– DERIVATIVES **glue-like** adjective, **gluey** adjective.
– ORIGIN Middle English: from Old French *glu* (noun), *gluer* (verb), from late Latin *glus*, *glut-*, from Latin *gluten*.

glue ear ▶ **noun** [mass noun] blocking of the Eustachian tube by mucus (occurring especially in children).

glue pot ▶ **noun** a pot with an outer container holding water, used to heat glue that sets when it cools.
■ Austral. informal an area of sticky mud.

glue-sniffing ▶ **noun** [mass noun] the practice of inhaling intoxicating fumes from the solvents in adhesives.

– DERIVATIVES **glue-sniffer** noun.

glug informal ▶ **verb** (**glugged**, **glugging**) [with obj. and adverbial of direction] pour or drink (liquid) with a hollow gurgling sound: *Jeff glugged whisky into glasses.*
▶ **noun** a hollow gurgling sound or series of sounds as of liquid being poured from a bottle.
■ an amount of liquid poured from a bottle: *a couple of good glugs of Dubonnet.*

– DERIVATIVES **gluggable** adjective.
– ORIGIN late 17th cent.: imitative.

Glühwein /ˈgluːvaɪn, German ˈglyːvaɪn/ ▶ **noun** [mass noun] mulled wine.
– ORIGIN German, from *glühen* 'to mull' + *Wein* 'wine'.

glum ▶ **adjective** (**glummer**, **glummest**) looking or feeling dejected; morose: *the princess looked glum but later cheered up.*

– DERIVATIVES **glumly** adverb, **glumness** noun.
– ORIGIN mid 16th cent.: related to dialect *glum* 'to frown', variant of GLOOM.

glume /gluːm/ ▶ **noun** Botany each of two membranous bracts surrounding the spikelet of a grass (forming the husk of a cereal grain) or one surrounding the florets of a sedge.
– ORIGIN late 18th cent.: from Latin *gluma* 'husk'.

gluon /ˈgluːɒn/ ▶ **noun** Physics a hypothetical massless subatomic particle believed to transmit the force binding quarks together in hadrons.
– ORIGIN 1970s: from GLUE + -ON.

glut ▶ **noun** an excessively abundant supply of something: *there is a glut of cars on the market.*
▶ **verb** (**glutted**, **glutting**) [with obj.] (usu. **be glutted**) supply or fill to excess: *the factories for recycling paper are glutted* | *he was glutting himself on alcohol.*
■ archaic satisfy fully: *he planned a treacherous murder to glut his desire for revenge.*

– ORIGIN Middle English: probably via Old French from Latin *gluttire* 'to swallow'; related to GLUTTON.

glutamate /ˈgluːtəmeɪt/ ▶ **noun** Biochemistry a salt or ester of glutamic acid.
■ [mass noun] glutamic acid, its salts, or its anion. ■ short for MONOSODIUM GLUTAMATE.

glutamic acid /gluːˈtamɪk/ ▶ **noun** [mass noun] Biochemistry an acidic amino acid which is a constituent of many proteins.
● Chem. formula: $HOOC(CH_2)_2(NH_2)COOH$.
– ORIGIN late 19th cent.: from GLUTEN + AMINE + -IC.

glutamine /ˈgluːtəmiːn/ ▶ **noun** Biochemistry a hydrophilic amino acid which is a constituent of most proteins.
● An amide of glutamic acid; chem. formula: $H_2NCOCH_2CH_2CH(NH_2)COOH$.
– ORIGIN late 19th cent.: blend of GLUTAMIC ACID and AMINE.

glutathione /ˌgluːtəˈθaɪəʊn/ ▶ **noun** [mass noun] Biochemistry a compound involved as a coenzyme in oxidation–reduction reactions in cells. It is a tripeptide derived from glutamic acid, cysteine, and glycine.

glute ▶ **noun** (usu. **glutes**) informal short for GLUTEUS.

gluten /ˈgluːt(ə)n/ ▶ **noun** [mass noun] a substance present in cereal grains, especially wheat, which is responsible for the elastic texture of dough. A mixture of two proteins, it causes illness in people with coeliac disease.
– ORIGIN late 16th cent. (originally denoting protein from animal tissue): via French from Latin, literally 'glue'.

gluteus /ˈgluːtɪəs, gluːˈtiːəs/ (also **gluteus muscle**) ▶ **noun** (pl. **glutei** /-tɪʌɪ, -tiːʌɪ/) any of three muscles in each buttock which move the thigh, the largest of which is the **gluteus maximus**.
– DERIVATIVES **gluteal** adjective.
– ORIGIN late 17th cent.: modern Latin, from Greek *gloutos* 'buttock'.

glutinous /ˈgluːtɪnəs/ ▶ **adjective** like glue in texture; sticky: *glutinous mud.*
– DERIVATIVES **glutinously** adverb, **glutinousness** noun.
– ORIGIN late Middle English: from Old French *glutineux* or Latin *glutinosus*, from *gluten* 'glue'.

glutton ▶ **noun** 1 an excessively greedy eater.
■ a person who is excessively fond of or always eager for something: *his depiction of himself as a glutton for poetry.*
2 another term for WOLVERINE.
– PHRASES **a glutton for punishment** a person who is always eager to undertake hard or unpleasant tasks.
– DERIVATIVES **gluttonize** (also **-ise**) verb, **gluttonous** adjective, **gluttonously** adverb.
– ORIGIN Middle English: from Old French *gluton*, from Latin *glutto(n-)* related to *gluttire* 'to swallow', *gluttus* 'greedy', and *gula* 'throat'.

gluttony ▶ **noun** [mass noun] habitual greed or excess in eating.
– ORIGIN Middle English: from Old French *glutonie*, from *gluton* 'glutton'.

glyceride /ˈglɪs(ə)rʌɪd/ ▶ **noun** a fatty acid ester of glycerol.

glycerine /ˈglɪs(ə)riːn, -ɪn/ (US **glycerin**) ▶ **noun** another term for GLYCEROL.
– ORIGIN mid 19th cent.: from French *glycérin*, from Greek *glukeros* 'sweet'.

glycerol /ˈglɪs(ə)rɒl/ ▶ **noun** a colourless, sweet, viscous liquid formed as a by-product in soap manufacture. It is used as an emollient and laxative, and for making explosives and antifreeze.
● A trihydric alcohol; chem. formula: $CH_2(OH)CH(OH)CH_2(OH)$.
– ORIGIN late 19th cent.: from GLYCERINE + -OL.

glyceryl /ˈglɪs(ə)rʌɪl, -rɪl/ ▶ **noun** [as modifier] Chemistry of or denoting a radical derived from glycerol by replacement of one or more hydrogen atoms: *glyceryl trinitrate.*
– ORIGIN late 19th cent.: from GLYCERINE + -YL.

glycine /ˈglʌɪsiːn/ ▶ **noun** [mass noun] Biochemistry the simplest naturally occurring amino acid, which is a constituent of most proteins.
● Chem. formula: H_2NCH_2COOH.
– ORIGIN mid 19th cent.: from Greek *glukus* 'sweet' + -INE[4].

glyco- ▶ **combining form** of, relating to, or producing sugar: *glycogenesis | glycoside.*
– ORIGIN from Greek *glukus* 'sweet'.

glycogen /ˈglʌɪkədʒ(ə)n/ ▶ **noun** [mass noun] Biochemistry a substance deposited in bodily tissues as a store of carbohydrates. It is a polysaccharide which forms glucose on hydrolysis.
– DERIVATIVES **glycogenic** /-ˈdʒɛnɪk/ adjective.

glycogenesis /ˌglʌɪkə(ʊ)ˈdʒɛnɪsɪs/ ▶ **noun** [mass noun] Biochemistry the formation of glycogen from sugar.

glycol /ˈglʌɪkɒl/ ▶ **noun** short for ETHYLENE GLYCOL.
■ Chemistry another term for DIOL.
– ORIGIN mid 19th cent. (applied to ethylene glycol): from GLYCERINE + -OL (originally intended to designate a substance intermediate between glycerine and alcohol).

glycolysis /glʌɪˈkɒlɪsɪs/ ▶ **noun** [mass noun] Biochemistry the breakdown of glucose by enzymes, releasing energy and pyruvic acid.
– DERIVATIVES **glycolytic** adjective /ˌglʌɪkəˈlɪtɪk/.

glycoprotein /ˌglʌɪkə(ʊ)ˈprəʊtiːn/ ▶ **noun** Biochemistry any of a class of proteins which have carbohydrate groups attached to the polypeptide chain.

glycosaminoglycan /ˌglʌɪkəʊsˌamɪnəʊˈglʌɪkan/ ▶ **noun** Biochemistry another term for MUCO-POLYSACCHARIDE.

glycoside /ˈglʌɪkə(ʊ)sʌɪd/ ▶ **noun** Biochemistry a compound formed from a simple sugar and another compound by replacement of a hydroxyl group in the sugar molecule. Many drugs and poisons derived from plants are glycosides.
– DERIVATIVES **glycosidic** adjective.
– ORIGIN late 19th cent.: from GLYCO- 'relating to sugar', on the pattern of *glucoside.*

glycosuria /ˌglʌɪkə(ʊ)ˈsjʊərɪə/ ▶ **noun** [mass noun] Medicine a condition characterized by an excess of sugar in the urine, typically associated with diabetes or kidney disease.
– DERIVATIVES **glycosuric** adjective.
– ORIGIN mid 19th cent.: from French *glycosurie*, from *glucos* 'glucose'.

Glyndebourne Festival /ˈglʌɪndbɔːn/ an annual festival of opera, held at the estate of Glyndebourne near Lewes, East Sussex.

Glyndwr /glɪnˈdʊr/ Welsh form of GLENDOWER.

glyph /glɪf/ ▶ **noun** 1 a hieroglyphic character or symbol; a pictograph: *flanges painted with esoteric glyphs.*
■ strictly, a sculptured symbol (e.g. as forming the ancient Mayan writing system). ■ Computing a small graphic symbol.
2 Architecture an ornamental carved groove or channel, as on a Greek frieze.
– DERIVATIVES **glyphic** adjective.
– ORIGIN late 18th cent. (in sense 2): from French *glyphe*, from Greek *gluphē* 'carving'.

glyphosate /ˈglʌɪfə(ʊ)seɪt/ ▶ **noun** [mass noun] a synthetic compound which is a non-selective systemic herbicide, particularly effective against perennial weeds.
● Alternative name: *N*-(**phosphonomethyl**) **glycine**; Chem. formula: $C_3H_8NO_5P$.

glyptic /ˈglɪptɪk/ ▶ **adjective** of or concerning carving or engraving.
– ORIGIN early 19th cent.: from French *glyptique* or Greek *gluptikos*, from *gluptēs* 'carver', from *gluphein* 'carve'.

glyptodont /ˈglɪptə(ʊ)dɒnt/ ▶ **noun** a fossil South American edentate mammal of the Cenozoic era, related to armadillos but much larger. Glyptodonts had fluted teeth and a body covered in a thick bony carapace.
● Family Glyptodontidae, order Xenarthra (or Edentata): several genera, including *Glyptodon.*
– ORIGIN mid 19th cent.: from Greek *gluptos* 'carved' (from *gluphein* 'carve') + *odous, odont-* 'tooth'.

glyptography /glɪpˈtɒgrəfi/ ▶ **noun** [mass noun] the art or scientific study of gem engraving.
– ORIGIN late 18th cent.: from Greek *gluptos* 'carved' (from *gluphein* 'carve') + -GRAPHY.

GM ▶ **abbreviation for** ■ general manager. ■ (in the US) General Motors. ■ (in the UK) George Medal. ■ Chess grandmaster. ■ (of a school in the UK) grant-maintained.

gm ▶ **abbreviation for** gram(s).

G-man ▶ **noun** 1 US informal an FBI agent. [ORIGIN: 1930s: probably an abbreviation of *Government man.*]
2 Irish a political detective. [ORIGIN: early 20th cent.: perhaps an arbitrary use of *G.*]

GMS ▶ **abbreviation for** grant maintained status (with reference to schools in the UK).

GMT ▶ **abbreviation for** Greenwich Mean Time.

GMWU ▶ **abbreviation for** (in the UK) General and Municipal Workers' Union.

gn ▶ **abbreviation for** guinea(s).

gnamma /ˈnamə/ (also **namma**) ▶ **noun** Austral. a natural hole in a rock in which rainwater collects.
– ORIGIN from Nyungar.

gnarl /nɑːl/ ▶ **noun** a rough, knotty protuberance, especially on a tree.
– ORIGIN early 19th cent.: back-formation from GNARLED.

gnarled ▶ **adjective** knobbly, rough, and twisted, especially with age: *the gnarled old oak tree.*
– ORIGIN early 17th cent.: variant of *knarled*, from KNAR.

gnarly ▶ **adjective** (**-ier**, **-iest**) 1 gnarled.
2 informal, chiefly N. Amer. difficult, dangerous, or challenging: *she battled through the gnarly first sequence.* [ORIGIN: originally surfers' slang, perhaps from the appearance of rough sea.]

▪unpleasant; unattractive: *train stations can be pretty gnarly places.*

gnash /naʃ/ ▶**verb** [with obj.] grind (one's teeth) together, typically as a sign of anger: *no doubt he is gnashing his teeth in rage.*
▪[no obj.] (of teeth) strike together; grind: *the dog's jaws were primed to gnash.*
– ORIGIN late Middle English: perhaps related to Old Norse *gnastan* 'a gnashing'.

gnashers ▶**plural noun** Brit. informal teeth.

gnat /nat/ ▶**noun** a small two-winged fly that resembles a mosquito. Gnats include both biting and non-biting forms, and they typically form large swarms.
• Several families, especially Culicidae (the biting gnats), which includes the **common gnat** (*Culex pipiens*).
▪a person or thing seen as tiny or insignificant, especially in comparison with something larger or more important: *I was only a gnat in the affair.*
– ORIGIN Old English *gnætt*, of Germanic origin; related to German *Gnitze*.

gnatcatcher ▶**noun** a tiny grey-backed New World songbird, with a long tail that is often cocked.
• Genus *Polioptila*, family Polioptilidae (or Sylviidae): several species.

gnathic /ˈnaθɪk, ˈneɪ-/ ▶**adjective** rare of or relating to the jaws.
– ORIGIN late 19th cent.: from Greek *gnathos* 'jaw' + **-IC**.

Gnathostomulida /ˌneɪθə(ʊ)stəʊˈmjʊlɪdə/ Zoology a minor phylum of minute marine worms which appear to be intermediate between coelenterates and flatworms.
– DERIVATIVES **gnathostomulid** /ˌneɪθə(ʊ)ˈstəʊmjʊlɪd/ noun & adjective.
– ORIGIN modern Latin (plural), from Greek *gnathos* 'jaw' + *stoma* 'mouth'.

gnaw /nɔː/ ▶**verb** [no obj.] bite at or nibble something persistently: *picking up the pig's foot, he* **gnawed at** *it.*
▪[with obj. and adverbial] bite at or nibble (something) until it reaches a specified size or state: *she had gnawed her fingers to the bone.* ▪ figurative (of something painful to the mind or body) cause persistent and wearing distress or anxiety: *the doubts continued to* **gnaw at** *me* | [as adj. **gnawing**] *that gnawing pain in her stomach.*
– DERIVATIVES **gnawingly** adverb.
– ORIGIN Old English *gnagen*, of Germanic origin; related to German *nagen*, ultimately imitative.

gneiss /nʌɪs/ ▶**noun** [mass noun] a metamorphic rock with a banded or foliated structure, typically coarse-grained and consisting mainly of feldspar, quartz, and mica.
– DERIVATIVES **gneissic** adjective, **gneissose** adjective.
– ORIGIN mid 18th cent.: from German, from Old High German *gneisto* 'spark' (because of the rock's sheen).

gnocchi /ˈn(j)ɒki, ˈgnɒki/ ▶**plural noun** (in Italian cooking) small dumplings made from potato, semolina, or flour, usually served with a sauce.
– ORIGIN Italian, plural of *gnocco*, alteration of *nocchio* 'knot in wood'.

gnome[1] /nəʊm/ ▶**noun** a legendary dwarfish creature supposed to guard the earth's treasures underground.
▪a small garden ornament in the form of a bearded man with a pointed hat. ▪ informal a small ugly person. ▪ informal a person regarded as having secret or sinister influence, especially in financial matters: *the gnomes of Zurich.*
– DERIVATIVES **gnomish** adjective.
– ORIGIN mid 17th cent.: from French, from modern Latin *gnomus*, a word used by Paracelsus as a synonym of *Pygmaeus*, denoting a mythical race of very small people said to inhabit parts of Ethiopia and India (compare with **PYGMY**).

gnome[2] /nəʊm, ˈnəʊmi/ ▶**noun** a short statement encapsulating a general truth; a maxim.
– ORIGIN late 16th cent.: from Greek *gnōmē* 'thought, opinion' (related to *gignōskein* 'know').

gnomic /ˈnəʊmɪk/ ▶**adjective** expressed in or of the nature of short, pithy maxims or aphorisms: *that most gnomic form, the aphorism.*
▪enigmatic; ambiguous: *I had to have the gnomic response interpreted for me.*
– DERIVATIVES **gnomically** adverb.
– ORIGIN early 19th cent.: from Greek *gnōmikos* (perhaps via French *gnomique*), from *gnōmē* 'thought, judgement', (plural) *gnōmai* 'sayings, maxims', related to *gignōskein* 'know'.

gnomon /ˈnəʊmɒn/ ▶**noun 1** the projecting piece on a sundial that shows the time by the position of its shadow.
▪Astronomy a structure, especially a column, used in observing the sun's meridian altitude.
2 Geometry the part of a parallelogram left when a similar parallelogram has been taken from its corner.
– DERIVATIVES **gnomonic** /-ˈmɒnɪk/ adjective.
– ORIGIN mid 16th cent.: via Latin from Greek *gnōmōn* 'indicator, carpenter's square' (related to *gignōskein* 'know').

gnosis /ˈnəʊsɪs/ ▶**noun** [mass noun] knowledge of spiritual mysteries.
– ORIGIN late 16th cent.: from Greek *gnōsis* 'knowledge' (related to *gignōskein* 'know').

gnostic /ˈnɒstɪk/ ▶**adjective** of or relating to knowledge, especially esoteric mystical knowledge.
▪(**Gnostic**) of or relating to Gnosticism.
▶**noun** (**Gnostic**) an adherent of Gnosticism.
– ORIGIN late 16th cent. (as a noun): via ecclesiastical Latin from Greek *gnōstikos*, from *gnōstos* 'known' (related to *gignōskein* 'know').

Gnosticism /ˈnɒstɪˌsɪz(ə)m/ ▶**noun** a prominent heretical movement of the 2nd-century Christian Church, partly of pre-Christian origin. Gnostic doctrine taught that the world was created and ruled by a lesser divinity, the demiurge, and that Christ was an emissary of the remote supreme divine being, esoteric knowledge (gnosis) of whom enabled the redemption of the human spirit.

gnotobiotic /ˌnəʊtə(ʊ)bʌɪˈɒtɪk/ ▶**adjective** Biology of, relating to, or denoting an environment for rearing or culturing organisms in which all the micro-organisms are either known or excluded.
– ORIGIN 1940s: from Greek *gnōtos* 'known' + **BIOTIC**.

GNP ▶**abbreviation for** gross national product.

Gnr ▶**abbreviation for** Gunner (in the British army).

gns ▶**abbreviation for** guineas.

gnu /(g)nuː, (g)njuː/ ▶**noun** a large dark antelope with a long head, a beard and mane, and a sloping back. Also called **WILDEBEEST**.
• Genus *Connochaetes*, family Bovidae: two species, in particular the abundant **brindled gnu** or blue wildebeest (*C. taurinus*).
– ORIGIN late 18th cent.: from Khoikhoi and San, perhaps imitative of the sound made by the animal when alarmed.

GNVQ ▶**abbreviation for** General National Vocational Qualification.

go[1] ▶**verb** (**goes, going**; past **went**; past participle **gone**)
1 [no obj., usu. with adverbial of direction] move from one place or point to another; travel: *he* **went out** *to the shops* | *she longs to* **go back** *home* | *we've a long way to go.*
▪travel a specified distance: *you just have to go a few miles to get to the road.* ▪ travel or move in order to engage in a specified activity or course of action: *let's* **go and** *have a pint* | [with infinitive] *we* **went to** *see her* | [with present participle] *she used to go hunting.* ▪ (**go to**) attend or visit for a particular purpose: *we went to the cinema* | *he went to Cambridge University.* ▪ [in imperative] begin motion (used in a starter's order to begin a race): *ready, steady, go!* ▪ (**go to**) (of a rank or honour) be allotted or awarded: *the top prize went to a twenty-four-year-old sculptor.* ▪ (**go into/to/towards**) (of a thing) contribute to or be put into (a whole); be used for or devoted to: *considerable effort went into making the operation successful.* ▪ pass a specified amount of time in a particular way or under particular circumstances: *sometimes they* **went for** *two months without talking.* ▪ used to indicate how many people a supply of food, money, or another resource is sufficient for or how much can be achieved using it: *the sale will* **go a long way towards** *easing the huge debt burden* | *a little luck can* **go a long way.** ▪ (of a thing) lie or extend in a certain direction: *the scar started just above her ankle and went all the way up inside her leg.* ▪ change in level, amount, or rank in a specified direction: *prices* **went up** *by 15 per cent.* ▪ informal used to emphasize the speaker's annoyance at a specified action or event: *then he* **goes and** *spoils it all* | [with present participle] *don't go poking your nose where you shouldn't.* ▪ informal said in various expressions when angrily or contemptuously dismissing someone: *go and get stuffed.*
2 [no obj.] leave; depart: *I really must go.*
▪(of time) pass or elapse: *the hours* **went by** | *three years* **went past.** ▪ come to an end; cease to exist: *a golden age that has now gone for good* | *11,500 jobs are due to go by next year.* ▪ leave or resign from a post: *I tried to persuade the Chancellor not to go.* ▪ be lost or stolen: *when he returned minutes later his equipment had gone.* ▪ cease operating or functioning: *the power went in our road last week.* ▪ die (used euphemistically): *I'd like to see my grandchildren before I go.* ▪ (of a thing) be sold: *the meat* **went to** *the butcher opposite the farm.* ▪ (of money) be spent, especially in a specified way: *the rest of his money* **went on** *medical expenses.*
3 (**be going to be/do something**) intend or be likely or intended to be or do something; be about to (used to express a future tense): *I'm going to be late for work* | *she's going to have a baby.*
4 [no obj., with complement] pass into a specified state, especially an undesirable one: *the food is going bad* | *her mind immediately went blank* | *he's gone crazy.*
▪(**go to/into**) enter into a specified state, institution, or course of action: *she turned over and went back to sleep* | *the car went into a spin.* ▪ happen, proceed, or be for a time in a specified condition: *no one went hungry in our house.* ▪ make a sound of a specified kind: *the engine went bang.* ▪ (of a bell or similar device) make a sound in functioning: *I heard the buzzer go four times.* ▪ [with direct speech] informal say: *the kids go, 'Yeah, sure.'* ▪ (**go by/under**) be known or called by (a specified name): *he now goes under the name Charles Perez.*
5 [no obj.] proceed in a specified way or have a specified outcome; turn out: *how did the weekend go?* | *it all* **went off** *smoothly.*
▪be successful, especially in being enjoyable or exciting: *the party hosts had to strive to make things go.* ▪ be acceptable or permitted: *underground events where* **anything goes.** ▪ (of a song, account, or similar) have a specified content or wording: *if you haven't heard it, the story goes like this.*
6 [no obj.] be harmonious, complementary, or matching: *rosemary* **goes with** *roast lamb* | *the earrings and the scarf don't really go.*
▪be found in the same place or situation; be associated: *cooking and eating* **go together.**
7 [no obj.] (of a machine or device) function: *my car won't go.*
▪continue in operation or existence: *the committee was* **kept going** *even when its existence could no longer be justified.*
8 [no obj.] (of an article) be regularly kept or put in a particular place: *remember which card goes in which slot.*
▪fit or be able to be accommodated in a particular place or space: *you're trying to squeeze a quart into a pint pot, and it just won't go.*
9 [no obj.] informal use a toilet; urinate or defecate.
▶**noun** (pl. **goes**) informal **1** an attempt or trial at something: *I thought I'd* **give it a go.**
▪a person's turn to use something or to move or act in a game: *I* **had a go on** *Nigel's racing bike* | *come on Tony, it's your go.* ▪ chiefly Brit. a state of affairs: *this seems a rum sort of go.* ▪ chiefly Brit. an attack of illness: *he's had this nasty go of dysentery.* ▪ N. Amer. a project or undertaking which has been approved: *tell them the project is a go.* ▪ chiefly Brit. used in reference to a single item, action, or spell of activity: *he put it to his lips then knocked it back in one go.*
2 [mass noun] spirit, animation, or energy: *there's no go in me at all these days.*
▪Brit. vigorous activity: *it's* **all go** *around here.*
▶**adjective** [predic.] informal functioning properly: *all systems go.*
– PHRASES **all the go** Brit. informal, dated in fashion. **as** (or **so**) **far as it goes** bearing in mind its limitations (said when qualifying praise of something): *the book is a useful catalogue as far as it goes.* **as —— go** compared to the average or typical one of the specified kind: *as castles go it is small and old.* **from the word go** informal from the very beginning. **go figure!** N. Amer. informal said to express the speaker's belief that something is amazing or incredible. **go great guns** see **GUN**. **go halves** (or **shares**) share something equally. **going!, gone!** an auctioneer's announcement that bidding is closing or closed. **going on ——** (Brit. also **going on for ——**) approaching a specified time, age, or amount: *I was going on fourteen when I went to my first gig.* **go (to) it** Brit. informal act in a vigorous, energetic, or dissipated way: *Go it, Dad! Give him what for!* **go it alone** see **ALONE**. **go to show** (or **prove**) (of an occurrence) serve as evidence or proof of something specified. **go well** S. African used to express good wishes to someone leaving. **have a go at** chiefly Brit. attack or criticize (someone): *she's always having a go at me.* **have —— going for one** informal used to indicate how much someone has in their favour or to their advantage: *Why did she do it? She had so much going for her.* **make a go of** informal be successful in (something): *he's determined to make a go of his marriage.* **on the go** informal very active or busy: *he's*

dead beat, he's been on the go all evening. **to be going on with** Brit. to start with; for the time being: *this is not a full critical appraisal but it will certainly do to be going on with.* **to go** chiefly N. Amer. (of food or drink from a restaurant or cafe) to be eaten or drunk off the premises: *order one large cheese-and-peppers pizza, to go.* **what goes around comes around** proverb the consequences of one's actions will have to be dealt with eventually. **who goes there?** said by a sentry as a challenge.

– ORIGIN Old English *gān*, of Germanic origin; related to Dutch *gaan* and German *gehen*; the form *went* was originally the past tense of **WEND**.

USAGE The use of **go** followed by **and**, as in *I must go and change* (rather than *I must go to change*), is extremely common but is regarded by some grammarians as an oddity. For more details, see **usage** at **AND**.

▶**go about 1** begin or carry on work at (an activity); busy oneself with: *you are going about this in the wrong way.* **2** Sailing change to an opposite tack.

go against oppose or resist: *he refused to go against the unions.* ■ be contrary to (a feeling or principle): *these tactics go against many of our instincts.* ■ (of a judgement, decision or result) be unfavourable for: *the tribunal's decision went against them.*

go ahead proceed or be carried out without hesitation: *the project will go ahead.*

go along with give one's consent or agreement to (a person or their views).

go around (of an aircraft) abort an approach to landing and prepare to make a fresh approach. See also ***go round***.

go around with be regularly in the company of: *he goes around with some of the local lads.*

go at energetically attack or tackle: *he went at things with a daunting eagerness.*

go back 1 (of a clock) be set to an earlier standard time, especially at the end of summertime. **2** (of two people) have known each each for a specified, typically long, period of time: *Victor and I go back a long way.*

go back on fail to keep (a promise): *he wouldn't go back on his word.*

go down 1 (of a ship or aircraft) sink or crash: *he saw eleven B-17s go down.* ■ be defeated in a contest: *they went down 2–1.* **2** (of a person, period, or event) be recorded or remembered in a particular way: *his name will now* ***go down in history.*** **3** be swallowed: *solids can sometimes go down much easier than liquids.* **4** (of a person, action, or work) elicit a specified reaction: *my slide shows went down reasonably well.* **5** N. Amer. informal happen: *you really don't know what's going down?* **6** Brit. informal leave a university, especially Oxford or Cambridge, after finishing one's studies. **7** Brit. informal be sent to prison.

go down on vulgar slang perform oral sex on.

go down with Brit. begin to suffer from (a specified illness): *I went down with an attack of bronchitis.*

go for 1 decide on; choose: *I wished that we had gone for plan B.* ■ tend to find (a particular type of person) attractive: *Dionne went for the outlaw type.* **2** attempt to gain or attain: *he went for a job as a delivery driver.* ■ **(go for it)** strive to the utmost to gain or achieve something (frequently said as an exhortation): *sounds like a good idea—go for it!* **3** launch oneself at (someone); attack: *she went for him with clawed hands.* **4** end up having a specified value or effect: *my good intentions* ***went for nothing.*** **5** apply to; have relevance for: *the same goes for money-grabbing lawyers.*

go forward (of a clock) be set to a later standard time, especially summertime.

go in for 1 enter (a contest) as a competitor: *he went in for the exam.* **2** like or habitually take part in (something, especially an activity): *I don't go in for the social whirl.*

go into 1 (especially of a vehicle) collide with. **2** investigate or enquire into (something): *there's no need to go into it now.* **3** (of a whole number) be capable of dividing another, typically without a remainder: *six into five won't go.*

go off 1 (of a gun, bomb, or similar device) explode or fire. ■ (of an alarm) begin to sound. ■ informal become suddenly angry; lose one's temper: *if you got in an argument with him he'd just go off.* **2** chiefly Brit. (especially of food) begin to decompose; become unfit for consumption. **3** informal, chiefly Brit. begin to dislike: *I went off men after my husband left me.* **4** go to sleep. **5** gradually cease to be felt: *I had a bad headache but it's going off now.*

go on 1 [often with present participle] continue or persevere: *I can't go on protecting you.* ■ talk at great length, especially tediously or angrily: *she* ***went on about*** *how lovely it would be to escape from the city.* ■ continue speaking or doing something after a short pause: [with direct speech] *'I don't understand,' she went on.* ■ informal said when encouraging someone or expressing disbelief: *go on, tell him!* **2** happen; take place: *God knows what went on there.* **3** [often with infinitive] proceed to do: *she went on to do postgraduate work.* **4** [usu. in negative] informal have a specified amount of care or liking for (something): *I heard this album a month or so and didn't go much on it.*

go out 1 (of a fire or light) be extinguished. **2** (of the tide) ebb; recede to low tide. **3** leave one's home to go to an entertainment or social event, typically in the evening: *I'm going out for dinner.* ■ carry on a regular romantic, and sometimes sexual, relationship: *he was* ***going out with*** *her best friend.* **4** used to convey someone's deep sympathy or similar feeling: *the Englishman's heart went out to the pitiful figure.* **5** Golf play the first nine holes in a round of eighteen holes. Compare with ***come home*** (see **HOME**). **6** (in some card games) be the first to dispose of all the cards in one's hand.

go over 1 examine, consider, or check the details of (something): *I want to go over these plans with you again.* **2** change one's allegiance or religion: *he* ***went over to*** *the pro-English party.* **3** (especially of an action or performance) be received in a specified way: *his earnestness would go over well in a courtroom.*

go round chiefly Brit. (chiefly US also **go around**) **1** spin: revolve: *the wheels were going round.* **2** (especially of food) be sufficient to supply everybody present: *there was barely enough food to go round.*

go through 1 undergo (a difficult or painful period or experience): *the country is going through a period of economic instability.* **2** search through or examine carefully or in sequence: *she started to go through the bundle of letters.* **3** (of a proposal or contract) be officially approved or completed: *the sale of the building is set to go through.* **4** informal use up or spend (available money or other resources). **5** (of a book) be successively published in (a specified number of editions): *within two years it went through thirty-one editions.* **6** Austral. informal leave hastily to avoid an obligation; abscond.

go to! archaic said to express disbelief, impatience, or admonition.

go under (of a business) become bankrupt. ■ (of a person) die or suffer an emotional collapse.

go up 1 (of a building or other structure) be built: *housing developments went up.* **2** explode or suddenly burst into flames: *last night two factories* ***went up in flames.*** **3** Brit. informal begin one's studies at a university, especially Oxford or Cambridge.

go with 1 give one's consent or agreement to (a person or their views). **2** have a romantic or sexual relationship with (someone).

go without suffer lack or deprivation: *I like to give my children what they want, even if I have to go without.*

go² ▶**noun** [mass noun] a Japanese board game of territorial possession and capture.

– ORIGIN late 19th cent.: Japanese, literally 'small stone', also the name of the game.

Goa /ˈɡəʊə/ a state on the west coast of India; capital, Panaji. Formerly a Portuguese territory, it was seized by India in 1961. It formed a Union Territory with Daman and Diu until 1987, when it was made a state.

– DERIVATIVES **Goan** adjective & noun, **Goanese** /ˌɡəʊəˈniːz/ adjective & noun.

goad /ɡəʊd/ ▶**noun** a spiked stick used for driving cattle.

■ a thing that stimulates someone into action: *for him the visit was a goad to renewed effort.*

▶**verb** [with obj.] provoke or annoy (someone) so as to stimulate some action or reaction: *he* ***goaded*** *her* ***on*** *to more daring revelations.*

■ [with obj. and adverbial of direction] drive or urge (an animal) on with a goad.

– ORIGIN Old English *gād*, of Germanic origin.

go-ahead informal ▶**noun** (usu. **the go-ahead**) permission to proceed: *the government had given the go-ahead for the power station.*

▶**adjective 1** enthusiastic about new projects; enterprising: *a young and go-ahead managing director.*

2 [attrib.] N. Amer. denoting the run, score, etc. which gives a team the lead in a game.

goal ▶**noun 1** (in football, rugby, hockey, and some other games) a pair of posts linked by a crossbar and typically with a net between, forming a space into or over which the ball has to be sent in order to score.

■ an instance of sending the ball into or over this space, especially as a unit of scoring in a game: *the decisive opening goal | we won by three goals to two.* ■ a cage or basket used similarly in other sports.

2 the object of a person's ambition or effort; an aim or desired result: *playing for Scotland has become the most important goal in his life.*

■ the destination of a journey: *the aircraft bumped towards our goal some 400 miles to the west.* ■ poetic/literary a point marking the end of a race.

– PHRASES **in goal** in the position of goalkeeper.

– DERIVATIVES **goalless** adjective.

– ORIGIN Middle English (in the sense 'limit, boundary'): of unknown origin.

goal area ▶**noun** Soccer a rectangular area in front of the goal from within which goal kicks must be taken.

goal average ▶**noun** [mass noun] Soccer the ratio of the numbers of goals scored for and against a team in a series of matches, sometimes used in deciding the team's position in a table.

goalball ▶**noun** [mass noun] a ball game for blind and visually handicapped players, played by teams of three. The object is to roll a large ball containing bells over a line at the end of the court.

■ [count noun] the ball used in this game.

goal difference ▶**noun** [mass noun] Soccer the difference between the number of goals scored for and against a team in a series of matches, sometimes used in deciding the team's position in a table.

goalie ▶**noun** informal term for **GOALKEEPER** or **GOALTENDER**.

goalkeeper ▶**noun** a player in soccer or field hockey whose special role is to stop the ball from entering the goal.

– DERIVATIVES **goalkeeping** noun.

goal kick ▶**noun 1** Soccer a free kick taken by the defending side from within their goal area after attackers send the ball over the byline.

2 Rugby an attempt to kick a goal.

– DERIVATIVES **goal-kicker** noun (Rugby), **goal-kicking** noun (Rugby).

goal line ▶**noun** a line across a football or hockey field at or near its end, on which the goal is placed or which acts as the boundary beyond which a try or touchdown is scored.

goalmouth ▶**noun** the area just in front of a goal in soccer or hockey.

goalpost ▶**noun** either of the two upright posts of a goal.

– PHRASES **move the goalposts** unfairly alter the conditions or rules of a procedure during its course.

goaltender ▶**noun** chiefly N. Amer. a goalkeeper, especially in ice hockey.

– DERIVATIVES **goaltending** noun.

goanna /ɡəʊˈanə/ ▶**noun** Australian term for **MONITOR** (in sense 4).

– ORIGIN mid 19th cent.: alteration of **IGUANA**.

go-around (also **go-round**) ▶**noun 1** a flight path typically taken by an aircraft after an aborted approach to landing.

2 US informal a confrontation; an argument.

goat ▶**noun 1** a hardy domesticated ruminant mammal that has backward curving horns and (in the male) a beard. It is kept for its milk and meat, and noted for its lively and frisky behaviour.

• *Capra hircus*, family Bovidae, descended from the wild bezoar.

■ a wild mammal related to this, such as the ibex, markhor, and tur. See also **MOUNTAIN GOAT**. ■ **(the Goat)** the zodiacal sign Capricorn or the constellation Capricornus.

2 a person likened to a goat, in particular:

■ a lecherous man. ■ Brit. informal a stupid person; a fool: *she was going to make a goat of herself.* ■ US a scapegoat.

– PHRASES **get someone's goat** informal irritate someone.

– DERIVATIVES **goatish** adjective, **goaty** adjective.

– ORIGIN Old English *gāt* 'nanny goat', of Germanic origin; related to Dutch *geit* and German *Geiss*, also to Latin *haedus* 'kid'.

goat-antelope ▸ noun a ruminant mammal of a group that combines the characteristics of both goats and antelopes.
● Subfamily Caprinae, family Bovidae: tribes Rupicaprini (the chamois, goral, serow, and mountain goat) and Ovibonini (the musk ox and takin).

goatee /gəʊˈtiː/ (also **goatee beard**) ▸ noun a small pointed beard like that of a goat.
– DERIVATIVES **goateed** adjective.

goatfish ▸ noun (pl. same or **-fishes**) North American term for RED MULLET.

goatherd ▸ noun a person who tends goats.
– ORIGIN Old English, from GOAT + obsolete *herd* 'herdsman'.

goat moth ▸ noun a large greyish moth, the caterpillar of which bores into wood and has a goat-like smell.
● *Cossus cossus*, family Cossidae.

goat's beard ▸ noun **1** a Eurasian plant of the daisy family, with slender grass-like leaves, yellow flowers that typically close at about midday, and downy fruits which resemble those of a dandelion.
● *Tragopogon pratensis*, family Compositae.
2 a plant of the rose family, with long plumes of white flowers, found in both Eurasia and North America.
● *Aruncus dioicus*, family Rosaceae.
– ORIGIN mid 16th cent.: translating Greek *tragopōgon* or Latin *Barba Capri*.

goatskin ▸ noun the skin of a goat.
■ [mass noun] such a skin, or leather made from it, as a material. ■ a garment or object made out of goatskin.

goat's rue ▸ noun a herbaceous plant of the pea family, which was formerly used in medicine, especially as a vermifuge.
● Two species in the family Leguminosae: a bushy Eurasian plant which is cultivated as an ornamental (*Galega officinalis*), and a North American plant with pink and yellow flowers and which smells of goats (*Tephrosia virginiana*).

goatsucker ▸ noun another term for NIGHTJAR.
– ORIGIN early 17th cent.: so named because the bird was thought to suck goats' udders.

goat willow ▸ noun a common European willow with broad leaves and soft fluffy catkins. Also called SALLOW² or PUSSY WILLOW.
● *Salix caprea*, family Salicaceae.

go-away bird ▸ noun a crested long-tailed African bird of the turaco family, with mainly grey plumage and a call that resembles the words 'go away'. Also called LOERIE or LOURIE in South Africa.
● Family Musophagidae: two genera and three species, in particular *Corythaixoides concolor*.

gob¹ ▸ noun informal, chiefly Brit. a person's mouth: *Jean told him to shut his big gob.*
– ORIGIN mid 16th cent.: perhaps from Scottish Gaelic *gob* 'beak, mouth'.

gob² informal ▸ noun **1** Brit. a lump or clot of a slimy or viscous substance: *a gob of phlegm.*
■ N. Amer. a small lump.
2 (**gobs of**) N. Amer. a lot of: *he wants to make gobs of money selling cassettes.*
▸ verb (**gobbed**, **gobbing**) [no obj.] Brit. spit.
– ORIGIN late Middle English: from Old French *gobe* 'mouthful, lump', from *gober* 'to swallow, gulp', perhaps of Celtic origin.

gob³ ▸ noun informal, dated an American sailor.
– ORIGIN early 20th cent.: of unknown origin.

gobbet /ˈɡɒbɪt/ ▸ noun a piece or lump of flesh, food, or other matter: *a torn-off gobbet of flesh.*
■ an extract from a text, especially one set for translation or comment in an examination: *the poetry was mainly seen as a quarry for gobbets.*
– ORIGIN Middle English: from Old French *gobet*, diminutive of *gobe* (see GOB²).

Gobbi /ˈɡɒbi/, Tito (1915–84), Italian operatic baritone. He was famous for his interpretations of Verdi's baritone roles, and for his performances in the title role of Berg's *Wozzeck* and as Scarpia in Puccini's *Tosca*.

gobble¹ ▸ verb [with obj.] eat (something) hurriedly and noisily: *one man gobbled up a kipper.*
■ use a large amount of (something) very quickly: *these old houses just gobble up money.* ■ (of a large organization or other body) incorporate or take over (a smaller one): *this small department was gobbled up by the Ministry of Transport.*
– ORIGIN early 17th cent.: probably from GOB².

gobble² ▸ verb [no obj.] (of a turkeycock) make a characteristic swallowing sound in the throat.
■ (of a person) make such a sound when speaking, especially when excited or angry: *she was gobbling to herself faintly in her distress.*
– ORIGIN late 17th cent.: imitative, perhaps influenced by GOBBLE¹.

gobbledegook /ˈɡɒb(ə)ldɪˌɡuːk, -ˌɡʊk/ (also **gobbledygook**) ▸ noun [mass noun] informal language that is meaningless or is made unintelligible by excessive use of abstruse technical terms; nonsense.
– ORIGIN 1940s (originally US): probably imitating a turkey's gobble.

gobbler¹ ▸ noun a person who eats greedily and noisily.

gobbler² ▸ noun N. Amer. informal a turkeycock.

gobdaw /ˈɡɒbdɔː/ ▸ noun informal, chiefly Irish a foolish or pretentious person.
– ORIGIN 1950s: of unknown origin; compare with Irish *gabhdán* 'gullible person'.

Gobelin /ˈɡɒb(ə)lã, ˈɡəʊb-, -lɪn/ (also **Gobelin tapestry**) ▸ noun a tapestry made at the Gobelins factory in Paris, or in imitation of one.

Gobelins /ˈɡɒb(ə)lãz, ˈɡəʊb-, -lɪnz, French ɡɔblɛ̃/ a tapestry and textile factory in Paris, established by the Gobelin family *c.*1440 and taken over by the French Crown in 1662. It was highly successful in the late 17th and 18th centuries, when designs by leading French painters were used, and tapestry panels became used as alternatives to oil paintings.

go-between ▸ noun an intermediary or negotiator.

gobi /ˈɡəʊbi/ ▸ noun Indian term for CAULIFLOWER or CABBAGE.
– ORIGIN Punjabi.

Gobi Desert /ˈɡəʊbi/ a barren plateau of southern Mongolia and northern China.

Gobineau /ˈɡɒbɪnəʊ, French ɡɔbino/, Joseph Arthur, Comte de (1816–82), French writer and anthropologist. His stated view that the races are innately unequal and that the white Aryan race is superior to all others later influenced the ideology and policies of the Nazis.

goblet ▸ noun a drinking glass with a foot and a stem.
■ archaic a metal or glass bowl-shaped drinking cup, sometimes with a foot and a cover. ■ Brit. a receptacle forming part of a liquidizer.
– ORIGIN late Middle English: from Old French *gobelet*, diminutive of *gobel* 'cup', of unknown origin.

goblet cell ▸ noun Anatomy a column-shaped cell found in the respiratory and intestinal tracts, which secretes the main component of mucus.

goblin ▸ noun a mischievous, ugly, dwarf-like creature of folklore.
– ORIGIN Middle English: from Old French *gobelin*, possibly related to German *Kobold* (see KOBOLD) or to Greek *kobalos* 'mischievous goblin'. In medieval Latin *Gobelinus* occurs as the name of a mischievous spirit, said to haunt Évreux in northern France in the 12th cent.

gobo¹ /ˈɡəʊbəʊ/ ▸ noun (pl. **-os**) a dark plate or screen used to shield a lens from light.
■ Theatre a partial screen used in front of a spotlight to project a shape. ■ a shield used to mask a microphone from extraneous noise.
– ORIGIN 1930s: of unknown origin, perhaps from *go between*.

gobo² /ˈɡəʊbəʊ/ ▸ noun [mass noun] a vegetable root used in Japanese and other oriental cookery.
– ORIGIN Japanese.

gobony /ɡɒˈbəʊni/ ▸ adjective Heraldry another term for COMPONY.

gobshite /ˈɡɒbʃʌɪt/ ▸ noun vulgar slang, chiefly Irish a stupid, foolish, or incompetent person.

gobsmacked ▸ adjective Brit. informal utterly astonished; astounded.
– DERIVATIVES **gobsmacking** adjective.
– ORIGIN 1980s: from GOB¹ + SMACK¹, with reference to being shocked by a blow to the mouth, or to clapping a hand to one's mouth in astonishment.

gobstopper ▸ noun chiefly Brit. a large hard spherical sweet.

goby /ˈɡəʊbi/ ▸ noun (pl. **-ies**) a small, usually marine fish that typically has a sucker on the underside.
● Family Gobiidae: numerous genera and species.

– ORIGIN mid 18th cent.: from Latin *gobius*, from Greek *kōbios*, denoting some kind of small fish.

go-by ▸ noun informal, dated (in phrase **give someone the go-by**) avoid or snub someone: *ministers from the former cabinet who were given the go-by have expressed resentment.*
■ end a romantic relationship with someone: *her young man's given her the go-by.*

GOC Brit. ▸ abbreviation for General Officer Commanding.

go-cart ▸ noun **1** variant spelling of GO-KART.
2 a pushchair. ■ archaic a baby walker.
– ORIGIN late 17th cent. (denoting a baby walker): from GO¹ (in the obsolete sense 'walk') + CART.

God ▸ noun **1** [without article] (in Christianity and other monotheistic religions) the creator and ruler of the universe and source of all moral authority; the supreme being.
2 (**god**) (in certain other religions) a superhuman being or spirit worshipped as having power over nature or human fortunes; a deity: *a moon god* | *an incarnation of the god Vishnu.*
■ an image, idol, animal, or other object worshipped as divine or symbolizing a god. ■ used as a conventional personification of fate: *he dialled the number and, the gods relenting, got through at once.*
3 (**god**) an adored, admired, or influential person: *he has little time for the fashion victims for whom he is a god.*
■ a thing accorded the supreme importance appropriate to a god: *don't make money your god.*
4 (**the gods**) informal the gallery in a theatre.
■ the people sitting in this area.
▸ exclamation used to express a range of emotions such as surprise, anger, and distress: *God, what did I do to deserve this?* | *my God! Why didn't you tell us sooner?*
■ to give emphasis to a statement or declaration: *God, how I hate that woman!*
– PHRASES **God's acre** archaic a churchyard. **for God's sake!** see SAKE¹ (sense 3). **God bless** an expression of good wishes on parting. **God damn (you, him,** etc) may (you, he, etc.) be damned. **God the Father** (in Christian doctrine) the first person of the Trinity, God as creator and supreme authority. **God forbid** see FORBID. **God grant** used to express a wish that something should happen: *God grant he will soon regain his freedom.* **God help (you, him,** etc.) used to express the belief that someone is in a difficult, dangerous, or hopeless situation: *God help anyone who tried to jolly me out of my bad mood.* **God the Son** (in Christian doctrine) Christ regarded as the second person of the Trinity; God as incarnate and resurrected saviour. **God willing** used to express the wish that one will be able to do as one intends or that something will happen as planned: *one day, God willing, she and John might have a daughter.* **in God's name** used in questions to emphasize anger or surprise: *what in God's name are you doing up there?* **in the lap of the gods** see LAP¹. **play God** behave as if all-powerful or supremely important. **please God** used to emphasize a strong wish or hope: *please God the money will help us find a cure.* **thank God** see THANK. **to God** used after a verb to emphasize a strong wish or hope: *I hope to God you've got something else to put on.* **with God** dead and in heaven.
– DERIVATIVES **godhood** noun, **godship** noun, **godward** adjective & adverb, **godwards** adverb.
– ORIGIN Old English, of Germanic origin; related to Dutch *god* and German *Gott*.

Godard /ˈɡɒdɑː, French ɡɔdaʁ/, Jean-Luc (b.1930), French film director. He was one of the leading figures of the *nouvelle vague*. His films include *Breathless* (1960), *Alphaville* (1965), and the more overtly political *Wind from the East* (1969).

Godavari /ɡəʊˈdɑːvəri/ a river in central India which rises in the state of Maharashtra and flows about 1,440 km (900 miles) south-east across the Deccan plateau to the Bay of Bengal.

God-awful ▸ adjective informal extremely unpleasant: *the most God-awful row.*

godchild ▸ noun (pl. **-children**) a person in relation to a godparent.

goddam (also **goddamn, goddamned**) ▸ adjective & adverb informal, chiefly US used for emphasis, especially to express anger or frustration.
– ORIGIN mid 17th cent.: abbreviation of *God damn (me).*

Goddard /ˈɡɒdɑːd/, Robert Hutchings (1882–1945), American physicist. He carried out pioneering work in rocketry, and designed and built the first successful liquid-fuelled rocket. NASA's Goddard Space Flight Center is named after him.

god-daughter ▶ noun a female godchild.

goddess ▶ noun a female deity: *a temple to Athena Nike, goddess of victory.*
■ a woman who is adored, especially for her beauty: *he had an affair with a screen goddess.*

Gödel /ˈɡɜːd(ə)l/, Kurt (1906–78), Austrian-born American mathematician. He made several important contributions to mathematical logic, especially the incompleteness theorem.

Gödel's incompleteness theorem see INCOMPLETENESS THEOREM.

godet /ɡəʊˈdɛt, ˈɡəʊdeɪ/ ▶ noun a triangular piece of material inserted in a dress, shirt, or glove to make it flared or for ornamentation.
– ORIGIN late 19th cent.: from French.

godetia /ɡə(ʊ)ˈdiːʃə/ ▶ noun a North American plant with showy lilac to red flowers.
● Genus *Clarkia* (or *Godetia*), family Onagraceae.
– ORIGIN modern Latin, named after Charles H. *Godet* (1797–1879), Swiss botanist.

go-devil ▶ noun N. Amer. chiefly historical a gadget used in farming, logging, or drilling for oil, in particular:
■ a crude sled, used chiefly for dragging logs. ■ a jointed apparatus for cleaning pipelines.

godfather ▶ noun 1 a male godparent.
2 a man who is influential in a movement or organization, through providing support for it or through playing a leading or innovatory part in it: *the godfather of alternative comedy.*
■ a person directing an illegal organization, especially a leader of the American Mafia.

God-fearing ▶ adjective earnestly religious: *an honest, God-fearing woman.*

godforsaken ▶ adjective lacking any merit or attraction: *what are you doing in this godforsaken place?*

God-given ▶ adjective received from God.
■ possessed by unquestionable right, as if by divine authority: *being my stepsister doesn't give you a God-given right to know all my business.*

Godhavn /ˈɡɒdˌhɑːv(ə)n/ a town in western Greenland, on the south coast of the island of Disko.

godhead ▶ noun (usu. **the Godhead**) God.
■ [mass noun] divine nature. ■ informal an adored, admired, or influential person; an idol.

Godiva /ɡəˈdʌɪvə/, Lady (d.1080), English noblewoman, wife of Leofric, Earl of Mercia. According to a 13th-century legend, she agreed to her husband's proposition that he would reduce unpopular taxes only if she rode naked on horseback through the marketplace of Coventry. According to later versions of the story, all the townspeople refrained from watching, except for peeping Tom, who was struck blind in punishment.

godless ▶ adjective not recognizing or obeying God: *the godless forces of communism.*
■ without a god: *humanity coming to terms with a godless world.* ■ profane; wicked.
– DERIVATIVES **godlessness** noun.

godlike ▶ adjective resembling God or a god in qualities such as power, beauty, or benevolence: *our parents are godlike figures to our childish eyes.*
■ befitting or appropriate to a god: *we act as though we have godlike powers to decide our own destiny.*

godly ▶ adjective (**godlier**, **godliest**) devoutly religious; pious: *how to live the godly life.*
– DERIVATIVES **godliness** noun.

god-man ▶ noun 1 Indian a holy man; a guru.
2 an incarnation of a god in human form.

godmother ▶ noun a female godparent.
■ a woman who is influential in a movement or organization, through providing support for it or through playing a leading or innovatory part in it: *the godmother of the regiment.*

godown /ˈɡəʊdaʊn, ɡəˈdaʊn/ ▶ noun (in east Asia, especially India) a warehouse.
– ORIGIN late 16th cent.: from Portuguese *gudão*, from Tamil *kiṭaṅku*, Malayalam *kiṭaṅṅu*, or Kannada *gaḍaṅgu* 'store, warehouse'.

godparent ▶ noun a person who presents a child at baptism, responding on their behalf and promising

to take responsibility for their religious education.

God Save the Queen (also **King**) ▶ noun the British national anthem.
– ORIGIN evidence suggests a 17th-cent. origin for the complete words and tune of the anthem. The ultimate origin is obscure: the phrase 'God save the King' occurs in various passages in the Old Testament, while as early as 1545 it was a watchword in the navy, with 'long to reign over us' as a countersign.

God's country (also **God's own country**) ▶ noun [in sing.] used especially with reference to the United States to express a sense of the country's beauty and excellence.

godsend ▶ noun a very helpful or valuable event, person, or thing: *these information packs are a godsend to schools.*
– ORIGIN early 19th cent.: from *God's send* 'what God has sent'.

God's gift ▶ noun chiefly Brit. the ideal or best possible person or thing for someone or something (used chiefly ironically or in negative statements): *he appeared to think he was God's gift to women.*

God slot ▶ noun informal a period in a broadcasting schedule regularly reserved for religious programmes.

godson ▶ noun a male godchild.

Godspeed ▶ exclamation dated an expression of good wishes to a person starting a journey.
– ORIGIN Middle English: from *God speed you* 'may God help you prosper'.

God squad ▶ noun informal used to refer to evangelical Christians, typically suggesting intrusive moralizing and proselytizing.

God's truth ▶ noun [mass noun] the absolute truth: *I loved him, that's God's truth.*

Godthåb /ˈɡɒdhɔːb/ former name (until 1979) for NUUK.

Godunov /ˈɡɒdʊnɒf/, Boris (1550–1605), tsar of Russia 1598–1605. A counsellor of Ivan the Terrible, he succeeded Ivan's son as tsar. His reign was marked by famine, doubts over his involvement in the earlier death of Ivan's eldest son, and the appearance of a pretender, the so-called False Dmitri.

Godwin, William (1756–1836), English social philosopher and novelist. He advocated a system of anarchism based on a belief in the goodness of human reason and on his doctrine of extreme individualism.

Godwin-Austen, Mount former name for K2.

godwit ▶ noun a large, long-legged wader with a long, slightly upturned or straight bill, and typically a reddish-brown head and breast in the breeding male.
● Genus *Limosa*, family Scolopacidae: four species.
– ORIGIN mid 16th cent.: of unknown origin.

Godwottery /ɡɒdˈwɒt(ə)ri/ ▶ noun [mass noun] Brit. humorous an affected quality of archaism, excessive fussiness, and sentimentality.
– ORIGIN 1930s: from the line 'A garden is a lovesome thing, God wot!', in T. E. Brown's poem *My Garden* (1876).

Goebbels /ˈɡɜːb(ə)lz/ (also **Göbbels**), (Paul) Joseph (1897–1945), German Nazi leader and politician. From 1933 Goebbels was Hitler's Minister of Propaganda, with control of the press, radio, and all aspects of culture, and manipulated these in order to further Nazi aims. He committed suicide rather than surrender to the Allies.

goer ▶ noun 1 [in combination] a person who attends a specified place or event, especially regularly: *churchgoers* | *a theatre-goer.*
2 [with adj.] informal a person or thing that goes in a specified way: *horse no. 7 is a fast goer.*
■ a project likely to be accepted or to succeed: *if the business is a goer, the entrepreneur moves on.*
3 informal a sexually unrestrained woman or girl.

Goering /ˈɡɜːrɪŋ/, Hermann Wilhelm (1893–1946), German Nazi leader and politician. Goering was responsible for the German rearmament programme, founder of the Gestapo, and from 1936 until 1943 directed the German economy. Sentenced to death at the Nuremberg war trials, he committed suicide in his cell.

Goes /ɡuːs/, Hugo van der (*fl. c.*1467–82), Flemish painter, born in Ghent. His best-known work is the

large-scale *Portinari Altarpiece* (1475), commissioned for a church in Florence.

goes third person singular present of GO[1].

goest /ˈɡəʊɪst/ archaic second person singular present of GO[1].

goeth /ˈɡəʊɪθ/ archaic third person singular present of GO[1].

Goethe /ˈɡɜːtə/, Johann Wolfgang von (1749–1832), German poet, dramatist, and scholar. Involved at first with the *Sturm und Drang* movement, Goethe changed to a more measured and classical style, as in the 'Wilhelm Meister' novels (1796–1829). Notable dramas: *Götz von Berlichingen* (1773), *Tasso* (1790), and *Faust* (1808–32).
– DERIVATIVES **Goethean** (also **Goethian**) adjective.

goethite /ˈɡɜːtʌɪt/ ▶ noun [mass noun] a dark or yellowish-brown mineral consisting of hydrated iron oxide, occurring typically as masses of fibrous crystals.
– ORIGIN early 19th cent.: from the name of J.W. von GOETHE + -ITE[1].

go-faster stripes ▶ plural noun striped stickers on the bodywork of a car, especially horizontally along the doors, intended to make it look more sporty.

gofer /ˈɡəʊfə/ (also **gopher**) ▶ noun informal, chiefly N. Amer. a person who runs errands, especially on a film set or in an office; a dogsbody.
– ORIGIN 1960s: from *go for* (i.e. go and fetch).

goffer /ˈɡɒfə/ ▶ verb [with obj.] [usu. as adj. **goffered**] treat (a lace edge or frill) with heated irons in order to crimp or flute it: *a goffered frill.*
■ [as adj. **goffered**] (of the gilt edges of a book) embossed with a repeating design.
▶ noun an iron used to crimp or flute lace.
– ORIGIN late 16th cent.: from French *gaufrer* 'stamp with a patterned tool', from *gaufre* 'honeycomb', from Middle Low German *wāfel* (see WAFFLE[2]).

Gog and Magog /ɡɒɡ, ˈmeɪɡɒɡ/ **1** in the Bible, the names of enemies of God's people. In Ezek. 38–9, Gog is apparently a ruler from the land of Magog, while in Rev. 20:8, Gog and Magog are nations under the dominion of Satan.
2 (in medieval legend) opponents of Alexander the Great, living north of the Caucasus.
3 two giant statues standing in Guildhall, London, representing either the last two survivors of a race of giants supposed to have inhabited Britain before Roman times, or Gogmagog, chief of the giants, and Corineus, a Roman invader.

go-getter ▶ noun informal an aggressively enterprising person.
– DERIVATIVES **go-getting** adjective.

gogga /ˈxɔxə, ˈxɒxə/ ▶ noun S. African informal an insect.
■ a person or thing regarded as dangerous or unwanted: *apartheid was a gogga that had outstayed its welcome.*
– ORIGIN Afrikaans, from Khoikhoi *xo-xon*, a collective term for slithering and creeping creatures.

goggle ▶ verb [no obj.] look with wide open eyes, typically in amazement or wonder: *they were goggling at me as if I was some kind of terrorist.*
■ (of the eyes) protrude or open wide.
▶ adjective [attrib.] (of the eyes) protuberant or rolling.
▶ noun 1 (**goggles**) close-fitting glasses with side shields, for protecting the eyes from glare, dust, water, etc.
■ informal glasses.
2 [in sing.] a stare with protruding eyes.
3 (**goggles**) the staggers (a disease of sheep).
– DERIVATIVES **goggled** adjective.
– ORIGIN Middle English (in the sense 'look to one side, squint'): probably from a base symbolic of oscillating movement.

goggle-box ▶ noun (**the goggle-box**) Brit. informal a television set.

goggle-eye ▶ noun any of a number of edible fishes with large eyes that occur widely on reefs in tropical and subtropical seas:
● a nocturnal fish related to the bigeye (*Priacanthus hamrur*, family Priacanthidae). ● (also **goggle-eye jack**) a fish often found in shoals (*Selar crumenophthalmus*, family Carangidae).

goggle-eyed ▶ adjective having staring or protuberant eyes, especially through astonishment.

go-go ▶ adjective [attrib.] **1** relating to or denoting an unrestrained and erotic style of dancing to popular music: *a go-go bar* | *go-go dancers.*
2 assertively dynamic: *the go-go bravado of the 1980s.*
▶ noun [mass noun] a style of popular music originating

in the black communities of Washington DC and characterized by an incessant funk beat.

– ORIGIN 1960s: reduplication of **GO**[1], perhaps influenced by **A GOGO**.

Gogol /ˈgəʊgɒl, ˈgɒg(ə)l/, Nikolai (Vasilevich) (1809–52), Russian novelist, dramatist, and short-story writer, born in Ukraine. His writings are satirical, often exploring themes of fantasy and the supernatural. Notable works: *The Government Inspector* (play, 1836), *Notes of a Madman* (short fiction, 1835), and *Dead Souls* (novel, 1842).

Goiânia /gɔɪˈɑːnɪə/ a city in south central Brazil, capital of the state of Goiás; pop. 998,500 (1990). Founded as a new city in 1933, it replaced the town of Goiás as state capital in 1942.

Goiás /gɔɪˈɑːs/ a state in south central Brazil; capital, Goiânia.

Goidelic /gɔɪˈdelɪk/ ▶ adjective of, relating to, or denoting the northern group of Celtic languages, including Irish, Scottish Gaelic, and Manx. Speakers of the Celtic precursor of the Goidelic languages may have invaded Ireland from Europe *c*.1000 BC, spreading into Scotland and the Isle of Man from the 5th century AD onwards. Compare with **BRYTHONIC**. Also called **Q-CELTIC**.
▶ noun [mass noun] these languages collectively.

going ▶ noun 1 an act or instance of leaving a place; a departure: *his going left an enormous gap in each of their lives.*
2 [in sing.] the condition of the ground viewed in terms of suitability for walking, riding, or other travel (used especially in the context of horse racing): *the going was ideal here, with short turf and a level surface.*
■ progress affected by such a condition: *the paths were covered with drifting snow and the going was difficult.* ■ conditions for, or progress in, an endeavour: *when the going gets tough, the tough get going.*
▶ adjective 1 [predic.] chiefly Brit. existing or available; to be had: *he asked if there were any other jobs going.*
2 [attrib.] (especially of a price) generally accepted as fair or correct; current: *people willing to work for the going rate.*

going away ▶ adjective [attrib.] (of a woman's clothes) to be worn while leaving for her honeymoon.
■ marking or celebrating a departure: *a going-away party.*
▶ adverb informal with victory assured before the end of a race or other sporting contest: *he caught the Nigerian coming around the final curve and won going away.*

going concern ▶ noun a business that is operating and making a profit.

going-over ▶ noun [in sing.] informal a thorough treatment, especially in cleaning or inspection: *give the place a going-over with the Hoover.*
■ a beating. ■ a heavy defeat: *Pontypool gave them a 35–6 going-over.*

goings-on ▶ plural noun events or behaviour, especially of an unusual or suspect nature.

goitre /ˈgɔɪtə/ (US **goiter**) ▶ noun a swelling of the neck resulting from enlargement of the thyroid gland: *a woman with a goitre* | [mass noun] *the belief that amber necklaces were good for curing goitre.*
– DERIVATIVES **goitred** adjective, **goitrous** adjective.
– ORIGIN early 17th cent.: from French, a back-formation from *goitreux* 'having a goitre', or from Old French *goitron* 'gullet', both based on Latin *guttur* 'throat'.

go-kart (also **go-cart**) ▶ noun a small racing car with a lightweight or skeleton body.
– DERIVATIVES **go-karting** noun.
– ORIGIN 1950s: *kart*, alteration of **CART**.

Gokhale /ˈgəʊkələɪ/, Gopal Krishna (1866–1915), Indian political leader and social reformer, president of the Indian National Congress from 1905. He was a leading advocate of Indian self-government through constitutional or moderate means.

Golan Heights /ˈgəʊlɑːn, ˈgəʊlən/ a range of hills on the border between Syria and Israel, north-east of the Sea of Galilee. Formerly under Syrian control, the area was occupied by Israel in 1967 and annexed in 1981. Negotiations for the withdrawal of Israeli troops from the region began in 1992.

Golconda /gɒlˈkɒndə/ ▶ noun a source of wealth, advantages, or happiness: *the posters calling*

emigrants from Europe to the Golconda of the American West.
– ORIGIN late 19th cent.: from the name of a city near Hyderabad, India, famous for its diamonds.

gold ▶ noun 1 [mass noun] a yellow precious metal, the chemical element of atomic number 79, valued especially for use in jewellery and decoration, and to guarantee the value of currencies. (Symbol: **Au**)
■ [with modifier] an alloy of this: *9-carat gold.*

> Gold is quite widely distributed in nature but economical extraction is only possible from deposits of the native metal or sulphide ores, or as a by-product of copper and lead mining. The use of the metal in coins is now limited, but it is also used in electrical contacts and (in some countries) as a filling for teeth.

2 [mass noun] a deep lustrous yellow or yellow-brown colour: *her eyes were light green and flecked with gold.*
3 [mass noun] coins or articles made of gold: *her ankles and wrists were glinting with gold.*
■ money in large sums; wealth: *he proved to be a rabid seeker for gold and power.* ■ a thing that is precious, beautiful, or brilliant: *they scout continents in search of the new green gold.* ■ [count noun] short for **GOLD MEDAL**.
4 the bullseye of an archery target.
– PHRASES **go gold** (of a recording) achieve sales meriting a gold disc. **pot** (or **crock**) **of gold** a large but distant or imaginary reward. [ORIGIN: with allusion to the story of a crock of gold supposedly to be found by anyone reaching the end of a rainbow.]
– ORIGIN Old English, of Germanic origin; related to Dutch *goud* and German *Gold*, from an Indo-European root shared by **YELLOW**.

gold-beater ▶ noun a person who beats gold out into gold leaf.

gold-beater's skin ▶ noun a membrane used to separate leaves of gold during beating.

gold beetle (also **goldbug**) ▶ noun N. Amer. a leaf beetle with metallic gold coloration.
● Several species in the family Chrysomelidae, in particular *Metriona bicolor*.

gold brick informal, chiefly US ▶ noun a thing that looks valuable, but is in fact worthless.
■ (also **gold-bricker**) a confidence trickster. ■ a lazy person.
▶ verb (**gold-brick**) [no obj.] invent excuses to avoid a task; shirk: *he wasn't goldbricking; he was really sick.*
■ [with obj.] swindle (someone).

goldbug ▶ noun chiefly US 1 informal an advocate of a single gold standard for currency.
■ a person favouring gold as an investment.
2 another term for **GOLD BEETLE**.

gold card ▶ noun a charge card or credit card issued to people with a high credit rating and giving benefits not available with the standard card.

Gold Coast 1 former name (until 1957) for **GHANA**.
2 a resort region on the east coast of Australia, to the south of Brisbane.

Gold Collar ▶ noun a classic greyhound race run annually in September at the Catford track in south London

goldcrest ▶ noun a very small Eurasian warbler with a black-bordered yellow or orange crest.
● *Regulus regulus*, family Sylviidae.

gold-digger ▶ noun informal a woman who goes out with men purely to extract money from them.

gold disc ▶ noun a framed golden disc awarded to a recording artist or group for sales of a recording exceeding a specified high figure.

gold dust ▶ noun [mass noun] 1 fine particles of gold.
■ a thing regarded as very valuable: *dollars are gold dust to the locals.*
2 a cultivated evergreen alyssum, with grey-green leaves and numerous small yellow flowers.
● *Alyssum saxatile*, family Cruciferae.

golden ▶ adjective 1 coloured or shining like gold: *curls of glossy golden hair* | *bake until golden.*
2 made or consisting of gold: *a golden crown.*
3 rare and precious, in particular:
■ (of a period) very happy and prosperous: *those golden days before World War I.* ■ (of an opportunity) very favourable: *a golden opportunity to boost foreign trade.*
– DERIVATIVES **goldenly** adverb.

golden age ▶ noun an idyllic, often imaginary past time of peace, prosperity, and happiness.
■ the period when a specified art, skill, or activity is at its peak: *the golden age of cinema.*

– ORIGIN mid 16th cent.: the Greek and Roman poets' name for the first period of history, when the human race lived in an ideal state.

golden ager ▶ noun N. Amer. used euphemistically or humorously to refer to an old person.

goldenback (also **golden-backed woodpecker**) ▶ noun an Asian woodpecker with a yellow back and wings.
● Genera *Dinopium* and *Chrysocolaptes*, family Picidae: three or four species.

golden boy ▶ noun informal a very popular or successful man: *the golden boy of British golf.*

golden calf ▶ noun (in the Bible) an image of gold in the shape of a calf, made by Aaron in response to the Israelites' plea for a god while they awaited Moses' return from Mount Sinai, where he was receiving the Ten Commandments (Exod. 32).
■ a false god, especially wealth as an object of worship.

golden cat ▶ noun a small forest-dwelling cat found in Africa and Asia.
● Genus *Felis*, family Felidae: the African *F. aurata*, with a chestnut to silver-grey coat, and the Asiatic *F. temmincki*, with a golden-brown coat and striped head.

golden chain ▶ noun the common laburnum.

Golden Delicious ▶ noun a widely grown dessert apple of a greenish-yellow, soft-fleshed variety.

golden eagle ▶ noun a large Eurasian and North American eagle with yellow-tipped head feathers in the mature adult.
● *Aquila chrysaetos*, family Accipitridae.

goldeneye ▶ noun (pl. same or **goldeneyes**) a migratory northern diving duck, the male of which has a dark head with a white cheek patch and yellow eyes.
● Genus *Bucephala*, family Anatidae: two species, in particular the **common goldeneye** (*B. clangula*).

Golden Fleece Greek Mythology the fleece of a golden ram, guarded by an unsleeping dragon, and sought and won by Jason with the help of Medea.
■ a goal that is highly desirable but difficult to achieve.

Golden Gate a deep channel connecting San Francisco Bay with the Pacific Ocean, spanned by the Golden Gate suspension bridge (completed 1937).

golden girl ▶ noun informal a very popular or successful young woman.

golden glow ▶ noun N. Amer. a tall rudbeckia with globular yellow flower heads.
● *Rudbeckia laciniata*, family Compositae.

golden goal ▶ noun (in some soccer and hockey competitions) the first goal scored during extra time which ends the match and gives victory to the scoring side.

golden goose ▶ noun a continuing source of wealth or profit that may be exhausted if it is misused: *they were killing the golden goose of tourism.* See also *kill the goose that lays the golden eggs* at **EGG**[1].

Golden Guernsey ▶ noun a goat of a golden breed with long silky hair, sometimes kept ornamentally.

golden hamster ▶ noun see **HAMSTER**.

golden handcuffs ▶ plural noun informal used to refer to benefits, typically deferred payments, provided by an employer to discourage an employee from taking employment elsewhere.

golden handshake ▶ noun informal a payment given to someone who is made redundant or retires early.

Golden Hind the ship in which Francis Drake circumnavigated the globe in 1577–80.
– ORIGIN named by Drake in honour of his patron, Sir Christopher Hatton (1540–91), whose crest was a golden hind.

Golden Horde the Tartar and Mongol army, led by descendants of Genghis Khan, that overran Asia and parts of eastern Europe in the 13th century and maintained an empire until around 1500 (so called from the richness of the leader's camp).

Golden Horn a curved inlet of the Bosporus forming the harbour of Istanbul. Turkish name **HALIÇ**.

golden jackal ▶ noun a jackal with a yellowish-golden coat, native to Africa, Asia, and SE Europe.
● *Canis aureus*, family Canidae.

golden jubilee ▶ noun the fiftieth anniversary of a significant event.

golden mean ▸ noun [in sing.] **1** the ideal moderate position between two extremes.
2 another term for GOLDEN SECTION.

golden mole ▸ noun a blind mole with an iridescent sheen to its coat, native to southern Africa.
● Family Chrysochloridae: several genera and species.

golden number ▸ noun the number showing a year's place in the Metonic lunar cycle and used to fix the date of Easter for that year.

golden oldie ▸ noun informal an old song or film that is still well known and popular.
■ a person who is no longer young but is still successful in their field.

golden orfe ▸ noun an orfe (fish) of an ornamental yellow variety, widely kept in aquaria and ponds.

golden oriole ▸ noun a Eurasian oriole with a melodious call, the male being bright yellow and black and the female mainly green.
● Oriolus oriolus, family Oriolidae.

golden parachute ▸ noun informal a large payment or other financial compensation guaranteed to a company executive if they should be dismissed as a result of a merger or takeover.

golden perch ▸ noun another term for CALLOP.

golden plover ▸ noun a North Eurasian and North American plover, with a gold-speckled back and black face and underparts in the breeding season.
● Genus Pluvialis, family Charadriidae: three species, in particular P. apricaria of Europe and P. dominica of Canada.

golden retriever ▸ noun a retriever of a breed with a thick golden-coloured coat.

goldenrod ▸ noun a plant of the daisy family, which bears tall spikes of small bright yellow flowers.
● Genus Solidago, family Compositae.

golden rule ▸ noun a basic principle which should always be followed to ensure success in general or in a particular activity.
■ the biblical rule of 'do as you would be done by' (Matt. 7:12).

goldenseal ▸ noun a North American woodland plant of the buttercup family, with a bright yellow root that is used in herbal medicine.
● Hydrastis canadensis, family Ranunculaceae.

golden section ▸ noun the division of a line so that the whole is to the greater part as that part is to the smaller part (i.e. in a ratio of 1 to ½ (√5 + 1)), a proportion which is considered to be particularly pleasing to the eye.

golden share ▸ noun Brit. a share in a company that gives control of at least 51 per cent of the voting rights, especially when held by the government.

Golden State informal name for CALIFORNIA.

golden syrup ▸ noun [mass noun] Brit. a pale treacle.

golden wattle ▸ noun an Australian acacia with golden flowers.
● Genus Acacia, family Leguminosae: A. pycnatha, whose flowers are used as Australia's national emblem, and A. longifolia.

golden wedding ▸ noun the fiftieth anniversary of a wedding.

goldfield ▸ noun a district in which gold is found as a mineral.

goldfinch ▸ noun a brightly coloured finch with yellow feathers in the plumage.
● Genus Carduelis, family Fringillidae: four species, especially the **Eurasian goldfinch** (C. carduelis) and the **American goldfinch** (C. tristis).
– ORIGIN late Old English goldfinc (see GOLD, FINCH).

goldfish ▸ noun (pl. same or **-fishes**) a small reddish-golden Eurasian carp, popular in ponds and aquaria. A long history of breeding in China and Japan has resulted in many varieties of form and colour.
● Carassius auratus, family Cyprinidae.

goldfish bowl ▸ noun chiefly Brit. a spherical glass container for goldfish.
■ figurative a place or situation lacking privacy: a goldfish bowl of publicity.

goldilocks ▸ noun **1** informal a person with golden hair.
2 a Eurasian woodland buttercup.
● Ranunculus auricomus, family Ranunculaceae.
3 a yellow-flowered European plant of the daisy family, resembling the Michaelmas daisy.
● Aster linosyris, family Compositae.

Golding, Sir William (Gerald) (1911–93), English novelist. He achieved literary success with his first novel Lord of the Flies (1954), about boys stranded on a desert island who revert to savagery. Other notable works: Rites of Passage (Booker Prize, 1980). Nobel Prize for Literature (1983).

gold leaf ▸ noun [mass noun] gold that has been beaten into a very thin sheet, used in gilding.
▸ verb (**gold-leaf**) [with obj.] apply a layer of gold leaf to.

Goldman, Emma (1869–1940), Lithuanian-born American political activist, involved in New York's anarchist movement and an opponent of US conscription. Notable works: Anarchism and Other Essays (1910) and My Disillusionment in Russia (1923).

Goldmark, Peter Carl (1906–77), Hungarian-born American inventor and engineer. He made the first colour television broadcast in 1940, invented the long-playing record in 1948, and pioneered video cassette recording.

gold medal ▸ noun a medal made of or coloured gold, customarily awarded for first place in a race or competition.

gold mine ▸ noun a place where gold is mined.
■ figurative a source of wealth, valuable information, or resources: this book is a gold mine of information.
– DERIVATIVES **gold miner** noun.

gold of pleasure ▸ noun [mass noun] a yellow-flowered Mediterranean plant of the cabbage family, which yields fibre, oilseed, and seed for cage birds.
● Camelina sativa, family Cruciferae.

gold plate ▸ noun [mass noun] a thin layer of gold, electroplated or otherwise applied as a coating to another metal.
■ objects coated with gold. ■ plates, dishes, etc. made of gold.
▸ verb (**gold-plate**) [with obj.] cover (something) with a thin layer of gold.

gold-plated ▸ adjective covered with a thin layer of gold: a gold-plated tiepin.
■ figurative likely to prove profitable; secure: houses are no longer the gold-plated investment they were.

gold record ▸ noun North American term for GOLD DISC.

gold reserve ▸ noun a quantity of gold held by a central bank to support the issue of currency.

gold rush ▸ noun a rapid movement of people to a newly discovered goldfield. The first major gold rush, to California in 1848, was followed by others in the US, Australia (1851–3), South Africa (1884), and Canada (Klondike, 1897–8).

Goldschmidt /ˈɡəʊldʃmɪt, German ˈɡɔltʃmɪt/, Victor Moritz (1888–1947), Swiss-born Norwegian chemist. Considered the founder of modern geochemistry, he carried out fundamental work on crystal structure, suggesting a law relating it to chemical composition. Goldschmidt used X-ray crystallography to determine the structure of many compounds.

Goldsmith, Oliver (1728–74), Irish novelist, poet, essayist, and dramatist. Notable works: The Vicar of Wakefield (novel, 1766), The Deserted Village (poem, 1770), and She Stoops to Conquer (play, 1773).

goldsmith ▸ noun a person who makes gold articles.
– ORIGIN late Old English (see GOLD, SMITH).

gold standard ▸ noun historical the system by which the value of a currency was defined in terms of gold, for which the currency could be exchanged. The gold standard was generally abandoned in the Depression of the 1930s.
■ figurative the best or most prestigious thing of its type: breast milk provides the gold standard by which infant feeds are measured.

Gold Stick ▸ noun [mass noun] (in the UK) a ceremonial officer in the Sovereign's household, entitled to carry a gilt rod on state occasions.

gold thread ▸ noun [mass noun] a plant of the buttercup family, which yields a yellow dye and is used in herbal medicine as a treatment for mouth ulcers. It grows in North America and NE Asia.
● Coptis trifolia, family Ranunculaceae.

goldwasser /ˈɡəʊldvasə, ˈɡɒl-/ ▸ noun [mass noun] a liqueur containing particles of gold leaf, originally made at Gdańsk in Poland.
– ORIGIN from German, literally 'gold water'.

goldwork ▸ noun [mass noun] gold objects collectively.

– DERIVATIVES **goldworking** noun.

Goldwyn, Samuel (1882–1974), Polish-born American film producer; born Schmuel Gelbfisz; changed to Samuel Goldfish then Goldwyn. With Louis B. Mayer, he founded the film company Metro-Goldwyn-Mayer (MGM) in 1924.

golem /ˈɡəʊləm, ˈɡɒl-/ ▸ noun (in Jewish legend) a clay figure brought to life by magic.
■ an automaton or robot.
– ORIGIN late 19th cent.: from Yiddish goylem, from Hebrew gōlem 'shapeless mass'.

golf ▸ noun **1** [mass noun] a game played on a large open-air course, in which a small hard ball is struck with a club into a series of small holes in the ground, the object being to use the fewest possible strokes to complete the course.

A golf course usually has 18 holes, each set in a smooth lawn (a green) separated from the others by stretches of smooth grass (fairways), rough ground, sand-filled bunkers, and other hazards. Various clubs are used to hit the ball from a tee towards the green, up to 450 m away, and then putt it into the hole.

2 a code word representing the letter G, used in radio communication.
▸ verb [no obj.] play golf: [as noun **golfing**] a week's golfing.
– ORIGIN late Middle English (originally Scots): perhaps related to Dutch kolf 'club, bat', used as a term in several Dutch games; golf, however, is recorded before these games.

golf ball ▸ noun a small hard ball used in the game of golf.
■ (**golfball**) a small metal globe used in some electric typewriters to carry the type.

golf cart ▸ noun a small motorized vehicle for golfers and their equipment.

golf club ▸ noun **1** a club used to hit the ball in golf, with a heavy wooden or metal head on a slender shaft.
2 an organization of members for playing golf.
■ the premises used by such an organization.

golf course ▸ noun a course on which golf is played.

golfer ▸ noun **1** a person who plays golf.
2 Brit. dated a cardigan.

golf links ▸ plural noun see LINKS.

golf shirt ▸ noun N. Amer. a light, short-sleeved shirt with a collar, typically of a knitted fabric and with buttons at the neck only.

golgappa /ɡəʊlˈɡʌpə/ ▸ noun another term for PANI PURI.
– ORIGIN from Hindi golgappā.

Golgi /ˈɡɒldʒi/, Camillo (1844–1926), Italian histologist and anatomist. He devised a staining technique to investigate nerve tissue, classified types of nerve cell, and described the structure in the cytoplasm of most cells, now named after him. Nobel Prize for Physiology or Medicine (1906).

Golgi body /ˈɡɒldʒi, -gi/ (also **Golgi apparatus**) ▸ noun Biology a complex of vesicles and folded membranes within the cytoplasm of most eukaryotic cells, involved in secretion and intracellular transport.

Golgotha /ˈɡɒlɡəθə/ the site of the crucifixion of Jesus; Calvary.
– ORIGIN from late Latin, via Greek from an Aramaic form of Hebrew gulgoleth 'skull' (see Matt. 27:33).

Goliath /ɡəˈlʌɪəθ/ (in the Bible) a Philistine giant, according to legend slain by David (1 Sam. 17), but according to another tradition slain by Elhanan (2 Sam. 21:19).

goliath beetle ▸ noun a very large, boldly marked tropical beetle related to the chafers, the male of which has a forked horn on the head.
● Genus Goliathus, family Scarabaeidae: several species, in particular G. giganteus of Africa, which is the largest known beetle.

goliath frog ▸ noun a giant frog of West Central Africa.
● Rana goliath, family Ranidae.

Gollancz /ˈɡɒlants/, Sir Victor (1893–1967), British publisher and philanthropist, founder of the charity War on Want.

golliwog ▸ noun a soft doll with bright clothes, a black face, and fuzzy hair.
– ORIGIN late 19th cent.: from Golliwogg, the name of a doll character in books by Bertha Upton (died 1912), American writer; perhaps suggested by GOLLY[1] and POLLIWOG.

gollop /ˈɡɒləp/ Brit. informal ▶ **verb** (**golloped**, **golloping**) [with obj.] swallow (food) hastily or greedily.
▶ **noun** a hasty gulp: *breathing great gollops of air.*
– ORIGIN early 19th cent.: perhaps from **GULP**, influenced by **GOBBLE**[1].

golly[1] (also **by golly**) ▶ **exclamation** informal, dated used to express surprise or delight: *'Golly! Is that the time?'*
– ORIGIN late 18th cent.: euphemism for **GOD**.

golly[2] ▶ **noun** (pl. **-ies**) Brit. informal short for **GOLLIWOG**.

GOM Brit. ▶ **abbreviation for** Grand Old Man, a name originally applied to Gladstone.

gombeen /ɡɒmˈbiːn/ ▶ **noun** [mass noun] [as modifier] Irish involved in the practice of usury: *a gombeen Dubliner.*
– ORIGIN mid 19th cent.: from Irish *gaimbín*, perhaps from the same Celtic source as medieval Latin *cambire* 'to change'.

Gomel /ˈɡomʲilʲ/ Russian name for **HOMEL**.

Gomorrah /ɡəˈmɒrə/ a town in ancient Palestine, probably south of the Dead Sea. According to Gen. 19:24, it was destroyed by fire from heaven, along with Sodom, for the wickedness of its inhabitants.

-gon ▶ **combining form** in nouns denoting plane figures with a specified number of angles: *hexagon | pentagon.*
– ORIGIN from Greek *-gōnos* '-angled'.

gonad /ˈɡəʊnad/ ▶ **noun** Physiology & Zoology an organ that produces gametes; a testis or ovary.
– DERIVATIVES **gonadal** /ɡə(ʊ)ˈneɪd(ə)l/ adjective.
– ORIGIN late 19th cent.: from modern Latin *gonades*, plural of *gonas*, from Greek *gonē* 'generation, seed'.

gonadotrophic hormone /ˌɡəʊnadə(ʊ)ˈtrəʊfɪk, -ˈtrɒfɪk/ (also **gonadotropic hormone** /-ˈtrəʊpɪk, -ˈtrɒpɪk/) ▶ **noun** another term for **GONADOTROPHIN**.

gonadotrophin /ˌɡəʊnadə(ʊ)ˈtrəʊfɪn/ (also **gonadotropin** /-ˈtrəʊpɪn, -ˈtrɒpɪn/) ▶ **noun** Biochemistry any of a group of hormones secreted by the pituitary which stimulate the activity of the gonads.

Goncharov /ˈɡɒntʃərɒf/, Ivan (Aleksandrovich) (1812–91), Russian novelist. His novel *Oblomov* (1857) is regarded as one of the greatest works of Russian realism.

Goncourt /ɡɒnˈkʊə, French ɡɔ̃kuʀ/, Edmond de (1822–96) and Jules de (1830–70), French novelists and critics. Working together, the brothers wrote art criticism, realist novels, and social history. In his will Edmond provided for the establishment of the Académie Goncourt, which awards the annual Prix Goncourt.

Gond /ɡɒnd, ɡəʊnd/ (also **Gondi** /ˈɡɒndi/) ▶ **noun** (pl. same) **1** a member of an indigenous people living in the hill forests of central India.
2 [mass noun] the Dravidian language of this people, with several highly differentiated dialects and about 2 million speakers.
▶ **adjective** of or relating to the Gonds or their language.
– ORIGIN from Sanskrit *goṇḍa*.

gondola /ˈɡɒndələ/ ▶ **noun** a light flat-bottomed boat used on Venetian canals, having a high point at each end and worked by one oar at the stern.
■ a cabin on a suspended ski lift. ■ (also **gondola car**) N. Amer. an open railway freight wagon. ■ an enclosed compartment suspended from an airship or balloon. ■ Brit. a free-standing block of shelves used to display goods in a supermarket.
– ORIGIN mid 16th cent.: from Venetian Italian, from Rhaeto-Romance *gondolà* 'to rock, roll'.

gondolier /ˌɡɒndəˈlɪə/ ▶ **noun** a person who propels and steers a gondola.
– ORIGIN early 17th cent.: via French from Italian *gondoliere*, from *gondola* (see **GONDOLA**).

Gondwana /ɡɒnˈdwɑːnə/ (also **Gondwanaland**) a vast continental area believed to have existed in the southern hemisphere and to have resulted from the break-up of Pangaea in Mesozoic times. It comprised the present Arabia, Africa, South America, Antarctica, Australia, and the peninsula of India.
– ORIGIN late 19th cent. (originally denoting any of a series of rocks in India, especially fluviatile shales and sandstones): from the name of a region in central northern India, from Sanskrit *goṇḍavana* 'forest of Gond'.

gone past participle of **GO**[1]. ▶ **adjective** [predic.] **1** no longer present; departed: *while you were gone | the bad old days are gone.*
■ no longer in existence; dead or extinct: *an aunt of mine, long since gone.* ■ informal in a trance or stupor, especially through exhaustion, drink, or drugs: *she sat, half-gone, on a folding chair.* ■ [attrib.] informal, chiefly US lost; hopeless: *spending time and effort on a gone sucker like Galindez.* ■ US informal, dated excellent; inspired: *a bunch of real gone cats.*
2 informal having reached a specified time in a pregnancy: *she is now four months gone.*
▶ **preposition** Brit. (of time) past: *it's gone half past eleven.*
■ (of age) older than: *she was gone sixty by then.*
– PHRASES **be gone on** informal be infatuated with: *I always knew he was awfully gone on you.* **gone away!** a huntsman's cry, indicating that a fox has been started.

gone goose ▶ **noun** informal, dated a person or thing that is beyond hope.

goner /ˈɡɒnə/ ▶ **noun** informal a person or thing that is doomed or cannot be saved.

gonfalon /ˈɡɒnf(ə)lən/ ▶ **noun** a banner or pennant, especially one with streamers, hung from a crossbar.
– DERIVATIVES **gonfalonier** /ˌɡɒnfələˈnɪə/ noun.
– ORIGIN late 16th cent.: from Italian *gonfalone*, from a Germanic compound whose second element is related to **VANE**.

gong ▶ **noun** **1** a metal disc with a turned rim, giving a resonant note when struck: *a dinner gong.*
2 Brit. informal a medal or decoration.
▶ **verb** [no obj.] sound a gong or make a sound like that of a gong being struck.
– ORIGIN early 17th cent.: from Malay *gong*, *gung*, of imitative origin.

gongoozler /ɡɒŋˈɡuːzlə/ ▶ **noun** informal an idle spectator.
– ORIGIN early 20th cent. (originally denoting a person who idly watched activity on a canal); rare before 1970: perhaps from Lincolnshire dialect *gawn* and *gooze* 'stare, gape'.

goniatite /ˈɡəʊnɪətʌɪt/ ▶ **noun** an ammonoid fossil of an early type found chiefly in the Devonian and Carboniferous periods, typically with simple angular suture lines. Compare with **AMMONITE** and **CERATITE**.
● Typified by the genus *Goniatites*, order Goniatitida.
– ORIGIN mid 19th cent.: from modern Latin *Goniatites*, from Greek *gōnia* 'angle'.

gonif /ˈɡɒnɪf/ (also **goniff**) ▶ **noun** N. Amer. informal a disreputable or dishonest person (often used as a general term of abuse).
– ORIGIN mid 19th cent.: from Yiddish *ganev*, from Hebrew *gannāḇ* 'thief'.

goniometer /ˌɡəʊnɪˈɒmɪtə/ ▶ **noun** an instrument for the precise measurement of angles, especially one used to measure the angles between the faces of crystals.
– DERIVATIVES **goniometric** adjective, **goniometrical** adjective, **goniometry** noun.
– ORIGIN mid 18th cent.: from French *goniomètre*, from Greek *gōnia* 'angle' + French *-mètre* '(instrument) measuring'.

gonna informal ▶ **contraction of** going to: *So what you gonna do now?*

gonococcus /ˌɡɒnəˈkɒkəs/ ▶ **noun** (pl. **gonococci** /-k(s)ʌɪ, -k(s)iː/) a bacterium which causes gonorrhoea.
● *Neisseria gonorrhoeae*, a Gram-negative diplococcus.
– DERIVATIVES **gonococcal** adjective.
– ORIGIN late 19th cent.: blend of **GONORRHOEA** and **COCCUS**.

gonolek /ˈɡɒnəlɛk/ ▶ **noun** an African shrike with a mainly black back and red underparts.
● Genus *Laniarius*, family Laniidae: three species, in particular the **common gonolek** (*L. barbarus*).

gonorrhoea /ˌɡɒnəˈrɪə/ (US **gonorrhea**) ▶ **noun** [mass noun] a venereal disease involving inflammatory discharge from the urethra or vagina.
– DERIVATIVES **gonorrhoeal** adjective.
– ORIGIN early 16th cent.: via late Latin from Greek *gonorrhoia*, from *gonos* 'semen' + *rhoia* 'flux'.

gonzo ▶ **adjective** informal, chiefly US of or associated with journalistic writing of an exaggerated, subjective, and fictionalized style.
■ bizarre or crazy: *the woman was either gonzo or stoned.*
– ORIGIN 1970s: perhaps from Italian *gonzo* 'foolish' or Spanish *ganso* 'goose, fool'.

goo ▶ **noun** [mass noun] informal **1** a sticky or slimy substance: *he tipped the greyish goo from the test tube.*
2 sickly sentiment.
– ORIGIN early 20th cent. (originally US): perhaps from *burgoo*, a nautical slang term for porridge, based on Persian *bulġūr* 'bruised grain'.

good ▶ **adjective** (**better**, **best**) **1** to be desired or approved of: *we live at peace with each other, which is good | a good quality of life.*
■ pleasing and welcome: *she was pleased to hear good news about him.* ■ expressing approval: *the play had good reviews.*
2 having the qualities required for a particular role: *the schools here are good.*
■ functioning or performed well: *good health | either she was feeling chastened or she was doing a good act.* ■ appropriate to a particular purpose: *this is a good month for planting seeds.* ■ (of language) with correct grammar and pronunciation: *she speaks good English.* ■ strictly adhering to or fulfilling all the principles of a particular cause, religion, or party: *a good Catholic girl.* ■ (of a ticket) valid: *the ticket is* **good for** *travel from May to September.*
3 possessing or displaying moral virtue: *I've met many good people who made me feel ashamed of my own shortcomings |* [as plural noun **the good**] *the rich and the good shared the same fate as the poor and the bad.*
■ showing kindness: *you are good—thank you.* ■ obedient to rules or conventions: *accustom the child to being rewarded for good behaviour.* ■ used to address or refer to people, especially in a patronizing or humorous way: *the good people of the city were disconcerted.* ■ commanding respect: *he was concerned with establishing and maintaining his good name.* ■ belonging or relating to a high social class: *he comes from a good family.*
4 giving pleasure; enjoyable or satisfying: *the streets fill up with people looking for a good time.*
■ pleasant to look at; attractive: *you're looking pretty good.* ■ (of food and drink) having a pleasant taste: *we had the beef, and very good it was.* ■ (of clothes) smart and suitable for formal wear: *he went upstairs to change out of his good suit.*
5 [attrib.] thorough: *now is the time to have a really good clear-up | have a good look around.*
■ used to emphasize that a number is at least as great as one claims: *they're a good twenty years younger.* ■ used to emphasize a following adjective: *we had a good long hug.* ■ fairly large: *a good crowd |* figurative *there's a good chance that we may be able to help you.*
6 used in conjunction with the name of God or a related expression as an exclamation of extreme surprise or anger: *good heavens!*
▶ **noun** **1** [mass noun] that which is morally right; righteousness: *a mysterious balance of good and evil.*
2 [mass noun] benefit or advantage to someone or something: *he is* **too clever for his own good.**
3 (**goods**) merchandise or possessions: *imports of luxury goods.*
■ Brit. things to be transported, as distinct from passengers: *a means of transporting passengers as well as goods |* [as modifier] *a goods train.* ■ (**the goods**) informal the genuine article.
▶ **adverb** informal well: *my mother could never cook this good.*
– PHRASES **all to the good** to be welcomed without qualification. **as good as —** very nearly —: *she's as good as here.* ■ used of a result which will inevitably follow: *if we pass on the information, he's as good as dead.* **be any** (or **no** or **much**) **good** have some (or none or a lot of) merit: *tell me whether that picture is any good.* ■ be of some (or none or a lot of) help in dealing with a situation: *it was no good trying to ward things off.* **be so good as** (or **be good enough**) **to do something** used to make a polite request: *would you be so good as to answer.* **be — to the good** have a specified net profit or advantage: *I came out £7 to the good.* **come up with** (or **deliver**) **the goods** informal do what is expected or required of one. **do good 1** act virtuously, especially by helping others. **2** make a helpful contribution to a situation: *could the discussion do any good?* **do someone good** be beneficial to someone, especially to their health: *the walk will do you good.* **for good** (**and all**) forever; definitively: *the experience almost frightened me away for good.* **get** (or **have**) **the goods on** informal obtain (or possess) information about (someone) which may be used to their detriment. **good and —** informal used as an intensifier before an adjective or adverb: *it'll be good and dark by then.* (**as**) **good as gold** (of a child) extremely well-behaved. (**as**) **good as new** in a very good condition or state, close to the original state again after damage, injury, or illness: *the skirt looked*

as good as new. **the Good Book** the Bible. **good for 1** having a beneficial effect on: *smoking is not good for the lungs.* **2** reliably providing: *they found him good for a laugh.* ■ sufficient to pay for: *his money was good for a bottle of whisky.* **good for** (or **on**) **you** (or **him, her,** etc.)! used as an exclamation of approval towards a person, especially for something that they have achieved: *'I'm having driving lessons and taking my test next month.' 'Good for you!'* **good oil** Austral. informal reliable information. [ORIGIN: figurative use referring to lubricating oil and the successful running of a machine.] **the Good Shepherd** a name for Jesus. [ORIGIN: with biblical allusion to John x. 1–16.] **good wine needs no bush** see WINE[1]. **a good word** words in recommendation or defence of a person: *I hoped you might put in a good word for me with your friends.* **have a good mind to do something** see MIND. **in someone's good books** see BOOK. **in good time 1** with no risk of being late: *I arrived in good time.* **2** (also **all in good time**) in due course but without haste: *you shall have a puppy all in good time.* **make good** be successful: *a college friend who made good in Hollywood.* **make something good 1** compensate for loss, damage, or expense: *if I scratched the table I'd make good the damage.* ■ repair or restore after damage: *make good the wall where you have buried the cable.* **2** fulfil a promise or claim: *I challenged him to make good his boast.* **one good turn deserves another** see TURN. **take something in good part** not be offended by something: *he took her abruptness in good part.* **up to no good** doing something wrong.
– ORIGIN Old English *gōd,* of Germanic origin; related to Dutch *goed* and German *gut.*

good afternoon ▶ exclamation expressing good wishes on meeting or parting in the afternoon.

Goodall, Jane (b.1934), English zoologist. After working with Louis Leakey in Tanzania from 1957, she made prolonged and intimate studies of chimpanzees at the Gombe Stream Reserve by Lake Tanganyika from 1970.

goodbye (US also **goodby**) ▶ exclamation used to express good wishes when parting or at the end of a conversation.
▶ noun (pl. **goodbyes**; US also **goodbys**) an instance of saying 'goodbye'; a parting: *a final goodbye.*
– ORIGIN late 16th cent.: contraction of *God be with you!,* with *good* substituted on the pattern of phrases such as *good morning.*

good day ▶ exclamation expressing good wishes on meeting or parting during the day.

good doer ▶ noun Brit. informal a thing, especially a cultivated plant or domesticated animal, that thrives or performs well without special attention.

good evening ▶ exclamation expressing good wishes on meeting or parting during the evening.

good fairy ▶ noun (in pantomimes and fairy stories) a fairy who helps and acts on behalf of the good characters.

good faith ▶ noun [mass noun] honesty or sincerity of intention: *the details contained in this brochure have been published in good faith.*

goodfella ▶ noun informal, chiefly N. Amer. a gangster, especially a member of a Mafia family.

good form ▶ noun [mass noun] behaviour that complies with current social conventions: *it wasn't considered good form to show too much enthusiasm.*

good-for-nothing ▶ adjective (of a person) worthless: *his good-for-nothing son.*
▶ noun a worthless person.

Good Friday ▶ noun the Friday before Easter Sunday, on which the Crucifixion of Christ is commemorated in the Christian Church. It is traditionally a day of fasting and penance.
– ORIGIN from GOOD, in the sense 'holy, observed as a holy day'.

good-hearted ▶ adjective kind and well meaning.
– DERIVATIVES **good-heartedness** noun.

Good Hope, Cape of see CAPE OF GOOD HOPE.

good humour ▶ noun [mass noun] a genial disposition or mood: *I admire your dignity and good humour.*

good-humoured ▶ adjective genial; cheerful.
– DERIVATIVES **good-humouredly** adverb.

goodie ▶ noun variant spelling of GOODY[1].

goodish ▶ adjective fairly good: *in goodish working order.*
■ fairly large: *a goodish portion.*

Good King Henry ▶ noun an edible plant of the goosefoot family, with large dark green leaves and insignificant clusters of flowers, native to Europe.
● *Chenopodium bonus-henricus,* family Chenopodiaceae.
– ORIGIN late 16th cent.: of unknown origin.

good-looking ▶ adjective (chiefly of a person) attractive.
– DERIVATIVES **good-looker** noun.

goodly ▶ adjective (**goodlier, goodliest**) **1** considerable in size or quantity: *we ran up a goodly drinks bill.*
2 archaic attractive, excellent, or admirable.
– DERIVATIVES **goodliness** noun.
– ORIGIN Old English *gōdlic* (see GOOD, -LY[1]).

Goodman, Benny (1909–86), American jazz clarinettist and bandleader; full name *Benjamin David Goodman;* known as **the King of Swing.** In 1934 he formed his own big band, which was the first to include both black and white musicians.

goodman ▶ noun (pl. **-men**) archaic, chiefly Scottish the male head of a household.

good money ▶ noun [mass noun] money that might usefully be spent elsewhere; hard-earned money: *I'm not going to pay good money for it.*
■ informal high wages: *I earn good money.*

good morning ▶ exclamation expressing good wishes on meeting or parting during the morning.

good nature ▶ noun a kind and unselfish disposition: *your boy has a good nature.*
– DERIVATIVES **good-natured** adjective, **good-naturedly** adverb.

goodness ▶ noun the quality of being good, in particular:
■ virtue; moral excellence: *a belief in the basic goodness of mankind.* ■ kindness; generosity: *he did it out of the goodness of his heart.* ■ the beneficial or nourishing element of food.
▶ exclamation (as a substitution for 'God') expressing surprise, anger, etc.: *goodness knows what her rent will be.*
– PHRASES **for goodness' sake** see SAKE[1]. **goodness of fit** Statistics the extent to which observed data matches the values expected by theory. **have the goodness to do something** used in exaggeratedly polite requests: *have the goodness to look at me when I'm speaking to you!*
– ORIGIN Old English *gōdnes* (see GOOD, -NESS).

Good News Bible ▶ noun a translation of the Bible in simple everyday English, published 1966–76 by the United Bible Societies.

goodnight ▶ exclamation expressing good wishes on parting at night or before going to bed.

goodo /ˈɡʊdəʊ/ ▶ adjective Austral./NZ informal good.

good-oh /ˈɡʊdəʊ, ɡʊdˈəʊ/ ▶ exclamation dated used to express pleasure or approval.

goods and chattels ▶ plural noun chiefly Law all kinds of personal possessions.

good-tempered ▶ adjective not easily irritated or made angry.
– DERIVATIVES **good-temperedly** adverb.

good-time ▶ adjective [attrib.] (of a person) recklessly pursuing pleasure.
■ (of music) intended purely to entertain.
– DERIVATIVES **good-timer** noun.

goodwife ▶ noun (pl. **-wives**) archaic, chiefly Scottish the female head of a household.

goodwill ▶ noun [mass noun] **1** friendly, helpful, or cooperative feelings or attitude: *the scheme is dependent on goodwill between the two sides* | [as modifier] *a goodwill gesture.*
2 the established reputation of a business regarded as a quantifiable asset, e.g. as represented by the excess of the price paid at a takeover for a company over its fair market value.

Goodwin Sands an area of sandbanks in the Strait of Dover. Often exposed at low tide, the sandbanks are a hazard to shipping.

Goodwood a racecourse in West Sussex, near Chichester. It is the scene of an annual summer race meeting.

good works ▶ plural noun charitable acts.

goody[1] ▶ noun (also **goodie**) (pl. **-ies**) informal **1** Brit. a good or favoured person, especially a hero in a story or film: *the goodies always won in the end.*
2 (usu. **goodies**) something attractive or desirable, especially something tasty or pleasant to eat.

▶ exclamation expressing childish delight: *goody, we can have a party.*

goody[2] ▶ noun (pl. **-ies**) archaic (often as a title prefixed to a surname) an elderly woman of humble station: *the tale of Goody Blake and Harry Gill.*
– ORIGIN mid 16th cent.: pet form of GOODWIFE; compare with HUSSY.

Goodyear, Charles (1800–60), American inventor. He developed the process of the vulcanization of rubber, after accidentally dropping some rubber mixed with sulphur and white lead on to a hot stove.

goody-goody informal ▶ noun a smug or obtrusively virtuous person.
▶ adjective smug or obtrusively virtuous.

gooey ▶ adjective (**gooier, gooiest**) informal soft and sticky.
■ mawkishly sentimental: *you can love somebody without going all gooey.*
– DERIVATIVES **gooeyness** noun.

goof informal, chiefly N. Amer. ▶ noun **1** a mistake: *he made one of the most embarrassing goofs of his tenure.*
2 a foolish or stupid person.
▶ verb [no obj.] **1** spend time idly or foolishly; fool around: *I was goofing around and broke my arm.*
■ (**goof off**) evade a duty; idle or shirk: *he was goofing off from incessant maths homework.* ■ (**goof on**) make fun of; ridicule: *Lew and I started goofing on Alison's friend.*
2 make a mistake; blunder: *you're scared to say yes in case you goof up.*
3 [with obj.] take a stupefying dose of (an illegal drug).
– ORIGIN early 20th cent.: of unknown origin; compare with GOOP[1].

goofball ▶ noun informal, chiefly N. Amer. **1** a naive or stupid person.
2 a narcotic drug in pill form, especially a barbiturate.

goof-off ▶ noun N. Amer. informal a person who is habitually lazy or does less than their fair share of work.

goof-up ▶ noun informal, chiefly N. Amer. a stupid mistake.

goofus /ˈɡuːfəs/ ▶ noun US informal a foolish or stupid person (often used as a general term of abuse).
– ORIGIN 1920s: based on GOOF.

goofy ▶ adjective (**goofier, goofiest**) informal **1** chiefly N. Amer. foolish; harmlessly eccentric.
2 having or displaying protruding or crooked front teeth.
3 (in surfing and other board sports) with the right leg in front of the left on the board.
– DERIVATIVES **goofily** adverb, **goofiness** noun.

goog ▶ noun Austral. informal an egg.
– PHRASES **(as) full as a goog** very drunk.
– ORIGIN early 20th cent.: abbreviation of *googie,* from Scots dialect *goggie,* child's word for an egg.

googly ▶ noun (pl. **-ies**) Cricket an off break bowled with an apparent leg-break action.
– ORIGIN early 20th cent.: of unknown origin.

googol /ˈɡuːɡɒl/ ▶ cardinal number equivalent to ten raised to the power of a hundred (10^{100}).
– ORIGIN 1940s: said to have been coined by the nine-year-old nephew of E. Kasner (1878–1955), American mathematician, at Kasner's request.

googolplex /ˈɡuːɡ(ə)lplɛks/ ▶ cardinal number equivalent to ten raised to the power of a googol.
– ORIGIN 1940s: from GOOGOL + -*plex* as in *multiplex.*

goo-goo informal ▶ adjective **1** amorously adoring: *making goo-goo eyes at him.*
2 (of speech or vocal sounds) childish or meaningless: *making soothing goo-goo noises.*
– ORIGIN early 20th cent.: possibly related to GOGGLE.

gook[1] /ɡuːk, ɡʊk/ ▶ noun offensive, chiefly US a foreigner, especially a person of SE Asian descent.
– ORIGIN 1930s: of unknown origin.

gook[2] /ɡuːk, ɡʊk/ ▶ noun [mass noun] informal a sloppy wet or viscous substance: *all that gook she kept putting on her face.*
– ORIGIN 1970s: variant of GUCK.

Goolagong /ˈɡuːləɡɒŋ/, Evonne, see CAWLEY.

goolie /ˈɡuːli/ (also **gooly**) ▶ noun (pl. **-ies**) **1** (usu. **goolies**) Brit. vulgar slang a testicle. [ORIGIN: 1930s: apparently of Indian origin; compare with Hindi *golī* 'bullet, ball, pill'.]
2 Austral. informal a stone or pebble. [ORIGIN: probably from an Aboriginal language of New South Wales.]

goombah /guːmˈbɑː/ ▶ noun N. Amer. informal an associate or accomplice, especially a senior member of a criminal gang.
– ORIGIN 1960s: probably a dialect alteration of Italian *compàre* 'godfather, friend, accomplice'.

goombay /ˈguːmbeɪ/ ▶ noun W. Indian a goatskin drum with a round or squared top, played with the hands.
■ a dance to such drums. ■ (chiefly in the Bahamas) a festival or season of such music and dance.
– ORIGIN perhaps from Kikongo *ngoma*, denoting a type of drum.

goon ▶ noun informal **1** a silly, foolish, or eccentric person.
2 chiefly N. Amer. a bully or thug, especially a member of an armed or security force: *a squad of army goons waving pistols*.
■ Brit. a guard in a German prisoner-of-war camp during the Second World War.
– ORIGIN mid 19th cent.: perhaps from dialect *gooney* 'booby'; influenced by the subhuman cartoon character 'Alice the *Goon*', created by E. C. Segar (1894–1938), American cartoonist.

goonda /ˈguːndə/ ▶ noun Indian a hired thug or bully.
– ORIGIN from Hindi *guṇḍā* 'rascal'.

gooney bird (also **goony bird**) ▶ noun chiefly US another term for an albatross of the North Pacific.
● Genus *Diomedea*, family Diomedeidae: the Laysan albatross (*D. immutabilis*) and the black-footed albatross (*D. nigripes*).
– ORIGIN mid 19th cent.: of unknown origin.

goop[1] ▶ noun informal a stupid person.
– DERIVATIVES **goopiness** noun, **goopy** adjective.
– ORIGIN early 20th cent. (originally US): of unknown origin; compare with **GOOF**.

goop[2] ▶ noun informal, chiefly N. Amer. another term for **GLOOP**.
– DERIVATIVES **goopiness** noun, **goopy** adjective.

Goorkha ▶ noun old-fashioned spelling of **GURKHA**.

goosander /guːˈsandə/ ▶ noun (pl. same or **goosanders**) a large Eurasian and North American merganser, the male of which has a dark green head and whitish underside.
● *Mergus merganser*, family Anatidae. North American name: **common merganser**.
– ORIGIN early 17th cent.: probably from **GOOSE** + *-ander* as in dialect *bergander* 'shelduck' (the colouring of the male goosander resembling that of the shelduck).

goose /guːs/ ▶ noun (pl. **geese** /giːs/) **1** a large waterbird with a long neck, short legs, webbed feet, and a short broad bill. Generally geese are larger than ducks and have longer necks and shorter bills.
● Several genera in the family Anatidae; most domesticated geese are descended from the greylag.
■ the female of such a bird. ■ [mass noun] the flesh of a goose as food.
2 informal a foolish person: *'Silly goose,' he murmured fondly*.
3 (pl. **gooses**) a tailor's smoothing iron.
▶ verb [with obj.] informal **1** poke (someone) in the bottom.
2 N. Amer. give (something) a boost; invigorate; increase: *the director goosed up the star's grosses by making him funny*.
– ORIGIN Old English *gōs*, of Germanic origin; related to Dutch *gans* and German *Gans*, from an Indo-European root shared by Latin *anser* and Greek *khēn*.

goose barnacle ▶ noun a stalked barnacle which hangs down from driftwood or other slow-moving floating objects, catching passing prey with its feathery legs.
● Genus *Lepas*, class Cirripedia.

gooseberry ▶ noun (pl. **-ies**) **1** a round edible yellowish-green or reddish berry with a thin translucent hairy skin.
2 the thorny European shrub which bears this fruit.
● *Ribes grossularia*, family Grossulariaceae.
3 Brit. informal a third person who stays in the company of two people, especially lovers, who would prefer to be alone: *they didn't want me playing gooseberry on their first date*. [ORIGIN: *gooseberry* from *gooseberry-picker*, referring to an activity as a pretext for the lovers to be together.]
– ORIGIN mid 16th cent.: the first element perhaps from **GOOSE**, or perhaps based on Old French *groseille*, altered because of an unexplained association with the bird.

goosebumps ▶ plural noun chiefly N. Amer. another term for **GOOSE PIMPLES**.

goose egg ▶ noun N. Amer. informal a zero score in a game.
– ORIGIN late 19th cent.: with reference to the shape of the zero; compare with **DUCK**[3].

goosefish ▶ noun (pl. same or **-fishes**) N. Amer. a bottom-dwelling anglerfish.
● Family Lophiidae: several species, in particular *Lophius americanus* of North American waters.

gooseflesh ▶ noun [mass noun] a pimply state of the skin with the hairs erect, produced by cold or fright.
– ORIGIN early 19th cent.: so named because the skin resembles that of a plucked goose.

goosefoot ▶ noun (pl. **goosefoots**) a plant of temperate regions with divided leaves which are said to resemble the foot of a goose. Some kinds are edible and many are common weeds.
● Genus *Chenopodium*, family Chenopodiaceae

goosegog /ˈɡʊzɡɒɡ, ˈɡuːsɡɒɡ/ ▶ noun Brit. informal a gooseberry.
– ORIGIN early 19th cent.: humorous alteration, *gog* being an altered form of **GOB**[2].

goosegrass ▶ noun [mass noun] a widely distributed scrambling plant related to bedstraws, with hooked bristles on the stem, leaves, and seeds which cling to fur and clothing. Also called **CLEAVERS**.
● *Galium aparine*, family Rubiaceae.

gooseneck ▶ noun a support or pipe curved like a goose's neck.
■ Sailing a metal fitting at the end of a boom, connecting it to a pivot or ring at the base of the mast.

goose pimples ▶ plural noun the pimples that form gooseflesh.

gooseskin ▶ noun another term for **GOOSEFLESH**.

goose-step ▶ noun a military marching step in which the legs are not bent at the knee.
▶ verb [no obj., with adverbial] march with such a step: *East German soldiers goose-stepped outside the monument*.

goosey (also **goosy**) ▶ adjective (**-ier**, **-iest**) having or showing a quality considered to be characteristic of a goose, especially foolishness or nervousness.
■ informal exhibiting gooseflesh: *I've gone all goosey*. ■ US informal sensitive to being tickled.

Goossens /ˈɡuːs(ə)nz/, Sir (Aynsley) Eugene (1893–1962), English conductor, violinist, and composer, of Belgian descent.

GOP ▶ abbreviation for Grand Old Party (the Republican Party in the US).

gopak /ˈɡəʊpak/ (also **hopak**) ▶ noun an energetic Ukrainian dance in duple time, traditionally performed by men.
– ORIGIN 1920s: via Russian, from Ukrainian *hopak*.

gopher /ˈɡəʊfə/ ▶ noun **1** (also **pocket gopher**) a burrowing rodent with fur-lined pouches on the outside of the cheeks, found in North and Central America.
● Family Geomyidae: several genera and species.
■ informal North American term for **GROUND SQUIRREL**.
2 (also **gopher tortoise**) a tortoise of dry sandy regions that excavates tunnels as shelter from the sun, native to the southern US.
● *Gopherus polyphemus*, family Testudinidae.
■ [usu. as modifier] N. Amer. any of a number of reptiles and amphibians that enter burrows.
3 (also **Gopher**) Computing a menu-based system which allows users of the Internet to search for and retrieve documents on topics of interest. [ORIGIN: 1990s: named after the gopher mascot of the University of Minnesota, US, where the system was invented.]
4 variant spelling of **GOFER**.
– ORIGIN late 18th cent.: perhaps from Canadian French *gaufre* 'honeycomb' (because the gopher 'honeycombs' the ground with its burrows).

gopher snake ▶ noun a large harmless yellowish-cream snake with darker markings, native to western North America.
● *Pituophis catenifer*, family Colubridae.
■ (also **blue gopher snake**) another term for **INDIGO SNAKE**.

Gopher State informal name for **MINNESOTA**.

gopher wood ▶ noun **1** [mass noun] (in biblical use) the timber from which Noah's ark was made, from an unidentified tree (Gen. 6:14).
2 (**gopherwood**) either of two North American trees:
● stinking cedar. ● yellow-wood.

– ORIGIN early 17th cent.: *gopher* from Hebrew *gōper*.

gopik /ˈɡəʊpɪk/ ▶ noun (pl. same or **gopiks**) a monetary unit of Azerbaijan, equal to one hundredth of a manat.

Gorakpur /ˈɡɔːrakˌpʊə/ an industrial city in NE India, in Uttar Pradesh near the border with Nepal; pop. 490,000 (1991).

goral /ˈɡɔːr(ə)l/ ▶ noun a long-haired goat-antelope with backward curving horns, found in mountainous regions of east Asia.
● Genus *Nemorhaedus*, family Bovidae: two species.
– ORIGIN mid 19th cent.: a local word in the Himalayas.

Gorbachev /ˈɡɔːbətʃɒf, ˌɡɔːbəˈtʃɒf/, Mikhail (Sergeevich) (b.1931), Soviet statesman, General Secretary of the Communist Party of the USSR 1985–91 and President 1988–91. His foreign policy brought about an end to the cold war, while within the USSR he introduced major reforms known as glasnost and perestroika. He resigned following an attempted coup and at a time of the Soviet republics' desire for autonomy. Nobel Peace Prize (1990).

Gorbals /ˈɡɔːb(ə)lz/ a district of Glasgow on the south bank of the River Clyde, formerly noted for its slums and tenement buildings.

gorblimey Brit. informal ▶ exclamation an expression of surprise or indignation.
▶ adjective [attrib.] common; lower class.
– ORIGIN late 19th cent.: alteration of *God blind me*; also in use as a noun in the early 20th cent. to denote various kinds of unusual clothing.

gorcock /ˈɡɔːkɒk/ ▶ noun Scottish & N. English the male of the red grouse.
– ORIGIN early 17th cent.: from *gor-* (of unknown origin) + **COCK**[1].

Gordian knot /ˈɡɔːdɪən/ ▶ noun an extremely difficult or involved problem.
– PHRASES **cut the Gordian knot** solve or remove a problem in a direct or forceful way, rejecting gentler or more indirect methods.
– ORIGIN mid 16th cent.: from the legend that *Gordius*, king of Gordium, tied an intricate knot and prophesied that whoever untied it would become the ruler of Asia. It was cut through with a sword by Alexander the Great.

gordian worm ▶ noun another term for **HORSEHAIR WORM**.

Gordimer /ˈɡɔːdɪmə/, Nadine (b.1923), South African novelist and short-story writer. Her experience of the effects of apartheid underlies much of her work. Notable novels: *The Conservationist* (Booker Prize, 1974). Nobel Prize for Literature (1991).

Gordium /ˈɡɔːdɪəm/ an ancient city of Asia Minor (now NW Turkey), the capital of Phrygia in the 8th and 9th centuries BC.

gordo /ˈɡɔːdəʊ/ ▶ noun Austral. a popular variety of grape.
– ORIGIN abbreviation of Spanish *gordo blanco*, literally 'fat white'.

Gordon, Charles George (1833–85), British general and colonial administrator. He made his name by crushing the Taiping Rebellion (1863–4) in China. In 1884 he fought Mahdist forces in Sudan led by Muhammad Ahmad (see **MAHDI**) but was trapped at Khartoum and killed.

Gordon Bennett ▶ exclamation expressing surprise, incredulity, or exasperation.
– ORIGIN 1890s: probably an alteration of **GORBLIMEY**, after James *Gordon Bennett* (1841–1918), American publisher and sports sponsor.

Gordon Riots a series of anti-Catholic riots in London in June 1780 in which about 300 people were killed. The riots were provoked by a petition presented to Parliament by Lord George Gordon (1751–93) against the relaxation of restrictions on the holding of landed property by Roman Catholics.

Gordon setter ▶ noun a setter of a black-and-tan breed, used as a gun dog.
– ORIGIN mid 19th cent.: named after the 4th Duke of *Gordon* (1743–1827), who promoted the breed.

Gordy /ˈɡɔːdi/, Berry, Jr (b.1929), American record producer. He founded the Motown record company in 1959.

gore[1] ▶ noun [mass noun] blood that has been shed,

especially as a result of violence: *the film omitted the blood and gore in order to avoid controversy.*
– ORIGIN Old English *gor* 'dung, dirt', of Germanic origin; related to Dutch *goor*, Swedish *gorr* 'muck, filth'. The current sense dates from the mid 16th cent.

gore² ▶ **verb** [with obj.] (of an animal such as a bull) pierce or stab with a horn or tusk.
– ORIGIN late Middle English (in the sense 'stab, pierce'): of unknown origin.

gore³ ▶ **noun** a triangular or tapering piece of material used in making a garment, sail, or umbrella.
▶ **verb** [with obj.] make with such a piece of material: [as adj. **gored**] *a gored skirt.*
– ORIGIN Old English *gāra* 'triangular piece of land', of Germanic origin; related to Dutch *geer* and German *Gehre*, also probably to Old English *gār* 'spear' (a spearhead being triangular).

Górecki /gəˈrɛtski/, Henryk (Mikołaj) (b.1933), Polish composer. His works, influenced by religious music, include the Third Symphony (1976), known as the *Symphony of Sorrowful Songs.*

g

Göreme /ˈgəːriːmi/ a valley in Cappadocia in central Turkey, noted for its cave dwellings hollowed out of the soft tufa rock. In the Byzantine era these contained hermits' cells, monasteries, and more than 400 churches.

Gore-tex /ˈgɔːtɛks/ ▶ **noun** [mass noun] trademark a synthetic waterproof fabric permeable to air and water vapour, used in outdoor and sports clothing.

gorge ▶ **noun 1** a narrow valley between hills or mountains, typically with steep rocky walls and a stream running through it.
2 archaic the throat.
■Falconry the crop of a hawk. ■ the contents of the stomach.
3 Architecture the neck of a bastion or other outwork; the rear entrance to a fortification.
4 a mass of ice obstructing a narrow passage, especially a river.
▶ **verb** [no obj.] eat a large amount greedily; fill oneself with food: *the river comes alive during March when fish gorge on caddis | we used to go to all the little restaurants there and gorge ourselves.*
– PHRASES **one's gorge rises** one is sickened or disgusted: *looking at it, Wendy felt her gorge rise.*
– DERIVATIVES **gorger** noun.
– ORIGIN Middle English (as a verb): from Old French *gorger*, from *gorge* 'throat', based on Latin *gurges* 'whirlpool'. The noun originally meant 'throat' and is from Old French *gorge*; sense 1 dates from the mid 18th cent.

gorged ▶ **adjective** [postpositive] Heraldry having the neck encircled by a coronet or collar, especially one of a specified tincture.
– ORIGIN early 17th cent.: from French *gorge* 'throat' + **-ED**¹.

gorgeous ▶ **adjective** beautiful; very attractive: *gorgeous colours and exquisite decoration.*
■informal very pleasant: *these jam tarts are gorgeous.*
– DERIVATIVES **gorgeously** adverb, **gorgeousness** noun.
– ORIGIN late 15th cent. (describing sumptuous clothing): from Old French *gorgias* 'fine, elegant', of unknown origin.

gorget /ˈgɔːdʒɪt/ ▶ **noun 1** historical an article of clothing that covered the throat.
■a piece of armour for the throat. ■ a wimple.
2 a patch of colour on the throat of a bird or other animal, especially a hummingbird.
– ORIGIN late Middle English (denoting a piece of armour protecting the throat): from Old French *gorgete*, from *gorge* 'throat' (see **GORGE**).

gorgio /ˈgɔːdʒɪəʊ/ ▶ **noun** (pl. **-os**) the gypsy name for a non-gypsy.
– ORIGIN from Romany *gorjo*.

gorgon /ˈgɔːg(ə)n/ ▶ **noun** Greek Mythology each of three sisters, Stheno, Euryale, and Medusa, with snakes for hair, who had the power to turn anyone who looked at them to stone. Medusa was killed by Perseus.
■a fierce, frightening, or repulsive woman.
– ORIGIN via Latin from Greek *Gorgō*, from *gorgos* 'terrible'.

gorgoneion /ˌgɔːgəˈnʌɪən/ ▶ **noun** (pl. **gorgoneia** /-ˈnʌɪə/) a representation of a gorgon's head.
– ORIGIN Greek, neuter of *gorgoneios* 'of or relating to a gorgon' (see **GORGON**).

gorgonian /gɔːˈgəʊnɪən/ Zoology ▶ **noun** a colonial coral of an order distinguished by having a horny tree-like skeleton, including the sea fans and precious red coral. Also called **HORNY CORAL**.
● Order Gorgonacea, class Anthozoa.
▶ **adjective** of or relating to gorgons or gorgonians.
– ORIGIN mid 19th cent.: from modern Latin *Gorgonia*, from Latin *Gorgo* (see **GORGON**), with reference to its petrifaction, + **-AN**.

Gorgonzola /ˌgɔːg(ə)nˈzəʊlə/ ▶ **noun** [mass noun] a type of rich, strong-flavoured Italian cheese with bluish-green veins.
– ORIGIN named after *Gorgonzola*, a village in northern Italy, where it was originally made.

gorilla ▶ **noun** a powerfully built great ape with a large head and short neck, found in the forests of central Africa. It is the largest living primate.
● *Gorilla gorilla*, family Pongidae: three races (two **lowland gorillas** and the **mountain gorilla**).
■informal a heavily built aggressive-looking man.
– ORIGIN from an alleged African word for a wild or hairy person, found in the Greek account of the voyage of the Carthaginian explorer Hanno in the 5th or 6th cent. BC; adopted in 1847 as the specific name of the ape.

Gorkhali /gɔːˈkɑːli/ ▶ **noun** variant spelling of **GURKHALI**.

Gorky¹ /ˈgɔːki/ former name (1932–91) for **NIZHNI NOVGOROD**.

Gorky² /ˈgɔːki/, Arshile (1904–48), Turkish-born American painter. An exponent of abstract expressionism, he is best known for his work of the early 1940s, for example *Waterfall* (1943).

Gorky³ /ˈgɔːki/, Maxim (1868–1936), Russian writer and revolutionary; pseudonym of *Aleksei Maksimovich Peshkov*. After the Revolution he was honoured as the founder of the new, officially sanctioned socialist realism. His best-known works include the play *The Lower Depths* (1901) and his autobiographical trilogy (1915–23).

Gorlovka /ˈgɒrləfkə/ Russian name for **HORLIVKA**.

gormandize /ˈgɔːm(ə)ndʌɪz/ (also **-ise**) ▶ **verb** variant spelling of **GOURMANDIZE**.
– DERIVATIVES **gormandizer** noun.

gormless ▶ **adjective** informal, chiefly Brit. lacking sense or initiative; foolish.
– DERIVATIVES **gormlessly** adverb, **gormlessness** noun.
– ORIGIN mid 18th cent. (originally as *gaumless*): from dialect *gaum* 'understanding' (from Old Norse *gaumr* 'care, heed') + **-LESS**.

Gorno-Altai /ˌgɔːnəʊalˈtʌɪ/ an autonomous republic in south central Russia, on the border with Mongolia; pop. 192,000 (1989); capital, Gorno-Altaisk.

Gorno-Altaisk /ˌgɔːnəʊalˈtʌɪsk/ a city in south central Russia, capital of the republic of Gorno-Altai; pop. 39,000 (1990). It was known as Ulala until 1932 and as Oirot-Tura from 1932 until 1948.

gorp ▶ **noun** [mass noun] N. Amer. informal another term for **TRAIL MIX**.

gorse ▶ **noun** [mass noun] a yellow-flowered shrub of the pea family, the leaves of which are modified to form spines, native to western Europe and North Africa.
● Genus *Ulex*, family Leguminosae: several species, in particular the common European *U. europaeus*, which grows widely in heathy places.
– DERIVATIVES **gorsy** adjective.
– ORIGIN Old English *gors*, *gorst*, from an Indo-European root meaning 'rough, prickly', shared by German *Gerste* and Latin *hordeum* 'barley'.

Gorsedd /ˈgɔːsɛð/ ▶ **noun** a council of Welsh or other Celtic bards and Druids, especially as meeting daily before the eisteddfod.
– ORIGIN Welsh, 'mound, throne, assembly'.

gory ▶ **adjective** (**-ier**, **-iest**) involving or showing violence and bloodshed: *a gory horror film.*
■covered in blood.
– PHRASES **the gory details** humorous the explicit details of something: *she told him the gory details of her past.*
– DERIVATIVES **gorily** adverb, **goriness** noun.

gosh ▶ **exclamation** informal used to express surprise or give emphasis: *gosh, we envy you.*
■chiefly N. Amer. used as a euphemism for 'God': *a gosh-awful team.*
– ORIGIN mid 18th cent.: euphemism for **GOD**.

goshawk /ˈgɒshɔːk/ ▶ **noun** a large short-winged hawk, resembling a large sparrowhawk.
● Genus *Accipiter*, family Accipitridae: several species, in particular the **northern goshawk** (*A. gentilis*) of Eurasia and North America.
– ORIGIN Old English *gōshafoc*, from *gōs* 'goose' + *hafoc* 'hawk'.

gosht /gəʊʃt/ ▶ **noun** [mass noun] Indian red meat (beef, lamb, or mutton): [as modifier] *gosht biryani.*
– ORIGIN from Hindi *gośt*.

gosling /ˈgɒzlɪŋ/ ▶ **noun** a young goose.
– ORIGIN Middle English (originally *gesling*): from Old Norse *gæslingr*, from *gás* 'goose' + **-LING**, later altered by association with **GOOSE**.

go-slow ▶ **noun** chiefly Brit. a strategy or tactic, especially a form of industrial action, in which work or progress is delayed or slowed down.

gospel ▶ **noun 1** the teaching or revelation of Christ: *it is the Church's mission to preach the gospel.*
■(also **gospel truth**) [mass noun] a thing that is absolutely true: *they say it's sold out, but don't take that as gospel.* ■ a set of principles or beliefs: *the new economics unit has produced what it reckons to be the approved gospel.*
2 (**Gospel**) the record of Christ's life and teaching in the first four books of the New Testament.
■each of these books. ■ a portion from one of these read at a church service.

> The four Gospels ascribed to St Matthew, St Mark, St Luke, and St John all give an account of the ministry, crucifixion, and resurrection of Christ, though the Gospel of John differs greatly from the other three. There are also several apocryphal gospels of later date.

3 (also **gospel music**) [mass noun] a fervent style of black American evangelical religious singing, developed from spirituals sung in Southern Baptist and Pentecostal Churches.
– ORIGIN Old English *gōdspel*, from *gōd* 'good' + *spel* 'news, a story' (see **SPELL²**), translating ecclesiastical Latin *bona annuntiatio* or *bonus nuntius*, used to gloss ecclesiastical Latin *evangelium*, from Greek *euangelion* 'good news' (see **EVANGEL**); after the vowel was shortened in Old English, the first syllable was mistaken for *god* 'God'.

gospelize ▶ **verb** [with obj.] rare preach the Gospel to; convert to Christianity.

gospeller (US **gospeler**) ▶ **noun** a person who zealously teaches or professes faith in the gospel.
■(in church use) the reader of the Gospel in a Communion service.

Gospel side ▶ **noun** (in a church) the north side of the altar, at which the Gospel is read.

goss ▶ **noun** Brit. informal gossip: *a bit of background goss.*
– ORIGIN late 20th cent.: abbreviation.

gossamer ▶ **noun** [mass noun] a fine, filmy substance consisting of cobwebs spun by small spiders, which is seen especially in autumn.
■used to refer to something very light, thin, and insubstantial or delicate: *in the light from the table lamp, his hair was blonde gossamer.*
▶ **adjective** [attrib.] made of or resembling gossamer: *gossamer wings.*
– DERIVATIVES **gossamery** adjective.
– ORIGIN Middle English: apparently from **GOOSE** + **SUMMER**¹, perhaps from the time of year around St Martin's summer, i.e. early November, when geese were eaten (gossamer being common then).

gossan /ˈgɒz(ə)n/ ▶ **noun** [mass noun] Geology & Mining an iron-containing secondary deposit, largely consisting of oxides and typically yellowish or reddish, occurring above a deposit of a metallic ore.
– ORIGIN late 18th cent.: of unknown origin.

gossip ▶ **noun** [mass noun] casual or unconstrained conversation or reports about other people, typically involving details which are not confirmed as being true: *he became the subject of much local gossip.*
■[in sing.] a conversation about such matters: *she just comes round here for a gossip.* ■ [count noun] chiefly derogatory a person who likes talking about other people's private lives.
▶ **verb** (**gossiped**, **gossiping**) [no obj.] engage in gossip: *they would start gossiping about her as soon as she left.*
– DERIVATIVES **gossiper** noun, **gossipy** adjective.
– ORIGIN late Old English *godsibb*, 'godfather, godmother, baptismal sponsor', literally 'a person related to one in God', from *god* 'God' + *sibb* 'a relative' (see **SIB**). In Middle English the sense was 'a close friend, a person with whom one gossips', hence 'a person who gossips', later (early 19th

cent.) 'idle talk' (from the verb, which dates from the early 17th cent.).

gossip column ▶ **noun** a section of a newspaper devoted to gossip about well-known people.
– DERIVATIVES **gossip columnist** noun.

gossoon /gɒˈsuːn/ ▶ **noun** Irish a lad.
– ORIGIN late 17th cent.: from French *garçon* 'boy'.

gossypol /ˈgɒsɪpɒl/ ▶ **noun** [mass noun] Chemistry a toxic crystalline compound present in cotton-seed oil.
• A polycyclic phenol; chem. formula: $C_{30}H_{30}O_8$.
– ORIGIN late 19th cent.: from modern Latin *Gossypium* (genus name), from Latin *gossypinum, -pion* 'cotton plant' (of unknown origin) + **-OL**.

got past and past participle of **GET**.

gotcha (also **gotcher**) informal ▶ **exclamation** I have got you (used to express satisfaction at having captured or defeated someone or uncovered their faults).
▶ **noun** an instance of publicly tricking someone or exposing them to ridicule, especially by means of an elaborate deception.
– ORIGIN 1930s: representing a pronunciation.

Göteborg /jœtəˈbɔrj/ Swedish name for **GOTHENBURG**.

Goth /gɒθ/ ▶ **noun 1** a member of a Germanic people that invaded the Roman Empire from the east between the 3rd and 5th centuries. The eastern division, the Ostrogoths, founded a kingdom in Italy, while the Visigoths went on to found one in Spain.
2 (**goth**) [mass noun] a style of rock music derived from punk, typically with apocalyptic or mystical lyrics.
■[count noun] a member of a subculture favouring black clothing, white and black make-up, and goth music.
– ORIGIN Old English *Gota*, superseded in Middle English by the adoption of late Latin *Gothi* (plural), from Greek *Gothoi*, from Gothic *Gutthiuda* 'the Gothic people'.

Gotha /ˈgəʊtə, ˈgəʊθə, German ˈgoːta/ a city in central Germany, in Thuringia; pop. 57,600 (1981). From 1640 until 1918 it was the residence of the dukes of Saxe-Gotha and Saxe-Coburg-Gotha.

Gotham 1 /ˈgəʊtəm/ a village in Nottinghamshire. It is associated with the folk tale *The Wise Men of Gotham*, in which the inhabitants of the village demonstrated cunning by feigning stupidity.
2 /ˈgɒθəm/ a nickname for New York City, used originally by Washington Irving and now associated with the Batman stories.

Gothenburg /ˈgɒθənbəːg/ a seaport in SW Sweden, on the Kattegat strait; pop. 433,000 (1990). It is the second largest city in Sweden. Swedish name **GÖTEBORG**.

Gothic ▶ **adjective 1** of or relating to the Goths or their extinct language, which belongs to the East Germanic branch of the Indo-European language family. It provides the earliest manuscript evidence of any Germanic language (4th–6th centuries AD).
2 of or in the style of architecture prevalent in western Europe in the 12th–16th centuries (and revived in the mid 18th to early 20th centuries), characterized by pointed arches, rib vaults, and flying buttresses, together with large windows and elaborate tracery. English Gothic architecture is divided into Early English, Decorated, and Perpendicular.
3 (also pseudo-archaic **Gothick**) belonging to or redolent of the Dark Ages; portentously gloomy or horrifying: *19th-century Gothic horror.*
4 (of lettering) of or derived from the angular style of handwriting with broad vertical downstrokes used in western Europe from the 13th century, including Fraktur and black-letter typefaces.
5 (**gothic**) of or relating to goths or their rock music.
▶ **noun** [mass noun] **1** the extinct language of the Goths.
2 the Gothic style of architecture.
3 Gothic type.
– DERIVATIVES **Gothically** adverb, **Gothicism** noun.
– ORIGIN from French *gothique* or late Latin *gothicus*, from *Gothi* (see **GOTH**). It was used in the 17th and 18th cents to mean 'not classical' (i.e. not Greek or Roman), and hence to refer to medieval architecture which did not follow classical models (sense 2) and a typeface based on medieval handwriting (sense 4).

gothic novel ▶ **noun** an English genre of fiction popular in the 18th to early 19th centuries, characterized by an atmosphere of mystery and horror and having a pseudo-medieval setting.

Gotland /ˈgɒtlənd/ an island and province of Sweden, in the Baltic Sea; pop. 57,100 (1990); capital, Visby.

gotta ▶ **contraction of** ■ have got a (not acceptable in standard use): *I gotta licence.* ■ have got to (not acceptable in standard use): *you gotta be careful.*

gotten N. Amer. past participle of **GET**.

USAGE As past participles of **get**, **got** and **gotten** both date back to Middle English. The form **gotten** is not used in British English but is very common in North American English, though even there it is often regarded as non-standard. In North American English, **got** and **gotten** are not identical in use. **Gotten** usually implies the process of obtaining something, as in *he had* **gotten** *us tickets for the show*, while **got** implies the state of possession or ownership, as in *I haven't* **got** *any money.*

Götterdämmerung /ˌgəːtəˈdɛmərʊŋ/ (in Germanic mythology) the downfall of the gods.
– ORIGIN German, literally 'twilight of the gods', popularized by Wagner's use of the word as the title of the last opera of the Ring cycle.

Göttingen /ˈgəːtɪŋən, German ˈgœtɪŋən/ a town in north central Germany, on the River Leine; pop. 124,000 (1991). It is noted for its university.

gouache /guːˈɑːʃ, gwɑːʃ/ ▶ **noun** [mass noun] a method of painting using opaque pigments ground in water and thickened with a glue-like substance.
■paint of this kind; opaque watercolour. ■ [count noun] a picture painted in this way.
– ORIGIN late 19th cent.: French, from Italian *guazzo*.

Gouda[1] /ˈgaʊdə/ a market town in the Netherlands, just north-east of Rotterdam; pop. 65,900 (1991).

Gouda[2] /ˈgaʊdə/ ▶ **noun** [mass noun] a flat round cheese with a yellow rind, originally made in Gouda.

gouge /gaʊdʒ, guːdʒ/ ▶ **noun 1** a chisel with a concave blade, used in carpentry, sculpture, and surgery.
2 an indentation or groove made by gouging.
▶ **verb** [with obj.] **1** make (a groove, hole, or indentation) with or as if with a gouge: *the channel had been gouged out by the ebbing water.*
■make a rough hole or indentation in (a surface), especially so as to mar or disfigure it: *he had wielded the blade inexpertly, gouging the grass in several places.* ■ (**gouge something out**) cut or force something out roughly or brutally: *one of the young man's eyes had been gouged out.* ■ [no obj.] Austral. dig for minerals, especially opal: *he was* **gouging for** *ore.*
2 N. Amer. informal overcharge; swindle: *the airline ends up gouging the very passengers it is supposed to assist.*
■(**gouge something out**) obtain money by swindling or extortion: *he'd gouged wads* **out of** *Morty.*
– DERIVATIVES **gouger** noun.
– ORIGIN late Middle English: from Old French, from late Latin *gubia*, *gulbia*, perhaps of Celtic origin; compare with Old Irish *gulba* 'beak' and Welsh *gylf* 'beak, pointed instrument'.

Gough Island /gɒf/ an island in the South Atlantic, south of Tristan da Cunha. In 1938 it became a dependency of the British Crown Colony of St Helena.

goujons /ˈguː(d)ʒɒnz/ ▶ **plural noun** Brit. deep-fried strips of chicken or fish.
– ORIGIN from French *goujon* 'gudgeon' (see **GUDGEON**[1]).

goulash /ˈguːlaʃ/ ▶ **noun 1** [mass noun] a highly seasoned Hungarian soup or stew of meat and vegetables, flavoured with paprika.
2 (in informal bridge) a redealing of the four hands (unshuffled, with each hand arranged in suits and order of value) after no player has bid. The cards are usually dealt in batches of five, five, and three, and the resulting hands may have very uneven distributions.
– ORIGIN from Hungarian *gulyás-hús*, from *gulyás* 'herdsman' + *hús* 'meat'; sense 2 (dating from the 1920s) is an extended use.

Gould[1] /guːld/, Glenn (Herbert) (1932–82), Canadian pianist and composer. Best known for his performances of works by Bach, he retired from the concert platform in 1964 to concentrate on recording and broadcasting.

Gould[2] /guːld/, John (1804–81), English bird artist. He produced many large illustrated volumes, though it is believed that many of the finest plates were actually drawn by Gould's wife and other employed artists.

Gould[3] /guːld/, Stephen Jay (b.1941), American palaeontologist. A noted popularizer of science, he has studied modifications of Darwinian evolutionary theory, proposed the concept of punctuated equilibrium, and written on the social context of scientific theory.

Gounod /ˈguːnəʊ, French guno/, Charles François (1818–93), French composer, conductor, and organist. He is best known for his opera *Faust* (1859).

goura /ˈgʊərə/ ▶ **noun** another term for **CROWNED PIGEON**.
– ORIGIN mid 19th cent.: modern Latin genus name, from a local word in New Guinea.

gourami /gʊ(ə)ˈrɑːmi, ˈgʊərəmi/ ▶ **noun** (pl. same or **gouramis**) a small brightly coloured Asian labyrinth fish, popular in aquaria. It builds a nest of bubbles, which is typically guarded by the male.
• Belontiidae and related families: several species.
– ORIGIN late 19th cent.: from Malay *gurami*.

gourd /gʊəd, gɔːd/ ▶ **noun 1** a fleshy, typically large fruit with a hard skin, some varieties of which are edible.
■a drinking container, water container, or ornament made from the hard hollowed and dried skin of this fruit.
2 a climbing or trailing plant which bears this fruit.
• Family Cucurbitaceae (the **gourd family**): several genera and species, including the coloured **ornamental gourds** (*Cucurbita pepo* var. *ovifera*). The gourd family also includes the marrows, squashes, pumpkins, melons, and cucumbers.
– PHRASES **out of one's gourd** N. Amer. informal out of one's mind; crazy. ■ under the influence of alcohol or drugs: *he was obviously stoned out of his gourd.*
– DERIVATIVES **gourdful** noun (pl. **-fuls**).
– ORIGIN Middle English: from Old French *gourde*, based on Latin *cucurbita*.

gourde /gʊəd/ ▶ **noun** the basic monetary unit of Haiti, equal to 100 centimes.
– ORIGIN the Franco-American name for a dollar.

gourmand /ˈgʊəmənd, ˈgɔː-/ ▶ **noun** a person who enjoys eating and often eats too much.
■a connoisseur of good food.
– DERIVATIVES **gourmandism** noun.
– ORIGIN late Middle English: from Old French, of unknown origin.

USAGE The words **gourmand** and **gourmet** overlap in meaning but are not identical. Both can be used to mean 'a connoisseur of good food' but **gourmand** is more usually used to mean 'a person who enjoys eating and often eats too much'.

gourmandize /ˌgʊəm(ə)nˈdiːz, ˈgɔː-/ (also **gormandize, -ise**) ▶ **verb** [no obj.] indulge in good eating; eat greedily.
▶ **noun** [mass noun] the action of indulging in or being a connoisseur of good eating.
– ORIGIN late Middle English (as a noun): from French *gourmandise*, from *gourmand*; the verb dates from the mid 16th cent.

gourmet /ˈgʊəmeɪ, ˈgɔː-/ ▶ **noun** a connoisseur of good food; a person with a discerning palate.
■[as modifier] of a kind or standard suitable for a gourmet: *a gourmet meal.*
– ORIGIN early 19th cent.: French, originally meaning 'wine taster', influenced by **GOURMAND**.

USAGE On the distinction between **gourmet** and **gourmand**, see usage at **GOURMAND**.

gout /gaʊt/ ▶ **noun 1** [mass noun] a disease in which defective metabolism of uric acid causes arthritis, especially in the smaller bones of the feet, deposition of chalk-stones, and episodes of acute pain.
2 poetic/literary a drop or spot, especially of blood, smoke, or flame: *gouts of flame and phlegm.*
– DERIVATIVES **goutiness** noun, **gouty** adjective.
– ORIGIN Middle English: from Old French *goute*, from medieval Latin *gutta*, literally 'drop' (because gout was believed to be caused by the dropping of diseased matter from the blood into the joints).

goutweed ▶ **noun** [mass noun] ground elder, which was formerly used to treat gout. Compare with **HERB GERARD**.

gov. ▶ **abbreviation for** ■ government. ■ governor.

govern /ˈgʌv(ə)n/ ▶ **verb** [with obj.] **1** conduct the policy, actions, and affairs of (a state, organization,

or people): *he was incapable of governing the country* | [as adj. **governing**] *the governing coalition.*
▪control, influence, or regulate (a person, action, or course of events): *the future of Jamaica will be governed by geography not history.* ▪ **(govern oneself)** conduct oneself, especially with regard to controlling one's emotions: *the rabbinic system that delineates how a devout Jew governs himself.*
2 constitute a law, rule, standard, or principle for: *constant principles govern the poetic experience.*
▪serve to decide (a legal case).
3 Grammar (of a word) require that (another word or group of words) be in a particular case: *the Latin preposition 'cum' governs nouns in the ablative.*
– DERIVATIVES **governability** noun, **governable** adjective.
– ORIGIN Middle English: from Old French *governer*, from Latin *gubernare* 'to steer, rule', from Greek *kubernan* 'to steer'.

governance ▶**noun** [mass noun] the action or manner of governing: *a more responsive system of governance will be required.*
▪archaic sway; control: *what, shall King Henry be a pupil still, **under** the surly Gloucester's **governance**?*
– ORIGIN Middle English: from Old French, from *governer* (see **GOVERN**).

governess ▶**noun** a woman employed to teach children in a private household.
▪used to refer to a woman who is overfastidious, strict, or prim.
– DERIVATIVES **governessy** adjective.
– ORIGIN Middle English (originally *governeress*, denoting a female ruler): from Old French *governeresse*, feminine of *governeour* 'governor', from Latin *gubernator*, from *gubernare* (see **GOVERN**).

governing body ▶**noun** a group of people who formulate the policy and direct the affairs of an institution in partnership with the managers, especially on a voluntary or part-time basis: *the school's governing body.*

government /ˈɡʌv(ə)nˌm(ə)nt, ˈɡʌvəm(ə)nt/ ▶**noun** **1** [treated as sing. or pl.] the governing body of a state; a particular ministry in office: *the government's economic record will undoubtedly cost them the seat* | [as modifier] *government controls.*
▪[mass noun] the system by which a state or community is governed: *recent cutbacks in government are making subsidies less available.* ▪ [mass noun] the action or manner of controlling or regulating a state, organization, or people: *rules for the government of the infirmary.*
2 Grammar the relation between a governed and a governing word.
– DERIVATIVES **governmental** adjective, **governmentally** adverb.
– ORIGIN Middle English: from Old French *governement*, from *governer* (see **GOVERN**).

Government House ▶**noun** Brit. the official residence of a governor, especially in a colony or Commonwealth state that regards the British monarch as head of state.

government issue ▶**adjective** (of equipment) provided by the government.

government paper ▶**noun** [mass noun] bonds or other promissory certificates issued by the government.

government securities ▶**plural noun** another term for **GOVERNMENT PAPER**.

government surplus ▶**noun** [mass noun] unused equipment sold by the government.

governor ▶**noun** **1** an official appointed to govern a town or region.
▪the elected executive head of a state of the US. ▪ the representative of the British Crown in a colony or in a Commonwealth state that regards the monarch as head of state.
2 the head of a public institution: *the governor of the Bank of England.*
▪a member of a governing body.
3 Brit. informal the person in authority; one's employer.
4 a device automatically regulating the supply of fuel, steam, or water to a machine, ensuring uniform motion or limiting speed.
– DERIVATIVES **governorate** noun, **governorship** noun.
– ORIGIN Middle English: from Old French *governeour*, from Latin *gubernator*, from *gubernare* (see **GOVERN**).

Governor General ▶**noun** (pl. **Governors General**) the chief representative of the Crown in a Commonwealth country of which the British monarch is head of state.
▪chiefly historical an analogous representative of another Crown.

govt ▶**abbreviation for** government: *local govt.*

gowan /ˈɡaʊən/ ▶**noun** Scottish & N. English a wild white or yellow flower, especially a daisy.
– ORIGIN mid 16th cent.: probably a variant of dialect *gollan*, denoting various yellow-flowered plants, perhaps related to Old English *golde* 'marigold'.

gowk /ɡaʊk/ ▶**noun** dialect **1** an awkward or foolish person (often as a general term of abuse).
2 a cuckoo.
– ORIGIN Middle English (in sense 2): from Old Norse *gaukr.*

gown ▶**noun** a long dress, typically having a close-fitting bodice and a flared or flowing skirt, worn on formal occasions: *a silk ball gown.*
▪a protective garment worn in hospital, either by a staff member during surgery or by a patient. ▪ a loose cloak indicating one's profession or status, worn by a lawyer, teacher, academic, or university student. ▪ [mass noun] the members of a university as distinct from the permanent residents of the university town: *the annual town versus gown cricket match.* Often contrasted with **TOWN**.
▶**verb** **(be gowned)** be dressed in a gown: *she was gowned in luminous silk.*
– ORIGIN Middle English: from Old French *goune*, from late Latin *gunna* 'fur garment'; probably related to Byzantine Greek *gouna* 'fur, fur-lined garment'.

Gowon /ˈɡəʊwɒn/, Yakubu (b.1934), Nigerian general and statesman, head of state 1966–75. Following the Biafran civil war (1967–70) he maintained a policy of 'no victor, no vanquished' which helped to reconcile the warring factions.

goy /ɡɔɪ/ ▶**noun** (pl. **goyim** /ˈɡɔɪɪm/ or **goys**) informal, offensive a Jewish name for a non-Jew.
– DERIVATIVES **goyish** adjective.
– ORIGIN from Hebrew *gōy* 'people, nation'.

Goya /ˈɡɔɪə/ (1746–1828), Spanish painter and etcher; full name *Francisco José de Goya y Lucientes*. He is famous for his works treating the French occupation of Spain (1808–14), including *The Shootings of May 3rd 1808* (painting, 1814) and *The Disasters of War* (etchings, 1810–14), depicting the cruelty and horror of war.

Gozo /ˈɡəʊzəʊ/ a Maltese island, to the north-west of the main island of Malta.

GP ▶**abbreviation for** ▪ general practitioner: *talk over any worries with your GP.* ▪ Grand Prix.

Gp Capt ▶**abbreviation for** Group Captain.

gph ▶**abbreviation for** gallons per hour.

GPI ▶**abbreviation for** general paralysis of the insane, a combination of dementia, weakness, speech and hearing difficulty, and other symptoms caused by affection of the brain in the late stages of syphilis.

gpm ▶**abbreviation for** gallons per minute.

GPO ▶**abbreviation for** ▪ historical (in the UK) General Post Office. ▪ (in the US) Government Printing Office.

GPS ▶**abbreviation for** Global Positioning System, an accurate worldwide navigational and surveying facility based on the reception of signals from an array of orbiting satellites.

GPU a Soviet secret police agency 1922–3. See also **OGPU**.
– ORIGIN abbreviation of Russian *Gosudarstvennoe politicheskoe upravlenie* 'State Political Directorate'.

GR ▶**abbreviation for** ▪ Greece (international vehicle registration). ▪ King George. [ORIGIN: from Latin *Georgius Rex.*]

gr. ▶**abbreviation for** ▪ grain(s). ▪ gram(s). ▪ grey. ▪ gross.

Graafian follicle /ˈɡrɑːfɪən/ ▶**noun** Physiology a fluid-filled structure in the mammalian ovary within which an ovum develops prior to ovulation.
– ORIGIN mid 19th cent.: named after R. de Graaf (1641–73), Dutch anatomist.

grab ▶**verb** **(grabbed, grabbing)** [with obj.] **1** grasp or seize suddenly and roughly: *she grabbed him by the shirt collar* | *she grabbed her keys and rushed out.*
▪[no obj.] **(grab at/for)** make a sudden snatch at: *he grabbed at the handle, missed, and nearly fell.* ▪ informal obtain or get (something) quickly or opportunistically, sometimes unscrupulously: *I'll grab another drink while there's still time* | *someone's grabbed my seat.* ▪ [no obj.] (of a brake on a vehicle) grip the wheel harshly or jerkily: *the brakes grabbed very badly.*
2 [usu. with negative or in questions] informal attract the attention of; make an impression on: *how does that grab you?*
▶**noun** **1** [in sing.] a quick sudden clutch or attempt to seize: *he **made a** lungeing **grab at** the pistol.*
2 a mechanical device for clutching, lifting, and moving things, especially materials in bulk.
▪[as modifier] denoting a bar or strap for people to hold on to for support or in a moving vehicle: *for elderly people, grab rails at strategic places are likely to prevent accidents.*
– PHRASES **up for grabs** informal available; obtainable: *great prizes up for grabs.*
– DERIVATIVES **grabber** noun.
– ORIGIN late 16th cent.: from Middle Low German and Middle Dutch *grabben*; perhaps related to **GRIP**, **GRIPE**, and **GROPE**.

grab bag ▶**noun** N. Amer. a lucky dip in which wrapped items are chosen by people at random.
▪an assortment of items in a sealed bag which one buys or is given without knowing what the contents are.

grabble ▶**verb** [no obj.] archaic feel or search with the hands; grope about.
▪sprawl or tumble on all fours.
– ORIGIN late 16th cent.: probably from Dutch *grabbelen* 'scramble for a thing', from Middle Dutch *grabben* (see **GRAB**).

grabby ▶**adjective** informal, chiefly US having or showing a selfish desire for something; greedy.
▪attracting attention; arousing people's interest: *a grabby angle on a news story.*

graben /ˈɡrɑːb(ə)n/ ▶**noun** (pl. same or **grabens**) Geology an elongated block of the earth's crust lying between two faults and displaced downwards relative to the blocks on either side, as in a rift valley.
– ORIGIN late 19th cent.: from German *Graben* 'a ditch'.

Gracchus /ˈɡrakəs/, Tiberius Sempronius (*c.*163–133 BC) and his brother Gaius Sempronius (*c.*153–121 BC), Roman tribunes; also known as **the Gracchi**. They were responsible for radical social and economic legislation, especially concerning the redistribution of land to the poor.

Grace, W. G. (1848–1915), English cricketer; full name *William Gilbert Grace*. In a first-class career that lasted until 1908, he made 126 centuries, scored 54,896 runs, and took 2,864 wickets. He twice captained England in test matches against Australia (1880 and 1882).

grace ▶**noun** [mass noun] **1** simple elegance or refinement of movement: *she moved through the water with effortless grace.*
▪courteous good will: *at least he has the grace to admit his debt to her.* ▪ **(graces)** an attractively polite manner of behaving: *she has all **the social graces**.*
2 (in Christian belief) the free and unmerited favour of God, as manifested in the salvation of sinners and the bestowal of blessings.
▪[count noun] a divinely given talent or blessing: *the scheme has proved to be a great grace for the Church.* ▪ the condition or fact of being favoured by someone: *he fell from grace with the tabloids after he was sent off for swearing.*
3 a period officially allowed for payment of a sum due or for compliance with a law or condition, especially an extended period granted as a special favour: *another three days' grace.*
4 a short prayer of thanks said before or after a meal: *before dinner the Reverend Newman said grace.*
5 **(His, Her,** or **Your Grace)** used as forms of description or address for a duke, duchess, or archbishop: *His Grace, the Duke of Atholl.*
▶**verb** [with obj. and adverbial] do honour or credit to (someone or something) by one's presence: *she bowed out from the sport she has graced for two decades.*
▪[with obj.] (of a person or thing) be an attractive presence in or on; adorn: *Ms Pasco has graced the front pages of magazines like Elle and Vogue.*
– PHRASES **be in someone's good** (or **bad**) **graces** be regarded by someone with favour (or disfavour). **there but for the grace of God (go I)** used to acknowledge one's good fortune in avoiding another's mistake or misfortune. **the (Three) Graces** Greek Mythology three beautiful goddesses

(Aglaia, Thalia, and Euphrosyne), daughters of Zeus. They were believed to personify and bestow charm, grace, and beauty. **with good** (or **bad**) **grace** in a willing and happy (or resentful and reluctant) manner.
– ORIGIN Middle English: via Old French from Latin *gratia*, from *gratus* 'pleasing, thankful'; related to **GRATEFUL**.

grace and favour ▶ **adjective** [attrib.] Brit. denoting accommodation occupied by permission of a sovereign or government.

graceful ▶ **adjective** having or showing grace or elegance: *she was a tall girl, slender and graceful.*
– DERIVATIVES **gracefully** adverb, **gracefulness** noun.

graceless ▶ **adjective** lacking grace, elegance, or charm.
– DERIVATIVES **gracelessly** adverb, **gracelessness** noun.

grace note ▶ **noun** Music an extra note added as an embellishment and not essential to the harmony or melody.

Gracias a Dios, Cape /ˌgrasɪas a ˈdiːɒs/ a cape forming the easternmost extremity of the Mosquito Coast in Central America, on the border between Nicaragua and Honduras.
– ORIGIN Spanish, literally 'thanks (be) to God', so named by Columbus, who, becalmed off the coast in 1502, was able to continue his voyage with the arrival of a following wind.

gracile /ˈgrasɪl, ˈgrasʌɪl/ ▶ **adjective** Anthropology (of a hominid species) of slender build.
■ (of a person) slender or thin, especially in a charming or attractive way.
– ORIGIN early 17th cent.: from Latin *gracilis* 'slender'.

gracilis /ˈgrasɪlɪs/ (also **gracilis muscle**) ▶ **noun** Anatomy a slender superficial muscle of the inner thigh.
– ORIGIN early 17th cent.: from Latin, literally 'slender'.

gracility /grəˈsɪlɪti/ ▶ **noun** [mass noun] formal **1** the state of being gracefully slender.
2 (with reference to a literary style) plain simplicity.

gracious ▶ **adjective** **1** courteous, kind, and pleasant, especially towards someone of lower social status: *smiling and gracious in defeat.*
■ elegant and tasteful, especially as exhibiting wealth or high social status: *the British painter specialized in gracious Victorian interiors | gracious living.*
2 (in Christian belief) showing divine grace: *I am saved by God's gracious intervention on my behalf.*
3 Brit. a polite epithet used of royalty or their acts: *the accession of Her present gracious Majesty.*
▶ **exclamation** expressing polite surprise.
– DERIVATIVES **graciously** adverb, **graciousness** noun.
– ORIGIN Middle English: via Old French from Latin *gratiosus*, from *gratia* 'esteem, favour' (see **GRACE**).

grackle ▶ **noun** **1** a songbird of the American blackbird family, the male of which has shiny black plumage with a blue-green sheen.
• Several genera and species, family Icteridae, in particular the **common grackle** (*Quiscalus quiscula*).
2 another term for an Asian mynah or starling, with mainly black plumage.
• *Gracula* and other genera, family Sturnidae; **southern grackle** is another term for the hill mynah.
– ORIGIN late 18th cent.: from modern Latin *Gracula*, from Latin *graculus* 'jackdaw'.

grad[1] ▶ **noun** informal term for **GRADUATE**.

grad[2] ▶ **abbreviation for** gradient.

gradable ▶ **adjective** Grammar denoting an adjective that can be used in the comparative and superlative and take a submodifier. Contrasted with **CLASSIFYING**.
– DERIVATIVES **gradability** noun.

gradate ▶ **verb** pass or cause to pass by gradations from one shade of colour to another: [no obj.] *the black background gradated toward a dark purple.*
■ [with obj.] arrange in steps or grades of size, amount, or quality: [as adj. **gradated**] *the Temple compound became a series of concentric circles of graded purity.*
– ORIGIN mid 18th cent.: back-formation from **GRADATION**.

gradation ▶ **noun** a scale or a series of successive changes, stages, or degrees: *the Act fails to provide both a clear and defensible gradation of offences.*
■ a stage or change in a such a scale or series: *minute gradations of distance.* ■ a minute change from one shade, tone, or colour to another: *amorphous shapes in subtle gradations of green and blue.* ■ (in historical linguistics) another term for **ABLAUT**.
– DERIVATIVES **gradational** adjective, **gradationally** adverb.
– ORIGIN mid 16th cent.: from Latin *gradatio(n-)*, based on *gradus* 'step'.

Grade, Lew, Baron Grade of Elstree (1906–98), British television producer and executive, born in Russia; born *Louis Winogradsky*. A pioneer of British commercial television, he served as president of ATV (Associated Television) from 1977 to 1982.

grade ▶ **noun** **1** a particular level of rank, quality, proficiency, intensity, or value: *sea salt is usually available in coarse or fine grades.*
■ a level in a salary or employment structure. ■ Brit. a level of importance allocated to a listed building: [as modifier] *a Grade I listed building.* ■ chiefly N. Amer. a mark indicating the quality of a student's work: *I got good grades last semester.* ■ Brit. an examination, especially in music: *I took grade five and got a distinction.* ■ N. Amer. (with specifying ordinal number) those pupils in a school or school system who are grouped by age or ability for teaching at a particular level for a year: *she teaches first grade.* ■ (in historical linguistics) a relative position in a series of forms involving ablaut. ■ Zoology a group of animals at a similar evolutionary level.
2 chiefly N. Amer. a gradient or slope: *just over the crest of a long seven per cent grade.*
3 [usu. as modifier] a variety of cattle produced by crossing with a superior breed: *grade stock.*
▶ **verb** [with obj.] (usu. **be graded**) **1** arrange in or allocate to grades; class or sort: *they are graded according to thickness* | [as adj. **graded**] *carefully graded exercises.*
■ chiefly N. Amer. give a mark to (a student or a piece of work).
2 [no obj.] pass gradually from one level, especially a shade of colour, into another: *the sky graded from blue at the top of the shot to white on the horizon.*
3 reduce (a road) to an easy gradient.
4 cross (livestock) with a superior breed.
– PHRASES **at grade** N. Amer. on the same level: *the crossing at grade of two streets.* **make the grade** informal succeed; reach the desired standard.
– ORIGIN early 16th cent.: from French, or from Latin *gradus* 'step'. Originally used as a unit of measurement of angles (a degree of arc), the term later referred to degrees of merit or quality.

grade crossing ▶ **noun** North American term for **LEVEL CROSSING**.

gradely ▶ **adjective** N. English fine; decent; respectable: *she were a gradely lass.*
– ORIGIN Middle English (originally in the sense 'excellent, noble'): from Old Norse *greithligr*, from *greithr* 'ready'.

grader ▶ **noun** **1** a person or thing that grades.
■ a wheeled machine for levelling the ground, especially in making roads.
2 [in combination] N. Amer. a pupil of a specified grade in a school: *first-grader.*

grade school ▶ **noun** N. Amer. elementary school.
– DERIVATIVES **grade schooler** noun.

gradience ▶ **noun** [mass noun] Linguistics the absence of a clear-cut boundary between one category and another, for example between *cup* and *mug* in semantics.

gradient /ˈgreɪdɪənt/ ▶ **noun** **1** an inclined part of a road or railway; a slope: *fail-safe brakes for use on steep gradients.*
■ the degree of such a slope: *the path becomes very rough as the gradient increases.* ■ Mathematics the degree of steepness of a graph at any point.
2 Physics an increase or decrease in the magnitude of a property (e.g. temperature, pressure, or concentration) observed in passing from one point or moment to another.
■ the rate of such a change. ■ Mathematics the vector formed by the operator ∇ acting on a scalar function at a given point in a scalar field.
– ORIGIN mid 19th cent.: from **GRADE**, on the pattern of *salient*.

gradine /grəˈdiːn/ (also **gradin** /ˈgreɪdɪn/) ▶ **noun** archaic a low step or ledge, especially one at the back of an altar.
– ORIGIN mid 19th cent.: from Italian *gradino*, diminutive of *grado* 'step'.

gradiometer /ˌgreɪdɪˈɒmɪtə/ ▶ **noun** a surveying instrument used for setting out or measuring the gradient of a slope.
■ Physics an instrument for measuring the gradient of an energy field, especially the horizontal gradient of the earth's gravitational or magnetic field.

gradual /ˈgradʒʊəl/ ▶ **adjective** taking place or progressing slowly or by degrees: *the gradual introduction of new methods.*
■ (of a slope) not steep or abrupt.
▶ **noun** (in the Western Christian Church) a response sung or recited between the Epistle and Gospel in the Mass.
■ a book of plainsong for the Mass.
– DERIVATIVES **gradually** adverb, **gradualness** noun.
– ORIGIN late Middle English: from medieval Latin *gradualis*, from Latin *gradus* 'step'. The original sense of the adjective was 'arranged in degrees'; the noun refers to the altar steps in a church, from which the antiphons were sung.

gradualism ▶ **noun** [mass noun] a policy of gradual reform rather than sudden change or revolution.
■ Biology the hypothesis that evolution proceeds chiefly by the accumulation of gradual changes (in contrast to the punctuationist model).
– DERIVATIVES **gradualist** noun, **gradualistic** adjective.

graduand /ˈgradʒʊand, -dj-, -ənd/ ▶ **noun** Brit. a person who is about to receive an academic degree.
– ORIGIN late 19th cent.: from medieval Latin *graduandus*, gerundive of *graduare* 'take a degree' (see **GRADUATE**).

graduate ▶ **noun** /ˈgradʒʊət, -djʊət/ a person who has successfully completed a course of study or training, especially a person who has been awarded an undergraduate or first academic degree.
■ N. Amer. a person who has received a high-school diploma: *she is 19, a graduate of Lincoln High.*
▶ **verb** /ˈgradʒʊeɪt, -djʊeɪt/ **1** [no obj.] successfully complete an academic degree, course of training, or (N. Amer.) high school: *he* ***graduated from*** *Glasgow University in 1990.*
■ [with obj.] N. Amer. confer a degree or other academic qualification on: *the school graduated more than one hundred arts majors in its first year.* ■ (**graduate to**) move up to (a more advanced level or position): *he started with motorbikes but now he's graduated to his first car.*
2 [with obj.] arrange in a series or according to a scale: [as adj. **graduated**] *a graduated tax.*
■ mark out (an instrument or container) in degrees or other proportionate divisions: *the stem was graduated with marks for each hour.*
3 [with obj.] change (something, typically colour or shade) gradually or step by step: *the colour is graduated from the middle of the frame to the top.*
– ORIGIN late Middle English: from medieval Latin *graduat-* 'graduated', from *graduare* 'take a degree', from Latin *gradus* 'degree, step'.

graduated pension ▶ **noun** (in the UK) a state pension paid under a system (in operation 1961–75) in which both contributions and payments were in proportion to wages or salary.

graduate school ▶ **noun** N. Amer. a department of a university for advanced work by graduates.

graduation ▶ **noun** [mass noun] **1** the receiving or conferring of an academic degree or diploma.
■ [count noun] the ceremony at which degrees are conferred.
2 the action of dividing into degrees or other proportionate divisions on a graduated scale.
■ [count noun] a mark on a container or instrument indicating a degree of quantity.

gradus /ˈgreɪdəs/ ▶ **noun** (pl. **graduses**) historical a manual of classical prosody formerly used in schools to help in writing Greek and Latin verse.
– ORIGIN mid 18th cent.: Latin, from *Gradus ad Parnassum* 'Step(s) to Parnassus', the title of one such manual.

Graecism /ˈgriːsɪz(ə)m, ˈgrʌɪ-/ (also **Grecism**) ▶ **noun** a Greek idiom or grammatical feature, especially as imitated in another language.
■ [mass noun] the Greek spirit, style, or mode of expression, especially as imitated in a work of art.
– ORIGIN late 16th cent.: from French *grécisme* or medieval Latin *Graecismus*, from *Graecus* (see **GREEK**).

Graeco- /ˈgriːkəʊ, ˈgrʌɪ-/ (also **Greco-**) ▶ **combining form** Greek; Greek and ...: *Graecophile | Graeco-Turkish.*
■ relating to Greece.
– ORIGIN from Latin *Graecus* (see **GREEK**).

g

Graeco-Roman (also **Greco-Roman**) ▶ **adjective** of or relating to the ancient Greeks and Romans.
■denoting a style of wrestling in which holds below the waist are prohibited.

Graf /grɑːf/, Steffi (b.1969), German tennis player; full name *Stephanie Graf*. She was ranked top women's player at the age of 16 and won her seventh Wimbledon singles title in 1996.

graffiti /grəˈfiːti/ ▶ **plural noun** (sing. **graffito** /-təʊ/) [treated as sing. or pl.] writing or drawings scribbled, scratched, or sprayed illicitly on a wall or other surface in a public place: *the walls were covered with graffiti* | [as modifier] *a graffiti artist.*
▶**verb** [with obj.] **1** write or draw graffiti on (something): *he and another artist graffitied an entire train.*
■write (words or drawings) as graffiti.
– DERIVATIVES **graffitist** noun.
– ORIGIN mid 19th cent.: from Italian (plural), from *graffio* 'a scratch'.

USAGE In Italian the word **graffiti** is a plural noun and its singular form is **graffito**. Traditionally, the same distinction has been maintained in English, so that **graffiti**, being plural, would require a plural verb: *the **graffiti were** all over the wall.* By the same token, the singular would require a singular verb: *there **was** a **graffito** on the wall.* Today, these distinctions survive in some specialist fields such as archaeology but sound odd to most native speakers. The most common modern use is to treat **graffiti** as if it were a mass noun, similar to a word like **writing**, and not to use **graffito** at all. In this case, **graffiti** takes a singular verb, as in *the **graffiti was** all over the wall.* Such uses are now widely accepted as standard, and may be regarded as part of the natural development of the language, rather than as mistakes. A similar process is going on with other words such as **agenda**, **data**, and **media**.

graft[1] ▶ **noun 1** Horticulture a shoot or scion inserted into a slit of stock, from which it receives sap.
■an instance of inserting a shoot or scion in this way.
2 Medicine a piece of living tissue that is transplanted surgically.
■a surgical operation in which tissue is transplanted.
▶**verb** [with obj. and adverbial] **1** Horticulture insert (a scion) as a graft: *it was common to graft different varieties on to a single tree trunk.*
■insert a graft on (a stock).
2 Medicine transplant (living tissue) as a graft: *they can graft a new hand on to the nerve ends.*
■figurative insert or fix (something) permanently to something else, typically in a way considered inappropriate: *western-style government could not easily be **grafted on to** a profoundly different country.*
– ORIGIN late Middle English *graff*, from Old French *grafe*, via Latin from Greek *graphion* 'stylus, writing implement' (with reference to the tapered tip of the scion), from *graphein* 'write'. The final *-t* is typical of phonetic confusion between *-f* and *-ft* at the end of words; compare with **TUFT**.

graft[2] Brit. informal ▶ **noun** [mass noun] hard work: *turning those dreams into reality was sheer hard graft.*
▶**verb** [no obj.] work hard: *I need people prepared to go out and graft.*
– DERIVATIVES **grafter** noun.
– ORIGIN mid 19th cent.: perhaps related to the phrase *spade's graft* 'the amount of earth that one stroke of a spade will move', based on Old Norse *grǫftr* 'digging'.

graft[3] ▶ **noun** [mass noun] practices, especially bribery, used to secure illicit gains in politics or business; corruption: *sweeping measures to curb official graft.*
■such gains: *government officials grow fat off bribes and graft.*
▶**verb** [no obj.] make money by shady or dishonest means.
– DERIVATIVES **grafter** noun.
– ORIGIN mid 19th cent.: of unknown origin.

Grafton /ˈgrɑːftən/, Augustus Henry Fitzroy, 3rd Duke of (1735–1811), British Whig statesman, Prime Minister 1768–70.

graft union ▶ **noun** the point on a plant where the graft is joined to the rootstock.

Graham[1], Martha (1893–1991), American dancer, teacher, and choreographer. She evolved a new dance language using more flexible movements intended to express psychological complexities and emotional power.

Graham[2], Thomas (1805–69), Scottish physical chemist. He studied diffusion and osmosis, coining the word *osmose* (now *osmosis*) and *colloid* in its modern chemical sense.

Graham[3], Billy (b.1918), American evangelical preacher; full name *William Franklin Graham*. He is world famous as a mass evangelist.

graham ▶ **adjective** [attrib.] N. Amer. denoting unsifted wholewheat flour, or biscuits or bread made from this: *a box of graham crackers.*
– ORIGIN mid 19th cent.: named after Sylvester *Graham* (1794–1851), an American advocate of dietary reform.

Grahame, Kenneth (1859–1932), Scottish-born writer of children's stories, resident in England from 1864. He is remembered for the children's classic *The Wind in the Willows* (1908).

Graham Land the northern part of the Antarctic Peninsula, the only part of Antarctica lying outside the Antarctic Circle. Discovered in 1831–2 by the English navigator John Biscoe (1794–1843), it now forms part of British Antarctic Territory, but is claimed also by Chile and Argentina.

Graham's law Chemistry a law stating that the rates of diffusion and effusion of a gas are inversely proportional to the square root of the density of the gas.
– ORIGIN mid 19th cent.: named after T. *Graham* (see **GRAHAM**[2]).

Grail (also **Holy Grail**) ▶ **noun** (in medieval legend) the cup or platter used by Christ at the Last Supper, and in which Joseph of Arimathea received Christ's blood at the Cross. Quests for it undertaken by medieval knights are described in versions of the Arthurian legends written from the early 13th century onward.
■figurative a thing which is being earnestly pursued or sought after: *profit has become the holy grail.*
– ORIGIN from Old French *graal*, from medieval Latin *gradalis* 'dish'.

grain ▶ **noun 1** [mass noun] wheat or any other cultivated cereal used as food.
■the seeds of such cereals: [as modifier] *grain exports.*
2 a single fruit or seed of a cereal: *a few grains of corn.*
■a small hard particle of a substance such as salt or sand: *a **grain** of salt.* ■ the smallest possible quantity or amount of a quality: *there wasn't **a grain of truth** in what he said.* ■ a discrete particle or crystal in a metal, igneous rock, etc., typically visible only when a surface is magnified. ■ a piece of solid propellant for use in a rocket engine.
3 (abbrev.: **gr.**) the smallest unit of weight in the troy and avoirdupois systems, equal to 1⁄5760 of a pound troy and 1⁄7000 of a pound avoirdupois (approximately 0.0648 grams). [ORIGIN: because originally the weight was equivalent to that of a grain of corn.]
4 [mass noun] the longitudinal arrangement or pattern of fibres in wood, paper, etc.: *he scored **along the grain** of the table with the knife.*
■roughness in texture of wood, stone, etc.; the arrangement and size of constituent particles: *the lighter, finer grain of the wood is attractive.* ■ the rough or wrinkled outer surface of leather, or of a similar artificial material. ■ Mining lamination or planes of cleavage in materials such as stone and coal. ■ Photography a granular appearance of a photograph or negative, which is in proportion to the size of the emulsion particles composing it.
5 archaic a person's character or natural tendency.
6 [mass noun] historical kermes or cochineal, or dye made from either of these. [ORIGIN: the kermes was thought to consist of grains.]
▶**verb** [with obj.] **1** (usu. **be grained**) give a rough surface or texture to: *her fingers were **grained with** chalk dust.*
■[no obj.] form into grains: *if the sugar does grain up, add more water.*
2 [usu. as noun **graining**] paint (especially furniture or interior surfaces) in imitation of the grain of wood or marble: *the art of graining and marbling.*
3 remove hair from (a hide): [as adj. **grained**] *the boots were of best grained leather.*
4 N. Amer. feed (a horse) on grain.
– PHRASES **against the grain** contrary to the natural inclination or feeling of someone or something: *it **goes against the grain** to tell outright lies.*
– DERIVATIVES **grained** adjective [usu. in combination] *coarse-grained sandstone*, **grainer** noun, **grainless** adjective.
– ORIGIN Middle English (originally in the sense 'seed, grain of corn'): from Old French *grain*, from Latin *granum*.

grain beetle ▶ **noun** a small beetle which infests grain stores and warehouses.
• Cucujidae and other families: several species, in particular the tropical **saw-toothed grain beetle** (*Oryzaephilus surinamensis*), now found worldwide.

grain borer ▶ **noun** a beetle that feeds on grain and rice and is a common pest of granaries and flour mills.
• Family Bostrichidae: several species, including the tropical **lesser grain borer** (*Rhizopertha dominica*), now found worldwide.

Grainger /ˈgreɪndʒə/, (George) Percy (Aldridge) (1882–1961), Australian-born American composer and pianist. From 1901 he lived in London, where he collected, edited, and arranged English folk songs. Notable works: *Shepherd's Hey* (1911).

grain leather ▶ **noun** [mass noun] leather dressed with the grain side outwards.

grain side ▶ **noun** the side of a hide on which the hair was.

grains of Paradise ▶ **plural noun** the seeds of a West African plant of the ginger family, resembling those of cardamom and used as a spice and in herbal medicine. Also called **MALAGUETTA**.
• The plant is *Aframomum melegueta*, family Zingiberaceae.

grain weevil ▶ **noun** a weevil that is a common pest of stored grain, which is eaten by the larvae.
• *Sitophilus granarius*, family Curculionidae.

grain whisky ▶ **noun** [mass noun] whisky made mainly from unmalted wheat or maize.

grainy ▶ **adjective** (**grainier**, **grainiest**) **1** granular: *a juicy, grainy texture.*
■Photography showing visible grains of emulsion, as characteristic of old photographs or modern high-speed film. ■ (of sound, especially recorded music or a voice) having a rough or gravelly quality: *the grainy sound of bootleg cassettes.* ■ (of food) containing whole grains: *a good grainy loaf.*
2 (of wood) having prominent grain.
– DERIVATIVES **graininess** noun.

gralloch /ˈgraləx/ ▶ **noun** [mass noun] the viscera of a dead deer.
▶**verb** [with obj.] disembowel (a deer that has been shot).
– ORIGIN mid 19th cent.: from Scottish Gaelic *grealach* 'entrails'.

gram[1] (Brit. also **gramme**) (abbrev.: **g**) ▶ **noun** a metric unit of mass equal to one thousandth of a kilogram.
– ORIGIN late 18th cent.: from French *gramme*, from late Latin *gramma* 'a small weight', from Greek.

gram[2] ▶ **noun** [mass noun] chickpeas or other pulses used as food.
– ORIGIN early 18th cent.: from Portuguese *grão*, from Latin *granum* 'grain'.

gram[3] ▶ **noun** variant of **GRAMMA**.

-gram[1] ▶ **combining form** in nouns denoting something written or recorded (especially in a certain way): *cryptogram* | *heliogram.*
– DERIVATIVES **-grammatic** combining form in corresponding adjectives.
– ORIGIN from Greek *gramma* 'thing written, letter of the alphabet', from *graphein* 'write'.

-gram[2] ▶ **combining form** in nouns denoting a person paid to deliver a novelty greeting or message as a humorous surprise for the recipient: *kissogram.*
– ORIGIN on the pattern of *telegram*.

gramadoelas /ˈxramadʊləz, -las/ (also **gamadoelas**) ▶ **plural noun** [treated as sing.] S. African informal wild, remote country: *they were stuck in the parched gramadoelas, kilometres from anywhere.*
– ORIGIN Afrikaans, of unknown origin.

gramicidin /ˌgramɪˈsʌɪdɪn/ ▶ **noun** [mass noun] Medicine an antibiotic with a wide range of activity, used in many medicinal preparations.
• This antibiotic is obtained from the bacterium *Bacillus brevis*.

graminaceous /ˌgramɪˈneɪʃəs/ ▶ **adjective** Botany of, relating to, or denoting plants of the grass family (Gramineae).
– ORIGIN mid 19th cent.: from Latin *gramen*, *gramin-* 'grass' + **-ACEOUS**.

graminivorous /ˌgramɪˈnɪv(ə)rəs/ ▶ **adjective** Zoology (of an animal) feeding on grass.
– ORIGIN mid 18th cent.: from Latin *gramen*, *gramin-* 'grass' + **-VOROUS**.

gramma (also **gram**) ▶ **noun** N. Amer. informal one's grandmother.

grammalogue /ˈgraməlɒg/ ▶ noun (in shorthand) a word represented by a single sign or symbol.
– ORIGIN mid 19th cent.: formed irregularly from Greek *gramma* 'letter of the alphabet, thing written' + *logos* 'word', on the pattern of words such as *catalogue*.

grammar ▶ noun 1 [mass noun] the whole system and structure of a language or of languages in general, usually taken as consisting of syntax and morphology (including inflections) and sometimes also phonology and semantics. ■ [usu. with modifier] a particular analysis of the system and structure of language or of a specific language. ■ [count noun] a book on grammar: *my old Latin grammar*. ■ a set of actual or presumed prescriptive notions about correct use of a language: *it was not bad grammar, just dialect*. ■ the basic elements of an area of knowledge or skill: *the grammar of wine*. ■ Computing a set of rules governing what strings are valid or allowable in a language or text.
2 Brit. informal a grammar school.
– ORIGIN late Middle English: from Old French *gramaire*, via Latin from Greek *grammatikē (tekhnē)* '(art) of letters', from *gramma*, *grammat-* 'letter of the alphabet, thing written'.

grammarian /grəˈmɛːrɪən/ ▶ noun a person who studies and writes about grammar.
– ORIGIN Middle English: from Old French *gramarien*, from *gramaire* (see GRAMMAR).

grammar school ▶ noun 1 (in the UK) a state secondary school to which pupils are admitted on the basis of ability. Since 1965 most have been absorbed into the comprehensive school system. ■ historical a school founded in or before the 16th century for teaching Latin, later becoming a secondary school teaching academic subjects.
2 US another term for ELEMENTARY SCHOOL.

grammatical /grəˈmatɪk(ə)l/ ▶ adjective of or relating to grammar: *grammatical analysis* | *the grammatical function of a verb*. ■ well formed; in accordance with the productive rules of the grammar of a language: *a grammatical sentence*.
– DERIVATIVES **grammaticality** noun, **grammatically** adverb, **grammaticalness** noun.
– ORIGIN early 16th cent.: from late Latin *grammaticalis*, via Latin from Greek *grammatikos*, from *gramma*, *grammatos* 'letter of the alphabet, thing written'.

grammaticalize (also **-ise**) ▶ verb [with obj.] Linguistics change (an element) from being one having lexical meaning into one having a largely grammatical function.
– DERIVATIVES **grammaticalization** noun.

gramme ▶ noun variant spelling of GRAM¹.

Grammy ▶ noun (pl. **Grammys** or **Grammies**) each of a number of annual awards given by the American National Academy of Recording Arts and Sciences for achievement in the record industry.
– ORIGIN 1950s: blend of GRAMOPHONE and EMMY.

Gram-negative ▶ adjective see GRAM STAIN.

gramophone ▶ noun old-fashioned term for RECORD PLAYER.
– DERIVATIVES **gramophonic** adjective.
– ORIGIN late 19th cent.: formed by inversion of elements of *phonogram* 'sound recording'.

gramophone record ▶ noun fuller form of RECORD (in sense 4).

gramp (also **gramps**, **grampy**) ▶ noun dialect or informal one's grandfather.
– ORIGIN late 19th cent.: contraction of GRANDPAPA.

Grampian /ˈgrampɪən/ a former local government region in NE Scotland, dissolved in 1996.

Grampian Mountains (also **the Grampians**) 1 a mountain range in north central Scotland. Its southern edge forms a natural boundary between the Highlands and the Lowlands.
2 a mountain range in SE Australia, in Victoria. It forms a spur of the Great Dividing Range at its western extremity.

Gram-positive ▶ adjective see GRAM STAIN.

grampus /ˈgrampəs/ ▶ noun (pl. **grampuses**) 1 a cetacean of the dolphin family, in particular: ■ another term for RISSO'S DOLPHIN. ■ another term for KILLER WHALE.
2 Brit. used in comparisons to convey the fact that someone is breathing heavily and loudly: *he was now puffing like a grampus*.
– ORIGIN early 16th cent.: alteration (by association with GRAND 'big') of Old French *grapois*, from

medieval Latin *craspiscis*, from Latin *crassus piscis* 'fat fish'.

Gramsci /ˈgramʃi/, Antonio (1891–1937), Italian political theorist and activist, co-founder and leader of the Italian Communist Party. Imprisoned in 1926 when the Fascists banned the Communist Party, he died shortly after his release. *Letters from Prison* (1947) remains an important work.

Gram stain ▶ noun [mass noun] Medicine a staining technique for the preliminary identification of bacteria, in which a violet dye is applied, followed by a decolorizing agent and then a red dye. The cell walls of certain bacteria (denoted **Gram-positive**) retain the first dye and appear violet, while those that lose it (denoted **Gram-negative**) appear red.
– ORIGIN late 19th cent.: named after Hans C. J. Gram (1853–1938), the Danish physician who devised the method.

gran ▶ noun informal, chiefly Brit. one's grandmother.
– ORIGIN mid 19th cent.: abbreviation.

grana /ˈɡrɑːnə, ˈɡreɪnə/ ▶ plural noun (sing. **granum**) Botany the stacks of thylakoids embedded in the stroma of a chloroplast.
– ORIGIN late 19th cent.: plural of Latin *granum* 'grain'.

Granada /grəˈnɑːdə, Spanish graˈnaða/ 1 a city in Andalusia in southern Spain; pop. 286,700 (1991). Founded in the 8th century, it became the capital of the Moorish kingdom of Granada in 1238. It is the site of the Alhambra palace.
2 a city in Nicaragua, on the NW shore of Lake Nicaragua; pop. 88,600 (1985). Founded by the Spanish in 1523, it is the oldest city in the country.

granadilla /ɡran-/ (also **grenadilla**) ▶ noun a passion fruit, or the fruit of a related plant. ● This fruit comes from plants of the genus *Passiflora*, family Passifloraceae, including the **giant granadilla** (*P. quadrangularis*), which has large pale fruits.
– ORIGIN late 16th cent.: Spanish, diminutive of *granada* 'pomegranate'.

granary ▶ noun (pl. **-ies**) 1 a storehouse for threshed grain. ■ a region producing large quantities of corn.
2 short for GRANARY BREAD.
– ORIGIN late 16th cent.: from Latin *granarium*, from *granum* 'grain'.

granary bread ▶ noun [mass noun] trademark a type of brown bread containing whole grains of wheat.

Gran Canaria /ˌɡran kəˈnɛːrɪə, Spanish ɡran kaˈnarja/ a volcanic island off the NW coast of Africa, one of the Canary Islands. Its chief town, Las Palmas, is the capital of the Canary Islands.

Gran Chaco /ɡran ˈtʃakəʊ/ (also **Chaco**) a lowland plain in central South America, extending from southern Bolivia through Paraguay to northern Argentina.

grand ▶ adjective 1 magnificent and imposing in appearance, size, or style: *a grand country house* | *the dinner party was very grand*. ■ designed to impress through scale or splendour: *make a grand gesture*. ■ (of a person) of high rank and with an appearance and manner appropriate to it: *she was such a grand lady*. ■ large or ambitious in scope or scale: *his grand design for the future of Europe* | *collecting on a grand scale*. ■ used in names of places or buildings to suggest size or splendour: *the Grand Canyon* | *the Grand Hotel*.
2 [attrib.] denoting the largest or most important item of its kind: *the grand entrance*. ■ of the highest rank (used especially in official titles): *the Grand Vizier*. ■ Law (of a crime) serious: *grand theft*. Compare with PETTY (in sense 2).
3 informal very good or enjoyable; excellent: *we had a grand day*.
4 [in combination] (in names of family relationships) denoting one generation removed in ascent or descent: *a grand-niece*.
▶ noun 1 (pl. same) informal a thousand dollars or pounds: *he gets thirty-five grand a year*.
2 a grand piano.
– PHRASES **a** (or **the**) **grand old man of** a man long and highly respected in (a particular field): *a grand old man of Scottish local government*.
– DERIVATIVES **grandly** adverb, **grandness** noun.
– ORIGIN Middle English: from Old French *grant*, *grand*, from Latin *grandis* 'full-grown, big, great'. The original uses were to denote family relationships (sense 4, following Old French usage) and as a title (*the Grand*, translating Old French *le*

Grand); hence the senses 'of the highest rank', 'of great importance'.

grandad (also **granddad**) ▶ noun 1 informal one's grandfather. ■ a form of address to an elderly man: *cheer up, grandad, it may never happen*.
2 [as modifier] denoting a style of shirt or shirt neckline with a collar in the form of a narrow upright band fastened with buttons.

grandam /ˈɡrandam/ (also **grandame**) ▶ noun archaic term for GRANDMOTHER. ■ an old woman. ■ a female ancestor.
– ORIGIN Middle English: from Anglo-Norman French *graund dame* (see GRAND, DAME). Of the English terms of relationship formed with *grand*, this is the oldest.

grand apartheid ▶ noun [mass noun] historical (in South Africa) a form of apartheid, prevalent in the 1960s and 1970s, which involved comprehensive racial segregation and measures such as the removal of black people from white areas and the creation of black homelands.

grand-aunt ▶ noun another term for GREAT-AUNT.

Grand Banks a submarine plateau of the continental shelf off the SE coast of Newfoundland, Canada. It is a meeting place of the warm Gulf Stream and the cold Labrador Current; this promotes the growth of plankton, making the waters an important feeding area for fish.

grand battement /ɡrɒ̃/ ▶ noun Ballet a movement in which both legs are kept straight and one leg is kicked outwards from the body and in again.

Grand Canal 1 a series of waterways in eastern China, extending from Beijing southwards to Hangzhou, a distance of 1,700 km (1,060 miles). Its original purpose was to transport rice from the river valleys to the cities. Its construction proceeded in stages between 486 BC and AD 1327.
2 the main waterway of Venice in Italy. It is lined on each side by fine palaces and spanned by the Rialto Bridge.

Grand Canyon a deep gorge in Arizona, formed by the Colorado River. It is about 440 km (277 miles) long, 8 to 24 km (5 to 15 miles) wide, and, in places, 1,800 m (6,000 ft) deep. The area was designated a national park in 1919.

Grand Canyon State informal name for ARIZONA.

grandchild ▶ noun (pl. **-children**) a child of one's son or daughter.

grand cross ▶ noun Astrology an arrangement of four planets in which each is in opposition to one other planet and square to the other two, forming a cross.

grand cru /ɡrɒ̃ ˈkruː French ɡrɑ̃ kry/ ▶ noun (pl. **grands crus** pronunc. same) (chiefly in French official classifications) a wine of the most superior grade, or the vineyard which produces it. Compare with PREMIER CRU.
– ORIGIN French, literally 'great growth'.

granddad ▶ noun variant spelling of GRANDAD.

granddaughter ▶ noun a daughter of one's son or daughter.

grand duchess ▶ noun the wife or widow of a grand duke. ■ a princess or noblewoman ruling over a territory in certain European countries. ■ historical a daughter (or son's daughter) of a Russian tsar.

grand duchy ▶ noun a state or territory ruled by a grand duke or duchess.

grand duke ▶ noun a prince or nobleman ruling over a territory in certain European countries. ■ historical a son (or son's son) of a Russian tsar.

Grande Comore /ˌɡrɒd kəˈmɔː/ the largest of the islands of the Comoros, off the NW coast of Madagascar; pop. 233,500 (1991); chief town (and capital of the Comoros), Moroni.

grande dame /ɡrɒd ˈdam/ ▶ noun a woman of influential position within a particular sphere: *the grande dame of British sculpture*.
– ORIGIN French, literally 'grand lady'.

grandee /ɡranˈdiː/ ▶ noun a Spanish or Portuguese nobleman of the highest rank. ■ a person of high rank or eminence: *several City grandees and eminent lawyers*.
– ORIGIN late 16th cent.: from Spanish and

Portuguese *grande* 'grand', used as a noun. The change of ending was due to association with **-EE**.

grande horizontale /ˌgrɒd ˌprizɒ̃'tɑːl/ ▶ **noun** (pl. **grandes horizontales** pronunc. same) humorous a prostitute.
– ORIGIN late 19th cent.: French, literally 'great horizontal'.

grandeur /'grandjə, -(d)ʒə/ ▶ **noun** [mass noun] splendour and impressiveness, especially of appearance or style: *the austere grandeur of mountain scenery.*
■ high rank or social importance: *for all their grandeur, the chancellors were still officials of the household.*
– ORIGIN late 16th cent. (denoting tall stature): from French, from *grand* 'great, grand' (see **GRAND**).

grandfather ▶ **noun** the father of one's father or mother.
■ the person who founded or originated something: *Freud is often called the grandfather of psychoanalysis.*
▶ **verb** [with obj.] N. Amer. informal exempt (someone or something) from a new law or regulation: *smokers who worked here before the ban have been grandfathered.*
– DERIVATIVES **grandfatherly** adjective.

grandfather clause ▶ **noun** N. Amer. informal a clause exempting certain pre-existing classes of people or things from the requirements of a piece of legislation.

grandfather clock ▶ **noun** a clock in a tall free-standing wooden case, driven by weights.

Grand Fleet historical the main British naval fleet, either that based at Spithead in the 18th century or that based at Scapa Flow in the First World War.

Grand Guignol /ˌgrɒ giː'njɒl, French grɑ̃ ɡiɲɔl/ ▶ **noun** a dramatic entertainment of a sensational or horrific nature, originally a sequence of short pieces as performed at the Grand Guignol theatre in Paris.
– ORIGIN French, literally 'Great Punch'.

grandiflora /ˌgrandɪ'flɔːrə/ ▶ **adjective** [attrib.] (of a cultivated plant) bearing large flowers.
▶ **noun** a grandiflora plant.
– ORIGIN early 20th cent.: modern Latin (often used in specific names of large-flowered plants), from Latin *grandis* 'great' + *flos, flor-* 'flower'.

grandiloquent /gran'dɪləkwənt/ ▶ **adjective** pompous or extravagant in language, style, or manner, especially in a way that is intended to impress: *a grandiloquent celebration of Spanish glory.*
– DERIVATIVES **grandiloquence** noun, **grandiloquently** adverb.
– ORIGIN late 16th cent.: from Latin *grandiloquus* literally 'grand-speaking', from *grandis* 'grand' + *loqui* 'speak'. The ending was altered in English by association with **ELOQUENT**.

Grand Inquisitor ▶ **noun** historical the director of the court of Inquisition, especially in Spain and Portugal.

grandiose /'grandɪəʊs/ ▶ **adjective** impressive or magnificent in appearance or style, especially pretentiously so: *the court's grandiose facade.*
■ conceived on a very grand or ambitious scale: *grandiose plans to reform the world.*
– DERIVATIVES **grandiosely** adverb, **grandiosity** noun.
– ORIGIN mid 19th cent.: from French, from Italian *grandioso*, from *grande* 'grand'.

grand jeté /ˌgrɒ ʒ(ə)'teɪ, ʒə'teɪ/ ▶ **noun** Ballet a jump in which a dancer springs from one foot to land on the other with one leg forward of their body and the other stretched backwards while in the air.

grand jury ▶ **noun** US Law a jury, normally of twenty-three jurors, selected to examine the validity of an accusation prior to trial.

grand larceny ▶ **noun** [mass noun] Law (in many US states and formerly in Britain) theft of personal property having a value above a legally specified amount.

grandma ▶ **noun** informal one's grandmother.

grand mal /grɒ 'mal/ ▶ **noun** [mass noun] a serious form of epilepsy with muscle spasms and prolonged loss of consciousness. Compare with **PETIT MAL**.
■ [count noun] an epileptic fit of this kind.
– ORIGIN late 19th cent.: from French, literally 'great sickness'.

grandmama (also **grandmamma**) ▶ **noun** archaic form of **GRANDMA**.

Grandma Moses see **MOSES**[2].

grand manner ▶ **noun** (**the grand manner**) a style

considered appropriate for noble and stately matters: *formal dining in the grand manner.*
■ (**the Grand Manner**) the lofty and rhetorical manner of historical painting exemplified by Raphael and Poussin.

Grand Marnier /grɒ 'mɑːnɪeɪ/ ▶ **noun** [mass noun] trademark an orange-flavoured cognac-based liqueur.
– ORIGIN French.

grand master ▶ **noun 1** (usu. **grandmaster**) a chess player of the highest class, especially one who has won an international tournament.
2 (**Grand Master**) the head of an order of chivalry or of Freemasons.

grandmother ▶ **noun** the mother of one's father or mother.
– PHRASES **teach one's grandmother to suck eggs** presume to advise a more experienced person.
– DERIVATIVES **grandmotherly** adjective.

grandmother clock ▶ **noun** a clock similar to a grandfather clock but about two thirds the size.

grandmother's footsteps ▶ **plural noun** [treated as sing.] Brit. a children's game in which one stands with their back to the others, who creep up with the aim of touching the lone child on the back without being seen to move whenever he or she unexpectedly turns around.

Grand National an annual horse race established in 1839, a steeplechase run over a course of 4 miles 856 yards (about 7,200 metres) with thirty jumps, at Aintree, Liverpool, in late March or early April.

grand-nephew ▶ **noun** another term for **GREAT-NEPHEW**.

grand-niece ▶ **noun** another term for **GREAT-NIECE**.

grand opera ▶ **noun** an opera on a serious theme in which the entire libretto (including dialogue) is sung.
■ [mass noun] the genre of such opera.

grandpa ▶ **noun** informal one's grandfather.

grandpapa ▶ **noun** old-fashioned term for **GRANDFATHER**.

grandpappy ▶ **noun** (pl. **-ies**) North American term for **GRANDFATHER**.

grandparent ▶ **noun** a parent of one's father or mother; a grandmother or grandfather.
– DERIVATIVES **grandparental** adjective, **grandparenthood** noun.

Grand Penitentiary ▶ **noun** (in the Roman Catholic Church) a cardinal presiding over the penitentiary.

grand piano ▶ **noun** a large, full-toned piano which has the body, strings, and soundboard arranged horizontally and in line with the keys and is supported by three legs.

Grand Prix /grɒ 'priː/ ▶ **noun** (pl. **Grands Prix** pronunc. same) an important sporting event in which participants compete for a major prize.
■ any of a series of motor-racing or motorcycling contests forming part of a world championship series, held in various countries under international rules. ■ (in full **Grand Prix de Paris**) an international horse race for three-year-olds, founded in 1863 and run annually in June at Longchamps, Paris.
– ORIGIN mid 19th cent.: French, literally 'great or chief prize'.

grand seigneur /ˌgrɒ seɪ'njɜː/ ▶ **noun** a man whose rank or position allows him to command others.
– ORIGIN French, literally 'great lord'.

grand serjeanty ▶ **noun** see **SERJEANTY**.

grand siècle /ˌgrɒ sɪ'ɛkl(ə), French grɑ̃ sjɛkl/ ▶ **noun** the reign of Louis XIV, seen as France's period of political and cultural pre-eminence.
– ORIGIN French, literally 'great century or age'.

grandsire ▶ **noun 1** archaic term for **GRANDFATHER**.
2 Bell-ringing a particular method of change-ringing involving an odd number of bells.

grand slam ▶ **noun** the winning of each of a group of major championships or matches in a particular sport in the same year, in particular in tennis, golf, or rugby union.
■ Bridge the bidding and winning of all thirteen tricks. ■ Baseball a home run hit when each of the three bases is occupied by a runner, thus scoring four runs.
– ORIGIN early 19th cent. (as a term in cards, especially bridge): from **SLAM**[2].

grandson ▶ **noun** the son of one's son or daughter.

grandstand ▶ **noun** the main stand, usually roofed, commanding the best view for spectators at racecourses or sports grounds.
■ [as modifier] (of a view) seen from an advantageous position, as if from a grandstand: *our balcony gave us a grandstand view of the arena.*
▶ **verb** [no obj.] [usu. as noun **grandstanding**] derogatory seek to attract applause or favourable attention from spectators or the media: *they accused him of political grandstanding.*

grandstand finish ▶ **noun** (in sport) a close or exciting finish to a race or competition.

grand total ▶ **noun** the final amount after everything is added up; the sum of other totals.

grand tour ▶ **noun** historical a cultural tour of Europe conventionally undertaken, especially in the 18th century, by a young man of the upper classes as a part of his education.

grand tourer ▶ **noun** dated a car designed for comfortable long-distance touring.

grand trine ▶ **noun** Astrology an arrangement of three planets in which each planet is in trine with the other two, forming an equilateral triangle.

grand-uncle ▶ **noun** another term for **GREAT-UNCLE**.

grand unified theory ▶ **noun** Physics a theory attempting to give a single explanation of the strong, weak, and electromagnetic interactions between subatomic particles.

grange ▶ **noun** [usu. in names] Brit. a country house with farm buildings attached: *Biddulph Grange.*
■ historical an outlying farm with tithe barns belonging to a monastery or feudal lord. ■ archaic a barn.
– ORIGIN Middle English (in the sense 'granary, barn'): from Old French, from medieval Latin *granica (villa)* 'grain house or farm', based on Latin *granum* 'grain'.

grangerize /'greɪn(d)ʒəraɪz/ (also **-ise**) ▶ **verb** [with obj.] [usu. as adj. **grangerized**] illustrate (a book) by later insertion of material, especially prints cut from other works.
– DERIVATIVES **grangerization** noun.
– ORIGIN late 19th cent.: from the name J. *Granger* (1723–76), English biographer.

graniferous /grə'nɪf(ə)rəs/ ▶ **adjective** Botany (of a plant) producing grain or a grain-like seed.
– ORIGIN mid 17th cent.: from Latin *granum* 'grain' + **-FEROUS**.

granita /grə'niːtə/ ▶ **noun** (pl. **granite** /-'niːteɪ/) a coarse Italian-style water ice.
■ a drink made with crushed ice.
– ORIGIN Italian.

granite /'granɪt/ ▶ **noun** [mass noun] a very hard, granular, crystalline, igneous rock consisting mainly of quartz, mica, and feldspar and often used as a building stone.
■ used in similes and metaphors to refer to something very hard and impenetrable: [as modifier] *a man with granite determination.*
– DERIVATIVES **granitic** adjective, **granitoid** adjective & noun.
– ORIGIN mid 17th cent.: from Italian *granito*, literally 'grained', from *grano* 'grain', from Latin *granum*.

Granite State informal name for **NEW HAMPSHIRE**.

graniteware ▶ **noun** [mass noun] a speckled form of earthenware imitating the appearance of granite.
■ a kind of enamelled ironware.

granitize (also **-ise**) ▶ **verb** [with obj.] [usu. as adj. **granitized**] Geology alter (rock) so as to give it a granitic character.
– DERIVATIVES **granitization** noun.

granivorous /grə'nɪv(ə)rəs/ ▶ **adjective** Zoology (of an animal) feeding on grain.
– DERIVATIVES **granivore** noun.
– ORIGIN mid 17th cent.: from Latin *granum* 'grain' + **-VOROUS**.

granny (also **grannie**) ▶ **noun** (pl. **-ies**) informal one's grandmother.
– ORIGIN mid 17th cent.: from *grannam* (representing a colloquial pronunciation of **GRANDAM**) + **-Y**[2].

granny bond ▶ **noun** Brit. informal a form of index-linked National Savings certificate, originally available only to pensioners.

granny flat ▶ **noun** informal a part of a house made

into self-contained accommodation suitable for an elderly relative.

granny gear ▶ noun informal the lowest gear on a bicycle.

granny glasses ▶ plural noun informal round steel-rimmed or gold-rimmed glasses.

granny knot ▶ noun a reef knot with the ends crossed the wrong way and therefore liable to slip.

Granny Smith ▶ noun a dessert apple of a bright green variety with crisp sharp-flavoured flesh, originating in Australia.
– ORIGIN late 19th cent.: named after Maria Ann (*Granny*) *Smith* (c.1801–1870), who first produced such apples.

granodiorite /ˌgranə(ʊ)'dʌɪərʌɪt/ ▶ noun [mass noun] Geology a coarse-grained plutonic rock containing quartz and plagioclase, between granite and diorite in composition.
– ORIGIN late 19th cent.: from GRANITE + DIORITE.

granola /grə'nəʊlə/ ▶ noun [mass noun] N. Amer. a kind of breakfast cereal resembling muesli.
■ [as modifier] chiefly derogatory denoting those with liberal or Green political views, typified as eating health foods.
– ORIGIN late 19th cent. (as a trademark): from *gran-* (representing GRANULAR or GRAIN) + *-ola* (suffix chiefly in US usage). The current term dates from the 1970s.

granolithic /ˌgranə(ʊ)'lɪθɪk/ ▶ adjective (of concrete) containing fine granite chippings or crushed granite, used to render floors and surfaces.
■ (of a floor or surface) rendered with such concrete.
▶ noun [mass noun] granolithic concrete or rendering.
– ORIGIN late 19th cent.: from *grano-* (irregular combining form from Latin *granum* 'grain') + Greek *lithos* 'stone' + -IC.

granophyre /ˈgranə(ʊ)ˌfʌɪə/ ▶ noun [mass noun] Geology a granitic rock consisting of intergrown feldspar and quartz crystals in a medium- to fine-grained groundmass.
– DERIVATIVES **granophyric** /ˌgranə(ʊ)'fɪrɪk/ adjective.
– ORIGIN late 19th cent.: from German *Granophyr*, from *Granit* 'granite'+ *Porphyr* (see PORPHYRY).

Grant[1], Cary (1904–86), British-born American actor; born *Alexander Archibald Leach*. He acted in more than seventy films, including *Holiday* (1938) and *The Philadelphia Story* (1940).

Grant[2], Duncan (James Corrow) (1885–1978), Scottish painter and designer, a pioneer of abstract art in Britain. He was a cousin of Lytton Strachey and a member of the Bloomsbury Group.

Grant[3], Ulysses S. (1822–85), American general and 18th President of the US 1869–77; born *Hiram Ulysses Grant*; full name *Ulysses Simpson Grant*. As supreme commander of the Unionist armies, he defeated the Confederate army in 1865 with a policy of attrition.

grant ▶ verb [with two objs] **1** agree to give or allow (something requested) to: *they were granted a meeting.*
■ give (a right, power, property, etc.) formally or legally to: *they will grant you asylum.*
2 agree or admit to (someone) that (something) is true: *he hasn't made much progress, I'll grant you that.*
▶ noun a sum of money given by an organization, especially a government, for a particular purpose.
■ [mass noun] formal the action of granting something: *we had to recommend the grant or refusal of broadcasting licences.* ■ Law a legal conveyance or formal conferment: *a grant of land | a grant of probate.*
– PHRASES **take someone or something for granted** fail to appreciate someone or something that is very familiar or obvious: *the comforts that people take for granted.* ■ (**take something for granted**) assume that something is true without questioning it: *people no longer took for granted everything about Christianity.*
– DERIVATIVES **grantable** adjective, **granter** noun.
– ORIGIN Middle English: from Old French *granter* 'consent to support', variant of *creanter* 'to guarantee', based on Latin *credere* 'entrust'.

grant aid Brit. ▶ noun [mass noun] financial assistance, especially money that is granted by central government to local government or an institution.
▶ verb (**grant-aid**) [with obj.] give such financial assistance to.

granted ▶ adverb [sentence adverb] admittedly; it is true (used to introduce a factor which is opposed to the main line of argument but is not regarded as so strong as to invalidate it): *granted, we are seeing the exceptional, but one fact must be faced.*
▶ conjunction (**granted that**) even assuming that: *granted that officers were used to making decisions, they still couldn't be expected to understand.*

grantee ▶ noun chiefly Law a person to whom a grant or conveyance is made.

Granth /grʌnt/ short for ADI GRANTH.

Grantha /ˈgrʌntə/ ▶ noun a southern Indian alphabet dating from the 5th century AD, used by Tamil brahmans for the Sanskrit transcriptions of their sacred books.
– ORIGIN from Sanskrit *grantha* (see GRANTH).

Granth Sahib another term for ADI GRANTH.

grant-in-aid ▶ noun (pl. **grants-in-aid**) an amount of money given to local government, an institution, or a particular scholar.

grant-maintained ▶ adjective Brit. (of a school) funded by central rather than local government, and self-governing.

grantor ▶ noun chiefly Law a person or institution that makes a grant or conveyance.

gran turismo /ˌgran tʊ'rɪzməʊ/ (abbrev.: GT) ▶ noun (pl. **-os**) a high-performance model of motor car.
– ORIGIN mid 20th cent.: Italian, literally 'great touring'.

granular ▶ adjective resembling or consisting of small grains or particles.
■ having a roughened surface or structure.
– DERIVATIVES **granularity** noun.
– ORIGIN late 18th cent.: from late Latin *granulum* (see GRANULE) + -AR[1].

granulate ▶ verb **1** [with obj.] [usu. as adj. **granulated**] form (something) into grains or particles: *granulated sugar.*
■ [no obj.] (of a substance) take the form of grains or particles: *the syrup would not granulate properly.*
2 [no obj.] [often as adj. **granulating**] Medicine (of a wound or lesion) form multiple small prominences as part of the healing process.
■ [as adj. **granulated**] chiefly Biology having a roughened surface: *the skin is densely granulated.*
– DERIVATIVES **granulation** noun, **granulator** noun.

granule /ˈgranjuːl/ ▶ noun a small compact particle of a substance: *coffee granules.*
– ORIGIN mid 17th cent.: from late Latin *granulum*, diminutive of Latin *granum* 'grain'.

granulite ▶ noun [mass noun] Geology a fine-grained granular metamorphic rock in which the main component minerals are typically feldspars and quartz.
– DERIVATIVES **granulitic** adjective.
– ORIGIN mid 19th cent.: from GRANULE + -ITE[1].

granulocyte /ˈgranjʊlə(ʊ)ˌsʌɪt/ ▶ noun Physiology a white blood cell with secretory granules in its cytoplasm, e.g. an eosinophil or a basophil.
– DERIVATIVES **granulocytic** adjective.
– ORIGIN early 20th cent.: from late Latin *granulum* 'granule' + -CYTE.

granuloma /ˌgranjʊ'ləʊmə/ ▶ noun (pl. **granulomas** or **granulomata** /-mətə/) Medicine a mass of granulation tissue, typically produced in response to infection, inflammation, or the presence of a foreign substance.
– DERIVATIVES **granulomatous** adjective.

granulometric /ˌgranjʊlə(ʊ)'mɛtrɪk/ ▶ adjective relating to the size distribution or measurement of grain sizes in sand, rock, or other deposits.

granum /ˈgrɑːnəm, ˈgreɪnəm/ singular form of GRANA.

Granville-Barker, Harley (1877–1946), English dramatist, critic, theatre director, and actor. His *Prefaces to Shakespeare* (1927–46) influenced subsequent interpretation of Shakespeare's work. Notable plays: *The Voysey Inheritance* (1905).

grape ▶ noun **1** a berry (typically green, purple, or black) growing in clusters on a grapevine, eaten as fruit and used in making wine.
■ (**the grape**) informal wine: *an exploration of the grape.*
2 short for GRAPESHOT.
– DERIVATIVES **grapey** (also **grapy**) adjective.
– ORIGIN Middle English (also in the Old French sense): from Old French, 'bunch of grapes', probably from *graper* 'gather (grapes)', from *grap* 'hook' (denoting an implement used in harvesting grapes), of Germanic origin.

grapefruit ▶ noun (pl. same) **1** a large round yellow citrus fruit with an acid juicy pulp.
2 the tree bearing this fruit.
● *Citrus paradisi*, family Rutaceae.
– ORIGIN early 19th cent.: from GRAPE + FRUIT (probably because the fruits grow in clusters).

grape hyacinth ▶ noun a small Eurasian plant of the lily family, with clusters of small globular blue flowers, cultivated as an ornamental or for use in perfume.
● Genus *Muscari*, family Liliaceae.

grape ivy ▶ noun an evergreen climbing plant of the vine family which is grown as a house plant.
● Genera *Cissus* and *Rhoicissus*, family Vitaceae: several species, in particular *C. rhombifolia* (or *R. rhomboidea*).

grapeseed oil ▶ noun [mass noun] oil extracted from the residue of grapes which have been juiced.

grapeshot ▶ noun [mass noun] historical ammunition consisting of a number of small iron balls fired together from a cannon.

grape sugar ▶ noun [mass noun] dextrose present in or derived from grapes.

grapevine ▶ noun **1** a vine native to both Eurasia and North America, especially one bearing fruit (grapes) used for eating or winemaking. Numerous cultivars and hybrids have been developed for the winemaking industry.
● Genus *Vitis*, family Vitaceae: many species, in particular *V. vinifera* and the American *V. labrusca*.
2 informal used to refer to the circulation of rumours and unofficial information: *I'd heard on the grapevine that the business was nearly settled.*

graph[1] /grɑːf, graf/ ▶ noun a diagram showing the relation between variable quantities, typically of two variables, each measured along one of a pair of axes at right angles.
■ Mathematics a collection of points whose coordinates satisfy a given relation.
▶ verb [with obj.] plot or trace on a graph.
– ORIGIN late 19th cent.: abbreviation of *graphic formula*.

graph[2] /grɑːf, graf/ ▶ noun Linguistics a visual symbol representing a unit of sound or other feature of speech. Graphs include not only letters of the alphabet but also punctuation marks.
– ORIGIN 1930s: from Greek *graphē* 'writing'.

-graph ▶ combining form **1** in nouns denoting something written or drawn in a specified way: *autograph.*
2 in nouns denoting an instrument that records: *seismograph.*
– ORIGIN from French *-graphe*, based on Greek *graphos* 'written, writing'.

grapheme /ˈgrafiːm/ ▶ noun Linguistics the smallest meaningful contrastive unit in a writing system. Compare with PHONEME.
– DERIVATIVES **graphemic** adjective, **graphemically** adverb, **graphemics** noun.
– ORIGIN 1930s: from GRAPH[2] + -EME.

-grapher ▶ combining form indicating a person concerned with a subject denoted by a noun ending in -graphy (such as *geographer* corresponding to *geography*).
– ORIGIN from Greek *-graphos* 'writer' + -ER[1].

graphic ▶ adjective **1** of or relating to visual art, especially involving drawing, engraving, or lettering: *his mature graphic work.*
■ giving a vivid picture with explicit detail: *he gave a graphic description of the torture.* ■ Computing of, relating to, or denoting a visual image: *graphic information such as charts and diagrams.*
2 of or in the form of a graph.
3 [attrib.] Geology of or denoting rocks having a surface texture resembling cuneiform writing.
▶ noun Computing a graphical item displayed on a screen or stored as data.
– DERIVATIVES **graphically** adverb, **graphicness** noun.
– ORIGIN mid 17th cent.: via Latin from Greek *graphikos*, from *graphē* 'writing, drawing'.

-graphic ▶ combining form in adjectives corresponding to nouns ending in -graphy (such as *demographic* corresponding to *demography*).
– DERIVATIVES **-graphically** combining form in corresponding adverbs.
– ORIGIN from or suggested by Greek *-graphikos*, from *graphē* 'writing, drawing'; partly from -GRAPHY or -GRAPH + -IC.

graphicacy /'grafɪkəsi/ ▶ noun [mass noun] the ability to understand and use a map or graph.
– ORIGIN 1960s: from **GRAPHIC**, on the pattern of *literacy* and *numeracy*.

graphical ▶ adjective **1** of, relating to, or in the form of a graph: *flow charts are graphical presentations.*
2 of or relating to visual art or computer graphics: *a high-resolution graphical display.*
– DERIVATIVES **graphically** adverb.

-graphical ▶ combining form equivalent to **-GRAPHIC**.

graphical user interface (abbrev. **GUI**) ▶ noun Computing a visual way of interacting with a computer using items such as windows, icons, and menus, used by most modern operating systems.

graphic arts ▶ plural noun the visual arts based on the use of line and tone rather than three-dimensional work or the use of colour.
■ [mass noun] (**graphic art**) the activity of practising these arts, especially as a subject of study.
– DERIVATIVES **graphic artist** noun.

graphic design ▶ noun [mass noun] the art or skill of combining text and pictures in advertisements, magazines, or books.
– DERIVATIVES **graphic designer** noun.

graphic equalizer ▶ noun an electronic device or computer program which allows the separate control of the strength and quality of selected frequency bands.

graphic novel ▶ noun a novel in comic-strip format.

graphics ▶ plural noun [usu. treated as sing.] **1** the products of the graphic arts, especially commercial design or illustration.
2 the use of diagrams in calculation and design.
3 (also **computer graphics**) [treated as pl.] visual images produced by computer processing.
■ [treated as sing.] the use of computers linked to display screens to generate and manipulate visual images.

graphics card ▶ noun Computing a printed circuit board that controls the output to a display screen.

graphics tablet ▶ noun Computing an input device consisting of a flat, pressure-sensitive pad which the user draws on or points at with a special stylus, to guide a pointer displayed on the screen.

graphite ▶ noun [mass noun] a grey crystalline allotropic form of carbon which occurs as a mineral in some rocks and can be made from coke. It is used as a solid lubricant, in pencils, and as a moderator in nuclear reactors.
– DERIVATIVES **graphitic** adjective.
– ORIGIN late 18th cent.: coined in German (*Graphit*), from Greek *graphein* 'write' (because of its use as pencil 'lead').

graphitize /'grafɪtʌɪz/ (also **-ise**) ▶ verb [with obj.] technical convert or be converted into graphite.
– DERIVATIVES **graphitization** noun.

graphology ▶ noun [mass noun] **1** the study of handwriting, for example as used to infer a person's character.
2 Linguistics the study of written and printed symbols and of writing systems.
– DERIVATIVES **graphological** adjective, **graphologist** noun.
– ORIGIN mid 19th cent.: from Greek *graphē* 'writing' + **-LOGY**.

graph paper ▶ noun [mass noun] paper printed with a network of small squares to assist the drawing of graphs or other diagrams.

graph theory ▶ noun [mass noun] the mathematical theory of the properties and applications of graphs.

-graphy ▶ combining form in nouns denoting: **1** a descriptive science: *geography.*
2 a technique of producing images: *radiography.*
3 a style or method of writing or drawing: *calligraphy.*
■ writing about (a specified subject): *hagiography.* ■ a written or printed list: *filmography.*
– ORIGIN from or suggested by Greek *-graphia* 'writing'.

grapnel /'grapn(ə)l/ ▶ noun a grappling hook.
■ a small anchor with several flukes.
– ORIGIN late Middle English: from an Anglo-Norman French diminutive of Old French *grapon*, of Germanic origin.

grappa /'grapə/ ▶ noun [mass noun] a brandy distilled from the fermented residue of grapes after they have been pressed in winemaking.
– ORIGIN Italian, literally 'grape stalk', of Germanic origin.

Grappelli /grə'pɛli/, Stephane (1908–97), French jazz violinist. With Django Reinhardt, he founded the group the Quintette du Hot Club de France in 1934.

grapple ▶ verb **1** [no obj.] engage in a close fight or struggle without weapons; wrestle: *passers-by grappled with the man after the knife attack.*
■ [with obj.] seize hold of (someone). ■ (**grapple with**) struggle with or work hard to deal with or overcome (a difficulty or challenge): *other towns are still grappling with the problem.*
2 [with obj.] archaic seize or hold with a grapnel.
▶ noun an act of grappling.
■ informal a wrestling match. ■ an instrument for catching hold of or seizing something; a grappling hook.
– DERIVATIVES **grappler** noun.
– ORIGIN Middle English (as a noun denoting a grappling hook): from Old French *grapil*, from Provençal, diminutive of *grapa* 'hook', of Germanic origin; related to **GRAPE**. The verb dates from the mid 16th cent.

grappling hook (also **grappling iron**) ▶ noun a device with iron claws, attached to a rope and used for dragging or grasping.

graptolite /'graptəlʌɪt/ ▶ noun a fossil marine invertebrate animal of the Palaeozoic era, forming mainly planktonic colonies and believed to be related to the pterobranchs.
● Class Graptolithina, phylum Hemichordata.
– ORIGIN mid 19th cent.: from Greek *graptos* 'marked with letters' + **-LITE**: so named because of the impressions left on hard shales, resembling markings with a slate pencil.

Grasmere /'grɑːsmɪə/ a village in Cumbria, beside a small lake of the same name; pop. 1,100 (1981). William and Dorothy Wordsworth lived there from 1799.

grasp /grɑːsp/ ▶ verb [with obj.] seize and hold firmly: *she grasped the bottle.*
■ [no obj.] (**grasp at**) try to seize hold of: *they grasped at each other with numbed fingers* | *they had grasped at any means to overthrow him.* ■ get mental hold of; comprehend fully: *the way in which children could grasp complex ideas.* ■ act decisively to the advantage of (something): *we must grasp the opportunities offered.*
▶ noun [in sing.] a firm hold or grip: *the child slipped from her grasp.*
■ a person's power or capacity to attain something: *he knew success was within his grasp.* ■ a person's understanding: *meanings that are beyond my grasp* | *his grasp of detail.*
– PHRASES **grasp at a straw** (or **straws**) see **STRAW**. **grasp the nettle** Brit. tackle a difficulty boldly. [ORIGIN: because a nettle stings when touched lightly, but not when grasped firmly.]
– DERIVATIVES **graspable** adjective, **grasper** noun.
– ORIGIN late Middle English: perhaps related to **GROPE**.

grasping ▶ adjective avaricious; greedy: *they were regarded as grasping landlords.*
– DERIVATIVES **graspingly** adverb, **graspingness** noun.

Grass /grɑːs, gras/, Günter (Wilhelm) (b.1927), German novelist, poet, and dramatist. Notable works: *The Tin Drum* (novel, 1959) and *The Flounder* (novel, 1977). He was awarded the 1999 Nobel Prize for Literature.

grass ▶ noun **1** [mass noun] vegetation consisting of typically short plants with long narrow leaves, growing wild or cultivated on lawns and pasture, and as a fodder crop.
■ ground covered with grass. ■ pasture land: *the farms were mostly given over to grass.*
2 the mainly herbaceous plant that constitutes such vegetation, which has jointed stems and spikes of small wind-pollinated flowers.

> Grasses belong to the large family Gramineae (or Poaceae), the **grass family**, and form the dominant vegetation of many areas of the world. The possession of a growing point that is mainly at ground level makes grasses suitable as the food of many grazing animals, and for use in lawns and playing fields.

3 [mass noun] informal cannabis.
4 Brit. informal a police informer. [ORIGIN: perhaps related to the 19th-cent. rhyming slang *grasshopper* 'copper'.]
▶ verb [with obj.] **1** (usu. **be grassed**) cover (an area of ground) with grass: *the railtracks were mostly grassed over.*
■ US feed (livestock) with grass.
2 [no obj.] Brit. informal inform the police of criminal activity or plans: *someone had grassed on the thieves.*
3 catch and bring (a fish) to the riverbank.
4 chiefly Rugby & Australian Rules knock (someone) down.
– PHRASES **at grass** grazing: *the mare will be out at grass during the day.* **the grass is always greener on the other side of the fence** proverb other people's lives or situations always seem better than your own. **not let the grass grow under one's feet** not delay in acting or taking an opportunity. **put out to grass** put (an animal) out to graze. ■ informal force (someone) to retire; make redundant.
– DERIVATIVES **grassless** adjective, **grass-like** adjective.
– ORIGIN Old English *græs*, of Germanic origin; related to Dutch *gras*, German *Gras*, also ultimately to **GREEN** and **GROW**.

grassbird ▶ noun a brown streaked warbler frequenting long grass and reed beds.
● Family Sylviidae: genus *Megalurus* of Australasia and Asia (also called **MARSHBIRD**), and *Sphenoeacus afer* of southern Africa.

grassbox ▶ noun a rigid receptacle on a lawnmower for collecting the cut grass.

grass carp ▶ noun a large Chinese freshwater fish, farmed for food in SE Asia and introduced elsewhere to control the growth of vegetation in waterways.
● *Ctenopharyngodon idella*, family Cyprinidae.

grasscloth ▶ noun [mass noun] a fine, light cloth resembling linen, woven from the fibres of the inner bark of the ramie plant.

Grasse /grɑːs, French gʀas/ a town near Cannes in SE France, centre of the French perfume industry; pop. 42,080 (1990).

grasshopper ▶ noun a plant-eating insect with long hind legs which are used for jumping and for producing a chirping sound, frequenting grassy places and low vegetation.
● Family Acrididae, order Orthoptera: many genera.

grasshopper mouse ▶ noun a mainly carnivorous North American mouse, with a stout body, grey or brownish fur, and a short white-tipped tail.
● Genus *Onychomys*, family Muridae: three species.

grasshopper warbler ▶ noun a secretive Eurasian warbler with a song that is a high-pitched mechanical-sounding trill.
● Genus *Locustella*, family Sylviidae: several species, in particular the widespread *L. naevia*.

grassland ▶ noun [mass noun] (also **grasslands**) a large open area of country covered with grass, especially one used for grazing: *rough grassland.*

grass of Parnassus ▶ noun a herbaceous plant of north temperate regions, which bears a solitary white flower.
● Genus *Parnassia*, family Saxifragaceae: several species, in particular *P. palustris.*

grass parrot (also **grass parakeet**) ▶ noun Austral. a small parrot frequenting grassy country.
● Family Psittacidae: several genera, in particular *Psephotus* and *Neophema.*

grass pea ▶ noun a plant of the pea family which is cultivated as food for animals and humans, though excessive consumption can lead to lathyrism. Also called **CHICKLING PEA**.
● *Lathyrus sativus*, family Leguminosae.

grassquit /'grɑːskwɪt/ ▶ noun a small Caribbean and tropical American songbird related to the buntings, the male being partly or mainly black.
● Family Emberizidae (subfamily Emberizinae): three genera, in particular *Tiaris*, and several species.

grass roots ▶ plural noun the most basic level of an activity or organization: [as modifier] *improving the game at grass-roots level.*
■ ordinary people regarded as the main body of an organization's membership: *you have lost touch with the grass roots of the party.*

grass sickness ▶ noun [mass noun] a disease of horses which affects the bowel and is usually fatal.

grass ski ▶ noun each of a pair of devices resembling caterpillar tracks, worn on the feet for going down grass-covered slopes as if on skis.
– DERIVATIVES **grass skiing** noun.

grass skirt ▶ noun a skirt made of long grass and

leaves fastened to a waistband, associated especially with female dancers from some Pacific islands.

grass snake ▶ noun a common harmless Eurasian snake that typically has a yellowish band around the neck and is often found in or near water.
● *Natrix natrix*, family Colubridae.
■ North American term for **GREEN SNAKE**.

grass tetany (also **grass staggers**) ▶ noun [mass noun] a disease of livestock caused by magnesium deficiency, occurring especially when there is a change from indoor feeding to outdoor grazing.

grass tree ▶ noun another term for **BLACKBOY**.

grassveld /'grɑːsfɛlt/ ▶ noun [mass noun] S. African uncultivated land on which the dominant vegetation type is indigenous grass.
– ORIGIN partly translating Afrikaans *grasveld* 'prairie'.

grass widow ▶ noun a woman whose husband is away often or for a prolonged period.
– ORIGIN early 16th cent. (denoting an unmarried woman with a child): from **GRASS** + **WIDOW**, perhaps from the idea of the couple having lain on the grass instead of in bed. The current sense dates from the mid 19th cent; compare with Dutch *grasweduwe* and German *Strohwitwe* 'straw widow'.

grassy ▶ adjective (**grassier**, **grassiest**) of or covered with grass: *grassy slopes*.
■ characteristic of grass: *an intense grassy green*. ■ tasting or smelling like grass: *try the pleasant, grassy Chablis*.
– DERIVATIVES **grassiness** noun.

grate[1] ▶ verb 1 [with obj.] reduce (something, especially food) to small shreds by rubbing it on a grater: *peel and roughly grate the carrots* | [as adj. **grated**] *grated cheese*.
2 [no obj.] make an unpleasant rasping sound: *the hinges of the door grated*.
■ (**grate against**) rub against something with such a sound: *his helmet grated against the top of the door*. ■ have an irritating effect: *he had a juvenile streak which grated on her nerves*.
– ORIGIN late Middle English: from Old French *grater*, of Germanic origin; related to German *kratzen* 'to scratch'.

grate[2] ▶ noun 1 the recess of a fireplace or furnace.
■ a metal frame confining fuel in a fireplace or furnace.
2 a grating.
– ORIGIN Middle English (meaning 'a grating'): from Old French, based on Latin *cratis* 'hurdle'.

grateful ▶ adjective feeling or showing an appreciation of kindness; thankful: *I'm terribly grateful to you for all your help*.
■ archaic received or experienced with gratitude; welcome: *enjoying the grateful shade*.
– DERIVATIVES **gratefully** adverb, **gratefulness** noun.
– ORIGIN mid 16th cent.: from obsolete *grate* 'pleasing, agreeable, thankful' (from Latin *gratus*) + **-FUL**.

grater ▶ noun a device having a surface covered with holes edged by slightly raised cutting edges, used for grating cheese and other foods.

graticule /'gratɪkjuːl/ ▶ noun technical a network of lines representing meridians and parallels, on which a map or plan can be represented.
■ a series of fine lines or fibres in the eyepiece of an optical device, such as a telescope or microscope, or on the screen of an oscilloscope, used as a measuring scale or an aid in locating objects.
– ORIGIN late 19th cent.: from French, from medieval Latin *graticula* 'a little grating', from Latin *craticula* 'gridiron', diminutive of *cratis* 'hurdle'.

gratify ▶ verb (**-ies**, **-ied**) [with obj.] (often **be gratified**) give (someone) pleasure or satisfaction: *I was gratified to see the coverage in May's issue* | [as adj. **gratifying**] *the results were gratifying*.
■ indulge or satisfy (a desire): *not all the sexual impulses can be gratified*.
– DERIVATIVES **gratification** noun, **gratifier** noun, **gratifyingly** adverb.
– ORIGIN late Middle English (in the sense 'make pleasing'): from French *gratifier* or Latin *gratificari* 'give or do as a favour', from *gratus* 'pleasing, thankful'.

gratin /'gratã, 'gratan/ ▶ noun a dish with a light browned crust of breadcrumbs or melted cheese.
– ORIGIN French, from *gratter*, earlier *grater* 'to grate'.

gratiné /ˌgratɪ'neɪ/ (also **gratinée**) ▶ adjective [postpositive] another term for **AU GRATIN**.
– DERIVATIVES **gratinéed** adjective.
– ORIGIN French, past participle of *gratiner* 'cook au gratin'.

grating[1] ▶ adjective sounding harsh and unpleasant: *her high, grating voice*.
■ irritating: *it has a smarty-pants tone which I found grating*.
– DERIVATIVES **gratingly** adverb.

grating[2] ▶ noun a framework of parallel or crossed bars, typically preventing access through an opening while permitting communication or ventilation.
■ (also **diffraction grating**) Optics a set of equally spaced parallel wires, or a surface ruled with equally spaced parallel lines, used to produce spectra by diffraction.

gratis /'gratɪs, 'grɑː-, 'greɪ-/ ▶ adverb without charge; free: *a monthly programme was issued gratis*.
▶ adjective given or done for nothing; free: *gratis copies*.
– ORIGIN late Middle English: from Latin, contraction of *gratiis* 'as a kindness', from *gratia* 'grace, kindness'.

gratitude ▶ noun [mass noun] the quality of being thankful; readiness to show appreciation for and to return kindness: *she expressed her gratitude to the committee for their support*.
– ORIGIN late Middle English: from Old French, or from medieval Latin *gratitudo*, from Latin *gratus* 'pleasing, thankful'.

gratuitous /grə'tjuːɪtəs/ ▶ adjective 1 uncalled for; lacking good reason; unwarranted: *gratuitous violence*.
2 given or done free of charge: *solicitors provide a form of gratuitous legal advice*.
– DERIVATIVES **gratuitously** adverb, **gratuitousness** noun.
– ORIGIN mid 17th cent.: from Latin *gratuitus* 'given freely, spontaneous' + **-OUS**.

gratuity /grə'tjuːɪti/ ▶ noun (pl. **-ies**) money given in return for some service or favour, in particular:
■ formal a tip given to a waiter, taxi driver, etc. ■ Brit. a sum of money paid to an employee at the end of a period of employment.
– ORIGIN late 15th cent. (denoting graciousness or favour): from Old French *gratuité* or medieval Latin *gratuitas* 'gift', from Latin *gratus* 'pleasing, thankful'.

graunch /grɔːn(t)ʃ/ ▶ verb [no obj.] Brit. informal make a crunching or grinding noise: *the wheels soon graunched against a broken stone wall*.
– ORIGIN late 19th cent. (originally Leicestershire dialect): imitative.

gravadlax /'gravəd,laks/ ▶ noun variant spelling of **GRAVLAX**.

gravamen /grə'veɪmɛn/ ▶ noun (pl. **gravamina** /-mɪnə/) chiefly Law the essence or most serious part of a complaint or accusation.
■ a grievance.
– ORIGIN early 17th cent. (as an ecclesiastical term denoting formal presentation of a grievance): from late Latin, literally 'physical inconvenience', from Latin *gravare* 'to load', from *gravis* 'heavy'.

grave[1] ▶ noun a place of burial for a dead body, typically a hole dug in the ground and marked by a stone or mound: *the coffin was lowered into the grave*.
■ (**the grave**) used as an allusive term for death: *life beyond the grave*. ■ a place where a broken piece of machinery or other discarded object lies: *lift the aircraft from its watery grave*.
– PHRASES **dig one's own grave** do something foolish which causes one to fail or be ruined. (**as**) **silent** (or **quiet**) **as the grave** extremely quiet. **take the** (or **one's** etc.) **secret to the grave** die without revealing a secret. **turn** (N. Amer. also **turn over**) **in one's grave** used to express the opinion that something would have caused anger or distress in someone who is now dead: *Bach must be turning in his grave at the vulgarities of the twentieth century*.
– ORIGIN Old English *græf*, of Germanic origin; related to Dutch *graf* and German *Grab*.

grave[2] ▶ adjective giving cause for alarm; serious: *a matter of grave concern*.
■ serious or solemn in manner or appearance; sombre: *his face was grave*.
▶ noun /grɑːv/ another term for **GRAVE ACCENT**.
– DERIVATIVES **gravely** adverb, **graveness** noun.
– ORIGIN late 15th cent. (originally of a wound in the

sense 'severe, serious'): from Old French *grave* or Latin *gravis* 'heavy, serious'.

grave[3] ▶ verb (past participle **graven** or **graved**) [with obj.] archaic engrave (an inscription or image) on a surface.
■ poetic/literary fix (something) indelibly in the mind: *the times are graven on my memory*.
– ORIGIN Old English *grafan* 'dig', of Germanic origin; related to German *graben*, Dutch *graven* 'dig' and German *begraben* 'bury', also to **GRAVE**[1] and **GROOVE**.

grave[4] ▶ verb [with obj.] historical clean (a ship's bottom) by burning off the accretions and then tarring it.
– ORIGIN late Middle English: perhaps from French dialect *grave*, variant of Old French *greve* 'shore' (because originally the ship would have been run aground).

grave accent /grɑːv/ ▶ noun a mark (`) placed over a vowel in some languages to indicate a feature such as altered sound quality, vowel length, or intonation.
– ORIGIN early 17th cent.: French *grave* (see **GRAVE**[2]).

grave goods ▶ plural noun Archaeology utilitarian and valuable objects deposited with bodies in prehistoric and ancient graves, probably intended for use in the afterlife.

gravel ▶ noun [mass noun] a loose aggregation of small water-worn or pounded stones.
■ a mixture of such stones with coarse sand, used for paths and roads and as an aggregate. ■ a stratum or deposit of such stones. ■ Medicine aggregations of crystals formed in the urinary tract.
▶ verb (**gravelled**, **gravelling**; US **graveled**, **graveling**) [with obj.] 1 cover (an area of ground) with gravel.
2 US informal make (someone) angry or annoyed: *the strike was badly organized and it gravelled him to involve himself in it*.
■ archaic make (someone) feel confused or puzzled.
– ORIGIN Middle English: from Old French, diminutive of *grave* (see **GRAVE**[4]).

gravel-blind ▶ adjective archaic almost completely blind.
– ORIGIN early 17th cent.: originally as *high-gravel-blind*, a humorous usage meaning 'more than sand-blind (= half-blind)', with reference to Shakespeare's *Merchant of Venice*.

gravelly ▶ adjective resembling, containing, or consisting of gravel: *a dry gravelly soil*.
■ (of a voice) deep and rough-sounding.

graven past participle of **GRAVE**[3].

graven image ▶ noun a carved idol or representation of a god used as an object of worship.
– ORIGIN with biblical allusion to Exod. 20:4.

Gravenstein /'grɑːvə(n)ˌstʌɪn/ ▶ noun an apple of a large variety having yellow, red-streaked skin. It is widely grown in North America, where it is used for cooking and as a dessert apple.
– ORIGIN early 19th cent.: the German form of *Graasten*, a village in Denmark formerly in Schleswig-Holstein, Germany.

graver ▶ noun a burin or other engraving tool.
■ archaic a person who engraves or carves.

Graves[1] /greɪvz/, Robert (Ranke) (1895–1985), English poet, novelist, and critic, known for his interest in classics and mythology. Notable prose works: *Goodbye to All That* (autobiography, 1929), *I, Claudius* (historical fiction, 1934), and *The White Goddess* (non-fiction, 1948).

Graves[2] /grɑːv, French grav/ ▶ noun [mass noun] a red or white wine from the district of Graves, to the south of Bordeaux in France.

Graves' disease ▶ noun [mass noun] a swelling of the neck and protrusion of the eyes resulting from an overactive thyroid gland. Also called **EXOPHTHALMIC GOITRE**.
– ORIGIN mid 19th cent.: named after Robert J. *Graves* (1796–1853), the Irish physician who first identified it.

graveside ▶ noun the ground around the edge of a grave.

gravestone ▶ noun an inscribed headstone marking a grave.

Gravettian /grə'vɛtɪən/ ▶ adjective Archaeology of, relating to, or denoting an Upper Palaeolithic culture in Europe following the Aurignacian, dated to about 28,000–19,000 years ago.

■[as noun **the Gravettian**] the Gravettian culture or period.
– ORIGIN 1930s: from *la Gravette*, an archaeological site in SW France, where objects from this culture were found.

graveyard ▶ noun a burial ground, especially one beside a church.

graveyard shift ▶ noun chiefly N. Amer. a work shift that runs through the early morning hours, typically covering the period between midnight and 8 a.m.

gravid /ˈɡravɪd/ ▶ adjective technical pregnant; carrying eggs or young.
■figurative full of meaning or a specified quality: *the scene is gravid with unease.*
– ORIGIN late 16th cent.: from Latin *gravidus* 'laden, pregnant', from *gravis* 'heavy'.

gravimeter /ɡrəˈvɪmɪtə/ ▶ noun an instrument for measuring the difference in the force of gravity from one place to another.
– DERIVATIVES **gravimetric** /ˌɡravɪˈmɛtrɪk/ adjective.
– ORIGIN late 18th cent.: from French *gravimètre*, from *grave* 'heavy' (from Latin *gravis*) + *-mètre* '(instrument) measuring'.

gravimetry /ɡrəˈvɪmɪtri/ ▶ noun [mass noun] Physics the measurement of weight.

graving dock ▶ noun another term for **DRY DOCK**.
– ORIGIN early 19th cent.: *graving* from **GRAVE**[4].

gravitas /ˈɡravɪtas, -tɑːs/ ▶ noun [mass noun] dignity, seriousness, or solemnity of manner: *a post for which he has the expertise and the gravitas.*
– ORIGIN Latin, from *gravis* 'serious'.

gravitate /ˈɡravɪteɪt/ ▶ verb [no obj., with adverbial] move towards or be attracted to a place, person, or thing: *young western Europeans will gravitate to Berlin.*
■Physics move, or tend to move, towards a centre of gravity or other attractive force. ■archaic descend or sink by the force of gravity.
– ORIGIN mid 17th cent.: from modern Latin *gravitat-*, from the verb *gravitare*, from Latin *gravitas* 'weight'.

gravitation ▶ noun [mass noun] movement, or a tendency to move, towards a centre of attractive force, as in the falling of bodies to the earth.
■Physics a force of attraction exerted by each particle of matter in the universe on every other particle: *the law of universal gravitation.* Compare with **GRAVITY**. ■figurative movement towards or attraction to something: *this recent gravitation towards the Continent.*
– DERIVATIVES **gravitational** adjective, **gravitationally** adverb.
– ORIGIN mid 17th cent.: from modern Latin *gravitatio(n-)*, from the verb *gravitare* (see **GRAVITATE**).

gravitational constant (abbrev.: **G**) ▶ noun Physics the constant in Newton's law of gravitation relating gravity to the masses and separation of particles, equal to 6.67×10^{-11} N m^2 kg^{-2}.

gravitational field ▶ noun Physics the region of space surrounding a body in which another body experiences a force of gravitational attraction.

gravitational lens ▶ noun Astronomy a region of space containing a massive object whose gravitational field distorts electromagnetic radiation passing through it in a similar way to a lens, sometimes producing a multiple image of a remote object.

graviton /ˈɡravɪtɒn/ ▶ noun Physics a hypothetical quantum of gravitational energy, regarded as a particle.
– ORIGIN 1940s: from **GRAVITATION** + **-ON**.

gravity ▶ noun [mass noun] **1** Physics the force that attracts a body towards the centre of the earth, or towards any other physical body having mass. For most purposes Newton's laws of gravity apply, with minor modifications to take the general theory of relativity into account.
■the degree of intensity of this, measured by acceleration.
2 extreme or alarming importance; seriousness: *crimes of the utmost gravity.*
■seriousness or solemnity of manner: *has the poet ever spoken with greater eloquence or gravity?*
– ORIGIN late 15th cent. (in sense 2): from Old French, or from Latin *gravitas* 'weight, seriousness', from *gravis* 'heavy'. Sense 1 dates from the 17th cent.

gravity feed ▶ noun [mass noun] a supply system making use of gravity to maintain the flow of material.
– DERIVATIVES **gravity-fed** adjective.

gravity wave ▶ noun Physics **1** a hypothetical wave carrying gravitational energy, postulated by Einstein to be emitted when a massive body is accelerated.
2 a wave propagated on a liquid surface or in a fluid through the effects of gravity.

gravlax /ˈɡravlaks/ (also **gravadlax**) ▶ noun [mass noun] a Scandinavian dish of dry-cured salmon marinated in herbs.
– ORIGIN Swedish, from *grav* 'trench' + *lax* 'salmon' (from the former practice of burying the salmon in salt in a hole in the ground).

gravure /ɡrəˈvjʊə/ ▶ noun short for **PHOTOGRAVURE**.

gravy ▶ noun (pl. **-ies**) **1** [mass noun] the fat and juices exuding from meat during cooking.
■a sauce made from these juices together with stock and other ingredients.
2 [mass noun] informal unearned or unexpected money.
– ORIGIN Middle English (denoting a spicy sauce): perhaps from a misreading (as *gravé*) of Old French *grané*, probably from *grain* 'spice', from Latin *granum* 'grain'.

gravy boat ▶ noun a long narrow jug used for serving gravy.

gravy train ▶ noun informal used to refer to a situation in which someone can make a lot of money for very little effort: *come to Hollywood and get on to the gravy train.*

Gray[1], Asa (1810–88), American botanist, author of many textbooks which greatly popularized botany. He supported Darwin's theories at a time when they were anathema to many.

Gray[2], Thomas (1716–71), English poet, best known for 'Elegy Written in a Country Church-Yard' (1751).

gray[1] (abbrev.: **Gy**) ▶ noun Physics the SI unit of the absorbed dose of ionizing radiation, corresponding to one joule per kilogram.
– ORIGIN 1970s: named after Louis H. *Gray* (1905–65), English radiobiologist.

gray[2] ▶ adjective US spelling of **GREY**.

graybeard ▶ noun US spelling of **GREYBEARD**.

Gray code ▶ noun a numerical code used in computing in which consecutive integers are represented by binary numbers differing in only one digit.
– ORIGIN mid 20th cent.: named after Frank *Gray* (1887–1969), American physicist.

graylag ▶ noun US spelling of **GREYLAG**.

grayling ▶ noun **1** an edible freshwater fish which is silvery-grey with horizontal violet stripes and has a long high dorsal fin, of both Eurasia and North America.
• Genus *Thymallus*, family Salmonidae: several species.
2 a mainly brown European butterfly which has wings with bright eyespots and greyish undersides.
• *Hipparchia semele*, subfamily Satyrinae, family Nymphalidae.
– ORIGIN Middle English: from *gray* (variant of **GREY**) + **-LING**.

grayscale ▶ noun US spelling of **GREYSCALE**.

graywacke ▶ noun US spelling of **GREYWACKE**.

Graz /ɡrɑːts/ a city in southern Austria, on the River Mur, capital of the state of Styria; pop. 232,155 (1991). It is the second largest city in Austria.

graze[1] ▶ verb [no obj.] (of cattle, sheep, etc.) eat grass in a field: *cattle **graze on** the open meadows.*
■[with obj.] (of an animal) feed on (grass or land covered by grass): *downland areas grazed by rabbits and sheep.* ■[with obj.] put (cattle, sheep, etc.) to feed on land covered by grass: *shepherds who grazed animals on common land.* ■informal (of a person) eat small quantities of food at frequent but irregular intervals: *advertisers should not encourage children to **graze on** snacks or sweets.* ■informal, chiefly US casually sample something: *we grazed up and down channels.*
– DERIVATIVES **grazer** noun.
– ORIGIN Old English *grasian*, from *græs* 'grass'.

graze[2] ▶ verb [with obj.] scrape the skin of (a part of the body) so as to break the surface but cause little or no bleeding: *she fell down and grazed her knees.*
■touch or scrape lightly in passing: *his hands just grazed hers.*
▶ noun a slight injury where the skin is scraped.
– ORIGIN late 16th cent.: perhaps a specific use of **GRAZE**[1].

grazier /ˈɡreɪzɪə/ ▶ noun a person who rears or fattens cattle or sheep for market.
– ORIGIN Middle English: from **GRASS** + **-IER**.

grazing ▶ noun [mass noun] grassland suitable for pasturage: *pastures and rough grazing.*

grease ▶ noun [mass noun] oily or fatty matter, in particular:
■a thick oily substance used as a lubricant: *axle grease.* ■oil or fat used or produced in cooking. ■oily matter in the hair, especially when applied as a dressing. ■the oily matter in unprocessed wool; lanolin.
▶ verb [with obj.] smear or lubricate with grease: [as adj. **greased**] *place on a greased baking sheet.*
– PHRASES **grease the palm of** informal bribe (someone). [ORIGIN: *grease* expressing the sense 'cause to run smoothly' and *palm*, by association with the taking of money.] **grease the skids** N. Amer. informal help matters run smoothly: *his mission was to use his budgetary skills to grease the skids for new projects.* **like greased lightning** informal extremely fast: *he leaped over the tailboard of the lorry like greased lightning.*
– DERIVATIVES **greaseless** adjective.
– ORIGIN Middle English: from Old French *graisse*, based on Latin *crassus* 'thick, fat'.

greaseball ▶ noun offensive, chiefly N. Amer. a foreigner, especially one of Mediterranean or Latin American origin.

grease gun ▶ noun a device for pumping grease under pressure to a particular point.

grease monkey ▶ noun informal, derogatory a mechanic.

greasepaint ▶ noun [mass noun] a waxy substance used as make-up by actors.

greaseproof ▶ adjective (especially of paper used in cooking) impermeable to oil or grease.

greaser ▶ noun **1** a motor mechanic or unskilled engineer on a ship.
■Brit. informal a scruffily dressed young man with long hair, especially a member of a motorcycle gang.
2 US informal, offensive a Hispanic American, especially a Mexican.
3 informal a gentle landing of an aircraft.

greasewood ▶ noun a resinous dwarf shrub of the goosefoot family, which yields hard yellow wood used chiefly for fuel. It grows in dry areas of the western US and is toxic to stock if eaten in large quantities.
• *Sarcobatus vermiculatus*, family Chenopodiaceae.

greasy ▶ adjective (**greasier**, **greasiest**) covered with an oily substance: *he wiped his greasy fingers.*
■producing more body oils than average: *greasy skin.* ■containing or cooked with too much oil or fat: *greasy food.* ■of or like grease: *their moisturizers don't feel greasy.* ■slippery: *the floor was greasy.* ■figurative (of a person or their manner) effusively polite in a way that is felt to be insincere and repulsive: *the greasy little man from the newspaper.*
– DERIVATIVES **greasily** adverb, **greasiness** noun.

greasy pole ▶ noun informal a pole covered with an oily substance to make it more difficult to climb or walk along, used especially as a form of entertainment.
■used to refer to the difficult route to the top of someone's profession: *he steadily climbed the greasy pole towards the job he coveted most.*

greasy spoon ▶ noun informal a cheap, run-down cafe or restaurant serving fried foods.

great ▶ adjective **1** of an extent, amount, or intensity considerably above the normal or average: *the article was of great interest | she showed great potential as an actor.*
■very large and imposing: *a great ocean between them.* ■[attrib.] used to reinforce another adjective of size or extent: *a great big grin | huge great hooks.* ■[attrib.] used to express surprise, admiration, or contempt, especially in exclamations: *you great oaf!* ■(also **greater**) [attrib.] used in names of animals or plants which are larger than similar kinds, e.g. **great tit**, **greater celandine**. ■(**Great**) [attrib.] [in place names] denoting the larger or largest part of a place: *Great Malvern.* ■(**Greater**) [attrib.] (of a city) including adjacent urban areas: *Greater Manchester.*
2 of ability, quality, or eminence considerably above the normal or average: *the great Italian conductor | we obeyed our great men and leaders | great art has the power to change lives.*
■(**the Great**) a title denoting the most important person of the name: *Alexander the Great.* ■informal very

good or satisfactory; excellent: *another great goal from Alan* | *he's a great bloke* | *wouldn't it be great to have him back?* | [as exclamation] *'Great!' said Tom.* ■ [predic.] informal (of a person) very skilled or capable in a particular area: *a brilliant man, great at mathematics.*
3 [attrib.] denoting the element of something that is the most important or the most worthy of consideration: *the great thing is the challenge.*
■ used to indicate that someone or something particularly deserves a specified description: *I was a great fan of Hank's.*
4 [in combination] (in names of family relationships) denoting one degree further removed upwards or downwards: *great-aunt* | *great-great-grandfather.*
▶ noun **1** a great or distinguished person: *the Beatles, Bob Dylan, all the greats.*
■ [as plural noun **the greats**] great people collectively: *the lives of the great, including Churchill and Newton.*
2 (**Greats**) another term for **LITERAE HUMANIORES**.
▶ adverb informal excellently; very well: *we played awful, they played great.*
– PHRASES **the great and the good** often ironic distinguished and worthy people collectively: *a non-departmental public body made up of the great and the good.* **great and small** of all sizes, classes, or types: *all creatures great and small.* **a great deal** see **DEAL**[1]. **a great many** see **MANY**. **a great one for** a habitual doer of; an enthusiast for: *my father was a great one for buying gadgets.* **Great Scott!** expressing surprise or amazement. [ORIGIN: arbitrary euphemism for *Great God!*] **to a great extent** in a substantial way; largely: *we are all to a great extent the product of our culture.*
– ORIGIN Old English *grēat* 'big', of West Germanic origin; related to Dutch *groot* and German *gross.*

great ape ▶ noun a large ape of a family closely related to humans, including the gorilla, orang-utan, and chimpanzees, but excluding the gibbons; an anthropoid ape.
● Family Pongidae, order Primates.

Great Attractor Astronomy a massive grouping of galaxies in the direction of the constellations Hydra and Centaurus, whose gravitational pull is thought to be responsible for deviations in the velocity of other galaxies.

great auk ▶ noun a large extinct flightless auk of the North Atlantic, resembling a giant razorbill. The great auk was the original 'penguin'; many were taken for food, and the last individuals were killed on an islet off Iceland in 1844.
● *Alca* (or *Pinguinus*) *impennis*, family Alcidae.

great-aunt ▶ noun an aunt of one's father or mother.

Great Australian Bight a wide bay on the south coast of Australia, part of the southern Indian Ocean.

Great Barrier Reef a coral reef in the western Pacific, off the coast of Queensland, Australia. It extends for about 2,000 km (1,250 miles), roughly parallel to the coast, and is the largest coral reef in the world.

Great Basin an arid region of the western US between the Sierra Nevada and the Rocky Mountains, including most of Nevada and parts of the adjacent states.

Great Bear Astronomy the constellation Ursa Major.

Great Bear Lake a large lake in the Northwest Territories, Canada. It drains into the Mackenzie River via the Great Bear River.

Great Bible ▶ noun the edition of the English Bible which Thomas Cromwell ordered in 1538 to be set up in every parish church. It was the work of Miles Coverdale, and was first issued in 1539.

Great Britain England, Wales, and Scotland considered as a unit. The name is also often used loosely to refer to the United Kingdom.

Great Charter another name for **MAGNA CARTA**.

great circle ▶ noun a circle on the surface of a sphere which lies in a plane passing through the sphere's centre. As it represents the shortest distance between any two points on a sphere, a great circle of the earth is the preferred route taken by a ship or aircraft.

greatcoat ▶ noun a long heavy overcoat.

great crested grebe ▶ noun a large grebe with a crest and ear ruffs in the breeding season, found from Europe to New Zealand.
● *Podiceps cristatus*, family Podicipedidae.

great crested newt ▶ noun another term for **CRESTED NEWT**.

Great Dane ▶ noun a dog of a very large, powerful, short-haired breed.

Great Depression see **DEPRESSION**.

Great Dismal Swamp (also **Dismal Swamp**) an area of swampland in SE Virginia and NE North Carolina.

Great Divide another name for **CONTINENTAL DIVIDE** or **GREAT DIVIDING RANGE**.

great divide ▶ noun a distinction regarded as significant and very difficult to ignore or overcome: *the great divide between workers and management.*
■ an event, date, or place seen as the point at which significant and irrevocable change occurs: *to our parents, the war was the great divide.* ■ the boundary between life and death: *she is still on the human side of the great divide.*

Great Dividing Range a mountain system in eastern Australia. Curving roughly parallel to the coast, it extends from eastern Victoria to northern Queensland. Also called **GREAT DIVIDE**.

Greater Antilles see **ANTILLES**.

Greater Bairam ▶ noun an annual Muslim festival held at the end of the Islamic year.

greater celandine ▶ noun a yellow-flowered Eurasian plant of the poppy family. Its toxic orange sap has long been used in herbal medicine, especially for disorders of the eyes and skin.
● *Chelidonium majus*, family Papaveraceae.

Greater London a metropolitan area comprising central London and the surrounding regions. It is divided administratively into the City of London, thirteen inner London boroughs, and twenty outer London boroughs.

Greater Manchester a metropolitan county of NW England including the city of Manchester and adjacent areas.

Greater Sunda Islands see **SUNDA ISLANDS**.

Great Exhibition the first international exhibition of the products of industry, promoted by Prince Albert and held in the Crystal Palace in London in 1851.

Great Fire another name for **FIRE OF LONDON**.

Great Glen a large fault valley in Scotland, extending from the Moray Firth south-west for 37 km (60 miles) to Loch Linnhe, and containing Loch Ness. Also called **GLEN MORE**.

Great Grimsby official name for **GRIMSBY**.

great-hearted ▶ adjective dated having a noble, generous, and courageous spirit.
– DERIVATIVES **great-heartedness** noun.

Great Indian Desert another name for **THAR DESERT**.

Great Lakes a group of five large interconnected lakes in central North America, consisting of Lakes Superior, Michigan, Huron, Erie, and Ontario, and constituting the largest area of fresh water in the world. Lake Michigan is wholly within the US, and the others lie on the Canada–US border. Connected to the Atlantic Ocean by the St Lawrence Seaway, the Great Lakes form an important commercial waterway.

Great Lake State informal name for **MICHIGAN**.

Great Land informal name for **ALASKA**.

Great Leap Forward an unsuccessful attempt made under Mao Zedong in China 1958–60 to hasten the process of industrialization and improve agricultural production by reorganizing the population into large rural collectives and adopting labour-intensive industrial methods.

greatly ▶ adverb by a considerable amount; very much: *I admire him greatly* | [as submodifier] *they now have greatly increased powers.*

Great Mother ▶ noun another name for **MOTHER GODDESS**.

Great Nebula Astronomy **1** (also **Great Nebula in Andromeda**) the Andromeda Galaxy.
2 (also **Great Nebula in Orion**) a bright emission nebula in Orion, visible to the naked eye.

great-nephew ▶ noun a son of one's nephew or niece.

greatness ▶ noun [mass noun] the quality of being great, in particular distinguished or eminent: *Elgar's greatness as a composer.*

great-niece ▶ noun a daughter of one's nephew or niece.

great northern diver ▶ noun a diving waterbird with a black streamlined head, breeding in northern North America, Greenland, and Iceland.
● *Gavia immer*, family Gaviidae. North American name: **common loon**.

Great Northern War a conflict 1700–21 in which Russia, Denmark, Poland, and Saxony opposed Sweden. The war resulted in Sweden losing her imperial possessions in central Europe, and Russia under Peter the Great becoming a major power in the Baltic.

great organ ▶ noun the chief keyboard in a large organ and its related pipes and mechanism.

Great Ouse another name for **OUSE** (in sense 1).

Great Plague a serious outbreak of bubonic plague in England in 1665–6, in which about one fifth of the population of London died. It was the last major outbreak in Britain.

Great Plains a vast area of plains to the east of the Rocky Mountains in North America, extending from the valleys of the Mackenzie River in Canada to southern Texas.

Great Rebellion the Royalist name for the English Civil War of 1642–51.

Great Red Spot Astronomy a weather system on the planet Jupiter which measures over 10,000 km across and has persisted at least since the beginning of telescopic observations.

Great Rift Valley a large system of rift valleys in eastern Africa and the Middle East, forming the most extensive such system in the world and running for some 4,285 km (3,000 miles) from the Jordan valley in Syria into Mozambique. It is marked by a chain of lakes and a series of volcanoes, including Mount Kilimanjaro.

Great Russian ▶ adjective & noun former term for **RUSSIAN** (language and people), as distinguished from other peoples and languages of the old Russian Empire.

Great St Bernard Pass see **ST BERNARD PASS**.

Great Salt Lake a salt lake in northern Utah, near Salt Lake City. With an area of some 2,590 sq. km (1,000 sq. miles), it is the largest salt lake in North America.

Great Sand Sea an area of desert in NE Africa, on the border between Libya and Egypt.

Great Sandy Desert 1 a large tract of desert in north central Western Australia.
2 another name for **RUB' AL KHALI**.

Great Schism 1 the breach between the Eastern and the Western Churches, traditionally dated to 1054 and becoming final in 1472.
2 the period 1378–1417, when the Western Church was divided by the creation of antipopes.

Great Seal ▶ noun a seal used for the authentication of state documents of the highest importance. That of the UK is held by the Lord Chancellor and that of the US by the Secretary of State.

great skua ▶ noun a large North Atlantic skua with mainly brown plumage, feeding by robbing other seabirds. Also called **BONXIE**.
● *Catharacta skua*, family Stercorariidae.

Great Slave Lake a large lake in the Northwest Territories in Canada. The deepest lake in North America, it reaches a depth of 615 m (2,015 ft). The Mackenzie River flows out of it.

great tit ▶ noun a tit (songbird) with a black head and white cheeks, occurring in many different races from western Europe to east Asia.
● *Parus major*, family Paridae.

Great Trek the northward migration 1835–7 of large numbers of Boers, discontented with British rule in the Cape, to the areas where they eventually founded the Transvaal Republic and Orange Free State.

great-uncle ▶ noun an uncle of one's mother or father.

Great Victoria Desert a desert region of Australia, which straddles the boundary between Western Australia and South Australia.

Great Wall of China a fortified wall in northern China, extending some 2,400 km (1,500 miles) from Kansu province to the Yellow Sea north of Beijing. It was first built *c*.210 BC, as a protection against nomad invaders. The present wall dates from the Ming dynasty.

Great War another name for **FIRST WORLD WAR**.

Great Wen an archaic nickname for London.

great white shark ▶ **noun** a large aggressive shark of warm seas, with a brownish or grey back, white underparts, and large triangular teeth. Also called **WHITE POINTER**, **MANEATER**.
● *Carcharodon carcharias*, family Lamnidae.

Great White Way nickname for **BROADWAY**.

greave ▶ **noun** historical a piece of armour used to protect the shin.
– ORIGIN Middle English: from Old French *greve* 'shin, greave', of unknown origin.

Greaves, Jimmy (b.1940), English footballer; full name *James Greaves*. He played as a striker for Chelsea, AC Milan, Tottenham Hotspur, and West Ham United and won 57 international caps (from 1959).

grebe /gri:b/ ▶ **noun** a diving waterbird with a long neck, lobed toes, and almost no tail, typically having bright breeding plumage used in display.
● Family Podicipedidae: several genera.
– ORIGIN mid 18th cent.: from French *grèbe* (term used in the Savoie region), of unknown origin.

grebo /'gri:bəʊ/ ▶ **noun** (pl. **-os**) [mass noun] a member of an urban youth cult favouring heavy metal, punk rock music, and long hair.
– ORIGIN 1980s: perhaps from **GREASER**, on the pattern of words such as *dumbo*.

Grecian ▶ **adjective** of or relating to ancient Greece, especially its architecture.
– ORIGIN late Middle English: from Old French *grecien*, from Latin *Graecia* 'Greece'.

Grecian nose ▶ **noun** a straight nose that continues the line of the forehead without a dip.

Grecism ▶ **noun** variant spelling of **GRAECISM**.

Greco- ▶ **combining form** variant spelling of **GRAECO-**.

Greco, El see **EL GRECO**.

Greco-Roman ▶ **adjective** variant spelling of **GRAECO-ROMAN**.

Greece a country in SE Europe; pop. 10,269,000 (1991); official language, Greek; capital, Athens.

The age of the classical city states, of which the most prominent were Athens and Sparta, reached its peak in the 5th century BC, after which Greece fell to Macedon and then became part of the Roman and Byzantine Empires. It was conquered by the Ottoman Turks in 1466 and remained under Turkish rule until the war of independence (1821–30), after which it became a kingdom. The monarchy was overthrown in a military coup in 1967; a civilian republic was established in 1974. Greece joined the EC in 1981.

greed ▶ **noun** [mass noun] intense and selfish desire for something, especially wealth, power, or food.
– ORIGIN late 16th cent.: back-formation from **GREEDY**.

greedy ▶ **adjective** (**greedier**, **greediest**) having an excessive desire or appetite for food.
■ having or showing an intense and selfish desire for something, especially wealth or power: *driven from their land by greedy developers*.
– DERIVATIVES **greedily** adverb, **greediness** noun.
– ORIGIN Old English *grǣdig*, of Germanic origin.

greegree ▶ **noun** variant spelling of **GRIS-GRIS**.

Greek ▶ **adjective** of or relating to Greece, its people, or their language. Compare with **HELLENIC**.
▶ **noun 1** a native or national of modern Greece, or a person of Greek descent.
■ a Greek-speaking person in the ancient world, especially a native of one of the city states of Greece and the eastern Mediterranean.
2 [mass noun] the ancient or modern language of Greece, the only representative of the Hellenic branch of the Indo-European family.

The ancient form of Greek was spoken in the southern Balkan peninsula from the 2nd millennium BC. The Greek alphabet, used from the 1st millennium BC onwards, was adapted from the Phoenician alphabet. The dialect of classical Athens formed the basis of the standard dialect (*koinē*) from the 3rd century BC onwards, and this remained as a literary language during the periods of the Byzantine Empire and Turkish rule (see **KATHAREVOUSA**). The colloquial language, however, continued to evolve independently (see **DEMOTIC**).

– PHRASES **beware** (or **fear**) **the Greeks bearing gifts** proverb if a rival or enemy shows one generosity or kindness, one should be suspicious of their motives. [ORIGIN: with allusion to Virgil's *Aeneid* (ii. 49).] **it's** (**all**) **Greek to me** informal I can't understand it at all.
– DERIVATIVES **Greekness** noun.
– ORIGIN Old English *Grēcas* 'the Greeks', from Latin *Graeci*, the name given by the Romans to the people who called themselves the Hellenes, from Greek *Graikoi*, which according to Aristotle was the prehistoric name of the Hellenes.

Greek Church another term for **GREEK ORTHODOX CHURCH**.

Greek coffee ▶ **noun** [mass noun] very strong black coffee served with the fine grounds in it.

Greek cross ▶ **noun** a cross of which all four arms are of equal length.

Greek fire ▶ **noun** [mass noun] historical a combustible composition emitted by a flame-throwing weapon, and used to set light to enemy ships. It was first used by the Greeks besieged in Constantinople (673–8). It ignited on contact with water, and was probably based on naphtha and quicklime.

Greek key ▶ **noun** a pattern of interlocking right-angled spirals.

Greek Orthodox Church (also **Greek Church**) the Eastern Orthodox Church which uses the Byzantine rite in Greek, in particular the national Church of Greece. See **ORTHODOX CHURCH**.

Greek salad ▶ **noun** a salad consisting of tomatoes, olives, and feta cheese.

green ▶ **adjective 1** of the colour between blue and yellow in the spectrum; coloured like grass or emeralds: *the leaves are bright green*.
■ consisting of fresh vegetables of this colour: *a green salad*. ■ denoting a light or flag of this colour used as a signal to proceed. ■ (of a ski run) of the lowest level of difficulty, as indicated by coloured markers on the run. ■ Physics denoting one of three colours of quark.
2 covered with grass, trees, or other plants: *proposals that would smother green fields with development*.
■ (usu. **Green**) concerned with or supporting protection of the environment as a political principle: *official Green candidates*. ■ (of a product) not harmful to the environment.
3 (of a plant or fruit) young or unripe: *green shoots*.
■ (of wood) unseasoned. ■ (of food or leather) not dried, smoked, or tanned. ■ (of a person) inexperienced, naive, or gullible: *a green recruit fresh from college*. ■ (of a memory) not fading: *clubs devoted to keeping green the memory of Sherlock Holmes*. ■ still strong or vigorous: *first there was green old age, hardly different from middle age*. ■ archaic (of a wound) fresh; not healed.
4 (of the complexion or a person) pale and sickly-looking: *'Are you all right?—You look absolutely green.'*
■ as a sign of jealousy or envy.
▶ **noun 1** [mass noun] green colour or pigment: *major roads are marked in green*.
■ green clothes or material: *two girls in red and green*. ■ green foliage or growing plants: *that lovely canopy of green over Stratford Road*. ■ informal, dated low-grade cannabis. ■ informal, dated money: *that's a lot of green*.
2 a green thing, in particular:
■ a green light. ■ the green ball in snooker.
3 a piece of public or common grassy land, especially in the centre of a village: *a house overlooking the green*.
■ an area of smooth, very short grass immediately surrounding a hole on a golf course.
4 (**greens**) green vegetables: *eat up your greens*.
■ (**one's greens**) Brit. informal, dated sexual intercourse.
5 (usu. **Green**) a member or supporter of an environmentalist group or party.
▶ **verb** make or become green, in particular:
■ [with obj.] make (an urban or desert area) more verdant by planting or encouraging trees or other greenery: *they were greening China's semi-arid Yellow River delta*. ■ [with obj.] make less harmful or more sensitive to the environment: *the importance of greening this industry*. ■ [no obj.] become green in colour, through age or by becoming covered with plants: *the roof was greening with lichen*.
– DERIVATIVES **greenish** adjective, **greenly** adverb, **greenness** noun.
– ORIGIN Old English *grēne* (adjective), *grēnian* (verb), of Germanic origin; related to Dutch *groen*, German *grün*, also to **GRASS** and **GROW**.

green algae ▶ **plural noun** photosynthetic algae which contain chlorophyll and store starch in discrete chloroplasts. They are eukaryotic and most live in fresh water, ranging from unicellular flagellates to more complex multicellular forms.
● Treated either as plants (division Chlorophyta) or as protozoans (phylum Chlorophyta, kingdom Protista). The classification of green algae is complex and under review.

Greenaway[1], Kate (1846–1901), English artist; full name *Catherine Greenaway*. She is known especially for her illustrations of children's books such as *Mother Goose* (1881).

Greenaway[2], Peter (b.1942), English film director. His contrived and controversial works explore sex, human mutability, and gamesmanship. Notable films: *The Draughtsman's Contract* (1982) and *The Cook, The Thief, His Wife, and Her Lover* (1989).

greenback ▶ **noun 1** US informal a dollar bill; a dollar: *purchased with our last greenback*.
2 informal an animal with a green back, especially a race of the cut-throat trout found only in Colorado, US.

green baize door ▶ **noun** see **BAIZE DOOR**.

green belt ▶ **noun 1** an area of open land around a city, on which building is restricted.
2 a green belt marking a level of proficiency in judo, karate, or other martial arts below that of a brown belt.
■ a person qualified to wear this.

Green Beret ▶ **noun** informal a British commando or a member of the US Army Special Forces.

Green Book ▶ **noun** Law (in England and Wales) a book setting out the procedural rules of the county courts, bound in green.

greenbottle ▶ **noun** a metallic green fly which sometimes lays eggs in wounds on sheep or other animals.
● Genus *Lucilia*, family Calliphoridae: several species, in particular the common *L. caesar*.

green box ▶ **noun** a set of farming subsidies in the EU that do not affect production levels or prices.

greenbul /'gri:nbʊl/ ▶ **noun** an African bulbul with an olive-green back.
● Family Pycnonotidae: several genera, in particular *Phyllastrephus* and *Pycnonotus*, and numerous species.

green card ▶ **noun 1** (in the UK) an international insurance document for motorists.
2 (in the US) a permit allowing a foreign national to live and work permanently in the US.

green channel ▶ **noun** (at a customs area in an airport or port) the passage which should be taken by arriving passengers who have no goods to declare.

green cheese ▶ **noun** [mass noun] unripened or unmatured cheese.

Green Cloth (in full **Board of Green Cloth**) ▶ **noun** (in the UK) the Lord Steward's department of the royal household.

green crop ▶ **noun** Brit. a crop used in a green or unripe state as fodder.

green dragon ▶ **noun** a North American arum with a large divided leaf, a greenish-cream spathe, and a very long white spadix. Also called **DRAGON ARUM**.
● *Arisaema dracontium*, family Araceae.

green drake ▶ **noun** Brit. the green subadult of certain mayflies.
● Genus *Ephemera*, family Ephemeridae.
■ an artificial fishing fly that imitates this.

Greene, (Henry) Graham (1904–91), English novelist. The moral paradoxes he saw in his Roman Catholic faith underlie much of his work. Notable works: *Brighton Rock* (1938), *The Power and the Glory* (1940), and *The Third Man* (written as a screenplay, and filmed in 1949; novel 1950).

green earth ▶ **noun** another term for **TERRE VERTE**.

Greener ▶ **noun** a type of shotgun.
– ORIGIN late 19th cent.: named after William *Greener* (1806–69) or his son William W. *Greener*, gunsmiths and authors.

greenery ▶ **noun** [mass noun] green foliage, growing plants, or vegetation.

greenery-yallery /ˌgri:nərɪ'jalərɪ/ ▶ **adjective** informal green and yellow: *the greenery-yallery dogwood*.
■ of or in the style of the 19th-century Aesthetic Movement (used to convey the idea of affectation): *a greenery-yallery fin-de-siècle lyricism*.
– ORIGIN late 19th cent.: from **GREEN** + *yaller* (variant of **YELLOW**), with reduplication of the suffix **-Y**[1].

greeneye ▶ **noun** a small slender-bodied fish with iridescent pale green eyes, occurring in deep waters of the western Atlantic.

● Family Chlorophthalmidae: two genera and several species.

green-eyed monster ▶ noun (**the green-eyed monster**) informal, humorous jealousy personified.
– ORIGIN from Shakespeare's *Othello* (III. 3. 166).

green fat ▶ noun [mass noun] the green gelatinous part of a turtle, highly regarded by gourmets.

green fee (US also **greens fee**) ▶ noun a charge for playing one round or session on a golf course.

greenfeed ▶ noun [mass noun] Austral./NZ forage grown to be fed fresh to livestock.

greenfield ▶ adjective [attrib.] relating to or denoting previously undeveloped sites for commercial development or exploitation.

greenfinch ▶ noun a Eurasian finch with green and yellow plumage.
● Genus *Carduelis*, family Fringillidae: three species, in particular the common *C. chloris* of Europe and the Middle East.

green fingers ▶ plural noun Brit. informal natural ability in growing plants.
– DERIVATIVES **green-fingered** adjective.

greenfly ▶ noun (pl. same or **-flies**) chiefly Brit. a green aphid which is a common pest of crops and garden plants.
● Several species in the family Aphididae.

greengage ▶ noun **1** a sweet greenish fruit resembling a small plum. Also called GAGE³.
2 the tree bearing this fruit.
● *Prunus domestica* subsp. *italica* (or *P. italica*), family Rosaceae.
– ORIGIN early 18th cent.: named after Sir William Gage (1657–1727), the English botanist who introduced it to England.

green goose ▶ noun a goose that is killed when under four months old and eaten without stuffing.

greengrocer ▶ noun Brit. a retailer of fruit and vegetables.
– DERIVATIVES **greengrocery** noun.

greenhead ▶ noun **1** (also **greenhead fly**) chiefly US a biting horsefly with green eyes.
● Genus *Chrysops*, family Tabanidae.
2 Austral. an ant with a green head and a painful sting.
● *Rhytidoponera metallica*, family Formicidae.

greenheart ▶ noun a South American evergreen tree of the laurel family, yielding hard greenish timber which is used for marine work because of its resistance to marine borers.
● *Ocotea rodiaei*, family Lauraceae.
■ [mass noun] this timber, or similar timber from various other tropical trees.

greenhide ▶ noun Austral. the untanned hide of an animal.

greenhorn ▶ noun informal, chiefly N. Amer. a person who is new to or inexperienced at a particular activity.

greenhouse ▶ noun a glass building in which plants are grown that need protection from cold weather.

greenhouse effect ▶ noun the trapping of the sun's warmth in a planet's lower atmosphere due to the greater transparency of the atmosphere to visible radiation from the sun than to infrared radiation emitted from the planet's surface.

On earth the increasing quantity of atmospheric carbon dioxide from the burning of fossil fuels, together with the release of other gases, is causing an increased greenhouse effect and leading to global warming. A greenhouse effect involving CO_2 is also responsible for the very high surface temperature of Venus. See also GLOBAL WARMING.

greenhouse gas ▶ noun a gas that contributes to the greenhouse effect by absorbing infrared radiation. Carbon dioxide and chlorofluorocarbons are examples of greenhouse gases.

greenie ▶ noun informal, often derogatory a person who campaigns for protection of the environment.

greening ▶ noun an apple of a variety that is green when ripe.
– ORIGIN early 17th cent. (originally denoting a kind of pear): probably from Middle Dutch *groeninc*, a kind of apple, from *groen* 'green'.

greenkeeper (N. Amer. also **greenskeeper**) ▶ noun a person employed to look after a golf course.

Greenland a large island lying to the north-east of North America and mostly within the Arctic Circle; pop. 55,100 (1993); capital, Nuuk (Godthåb). Danish name GRØNLAND; called in Inuit KALAALLIT NUNAAT.

Only 5 per cent of Greenland is habitable; the population is largely Inuit. Formerly a Norse and a Danish settlement, Greenland became a dependency of Denmark in 1953 with internal autonomy from 1979. It withdrew from the EC in 1985.

– DERIVATIVES **Greenlander** noun.

Greenland halibut ▶ noun an edible halibut with a black or dark brown upper side, which is found in cold deep waters of the north.
● *Reinhardtius hippoglossoides*, family Pleuronectidae.

Greenlandic /griːˈlandɪk/ ▶ noun [mass noun] a dialect of the Inuit (Eskimo) language which is one of the official languages of Greenland (the other being Danish).

Greenland right whale (also **Greenland whale**) ▶ noun another term for BOWHEAD.

Greenland Sea a sea which lies between the east coast of Greenland and the Svalbard archipelago, forming part of the Arctic Ocean.

green leek ▶ noun Austral. a green-faced or mainly green parrot.
● Family Psittacidae: several species, e.g. the superb parrot (*Polytelis swainsonii*).

greenlet /ˈgriːnlɪt/ ▶ noun a small warbler-like vireo with drab plumage, found in Central and South America.
● Genus *Hylophilus*, family Vireonidae: several species.

green light ▶ noun a green traffic light giving permission to proceed.
■ figurative permission to go ahead with a project: *the Secretary of State has* **given the green light for** *a wind-farm development*.
▶ verb (**green-light**) [with obj.] chiefly N. Amer. give permission to go ahead with (a project, especially a film).

greenling ▶ noun a spiny-finned edible fish of the North Pacific.
● Family Hexagrammidae: two genera and several species, including the lingcod.

green lizard ▶ noun a lizard that is typically green with (especially in the male) a blue throat, native to Europe and SW Asia.
● *Lacerta viridis*, family Lacertidae.

greenmail ▶ noun [mass noun] Stock Exchange the practice of buying enough shares in a company to threaten a takeover, forcing the owners to buy them back at a higher price in order to retain control.
– DERIVATIVES **greenmailer** noun.
– ORIGIN 1980s: blend of GREEN and BLACKMAIL.

green man ▶ noun **1** (in the UK) a symbol of an illuminated green human figure at a pedestrian crossing, indicating that it is safe to cross the road.
2 historical a man dressed up in greenery to represent a wild man of the woods or seasonal fertility.
■ a carved image of this, often seen in medieval English churches as a human face with branches and foliage growing out of the mouth.

green manure ▶ noun [mass noun] a fertilizer consisting of growing plants that are ploughed back into the soil.

green monkey ▶ noun a common African guenon with greenish-brown upper parts and a black face. Compare with GRIVET and VERVET.
● *Cercopithecus aethiops*, family Cercopithecidae, in particular the race *C. a. sabaeus* of West Africa, which is often tamed.

Green Mountain State informal name for VERMONT.

Greenock /ˈgriːnək/ a port in west central Scotland, on the Firth of Clyde; pop. 55,000 (1991).

greenockite /ˈgriːnəkʌɪt/ ▶ noun [mass noun] a mineral consisting of cadmium sulphide which typically occurs as a yellow crust on zinc ores.
– ORIGIN mid 19th cent.: from the name of Lord Greenock, who later became Earl Cathcart (1783–1859), + -ITE¹.

Green Paper ▶ noun (in the UK) a preliminary report of government proposals that is published in order to provoke discussion.

Green Party ▶ noun an environmentalist political party.

Greenpeace an international organization that campaigns actively but non-violently for conservation of the environment and the preservation of endangered species.

green pepper ▶ noun the unripe fruit of a sweet pepper, which is mild in flavour and widely used in cookery.

■ the plant which yields this fruit. See CAPSICUM.

green pigeon ▶ noun a fruit-eating pigeon with mainly green plumage occurring in the Old World tropics.
● Genus *Treron*, family Columbidae: many species. See also FRUIT PIGEON.

green plover ▶ noun Brit. the northern lapwing.

green pound ▶ noun the exchange rate for the pound applied to payments for agricultural produce in the EU.

green revolution ▶ noun **1** a large increase in crop production in developing countries achieved by the use of artificial fertilizers, pesticides, and high-yield crop varieties.
2 a dramatic rise in concern about the environment in industrialized countries.

green room ▶ noun a room in a theatre or studio in which performers can relax when they are not performing.

greensand ▶ noun [mass noun] Geology a greenish kind of sandstone, often loosely consolidated.
■ (usu. **the Greensand**) a stratum largely composed of such sandstone, deposited during the Cretaceous period and often underlying chalk.

greens fee ▶ noun US term for GREEN FEE.

greenshank ▶ noun a large sandpiper with long greenish legs and grey plumage, breeding in northern Eurasia and North America.
● Genus *Tringa*, family Scolopacidae: two species, in particular *T. nebularia*.

greenskeeper ▶ noun North American term for GREENKEEPER.

green snake ▶ noun a harmless American snake with a green back and white or yellowish underparts.
● Genus *Opheodrys*, family Colubridae: two species.

green space ▶ noun an area of grass, trees, or other vegetation set apart for recreational or aesthetic purposes in an otherwise urban environment.

greenstick fracture ▶ noun a fracture of the bone, occurring typically in children, in which one side of the bone is broken and the other only bent.

greenstone ▶ noun [mass noun] Geology a greenish igneous rock containing feldspar and hornblende.
■ chiefly NZ a variety of jade.

greensward /ˈgriːnˌswɔːd/ ▶ noun [mass noun] archaic or poetic/literary grass-covered ground.

green tea ▶ noun [mass noun] tea made from unfermented leaves that is pale in colour and slightly bitter in flavour, produced mainly in China and Japan. Compare with BLACK TEA.

green thumb ▶ noun North American term for GREEN FINGERS.

green turtle ▶ noun a sea turtle with an olive-brown shell, often living close to the coast and extensively hunted for food.
● *Chelonia mydas*, family Cheloniidae.

green vitriol ▶ noun [mass noun] archaic crystalline ferrous sulphate.

greenware ▶ noun [mass noun] unfired pottery.

greenway ▶ noun US a strip of undeveloped land near an urban area, set aside for recreational use or environmental protection.

Greenwich /ˈgrɛnɪtʃ, ˈgrɪnɪdʒ/ a London borough on the south bank of the Thames, the original site of the Royal Greenwich Observatory.

Greenwich Mean Time (abbrev.: **GMT**) (also **Greenwich time**) the mean solar time at the Greenwich meridian, adopted as the standard time in a zone that includes the British Isles.

Greenwich meridian ▶ noun the prime meridian, which passes through the former Royal Observatory at Greenwich. It was adopted internationally as the zero of longitude in 1884.

Greenwich Village a district of New York City on the lower west side of Manhattan, traditionally associated with writers, artists, and musicians.

greenwood ▶ noun archaic a wood or forest in leaf (regarded as the typical scene of medieval outlaw life).

green woodpecker ▶ noun a large green and yellow woodpecker with a red crown and a laughing call, found from Europe to central Asia.
● *Picus viridis*, family Picidae.

greeny ▶ **adjective** [often in combination] slightly green: *the greeny-brown surface of the stone.*

Greer, Germaine (b.1939), Australian feminist and writer. She first achieved recognition with her influential book *The Female Eunuch* (1970), an analysis of women's subordination in a male-dominated society.

greet[1] ▶ **verb** [with obj.] give a polite word or sign of welcome or recognition to (someone) on meeting. ■ [with obj. and adverbial] receive or acknowledge (something) in a specified way: *everyone present greeted this idea warmly.* ■ (of a sight or sound) become apparent to or be noticed by (someone) on arrival somewhere: *you're greeted with a delightful confusion of aromas.*
– ORIGIN Old English *grētan* 'approach, attack, or salute', of West Germanic origin; related to Dutch *groeten* and German *grüssen* 'greet'.

greet[2] ▶ **verb** [no obj.] Scottish weep; cry: *he sat down on the armchair and started to greet.*
– ORIGIN Old English, partly from *grētan* 'cry out, rage', partly from *grēotan* 'lament', both of Germanic origin.

greeter ▶ **noun** chiefly US a person employed to greet customers at a shop, restaurant, or other business.

greeting ▶ **noun** a polite word or sign of welcome or recognition: *Mandy shouted a greeting.* ■ [mass noun] the action of giving such a sign: *she raised her hand* ***in greeting***. ■ (usu. **greetings**) a formal expression of goodwill, said on meeting or in a written message: *warm greetings to you all.*

greetings card (US **greeting card**) ▶ **noun** a decorative card sent to convey good wishes.

gregarine /ˈɡrɛɡərʌɪn/ Zoology ▶ **adjective** of or relating to a group of microscopic worm-like protozoans that are internal parasites of insects, annelids, and other invertebrates. ■ (of movement) slow and gliding, as seen in these protozoans.
▶ **noun** a gregarine protozoan.
• Class Gregarina (or subclass Gregarinidia), phylum Sporozoa, kingdom Protista.
– ORIGIN mid 19th cent.: from modern Latin *Gregarina*, from Latin *gregarius* (see **GREGARIOUS**).

gregarious /ɡrɪˈɡɛːrɪəs/ ▶ **adjective** (of a person) fond of company; sociable: *he was a popular and gregarious man.* ■ (of animals) living in flocks or loosely organized communities: *gregarious species forage in flocks from colonies or roosts.* ■ (of plants) growing in open clusters or in pure associations.
– DERIVATIVES **gregariously** adverb, **gregariousness** noun.
– ORIGIN mid 17th cent.: from Latin *gregarius* (from *grex, greg-* 'a flock') + **-OUS**.

Gregorian calendar /ɡrɪˈɡɔːrɪən/ ▶ **noun** the calendar introduced in 1582 by Pope Gregory XIII, as a modification of the Julian calendar.

To bring the calendar back into line with the solar year, 10 days were suppressed, and centenary years were only made leap years if they were divisible by 400. Scotland adopted the Gregorian calendar in 1600, but England and Wales did not follow suit until 1752 (by which time 11 days had to be suppressed). At the same time New Year's Day was changed from 25 March to 1 January, and dates using the new calendar were designated 'New Style'.

Gregorian chant ▶ **noun** [mass noun] church music sung as a single vocal line in free rhythm and a restricted scale (plainsong), in a style developed for the medieval Latin liturgy.
– ORIGIN mid 18th cent.: named after St Gregory the Great (in Latin *Gregorius*), who is said to have standardized it.

Gregorian telescope ▶ **noun** an early reflecting telescope in which light reflected from a concave elliptical secondary mirror passes through a hole in the primary mirror. It was rendered obsolete by the introduction of Newtonian and Cassegrain telescopes.
– ORIGIN mid 18th cent.: named after James Gregory (1638–75), the Scottish mathematician who invented it.

Gregory, St (*c.*540–604), pope (as Gregory I) 590–604 and Doctor of the Church; known as St Gregory the Great. An important reformer, he did much to establish the temporal power of the papacy. He sent St Augustine to England to lead the country's conversion to Christianity, and is also credited with the introduction of Gregorian chant. Feast day, 12 March.

Gregory of Nazianzus, St /ˌnazɪˈanzəs/ (329–89), Doctor of the Church, bishop of Constantinople. With St Basil and St Gregory of Nyssa he was an upholder of Orthodoxy against the Arian and Apollinarian heresies, and influential in restoring adherence to the Nicene Creed. Feast day (in the Eastern Church) 25 and 30 January; (in the Western Church) 2 January (formerly 9 May).

Gregory of Nyssa, St /ˈnɪsə/ (*c.*330–*c.*395), Doctor of the Eastern Church, bishop of Nyssa in Cappadocia. The brother of St Basil, he was an Orthodox follower of Origen and joined with St Basil and St Gregory of Nazianzus in opposing Arianism. Feast day, 9 March.

Gregory of Tours, St /tʊə/ (*c.*540–94), Frankish bishop and historian. He was elected bishop of Tours in 573; his writings provide the chief authority for the early Merovingian period of French history. Feast day, 17 November.

greisen /ˈɡrʌɪz(ə)n/ ▶ **noun** [mass noun] Geology a light-coloured rock containing quartz, mica, and fluorine-rich minerals, resulting from the alteration of granite by hot vapour from magma.
– ORIGIN late 19th cent.: from German, probably a dialect word, from *greis* 'grey with age'.

gremlin ▶ **noun** informal an imaginary mischievous sprite regarded as responsible for an unexplained problem or fault, especially a mechanical or electronic one: *a gremlin in my computer omitted a line.* ■ such a problem or fault.
– ORIGIN 1940s: perhaps suggested by **GOBLIN**.

Grenache /ɡrəˈnaʃ/ ▶ **noun** [mass noun] a variety of black wine grape native to the Languedoc-Roussillon region of France. ■ a sweet red dessert wine made from this grape.
– ORIGIN French.

Grenada /ɡrəˈneɪdə/ a country in the Caribbean, consisting of the island of Grenada (the southernmost of the Windward Islands) and the southern Grenadine Islands; pop. 94,800 (1991); languages, English (official), English Creole; capital, St George's.

The island of Grenada was sighted in 1498 by Columbus. Colonized by the French, it was ceded to Britain in 1763, recaptured by the French, and restored to Britain in 1783. It became an independent Commonwealth state in 1974. Seizure of power by a left-wing military group in 1983 prompted an invasion by the US and some Caribbean countries; they withdrew in 1985.

– DERIVATIVES **Grenadian** adjective & noun.

grenade /ɡrəˈneɪd/ ▶ **noun** a small bomb thrown by hand or launched mechanically. ■ a glass receptacle containing chemicals which are released when the receptacle is thrown and broken, used for testing drains and extinguishing fires.
– ORIGIN mid 16th cent. (in the sense 'pomegranate'): from French, alteration of Old French (*pome*) *grenate* (see **POMEGRANATE**), on the pattern of Spanish *granada*. The bomb was so named because of its shape, supposedly resembling a pomegranate.

grenadier /ˌɡrɛnəˈdɪə/ ▶ **noun** **1** historical a soldier armed with grenades. ■ (**Grenadiers** or **Grenadier Guards**) (in the UK) the first regiment of the royal household infantry.
2 a common bottom-dwelling fish with a large head, a long tapering tail, and typically a luminous gland on the belly. Also called **RAT-TAIL**.
• Family Macrouridae: numerous genera and species.
3 a reddish-brown African waxbill with a red bill and a bright blue rump.
• Genus *Uraeginthus*, family Estrildidae: the **common grenadier** (*U. granatina*), with violet cheeks, and the **purple grenadier** (*U. ianthinogaster*), with a blue belly.
– ORIGIN late 17th cent.: from French, from *grenade* (see **GRENADE**).

grenadilla /ˌɡrɛnəˈdɪlə/ ▶ **noun** variant spelling of **GRANADILLA**.

grenadine[1] /ˈɡrɛnədiːn/ ▶ **noun** [mass noun] a sweet cordial made in France from pomegranates.
– ORIGIN French, from *grenade* 'pomegranate' (see **GRENADE**).

grenadine[2] /ˈɡrɛnədiːn/ ▶ **noun** [mass noun] dress fabric of loosely woven silk or silk and wool.
– ORIGIN mid 19th cent.: from French (earlier *grenade*), 'grained silk', from *grenu* 'grained', from *grain* 'grain'.

Grenadine Islands /ˈɡrɛnədiːn/ (also **the Grenadines**) a chain of small islands in the Caribbean, part of the Windward Islands. They are divided administratively between St Vincent and Grenada.

Grendel /ˈɡrɛnd(ə)l/ the water monster killed by Beowulf in the Old English epic poem *Beowulf*.

Grenfell /ˈɡrɛnf(ə)l/, Joyce (Irene Phipps) (1910–79), English entertainer and writer. She appeared in revues, one-woman shows, and films, in which she specialized in portraying gauche female characters.

Grenoble /ɡrəˈnəʊb(ə)l, French ɡʀənɔbl/ a city in SE France; pop. 153,970 (1991). It is an important industrial city.

Grenville /ˈɡrɛnvɪl/, George (1712–70), British Whig statesman, Prime Minister 1763–5.

Gresham /ˈɡrɛʃəm/, Sir Thomas (*c.*1519–79), English financier. He founded the Royal Exchange in 1566 and served as the chief financial adviser to the Elizabethan government.

Gresham's law Economics the tendency for money of lower intrinsic value to circulate more freely than money of higher intrinsic and equal nominal value (often expressed as 'Bad money drives out good').

Gresley /ˈɡrɛzli/, Sir (Herbert) Nigel (1876–1941), British railway engineer. He is most famous for designing express steam locomotives, such as the A4 class exemplified by the *Mallard*.

Gretna Green a village in Scotland just north of the English border near Carlisle, formerly a popular place for runaway couples from England to be married without the parental consent required in England for people under a certain age.

Gretzky /ˈɡrɛtski/, Wayne (b.1961), Canadian ice-hockey player. He is the all-time leading point-scorer in the National Hockey League, and was voted Most Valuable Player nine times.

Greuze /ɡrəːz, French ɡʀøz/, Jean-Baptiste (1725–1805), French painter, noted for his genre paintings and portraits.

grevillea /ɡrɪˈvɪlɪə/ ▶ **noun** an evergreen tree or shrub which bears conspicuous flowers that lack petals, most kinds of which are native to Australia.
• Genus *Grevillea*, family Proteaceae.
– ORIGIN modern Latin, named after Charles F. *Greville* (1749–1809), Scottish horticulturalist.

grew past of **GROW**.

Grey[1], Charles, 2nd Earl (1764–1845), British statesman, Prime Minister 1830–4. His government passed the first Reform Act (1832) as well as important factory legislation and the Act abolishing slavery throughout the British Empire.

Grey[2], Lady Jane (1537–54), niece of Henry VIII, queen of England 9–19 July 1553. In 1553, to ensure a Protestant succession, John Dudley, the Duke of Northumberland, forced Jane to marry his son and persuaded the dying Edward VI to name Jane as his successor. She was quickly deposed by forces loyal to Edward's (Catholic) sister Mary, who had popular support, and executed the following year.

Grey[3], Zane (1872–1939), American writer; born *Pearl Grey*. He wrote fifty-four westerns in a somewhat romanticized and formulaic style, which sold over 13 million copies during his lifetime.

grey (US **gray**) ▶ **adjective** **1** of a colour intermediate between black and white, as of ashes or lead: *grey flannel trousers.* ■ (of hair) turning grey or white with age: *a grey beard.* ■ (of a person) having grey hair: [as complement] *he is getting on a bit, and going grey.* ■ informal, chiefly N. Amer. relating to old people, especially when seen as an oppressed group: *grey power.* ■ (of the weather) cloudy and dull; without sun: *a cold, grey November day.* ■ (of a person's face) pale, as through tiredness, age, or illness: *a few people, their faces grey and bitter.*
2 dull and nondescript; without interest or character: *grey, faceless men | the grey daily routine.*
3 (of financial or trading activity) not accounted for in official statistics: *the grey economy.*
4 S. African of or relating to a residential area in which people of differing ethnic backgrounds live as neighbours: *a grey Cape Town suburb.*
▶ **noun** **1** [mass noun] grey colour or pigment: *dirty intermediate tones of grey.* ■ grey clothes or material: *the gentleman in grey.* ■ grey hair: *he sighed at the amount of grey at his temple.*
2 a grey thing or animal, in particular a grey or white horse.
▶ **verb** [no obj.] (especially of hair) become grey with

age: *he had put on weight and greyed somewhat* | [as adj.] **greying** *a man of about fifty with greying hair.*
■(of a person or group) become older; age: [as adj.] **greying** *a greying workforce.*
– DERIVATIVES **greyish** adjective, **greyly** adverb, **greyness** noun.
– ORIGIN Old English *græg*, of Germanic origin; related to Dutch *grauw* and German *grau.*

grey area ▸ noun an ill-defined situation or field not readily conforming to a category or to an existing set of rules: *grey areas in the legislation have still to be clarified.*

greybeard (US **graybeard**) ▸ noun **1** humorous or derogatory an old man.
2 archaic a large stoneware jug used for holding spirits.

grey drake ▸ noun Brit. the greyish gravid female of certain mayflies.
● Genus *Ephemera*, family Ephemeridae.
■an artificial fishing fly that imitates this.

grey eminence ▸ noun another term for ÉMINENCE GRISE.

Grey Friar ▸ noun a Franciscan friar.
– ORIGIN Middle English: so named because of the colour of the order's habit.

grey goose ▸ noun a goose of a group distinguished by having mainly grey plumage.
● Genus *Anser*, family Anatidae: several species, e.g. greylag and white-fronted geese.

greyhen ▸ noun the female of the black grouse.

greyhound ▸ noun a dog of a tall, slender breed having keen sight and capable of high speed, used since ancient times for hunting small game and now chiefly in racing and coursing.
– ORIGIN Old English *grīghund*; the first element, related to Old Norse *grey* 'bitch', is of unknown origin.

greyhound racing ▸ noun [mass noun] a sport in which greyhounds race around a circular or oval track in pursuit of a moving dummy hare and spectators bet on the outcome.

grey jay ▸ noun a fluffy long-tailed jay with dark grey upper parts and a whitish face, found in Canada and the north-western US.
● *Perisoreus canadensis*, family Corvidae.

grey kangaroo ▸ noun a large forest-dwelling kangaroo native to Australia.
● Genus *Macropus*, family Macropodidae: the eastern *M. giganteus* (also called FORESTER), with silvery-grey fur, and the western *M. fuliginosus*, with brownish fur.

grey knight ▸ noun Stock Exchange a person or company making a possibly hostile counter offer for a company already facing a hostile takeover bid.
– ORIGIN by association with BLACK KNIGHT and WHITE KNIGHT.

greylag (also **greylag goose**) ▸ noun a large goose with mainly grey plumage, which is native to Eurasia and is the ancestor of the domestic goose.
● *Anser anser*, family Anatidae
– ORIGIN early 18th cent.: probably from GREY + dialect *lag* 'goose', of unknown origin.

grey matter ▸ noun [mass noun] the darker tissue of the brain and spinal cord, consisting mainly of nerve cell bodies and branching dendrites. Compare with WHITE MATTER.
■informal intelligence: *I wish I had a little of her grey matter.*

grey mullet ▸ noun a thick-bodied, blunt-headed fish that typically lives in inshore or estuarine waters and is a valued food fish.
● Family Mugilidae: several genera and species.

grey nurse ▸ noun see NURSE².

grey parrot (also **African grey parrot**) ▸ noun a parrot of western equatorial Africa, with grey plumage and a red tail, often kept as a pet for its mimicking abilities.
● *Psittacus erithacus*, family Psittacidae.

greyscale ▸ noun Computing a range of grey shades from white to black, as used in a monochrome display or printout: [as modifier] *a greyscale scanner.*

grey seal ▸ noun a large seal with a spotted greyish coat and a convex profile, found commonly in the North Atlantic. Also called ATLANTIC SEAL.
● *Halichoerus grypus*, family Phocidae.

grey squirrel ▸ noun an American tree squirrel with mainly grey fur.
● Genus *Sciurus*, family Sciuridae: four species, in particular

Sciurus carolinensis, native to eastern North America and introduced to Britain and elsewhere.

greywacke /ˈɡreɪwakə/ (US **graywacke**) ▸ noun [mass noun] Geology a dark coarse-grained sandstone containing more than 15 per cent clay.
– ORIGIN late 18th cent. (as *grauwacke*): from German *Grauwacke*, from *grau* 'grey' + WACKE. The Anglicized form dates from the early 19th cent.

grey water ▸ noun [mass noun] technical the relatively clean waste water from baths, sinks, washing machines, and other kitchen appliances. Compare with BLACK WATER.

grey whale ▸ noun a mottled grey baleen whale that typically has heavy encrustations of barnacles on the skin, commonly seen in coastal waters of the NE Pacific.
● *Eschrichtius robustus*, the only member of the family Eschrichtiidae.

grey wolf ▸ noun another term for TIMBER WOLF.

gribble ▸ noun a small marine isopod crustacean that bores into submerged wooden structures, often causing damage to pier timbers.
● *Limnoria lignorum*, order Isopoda.
– ORIGIN late 18th cent.: perhaps related to the verb GRUB.

gricer /ˈɡrʌɪsə/ ▸ noun Brit. informal an obsessive or fanatical railway enthusiast.
– ORIGIN 1960s: origin uncertain; said to be a humorous representation of a received pronunciation of *grouser* 'grouse-shooter'.

grid ▸ noun **1** a framework of spaced bars that are parallel to or cross each other; a grating: *the metal grids had been pulled across the foyer.*
2 a network of lines that cross each other to form a series of squares or rectangles: *a grid of tree-lined streets.*
■a network of cables or pipes for distributing power, especially high-voltage transmission lines for electricity: *the second reactor was not connected to the grid until 1985.* ■ a network of regularly spaced lines on a map that cross one another at right angles and are numbered to enable the precise location of a place. ■a pattern of lines marking the starting places on a motor-racing track: *first away from the grid.* ■ Electronics an electrode placed between the cathode and anode of a thermionic valve or cathode ray tube, serving to control or modulate the flow of electrons.
▸ verb [with obj.] [usu. as adj. **gridded**] put into or set out as a grid: *a well-planned core of gridded streets.*
– ORIGIN mid 19th cent.: back-formation from GRIDIRON.

grid bias ▸ noun Electronics a fixed voltage applied between the cathode and the control grid of a thermionic valve which determines its operating conditions.

gridder ▸ noun US an American football player.

griddle ▸ noun **1** a circular iron plate that is heated and used for cooking food: [as modifier] *griddle cakes.*
2 historical a miner's wire-bottomed sieve.
▸ verb [with obj.] **1** cook on a griddle: [as adj. **griddled**] *griddled corn cakes.*
2 historical screen (ore) with a griddle: *black copper ore is generally griddled out.*
– ORIGIN Middle English (denoting a gridiron): from Old French *gredil*, from Latin *craticula*, diminutive of *cratis* 'hurdle'; related to CRATE, GRATE², and GRILL¹.

gridiron /ˈɡrɪdʌɪən/ ▸ noun **1** a frame of parallel bars or beams, typically in two sets arranged at right angles, in particular:
■a frame of parallel metal bars used for grilling meat or fish over an open fire. ■ a frame of parallel beams for supporting a ship in dock. ■ (in the theatre) a framework over a stage supporting scenery and lighting.
2 a field for American football, marked with regularly spaced parallel lines.
■[mass noun] N. Amer. the game of American football: [as modifier] *the national gridiron season.*
3 another term for GRID (in sense 2).
– ORIGIN Middle English *gredire*, alteration of *gredile* 'griddle' by association with IRON.

gridlock ▸ noun **1** a traffic jam affecting a whole network of intersecting streets.
2 another term for DEADLOCK (in sense 1).
– DERIVATIVES **gridlocked** adjective.

grid reference ▸ noun a map reference indicating a location in terms of a series of vertical and

horizontal grid lines identified by numbers or letters.

grief ▸ noun [mass noun] deep or intense sorrow, especially caused by someone's death: *she was overcome with grief.*
■informal trouble or annoyance: *they won't give you any grief in the next few days.*
– PHRASES **come to grief** have an accident; meet with disaster: *many a ship has come to grief along this shore.* **good grief!** an exclamation of surprise or alarm.
– ORIGIN Middle English: from Old French *grief*, from *grever* 'to burden' (see GRIEVE¹).

grief-stricken ▸ adjective overcome with deep or intense sorrow.

Grieg /ɡriːɡ/, Edvard (1843–1907), Norwegian composer, conductor, and violinist. Famous works include the Piano Concerto in A minor (1869) and the incidental music to Ibsen's play *Peer Gynt* (1876).

Grierson /ˈɡriːəs(ə)n/, John (1898–1972), Scottish film director and producer. A pioneer in British documentary film-making, he made his name with *Drifters* (1928), before heading the GPO Film Unit (1933–9) and establishing the National Film Board of Canada (1939).

grievance ▸ noun a real or imagined wrong or other cause for complaint or protest, especially unfair treatment: *failure to redress genuine grievances.*
■a feeling of resentment over something believed to be wrong or unfair: *he was nursing a grievance.*
– ORIGIN Middle English (also in the sense 'injury'): from Old French *grevance*, from *grever* 'to burden' (see GRIEVE¹).

grieve¹ ▸ verb [no obj.] suffer grief: *she grieved for her father.*
■[with obj.] feel grief for or because of: *she did not have the opportunity to grieve her mother's death.* ■ [with obj.] cause great distress to (someone): *Dolly was deeply grieved* | [with obj. and infinitive] *it grieves me to think of you in that house alone.*
– DERIVATIVES **griever** noun.
– ORIGIN Middle English (also in the sense 'harm, oppress'): from Old French *grever* 'burden, encumber', based on Latin *gravare*, from *gravis* 'heavy, grave' (see GRAVE²).

grieve² ▸ noun Scottish an overseer, manager, or bailiff on a farm.
– ORIGIN late 15th cent.: related to REEVE¹.

grievous ▸ adjective formal (of something bad) very severe or serious: *his death was a grievous blow* | *the American fleet suffered grievous losses.*
– DERIVATIVES **grievously** adverb, **grievousness** noun.
– ORIGIN Middle English: from Old French *greveus*, from *grever* (see GRIEVE¹).

grievous bodily harm (abbrev.: GBH) ▸ noun [mass noun] Law serious physical injury inflicted on a person by the deliberate action of another. Compare with ACTUAL BODILY HARM.

griff ▸ noun [mass noun] informal, dated news or reliable information.
– ORIGIN late 19th cent.: abbreviation of the slang term *griffin* 'a betting tip', of unknown origin.

griffin (also **gryphon**, **griffon**) ▸ noun a mythical creature with the head and wings of an eagle and the body of a lion, typically depicted with pointed ears and with the eagle's legs taking the place of the forelegs.
– ORIGIN Middle English: from Old French *grifoun*, based on late Latin *gryphus*, via Latin from Greek *grups, grup-.*

Griffith¹, Arthur (1872–1922), Irish nationalist leader and statesman, President of the Irish Free State 1922. In 1905 he founded and became president of Sinn Fein. He became Vice-President of the newly declared Irish Republic in 1919 and negotiated the Anglo-Irish Treaty (1921).

Griffith², D. W. (1875–1948), American film director; full name *David Lewelyn Wark Griffith*. A pioneer in film, he is responsible for introducing many cinematic techniques, including flashback and fade-out. Notable films: *The Birth of a Nation* (1915), *Intolerance* (1916), and *Broken Blossoms* (1919).

griffon /ˈɡrɪf(ə)n/ ▸ noun **1** a dog of any of several terrier-like breeds originating in NW Europe.
■(also **Brussels griffon**) a dog of a toy breed with a flat face and upturned chin.
2 (also **griffon vulture**) a large Old World vulture with predominantly pale brown plumage.

● Genus *Gyps*, family Accipitridae: four species, in particular the Eurasian *G. fulvus* and the African **Ruppell's griffon** (*G. ruepelli*).

3 variant spelling of **GRIFFIN**.

– ORIGIN Middle English (in senses 2 and 3): variant of **GRIFFIN**; sense 1 was adopted from French in the 18th cent.

grift N. Amer. informal ▶ **verb** [no obj.] engage in petty swindling.
▶ **noun** a petty swindle.
– DERIVATIVES **grifter** noun.
– ORIGIN early 20th cent.: alteration of **GRAFT**[2].

grig ▶ **noun** dialect **1** a small eel.
2 a grasshopper or cricket.
– PHRASES **(as) merry** (or **lively**) **as a grig** full of fun; extravagantly lively.
– ORIGIN Middle English (in the sense 'dwarf'): of unknown origin.

gri-gri ▶ **noun** variant spelling of **GRIS-GRIS**.

grike /ɡrʌɪk/ (also **gryke**) ▶ **noun** a fissure separating blocks or clints in a limestone pavement.
– ORIGIN late 18th cent. (originally northern English dialect): of unknown origin.

g

grill[1] ▶ **noun** Brit. a device on a cooker that radiates heat downwards for cooking food.
■ a gridiron used for cooking food on an open fire. ■ a dish of food, especially meat, cooked using a grill. ■ (also **grill room**) a restaurant serving grilled food.
▶ **verb** **1** [with obj.] cook (something) using a grill: *grill the trout for about five minutes.*
2 [with obj.] informal subject (someone) to intense questioning or interrogation: *my father grilled us about what we had been doing* | [as noun **grilling**] *they faced a grilling over the latest results.*
– DERIVATIVES **griller** noun.
– ORIGIN mid 17th cent.: from French *gril* (noun), *griller* (verb), from Old French *graille* 'grille'.

grill[2] ▶ **noun** variant spelling of **GRILLE**.

grillade /ɡrɪˈleɪd, -ˈjɑːd, ˈɡriːɑːd/ ▶ **noun** (often **grillades**) a kind of meat stew usually made with beef steak, typical of French regional and Cajun cookery.
– ORIGIN French.

grillage /ˈɡrɪlɪdʒ/ ▶ **noun** a heavy framework of cross-timbering or metal beams forming a foundation for building on difficult ground.
– ORIGIN late 18th cent.: from French (see **GRILLE**, **-AGE**).

grille (also **grill**) ▶ **noun** a grating or screen of metal bars or wires, placed in front of something as protection or to allow ventilation or discreet observation.
– ORIGIN mid 17th cent.: from French, from medieval Latin, *craticula*, diminutive of *cratis* 'hurdle'; related to **CRATE**, **GRATE**[2], and **GRIDDLE**.

grill room ▶ **noun** see **GRILL**[1].

grilse /ɡrɪls/ ▶ **noun** a salmon that has returned to fresh water after a single winter at sea.
– ORIGIN late Middle English: of unknown origin.

grim ▶ **adjective** (**grimmer**, **grimmest**) forbidding or uninviting: *his grim expression* | *long rows of grim, dark housing developments.*
■ (of humour) lacking genuine levity; mirthless; black: *some moments of grim humour.* ■ unappealing or unattractive: *a grim goalless draw in appalling weather.* ■ depressing or worrying to consider: *the grim news of the murder.* ■ unrelentingly harsh; merciless or severe: *few creatures are able to thrive in this grim and hostile land.*
– PHRASES **like** (or **for**) **grim death** with great determination: *we had to hold on like grim death.*
– DERIVATIVES **grimly** adverb, **grimness** noun.
– ORIGIN Old English, of Germanic origin; related to Dutch *grim* and German *grimm*.

grimace /ɡrɪˈmeɪs, ˈɡrɪməs/ ▶ **noun** an ugly, twisted expression on a person's face, typically expressing disgust, pain, or wry amusement: *she gave a grimace of pain.*
▶ **verb** [no obj.] make a grimace: *I sipped the coffee and grimaced.*
– DERIVATIVES **grimacer** noun.
– ORIGIN mid 17th cent.: from French, from Spanish *grimazo* 'caricature', from *grima* 'fright'.

Grimaldi[1] /ɡrɪˈmaldi/, Francesco Maria (1618–63), Italian physicist and astronomer, who discovered the diffraction of light and verified Galileo's law of the uniform acceleration of falling bodies.

Grimaldi[2] /ɡrɪˈmaldi/, Joseph (1779–1837), English circus entertainer, who created the role of the circus clown. He performed at Covent Garden, where he became famous for his acrobatic skills.

grimalkin /ɡrɪˈmalkɪn, -ˈmɔːl-/ ▶ **noun** archaic a cat (used especially in reference to its characteristically feline qualities).
■ a spiteful old woman.
– ORIGIN late 16th cent.: from **GREY** + *Malkin* (pet form of the given name *Matilda*).

grime ▶ **noun** [mass noun] dirt ingrained on the surface of something, especially clothing, a building, or the skin.
▶ **verb** [with obj.] (usu. **be grimed**) blacken or make dirty with grime: *windows grimed like a coal miner's goggles.*
– ORIGIN Middle English: from Middle Low German and Middle Dutch.

Grimm /ɡrɪm/, Jacob (Ludwig Carl) (1785–1863) and Wilhelm (Carl) (1786–1859), German philologists and folklorists. In 1852 the brothers jointly inaugurated a dictionary of German on historical principles, which was eventually completed by other scholars in 1960. They also compiled an anthology of German fairy tales, which appeared in three volumes between 1812 and 1822.

Grimm's law Linguistics the observation that certain Indo-European consonants (mainly stops) undergo regular changes in the Germanic languages which are not seen in others such as Greek or Latin. Examples include *p* becoming *f* so that Latin *pedem* corresponds to English *foot* and German *Fuss*. The principle was set out by Jacob Grimm in his German grammar (2nd edition, 1822).

grimoire /ɡrɪmˈwɑː/ ▶ **noun** a book of magic spells and invocations.
– ORIGIN mid 19th cent.: French, alteration of *grammaire* 'grammar'.

Grimond /ˈɡrɪmənd/, Jo, Baron (1913–93), British Liberal politician, leader of the Liberal Party 1956–67; full name *Joseph Grimond*.

Grim Reaper ▶ **noun** a personification of death in the form of a cloaked skeleton wielding a large scythe.

Grimsby /ˈɡrɪmzbi/ a port on the south shore of the Humber estuary, administrative centre of North East Lincolnshire; pop. 88,900 (1991). Official name **GREAT GRIMSBY**.

grimy ▶ **adjective** (**grimier**, **grimiest**) covered with or characterized by grime: *the grimy industrial city.*
– DERIVATIVES **grimily** adverb, **griminess** noun.

grin ▶ **verb** (**grinned**, **grinning**) [no obj.] smile broadly, especially in an unrestrained manner and with the mouth open: *Dennis appeared, grinning cheerfully.*
■ grimace or appear to grimace grotesquely in a way that reveals the teeth: [as adj. **grinning**] *a grinning skull.*
▶ **noun** a broad smile: *'OK,' he said with a grin.*
– PHRASES **grin and bear it** suffer pain or misfortune in a stoical manner.
– DERIVATIVES **grinner** noun, **grinningly** adverb.
– ORIGIN Old English *grennian* 'bare the teeth in pain or anger', of Germanic origin; probably related to **GROAN**.

grind ▶ **verb** (past and past participle **ground**) **1** [with obj.] reduce (something) to small particles or powder by crushing it: *grind some black pepper over the salad* | *mother preferred to* **grind up** *the rice prior to boiling.*
■ [no obj.] (of a mill or machine) work with a crushing action: *the old mill was grinding again.* ■ sharpen, smooth, or produce (something) by crushing or by friction: *power from a waterwheel was used to grind cutlery.* ■ operate (a mill or machine) by turning the handle: *she was grinding a coffee mill.*
2 rub or cause to rub together gratingly: [no obj.] *tectonic plates that inexorably grind against each other* | [with obj.] *he keeps me awake at night, grinding his teeth.*
■ [no obj., with adverbial] move noisily and laboriously, especially when impeded by friction: *the truck was grinding slowly up the hill.*
3 [no obj.] informal (of a dancer) rotate the hips: *go-go girls grinding to blaring disco.*
■ Brit. vulgar slang, dated have sexual intercourse.
▶ **noun** [in sing.] **1** a crushing or grating sound or motion: *the crunch and grind of bulldozers* | figurative *the slow grind of the US legal system.*
■ hard dull work: *relief from the daily grind.* ■ the size of ground particles: *only the right grind gives you all the fine flavour.*
2 informal a dancer's rotary movement of the hips: *a bump and grind.*
■ Brit. vulgar slang, dated an act of sexual intercourse.
– PHRASES **grind to a halt** (or **come to a grinding halt**) move more and more slowly and then stop.
– ORIGIN Old English *grindan*, probably of Germanic origin. Although no cognates are known, it may be distantly related to Latin *frendere* 'rub away, gnash'.
▶ **grind away** work or study hard.
grind someone down wear someone down with continuous harsh or oppressive treatment: *mundane everyday things which just grind people down.*
grind on continue for a long time in a wearying or tedious way: *the rail talks grind on.*
grind something out produce something dull or tedious slowly and laboriously: *I must grind out some more fiction.*

grinder ▶ **noun** **1** a machine used for grinding something: *a coffee grinder.*
■ a person employed to grind cutlery, tools, or cereals.
2 a molar tooth.
■ (**grinders**) informal the teeth.
3 US informal another name for **HOAGIE**.

grinding ▶ **adjective** [attrib.] **1** (of a state) oppressive, tedious, and seemingly without end: *grinding poverty.*
2 (of a sound or motion) harsh and grating: *the grinding roar of the lorries.*
– DERIVATIVES **grindingly** adverb.

grinding wheel ▶ **noun** a wheel used for cutting, grinding, or finishing metal or other objects, and typically made of abrasive particles bonded together.

grindstone ▶ **noun** a thick disc of stone or other abrasive material mounted so as to revolve, used for grinding, sharpening, or polishing metal objects.
■ rare another term for **MILLSTONE**.
– PHRASES **keep one's nose to the grindstone** work hard and continuously.

gringo /ˈɡrɪŋɡəʊ/ ▶ **noun** (pl. **-os**) informal a white person from an English-speaking country (used in Spanish-speaking countries, chiefly Central and South America).
– ORIGIN Spanish, literally 'foreign, foreigner, or gibberish'.

griot /ˈɡriːəʊ/ ▶ **noun** a member of a class of travelling poets, musicians, and storytellers who maintain a tradition of oral history in parts of West Africa.
– ORIGIN French, earlier *guiriot*, perhaps from Portuguese *criado*.

grip ▶ **verb** (**gripped**, **gripping**) [with obj.] **1** take and keep a firm hold of; grasp tightly: *his knuckles were white as he gripped the steering wheel.*
■ [no obj.] maintain a firm contact, especially by friction: *a sole that really grips well on wet rock.*
2 (of a feeling or emotion) deeply affect (someone): *she was gripped by a feeling of excitement.*
■ (of an illness or unwelcome situation) afflict strongly: *the country was gripped by recession.* ■ compel the attention or interest of: [as adj. **gripping**] *a gripping TV thriller.*
▶ **noun** **1** [in sing.] a firm hold; a tight grasp or clasp: *his arm was held in a vice-like grip* | figurative *the icy grip of winter.*
■ a manner of grasping or holding something: *I've changed my grip and my backswing.* ■ [mass noun] the ability of something, especially a wheel or shoe, to maintain a firm contact with a surface: *these shoes have got no grip.* ■ [in sing.] an effective form of control over something: *our firm* **grip on** *inflation.* ■ [in sing.] an intellectual understanding of something: *you've got a pretty good* **grip on** *what's going on.*
2 a part or attachment by which something is held in the hand: *handlebar grips.*
■ a hairgrip.
3 a travelling bag: *a grip crammed with new clothes.*
4 an assistant in a theatre; a stage hand.
■ a member of a camera crew responsible for moving and setting up equipment.
5 Austral. informal a job or occupation.
– PHRASES **come** (or **get**) **to grips with** engage in combat with: *British forces never came to grips with the enemy.* ■ begin to deal with or understand: *a real tough problem to come to grips with.* **get a grip** [usu. in imperative] informal keep or recover one's self-control: *get a grip, guys!* **get** (or **take**) **a grip on** take control of: *hypochondria began to take a grip on him.* **in the grip of** dominated or affected by something undesirable or adverse: *Britain was in the grip of a nostalgia boom.* **lose one's grip** become unable to understand or control one's situation: *an elderly person who seems to be losing his grip.*
– DERIVATIVES **gripper** noun, **grippingly** adverb.

– ORIGIN Old English *grippa* (verb), *gripe* 'grasp, clutch' (noun), *gripa* 'handful, sheath'; related to **GRIPE**.

gripe ▶ verb **1** [reporting verb] informal express a complaint or grumble about something, especially something trivial: [no obj.]: *he griped about empty counters in butchers' shops* | [with direct speech] *'Holidays make no difference to Simon,' Pat griped.* **2** [with obj.] affect with gastric or intestinal pain: *it gripes my belly like a green apple* | [as adj. **griping**] *then the griping pains started.* **3** [with obj.] archaic grasp tightly; clutch: *Hilyard griped his dagger.* **4** [with obj.] Nautical secure (a boat) with gripes. **5** [no obj.] Sailing (of a ship) turn to face the wind in spite of the helm. ▶ noun **1** informal a complaint, especially a trivial one: *my only gripe is that it could have been bigger.* **2** [mass noun] gastric or intestinal pain; colic. **3** archaic an act of grasping tightly. **4** (**gripes**) Nautical lashings securing a boat in its place on deck or in davits. – DERIVATIVES **griper** noun. – ORIGIN Old English *grīpan* 'grasp, clutch', of Germanic origin; related to Dutch *grijpen*, German *greifen* 'seize', also to **GRIP** and **GROPE**. Sense 2 dates from the 17th cent.; sense 1, of US origin, dates from the 1930s.

gripe water ▶ noun [mass noun] Brit. trademark a solution given to babies for the relief of colic, wind, and indigestion.

grippe /grɪp/ ▶ noun old-fashioned term for **INFLUENZA**. – ORIGIN late 18th cent.: French, from *gripper* 'seize'.

grippy ▶ adjective (of a wheel or shoe) able to grip a surface well: *a very comfortable boot with a grippy rubber sole.* ■(of a surface) easy to grip.

Griqua /ˈɡriːkwə/ ▶ noun (pl. same or **Griquas**) a member of a people of mixed European and Khoikhoi origin, living mainly in the Cape Province of South Africa. – ORIGIN the name in Nama.

Gris /griːs/, Juan (1887–1927), Spanish painter; born *José Victoriano Gonzales*. His main contribution was to the development of the later phase of synthetic cubism. His work features the use of collage and paint in simple fragmented shapes.

grisaille /grɪˈzeɪl, -ˈlɪ/ ▶ noun [mass noun] Art a method of painting in grey monochrome, typically to imitate sculpture. ■[count noun] a painting or stained-glass window in this style. – ORIGIN mid 19th cent.: French, from *gris* 'grey'.

griseofulvin /ˌɡrɪzɪə(ʊ)ˈfʊlvɪn/ ▶ noun [mass noun] Medicine an antibiotic used against fungal infections of the hair and skin. ■This antibiotic is obtained from the mould *Penicillium griseofulvum*. – ORIGIN 1930s: from the modern Latin binomial, from medieval Latin *griseus* 'greyish' + Latin *fulvus* 'reddish yellow'.

grisette /grɪˈzɛt/ ▶ noun **1** a common edible woodland mushroom with a brown or grey cap, a slender stem, and white gills. ■*Amanita vaginata* and *A. fulva*, family Amanitaceae, class Hymenomycetes. **2** dated a young working-class Frenchwoman. – ORIGIN French, from *gris* 'grey' + the diminutive suffix *-ette*; in sense 2 the term derives from the grey dress material typically worn by such women; sense 1 is an extended use.

gris-gris /ˈɡriːɡriː/ (also **gri-gri**, **greegree**) ▶ noun (pl. same) an African or Caribbean charm or amulet. ■[mass noun] the use of such charms, especially in voodoo: [as modifier] *the New Orleans gris-gris traditions.* – ORIGIN late 17th cent.: from French *grisgris*, of West African origin.

griskin /ˈɡrɪskɪn/ ▶ noun [mass noun] Brit. the lean part of a loin of pork. – ORIGIN late 17th cent.: perhaps from archaic *grice* 'pig' + **-KIN**.

grisly /ˈɡrɪzli/ ▶ adjective (**grislier**, **grisliest**) causing horror or disgust: *the town was shaken by a series of grisly crimes.* – DERIVATIVES **grisliness** noun. – ORIGIN Old English *grislic* 'terrifying', of Germanic origin; related to Dutch *griezelig*.

grison /ˈɡrɪz(ə)n, ˈɡrʌɪs(ə)n/ ▶ noun a weasel-like mammal with dark fur and a white stripe across the forehead, found in Central and South America. ●Genus *Galictis*, family Mustelidae: two species. – ORIGIN late 18th cent.: from French, from *gris* 'grey'.

grissini /ɡrɪˈsiːni/ ▶ plural noun thin, crisp Italian breadsticks. – ORIGIN Italian.

grist ▶ noun [mass noun] corn that is ground to make flour. ■malt crushed to make mash for brewing. ■figurative useful material, especially to back up an argument: *the research provided the most sensational grist for opponents of tobacco.* – PHRASES **grist to the mill** useful experience, material, or knowledge. – ORIGIN Old English 'grinding', of Germanic origin; related to **GRIND**.

gristle /ˈɡrɪs(ə)l/ ▶ noun [mass noun] cartilage, especially when found as tough inedible tissue in meat. – DERIVATIVES **gristly** adjective. – ORIGIN Old English, of unknown origin.

gristmill ▶ noun a mill for grinding corn.

grit ▶ noun [mass noun] **1** small loose particles of stone or sand: *she had a bit of grit in her eye.* ■[as modifier] (with numeral) indicating the grade of fineness of an abrasive: *400 grit paper.* ■(also **gritstone**) a coarse sandstone: [count noun] *layers of impervious shales and grits.* **2** courage and resolve; strength of character: *he displayed the true grit of the navy pilot he used to be.* ▶ verb (**gritted**, **gritting**) [with obj.] **1** clench (the teeth), especially in order to keep one's resolve when faced with an unpleasant or painful duty: figurative *Parliament must grit its teeth and take action* | [as adj. **gritted**] *'Not here,' he said through gritted teeth.* **2** spread grit and often salt on (an icy road). **3** [no obj.] move with or make a grating sound: *fine red dust that gritted between the teeth.* – ORIGIN Old English *grēot* 'sand, gravel', of Germanic origin; related to German *Griess*, also to **GROATS**.

grits ▶ plural noun [also treated as sing.] US a dish of coarsely ground corn (maize) kernels boiled with water or milk. ■coarsely ground corn kernels from which this dish is made. – ORIGIN Old English *grytt*, *grytte* 'bran, mill dust', of Germanic origin: related to Dutch *grutten*, German *Grütze*, also to **GROATS**.

gritter ▶ noun Brit. a vehicle or machine for spreading grit and often salt on roads in icy or potentially icy weather.

gritty ▶ adjective (**grittier**, **grittiest**) **1** containing or covered with grit. **2** showing courage and resolve: *a typically gritty performance by the British player.* ■tough and uncompromising: *a gritty look at urban life.* – DERIVATIVES **grittily** adverb, **grittiness** noun.

Grivas /ˈɡriːvəs/, George (Theodorou) (1898–1974), Greek Cypriot patriot and soldier. A supporter of the union of Cyprus with Greece, he led the guerrilla campaign against British rule, which culminated in the country's independence in 1959.

grivet /ˈɡrɪvɪt/ (also **grivet monkey**) ▶ noun a common African guenon with greenish-brown upper parts and a black face. Compare with **GREEN MONKEY** and **VERVET**. ●*Cercopithecus aethiops*, family Cercopithecidae, in particular the race *C. a. aethiops* of Ethiopia and Sudan, with long white cheek tufts. – ORIGIN mid 19th cent.: from French, of unknown origin.

grizzle[1] ▶ verb [no obj.] informal, chiefly Brit. (of a child) cry fretfully: [as adj. **grizzling**] *a grizzling baby* | [as noun **grizzling**] *no grizzling, now!* ■complain; grumble. – DERIVATIVES **grizzler** noun. – ORIGIN mid 18th cent. (in the sense 'show the teeth, grin'): of unknown origin.

grizzle[2] ▶ adjective [often in combination] (especially of hair or fur) having dark and white hairs mixed: *grizzle-haired.* ▶ noun [mass noun] a mixture of dark and white hairs. – ORIGIN Middle English: from Old French *grisel*, from *gris* 'grey'.

grizzled ▶ adjective having or streaked with grey hair: *grizzled hair.*

– ORIGIN late Middle English: from the adjective **GRIZZLE**[2] + **-ED**[1].

grizzly (also **grizzly bear**) ▶ noun (pl. **-ies**) an animal of a large race of the brown bear native to North America. ●*Ursus arctos horribilis*, family Ursidae. – ORIGIN early 19th cent.: *grizzly* from **GRIZZLE**[2].

groan ▶ verb [no obj.] make a deep inarticulate sound in response to pain or despair: *Marty groaned and pulled the blanket over his head.* ■[with direct speech] say something in a despairing or miserable tone: *'Oh God! I groaned.* ■complain; grumble: *they were moaning and groaning about management.* ■(of a thing) make a low creaking or moaning sound when pressure or weight is applied: *James slumped back into his chair, making it groan and bulge.* ■(**groan beneath/under**) figurative be oppressed by: *families groaning under mortgage increases.* ▶ noun a deep inarticulate sound made in pain or despair. ■a complaint: *able to listen with sincerity to everyone's moans and groans.* ■a low creaking or moaning sound made by an object or device under pressure: *the protesting groan of timbers.* – DERIVATIVES **groaner** noun, **groaningly** adverb. – ORIGIN Old English *grānian*, of Germanic origin; related to German *greinen* 'grizzle, whine', *grinsen* 'grin', also probably to **GRIN**.

groat ▶ noun historical any of various medieval European coins, in particular an English silver coin worth four old pence, issued between 1351 and 1662. ■[in sing.] [with negative] archaic a small sum: *I do not care a groat.* – ORIGIN from Middle Dutch *groot* or Middle Low German *grōte* 'great, thick', hence 'thick penny'; compare with **GROSCHEN**.

groats ▶ plural noun hulled or crushed grain, especially oats. – ORIGIN late Old English *grotan* (plural): related to **GRIT** and **GRITS**.

Gro-bag ▶ noun trademark for **GROWBAG**.

grocer ▶ noun a person who sells food and small household goods. – ORIGIN Middle English (originally 'a person who sold things in the gross' (i.e. in large quantities)): from Old French *grossier*, from medieval Latin *grossarius*, from late Latin *grossus* 'gross'.

grocery ▶ noun (pl. **-ies**) a grocer's shop or business. ■(**groceries**) items of food sold in such a shop.

groceteria /ˌɡrəʊsəˈtɪːrɪə/ ▶ noun N. Amer. a small grocery.

grockle ▶ noun Brit. informal, often derogatory a holidaymaker at an English resort, especially one in the West Country. – ORIGIN an invented word, originally a fantastic creature in a children's comic, adopted arbitrarily and popularized by the film *The System* (1962).

Grodno /ˈɡrɒdnə/ Russian name for **HRODNA**.

grog ▶ noun [mass noun] spirits (originally rum) mixed with water. ■informal, chiefly Austral./NZ alcoholic drink, especially beer. ■ crushed unglazed pottery or brick used as an additive in plaster or clay. – ORIGIN mid 18th cent.: said to be from *Old Grog*, the reputed nickname (because of his grogram cloak) of Admiral Vernon (1684–1757), who in 1740 first ordered diluted (instead of neat) rum to be served out to sailors.

groggy ▶ adjective (**groggier**, **groggiest**) dazed, weak, or unsteady, especially from illness, intoxication, sleep, or a blow: *the sleeping pills had left her feeling groggy.* – DERIVATIVES **groggily** adverb, **grogginess** noun.

grogram /ˈɡrɒɡrəm/ ▶ noun [mass noun] a coarse fabric made of silk, often combined with mohair or wool and stiffened with gum. – ORIGIN mid 16th cent.: from French *gros grain* 'coarse grain' (see also **GROSGRAIN**).

groin[1] ▶ noun **1** the area between the abdomen and the thigh on either side of the body. ■informal the region of the genitals: *he took a pace back and kicked him in the groin.* **2** Architecture a curved edge formed by two intersecting vaults. – ORIGIN late Middle English *grynde*, perhaps from Old English *grynde* 'depression, abyss'.

groin[2] ▶ noun US term for **GROYNE**.

groined ▶ adjective Architecture (of a vault) formed by

the intersection of two barrel vaults, usually with plain groins without ribs.

grok ▶ **verb** (**grokked**, **grokking**) [with obj.] US informal understand (something) intuitively or by empathy: *because of all the commercials, children grok things immediately.*
■[no obj.] empathize or communicate sympathetically; establish a rapport.
– ORIGIN mid 20th cent.: a word invented by Robert Heinlein (born 1907), American author.

grommet /ˈɡrɒmɪt/ ▶ **noun 1** an eyelet placed in a hole in a sheet or panel to protect or insulate a rope or cable passed through it or to prevent the sheet or panel from being torn.
2 Medicine a tube surgically implanted in the eardrum, typically to drain fluid from the middle ear.
– ORIGIN early 17th cent. (in nautical use in the sense 'a circle of rope used as a fastening'): from obsolete French *grommette*, from *gourmer* 'to curb', of unknown ultimate origin. Current senses date from the mid 20th cent.

gromwell ▶ **noun** a widely distributed plant of the borage family, typically having white or blue flowers which are followed by smooth hard nutlets.
• Genus *Lithospermum*, family Boraginaceae: several species, in particular the common Eurasian *L. officinale*.
– ORIGIN Middle English: from Old French *gromil*, probably from a medieval Latin phrase meaning 'crane's millet'.

Gromyko /ɡrəˈmiːkəʊ/, Andrei (Andreevich) (1909–89), Soviet statesman, Foreign minister 1957–85, President of the USSR 1985–8. His appointment to the presidency (largely a formal position) by Gorbachev was widely interpreted as a manoeuvre to reduce Gromyko's influence and make possible an ending of the cold war.

Groningen /ˈɡrəʊnɪŋən, ˈɡrɒn-/ a city in the northern Netherlands, capital of a province of the same name; pop. 168,700 (1991).

Grønland /ˈɡrœnlan/ Danish name for **GREENLAND**.

groom ▶ **verb** [with obj.] **1** look after the coat of (a horse, dog, or other animal) by brushing and cleaning it: *you must be prepared to spend time grooming your dog.*
■(of an animal) clean the fur or skin of: *their main preoccupation is licking and* **grooming themselves**. ■ give a neat and tidy appearance to (someone): [as noun **grooming**] *she pays great attention to make-up, grooming, and clothes.* ■ look after (a lawn, ski slope, or other surface).
2 prepare or train (someone) for a particular purpose or activity: *star pupils who are* **groomed for** *higher things.*
▶ **noun 1** a person employed to take care of horses.
2 a bridegroom.
3 Brit. any of various officials of the royal household.
– ORIGIN Middle English (in the sense 'boy', later 'man, male servant'): of unknown origin.

groomsman ▶ **noun** (pl. **-men**) a male friend officially attending the bridegroom at a wedding.

groove ▶ **noun 1** a long, narrow cut or depression, especially one made to guide motion or receive a corresponding ridge.
■a spiral track cut in a gramophone record, into which the stylus fits. ■ Baseball, informal the centre of the strike zone (where the ball is easiest to hit). ■ Climbing an indentation where two planes of rock meet at an angle of more than 120°.
2 an established routine or habit: *his thoughts were slipping* **into a** *familiar* **groove**.
3 informal a rhythmic pattern in popular or jazz music: *the groove laid down by the drummer and bassist is tough and funky.*
▶ **verb 1** [with obj.] make a groove or grooves in: *deep lines grooved her face.*
2 [no obj.] informal dance or listen to popular or jazz music, especially that with an insistent rhythm: *they were* **grooving to** *Motown.*
■dated play such music in an accomplished and stylish manner: *the rhythm section grooves in the true Basie manner.* ■ enjoy oneself: *Harley relaxed and began to groove.*
3 [with obj.] Baseball, informal pitch (a ball) in the centre of the strike zone.
■N. Amer. (in the context of other sports) kick or throw (the ball) successfully; score (a goal) with stylish ease: *the San Diego kicker grooved the winning field goal.*
– PHRASES **in** (or **into**) **the groove** informal performing consistently well or confidently: *it might take me a couple of races to get back into the groove.* ■ indulging in relaxed and spontaneous enjoyment, especially dancing: *get into the groove!*
– ORIGIN Middle English (denoting a mine or shaft): from Dutch *groeve* 'furrow, pit'; related to **GRAVE**[1].

grooved ▶ **adjective 1** provided with or having a groove or grooves.
2 informal (of a sports player's action) so well-practised as to be automatic: *expert players play regularly and have grooved strokes.*

grooved ware ▶ **noun** [mass noun] Archaeology prehistoric pottery of the mid to late Neolithic in Britain (*c.*3300–2100 BC), characterized by a flat base and decorated chiefly with grooves and straight lines.

grooving saw ▶ **noun** a circular saw used for cutting grooves.

groovy ▶ **adjective** (**groovier**, **grooviest**) informal, dated or humorous fashionable and exciting: *sporting a groovy new haircut.*
■enjoyable and excellent: *he played all the remarkably groovy guitar parts himself.*
– DERIVATIVES **groovily** adverb, **grooviness** noun.

grope ▶ **verb 1** [no obj., with adverbial] feel about or search blindly or uncertainly with the hands: *she got up and* **groped for** *her spectacles.*
■(**grope for**) search mentally with hesitation or uncertainty for (a word or answer): *she was groping for the words which would express what she thought* | [as adj. **groping**] *their groping attempts to create a more meaningful existence.* ■ move along with difficulty by feeling objects as one goes: *she blew out the candle and* **groped her way** *to the door.*
2 [with obj.] informal feel or fondle (someone) for sexual pleasure, especially against their will: *he was accused of groping office girls.*
▶ **noun** an act of fondling someone for sexual pleasure: *she and Steve sneaked off for a quick grope.*
– DERIVATIVES **gropingly** adverb.
– ORIGIN Old English *grāpian*, of West Germanic origin; related to **GRIPE**.

groper[1] ▶ **noun 1** chiefly Austral. variant spelling of **GROUPER**.
2 (also **blue groper**) a large Australian wrasse which is a popular sporting fish.
• *Achoerodus gouldii*, family Labridae.

groper[2] ▶ **noun 1** a person who feels or fondles someone for sexual pleasure, especially against their will.
2 Austral. informal short for **SANDGROPER**.

Gropius /ˈɡrəʊpɪəs/, Walter (1883–1969), German-born American architect. He was the first director of the Bauhaus School of Design (1919–28) and a pioneer of the international style. He settled in the US in 1938, where he was professor of architecture at Harvard University until 1952.

grosbeak /ˈɡrəʊsbiːk/ ▶ **noun** a finch or related songbird with a stout conical bill and typically brightly coloured plumage.
• Several genera in the family Fringillidae and subfamily Cardinalinae (family Emberizidae); the **white-fronted grosbeak** or **grosbeak weaver** (*Amblyospiza albifrons*) belongs to the family Ploceidae.
– ORIGIN late 17th cent.: from French *grosbec*, from *gros* 'big, fat' + *bec* 'beak'.

groschen /ˈɡrəʊʃ(ə)n, ˈɡrɒʃ(ə)n/ ▶ **noun** (pl. same) a former monetary unit of Austria, equal to one hundredth of a schilling.
■historical a small German silver coin. ■ informal a German ten-pfennig piece.
– ORIGIN German, from Middle High German *grosse*, from medieval Latin (*denarius*) *grossus* 'thick (penny)'; compare with **GROAT**.

grosgrain /ˈɡrəʊɡreɪn/ ▶ **noun** a heavy ribbed fabric, typically of silk or rayon.
– ORIGIN mid 19th cent.: French, 'coarse grain' (see also **GROGRAM**).

gros point /ɡrəʊ ˈpwã/ ▶ **noun** [mass noun] a type of needlepoint embroidery consisting of stitches crossing two or more threads of the canvas in each direction.
– ORIGIN mid 19th cent.: French, literally 'large stitch', from *gros point de Venise*, a type of lace originally from Venice, worked in bold relief. The current sense dates from the 1930s.

gross ▶ **adjective 1** unattractively large or bloated: *I feel fat, gross—even my legs feel flabby.*
■large-scale; not fine or detailed: *at the gross anatomical level.* ■ vulgar; unrefined: *the duties we felt called upon to perform towards our inferiors were only gross, material ones.* ■ informal very unpleasant; repulsive: *I think they're completely disgusting, gross.* ■(in a negative context) complete; blatant: *a gross exaggeration.*
2 (of income, profit, or interest) without deduction of tax or other contributions; total: *the gross amount of the gift was £1,000* | *the current rate of interest is about 6.1 per cent gross.* Often contrasted with **NET**[2] (in sense 1).
■(of weight) including contents, fittings, wrappings, or other variable items; overall: *a projected gross take-off weight of 500,000 pounds.* ■ (of a score in golf) as actually played, without taking handicap into account.
▶ **adverb** without tax or other contributions having been deducted.
▶ **verb** [with obj.] produce or earn (an amount of money) as gross profit or income: *the film went on to gross $8 million in the US.*
■(**gross something up**) add deductions such as tax to a net amount: *all commuting costs were grossed up for tax and National Insurance deductions.*
▶ **noun 1** (pl. same) an amount equal to twelve dozen; 144: *fifty-five gross of tins of processed milk.* [ORIGIN: From French *grosse douzaine*, literally 'large dozen'.]
2 (pl. **grosses**) a gross profit or income: *the box office grosses mounted.*
– PHRASES **by the gross** figurative in large numbers or amounts: *impoverished Mexicans who were arrested here by the gross.*
– DERIVATIVES **grossly** adverb [as submodifier] *Freda was grossly overweight*, **grossness** noun.
– ORIGIN Middle English (in the sense 'thick, massive, bulky'): from Old French *gros*, *grosse* 'large', from late Latin *grossus*.
▶**gross someone out** informal, chiefly N. Amer. disgust someone with repulsive or obscene behaviour or appearance.

gross domestic product (abbrev.: **GDP**) ▶ **noun** the total value of goods produced and services provided in a country during one year. Compare with **GROSS NATIONAL PRODUCT**.

Grosseteste /ˈɡrəʊstɛst/, Robert (*c.*1175–1253), English churchman, philosopher, and scholar. His experimental approach to science, especially in optics and mathematics, inspired his pupil Roger Bacon.

Grossglockner /ˈɡrəʊsˌɡlɒknə/ the highest mountain in Austria, in the eastern Tyrolean Alps, rising to a height of 3,797 m (12,457 ft).

gross national product (abbrev.: **GNP**) ▶ **noun** the total value of goods produced and services provided by a country during one year, equal to the gross domestic product plus the net income from foreign investments.

gross-out ▶ **noun** informal, chiefly N. Amer. something disgusting or repellent: [as modifier] *the movie features several gross-out scenes.*

gross ton ▶ **noun** see **TON**[1] (sense 1).

grossular /ˈɡrɒsjʊlə/ ▶ **noun** [mass noun] a mineral of the garnet group, consisting essentially of calcium aluminium silicate.
– ORIGIN early 19th cent.: from modern Latin *grossularia* 'gooseberry'. The yellow-green variety is sometimes known as *gooseberry garnet*.

Gros Ventre /ɡrəʊ ˈvɒntrə/ ▶ **noun** (pl. **Gros Ventres**) another term for **HIDATSA**.
– ORIGIN French, literally 'big belly'.

Grosz /ɡrəʊs, German ɡrɔs/, George (1893–1959), German painter and draughtsman. His satirical drawings and paintings characteristically depict a decadent society in which gluttony and depraved sensuality are juxtaposed with poverty and disease.

grosz /ɡrɔːʃ/ ▶ **noun** (pl. **groszy** or **grosze**) a monetary unit in Poland, equal to one hundredth of a zloty.
– ORIGIN Polish; compare with **GROSCHEN**.

grot[1] ▶ **noun** [mass noun] Brit. informal something unpleasant, dirty, or of poor quality; rubbish.
– ORIGIN 1960s: back-formation from **GROTTY**.

grot[2] ▶ **noun** poetic/literary a grotto.
– ORIGIN early 16th cent.: from French *grotte*, from Italian *grotta*, via Latin from Greek *kruptē* 'vault, crypt'.

grotesque /ɡrə(ʊ)ˈtɛsk/ ▶ **adjective** comically or repulsively ugly or distorted: *grotesque facial distortions.*
■incongruous or inappropriate to a shocking degree: *a lifestyle of grotesque luxury.*
▶ **noun 1** a very ugly or comically distorted figure, creature, or image: *the rods are carved in the form of a series of gargoyle faces and grotesques.*

■(**the grotesque**) that which is grotesque: *images of the macabre and the grotesque.* ■[mass noun] a style of decorative painting or sculpture consisting of the interweaving of human and animal forms with flowers and foliage.
2 [mass noun] Printing a family of 19th-century sans serif typefaces.
– DERIVATIVES **grotesquely** adverb, **grotesqueness** noun.
– ORIGIN mid 16th cent. (as noun): from French *crotesque* (the earliest form in English), from Italian *grottesca*, from *opera* or *pittura grottesca* 'work or painting resembling that found in a grotto'; 'grotto' here probably denoted the rooms of ancient buildings in Rome which had been revealed by excavations, and which contained murals in the grotesque style.

grotesquerie /ɡrəʊˈtɛskəri/ ▶ **noun** (pl. **-ies**) [mass noun] grotesque quality or grotesque things collectively: *living in a world of grotesquerie and make-believe.*
■[count noun] a grotesque figure, object, or action.
– ORIGIN late 17th cent.: French (see **GROTESQUE**).

Grotius /ˈɡrəʊtɪəs/, Hugo (1583–1645), Dutch jurist and diplomat; Latinized name of *Huig de Groot*. His legal treatise *De Jure Belli et Pacis* (1625) established the basis of modern international law.

grotto ▶ **noun** (pl. **-oes** or **-os**) a small picturesque cave, especially an artificial one in a park or garden.
■an indoor structure resembling a cave: *visits to Father Christmas's grotto.*
– DERIVATIVES **grottoed** adjective.
– ORIGIN early 17th cent.: from Italian *grotta*, via Latin from Greek *kruptē* (see **CRYPT**).

grotty ▶ **adjective** (**grottier**, **grottiest**) Brit. informal unpleasant and of poor quality: *a grotty little hotel.*
■[as complement] unwell: *if the person feels very grotty, it is probably true influenza.*
– DERIVATIVES **grottiness** noun.
– ORIGIN 1960s: from **GROTESQUE** + **-Y**[1].

grouch /ɡraʊtʃ/ ▶ **noun** a habitually grumpy person: *rock's foremost poet and ill-mannered grouch.*
■a complaint or grumble: *my only real grouch was that the children's chorus was far less easy on the ear.* ■ a fit of grumbling or sulking: *he's in a thundering grouch.*
▶ **verb** [no obj.] voice one's discontent in an ill-tempered manner; grumble: *there's not a lot to grouch about.*
– ORIGIN late 19th cent.: variant of obsolete *grutch*, from Old French *grouchier* 'to grumble, murmur', of unknown origin. Compare with **GRUDGE**.

grouchy ▶ **adjective** (**grouchier**, **grouchiest**) irritable and bad-tempered; grumpy; complaining: *the old man grew sulky and grouchy.*
– DERIVATIVES **grouchily** adverb, **grouchiness** noun.

ground[1] ▶ **noun 1** [in sing.] the solid surface of the earth: *he lay on the ground.*
■[mass noun] a limited or defined extent of the earth's surface; land: *an adjoining area of ground had been purchased.* ■ [mass noun] land of a specified kind: *my feet squelched over marshy ground.* ■ [count noun] an area of land or sea used for a specified purpose: *shore dumping can pollute fishing grounds and beaches.* ■ (**grounds**) an area of enclosed land surrounding a large house or other building: *the house stands in seven acres of grounds.* ■ Brit. the floor of a room: *the device fell to the ground, where it exploded, blowing a hole in the floor.* ■ [as modifier] (in aviation) of or relating to the ground rather than the air (with particular reference to the maintenance and servicing of an aircraft on the ground): *ground staff | ground crew.* ■ [as modifier] (of an animal) living on or in the ground. ■ [as modifier] (of a fish) bottom-dwelling. ■ [as modifier] (of a plant) low-growing, especially in relation to similar plants.
2 [mass noun] an area of knowledge or subject of discussion or thought: *third-year courses typically cover less ground and go into more depth* | [count noun] *he shifted the argument on to theoretical grounds of his own choosing.*
3 (**grounds**) factors forming a basis for action or the justification for a belief: *there are some grounds for optimism* | *they called for a retrial on the grounds of the new evidence.*
4 chiefly Art a prepared surface to which paint is applied.
■a substance used to prepare a surface for painting. ■ (in embroidery or ceramics) a plain surface to which decoration is applied. ■ a piece of wood fixed to a wall as a base for boards, plaster, or joinery.
5 Music short for **GROUND BASS**.
6 (**grounds**) solid particles, especially of coffee, which form a residue; sediment.
7 N. Amer. electrical connection to the earth. See **EARTH** (in sense 3).
▶ **verb** [with obj.] **1** (often **be grounded**) prohibit or prevent (a pilot or an aircraft) from flying: *a bitter wind blew from the north-east and the bombers were grounded.*
■informal, chiefly N. Amer. (of a parent) refuse to allow (a child) to go out socially as a punishment.
2 run (a ship) aground: *rather than be blown up, Muller grounded his ship on a coral reef and surrendered.*
■[no obj.] (of a ship) go aground: *the larger ships grounded on the river bed at low tide.*
3 (usu. **be grounded in**) give (something abstract) a firm theoretical or practical basis: *the study of history must be grounded in a thorough knowledge of the past.*
■instruct (someone) thoroughly in a subject: *Eva's governess grounded her in Latin, Greek, and Italian.*
4 place or lay (something) on the ground or touch the ground with it: *he was penalized two strokes for grounding his club in a bunker.*
5 N. Amer. connect (an electrical device) with the ground.
– PHRASES **be thick** (or **thin**) **on the ground** existing (or not existing) in large numbers or amounts: *new textbooks on particle physics are thin on the ground.* **break ground** N. Amer. **1** do preparatory digging or other work prior to building or planting something. **2** another term for ***break new ground*** below. **break new** (or **fresh**) **ground** do something innovative which is considered an advance or positive benefit. **cut the ground from under someone's feet** do something which leaves someone without a reason or justification for their actions or opinions. **from the ground up** informal completely or complete: *they needed a rethink of their doctrine from the ground up.* **gain ground** become more popular or accepted: *new moral attitudes are gaining ground.* **gain ground on** get closer to someone or something one is pursuing or with whom one is competing: *the dollar gained ground on all other major currencies.* **get in on the ground floor** informal become part of an enterprise in its early stages. **get off the ground** (or **get something off the ground**) start or cause to start happening or functioning successfully: *he doesn't appreciate the steps he must take to get the negotiations off the ground.* **give** (or **lose**) **ground** retreat or lose one's advantage during a conflict or competition: *he refused to give ground on this issue.* **go to ground** (of a fox or other animal) enter its earth or burrow. ■ figurative (of a person) hide or become inaccessible, especially for a long time: *he had gone to ground following the presidential coup.* **hold** (or **stand**) **one's ground** not retreat or lose one's advantage during a conflict or competition: *you will be able to hold your ground and resist the enemy's attack.* **make up ground** get closer to someone ahead in a race or competition. **on the ground** in a place where real, practical work is done: *the troops on the ground are cynical.* **on one's own ground** in one's own territory or concerning one's own range of knowledge or experience: *I feel reasonably relaxed if I'm interviewed on my own ground.* **prepare the ground** make it easier for something to occur or be developed: *parliament approved a series of measures intended to prepare the ground for the new economic structure.* **run someone/thing to ground** see **RUN**. **work** (or **run**) **oneself into the ground** exhaust oneself by working or running very hard.
– ORIGIN Old English *grund*, of Germanic origin; related to Dutch *grond* and German *Grund*.
▶**ground out** Baseball (of a batter) be put out because of hitting a ground ball to a fielder who throws it to first base before the batter touches that base: *he grounded out to shortstop.*

ground[2] past and past participle of **GRIND**.
▶ **adjective** [attrib.] reduced to fine particles by crushing or mincing: *ground cumin.*
■shaped, roughened, or polished by grinding: *the thick opaque ground perimeter of the lenses.*
– PHRASES **ground down** exhausted or worn down.

groundbait ▶ **noun** [mass noun] Brit. bait thrown into the water while fishing (as distinct from hookbait).
– DERIVATIVES **groundbaiting** noun.

ground ball ▶ **noun** Baseball a ball hit along the ground.

ground bass ▶ **noun** Music a short theme, usually in the bass, which is constantly repeated as the other parts of the music vary.

ground beetle ▶ **noun** any of a number of beetles that live mainly on or near the ground, in particular:
● a fast-running predatory beetle, typically black in colour (family Carabidae). ● (**nocturnal ground beetle**) another term for **DARKLING BEETLE**.

ground-breaking ▶ **adjective** breaking new ground; innovative; pioneering.
– DERIVATIVES **ground-breaker** noun.

ground cherry ▶ **noun** an American plant of the nightshade family which resembles the Cape gooseberry.
● Genus *Physalis*, family Solanaceae: several species, in particular *P. pruinosa*, which yields edible fruit.

ground control ▶ **noun** [treated as sing. or pl.] the personnel and equipment that monitor and direct the flight and landing of aircraft or spacecraft.
– DERIVATIVES **ground controller** noun.

ground cover ▶ **noun** [mass noun] low-growing, spreading plants that help to stop weeds growing.

ground dove ▶ **noun** a small dove that spends much of its time on the ground, feeding and frequently nesting there.
● *Columbina*, *Gallicolumba*, and related genera, family Columbidae: several species, including the **common ground dove** (*C. passerina*) of North and Central America.

ground effect ▶ **noun** the effect of added aerodynamic buoyancy produced by a cushion of air below a vehicle moving close to the ground.

ground elder ▶ **noun** a common weed of the parsley family, with leaves that resemble those of the elder and spreading underground stems, native to Europe.
● *Aegopodium podagraria*, family Umbelliferae: a variegated cultivar is sometimes grown as ground cover.

grounder ▶ **noun** Baseball a ground ball.

ground floor ▶ **noun** the floor of a building at ground level.

ground frost ▶ **noun** [mass noun] Brit. frost formed on the surface of the ground or in the top layer of soil.

ground game ▶ **noun** [mass noun] **1** game animals such as rabbits and hares that live in the ground.
2 American Football play consisting of running to advance the ball.

ground glass ▶ **noun** [mass noun] **1** glass with a smooth ground surface that renders it non-transparent while retaining its translucency.
2 glass ground into an abrasive powder.

groundhog ▶ **noun** North American term for **WOODCHUCK**.

Groundhog Day ▶ **noun** (in the US) 2 February, when the groundhog is said to come out of its hole at the end of hibernation. If the animal sees its shadow—i.e. if the weather is sunny—it is said to portend six weeks more of winter weather.

groundhopper ▶ **noun** a small predominantly brown insect that resembles a grasshopper and has well-developed wings.
● Family Tetrigidae, order Orthoptera: several species, including the European **common groundhopper** (*Tetrix undulata*).

grounding ▶ **noun** [in sing.] basic training or instruction in a subject: *every child needs a good grounding in science and technology.*

ground ivy ▶ **noun** a creeping plant of the mint family, with bluish-purple flowers, native to Europe where it commonly grows on hedge-banks and in woodland.
● *Glechoma hederacea*, family Labiatae.

groundless ▶ **adjective** not based on any good reason: *your fears are quite groundless.*
– DERIVATIVES **groundlessly** adverb, **groundlessness** noun.
– ORIGIN Old English *grundlēas* (see **GROUND**[1], **-LESS**).

ground level ▶ **noun 1** the level of the ground: [as modifier] *ground-level ozone pollution.*
■the ground floor of a building.
2 Physics another term for **GROUND STATE**.

groundling /ˈɡraʊn(d)lɪŋ/ ▶ **noun 1** a spectator or reader of inferior taste (originally a member of the part of a theatre audience that traditionally stood in the pit beneath the stage): *Dante is not for groundlings.* [ORIGIN: with reference to Shakespeare's *Hamlet* III. ii. 11.]
2 a person on the ground as opposed to one in a spacecraft or aircraft.
3 a fish that lives at the bottom of lakes and streams, especially a gudgeon or loach.
4 a creeping or dwarf plant.
– ORIGIN early 17th cent. (denoting a fish): from

g

GROUND[1] + **-LING**; compare with Dutch *grondeling*, German *Gründling* 'gudgeon'.

ground loop ▸ noun **1** a violent, uncontrolled swinging movement of an aircraft while landing, taking off, or taxiing.
2 North American term for **EARTH LOOP**.
▸ verb (**ground-loop**) [no obj.] (of an aircraft) make a ground loop.

groundmass ▸ noun [in sing.] Geology the compact, finer-grained material in which the crystals are embedded in a porphyritic rock.

groundnut ▸ noun **1** another term for **PEANUT**.
2 a North American plant of the pea family, which yields a sweet edible tuber.
● Genus *Apios*, family Leguminosae: several species, in particular *A. tuberosa*.

groundout ▸ noun Baseball a play in which a batter is put out by hitting a ground ball to a fielder who throws it to first base before the batter touches that base.

ground pine ▸ noun **1** a small yellow-flowered Eurasian plant of the mint family, which resembles a pine seedling in appearance and smell.
● *Ajuga chamaepitys*, family Labiatae.
2 a North American clubmoss with small shiny leaves, resembling a miniature conifer and growing typically in coniferous woodland.
● Genus *Lycopodium*, family Lycopodiaceae: several species, in particular *L. obscurum* and *L. tristachyum*.

ground plan ▸ noun the plan of a building at ground level.
■ the general outline or basis of a scheme.

ground provisions ▸ plural noun W. Indian starchy root crops such as yams and sweet potatoes.

ground rent ▸ noun [mass noun] Brit. rent paid under the terms of a lease by the owner of a building to the owner of the land on which it is built.

ground rule ▸ noun (usu. **ground rules**) a basic principle: *some ground rules for assessing new machines.*

ground run ▸ noun the movement of an aircraft along the ground just before take-off or just after landing.

groundsel /ˈɡraʊn(d)s(ə)l/ ▸ noun a widely distributed plant of the daisy family, with yellow rayless flowers.
● Genus *Senecio*, family Compositae: several species, in particular the **common groundsel** (*S. vulgaris*), which is a common weed. See also **GIANT GROUNDSEL**.
– ORIGIN Old English *gundæswelgiæ* (later *grundeswylige*), probably from *gund* 'pus' + *swelgan* 'to swallow' (with reference to its use in poultices). The later form may be by association with **GROUND**, and refer to the plant's rapid growth.

groundsheet ▸ noun a waterproof sheet spread on the ground inside a tent.

groundskeeper ▸ noun North American term for **GROUNDSMAN**.

ground sloth ▸ noun an extinct terrestrial edentate mammal of the Cenozoic era in America, typically of very large size.
● Order Xenarthra (or Edentata). See **MEGATHERIUM**, **MYLODON**.

groundsman ▸ noun (pl. **-men**) Brit. a person who maintains a sports ground, a park, or the grounds of a school or other institution.

ground speed ▸ noun an aircraft's speed relative to the ground. Compare with **AIRSPEED**.

ground squirrel ▸ noun a burrowing squirrel that is typically highly social, found chiefly in North America and northern Eurasia, where it usually hibernates in winter. Also called **GOPHER** in North America.
● *Spermophilus* and other genera, family Sciuridae: many species, including the sousliks and chipmunks.

ground state ▸ noun Physics the lowest energy state of an atom or other particle.

groundstroke ▸ noun Tennis a stroke played after the ball has bounced, as opposed to a volley.

groundswell /ˈɡraʊn(d)swɛl/ ▸ noun [in sing.] **1** a build-up of opinion or feeling in a large section of the population: *an unexpected groundswell of opposition developed.*
2 a large or extensive swell in the sea.

ground tackle ▸ noun [mass noun] the equipment used to anchor or moor a boat or ship.

groundwater ▸ noun [mass noun] water held

underground in the soil or in pores and crevices in rock.

ground wave ▸ noun a radio wave which reaches a receiver from a transmitter directly, without reflection from the ionosphere.

groundwork ▸ noun [mass noun] preliminary or basic work: *the inquiry's findings are expected to lay the groundwork for a complete overhaul of the system.*

ground zero ▸ noun [in sing.] the point on the earth's surface directly above or below an exploding nuclear bomb.
■ figurative a starting point or base for some activity: *if you're starting at ground zero in terms of knowledge, go to the library.*

group ▸ noun [treated as sing. or pl.] a number of people or things that are located close together or are considered or classed together: *these bodies fall into four distinct groups.*
■ a number of people that work together or share certain beliefs: *I now belong to my local drama group.* ■ a commercial organization consisting of several companies under common ownership. ■ a number of musicians who play popular music together. ■ Military a division of an air force, usually consisting of two or more stations. ■ Art two or more figures or objects forming a design. ■ Linguistics (in systemic grammar) a level of structure between clause and word, broadly corresponding to phrase in other grammars. ■ Chemistry a set of elements occupying a column in the periodic table and having broadly similar properties arising from their similar electronic structure. ■ Chemistry a combination of atoms having a recognizable identity in a number of compounds. ■ Mathematics a set of elements, together with an associative binary operation, which contains an inverse for each element and an identity element.
▸ verb [with obj. and adverbial] (often **be grouped**) put together or place in a group or groups: *three wooden chairs were grouped around a dining table.*
■ put into categories; classify: *we group them into species merely as a convenience.* ■ [no obj., with adverbial] form a group or groups: *many growers began to group together to form cooperatives.*
– ORIGIN late 17th cent.: from French *groupe*, from Italian *gruppo*, of Germanic origin; related to **CROP**.

group area ▸ noun (in South Africa during the apartheid era) a residential area demarcated by law for occupation by an official ethnic group.

group captain ▸ noun a rank of officer in the RAF, above wing commander and below air commodore.

group dynamics ▸ plural noun [also treated as sing.] Psychology the processes involved when people in a group interact with each other, or the study of these.

grouper (chiefly Austral. also **groper**) ▸ noun a large or very large heavy-bodied fish of the sea bass family, with a big head and wide mouth, found in warm seas.
● Family Serranidae: several genera, in particular *Epinephelus* and *Mycteroperca*.
– ORIGIN early 17th cent.: from Portuguese *garoupa*, probably from a local term in South America.

group home ▸ noun a home where a small number of unrelated people in need of care, support, or supervision, such as the elderly or the mentally ill, can live together.

groupie ▸ noun informal a person, especially a young woman, who regularly follows a pop group or other celebrity in the hope of meeting or getting to know them.

grouping ▸ noun a set of people acting together with a common interest or purpose, especially within a larger organization: *a grouping of left-wing trade union leaders.*
■ [mass noun] the arrangement or formation of people or things in a group or groups: *an alternative form of ability grouping.*

Group of Eight (abbrev.: **G8**) the eight leading industrial nations (the US, Japan, France, the UK, Canada, Italy, and Russia), whose heads of government meet regularly.

Group of Seven a group of Canadian landscape painters, officially established in 1920, who formed the first major national movement in Canadian art. Their work exhibited a bold and colourful expressionistic style.

Group of Seventy-Seven the developing countries of the world.

Group of Three the three largest industrialized economies (the US, Germany, and Japan).

group practice ▸ noun a medical practice run by several doctors.

groupset ▸ noun the brakes and gears for a bicycle.

group therapy ▸ noun [mass noun] a form of psychiatric therapy in which patients meet to describe and discuss their problems.

groupthink ▸ noun [mass noun] chiefly N. Amer. the practice of thinking or making decisions as a group that results in unchallenged, poor-quality decision-making: *there's always a danger of groupthink when two leaders are so alike.*
– ORIGIN late 20th cent.: on the pattern of *doublethink*.

groupuscule /ˈɡruːpəˌskjuːl/ ▸ noun a political or religious splinter group.
– ORIGIN mid 20th cent.: from French, diminutive of *groupe* 'group'.

group velocity ▸ noun Physics the speed at which the energy of a wave travels.

groupware ▸ noun [mass noun] Computing software designed to facilitate collective working by a number of different users.

group work ▸ noun [mass noun] Brit. work done by a group in collaboration.

grouse[1] ▸ noun (pl. same) a medium to large game bird with a plump body and feathered legs, the male being larger and more conspicuously coloured than the female.
● Family Tetraonidae (or Phasianidae): several genera, especially *Lagopus* and *Tetrao*. The family also includes ptarmigans, capercaillies, and prairie chickens.
■ [mass noun] the flesh of this bird as food.
– ORIGIN early 16th cent.: perhaps related to medieval Latin *gruta* or to Old French *grue* 'crane'.

grouse[2] ▸ verb [no obj.] complain pettily; grumble: *she heard him grousing about his assistant.*
▸ noun a grumble or complaint: *our biggest grouse was about the noise of construction work.*
– DERIVATIVES **grouser** noun.
– ORIGIN early 19th cent.: of unknown origin; compare with **GROUCH**.

grouse[3] ▸ adjective Austral./NZ informal very good (used as a general term of approval): *the car was a grouse tomato red which everyone liked.*
– ORIGIN 1920s: of unknown origin.

grouse moor ▸ noun an area of managed moorland for the shooting of red grouse.

grout[1] /ɡraʊt/ ▸ noun [mass noun] a mortar or paste for filling crevices, especially the gaps between wall or floor tiles.
▸ verb [with obj.] fill in with grout: *the gaps are grouted afterwards.*
– ORIGIN mid 17th cent.: perhaps from obsolete *grout* 'sediment', (plural) 'dregs', or related to French dialect *grouter* 'grout a wall'.

grout[2] /ɡraʊt/ ▸ noun (**grouts**) archaic sediment; dregs; grounds: *old women told fortunes in grouts of tea.*
– ORIGIN Old English *grūt*, of Germanic origin; related to Dutch *gruit* 'dregs', German *Grauss* 'grain, weak beer', also to **GRITS** and **GROATS**. The original meaning was 'coarse meal, groats', also denoting the infusion of malt which was fermented to make beer, hence, in Middle English, 'sediment'.

grouter[1] ▸ noun a tool used for grouting tiles.

grouter[2] ▸ noun Austral. informal a lucky but unfair advantage: *he has managed to come in on the grouter with a borrowed pound.*
– ORIGIN early 20th cent.: of unknown origin.

grouting ▸ noun [mass noun] grout, especially when hardened.

Grove, Sir George (1820–1900), English musicologist. He was the founder and first editor of the multi-volume *Dictionary of Music and Musicians* (1879–89) and served as the first director of the Royal College of Music (1883–94).

grove ▸ noun a small wood, orchard, or group of trees: *an olive grove* | [in place names] *Ladbroke Grove.*
– DERIVATIVES **grovy** adjective.
– ORIGIN Old English *grāf*, of Germanic origin.

grovel ▸ verb (**grovelled**, **grovelling**; US **groveled**, **groveling**) [no obj.] lie or move abjectly on the ground with one's face downwards: *he grovelled in agony as the driver lashed him repeatedly.*
■ act in an obsequious manner in order to obtain someone's forgiveness or favour: *everyone expected me*

to grovel with gratitude | [as adj. **grovelling**] *his grovelling references to 'great' historians and their 'brilliant' works.*

– DERIVATIVES **groveller** noun, **grovellingly** adverb.

– ORIGIN Middle English: back-formation from the obsolete adverb *grovelling*, from obsolete *groof, grufe* 'the face or front' (in the phrase *on grufe*, from Old Norse *á grúfu* 'face downwards') + the suffix *-ling*.

groves of Academe /ˈakədiːm/ ▶ **plural noun** the academic world.

– ORIGIN translating Horace's *silvas Academi*.

grow /ɡrəʊ/ ▶ **verb** (past **grew** /ɡruː/; past participle **grown** /ɡrəʊn/) [no obj.] **1** (of a living thing) undergo natural development by increasing in size and changing physically; progress to maturity: *he would watch Nick grow to manhood* | [as adj. **growing**] *the linguistic skills acquired by the growing child* | [as adj. **grown**] *the stupidity of grown men kicking a ball into a net.*

■ (of a plant) germinate and develop: *it will even grow in plain gravel or sand.* ■ [with obj.] produce by cultivation: *more and more land was needed to grow crops for export.* ■ [with obj.] allow or cause (a part of the body) to grow or develop: [with obj. and complement] *she grew her hair long.* ■ (of something abstract) come into existence and develop: *an awareness of politics* **grows out of** *individuals' perception of the world around them.*

2 become larger or greater over a period of time; increase: *turnover grew to more than $100,000 within three years* | [as adj. **growing**] *a growing number of people are coming to realize this.*

■ [with obj.] chiefly N. Amer. cause (something, especially a business) to expand or increase.

3 [with complement] become gradually or increasingly: *sharing our experiences we grew braver.*

■ [with infinitive] (of a person) come to feel or know something over time: *supposing we had grown to know and love nuclear power.* ■ (**grow apart**) (of two or more people) become gradually estranged. ■ (**grow away from**) become gradually separated from (one's family, friends, or background): *emotionally his family had grown away from him.*

– PHRASES **grow on trees** [usu. with negative] informal be plentiful or easily obtained: *sponsorship money doesn't grow on trees in the States.*

– DERIVATIVES **growable** adjective.

– ORIGIN Old English *grōwan* (originally referring chiefly to plants), of Germanic origin; related to Dutch *groeien*, also to **GRASS** and **GREEN**.

▶ **grow into** become as a result of natural development or gradual increase: *Barrow-in-Furness grew into a fishing village of about three hundred people by the 1840s.* ■ become large enough to wear (a garment) comfortably.

grow on become gradually more appealing to (someone): *this stuff grows on you.*

grow out disappear because of normal growth: *Colette's old perm had almost grown out.*

grow out of become too large to wear (a garment): *blazers that they grew out of.* ■ become too mature to retain (a childish habit): *most children grow out of tantrums by the time they're three.*

grow up advance to maturity; spend one's childhood and adolescence: *a young Muslim woman who grew up in Britain.* ■ [often in imperative] begin to behave or think sensibly and realistically: *grow up, sister, and come into the real world.* ■ arise; develop: *a school of painting grew up in Cuzco.*

growbag (also trademark **Gro-bag**) ▶ **noun** Brit. a bag containing potting compost for growing plants such as tomatoes in.

grower ▶ **noun 1** a person who grows a particular type of crop: *a fruit grower.*

2 [with adj.] a plant that grows in a specified way: *a fast grower.*

growing bag ▶ **noun** Brit. another term for **GROWBAG**.

growing pains ▶ **plural noun** neuralgic pains which occur in the limbs of some young children.

■ figurative the difficulties experienced in the early stages of an enterprise: *the growing pains of a young republic.*

growing point ▶ **noun** the point at which growth originates.

■ Botany the meristem region at the apex of a plant shoot at which continuous cell division and differentiation occur.

growing season ▶ **noun** the part of the year during which rainfall and temperature allow plants to grow: *a short growing season.*

growl ▶ **verb** [no obj.] (of an animal, especially a dog) make a low guttural sound of hostility in the throat: *the dogs yapped and growled about his heels.*

■ [with direct speech] (of a person) say something in a low grating voice, typically in a threatening manner: *'Keep out of this,' he growled.* ■ (of a thing) make a low or harsh rumbling sound, typically one that is felt to be threatening: *thunder growls without warning from a summer sky.*

▶ **noun** a low guttural sound made in the throat, especially by a dog.

■ a similar sound made by a person, especially to express hostility or anger. ■ [in sing.] a low throaty sound made by a machine or engine: *the growl of diesel engines.*

– DERIVATIVES **growlingly** adverb.

– ORIGIN mid 17th cent.: probably imitative.

growler ▶ **noun 1** a person or thing that growls.

2 a small iceberg that rises little above the water.

3 archaic, informal a four-wheeled hansom cab.

4 US informal a pail or other container used for carrying drink, especially draught beer.

growmore ▶ **noun** [mass noun] Brit. a balanced inorganic fertilizer of a standard kind.

grown past participle of **GROW**.

grown-up ▶ **adjective** adult: *Joe is married with two grown-up children.*

■ suitable for or characteristic of an adult: *it seems a grown-up thing to do.*

▶ **noun** an adult (especially a child's word): *I don't like it when grown-ups get all serious.*

growth ▶ **noun 1** [mass noun] the process of increasing in physical size: *the upward growth of plants* | *the growth of the city affects the local climate.*

■ the process of developing or maturing physically, mentally, or spiritually: *keeping a journal can be a vital step in our personal growth.* ■ the increase in number and spread of small or microscopic organisms: *some additives slow down the growth of micro-organisms.* ■ the process of increasing in amount, value, or importance: *the rates of population growth are lowest in the north.* ■ increase in economic value or activity: *the government aims to get growth back into the economy.*

2 something that has grown or is growing: *a day's growth of unshaven stubble on his chin.*

■ Medicine & Biology a tumour or other abnormal formation.

3 a vineyard or crop of grapes of a specified classification of quality, or a wine from it.

growth factor ▶ **noun** Biology a substance, such as a vitamin or hormone, which is required for the stimulation of growth in living cells.

growth hormone ▶ **noun** a hormone which stimulates growth in animal or plant cells, especially (in animals) that secreted by the pituitary gland.

growth industry ▶ **noun** an industry that is developing particularly rapidly.

growth ring ▶ **noun** a concentric layer of wood, shell, or bone developed during an annual or other regular period of growth.

growth stock ▶ **noun** a company stock that tends to increase in capital value rather than yield high income.

groyne (US **groin**) ▶ **noun** a low wall or sturdy timber barrier built out into the sea from a beach to check erosion and drifting.

– ORIGIN late 16th cent.: from dialect *groin* 'snout', from Old French *groign*, from late Latin *grunium* 'pig's snout', from Latin *grunnire* 'to grunt'.

grozing iron /ˈɡrəʊzɪŋ/ ▶ **noun** chiefly historical a pair of pliers for clipping the edges of pieces of glass.

■ historical a tool for smoothing soldered joints in lead pipes.

– ORIGIN Middle English: *grozing* from Middle Dutch, from the stem of *gruizen* 'crush, trim glass', from *gruis* 'fragments'.

Grozny /ˈɡrɒzni/ a city in SW Russia, near the border with Georgia, capital of Chechnya; pop. 401,000 (est. 1990).

GRP ▶ **abbreviation for** glass-reinforced plastic.

grt ▶ **abbreviation for** gross registered tonnage, a measure of a ship's size found by dividing the volume of the space enclosed by its hull (measured in cubic feet) by one hundred.

grub ▶ **noun 1** the larva of an insect, especially a beetle.

■ a maggot or small caterpillar.

2 [mass noun] informal food: *a popular bar serving excellent pub grub.*

▶ **verb** (**grubbed**, **grubbing**) [no obj., with adverbial] **1** dig or poke superficially at the earth; dig shallowly in soil: *the damage done to pastures by badgers* **grubbing for** *worms.*

■ [with obj.] remove (something) from the earth by digging it up: *all the vines are* **grubbed up** *and the land left fallow for a few years.* ■ [with obj.] clear (the ground) of roots and stumps: [as noun **grubbing**] *construction operations including clearing and grubbing.*

2 search for something in a clumsy and unmethodical manner; rummage: *I began grubbing about in the waste-paper basket to find the envelope.*

■ do demeaning or humiliating work in order to achieve something: *she has achieved material independence without having to* **grub for** *it.* ■ [with obj.] achieve or acquire (something) in such a way: *they were grubbing a living from garbage pails.*

– ORIGIN Middle English: perhaps related to Dutch *grobbelen*, also to **GRAVE**[1].

grubber ▶ **noun 1** [usu. in combination] a person who is determined to acquire or amass something, especially in a ruthless or unscrupulous manner: *a money-grubber* | *a vote-grubber.*

2 [with modifier] an implement for digging up plants: *a daisy-grubber.*

3 Cricket a ball that is bowled along the ground.

■ (also **grubber kick**) Rugby a forward kick of the ball along the ground.

grubby ▶ **adjective** (**grubbier**, **grubbiest**) dirty; grimy: *the grubby face of a young boy.*

■ figurative disreputable; sordid: *grubby little moneylenders.*

– DERIVATIVES **grubbily** adverb, **grubbiness** noun.

grub screw ▶ **noun** Brit. a small headless screw, used typically to attach a handle or cam to a spindle.

grubstake N. Amer. informal ▶ **noun** an amount of material, provisions, or money supplied to an enterprise (originally a prospector for ore) in return for a share in the resulting profits.

▶ **verb** [with obj.] provide with a grubstake.

Grub Street ▶ **noun** used in reference to a world or class of impoverished journalists and writers.

– ORIGIN the name of a street (later Milton Street) in Moorgate, London, inhabited by such authors in the 17th cent.

grudge ▶ **noun** a persistent feeling of ill will or resentment resulting from a past insult or injury: *a former employee who might* **harbour a grudge against** *the company.*

▶ **verb** [with obj.] be resentfully unwilling to give, grant, or allow (something): *he grudged the work and time that the meeting involved.*

■ [with two objs] [usu. with negative] feel resentful that (someone) has achieved (something): *I don't grudge him his moment of triumph.*

– PHRASES **bear** (or **owe**) **someone a grudge** maintain a feeling of ill will or resentment towards someone.

– DERIVATIVES **grudger** noun.

– ORIGIN late Middle English: variant of obsolete *grutch* 'complain, murmur, grumble', from Old French *grouchier*, of unknown origin. Compare with **GROUCH**.

grudge match ▶ **noun** a contest or other competitive situation based on personal antipathy between the participants.

grudging ▶ **adjective** given, granted, or allowed only reluctantly or resentfully: *a grudging apology.*

■ (of a person) reluctant or resentfully unwilling to give, grant, or allow something: *Oliver was grudging about accepting Wickham's innocence.*

– DERIVATIVES **grudgingly** adverb, **grudgingness** noun.

gruel ▶ **noun** [mass noun] a thin liquid food of oatmeal or other meal boiled in milk or water.

– ORIGIN Middle English: from Old French, of Germanic origin.

gruelling (US **grueling**) ▶ **adjective** extremely tiring and demanding: *a gruelling schedule.*

– DERIVATIVES **gruellingly** adverb.

– ORIGIN mid 19th cent.: from the verb *gruel* 'exhaust, punish', from an old phrase *get one's gruel* 'receive one's punishment'.

gruesome ▶ **adjective** causing repulsion or horror; grisly: *the most gruesome murder.*

■ informal extremely unpleasant: *gruesome catering.*

– DERIVATIVES **gruesomely** adverb, **gruesomeness** noun.

– ORIGIN late 16th cent.: from Scots *grue* 'to feel horror, shudder' (of Scandinavian origin) + **-SOME**[1]. Rare before the late 18th cent., the word was popularized by Sir Walter Scott.

gruff ▶ adjective abrupt or taciturn in manner: *penetrate a fairly gruff exterior and you will find him affable.*
■ (of a voice) rough and low in pitch: *she spoke with a gruff, masculine voice.*
– DERIVATIVES **gruffly** adverb, **gruffness** noun.
– ORIGIN late 15th cent. (in the sense 'coarse-grained'): from Flemish and Dutch *grof* 'coarse, rude', of West Germanic origin.

grumble ▶ verb [reporting verb] complain or protest about something in a bad-tempered but typically muted way: [with clause] *his father was grumbling that he hadn't heard a word from him* | [with obj.] *he grumbled something about the decision being unnecessary.*
■ [no obj.] make a low rumbling sound: *thunder was grumbling somewhere in the distance.* ■ [no obj.] (of an internal organ) give intermittent discomfort: [as adj. **grumbling**] *a grumbling appendix.*
▶ noun a complaint: *the main grumble is that he spends too much time away.*
■ a low rumbling sound.
– DERIVATIVES **grumbler** noun, **grumblingly** adverb, **grumbly** adjective.
– ORIGIN late 16th cent.: from obsolete *grumme* (probably of Germanic origin and related to Dutch *grommen*) + -LE⁴.

grump informal ▶ noun a grumpy person.
■ a fit of sulking: *the parish priest was in such a grump about the contributions to a new altar.*
▶ verb [no obj.] act in a sulky, grumbling manner: *he grumped at me when I moved the papers.*
– DERIVATIVES **grumpish** adjective, **grumpishly** adverb.
– ORIGIN early 18th cent.: imitating inarticulate sounds expressing displeasure.

grumpy ▶ adjective (**grumpier**, **grumpiest**) bad-tempered and sulky.
– DERIVATIVES **grumpily** adverb, **grumpiness** noun.

Grundy ▶ noun see MRS GRUNDY.

Grünewald /ˈgruːnəˌvald, German ˈgryːnəvalt/, Mathias (c.1460–1528), German painter; born *Mathis Nithardt*; also called **Mathis Gothardt**. His most famous work is the nine-panel *Isenheim Altar* (completed 1516).

grunge ▶ noun [mass noun] **1** chiefly N. Amer. grime; dirt. **2** (also **grunge rock**) a style of rock music characterized by a raucous guitar sound and lazy vocal delivery.
■ the fashion associated with this music, including loose, layered clothing and ripped jeans.
– DERIVATIVES **grunginess** noun, **grungy** adjective.
– ORIGIN 1970s: back-formation from *grungy*, perhaps suggested by GRUBBY and DINGY.

grunion /ˈgrʌnjən/ ▶ noun a small, slender Californian fish that swarms on to beaches at night to spawn. The eggs are buried in the sand and the young fish are swept out to sea on the following spring tide.
● *Leuresthes tenuis*, family Atherinidae.
– ORIGIN early 20th cent.: probably from Spanish *gruñón* 'grunter'.

grunt ▶ verb [no obj.] (of an animal, especially a pig) make a low, short guttural sound.
■ (of a person) make a low inarticulate sound resembling this, typically to express effort or indicate assent: *Graham grunted and heaved as he helped the masons fit a huge slab of stone into place.*
▶ noun **1** a low, short guttural sound made by an animal or a person. **2** informal, chiefly N. Amer. a low-ranking or unskilled soldier or other worker: *he went from grunt to senior executive vice-president in less than five years* | [as modifier] *grunt work.* [ORIGIN: alteration of *ground*, from *ground man* (with reference to unskilled railway work before progressing to lineman).] **3** [mass noun] informal power, especially that of a motor vehicle: *what the big wagon needs is grunt, and the turbo does the business.* **4** an edible shoaling fish of tropical inshore waters and coral reefs, able to make a loud noise by grinding its teeth and amplifying the sound in the swim bladder.
● Family Pomadasyidae: numerous genera and species.
– ORIGIN Old English *grunnettan*, of Germanic origin and related to German *grunzen*; probably originally imitative.

grunter ▶ noun a fish that makes a grunting noise, especially when caught, in particular:
■ a mainly marine fish of warm waters (family Theraponidae: several genera). ■ another term for GRUNT (in sense 4).

gruntled ▶ adjective humorous pleased, satisfied, and contented.
– ORIGIN 1930s: back-formation from DISGRUNTLED.

Grus /grʌs/ Astronomy a small southern constellation (the Crane), south of Piscis Austrinus.
■ [as genitive **Gruis** /ˈgruːɪs/] used with preceding letter or numeral to designate a star in this constellation: *the star Delta Gruis.*
– ORIGIN Latin.

Gruyère /ˈgruːjɛː/ ▶ noun [mass noun] a firm, tangy cheese.
– ORIGIN named after *Gruyère*, a district in Switzerland, where it was first made.

gryke ▶ noun variant spelling of GRIKE.

gryphon ▶ noun variant spelling of GRIFFIN.

grysbok /ˈgrʌɪsbɒk, ˈxrɛɪs-/ ▶ noun a small mainly nocturnal antelope with small vertical horns and a slightly arched back, found in SW Africa.
● Genus *Raphicerus*, family Bovidae: two species.
– ORIGIN late 18th cent.: from Afrikaans, from Dutch *grijs* 'grey' + *bok* 'buck'.

Grytviken /ˈgrɪtˌviːkən/ the chief settlement on the island of South Georgia, in the South Atlantic, a former whaling station.

gs historical ▶ abbreviation for guineas.

GSM ▶ abbreviation for Global System (or Standard) for Mobile, a standardized international system for digital mobile telecommunication.

gsm ▶ abbreviation for grams per square metre, a measure of weight for paper: *100 gsm paper.*

GSOH ▶ abbreviation for good sense of humour (used in personal advertisements).

G spot ▶ noun a sensitive area of the anterior wall of the vagina believed by some to be highly erogenous and capable of ejaculation.
– ORIGIN 1944: *G* from *Gräfenberg*, because first described by Gräfenberg and Dickinson in the *Western Journal of Surgery*.

GSR ▶ abbreviation for galvanic skin response.

GST ▶ abbreviation for (in New Zealand and Canada) Goods and Services Tax, a broadly applied value added tax.

Gstaad /gəˈʃtɑːt, German kʃtaːt/ a winter-sports resort in western Switzerland.

G-string (also **gee-string**) ▶ noun a garment consisting of a narrow strip of cloth that covers the genitals and is attached to a waistband, worn as underwear or by striptease performers.

G-suit ▶ noun a garment with pressurized pouches that are inflatable with air or fluid, worn by fighter pilots and astronauts to enable them to withstand high gravitational forces.
– ORIGIN 1940s: from *g* (symbol of *gravity*) + SUIT.

GT ▶ adjective denoting a high-performance car: *GT cars.*
▶ noun a high-performance car.
– ORIGIN 1960s: abbreviation of Italian GRAN TURISMO.

Gt ▶ abbreviation for Great: *Gt Britain.*

GTi ▶ adjective denoting a high-performance car with a fuel-injected engine: *a Peugeot 205 GTi.*
▶ noun a car of this type.
– ORIGIN late 20th cent.: from GT + *i* for injection.

guacamole /ˌgwɑːkəˈməʊleɪ, -li/ ▶ noun [mass noun] a dish of mashed avocado mixed with chopped onion, chilli peppers, and seasoning.
– ORIGIN Latin American Spanish, from Nahuatl *ahuacamolli*, from *ahuacatl* 'avocado' + *molli* 'sauce'.

guacharo /ˈgwɑːtʃərəʊ/ ▶ noun (pl. **-os**) North American term for OILBIRD.
– ORIGIN early 19th cent.: from Spanish *guáchero*, of South American origin.

Guadalajara /ˌgwɑːdələˈhɑːrə/ **1** a city in central Spain, to the north-east of Madrid; pop. 67,200 (1991). **2** a city in west central Mexico, capital of the state of Jalisco; pop. 2,846,720 (1990).

Guadalcanal /ˌgwɑːdəlkəˈnal/ an island in the western Pacific, the largest of the Solomon Islands; pop. 71,300 (est. 1987). During the Second World War it was the scene of the first major US offensive against the Japanese (August 1942).

Guadalquivir /ˌgwɑːdəlkɪˈvɪə, Spanish gwaðalkiˈβir/ a river of Andalusia in southern Spain. It flows for 657 km (410 miles) through Cordoba and Seville to reach the Atlantic north-west of Cadiz.

Guadeloupe /ˌgwɑːdəˈluːp, French gwadlup/ a group of islands in the Lesser Antilles, forming an overseas department of France; pop. 387,030 (1991); languages, French (official), French Creole; capital, Basse-Terre.
– DERIVATIVES **Guadeloupian** adjective & noun.

Guadiana /ˌgwɑːdɪˈɑːnə/ a river of Spain and Portugal. Rising in a plateau region south-east of Madrid, it flows south-westwards for some 580 km (360 miles), entering the Atlantic at the Gulf of Cadiz. For the last part of its course it forms the border between Spain and Portugal.

guaiac /ˈgwʌɪak/ ▶ noun [mass noun] brown resin obtained from guaiacum trees, used as a flavouring and in varnishes.

guaiacol /ˈgwʌɪəkɒl/ ▶ noun Chemistry an oily yellow liquid with a penetrating odour, obtained by distilling wood tar or guaiac, used as a flavouring and an expectorant.
● Alternative name: o-**methoxyphenol**; chem. formula: $HOC_6H_4OCH_3$.
– ORIGIN mid 19th cent.: from GUAIACUM + -OL.

guaiacum /ˈgwʌɪəkəm/ ▶ noun an evergreen tree of the Caribbean and tropical America, formerly important for its hard, heavy, oily timber but now scarce. Also called LIGNUM VITAE.
● *Guaiacum officinale* and *G. sanctum*, family Zygophyllaceae.
■ another term for GUAIAC.
– ORIGIN mid 16th cent.: modern Latin, via Spanish from Taino *guayacan*.

Guam /gwɑːm/ the largest and southernmost of the Mariana Islands, administered as an unincorporated territory of the US; pop. 132,000 (1990); languages, English (official), Austronesian languages; capital, Agaña. Guam was ceded to the US by Spain in 1898.
– DERIVATIVES **Guamanian** /gwɑːˈmeɪnɪən/ adjective & noun.

guan /gwɑːn/ ▶ noun a large pheasant-like tree-dwelling bird of tropical American rainforests.
● Family Cracidae (the **guan family**): several genera, especially *Penelope*. The guan family also includes curassows and chachalacas.
– ORIGIN late 17th cent.: via American Spanish from Miskito *kwamu*.

guanaco /gwəˈnɑːkəʊ/ ▶ noun (pl. **-os**) a wild Andean mammal similar to the domestic llama, which is probably derived from it. It has a valuable pale brown pelt.
● *Lama guanicoe*, family Camelidae.
– ORIGIN early 17th cent.: via Spanish from Quechua *huanacu*.

Guanajuato /ˌgwɑːnəˈhwɑːtəʊ/ a state of central Mexico.
■ its capital city; pop. 45,000 (est. 1983). The city developed as a silver-mining centre after a rich vein of silver was discovered there in 1558.

Guangdong /gwaŋˈdʊŋ/ (also **Kwangtung**) province of southern China, on the South China Sea; capital, Guangzhou (Canton).

Guangxi Zhuang /ˌgwaŋʃiː ˈʒwaŋ/ (also **Kwangsi Chuang**) an autonomous region of southern China, on the Gulf of Tonkin; capital, Nanning.

Guangzhou /gwaŋˈdʒəʊ/ (also **Kwangchow**) a city in southern China, the capital of Guangdong province; pop. 3,918,000 (1990). It is the leading industrial and commercial centre of southern China. Also called CANTON.

guanidine /ˈgwɑːnɪdiːn/ ▶ noun [mass noun] Chemistry a strongly basic crystalline compound, used in organic synthesis.
● An imide derived from urea; Chem. formula: $HNC(NH_2)_2$.
– ORIGIN mid 19th cent.: from GUANO + -IDE + -INE⁴.

guanine /ˈgwɑːniːn/ ▶ noun [mass noun] Biochemistry a compound that occurs in guano and fish scales, and is one of the four constituent bases of nucleic acids. A pure derivative, it is paired with cytosine in double-stranded DNA.
● Alternative name: 6-**oxy-2-aminopurine**; chem. formula: $C_5H_5N_5O$.
– ORIGIN mid 19th cent.: from GUANO + -INE⁴.

guano /ˈgwɑːnəʊ/ ▶ noun (pl. **-os**) [mass noun] the excrement of seabirds, occurring in thick deposits notably on the islands off Peru and Chile, and used as fertilizer.
■ an artificial fertilizer resembling natural guano, especially one made from fish.
– ORIGIN early 17th cent.: from Spanish, or from

Latin American Spanish *huano*, from Quechua *huanu* 'dung'.

guanosine /ˈɡwɑːnəsiːn/ ▶ **noun** [mass noun] Biochemistry a compound consisting of guanine combined with ribose, present in all living tissue in combined form as nucleotides.
– ORIGIN early 20th cent.: from **GUANINE**, with the insertion of **-OSE**².

Guantánamo Bay /ɡwɑːnˈtɑːnəməʊ/ a bay on the SE coast of Cuba. It is the site of a US naval base established in 1903.

guar /ɡwɑː/ ▶ **noun** a drought-resistant plant of the pea family, which is grown as a vegetable and fodder crop and as a source of guar gum, native to dry regions of Africa and Asia. Also called **CLUSTER BEAN**.
• *Cyamopsis tetragonoloba*, family Leguminosae.
■(also **guar flour** or **guar gum**) [mass noun] a fine powder obtained by grinding guar seeds, which is used in the food, paper, and other industries.
– ORIGIN late 19th cent.: from Hindi *guār*.

guarache /ɡwəˈrɑːtʃi/ ▶ **noun** variant spelling of **HUARACHE**.

Guarani /ˌɡwɑːrəˈniː/ ▶ **noun** (pl. same) **1** a member of an American Indian people of Paraguay and adjacent regions.
2 [mass noun] the language of this people, which has over 3 million speakers. It is one of the main divisions of the Tupi-Guarani language family and is a national language of Paraguay.
3 (**guarani**) the basic monetary unit of Paraguay, equal to 100 centimos.
▶ **adjective** of or relating to the Guarani or their language.
– ORIGIN Spanish.

guarantee ▶ **noun** a formal promise or assurance (typically in writing) that certain conditions will be fulfilled, especially that a product will be repaired or replaced if not of a specified quality and durability: *we offer a 10-year* ***guarantee against*** *rusting.*
■something that gives a certainty of outcome: *supervision can't be a* ***guarantee against*** *a new offence.* ■ variant spelling of **GUARANTY**. ■ less common term for **GUARANTOR**.
▶ **verb** (**guarantees**, **guaranteed**, **guaranteeing**) [no obj.] provide a formal assurance or promise, especially that certain conditions will be fulfilled relating to a product, service, or transaction: [with infinitive] *the company guarantees to refund your money.*
■[with obj.] provide such an assurance regarding (something, especially a product): *the cooker is guaranteed for five years* | [as adj. **guaranteed**] *the guaranteed bonus is not very high.* ■ [with obj.] provide financial security for; underwrite: *a demand that £100,000 be deposited to guarantee their costs.* ■ [with obj.] promise with certainty: *no one can guarantee a profit on stocks and shares.*
– ORIGIN late 17th cent. (in the sense 'guarantor'): perhaps from Spanish *garante*, corresponding to French *garant* (see **WARRANT**), later influenced by French *garantie* 'guaranty'.

guarantee fund ▶ **noun** a sum of money pledged as a contingent indemnity for loss.

guarantor /ˌɡar(ə)nˈtɔː/ ▶ **noun** a person, organization, or thing that gives or acts as a guarantee: *the role of the police as guarantors of public order.*
■Law a person or organization who provides a guaranty.

guaranty /ˈɡar(ə)nti/ (also **guarantee**) ▶ **noun** (pl. **-ies**) an undertaking to answer for the payment of a debt or for the performance of an obligation by another person liable in the first instance.
■a thing serving as security for such an undertaking.
– ORIGIN early 16th cent.: from Old French *garantie*, from *garantir*; related to **WARRANT**.

guard ▶ **verb** [with obj.] watch over to keep safe: *they were sent to* ***guard*** *villagers* ***from*** *attack by bandits.*
■watch over in order to control entry and exit: *the gates were guarded by uniformed soldiers.* ■ watch over (someone) to prevent them from escaping: *police officers were guarding inmates who cannot be accommodated in prison.* ■ [no obj.] (**guard against**) take precautions against: *farmers must guard against sudden changes in the market.* ■ protect against damage or harm: *the company fiercely guarded its independence.* ■ Basketball stay close to (an opponent) in order to prevent them getting or passing the ball.
▶ **noun 1** a person who keeps watch, especially a soldier or other person formally assigned to protect a person or to control access to a place: *a security guard* | [as modifier] *he distracted the soldier on guard duty.*
■[treated as sing. or pl.] a body of soldiers serving to protect a place or person: *the hound belonged to a member of the castle's guard.* ■ (**Guards**) the household troops of the British army. ■ N. Amer. a prison warder. ■ Brit. an official who rides on and is in general charge of a train. ■ American Football each of two players either side of the centre. ■ Basketball each of two players chiefly responsible for marking opposing players.
2 a device worn or fitted to prevent injury or damage: *a retractable blade guard.*
3 a defensive posture that is adopted in a boxing or martial arts contest or in a fight: *this kick can curl around an otherwise effective guard.*
■a state of caution, vigilance, or preparedness against adverse circumstances: *he let his guard slip enough to make some unwise comments.*
– PHRASES **guard of honour** a group of soldiers ceremonially welcoming an important visitor. **keep** (or **stand**) **guard** act as a guard. **off guard** unprepared for some surprise or difficulty: *the government was caught off guard by the unexpected announcement.* **on guard** on duty to protect or defend something. ■ (also **on one's guard**) prepared for any contingency; vigilant: *we must be* ***on guard against*** *such temptation.* **raise one's guard** adopt a defensive posture. **take guard** Cricket (of a batsman) stand in position ready to receive the ball, especially having asked the umpire to check the position of one's bat with respect to the stumps. **under guard** being guarded: *he was held in an empty stable under guard.*
– ORIGIN late Middle English (in the sense 'care, custody'): from Old French *garde* (noun), *garder* (verb), of West Germanic origin. Compare with **WARD**.

guardant /ˈɡɑːd(ə)nt/ ▶ **adjective** [usu. postpositive] Heraldry (especially of an animal) depicted with the body sideways and the face towards the viewer: *three lions passant guardant.*
– ORIGIN late 16th cent.: from French *gardant* 'guarding', from *garder* 'to guard'.

guard cell ▶ **noun** Botany each of a pair of curved cells that surround a stoma, becoming larger or smaller according to the pressure within the cells.

guarded ▶ **adjective** cautious and having possible reservations: *he has given a guarded welcome to the idea.*
– DERIVATIVES **guardedly** adverb, **guardedness** noun.

guardee ▶ **noun** Brit. informal a guardsman, especially one seen as representing smartness or elegance.

guard hair ▶ **noun** [mass noun] long, coarse hair forming an animal's outer fur.

guardhouse ▶ **noun** a building used to accommodate a military guard or to detain military prisoners.

Guardi /ˈɡwɑːdi, Italian ˈɡwardi/, Francesco (1712–93), Italian painter. A pupil of Canaletto, he produced paintings of Venice notable for their free handling of light and atmosphere.

guardian ▶ **noun** a defender, protector, or keeper: *self-appointed guardians of public morality.*
■a person who looks after and is legally responsible for someone who is unable to manage their own affairs, especially a child whose parents have died. ■ the superior of a Franciscan convent.
– DERIVATIVES **guardianship** noun.
– ORIGIN late Middle English: from Old French *garden*, of Germanic origin; compare with **WARD** and **WARDEN**. The ending was altered by association with **-IAN**.

guardian angel ▶ **noun** a spirit that is thought to watch over and protect a person or place.

guard rail ▶ **noun** a rail that prevents people from falling off or being hit by something.
■North American term for **CRASH BARRIER**.

guard ring ▶ **noun** a ring-shaped electrode used to limit the extent of an electric field, especially in a capacitor.

guardroom ▶ **noun** a room in a military base used to accommodate a guard or detain prisoners.

guardsman ▶ **noun** (pl. **-men**) (in the UK) a soldier of a regiment of Guards.
■(in the US) a member of the National Guard.

guard's van ▶ **noun** Brit. a carriage or wagon occupied by the guard on a train.

Guarneri /ɡwɑːˈnɛːri/, Giuseppe (1687–1744), Italian violin-maker; known as **del Gesù**. He is the most famous of a family of three generations of violin-makers based in Cremona.

Guatemala /ˌɡwɑːtəˈmɑːlə/ a country in Central America, bordering on the Pacific Ocean and with a short coastline on the Caribbean Sea; pop. 10,621,200 (est. 1995); official language, Spanish; capital, Guatemala City.

A former centre of Mayan civilization, Guatemala was conquered by the Spanish in 1523–4. After independence it formed the core of the short-lived United Provinces of Central America (1828–38) before becoming an independent republic in its own right.

– DERIVATIVES **Guatemalan** adjective & noun.

Guatemala City the capital of Guatemala; pop. 1,167,495 (est. 1995). Situated at an altitude of 1,500 m (4,920 ft) in the central highlands, the city was founded in 1776 to replace the former capital, Antigua Guatemala, which was destroyed by an earthquake in 1773.

guava /ˈɡwɑːvə/ ▶ **noun 1** an edible pale orange tropical fruit with pink juicy flesh and a strong sweet aroma.
2 the small tropical American tree which bears this fruit.
• Genus *Psidium*, family Myrtaceae: several species, in particular *P. guajava*.
– ORIGIN mid 16th cent.: from Spanish *guayaba*, probably from Taino.

Guayaquil /ˌɡwʌjəˈkiːl/ a seaport in Ecuador, the country's principal port and second largest city; pop. 1,877,030 (est. 1995).

guayule /ɡwʌɪˈuːli/ ▶ **noun** a silver-leaved Mexican shrub of the daisy family which yields large amounts of latex.
• *Parthenium argentatum*, family Compositae.
■[mass noun] a rubber substitute made from this latex.
– ORIGIN early 20th cent.: via Latin American Spanish from Nahuatl *cuauhuli*.

gubbins ▶ **plural noun** [treated as sing. or pl.] Brit. informal miscellaneous items; paraphernalia: *businesses who don't want to get their hands grubby with all the technical gubbins.*
■[treated as sing.] a gadget: *a little gubbins he had made as a boy.*
– ORIGIN mid 16th cent. (in the sense 'fragments'): from obsolete *gobbon* 'piece, slice, gob', from Old French; probably related to **GOBBET**. Current senses date from the early 20th cent.

gubernatorial /ˌɡ(j)uːbənəˈtɔːrɪəl/ ▶ **adjective** of or relating to a governor, particularly that of a state in the US: *a gubernatorial election.*
– ORIGIN mid 18th cent.: from Latin *gubernator* 'governor', (from *gubernare* 'steer, govern', from Greek *kubernan* 'to steer') + **-IAL**.

guck ▶ **noun** [mass noun] N. Amer. informal a slimy, dirty, or otherwise unpleasant substance: *he got mud and cow guck all over his white jersey.*
– ORIGIN possibly a blend of **GOO** and **MUCK**.

guddle Scottish ▶ **verb** [no obj.] fish with the hands by groping under the stones or banks of a stream.
■[with obj.] catch (a fish) in such a way.
▶ **noun** a muddle; a mess.
– DERIVATIVES **guddler** noun.
– ORIGIN mid 17th cent.: of unknown origin.

gudgeon¹ /ˈɡʌdʒ(ə)n/ ▶ **noun 1** a small edible European freshwater fish, often used as bait by anglers.
• *Gobio gobio*, family Cyprinidae.
2 archaic a credulous or easily fooled person.
– ORIGIN late Middle English: from Old French *goujon*, from Latin *gobio(n-)*, from *gobius* 'goby'.

gudgeon² /ˈɡʌdʒ(ə)n/ ▶ **noun** a pivot or spindle on which a bell or other object swings or rotates.
■the tubular part of a hinge into which the pin fits to unite the joint. ■ a socket at the stern of a boat, into which a rudder is fitted. ■ a pin holding two blocks of stone together.
– ORIGIN Middle English: from Old French *goujon*, diminutive of *gouge* (see **GOUGE**).

gudgeon pin ▶ **noun** a pin holding a piston rod and a connecting rod together.

Gudrun /ˈɡʊdruːn/ (in Norse legend) the Norse equivalent of Kriemhild, wife of Sigurd and later of Atli (Attila the Hun).

guelder rose /ˈɡɛldə/ ▶ **noun** a deciduous Eurasian shrub with flattened heads of fragrant creamy-white flowers, followed by clusters of translucent red berries.

• *Viburnum opulus*, family Caprifoliaceae. See also **SNOWBALL TREE**.

– ORIGIN late 16th cent.: from Dutch *geldersche roos* 'rose of *Gelderland*' (see **GELDERLAND**).

Guelph /gwɛlf/ ▶ **noun 1** a member of one of two great factions in Italian medieval politics, traditionally supporting the Pope against the Holy Roman emperor. Compare with **GHIBELLINE**.
2 a member of a princely family of Swabian origin from which the British royal house is descended through George I.
– DERIVATIVES **Guelphic** adjective.
– ORIGIN from Italian *Guelfo*, from Middle High German *Welf*, the name of the founder of one of the two great rival dynasties in the Holy Roman Empire.

guenon /gəˈnɒn/ ▶ **noun** an African monkey found mainly in forests, with a long tail and typically a brightly coloured coat. The male is much larger than the female.
• Genus *Cercopithecus*, family Cercopithecidae: several species, including the vervet, mona, and Diana monkeys.
– ORIGIN mid 19th cent.: from French, of unknown origin.

guerdon /ˈgəːd(ə)n/ chiefly archaic ▶ **noun** a reward or recompense.
▶ **verb** [with obj.] give a reward to (someone): *there might come a time in which he should guerdon them.*
– ORIGIN late Middle English: from Old French, from medieval Latin *widerdonum*, alteration (by association with Latin *donum* 'gift') of a West Germanic compound represented by Old High German *widarlōn* 'repayment'.

Guericke /ˈgɛːrɪkə/, Otto von (1602–86), German engineer and physicist. He was the first to investigate the properties of a vacuum, and he devised the Magdeburg hemispheres to demonstrate atmospheric pressure.

Guernica /gəːˈniːkə, ˈgəːnɪkə/ a town in the Basque Provinces of northern Spain, to the east of Bilbao; pop. 17,840 (1981). Formerly the seat of a Basque parliament, it was bombed in 1937, during the Spanish Civil War, by German planes in support of Franco, an event depicted in a famous painting by Picasso. Full name **GUERNICA Y LUNO** /iː ˈluːnəʊ/.

Guernsey[1] /ˈgəːnzi/ an island in the English Channel, to the north-west of Jersey; pop. 58,870 (1991); capital, St Peter Port. It is the second largest of the Channel Islands.

Guernsey[2] /ˈgəːnzi/ ▶ **noun** (pl. **-eys**) **1** an animal of a breed of dairy cattle from Guernsey, noted for producing rich, creamy milk.
2 (**guernsey**) a thick sweater made with oiled navy-blue wool and originally worn by fishermen.
■ Austral. a football jumper, especially one of the sleeveless kind worn by Australian Rules players.
– PHRASES **get a guernsey** Austral. informal be selected for a football team. ■ gain recognition or approbation: *the papers weren't going to give him a guernsey, no matter how brilliant he might be.*

Guernsey lily ▶ **noun** a nerine with large heads of pink lily-like flowers. Native to South Africa, it has long been cultivated and was first described in Guernsey.
• *Nerine sarniensis*, family Liliaceae (or Amaryllidaceae).

Guerrero /gɛˈrɛːrəʊ/ a state of SW central Mexico, on the Pacific coast; capital, Chilpancingo.

guerrilla /gəˈrɪlə/ (also **guerilla**) ▶ **noun** a member of a small independent group taking part in irregular fighting, typically against larger regular forces: *this small town fell to the guerrillas* | [as modifier] *guerrilla warfare.*
– ORIGIN early 19th cent. (introduced during the Peninsular War): from Spanish, diminutive of *guerra* 'war'.

guess ▶ **verb** [with obj.] estimate or suppose (something) without sufficient information to be sure of being correct: *she guessed the child's age at 14 or 15* | [with clause] *he took her aside and I guessed that he was offering her a job.*
■ (**guess at**) make a conjecture about: *their motives he could only guess at.* ■ correctly conjecture or perceive: [with clause] *she's guessed where we're going.* ■ [in imperative] used to introduce something considered surprising or exciting: *guess what I've just seen!* ■ (**I guess**) informal used to indicate that although one thinks or supposes something, it is without any great conviction or strength of feeling: [with clause] *I guess I'd better tell you everything.*
▶ **noun** an estimate or conjecture: *my guess is that within a year we will have a referendum.*
– PHRASES **anybody's** (or **anyone's**) **guess** very difficult or impossible to determine: *how well the system will work is anybody's guess.* **keep someone guessing** informal leave someone uncertain or in doubt as to one's intentions or plans.
– DERIVATIVES **guessable** adjective, **guesser** noun.
– ORIGIN Middle English: origin uncertain; perhaps from Dutch *gissen*, and probably related to **GET**.

guesstimate (also **guestimate**) informal ▶ **noun** /ˈgɛstɪmət/ an estimate based on a mixture of guesswork and calculation.
▶ **verb** /ˈgɛstɪmeɪt/ [with obj.] form such an estimate of: *the task is to guesstimate the total vote.*
– ORIGIN 1930s (originally US): blend of **GUESS** and **ESTIMATE**.

guesswork ▶ **noun** [mass noun] the process or results of guessing.

guest ▶ **noun** a person who is invited to visit the home of or take part in a function organized by another: *I have two guests coming to dinner tonight* | [as modifier] *a guest bedroom.*
■ a person invited to participate in an official event: *he went to Moscow as a guest of the Young Pioneers* | [as modifier] *a guest speaker.* ■ a person invited to take part in a radio or television programme, sports event, or other entertainment: *a regular guest on the morning show* | [as modifier] *a guest appearance.* ■ a person lodging at a hotel or boarding house: *a reduction for guests staying seven nights or more.* ■ chiefly US a customer at a restaurant. ■ Entomology a small invertebrate that lives unharmed within an ants' nest.
▶ **verb** [no obj.] informal appear as a guest: *he* ***guested on*** *one of her early albums.*
– PHRASES **be my guest** informal please do: *May I choose the restaurant? Be my guest!* **guest of honour** the most important guest at an occasion.
– ORIGIN Middle English: from Old Norse *gestr*, of Germanic origin; related to Dutch *gast* and German *Gast*, from an Indo-European root shared by Latin *hostis* 'enemy' (originally 'stranger').

guest beer ▶ **noun** Brit. (in a tied public house) a beer offered in addition to those produced by the brewery.
■ (in a free house) a beer available only temporarily.

guest house ▶ **noun** a private house offering accommodation to paying guests.

guestimate ▶ **noun** & **verb** variant spelling of **GUESSTIMATE**.

guest rope ▶ **noun** a second rope fastened to a boat in tow to keep it steady.
■ a rope slung outside a ship to give a hold for boats coming alongside.
– ORIGIN early 17th cent.: of unknown origin.

guest worker ▶ **noun** English term for **GASTARBEITER**.
– ORIGIN 1960s: translation of the German.

Guevara /gəˈvɑːrə, Spanish geˈβara/, Che (1928–67), Argentinian revolutionary and guerrilla leader; full name *Ernesto Guevara de la Serna*. He played a significant part in the Cuban revolution (1956–9) and became a government minister under Castro. He was captured and executed by the Bolivian army while training guerrillas for a planned uprising in Bolivia.

guff ▶ **noun 1** [mass noun] informal trivial or worthless talk or ideas.
2 Scottish an unpleasant smell.
– ORIGIN early 19th cent. (in the sense 'puff, whiff of a bad smell'): imitative.

guffaw /gəˈfɔː/ ▶ **noun** a loud and boisterous laugh.
▶ **verb** [no obj.] laugh in such a way: *both men guffawed at the remark.*
– ORIGIN early 18th cent. (originally Scots): imitative.

Guggenheim /ˈgʊgənhʌɪm/, Meyer (1828–1905), Swiss-born American industrialist. With his seven sons he established large mining and metal-processing companies. His son **Solomon** (1861–1949) set up several foundations providing support for the arts, including the Guggenheim Museum in New York.

GUI Computing ▶ **abbreviation for** graphical user interface.

Guiana /gɪˈɑːnə, gʌɪˈanə/ a region in northern South America, bounded by the Orinoco, Negro, and Amazon Rivers and the Atlantic Ocean. It now comprises Guyana, Suriname, French Guiana, and the Guiana Highlands.

Guiana Highlands a mountainous plateau region of northern South America, lying between the Orinoco and Amazon River basins, largely in SE Venezuela and northern Brazil. Its highest peak is Roraima (2,774 m; 9,094 ft).

guid /gɪd/ ▶ **noun** Scottish form of **GOOD**.

guidance ▶ **noun** [mass noun] **1** advice or information aimed at resolving a problem or difficulty, especially as given by someone in authority: *he looked to his father for inspiration and guidance.*
2 the directing of the motion or position of something, especially a missile: *a glide missile with television guidance.*

guide ▶ **noun 1** a person who advises or shows the way to others: *this lady is going to act as our guide for the rest of the tour.*
■ a professional mountain climber in charge of a group. ■ (**Guide**) chiefly Brit. a member of the Guides Association.
2 a thing that helps someone to form an opinion or make a decision or calculation: *here is a* ***guide to*** *the number of curtain hooks you will need.*
■ a principle or standard of comparison: *as a guide, there are roughly six glasses to a bottle.* ■ a book, document, or display providing information on a subject or about a place: *a TV guide.*
3 a structure or marking which directs the motion or positioning of something: *the guides for the bolt needed straightening.*
▶ **verb 1** [with obj. and adverbial of direction] show or indicate the way to (someone): *he guided her to the front row and sat beside her.*
■ [with obj.] direct the motion or positioning of (something): *the groove in the needle guides the thread.*
2 [with obj.] direct or have an influence on the course of action of (someone or something): *he guided the team to a second successive win in the tournament.*
– DERIVATIVES **guidable** adjective, **guider** noun.
– ORIGIN late Middle English: from Old French *guide* (noun), *guider* (verb), of Germanic origin; related to **WIT**[2].

guidebook ▶ **noun** a book of information about a place, designed for the use of visitors or tourists.

guided ▶ **adjective** conducted by a guide: *a guided tour of the castle.*
■ directed by remote control or by internal equipment: *a guided missile.*

guide dog ▶ **noun** a dog that has been trained to lead a blind person.

guideline ▶ **noun** a general rule, principle, or piece of advice.

guide number ▶ **noun** Photography a measure of the power of a flashgun expressed in metres or feet.

guidepost ▶ **noun** archaic term for **SIGNPOST**.

Guider (also **Guide Guider**) ▶ **noun** Brit. an adult leader in the Guides Association.

guide rope ▶ **noun** a rope used to guide the movement of the load of a crane.

Guides Association (in the UK) an organization for girls, corresponding to the Scout Association. Formerly (until 1992) called **GIRL GUIDES ASSOCIATION**.

It was established in 1910 by Lord Baden-Powell with his wife and sister. The three sections into which it is divided, originally Brownies, Guides, and Rangers, are now called Brownie Guides (7–11 years), Guides (10–16 years), and Ranger Guides (14–19 years). Similar organizations exist in many countries worldwide under the aegis of the World Association of Girl Guides and Girl Scouts, formed in 1928.

guideway ▶ **noun** a groove or track along which something moves.

guidon /ˈgʌɪd(ə)n/ ▶ **noun** a pennant that narrows to a point or fork at the free end, especially one used as the standard of a light cavalry regiment.
– ORIGIN mid 16th cent.: from French, from Italian *guidone*, from *guida* 'a guide'.

Guienne variant spelling of **GUYENNE**.

Guignol /giːˈnjɒl, French giɲɔl/ the bloodthirsty chief character in a French puppet show of that name which is similar to Punch and Judy. See also **GRAND GUIGNOL**.

guild (also **gild**) ▶ **noun** a medieval association of craftsmen or merchants, often having considerable power.
■ an association of people for mutual aid or the pursuit of a common goal. ■ Ecology a group of species

that have similar requirements and play a similar role within a community.
– ORIGIN late Old English: probably from Middle Low German and Middle Dutch *gilde*, of Germanic origin; related to **YIELD**.

guilder /ˈgɪldə/ ▶ noun (pl. same or **guilders**) (until the introduction of the euro in 2002) the basic monetary unit of the Netherlands, equal to 100 cents.
■historical a gold or silver coin formerly used in the Netherlands, Germany, and Austria.
– ORIGIN alteration of Dutch *gulden* (see **GULDEN**).

Guildford /ˈgɪlfəd/ a town in southern England; pop. 63,090 (1981).

guildhall ▶ noun a building used as the meeting place of a guild or corporation.
■Brit. a town hall. ■(**the Guildhall**) the hall of the Corporation of the City of London, used for ceremonial occasions.

guile /gʌɪl/ ▶ noun [mass noun] sly or cunning intelligence: *he used all his guile and guts to free himself from the muddle he was in.*
– DERIVATIVES **guileful** adjective, **guilefully** adverb.
– ORIGIN Middle English: from Old French, probably from Old Norse; compare with **WILE**.

guileless ▶ adjective devoid of guile; innocent and without deception: *his face, once so open and guileless.*
– DERIVATIVES **guilelessly** adverb, **guilelessness** noun.

Guilin /gweɪˈlɪn/ (also **Kweilin**) a city in southern China, on the Li River, in the autonomous region of Guangxi Zhuang; pop. 552,300 (1990).

Guillain–Barré syndrome /ˌgɪjãˈbareɪ/ ▶ noun [mass noun] Medicine an acute form of polyneuritis, often preceded by a respiratory infection, causing weakness and often paralysis of the limbs.
– ORIGIN 1916: named after Georges *Guillain* (1876–1961) and Jean *Barré* (1880–1967), two of those who first described the syndrome.

guillemot /ˈgɪlɪmɒt/ ▶ noun an auk with a narrow pointed bill, typically nesting on cliff ledges.
• Family Alcidae, genera *Uria* (white-breasted) and *Cepphus* (black-breasted): five species. Compare with **MURRE**.
– ORIGIN late 17th cent.: from French, diminutive of *Guillaume* 'William'.

guilloche /gɪˈləʊʃ, -ˈlɒʃ/ ▶ noun [mass noun] ornamentation resembling braided or interlaced ribbons.
– ORIGIN mid 19th cent.: from French *guillochis*, denoting the ornamentation, or *guilloche*, a carving tool.

guillotine /ˈgɪlətiːn, gɪləˈtiːn/ ▶ noun a machine with a heavy blade sliding vertically in grooves, used for beheading people.
■a device for cutting that incorporates a descending or sliding blade, used typically for cutting paper, card, or sheet metal. ■a surgical instrument with a sliding blade used typically for the removal of the tonsils. ■Brit. (in parliament) a procedure used to prevent delay in the discussion of a legislative bill by fixing times at which various parts of it must be voted on: [as modifier] *a guillotine motion.*
▶ verb [with obj.] execute (someone) by guillotine.
■Brit. (in parliament) end discussion by applying a guillotine to (a bill or debate).
– ORIGIN late 18th cent.: from French, named after Joseph-Ignace *Guillotin* (1738–1814), the French physician who recommended its use for executions in 1789.

guilt ▶ noun [mass noun] the fact of having committed a specified or implied offence or crime: *it is the duty of the prosecution to prove the prisoner's guilt.*
■a feeling of having committed wrong or failed in an obligation: *he remembered with sudden guilt the letter from his mother that he had not yet read.*
– PHRASES **guilt by association** guilt ascribed to someone not because of any evidence but because of their association with an offender.
– ORIGIN Old English *gylt*, of unknown origin.

guiltless ▶ adjective having no guilt; innocent: *people are forever criticizing the service, and I am not myself guiltless in this.*
– DERIVATIVES **guiltlessly** adverb, **guiltlessness** noun.

guilt trip ▶ noun an experience of feeling guilty about something, especially when such guilt is excessive, self-indulgent, or unfounded: *we want no guilt trips about taking part in the war.*
▶ verb (**guilt-trip**) [with obj.] make (someone) feel guilty, especially in order to induce them to do something: *a pay increase will not guilt-trip them into improvements.*

guilty ▶ adjective (**guiltier**, **guiltiest**) culpable of or responsible for a specified wrongdoing: *the police will soon discover who the guilty party is* | *he was found* ***guilty of*** *manslaughter* | *he found them* ***guilty on*** *a lesser charge.* See also **FIND**, **PLEAD**.
■justly chargeable with a particular fault or error: *she was guilty of a serious error of judgement.* ■conscious of or affected by a feeling of guilt: *Joe felt guilty at having deceived the family* | *he wrestled with a guilty conscience after his adultery.* ■involving a feeling or a judgement of guilt: *I have no guilty secret to reveal* | *a guilty verdict.*
– PHRASES **not guilty** innocent, especially of a formal charge: [as modifier] *the judge directed the jury to return a not guilty verdict.*
– DERIVATIVES **guiltily** adverb, **guiltiness** noun.
– ORIGIN Old English *gyltig* (see **GUILT**, **-Y**[1]).

guimp ▶ noun variant spelling of **GIMP**[1] and **GUIMPE**.

guimpe /gɪmp/ (also **guimp**) ▶ noun historical a high-necked blouse or undergarment worn showing beneath a low-necked dress.
– ORIGIN mid 19th cent.: from French; related to German *Wimpel*, Dutch *wimpel* 'pennant, streamer', also to **WIMPLE** and the rare word *gimp* 'nun's neckerchief'.

Guinea /ˈgɪni/ a country on the west coast of Africa; pop. 6,909,300 (est. 1990); languages, French (official), Fulani, Malinke, and other languages; capital, Conakry.

> Part of a feudal Fulani empire from the 16th century, Guinea was colonized by France, becoming part of French West Africa. It became an independent republic in 1958.

– DERIVATIVES **Guinean** adjective & noun.

guinea /ˈgɪni/ (abbrev.: **gn.**) ▶ noun Brit. the sum of £1.05 (21 shillings in pre-decimal currency), now used mainly for determining professional fees and auction prices.
■historical a former British gold coin that was first minted in 1663 from gold imported from West Africa, with a value that was later fixed at 21 shillings. It was replaced by the sovereign from 1817.
– ORIGIN named after **GUINEA** in West Africa.

Guinea, Gulf of a large inlet of the Atlantic Ocean bordering on the southern coast of West Africa.

Guinea-Bissau /ˌgɪnɪbɪˈsaʊ/ a country on the west coast of Africa, between Senegal and Guinea; pop. 1,000,000 (est. 1990); languages, Portuguese (official), West African languages, Creoles; capital, Bissau.

> The area was explored by the Portuguese in the 15th century and was a centre of the slave trade. Formerly called Portuguese Guinea, it became a colony in 1879, and the independent republic of Guinea-Bissau in 1974.

guineafowl ▶ noun (pl. same) a large African game bird with slate-coloured, white-spotted plumage and a loud call. It is sometimes domesticated.
• Family Numididae (or Phasianidae): several genera and species, e.g. the **helmeted guineafowl** (*Numida meleagris*).

guinea pig ▶ noun a domesticated tailless South American cavy, originally raised for food. It no longer occurs in the wild and is now typically kept as a pet or for laboratory research.
• *Cavia porcellus*, family Caviidae.
■a person or thing used as a subject for experiment.

Guinea worm ▶ noun a very long parasitic nematode worm which lives under the skin of infected humans and other mammals in rural Africa and Asia.
• *Dracunculus medinensis*, class Phasmida.

guinep /gɪˈnɛp/ ▶ noun see **GENIP** (sense 2).

Guinevere /ˈgwɪnɪvɪə/ (in Arthurian legend) the wife of King Arthur and mistress of Lancelot.

Guinness /ˈgɪnɪs/, Sir Alec (1914–2000), English actor. He gave memorable performances in the films *Bridge on the River Kwai* (1957) and *Star Wars* (1977) and as espionage chief George Smiley in television versions of John Le Carré's books.

guipure /gɪˈpjʊə/ ▶ noun [mass noun] a heavy lace consisting of embroidered motifs held together by large connecting stitches.
– ORIGIN mid 19th cent.: from French, from *guiper* 'cover with silk', of Germanic origin.

guiro /ˈgwɪərəʊ/ ▶ noun (pl. **-os**) a musical instrument with a serrated surface which gives a rasping sound when scraped with a stick, originally made from an elongated gourd and used in Latin American music.
– ORIGIN Spanish, 'gourd'.

guise /gʌɪz/ ▶ noun an external form, appearance, or manner of presentation, typically concealing the true nature of something: *he visited* ***in the guise of*** *an inspector* | *sums paid* ***under the guise of*** *consultancy fees.*
– ORIGIN Middle English: from Old French, of Germanic origin; related to **WISE**[2].

guiser /ˈgʌɪzə/ ▶ noun archaic a mummer in a folk play performed especially at Christmas or Halloween.
– ORIGIN late 15th cent.: from the archaic verb *guise* 'dress fantastically', from the noun **GUISE**.

guitar ▶ noun a stringed musical instrument, with a fretted fingerboard, typically incurved sides, and six or twelve strings, played by plucking or strumming with the fingers or a plectrum. See also **ELECTRIC GUITAR**.
– DERIVATIVES **guitarist** noun.
– ORIGIN early 17th cent.: from Spanish *guitarra* (partly via French), from Greek *kithara*, denoting an instrument similar to the lyre.

guitarfish ▶ noun (pl. same or **-fishes**) a fish of shallow warm seas, related to the rays and having a guitar-like body shape.
• Several species in the family Rhinobatidae, including *Rhinobatus rhinobatus*, common in European waters, and the **Chinese guitarfish** (*Platyrhina sinensis*, family Platyrhinidae).

guiver ▶ noun variant spelling of **GUYVER**.

Guiyang /gweɪˈjaŋ/ (also **Kweiyang**) an industrial city in southern China, capital of Guizhou province; pop. 1,490,000 (est. 1989).

Guizhou /gweɪˈdʒəʊ/ (also **Kweichow**) a province of southern China; capital, Guiyang.

Gujarat /ˌgʊdʒəˈrɑːt/ a state in western India, with an extensive coastline on the Arabian Sea; capital, Gandhinagar. Formed in 1960 from the northern and western parts of the former state of Bombay, it is one of the most industrialized parts of the country.

Gujarati /ˌguːdʒəˈrɑːti, ˌgʊ-/ (also **Gujerati**) ▶ noun (pl. **Gujaratis**) **1** a native or inhabitant of Gujarat. **2** [mass noun] the Indic language of the Gujaratis, spoken by about 45 million people.
▶ adjective of or relating to this people or their language.

Gujranwala /ˌgʊdʒrənˈwɑːlə/ a city in Pakistan, in Punjab province, north-west of Lahore; pop. 597,000 (1981). It was the birthplace of the Sikh ruler Ranjit Singh, and was an important centre of Sikh influence in the early 19th century.

Gujrat /gʊdʒˈrɑːt/ a city in Pakistan, in Punjab province, north of Lahore; pop. 154,000 (1981).

gulab jamun /gʊˌlɑːb ˈdʒɑːmʌn/ ▶ noun an Indian sweet consisting of a ball of deep-fried paneer boiled in a sugar syrup.
– ORIGIN from Hindi *gulāb* 'rose water' and *jāmun* 'fruit'.

Gulag /ˈguːlag/ ▶ noun [in sing.] a system of labour camps maintained in the Soviet Union from 1930 to 1955 in which many people died.
■(**gulag**) [count noun] a camp in this system, or any political labour camp.
– ORIGIN Russian, from *G(lavnoe) u(pravlenie ispravitel'no-trudovykh) lag(ereĭ)* 'Chief Administration for Corrective Labour Camps'.

gular /ˈgjuːlə/ Zoology ▶ adjective of, relating to, or situated on the throat of an animal, especially a reptile, fish, or bird.
▶ noun a plate or scale on the throat of a reptile or fish.
– ORIGIN early 19th cent.: from Latin *gula* 'throat' + **-AR**[1].

Gulbarga /gʊlˈbɑːgə/ a city in south central India, in the state of Karnataka; pop. 303,000 (1991). Formerly the seat of the Bahmani kings of the Deccan (1347–*c*.1424), it is now a centre of the cotton trade.

Gulbenkian /gʊlˈbɛŋkɪən/, Calouste Sarkis (1869–1955), Turkish-born British oil magnate and philanthropist, of Armenian descent. He founded the Gulbenkian Foundation, to which he left his large fortune and art collection.

gulch /gʌltʃ/ ▶ noun N. Amer. a narrow and steep-sided ravine marking the course of a fast stream.
– ORIGIN mid 19th cent.: perhaps from dialect *gulch* 'to swallow'.

gulden /ˈɡʊld(ə)n/ ▸ noun (pl. same or **guldens**) another term for **GUILDER**.
– ORIGIN Dutch and German, literally 'golden'.

gules /ɡjuːlz/ ▸ noun [mass noun] red, as a heraldic tincture: [postpositive] *sword and long cross gules.*
– ORIGIN Middle English: from Old French *goles* (plural of *gole* 'throat', from Latin *gula*), used to denote pieces of red-dyed fur used as a neck ornament.

gulf ▸ noun 1 a deep inlet of the sea almost surrounded by land, with a narrow mouth.
■ **(the Gulf)** informal name for **PERSIAN GULF**.
2 a deep ravine, chasm, or abyss.
■ figurative a large difference or division between two people or groups, or between viewpoints, concepts, or situations: *a wide gulf between theory and practice.*
– ORIGIN late Middle English: from Old French *golfe*, from Italian *golfo*, based on Greek *kolpos* 'bosom, gulf'.

Gulf of Aden, Gulf of Boothia, etc. see **ADEN, GULF OF; BOOTHIA, GULF OF;** etc.

Gulf States 1 the states bordering on the Persian Gulf (Iran, Iraq, Kuwait, Saudi Arabia, Bahrain, Qatar, the United Arab Emirates, and Oman).
2 the states of the US bordering on the Gulf of Mexico (Florida, Alabama, Mississippi, Louisiana, and Texas).

Gulf Stream a warm ocean current which flows from the Gulf of Mexico parallel with the American coast towards Newfoundland, continuing across the Atlantic Ocean towards NW Europe as the North Atlantic Drift.

Gulf War 1 another name for **IRAN–IRAQ WAR**.
2 the war of January and February 1991 in which an international coalition of forces assembled in Saudi Arabia under the auspices of the United Nations forced the withdrawal of Saddam Hussein's Iraqi forces from Kuwait, which they had invaded and occupied in August 1990.

Gulf War syndrome ▸ noun [mass noun] a medical condition affecting many veterans of the 1991 Gulf War, causing fatigue, chronic headaches, and skin and respiratory disorders. Its origin is uncertain, though it has been attributed to exposure to a combination of pesticides, vaccines, and other chemicals.

gulfweed ▸ noun another term for **SARGASSUM**.

gull¹ ▸ noun a long-winged web-footed seabird with a raucous call, typically having white plumage with a grey or black mantle.
● Family Laridae: several genera, in particular *Larus*, and numerous species.
– ORIGIN late Middle English: of Celtic origin; related to Welsh *gwylan* and Breton *gwelan*.

gull² ▸ verb [with obj.] fool or deceive (someone): *British workers had been gulled into inflicting poverty and deprivation upon themselves.*
▸ noun a person who is fooled or deceived.
– ORIGIN late 16th cent.: of unknown origin.

Gullah /ˈɡʌlə/ ▸ noun 1 a member of a black people living on the coast of South Carolina and nearby islands.
2 [mass noun] the Creole language of this people, having an English base with elements from various West African languages. It has about 125,000 speakers.
▸ adjective of or relating to this people or their language.
– ORIGIN perhaps a shortening of *Angola*, or from *Gola*, the name of an agricultural people of Liberia and Sierra Leone.

gullery ▸ noun (pl. **-ies**) a breeding colony, breeding place, or roost of gulls.

gullet ▸ noun the passage by which food passes from the mouth to the stomach; the oesophagus.
– ORIGIN late Middle English: from Old French *goulet*, diminutive of *goule* 'throat', from Latin *gula*.

gulley ▸ noun (pl. **-eys**) variant spelling of **GULLY**.

gullible ▸ adjective easily persuaded to believe something; credulous: *an attempt to persuade a gullible public to spend their money.*
– DERIVATIVES **gullibility** noun, **gullibly** adverb.
– ORIGIN early 19th cent.: from **GULL²** + **-IBLE**.

gull wing ▸ noun [as modifier] (of a door on a car or aircraft) opening upwards: *gull-wing doors.*

gully ▸ noun (pl. **-ies**) 1 (also **gulley**) a water-worn ravine.

■ a deep artificial channel serving as a gutter or drain.
■ Austral./NZ a river valley.
2 (also **gali**) Indian an alley. [ORIGIN: from Hindi *galī*.]
3 Cricket a fielding position on the off side between point and the slips.
■ a fielder at this position.
▸ verb (also **gulley**) [with obj.] [usu. as adj. **gullied**] erode gullies into (land) by water action: *he began to pick his way over the gullied landscape.*
– ORIGIN mid 16th cent. (in the sense 'gullet'): from French *goulet* (see **GULLET**).

gulp ▸ verb [with obj.] swallow (drink or food) quickly or in large mouthfuls, often audibly: *he smiled and gulped his tea.*
■ breathe (air) deeply and quickly: *we emerged to gulp great lungfuls of cold night air.* ■ [no obj.] make effortful breathing or swallowing movements, typically in response to strong emotion: *fumes seeped in until she was forced to gulp for air* | *she gulped back the tears.*
▸ noun an act of gulping food or drink: *she swallowed the rest of the coffee with a gulp.*
■ a large mouthful of liquid hastily drunk: *Titch took a gulp of beer and wiped his mouth on his sleeve.* ■ a large quantity of air breathed in. ■ a swallowing movement of the throat: *the chairman gave an audible gulp.*
– PHRASES **at a gulp** with one gulp: *having emptied his glass at a gulp, Roger pulled out a cigar.*
– DERIVATIVES **gulpy** adjective.
– ORIGIN Middle English: probably from Middle Dutch *gulpen*, of imitative origin.

gulper (also **gulper eel**) ▸ noun a deep-sea eel with very large jaws that open to give an enormous gape and with eyes near the tip of the snout.
● Order Saccopharyngiformes: several families.

GUM ▸ abbreviation for genito-urinary medicine.

gum¹ ▸ noun 1 [mass noun] a viscous secretion of some trees and shrubs that hardens on drying but is soluble in water, and from which adhesives and other products are made. Compare with **RESIN**.
■ glue that is used for sticking paper or other light materials together. ■ a sticky secretion collecting in the corner of the eye.
■ short for **CHEWING GUM** or **BUBBLE GUM**. ■ [count noun] a firm, jelly-like translucent sweet made with gelatin or gum arabic. ■ [count noun] a gum tree, especially a eucalyptus. See also **SWEET GUM**.
2 North American term for **GUMBOOT**.
▸ verb (**gummed**, **gumming**) [with obj.] cover with gum or glue: [as adj. **gummed**] *gummed paper.*
■ [with obj. and adverbial] fasten with gum or glue: *the receipts are gummed into a special book.* ■ (**gum something up**) clog up a mechanism and prevent it from working properly: *open and close the valves to make sure they don't get gummed up.*
– ORIGIN Middle English: from Old French *gomme*, based on Latin *gummi*, from Greek *kommi*, from Egyptian *kemai.*

gum² ▸ noun the firm area of flesh around the roots of the teeth in the upper or lower jaw: *a tooth broken off just above the gum* | [as modifier] *gum disease.*
– ORIGIN Old English *gōma* 'inside of the mouth or throat', of Germanic origin; related to German *Gaumen* 'roof of the mouth'.

gum³ ▸ noun (in phrase **by gum!**) chiefly N. English an exclamation used for emphasis.
– ORIGIN early 19th cent.: euphemistic alteration of *God.*

gum arabic ▸ noun [mass noun] a gum exuded by some kinds of acacia and used as glue and in incense.

gum benjamin ▸ noun another term for **BENZOIN** (in sense 1).

gum benzoin ▸ noun see **BENZOIN** (sense 1).

gumbo ▸ noun (pl. **-os**) [mass noun] N. Amer. 1 okra, especially the gelatinous pods used in cooking.
■ (in Cajun cooking) a spicy chicken or seafood soup thickened typically with okra or rice.
2 (**Gumbo**) a French-based patois spoken by some blacks and Creoles in Louisiana.
3 a fine clayey soil that becomes sticky and impervious when wet.
4 a type of Cajun music consisting of a lively blend of styles and sounds: *New Orleans syncopated gumbo.*
– ORIGIN early 19th cent.: from the Angolan word *kingombo* 'okra'.

gumboil ▸ noun a small swelling formed on the gum over an abscess at the root of a tooth.

gumboot ▸ noun (usu. **gumboots**) dated, chiefly Brit. a long rubber boot; a wellington.

gumboot dance ▸ noun (in South Africa) a dance developed and performed by mineworkers, mimicking military marching.

gumdrop ▸ noun a firm, jelly-like translucent sweet made with gelatin or gum arabic.

gumma /ˈɡʌmə/ ▸ noun (pl. **gummas** or **gummata** /-mətə/) Medicine a small soft swelling which is characteristic of the late stages of syphilis and occurs in the connective tissue of the liver, brain, testes, and heart.
– DERIVATIVES **gummatous** adjective.
– ORIGIN early 18th cent.: modern Latin, from Latin *gummi* (see **GUM¹**).

gummosis /ɡəˈməʊsɪs/ ▸ noun [mass noun] the copious production and exudation of gum by a diseased or damaged tree, especially as a symptom of a disease of fruit trees.

gummy¹ ▸ adjective (**gummier**, **gummiest**) viscous; sticky.
■ covered with or exuding a viscous substance: *his eyes are all gummy.*
– DERIVATIVES **gumminess** noun.

gummy² ▸ adjective (**gummier**, **gummiest**) toothless: *a gummy grin.*
▸ noun (pl. **-ies**) 1 (also **gummy shark**) a small edible shark of Australasian coastal waters, with rounded teeth that it uses to crush hard-shelled prey.
● *Mustelus antarcticus*, family Triakidae.
2 Austral./NZ a sheep that has lost or is losing its teeth.
– DERIVATIVES **gummily** adverb.

gum olibanum ▸ noun another term for **FRANKINCENSE**.

gum opopanax ▸ noun see **OPOPANAX** (sense 2).

gumption /ˈɡʌm(p)ʃ(ə)n/ ▸ noun [mass noun] informal shrewd or spirited initiative and resourcefulness: *his new wife had the gumption to put her foot down and head Dan off from those crazy schemes.*
– ORIGIN early 18th cent. (originally Scots): of unknown origin.

gum resin ▸ noun [mass noun] a plant secretion consisting of resin mixed with gum.

gum sandarac ▸ noun see **SANDARAC**.

gumshield ▸ noun a pad or plate held in the mouth by a sports player to protect the teeth and gums.

gumshoe ▸ noun N. Amer. informal a detective.
– ORIGIN early 20th cent.: from *gumshoes* in the sense 'sneakers', suggesting stealth.

gum tragacanth ▸ noun see **TRAGACANTH**.

gum tree ▸ noun a tree that exudes gum, especially a eucalyptus.
– PHRASES **up a gum tree** Brit. informal in or into a predicament: *offers of devolution will lead ministers straight up a gum tree.*

gum turpentine ▸ noun see **TURPENTINE**.

gun ▸ noun a weapon incorporating a metal tube from which bullets, shells, or other missiles are propelled by explosive force, typically making a characteristic loud, sharp noise.
■ a device for discharging something (e.g. insecticide, grease, or electrons) in a required direction. ■ N. Amer. a gunman: *a hired gun.* ■ Brit. a member of a shooting party. ■ (**guns**) Nautical slang, dated used as a nickname for a ship's gunnery officer. ■ a starting pistol used in athletics. ■ the firing of a piece of artillery as a salute or signal: *the boom of the one o'clock gun echoed across the river.*
▸ verb (**gunned**, **gunning**) [with obj.] 1 (**gun someone down**) shoot someone with a gun: *they were gunned down by masked snipers.*
2 informal cause (an engine) to race: *as Neil gunned the engine the boat jumped forward.*
■ [with obj. and adverbial of direction] accelerate (a vehicle): *he gunned the car away from the kerb.*
– PHRASES **big gun** informal an important or powerful person. **go great guns** informal proceed forcefully, vigorously, or successfully: *the film industry has been going great guns recently.* **jump the gun** informal act before the proper or appropriate time. **stick to one's guns** informal refuse to compromise or change, despite criticism: *we have stuck to our guns on that issue.* **top gun** a (or the) most important or powerful person: *the top guns in contention for the coveted post of chairman.* **under the gun** N. Amer. informal under great pressure: *manufacturers are under the gun to offer alternatives.*

g

– DERIVATIVES **gunless** adjective, **gunned** adjective [in combination] *a heavy-gunned ship.*

– ORIGIN Middle English *gunne, gonne,* perhaps from a pet form of the Scandinavian name *Gunnhildr,* from *gunnr + hildr,* both meaning 'war'.

▶ **gun for** pursue or act against (someone) with hostility: *the Republican candidate was gunning for his rival over campaign payments.* ■ seek out or strive for (something) determinedly: *he had been gunning for a place in the squad.*

gunboat ▶ noun a small fast ship mounting guns, for use in shallow coastal waters and rivers.

gunboat diplomacy ▶ noun [mass noun] foreign policy that is supported by the use or threat of military force.

gun carriage ▶ noun a wheeled support for a piece of artillery.

guncotton ▶ noun [mass noun] a highly nitrated form of nitrocellulose, used as an explosive.

gun deck ▶ noun a deck on a ship on which guns are placed.
■ historical the lowest such deck on a ship of the line.

gundi /ˈgʌndi/ ▶ noun (pl. **gundis**) a small gregarious rodent living on rocky outcrops in the deserts of North and East Africa.
● Family Ctenodactylidae: four genera and several species.

– ORIGIN late 18th cent.: from North African Arabic.

gun dog ▶ noun a dog trained to retrieve game for a gamekeeper or the members of a shoot.

gundy /ˈgʌndi/ ▶ noun (in phrase **no good to gundy**) Austral. informal no good at all.

– ORIGIN of unknown origin.

gunfight ▶ noun a fight involving an exchange of fire with guns.

– DERIVATIVES **gunfighter** noun.

gunfire ▶ noun [mass noun] the repeated firing of a gun or guns: *they'd been caught up in gunfire in Beirut.*

gunge Brit. informal ▶ noun [mass noun] a sticky, viscous, and unpleasantly messy material.
▶ verb (**gunged, gungeing**) [with obj.] (**gunge something up**) clog or obstruct with gunge.

– DERIVATIVES **gungy** adjective.

– ORIGIN 1960s: perhaps suggested by **GOO** and **GUNK**.

gung-ho /ˌgʌŋˈhəʊ/ ▶ adjective unthinkingly enthusiastic and eager, especially about taking part in fighting or warfare: *the gung-ho tabloids have wrapped themselves in the Union Jack.*

– ORIGIN Second World War: from Chinese *gōnghé,* taken to mean 'work together' and adopted as a slogan by US Marines.

gunite /ˈgʌnʌɪt/ ▶ noun [mass noun] a mixture of cement, sand, and water applied through a pressure hose, producing a dense hard layer of concrete used in building for lining tunnels and structural repairs.

– ORIGIN early 20th cent.: from **GUN** + **-ITE**[1].

gunk ▶ noun [mass noun] informal unpleasantly sticky or messy substance.

– ORIGIN 1930s (originally US): the proprietary name of a detergent.

gunkhole informal, chiefly N. Amer. ▶ noun a shallow inlet or cove that is difficult or dangerous to navigate.
▶ verb [no obj., with adverbial of direction] cruise in and out of such inlets or coves: *they were gunkholing through the coral archipelago.*

– ORIGIN early 20th cent.: of unknown origin.

gunlock ▶ noun a mechanism by which the charge of a gun is exploded.

gunmaker ▶ noun a manufacturer of guns.

gunman ▶ noun (pl. **-men**) a man who uses a gun to commit a crime or terrorist act: *a gang of masked gunmen.*

gunmetal ▶ noun [mass noun] a grey corrosion-resistant form of bronze containing zinc.
■ a dull bluish-grey colour: [as modifier] *the river glinted brass under a gunmetal sky.*

gun microphone ▶ noun a highly directional microphone with an elongated barrel which can be directed from a distance at a localized sound source.

gun moll ▶ noun informal a gangster's mistress or girlfriend.

Gunn, Thom (b.1929), English poet, resident in California from 1954; full name *Thomson William Gunn.* His works, written in a predominantly low-key, laconic, and colloquial style, include *Fighting*

Terms (1954), *My Sad Captains* (1961), and *The Passages of Joy* (1982).

gunnel[1] /ˈgʌn(ə)l/ ▶ noun an elongated laterally compressed fish with a dorsal fin that runs along most of the back and reduced or absent pelvic fins. It occurs in cool inshore waters of the northern hemisphere.
● Family Pholidae: two genera and several species.

– ORIGIN late 17th cent.: of unknown origin.

gunnel[2] ▶ noun variant spelling of **GUNWALE**.

Gunnell /ˈgʌn(ə)l/, Sally (Jane Janet) (b.1966), English athlete. She won the Olympic gold in the 400-metres hurdles in 1992 and the world championship title the following year.

gunner ▶ noun **1** a serviceman who operates or specializes in guns, in particular:
■ (in the British army) an artillery soldier (used especially as an official term for a private). ■ historical a naval warrant officer in charge of a ship's guns, gun crews, and ordnance stores. ■ a member of an aircraft crew who operates a gun, especially (formerly) in a gun turret on a bomber.
2 a person who hunts game with a gun.

gunnera /ˈgʌn(ə)rə, gʌˈnɪərə/ ▶ noun a South American plant with extremely large leaves that resemble rhubarb and which is grown as a waterside ornamental.
● Genus *Gunnera,* family Gunneraceae: several species, in particular *G. manicata* and *G. tinctoria.*

– ORIGIN modern Latin, named after Johann E. *Gunnerus* (1718–73), Norwegian botanist.

gunnery ▶ noun [mass noun] the design, manufacture, or firing of heavy guns: *a pioneer of naval gunnery.*

gunnery sergeant ▶ noun a rank of non-commissioned officer in the US marines, above staff sergeant and below master sergeant.

gunny /ˈgʌni/ ▶ noun [mass noun] chiefly N. Amer. coarse sacking, typically made of jute fibre.

– ORIGIN early 18th cent.: from Marathi *gōnī,* from Sanskrit *goṇī* 'sack'.

gunplay ▶ noun [mass noun] chiefly N. Amer. the use of guns: *the struggle started with skirmishes and some scattered gunplay.*

gunpoint ▶ noun (in phrase **at gunpoint**) while threatening someone or being threatened with a gun: *two robbers held a family at gunpoint while they searched their house.*

gun port ▶ noun see **PORT**[4].

gunpowder ▶ noun [mass noun] **1** an explosive consisting of a powdered mixture of saltpetre, sulphur, and charcoal. The earliest known propellant explosive, gunpowder has now largely been superseded by high explosives, although it is still used for quarry blasting and in fuses and fireworks.
2 a fine green China tea of granular appearance.

Gunpowder Plot a conspiracy by a small group of Catholic extremists to blow up James I and his Parliament on 5 November 1605.

The plot is commemorated by the traditional searching of the vaults before the opening of each session of Parliament, and by bonfires and fireworks, with the burning of an effigy of Guy Fawkes, one of the conspirators, annually on 5 November.

gunroom ▶ noun **1** a room used for storing sporting guns in a house.
2 Brit. dated a set of quarters for midshipmen or other junior officers in a warship.

gunrunner ▶ noun a person engaged in the illegal sale or importing of firearms.

– DERIVATIVES **gunrunning** noun.

gunsel /ˈgʌns(ə)l/ ▶ noun US informal a criminal carrying a gun.

– ORIGIN early 20th cent. (denoting a homosexual youth): from Yiddish *gendzel* 'little goose', influenced in sense by **GUN**.

gunship ▶ noun a heavily armed helicopter.

gunshot ▶ noun a shot fired from a gun.
■ [mass noun] archaic the range of a gun: *we bore down and came nearly within gunshot.*

gun-shy ▶ adjective (especially of a hunting dog) alarmed at the report of a gun.
■ figurative nervous and apprehensive.

gunsight ▶ noun a device on a gun that enables it to be aimed accurately.

gunslinger ▶ noun informal a man who carries a gun and shoots well.
■ figurative a forceful and adventurous participant in a

particular sphere: *the heroes of Wall Street were hip young gunslingers.*

– DERIVATIVES **gunslinging** adjective.

gunsmith ▶ noun a person who makes, sells, and repairs small firearms.

gunstock ▶ noun the wooden stock or support to which the barrel of a gun is attached.

gunter ▶ noun Sailing a fore-and-aft sail whose spar is nearly vertical, so that the sail is nearly triangular.
■ (also **gunter rig**) historical a type of rig in which the topmast slides up and down the lower mast on rings.

– DERIVATIVES **gunter-rigged** adjective.

– ORIGIN late 18th cent.: named after E. *Gunter* (see **GUNTER'S CHAIN**).

Gunter's chain /ˈgʌntəz/ ▶ noun Surveying a former measuring instrument 66 ft (20.1 m) long, subdivided into 100 links, each of which is a short section of wire connected to the next link by a loop. It has now been superseded by the steel tape and electronic equipment.
■ this length as a unit, equal to ¹⁄₁₀ furlong or ¹⁄₈₀ mile. Also called **CHAIN**.

– ORIGIN late 17th cent.: named after Edmund *Gunter* (1581–1626), the English mathematician who devised it.

Gunther /ˈgʊntə/ (in the Nibelungenlied) the husband of Brunhild and brother of Kriemhild, by whom he was beheaded in revenge for Siegfried's murder.

Guntur /ˈgʊntʊə/ a city in eastern India, in Andhra Pradesh; pop. 471,000 (1991).

gunwale /ˈgʌn(ə)l/ (also **gunnel**) ▶ noun (often **gunwales**) the upper edge or planking of the side of a boat or ship.

– PHRASES **to the gunwales** informal so as to be almost overflowing: *the car is stuffed to the gunwales with camera equipment.*

– ORIGIN late Middle English: from **GUN** + **WALE** (because it was formerly used to support guns).

gunyah /ˈgʌnjə/ ▶ noun Austral. an Aboriginal bush hut, typically made of sheets of bark and branches.

– ORIGIN from Dharuk *ganya* 'house, hut'.

Günz /gʊnts/ ▶ noun [usu. as modifier] Geology a Middle Pleistocene glaciation in the Alps, preceding the Mindel and possibly corresponding to the Menapian of northern Europe.
■ the system of deposits laid down at this time.

– ORIGIN early 20th cent.: named after a river near the Alps in southern Germany.

Guomindang /ˌgwəʊmɪnˈdaŋ/ variant spelling of **KUOMINTANG**.

guppy /ˈgʌpi/ ▶ noun (pl. **-ies**) a small live-bearing freshwater fish widely kept in aquaria. Native to tropical America, it has been introduced elsewhere to control mosquito larvae.
● *Poecilia reticulata,* family Poeciliidae.

– ORIGIN 1920s: named after R. J. Lechmere *Guppy* (1836–1916), a Trinidadian clergyman who sent the first specimen to the British Museum.

Gupta /ˈgʊptə/ a Hindu dynasty established in AD 320 by Chandragupta I in Bihar. At one stage it ruled most of the north of the Indian subcontinent, but it began to disintegrate towards the end of the 5th century.

– DERIVATIVES **Guptan** adjective.

Gur /gʊə/ ▶ noun [mass noun] a branch of the Niger-Congo family of languages, spoken in parts of West Africa. It includes More and Senufo. Also called **VOLTAIC**.
▶ adjective of, relating to, or denoting this group of languages.

gur /gʊr/ ▶ noun [mass noun] (in the Indian subcontinent) a type of unrefined, solid brown sugar made from boiling sugar cane juice until dry.

– ORIGIN from Hindi *gur* and Marathi *gūr,* from Sanskrit *guḍa.*

Gurdjieff /ˈgɜːdʒɛf/, George (Ivanovich) (1877–1949), Russian spiritual leader and occultist. He founded the Institute for the Harmonious Development of Man in Paris (1922).

gurdwara /gʊəˈdwɑːrə, gəˈdwɑːrə/ ▶ noun a Sikh place of worship.

– ORIGIN from Punjabi *gurduārā,* from Sanskrit *guru* 'teacher' + *dvāra* 'door'.

gurgle ▶ verb [no obj.] make a hollow bubbling sound like that made by water running out of a bottle: *my stomach gurgled* | [as adj.] **gurgling**] *a faint gurgling noise.*

▪[with adverbial of direction] (of a liquid) run or flow with such a sound: *chemicals gurgle down a drain straight into the sewers.*
▶**noun** a gurgling sound: *Catherine gave a gurgle of laughter.*
– ORIGIN late Middle English: imitative, or directly from Dutch *gorgelen*, German *gurgeln*, or medieval Latin *gurgulare*, all from Latin *gurgulio* 'gullet'.

gurjun /ˈgəːdʒ(ə)n/ ▶**noun** a large tree which yields light absorbent timber and a resin that was formerly used medicinally and as a varnish. It is native to SE Asia and parts of the Pacific. See also **KERUING**.
• Genus *Dipterocarpus*, family Dipterocarpaceae: several species.
▪(also **gurjun oil** or **balsam**) [mass noun] the viscid resin of this tree.
– ORIGIN mid 19th cent.: from Bengali *garjan*.

Gurkha /ˈgəːkə, ˈgʊəkə/ ▶**noun** a member of any of several peoples of Nepal noted for their military prowess.
▪a member of a regiment in the British army established specifically for Nepalese recruits in the mid 19th century.
– ORIGIN name of a locality, from Sanskrit *gorakṣa* 'cowherd' (from *go* 'cow' + *rakṣ-* 'protect'), used as an epithet of their patron deity.

Gurkhali /gəːˈkɑːli/ (also **Gorkhali**) ▶**noun** another term for **NEPALI** (the language).

Gurmukhi /ˈgʊəmʊki/ ▶**noun** the script used by Sikhs for writing Punjabi.
▪the Punjabi language as written in this script.
– ORIGIN Punjabi, from Sanskrit *guru* (see **GURU**) + *mukha* 'mouth'.

gurn /gəːn/ (also **girn**) ▶**verb** [no obj.] **1** Brit. pull a grotesque face: *they proceeded to camp it up and gurn around the stage.*
2 (usu. **girn**) chiefly Scottish & Irish complain peevishly.
– DERIVATIVES **gurner** noun.
– ORIGIN early 20th cent.: dialect variant of **GRIN**.

gurnard /ˈgəːnəd/ ▶**noun** a bottom-dwelling fish of coastal waters, with a heavily boned head and three finger-like pectoral rays which it uses for searching for food and for walking on the seabed.
• Family Triglidae: several genera and many species, including the common European *Eutrigla gurnardus*.
– ORIGIN Middle English: from Old French *gornart*, from *grondir* 'to grunt', from Latin *grundire*, *grunnire*.

Gurney /ˈgəːni/, Ivor (Bertie) (1890–1937), English poet and composer. He fought on the Western Front during the First World War, and wrote the verse collections *Severn and Somme* (1917) and *War's Embers* (1919).

gurney /ˈgəːni/ ▶**noun** (pl. **-eys**) chiefly N. Amer. a wheeled stretcher used for transporting hospital patients.
– ORIGIN late 19th cent.: apparently named after J. T. *Gurney* of Boston, Massachusetts, patentee of a new cab design in 1883.

gurry /ˈgʌri/ ▶**noun** [mass noun] chiefly N. Amer. fish or whale offal.
– ORIGIN late 18th cent.: of unknown origin.

guru /ˈgʊruː, ˈguːruː/ ▶**noun** a Hindu spiritual teacher.
▪each of the ten first leaders of the Sikh religion. ▪ an influential teacher or popular expert: *a management guru.*
– ORIGIN from Hindi and Punjabi, from Sanskrit *guru* 'weighty, grave' (compare with Latin *gravis*), hence 'elder, teacher'.

gush ▶**verb** [no obj.] **1** [with adverbial of direction] (of a liquid) flow out in a rapid and plentiful stream, often suddenly: *William watched the murky liquid gushing out* | figurative *words gushed out incontinently.*
▪[with obj. and adverbial of direction] send out in a rapid and plentiful stream.
2 speak or write with effusiveness or exaggerated enthusiasm: *a nice old lady reporter who covers the art openings and gushes about everything.*
▶**noun 1** a rapid and plentiful stream or burst.
2 [mass noun] exaggerated effusiveness or enthusiasm.
– DERIVATIVES **gushingly** adverb.
– ORIGIN late Middle English: probably imitative.

gusher ▶**noun 1** an oil well from which oil flows profusely without being pumped.
▪a thing from which a liquid flows profusely.
2 an effusive person: *the earnest, ingratiating gusher of numerous television interviews.*

gushy ▶**adjective** (**gushier**, **gushiest**) excessively effusive: *her gushy manner.*
– DERIVATIVES **gushily** adverb, **gushiness** noun.

gusset /ˈgʌsɪt/ ▶**noun** a piece of material sewn into a garment to strengthen or enlarge a part of it, such as the collar of a shirt or the crotch of an undergarment.
▪a bracket strengthening an angle of a structure.
– DERIVATIVES **gusseted** adjective.
– ORIGIN late Middle English: from Old French *gousset*, diminutive of *gousse* 'pod, shell', of unknown origin.

gussy ▶**verb** (**-ies**, **-ied**) [with obj.] (**gussy someone/thing up**) informal, chiefly N. Amer. make more attractive, especially in a showy or gimmicky way: *shopkeepers gussied up their window displays.*
– ORIGIN 1940s: perhaps from *Gussie*, pet form of the given name *Augustus*.

gust ▶**noun** a brief, strong rush of wind.
▪a burst of something such as rain, sound, or emotion: *gusts of rain lashed down the narrow alleys.*
▶**verb** [no obj.] (of the wind) blow in gusts: *the wind was gusting through the branches of the tree.*
– ORIGIN late 16th cent.: from Old Norse *gustr*, related to *gjósa* 'to gush'.

gustation ▶**noun** [mass noun] formal the action or faculty of tasting.
– DERIVATIVES **gustative** adjective.
– ORIGIN late 16th cent.: from Latin *gustatio(n-)*, from *gustare* 'to taste', from *gustus* 'taste'.

gustatory /gʌˈsteɪt(ə)ri, ˈgʌstət(ə)ri/ ▶**adjective** formal concerned with tasting or the sense of taste: *gustatory delights.*

Gustavus Adolphus /gʊˌstɑːvəs əˈdɒlfəs/ (1594–1632), king of Sweden 1611–32. His repeated victories in battle made Sweden a European power, and in 1630 he intervened on the Protestant side in the Thirty Years War. His domestic reforms laid the foundation of the modern state.

gusto ▶**noun** (pl. **-os** or **-oes**) [mass noun] **1** enjoyment or vigour in doing something; zest: *she sang it with gusto.*
▪[in sing.] archaic a relish or liking: *he had a particular gusto for those sort of performances.*
2 archaic style of artistic execution.
– ORIGIN early 17th cent.: from Italian, from Latin *gustus* 'taste'.

gusty ▶**adjective** (**gustier**, **gustiest**) **1** characterized by or blowing in gusts: *a gusty morning.*
2 having or showing gusto: *gusty female vocals.*
– DERIVATIVES **gustily** adverb, **gustiness** noun.

gut ▶**noun 1** (also **guts**) the stomach or belly: *a painful stabbing feeling in his gut.*
▪Medicine & Biology the lower alimentary canal or a part of this; the intestine: *microbes which naturally live in the human gut.* ▪ (**guts**) entrails that have been removed or exposed in violence or by a butcher. ▪ (**guts**) the internal parts or essence of something: *the guts of a modern computer.* ▪ (**guts**) [with modifier] used to form names attributing negative characteristics to people: *what's the matter with you, misery guts?* | *greedy guts.*
2 (**guts**) informal personal courage and determination; toughness of character: *she had both more brains and more guts than her husband* | *you just haven't got the guts to admit it.*
▪[as modifier] informal (of a feeling or reaction) based on a deep-seated emotional response rather than considered thought; instinctive: *a gut feeling.*
3 [mass noun] fibre made from the intestines of animals, used especially for violin or racket strings or for surgical use: [as modifier] *gut strings.*
4 a narrow passage or strait.
▶**verb** (**gutted**, **gutting**) [with obj.] take out the intestines and other internal organs of (a fish or other animal) before cooking it.
▪remove or destroy completely the internal parts of (a building or other structure): *the fire gutted most of the factory.* ▪ remove or extract the most important parts of (something) in a damaging or destructive manner: *watching in silence while arts budgets were gutted.*
– PHRASES **bust a gut** informal make a strenuous effort: *a problem which nobody is going to bust a gut trying to solve.* —— **one's guts out** used to indicate that the specified action is done or performed as hard as possible: *he ran his guts out and finished fourth.* **hate someone's guts** informal feel a strong hatred for someone. **have someone's guts for garters** informal, chiefly humorous punish someone severely: *if Jake found out he would have her guts for garters!* **sweat** (or **work**) **one's guts out** informal work extremely hard.
– ORIGIN Old English *guttas* (plural), probably related to *gēotan* 'pour'.

gutbucket informal ▶**noun 1** [as modifier] chiefly N. Amer. (of jazz or blues) raw and spirited in style: *his gutbucket guitar solos.* [ORIGIN: early 20th cent.: perhaps from the earlier denotation of a one-stringed plucked instrument, with reference to its construction, or referring to the bucket which caught *gutterings* (streams of liquid) from beer barrels in low-class saloons where such music was played.]
2 Brit. a glutton.

Gutenberg /ˈguːt(ə)nbəːg, German ˈguːtnbɛrk/, Johannes (*c.*1400–68), German printer. He was the first in the West to print using movable type and was the first to use a press. By *c.*1455 he had produced what later became known as the Gutenberg Bible.

Gutenberg Bible ▶**noun** the edition of the Bible (Vulgate version) completed by Johannes Gutenberg in about 1455 in Mainz, Germany. It is the first complete book extant in the West and is also the earliest to be printed from movable type.

gut flora ▶**plural noun** another term for **INTESTINAL FLORA**.

Guthrie /ˈgʌθri/, Woody (1912–1967), American folk singer and songwriter; full name *Woodrow Wilson Guthrie*. His radical politics and the rural hardships of the Depression inspired many of his songs.

Guthrie test ▶**noun** Medicine a routine blood test carried out on babies a few days after birth to detect the condition phenylketonuria.
– ORIGIN named after Robert *Guthrie* (born 1916), American microbiologist.

Gutiérrez /ˌgʊtɪˈɛːrəz, Spanish guˈtjerres, -rreθ/, Gustavo (b.1928), Peruvian theologian. He was an important figure in the emergence of liberation theology in Latin America, outlining its principles in *A Theology of Liberation* (1971).

gutless ▶**adjective** informal lacking courage or determination.
– DERIVATIVES **gutlessly** adverb, **gutlessness** noun.

gut-rot ▶**noun** [mass noun] Brit. informal **1** another term for **ROTGUT**.
2 a stomach upset.

gutser /ˈgʌtsə/ (also **gutzer**) ▶**noun** Austral./NZ informal a heavy fall or collision.
– PHRASES **come a gutser** suffer a failure or defeat.
– ORIGIN early 20th cent.: from the noun **GUT**.

gutsy ▶**adjective** (**gutsier**, **gutsiest**) informal **1** showing courage, determination, and spirit: *she gave a gutsy performance in the tennis tournament.*
▪(of food or drink) strongly flavoursome: *a smooth Bordeaux that is gutsy enough to accompany steak.*
2 greedy.
– DERIVATIVES **gutsily** adverb, **gutsiness** noun.

gutta-percha /ˌgʌtəˈpəːtʃə/ ▶**noun** [mass noun] a hard tough thermoplastic substance which is the coagulated latex of certain Malaysian trees. It consists chiefly of a hydrocarbon isomeric with rubber and is now used chiefly in dentistry and for electrical insulation.
• This substance is obtained from trees of the genus *Palaquium*, family Sapotaceae, in particular *P. gutta*.
– ORIGIN mid 19th cent.: from Malay *getah perca*, from *getah* 'gum' + *perca* 'strips of cloth' (which it resembles), altered by association with obsolete *gutta* 'gum', from Latin *gutta* 'a drop'.

guttate /ˈgʌteɪt/ ▶**adjective** chiefly Biology having drops or drop-like markings.
▪in the form of or resembling drops.
– ORIGIN early 19th cent.: from Latin *guttatus* 'speckled', from *gutta* 'a drop'.

guttation /gʌˈteɪʃ(ə)n/ ▶**noun** [mass noun] the secretion of droplets of water from the pores of plants.
– ORIGIN late 19th cent.: from Latin *gutta* 'drop' + **-ATION**.

gutted ▶**adjective** Brit. informal bitterly disappointed or upset: *I know how gutted the players must feel.*

gutter ▶**noun** a shallow trough fixed beneath the edge of a roof for carrying off rainwater.
▪a channel at the side of a street for carrying off rainwater. ▪ (**the gutter**) used to refer to a poor or squalid background or environment: *only moneyed privilege had kept him out of the gutter.* ▪ technical a

groove or channel for flowing liquid. ■ the blank space between facing pages of a book or between adjacent columns of type or stamps in a sheet.

▶ **verb 1** [no obj.] (of a candle or flame) flicker and burn unsteadily: *the candles had almost guttered out.*
2 [with obj.] archaic channel or furrow with something such as streams or tears: *my cheeks are guttered with tears.*
■ [no obj.] (**gutter down**) stream down: *the raindrops gutter down her visage.*
– ORIGIN Middle English: from Old French *gotiere*, from Latin *gutta* 'a drop'; the verb dates from late Middle English, originally meaning 'cut grooves in' and later (early 18th cent.) used of a candle which melts rapidly because it has become channelled on one side.

guttering ▶ **noun** [mass noun] chiefly Brit. the gutters of a building.
■ material used to make gutters.

gutter press ▶ **noun** (**the gutter press**) chiefly Brit. reporters or newspapers engaging in sensational journalism, especially accounts of the private lives of public figures.

guttersnipe ▶ **noun** derogatory a street urchin.

guttural /ˈɡʌt(ə)r(ə)l/ ▶ **adjective** (of a speech sound) produced in the throat; harsh-sounding.
■ (of a manner of speech) characterized by the use of such sounds: *his parents' guttural central European accent.*
▶ **noun** a guttural consonant (e.g. *k*, *g*) or other speech sound.
– DERIVATIVES **gutturally** adverb.
– ORIGIN late 16th cent.: from French, or from medieval Latin *gutturalis*, from Latin *guttur* 'throat'.

gutty[1] ▶ **noun** Irish & Scottish informal a plimsoll.

gutty[2] ▶ **adjective** (**-ier**, **-iest**) N. Amer. informal gutsy.

gutzer ▶ **noun** variant spelling of **GUTSER**.

guv ▶ **noun** Brit. informal (as a form of address) sir: *'Excuse me, guv,' he began.*
– ORIGIN late 19th cent.: abbreviation of **GUV'NOR**.

guv'nor ▶ **noun** Brit. informal a man in a position of authority such as one's employer or father (often used as a term of address): *I had a lecture from the guv'nor | spare a tanner, guv'nor.*
– ORIGIN mid 19th cent.: representing a non-standard or colloquial pronunciation.

GUY ▶ **abbreviation for** Guyana (international vehicle registration).

guy[1] ▶ **noun 1** informal a man: *he's a nice guy.* [ORIGIN: originally a US usage.]
■ (**guys**) chiefly N. Amer. people of either sex: *you guys want some coffee?*
2 Brit. a figure representing Guy Fawkes, burnt on a bonfire on Guy Fawkes' Night, and often displayed by children begging for money for fireworks.
▶ **verb** [with obj.] make fun of; ridicule: *he didn't realize I was guying the whole idea.*
– ORIGIN early 19th cent. (in sense 2): named after *Guy* Fawkes (see **GUNPOWDER PLOT**).

guy[2] ▶ **noun** a rope or line fixed to the ground to secure a tent or other structure.
▶ **verb** [with obj.] secure with a line or lines: *it was set on concrete footings and guyed with steel cable.*
– ORIGIN late Middle English: probably of Low German origin; related to Dutch *gei* 'brail' and German *Geitaue* 'brails'.

Guyana /ɡʌɪˈanə/ a country on the NE coast of South America; pop. 737,950 (est. 1992); languages, English (official), English Creole, Hindi; capital, Georgetown. Official name **COOPERATIVE REPUBLIC OF GUYANA**.

> The Spaniards explored the area in 1499, and the Dutch settled there in the 17th century. It was occupied by the British from 1796 and established, with adjacent areas, as the colony of British Guiana in 1831. In 1966 it became an independent Commonwealth state.

– DERIVATIVES **Guyanese** /ˌɡʌɪəˈniːz/ adjective & noun.
– ORIGIN from an American Indian word meaning 'land of waters'.

Guyenne /ɡiːˈɛn/ (also **Guienne**) a region and former province of southern France, stretching from the Bay of Biscay to the SW edge of the Massif Central.

Guy Fawkes Night ▶ **noun** another term for **BONFIRE NIGHT**.

guyot /ˈɡiːəʊ/ ▶ **noun** Geology a seamount with a flat top.
– ORIGIN 1940s: named after Arnold H. *Guyot* (1807–84), Swiss geographer.

guyver /ˈɡʌɪvə/ (also **guiver** or **gyver**) ▶ **noun** [mass noun] Austral./NZ informal ingratiating or affected speech or behaviour: *I couldn't want you to get stuck-up and start putting on the guyver.*
– ORIGIN mid 19th cent.: of unknown origin.

guzzle ▶ **verb** [with obj.] eat or drink (something) greedily: *he would guzzle his ale* | figurative *this car guzzles petrol.*
– DERIVATIVES **guzzler** noun.
– ORIGIN late 16th cent.: perhaps from Old French *gosillier* 'chatter, vomit', from *gosier* 'throat', from late Latin *geusiae* 'cheeks'.

Gvozdena Vrata /ˌɡvɒzdɛnə ˈvrɑːtə/ Serbo-Croat name for **IRON GATE**.

GVW US ▶ **abbreviation for** gross vehicle weight.

Gwalior /ˈɡwɑːlɪɔː/ a city in a district of the same name in Madhya Pradesh, central India; pop. 693,000 (1991), noted for its 6th-century fortress.

Gwent /ɡwɛnt/ a former county of SE Wales, formed in 1974 from most of Monmouthshire, part of Breconshire, and Newport, and dissolved in 1996.

Gwynedd /ˈɡwɪnɛð/ a county of NW Wales, formed in 1974 from Anglesey, Caernarfonshire, part of Denbighshire, and most of Merionethshire and re-formed in 1996 with a smaller area; administrative centre, Caernarfon.
■ a former principality of North Wales. Powerful in the mid 13th century under Llewelyn, it was finally subjugated by the English forces of Edward I in 1282, following Llewelyn's death.

gwyniad /ˈɡwɪnɪad/ ▶ **noun** a powan (fish) of a variety occurring only in Bala Lake in North Wales.
– ORIGIN early 17th cent.: Welsh, from *gwyn* 'white'.

Gwynn, Nell (1650–87), English actress; full name *Eleanor Gwynn*. Originally an orange-seller, she became famous as a comedienne at the Theatre Royal, Drury Lane, London. She was a mistress of Charles II.

Gy Physics ▶ **abbreviation for** gray(s).

Gyandzhe /ˈɡʲandʒə/ Russian name for **GÄNCÄ**.

gybe /dʒʌɪb/ (US **jibe**) Sailing ▶ **verb** [no obj.] change course by swinging the sail across a following wind: *they gybed, and slewed round.*
■ [with obj.] swing (a sail or boom) across the wind in such a way. ■ (of a sail or boom) swing or be swung across the wind: [as adj. **gybing**] *the skipper was hit by a gybing boom.*
▶ **noun** an act or instance of gybing.
– ORIGIN late 17th cent.: from obsolete Dutch *gijben*.

gym ▶ **noun** informal **1** a gymnasium.
2 [mass noun] gymnastics: *I can't do gym today.*
– ORIGIN late 19th cent.: abbreviation.

gymkhana /dʒɪmˈkɑːnə/ ▶ **noun 1** an equestrian day event comprising races and other competitions on horseback, typically for children.
2 Indian a public place with facilities for athletics.
– ORIGIN mid 19th cent.: from Urdu *gendkānah* 'racket court', from Hindi *gemd* 'ball' + Persian *kānah* 'house', altered by association with **GYMNASTIC**.

gymnasium /dʒɪmˈneɪzɪəm/ ▶ **noun** (pl. **gymnasiums** or **gymnasia** /-zɪə/) **1** a room or building equipped for gymnastics, games, and other physical exercise.
2 /also ɡɪmˈnɑːzɪəm/ a school in Germany, Scandinavia, or central Europe that prepares pupils for university entrance.
– DERIVATIVES **gymnasial** adjective (only in sense 2).
– ORIGIN late 16th cent.: via Latin from Greek *gumnasion*, from *gumnazein* 'exercise naked', from *gumnos* 'naked'.

gymnast ▶ **noun** a person trained in or skilled in gymnastics.
– ORIGIN late 16th cent.: from French *gymnaste* or Greek *gumnastēs* 'trainer of athletes', from *gumnazein* 'exercise naked' (see **GYMNASIUM**).

gymnastic ▶ **adjective** of or relating to gymnastics: *a gymnastic display.*
– DERIVATIVES **gymnastically** adverb.

gymnastics ▶ **plural noun** [also treated as sing.] exercises developing or displaying physical agility and coordination. The modern sport of gymnastics typically involves exercises on bars, beam, floor, and vaulting horse.
■ [with adj.] other physical or mental agility of a specified kind: *these vocal gymnastics make the music unforgettable.*

gymno- /ˈdʒɪmnəʊ/ ▶ **combining form** bare; naked: *gymnosophist | gymnosperm.*
– ORIGIN from Greek *gumnos* 'naked'.

gymnogene /ˈdʒɪmnə(ʊ)dʒiːn/ ▶ **noun** a name used in Africa for the harrier hawk.
– ORIGIN late 19th cent.: from modern Latin *Gymnogenys* (former genus name), literally 'bare-chinned'.

gymnosophist /dʒɪmˈnɒsəfɪst/ ▶ **noun** a member of an ancient Hindu sect who wore very little clothing and were given to asceticism and contemplation.
– DERIVATIVES **gymnosophy** noun.
– ORIGIN late Middle English: from French *gymnosophiste*, via Latin from Greek *gumnosophistai* (plural), from *gumnos* 'naked' + *sophistēs* 'teacher of philosophy, sophist' (see **SOPHIST**).

gymnosperm /ˈdʒɪmnə(ʊ)spəːm/ ▶ **noun** Botany a plant of a group that comprises those that have seeds unprotected by an ovary or fruit, including the conifers, cycads, and ginkgo. Compare with **ANGIOSPERM**.
● Subdivision Gymnospermae, division Spermatophyta.
– DERIVATIVES **gymnospermous** /-ˈspəːməs/ adjective.

gymnure /ˈɡɪmnjʊə/ ▶ **noun** another term for **MOONRAT**.
– ORIGIN late 19th cent.: from modern Latin *Gymnura* (former genus name), from Greek *gumnos* 'naked' + *oura* 'tail'.

gymslip ▶ **noun** Brit. a sleeveless belted tunic reaching from the shoulder to the knee, formerly worn by schoolgirls.

gynaeceum /dʒʌɪˈniːsɪəm, ɡ-/ ▶ **noun** (pl. **gynaecea**) a part of a building set apart for women in an ancient Greek or Roman house.
– ORIGIN Latin, from Greek.

gynaeco- /ˈɡʌɪnɪkɒ, ɡʌɪˈniːkəʊ, dʒ-/ (US **gyneco-**) ▶ **combining form** relating to women; female: *gynaecocracy | gynaecophobia.*
– ORIGIN from Greek *gunē*, *gunaik-* 'woman, female'.

gynaecocracy /ˌɡʌɪnɪˈkɒkrəsi, dʒ-/ (US **gynecocracy**) ▶ **noun** another term for **GYNARCHY**.

gynaecology /ˌɡʌɪnɪˈkɒlədʒi, dʒ-/ (US **gynecology**) ▶ **noun** [mass noun] the branch of physiology and medicine which deals with the functions and diseases specific to women and girls, especially those affecting the reproductive system.
– DERIVATIVES **gynaecologic** adjective, **gynaecological** adjective, **gynaecologically** adverb, **gynaecologist** noun.

gynaecomastia /ˌɡʌɪnɪkə(ʊ)ˈmastɪə, ɡʌɪˈniːkə(ʊ)-, dʒ-/ (US **gynecomastia**) ▶ **noun** [mass noun] Medicine enlargement of a man's breasts, usually due to hormone imbalance or hormone therapy.

gynaecophobia /ˌɡʌɪnɪkə(ʊ)ˈfəʊbɪə, ɡʌɪˈniːkə(ʊ)-, dʒ-/ (US **gynecophobia**) ▶ **noun** another term for **GYNOPHOBIA**.

gynandromorph /dʒɪˈnandrəmɔːf, ɡʌɪ-/ ▶ **noun** Zoology & Medicine an abnormal individual, especially an insect, having some male and some female characteristics.
– DERIVATIVES **gynandromorphic** adjective, **gynandromorphy** noun.
– ORIGIN late 19th cent.: from Greek *gunandros* 'of doubtful sex' (see **GYNANDROUS**) + *morphē* 'form'.

gynandrous /dʒɪˈnandrəs, ɡʌɪ-/ ▶ **adjective** Botany (of a flower) having stamens and pistil united in one column, as in orchids.
■ (of a person or animal) hermaphrodite.
– ORIGIN early 19th cent.: from Greek *gunandros* 'of doubtful sex' (from *gunē* 'woman' + *anēr*, *andr-* 'man, male') + **-OUS**.

gynarchy /ˈɡʌɪnɑːki, ˈdʒʌɪ-/ ▶ **noun** (pl. **-ies**) [mass noun] rule by women or a woman.

gyneco- ▶ **combining form** US spelling of **GYNAECO-**.

gynocentric /ˌɡʌɪnə(ʊ)ˈsɛntrɪk, ˌdʒʌɪ-/ ▶ **adjective** centred on or concerned exclusively with women; taking a female (or specifically a feminist) point of view.

gynoecium /ɡʌɪˈniːsɪəm, dʒ-/ ▶ **noun** (pl. **gynoecia** /-sɪə/) Botany the female part of a flower, consisting of one or more carpels.
– ORIGIN mid 19th cent.: modern Latin, from Greek *gunaikeion* 'women's apartments', from *gunē*, *gunaik-* 'woman, female' + *oikos* 'house'.

gynophobia /ˌɡʌɪnə(ʊ)ˈfəʊbɪə, ˌdʒʌɪ-/ ▶ **noun** extreme or irrational fear of women or of the female.
– DERIVATIVES **gynophobic** adjective.

-gynous ▶ **combining form** Botany having female

g

organs or pistils of a specified kind or number: *epigynous*.
– ORIGIN based on modern Latin *-gynus* (from Greek *-gunos*, from *gunē* 'woman') + **-OUS**.

gyp[1] /dʒɪp/ (also **gip**) ▶ noun [mass noun] Brit. informal pain or discomfort: *one of her Achilles tendons had begun giving her gyp.*
– ORIGIN late 19th cent.: perhaps from *gee-up* (see **GEE**[2]).

gyp[2] /dʒɪp/ ▶ noun Brit. a college servant at the Universities of Cambridge and Durham.
– ORIGIN mid 18th cent.: perhaps from obsolete *gippo* 'menial kitchen servant', originally denoting a man's short tunic, from obsolete French *jupeau*.

gyp[3] /dʒɪp/ informal ▶ verb (**gypped**, **gypping**) [with obj.] cheat or swindle (someone): *that's salesmanship, you have to gyp people into buying stuff they don't like.*
▶ noun an act of cheating; a swindle.
– ORIGIN late 19th cent.: of unknown origin.

gyppo /'dʒɪpəʊ/ (also **gippo**) ▶ noun (pl. **-os**) informal, derogatory a gypsy.

gyppy tummy ▶ noun variant spelling of **GIPPY TUMMY**.

gypsophila /dʒɪp'sɒfɪlə/ ▶ noun a plant of the genus *Gypsophila* in the pink family, especially (in gardening) baby's breath.
– ORIGIN modern Latin, from Greek *gupsos* 'chalk, gypsum' + *philos* 'loving'.

gypsum /'dʒɪpsəm/ ▶ noun [mass noun] a soft white or grey mineral consisting of hydrated calcium sulphate. It occurs chiefly in sedimentary deposits and is used to make plaster of Paris and fertilizers, and in the building industry.
– DERIVATIVES **gypsiferous** /-'sɪf(ə)rəs/ adjective.
– ORIGIN late Middle English: from Latin, from Greek *gupsos*.

gypsum board ▶ noun North American term for **PLASTERBOARD**.

gypsy (also **gipsy**) ▶ noun (pl. **-ies**) a member of a travelling people with dark skin and hair, speaking a language (Romany) related to Hindi, and traditionally living by seasonal work, itinerant trade, and fortune-telling. Gypsies are now found mostly in Europe, parts of North Africa, and North America, but are believed to have originated in the Indian subcontinent.
– DERIVATIVES **gypsyish** adjective.
– ORIGIN mid 16th cent.: originally *gipcyan*, short for **EGYPTIAN** (because gypsies were popularly supposed to have come from Egypt).

gypsy moth ▶ noun a tussock moth having a brown male and larger white female, the latter being fully winged but flightless. The caterpillar can be a serious pest of orchards and woodland.
● *Lymantria dispar*, family Lymantriidae.

gypsywort (also **gipsywort**) ▶ noun a white-flowered Eurasian plant of the mint family, which grows in damp habitats.
● *Lycopus europaeus*, family Labiatae.
– ORIGIN late 18th cent.: so named because it was reputed to have been used by gypsies to stain the skin brown.

gyral /'dʒaɪr(ə)l/ ▶ adjective chiefly Anatomy of or relating to a gyrus or gyri.

gyrate ▶ verb move or cause to move rapidly in a circle or spiral: [no obj.] *their wings gyrate through the water like paddle wheels.*
■ [no obj.] dance in a wild or suggestive manner: *strippers gyrated to rock music on a low stage.*
– DERIVATIVES **gyration** noun, **gyrator** noun.
– ORIGIN early 19th cent.: from Latin *gyrat-* 'revolved', from the verb *gyrare*, from Greek *guros* 'a ring'.

gyratory /dʒaɪ'reɪt(ə)ri, 'dʒaɪrət-/ ▶ adjective of or involving circular or spiral motion.
▶ noun (pl. **-ies**) a road junction or traffic system requiring the circular movement of traffic, larger or more complex than an ordinary roundabout.

gyre /'dʒaɪə, 'gaɪə/ ▶ verb [no obj.] poetic/literary whirl; gyrate: *a swarm of ghosts gyred around him.*
▶ noun a spiral; a vortex.
■ Geography a circular pattern of currents in an ocean basin: *the central North Pacific gyre.*
– ORIGIN late Middle English (in the sense 'whirl (someone or something) round': from late Latin *gyrare*, from Latin *gyrus* 'a ring', from Greek *guros*. The noun is from Latin *gyrus*.

gyrfalcon /'dʒɜː,fɔː(l)k(ə)n, -,fɒlk(ə)n/ ▶ noun the largest falcon, found in arctic regions and occurring in several colour forms, one of which is mainly white.
● *Falco rusticolus*, family Falconidae.
– ORIGIN Middle English: from Old French *gerfaucon*, of Germanic origin. The first element is probably related to Old High German *gēr* 'spear'; the spelling *gyr-* arose from a mistaken idea that the bird's name came from Latin *gyrare* 'revolve'.

gyri plural form of **GYRUS**.

gyro[1] /'dʒaɪrəʊ/ ▶ noun (pl. **-os**) short for **GYROSCOPE** or **GYROCOMPASS**.

gyro[2] /'dʒaɪrəʊ/ ▶ noun (pl. **-os**) N. Amer. a sandwich made with slices of spiced meat cooked on a spit, served with salad in pitta bread.
– ORIGIN 1970s: from modern Greek *guros* 'turning'.

gyro- /'dʒaɪrəʊ/ ▶ combining form 1 relating to rotation: *gyromagnetic.*
2 gyroscopic: *gyrostabilizer.*
– ORIGIN from Greek *guros* 'a ring'.

gyrocompass ▶ noun a non-magnetic compass in which the direction of true north is maintained by a continuously driven gyroscope whose axis is parallel to the earth's axis of rotation.

gyrocopter ▶ noun a small, light single-seater autogiro.
– ORIGIN from **GYRO-** 'relating to rotation', on the pattern of *helicopter.*

gyromagnetic ▶ adjective 1 Physics of or relating to the magnetic and mechanical properties of a rotating charged particle.
2 (of a compass) combining a gyroscope and a normal magnetic compass.

gyron /'dʒaɪr(ə)n/ ▶ noun Heraldry a triangular ordinary formed by two lines from the edge of the shield meeting at the fess point at 45 degrees.
– ORIGIN late 16th cent.: from Old French *giron* 'gusset'.

gyronny /dʒaɪ'rɒni/ ▶ adjective Heraldry (of a shield) divided into eight gyrons by straight lines all crossing at the fess point.
– ORIGIN late Middle English: from French *gironné*, from *giron* (see **GYRON**).

gyropilot ▶ noun a gyrocompass used to provide automatic steering for a ship or aircraft.

gyroplane ▶ noun an autogiro or similar aircraft.

gyroscope ▶ noun a device consisting of a wheel or disc mounted so that it can spin rapidly about an axis which is itself free to alter in direction. The orientation of the axis is not affected by tilting of the mounting, so gyroscopes can be used to provide stability or maintain a reference direction, in navigation systems, automatic pilots, and stabilizers.
– DERIVATIVES **gyroscopic** adjective, **gyroscopically** adverb.
– ORIGIN mid 19th cent.: from French, from Greek *guros* 'a ring' + modern Latin *scopium* (see **-SCOPE**).

gyrostabilizer ▶ noun a gyroscopic device for maintaining the equilibrium of something such as a ship, aircraft, or platform.

gyrus /'dʒaɪrəs/ ▶ noun (pl. **gyri** /-rʌɪ/) Anatomy a ridge or fold between two clefts on the cerebral surface in the brain.
– ORIGIN mid 19th cent.: from Latin, from Greek *guros* 'a ring'.

Gy Sgt ▶ abbreviation for Gunnery Sergeant.

gyttja /'jɪtʃə/ ▶ noun [mass noun] Geology sediment rich in organic matter deposited at the bottom of a eutrophic lake.
– ORIGIN late 19th cent.: Swedish, literally 'mud, ooze'.

Gyumri /'gjʊmri/ an industrial city in NW Armenia, close to the border with Turkey; pop. 123,000 (1990). Founded as a fortress in 1837, the city was destroyed by an earthquake in 1926 and again in 1988. It was formerly called Aleksandropol (1840–1924) and Leninakan (1924–91). Russian name **KUMAYRI**.

gyve /dʒaɪv, gaɪv/ ▶ noun (usu. **gyves**) archaic a fetter or shackle.
– DERIVATIVES **gyved** adjective.
– ORIGIN Middle English: of unknown origin.

gyver ▶ noun variant spelling of **GUIVER**.

Hh

H¹ (also **h**) ▶ noun (pl. **Hs** or **H's**) **1** the eighth letter of the alphabet.
■ denoting the next after G in a set of items, categories, etc. ■ (**h**) Chess denoting the file on the right-hand edge of the board, as viewed from White's side.
2 (**H**) a shape like that of a capital H.
3 (**H**) Music (in the German system) the note B natural.

H² ▶ abbreviation for ■ hard (used in describing grades of pencil lead): *a 2H pencil.* ■ height (in giving the dimensions of an object). ■ Physics henry(s). ■ informal heroin. ■ Hungary (international vehicle registration). ■ Brit. (on signs in the street) hydrant.
▶ symbol for ■ Chemistry enthalpy. ■ the chemical element hydrogen. ■ Physics magnetic field strength.

h ▶ abbreviation for ■ (in measuring the height of horses) hand(s). ■ [in combination] (in units of measurement) hecto-: *wine production reached 624,000 hl last year.* ■ Brit. (with reference to sporting fixtures) home. ■ horse. ■ (especially with reference to water) hot: *nine rooms, all with h & c.* ■ hour(s): *breakfast at 0700 h.*
▶ symbol for ■ Physics Planck's constant. ■ (**h**) Physics Planck's constant divided by 2π.

ha¹ (also **hah**) ▶ exclamation used to express surprise, suspicion, triumph, or some other powerful emotion.
▶ verb see **hum and haw** at **HUM¹**.
– ORIGIN natural utterance: first recorded in Middle English.

ha² ▶ abbreviation for hectare(s).

haaf /hɑːf, haf/ ▶ noun (**the haaf**) (in Orkney and Shetland) the area of sea used for deep-sea fishing.
– ORIGIN late 18th cent.: from Old Norse *haf* 'high sea, ocean'; related to Danish *hav* and Swedish *haf*.

haar /hɑː/ ▶ noun a cold sea fog on the east coast of England or Scotland.
– ORIGIN late 17th cent.: perhaps from Old Norse *hárr* 'hoar, hoary'.

Haarlem /ˈhɑːləm/ a city in the Netherlands, near Amsterdam; pop. 148,470 (1991). It is the capital of the province of North Holland and the commercial centre of the Dutch bulb industry.

Hab. ▶ abbreviation for Habakkuk (in biblical references).

Habakkuk /ˈhabəkək, həˈbak-/ a Hebrew minor prophet, probably of the 7th century BC.
■ a book of the Bible containing his prophecies.

habanera /ˌhabəˈnɛːrə, ˌɑːbə-/ ▶ noun a Cuban dance in slow duple time.
– ORIGIN late 19th cent.: Spanish, short for *danza habanera* 'dance of Havana'.

Habanero /ˌabəˈnɛːrəʊ/ ▶ noun North American term for **SCOTCH BONNET**.
– ORIGIN Spanish, literally 'of Havana'.

habdabs ▶ plural noun variant spelling of **ABDABS**.

Habdalah /hɑːvˈdɑːlə/ (also **Havdalah**) ▶ noun a Jewish religious ceremony or formal prayer marking the end of the Sabbath.
– ORIGIN from Hebrew *haḇdālāh* 'separation, division'.

habeas corpus /ˌheɪbɪəs ˈkɔːpəs/ ▶ noun [mass noun] Law a writ requiring a person under arrest to be brought before a judge or into court, especially to secure the person's release unless lawful grounds are shown for their detention.
■ the legal right to apply for such a writ.
– ORIGIN late Middle English: Latin, literally 'thou shalt have the body (in court)'.

habendum /həˈbɛndəm/ ▶ noun Law the part of a deed or conveyance which states the estate or quantity of interest to be granted, e.g. the term of a lease.
– ORIGIN Latin, literally 'that is to be had', gerundive of *habere* 'have'.

haberdasher /ˈhabəˌdaʃə/ ▶ noun **1** Brit. a dealer in dressmaking and sewing goods.
2 N. Amer. a dealer in men's clothing.
– ORIGIN Middle English: probably based on Anglo-Norman French *hapertas*, perhaps the name of a fabric, of unknown origin. In early use the term denoted a dealer in a variety of household goods, later also specifically a hatter. Current senses date from the early 17th cent.

haberdashery ▶ noun (pl. **-ies**) [mass noun] the goods and wares sold by a haberdasher.
■ [count noun] the shop of a haberdasher.

habergeon /ˈhabədʒ(ə)n, həˈbəːdʒ(ə)n/ ▶ noun historical a sleeveless coat of mail or scale armour.
– ORIGIN Middle English: from Old French *haubergeon*, from *hauberc* (see **HAUBERK**), originally denoting a garment protecting the neck; compare with Dutch *halsberg*.

Habermas /ˈhɑːbəmas/, Jürgen (b.1929), German social philosopher. A leading figure of the Frankfurt School, he developed its cultural reappraisal of Marxism and is especially noted for his work on communication theory.

Haber process /ˈhɑːbə/ (also **Haber–Bosch process**) ▶ noun [mass noun] an industrial process for producing ammonia from nitrogen and hydrogen, using an iron catalyst at high temperature and pressure.
– ORIGIN named after Fritz *Haber* (1868–1934) and Carl *Bosch* (1874–1940), German chemists.

habile /ˈhabɪl/ ▶ adjective rare deft; skilful.
– ORIGIN late Middle English: variant of **ABLE**. The spelling change in the 16th and 17th cents was due to association with French *habile* and Latin *habilis*.

habiliment /həˈbɪlɪm(ə)nt/ ▶ noun (usu. **habiliments**) archaic clothing.
– ORIGIN late Middle English (in the general sense 'outfit, attire'): from Old French *habillement*, from *habiller* 'fit out', from Latin *habilis* (see **ABLE**).

habilitate /həˈbɪlɪteɪt/ ▶ verb [no obj.] qualify for office, especially as a teacher in a German university.
– DERIVATIVES **habilitation** noun.
– ORIGIN early 17th cent.: from medieval Latin *habilitat-* 'made able', from the verb *habilitare*, from *habilitas* (see **ABILITY**).

habit ▶ noun **1** a settled or regular tendency or practice, especially one that is hard to give up: *this can develop into a bad habit* | [mass noun] *we stayed together out of habit.*
■ informal an addictive practice, especially one of taking drugs: *a cocaine habit.* ■ Psychology an automatic reaction to a specific situation. ■ [mass noun] general shape or mode of growth, especially of a plant or a mineral: *a shrub of spreading habit.*
2 a long, loose garment worn by a member of a religious order.
■ short for **RIDING HABIT**. ■ [mass noun] archaic dress; attire.
3 archaic a person's bodily condition or constitution.
▶ verb [with obj.] (usu. **be habited**) archaic dress; clothe: *a boy habited as a serving lad.*
– PHRASES **break** (or informal **kick**) **the habit** stop engaging in a habitual practice.
– ORIGIN Middle English: from Old French *abit*, *habit*, from Latin *habitus* 'condition, appearance', from *habere* 'have, consist of'. The term originally meant 'dress, attire', later coming to denote physical or mental constitution.

habitable ▶ adjective suitable or good enough to live in.
– DERIVATIVES **habitability** noun.
– ORIGIN late Middle English: via Old French from Latin *habitabilis*, from *habitare* 'possess, inhabit'.

habitant ▶ noun **1** /abiˈtɒ̃/ [often as modifier] an early French settler in Canada (especially Quebec) or Louisiana: *the habitant farmhouses of old Quebec.*
2 /ˈhabɪt(ə)nt/ archaic an inhabitant.
– ORIGIN late Middle English (in sense 2): from Old French, from *habiter*, from Latin *habitare* 'inhabit'.

habitat ▶ noun the natural home or environment of an animal, plant, or other organism: *wild chimps in their natural habitat.*
■ informal a person's usual or preferred surroundings.
– ORIGIN late 18th cent.: from Latin, literally 'it dwells', from *habitare* (see **HABITABLE**).

habitation ▶ noun [mass noun] the state or process of living in a particular place: *signs of human habitation.*
■ [count noun] formal a place in which to live; a house or home.
– DERIVATIVES **habitative** adjective.
– ORIGIN late Middle English: via Old French from Latin *habitatio(n-)*, from *habitare* 'inhabit'.

habit-forming ▶ adjective (of a drug or activity) addictive.

habitual /həˈbɪtʃʊəl, -tjʊəl/ ▶ adjective done or doing constantly or as a habit: *a habitual late sleeper* | *this pattern of behaving can become habitual.*
■ regular; usual: *his habitual dress.*
– DERIVATIVES **habitually** adverb.
– ORIGIN late Middle English (in the sense 'part of one's character'): from medieval Latin *habitualis*, from *habitus* 'condition, appearance' (see **HABIT**).

habituate ▶ verb chiefly Zoology make or become accustomed or used to something: [with obj.] *she had habituated the chimps to humans.*
– ORIGIN late 15th cent.: from late Latin *habituat-* 'accustomed', from the verb *habituare*, from *habitus* (see **HABIT**).

habituation ▶ noun [mass noun] the action of habituating or the condition of being habituated.
■ Psychology the diminishing of an innate response to a frequently repeated stimulus.
– ORIGIN late Middle English (in the sense 'formation of habit'): from French or from Latin *habituatio(n-)*, from late Latin *habituare* (see **HABITUATE**).

habitude ▶ noun rare a habitual tendency or way of behaving.

– ORIGIN late Middle English: via Old French from Latin *habitudo*, from *habere* 'have' (compare with **HABIT**).

habitué /(h)ə'bɪtjʊeɪ/ ▶ noun a resident of or frequent visitor to a particular place: *an habitué of the West End*.
– ORIGIN early 19th cent.: French, literally 'accustomed', past participle of *habituer*.

habitus /'habɪtəs/ ▶ noun [mass noun] chiefly Medicine & Psychology general constitution, especially bodily build.
– ORIGIN late 19th cent.: from Latin.

haboob /hə'buːb/ ▶ noun a violent and oppressive wind blowing in summer in Sudan and elsewhere, bringing sand from the desert.
– ORIGIN late 19th cent.: from Arabic *habūb* 'blowing furiously'.

Habsburg /'hapsbəːg/ (also **Hapsburg**) one of the principal dynasties of central Europe from medieval to modern times.

The family established a hereditary monarchy in Austria in 1282 and secured the title of Holy Roman emperor from 1452. Austrian and Spanish branches were created when Charles divided the territories between his son Philip II and his brother Ferdinand; the Habsburgs ruled Spain 1504–1700, while Habsburg rule in Austria ended with the collapse of Austria–Hungary in 1918.

háček /'hɑːtʃɛk, 'ha-/ ▶ noun a diacritic mark (ˇ) placed over a letter to indicate modification of the sound in Slavic and other languages.
– ORIGIN Czech, diminutive of *hák* 'hook'.

hacendado /ˌasɛn'dɑːdəʊ, Spanish aθen'daðo, asen-/ (also **haciendado** /ˌasjɛn-, Spanish aθjen-, asjen-/) ▶ noun (pl. **-os**) the owner of a hacienda.
– ORIGIN Spanish.

hachures /ha'ʃjʊəz/ ▶ plural noun parallel lines used in hill-shading on maps, their closeness indicating steepness of gradient.
– DERIVATIVES **hachured** adjective.
– ORIGIN mid 19th cent.: from French, from *hacher* (see **HATCH**³).

hacienda /ˌhasɪ'ɛndə, Spanish a'θjenda, a'sjenda/ ▶ noun (in Spanish-speaking countries or regions) a large estate or plantation with a dwelling house.
– ORIGIN Spanish, from Latin *facienda* 'things to be done', from *facere* 'make, do'.

hack¹ ▶ verb 1 [with obj.] cut with rough or heavy blows: *hack off the dead branches* | [no obj.] *men hack at the coalface*.
■ kick wildly or roughly: *he had to race from his line to hack the ball into the stand*.
2 [no obj.] use a computer to gain unauthorized access to data in a system: *they hacked into a bank's computer*.
[with obj.] gain unauthorized access to (data in a computer): *hacking private information from computers*.
3 [usu. with negative] (**hack it**) informal manage; cope: *lots of people leave because they can't hack it*.
▶ noun 1 a rough cut, blow, or stroke: *he was sure one of us was going to take a hack at him*.
■ (in sport) a kick or a stroke with a stick inflicted on another player. ■ a notch cut in the ice, or a peg inserted, to steady the foot when delivering a stone in curling. ■ a tool for rough striking or cutting, e.g. a mattock or a miner's pick. ■ archaic a gash or wound.
2 informal an act of computer hacking.
■ a piece of computer code which performs some function, especially an unofficial alternative or addition to a commercial program: *freeware and shareware hacks*.
– PHRASES **hacking cough** a short, dry, frequent cough.
– ORIGIN Old English *haccian* 'cut in pieces', of West Germanic origin; related to Dutch *hakken* and German *hacken*.
▶ **hack around** N. Amer. pass one's time idly or with no definite purpose.
hack someone off informal annoy or infuriate someone.

hack² ▶ noun 1 a writer or journalist producing dull, unoriginal work: [as modifier] *a hack scriptwriter*.
■ a person who does dull routine work.
2 a horse for ordinary riding.
■ a good-quality lightweight riding horse, especially one used in the show ring. ■ a ride on a horse. ■ an inferior or worn-out horse. ■ a horse let out for hire.
3 N. Amer. a taxi.
▶ verb [no obj.] [usu. as noun **hacking**] ride a horse for pleasure or exercise.

– DERIVATIVES **hackery** noun.
– ORIGIN Middle English (in sense 2): abbreviation of **HACKNEY**. Sense 1 dates from the late 17th cent.

hack³ ▶ noun 1 Falconry a board on which a hawk's meat is laid.
2 a wooden frame for drying bricks, cheeses, etc.
■ a pile of bricks stacked up to dry before firing.
– PHRASES **at hack** (of a young hawk) given partial liberty but not yet allowed to hunt for itself.
– ORIGIN late Middle English (denoting the lower half of a divided door): variant of **HATCH**¹.

hackamore /'hakəmɔː/ ▶ noun a bitless bridle which operates by exerting pressure on the horse's nose.
– ORIGIN mid 19th cent.: perhaps from Spanish *jaquima*, earlier *xaquima* 'halter'.

hackberry ▶ noun (pl. **-ies**) a tree of the elm family which has leaves that resemble those of nettles, found in both tropical and temperate regions. See also **NETTLE TREE**.
● Genus *Celtis*, family Ulmaceae: several species, in particular the **North American hackberry** (*C. occidentalis*), which bears purple edible berries.
■ the berry of this tree.
– ORIGIN mid 18th cent.: variant of northern English dialect *hagberry*, of Scandinavian origin.

hacker ▶ noun 1 informal a person who uses computers to gain unauthorized access to data.
2 a person or thing that hacks or cuts roughly.

hackette ▶ noun informal, chiefly derogatory a female journalist.

hacking jacket ▶ noun a riding jacket with slits at the side or back.

hackle ▶ noun 1 (**hackles**) erectile hairs along the back of a dog or other animal, which rise when it is angry or alarmed.
■ the hairs on the back of a person's neck, thought of as being raised when the person is angry or hostile: *she felt her hackles rise in anger*.
2 (often **hackles**) a long, narrow feather on the neck or saddle of a domestic cock or other bird.
■ Fishing a feather wound around a fishing fly so that its filaments are splayed out. ■ [mass noun] such feathers collectively. ■ a bunch of feathers in a military headdress, for example of a regiment of fusiliers or the Black Watch.
3 a steel comb for dressing flax.
▶ verb [with obj.] dress or comb with a hackle.
– ORIGIN late Middle English (in sense 2): variant of **HATCHEL**.

hackmatack /'hakmətak/ ▶ noun any of a number of North American coniferous trees, in particular the tamarack.
– ORIGIN late 18th cent.: perhaps from Western Abnaki.

hackney ▶ noun (pl. **-eys**) historical a horse or pony of a light breed with a high-stepping trot, used in harness.
■ [usu. as modifier] a horse-drawn vehicle kept for hire: *a hackney coach*.
– ORIGIN Middle English: probably from *Hackney* in East London, where horses were pastured. The term originally denoted an ordinary riding horse (as opposed to a war horse or draught horse), especially one available for hire: hence *hackney carriage* or *coach*, and the verb *hackney* meaning 'use (a horse) for general purposes', later 'make commonplace by overuse' (see **HACKNEYED**).

hackney carriage ▶ noun Brit. the official term for a taxi.

hackneyed ▶ adjective (of a phrase or idea) lacking import through having been overused; unoriginal and trite: *hackneyed old sayings*.

hacksaw ▶ noun a saw with a narrow fine-toothed blade set in a frame, used especially for cutting metal.
▶ verb (past participle **-sawn** or **-sawed**) [with obj.] cut (something) using a hacksaw.

had past and past participle of **HAVE**.

hadada /'hɑːdədɑː/ (also **hadeda**, **hadada ibis**) ▶ noun a large grey-brown African ibis with iridescent patches on the wings and a loud, harsh call.
● *Bostrychia* (or *Hagedashia*) *hagedash*, family Threskiornithidae.
– ORIGIN late 18th cent.: imitative of its call.

hadal /'heɪdəl/ ▶ adjective of or relating to the zone of the sea greater than 6000 m in depth (chiefly oceanic trenches).

– ORIGIN mid 20th cent.: from **HADES** + **-AL**.

hadda informal ▶ contraction of had to.

haddock ▶ noun (pl. same) a silvery-grey bottom-dwelling fish of North Atlantic coastal waters, related to the cod. It is popular as a food fish and is of great commercial value.
● *Melanogrammus aeglefinus*, family Gadidae.
– ORIGIN Middle English: from Anglo-Norman French *hadoc*, from Old French *hadot*, of unknown origin.

hade /heɪd/ Geology ▶ noun the inclination of a mineral vein or fault from the vertical.
▶ verb [no obj.] (of a shaft, vein, or fault) incline from the vertical.
– ORIGIN late 17th cent.: perhaps a dialect form of the verb **HEAD**.

hadeda ▶ noun variant spelling of **HADADA**.

Hades /'heɪdiːz/ Greek Mythology the underworld; the abode of the spirits of the dead.
■ the god of the underworld, one of the sons of Cronus. Also called **PLUTO**.
– DERIVATIVES **Hadean** adjective.
– ORIGIN from Greek *Haidēs*, of unknown origin.

Hadhramaut /ˌhɑːdrə'maʊt, -'mɔːt/ a narrow region on the southern coast of Yemen, separating the Gulf of Aden from the desert land of the southern Arabian peninsula.

Hadith /ha'diːθ/ ▶ noun (pl. same or **Hadiths**) a collection of traditions containing sayings of the prophet Muhammad which, with accounts of his daily practice (the Sunna), constitute the major source of guidance for Muslims apart from the Koran.
■ one of these sayings.
– ORIGIN from Arabic *ḥadīṯ* 'tradition'.

Hadlee /'hadli/, Sir Richard (John) (b.1951), New Zealand cricketer. An all-rounder, he took a record of 431 test wickets during his career.

Hadley cell ▶ noun Meteorology a large-scale atmospheric convection cell in which air rises at the equator and sinks at medium latitudes, typically about 30° north or south.
– ORIGIN 1950s: named after George *Hadley* (1685–1768), English scientific writer.

hadn't ▶ contraction of had not.

Hadrian /'heɪdrɪən/ (AD 76–138), Roman emperor 117–138; full name *Publius Aelius Hadrianus*. The adopted successor of Trajan, he toured the provinces of the Empire and secured the frontiers.

Hadrian's Wall a Roman defensive wall across northern England, stretching from the Solway Firth in the west to the mouth of the River Tyne in the east (about 120 km, 74 miles). It was begun in AD 122, after the emperor Hadrian's visit, to defend the province of Britain against invasions by tribes from the north.

hadron /'hadrɒn/ ▶ noun Physics a subatomic particle of a type including the baryons and mesons, which can take part in the strong interaction.
– DERIVATIVES **hadronic** adjective.
– ORIGIN 1960s: from Greek *hadros* 'bulky' + **-ON**.

hadrosaur /'hadrəsɔː/ ▶ noun a large herbivorous mainly bipedal dinosaur of the late Cretaceous period, with jaws flattened like the bill of a duck. Also called **DUCK-BILLED DINOSAUR**.
● Family Hadrosauridae, infraorder Ornithopoda, order Ornithischia.
– ORIGIN late 19th cent.: from modern Latin *Hadrosaurus* (genus name), from Greek *hadros* 'thick, stout' + *sauros* 'lizard'.

hadst archaic second person singular past of **HAVE**.

haecceity /hɛk'siːɪti, hiːk-/ ▶ noun [mass noun] Philosophy that property or quality of a thing by virtue of which it is unique or describable as 'this (one)'.
■ the property of being a unique and individual thing.
– ORIGIN mid 17th cent.: from medieval Latin *haecceitas*, from Latin *haec*, feminine of *hic* 'this'.

Haeckel /'hɛk(ə)l/, Ernst Heinrich (1834–1919), German biologist and philosopher. He popularized Darwin's theories and saw evolution as providing a framework for describing the world, with the German Empire representing the highest evolved form of a civilized nation.

haem /hiːm/ (US **heme**) ▶ noun [mass noun] Biochemistry an iron-containing compound of the porphyrin class which forms the non-protein part of haemoglobin and some other biological molecules.

– ORIGIN 1920s: back-formation from **HAEMOGLOBIN**.

haemagglutination /ˌhiːməgluːtɪˈneɪʃ(ə)n/ (US **hemagglutination**) ▶ noun [mass noun] Medicine & Biology the clumping together of red blood cells.

haemagglutinin /ˌhiːməˈgluːtɪnɪn/ (US **hemagglutinin**) ▶ noun Medicine & Biology a substance, such as a viral protein, which causes haemagglutination.

haemal /ˈhiːm(ə)l/ (US **hemal**) ▶ adjective Physiology of or concerning the blood.
■ Zoology situated on the same side of the body as the heart and major blood vessels (i.e. in chordates, ventral).
– ORIGIN mid 19th cent.: from Greek *haima* 'blood' + **-AL**.

haemangioma /ˌhiːmandʒɪˈəʊmə/ (US **hemangioma**) ▶ noun (pl. **haemangiomas** or **haemangiomata** /-mətə/) Medicine a benign tumour of blood vessels, often forming a red birthmark.

haematemesis /ˌhiːməˈtɛmɪsɪs/ (US **hematemesis**) ▶ noun [mass noun] Medicine the vomiting of blood.
– ORIGIN early 19th cent.: from **HAEMATO-** 'of blood' + Greek *emesis* 'vomiting'.

haematic /hɪˈmatɪk/ (US **hematic**) ▶ adjective Medicine, dated of, relating to, or affecting the blood.
– ORIGIN mid 19th cent.: from Greek *haimatikos*, from *haima, haimat-* 'blood'.

haematin /ˈhiːmətɪn/ (US **hematin**) ▶ noun [mass noun] Biochemistry a bluish-black compound derived from haemoglobin by removal of the protein part and oxidation of the iron atom.
– ORIGIN mid 19th cent.: from Greek *haima, haimat-* 'blood' + **-IN**[1].

haematite /ˈhiːmətʌɪt/ (US **hematite**) ▶ noun a reddish-black mineral consisting of ferric oxide. It is an important ore of iron.
– ORIGIN late Middle English: via Latin from Greek *haimatitēs (lithos)* 'blood-like (stone)', from *haima, haimat-* 'blood'.

haemato- (US **hemato-**) ▶ combining form of or relating to the blood: *haematoma*.
– ORIGIN from Greek *haima, haimat-* 'blood'.

haematocele /ˈhiːmətə(ʊ)siːl/ (US **hematocele**) ▶ noun Medicine a swelling caused by blood collecting in a body cavity.

haematocrit /ˈhiːmətə(ʊ)krɪt/ (US **hematocrit**) ▶ noun Physiology the ratio of the volume of red blood cells to the total volume of blood.
■ an instrument for measuring this, typically by centrifugation.
– ORIGIN late 19th cent.: from **HAEMATO-** 'of blood' + Greek *kritēs* 'judge'.

haematogenous /ˌhiːməˈtɒdʒɪnəs/ (US **hematogenous**) ▶ adjective Medicine originating in or carried by the blood.

haematology /ˌhiːməˈtɒlədʒi/ (US **hematology**) ▶ noun [mass noun] the study of the physiology of the blood.
– DERIVATIVES **haematologic** adjective, **haematological** adjective, **haematologist** noun.

haematoma /ˌhiːməˈtəʊmə/ (US **hematoma**) ▶ noun (pl. **haematomas** or **haematomata** /-mətə/) Medicine a solid swelling of clotted blood within the tissues.

haematophagous /ˌhiːməˈtɒfəgəs/ (US **hematophagous**) ▶ adjective (of an animal, especially an insect or tick) feeding on blood.

haematopoiesis /ˌhiːmatə(ʊ)pɔɪˈiːsɪs/ (US **hematopoiesis**) ▶ noun another term for **HAEMOPOIESIS**.
– DERIVATIVES **haematopoietic** adjective.

haematoxylin /ˌhiːməˈtɒksɪlɪn/ (US **hematoxylin**) ▶ noun [mass noun] Chemistry a colourless compound present in logwood, which is easily converted into blue, red, or purple dyes and is used as a biological stain.
● A phenol; chem. formula: $C_{16}H_{14}O_6$.
– ORIGIN mid 19th cent.: from modern Latin *Haematoxylum* (genus name), from **HAEMATO-** 'of blood' + Greek *xulon* 'wood'.

haematuria /ˌhiːməˈtjʊərɪə/ (US **hematuria**) ▶ noun [mass noun] Medicine the presence of blood in urine.

-haemia ▶ combining form variant spelling of **-AEMIA**.

haemo- (US **hemo-**) ▶ combining form equivalent to **HAEMATO-**.
– ORIGIN from Greek *haima* 'blood'.

haemochromatosis /ˌhiːmə(ʊ)krəʊməˈtəʊsɪs/ (US **hemochromatosis**) ▶ noun [mass noun] Medicine a hereditary disorder in which iron salts are deposited in the tissues, leading to liver damage, diabetes mellitus, and bronze discoloration of the skin.

haemocoel /ˈhiːməsiːl/ (US **hemocoel**) ▶ noun Zoology the primary body cavity of most invertebrates, containing circulatory fluid.
– ORIGIN late 19th cent.: from **HAEMO-** 'of blood' + Greek *koilos* 'hollow, cavity'.

haemocyanin /ˌhiːmə(ʊ)ˈsʌɪənɪn/ (US **hemocyanin**) ▶ noun [mass noun] Biochemistry a protein containing copper, responsible for transporting oxygen in the blood plasma of arthropods and molluscs.
– ORIGIN mid 19th cent.: from **HAEMO-** 'of blood' + **CYAN-** + **-IN**[1].

haemocytometer /ˌhiːmə(ʊ)sʌɪˈtɒmɪtə/ (US **hemocytometer**) ▶ noun an instrument for visual counting of the number of cells in a blood sample or other fluid under a microscope.

haemodialysis /ˌhiːmə(ʊ)dʌɪˈalɪsɪs/ (US **hemodialysis**) ▶ noun (pl. **haemodialyses** /-siːz/) Medicine kidney dialysis.

haemodynamic (US **hemodynamic**) ▶ adjective Physiology of or relating to the flow of blood within the organs and tissues of the body.
– DERIVATIVES **haemodynamically** adverb, **haemodynamics** noun.

haemoglobin /ˌhiːməˈgləʊbɪn/ (US **hemoglobin**) ▶ noun [mass noun] Biochemistry a red protein responsible for transporting oxygen in the blood of vertebrates. Its molecule comprises four subunits, each containing an iron atom bound to a haem group.
– ORIGIN mid 19th cent.: a contracted form of *haematoglobulin*, in the same sense.

haemoglobinopathy /ˌhiːmə,gləʊbɪˈnɒpəθi/ (US **hemoglobinopathy**) ▶ noun (pl. **-ies**) Medicine a hereditary condition involving an abnormality in the structure of haemoglobin.

haemoglobinuria /ˌhiːmə,gləʊbɪˈnjʊərɪə/ (US **hemoglobinuria**) ▶ noun [mass noun] Medicine excretion of free haemoglobin in the urine.

haemolymph /ˈhiːmə(ʊ)lɪmf/ (US **hemolymph**) ▶ noun [mass noun] a fluid equivalent to blood in most invertebrates, occupying the haemocoel.

haemolysis /hiːˈmɒlɪsɪs/ (US **hemolysis**) ▶ noun [mass noun] the rupture or destruction of red blood cells.

haemolytic /ˌhiːməˈlɪtɪk/ (US **hemolytic**) ▶ adjective Medicine relating to or involving the rupture or destruction of red blood cells: *haemolytic anaemia*.

haemolytic disease of the newborn ▶ noun [mass noun] Medicine a severe form of anaemia caused in a fetus or newborn infant by incompatibility with the mother's blood type, typically when the mother is rhesus negative and produces antibodies which attack rhesus positive fetal blood through the placenta. Also called **ERYTHROBLASTOSIS**.

haemophilia /ˌhiːməˈfɪlɪə/ (US **hemophilia**) ▶ noun [mass noun] a medical condition in which the ability of the blood to clot is severely reduced, causing the sufferer to bleed severely from even a slight injury. The condition is typically caused by a hereditary lack of a coagulation factor, most often factor VIII.
– DERIVATIVES **haemophiliac** noun, **haemophilic** adjective.

haemopoiesis /ˌhiːmə(ʊ)pɔɪˈiːsɪs/ (US **hemopoiesis**) ▶ noun [mass noun] the production of blood cells and platelets, which occurs in the bone marrow.
– DERIVATIVES **haemopoietic** adjective.
– ORIGIN early 20th cent.: from **HAEMO-** 'of blood' + Greek *poiēsis* 'making'.

haemoptysis /hiːˈmɒptɪsɪs/ (US **hemoptysis**) ▶ noun [mass noun] the coughing up of blood.
– ORIGIN mid 17th cent.: from modern Latin *hemoptysis*, from **HAEMO-** 'of blood' + Greek *ptusis* 'spitting'.

haemorrhage /ˈhɛmərɪdʒ/ (US **hemorrhage**) ▶ noun an escape of blood from a ruptured blood vessel, especially when profuse.
■ a damaging loss of valuable people or resources suffered by an organization, group, or state: *a haemorrhage of highly qualified teachers.*
▶ verb [no obj.] (of a person) suffer a haemorrhage: *he had begun haemorrhaging in the night.*
■ [with obj.] expend (money) in large amounts in a seemingly uncontrollable manner.
– ORIGIN late 17th cent. (as a noun): alteration of obsolete *haemorrhagy*, via Latin from Greek *haimorrhagia*, from *haima* 'blood' + the stem of *rhēgnunai* 'burst'.

haemorrhagic /ˌhɛməˈradʒɪk/ (US **hemorrhagic**) ▶ adjective accompanied by or produced by haemorrhage: *a viral haemorrhagic fever | haemorrhagic colitis.*

haemorrhoid /ˈhɛmərɔɪd/ (US **hemorrhoid**) ▶ noun (usu. **haemorrhoids**) a swollen vein or group of veins in the region of the anus. Also (collectively) called **PILES**.
– DERIVATIVES **haemorrhoidal** adjective.
– ORIGIN late Middle English: via Old French and Latin from Greek *haimorrhoides (phlebes)* 'bleeding (veins)', from *haima* 'blood' + an element related to *rhein* 'to flow'.

haemostasis /ˌhiːmə(ʊ)ˈsteɪsɪs/ (US **hemostasis**) ▶ noun [mass noun] Medicine the stopping of a flow of blood.
– DERIVATIVES **haemostatic** adjective.

haemostat /ˈhiːməstat/ (US **hemostat**) ▶ noun Medicine an instrument for preventing blood flow by compression of a blood vessel.

haere mai /ˌhʌɪrə ˈmʌɪ/ ▶ exclamation used as a Maori greeting.
– ORIGIN Maori, literally 'come hither'.

hafiz /ˈhɑːfɪz/ ▶ noun a Muslim who knows the Koran by heart.
– ORIGIN Persian, from Arabic *ḥāfiẓ* 'guardian', from *ḥāfiẓa* 'guard, know by heart'.

Haflinger /ˈhaflɪŋə/ ▶ noun a draught pony of a sturdy chestnut breed with a flaxen mane and tail.
– ORIGIN late 19th cent.: German, from *Hafling*, the name of a Tyrolean village where the breed originated.

hafnium /ˈhafnɪəm/ ▶ noun [mass noun] the chemical element of atomic number 72, a hard silver-grey metal of the transition series, resembling and often occurring with zirconium. (Symbol: **Hf**)
– ORIGIN 1920s: modern Latin, from *Hafnia*, Latinized form of Danish *Havn*, former name of Copenhagen.

haft /hɑːft/ ▶ noun the handle of a knife, axe, or spear.
▶ verb [with obj.] [often as adj. **hafted**] provide (a blade, axe head, or spearhead) with a haft.
– ORIGIN Old English *hæft*, of Germanic origin: related to Dutch *heft, hecht* and German *Heft*, also to **HEAVE**.

Haftorah /hɑːˈtɔːrɑː/ (also **Haphtarah** or **Haphtorah**) ▶ noun (pl. **Haftoroth** /-rəʊt/) Judaism a short reading from the Prophets which follows the reading from the Law in a Jewish synagogue.
– ORIGIN from Hebrew *hapṭārāh* 'dismissal'.

Hag. ▶ abbreviation for Haggai (in biblical references).

hag[1] ▶ noun **1** a witch, especially one in the form of an ugly old woman (often used as a term of disparagement for a woman): *a fat old hag in a dirty apron.*
2 short for **HAGFISH**.
– DERIVATIVES **haggish** adjective.
– ORIGIN Middle English: perhaps from Old English *hægtesse, hegtes*, related to Dutch *heks* and German *Hexe* 'witch', of unknown ultimate origin.

hag[2] ▶ noun Scottish & N. English **1** (also **peat hag**) an overhang of peat.
2 a soft place on a moor or a firm place in a bog.
– ORIGIN Middle English (denoting a gap in a cliff): from Old Norse *hǫgg* 'gap', from *hǫggva* 'hack, hew'.

Hagar /ˈheɪɡɑː/ (in the Bible and in Islamic tradition) the mother of Ishmael (Ismail), son of Abraham.

Hagen /ˈhɑːɡ(ə)n/ an industrial city in NW Germany, in North Rhine-Westphalia; pop. 214,085 (1991).

hagfish ▶ noun (pl. same or **-fishes**) a primitive jawless marine vertebrate distantly related to the lampreys, with a slimy eel-like body, a slit-like mouth surrounded by barbels, and a rasping tongue used for feeding on dead or dying fish.
● Class Myxini and family Myxinidae: several genera, in particular *Myxine*, and numerous species.
– ORIGIN early 17th cent.: from **HAG**[1] + **FISH**[1].

Haggadah /həˈɡɑːdə, haɡaˈdɑː/ (also **Aggadah**) ▶ noun (pl. **Haggadoth** or **Haggadot** /-dəʊt/) Judaism **1** the text recited at the Seder on the first two

nights of the Jewish Passover, including a narrative of the Exodus.
2 a legend, parable, or anecdote used to illustrate a point of the Law in the Talmud.
■[mass noun] this (non-legal) element of the Talmud. Compare with HALACHA.
– DERIVATIVES **Haggadic** /-'gadık, -'gɑːdık/ adjective, **Haggadist** noun.
– ORIGIN from Hebrew *Haggāḏāh*, 'tale, parable', from *higgīd* 'tell, expound'.

Haggai /'hageɪ,ʌɪ/ a Hebrew minor prophet of the 6th century BC.
■a book of the Bible containing his prophecies of a glorious future in the Messianic age.

Haggard, Sir (Henry) Rider (1856–1925), English novelist. He is famous for adventure novels such as *King Solomon's Mines* (1885) and *She* (1889).

haggard ▶ adjective **1** looking exhausted and unwell, especially from fatigue, worry, or suffering: *I trailed on behind, haggard and dishevelled.*
2 (of a hawk) caught for training as a wild adult of more than twelve months. Compare with PASSAGE HAWK.
▶ noun a haggard hawk.
– DERIVATIVES **haggardly** adverb, **haggardness** noun.
– ORIGIN mid 16th cent. (used in falconry): from French *hagard*; perhaps related to HEDGE; later influenced by HAG¹.

haggis ▶ noun (pl. same) a Scottish dish consisting of a sheep's or calf's offal mixed with suet, oatmeal, and seasoning and boiled in a bag, traditionally one made from the animal's stomach.
– ORIGIN late Middle English: probably from earlier *hag* 'hack, hew', from Old Norse *hǫggva*.

haggle ▶ verb [no obj.] dispute or bargain persistently, especially over the cost of something: *the two sides are haggling over television rights.*
▶ noun a period of such bargaining.
– DERIVATIVES **haggler** noun.
– ORIGIN late 16th cent. (in the sense 'hack, mangle'): from Old Norse *hǫggva* 'hew'.

Hagia Sophia /ˌhagɪə səˈfiːə/ another name for ST SOPHIA.
– ORIGIN Greek, literally 'holy wisdom'.

hagio- ▶ combining form relating to saints or holiness: *hagiographer.*
– ORIGIN from Greek *hagios* 'holy'.

Hagiographa /ˌhagɪˈɒgrəfə/ ▶ plural noun the books of the Bible comprising the last of the three major divisions of the Hebrew scriptures, other than the Law and the Prophets. The books of the Hagiographa are: Ruth, Psalms, Job, Proverbs, Ecclesiastes, Song of Solomon, Lamentations, Daniel, Esther, Ezra-Nehemiah, and Chronicles. Also called **the Writings**.
– ORIGIN via late Latin from Greek.

hagiographer /ˌhagɪˈɒgrəfə/ ▶ noun **1** a writer of the lives of the saints.
■derogatory a person who writes in an adulatory way about someone else, especially in a biography.
2 Theology a writer of any of the Hagiographa.

hagiography /ˌhagɪˈɒgrəfi/ ▶ noun [mass noun] the writing of the lives of the saints.
■derogatory adulatory writing about another person. ■ [count noun] a biography idealizing its subject.
– DERIVATIVES **hagiographic** adjective, **hagiographical** adjective.

hagiolatry /ˌhagɪˈɒlətri/ ▶ noun [mass noun] the worship of saints.
■derogatory undue veneration of a famous person.

hagiology /ˌhagɪˈɒlədʒi/ ▶ noun [mass noun] literature dealing with the lives and legends of saints.
– DERIVATIVES **hagiological** adjective, **hagiologist** noun.

hagioscope /'hagɪəskəʊp/ ▶ noun another term for SQUINT (in sense 3).

hag-ridden ▶ adjective afflicted by nightmares or anxieties: *he was hag-ridden by his early success.*

Hague /heɪg/ (**The Hague**) the seat of government and administrative centre of the Netherlands, on the North Sea coast, capital of the province of South Holland; pop. 444,240 (1991). The International Court of Justice is based there. Dutch name DEN HAAG; also called 'S-GRAVENHAGE.

hah ▶ exclamation variant spelling of HA¹.

ha-ha ▶ noun a ditch with a wall on its inner side below ground level, forming a boundary to a park or garden without interrupting the view.
– ORIGIN early 18th cent.: from French, said to be from the cry of surprise on suddenly encountering such an obstacle.

ha ha ▶ exclamation used to represent laughter or open amusement.
– ORIGIN natural utterance: first recorded in Old English (compare with HA¹).

haham /'hɑːhəm/ (also **chacham**) ▶ noun a spiritual leader among Sephardic Jews, or, more generally, a person learned in Jewish law.
– ORIGIN from Hebrew *ḥāḵām* 'wise'.

Hahn /hɑːn/, Otto (1879–1968), German chemist, co-discoverer of nuclear fission. Together with Lise Meitner he discovered the new element protactinium in 1917. The pair discovered nuclear fission in 1938 with **Fritz Strassmann** (1902–80). Nobel Prize for Chemistry (1944).

hahnium /'hɑːnɪəm/ ▶ noun [mass noun] the name formerly proposed by the American Chemical Society for the chemical element of atomic number 105 (**dubnium**), and by IUPAC for element 108 (**hassium**).
– ORIGIN 1970s: named in honour of O. HAHN.

Haida /'hʌɪdə/ ▶ noun (pl. same or **Haidas**) **1** a member of an American Indian people living on the Pacific coast of Canada.
2 [mass noun] the language of this people, now almost extinct.
▶ adjective of or relating to this people or their language.
– ORIGIN the name in Haida, literally 'people'.

Haifa /'hʌɪfə/ the chief port of Israel, in the north-west of the country on the Mediterranean coast; pop. 248,200 (est. 1993).

Haig, Douglas, 1st Earl Haig of Bemersyde (1861–1928), British Field Marshal. During the First World War he served as Commander-in-Chief of British forces in France, maintaining a strategy of attrition throughout his command.

haik /heɪk, 'hɑːɪk/ (also **haick**) ▶ noun a large outer wrap, typically white, worn by people from North Africa.
– ORIGIN early 18th cent.: from Arabic *ḥā'ik*.

Haikou /hʌɪ'kəʊ/ the capital of Hainan autonomous region, a port on the NE coast of Hainan island; pop. 410,000 (1990).

haiku /'hʌɪkuː/ ▶ noun (pl. same or **haikus**) a Japanese poem of seventeen syllables, in three lines of five, seven, and five, traditionally evoking images of the natural world.
■an English imitation of this.
– ORIGIN Japanese, contracted form of *haikai no ku* 'light verse'.

hail¹ ▶ noun [mass noun] pellets of frozen rain which fall in showers from cumulonimbus clouds.
■[in sing.] a large number of things hurled forcefully through the air, especially with intent to harm: *a hail of bullets.*
▶ verb [no obj.] (**it hails**, **it is hailing**, etc.) hail falls: *it hailed so hard we had to stop.*
– ORIGIN Old English *hagol*, *hægl* (noun), *hagalian* (verb), of Germanic origin; related to Dutch *hagel* and German *Hagel*.

hail² ▶ verb [with obj.] **1** call out to (someone) to attract attention: *I hailed her in English.*
■signal (an approaching taxi) to stop.
2 [with obj.] (often **be hailed**) acclaim enthusiastically as being a specified thing: *he has been hailed as the new James Dean.*
3 [no obj.] (**hail from**) have one's home or origins in (a place): *they hail from Turkey.*
▶ exclamation archaic expressing greeting or acclaim: *hail, Caesar!*
▶ noun a shout or call used to attract attention.
– PHRASES **within hail** at a distance within which someone may be called to; within earshot.
– DERIVATIVES **hailer** noun.
– ORIGIN Middle English: from the obsolete adjective *hail* 'healthy' (occurring in greetings and toasts, such as *wæs hæil*: see WASSAIL), from Old Norse *heill*, related to HALE¹ and WHOLE.

Haile Selassie /ˌhʌɪli səˈlasi/ (1892–1975), emperor of Ethiopia 1930–74; born *Tafari Makonnen*. In exile in Britain during the Italian occupation of Ethiopia (1936–41), he was restored to the throne by the Allies and ruled until deposed by a military coup. He is revered by the Rastafarian religious sect.

hail-fellow-well-met ▶ adjective showing excessive familiarity: *Arnold was very cheerful in a hail-fellow-well-met sort of way.*

Hail Mary ▶ noun (pl. **Hail Marys**) a prayer to the Virgin Mary used chiefly by Roman Catholics, beginning with part of Luke 1:28. Also called AVE MARIA.

hailstone ▶ noun a pellet of hail.

Hailwood, Mike (1940–81), English racing motorcyclist; full name *Stanley Michael Bailey Hailwood*. He won the Isle of Man TT a record fourteen times and was world champion nine times in three different classes.

Hainan /hʌɪ'nan/ an island in the South China Sea, forming an autonomous region of China; pop. 6,420,000 (1990); capital, Haikou.

Hainaut /eɪ'nəʊ, '(h)enəʊ/ a province of southern Belgium; capital, Mons.

Haiphong /hʌɪ'fɒŋ/ a port in northern Vietnam, on the delta of the Red River in the Gulf of Tonkin; pop. 783,100 (est. 1992).

hair ▶ noun **1** any of the fine thread-like strands growing from the skin of humans, mammals, and some other animals.
■a similar strand growing from the epidermis of a plant, or forming part of a living cell. ■ (**a hair**) a very small quantity or extent: *his magic takes him a hair above the competition.*
2 [mass noun] such strands collectively, especially those growing on a person's head: *a woman with shoulder-length fair hair.*
– PHRASES **hair of the dog** informal an alcoholic drink taken to cure a hangover. [ORIGIN: from *hair of the dog that bit you*, formerly recommended as an efficacious remedy for the bite of a mad dog.] **a hair's breadth** a very small amount or margin: *you escaped death by a hair's breadth.* **in** (or **out of**) **someone's hair** informal annoying (or ceasing to annoy) someone: *they sent him to America, just to get him out of their hair.* **keep your hair on!** Brit. informal used to urge someone not to panic or lose their temper. **let one's hair down** informal behave wildly or uninhibitedly. **make someone's hair stand on end** alarm or horrify someone. **not turn a hair** remain apparently unmoved or unaffected. **split hairs** make small and overfine distinctions.
– DERIVATIVES **haired** adjective [in combination] *a curly-haired boy*, **hairless** adjective, **hair-like** adjective.
– ORIGIN Old English *hær*, of Germanic origin; related to Dutch *haar* and German *Haar*.

hairband ▶ noun a band for securing or tying back one's hair.

hairbrush ▶ noun a brush for smoothing a person's hair.

haircloth ▶ noun [mass noun] stiff cloth woven with a cotton or linen warp and horsehair weft.

haircut ▶ noun the style in which a person's hair is cut.
■an act of cutting a person's hair.

hairdo ▶ noun (pl. **-os**) informal an act of styling a woman's hair.
■the style of a woman's hair.

hairdresser ▶ noun a person who cuts and styles hair as an occupation.
– DERIVATIVES **hairdressing** noun.

hairdryer (also **hairdrier**) ▶ noun an electrical device for drying a person's hair by blowing warm air over it.

hair grass ▶ noun [mass noun] a slender-stemmed grass of temperate and cool regions.
● *Deschampsia*, *Aira*, and other genera, family Gramineae.

hairgrip ▶ noun Brit. a flat hairpin with the ends close together.

hairless bat ▶ noun an almost hairless black free-tailed bat found in SE Asia.
● Genus *Cheiromeles*, family Molossidae: two species, in particular *C. torquatus*.

hairline ▶ noun **1** the edge of a person's hair, especially on the forehead.
2 [as modifier] very thin or fine: *a hairline fracture.*

hairnet ▶ noun a piece of fine meshwork for confining the hair.

hairpiece ▶ noun a patch or bunch of false hair used to augment a person's natural hair.

hairpin ▶ noun a U-shaped pin for fastening the hair.

hairpin bend ▶ noun Brit. a sharp U-shaped bend in a road.

hair-raising ▶**adjective** extremely alarming, astonishing, or frightening: *hair-raising adventures.*

hair shirt ▶**noun** a shirt of haircloth, formerly worn by penitents and ascetics.
▶**adjective** (**hair-shirt** or **hair-shirted**) austere and self-sacrificing.

hairslide ▶**noun** Brit. a clip for keeping a woman's hair in position.

hair space ▶**noun** Printing a very thin space between letters or words.

hair-splitting ▶**adjective** characterized by or fond of small and overfine distinctions: *the legal experts have a particularly hair-splitting mentality.*
▶**noun** [mass noun] the action of making small and overfine distinctions; quibbling.
– DERIVATIVES **hair-splitter** noun.

hairspray ▶**noun** [mass noun] a solution sprayed on to a person's hair to keep it in place.

hairspring ▶**noun** a slender flat coiled spring regulating the movement of the balance wheel in a watch.

hairstreak ▶**noun** a butterfly with a narrow streak or row of dots on the underside of the hindwing and a small tail-like projection on the hindwing.
• Many genera in the family Lycaenidae.

hairstyle ▶**noun** a particular way in which a person's hair is cut or arranged.

hairstylist ▶**noun** a person who cuts and styles people's hair professionally.
– DERIVATIVES **hairstyling** noun.

hair trigger ▶**noun** a trigger of a firearm set for release at the slightest pressure.
■[as modifier] figurative liable to change suddenly and violently: *a hair-trigger temperament.*

hair worm ▶**noun** another term for **HORSEHAIR WORM**.

hairy ▶**adjective** (**hairier**, **hairiest**) **1** covered with hair, especially thick or long hair: *a hairy chest.*
■having a rough feel or appearance suggestive of coarse hair: *a hairy tweed coat and skirt.*
2 informal alarming and difficult: *we drove up yet another hairy mountain road.*
– DERIVATIVES **hairily** adverb, **hairiness** noun.

Haiti /ˈheɪti/ a country in the Caribbean, occupying the western third of the island of Hispaniola; pop. 7,041,000 (est. 1994); official languages, Haitian Creole, French; capital, Port-au-Prince.

The area was ceded to France by Spain in 1697, and many slaves were imported from West Africa to work on sugar plantations. In 1791 the slaves rose in rebellion under Toussaint L'Ouverture, and in 1804 the colony was proclaimed an independent state under the name of Haiti. It was administered by the US 1915–34 after a succession of corrupt dictatorships. From 1957 to 1986 the country was under the oppressive dictatorship of the Duvalier family. Haiti's first democratically chosen President was elected in 1990 but overthrown by the military the following year; democracy was restored by US and UN intervention in 1994.

Haitian /ˈheɪʃɪən, -ʃ(ə)n/ ▶**adjective** of or relating to Haiti, its inhabitants, or their language.
▶**noun 1** a native or inhabitant of Haiti.
2 (also **Haitian Creole**) [mass noun] the French-based Creole language spoken in Haiti.

Haitink /ˈhʌɪtɪŋk/, Bernard (Johann Herman) (b.1929), Dutch conductor, principal conductor of the London Philharmonic Orchestra 1967–79 and musical director of Glyndebourne (1977–87) and Covent Garden (from 1987).

haji /ˈhadʒiː/ (also **hajji**) ▶**noun** (pl. **hajis**) a Muslim who has been to Mecca as a pilgrim: [as title] *Haji Hadi.*
– ORIGIN from Persian and Turkish *ḥājjī*, *ḥājī*, from Arabic *ḥajj* (see **HAJJ**).

hajj /hadʒ/ (also **haj**) ▶**noun** the Muslim pilgrimage to Mecca which takes place in the last month of the year, and which all Muslims are expected to make at least once during their lifetime.
– ORIGIN from Arabic *(al-) ḥajj* '(the Great) Pilgrimage'.

haka /ˈhɑːkə/ ▶**noun** a Maori ceremonial war dance involving chanting, an imitation of which is performed by New Zealand rugby teams before a match.
– ORIGIN Maori.

hakama /ˈhakəmə, ˈhɑː-/ ▶**noun** [treated as sing. or pl.] loose trousers with many pleats in the front, forming part of Japanese formal dress.
– ORIGIN mid 19th cent.: Japanese.

hake ▶**noun 1** a large-headed elongated fish with long jaws and strong teeth. It is a valuable commercial food fish.
• Family Merlucciidae and genus *Merluccius*: several species, including the **European hake** (*M. merluccius*).
2 any of a number of similar fishes related to the true hakes.
• Species in several families, especially in the NW Atlantic genus *Urophycis* (family Phycidae).
– ORIGIN Middle English: perhaps from Old English *haca* 'hook'.

Hakenkreuz /ˈhɑːk(ə)nˌkrɔɪts, German ˈhaːkən-ˌkrɔyts/ ▶**noun** a swastika, especially in its clockwise form as a Nazi symbol.
– ORIGIN German, from *Haken* 'hook' + *Kreuz* 'cross'.

hakim /haˈkiːm/ ▶**noun 1** a physician using traditional remedies in India and Muslim countries. [ORIGIN: from Arabic *ḥakīm* 'wise man, physician'.]
2 a judge, ruler, or governor in India and Muslim countries. [ORIGIN: from Arabic *ḥākim* 'ruler'.]

Hakka /ˈhakə/ ▶**noun 1** a member of a people of SE China who migrated from the north during the 12th century.
2 [mass noun] the dialect of Chinese spoken by this people, with about 27 million speakers. Also called **KEJIA**.
▶**adjective** of or relating to this people or their language.
– ORIGIN from Chinese (Cantonese dialect) *haàk ka* 'stranger'.

Hakluyt /ˈhakluːt/, Richard (*c.*1552–1616), English geographer and historian. He compiled *Principal Navigations, Voyages, and Discoveries of the English Nation* (1598), a collection of accounts of great voyages of discovery.

Hakodate /ˌhɑːkəʊˈdɑːteɪ/ a port in northern Japan, on the southern tip of the island of Hokkaido; pop. 307,000 (1990).

Halab /hɑːˈlɑːb/ Arabic name for **ALEPPO**.

Halacha /ˌhalɑːˈxɑː, həˈlɑːkə/ (also **Halakah**) ▶**noun** [mass noun] Jewish law and jurisprudence, based on the Talmud.
– DERIVATIVES **Halachic** adjective.
– ORIGIN from Hebrew *hălāḵāh* 'law'.

Halafian /həˈlɑːfɪən/ ▶**adjective** Archaeology of, relating to, or denoting a prehistoric culture extending from Syria to the Mediterranean coast and eastern Turkey (late 6th and early 5th millennium BC). This culture is identified primarily by the use of polychrome pottery (**Halaf ware**).
■[as noun **the Halafian**] the Halafian culture or period.
– ORIGIN 1930s: from the place name Tell *Halaf* (in NE Syria, where the pottery was first discovered) + **-IAN**.

halal /həˈlɑːl/ ▶**adjective** denoting or relating to meat prepared as prescribed by Muslim law: *halal butchers.*
■religiously acceptable according to Muslim law: *halal banking.*
▶**noun** [mass noun] halal meat.
– ORIGIN mid 19th cent.: from Arabic *ḥalāl* 'according to religious law'.

halala /həˈlɑːlə/ ▶**noun** (pl. same or **halalas**) a monetary unit of Saudi Arabia, equal to one hundredth of a rial.
– ORIGIN Arabic.

halation /həˈleɪʃ(ə)n/ ▶**noun** [mass noun] the spreading of light beyond its proper boundaries to form a fog round the edges of a bright image in a photograph or on a television screen.
– ORIGIN mid 19th cent.: formed irregularly from **HALO** + **-ATION**.

halberd /ˈhalbəːd/ (also **halbert**) ▶**noun** historical a combined spear and battleaxe.
– ORIGIN late 15th cent.: from French *hallebarde*, from Italian *alabarda*, from Middle High German *helmbarde* (from *helm* 'handle' + *barde* 'hatchet').

halberdier /ˌhalbəˈdɪə/ ▶**noun** historical a man armed with a halberd.
– ORIGIN early 16th cent.: from French *hallebardier*, from *hallebarde* (see **HALBERD**).

halcyon /ˈhalsɪən, -ʃ(ə)n/ ▶**adjective** denoting a period of time in the past that was idyllically happy and peaceful: *the halcyon days of the mid 1980s, when profits were soaring.*
▶**noun 1** a tropical Asian and African kingfisher with brightly coloured plumage.
• Genus *Halcyon*, family Alcedinidae: many species.
2 a mythical bird said by ancient writers to breed in a nest floating at sea at the winter solstice, charming the wind and waves into calm.
– ORIGIN late Middle English (in the mythological sense): via Latin from Greek *alkuōn* 'kingfisher' (also *halkuōn*, by association with *hals* 'sea' and *kuōn* 'conceiving').

Haldane /ˈhɔːldeɪn/, J. B. S. (1892–1964), Scottish mathematical biologist; full name *John Burdon Sanderson Haldane*. As well as contributing to the development of population genetics, Haldane became well known as a popularizer of science and as an outspoken Marxist.

haldi /ˈhʌldi/ ▶**noun** Indian term for **TURMERIC**.
– ORIGIN via Hindi from Sanskrit *haridrā*.

Hale, George Ellery (1868–1938), American astronomer. He discovered that sunspots are associated with strong magnetic fields and invented the spectroheliograph. He also initiated the construction of several large telescopes.

hale¹ ▶**adjective** (of an old person) strong and healthy: *only just sixty, very* **hale and hearty**.
– ORIGIN Old English, northern variant of *hāl* 'whole'.

hale² ▶**verb** [with obj. and adverbial of direction] archaic drag or draw forcibly: *he haled an old man out of the audience.*
– ORIGIN Middle English: from Old French *haler*, from Old Norse *hala*.

h

Hale–Bopp a periodic comet which passed close to the sun in the spring of 1997 and was one of the brightest of the 20th century.
– ORIGIN named after Alan Hale and Thomas *Bopp*, the American astronomers who discovered it (independently of each other).

haler /ˈhɑːlə/ ▶**noun** (pl. same or **haleru** /ˈhɑːləruː/) a monetary unit of the Czech Republic and Slovakia, equal to one hundredth of a koruna.
– ORIGIN from Czech *haléř*, from Middle High German *haller*, from *Schwäbisch Hall*, a town in Germany where coins were minted.

halesome ▶**adjective** chiefly Scottish wholesome: *the friendly pub and halesome fare.*

Halesowen /heɪlzˈəʊɪn/ an engineering town in the west Midlands; pop. 57,530 (1981).

Haley /ˈheɪli/, Bill (1925–81), American rock-and-roll singer; full name *William John Clifton Haley*. His song 'Rock Around the Clock' (1954) was the first to popularize rock and roll.

half ▶**noun** (pl. **halves**) either of two equal or corresponding parts into which something is or can be divided: *two and a half years | the northern half of the island | divided* **in half** | *reduced* **by half**.
■either of two equal periods of time into which a sports game or a performance is divided. ■ Brit. informal half a pint of beer or a similar drink: ***a half of*** *bitter.* ■ informal a half-price fare or ticket, especially for a child. ■ Golf a score for an individual hole that is the same as one's opponent's. ■ short for **HALFBACK**.
▶**predeterminer**, **pronoun**, & **adjective** an amount equal to a half: [as predeterminer] *half an hour | almost half the children turned up* | [as pronoun] ***half of*** *the lectures are delivered by him* | [as adj.] *the last half century.*
■amounting to a part thought of as roughly a half: [as predeterminer] *half the audience were blubbing away* | [as pronoun] ***half of*** *them are gatecrashers.*
▶**adverb** to the extent of half: *the glass was half full.*
■[often in combination] to a certain extent; partly: *the chicken is half-cooked.*
– PHRASES **a —— and a half** informal used to indicate that one considers a particular person or thing to be an impressive example of their kind: *Aunt Edie was a woman and a half.* **at half cock** see **HALF-COCK**. **half the battle** see **BATTLE**. **half a chance** informal the slightest opportunity: *given half a chance he can make anything work.* **half an eye** see **EYE**. **the half of it** [usu. with negative] informal the most important part or aspect of something: *you don't know the half of it.* **half one** (**two**, etc.) informal way of saying *half past one* (*two*, etc.). **half past one** (**two**, etc.) thirty minutes after one (two, etc.) o'clock. **half the time** see **TIME**. **not do things by halves** do things thoroughly or extravagantly. **not half 1** not nearly: *he is not half such a fool as they thought.* **2** informal not at all: *the players are not half bad.* **3** Brit. informal to an extreme degree; very much so: *she didn't half flare up!* **too —— by half** used to emphasize something bad: *the idea seems too superstitious by half.*
– ORIGIN Old English *half*, *healf*, of Germanic origin; related to Dutch *half* and German *halb* (adjectives).

The earliest meaning of the Germanic base was 'side', also a noun sense in Old English.

half a crown ▶ noun another term for **HALF-CROWN**.

half a dozen ▶ noun another term for **HALF-DOZEN**.

half-and-half ▶ adverb & adjective in equal parts: [as adv.] views were split almost exactly half-and-half | [as adj.] a half-and-half mixture.
▶ noun [mass noun] N. Amer. a mixture of milk and cream.

half-arsed (US **-assed**, **-ass**) ▶ adjective vulgar slang incompetent; inadequate.

halfback ▶ noun a player in a ball game such as soccer, rugby, or field hockey whose position is between the forwards and fullbacks.

half-baked ▶ adjective (of an idea or philosophy) not fully thought through; lacking a sound basis: half-baked notions of Teutonic superiority.
■ foolish: half-baked visionaries without a mission.

half-ball ▶ noun Billiards & Snooker a stroke in which the centre of the cue ball is aimed at the edge of the object ball: [as modifier] a half-ball shot.

halfbeak ▶ noun a slender shoaling fish of coastal areas, with small pectoral fins and the lower jaw lengthened into a beak. It is related to the flying fishes and often skitters along the surface. Also called **GARFISH** in Australia and New Zealand.
● Several genera and species in the family Exocoetidae, including the widely distributed Euleptorhamphus viridis.

half binding ▶ noun [mass noun] a type of bookbinding in which the spine and corners are bound in one material (typically leather) and the rest of the cover in another.
– DERIVATIVES **half-bound** adjective.

half blood ▶ noun **1** [mass noun] the relationship between people having one parent in common: brothers and sisters of the half blood.
■ [count noun] a person related to another in this way.
2 offensive another term for **HALF-BREED**.
– DERIVATIVES **half-blooded** adjective (only in sense 2).

half-blue ▶ noun Brit. a person who has represented Oxford or Cambridge University in a minor sport or as a second choice in any sport.
■ the distinction gained in this way.

half board ▶ noun [mass noun] Brit. provision of bed, breakfast, and one main meal at a hotel or guest house: guests on half board.

half-boot ▶ noun a boot that reaches up to the calf.

half-bottle ▶ noun a bottle that is half the standard size.

half-breed ▶ noun offensive a person whose parents are of different races, especially the offspring of an American Indian and a person of white European ancestry.

half-brother ▶ noun a brother with whom one has only one parent in common.

half-butt ▶ noun a long billiard cue about 2.4 m (8 feet) in length.

half-caste ▶ noun offensive a person whose parents are of different races.

half-century ▶ noun a period of fifty years.
■ a score of fifty in a sporting event, especially a batsman's score of fifty in cricket.

half-cock ▶ noun the partly raised position of the cock of a gun.
– PHRASES **at half-cock** (of a gun) with the cock partly raised. ■ figurative when only partly ready: the postponement saved the army from setting off another attack at half-cock.
– DERIVATIVES **half-cocked** adjective.

half-crown (also **half a crown**) ▶ noun a former British coin and monetary unit equal to two shillings and sixpence (12½p).

half-cut ▶ adjective Brit. informal drunk.

half-deck ▶ noun a deck reaching half the length of a ship or boat, fore or aft.
– DERIVATIVES **half-decked** adjective.

half-door ▶ noun a door of half the usual size, typically covering the bottom half of an opening (e.g. in a stable).

half-dozen (also **half a dozen**) ▶ noun a set or group of six: a half-dozen slices of smoked salmon.

half-duplex ▶ adjective (of a communications system or computer circuit) allowing the transmission of signals in both directions but not simultaneously.

half-hardy ▶ adjective (of a plant) able to grow outdoors at all times except in severe frost: a half-hardy annual.

half-hear ▶ verb [with obj.] [usu. as adj. **half-heard**] hear (something) without being completely aware of it or without being able to make it out fully: half-heard conversations.

half-hearted ▶ adjective without enthusiasm or energy: a half-hearted attempt.
– DERIVATIVES **half-heartedly** adverb, **half-heartedness** noun.

half hitch ▶ noun a knot formed by passing the end of a rope round its standing part and then through the loop.

half holiday ▶ noun a day of which either the morning or (usually) the afternoon is taken as a holiday, especially at school.

half-hose ▶ noun [mass noun] socks covering the lower leg.

half-hour ▶ noun (also **half an hour**) a period of thirty minutes: buses run every half-hour.
■ a point in time thirty minutes after any full hour of the clock: the library clock struck the half-hour.
– DERIVATIVES **half-hourly** adjective & adverb.

half-hunter ▶ noun a pocket watch with a hinged cover in the middle of which a small opening or window allows one to read the approximate time.

half-inch ▶ noun a unit of length half as large as an inch.
▶ verb [with obj.] Brit. informal steal: she had her handbag half-inched. [ORIGIN: 1920s: rhyming slang for 'pinch'.]

half-integer ▶ noun a number obtained by dividing an odd integer by two (½, 1½, 2½, etc.).
– DERIVATIVES **half-integral** adjective.

half landing ▶ noun Brit. an area of floor where a flight of stairs turns through 180 degrees.

half-lap ▶ noun another term for **LAP JOINT**.

half-length ▶ adjective of approximately half the normal length.
■ (of a painting or sculpture) showing a person down to their waist.
▶ noun a painting or sculpture of a person down to their waist.

half-life ▶ noun the time taken for the radioactivity of a specified isotope to fall to half its original value.
■ the time required for any specified property (e.g. the concentration of a substance in the body) to decrease by half.

half-light ▶ noun [mass noun] dim light such as at dusk: the trees had a slightly spooky look in the half-light.

half mast ▶ noun the position of a flag which is being flown some way below the top of its staff as a mark of respect for a person who has died: each club flew its flag at half mast.
■ chiefly humorous a position lower than normal or acceptable, especially for clothes: his tie was at half mast.

half measure ▶ noun (usu. **half measures**) an action or policy that is not forceful or decisive enough: there are no half measures with this company.

half-moon ▶ noun the moon when only half its illuminated surface is visible from the earth; the first or last quarter.
■ the time when this occurs. ■ a semicircular or crescent-shaped object: [as modifier] half-moon spectacles.

half-move ▶ noun Chess a move made by one player (especially in the context of the analysis of play made by a chess-playing computer program).

half nelson ▶ noun see **NELSON**.

half note ▶ noun Music, chiefly N. Amer. a minim.

half pay ▶ noun [mass noun] half of a person's normal or previous salary or wages, especially as paid to military officers on retirement: he retired from the army as captain on half pay.

halfpenny /ˈheɪpni/ (also **ha'penny**) ▶ noun (pl. for separate coins **-pennies**, for a sum of money **-pence** /ˈheɪp(ə)ns/) a former British coin equal to half an old or new penny. The last halfpenny was withdrawn in 1984.

halfpennyworth /ˈheɪpθ, ˈheɪpnɪˌwəθ/ (also **ha'p'orth**) ▶ noun Brit. as much as could be bought for a halfpenny.
■ [usu. with negative] (**ha'p'orth**) informal a negligible amount: he's never done a ha'p'orth of bother.
– PHRASES **don't spoil the ship for a ha'p'orth of tar**

proverb don't risk the failure of a large project by trying to economize on trivial things. [ORIGIN: referring to the use of tar to keep flies off sores on sheep (from dialect pronunciation of sheep as ship).]

half-pie ▶ adjective NZ informal imperfect; mediocre.
– ORIGIN pie perhaps from Maori pai 'good'.

half-pipe ▶ noun a channel made of concrete or cut into the snow with a U-shaped cross section, used by skateboarders, rollerbladers, or snowboarders to perform jumps and other manoeuvres.

half plate ▶ noun Brit. a photographic plate measuring 4¾ × 6½ inches (c.16.5 × 10.8 cm).

half-price ▶ adjective & adverb costing half the normal price: [as adj.] half-price admission | [as adv.] a brooch I bought half-price in the sale.
▶ noun half the usual price: many shoes at half price.

half relief ▶ noun [mass noun] a method of moulding, carving, or stamping in relief a design in which figures project to half their true proportions.
■ [count noun] a sculpture or carving in half relief.

half-round ▶ adjective semicircular.
■ (of a file) having one flat side and the other rounded.

half seas over ▶ adjective [predic.] Brit. informal, dated fairly drunk.

half-sister ▶ noun a sister with whom one has only one parent in common.

half-sovereign ▶ noun a former British gold coin worth ten shillings (50p).

half-standard ▶ noun a tree or shrub that grows on an erect stem of half height and stands alone without support.

half step ▶ noun Music a semitone.

half-term ▶ noun Brit. a short holiday about halfway through a school term: I'm not coming home at half-term.

half-tester ▶ noun historical a canopy extending over half the length of a bed.
■ a bed with such a canopy.

half-timbered ▶ adjective having walls with a timber frame and a brick or plaster filling.
– DERIVATIVES **half-timbering** noun.

half-time ▶ noun the time at which half of a game or contest is completed, especially when marked by an interval: Spain led 9–7 at half-time.

half-title ▶ noun the title of a book, printed on the right-hand page before the title page.
■ the title of a section of a book printed on the right-hand page before it. ■ a page on which a title of either of these kinds is printed.

half-tone ▶ noun **1** [usu. as modifier] a reproduction of a photograph or other image in which the various tones of grey or colour are produced by variously sized dots of ink: half-tone illustrations.
2 Music, chiefly US a semitone.

half-track ▶ noun a military or other vehicle with wheels at the front and caterpillar tracks at the rear.

half-truth ▶ noun a statement that conveys only part of the truth, especially one used deliberately in order to deceive someone.

half-uncial ▶ adjective of a style of medieval letter showing features of both uncial and cursive script.
▶ noun a letter in such a style.

half-volley ▶ noun (chiefly in tennis or soccer) a strike or kick of the ball made immediately after it bounces off the ground.

halfway ▶ adverb & adjective at or to a point equidistant between two others: [as adv.] he stopped halfway down the passage | [as adj.] during the night we passed Kingoonya, the halfway mark.
■ in the middle of a period of time: [as adv.] halfway through the night. ■ [as adv.] to some extent: I'm incapable of doing anything even halfway decent.

halfway house ▶ noun [in sing.] the halfway point in a progression.
■ a compromise between two different or opposing views or courses of action: the formula seems a good halfway house and avoids another row. ■ a centre for rehabilitating former prisoners, psychiatric patients, or others unused to non-institutional life. ■ historical an inn midway between two towns.

halfway line ▶ noun a line across a sports field midway between the ends.

halfwit ▶ noun informal a foolish or stupid person.
– DERIVATIVES **half-witted** adjective, **half-wittedly** adverb, **half-wittedness** noun.

half-yearly ▶ adjective & adverb at intervals of six

months: [as adj.] *the loan was to be repaid by 80 half-yearly instalments* | [as adv.] *the interest will be paid half-yearly in June and December.*
■[as adj.] relating to half a financial year: *half-yearly sales.*

halibut /ˈhalɪbət/ ▶ **noun** (pl. same) a northern marine fish which is the largest of the flatfishes and important as a food fish.
• Genus *Hippoglossus*, family Pleuronectidae: *H. hippoglossus* of the Atlantic and *H. stenolepis* of the Pacific. See also **GREENLAND HALIBUT**.
■used in names of large edible flatfishes of other families, e.g. **Queensland halibut**.
– ORIGIN late Middle English: from *haly* 'holy' + obsolete *butt* 'flatfish' (because it was often eaten on holy days).

Haliç /haˈliːtʃ/ Turkish name for **GOLDEN HORN**.

Halicarnassus /ˌhalɪkɑːˈnasəs/ an ancient Greek city on the SW coast of Asia Minor, at what is now the Turkish city of Bodrum. It is the site of the Mausoleum of Halicarnassus, one of the Seven Wonders of the World.

halide /ˈheɪlʌɪd/ ▶ **noun** Chemistry a binary compound of a halogen with another element or group.

Halifax /ˈhalɪfaks/ **1** the capital of Nova Scotia, Canada; pop. 67,800 (1991); metropolitan areas pop. 320,500. It is Canada's principal ice-free port on the Atlantic coast. [ORIGIN: named after George Montagu Dunk (1716–71), the second earl of *Halifax*.]
2 a town in northern England, on the River Calder, formerly in Yorkshire; pop. 77,350 (1981).

halite /ˈhalʌɪt/ ▶ **noun** [mass noun] sodium chloride as a mineral, typically occurring as colourless cubic crystals; rock salt.
– ORIGIN mid 19th cent.: from Greek *hals* 'salt' + **-ITE**[1].

halitosis /ˌhalɪˈtəʊsɪs/ ▶ **noun** technical term for **BAD BREATH**.
– ORIGIN late 19th cent.: from Latin *halitus* 'breath' + **-OSIS**.

Hall, (Marguerite) Radclyffe (1883–1943), English novelist and poet. She is chiefly remembered for her novel *The Well of Loneliness* (1928), an exploration of a lesbian relationship, which caused outrage and was banned in Britain for many years.

hall ▶ **noun 1** the room or space just inside the front entrance of a house or flat: *an entrance hall.*
■N. Amer. a corridor or area on to which rooms open.
2 a large room for meetings, concerts, or other events: [in names] *the Royal Albert Hall.*
■a large public room in a mansion or palace used for receptions and banquets. ■ the room used for meals in a college, university, or school: *he dined* ***in hall.*** ■(also **hall of residence**) chiefly Brit. a university building containing rooms for students to live in. ■ the principal living room of a medieval house. ■ the building of a guild.
3 [usu. in names] Brit. a large country house, especially one with a landed estate: *Darlington Hall.*
– ORIGIN Old English *hall, heall* (originally denoting a roofed space, located centrally, for the communal use of a tribal chief and his people); of Germanic origin and related to German *Halle*, Dutch *hall*, also to Norwegian and Swedish *hall*.

Halle /ˈhalə/ a city in east central Germany, on the River Saale, in Saxony-Anhalt; pop. 303,000 (1991).

Hallé /ˈhaleɪ/, Sir Charles (1819–95), German-born pianist and conductor; born *Karl Halle*. He left Paris in 1848 and settled in Manchester, where he founded the Hallé Orchestra (1858).

Hall effect ▶ **noun** Physics the production of a potential difference across an electrical conductor when a magnetic field is applied in a direction perpendicular to that of the flow of current.
– ORIGIN early 20th cent.: named after Edwin H. *Hall* (1855–1938), American physicist.

Hallel /ˈhalɛl, haˈleɪl/ ▶ **noun** (usu. **the Hallel**) a portion of the service for certain Jewish festivals, consisting of Psalms 113–118: [as modifier] *the Hallel psalms.*
– ORIGIN from Hebrew *hallēl* 'praise'.

hallelujah /ˌhalɪˈluːjə/ (also **alleluia**) ▶ **exclamation** God be praised (uttered in worship or as an expression of rejoicing).
▶**noun** an utterance of the word 'hallelujah' as an expression of worship or rejoicing.
■(usu. **alleluia**) a piece of music or church liturgy containing this: *the Gospel comes after the Alleluia verse.*
– ORIGIN Old English, via ecclesiastical Latin *alleluia* from Greek *allēlouia* (in the Septuagint), or (from the 16th century) directly from Hebrew *hallĕlūyāh* 'praise ye the Lord'.

Haller /ˈhalə/, Albrecht von (1708–77), Swiss anatomist and physiologist. He pioneered the study of neurology and experimental physiology and wrote the first textbook of physiology.

Halley /ˈhali, ˈhɔːli/, Edmond (1656–1742), English astronomer and mathematician. He is best known for identifying a bright comet (later named after him), and for successfully predicting its return.

Halley's Comet a periodical comet with an orbital period of about 76 years, its reappearance in 1758–9 having been predicted by Edmond Halley. It was first recorded in 240 BC and last appeared, rather faintly, in 1985–6.

Halliday /ˈhalɪdeɪ/, Michael Alexander Kirkwood (b.1925), English linguist. He built on the work of J. R. Firth in pursuit of a psychologically and sociologically realistic overall theory of language and its functions.

hallmark ▶ **noun** a mark stamped on articles of gold, silver, or platinum by the British assay offices, certifying their standard of purity.
■a distinctive feature, especially one of excellence: *the tiny bubbles are the hallmark of fine champagnes.*
▶**verb** [with obj.] stamp with a hallmark.
■designate as distinctive, especially for excellence.
– ORIGIN early 18th cent. (as a noun): from *Goldsmiths' Hall* in London, where articles were tested and stamped with such a mark.

hallo ▶ **exclamation**, **noun**, & **verb** variant spelling of **HELLO**.

Hall of Fame a national memorial in New York City containing busts and memorials honouring the achievements of famous Americans.
■[as noun] chiefly N. Amer. the class or category of those who have excelled in a particular activity: *the Hockey Hall of Fame.*
– DERIVATIVES **Hall of Famer** noun.

hall of residence ▶ **noun** see **HALL** (sense 2).

halloo ▶ **exclamation** used to incite dogs to the chase during a hunt.
■used to attract someone's attention.
▶**noun** a cry of 'halloo'.
▶**verb** (**halloos, hallooed**) [no obj.] cry or shout 'halloo' to attract attention or to give encouragement to dogs in hunting.
■[with obj.] shout to (someone) to attract their attention.
– ORIGIN mid 16th cent.: probably from the rare verb *hallow* 'pursue or urge on with shouts', from imitative Old French *haloer*.

hallow /ˈhaləʊ/ ▶ **verb** [with obj.] honour as holy: *the Ganges is hallowed as a sacred, cleansing river* | [as adj. **hallowed**] *hallowed ground.*
■formal make holy; consecrate. ■[as adj. **hallowed**] greatly revered or respected: *the hallowed turf of Wimbledon.*
▶**noun** archaic a saint or holy person.
– ORIGIN Old English *hālgian* (verb), *hālga* (noun), of Germanic origin; related to Dutch and German *heiligen*, also to **HOLY**.

Halloween (also **Hallowe'en**) ▶ **noun** the night of 31 October, the eve of All Saints' Day. Halloween is of pre-Christian origin, being associated with the Celtic festival Samhain, when ghosts and spirits were thought to be abroad. Adopted as a Christian festival, it gradually became a secular rather than a Christian observance, involving dressing up and the wearing of masks.
– ORIGIN late 18th cent.: contraction of *All Hallow Even* (see **HALLOW, EVEN**[2]).

Hallowes /ˈhaləʊz/, Odette (1912–95), French heroine of the Second World War; born *Marie Céline*. She worked as a British secret agent in occupied France from 1942 until captured in 1943. Imprisoned for two years, she refused to betray her associates in spite of torture and was awarded the George Cross in 1946.

hall porter ▶ **noun** Brit. a concierge or a person who carries guests' luggage in a hotel.

hallstand (US **hall tree**) ▶ **noun** a coat stand in the hall of a house.

Hallstatt /ˈhalʃtat/ ▶ **noun** [usu. as modifier] Archaeology a cultural phase of the late Bronze Age and early Iron Age in Europe (*c.*1200–600 BC in temperate continental areas), preceding the La Tène period. It is generally equated with the Urnfield complex and is associated with the early Celts.
– ORIGIN mid 19th cent.: the name of a village in Austria, site of a burial ground of this period.

halluces plural form of **HALLUX**.

hallucinate /həˈluːsɪneɪt/ ▶ **verb** [no obj.] experience a seemingly real perception of something not actually present, typically as a result of a mental disorder or of taking drugs: *they thought he was seeing things, hallucinating.*
■[with obj.] experience a hallucination of (something).
– DERIVATIVES **hallucinant** adjective & noun, **hallucinator** noun.
– ORIGIN mid 17th cent. (in the sense 'be deceived, have illusions'): from Latin *hallucinat-* 'gone astray in thought', from the verb *hallucinari*, from Greek *alussein* 'be uneasy or distraught'.

hallucination ▶ **noun** an experience involving the apparent perception of something not present: *he continued to suffer from horrific hallucinations.*

hallucinatory /həˈluːsɪnəˌt(ə)ri/ ▶ **adjective** of or resembling a hallucination: *a hallucinatory fantasy.*
■inducing hallucinations: *a hallucinatory drug.*

hallucinogen /həˈluːsɪnədʒ(ə)n/ ▶ **noun** a drug that causes hallucinations, such as LSD.
– DERIVATIVES **hallucinogenic** adjective.

hallux /ˈhaləks/ ▶ **noun** (pl. **halluces** /-jʊsiːz, -ləsiːz/) Anatomy a person's big toe.
■Zoology the innermost digit of the hind foot of vertebrates.
– ORIGIN mid 19th cent.: modern Latin alteration of medieval Latin *allex*, Latin *hallus*.

hallway ▶ **noun** another term for **HALL** (in sense 1).

halma /ˈhalmə/ ▶ **noun** [mass noun] a game played by two or four people using a board of 256 squares, with pieces advancing from one corner to the opposite corner by being moved over other pieces into vacant squares.
– ORIGIN late 19th cent.: from Greek, literally 'leap'.

Halmahera /ˌhalməˈhɪərə/ the largest of the Molucca Islands.

halo /ˈheɪləʊ/ ▶ **noun** (pl. **-oes** or **-os**) a disc or circle of light shown surrounding or above the head of a saint or holy person to represent their holiness.
■figurative the glory associated with an idealized person or thing: *he has long since lost his halo for many ordinary Russians.* ■ a circle or ring of something resembling a halo: *their frizzy haloes of hair.* ■ a circle of white or coloured light round the sun, moon, or other luminous body caused by refraction through ice crystals in the atmosphere.
▶**verb** (**-oes, -oed**) [with obj.] (usu. **be haloed**) surround with or as if with a halo.
– ORIGIN mid 16th cent. (denoting a circle of light round the sun etc.): from medieval Latin, from Latin *halos*, from Greek *halōs* 'disc of the sun or moon'.

halo- /ˈheɪləʊ/ ▶ **combining form 1** relating to salinity: *halophile.* [ORIGIN: from Greek *hals, halo-* 'salt'.]
2 representing **HALOGEN**.

halocarbon ▶ **noun** Chemistry a CFC or other compound in which the hydrogen of a hydrocarbon is replaced by halogens.

halo effect ▶ **noun** the tendency for an impression created in one area to influence opinion in another area.

haloform ▶ **noun** Chemistry a compound derived from methane by substituting three hydrogen atoms by halogen atoms, e.g. chloroform.
– ORIGIN 1930s: from **HALOGEN**, on the pattern of *chloroform*.

halogen /ˈhalədʒ(ə)n, ˈheɪl-/ ▶ **noun** Chemistry any of the elements fluorine, chlorine, bromine, iodine, and astatine, occupying group VIIA (17) of the periodic table. They are reactive non-metallic elements which form strongly acidic compounds with hydrogen from which simple salts can be made.
■[as modifier] denoting lamps and radiant heat sources using a filament surrounded by the vapour of iodine or another halogen: *a halogen bulb.*
– DERIVATIVES **halogenic** adjective.
– ORIGIN mid 19th cent.: from Greek *hals, halo-* 'salt' + **-GEN**.

halogenate /həˈlɒdʒɪneɪt/ ▶ **verb** [with obj.] [usu. as adj. **halogenated**] Chemistry introduce one or more halogen atoms into (a compound or molecule), usually in place of hydrogen.
– DERIVATIVES **halogenation** noun.

a cat | ɑː arm | ɛ bed | ɛː hair | ə ago | əː her | ɪ sit | i cosy | iː see | ɒ hot | ɔː saw | ʌ run | ʊ put | uː too | ʌɪ my | aʊ how | eɪ day | əʊ no | ɪə near | ɔɪ boy | ʊə poor | ʌɪə fire | aʊə sour

halon /ˈheɪlɒn/ ▶ noun any of a number of unreactive gaseous compounds of carbon with bromine and other halogens, used in fire extinguishers, but now known to damage the ozone layer.
– ORIGIN 1960s: from **HALOGEN** + **-ON**.

haloperidol /ˌhaləʊˈpɛrɪdɒl, ˌheɪlə(ʊ)-/ ▶ noun [mass noun] Medicine a synthetic antidepressant drug used chiefly in the treatment of psychotic conditions.
– ORIGIN 1960s: blend of **HALOGEN** and **PIPERIDINE** + **-OL**.

halophile /ˈhalə(ʊ)fʌɪl, ˈheɪl-/ ▶ noun Ecology an organism, especially a micro-organism, that grows in or can tolerate saline conditions.
– DERIVATIVES **halophilic** adjective.

halophyte /ˈhaləfʌɪt, ˈheɪl-/ ▶ noun Botany a plant adapted to growing in saline conditions, as in a salt marsh.

halothane /ˈhalə(ʊ)θeɪn/ ▶ noun [mass noun] Medicine a volatile synthetic organic compound used as a general anaesthetic.
● Chem. formula: $CF_3CHBrCl$.
– ORIGIN 1950s: blend of **HALOGEN** and **ETHANE**.

Hals /hals/, Frans (c.1580–1666), Dutch portrait and genre painter. He endowed his portraits with vitality, departing from conventional portraiture with works such as *The Banquet of the Officers of the St George Militia Company* (1616) and *The Laughing Cavalier* (1624).

Hälsingborg /ˌhɛlsɪŋˈbɔrj/ Swedish name for **HELSINGBORG**.

halt¹ ▶ verb bring or come to an abrupt stop: [with obj.] *there is growing pressure to halt the bloodshed* | [no obj.] *she halted in mid sentence*.
■ [in imperative] used as a military command to bring marching soldiers to a stop: *company, halt!*
▶ noun a suspension of movement or activity, typically a temporary one: *a halt in production* | *a bus screeched to a halt*.
■ Brit. a minor stopping place on a local railway line.
– PHRASES **call a halt** demand or order a stop: *he decided to **call a halt** to all further discussion*.
– ORIGIN late 16th cent.: originally in the phrase *make halt*, from German *haltmachen*, from *halten* 'to hold'.

halt² archaic ▶ adjective lame.
▶ verb [no obj.] walk with a limp: *he halted slightly in his walk*.
– ORIGIN Old English *healtian* (verb), *halt*, *healt* (adjective), of Germanic origin.

halter ▶ noun 1 a rope or strap placed around the head of a horse or other animal, used for leading or tethering it.
■ archaic a rope with a noose for hanging a person.
2 [usu. as modifier] a strap by which the bodice of a sleeveless dress or top is fastened or held behind at the neck, leaving the shoulders and back bare: *tourists in halter tops and shorts*.
▶ verb [with obj.] put a halter on (an animal).
■ archaic hang (someone).
– ORIGIN Old English *hælftre*, of Germanic origin, meaning 'something to hold things by'; related to German *Halfter*, also to **HELVE**.

halter-break ▶ verb [with obj.] accustom (a young horse) to wearing and being handled in a halter.

haltere /ˈhaltɪə/ ▶ noun (usu. **halteres**) Entomology the balancing organ of a two-winged fly, seen as either of a pair of knobbed filaments that take the place of the hindwings, vibrating during flight.
– ORIGIN mid 16th cent. (originally plural, denoting a pair of weights like dumb-bells held in the hands to give impetus when jumping): from Greek *haltēres* (plural), from *hallesthai* 'to leap'.

halter-neck ▶ adjective [attrib.] (of a woman's garment) held up by a strap around the neck.
▶ noun a garment with such a neckline.

halting ▶ adjective slow and hesitant, especially through lack of confidence; faltering: *she speaks halting English with a heavy accent*.
– DERIVATIVES **haltingly** adverb.

halva /ˈhalvɑː, -və/ (also **halvah**) ▶ noun [mass noun] a Middle Eastern sweet made of sesame flour and honey.
– ORIGIN Yiddish, or from Turkish *helva*, from Arabic and Persian *ḥalwā* 'sweetmeat'.

halve ▶ verb [with obj.] 1 divide into two parts of equal or roughly equal size: *halve the aubergine lengthways*.
■ reduce or be reduced by half: [no obj.] *pre-tax profits nearly halved to £5 m* | [with obj.] *his pledge to halve the deficit over the next four years*. ■ share (something)

equally with another person: *she insisted on halving the bill*. ■ Golf use the same number of strokes as one's opponent and thus draw (a hole or match).
2 [usu. as noun **halving**] fit (crossing timbers) together by cutting out half the thickness of each.
– ORIGIN Middle English: from **HALF**.

halvers /ˈhɑːvəz/ ▶ plural noun (in phrase **go halvers**) informal, chiefly Scottish, N. English, & N. Amer. agree to have a half share each.

halves plural form of **HALF**.

halwa /ˈhalwɑː/ (also **halwah**) ▶ noun [mass noun] a sweet Indian dish consisting of carrots or semolina boiled with milk, almonds, sugar, butter, and cardamom.
– ORIGIN from Arabic, literally 'sweetmeat'.

halyard /ˈhaljəd/ ▶ noun a rope used for raising and lowering a sail, yard, or flag on a sailing ship.
– ORIGIN late Middle English *halier*, from **HALE²** + **-IER**. The change in the ending in the 18th cent. was due to association with **YARD¹**.

Ham /ham/ (in the Bible) a son of Noah (Gen. 10:1), traditional ancestor of the Hamites.

ham¹ ▶ noun 1 [mass noun] meat from the upper part of a pig's leg salted and dried or smoked: *thin slices of ham* | [count noun] *a honey-baked ham*.
2 (**hams**) the back of the thigh or the thighs and buttocks: *he squatted down on his hams*.
– ORIGIN Old English *ham*, *hom* (originally denoting the back of the knee), from a Germanic base meaning 'be crooked'. In the late 15th cent. the term came to denote the back of the thigh, hence the thigh or hock of an animal.

ham² ▶ noun 1 [usu. as modifier] an excessively theatrical actor: *ham actors*.
■ [mass noun] excessively theatrical acting.
2 (also **radio ham**) informal an amateur radio operator.
▶ verb (**hammed**, **hamming**) [no obj.] informal overact: *he was hamming it up, doing all the voices and the effects*.
– ORIGIN late 19th cent. (originally US): perhaps from the first syllable of **AMATEUR**; compare with the US slang term *hamfatter* 'inexpert performer'. Sense 2 dates from the early 20th cent.

Hama /ˈhɑːmɑː/ (also **Hamah**) an industrial city in western Syria, on the River Orontes; pop. 229,000 (1993). It was the centre of an Aramaean kingdom in the 11th century BC. Much of the modern city was destroyed during an unsuccessful uprising against the government in 1982.

Hamada /ˈhamədə/, Shoji (1894–1978), Japanese potter. He collaborated with Bernard Leach, working mainly in stoneware to produce utilitarian items of unpretentious simplicity.

hamadryad /ˌhaməˈdrʌɪad, -ad/ ▶ noun 1 Greek & Roman Mythology a nymph who lives in a tree and dies when the tree dies.
2 another term for **KING COBRA**.
– ORIGIN via Latin from Greek *Hamadruas*, from *hama* 'together' + *drus* 'tree'.

hamadryas /ˌhaməˈdrʌɪas, -as/ (also **hamadryas baboon**) ▶ noun a large Arabian and NE African baboon, the male of which has a silvery-grey cape of hair and a naked red face and rump. It was held sacred in ancient Egypt.
● *Papio hamadryas*, family Cercopithecidae.
– ORIGIN 1930s: modern Latin (see **HAMADRYAD**).

Hamah variant spelling of **HAMA**.

Hamamatsu /ˌhaməˈmatsuː/ an industrial city on the southern coast of the island of Honshu, Japan; pop. 535,000 (1990).

hamamelis /ˌhaməˈmiːlɪs/ ▶ noun the witch hazel.
– ORIGIN mid 18th cent.: modern Latin (genus name), from Greek *hamamēlis* 'medlar'.

hamartia /həˈmɑːtɪə/ ▶ noun a fatal flaw leading to the downfall of a tragic hero or heroine.
– ORIGIN late 18th cent.: Greek, 'fault, failure, guilt'; the term was used in Aristotle's *Poetics* with reference to ancient Greek tragedy.

Hamas /ˈhamas/ a Palestinian Islamic fundamentalist movement that has become a focus for Arab resistance in the Israeli-occupied territories. It opposes peace with Israel and has come into conflict with the more moderate Palestine Liberation Organization.

hamate /ˈheɪmət/ (also **hamate bone**) ▶ noun Anatomy a carpal bone situated on the lower outside edge of the hand. It has a hook-shaped projection on the

palmar side to which muscles of the little finger are attached.
– ORIGIN early 18th cent.: from Latin *hamatus* 'hooked', from *hamus* 'hook'.

hamba /ˈhambə/ ▶ verb [no obj., often in imperative] S. African go away: *hamba—can't you see I'm busy?*
– ORIGIN Xhosa and Zulu.

hambone /ˈhambəʊn/ ▶ noun N. Amer. informal an inferior actor or performer, especially one who uses a spurious black accent.

Hamburg¹ /ˈhambəːg, German ˈhambʊrk/ a port in northern Germany, on the River Elbe; pop. 1,668,760 (1991). Founded by Charlemagne in the 9th century, it is now the largest port in Germany, with extensive shipyards.

Hamburg² /ˈhambəːg/ ▶ noun 1 (also **Hamburg steak**) N. Amer. another term for **HAMBURGER**.
2 (also **Black** or **Muscat Hamburg**) a black variety of grape of German origin, specially adapted to hothouse cultivation.
– ORIGIN from **HAMBURG¹**.

hamburger ▶ noun a round patty of minced beef, fried or grilled and typically served in a bread roll.
– ORIGIN late 19th cent. (originally US): from German, from **HAMBURG¹**.

hamel /ˈhaməl, ˈhɑːməl/ ▶ noun S. African a castrated ram.
– ORIGIN Afrikaans.

Hameln /ˈhɑːm(ə)ln/ (also **Hamelin** /ˈhamlɪn/) a town in NW Germany, in Lower Saxony, on the River Weser; pop. 57,000 (1983). A medieval market town, it is the setting of the legend of the Pied Piper of Hamelin.

hamerkop ▶ noun variant spelling of **HAMMERKOP**.

hames /heɪmz/ ▶ plural noun two curved pieces of iron or wood forming or attached to the collar of a draught horse, to which the traces are attached.
– ORIGIN Middle English: from Middle Dutch.

ham-fisted ▶ adjective informal clumsy; bungling: *a ham-fisted attempt*.
– DERIVATIVES **ham-fistedly** adverb, **ham-fistedness** noun.

ham-handed ▶ adjective another term for **HAM-FISTED**.
– DERIVATIVES **ham-handedly** adverb, **ham-handedness** noun.

Hamhung /ˈhamhʌŋ/ an industrial city in eastern North Korea; pop. 775,000 (est. 1984). It was the centre of government of NE Korea during the Yi dynasty of 1392–1910.

Hamilcar /haˈmɪlkɑː, ˈhamɪlˌkɑː/ (c.270–229 BC), Carthaginian general, father of Hannibal. He fought Rome in the first Punic War and negotiated the terms of peace after Carthaginian defeat.

Hamilton¹ 1 a town in South Lanarkshire, southern Scotland, near Glasgow; pop. 50,000 (1991).
2 a port and industrial city in southern Canada, at the western end of Lake Ontario; pop. 318,500 (1991); metropolitan area pop. 599,760.
3 a city on North Island, New Zealand; pop. 148,625 (1991).
4 the capital of Bermuda; pop. 1,100 (1991).

Hamilton², Alexander (c.1757–1804), American Federalist politician. He established the US central banking system, and advocated strong central government. He was killed in a duel with Aaron Burr.

Hamilton³, Sir Charles (1900–78), New Zealand inventor and motor-racing driver, best known for his development of the jet boat.

Hamilton⁴, Lady Emma (c.1765–1815), English beauty and mistress of Lord Nelson; born *Amy Lyon*. She met Lord Nelson while married to Sir William Hamilton, the British ambassador to Naples. She had a daughter by Nelson in 1801 and lived with him after her husband's death in 1803.

Hamilton⁵, Sir William Rowan (1806–65), Irish mathematician and theoretical physicist. Hamilton made influential contributions to optics and to the foundations of algebra and quantum mechanics.

Hamiltonian /ˌham(ɪ)lˈtəʊnɪən/ ▶ adjective 1 Physics & Mathematics of, relating to, or invented by the mathematician Sir W. R. Hamilton, especially denoting concepts employed in the wave-mechanical description of particles.

2 of or relating to the American statesman Alexander Hamilton or his doctrines.

▶**noun 1** (also **hamiltonian**) Physics & Mathematics a Hamiltonian operator or function.
2 a follower or adherent of Alexander Hamilton or his doctrines.
– DERIVATIVES **Hamiltonianism** noun (only in sense 2).

Hamite /ˈhamʌɪt/ ▶**noun** a member of a group of North African peoples, including the ancient Egyptians and Berbers, supposedly descended from Ham, son of Noah.

Hamitic /həˈmɪtɪk/ ▶**adjective** historical of or denoting a hypothetical language family formerly proposed to comprise Berber, ancient Egyptian, the Cushitic languages, and the Chadic languages. These are now recognized as independent branches of the Afro-Asiatic family.
– ORIGIN from **HAMITE** + -IC.

Hamito-Semitic /ˌhamɪtəʊsɪˈmɪtɪk/ ▶**adjective** former term for **AFRO-ASIATIC**.

Hamlet a legendary prince of Denmark, hero of a tragedy by Shakespeare.
– PHRASES **Hamlet without the Prince** a performance or event taking place without the principal actor or central figure.

hamlet ▶**noun** a small settlement, generally one smaller than a village, and strictly (in Britain) one without a church.
– ORIGIN Middle English: from Old French *hamelet*, diminutive of *hamel* 'little village'; related to **HOME** (*hám* in Old English).

Hamm /ham/ an industrial city in NW Germany, in North Rhine-Westphalia, on the Lippe River; pop. 180,320 (1991).

Hammarskjöld /ˈhaməˌʃʊld/, Dag (Hjalmar Agne Carl) (1905–61), Swedish diplomat and politician. As Secretary General of the United Nations (1953–61) he was influential in the establishment of the UN emergency force in Sinai and Gaza (1956), and also initiated peace moves in the Middle East (1957–8). He was posthumously awarded the 1961 Nobel Peace Prize.

hammer ▶**noun 1** a tool with a heavy metal head mounted at right angles at the end of a handle, used for jobs such as breaking things and driving in nails.
■ a machine with a metal block for giving a heavy blow to something. ■ an auctioneer's mallet for indicating by a sharp tap that an article is sold. ■ a part of a mechanism that hits another part to make it work, such as one exploding the charge in a gun or one striking the strings of a piano.
2 a metal ball of about 7 kg attached to a wire for throwing in an athletic contest.
■ (**the hammer**) the sport of throwing such a ball.
3 another term for **MALLEUS**.
▶**verb** [with obj.] **1** hit or beat (something) repeatedly with a hammer or similar object.
■ [no obj.] strike or knock at or on something violently with one's hand or with a hammer or other object: *she hammered on his door.* ■ [no obj.] (**hammer away**) work hard and persistently: *they must hammer away at these twin themes day after day.* ■ [with obj. and adverbial] drive or secure (something) by striking with or as if with a hammer: *he hammered the tack in | he was hammering leather soles on to a pair of small boots.* ■ (**hammer something in/into**) inculcate forcefully or repeatedly: *a commercial image that was hammered into English consciousness.*
2 informal attack or criticize forcefully and relentlessly: *he got hammered for an honest mistake.*
■ utterly defeat in a game or contest: *they hammered St Mirren 4–0.*
3 Stock Exchange declare (a person or company) a defaulter.
■ informal beat down the price of (a stock): *sceptical investors hammered the computer company's stock.* [ORIGIN: from the practice of striking three strokes with a mallet on the side of a rostrum in the Stock Exchange before a formal declaration of default.]
– PHRASES **come** (or **go**) **under the hammer** be sold at an auction. **hammer and tongs** informal energetically, enthusiastically, or with great vehemence: *racehorses going at it hammer and tongs.* **hammer something home** see **HOME**.
– DERIVATIVES **hammerless** adjective.
– ORIGIN Old English *hamor*, *hamer*, of Germanic origin: related to Dutch *hamer*, German *Hammer*,

and Old Norse *hamarr* 'rock'. The original sense was probably 'stone tool'.

▶**hammer something out 1** make something by shaping metal with a hammer. **2** laboriously work out the details of a plan or agreement: *a deal was being hammered out with the Dutch museums.* **3** play a tune loudly or clumsily, especially on the piano.

hammer and sickle ▶**noun** the symbols of the industrial worker and the peasant used as the emblem of the former USSR and of international communism.

hammer beam ▶**noun** a short wooden beam (typically carved) projecting from a wall to support either a principal rafter or one end of an arch.

hammer drill ▶**noun** a power drill that works by delivering a rapid succession of blows, used chiefly for drilling in masonry or rock.

Hammerfest /ˈhaməfɛst/ a port in northern Norway, on Kvaløy island; pop. 6,900 (1991). It is the northernmost town in Europe.

hammerhead ▶**noun 1** (also **hammerhead shark**) a shark of tropical and temperate oceans that has flattened blade-like extensions on either side of the head, with the eyes and nostrils placed at or near the ends.
● Family Sphyrnidae and genus *Sphyrna*: several species.
2 another term for **HAMMERKOP**.

hammering ▶**noun 1** [mass noun] the action of hammering something or the sound of such an action.
2 informal a heavy defeat: *the 7–0 hammering by the league leaders.*
– PHRASES **take a hammering** be subjected to a heavy defeat or harsh treatment.

hammerkop /ˈhaməkɒp/ (also **hamerkop**) ▶**noun** a brown African marshbird related to the storks, which has a crest that looks like a backward projection of the head, and constructs an enormous nest.
● *Scopus umbretta*, the only member of the family Scopidae.
– ORIGIN mid 19th cent.: from Afrikaans *hamerkop*, from *hamer* 'hammer' + *kop* 'head'.

hammerlock ▶**noun** an armlock in which a person's arm is bent up behind their back.

hammer price ▶**noun** the price realized by an item sold at auction.

Hammerstein /ˈhaməstʌɪn/, Oscar (1895–1960), American librettist; full name *Oscar Hammerstein II*. He collaborated with various composers, most notably Richard Rodgers, with whom he wrote *Oklahoma!* (1943), *South Pacific* (1949), and *The Sound of Music* (1959).

hammer toe ▶**noun** a toe that is bent permanently downwards, typically as a result of pressure from footwear.

Hammett /ˈhamɪt/, (Samuel) Dashiell (1894–1961), American novelist. He developed the hard-boiled style of detective fiction in works such as *The Maltese Falcon* (1930) and *The Thin Man* (1932).

hammock ▶**noun** a bed made of canvas or of rope mesh and suspended by cords at the ends, used as garden furniture or on board ship.
– ORIGIN mid 16th cent. (in the Spanish form *hamaca*): via Spanish from Taino *hamaka*; the ending was altered in the 16th cent. by association with -OCK.

Hammond, Dame Joan (1912–96), Australian operatic soprano, born in New Zealand.

Hammond organ ▶**noun** trademark a type of electronic organ.
– ORIGIN 1930s: named after Laurens *Hammond* (1895–1973), American mechanical engineer.

Hammurabi /ˌhamʊˈrɑːbi/ (d.1750 BC), the sixth king of the first dynasty of Babylonia, reigned 1792–1750 BC. He extended the Babylonian empire and instituted one of the earliest known collections of laws.

hammy ▶**adjective** (**hammier**, **hammiest**) **1** informal (of acting or an actor) exaggerated or over-theatrical: *there is some hammy acting.*
2 (of a hand or thigh) thick and solid.
– DERIVATIVES **hammily** adverb, **hamminess** noun.

Hamnett /ˈhamnɪt/, Katharine (b.1952), English fashion designer.

hamper[1] ▶**noun** a basket with a carrying handle and a hinged lid, used for food, cutlery, and plates on a picnic: *a picnic hamper.*

■ N. Amer. a large basket with a lid used for laundry: *a laundry hamper.* ■ Brit. a box containing food and drink for a special occasion: *a Christmas food hamper.*
– ORIGIN Middle English (denoting any large case or casket): from Anglo-Norman French *hanaper* 'case for a goblet', from Old French *hanap* 'goblet', of Germanic origin.

hamper[2] ▶**verb** [with obj.] (often **be hampered**) hinder or impede the movement or progress of: *their work is hampered by lack of funds.*
▶**noun** [mass noun] Nautical necessary but cumbersome equipment on a ship.
– ORIGIN late Middle English (in the sense 'shackle, entangle, catch'): perhaps related to German *hemmen* 'restrain'.

Hampshire[1] a county on the coast of southern England; county town, Winchester.

Hampshire[2] ▶**noun** a pig of a black breed with a white saddle and prick ears.

Hampstead a residential suburb of NW London.

Hampton a city in SE Virginia, on the harbour of Hampton Roads, on Chesapeake Bay; pop. 133,790 (1990).

Hampton Court a palace on the north bank of the Thames in the borough of Richmond-upon-Thames, London, a favourite royal residence until the reign of George II. Its gardens contain a well-known maze.

Hampton Roads a deep-water estuary 6 km (4 miles) long, formed by the James River where it joins Chesapeake Bay, on the Atlantic coast in SE Virginia.

hamster ▶**noun** a solitary burrowing rodent with a short tail and large cheek pouches for carrying food, native to Europe and North Asia.
● Subfamily Cricetinae, family Muridae: several genera and species, in particular the **golden hamster** (*Mesocricetus auratus*), often kept as a pet or laboratory animal, and the **common hamster** (*Cricetus cricetus*).
– ORIGIN early 17th cent.: from German, from Old High German *hamustro* 'corn-weevil'.

hamstring ▶**noun** any of five tendons at the back of a person's knee: *he pulled a hamstring.*
■ the great tendon at the back of a quadruped's hock.
▶**verb** (past and past participle **hamstrung**) [with obj.] cripple (a person or animal) by cutting their hamstrings.
■ (usu. **be hamstrung**) severely restrict the efficiency or effectiveness of: *we were hamstrung by a total lack of knowledge.*

Hamsun /ˈhamsʊn/, Knut (1859–1952), Norwegian novelist; pseudonym of *Knut Pedersen*. Notable works: *Hunger* (1890) and *Growth of the Soil* (1917). Nobel Prize for Literature (1920).

hamulus /ˈhamjʊləs/ ▶**noun** (pl. **hamuli** /-lʌɪ, -liː/) Anatomy & Zoology a small hook or hook-like projection, especially one of a number linking the fore- and hindwings of a bee or wasp.
– ORIGIN early 18th cent.: from Latin, diminutive of *hamus* 'hook'.

hamza /ˈhamzə/ ▶**noun** (in Arabic script) a symbol representing a glottal stop.
■ such a sound.
– ORIGIN Arabic, literally 'compression'.

Han /han/ **1** the Chinese dynasty that ruled from 206 BC until AD 220 with only a brief interruption. During this period Chinese rule was extended over Mongolia, Confucianism was recognized as the state philosophy, and detailed historical records were kept.
2 the dominant ethnic group in China.

Hancock, Tony (1924–68), English comedian; full name *Anthony John Hancock*. He made his name in 1954 with the radio series *Hancock's Half Hour*, which was later adapted to television (1956–61).

hand ▶**noun 1** the end part of a person's arm beyond the wrist, including the palm, fingers, and thumb: *she placed the money on the palm of her hand | he was leading her by the hand.*
■ a similar prehensile organ forming the end part of a limb of various mammals, such as that on all four limbs of a monkey. ■ W. Indian a person's arm, including the hand. ■ [as modifier] operated by or held in the hand: *hand luggage.* ■ [as modifier or in combination] done or made manually rather than by machine: *hand signals | a hand-stitched quilt.* ■ [in sing.] informal a round of applause: *his fans gave him a big hand.* ■ dated a pledge of marriage by a woman: *he wrote to request the hand of her daughter in marriage.*
2 something resembling a hand in form or position, in particular:

■ a pointer on a clock or watch indicating the passing of units of time: *the second hand.* ■ a bunch of bananas. ■ Brit. a forehock of pork.

3 (**hands**) used in reference to the power to direct something: *the day-to-day running of the house was in her hands | taking the law into their own hands.* ■ (usu. **a hand**) an active role in influencing something: *he **had** a big **hand in** organizing the event.* ■ (usu. **a hand**) help in doing something: *do you need a hand?* ■ a person's workmanship, especially in artistic work: *this should be a clue in attributing other work to his hand.* ■ a person's handwriting: *he inscribed the statement in a bold hand.* ■ [with adj.] a person who does something to a specified standard: *I'm a great **hand at** inventing.*

4 a person who engages in manual labour, especially in a factory, on a farm, or on board a ship: *a factory hand | the ship was lost with all hands.*

5 the set of cards dealt to a player in a card game. ■ a round or short spell of play in a card game: *they played **a hand of** whist.* ■ Bridge the cards held by declarer as opposed to those in the dummy.

6 a unit of measurement of a horse's height, equal to 4 inches (10.16 cm). [ORIGIN: denoting the breadth of a hand, formerly used as a more general lineal measure and taken to equal three inches.]

▶ **verb 1** [with two objs] pick (something) up and give to (someone): *he handed each man a glass | I handed the trowel back to him.* ■ informal make (abusive, untrue, or otherwise objectionable remarks) to (someone): *all the yarns she'd been handing me.* ■ informal make (something) very easily obtainable for (someone): *it was a win handed to him on a plate.*

2 [with obj. and adverbial of direction] hold the hand of (someone) in order to help them move in the specified direction: *he handed him into a carriage.*

3 [with obj.] Sailing take in or furl (a sail): ***hand in** the main!*

– PHRASES **all hands on deck** a cry or signal used on board ship, typically in an emergency, to indicate that all crew members are to go on deck. ■ used to indicate that the involvement of all members of a team is required: *it was all hands on deck getting breakfast ready.* **at hand** close by: *a mortar burst close at hand.* ■ readily accessible when needed. ■ close in time; about to happen: *a breakthrough in combating the disease may be at hand.* **at** (or **by**) **the hands** (or **hand**) **of** through the agency of: *tests he would undergo at the hands of a senior neurologist.* **bind** (or **tie**) **someone hand and foot** tie someone's hands and feet together. **by hand** by a person and not a machine: *the crop has to be harvested by hand.* **get** (or **keep**) **one's hand in** become (or remain) practised in something. **give** (or **lend**) **a hand** assist in an action or enterprise. **hand in glove** in close collusion or association: *they were working **hand in glove with** our enemies.* **hand in hand** (of two people) with hands joined, especially as a mark of affection. ■ figurative closely associated: *she had the confidence that usually **goes hand in hand with** experience.* (**from**) **hand to mouth** satisfying only one's immediate needs because of lack of money for future plans and investments: *they were flat broke and living hand to mouth |* [as modifier] *a hand-to-mouth existence.* **hands down** easily and decisively: *Swindon won hands down … 4–1.* **hands off** used as a warning not to touch or interfere with something: *hands off that cake tin!* ■ [as adj. **hands-off**] not involving or requiring direct control or intervention: *a hands-off management style.* **hands-on** involving or offering active participation rather than theory: *hands-on in-service training.* ■ Computing involving or requiring personal operation at a keyboard. **a hand's turn** [usu. with negative] informal a stroke of work: *they sit there without doing a hand's turn.* **hands up!** used as an instruction to raise one's hands in surrender or to signify assent or participation: *hands up who saw the programme!* **have one's hands full** have as much work as one can do. **have one's hands tied** informal be unable to act freely. **have to hand it to someone** informal used to acknowledge the merit or achievement of someone: *I've got to hand it to you—you've got the magic touch.* **in hand 1** receiving or requiring immediate attention: *he threw himself into the work in hand.* ■ in progress: *negotiations are now well in hand.* **2** ready for use if required; in reserve: *he had £1,000 of borrowed cash in hand.* **3** under one's control: *the police had the situation well in hand.* ■ (of land) farmed directly by its owner and not let to tenants. **in safe hands** protected by someone trustworthy from harm or damage: *the future of the cathedral is in safe hands.* **make** (or **lose** or **spend**) **money hand over fist** informal make (or lose or spend) money very rapidly. **many hands make light work** proverb a task is soon accomplished if several people help. **off someone's hands** not having to be dealt with or looked after by the person specified: *they just want the problem off their hands.* **on every hand** all around: *new technologies were springing up on every hand.* **on hand** present, especially for a specified purpose: *her trainer was on hand to give advice.* ■ readily available. ■ needing to be dealt with: *they had many urgent and pressing matters on hand.* **on someone's hands** used to indicate that someone is responsible for dealing with someone or something: *he has a difficult job on his hands.* ■ used to indicate that someone is to blame for something: *he has my son's blood on his hands.* ■ at someone's disposal: *since I retired I've had more time on my hands.* **on the one** (or **the other**) **hand** used to present factors which are opposed or which support opposing opinions: *a conflict between their rationally held views on the one hand and their emotions and desires on the other.* **out of hand 1** not under control. **2** without taking time to think: *they rejected negotiations out of hand.* **the right hand doesn't know what the left hand's doing** used to convey that there is a state of confusion within a group or organization. **a safe pair of hands** (in a sporting context) used to refer to someone who is reliable when catching a ball. ■ used to denote someone who is capable, reliable, or trustworthy in the management of a situation. **set** (or **put**) **one's hand to** start work on. **stay someone's hand** restrain someone from acting. **take a hand** become influential in determining something; intervene: *fate was about to **take a hand in** the outcome of the championship.* **to hand** within easy reach: *have a pen and paper to hand.* **turn one's hand to** undertake (an activity different from one's usual occupation). **wait on someone hand and foot** attend to all someone's needs or requests, especially when this is regarded as unreasonable. **with one hand** (**tied**) **behind one's back** with serious limitations or restrictions: *at the moment, the police are tackling record crime rates with one hand tied behind their back.* ■ used to indicate that one could do something without any difficulty: *I could do her job with one hand tied behind my back.*

– DERIVATIVES **handless** adjective.

– ORIGIN Old English *hand, hond*, of Germanic origin; related to Dutch *hand* and German *Hand*.

▶ **hand something down 1** pass something on to a younger person or a successor: *songs are handed down from mother to daughter.* **2** announce something, especially a judgement or sentence, formally or publicly.

hand something in give something to a person in authority for their attention.

hand someone off Rugby push away a tackling opponent with one's hand.

hand something on pass something to the next person in a series or succession: *he had handed on the family farm to his son.* ■ pass responsibility for something to someone else; delegate.

hand something out 1 give a share of something or one of a set of things to each of a number of people; distribute: *they handed out free drinks to everyone.* **2** impose or inflict a penalty or misfortune on someone.

hand over pass responsibility to someone else: *he will soon **hand over to** a new director.*

hand someone/thing over give someone or something, or the responsibility for someone or something, to someone else.

hand something round (or N. Amer. **around**) offer something to each of a number of people in turn: *a big box of chocolates was handed round.*

handbag ▶ **noun** Brit. a small bag used by a woman to carry everyday personal items.

handball ▶ **noun** [mass noun] **1** a game similar to fives, in which the ball is hit with the hand in a walled court. ■ a team game similar to soccer in which the ball is thrown or hit with the hands rather than kicked.
2 Soccer touching of the ball with the hand or arm, constituting a foul.

handbasin ▶ **noun** Brit. a washbasin.

handbell ▶ **noun** a small bell with a handle or strap, especially one of a set tuned to a range of notes and played by a group of people.

handbill ▶ **noun** a small printed advertisement or other notice distributed by hand.

handbook ▶ **noun** a book giving information such as facts on a particular subject or instructions for operating a machine.

handbrake ▶ **noun** a brake operated by hand, used to hold an already stationary vehicle.

handbrake turn ▶ **noun** a skidding turn in a fast-moving car, typically through 180°, effected by a sudden application of the handbrake.

h & c Brit. ▶ **abbreviation for** hot and cold (used in describing the water supply to a hotel bedroom or a room in a house): *all rooms have h & c.*

handcar ▶ **noun** N. Amer. a light railway vehicle propelled by cranks or levers and used by workers for inspecting the track.

handcart ▶ **noun** a small cart pushed or drawn by hand, used for delivering merchandise or luggage.

handclap ▶ **noun** a clap of the hands.

handcraft ▶ **verb** [with obj.] [usu. as adj. **handcrafted**] make skilfully by hand: *a handcrafted rocking chair.*
▶ **noun** another term for **HANDICRAFT**.

hand crank ▶ **noun** a crank that is turned by hand.
▶ **verb** (**hand-crank**) [with obj.] operate (a device) by turning a crank by hand.

hand cream ▶ **noun** a moisturizing cream for the hands.

handcuff ▶ **noun** (**handcuffs**) a pair of lockable linked metal rings for securing a prisoner's wrists.
▶ **verb** [with obj.] put handcuffs on (someone): *he was led into court **handcuffed to** a policeman.*

-handed ▶ **combining form 1** for or involving a specified number of hands: *a two-handed back-hand.*
2 chiefly using or designed for use by the hand specified: *a right-handed batsman | a left-handed guitar.*
3 having hands as specified: *the burglar left empty-handed.*

– DERIVATIVES **-handedly** adverb, **-handedness** noun.

Handel /ˈhand(ə)l/, George Frederick (1685–1759), German-born composer and organist, resident in England from 1712; born *Georg Friedrich Händel*. A prolific composer, he is chiefly remembered for his choral works, especially the oratorio *Messiah* (1742), and, for orchestra, his *Water Music* suite (c.1717) and *Music for the Royal Fireworks* (1749).

handful ▶ **noun** (pl. **-fuls**) **1** a quantity that fills the hand: *a small **handful of** fresh coriander.* ■ a small number or amount: *controlled ultimately by a **handful of** firms.*
2 informal a person who is very difficult to deal with or control: *the kids could be such a handful.*

hand gallop ▶ **noun** [in sing.] an easily controlled gallop.

hand grenade ▶ **noun** a hand-thrown grenade.

handgrip ▶ **noun 1** a handle for holding something by.
2 a grasp with the hand, especially considered in terms of its strength, as in a handshake.
3 a soft bag with handles for carrying belongings in on a journey.

handgun ▶ **noun** a gun designed for use by one hand, chiefly either a pistol or a revolver.

hand-held ▶ **adjective** designed to be held in the hand: *a hand-held camera.*
▶ **noun** a small computer that can be used in the hand.

handhold ▶ **noun** something for a hand to grip on.

hand-hot ▶ **adjective** (especially of water) hot, but not too hot to put one's hands into.

handicap ▶ **noun** a condition that markedly restricts a person's ability to function physically, mentally, or socially: *he was born with a significant visual handicap.* ■ a circumstance that makes progress or success difficult: *a criminal conviction is a handicap and a label that may stick forever.* ■ a disadvantage imposed on a superior competitor in sports such as golf, horse racing, and competitive sailing in order to make the chances more equal. ■ a race or contest in which such a disadvantage is imposed: [in names] *the National Hunt Handicap Chase.* ■ the extra weight allocated to be carried in a race by a racehorse on the basis of its previous form to make its chances of winning the same as those of the other horses. ■ the number of strokes by which a golfer normally exceeds par for a course (used as a method of enabling players of unequal ability to compete with each other): *he plays off a handicap of 10.*

▸ **verb** (**handicapped**, **handicapping**) [with obj.] act as an impediment to: *lack of funding has handicapped the development of research.*

■ place (someone) at a disadvantage: *without a good set of notes you will handicap yourself when it comes to exams.*

– PHRASES **out of the handicap** Horse Racing having a handicap rating that would merit carrying a weight below the minimum specified for a race.

– ORIGIN mid 17th cent.: from the phrase *hand in cap*; originally a pastime in which one person claimed an article belonging to another and offered something in exchange, any difference in value being decided by an umpire. All three deposited forfeit money in a cap; the two opponents showed their agreement or disagreement with the valuation by bringing out their hands either full or empty. If both were the same, the umpire took the forfeit money; if not it went to the person who accepted the valuation. The term *handicap race* was applied (late 18th cent.) to a horse race in which an umpire decided the weight to be carried by each horse, the owners showing acceptance or dissent in a similar way; hence in the late 19th cent. *handicap* came to mean the extra weight given to the superior horse.

handicap mark ▸ **noun** see **MARK**[1] (sense 3).

handicapped ▸ **adjective** (of a person) having a condition that markedly restricts their ability to function physically, mentally, or socially: *a special school for handicapped children.*

> **USAGE** The word **handicapped** is first recorded in the early 20th century in the sense referring to a person's mental or physical disabilities. It was the standard term in British English until relatively recently but, like many terms in this sensitive field, its prominence has been short-lived. In reference to physical disability, it is now rather dated and may even be found offensive. It has been superseded by more recent terms such as **disabled**.

handicapper ▸ **noun** a person appointed to fix or assess a competitor's handicap, especially in golf or horse racing.

■ [usu. in combination] a person or horse having a specified handicap: *a three-handicapper.*

handicraft ▸ **noun** (often **handicrafts**) a particular skill of making decorative domestic or other objects by hand: *the traditional handicrafts of this region* | [mass noun] *teachers of drawing, design, and handicraft* | [as modifier] *handicraft workshops.*

■ an object made using a skill of this kind.

– ORIGIN Middle English: alteration of **HANDCRAFT**, on the pattern of *handiwork.*

handiwork ▸ **noun** [mass noun] **1** (**one's handiwork**) something that one has made or done: *the dressmakers stood back to survey their handiwork.*
2 making things by hand, considered as a subject of instruction.

– ORIGIN Old English *handgeweorc*, from **HAND** + *geweorc* 'something made', interpreted in the 16th cent. as *handy* + *work.*

handjob ▸ **noun** vulgar slang an act of male masturbation, especially as performed on a man by someone else.

handkerchief /ˈhaŋkətʃɪf/ ▸ **noun** (pl. **handkerchiefs** or **handkerchieves** /-tʃiːvz/) a square of cotton or other finely woven material intended for wiping one's nose.

– ORIGIN mid 16th cent.: from **HAND** + **KERCHIEF**.

handkerchief tree ▸ **noun** another term for **DOVE TREE**.

handle ▸ **verb** [with obj.] **1** feel or manipulate with the hands: *heavy paving slabs can be difficult to handle* | *people who handle food.*

■ (chiefly in soccer) touch (the ball) with the hand or lower arm in contravention of the rules. ■ drive or control (a vehicle). ■ [no obj., with adverbial] (of a vehicle) respond in a specified manner when being driven or controlled: *the new model does not handle nearly so well.*
2 manage (a situation or problem): *a lawyer's ability to handle a case properly.*

■ informal deal with (someone or something): *I don't think I could handle it if they turned me down.* ■ have the resources to cope with: *more orders than I can handle.* ■ control or manage commercially: *the advertising company that is handling the account.* ■ [with adverbial] (**handle oneself**) conduct oneself in a specified manner: *he handled himself with considerable aplomb.*

■ (**handle oneself**) informal defend oneself physically or verbally: *I can handle myself in a fight.*
3 process: *the airport expects to handle almost 250,000 passengers this weekend.*

■ receive or deal in (stolen goods): *he admitted handling the stolen chequebook.*

▸ **noun** **1** the part by which a thing is held, carried, or controlled: *a holdall with two carrying handles.*

■ (**a handle on**) figurative a means of understanding, controlling, or approaching a person or situation: *it'll give people some kind of handle on these issues.*
2 informal the name of a person or place: *that's some handle for a baby.*
3 [in sing.] the feel of goods, especially textiles, when handled: *fabrics with a softer handle.*
4 [in sing.] US informal the total amount of money bet over a particular time (typically at a casino) or at a particular sporting event: *the monthly handle of a couple of casinos in Las Vegas.*

– DERIVATIVES **handleability** /-ˈbɪlɪti/ noun, **handleable** adjective, **handled** adjective [in combination] *a side-handled baton,* **handleless** adjective.

– ORIGIN Old English *handle* (noun), *handlian* (verb), from **HAND**.

handlebar ▸ **noun** (usu. **handlebars**) the steering bar of a bicycle, motorbike, scooter, or other vehicle, with a handgrip at each end.

handlebar moustache ▸ **noun** a wide, thick moustache with the ends curving slightly upwards.

handler ▸ **noun** **1** [usu. with modifier] a person who handles or deals with certain articles or commodities: *a baggage handler* | *a food handler.*

■ a device which handles certain articles or substances. ■ Brit. a person who assists in the trafficking of stolen property or drugs.
2 a person who trains or has charge of an animal, in particular a police officer in charge of a dog.
3 a person who trains or manages another person, in particular:

■ a person who trains and acts as second to a boxer. ■ a publicity agent. ■ a person who directs the activities of a spy or other freelance agent.

Handley Page, Frederick, see **PAGE**.

handlist ▸ **noun** a short list of something such as essential reading or the items in a collection.

handmade ▸ **adjective** made by hand, not by machine, and typically therefore of superior quality: *his expensive handmade leather shoes.*

handmaid ▸ **noun** a female servant.

■ a subservient partner or element.

handmaiden ▸ **noun** another term for **HANDMAID**.

hand-me-down ▸ **noun** (usu. **hand-me-downs**) a garment or other item that has been passed on from another person.

handoff ▸ **noun** American Football an exchange made by handing the ball to a teammate.

handout ▸ **noun** **1** a quantity of financial or other material aid given to a person or organization: *dependence on central government handouts.*
2 printed information provided free of charge, especially to accompany a lecture or advertise something.

handover ▸ **noun** chiefly Brit. an act or instance of handing something over.

hand-pick ▸ **verb** [with obj.] [usu. as adj. **hand-picked**] select carefully with a particular purpose in mind: *a small hand-picked group of MPs.*

hand plant ▸ **noun** a jump or other manoeuvre in skateboarding and snowboarding involving the use of a hand to push away from a surface.

handprint ▸ **noun** the mark left by the impression of a hand.

handpump ▸ **noun** a pump operated by hand, especially for drawing well water or draught beer.

handrail ▸ **noun** a rail fixed to posts or a wall for people to hold on to for support.

handsaw ▸ **noun** a wood saw worked by one hand.

handsel ▸ **noun** & **verb** variant spelling of **HANSEL**.

handset ▸ **noun** the part of a telephone that is held up to speak into and listen to.

■ a hand-held controller for a piece of electronic equipment, such as a television or video recorder.

handshake ▸ **noun** an act of shaking a person's hand with one's own as a greeting.

■ a person's particular way of doing this: *her handshake was warm and firm.* ■ Computing an exchange of standardized signals between devices in a computer network regulating the transfer of data.

handshaking ▸ **noun** [mass noun] the action of shaking hands with a person.

■ Computing the action of exchanging standardized signals between devices in a computer network to regulate the transfer of data. ■ Computing a system of such standardized signals.

handsome ▸ **adjective** (**handsomer**, **handsomest**)
1 (of a man) good-looking.

■ (of a woman) striking and imposing rather than conventionally pretty. ■ (of a thing) well made, imposing, and of obvious quality: *handsome cookery books* | *a handsome country town.*
2 (of a number, sum of money, or margin) substantial: *elected by a handsome majority.*

– PHRASES **handsome is as handsome does** proverb character and behaviour are more important than appearance.

– DERIVATIVES **handsomely** adverb, **handsomeness** noun.

– ORIGIN Middle English: from **HAND** + -**SOME**[1]. The original sense was 'easy to handle or use', hence 'suitable' and 'apt, clever' (mid 16th cent.), giving rise to the current appreciatory senses (late 16th cent.).

handspike ▸ **noun** historical a wooden rod with an iron tip, used as a lever on board ship and by artillery soldiers.

handspring ▸ **noun** a jump through the air on to one's hands followed by another on to one's feet.

handstand ▸ **noun** an act of balancing on one's hands with one's feet in the air or against a wall.

handstroke ▸ **noun** Bell-ringing a pull of the sally of the rope so as to swing the bell through a full circle. Compare with **BACKSTROKE**.

hand-to-hand ▸ **adjective** (of fighting) at close quarters: *hand-to-hand fighting.*

hand tool ▸ **noun** a tool held in the hand and operated without electricity or other power.

handwork ▸ **noun** [mass noun] work done with the hands: *the transition from handwork to machine production.*

– DERIVATIVES **handworked** adjective.

handwriting ▸ **noun** [mass noun] writing with a pen or pencil.

■ a person's particular style of writing: *her handwriting was small and neat.*

handwritten ▸ **adjective** written with a pen, pencil, or other hand-held implement.

Handy, W. C. (1873–1958), American blues musician; full name *William Christopher Handy.* He set up a music-publishing house in 1914, and his transcriptions of traditional blues helped establish the pattern of the modern twelve-bar blues.

handy ▸ **adjective** (**handier**, **handiest**) **1** convenient to handle or use; useful: *a handy desktop encyclopedia* | *handy for everyday use.*
2 ready to hand: *keep credit cards handy.*

■ placed or occurring conveniently: *a hotel in a handy central location.*
3 skilful: *he's handy with a needle.*

– PHRASES **come in handy** informal turn out to be useful: *the sort of junk that might come in handy one day.*

– DERIVATIVES **handily** adverb, **handiness** noun.

handyman ▸ **noun** (pl. **-men**) a person able or employed to do occasional domestic repairs and minor renovations.

hanepoot /ˈhɑːnəˌpʊət/ ▸ **noun** [mass noun] a variety of muscat grape, Muscat d'Alexandrie, grown in South Africa.

■ a sweet wine made from this grape, unfortified for table use, and fortified as a muscatel dessert wine.

– ORIGIN Afrikaans, from Dutch *haan* 'cock' + *poot* 'foot'.

hang ▸ **verb** (past and past participle **hung** except in sense 2) **1** suspend or be suspended from above with the lower part dangling free: [with obj.] *that's where people are supposed to hang their washing* | [no obj.] *he stood swaying, his arms hanging limply by his sides.*

■ attach or be attached to a hook on a wall: [with obj.] *we could just hang the pictures on the walls* | [no obj.] *the room in which the pictures will hang.* ■ (**be hung with**) be adorned with pictures or other decorations: *the walls of her hall were hung with examples of her work.* ■ attach or be attached so as to allow free movement about the point of attachment: [with obj.] *a long time was spent hanging a couple of doors* | [no obj., with complement] *she just sat with her mouth hanging open.* ■ [with obj.] attach (meat or game) to a hook and leave it until dry, tender, or high. ■ [no obj., with adverbial] (of fabric or a garment) fall or drape from a fixed point in a specified way: *this blend of silk and wool hangs well and resists creases.* ■ [with obj.] paste (wallpaper) to a wall. ■ N. Amer. informal way of saying **hang around** (in sense 2) or **hang out** (in sense 3).

2 (past and past participle **hanged**) [with obj.] kill (someone) by tying a rope attached from above around their neck and removing the support from beneath them (often used as a form of capital punishment): *he was hanged for murder | she hanged herself in her cell on 19 February.*
■ [no obj.] be killed in such a way: *both men were sentenced to hang.* ■ dated used in expressions as a mild oath: [no obj.] *they could all go hang* | [with obj.] *I'm hanged if I know.*

3 [no obj., with adverbial of place] remain static in the air: *a black pall of smoke hung over Valletta.*
■ be present or imminent, especially oppressively or threateningly: *a sense of dread hung over him for days.* ■ [with obj.] Baseball deliver (a pitch) which does not change direction and is easily hit by a batter.

4 Computing come or cause to come unexpectedly to a state in which no further operations can be carried out.

▶ **noun** [in sing.] a downward droop or bend: *the bullish hang of his head.*
■ the way in which something hangs: *the hang of one's clothes.* ■ the way in which pictures are displayed in an exhibition.

▶ **exclamation** S. African, dated used to express a range of strong emotions from enthusiasm to anger: *hang, but I loved those soldiers!*

– PHRASES **get the hang of** informal learn how to operate or do (something): *it's all quite simple when you get the hang of it.* **hang by a thread** see THREAD. **hang fire** delay or be delayed in taking action or progressing. **hang one's hat** N. Amer. informal be resident. **hang heavily** (or **heavy**) (of time) pass slowly. **hang in the air** remain unresolved: *the success of the Green movement has left that rather uncomfortable question hanging in the air.* **hang a left** (or **right**) informal, chiefly US make a left (or right) turn. **hang loose** see LOOSE. **(a) hang of** S. African informal to a very high degree; very great: *we had to walk a hang of a long way.* [ORIGIN: *hang*, a euphemism for *hell*, apparently from New Zealand English.] **hang someone out to dry** informal, chiefly N. Amer. leave someone in a difficult or vulnerable situation. **hang ten** Surfing ride a surfboard with all ten toes curled over the board's front edge. **hang tough** N. Amer. be or remain inflexible or firmly resolved. **let it all hang out** informal be very relaxed or uninhibited. **not care** (or **give**) **a hang** informal not care at all: *people just don't give a hang about plants.* **you may** (or **might**) **as well be hanged for a sheep as for a lamb** proverb if the penalty for two offences is the same, you might as well commit the more serious one, especially if it brings more benefit.

– ORIGIN Old English *hangian* (intransitive verb), of West Germanic origin, related to Dutch and German *hangen*, reinforced by the Old Norse transitive verb *hanga*.

USAGE In modern English **hang** has two past tense and past participle forms: **hanged** and **hung**. **Hung** is the normal form in most general uses, e.g. *they* **hung** *out the washing; she* **hung** *around for a few minutes; he had* **hung** *the picture over the fireplace*, but **hanged** is the form normally used in reference to execution by hanging: *the prisoner was* **hanged**. The reason for this distinction is a complex historical one: **hanged**, the earlier form, was superseded by **hung** sometime after the 16th century; it is likely that the retention of **hanged** for the execution sense may have to do with the tendency of archaic forms to remain in the legal language of the courts.

▶ **hang around** (or **round** or Brit. **about**) **1** loiter; wait around: *undercover officers spent most of their time hanging around bars.* ■ informal wait: [in imperative] *hang about, you see what it says here?* **2** (**hang around with**) associate with (someone): *I hung around with the thugs.*

hang back remain behind: *Stephen hung back for fear of being seen.* ■ show reluctance to act or move: *I do not believe that our European neighbours will hang back from this.*

hang in informal, chiefly N. Amer. remain persistent and determined in difficult circumstances: *in the second half, we just had to hang in there.*

hang on 1 hold tightly: *he hung on to the back of her coat.* ■ informal remain firm or persevere, especially in difficult circumstances: *United hung on for victory.* ■ (**hang on to**) keep; retain: *he is determined to hang on to his job.* **2** informal wait for a short time: *hang on a minute—do you think I might have left anything out?* ■ (on the telephone) remain connected until one is able to talk to a particular person. **3** be contingent or dependent on: *the future of Europe should not hang on a referendum by the French.* **4** listen closely to: *she hung on his every word.*

hang something on informal attach the blame for something to (someone).

hang out 1 (of washing) hang from a clothes line to dry. **2** protrude and hang loosely downwards: *chaps in jeans with their shirts hanging out.* ■ (**hang out of**) lean out of: *he was found after the collision hanging out of the defendant's car.* **3** informal spend time relaxing or enjoying oneself: *musicians hang out with their own kind.*

hang something out hang something on a line or pole or from a window.

hang together 1 make sense; be consistent: *it helps the speech to hang together.* **2** (of people) remain associated; help or support each other.

hang up 1 hang from a hook: *your dressing gown's hanging up behind the door.* **2** end a telephone conversation by cutting the connection. ■ (**hang up on**) end a telephone conversation with (someone) by abruptly and unexpectedly cutting the connection.

hang something up hang something on a hook: *Jamie hung up our jackets.* ■ informal cease or retire from the activity associated with the garment or object specified: *the midfielder has finally decided to hang up his boots.*

hangar /ˈhaŋə/ ▶ **noun** a large building with extensive floor area, typically for housing aircraft.
– DERIVATIVES **hangarage** noun.
– ORIGIN late 17th cent. (in the sense 'shelter'): from French; probably from Germanic bases meaning 'hamlet' and 'enclosure'.

Hangchow /haŋˈtʃaʊ/ variant of HANGZHOU.

hangdog ▶ **adjective** having a dejected or guilty appearance; shamefaced: *the hangdog look of a condemned man.*

hanger[1] ▶ **noun 1** [in combination] a person who hangs something: *a wallpaper-hanger.*
2 (also **coat hanger**) a shaped piece of wood, plastic, or metal with a hook at the top, from which clothes may be hung in order to keep them in shape and free of creases.

hanger[2] ▶ **noun** Brit. a wood on the side of a steep hill.
– ORIGIN Old English *hangra*, from *hangian* 'hang'.

hanger-on ▶ **noun** (pl. **hangers-on**) a person who associates with another person or a group in a sycophantic manner or for the purpose of gaining some personal advantage.

hang-glider ▶ **noun** an unpowered flying apparatus for a single person, consisting of a frame with a fabric aerofoil stretched over it. The operator is suspended from a harness below and controls flight by body movement.
■ a person flying such an apparatus.
– DERIVATIVES **hang-glide** verb, **hang-gliding** noun.

hangi /ˈhaŋi, ˈhɑːŋi/ ▶ **noun** NZ a pit in which food is cooked on heated stones.
■ [mass noun] the food cooked in such a pit. ■ a meal or gathering at which such food is cooked and served.
– ORIGIN Maori.

hanging ▶ **noun 1** [mass noun] the practice of hanging condemned people as a form of capital punishment.
2 a decorative piece of fabric or curtain hung on the wall of a room or around a bed.
▶ **adjective** [attrib.] suspended in the air: *hanging palls of smoke.*
■ situated or designed so as to appear to hang down: *hanging gardens.*

hanging basket ▶ **noun** a basket or similar container which can be suspended from a building by a small rope or chain and in which decorative flowering plants are grown.

Hanging Gardens of Babylon legendary terraced gardens at Babylon, watered by pumps from the Euphrates, whose construction was ascribed to Nebuchadnezzar (*c.*600 BC). They were one of the Seven Wonders of the World.

hanging paragraph ▶ **noun** a paragraph in which all lines except the first are indented.

hanging valley ▶ **noun** a valley which is cut across by a deeper valley or a cliff.

hangman ▶ **noun** (pl. **-men**) an executioner who hangs condemned people.
■ [mass noun] a game for two in which one player tries to guess the letters of a word, and failed attempts are recorded by drawing a gallows and someone hanging on it, line by line.

hangnail ▶ **noun** a piece of torn skin at the root of a fingernail.
– ORIGIN late 17th cent.: alteration of *agnail* 'painful swelling around a nail' (from Old English *angnægl*, denoting a corn on the toe), influenced by HANG.

hang-out ▶ **noun** informal a place one lives in or frequently visits.

hangover ▶ **noun** a severe headache or other after-effects caused by drinking an excess of alcohol.
■ a thing that has survived from the past: *a hangover from the Sixties.*

Hang Seng index /haŋ ˈsɛŋ/ a figure indicating the relative price of shares on the Hong Kong Stock Exchange.
– ORIGIN named after the *Hang Seng Bank* in Hong Kong, where it was devised.

hang-up ▶ **noun** informal an emotional problem or inhibition: *people with hang-ups about their age.*

Hangzhou /haŋˈdʒəʊ/ (also **Hangchow**) the capital of Zhejiang province in eastern China, situated on Hangzhou Bay, an inlet of the Yellow Sea, at the southern end of the Grand Canal; pop. 2,589,500 (1990).

hank ▶ **noun 1** a coil or skein of wool, hair, or other material: *a thick* **hank of** *her blonde hair.*
2 a measurement of the length per unit mass of cloth or yarn, which varies according to the type being measured. For example it is equal to 840 yards for cotton yarn and 560 yards for worsted.
3 Sailing a ring for securing a staysail to the stay.
– ORIGIN Middle English: from Old Norse *hǫnk*; compare with Swedish *hank* 'string' and Danish *hank* 'handle'.

hanker ▶ **verb** [no obj.] (**hanker after/for/to do something**) feel a strong desire for or to do something: *he hankered after a lost golden age | she hankered to go back* | [as noun **hankering**] *a hankering after familiar music.*
– DERIVATIVES **hankerer** noun.
– ORIGIN early 17th cent.: probably related to HANG; compare with Dutch *hunkeren*.

Hanks /haŋks/, Tom (b.1956), American actor; full name *Thomas J. Hanks*. He won Oscars for his performances in *Philadelphia* (1993) and *Forrest Gump* (1994).

hanky (also **hankie**) ▶ **noun** (pl. **-ies**) informal a handkerchief.
– ORIGIN late 19th cent.: abbreviation.

hanky-panky ▶ **noun** [mass noun] informal, humorous behaviour, in particular sexual or legally dubious behaviour, considered improper but not seriously so: *suspicions of financial hanky-panky.*
– ORIGIN mid 19th cent.: perhaps an alteration of HOKEY-POKEY.

Hannibal /ˈhanɪb(ə)l/ (247–182 BC), Carthaginian general. In the second Punic War he attacked Italy via the Alps, repeatedly defeating the Romans, but failed to take Rome itself.

Hanoi /haˈnɔɪ/ the capital of Vietnam, situated on the Red River in the north of the country; pop. 1,089,700 (1989). It was the capital of French Indo-China from 1887 to 1946 and of North Vietnam before the reunification of North and South Vietnam.

Hanover /ˈhanə(ʊ)və/ an industrial city in NW Germany, on the Mittelland Canal; pop. 517,480 (1991). It is the capital of Lower Saxony. German name HANNOVER /haˈnoːfɐ/.
■ a former state and province in northern Germany. In 1714 the Elector of Hanover succeeded to the British throne as George I, and from then until the accession of Victoria (1837) the same monarch ruled both Britain and Hanover. ■ the British royal house from 1714 to the death of Queen Victoria in 1901.

Hanoverian /ˌhanə(ʊ)ˈvɪərɪən/ ▶ **adjective** of or relating to the royal house of Hanover.
▶ **noun 1** (usu. **the Hanoverians**) any of the British sovereigns from George I to Victoria.
2 a medium-built horse of a German breed, developed for use both as a riding horse and in harness.

b **but** | d **dog** | f **few** | g **get** | h **he** | j **yes** | k **cat** | l **leg** | m **man** | n **no** | p **pen** | r **red** | s **sit** | t **top** | v **voice** | w **we** | z **zoo** | ʃ **she** | ʒ **decision** | θ **thin** | ð **this** | ŋ **ring** | x **loch** | tʃ **chip** | dʒ **jar**

Hansard /ˈhansɑːd, -səd/ ▶ noun the official verbatim record of debates in the British, Canadian, Australian, or New Zealand parliament.
– ORIGIN late 19th cent.: named after Thomas C. Hansard (1776–1833), an English printer whose company originally printed it.

Hanse /ˈhansə/ ▶ noun a medieval guild of merchants.
■ (the Hanse) the Hanseatic League. ■ a fee payable to a guild of merchants.
– ORIGIN Middle English: from Old French hanse 'guild, company', from Old High German hansa 'company, troop'.

Hanseatic League /ˌhansɪˈatɪk/ a medieval association of north German cities, formed in 1241 and surviving until the 19th century. In the later Middle Ages it included over 100 towns and functioned as an independent political power.
– ORIGIN Hanseatic from medieval Latin Hanseaticus, from hansa (see HANSE).

hansel /ˈhans(ə)l/ (also **handsel**) archaic or US ▶ noun a gift given at the beginning of the year or to mark an acquisition or the start of an enterprise, supposedly to bring good luck.
■ the first instalment of a payment.
▶ verb (**hanselled, hanselling**; US **hanseled, hanseling**) [with obj.] give a hansel to: the practice of hanselling the master still flourished in Scotland.
■ inaugurate (something), especially by being the first to try it: a floodlit fixture to officially hansel the completed stadium.
– ORIGIN Middle English (denoting luck): apparently related to late Old English handselen 'giving into a person's hands', and Old Norse handsal 'giving of the hand to seal a promise', from HAND + an element related to SELL; the notion of 'luck', however, is not present in these words.

Hansen's disease /ˈhans(ə)nz/ ▶ noun another term for LEPROSY.
– ORIGIN 1930s: named after Gerhard H. A. Hansen (1841–1912), the Norwegian physician who discovered the causative agent of the disease.

hansom /ˈhans(ə)m/ (also **hansom cab**) ▶ noun historical a two-wheeled horse-drawn cab accommodating two inside, with the driver seated behind.
– ORIGIN mid 19th cent.: named after Joseph A. Hansom (1803–82), English architect, patentee of such a cab in 1834.

hantavirus /ˈhantəˌvʌɪrəs/ ▶ noun a virus of a genus carried by rodents and causing various febrile haemorrhagic diseases, often with kidney damage or failure.
– ORIGIN 1980s: from Hantaan (the name of a river in Korea where the virus was first isolated) + VIRUS.

Hants ▶ abbreviation for Hampshire.

Hanukkah /ˈhanʊkə, x-/ (also **Chanukkah**) ▶ noun a lesser Jewish festival, lasting eight days from the 25th day of Kislev (in December) and commemorating the rededication of the Temple in 165 BC by the Maccabees after its desecration by the Syrians. It is marked by the successive kindling of eight lights.
– ORIGIN from Hebrew ḥănukkāh 'consecration'.

Hanuman /ˌhʌnʊˈmɑːn/ Hinduism a semi-divine being of monkey-like form, whose exploits are described in the Ramayana.
– ORIGIN from Sanskrit hanumant 'large-jawed'.

hanuman /ˌhʌnʊˈmɑːn/ (also **hanuman langur**) ▶ noun a pale-coloured langur monkey of the Indian subcontinent, venerated by Hindus.
● Presbytis entellus, family Cercopithecidae.

Haora variant spelling of HOWRAH.

hap archaic ▶ noun [mass noun] luck; fortune.
■ [count noun] a chance occurrence, especially an event that is considered unlucky.
▶ verb (**happed, happing**) [no obj.] come about by chance: what can hap to him worthy to be deemed evil?
■ [with infinitive] have the fortune or luck to do something: where'er I happ'd to roam.
– ORIGIN Middle English: from Old Norse happ.

hapax legomenon /ˌhapaks lɪˈɡɒmɪnɒn/ ▶ noun (pl. **hapax legomena** /-mɪnə/) a term of which only one instance of use is recorded.
– ORIGIN mid 17th cent.: Greek, 'a thing said once', from hapax 'once' and the passive participle of legein 'to say'.

ha'penny ▶ noun variant spelling of HALFPENNY.

haphazard /hapˈhazəd/ ▶ adjective lacking any

obvious principle of organization: the music business works in a haphazard fashion.
– DERIVATIVES **haphazardly** adverb, **haphazardness** noun.
– ORIGIN late 16th cent.: from HAP + HAZARD.

Haphtarah /ˌhɑːftɑːˈrɑː/ (also **Haphtorah**) ▶ noun (pl. **Haphtaroth, Haphtoroth** /-rəʊt/) variant spelling of HAFTORAH.

hapless ▶ adjective (especially of a person) unfortunate: they stoned the hapless farmer to death.
– DERIVATIVES **haplessly** adverb, **haplessness** noun.
– ORIGIN late Middle English: from HAP (in the early sense 'good fortune') + -LESS.

haplo- ▶ combining form single; simple: haplography | haploid.
– ORIGIN from Greek haploos 'single'.

haplochromine /ˌhaplə(ʊ)ˈkrəʊmʌɪn/ Zoology ▶ adjective of, relating to, or denoting cichlid fishes of a large and diverse group that are particularly abundant in the large lakes of East Africa.
▶ noun a haplochromine fish.
● Haplochromis and related genera, family Cichlidae.
– ORIGIN from the modern Latin genus name.

haplodiploid /ˌhaplə(ʊ)ˈdɪplɔɪd/ ▶ adjective Biology denoting or possessing a genetic system in which females develop from fertilized (diploid) eggs and males from unfertilized (haploid) ones.

haplography /hapˈlɒɡrəfi/ ▶ noun [mass noun] the inadvertent omission of a repeated letter or letters in writing (e.g. writing philogy for philology).
– ORIGIN late 19th cent.: from Greek haploos 'single' + -GRAPHY.

haploid /ˈhaplɔɪd/ Genetics ▶ adjective (of a cell or nucleus) having a single set of unpaired chromosomes. Compare with DIPLOID.
■ (of an organism or part) composed of haploid cells.
▶ noun a haploid organism or cell.
– DERIVATIVES **haploidy** noun.
– ORIGIN early 20th cent.: from Greek haploos 'single' + -OID.

haplology /hapˈlɒlədʒi/ ▶ noun the omission of one occurrence of a sound or syllable which is repeated within a word (e.g. in February pronounced as /ˈfɛbri/).
– ORIGIN late 19th cent.: from Greek haploos 'single' + -LOGY.

haplontic /hapˈlɒntɪk/ ▶ adjective Genetics (chiefly of an alga or other lower plant) having a life cycle in which the main form is haploid, with a diploid zygote being formed only briefly. Compare with DIPLONTIC and DIPLOHAPLONTIC.
– DERIVATIVES **haplont** noun.

ha'p'orth ▶ noun variant spelling of HALF-PENNYWORTH.

happen ▶ verb [no obj.] **1** take place; occur: the afternoon when the disturbance happened.
■ ensue as an effect or result of an action or event: this is what happens when the mechanism goes wrong. ■ [with infinitive] chance to do something or come about: we just happened to meet Paul | there happens to be a clash of personalities. ■ [with clause] come about by chance: it just so happened that she turned up that afternoon. ■ (happen on) find or come across by chance. ■ [with infinitive] used as a polite formula in questions: do you happen to know who her doctor is?
2 (happen to) be experienced by (someone); befall: the same thing happened to me.
■ become of: I don't care what happens to the money.
▶ adverb [sentence adverb] N. English perhaps; maybe: happen I'll go back just for a while.
– PHRASES **as it happens** actually; as a matter of fact: we've got a room vacant, as it happens.
– ORIGIN late Middle English (superseding the verb hap): from the noun HAP + -EN¹.

happening ▶ noun **1** an event or occurrence: altogether it was an eerie happening.
2 a partly improvised or spontaneous piece of theatrical or other artistic performance, typically involving audience participation: a multimedia happening.
▶ adjective informal fashionable; trendy: nightclubs for the young are the happening thing.

happenstance /ˈhap(ə)nˌstans/ ▶ noun [mass noun] chiefly N. Amer. coincidence: it was just happenstance that I happened to be there | [count noun] an untoward happenstance for Trudy.
– ORIGIN late 19th cent.: blend of HAPPEN and CIRCUMSTANCE.

happi /ˈhapi/ (also **happi coat**) ▶ noun (pl. **happis**) a loose informal Japanese coat.
– ORIGIN late 19th cent.: Japanese.

happily ▶ adverb in a happy way.
■ [sentence adverb] it is fortunate that: happily, today's situation is very different.

happy ▶ adjective (**happier, happiest**) **1** feeling or showing pleasure or contentment: Melissa came in looking happy and excited | [with clause] we're just happy that he's still alive | [with infinitive] they are happy to see me doing well.
■ [predic.] (**happy about**) having a sense of trust and confidence in (a person, arrangement, or situation): he was not happy about the proposals. ■ [predic.] (**happy with**) satisfied with the quality or standard of: I'm happy with his performance. ■ [with infinitive] willing to do something: we will be happy to advise you. ■ [attrib.] used in greetings: happy Christmas | happy birthday. ■ [attrib.] fortunate and convenient: he had the happy knack of making people like him.
2 [in combination] informal inclined to use a specified thing excessively or at random: bomb-happy.
– PHRASES (**as**) **happy as a sandboy** (or Brit. **Larry** or N. Amer. **a clam**) extremely happy. **happy hunting ground** a place where success or enjoyment is obtained. [ORIGIN: originally referring to the optimistic hope of American Indians for good hunting grounds in the afterlife.]
– DERIVATIVES **happiness** noun.
– ORIGIN Middle English (in the sense 'lucky'): from the noun HAP + -Y¹.

happy-clappy informal, derogatory ▶ adjective belonging to or characteristic of a Christian group whose worship is marked by enthusiasm and spontaneity.
▶ noun (pl. **-ies**) a member of such a Christian group.

happy event ▶ noun humorous the birth of a child.

happy families ▶ noun [mass noun] Brit. a children's card game played with special cards in sets of four, each depicting members of a 'family', the object being to acquire as many sets as possible.

happy-go-lucky ▶ adjective cheerfully unconcerned about the future: a happy-go-lucky, relaxed attitude.

happy hour ▶ noun a period of the day when drinks are sold at reduced prices in a bar or other licensed establishment.

happy medium ▶ noun a satisfactory compromise: you have to strike a happy medium between looking like royalty and looking like a housewife.

Hapsburg /ˈhapsbəːɡ/ variant spelling of HABSBURG.

hapten /ˈhaptən/ ▶ noun Physiology a small molecule which, when combined with a larger carrier such as a protein, can elicit the production of antibodies which bind specifically to it (in the free or combined state).
– ORIGIN early 20th cent.: from Greek haptein 'fasten'.

haptic /ˈhaptɪk/ ▶ adjective technical of or relating to the sense of touch, in particular relating to the perception and manipulation of objects using the senses of touch and proprioception.
– ORIGIN late 19th cent.: from Greek haptikos 'able to touch or grasp', from haptein 'fasten'.

haptoglobin /ˌhaptə(ʊ)ˈɡləʊbɪn/ ▶ noun [mass noun] Biochemistry a protein present in blood serum which binds to and removes free haemoglobin from the bloodstream.
– ORIGIN 1940s: from Greek haptein 'fasten' + (haemo)globin.

hapu /ˈhɑːpuː/ ▶ noun NZ a division of a Maori people or community.
– ORIGIN Maori.

hara-kiri /ˌharəˈkɪri/ ▶ noun [mass noun] ritual suicide by disembowelment with a sword, formerly practised in Japan by samurai as an honourable alternative to disgrace or execution.
■ figurative ostentatious or ritualized self-destruction.
– ORIGIN mid 19th cent.: colloquial Japanese, from hara 'belly' + kiri 'cutting'.

haram /hɑːˈrɑːm/ ▶ adjective forbidden or proscribed by Islamic law.
– ORIGIN from Arabic ḥarām 'forbidden'.

harangue /həˈraŋ/ ▶ noun a lengthy and aggressive speech.
▶ verb [with obj.] lecture (someone) at length in an aggressive and critical manner: he harangued the public on their ignorance.

a cat | ɑː arm | ɛ bed | ɛː hair | ə ago | əː her | ɪ sit | i cosy | iː see | ɒ hot | ɔː saw | ʌ run | ʊ put | uː too | ʌɪ my | aʊ how | eɪ day | əʊ no | ɪə near | ɔɪ boy | ʊə poor | ʌɪə fire | aʊə sour

– DERIVATIVES **haranguer** noun.
– ORIGIN late Middle English: from Old French *arenge*, from medieval Latin *harenga*, perhaps of Germanic origin. The spelling was later altered to conform with French *harangue* (noun), *haranguer* (verb).

Harappa /həˈrapə/ an ancient city of the Indus valley civilization (c.2600–1700 BC), in northern Pakistan. The site of the ruins was discovered in 1920.

Harare /həˈrɑːri/ the capital of Zimbabwe; pop. 1,184,170 (1992). Former name (until 1982) **SALISBURY**.

harass /ˈharəs, həˈras/ ▶ **verb** [with obj.] subject to aggressive pressure or intimidation: *a warning to men harassing girls at work.*
■ make repeated small-scale attacks on (an enemy): *the squadron's task was to harass the retreating enemy forces.* ■ [as adj. **harassed**] feeling or looking strained by having too many demands made on one.
– DERIVATIVES **harasser** noun, **harassingly** adverb, **harassment** noun.
– ORIGIN early 17th cent.: from French *harasser*, from *harer* 'set a dog on', from Germanic *hare*, a cry urging a dog to attack.

h

USAGE There are two possible pronunciations of the word **harass**: one with the stress on the **har-** and the other with the stress on the **-rass**. The former pronunciation is the older one and is regarded by some people as the only correct one, especially in British English. However, the pronunciation with the stress on the second syllable **-rass** is very common and is now accepted as a standard alternative.

Harbin /hɑːˈbiːn, -ˈbɪn/ the capital of Heilongjiang province in NE China, on the Songhua River; pop. 3,597,400 (1990).

harbinger /ˈhɑːbɪn(d)ʒə/ ▶ **noun** a person or thing that announces or signals the approach of another: *witch hazels are the harbingers of spring.*
■ a forerunner of something.
– ORIGIN Middle English: from Old French *herbergere*, from *herbergier* 'provide lodging for', from *herberge* 'lodging', from Old Saxon *heriberga* 'shelter for an army, lodging' (from *heri* 'army' + a Germanic base meaning 'fortified place'), related to **HARBOUR**. The term originally denoted a person who provided lodging, later one who went ahead to find lodgings for an army or for a nobleman and his retinue, hence, a herald (mid 16th cent.).

harbour (US **harbor**) ▶ **noun** a place on the coast where ships may moor in shelter, especially one protected from rough water by piers, jetties, and other artificial structures.
■ figurative a place of refuge: *the offered harbour of his arms.*
▶ **verb** [with obj.] **1** keep (a thought or feeling, typically a negative one) in one's mind, especially secretly: *she started to harbour doubts about the wisdom of their journey.*
2 give a home or shelter to: *woodlands that once harboured a colony of red deer.*
■ shelter or hide (a criminal or wanted person): *he was suspected of harbouring an escaped prisoner.* ■ carry the germs of (a disease).
3 [no obj.] archaic (of a ship or its crew) moor in a harbour: *he might have harboured in Falmouth.*
– DERIVATIVES **harbourless** adjective.
– ORIGIN late Old English *herebeorg* 'shelter, refuge', *herebeorgian* 'occupy shelter', of Germanic origin; related to Dutch *herberge* and German *Herberge*, also to French *auberge* 'inn'; see also **HARBINGER**.

harbourage (US **harborage**) ▶ **noun** a harbour or other place of shelter.

harbour master (US **harbormaster**) ▶ **noun** an official in charge of a harbour.

harbour seal ▶ **noun** North American term for **COMMON SEAL**[1].

hard ▶ **adjective 1** solid, firm, and rigid; not easily broken, bent, or pierced: *a hard mattress | rub the varnish down when it's hard.*
■ (of a person) not showing any signs of weakness; tough: *only a handful are hard enough to join the SAS.* ■ (of information) reliable, especially because based on something true or substantiated: *hard facts about the underclass are maddeningly elusive.* ■ (of a subject of study) dealing with precise and verifiable facts: *efforts to turn psychology into hard science.* ■ (of a consonant) pronounced as a velar plosive (as *c* in *cat*, *g* in *go*). ■ (of prices of shares, commodities, etc.) high and stable; firm. ■ (of science fiction) scientifically accurate rather than purely fantastic or whimsical: *a hard SF novel.*
2 requiring a great deal of endurance or physical or mental effort: *airship-flying was pretty hard work* | [with infinitive] *she found it hard to believe that he could be involved.*
■ putting a lot of energy into an activity: *he'd been a hard worker all his life | everyone has been hard at work.* ■ difficult to bear; causing suffering: *times were hard at the end of the war | he'd had a hard life.* ■ not showing sympathy or affection; strict: *he can be such a hard taskmaster.* ■ denoting an extreme or dogmatic faction within a political party: *the hard left.* ■ (of a season or the weather) severe: *it's been a long, hard winter.* ■ harsh or unpleasant to the senses: *the hard light of morning.* ■ (of wine) harsh or sharp to the taste, especially because of tannin.
3 done with a great deal of force or strength: *a hard whack.*
4 very potent, powerful, or intense, in particular:
■ (of liquor) strongly alcoholic; spirit rather than beer or wine. ■ (of a drug) potent and addictive. ■ (of water) containing mineral salts that make lathering difficult. ■ (of radiation) highly penetrating. ■ (of pornography) highly obscene and explicit.
▶ **adverb 1** with a great deal of effort: *they work hard at school.*
■ with a great deal of force; violently: *it was raining hard.*
2 so as to be solid or firm: *the mortar has set hard.*
3 to the fullest extent possible: *put the wheel* **hard over** *to starboard.*
▶ **noun** Brit. a road leading down across a foreshore.
– PHRASES **be hard on 1** treat or criticize (someone) severely: *you're being too hard on her.* **2** be difficult for or unfair to: *I think the war must have been hard on her.* **3** be likely to hurt or damage: *the monitor flickers, which is hard on the eyes.* **be hard put (to it)** [usu. with infinitive] find it very difficult: *you'll be hard put to find a better compromise.* **give someone a hard time** informal deliberately make a situation difficult for someone. **go hard with** dated turn out to (someone's) disadvantage: *it would go hard with the poor.* **hard and fast** [usu. with negative] (of a rule or a distinction made) fixed and definitive. **hard as nails** see **NAIL**. **hard at it** informal busily working or occupied: *they were hard at it with brooms and mops.* **hard by** close to: *he lived hard by the cathedral.* **hard done by** Brit. harshly or unfairly treated: *she would be justified in feeling hard done by.* **hard feelings** [usu. with negative] feelings of resentment: *there are* **no hard feelings** *and we wish him well.* **hard going** difficult to understand or enjoy: *the studying is at times hard going.* **hard hit** badly affected: *Trinidad had been hard hit by falling oil prices.* **hard luck** (or **lines**) Brit. informal used to express sympathy or commiserations: ironic *if you don't like it then hard luck.* **a hard nut to crack** informal a person or thing that is difficult to understand or influence. **hard of hearing** not able to hear well. **hard on** (or **upon**) close to; following soon after: **hard on the heels of** *Wimbledon comes the Henley Regatta.* **hard up** informal short of money: *I'm too hard up to buy fancy clothes.* **the hard way** through suffering or learning from the unpleasant consequences of mistakes: *his reputation was earned the hard way.* **play hard to get** informal deliberately adopt an aloof or uninterested attitude, typically in order to make oneself more attractive or interesting. **put the hard word on** Austral./NZ informal ask a favour of (someone), especially a sexual or financial one.
– DERIVATIVES **hardish** adjective, **hardness** noun.
– ORIGIN Old English *hard*, *heard*, of Germanic origin; related to Dutch *hard* and German *hart*.

hardback ▶ **adjective** (of a book) bound in stiff covers.
▶ **noun** a book bound in stiff covers.
– PHRASES **in hardback** in an edition bound in stiff covers: *it was first published in hardback in 1981.*

hardball ▶ **noun** [mass noun] N. Amer. baseball, especially as contrasted with softball.
■ informal uncompromising and ruthless methods or dealings, especially in politics: *the leadership played hardball to win the vote.*

hardbitten ▶ **adjective** tough and cynical: *a hardbitten war reporter.*

hardboard ▶ **noun** [mass noun] stiff board made of compressed and treated wood pulp.

hard-boiled ▶ **adjective 1** (of an egg) boiled until the white and the yolk are solid.
2 (of a person) tough and cynical.
■ denoting a tough, realistic style of detective fiction set in a world permeated by corruption and deceit: *a hard-boiled thriller.*

hard case ▶ **noun** informal a tough or intractable person.
■ Austral./NZ an amusing or eccentric person.

hard cash ▶ **noun** [mass noun] negotiable coins and banknotes as opposed to other forms of payment.

hard cheese ▶ **noun** see **CHEESE**[1].

hard clam ▶ **noun** another term for **QUAHOG**.

hard coal ▶ **noun** another term for **ANTHRACITE**.

hard-code ▶ **verb** [with obj.] Computing fix (data or parameters) in a program in such a way that they cannot easily be altered by the user.

hard copy ▶ **noun** a printed version on paper of data held in a computer.

hard core ▶ **noun 1** the most active, committed, or doctrinaire members of a group or movement: *there is always a hard core of trusty stalwarts* | [as modifier] *a hard-core following.*
■ [mass noun] popular music that is experimental in nature and typically characterized by high volume and aggressive presentation. ■ [mass noun] pornography of a very explicit kind: [as modifier] *hard-core porn.*
2 [mass noun] Brit. broken bricks, rubble, or similar solid material used as a filling or foundation in building.

hardcover ▶ **adjective** & **noun** chiefly N. Amer. another term for **HARDBACK**.

hard currency ▶ **noun** [mass noun] currency that is not likely to depreciate suddenly or to fluctuate greatly in value.

hard disk ▶ **noun** Computing a rigid non-removable magnetic disk with a large data storage capacity.

hard doer ▶ **noun** see **DOER**.

hard drive ▶ **noun** another term for **HARD DISK**.

hard-earned ▶ **adjective** having taken a great deal of effort to earn or acquire: *hard-earned money.*

harden ▶ **verb** make or become hard or harder: [no obj.] *wait for the glue to harden* | [with obj.] *bricks which seem to have been hardened by firing.*
■ make or become more severe and less sympathetic: [with obj.] *she hardened her heart.* ■ make or become tougher and more clearly defined: [no obj.] *suspicion* **hardened into** *certainty.* ■ [no obj.] (of prices of shares, commodities, etc.) rise and remain steady at a higher level.
– PHRASES **hardening of the arteries** another term for **ARTERIOSCLEROSIS**.
– DERIVATIVES **hardener** noun.
▶ **harden something off** inure a plant to cold by gradually increasing its exposure to it.

hardened ▶ **adjective 1** having become or been made hard or harder: *hardened steel.*
■ strengthened or made secure against attack, especially by nuclear weapons: *the silos are* **hardened against** *air attack.*
2 [attrib.] very experienced in a particular job or activity and therefore not easily upset by its more unpleasant aspects: *hardened police officers* | [in combination] *a battle-hardened veteran.*
■ utterly fixed in a habit or way of life seen as bad: *hardened criminals | a hardened liar.*

hard error ▶ **noun** Computing an error or hardware fault causing failure of a program or operating system, especially one that gives no option of recovery.

hard fern ▶ **noun** a European fern of heathy places, which has long, narrow leathery fronds consisting of a row of thin lobes on each side of the stem.
• *Blechnum spicant*, family Blechnaceae.

hard hat ▶ **noun** a rigid protective helmet, as worn by factory and building workers.
■ informal a worker who wears a hard hat. ■ informal, chiefly US a person with reactionary or conservative views.

hardhead ▶ **noun 1** an Australasian diving duck related to the pochard, with mainly dark brown plumage.
• *Aythya australis*, family Anatidae. Alternative name: **white-eyed duck**.
2 (also **hardhead catfish**) a marine catfish, the male of which incubates the eggs inside its mouth. It occurs along the Atlantic coast of North America.
• *Arius felis*, family Ariidae.

hard-headed ▶ **adjective** practical and realistic; not sentimental: *a hard-headed businessman.*
– DERIVATIVES **hard-headedly** adverb, **hard-headedness** noun.

hardheads (also **hardhead**) ▶ plural noun [treated as sing.] Brit. another term for KNAPWEED.

hard-hearted ▶ adjective incapable of being moved to pity or tenderness; unfeeling.
– DERIVATIVES **hard-heartedly** adverb, **hard-heartedness** noun.

hard-hitting ▶ adjective uncompromisingly direct and honest, especially in revealing unpalatable facts: *a hard-hitting anti-fox-hunting poster.*

Hardie, (James) Keir (1856–1915), Scottish Labour politician. A miner before becoming an MP in 1892, he became the first leader of both the Independent Labour Party (1893) and the Labour Party (1906).

hardihood ▶ noun [mass noun] dated boldness; daring.

Harding, Warren (Gamaliel) (1865–1923), American Republican statesman, 29th President of the US 1921–3.

hard labour ▶ noun [mass noun] heavy manual work as a punishment.

hard landing ▶ noun a clumsy or rough landing of an aircraft.
■ an uncontrolled landing in which a spacecraft crashes on to the surface of a planet or moon and is destroyed.

hard line ▶ noun an uncompromising adherence to a firm policy: *he is known to take a hard line on sentencing policy for murder.*
▶ adjective uncompromising; strict: *a hard-line party activist.*

hardliner ▶ noun a member of a group, typically a political group, who adheres uncompromisingly to a set of ideas or policies.

hard-luck story ▶ noun an account of one's problems intended to gain someone else's sympathy or help.

hardly ▶ adverb **1** scarcely (used to qualify a statement by saying that it is true to an insignificant degree): *it is hardly bigger than a credit card.*
■ only a very short time before: *the party had hardly started when the police arrived.* ■ only with great difficulty: *she could hardly sit up straight.* ■ no or not (suggesting surprise at or disagreement with a statement): *I hardly think so.*
2 archaic harshly: *the rule worked hardly.*
– PHRASES **hardly any** almost no: *they sold hardly any books.* ■ almost none: *hardly any had previous convictions.* **hardly ever** very rarely: *we hardly ever see them.*

> USAGE Words like **hardly**, **scarcely**, and **rarely** should not be used with negative constructions. Thus, it is correct to say *I can hardly wait* but incorrect to say *I can't hardly wait*. This is because adverbs like **hardly** are treated as if they were negatives, and it is a well-known grammatical rule of standard English that double negatives (i.e. in this case having **hardly** and **not** in the same clause) are not acceptable. Words like **hardly** behave as negatives in other respects as well, as for example in combining with words like **any** or **at all**, which normally only occur where a negative is present (thus, standard usage is *I've got hardly any money* but not *I've got any money*). See also usage at DOUBLE NEGATIVE.

hard-nosed ▶ adjective informal realistic and determined; tough-minded: *the hard-nosed, tough approach.*

hard nut ▶ noun Brit. informal a tough, aggressive, or insensitive person: *a local hard nut awaiting trial for murder.*

hard-on ▶ noun vulgar slang an erection of the penis.

hard pad ▶ noun [mass noun] hardening of the pads of the feet, a symptom of distemper in dogs and other animals.

hard palate ▶ noun the bony front part of the palate.

hardpan ▶ noun [mass noun] a hardened impervious layer, typically of clay, occurring in or below the soil and impairing drainage and plant growth.

hard-paste ▶ adjective denoting true porcelain made of fusible and infusible materials (usually kaolin and china stone) fired at a high temperature. Developed in early medieval China, it was not made in Europe until the early 18th century.

hard-pressed ▶ adjective **1** closely pursued: *the hard-pressed French infantry.*
2 burdened with urgent business: *training centres are hard-pressed and insufficient in numbers.*

■ in difficulties: [with infinitive] *the staff were hard-pressed to give even basic care.*

hard rock ▶ noun [mass noun] highly amplified rock music with a heavy beat.

hard roe ▶ noun see ROE[1].

hard sauce ▶ noun [mass noun] a sauce of butter and sugar, typically with brandy, rum, or vanilla added.

hard sell ▶ noun (often **the hard sell**) a policy or technique of aggressive salesmanship or advertising: *they invited 1,000 participants and gave them the hard sell.*

hard-shell ▶ adjective [attrib.] **1** having a hard shell or outer casing: *a hard-shell suitcase.*
2 chiefly US rigid or uncompromising, especially in fundamentalist religious belief.

hardshell clam ▶ noun another term for QUAHOG.

hardship ▶ noun [mass noun] severe suffering or privation: *intolerable levels of hardship* | [count noun] *the shared hardships of wartime.*

hard shoulder ▶ noun Brit. a hardened strip alongside a motorway for stopping on in an emergency.

hardstanding ▶ noun [mass noun] Brit. ground surfaced with a hard material for parking vehicles on.

hardstone ▶ noun [mass noun] precious or semi-precious stone used for intaglio, mosaic work, etc.

hard stuff ▶ noun (**the hard stuff**) informal strong alcoholic drink.

hard tack ▶ noun [mass noun] archaic hard dry bread or biscuit, especially as rations for sailors or soldiers.

hardtop ▶ noun **1** a motor vehicle with a rigid roof which in some cases is detachable.
■ a roof of this type.
2 (also **hardtop road**) Canadian a metalled road.

Hardwar /hɑːˈdwɑː/ a city in Uttar Pradesh, northern India, on the River Ganges; pop. 188,960 (1991). It is a place of Hindu pilgrimage.

hardware ▶ noun [mass noun] tools, machinery, and other durable equipment: *tanks and other military hardware.*
■ the machines, wiring, and other physical components of a computer or other electronic system. Compare with SOFTWARE. ■ tools, implements, and other items used in home life and activities such as gardening.

hard-wearing ▶ adjective able to stand much wear: *a hard-wearing fabric.*

hard wheat ▶ noun [mass noun] wheat of a variety having a hard grain rich in gluten.

hard-wired ▶ adjective Electronics involving or achieved by permanently connected circuits rather than software.
– DERIVATIVES **hard-wire** verb & adjective.

hardwood ▶ noun [mass noun] **1** the wood from a broadleaved tree (such as oak, ash, or beech) as distinguished from that of conifers.
■ [count noun] a tree producing such wood.
2 (in gardening) mature growth on shrubs and other plants from which cuttings may be taken.

hard-working ▶ adjective (of a person) tending to work with energy and commitment; diligent.

Hardy[1], Oliver, see LAUREL AND HARDY.

Hardy[2], Thomas (1840–1928), English novelist and poet. Much of his work deals with the struggle against the indifferent force that inflicts the sufferings and ironies of life. Notable novels: *The Mayor of Casterbridge* (1886), *Tess of the D'Urbervilles* (1891), and *Jude the Obscure* (1896).

hardy ▶ adjective (**hardier**, **hardiest**) capable of enduring difficult conditions; robust.
■ (of a plant) able to survive outside during winter.
– DERIVATIVES **hardily** adverb, **hardiness** noun.
– ORIGIN Middle English (in the sense 'bold, daring'): from Old French *hardi*, past participle of *hardir* 'become bold', of Germanic origin; related to HARD.

Hare[1], Sir David (b.1947), English dramatist and director. He is noted for political dramas, such as *Plenty* (1978), centring around intense, self-destructive characters. He has also written and directed films including *Wetherby* (1985) and *Paris by Night* (1988).

Hare[2], William, see BURKE[4].

hare ▶ noun a fast-running, long-eared mammal that resembles a large rabbit, having very long hind legs and typically found in grassland or open woodland.
● *Lepus* and other genera, family Leporidae: several species.
■ (also **electric hare**) a dummy hare propelled around the track in greyhound racing.
▶ verb [no obj., with adverbial of direction] run with great speed: *he hared off between the trees.*
– PHRASES **run with the hare and hunt with the hounds** Brit. try to remain on good terms with both sides in a conflict or dispute. **start a hare** Brit. dated raise a topic of conversation.
– ORIGIN Old English *hara*, of Germanic origin: related to Dutch *haas* and German *Hase*.

hare and hounds ▶ noun [mass noun] a game, especially a paperchase, in which a group of people chase another person or group across the countryside.

harebell ▶ noun a widely distributed bellflower with slender stems and pale blue flowers in late summer. Also called BLUEBELL, especially in Scotland.
● *Campanula rotundifolia*, family Campanulaceae.
– ORIGIN Middle English: probably so named because it is found growing in places frequented by hares.

hare-brained ▶ adjective rash; ill-judged.

Haredi /haˈrɛdi/ ▶ noun (pl. **Haredim** /-dɪm/) a member of any of various Orthodox Jewish sects characterized by strict adherence to the traditional form of Jewish law and rejection of modern secular culture, many of whom do not recognize the modern state of Israel as a spiritual authority.
– ORIGIN Hebrew, literally 'one who trembles (in awe at the word of God)'.

Harefoot, Harold, see HAROLD.

Hare Krishna /ˌhɑːri ˈkrɪʃnə, ˌhɑːreɪ/ ▶ noun a member of the International Society for Krishna Consciousness, a religious sect based mainly in the US and other Western countries. Its devotees typically wear saffron robes, favour celibacy, practise vegetarianism, and chant mantras based on the name of the Hindu god Krishna.
■ [mass noun] this sect.
– ORIGIN 1960s: Sanskrit, literally 'O Vishnu Krishna', the words of a devotional chant.

harelip ▶ noun another term for CLEFT LIP.
– DERIVATIVES **harelipped** adjective.
– ORIGIN mid 16th cent.: from a perceived resemblance to the mouth of a hare.

> USAGE Use of the word **harelip** can cause offence and should be avoided; use **cleft lip** instead.

harem /ˈhɑːriːm, hɑːˈriːm, ˈhɛːrəm/ ▶ noun **1** the separate part of a Muslim household reserved for wives, concubines, and female servants.
2 the wives (or concubines) of a polygamous man.
■ a group of female animals sharing a single mate.
– ORIGIN mid 17th cent. (in sense 1): from Arabic *ḥaram, ḥarīm*, literally 'prohibited, prohibited place' (hence 'sanctuary, women's quarters, women'), from *ḥarama* 'be prohibited'.

hare's-foot (also **hare's-foot clover**) ▶ noun a slender clover which has soft hairs around the flowers.
● *Trifolium arvense*, family Leguminosae.

hare's-tail (also **hare's-tail grass**) ▶ noun a Mediterranean grass with white silky flowering heads and woolly grey-green leaves.
● *Lagurus ovatus*, family Gramineae.

hare wallaby ▶ noun a small, agile, fast-moving Australian wallaby with orange rings of fur around the eyes.
● Genera *Lagorchestes* and *Lagostrophus*, family Macropodidae: several species.

harewood ▶ noun [mass noun] stained sycamore wood used for making furniture.
– ORIGIN late 17th cent.: from German dialect *Ehre* (from Latin *acer* 'maple') + WOOD.

Hargeisa /hɑːˈɡeɪsə/ (also **Hargeysa**) a city in NW Somalia; pop. 400,000 (est.).

Hargreaves, James (1720–78), English inventor. A pioneer of the Lancashire cotton industry, he invented the spinning jenny (*c*.1764).

haricot /ˈharɪkəʊ/ (also **haricot bean**) ▶ noun **1** a French bean of a variety with small white seeds.
2 the dried seed of this bean used as a vegetable.
– ORIGIN mid 17th cent.: French, perhaps from Aztec *ayacotli*.

Harijan /ˈhʌrɪdʒ(ə)n, ˈharɪdʒan/ ▶ noun dated a

member of a hereditary Hindu group of the lowest social and ritual status. See **UNTOUCHABLE**.
– ORIGIN from Sanskrit *harijana*, literally 'a person dedicated to Vishnu', from *Hari* 'Vishnu' + *jana* 'person'. The term was adopted and popularized by Gandhi.

harissa /ˈarɪsə/ ▶ noun [mass noun] a hot sauce or paste used in North African cuisine, made from chilli peppers, paprika, and olive oil.
– ORIGIN from Arabic.

hark ▶ verb [no obj., usu. in imperative] poetic/literary listen: *Hark! He knocks.*
■(**hark at**) informal used to draw attention to someone who has said or done something considered to be foolish or silly: *just hark at you, speaking all lah-de-dah!*
– ORIGIN Middle English: of Germanic origin; related to German *horchen*, also to **HEARKEN**.
▶**hark back** mention or remember something from the past: *if it was such a rotten holiday, why hark back to it?* [ORIGIN: originally a hunting term, used of hounds retracing their steps to find a lost scent.]
hark back to evoke (an older style or genre): *paintings that hark back to Constable and Turner.*

harken ▶ verb variant spelling of **HEARKEN**.

Harlech /ˈhɑːlɛk, -lɛx/ a village on the west coast of Wales, in Gwynedd; pop. 1,313 (1989). It is noted for the ruins of its 13th-century castle.

Harlem /ˈhɑːləm/ a district of New York City, situated to the north of 96th Street in NE Manhattan. It has a large black population and in the 1920s and 1930s was noted for its nightclubs and jazz bands.

Harlem Renaissance a movement in US literature in the 1920s which centred on Harlem and was an early manifestation of black consciousness in the US. The movement included writers such as Langston Hughes and Zora Neale Hurston.

harlequin /ˈhɑːlɪkwɪn/ ▶ noun 1 (**Harlequin**) a mute character in traditional pantomime, typically masked and dressed in a diamond-patterned costume.
■historical a stock comic character in Italian *commedia dell'arte*.
2 (also **harlequin duck**) a small duck of fast-flowing streams around the Arctic and North Pacific, the male having mainly grey-blue plumage with bold white markings.
● *Histrionicus histrionicus*, family Anatidae.
▶ adjective in varied colours; variegated.
– ORIGIN late 16th cent.: from obsolete French, from earlier *Herlequin* (or *Hellequin*), the name of the leader of a legendary troop of demon horsemen; perhaps ultimately related to Old English *Herla cyning* 'King Herla', a mythical figure sometimes identified with Woden.

harlequinade /ˌhɑːlɪkwɪˈneɪd/ ▶ noun historical the section of a traditional pantomime in which Harlequin played a leading role.
■dated a piece of buffoonery.
– ORIGIN late 18th cent.: from French *arlequinade*, from (*h*)*arlequin* (see **HARLEQUIN**).

harlequin fish ▶ noun a small brightly coloured freshwater fish of SE Asia, popular in aquaria.
● *Rasbora heteromorpha*, family Cyprinidae.

Harley Street a street in central London where many eminent physicians and surgeons have consulting rooms.

harlot /ˈhɑːlət/ ▶ noun archaic a prostitute or promiscuous woman.
– DERIVATIVES **harlotry** noun.
– ORIGIN Middle English (denoting a vagabond or beggar, later a lecherous man or woman): from Old French *harlot, herlot* 'young man, knave, vagabond'.

Harlow[1] a town in west Essex, north of London; pop. 79,520 (1981). It was designated as a new town in 1947.

Harlow[2], Jean (1911–37), American film actress; born *Harlean Carpenter*. Her six films with Clark Gable included *Red Dust* (1932) and *Saratoga* (1937).

harm ▶ noun [mass noun] physical injury, especially that which is deliberately inflicted: *it's fine as long as no one is inflicting harm on anyone else.*
■material damage: *it's unlikely to do much harm to the engine.* ■actual or potential ill effect or danger: *I can't see any harm in it.*
▶ verb [with obj.] physically injure: *the villains didn't harm him.*
■damage the health of: *smoking when pregnant can*

harm your baby. ■ have an adverse effect on: *this could harm his World Cup prospects.*
– PHRASES **come to no harm** be unhurt or undamaged. **do more harm than good** inadvertently make a situation worse rather than better. **no harm done** used to reassure someone that what they have done has caused no real damage or problems. **out of harm's way** in a safe place.
– ORIGIN Old English *hearm* (noun), *hearmian* (verb), of Germanic origin; related to German *Harm* and Old Norse *harmr* 'grief, sorrow'.

harmattan /hɑːˈmat(ə)n/ ▶ noun a very dry, dusty easterly or north-easterly wind on the West African coast, occurring from December to February.
– ORIGIN late 17th cent.: from Twi *haramata*.

harmful ▶ adjective causing or likely to cause harm: *shield the planet from harmful cosmic rays | sugars which can be harmful to the teeth.*
– DERIVATIVES **harmfully** adverb, **harmfulness** noun.

harmless ▶ adjective not able or likely to cause harm: *the venom of most spiders is harmless to humans.*
■inoffensive: *as an entertainer, he's pretty harmless.*
– DERIVATIVES **harmlessly** adverb, **harmlessness** noun.

harmolodics /ˌhɑːməˈlɒdɪks/ ▶ plural noun [treated as sing.] a form of free jazz in which musicians improvise simultaneously on a melodic line at various pitches.
– DERIVATIVES **harmolodic** adjective.
– ORIGIN 1970s: coined by the American saxophonist Ornette Coleman (b. 1930) and said to be a blend of *harmony, movement,* and *melodic.*

harmonic /hɑːˈmɒnɪk/ ▶ adjective 1 of, relating to, or characterized by musical harmony: *a basic four-chord harmonic sequence.*
■Music relating to or denoting a harmonic or harmonics.
2 Mathematics of or relating to a harmonic series or progression.
■Physics of or relating to component frequencies of a complex oscillation or wave. ■ Astrology using or produced by the application of a harmonic: *harmonic charts.*
▶noun 1 Music an overtone accompanying a fundamental tone at a fixed interval, produced by vibration of a string, column of air, etc. in an exact fraction of its length.
■a note produced on a musical instrument as an overtone, e.g. by lightly touching a string while sounding it.
2 Physics a component frequency of an oscillation or wave.
■Astrology a division of the zodiacal circle by a specified number, used in the interpretation of a birth chart.
– DERIVATIVES **harmonically** adverb.
– ORIGIN late 16th cent. (in the sense 'relating to music, musical'): via Latin from Greek *harmonikos*, from *harmonia* (see **HARMONY**).

harmonica /hɑːˈmɒnɪkə/ ▶ noun a small rectangular wind instrument with a row of metal reeds along its length, held against the lips and moved from side to side to produce different notes by blowing or sucking. Also called **MOUTH ORGAN**.
– ORIGIN mid 18th cent.: from Latin, feminine singular or neuter plural of *harmonicus* 'musical' (see **HARMONIC**).

harmonic minor (also **harmonic minor scale**) ▶ noun Music a scale containing a minor third, minor sixth, and major seventh, forming the basis of conventional harmony in minor keys.

harmonic motion ▶ noun another term for **SIMPLE HARMONIC MOTION**.

harmonic progression ▶ noun 1 Music a series of chord changes forming the underlying harmony of a piece of music.
2 Mathematics a sequence of quantities whose reciprocals are in arithmetic progression (e.g. 1, ⅓, ⅙, ⅐, etc.).

harmonic series ▶ noun 1 Music a set of frequencies consisting of a fundamental and the harmonics related to it by an exact fraction.
2 Mathematics a series of values in harmonic progression.

harmonious ▶ adjective tuneful; not discordant: *harmonious music.*
■forming a pleasing or consistent whole: *the decor is a harmonious blend of traditional and modern.* ■ free from disagreement or dissent: *harmonious relationships.*

– DERIVATIVES **harmoniously** adverb, **harmoniousness** noun.

harmonist ▶ noun a person skilled in musical harmony.

harmonium /hɑːˈməʊnɪəm/ ▶ noun a keyboard instrument in which the notes are produced by air driven through metal reeds by foot-operated bellows.
– ORIGIN mid 19th cent.: from French, from Latin *harmonia* (see **HARMONY**) or Greek *harmonios* 'harmonious'.

harmonize (also **-ise**) ▶ verb [with obj.] add notes to (a melody) to produce harmony.
■[no obj.] produce a pleasing visual combination: *steeply pitched roofs which harmonize with the form of the main roof.* ■ make consistent: *plans to harmonize the railways of Europe.*
– DERIVATIVES **harmonization** noun.
– ORIGIN late 15th cent. (in the sense 'sing or play in harmony'): from French *harmoniser*, from *harmonie* (see **HARMONY**).

harmony ▶ noun (pl. **-ies**) [mass noun] 1 the combination of simultaneously sounded musical notes to produce chords and chord progressions having a pleasing effect: *the piece owes its air of tranquillity largely to the harmony* | [count noun] *an exciting variety of improvised harmonies.*
■the study or composition of musical harmony. ■ the quality of forming a pleasing and consistent whole: *delightful cities where old and new blend in harmony.* ■ [count noun] an arrangement of the four Gospels, or of any parallel narratives, which presents a single continuous narrative text.
2 agreement or concord: *man and machine in perfect harmony.*
– PHRASES **harmony of the spheres** see **SPHERE**.
– ORIGIN late Middle English: via Old French from Latin *harmonia* 'joining, concord', from Greek, from *harmos* 'joint'.

Harmsworth, Alfred Charles William, see **NORTHCLIFFE**.

harness ▶ noun a set of straps and fittings by which a horse or other draught animal is fastened to a cart, plough, etc. and is controlled by its driver.
■an arrangement of straps for fastening something such as a parachute to a person's body or for restraining a young child.
▶ verb [with obj.] 1 put a harness on (a horse or other draught animal).
■(**harness something to**) attach a draught animal to (something) by a harness: *the horse was harnessed to two long shafts.*
2 control and make use of (natural resources), especially to produce energy: *attempts to harness solar energy* | figurative *harnessing the creativity of graduates.*
– PHRASES **in harness** (of a horse or other animal) used for driving or draught work. ■ in the routine of daily work: *a man who died in harness far beyond the normal age of retirement.* ■ working closely with someone to achieve something: *local and central government should work in harness.*
– DERIVATIVES **harnesser** noun.
– ORIGIN Middle English: from Old French *harneis* 'military equipment', from Old Norse, from *herr* 'army' + *nest* 'provisions'.

harness racing ▶ noun another term for **TROTTING**.

Harold the name of two kings of England:
■Harold I (d.1040), reigned 1035–40; known as **Harold Harefoot**. An illegitimate son of Canute, he came to the throne when his half-brother Hardecanute (Canute's legitimate heir) was king of Denmark and thus absent when Canute died.
■Harold II (c.1019–66), reigned 1066, the last Anglo-Saxon king of England. Succeeding Edward the Confessor, he was faced with two invasions within months of his accession. He resisted his half-brother Tostig and the Norse king Harald Hardrada at Stamford Bridge, but was killed and his army defeated by William of Normandy at the Battle of Hastings.

Haroun-al-Raschid /haˌruːn ˌalraˈʃiːd/ variant spelling of **HARUN AR-RASHID**.

harp ▶ noun 1 a musical instrument, roughly triangular in shape, consisting of a frame supporting a graduated series of parallel strings, played by plucking with the fingers. The modern orchestral harp has an upright frame, with pedals which enable the strings to be retuned to different keys.

2 (also **harp shell** or **harp snail**) a marine mollusc which has a large vertically ribbed shell with a wide aperture, found chiefly in the Indo-Pacific.
● Family Harpidae, class Gastropoda.
▶ verb [no obj.] **1** (**harp on**) talk or write persistently and tediously on a particular topic: *guys who are constantly harping on about the war.*
2 archaic play on a harp.
– ORIGIN Old English *hearpe*, of Germanic origin; related to Dutch *harp* and German *Harfe*.

harper ▶ noun a musician, especially a folk musician, who plays a harp.

Harpers Ferry a small town in Jefferson County, West Virginia. It is famous for a raid in October 1859 in which John Brown and a group of abolitionists captured a Federal arsenal located there.

harpist ▶ noun a musician who plays a harp.

Harpocrates /haːˈpɒkrətiːz/ Greek name for **HORUS**.

harpoon ▶ noun a barbed spear-like missile attached to a long rope and thrown by hand or fired from a gun, used for catching whales and other large sea creatures.
▶ verb [with obj.] spear (something) with a harpoon.
– DERIVATIVES **harpooner** noun.
– ORIGIN early 17th cent. (denoting a barbed dart or spear): from French *harpon*, from *harpe* 'dog's claw, clamp', via Latin from Greek *harpē* 'sickle'.

harpoon gun ▶ noun a type of gun used for firing harpoons.

harp seal ▶ noun a slender North Atlantic seal that typically has a dark harp-shaped mark on its grey back.
● *Phoca groenlandica*, family Phocidae.

harp shell ▶ noun see **HARP** (sense 2).

harpsichord /ˈhaːpsɪkɔːd/ ▶ noun a keyboard instrument with horizontal strings which run perpendicular to the keyboard in a long tapering case, and are plucked by points of quill, leather, or plastic operated by depressing the keys. It is used chiefly in European classical music of the 16th to 18th centuries.
– DERIVATIVES **harpsichordist** noun.
– ORIGIN early 17th cent.: from obsolete French *harpechorde*, from late Latin *harpa* 'harp' + *chorda* 'string' (the insertion of the letter *s* being unexplained).

harp snail ▶ noun see **HARP** (sense 2).

harpy ▶ noun (pl. **-ies**) Greek & Roman Mythology a rapacious monster described as having a woman's head and body and a bird's wings and claws or depicted as a bird of prey with a woman's face.
■ a grasping, unscrupulous woman.
– ORIGIN late Middle English: from Latin *harpyia*, from Greek *harpuiai* 'snatchers'.

harpy eagle ▶ noun a very large crested eagle of tropical rainforests, often preying on monkeys.
● Family Accipitridae: *Harpia harpyja* of South America, the largest eagle, and *Harpyopsis novaeguineae* of New Guinea.

harquebus /ˈhaːkwɪbəs/ (also **arquebus**) ▶ noun historical an early type of portable gun supported on a tripod or a forked rest.
– ORIGIN mid 16th cent.: from French *harquebuse*, based on Middle Low German *hakebusse*, from *hake* 'hook' + *busse* 'gun'.

harridan /ˈharɪd(ə)n/ ▶ noun a strict, bossy, or belligerent old woman: *a bullying old harridan.*
– ORIGIN late 17th cent. (originally slang): perhaps from French *haridelle* 'old horse'.

harrier[1] ▶ noun a person who engages in persistent attacks on others or incursions into their land.

harrier[2] ▶ noun a hound of a breed used for hunting hares.
■ (**Harriers**) used in the names of teams of cross-country runners: *Durham City Harriers.*
– ORIGIN late Middle English *hayrer*, from **HARE** + **-ER**[1]. The spelling change was due to association with **HARRIER**[1].

harrier[3] ▶ noun a long-winged, slender-bodied bird of prey with low quartering flight.
● Genus *Circus*, family Accipitridae: several species.
– ORIGIN mid 16th cent. (as *harrower*): from *harrow* 'harry, rob' (variant of **HARRY**). The spelling change in the 17th cent. was due to association with **HARRIER**[1].

harrier hawk ▶ noun an African bird of prey with

a bare yellow face, resembling a goshawk but flying like a harrier.
● Genus *Polyboroides*, family Accipitridae: two species, in particular *P. typus.*

Harris[1] the southern part of the island of Lewis and Harris in the Outer Hebrides.

Harris[2], Sir Arthur Travers (1892–1984), British Marshal of the RAF; known as **Bomber Harris**. As Commander-in-Chief of Bomber Command (1942–5) in the Second World War he organized mass bombing raids against German towns which resulted in large-scale civilian casualties.

Harris[3], Frank (1856–1931), Irish writer; born *James Thomas Harris*. He gained a reputation as a fearless journalist and edited the periodical *Saturday Review* (1894–8). His autobiography *My Life and Loves* (1923–7) became notorious for its unreliability and sexual frankness.

Harrisburg /ˈharɪsbəːg/ the state capital of Pennsylvania, on the Susquehanna River; pop. 52,370 (1990). The nearby nuclear power station at Three Mile Island suffered a serious accident in 1979.

Harris' hawk (also **Harris hawk**) ▶ noun a large chocolate-brown buzzard with chestnut shoulder patches, popular with falconers. It occurs in arid country from the southern US to South America and frequently nests in tall cacti.
● *Parabuteo unicinctus*, family Accipitridae.

Harrison[1], Benjamin (1833–1901), American Republican statesman, 23rd President of the US 1889–93.

Harrison[2], George (b.1943), English rock and pop guitarist, the lead guitarist of the Beatles.

Harrison[3], Sir Rex (1908–90), English actor; full name *Reginald Carey Harrison*. Notable films: *Blithe Spirit* (1944), *My Fair Lady* (1964), and *Dr Dolittle* (1967).

Harrison[4], William Henry (1773–1841), American Whig statesman, 9th President of the US, 1841. He died of pneumonia a month after his inauguration.

Harris tweed ▶ noun [mass noun] trademark handwoven tweed made in the Outer Hebrides in Scotland, especially on the island of Lewis and Harris.

Harrod /ˈharəd/, Charles Henry (1800–85), English grocer and tea merchant. In 1853 he took over a shop in Knightsbridge, London, which, after expansion by his son **Charles Digby Harrod** (1841–1905), became a prestigious department store.

Harrovian /həˈrəʊvɪən/ ▶ noun a past or present member of Harrow School.
– ORIGIN early 19th cent.: from modern Latin *Harrovia* 'Harrow' + **-AN**.

harrow ▶ noun an implement consisting of a heavy frame set with teeth or tines which is dragged over ploughed land to break up clods, remove weeds, and cover seed.
▶ verb [with obj.] **1** draw a harrow over (land).
2 cause distress to: *Todd could take it, whereas I'm harrowed by it* | [as adj.] **harrowing**] *a harrowing film about racism and violence.*
– DERIVATIVES **harrower** noun, **harrowingly** adverb.
– ORIGIN Middle English: from Old Norse *herfi*; obscurely related to Dutch *hark* 'rake'.

Harrowing of Hell (in medieval Christian theology) the defeat of the powers of evil and the release of its victims by the descent of Christ into hell after his death.
– ORIGIN Middle English: *harrowing* from *harrow*, by-form of the verb **HARRY**.

Harrow School a boys' public school in NW London, founded under Queen Elizabeth I in 1571.

harrumph /həˈrʌmf/ ▶ verb [no obj.] clear the throat noisily.
■ grumpily express dissatisfaction or disapproval: *sceptics tend to harrumph at case histories like this.*
▶ noun a noisy clearing of the throat.
■ a grumpy expression of dissatisfaction or disapproval.
– ORIGIN 1930s: imitative.

harry ▶ verb (**-ies**, **-ied**) [with obj.] persistently carry out attacks on (an enemy or an enemy's territory).
■ persistently harass: *the government is being mercilessly harried by a new lobby.*
– ORIGIN Old English *herian, hergian*, of Germanic origin, probably influenced by Old French *harier*, in the same sense.

harsh ▶ adjective **1** unpleasantly rough or jarring to

the senses: *drenched in a harsh white neon light* | *harsh guttural shouts.*
2 cruel or severe: *a time of harsh military discipline.*
■ (of a climate or conditions) difficult to survive in; hostile: *the harsh environment of the desert.* ■ (of reality or a fact) grim and unpalatable: *the harsh realities of the world news.* ■ having an undesirably strong effect: *she finds soap too harsh and drying.*
– DERIVATIVES **harshen** verb, **harshly** adverb, **harshness** noun.
– ORIGIN Middle English: from Middle Low German *harsch* 'rough', literally 'hairy', from *haer* 'hair'.

harslet /ˈhaːslɪt/ ▶ noun variant spelling of **HASLET**.

hart ▶ noun an adult male deer, especially a red deer over five years old.
– ORIGIN Old English *heorot, heort*, of Germanic origin; related to Dutch *hert* and German *Hirsch*.

hartal /ˈhaːtaːl, ˈhəːtaːl/ ▶ noun (in the Indian subcontinent) a closure of shops and offices as a protest or a mark of sorrow.
– ORIGIN from Hindi *hartāl, hattāl*, literally 'locking of shops', from Sanskrit *haṭṭa* 'market' + Hindi *tāla* 'lock'.

Harte /haːt/, (Francis) Bret (1836–1902), American short-story writer and poet. He is chiefly remembered for his stories about life in a Californian gold-mining settlement.

hartebeest[1] /ˈhaːtɪbiːst/ ▶ noun a large African antelope with a long head and sloping back, related to the gnus.
● Genera *Alcelaphus, Damaliscus*, and *Sigmoceros*, family Bovidae: three or four species, in particular the **red hartebeest** (*A. buselaphus*), which typically has a reddish-brown coat.
– ORIGIN late 18th cent.: from South African Dutch, from Dutch *hert* 'hart' + *beest* 'beast'.

hartebeest[2] /ˈhaːtɪbiːst/ ▶ adjective S. African (of a house, hut, or shelter) simply constructed, typically with a thatched roof and walls made of reed or wattle and daub.
– ORIGIN a loan translation of South African Dutch *hardebies* 'hard reed'. Folk etymology connects the shelter with hartebeest hunting.

Hartford the state capital of Connecticut, situated on the Connecticut River; pop. 139,740 (1990).

Hartlepool /ˈhaːtlɪˌpuːl/ a port on the North Sea coast of NE England; pop. 92,130 (1981).

Hartley, L. P. (1895–1972), English novelist and short-story writer; full name *Leslie Poles Hartley*. Much of his work deals with memory and the effects of childhood experience on adult life and character. Notable novels: *The Shrimp and the Anemone* (1944) and *The Go-Between* (1953).

Hartnell /ˈhaːtn(ə)l/, Sir Norman (1901–79), English couturier. He is remembered especially as the dressmaker to Queen Elizabeth II (whose coronation gown he designed) and the Queen Mother.

hartshorn /ˈhaːtsˌhɔːn/ (also **spirit of hartshorn**) ▶ noun [mass noun] archaic aqueous ammonia solution used as smelling salts, formerly prepared from the horns of deer.
– ORIGIN Old English *heortes horn* (see **HART**, **HORN**).

hart's tongue (also **hart's tongue fern**) ▶ noun a common European fern whose long, narrow undivided fronds are said to resemble the tongues of deer.
● *Phyllitis* (or *Asplenium*) *scolopendrium*, family Aspleniaceae.

harum-scarum /ˌhɛːrəmˈskɛːrəm/ ▶ adjective reckless; impetuous: *a wild harum-scarum youth.*
▶ noun such a person.
– ORIGIN late 17th cent. (as an adverb): reduplication based on **HARE** and **SCARE**.

Harun ar-Rashid /haˌruːn ˌaːraˈfiːd/ (also **Haroun-al-Raschid**) (763–809), fifth Abbasid caliph of Baghdad 786–809. The most powerful of the Abbasid caliphs, he was made famous by his portrayal in the *Arabian Nights.*

haruspex /həˈrʌspɛks/ ▶ noun (pl. **haruspices** /-spiːsiːz/) (in ancient Rome) a religious official who interpreted omens by inspecting the entrails of sacrificial animals.
– DERIVATIVES **haruspicy** /həˈrʌspɪsi/ noun.
– ORIGIN Latin, from an unrecorded element meaning 'entrails' (related to Sanskrit *hirā* 'artery') + *-spex* (from *specere* 'look at').

Harvard classification ▶ noun Astronomy a system of classification of stars based on their spectral types, the chief classes (O, B, A, F, G, K, M)

forming a series from very hot bluish-white stars to cool dull red stars.
– ORIGIN 1960s: named after the observatory at **HARVARD UNIVERSITY**, where it was devised.

Harvard University /ˈhɑːvəd/ the oldest American university, founded in 1636 at Cambridge, Massachusetts.
– ORIGIN named after John *Harvard* (1607–38), an English settler who bequeathed his library and half his estate to the university.

harvest ▶ noun the process or period of gathering in crops: *helping with the harvest.*
■ the season's yield or crop: *a poor harvest.* ■ a quantity of animals caught or killed for human use: *a limited harvest of wild mink.* ■ figurative the product or result of an action: *in terms of science, Apollo yielded a meagre harvest.*
▶ verb [with obj.] gather (a crop) as a harvest: [as noun **harvesting**] *after harvesting, most of the crop is stored in large buildings.*
■ catch or kill (animals) for human consumption or use. ■ remove (cells, tissue, or an organ) from a person or animal for experimental or transplantation purposes. ■ figurative gain (something) as the result of an action: *he harvested a hat-trick of honours.*
– DERIVATIVES **harvestable** adjective, **harvester** noun.
– ORIGIN Old English *hærfest* 'autumn', of Germanic origin; related to Dutch *herfst* and German *Herbst*, from an Indo-European root shared by Latin *carpere* 'pluck' and Greek *karpos* 'fruit'.

harvester ant ▶ noun an ant that gathers and stores seeds and grain as a communal food source for the colony.
● *Messor* and other genera, family Formicidae.

harvest festival ▶ noun a celebration of the annual harvest, especially (in Britain) one held in schools and as a service in Christian churches, to which gifts of food are brought for the poor.

harvest home ▶ noun the gathering in of the final part of the year's harvest.
■ a festival marking the end of the harvest period.

harvestman ▶ noun (pl. **-men**) an arachnid with a globular body and very long thin legs, typically living in leaf litter and on tree trunks.
● Order Opiliones: three suborders.

harvest mite ▶ noun a minute mite whose parasitic larvae live on or under the skin of warm-blooded animals where they cause irritation and dermatitis, and sometimes transmit scrub typhus.
● Genus *Trombicula*, family Trombiculidae: many species, including the European *T. autumnalis*, which is common at harvest time.

harvest moon ▶ noun the full moon that is seen nearest to the time of the autumn equinox.

harvest mouse ▶ noun **1** a small North Eurasian mouse with a prehensile tail, nesting among the stalks of growing cereals and other vegetation.
● *Micromys minutus*, family Muridae.
2 a nocturnal mouse found in North and Central America.
● Genus *Reithrodontomys*, family Muridae: several species.

Harvey, William (1578–1657), English physician, discoverer of the circulation of the blood. In *De Motu Cordis* (1628) Harvey described the motion of the heart and concluded that the blood left through the arteries and returned to the heart through the veins after it had passed through the flesh.

Harvey Wallbanger ▶ noun a cocktail made from vodka or gin, orange juice, and Galliano.

Harwich /ˈharɪtʃ/ a port in Essex, on the North Sea coast of SE England; pop. 17,330 (1981).

Haryana /ˌhʌrɪˈɑːnə/ a state of northern India; capital, Chandigarh. It was formed in 1966, largely from Hindi-speaking parts of the former state of Punjab.

harzburgite /ˈhɑːtsbəˌɡʌɪt/ ▶ noun [mass noun] Geology a plutonic rock of the peridotite group consisting largely of orthopyroxene and olivine.
– ORIGIN late 19th cent.: from *Harzburg*, the name of a town in Germany, + **-ITE**[1].

Harz Mountains /hɑːts/ a range of mountains in central Germany, the highest of which is the Brocken.

has third person singular present of **HAVE**.

has-been ▶ noun informal, derogatory a person or thing considered to be outmoded or no longer of any significance: *a political has-been.*

Hasdrubal[1] /ˈhazdrʊb(ə)l/ (d.221 BC), Carthaginian general. He accompanied his father-in-law, Hamilcar, to Spain in 237 and advanced the Carthaginian boundary to the Ebro.

Hasdrubal[2] /ˈhazdrʊb(ə)l/ (d.207 BC), Carthaginian general. The younger brother of Hannibal, he was left in command of Carthaginian forces in Spain after Hannibal departed for Italy in 218.

Hašek /ˈhaʃɛk/, Jaroslav (1883–1923), Czech novelist and short-story writer. His unfinished four-volume comic novel satirizing military life and bureaucracy appeared in Britain in a bowdlerized form as *The Good Soldier Schweik* (1930).

hash[1] ▶ noun a dish of cooked meat cut into small pieces and recooked, usually with potatoes.
■ N. Amer. a finely chopped mixture: *a hash of raw tomatoes, chillies, and coriander.* ■ a mixture of jumbled incongruous things; a mess.
▶ verb [with obj.] **1** make (meat or other food) into a hash.
■ N. Amer. chop (meat or vegetables).
2 (**hash something out**) come to agreement on something after lengthy and vigorous discussion.
– PHRASES **make a hash of** informal make a mess of; bungle. **settle someone's hash** informal deal with and subdue someone in no uncertain manner.
– ORIGIN late 16th cent. (as a verb): from French *hacher*, from *hache* (see **HATCHET**).

hash[2] ▶ noun informal short for **HASHISH**.

hash[3] (also **hash sign**) ▶ noun the symbol #.
– ORIGIN 1980s: probably from **HATCH**[3], altered by folk etymology.

hash browns (also **hashed browns**) ▶ plural noun chiefly N. Amer. a dish of cooked potatoes, typically with onions added, that have been chopped into small pieces then fried until brown.

Hashemite /ˈhaʃɪmʌɪt/ ▶ noun a member of an Arab princely family claiming descent from Hashim, great-grandfather of Muhammad.
▶ adjective of or relating to this family.

Hashemite Kingdom of Jordan official name for **JORDAN**[1] (in sense 1).

hash house ▶ noun informal, chiefly N. Amer. a cheap eating house.

Hashimoto's disease /ˌhaʃɪˈməʊtəʊz/ ▶ noun [mass noun] an autoimmune disease causing chronic inflammation and consequential failure of the thyroid gland.
– ORIGIN 1930s: named after Hakaru *Hashimoto* (1881–1934), Japanese surgeon.

hashish /ˈhaʃiːʃ, -ʃɪʃ, haˈʃiːʃ/ ▶ noun [mass noun] cannabis.
– ORIGIN late 16th cent.: from Arabic *ḥašīš* 'dry herb, powdered hemp leaves'.

Hasid /ˈhasɪd/ (also **Chasid**, **Chassid**, or **Hassid**) ▶ noun (pl. **Hasidim**) **1** a member of a strictly orthodox Jewish sect in Palestine in the 3rd and 2nd centuries BC which opposed Hellenizing influences on their faith and supported the Maccabean revolt.
2 an adherent of Hasidism.
– DERIVATIVES **Hasidic** /-ˈsɪdɪk/ adjective.
– ORIGIN from Hebrew *ḥāsīḏ* 'pious'.

Hasidism /ˈhasɪˌdɪz(ə)m/ (also **Chasidism**, **Chassidism**, or **Hassidism**) ▶ noun [mass noun] a mystical Jewish movement founded in Poland in the 18th century in reaction to the rigid academicism of rabbinical Judaism. The movement declined sharply in the 19th century, but fundamentalist communities developed from it, and Hasidism is still influential in Jewish life, particularly in Israel and New York.

haslet /ˈhazlɪt, ˈheɪzlɪt/ (also **harslet**) ▶ noun [mass noun] chiefly Brit. a cold meat preparation consisting of chopped or minced pork offal compressed into a loaf before being cooked.
– ORIGIN late Middle English (originally denoting meat for roasting): from Old French *hastelet*, diminutive of *haste* 'roast meat, spit', probably of Germanic origin and related to Dutch *harst* 'sirloin'.

Hasmonean /ˌhazməˈnɪən/ ▶ adjective of or relating to the Jewish dynasty established by the Maccabees.
▶ noun a member of this dynasty.
– ORIGIN from modern Latin *Asmonaeus* (from Greek

Asamonaios, the grandfather of Mattathias, head of the Maccabees in the 2nd cent. BC) + **-AN**.

hasn't ▶ contraction of has not.

hasp /hɑːsp/ ▶ noun a slotted hinged metal plate that forms part of a fastening for a door or lid and is fitted over a metal loop and secured by a pin or padlock.
■ a similar metal plate on a trunk or suitcase with a projecting piece which is secured by the lock.
▶ verb [with obj.] archaic lock (a door, window, or lid) by securing the hasp over the loop of the fastening.
– ORIGIN Old English *hæpse*, *hæsp*, of Germanic origin; related to Dutch *haspel* and German *Haspe*.

Hasselt /ˈhaselt/ a city in NE Belgium, on the River Demer, capital of the province of Limburg; pop. 66,610 (1991).

Hassid ▶ noun variant spelling of **HASID**.

Hassidism ▶ noun variant spelling of **HASIDISM**.

hassium /ˈhasɪəm/ ▶ noun [mass noun] the chemical element of atomic number 108, a very unstable element made by high-energy atomic collisions. (Symbol: **Hs**) See also **HAHNIUM**.
– ORIGIN modern Latin, from Latin *Hassias* 'Hesse' (the German state); it was discovered in Darmstadt in 1984.

hassle informal ▶ noun [mass noun] irritating inconvenience: *the hassle of child care* | [count noun] *travelling can be a hassle.*
■ deliberate harassment: *when I told them I would not work on Sundays I got hassle.* ■ [count noun] N. Amer. a disagreement; a quarrel.
▶ verb [with obj.] harass; pester: *you want to sit and relax and not get hassled.*
– ORIGIN late 19th cent. (originally dialect in the sense 'hack or saw at'): of unknown origin, perhaps a blend of **HAGGLE** and **TUSSLE**.

hassock /ˈhasək/ ▶ noun **1** a thick, firmly padded cushion, in particular:
■ chiefly Brit. a cushion for kneeling on in church, while at prayer. ■ N. Amer. a footstool.
2 a firm clump of grass or matted vegetation in marshy or boggy ground.
– ORIGIN Old English *hassuc* (in sense 2), of unknown origin.

hast archaic second person singular present of **HAVE**.

hastate /ˈhasteɪt/ ▶ adjective Botany (of a leaf) having a narrow triangular shape like that of a spearhead.
– ORIGIN late 18th cent.: from Latin *hastatus*, from *hasta* 'spear'.

haste ▶ noun [mass noun] excessive speed or urgency of movement or action; hurry: *working with feverish haste* | *I write in haste.*
▶ verb archaic term for **HASTEN**.
– PHRASES **make haste** dated hurry; hasten: *I make haste to seal this.* **more haste, less speed** proverb you make better progress with a task if you don't try to do it too quickly.
– ORIGIN Middle English: from Old French *haste* (noun), *haster* (verb), of Germanic origin.

hasten ▶ verb [no obj., with infinitive] be quick to do something: *he hastened to refute the assertion.*
■ [with adverbial of direction] move or travel hurriedly: *we hastened back to Paris.* ■ [with obj.] cause (something, especially something undesirable) to happen sooner than it otherwise would.
– ORIGIN mid 16th cent.: extended form of **HASTE**, on the pattern of verbs in **-EN**[1].

Hastings, Warren (1732–1818), British colonial administrator. India's first Governor General (1774–1784), he introduced vital administrative reforms. He was later impeached for corruption but acquitted after a seven-year trial.

Hastings, Battle of a decisive battle which took place in 1066 just north of the town of Hastings, East Sussex. William the Conqueror defeated the forces of the Anglo-Saxon king Harold II; Harold died in the battle, leaving the way open for the Norman Conquest of England.

hasty ▶ adjective (**hastier**, **hastiest**) done or acting with excessive speed or urgency; hurried: *a hasty attempt to defuse the situation* | *hasty decisions.*
■ archaic quick-tempered.
– DERIVATIVES **hastily** adverb, **hastiness** noun.
– ORIGIN Middle English: from Old French *hasti*, *hastif*, from *haste* (see **HASTE**).

hasty pudding ▶ noun [mass noun] a pudding containing wheat flour or (in North America) maize flour stirred to a thick batter in boiling milk or water.

hat ▶ **noun** a shaped covering for the head worn for warmth, as a fashion item, or as part of a uniform.
▪used to refer to a particular role or occupation of someone who has more than one: *wearing her scientific hat she is director of a pharmacology research group.*
– PHRASES **hats off to ——** used to express admiration for someone who has achieved something or done something praiseworthy: *hats off to them for agreeing to work for the day to raise money.* **keep something under one's hat** keep something a secret. **pass the hat round** (or N. Amer. **pass the hat**) collect contributions of money from a number of people for a specific purpose. **pick something out of a hat** select something, especially the winner of a contest, at random. **take one's hat off to** used to state one's admiration for (someone who has achieved something). **throw one's hat in** (or **into**) **the ring** express willingness to take up a challenge.
– DERIVATIVES **hatful** noun (pl. **-fuls**), **hatless** adjective, **hatted** adjective.
– ORIGIN Old English *hætt*, of Germanic origin; related to Old Norse *hǫttr* 'hood', also to **HOOD**[1].

hatband ▶ **noun** a decorative ribbon encircling a hat, held in position above the brim.

hatbox ▶ **noun** a large cylindrical box used to protect a hat when being transported or stored.

hatch[1] ▶ **noun** an opening of restricted size allowing for passage from one area to another, in particular:
▪a door in an aircraft, spacecraft, or submarine. ▪ an opening in the deck of a boat or ship leading to the cabin or a lower level: *a cargo hatch.* ▪ an opening in a ceiling leading to a loft. ▪ an opening in a kitchen wall for serving or selling food through: *a service hatch.* ▪ the rear door of a hatchback car. ▪ short for **HATCHBACK**.
– PHRASES **down the hatch** informal used to express friendly feelings towards one's companions before drinking. **under** (**the**) **hatches** below deck in a ship.
– ORIGIN Old English *hæcc* (denoting the lower half of a divided door), of Germanic origin; related to Dutch *hek* 'paling, screen'.

hatch[2] ▶ **verb 1** [no obj.] (of a young bird, fish, or reptile) emerge from its egg: *ten little chicks **hatched out**.*
▪(of an egg) open and produce a young animal: *eggs need to be put in a warm place to hatch.* ▪ [with obj.] incubate (an egg). ▪ [with obj.] cause (a young animal) to emerge from its egg: *our penguins were hatched and hand-reared here.*
2 [with obj.] conspire to devise (a plot or plan): *the little plot that you and Sylvia **hatched up** last night.*
▶ **noun** a newly hatched brood: *a hatch of mayflies.*
– ORIGIN Middle English *hacche*; related to Swedish *häcka* and Danish *hække*.

hatch[3] ▶ **verb** [with obj.] (in fine art and technical drawing) shade (an area) with closely drawn parallel lines: [as noun **hatching**] *the miniaturist's use of hatching and stippling.*
– ORIGIN late 15th cent. (in the sense 'inlay with strips of metal'): from Old French *hacher*, from *hache* (see **HATCHET**).

hatchback ▶ **noun** a car with a door across the full width at the back end that opens upwards to provide easy access for loading.

hatchel /ˈhatʃ(ə)l/ ▶ **noun** another term for **HACKLE** (in sense 3).
▶ **verb** another term for **HACKLE**.
– ORIGIN Middle English *hechele*, of West Germanic origin, related to **HOOK**.

hatchery ▶ **noun** (pl. **-ies**) an installation or building in which the hatching of fish or poultry eggs is artificially controlled for commercial purposes.

hatchet ▶ **noun** a small axe with a short handle for use in one hand.
– ORIGIN Middle English: from Old French *hachette*, diminutive of *hache* 'axe', from medieval Latin *hapia*, of Germanic origin.

hatchet-faced ▶ **adjective** informal (especially of someone with a narrow face or sharp features) having a grim or hostile expression.

hatchetfish ▶ **noun** (pl. same or **-fishes**) a deep-bodied laterally compressed tropical freshwater fish of the New World. It is able to fly short distances above the surface of the water by beating its broad pectoral fins.
• Family Gasteropelecidae: three genera, in particular *Gasteropelecus*, and several species.

hatchet job ▶ **noun** informal a fierce verbal attack on someone or their work, especially in print.
▪the dismissal of a number of people from an organization.

hatchet man ▶ **noun** informal a person employed to carry out controversial or disagreeable tasks, such as the dismissal of a number of people from employment.
▪a person who writes fierce attacks on others or their work.
– ORIGIN late 19th cent. (originally US): figuratively, from an early use denoting a hired Chinese assassin.

hatchling ▶ **noun** a young animal that has recently emerged from its egg.

hatchment ▶ **noun** a large tablet, typically diamond-shaped, bearing the coat of arms of someone who has died, displayed in their honour.
– ORIGIN early 16th cent.: probably from obsolete French *hachement*, from Old French *acesmement* 'adornment'.

hatchway ▶ **noun** an opening or hatch, especially in a ship's deck.

hate ▶ **verb** [with obj.] feel intense or passionate dislike for (someone): *the boys hate each other | he was particularly hated by the extreme right.*
▪have a strong aversion to (something): *he hates flying* | [with infinitive] *I'd hate to live there.* ▪ [with infinitive] used politely to express one's regret or embarrassment at doing something: *I hate to bother you.*
▶ **noun** [mass noun] intense or passionate dislike: *feelings of hate and revenge.*
▪[as modifier] denoting hostile actions motivated by intense dislike or prejudice: *a hate campaign.* ▪ [count noun] informal a hated person or thing: *Richard's **pet hate** is filling in his tax returns.*
– DERIVATIVES **hatable** (also **hateable**) adjective, **hater** noun.
– ORIGIN Old English *hatian* (verb), *hete* (noun), of Germanic origin; related to Dutch *haten* (verb) and German *hassen* (verb), *Hass* 'hatred'.

hateful ▶ **adjective** arousing, deserving of, or filled with hatred.
▪informal very unpleasant: *a hateful dress.*
– DERIVATIVES **hatefully** adverb, **hatefulness** noun.

hate mail ▶ **noun** [mass noun] hostile and sometimes threatening letters sent, usually anonymously, to an individual or group.

hath archaic third person singular present of **HAVE**.

Hathaway /ˈhaθəweɪ/, Anne (*c.*1557–1623), the wife of Shakespeare, whom she married in 1582.

hatha yoga /ˌhʌtə, ˌhaθə/ ▶ **noun** [mass noun] a system of physical exercises and breathing control used in yoga.
– ORIGIN from Sanskrit *haṭha* 'force' and **YOGA**.

Hathor /ˈhaθɔː/ Egyptian Mythology a sky goddess, the patron of love and joy, represented variously as a cow, with a cow's head or ears, or with a solar disc between a cow's horns.

hatpin ▶ **noun** a long pin, typically with an ornamental head, that holds a woman's hat in position by securing it to her hair.

hatred ▶ **noun** [mass noun] intense dislike or ill will: *racial hatred | his murderous hatred of his brother.*
– ORIGIN Middle English: from **HATE** + *-red* (from Old English *rǣden* 'condition').

Hatshepsut /hatˈʃɛpsʊt/ (d.1482 BC), Egyptian queen of the 18th dynasty, reigned *c.*1503–1482 BC. On the death of her husband Tuthmosis II she became regent for her nephew Tuthmosis III. She then named herself Pharaoh and was often portrayed as male.

hatstand ▶ **noun** a tall free-standing post fitted with large hooks for hanging hats on.

hatter ▶ **noun** a person who makes and sells hats.

Hatti ▶ **plural noun** the ancient Anatolian people whose language was Hattic.
– ORIGIN Assyrian and Hittite.

Hattic /ˈhatɪk/ ▶ **noun** [mass noun] an ancient language of NW Anatolia, spoken in the 3rd millennium BC, in which a few cuneiform tablets survive, some bilingual with Hittite. It was neither an Indo-European nor a Semitic language, but it had a strong influence on the vocabulary of Hittite, which eventually displaced it.
▶ **adjective** of or relating to this language or the people who spoke it.
– DERIVATIVES **Hattian** adjective.

hat-trick ▶ **noun** three successes of the same kind, especially consecutive ones within a limited period.
▪(chiefly in soccer) the scoring of three goals in a game by one player. ▪ (in cricket) the taking of three wickets by the same bowler with successive balls.
– ORIGIN late 19th cent.: originally referring to the club presentation of a new hat (or some equivalent) to a bowler taking three wickets successively.

Hattusa /ˈhatʊsə/ the capital of the ancient Hittite empire, situated in central Turkey about 35 km (22 miles) east of Ankara.

hauberk /ˈhɔːbəːk/ ▶ **noun** historical a piece of armour originally covering only the neck and shoulders but later consisting of a full-length coat of mail or military tunic.
– ORIGIN Middle English: from Old French *hauberc*, *hausberc*, originally denoting protection for the neck, of Germanic origin.

haugh /hɔː, hɑːx/ ▶ **noun** Scottish & N. English a piece of flat alluvial land by the side of a river, forming part of the floor of the river valley.
– ORIGIN Middle English: probably from Old English *healh* 'corner, nook', related to *holh* 'hollow'.

haughty ▶ **adjective** (**haughtier**, **haughtiest**) arrogantly superior and disdainful: *a look of haughty disdain | a haughty British aristocrat.*
– DERIVATIVES **haughtily** adverb, **haughtiness** noun.
– ORIGIN mid 16th cent.: extended form of obsolete *haught*, earlier *haut*, from Old French, from Latin *altus* 'high'.

Hau-Hauism /ˈhaʊˌhaʊɪʒ(ə)m/ ▶ **noun** [mass noun] a 19th-century Maori religion promising eternal salvation from the white man.
– ORIGIN from Maori *Hau Hau* + **-ISM**.

haul ▶ **verb 1** [with obj. and adverbial] (of a person) pull or drag with effort or force: *he hauled his bike out of the shed.*
▪(**haul oneself**) propel or pull oneself with difficulty: *he hauled himself along the cliff face.* ▪ informal force (someone) to appear for reprimand or trial: *he is to be **hauled before** the Press Council.* ▪ [no obj., with adverbial] (of a person) pull hard: *she **hauled on** the reins.*
2 [with obj.] (of a vehicle) pull (an attached trailer or carriage) behind it: *the engine hauls the overnight sleeper from London Euston.*
▪transport in a lorry or cart: *he made a living hauling coal.*
3 [no obj., with adverbial of direction] (especially of a sailing ship) make an abrupt change of course.
▶ **noun 1** a quantity of something that has been stolen or is possessed illegally: *they escaped with a haul of antiques.*
▪the number of points, medals, or titles won by a person or team in a sporting event or over a period. ▪ a number of fish caught.
2 a distance to be traversed: *the thirty-mile haul to Tamanrasset.*
– PHRASES **haul ass** N. Amer. informal move or leave fast. **haul off** N. Amer. informal leave; depart. ▪ withdraw a little in preparation for some action: *he hauled off and smacked the kid.* **haul someone over the coals** see **COAL**.
– ORIGIN mid 16th cent. (originally in the nautical sense 'trim sails for sailing closer to the wind'): variant of **HALE**[2].

haulage ▶ **noun** [mass noun] the action or process of hauling.
▪the commercial transport of goods: *road haulage.* ▪ a charge for such transport.

hauler ▶ **noun** North American term for **HAULIER**.
▪a lorry used for the transport of goods or materials.

haulier /ˈhɔːlɪə/ ▶ **noun** Brit. a person or company employed in the transport of goods or materials by road: *a major haulier between Europe and Asia.*
▪a miner who is responsible for transporting coal within a mine.

haulm /hɔːm/ ▶ **noun** a stalk or stem.
▪[mass noun] the stalks or stems collectively of peas, beans, or potatoes without the pods or tubers, as used for bedding: *potato haulm.*
– ORIGIN Old English *healm*, *halm*, of Germanic origin; related to Dutch *halm* and German *Halm*, from an Indo-European root shared by Latin *culmus* 'stalk' and Greek *kalamos* 'reed'.

haunch ▶ **noun** **1** a buttock and thigh considered together, in a human or animal.
■[mass noun] the leg and loin of an animal, especially a deer, as food: *haunch of venison.*
2 Architecture the side of an arch, between the crown and the pier.
– PHRASES **sit on one's haunches** squat with the haunches resting on the backs of the heels.
– ORIGIN Middle English: from Old French *hanche*, of Germanic origin.

haunt ▶ **verb** [with obj.] (of a ghost) manifest itself at (a place) regularly: *a grey lady who haunts the chapel.*
■(of a person) frequent (a place): *he haunts street markets.* ■ be persistently and disturbingly present, especially in someone's mind: *cities haunted by the shadow of cholera | the sight haunted me for years.*
▶ **noun** a place frequented by a specified person: *a favourite haunt of artists of the time.*
– DERIVATIVES **haunter** noun.
– ORIGIN Middle English (in the sense 'frequent (a place)'): from Old French *hanter*, of Germanic origin; distantly related to **HOME**.

haunted ▶ **adjective** (of a place) frequented by a ghost: *a reputedly haunted room in the castle.*
■having or showing signs of mental anguish or torment: *the hollow cheeks, the haunted eyes.*

h

haunting ▶ **adjective** poignant; evocative: *the sweet haunting sound of pan pipes.*
– DERIVATIVES **hauntingly** adverb.

Hauptmann /ˈhaʊtman/, Gerhart (1862–1946), German dramatist. An early pioneer of naturalism, he is known for *Before Sunrise* (1889) and *The Ascension of Joan* (1893). Nobel Prize for Literature (1912).

haurient /ˈhɔːrɪənt/ ▶ **adjective** [postpositive] Heraldry (of a fish or marine creature) depicted swimming vertically, typically with the head upwards.
– ORIGIN late 16th cent.: from Latin *haurient-* 'drawing in (air, water, etc.)', from the verb *haurire*.

Hausa /ˈhaʊsə/ ▶ **noun** (pl. same or **Hausas**) **1** a member of a people of northern Nigeria and adjacent regions.
2 [mass noun] the Chadic language of this people. It is spoken by some 30 million people, mainly in Nigeria and Niger, and is widely used as a lingua franca in parts of West Africa.
▶ **adjective** of or relating to this people or their language.
– ORIGIN the name in Hausa.

hausfrau /ˈhaʊsfraʊ/ ▶ **noun** a German housewife.
■informal a woman regarded as overly domesticated or efficient.
– ORIGIN late 18th cent.: from German, from *Haus* 'house' + *Frau* 'woman, wife'.

haustellum /hɔːˈstɛləm/ ▶ **noun** (pl. **haustella**) Zoology the sucking organ or proboscis of an insect or crustacean.
– DERIVATIVES **haustellate** /ˈhɔːstələt, -leɪt/ adjective.
– ORIGIN early 19th cent.: modern Latin diminutive of *haustrum* 'scoop', from *haust-* 'drawn in', from the verb *haurire*.

haustorium /hɔːˈstɔːrɪəm/ ▶ **noun** (pl. **haustoria** /-rɪə/) Botany a slender projection from the root of a parasitic plant, such as a dodder, or from the hyphae of a parasitic fungus, enabling the parasite to penetrate the tissues of its host and absorb nutrients from it.
– DERIVATIVES **haustorial** adjective.
– ORIGIN late 19th cent.: modern Latin, from Latin *haustor* 'thing that draws in', from the verb *haurire*.

hautboy /ˈ(h)əʊbɔɪ/ ▶ **noun** archaic form of **OBOE**.
– ORIGIN mid 16th cent.: from French *hautbois*, from *haut* 'high' + *bois* 'wood'.

haute bourgeoisie /ˌəʊt bʊəʒwɑːˈziː/ ▶ **noun** (**the haute bourgeoisie**) [treated as sing. or pl.] the upper middle class.
– ORIGIN French, literally 'high bourgeoisie'.

haute couture /ˌəʊt kʊˈtjʊə/ ▶ **noun** [mass noun] the designing and making of high-quality fashionable clothes by leading fashion houses, especially to order.
■fashion houses who engage in such work. ■ clothes of this kind.
– ORIGIN French, literally 'high dressmaking'.

haute cuisine /ˌəʊt kwɪˈziːn/ ▶ **noun** [mass noun] the preparation and cooking of high-quality food following the style of traditional French cuisine.
■food produced in such a way.
– ORIGIN French, literally 'high cookery'.

haute école /ˌəʊt eɪˈkɒl/ ▶ **noun** [mass noun] the art or practice of advanced classical dressage.
– ORIGIN French, literally 'high school'.

Haute-Normandie /əʊtˈnɔːməndi, French ˈotnɔʀmɑ̃di/ a region of northern France, on the coast of the English Channel, including the city of Rouen.

hauteur /əʊˈtəː, French ˈotœʀ/ ▶ **noun** [mass noun] proud haughtiness of manner.
– ORIGIN French, from *haut* 'high'.

haut monde /əʊ ˈmɒ̃d/ ▶ **noun** (**the haut monde**) fashionable society.
– ORIGIN French, literally 'high world'.

haut-relief /ˌəʊrɪˈliːf/ ▶ **noun** [mass noun] Sculpture another term for ***high relief*** (see **RELIEF** in sense 4).
■[count noun] a sculpture or carving in high relief.
– ORIGIN mid 19th cent.: French, literally 'high relief'.

havala /hʌˈveɪlə/ ▶ **noun** [mass noun] Indian an unofficial or illegal way of changing foreign currency.
– ORIGIN from Hindi *havālā*.

Havana[1] /həˈvanə/ the capital of Cuba, situated on the north coast; pop. 2,160,300 (est. 1992). It was founded in 1515 by Diego Velázquez de Cuéllar. Spanish name **La Habana**.

Havana[2] /həˈvanə/ ▶ **noun** a cigar made in Cuba or from Cuban tobacco.

Havant /ˈhav(ə)nt/ a town in SE Hampshire; pop. 50,220 (1981).

Havdalah ▶ **noun** variant spelling of **HABDALAH**.

have ▶ **verb** (**has**; past and past participle **had**)
▶ **verb** [with obj.] **1** (also **have got**) possess, own, or hold: *he had a new car and a boat | have you got a job yet? | I don't have that much money on me.*
■possess or be provided with (a quality, characteristic, or feature): *the ham had a sweet, smoky flavour | she's got blue eyes | the house has gas-fired central heating.* ■ (**have oneself**) informal, chiefly N. Amer. provide or indulge oneself with (something): *he had himself two highballs.* ■ be made up of; comprise: *in 1989 the party had 10,000 members.* ■ used to indicate a particular relationship: *he's got three children | do you have a client named Peters?* ■ be able to make use of (something available or at one's disposal): *how much time have I got for the presentation?* ■ have gained (a qualification): *he's got a BA in English.* ■ possess as an intellectual attainment; know (a language or subject): *he knew Latin and Greek; I had only a little French.*
2 experience; undergo: *I went to a few parties and had a good time | I was having difficulty in keeping awake.*
■(also **have got**) suffer from (an illness, ailment, or disability): *I've got a headache.* ■ (also **have got**) let (a feeling or thought) come into one's mind; hold in the mind: *he had the strong impression that someone was watching him | we've got a few ideas we're kicking around.* ■ [with past participle] experience or suffer the specified action happening or being done to (something): *she had her bag stolen.* ■ [with obj. and complement] cause (someone or something) to be in a particular state or condition: *I want to have everything ready in good time | I had the TV on with the sound turned down.* ■ (also **have got**) informal have put (someone) at a disadvantage in an argument (said either to acknowledge that one has no answer to a point or to show that one knows one's conversant has no answer): *you've got me there; I've never given the matter much thought.* ■ [with past participle] cause (something) to be done for one by someone else: *it is advisable to have your carpet laid by a professional.* ■ tell or arrange for (someone) to do something for one: [with obj. and infinitive] *he had his bodyguards throw Chris out | she's always having the builders in to do something or other.* ■ (usu. **be had**) informal cheat or deceive (someone): *I realized I'd been had.* ■ vulgar slang have sexual intercourse with.
3 (**have to** or **have got to do something**) be obliged or find it necessary to do the specified thing: *you don't have to accept this situation | sorry, we've got to dash.*
■[with obj. and usu. with infinitive] need or be obliged to do (something): *he's got a lot to do.* ■ be strongly recommended to do something: *if you think that place is great, you have to try our summer house.* ■ be certain or inevitable to happen or be the case: *there has to be a catch.*
4 perform the action indicated by the noun specified (used especially in spoken English as an alternative to a more specific verb): *he had a look round | the colour green has a restful effect.*
■organize and bring about: *are you are going to have a party?* ■ eat or drink: *they had beans on toast.* ■ give birth to or be due to give birth to: *she's going to have a baby.*
5 (also **have got**) show (a personal attribute or quality) by one's actions or attitude: *he had little patience with technological gadgetry |* [with obj. and infinitive] *you never even phoned, and now you've got the cheek to come back.*
■[often in imperative] exercise or show (mercy, pity, etc.) towards another person: *God have mercy on me!* ■ [with negative] not accept; refuse to tolerate: *I can't have you insulting Tom like that.*
6 (also **have got**) [with obj. and adverbial of place] place or keep (something) in a particular position: *Mary had her back to me | I soon had the trout in a net.*
■hold or grasp (someone or something) in a particular way: *he had me by the throat.*
7 be the recipient of (something sent, given, or done): *she had a letter from Mark.*
■take or invite into one's home so as to provide care or entertainment, especially for a limited period: *we're having the children for the weekend.*
▶ **auxiliary verb** used with a past participle to form the perfect, pluperfect, and future perfect tenses, and the conditional mood: *I have finished | he had asked her | she will have left by now | I could have helped, had I known | 'Have you seen him?' 'Yes, I have.'*
▶ **noun** **1** (**the haves**) informal people with plenty of money and possessions: *an increasing gap between the haves and have-nots.*
2 [in sing.] Brit. informal, dated a swindle.
– PHRASES **have a care** (or **an eye** etc.) see **CARE**, **EYE**, etc. **have got it bad** (or **badly**) informal be very powerfully affected emotionally, especially by love. ■ be in a situation where one is treated badly or exploited. **have had it** informal **1** be in a very poor condition; be beyond repair or past its best: *the car had had it.* ■ be extremely tired. ■ have lost all chance of survival: *when the lorry smashed into me, I thought I'd had it.* **2** be unable to tolerate someone or something any longer: ***I've had it with*** *him—he's humiliated me once too often!* **have it** **1** [with clause] express the view that (used to indicate that the speaker is reporting something which they do not necessarily believe to be fact): *rumour had it that although he lived in a derelict house, he was really very wealthy.* **2** win a decision, especially after a vote: *the ayes have it.* **3** have found the answer to something: *'I have it!' Rosa exclaimed.* **have it away** (**on one's toes**) Brit. informal leave quickly. **have it away** (or **off**) Brit. vulgar slang have sexual intercourse. **have it both ways** see **BOTH**. **have** (**got**) **it in for** informal feel a particular dislike of (someone) and behave in a hostile manner towards them. **have** (**got**) **it in one** (**to do something**) informal have the capacity or potential (to do something): *everyone thinks he has it in him to produce a literary classic.* **have it out** informal attempt to resolve a contentious matter by confronting someone and engaging in a frank discussion or argument: *give her the chance of a night's rest before you* ***have it out with*** *her.* **have a nice day** chiefly US used to express good wishes when parting. **have** (**got**) **nothing on** informal **1** be not nearly as good as (someone or something), especially in a particular respect. **2** (**have nothing** or **something on someone**) know nothing (or something) discreditable or incriminating about someone: *I am not worried—they've got nothing on me.* **have nothing to do with** see **DO**[1]. **have one too many** see **MANY**. **have** (**got**) **something to oneself** be able to to use, occupy, or enjoy something without having to share it with anyone else. **have —— to do with** see **DO**[1].
– ORIGIN Old English *habban*, of Germanic origin; related to Dutch *hebben* and German *haben*, also probably to **HEAVE**.

USAGE 1 **Have** and **have got**: there is a great deal of debate on the difference between these two forms; a traditional view is that **have got** is chiefly British, but not correct in formal writing, while **have** is chiefly American. Actual usage is more complicated: **have got** is in fact also widely used in US English. In both British and US usage **have** is more formal than **have got** and it is more appropriate in writing to use constructions such as **don't have** rather than **haven't got**.
2 A common mistake is to write the word **of** instead of **have** or **'ve**: *I **could of** told you that* instead of *I **could've** told you that.* The reason for the mistake is that the pronunciation of **have** in unstressed contexts is the same as that of **of**, and the two words are confused when it comes to writing them down. The error was recorded as early as 1837 and, though common, is unacceptable in standard English.
3 Another controversial issue is the insertion of **have** where it is superfluous, as for example *I might have*

missed it if you **hadn't have** pointed it out (rather than the standard ... if you **hadn't** pointed it out). This construction has been around since at least the 15th and 16th centuries, but only where a hypothetical situation is presented (e.g. statements starting with **if**). More recently, there has been speculation among grammarians and linguists that this insertion of **have** may represent a kind of subjunctive and is actually making a useful distinction in the language. However, it is still regarded as an error in standard English.

▶**have at** tackle or attack forcefully or aggressively.
have someone on Brit. informal try to make someone believe something that is untrue, especially as a joke: *that's just too neat—you're having me on.*
have (got) something on 1 be wearing something: *she had a blue dress on.* **2** Brit. be committed to an arrangement: *I've got a lot on at the moment.*
have something out undergo an operation to extract a part of one's body.
have someone up (usu. **be had up**) Brit. informal bring someone before a court of justice to answer for an alleged offence: *you can* **be had up** *for blackmail.*

Havel /ˈhɑːv(ə)l/, Václav (b.1936), Czech dramatist and statesman, President of Czechoslovakia 1989–92 and of the Czech Republic since 1993. His plays, such as *The Garden Party* (1963), were critical of totalitarianism and he was twice imprisoned as a dissident. He was elected president following the velvet revolution.

haveli /ˌhʌvəˈliː/ ▶**noun** (pl. **havelis**) Indian a mansion.
– ORIGIN via Hindi from Arabic *havelī.*

haven ▶**noun** a place of safety or refuge: *a haven for wildlife.*
■an inlet providing shelter for ships or boats; a harbour or small port.
– ORIGIN late Old English *hæfen*, from Old Norse *hǫfn*; related to Dutch *haven*, German *Hafen* 'harbour'.

have-nots ▶**plural noun** (usu. **the have-nots**) informal economically disadvantaged people.

haven't ▶**contraction of** have not.

haver /ˈheɪvə/ ▶**verb** [no obj.] Scottish talk foolishly; babble: *Tom havered on.*
■Brit. act in a vacillating or indecisive manner: [as noun **havering**] *she was exasperated by all this havering.*
▶**noun** [mass noun] (also **havers**) Scottish foolish talk; nonsense.
– ORIGIN early 18th cent.: of unknown origin.

haversack /ˈhavəsak/ ▶**noun** a small, stout bag carried on the back or over the shoulder, used especially by soldiers and walkers.
– ORIGIN mid 18th cent.: from French *havresac*, from obsolete German *Habersack*, denoting a bag used by soldiers to carry oats as horse feed, from dialect *Haber* 'oats' + *Sack* 'sack, bag'.

Haversian canal /həˈvəːʃ(ə)n/ ▶**noun** Anatomy any of the minute tubes which form a network in bone and contain blood vessels.
– ORIGIN mid 19th cent.: named after Clopton *Havers* (1650–1702), English anatomist.

haversine /ˈhavəsʌɪn/ (also **haversin**) ▶**noun** Mathematics half of a versed sine.
– ORIGIN late 19th cent.: contraction of *half versed sine.*

havildar /ˈhavɪldɑː/ ▶**noun** (in the Indian subcontinent) a soldier or police officer corresponding to a sergeant.
– ORIGIN from Urdu *hawildār*, from Persian *ḥawāldār* 'trust-holder', from *ḥawāl* (from Arabic *ḥawāl* 'charge, assignment') + *-dār* 'holder'.

havoc ▶**noun** [mass noun] widespread destruction: *the hurricane ripped through Florida causing havoc.*
■great confusion or disorder: *schoolchildren wreaking havoc in the classroom.*
▶**verb** (**havocked**, **havocking**) [with obj.] archaic lay waste to; devastate.
– PHRASES **play havoc with** completely disrupt; cause serious damage to: *shift work plays havoc with the body clock.*
– ORIGIN late Middle English: from Anglo-Norman French *havok*, alteration of Old French *havot*, of unknown origin. The word was originally used in the phrase *cry havoc* (Old French *crier havot*) 'to give an army the order *havoc*', which was the signal for plundering.

haw¹ ▶**noun** the red fruit of the hawthorn.
– ORIGIN Old English *haga*, of Germanic origin; probably related to **HEDGE** (compare with Dutch *haag* 'hedge').

haw² ▶**noun** the third eyelid or nictitating membrane in certain mammals, especially dogs and cats.
– ORIGIN late Middle English (denoting a discharge from the eye): of unknown origin.

haw³ ▶**verb** see ***hum and haw*** at **HUM¹**.

Hawaii /həˈwʌɪi/ a state of the US comprising a group of over twenty islands in the North Pacific; capital, Honolulu (on Oahu); pop. 1,108,230 (1990). First settled by Polynesians, Hawaii was discovered by Captain James Cook in 1778. It was annexed by the US in 1898 and became the 50th state in 1959. Former name **SANDWICH ISLANDS**.
■the largest island in the state of Hawaii.

Hawaiian ▶**noun 1** a native or inhabitant of Hawaii.
2 [mass noun] the Austronesian language of Hawaii, now spoken by fewer than 2,000 people.
▶**adjective** of or relating to Hawaii, its people, or their language.
■Geology relating to or denoting a type of volcanic eruption in which very fluid basaltic lava is produced, as is typical of volcanoes in Hawaii.

Hawaiian goose ▶**noun** a rare goose native to Hawaii, now breeding chiefly in captivity. Also called **NENE**.
• *Branta sandvicensis*, family Anatidae.

Hawaiian guitar ▶**noun** a steel-stringed guitar in which a characteristic glissando effect is produced by sliding a metal bar along the strings as they are plucked.

Hawaiian honeycreeper ▶**noun** see **HONEYCREEPER** (sense 2).

hawfinch ▶**noun** a large Old World finch with a massive bill for cracking open cherry stones and other hard seeds.
• Genus *Coccothraustes*, family Fringillidae: three species, in particular the widespread *C. coccothraustes*.
– ORIGIN late 17th cent.: from **HAW¹** + **FINCH**.

hawk¹ ▶**noun 1** a diurnal bird of prey with broad rounded wings and a long tail, typically taking prey by surprise with a short chase. Compare with **FALCON**.
• Family Accipitridae: several genera, especially *Accipiter*, which includes the sparrowhawk and goshawk.
■N. Amer. a bird of prey related to the buzzards. ■ Falconry any diurnal bird of prey used in falconry.
2 a person who advocates an aggressive or warlike policy, especially in foreign affairs. Compare with **DOVE¹** (in sense 2).
3 used in names of hawkmoths, e.g. **eyed hawk**.
▶**verb** [no obj.] **1** (of a person) hunt game with a trained hawk: *he spent the afternoon hawking.*
2 (of a bird or dragonfly) hunt on the wing for food: *swifts hawked low over the water* | [with obj.] *dragonflies hawk and feed on flies.*
– PHRASES **have eyes like a hawk** miss nothing of what is going on around one. **watch someone like a hawk** keep a vigilant eye on someone, especially to check that they do nothing wrong.
– DERIVATIVES **hawkish** adjective, **hawkishly** adverb, **hawkishness** noun, **hawklike** adjective.
– ORIGIN Old English *hafoc, heafoc*, of Germanic origin; related to Dutch *havik* and German *Habicht*.

hawk² ▶**verb** [with obj.] carry about and offer (goods) for sale, typically advertising them by shouting: *street traders were hawking costume jewellery.*
– ORIGIN late 15th cent.: back-formation from **HAWKER¹**.

hawk³ ▶**verb** [no obj.] clear the throat noisily: *he hawked and spat into the flames.*
■[with obj.] (**hawk something up**) bring phlegm up from the throat.
– ORIGIN late 16th cent.: probably imitative.

hawk⁴ ▶**noun** a plasterer's square board with a handle underneath for carrying plaster or mortar.
– ORIGIN late Middle English: of unknown origin.

hawkbit ▶**noun** a Eurasian plant of the daisy family which resembles a dandelion, with a rosette of leaves and yellow flowers.
• Genus *Leontodon*, family Compositae.
– ORIGIN early 18th cent.: blend of **HAWKWEED** and **DEVIL'S BIT**.

Hawke, Bob (b.1929), Australian Labor statesman, Prime Minister 1983–91; full name *Robert James Lee Hawke*. During his premiership he pursued an economic programme based on free-market policies and tax reform.

hawk eagle ▶**noun** a small tropical eagle with broad wings and a long tail, and typically a crest.
• Genera *Spizaetus* and *Spizastur*, family Accipitridae: several species.

Hawke Bay a bay on the east coast of North Island, New Zealand.

hawker¹ ▶**noun** a person who travels about selling goods, typically advertising them by shouting.
– ORIGIN early 16th cent.: probably from Low German or Dutch and related to **HUCKSTER**.

hawker² ▶**noun 1** a falconer.
2 a slender-bodied dragonfly that remains airborne for long periods, typically patrolling a particular stretch of water.
• Aeshnidae, Gomphidae, and other families, order Odonata: several genera.
– ORIGIN Old English *hafocere*, from *hafoc* 'hawk'.

Hawke's Bay an administrative region on the eastern coast of North Island, New Zealand.

hawk-eyed ▶**adjective** having very good eyesight.
■watching carefully; vigilant: *a hawk-eyed policeman saved the lives of dozens of shoppers.*

Hawkeye State informal name for **IOWA**.

hawkfish ▶**noun** (pl. same or **-fishes**) a small tropical marine fish found chiefly in the Indo-Pacific region. It typically lives in shallow water and adopts a distinctive perching or 'hovering' position just above coral.
• Family Cirrhitidae: three genera and several species.

Hawking, Stephen (William) (b.1942), English theoretical physicist. His main work has been on space-time, quantum mechanics, and black holes. His book *A Brief History of Time* (1988) proved a popular best-seller.

Hawking radiation ▶**noun** [mass noun] Physics electromagnetic radiation which, according to theory, should be emitted by a black hole. The radiation is due to the black hole capturing one of a particle-antiparticle pair created spontaneously near to the event horizon.

Hawkins¹, Coleman (Randolph) (1904–69), American jazz saxophonist.

Hawkins² (also **Hawkyns**), Sir John (1532–95), English sailor. Involved in the slave trade and privateering, he later helped build up the fleet which defeated the Spanish Armada in 1588.

hawkmoth ▶**noun** a large swift-flying moth with a stout body and narrow forewings, typically feeding on nectar while hovering. The large caterpillar bears a spike at the rear end. Called **SPHINX** in North America.
• Family Sphingidae: several genera and many species.

hawk-nosed ▶**adjective** (of a person) having a nose which is curved like a hawk's beak.

hawk owl ▶**noun** a hawklike owl with a small head and long tail, and typically an obscure facial disc.
• Family Strigidae: three genera, including *Ninox* (several species in Asia and Australasia) and *Surnia*, in particular the diurnal *S. ulula* of northern coniferous forests.

Hawks, Howard (Winchester) (1896–1977), American film director, producer, and screenwriter. He directed such films as *The Big Sleep* (1946), *Gentlemen Prefer Blondes* (1953), and *Rio Bravo* (1959).

hawksbeard ▶**noun** a plant of the daisy family which resembles a dandelion but has a branched stem with several flowers.
• Genus *Crepis*, family Compositae.

hawksbill (also **hawksbill turtle**) ▶**noun** a small tropical sea turtle with hooked jaws and overlapping horny plates on the shell, extensively hunted as the traditional source of tortoiseshell.
• *Eretmochelys imbricata*, family Cheloniidae.

hawkshaw ▶**noun** informal, dated a detective.
– ORIGIN early 20th cent.: from the name of a detective in the play *The Ticket-of-Leave Man* by Tom Taylor (1817–80), English dramatist; also portrayed in the comic strip *Hawkshaw the Detective* by Augustus Charles ('Gus') Mager (1878–1956), American cartoonist.

Hawksmoor, Nicholas (1661–1736), English architect. Having become a clerk to Sir Christopher Wren in 1679, in 1690 he went on to work with Vanbrugh at Castle Howard and Blenheim Palace. He later designed six London churches.

hawkweed ▶**noun** [mass noun] a widely distributed plant of the daisy family, which typically has yellow dandelion-like flower heads and often grows as a weed.
• Genus *Hieracium*, family Compositae.

– ORIGIN late Old English, rendering Latin *hieracium*, based on Greek *hierax* 'hawk'.

Hawkyns variant spelling of **HAWKINS**[2].

Haworth /ˈhaʊwəθ/, Sir Walter Norman (1883–1950), English organic chemist. He was a pioneer in carbohydrate chemistry and was the first person to make a vitamin artificially when he synthesized vitamin C. Nobel Prize for Chemistry (1937).

hawse /hɔːz/ ▶ noun the part of a ship's bows through which the anchor cables pass.
■ the space between the head of an anchored vessel and the anchors.
– PHRASES **a foul hawse** a situation in which an anchored ship's port and starboard cables are crossed.
– ORIGIN late Middle English *halse*, probably from Old Norse *háls* 'neck, ship's bow'.

hawse hole ▶ noun a hole in the deck of a ship through which an anchor cable passes.

hawsepipe ▶ noun an inclined pipe leading from a hawse hole to the side of a ship, containing the shank of the anchor when the anchor is raised.

hawser /ˈhɔːzə/ ▶ noun a thick rope or cable for mooring or towing a ship.
– ORIGIN Middle English: from Anglo-Norman French *haucer*, from Old French *haucier* 'to hoist', based on Latin *altus* 'high'.

hawser-laid ▶ adjective another term for **CABLE-LAID**.

hawthorn ▶ noun a thorny shrub or tree of the rose family, with white, pink, or red blossom and small dark red fruits (haws). Native to north temperate regions, it is commonly used for hedging in Britain. Also called **MAY**, **QUICKTHORN**, or **WHITETHORN**.
● Genus *Crataegus*, family Rosaceae: many species, in particular the European **common hawthorn** (*C. monogyna*).
– ORIGIN Old English *hagathorn*, probably meaning literally 'hedge thorn' (see **HAW**[1], **THORN**); related to Dutch *haagdoorn*, German *Hagedorn*.

Hawthorne, Nathaniel (1804–64), American novelist and short-story writer. Much of his fiction explores guilt, sin, and morality. Notable works: *Twice-Told Tales* (short stories, 1837) and *The House of Seven Gables* (novel, 1851).

Hawthorne effect ▶ noun [mass noun] the alteration of behaviour by the subjects of a study due to their awareness of being observed.
– ORIGIN 1960s: from *Hawthorne*, the name of one of the Western Electric Company's plants in Chicago, where the phenomenon was first observed in the 1920s.

Hay, Will (1888–1949), English actor and comedian; full name *William Thomson Hay*. He is remembered for his screen characterizations of incompetent authority figures. His films include *Oh, Mr Porter!* (1937) and *My Learned Friend* (1944).

hay[1] ▶ noun [mass noun] grass that has been mown and dried for use as fodder.
– PHRASES **hit the hay** informal go to bed. **make hay (while the sun shines)** proverb make good use of an opportunity while it lasts.
– ORIGIN Old English *hēg, hīeg, hīg*, of Germanic origin; related to Dutch *hooi* and German *Heu*, also to **HEW**.

hay[2] ▶ noun a country dance with interweaving steps similar to a reel.
■ a winding figure in such a dance.
– ORIGIN early 16th cent.: from an obsolete sense 'a kind of dance' of French *haie* 'hedge', figuratively 'row of people lining the route of a procession'.

haybox ▶ noun historical a box stuffed with hay in which heated food was left to continue cooking.

haycock ▶ noun a conical heap of hay in a field.

Hay diet ▶ noun a diet in which carbohydrates are eaten at separate times from fruit and proteins, in the belief that this aids digestion.
– ORIGIN 1930s: named after William Howard Hay (1866–1940), the American physician who devised it.

Haydn /ˈhaɪd(ə)n/, Franz Joseph (1732–1809), Austrian composer. A major exponent of the classical style, he taught both Mozart and Beethoven. His work includes 108 symphonies, 67 string quartets, 12 masses, and the oratorio *The Creation* (1796–8).

Hayek /ˈhʌɪɛk/, Friedrich August von (1899–1992), Austrian-born British economist. Strongly opposed to Keynesian economics, he was a leading advocate of the free market. Nobel Prize for Economics (1974).

Hayes, Rutherford (Birchard) (1822–93), American Republican statesman, 19th President of the US 1877–81. His administration brought the Reconstruction era in the South to an end.

hay fever ▶ noun [mass noun] an allergy caused by pollen or dust in which the mucous membranes of the eyes and nose are inflamed, causing running at the nose and watery eyes.

haying ▶ noun [mass noun] the activity of mowing and drying grass to make hay.

haylage /ˈheɪlɪdʒ/ ▶ noun [mass noun] silage made from grass which has been partially dried.
– ORIGIN 1960s: blend of **HAY**[1] and **SILAGE**.

hayloft ▶ noun a loft over a stable used for storing hay or straw.

haymaker ▶ noun **1** a person who is involved in making hay, especially one who tosses and spreads it to dry after mowing.
■ an apparatus for shaking and drying hay.
2 informal a forceful blow.

haymaking ▶ noun [mass noun] the activity of making hay from grass grown for fodder.

haymow /ˈheɪmaʊ/ ▶ noun a stack of hay or part of a barn in which hay is stored.

hayrick ▶ noun another term for **HAYSTACK**.

hayride ▶ noun chiefly N. Amer. a ride taken for pleasure in a wagon carrying hay.

hayseed ▶ noun **1** [mass noun] grass seed obtained from hay.
2 informal, chiefly N. Amer. a person from the country, especially a simple, unsophisticated one.

haystack ▶ noun a packed pile of hay, typically with a pointed or ridged top.

haywire ▶ adjective informal erratic; out of control: *her imagination had gone haywire*.
– ORIGIN early 20th cent. (originally US): from **HAY**[1] + **WIRE**, from the use of hay-baling wire in makeshift repairs.

Hayworth, Rita (1918–87), American actress and dancer; born *Margarita Carmen Cansino*. She achieved stardom in film musicals such as *Cover Girl* (1944) before going on to play roles in *film noir*, notably in *Gilda* (1946) and *The Lady from Shanghai* (1948).

hazard /ˈhazəd/ ▶ noun **1** a danger or risk: *the hazards of childbirth*.
■ a potential source of danger: *a fire hazard | a health hazard*. ■ a permanent feature of a golf course which presents an obstruction to playing a shot, such as a bunker or stream.
2 [mass noun] poetic/literary chance; probability: *we can form no calculation concerning the laws of hazard*.
3 [mass noun] a gambling game using two dice, in which the chances are complicated by arbitrary rules.
4 (in real tennis) each of the winning openings in the court.
5 Billiards a stroke with which a ball is pocketed.
■ (**losing hazard**) the pocketing of the cue ball off another ball. ■ (**winning hazard**) the pocketing of the object ball.
▶ verb [with obj.] **1** venture to say (something): *he hazarded a guess*.
2 put (something) at risk of being lost: *the cargo business is too risky to hazard money on*.
– ORIGIN Middle English (in sense 3): from Old French *hasard*, from Spanish *azar*, from Arabic *az-zahr* 'chance, luck', from Persian *zār* or Turkish *zar* 'dice'.

hazard lights (also **hazard warning lights**) ▶ plural noun yellow flashing indicator lights on a vehicle, switched on simultaneously as a warning that the vehicle is stationary or unexpectedly slowing down or reversing.

hazardous ▶ adjective risky; dangerous: *we work in hazardous conditions | it is hazardous to personal safety*.
– DERIVATIVES **hazardously** adverb, **hazardousness** noun.
– ORIGIN mid 16th cent.: from French *hasardeux*, from *hasard* 'chance' (see **HAZARD**).

hazard pay ▶ noun US term for **DANGER MONEY**.

Hazchem /ˈhazkɛm/ ▶ noun [as modifier] denoting a system of labelling hazardous chemicals, especially during transportation.
– ORIGIN 1970s: from *hazardous chemical*.

haze[1] ▶ noun a slight obscuration of the lower atmosphere, typically caused by fine suspended particles.
■ a very tenuous cloud of something such as vapour or smoke in the air: *a faint haze of steam*. ■ [in sing.] figurative a state of mental obscurity or confusion: *through an alcoholic haze*.
– ORIGIN early 18th cent. (originally denoting fog or hoar frost): probably a back-formation from **HAZY**.

haze[2] ▶ verb N. Amer. **1** [with obj.] force (a new recruit in the military or a potential recruit to a university fraternity) to perform strenuous, humiliating, or dangerous tasks: *rookies were mercilessly hazed*.
2 [with obj. and adverbial of direction] drive (cattle) in a specified direction while on horseback.
– ORIGIN late 17th cent. (originally Scots and dialect in the sense 'frighten, scold, or beat'): perhaps related to obsolete French *haser* 'tease or insult'.

hazel ▶ noun **1** a temperate shrub or small tree with broad leaves, bearing prominent male catkins in spring and round hard-shelled edible nuts in autumn.
● Genus *Corylus*, family Betulaceae: several species, in particular the common **Eurasian hazel** (*C. avellana*), formerly widely managed as coppice.
2 [mass noun] a reddish-brown or greenish-brown colour, especially of someone's eyes.
– ORIGIN Old English *hæsel*, of Germanic origin; related to Dutch *hazelaar* 'hazel tree', *hazelnoot* 'hazelnut', and German *Hasel*, from an Indo-European root shared by Latin *corylus*.

hazel grouse ▶ noun a small Eurasian woodland grouse with mainly greyish plumage.
● *Bonasa bonasia*, family Tetraonidae (or Phasianidae).

hazelnut ▶ noun a round brown hard-shelled nut that is the edible fruit of the hazel.

Hazlitt /ˈhazlɪt, ˈheɪz-/, William (1778–1830), English essayist and critic. His diverse essays, collected in *Table Talk* (1821), were marked by a clarity and conviction which brought new vigour to English prose writing.

hazy ▶ adjective (**hazier**, **haziest**) covered by a haze: *it was a beautiful day but quite hazy*.
■ vague, indistinct, or ill-defined: *hazy memories | the picture we have of him as a man is extremely hazy*.
– DERIVATIVES **hazily** adverb, **haziness** noun.
– ORIGIN early 17th cent. (in nautical use in the sense 'foggy'): of unknown origin.

hazzan /xaˈzɑːn, ˈhɑːz(ə)n/ ▶ noun (pl. **hazzanim**) another term for **CANTOR** (in sense 1).
– ORIGIN mid 17th cent.: from Hebrew *ḥazzān* 'cantor', possibly from Assyrian *hazannu* 'mayor, village headman'.

HB ▶ abbreviation for ■ half board. ■ (also **hb**) hardback. ■ hard black (used in describing a medium grade of pencil lead). ■ the political wing of the Basque separatist organization ETA. [ORIGIN: abbreviation of Basque *Herri Batasuna* 'United People'.]

Hb ▶ symbol for haemoglobin.

HBM Brit. ▶ abbreviation for Her or His Britannic Majesty (or Majesty's).

H-bomb ▶ noun another term for **HYDROGEN BOMB**.
– ORIGIN 1950s: from **H**[2] (denoting hydrogen) + **BOMB**.

HC ▶ abbreviation for ■ Holy Communion. ■ (in the UK) House of Commons. ■ hydrocarbon: *increasing fuel efficiency decreases the levels of HC*.

h.c. ▶ abbreviation for honoris causa.

HCF ▶ abbreviation for Mathematics highest common factor.

HCFC ▶ abbreviation for hydrochlorofluorocarbon.

H.D. see **DOOLITTLE**.

HDD Computing ▶ abbreviation for hard disk drive.

HDTV ▶ abbreviation for high-definition television, using more lines per frame to give a sharper image.

HE ▶ abbreviation for ■ high explosive. ■ His Eminence. ■ His or Her Excellency.

He ▶ symbol for the chemical element helium.

he ▶ pronoun [third person singular] used to refer to a man, boy, or male animal previously mentioned or easily identified: *everyone liked my father—he was the perfect gentleman*.
■ used to refer to a person or animal of unspecified sex (in modern use, now chiefly replaced by 'he or she' or 'they': see usage note below): *every child needs to know that he is loved*. ■ any person (in modern use,

now chiefly replaced by 'anyone' or 'the person': see usage note below): *he who is silent consents.*

▶**noun** [in sing.] a male; a man: *is that a he or a she?*

■[in combination] male: *a he-goat.*

– ORIGIN Old English *he, hē*, of Germanic origin; related to Dutch *hij*.

USAGE 1 For a discussion of *I am older than* **he** versus *I am older than* **him**, see **usage** at **PERSONAL PRONOUN**.

2 Until recently, **he** was used uncontroversially to refer to a person of unspecified sex, as in *every child needs to know that* **he** *is loved.* In the 20th century, this use has become problematic and has become a hallmark of old-fashioned language or sexism in language. Use of **they** as an alternative to **he** in this sense (*everyone needs to feel that* **they** *matter*) has been in use since the 18th century, in contexts where it occurs after an indefinite pronoun such as **everyone** or **someone**. It is becoming more and more accepted both in speech and in writing, and is used as the norm in this dictionary. Another alternative is **he or she**, though this can become tiresomely long-winded when used frequently.

Head, Edith (b.1907), American costume designer. She worked on a wide range of films, winning Oscars for costume design in *All About Eve* (1950) and *The Sting* (1973).

head ▶**noun** **1** the upper part of the human body, or the front or upper part of the body of an animal, typically separated from the rest of the body by a neck, and containing the brain, mouth, and sense organs.

■the head regarded as the location of intellect, imagination, and memory: *whatever comes into my head.* ■(**head for**) an aptitude for or tolerance of: *she had a good head for business | a head for heights.* ■informal a headache, especially one resulting from intoxication. ■the height or length of a head as a measure: *he was beaten by a head.* ■(**heads**) the side of a coin bearing the image of a head (used when tossing a coin to determine a winner): *heads or tails?* ■the antlers of a deer.

2 a thing having the appearance of a head either in form or in relation to a whole, in particular:

■the cutting, striking, or operational end of a tool, weapon, or mechanism. ■the flattened or knobbed end of a nail, pin, screw, or match. ■the ornamented top of a pillar or column. ■a compact mass of leaves or flowers at the top of a stem, especially a capitulum: *huge heads of fluffy cream flowers.* ■the edible leafy part at the top of the stem of such green vegetables as cabbage and lettuce. ■one saleable unit of certain vegetables, such as cabbage or celery.

3 the front, forward, or upper part or end of something, in particular:

■the upper end of a table or bed: *he sat down at the head of the cot.* ■the upper horizontal part of a window frame or door frame. ■the flat end of a cask or drum. ■the front of a queue or procession. ■the top of a page. ■short for **HEADLINE**. ■the top of a flight of stairs or steps. ■the source of a river or stream. ■the end of a lake or inlet at which a river enters. ■[usu. in place names] a promontory: *Beachy Head.* ■the top of a ship's mast. ■the bows of a ship. ■the fully developed top of a boil or spot. ■the foam on top of a glass of beer, or the cream on the top of milk. ■short for **CYLINDER HEAD**.

4 a person in charge of something; a director or leader: *the head of the Dutch Catholic Church.*

■Brit. short for **HEADMASTER**, **HEADMISTRESS**, or **HEAD TEACHER**.

5 Grammar the word that governs all the other words in a phrase in which it is used, having the same grammatical function as the whole phrase.

6 a person considered as a numerical unit: *they paid fifty pounds a head.*

■[treated as pl.] a number of cattle or game as specified: *seventy head of dairy cattle.*

7 a component in an audio, video, or information system by which information is transferred from an electrical signal to the recording medium, or vice versa.

■the part of a record player that holds the playing cartridge and stylus. ■short for **PRINTHEAD**.

8 a body of water kept at a particular height in order to provide a supply at sufficient pressure: *an 8 m head of water in the shafts.*

■the pressure exerted by such water or by a confined body of steam: *a good head of steam on the gauge.*

9 Nautical slang a toilet, especially on a ship.

10 [mass noun] Geology a superficial deposit of rock fragments, formed at the edge of an ice sheet by repeated freezing and thawing and then moved downhill.

▶**adjective** [attrib.] chief; principal: *the head waiter.*

▶**verb** [with obj.] **1** be in the leading position on: *the St George's Day procession was headed by the mayor.*

■be in charge of: *an organizational unit headed by a line manager | she* **headed up** *the Jubilee Year programme.*

2 (usu. **be headed**) give a title or caption to: *an article headed 'The Protection of Human Life'.*

■[as adj. **headed**] having a printed heading, typically the name and address of a person or organization: *headed notepaper.*

3 [no obj., with adverbial of direction] (also chiefly US **be headed**) move in a specified direction: *he was* **heading for** *the exit | we were headed in the wrong direction.*

■(**head for**) appear to be moving inevitably towards (something, especially something undesirable): *the economy is heading for recession.* ■[with obj. and adverbial of direction] direct or steer in a specified direction: *she headed the car towards them.*

4 Soccer shoot or pass (the ball) with the head: *a corner kick that he headed into the net.*

5 lop off the upper part or branches of (a plant or tree).

6 [no obj.] (of a lettuce or cabbage) form a head.

– PHRASES **be banging** (or **knocking**) **one's head against a brick wall** be doggedly attempting the impossible and suffering in the process. **bang** (or **knock**) **people's heads together** reprimand people severely, especially in an attempt to stop them arguing. **be hanging over someone's head** (of something unpleasant) threaten to affect someone at any moment. **be on someone's** (**own**) **head** be someone's sole responsibility. **bite** (or **snap**) **someone's head off** reply sharply and brusquely to someone. **by the head** Nautical (of a boat or ship) deeper in the water forward than astern: *the Boy Andrew went down by the head.* **come to a head** reach a crisis: *the violence came to a head with the deaths of six youths.* **do someone's head in** Brit. informal cause someone to feel annoyed, confused, or frustrated. **enter someone's head** [usu. with negative] occur to someone: *such an idea never entered my head.* **from head to toe** (or **foot**) all over one's body: *I was shaking from head to toe.* **get one's head down** Brit. informal **1** sleep. **2** concentrate on the task in hand. **get one's head round** (or **around**) [usu. with negative] informal understand or come to terms with something: *I just can't get my head around this idea.* **give someone his** (or **her**) **head** allow someone complete freedom of action. **give someone head** vulgar slang perform oral sex on someone. **go to someone's head** (of alcohol) make someone dizzy or slightly drunk. ■(of success) make someone conceited. **get something into one's** (or **someone's**) **head** come (or cause someone) to realize or understand: *when will you get it into your head that it's the project that counts not me?* **hang one's head** (**in shame**) be deeply ashamed. **head of hair** the hair on a person's head, regarded in terms of its appearance or quantity: *he had a fine head of hair.* **head and shoulders above** informal by far superior to. **—— one's head off** talk, laugh, etc. unrestrainedly: *he was drunk as a newt and singing his head off.* **head over heels 1** turning over completely in forward motion, as in a somersault. **2** (also **head over heels in love**) madly in love: *I immediately* **fell head over heels for** *Don.* **a head start** an advantage granted or gained at the beginning of something: *our fine traditions give us a* **head start** *on the competition.* **heads I win, tails you lose** I win whatever happens. **heads will roll** people will be dismissed or forced to resign. **hold** (or **put**) **a gun** (or **a pistol**) **to someone's head** force someone to do something by using threats. **hold up one's head** (or **hold one's head high**) be confident or unashamed: *under the circumstances I would find it impossible to hold my head up in the town.* **in one's head** by mental process without use of physical aids: *the piece he'd already written in his head.* **keep one's head** remain calm. **keep one's head above water** avoid succumbing to difficulties, typically debt. **keep one's head down** remain inconspicuous in difficult or dangerous times. **knock something on the head** dismiss an idea, project, or rumour once and for all. **lose one's head** lose self-control; panic. **make head or tail of** [usu. with negative] understand at all: *we couldn't make head nor tail of the answer.* **off** (or **out of**) **one's head** informal crazy: *my old man's* **going off his head**, *you know.* ■extremely drunk or severely under the influence of drugs. **off the top of one's head** without careful thought or investigation. **over someone's head 1** (also **above someone's head**) beyond someone's ability to understand: *the discussion was over my head, I'm afraid.* **2** without someone's knowledge or involvement, especially when they have a right to it: *the deal was struck over the heads of the regions concerned.* ■with disregard for someone else's (stronger) claim: *his promotion over the heads of more senior colleagues.* **put their** (or **our** or **your**) **heads together** consult and work together: *they forced the major banks to put their heads together to sort it out.* **put something into someone's head** suggest something to someone: *who's been putting ideas into your head?* **standing on one's head** with no difficulty at all: *I could design this garden standing on my head.* **stand** (or **turn**) **something on its head** completely reverse the principles or interpretation of an idea or argument. **take it into one's head to do something** impetuously decide to do something. **turn someone's head** make someone conceited. **turn heads** attract a great deal of attention or interest: *she recently turned heads with a nude scene.*

– DERIVATIVES **headed** adjective [in combination] *bald-headed men | woolly-headed New Age thinking,* **headless** adjective.

– ORIGIN Old English *hēafod*, of Germanic origin; related to Dutch *hoofd* and German *Haupt*.

▶**head someone/thing off** intercept and turn aside: *he ran up the road to head off approaching cars.*

■forestall: *they headed off a row by ordering further study of both plans.*

head up Sailing steer towards the wind.

-head[1] ▶**suffix** equivalent to **-HOOD**.

– ORIGIN Middle English *-hed, -hede*.

-head[2] ▶**combining form** **1** denoting the front, forward, or upper part or end of a specified thing: *spearhead | masthead.*

2 in nouns used informally to express disparagement of a person: *airhead | dumbhead.*

3 in nouns used informally to denote an addict or habitual user of a specified drug: *crackhead.*

headache ▶**noun** a continuous pain in the head.

■informal a thing or person that causes worry or trouble; a problem: *an administrative headache.*

– DERIVATIVES **headachy** adjective.

headage ▶**noun** [mass noun] [often as modifier] the number of animals held as stock on a farm.

headband ▶**noun** **1** a band of fabric worn around the head as a decoration or to keep the hair or perspiration off the face.

2 an ornamental strip of coloured silk fastened to the top of the spine of a book.

headbanger ▶**noun** informal **1** a fan or performer of heavy metal music.

2 a mad or eccentric person.

headbanging ▶**noun** [mass noun] violent rhythmic shaking of the head by fans of heavy metal music.

■violent rocking of the body and shaking or knocking of the head, by children or mentally disordered adults.

headboard ▶**noun** **1** an upright panel forming or placed behind the head of a bed.

2 a board on the front of a train bearing the name of the route or service for which it is being used.

3 Sailing a reinforcement at the top of a triangular sail such as a mainsail.

headbutt ▶**noun** an aggressive and forceful thrust with the top of the head, especially into the face or body of another person.

▶**verb** [with obj.] attack (someone) with such a thrust of the head.

head case ▶**noun** informal a mentally ill or unstable person.

headcheese ▶**noun** North American term for **BRAWN** (sense 2).

headcount ▶**noun** an instance of counting the number of people present.

■a total number of people, especially the number of people employed in a particular organization.

headdress ▶**noun** an ornamental covering or band for the head, especially one worn on ceremonial occasions.

headend ▶**noun** a control centre in a cable television system where various signals are brought together and monitored before being introduced into the cable network.

header ▶ noun **1** Soccer a shot or pass made with the head.
2 informal a headlong fall or dive.
3 a brick or stone laid at right angles to the face of a wall. Compare with STRETCHER (in sense 4).
4 (also **header tank**) a raised tank of water maintaining pressure in a plumbing system.
5 a line or block of text appearing at the top of each page of a book or document. Compare with FOOTER[1] (in sense 3).

head first ▶ adjective & adverb with the head in front of the rest of the body: [as adv.] *she dived head first into the water* | [as attrib. adj.] *a head-first slide.*
■without sufficient forethought.

head gasket ▶ noun the gasket which fits between the cylinder head and the cylinders or cylinder block in an internal-combustion engine.

headgear ▶ noun [mass noun] hats, helmets, and other items worn on the head: *protective headgear.*

headhunt ▶ verb [with obj.] [as noun **headhunting**] the practice among some peoples of collecting the heads of dead enemies as trophies.
■(often **be headhunted**) identify and approach (a suitable person employed elsewhere) to fill a business position.
– DERIVATIVES **headhunter** noun.

heading ▶ noun **1** a title at the head of a page or section of a book: *chapter headings.*
■a division or section of a subject; a class or category: *this topic falls under four main headings.*
2 a direction or bearing: *he crawled on a heading of 90 degrees until he came to the track.*
3 a horizontal passage made in preparation for building a tunnel.
■Mining another term for DRIFT (in sense 4).
4 a strip of cloth at the top of a curtain above the hooks or wire by which it is suspended.

headland ▶ noun **1** a narrow piece of land that projects from a coastline into the sea.
2 a strip of land left unploughed at the end of a field.

headlight (also **headlamp**) ▶ noun a powerful light at the front of a motor vehicle or railway engine.

headline ▶ noun a heading at the top of an article or page in a newspaper or magazine: *a front-page headline.*
■(**the headlines**) the most important items of news in a newspaper or in a broadcast news bulletin: *issues that are never long out of the headlines* | *the war at sea began to hit the headlines.*
▶verb **1** [with obj. and complement] provide with a headline: *a feature that was headlined 'Invest in your Future'.*
2 [with obj.] appear as the star performer at (a concert): *Nirvana headlined the 1992 Reading Festival* | [no obj.] *they are headlining at the Town & Country club.*

head line ▶ noun (in palmistry) the lower of the two horizontal lines that cross the palm of the hand, linked to the nature and strength of a person's mental faculties.

headliner ▶ noun a performer or act that is promoted as the star attraction on a bill.

headlock ▶ noun a method of restraining someone by holding an arm firmly around their head, especially as a hold in wrestling.

headlong ▶ adverb & adjective **1** [as adv.] with the head foremost: *he fell headlong into the tent.*
2 in a rush; with reckless haste: [as attrib. adj.] *a headlong dash through the house* | [as adv.] *those who rush headlong to join in the latest craze.*
– ORIGIN Middle English *headling* (from HEAD + the adverbial suffix *-ling*), altered in late Middle English by association with -LONG.

head louse ▶ noun a louse which infests the hair of the human head and is especially common among schoolchildren.
● *Pediculus humanus capitis*, family Pediculidae, order Anoplura. See also BODY LOUSE.

headman ▶ noun (pl. **-men**) the chief or leader of a community or tribe.

headmaster ▶ noun chiefly Brit. a man who is the head teacher in a school.
– DERIVATIVES **headmasterly** adjective.

headmistress ▶ noun chiefly Brit. a woman who is the head teacher in a school.
– DERIVATIVES **headmistressy** adjective.

headmost ▶ adjective archaic (chiefly of a ship) holding a position in advance of others; foremost.

headnote ▶ noun a note inserted at the head of an article or document, summarizing or commenting on the content.
■Law a summary of a decided case prefixed to the case report, setting out the principles behind the decision and an outline of the facts.

head of state ▶ noun the chief public representative of a country, such as a president or monarch, who may also be the head of government.

head-on ▶ adjective & adverb **1** with or involving the front of a vehicle: [as attrib. adj.] *a head-on collision* | [as adv.] *they hit a bus head-on.*
2 with or involving direct confrontation: [as attrib. adj.] *trying to avoid a head-on clash.*

headphones ▶ plural noun a pair of earphones joined by a band placed over the head, for listening to audio signals such as music or speech.

headpiece ▶ noun **1** a device worn on the head as an ornament or to serve a function.
2 an illustration or ornamental motif printed at the head of a chapter in a book.
3 the part of a halter or bridle that fits over the top of a horse's head behind the ears.

headquarter ▶ verb [with obj. and adverbial of place] (usu. **be headquartered**) provide (an organization) with headquarters at a specified location: *Unesco is headquartered in Paris.*

headquarters ▶ noun [treated as sing. or pl.] the premises occupied by a military commander and the commander's staff.
■the place or building serving as the managerial and administrative centre of an organization.

headrail ▶ noun a horizontal rail at the top of something.

headrest ▶ noun a padded part extending from or fixed to the back of a seat or chair, designed to support the head.

headroom ▶ noun [mass noun] the space between the top of a vehicle or a person's head and the roof, ceiling, or other structure above.

headsail /ˈhedseɪl, -s(ə)l/ ▶ noun a sail on a ship's foremast or bowsprit.

headscarf ▶ noun (pl. **-scarves**) a square of fabric worn as a covering for the head, often folded into a triangle and knotted under the chin.

head sea ▶ noun a mass of waves coming from directly in front of a ship: *we tried out the boat in a steep head sea.*

headset ▶ noun **1** a set of headphones, typically with a microphone attached, used especially in telephony and radio communication.
2 the bearing assembly which links the front fork of a bicycle to its frame.

headship ▶ noun the position of leader or chief.
■chiefly Brit. the position of head teacher in a school.

headshrinker ▶ noun historical a headhunter who preserved and shrank the heads of his dead enemies.
■informal, chiefly N. Amer. a psychiatrist. Compare with SHRINK.

headsman ▶ noun (pl. **-men**) historical **1** a man who was responsible for beheading condemned prisoners.
2 a person in command of a whaling boat.

headspring ▶ noun **1** a spring that is the main source of a stream.
2 a somersault similar to a handspring, except that the performer lands on the head as well as the hands.

headsquare ▶ noun another term for HEADSCARF.

headstall /ˈhedstɔːl/ ▶ noun chiefly N. Amer. **1** a head collar or halter.
2 another term for HEADPIECE (in sense 3).

headstander ▶ noun a small deep-bodied freshwater fish of the Amazon region, popular in aquaria. It swims and feeds at an oblique angle with the head down.
● Genus *Abramites*, family Anostomidae: two species.

headstay ▶ noun another term for FORESTAY.

headstock ▶ noun **1** a set of bearings in a machine, supporting a revolving part.
■the widened piece at the end of the neck of a guitar, to which the tuning pegs are fixed.
2 the horizontal end member of the underframe of a railway vehicle.

headstone ▶ noun a slab of stone set up at the head of a grave, typically inscribed with the name of the dead person.

headstream ▶ noun a headwater stream.

headstrong ▶ adjective energetically wilful and determined: *the headstrong impulsiveness of youth.*

heads-up N. Amer. informal ▶ noun an advance warning of something: *the heads-up came just in time to stop the tanks from launching the final assault.*
▶ adjective [attrib.] showing alertness or perceptiveness: *they played a very heads-up game.*

head teacher ▶ noun the teacher in charge of a school.

head-to-head ▶ adjective & adverb involving two parties confronting each other: [as adj.] *a head-to-head battle with discounters.*
▶ noun a conversation, confrontation, or contest between two parties.

head-turning ▶ adjective extremely noticeable or attractive.

head-up display (N. Amer. also **heads-up display**) ▶ noun a display of instrument readings in an aircraft or vehicle that can be seen without lowering the eyes, typically through being projected on to the windscreen or visor.

head voice ▶ noun [in sing.] one of the high registers of the voice in speaking or singing, above chest voice.

headward ▶ adjective in the region or direction of the head.
■Geology denoting erosion by a stream or river occurring progressively upstream from the original source.
▶ adverb (also **headwards**) towards the head.

headwater ▶ noun (usu. **headwaters**) a tributary stream of a river close to or forming part of its source.

headway ▶ noun **1** [mass noun] forward movement or progress: *they appear to be making headway in bringing the rebels under control* | *the ship was making very little headway against heavy seas.*
2 the average interval between trains or buses on a regular service: *a six-minute headway.*

headwind ▶ noun a wind blowing from directly in front, opposing forward motion.

headword ▶ noun a word which begins a separate entry in a reference work.

headwork ▶ noun **1** [mass noun] activities taxing the mind; mental work.
2 (**headworks**) apparatus for controlling the flow of water in a river or canal.

heady ▶ adjective (**headier**, **headiest**) (of liquor) potent; intoxicating: *several bottles of heady local wine.*
■having a strong or exhilarating effect: *the heady days of the birth of the women's movement* | *a heady, exotic perfume.*
– DERIVATIVES **headily** adverb, **headiness** noun.

heal ▶ verb [with obj.] (of a person or treatment) cause (a wound, injury, or person) to become sound or healthy again: *his concern is to heal sick people* | [as adj. **healing**] *a healing experience* | [as noun **healing**] *the gift of healing.*
■[no obj.] become sound or healthy again: *he would have to wait until his knee had healed.* ■alleviate (a person's distress or anguish). ■correct or put right (an undesirable situation): *the rift between them was never really healed.*
– DERIVATIVES **healable** adjective, **healer** noun.
– ORIGIN Old English *hǣlan* (in the sense 'restore to sound health'), of Germanic origin; related to Dutch *heelen* and German *heilen*, also to WHOLE.

heal-all ▶ noun a universal remedy; a panacea.
■informal any of a number of medicinal plants, especially roseroot and self-heal.

heald /hiːld/ ▶ noun another term for HEDDLE.
– ORIGIN Old English *hefel, hefeld* 'the warp and weft', of Germanic origin, from a base meaning 'raise'. The current sense dates from the mid 18th cent.

health ▶ noun [mass noun] the state of being free from illness or injury: *he was restored to health* | [as modifier] *a health risk.*
■a person's mental or physical condition: *bad health forced him to retire* | figurative *a standard for measuring the financial health of a company.* ■(**your health** or **your good health**) used to express friendly feelings towards one's companions before drinking.
– ORIGIN Old English *hǣlth*, of Germanic origin; related to WHOLE.

health centre ▶ noun a building or establishment

housing local medical services or the practice of a group of doctors.

health certificate ▶ **noun** a certificate attesting a person's good health, sometimes required when travelling between states or countries.

health farm ▶ **noun** a residential establishment where people seek improved health by a regimen of dieting, exercise, and treatment.

health food ▶ **noun** [mass noun] natural food that is thought to have health-giving qualities.

healthful ▶ **adjective** having or conducive to good health: *healthful methods of cooking vegetables.*

– DERIVATIVES **healthfully** adverb, **healthfulness** noun.

health physics ▶ **plural noun** [treated as sing.] the branch of radiology that deals with the health of people working with radioactive materials.

health service ▶ **noun** a public service providing medical care.

■(**the health service**) Brit. short for **NATIONAL HEALTH SERVICE**.

health visitor ▶ **noun** Brit. a trained nurse who visits people in their homes to assist or advise the chronically ill or parents with very young children.

healthy ▶ **adjective** (**healthier**, **healthiest**) in good health: *feeling fit and healthy.*

■(of a part of the body) not diseased: *healthy cells.* ■ indicative of, conducive to, or promoting good health: *a healthy appetite | a healthy balanced diet.* ■ (of a person's attitude) sensible and well balanced: *a healthy contempt for authority.* ■ figurative in a good condition: *the family is the basis of any healthy society.* ■ desirable; beneficial: *healthy competition.* ■ of a very satisfactory size or amount: *making a healthy profit.*

– DERIVATIVES **healthily** adverb, **healthiness** noun.

Heaney /ˈhiːni/, Seamus (Justin) (b.1939), Irish poet. Born in Northern Ireland, in 1972 he took Irish citizenship. Notable works: *North* (1975) and *The Haw Lantern* (1987). Nobel Prize for Literature (1995).

heap ▶ **noun** an untidy collection of things piled up haphazardly: *she rushed out, leaving her clothes in a heap on the floor | a disordered* ***heap of*** *boxes.*

■a mound or pile of a particular substance: ***a heap of*** *gravel.* ■ informal an untidy or dilapidated place or vehicle: *they climbed back in the heap and headed home.* ■ (**a heap of/heaps of**) informal a large amount or number of something: *we have heaps of room.*

▶ **adverb** (**heaps**) informal a great deal: *'How do you like Maggie?' 'I like you heaps better!'*

▶ **verb** [with obj.] put in a pile or mound: *she heaped logs on the fire |* ***heaped up*** *in one corner was a pile of junk.*

■(**heap something with**) load something copiously with: *he heaped his plate with rice.* ■ (**heap something on/upon**) bestow praise, abuse, or criticism liberally on: *they once heaped praise on her.* ■ [as adj. **heaped**] Brit. (of a spoon or other container) with the contents piled above the brim or edge. ■ [no obj.] form a heap: *clouds heaped higher in the west.*

– PHRASES **at the top** (or **bottom**) **of the heap** (of a person) at the highest (or lowest) point of a society or organization. **be struck all of a heap** informal be extremely disconcerted. **heap coals of fire on someone's head** Brit. go out of one's way to cause someone remorse. [ORIGIN: with biblical allusion to Rom. 12:20.] **in a heap** (of a person) with the body completely limp: *he landed in a heap at the bottom of the stairs.*

– ORIGIN Old English *hēap* (noun), *hēapian* (verb), of Germanic origin; related to Dutch *hoop* and German *Haufen*.

hear ▶ **verb** (past and past participle **heard**) [with obj.] perceive with the ear the sound made by (someone or something): *behind her she could hear men's voices |* [with obj. and infinitive] *she had never been heard to complain |* [no obj.] *he did not hear very well.*

■be told or informed of: *have you heard the news? |* [with clause] *they heard that I had moved |* [no obj.] *I was shocked to* ***hear of*** *her death.* ■ [no obj.] (**have heard of**) be aware of; know of the existence of: *nobody had ever heard of my college.* ■ [no obj.] (**hear from**) be contacted by (someone), especially by letter or telephone: *if you would like to join the committee, we would love to hear from you.* ■ listen or pay attention to: [with clause] *she just doesn't hear what I'm telling her.* ■ (**hear someone out**) listen to all that someone has to say: *Joseph gravely heard them out but never offered advice.* ■ [no obj.] (**will/would not hear of**) will or would not allow or agree to: *I won't hear of such idiocy.* ■ Law listen to and judge (a case or plaintiff): *an all-woman jury heard the case.* ■ listen to and grant (a prayer): *our Heavenly Father has heard our prayers.*

– PHRASES **be hearing things** see **THING**. **be unable to hear oneself think** informal used to complain about very loud noise or music: *I hate bars where you can't hear yourself think.* **hear! hear!** used to express one's wholehearted agreement, especially with something said in a speech. **hear say** (or **tell**) **of** (or **that**) be informed of or that: *I heard tell that he went out west.*

– DERIVATIVES **hearable** adjective, **hearer** noun.

– ORIGIN Old English *hīeran*, *hēran*, of Germanic origin; related to Dutch *hooren* and German *hören*.

Heard and McDonald Islands a group of uninhabited islands in the southern Indian Ocean, administered by Australia since 1947 as an external territory.

hearing ▶ **noun 1** [mass noun] the faculty of perceiving sounds: *people who have very acute hearing.*

■the range within which sounds may be heard; earshot: *she had moved out of hearing.*

2 an opportunity to state one's case: *I think I had a fair hearing.*

■Law an act of listening to evidence in a court of law or before an official, especially a trial before a judge without a jury.

hearing aid ▶ **noun** a small device which fits on the ear, worn by a partially deaf person to amplify sound.

hearing dog ▶ **noun** a dog trained to alert the deaf or hard of hearing to such sounds as the ringing of an alarm, doorbell, or telephone.

hearken /ˈhɑːk(ə)n/ (also **harken**) ▶ **verb** [no obj.] archaic listen: *he refused to* ***hearken to*** *Sir Thomas's words of wisdom.*

– ORIGIN Old English *heorcnian*; probably related to **HARK**. The spelling with *ea* (dating from the 16th cent.) is due to association with **HEAR**.

▶**hearken back** another way of saying ***hark back*** (see **HARK**).

hearsay ▶ **noun** [mass noun] information received from other people which one cannot adequately substantiate; rumour: *according to hearsay, Bez had managed to break his arm.*

■Law the report of another person's words by a witness, which is usually disallowed as evidence in a court of law.

hearsay evidence ▶ **noun** [mass noun] Law evidence given by a witness based on information received from others rather than personal knowledge.

hearse /həːs/ ▶ **noun** a vehicle for conveying the coffin at a funeral.

– ORIGIN Middle English: from Anglo-Norman French *herce* 'harrow, frame', from Latin *hirpex* 'a kind of large rake', from Oscan *hirpus* 'wolf' (with reference to the teeth). The earliest recorded sense in English is 'latticework canopy placed over the coffin (whilst in church) of a distinguished person', but this probably arose from the late Middle English sense 'triangular frame (shaped like the ancient harrow) for carrying candles at certain services'. The current sense dates from the mid 17th cent.

Hearst /həːst/, William Randolph (1863–1951), American newspaper publisher and tycoon. His introduction of features such as large headlines and sensational crime reporting revolutionized American journalism. He was the model for the central character of Orson Welles's film *Citizen Kane* (1941).

heart ▶ **noun 1** a hollow muscular organ that pumps the blood through the circulatory system by rhythmic contraction and dilation. In vertebrates there may be up to four chambers (as in humans), with two atria and two ventricles.

■the region of the chest above the heart: *holding hand on heart for the Pledge of Allegiance.* ■ the heart regarded as the centre of a person's thoughts and emotions, especially love or compassion: *hardening his heart, he ignored her entreaties | he poured out his heart to me |* [mass noun] *he has no heart.* ■ [mass noun] one's mood or feeling: *they had a change of heart | they found him well and* ***in good heart.*** ■ [mass noun] courage or enthusiasm: *they may* ***lose heart*** *as the work mounts up | Mary* ***took heart*** *from the encouragement handed out | I put my* ***heart and soul*** *into it and then got fired.*

2 the central or innermost part of something: *right in the heart of the city.*

■the vital part or essence: *the heart of the matter.* ■ the close compact head of a cabbage or lettuce.

3 a conventional representation of a heart with two equal curves meeting at a point at the bottom and a cusp at the top.

■(**hearts**) one of the four suits in a conventional pack of playing cards, denoted by a red figure of such a shape. ■ a card of this suit. ■ (**hearts**) a card game similar to whist, in which players attempt to avoid taking tricks containing a card of this suit.

4 [usu. with modifier] the condition of agricultural land as regards fertility.

– PHRASES **after one's own heart** of the type that one likes or understands best; sharing one's tastes. **at heart** in one's real nature, in contrast to how one may appear: *he's a good lad at heart.* **break someone's heart** overwhelm someone with sadness. **by heart** from memory. **close** (or **dear**) **to** (or **near**) **one's heart** of deep interest and concern to one. **from the** (**bottom of one's**) **heart** with sincere feeling: *their warmth and hospitality is right from the heart.* **give** (or **lose**) **one's heart to** fall in love with. **have a heart** [often in imperative] be merciful; show pity. **have a heart of gold** have a generous nature. **have the heart to do something** [usu. with negative] be insensitive or hard-hearted enough to do something: *I don't have the heart to tell her.* **have** (or **put**) **one's heart in** be (or become) keenly involved in or committed to (an enterprise). **have one's heart in one's mouth** be greatly alarmed or apprehensive. **have one's heart in the right place** be sincere or well intentioned. **heart of stone** a stern or cruel nature. **hearts and flowers** used in allusion to extreme sentimentality. **hearts and minds** used in reference to emotional and intellectual support or commitment: *a campaign to win the hearts and minds of America's college students.* **one's heart's desire** a person or thing that one greatly wishes for. **one's heartstrings** used in reference to one's deepest feelings of love or compassion: *the kitten's pitiful little squeak* ***tugged at her heartstrings.*** **in one's heart of hearts** in one's inmost feelings. **take something to heart** take criticism seriously and be affected or upset by it. **wear one's heart on one's sleeve** make one's feelings apparent. **with all one's heart** (or **one's whole heart**) sincerely; completely.

– DERIVATIVES **hearted** adjective [in combination] *a generous-hearted woman.*

– ORIGIN Old English *heorte*, of Germanic origin; related to Dutch *hart* and German *Herz*, from an Indo-European root shared by Latin *cor*, *cord-* and Greek *kēr*, *kardia*.

heartache ▶ **noun** [mass noun] emotional anguish or grief, typically caused by the loss or absence of someone loved.

heart attack ▶ **noun** a sudden occurrence of coronary thrombosis, typically resulting in the death of part of a heart muscle and sometimes fatal.

heartbeat ▶ **noun** the pulsation of the heart.

■(usu. **heartbeats**) a single pulsation of the heart: *her heartbeats steadied.* ■ figurative a person or thing providing or representing an animating or vital unifying force: *Ontario has long been the commercial heartbeat of Canada.*

– PHRASES **a heartbeat** (**away**) **from** very close to; on the verge of: *laughter was only a heartbeat from tears.*

heartbreak ▶ **noun** [mass noun] overwhelming distress: *an unforgettable tale of joy and heartbreak.*

heartbreaker ▶ **noun 1** a person who is very attractive but who is irresponsible in emotional relationships.

2 a story or event which causes overwhelming distress.

heartbreaking ▶ **adjective** causing overwhelming distress; very upsetting.

– DERIVATIVES **heartbreakingly** adverb [as submodifier] *the children's expectations were heartbreakingly wrong.*

heartbroken ▶ **adjective** (of a person) suffering from overwhelming distress; very upset: *he was* ***heartbroken at*** *the thought of leaving the house.*

heartburn ▶ **noun** [mass noun] a form of indigestion felt as a burning sensation in the chest, caused by acid regurgitation into the oesophagus.

hearten ▶ **verb** [with obj.] (usu. **be heartened**) make more cheerful or confident: [with obj. and infinitive] *she was heartened to observe that the effect was faintly comic |* [as adj. **heartening**] *this is the most heartening news of all.*

– DERIVATIVES **hearteningly** adverb.

heart failure ▶ **noun** [mass noun] severe failure of the heart to function properly, especially as a cause of death: *her mother had died of heart failure.*

heartfelt ▶ adjective (of a feeling or its expression) sincere; deeply and strongly felt: *our heartfelt thanks.*

hearth /hɑːθ/ ▶ noun the floor of a fireplace: *a cheerful fire burning in the hearth.*
■ the area in front of a fireplace: *they were sitting around the hearth.* ■ used as a symbol of one's home: *he left hearth and home to train in Denmark.* ■ the base or lower part of a furnace, where molten metal collects.
– ORIGIN Old English *heorth*, of West Germanic origin; related to Dutch *haard* and German *Herd.*

hearthrug ▶ noun a rug laid in front of a fireplace to protect the carpet or floor.

hearthstone ▶ noun a flat stone forming a hearth or part of a hearth.

heartily ▶ adverb **1** in a hearty manner: *she laughed heartily | they dined heartily.*
2 [as submodifier] very; to a great degree (especially with reference to personal feelings): *they were heartily sick of the whole subject.*

heartland ▶ noun (also **heartlands**) the central or most important part of a country, area, or field of activity.
■ the centre of support for a belief or movement: *the heartland of the rebel cause.*

heartless ▶ adjective displaying a complete lack of feeling or consideration: *heartless thieves stole the pushchair of a two-year-old boy.*
– DERIVATIVES **heartlessly** adverb, **heartlessness** noun.

heart line ▶ noun (in palmistry) the upper of the two horizontal lines that cross the palm of the hand, linked to a person's physical health and ability to form emotional relationships.

heart-lung machine ▶ noun a machine that temporarily takes over the functions of the heart and lungs, especially during heart surgery.

Heart of Dixie informal name for **ALABAMA**.

heart of palm ▶ noun the edible bud of a palm tree.

heart-rending ▶ adjective (of a story or event) causing great sadness or distress.
– DERIVATIVES **heart-rendingly** adverb.

heart's-blood ▶ noun [mass noun] archaic the blood, as being necessary for life.

heart-searching ▶ noun [mass noun] thorough, typically painful examination of one's feelings and motives: *I began to write, but not without much heart-searching.*

heartsease /ˈhɑːtsiːz/ (also **heart's-ease**) ▶ noun a wild European pansy which typically has purple and yellow flowers. It has given rise to hybrids from which most garden pansies were developed.
● *Viola tricolor,* family Violaceae.
– ORIGIN late Middle English: origin uncertain, the term being applied by herbalists to both the pansy and the wallflower in the 16th cent.

heartsick (also **heartsore**) ▶ adjective chiefly poetic/literary very despondent, typically from grief or loss of love.
– DERIVATIVES **heartsickness** noun.

heart-stopping ▶ adjective thrilling; full of suspense.
– DERIVATIVES **heart-stopper** noun, **heart-stoppingly** adverb.

heart-throb ▶ noun informal a man, typically a celebrity, whose good looks excite rather immature romantic feelings in women.

heart-to-heart ▶ adjective (of a conversation) candid, intimate, and personal: *a heart-to-heart chat.*
▶ noun such a conversation.

heart urchin ▶ noun a heart-shaped burrowing sea urchin which has a thick covering of fine spines on the shell, giving it a furry appearance.
● Class Echinoidea, order Spatangoida.

heart-warming ▶ adjective emotionally rewarding or uplifting.

heartwood ▶ noun [mass noun] the dense inner part of a tree trunk, yielding the hardest timber.

hearty ▶ adjective (**heartier**, **heartiest**) **1** (of a person or their behaviour) loudly vigorous and cheerful: *a hearty and boisterous character | he sang in a hearty baritone.*
■ (of a feeling or an opinion) heartfelt: *he expressed his hearty agreement | hearty congratulations.* ■ (of a

person) strong and healthy: *a formidably hearty spinster of fifty-five.*
2 (of food) wholesome and substantial.
■ (of a person's appetite) robust and healthy: *Jim goes for a long walk to work up a hearty appetite for dinner.*
▶ noun Brit. informal **1** a vigorously cheerful and sporty person.
2 (usu. **me hearties**) a form of address ascribed to sailors.
– DERIVATIVES **heartiness** noun.

heat ▶ noun [mass noun] **1** the quality of being hot; high temperature: *it is sensitive to both heat and cold.*
■ Physics heat seen as a form of energy arising from the random motion of the molecules of bodies, which may be transferred by conduction, convection, or radiation. ■ hot weather conditions: *the oppressive heat was making both men sweat.* ■ a source or level of heat for cooking: *remove from the heat and beat in the butter.* ■ a spicy quality in food that produces a burning sensation in the mouth: *chilli peppers add taste and heat to food.* ■ technical the amount of heat that is needed to cause a specific process or is evolved in such a process: *the heat of formation.* ■ [count noun] technical a single operation of heating something, especially metal in a furnace.
2 intensity of feeling, especially of anger or excitement: *conciliation services are designed to take the heat out of disputes.*
■ (**the heat**) informal intensive and unwelcome pressure or criticism, especially from the authorities: *a flurry of legal proceedings turned up the heat in the dispute | the heat is on.*
3 [count noun] a preliminary round in a race or contest: *winners of the regional heats.*
▶ verb make or become hot or warm: [with obj.] *the room faces north and is difficult to heat* | [no obj.] *the pipes expand as they heat up.*
■ [no obj.] (**heat up**) (of a person) become excited or impassioned. ■ [no obj.] (**heat up**) become more intense and exciting: *the action really begins to heat up.* ■ [with obj.] archaic inflame; excite: *this discourse had heated them.*
– PHRASES **if you can't stand the heat, get out of the kitchen** proverb if you can't deal with the pressures and difficulties of a situation or task, you should leave others to deal with it rather than complaining. **in the heat of the moment** while temporarily angry, excited, or engrossed, and without stopping for thought. **on** (or US **in**) **heat** (of a female mammal) in the receptive period of the sexual cycle; in oestrus.
– ORIGIN Old English *hǣtu* (noun), *hǣtan* (verb), of Germanic origin; related to Dutch *hitte* (noun) and German *heizen* (verb), also to **HOT**.

heat barrier ▶ noun the limitation of the speed of an aircraft or other flying object by heat resulting from air friction.

heat capacity ▶ noun another term for **THERMAL CAPACITY**.

heat death ▶ noun Physics a state of uniform distribution of energy, especially viewed as a possible fate of the universe. It is a corollary of the second law of thermodynamics.

heated ▶ adjective **1** made warm or hot: *a heated swimming pool.*
2 inflamed with passion or conviction: *she had a heated argument with an official.*
– DERIVATIVES **heatedly** adverb.

heat engine ▶ noun a device for producing motive power from heat.

heater ▶ noun **1** a person or thing that heats, in particular a device for warming the air or water: *a wall-mounted electric heater | a gas water heater.*
■ Electronics a conductor used for indirect heating of the cathode of a thermionic valve.
2 Baseball a fast ball.
3 N. Amer. informal, dated a gun.

heat-exchanger ▶ noun a device for transferring heat from one medium to another.

Heath, Sir Edward (Richard George) (b.1916), British Conservative statesman, Prime Minister 1970–4. He negotiated Britain's entry into the European Economic Community and faced problems caused by a marked increase in oil prices. Attempts to restrain wage rises led to widespread strikes and he lost a general election after a second national coal strike.

heath ▶ noun **1** chiefly Brit. an area of open uncultivated land, typically on acid sandy soil, with characteristic vegetation of heather, gorse, and coarse grasses.

■ [mass noun] Ecology vegetation dominated by dwarf shrubs of the heather family: [as modifier] *heath vegetation.*
2 a dwarf shrub with small leathery leaves and small pink or purple bell-shaped flowers, characteristic of heathland and moorland.
● *Erica* and related genera, family Ericaceae: many species, including the common European **cross-leaved heath** (*E. tetralix*).
3 a small light brown and orange European butterfly which typically has eyespots on the wings, the caterpillar feeding on grasses.
● Genus *Coenonympha,* subfamily Satyrinae, family Nymphalidae: several species, including the common **small heath** (*C. pamphilus*).
4 a yellowish-brown chiefly day-flying European moth of heathland and grassland.
● Several species in the family Geometridae, including the common heath (*Ematurga atomaria*).
– DERIVATIVES **heathy** adjective.
– ORIGIN Old English *hǣth*, of Germanic origin; related to Dutch *heide* and German *Heide.*

heat haze ▶ noun an obscuration of the atmosphere in hot weather, especially a shimmering in the air near the ground that distorts distant views.

heathen /ˈhiːð(ə)n/ ▶ noun chiefly derogatory a person who does not belong to a widely held religion (especially one who is not a Christian, Jew, or Muslim) as regarded by those who do: *bringing Christianity to the heathens.*
■ a follower of a polytheistic religion; a pagan. ■ [mass noun] (**the heathen**) heathen people collectively, especially (in biblical use) those who did not worship the God of Israel. ■ informal an unenlightened person; a person regarded as lacking culture or moral principles.
▶ adjective of or relating to heathens: *heathen gods.*
– DERIVATIVES **heathendom** noun, **heathenish** adjective, **heathenism** noun.
– ORIGIN Old English *hǣthen*, of Germanic origin; related to Dutch *heiden* and German *Heide*; generally regarded as a specifically Christian use of a Germanic adjective meaning 'inhabiting open country', from the base of **HEATH**.

heather ▶ noun [mass noun] a purple-flowered Eurasian heath that grows abundantly on moorland and heathland. Many ornamental varieties have been developed. Also called **LING**.
● *Calluna vulgaris,* family Ericaceae (the **heather family**). This family includes the rhododendrons and azaleas as well as the bilberries and many other berry-bearing dwarf shrubs.
■ informal any similar plant of this family; a heath.
– DERIVATIVES **heathery** adjective.
– ORIGIN Old English *hadre, hedre* (recorded in place names), of unknown origin. The word was chiefly Scots until the 16th cent.; the change in the first syllable in the 18th cent. was due to association with **HEATH**.

heathland ▶ noun [mass noun] (also **heathlands**) an extensive area of heath: *1,000 acres of heathland.*

Heath Robinson ▶ adjective Brit. ingeniously or ridiculously over-complicated in design or construction: *a vast Heath Robinson mechanism.*
– ORIGIN early 20th cent.: named after W. Heath Robinson (see **ROBINSON**²).

Heathrow an international airport situated 25 km (15 miles) west of the centre of London.

heating ▶ noun [mass noun] the imparting or generation of heat.
■ equipment or devices used to provide heat, especially to a building: *we had no heating in our bedrooms.*

heat lamp ▶ noun an electrical device with a bulb that emits mainly heat rather than light, used as a heat source.

heatproof ▶ adjective able to resist great heat.

heat pump ▶ noun a device that transfers heat from a colder area to a hotter area by using mechanical energy, as in a refrigerator.

heat-resistant ▶ adjective another term for **HEATPROOF**.
■ not easily becoming hot.

heat-seeking ▶ adjective (of a missile) able to detect and home in on infrared radiation emitted by a target, such as the exhaust vent of a jet aircraft.

heat shield ▶ noun a device or coating for protection from excessive heat.
■ an outer covering on a spacecraft, especially on the nose cone and leading edges, to protect it from the

heat generated during re-entry into the earth's atmosphere.

heat sink ▶ **noun** a device or substance for absorbing excessive or unwanted heat.

heatstroke ▶ **noun** [mass noun] a condition marked by fever and often by unconsciousness, caused by failure of the body's temperature-regulating mechanism when exposed to excessively high temperatures.

heat treatment ▶ **noun** [mass noun] the use of heat for therapeutic purposes in medicine or to modify the properties of a material, especially in metallurgy.
– DERIVATIVES **heat-treat** verb.

heatwave ▶ **noun** a prolonged period of abnormally hot weather.

heave /hiːv/ ▶ **verb** (past and past participle **heaved** or chiefly Nautical **hove**) **1** [with obj. and adverbial of direction] lift or haul (a heavy thing) with great effort: *she heaved the sofa back into place | he* ***heaved himself*** *out of bed.*
■ Nautical pull, raise, or move (a boat or ship) by hauling on a rope or ropes. ■ informal throw (something heavy): *she heaved half a brick at him.*
2 [with obj.] produce (a sigh): *he heaved a euphoric sigh of relief.*
3 [no obj.] rise and fall rhythmically or spasmodically: *his shoulders heaved as he panted.*
■ make an effort to vomit; retch: *my stomach heaved.*
▶ **noun 1** an act of heaving, especially a strong pull.
■ Geology a sideways displacement in a fault.
2 (**heaves**) another term for **COPD** of horses.
– PHRASES **heave in sight** (or **into view**) chiefly Nautical come into view: *they held out until a British fleet hove in sight.*
– DERIVATIVES **heaver** noun.
– ORIGIN Old English *hebban*, of Germanic origin; related to Dutch *heffen* and German *heben* 'lift up'.
▶ **heave to** Nautical (of a boat or ship) come to a stop, especially by turning across the wind leaving the headsail backed.

heave-ho ▶ **exclamation** a cry emitted when doing actions that take physical effort.
▶ **noun** such an exclamation.
■ (**the heave-ho**) expulsion or elimination from an institution, association, or contest: *conjecture over who'll* ***get the heave-ho.***
– ORIGIN late Middle English: from *heave!* (imperative) + **HO**[2], originally in nautical use when hauling a rope.

heaven ▶ **noun 1** a place regarded in various religions as the abode of God (or the gods) and the angels, and of the good after death, often traditionally depicted as being above the sky.
■ God (or the gods): *Constantine was persuaded that disunity in the Church was displeasing to heaven.* ■ Theology a state of being eternally in the presence of God after death. ■ informal a place, state, or experience of supreme bliss: *lying by the pool with a good book is my idea of heaven.* ■ used in various exclamations as a substitute for 'God': *heaven knows! | good heavens!*
2 (often **heavens**) poetic/literary the sky, especially perceived as a vault in which the sun, moon, stars, and planets are situated: *Galileo used a telescope to observe the heavens.*
– PHRASES **the heavens open** it suddenly starts to rain very heavily. **in seventh heaven** in a state of ecstasy. **move heaven and earth to do something** make extraordinary efforts to do a specified thing: *if he had truly loved her he would have moved heaven and earth to get her back.* **stink** (or **smell**) **to high heaven** have a very strong and unpleasant odour.
– DERIVATIVES **heavenward** adjective & adverb, **heavenwards** adverb.
– ORIGIN Old English *heofon*, of Germanic origin; related to Dutch *hemel* and German *Himmel*.

heavenly ▶ **adjective 1** of heaven; divine: *heavenly Father.*
2 of the heavens or sky: *heavenly constellations.*
3 informal very pleasing; wonderful: *their shampoos smell heavenly | it was a heavenly morning for a ride.*
– DERIVATIVES **heavenliness** noun.
– ORIGIN Old English *heofonlic* (see **HEAVEN**, **-LY**[1]).

heavenly body ▶ **noun** a planet, star, or other celestial body.

heavenly host ▶ **noun** a literary or biblical term for the angels.

heaven-sent ▶ **adjective** (of an event or opportunity) occurring at a very favourable time; very opportune.

heavier-than-air ▶ **adjective** (of an aircraft) weighing more than the air it displaces.

heaving ▶ **adjective** Brit. informal (of a place) extremely crowded: *the foyer was absolutely heaving with people.*

heaving line ▶ **noun** a lightweight line with a weight at the end, made to be thrown between a ship and the shore, or from one ship to another, and used to pull a heavier line across.

Heaviside /ˈhɛvɪsʌɪd/, Oliver (1850–1925), English physicist and electrical engineer, important in the development of telephone communication and telegraphy. In 1902 he suggested (independently of A. E. Kennelly) the existence of a layer in the atmosphere responsible for reflecting radio waves back to earth.

Heaviside layer (also **Heaviside–Kennelly layer**) ▶ **noun** another name for **E-LAYER**.
– ORIGIN early 20th cent.: named after O. **HEAVISIDE** and A. E. **KENNELLY**.

heavy ▶ **adjective** (**heavier**, **heaviest**) **1** of great weight; difficult to lift or move: *a heavy and bulky load | the pan was too heavy for me to carry.*
■ used in questions about weight: *how heavy is it?* ■ [attrib.] (of a class of thing) above the average weight; large of its kind: *heavy artillery | heavy woollens.* ■ [predic.] weighed down; full of something: *branches* ***heavy with*** *blossoms.* ■ (of a person's head or eyes) feeling weighed down by weariness: *a heavy head.* ■ Physics of or containing atoms of an isotope of greater than the usual mass. See also **HEAVY WATER**.
2 of great density; thick or substantial: *heavy grey clouds | heavy horn-rimmed glasses.*
■ (of food or a meal) hard to digest; too filling. ■ (of ground or soil) hard to travel over or work with because muddy or full of clay. ■ not delicate or graceful; coarse: *he had a big moustache and heavy features.* ■ moving slowly or with difficulty: *steering that is heavy when parking.* ■ intellectually slow. ■ (of a smell) overpowering: *the air was heavy with the sweet odour of apples.* ■ (of the sky) full of dark clouds; oppressive: *a heavy thundery sky.*
3 of more than the usual size, amount, or force: *a heavy cold | rush hour traffic was heavy and I was delayed.*
■ (**heavy on**) using a lot of: *stories heavy on melodrama.* ■ doing something to excess: *a heavy smoker.*
4 striking or falling with force: *a heavy blow to the head | we had heavy overnight rain.*
■ causing a strong impact: *a heavy fall.* ■ (of music, especially rock) having a strong bass component and a forceful rhythm.
5 needing much physical effort: *heavy work like repairing pathways.*
■ mentally oppressive; hard to endure: *a heavy burden of responsibility.* ■ very important or serious: *a heavy discussion.* ■ (of a literary work) hard to read or understand because overly serious or difficult. ■ feeling or expressing grief: *I left him with a heavy heart.* ■ informal (of a situation) serious and hard to deal with: *things were getting pretty heavy.* ■ informal (of a person) strict or harsh: *the police were really getting heavy.*
▶ **noun** (pl. **-ies**) **1** a thing, such as a vehicle, that is large or heavy of its kind.
■ informal a large, strong man, especially one hired for protection: *I needed money to pay off the heavies.* ■ (**heavies**) Brit. informal serious newspapers: *reporters from the Sunday heavies.* ■ informal an important person: *music business heavies.*
2 [mass noun] chiefly Scottish strong beer, especially bitter: *a pint of heavy.*
▶ **adverb** [usu. in combination] heavily: *heavy-built birds | heavy-laden.*
– PHRASES **heavy going** used in reference to a person or situation that is difficult or boring to deal with: *she found Hilary heavy going.* **make heavy weather of** see **WEATHER**.
– DERIVATIVES **heavily** adverb, **heaviness** noun, **heavyish** adjective.
– ORIGIN Old English *hefig*, of Germanic origin; related to Dutch *hevig*, also to **HEAVE**.

heavy breathing ▶ **noun** [mass noun] breathing that is audible through being deep or laboured, especially in sleep or as a result of exertion.

heavy chemicals ▶ **plural noun** bulk chemicals used in industry and agriculture.

heavy cream ▶ **noun** North American term for **DOUBLE CREAM**.

heavy-duty ▶ **adjective** (of material or an article) designed to withstand the stresses of demanding use: *heavy-duty rubber gloves.*
■ informal intense, important, or abundant: *she did some heavy-duty cleaning.*

heavy-footed ▶ **adjective** slow and laborious in movement: *the All Blacks make the Lions' pack look heavy-footed.*

heavy-handed ▶ **adjective** clumsy, insensitive, or overly forceful: *heavy-handed policing.*
■ using too much of something: *beware of being heavy-handed with the flour.*
– DERIVATIVES **heavy-handedly** adverb, **heavy-handedness** noun.

heavy-hearted ▶ **adjective** feeling depressed or melancholy.

heavy horse ▶ **noun** a large, strong, heavily built horse of a type or breed used for draught work.

heavy hydrogen ▶ **noun** another term for **DEUTERIUM**.

heavy industry ▶ **noun** [mass noun] the manufacture of large, heavy articles and materials in bulk.

heavy metal ▶ **noun 1** a metal of relatively high density, or of high relative atomic weight.
2 [mass noun] a type of highly amplified harsh-sounding rock music with a strong beat, characteristically using violent or fantastic imagery.

heavy oil ▶ **noun** any of the relatively dense hydrocarbons (denser than water) derived from petroleum, coal tar, and similar materials.

heavy petting ▶ **noun** [mass noun] erotic contact between two people involving stimulation of the genitals but stopping short of intercourse.

heavy water ▶ **noun** [mass noun] water in which the hydrogen in the molecules is partly or wholly replaced by the isotope deuterium, used especially as a moderator in nuclear reactors.

heavyweight ▶ **noun 1** [mass noun] a weight in boxing and other sports, typically the heaviest category. In the amateur boxing scale it ranges from 81 to 91 kg.
■ [count noun] a boxer or other competitor of this weight.
2 a person or thing of above-average weight.
■ [often with modifier] a person of influence or importance, especially in a particular sphere: *a political heavyweight with national recognition.*
▶ **adjective** of above-average weight.
■ serious, important, or influential: *heavyweight news coverage.*

Heb. ▶ **abbreviation for** ■ Epistle to the Hebrews (in biblical references). ■ Hebrew.

hebdomadal /hɛbˈdɒməd(ə)l/ ▶ **adjective** formal weekly (used especially of organizations which meet weekly): *Oxford University's Hebdomadal Council.*
– ORIGIN early 17th cent. (in the sense 'lasting seven days'): from late Latin *hebdomadalis*, from Greek *hebdomas*, *hebdomad-* 'the number seven, seven days', from *hepta* 'seven'.

Hebe[1] /ˈhiːbi/ **1** Greek Mythology the daughter of Hera and Zeus, and cup-bearer of the gods.
2 Astronomy asteroid 6, discovered in 1847 (diameter 192 km).
– ORIGIN from Greek *hēbē* 'youthful beauty'.

Hebe[2] /hiːb/ ▶ **noun** US informal, offensive a Jewish person.
– ORIGIN early 20th cent.: abbreviation of **HEBREW**.

hebe /hiːbi/ ▶ **noun** an evergreen flowering shrub with spikes of mauve, pink, or white flowers, native to New Zealand and widely grown as an ornamental.
● Genus *Hebe* (formerly *Veronica*), family Scrophulariaceae.
– ORIGIN modern Latin, named after the goddess *Hebe* (see **HEBE**[1]).

Hebei /həˈbeɪ/ (also **Hopeh**) a province of NE central China; capital, Shijiazhuang.

hebephrenia /ˌhiːbɪˈfriːnɪə/ ▶ **noun** [mass noun] a form of chronic schizophrenia involving disordered thought, inappropriate emotions, hallucinations, and bizarre behaviour.
– DERIVATIVES **hebephrenic** /-ˈfrɛnɪk/ adjective & noun.
– ORIGIN late 19th cent. (originally associated with behaviour in puberty): from **HEBE**[1] + Greek *phrēn* 'mind' + **-IA**[1].

hebetude /ˈhɛbɪtjuːd/ ▶ **noun** [mass noun] poetic/literary the state of being dull or lethargic.
– ORIGIN early 17th cent.: from late Latin *hebetudo*, from *hebes*, *hebet-* 'blunt'.

Hebraic /hɪˈbreɪɪk/ ▶ **adjective** of Hebrew or the Hebrews: *a student of Hebraic religious literature.*
– DERIVATIVES **Hebraically** adverb.

h

– ORIGIN via Christian Latin from late Greek *Hebraikos*, from *Hebraios* (see **HEBREW**).

Hebraism /ˈhiːbreɪɪz(ə)m/ ▶ **noun 1** a Hebrew idiom or expression.
2 [mass noun] the Jewish religion, culture, or character.
– DERIVATIVES **Hebraistic** adjective, **Hebraize** (also **-ise**) verb.
– ORIGIN late 16th cent.: from French *hébraïsme* or modern Latin *Hebraismus*, from late Greek *Hebraïsmos*, from *Hebraios* (see **HEBREW**).

Hebraist /ˈhiːbreɪɪst/ ▶ **noun** a scholar of the Hebrew language.

Hebrew /ˈhiːbruː/ ▶ **noun 1** a member of an ancient people living in what is now Israel and Palestine and, according to biblical tradition, descended from the patriarch Jacob, grandson of Abraham. After the Exodus (*c*.1300 BC) they established the kingdoms of Israel and Judah, and their scriptures and traditions form the basis of the Jewish religion.
■old-fashioned and sometimes offensive term for **JEW**.
2 [mass noun] the Semitic language of this people, in its ancient or modern form.
▶ **adjective 1** of or in Hebrew.
2 of the Hebrews or the Jews.

Hebrew is written from right to left in a characteristic alphabet of twenty-two consonants, the vowels sometimes being marked by additional signs. From about AD 500 it was almost entirely restricted to Jewish religious use, but it was revived as a spoken language in the 19th century and, with a vocabulary extended by borrowing from contemporary languages, is now the official language of the state of Israel.

– ORIGIN from Old French *Ebreu*, via Latin from late Greek *Hebraios*, from Aramaic *ʿibray*, based on Hebrew *ʿibrî* understood to mean 'one from the other side (of the river)'.

Hebrew Bible the sacred writings of Judaism, called by Christians the Old Testament, and comprising the Law (Torah), the Prophets, and the Hagiographa or Writings.

Hebrews, Epistle to the a book of the New Testament, traditionally included among the letters of St Paul but now generally held to be non-Pauline.

Hebrides /ˈhɛbrɪdiːz/ a group of about 500 islands off the NW coast of Scotland. Also called **WESTERN ISLES**.

The **Inner Hebrides** include the islands of Skye, Mull, Jura, Islay, Iona, Coll, Eigg, Rhum, Staffa, and Tiree. The Little Minch separates this group from the **Outer Hebrides**, which include the islands of Lewis and Harris, North and South Uist, Benbecula, Barra, and the isolated St Kilda group. The shipping forecast area **Hebrides** covers an area of the Atlantic off the NW coast of Scotland.

– DERIVATIVES **Hebridean** noun & adjective.

Hebron /ˈhɛbrɒn/ a Palestinian city on the West Bank of the Jordan; pop. 75,000 (est. 1984). As the home of Abraham it is a holy city of both Judaism and Islam. Israeli forces withdrew from all but a small part of the city in 1997.

Hebros /ˈhiːbrəs/ (also **Hebrus**) ancient Greek name for **MARITSA**.

Hecate /ˈhɛkəti/ Greek Mythology a goddess of dark places, often associated with ghosts and sorcery. She is frequently identified with Artemis and Selene.

hecatomb /ˈhɛkətuːm/ ▶ **noun** (in ancient Greece or Rome) a great public sacrifice, originally of a hundred oxen.
■figurative an extensive loss of life for some cause.
– ORIGIN late 16th cent.: via Latin from Greek *hekatombē* (from *hekaton* 'hundred' + *bous* 'ox').

heck ▶ **exclamation** expressing surprise, frustration, or dismay: *oh heck, I can't for the life of me remember.*
■**(the heck)** used for emphasis in questions and exclamations: *what the heck's the matter?*
– PHRASES **a heck of a ——** used for emphasis in various statements or exclamations: *it was a heck of a lot of money.*
– ORIGIN late 19th cent. (originally northern English dialect): euphemistic alteration of **HELL**.

heckelphone /ˈhɛk(ə)lfəʊn/ ▶ **noun** a woodwind instrument resembling a large oboe, with a range about an octave lower.
– ORIGIN early 20th cent.: from German *Heckelphon*, named after Wilhelm *Heckel* (1856–1909), German instrument-maker, on the pattern of *saxophone*.

heckle ▶ **verb** [with obj.] **1** interrupt (a public speaker) with derisive or aggressive comments or abuse: *he was booed and heckled when he tried to address the demonstrators* | [no obj.] *women round him started heckling.*
2 dress (flax or hemp) to split and straighten the fibres for spinning.
▶ **noun** a heckling comment: *heckles of 'Get stuffed!'*
– DERIVATIVES **heckler** noun.
– ORIGIN Middle English (in sense 2): from *heckle* 'flax comb', a northern and eastern form of **HACKLE**. The sense 'interrupt (a public speaker) with aggressive questions' arose in the mid 17th cent.; for the development in sense, compare with **TEASE**.

hectare /ˈhɛktɛː, -ɑː/ (abbrev.: **ha**) ▶ **noun** a metric unit of square measure, equal to 100 ares (2.471 acres or 10,000 square metres).
– DERIVATIVES **hectarage** noun.
– ORIGIN early 19th cent.: from French, formed irregularly from Greek *hekaton* 'hundred' + **ARE**[2].

hectic ▶ **adjective 1** full of incessant or frantic activity: *a hectic business schedule.*
2 Medicine, archaic relating to, affected by, or denoting a regularly recurrent fever typically accompanying tuberculosis, with flushed cheeks and hot, dry skin.
▶ **noun** Medicine, archaic a hectic fever or flush.
■a patient suffering from such a fever.
– DERIVATIVES **hectically** adverb.
– ORIGIN late Middle English *etik*, via Old French from late Latin *hecticus*, from Greek *hektikos* 'habitual', from *hexis* 'habit, state of mind or body'. The original specific association with the symptoms of tuberculosis (*hectic fever*) gave rise to the early 20th-cent. sense 'characterized by feverish activity'.

hecto- ▶ **combining form** (used commonly in units of measurement) a hundred: *hectometre.*
– ORIGIN from French, formed irregularly by contraction of Greek *hekaton* 'hundred'.

hectocotylus /ˌhɛktə(ʊ)ˈkɒtɪləs/ ▶ **noun** (pl. **hectocotyli** /-lʌɪ, -liː/) Zoology a modified arm used by male octopuses and some other cephalopods to transfer sperm to the female.
– ORIGIN mid 19th cent.: modern Latin, from **HECTO-** 'hundred' + Greek *kotulē* 'hollow thing', a name given by Cuvier to what he mistakenly took to be a genus of parasitic worms.

hectogram (also **hectogramme**) (abbrev.: **hg**) ▶ **noun** a metric unit of mass equal to one hundred grams.

hectolitre /ˈhɛktə(ʊ),liːtə/ (US **hectoliter**) (abbrev.: **hl**) ▶ **noun** a metric unit of capacity equal to one hundred litres, used especially for wine, beer, grain, and other agricultural produce.

hectometre /ˈhɛktə(ʊ),miːtə/ (US **hectometer**) (abbrev.: **hm**) ▶ **noun** a metric unit of length equal to one hundred metres.

Hector /ˈhɛktə/ Greek Mythology a Trojan warrior, son of Priam and Hecuba and husband of Andromache. He was killed by Achilles, who dragged his body behind his chariot three times round the walls of Troy.

hector /ˈhɛktə/ ▶ **verb** [with obj.] talk to (someone) in a bullying way: *she doesn't hector us about giving up things* | [as adj. **hectoring**] *a brusque, hectoring manner.*
– DERIVATIVES **hectoringly** adverb.
– ORIGIN late Middle English: from the Latin name **HECTOR**. Originally denoting a hero, the sense later became 'braggart or bully' (applied in the late 17th cent. to a member of a gang of London youths), hence 'talk to in a bullying way'.

Hecuba /ˈhɛkjʊbə/ Greek Mythology a Trojan woman, the wife of Priam and mother of children including Hector, Paris, Cassandra, and Troilus.

he'd ▶ **contraction of** ■ he had: *he'd seen all he wanted.* ■ he would: *he'd like to see you.*

heddle /ˈhɛd(ə)l/ ▶ **noun** a looped wire or cord with an eye in the centre through which a warp yarn is passed in a loom before going through the reed to control its movement and divide the threads.
– ORIGIN early 16th cent.: apparently from an alteration of Old English *hefeld* (see **HEALD**).

heder /ˈhɛdə, ˈxɛdə/ ▶ **noun** (pl. **hedarim** /hɛˈdɑːrɪm, xɛ-/ or **heders**) variant spelling of **CHEDER**.

hedge ▶ **noun** a fence or boundary formed by closely growing bushes or shrubs: *a privet hedge.*
■a contract entered into or asset held as a protection against possible financial loss: *he sees the new fund as an excellent* **hedge against** *a fall in sterling.* ■ a word or phrase used to allow for additional possibilities or to avoid over-precise commitment, for example *etc.*, *often*, *usually*, or *sometimes*.
▶ **verb** [with obj.] **1** (often **be hedged**) surround or bound with a hedge: *a garden hedged with yew.*
■**(hedge something in)** enclose.
2 limit or qualify (something) by conditions or exceptions: *they* **hedged** *their story* **about** *with provisos.*
■[no obj.] avoid making a definite decision, statement, or commitment: *he hedged at every new question.*
3 protect (one's investment or an investor) against loss by making balancing or compensating contracts or transactions.
– PHRASES **hedge one's bets** avoid committing oneself when faced with a difficult choice.
– DERIVATIVES **hedger** noun.
– ORIGIN Old English *hegg*, of Germanic origin; related to Dutch *heg* and German *Hecke*.

hedge brown ▶ **noun** another term for **GATEKEEPER** (in sense 2).

hedge garlic ▶ **noun** another term for **JACK-BY-THE-HEDGE**.

hedgehog ▶ **noun** a nocturnal insectivorous Old World mammal with a spiny coat and short legs, able to roll itself into a ball for defence.
• Family Erinaceidae: four genera and several species, including the common *Erinaceus europaeus* of western and northern Europe.
■any other animal covered with spines, especially (N. Amer.) a porcupine. ■ used in names of plants or fruits resembling a hedgehog in having spines or prickles, e.g. **hedgehog cactus**, **hedgehog holly**.
– ORIGIN late Middle English: from **HEDGE** (from its habitat) + **HOG** (from its piglike snout).

hedgehog fungus ▶ **noun** an edible mushroom which has a cap with a lobed fleshy margin, the underside of which bears downward-pointing spore-bearing spines, common in both Eurasia and North America.
• *Hydnum repandum*, family Hydnaceae, class Hymenomycetes.

hedge-hop ▶ **verb** [no obj., with adverbial of direction] fly an aircraft at a very low altitude.
– DERIVATIVES **hedge-hopper** noun.

hedge-laying ▶ **noun** the process of making or maintaining a hedge by weaving partly cut branches through the upright stems of a row of shrubs.

hedgerow ▶ **noun** a rough or mixed hedge of wild shrubs and occasional trees, typically bordering a road or field.
– ORIGIN Old English: from **HEDGE** + obsolete *rew* 'hedgerow', assimilated to **ROW**[1].

hedge sparrow ▶ **noun** another term for **DUNNOCK**.

hedge-trimmer ▶ **noun** an electric tool with a blade like a chainsaw, used for cutting back bushes, shrubs, and hedges.

hedging ▶ **noun** [mass noun] the planting or trimming of hedges: *contract work for hedging and ditching.*
■bushes and shrubs planted to form hedges.

hedonic /hiːˈdɒnɪk, hɛ-/ ▶ **adjective** technical relating to, characterized by, or considered in terms of pleasant (or unpleasant) sensations.
– ORIGIN mid 17th cent.: from Greek *hēdonikos*, from *hēdonē* 'pleasure'.

hedonism /ˈhiːd(ə)nɪz(ə)m, ˈhɛ-/ ▶ **noun** [mass noun] the pursuit of pleasure; sensual self-indulgence.
■the ethical theory that pleasure (in the sense of the satisfaction of desires) is the highest good and proper aim of human life.
– DERIVATIVES **hedonist** noun, **hedonistic** adjective, **hedonistically** adverb.
– ORIGIN mid 19th cent.: from Greek *hēdonē* 'pleasure' + **-ISM**.

-hedron ▶ **combining form** (pl. **-hedra** or **-hedrons**) in nouns denoting geometrical solids having a specified number of plane faces: *decahedron.*
■denoting geometrical solids having faces of a specified shape: *rhombohedron.*
– DERIVATIVES **-hedral** combining form in corresponding adjectives.
– ORIGIN from Greek *hedra* 'seat, base'.

heebie-jeebies ▶ **plural noun** (**the heebie-jeebies**) informal a state of nervous fear or anxiety: *it takes a lot more than a measly poltergeist to* **give me the heebie-jeebies**.
– ORIGIN 1920s (originally US): of unknown origin.

heed ▶ **verb** [with obj.] pay attention to; take notice of: *he should have heeded the warnings.*
▶ **noun** [mass noun] careful attention: *if he heard, he* **paid no heed** | *we must* **take heed of** *the suggestions.*
– ORIGIN Old English *hēdan* (originally intransitive), of West Germanic origin; related to Dutch *hoeden* and German *hüten*.

heedful ▶ **adjective** aware of and attentive to: *he is* **heedful of** *his own intuitions.*
– DERIVATIVES **heedfully** adverb, **heedfulness** noun.

heedless ▶ **adjective** showing a reckless lack of care or attention: *'Elaine!' she shouted,* **heedless of** *attracting unwanted attention* | *his heedless impetuosity.*
– DERIVATIVES **heedlessly** adverb, **heedlessness** noun.

hee-haw ▶ **noun** the loud, harsh cry of a donkey or mule.
■ [as modifier] US informal relating to or denoting unsophisticated rural humour and attitudes.
▶ **verb** [no obj.] make the loud, harsh cry of a donkey or mule.
– ORIGIN early 19th cent.: imitative.

heel[1] ▶ **noun 1** the back part of the foot below the ankle.
■ a corresponding part of the foot in vertebrate animals. ■ the part of the palm of the hand next to the wrist: *he rubbed the heel of his hand against the window.* ■ the part of a shoe or boot supporting the heel: *shoes with low heels.* ■ the part of a sock covering the heel. ■ (**heels**) high-heeled shoes.
2 a thing resembling a heel in form or position, in particular:
■ the end of a violin bow at which it is held. ■ the part of the head of a golf club nearest the shaft. ■ a crusty end of a loaf of bread, or the rind of a cheese. ■ a piece of the main stem of a plant left attached to the base of a cutting.
3 informal, dated an inconsiderate or untrustworthy person: *what kind of a heel do you think I am?*
4 [as exclamation] a command to a dog to walk close behind its owner.
▶ **verb** [with obj.] **1** fit or renew a heel on (a shoe or boot).
2 Rugby push or kick (the ball) out of the back of the scrum with one's heel.
3 Golf strike (the ball) with the heel of the club.
4 [no obj.] touch the ground with the heel when dancing.
– PHRASES **at** (or **to**) **heel** (of a dog) close to and slightly behind its owner. **at** (or **on**) **the heels of** following closely after: *he headed off with Sammy at his heels.* **bring someone to heel** bring someone under control. **cool** (or Brit. **kick**) **one's heels** be kept waiting. **down at heel** (of a shoe) with the heel worn down. ■ having a poor, shabby appearance. **kick up one's heels** chiefly N. Amer. have a lively, enjoyable time. **set** (or **rock**) **someone back on their heels** astonish or discomfit someone. **take to one's heels** run away. **turn on one's heel** turn sharply round. **under the heel of** dominated or controlled by: *the Greeks spent several centuries under the heel of the Ottoman Empire.*
– DERIVATIVES **heeled** adjective [in combination] *high-heeled shoes*, **heelless** adjective.
– ORIGIN Old English *hēla*, *hǣla*, of Germanic origin; related to Dutch *hiel*, also to **HOUGH**.

heel[2] ▶ **verb** [no obj.] (of a boat or ship) lean over owing to the pressure of wind or an uneven load. Compare with **LIST**[2].
■ [with obj.] cause (a boat or ship) to lean over in such a way.
▶ **noun** an instance of a ship leaning over in such a way.
■ [mass noun] the degree of incline of a ship's leaning measured from the vertical.
– ORIGIN late 16th cent.: from obsolete *heeld*, *hield* 'incline', of Germanic origin; related to Dutch *hellen*.

heel[3] ▶ **verb** [with obj.] (**heel something in**) set a plant in the ground and cover its roots.
– ORIGIN Old English *helian* 'cover, hide', of Germanic origin, from an Indo-European root shared by Latin *celare* 'hide'.

heelball ▶ **noun** [mass noun] a mixture of hard wax and lampblack used by shoemakers for polishing.
■ this or a similar mixture used in brass rubbing.

heel bar ▶ **noun** a small shop or stall where shoes are repaired, especially while the customer waits.

heel bone ▶ **noun** the calcaneum.

heeltap ▶ **noun 1** one of the layers of leather or other material of which a shoe heel is made.
2 dated an amount of liquor left at the bottom of a glass after drinking.

Hefei /hɛˈfeɪ/ (also **Hofei**) an industrial city in eastern China, capital of Anhui province; pop. 1,541,000 (1990).

heft ▶ **verb** [with obj. and adverbial] lift or carry (something heavy): *Donald hefted a stone jar of whisky into position.*
■ lift or hold (something) in order to test its weight: *Aileen hefted the gun in her hand.*
▶ **noun** [mass noun] chiefly N. Amer. the weight of someone or something.
■ figurative ability or influence: *his colleagues wonder if he has the intellectual heft for his new job.*
– ORIGIN late Middle English (as a noun): probably from **HEAVE**, on the pattern of words such as *cleft* and *weft*.

hefty ▶ **adjective** (**heftier**, **heftiest**) large, heavy, and powerful: *a hefty young chap.*
■ (of a number or amount) impressively large: *a hefty 10 million* | *hefty Christmas bonuses.*
– DERIVATIVES **heftily** adverb, **heftiness** noun.

Hegel /ˈheɪɡ(ə)l/, Georg Wilhelm Friedrich (1770–1831), German philosopher. In his *Science of Logic* (1812–16) Hegel described the three-stage process of dialectical reasoning, on which Marx based his theory of dialectical materialism. He believed that history, the evolution of ideas, and human consciousness all develop through idealist dialectical processes as part of the Absolute or God coming to know itself.
– DERIVATIVES **Hegelian** /heɪˈɡiːlɪən, hɪ-, -ˈɡeɪl-/ adjective & noun, **Hegelianism** noun.

hegemonic /ˌhɛdʒɪˈmɒnɪk, ˌhɛɡɪ-/ ▶ **adjective** ruling or dominant in a political or social context: *the bourgeoisie constituted the hegemonic class.*
– ORIGIN mid 17th cent.: from Greek *hēgemonikos* 'capable of commanding', from *hēgemōn* (see **HEGEMONY**).

hegemony /hɪˈdʒɛməni, -ˈɡɛ-/ ▶ **noun** [mass noun] leadership or dominance, especially by one state or social group over others: *Germany was united under Prussian hegemony after 1871.*
– ORIGIN mid 16th cent.: from Greek *hēgemonia*, from *hēgemōn* 'leader', from *hēgeisthai* 'to lead'.

Hegira /ˈhɛdʒɪrə/ (also **Hejira** or **Hijra**) ▶ **noun** Muhammad's departure from Mecca to Medina in AD 622, prompted by the opposition of the merchants of Mecca and marking the consolidation of the first Muslim community.
■ the Muslim era reckoned from this date: *the second century of the Hegira.* See also **AH**. ■ (**hegira**) an exodus or migration.
– ORIGIN via medieval Latin from Arabic *hijra* 'departure', from *hajara* 'emigrate'.

heiau /ˈheɪaʊ/ ▶ **noun** (pl. same or **heiaus**) an ancient Hawaiian temple or sacred site.
– ORIGIN Hawaiian.

Heidegger /ˈhʌɪˌdɛɡə/, Martin (1889–1976), German philosopher. In *Being and Time* (1927) he examined the ontology of Being, in particular human existence as involvement with a world of objects (*Dasein*). His writings on *Angst* (dread) as a fundamental part of human consciousness due to radical freedom of choice and awareness of death had a strong influence on existentialist philosophers such as Sartre.

Heidelberg /ˈhʌɪd(ə)lbəːɡ, German ˈhaɪdlbɛrk/ a city in SW Germany, on the River Neckar in Baden-Württemberg; pop. 139,390 (1991). Its university is the oldest in Germany.

heifer /ˈhɛfə/ ▶ **noun** a female domestic bovine animal (i.e. a cow in the broad sense) that has not borne a calf, or has borne only one calf. Often contrasted with **cow**[1] in the stricter sense.
– ORIGIN Old English *heahfore*, of unknown origin.

heigh ▶ **exclamation** archaic expressing encouragement or enquiry.
– ORIGIN natural utterance: first recorded in Middle English.

heigh-ho /heɪˈhəʊ/ ▶ **exclamation** informal expressing boredom, resignation, or jollity: *heigh-ho—then it is foot slogging again* | *how pleasant it is to have money, heigh-ho!*

height ▶ **noun 1** [mass noun] the measurement from base to top or (of a standing person) from head to foot: *columns rising to 65 feet* **in height** | *both men were of middle height.*
■ elevation above ground or a recognized level (typically sea level): *the glider is gaining height.* ■ the quality of being tall or high: *her height marked her out from other women.*
2 a high place or area: *he's terrified of heights.*
3 the most intense part or period of something: *the* **height of** *the tourist season* | **at the height of** *his career* | *they* **took** *consumerism* **to new heights**.
■ an extreme instance or example of something: *it would be* **the height of** *bad manners not to attend the wedding.*
– ORIGIN Old English *hēhthu* (in the sense 'top of something'), of Germanic origin; related to Dutch *hoogte*, also to **HIGH**.

heighten ▶ **verb** [with obj.] make (something) higher.
■ make or become more intense: [with obj.] *the pleasure was heightened by the sense of guilt that accompanied it* | [as adj. **heightened**] *the heightened colour of her face* | [no obj.] *concern over CFCs has heightened.*

height of land ▶ **noun** N. Amer. a watershed.

Heilbronn /ˈhʌɪlbrɒn, German haɪlˈbrɔn/ a city in SW Germany, on the River Neckar in Baden-Württemberg; pop. 117,430 (1991).

Heilong /heɪˈlʊŋ/ Chinese name for **AMUR**.

Heilongjiang /ˌheɪlʊŋdʒɪˈaŋ/ (also **Heilungkiang** /ˌheɪlʊŋkɪˈaŋ/) a province of NE China, on the Russian frontier; capital, Harbin.

Heimlich procedure /ˈhʌɪmlɪç/ (also **Heimlich manoeuvre**) ▶ **noun** a first-aid procedure for dislodging an obstruction from a person's windpipe in which a sudden strong pressure is applied on their abdomen, between the navel and the ribcage.
– ORIGIN 1970s: named after Henry J. *Heimlich* (born 1920), the American doctor who developed the procedure.

Heine /ˈhʌɪnə/, (Christian Johann) Heinrich (1797–1856), German poet; born *Harry Heine*. Much of his early lyric poetry was set to music by Schumann and Schubert. In 1830 Heine emigrated to Paris, where his works became more political.

heinie /ˈhʌɪni/ ▶ **noun** US informal a person's buttocks.
– ORIGIN 1960s: alteration of **HINDER**[2], variant of **HIND**[1].

heinous /ˈheɪnəs, ˈhiːnəs/ ▶ **adjective** (of a person or wrongful act, especially a crime) utterly odious or wicked: *a battery of heinous crimes.*
– DERIVATIVES **heinously** adverb, **heinousness** noun.
– ORIGIN late Middle English: from Old French *haineus*, from *hair* 'to hate', of Germanic origin.

Heinz /hʌɪnz/, Henry John (1844–1919), American food manufacturer. In 1869 he established a family firm for the manufacture and sale of processed foods. Heinz devised the marketing slogan '57 Varieties' in 1896.

heir /ɛː/ ▶ **noun** a person legally entitled to the property or rank of another on that person's death: *his eldest son and heir* | *she aspired to marry the heir to the throne.*
■ figurative a person inheriting and continuing the legacy of a predecessor: *they saw themselves as the true heirs of the Enlightenment.*
– DERIVATIVES **heirdom** noun, **heirless** adjective, **heirship** noun.
– ORIGIN Middle English: via Old French from Latin *heres*.

heir apparent ▶ **noun** (pl. **heirs apparent**) an heir whose claim cannot be set aside by the birth of another heir. Compare with **HEIR PRESUMPTIVE**.
■ figurative a person who is most likely to succeed to the place of another.

heir-at-law ▶ **noun** (pl. **heirs-at-law**) an heir by right of blood, especially to the real property of an intestate.

heiress ▶ **noun** a female heir, especially to vast wealth.

heirloom ▶ **noun** a valuable object that has belonged to a family for several generations.
– ORIGIN late Middle English: from **HEIR** + **LOOM**[1] (which formerly had the senses 'tool, heirloom').

heir presumptive ▶ **noun** (pl. **heirs presumptive**) an heir whose claim may be set aside by the birth of another heir. Compare with **HEIR APPARENT**.

Heisenberg /ˈhʌɪz(ə)nbəːɡ, German ˈhaɪznbɛrk/, Werner Karl (1901–76), German mathematical physicist and philosopher. He developed a system of quantum mechanics based on matrix algebra in which he states his famous uncertainty principle (1927). For this and his discovery of the allotropic forms of hydrogen he was awarded the 1932 Nobel Prize for Physics.

heist /hʌɪst/ informal, chiefly N. Amer. ▶ **noun** a robbery: *a diamond heist.*
▶ **verb** [with obj.] steal: *he heisted a Pontiac.*
– ORIGIN mid 19th cent.: representing a local pronunciation of **HOIST**.

hei-tiki /heɪˈtɪki/ ▶ **noun** a greenstone neck ornament worn by Maoris.
– ORIGIN Maori, from *hei* 'hang' + *tiki* 'image'.

Hejaz /hɪˈdʒaz/ (also **Hijaz**) a coastal region of western Saudi Arabia, extending along the Red Sea.

Hejira ▶ **noun** variant spelling of **HEGIRA**.

Hekla /ˈhɛklə/ an active volcano in SW Iceland, rising to a height of 1,491 m (4,840 ft).

HeLa cells /ˈhiːlə/ ▶ **plural noun** human epithelial cells of a strain maintained in tissue culture since 1951 and used in research especially in virology.
– ORIGIN 1950s: from the name of *Henrietta Lacks*, whose cervical carcinoma provided the original cells.

held past and past participle of **HOLD**[1].

Heldentenor /ˈhɛld(ə)nˌtɛnɔː/ ▶ **noun** a powerful tenor voice suitable for heroic roles in opera.
■ a singer with such a voice.
– ORIGIN 1920s: German, literally 'hero tenor'.

Helen Greek Mythology the daughter of Zeus and Leda, born from an egg. In the Homeric poems she was the outstandingly beautiful wife of Menelaus, and her abduction by Paris (to whom she had been promised, as a bribe, by Aphrodite) led to the Trojan War.

Helena /ˈhɛlɪnə/ the state capital of Montana; pop. 24,570 (1990).

Helena, St /ˈhɛlɪnə/ (*c.*255–*c.*330 AD), Roman empress and mother of Constantine the Great. In 326 she visited the Holy Land and founded basilicas on the Mount of Olives and at Bethlehem. She is credited with the finding of the cross on which Christ was crucified. Feast day (in the Eastern Church) 21 May; (in the Western Church) 18 August.

helenium /hɛˈliːnɪəm/ ▶ **noun** an American plant of the daisy family, which bears many red to yellow flowers, each having a prominent central disc.
● Genus *Helenium*, family Compositae.
– ORIGIN modern Latin, from Greek *helenion*. The term originally denoted the herb *elecampane*, possibly in commemoration of Helen of Troy (said to have planted elecampane on the island of Pharos); the current designation was adopted by Linnaeus in the 18th cent.

Helgoland /ˈhɛlgolant/ German name for **HELIGOLAND**.

heli- ▶ **combining form** relating to helicopters: *heli-skiing | helipad.*

heliacal rising /hɪˈlʌɪək(ə)l/ ▶ **noun** the rising of a celestial object at the same time as the sun, or its first visible rising after a period of invisibility due to conjunction with the sun. The last setting before such a period is the **heliacal setting**.
– ORIGIN early 17th cent.: *heliacal*, via late Latin from Greek *hēliakos* (from *hēlios* 'sun') + **-AL**.

helianthemum /ˌhiːlɪˈanθɪməm/ ▶ **noun** a low evergreen shrub with saucer-shaped flowers, which is grown as an ornamental. Also called **ROCK ROSE**.
● Genus *Helianthemum*, family Cistaceae.
– ORIGIN modern Latin, from Greek *hēlios* 'sun' + *anthemon* 'flower' (because the flowers open in sunlight).

helianthus /ˌhiːlɪˈanθəs/ ▶ **noun** a plant of the genus *Helianthus* in the daisy family, especially (in gardening) a sunflower.
– ORIGIN modern Latin, from Greek *hēlios* 'sun' + *anthos* 'flower'.

helical /ˈhɛlɪk(ə)l, ˈhiː-/ ▶ **adjective** having the shape or form of a helix; spiral: *helical molecules.*
– DERIVATIVES **helically** adverb.

helices plural form of **HELIX**.

helichrysum /ˌhɛlɪˈkrʌɪsəm/ ▶ **noun** an Old World plant of the daisy family. Some kinds are grown as everlastings, retaining their shape and colour when dried.
● Genus *Helichrysum*, family Compositae.
– ORIGIN Latin, from Greek *helikhrusos*, from *helix* 'spiral' + *khrusos* 'gold'. It originally denoted a yellow-flowered plant, possibly *Helichrysum stoechas*.

helicity /hiːˈlɪsɪti/ ▶ **noun** [mass noun] **1** chiefly Biochemistry helical character, especially of DNA.
2 Physics a combination of the spin and the linear motion of a subatomic particle.
– ORIGIN 1950s (in sense 2): from Latin *helix*, *helic-* 'spiral' + **-ITY**.

helicoid /ˈhiːlɪkɔɪd/ ▶ **adjective** of the form of a helix or helicoid.
▶ **noun** an object of spiral or helical shape.
■ Geometry a surface formed by simultaneously moving a straight line along an axis and rotating it around it (like a screw thread).
– DERIVATIVES **helicoidal** adjective.
– ORIGIN late 17th cent.: from Greek *helikoeidēs* 'of spiral form', from *helix*, *helik-* (see **HELIX**).

helicon /ˈhɛlɪk(ə)n/ ▶ **noun** a large spiral bass tuba played encircling the player's head and resting on the shoulder.
– ORIGIN late 19th cent.: from Latin, associated with **HELIX**.

heliconia /ˌhɛlɪˈkəʊnɪə/ ▶ **noun** a large-leaved tropical American plant which bears spectacular flowers with brightly coloured bracts.
● Genus *Heliconia*, family Heliconiaceae (formerly Musaceae): many species, including the lobster claw.

Helicon, Mount /ˈhɛlɪk(ə)n/ a mountain in Boeotia, central Greece, to the north of the Gulf of Corinth, rising to 1,750 m (5741 ft). It was believed by the ancient Greeks to be the home of the Muses.

helicopter ▶ **noun** a type of aircraft which derives both lift and propulsion from one or two sets of horizontally revolving overhead rotors. It is capable of moving vertically and horizontally, the direction of motion being controlled by the pitch of the rotor blades. Compare with **AUTOGIRO**.
▶ **verb** [with obj. and adverbial of direction] transport by helicopter.
■ [no obj., with adverbial of direction] fly somewhere in a helicopter.
– ORIGIN late 19th cent.: from French *hélicoptère*, from Greek *helix* 'spiral' + *pteron* 'wing'.

helictite /hɛˈlɪktʌɪt/ ▶ **noun** Geology a distorted form of stalactite, typically resembling a twig.
– ORIGIN late 19th cent.: from Greek *heliktos* 'twisted', on the pattern of *stalactite*.

Heligoland /ˈhɛlɪgəʊland/ a small island in the North Sea off the coast of Germany, one of the North Frisian Islands. The island was Danish from 1714 until seized by the British navy in 1807 and later ceded officially to Britain. In 1890 it was returned to Germany. German name **HELGOLAND**.

helio- /ˈhiːlɪəʊ/ ▶ **combining form** of or relating to the sun: *heliogravure | heliostat.*
– ORIGIN from Greek *hēlios* 'sun'.

heliocentric ▶ **adjective** having or representing the sun as the centre, as in the accepted astronomical model of the solar system. Compare with **GEOCENTRIC**.
■ Astronomy measured from or considered in relation to the centre of the sun: *heliocentric distance.*
– DERIVATIVES **heliocentrically** adverb.

Heliogabalus /ˌhiːlɪəˈgabələs/ (also **Elagabalus**) (AD 204–22), Roman emperor 218–22; born *Varius Avitus Bassianus*. He took his name from the Syro-Phoenician sun god Elah-Gabal, of whom he was a hereditary priest. He became notorious for his dissipated lifestyle and neglect of state affairs; he and his mother were both murdered.

heliogram ▶ **noun** a message sent by reflecting sunlight in flashes from a movable mirror.

heliograph ▶ **noun 1** a signalling device by which sunlight is reflected in flashes from a movable mirror.
■ a message sent in such a way; a heliogram.
2 a telescopic apparatus for photographing the sun.
3 historical a type of early photographic engraving made using a sensitized silver plate and an asphalt or bitumen varnish.
▶ **verb** [with obj.] **1** dated send (a message) by heliograph.
2 historical take a heliographic photograph of.
– DERIVATIVES **heliographic** adjective, **heliography** noun.

heliogravure /ˌhiːlɪəʊgrəˈvjʊə/ ▶ **noun** another term for **PHOTOGRAVURE**.

heliometer /ˌhiːlɪˈɒmɪtə/ ▶ **noun** Astronomy a refracting telescope with a split objective lens, used for finding the angular distance between two stars.
– ORIGIN mid 18th cent.: from **HELIO-** 'of the sun' + **-METER** (because it was originally used for measuring the diameter of the sun).

heliopause ▶ **noun** Astronomy the boundary of the heliosphere.

Heliopolis /ˌhiːlɪˈɒpəlɪs/ **1** an ancient Egyptian city situated near the apex of the Nile delta at what is now Cairo. It was the original site of the obelisks known as Cleopatra's Needles.
2 ancient Greek name for **BAALBEK**.
– ORIGIN from Greek *hēlios* 'sun' + *polis* 'city'.

Helios /ˈhiːlɪɒs/ Greek Mythology the sun personified as a god, father of Phaethon. He is generally represented as a charioteer driving daily from east to west across the sky.
– ORIGIN Greek *hēlios* 'sun'.

heliosphere ▶ **noun** Astronomy the region of space, encompassing the solar system, in which the solar wind has a significant influence.
– DERIVATIVES **heliospheric** adjective.

heliostat /ˈhiːlɪə(ʊ)stat/ ▶ **noun** an apparatus containing a movable mirror, used to reflect sunlight in a fixed direction.

heliotherapy ▶ **noun** [mass noun] the therapeutic use of sunlight.

heliotrope /ˈhiːlɪətrəʊp, ˈhɛl-/ ▶ **noun** a plant of the borage family, cultivated for its fragrant purple or blue flowers which are used in perfume.
● Genus *Heliotropium*, family Boraginaceae.
■ [mass noun] a light purple colour, similar to that typical of heliotrope flowers.
– ORIGIN Old English *eliotropus* (originally applied to various plants whose flowers turn towards the sun), via Latin from Greek *hēliotropion* 'plant turning its flowers to the sun', from *hēlios* 'sun' + *trepein* 'to turn'. The spelling was influenced by French *héliotrope*.

heliotropism /ˌhiːlɪə(ʊ)ˈtrəʊpɪz(ə)m/ ▶ **noun** [mass noun] Botany the directional growth of a plant in response to sunlight. Compare with **PHOTOTROPISM**.
■ Zoology the tendency of an animal to move towards light.
– DERIVATIVES **heliotropic** adjective.

Heliozoa /ˌhiːlɪə(ʊ)ˈzəʊə/ Zoology a phylum of single-celled aquatic animals that are related to the radiolarians. They have a spherical shell with fine radiating needle-like projections.
● Class Heliozoa, phylum Actinopoda, kingdom Protista.
– DERIVATIVES **heliozoan** noun & adjective.
– ORIGIN modern Latin (plural), from Greek *hēlios* 'sun' + *zōion* 'animal'.

helipad ▶ **noun** a landing and take-off area for helicopters.

heliport ▶ **noun** an airport or landing place for helicopters.
– ORIGIN 1940s: from **HELI-** + **PORT**[1], on the pattern of *airport*.

heli-skiing ▶ **noun** [mass noun] skiing in which the skier is taken up the mountain by helicopter.
– DERIVATIVES **heli-ski** verb, **heli-skier** noun.

helium /ˈhiːlɪəm/ ▶ **noun** [mass noun] the chemical element of atomic number 2, an inert gas which is the lightest member of the noble gas series. (Symbol: **He**)

Helium occurs in traces in air, and more abundantly in natural gas deposits. It is used as a lifting gas for balloons and airships, and liquid helium (boiling point: 4.2 kelvins, −268.9°C) is used as a coolant. Helium is produced in stars as the main product of the thermonuclear fusion of hydrogen, and is the second most abundant element in the universe after hydrogen.

– ORIGIN late 19th cent.: modern Latin, from Greek *hēlios* 'sun', because its existence was inferred from an emission line in the sun's spectrum.

helix /ˈhiːlɪks/ ▶ **noun** (pl. **helices** /ˈhiːlɪsiːz, ˈhɛl-/) an object having a three-dimensional shape like that of a wire wound uniformly in a single layer around a cylinder or cone, as in a corkscrew or spiral staircase.
■ Geometry a curve on a conical or cylindrical surface which would become a straight line if the surface were unrolled into a plane. ■ Biochemistry an extended spiral chain of atoms in a protein, nucleic acid, or other polymeric molecule. ■ Architecture a spiral ornament. ■ Anatomy the rim of the external ear.
– ORIGIN mid 16th cent. (in the architectural sense 'spiral ornament'): via Latin from Greek.

hell ▶ noun a place regarded in various religions as a spiritual realm of evil and suffering, often traditionally depicted as a place of perpetual fire beneath the earth where the wicked are punished after death.

■ a state or place of great suffering; an unbearable experience: *I've been through hell | he made her life hell.*
▶ exclamation used to express annoyance or surprise or for emphasis: *oh, hell—where will this all end? | hell, no, we were all married.*
■ (the hell) informal expressing anger, contempt, or disbelief: *who the hell are you? | the hell you are!*
– PHRASES **all hell broke** (or **was let**) **loose** informal suddenly there was pandemonium. (**as**) —— **as hell** informal used for emphasis: *he's as guilty as hell.* **be hell on** informal be very unpleasant or harmful to: *a sensitive liberal mentality can be hell on a marriage.* **come hell or high water** whatever difficulties may occur. **for the hell of it** informal just for fun: *she walked on window ledges for the hell of it.* —— **from hell** informal an extremely unpleasant or troublesome instance or example of something: *wives from hell.* **get hell** informal be severely reprimanded: *she got hell on the way home.* **get the hell out** (**of**) informal escape from (a place or situation) very quickly: *let's all get the hell out of here.* **give someone hell** informal severely reprimand or make things very unpleasant for someone. **go to hell** informal used to express angry rejection of someone or something. **go to** (or **through**) **hell and back** endure an extremely unpleasant or difficult experience. **go to hell in a handbasket** N. Amer. informal undergo a rapid process of deterioration. **hell for leather** as fast as possible. **hell's bells** informal an exclamation of annoyance or anger. **hell hath no fury like a woman scorned** proverb a woman who has been rejected by a man can be ferociously angry and vindictive. **a** (or **one**) **hell of a** —— informal used to emphasize something very bad or great: *it cost us a hell of a lot of money.* **hell's half acre** N. Amer. a great distance. **like hell** informal **1** very fast, much, hard, etc. (used for emphasis): *it hurts like hell.* **2** used in ironic expressions of scorn or disagreement: *like hell, he thought.* **not a hope in hell** informal no chance at all. **play hell** (or **merry hell**) informal make a fuss; create havoc. ■ cause damage: *the rough road played hell with the tyres.* **the road to hell is paved with good intentions** proverb promises and plans must be put into action, otherwise they are useless. **there will be hell to pay** informal serious trouble will occur as a result of a previous action. **to hell** used for emphasis: *damn it to hell.* **to hell with** informal expressing one's scorn or lack of concern for (someone or something). **until** (or **till**) **hell freezes over** for an extremely long time or forever. **what the hell** informal it doesn't matter.
– DERIVATIVES **hellward** adverb & adjective.
– ORIGIN Old English *hel*, *hell*, of Germanic origin; related to Dutch *hel* and German *Hölle*, from an Indo-European root meaning 'to cover or hide'.

he'll ▶ contraction of he shall; he will.

hellacious /hɛˈleɪʃəs/ ▶ adjective N. Amer. informal very great, bad, or overwhelming: *there was this hellacious hailstorm.*
– DERIVATIVES **hellaciously** adverb.
– ORIGIN 1930s: from **HELL** + **-ACIOUS**, perhaps suggested by *bodacious.*

Helladic /hɛˈladɪk/ ▶ adjective Archaeology of, relating to, or denoting the Bronze Age cultures of mainland Greece (c.3000–1050 BC), of which the latest period is equivalent to the Mycenaean age.
– ORIGIN early 19th cent.: from Greek *Helladikos*, from *Hellas*, *Hellad-* 'Greece'.

Hellas /ˈhɛlas/ Greek name for **GREECE**.

hellbender ▶ noun an aquatic giant salamander with greyish skin and a flattened head, native to North America.
● *Cryptobranchus alleganiensis*, family Cryptobranchidae.

hell-bent ▶ adjective [predic.] determined to achieve something at all costs: *why are you hell-bent on leaving?*

hellcat ▶ noun a spiteful, violent woman.

hellebore /ˈhɛlɪbɔː/ ▶ noun a poisonous winter-flowering Eurasian plant of the buttercup family, typically having coarse divided leaves and large white, green, or purplish flowers.
● Genus *Helleborus*, family Ranunculaceae: several species, including the Christmas rose.
■ a false helleborine.
– ORIGIN Old English (denoting any of various plants supposed to cure madness), from Old French *ellebre*, *elebore* or medieval Latin *eleborus*, via Latin from Greek *helleboros.*

helleborine /ˈhɛlɪbəˌriːn, -ˌrʌɪn/ ▶ noun a mainly woodland orchid occurring chiefly in north temperate regions. See also **FALSE HELLEBORINE**.
● Two genera in the family Orchidaceae: *Epipactis* (with greenish or reddish flowers that are sometimes self-fertilized) and *Cephalanthera* (with larger white or pink flowers).
– ORIGIN late 16th cent.: French or Latin, from Greek *helleborinē*, a plant like hellebore, from *helleboros* 'hellebore'.

Hellen /ˈhɛlɪn/ Greek Mythology the son or brother of Deucalion and ancestor of all the Hellenes or Greeks.

Hellene /ˈhɛliːn/ ▶ noun an ancient Greek.
■ a native of modern Greece (chiefly in the title of the now exiled royal family): *the King of the Hellenes.*
– ORIGIN from Greek *Hellēn* 'a Greek'. Compare with **HELLEN**.

Hellenic /hɛˈlɛnɪk, -ˈliːnɪk/ ▶ adjective Greek.
■ Archaeology relating to or denoting Iron Age and Classical Greek culture (between Helladic and Hellenistic).
▶ noun [mass noun] the branch of the Indo-European language family comprising classical and modern Greek.
■ the Greek language.
– ORIGIN from Greek *Hellēnikos*, from *Hellēn* (see **HELLENE**).

Hellenism /ˈhɛlɪnɪz(ə)m/ ▶ noun [mass noun] the national character or culture of Greece, especially ancient Greece.
■ the study or imitation of ancient Greek culture.
– DERIVATIVES **Hellenist** noun, **Hellenization** noun, **Hellenize** (also **-ise**) verb, **Hellenizer** noun.
– ORIGIN early 17th cent. (denoting a Greek phrase or idiom): from Greek *Hellēnismos*, from *Hellēnizein* 'speak Greek, make Greek', from *Hellēn* 'a Greek'.

Hellenistic ▶ adjective of or relating to Greek history, language, and culture from the death of Alexander the Great to the defeat of Cleopatra and Mark Antony by Octavian in 31 BC. During this period Greek culture flourished, spreading through the Mediterranean and into the Near East and Asia and centring on Alexandria in Egypt and Pergamum in Turkey.

Heller, Joseph (1923–99), American novelist. His experiences in the US air force during the Second World War inspired his best-known novel *Catch-22* (1961), an absurdist black comedy satirizing war and the source of the expression 'catch-22'.

heller /ˈhɛlə/ ▶ noun (pl. same or **hellers**) a former German or Austrian coin of low value.
■ another term for **HALER**.
– ORIGIN from German *Heller*, earlier *haller* (see **HALER**).

Hellespont /ˈhɛlɪspɒnt/ the ancient name for the Dardanelles, named after the legendary Helle, who fell into the strait and was drowned while escaping with her brother Phrixus from their stepmother, Ino, on a golden-fleeced ram.

hellfire ▶ noun [mass noun] the fire or fires regarded as existing in hell: *threats of hellfire and damnation.*

hellgrammite /ˈhɛlɡrəmʌɪt/ ▶ noun N. Amer. the aquatic larva of a dobsonfly, often used as fishing bait.
– ORIGIN mid 19th cent.: of unknown origin.

hellhole ▶ noun an oppressive or unbearable place.

hellhound ▶ noun a demon in the form of a dog.

hellion /ˈhɛljən/ ▶ noun N. Amer. informal a rowdy, mischievous, or trouble-making person, especially a child.
– ORIGIN mid 19th cent.: perhaps from dialect *hallion* 'a worthless fellow', changed by association with **HELL**.

hellish ▶ adjective of or like hell: *an unearthly, hellish landscape.*
■ informal extremely difficult or unpleasant: *it had been a hellish week.*
▶ adverb [as submodifier] Brit. informal extremely (used for emphasis): *it was hellish expensive.*
– DERIVATIVES **hellishly** adverb [as submodifier] *a hellishly dull holiday,* **hellishness** noun.

Hellman /ˈhɛlmən/, Lillian (Florence) (1907–84), American dramatist. Her plays, such as *The Children's Hour* (1934) and *The Little Foxes* (1939), often reflected her socialist and feminist concerns. She lived with the detective-story writer Dashiell Hammett, and both were blacklisted during the McCarthy era.

hello (also **hallo** or **hullo**) ▶ exclamation used as a greeting: *hello there, Katie!*
■ used to begin a telephone conversation: *Hello? Connor speaking.* ■ Brit. used to express surprise: *hello, what's all this then?* ■ used as a cry to attract someone's attention: *'Hello below!' he cried.*
▶ noun (pl. **-os**) an utterance of 'hello'; a greeting.
▶ verb (**-oes, -oed**) [no obj.] say or shout 'hello'; greet someone.
– ORIGIN late 19th cent.: variant of earlier *hollo*; related to **HOLLA**.

hellraiser ▶ noun a person who causes trouble by drinking, being violent, or otherwise behaving outrageously.
– DERIVATIVES **hellraising** adjective & noun.

Hell's Angel ▶ noun a member of any of a number of gangs ('chapters') of male motorcycle enthusiasts, first formed in California in the 1950s and originally notorious for lawless behaviour.

Hell's Canyon a chasm in Idaho, cut by the Snake River and forming the deepest gorge in the US. Flanked by the Seven Devils Mountains, the canyon drops to a depth of 2,433 m (7,900 ft).

helluva ▶ contraction of a hell of a (representing a non-standard pronunciation): *I'm in a helluva mess.*

helm¹ ▶ noun (**the helm**) a tiller or wheel for steering a ship or boat.
■ figurative a position of leadership: *they are family-run empires whose founders remain at the helm.* ■ Nautical a helmsman.
▶ verb [with obj.] steer (a boat or ship).
■ figurative manage the running of: *the magazine he helmed in the late eighties.*
– ORIGIN Old English *helma*; probably related to **HELVE**.

helm² ▶ noun archaic a helmet.
– DERIVATIVES **helmed** adjective.
– ORIGIN Old English, of Germanic origin; related to Dutch *helm* and German *Helm*, also to **HELMET**, from an Indo-European root meaning 'to cover or hide'.

Helmand /ˈhɛlmənd/ the longest river in Afghanistan. Rising in the Hindu Kush, it flows 1,125 km (700 miles), generally south-west, before emptying into marshland near the Iran–Afghanistan frontier.

helmet ▶ noun **1** a hard or padded protective hat, various types of which are worn by soldiers, police officers, motorcyclists, sports players, and others. **2** Botany the arched upper part (galea) of the corolla in some flowers, especially those of the mint and orchid families. **3** (also **helmet shell**) a predatory mollusc with a squat heavy shell, which lives in tropical and temperate seas and preys chiefly on sea urchins.
● Family Cassidae, class Gastropoda.
– DERIVATIVES **helmeted** adjective.
– ORIGIN late Middle English: from Old French, diminutive of *helme*, of Germanic origin; related to **HELM²**.

helmet bird ▶ noun a heavily built Madagascan bird of the vanga shrike family, with a very large deep bill.
● *Euryceros prevostii*, family Vangidae.

Helmholtz /ˈhɛlmhɒlts/, Hermann Ludwig Ferdinand von (1821–94), German physiologist and physicist. He formulated the principle of the conservation of energy in 1847. Other achievements include his studies in sense perception, hydrodynamics, and non-Euclidean geometry.

helminth /ˈhɛlmɪnθ/ ▶ noun a parasitic worm; a fluke, tapeworm, or nematode.
– DERIVATIVES **helminthic** adjective.
– ORIGIN mid 19th cent.: from Greek *helmins*, *helminth-* 'intestinal worm'.

helminthiasis /ˌhɛlmɪnˈθʌɪəsɪs/ ▶ noun [mass noun] Medicine infestation with parasitic worms.

helminthology /ˌhɛlmɪnˈθɒlədʒi/ ▶ noun [mass noun] the study of parasitic worms.
– DERIVATIVES **helminthological** adjective, **helminthologist** noun.

Helmont /ˈhɛlmɒnt/, Joannes Baptista van (1577–1644), Belgian chemist and physician. He made early studies on the conservation of matter, was the first to distinguish gases, and coined the word *gas*.

helmsman ▶ noun (pl. **-men**) a person who steers a ship or boat.

Héloïse /ˈɛləʊiːz/ (1098–1164), French abbess. She is known for her tragic love affair with the theologian Abelard, which began after she became his pupil. When the affair came to light, Abelard persuaded her to enter a convent; she later became abbess of the community of Paraclete. See also **ABELARD**.

helot /ˈhɛlət/ ▶ **noun** a member of a class of serfs in ancient Sparta, intermediate in status between slaves and citizens.
■ a serf or slave.
– DERIVATIVES **helotage** noun, **helotism** noun, **helotry** noun.
– ORIGIN via Latin from Greek *Heilōtes* (plural), traditionally taken as referring to *Helos*, a Laconian town whose inhabitants were enslaved.

help ▶ **verb** [with obj.] **1** make it easier for (someone) to do something by offering them one's services or financial or material aid: *they helped her with domestic chores* | [with obj. and infinitive] *she helped him find a buyer* | [no obj.] *the teenager* ***helped out*** *in the corner shop.*
■ improve (a situation or problem); be of benefit to: *upbeat comments about prospects helped confidence* | [no obj.] *legislation to fit all new cars with catalytic converters will help.* ■ [with obj. and adverbial of direction] assist (someone) to move in a specified direction: *I helped her up.* ■ (**help someone on/off with**) assist someone to put on or take off (a garment). ■ relieve the symptoms of (an ailment): *sore throats can be helped by gargles.*
2 (**help someone to**) serve someone with (food or drink): *she* ***helped herself*** *to a biscuit.*
■ (**help oneself**) take something without permission: *he* ***helped himself to*** *the wages she had brought home.*
3 (**can/could not help**) cannot or could not avoid: *he could not help laughing* | *it cannot be helped.*
■ (**can/could not help oneself**) cannot or could not stop oneself from acting in a certain way: *she couldn't help herself; she burst into tears.*
▶ **noun** [mass noun] assistance: *I asked for help from my neighbours* | *thank you for your help.*
■ [in sing.] a person or thing that helps: *he was a great help.* ■ [count noun] a domestic servant or employee. ■ [as plural noun **the help**] a group of such employees working for one employer. ■ [as modifier] giving assistance to a computer user in the form of displayed instructions: *a help menu.*
▶ **exclamation** used as an appeal for urgent assistance: *Help! I'm drowning!*
– PHRASES **a helping hand** assistance: *she was always ready to lend a helping hand.* **so help me** (**God**) used to emphasize that one means what one is saying. **there is no help for it** there is no way of avoiding or remedying a situation.
– DERIVATIVES **helper** noun.
– ORIGIN Old English *helpan* (verb), *help* (noun), of Germanic origin; related to Dutch *helpen* and German *helfen*.

help desk ▶ **noun** a service providing information and support to the users of a computer network.

helper cell ▶ **noun** Physiology a T-lymphocyte that influences or controls the differentiation or activity of other cells of the immune system.

helpful ▶ **adjective** giving or ready to give help: *people are friendly and helpful* | *helpful staff.*
■ useful: *we find it very helpful to receive comments.*
– DERIVATIVES **helpfully** adverb, **helpfulness** noun.

helping ▶ **noun** a portion of food served to one person at one time: *there will be enough for six to eight helpings* | *she asked for a second helping of spinach.*

helpless ▶ **adjective** unable to defend oneself or to act without help: *the cubs are born blind and helpless.*
■ uncontrollable: *they burst into helpless laughter.*
– DERIVATIVES **helplessly** adverb, **helplessness** noun.

helpline ▶ **noun** a telephone service providing help with problems.

Helpmann /ˈhɛlpmən/, Sir Robert (Murray) (1909–86), Australian ballet dancer, choreographer, director, and actor. He joined the Vic-Wells Ballet shortly after coming to England in 1933, and in 1935 began a long partnership with Margot Fonteyn.

helpmate (also **helpmeet**) ▶ **noun** a helpful companion or partner, especially one's husband or wife.
– ORIGIN late 17th cent. (as *helpmeet*): from an erroneous reading of Gen. 2:18, 20, where Adam's future wife is described as 'an help meet for him' (i.e. a suitable helper for him). The variant *helpmate* came into use in the early 18th cent.

Helsingborg /ˈhɛlsɪŋbɔːg/ a port in southern Sweden, situated on the Øresund opposite Elsinore in Denmark; pop. 109,270 (1990). Swedish name **HÄLSINGBORG**.

Helsingør /ˌhɛlsɛŋˈøːr/ Danish name for **ELSINORE**.

Helsinki /ˈhɛlsɪŋki, hɛlˈsɪŋki/ the capital of Finland, a port in the south on the Gulf of Finland; pop. 492,400 (1990). Swedish name **HELSINGFORS** /ˌhɛlsɪŋˈfɔrs/.

helter-skelter ▶ **adjective** & **adverb** in disorderly haste or confusion: [as adj.] *the helter-skelter dash to unity* | [as adv.] *hurtling helter-skelter down the pavement.*
▶ **noun 1** Brit. a tall spiral slide winding around a tower at a fair.
2 [in sing.] disorder; confusion: *the helter-skelter of a school day.*
– ORIGIN late 16th cent. (as an adverb): a rhyming jingle of unknown origin, perhaps symbolic of running feet or from Middle English *skelte* 'hasten'.

helve /hɛlv/ ▶ **noun** the handle of a weapon or tool.
– ORIGIN Old English *helfe*, of Germanic origin; related to **HALTER**.

Helvetia /hɛlˈviːʃə/ Latin name for **SWITZERLAND**.

Helvetian chiefly historical ▶ **adjective** Swiss.
▶ **noun** a native of Switzerland.

Helvetic /hɛlˈvɛtɪk/ ▶ **adjective** & **noun** another term for **HELVETIAN**.

hem¹ ▶ **noun** the edge of a piece of cloth or clothing which has been turned under and sewn.
▶ **verb** (**hemmed**, **hemming**) [with obj.] **1** turn under and sew the edge of (a piece of cloth).
2 (**hem someone/thing in**) (usu. **be hemmed in**) surround and restrict the space or movement of: *he was hemmed in by the tables.*
– ORIGIN Old English 'the border of a piece of cloth', of West Germanic origin. The verb senses date from the mid 16th cent.

hem² ▶ **exclamation** used in writing to indicate a sound made when coughing or clearing the throat to attract someone's attention or express hesitation.
▶ **noun** an utterance of such a sound.
▶ **verb** (**hemmed**, **hemming**) [no obj.] archaic make such a sound when hesitating or as a signal.
– PHRASES **hem and haw** another way of saying **HUM AND HAW** (see **HUM¹**).
– ORIGIN late 15th cent.: imitative.

hemagglutination etc. ▶ **noun** US spelling of **HAEMAGGLUTINATION** etc.

he-man ▶ **noun** informal a well-built, muscular man, especially one who is ostentatiously so.

hemato- ▶ **combining form** US spelling of **HAEMATO-**.

heme ▶ **noun** US spelling of **HAEM**.

Hemel Hempstead /ˌhɛm(ə)l ˈhɛmpstɪd/ a town in SE England, in Hertfordshire; pop. 80,340 (1981). It was designated as a new town in 1947.

hemerocallis /ˌhɛm(ə)rə(ʊ)ˈkalɪs/ ▶ **noun** (pl. same) a plant of a genus that comprises the day lilies.
• Genus *Hemerocallis*, family Liliaceae.
– ORIGIN modern Latin, from Greek *hēmerokallis* 'a lily that flowers for a day', from *hēmera* 'day' + *kallos* 'beauty'.

hemi- ▶ **prefix** half: *hemicylindrical* | *hemiplegia.*
– ORIGIN from Greek *hēmi-*; related to Latin *semi-*.

-hemia ▶ **combining form** US spelling of **-AEMIA**.

hemianopia /ˌhɛmɪəˈnəʊpɪə/ (also **hemianopsia** /-ˈnɒpsɪə/) ▶ **noun** [mass noun] blindness over half the field of vision.

hemicellulose ▶ **noun** Biochemistry any of a class of substances which occur as constituents of the cell walls of plants and are polysaccharides of simpler structure than cellulose.
– ORIGIN late 19th cent.: coined in German from **HEMI-** + **CELLULOSE**.

Hemichordata /ˌhɛmɪkɔːˈdeɪtə/ Zoology a small phylum of marine invertebrates that comprises the acorn worms.
– DERIVATIVES **hemichordate** noun & adjective.
– ORIGIN modern Latin (see **HEMI-**, **CHORDATA**).

hemicycle ▶ **noun** a semicircular shape or structure.

hemicylindrical ▶ **adjective** having the shape of half a cylinder (divided lengthways).

hemidemisemiquaver /ˌhɛmɪdɛmɪˈsɛmɪkweɪvə/ ▶ **noun** Music, chiefly Brit. a note with the time value of half a demisemiquaver, represented by a large dot with a four-hooked stem. Also called **SIXTY-FOURTH NOTE**.

hemihydrate /ˌhɛmɪˈhʌɪdreɪt/ ▶ **noun** Chemistry a crystalline hydrate containing one molecule of water for every two molecules of the compound in question.

hemimetabolous /ˌhɛmɪmɛˈtabələs/ ▶ **adjective** Entomology (of an insect) having no pupal stage in the transition from larva to adult.
– DERIVATIVES **hemimetabolic** adjective.

hemimorphite /ˌhɛmɪˈmɔːfʌɪt/ ▶ **noun** [mass noun] a mineral consisting of hydrated zinc silicate, typically occurring as flat white prisms.

Hemingway, Ernest (Miller) (1899–1961), American novelist, short-story writer, and journalist. He achieved success with *The Sun Also Rises* (1926), which reflected the disillusionment of the post-war 'lost generation'. Other notable works: *A Farewell to Arms* (1929), *For Whom the Bell Tolls* (1940), and *The Old Man and the Sea* (1952, Pulitzer Prize 1953). Nobel Prize for Literature (1954).

hemiola /ˌhɛmɪˈəʊlə/ ▶ **noun** Music a musical figure in which, typically, two groups of three beats are replaced by three groups of two beats, giving the effect of a shift between triple and duple metre.
– ORIGIN late Middle English: via medieval Latin from Greek *hēmiolia* 'in the ratio of one and a half to one' (from *hēmi-* 'half' + *holos* 'whole').

hemiparasite ▶ **noun** Botany a plant which obtains or may obtain part of its food by parasitism, e.g. mistletoe, which also photosynthesizes.

hemiparesis /ˌhɛmɪpəˈriːsɪs/ ▶ **noun** another term for **HEMIPLEGIA**.

hemipenis /ˈhɛmɪpiːnɪs/ ▶ **noun** (pl. **hemipenes**) Zoology each of the paired male reproductive organs in snakes and lizards.

hemiplegia /ˌhɛmɪˈpliːdʒə/ ▶ **noun** [mass noun] Medicine paralysis of one side of the body.
– DERIVATIVES **hemiplegic** noun & adjective.
– ORIGIN early 17th cent.: modern Latin, from Greek *hēmiplēgia*, from *hemi-* 'half' + *plēgē* 'stroke'.

hemipode /ˈhɛmɪpəʊd/ ▶ **noun** another term for **BUTTON-QUAIL**.
– ORIGIN mid 19th cent.: from modern Latin *Hemipodius* (former genus name), from Greek *hemi-* 'half' + *pous, pod-* 'foot'.

Hemiptera /hɛˈmɪpt(ə)rə/ Entomology a large order of insects that comprises the true bugs, which include aphids, cicadas, leafhoppers, and many others. They have piercing and sucking mouthparts and incomplete metamorphosis. See also **HETEROPTERA**, **HOMOPTERA**.
■ [as plural noun **hemiptera**] insects of this order; true bugs.
– DERIVATIVES **hemipteran** noun & adjective, **hemipterous** adjective.
– ORIGIN modern Latin (plural), from Greek *hemi-* 'half' + *pteron* 'wing' (because of the forewing structure, partly hardened at the base and partly membranous).

hemisphere ▶ **noun** a half of a sphere.
■ a half of the earth, usually as divided into northern and southern halves by the equator, or into western and eastern halves by an imaginary line passing through the poles. ■ a half of the celestial sphere. ■ (also **cerebral hemisphere**) each of the two parts of the cerebrum (left and right) in the brain of a vertebrate.
– DERIVATIVES **hemispheric** adjective, **hemispherical** adjective, **hemispherically** adverb.
– ORIGIN late Middle English (in the sense 'half the celestial sphere, the sky'): from Old French *emisphere*, via Latin from Greek *hēmisphairion*, from *hēmi-* 'half' + *sphaira* 'sphere'.

hemistich /ˈhɛmɪstɪk/ ▶ **noun** (chiefly in Old English verse) a half of a line of verse.
– ORIGIN late 16th cent.: via late Latin from Greek *hēmistikhion*, from *hemi-* 'half' + *stikhos* 'row, line of verse'.

Hemkund, Lake /hɛmˈkʊnd/ a lake in northern India, in the Himalayan foothills of Uttar Pradesh. It is regarded as holy by the Sikhs.

hemline ▶ **noun** the level of the lower edge of a garment such as a skirt, dress, or coat.

hemlock ▶ **noun 1** a highly poisonous European

plant of the parsley family, with a purple-spotted stem, fern-like leaves, small white flowers, and an unpleasant smell.
• *Conium maculatum*, family Umbelliferae.
■[mass noun] a sedative or poisonous potion obtained from this plant.
2 (also **hemlock fir** or **spruce**) a coniferous North American tree with dark green foliage which is said to smell like hemlock when crushed, grown chiefly for timber.
• Genus *Tsuga*, family Pinaceae: several species.
– ORIGIN Old English *hymlice, hemlic*, of unknown origin.

hemo- ▶ **combining form** US spelling of **HAEMO-**.

hemp ▶ **noun** (also **Indian hemp**) [mass noun] the cannabis plant, especially when grown for fibre.
■the fibre of this plant, extracted from the stem and used to make rope, stout fabrics, fibreboard, and paper. ■ used in names of other plants that yield fibre, e.g. **Manila hemp**. ■ the drug cannabis.
– DERIVATIVES **hempen** adjective (archaic).
– ORIGIN Old English *henep, hænep*, of Germanic origin; related to Dutch *hennep* and German *Hanf*, also to Greek *kannabis*.

hemp agrimony ▶ **noun** an erect Eurasian plant of the daisy family, resembling a valerian, with clusters of pale purple flowers and hairy stems.
• *Eupatorium cannabinum*, family Compositae.

hemp-nettle ▶ **noun** a nettle-like Eurasian plant of the mint family.
• Genus *Galeopsis*, family Labiatae.

hempseed /ˈhɛmpsiːd/ ▶ **noun** [mass noun] the seed of hemp, particularly as used for fishing bait.

hemstitch ▶ **noun** a decoration used on woven fabric, especially alongside a hem, in which several adjacent threads are pulled out and the crossing threads are tied into bunches, making a row of small openings.
▶ **verb** [with obj.] incorporate such a decoration in the hem of (a piece of cloth or clothing).

hen ▶ **noun** a female bird, especially of a domestic fowl.
■(**hens**) domestic fowls of either sex. ■ used in names of birds, especially waterbirds of the rail family, e.g. **moorhen**, **native hen**. ■ a female lobster, crab, or salmon. ■ Scottish used as an affectionate term of address to a girl or woman.
– PHRASES **as rare** (or **scarce**) **as hen's teeth** extremely rare.
– ORIGIN Old English *henn*, of Germanic origin; related to Dutch *hen* and German *Henne*.

Henan /həˈnan/ (also **Honan**) a province of NE central China; capital, Zhengzhou.

hen and chickens ▶ **noun** any of a number of plants producing additional small flower heads or offshoots.
• Several species, especially the houseleek *Jovibarba sobilifera* (family Crassulaceae).

henbane /ˈhɛnbeɪn/ ▶ **noun** a coarse and poisonous Eurasian plant of the nightshade family, with sticky hairy leaves and an unpleasant smell.
• *Hyoscyamus niger*, family Solanaceae.
■[mass noun] a narcotic drink prepared from this plant.

henbit /ˈhɛnbɪt/ ▶ **noun** a dead-nettle with purple flowers and partly prostrate stems, native to Eurasia.
• Genus *Lamium*, family Labiatae: several species, in particular *L. amplexicaule*.
– ORIGIN late 16th cent.: apparently a translation of Low German or Dutch *hoenderbeet*.

hence ▶ **adverb** **1** as a consequence; for this reason: *many vehicle journeys (and hence a lot of pollution) would be saved | he was a tiny, slight figure, hence his sobriquet, 'the Little Wonder'.*
2 in the future (used after a period of time): *two years hence they might say something quite different.*
3 (also **from hence**) archaic from here: *hence, be gone.*
– ORIGIN Middle English *hennes* (in sense 3): from earlier *henne* (from Old English *heonan*, of Germanic origin, related to **HE**) + **-S**[3] (later respelled *-ce* to denote the unvoiced sound).

henceforth (also **henceforward**) ▶ **adverb** from this or that time on: *henceforth, parties which fail to get 5% of the vote will not be represented in parliament.*

henchman ▶ **noun** (pl. **-men**) chiefly derogatory a faithful follower or political supporter, especially one prepared to engage in crime or dishonest practices by way of service.
■historical a squire or page of honour to a person of rank. ■ (in Scotland) the principal attendant of a Highland chief.
– ORIGIN Middle English, from Old English *hengest* 'male horse' + **MAN**, the original sense being probably 'groom'. In the mid 18th cent. the sense 'principal attendant of a Highland chief' was popularized by Sir Walter Scott, whence the current (originally US) usage.

hendeca- /ˈhɛndɛkə, hɛnˈdɛkə/ ▶ **combining form** eleven; having eleven: *hendecasyllable.*
– ORIGIN from Greek *hendeka* 'eleven'.

hendecagon /hɛnˈdɛkəg(ə)n/ ▶ **noun** a plane figure with eleven straight sides and angles.
– DERIVATIVES **hendecagonal** adjective /ˌhɛndɪˈkag(ə)n(ə)l/.
– ORIGIN early 18th cent.: from **HENDECA-** 'eleven' + **-GON**, on the pattern of words such as *polygon*.

hendecasyllable /ˌhɛndɛkəˈsɪləb(ə)l/ ▶ **noun** Prosody a line of verse containing eleven syllables.
– DERIVATIVES **hendecasyllabic** adjective.

hendiadys /hɛnˈdʌɪədɪs/ ▶ **noun** [mass noun] the expression of a single idea by two words connected with 'and', e.g. *nice and warm*, when one could be used to modify the other, as in *nicely warm*.
– ORIGIN late 16th cent.: via medieval Latin from Greek *hen dia duoin* 'one thing by two'.

Hendrix, Jimi (1942–70), American rock guitarist and singer; full name *James Marshall Hendrix*. Remembered for the flamboyance and originality of his improvisations, he greatly widened the scope of the electric guitar. Notable songs: 'Purple Haze' (1967), 'All Along the Watchtower' (1968).

Hendry, Stephen (Gordon) (b.1969), Scottish snooker player. He became the youngest world snooker champion in 1990. He regained the title in 1992 and in 1996 won it for the sixth time.

henequen /ˈhɛnɪkɛn/ ▶ **noun** [mass noun] **1** a fibre resembling sisal, which is chiefly used for binder twine and paper pulp.
2 a Central American agave from which such fibre is obtained.
• *Agave fourcroydes*, family Agavaceae.
– ORIGIN early 17th cent.: from Spanish *jeniquen*, from a local word.

henge /hɛn(d)ʒ/ ▶ **noun** a prehistoric monument consisting of a circle of stone or wooden uprights.
– ORIGIN mid 18th cent.: back-formation from **STONEHENGE**.

Hengist and Horsa /ˈhɛŋgɪst, ˈhɔːsə/ (d.488 & d.455), semi-mythological Jutish leaders. According to Bede the brothers were invited to Britain by the British king Vortigern in 449 to assist in defeating the Picts and later established an independent Anglo-Saxon kingdom in Kent.

hen harrier ▶ **noun** a widespread harrier of open country, the male of which is mainly pale grey and the female brown.
• *Circus cyaneus*, family Accipitridae. North American name: **marsh hawk**, **northern harrier**.
– ORIGIN mid 16th cent.: so named because it was believed to prey on poultry.

Henle's loop ▶ **noun** another term for **LOOP OF HENLE**.

Henley Royal Regatta the oldest rowing regatta in Europe, inaugurated in 1839 at Henley-on-Thames, Oxfordshire, and held annually in the first week in July.

henna ▶ **noun** [mass noun] **1** the powdered leaves of a tropical shrub, used as a dye to colour the hair and decorate the body.
2 the Old World shrub which produces these leaves, with small pink, red, or white flowers.
• *Lawsonia inermis*, family Lythraceae.
▶ **verb** (**hennas**, **hennaed**, **hennaing**) [with obj.] dye (hair) with henna.
– ORIGIN early 17th cent.: from Arabic *ḥinnā'*.

hen night ▶ **noun** Brit. informal a celebration held for a woman who is about to get married, attended only by women.

henotheism /ˈhɛnəʊˌθiːɪz(ə)m/ ▶ **noun** [mass noun] adherence to one particular god out of several, especially by a family, tribe, or other group.
– ORIGIN mid 19th cent.: from Greek *heis, henos* 'one' + *theos* 'god' + **-ISM**.

hen party ▶ **noun** informal a social gathering of women, especially a hen night.

henpeck ▶ **verb** [with obj.] [usu. as adj. **henpecked**] (of a woman) continually criticize and order about (her husband or other male partner): *henpecked husbands.*

Henri /ˈhɛnri/, Robert (1865–1929), American painter. An advocate of realism, he believed that the artist must be a social force. The Ashcan School of painters was formed largely as a result of his influence.

Henrician /hɛnˈrɪʃɪən/ ▶ **adjective** of or relating to the reign and policies of Henry VIII of England.

Henrietta Maria (1609–69), daughter of Henry IV of France, queen consort of Charles I of England 1625–49. Her Roman Catholicism heightened public anxieties about the court's religious sympathies and was a contributory cause of the English Civil War.

Henry[1] the name of eight kings of England:
■**Henry I** (1068–1135), youngest son of William I, reigned 1100–35. His only son drowned in 1120, and although Henry extracted an oath of loyalty to his daughter Matilda from the barons in 1127, his death was followed almost immediately by the outbreak of civil war.
■**Henry II** (1133–89), son of Matilda, reigned 1154–89. The first Plantagenet king, he restored order after the reigns of Stephen and Matilda. Opposition to his policies on reducing the power of the Church was led by Thomas à Becket, who was eventually murdered by four of Henry's knights.
■**Henry III** (1207–72), son of John, reigned 1216–72. His ineffectual government caused widespread discontent, ending in Simon de Montfort's defeat and capture of Henry in 1264. Although he was restored a year later, real power resided with his son, who eventually succeeded him as Edward I.
■**Henry IV** (1367–1413), son of John of Gaunt, reigned 1399–1413; known as **Henry Bolingbroke**. He overthrew Richard II, establishing the Lancastrian dynasty. His reign was marked by rebellion in Wales and the north, where the Percy family raised several uprisings.
■**Henry V** (1387–1422), son of Henry IV, reigned 1413–22. He renewed the Hundred Years War soon after coming to the throne and defeated the French at Agincourt in 1415.
■**Henry VI** (1421–71), son of Henry V, reigned 1422–61 and 1470–1. He was unfit to rule effectively on his own due to a recurrent mental illness. Government by the monarchy became increasingly unpopular and after intermittent civil war with the House of York (the Wars of the Roses), Henry was deposed in 1461 by Edward IV. He briefly regained his throne following a Lancastrian uprising.
■**Henry VII** (1457–1509), the first Tudor king, son of Edmund Tudor, Earl of Richmond, reigned 1485–1509; known as **Henry Tudor**. Although the grandson of Owen Tudor, he inherited the Lancastrian claim to the throne through his mother, a great-granddaughter of John of Gaunt. He defeated Richard III at Bosworth Field and eventually established an unchallenged Tudor dynasty.
■**Henry VIII** (1491–1547), son of Henry VII, reigned 1509–47. Henry had six wives (Catherine of Aragon, Anne Boleyn, Jane Seymour, Anne of Cleves, Catherine Howard, Katherine Parr); he executed two and divorced two. His first divorce, from Catherine of Aragon, was opposed by the Pope, leading to England's break with the Roman Catholic Church.

Henry[2] (1394–1460), Portuguese prince; known as **Henry the Navigator**. The third son of John I of Portugal, he organized many voyages of discovery, most notably south along the African coast, thus laying the foundation for Portuguese imperial expansion round Africa to the Far East.

Henry[3] the name of seven kings of the Germans, six of whom were also Holy Roman emperors:
■**Henry I** (*c.*876–936), reigned 919–36; known as **Henry the Fowler**. He waged war successfully against the Slavs in Brandenburg, the Magyars, and the Danes.
■**Henry II** (973–1024), reigned 1002–24, Holy Roman Emperor 1014–24; also known as **Saint Henry**.
■**Henry III** (1017–56), reigned 1039–56, Holy Roman emperor 1046–56. He brought stability and prosperity to the empire, defeating the Czechs and fixing the frontier between Austria and Hungary.
■**Henry IV** (1050–1106), son of Henry III, reigned 1056–1105, Holy Roman emperor 1084–1105. Increasing conflict with Pope Gregory VII led Henry to call a council in 1076 to depose the Pope, who excommunicated Henry. Henry obtained absolution by doing penance before Gregory in 1077 but managed to depose him in 1084.
■**Henry V** (1086–1125), reigned 1099–1125, Holy Roman Emperor 1111–25.
■**Henry VI** (1165–97), reigned 1169–97, Holy Roman Emperor 1191–7.

■Henry VII (c.1269/74–1313), reigned 1308–13, Holy Roman Emperor 1312–3.

Henry[4], O (1862–1910), American short-story writer; pseudonym of *William Sydney Porter*. Jailed for embezzlement in 1898, he started writing short stories in prison. Collections include *Cabbages and Kings* (1904) and *The Voice of the City* (1908).

henry (abbrev.: **H**) ▶ noun (pl. **henries** or **henrys**) Physics the SI unit of inductance, equal to an electromotive force of one volt in a closed circuit with a uniform rate of change of current of one ampere per second.
– ORIGIN late 19th cent.: named after Joseph *Henry* (1797–1878), the American physicist who discovered the phenomenon.

Henry Bolingbroke, Henry IV of England (see **HENRY**[1]).

Henry IV (1553–1610), king of France 1589–1610; known as **Henry of Navarre**. Although leader of Huguenot forces in the latter stages of the French Wars of Religion, on succeeding the Catholic Henry III he became Catholic himself in order to guarantee peace. He established religious freedom with the Edict of Nantes (1598) and restored order after the prolonged civil war.

Henry's law Chemistry a law stating that the mass of a dissolved gas in a given volume of solvent at equilibrium is proportional to the partial pressure of the gas.
– ORIGIN late 19th cent.: named after William *Henry* (1774–1836), English chemist.

Henry the Fowler, Henry I, king of the Germans (see **HENRY**[3]).

Henry Tudor, Henry VII of England (see **HENRY**[1]).

Henze /ˈhɛntsə/, Hans Werner (b.1926), German composer and conductor. His diverse works are influenced by serialism, classical composers, and Italian opera, and sometimes reflect his left-wing ideals, as in *The Raft of the Medusa* (1968) (a requiem for Che Guevara).

hep[1] ▶ adjective old-fashioned term for **HIP**[3].

hep[2] ▶ noun archaic or dialect term for **HIP**[2].

heparin /ˈhɛpərɪn/ ▶ noun [mass noun] Biochemistry a compound occurring in the liver and other tissues which inhibits blood coagulation. A sulphur-containing polysaccharide, it is used as an anticoagulant in the treatment of thrombosis.
– ORIGIN early 20th cent.: via late Latin from Greek *hēpar* 'liver' + **-IN**[1].

heparinize (also **-ise**) ▶ verb [with obj.] add heparin to (blood or a container about to be filled with blood) to prevent it from coagulating.
– DERIVATIVES **heparinization** noun.

hepatic /hɪˈpatɪk/ ▶ adjective of or relating to the liver: *right and left hepatic ducts.*
▶ noun Botany less common term for **LIVERWORT**.
– ORIGIN late Middle English: via Latin from Greek *hēpatikos*, from *hēpar*, *hēpat-* 'liver'.

hepatica /hɪˈpatɪkə/ ▶ noun a plant of the buttercup family, with anemone-like flowers, native to north temperate regions.
● Genus *Hepatica*, family Ranunculaceae.
– ORIGIN from medieval Latin *hepatica (herba)* 'plant having liver-shaped parts, or one used to treat liver diseases', feminine of *hepaticus* (see **HEPATIC**).

Hepaticae /hɛˈpatɪkiː/ Botany a class of lower plants that comprises the liverworts.
– ORIGIN modern Latin (plural), from Greek *hēpar*, *hēpat-* 'liver'.

hepatic portal vein ▶ noun see **PORTAL VEIN**.

hepatitis /ˌhɛpəˈtʌɪtɪs/ ▶ noun [mass noun] a disease characterized by inflammation of the liver.
– ORIGIN early 18th cent.: modern Latin, from Greek *hēpar*, *hēpat-* 'liver' + **-ITIS**.

hepatitis A ▶ noun [mass noun] a form of viral hepatitis transmitted in food, causing fever and jaundice.

hepatitis B ▶ noun [mass noun] a severe form of viral hepatitis transmitted in infected blood, causing fever, debility, and jaundice.

hepatitis C ▶ noun [mass noun] a form of viral hepatitis transmitted in infected blood, causing chronic liver disease. It was formerly called non-A, non-B hepatitis.

hepato- /ˈhɛpətəʊ, hɛˈpatə(ʊ)-/ ▶ combining form of or relating to the liver.
– ORIGIN from Greek *hēpar*, *hēpat-* 'liver'.

hepatocyte /ˈhɛpətəʊsʌɪt, hɛˈpatə(ʊ)-/ ▶ noun Physiology a liver cell.

hepatoma /ˌhɛpəˈtəʊmə/ ▶ noun (pl. **hepatomas** or **hepatomata** /-mətə/) Medicine a cancer of the cells of the liver.

hepatomegaly /ˌhɛpətəʊˈmɛgəli, hɛˌpatəʊ-/ ▶ noun [mass noun] Medicine abnormal enlargement of the liver.

hepatopancreas /ˌhɛpətəʊˈpaŋkrɪəs, hɛˌpatəʊ-/ ▶ noun technical term for **DIGESTIVE GLAND**.

hepatotoxic /ˌhɛpətəʊˈtɒksɪk, hɛˌpatəʊ-/ ▶ adjective damaging or destructive to liver cells.
– DERIVATIVES **hepatotoxicity** noun, **hepatotoxin** noun.

Hepburn[1] /ˈhɛpbəːn/, Audrey (1929–93), British actress, born in Belgium. After pursuing a career as a stage and film actress in England, she moved to Hollywood, where she starred in such films as *Roman Holiday* (1953), for which she won an Oscar, and *My Fair Lady* (1964).

Hepburn[2] /ˈhɛpbəːn/, Katharine (b.1909), American actress. She starred in a wide range of films, often opposite Spencer Tracy; films include *Woman of the Year* (1942), *The African Queen* (1951), and *On Golden Pond* (1981), for which she won her fourth Oscar.

hepcat ▶ noun informal, dated a stylish or fashionable person, especially in the sphere of jazz or popular music.
– ORIGIN 1930s: from **HEP**[1] + **CAT**[1].

Hephaestus /hɪˈfiːstəs/ Greek Mythology the god of fire and of craftsmen, son of Zeus and Hera. He was a divine metalworker who was lame as the result of having interfered in a quarrel between his parents. Roman equivalent **VULCAN**.

Hepplewhite /ˈhɛp(ə)lwʌɪt/, George (d.1786), English cabinetmaker and furniture designer. The posthumously published book of his designs, *The Cabinetmaker and Upholsterer's Guide* (1788), contains almost 300 designs, characterized by light and elegant lines, which sum up neoclassical taste.

hepta- ▶ combining form seven; having seven: *heptagon* | *heptathlon*.
– ORIGIN from Greek *hepta* 'seven'.

heptachlor /ˈhɛptəklɔː/ ▶ noun [mass noun] a chlorinated hydrocarbon used as an insecticide.
● Chem. formula: $C_{10}H_5Cl_7$.

heptad /ˈhɛptad/ ▶ noun technical a group or set of seven.
– ORIGIN mid 17th cent.: from Greek *heptas*, *heptad-*, from *hepta* 'seven'.

heptagon /ˈhɛptəg(ə)n/ ▶ noun a plane figure with seven straight sides and angles.
– DERIVATIVES **heptagonal** adjective.
– ORIGIN late 16th cent.: from Greek *heptagonon*, neuter (used as a noun) of *heptagonos* 'seven-angled'.

heptahedron /ˌhɛptəˈhiːdrən, -ˈhɛd-/ ▶ noun (pl. **heptahedra** or **heptahedrons**) a solid figure with seven plane faces.
– DERIVATIVES **heptahedral** adjective.
– ORIGIN late 17th cent.: from **HEPTA-** 'seven' + **-HEDRON**, on the pattern of words such as *polyhedron*.

heptamerous /hɛpˈtamərəs/ ▶ adjective Botany & Zoology having parts arranged in groups of seven.
■consisting of seven joints or parts.

heptameter /hɛpˈtamɪtə/ ▶ noun Prosody a line of verse consisting of seven metrical feet.
– ORIGIN late 19th cent.: via late Latin from Greek *heptametron*, from *hepta-* 'seven' + *metron* 'measure'.

heptane /ˈhɛpteɪn/ ▶ noun Chemistry a colourless liquid hydrocarbon of the alkane series, present in petroleum spirit.
● Chem. formula: C_7H_{16}; several isomers, especially the straight-chain isomer (*n*-**heptane**).
– ORIGIN late 19th cent.: from **HEPTA-** 'seven' (denoting seven carbon atoms) + **-ANE**[2].

heptarchy /ˈhɛptɑːki/ ▶ noun (pl. **-ies**) a state or region consisting of seven smaller, autonomous regions.
■[mass noun] government by seven rulers.
– DERIVATIVES **heptarchic** /-ˈtɑːkɪk/ adjective, **heptarchical** /-ˈtɑːkɪk(ə)l/ adjective.
– ORIGIN late 16th cent.: from **HEPTA-** 'seven' + Greek *arkhia* 'rule', on the pattern of *tetrarchy*.

Heptateuch /ˈhɛptətjuːk/ ▶ noun the first seven books of the Bible (Genesis to Judges) collectively.
– ORIGIN late 17th cent.: via late Latin from Greek

heptateukhos, from *hepta* 'seven' + *teukhos* 'book, volume'.

heptathlon /hɛpˈtaθlɒn, -lən/ ▶ noun an athletic event, in particular one for women, in which each competitor takes part in the same prescribed seven events (100 metres hurdles, high jump, shot-put, 200 metres, long jump, javelin, and 800 metres).
– DERIVATIVES **heptathlete** noun.
– ORIGIN 1970s: from **HEPTA-** 'seven' + Greek *athlon* 'contest', on the pattern of words such as *decathlon*.

heptavalent /ˌhɛptəˈveɪl(ə)nt/ ▶ adjective Chemistry having a valency of seven.

heptyl /ˈhɛptʌɪl, -tɪl/ ▶ noun [as modifier] Chemistry of or denoting an alkyl radical —C_7H_{15}, derived from heptane.

Hepworth, Dame (Jocelyn) Barbara (1903–75), English sculptor. A pioneer of abstraction in British sculpture, she worked in wood, stone, and bronze and is noted for her simple monumental works in landscape and architectural settings, including *The Family of Man* (nine-piece group, 1972).

her ▶ pronoun [third person singular] **1** used as the object of a verb or preposition to refer to a female person or animal previously mentioned or easily identified: *she knew I hated her* | *I told Hannah I would wait for her.* Compare with **SHE**.
■referring to a ship, country, or other inanimate thing regarded as female: *the crew tried to sail her through a narrow gap.* ■ used after the verb 'to be' and after 'than' or 'as': *it must be her* | *he was younger than her.* See **usage** below.
2 archaic or N. Amer. dialect herself: *peevishly she flung her on her face.*
▶possessive determiner **1** belonging to or associated with a female person or animal previously mentioned or easily identified: *Patricia loved her job.*
■belonging to or associated with a ship, country, or other inanimate thing regarded as female.
2 (**Her**) used in titles: *Her Majesty* | *Her Royal Highness.*
– PHRASES **her indoors** Brit. informal, humorous one's wife.
– ORIGIN Old English *hire*, genitive and dative of *hīo*, *hēo* 'she'.

USAGE Is it incorrect to say *I am older than her* (rather than *I am older than she*) or *it's her all right* (rather than *it's she all right*) and, if so, why? For a discussion of this issue, see **usage** at **PERSONAL PRONOUN**.

Hera /ˈhɪərə/ Greek Mythology a powerful goddess, the wife and sister of Zeus and the daughter of Cronus and Rhea. She was worshipped as the queen of heaven and as a marriage goddess. Roman equivalent **JUNO**.
– ORIGIN from Greek *Hēra* 'lady', feminine of *hērōs* 'hero', perhaps used as a title.

Heracles /ˈhɛrəkliːz/ Greek form of **HERCULES**.

Heraclitus /ˌhɛrəˈklʌɪtəs/ (c.500 BC), Greek philosopher. He believed that fire is the origin of all things and that permanence is an illusion, everything being in a (harmonious) process of constant change.

Heraklion /hɪˈraklɪən/ the capital of Crete, a port on the north coast of the island; pop. 117,000 (1991). Greek name **IRÁKLION**.

herald ▶ noun **1** an official employed to oversee state ceremonial, precedence, and the use of armorial bearings, and (historically) to make proclamations, carry ceremonial messages, and oversee tournaments.
■(in the UK) an official of the College of Arms or the Lyon Court ranking above a pursuivant.
2 a person or thing viewed as a sign that something is about to happen: *they considered the first primroses as the herald of spring.*
3 a brown moth with dull orange markings, often hibernating in houses and old buildings.
● *Scoliopteryx libatrix*, family Noctuidae.
▶verb [with obj.] be a sign that (something) is about to happen: *the speech heralded a change in policy.*
■(usu. **be heralded**) acclaim: *the band have been heralded as the great hope for the nineties.*
– ORIGIN Middle English: from Old French *herault* (noun), *herauder* (verb), of Germanic origin.

heraldic /hɛˈraldɪk/ ▶ adjective of or relating to heraldry.
– DERIVATIVES **heraldically** adverb.

heraldist ▶ noun an expert in heraldry.

heraldry ▶ noun [mass noun] the system by which

coats of arms and other armorial bearings are devised, described, and regulated.
■armorial bearings or other heraldic symbols. ■colourful ceremony: *all the pomp and heraldry provided a splendid pageant.*

Heralds' College informal name for **COLLEGE OF ARMS**.

Herat /hə'rat/ a city in western Afghanistan; pop. 177,300 (est. 1988).

herb ▶**noun 1** any plant with leaves, seeds, or flowers used for flavouring, food, medicine, or perfume: *bundles of dried herbs* | [as modifier] *a herb garden.*
2 Botany any seed-bearing plant which does not have a woody stem and dies down to the ground after flowering.
– ORIGIN Middle English: via Old French from Latin *herba* 'grass, green crops, herb'. Although *herb* has always been spelled with an *h*, pronunciation without it was usual until the 19th cent. and is still standard in the US.

herbaceous /həː'beɪʃəs/ ▶**adjective** of, denoting, or relating to herbs (in the botanical sense).
– ORIGIN mid 17th cent.: from Latin *herbaceus* 'grassy' (from *herba* 'grass, herb') + **-OUS**.

herbaceous border ▶**noun** a garden border containing herbaceous, typically perennial, flowering plants.

herbaceous perennial ▶**noun** a plant whose growth dies down annually but whose roots or other underground parts survive.

herbage ▶**noun** [mass noun] herbaceous vegetation.
■the succulent part of this vegetation, used as pasture. ■historical the right of pasture on another person's land.
– ORIGIN late Middle English: from Old French *erbage*, based on Latin *herba* 'herb, grass, crops'.

herbal ▶**adjective** relating to or made from herbs, especially those used in cooking and medicine: *herbal lore* | *herbal remedies.*
▶**noun** a book that describes herbs and their culinary and medicinal properties.
– ORIGIN early 16th cent. (as a noun): from medieval Latin *herbalis* (adjective), from Latin *herba* 'grass, herb'.

herbalism ▶**noun** [mass noun] the study or practice of the medicinal and therapeutic use of plants, now especially as a form of alternative medicine.

herbalist ▶**noun** a practitioner of herbalism.
■a dealer in medicinal herbs. ■an early botanical writer.

herbarium /həː'bɛːrɪəm/ ▶**noun** (pl. **herbaria** /-rɪə/) a systematically arranged collection of dried plants.
■a room or building housing such a collection. ■a box, cabinet, or other receptacle in which dried plants are kept.
– ORIGIN late 18th cent.: from late Latin, from Latin *herba* 'grass, herb'.

herbary ▶**noun** (pl. **-ies**) archaic a herb garden.

herb bennet ▶**noun** another term for **WOOD AVENS**.
– ORIGIN late Middle English: from Old French *herbe beneite*, from medieval Latin *herba benedicta* 'blessed herb' (apparently first applied to a plant thought to ward off the Devil).

herb Christopher ▶**noun** the common Eurasian baneberry.
– ORIGIN late 16th cent.: translation of medieval Latin *herba Christophori* 'herb of St Christopher' (see **CHRISTOPHER, ST**).

herbed ▶**adjective** (of food) cooked, flavoured, or seasoned with herbs.

Herbert[1], Sir A. P. (1890–1970), English writer and politician; full name *Alan Patrick Herbert*. He wrote novels, items for the magazine *Punch*, and libretti for comic operas. As an MP, he was best known for campaigning to reform the divorce laws.

Herbert[2], George (1593–1633), English metaphysical poet. He was vicar of Bemerton, near Salisbury; his poems are pervaded by simple piety and reflect the spiritual conflicts he experienced before submitting his will to God.

herb Gerard /'dʒɛrɑːd/ ▶**noun** ground elder, which was formerly used to treat gout. Compare with **GOUTWEED**.
– ORIGIN named after St *Gerard* of Toul (*c.*935–94), invoked against gout.

herbicide /'həːbɪsʌɪd/ ▶**noun** a substance that is toxic to plants and is used to destroy unwanted vegetation.

herbivore /'həːbɪvɔː/ ▶**noun** an animal that feeds on plants.
– DERIVATIVES **herbivorous** /-'bɪv(ə)rəs/ adjective.
– ORIGIN mid 19th cent.: from Latin *herba* 'herb' + *-vore* (see **-VOROUS**).

herb Paris ▶**noun** a European woodland plant of the lily family, which has a single unbranched stem bearing a green and purple flower above four unstalked leaves.
• *Paris quadrifolia*, family Liliaceae (or Trilliaceae).
– ORIGIN translating medieval Latin *herba paris*, probably literally 'herb of a pair', referring to the resemblance of the four leaves to a true-love knot.

herb Robert ▶**noun** a common cranesbill with pungent-smelling red-stemmed leaves and pink flowers, native to north temperate regions.
• *Geranium robertianum*, family Geraniaceae.
– ORIGIN translating medieval latin *herba Roberti*, variously supposed to refer to *Robert* Duke of Normandy, St *Robert*, or St Rupert.

herb tea ▶**noun** an infusion of herbs as a refreshing or medicinal drink.

herby ▶**adjective** (**herbier**, **herbiest**) (of food or drink) containing or tasting or smelling of herbs.

Hercegovina variant spelling of **HERZEGOVINA**.

Herculaneum /ˌhəːkjʊ'leɪnɪəm/ an ancient Roman town, near Naples, on the lower slopes of Vesuvius. The volcano's eruption in AD 79 buried it deeply under volcanic ash, along with Pompeii, and thus largely preserved it until its accidental rediscovery by a well-digger in 1709.

Herculean /ˌhəːkjʊ'liːən, həː'kjuːlɪən/ ▶**adjective** requiring great strength or effort: *a Herculean task.*
■(of a person) muscular and strong.
– ORIGIN late 16th cent. (in the sense 'relating to Hercules'): from Latin *Herculeus* 'Hercules' + **-AN**.

Hercules /'həːkjʊliːz/ **1** Greek & Roman Mythology a hero of superhuman strength and courage who performed twelve immense tasks or 'labours' imposed on him and who after death was ranked among the gods.
■[as noun **a Hercules**] a man of exceptional strength or size.
2 Astronomy a large northern constellation, said to represent the kneeling figure of Hercules. It contains the brightest globular cluster in the northern hemisphere, but no bright stars.
■[as genitive **Herculis** /'həːkjʊlɪs/] used with preceding letter or numeral to designate a star in this constellation: *the star Delta Herculis.*
– ORIGIN Latin, from Greek *Hēraklēs*.

Hercules beetle ▶**noun** a very large tropical American rhinoceros beetle, the male of which has two long curved horns extending from the head and one from the thorax.
• *Dynastes hercules*, family Scarabaeidae.

Hercules' club ▶**noun** either of two tall prickly shrubs or small trees of the US:
• the southern prickly ash (*Zanthoxylum clava-herculis*, family Rutaceae). • another term for **DEVIL'S WALKING STICK**.

Hercynian /həː'sɪnɪən/ ▶**adjective** Geology of, relating to, or denoting a prolonged mountain-forming period (orogeny) in western Europe, eastern North America, and the Andes in the Upper Palaeozoic era, especially the Carboniferous and Permian periods.
■[as noun **the Hercynian**] the Hercynian orogeny.
– ORIGIN late 16th cent.: from Latin *Hercynia silva*; originally used by the ancient writers to designate an area of forested mountains in central Germany; later (from the late 19th cent.) applied in geology to the Harz Mountains formed in the Hercynian period.

herd ▶**noun** a large group of animals, especially hoofed mammals, that live, feed, or migrate together or are kept together as livestock: *a herd of elephants* | *large farms with big dairy herds.*
■derogatory a large group of people, typically with a shared characteristic: *I dodged herds of joggers and cyclists* | *he is not of the common herd.*
▶**verb** [with adverbial of direction] move in a particular direction: [with obj.] *the visitors were herded into two large halls* | [no obj.] *we all herded into a storage room.*
■[with obj.] keep or look after (livestock).
– ORIGIN Old English *heord*, of Germanic origin; related to German *Herde*.

herd book ▶**noun** Brit. a book recording the pedigrees of cattle, goats, or other livestock.

herdboy ▶**noun** a boy who looks after a herd of livestock.

herder ▶**noun** a person who looks after a herd of livestock or makes a living from keeping livestock, especially in open country.

herd instinct ▶**noun** an inclination in people or animals to behave or think like the majority.

herdsman ▶**noun** (pl. **-men**) the owner or keeper of a herd of domesticated animals.
■(**the Herdsman**) the constellation Boötes.

Herdwick /'həːdwɪk/ ▶**noun** a sheep of a hardy mountain breed from the north of England.
– ORIGIN early 19th cent.: from (now obsolete) *herdwick* 'pasture ground' (see **HERD**, **WICK**[2]), perhaps because this breed originated in the pasture grounds of Furness Abbey.

here ▶**adverb 1** in, at, or to this place or position: *they have lived here most of their lives* | *we leave here on the sixteenth* | [after prep.] *I'm getting out of here.*
■used when pointing or gesturing to indicate the place in mind: *sign here* | *I have here a letter from the chief.* ■used to draw attention to someone or something that has just arrived: ***here's*** *my brother* | ***here comes*** *the bus.* ■[with infinitive] used to indicate one's role in a particular situation: *I'm here to help you.* ■used to refer to existence in the world in general: *what are we all doing here?*
2 (usu. **here is/are**) used when introducing something or someone: *here's a dish that is simple and quick to make.*
■used when giving something to someone: *here's the money I promised you.*
3 used when indicating a time or situation that has arrived or is happening: *here is your opportunity.*
■used to refer to a particular point or aspect reached in an argument, situation, or activity: *here lies the key to the recovery* | *here we encounter the main problem.*
▶**exclamation 1** used to attract someone's attention: *here, let me hold it* | *here, what's going on?*
2 indicating one's presence in a roll-call.
– PHRASES **here and now** at this very moment; at the present time: *we're going to settle this here and now* | [as noun] *our obsession with* ***the here and now.*** **here and there** in various places: *small bushes scattered here and there.* **here goes** an expression indicating that one is about to start something difficult or exciting. **here's to someone/thing** used to wish health or success before drinking: *here's to us!* | *here's to your safe arrival.* **here today, gone tomorrow** soon over or forgotten; short-lived. **here we are** said on arrival at one's destination. **here we go again** said to indicate that the same events, typically undesirable ones, are recurring. **neither here nor there** of no importance or relevance.
– ORIGIN Old English *hēr*, of Germanic origin; related to Dutch and German *hier*, also to **HE**.

hereabouts (also **hereabout**) ▶**adverb** near this place: *there is little natural water hereabouts.*

hereafter ▶**adverb** formal from now on: *nothing I say hereafter is intended to relate to the second decision.*
■at some time in the future: *this court is in no way prejudging any such defence which may hereafter be raised.* ■after death: *a sermon about hope of* ***life hereafter.***
▶**noun** (**the hereafter**) life after death: *suffering is part of our preparation for the hereafter.*

hereat ▶**adverb** archaic as a result of this: *greatly distressed hereat, they declared themselves to deserve a fine.*

hereby ▶**adverb** formal as a result of this document or utterance: *all such warranties are hereby excluded.*

hereditable /hɪ'rɛdɪtəb(ə)l/ ▶**adjective** less common term for **HERITABLE**.
– ORIGIN late Middle English: from Old French, or from medieval Latin *hereditabilis*, from ecclesiastical Latin *hereditare* 'inherit', from Latin *heres*, *hered-* 'heir'.

hereditament /ˌhɛrɪ'dɪtəm(ə)nt, hɪ'rɛdɪt-/ ▶**noun** Law, dated any item of property, either a **corporeal hereditament** (land or a building) or an **incorporeal hereditament** (such as a rent or a right of way).
■an item of inheritance.
– ORIGIN late Middle English: from medieval Latin *hereditamentum*, from ecclesiastical Latin *hereditare* 'inherit', from Latin *heres*, *hered-* 'heir'.

hereditarian /hɪˌrɛdɪ'tɛːrɪən/ ▶**adjective** of or relating to the theory or belief that heredity is the

primary influence on human behaviour, intelligence, or other characteristics.
▶noun an advocate of such a view.
– DERIVATIVES **hereditarianism** noun.

hereditary /hɪˈrɛdɪt(ə)ri/ ▶adjective (of a title, office, or right) conferred by or based on inheritance: *the Queen's hereditary right to the throne.* ■[attrib.] (of a person) holding a position by inheritance: *a hereditary peer.* ■(of a characteristic or disease) determined by genetic factors and therefore able to be passed on from parents to their offspring or descendants. ■of or relating to inheritance: *the main objection to the hereditary principle is that such peers are not elected.* ■Mathematics (of a set) defined such that every element which has a given relation to a member of the set is also a member of the set.
– DERIVATIVES **hereditarily** adverb, **hereditariness** noun.
– ORIGIN late Middle English: from Latin *hereditarius*, from *hereditas* (see **HEREDITY**).

heredity /hɪˈrɛdɪti/ ▶noun [mass noun] **1** the passing on of physical or mental characteristics genetically from one generation to another. ■a person's ancestry: *he wears a Cossack tunic to emphasize his Russian heredity.* **2** inheritance of title, office, or right: *a second chamber whose membership is largely based on heredity.*
– ORIGIN late 18th cent.: from French *hérédité*, from Latin *hereditas* 'heirship', from *heres, hered-* 'heir'.

Hereford[1] /ˈhɛrɪfəd/ a city in west central England, administrative centre of the county of Herefordshire, on the River Wye; pop. 49,800 (1991).

Hereford[2] /ˈhɛrɪfəd/ ▶noun an animal of a breed of red and white beef cattle.

Hereford and Worcester a former county of west central England, formed in 1974 from the counties of Herefordshire and Worcestershire, which were reinstated in 1998.

Herefordshire a county of west central England, between 1974 and 1998 part of the county of Hereford and Worcester.

herein ▶adverb formal in this document or book. ■used to introduce something that depends on or arises from what has just been mentioned: *the statues are sensual to the point of erotic and herein lies their interest.*

hereinafter ▶adverb formal further on in this document: *grievous bodily harm (hereinafter GBH).*

hereinbefore ▶adverb formal before this point in this document.

hereof ▶adverb formal of this document: *in accordance with section 17 hereof.*

Herero /həˈrɛːrəʊ, -ˈrɪərəʊ/ ▶noun (pl. same or **-os**) **1** a member of a people living in Namibia, Angola, and Botswana. **2** [mass noun] the Bantu language of this people, with about 75,000 speakers.
▶adjective of or relating to the Herero or their language.
– ORIGIN a local name, from *Otshi-Herero*, the Herero word for the language.

heresiarch /hɛˈriːzɪɑːk/ ▶noun the founder of a heresy or the leader of a heretical sect.
– ORIGIN mid 16th cent.: via ecclesiastical Latin from ecclesiastical Greek *hairesiarkhēs* 'leader of a sect', from *hairesis* 'heretical sect, heresy' + *arkhēs* 'ruler'.

heresy /ˈhɛrɪsi/ ▶noun (pl. **-ies**) [mass noun] belief or opinion contrary to orthodox religious (especially Christian) doctrine: *Huss was burned for heresy* | [count noun] *the doctrine was denounced as a heresy by the pope.* ■opinion profoundly at odds with what is generally accepted: *the heresy of being uncommitted to the right political dogma* | [count noun] *the politician's heresies became the conventional wisdom of the day.*
– ORIGIN Middle English: from Old French *heresie*, based on Latin *haeresis*, from Greek *hairesis* 'choice' (in ecclesiastical Greek 'heretical sect'), from *haireomai* 'choose'.

heretic /ˈhɛrɪtɪk/ ▶noun a person believing in or practising religious heresy. ■a person holding an opinion at odds with what is generally accepted.
– DERIVATIVES **heretical** /hɪˈrɛtɪk(ə)l/ adjective, **heretically** adverb.
– ORIGIN Middle English: from Old French *heretique*, via ecclesiastical Latin from Greek *hairetikos* 'able to choose' (in ecclesiastical Greek, 'heretical'), from *haireomai* 'choose'.

hereto ▶adverb formal to this matter or document: *the written consent of each of the parties hereto* | *hereto is appended an estimate of the cost.*

heretofore ▶adverb formal before now: *diseases that heretofore were usually confined to rural areas.*

hereunder ▶adverb formal as provided for under the terms of this document: *all expenses incurred hereunder by the bank shall be recoverable.* ■further on in a document.

hereunto ▶adverb archaic or formal to this document: *signed in the presence of us both who have hereunto subscribed our names as witnesses.*

hereupon ▶adverb archaic after or as a result of this.

Hereward the Wake /ˈhɛrɪwəd/ (11th century), semi-legendary Anglo-Saxon rebel leader. A leader of Anglo-Saxon resistance to William I's new Norman regime, he is thought to have been responsible for an uprising centred on the Isle of Ely in 1070.
– ORIGIN *the Wake* apparently in the sense 'the watchful one'.

herewith ▶adverb formal with this letter: *I enclose herewith a copy of this discussion document.*

heriot /ˈhɛrɪət/ ▶noun Brit. historical a tribute paid to a lord out of the belongings of a tenant who died, often consisting of a live animal or, originally, military equipment that he had been lent during his lifetime.
– ORIGIN Old English *heregeatwa*, from *here* 'army' + *geatwa* 'trappings'.

heritable ▶adjective able to be inherited, in particular: ■Biology (of a characteristic) transmissible from parent to offspring. ■Law (of property) capable of being inherited by heirs-at-law. Compare with **MOVABLE** (in sense 2).
– DERIVATIVES **heritability** noun, **heritably** adverb.
– ORIGIN late Middle English: from Old French *heriter* 'inherit', from ecclesiastical Latin *hereditare*, from Latin *heres, hered-* 'heir'.

heritage ▶noun [in sing.] **1** property that is or may be inherited; an inheritance. ■valued objects and qualities such as historic buildings, unspoilt countryside, and cultural traditions that have been passed down from previous generations: *Europe's varied cultural heritage* | [mass noun] *the estuary has a sense of history and heritage.* ■[as modifier] denoting or relating to things of special architectural, historical, or natural value that are protected and preserved for the nation: *a heritage centre* | *heritage buildings.* ■[as modifier] N. Amer. (of a plant variety) not hybridized with another; old-fashioned: *heritage roses.* **2** archaic a special or individual possession; an allotted portion: *God's love remains your heritage.* ■God's chosen people (the people of Israel, or the Christian Church).
– ORIGIN Middle English: from Old French *heritage*, from *heriter* 'inherit' (see **HERITABLE**).

heritor /ˈhɛrɪtə/ ▶noun Scots Law a proprietor of a heritable object. ■a person who inherits.
– ORIGIN late Middle English: from Anglo-Norman French *heriter*, based on Latin *hereditarius* (see **HEREDITARY**). The spelling change in the 16th cent. was by association with words ending in **-OR**[1].

herky-jerky /ˈhəːkɪˌdʒəːki/ ▶adjective N. Amer. informal characterized by or moving in sudden stops and starts: *herky-jerky black and white newsreels.*
– ORIGIN late 20th cent.: reduplication of **JERKY**.

herl /həːl/ ▶noun a barb or filament of a feather used in dressing a fishing fly.
– ORIGIN late Middle English: apparently of Germanic origin and related to Middle Low German *harle*.

herm /həːm/ ▶noun a squared stone pillar with a carved head on top (typically of Hermes), used in ancient Greece as a boundary marker or a signpost.
– ORIGIN from the Greek name **HERMES**.

hermaphrodite /həːˈmafrədʌɪt/ ▶noun a person or animal having both male and female sex organs or other sexual characteristics, either abnormally or (in the case of some organisms) as the natural condition. ■Botany a plant having stamens and pistils in the same flower. ■archaic a person or thing combining opposite qualities or characteristics.
▶adjective of or denoting a person, animal, or plant of this kind: *hermaphrodite creatures in classical sculpture.*
– DERIVATIVES **hermaphroditic** adjective, **hermaphroditical** adjective, **hermaphroditism** noun.
– ORIGIN late Middle English: via Latin from Greek *hermaphroditos* (see **HERMAPHRODITUS**).

hermaphrodite brig ▶noun a two-masted sailing ship with a square-rigged foremast and, on the mainmast, a square topsail above a fore-and-aft gaff mainsail.

Hermaphroditus /həˌmafrəˈdʌɪtəs/ Greek Mythology a son of Hermes and Aphrodite, with whom the nymph Salmacis fell in love and prayed to be forever united. As a result Hermaphroditus and Salmacis became joined in a single body which retained characteristics of both sexes.

hermeneutic /ˌhəːmɪˈnjuːtɪk/ ▶adjective concerning interpretation, especially of the Bible or literary texts.
▶noun a method or theory of interpretation.
– DERIVATIVES **hermeneutical** adjective, **hermeneutically** adverb.
– ORIGIN late 17th cent.: from Greek *hermēneutikos*, from *hermēneuein* 'interpret'.

hermeneutics ▶plural noun [usu. treated as sing.] the branch of knowledge that deals with interpretation, especially of the Bible or literary texts.

Hermes /ˈhəːmiːz/ Greek Mythology the son of Zeus and Maia, the messenger of the gods, and god of merchants, thieves, and oratory. He was portrayed as a herald equipped for travelling, with broad-brimmed hat, winged shoes, and a winged rod. Roman equivalent **MERCURY**.
– ORIGIN probably from Greek *herma* 'heap of stones': from early times he was represented by a carved stock or stone and was identified with **THOTH**.

Hermes Trismegistus /ˌtrɪsməˈdʒɪstəs/ a legendary figure regarded by Neoplatonists and others as the author of certain works on astrology, magic, and alchemy.
– ORIGIN Latin, 'thrice-greatest Hermes', in reference to **THOTH**, identified with **HERMES**.

hermetic /həːˈmɛtɪk/ ▶adjective **1** (of a seal or closure) complete and airtight. ■insulated or protected from outside influences: *a hermetic society.* **2** (also **Hermetic**) of or relating to an ancient occult tradition encompassing alchemy, astrology, and theosophy. ■esoteric; cryptic: *obscure and hermetic poems.*
– DERIVATIVES **hermetically** adverb, **hermeticism** noun.
– ORIGIN mid 17th cent. (in sense 2): from modern Latin *hermeticus*, from **HERMES**, identified with **THOTH**, regarded as the founder of alchemy and astrology.

hermit ▶noun **1** a person living in solitude as a religious discipline. ■any person living in solitude or seeking to do so. **2** a hummingbird found in the shady lower layers of tropical forests, foraging along a regular route. • *Phaethornis* and other genera, family Trochilidae: several species.
– DERIVATIVES **hermitic** adjective.
– ORIGIN Middle English: from Old French *hermite*, from late Latin *eremita*, from Greek *erēmitēs*, from *erēmos* 'solitary'.

hermitage ▶noun **1** the dwelling of a hermit, especially when small and remote. **2** (**the Hermitage**) a major art museum in St Petersburg, Russia, containing among its collections those begun by Catherine the Great. [ORIGIN: named with reference to the 'retreat' in which the empress displayed her treasures to her friends.]
– ORIGIN Middle English: from Old French, from *hermite* (see **HERMIT**).

hermit crab ▶noun a crab with a soft asymmetrical abdomen, which lives in a cast-off mollusc shell for protection. In several kinds the shell becomes covered with sponges, sea anemones, or bryozoans. • Superfamily Paguroidea.

Hermitian /həːˈmɪtɪən/ ▶adjective Mathematics denoting or relating to a matrix in which those pairs of elements which are symmetrically placed with respect to the principal diagonal are complex conjugates.
– ORIGIN early 20th cent.: from the name of Charles *Hermite* (1822–1905), French mathematician, + **-IAN**.

hermit thrush ▶ **noun** a small migratory North American thrush, noted for its melodious song.
• *Catharus guttatus*, family Turdidae.

Hermosillo /ˌɛːməˈsiːjəʊ, -ˈsiːljəʊ/ a city in NW Mexico, capital of the state of Sonora; pop. 449,470 (1990).

hernia /ˈhəːnɪə/ ▶ **noun** (pl. **hernias** or **herniae** /-nɪiː/) a condition in which part of an organ is displaced and protrudes through the wall of the cavity containing it (often involving the intestine at a weak point in the abdominal wall).
– DERIVATIVES **hernial** adjective.
– ORIGIN late Middle English: from Latin.

herniate /ˈhəːnɪeɪt/ ▶ **verb** [no obj.] [usu. as adj. **herniated**] (of an organ) suffer a hernia: *a herniated disc.*
– DERIVATIVES **herniation** noun.

Herning /ˈhəːnɪŋ/ a city in central Jutland, Denmark; pop. 56,690 (1991).

Hero[1] Greek Mythology a priestess of Aphrodite at Sestos on the European shore of the Hellespont, whose lover Leander, a youth of Abydos on the opposite shore, swam the strait nightly to visit her. One stormy night he was drowned and Hero in grief threw herself into the sea.

Hero[2] (1st century), Greek mathematician and inventor; known as **Hero of Alexandria**. His surviving works are important as a source for ancient practical mathematics and mechanics. He described a number of hydraulic, pneumatic, and other mechanical devices, including elementary applications of the power of steam.

hero ▶ **noun** (pl. **-oes**) a person, typically a man, who is admired or idealized for their courage, outstanding achievements, or noble qualities: *a war hero.*
■ the chief male character in a book, play, or film, who is typically identified with good qualities, and with whom the reader is expected to sympathize. ■ (in mythology and folklore) a person of superhuman qualities and often semi-divine origin, in particular one of those whose exploits and dealings with the gods were the subject of ancient Greek myths and legends. ■ (also **hero sandwich**) chiefly N. Amer. another term for **HOAGIE**.
– ORIGIN Middle English (with mythological reference): via Latin from Greek *hērōs*.

Herod /ˈhɛrəd/ the name of four rulers of ancient Palestine:
■ **Herod the Great** (*c.*74–4 BC), ruled 37–4 BC. According to the New Testament, Jesus was born during his reign, and he ordered the massacre of the innocents (Matt. 2:16).
■ **Herod Antipas** (22 BC–*c.*40 AD), son of Herod the Great, tetrarch of Galilee and Peraea 4 BC–AD 40. He married Herodias and was responsible for the beheading of John the Baptist. According to the New Testament (Luke 23:7), Pilate sent Jesus to be questioned by him before the Crucifixion.
■ **Herod Agrippa I** (10 BC–AD 44), grandson of Herod the Great, king of Judaea AD 41–4. He imprisoned St Peter and put St James the Great to death.
■ **Herod Agrippa II** (AD 27–*c.*93), son of Herod Agrippa I, king of various territories in northern Palestine 50–*c.*93. He presided over the trial of St Paul (Acts 25:13 ff.).
– DERIVATIVES **Herodian** /hɛˈrəʊdɪən/ adjective & noun.

Herodotus /hɪˈrɒdətəs/ (5th century BC), Greek historian. He was the first historian to collect his materials systematically, test their accuracy to a certain extent, and arrange them in a well-constructed and vivid narrative.

heroic ▶ **adjective** having the characteristics of a hero or heroine; very brave: *heroic deeds | a few heroic individuals.*
■ of or representing heroes or heroines: *early medieval heroic poetry.* ■ (of language or a work of art) grand or grandiose in scale or intention: *one passes under pyramids and obelisks, all on a heroic scale.* ■ Sculpture (of a statue) larger than life size but less than colossal.
▶ **noun** (**heroics**) **1** behaviour or talk that is bold or dramatic, especially excessively or unexpectedly so: *the makeshift team performed heroics.*
2 short for **HEROIC VERSE**.
– DERIVATIVES **heroically** adverb.
– ORIGIN late Middle English: from Old French *heroique* or Latin *heroicus*, from Greek *hērōikos* 'relating to heroes', from *hērōs* 'hero'.

heroic age ▶ **noun** the period in Greek history and legend before the Trojan War and its aftermath, in which the legends of the heroes were set.

heroic couplet ▶ **noun** (in verse) a pair of rhyming iambic pentameters, much used by Chaucer and the poets of the 17th and 18th centuries such as Alexander Pope.

heroic verse ▶ **noun** [mass noun] a type of verse used for epic or heroic subjects, such as the hexameter, iambic pentameter, or alexandrine.

heroin ▶ **noun** [mass noun] a highly addictive analgesic drug derived from morphine, often used illicitly as a narcotic producing euphoria.
• Alternative name: **diacetylmorphine**; chem. formula: $C_{17}H_{17}NO(C_2H_3O_2)_2$.
– ORIGIN late 19th cent.: from German *Heroin*, from Latin *heros* 'hero' (because of its effects on the user's self-esteem).

heroine ▶ **noun** a woman admired or idealized for her courage, outstanding achievements, or noble qualities: *she was the heroine of a materialist generation.*
■ the chief female character in a book, play, or film, who is typically identified with good qualities, and with whom the reader is expected to sympathize. ■ (in mythology and folklore) a woman of superhuman qualities and often semi-divine origin, in particular one whose dealings with the gods were the subject of ancient Greek myths and legends.
– ORIGIN mid 17th cent. (in the sense 'demi-goddess, venerated woman'): from French *héroïne* or Latin *heroina*, from Greek *hērōinē*, feminine of *hērōs* 'hero'.

heroism ▶ **noun** [mass noun] great bravery.
– ORIGIN early 18th cent.: from French *héroïsme*, from *héros*, from Latin *heros* (see **HERO**).

heroize /ˈhɪərəʊʌɪz, ˈhɛr-/ (also **-ise**) ▶ **verb** [with obj.] (often **be heroized**) treat or represent as a hero: *the father is heroized for long forbearance.*

heron ▶ **noun** a large fish-eating wading bird with long legs, a long S-shaped neck, and a long pointed bill.
• Family Ardeidae (the **heron family**): several genera and numerous species, e.g. the Old World **grey heron** (*Ardea cinerea*). The heron family also includes the bitterns and egrets.
– ORIGIN Middle English: from Old French, of Germanic origin.

heronry ▶ **noun** (pl. **-ies**) a breeding colony of herons, typically in a group of trees.

Herophilus /hɪəˈrɒfɪləs/ (4th–3rd centuries BC), Greek anatomist. He is regarded as the father of human anatomy for his fundamental discoveries concerning the anatomy of the brain, eye, and reproductive organs. Herophilus also studied the physiology of nerves, arteries, and veins.

hero's welcome ▶ **noun** an enthusiastic welcome for someone who has done something brave or praiseworthy.

hero worship ▶ **noun** [mass noun] excessive admiration for someone.
■ (in ancient Greece) the worship of superhuman heroes.
▶ **verb** (**hero-worship**) [with obj.] admire (someone) excessively.
– DERIVATIVES **hero-worshipper** noun.

herp ▶ **noun** short for **HERPTILE**.

herpes /ˈhəːpiːz/ ▶ **noun** [mass noun] any of a group of virus diseases caused by herpesviruses, affecting the skin (often with blisters) or the nervous system.
– DERIVATIVES **herpetic** adjective.
– ORIGIN late Middle English (originally used also of other skin conditions): via Latin from Greek *herpēs* 'shingles', literally 'creeping', from *herpein* 'to creep'.

herpes simplex ▶ **noun** [mass noun] a viral infection caused by a group of herpesviruses, which may produce cold sores, genital inflammation, or conjunctivitis.

herpesvirus /ˈhəːpiːzˌvʌɪrəs/ ▶ **noun** Medicine any of a group of DNA viruses causing herpes and other diseases.

herpes zoster /ˈzɒstə/ ▶ **noun** [mass noun] medical name for **SHINGLES**.
■ a herpesvirus that causes shingles and chickenpox.
– ORIGIN late Middle English: from **HERPES** and Latin *zoster*, from Greek *zōstēr* 'girdle, shingles'.

herpetofauna /ˈhəːpɪtə(ʊ),fɔːnə/ ▶ **noun** [mass noun] Zoology the reptiles and amphibians of a particular region, habitat, or geological period.
– DERIVATIVES **herpetofaunal** adjective.
– ORIGIN modern Latin, from Greek *herpeton* 'creeping thing, reptile' + **FAUNA**.

herpetology /ˌhəːpɪˈtɒlədʒi/ ▶ **noun** [mass noun] the branch of zoology concerned with reptiles and amphibians.
– DERIVATIVES **herpetological** adjective, **herpetologist** noun.
– ORIGIN early 19th cent.: from Greek *herpeton* 'reptile' (from *herpein* 'to creep') + **-LOGY**.

herptile /ˈhəːptʌɪl/ ▶ **noun** a reptile or amphibian.
– ORIGIN blend of **HERPETOLOGY** and **REPTILE**.

Herr /hɛː, German hɛr/ ▶ **noun** (pl. **Herren** /ˈhɛr(ə)n/) a title or form of address used of or to a German-speaking man, corresponding to *Mr* and also used before a rank or occupation.
■ a German man.
– ORIGIN German, from Old High German *hērro*, comparative of *hēr* 'exalted'.

Herrenvolk /ˈhɛr(ə)nfɒlk, -fəʊk/ ▶ **noun** the German nation as considered by the Nazis to be innately superior to others.
– ORIGIN German, 'master race', from *Herr* 'master' + *Volk* 'people, folk'.

Herrick /ˈhɛrɪk/, Robert (1591–1674), English poet. He is best known for his collection *Hesperides* (1648), containing both secular and religious poems.

herring ▶ **noun** a fairly small silvery fish which is most abundant in coastal waters and is of great commercial importance in many parts of the world.
• *Clupea* and other genera, family Clupeidae (the **herring family**): several species, in particular (*C. harengus*), of the North Atlantic. The herring family also includes the sprats, shads, and pilchards.
– ORIGIN Old English *hǣring*, *hēring*, of West Germanic origin; related to Dutch *haring* and German *Hering*.

herringbone ▶ **noun** [mass noun] [usu. as modifier] **1** an arrangement or design consisting of columns of short parallel lines, with all the lines in one column sloping one way and all the lines in the next column sloping the other way so as to resemble the bones in a fish, used especially in the weave of cloth or the placing of bricks: *a grey herringbone tweed jacket.*
■ (also **herringbone stitch**) a cross stitch with a pattern resembling such an arrangement, used in embroidery or for securing an edge.
2 Skiing a method of ascending a slope by walking facing up it with the skis pointing outwards.
▶ **verb 1** [with obj.] mark with a herringbone pattern.
■ work with a herringbone stitch.
2 [no obj., with adverbial of direction] Skiing ascend a slope using the herringbone technique.

herringbone parlour ▶ **noun** a milking parlour in which the cows stand at an angle along each side of a central operator's pit, forming a herringbone pattern.

herring gull ▶ **noun** a gull with grey black-tipped wings, abundant and widespread in both Eurasia and North America.
• *Larus argentatus*, family Laridae.

Herriot /ˈhɛrɪət/, James (1916–1995), English short-story writer and veterinary surgeon; pseudonym of *James Alfred Wight*. His experiences as a vet in North Yorkshire inspired a series of stories including *All Creatures Great and Small* (1972).

Herrnhuter /ˈhɛːnhuːtə, ˈhɛːr(ə)n-/ ▶ **noun** a member of a Moravian Church.
– ORIGIN mid 18th cent.: German, from *Herrnhut* (literally 'the Lord's keeping'), the name of the first German settlement of the Moravian Church.

hers ▶ **possessive pronoun** used to refer to a thing or things belonging to or associated with a female person or animal previously mentioned: *his eyes met hers | the choice was hers | friends **of hers** warned her.*

Herschel[1] /ˈhəːʃ(ə)l/, Sir (Frederick) William (1738–1822), German-born British astronomer. His cataloguing of the skies resulted in the discovery of the planet Uranus. He was the first to appreciate the great remoteness of stars and developed the idea that the sun belongs to the star system of the Milky Way.

Herschel[2] /ˈhəːʃ(ə)l/, Sir John (Frederick William) (1792–1871), English astronomer and physicist, son of William. He extended the sky survey to the southern hemisphere, carried out pioneering work in photography, and made contributions to meteorology and geophysics.

herself ▶ **pronoun** [third person singular] **1** [reflexive] used as the object of a verb or preposition to refer to a female person or animal previously mentioned as

the subject of the clause: *she had to defend herself* | *Jo made herself a cup of tea.*
2 [emphatic] she or her personally (used to emphasize a particular female person or animal mentioned): *she told me herself.*
– ORIGIN Old English (see HER, SELF).

herstory /ˈhəːst(ə)ri/ ▶ noun (pl. **-ies**) [mass noun] history viewed from a female or specifically feminist perspective.
– ORIGIN 1970s: from HER + STORY[1], analogous formation based on the form *history*.

Hertford /ˈhɑːtfəd/ the county town of Hertfordshire; pop. 21,400 (1981).

Hertfordshire a county of SE England, one of the Home Counties; county town, Hertford.

Herts. /hɑːts/ ▶ abbreviation for Hertfordshire.

Hertz /həːts, German hɛrts/, Heinrich Rudolf (1857–94), German physicist and pioneer of radio communication. He continued the work of Maxwell on electromagnetic waves and was the first to broadcast and receive radio waves. Hertz also showed that light and radiant heat were electromagnetic in nature.

hertz /həːts/ (abbrev.: **Hz**) ▶ noun (pl. same) the SI unit of frequency, equal to one cycle per second.
– ORIGIN late 19th cent.: named after H. R. HERTZ.

Hertzian wave /ˈhəːtsɪən/ ▶ noun former term for RADIO WAVE.

Hertzsprung–Russell diagram /ˈhəːts,sprʌŋ/ ▶ noun Astronomy a two-dimensional graph, devised independently by Ejnar Hertzsprung (1873–1967) and Henry Norris Russell (1877–1957), in which the absolute magnitudes of stars are plotted against their spectral types. Stars are found to occupy only certain regions of such a diagram.

Herut /heˈruːt/ a right-wing Israeli political party founded by Menachem Begin in 1948, from the remains of the Irgun group. Herut was one of the parties that combined to form the Likud coalition in 1973.
– ORIGIN Hebrew, 'freedom'.

Herzegovina /ˌhɛːtsəˈɡɒvɪnə, -ɡəˈviːnə/ (also **Hercegovina**) a region in the Balkans forming the southern part of Bosnia–Herzegovina and separated from the Adriatic by part of Croatia. Its chief town is Mostar.
– DERIVATIVES **Herzegovinian** adjective & noun.

Herzl /ˈhəːts(ə)l/, Theodor (1860–1904), Hungarian-born journalist, dramatist, and Zionist leader. The founder of the Zionist movement (1897), he worked for most of his life as a writer and journalist in Vienna.

Herzog /ˈhəːtsɒɡ, German ˈhɛrtsɔːk/, Werner (b.1942), German film director; born *Werner Stipetic*. Themes of remoteness in time and space are dominant elements throughout his films, which include *Aguirre, Wrath of God* (1972) and *Fitzcarraldo* (1982).

he's ▶ contraction of ■ he is: *he's going to speak.* ■ he has: *he's given up his job.*

Heshvan /ˈhɛʃv(ə)n/ ▶ noun variant spelling of HESVAN.

Hesiod /ˈhiːsɪəd/ (c.700 BC), Greek poet. One of the earliest known Greek poets, he wrote the *Theogony*, a hexametric poem on the genealogies of the gods, and *Works and Days*, which gave moral and practical advice and was the chief model for later ancient didactic poetry.

hesitant ▶ adjective tentative, unsure, or slow in acting or speaking: *clients are hesitant about buying* | *her slow, hesitant way of speaking.*
– DERIVATIVES **hesitance** noun, **hesitancy** noun, **hesitantly** adverb.
– ORIGIN late Middle English: from Latin *haesitant-* 'being undecided', from the verb *haesitare* (see HESITATE).

hesitate ▶ verb [no obj.] pause before saying or doing something, especially through uncertainty: *she hesitated, unsure of what to say* | *one hesitates over publicizing these things.* ■ [with infinitive] be reluctant to do something: *he hesitated to spoil the mood by being inquisitive.*
– PHRASES **he who hesitates is lost** proverb delay or vacillation may have unfortunate or disastrous consequences.
– DERIVATIVES **hesitater** noun, **hesitatingly** adverb.
– ORIGIN early 17th cent.: from Latin *haesitat-* 'stuck

fast, left undecided', from the verb *haesitare*, from *haerere* 'stick, stay'.

hesitation ▶ noun [mass noun] the action of pausing or hesitating before saying or doing something: *she answered without hesitation.*
■ [usu. with negative] doubt or reluctance: *I have no hesitation in recommending him.*
– ORIGIN early 17th cent.: from Latin *haesitatio(n)-*, from *haesitare* (see HESITATE).

Hesperian /hɛˈspɪərɪən/ ▶ adjective Greek Mythology of or concerning the Hesperides.
■ poetic/literary western.
– ORIGIN late 15th cent.: from Latin *hesperius* (from Greek *Hesperia*, from *hesperos* 'land of the west', from *hesperos* 'western' (see HESPERUS)) + -AN.

Hesperides /hɛˈspɛrɪdiːz/ Greek Mythology a group of nymphs who were guardians, with the aid of a watchful dragon, of a tree of golden apples in a garden located beyond the Atlas Mountains at the western border of Oceanus, the river encircling the world. One of the labours of Hercules was to fetch the golden apples.

hesperidium /ˌhɛspəˈrɪdɪəm/ ▶ noun (pl. **hesperidia** /-dɪə/) Botany a fruit with sectioned pulp inside a separable rind, e.g. an orange or grapefruit.
– ORIGIN mid 19th cent.: based on *Hesperideae*, former name of an order of plants containing citrus fruits, named after the golden apples of the Hesperides (see HESPERIDES) + -IUM.

Hesperus /ˈhɛspərəs/ ▶ noun poetic/literary the planet Venus.
– ORIGIN Latin, from Greek *hesperos* 'western', (as a noun) 'the evening star'.

Hess[1] /hɛs/, Dame Myra (1890–1965), English pianist. She was noted for her performances of the music of Schumann, Beethoven, Mozart, and Bach.

Hess[2] /hɛs/, Victor Francis (1883–1964), Austrian-born American physicist; born *Victor Franz Hess*. He showed that some ionizing radiation (later termed cosmic rays) was extraterrestrial in origin but did not come from the sun. Nobel Prize for Physics (1936, shared with C. D. Anderson).

Hess[3] /hɛs/, (Walther Richard) Rudolf (1894–1987), German Nazi politician, deputy leader of the Nazi Party 1934–41. In 1941, secretly and on his own initiative, he parachuted into Scotland to negotiate peace with Britain. He was imprisoned for the duration of the war and, at the Nuremberg war trials, sentenced to life imprisonment in Spandau prison, Berlin, where he died.

Hesse[1] /hɛs/ a state of western Germany; capital, Wiesbaden. German name **HESSEN** /ˈhɛsn/.
– DERIVATIVES **Hessian** adjective & noun.

Hesse[2] /hɛs, ˈhɛsə/, Hermann (1877–1962), German-born Swiss novelist and poet. His work reflects his interest in spiritual values as expressed in Eastern religion and his involvement in Jungian analysis. Notable works: *Siddhartha* (1922), *Der Steppenwolf* (1927), and *The Glass Bead Game* (1943). Nobel Prize for Literature (1946).

hessian ▶ noun [mass noun] a strong, coarse fabric made from hemp or jute, used for sacks.
– ORIGIN late 19th cent.: from *Hesse* (see HESSE[1]) + -IAN.

Hessian boot ▶ noun a high tasselled leather boot, originally worn by Hessian troops.

Hessian fly ▶ noun a gall midge whose larvae are a pest of cereal crops, occurring in all wheat-growing areas.
● *Mayetiola destructor*, family Cecidomyiidae.
– ORIGIN late 18th cent.: so named because it was supposed (erroneously) to have been carried to America by Hessian troops during the War of Independence.

hest ▶ noun archaic form of BEHEST.
– ORIGIN Old English *hæs*, of Germanic origin; related to HIGHT. The spelling change in Middle English was by association with abstract nouns ending in *-t*.

Hesvan /ˈhɛsv(ə)n/ (also **Chesvan, Heshvan**) ▶ noun (in the Jewish calendar) the second month of the civil and eighth of the religious year, usually coinciding with parts of October and November.
– ORIGIN from Hebrew *ḥešwān*.

Hesychast /ˈhɛsɪkast/ ▶ noun historical a member of a movement dedicated to interior prayer, originating among the Orthodox monks of Mount Athos in the 14th century.

– ORIGIN mid 19th cent.: from late Greek *hēsukhastēs* 'hermit', from *hēsukhazein* 'be still', from *hēsukhos* 'still'.

het ▶ adjective & noun informal short for HETERO-SEXUAL.

hetaera /hɪˈtɪərə/ (also **hetaira** /-ˈtʌɪrə/) ▶ noun (pl. **hetaeras** or **hetaerae** /-ˈtɪəriː/ or **hetairas** or **hetairai** /-ˈtʌɪrʌɪ/) a courtesan or mistress, especially one in ancient Greece akin to the modern geisha.
– ORIGIN from Greek *hetaira*, feminine of *hetairos* 'companion'.

hetero /ˈhɛt(ə)rəʊ/ ▶ adjective & noun informal short for HETEROSEXUAL.

hetero- ▶ combining form other; different: *heteropolar* | *heterosexual*. Often contrasted with HOMO-.
– ORIGIN from Greek *heteros* 'other'.

heteroaromatic /ˌhɛtərəʊarəˈmatɪk/ ▶ adjective Chemistry denoting an organic compound with a ring structure which is both heterocyclic and aromatic.

heterocercal /ˌhɛtərəʊˈsəːkəl/ ▶ adjective Zoology (of a fish's tail) having unequal upper and lower lobes, usually with the vertebral column passing into the upper. Contrasted with DIPHYCERCAL, HOMOCERCAL.
– ORIGIN mid 19th cent.: from HETERO- 'other' + Greek *kerkos* 'tail'.

heterochromatic /ˌhɛt(ə)rəʊkrəˈmatɪk/ ▶ adjective
1 of several different colours or (in physics) wavelengths.
2 Biochemistry of or relating to heterochromatin.

heterochromatin /ˌhɛtərəʊˈkrəʊmətɪn/ ▶ noun [mass noun] Biology chromosome material of different density from normal (usually greater), in which the activity of the genes is modified or suppressed. Compare with EUCHROMATIN.

heteroclite /ˈhɛt(ə)rə(ʊ)klʌɪt/ formal ▶ adjective abnormal or irregular.
▶ noun an abnormal thing or person.
■ an irregularly declined word, especially a Greek or Latin noun.
– DERIVATIVES **heteroclitic** adjective.
– ORIGIN late 15th cent.: via late Latin from Greek *heteroklitos*, from *heteros* 'other' + *-klitos* 'inflected' (from *klinein* 'to lean, inflect').

heterocyclic /ˌhɛt(ə)rə(ʊ)ˈsʌɪklɪk, -ˈsɪklɪk/ ▶ adjective Chemistry denoting a compound whose molecule contains a ring of atoms of at least two elements (one of which is generally carbon).

heterodox /ˈhɛt(ə)rə(ʊ)dɒks/ ▶ adjective not conforming with accepted or orthodox standards or beliefs: *heterodox views.*
– DERIVATIVES **heterodoxy** noun.
– ORIGIN early 17th cent. (originally as a noun denoting an unorthodox opinion): via late Latin from Greek *heterodoxos*, from *heteros* 'other' + *doxa* 'opinion'.

heterodyne /ˈhɛt(ə)rə(ʊ)dʌɪn/ Electronics ▶ adjective of or relating to the production of a lower frequency from the combination of two almost equal high frequencies, as used in radio transmission.
▶ verb [with obj.] combine (a high-frequency signal) with another to produce a lower frequency in this way.
– ORIGIN early 20th cent.: from HETERO- 'other' + *-dyne*, suffix formed irregularly from Greek *dunamis* 'power'.

heterogametic /ˌhɛt(ə)rə(ʊ)ɡəˈmɛtɪk/ ▶ adjective Biology denoting the sex which has sex chromosomes that differ in morphology, resulting in two different kinds of gamete, e.g. (in mammals) the male and (in birds) the female. The opposite of HOMOGAMETIC.

heterogamy /ˌhɛt(ə)rəˈrɒɡəmi/ ▶ noun [mass noun] **1** chiefly Zoology the alternation of generations, especially between sexual and parthenogenetic generations.
2 Botany a state in which the flowers of a plant are of two or more types. Compare with HOMOGAMY (in sense 2).
■ another term for ANISOGAMY.
3 marriage between people from different sociological or educational backgrounds. Compare with HOMOGAMY (in sense 1).
– DERIVATIVES **heterogamous** adjective.

heterogeneous /ˌhɛt(ə)rə(ʊ)ˈdʒiːnɪəs, -ˈdʒɛn-/ ▶ adjective diverse in character or content: *a large and heterogeneous collection.*
■ Chemistry of or denoting a process involving substances in different phases (solid, liquid, or gaseous):

heterogeneous catalysis. ■ Mathematics incommensurable through being of different kinds, degrees, or dimensions.
– DERIVATIVES **heterogeneity** /-dʒɪˈniːɪti, -ˈneɪti/ noun, **heterogeneously** adverb, **heterogeneousness** noun.
– ORIGIN early 17th cent.: from medieval Latin *heterogeneus*, from Greek *heterogenēs*, from *heteros* 'other' + *genos* 'a kind'.

USAGE The correct spelling is **heterogeneous** but a fairly common misspelling is **heterogenous**. The reason for the error probably relates to the pronunciation, which, in rapid speech, often misses out the extra e. In the British National Corpus, the misspelling occurs in 5 per cent of citations for the word.

heteroglossia /ˌhɛtərəʊˈɡlɒsɪə/ ▶ noun [mass noun] the presence of two or more voices or expressed viewpoints in a text or other artistic work.

heterograft ▶ noun another term for XENOGRAFT.

heterologous /ˌhɛtəˈrɒləɡəs/ ▶ adjective chiefly Medicine & Biology not homologous: *heterologous antiserum*.
– DERIVATIVES **heterology** noun.

heteromerous /ˌhɛtəˈrɒm(ə)rəs/ ▶ adjective Biology having or composed of parts that differ in number or position.

heteromorphic /ˌhɛt(ə)rə(ʊ)ˈmɔːfɪk/ ▶ adjective Biology occurring in two or more different forms, especially at different stages in the life cycle.
– DERIVATIVES **heteromorph** noun, **heteromorphy** noun.

heteromorphism /ˌhɛt(ə)rə(ʊ)ˈmɔːfɪz(ə)m/ ▶ noun [mass noun] Biology the quality or condition of existing in various forms: *chromosomal heteromorphism*.

heteronomous /ˌhɛtəˈrɒnəməs/ ▶ adjective subject to a law or standard external to itself.
■ (in Kantian moral philosophy) acting in accordance with one's desires rather than reason or moral duty. Compare with AUTONOMOUS. ■ subject to different laws.
– DERIVATIVES **heteronomy** noun.

heteronym /ˈhɛtərə(ʊ)nɪm/ ▶ noun Linguistics **1** each of two or more words which are spelled identically but have different sounds and meanings, such as *tear* meaning 'rip' and *tear* meaning 'liquid from the eye'.
2 each of two or more words which are used to refer to the identical thing in different geographical areas of a speech community, such as *nappy* and *diaper*.
3 each of two words having the same meaning but derived from unrelated sources, for example *preface* and *foreword*. Contrasted with PARONYM.
– DERIVATIVES **heteronymic** adjective, **heteronymous** adjective.

heteropolar /ˌhɛtərəʊˈpəʊlə/ ▶ adjective chiefly Physics characterized by opposite or alternating polarity.
■ (especially of an electric motor) with an armature passing north and south magnetic poles alternately.

Heteroptera /ˌhɛtəˈrɒpt(ə)rə/ ▶ plural noun Entomology a group of true bugs comprising those in which the forewings are non-uniform, having a thickened base and membranous tip. The predatory and water bugs belong to this group, as well as many plant bugs. Compare with HOMOPTERA.
● Suborder Heteroptera, order Hemiptera.
■ [as plural noun **heteroptera**] bugs of this group.
– DERIVATIVES **heteropteran** noun & adjective, **heteropterous** adjective.
– ORIGIN modern Latin (plural), from Greek *heteros* 'other' + *pteron* 'wing'.

heterosexism ▶ noun [mass noun] discrimination or prejudice against homosexuals on the assumption that heterosexuality is the normal sexual orientation.
– DERIVATIVES **heterosexist** adjective.

heterosexual ▶ adjective (of a person) sexually attracted to people of the opposite sex.
■ involving or characterized by sexual attraction between people of the opposite sex: *heterosexual relationships*.
▶ noun a heterosexual person.
– DERIVATIVES **heterosexuality** noun, **heterosexually** adverb.

heterosis /ˌhɛtəˈrəʊsɪs/ ▶ noun technical term for HYBRID VIGOUR.
– ORIGIN early 20th cent.: from Greek *heterōsis* 'alteration', from *heteros* 'other'.

heterostyly /ˈhɛtərə(ʊ)ˌstʌɪli/ ▶ noun [mass noun] Botany the condition (e.g. in primroses) of having styles of different lengths relative to the stamens in the flowers of different individual plants, to reduce self-fertilization.
– DERIVATIVES **heterostylous** adjective.
– ORIGIN late 19th cent.: from HETERO- 'different' + Greek *stulos* 'column' + -Y³.

heterotic /ˌhɛtəˈrɒtɪk/ ▶ adjective **1** Biology of or relating to hybrid vigour (heterosis).
2 Physics of or relating to a theory of cosmic strings combining elements of two earlier models.

heterotransplant ▶ noun another term for XENOGRAFT.

heterotroph /ˈhɛt(ə)rə(ʊ)trəʊf, -ˈtrɒf/ ▶ noun Biology an organism deriving its nutritional requirements from complex organic substances. Compare with AUTOTROPH.
– DERIVATIVES **heterotrophic** adjective, **heterotrophy** noun.
– ORIGIN early 20th cent.: from HETERO- 'other' + Greek *trophos* 'feeder'.

heterozygote /ˌhɛt(ə)rə(ʊ)ˈzʌɪɡəʊt/ ▶ noun Genetics an individual having two different alleles of a particular gene or genes, and so giving rise to varying offspring. Compare with HOMOZYGOTE.
– DERIVATIVES **heterozygosity** noun, **heterozygous** adjective.

hetman /ˈhɛtmən/ ▶ noun (pl. **-men**) a Polish or Cossack military commander.
– ORIGIN Polish, probably from German *Hauptmann* 'captain'.

het up ▶ adjective [predic.] informal angry and agitated: *her husband is all het up about something*.
– ORIGIN mid 19th cent.: from dialect *het* 'heated, hot', surviving in Scots and northern English dialect.

heuchera /ˈhɔɪkərə, ˈhjuːk-/ ▶ noun a North American plant with dark green round or heart-shaped leaves and slender stems of tiny flowers.
● Genus *Heuchera*, family Saxifragaceae: many species, in particular *H. sanguinea*, with many ornamental cultivars.
– ORIGIN modern Latin, named after Johann H. von *Heucher* (1677–1747), German botanist.

heuriger /ˈhɔɪrɪɡə/ (also **heurige**) ▶ noun (pl. **heurigen** /-ɡ(ə)n/) [mass noun] (especially in Austria) wine from the latest harvest.
■ [count noun] an establishment where this is served.
– ORIGIN Austrian German, literally 'this year's (wine)'.

heuristic /ˌhjʊ(ə)ˈrɪstɪk/ ▶ adjective enabling a person to discover or learn something for themselves.
■ Computing proceeding to a solution by trial and error or by rules that are only loosely defined.
▶ noun a heuristic process or method.
■ (**heuristics**) [usu. treated as sing.] the study and use of heuristic techniques.
– DERIVATIVES **heuristically** adverb.
– ORIGIN early 19th cent.: formed irregularly from Greek *heuriskein* 'find'.

hevea /ˈhiːvɪə/ ▶ noun a South American tree of a genus which comprises the rubber trees.
● Genus *Hevea*, family Euphorbiaceae.
– ORIGIN modern Latin, from Quechua *hyeve*.

Hevesy /ˈhɛvəʃi/, George Charles de (1885–1966), Hungarian-born radiochemist. He studied radioisotopes and invented the technique of labelling with isotopic tracers. Hevesy was also co-discoverer of the element hafnium (1923). Nobel Prize for Chemistry (1943).

HEW ▶ abbreviation for (the US Department of) Health, Education, and Welfare.

hew /hjuː/ ▶ verb (past participle **hewn** or **hewed**) **1** [with obj.] chop or cut (something, especially wood or coal) with an axe, pick, or other tool: *master carpenters would hew the logs with an axe*.
■ (usu. **be hewn**) make or shape (something) by cutting or chopping a material such as wood or stone: *a seat hewn out of a fallen tree trunk*.
2 [no obj.] (**hew to**) N. Amer. conform or adhere to: *his administration would hew to high ethical standards*.
– ORIGIN Old English *hēawan*, of Germanic origin; related to Dutch *houwen* and German *hauen*.

hewer ▶ noun dated a person who cuts wood, stone, or other materials.
■ a miner who cuts coal from a seam.
– PHRASES **hewers of wood and drawers of water**

menial drudges; labourers. [ORIGIN: with biblical allusion to Josh. 9:21.]

hex¹ chiefly N. Amer. ▶ verb [with obj.] cast a spell on; bewitch: *he hexed her with his fingers*.
▶ noun a magic spell; a curse: *a death hex*.
■ a witch.
– ORIGIN mid 19th cent. (as a verb): from Pennsylvanian German *hexe* (verb), *Hex* (noun), from German *hexen* (verb), *Hexe* (noun).

hex² ▶ adjective & noun short for HEXADECIMAL.

hexa- (also **hex-** before a vowel) ▶ combining form six; having six.
– ORIGIN from Greek *hex* 'six'.

hexachord /ˈhɛksəkɔːd/ ▶ noun a musical scale of six notes with a semitone between the third and fourth. An overlapping series of seven such scales starting on G, C, and F formed the basis of medieval music theory.

hexad /ˈhɛksad/ ▶ noun technical a group or set of six.
– ORIGIN mid 17th cent. (denoting a series of six numbers): from Greek *hexas*, *hexad-*, from *hex* 'six'.

hexadecimal /ˌhɛksəˈdɛsɪm(ə)l/ ▶ adjective Computing relating to or using a system of numerical notation that has 16 rather than 10 as its base.
– DERIVATIVES **hexadecimally** adverb.

hexagon /ˈhɛksəɡ(ə)n/ ▶ noun a plane figure with six straight sides and angles.
– DERIVATIVES **hexagonal** adjective.
– ORIGIN late 16th cent.: via late Latin from Greek *hexagōnon*, neuter (used as a noun) of *hexagōnos* 'six-angled'.

hexagram ▶ noun a figure formed of six straight lines, in particular:
■ a star-shaped figure formed by two intersecting equilateral triangles. ■ any of a set of sixty-four figures made up of six parallel whole or broken lines, occurring in the ancient Chinese *I Ching*.
– ORIGIN mid 19th cent.: from HEXA- 'six' + Greek *gramma* 'line'.

hexahedron /ˌhɛksəˈhiːdrən, -ˈhɛd-/ ▶ noun (pl. **hexahedra** or **hexahedrons**) a solid figure with six plane faces.
– DERIVATIVES **hexahedral** adjective.
– ORIGIN late 16th cent.: from Greek *hexaedron*, neuter (used as a noun) of *hexaedros* 'six-faced'.

hexamerous /hɛkˈsam(ə)rəs/ ▶ noun Botany & Zoology having parts arranged in groups of six.
■ consisting of six joints or parts.

hexameter /hɛkˈsamɪtə/ ▶ noun Prosody a line of verse consisting of six metrical feet.
– ORIGIN late Middle English: from Latin, from Greek *hexametros* 'of six measures' (from *hex* 'six' + *metron* 'measure'.

hexane /ˈhɛkseɪn/ ▶ noun Chemistry a colourless liquid hydrocarbon of the alkane series, present in petroleum spirit.
● Chem. formula: C_6H_{14}; five isomers, especially the straight-chain isomer (*n*-hexane).
– ORIGIN late 19th cent.: from HEXA- 'six' (denoting six carbon atoms) + -ANE².

hexapla /ˈhɛksəplə/ ▶ noun a sixfold text in parallel columns, especially of the Old Testament.
– ORIGIN early 17th cent. (originally referring to Origen's edition of the Old Testament): from Greek, neuter plural of *hexaploos* 'sixfold', from *hex* 'six' + *ploos* 'fold'.

hexaploid /ˈhɛksəplɔɪd/ Genetics ▶ adjective (of a cell or nucleus) containing six homologous sets of chromosomes.
■ (of an organism or species) composed of hexaploid cells.
▶ noun a hexaploid organism, variety, or species.
– DERIVATIVES **hexaploidy** noun.

Hexapoda /hɛkˈsapədə/ Entomology a class of six-legged arthropods that comprises the insects. The name is used as another term for Insecta, especially when the primitive apterygotes are not considered to be true insects.
– DERIVATIVES **hexapod** noun.
– ORIGIN modern Latin (plural), from Greek *hexapous*, *hexapod-*, from *hex* 'six' + *pous* 'foot'.

hexastyle /ˈhɛksəstʌɪl/ Architecture ▶ noun a six-columned portico.
▶ adjective (of a portico) having six columns.
– ORIGIN early 18th cent.: from Greek *hexastulos*, from *hex* 'six' + *stulos* 'column'.

Hexateuch /ˈhɛksətjuːk/ ▶ noun the first six books of the Bible (Genesis to Joshua) collectively.

– ORIGIN late 19th cent.: from **HEXA-** 'six' + Greek *teukhos* 'book'.

hexavalent /ˌhɛksəˈveɪl(ə)nt/ ▶ **adjective** Chemistry having a valency of six.

hexose /ˈhɛksəʊz, -s/ ▶ **noun** Chemistry any of the class of simple sugars whose molecules contain six carbon atoms, such as glucose and fructose. They generally have the chemical formula $C_6H_{12}O_6$.
– ORIGIN late 19th cent.: from **HEXA-** 'six' + **-OSE**[2].

hexyl /ˈhɛksʌɪl, -sɪl/ ▶ **noun** [as modifier] Chemistry of or denoting an alkyl radical $—C_6H_{13}$, derived from hexane.

hey ▶ **exclamation** used to attract attention, to express surprise, interest, or annoyance, or to elicit agreement: *hey, what's going on here?*
– PHRASES **hey up** Brit. informal used as a greeting or as a way of drawing attention to something: *Hey up, Margaret!* | *Hey up! Here's the cops!* **what the hey** N. Amer. informal used as a euphemism for 'what the hell'.
– ORIGIN natural exclamation: first recorded in Middle English.

heyday ▶ **noun** (usu. **one's heyday**) the period of a person's or thing's greatest success, popularity, activity, or vigour: *the paper has lost millions of readers since its heyday in 1964.*
– ORIGIN late 16th cent. (denoting good spirits or passion): from archaic *heyday!*, an exclamation of joy, surprise, etc.

Heyer /ˈheɪə/, Georgette (1902–74), English novelist. She is noted especially for her historical novels, which include numerous Regency romances such as *Regency Buck* (1935).

Heyerdahl /ˈheɪədɑːl/, Thor (b.1914), Norwegian anthropologist. He is noted for his ocean voyages in primitive craft to demonstrate his theories of cultural diffusion, the best known of which was that of the balsa raft *Kon-Tiki* from Peru to the islands east of Tahiti in 1947.

hey presto ▶ **exclamation** Brit. a phrase announcing the successful completion of a trick, or to suggest that something has been done so easily that it seems to be magic: *press the start button and, hey presto, a copy comes out the other end.*

Hezbollah /ˌhɛzbəˈlɑː, ˈhɛzbɒlə/ (also **Hizbullah**) an extremist Shiite Muslim group which has close links with Iran, created after the Iranian revolution of 1979 and active especially in Lebanon.
– ORIGIN from Arabic *ḥizbullāh* 'Party of God', from *ḥezb* 'party' + *'allāh* (see **ALLAH**).

HF Physics ▶ **abbreviation for** high frequency.

Hf ▶ **symbol for** the chemical element hafnium.

hf ▶ **abbreviation for** half.

HFC ▶ **abbreviation for** hydrofluorocarbon.

HG Brit. ▶ **abbreviation for** ■ Her or His Grace. ■ historical Home Guard: *Captain Drummond (HG).*

Hg ▶ **symbol for** the chemical element mercury.
– ORIGIN abbreviation of modern Latin *hydrargyrum*.

hg ▶ **abbreviation for** hectogram(s).

HGH ▶ **abbreviation for** human growth hormone.

HGV Brit. ▶ **abbreviation for** heavy goods vehicle.

HH ▶ **abbreviation for** ■ Brit. Her or His Highness. ■ His Holiness. ■ (used in describing grades of pencil lead) extra hard.

hh. ▶ **abbreviation for** hands (as a unit of measurement of a horse's height).

hhd ▶ **abbreviation for** hogshead(s).

H-hour ▶ **noun** the time of day at which an attack, landing, or other military operation is scheduled to begin.
– ORIGIN First World War: from *H* (for *hour*) + **HOUR**.

HI ▶ **abbreviation for** Hawaii (in official postal use).

hi ▶ **exclamation** informal used as a friendly greeting or to attract attention: *'Hi there. How was the flight?'*
– ORIGIN natural exclamation: first recorded in late Middle English.

hiatus /hʌɪˈeɪtəs/ ▶ **noun** (pl. **hiatuses**) [usu. in sing.] a pause or gap in a sequence, series, or process: *there was a brief hiatus in the war with France.*
■ Prosody & Grammar a break between two vowels coming together but not in the same syllable, as in *the ear* and *cooperate*.
– DERIVATIVES **hiatal** adjective.
– ORIGIN mid 16th cent. (originally denoting a physical gap or opening): from Latin, literally 'gaping', from *hiare* 'gape'.

hiatus hernia (also **hiatal hernia**) ▶ **noun** Medicine the protrusion of an organ, typically the stomach, through the oesophageal opening in the diaphragm.

Hiawatha /ˌhʌɪəˈwɒθə/ a legendary 16th-century North American Indian teacher and chieftain, hero of a narrative poem by Henry Wadsworth Longfellow called *The Song of Hiawatha* (1855).

Hib ▶ **noun** a bacterium that causes infant meningitis.
• *Haemophilus influenzae* type B.
– ORIGIN late 20th cent.: acronym.

hiba /ˈhiːbə/ ▶ **noun** a Japanese conifer with evergreen scale-like leaves which form flattened sprays of foliage, widely planted as an ornamental and yielding durable timber.
• *Thujopsis dolabrata*, family Cupressaceae.
– ORIGIN Japanese.

hibachi /hɪˈbatʃi, ˈhɪbətʃi/ ▶ **noun** (pl. **hibachis**) a portable cooking apparatus similar to a small barbecue.
■ (in Japan) a large earthenware pan or brazier in which charcoal is burnt to provide indoor heating.
– ORIGIN mid 19th cent.: Japanese *hibachi*, *hi-hachi*, from *hi* 'fire' + *hachi* 'bowl, pot'.

hibakusha /ˈhɪbəˌkuːʃə/ ▶ **noun** (pl. same) (in Japan) a survivor of either of the atomic explosions at Hiroshima or Nagasaki in 1945.
– ORIGIN mid 20th cent.: Japanese, from *hi* 'suffer' + *baku* 'explosion' + *sha* 'person'.

hibernate ▶ **verb** [no obj.] (of an animal or plant) spend the winter in a dormant state.
■ figurative (of a person) remain inactive or indoors for an extended period: *the pilots who have been hibernating during the winter months get their gliders out again.*
– DERIVATIVES **hibernation** noun, **hibernator** noun.
– ORIGIN early 19th cent.: from Latin *hibernare*, from *hiberna* 'winter quarters', from *hibernus* 'wintry'.

Hibernian /hʌɪˈbəːnɪən/ ▶ **adjective** of or concerning Ireland (now chiefly used in names): *the Royal Hibernian Academy.*
▶ **noun** a native of Ireland (now chiefly used in names): *the Ancient Order of Hibernians.*
– ORIGIN from Latin *Hibernia* (alteration of *Iverna*, from Greek *I(w)ernē*, of Celtic origin; related to Irish *Ériu*, *Éirinn* 'Ireland': see **EIRE**, **ERIN**) + **-AN**.

Hibernianism (also **Hibernicism**) ▶ **noun** an Irish idiom or expression.

Hiberno- /hʌɪˈbəːnəʊ/ ▶ **combining form** Irish; Irish and ...: *Hiberno-English.*
■ relating to Ireland.
– ORIGIN from medieval Latin *Hibernus* 'Irish'; see also **HIBERNIAN**.

hibiscus /hɪˈbɪskəs/ ▶ **noun** a plant of the mallow family, grown in warm climates for its large brightly coloured flowers or for products such as fibre or timber.
• Genus *Hibiscus*, family Malvaceae: many species, including the rose mallow.
– ORIGIN Latin, from Greek *hibiskos*, which Dioscorides identified with the marsh mallow.

hic ▶ **exclamation** used in writing to express the sound of a hiccup, especially a drunken one.
– ORIGIN late 19th cent.: imitative.

hiccup (also **hiccough** (pronunc. same)) ▶ **noun** an involuntary spasm of the diaphragm and respiratory organs, with a sudden closure of the glottis and a characteristic sound like that of a cough.
■ (**hiccups**) an attack of such spasms occurring repeatedly for some time: *then she got hiccups.* ■ a temporary or minor difficulty or setback: *just a little hiccup in our usual wonderful service.*
▶ **verb** (**hiccuped**, **hiccuping**) [no obj.] suffer from or make the sound of a hiccup or series of hiccups.
– DERIVATIVES **hiccupy** adjective.
– ORIGIN late 16th cent.: imitative; the form *hiccough* arose by association with **COUGH**.

hic jacet /hɪk ˈdʒeɪsɛt, ˈjakɛt/ ▶ **noun** poetic/literary an epitaph.
– ORIGIN Latin, 'here lies', the first two words of a Latin epitaph.

hick ▶ **noun** informal, chiefly N. Amer. a person who lives in the country, regarded as being unintelligent or parochial: [as modifier] *she puts on a hick accent.*
– ORIGIN mid 16th cent.: pet form of the given name *Richard*.

hickey ▶ **noun** (pl. **-eys**) **1** N. Amer. informal a gadget.
2 a blemish in printing, especially an uninked area in a solid, caused by a piece of dirt.
■ N. Amer. informal a skin blemish, especially a mark caused by a love bite.
– ORIGIN early 20th cent.: of unknown origin.

Hickok, James Butler (1837–76), American frontiersman and marshal; known as **Wild Bill Hickok**. The legend of his invincibility in his encounters with frontier desperadoes became something of a challenge to gunmen, and he was eventually murdered at Deadwood, South Dakota.

hickory ▶ **noun** **1** a chiefly North American tree of the walnut family, which yields useful timber and typically bears edible nuts.
• Genus *Carya*, family Juglandaceae: several species, including the **shagbark hickory** (*C. ovata*), with shaggy peeling bark. See also **PECAN**.
■ a stick made of hickory wood.
2 (also **hickory wattle**) Austral. an acacia tree that yields tough, close-grained timber.
• Genus *Acacia*, family Leguminosae: several species, in particular *A. implexa*.
– ORIGIN late 17th cent.: abbreviation of *pohickery*, the local Virginian name, from Algonquian *pawcohiccora*.

Hicks, Sir John Richard (1904–89), English economist. He did pioneering work on general economic equilibrium (the theory that economic forces tend to balance one another rather than simply reflect cyclical trends), for which he shared a Nobel Prize with K. J. Arrow in 1972.

hid past of **HIDE**[1].

Hidalgo /hɪˈdalgəʊ/ a state of southern Mexico; capital, Pachuca de Soto.

hidalgo /hɪˈdalgəʊ/ ▶ **noun** (pl. **-os**) a gentleman in a Spanish-speaking country.
– ORIGIN late 16th cent.: Spanish, from *hijo de algo*, literally 'son of something' (i.e. of an important person).

Hidatsa /hɪˈdatsə/ ▶ **noun** (pl. same or **Hidatsas**) **1** a member of an American Indian people living on the upper Missouri River.
2 [mass noun] the Siouan language of this people, now almost extinct.
▶ **adjective** of or relating to this people or their language.
– ORIGIN from Hidatsa *hiratsa* 'willow wood lodge'.

hidden past participle of **HIDE**[1]. ▶ **adjective** kept out of sight; concealed: *hidden dangers* | *her hidden feelings.*
– DERIVATIVES **hiddenness** noun.

hidden agenda ▶ **noun** a secret or ulterior motive for something.

hiddenite /ˈhɪd(ə)nʌɪt/ ▶ **noun** [mass noun] a rare green gem variety of spodumene.
– ORIGIN late 19th cent.: named after William E. Hidden (1832–1918), American mineralogist.

hidden reserves ▶ **plural noun** a company's funds that are not declared on its balance sheet.
■ mental or physical capabilities beyond those normally available to someone: *hidden reserves of power.*

hide[1] ▶ **verb** (past **hid**; past participle **hidden**) [with obj.] put or keep out of sight; conceal from the view or notice of others: *he hid the money in the house* | *they swept up the pieces and hid them* ***away***.
■ (of a thing) prevent (someone or something) from being seen: *clouds rolled up and hid the moon.* ■ keep secret or unknown: *Herbert could hardly hide his dislike.* ■ [no obj.] conceal oneself: *Juliet's first instinct was to hide under the blankets* | *he had a little money and could* ***hide out*** *until the end of the month.* ■ [no obj.] (**hide behind**) use (someone or something) to protect oneself from criticism or punishment, especially in a way considered cowardly or unethical: *companies and manufacturers with poor security can hide behind the law.*
▶ **noun** Brit. a camouflaged shelter used to get a close view of wildlife.
– PHRASES **hide one's head** cover up one's face or keep out of sight, especially from shame. **hide one's light under a bushel** keep quiet about one's talents or accomplishments. [ORIGIN: with biblical allusion to Matt. 15.]
– DERIVATIVES **hider** noun.
– ORIGIN Old English *hȳdan*, of West Germanic origin.

hide[2] ▶ **noun** the skin of an animal, especially when tanned or dressed.
■ used to refer to a person's ability to withstand

criticisms or insults: *'I'm sorry I called you a pig.' 'My hide's thick enough; it didn't bother me.'*

– PHRASES **hide or hair of someone** [with negative] the slightest sight or trace of someone: *I could find neither hide nor hair of him.* **save one's hide** escape from danger or difficulty. **tan** (or **whip**) **someone's hide** beat or flog someone. ■ punish someone severely.

– DERIVATIVES **hided** adjective.

– ORIGIN Old English *hȳd*, of Germanic origin; related to Dutch *huid* and German *Haut*.

hide³ ▶ **noun** a former measure of land used in England, typically equal to between 60 and 120 acres, being the amount that would support a family and its dependants.

– ORIGIN Old English *hīd*, *hīgid*, from the base of *hīgan*, *hīwan* 'household members', of Germanic origin.

hide-and-seek ▶ **noun** [mass noun] a children's game in which one or more players hide and the other or others have to look for them.

hideaway ▶ **noun** a place used for hiding in, especially as a retreat from other people.

hide beetle ▶ **noun** a dull brown scavenging beetle that feeds on stored hides and dried meat and may be a serious pest of warehouses.

● *Dermestes maculatus*, family Dermestidae.

hidebound ▶ **adjective** unwilling or unable to change because of tradition or convention: *you are hidebound by your petty laws.*

– ORIGIN mid 16th cent. (as a noun denoting a condition of cattle): from **HIDE**² + **BOUND**⁴. The earliest sense of the adjective (referring to cattle) was extended to emaciated human beings, and then applied figuratively in the sense 'narrow, cramped, or bigoted in outlook'.

hideous ▶ **adjective** ugly or disgusting to look at: *his smile made him look more hideous than ever.*

■ extremely unpleasant: *the whole hideous story.*

– DERIVATIVES **hideously** adverb [as submodifier] *a hideously expensive camera*, **hideousness** noun.

– ORIGIN Middle English: from Old French *hidos*, *hideus*, from *hide*, *hisde* 'fear', of unknown origin.

hideout ▶ **noun** a hiding place, especially one used by someone who has broken the law.

hidey-hole (also **hidy-hole**) ▶ **noun** informal a place for hiding something or oneself in, especially as a retreat from other people.

hiding¹ ▶ **noun** informal a physical beating: *they took off after him, caught him, and gave him a hiding.*

■ figurative a severe defeat: *if they'd played badly they might have expected a hiding.*

– PHRASES **be on a hiding to nothing** Brit. be unlikely to succeed, or be unlikely to gain much advantage if one does.

– ORIGIN early 19th cent.: from **HIDE**² + **-ING**¹.

hiding² ▶ **noun** [mass noun] the action of concealing someone or something.

■ the state of being hidden: *the shipowner had gone into hiding.*

– ORIGIN Middle English: from **HIDE**¹ + **-ING**¹.

hiding place ▶ **noun** a place for concealing someone or something.

hidrosis /hɪˈdrəʊsɪs/ ▶ **noun** [mass noun] Medicine sweating.

– DERIVATIVES **hidrotic** adjective.

– ORIGIN mid 19th cent.: from Greek *hidrōsis*, from *hidrōs* 'sweat'.

hie /hʌɪ/ ▶ **verb** (**hies**, **hied**, **hieing** or **hying**) [no obj., with adverbial of direction] archaic go quickly: *I hied down to New Orleans* | *I* **hied me** *to a winehouse.*

– ORIGIN Middle English: from Old English *hīgian* 'strive, pant', of unknown origin.

hielaman /ˈhiːləmən/ ▶ **noun** an Australian Aboriginal shield made of bark or wood.

– ORIGIN from Dharuk *yilimang*.

hierarch /ˈhʌɪərɑːk/ ▶ **noun** a chief priest, archbishop, or other leader.

– ORIGIN late Middle English: via medieval Latin from Greek *hierarkhēs*, from *hieros* 'sacred' + *arkhēs* 'ruler'.

hierarchical ▶ **adjective** of the nature of a hierarchy; arranged in order of rank: *the hierarchical bureaucracy of a local authority.*

– DERIVATIVES **hierarchically** adverb.

hierarchy /ˈhʌɪərɑːki/ ▶ **noun** (pl. **-ies**) a system or organization in which people or groups are ranked one above the other according to status or authority.

■ (**the hierarchy**) the clergy of the Catholic Church or of an episcopal Church; the religious authorities. ■ (**the hierarchy**) the upper echelons of a hierarchical system; those in authority: *the magazine was read quite widely even by some of the hierarchy.* ■ an arrangement or classification of things according to relative importance or inclusiveness: *a taxonomic hierarchy of phyla, classes, orders, families, genera, and species.* ■ Theology the traditional system of orders of angels and other heavenly beings.

– DERIVATIVES **hierarchic** adjective, **hierarchization** noun, **hierarchize** (also **-ise**) verb.

– ORIGIN late Middle English: via Old French and medieval Latin from Greek *hierarkhia*, from *hierarkhēs* 'sacred ruler' (see **HIERARCH**). The earliest sense was 'system of orders of angels and heavenly beings'; the other senses date from the 17th cent.

hieratic /ˌhʌɪəˈratɪk/ ▶ **adjective** of or concerning priests: *he raised both his arms in an outlandish hieratic gesture.*

■ of or in the ancient Egyptian writing of abridged hieroglyphics used by priests. Compare with **DEMOTIC**. ■ of or concerning Egyptian or Greek styles of art adhering to early methods as laid down by religious tradition.

– DERIVATIVES **hieratically** adverb.

– ORIGIN mid 17th cent. (earlier as *hieratical*): via Latin from Greek *hieratikos*, from *hierasthai* 'be a priest', from *hiereus* 'priest', *hieros* 'sacred'.

hiero- /ˈhʌɪrəʊ/ ▶ **combining form** sacred; holy.

– ORIGIN from Greek *hieros* 'sacred'.

hierocracy /hʌɪˈrɒkrəsi/ ▶ **noun** (pl. **-ies**) [mass noun] rule by priests.

■ [count noun] a ruling body composed of priests.

– DERIVATIVES **hierocratic** adjective.

hieroglyph /ˈhʌɪrəglɪf/ ▶ **noun** a stylized picture of an object representing a word, syllable, or sound, as found in ancient Egyptian and certain other writing systems.

– ORIGIN late 16th cent.: back-formation from **HIEROGLYPHIC**.

hieroglyphic ▶ **noun** (**hieroglyphics**) writing consisting of hieroglyphs.

■ enigmatic or incomprehensible symbols or writing: *tattered notebooks filled with illegible hieroglyphics.*

▶ **adjective** of or written in hieroglyphs.

■ (especially in art) stylized, symbolic, or enigmatic in effect.

– DERIVATIVES **hieroglyphical** adjective, **hieroglyphically** adverb.

– ORIGIN late 16th cent.: from French *hiéroglyphique*, from Greek *hieroglyphikos*, from *hieros* 'sacred' + *gluphē* 'carving'.

hierogram /ˈhʌɪrə(ʊ)gram/ ▶ **noun** a sacred inscription or symbol.

hierolatry /ˌhʌɪəˈrɒlətri/ ▶ **noun** [mass noun] the worship of saints or sacred things.

hierology /hʌɪˈrɒlədʒi/ ▶ **noun** [mass noun] sacred literature or lore.

hierophant /ˈhʌɪrə(ʊ)fant/ ▶ **noun** a person, especially a priest, who interprets sacred mysteries or esoteric principles.

– DERIVATIVES **hierophantic** adjective.

– ORIGIN late 17th cent.: via late Latin from Greek *hierophantēs*, from *hieros* 'sacred' + *phainein* 'show, reveal'.

hi-fi informal ▶ **adjective** of, used for, or relating to the reproduction of music or other sound with high fidelity.

▶ **noun** (pl. **hi-fis**) a set of equipment for high-fidelity sound reproduction.

– ORIGIN 1950s: abbreviation of **HIGH FIDELITY**.

higgle ▶ **verb** archaic spelling of **HAGGLE**.

higgledy-piggledy ▶ **adverb** & **adjective** in confusion or disorder: [as adv.] *bits of paper hanging higgledy-piggledy on the furniture and walls* | [as adj.] *a higgledy-piggledy mountain of newspapers.*

– ORIGIN late 16th cent.: rhyming jingle, probably with reference to the irregular herding together of pigs.

higgler ▶ **noun** W. Indian a person who travels around selling small items; a pedlar.

Higgs (also **Higgs boson** or **Higgs particle**) ▶ **noun** Physics a subatomic particle whose existence is predicted by the theory which unified the weak and electromagnetic interactions.

– ORIGIN 1970s: named after Peter W. *Higgs* (born 1929), English physicist.

high ▶ **adjective 1** of great vertical extent: *the top of a high mountain* | *the mast was higher than the tallest building in the city.*

■ (after a measurement and in questions) measuring a specified distance from top to bottom: *a tree forty feet high.* ■ far above ground, sea level, or another point of reference: *a palace high up on a hill.* ■ extending above the normal or average level: *a round face with a high forehead.* ■ [attrib.] (of territory or landscape) inland and well above sea level: *high prairies.* ■ near to the top of a real or notional list in order of rank or importance: *financial security is* **high on** *your list of priorities.* ■ [attrib.] performed at, to, or from a considerable height: *high diving.*

2 great, or greater than normal, in quantity, size, or intensity: *a high temperature* | *sweets and chocolate are very* **high in** *calories.*

■ of large numerical or monetary value: *they had been playing for high stakes.* ■ very favourable: *she had no very high opinion of men.* ■ extreme in religious or political views: *a man of high Tory opinions.* ■ (of a period or movement) at its peak: *high summer.* ■ (of latitude) close to 90°; near the North or South Pole: *high southern latitudes.*

3 great in rank or status: *both held high office under Lloyd George.*

■ ranking above others of the same kind: *the last High King of Ireland.* ■ morally or culturally superior: *they believed that Nature was driven by something higher than mere selfishness.*

4 (of a sound or note) having a frequency at the upper end of the auditory range: *a high, squeaky voice.*

■ (of a singer or instrument) producing notes of relatively high pitch: *a high soprano voice.*

5 [predic.] informal excited; euphoric: *she wasn't tipsy, just a little high.*

■ intoxicated with drugs: *some of them were already* **high on** *alcohol and Ecstasy.*

6 [predic.] unpleasantly strong-smelling, in particular (of food) beginning to go bad.

■ (of game) slightly decomposed and so ready to cook.

7 Phonetics (of a vowel) produced with the tongue relatively near the palate.

▶ **noun 1** a high point, level, or figure: *commodity prices were actually at a rare high.*

■ a notably happy or successful moment: *the highs and lows of life.* ■ a high-frequency sound or musical note. ■ an area of high barometric pressure; an anticyclone.

2 [usu. in sing.] informal a state of high spirits or euphoria, especially one induced by drugs: *if the stable is doing well then everybody's* **on a high**.

3 informal, chiefly N. Amer. high school: *I go to junior high.*

4 a high power setting: *the vent blower was on high.*

■ top gear in a motor vehicle.

▶ **adverb 1** at or to a considerable or specified height: *the sculpture stood about five feet high.*

2 highly: *he ranked high among the pioneers of twentieth-century chemical technology.*

■ at a high price: *buying shares low and selling them high.*

3 (of a sound) at or to a high pitch.

– PHRASES **ace** (or **king** or **queen** etc.) **high** (in card games) having the ace (or another specified card) as the highest-ranking. **from on high** from a very high place. ■ from remote high authority or heaven: *central government programmes coming down from on high.* **high and dry** out of the water, especially the sea as it retreats. ■ in a difficult position, especially without resources: *your family would be* **left high and dry** *by the death of the breadwinner.* **high and low** in many different places: *I* **searched high and low** *for a new teacher.* **high and mighty** important and influential: *the accursed high and mighty elite.* ■ informal thinking or acting as though one is more important than others. **the high ground** a position of superiority (originally in military conflict): *if he turns it down, he will have lost the moral high ground to the president.* **a high old ——** [attrib.] informal used for emphasis: *a high old time of it we all had.* **high, wide, and handsome** informal expansive and impressive. [ORIGIN: from *Arizona Nights* by Stewart E. White (1873–1946), American author.] **it is high time that ——** it is past the time when something should have happened or been done: *it was high time that she faced facts.* **on high** in or to heaven or a high place: *a spotter plane circling on high.* **on one's high horse** informal used to refer to someone behaving in an arrogant or pompous manner. **run high** (of a river) be full and close to overflowing, with a strong

current. ■ (of feelings) be intense: *passions run high when marriages break up and children are involved.*
– ORIGIN Old English *hēah*, of Germanic origin; related to Dutch *hoog* and German *hoch*.

high altar ▶ noun the chief altar of a church, typically in the chancel.

highball N. Amer. ▶ noun **1** a drink consisting of a spirit, especially whisky, and a mixer such as soda or ginger ale, served with ice in a tall glass. **2** informal a railway signal to proceed.
▶ verb [no obj., with adverbial of direction] informal travel fast: *they highballed north.*

high-band ▶ adjective relating to or denoting a video system using a relatively high carrier frequency, which allows more bandwidth for the signal.

highbinder /ˈhaɪbaɪndə/ ▶ noun US informal an unscrupulous person, especially a corrupt politician.
■ an assassin, especially one belonging to a Chinese-American criminal organization.
– ORIGIN early 19th cent.: first recorded as *Highbinders*, the name of a New York gang.

high-born ▶ adjective having noble parents: *a high-born Portuguese family.*

highboy ▶ noun N. Amer. a tall chest of drawers on legs.

highbrow ▶ adjective often derogatory scholarly or rarefied in taste: *innovatory art had a small, mostly highbrow following.*
▶ noun a person of this type.

high chair ▶ noun a chair with long legs for a baby or small child, fitted with a tray that is used like a table at mealtimes.

High Church ▶ adjective of or adhering to a tradition within the Anglican Church emphasizing ritual, priestly authority, sacraments, and historical continuity with Catholic Christianity. Compare with LOW CHURCH, BROAD CHURCH.
▶ noun [treated as sing. or pl.] the principles or adherents of this tradition.
– DERIVATIVES **High Churchman** noun.

high-class ▶ adjective of a high standard, quality, or social class: *a high-class boarding school.*

high colour (also **high colouring**) ▶ noun a flushed complexion: *he had a high colour to his cheeks.*

high command ▶ noun the commander-in-chief and associated senior staff of an army, navy, or air force.

high commission ▶ noun an embassy of one Commonwealth country in another.
– DERIVATIVES **high commissioner** noun.

high court ▶ noun a supreme court of justice.
■ (in full **High Court of Justice**) (in England and Wales) the court of unlimited civil jurisdiction forming part of the Supreme Court and comprising three divisions: Queen's Bench, Chancery, and the Family Division. ■ (in full **High Court of Justiciary**) the supreme criminal court of Scotland.

High Court of Parliament ▶ noun (in the UK) formal term for PARLIAMENT.

high day ▶ noun Brit. the day of a religious festival.
– PHRASES **high days and holidays** informal special occasions: *the drawing room is used only on high days and holidays.*

high-dependency ▶ adjective [attrib.] Brit. of or relating to hospital patients requiring a high level of medical treatment and supervision.

high-end ▶ adjective [attrib.] denoting the most expensive of a range of products.

high enema ▶ noun an enema delivered into the colon.

Higher ▶ noun (in Scotland) the more advanced of the two main levels of the Scottish Certificate of Education. Compare with ORDINARY GRADE.

higher animals ▶ plural noun animals of relatively advanced or developed characteristics, such as mammals and other vertebrates.

higher court ▶ noun Law a court that can overrule the decision of another.

higher criticism ▶ noun [mass noun] the study of the literary methods and sources discernible in a text, especially as applied to biblical writings.

higher education ▶ noun [mass noun] education at universities or similar educational establishments, especially to degree level.

higher mathematics ▶ plural noun [usu. treated as sing.] advanced mathematics, such as number theory and topology, as taught at university level.

higher plants ▶ plural noun plants of relatively complex or advanced characteristics, especially vascular plants (including flowering plants).

higher-up ▶ noun informal a senior person in an organization.

highest common factor (abbrev.: HCF) ▶ noun the highest number that can be divided exactly into each of two or more numbers.

high explosive ▶ noun a chemical explosive of the kind used in shells and bombs, which is more rapid and destructive in its effects than gunpowder.

highfalutin /ˌhaɪfəˈluːtɪn/ (also **highfaluting** /-tɪŋ/) ▶ adjective informal (especially of speech, writing, or ideas) pompous or pretentious: *you don't want any highfalutin jargon.*
– ORIGIN mid 19th cent. (originally US): perhaps from HIGH + *fluting* (present participle of FLUTE).

high fashion ▶ noun another term for HAUTE COUTURE.

high fidelity ▶ noun [mass noun] the reproduction of sound with little distortion, giving a result very similar to the original.

high finance ▶ noun [mass noun] financial transactions involving large sums.

high five informal, chiefly N. Amer. ▶ noun a gesture of celebration or greeting in which two people slap each other's palms with their arms raised: *he grinned and gave him a high five.*
▶ verb (**high-five**) [with obj.] greet with such a gesture.

high-flown ▶ adjective (especially of language or ideas) extravagant and grand-sounding.

high-flyer (also **high-flier**) ▶ noun a person who is or has the potential to be very successful, especially academically or in business.
– DERIVATIVES **high-flying** adjective.

high forest ▶ noun [mass noun] forest consisting of tall trees.
■ Forestry forest raised wholly or mainly from seed, especially as opposed to pollarded or coppiced forest.

high frequency ▶ noun (in radio) a frequency of 3–30 megahertz.

high gear ▶ noun a gear that causes a wheeled vehicle to move fast, due to a high ratio between the speed of the wheels and that of the mechanism driving them.

High German ▶ noun [mass noun] the standard literary and spoken form of German, originally used in the highlands in the south of Germany. The establishment of this form as a standard language owes much to the biblical translations of Martin Luther in the 16th century. See also MIDDLE HIGH GERMAN, OLD HIGH GERMAN.

high-grade ▶ adjective of very good quality: *high-grade steel.*

high-handed ▶ adjective using power or authority without considering the feelings of others: *a fairly high-handed decision.*
– DERIVATIVES **high-handedly** adverb, **high-handedness** noun.

high hat ▶ noun **1** a tall hat, especially a top hat. ■ N. Amer. informal a snobbish or supercilious person. **2** (**high-hat**) variant form of HI-HAT. **3** a silvery marine fish with longitudinal brown stripes and a long upright dorsal fin, found in shallow rocky waters of the Caribbean.
● *Equetus acuminatus*, family Sciaenidae.
▶ adjective (**high-hat**) N. Amer. informal snobbish.
▶ verb (**high-hat**) (**-hatted**, **-hatting**) [with obj.] N. Amer. informal act in a snobbish or supercilious manner towards (someone).

high heels ▶ plural noun tall, thin heels on women's shoes.
– DERIVATIVES **high-heeled** adjective.

High Holidays (also **High Holy Days**) ▶ plural noun the Jewish festivals of Yom Kippur and Rosh Hashana. Also called DAYS OF AWE.

high hurdles ▶ plural noun [treated as sing.] a race in which runners jump over hurdles 42 inches (107 cm) high.
– DERIVATIVES **high hurdler** noun.

high-impact ▶ adjective [attrib.] **1** (of plastic or a similar substance) able to withstand great impact without breaking. **2** denoting exercises, typically aerobics, that place a great deal of stress on the body.

high jinks ▶ plural noun boisterous fun: *high jinks behind the wheel of a car.*
– ORIGIN late 17th cent.: see JINK.

high jump ▶ noun (**the high jump**) an athletic event in which competitors jump high over a bar which is raised until only one competitor can jump it without dislodging it.
– PHRASES **be for the high jump** Brit. informal be about to be severely reprimanded or punished.
– DERIVATIVES **high jumper** noun.

high-key (also **high-keyed**) ▶ adjective Art & Photography having a predominance of light or bright tones.

high kick ▶ noun a kick with the foot high in the air, for example in dancing or martial arts.
– DERIVATIVES **high-kicking** adjective.

highland ▶ noun **1** [mass noun] (also **highlands**) an area of high or mountainous land: *the highlands of Madagascar* | [as modifier] *a highland region of Vietnam.* **2** (**the Highlands**) the mountainous part of Scotland, to the north of Glasgow and Stirling, often associated with Gaelic culture: [as modifier] *a Highland regiment.*
■ (**Highland**) an administrative region of northern Scotland; administrative centre, Inverness.
– DERIVATIVES **highlander** noun, **highlandman** noun (pl. **-men**).
– ORIGIN Old English *hēahland* 'a high promontory' (see HIGH, LAND).

Highland cattle ▶ plural noun animals of a shaggy-haired breed of cattle with long, curved widely spaced horns.

Highland clearances the forced removal of crofters from their land in the Highlands of Scotland in the late 18th and early 19th centuries. The clearances, carried out by landlords wanting to install sheep and deer on their estates, led to extreme hardship as well as to widespread emigration to North America and elsewhere.

Highland dress ▶ noun [mass noun] clothing in the traditional style of the Scottish Highlands, now chiefly worn on formal occasions and including the kilt.

Highland fling ▶ noun a vigorous Scottish dance consisting of a series of complex steps performed solo, originally to celebrate victory.

Highland Games ▶ plural noun a meeting for athletic events, playing of the bagpipes, and dancing, held in the Scottish Highlands or by Scots elsewhere.

highland moccasin ▶ noun the North American copperhead snake.

Highland pony ▶ noun a large stocky pony of a strong breed with a long mane and tail, originally from Scotland.

high-level ▶ adjective at or of a level above that which is normal or average: *a high-level cistern* | *high-level crop production.*
■ relating to or involving people of high administrative rank or great authority: *high-level negotiations.* ■ Computing denoting a programming language (e.g. BASIC or Pascal) that is relatively accessible to the user, having instructions that resemble an existing language such as English. ■ (of nuclear waste) highly radioactive and requiring long-term storage in isolation.

high life ▶ noun [mass noun] **1** (also **high living**) an extravagant social life as enjoyed by the wealthy. **2** (usu. **highlife**) a style of dance music of West African origin, influenced by rock and jazz.

highlight ▶ noun **1** an outstanding part of an event or period of time: *he views that season as the highlight of his career.*
■ (**highlights**) the best parts of a sporting or other event edited for broadcasting or recording. **2** a bright or reflective area in a painting, picture, or design.
■ (usu. **highlights**) a bright tint in the hair, especially one produced by bleaching or dyeing.
▶ verb [with obj.] **1** (usu. **be highlighted**) pick out and emphasize: *the issues highlighted by the report.*
■ make visually prominent: *a vast backdrop with the colourful logo highlighted with lasers.* ■ mark with a highlighter: *a photocopy with sections highlighted in green.* **2** create highlights in (hair).

highlighter ▶ noun **1** a broad marker pen used to overlay transparent fluorescent colour on text or a part of an illustration, leaving it legible and emphasized.

2 a cosmetic that is lighter than the wearer's foundation or skin, used to emphasize features such as the eyes or cheekbones.

high-low ▶ noun historical a lace-up boot with a low heel, reaching to the ankle, worn by the military in the 18th and early 19th centuries.

highly ▶ adverb to a high degree: [as submodifier] *a highly dangerous substance* | *highly paid people.*
■ high in a hierarchy: *a highly placed British official.*
■ favourably: *he was highly regarded by his colleagues.*
– ORIGIN Old English *hēalice* (see HIGH, -LY¹).

highly strung ▶ adjective Brit. very nervous and easily upset.

High Mass ▶ noun a Roman Catholic or Anglo-Catholic mass with full ceremonial, including music and incense and typically having the assistance of a deacon and subdeacon.

high-minded ▶ adjective having strong moral principles: *rich high-minded Victorians.*
– DERIVATIVES **high-mindedly** adverb, **high-mindedness** noun.

high muck-a-muck (also **high muckety-muck**) ▶ noun N. Amer. informal a person in a position of authority, especially one who is overbearing or conceited.
– ORIGIN mid 19th cent.: perhaps from Chinook *hiyu* 'plenty' + *muckamuck* 'food', from Nootka *ḥayo* 'ten' + *ma·ho·maq·* 'choice wheatmeal', with *high* substituted for *hiyu.*

highness ▶ noun **1** (**His/Your** etc. **Highness**) a title given to a person of royal rank, or used in addressing them: *I am most grateful, Your Highness.*
2 [mass noun] the state of being high: *the highness of her cheekbones.*
– ORIGIN Old English *hēanes* (see HIGH, -NESS).

high noon ▶ noun **1** midday.
2 an event or confrontation which is likely to decide the final outcome of a situation: *the high noon of his quest for the presidential nomination.* [ORIGIN: popularized by the film *High Noon* (1952).]

high note ▶ noun a successful point in an event or period of time: *he wants to end his managerial career on a high note.*

high-octane ▶ adjective denoting petrol having a high octane number and thus good anti-knock properties.
■ figurative powerful or dynamic: *a high-octane forty-year-old.*

high-pass ▶ adjective Electronics (of a filter) transmitting all frequencies above a certain value.

high-pitched ▶ adjective **1** (of a sound) high.
2 (of a roof) steep.
3 (of a battle or dispute) intense.

high places ▶ plural noun positions of power or authority: *people in high places were taking note.*

high point ▶ noun the most enjoyable or significant part of an experience or period of time: *the English lesson was the high point of the morning.*

high polymer ▶ noun a polymer having a high molecular weight, such as those used in plastics and resins.

high-powered (also **high-power**) ▶ adjective (of a machine or device) having greater than normal strength or capabilities: *a high-powered rifle.*
■ dynamic and capable: *a high-powered delegation.*

high priest ▶ noun a chief priest of a non-Christian religion, in particular:
■ the chief priest of the historic Jewish religion. ■ the head of a religious cult or similar group. ■ figurative a chief advocate of a belief or practice: *the high priest of the drug culture.*

high priestess ▶ noun a female high priest.

high profile ▶ noun [in sing.] a position attracting much attention or publicity: *people who have a high profile in the community.*
▶ adjective attracting much attention or publicity: *a high-profile military presence.*

high relief ▶ noun see RELIEF (sense 4).

High Renaissance see RENAISSANCE.

high-res ▶ adjective variant spelling of HI-RES.

high-rise ▶ adjective (of a building) having many storeys: *a high-rise block of flats.*
■ taller or set higher than normal: *high-rise handlebars.*
▶ noun a building with many storeys.

high road ▶ noun a main road: [in place names] *Kilburn High Road.*
■ figurative, N. Amer. a morally superior approach towards something: *he is winning support for taking the high road in refusing to be drawn into negative campaigning.*
■ a direct or certain route or course.

high roller ▶ noun informal, chiefly N. Amer. a person who gambles or spends large sums of money.
– DERIVATIVES **high-rolling** adjective.
– ORIGIN with reference to rolling dice.

high school ▶ noun **1** N. Amer. a secondary school.
2 (in the UK) used chiefly in names of grammar schools or independent fee-paying secondary schools, or for the lower years of a secondary school: *Wycombe High School.*
– DERIVATIVES **high schooler** noun.

high seas ▶ plural noun (**the high seas**) the open ocean, especially that not within any country's jurisdiction.

high season ▶ noun Brit. the most popular time of year at a resort, hotel, or tourist attraction, when prices are highest.

high-security ▶ adjective extremely secure: *a high-security jail.*

high sheriff ▶ noun see SHERIFF.

high sign ▶ noun N. Amer. informal a surreptitious gesture, often pre-arranged, giving warning or indicating that all is well: *I'm getting the high sign from my secretary—gotta go.*

Highsmith, Patricia (1921–95), American writer of detective fiction; born *Patricia Plangman*. Her novels are noted for their black humour, particularly those featuring Tom Ripley, an amoral anti-hero resident in France. *Strangers on a Train* (1949) was filmed by Alfred Hitchcock in 1951.

high society ▶ noun see SOCIETY (sense 1).

high-sounding ▶ adjective (of language or ideas) extravagant and grand-sounding.

high-speed ▶ adjective moving, operating, or happening very quickly: *high-speed travel.*
■ (of photographic film) needing little light or only short exposure. ■ (of steel) suitable for drill bits and other tools that cut so fast that they become red-hot.

high spirits ▶ plural noun (also **high spirit**) lively and cheerful behaviour or mood: *the team returned in high spirits.*
– DERIVATIVES **high-spirited** adjective, **high-spiritedness** noun.

high spot ▶ noun the most enjoyable or significant part of an experience or period of time: *the high spot of the tour was to be an audience with the Pope.*
– PHRASES **hit the high spots** informal visit the most exciting places in town.

high-stick ▶ verb [with obj.] [often as noun **high-sticking**] Ice Hockey strike (an opponent) on or above the shoulders with one's stick, for which a penalty may be assessed.

high street ▶ noun Brit. the main street of a town, especially as the traditional site for most shops, banks, and other businesses.
■ [as modifier] (of retail goods) catering to the needs of the ordinary public: *high-street fashion.*

high-strung ▶ adjective chiefly N. Amer. another term for HIGHLY STRUNG.

hight /haɪt/ ▶ adjective [predic.] archaic or poetic/literary named: *a little pest, hight Tommy Moore.*
– ORIGIN Middle English, from Old English *heht*, past tense of *hātan* 'command, call, or name', of Germanic origin; related to Dutch *heten* and German *heissen.*

high table ▶ noun Brit. a table in a dining hall, typically on a platform, for the most important people, such as the fellows of a college: *I sat at high table.*

hightail ▶ verb [no obj., with adverbial of direction] informal, chiefly N. Amer. move or travel fast: *they hightailed it to India.*

high tea ▶ noun Brit. a meal eaten in the late afternoon or early evening, typically consisting of a cooked dish, bread and butter, and tea.

high-tech (also **hi-tech**) ▶ adjective employing, requiring, or involved in high technology: *a high-tech security system.*
■ (chiefly in architecture and interior design) using styles and materials, such as steel, glass, and plastic, that are associated with industrial use.
▶ noun (**high tech**) short for HIGH TECHNOLOGY.

high technology ▶ noun [mass noun] advanced technological development, especially in electronics: [as modifier] *high-technology weapons.*

high-tensile ▶ adjective (of metal) very strong under tension: *high-tensile steel.*

high tension ▶ noun another term for HIGH VOLTAGE.

high-test ▶ adjective US (of petrol) high-octane.
■ meeting very high standards: *a high-test office.*

high-ticket ▶ adjective another term for BIG-TICKET.

high tide ▶ noun the state of the tide when at its highest level: *at high tide you have to go inland.*
■ the highest point of something: *the high tide of nationalism.*

high-toned ▶ adjective chiefly N. Amer. stylish or superior: *an oasis of classily high-toned culture.*

high-top ▶ adjective denoting a soft-soled sports shoe with a laced upper that extends some distance above the wearer's ankle.
▶ noun (**high-tops**) a pair of such shoes.

high treason ▶ noun see TREASON.

high-up ▶ noun informal a senior person in an organization.

high voltage ▶ noun an electrical potential large enough to cause injury or damage.

high water ▶ noun another term for HIGH TIDE.

high-water mark ▶ noun the level reached by the sea at high tide, or by a lake or river in time of flood.
■ a maximum recorded level or value: *unemployment and crime both stand at a high-water mark.*

highway ▶ noun chiefly N. Amer. a main road, especially one connecting major towns or cities: *a six-lane highway* | figurative *the highway to success.*
■ (chiefly in official use) a public road: *the Highways Department.* ■ Computing a pathway connecting parts of one computer system or between different systems.

Highway Code (in the UK) the official set of rules and guidance for road users.

highwayman ▶ noun (pl. **-men**) historical a man, typically on horseback, who held up travellers at gunpoint in order to rob them.

high wire ▶ noun a high tightrope.
■ [as modifier] figurative requiring great skill or judgement: *it will take a financial high-wire balancing act to fund the requirements.*

high words ▶ plural noun archaic angry words: *high words passed between them.*

high yellow US offensive ▶ adjective denoting a light-skinned person with one black and one white parent.
▶ noun a person of this kind.

HIH Brit. ▶ abbreviation for Her or His Imperial Highness.

hi-hat (also **high-hat**) ▶ noun a pair of foot-operated cymbals forming part of a drum kit.

hijack ▶ verb [with obj.] illegally seize (an aircraft, ship, or vehicle) while in transit and force it to go to a different destination or use it for one's own purposes: *three armed men hijacked a white van* | [as noun **hijacking**] *an eight-hour hijacking.*
■ steal (goods) by seizing them in transit. ■ take over (something) and use it for a different purpose: *the organization had been hijacked by extremists.*
▶ noun an incident or act of hijacking.
– DERIVATIVES **hijacker** noun.
– ORIGIN 1920s (originally US): of unknown origin.

Hijaz variant spelling of HEJAZ.

Hijra /ˈhɪdʒrə/ ▶ noun variant spelling of HEGIRA.

hijra /ˈhɪdʒrə/ ▶ noun Indian a transvestite or eunuch.
– ORIGIN Hindi.

hike ▶ noun **1** a long walk or walking tour.
■ informal a long distance: *it's such a hike from Adelaide to Perth.*
2 a sharp increase, especially in price: *fears of a hike in interest rates.*
▶ verb **1** [no obj., with adverbial of direction] walk for a long distance, especially across country: *they hiked across the moors for miles* | [as noun **hiking**] *she enjoys hiking and climbing in her spare time.*
2 [with obj.] pull or lift up (something, especially clothing): *Roy hiked up his trousers to reveal his socks.*
■ increase (something, especially a price) sharply: *the government hiked up the price of milk by 40 per cent.*
– PHRASES **take a hike** [usu. in imperative] informal, chiefly US

go away (used as an expression of irritation or annoyance).
– DERIVATIVES **hiker** noun.
– ORIGIN early 19th cent. (originally dialect, as a verb): of unknown origin.

hila plural form of **HILUM**.

hilar /ˈhʌɪlə/ ▶ adjective Anatomy & Botany of or relating to a hilus or hilum.

hilarious /hɪˈlɛːrɪəs/ ▶ adjective extremely amusing: *her hilarious novel.*
■ boisterously merry: *an old man was in hilarious conversation with three young men.*
– DERIVATIVES **hilariously** adverb.
– ORIGIN early 19th cent.: from Latin *hilaris* (from Greek *hilaros* 'cheerful') + -OUS. The sense 'exceedingly amusing' dates from the 1920s.

hilarity /hɪˈlarɪti/ ▶ noun [mass noun] extreme amusement, especially when expressed by laughter: *his incredulous expression was the cause of much hilarity.*
■ boisterous merriment: *the noisy hilarity of the streets.*
– ORIGIN late Middle English (in the sense 'cheerfulness'): from French *hilarité*, from Latin *hilaritas* 'cheerfulness, merriment', from *hilaris* (see **HILARIOUS**).

Hilary, St (c.315–c.367), French bishop. In c.350 he was appointed bishop of Poitiers, in which position he became a leading opponent of Arianism. Feast day, 13 January.

Hilary term ▶ noun Brit. (in some universities) the university term beginning in January.
– ORIGIN late Middle English: named after *Hilarius* (see **HILARY, ST**).

Hilbert space ▶ noun Mathematics an infinite-dimensional analogue of Euclidean space.
– ORIGIN early 20th cent.: named after David *Hilbert* (1862–1943), German mathematician.

Hilda, St (614–80), English abbess. Related to the Anglo-Saxon kings of Northumbria, she founded a monastery for both men and women at Whitby around 658, and was one of the leaders of the Celtic Church delegation at the Synod of Whitby. Feast day, 17 November.

Hildegard of Bingen, St /ˈhɪldəɡɑːd, ˈbɪŋən/ (1098–1179), German abbess, scholar, composer, and mystic. A nun of the Benedictine order, she wrote scientific works, poetry, and music, and described her mystical experiences in *Scivias*.

Hildesheim /ˈhɪldəsˌhʌɪm/ an industrial city in Lower Saxony, NW Germany; pop. 106,000 (1991).

Hiligaynon /ˌhɪlɪˈɡeɪnən/ ▶ noun (pl. same or **Hiligaynons**) 1 a member of a people inhabiting Panay, Negros, and other islands in the central Philippines.
2 [mass noun] the Austronesian language of this people, with about 5 million speakers. Also called **ILONGGO**.
▶ adjective of or relating to this people or their language.

Hill¹, Benny (1925–92), English comedian; born *Alfred Hawthorne*. His risqué humour, as seen in the series *The Benny Hill Show*, had an international appeal.

Hill², Damon (b.1960), English motor-racing driver. Son of Graham Hill, he won the Formula One world championship in 1996.

Hill³, (Norman) Graham (1929–75), English motor-racing driver. He became Formula One world champion in 1962 and 1975.

Hill⁴, Octavia (1838–1912), English housing reformer and co-founder of the National Trust (1895).

Hill⁵, Sir Rowland (1795–1879), English educationist, administrator, and inventor. He is chiefly remembered for his introduction of the penny postage-stamp system in 1840.

hill ▶ noun a naturally raised area of land, not as high or craggy as a mountain.
■ a sloping piece of road: *they were climbing a steep hill in low gear.* ■ a heap or mound of something: *a hill of sliding shingle.*
▶ verb [with obj.] form (something) into a heap.
■ bank up (a plant) with soil: *if frost threatens our new plants, we hill them up.*
– PHRASES **a hill of beans** [with negative] N. Amer. informal a thing of little value: *the problems of one old actor don't amount to a hill of beans.* **over the hill** informal old and past one's best.
– ORIGIN Old English *hyll*, of Germanic origin; from

an Indo-European root shared by Latin *collis* and Greek *kolōnos* 'hill'.

Hillary, Sir Edmund (Percival) (b.1919), New Zealand mountaineer and explorer. In 1953 Hillary and Tenzing Norgay were the first people to reach the summit of Mount Everest, as members of a British expedition.

hillbilly ▶ noun (pl. **-ies**) US 1 informal, usu. derogatory an unsophisticated country person, as associated originally with the remote regions of the Appalachians.
2 old-fashioned term for **COUNTRY MUSIC**.
– ORIGIN early 20th cent.: from **HILL** + *Billy* (pet form of the given name *William*).

hill climb ▶ noun a race for vehicles up a steep hill.
– DERIVATIVES **hill-climber** noun, **hill-climbing** noun.

hill figure ▶ noun an outline of a horse, human, or other design cut into the turf of a hill, especially in the chalk downs of southern England, and visible from a distance as a white figure. The oldest of these (the White Horse at Uffington, Oxfordshire) is prehistoric.

hill fort ▶ noun a fort built on a hill, in particular an area on a hilltop enclosed by a system of defensive banks and ditches, as used by Iron Age peoples in NW Europe.

hillman ▶ noun (pl. **-men**) an inhabitant of hilly country.

hillock ▶ noun a small hill or mound.
– DERIVATIVES **hillocky** adjective.

hillside ▶ noun the sloping side of a hill.

hillstar ▶ noun a hummingbird that typically lives at high altitude, especially in the Andes, and is adapted to the harsher climate there.
● Family Trochilidae: two genera, in particular *Oreotrochilus*, and five species.

hill station ▶ noun a town in the low mountains of the Indian subcontinent, popular as a holiday resort during the hot season.

hilltop ▶ noun the summit of a hill.

hillwalking ▶ noun [mass noun] the pastime of walking in hilly country.
– DERIVATIVES **hillwalker** noun.

hilly ▶ adjective (**hillier**, **hilliest**) having many hills.
– DERIVATIVES **hilliness** noun.

hilt ▶ noun the handle of a weapon or tool, especially a sword, dagger, or knife.
– PHRASES (**up**) **to the hilt** completely: *the estate was mortgaged up to the hilt.*
– DERIVATIVES **hilted** adjective.
– ORIGIN Old English *hilt*, *hilte*, of Germanic origin.

hilum /ˈhʌɪləm/ ▶ noun (pl. **hila** /-lə/) Botany the scar on a seed marking the point of attachment to its seed vessel.
■ a point in a starch granule around which the layers of starch are deposited. ■ Anatomy another term for **HILUS**.
– ORIGIN mid 17th cent. (in the Latin sense): from Latin, literally 'little thing, trifle', once thought to mean 'that which sticks to a bean', hence the current sense (mid 18th cent.).

hilus /ˈhʌɪləs/ ▶ noun (pl. **hili** /ˈhʌɪlʌɪ/) Anatomy an indentation in the surface of a kidney, spleen, or other organ, where blood vessels, ducts, nerve fibres, etc. enter or leave it.
– ORIGIN mid 19th cent.: modern Latin, alteration of **HILUM**.

Hilversum /ˈhɪlvəsəm/ a town in the Netherlands, in North Holland province, near Amsterdam; pop. 84,600 (1991). It is the centre of the Dutch radio and television network.

HIM Brit. ▶ abbreviation for Her or His Imperial Majesty.

him ▶ pronoun [third person singular] 1 used as the object of a verb or preposition to refer to a male person or animal previously mentioned or easily identified: *his wife survived him | he took the children with him.* Compare with **HE**.
■ referring to a person or animal of unspecified sex: *withdrawing your child from school to educate him at home may seem drastic.* ■ used after the verb 'to be' and after 'than' or 'as': *that's him all right | I could never be as good as him.*
2 archaic or N. Amer. dialect himself: *in the depths of him, he too didn't want to go.*
– ORIGIN Old English, dative singular form of *he*, *hē* 'he' and *hit* 'it'.

USAGE Why do people tell us that it is wrong to say *I could never be as good as* **him** (rather than *I could never be as good as* **he**)? If they are right, why does **he** in this context sound so odd? For a discussion of this issue, see usage at **PERSONAL PRONOUN**.

Himachal Pradesh /hɪˌmɑːtʃəl prəˈdɛʃ/ a mountainous state in northern India; capital, Simla.

Himalayan ▶ adjective of or relating to the Himalayas: *the Himalayan foothills.*
▶ noun North American term for **COLOURPOINT**.

Himalayas /ˌhɪməˈleɪəz, hɪˈmɑːljəz/ a vast mountain system in southern Asia, extending 2,400 km (1,500 miles) from Kashmir eastwards to Assam.

The Himalayas consist of a series of parallel ranges rising up from the Ganges basin to the Tibetan plateau, at over 3,000 m above sea level. The backbone is the Great Himalayan Range, the highest mountain range in the world, with several peaks rising to over 7,700 m (25,000 ft), the highest being Mount Everest.

– ORIGIN from Sanskrit *Himālaya*, from *hima* 'snow' + *ālaya* 'abode'.

himation /hɪˈmatɪɒn/ ▶ noun an outer garment worn by the ancient Greeks over the left shoulder and under the right.
– ORIGIN Greek.

Himmler /ˈhɪmlə/, Heinrich (1900–45), German Nazi leader, chief of the SS (1929–45) and of the Gestapo (1936–45). He established and oversaw the systematic genocide of over 6 million Jews and other disfavoured groups between 1941 and 1945. Captured by British forces in 1945, he committed suicide.

Hims /hɪms, hɪmz/ variant form of **HOMS**.

himself ▶ pronoun [third person singular] 1 [reflexive] used as the object of a verb or preposition to refer to a male person or animal previously mentioned as the subject of the clause: *the steward introduced himself as Pete | he ought to be ashamed of himself.*
2 [emphatic] he or him personally (used to emphasize a particular male person or animal mentioned): *Thomas himself laid down what we should do.*
■ chiefly Irish a third party of some importance, especially the master of the house: *I'll mention it to himself.*
– ORIGIN Old English (see **HIM**, **SELF**).

Himyarite /ˈhɪmjərʌɪt/ ▶ noun a member of an ancient people of the SW part of the Arabian peninsula, who ruled much of southern Arabia before the 6th century AD.
▶ adjective of or relating to this people.
– ORIGIN from the name *Himyar* (the name of a traditional king of Yemen) + -ITE¹.

hin ▶ noun a Hebrew unit of liquid capacity equal to approximately 5 litres (about one gallon).
– ORIGIN late Middle English: from biblical Hebrew *hīn*.

Hinault /ˈiːnəʊ, French ino/, Bernard (b.1954), French racing cyclist. He won the Tour de France five times between 1978 and 1985 and won the Tour of Italy three times between 1980 and 1985.

Hinayana /ˌhiːnəˈjɑːnə/ (also **Hinayana Buddhism**) ▶ noun [mass noun] a name given by the followers of Mahayana Buddhism to the more orthodox schools of early Buddhism. The tradition died out in India, but it survived in Ceylon (Sri Lanka) as the Theravada school and was taken from there to other regions of SE Asia. See **THERAVADA**.
– ORIGIN from Sanskrit *hīna* 'lesser' + *yāna* 'vehicle'.

hind¹ ▶ adjective [attrib.] (especially of a bodily part) situated at the back; posterior: *a hind leg.*
– PHRASES **on one's hind legs** see **LEG**.
– ORIGIN Middle English: perhaps shortened from Old English *behindan* (see **BEHIND**).

hind² ▶ noun a female deer, especially a red deer or sika in and after the third year.
– ORIGIN Old English, of Germanic origin; related to Dutch *hinde* and German *Hinde*, from an Indo-European root meaning 'hornless', shared by Greek *kemas* 'young deer'.

hind³ ▶ noun archaic, chiefly Scottish a skilled farm worker, typically married and with a tied cottage.
■ a farm steward or bailiff. ■ a peasant or rustic.
– ORIGIN late Old English *hīne* 'household servants', apparently from *hīgna*, *hīna*, genitive plural of *hīgan*, *hīwan* 'family members'.

hind- ▶ combining form (added to nouns) at the back; posterior: *hindquarters | hindwing.*

hindbrain ▶ noun the lower part of the brainstem,

comprising the cerebellum, pons, and medulla oblongata. Also called **RHOMBENCEPHALON**.

Hindemith /ˈhɪndəmɪt/, Paul (1895–1963), German composer. A leading figure in the neoclassical trend which began in the 1920s and an exponent of *Gebrauchsmusik* ('utility music'), he believed that music should have a social purpose. Notable works: *Mathis der Maler* (opera, 1938).

Hindenburg[1] /ˈhɪndn̩ˌbʊrk/ former German name (1915–45) for **ZABRZE**.

Hindenburg[2] /ˈhɪndənˌbəːɡ, German ˈhɪndn̩ˌbʊrk/, Paul Ludwig von Beneckendorff und von (1847–1934), German Field Marshal and statesman, President of the Weimar Republic 1925–34. Elected President in 1925 and re-elected in 1932, he reluctantly appointed Hitler as Chancellor in 1933.

Hindenburg Line (in the First World War) a German fortified line of defence on the Western Front to which Paul von Hindenburg directed retreat and which was not breached until near the end of the war. Also called **SIEGFRIED LINE**.

hinder[1] /ˈhɪndə/ ▶ **verb** [with obj.] create difficulties for (someone or something), resulting in delay or obstruction: *his disability **hinders** him **from** using the usual facilities.*
– ORIGIN Old English *hindrian* 'injure or damage', of Germanic origin; related to German *hindern*, also to **BEHIND**.

hinder[2] /ˈhʌɪndə/ ▶ **adjective** [attrib.] (especially of a bodily part) rear; hind: *the hinder end of its body.*
– ORIGIN Middle English: perhaps from Old English *hinderweard* 'backward', related to **BEHIND**.

Hindi /ˈhɪndi/ ▶ **noun** [mass noun] the most widely spoken language of northern India, with over 200 million speakers; one of the official languages of India. It is an Indic language derived from Sanskrit and is written in the Devanagari script.
▶ **adjective** of or relating to Hindi.
– ORIGIN from Urdu *hindī*, from *Hind* 'India'.

hindmost ▶ **adjective** furthest back: *the hindmost attendant.*

Hindoo ▶ **noun** & **adjective** archaic spelling of **HINDU**.

hindquarters ▶ **plural noun** the hind legs and adjoining parts of a quadruped.

hindrance /ˈhɪndr(ə)ns/ ▶ **noun** a thing that provides resistance, delay, or obstruction to something or someone: ***a hindrance to** the development process* | [mass noun] *the visitor can wander around without hindrance.*

hindsight ▶ **noun** [mass noun] understanding of a situation or event only after it has happened or developed: ***with hindsight**, I should never have gone.*

Hindu /ˈhɪnduː, hɪnˈduː/ ▶ **noun** (pl. **Hindus**) a follower of Hinduism.
▶ **adjective** of or relating to Hindus or Hinduism.
– ORIGIN Urdu, from Persian *hindū*, from *Hind* 'India'.

Hinduism ▶ **noun** [mass noun] a major religious and cultural tradition of the Indian subcontinent, which developed from Vedic religion.

> Hinduism is practised primarily in India, Bangladesh, Sri Lanka, and Nepal. It is a diverse family of devotional and ascetic cults and philosophical schools, all sharing a belief in reincarnation and involving the worship of one or more of a large pantheon of gods and goddesses, including Brahma, Shiva, and Vishnu (incarnate as Rama and Krishna), Kali, Durga, Parvati, and Ganesh. Hindu society was traditionally based on a caste system.

– DERIVATIVES **Hinduize** (also **-ise**) verb.

Hindu Kush /ˌhɪnduː ˈkuːʃ, ˈkʊʃ/ a range of high mountains in northern Pakistan and Afghanistan, forming a westward continuation of the Himalayas. Several peaks exceed 6,150 m (20,000 ft), the highest being Tirich Mir.

Hindustan /ˌhɪndʊˈstɑːn, -ˈstan/ historical the Indian subcontinent in general, more specifically that part of India north of the Deccan, especially the plains of the Ganges and Jumna Rivers.

Hindustani /ˌhɪndʊˈstɑːni/ ▶ **noun** [mass noun] a group of mutually intelligible languages and dialects spoken in NW India, principally Hindi and Urdu.
■ the Delhi dialect of Hindi, widely used throughout India as a lingua franca.
▶ **adjective** of or relating to the culture of NW India: *Hindustani classical music.*

> **USAGE** **Hindustani** was the usual term in the 18th and 19th centuries for the native language of NW India. The usual modern term is **Hindi** (or **Urdu** in Muslim contexts), although **Hindustani** is still used to refer to the dialect of Hindi spoken around Delhi, which is widely used throughout India as a lingua franca.

Hindutva /hɪnˈdʊtvə/ ▶ **noun** [mass noun] Indian a very strong or aggressive sense of Hindu identity, seeking the creation of a Hindu state.
– ORIGIN Hindi.

hindwing ▶ **noun** either of the two back wings of a four-winged insect.

hinge ▶ **noun** a movable joint or mechanism on which a door, gate, or lid swings as it opens and closes or which connects linked objects.
■ Biology a natural joint that performs a similar function, for example that of a bivalve shell. ■ a central point or principle on which everything depends: *this span can be called the hinge of history.*
▶ **verb** (**hingeing** or **hinging**) [with obj.] (usu. **be hinged**) attach or join with or as if with a hinge: *the ironing board was set into the wall and hinged at the bottom* | [as adj. **hinged**] *a pocket watch with a hinged lid.*
■ [no obj., with adverbial of direction] (of a door or part of a structure) hang and turn on a hinge: *the skull's jaw hinged down.* ■ [no obj.] (**hinge on**) depend entirely on: *the future of the industry could hinge on the outcome of next month's election.*
– DERIVATIVES **hingeless** adjective.
– ORIGIN Middle English *henge*; related to **HANG**.

hinky ▶ **adjective** (**-ier**, **-iest**) US informal (of a person) dishonest or suspect.
■ (of an object) unreliable: *my brakes are a little hinky.*
– ORIGIN 1950s: of obscure origin.

hinny[1] ▶ **noun** (pl. **-ies**) the offspring of a female donkey and a male horse.
– ORIGIN early 17th cent.: via Latin from Greek *hinnos*.

hinny[2] (also **hinnie**) ▶ **noun** (pl. **-ies**) Scottish & N. English used as a term of endearment.
– ORIGIN early 19th cent.: variant of **HONEY**.

hinoki /hɪˈnəʊki/ ▶ **noun 1** [mass noun] the valuable timber of a Japanese cypress.
2 (also **hinoki cypress**) the tall slow-growing tree that yields this timber and has bright green leaves.
• *Chamaecyparis obtusa*, family Cupressaceae.
– ORIGIN early 18th cent.: from Japanese.

hint ▶ **noun** a slight or indirect indication or suggestion: *he has given no **hint of** his views.*
■ a small piece of practical information or advice: *handy hints about what to buy.* ■ a very small trace of something: *Randall smiled with **a hint of** mockery.*
▶ **verb** [no obj.] suggest or indicate something indirectly or covertly: *the Minister **hinted at** a possible change of heart* | [with clause] *Edwards has hinted that he will dispose of his majority shareholding.*
■ (**hint at**) (of a thing) be a slight or possible indication of: *the restrained fronts of the terraced houses only hinted at the wealth within.*
– PHRASES **take a** (or **the**) **hint** understand and act on a hint: *she tried to put him off but he didn't take the hint.*
– ORIGIN early 17th cent. (in the sense 'occasion, opportunity'): apparently from obsolete *hent* 'grasp, get hold of', from Old English *hentan*, of Germanic origin; related to **HUNT**. The basic notion is 'something that may be taken advantage of'.

hinterland /ˈhɪntəland/ ▶ **noun** [usu. in sing.] the remote areas of a country away from the coast or the banks of major rivers.
■ the area around or beyond a major town, coastal stretch, or river: *a market town serving its rich agricultural hinterland.* ■ figurative an area lying beyond what is visible or known: *the strange hinterland where life begins and ends.*
– ORIGIN late 19th cent.: from German, from *hinter* 'behind' + *Land* 'land'.

hip[1] ▶ **noun 1** a projection of the pelvis and upper thigh bone on each side of the body in human beings and quadrupeds.
■ (**hips**) the circumference of the body at the buttocks: *a sweater tied round the hips.* ■ a person's hip joint: *she went into a fence and dislocated her hip.*
2 the sharp edge of a roof from the ridge to the eaves where the two sides meet.
– PHRASES **on the hip** archaic at a disadvantage.
– ORIGIN Old English *hype*, of Germanic origin; related to Dutch *heup* and German *Hüfte*, also to **HOP**[1].

hip[2] (also **rose hip**) ▶ **noun** the fruit of a rose, especially a wild kind.
– ORIGIN Old English *hēope*, *hīope*, of West Germanic origin; related to Dutch *joop* and German *Hiefe*.

hip[3] ▶ **adjective** (**hipper**, **hippest**) informal following the latest fashion, especially in popular music and clothes: *it's becoming hip to be environmentally conscious.*
■ understanding; aware: *he's trying to show how **hip** he is **to** Americana.*
– DERIVATIVES **hipness** noun.
– ORIGIN early 20th cent. (originally US): of unknown origin.

hip[4] ▶ **exclamation** introducing a communal cheer: *hip hip hooray!*
– ORIGIN mid 18th cent.: of unknown origin.

hip bath ▶ **noun** a portable bath large enough to sit rather than lie down in.

hip bone ▶ **noun** a large bone forming the main part of the pelvis on each side of the body and consisting of the fused ilium, ischium, and pubis. Also called **INNOMINATE BONE**.

hip flask ▶ **noun** a small flask for spirits, of a kind intended to be carried in a hip pocket.

hip hop ▶ **noun** [mass noun] a style of popular music of US black and Hispanic origin, featuring rap with an electronic backing.
– ORIGIN 1980s: reduplication probably based on **HIP**[3].

hip-huggers ▶ **plural noun** women's trousers fitting tightly at the hips.

hip joint ▶ **noun** the ball-and-socket joint connecting a leg to the trunk of the body, in which the head of the thigh bone fits into the socket of the ilium.

Hipparchus /hɪˈpɑːkəs/ (*c.*170–after 126 BC), Greek astronomer and geographer. He is best known for his discovery of the precession of the equinoxes and is credited with the invention of trigonometry.

hippeastrum /ˌhɪpɪˈastrəm/ ▶ **noun** see **AMARYLLIS**.
– ORIGIN modern Latin, from Greek *hippeus* 'horseman' (the leaves appearing to ride on one another) + *astron* 'star' (from the flower-shape).

hipped[1] ▶ **adjective 1** [in combination] (of a person or animal) having hips of a specified kind: *a thin-hipped girl.*
2 (of a roof) having a sharp edge from the ridge to the eaves where the two sides meet.

hipped[2] ▶ **adjective** [predic.] (**hipped on**) informal, chiefly N. Amer. obsessed or infatuated with: *hipped on discipline.*
– ORIGIN 1920s.: from **HIP**[3], or as the past participle of *hip* 'make someone hip (i.e. aware).'

hipped roof ▶ **noun** another term for **HIP ROOF**.

hipper ▶ **noun** Austral. a soft pad used to protect a person's hip when sleeping on the ground.

hippie ▶ **noun** & **adjective** variant spelling of **HIPPY**[1].

hippo ▶ **noun** (pl. same or **-os**) informal term for **HIPPOPOTAMUS**.

hippocampus /ˌhɪpə(ʊ)ˈkampəs/ ▶ **noun** (pl. **hippocampi** /-pi, -pʌɪ/) Anatomy the elongated ridges on the floor of each lateral ventricle of the brain, thought to be the centre of emotion, memory, and the autonomic nervous system.
– ORIGIN late 16th cent.: via Latin from Greek *hippokampos*, from *hippos* 'horse' + *kampos* 'sea monster'.

hip pocket ▶ **noun** a pocket in the back of a pair of trousers.
– PHRASES **in someone's hip pocket** N. Amer. completely under someone's control.

hippocras /ˈhɪpəkras/ ▶ **noun** [mass noun] historical wine flavoured with spices.
– ORIGIN late Middle English: from Old French *ipocras* 'Hippocrates' (see **HIPPOCRATES**), translating medieval Latin *vinum Hippocraticum* 'Hippocratic wine' (because it was strained through a filter called a *Hippocrates' sleeve*).

Hippocrates /hɪˈpɒkrətiːz/ (*c.*460–377 BC), Greek physician, traditionally regarded as the father of medicine. His name is associated with the medical profession's Hippocratic oath from his attachment to a body of ancient Greek medical writings, probably none of which was written by him.

Hippocratic oath /ˌhɪpəˈkratɪk/ ▶ **noun** an oath stating the obligations and proper conduct of doctors, formerly taken by those beginning medical

practice. Parts of the oath are still used in some medical schools.
– ORIGIN mid 18th cent.: *Hippocratic* from medieval Latin *Hippocraticus* 'relating to Hippocrates' (see **HIPPOCRATES**).

Hippocrene /ˈhɪpəkriːn/ ▶ **noun** [mass noun] poetic/literary used to refer to poetic or literary inspiration.
– ORIGIN early 17th cent.: via Latin from Greek *Hippokrēnē, Hippou krēnē*, literally 'fountain of the horse' (from *hippos* 'horse' + *krēnē* 'fountain'), the name of a fountain on Mount Helicon sacred to the Muses, which according to legend was produced by a stroke of Pegasus' hoof.

hippodrome /ˈhɪpədrəʊm/ ▶ **noun 1** [as name] a theatre or concert hall: *the Birmingham Hippodrome.*
2 (in ancient Greece or Rome) a course for chariot or horse races.
– ORIGIN late 16th cent. (in sense 2): from French, via Latin from Greek *hippodromos*, from *hippos* 'horse' + *dromos* 'race, course'. The early sense led to the term's use as a grandiose name for a modern circus, later applied to other places of popular entertainment (sense 1, late 19th cent.).

hippogriff /ˈhɪpə(ʊ)ɡrɪf/ (also **hippogryph**) ▶ **noun** a mythical creature with the body of a horse and the wings and head of an eagle, born of the union of a male griffin and a filly.
– ORIGIN mid 17th cent.: from French *hippogriffe*, from Italian *ippogrifo*, from Greek *hippos* 'horse' + Italian *grifo* 'griffin'.

Hippolytus /hɪˈpɒlɪtəs/ Greek Mythology the son of Theseus, banished and cursed by his father after being accused by Phaedra of rape. He was killed when a sea monster, sent by Poseidon in response to the curse, frightened his horses as he drove his chariot along a seashore.

hippopotamus /ˌhɪpəˈpɒtəməs/ ▶ **noun** (pl. **hippopotamuses** or **hippopotami** /-mʌɪ/) a large thick-skinned semiaquatic African mammal, with massive jaws and large tusks.
• Family Hippopotamidae: the very large *Hippopotamus amphibius*, frequenting rivers and lakes, and the smaller **pygmy hippopotamus** (*Choeropsis liberiensis*), frequenting forests near fresh water in West Africa.
– ORIGIN Middle English: via Latin from Greek *hippopotamos*, earlier *hippos ho potamios* 'river horse' (from *hippos* 'horse', *potamos* 'river').

Hippo Regius /ˌhɪpəʊ ˈriːdʒɪəs/ see **ANNABA**.

hippuric acid /hɪˈpjʊərɪk/ ▶ **noun** [mass noun] Biochemistry a compound formed in metabolism and present in the urine of herbivores and other mammals.
• A benzoyl derivative of glycine; chem. formula: $C_6H_5CONHCH_2COOH$.
– DERIVATIVES **hippurate** noun.
– ORIGIN mid 19th cent.: *hippuric* from Greek *hippos* 'horse' + *ouron* 'urine' + **-IC**.

hippus /ˈhɪpəs/ ▶ **noun** [mass noun] Medicine spasmodic or rhythmic contraction of the pupil of the eye, a symptom of some neurological conditions.
– ORIGIN late 17th cent.: modern Latin, from Greek *hippos* 'tremor of the eyes'.

hippy[1] (also **hippie**) ▶ **noun** (pl. **-ies**) (especially in the 1960s) a person of unconventional appearance, typically having long hair and wearing beads, associated with a subculture involving a rejection of conventional values and the taking of hallucinogenic drugs.
▶ **adjective** of or relating to hippies or the subculture associated with them: *hippy philosophy.*
– DERIVATIVES **hippiedom** noun, **hippiness** noun, **hippyish** adjective.
– ORIGIN 1950s: from **HIP**[3] + **-Y**[1].

hippy[2] ▶ **adjective** (of a woman) having large hips.

hippy-dippy ▶ **adjective** informal rejecting conventional practices or behaviour in a way perceived to be vague and unconsidered or foolishly idealistic.

hip roof (also **hipped roof**) ▶ **noun** a roof with a sharp edge or edges from the ridge to the eaves where the two sides meet.

hipshot ▶ **adjective** & **adverb** chiefly N. Amer. having a dislocated hip.
■ [as adv.] having a posture with one hip lower than the other.

hipster[1] ▶ **adjective** Brit. (of a garment) having the waistline at the hips rather than the waist.
▶ **noun** (**hipsters**) trousers with such a waistline.

hipster[2] ▶ **noun** informal a person who follows the latest trends and fashions.
– DERIVATIVES **hipsterism** noun.
– ORIGIN 1940s (used originally as an equivalent term to **HEPCAT**): from **HIP**[3] + **-STER**.

hiragana /ˌhɪrəˈɡɑːnə, ˌhɪərə-/ ▶ **noun** [mass noun] the more cursive form of kana (syllabic writing) used in Japanese, primarily used for function words and inflections. Compare with **KATAKANA**.
– ORIGIN Japanese, 'plain kana'.

hircine /ˈhəːsʌɪn/ ▶ **adjective** archaic of or resembling a goat.
– ORIGIN mid 17th cent.: from Latin *hircinus*, from *hircus* 'he-goat'.

hire ▶ **verb** [with obj.] **1** chiefly Brit. obtain the temporary use of (something) for an agreed payment: *she had to hire a dress for the wedding.*
■ (**hire something out**) grant the temporary use of something for an agreed payment: *most train stations hire out cycles.*
2 employ (someone) for wages: *management hired and fired labour in line with demand.*
■ employ for a short time to do a particular job: *don't hire a babysitter who's under 16* | [as adj. **hired**] *a hired assassin.* ■ (**hire oneself out**) make oneself available for temporary employment.
▶ **noun 1** [mass noun] the action of hiring someone or something: *the agreed rate for the hire of the machine* | [as modifier] *a hire charge.*
2 N. Amer. a recently recruited employee.
– PHRASES **for** (or **on**) **hire** available to be hired.
– DERIVATIVES **hireable** (US also **hirable**) adjective, **hirer** noun.
– ORIGIN Old English *hȳrian* 'employ (someone) for wages', *hȳr* 'payment under contract for the use of something', of West Germanic origin; related to Dutch *huren* (verb), *huur* (noun).

hire car ▶ **noun** Brit. a car hired, or available for hire.

hired girl ▶ **noun** N. Amer. a female domestic servant.

hired hand ▶ **noun** a person hired to do short-term manual work.

hired man ▶ **noun** N. Amer. a male domestic servant.

hireling ▶ **noun** chiefly derogatory a person employed to undertake menial work, especially on a casual basis.
– ORIGIN mid 16th cent.: from **HIRE** + **-LING**, on the pattern of Dutch *huurling*.

hire purchase ▶ **noun** [mass noun] Brit. a system by which someone pays for a thing in regular instalments while having the use of it.

hi-res (also **high-res**) ▶ **adjective** informal (of a display or a photographic or video image) showing a large amount of detail.
– ORIGIN late 20th cent.: from *high-resolution*.

Hiri Motu ▶ **noun** see **MOTU** (sense 2).

Hirohito /ˌhɪrəˈhiːtəʊ/ (1901–89), emperor of Japan 1926–89; full name *Michinomiya Hirohito*. Regarded as the 124th direct descendant of Jimmu, he refrained from involvement in politics, though he was instrumental in obtaining Japan's agreement to the unconditional surrender which ended the Second World War. In 1946 the new constitution imposed by America obliged him to renounce his divinity and become a constitutional monarch.

hirola /hɪˈrəʊlə/ ▶ **noun** a rare yellowish-brown antelope native to Kenya and Somalia.
• *Damaliscus hunteri*, family Bovidae. Alternative name: **Hunter's hartebeest**.
– ORIGIN late 19th cent.: from Oromo.

Hiroshima /hɪˈrɒʃɪmə, ˌhɪrəˈʃiːmə/ a city on the south coast of the island of Honshu, western Japan, capital of Chugoku region; pop. 1,086,000 (1990). It was the target of the first atom bomb, which was dropped by the United States on 6 August 1945 and resulted in the deaths of about one third of the city's population of 300,000. Together with a second attack, on Nagasaki three days later, this led to Japan's surrender and the end of the Second World War.

hirple /ˈhəːp(ə)l/ ▶ **verb** [no obj., with adverbial of direction] chiefly Scottish & N. English walk lamely; hobble.
– ORIGIN late 15th cent.: of unknown origin.

Hirschsprung's disease /ˈhɪəʃˌ(s)prʊŋz/ ▶ **noun** [mass noun] a congenital condition in which the rectum and part of the colon fail to develop a normal system of nerves, and consequently faeces accumulate in the colon following birth.
– ORIGIN early 20th cent.: named after Harald *Hirschsprung* (1830–1916), Danish paediatrician.

hirsute /ˈhəːsjuːt/ ▶ **adjective** formal, often humorous hairy: *their hirsute chests.*
– DERIVATIVES **hirsuteness** noun.
– ORIGIN early 17th cent.: from Latin *hirsutus*.

hirsutism /ˈhəːsjuːtɪz(ə)m/ ▶ **noun** [mass noun] Medicine abnormal growth of hair on a woman's face and body.

hirundine /ˈhɪrʌndʌɪn, hɪˈrʌndʌɪn/ ▶ **noun** Ornithology a songbird of the swallow family (Hirundinidae).
– ORIGIN mid 19th cent.: from Latin *hirundo* 'swallow' + **-INE**[1].

his ▶ **possessive determiner 1** belonging to or associated with a male person or animal previously mentioned or easily identified: *James sold his business.*
■ belonging to or associated with a person or animal of unspecified sex (in modern use chiefly replaced by 'his or her' or 'their'): *any child with delayed speech should have his hearing checked.* See **usage** at **HE**.
2 (**His**) used in titles: *His Excellency* | *His Lordship.*
▶ **possessive pronoun** used to refer to a thing or things belonging to or associated with a male person or animal previously mentioned: *he took my hand in his* | *some friends of his.*
– PHRASES **his and hers** (of matching items) for husband and wife, or men and women: *his and hers towels.*
– ORIGIN Old English, genitive singular form of *he, hē* 'he' and *hit* 'it'.

Hispanic /hɪˈspanɪk/ ▶ **adjective** of or relating to Spain or to Spanish-speaking countries, especially those of Central and South America.
■ of or relating to Spanish-speaking people or their culture, especially in the US.
▶ **noun** a Spanish-speaking person, especially one of Latin American descent, living in the US.
– DERIVATIVES **Hispanicize** (also **-ise**) verb.
– ORIGIN from Latin *Hispanicus*, from *Hispania* 'Spain'.

USAGE In the US, **Hispanic** is the standard accepted term when referring to Spanish-speaking people living in the US. Other, more specific, terms such as **Latino** and **Chicano** are also used where occasion demands.

Hispanic American ▶ **noun** a US citizen or resident of Hispanic descent.
▶ **adjective** of or relating to Hispanic Americans.

Hispaniola /ˌhɪspanˈjəʊlə/ an island of the Greater Antilles in the Caribbean, divided into the states of Haiti and the Dominican Republic. After its European discovery by Columbus in 1492, Hispaniola was colonized by the Spaniards, who ceded the western part (now Haiti) to France in 1697.

Hispanist /ˈhɪspənɪst/ (also **Hispanicist** /hɪˈspanɪsɪst/) ▶ **noun** an expert in or student of the language, literature, and civilization of Spain and the Spanish-speaking countries of South America.

Hispano- /hɪˈspanəʊ/ ▶ **combining form** Spanish; Spanish and ...: *Hispano-Argentine.*
■ relating to Spain.
– ORIGIN from Latin *Hispanus* 'Spanish'.

hispid /ˈhɪspɪd/ ▶ **adjective** Botany & Zoology covered with stiff hair or bristles.
– ORIGIN mid 17th cent.: from Latin *hispidus*.

hiss ▶ **verb** [no obj.] make a sharp sibilant sound as of the letter *s*: *the escaping gas was now hissing.*
■ (of a person) make such a sound as a sign of disapproval or derision: *the audience hissed loudly at the mention of his name.* ■ [with obj.] express disapproval of (someone) by making such a sound: *he was hissed off the stage.* ■ [reporting verb] whisper something in an urgent or angry way: *he hissed at them to be quiet* | [with direct speech] *'Get back!' he hissed.*
▶ **noun** a sharp sibilant sound: *the spit and hiss of a cornered cat.*
■ a sound such as this used as an expression of disapproval or derision: *a hiss of annoyance.* ■ [mass noun] electrical interference at audio frequencies: *tape hiss.*
– ORIGIN late Middle English (as a verb): imitative.

hisself ▶ **pronoun** non-standard spelling of **HIMSELF**, used in representing informal or dialect speech.

hist ▶ **exclamation** archaic used to attract attention or call for silence.
– ORIGIN natural exclamation: first recorded in English in the late 16th cent.

hist- ▶ **combining form** variant spelling of **HISTO-** shortened before a vowel (as in *histidine*).

histamine /ˈhɪstəmiːn/ ▶ **noun** [mass noun] Biochemistry a

compound which is released by cells in response to injury and in allergic and inflammatory reactions, causing contraction of smooth muscle and dilation of capillaries.
● A heterocyclic amine; chem. formula: $C_5H_9N_3$.
– DERIVATIVES **histaminic** adjective.
– ORIGIN early 20th cent.: blend of **HISTIDINE** and **AMINE**.

histidine /ˈhɪstɪdiːn/ ▶ **noun** [mass noun] Biochemistry a basic amino acid which is a constituent of most proteins. It is an essential nutrient in the diet of vertebrates, and is the source from which histamine is derived in the body.
● Chem. formula: $C_6H_9N_3O_2$.
– ORIGIN late 19th cent.: from Greek *histos* 'web, tissue' + **-IDE** + **-INE**[4].

histiocyte /ˈhɪstɪə(ʊ)sʌɪt/ ▶ **noun** Physiology a stationary phagocytic cell present in connective tissue.
– ORIGIN early 20th cent.: from Greek *histion* (diminutive of *histos* 'tissue, web') + **-CYTE**.

histo- /ˈhɪstəʊ/ (also **hist-** before a vowel) ▶ **combining form** Biology relating to organic tissue: *histochemistry* | *histocompatibility*.
– ORIGIN from Greek *histos* 'web, tissue'.

histochemistry ▶ **noun** [mass noun] the branch of science concerned with the identification and distribution of the chemical constituents of tissues by means of stains, indicators, and microscopy.
– DERIVATIVES **histochemical** adjective.

histocompatibility ▶ **noun** [mass noun] Medicine compatibility between the tissues of different individuals, so that one accepts a graft from the other without giving an immune reaction.

histogenesis /ˌhɪstə(ʊ)ˈdʒɛnɪsɪs/ ▶ **noun** [mass noun] Biology the differentiation of cells into specialized tissues and organs during growth.
– DERIVATIVES **histogenetic** adjective.

histogeny /hɪˈstɒdʒɪni/ ▶ **noun** another term for **HISTOGENESIS**.
– DERIVATIVES **histogenic** adjective.

histogram ▶ **noun** Statistics a diagram consisting of rectangles whose area is proportional to the frequency of a variable and whose width is equal to the class interval.
– ORIGIN late 19th cent.: from Greek *histos* 'mast, web' + **-GRAM**[1].

histology /hɪˈstɒlədʒi/ ▶ **noun** [mass noun] Biology the study of the microscopic structure of tissues.
– DERIVATIVES **histological** adjective, **histologist** noun.

histolysis /hɪˈstɒlɪsɪs/ ▶ **noun** [mass noun] Biology the breaking down of tissues (e.g. during animal metamorphosis).
– DERIVATIVES **histolytic** adjective.

histone /ˈhɪstəʊn/ ▶ **noun** Biochemistry any of a group of basic proteins found in chromatin.
– ORIGIN late 19th cent.: coined in German, perhaps from Greek *histanai* 'arrest' or from *histos* 'web, tissue'.

histopathology ▶ **noun** [mass noun] the study of changes in tissues caused by disease.
– DERIVATIVES **histopathological** adjective, **histopathologist** noun.

histoplasmosis /ˌhɪstəʊplazˈməʊsɪs/ ▶ **noun** [mass noun] Medicine infection by a fungus found in the droppings of birds and bats in humid areas. It is not serious if confined to the lungs but can be fatal if spread throughout the body.
● The fungus is *Histoplasma capsulatum*.

historian ▶ **noun** an expert in or student of history, especially that of a particular period, geographical region, or social phenomenon: *a military historian*.
– ORIGIN late Middle English: from Old French *historien*, from Latin *historia* (see **HISTORY**).

historiated /hɪˈstɔːrɪeɪtɪd/ ▶ **adjective** (of an initial letter in an illuminated manuscript) decorated with designs representing scenes from the text.
– ORIGIN late 19th cent.: from French *historié*, past participle of *historier* in an obsolete sense 'illustrate', from medieval Latin *historiare*, from *historia* (see **HISTORY**).

historic ▶ **adjective** **1** famous or important in history, or potentially so: *we are standing on a historic site* | *a time of historic change*.
■ archaic of or concerning history; of the past: *eruptions in historic times*.
2 Grammar (of a tense) used in the narration of past events, especially Latin and Greek imperfect and pluperfect.
– ORIGIN early 17th cent. (in the sense 'relating to or in accordance with history'): via Latin from Greek *historikos*, from *historia* 'narrative, knowing by enquiry' (see **HISTORY**).

USAGE On the use of *an historic moment* or *a historic moment*, see **usage** at **AN**.

historical ▶ **adjective** of or concerning history; concerning past events: *historical evidence*.
■ belonging to the past, not the present: *famous historical figures*. ■ (especially of a novel or film) set in the past. ■ (of the study of a subject) based on an analysis of its development over a period: *for the Darwinians, biogeography became a historical science*.
– ORIGIN late Middle English: via Latin from Greek *historikos* (see **HISTORIC**).

USAGE On the use of *an historical event* or *a historical event*, see **usage** at **AN**.

historical linguistics ▶ **plural noun** [treated as sing.] the study of the history and development of languages.

historically ▶ **adverb** with reference to past events: *a historically accurate picture of the time*.
■ [sentence adverb] in the past: *historically, government policy has favoured urban dwellers*.

historical materialism ▶ **noun** another term for **DIALECTICAL MATERIALISM**.

historicism ▶ **noun** [mass noun] **1** the theory that social and cultural phenomena are determined by history.
■ the belief that historical events are governed by laws.
2 the tendency to regard historical development as the most basic aspect of human existence.
3 chiefly derogatory (in artistic and architectural contexts) excessive regard for past styles.
– DERIVATIVES **historicist** noun.
– ORIGIN late 19th cent.: from **HISTORIC**, translating German *Historismus*.

historicity /ˌhɪstəˈrɪsɪti/ ▶ **noun** [mass noun] historical authenticity: *the historicity of bible narrative*.

historicize (also **-ise**) ▶ **verb** [with obj.] treat or represent as historical.
– DERIVATIVES **historicization** noun.

historic present ▶ **noun** [mass noun] Grammar the present tense used instead of the past in vivid narrative, especially in titles, such as 'The Empire Strikes Back', and informally in speech, e.g. 'so I say to him'.

historiography /hɪˌstɔːrɪˈɒɡrəfi, -ˌstɒrɪ-/ ▶ **noun** [mass noun] the study of the writing of history and of written histories.
■ the writing of history.
– DERIVATIVES **historiographer** noun, **historiographic** adjective, **historiographical** adjective.
– ORIGIN mid 16th cent.: via medieval Latin from Greek *historiographia*, from *historia* 'narrative, history' + *-graphia* 'writing'.

history ▶ **noun** (pl. **-ies**) **1** [mass noun] the study of past events, particularly in human affairs: *medieval European history*.
■ the past considered as a whole: *letters that have changed the course of history*.
2 the whole series of past events connected with someone or something: *the history of the Empire*.
■ an eventful past: *the group has quite a history*. ■ a past characterized by a particular thing: *his family had a history of insanity*.
3 a continuous, typically chronological, record of important or public events or of a particular trend or institution: *a history of the labour movement*.
■ a historical play: *Shakespeare's comedies, histories, and tragedies*.
– PHRASES **be history** be perceived as no longer relevant to the present: *the mainframe will soon be history* | *I was making a laughing stock of myself, but that's history now*. ■ informal used to indicate imminent departure, dismissal, or death: *an inch either way and you'd be history*. **go down in history** be remembered or recorded in history. **make history** do something that is remembered in or influences the course of history. **the rest is history** used to indicate that the events succeeding those already related are so well known that they need not be recounted again: *they teamed up, discovered that they could make music, and the rest is history*.
– ORIGIN late Middle English (also as a verb): via Latin from Greek *historia* 'finding out, narrative, history', from *histōr* 'learned, wise man', from an Indo-European root shared by **WIT**[2].

histosol /ˈhɪstəsɒl/ ▶ **noun** Soil Science a soil of an order comprising peaty soils, with a deep surface layer of purely organic material.

histrionic /ˌhɪstrɪˈɒnɪk/ ▶ **adjective** overly theatrical or melodramatic in character or style: *a histrionic outburst*.
■ formal of or concerning actors or acting: *histrionic talents*. ■ Psychiatry denoting a personality disorder marked by shallow volatile emotions and attention-seeking behaviour.
▶ **noun** **1** (**histrionics**) exaggerated dramatic behaviour designed to attract attention.
■ dramatic performance; theatre.
2 archaic an actor.
– DERIVATIVES **histrionically** adverb.
– ORIGIN mid 17th cent. (in the sense 'dramatically exaggerated, hypocritical'): from late Latin *histrionicus*, from Latin *histrio(n-)* 'actor'.

hit ▶ **verb** (**hitting**; past and past participle **hit**) [with obj.] **1** bring one's hand or a tool or weapon into contact with (someone or something) quickly and forcefully: *the woman hit her child for stealing sweets* | [no obj.] *the police **hit out** with truncheons*.
■ accidentally strike (part of one's body) against something, often causing injury: *she fainted and **hit** her head **on** the metal bedstead*. ■ (of a moving object or body) come into contact with (someone or something stationary) quickly and forcefully: *a car hit the barrier*. ■ informal touch or press (part of a machine or other device) in order to work it: *he picked up the phone and hit several buttons*.
2 cause harm or distress to: *the area has been badly hit by pit closures*.
■ [no obj.] (**hit out**) make a strongly worded criticism or attack: *he **hit out at** suppliers for hyping their products*. ■ (of a disaster) occur in and cause damage to (an area) suddenly: *the country was hit by a major earthquake*. ■ informal, chiefly US attack and rob or kill: *if they're cops, maybe it's not a good idea to have them hit*. ■ informal be affected by (an unfortunate and unexpected circumstance or event): *the opening of the town centre hit a snag*.
3 (of a missile or a person aiming one) strike (a target): *the sniper fired and hit a third man*.
■ informal reach (a particular level, point, or figure): *his career hit rock bottom*. ■ arrive at (a place): *it was still night when we hit the outskirts of London*. ■ informal go to (a place): *we hit a diner for coffee and doughnuts*. ■ be suddenly and vividly realized by: [with obj. and clause] *it hit her that I wanted to settle down here*. ■ [no obj.] informal (of a piece of music, film, or play) be successful: *actors are promised a pay increase if a show hits*. ■ [no obj.] take effect: *we sat waiting for the caffeine to hit*. ■ informal give (someone) a dose of a drug or an alcoholic drink. ■ informal (of a product) become available and make an impact on: *the latest board game to hit the market*. ■ informal used to express the idea that someone is taking up a pursuit or taking it seriously: *more and more teenagers are hitting the books*. ■ (**hit someone for/up for**) informal, chiefly US ask someone for: *she was waiting for the right moment to hit her mother for some cash*.
4 propel (a ball) with a bat, racket, stick, etc. to score runs or points in a game.
■ score (runs or points) in this way: *he had hit 25 home runs*.
▶ **noun** **1** an instance of striking or being struck: *few structures can withstand a hit from a speeding car*.
■ a verbal attack: *he could not resist a **hit at** his friend's religiosity*. ■ informal, chiefly US a murder, typically one planned and carried out by a criminal organization. ■ Baseball short for **BASE HIT**.
2 an instance of striking the target aimed at: *one of the bombers had scored a direct hit*.
■ a successful venture, especially in entertainment: *he was the director of many big hits* | [as modifier] *a hit comedy*. ■ a successful pop record or song. ■ informal a successful and popular person or thing: *handsome, smiling, and smart, he was an immediate hit*. ■ Computing an instance of identifying an item of data which matches the requirements of a search.
3 informal a dose of a narcotic drug.
– PHRASES **hit-and-miss** done or occurring at random: *picking a remedy can be a bit hit-and-miss*. **hit-and-run** denoting a person who causes accidental or wilful damage and escapes before being discovered, or damage caused in this way: *he was struck by a hit-and-run driver*. **hit someone below the belt** Boxing give one's opponent an illegal low blow. ■ behave unfairly, especially so as to gain an unfair advantage. **hit the bottle** see **BOTTLE**. **hit someone for six** Brit. affect someone very severely.

[ORIGIN: with allusion to a forceful hit that scores six runs in cricket.] **hit the ground running** informal start something and proceed at a fast pace with enthusiasm. **hit the hay** see HAY[1]. **hit home** see HOME. **hit it off** informal be naturally friendly or well suited. **hit the jackpot** see JACKPOT. **hit the mark** be successful in an attempt or accurate in a guess. **hit the nail on the head** find exactly the right answer. **hit-or-miss** as likely to be unsuccessful as successful: *her work can be hit-or-miss.* **hit the right note** see NOTE. **hit the road** (or US **trail**) informal set out on a journey. **hit the roof** see ROOF. **hit the sack** see SACK[1]. **hit the spot** see SPOT. **hit wicket** Cricket the action of a batsman stepping on or knocking over the wicket, resulting in their dismissal. **make a hit** be successful or popular: *you made a big hit with her.*
– DERIVATIVES **hitter** noun.
– ORIGIN late Old English *hittan* (in the sense 'come upon, find'), from Old Norse *hitta* 'come upon, meet with', of unknown origin.

▶ **hit on** (or **upon**) **1** discover or think of, especially by chance: *she hit on a novel idea for fund-raising.* **2** N. Amer. informal make sexual advances towards. ■ attempt to get something, typically money, from someone: *he hit on family members.*
hit something up Cricket score runs energetically.

hitch ▶ verb **1** [with obj., and adverbial of direction] move (something) into a different position with a jerk: *she hitched the blanket around him* | *he hitched his pants up.*
2 [no obj.] informal travel by hitch-hiking. ■ [with obj.] obtain (a lift) by hitch-hiking. **3** [with obj.] fasten or tether with a rope: *he returned to where he had hitched his horse.* ■ harness (a draught animal or team): *Thomas hitched the pony to his cart.*
▶ noun **1** a temporary interruption or problem: *everything went without a hitch.* **2** a knot of a particular kind, typically one used for fastening a rope to something else. ■ N. Amer. a device for attaching one thing to another, especially the tow bar of a motor vehicle. **3** informal an act of hitch-hiking. **4** N. Amer. informal a period of service: *his 12-year hitch in the navy.*
– PHRASES **get hitched** informal marry. **hitch one's wagon to a star** try to succeed by forming a relationship with someone who is already successful.
– ORIGIN Middle English (in the sense 'lift up with a jerk'): of unknown origin.

Hitchcock, Sir Alfred (Joseph) (1899–1980), English film director. Acclaimed in Britain for films such as *The Thirty-Nine Steps* (1935), he moved to Hollywood in 1939. Among his later works, notable for their suspense and their technical ingenuity, are the thrillers *Strangers on a Train* (1951), *Psycho* (1960), and *The Birds* (1963).

Hitchens /ˈhɪtʃɪnz/, Ivon (1893–1979), English painter. He is known chiefly for landscapes represented in an almost abstract style using areas of vibrant colour.

hitcher ▶ noun a hitch-hiker.

hitch-hike ▶ verb [no obj.] travel by getting free lifts in passing vehicles: *we hitch-hiked up to Scotland.*
▶ noun a journey made by hitch-hike.
– DERIVATIVES **hitch-hiker** noun.

Hite, Shere (b.1942), American feminist. She published her research into sex, gender definition, and private life in the ground-breaking work *The Hite Report on Female Sexuality* (1976), based on the responses of thousands of people to anonymous questionnaires.

hi-tech ▶ adjective variant spelling of HIGH-TECH.

hither ▶ adverb archaic or poetic/literary to or towards this place: *I little knew then that such calamity would summon me hither!*
▶ adjective archaic situated on this side: *the hither side of Severn.*
– ORIGIN Old English *hider*, of Germanic origin; related to HE and HERE.

hither and thither (also **hither and yon**) ▶ adverb in various directions, especially in a disorganized way: *the entire household ran hither and thither.*

hitherto ▶ adverb until now or until the point in time under discussion: *hitherto part of French West Africa, Benin achieved independence in 1960.*

hitherward ▶ adverb archaic to or towards this place.

Hitler, Adolf (1889–1945), Austrian-born Nazi leader, Chancellor of Germany 1933–45.
■ [as noun **a Hitler**] a person with authoritarian or tyrannical characteristics: *little Hitlers of the Trade Union movement.*

He co-founded the National Socialist German Workers' (Nazi) Party in 1919, and came to prominence through his powers of oratory. While imprisoned for an unsuccessful putsch in Munich (1923–4) he wrote *Mein Kampf* (1925), an exposition of his political ideas. Becoming Chancellor in 1933, he established the totalitarian Third Reich. His expansionist foreign policy precipitated the Second World War, while his fanatical anti-Semitism led to the Holocaust.

– DERIVATIVES **Hitlerian** adjective, **Hitlerism** noun, **Hitlerite** noun & adjective.

Hitler moustache ▶ noun a small square moustache like that worn by Adolf Hitler.

Hitler salute ▶ noun another term for NAZI SALUTE.

hit list ▶ noun a list of people to be killed for criminal or political reasons: *a terrorist hit list.*

hit man ▶ noun informal a person who is paid to kill someone, especially for a criminal or political organization.

hit-out ▶ noun Austral. **1** Australian Rules an instance of hitting the ball towards a teammate after it has been bounced by the umpire or at a boundary throw-in. **2** informal a brisk run.

hit parade ▶ noun dated a weekly listing of the current best-selling pop records.

hit squad ▶ noun a team of assassins.

Hittite /ˈhɪtʌɪt/ ▶ noun **1** a member of an ancient people who established an empire in Asia Minor and Syria that flourished from c.1700 to c.1200 BC. ■ a subject of this empire or one of their descendants, including a Canaanite or Syrian people mentioned in the Bible (11th to 8th century BC). **2** [mass noun] the language of the Hittites, the oldest attested Indo-European language. Written in both hieroglyphic and cuneiform scripts, it was deciphered in the early 20th century.
▶ adjective of or relating to the Hittites, their empire, or their language.
– ORIGIN from Hebrew *Ḥittīm*, ultimately from Hittite *Ḥatti.*

HIV ▶ abbreviation for human immunodeficiency virus, a retrovirus which causes Aids.

hive ▶ noun a beehive. ■ the bees in a hive. ■ a thing that has the domed shape of a beehive. ■ figurative a place in which people are busily occupied: *the kitchen became a hive of activity.*
▶ verb [with obj.] place (bees) in a hive. ■ [no obj.] (of bees) enter a hive.
– ORIGIN Old English *hȳf*, of Germanic origin.
▶ **hive something off** chiefly Brit. (especially in business) separate something from a larger group or organization, especially from public to private ownership: *the weekly magazine hived off by the BBC.*

hive bee ▶ noun see BEE (sense 1).

hives ▶ plural noun [treated as sing. or pl.] another term for URTICARIA.
– ORIGIN early 16th cent. (originally Scots, denoting various conditions causing a rash, especially in children): of unknown origin.

HIV-positive ▶ adjective having had a positive result in a blood test for the Aids virus HIV.

hiya ▶ exclamation an informal greeting.
– ORIGIN 1940s: alteration of *how are you?*

Hizbullah /ˌhɪzbʊˈlɑː, ˈhɪzbʊlə/ variant spelling of HEZBOLLAH.

HK ▶ abbreviation for Hong Kong.

HKJ ▶ abbreviation for Jordan (international vehicle registration).
– ORIGIN from *Hashemite Kingdom of Jordan.*

HL ▶ abbreviation for (in the UK) House of Lords.

hl ▶ abbreviation for hectolitre(s).

HM ▶ abbreviation for ■ headmaster or headmistress. ■ Brit. heavy metal (music). ■ (in the UK) Her (or His) Majesty('s): *HM Forces.*

hm ▶ abbreviation for hectometre(s).

h'm (also **hmm**) ▶ exclamation & noun variant spelling of HEM[2], HUM[1].

HMG ▶ abbreviation for (in the UK) Her or His Majesty's Government.

HMI historical ▶ abbreviation for (in the UK) Her or His Majesty's Inspector (of Schools).

Hmong /hmɒŋ/ ▶ noun (pl. same) **1** a member of a people living in isolated mountain villages throughout SE Asia. **2** [mass noun] the language of this people, occurring in a large number of highly distinct dialects.
▶ adjective relating to or denoting this people or their language.

USAGE The term **Hmong** is now usually preferred, as being the name the people use with reference to themselves, though the Chinese name **Miao** (or, in SE Asia, **Meo**) was until recently more common in English contexts.

HMS ▶ abbreviation for Her or His Majesty's Ship, used in the names of ships in the British navy: *HMS Ark Royal.*

HMSO ▶ abbreviation for (in the UK) Her or His Majesty's Stationery Office, which publishes official government documents and legislation.

HNC ▶ abbreviation for (in the UK) Higher National Certificate.

HND ▶ abbreviation for (in the UK) Higher National Diploma.

Ho ▶ symbol for the chemical element holmium.

ho[1] (also **hoe**) ▶ noun (pl. **-os** or **-oes**) black slang a prostitute. ■ derogatory a woman.
– ORIGIN 1960s: representing a dialect pronunciation of WHORE.

ho[2] ▶ exclamation **1** an expression of surprise, admiration, triumph, or derision: *Ho! I'll show you.* ■ [in combination] used as the second element of various exclamations: *what ho!* | *heave ho.* **2** used to call for attention: *ho there!* ■ [in combination] chiefly Nautical used to draw attention to something: *land ho!*
– ORIGIN natural exclamation: first recorded in Middle English.

ho. ▶ abbreviation for house.

hoagie /ˈhəʊɡi/ ▶ noun (pl. **-ies**) chiefly N. Amer. a sandwich made of a long roll filled with meat, cheese, and salad. ■ (also **hoagie roll**) a bread roll used for such a sandwich.
– ORIGIN of unknown origin.

hoar /hɔː/ archaic or poetic/literary ▶ adjective greyish white; grey or grey-haired with age.
▶ noun [mass noun] hoar frost.
– ORIGIN Old English *hār*, of Germanic origin; related to German *hehr* 'majestic, noble'.

hoard ▶ noun a stock or store of money or valued objects, typically one that is secret or carefully guarded: *he came back to rescue his little hoard of gold.* ■ an ancient store of coins or other valuable artefacts: *a hoard of Romano-British bronzes.* ■ an amassed store of useful information or facts, retained for future use: *a hoard of secret information about his work.*
▶ verb [with obj.] amass (money or valued objects) and hide or store away: *thousands of antiques hoarded by a compulsive collector.* ■ accumulate a supply of (something) in a time of scarcity: *many of the boat people had hoarded rations.* ■ reserve in the mind for future use: [as adj. **hoarded**] *a year's worth of hoarded resentments and grudges.*
– DERIVATIVES **hoarder** noun.
– ORIGIN Old English *hord* (noun), *hordian* (verb), of Germanic origin; related to German *Hort* (noun), *horten* (verb).

USAGE The words **hoard** and **horde** have some similarities in meaning and are pronounced the same, so they are therefore sometimes confused. A **hoard** is 'a secret stock or store of something', as in *a hoard of treasure*, while a **horde** is a disparaging word for 'a large group of people', as in *hordes of fans descended on the stage*. Instances of **hoard** being used instead of **horde** are not uncommon: around 10 per cent of citations for **hoard** in the British National Corpus are for the incorrect use.

hoarding ▶ noun Brit. a large board in a public place, used to display advertisements. ■ a temporary board fence erected round a building site.
– ORIGIN early 19th cent.: from obsolete *hoard* in the same sense (probably based on Old French *hourd*; related to HURDLE) + -ING[1].

hoar frost ▶ noun [mass noun] a greyish-white

crystalline deposit of frozen water vapour formed in clear still weather on vegetation, fences, etc.

hoarhound ▶ noun variant spelling of **HOREHOUND**.

hoarse ▶ adjective (of a person's voice) sounding rough and harsh, typically as the result of a sore throat or of shouting: *a hoarse whisper.*
– DERIVATIVES **hoarsely** adverb, **hoarsen** verb, **hoarseness** noun.
– ORIGIN Old English *hās*, of Germanic origin; related to Dutch *hees*. The spelling with *r* was influenced in Middle English by an Old Norse cognate.

hoarstone ▶ noun Brit. (now only in place names) an ancient boundary stone.

hoary ▶ adjective (**hoarier**, **hoariest**) **1** greyish-white: *hoary cobwebs.*
■ (of a person) having grey or white hair; aged: *young lasses imprisoned by hoary old husbands.* ■ [attrib.] used in names of animals and plants covered with whitish fur or short hairs, e.g. **hoary bat**, **hoary cress**.
2 old and trite: *the hoary old adage often used by Fleet Street editors.*
– DERIVATIVES **hoarily** adverb, **hoariness** noun.

hoary marmot ▶ noun a large stocky greyish-brown marmot with a whistling call, found in the mountains of north-western North America.
● *Marmota caligata*, family Sciuridae.

hoatzin /həʊˈatsɪn/ ▶ noun a large tree-dwelling tropical American bird with weak flight. Young hoatzins have hooked claws on their wings, enabling them to climb about among the branches.
● *Opisthocomus hoazin*, the only member of the family Opisthocomidae (order Galliformes or Cuculiformes).
– ORIGIN mid 17th cent.: from American Spanish, from Nahuatl *uatzin*, probably imitative of its call.

hoax ▶ noun a humorous or malicious deception: *they recognized the plan as a hoax* | [as modifier] *he was accused of making hoax calls.*
▶ verb [with obj.] deceive with a hoax.
– DERIVATIVES **hoaxer** noun.
– ORIGIN late 18th cent. (as a verb): probably a contraction of **HOCUS**.

hob[1] ▶ noun **1** Brit. a cooking appliance, or the flat top part of a cooker, with hotplates or burners.
■ a flat metal shelf at the side of a fireplace, having its surface level with the top of the grate and used especially for heating pans.
2 a machine tool used for cutting gears or screw threads.
3 a peg or pin used as a mark in throwing games.
– ORIGIN late 16th cent. (in sense 3): alteration of **HUB**. Sense 1, 'metal shelf by a fireplace', dates from the late 17th cent.

hob[2] ▶ noun **1** a male ferret. Compare with **GILL**[4] (in sense 2).
2 archaic or dialect a sprite or hobgoblin.
– PHRASES **play** (or **raise**) **hob** N. Amer. cause mischief.
– ORIGIN late Middle English (in the sense 'country fellow'): pet form of *Rob*, short for *Robin* or *Robert*, often referring specifically to **ROBIN GOODFELLOW**.

Hobart /ˈhəʊbɑːt/ the capital and chief port of Tasmania; pop. 127,130 (1991).
– ORIGIN named after Lord *Hobart* (1760–1816), Secretary of State for the Colonies.

Hobbema /ˈhɒbəmə/, Meindert (1638–1709), Dutch landscape painter. A pupil of Jacob van Ruisdael, he was one of the last 17th-century Dutch landscape painters.

Hobbes /hɒbz/, Thomas (1588–1679), English philosopher. Hobbes was a materialist, claiming that there was no more to the mind than the physical motions discovered by science, and he believed that human action was motivated entirely by selfish concerns, notably fear of death. In *Leviathan* (1651) he argued that absolute monarchy was the most rational, hence desirable, form of government.
– DERIVATIVES **Hobbesian** adjective.

hobbit ▶ noun a member of an imaginary race similar to humans, of small size and with hairy feet, in stories by J. R. R. Tolkien.
– ORIGIN 1937: invented by Tolkien in his book *The Hobbit*, and said by him to mean 'hole-dweller'.

hobble ▶ verb **1** [no obj., with adverbial of direction] walk in an awkward way, typically because of pain from an injury: *he was hobbling around on crutches.*
■ figurative proceed haltingly in action or speech: *inertia and habit will keep it hobbling along.*
2 [with obj.] (often **be hobbled**) tie or strap together

(the legs of a horse or other animal) to prevent it from straying. [ORIGIN: variant of **HOPPLE**.]
■ cause (a person or animal) to limp: *Johnson was still hobbled slightly by an ankle injury.* ■ figurative be or cause a problem for: *cotton farmers were hobbled by low prices.*
▶ noun **1** [in sing.] an awkward way of walking, typically due to pain from an injury: *he finished the match almost reduced to a hobble.*
2 a rope or strap used for hobbling a horse or other animal.
– DERIVATIVES **hobbler** noun.
– ORIGIN Middle English: probably of Dutch or Low German origin and related to Dutch *hobbelen* 'rock from side to side'.

hobblebush ▶ noun a North American viburnum which bears clusters of white or pink flowers and purple-black berries.
● *Viburnum alnifolium*, family Caprifoliaceae.

hobbledehoy /ˈhɒb(ə)ldɪˌhɔɪ/ informal, dated ▶ noun a clumsy or awkward youth.
▶ adjective awkward or clumsy: *his hobbledehoy hands.*
– ORIGIN mid 16th cent.: of unknown origin.

hobble skirt ▶ noun a style of skirt so narrow at the hem as to impede walking, popular in the 1910s.

Hobbs, Sir Jack (1882–1963), English cricketer; full name *John Berry Hobbs*. During his career (1905–1934) he scored 61,237 runs and 197 centuries, and made 61 test appearances for England.

hobby[1] ▶ noun (pl. **-ies**) **1** an activity done regularly in one's leisure time for pleasure: *her hobbies are reading and gardening.*
2 archaic a small horse or pony.
■ historical an early type of velocipede.
– ORIGIN late Middle English *hobyn*, *hoby*, from pet forms of the given name *Robin*. Originally in sense 2 (compare with **DOBBIN**), it later came to denote a toy horse or hobby horse, hence 'a pastime, something done for pleasure'.

hobby[2] ▶ noun (pl. **-ies**) a migratory Old World falcon with long narrow wings, catching dragonflies and birds on the wing.
● Genus *Falco*, family Falconidae: four species, e.g. the (**northern**) **hobby** (*F. subbuteo*) of Eurasia.
– ORIGIN late Middle English: from Old French *hobet*, diminutive of *hobe* 'falcon'.

hobby horse ▶ noun **1** a child's toy consisting of a stick with a model of a horse's head at one end.
■ a rocking horse. ■ a model of a horse or a horse's head, typically of wicker, used in morris dancing or pantomime.
2 a preoccupation; a favourite topic: *scientific visualization is another of his hobby horses.*

hobbyist ▶ noun a person who pursues a particular hobby: *a computer hobbyist.*

hobday ▶ verb [with obj.] Brit. operate on (a horse) to improve its breathing by pinning back the vocal fold in the larynx.
– ORIGIN 1930s: named after Sir Frederick T. G. *Hobday* (1869–1939), the British veterinary surgeon who introduced the technique.

hobgoblin ▶ noun (in mythology and fairy stories) a mischievous imp or sprite.
■ a fearsome mythical creature.
– ORIGIN mid 16th cent.: from **HOB**[2] + **GOBLIN**.

hobnail ▶ noun a short heavy-headed nail used to reinforce the soles of boots.
■ a blunt projection, especially in cut or moulded glassware. ■ [mass noun] glass decorated with such projections.
– DERIVATIVES **hobnailed** adjective.
– ORIGIN late 16th cent.: from **HOB**[1] + **NAIL**.

hobnail liver (also **hobnailed liver**) ▶ noun a liver having many small knobbly projections due to cirrhosis.

hobnob ▶ verb (**hobnobbed**, **hobnobbing**) [no obj.] informal mix socially, especially with those of perceived higher social status: *he was hobnobbing with the great and good.*
– ORIGIN early 19th cent. (in the sense 'drink together'): from archaic *hob or nob*, *hob and nob*, probably meaning 'give and take', used by two people drinking to each other's health, from dialect *hab nab* 'have or not have'.

hobo ▶ noun (pl. **-oes** or **-os**) N. Amer. a homeless person or migrant worker; a tramp.
– ORIGIN late 19th cent.: of unknown origin.

Hobson's choice ▶ noun a choice of taking what is available or nothing at all.

– ORIGIN mid 17th cent.: named after Thomas *Hobson* (1554–1631), a Cambridge carrier who hired out horses, giving the customer the 'choice' of the one nearest the door or none at all.

Ho Chi Minh /ˌhəʊ tʃiː ˈmɪn/, Vietnamese communist statesman (1890–1969), President of North Vietnam 1954–69; born *Nguyen That Thanh*. He led the Vietminh against the Japanese during the Second World War, fought the French until they were defeated in 1954 and Vietnam was divided into North and South Vietnam, and deployed his forces in the guerrilla struggle that became the Vietnam War.

Ho Chi Minh City official name (since 1975) for **SAIGON**.

hock[1] ▶ noun **1** the joint in a quadruped's hind leg between the knee and the fetlock, the angle of which points backwards.
2 a knuckle of meat, especially of pork or ham.
– ORIGIN late Middle English: variant of **HOUGH**.

hock[2] ▶ noun [mass noun] Brit. a dry white wine from the German Rhineland.
– ORIGIN abbreviation of obsolete *hockamore*, alteration of German *Hochheimer* (*Wein*) '(wine) from Hochheim'.

hock[3] ▶ verb [with obj.] informal deposit (an object) with a pawnbroker as security for money lent.
– PHRASES **in hock** having been pawned. ■ in debt: *East European states in hock to Western bankers.*
– ORIGIN mid 19th cent. (in the phrase *in hock*): from Dutch *hok* 'hutch, prison, debt'.

hocket ▶ noun Music a spasmodic or interrupted effect in medieval and contemporary music, produced by dividing a melody between two parts, notes in one part coinciding with rests in the other.
– DERIVATIVES **hocketing** noun.
– ORIGIN late 18th cent.: from French *hoquet* 'hiccup'; in Old French the sense was 'hitch, sudden interruption' which also existed in Middle English.

hockey[1] /ˈhɒki/ ▶ noun [mass noun] a team game played between two teams of eleven players each, using hooked sticks with which the players try to drive a small hard ball towards goals at opposite ends of a field. It is also called **field hockey** to distinguish it from **ice hockey**.
– ORIGIN early 16th cent.: of unknown origin.

hockey[2] /ˈɒki, ˈhɒki/ ▶ noun variant spelling of **OCHE**.

Hockney, David (b.1937), English painter and draughtsman. He is best known for his association with pop art and for his Californian work of the mid 1960s, which depicts flat, almost shadowless architecture, lawns, and swimming pools.

Hocktide ▶ noun (in England) a religious festival formerly kept on the second Monday and Tuesday after Easter, during which, in pre-Reformation times, money was raised for church and parish purposes.
– ORIGIN of unknown origin.

hocus /ˈhəʊkəs/ ▶ verb (**hocussed**, **hocussing** or **hocused**, **hocusing**) [with obj.] archaic **1** deceive (someone).
2 stupefy (someone) with drugs, typically for a criminal purpose.
■ drug (liquor): *you shall hocus his drink.*
– ORIGIN late 17th cent.: from an obsolete noun *hocus* 'trickery', from **HOCUS-POCUS**.

hocus-pocus ▶ noun [mass noun] meaningless talk or activity, often designed to draw attention away from and disguise what is actually happening: *some people still view psychology as a lot of hocus-pocus.*
■ a form of words often used by a person performing conjuring tricks.
– ORIGIN early 17th cent.: from *hax pax max Deus adimax*, a pseudo-Latin phrase used as a magic formula by conjurors.

hod ▶ noun a builder's V-shaped open trough on a pole, used for carrying bricks and other building materials.
■ a coal scuttle.
– ORIGIN late 16th cent.: variant of northern English dialect *hot* 'a basket for carrying earth', from Old French *hotte* 'pannier', probably of Germanic origin.

hodden /ˈhɒd(ə)n/ ▶ noun [mass noun] chiefly Scottish & N. English a coarse woollen cloth.
– ORIGIN late 16th cent.: of unknown origin.

Hodeida /həʊˈdeɪdə/ the chief port of Yemen, on

the Red Sea; pop. 246,000 (est. 1993). Arabic name **AL-HUDAYDA**.

Hodge ▶ noun Brit. archaic used as a name for a typical English agricultural labourer.
– ORIGIN late Middle English: pet form of the given name *Roger*.

hodgepodge ▶ noun US variant of **HOTCHPOTCH**.
– ORIGIN late Middle English: changed by association with **HODGE**.

Hodgkin[1], Sir Alan Lloyd (1914–98), English physiologist. With Andrew Huxley he demonstrated the role of sodium and potassium ions in the transmission of nerve impulses between cells. Nobel Prize (1963).

Hodgkin[2], Dorothy (Crowfoot) (1910–94), British chemist. She developed Sir Lawrence Bragg's X-ray diffraction technique for investigating the structure of crystals and applied it to complex organic compounds. Using this method she determined the structures of penicillin, vitamin B_{12}, and insulin. Nobel Prize for Chemistry (1964).

Hodgkin's disease ▶ noun [mass noun] a malignant though often curable disease of lymphatic tissues typically causing painless enlargement of the lymph nodes, liver, and spleen.
– ORIGIN mid 19th cent.: named after Thomas *Hodgkin* (1798–1866), the English physician who first described it.

hodiernal /ˌhɒdɪˈɜːn(ə)l, ˌhəʊdɪ-/ ▶ adjective rare of or relating to the present day.
– ORIGIN mid 17th cent.: from Latin *hodiernus* (from *hodie* 'today') + **-AL**.

hodman ▶ noun (pl. **-men**) Brit. a labourer who carries a hod.

hodograph /ˈhɒdəɡrɑːf/ ▶ noun Mathematics a curve the radius vector of which represents in magnitude and direction the velocity of a moving object.
– ORIGIN mid 19th cent.: from Greek *hodos* 'way' + **-GRAPH**.

hodoscope /ˈhɒdəskəʊp/ ▶ noun Physics an instrument for observing the paths of subatomic particles, especially those arising from cosmic rays.
– ORIGIN early 20th cent. (denoting a microscope for examination of light paths in crystals): from Greek *hodos* 'way' + **-SCOPE**. The current sense dates from the 1950s.

Hoe, Richard March (1812–86), American inventor and industrialist. In 1846 he became the first printer to develop a successful rotary press, which greatly increased the speed of printing.

hoe[1] ▶ noun a long-handled gardening tool with a thin metal blade, used mainly for weeding.
▶ verb (**-oes, -oed, -oeing**) [with obj.] use a hoe to dig (earth) or thin out or dig up (plants).
– DERIVATIVES **hoer** noun.
– ORIGIN Middle English: from Old French *houe*, of Germanic origin; related to German *Haue*, also to **HEW**.
■ **hoe in** Austral./NZ informal eat eagerly.
■ **hoe into** Austral./NZ informal attack or criticize.

hoe[2] ▶ noun variant spelling of **HO**[1].

hoecake ▶ noun US a coarse cake of maize flour, originally baked on the blade of a hoe.

hoedown ▶ noun N. Amer. a social gathering at which lively folk dancing takes place.
■ a lively folk dance.

Hoek van Holland /ˌhuk van ˈhɒlant/ Dutch name for **HOOK OF HOLLAND**.

Hofei /həʊˈfeɪ/ variant of **HEFEI**.

Hoffa /ˈhɒfə/, Jimmy (1913–c.75), American trade union leader; full name *James Riddle Hoffa*. President of the Teamsters union from 1957, he was imprisoned in 1967–71 for attempted bribery of a federal court judge, fraud, and looting pension funds. He disappeared in 1975, and is thought to have been murdered.

Hoffman /ˈhɒfmən/, Dustin (Lee) (b.1937), American actor. A versatile method actor, he won Oscars for *Kramer vs Kramer* (1979) and *Rain Man* (1989). Other notable films: *The Graduate* (1967) and *Tootsie* (1983).

Hoffmann /ˈhɒfmən/, E. T. A. (1776–1822), German novelist, short-story writer, and music critic; full name *Ernst Theodor Amadeus Hoffmann*. His extravagantly fantastic stories provided the inspiration for Offenbach's opera *Tales of Hoffmann* (1881).

Hofmannsthal /ˈhɒfmənsˌtɑːl, German ˈhoːf-

mansˌtaːl/, Hugo von (1874–1929), Austrian poet and dramatist. He wrote the libretti for many of the operas of Richard Strauss, including *Elektra* (1909). With Strauss and Max Reinhardt he helped found the Salzburg Festival.

hog ▶ noun **1** a domesticated pig, especially a castrated male reared for slaughter.
■ a feral pig. ■ a wild animal of the pig family, for example a warthog. ■ informal a greedy person.
2 (also **hogg**) dialect a young sheep before the first shearing.
▶ verb (**hogged, hogging**) [with obj.] **1** informal keep or use all of (something) for oneself in an unfair or selfish way: *he never hogged the limelight.*
2 (usu. **be hogged**) distort (a ship) by supporting it in the centre and allowing the bow and stern to droop.
– PHRASES **go the whole hog** informal do something completely or thoroughly. [ORIGIN: of several origins suggested, one interprets *hog* as the American slang term for a ten cent piece; another refers the idiom to one of Cowper's poems (1779), which discusses Muslim uncertainty about which parts of the pig are acceptable as food, leading to the 'whole hog' being eaten, because of confusion over Mohammed's teaching.] **live high on** (or **off**) **the hog** N. Amer. informal have a luxurious lifestyle.
– DERIVATIVES **hogger** noun, **hoggery** noun, **hoggish** adjective, **hoggishly** adverb, **hog-like** adjective.
– ORIGIN late Old English *hogg, hocg*, perhaps of Celtic origin and related to Welsh *hwch* and Cornish *hoch* 'pig, sow'.

hogan /ˈhəʊɡ(ə)n/ ▶ noun a traditional Navajo Indian hut of logs and earth.
– ORIGIN Navajo.

Hogarth /ˈhəʊɡɑːθ/, William (1697–1764), English painter and engraver. Notable works include his series of engravings on 'modern moral subjects', such as *A Rake's Progress* (1735), which satirized the vices of both high and low life in 18th-century England.
– DERIVATIVES **Hogarthian** adjective.

hogback (also **hog's back**) ▶ noun a long hill or mountain ridge with steep sides.

hog badger ▶ noun a badger with a long mobile snout and dark facial stripes, found in the forests of east Asia.
● *Arctonyx collaris*, family Mustelidae.

hog deer ▶ noun a short-legged heavily built deer having a yellow-brown coat with darker underparts, found in grasslands and paddy fields in SE Asia.
● *Cervus porcinus*, family Cervidae.

hogfish ▶ noun (pl. same or **-fishes**) a colourful wrasse that occurs chiefly in the warm waters of the western Atlantic, often acting as a cleaner fish for other species.
● Several genera and species in the family Labridae, in particular the large edible *Lachnolaimus maximus*.

Hogg, James (1770–1835), Scottish poet. A shepherd in the Ettrick Forest whose poetic talent was discovered by Sir Walter Scott, he is best known today for his prose work *The Confessions of a Justified Sinner* (1824).

hogg ▶ noun variant spelling of **HOG** (in sense 2).

Hoggar Mountains /ˈhɒɡə/ a mountain range in the Saharan desert of southern Algeria, rising to a height of 2,918 m (9,573 ft) at Tahat. Also called **AHAGGAR MOUNTAINS**.

hogget /ˈhɒɡɪt/ ▶ noun Brit. a yearling sheep.
■ NZ a lamb between weaning and first shearing.
– ORIGIN late Middle English (applied also to a young boar): from **HOG** + **-ET**[1].

hoggin ▶ noun [mass noun] a mixture of sand and gravel, used especially as hard core in road-building.
– ORIGIN mid 19th cent.: of unknown origin.

hog line ▶ noun Curling a line marked across either end of a curling rink at one sixth of the rink's length from the tee. No sweeping is allowed until a stone has crossed the first line.

Hogmanay /ˈhɒɡməneɪ, ˌhɒɡməˈneɪ/ ▶ noun (in Scotland) New Year's Eve, and the celebrations that take place at this time.
– ORIGIN early 17th cent.: perhaps from *hoguinané*, Norman French form of Old French *aguillanneuf* 'last day of the year, new year's gift'.

hog-nosed bat ▶ noun a tiny insectivorous bat with a piglike nose and no tail, native to Thailand. It is the smallest known bat.
● *Craseonycteris thonglongyai*, the only member of the family Craseonycteridae.

hog-nosed skunk ▶ noun an American skunk with a bare elongated snout and a black face, found in rugged terrain.
● Genus *Conepatus*, family Mustelidae: several species.

hognose snake (also **hog-nosed snake**) ▶ noun a harmless burrowing American snake with an upturned snout. When threatened it inflates itself with air and hisses, and may feign death. Also called **PUFF ADDER** in North America.
● Genus *Heterodon*, family Colubridae: several species.

hognut ▶ noun another term for **EARTHNUT** (in sense 1).

hog plum ▶ noun a tropical tree which bears edible plum-like fruit, in particular:
● a Caribbean tree with yellow fruit (*Spondias mombin*, family Anacardiaceae). ● (**American hog plum**) an American tree with bitter fruit and timber that is used as a sandalwood substitute (*Ximenia americana*, family Olacaceae).
– ORIGIN late 17th cent.: so named because the fruit is common food for hogs in the West Indies and Brazil.

hog's back ▶ noun variant spelling of **HOGBACK**.

hogshead (abbrev.: **hhd**) ▶ noun a large cask.
■ a measure of capacity for wine, equal to 52.5 imperial gallons or 63 US gallons (238.7 litres). ■ a measure of capacity for beer, equal to 54 imperial gallons or 64 US gallons (245.5 litres).
– ORIGIN Middle English: from **HOG** + **HEAD**; the reason for the term is unknown.

hog-tie ▶ verb N. Amer. [with obj.] secure by fastening the hands and feet or all four feet together.
■ figurative impede or hinder greatly.

hogwash ▶ noun [mass noun] informal nonsense.
– ORIGIN mid 15th cent.: from **HOG** + **WASH**; the original sense was 'kitchen swill for pigs'.

hogweed ▶ noun [mass noun] a large, coarse, white-flowered weed of the parsley family, native to north temperate regions and formerly used as forage for pigs.
● Genus *Heracleum*, family Umbelliferae: several species, in particular the common European *H. sphondylium* and the introduced **giant hogweed** (*H. mantegazzianum*).

hog-wild ▶ adjective N. Amer. informal out of control.

Hohenstaufen /ˈhəʊənˌʃtaʊf(ə)n, German ˈhoːənˌʃtaʊfn/ a German dynastic family, some of whom ruled as Holy Roman emperors between 1138 and 1254, among them Frederick I (Barbarossa).

Hohenzollern /ˈhəʊənˌzɒlən, German ˌhoːənˈtsɔlən/ a German dynastic family from which came the kings of Prussia from 1701 to 1918 and German emperors from 1871 to 1918.

Hohhot /həʊˈhɒt/ (also **Huhehot**) the capital of Inner Mongolia autonomous region, NE China; pop. 1,206,000 (1990). Former name (until 1954) **KWESUI**.

ho ho ▶ exclamation representing deep, exuberant laughter.
■ used to express triumph, especially at discovery: *Ho ho! A stranger in our midst!*
– ORIGIN mid 16th cent.: reduplication of **HO**[2].

ho-hum ▶ exclamation used to express boredom or resignation.
▶ adjective boring: *a ho-hum script.*
– ORIGIN 1920s: imitative of a yawn.

hoick Brit. informal ▶ verb [with obj. and adverbial of direction] lift or pull abruptly or with effort: *she hoicked her bag on to the desk.*
▶ noun an abrupt pull.
– ORIGIN late 19th cent.: perhaps a variant of **HIKE**.

hoicks /hɔɪks/ ▶ exclamation variant of **YOICKS**.

hoi polloi /ˌhɔɪ pɒˈlɔɪ/ ▶ plural noun (usu. **the hoi polloi**) derogatory the masses; the common people: *avoid mixing with the hoi polloi.*
– ORIGIN mid 17th cent.: Greek, literally 'the many'.

USAGE 1 To those in the know, **hoi** is the Greek word for the definite article **the** (nominative masculine plural); the phrase **hoi polloi** thus translates as 'the many'. This knowledge has led some traditionalists to insist that **hoi polloi** should not be used in English with **the**, since that would be to state the word **the** twice. Such arguments miss the point: once established in English, expressions such as **hoi polloi** are treated as a fixed unit and are subject to the rules and conventions of English. Evidence shows that use with **the** has now become an accepted part of standard English usage.
2 Hoi polloi is sometimes used incorrectly to mean 'upper class', i.e. the exact opposite of its normal meaning. It seems likely that the confusion arose by association with the similar-sounding but otherwise unrelated word **hoity-toity**.

hoisin /'hɔɪzɪn/ (also **hoisin sauce**) ▶ **noun** [mass noun] a sweet, spicy dark red sauce made from soya beans, vinegar, sugar, garlic, and various spices, widely used in southern Chinese cooking.

hoist ▶ **verb** [with obj.] raise (something) by means of ropes and pulleys: *a white flag was hoisted.*
■[with obj. and adverbial] raise or haul up: *she hoisted her backpack on to her shoulder.*
▶ **noun 1** an act of raising or lifting something.
■figurative an act of increasing something: *the government's interest rate hoist.* ■ an apparatus for lifting or raising something.
2 the part of a flag nearest the staff.
3 a group of flags raised as a signal.
– PHRASES **hoist one's flag** (of an admiral) take up command. **hoist the flag** stake one's claim to discovered territory by displaying a flag. **hoist with one's own petard** see **PETARD**.
– DERIVATIVES **hoister** noun.
– ORIGIN late 15th cent.: alteration of dialect *hoise*, probably from Dutch *hijsen* or Low German *hiesen*, but recorded earlier.

hoity-toity ▶ **adjective 1** haughty; snobbish: *a hoity-toity little madam.*
2 archaic frolicsome.
– ORIGIN mid 17th cent. (in the sense 'boisterous or silly behaviour'): from obsolete *hoit* 'indulge in riotous mirth', of unknown origin.

hok /hɒk, hɔːk/ (also **hokkie**) ▶ **noun** S. African an enclosure for domestic animals.
■a small hut.
– ORIGIN Afrikaans.

Hokan /'həʊkan/ ▶ **adjective** relating to or denoting a group of American Indian languages of California and western Mexico, considered as a possible language family. They include Yuman, Mojave, and several other languages now extinct or almost so.
▶ **noun** [mass noun] this hypothetical language family.
– ORIGIN from Hokan *hok* 'about two' + **-AN**.

hoke /həʊk/ ▶ **verb** [with obj.] informal, chiefly N. Amer. (of an actor) act (a part) in an insincere, sentimental, or melodramatic manner: *just try it straight—don't* ***hoke*** *it up.*
– ORIGIN early 20th cent.: back-formation from **HOKUM**.

hokey ▶ **adjective** (**hokier**, **hokiest**) N. Amer. informal mawkishly sentimental: *a hokey tear jerker.*
■noticeably contrived: *a hokey country-western accent.*
– DERIVATIVES **hokeyness** (also **hokiness**) noun.
– ORIGIN 1940s: from **HOKUM** + **-Y**[1].

hokey-cokey ▶ **noun** a communal dance performed in a circle with synchronized shaking of the limbs in turn, accompanied by a simple song.
– ORIGIN 1940s: perhaps from **HOCUS-POCUS**.

hokey-pokey ▶ **noun** informal **1** [mass noun] dated ice cream sold on the street, especially by Italian street vendors.
2 (**the hokey-pokey**) US term for **HOKEY-COKEY**.
– ORIGIN late 19th cent.: of unknown origin.

hoki /'həʊki/ ▶ **noun** an edible marine fish related to the hakes, found off the southern coasts of New Zealand.
• *Macruronus novaezeelandiae*, family Macruronidae.
– ORIGIN late 19th cent.: from Maori.

Hokkaido /hɒ'kʌɪdəʊ/ the most northerly of the four main islands of Japan, constituting an administrative region; pop. 5,644,000 (1990); capital, Sapporo.

hokku /'hɒkuː/ ▶ **noun** (pl. same) another term for **HAIKU**.
– ORIGIN Japanese, literally 'opening verse' (of a linked sequence of comic verses).

hokonui /'hɒkənʊi/ ▶ **noun** [mass noun] NZ illicitly distilled spirits, especially whisky.
– ORIGIN from a Maori place name.

hokum /'həʊkəm/ ▶ **noun** [mass noun] informal nonsense: *they dismissed such corporate homilies as boardroom hokum.*
■trite, sentimental, or unrealistic situations and dialogue in a film, play, or piece of writing: *classic B-movie hokum.*
– ORIGIN early 20th cent.: of unknown origin.

Hokusai /'həʊkʊsʌɪ, ˌhəʊkʊ'sʌɪ/, Katsushika (1760–1849), Japanese painter and wood engraver. A leading artist of the *ukiyo-e* school, he represented aspects of Japanese everyday life in his woodcuts and strongly influenced European Impressionist artists.

Holarctic /hə(ʊ)'lɑːktɪk/ ▶ **adjective** Zoology of, relating to, or denoting a zoogeographical region comprising the Nearctic and Palaearctic regions combined. The two continents have been linked intermittently by the Bering land bridge, and the faunas are closely related.
■[as noun **the Holarctic**] the Holarctic region.
– ORIGIN late 19th cent.: from **HOLO-** 'whole' + **ARCTIC**.

Holbein /'hɒlbʌɪn/, Hans (1497–1543), German painter and engraver; known as **Holbein the Younger**. He became a well-known court portraitist in England and was commissioned by Henry VIII to supply portraits of the king's prospective brides. Notable works: *Dance of Death* (series of woodcuts, *c.*1523–6); *Anne of Cleves* (miniature, 1539).

hold[1] ▶ **verb** (past and past participle **held**) **1** [with obj.] grasp, carry, or support with one's arms or hands: *she was holding a brown leather suitcase* | [no obj.] *he* ***held on to*** *the back of a chair.*
■[with obj. and adverbial] keep or sustain in a specified position: *I held the door open for him* | figurative *the people are* ***held down*** *by a repressive military regime.* ■ embrace (someone): *Mark pulled her into his arms and held her close.* ■ (**hold something up**) support and prevent from falling: *concrete pillars hold up the elevated section of the railway.* ■ be able to bear (the weight of a person or thing): *I reached up to the nearest branch which seemed likely to hold my weight.* ■ (of a vehicle) maintain close contact with (the road), especially when driven at speed: *the car holds the corners very well.* ■ (of a ship or an aircraft) continue to follow (a particular course): *the ship is holding a south-easterly course.* ■ [no obj., with adverbial of direction] archaic keep going in a particular direction: *he* ***held on his way,*** *close behind his friend.*
2 [with obj.] keep or detain (someone): *the police were holding him on a murder charge* | [with obj. and complement] *she was held prisoner for two days.*
■keep possession of (something), typically in the face of a challenge or attack: *the rebels held the town for many weeks* | [no obj.] *White managed to* ***hold on to*** *his lead.* ■ keep (someone's interest or attention). ■ (of a singer or musician) sustain (a note). ■ stay or cause to stay at a certain value or level: [no obj.] *MCI shares held at 77p* | [with obj.] *he is determined to hold down inflation.* ■ (in sport) manage to achieve a draw against (opponents thought likely to win): *AC Milan were* ***held to a*** *1–1* ***draw*** *by Udinese.*
3 [no obj.] remain secure, intact, or in position without breaking or giving way: *the boat's anchor would not hold.*
■(of a favourable condition or situation) continue without changing: *let's hope her luck holds.* ■ be or remain valid or available: *I'll have that coffee now, if the offer still holds.* ■ (of an argument or theory) be logical, consistent, or convincing: *their views still seem to* ***hold up*** *extremely well.* ■ (**hold to**) refuse to abandon or change (a principle or opinion). ■ [with obj.] (**hold someone to**) cause someone to adhere to (a commitment).
4 [with obj.] contain or be capable of containing (a specified amount): *the tank held twenty-four gallons.*
■be able to drink (a reasonable amount of alcohol) without becoming drunk or suffering any ill effects: *I can hold my drink as well as anyone.* ■ have or be characterized by: *I don't know what the future holds.*
5 [with obj.] have in one's possession: *the managing director still holds fifty shares in the company.*
■[no obj.] N. Amer. informal be in possession of illegal drugs: *he was holding, and the police hauled him off to jail.* ■ have or occupy (a job or position). ■ [with obj.] have or adhere to (a belief or opinion): *I feel nothing but pity for someone who holds such chauvinistic views* | [with clause] *they hold that all literature is empty of meaning.* ■ [with obj. and complement] consider (someone) to be responsible or liable for a particular situation: *you can't hold yourself responsible for what happened.* ■ (**hold someone/thing in**) regard someone or something with (a specified feeling): *the speed limit is held in contempt by many drivers.* ■ [with clause] (of a judge or court) rule; decide: *the Court of Appeal held that there was no evidence to support the judge's assessment.*
6 [with obj.] keep or reserve for someone: *a booking can be held for twenty-four hours.*
■prevent from going ahead or occurring: *hold your fire!* ■ maintain (a telephone connection) until the person one has telephoned is free to speak: *please* ***hold the line,*** *and I'll see if he's available* | [no obj.] *will you hold?* ■ N. Amer. informal refrain from adding or using (something, typically an item of food or drink): *a strawberry margarita, but hold the tequila.* ■ (**hold it**) informal used as a way of exhorting someone to wait or to stop doing something: *hold it right there, mate!* ■ [no obj.] archaic restrain oneself.
7 [with obj.] arrange and take part in (a meeting or conversation): *a meeting was held at the church.*
▶ **noun 1** an act or manner of grasping something; a grip: *he* ***caught hold of*** *her arm* | *he lost his hold and fell.*
■a particular way of grasping or restraining someone, especially an opponent in wrestling or judo. ■ a place where one can grip with one's hands or feet while climbing: *he felt carefully with his feet for a hold and swung himself up.* ■ a way of influencing someone: *he discovered that Tom had some kind of* ***hold over*** *his father.* ■ a degree of power or control: *military forces tightened their* ***hold on*** *the capital.*
2 archaic a fortress.
– PHRASES **be left holding the baby** (or US **bag**) informal be left with an unwelcome responsibility, typically without warning. **don't hold your breath** see **BREATH**. **get hold of** grasp (someone or something) physically. ■ grasp (something) intellectually; understand. ■ informal obtain: *if you can't get hold of ripe tomatoes, add some tomato purée.* ■ informal find or manage to contact (someone): *I'll try and get hold of Mark.* **hold someone/thing at bay** see **BAY**[5]. **hold one's breath** see **BREATH**. **hold someone/thing cheap** archaic have a low opinion of someone or something. **hold court** be the centre of attention amidst a crowd of one's admirers. **hold someone/thing dear** care for or value someone or something greatly: *fidelity is something most of us hold dear.* **hold fast** remain tightly secured: *the door held fast, obviously locked.* ■ continue to believe in or adhere to an idea or principle: *it is important that we* ***hold fast to*** *the policies.* **hold the field** see **FIELD**. **hold the fort** take responsibility for a situation while another person is temporarily absent. **hold good** (or **true**) remain true or valid: *his views still hold true today.* **hold one's ground** see **GROUND**[1]. **hold someone's hand** give a person comfort, guidance, or moral support in a difficult situation. **hold hands** (of two or more people) clasp each other by the hand, typically as a sign of affection. **hold hard** Brit. used as a way of exhorting someone to stop or wait: *here, hold hard a minute.* **hold someone/thing harmless** Law indemnify. **hold one's horses** [usu. as imperative] informal wait a moment. **hold the line** not yield to the pressure of a difficult situation: *France's central bank would hold the line.* **hold one's nose** squeeze one's nostrils with one's fingers in order to avoid inhaling an unpleasant smell. **hold one's own** see **OWN**. **hold one's peace** see **PEACE**. **hold (one's) serve** (or **service**) (in tennis and other racket sports) win a game in which one is serving. **hold the stage** see **STAGE**. **hold sway** see **SWAY**. **hold thumbs** S. African fold one's fingers over one's thumb to bring good luck. **hold someone to bail** Law bind by bail. **hold one's tongue** [often in imperative] informal remain silent. **hold someone/thing to ransom** see **RANSOM**. **hold up one's head** (or **hold one's head high**) see **HEAD**. **hold water** [often with negative] (of a statement, theory, or line of reasoning) appear to be valid, sound, or reasonable: *this argument just does not hold water.* **no holds barred** (in wrestling) with no restrictions on the kinds of holds that are used. ■ figurative used to convey that no rules or restrictions apply in a conflict or dispute: *no-holds-barred military action.* **on hold** waiting to be connected while making a telephone call. ■ temporarily not being dealt with or pursued: *he has had to* ***put*** *his career* ***on hold.*** **take hold** start to have an effect: *the reforms of the late nineteenth century had taken hold.* **there is no holding someone** used to convey that someone is particularly determined or cannot be prevented from doing something: *there's no holding you these days.*
– DERIVATIVES **holdable** adjective.
– ORIGIN Old English *haldan*, *healdan*, of Germanic

h

origin; related to Dutch *houden* and German *halten*; the noun is partly from Old Norse *hald* 'hold, support, custody'.

▶**hold something against** allow past actions or circumstances to have a negative influence on one's present attitude towards (someone): *he knew that if he failed her, she would hold it against him forever.* **hold back** hesitate to act or speak: *he held back, remembering the mistake he had made before.* **hold someone/thing back** prevent or restrict the advance, progress, or development of someone or something: *Jane struggled to hold back the tears.* ■ (**hold something back**) refuse or be unwilling to make something known: *you're not holding anything back from me, are you?* **hold something down** informal succeed in keeping a job or position for a period of time. **hold forth** talk lengthily, assertively, or tediously about a subject: *he was* ***holding forth on*** *the merits of the band's debut LP.* **hold off** (of bad weather) fail to occur. ■ delay or postpone an action or decision. **hold someone/thing off** resist an attacker or challenge: *he held off a late challenge by Vose to win by thirteen seconds.* **hold on 1** [often in imperative] wait; stop: *hold on a minute, I'll be right back!* **2** endure or keep going in difficult circumstances: *if only they could hold on a little longer.* **hold on to** keep: *the industry is trying to hold on to experienced staff.* **hold out** resist or survive in dangerous or difficult circumstances: *British troops* ***held out against*** *constant attacks.* ■ continue to be sufficient: *we can stay here for as long as our supplies hold out.* **hold out for** continue to demand (a particular thing), refusing to accept what has been offered: *he is holding out for a guaranteed 7 per cent raise.* **hold out on** informal refuse to give something, typically information, to (someone). **hold something out** offer a chance or hope: *a new drug may hold out hope for patients with lung cancer.* **hold something over 1** postpone something. **2** use a fact or piece of information to threaten or intimidate (someone). **hold together** (or **hold something together**) remain or cause to remain united: *if your party holds together, you will probably win.* **hold up** remain strong or vigorous: *the Labour vote held up well.* **hold someone/thing up 1** delay or block the movement or progress of someone or something: *our return flight was held up for seven hours.* **2** rob someone or something using the threat of force or violence: *a masked raider held up the post office.* **3** present or expose someone or something as an example or for particular treatment: *they were* ***held up to*** *public ridicule.* **4** Bridge refrain from playing a winning card for tactical reasons. **hold with** [with negative] informal approve of: *I don't hold with fighting or violence.*

hold² ▶ **noun** a large compartment or space in the lower part of a ship or aircraft in which cargo is stowed.
– ORIGIN late 16th cent.: from obsolete *holl*, from Old English *hol* (see **HOLE**). The addition of *-d* was due to association with **HOLD**¹.

holdall ▶ **noun** Brit. a large rectangular bag with handles and a shoulder strap, used for carrying clothes and other personal belongings.

holdback ▶ **noun** a thing serving to hold something else in place: *a curtain holdback.*
■ a sum of money withheld under certain conditions.

holder ▶ **noun 1** a device or implement for holding something: [in combination] *a cigarette-holder.*
2 a person that holds something: *a British passport holder | holders of two American hostages.*
■ the possessor of a trophy, championship, or record.
3 a smallholder.

Hölderlin /ˈhəːldəlɪn, German ˈhœldɐliːn/, (Johann Christian) Friedrich (1770–1843), German poet. Most of his poems express a romantic yearning for harmony with nature and beauty. While working as a tutor he fell in love with his employer's wife, who is portrayed in his novel *Hyperion* (1797–9).

holdfast ▶ **noun** a firm grip.
■ a staple or clamp securing an object to a wall or other surface. ■ Biology a stalked organ by which an alga or other simple aquatic plant or animal is attached to a substrate.

holding ▶ **noun 1** an area of land held by lease.
■ the tenure of such land.
2 (**holdings**) stocks, property, and other financial assets in someone's possession: *commercial property holdings.*

holding company ▶ **noun** a company created to buy and possess the shares of other companies, which it then controls.

holding ground ▶ **noun** Nautical an area of seabed where an anchor will hold.

holding operation ▶ **noun** a course of action designed to maintain the status quo under difficult circumstances.

holding pattern ▶ **noun** the flight path maintained by an aircraft awaiting permission to land.

holding tank ▶ **noun** a large container in which liquids are temporarily held.

holdout ▶ **noun** chiefly N. Amer. an act of resisting something or refusing to accept what is offered: *a defiant holdout against a commercial culture.*
■ a person or organization acting in such a way.

holdover ▶ **noun** chiefly N. Amer. a person or thing surviving from an earlier time, especially someone surviving in office: *Young is the only holdover from the 1988 team.*

hold-up ▶ **noun 1** a situation that causes delay, especially to a car journey.
2 a robbery conducted with the use of threats or violence: *the shocked victims of an armed hold-up.*
3 (usu. **hold-ups**) a stocking held up by an elasticated top rather than by suspenders.

hole ▶ **noun 1** a hollow place in a solid body or surface: *he managed to dig out a small snow hole.*
■ an animal's burrow. ■ an aperture passing through something: *he had a hole in his sock.* ■ a cavity or receptacle on a golf course, typically one of eighteen or nine, into which the ball must be hit. ■ a cavity of this type as representing a division of a golf course or of play in golf: *Stephen lost the first three holes to Eric.* ■ Physics a position from which an electron is absent, especially one regarded as a mobile carrier of positive charge in a semiconductor. ■ [in place names] a valley: *Seaton Hole.*
2 informal a small or unpleasant place: *she had wasted a whole lifetime in this hole of a town.*
■ informal an awkward situation: *get yourself out of a hole.*
▶ **verb** [with obj.] **1** make a hole or holes in: *a fuel tank was holed by the attack and a fire started.*
2 Golf hit (the ball) so that it falls into a hole: *alternate shots from each partner until the ball is holed |* [no obj.] *he* ***holed in one*** *at the third.*
– PHRASES **blow a hole in** ruin the effectiveness of (something): *the amendment could blow a hole in the legislation.* **in the hole** N. Amer. informal in debt: *we're still three thousand dollars in the hole.* **in holes** worn so much that holes have formed: *my clothes are in holes.* **make a hole in** use a large amount of: *holidays can make a big hole in your savings.* **need something like a hole in the head** informal used to emphasize that someone has absolutely no need or desire for something.
– DERIVATIVES **holey** adjective.
– ORIGIN Old English *hol* (noun), *holian* (verb), of Germanic origin; related to Dutch *hol* (noun) 'cave', (adjective) 'hollow', and German *hohl* 'hollow', from an Indo-European root meaning 'cover, conceal'.
▶**hole out 1** Golf send the ball into a hole. **2** Cricket (of a batsman) hit the ball to a fielder and be caught. **hole up** informal hide oneself: *I holed up for two days in a tiny cottage in Snowdonia.*

hole-and-corner ▶ **adjective** attempting to avoid public notice; secret: *a hole-and-corner wedding.*

hole card ▶ **noun** (in stud poker) a card which has been dealt face down.
■ figurative, chiefly US a thing that is kept secret until it can be used to one's own advantage.

hole-in-one ▶ **noun** (pl. **holes-in-one**) Golf a shot that enters the hole from the tee with no intervening shots.

hole in the heart ▶ **noun** Medicine a congenital defect in the heart septum, resulting in inadequate circulation of oxygenated blood (a cause of blue baby syndrome).

hole in the wall ▶ **noun** informal **1** Brit. an automatic cash dispenser installed in the outside wall of a bank.
2 a small dingy bar, shop, or restaurant.

hole saw ▶ **noun** a tool for making circular holes, consisting of a metal cylinder with a toothed edge.

Holi /ˈhəʊliː/ ▶ **noun** a Hindu spring festival celebrated in February or March in honour of Krishna.
– ORIGIN via Hindi from Sanskrit *holī*.

Holiday /ˈhɒlɪdeɪ/, Billie (1915–59), American jazz singer; born *Eleanora Fagan*. She began her recording career with Benny Goodman's band in 1933, going on to perform with many small jazz groups.

holiday chiefly Brit. ▶ **noun** (often **holidays**) an extended period of recreation, especially one spent away from home or in travelling: *I spent my summer holidays on a farm | Fred was* ***on holiday*** *in Spain.*
■ a day of festivity or recreation when no work is done: *25 December is an official public holiday.* ■ [as modifier] characteristic of a holiday; festive: *a holiday atmosphere.*
▶ **verb** [no obj., with adverbial of place] spend a holiday in a specified place: *he is* ***holidaying in*** *Italy.*
– ORIGIN Old English *hāligdæg* 'holy day'.

holiday camp ▶ **noun** Brit. a site for holidaymakers with accommodation, entertainment, and leisure facilities.

holidaymaker ▶ **noun** Brit. a person on holiday away from home.

holiday season ▶ **noun** (in the US) the period of time from Thanksgiving until New Year, including such religious and secular festivals as Christmas, Hanukkah, and Kwanzaa.

holiday village ▶ **noun** Brit. a large, modern holiday camp.

holier-than-thou ▶ **adjective** characterized by an attitude of moral superiority: *they had quite a critical, holier-than-thou approach.*

holiness ▶ **noun** [mass noun] the state of being holy: *a life of holiness and total devotion to God.*
■ (**His/Your Holiness**) a title given to the Pope, Orthodox patriarchs, and the Dalai Lama, or used in addressing them. ■ [as modifier] denoting a Christian renewal movement originating in the mid 19th century among Methodists in the US, emphasizing the Wesleyan doctrine of the sanctification of believers.
– ORIGIN Old English *hālignes* (see **HOLY, -NESS**).

Holinshed /ˈhɒlɪnʃɛd/, Raphael (died *c.*1580), English chronicler. Although the named compiler of *The Chronicles of England, Scotland, and Ireland* (1577), Holinshed wrote only the *Historie of England* and had help with the remainder. The revised (1587) edition was used by Shakespeare.

holism /ˈhəʊlɪz(ə)m, ˈhɒl-/ ▶ **noun** [mass noun] chiefly Philosophy the theory that parts of a whole are in intimate interconnection, such that they cannot exist independently of the whole, or cannot be understood without reference to the whole, which is thus regarded as greater than the sum of its parts. Holism is often applied to mental states, language, and ecology. The opposite of **ATOMISM**.
■ Medicine the treating of the whole person, taking into account mental and social factors, rather than just the symptoms of a disease.
– DERIVATIVES **holist** adjective & noun.
– ORIGIN 1920s: from **HOLO-** 'whole' + **-ISM**; coined by J. C. Smuts to designate the tendency in nature to produce organized 'wholes' (bodies or organisms) from the ordered grouping of units.

holistic /həʊˈlɪstɪk, hɒ-/ ▶ **adjective** chiefly Philosophy characterized by understanding the parts of something to be intimately interconnected and explicable only by reference to the whole.
■ Medicine characterized by the treatment of the whole person, taking into account mental and social factors, rather than just the symptoms of a disease.
– DERIVATIVES **holistically** adverb.

holla /ˈhɒlə/ ▶ **exclamation** archaic used to call attention to something: *'Holla! what storm is this?'*
– ORIGIN early 16th cent. (as an order to stop or cease): from French *holà*, from *ho* 'ho!' + *là* 'there'.

Holland another name for the **NETHERLANDS**.
■ a former province of the Netherlands, comprising the coastal parts of the country. It is now divided into **North Holland** and **South Holland**.

holland ▶ **noun** [mass noun] a kind of smooth, hard-wearing linen fabric, used chiefly for window blinds and furniture covering.
– ORIGIN Middle English: from **HOLLAND**, the name of a former province of the Netherlands where the

cloth was made, from Dutch, earlier *Holtlant* (from *holt* 'wood' + *-lant* 'land').

hollandaise sauce /ˌhɒlənˈdeɪz, ˈhɒlənˌdeɪz/ ▶ **noun** [mass noun] a creamy sauce of melted butter, egg yolks, and vinegar, served especially with fish.
– ORIGIN French *hollandaise*, feminine of *hollandais* 'Dutch', from *Hollande* 'Holland'.

Hollander ▶ **noun** dated a native of the Netherlands.

Hollands ▶ **noun** [mass noun] archaic Dutch gin.
– ORIGIN from archaic Dutch *hollandsch genever* (earlier form of *hollands jenever*) 'Dutch gin'.

holler informal ▶ **verb** [no obj.] (of a person) give a loud shout or cry: *he hollers when he wants feeding* | [with direct speech] *'I can't get down,' she hollered.*
▶ **noun** a loud cry or shout.
▪(also **field holler**) chiefly US a melodic cry with abrupt or swooping changes of pitch, used originally by black slaves at work in the fields and later contributing to the development of the blues.
– ORIGIN late 17th cent. (as a verb): variant of the rare verb *hollo*; related to **HALLOO**.

Hollerith /ˈhɒlərɪθ/, Herman (1860–1929), American engineer. He invented a tabulating machine using punched cards for computation, an important precursor of the electronic computer, and founded a company that later expanded to become the IBM Corporation.

hollow ▶ **adjective** **1** having a hole or empty space inside: *each fibre has a hollow core.*
▪having a depression in its surface; concave: *hollow cheeks.* ▪ (of a sound) echoing, as though made in or on an empty container: *a hollow cough.*
2 without significance: *the result was a hollow victory.*
▪insincere: *a hollow promise.*
▶ **noun** a hole or depression in something: *a hollow at the base of a large tree.*
▪a hole or enclosed space within something: *he held them in the hollow of his hand.* ▪ a small valley: *a village nestled in a hollow in the Cotswolds.*
▶ **verb** [with obj.] form by making a hole: *a tunnel was* **hollowed out** *in a mountain range.*
▪make a depression in: *Flora's laugh hollowed her cheeks.*
– PHRASES **beat someone hollow** defeat or surpass someone completely or thoroughly.
– DERIVATIVES **hollowly** adverb, **hollowness** noun.
– ORIGIN Old English *holh* 'cave'; obscurely related to **HOLE**.

hollow-eyed ▶ **adjective** (of a person) having deeply sunk eyes, typically as a result of illness or tiredness.

hollow-hearted ▶ **adjective** archaic insincere; false.

hollow square ▶ **noun** historical a body of infantry drawn up in a square with a space in the middle.

hollowware ▶ **noun** [mass noun] hollow articles of cookware or crockery, such as pots, kettles, and jugs.

Holly, Buddy (1936–59), American rock-and-roll singer, guitarist, and songwriter; born *Charles Hardin Holley*. He recorded such hits as 'That'll be the Day' with his band, The Crickets, before going solo in 1958. He was killed in an aircraft crash.

holly ▶ **noun** a widely distributed evergreen shrub, typically having prickly dark green leaves, small white flowers, and red berries.
• Genus *Ilex*, family Aquifoliaceae: many species, in particular *I. aquifolium*.
▪[mass noun] the branches, foliage, and berries of this plant used as decorations at Christmas.
– ORIGIN Middle English *holi*, shortened form of Old English *holegn*, *holen*, of Germanic origin; related to German *Hulst*.

holly fern ▶ **noun** a small shield fern which has narrow glossy fronds with a double row of stiff bristle-edged lobes, found chiefly in mountainous areas of both Eurasia and North America.
• Several species in the genus *Polystichum*, family Dryopteridaceae, in particular the widespread *P. lonchitis*.

hollyhock ▶ **noun** a tall Eurasian plant of the mallow family, with large showy flowers.
• *Alcea rosea*, family Malvaceae.
– ORIGIN Middle English: from **HOLY** + obsolete *hock* 'mallow', of unknown origin. It originally denoted the marsh mallow which has medicinal uses (hence, perhaps, the use of 'holy'); the current sense dates from the mid 16th cent.

holly oak ▶ **noun** the holm oak or the kermes oak, both of which have tough evergreen leaves that are reminiscent of those of holly.

Hollywood a district of Los Angeles, the principal centre of the American film industry.
▪the American film industry and the lifestyles of the people associated with it: *he was never seduced by the glitz and money of Hollywood.*

holm /həʊm/ (also **holme**) ▶ **noun** Brit. an islet, especially in a river or near a mainland.
▪a piece of flat ground by a river, which is submerged in time of flood.
– ORIGIN Old English, from Old Norse *holmr*; more frequently used in Scotland and northern England, but found in place names throughout Britain.

Holmes[1] /həʊmz/, Arthur (1890–1965), English geologist and geophysicist. He pioneered the isotopic dating of rocks and was one of the first supporters of the theory of continental drift. His *Principles of Physical Geology* (1944) became a standard text.

Holmes[2] /həʊmz/, Oliver Wendell (1809–94), American physician, poet, and essayist. His best-known literary works are the humorous essays known as 'table talks', which began with *The Autocrat of the Breakfast Table* (1857–8).

Holmes[3] /həʊmz/, Sherlock, an extremely perceptive private detective in stories by Sir Arthur Conan Doyle.
– DERIVATIVES **Holmesian** adjective.

holmium /ˈhəʊlmɪəm/ ▶ **noun** [mass noun] the chemical element of atomic number 67, a soft silvery-white metal of the lanthanide series. (Symbol: **Ho**)
– ORIGIN late 19th cent.: modern latin, from *Holmia*, Latinized form of *Stockholm*, the capital of Sweden (because many minerals of the yttrium group, to which holmium belongs, are found in that area); discovered by P.T. Cleve, Swedish chemist.

holm oak ▶ **noun** an evergreen southern European oak, which has dark green glossy leaves. Also called **EVERGREEN OAK** or **ILEX**.
• *Quercus ilex*, family Fagaceae.
– ORIGIN late Middle English: *holm*, alteration of dialect *hollin*, from Old English *holen* 'holly'.

holo /ˈhɒləʊ/ ▶ **noun** (pl. **-os**) informal a hologram.

holo- ▶ **combining form** whole; complete: *holocaust* | *holophytic.*
– ORIGIN from Greek *holos* 'whole'.

holocaust /ˈhɒləkɔːst/ ▶ **noun** **1** destruction or slaughter on a mass scale, especially caused by fire or nuclear war: *a nuclear holocaust* | [mass noun] *the threat of imminent holocaust.*
▪(**the Holocaust**) the mass murder of Jews under the German Nazi regime during the period 1941–45. More than 6 million European Jews, as well as members of other persecuted groups, were murdered at concentration camps such as Auschwitz.
2 historical a Jewish sacrificial offering which is burnt completely on an altar.
– ORIGIN Middle English: from Old French *holocauste*, via late Latin from Greek *holokauston*, from *holos* 'whole' + *kaustos* 'burnt' (from *kaiein* 'burn').

Holocene /ˈhɒləsiːn/ ▶ **adjective** Geology of, relating to, or denoting the present epoch, which is the second epoch in the Quaternary period and followed the Pleistocene. Also called **RECENT**.
▪[as noun **the Holocene**] the Holocene epoch or the system of deposits laid down during this time.

> The Holocene epoch has lasted from about 10,000 years ago to the present day. It covers the period since the ice retreated after the last glaciation and it is sometimes regarded as just another interglacial period.

– ORIGIN late 19th cent.: coined in French from **HOLO-** 'whole' + Greek *kainos* 'new'.

holoenzyme /ˌhɒləʊˈɛnzʌɪm/ ▶ **noun** Biochemistry a biochemically active compound formed by the combination of an enzyme with a coenzyme.

Holofernes /ˌhɒləˈfəːniːz, həˈlɒfəˌniːz/ (in the Apocrypha) the Assyrian general of Nebuchadnezzar's forces, who was killed by Judith (Judith 4:1 ff.).

hologram /ˈhɒləgram/ ▶ **noun** a three-dimensional image formed by the interference of light beams from a laser or other coherent light source.
▪a photograph of an interference pattern which, when suitably illuminated, produces a three-dimensional image.

holograph /ˈhɒləgrɑːf/ ▶ **noun** a manuscript handwritten by the person named as its author.
– ORIGIN early 17th cent.: from French *holographe*, or via late Latin from Greek *holographos*, from *holos* 'whole' + *-graphos* 'written, writing'.

holography /hɒˈlɒgrəfi/ ▶ **noun** [mass noun] the study or production of holograms.
– DERIVATIVES **holographic** adjective, **holographically** adverb.

holophrasis /ˌhɒləʊˈfreɪsɪs/ ▶ **noun** [mass noun] the expression of a whole phrase in a single word, for example *howdy* for *how do you do.*
▪the learning of linguistic elements as whole chunks by very young children acquiring their first language, for example *it's all gone* learned as *allgone*.
– DERIVATIVES **holophrase** noun, **holophrastic** adjective.

holophytic /ˌhɒlə(ʊ)ˈfɪtɪk/ ▶ **adjective** Biology (of a plant or protozoan) able to synthesize complex organic compounds by photosynthesis.

holothurian /ˌhɒlə(ʊ)ˈθjʊərɪən/ ▶ **noun** Zoology a sea cucumber.
– ORIGIN mid 19th cent.: from the modern Latin genus name *Holothuria* (from Greek *holothourion*, denoting a kind of zoophyte) + **-AN**.

Holothuroidea /ˌhɒlə(ʊ)θjʊəˈrɔɪdɪə/ Zoology a class of echinoderms that comprises the sea cucumbers.
– DERIVATIVES **holothuroid** /ˈhɒlə(ʊ)θjʊərɔɪd/ noun & adjective.
– ORIGIN modern Latin (plural), based on Greek *holothourion* (see **HOLOTHURIAN**).

holotype /ˈhɒlətʌɪp/ ▶ **noun** Botany & Zoology a single type specimen upon which the description and name of a new species is based. Compare with **SYNTYPE**.

hols ▶ **plural noun** Brit. informal holidays.
– ORIGIN early 20th cent.: abbreviation.

Holst /həʊlst/, Gustav (Theodore) (1874–1934), English composer, of Swedish and Russian descent. He made his reputation with the orchestral suite *The Planets* (1914–16). Other notable works: *Choral Hymns from the Rig Veda* (1908–12).

Holstein[1] /ˈhɒlstʌɪn, -ʃtʌɪn/ a former duchy of the German kingdom of Saxony, situated in the southern part of the Jutland peninsula. A duchy of Denmark from 1474, it was taken by Prussia in 1866 and incorporated with the neighbouring duchy of Schleswig as the province of Schleswig-Holstein.

Holstein[2] /ˈhɒlstʌɪn, -iːn/ ▶ **noun** an animal of a typically black-and-white breed of large dairy cattle.

Holsteinian /hɒlˈstʌɪnɪən/ ▶ **adjective** Geology of, relating to, or denoting an interglacial period of the Pleistocene in northern Europe, following the Elster glaciation and corresponding to the Hoxnian in Britain.
▪[as noun **the Holsteinian**] the Holsteinian interglacial or the system of deposits laid down during it.
– ORIGIN 1960s: from **HOLSTEIN**[1] + **-IAN**.

holster /ˈhəʊlstə, ˈhɒl-/ ▶ **noun** a holder for carrying a handgun or other firearm, typically made of leather and worn on a belt or under the arm: *a shoulder holster.*
▶ **verb** [with obj.] put (a gun) into its holster.
– ORIGIN mid 17th cent.: corresponding to and contemporary with Dutch *holster*, of unknown origin.

holt[1] /həʊlt/ ▶ **noun** **1** the den of an otter.
2 dialect, chiefly US a grip or hold.
– ORIGIN late Middle English (in sense 2): variant of **HOLD**[1].

holt[2] /həʊlt/ ▶ **noun** archaic or dialect a wood or wooded hill.
– ORIGIN Old English, of Germanic origin; related to Middle Dutch *hout* and German *Holz*, from an Indo-European root shared by Greek *klados* 'twig'.

holus-bolus /ˌhəʊləsˈbəʊləs/ ▶ **adverb** Canadian or archaic all at once: *swallowing every proposal that is made holus-bolus.*
– ORIGIN mid 19th cent. (originally dialect): perhaps pseudo-Latin for 'whole bolus, whole lump'.

holy ▶ **adjective** (**holier**, **holiest**) **1** dedicated or consecrated to God or a religious purpose; sacred: *the Holy Bible* | *the holy month of Ramadan.*
▪(of a person) devoted to the service of God: *saints and holy men.* ▪ morally and spiritually excellent: *I do not lead a holy life.*
2 dated or humorous used in exclamations of surprise or dismay: *holy smoke!*
– ORIGIN Old English *hālig*, of Germanic origin; related to Dutch and German *heilig*, also to **WHOLE**.

h

Holy Alliance a loose alliance of European powers pledged to uphold the principles of the Christian religion. It was proclaimed at the Congress of Vienna (1814–15) by the emperors of Austria and Russia and the king of Prussia and was joined by most other European monarchs.

Holy Ark ▶ noun see **ARK** (sense 2).

holy city ▶ noun a city held sacred by the adherents of a religion.
■ (**the Holy City**) Jerusalem. ■ (**the Holy City**) (in Christian tradition) Heaven.

Holy Communion ▶ noun see **COMMUNION** (sense 2).

Holy Cross Day ▶ noun the day on which the feast of the Exaltation of the Cross is held, 14 September.

holy day ▶ noun a day on which a religious observance is held.

Holy Family Christ as a child with Mary and Joseph (and often also others such as John the Baptist or St Anne), especially as a subject for a painting.

Holy Father ▶ noun the Pope.

Holy Ghost ▶ noun another term for **HOLY SPIRIT**.

Holy Grail ▶ noun see **GRAIL**.

Holyhead /ˈhɒlɪhɛd/ a port on Holy Island in Wales, off Anglesey; pop. 12,652 (1981). It is the chief port for ferries between the British mainland and Ireland.

Holy Innocents' Day ▶ noun see **INNOCENTS' DAY**.

Holy Island 1 another name for **LINDISFARNE**.
2 a small island off the western coast of Anglesey in North Wales. It contains the ferry port of Holyhead. Welsh name **CAERGYBI**.

Holy Joe ▶ noun informal a sanctimonious or pious man.
■ a clergyman.
– ORIGIN late 19th cent.: originally nautical slang.

Holy Land a region on the eastern shore of the Mediterranean, in what is now Israel and Palestine, revered by Christians as the place in which Christ lived and taught, by Jews as the land given to the people of Israel, and by Muslims.
■ a region similarly revered, for example, Arabia in Islam.

Holy League any of various European alliances sponsored by the papacy during the 15th, 16th, and 17th centuries. They include the League of 1511–13, formed by Pope Julius II to expel Louis XII of France from Italy, and the French Holy League (also called the Catholic League) of 1576 and 1584, a Catholic extremist league formed during the French Wars of Religion.

Holy Name ▶ noun (especially in the Catholic Church) the name of Jesus as an object of formal devotion.

Holyoake /ˈhəʊlɪəʊk/, Sir Keith (Jacka) (1904–83), New Zealand statesman, Prime Minister 1957 and 1960–72, Governor General 1977–80.

Holy Office the ecclesiastical court of the Roman Catholic Church established as the final court of appeal in trials of heresy. Formed in 1542 as part of the Inquisition, it was renamed the Sacred Congregation for the Doctrine of the Faith in 1965.

holy of holies ▶ noun the inner chamber of the sanctuary in the Jewish Temple in Jerusalem, separated by a veil from the outer chamber. It was reserved for the presence of God and could be entered only by the High Priest on the Day of Atonement.
■ a place regarded as most sacred or special: *she had done the wrong thing, venturing into this holy of holies.*

holy orders ▶ plural noun the sacrament or rite of ordination as a member of the clergy, especially in the grades of bishop, priest, or deacon.
– PHRASES **in holy orders** having the status of an ordained member of the clergy. **take holy orders** become an ordained member of the clergy.

holy place ▶ noun a place revered as holy, typically one to which religious pilgrimage is made.
■ historical the outer chamber of the sanctuary in the Jewish Temple in Jerusalem.

holy roller ▶ noun informal, derogatory a member of an evangelical Christian group which expresses religious fervour by frenzied excitement or trances.

Holy Roman Empire the empire set up in western Europe following the coronation of Charlemagne as emperor in the year 800. It was created by the medieval papacy in an attempt to unite Christendom under one rule. At times the territory of the empire was extensive and included Germany, Austria, Switzerland, and parts of Italy and the Netherlands.

Holy Rood Day ▶ noun **1** the day on which the feast of the Invention of the Cross is held, 3 May.
2 another term for **HOLY CROSS DAY**.

Holy Sacrament ▶ noun see **SACRAMENT**.

Holy Saturday ▶ noun the Saturday preceding Easter Sunday. Also called **EASTER EVE** or **EASTER SATURDAY**.

Holy Scripture ▶ noun [mass noun] the sacred writings of Christianity contained in the Bible.

Holy See the papacy or the papal court; those associated with the Pope in the government of the Roman Catholic Church at the Vatican. Also called **SEE OF ROME**.

Holy Sepulchre the place in which the body of Jesus was laid after being taken down from the Cross.
■ the church in Jerusalem erected over the traditional site of this tomb.

Holy Spirit ▶ noun (in Christianity) the third person of the Trinity; God as spiritually active in the world.

Holy Spirit Association for the Unification of World Christianity another name for **UNIFICATION CHURCH**.

holystone /ˈhəʊlɪstəʊn/ chiefly historical ▶ noun a piece of soft sandstone used for scouring the decks of ships.
▶ verb [with obj.] scour (a deck) with a holystone.
– ORIGIN early 19th cent.: probably from **HOLY** + **STONE**. Sailors called the stones 'bibles' or 'prayer books', perhaps because they scrubbed the decks on their knees.

holy terror ▶ noun see **TERROR** (sense 2).

Holy Thursday ▶ noun **1** (chiefly in the Roman Catholic Church) Maundy Thursday.
2 dated (in the Anglican Church) Ascension Day.

Holy Trinity ▶ noun see **TRINITY**.

holy war ▶ noun a war declared or waged in support of a religious cause.

holy water ▶ noun [mass noun] water blessed by a priest and used in religious ceremonies.

Holy Week ▶ noun the week before Easter, starting on Palm Sunday.

Holy Writ ▶ noun [mass noun] Holy Bible.
■ writings or sayings of unchallenged authority.

Holy Year ▶ noun (in the Roman Catholic Church) a period of remission from the penal consequences of sin, granted under certain conditions for a year usually at intervals of twenty-five years.

hom /həʊm/ (also **homa** /ˈhəʊmə/) ▶ noun the soma plant.
■ [mass noun] the juice of this plant as a sacred drink of the Parsees.
– ORIGIN mid 19th cent.: from Persian *hūm* or Avestan *haoma*.

homage /ˈhɒmɪdʒ/ ▶ noun [mass noun] special honour or respect shown publicly: *they* ***paid homage to*** *the local boy who became President* | [count noun] *Daniel's films were a* ***homage to*** *her.*
■ formal public acknowledgement of feudal allegiance: *a man doing* ***homage to*** *his personal lord.*
– ORIGIN Middle English: Old French, from medieval Latin *hominaticum*, from Latin *homo, homin-* 'man' (the original use of the word denoted the ceremony by which a vassal declared himself to be his lord's 'man').

hombre /ˈɒmbreɪ/ ▶ noun informal, chiefly US a man, especially one of a particular type: *the Raiders quarterback is one tough hombre.*
– ORIGIN mid 19th cent. (originally denoting a man of Spanish descent): Spanish, 'man', from Latin *homo, homin-*.

homburg /ˈhɒmbəːg/ ▶ noun a man's felt hat having a narrow curled brim and a tapered crown with a lengthwise indentation.
– ORIGIN late 19th cent.: named after *Homburg*, a town in western Germany, where such hats were first worn.

home ▶ noun **1** the place where one lives permanently, especially as a member of a family or household: *I was nineteen when I left home and went to college* | *they have made Provence their home.*
■ the family or social unit occupying such a place: *he came from a good home and was well educated.* ■ a house or flat considered as a commercial property: *low-cost homes for first-time buyers.* ■ a place where something flourishes, is most typically found, or from which it originates: *Piedmont is the home of Italy's finest red wines.* ■ informal a place where an object is kept.
2 an institution for people needing professional care or supervision: *an old people's home.*
3 the finishing point in a race: *he was four fences from home.*
■ (in games) the place where a player is free from attack. ■ (in lacrosse) each of the three players stationed nearest their opponents' goal. ■ Baseball short for **HOME PLATE**. ■ a match played or won by a team on their own ground.
▶ adjective [attrib.] **1** of or relating to the place where one lives: *I don't have your home address.*
■ made, done, or intended for use in the place where one lives: *traditional home cooking.* ■ relating to one's own country and its domestic affairs: *we need to stimulate demand within the UK home market.*
2 (of a sports team or player) belonging to the country or locality in which a sporting event takes place: *the home side.*
■ played on or connected with a team's own ground: *their first home match of the season.*
3 N. Amer. denoting the administrative centre of an organization: *the company has moved its home office.*
▶ adverb to the place where one lives: *what time did he get home last night?*
■ in or at the place where one lives: *I stayed home with the kids.* ■ to the end or conclusion of a race or something difficult: *the favourite romped home six lengths clear.* ■ to the intended or correct position: *he slid the bolt home noisily.*
▶ verb [no obj.] **1** (of an animal) return by instinct to its territory after leaving it: *a dozen geese homing to their summer nesting grounds.*
■ (of a pigeon bred for long-distance racing) fly back to or arrive at its loft after being released at a distant point.
2 (**home in on**) move or be aimed towards (a target or destination) with great accuracy: *more than 100 missiles were launched, homing in on radar emissions.*
■ focus attention on: *a teaching style which homes in on what is of central importance for each pupil.*
3 [with obj.] provide (an animal) with a home as a pet.
– PHRASES **at home** in one's own house. ■ in one's own neighbourhood, town, or country: *he has been consistently successful both at home and abroad.* ■ comfortable and at ease in a place or situation: *sit down and* ***make yourself at home.*** ■ confident or relaxed about doing or using something: *he was quite at home talking about Eisenstein or Brecht.* ■ ready to receive and welcome visitors: *she took to her room and was not* ***at home to*** *friends.* ■ (with reference to sports fixtures) at a team's own ground: *Spurs drew 1–1 at home to Leeds.* **bring something home to** make (someone) realize the full significance of something: *her first-hand account brought home to me the pain of the experience.* **close** (or **near**) **to home** (of a remark or topic of discussion) relevant or accurate to the point that one feels uncomfortable or embarrassed. **come home** Golf play the second nine holes in a round of eighteen holes. Compare with ***go out*** (see **GO**[1]). **come home to someone** (of the significance of something) become fully realized by someone: *the full enormity of what was happening came home to Sara.* **drive** (or **hammer** or **press** or **ram**) **something home** make something clearly and fully understood by the use of repeated or forcefully direct arguments. **hit** (or **strike**) **home** (of a blow or a missile) reach an intended target. ■ (of words) have the intended, especially unsettling or painful, effect on their audience: *she could see that her remark had hit home.* ■ (of the significance or true nature of a situation) become fully realized by someone: *the full impact of life as a celebrity began to hit home.* **home and dry** (US **home free**, Austral./NZ **home and hosed**) chiefly Brit. having successfully achieved or being within sight of achieving one's objective: *at 3–0 up they should have been home and dry.* **a home from** (or N. Amer. **away from**) **home** a place where one is as happy, relaxed, or comfortable as in one's own home. **home is where the heart is** proverb your home will always be the place for which you feel the deepest affection, no matter where you are. **home, James (and don't spare the horses)!** dated used as a humorous way of

exhorting the driver of a vehicle to drive home quickly. **home sweet home** used as an expression of one's pleasure or relief at being in or returning to one's own home. **when ——'s at home** Brit. used to add humorous emphasis to a question about someone's identity: *who's Peter when he's at home?*
– DERIVATIVES **homelike** adjective.
– ORIGIN Old English *hām*, of Germanic origin; related to Dutch *heem* and German *Heim*.

home banking ▶ noun [mass noun] a system of banking whereby transactions are performed directly by telephone or via a computer and modem.

home bird ▶ noun Brit. informal another term for **HOMEBODY**.

homebody ▶ noun (pl. **-ies**) informal, chiefly N. Amer. a person who likes to stay at home, especially one who is perceived as unadventurous.

homeboy ▶ noun informal, chiefly US & S. African a young acquaintance from one's own town or neighbourhood, or from the same social background.
■ (especially among urban black people) a member of a peer group or gang. ■ a performer of rap music.

home brew ▶ noun [mass noun] beer or other alcoholic drink brewed at home.
■ [as modifier] informal, chiefly US made at home, rather than in a shop or factory: *home-brew software.*
– DERIVATIVES **home-brewed** adjective.

homebuyer ▶ noun a person who buys a house or flat.

home cinema ▶ noun [mass noun] chiefly Brit. television and video equipment designed to reproduce at home the experience of being in a cinema, typically including stereo speakers and a widescreen set.

homecoming ▶ noun an instance of returning home.
■ N. Amer. a reunion of former students of a university, college, or high school.

Home Counties the English counties surrounding London, into which London has extended. They comprise chiefly Essex, Kent, Surrey, and Hertfordshire.

home economics ▶ plural noun [often treated as sing.] cookery and other aspects of household management, especially as taught at school.

home farm ▶ noun chiefly Brit. & S. African a farm on an estate that is set aside to provide produce for the owner of the estate.

home fries (also **home-fried potatoes**) ▶ plural noun N. Amer. fried sliced potatoes.

homegirl ▶ noun a female equivalent of a homeboy.

home-grown ▶ adjective grown or produced in one's own garden or country rather than abroad.
■ belonging to one's own particular locality or country: *home-grown talent.*

Home Guard the British citizen army organized in 1940 to defend the UK against invasion, finally disbanded in 1957.

home help ▶ noun Brit. a person employed, especially by a local authority, to help in another's home.
■ [mass noun] a service by which such people are provided.

home key ▶ noun 1 Music the basic key in which a work is written.
2 a key on a computer or typewriter keyboard which acts as the base position for one's fingers in touch-typing.

Homel /'homɪl/ an industrial city in SE Belarus; pop. 506,100 (1990). Russian name **GOMEL**.

homeland ▶ noun a person's or a people's native land: *he left his homeland to settle in London.*
■ an autonomous or semi-autonomous state occupied by a particular people: *their political aim is a separate Tamil homeland.* ■ historical any of ten partially self-governing areas in South Africa designated for particular indigenous African peoples under the former policy of separate development.

homeless ▶ adjective (of a person) without a home, and therefore typically living on the streets: *the plight of young . homeless people* | [as noun **the homeless**] *charities for the homeless.*
– DERIVATIVES **homelessness** noun.

home loan ▶ noun a loan advanced to a person to assist in buying a house or flat.

homely ▶ adjective (**homelier**, **homeliest**) 1 Brit. (of a place or surroundings) simple but cosy and comfortable, as in one's own home: *a modern hotel with a homely atmosphere.*
■ unsophisticated and unpretentious: *homely pleasures.*
2 N. Amer. (of a person) unattractive in appearance.
– DERIVATIVES **homeliness** noun.

home-made ▶ adjective made at home, rather than in a shop or factory: *home-made bread.*

homemaker ▶ noun a person, especially a housewife, who manages a home.

home-making ▶ noun [mass noun] the creation and management of a home, especially as a pleasant place in which to live.

home movie ▶ noun a film made at home or without professional equipment or expertise.

homeobox /ˌhɒmɪə(ʊ)'bɒks, ˌhəʊm-/ (also **homoeobox**) ▶ noun Genetics any of a class of closely similar sequences which occur in various genes and are involved in regulating embryonic development in a wide range of species.
– ORIGIN 1980s: from *homeotic* (see **HOMEOSIS**) + the noun **BOX**[1]; first discovered in homeotic genes of *Drosophila* fruit flies.

Home Office the British government department dealing with domestic affairs, including law and order, immigration, and broadcasting, in England and Wales.

Home of the Hirsel of Coldstream /'hɜː:s(ə)l/, Baron, see **DOUGLAS-HOME**.

homeomorphism /ˌhɒmɪə(ʊ)'mɔːfɪz(ə)m, ˌhəʊm-/ ▶ noun Mathematics an instance of topological equivalence.
– DERIVATIVES **homeomorphic** adjective.

homeopath /'həʊmɪəpaθ, 'hɒm-/ (also **homoeopath**) ▶ noun a person who offers treatment by homeopathy.
– ORIGIN mid 19th cent.: from German *Homöopath* (see **HOMEOPATHY**).

homeopathy /ˌhəʊmɪ'ɒpəθi, hɒm-/ (also **homoeopathy**) ▶ noun a system of complementary medicine in which disease is treated by minute doses of natural substances that in a healthy person would produce symptoms of disease. Often contrasted with **ALLOPATHY**.
– DERIVATIVES **homeopathic** adjective, **homeopathically** adverb, **homeopathist** noun.
– ORIGIN early 19th cent.: coined in German from Greek *homoios* 'like' + *patheia* (see **-PATHY**).

homeosis /ˌhɒmɪ'əʊsɪs/ (also **homoeosis**) ▶ noun (pl. **homeoses** /-siːz/) Biology the replacement of part of one segment of an insect or other segmented animal by a structure characteristic of a different segment, especially through mutation.
– DERIVATIVES **homeotic** adjective.
– ORIGIN late 19th cent.: from Greek *homoiōsis* 'becoming like', from *homoios* 'like'.

homeostasis /ˌhɒmɪə(ʊ)'steɪsɪs, ˌhəʊm-/ (also **homoeostasis**) ▶ noun (pl. **homeostases** /-siːz/) the tendency towards a relatively stable equilibrium between interdependent elements, especially as maintained by physiological processes.
– DERIVATIVES **homeostatic** adjective.
– ORIGIN 1920s: modern Latin, from Greek *homoios* 'like' + **-STASIS**.

homeotherm /'hɒmɪə(ʊ),θɜːm/ (also **homoiotherm**) ▶ noun Zoology an organism that maintains its body temperature at a constant level, usually above that of the environment, by its metabolic activity. Often contrasted with **POIKILOTHERM**; compare with **WARM-BLOODED**.
– DERIVATIVES **homeothermal** adjective, **homeothermic** adjective, **homeothermy** noun.
– ORIGIN late 19th cent.: modern Latin, from Greek *homoios* 'like' + *thermē* 'heat'.

homeowner ▶ noun a person who owns their own home.

home page ▶ noun Computing an individual's or organization's introductory document on the World Wide Web.

home plate ▶ noun Baseball the five-sided white rubber plate-like base next to which the batter stands and which must be touched in scoring a run.

home port ▶ noun the port from which a ship originates.

Homer[1] /'həʊmə/ (8th century BC), Greek epic poet. He is traditionally held to be the author of the *Iliad*

and the *Odyssey*, though modern scholarship has revealed the place of the Homeric poems in a pre-literate oral tradition. In later antiquity Homer was regarded as the greatest poet, and his poems were constantly used as a model and source by others.
– PHRASES **Homer sometimes nods** proverb even the most gifted person occasionally makes mistakes.

Homer[2] /'həʊmə/, Winslow (1836–1910), American painter. He is best known for his seascapes, such as *Cannon Rock* (1895), painted in a vigorous naturalistic style considered to express the American pioneering spirit.

homer ▶ noun 1 Baseball a home run.
2 a homing pigeon.
3 informal a referee or official who is thought to favour the team playing at home.

home range ▶ noun Zoology an area over which an animal or group of animals regularly travels in search of food or mates, and which may overlap with those of neighbouring animals or groups of the same species.

Homeric /həʊ'mɛrɪk/ ▶ adjective of or in the style of Homer or the epic poems ascribed to him.
■ of Bronze Age Greece as described in these poems: *the mists of the Homeric age.* ■ epic and large-scale: *some of us exert a Homeric effort.*
– ORIGIN via Latin from Greek *Homērikos*, from *Homēros* (see **HOMER**[1]).

home rule ▶ noun [mass noun] the government of a colony, dependent country, or region by its own citizens, in particular as advocated for Ireland 1870–1914.

> The campaign for Irish home rule was one of the dominant forces in British politics in the late 19th and early 20th centuries, particularly in that Irish nationalists frequently held the balance of power in the House of Commons. A Home Rule Act was finally passed in 1914 but was suspended until after the First World War; after the Easter Rising of 1916 and Sinn Fein's successes in the general election of 1918, southern Ireland became the Irish Free State in 1921.

home run ▶ noun Baseball a hit that allows the batter to make a complete circuit of the bases and score a run.

home-schooling ▶ noun [mass noun] chiefly US the education of a child at home by their parents.
– DERIVATIVES **home-school** verb, **home-schooler** noun.

Home Secretary ▶ noun (in the UK) the Secretary of State in charge of the Home Office.

Home Service one of the original programme services of the BBC (renamed *Radio 4*).

home shopping ▶ noun [mass noun] shopping carried out from one's own home by ordering goods advertised in a catalogue or on a television channel, or by using various electronic media.
– DERIVATIVES **home shopper** noun.

homesick ▶ adjective experiencing a longing for one's home during a period of absence from it: *he was homesick for America after five weeks in Europe.*
– DERIVATIVES **homesickness** noun.

home signal ▶ noun Brit. a railway signal controlling entry to the immediate section of the line.

homesite ▶ noun N. Amer. & Austral./NZ a building plot.

homespun ▶ adjective 1 simple and unsophisticated: *homespun philosophy.*
2 (of cloth or yarn) made or spun at home.
■ denoting a coarse handwoven fabric similar to tweed.
▶ noun [mass noun] cloth of this type: *clad in homespun.*

homestead ▶ noun 1 a house, especially a farmhouse, and outbuildings.
■ Austral./NZ the owner's residence on a sheep or cattle station.
2 N. Amer. historical an area of land (usually 160 acres) granted to a settler as a home.
3 (in South Africa) a hut or cluster of huts occupied by one family or clan, standing alone or as part of a traditional African village.
– DERIVATIVES **homesteader** noun.
– ORIGIN Old English *hāmstede* 'a settlement' (see **HOME**, **STEAD**).

homesteading ▶ noun [mass noun] N. Amer. life as a settler on a homestead.
■ the granting of homesteads to settlers.

home straight (also **home stretch**) ▶ noun the concluding stretch of a racecourse.
■ figurative the last part of an activity or campaign: *heading down the home stretch to Tuesday's final.*

homestyle ▶ adjective [attrib.] N. Amer. (especially of food) such as would be made or provided at home; simple and unpretentious.

home theater ▶ noun North American term for HOME CINEMA.

home truth ▶ noun (usu. **home truths**) an unpleasant fact about oneself, especially as pointed out by another person: *what he needed was someone to tell him a few home truths.*

home unit ▶ noun Austral. a flat, especially one occupied by the owner, that is one of several in a large building.

homeward ▶ adverb (also **homewards**) towards home: *setting off homeward.*
▶ adjective going or leading towards home: *their homeward journey.*
– ORIGIN Old English *hāmweard* (see HOME, -WARD).

homeward-bound ▶ adjective on the way home: *the next day we were homeward-bound.*

homework ▶ noun [mass noun] school work that a pupil is required to do at home.
■ work or study done in preparation for a certain event or situation: *he had evidently done his homework and read his predecessor's reports.* ■ paid work carried out in one's own home, especially low-paid piecework.

homeworker ▶ noun a person who works from home, especially doing low-paid piecework.

homey (also **homy**) ▶ adjective (**homier**, **homiest**) (of a place or surroundings) pleasantly comfortable and cosy.
■ unsophisticated; unpretentious: *an idealized vision of traditional peasant life as simple and homey.*
– DERIVATIVES **homeyness** (also **hominess**) noun.

homicidal ▶ adjective of, relating to, or tending towards murder: *he had homicidal tendencies.*

homicide ▶ noun [mass noun] the deliberate and unlawful killing of one person by another; murder: *he was charged with homicide* | [count noun] *knives account for a third of all homicides.*
■ (**Homicide**) chiefly US the police department that deals with such crimes: *a man from Homicide.* ■ [count noun] dated a murderer.
– ORIGIN Middle English: from Old French, from Latin *homicidium*, from *homo, homin-* 'man'.

homie (also **homey**) ▶ noun (pl. **-ies**) informal, chiefly US a homeboy or homegirl.

homiletic /ˌhɒmɪˈlɛtɪk/ ▶ adjective of the nature of or characteristic of a homily: *homiletic literature.*
▶ noun (**homiletics**) the art of preaching or writing sermons: *the teaching of homiletics.*
– ORIGIN mid 17th cent.: via late Latin from Greek *homilētikos*, from *homilein* 'converse with, consort', from *homilia* (see HOMILY).

homiliary /hɒˈmɪlɪəri/ ▶ noun (pl. **-ies**) historical a book of homilies.
– ORIGIN mid 19th cent.: from medieval Latin *homiliarius*, from ecclesiastical Latin *homilia* (see HOMILY).

homily /ˈhɒmɪli/ ▶ noun (pl. **-ies**) a religious discourse which is intended primarily for spiritual edification rather than doctrinal instruction.
■ a tedious moralizing discourse: *she delivered her homily about the need for patience.*
– DERIVATIVES **homilist** noun.
– ORIGIN late Middle English: via Old French from ecclesiastical Latin *homilia*, from Greek, 'discourse, conversation' (in ecclesiastical use, 'sermon'), from *homilos* 'crowd'.

homing ▶ adjective relating to an animal's ability to return to a place or territory after travelling a distance away from it: *a strong homing instinct.*
■ (of a pigeon) trained to fly home from a great distance and bred for long-distance racing. ■ (of a weapon or piece of equipment) fitted with an electronic device that enables it to find and hit a target.

hominid /ˈhɒmɪnɪd/ ▶ noun Zoology a primate of a family (Hominidae) which includes humans and their fossil ancestors.
– ORIGIN late 19th cent.: from modern Latin *Hominidae* (plural), from Latin *homo, homin-* 'man'.

hominoid /ˈhɒmɪnɔɪd/ Zoology ▶ noun a primate of a group that includes humans, their fossil ancestors, and the great apes.
● Superfamily Hominoidea: families Hominidae and Pongidae.
▶ adjective of or relating to primates of this group; hominid or pongid.
– ORIGIN early 20th cent.: from Latin *homo, homin-* 'human being' + -OID.

hominy /ˈhɒmɪni/ ▶ noun [mass noun] US coarsely ground corn (maize) used to make grits: [as modifier] *hominy grits.*
– ORIGIN shortened from Virginia Algonquian *uskatahomen.*

Homo /ˈhəʊməʊ, ˈhɒməʊ/ the genus of primates of which modern humans (Homo sapiens) are the present-day representatives.
■ [with Latin or pseudo-Latin modifier] denoting kinds of modern human, often humorously: *a textbook example of Homo neuroticus.*

The genus *Homo* is believed to have existed for at least two million years, and modern humans (*H. sapiens sapiens*) first appeared in the Upper Palaeolithic. Among several extinct species are *H. habilis, H. erectus,* and *H. neanderthalensis.*

– ORIGIN Latin, 'man'.

homo /ˈhəʊməʊ/ informal, chiefly derogatory ▶ noun (pl. **-os**) a homosexual man.
▶ adjective homosexual.
– ORIGIN 1920s: abbreviation.

homo- ▶ combining form **1** same: *homogametic.*
2 relating to homosexual love: *homoerotic.* Often contrasted with HETERO-.
– ORIGIN from Greek *homos* 'same'.

homocentric¹ ▶ adjective having the same centre.

homocentric² ▶ adjective another term for ANTHROPOCENTRIC.

homocercal /ˌhɒmə(ʊ)ˈsəːk(ə)l, ˌhəʊm-/ ▶ adjective Zoology (of a fish's tail) appearing outwardly symmetrical but with the backbone passing into the upper lobe, as in all higher fish. Contrasted with DIPHYCERCAL, HETEROCERCAL.
– ORIGIN mid 19th cent.: from HOMO- 'same' + Greek *kerkos* 'tail' + -AL.

homocysteine /ˌhɒmə(ʊ)ˈsɪstiːn, ˌhəʊm-, -tɪn, -tem, -tiːn/ ▶ noun [mass noun] Biochemistry an amino acid which occurs in the body as an intermediate in the metabolism of methionine and cysteine.
● Chem. formula: $HSCH_2CH_2CH(NH_2)COOH$.

homoeobox ▶ noun variant spelling of HOMEOBOX.

homoeopath ▶ noun variant spelling of HOMEOPATH.

homoeopathy ▶ noun variant spelling of HOMEOPATHY.

homoeosis ▶ noun (pl. **homoeoses**) variant spelling of HOMEOSIS.

homoeostasis ▶ noun (pl. **homoeostases**) variant spelling of HOMEOSTASIS.

homoerotic /ˌhəʊmə(ʊ)ɪˈrɒtɪk, ˌhɒmə(ʊ)-/ ▶ adjective concerning or arousing sexual desire centred on a person of the same sex: *homoerotic images.*

homogametic /ˌhɒmə(ʊ)ɡəˈmɛtɪk, -ˈmiːtɪk, ˌhəʊm-/ ▶ adjective Biology denoting the sex which has sex chromosomes that do not differ in morphology, resulting in only one kind of gamete, e.g. (in mammals) the female and (in birds) the male. The opposite of HETEROGAMETIC.

homogamy /hɒˈmɒɡəmi/ ▶ noun [mass noun] **1** Biology inbreeding, especially as a result of isolation.
■ marriage between people from similar sociological or educational backgrounds. Compare with HETEROGAMY (in sense 3).
2 Botany a state in which the flowers of a plant are all of one type (either hermaphrodite or of the same sex). Compare with HETEROGAMY (in sense 2).
3 Botany the simultaneous ripening of the stamens and pistils of a flower, ensuring self-pollination. Compare with DICHOGAMY.
– DERIVATIVES **homogamous** adjective.
– ORIGIN late 19th cent.: from HOMO- 'same' + Greek *gamos* 'marriage'.

homogenate /həˈmɒdʒɪneɪt/ ▶ noun Biology a suspension of cell fragments and cell constituents obtained when tissue is homogenized.

homogeneous /ˌhɒmə(ʊ)ˈdʒiːnɪəs, -ˈdʒɛn-, ˌhəʊm-/ ▶ adjective of the same kind; alike: *if all jobs and workers were homogeneous.*
■ consisting of parts all of the same kind: *a homogeneous society.* ■ Mathematics containing terms all of the same degree.
– DERIVATIVES **homogeneity** /-dʒɪˈniːɪti, -dʒɪˈneɪti/ noun, **homogeneously** adverb, **homogeneousness** noun.
– ORIGIN early 17th cent. (as *homogeneity*): from medieval Latin *homogeneus*, from Greek *homogenēs*, from *homos* 'same' + *genos* 'race, kind'.

USAGE The correct spelling is **homogeneous** but a common misspelling is **homogenous**. The reason for the error probably relates to the *pronunciation*, in which the *e* is often missed out, but it may also have arisen through confusion with other words such as **homogenize**.

homogenize (also **-ise**) ▶ verb [with obj.] **1** subject (milk) to a process in which the fat droplets are emulsified and the cream does not separate: [as adj. **homogenized**] *homogenized milk.*
■ Biology prepare a suspension of cell constituents from (tissue) by physical treatment in a liquid.
2 make uniform or similar.
– DERIVATIVES **homogenization** /-ˈzeɪʃ(ə)n/ noun, **homogenizer** noun.

homogenous /həˈmɒdʒɪnəs/ ▶ adjective Biology old-fashioned term for HOMOLOGOUS.
– ORIGIN late 19th cent.: from HOMO- 'same' + Greek *genos* 'race, kind' + -OUS.

homograft /ˈhɒməɡrɑːft, ˈhəʊm-/ ▶ noun a tissue graft from a donor of the same species as the recipient. Compare with ALLOGRAFT.

homograph ▶ noun each of two or more words spelled the same but not necessarily pronounced the same and having different meanings and origins (e.g. BOW¹ and BOW²).
– DERIVATIVES **homographic** adjective.

homoiotherm /ˈhɒmɔɪə(ʊ)ˌθəːm/ ▶ noun variant spelling of HOMEOTHERM.

homoiousian /ˌhɒmɔɪˈuːsɪən, -ˈaʊ-, -z-/ ▶ noun historical a person who held that God the Father and God the Son are of like but not identical substance. Compare with HOMOOUSIAN.
– ORIGIN late 17th cent. (as an adjective in the sense 'of similar but not identical substance'): via ecclesiastical Latin from Greek *homoiousios*, from *homoios* 'like' + *ousia* 'essence, substance'. The noun dates from the mid 18th cent.

homolog ▶ noun US variant spelling of HOMOLOGUE.

homologate /həˈmɒləɡeɪt/ ▶ verb [with obj.] formal express agreement with or approval of.
■ approve (a car, boat, or engine) for sale in a particular market or use in a particular class of racing.
– DERIVATIVES **homologation** noun.
– ORIGIN late 16th cent.: from medieval Latin *homologat-* 'agreed', from the verb *homologare*, from Greek *homologein* 'confess'.

homologize /həˈmɒlədʒʌɪz/ (also **-ise**) ▶ verb [with obj.] formal make or show to have the same relation, relative position, or structure.

homologous /həˈmɒləɡəs/ ▶ adjective having the same relation, relative position, or structure, in particular:
■ (of organs) similar in position, structure, and evolutionary origin but not necessarily in function: *a seal's flipper is homologous with the human arm.* Often contrasted with ANALOGOUS. ■ Biology (of chromosomes) pairing at meiosis and having the same structural features and pattern of genes. ■ Chemistry (of a series of chemical compounds) having the same functional group but differing in composition by a fixed group of atoms.
– ORIGIN mid 17th cent.: via medieval Latin from Greek *homologos* 'agreeing, consistent', from *homos* 'same' + *logos* 'ratio, proportion'.

homologue /ˈhɒməlɒɡ/ (US **homolog**) ▶ noun technical a homologous thing.
– ORIGIN mid 19th cent.: from French, from Greek *homologos* (see HOMOLOGOUS).

homology /həˈmɒlədʒi/ ▶ noun [mass noun] the quality or condition of being homologous.

homomorphic ▶ adjective technical of the same or similar form.
■ Mathematics of, relating to, or of the nature of a homomorphism.
– DERIVATIVES **homomorphically** adverb.

homomorphism ▶ noun Mathematics a transformation of one set into another that preserves in the second set the relations between elements of the first.

homonym /ˈhɒmənɪm/ ▶ noun each of two or more words having the same spelling and pronunciation but different meanings and origins (e.g. POLE¹ and POLE²).
■ Biology a Latin name which is identical to that of a different organism, the newer of the two names being invalid.

– DERIVATIVES **homonymic** adjective, **homonymous** adjective, **homonymy** noun.
– ORIGIN late 17th cent.: via Latin from Greek *homōnumon*, neuter of *homōnumos* 'having the same name', from *homos* 'same' + *onoma* 'name'.

homoousian /ˌhɒməʊˈuːsɪən, -ˈaʊ-, -z-, ˌhɒməʊˈ-/ (also **homousian**) ▶ noun historical a person who held that God the Father and God the Son are of the same substance. Compare with **HOMOIOUSIAN**.
– ORIGIN mid 16th cent.: from ecclesiastical Latin *homousianus*, from *homousius*, from Greek *homoousios*, from *homos* 'same' + *ousia* 'essence', substance'.

homophobia /ˌhɒməˈfəʊbɪə, ˌhəʊmə-/ ▶ noun [mass noun] an extreme and irrational aversion to homosexuality and homosexual people.
– DERIVATIVES **homophobe** noun, **homophobic** adjective.
– ORIGIN 1960s: from **HOMOSEXUAL** + **-PHOBIA**.

homophone /ˈhɒməfəʊn, ˈhəʊm-/ ▶ noun each of two or more words having the same pronunciation but different meanings, origins, or spelling (e.g. **NEW** and **KNEW**).
  ▪each of a set of symbols denoting the same sound or group of sounds.

homophonic ▶ adjective 1 Music characterized by the movement of accompanying parts in the same rhythm as the melody. Often contrasted with **POLYPHONIC**.
  2 another term for **HOMOPHONOUS** (in sense 2).
– DERIVATIVES **homophonically** adverb.

homophonous /həˈmɒf(ə)nəs/ ▶ adjective 1 (of music) homophonic.
  2 (of a word or words) having the same pronunciation as another or others but different meaning, origin, or spelling.
– DERIVATIVES **homophony** noun.

homopolar ▶ adjective having equal or constant electrical polarity.
  ▪(of an electric generator) producing direct current without the use of commutators.

Homoptera /hɒˈmɒpt(ə)rə/ Entomology a group of true bugs comprising those in which the forewings are uniform in texture. Plant bugs such as aphids, whitefly, scale insects, and cicadas belong to this group. Compare with **HETEROPTERA**.
  ●Suborder Homoptera, order Hemiptera.
  ▪[as plural noun] **homoptera** bugs of this group.
– DERIVATIVES **homopteran** noun & adjective, **homopterous** adjective.
– ORIGIN modern Latin (plural), from **HOMO-** 'equal' + Greek *pteron* 'wing'.

homorganic /ˌhɒmɔːˈɡanɪk/ ▶ adjective denoting sets of speech sounds that are produced using the same vocal organs, e.g. *p*, *b*, and *m*.

Homo sapiens /ˌhəʊməʊ ˈsapɪɛnz, ˌhɒməʊ/ the primate species to which modern humans belong; humans regarded as a species. See also **HOMO**.
  ▪a member of this species.
– ORIGIN Latin, literally 'wise man'.

homosexual /ˌhɒmə(ʊ)ˈsɛksjʊəl, ˌhəʊm-, -ʃʊəl/ ▶ adjective (of a person) sexually attracted to people of one's own sex.
  ▪involving or characterized by sexual attraction between people of the same sex: *homosexual desire*.
  ▶ noun a person who is sexually attracted to people of their own sex.
– DERIVATIVES **homosexuality** noun, **homosexually** adverb.
– ORIGIN late 19th cent.: from **HOMO-** 'same' + **SEXUAL**.

homosocial ▶ adjective of or relating to social interaction between members of the same sex, typically men.

homotransplant ▶ noun another term for **ALLOGRAFT**.

homousian ▶ noun variant spelling of **HOMOOUSIAN**.

homozygote /ˌhɒmə(ʊ)ˈzaɪɡəʊt, ˌhəʊm-/ ▶ noun Genetics an individual having two identical alleles of a particular gene or genes and so breeding true for the corresponding characteristic. Compare with **HETEROZYGOTE**.
– DERIVATIVES **homozygosity** noun, **homozygous** adjective.

Homs /hɒms, hɒmz/ (also **Hims**) an industrial city in western Syria, on the River Orontes; pop. 537,000 (1993). It was named in 636 by the Muslims and occupies the site of ancient Emesa.

homunculus /hɒˈmʌŋkjʊləs/ (also **homuncule** /-kjuːl/) ▶ noun (pl. **homunculi** /-laɪ/ or **homuncules**) a very small human or humanoid creature.
  ▪historical a microscopic but fully formed human being from which a fetus was formerly believed to develop.
– ORIGIN mid 17th cent.: from Latin, diminutive of *homo*, *homin-* 'man'.

homy ▶ adjective variant spelling of **HOMEY**.

Hon ▶ abbreviation for ▪ (in official job titles) Honorary: *the Hon Secretary*. ▪ (in titles of the British nobility, members of parliament and some other politicians, and (in the US) judges) Honourable: *the Hon Charles Rothschild*.

hon ▶ noun informal short for **HONEY** (as a form of address): *It wouldn't interest you, hon*.

Honan /həˈnan/ **1** variant of **HENAN**.
  2 former name for **LUOYANG**.

honcho /ˈhɒn(t)ʃəʊ/ informal ▶ noun (pl. **-os**) a leader or manager; the person in charge: *the company's head honcho in the US*.
  ▶ verb (**-oes, -oed**) [with obj.] N. Amer. be in charge of (a project or situation).
– ORIGIN 1940s: from Japanese *hanchō* 'group leader', a term brought back to the US by servicemen stationed in Japan during the occupation following the Second World War.

Honda /ˈhɒndə/, Soichiro (1906–92), Japanese motor manufacturer. Opening his first factory in 1934, he began motorcycle manufacture in 1948 and expanded into car production during the 1960s.

Honduras /hɒnˈdjʊərəs/ a country of Central America, bordering on the Caribbean Sea and with a short coastline on the Pacific Ocean; pop. 5,294,000 (est. 1994); official language, Spanish; capital, Tegucigalpa. See also **BRITISH HONDURAS**.

Honduras was at the southern limit of the Mayan empire. It was encountered by Columbus in 1502, and became a Spanish colony. In 1821 Honduras became an independent republic, and was part of the United Provinces of Central America between 1823 and 1838.

– DERIVATIVES **Honduran** adjective & noun.

hone ▶ verb [with obj.] sharpen with a whetstone.
  ▪(usu. **be honed**) make sharper or more focused or efficient: *their appetites were honed by fresh air and exercise*.
  ▶ noun a whetstone, especially one used to sharpen razors.
  ▪[mass noun] the stone of which whetstones are made.
– ORIGIN Middle English: from Old English *hān* 'stone', of Germanic origin; related to Old Norse *hein*.

Honecker /ˈhɒnɪkə, German ˈhoːnɛkɐ/, Erich (1912–94), East German communist statesman, head of state 1976–89. His repressive regime was marked by a close allegiance to the Soviet Union. He was ousted in 1989 as communism collapsed throughout eastern Europe.

Honegger /ˈhɒnɪɡə, French ɔnɛɡɛʀ/, Arthur (1892–1955), French composer, of Swiss descent. He lived and worked chiefly in Paris, where he became a member of the anti-romantic group Les Six. His first major success was the orchestral work *Pacific 231* (1924).

honest ▶ adjective free of deceit and untruthfulness; sincere: *I haven't been totally honest with you*.
  ▪morally correct or virtuous: *I did the only right and honest thing*. ▪ [attrib.] fairly earned, especially through hard work: *struggling to make an honest living*. ▪ (of an action) blameless or well intentioned even if unsuccessful or misguided: *he'd made an honest mistake*. ▪ [attrib.] simple, unpretentious, and unsophisticated: *good honest food with no gimmicks*.
  ▶ adverb [sentence adverb] informal used to persuade someone of the truth of something: *you'll like it when you get there, honest*.
– PHRASES **earn** (or **turn**) **an honest penny** earn money fairly. **make an honest woman of** dated or humorous marry a woman, especially to avoid scandal if she is pregnant. [ORIGIN **honest** here originally meant 'respectable', but was probably associated with the archaic sense 'chaste, virtuous'.] **to be honest** speaking frankly: *to be honest, I expected to play worse*.
– ORIGIN Middle English (originally in the sense 'held in or deserving of honour'): via Old French from Latin *honestus*, from *honos* (see **HONOUR**).

honest broker ▶ noun an impartial mediator in international, industrial, or other disputes.
– ORIGIN late 19th cent.: translating German *ehrlicher*

Makler with reference to **BISMARCK[2]**, under whom Germany was united.

honestly ▶ adverb **1** in a truthful, fair, or honourable way: *he'd come by the money honestly*.
  2 used to emphasize the sincerity of an opinion, belief, or feeling: *she honestly believed that she was making life easier for Jack*.
  ▪[sentence adverb] used to emphasize the sincerity or truthfulness of a statement: *honestly, darling, I'm not upset*. ▪ [sentence adverb] used to indicate the speaker's disapproval, annoyance, or impatience: *honestly, that man is the absolute limit!*

honest-to-God informal ▶ adjective [attrib.] genuine; real: *an honest-to-God celebrity*.
  ▶ adverb genuinely; really: [as exclamation] *'You mean you didn't know?' 'Honest to God!'*

honest-to-goodness ▶ adjective [attrib.] plain, genuine, and straightforward: *an honest-to-goodness family holiday in the sun*.

honesty ▶ noun [mass noun] **1** the quality of being honest: *they spoke with convincing honesty about their fears* | *it was not, in all honesty, an auspicious debut*.
  2 a European plant with purple or white flowers and round, flat, translucent seed pods which are used for indoor flower arrangements.
  ●Genus *Lunaria*, family Cruciferae.
– PHRASES **honesty is the best policy** proverb there are often practical as well as moral reasons for being honest.
– ORIGIN Middle English: from Old French *honeste*, from Latin *honestas*, from *honestus* (see **HONEST**). The original sense was 'honour, respectability', later 'decorum, virtue, chastity'. The plant is so named from its seed pods, translucency symbolizing lack of deceit.

honewort /ˈhəʊnwəːt/ ▶ noun a wild plant of the parsley family.
  ● Two species in the family Umbelliferae: *Cryptotaenia canadensis*, a native of North America and east Asia which is cultivated for food in Japan, and *Trinia glauca*, a small European plant.
– ORIGIN mid 17th cent.: from obsolete *hone* 'swelling' (for which the plant was believed to be a remedy) + **WORT**.

honey ▶ noun (pl. **-eys**) **1** [mass noun] a sweet, sticky yellowish-brown fluid made by bees and other insects from nectar collected from flowers.
  ▪a yellowish-brown or golden colour: [as modifier] *her honey skin*. ▪ any sweet substance similar to bees' honey.
  2 informal an excellent example of something: *it's one honey of an adaptation*.
  ▪chiefly N. Amer. darling; sweetheart (usually as a form of address): *hi, honey!*
– ORIGIN Old English *hunig*, of Germanic origin; related to Dutch *honig* and German *Honig*.

honey ant ▶ noun another term for **HONEYPOT ANT**.

honey badger ▶ noun another term for **RATEL**.

honeybee ▶ noun see **BEE** (sense 1).

honeybird ▶ noun a small, drab African bird of the honeyguide family.
  ● Genus *Prodotiscus*, family Indicatoridae: three species.

honey bucket ▶ noun N. Amer. informal a toilet which does not use water and has to be emptied manually.

honeybun (also **honeybunch**) ▶ noun N. Amer. informal darling (used as a form of address).

honey buzzard ▶ noun a large Eurasian bird of prey resembling a buzzard, having a small head and long tail, feeding on the larvae, pupae, adults, and nests of bees and wasps.
  ● Genus *Pernis*, family Accipitridae: three species, in particular *P. apivorus*.

honeycomb ▶ noun **1** a structure of hexagonal cells of wax, made by bees to store honey and eggs.
  2 a structure of adjoining cavities or cells: *a honeycomb of caves*.
  ▪a mass of cavities produced by corrosion or dissolution: [as modifier] *honeycomb weathering*. ▪ a raised hexagonal or cellular pattern on the face of a fabric.
  3 [mass noun] tripe from the second stomach of a ruminant.
  ▶ verb [with obj.] fill with cavities or tunnels: *whole hillsides were honeycombed with mines*.
  ▪corrode (something) internally, forming small cavities in it. ▪ figurative infiltrate and undermine: *their men honeycombed the army*.
– ORIGIN Old English *hunigcamb* (see **HONEY**, **COMB**).

honeycreeper ▶ noun **1** a tropical American

tanager with a long curved bill, feeding on nectar and insects.
• Genera *Cyanerpes* and *Chlorophanes*, family Emberizidae (subfamily Thraupinae): five species.
2 (also **Hawaiian honeycreeper**) a Hawaiian songbird of variable appearance and with a specialized bill, several kinds of which are now endangered.
• Family Drepanididae (or Fringillidae): several genera and species, often with Hawaiian names such as the iiwi and ou.

honeydew ▶ **noun 1** [mass noun] a sweet, sticky substance excreted by aphids and often deposited on leaves and stems.
■ poetic/literary an ideally sweet substance.
2 (also **honeydew melon**) a melon of a variety with smooth pale skin and sweet green flesh.

honeyeater ▶ **noun** an Australasian songbird with a long brush-like tongue for feeding on nectar.
• Family Meliphagidae: numerous species and genera.

honeyed (also **honied**) ▶ **adjective** (of food) containing or coated with honey.
■ having a rich sweetness of taste or smell: *as the wine matures it becomes more honeyed.* ■ having a golden or warm yellow colour. ■ figurative (of a person's words or tone of voice) soothing, soft, and intended to please or flatter: *he wooed her with honeyed words.*

honey fungus (also **honey mushroom**) ▶ **noun** a widespread parasitic fungus that produces clumps of honey-coloured toadstools at the base of trees. The black string-like hyphae invade a tree, causing decay or death and spreading out to other trees.
• *Armillaria mellea*, family Tricholomataceae, class Hymenomycetes.

honeyguide ▶ **noun 1** a small bird of the Old World tropics, typically having drab plumage and feeding chiefly on beeswax and bee grubs. Two African kinds attract humans and other mammals, especially honey badgers, to bee nests.
• Family Indicatoridae: four genera, especially *Indicator*.
2 Botany a marking on the petal of a flower thought to guide pollinating insects to nectar.

honey locust ▶ **noun** a spiny tree of the pea family, grown as an ornamental for its fern-like foliage.
• Genus *Gleditsia*, family Leguminosae: several species, in particular the North American *G. triacanthos*, the pods of which contain a sweet pulp.

honeymoon ▶ **noun** a holiday spent together by a newly married couple: *they flew to the West Indies on honeymoon.*
■ [often as modifier] figurative an initial period of enthusiasm or goodwill, typically at the start of a new job: *the new President's honeymoon period.*
▶ **verb** [no obj., with adverbial of place] spend a honeymoon: *they are honeymooning in the south of France.*
– DERIVATIVES **honeymooner** noun.
– ORIGIN mid 16th cent. (originally denoting the period of time following a wedding): from **HONEY** + **MOON**. The original reference was to affection waning like the moon, but later the sense became 'the first month after marriage'.

honey parrot ▶ **noun** Australian term for **LORIKEET**.

honey possum ▶ **noun** a tiny shrew-like marsupial with a long pointed snout and a prehensile tail, found only in SW Australia, where it feeds exclusively upon nectar and pollen.
• *Tarsipes rostratus*, the only member of the family Tarsipedidae.

honeypot ▶ **noun** a container in which honey is kept: *she always had men hovering round her like bees round a honeypot.*
■ figurative a place to which many people are attracted: *the tourist honeypot of St Ives.* ■ vulgar slang a woman's genitals.

honeypot ant ▶ **noun** an ant that stores large amounts of honeydew and nectar in its elastic abdomen, which becomes greatly distended. This is then fed to nest mates by regurgitation.
• *Myrmecocystus* and other genera, family Formicidae.

honeysucker ▶ **noun** any of a number of long-billed birds which feed on nectar, especially (in South Africa) a sunbird.

honeysuckle ▶ **noun** a widely distributed climbing shrub with tubular flowers that are typically fragrant and of two colours or shades, opening in the evening for pollination by moths.
• Genus *Lonicera*, family Caprifoliaceae (the **honeysuckle family**): many species, including the Eurasian **common honeysuckle** (*L. periclymenum*) and many cultivars. The honeysuckle family also includes such berry-bearing shrubs as guelder rose, elder, and snowberry.
– ORIGIN Middle English *honysoukil*, extension of *honysouke*, from Old English *hunigsūce* (see **HONEY**, **SUCK**). It originally denoted tubular flowers, such as the red clover, which are sucked for their nectar.

honeywort ▶ **noun** a Mediterranean plant of the borage family, with greyish-green leaves and tubular yellow or purple flowers that are a favoured source of nectar for bees.
• Genus *Cerinthe*, family Boraginaceae: several species, in particular the yellow-flowered *C. major*.

hongi /ˈhɒŋi/ ▶ **noun** NZ (usu. **the hongi**) a traditional Maori greeting in which people press their noses together.
– ORIGIN Maori.

Hong Kong a former British dependency on the SE coast of China, returned to China in 1997; pop. 5,900,000 (est. 1990); official languages, English and Cantonese; capital, Victoria.

The area comprises Hong Kong Island, ceded by China in 1841, the Kowloon peninsula, ceded in 1860, and the New Territories, additional areas of the mainland which were leased for 99 years in 1898. Hong Kong has become one of the world's major financial and manufacturing centres, with the third largest container port in the world.

Honiara /ˌhəʊnɪˈɑːrə/ a port and the capital of the Solomon Islands, situated on the NW coast of the island of Guadalcanal; pop. 35,290 (1990).

honied ▶ **adjective** variant spelling of **HONEYED**.

honi soit qui mal y pense /ɒni ˌswɑː kiː mal iː ˈpɒ̃s/ ▶ **exclamation** shame on him who thinks evil of it (the motto of the Order of the Garter).
– ORIGIN French.

Honiton lace /ˈhɒnɪt(ə)n, ˈhʌn-/ ▶ **noun** [mass noun] lace consisting of floral sprigs hand sewn on to fine net or joined by lacework.
– ORIGIN mid 19th cent.: from *Honiton*, the name of a town in Devon.

honk ▶ **noun** the cry of a wild goose.
■ the harsh sound of a car horn.
▶ **verb** [no obj.] **1** emit such a cry or sound.
■ [with obj.] cause (a car horn) to make such a sound.
■ [with obj.] express by sounding a car horn: *taxi drivers honking their support.*
2 Brit. informal vomit.
– ORIGIN mid 19th cent.: imitative.

honker ▶ **noun** a person or thing that honks.
■ informal, chiefly N. Amer. a wild goose.

honky ▶ **noun** (pl. **-ies**) N. Amer. informal a derogatory term used by black people for a white person or for white people collectively.
– ORIGIN 1960s: of unknown origin.

honky-tonk ▶ **noun** informal **1** chiefly US a cheap or disreputable bar, club, or dance hall.
■ [as modifier] squalid and disreputable: *a honky-tonk beach resort.*
2 [mass noun] [often as modifier] ragtime piano music.
– ORIGIN late 19th cent.: of unknown origin.

honnête homme /ˌɒnɛt ˈɒm/ ▶ **noun** (usu. **the honnête homme**) a decent, cultivated man of the world; a gentleman.
– ORIGIN French, literally 'honest man'.

Honolulu /ˌhɒnəˈluːluː/ the state capital and principal port of Hawaii, situated on the SE coast of the island of Oahu; pop. 836,230 (1990).

honor ▶ **noun** & **verb** US spelling of **HONOUR**.

honorable ▶ **adjective** US spelling of **HONOURABLE**.

honorand /ˈɒnərand/ ▶ **noun** a person to be publicly honoured, especially with an honorary degree.
– ORIGIN 1950s: from Latin *honorandus* 'to be honoured', gerundive of *honorare* 'to honour', from *honor* 'honour'.

honorarium /ˌɒnəˈrɛːrɪəm/ ▶ **noun** (pl. **honorariums** or **honoraria** /-rɪə/) a payment given for professional services that are rendered nominally without charge.
– ORIGIN mid 17th cent.: from Latin, denoting a gift made on being admitted to public office, from *honorarius* (see **HONORARY**).

honorary ▶ **adjective 1** conferred as an honour, without the usual requirements or functions: *an honorary doctorate.*
■ (of a person) holding such a title or position: *he was elected an honorary fellow of the Royal College of Surgeons.*
2 Brit. (of an office or its holder) unpaid: *Honorary Secretary of the Association.*
– ORIGIN early 17th cent.: from Latin *honorarius*, from *honor* 'honour'.

honorific ▶ **adjective** given as a mark of respect: *he was elevated to the honorific status of 'Dom'.*
■ (of an office or post) given as a mark of respect, but having few or no duties. ■ denoting a form of address showing respect: *an honorific title for addressing women.*
▶ **noun** a title or word implying or expressing respect.
– DERIVATIVES **honorifically** adverb.
– ORIGIN mid 17th cent.: from Latin *honorificus*, from *honor* 'honour'.

honoris causa /ɒˌnɔːrɪs ˈkaʊzə/ ▶ **adverb** (especially of a degree awarded without examination) as a mark of esteem: *the artist has been awarded the degree honoris causa.*
– ORIGIN Latin, literally 'for the sake of honour'.

honour (US **honor**) ▶ **noun 1** [mass noun] high respect; esteem: *his portrait hangs in the place of honour.*
■ [in sing.] a person or thing that brings credit: *you are an honour to our profession.* ■ adherence to what is right or to a conventional standard of conduct: *I must as a matter of honour avoid any taint of dishonesty.*
2 a privilege: *Mrs Young had* **the honour of** *being received by the Queen.*
■ an exalted position: *the honour of being horse of the year.* ■ a thing conferred as a distinction, especially an official award for bravery or achievement: *the highest military honours.* ■ (**honours**) a special distinction for proficiency in an examination: *she passed with honours.* ■ (**honours**) a course of degree studies more specialized than for an ordinary pass: [as modifier] *an honours degree in mathematics.* ■ (**His**, **Your**, etc. **Honour**) a title of respect given to or used in addressing a circuit judge, a US mayor, and (in Irish or rustic speech) any person of rank. ■ Golf the right of driving off first, having won the previous hole.
3 dated a woman's chastity or her reputation for this: *she died defending her honour.*
4 Bridge an ace, king, queen, jack, or ten.
■ (**honours**) possession in one's hand of at least four of the ace, king, queen, jack, and ten of trumps, or of all four aces in no trumps, for which a bonus is scored. ■ (in whist) an ace, king, queen, or jack of trumps.
▶ **verb** [with obj.] **1** regard with great respect: *Joyce has now learned to honour her father's memory* | [as adj. **honoured**] *an honoured guest.*
■ (often **be honoured**) pay public respect to: *talented writers were honoured at a special ceremony.* ■ grace; privilege: *the Princess* **honoured** *the ball* **with** *her presence* | [as adj. **honoured**] *I felt honoured to be invited.*
2 fulfil (an obligation) or keep (an agreement): *make sure the franchisees honour the terms of the contract.*
■ accept (a bill) or pay (a cheque) when due: *the bank informed him that the cheque would not be honoured.*
– PHRASES **do the honours** informal perform a social duty or small ceremony for others (often used to describe the serving of food or drink to a guest). **honour bright** Brit. dated on my honour: *I'll never do it again, honour bright, I won't.* [ORIGIN: from Thomas Moore's *Tom Cribb's Memorial to Congress* (1819).] **honours are even** Brit. there is equality in the contest: *they are meeting in the final for the fifth time with honours even.* **in honour bound** another way of saying **ON ONE'S HONOUR**. **in honour of** as a celebration of or expression of respect for. **on one's honour** under a moral obligation: *they are on their honour as gentlemen not to cheat.* **on** (or **upon**) **my honour** used as an expression of sincerity: *I promise on my honour.* **there's honour among thieves** proverb dishonest people may have certain standards of behaviour which they will respect.
– ORIGIN Middle English: from Old French *onor* (noun), *onorer* (verb), from Latin *honor*.

honourable (US **honorable**) ▶ **adjective 1** bringing or worthy of honour: *this is the only honourable course* | *a decent and honourable man.*
■ formal or humorous (of the intentions of a man courting a woman) directed towards marriage: *the young man's intentions had been honourable.*
2 (**Honourable**) used as a title indicating eminence or distinction, given to certain high officials, the children of certain ranks of the nobility, and MPs: *the Honourable Alan Simpson, US Senator.*
– DERIVATIVES **honourableness** noun, **honourably** adverb.
– ORIGIN Middle English: via Old French from Latin *honorabilis*, from *honor* 'honour'.

honourable mention ▶ **noun** a commendation given to a candidate in an examination or competition who is not awarded a prize.

honour point ▶ **noun** Heraldry the point halfway between the top of a shield and the fess point.

honours list ▶ noun a publicly issued list of people and the distinctions they are to be awarded.

honours of war ▶ plural noun privileges granted to a capitulating force, for example that of marching out with colours flying.

honour system ▶ noun [in sing.] a system of payment or examinations which relies solely on the honesty of those concerned.

Hon. Sec. ▶ abbreviation for honorary secretary.

Honshu /ˈhɒnʃuː/ the largest of the four main islands of Japan; pop 99,254,000 (1990).

Hooch, Pieter de, see **DE HOOCH**.

hooch /huːtʃ/ (also **hootch**) ▶ noun [mass noun] informal alcoholic liquor, especially inferior or illicit whisky.
– ORIGIN late 19th cent.: abbreviation of *Hoochinoo*, the name of an Alaskan Indian people who made liquor.

Hood, Thomas (1799–1845), English poet and humorist. He wrote much humorous verse but is chiefly remembered for serious poems such as 'The Song of the Shirt'.

hood[1] ▶ noun 1 a covering for the head and neck with an opening for the face, typically forming part of a coat or cloak.
■a separate garment similar to this worn over a university gown or a surplice to indicate the wearer's degree. ■ Falconry a leather covering for a hawk's head.
2 a thing resembling a hood in shape or use, in particular:
■Brit. a folding waterproof cover of a motor car, pram, etc. ■ N. Amer. the bonnet of a motor vehicle. ■a canopy to protect users of machinery or to remove fumes from it. ■ a hood-like structure or marking on the head or neck of an animal. ■ the upper part of the flower of a plant such as a dead-nettle. ■a tubular attachment to keep stray light out of a camera lens: *a lens hood.*
▶ verb [with obj.] put a hood on or over.
– DERIVATIVES **hoodless** adjective, **hood-like** adjective.
– ORIGIN Old English *hōd*, of West Germanic origin; related to Dutch *hoed*, German *Hut* 'hat', also to **HAT**.

hood[2] ▶ noun informal, chiefly US a gangster or similar violent criminal.
– ORIGIN 1930s: abbreviation of **HOODLUM**.

hood[3] (also **'hood**) ▶ noun informal, chiefly US a neighbourhood, especially one's own neighbourhood: *I've lived in the hood for 15 years.*
– ORIGIN 1970s: shortening of **NEIGHBOURHOOD**.

-hood ▶ suffix forming nouns: 1 denoting a condition or quality: *falsehood | womanhood.*
2 denoting a collection or group: *brotherhood.*
– ORIGIN Old English *-hād*, originally an independent noun meaning 'person, condition, quality'.

hooded ▶ adjective (of an article of clothing) having a hood: *a hooded cloak.*
■(of a person) wearing a hood: *a hooded figure.* ■ (of eyes) having thick, drooping upper eyelids resembling hoods: *a dark man with hooded eyes stalked her.*

hooded crow ▶ noun a bird of the North and East European race of the carrion crow, having a grey body with a black head, wings, and tail.
• *Corvus corone cornix*, family Corvidae.

hooded seal ▶ noun a seal with a grey and white blotched coat, found in the Arctic waters of the North Atlantic. The male has a nasal sac that is inflated into a hood during display.
• *Cystophora cristata*, family Phocidae.

hoodie ▶ noun Scottish term for **HOODED CROW**.

hoodlum /ˈhuːdləm/ ▶ noun a person who engages in crime and violence; a hooligan or gangster.
– ORIGIN late 19th cent. (originally US): of unknown origin.

hood mould (also **hood moulding**) ▶ noun Architecture another term for **DRIPSTONE** (in sense 1).

hoodoo ▶ noun 1 [mass noun] voodoo; witchcraft.
■[count noun] a run of bad luck associated with a person or activity: *when is this hoodoo going to end?* ■ [count noun] a person or thing that brings or causes bad luck.
2 chiefly N. Amer. a column or pinnacle of weathered rock: *a towering sandstone hoodoo.*
▶ verb (**hoodoos, hoodooed**) [with obj.] bewitch: *she's hoodooed you.*
■bring bad luck to: *a fine player, but repeatedly hoodooed.*
– ORIGIN late 19th cent. (originally US): apparently an alteration of **VOODOO**. It originally denoted a person who practised voodoo, hence a hidden cause of bad luck (sense 1). Sense 2 is apparently due to the resemblance of the rock column to a strange human form, often topped by an overhanging 'hat' of harder rock.

hoodwink ▶ verb [with obj.] deceive or trick (someone): *staff were **hoodwinked into** thinking the cucumber was a sawn-off shotgun.*
– ORIGIN mid 16th cent. (originally in the sense 'to blindfold'): from the noun **HOOD**[1] + an obsolete sense of **WINK** 'close the eyes'.

hooey ▶ noun [mass noun] informal nonsense: *the emphasis on family is pretentious hooey.*
– ORIGIN 1920s (originally US): of unknown origin.

hoof ▶ noun (pl. **hoofs** or **hooves**) the horny part of the foot of an ungulate animal, especially a horse: *there was a clatter of hoofs as a rider came up to them.*
▶ verb [with obj.] informal 1 kick (a ball) powerfully.
2 (**hoof it**) go on foot.
■dance: *we hoof it reasonably fancily, and no one guffaws.*
– PHRASES **on the hoof** 1 (of livestock) not yet slaughtered. 2 informal without great thought or preparation: *policy was made on the hoof.*
– DERIVATIVES **hoofed** adjective.
– ORIGIN Old English *hōf*, of Germanic origin; related to Dutch *hoef* and German *Huf*.

hoofer ▶ noun informal a professional dancer.

hoof fungus ▶ noun another term for **TINDER FUNGUS**.

Hooghly /ˈhuːgli/ (also **Hugli**) the most westerly of the rivers of the Ganges delta, in West Bengal, India. It flows for 192 km (120 miles) into the Bay of Bengal and is navigable to Calcutta.

hoo-ha ▶ noun [in sing.] informal a commotion; a fuss: *the book was causing such a hoo-ha.*
– ORIGIN 1930s: of unknown origin.

hook ▶ noun 1 a piece of metal or other material, curved or bent back at an angle, for catching hold of or hanging things on: *a picture hook.*
■(also **fish-hook**) a bent piece of metal, typically barbed and baited, for catching fish. ■a cradle on which a telephone receiver rests. ■ figurative a thing designed to catch people's attention: *companies are looking for a sales hook.* ■a chorus or repeated instrumental passage in a piece of music, especially a pop or rock song, which gives it immediate appeal and makes it easy to remember.
2 a curved cutting instrument, especially as used for reaping or shearing.
3 a short swinging punch made with the elbow bent and rigid, especially in boxing: *a perfectly timed right hook to the chin.*
■Cricket a stroke made to the on side with a horizontal or slightly upward swing of the bat at shoulder height. ■ Golf a stroke which makes the ball deviate in flight in the direction of the follow-through (from right to left for a right-handed player), typically inadvertently.
4 a curved stroke in handwriting, especially as made in learning to write.
■Music an added stroke transverse to the stem in the symbol for a quaver or other note.
5 [usu. in place names] a curved promontory or sand spit.
▶ verb 1 [with obj. and adverbial] attach or fasten with a hook or hooks: *the truck had a red lamp hooked to its tailgate | she tried to **hook up** her bra.*
■[no obj., with adverbial of place] be or become attached with a hook: *a ladder that hooks over the roof ridge.* ■ bend or be bent into the shape of a hook so as to fasten around or to an object: [with obj.] *he hooked his thumbs in his belt* | [no obj.] *her legs hooked around mine.* ■ [with obj.] Rugby secure (the ball) and pass it backward with the foot in the scrum.
2 [with obj.] catch with a hook: *he hooked a 24 lb pike.*
■informal (usu. **be hooked**) captivate: *I was hooked by John's radical zeal.* ■ archaic, informal steal.
3 [with obj.] Cricket hit (the ball) round to the on side with a horizontal or slightly upward swing of the bat at shoulder height; hit a ball delivered by (the bowler) with such a stroke.
■Golf strike (the ball) or play (a stroke) so that the ball deviates in the direction of the follow-through, typically inadvertently. ■ [no obj.] Boxing punch one's opponent with the elbow bent and rigid.
4 [often in imperative] (**hook it**) Brit. informal, dated run away.
– PHRASES **by hook or by crook** by any possible means: *the government intends, by hook or by crook, to hold on to the land.* **get one's hooks into** informal get hold of: *they were going to move out rather than let Mel get his hooks into them.* **get** (or **give someone**) **the hook** N. Amer. informal be dismissed (or dismiss someone) from a job. **hook, line, and sinker** used to emphasize that someone has been completely deceived or tricked: *he fell hook, line, and sinker for this year's April Fool joke.* [ORIGIN: with allusion to the taking of bait by a fish.] **off the hook 1** informal no longer in difficulty or trouble: *I lied to get him off the hook.* **2** (of a telephone receiver) not on its rest, and so preventing incoming calls. **on the hook for** N. Amer. informal (in a financial context) responsible for: *he's on the hook for about $9.5 million.* **on one's own hook** informal, dated, chiefly US on one's own account; by oneself. **sling one's hook** [usu. in imperative] Brit. informal leave; go away.
– DERIVATIVES **hookless** adjective, **hooklet** noun, **hook-like** adjective.
– ORIGIN Old English *hōc*, of Germanic origin; related to Dutch *hoek* 'corner, angle, projecting piece of land', also to German *Haken* 'hook'.
▶**hook someone/thing up** (or **hook up**) link or be linked to electronic equipment: *Ali was hooked up to an electrocardiograph.*

hookah /ˈhʊkə/ ▶ noun an oriental tobacco pipe with a long, flexible tube which draws the smoke through water contained in a bowl.
– ORIGIN mid 18th cent.: from Urdu, from Arabic *ḥuḳḳa* 'casket, jar'.

hook and eye ▶ noun a small metal hook and loop used together as a fastener on a garment.

hookbait ▶ noun Brit. bait attached to a hook for fishing (as distinct from groundbait).

Hooke, Robert (1635–1703), English scientist. He formulated the law of elasticity (Hooke's law), proposed an undulating theory of light, introduced the term *cell* to biology, postulated elliptical orbits for the earth and moon, and proposed the inverse square law of gravitational attraction. He also invented or improved many scientific instruments and mechanical devices, and designed a number of buildings in London after the Great Fire.

hooked ▶ adjective 1 having a hook or hooks: *a hooked gold earring.*
■curved like a hook: *a golden eagle with hooked beak.*
2 informal captivated; absorbed: *cricket fans are currently **hooked on** a series of college matches.*
■addicted: *a girl who got **hooked on** cocaine.*
3 (of a rug or mat) made by pulling woollen yarn through canvas with a hook.

Hooker, Sir Joseph Dalton (1817–1911), English botanist and pioneer in plant geography. Hooker applied Darwin's theories to plants and, with **George Bentham** (1800–84), he produced a work on classification, *Genera Plantarum* (1862–83).

hooker[1] ▶ noun 1 Rugby the player in the middle of the front row of the scrum, who tries to hook the ball.
2 informal, chiefly N. Amer. a prostitute.

hooker[2] ▶ noun a one-masted sailing boat of a kind used especially in Ireland for fishing.
■Nautical, informal an old boat.
– ORIGIN mid 17th cent.: from Dutch *hoeker*, from *hoek* 'hook' (used earlier in *hoekboot*, denoting a two-masted Dutch fishing vessel).

hooker[3] ▶ noun N. Amer. informal a glass or drink of undiluted brandy, whisky, or other alcoholic spirit.
– ORIGIN mid 19th cent.: of unknown origin.

Hooke's law Physics a law stating that the strain in a solid is proportional to the applied stress within the elastic limit of that solid.

hookey (also **hooky**) ▶ noun (in phrase **play hookey**) N. Amer. informal play truant.
– ORIGIN mid 19th cent. (originally US): of unknown origin.

hook nose ▶ noun a prominent aquiline nose.
– DERIVATIVES **hook-nosed** adjective.

Hook of Holland a cape and port of the Netherlands, near The Hague, linked by ferry to Harwich, Hull, and Dublin. Dutch name **HOEK VAN HOLLAND**.

hook shot ▶ noun Basketball a twisting shot started with the player's back to the basket, and completed as they pivot round towards the basket.

hooktip ▶ noun a slender moth which has hooked tips to the forewings. The caterpillar tapers to a point at the rear and rests with both ends raised.
• Family Drepanidae: *Drepana* and other genera.

hook-up ▶ noun a connection or link, especially to

mains electricity or for communications or broadcasting equipment.

hookworm ▶ **noun** a parasitic nematode worm which inhabits the intestines of humans and other animals. It has hook-like mouthparts with which it attaches itself to the wall of the gut, puncturing the blood vessels and feeding on the blood.
• *Ancylostoma, Uncinaria, Necator,* and other genera, class Phasmida, including *N. americanus*, which infects millions of people in the tropics.
■ [mass noun] a disease caused by an infestation of hookworms, often resulting in severe anaemia.

hooky[1] ▶ **adjective** (of a tune or a component of a tune) having immediate appeal and easy to remember: *a hooky bass line.*

hooky[2] ▶ **noun** variant spelling of **HOOKEY**.

hooley ▶ **noun** (pl. **-eys**) informal, chiefly Irish a wild or noisy party.
– ORIGIN late 19th cent.: of unknown origin.

hooligan ▶ **noun** a violent young troublemaker, typically one of a gang: *a football hooligan.*
– DERIVATIVES **hooliganism** noun.
– ORIGIN late 19th cent.: perhaps from *Hooligan*, the surname of a fictional rowdy Irish family in a music-hall song of the 1890s, also of a character in a cartoon.

hoolock /ˈhuːlək/ (also **hoolock gibbon**) ▶ **noun** a gibbon with white eyebrows, the male of which has black fur and the female golden, found from NE India to Burma.
• *Hylobates hoolock*, family Hylobatidae.
– ORIGIN early 19th cent.: perhaps from Bengali and imitative of its cry.

hoon Austral./NZ informal ▶ **noun** a lout.
▶ **verb** [no obj.] behave like a lout.
– ORIGIN 1930s: of unknown origin.

hoop ▶ **noun** 1 a circular band of metal, wood, or similar material, especially one used for binding the staves of barrels or forming part of a framework.
■ a large ring used as a toy by being bowled along. ■ a large ring, typically with paper stretched over it, for circus performers to jump through. ■ historical a circle of flexible material used for expanding a woman's petticoat or skirt. ■ (also **hoop petticoat**) historical a petticoat expanded with such hoops. ■ chiefly Brit. an arch of metal through which the balls are hit in croquet.
2 a horizontal band of a contrasting colour on a sports shirt or jockey's cap.
■ Austral. informal a jockey.
▶ **verb** [with obj.] bind or encircle with or as with hoops.
– PHRASES **put someone** (or **go**) **through the hoops** make someone undergo (or be made to undergo) a difficult and gruelling test or series of tests.
– DERIVATIVES **hooped** adjective.
– ORIGIN late Old English *hōp*, of West Germanic origin; related to Dutch *hoep*.

hooper ▶ **noun** old-fashioned term for **COOPER**.
– ORIGIN Middle English: from **HOOP**.

hoop iron ▶ **noun** [mass noun] flattened iron in long thin strips used for binding together the staves of casks or tubs.

hoopla /ˈhuːplɑː/ ▶ **noun** 1 Brit. a game in which rings are thrown from behind a line in an attempt to encircle one of several prizes.
2 [mass noun] informal unnecessary fuss surrounding something.

hoopoe /ˈhuːpuː, -pəʊ/ ▶ **noun** a salmon-pink Eurasian bird with a long downcurved bill, a large erectile crest, and black-and-white wings and tail.
• *Upupa epops*, the only member of the family Upupidae.
– ORIGIN mid 17th cent.: alteration of obsolete *hoop*, from Old French *huppe*, from Latin *upupa*, imitative of the bird's call.

hoop petticoat ▶ **noun** see **HOOP** (sense 1).

hooray ▶ **exclamation** 1 another word for **HURRAH**.
2 Austral./NZ goodbye.

Hooray Henry ▶ **noun** (pl. **Hooray Henrys** or **Hooray Henries**) Brit. informal a lively but ineffectual young upper-class man.

hooroo /hʌˈruː/ (also **hurroo**) ▶ **exclamation** & **noun** Australian word for **HOORAY**.

hoosegow /ˈhuːsgaʊ/ ▶ **noun** informal, chiefly US a prison.
– ORIGIN early 20th cent.: via Latin American Spanish from Spanish *juzgado* 'tribunal', from Latin *judicatum* 'something judged', neuter past participle of *judicare*.

Hoosier /ˈhuːʒɪə/ ▶ **noun** US a native or inhabitant of the state of Indiana, US.
– ORIGIN early 19th cent.: of unknown origin.

Hoosier State informal name for **INDIANA**.

hoot ▶ **noun** a deep or medium-pitched musical sound, often wavering or syncopated, which is the typical call of many kinds of owl.
■ a similar but typically more raucous sound made by a horn, siren, or steam whistle. ■ a shout expressing scorn or disapproval: *there were hoots of derision.* ■ a short outburst of laughter: *the audience broke into hoots of laughter.* ■ (**a hoot**) informal an amusing situation or person: *your mum's a real hoot.*
▶ **verb** [no obj.] (of an owl) utter a hoot.
■ (of a person) make loud sounds of scorn, disapproval, or merriment: *she began to hoot with laughter.* ■ (**hoot something down**) express loud scornful disapproval of something: *his questions were hooted down or answered obscenely.* ■ (of a horn, siren, etc.) make a hoot. ■ [with obj.] (of the driver of a vehicle) sound (the horn).
– PHRASES **not care** (or **give**) **a hoot** (or **two hoots**) informal not care at all.
– ORIGIN Middle English (in the sense 'make sounds of derision'): perhaps imitative.

hootch ▶ **noun** variant spelling of **HOOCH**.

hootenanny /ˈhuːt(ə)ˌnani/ ▶ **noun** (pl. **-ies**) informal, chiefly US an informal gathering with folk music.
– ORIGIN 1920s (originally US, denoting a gadget or 'thingummy'): of unknown origin.

hooter ▶ **noun** 1 Brit. a siren or steam whistle, especially one used as a signal for work to begin or cease.
■ the horn of a motor vehicle.
2 informal a person's nose.
3 (**hooters**) N. Amer. vulgar slang a woman's breasts.

hoots ▶ **exclamation** Scottish & N. English archaic or humorous expressing dissatisfaction or impatience: *'Och, noo, hoots, Hamish! Wull yee no sing us a song?'*
– ORIGIN natural exclamation: first recorded in English in the mid 16th cent. as *hoot*; the form *hoots* dates from the early 19th cent.

Hoover[1], Herbert (Clark) (1874–1964), American Republican statesman, 31st President of the US 1929–33. As President he was faced with the long-term problems of the Depression.

Hoover[2], J. Edgar (1895–1972), American lawyer and director of the FBI 1924–72; full name *John Edgar Hoover*. He reorganized the FBI into an efficient, scientific law-enforcement agency, but came under criticism for the organization's role during the McCarthy era.

Hoover[3], William (Henry) (1849–1932), American industrialist. In 1908 he bought the patent of a lightweight electric cleaning machine and formed a company to manufacture it with great success. In 1910 the company was renamed Hoover.

Hoover[4] Brit. ▶ **noun** trademark a vacuum cleaner, properly one made by the Hoover company.
▶ **verb** (**hoover**) [with obj.] clean (something) with a vacuum cleaner: *he was hoovering the stairs.*
■ (**hoover something up**) suck something up with or as if with a vacuum cleaner: *hoover up all the dust.*
– ORIGIN 1920s: named after W.H. **HOOVER**[3].

Hooverville ▶ **noun** (in the US) a shanty town built by unemployed and destitute people during the Depression of the early 1930s.
– ORIGIN named after H.C. **HOOVER**[1], during whose presidency such accommodation was built (see also **-VILLE**).

hooves plural form of **HOOF**.

hop[1] ▶ **verb** (**hopped**, **hopping**) [no obj., with adverbial of direction] (of a person) move by jumping on one foot: *he hopped along beside her.*
■ (of a bird or other animal) move by jumping with two or all feet at once: *a blackbird was hopping around in the sun.* ■ spring or leap a short distance with one jump: *he hopped down from the rock.* ■ [with obj.] jump over (something): *the cow hopped the fence.* ■ informal make a quick trip: *she hopped over the Atlantic for a bit of shopping.* ■ (**hop it**) Brit. informal go away quickly. ■ make a quick change of position, location, or activity: *over the years he hopped from one department to another.* ■ [with obj.] informal jump on to (a moving vehicle): *ex-soldiers looking for work hopped freights heading west.* ■ [usu. as noun, in combination **-hopping**] (of an aircraft or ferry) pass quickly from one place to another: *two-week island-hopping packages.*
▶ **noun** 1 a hopping movement.
■ a short journey or distance: *a short hop by cab from Soho.*
2 an informal dance.
– PHRASES **hop, skip** (or **step**), **and jump** 1 old-fashioned term for **TRIPLE JUMP**. 2 informal a short distance: *it's just a hop, skip, and jump from my home town.* **hop the twig** (or **stick**) Brit. informal depart suddenly or die. **on the hop** Brit. informal 1 unprepared: *he was caught on the hop.* 2 bustling about; busy: *we were always kept on the hop.*
– ORIGIN Old English *hoppian*, of Germanic origin; related to German dialect *hopfen* and German *hopsen*.
▶ **hop in** (or **out**) informal get into (or out of) a car: *hop in then and we'll be off.*

hop[2] ▶ **noun** a twining climbing plant native to north temperate regions. Hops are cultivated for the cone-like flowers borne by the female plant, which are used in brewing beer.
• *Humulus lupulus*, family Cannabaceae (or Cannabidaceae).
■ (**hops**) the dried cone-like flowers of this plant, used in brewing to give a bitter flavour and as a mild sterilant. ■ (**hops**) Austral./NZ informal beer. ■ [mass noun] US informal, dated a narcotic drug, especially opium.
▶ **verb** (**hopped**, **hopping**) 1 [with obj.] flavour with hops: *a strong dark beer, heavily hopped.*
2 (**be hopped up**) informal be stimulated or intoxicated by or as if by a narcotic drug.
– DERIVATIVES **hoppy** adjective.
– ORIGIN late Middle English *hoppe* (in the sense 'ripened hop cones for flavouring malt liquor'), from Middle Low German or Middle Dutch.

hopak ▶ **noun** variant spelling of **GOPAK**.

hop back ▶ **noun** a container with a perforated bottom for straining off the hops in the manufacture of beer.

hop bine (also **hop bind**) ▶ **noun** the climbing stem of the hop.

Hope, Bob (b.1903), British-born American comedian; born *Leslie Townes Hope*. He often adopted the character of a cowardly incompetent, cheerfully failing to become a romantic hero, as in the series of *Road* films (1940–62).

hope ▶ **noun** [mass noun] 1 a feeling of expectation and desire for a certain thing to happen: *he looked through her belongings in the hope of coming across some information* | [count noun] *I had high hopes of making the Olympic team.*
■ [count noun] a person or thing that may help or save someone: *their only hope is surgery.* ■ grounds for believing that something good may happen: *he does see some hope for the future.*
2 archaic a feeling of trust.
▶ **verb** [no obj.] want something to happen or be the case: *he's hoping for an offer of compensation* | [with clause] *I hope that the kids are OK.*
■ [with infinitive] intend if possible to do something: *we're hoping to address all these issues.*
– PHRASES **hope against hope** cling to a mere possibility: *they were hoping against hope that he would find a way out.* **hope for the best** hope for a favourable outcome. **hope springs eternal in the human breast** proverb it is human nature to always find fresh cause for optimism. **not a** (or **some**) **hope** informal no chance at all.
– DERIVATIVES **hoper** noun.
– ORIGIN late Old English *hopa* (noun), *hopian* (verb), of Germanic origin; related to Dutch *hoop* (noun), *hopen* (verb), and German *hoffen* (verb).

hope chest ▶ **noun** N. Amer. a chest containing household linen and clothing stored by a woman in preparation for her marriage.

hopeful ▶ **adjective** feeling or inspiring optimism about a future event: *a hopeful sign* | [with clause] *he remained hopeful that something could be worked out.*
▶ **noun** a person likely or hoping to succeed: *promotion hopefuls Huddersfield.*
– DERIVATIVES **hopefulness** noun.

hopefully ▶ **adverb** 1 in a hopeful manner: *he rode on hopefully.*
2 [sentence adverb] it is to be hoped that: *hopefully it should be finished by next year.*

b **b**ut | d **d**og | f **f**ew | g **g**et | h **h**e | j **y**es | k **c**at | l **l**eg | m **m**an | n **n**o | p **p**en | r **r**ed | s **s**it | t **t**op | v **v**oice | w **w**e | z **z**oo | ʃ **sh**e | ʒ deci**s**ion | θ **th**in | ð **th**is | ŋ ri**ng** | x lo**ch** | tʃ **ch**ip | dʒ **j**ar

USAGE The traditional sense of **hopefully**, 'in a hopeful manner', has been used since the 17th century. In the second half of the 20th century a new use as a sentence adverb arose, meaning 'it is to be hoped that', as in ***hopefully**, we'll see you tomorrow*. This second use is now much commoner than the first use, accounting for more than 90 per cent of citations for **hopefully** in the British National Corpus. It is, however, widely believed to be incorrect. Why should this be? People do not criticize other sentence adverbs, e.g. **sadly** (as in ***sadly**, her father died last year*) or **fortunately** (as in ***fortunately**, he recovered*). Part of the reason is that **hopefully** is a rather odd sentence adverb: while many others, such as **sadly**, **regrettably**, and **clearly**, may be paraphrased as 'it is sad/regrettable/clear that ...', this is not possible with **hopefully**. Nevertheless, it is clear that use of **hopefully** has become a shibboleth of 'correctness' in the language in the late 20th century—even if the arguments on which this is based are not particularly strong—and it is wise to be aware of this in formal or written contexts.

Hopeh /həʊˈpeɪ/ variant of **HEBEI**.

hopeless ▶ **adjective** **1** feeling or causing despair: *Jess looked at him in mute hopeless appeal.*
2 inadequate; incompetent: *I'm **hopeless at** names.*
– DERIVATIVES **hopelessly** adverb, **hopelessness** noun.

hophead ▶ **noun** informal **1** US a drug addict.
2 Austral./NZ a heavy drinker.

Hopi /ˈhəʊpi/ ▶ **noun** (pl. same or **Hopis**) **1** a member of a Pueblo Indian people living chiefly in NE Arizona.
2 [mass noun] the Uto-Aztecan language of this people, with around 2,000 speakers.
▶ **adjective** of or relating to this people or their language.
– ORIGIN the name in Hopi.

Hopkins[1], Sir Anthony (Philip) (b.1937), Welsh actor, a US citizen from 2000. He won an Oscar for his performance in *The Silence of the Lambs* (1991). Other notable films: *The Elephant Man* (1980) and *The Remains of the Day* (1993).

Hopkins[2] Sir Frederick Gowland (1861–1947), English biochemist. He carried out pioneering work on 'accessory food factors' essential to the diet, later called vitamins. Nobel Prize for Physiology or Medicine (1929).

Hopkins[3], Gerard Manley (1844–89), English poet. Becoming a Jesuit in 1868, he wrote little poetry until 1876, when a shipwreck inspired him to write 'The Wreck of the Deutschland'. Like his poems 'Windhover' and 'Pied Beauty' (both 1877), it makes use of Hopkins's 'sprung rhythm' technique.

hoplite /ˈhɒplʌɪt/ ▶ **noun** a heavily armed foot soldier of ancient Greece.
– ORIGIN from Greek *hoplitēs*, from *hoplon* 'weapon'.

hop merchant ▶ **noun** North American term for **COMMA** (in sense 3).

Hopper, Edward (1882–1967), American realist painter. He is best known for his mature works, such as *Early Sunday Morning* (1930), often depicting isolated figures in bleak scenes from everyday urban life.

hopper[1] ▶ **noun** **1** a container for a bulk material such as grain, rock, or rubbish, typically one that tapers downward and is able to discharge its contents at the bottom.
■ chiefly historical a tapering container, working with a hopping motion, through which grain passed into a mill. ■ a railway wagon able to discharge coal or other bulk material through its floor. ■ a barge for carrying away mud or sediment from a dredging-machine and discharging it. ■ (also **hopper head**) a container at the top of a vertical pipe which receives water from a gutter or waste pipe.
2 a person or thing that hops.
■ informal a person who makes a series of short trips: *an island hopper.* ■ a hopping insect, especially a young locust.

hopper[2] ▶ **noun** a person who picks hops.

hopping ▶ **adjective** informal, chiefly N. Amer. very active or lively: *the delis do a hopping lunch business.*
– PHRASES **hopping mad** informal extremely angry.

hopping john ▶ **noun** [mass noun] (in the southern US and Caribbean) a stew of rice with black-eyed beans or peas, often also containing bacon and red peppers.

hopping mouse ▶ **noun** an Australian mouse with elongated hindlimbs and feet for jumping.
• Genus *Notomys*, family Muridae: several species.

hopple ▶ **verb** & **noun** Riding another term for **HOBBLE** (in sense 2).
– ORIGIN late 16th cent.: probably of Low German origin and related to early Flemish *hoppelen* and Middle Dutch *hobelen* 'jump, dance'; compare with **HOBBLE**.

hopsack ▶ **noun** [mass noun] a coarse clothing fabric of a loose plain weave.
■ [count noun] a coarse hemp sack used for hops.

hopscotch ▶ **noun** [mass noun] a children's game in which each child by turn hops into and over squares marked on the ground to retrieve a marker thrown into one of these squares.
– ORIGIN early 19th cent.: from **HOP**[1] + **SCOTCH**[1].

hop tree ▶ **noun** a North American shrub or small tree with bitter fruit that was formerly used in brewing as a substitute for hops.
• *Ptelea trifoliata*, family Rutaceae.

hora /ˈhɔːrə/ (also **horah**) ▶ **noun** a Romanian or Israeli dance in which the performers form a ring.
– ORIGIN late 19th cent.: from Romanian *horă*, Hebrew *hōrāh*.

Horace /ˈhɒrɪs/ (65–8 BC), Roman poet of the Augustan period; full name *Quintus Horatius Flaccus*. A notable satirist and literary critic, he is best known for his *Odes*, much imitated by later ages, especially by the poets of 17th-century England. His other works include *Satires* and *Ars Poetica*.

horal /ˈhɔːr(ə)l/ ▶ **adjective** of or relating to an hour or hours; hourly.
– ORIGIN early 18th cent.: from late Latin *horalis*, from Latin *hora* 'hour'.

horary /ˈhɔːrəri/ ▶ **adjective** archaic of or relating to hours as measurements of time.
■ occurring every hour: *I took horary observations of the barometer.* ■ Astrology relating to or denoting a branch of astrology in which answers are given to questions using a chart drawn up for the time a question is posed.
– ORIGIN early 17th cent.: from medieval Latin *horarius*, from Latin *hora* 'hour'.

Horatian /həˈreɪʃ(ə)n, -ʃɪən/ ▶ **adjective** of or relating to the Roman poet Horace or his work.
■ (of an ode) of several stanzas each of the same metrical pattern.

horchata /ɔːˈtʃɑːtə/ ▶ **noun** [mass noun] (in Spain and Latin American countries) an almond-flavoured soft drink.
– ORIGIN Spanish.

horde ▶ **noun** **1** chiefly derogatory a large group of people: *a **horde of** beery rugby fans.*
■ an army or tribe of nomadic warriors: *Tartar hordes.*
2 Anthropology a loosely knit small social group typically consisting of about five families.
– ORIGIN mid 16th cent. (originally denoting a tribe or troop of Tartar or other nomads): from Polish *horda*, from Turkish *ordu* '(royal) camp'.

USAGE The words **hoard** and **horde** are quite distinct; see **usage** at **HOARD**.

Hordern /ˈhɔːd(ə)n/, Sir Michael (Murray) (1911–95), English actor. He built a strong reputation in the classical theatre, playing the title role in *King Lear* (1960). He also acted in modern plays and made many film and television appearances.

horehound /ˈhɔːhaʊnd/ (also **hoarhound**) ▶ **noun** a strong-smelling hairy plant of the mint family, with a tradition of use in medicine.
• Two species in the family Labiatae: **white horehound** (*Marrubium vulgare*), a widely distributed plant traditionally used as a medicinal herb, and **black horehound** (*Ballota nigra*), a Eurasian plant which was formerly reputed to cure the bite of a mad dog.
■ [mass noun] the bitter aromatic juice of white horehound, used especially in the treatment of coughs and colds.
– ORIGIN Old English *hāre hūne*, from *hār* (see **HOAR**) + *hūne*, the name of the white horehound, also applied to related plants.

horizon ▶ **noun** **1** [usu. in sing.] the line at which the earth's surface and the sky appear to meet: *the sun rose above the horizon.*
■ (also **apparent horizon**) the circular boundary of the part of the earth's surface visible from a particular point, ignoring irregularities and obstructions. ■ (also **true horizon**) Astronomy a great circle of the celestial sphere, the plane of which passes through the centre of the earth and is parallel to that of the apparent horizon of a place.
2 (often **horizons**) the limit of a person's mental perception, experience, or interest: *she wanted to leave home and broaden her horizons.*
3 Geology a layer of soil or rock, or a set of strata, with particular characteristics.
■ Archaeology a level of an excavated site representing a particular period.
– PHRASES **on the horizon** just imminent or becoming apparent: *trouble could be on the horizon.*
– ORIGIN late Middle English: via Old French from late Latin *horizon*, from Greek *horizōn* (*kuklos*) 'limiting (circle)'.

horizontal ▶ **adjective** **1** parallel to the plane of the horizon; at right angles to the vertical: *a horizontal line.*
■ (of machinery) having its parts working in a horizontal direction: *a horizontal steam engine.*
2 uniform; based on uniformity: *horizontal expansion of the international community.*
■ combining firms engaged in the same stage or type of production: *a horizontal merger.* ■ involving social groups of equal status: *horizontal class loyalties.*
3 of or at the horizon: *the horizontal moon.*
▶ **noun** a horizontal line, plane, etc.
– DERIVATIVES **horizontality** noun, **horizontally** adverb.
– ORIGIN mid 16th cent. (in sense 3): from French, or from modern Latin *horizontalis*, from late Latin *horizon, horizont-* (see **HORIZON**).

Horkheimer /ˈhɔːkˌhʌɪmə, German ˈhɔrkˌhaɪmɐ/, Max (1895–1973), German philosopher and sociologist. A leading figure of the Frankfurt School, he wrote *Dialectic of the Enlightenment* (1947), with his colleague Theodor Adorno, and *Critical Theory* (1968).

Horlicks ▶ **noun** [mass noun] trademark a drink made from malted milk powder.
– PHRASES **make a Horlicks of** Brit. informal make a mess of.
– ORIGIN late 19th cent.: named after James and William *Horlick*, British-born brothers whose company first manufactured the drink in the US.

Horlivka /ˈhɔːljuːkə/ an industrial city in SE Ukraine, in the Donets Basin; pop. 337,900 (1990). Russian name **GORLOVKA**.

hormone ▶ **noun** Physiology a regulatory substance produced in an organism and transported in tissue fluids such as blood or sap to stimulate specific cells or tissues into action.
■ a synthetic substance with a similar effect. ■ (**hormones**) a person's sex hormones as held to influence behaviour or mood.
– DERIVATIVES **hormonal** adjective.
– ORIGIN early 20th cent.: from Greek *hormōn*, present participle of *horman* 'impel, set in motion'.

hormone replacement therapy (abbrev.: **HRT**) ▶ **noun** [mass noun] treatment with oestrogens with the aim of alleviating menopausal symptoms or osteoporosis.

Hormuz /ˈhɔːmuːz, hɔːˈmuːz/ (also **Ormuz**) an Iranian island at the mouth of the Persian Gulf, in the Strait of Hormuz. It is the site of an ancient city, which was an important centre of commerce in the Middle Ages.

Hormuz, Strait of a strait linking the Persian Gulf with the Gulf of Oman, which leads to the Arabian Sea, and separating Iran from the Arabian peninsula. It is of strategic and economic importance as a waterway through which sea traffic to and from the oil-rich states of the Gulf must pass.

horn ▶ **noun** **1** a hard permanent outgrowth, often curved and pointed, found in pairs on the heads of cattle, sheep, goats, giraffes, etc. and consisting of a core of bone encased in keratinized skin.
■ a woolly keratinized outgrowth, occurring singly or one behind another, on the snout of a rhinoceros. ■ a deer's antler. ■ a horn-like projection on the head of another animal, e.g. a snail's tentacle or the tuft of a horned owl. ■ [mass noun] W. Indian marital infidelity: *she took endless horn and pressure, but now she can't take it any more and wants a divorce.* ■ (**horns**) archaic a pair of horns as an emblem of a cuckold.
2 [mass noun] the substance of which horns are composed: *powdered rhino horn.*
■ [count noun] a receptacle or instrument made of horn, such as a drinking container or powder flask.

3 a thing resembling or compared to a horn in shape.
■ a horn-shaped projection. ■ a sharp promontory or mountain peak. ■ (**the Horn**) Cape Horn. ■ an arm or branch of a river or bay. ■ the extremity of the moon or other crescent. ■ Brit. vulgar slang an erect penis.
4 a wind instrument, conical in shape or wound into a spiral, originally made from an animal horn (now typically brass) and played by lip vibration.
■ short for **FRENCH HORN**.
5 an instrument sounding a warning or other signal: *a car horn*.
▶ **verb** [with obj.] **1** (of an animal) butt or gore with the horns.
2 W. Indian be unfaithful to (one's husband or wife): *all the time he was horning his wife*.
– PHRASES **blow** (or **toot**) **one's own horn** N. Amer. informal talk boastfully about oneself or one's achievements. **draw** (or **pull**) **in one's horns** become less assertive or ambitious. **on the horn** N. Amer. informal on the telephone: *she got on the horn to complain*. **on the horns of a dilemma** faced with a decision involving equally unfavourable alternatives.
– DERIVATIVES **hornist** noun (only in sense 4), **hornless** adjective, **horn-like** adjective.
– ORIGIN Old English, of Germanic origin; related to Dutch *hoorn* and German *Horn*, from an Indo-European root shared by Latin *cornu* and Greek *keras*.
▶ **horn in** informal intrude; interfere.

Horn, Cape the southernmost point of South America, on a Chilean island south of Tierra del Fuego. The region is notorious for its storms, and until the opening of the Panama Canal in 1914 constituted the only sea route between the Atlantic and Pacific Oceans. Also called **THE HORN**.
– ORIGIN named after *Hoorn*, the birthplace of the Dutch navigator William C. Schouten who discovered it in 1616.

hornbeam ▶ **noun** a deciduous tree of north temperate regions, with oval serrated leaves, inconspicuous drooping flowers, and tough winged nuts. It yields hard pale timber.
● Genus *Carpinus*, family Betulaceae: several species, including the common Eurasian *C. betulus*, with a silvery-grey bark, and the **American hornbeam** (*C. caroliniana*).
– ORIGIN late Middle English: so named because of the tree's hard, close-grained wood.

hornbill ▶ **noun** a medium to large tropical Old World bird, having a very large curved bill that typically has a large horny or bony casque. The male often seals up the female inside the nest hole.
● Family Bucerotidae: several genera and numerous species, e.g. the **great Indian hornbill** (*Buceros bicornis*).

hornblende /ˈhɔːnblɛnd/ ▶ **noun** [mass noun] a dark brown, black, or green mineral consisting of a silicate of calcium, magnesium, and iron, occurring in many igneous and metamorphic rocks.
– ORIGIN late 18th cent.: from German, from *Horn* 'horn' + *blende* (see **BLENDE**).

hornbook ▶ **noun** historical a teaching aid consisting of a leaf of paper showing the alphabet, and often the ten digits and the Lord's Prayer, mounted on a wooden tablet and protected by a thin plate of horn.
■ Law, N. Amer. a brief treatise summarizing important cases or legal points.

horned ▶ **adjective 1** having a horn or horns: *horned cattle* | [in combination] *a long-horned bison*.
2 [attrib.] poetic/literary crescent-shaped: *the horned moon*.

horned grebe ▶ **noun** North American term for **SLAVONIAN GREBE**.

horned lark ▶ **noun** North American term for **SHORELARK**.

horned lizard ▶ **noun** another term for **HORNED TOAD** (in sense 1).

horned owl (also **great horned owl**) ▶ **noun** a large owl found throughout North and South America, with horn-like ear tufts.
● *Bubo virginianus*, family Strigidae.

horned poppy ▶ **noun** a Eurasian poppy with greyish-green lobed leaves, large flowers, and a long curved seed capsule.
● Genus *Glaucium*, family Papaveraceae: several species, in particular the **yellow horned poppy** (*G. flavum*).

horned toad ▶ **noun 1** an American lizard that somewhat resembles a toad, with spiny skin and large spines on the head, typically occurring in dry open country. Also called **HORNED LIZARD**.
● Genus *Phrynosoma*, family Iguanidae: several species, in particular *P. cornutum*.
2 a large toad with horn-shaped projections of skin over the eyes, in particular:
● a SE Asian toad (*Megophrys* and other genera, family Peltobatidae). ● a South American toad (*Ceratophrys* and other genera, family Leptodactylidae).

horned viper ▶ **noun** a venomous nocturnal snake with an upright projection over each eye, native to the sandy deserts of North Africa and Arabia. It moves in the same way as the sidewinder.
● *Cerastes cerastes*, family Viperidae.

hornero /hɔːˈnɛːrəʊ/ ▶ **noun** (pl. **-os**) a tropical American bird of the ovenbird family, often building its oven-like mud nest on the top of a fence post. Also called **OVENBIRD**.
● Genus *Furnarius*, family Furnariidae: several species, in particular the **rufous hornero** (*F. rufus*).
– ORIGIN late 19th cent.: from Spanish, literally 'baker'.

Horner's syndrome ▶ **noun** [mass noun] Medicine a condition marked by a contracted pupil, drooping upper eyelid, and local inability to sweat on one side of the face, caused by damage to sympathetic nerves on that side of the neck.
– ORIGIN early 20th cent.: named after Johann F. *Horner* (1831–86), Swiss ophthalmologist.

hornet ▶ **noun** a large, fairly docile wasp which is typically red and yellow or red and black and typically nests in hollow trees.
● *Vespa* and other genera, family Vespidae: several species, including the European *V. crabro*.
– PHRASES **a hornets' nest** a situation fraught with difficulties or complications: *the move has* **stirred up** *a hornet's nest of academic fear and loathing*.
– ORIGIN Old English *hyrnet*, of Germanic origin; related to German *Hornisse*. The form of the word was probably influenced by Middle Dutch and Middle Low German *hornte*.

hornet moth ▶ **noun** a clearwing moth which resembles a hornet, with larvae that burrow under tree bark.
● Several species in the family Sesiidae, including *Sesia apiformis*, which can be a pest of poplars.

hornfels /ˈhɔːnfɛlz/ ▶ **noun** [mass noun] a dark, fine-grained metamorphic rock consisting largely of quartz, mica, and particular feldspars.
– ORIGIN mid 19th cent.: from German, literally 'horn rock'.

Horn of Africa a peninsula of NE Africa, comprising Somalia and parts of Ethiopia. It lies between the Gulf of Aden and the Indian Ocean. Also called **SOMALI PENINSULA**.

horn of plenty ▶ **noun 1** a cornucopia.
2 an edible woodland mushroom with a funnel-shaped cap that bears spores on its greyish outer surface, found in both Eurasia and North America.
● *Craterellus cornucopioides*, family Cantharellaceae, class Hymenomycetes.

hornpipe ▶ **noun** a lively dance associated with sailors, typically performed by one person.
■ a piece of music for such a dance.
– ORIGIN late Middle English (denoting a wind instrument made of horn, played to accompany dancing): from **HORN** + **PIPE**.

horn-rimmed ▶ **adjective** (of glasses) having rims made of horn or a similar substance.

horn shell ▶ **noun** a mollusc with a long tapering shell, occurring in brackish and marine waters.
● Families Potamididae and Cerithidae, class Gastropoda.

hornswoggle /ˈhɔːnswɒg(ə)l/ ▶ **verb** [with obj.] (usu. **be hornswoggled**) informal, chiefly N. Amer. get the better of (someone) by cheating or deception.
– ORIGIN early 19th cent. (originally US): of unknown origin.

horntail ▶ **noun** a large wasp-like sawfly which deposits its eggs inside trees and timber. It has a long egg-laying tube but no sting. Also called **WOODWASP**.
● Family Siricidae, suborder Symphyta, order Hymenoptera: several species.

Hornung /ˈhɔːnʊŋ/, Ernest William (1866–1921), English novelist. He was the creator of the gentleman burglar Raffles, who first featured in *The Amateur Cracksman* (1899).

hornworm ▶ **noun** N. Amer. the caterpillar of a hawkmoth, which has a spike or 'horn' on its tail.
● Family Sphingidae: several genera and many species, in particular pests like the **tobacco hornworm** (*Manduca sexta*) and the **tomato hornworm** (*M. quinquemaculata*).

hornwort ▶ **noun** a submerged aquatic plant with narrow forked leaves that become translucent and horny as they age, occurring worldwide.
● Family Ceratophyllaceae and genus *Ceratophyllum*: two or more species, in particular *C. demersum*.

horny ▶ **adjective** (**hornier**, **horniest**) **1** of or resembling horn: *a horny beak* | *horny nails*.
■ hard and rough: *horny hands* | *horny, dry skin*.
2 informal feeling or arousing sexual excitement.
– DERIVATIVES **horniness** noun.

horny coral ▶ **noun** see **CORAL** (sense 2).

horologe /ˈhɒrəlɒdʒ/ ▶ **noun** archaic a timepiece.
– ORIGIN late Middle English: from Old French, via Latin from Greek *hōrologion*, from *hōra* 'time' + *-logos* '-telling'.

Horologium /ˌhɒrəˈləʊdʒɪəm, -ˈlɒdʒ-/ Astronomy a faint southern constellation (the Clock), between Hydrus and Eridanus.
■ [as genitive **Horologii** /ˌhɒrəˈləʊdʒɪʌɪ, -dʒiː, -ˈlɒdʒ-/] used with preceding letter or numeral to designate a star in this constellation: *the star R Horologii*.
– ORIGIN Latin.

horology /hɒˈrɒlədʒi/ ▶ **noun** [mass noun] the study and measurement of time.
■ the art of making clocks and watches.
– DERIVATIVES **horologer** noun, **horologic** adjective, **horological** adjective, **horologist** noun.
– ORIGIN early 19th cent.: from Greek *hōra* 'time' + **-LOGY**.

horopter /hɒˈrɒptə/ ▶ **noun** Optics a line or surface containing all those points in space of which images fall on corresponding points of the retinas of the two eyes.
– ORIGIN early 18th cent.: from Greek *horos* 'limit' + *optēr* 'person who looks'.

horoscope ▶ **noun** Astrology a forecast of a person's future, typically including a delineation of character and circumstances, based on the relative positions of the stars and planets at the time of that person's birth.
■ a short forecast for people born under a particular sign, especially as published in a newspaper or magazine. ■ a birth chart. See **CHART**.
– DERIVATIVES **horoscopic** /-ˈskɒpɪk/ adjective, **horoscopy** /hɒˈrɒskəpi/ noun.
– ORIGIN Old English: via Latin from Greek *hōroskopos*, from *hōra* 'time' + *skopos* 'observer'.

Horowitz /ˈhɒrəvɪts/, Vladimir (1904–89), Russian pianist. He first toured the US in 1928, and settled there soon afterwards. A leading international virtuoso, he was best known for his performances of Scarlatti, Liszt, Scriabin, and Prokofiev.

horrendous /hɒˈrɛndəs/ ▶ **adjective** extremely unpleasant, horrifying, or terrible: *she suffered horrendous injuries*.
– DERIVATIVES **horrendously** adverb.
– ORIGIN mid 17th cent.: from Latin *horrendus* (gerundive of *horrere* '(of hair) stand on end') + **-OUS**.

horrent /ˈhɒr(ə)nt/ ▶ **adjective** poetic/literary **1** (of a person's hair) standing on end.
2 feeling or expressing horror: *a horrent cry*.
– ORIGIN mid 17th cent.: from Latin *horrent-* '(of hair) standing on end', from the verb *horrere*.

horrible ▶ **adjective** causing or likely to cause horror; shocking: *a horrible massacre*.
■ informal very unpleasant: *the tea tasted horrible*.
– DERIVATIVES **horribleness** noun, **horribly** adverb [as submodifier] *the plan had gone horribly wrong*.
– ORIGIN Middle English: via Old French from Latin *horribilis*, from *horrere* 'tremble, shudder' (see **HORRID**).

horrid ▶ **adjective 1** causing horror: *a horrid nightmare*.
■ informal very unpleasant or disagreeable: *the teachers at school were horrid* | *a horrid brown colour*.
2 poetic/literary rough; bristling.
– DERIVATIVES **horridly** adverb, **horridness** noun.
– ORIGIN late 16th cent. (in the sense 'rough, bristling'): from Latin *horridus*, from *horrere* 'tremble, shudder, (of hair) stand on end'.

horrific ▶ **adjective** causing horror: *horrific injuries*.
– DERIVATIVES **horrifically** adverb.
– ORIGIN mid 17th cent.: from Latin *horrificus*, from *horrere* 'tremble, shudder' (see **HORRID**).

horrify ▶ **verb** (**-ies**, **-ied**) [with obj.] (usu. **be horrified**) fill with horror; shock greatly: *they were horrified by* *the very idea* | [as adj. **horrified**] *the horrified spectators* | [as adj. **horrifying**] *a horrifying incident.*

– DERIVATIVES **horrification** noun, **horrifiedly** adverb, **horrifyingly** adverb [as submodifier] *horrifyingly flimsy boats.*

– ORIGIN late 18th cent.: from Latin *horrificare*, from *horrificus* (see HORRIFIC).

horripilation /hɒˌrɪpɪˈleɪʃ(ə)n/ ▶ noun [mass noun] poetic/literary the erection of hairs on the skin due to cold, fear, or excitement.

– DERIVATIVES **horripilate** verb.

– ORIGIN mid 17th cent.: from late Latin *horripilatio(n-)*, from Latin *horrere* 'stand on end' (see HORRID) + *pilus* 'hair'.

horror ▶ noun **1** [mass noun] an intense feeling of fear, shock, or disgust: *children screamed in horror.*

■ a thing causing such a feeling: *photographs showed the horror of the tragedy* | [count noun] *the horrors of civil war.* ■ a literary or film genre concerned with arousing such feelings: [as modifier] *a horror film.* ■ intense dismay: *to her horror she found that a thief had stolen the machine.* ■ [as exclamation] (**horrors**) chiefly humorous used to express dismay: *horrors, two buttons were missing!* ■ [in sing.] intense dislike: *many have a horror of consulting a dictionary.* ■ (**the horrors**) an attack of extreme nervousness or anxiety: *the mere thought of it gives me the horrors.*

2 informal a bad or mischievous person, especially a child: *that little horror Zach was around.*

– ORIGIN Middle English: via Old French from Latin *horror*, from *horrere* 'tremble, shudder' (see HORRID).

horror-struck (also **horror-stricken**) ▶ adjective (of a person) briefly paralysed with horror or shock.

horror vacui /ˌhɒrə ˈvakjuːʌɪ/ ▶ noun [in sing.] a fear or dislike of leaving empty spaces, especially in an artistic composition.

– ORIGIN modern Latin, 'horror of a vacuum'.

Horsa see HENGIST AND HORSA.

hors concours /ˌɔː kɒ̃ˈkʊə/ ▶ adjective **1** poetic/literary unrivalled; unequalled: *most husbands are fools, but that one was hors concours.*

2 formal (of an exhibit or exhibitor) not competing for a prize.

– ORIGIN French, literally 'out of the competition'.

hors de combat /ˌɔː də ˈkɒbaː/ ▶ adjective out of action due to injury or damage: *their pilots had been rendered temporarily hors de combat.*

– ORIGIN French, literally 'out of the fight'.

hors d'oeuvre /ɔː ˈdəːv, ˈdɜːvr(ə)/ ▶ noun (pl. same or **hors d'oeuvres** pronunc. same or /ˈdɜːvz/) a small savoury dish, typically one served as an appetizer at the beginning of a meal.

– ORIGIN French, literally 'outside the work'.

horse ▶ noun **1** a solid-hoofed plant-eating domesticated mammal with a flowing mane and tail, used for riding, racing, and to carry and pull loads.

● *Equus caballus*, family Equidae (the **horse family**), descended from the wild Przewalski's horse. The horse family also includes the asses and zebras.

■ an adult male horse; a stallion or gelding. ■ a wild mammal of the horse family. ■ [treated as sing. or pl.] cavalry: *forty horse and sixty foot.*

2 a frame or structure on which something is mounted or supported, especially a sawhorse.

■ Nautical a horizontal bar, rail, or rope in the rigging of a sailing ship for supporting something. ■ short for VAULTING HORSE.

3 [mass noun] informal heroin.

4 informal a unit of horsepower: *the huge 63-horse 701-cc engine.*

5 Mining an obstruction in a vein.

▶ verb [with obj.] (usu. **be horsed**) provide (a person or vehicle) with a horse or horses.

– PHRASES **don't change horses in midstream** proverb choose a sensible moment to change your mind. **from the horse's mouth** (of information) from the person directly concerned or another authoritative source. **horses for courses** Brit. proverb different people are suited to different things or situations. **to horse** (as a command) mount your horses! **you can lead** (or **take**) **a horse to water but you can't make him drink** proverb you can give someone an opportunity, but you can't force them to take it.

– DERIVATIVES **horseless** adjective, **horse-like** adjective.

– ORIGIN Old English *hors*, of Germanic origin; related to Dutch *ros* and German *Ross*.

▶ **horse around** (or **about**) informal fool about.

horse-and-buggy ▶ adjective [attrib.] N. Amer. old-fashioned: *horse-and-buggy technology.*

horseback ▶ adjective & adverb mounted on a horse: [as adj.] *a horseback parade* | [as adv.] *they rode horseback along the trail.*

– PHRASES **on horseback** mounted on a horse.

horsebean ▶ noun a field bean of a variety with relatively large seeds, used for feeding stock.

horse-block ▶ noun archaic term for MOUNTING BLOCK.

horsebox ▶ noun Brit. a motorized vehicle equipped with a compartment or container for transporting one or more horses.

horse brass ▶ noun see BRASS.

horse chestnut ▶ noun a deciduous tree with large leaves of five leaflets, conspicuous sticky winter buds, and upright conical clusters of white, pink, or red flowers. It bears nuts (conkers) enclosed in a fleshy case.

● Genus *Aesculus*, family Hippocastanaceae: several species, in particular *A. hippocastanum*, native east of the Balkans and widely planted.

■ another term for CONKER.

– ORIGIN late 16th cent.: translating (now obsolete) botanical Latin *Castanea equina*; its fruit is said to have been an Eastern remedy for chest diseases in horses.

horse cloth ▶ noun a cloth used to cover a horse, or as part of its trappings.

horse-coper ▶ noun Brit. archaic a person who buys and sells horses.

horse-drawn ▶ adjective (of a vehicle) pulled by a horse or horses: *a horse-drawn carriage.*

horseflesh ▶ noun [mass noun] horses considered collectively.

horsefly ▶ noun (pl. **-flies**) a stoutly built fly, the female of which is a bloodsucker and inflicts painful bites on horses and other large mammals including humans.

● Family Tabanidae: numerous species, in particular the common European *Haematopota pluvialis*.

Horse Guards ▶ plural noun (in the UK) the mounted squadrons provided from the Household Cavalry for ceremonial duties.

horsehair ▶ noun [mass noun] hair from the mane or tail of a horse, typically used in furniture for padding.

horsehair worm ▶ noun a long slender worm related to the nematodes, the larvae being parasites of arthropods and the adults living in water or damp soil.

● Phylum Nematomorpha: two classes.

Horsehead Nebula Astronomy a dust nebula in the shape of a horse's head, forming a dark silhouette against a bright emission nebula in Orion.

horse latitudes ▶ plural noun a belt of calm air and sea occurring in both the northern and southern hemispheres between the trade winds and the westerlies.

– ORIGIN late 18th cent.: of uncertain origin.

horse laugh ▶ noun a loud, coarse laugh.

horseleech ▶ noun a large predatory leech of freshwater and terrestrial habitats which feeds on carrion and small invertebrates.

● Genus *Haemopis*, family Hirudidae.

horseless ▶ adjective [attrib.] (of a vehicle) not drawn by a horse or horses: *a horseless cabriolet.*

horseless carriage ▶ noun archaic or humorous a motor car.

horse mackerel ▶ noun a shoaling edible fish of the eastern Atlantic, which is commercially fished in southern African waters. Also called SCAD.

● *Trachurus trachurus*, family Carangidae.

horseman ▶ noun (pl. **-men**) a rider on horseback, especially a skilled one.

horsemanship ▶ noun [mass noun] the art or practice of riding on horseback.

horsemint ▶ noun a tall coarse kind of mint.

● Genera *Mentha* and *Monarda*, family Labiatae: several species and hybrids, including the European *Mentha longifolia* and the North American *Monarda punctata*.

– ORIGIN Middle English: from HORSE (often used in the names of plants to denote a coarse variety) + MINT.

horse mushroom ▶ noun a large edible mushroom with a creamy-white cap and pinkish-grey gills, found in grassland in both Eurasia and North America.

● *Agaricus arvensis*, family Agaricaceae, class Hymenomycetes.

horse mussel ▶ noun a large marine mussel which may occur in very large populations in food-rich waters.

● Genus *Modiolus*, family Mytilidae.

Horsens /ˈhɔːs(ə)nz/ a port on the east coast of Denmark, situated at the head of Horsens Fjord; pop. 55,210 (1990).

horse opera ▶ noun N. Amer. informal a western film.

horse pistol ▶ noun historical a large pistol carried at the pommel of the saddle by a rider.

horseplay ▶ noun [mass noun] rough, boisterous play: *this ridiculous horseplay has gone far enough.*

horseplayer ▶ noun N. Amer. a person who regularly bets on horse races.

horsepower (abbrev.: **h.p.**) ▶ noun (pl. same) an imperial unit of power equal to 550 foot-pounds per second (about 750 watts).

■ the power of an engine measured in terms of this: *a strong 140-horsepower engine.* See also BRAKE HORSEPOWER.

horse racing ▶ noun [mass noun] the sport in which horses and their riders take part in races, either on a flat course or over hurdles or fences, typically with substantial betting on the outcome.

horseradish ▶ noun a European plant of the cabbage family, with long dock-like leaves, grown for its pungent root.

● *Armoracia rusticana*, family Cruciferae.

■ [mass noun] this root, which is scraped or grated as a condiment and often made into a sauce.

horse sense ▶ noun [mass noun] informal common sense.

horseshit ▶ noun [mass noun] vulgar slang, chiefly N. Amer. **1** horse dung.

2 nonsense.

horseshoe ▶ noun a shoe for a horse formed of a narrow band of iron in the form of an extended circular arc and secured to the hoof with nails.

■ a shoe of this kind or a representation of one, regarded as bringing good luck. ■ something resembling this in shape: [as modifier] *a horseshoe bend.* ■ (**horseshoes**) [treated as sing.] chiefly N. Amer. a game resembling quoits in which horseshoes are thrown at a peg.

horseshoe bat ▶ noun an insectivorous Old World bat with a horseshoe-shaped ridge on the nose.

● Family Rhinolophidae and genus *Rhinolophus*: numerous species.

horseshoe crab ▶ noun a large marine arthropod with a domed horseshoe-shaped shell, a long tail-spine, and ten legs, little changed since the Devonian.

● Class Merostomata, subphylum Chelicerata: four species, in particular the North American *Limulus polyphemus*.

horse-shoeing ▶ noun [mass noun] the skill or activity of shoeing horses; farriery.

horseshoe worm ▶ noun a worm-like tube-dwelling marine animal with a conspicuous horseshoe-shaped ring of ciliated tentacles (lophophore) around the mouth, extended for filter-feeding.

● Phylum Phoronida.

horse's neck ▶ noun informal a drink consisting of ginger ale, a twist of lemon peel, and spirits, typically brandy.

horsetail ▶ noun a plant with a hollow jointed stem which bears whorls of narrow leaves, producing spores in cones at the tips of the shoots.

● Genus *Equisetum*, the only surviving genus of the family Equisetaceae and class Sphenopsida, division Pteridophyta.

horse-trading ▶ noun [mass noun] the buying and selling of horses.

■ hard and shrewd bargaining, typically in politics.

– DERIVATIVES **horse-trade** verb, **horse-trader** noun.

horse walker ▶ noun a mechanically rotating arm or cage to which horses are tied in order to exercise.

horsewhip ▶ noun a long whip used for driving and controlling horses.

▶ verb (**-whipped**, **-whipping**) [with obj.] beat with such a whip: *she would horsewhip them mercilessly.*

horsewoman ▶ noun (pl. **-women**) a woman who rides on horseback, especially a skilled one.

horsey (also **horsy**) ▶ **adjective** (**horsier**, **horsiest**) **1** of or resembling a horse: *she had a long horsey face.* **2** concerned with or devoted to horses or horse racing: *the horsey fraternity.*
– DERIVATIVES **horsily** adverb, **horsiness** noun.

horst /hɔːst/ ▶ **noun** Geology a raised elongated block of the earth's crust lying between two faults.
– ORIGIN late 19th cent.: from German *Horst* 'heap'.

Horst Wessel Song /hɔːst 'vɛs(ə)l, German ˌhɔrst 'vɛsl/ the official song of the Nazi Party in Germany. The words were written by Horst Wessel (1907–30), a member of Hitler's Storm Troops killed by political enemies and regarded as a Nazi martyr.

Horta /'ɔːtə, French 'ɔʀta/, Victor (1861–1947), Belgian architect. He was a leading figure in art nouveau architecture and his work was notable for its innovative use of iron and glass.

hortatory /'hɔːtət(ə)ri/ ▶ **adjective** tending or aiming to exhort: *the hortatory moralism of many contemporary churchmen.*
– DERIVATIVES **hortation** noun, **hortative** adjective.
– ORIGIN late 16th cent.: from Latin *hortatorius*, from *hortari* 'exhort'.

hortensia /hɔː'tɛnsɪə/ ▶ **noun** a hydrangea of a group of varieties that have large rounded flower heads composed chiefly of sterile florets. Compare with LACECAP.
• *Hydrangea macrophylla* vars., family Hydrangeaceae.
– ORIGIN late 18th cent.: modern Latin, named after *Hortense*, wife of J.-A. Lepaute (1720–c.1787), French clockmaker.

horticulture /'hɔːtɪˌkʌltʃə/ ▶ **noun** [mass noun] the art or practice of garden cultivation and management.
– DERIVATIVES **horticultural** adjective, **horticulturalist** noun, **horticulturist** noun.
– ORIGIN late 17th cent.: from Latin *hortus* 'garden', on the pattern of *agriculture*.

hortus siccus /ˌhɔːtəs 'sɪkəs/ ▶ **noun** (pl. **horti sicci** /ˌhɔːtʌɪ 'sɪkʌɪ, -tiː, -kiː/) an arranged collection of dried plants; a herbarium.
– ORIGIN Latin, literally 'dry garden'.

Horus /'hɔːrəs/ Egyptian Mythology a god regarded as the protector of the monarchy, and typically represented as a falcon-headed man. He assumed various aspects: in the myth of Isis and Osiris he was the posthumous son of the latter, whose murder he avenged.

Hos. ▶ **abbreviation for** Hosea (in biblical references).

hosanna (also **hosannah**) ▶ **exclamation** (especially in biblical, Judaic, and Christian use) used to express adoration, praise, or joy.
▶ **noun** an expression of adoration, praise, or joy.
– ORIGIN Old English, via late Latin from Greek *hōsanna*, from Rabbinical Hebrew *hôša'nā*, abbreviation of biblical *hôšî'â-nnā* 'save, we pray' (Ps. 118:25).

hose ▶ **noun 1** a flexible tube conveying water, used chiefly for watering plants and in firefighting. **2** [treated as pl.] stockings, socks, and tights (especially in commercial use): *her hose had been laddered.* ■ historical breeches: *Elizabethan doublet and hose.*
▶ **verb** [with obj.] water, spray, or drench with a hose: *he was hosing down the driveway.*
– ORIGIN Old English *hosa*, of Germanic origin; related to Dutch *hoos* 'stocking, water-hose' and German *Hosen* 'trousers'. Originally singular, the term denoted a covering for the leg, sometimes including the foot but sometimes reaching only as far as the ankle.

Hosea /həʊ'zɪə/ a Hebrew minor prophet of the 8th century BC.
■ a book of the Bible containing his prophecies.

hose-in-hose ▶ **adjective** (especially of a polyanthus or other primula) having petal-like sepals, and so appearing to have one corolla within another.

hosel /'həʊz(ə)l/ ▶ **noun** the socket of a golf club head which the shaft fits into.
– ORIGIN late 16th cent.: diminutive of HOSE, in the dialect sense 'sheathing'.

hosepipe ▶ **noun** British term for HOSE (in sense 1).

hosier /'həʊzɪə/ ▶ **noun** a manufacturer or seller of hosiery.

hosiery ▶ **noun** [mass noun] stockings, socks, and tights collectively.

hospice ▶ **noun** a home providing care for the sick or terminally ill.
■ archaic a lodging for travellers, especially one run by a religious order.
– ORIGIN early 19th cent.: from French, from Latin *hospitium*, from *hospes*, *hospit-* (see HOST[1]).

hospitable /hɒ'spɪtəb(ə)l, 'hɒspɪt-/ ▶ **adjective** friendly and welcoming to strangers or guests: *two friendly, hospitable brothers run the hotel.*
■ (of an environment) pleasant and favourable for living in: *the Sonoran desert is one of the least hospitable places on earth.*
– DERIVATIVES **hospitably** adverb.
– ORIGIN late 16th cent.: from French, from obsolete *hospiter* 'receive a guest', from medieval Latin *hospitare* 'entertain', from *hospes*, *hospit-* (see HOST[1]).

hospital ▶ **noun 1** an institution providing medical and surgical treatment and nursing care for sick or injured people. **2** historical a hospice, especially one run by the Knights Hospitallers. **3** [usu. in names] Law, Brit. a charitable institution for the education of the young: *Christ's Hospital.*
– ORIGIN Middle English (in sense 2): via Old French from medieval Latin *hospitale*, neuter of Latin *hospitalis* 'hospitable', from *hospes*, *hospit-* (see HOST[1]).

hospital corners ▶ **plural noun** overlapping folds used to tuck sheets neatly and securely under the mattress at the corners, in a manner typically used by nurses.

hospitaler ▶ **noun** US spelling of HOSPITALLER.

hospital fever ▶ **noun** [mass noun] historical louse-borne typhus acquired in overcrowded, insanitary conditions in an old-fashioned hospital.

hospitalism ▶ **noun** [mass noun] the adverse effects of a prolonged stay in hospital, such as developmental retardation in children.

hospitality ▶ **noun** [mass noun] the friendly and generous reception and entertainment of guests, visitors, or strangers.
– ORIGIN late Middle English: from Old French *hospitalite*, from Latin *hospitalitas*, from *hospitalis* 'hospitable' (see HOSPITAL).

hospitalize (also **-ise**) ▶ **verb** [with obj.] (usu. **be hospitalized**) admit or cause (someone) to be admitted to hospital for treatment: *Casey was hospitalized for chest pains.*
– DERIVATIVES **hospitalization** noun.

hospitaller /'hɒspɪt(ə)lə/ (US **hospitaler**) ▶ **noun** a member of a charitable religious order, originally the Knights Hospitallers.
– ORIGIN Middle English: from Old French *hospitalier*, from medieval Latin *hospitalarius*, from *hospitale* (see HOSPITAL).

hospital pass ▶ **noun** Rugby a pass to a player likely to be tackled heavily as soon as the ball is received.

hospital ship ▶ **noun** a ship which functions as a hospital, especially to receive or take home sick or wounded military personnel.

hospital trust ▶ **noun** (in the UK) a National Health Service hospital which has opted to withdraw from local authority control and be managed by a trust instead.

hospodar /'hɒspədɑː/ ▶ **noun** historical a governor of Wallachia and Moldavia under the Ottoman Porte.
– ORIGIN from Romanian, from Ukrainian *hospodar*; related to Russian *gospodar'*, from *gospod'* 'lord'.

hoss ▶ **noun** non-standard spelling of HORSE, used in representing dialect or informal US speech.

host[1] ▶ **noun 1** a person who receives or entertains other people as guests.
■ a person, place, or organization that holds and organizes an event to which others are invited: *Innsbruck once* **played host to** *the Winter Olympics.* ■ an area in which particular living things are found: *Australia is* **host to** *some of the world's most dangerous animals.* ■ often humorous the landlord or landlady of a pub: **mine host** *raised his glass of whisky.* ■ the presenter of a television or radio programme. **2** Biology an animal or plant on or in which a parasite or commensal organism lives. ■ (also **host cell**) a living cell in which a virus multiplies. ■ an animal or person that has received transplanted tissue or a transplanted organ. **3** (also **host computer**) a computer which mediates multiple access to databases mounted on it or provides other services to a computer network.
▶ **verb** [with obj.] act as host at (an event) or for (a television or radio programme).
– ORIGIN Middle English: from Old French *hoste*, from Latin *hospes*, *hospit-* 'host, guest'.

host[2] ▶ **noun** (**a host/hosts of**) a large number of people or things: *a host of memories rushed into her mind.*
■ archaic an army. ■ poetic/literary (in biblical use) the sun, moon, and stars: *the starry host of heaven.* ■ another term for HEAVENLY HOST. See also ***Lord of hosts*** at LORD.
– ORIGIN Middle English: from Old French *ost*, *hoost*, from Latin *hostis* 'stranger, enemy' (in medieval Latin 'army').

host[3] ▶ **noun** (usu. **the Host**) the bread consecrated in the Eucharist: *the elevation of the Host.*
– ORIGIN Middle English: from Old French *hoiste*, from Latin *hostia* 'victim'.

hosta /'hɒstə/ ▶ **noun** an East Asian plant cultivated in the West for its shade-tolerant foliage and loose clusters of tubular mauve or white flowers.
• Genus *Hosta* (formerly *Funkia*), family Liliaceae.
– ORIGIN modern Latin, named after Nicolaus T. Host (1761–1834), Austrian physician.

hostage ▶ **noun** a person seized or held as security for the fulfilment of a condition.
– PHRASES **hold** (or **take**) **someone hostage** seize and keep someone as a hostage. **a hostage to fortune** an act, commitment, or remark which is regarded as unwise because it invites trouble or could prove difficult to live up to: *making objectives explicit is to* **give a hostage to fortune**.
– ORIGIN Middle English: from Old French, based on late Latin *obsidatus* 'the state of being a hostage' (the earliest sense in English), from Latin *obses*, *obsid-* 'hostage'.

hostel ▶ **noun** an establishment which provides cheap food and lodging for a specific group of people, such as students, workers, or travellers.
■ S. African a single-sex barracks or dormitory for black migrant workers in urban areas or for mineworkers. ■ short for YOUTH HOSTEL. ■ archaic an inn providing accommodation.
– ORIGIN Middle English (in the general sense 'lodging, place to stay)' : from Old French, from medieval Latin *hospitale* (see HOSPITAL).

hostelling (US **hosteling**) ▶ **noun** [mass noun] the practice of staying in youth hostels when travelling.
– DERIVATIVES **hosteller** noun.

hostelry ▶ **noun** (pl. **-ies**) archaic or humorous an inn or pub.
– ORIGIN late Middle English: from Old French *hostelerie* from *hostelier* 'innkeeper', from *hostel* (see HOSTEL).

hostess ▶ **noun** a woman who receives or entertains guests.
■ a woman employed to welcome and entertain customers at a nightclub, bar, or dance hall. ■ a stewardess on an aircraft, train, etc. ■ a woman who introduces a television or radio programme: *a game-show hostess.*
– ORIGIN Middle English: from Old French *(h)ostesse*, feminine of *(h)oste* (see HOST[1]).

hostess trolley ▶ **noun** a trolley, typically with electric plate-warmers, for holding food to be served at table.

hostie ▶ **noun** (pl. **-ies**) Austral./NZ informal an air hostess.
– ORIGIN 1960s: abbreviation.

hostile ▶ **adjective** unfriendly; antagonistic: *a hostile audience | he wrote a ferociously hostile attack.*
■ of or belonging to a military enemy: *hostile aircraft.* ■ [predic.] opposed: *people are very* **hostile to** *the idea.* ■ (of a takeover bid) opposed by the company to be bought.
– DERIVATIVES **hostilely** adverb.
– ORIGIN late 16th cent.: from French, or from Latin *hostilis*, from *hostis* 'stranger, enemy'.

hostile witness ▶ **noun** Law a witness who is antagonistic to the party calling them and, being unwilling to tell the truth, may have to be cross-examined by the party.

hostility ▶ **noun** (pl. **-ies**) [mass noun] hostile behaviour; unfriendliness or opposition: *their* **hostility to** *all outsiders.*
■ [count noun] (**hostilities**) acts of warfare: *he called for an immediate cessation of hostilities.*
– ORIGIN late Middle English: from French *hostilité* or late Latin *hostilitas*, from Latin *hostilis* (see HOSTILE).

hostler ▶ **noun** variant spelling of OSTLER.

hot ▶ **adjective** (**hotter**, **hottest**) **1** having a high

degree of heat or a high temperature: *it was hot inside the hall | basking under a hot sun.*
■ feeling or producing an uncomfortable sensation of heat: *she felt hot and her throat was parched.* ■ (of food or drink) prepared by heating and served without cooling. ■ informal (of an electric circuit) at a high voltage; live. ■ informal radioactive.
2 (of food) containing or consisting of pungent spices or peppers which produce a burning sensation when tasted: *a very hot dish cooked with green chilli.*
3 passionately enthusiastic, eager, or excited: *girls **hot for** glamour, travel, and rich husbands.*
■ lustful, amorous, or erotic: *steamy bed scenes which may be too hot for young fans.* ■ angry, indignant, or upset: *her reply came boiling out of her, hot with rage.* ■ (of music, especially jazz) strongly rhythmical and excitingly played: *hot salsa and lambada dancing.*
4 involving much activity, debate, or intense feeling: *the environment has become a very hot issue.*
■ (especially of news) fresh or recent and therefore of great interest: *have I got some hot gossip for you!* ■ currently popular, fashionable, or in demand: *the band are a hot draw.* ■ difficult to deal with; awkward or dangerous: *he found my story simply too hot to handle.* ■ (of a hit or return in ball games) difficult for an opponent to deal with. ■ Hunting (of the scent) fresh and strong, indicating that the quarry has passed recently. ■ informal (of goods) stolen and difficult to dispose of because easily identifiable. ■ informal (of a person) wanted by the police. ■ [predic.] (in children's games) very close to finding or guessing something.
5 informal very knowledgeable or skilful: *Tony is very **hot on** local history.*
■ [predic.] [usu. with negative] good; promising: *this is not so **hot for** business.* ■ [predic.] (**hot on**) informal considering as very important; strict about: *local customs officers are hot on confiscations.*
▶ **verb** (**hotted**, **hotting**) W. Indian make or become hot: [with obj.] *I hot some water quick and wash my hands.*
– PHRASES **go hot and cold** experience a sudden feeling of fear, anxiety, or shock. **have the hots for** informal be sexually attracted to. **hot and bothered** see **BOTHER**. **hot and heavy** N. Amer. informal intense; with intensity: *the competition became very hot and heavy.* **hot on the heels of** following closely: *critique followed hot on the heels of this pioneering work.* **hot to trot** informal ready and eager to engage in an activity. **hot under the collar** informal angry, resentful, or embarrassed. **in hot pursuit** following closely and eagerly. **in hot water** informal in a situation of difficulty, trouble, or disgrace: *he **landed in hot water** for an alleged V-sign to the fans.* **make it** (or **things**) **hot for someone** informal persecute someone.
– DERIVATIVES **hotness** noun, **hottish** adjective.
– ORIGIN Old English *hāt*, of Germanic origin; related to Dutch *heet* and German *heiss*.
▶ **hot up** (or **hot something up**) Brit. informal become or make hot: *he hotted up the flask in Daisy's hand.* ■ become or make more active, lively, or exciting: *the championship contest hotted up.*

hot air ▶ **noun** [mass noun] informal empty talk that is intended to impress: *they dismissed the theory as a load of hot air.*

hot-air gun ▶ **noun** see **AIR GUN** (sense 2).

hotbed ▶ **noun** a bed of earth heated by fermenting manure, for raising or forcing plants.
■ an environment promoting the growth of something, especially something unwelcome: *the country was **a hotbed of** revolt and dissension.*

hot-blooded ▶ **adjective** lustful; passionate: *hot-blooded Latin lovers.*

hot button ▶ **noun** N. Amer. informal [often as modifier] a topic or issue that is highly charged emotionally or politically: *the hot-button issue of nuclear waste disposal.*

hot cathode ▶ **noun** a cathode designed to be heated in order to emit electrons.

hotchpot ▶ **noun 1** [mass noun] Law the reunion and blending together of properties for the purpose of securing equal division, especially of the property of an intestate parent.
2 variant spelling of **HOTCHPOTCH**.
– ORIGIN late Middle English (in sense 2): from Anglo-Norman French and Old French *hochepot*, from *hocher* 'to shake' (probably of Low German origin) + *pot* 'pot'.

hotchpotch (N. Amer. **hodgepodge**) ▶ **noun** [in sing.] a confused mixture: *a **hotchpotch of** uncoordinated services.*
■ a mutton stew with mixed vegetables.
– ORIGIN late Middle English: variant of **HOTCHPOT**.

hot cross bun ▶ **noun** a bun marked with a cross and containing dried fruit, traditionally eaten on Good Friday.

hot dark matter ▶ **noun** see **DARK MATTER**.

hot-desking ▶ **noun** [mass noun] the practice in an office of allocating desks to workers when they are required or on a rota system, rather than giving each worker their own desk.

hot dog ▶ **noun 1** a hot sausage served in a long, soft roll.
2 N. Amer. informal a person, especially a skier or surfer, who performs stunts or tricks.
▶ **exclamation** N. Amer. informal used to express delight or enthusiastic approval.
▶ **verb** (**hotdog**) (**-dogged**, **-dogging**) [no obj.] N. Amer. informal perform stunts or tricks: *he chastised the dancers who'd been hotdogging.*
– DERIVATIVES **hotdogger** noun.

hotel ▶ **noun 1** an establishment providing accommodation, meals, and other services for travellers and tourists, by the night.
■ chiefly Austral./NZ a public house.
2 a code word representing the letter H, used in radio communication.
– ORIGIN mid 18th cent.: from French *hôtel*, from Old French *hostel* (see **HOSTEL**).

USAGE The normal pronunciation of **hotel** sounds the **h-**, which means that the preceding indefinite article is **a**. However, the older pronunciation without the **h-** is still sometimes heard, and gives rise to the preceding indefinite article being **an**. For a discussion of this, see **usage** at **AN**.

hotelier ▶ **noun** a person who owns or manages a hotel.
– ORIGIN early 20th cent.: from French *hôtelier*, from Old French *hostelier* 'innkeeper' (see **HOSTELRY**).

hot favourite ▶ **noun** a competitor who is strongly fancied to win a race or other contest.

hot flash ▶ **noun** chiefly N. Amer. another term for **HOT FLUSH**.

hot flush ▶ **noun** see **FLUSH**[1] (sense 1).

hotfoot ▶ **adverb** in eager haste: *he rushed hotfoot to the planning office to object.*
▶ **verb** (**hotfoot it**) [with adverbial of direction] walk or run quickly and eagerly: *we hotfooted it after him.*

hot gospel ▶ **noun** [mass noun] informal the fervent propounding of religious beliefs; zealous evangelism.
– DERIVATIVES **hot gospeller** noun.

hothead ▶ **noun** a person who is impetuous or easily becomes angry and violent.
– DERIVATIVES **hot-headed** adjective, **hot-headedly** adverb, **hot-headedness** noun.

hothouse ▶ **noun** a heated building, typically largely of glass, for rearing plants out of season or in a climate colder than is natural for them.
■ figurative an environment that encourages the rapid growth or development of someone or something, especially in a stifling or intense way: [as modifier] *the hothouse atmosphere of the college.*
▶ **verb** [with obj.] educate or teach (a child) to a high level at an earlier age than is usual.

hot key ▶ **noun** Computing a key or a combination of keys providing quick access to a particular function within a program.

hotline ▶ **noun** a direct telephone line set up for a specific purpose, especially for use in emergencies or for communication between heads of government.

hot link Computing ▶ **noun** a connection between documents or applications, which enables material from one source to be incorporated into another, in particular a facility which automatically updates material in a document when an alteration is made to the document from which it originated.
■ a hypertext link.
▶ **verb** (**hot-link**) [with obj.] connect (two documents) by means of a hot link.

hot list ▶ **noun** a list of currently popular, fashionable, or important people or things: *the Hollywood hot list.*
■ Computing a personal list of favourite or most frequently accessed web sites compiled by an Internet user. ■ a list of tasks taking priority over others.

hotly ▶ **adverb** in a passionate, excited, or angry way: *the rumours were hotly denied | hotly debated issues.*
■ closely and with determination: *he rushed out, hotly pursued by Boris.*

hot metal ▶ **noun** a typesetting technique in which type is newly made each time from molten metal, cast by a composing machine.

hot money ▶ **noun** [mass noun] capital which is frequently transferred between financial institutions in an attempt to maximize interest or capital gain.

hot pants ▶ **plural noun** very tight, brief women's shorts, worn as a fashion garment.

hotplate ▶ **noun** a flat heated surface (or a set of these), typically metal or ceramic, used for cooking food or keeping it hot.

hotpot ▶ **noun** Brit. a casserole of meat and vegetables, typically with a covering layer of sliced potato.

hot potato ▶ **noun** informal a controversial issue or situation which is awkward or unpleasant to deal with: *dog registration has become a political hot potato.*

hot press ▶ **noun** a device in which paper or cloth is pressed between glazed boards and hot metal plates in order to produce a smooth or glossy surface.
■ a similar apparatus used in making plywood.
▶ **verb** (**hot-press**) [with obj.] press with such a device.

hot rod ▶ **noun** a motor vehicle that has been specially modified to give it extra power and speed.
▶ **verb** (**hot-rod**) (**-rodded**, **-rodding**) **1** [with obj.] modify (a vehicle or other device) to make it faster or more powerful.
2 [no obj.] drive a hot rod.
– DERIVATIVES **hot-rodder** noun.

hot seat ▶ **noun** (**the hot seat**) informal **1** the position of a person who carries full responsibility for something, including facing criticism or being answerable for decisions or actions: *it's been a bad week for the men **in the hot seat**.*
2 chiefly US the electric chair.

hot shoe ▶ **noun** Photography a socket on a camera with direct electrical contacts for an attached flash gun or other accessory.

hot-short ▶ **adjective** (of a metal) brittle when hot.
– ORIGIN late 18th cent.: from **HOT** + *short* suggested by the earlier *red-short*, from Swedish *rödskör* (from *röd* 'red' + *skör* 'brittle').

hotshot ▶ **noun** informal an important or exceptionally able person.
■ a sports player with a good shot or aim.

hot spot ▶ **noun** a small area or region with a relatively hot temperature in comparison to its surroundings.
■ Geology an area of volcanic activity, especially where this is isolated. ■ figurative a place of significant activity or danger. ■ Computing an area on the screen which can be clicked on to start an operation such as loading a file.

hot spring ▶ **noun** a spring of naturally hot water, typically heated by subterranean volcanic activity.

Hotspur /ˈhɒtspəː/ the nickname of Sir Henry Percy (see **PERCY**).

hotspur /ˈhɒtspəː, -spə/ ▶ **noun** archaic a rash, impetuous person.
– ORIGIN late Middle English: literally 'a person whose spur is hot from rash or constant riding'.

hot-stove ▶ **adjective** [attrib.] N. Amer. denoting a discussion about a favourite sport carried on during the off season: *hot-stove speculation.*
– ORIGIN 1950s: by association with discussions conducted around a heater in the winter.

hot stuff ▶ **noun** [mass noun] informal used to refer to a person or thing of outstanding quality, interest, or talent: *he's hot stuff at arithmetic.*
■ used to refer to a sexually exciting person, film, book, etc.: *Jill was reputed to be hot stuff.*

hot-swap ▶ **verb** [with obj.] informal fit or replace (a computer part) with the power still connected.
– DERIVATIVES **hot-swappable** adjective.

hotsy-totsy ▶ **adjective 1** US informal, dated used as a term of approval: *hotsy-totsy rhythms thrill the air.*
2 US term for **HOITY-TOITY**.
– ORIGIN early 20th cent.: reduplication of **HOT**, a fanciful formation by Billie de Beck, American cartoonist.

hot-tempered ▶ **adjective** easily angered; quick-tempered.

Hottentot /ˈhɒt(ə)ntɒt/ ▶ **noun** & **adjective** used to refer to Khoikhoi peoples.
– ORIGIN Dutch, perhaps a repetitive formula in a Nama dancing-song, transferred by Dutch sailors to the people themselves, or from German *hotterentotteren* 'stutter' (with reference to their click language).

USAGE The word **Hottentot** is first recorded in the late 17th century and was a name applied by white Europeans to the Khoikhoi. It is now regarded as offensive with reference to people and should always be avoided in favour of **Khoikhoi** or the names of the particular peoples. The only standard use for **Hottentot** in modern use is in the names of animals and plants.

Hottentot fig ▶ **noun** a succulent mat-forming plant with bright yellow or lilac daisy-like flowers and edible fruit. It is native to South Africa and frequently naturalized on coastal cliffs in Europe.
● *Carpobrotus* (formerly *Mesembryanthemum*) *edulis*, family Aizoaceae.

hot ticket ▶ **noun** informal a person or thing that is much in demand: *he's the current hot ticket on the hard-core hip-hop block* | [as modifier] *a hot-ticket invitation.*

hottie (also **hotty**) ▶ **noun** (pl. **-ies**) Brit. informal a hot-water bottle.

hotting ▶ **noun** [mass noun] Brit. informal joyriding in stolen high-performance cars, especially for elaborate and dangerous display.
– DERIVATIVES **hotter** noun.

hot tub ▶ **noun** a large tub filled with hot aerated water used for recreation or physical therapy.

hot war ▶ **noun** a war with active military hostilities.

hot-water bottle (US also **hot-water bag**) ▶ **noun** a flat, oblong container, typically made of rubber, that is filled with hot water and used for warmth, especially for warming a bed.

hot-wire ▶ **adjective** [attrib.] (of an electrical instrument) depending on the expansion of a wire when heated or on a change in the electrical resistance of a wire when heated or cooled: *a hot-wire detector.*
▶ **verb** [with obj.] informal start the engine of (a vehicle) by bypassing the ignition system, typically in order to steal it.

houbara /huːˈbɑːrə/ (also **houbara bustard**) ▶ **noun** a bustard of arid open country and semi-desert, found from the Canary Islands to central Asia and threatened by hunting.
● *Chlamydotis undulata*, family Otidae.
– ORIGIN early 19th cent.: modern Latin, from Arabic *ḥubārā*.

Houdini /huːˈdiːni/, Harry (1874–1926), Hungarian-born American magician and escape artist; born *Erik Weisz*. In the early 1900s he became famous for his ability to escape from all kinds of bonds and containers, from prison cells to aerially suspended straitjackets.
■ [as noun] a person skilled at escaping: *you're a regular Houdini.* ■ an ingenious escape: *he will have to* **do a Houdini** *to escape from me.*

hough /hɒk/ Brit. ▶ **noun** variant spelling of **HOCK**[1] (in sense 1).
■ a joint of meat consisting of the part extending from the hock some way up the leg.
▶ **verb** [with obj.] archaic disable (a person or animal) by cutting the hamstrings.
– ORIGIN Old English *hōh* 'heel', of Germanic origin; related to **HEEL**.

hoummos ▶ **noun** variant spelling of **HUMMUS**.

hound ▶ **noun** a dog of a breed used for hunting, especially one able to track by scent.
■ [with modifier] a person keen in pursuit of something: *he has a reputation as a publicity hound.* ■ a pursuing runner in the game of hare and hounds. ■ informal, dated a despicable or contemptible man. ■ used in names of dogfishes, e.g. **nurse hound**, **smooth hound**.
▶ **verb** [with obj.] harass or persecute (someone) relentlessly: *she was hounded by the Italian press* | *his opponents used the allegations to* **hound** *him* **out of** *office.*
■ pursue relentlessly: *he led the race from start to finish but was hounded all the way by Phillips.*
– PHRASES **ride to hounds** see **RIDE**.
– ORIGIN Old English *hund* (in the general sense 'dog'), of Germanic origin; related to Dutch *hond* and German *Hund*, from an Indo-European root shared by Greek *kuōn*, *kun-* 'dog'.

houndfish ▶ **noun** (pl. same or **-fishes**) a large garfish of warm inshore waters, which leaps from the water and skitters over the surface when disturbed.
● Genus *Tylosaurus*, family Belonidae: several species.

hound's tongue ▶ **noun** a tall plant of the borage family, which bears long silky hairs, small purplish flowers, and tongue-shaped leaves, and has a mousy smell.
● *Cynoglossum officinale*, family Boraginaceae.

houndstooth ▶ **noun** a large check pattern with notched corners suggestive of a canine tooth, typically used in cloth for jackets and suits.

houngan /ˈhuːŋg(ə)n/ ▶ **noun** a voodoo priest.
– ORIGIN early 20th cent.: from Fon, from *hun*, a deity represented by a fetish, + *ga* 'chief'.

hour ▶ **noun 1** a period of time equal to a twenty-fourth part of a day and night and divided into 60 minutes: *York is within an hour's drive* | *rates of pay were low, starting at £1.20 an hour* | [as modifier, usu. with preceding numeral] *a two-hour operation.*
■ a more indefinite period of time: *during the early hours of the morning.* ■ the distance travelled in one hour: *by car Hull is only an hour away.*
2 a point in time: *I wondered if my last hour had come.*
■ a time of day or night: *you can't turn him away at this hour.* ■ a time of day specified as an exact number of hours from midnight or midday: *the clock in the sitting room* **struck the hour.** ■ (**hours**) [with preceding numeral] a time so specified on the 24-hour clock: *the first bomb fell at 0051 hours.* ■ the time as formerly reckoned from sunrise: *it was about the ninth hour.* ■ the appropriate time for some specific action: *now that the hour had come, David decided he could not face it.*
3 [usu. with modifier] a period set aside for some purpose or marked by some activity: *leisure hours.*
■ (**hours**) a fixed period of time for an activity, such as work, use of a building, etc.: *licensing hours.*
4 (usu. **hours**) (in the Western (Latin) Church) a short service of psalms and prayers to be said at a particular time of day, especially in religious communities.
5 Astronomy 15° of longitude or right ascension (one twenty-fourth part of a circle).
– PHRASES **all hours** most of the time, especially outside the time considered usual for something: *teenagers expect to be allowed to stay out* **to all hours.** **keep late** (or **regular**) **hours** do the same thing, typically getting up and going to bed, late or at the same time every day. **on the hour 1** at an exact hour, or on each hour, of the day or night. **2** after a period of one hour. **within the hour** after less than an hour.
– ORIGIN Middle English: from Anglo-Norman French *ure*, via Latin from Greek *hōra* 'season, hour'.

hourglass ▶ **noun** an invertible device with two connected glass bulbs containing sand that takes an hour to pass from the upper to the lower bulb.
■ [as modifier] shaped like such a device: *her hourglass figure.*

houri /ˈhʊəri/ ▶ **noun** (pl. **houris**) a beautiful young woman, especially one of the virgin companions of the faithful in the Muslim Paradise.
– ORIGIN mid 18th cent.: from French, from Persian *ḥūrī*, from Arabic *ḥūr*, plural of *'aḥwar* 'having eyes with a marked contrast of black and white'.

hour-long ▶ **adjective** [attrib.] lasting for one hour.

hourly ▶ **adjective 1** done or occurring every hour: *there is an hourly bus service.*
■ (with numeral or fraction) occurring at intervals measured in hours: *receiving six hourly doses of morphine* | *trains run at half-hourly intervals.*
2 reckoned hour by hour: *to introduce standard fees instead of hourly rates.*
▶ **adverb 1** every hour: *sunscreens should be applied hourly* | *a train runs hourly from 7 a.m. to 8 p.m.*
■ (with numeral or fraction) at intervals measured in hours: *temperature should be recorded four-hourly.*
2 by the hour: *hourly paid workers.*
3 very frequently; continually: *her curiosity was mounting hourly.*

house ▶ **noun** /haʊs/ **1** a building for human habitation, especially one that is lived in by a family or small group of people and consists of a ground floor and one or more upper storeys.
■ the people living in such a building; a household: *make yourself scarce before you wake the whole house.* ■ (often **House**) a family or family lineage, especially a noble or royal one; a dynasty: *the power and prestige of the house of Stewart.* ■ chiefly Scottish a dwelling that is one of several in a building. ■ [with modifier] a building in which animals live or in which things are kept: *a reptile house.*
2 a building in which people meet for a particular activity: *a house of prayer.*
■ a firm or institution: *a fashion house.* ■ (**the House**) Brit. informal the Stock Exchange. ■ a restaurant or inn: [as modifier] *a carafe of house red.* ■ a host or proprietor: *help yourself to a drink, compliments of the house!* ■ dated a brothel. ■ a theatre: *a hundred musicians performed in front of a full house.* ■ an audience in a theatre, cinema, or concert venue: *the house burst into applause.* ■ Brit. a performance in a theatre or cinema: *tickets for the first house.*
3 a religious community that occupies a particular building: *the Cistercian house at Clairvaux.*
■ chiefly Brit. a body of pupils living in the same building at a boarding school. ■ chiefly Brit. one of a number of groups into which pupils at a day school are divided for games or competition. ■ Brit. formal a college of a university.
4 a legislative or deliberative assembly: *the sixty-member National Council, the country's upper house.*
■ (**the House**) (in the UK) the House of Commons or Lords; (in the US) the House of Representatives. ■ used in formal debates that mimic the procedures of a legislative assembly: *a debate on the motion 'This house would legalize cannabis'.*
5 (also **house music**) [mass noun] a style of popular dance music typically using drum machines, synthesized bass lines, sparse repetitive vocals, and a fast beat.
6 Astrology a twelfth division of the celestial sphere, based on the positions of the ascendant and midheaven at a given time and place, and determined by any of a number of methods.
■ such a division represented as a sector on an astrological chart, used in allocating elements of character and circumstance to different spheres of human life.
7 [mass noun] Brit. old-fashioned term for **BINGO**.
■ [as exclamation] used by a bingo-player to announce that they have won.
▶ **adjective** [attrib.] **1** (of an animal or plant) kept in, frequenting, or infesting buildings.
2 of or relating to medical staff resident at a hospital.
3 of or relating to a firm, institution, or society: *a house journal.*
■ (of a band or group) resident or regularly performing in a club or other venue.
▶ **verb** /haʊz/ [with obj.] **1** provide (a person or animal) with shelter or accommodation: *they converted a disused cinema to house twelve employees.*
2 provide space for; accommodate: *the museum houses a collection of Roman sculpture.*
■ enclose or encase (something): *the radar could be housed in a pod beneath the engine.* ■ fix (something) in a socket or mortise.
– PHRASES **as safe as houses** Brit. thoroughly or completely safe. **get on** (or **along**) **like a house on fire** informal have a very good and friendly relationship. **go** (**all**) **round the houses** take a circuitous route to one's destination. ■ take an unnecessarily long time to get to the point. **house and home** a person's home (used for emphasis): *some people sell house and home to sit in a boat writing books.* **a house divided cannot stand** proverb a group or organization weakened by internal dissensions will be unable to withstand external pressures. **house of cards** a structure built out of playing cards precariously balanced together. ■ used to refer to an insubstantial or insecure situation or scheme: *the special constitutional arrangement collapsed like a house of cards.* **keep** (or **make**) **a House** Brit. secure the presence of enough members for a quorum in the House of Commons. **keep house** do the cooking, cleaning, and other tasks involved in the running of a household. **keep** (**to**) **the house** stay indoors. **on the house** (of a drink or meal in a bar or restaurant) at the management's expense; free. **play house** (of a child) play at being a family in its home. **put** (or **set** or **get**) **one's house in order** make necessary reforms: *the Americans need to get their own economic house in order.* **set up house** make one's home in a specified place.
– DERIVATIVES **houseful** noun (pl. **-fuls**), **houseless** adjective.
– ORIGIN Old English *hūs* (noun), *hūsian* (verb), of Germanic origin; related to Dutch *huis*, German

Haus (nouns), and Dutch *huizen*, German *hausen* (verbs).

house agent ▶ noun Brit. another term for *estate agent* (see ESTATE AGENCY).

house arrest ▶ noun [mass noun] the state of being kept as a prisoner in one's own house, rather than in a prison: *she was placed under house arrest.*

houseboat ▶ noun a boat which is or can be moored for use as a dwelling.

housebound ▶ adjective unable to leave one's house, typically due to illness or old age.

houseboy ▶ noun a boy or man employed to undertake domestic duties.

housebreak ▶ verb chiefly N. Amer. another term for HOUSE-TRAIN.

housebreaking ▶ noun [mass noun] Law, Brit. the action of breaking into a building, especially in daytime, to commit a crime. In 1968 it was replaced as a statutory crime (in England and Wales only) by burglary.
– DERIVATIVES **housebreaker** noun.

housecarl /ˈhaʊskɑːl/ (also **housecarle**) ▶ noun historical a member of the bodyguard of a Danish or English king or noble.
– ORIGIN late Old English *hūscarl*, from Old Norse *húskarl* 'manservant', (plural) 'retinue, bodyguard', from *hús* 'house' + *karl* 'man'.

house church ▶ noun 1 a charismatic Church independent of traditional denominations.
2 a group meeting for Christian worship in a private house.

housecoat ▶ noun a woman's long, loose, lightweight robe for informal wear around the house.

house cricket ▶ noun a chiefly nocturnal cricket with a birdlike warble, native to North Africa and SW Asia. It has become established in warm buildings throughout Europe.
● *Acheta domesticus*, family Gryllidae.

house dog ▶ noun a dog kept to guard a house.

housefather ▶ noun a man in charge of and living in a boarding school house or children's home.

house finch ▶ noun a red-breasted brown finch, now common from Canada to Mexico and sometimes regarded as a pest.
● *Carpodacus mexicanus*, family Fringillidae.

house flag ▶ noun a flag indicating the company that a ship belongs to.

housefly ▶ noun (pl. **-flies**) a common small fly occurring worldwide in and around human habitation. Its eggs are laid in decaying material, and the fly can be a health hazard due to its contamination of food.
● *Musca domestica*, family Muscidae.

house gecko ▶ noun a large-eyed nocturnal gecko of the Old World tropics, occupying a range of habitats including houses.
● *Hemidactylus*, *Gehyra*, and other genera, family Gekkonidae: several species, including *H. mabouia* of Africa and tropical America, and *G. mutilata* of Asia.

house guest ▶ noun a guest staying for some days in a private house.

household ▶ noun a house and its occupants regarded as a unit: *the whole household was asleep* | [as modifier] *household bills.*
■ (the **Household**) [usu. in titles] chiefly Brit. the establishment and affairs of a royal household: *Controller of the Household.*

Household Cavalry (in the British army) the two cavalry regiments with responsibility for guarding the monarch and royal palaces (and otherwise acting as part of the Royal Armoured Corps).

householder ▶ noun a person who owns or rents a house; the head of a household.

household gods ▶ plural noun gods presiding over a household, especially (in Roman History) the lares and penates.
■ figurative possessions held in esteem: *the Fairley household gods—portraits and an assortment of silver.*

household name (also **household word**) ▶ noun a person or thing that is well known by the public.

household troops ▶ plural noun (in the UK) troops nominally employed to guard the sovereign.

house-hunt ▶ verb [no obj.] seek a house to buy or rent and live in.
– DERIVATIVES **house-hunter** noun.

house husband ▶ noun a man who lives with a partner and carries out household duties traditionally done by a housewife rather than going out to work.

housekeeper ▶ noun a person, typically a woman, employed to manage a household.
– DERIVATIVES **housekeep** verb (dated).

housekeeping ▶ noun [mass noun] **1** the management of household affairs.
■ money set aside or given for such a purpose: *writing barely pays my part of the housekeeping.*
2 operations such as maintenance or record-keeping in a computer or organization which make work possible but do not directly constitute its performance.
■ Biology the regulation of metabolic functions that are common to all cells: [as modifier] *housekeeping genes.*

houseleek /ˈhaʊsliːk/ ▶ noun a succulent European plant with rosettes of fleshy leaves and small pink flowers. Houseleeks grow on walls and roofs, and are popular cultivated plants.
● *Sempervivum* and related genera, family Crassulaceae: several species, in particular *S. tectorum.*

house lights ▶ plural noun the lights in the auditorium of a theatre.

housemaid ▶ noun a female domestic employee, especially one who cleans reception rooms and bedrooms.

housemaid's knee ▶ noun [mass noun] inflammation of the fluid-filled cavity covering the kneecap (bursitis), often due to excessive kneeling.

houseman ▶ noun (pl. **-men**) **1** Brit. another term for HOUSE OFFICER.
2 N. Amer. another term for HOUSEBOY.

house martin ▶ noun a black-and-white Eurasian songbird of the swallow family, often building its mud nest on the walls of buildings.
● Genus *Delichon*, family Hirundinidae: three species, in particular the widespread *D. urbica.*

housemaster ▶ noun a male teacher in charge of a house at a boarding school.

housemistress ▶ noun a female teacher in charge of a house at a boarding school.

housemother ▶ noun a woman in charge of and living in a boarding school house or children's home.

house mouse ▶ noun a greyish-brown mouse found abundantly as a scavenger in human dwellings. It is widely kept as a pet or experimental animal, and has been bred in many varieties.
● *Mus musculus*, family Muridae.

house music ▶ noun see HOUSE (sense 5).

House of Commons (in the UK) the elected chamber of Parliament.

house of correction ▶ noun **1** historical an institution where vagrants and minor offenders were confined and set to work.
2 (in the US) an institution for the short-term confinement of minor offenders.

house officer ▶ noun Brit. a recent medical graduate receiving supervised training in a hospital and acting as an assistant physician or surgeon.

house of God ▶ noun a place of religious worship, especially a church.

house of ill fame (also **house of ill repute**) ▶ noun archaic or humorous a brothel.

House of Keys (in the Isle of Man) the elected chamber of Tynwald.

House of Lords (in the UK) the chamber of Parliament composed of peers and bishops.
■ a committee of specially qualified members of this, appointed as the ultimate judicial appeal court of England and Wales.

House of Representatives the lower house of the US Congress and other legislatures.

houseparent ▶ noun a housemother or housefather.

house party ▶ noun a party at which the guests stay at a house overnight or for a few days, especially one held in a country house.

house plant ▶ noun a plant which is grown indoors.

house-proud ▶ adjective attentive to, or preoccupied with, the care and appearance of one's home.

house rat ▶ noun another term for BLACK RAT, especially in South Asia.

houseroom ▶ noun [mass noun] space or accommodation in one's house.
– PHRASES **not give something houseroom** Brit. be unwilling to have or consider something.

house-sit ▶ verb [no obj.] live in and look after a house while its owner is away.
– DERIVATIVES **house-sitter** noun.

Houses of Parliament (in the UK) the Houses of Lords and Commons regarded together, or the building where they meet (the Palace of Westminster).

house sparrow ▶ noun a common brown and grey sparrow that nests in the eaves and roofs of houses, common from Europe to southern Asia and introduced elsewhere.
● *Passer domesticus*, family Passeridae (or Ploceidae).

house spider ▶ noun a large spider which frequently lives in houses, where it builds a sheet-like web.
● a common European spider which builds a large web with a tubular retreat in one corner (genus *Tegenaria*, family Agelenidae). ● a common North American spider (*Achaearanea tepidariorum*, family Theridiidae).

house style ▶ noun a company's preferred manner of presentation and layout of written material.

house-to-house ▶ adjective & adverb performed at or taken to each house in turn: [as adj.] *house-to-house inquiries* | [as adv.] *troops searched house-to-house for agitators.*
▶ noun [in sing.] a house-to-house collection, inquiry, or search.

housetop ▶ noun the outer surface of the roof of a house.
– PHRASES **shout something from the housetops** old-fashioned way of saying *shout something from the rooftops* (see SHOUT).

house-train ▶ verb [with obj.] chiefly Brit. train (a pet) to excrete outside the house or only in a special place.
■ informal, humorous teach (someone) good manners or tidiness.

House Un-American Activities Committee (abbrev.: **HUAC**) a committee of the US House of Representatives established in 1938 to investigate subversives. It became notorious for its zealous investigations of alleged communists, particularly in the late 1940s, although it was originally intended to pursue Fascists also.

house-warming ▶ noun [usu. as modifier] a party celebrating a move to a new home: *a house-warming party.*

housewife ▶ noun (pl. **-wives**) **1** a married woman whose main occupation is caring for her family, managing household affairs, and doing housework.
2 /ˈhʌzɪf/ a small case for needles, thread, and other small sewing items.
– DERIVATIVES **housewifely** adjective, **housewifery** noun.
– ORIGIN Middle English *husewif* (see HOUSE, WIFE).

housework ▶ noun [mass noun] regular work done in housekeeping, such as cleaning, shopping, and cooking.

housey ▶ adjective Brit. informal in the style of house music.

housey-housey (also **housie-housie**) ▶ noun Brit. old-fashioned term for BINGO.

housing[1] ▶ noun **1** [mass noun] houses and flats considered collectively: [as modifier] *a housing development.*
■ the provision of accommodation: [as modifier] *a housing association.*
2 a rigid casing that encloses and protects a piece of moving or delicate equipment.
■ a structure that supports and encloses the bearings at the end of an axle or shaft.
3 a recess or groove cut in one piece of wood to allow another piece to be attached to it.

housing[2] ▶ noun archaic a cloth covering put on a horse for protection or ornament.
– ORIGIN late Middle English (in the general sense 'covering'): from Old French *houce*, from medieval Latin *hultia*, of Germanic origin.

housing estate ▶ noun Brit. a residential area in which the houses have all been planned and built at the same time.

Housman /ˈhaʊsmən/, A. E. (1859–1936), English

poet and classical scholar; full name *Alfred Edward Housman*. He is now chiefly remembered for the poems collected in *A Shropshire Lad* (1896), a series of nostalgic verses largely based on ballad forms.

Houston /ˈh(j)uːst(ə)n/ an inland port of Texas, linked to the Gulf of Mexico by the Houston Ship Canal; pop. 1,630,550 (1990). Since 1961 it has been a centre for space research and manned space flight; it is the site of the NASA Space Centre.
– ORIGIN named after Samuel *Houston* (1793–1863), an American politician and military leader who led the struggle to win control of Texas and make it part of the US.

houting /ˈhaʊtɪŋ/ ▶ **noun** a migratory whitefish with a pointed snout. Now rare, it is found mainly in the Baltic and adjacent rivers.
• *Coregonus oxyrhinchus*, family Salmonidae.
– ORIGIN late 19th cent.: from Dutch, from Middle Dutch *houtic*, of unknown origin.

Hove a resort on the southern coast of England, a city (with Brighton) from 2000; pop. 67,140 (1981).

hove chiefly Nautical past of **HEAVE**.

hovel ▶ **noun 1** a small squalid, unpleasant, or simply constructed dwelling.
■archaic an open shed or outhouse, used for sheltering cattle or storing grain or tools.
2 historical a conical building enclosing a kiln.
– ORIGIN late Middle English: of unknown origin.

hover ▶ **verb** [no obj., with adverbial] remain in one place in the air: *Army helicopters hovered overhead.*
■remain poised in one place, typically with slight but undirected movement: *her hand* ***hovered over*** *the console.* ■ (of a person) wait or linger close at hand in a tentative or uncertain manner: *she hovered anxiously in the background.* ■ remain at or near a particular level: *inflation will hover around the 4 per cent mark.* ■ remain in a state that is between two specified states or kinds of things: *his expression* ***hovered between*** *cynicism and puzzlement.*
▶ **noun** [in sing.] an act of remaining in the air in one place.
– DERIVATIVES **hoverer** noun.
– ORIGIN late Middle English: from archaic *hove* 'hover, linger', of unknown origin.

hovercraft ▶ **noun** (pl. same) a vehicle or craft that travels over land or water on a cushion of air provided by a downward blast. A design was first patented by Christopher Cockerell in 1955.

hoverfly ▶ **noun** (pl. **-flies**) a fly which frequently hovers motionless in the air and feeds on the nectar of flowers. Most hoverflies are black and yellow, patterned to mimic various bees and wasps.
• Family Syrphidae: numerous genera and species.

hoverport ▶ **noun** a terminal for hovercraft.

hovertrain ▶ **noun** a train that travels on a cushion of air.

how¹ ▶ **adverb** [usu. interrogative adverb] **1** in what way or manner; by what means: *how does it work?* | *he did not know how he ought to behave* | [with infinitive] *he showed me how to adjust the focus.*
2 used to ask about the condition or quality of something: *how was your holiday?* | *how did they play?*
■used to ask about someone's physical or mental state: *how are the children?* | *I asked how he was doing.*
3 [with adj. or adv.] used to ask about the extent or degree of something: *how old are you?* | *how long will it take?* | *I wasn't sure how fast to go.*
■used to express a strong feeling such as surprise about the extent of something: *how kind it was of him* | *how I wish I had been there!*
4 [relative adverb] the way in which; that: *she told us how she had lived out of a suitcase for a week.*
■in any way in which; however: *I'll do business how I like.*
– PHRASES **and how!** informal very much so (used to express strong agreement): *'Did you miss me?' 'And how!'* **here's how!** dated said when drinking someone's health. **how about 1** used to make a suggestion or offer: *how about a drink?* **2** used when asking for information or an opinion on something: *how about your company?* **the how and why** the methods and reasons for doing something: *tonight's edition demystifies the how and why of television ratings.* **how come?** see **COME**. **how do?** an informal greeting on being introduced to a stranger. **how do you do?** a formal greeting. **how many** what number: *how many books did you sell?* **how much** what amount or price: *how much did I win?* **how now?** archaic what is the meaning of this? **how so?** how can you show that that is so? **how's that?** Cricket is the batsman out or not? (said to an umpire). **how's that for ——?** isn't that a remarkable instance of ——?: *how's that for stereotypical thinking?*
– ORIGIN Old English *hū*, of West Germanic origin; related to Dutch *hoe*, also to **WHO** and **WHAT**.

how² ▶ **exclamation** a greeting attributed to North American Indians (used in humorous imitation).
– ORIGIN early 19th cent.: perhaps from Sioux *háo* or Omaha *hou*.

Howard¹, Catherine (*c.*1521–42), fifth wife of Henry VIII. She married Henry soon after his divorce from Anne of Cleves in 1540. Accused of infidelity, she confessed and was beheaded.

Howard², John (1726–90), English philanthropist and prison reformer. His tour of British prisons in 1773 culminated in two Acts of Parliament setting down sanitary standards; his work *The State of Prisons in England and Wales* (1777) gave further impetus to the movement for improvements in prisons.

Howard³, John (Winston) (b.1939), Australian Liberal statesman, Prime Minister from 1996 with a Liberal–National Party coalition.

Howard⁴, Leslie (1893–1943), English actor; born *Leslie Howard Stainer*. He was best known for his roles as the archetypal English gentleman in films such as *The Scarlet Pimpernel* (1935) and *Pygmalion* (1938).

Howard⁵, Trevor (Wallace) (1916–88), English actor. He starred in *Brief Encounter* (1945) and *The Third Man* (1949) and later played character roles in films such as *Gandhi* (1982).

howbeit ▶ **adverb** archaic nevertheless; however: *howbeit, I've no proof of the thing.*

howdah /ˈhaʊdə/ ▶ **noun** (in the Indian subcontinent) a seat for riding on the back of an elephant or camel, typically with a canopy and accommodating two or more people.
– ORIGIN from Urdu *haudah*, from Arabic *hawdaj* 'litter'.

how-do-you-do (also **how-de-do** or **how-d'ye-do**) ▶ **noun** [in sing.] informal an awkward, messy, or annoying situation: *a fine how-do-you-do that would be!*

howdy ▶ **exclamation** N. Amer. an informal friendly greeting, particularly associated with the western US states: *howdy, stranger.*
– ORIGIN early 19th cent.: alteration of *how d'ye*.

Howe, Elias (1819–67), American inventor. In 1846 he patented the first sewing machine. Its principles were adapted by Isaac Merrit Singer and others in violation of Howe's patent rights, and it took a seven-year litigation battle to secure the royalties.

howe¹ ▶ **noun** N. English a tumulus or barrow.
■[in place names] a hill.
– ORIGIN Middle English: from Old Norse *haugr* 'mound', from a Germanic base meaning 'high'.

howe² ▶ **noun** Scottish & N. English a hollow place; a depression.
– ORIGIN late Middle English: variant of Old English *hol* (see **HOLE**).

howe'er /haʊˈɛː/ poetic/literary ▶ **contraction of** however.

however ▶ **adverb 1** used to introduce a statement that contrasts with or seems to contradict something that has been said previously: *People tend to put on weight in middle age. However, gaining weight is not inevitable.*
2 [relative adverb] in whatever way; regardless of how: *however you look at it, you can't criticize that.*
■[with adj. or adv.] to whatever extent: *he was hesitant to take the risk, however small.*

USAGE When **ever** is used for emphasis after **how** or **why**, it should be written as a separate word. Thus it is correct to write ***how ever did you manage?*** rather than ***however did you manage?*** (as distinct from other uses of the adverb **however**, which is always written as one word). However, with other words such as **what**, **where**, and **who**, the situation is not clear-cut: both two-word and one-word forms (both **what ever** and **whatever**, and so on) are well represented, and neither is regarded as particularly more correct than the other.

howff /haʊf/ ▶ **noun** Scottish a favourite meeting place or haunt, especially a public house.
– ORIGIN mid 16th cent. (as the name of the main burial ground in Dundee): of unknown origin.

howitzer /ˈhaʊɪtsə/ ▶ **noun** a short gun for firing shells on high trajectories at low velocities.
– ORIGIN late 17th cent.: from Dutch *houwitser*, from German *Haubitze*, from Czech *houfnice* 'catapult'.

howk /haʊk/ ▶ **verb** [with obj., and adverbial] chiefly Scottish dig out or up: *deep in their trenches the men stood,* ***howking out*** *the brown earth.*
■[no obj., with adverbial] search about by digging or rummaging: *Frankie howked among the beer cans.*
– ORIGIN late Middle English *holk*: related to Middle Low German *holken* 'to hollow', and **HOLE**.

howl ▶ **noun** a long, loud, doleful cry uttered by an animal such as a dog or wolf.
■a loud cry of pain, fear, anger, amusement, or derision: *he let out a* ***howl of*** *anguish* | figurative *I got* ***howls of*** *protest from readers.* ■ [in sing.] a prolonged wailing noise such as that made by a strong wind: *they listened to* ***the howl of*** *the gale.* ■ Electronics a wailing noise in a loudspeaker due to electrical or acoustic feedback.
▶ **verb** [no obj.] make a howling sound: *he howled in agony* | *the wind howled around the house.*
■weep and cry out loudly: *a baby started to howl.* ■ [with obj.] (**howl someone down**) shout in disapproval in order to prevent a speaker from being heard: *they howled me down and called me a chauvinist.*
– ORIGIN Middle English *houle* (verb), probably imitative.

howler ▶ **noun 1** informal a very stupid or glaring mistake, especially an amusing one.
2 a person or animal that howls.
3 (also **howler monkey**) a fruit-eating monkey with a prehensile tail and a loud howling call, native to the forests of tropical America.
• Genus *Alouatta*, family Cebidae: several species.

howlet ▶ **noun** chiefly Scottish an owl or owlet.
– ORIGIN late 15th cent.: diminutive of **OWL**, assimilated to the verb **HOWL**.

howling ▶ **adjective** [attrib.] **1** producing a long, loud, doleful cry or wailing sound.
■archaic filled with or characterized by such sounds: *the howling wilderness.*
2 informal extreme; great: *the meal was a howling success.*

howling dervish ▶ **noun** see **DERVISH**.

Howrah /ˈhaʊrə/ (also **Haora**) a city in eastern India; pop. 947,000 (1991). It is situated on the Hooghly River opposite Calcutta.

howsoe'er /ˌhaʊsəʊˈɛː/ poetic/literary ▶ **contraction of** howsoever.

howsoever formal or archaic ▶ **adverb** [with adj. or adv.] to whatever extent: *any quantity howsoever small.*
▶ **conjunction** in whatever way; regardless of how: *howsoever it came into being, it is good to look at.*

how-to informal ▶ **adjective** [attrib.] providing detailed and practical advice: *read a how-to book.*
▶ **noun** (pl. **-os**) a book, video, or training event that provides such advice.
■(**how-tos**) the correct procedures for a particular activity: *you will discover the how-tos of freehand drawing.*

howtowdie /haʊˈtaʊdi/ ▶ **noun** [mass noun] a Scottish dish of boiled chicken served with spinach and poached eggs.
– ORIGIN early 19th cent.: probably from Old French *estaudeau*, denoting a young chicken for the stew pot.

howzat ▶ **exclamation** Cricket shortened form of ***how's that*** (see **HOW¹**).

howzit ▶ **exclamation** S. African informal **1** used as a greeting, equivalent to 'hello' or 'how are you?'.
2 used to make a suggestion or request: *howzit for a small loan?*
– ORIGIN contraction of *how is it?*

Hoxha /ˈhɒdʒə/, Enver (1908–85), Albanian statesman, founder of the Albanian Communist Party 1941, Prime Minister 1944–54, and First Secretary of the Albanian Communist Party 1954–85. He rigorously isolated Albania from Western influences and implemented a Stalinist programme of nationalization and collectivization.

Hoxnian /ˈhɒksnɪən/ ▶ **adjective** Geology of, relating to, or denoting an interglacial period of the Pleistocene in Britain, following the Anglian glaciation and identified with the Holsteinian of northern Europe.
■[as noun **the Hoxnian**] the Hoxnian interglacial or the system of deposits laid down during it.
– ORIGIN 1950s: from *Hoxne*, the name of a village in Suffolk, + **-IAN**.

hoy¹ ▶ **exclamation** used to attract someone's attention: *'Hoy! Look!'*
▶ **noun** [mass noun] Austral. a game resembling bingo, using playing cards.
– ORIGIN natural exclamation: first recorded in late Middle English.

hoy² ▶ **noun** historical a small coastal sailing vessel, typically single-masted.
– ORIGIN Middle English: from Middle Dutch *hoei*, of unknown origin.

hoy³ ▶ **verb** [with obj.] Austral. & N. English informal throw.
– ORIGIN mid 19th cent.: of unknown origin.

hoya /'hɔɪə/ ▶ **noun** a climbing or sprawling evergreen shrub with ornamental foliage and waxy flowers, native to SE Asia and the Pacific and grown as a greenhouse or indoor plant.
● Genus *Hoya*, family Asclepiadaceae.
– ORIGIN modern Latin, named after Thomas *Hoy* (c.1750–c.1821), English gardener.

hoyden /'hɔɪd(ə)n/ ▶ **noun** dated a boisterous girl.
– DERIVATIVES **hoydenish** adjective.
– ORIGIN late 16th cent. (denoting a rude or ignorant man): probably from Middle Dutch *heiden* (see **HEATHEN**).

Hoyle¹, Sir Fred (b.1915), English astrophysicist and writer. He was one of the proponents of the steady state theory of cosmology, and, mainly with the American physicist **William A. Fowler** (1911–95), described the processes of nucleosynthesis inside stars. His later work has included the controversial suggestions that life on the earth has an extraterrestrial origin, and that some viruses arrive from space.

Hoyle² ▶ **noun** (in phrase **according to Hoyle**) according to plan or the rules.
– ORIGIN early 20th cent.: from the name of Edmond *Hoyle* (1672–1769), English writer on card games.

h.p. (also **HP**) ▶ **abbreviation for** ■ high pressure. ■ Brit. hire purchase. ■ horsepower.

HPV ▶ **abbreviation for** human papilloma virus.

HQ ▶ **abbreviation for** headquarters.

HR US ▶ **abbreviation for** House of Representatives.

hr ▶ **abbreviation for** hour.

Hradec Králové /ˌhraˈdɛts ˈkraːlɔveɪ/ a town in the northern Czech Republic, capital of East Bohemia region on the River Elbe; pop. 161,960 (1991). German name **KÖNIGGRÄTZ**.

HRH Brit. ▶ **abbreviation for** Her or His Royal Highness (as a title): *HRH Prince Philip.*

Hrodna /'hrɒdnə/ a city in western Belarus, on the Neman River near the borders with Poland and Lithuania; pop. 277,000 (1990). Russian name **GRODNO**.

hrs ▶ **abbreviation for** hours.

HRT ▶ **abbreviation for** hormone replacement therapy.

Hrvatska /ˈhˈrva:tska:/ Croatian name for **CROATIA**.

Hs ▶ **symbol for** the chemical element hassium.

HSE ▶ **abbreviation for** (in the UK) Health and Safety Executive.

HSH ▶ **abbreviation for** Her or His Serene Highness (as a title): *HSH Prince Rainer.*

Hsia-men variant of **XIAMEN**.

Hsian variant of **XIAN**.

Hsiang variant of **XIANG**.

Hsining variant of **XINING**.

HST ▶ **abbreviation for** ■ (in the UK) high-speed train, a design of express passenger train with integral diesel engines at either end. ■ Hubble Space Telescope.

Hsu-chou /ʃuːˈtʃaʊ/ variant of **XUZHOU**.

HT ▶ **abbreviation for** (electrical) high tension.

HTML ▶ **noun** [mass noun] Computing Hypertext Mark-up Language, a standardized system for tagging text files to achieve font, colour, graphic, and hyperlink effects on World Wide Web pages.

HTTP Computing ▶ **abbreviation for** Hypertext Transport (or Transfer) Protocol, the data transfer protocol used on the World Wide Web.

HUAC ▶ **abbreviation for** House Un-American Activities Committee.

Huainan /hwaɪˈnan/ a city in the province of Anhui, in east central China; pop. 1,228,000 (1990).

Huallaga /hwaˈjaːgə/ a river in central Peru, one of the headwaters of the Amazon. Rising in the central Andes, it flows, generally north-eastwards, for 1,100 km (700 miles) and emerges into the Amazon Basin at Lagunas.

Huambo /'hwambəʊ/ a city in the mountains in western Angola; pop. 400,000 (est. 1995). Founded in 1912, it was known by its Portuguese name of Nova Lisboa until 1978.

Huang Hai /hwaŋ 'hʌɪ/ Chinese name for **YELLOW SEA**.

Huang Ho /hwaŋ 'həʊ/ (also **Huang He** /'hi:/) Chinese name for **YELLOW RIVER**.

huarache /waˈrɑːtʃi/ (also **guarache**) ▶ **noun** a leather-thonged sandal, originally worn by Mexican Indians.
– ORIGIN late 19th cent.: Mexican Spanish.

Huascarán /ˌhwaskəˈraːn/ an extinct volcano in the Peruvian Andes, west central Peru, rising to 6,768 m (22,205 ft). It is the highest peak in Peru.

hub ▶ **noun** the central part of a wheel, rotating on or with the axle, and from which the spokes radiate.
■ a place or thing which forms the effective centre of an activity, region, or network: *the kitchen was the hub of family life.*
– PHRASES **hub-and-spoke** denoting a system of air transportation in which local airports offer flights to a central airport where international or long-distance flights are available.
– ORIGIN early 16th cent. (denoting a shelf at the side of a fireplace used for heating pans): of unknown origin (compare with **HOB¹**).

hubba hubba ▶ **exclamation** N. Amer. informal used to express approval, excitement, or enthusiasm, especially with regard to a person's appearance.
– ORIGIN 1940s: of unknown origin.

Hubbard squash /'hʌbəd/ ▶ **noun** a winter squash of a variety with a green or yellow rind and yellow flesh.

Hubble, Edwin Powell (1889–1953), American astronomer. He studied galaxies and devised a classification scheme for them. In 1929 he proposed what is now known as Hubble's law with its constant of proportionality (Hubble's constant).

hubble-bubble ▶ **noun** a hookah.
– ORIGIN mid 17th cent.: imitative repetition of **BUBBLE**.

Hubble classification Astronomy a simple method of describing the shapes of galaxies, using subdivisions of each of four basic types (elliptical, spiral, barred spiral, and irregular). Hubble's suggestion that they form an evolutionary sequence is no longer accepted.

Hubble's constant Astronomy the ratio of the speed of recession of a galaxy (due to the expansion of the universe) to its distance from the observer. The reciprocal of the constant is called **Hubble time** and represents the length of time for which the universe has been expanding, and hence the age of the universe.

Hubble's law Astronomy a law stating that the red shifts in the spectra of distant galaxies (and hence their speeds of recession) are proportional to their distance.

Hubble Space Telescope an orbiting astronomical observatory launched in 1990. The telescope's fine high-resolution images are far better than can be obtained from the earth's surface.

hubbub ▶ **noun** [in sing.] a chaotic din caused by a crowd of people: *a hubbub of laughter and shouting.*
■ a busy, noisy situation: *she fought through the hubbub.*
– ORIGIN mid 16th cent.: perhaps of Irish origin; compare with the Irish exclamations *ababú, abú,* used in battle cries.

hubby ▶ **noun** (pl. **-ies**) informal a husband.
– ORIGIN late 17th cent.: familiar abbreviation.

hubcap ▶ **noun** a metal or plastic cover for the hub of a motor vehicle's wheel.

Hubei /huːˈbeɪ/ (also **Hupeh**) a province of eastern China; capital, Wuhan.

Hubli /'huːbli/ (also **Hubli-Dharwad** /daˈwaːd/, **Hubli-Dharwar** /-ˈwaː/) a city in SW India; pop. 648,000 (1991). It was united with the adjacent city of Dharwad in 1961.

hubris /'hjuːbrɪs/ ▶ **noun** [mass noun] excessive pride or self-confidence.
■ (in Greek tragedy) excessive pride towards or defiance of the gods, leading to nemesis.
– DERIVATIVES **hubristic** adjective.
– ORIGIN Greek.

huchen /'huːk(ə)n/ ▶ **noun** (pl. same) a large, slender non-migratory fish of the salmon family, which lives only in the Danube River system.
● *Hucho hucho,* family Salmonidae.
– ORIGIN early 20th cent.: from German.

huckaback ▶ **noun** [mass noun] a strong linen or cotton fabric with a rough surface, used for towelling and glass cloths.
– ORIGIN late 17th cent.: of unknown origin.

huckleberry ▶ **noun 1** a soft edible blue-black fruit resembling a currant.
2 the low-growing North American plant of the heather family which bears this fruit.
● Genus *Gaylussacia,* family Ericaceae.
– ORIGIN late 16th cent.: probably originally a dialect name for the bilberry (though early evidence is lacking), from dialect *huckle* 'hip, haunch' (because of the plant's jointed stems).

huckster ▶ **noun** a person who sells small items, either door-to-door or from a stall or small shop.
■ a mercenary person keen to make a profit out of anything. ■ N. Amer. a publicity agent or advertising copywriter, especially for radio or television.
▶ **verb** [no obj.] chiefly N. Amer. bargain; haggle.
■ [with obj.] promote or sell (something, typically a product of questionable value).
– DERIVATIVES **hucksterism** noun.
– ORIGIN Middle English (in the sense 'retailer at a stall, hawker'): probably of Low German origin.

HUD ▶ **abbreviation for** head-up display.

Huddersfield a. town in northern England, formerly in Yorkshire; pop. 148,540 (1981).

huddle ▶ **verb** [no obj., with adverbial] crowd together; nestle closely: *they huddled together for warmth.*
■ curl one's body into a small space: *she huddled up close to him.* ■ [with obj. and adverbial] Brit. heap together in a disorderly manner: *a man with his clothes all huddled on anyhow.*
▶ **noun** a crowded or confused mass of people or things: *they stood in a huddle.*
■ a brief gathering of players during a game to receive instructions, especially in American Football. ■ [mass noun] archaic confusion; bustle.
– PHRASES **go into a huddle** informal get close to one or more people so as to speak about private or secret matters.
– ORIGIN late 16th cent. (in the sense 'conceal'): perhaps of Low German origin.

Hudson¹, Henry (c.1565–1611), English explorer. He discovered the North American bay, river, and strait which bear his name. In 1610 he attempted to winter in Hudson Bay, but his crew mutinied and set Hudson and a few companions adrift, never to be seen again.

Hudson², William Henry (1841–1922), British naturalist and writer, born in Argentina. A prolific author, he was an astute observer and lover of nature. Notable works: *The Naturalist in La Plata* (1892) and *Nature in Downland* (1900).

Hudson Bay a large inland sea in NE Canada. It is the largest inland sea in the world and is connected to the North Atlantic Ocean via the Hudson Strait.
– ORIGIN named after the explorer Henry *Hudson* (see **HUDSON¹**), who discovered it in 1610.

Hudsonian /hʌdˈsəʊnɪən/ ▶ **adjective** of or relating to Hudson Bay and the surrounding land.
■ Biology denoting a biogeographical zone represented by the territory around the bay (north of the tree line from Labrador to Alaska).

Hudson River a river of eastern North America, which rises in the Adirondack Mountains and flows southwards for 560 km (350 miles) into the Atlantic at New York.
– ORIGIN named after Henry *Hudson* (see **HUDSON¹**), who, in 1609 sailed 240 km (150 miles) up the river as far as Albany.

Hudson's Bay blanket ▶ **noun** Canadian a durable woollen blanket, typically with a coloured border.
– ORIGIN late 19th cent.: originally sold by the *Hudson's Bay* Company and frequently used as material for coats.

Hudson's Bay Company a British colonial trading company set up in 1670 and granted all lands draining into Hudson Bay for purposes of commercial exploitation, principally trade in fur. The company handed over control to the new Canadian government in 1870 and is now a Canadian retail and wholesale operation.

Hué /hweɪ/ a city in central Vietnam; pop. 219,150 (est. 1992).

hue ▶ **noun** a colour or shade: *her face lost its golden hue* | [mass noun] *verdigris is greenish-yellow in hue.*
■ the attribute of a colour by virtue of which it is discernible as red, green, etc., and which is dependent on its dominant wavelength, and independent of intensity or lightness. ■ figurative character; aspect: *men of all political hues submerged their feuds.*
– DERIVATIVES **hued** adjective [in combination] *rainbow-hued*, **hueless** adjective.
– ORIGIN Old English *hīw, hēow* (also 'form, appearance', obsolete except in Scots), of Germanic origin; related to Swedish *hy* 'skin, complexion'. The sense 'colour, shade' dates from the mid 19th cent.

hue and cry ▶ **noun** a loud clamour or public outcry.
■ historical a loud cry calling for the pursuit and capture of a criminal. In former English law, the cry had to be raised by the inhabitants of a hundred in which a robbery had been committed, if they were not to become liable for the damages suffered by the victim.
– ORIGIN late Middle English: from the Anglo-Norman French legal phrase *hu e cri*, literally 'outcry and cry', from Old French *hu* 'outcry' (from *huer* 'to shout').

huff ▶ **verb** [no obj.] blow out loudly; puff: *he was huffing under a heavy load.*
■ [with obj.] express (one's annoyance or offence): *he huffed out his sudden irritation.* ■ [with obj.] (in draughts) remove (an opponent's piece that could have made a capture) from the board as a forfeit. [ORIGIN: from the former practice of blowing on the piece.]
▶ **noun** [usu. in sing.] a fit of petty annoyance: *she walked off in a huff.*
– PHRASES **huff and puff** breathe heavily with exhaustion. ■ express one's annoyance in an obvious or threatening way.
– DERIVATIVES **huffish** adjective.
– ORIGIN late 16th cent.: imitative of the sound of blowing.

huffy ▶ **adjective** (**huffier**, **huffiest**) annoyed or irritated and quick to take offence at petty things.
– DERIVATIVES **huffily** adverb, **huffiness** noun.

hug ▶ **verb** (**hugged**, **hugging**) [with obj.] squeeze (someone) tightly in one's arms, typically to express affection: *he hugged her close to him* | *people kissed and hugged each other.*
■ hold (something) closely or tightly around or against part of one's body: *he hugged his knees to his chest.* ■ fit tightly round: *a pair of jeans that hugged the contours of his body.* ■ keep close to: *I headed north, hugging the coastline all the way.* ■ (**hug oneself**) congratulate or be pleased with oneself: *she hugged herself with secret joy.* ■ cherish or cling to (something such as a belief): *a boy hugging a secret.*
▶ **noun** an act of holding someone tightly in one's arms, typically to express affection.
■ a squeezing grip in wrestling.
– DERIVATIVES **huggable** adjective.
– ORIGIN mid 16th cent.: probably of Scandinavian origin and related to Norwegian *hugga* 'comfort, console'.

huge ▶ **adjective** (**huger**, **hugest**) extremely large; enormous: *a huge area* | *he made a huge difference to the team.*
– DERIVATIVES **hugeness** noun.
– ORIGIN Middle English: shortening of Old French *ahuge*, of unknown origin.

hugely ▶ **adverb** [often as submodifier] very much; to a very great extent: *a hugely expensive house.*

hugger-mugger ▶ **adjective 1** confused; disorderly: *a spirit of careless frivolity where all was hugger-mugger.*
2 secret; clandestine.
▶ **noun** [mass noun] **1** confusion; muddle.
2 secrecy.
– ORIGIN early 16th cent. (in sense 2 of the noun): probably related to **HUDDLE** and to dialect *mucker* 'hoard money, conceal'. This is one of a number of similar formations from late Middle English to the 16th cent., including *hucker-mucker* and *hudder-mudder*, with the basic sense 'secrecy, concealment'.

Huggins, Sir William (1824–1910), British astronomer. He pioneered spectroscopic analysis in astronomy, showing that nebulae are composed of luminous gas. He discovered the red shift in stellar spectra, attributing it to the Doppler effect and using it to measure recessional velocities.

Hughes[1], Ted (1930–98), English poet; full name *Edward James Hughes*. His vision of the natural world as a place of violence, terror, and beauty pervades his work. He was appointed Poet Laureate in 1984. Hughes was married to Sylvia Plath.

Hughes[2], Howard (Robard) (1905–76), American industrialist, film producer, and aviator. He made his fortune through the Hughes Tool Company, made his debut as a film director in 1926, and from 1935 to 1938 broke many world aviation records. For the last twenty-five years of his life he lived as a recluse.

Hughes[3], (James Mercer) Langston (1902–67), American writer. He began a prolific literary career with *The Weary Blues* (1926), a series of poems on black themes using blues and jazz rhythms. Other poetry collections include *The Negro Mother* (1931).

Hughie ▶ **noun** Austral./NZ informal an imaginary being held to be responsible for the weather.
– ORIGIN early 20th cent.: diminutive of the given name *Hugh*.

Hugli variant spelling of **HOOGHLY**.

Hugo /ˈhjuːɡəʊ, French ˈyɡo/ Victor (1802–85), French poet, novelist, and dramatist; full name *Victor-Marie Hugo*. A leading figure of French romanticism, he brought a new freedom to French poetry, and his belief that theatre should express both the grotesque and the sublime of human existence overturned existing conventions. His political and social concern is shown in his novels. Notable works: *Hernani* (drama, 1830) and *Les Misérables* (novel, 1862).

Huguenot /ˈhjuːɡənəʊ, -nɒt/ ▶ **noun** a French Protestant of the 16th–17th centuries. Largely Calvinist, the Huguenots suffered severe persecution at the hands of the Catholic majority, and many thousands emigrated from France.
– ORIGIN French, alteration (by association with the name of a Geneva burgomaster, Besançon *Hugues*) of *eiguenot*, from Dutch *eedgenot*, from Swiss German *Eidgenoss* 'confederate', from *Eid* 'oath' + *Genoss* 'associate'.

huh ▶ **exclamation** used to express scorn, anger, disbelief, surprise, or amusement: *'Huh,' she snorted, 'Over my dead body!'*
■ used in questions to invite agreement or further comment or to express a lack of understanding: *pretty devastating, huh?*
– ORIGIN natural utterance: first recorded in English in the early 17th cent.

Huhehot /ˌhuːheɪˈhɒt/ variant of **HOHHOT**.

hui /ˈhuːi/ ▶ **noun** (pl. **huis** or **huies**) (in New Zealand) a large social or ceremonial gathering.
■ (in Hawaii) a formal club or association.
– ORIGIN Maori and Hawaiian.

huia /ˈhuːɪə/ ▶ **noun** an extinct New Zealand wattlebird with glossy black plumage, the female having a much longer and more curved bill than the male. The tail feathers were formerly prized by Maoris, and the last huia was seen in 1907.
• *Heteralocha acutirostris*, family Callaeidae.
– ORIGIN mid 19th cent.: from Maori, imitative of its cry.

hula /ˈhuːlə/ (also **hula-hula**) ▶ **noun** a dance performed by Hawaiian women, characterized by six basic steps, undulating hips, and gestures symbolizing or imitating natural phenomena or historical or mythological subjects.
– ORIGIN early 19th cent.: Hawaiian.

hula hoop (also US trademark **Hula-Hoop**) ▶ **noun** a large hoop spun round the body by gyrating the hips, for play or exercise.

hula skirt ▶ **noun** a long grass skirt as worn by a hula dancer.

hulk ▶ **noun 1** an old ship stripped of fittings and permanently moored, especially for use as storage or (formerly) as a prison.
■ any large disused structure: *hulks of abandoned machinery.*
2 a large or unwieldy boat or other object.
■ a large, clumsy-looking person: *a six-foot hulk of a man.*
– ORIGIN Old English *hulc* 'fast ship', probably reinforced in Middle English by Middle Low German and Middle Dutch *hulk*; probably of Mediterranean origin and related to Greek *holkas* 'cargo ship'.

hulking ▶ **adjective** informal (of a person or object) very large, heavy, or clumsy: *a hulking young man.*

Hull a city and port in NE England, situated at the junction of the Hull and Humber Rivers; pop. 252,200 (1991). Official name **KINGSTON-UPON-HULL**.

hull[1] ▶ **noun** the main body of a ship or other vessel, including the bottom, sides, and deck but not the masts, superstructure, rigging, engines, and other fittings.
▶ **verb** [with obj.] (usu. **be hulled**) hit and pierce the hull of (a ship) with a shell or other missile.
– DERIVATIVES **hulled** adjective [in combination] *a wooden-hulled narrowboat.*
– ORIGIN Middle English: perhaps the same word as **HULL**[2], or related to **HOLD**[2].

hull[2] ▶ **noun** the outer covering of a fruit or seed, especially the pod of peas and beans, or the husk of grain.
■ the green calyx of a strawberry or raspberry.
▶ **verb** [with obj.] [usu. as adj. **hulled**] remove the hulls from (fruit, seeds, or grain).
– ORIGIN Old English *hulu*, of Germanic origin; related to Dutch *huls*, German *Hülse* 'husk, pod', and German *Hülle* 'covering', also to **HEEL**[3].

hullabaloo ▶ **noun** [in sing.] informal a commotion; a fuss: *remember all the hullabaloo over the golf ball?*
– ORIGIN mid 18th cent.: reduplication of *hallo, hullo*, etc.

hullo ▶ **exclamation** variant spelling of **HELLO**.
– ORIGIN first recorded, in this form, in T. Hughes' *Tom Brown's Schooldays* (1857).

hum[1] ▶ **verb** (**hummed**, **humming**) [no obj.] **1** make a low, steady continuous sound like that of a bee: *the computers hummed.*
■ sing with closed lips: *he hummed softly to himself* | [with obj.] *she was humming a cheerful tune.* ■ (of a place) be filled with a low, steady continuous sound: *the room hummed with an expectant murmur.* ■ informal be in a state of great activity: *the repair shops are humming as the tradesmen set about their various tasks.*
2 Brit. informal smell unpleasant: *when the wind drops this stuff really hums.*
▶ **noun** [in sing.] a low, steady continuous sound: *the hum of insects* | *a low hum of conversation.*
■ an unwanted low-frequency noise in an amplifier caused by variation of electric current, especially the alternating frequency of the mains.
– PHRASES **hum and haw** (or **ha**) Brit. hesitate; be indecisive.
– DERIVATIVES **hummable** adjective, **hummer** noun.
– ORIGIN late Middle English: imitative.

hum[2] ▶ **exclamation** used to express hesitation or dissent.
– ORIGIN mid 16th cent.: imitative; related to the verb **HUM**[1].

human ▶ **adjective** of, relating to, or characteristic of humankind or people: *the human body* | *the survival of the human race.*
■ of or characteristic of people as opposed to God or animals or machines, especially in being susceptible to weaknesses: *they are only human and therefore mistakes do occur* | *the risk of human error.* ■ of or characteristic of people's better qualities, such as kindness or sensitivity: *the human side of politics is getting stronger.* ■ Zoology of or belonging to the genus *Homo*.
▶ **noun** a human being, especially a person as distinguished from an animal or (in science fiction) an alien.
– DERIVATIVES **humanness** noun.
– ORIGIN late Middle English *humaine*, from Old French *humain(e)*, from Latin *humanus*, from *homo* 'man, human being'. The present spelling became usual in the 18th cent.; compare with **HUMANE**.

human being ▶ **noun** a man, woman, or child of the species *Homo sapiens*, distinguished from other animals by superior mental development, power of articulate speech, and upright stance.

human capital ▶ **noun** [mass noun] the skills, knowledge, and experience possessed by an individual or population, viewed in terms of their value or cost to an organization or country.

human chain ▶ **noun** a line of people formed for passing things quickly from one site to another.

■a line or circle of people linking hands in a protest or demonstration.

humane /hjʊ'meɪn/ ▶ adjective **1** having or showing compassion or benevolence: *regulations ensuring the humane treatment of animals.*
■inflicting the minimum of pain: *humane methods of killing.*
2 formal (of a branch of learning) intended to have a civilizing or refining effect on people.
– DERIVATIVES **humanely** adverb, **humaneness** noun.
– ORIGIN late Middle English: the earlier form of **HUMAN**, restricted to the senses above in the 18th cent.

humane killer ▶ noun Brit. an instrument for the painless slaughter of animals.

human engineering ▶ noun [mass noun] the management of industrial labour, especially as regards relationships between people and machines.

Human Genome Project an international project to chart the entire genetic material of a human being, the first draft of which was completed in 2000.

human geography ▶ noun [mass noun] the branch of geography dealing with how human activity affects or is influenced by the earth's surface.

human interest ▶ noun [mass noun] the aspect of a story in the media that interests people because it describes the experiences or emotions of individuals to which others can relate.

humanism ▶ noun [mass noun] an outlook or system of thought attaching prime importance to human rather than divine or supernatural matters. Humanist beliefs stress the potential value and goodness of human beings, emphasize common human needs, and seek solely rational ways of solving human problems.
■(often **Humanism**) a Renaissance cultural movement which turned away from medieval scholasticism and revived interest in ancient Greek and Roman thought. ■(among some contemporary writers) a system of thought criticized as being centred on the notion of the rational, autonomous self and ignoring the unintegrated and conditioned nature of the individual.
– DERIVATIVES **humanist** noun & adjective, **humanistic** adjective, **humanistically** adverb.

humanitarian /hjʊˌmanɪˈtɛːrɪən/ ▶ adjective concerned with or seeking to promote human welfare: *groups sending humanitarian aid | a humanitarian organization.*
▶ noun a person who seeks to promote human welfare; a philanthropist.
– DERIVATIVES **humanitarianism** noun.

USAGE Sentences such as *this is the worst humanitarian disaster this country has seen* are a loose use of the adjective **humanitarian** to mean 'human'. This use is quite common, especially in journalism, but is not generally considered good style.

humanity ▶ noun (pl. **-ies**) [mass noun] **1** the human race; human beings collectively: *appalling crimes against humanity.*
■the fact or condition of being human; human nature: *the humanity of Christ.*
2 humaneness; benevolence: *he praised them for their standards of humanity, care, and dignity.*
3 (**humanities**) learning or literature concerned with human culture, especially literature, history, art, music, and philosophy.
– ORIGIN Middle English: from Old French *humanite*, from Latin *humanitas*, from *humanus* (see **HUMAN**).

humanize (also **-ise**) ▶ verb [with obj.] **1** make (something) more humane or civilized: *his purpose was to humanize prison conditions.*
2 give (something) a human character.
– DERIVATIVES **humanization** noun.
– ORIGIN early 17th cent.: from French *humaniser*, from Latin *humanus* (see **HUMAN**).

humankind ▶ noun [mass noun] human beings considered collectively (used as a neutral alternative to 'mankind'): *the origin of humankind.*

humanly ▶ adverb **1** from a human point of view; in a human manner: *they can grow both humanly and spiritually.*
■by human means; within human ability: *we did all that was humanly possible.*
2 chiefly archaic with human feeling or kindness.

human nature ▶ noun [mass noun] the general psychological characteristics, feelings, and behavioural traits of humankind, regarded as

shared by all humans: *he had a poor opinion of human nature.*

humanoid /ˈhjuːmənɔɪd/ ▶ adjective having an appearance or character resembling that of a human.
▶ noun (especially in science fiction) a being resembling a human in its shape.

human relations ▶ plural noun relations with or between people, particularly the treatment of people in a professional context.

human resources ▶ plural noun the personnel of a business or organization, especially when regarded as a significant asset.

human right ▶ noun (usu. **human rights**) a right which is believed to belong justifiably to every person: *a flagrant disregard for basic human rights.*

human shield ▶ noun a person or group of people held near a potential target to deter attack.

Humber /ˈhʌmbə/ an estuary in NE England. It is formed at the junction of the Rivers Ouse and Trent, near Goole, and flows 60 km (38 miles) eastwards to enter the North Sea at Spurn Head. It has the major port of Hull on its north bank and is spanned by the world's second-largest suspension bridge, opened in 1981 and having a span of 1,410 m (4,626 ft).
■a shipping forecast area covering an area of the North Sea off eastern England, extending roughly from north Norfolk to Flamborough Head.

Humberside a former county of NE England, formed in 1974 from parts of the East and West Ridings of Yorkshire and the northern part of Lincolnshire. It was dissolved in 1996.

humble ▶ adjective (**humbler**, **humblest**) **1** having or showing a modest or low estimate of one's own importance: *I felt very humble when meeting her.*
■(of an action or thought) offered with or affected by such an estimate of one's own importance: *my humble apologies.*
2 of low social, administrative, or political rank: *she came from a humble, unprivileged background.*
■(of a thing) of modest pretensions or dimensions: *he built the business empire from humble beginnings.*
▶ verb [with obj.] lower (someone) in dignity or importance: *I knew he had humbled himself to ask for my help.*
■(usu. **be humbled**) decisively defeat (another team or competitor, typically one which was previously thought to be superior).
– PHRASES **eat humble pie** make a humble apology and accept humiliation. [ORIGIN: *humble pie* is from a pun based on **UMBLES** 'offal', considered inferior food.] **my humble abode** used to refer to one's home with an ironic or humorous show of modesty or humility. **your humble servant** archaic or humorous used at the end of a letter or as a form of ironic courtesy: *your most humble servant, George Porter.*
– DERIVATIVES **humbleness** noun, **humbly** adverb.
– ORIGIN Middle English: from Old French, from Latin *humilis* 'low, lowly', from *humus* 'ground'.

humble-bee ▶ noun another term for **BUMBLEBEE**.
– ORIGIN late Middle English: probably from Middle Low German *hummelbē*, from *hummel* 'to buzz' + *bē* 'bee'.

Humboldt /ˈhʌmbɒlt/, Friedrich Heinrich Alexander, Baron von (1769–1859), German explorer and scientist. He travelled in Central and South America (1799–1804) and wrote on natural history, meteorology, and physical geography.

Humboldt Current another name for **PERUVIAN CURRENT**.

humbug ▶ noun **1** [mass noun] deceptive or false talk or behaviour: *his comments are sheer humbug.*
■[count noun] a hypocrite: *you see what a humbug I am.*
2 Brit. a boiled sweet, especially one flavoured with peppermint.
▶ verb (**humbugged**, **humbugging**) [with obj.] deceive; trick: *poor Dave is easily humbugged.*
■[no obj.] dated act like a fraud or sham.
– DERIVATIVES **humbuggery** noun.
– ORIGIN mid 18th cent. (in the senses 'hoax, trick' and 'deceiver'): of unknown origin.

humdinger /hʌmˈdɪŋə/ ▶ noun informal a remarkable or outstanding person or thing of its kind: *a humdinger of a funny story.*
– ORIGIN early 20th cent. (originally US): of unknown origin.

humdrum ▶ adjective lacking excitement or variety; dull; monotonous: *humdrum routine work.*

▶ noun [mass noun] dullness; monotony: *an escape from the humdrum of his life.*
– ORIGIN mid 16th cent.: probably a reduplication of **HUM**[1].

Hume /hjuːm/, David (1711–76), Scottish philosopher, economist, and historian. He rejected the possibility of certainty in knowledge and claimed that all the data of reason stem from experience. Notable works: *A Treatise of Human Nature* (1739–40) and *History of England* (1754–62).
– DERIVATIVES **Humean** /ˈhjuːmɪən/ adjective & noun.

humectant /hjʊˈmɛkt(ə)nt/ ▶ adjective retaining or preserving moisture.
▶ noun a substance, especially a skin lotion or a food additive, used to reduce the loss of moisture.
– ORIGIN early 19th cent. (denoting a moistening agent): from Latin *humectant-* 'moistening', from the verb *humectare*, from *humectus* 'moist, wet', from *humere* 'be moist'.

humeral /ˈhjuːm(ə)r(ə)l/ ▶ adjective [attrib.] **1** of or relating to the humerus of a human or other vertebrate: *a humeral fracture.*
■Entomology of, relating to, or in the region of the humerus of an insect: *a humeral lobe.*
2 (in Catholic use) denoting a plain vestment worn around the shoulders when administering the sacrament.
– ORIGIN late 16th cent.: from French, or from late Latin *humeralis*, from Latin *humerus* (see **HUMERUS**).

humerus /ˈhjuːm(ə)rəs/ ▶ noun (pl. **humeri** /-rʌɪ/) Anatomy the bone of the upper arm or forelimb, forming joints at the shoulder and the elbow.
■Entomology a structure in an insect involving, or in the region of, the front basal corners of the wings or wing cases.
– ORIGIN late Middle English: from Latin, 'shoulder'.

humic /ˈhjuːmɪk/ ▶ adjective [attrib.] relating to or consisting of humus: *humic acids.*

humid /ˈhjuːmɪd/ ▶ adjective marked by a relatively high level of water vapour in the atmosphere: *a hot and humid day.*
– DERIVATIVES **humidly** adverb.
– ORIGIN late Middle English: from French *humide* or Latin *humidus*, from *humere* 'be moist'.

humidifier ▶ noun a device for keeping the atmosphere moist in a room.

humidify ▶ verb (**-ies**, **-ied**) [with obj.] [often as adj. **humidified**] increase the level of moisture in (air).
– DERIVATIVES **humidification** noun.

humidistat /hjʊˈmɪdɪstat/ ▶ noun a machine or device which automatically regulates the humidity of the air in a room or building.

humidity ▶ noun (pl. **-ies**) [mass noun] the state or quality of being humid.
■a quantity representing the amount of water vapour in the atmosphere or a gas: *the temperature is seventy-seven, the humidity in the low thirties.* ■atmospheric moisture.
– ORIGIN late Middle English: from Old French *humidite* or Latin *humiditas*, from *humidus* (see **HUMID**).

humidor /ˈhjuːmɪdɔː/ ▶ noun an airtight container for keeping cigars or tobacco moist.
– ORIGIN early 20th cent.: from **HUMID**, on the pattern of *cuspidor*.

humify /ˈhjuːmɪfʌɪ/ ▶ verb (**-ies**, **-ied**) [with obj.] convert (plant remains) into humus.
– DERIVATIVES **humification** noun.

humiliate ▶ verb [with obj.] make (someone) feel ashamed and foolish by injuring their dignity and self-respect, especially publicly: *you'll humiliate me in front of the whole school!* | [as adj. **humiliating**] *a humiliating election defeat.*
– DERIVATIVES **humiliatingly** adverb, **humiliation** noun, **humiliator** noun.
– ORIGIN mid 16th cent. (in the sense 'bring low'): from late Latin *humiliat-* 'made humble', from the verb *humiliare*, from *humilis* (see **HUMBLE**). The current sense dates from the mid 18th cent.

humility ▶ noun [mass noun] a modest or low view of one's own importance; humbleness.
– ORIGIN Middle English: from Old French *humilite*, from Latin *humilitas*, from *humilis* (see **HUMBLE**).

Humint /ˈhjuːmɪnt/ ▶ noun [mass noun] covert intelligence-gathering by agents or others.
– ORIGIN late 20th cent.: from *human intelligence*.

hummel /ˈhʌm(ə)l/ Scottish & N. English ▶ adjective (of a cow or stag) lacking horns or antlers.

▶ **noun** a stag which has failed to grow antlers, typically as a result of malnutrition when young.
– ORIGIN late 15th cent. (describing grain in the sense 'awnless'): related to Low German *hummel*, *hommel* 'hornless animal'.

hummingbird ▶ **noun** a small nectar-feeding tropical American bird that is able to hover and fly backwards, and typically has colourful iridescent plumage.
• Family Trochilidae: many genera and numerous species.
– ORIGIN mid 17th cent.: so named because of the humming sound produced by the rapid vibration of the bird's wings.

hummingbird hawkmoth ▶ **noun** a migratory day-flying hawkmoth that makes an audible hum while hovering in front of flowers to feed on nectar.
• *Macroglossum stellatarum*, family Sphingidae.

hummock ▶ **noun** a hillock, knoll, or mound.
■ a hump or ridge in an ice field. ■ N. Amer. a piece of forested ground rising above a marsh.
– DERIVATIVES **hummocky** adjective.
– ORIGIN mid 16th cent. (originally in nautical use denoting a small hillock on the coast): of unknown origin.

hummus /ˈhʊməs/ (also **hoummos** or **humous**) ▶ **noun** [mass noun] a thick paste or spread made from ground chickpeas and sesame seeds, olive oil, lemon, and garlic, made originally in the Middle East.
– ORIGIN from Arabic *ḥummuṣ*.

humongous /hjuːˈmʌŋɡəs/ (also **humungous**) ▶ **adjective** informal huge; enormous: *a humongous steak.*
– ORIGIN 1970s (originally US): possibly based on **HUGE** and **MONSTROUS**, influenced by the stress pattern of *stupendous*.

humor ▶ **noun** US spelling of **HUMOUR**.

humoral /ˈhjuːm(ə)r(ə)l/ ▶ **adjective** Medicine of or relating to the body fluids, especially with regard to immune responses involving antibodies in body fluids as distinct from cells (see **CELL-MEDIATED**).
■ historical of or relating to the four bodily humours. ■ Medicine, historical (of diseases) caused by or attributed to a disordered state of body fluids or (formerly) the bodily humours.
– ORIGIN late Middle English (in the general sense 'relating to bodily fluids'): from Old French, or from medieval Latin *humoralis*, from Latin *humor* 'moisture' (see **HUMOUR**).

humoresque /ˌhjuːməˈrɛsk/ ▶ **noun** a short, lively piece of music.
– ORIGIN late 19th cent.: from German *Humoreske*, from *Humor* 'humour'.

humorist ▶ **noun** a humorous writer, performer, or artist.

humorous ▶ **adjective** causing light-hearted laughter and amusement; comic: *a humorous and entertaining talk.*
■ having or showing a sense of humour: *his humorous grey eyes.*
– DERIVATIVES **humorously** adverb, **humorousness** noun.

humour (US **humor**) ▶ **noun** [mass noun] **1** the quality of being amusing or comic, especially as expressed in literature or speech: *his tales are full of humour.*
■ the ability to perceive or express humour or to appreciate a joke: *their inimitable brand of humour* | *she has a great **sense of humour**.*
2 a mood or state of mind: *her **good humour** vanished* | *the clash hadn't improved his humour.*
■ [count noun] archaic an inclination or whim.
3 (also **cardinal humour**) [count noun] historical each of the four chief fluids of the body (blood, phlegm, yellow bile (choler), and black bile (melancholy)) that were thought to determine a person's physical and mental qualities by the relative proportions in which they were present.
▶ **verb** [with obj.] comply with the wishes of (someone) in order to keep them content, however unreasonable such wishes might be: *she was always humouring him to prevent trouble.*
■ archaic adapt or accommodate oneself to (something).
– PHRASES **out of humour** in a bad mood.
– DERIVATIVES **humourless** adjective, **humourlessly** adverb, **humourlessness** noun.
– ORIGIN Middle English: via Old French from Latin *humor* 'moisture', from *humere* (see **HUMID**). The original sense was 'bodily fluid' (surviving in *aqueous humour* and *vitreous humour*, fluids in the eyeball); it was used specifically for any of the cardinal humours (sense 3), whence 'mental disposition' (thought to be caused by the relative proportions of the humours). This led, in the 16th cent., to the senses 'state of mind, mood' (sense 2) and 'whim, fancy', hence *to humour someone* 'to indulge a person's whim'. Sense 1 dates from the late 16th cent.

humous /ˈhjuːməs/ ▶ **noun** variant spelling of **HUMMUS**.

hump ▶ **noun** a rounded protuberance found on the back of a camel or other animal or as an abnormality on a person's back.
■ a rounded raised mass of earth or land. ■ a mound over which railway vehicles are pushed so as to run by gravity over points to the required place in a marshalling yard.
▶ **verb 1** [with obj. and adverbial of direction] informal lift or carry (a heavy object) with difficulty: *he continued to hump cases up and down the hotel corridor.*
2 [with obj.] make hump-shaped.
3 [no obj.] vulgar slang have sexual intercourse.
– PHRASES **get** (or **have**) **the hump** Brit. informal become or be annoyed or irritated. **over the hump** over the worst or most difficult part of something.
– DERIVATIVES **humped** adjective *a humped back*, **humpless** adjective, **humpy** adjective (**humpier**, **humpiest**).
– ORIGIN early 18th cent.: probably related to Low German *humpe* 'hump', also to Dutch *homp*, Low German *humpe* 'lump, hunk (of bread)'.

humpback ▶ **noun 1** (also **humpback whale**) a baleen whale which has a hump (instead of a dorsal fin) and long white flippers. It is noted for its lengthy vocalizations or 'songs'.
• *Megaptera novaeangliae*, family Balaenopteridae.
2 (also **humpback salmon**) a small salmon with dark spots on the back, native to the North Pacific and introduced into the NW Atlantic. Also called **PINK SALMON**.
• *Oncorhynchus gorbuscha*, family Salmonidae.
3 another term for **HUNCHBACK**.
– DERIVATIVES **humpbacked** adjective.

humpback bridge ▶ **noun** Brit. a small road bridge with a steep ascent and descent.

Humperdinck /ˈhʌmpədɪŋk, ˈhʊm-/, Engelbert (1854–1921), German composer. Influenced by Wagner, he is remembered as the composer of the opera *Hänsel und Gretel* (1893).

humph ▶ **exclamation** used to express slightly scornful doubt or dissatisfaction.
– ORIGIN natural utterance: first recorded in English in the mid 16th cent.

humpty-dumpty ▶ **noun** (pl. **-ies**) informal **1** a fat, rotund person.
2 a person or thing that once overthrown cannot be restored.
– ORIGIN late 18th cent.: from the egg-like nursery-rhyme character *Humpty-Dumpty*, who fell off a wall and could not be put together again.

humungous ▶ **adjective** variant spelling of **HUMONGOUS**.

humus /ˈhjuːməs/ ▶ **noun** [mass noun] the organic component of soil, formed by the decomposition of leaves and other plant material by soil micro-organisms.
– ORIGIN late 18th cent.: from Latin, 'soil'.

Humvee /ˈhʌmviː/ ▶ **noun** trademark, chiefly N. Amer. a modern military jeep.
– ORIGIN late 20th cent.: alteration, from the initials of *high-mobility multi-purpose vehicle*.

Hun ▶ **noun 1** a member of a warlike Asiatic nomadic people who invaded and ravaged Europe in the 4th–5th centuries.
■ a reckless or uncivilized destroyer of something.
2 informal, derogatory a German (especially in military contexts during the First and Second World Wars).
■ (**the Hun**) Germans collectively.
– DERIVATIVES **Hunnish** adjective.
– ORIGIN Old English *Hūne*, *Hūnas* (plural), from late Latin *Hunni*, from Greek *Hounnoi*, of Middle Iranian origin.

Hunan /huːˈnan/ a province of east central China; capital, Changsha.

hunch ▶ **verb** [with obj.] raise (one's shoulders) and bend the top of one's body forward: *he thrust his hands in his pockets, hunching his shoulders* | [no obj.] *he **hunched over** his glass.*
■ [no obj.] bend one's body into a huddled position: *I **hunched up** as small as I could.*
▶ **noun 1** a feeling or guess based on intuition rather than known facts: *she was acting **on a hunch**.*
2 a humped position or thing: *the hunch of his back.*
3 chiefly dialect a thick piece; a hunk: *a **hunch of** bread.*
– ORIGIN late 15th cent.: of unknown origin. The original meaning was 'push, shove' (noun and verb), a sense retained now in Scots as a noun, and in US dialect as a verb. Sense 1 of the noun derives probably from a US sense of the verb 'nudge someone in order to draw attention to something'.

hunchback ▶ **noun** a back deformed by a sharp forward angle, forming a hump, typically caused by collapse of a vertebra.
■ often offensive a person with such a deformity.
– DERIVATIVES **hunchbacked** adjective.

hundred ▶ **cardinal number** (pl. **hundreds** or (with numeral or quantifying word) **hundred**) (**a/one hundred**) the number equivalent to the product of ten and ten; ten more than ninety; 100: *a hundred yards away* | *there are just a hundred of us here.* (Roman numeral: **c** or **C**.)
■ (**hundreds**) the numbers from one hundred to 999: *an unknown number, probably in the hundreds, had already been lost.* ■ (**hundreds**) several hundred things or people: *it cost hundreds of pounds.* ■ (usu. **hundreds**) informal an unspecified large number: *hundreds of letters poured in.* ■ (**the —— hundreds**) the years of a specified century: *the early nineteen hundreds.* ■ one hundred years old: *you must be over a hundred!* ■ one hundred miles per hour. ■ Cricket a batsman's score of a hundred runs or more. ■ (chiefly in spoken English) used to express whole hours in the twenty-four-hour system: *twelve hundred hours.*
▶ **noun** Brit. historical a subdivision of a county or shire, having its own court: *Wantage Hundred.*
– PHRASES **a** (or **one**) **hundred per cent** entirely; completely: *I'm not a hundred per cent sure.* ■ [usu. with negative] informal completely fit and healthy: *she did not feel one hundred per cent.* ■ informal maximum effort and commitment: *he always gave one hundred per cent for United.*
– DERIVATIVES **hundredfold** adjective & adverb, **hundredth** ordinal number.
– ORIGIN late Old English, from *hund* 'hundred' (from an Indo-European root shared with Latin *centum* and Greek *hekaton*) + a second element meaning 'number'; of Germanic origin and related to Dutch *honderd* and German *hundert*. The noun sense 'subdivision of a county' is of uncertain origin: it may originally have been equivalent to a hundred hides of land (see **HIDE**[3]).

Hundred Flowers a period of debate in China 1956–7, when, under the slogan 'Let a hundred flowers bloom and a hundred schools of thought contend', citizens were invited to voice their opinions of the communist regime. It was forcibly ended after social unrest and fierce criticism of the government, with those who had voiced their opinions being prosecuted.

hundreds and thousands ▶ **plural noun** Brit. tiny sugar beads of varying colours used for decorating cakes and desserts.

hundredweight (abbrev.: **cwt.**) ▶ **noun** (pl. same or **-weights**) a unit of weight equal to one twentieth of an imperial or metric ton, in particular:
■ (also **long hundredweight**) Brit. equal to 112 lb avoirdupois (about 50.8 kg). ■ (also **short hundredweight**) US equal to 100 lb (about 45.4 kg). ■ (also **metric hundredweight**) equal to 50 kg.

Hundred Years War a war between France and England, conventionally dated 1337–1453.

The war consisted of a series of conflicts in which successive English kings attempted to dominate France and included an early string of English military successes, most notably Crécy and Poitiers. In 1415 England, under Henry V, delivered a crushing victory at Agincourt and occupied much of northern France, but, with the exception of Calais, all English conquests had been lost by 1453.

hung past and past participle of **HANG**. ▶ **adjective 1** (of an elected body) having no political party with an overall majority: *a hung parliament.*
■ (of a jury) unable to agree on a verdict.
2 [predic.] (**hung up**) informal emotionally confused or disturbed: *people are hung up in all sorts of ways.*
■ (**hung up about/on**) have a psychological or emotional obsession or problem about: *guys are so hung up about the way they look.*
3 [predic.] informal used especially in similes to refer to the size of a man's penis.

Hungarian /hʌŋˈɡɛːrɪən/ ▶ **adjective** of or relating to Hungary, its people, or their language.
▶ **noun 1** a native or national of Hungary.
■ a person of Hungarian descent.
2 [mass noun] the official language of Hungary, spoken also by some 2.5 million people in Romania. Hungarian is a Finno-Ugric language and is the only major language of the Ugric branch. Also called **MAGYAR**.
– ORIGIN from medieval Latin *Hungarī* (a name given to the Hungarians, who called themselves the Magyar) + **-AN**.

Hungary a country in central Europe; pop. 10,600,000 (est. 1990); official language, Hungarian; capital, Budapest. Hungarian name **MAGYARORSZÁG**.

Hungary was conquered by the Habsburgs in the 17th century, becoming an equal partner in the Austro-Hungarian empire in 1867. Following the collapse of the empire in 1918, Hungary became an independent kingdom. After participation in the Second World War on the Axis side, Hungary was occupied by the USSR, and became a communist state. A liberal reform movement was crushed by Soviet troops in 1956, but the communist system was abandoned in 1989.

– ORIGIN from medieval Latin *Hungaria* (see also **HUNGARIAN**).

hunger ▶ **noun** [mass noun] a feeling of discomfort or weakness caused by lack of food, coupled with the desire to eat: *she was faint with hunger.*
■ a severe lack of food: *they died from cold and hunger.* ■ a strong desire or craving: *her* ***hunger for*** *knowledge.*
▶ **verb** [no obj.] **1** (**hunger after/for**) have a strong desire or craving for: *all actors hunger for such a role.*
2 archaic feel or suffer hunger through lack of food.
– ORIGIN Old English *hungor* (noun), *hyngran* (verb), of Germanic origin; related to Dutch *honger* and German *Hunger.*

hunger march ▶ **noun** a march undertaken by a group of people in protest against unemployment or poverty, especially any of those by unemployed workers in Britain during the 1920s and 1930s.
– DERIVATIVES **hunger marcher** noun.

hunger strike ▶ **noun** a prolonged refusal to eat, carried out as a protest, typically by a prisoner.
– DERIVATIVES **hunger striker** noun.

hung-over ▶ **adjective** suffering from a hangover after drinking alcohol.

hungry ▶ **adjective** (**hungrier**, **hungriest**) feeling or displaying the need for food: *I was feeling ravenously hungry | children with hungry looks on their faces.*
■ [attrib.] causing hunger: *I always find art galleries hungry work.* ■ having a strong desire or craving: *a party* ***hungry for*** *power* | [in combination] *grasping, power-hungry individuals.* ■ Austral. mean.
– DERIVATIVES **hungrily** adverb, **hungriness** noun.
– ORIGIN Old English *hungrig*, of West Germanic origin; related to Dutch *hongerig*, German *hungrig*, also to **HUNGER**.

hunk ▶ **noun 1** a large piece of something, especially one of food cut or broken off a larger piece: ***a hunk of*** *bread.*
2 informal a sexually attractive man, especially a large, strong one.
– DERIVATIVES **hunky** adjective (**hunkier**, **hunkiest**).
– ORIGIN early 19th cent.: probably of Dutch or Low German origin.

hunker ▶ **verb** [no obj.] squat or crouch down low: *he* ***hunkered down*** *beside her.*
■ figurative apply oneself seriously to a task: *students* ***hunkered down*** *to prepare for the examinations.*
– ORIGIN early 18th cent.: probably related to Dutch *huiken* and German *hocken.*

hunkers ▶ **plural noun** informal haunches: *sitting on his hunkers.*
– ORIGIN mid 18th cent. (originally Scots): from **HUNKER**.

hunky-dory ▶ **adjective** informal fine; going well: *everything is hunky-dory.*
– ORIGIN mid 19th cent. (originally US): *hunky* from Dutch *honk* 'home, base' (in games); the origin of *dory* is unknown.

Hunt, (William) Holman (1827–1910), English painter, one of the founders of the Pre-Raphaelite Brotherhood. He painted biblical scenes with extensive use of symbolism. Notable works: *The Light of the World* (1854) and *The Scapegoat* (1855).

hunt ▶ **verb 1** [with obj.] pursue and kill (a wild animal) for sport or food: *in the autumn they hunted deer* | [no obj.] *they hunted and fished.*
■ chiefly Brit. pursue (a wild animal, especially a fox or deer) on horseback using hounds. ■ Brit. use (a hound or a horse) for hunting. ■ (of an animal) chase and kill (its prey): *mice are hunted by weasels and foxes* | [no obj.] *lionesses hunt in groups.* ■ [no obj.] try to find someone or something by searching carefully: *he desperately* ***hunted for*** *a new job.* ■ (**hunt something out/up**) search for something until it is found. ■ [with obj.] (of the police) search for (a criminal): *the gang is being hunted by police* | [no obj.] *police are* ***hunting for*** *her attacker.* ■ (**hunt someone down**) pursue and capture someone.
2 [no obj.] (of a machine, instrument needle, or system) oscillate about a desired speed, position, or state.
■ (of an aircraft or rocket) oscillate about a mean flight path.
3 [no obj.] (**hunt down/up**) (in change-ringing) move the place of a bell in a simple progression.
▶ **noun 1** an act of hunting wild animals or game.
■ an association of people who meet regularly to hunt, especially with hounds. ■ an area where hunting takes place. ■ a search: *police launched a* ***hunt for*** *the killer.*
2 an oscillating motion about a desired speed, position, or state.
– ORIGIN Old English *huntian*, of Germanic origin. The sense in change-ringing dates from the late 17th cent., and is probably based on the idea of the bells pursuing one another; it gave rise to the sense 'oscillate about a desired speed' (late 19th cent.).

hunt-and-peck ▶ **adjective** denoting or using an inexpert form of typing in which only one or two fingers are used: *hunt-and-peck computer users.*

huntaway ▶ **noun** NZ a dog trained to drive sheep forward.

hunted ▶ **adjective** being pursued or searched for: *they ran like hunted hares.*
■ appearing worn or harassed as if one is being pursued: *his eyes had a hunted look.*

Hunter, John (1728–93), Scottish anatomist, regarded as a founder of scientific surgery. He also made valuable investigations in pathology, physiology, dentistry, and biology.

hunter ▶ **noun 1** a person or animal that hunts: *a deer hunter.*
■ a person searching for something: *a bargain hunter.* ■ a horse of a breed developed for stamina in fox-hunting and ability to jump obstacles. ■ (**the Hunter**) the constellation Orion.
2 a watch with a hinged cover protecting the glass.

hunter-gatherer ▶ **noun** a member of a nomadic people who live chiefly by hunting and fishing, and harvesting wild food.

hunter-killer ▶ **adjective** (of a naval vessel, especially a submarine) equipped to locate and destroy enemy vessels, especially other submarines.

hunter's moon ▶ **noun** the first full moon after a harvest moon.

hunting ▶ **noun** [mass noun] **1** the activity of hunting wild animals or game, especially for food or sport.
2 (also **plain hunting**) Bell-ringing a simple system of changes in which bells move through the order in a regular progression.

hunting box ▶ **noun** Brit. historical a small house or lodge used by hunters.

hunting crop (also **hunting whip**) ▶ **noun** a short rigid riding whip with a handle at right angles to the stock and a long leather thong, used chiefly in hunting.

hunting dog ▶ **noun 1** (also **Cape hunting dog**) an African wild dog that has a dark coat with pale markings and a white-tipped tail, living and hunting in packs.
● *Lycaon pictus*, family Canidae. Alternative name: **African wild dog.**
2 a dog of a breed developed for hunting.

Huntingdon[1] a town in Cambridgeshire, on the River Ouse; pop. 17,600 (1981).

Huntingdon[2], Selina Hastings, Countess of (1707–91), English religious leader; born *Selina Shirley.* She was instrumental in introducing Methodism to the upper classes and established many chapels and a training college for ministers.

Huntingdonshire a former county of SE England. It became part of Cambridgeshire in 1974.

hunting ground ▶ **noun** a place used or suitable for hunting.
■ figurative a place where people can observe or acquire what they want: *the circuit is a favourite hunting ground for talent scouts.*

hunting horn ▶ **noun** a straight horn blown to give signals during hunting.

hunting pink ▶ **noun** see **PINK**[1] (sense 1).

Huntington a city in West Virginia, on the Ohio River; pop. 54,840 (1990).

Huntington Beach a city on the Pacific coast, to the south of Long Beach, in southern California; pop. 181,520 (1990). It is noted as a surfing locality.

Huntington's chorea ▶ **noun** [mass noun] a hereditary disease marked by degeneration of the brain cells and causing chorea and progressive dementia.
– ORIGIN late 19th cent.: named after George *Huntington* (1851–1916), the American neurologist who first described it.

hunting whip ▶ **noun** another term for **HUNTING CROP**.

huntress ▶ **noun** a woman who hunts.

hunt saboteur ▶ **noun** a person who attempts to disrupt a hunt.

huntsman ▶ **noun** (pl. **-men**) a person who hunts.
■ a hunt official in charge of hounds.

Huntsville a city in northern Alabama; pop. 159,790 (1990).

hunyak /ˈhʌnjak/ ▶ **noun** N. Amer. informal, derogatory a person of Hungarian or central European origin, especially an immigrant.
– ORIGIN early 20th cent.: alteration of **HUNGARIAN**, on the pattern of *Polack.*

Huon pine /ˈhjuːɒn/ ▶ **noun** a tall Tasmanian conifer which has yew-like berries and fragrant red timber.
● *Dacrydium franklinii*, family Podocarpaceae.
– ORIGIN early 19th cent.: from *Huon*, the name of a river in the south of Tasmania.

Hupeh /huːˈpeɪ/ variant of **HUBEI**.

hurdle ▶ **noun 1** an upright frame, typically one of a series, which athletes in a race must jump over.
■ (**hurdles**) a hurdle race: *the 100 m hurdles.*
2 an obstacle or difficulty: *there are many hurdles to overcome.*
3 a portable rectangular frame strengthened with withies or wooden bars, used as a temporary fence.
■ a horse race over a series of such frames: *a handicap hurdle.* ■ Brit. historical a frame on which traitors were dragged to execution.
▶ **verb 1** [no obj.] [often as noun **hurdling**] take part in a race that involves jumping hurdles.
■ [with obj.] jump over (a hurdle or other obstacle) while running.
2 [with obj.] enclose or fence off with hurdles.
– ORIGIN Old English *hyrdel* 'temporary fence', of Germanic origin; related to Dutch *horde* and German *Hürde.*

hurdler ▶ **noun** an athlete, dog, or horse that runs in hurdle races.

hurdy-gurdy /ˈhəːdɪˌɡəːdi/ ▶ **noun** (pl. **-ies**) a musical instrument with a droning sound played by turning a handle, which is typically attached to a rosined wheel sounding a series of drone strings, with keys worked by the left hand.
■ informal a barrel organ.
– ORIGIN mid 18th cent.: probably imitative of the sound of the instrument.

hurl ▶ **verb** [with obj. and adverbial of direction] throw (an object) with great force: *rioters hurled a brick through the windscreen of a car.*
■ push or impel (someone) violently: *she was hurled against the car* | figurative *he hurled himself into the job with enthusiasm.* ■ utter (abuse) vehemently: *the demonstrators hurled abuse at councillors.* ■ [no obj.] informal vomit: *it made me want to hurl.*
▶ **noun** Scottish informal a ride in a vehicle; a lift.
– ORIGIN Middle English: probably imitative, but corresponding in form and partly in sense with Low German *hurreln.*

hurler ▶ **noun 1** N. Amer. informal a baseball pitcher.
2 a player of hurling.

Hurler's syndrome /ˈhəːləz/ ▶ **noun** [mass noun] Medicine a defect in metabolism arising from congenital absence of an enzyme, causing accumulation of lipids and mucopolysaccharides, and resulting in mental retardation, a protruding abdomen, and bone deformities including an abnormally large head. Also called **GARGOYLISM**.
– ORIGIN 1930s: named after Gertrud *Hurler* (1889–1965), the Austrian paediatrician who first described it.

hurley ▶ **noun** a stick used in the game of hurling.

a cat | ɑː arm | ɛ bed | ɛː hair | ə ago | əː her | ɪ sit | i cosy | iː see | ɒ hot | ɔː saw | ʌ run | ʊ put | uː too | ʌɪ my | aʊ how | eɪ day | əʊ no | ɪə near | ɔɪ boy | ʊə poor | ʌɪə fire | aʊə sour

■[mass noun] another term for **HURLING**.
– ORIGIN early 19th cent.: from the verb **HURL**.

hurling ▶ **noun** [mass noun] an Irish game resembling hockey, played with a shorter stick with a broader oval blade. It is the national game of Ireland and may date back to the 2nd millennium BC.

hurly-burly ▶ **noun** [mass noun] busy, boisterous activity: *the hurly-burly of school life.*
– ORIGIN Middle English: reduplication based on **HURL**.

Huron /ˈhjʊərɒn/ ▶ **noun** (pl. same or **Hurons**) **1** a member of a confederation of native North American peoples formerly living in the region east of Lake Huron and now settled mainly in Oklahoma and Quebec.
2 [mass noun] the extinct Iroquoian language of any of these peoples.
▶ **adjective** of or relating to these peoples or their language.
– ORIGIN French, literally 'having hair standing in bristles on the head', from Old French *hure* 'head of a wild boar', of unknown ultimate origin.

Huron, Lake the second largest of the five Great Lakes of North America, on the border between Canada and the US.

h

hurrah (also **hooray**, **hurray**) ▶ **exclamation** used to express joy or approval: *Hurrah! She's here at last!*
▶ **noun** an utterance of the word 'hurrah'.
▶ **verb** [no obj.] shout 'hurrah'.
– ORIGIN late 17th cent.: alteration of archaic *huzza*; perhaps originally a sailors' cry when hauling.

Hurri /ˈhʌri/ ▶ **plural noun** the Hurrian people collectively.
– ORIGIN the name in Hittite and Akkadian.

Hurrian /ˈhʌrɪən/ ▶ **adjective** of, relating to, or denoting an ancient people, originally from Armenia, who settled in Syria and northern Mesopotamia during the 3rd–2nd millennia BC and were later absorbed by the Hittites and Assyrians.
▶ **noun** **1** a member of this people.
2 [mass noun] the language of the Hurrians, written in cuneiform and of unknown affinity (it is not Indo-European or Semitic).

hurricane /ˈhʌrɪk(ə)n, -keɪn/ ▶ **noun** a storm with a violent wind, in particular a tropical cyclone in the Caribbean.
■a wind of force 12 on the Beaufort scale (equal to or exceeding 64 knots or 118 kph). ■ figurative a violent uproar or outburst: *the manager resigned in a hurricane of disagreement.*
– ORIGIN mid 16th cent.: from Spanish *huracán*, probably from Taino *hurakán* 'god of the storm'.

hurricane deck ▶ **noun** a covered deck at or near the top of a ship's superstructure.

hurricane lamp ▶ **noun** an oil lamp with a glass chimney, designed to protect the flame even in high winds.

hurricane tape ▶ **noun** [mass noun] US a strong type of adhesive tape used on windows to keep the glass in place if it is broken by strong winds.

hurroo ▶ **exclamation** & **noun** variant spelling of **HOOROO**.

hurry ▶ **verb** (**-ies**, **-ied**) [no obj.] move or act with great haste: *we'd better hurry* | *servants hurried around.*
■[often in imperative] (**hurry up**) do something more quickly: *hurry up and finish your meal.* ■ [with obj.] cause to move or proceed with haste: *she hurried him across the landing.* ■ [with obj.] (often **be hurried**) do or finish (something) quickly, typically too quickly: *formalities were hurried over* | [as adj. **hurried**] *I ate a hurried breakfast.*
▶ **noun** [mass noun] great haste: *in my hurry to leave I knocked over a pile of books.*
■[with negative and in questions] a need for haste; urgency: *there's no hurry to get back* | *relax, what's the hurry?*
– PHRASES **in a hurry** rushed; in a rushed manner: *I'm in rather a hurry.* ■ eager to get a thing done quickly: *no one seemed in a hurry for the results.* ■ [usu. with negative] informal easily; readily: *an experience you won't forget in a hurry.*
– DERIVATIVES **hurriedly** adverb, **hurriedness** noun.
– ORIGIN late 16th cent. (as a verb): imitative.

hurry scurry archaic ▶ **noun** [mass noun] disorderly haste; confused hurrying.
▶ **adjective** & **adverb** with hurry and confusion.
– ORIGIN mid 18th cent.: reduplication of **HURRY**.

hurry-up ▶ **adjective** [attrib.] US informal showing, involving, or requiring haste or urgency.

hurst ▶ **noun** a hillock.
■a sandbank in the sea or a river. ■ [usu. in place names] a wood or wooded rise: *Cumnor Hurst.*
– ORIGIN Old English *hyrst*, of Germanic origin; related to German *Horst*.

Hurston /ˈhəːst(ə)n/, Zora Neale (1901–60), American novelist. Her novels reflect her interest in folklore, especially that of the Deep South. Notable works: *Jonah's Gourd Vine* (1934) and *Seraph on the Suwanee* (1948).

hurt ▶ **verb** (past and past participle **hurt**) [with obj.] cause physical pain or injury to: *Ow! You're hurting me!* | [no obj.] *does acupuncture hurt?*
■[no obj.] (of a part of the body) suffer pain: *my back hurts.* ■ cause mental pain or distress to (a person or their feelings): *she didn't want to hurt his feelings.* ■ [no obj.] (of a person) feel mental pain or distress: *he was hurting badly, but he smiled through his tears.* ■ be detrimental to: *high interest rates are hurting the local economy.* ■ [no obj.] (**hurt for**) US informal have a pressing need for: *Frank wasn't hurting for money.*
▶ **noun** [mass noun] physical injury; harm.
■mental pain or distress: *the hurt of being constantly ignored* | [count noun] *wariness that masked a hurt.*
– ORIGIN Middle English (originally in the senses 'to strike' and 'a blow'): from Old French *hurter* (verb), *hurt* (noun), perhaps ultimately of Germanic origin.

hurtful ▶ **adjective** causing distress to someone's feelings: *his hurtful remarks.*
– DERIVATIVES **hurtfully** adverb, **hurtfulness** noun.

hurtle ▶ **verb** [no obj., with adverbial of direction] move at a great speed, typically in a wildly uncontrolled manner: *a runaway car hurtled towards them.*
■[with obj. and adverbial of direction] cause to move in such a way.
– ORIGIN Middle English (in the sense 'strike against, collide with'): frequentative of **HURT**.

Husain variant spelling of **HUSSEIN**[2], **HUSSEIN**[3].

Husák /ˈhuːsak/, Gustáv (1913–91), Czechoslovak statesman, leader of the Communist Party of Czechoslovakia 1969–87 and President 1975–89. He succeeded Alexander Dubček following the Prague Spring of 1968 and purged the party of its reformist elements.

husband ▶ **noun** a married man considered in relation to his wife: *she and her husband are both retired.*
▶ **verb** [with obj.] use (resources) economically: *the need to husband his remaining strength.*
– DERIVATIVES **husbander** noun (rare), **husbandhood** noun, **husbandless** adjective, **husbandly** adjective.
– ORIGIN late Old English (in the senses 'male head of a household' and 'manager, steward', from Old Norse *húsbóndi* 'master of a house', from *hús* 'house' + *bóndi* 'occupier and tiller of the soil'. The original sense of the verb was 'till, cultivate'.

husbandman ▶ **noun** (pl. **-men**) archaic a person who cultivates the land; a farmer.
– ORIGIN Middle English (originally in northern English use denoting the holder of a *husbandland*, i.e. manorial tenancy): from **HUSBAND** in the obsolete sense 'farmer' + **MAN**.

husbandry ▶ **noun** [mass noun] **1** the care, cultivation, and breeding of crops and animals: *crop husbandry.*
2 management and conservation of resources.
– ORIGIN Middle English: from **HUSBAND** in the obsolete sense 'farmer' + **-RY**; compare with **HUSBANDMAN**.

hush ▶ **verb** [with obj.] make (someone) be quiet or stop talking: *he placed a finger before pursed lips to hush her.*
■[no obj., often in imperative] be quiet: *Hush! Someone will hear you.* ■ (**hush something up**) suppress public mention of something: *management took steps to hush up the dangers.*
▶ **noun** [in sing.] a silence: *a hush descended over the crowd.*
– ORIGIN mid 16th cent.: back-formation from obsolete *husht* 'silent, hushed' (taken to be a past participle), from an interjection *husht* 'quiet!'.

hushaby (also **hushabye**) ▶ **exclamation** archaic used to lull a child.

hushed ▶ **adjective** having a calm and still silence: *he addressed the hushed courtroom.*
■(of a voice or conversation) quiet and serious.

hush-hush ▶ **adjective** informal (especially of an official plan or project) highly secret or confidential: *a hush-hush research unit.*

hush money ▶ **noun** [mass noun] informal money paid to someone to prevent them from disclosing embarrassing or discreditable information.

hush puppy ▶ **noun** [mass noun] US maize bread which has been quickly deep-fried.

husk[1] ▶ **noun** the dry outer covering of some fruits or seeds.
■a dry or rough outer layer or coating, especially when it is empty of its contents: *the husks of dead bugs* | figurative *he had sapped her strength and left her a used-up husk.*
▶ **verb** [with obj.] remove the husk or husks from.
– ORIGIN late Middle English: probably from Low German *hūske* 'sheath', literally 'little house'.

husk[2] ▶ **noun** [mass noun] **1** bronchitis in cattle, sheep, or swine caused by parasitic infestation, typically marked by a husky cough.
2 huskiness: *the husk in her voice.*
▶ **verb** [with direct speech] say something in a husky voice: *'What big blue eyes you have,' husked Lorenzo.*
– ORIGIN early 18th cent.: partly from **HUSKY**[1], partly from the earlier verb *husk* '(of a farm animal) cough'.

husky[1] ▶ **adjective** (**huskier**, **huskiest**) **1** (of a voice or utterance) sounding low-pitched and slightly hoarse.
2 strong; hefty: *Paddy looked a husky, strong guy.*
3 like or consisting of a husk or husks.
– DERIVATIVES **huskily** adverb, **huskiness** noun.

husky[2] ▶ **noun** (pl. **-ies**) a powerful dog of a breed with a thick double coat which is typically grey, used in the Arctic for pulling sledges.
– ORIGIN mid 19th cent. (originally denoting the Eskimo language or an Eskimo): abbreviation of obsolete *Ehuskemay* or Newfoundland dialect *Huskemaw* 'Eskimo', probably from Montagnais (see **ESKIMO**). The term replaced the 18th-cent. term *Eskimo dog*.

Huss /hʌs/, John (*c.*1372–1415), Bohemian religious reformer; Czech name *Jan Hus*. A rector of Prague University, he supported the views of Wyclif, attacked ecclesiastical abuses, and was excommunicated in 1411. He was later tried and burnt at the stake. See also **HUSSITE**.

huss /hʌs/ ▶ **noun** Brit. a dogfish, especially the nurse hound (also called **BULL HUSS**).
• Genus *Scyliorhinus*, family Scyliorhinidae.
– ORIGIN Middle English *husk*, of unknown origin.

hussar /hʊˈzɑː/ ▶ **noun** historical a soldier in a light cavalry regiment which had adopted a dress uniform modelled on that of the Hungarian hussars (now only in titles): *the Queens Royal Irish Hussars.*
■(in the 15th century) a Hungarian light horseman.
– ORIGIN from Hungarian *huszár*, from Old Serbian *husar*, from Italian *corsaro* (see **CORSAIR**).

Hussein[1], Abdullah ibn, see **ABDULLAH IBN HUSSEIN**.

Hussein[2] /hʊˈseɪn/ (also **Husain**), ibn Talal (1935–99), king of Jordan from 1953. Throughout his reign Hussein sought to maintain good relations both with the West and with other Arab nations, but his moderate policies created problems with Palestinian refugees from Israel within Jordan. During the Gulf War he supported Iraq, but in 1994 he signed a treaty normalizing relations with Israel.

Hussein[3] /hʊˈseɪn/ (also **Husain**), Saddam (b.1937), Iraqi President, Prime Minister, and head of the armed forces since 1979; full name *Saddam bin Hussein at-Takriti*. During his presidency Iraq fought a war with Iran (1980–8) and invaded Kuwait (1990), from which Iraqi forces were expelled in the Gulf War of 1991. He also ordered punitive attacks on Kurdish rebels in the north of Iraq and on the Marsh Arabs in the south.

Husserl /ˈhʊsəːl, German ˈhʊsɐl/, Edmund (Gustav Albrecht) (1859–1938), German philosopher. His work forms the basis of the school of phenomenology; he rejected metaphysical assumptions about what actually exists, and explanations of why it exists, in favour of pure subjective consciousness as the condition for all experience, with the world as the object of this consciousness.

Hussite /ˈhʌsʌɪt/ ▶ **noun** a member or follower of the religious movement begun by John Huss. After Huss's execution the Hussites took up arms against the Holy Roman Empire and demanded a set of reforms that anticipated the Reformation. Most of the demands were granted (1436), and a Church

was established that remained independent of the Roman Catholic Church until 1620.
▶ **adjective** of or relating to the Hussites.
– DERIVATIVES **Hussitism** noun.

hussy ▶ **noun** (pl. **-ies**) an impudent or immoral girl or woman: *that brazen little hussy!*
– ORIGIN late Middle English: contraction of **HOUSEWIFE** (the original sense); the current sense dates from the mid 17th cent.

hustings ▶ **noun** (pl. same) a meeting at which candidates in an election address potential voters.
■ the campaigning associated with an election: *the Chancellor did not perform well at the hustings.*
– ORIGIN late Old English *husting* 'deliberative assembly, council', from Old Norse *hústhing* 'household assembly held by a leader', from *hús* 'house' + *thing* 'assembly, parliament'; *hustings* was applied in Middle English to the highest court of the City of London, presided over by the Recorder of London. Subsequently it denoted the platform in the Guildhall where the Lord Mayor and aldermen presided, and (early 18th cent.) a temporary platform on which parliamentary candidates were nominated; hence the sense 'electoral proceedings'.

hustle ▶ **verb 1** [with obj.] push roughly; jostle: *they were hissed and hustled as they went in.*
■ [with obj. and adverbial of direction] force (someone) to move hurriedly or unceremoniously in a specified direction: *I was hustled away to a cold cell.* ■ [no obj., with adverbial of direction] push one's way; bustle: *Stockwell hustled into the penalty area.*
2 [with obj.] informal, chiefly N. Amer. obtain by forceful action or persuasion.
■ (**hustle someone into**) coerce or pressure someone into doing or choosing something. ■ sell aggressively: *he hustled his company's oil around the country.* ■ steal; swindle: *Linda hustled money from men she met.*
3 [no obj.] N. Amer. informal engage in prostitution.
▶ **noun 1** [mass noun] busy movement and activity: *the **hustle and bustle** of the big cities.*
2 N. Amer. informal a fraud or swindle.
– PHRASES **hustle one's butt** (or vulgar slang **ass**) N. Amer. informal move or act quickly.
– ORIGIN late 17th cent. (originally in the sense 'shake, toss'): from Middle Dutch *hutselen*. The senses 'sell aggressively', 'swindle' were adopted from US usage. Sense 3 dates from the early 20th cent.

hustler ▶ **noun** informal, chiefly N. Amer. an enterprising and often dishonest person, especially one trying to sell something.
■ a prostitute.

Huston /ˈhjuːst(ə)n/, John (1906–87), American-born film director, an Irish citizen from 1964. He made his debut as a film director in 1941 with *The Maltese Falcon*. Other notable films: *The African Queen* (1951) and *Prizzi's Honor* (1985).

hut ▶ **noun** a small single-storey building of simple or crude construction, serving as a poor, rough, or temporary house or shelter.
▶ **verb** (**hutted**, **hutting**) [with obj.] provide with huts: [as adj. **hutted**] *a hutted encampment.*
– DERIVATIVES **hut-like** adjective.
– ORIGIN mid 16th cent. (in the sense 'temporary wooden shelter for troops'): from French *hutte*, from Middle High German *hütte*.

hutch ▶ **noun 1** a box or cage, typically with a wire mesh front, for keeping rabbits, ferrets, or other small domesticated animals: *a rabbit hutch.*
2 N. Amer. a storage chest.
■ a cupboard or dresser typically with open shelves above.
– ORIGIN Middle English: from Old French *huche*, from medieval Latin *hutica*, of unknown origin. The original sense was 'storage chest', surviving in North American usage (sense 2).

hutia /hʌˈtiːə/ ▶ **noun** a rodent resembling a cavy, with short legs and tail, found only in the Caribbean.
• Family Capromyidae: two genera, in particular *Capromys*, and several species, some of which are now extinct.
– ORIGIN mid 16th cent.: from Spanish, from Taino *huti*, *cuti*.

hutment ▶ **noun** Military an encampment of huts.

Hutterite /ˈhʌtərʌɪt/ ▶ **noun** a member of either an Anabaptist Christian sect established in Moravia in the early 16th century, or a North American community holding similar beliefs and practising a very old-fashioned communal way of life.
▶ **adjective** of or relating to Hutterites or their beliefs and practices.
– ORIGIN from the name of Jacob Hutter (died 1536), a Moravian Anabaptist, + **-ITE**[1].

Hutton[1], James (1726–97), Scottish geologist. Although controversial at the time, his description of the processes that have shaped the surface of the earth is now accepted as showing that it is very much older than had previously been believed.

Hutton[2], Sir Leonard (1916–90), English cricketer. He played for Yorkshire (1934–55) and for England (1937–55), scoring a record 364 in the 1938 test against Australia.

Hutu /ˈhuːtuː/ ▶ **noun** (pl. same or **Hutus** or **Bahutu** /bəˈhuːtuː/) a member of a Bantu-speaking people forming the majority population in Rwanda and Burundi. They are traditionally a farming people, and were historically dominated by the Tutsi people; the antagonism between the peoples led in 1994 to large-scale ethnic violence, especially in Rwanda.
▶ **adjective** of or relating to this people.
– ORIGIN a local name.

Huxley[1] /ˈhʌksli/, Aldous (Leonard) (1894–1963), English novelist and essayist. After writing *Antic Hay* (1923) and *Brave New World* (1932), in 1937 he moved to California, where in 1953 he experimented with psychedelic drugs, writing of his experiences in *The Doors of Perception* (1954).

Huxley[2] /ˈhʌksli/, Andrew Fielding (b.1917), English physiologist, the grandson of Thomas Henry Huxley. He worked with Sir Alan Hodgkin on the physiology of nerve transmission.

Huxley[3] /ˈhʌksli/, Sir Julian (1887–1975), English biologist, the grandson of Thomas Henry Huxley. He studied animal behaviour and was a notable interpreter of science to the public.

Huxley[4] /ˈhʌksli/, Thomas Henry (1825–95), English biologist. A surgeon and leading supporter of Darwinism, he coined the word *agnostic* to describe his own beliefs. Notable works: *Man's Place in Nature* (1863).

Huygens[1] /ˈhʌɪgənz/ , Christiaan (1629–95), Dutch physicist, mathematician, and astronomer. His wave theory of light enabled him to explain reflection and refraction. He also patented a pendulum clock, improved the lenses of his telescope, discovered a satellite of Saturn, and recognized the nature of Saturn's rings, which had eluded Galileo.

Huygens[2] a European space probe which is part of the Cassini spacecraft, due to detach from the orbiter and land on Saturn's moon Titan in 2004.

Huygens eyepiece ▶ **noun** Optics a simple eyepiece consisting of two separate planoconvex lenses, used chiefly in refracting telescopes of long focal length.

huzza /hʊˈzɑː/ (also **huzzah**) archaic ▶ **exclamation** used to express approval or delight.
▶ **verb** (**huzzaed**, **huzzaing**) [no obj.] cry 'huzza'.
– ORIGIN late 16th cent.: perhaps used originally as a sailor's cry when hauling.

Hwange /ˈhwaŋgi/ a town in western Zimbabwe; pop. 39,000 (1982). Nearby is the Hwange National Park, established as a game reserve in 1928. Former name (until 1982) **WANKIE**.

HWM ▶ **abbreviation for** high-water mark.

hwyl /ˈhuːɪl/ ▶ **noun** [mass noun] (in Welsh use) a stirring feeling of emotional motivation and energy.
– ORIGIN Welsh.

hyacinth /ˈhʌɪəsɪnθ/ ▶ **noun 1** a bulbous plant of the lily family, with strap-like leaves and a compact spike of bell-shaped fragrant flowers. Native to western Asia, hyacinths are cultivated outdoors and as house plants.
• Genus *Hyacinthus*, family Liliaceae: several species, in particular *H. orientalis*, from which the common large-flowered cultivars are derived.
■ [mass noun] a light purplish-blue colour typical of some hyacinth flowers.
2 another term for **JACINTH**.
– DERIVATIVES **hyacinthine** /-ˈsɪnθiːn, -θʌɪn/ adjective.
– ORIGIN mid 16th cent. (denoting a gem): from French *hyacinthe*, via Latin from Greek *huakinthos*, denoting any of various plants identified with the flower in the myth of **HYACINTHUS**, and a gem (perhaps the sapphire). The current sense dates from the late 16th cent.

Hyacinthus /ˌhʌɪəˈsɪnθəs/ Greek Mythology a beautiful boy whom the god Apollo loved but killed accidentally with a discus. From his blood Apollo caused the hyacinth to spring up.

Hyades /ˈhʌɪədiːz/ Astronomy an open star cluster in the constellation Taurus, appearing to surround the bright star Aldebaran.
– ORIGIN from Greek *Huades*, by folk etymology from *huein* 'to rain', but perhaps from *hus* 'pig', the Latin name of the constellation being *Suculae* 'little pigs'.

hyaena ▶ **noun** variant spelling of **HYENA**.

hyalin /ˈhʌɪəlɪn/ ▶ **noun** [mass noun] Physiology a clear substance produced especially by the degeneration of epithelial or connective tissues.
– ORIGIN mid 19th cent.: via Latin from Greek *hualinos*, from *hualos* 'glass'.

hyaline /ˈhʌɪəlɪn, -iːn, -ʌɪn/ ▶ **adjective** Anatomy & Zoology having a glassy, translucent appearance.
■ relating to, consisting of, or characterized by hyaline material.
▶ **noun 1** (**the hyaline**) poetic/literary a thing that is clear and translucent like glass, especially a smooth sea or a clear sky.
2 another term for **HYALIN**.
– ORIGIN mid 17th cent.: from Latin *hyalinus* (see **HYALIN**).

hyaline cartilage ▶ **noun** [mass noun] a translucent bluish-white type of cartilage present in the joints, the respiratory tract, and the immature skeleton.

hyaline membrane disease ▶ **noun** [mass noun] a condition in newborn babies in which the lungs are deficient in surfactant, which prevents their proper expansion and causes the formation of hyaline material in the lung spaces. Also called **RESPIRATORY DISTRESS SYNDROME**.

hyalite /ˈhʌɪəlʌɪt/ ▶ **noun** [mass noun] a translucent, colourless variety of opal.
– ORIGIN late 18th cent.: from Greek *hualos* 'glass' + **-ITE**[1].

hyaloid /ˈhʌɪəlɔɪd/ ▶ **adjective** Anatomy glassy; transparent.
– ORIGIN mid 19th cent.: from French *hyaloïde*, or via late Latin from Greek *hualoeidēs* 'like glass', from *hualos* 'glass'.

hyaloid membrane ▶ **noun** a thin transparent membrane enveloping the vitreous humour of the eye.

hyaluronic acid /ˌhʌɪəljʊəˈrɒnɪk/ ▶ **noun** [mass noun] Biochemistry a viscous fluid carbohydrate present in connective tissue, synovial fluid, and the humours of the eye.
– DERIVATIVES **hyaluronate** noun.
– ORIGIN 1930s: *hyaluronic* from a blend of **HYALOID** and **URONIC ACID**.

hybrid /ˈhʌɪbrɪd/ ▶ **noun** a thing made by combining two different elements; a mixture: *the final text is a **hybrid** of the stage play and the film.*
■ Biology the offspring of two plants or animals of different species or varieties, such as a mule: *a hybrid of wheat and rye.* ■ offensive a person of mixed racial or cultural origin. ■ a word formed from elements taken from different languages, for example *television* (*tele-* from Greek, *vision* from Latin).
▶ **adjective** of mixed character; composed of mixed parts: *Mexico's hybrid post-conquest culture.*
■ bred as a hybrid from different species or varieties: *a hybrid variety | hybrid offspring.*
– DERIVATIVES **hybridism** noun, **hybridity** noun.
– ORIGIN early 17th cent. (as a noun): from Latin *hybrida* 'offspring of a tame sow and wild boar, child of a freeman and slave, etc.'

hybridize (also **-ise**) ▶ **verb** [with obj.] cross-breed (individuals of two different species or varieties).
■ [no obj.] (of an animal or plant) breed with an individual of another species or variety.
– DERIVATIVES **hybridizable** adjective, **hybridization** noun.

hybrid vigour ▶ **noun** [mass noun] Genetics the tendency of a cross-bred individual to show qualities superior to those of both parents. Also called **HETEROSIS**.

hydantoin /hʌɪˈdantəʊɪn/ ▶ **noun** Chemistry a crystalline compound present in sugar beet and used in the manufacture of some anticonvulsant drugs.
• A cyclic derivative of urea; chem. formula: $C_3H_4N_2O_2$.
– ORIGIN mid 19th cent.: from Greek *hudōr* 'water' + *allantoic* (see **ALLANTOIS**) + **-IN**[1].

hydathode /ˈhʌɪdəθəʊd/ ▶ **noun** Botany a modified

pore, especially on a leaf, which exudes drops of water.
– ORIGIN late 19th cent.: from Greek *hudōr, hudat-* 'water' + *hodos* 'way'.

hydatid /ˈhʌɪdətɪd/ ▸ noun Medicine a cyst containing watery fluid.
■ such a cyst formed by and containing a tapeworm larva. ■ a tapeworm larva.
– ORIGIN late 17th cent.: from modern Latin *hydatis*, from Greek *hudatis, hudatid-* 'watery vesicle', from *hudōr, hudat-* 'water'.

hydatidiform mole /ˌhʌɪdəˈtɪdɪfɔːm/ ▸ noun Medicine a cluster of fluid-filled sacs formed in the womb by the degeneration of chorionic tissue around an aborting embryo.

Hyde[1], Edward, see CLARENDON.

Hyde[2], Mr, see JEKYLL[1].

Hyde Park the largest British royal park, in west central London. It contains the Serpentine, Marble Arch, the Albert Memorial, and Speakers' Corner.

Hyderabad /ˈhʌɪdərəbad/ **1** a city in central India, capital of the state of Andhra Pradesh; pop. 3,005,000 (1991).
2 a former large princely state of south central India, divided in 1956 between Maharashtra, Mysore, and Andhra Pradesh.
3 a city in SE Pakistan, in the province of Sind, on the River Indus; pop. 1,000,000 (est. 1991).

hydr- ▸ combining form variant spelling of HYDRO- shortened before a vowel (as in *hydraulic*).

Hydra /ˈhʌɪdrə/ **1** Greek Mythology a many-headed snake whose heads grew again as they were cut off, killed by Hercules.
■ [as noun **hydra**] a thing which is hard to overcome or resist because of its pervasive or enduring quality or its many aspects.
2 Astronomy the largest constellation (the Water Snake or Sea Monster), said to represent the beast slain by Hercules. Its few bright stars are close to the celestial equator. Compare with HYDRUS.
■ [as genitive **Hydrae** /ˈhʌɪdriː/] used with preceding letter or numeral to designate a star in this constellation: *the star Beta Hydrae.*
– ORIGIN via Latin from Greek *hudra.*

hydra ▸ noun a minute freshwater coelenterate with a stalk-like tubular body and a ring of tentacles around the mouth.
● Genus *Hydra,* class Hydrozoa.
– ORIGIN via Latin from Greek *hudra* 'water snake' (see HYDRA), named by Linnaeus because, if cut into pieces, each section can grow into a whole animal.

hydramnios /hʌɪˈdramnɪɒs/ ▸ noun [mass noun] Medicine a condition in which excess amniotic fluid accumulates during pregnancy.

hydrangea /hʌɪˈdreɪn(d)ʒə/ ▸ noun a shrub or climbing plant with rounded or flattened flowering heads of small florets, native to Asia and America.
● Genus *Hydrangea,* family Hydrangeaceae: many species, in particular the **common hydrangea** (*H. macrophylla*), with flowers that are typically blue, but often pink on alkaline soils.
– ORIGIN modern Latin, from Greek *hudro-* 'water' + *angeion* 'vessel' (from the cup shape of its seed capsule).

hydrant /ˈhʌɪdr(ə)nt/ ▸ noun a water pipe, especially one in a street, with a nozzle to which a fire hose can be attached.
– ORIGIN early 19th cent. (originally US): formed irregularly from HYDRO- 'relating to water' + -ANT.

hydrate ▸ noun /ˈhʌɪdreɪt/ Chemistry a compound, typically a crystalline one, in which water molecules are chemically bound to another compound or an element.
▸ verb /hʌɪˈdreɪt/ [with obj.] cause to absorb water.
■ Chemistry combine chemically with water molecules: [as adj. **hydrated**] *hydrated silicate crystals.*
– DERIVATIVES **hydratable** adjective, **hydration** noun, **hydrator** noun.
– ORIGIN early 19th cent.: coined in French from Greek *hudōr* 'water'.

hydraulic /hʌɪˈdrɔːlɪk, hʌɪˈdrɒlɪk/ ▸ adjective
1 denoting, relating to, or operated by a liquid moving in a confined space under pressure: *hydraulic fluid* | *hydraulic lifting gear.*
2 of or relating to the science of hydraulics.
3 (of cement) hardening under water.
– DERIVATIVES **hydraulically** adverb.
– ORIGIN early 17th cent.: via Latin from Greek *hudraulikos,* from *hudro-* 'water' + *aulos* 'pipe'.

hydraulic fracturing ▸ noun [mass noun] the forcing open of fissures in subterranean rocks by introducing liquid at high pressure, especially to extract oil or gas.

hydraulic ram ▸ noun an automatic pump in which a large volume of water flows through a valve which it periodically forces shut, the sudden pressure change being used to raise a smaller volume of water to a higher level.

hydraulics ▸ plural noun **1** [usu. treated as sing.] the branch of science and technology concerned with the conveyance of liquids through pipes and channels, especially as a source of mechanical force or control.
2 hydraulic systems, mechanisms, or forces.

hydrazine /ˈhʌɪdrəziːn/ ▸ noun [mass noun] Chemistry a colourless volatile alkaline liquid with powerful reducing properties, used in chemical synthesis and in some kinds of rocket fuels.
● Chem. formula: N_2H_4.
– ORIGIN late 19th cent.: from HYDROGEN + AZO- + -INE[4].

hydria /ˈhʌɪdrɪə/ ▸ noun (pl. **hydriae** or **hydriai**) Archaeology an ancient Greek pitcher with three handles.
– ORIGIN via Latin from Greek *hudria.*

hydric /ˈhʌɪdrɪk/ ▸ adjective Ecology (of an environment or habitat) containing plenty of moisture; very wet. Compare with MESIC[1] and XERIC.
– ORIGIN early 20th cent.: from HYDRO- + -IC.

hydride /ˈhʌɪdrʌɪd/ ▸ noun [mass noun] Chemistry a binary compound of hydrogen with a metal.

hydriodic acid /ˌhʌɪdrɪˈɒdɪk, -ʌɪˈɒdɪk/ ▸ noun [mass noun] Chemistry a strongly acidic solution of the gas hydrogen iodide in water.
● Chem. formula: HI.
– ORIGIN early 19th cent.: *hydriodic* from a blend of HYDROGEN and IODINE.

hydro ▸ noun (pl. **-os**) **1** Brit. a hotel or clinic originally providing hydropathic treatment.
2 a hydroelectric power plant.
■ [mass noun] hydroelectricity. ■ Canadian electricity.
– ORIGIN late 19th cent.: abbreviation.

hydro- (also **hydr-**) ▸ combining form **1** water; relating to water: *hydraulic* | *hydrocolloid.*
■ Medicine affected with an accumulation of serous fluid: *hydrocephalus.*
2 Chemistry combined with hydrogen: *hydrocarbon.*
– ORIGIN from Greek *hudōr* 'water'.

hydrobromic acid /ˌhʌɪdrə(ʊ)ˈbrəʊmɪk/ ▸ noun [mass noun] Chemistry a strongly acidic solution of the gas hydrogen bromide in water.
● Chem. formula: HBr.

hydrocarbon ▸ noun Chemistry a compound of hydrogen and carbon, such as any of those which are the chief components of petroleum and natural gas.

hydrocele /ˈhʌɪdrə(ʊ)siːl/ ▸ noun [mass noun] Medicine the accumulation of serous fluid in a body sac.

hydrocephalus /ˌhʌɪdrə(ʊ)ˈsɛf(ə)ləs, -ˈkɛf-/ ▸ noun [mass noun] Medicine a condition in which fluid accumulates in the brain, typically in young children, enlarging the head and sometimes causing brain damage.
– DERIVATIVES **hydrocephalic** adjective, **hydrocephaly** noun.
– ORIGIN late 17th cent.: modern Latin, from Greek *hudrokephalon,* from *hudro-* 'water' + *kephalē* 'head'.

hydrochloric acid ▸ noun [mass noun] Chemistry a strongly acidic solution of the gas hydrogen chloride in water.
● Chem. formula: HCl.

hydrochloride ▸ noun Chemistry a compound of a particular organic base with hydrochloric acid: [with modifier] *cocaine hydrochloride.*

hydrochlorofluorocarbon /ˌhʌɪdrəˌklɔːrə(ʊ)ˈfluərə(ʊ)kɑːbən, -ˌflɔːrə(ʊ)-/ (abbrev. **HCFC**) ▸ noun Chemistry any of a class of inert compounds of carbon, hydrogen, chlorine, and fluorine, used in place of CFCs as being somewhat less destructive to the ozone layer.

hydrocolloid /ˌhʌɪdrə(ʊ)ˈkɒlɔɪd/ ▸ noun a substance which forms a gel in the presence of water, examples of which are used in surgical dressings and in various industrial applications.

hydrocortisone ▸ noun [mass noun] Biochemistry a steroid hormone produced by the adrenal cortex

and used medicinally to treat inflammation resulting from eczema and rheumatism.

hydroculture ▸ noun another term for HYDROPONICS.

hydrocyanic acid /ˌhʌɪdrə(ʊ)sʌɪˈanɪk/ ▸ noun [mass noun] Chemistry a highly poisonous acidic solution of hydrogen cyanide in water.

hydrodynamics ▸ plural noun [treated as sing.] the branch of science concerned with forces acting on or exerted by fluids (especially liquids).
– DERIVATIVES **hydrodynamic** adjective, **hydro-dynamical** adjective, **hydrodynamicist** noun.
– ORIGIN late 18th cent.: from modern Latin *hydrodynamica,* from Greek *hudro-* 'water' + *dunamikos* (see DYNAMIC).

hydroelectric ▸ adjective relating to or denoting the generation of electricity using flowing water (typically from a reservoir held behind a dam or barrage) to drive a turbine which powers a generator.
– DERIVATIVES **hydroelectricity** noun.

hydrofluoric acid /ˌhʌɪdrə(ʊ)ˈflʊərɪk/ ▸ noun [mass noun] Chemistry an acidic, extremely corrosive, solution of the liquid hydrogen fluoride in water.
● Chem. formula: HF.

hydrofluorocarbon /ˌhʌɪdrə(ʊ)ˈflʊərə(ʊ)ˌkɑːb(ə)n, -ˈflɔː-/ (abbrev.: **HFC**) ▸ noun Chemistry any of a class of partly chlorinated and fluorinated hydrocarbons, used as an alternative to CFCs in foam production, refrigeration, and other processes.

hydrofoil ▸ noun a boat whose hull is fitted underneath with shaped vanes (foils) which lift the hull clear of the water at speed.
■ another term for FOIL[4].
– ORIGIN 1920s: from HYDRO- 'relating to water', on the pattern of *aerofoil.*

hydrofracturing ▸ noun another term for HYDRAULIC FRACTURING.

hydrogel ▸ noun a gel in which the liquid component is water.

hydrogen /ˈhʌɪdrədʒ(ə)n/ ▸ noun [mass noun] a colourless, odourless, highly flammable gas, the chemical element of atomic number 1. (Symbol: **H**)

Hydrogen is the lightest of the chemical elements and has the simplest atomic structure, a single electron orbiting a nucleus consisting of a single proton. It is by far the commonest element in the universe, although not on the earth, where it occurs chiefly combined with oxygen as water.

– DERIVATIVES **hydrogenous** /-ˈdrɒdʒɪnəs/ adjective.
– ORIGIN late 18th cent.: coined in French from Greek *hudro-* 'water' + *-genēs* (see -GEN).

hydrogenase /hʌɪˈdrɒdʒəneɪz/ ▸ noun [usu. with modifier] Biochemistry an enzyme which catalyses the reduction of a particular substance by hydrogen.

hydrogenate /hʌɪˈdrɒdʒəneɪt, ˈhʌɪdrədʒəneɪt/ ▸ verb [with obj.] [often as adj. **hydrogenated**] charge with or cause to combine with hydrogen.
– DERIVATIVES **hydrogenation** noun.

hydrogen bomb ▸ noun an immensely powerful bomb whose destructive power comes from the rapid release of energy during the nuclear fusion of isotopes of hydrogen (deuterium and tritium), using an atom bomb as a trigger.

hydrogen bond ▸ noun Chemistry a weak bond between two molecules resulting from an electrostatic attraction between a proton in one molecule and an electronegative atom in the other.

hydrogen cyanide ▸ noun [mass noun] Chemistry a highly poisonous gas or volatile liquid with an odour of bitter almonds, made by the action of acids on cyanides.
● Chem. formula: HCN.

hydrogen peroxide ▸ noun [mass noun] Chemistry a colourless viscous unstable liquid with strong oxidizing properties, used in some disinfectants and bleaches.
● Chem. formula: H_2O_2.

hydrogen sulphide ▸ noun [mass noun] Chemistry a colourless poisonous gas with a smell of bad eggs, made by the action of acids on sulphides.
● Chem. formula: H_2S.

hydrogeology ▸ noun [mass noun] the branch of geology concerned with water occurring underground or on the surface of the earth.
– DERIVATIVES **hydrogeological** adjective, **hydrogeologist** noun.

hydrography /hʌɪˈdrɒɡrəfi/ ▸ noun [mass noun] the

science of surveying and charting bodies of water, such as seas, lakes, and rivers.
– DERIVATIVES **hydrographer** noun, **hydrographic** adjective, **hydrographical** adjective, **hydrographically** adverb.

hydroid /ˈhʌɪdrɔɪd/ Zoology ▶ noun a coelenterate of an order which includes the hydras. They are distinguished by the dominance of the polyp phase.
● Order Hydroida, class Hydrozoa.
▶ adjective of or relating to coelenterates of this group.
■ another term for **POLYPOID** (in sense 1).
– ORIGIN mid 19th cent.: from **HYDRA** + **-OID**.

hydrolase /ˈhʌɪdrəleɪz/ ▶ noun [usu. with modifier] Biochemistry an enzyme that catalyses the hydrolysis of a particular substrate.

hydrology ▶ noun [mass noun] the branch of science concerned with the properties of the earth's water, and especially its movement in relation to land.
– DERIVATIVES **hydrologic** adjective, **hydrological** adjective, **hydrologically** adverb, **hydrologist** noun.

hydrolysate /hʌɪˈdrɒlɪseɪt/ ▶ noun Chemistry a substance produced by hydrolysis.

hydrolyse /ˈhʌɪdrəlʌɪz/ (also **hydrolyze**) ▶ verb [with obj.] Chemistry break down (a compound) by chemical reaction with water.
■ [no obj.] undergo this process.

hydrolysis /hʌɪˈdrɒlɪsɪs/ ▶ noun [mass noun] Chemistry the chemical breakdown of a compound due to reaction with water.
– DERIVATIVES **hydrolytic** adjective.

hydromagnetics ▶ plural noun another term for **MAGNETOHYDRODYNAMICS**.
– DERIVATIVES **hydromagnetic** adjective.

hydromassage ▶ noun [mass noun] massage using jets of water, as a health or beauty treatment.

hydromechanics ▶ plural noun [treated as sing.] the mechanics of liquids; hydrodynamics, especially in relation to mechanical applications.
– DERIVATIVES **hydromechanical** adjective.

hydromedusa /ˌhʌɪdrəʊmɪˈdjuːzə/ ▶ noun (pl. **hydromedusae**) Zoology the medusoid phase of a hydroid coelenterate.

hydromel /ˈhʌɪdrəmel/ ▶ noun [mass noun] historical a drink similar to mead, made with fermented honey and water.
– ORIGIN late Middle English: from Latin, from Greek hudromeli, from hudro- 'water' + meli 'honey'.

hydrometeor ▶ noun Meteorology an atmospheric phenomenon or entity involving water or water vapour, such as rain or a cloud.

hydrometer /hʌɪˈdrɒmɪtə/ ▶ noun an instrument for measuring the density of liquids.
– DERIVATIVES **hydrometric** adjective, **hydrometry** noun.

hydronic /hʌɪˈdrɒnɪk/ ▶ adjective denoting a cooling or heating system in which heat is transported using circulating water.

hydronium ion /hʌɪˈdrəʊnɪəm/ ▶ noun Chemistry another term for **HYDROXONIUM ION**.
– ORIGIN early 20th cent.: hydronium, from German (a contraction).

hydropathy /hʌɪˈdrɒpəθi/ ▶ noun [mass noun] the treatment of illness through the use of water, either internally or through external means such as steam baths (not now a part of orthodox medicine). Compare with **HYDROTHERAPY**.
– DERIVATIVES **hydropathic** adjective, **hydropathist** noun.
– ORIGIN mid 19th cent.: from **HYDRO-** 'of water', on the pattern of allopathy and homeopathy.

hydrophilic /ˌhʌɪdrə(ʊ)ˈfɪlɪk/ ▶ adjective having a tendency to mix with, dissolve in, or be wetted by water. The opposite of **HYDROPHOBIC**.
– DERIVATIVES **hydrophilicity** noun.

hydrophilous /hʌɪˈdrɒfɪl(ə)s/ ▶ adjective Botany (of a plant) water-pollinated.
– DERIVATIVES **hydrophily** noun.

hydrophobia /ˌhʌɪdrə(ʊ)ˈfəʊbɪə/ ▶ noun [mass noun] extreme or irrational fear of water, especially as a symptom of rabies in humans.
■ rabies, especially in humans.
– ORIGIN late Middle English: via late Latin from Greek hudrophobia, from hudro- 'water' + phobos 'fear'.

hydrophobic ▶ adjective 1 tending to repel or fail to mix with water. The opposite of **HYDROPHILIC**.

2 of or suffering from hydrophobia.
– DERIVATIVES **hydrophobicity** noun.

hydrophone ▶ noun a microphone which detects sound waves under water.

hydrophyte ▶ noun Botany a plant which grows only in or on water.
– DERIVATIVES **hydrophytic** adjective.

hydroplane ▶ noun 1 a light fast motor boat designed to skim over the surface of water.
2 a fin-like attachment which enables a moving submarine to rise or fall in the water.
3 US a seaplane.
▶ verb chiefly N. Amer. another term for **AQUAPLANE**.

hydroponics /ˌhʌɪdrə(ʊ)ˈpɒnɪks/ ▶ plural noun [treated as sing.] the process of growing plants in sand, gravel, or liquid, with added nutrients but without soil.
– DERIVATIVES **hydroponic** adjective, **hydroponically** adverb.
– ORIGIN 1930s: from **HYDRO-** 'of water' + Greek ponos 'labour' + **-ICS**.

hydropower ▶ noun [mass noun] hydroelectric power.

hydroquinone /ˌhʌɪdrə'kwɪnəʊn/ ▶ noun [mass noun] Chemistry a crystalline compound made by the reduction of benzoquinone.
● Alternative name: **benzene-1,4-diol**; chem. formula: $C_6H_4(OH)_2$.

hydrospeed (also **hydrospeeding**) ▶ noun [mass noun] a sport or leisure activity that involves jumping into fast-flowing white water and being carried along at high speed while buoyed up by a float.

hydrosphere ▶ noun (usu. **the hydrosphere**) all the waters on the earth's surface, such as lakes and seas, and sometimes including water over the earth's surface, such as clouds.

hydrostatic ▶ adjective relating to or denoting the equilibrium of liquids and the pressure exerted by liquid at rest.
– DERIVATIVES **hydrostatical** adjective, **hydrostatically** adverb.
– ORIGIN late 17th cent.: probably from Greek hudrostatēs 'hydrostatic balance', from hudro- 'water' + statikos (see **STATIC**).

hydrostatics ▶ plural noun [treated as sing.] the branch of mechanics concerned with the hydrostatic properties of liquids.

hydrosulphite /ˌhʌɪdrə(ʊ)ˈsʌlfʌɪt/ ▶ noun another term for **DITHIONITE**.

hydrotherapy ▶ noun another term for **HYDROPATHY**.
■ [mass noun] the use of exercises in a pool as part of treatment for conditions such as arthritis or partial paralysis: [as modifier] a hydrotherapy pool.
– DERIVATIVES **hydrotherapist** noun.

hydrothermal ▶ adjective of, relating to, or denoting the action of heated water in the earth's crust.
– DERIVATIVES **hydrothermally** adverb.

hydrothermal vent ▶ noun an opening in the sea floor out of which heated mineral-rich water flows.

hydrothorax ▶ noun [mass noun] the condition of having fluid in the pleural cavity.

hydrotropism /hʌɪˈdrɒtrəpɪz(ə)m/ ▶ noun [mass noun] Botany the growth or turning of plant roots towards or away from moisture.

hydrous ▶ adjective chiefly Chemistry & Geology containing water as a constituent: a hydrous lava flow.
– ORIGIN early 19th cent.: from Greek hudro- 'water' + **-OUS**.

hydroxide ▶ noun Chemistry a compound of a metal with the hydroxide ion OH^- (as in many alkalis) or the group —OH.

hydroxonium ion /ˌhʌɪdrɒkˈsəʊnɪəm/ ▶ noun Chemistry the ion H_3O^+, consisting of a protonated water molecule and present in all aqueous acids.
– ORIGIN 1920s: hydroxonium from **HYDRO-** (relating to hydrogen) + **OXY-**[2] + the suffix -onium (from **AMMONIUM**).

hydroxy- ▶ combining form Chemistry representing **HYDROXYL** or **HYDROXIDE**: hydroxyapatite.

hydroxyapatite /ˌhʌɪdrɒksɪˈapətʌɪt/ ▶ noun [mass noun] a mineral related to apatite which is the main inorganic constituent of tooth enamel and bone, although it is rare in rocks.

hydroxyl /hʌɪˈdrɒksʌɪl, -sɪl/ ▶ noun [as modifier] Chemistry of or denoting the radical —OH, present in alcohols and many other organic compounds: a hydroxyl group.
– ORIGIN mid 19th cent.: from a blend of **HYDROGEN** and **OXYGEN**, + **-YL**.

hydroxylate /hʌɪˈdrɒksɪleɪt/ ▶ verb [with obj.] [often as adj. **hydroxylated**] Chemistry introduce a hydroxyl group into (a molecule or compound).
– DERIVATIVES **hydroxylation** noun.

Hydrozoa /ˌhʌɪdrə(ʊ)ˈzəʊə/ Zoology a class of coelenterates which includes hydras and Portuguese men-of-war. Many of them are colonial and some kinds have both polypoid and medusoid phases.
– DERIVATIVES **hydrozoan** noun & adjective.
– ORIGIN modern Latin (plural), from **HYDRO-** 'water' + Greek zōion 'animal'.

Hydrus /ˈhʌɪdrəs/ Astronomy an inconspicuous southern constellation (the Water Snake), between the star Achernar and the south celestial pole. Compare with **HYDRA** (in sense 2).
■ [as genitive **Hydri** /ˈhʌɪdrʌɪ/] used with preceding letter or numeral to designate a star in this constellation: the star Delta Hydri.
– ORIGIN Latin, from Greek hudros.

hyena (also **hyaena**) ▶ noun a doglike African mammal with forelimbs that are longer than the hindlimbs and an erect mane. Hyenas are noted as scavengers but most are also effective hunters.
● Family Hyaenidae: two genera, in particular Hyaena, and three species.
– ORIGIN Middle English: via Latin from Greek huaina, feminine of hus 'pig' (the transference of the term probably being because the animal's mane was thought to resemble a hog's bristles).

hygiene ▶ noun [mass noun] conditions or practices conducive to maintaining health and preventing disease, especially through cleanliness: poor standards of food hygiene | personal hygiene.
– ORIGIN late 16th cent.: via French from modern Latin hygieina, from Greek hugieinē (tekhnē) '(art) of health', from hugiēs 'healthy'.

hygienic ▶ adjective conducive to maintaining health and preventing disease, especially by being clean; sanitary: hygienic conditions.
– DERIVATIVES **hygienically** adverb.

hygienist ▶ noun a specialist in the promotion of clean conditions for the preservation of health.

hygro- ▶ combining form relating to moisture: hygrometer.
– ORIGIN from Greek hugros 'wet'.

hygrometer /hʌɪˈgrɒmɪtə/ ▶ noun an instrument for measuring the humidity of the air or a gas.
– DERIVATIVES **hygrometric** adjective, **hygrometry** noun.

hygrophilous /hʌɪˈgrɒfɪləs/ ▶ adjective Botany (of a plant) growing in damp conditions.

hygrophyte /ˈhʌɪgrəfʌɪt/ ▶ noun Botany a plant which grows in wet conditions.

hygroscope /ˈhʌɪgrə(ʊ)skəʊp/ ▶ noun an instrument which gives an indication of the humidity of the air.

hygroscopic ▶ adjective (of a substance) tending to absorb moisture from the air.
■ relating to humidity or its measurement.
– DERIVATIVES **hygroscopically** adverb.

hying present participle of **HIE**.

Hyksos /ˈhɪksɒs/ ▶ plural noun a people of mixed Semitic and Asian descent who invaded Egypt and settled in the Nile delta c.1640 BC. They formed the 15th and 16th dynasties of Egypt and ruled a large part of the country until driven out c.1532 BC.
– ORIGIN from Greek Huksōs (interpreted by Manetho as 'shepherd kings' or 'captive shepherds'), from Egyptian heqa khoswe 'foreign rulers'.

hyla /ˈhʌɪlə/ ▶ noun a tree frog of a widespread genus, typically bright green in colour.
● Genus Hyla, family Hylidae: many species.
– ORIGIN modern Latin, from Greek hulē 'timber'.

hylo- ▶ combining form of or relating to matter: hylozoism.
– ORIGIN from Greek hulē 'matter'.

hylomorphism /ˌhʌɪlə(ʊ)ˈmɔːfɪz(ə)m/ ▶ noun [mass noun] Philosophy the doctrine that physical objects result from the combination of matter and form.
– DERIVATIVES **hylomorphic** adjective.
– ORIGIN late 19th cent.: from **HYLO-** 'matter' + Greek morphē 'form'.

hylozoism /ˌhʌɪlə(ʊ)ˈzəʊɪz(ə)m/ ▶ noun [mass noun] Philosophy the doctrine that all matter has life.
– ORIGIN late 17th cent.: from HYLO- 'matter' + Greek zōē 'life'.

hymen /ˈhʌɪmən/ ▶ noun a membrane which partially closes the opening of the vagina and whose presence is traditionally taken to be a mark of virginity.
– DERIVATIVES **hymenal** adjective.
– ORIGIN mid 16th cent.: via late Latin from Greek humēn 'membrane'.

hymeneal /ˌhʌɪmɪˈniːəl/ ▶ adjective poetic/literary of or concerning marriage.
– ORIGIN early 17th cent.: from Latin hymenaeus, from Hymen (from Greek Humēn), the name of the god of marriage, + -AL.

hymenium /hʌɪˈmiːnɪəm/ ▶ noun (pl. **hymenia** /-nɪə/) Botany (in higher fungi) a surface consisting mainly of spore-bearing structures (asci or basidia).
– DERIVATIVES **hymenial** adjective.
– ORIGIN early 19th cent.: from Greek humenion, diminutive of humēn 'membrane'.

Hymenoptera /ˌhʌɪmɪˈnɒpt(ə)rə/ Entomology a large order of insects that includes the bees, wasps, ants, and sawflies. They have four transparent wings and the females typically have a sting.
■ [as plural noun **hymenoptera**] insects of this order.
– DERIVATIVES **hymenopteran** noun & adjective, **hymenopterous** adjective.
– ORIGIN modern Latin (plural), from Greek humenopteros 'membrane-winged', from humēn 'membrane' + pteron 'wing'.

Hymie /ˈhʌɪmi/ ▶ noun US informal an offensive term for a Jewish person.
– ORIGIN 1980s: colloquial abbreviation of the Jewish male given name Hyman.

hymn ▶ noun a religious song or poem, typically of praise to God or a god: a Hellenistic hymn to Apollo.
■ a formal song sung during Christian worship, typically by the whole congregation. ■ a song, text, or other composition praising or celebrating someone or something: the book is a hymn to the glories of the English public school.
▶ verb **1** [with obj.] praise or celebrate (something): Johnson's reply hymns education.
2 [no obj.] rare sing hymns.
– DERIVATIVES **hymnic** /ˈhɪmnɪk/ adjective.
– ORIGIN Old English, via Latin from Greek humnos 'ode or song in praise of a god or hero', used in the Septuagint to translate various Hebrew words, and hence in the New Testament and other Christian writings.

hymnal /ˈhɪmn(ə)l/ ▶ noun a book of hymns.
▶ adjective of hymns: hymnal music.
– ORIGIN late 15th cent.: from medieval Latin hymnale, from Latin hymnus (see HYMN).

hymnary /ˈhɪmnəri/ ▶ noun (pl. **-ies**) another term for HYMNAL.

hymnody /ˈhɪmnədi/ ▶ noun [mass noun] the singing or composition of hymns.
– DERIVATIVES **hymnodist** noun.
– ORIGIN early 18th cent.: via medieval Latin from Greek humnōidia, from humnos 'hymn'.

hymnographer /hɪmˈnɒɡrəfə/ ▶ noun a writer of hymns.
– DERIVATIVES **hymnography** noun.
– ORIGIN early 17th cent.: from Greek humnographos, from humnos 'hymn' + graphos 'writer'.

hymnology /hɪmˈnɒlədʒi/ ▶ noun [mass noun] the study or composition of hymns.
– DERIVATIVES **hymnological** adjective, **hymnologist** noun.
– ORIGIN mid 17th cent.: originally from Greek humnologia 'hymn-singing', the early sense until the mid 19th cent.

hyoid /ˈhʌɪɔɪd/ Anatomy & Zoology ▶ noun (also **hyoid bone**) a U-shaped bone in the neck which supports the tongue.
▶ adjective of or relating to this bone or structures associated with it.
– ORIGIN early 19th cent.: via French from modern Latin hyoïdes, from Greek huoeidēs 'shaped like the letter upsilon (υ).

hyoscine /ˈhʌɪəsiːn/ ▶ noun [mass noun] Chemistry a poisonous plant alkaloid used as an antiemetic in motion sickness and as a preoperative medication for examination of the eye.
● Chem. formula: $C_{17}H_{21}NO_4$. It is obtained chiefly from plants of the genus Scopolia, family Solanaceae.

– ORIGIN late 19th cent.: from modern Latin hyoscyamus (see HYOSCYAMINE) + -INE⁴.

hyoscyamine /ˌhʌɪə(ʊ)ˈsʌɪəmiːn/ ▶ noun [mass noun] Chemistry a poisonous compound present in henbane, with similar properties to hyoscine.
● Chem. formula: $C_{17}H_{23}NO_3$.
– ORIGIN mid 19th cent.: from modern Latin hyoscyamus (from Greek huoskuamos 'henbane', from hus, huos 'pig' + kuamos 'bean') + -INE⁴.

hyp- ▶ combining form variant spelling of HYPO- shortened before a vowel or h (as in hypaesthesia).

hypaesthesia /ˌhʌɪpiːsˈθiːzɪə, -pɛs-/ (US **hypesthesia**) ▶ noun [mass noun] a diminished capacity for physical sensation, especially of the skin.
– DERIVATIVES **hypaesthetic** adjective.
– ORIGIN late 19th cent.: from HYPO- 'below' + Greek aisthēsis 'sensation'.

hypaethral /hʌɪˈpiːθr(ə)l, hɪ-/ (also **hypethral**) ▶ adjective (of a classical building) having no roof; open to the sky: the hypaethral temple.
– ORIGIN late 18th cent.: via Latin from Greek hupaithros (from hupo 'under' + aithēr 'air') + -AL.

hypallage /hʌɪˈpalədʒi, hɪ-/ ▶ noun Rhetoric a transposition of the natural relations of two elements in a proposition, for example in the sentence 'Melissa shook her doubtful curls'.
– ORIGIN late 16th cent.: via late Latin from Greek hupallagē, from hupo 'under' + allassein 'to exchange'.

hypalon /ˈhʌɪpəlɒn/ ▶ noun [mass noun] trademark a kind of synthetic rubber made of chlorinated and sulphonated polyethylene.
– ORIGIN mid 20th cent.: of unknown origin.

hypanthium /hɪˈpanθɪəm, hʌɪ-/ ▶ noun (pl. **hypanthia**) Botany a cup-like or tubular enlargement of the receptacle of a flower, loosely surrounding the gynoecium or united with it.

Hypatia /hʌɪˈpeɪʃɪə/ (c.370–415), Greek philosopher, astronomer, and mathematician. Head of the Neoplatonist school at Alexandria, she wrote several learned treatises as well as devising inventions such as an astrolabe.

hype¹ informal ▶ noun [mass noun] extravagant or intensive publicity or promotion: she relied on hype and television to stoke up interest in her music.
■ [count noun] a deception carried out for the sake of publicity.
▶ verb [with obj.] promote or publicize (a product or idea) intensively, often exaggerating its importance or benefits.
– ORIGIN 1920s (originally US in the sense 'short-change, cheat', or 'person who cheats etc.'): of unknown origin.

hype² informal ▶ noun a hypodermic needle or injection.
■ a drug addict.
▶ verb [with obj.] (usu. **be hyped up**) stimulate or excite (someone): I was hyped up because I wanted to do well.
– ORIGIN 1920s (originally US): abbreviation of HYPODERMIC.

hyper ▶ adjective informal hyperactive or unusually energetic: eating sugar makes you hyper.
– ORIGIN 1940s: abbreviation of HYPERACTIVE.

hyper- ▶ prefix **1** over; beyond; above: hypernym.
■ exceeding: hypersonic. ■ excessively; above normal: hyperthyroidism.
2 relating to hypertext: hyperlink.
– ORIGIN from Greek huper 'over, beyond'.

hyperactive ▶ adjective abnormally or extremely active: a hyperactive pituitary gland.
■ (of a child) showing constantly active and sometimes disruptive behaviour.
– DERIVATIVES **hyperactivity** noun.

hyperaemia /ˌhʌɪpəˈriːmɪə/ (US **hyperemia**) ▶ noun [mass noun] Medicine an excess of blood in the vessels supplying an organ or other part of the body.
– DERIVATIVES **hyperaemic** adjective.
– ORIGIN mid 19th cent.: from HYPER- 'above normal' + -AEMIA.

hyperaesthesia /ˌhʌɪpəriːsˈθiːzɪə, -ɛsˈθiː-/ (US **hyperesthesia**) ▶ noun [mass noun] Medicine excessive physical sensitivity, especially of the skin.
– DERIVATIVES **hyperaesthetic** adjective.
– ORIGIN mid 19th cent.: from HYPER- 'above normal' + Greek aisthēsis 'sensation'.

hyperalgesia /ˌhʌɪpəralˈdʒiːzɪə/ ▶ noun [mass noun] Medicine abnormally heightened sensitivity to pain.
– DERIVATIVES **hyperalgesic** adjective.

hyperalimentation ▶ noun [mass noun] Medicine artificial supply of nutrients, typically intravenously.

hyperbaric /ˌhʌɪpəˈbarɪk/ ▶ adjective of or involving a gas at a pressure greater than normal.
– ORIGIN 1960s: from HYPER- 'above normal' + Greek baros 'heavy'.

hyperbaton /hʌɪˈpəːbətɒn/ ▶ noun Rhetoric an inversion of the normal order of words, especially for the sake of emphasis, as in the sentence 'this I must see'.
– ORIGIN mid 16th cent.: via Latin from Greek huperbaton 'overstepping' (from huper 'over, above' + bainein 'go, walk').

hyperbola /hʌɪˈpəːbələ/ ▶ noun (pl. **hyperbolas** or **hyperbolae** /-liː/) a symmetrical open curve formed by the intersection of a cone with a plane at a smaller angle with its axis than the side of the cone.
■ Mathematics the pair of such curves formed by the intersection of a plane with two equal cones on opposite sides of the same vertex.
– ORIGIN mid 17th cent.: modern Latin, from Greek huperbolē 'excess' (from huper 'above' + ballein 'to throw').

hyperbole /hʌɪˈpəːbəli/ ▶ noun [mass noun] exaggerated statements or claims not meant to be taken literally.
– DERIVATIVES **hyperbolical** adjective, **hyperbolically** adverb, **hyperbolism** noun.
– ORIGIN late Middle English: via Latin from Greek huperbolē (see HYPERBOLA).

hyperbolic /ˌhʌɪpəˈbɒlɪk/ ▶ adjective **1** of or relating to a hyperbola.
■ Mathematics (of a function, e.g. cosine) having the same relation to a rectangular hyperbola as the unqualified function does to a circle.
2 (of language) exaggerated; hyperbolical.

hyperboloid /hʌɪˈpəːbəlɔɪd/ ▶ noun a solid or surface having plane sections that are hyperbolas, ellipses, or circles.
– DERIVATIVES **hyperboloidal** adjective.

hyperborean /ˌhʌɪpəbɔːˈriːən, -ˈbɔːrɪən/ poetic/literary ▶ noun an inhabitant of the extreme north.
■ (Hyperborean) Greek Mythology a member of a race worshipping Apollo and living in a land of sunshine and plenty beyond the north wind.
▶ adjective of or relating to the extreme north.
– ORIGIN late Middle English: from late Latin hyperboreanus, from Greek huperboreos, from huper 'beyond' + boreas 'north wind'.

hypercholesterolaemia /ˌhʌɪpəkəˌlɛstərəˈliːmɪə/ (US **hypercholesterolemia**) ▶ noun [mass noun] Medicine an excess of cholesterol in the bloodstream.
– ORIGIN late 19th cent.: from HYPER- 'above normal' + CHOLESTEROL + -AEMIA.

hypercorrection ▶ noun [mass noun] the use of an erroneous word form or pronunciation based on a false analogy with a correct or prestigious form, such as the pronunciation of Munich with a soft /ç/ at the end, as if it were the German name for the city.
– DERIVATIVES **hypercorrect** adjective.

hypercritical ▶ adjective excessively and unreasonably critical, especially of small faults.
– DERIVATIVES **hypercritically** adverb.

hypercube ▶ noun a geometrical figure in four or more dimensions which is analogous to a cube in three dimensions.

hyperdrive ▶ noun (in science fiction) a supposed propulsion system for travel in hyperspace.

hyperemia ▶ noun US spelling of HYPERAEMIA.

hyperesthesia ▶ noun US spelling of HYPERAESTHESIA.

hyperextend ▶ verb [with obj.] forcefully extend a limb or joint beyond its normal limits, either in exercise or therapy or so as to cause injury.
– DERIVATIVES **hyperextension** noun.

hyperfocal distance ▶ noun the distance between a camera lens and the closest object which is in focus when the lens is focused at infinity.

hypergamy /hʌɪˈpəːɡəmi/ ▶ noun [mass noun] the action of marrying a person of a superior caste or class.
– ORIGIN late 19th cent.: from HYPER- 'above' + Greek gamos 'marriage'.

hyperglycaemia /ˌhʌɪpəɡlʌɪˈsiːmɪə/ (US **hyperglycemia**) ▶ noun [mass noun] Medicine an excess

of glucose in the bloodstream, often associated with diabetes mellitus.
– DERIVATIVES **hyperglycaemic** adjective.
– ORIGIN late 19th cent.: from **HYPER-** 'above normal' + **GLYCO-** + **-AEMIA**.

hypergolic /ˌhʌɪpəˈɡɒlɪk/ ▶ adjective (of a rocket propellant) igniting spontaneously on mixing with another substance.
– ORIGIN 1940s: from German *Hypergol*, probably from **HYPER-** 'beyond' + Greek *ergon* 'work' + **-OL**.

hypericum /hʌɪˈpɛrɪkəm/ ▶ noun a yellow-flowered plant of a genus that includes the St John's worts, tutsan, and rose of Sharon.
● Genus *Hypericum*, family Guttiferae.
– ORIGIN Latin, from Greek *hupereikon*, from *huper* 'over, above' + *ereikē* 'heath'.

hyperimmune ▶ adjective Medicine having a high concentration of antibodies produced in reaction to repeated injections of an antigen.
– DERIVATIVES **hyperimmunized** adjective.

hyperinflation ▶ noun [mass noun] monetary inflation occurring at a very high rate.

Hyperion /hʌɪˈpɪərɪən/ Astronomy a satellite of Saturn, the sixteenth closest to the planet, discovered in 1848 and having an irregular shape.
– ORIGIN named after a Titan of Greek mythology.

hyperkeratosis /ˌhʌɪpərkɛrəˈtəʊsɪs/ ▶ noun [mass noun] Medicine abnormal thickening of the outer layer of the skin.

hyperkinesis /ˌhʌɪpəkɪˈniːsɪs, -kʌɪ-/ (also **hyperkinesia**) ▶ noun [mass noun] **1** Medicine muscle spasm.
2 Psychiatry a disorder of children marked by hyperactivity and inability to concentrate.
– ORIGIN mid 19th cent.: from **HYPER-** 'above normal' + Greek *kinēsis* 'motion'.

hyperkinetic /ˌhʌɪpəkɪˈnɛtɪk, -kʌɪ-/ ▶ adjective frenetic; hyperactive.
■ of or affected with hyperkinesis.

hyperlink Computing ▶ noun a link from a hypertext file or document to another location or file, typically activated by clicking on a highlighted word or image at a particular location on the screen.
▶ verb [with obj.] link (a file) in this way: *thumbnail images which are hyperlinked to a larger image.*

hyperlipaemia /ˌhʌɪpəlɪˈpiːmɪə/ (US **hyperlipemia**) ▶ noun [mass noun] Medicine an abnormally high concentration of fats or lipids in the blood.
– DERIVATIVES **hyperlipaemic** adjective.

hyperlipidaemia /ˌhʌɪpəˌlɪpɪˈdiːmɪə/ (US **hyperlipidemia**) ▶ noun another term for **HYPERLIPAEMIA**.
– DERIVATIVES **hyperlipidaemic** adjective.

hypermarket ▶ noun chiefly Brit. a very large self-service store with a wide range of goods and a large car park, typically situated outside a town.
– ORIGIN 1970s: translation of French *hypermarché*, from **HYPER-** 'beyond, exceeding' + *marché* 'market'.

hypermedia ▶ noun [mass noun] Computing an extension to hypertext providing multimedia facilities, such as those handling sound and video.
– ORIGIN 1960s: from **HYPER-** 'above, beyond' + **MEDIA**[1].

hypermetropia /ˌhʌɪpəmɪˈtrəʊpɪə/ ▶ noun [mass noun] long-sightedness.
– DERIVATIVES **hypermetropic** adjective.
– ORIGIN mid 19th cent.: from Greek *hupermetros* 'beyond measure' (from *huper* 'over, above' + *metron* 'measure') + *ōps* 'eye'.

hypermnesia /ˌhʌɪpəmˈniːzɪə/ ▶ noun [mass noun] unusual power or enhancement of memory, typically under abnormal conditions such as trauma, hypnosis, or narcosis.

hypermutable ▶ adjective Genetics of or in a state in which mutation is abnormally frequent.
– DERIVATIVES **hypermutation** noun.

hypernym /ˈhʌɪpənɪm/ ▶ noun a word with a broad meaning which more specific words fall under; a superordinate. For example, *colour* is a hypernym of *red*. Contrasted with **HYPONYM**.
– ORIGIN 1970s: from **HYPER-** 'beyond', on the pattern of *hyponym*.

hyperon /ˈhʌɪp(ə)rɒn/ ▶ noun Physics an unstable subatomic particle classified as a baryon, heavier than the neutron and proton.
– ORIGIN 1950s: from **HYPER-** 'beyond, over' + **-ON**.

hyperopia /ˌhʌɪpərˈəʊpɪə/ ▶ noun another term for **HYPERMETROPIA**.
– DERIVATIVES **hyperopic** adjective.
– ORIGIN late 19th cent.: from **HYPER-** 'beyond' + Greek *ōps* 'eye'.

hyperparasite ▶ noun Biology a parasite whose host is itself a parasite.
– DERIVATIVES **hyperparasitic** adjective, **hyperparasitism** noun.

hyperparathyroidism /ˌhʌɪpəˌparəˈθʌɪrɔɪdɪz(ə)m/ ▶ noun [mass noun] Medicine an abnormally high concentration of parathyroid hormone in the blood, resulting in weakening of the bones through loss of calcium.
– DERIVATIVES **hyperparathyroid** adjective.

hyperplasia /ˌhʌɪpəˈpleɪzɪə/ ▶ noun [mass noun] Medicine & Biology the enlargement of an organ or tissue caused by an increase in the reproduction rate of its cells, often as an initial stage in the development of cancer.
– ORIGIN mid 19th cent.: from **HYPER-** 'beyond' + Greek *plasis* 'formation'.

hyperreal ▶ adjective **1** exaggerated in comparison to reality.
2 (of artistic representation) extremely realistic in detail.
– DERIVATIVES **hyperrealism** noun, **hyperrealist** adjective, **hyperrealistic** adjective, **hyperreality** noun.

hypersensitive ▶ adjective abnormally or excessively sensitive, either psychologically or in physical response.
– DERIVATIVES **hypersensitiveness** noun, **hypersensitivity** noun.

hypersonic ▶ adjective **1** relating to speeds of more than five times the speed of sound (Mach 5).
2 relating to sound frequencies above about a thousand million hertz.
– DERIVATIVES **hypersonically** adverb.
– ORIGIN 1930s (in sense 2): from **HYPER-** 'beyond, exceeding', on the pattern of *supersonic* and *ultrasonic*.

hyperspace ▶ noun [mass noun] space of more than three dimensions.
■ (in science fiction) a notional space–time continuum in which it is possible to travel faster than light.
– DERIVATIVES **hyperspatial** adjective.

hypersthene /ˈhʌɪpəsθiːn/ ▶ noun [mass noun] a greenish rock-forming mineral of the orthopyroxene class, consisting of a magnesium iron silicate.
– ORIGIN early 19th cent.: coined in French, from **HYPER-** 'exceeding' + Greek *sthenos* 'strength' (because it is harder than hornblende).

hypertension ▶ noun [mass noun] Medicine abnormally high blood pressure.
■ a state of great psychological stress.

hypertensive ▶ adjective exhibiting hypertension.
▶ noun Medicine a person with high blood pressure.

hypertext ▶ noun [mass noun] Computing a software system allowing extensive cross-referencing between related sections of text and associated graphic material.
■ [count noun] a document presented on a computer in this way.

hyperthermia /ˌhʌɪpəˈθəːmɪə/ ▶ noun [mass noun] Medicine the condition of having a body temperature greatly above normal.
– DERIVATIVES **hyperthermic** adjective.
– ORIGIN late 19th cent.: from **HYPER-** 'beyond' + Greek *thermē* 'heat'.

hyperthyroidism /ˌhʌɪpəˈθʌɪrɔɪdɪz(ə)m/ ▶ noun [mass noun] Medicine overactivity of the thyroid gland, resulting in a rapid heartbeat and an increased rate of metabolism. Also called **THYROTOXICOSIS**.
– DERIVATIVES **hyperthyroid** adjective, **hyperthyroidic** adjective.

hypertonic /ˌhʌɪpəˈtɒnɪk/ ▶ adjective having increased pressure or tone, in particular:
■ Biology having a higher osmotic pressure than a particular fluid, typically a body fluid or intracellular fluid. ■ Physiology of or in a state of abnormally high muscle tone.
– DERIVATIVES **hypertonia** noun (only of muscles), **hypertonicity** noun.

hypertrophy /hʌɪˈpəːtrəfi/ ▶ noun [mass noun] Physiology the enlargement of an organ or tissue from the increase in size of its cells.

– DERIVATIVES **hypertrophic** adjective, **hypertrophied** adjective.
– ORIGIN mid 19th cent.: from **HYPER-** 'beyond, exceeding' + Greek *-trophia* 'nourishment'.

hyperventilate ▶ verb [no obj.] breathe at an abnormally rapid rate, so increasing the rate of loss of carbon dioxide.
■ [with obj.] (usu. **be hyperventilated**) cause to breathe in such a way. ■ [as adj. **hyperventilated**] figurative inflated or pretentious in style; overblown.
– DERIVATIVES **hyperventilation** noun.

hypesthesia ▶ noun US spelling of **HYPAESTHESIA**.

hypethral ▶ adjective variant spelling of **HYPAETHRAL**.

hypha /ˈhʌɪfə/ ▶ noun (pl. **hyphae** /-fiː/) Botany each of the branching filaments that make up the mycelium of a fungus.
– DERIVATIVES **hyphal** adjective.
– ORIGIN mid 19th cent.: modern Latin, from Greek *huphē* 'web'.

Hyphasis /ˈhʌɪfəsɪs/ ancient Greek name for **BEAS**.

hyphen /ˈhʌɪf(ə)n/ ▶ noun the sign (-) used to join words to indicate that they have a combined meaning or that they are linked in the grammar of a sentence (as in *pick-me-up*, *rock-forming*), to indicate the division of a word at the end of a line, or to indicate a missing or implied element (as in *short- and long-term*).
▶ verb another term for **HYPHENATE**.
– ORIGIN early 17th cent.: via late Latin from Greek *huphen* 'together', from *hupo* 'under' + *hen* 'one'.

hyphenate ▶ verb [with obj.] write with a hyphen: [as adj. **hyphenated**] *a hyphenated surname.*
– DERIVATIVES **hyphenation** noun.

hyphenated American ▶ noun US informal an American citizen who can trace their ancestry to another, specified part of the world, such as an African American or an Irish American (so called because terms like *African American* are often written with a hyphen).

hypnagogic /ˌhɪpnəˈɡɒdʒɪk/ (also **hypnogogic**) ▶ adjective Psychology of or relating to the state immediately before falling asleep.
– ORIGIN late 19th cent.: from French *hypnagogique*, from Greek *hupnos* 'sleep' + *agōgos* 'leading' (from *agein* 'to lead').

hypno- ▶ combining form relating to sleep: *hypnopaedia.*
■ relating to hypnosis: *hypnotherapy.*
– ORIGIN from Greek *hupnos* 'sleep'.

hypnopaedia /ˌhɪpnəʊˈpiːdɪə/ (US **hypnopedia**) ▶ noun [mass noun] learning by hearing while asleep or under hypnosis.

hypnopompic /ˌhɪpnə(ʊ)ˈpɒmpɪk/ ▶ adjective Psychology of or relating to the state immediately preceding waking up.
– ORIGIN early 20th cent.: from Greek *hupnos* 'sleep' + *pompē* 'sending away' + **-IC**.

Hypnos /ˈhɪpnɒs/ Greek Mythology the god of sleep, son of Nyx (Night).
– ORIGIN from Greek *hupnos* 'sleep'.

hypnosis ▶ noun [mass noun] the induction of a state of consciousness in which a person apparently loses the power of voluntary action and is highly responsive to suggestion or direction. Its use in therapy, typically to recover suppressed memories or to allow modification of behaviour by suggestion, has been revived but is still controversial.
■ this state of consciousness.
– ORIGIN late 19th cent.: from Greek *hupnos* 'sleep' + **-OSIS**.

hypnotherapy ▶ noun [mass noun] the use of hypnosis as a therapeutic technique.
– DERIVATIVES **hypnotherapist** noun.

hypnotic ▶ adjective **1** of, producing, or relating to hypnosis: *a hypnotic state.*
■ exerting a compelling, fascinating, or soporific effect: *her voice had a hypnotic quality.*
2 Medicine (of a drug) sleep-inducing.
▶ noun **1** Medicine a sleep-inducing drug.
2 a person under or open to the influence of hypnotism.
– DERIVATIVES **hypnotically** adverb.
– ORIGIN early 17th cent.: from French *hypnotique*, via late Latin from Greek *hupnōtikos* 'narcotic, causing sleep', from *hupnoun* 'put to sleep', from *hupnos* 'sleep'.

hypnotism ▶ noun [mass noun] the study or practice of hypnosis.
– DERIVATIVES **hypnotist** noun.

hypnotize (also **-ise**) ▶ verb [with obj.] produce a state of hypnosis in (someone): *a witness had been hypnotized to enhance his memory.*
■ capture the whole attention of (someone); fascinate: *the barman seemed hypnotized by the pub's female singer.*
– DERIVATIVES **hypnotizable** adjective.

hypo¹ ▶ noun [mass noun] Photography the chemical sodium thiosulphate (formerly called hyposulphite) used as a photographic fixer.
– ORIGIN mid 19th cent.: abbreviation of *hyposulphite.*

hypo² ▶ noun (pl. **-os**) informal term for **HYPODERMIC.**
– ORIGIN early 20th cent.: abbreviation.

hypo³ ▶ noun (pl. **-os**) informal an attack of hypoglycaemia.
– ORIGIN late 20th cent.: abbreviation.

hypo- (also **hyp-**) ▶ prefix under: *hypodermic.*
■ below normal: *hypoglycaemia.* ■ slightly: *hypomanic.* ■ Chemistry containing an element with an unusually low valency: *hypochlorous.*
– ORIGIN from Greek *hupo* 'under'.

hypo-allergenic ▶ adjective (especially of cosmetics and textiles) relatively unlikely to cause an allergic reaction.

hypoblast /'hʌɪpə(ʊ)blast/ ▶ noun Biology former term for **ENDODERM.**

hypocalcaemia /ˌhʌɪpəʊkal'siːmɪə/ (US **hypocalcemia**) ▶ noun [mass noun] Medicine deficiency of calcium in the bloodstream.

hypocaust /'hʌɪpə(ʊ)kɔːst/ ▶ noun a hollow space under the floor of an ancient Roman building, into which hot air was sent for heating a room or bath.
– ORIGIN from Latin *hypocaustum,* from Greek *hupokauston* 'place heated from below', from *hupo* 'under' + *kau-* (base of *kaiein* 'to burn').

hypochlorous acid /ˌhʌɪpə(ʊ)'klɔːrəs/ ▶ noun [mass noun] Chemistry a weak acid with oxidizing properties formed when chlorine dissolves in cold water and used in bleaching and water treatment.
● Chem. formula: HOCl.
– DERIVATIVES **hypochlorite** noun.
– ORIGIN mid 19th cent.: *hypochlorous* from **HYPO-** (denoting an element in a low valency) + **CHLORINE** + **-OUS.**

hypochondria /ˌhʌɪpə'kɒndrɪə/ ▶ noun [mass noun] abnormal anxiety about one's health, especially with an unwarranted fear that one has a serious disease.
– ORIGIN late Middle English (in the Greek sense): via late Latin from Greek *hupokhondria,* denoting the soft body area below the ribs, from *hupo* 'under' + *khondros* 'sternal cartilage'. Melancholy was originally thought to arise from the liver, gall bladder, spleen, etc.

hypochondriac ▶ noun a person who is abnormally anxious about their health.
▶ adjective another term for **HYPOCHONDRIACAL.**
– ORIGIN late 16th cent.: coined in French from Greek *hupokhondriakos,* from *hupokhondria* (see **HYPOCHONDRIA**).

hypochondriacal /ˌhʌɪpə(ʊ)kɒn'drʌɪək(ə)l/ ▶ adjective of or affected by hypochondria.

hypochondriasis /ˌhʌɪpə(ʊ)kɒn'drʌɪəsɪs/ ▶ noun technical term for **HYPOCHONDRIA.**

hypocoristic /ˌhʌɪpə(ʊ)kə'rɪstɪk/ ▶ adjective denoting or of the nature of a pet name or diminutive form of a name.
▶ noun a hypocoristic name or form.
– DERIVATIVES **hypocorism** noun.
– ORIGIN mid 19th cent.: from Greek *hupokorisma,* from *hupokorizesthai* 'play the child', from *hupo* 'under' + *korē* 'child'.

hypocotyl /ˌhʌɪpə(ʊ)'kɒtɪl/ ▶ noun Botany the part of the stem of an embryo plant beneath the stalks of the seed-leaves or cotyledons and directly above the root.

hypocrisy ▶ noun (pl. **-ies**) [mass noun] the practice of claiming to have higher standards or beliefs than is the case.
– ORIGIN Middle English: from Old French *ypocrisie,* via ecclesiastical Latin, from Greek *hupokrisis* 'acting of a theatrical part', from *hupokrinesthai* 'play a part, pretend', from *hupo* 'under' + *krinein* 'decide, judge'.

hypocrite ▶ noun a person who indulges in hypocrisy.
– DERIVATIVES **hypocritical** adjective, **hypocritically** adverb.
– ORIGIN Middle English: from Old French *ypocrite,* via ecclesiastical Latin from Greek *hupokritēs* 'actor', from *hupokrinesthai* (see **HYPOCRISY**).

hypocycloid /ˌhʌɪpə(ʊ)'sʌɪklɔɪd/ ▶ noun Mathematics the curve traced by a point on the circumference of a circle which is rolling on the interior of another circle.
– DERIVATIVES **hypocycloidal** adjective.

hypodermic ▶ adjective [attrib.] Medicine of or relating to the region immediately beneath the skin.
■ (of a needle or syringe) used to inject a drug or other substance beneath the skin. ■ (of a drug or other substance or its application) injected beneath the skin.
▶ noun a hypodermic syringe or injection.
– DERIVATIVES **hypodermically** adverb.
– ORIGIN mid 19th cent.: from **HYPO-** 'under' + Greek *derma* 'skin' + **-IC.**

hypogastrium /ˌhʌɪpə(ʊ)'gastrɪəm/ ▶ noun (pl. **hypogastria** /-rɪə/) Anatomy the part of the central abdomen which is situated below the region of the stomach.
– DERIVATIVES **hypogastric** adjective.
– ORIGIN late 17th cent.: modern Latin, from Greek *hupogastrion,* from *hupo* 'under' + *gastēr* 'belly'.

hypogeal /ˌhʌɪpə(ʊ)'dʒiːəl/ (also **hypogean**) ▶ adjective Botany underground; subterranean. Compare with **EPIGEAL.**
■ (of seed germination) with the seed leaves remaining below the ground.
– ORIGIN late 17th cent.: via late Latin from Greek *hupogeios* (from *hupo* 'under' + *gē* 'earth') + **-AL.**

hypogene /ˌhʌɪpə(ʊ)'dʒiːn/ ▶ adjective Geology producing or occurring under the surface of the earth.
– DERIVATIVES **hypogenic** adjective.
– ORIGIN mid 19th cent.: from **HYPO-** 'under' + Greek *genēs* '-born, of a certain kind'.

hypogeum /ˌhʌɪpə(ʊ)'dʒiːəm/ ▶ noun (pl. **hypogea**) an underground chamber.
– ORIGIN mid 17th cent.: from Latin, from Greek *hupogeion,* neuter of *hupogeios* 'underground'.

hypoglossal nerve /ˌhʌɪpə(ʊ)'glɒs(ə)l/ ▶ noun Anatomy each of the twelfth pair of cranial nerves, supplying the muscles of the tongue.
– ORIGIN mid 19th cent.: *hypoglossal* from **HYPO-** 'under' + Greek *glōssa* 'tongue' + **-AL.**

hypoglycaemia /ˌhʌɪpə(ʊ)glʌɪ'siːmɪə/ (US **hypoglycemia**) ▶ noun [mass noun] Medicine deficiency of glucose in the bloodstream.
– DERIVATIVES **hypoglycaemic** adjective.
– ORIGIN late 19th cent.: from **HYPO-** 'below' + **GLYCO-** + **-AEMIA.**

hypogonadism /ˌhʌɪpə(ʊ)'gəʊnadɪz(ə)m/ ▶ noun [mass noun] Medicine reduction or absence of hormone secretion or other physiological activity of the gonads (testes or ovaries).
– DERIVATIVES **hypogonadal** adjective, **hypogonadic** noun & adjective.

hypogynous /hʌɪ'pɒdʒɪnəs/ ▶ adjective Botany (of a plant or flower) having the stamens and other floral parts situated below the carpels (or gynoecium). Compare with **EPIGYNOUS, PERIGYNOUS.**
– DERIVATIVES **hypogyny** noun.
– ORIGIN early 19th cent.: from modern Latin *hypogynus,* from **HYPO-** 'below' + *gunē* 'woman' (used to represent 'pistil') + **-OUS.**

hypoid /'hʌɪpɔɪd/ (also **hypoid gear**) ▶ noun a bevel wheel with teeth engaging with a spiral pinion mounted at right angles to the wheel's axis, used to connect non-intersecting shafts in vehicle transmissions and other mechanisms.
– ORIGIN 1920s: perhaps a contraction of **HYPERBOLOID.**

hypokalaemia /ˌhʌɪpəʊkə'liːmɪə/ (US **hypokalemia**) ▶ noun [mass noun] Medicine deficiency of potassium in the bloodstream.
– DERIVATIVES **hypokalaemic** adjective.
– ORIGIN 1940s: from **HYPO-** 'below' + modern Latin *kalium* 'potassium'.

hypolimnion /ˌhʌɪpə(ʊ)'lɪmnɪən/ ▶ noun (pl. **hypolimnia** /-nɪə/) the lower layer of water in a stratified lake, typically cooler than the water above and relatively stagnant.
– ORIGIN early 20th cent.: from **HYPO-** 'below' + Greek *limnion* (diminutive of *limnē* 'lake').

hypomagnesaemia /ˌhʌɪpə(ʊ)ˌmagnɪ'ziːmɪə/ (US **hypomagnesemia**) ▶ noun [mass noun] Medicine & Veterinary Medicine deficiency of magnesium in the blood, important in cattle as the cause of grass tetany.
– DERIVATIVES **hypomagnesaemic** adjective.

hypomania ▶ noun [mass noun] Psychiatry a mild form of mania, marked by elation and hyperactivity.
– DERIVATIVES **hypomanic** adjective.

hyponym /'hʌɪpə(ʊ)nɪm/ ▶ noun a word of more specific meaning than a general or superordinate term applicable to it. For example, *spoon* is a hyponym of *cutlery.* Contrasted with **HYPERNYM.**
– DERIVATIVES **hyponymy** noun.

hypoparathyroidism /ˌhʌɪpəʊˌparə'θʌɪrɔɪdɪz(ə)m/ ▶ noun [mass noun] Medicine diminished concentration of parathyroid hormone in the blood, which causes deficiencies of calcium and phosphorus compounds in the blood and results in muscular spasms.
– DERIVATIVES **hypoparathyroid** adjective.

hypophysis /hʌɪ'pɒfɪsɪs/ ▶ noun (pl. **hypophyses** /-siːz/) Anatomy technical term for **PITUITARY.**
– DERIVATIVES **hypophyseal** /ˌhʌɪpə(ʊ)'fɪzɪəl/ (also **hypophysial**) adjective.
– ORIGIN late 17th cent.: modern Latin, from Greek *hupophusis* 'offshoot', from *hupo* 'under' + *phusis* 'growth'.

hypopituitarism /ˌhʌɪpəʊpɪ'tjuːɪt(ə)rɪz(ə)m/ ▶ noun [mass noun] Medicine diminished hormone secretion by the pituitary gland, causing dwarfism in children and premature ageing in adults.
– DERIVATIVES **hypopituitary** adjective.

hypospadias /ˌhʌɪpəʊ'speɪdɪəs/ ▶ noun [mass noun] Medicine a congenital condition in males in which the opening of the urethra is on the underside of the penis.
– ORIGIN early 19th cent.: from Greek *hupospadias* 'person having hypospadias'.

hypospray ▶ noun (chiefly in science fiction) a device used to introduce a drug or other substance into the body through the skin without puncturing it.

hypostasis /hʌɪ'pɒstəsɪs/ ▶ noun (pl. **hypostases** /-siːz/) 1 [mass noun] Medicine the accumulation of fluid or blood in the lower parts of the body or organs under the influence of gravity, as occurs in cases of poor circulation or after death.
2 Philosophy an underlying reality or substance, as opposed to attributes or to that which lacks substance.
■ Theology (in trinitarian doctrine) each of the three persons of the Trinity, as contrasted with the unity of the Godhead. ■ [in sing.] Theology the single person of Christ, as contrasted with his dual human and divine nature.
– ORIGIN early 16th cent. (in theological use): via ecclesiastical Latin from Greek *hupostasis* 'sediment', later 'essence, substance', from *hupo* 'under' + *stasis* 'standing'.

hypostasize (also **-ise**) ▶ verb [with obj.] formal treat or represent (something abstract) as a concrete reality.

hypostatic /ˌhʌɪpə(ʊ)'statɪk/ ▶ adjective Theology relating to the persons of the Trinity.
– DERIVATIVES **hypostatical** adjective.

hypostatic union ▶ noun Theology the combination of divine and human natures in the single person of Christ.

hypostatize ▶ verb North American term for **HYPOSTASIZE.**

hypostyle /'hʌɪpə(ʊ)stʌɪl/ ▶ adjective Architecture (of a building) having a roof supported by pillars, typically in several rows.
▶ noun a building having such a roof.
– ORIGIN mid 19th cent.: from Greek *hupostulos,* from *hupo* 'under' + *stulos* 'column'.

hypotaxis /ˌhʌɪpə(ʊ)'taksɪs/ ▶ noun [mass noun] Grammar the subordination of one clause to another. Contrasted with **PARATAXIS.**
– DERIVATIVES **hypotactic** adjective.
– ORIGIN late 19th cent.: from Greek *hupotaxis,* from *hupo* 'under' + *taxis* 'arrangement'.

hypotension ▶ noun [mass noun] abnormally low blood pressure.

hypotensive ▸ **adjective** lowering the blood pressure: *hypotensive drugs* | *the hypotensive effect.*
■ relating to or suffering from abnormally low blood pressure.

hypotenuse /hʌɪˈpɒtənjuːz, -s/ ▸ **noun** the longest side of a right-angled triangle, opposite the right angle.
– ORIGIN late 16th cent.: via Latin *hypotenusa* from Greek *hupoteinousa* (*grammē*) 'subtending (line)', from the verb *hupoteinein* (from *hupo* 'under' + *teinein* 'stretch').

hypothalamus /ˌhʌɪpə(ʊ)ˈθaləməs/ ▸ **noun** (pl. **hypothalami** /-mʌɪ/) Anatomy a region of the forebrain below the thalamus which coordinates both the autonomic nervous system and the activity of the pituitary, controlling body temperature, thirst, hunger, and other homeostatic systems, and involved in sleep and emotional activity.
– DERIVATIVES **hypothalamic** adjective.

hypothec /hʌɪˈpɒθɪk, ˈhʌɪ-/ ▸ **noun** (in Roman and Scots law) a right established by law over a debtor's property that remains in the debtor's possession.
– DERIVATIVES **hypothecary** /hʌɪˈpɒθɪk(ə)ri/ adjective.
– ORIGIN early 16th cent.: from French *hypothèque*, via late Latin from Greek *hupothēkē* 'deposit' (from *hupo* 'under' + *tithenai* 'to place').

hypothecate /hʌɪˈpɒθɪkeɪt/ ▸ **verb** [with obj.] pledge (money) by law to a specific purpose.
– DERIVATIVES **hypothecation** noun.
– ORIGIN early 17th cent.: from medieval Latin *hypothecat-* 'given as a pledge', from the verb *hypothecare*, based on Greek *hupothēkē* (see **HYPOTHEC**).

hypothermia /ˌhʌɪpə(ʊ)ˈθəːmɪə/ ▸ **noun** [mass noun] the condition of having an abnormally (typically dangerously) low body temperature.
– ORIGIN late 19th cent.: from **HYPO-** 'below' + Greek *thermē* 'heat'.

hypothesis /hʌɪˈpɒθɪsɪs/ ▸ **noun** (pl. **hypotheses** /-siːz/) a supposition or proposed explanation made on the basis of limited evidence as a starting point for further investigation: *his 'steady state' hypothesis of the origin of the universe.*
■ Philosophy a proposition made as a basis for reasoning, without any assumption of its truth.
– ORIGIN late 16th cent.: via late Latin from Greek *hupothesis* 'foundation', from *hupo* 'under' + *thesis* 'placing'.

hypothesis testing ▸ **noun** [mass noun] Statistics the theory, methods, and practice of testing a hypothesis by comparing it with the null hypothesis. The null hypothesis is only rejected if its probability falls below a predetermined significance level, in which case the hypothesis being tested is said to have that level of significance.

hypothesize (also **-ise**) ▸ **verb** [with obj.] put (something) forward as a hypothesis.
– DERIVATIVES **hypothesizer** noun.

hypothetical /ˌhʌɪpəˈθɛtɪk(ə)l/ ▸ **adjective** of or based on or serving as a hypothesis: *that option is merely hypothetical at this juncture.*
■ supposed but not necessarily real or true: *the hypothetical tenth planet.* ■ Logic denoting or containing a proposition of the logical form *if p then q.*
▸ **noun** (usu. **hypotheticals**) a hypothetical proposition or statement.
– DERIVATIVES **hypothetically** adverb [sentence adverb] *hypothetically, varying interpretations of the term are possible.*

hypothetical imperative ▸ **noun** Philosophy a moral obligation that applies only if one desires the implicated goal.

hypothetico-deductive ▸ **adjective** Philosophy of or relating to the testing of the consequences of hypotheses, to determine whether the hypotheses themselves are false or acceptable.

hypothyroidism /ˌhʌɪpəʊˈθʌɪrɔɪdɪz(ə)m/ ▸ **noun** [mass noun] Medicine abnormally low activity of the thyroid gland, resulting in retardation of growth and mental development in children and adults.

– DERIVATIVES **hypothyroid** noun & adjective.

hypotonic /ˌhʌɪpə(ʊ)ˈtɒnɪk/ ▸ **adjective** having reduced pressure or tone, in particular:
■ Biology having a lower osmotic pressure than a particular fluid, typically a body fluid or intracellular fluid. ■ Physiology of or in a state of abnormally low muscle tone.
– DERIVATIVES **hypotonia** noun, **hypotonicity** noun.

hypoventilation ▸ **noun** [mass noun] Medicine breathing at an abnormally slow rate, resulting in an increased amount of carbon dioxide in the blood.

hypovolaemia /ˌhʌɪpə(ʊ)vəˈliːmɪə/ (US **hypovolemia**) ▸ **noun** [mass noun] Medicine a decreased volume of circulating blood in the body.
– DERIVATIVES **hypovolaemic** adjective.
– ORIGIN early 20th cent.: from **HYPO-** 'under' + **VOLUME** + Greek *haima* 'blood'.

hypoxaemia /ˌhʌɪpɒkˈsiːmɪə/ (US **hypoxemia**) ▸ **noun** [mass noun] Medicine an abnormally low concentration of oxygen in the blood.
– ORIGIN late 19th cent.: from **HYPO-** (denoting an element in a low valency) + **OXYGEN** + **-AEMIA**.

hypoxanthine /ˌhʌɪpəʊˈzanθiːn/ ▸ **noun** [mass noun] Biochemistry a compound which is an intermediate in the metabolism of purines in animals and occurs in plant tissues.
● Alternative name: **6-hydroxypurine**; chem. formula: $C_5H_4N_4O$.

hypoxia /hʌɪˈpɒksɪə/ ▸ **noun** [mass noun] Medicine deficiency in the amount of oxygen reaching the tissues.
– DERIVATIVES **hypoxic** adjective.
– ORIGIN 1940s: from **HYPO-** (denoting an element in a low valency) + **OXYGEN** + **-IA**[1].

hypsilophodont /ˌhɪpsɪˈlɒfədɒnt/ (also **hypsilophodontid** /ˌhɪpsɪˌlɒfəˈdɒntɪd/) ▸ **noun** a small bipedal herbivorous dinosaur of the late Jurassic and Cretaceous periods, adapted for swift running.
● Family Hypsilophodontidae, infraorder Ornithopoda, order Ornithischia.
– ORIGIN late 19th cent.: from modern Latin *Hypsilophodontidae*, from Greek *hupsilophos* 'high-crested' + *odous, odont-* 'tooth'.

hypso- ▸ **combining form** relating to height or elevation: *hypsometer.*
– ORIGIN from Greek *hupsos* 'height'.

hypsography /hɪpˈsɒɡrəfi/ ▸ **noun** [mass noun] the branch of geography concerned with the determination and mapping of the relative elevation of areas of land.
– DERIVATIVES **hypsographic** adjective, **hypsographical** adjective.

hypsometer /hɪpˈsɒmɪtə/ ▸ **noun** a device for calibrating thermometers at the boiling point of water at a known height above sea level or for estimating height above sea level by finding the temperature at which water boils.

hypsometric /ˌhɪpsə(ʊ)ˈmɛtrɪk/ ▸ **adjective** of or relating to the use of the hypsometer; hypsographic.

Hyracoidea /ˌhʌɪraˈkɔɪdɪə/ Zoology a small order of mammals that comprises the hyraxes.
– DERIVATIVES **hyracoid** noun & adjective.
– ORIGIN modern Latin (plural), based on Greek *hurax, hurak-* (see **HYRAX**).

hyracotherium /ˌhʌɪrəkə(ʊ)ˈθɪərɪəm/ ▸ **noun** the earliest fossil ancestor of the horse, which was a small forest animal of the Eocene epoch, with four toes on the front feet and three on the back.
● Genus *Hyracotherium*, family Equidae.
– ORIGIN modern Latin: from *hyraco-* (combining form from **HYRAX**) + Greek *thērion* 'wild animal'.

hyrax /ˈhʌɪraks/ ▸ **noun** a small herbivorous mammal with a compact body and a very short tail, found in arid country in Africa and Arabia. The nearest relatives to hyraxes are the elephants and other subungulates.
● Family Procaviidae and order Hyracoidea: three genera and several species.
– ORIGIN mid 19th cent.: modern Latin, from Greek *hurax* 'shrew-mouse'.

hyson /ˈhʌɪs(ə)n/ ▸ **noun** [mass noun] a type of green China tea.
– ORIGIN mid 18th cent.: from Chinese *xīchūn*, literally 'bright spring'.

hyssop /ˈhɪsəp/ ▸ **noun 1** a small bushy aromatic plant of the mint family, the bitter minty leaves of which are used in cookery and herbal medicine.
● *Hyssopus officinalis*, family Labiatae.
2 (in biblical use) a wild shrub of uncertain identity whose twigs were used for sprinkling in ancient Jewish rites of purification.
– ORIGIN Old English *hysope* (reinforced in Middle English by Old French *ysope*), via Latin from Greek *hyssōpos*, of Semitic origin.

hysterectomize ▸ **verb** [with obj.] perform a hysterectomy on (a woman).

hysterectomy /ˌhɪstəˈrɛktəmi/ ▸ **noun** (pl. **-ies**) a surgical operation to remove all or part of the womb.
– ORIGIN late 19th cent.: from Greek *hustera* 'womb' + **-ECTOMY**.

hysteresis /ˌhɪstəˈriːsɪs/ ▸ **noun** [mass noun] Physics the phenomenon in which the value of a physical property lags behind changes in the effect causing it, as for instance when magnetic induction lags behind the magnetizing force.
– ORIGIN late 19th cent.: from Greek *husterēsis* 'shortcoming, deficiency', from *husterein* 'be behind', from *husteros* 'late'.

hysteria ▸ **noun** [mass noun] exaggerated or uncontrollable emotion or excitement, especially among a group of people: *the anti-Semitic hysteria of the 1890s.*
■ Psychiatry a psychological disorder (not now regarded as a single definite condition) whose symptoms include conversion of psychological stress into physical symptoms (somatization), selective amnesia, shallow volatile emotions, and overdramatic or attention-seeking behaviour. The term has a controversial history as it was formerly regarded as a disease specific to women.
– ORIGIN early 19th cent.: from Latin *hystericus* (see **HYSTERIC**).

hysteric ▸ **noun 1** (**hysterics**) informal a wildly emotional and exaggerated reaction: *the widow had hysterics and the inquest was wrapped up quickly.*
■ uncontrollable laughter: *this started them both giggling and they fled upstairs in hysterics.*
2 a person suffering from hysteria.
▸ **adjective** another term for **HYSTERICAL** (in sense 2).
– ORIGIN mid 17th cent. (as an adjective): via Latin from Greek *husterikos* 'of the womb', from *hustera* 'womb' (hysteria being thought to be specific to women and associated with the womb).

hysterical ▸ **adjective 1** deriving from or affected by uncontrolled extreme emotion: *hysterical laughter* | *the band were mobbed by hysterical fans.*
■ informal extremely funny: *her attempts to teach them to dance were hysterical.*
2 Psychiatry relating to, associated with, or suffering from hysteria: *the doctor thinks the condition is partly hysterical.*
■ another term for **HISTRIONIC** (denoting personality disorder).
– DERIVATIVES **hysterically** adverb [as submodifier] *isn't it hysterically funny?*

hysteron proteron /ˌhɪstərɒn ˈprɒtərɒn/ ▸ **noun** Rhetoric a figure of speech in which what should come last is put first, i.e. an inversion of the natural order, for example 'I die! I faint! I fail!'.
– ORIGIN mid 16th cent.: late Latin, from Greek *husteron proteron* 'the latter (put in place of) the former'.

Hystricomorpha /ˌhɪstrɪkə(ʊ)ˈmɔːfə/ Zoology a major division of the rodents which includes the guinea pigs, coypu, porcupines and their relatives. They occur chiefly in South America.
● Suborder Hystricomorpha, order Rodentia.
– DERIVATIVES **hystricomorph** noun & adjective.
– ORIGIN modern Latin (plural), from Latin *hystrix, hystric-* 'porcupine' (from Greek *hustrix*) + *morphē* 'form'.

Hytrel /ˈhʌɪtrɛl/ ▸ **noun** [mass noun] trademark a strong, flexible synthetic resin used in shoes, sports equipment, and other manufactured articles.

Hz ▸ abbreviation for hertz.

Ii

I¹ (also **i**) ▶ noun (pl. **Is** or **I's**) **1** the ninth letter of the alphabet.
▪ denoting the next after H in a set of items, categories, etc.
2 the Roman numeral for one.
– PHRASES **dot the i's and cross the t's** see DOT¹.

I² ▶ pronoun [first person singular] used by a speaker to refer to himself or herself: *accept me for what I am.*
▶ noun (**the I**) Philosophy (in metaphysics) the subject or object of self-consciousness; the ego.
– ORIGIN Old English, of Germanic origin; related to Dutch *ik* and German *ich*, from an Indo-European root shared by Latin *ego* and Greek *egō.*

USAGE Why is it incorrect to say *between you and I* (rather than *between you and me*)? Why is it also incorrect to say *John and me went to the shops* (instead of *John and I went to the shops*)? Is it correct or incorrect to say *she's much better than me* or should it be *she's much better than I*? For a discussion of such questions, see usage at **BETWEEN** and **PERSONAL PRONOUN**.

I³ ▶ abbreviation for ▪ (**I.**) Island(s) or Isle(s) (chiefly on maps). ▪ Italy (international vehicle registration).
▶ symbol for ▪ electric current: *V = I/R.* ▪ the chemical element iodine.

i ▶ symbol for (*i*) Mathematics the imaginary quantity equal to the square root of minus one. Compare with **J**.

-i¹ ▶ suffix forming the plural: **1** of nouns adopted from Latin ending in *-us: foci | timpani.*
2 of nouns adopted from Italian ending in *-e* or *-o: dilettanti.*

USAGE Many nouns derived from a foreign language retain their foreign plural, at least when they first enter English and particularly if they belong to a specialist field. Over time, it is quite normal for a word in general use to acquire a regular English plural, however. This may coexist with the foreign plural (e.g. **cactus**, plural **cacti** or **cactuses**) or it may actually oust a foreign plural (**octopus**, plural **octopuses** rather than **octopodes**).

-i² ▶ suffix forming adjectives from names of countries or regions in the Near or Middle East: *Azerbaijani | Pakistani.*
– ORIGIN from Semitic and Indo-Iranian adjectival endings.

-i- ▶ suffix a connecting vowel chiefly forming words ending in *-ana, -ferous, -fic, -form, -fy, -gerous, -vorous.* Compare with **-O-**.

IA ▶ abbreviation for Iowa (in official postal use).

Ia ▶ abbreviation for Iowa.

-ia¹ ▶ suffix **1** forming nouns adopted unchanged from Latin or Greek (such as *mania, militia*), and modern Latin terms (such as *utopia*).
2 forming names of:
▪ Medicine states and disorders: *anaemia | diphtheria.* ▪ Botany & Zoology genera and higher groups: *dahlia | Latimeria.*
3 forming names of countries: *India.*
– ORIGIN representing Latin or Greek endings.

-ia² ▶ suffix forming noun plurals: **1** from Greek neuter nouns ending in *-ion* or from those in Latin ending in *-ium* or *-e: paraphernalia | regalia.*
2 Zoology in the names of classes: *Reptilia.*

IAA Biochemistry ▶ abbreviation for indoleacetic acid.

IAEA ▶ abbreviation for International Atomic Energy Agency.

-ial ▶ suffix forming adjectives such as *celestial, primordial.*
– ORIGIN from French *-iel* or Latin *-ialis.*

iamb /'ʌɪam(b)/ ▶ noun Prosody another term for **IAMBUS**.

iambic /ʌɪ'ambɪk/ ▶ adjective Prosody of or using iambuses: *iambic pentameters.*
▶ noun a verse using iambuses.
▪ (**iambics**) verse of this kind.
– ORIGIN mid 16th cent.: from French *iambique*, via late Latin from Greek *iambikos*, from *iambos* (see **IAMBUS**).

iambus /ʌɪ'ambəs/ ▶ noun (pl. **iambuses** or **iambi** /-bʌɪ/) Prosody a metrical foot consisting of one short (or unstressed) syllable followed by one long (or stressed) syllable.
– ORIGIN late 16th cent.: Latin, from Greek *iambos* 'iambus, lampoon', from *iaptein* 'attack verbally' (because the iambic trimeter was first used by Greek satirists).

-ian ▶ suffix forming adjectives and nouns such as *antediluvian* and *Bostonian*. Compare with **-AN**.
– ORIGIN from French *-ien* or Latin *-ianus.*

Iapetus /ʌɪ'apɪtəs/ Astronomy a satellite of Saturn, the seventeenth closest to the planet, having one bright icy side and one very dark side, discovered by Cassini in 1671 (diameter 1,440 km).
– ORIGIN named after a Titan of Greek mythology, son of Uranus (Heaven) and Gaia (Earth).

Iaşi /'jaʃi/ a city in eastern Romania; pop. 337,600 (1993). From 1565 to 1859 it was the capital of the principality of Moldavia. German name **JASSY**.

-iasis ▶ suffix a common form of **-ASIS**.

IATA /ʌɪ'ɑːtə/ ▶ abbreviation for International Air Transport Association.

iatro- /ʌɪ'atrəʊ/ ▶ combining form relating to a physician or to medical treatment: *iatrogenic.*
– ORIGIN from Greek *iatros* 'physician', from *iasthai* 'heal'.

iatrochemistry ▶ noun [mass noun] historical a school of thought of the 16th and 17th centuries which sought to understand medicine and physiology in terms of chemistry.
– DERIVATIVES **iatrochemical** adjective, **iatrochemist** noun.

iatrogenic /ʌɪˌatrə(ʊ)'dʒɛnɪk/ ▶ adjective of or relating to illness caused by medical examination or treatment.
– DERIVATIVES **iatrogenesis** noun.

IB ▶ abbreviation for International Baccalaureate.

ib. ▶ adverb short for IBID.

IBA ▶ abbreviation for (in the UK) Independent Broadcasting Authority.

Ibadan /ɪ'bad(ə)n/ the second-largest city of Nigeria, situated 160 km (100 miles) north-east of Lagos; pop. 1,295,000 (1991).

Iban /'iːban/ ▶ noun (pl. same) **1** a member of an indigenous people of Kalimantan and Sarawak. Also called **SEA DAYAK**.
2 [mass noun] the Austronesian language of this people, spoken by around 380,000 people.
▶ adjective of or relating to the Iban or their language.

– ORIGIN the name in Iban.

Ibárruri Gómez /ɪˌbɑːrʊrɪ 'gəʊmɛz, Spanish i'barruri 'gomeθ, -mes/, Dolores (1895–1989), Spanish communist politician and leader of the Republicans during the Spanish Civil War; known as La Pasionaria.

I-beam ▶ noun a girder which has the shape of an I when viewed in section.

Iberia /ʌɪ'bɪərɪə/ the ancient name for the Iberian peninsula.
– ORIGIN Latin, literally 'the country of the *Iberi* or *Iberes*', from Greek *Ibēres* 'Spaniards'.

Iberian ▶ adjective relating to or denoting Iberia, or the countries of Spain and Portugal.
▶ noun **1** a native of Iberia, especially in ancient times.
2 [mass noun] the extinct Romance language spoken in the Iberian peninsula in late classical times. It forms an intermediate stage between Latin and modern Spanish, Catalan, and Portuguese. Also called **IBERO-ROMANCE**.
3 [mass noun] the extinct Celtic language spoken in the Iberian peninsula in ancient times, known only from a few inscriptions, place names, and references by Latin authors. Also called **CELTIBERIAN**.

Iberian peninsula the extreme SW peninsula of Europe, containing present-day Spain and Portugal. It was colonized by Carthage until the third Punic War (149–146 BC), after which it came increasingly under Roman influence. It was invaded by the Visigoths in the 4th–5th centuries AD and by the Moors in the 8th century.

iberis /ʌɪ'bɪərɪs/ ▶ noun (pl. same) a plant of a genus that comprises the candytufts.
● Genus *Iberis*, family Cruciferae.
– ORIGIN modern Latin, probably from Greek *ibēris*, denoting a kind of pepperwort.

Ibero- /ʌɪ'bɪərəʊ/ ▶ combining form Iberian; Iberian and …: *Ibero-Roman.*
▪ relating to Iberia.

Ibero-Romance ▶ noun another term for **IBERIAN** (in sense 2).

ibex /'ʌɪbɛks/ ▶ noun (pl. **ibexes**) a wild goat with long, thick ridged horns and a beard, found in the mountains of the Alps, Pyrenees, central Asia, and Ethiopia.
● Genus *Capra*, family Bovidae: the widespread *C. ibex*, and the **Spanish ibex** (*C. pyrenaica*) of the Pyrenees.
– ORIGIN early 17th cent.: from Latin.

IBF ▶ abbreviation for International Boxing Federation.

Ibibio /ˌɪbɪ'biːəʊ/ ▶ noun (pl. same or **-os**) **1** a member of a people of southern Nigeria.
2 [mass noun] the language of this people, belonging to the Benue-Congo group and closely related to Efik. It has around 2 million speakers.
▶ adjective of or relating to this people or their language.
– ORIGIN the name in Ibibio.

ibid. /'ɪbɪd/ (also **ib.**) ▶ adverb in the same source (used to save space in textual references to a quoted work which has been mentioned in a previous reference).

– ORIGIN abbreviation of Latin *ibidem* 'in the same place'.

-ibility ▶ **suffix** forming nouns corresponding to adjectives ending in *-ible* (such as *accessibility* corresponding to *accessible*).
– ORIGIN from French *-ibilité* or Latin *-ibilitas*.

I.Biol. ▶ **abbreviation for** (in the UK) Institute of Biology.

ibis /ˈʌɪbɪs/ ▶ **noun** (pl. **ibises**) a large wading bird with a long downcurved bill, long neck, and long legs.
• Family Threskiornithidae: several genera and species, including the **sacred ibis**.
– ORIGIN late Middle English: via Latin from Greek.

ibisbill ▶ **noun** an upland wading bird of central Asia, with a long downcurved bill and black, white, and blue-grey plumage on the head and breast.
• *Ibidorhyncha struthersii*, the only member of the family Ibidorhynchidae.

Ibiza /ɪˈbiːθə, Spanish iˈβiθa, -sa/ the westernmost of the Balearic Islands.
■ its capital city and port; pop. 25,490 (1981).
– DERIVATIVES **Ibizan** adjective & noun.

Ibizan hound ▶ **noun** a dog of a breed of hound from Ibiza, characterized by large, pointed, pricked ears and white, fawn, or reddish-brown colouring.

-ible ▶ **suffix** forming adjectives: **1** able to be: *audible* | *defensible*.
2 suitable for being: *reversible* | *edible*.
3 causing: *terrible* | *horrible*.
4 having the quality to: *descendible* | *passible*.
– ORIGIN from French *-ible* or Latin *-ibilis*.

-ibly ▶ **suffix** forming adverbs corresponding to adjectives ending in *-ible* (such as *audibly* corresponding to *audible*).

IBM ▶ **abbreviation for** International Business Machines, a leading American computer manufacturer.

Ibn Batuta /ˌɪb(ə)n bɑːˈtuːtɑː/ (*c.*1304–68), Arab explorer. From 1325 to 1354 he journeyed through North and West Africa, India, and China, and wrote a vivid account of his travels in the *Rihlah*.

ibn Hussein, Abdullah, see **ABDULLAH IBN HUSSEIN**.

Ibo /ˈiːbəʊ/ ▶ **noun** & **adjective** see **IGBO**.

ibogaine /ɪˈbəʊɡəˌiːn/ ▶ **noun** [mass noun] a hallucinogenic compound derived from the roots of a West African shrub, sometimes used as a treatment for heroin or cocaine addiction.
• The shrub is *Tabernanthe iboga*, family Apocynaceae.
– ORIGIN from a blend of *iboga* (local name for the compound) and **COCAINE**.

IBRD ▶ **abbreviation for** International Bank for Reconstruction and Development.

IBS ▶ **abbreviation for** irritable bowel syndrome.

Ibsen /ˈɪbs(ə)n/, Henrik (1828–1906), Norwegian dramatist. He is credited with being the first major dramatist to write tragedy about ordinary people in prose. Ibsen's later works, such as *The Master Builder* (1892), deal increasingly with the forces of the unconscious and were admired by Sigmund Freud. Other notable works: *Peer Gynt* (1867), *A Doll's House* (1879), *Ghosts* (1881).

ibuprofen /ˌʌɪbjuːˈprəʊf(ə)n/ ▶ **noun** [mass noun] a synthetic compound used widely as an analgesic and anti-inflammatory drug.
• Alternative name: **2-(4-isobutylphenyl) propionic acid**; chem. formula: $C_{13}H_{18}O_2$.
– ORIGIN 1960s: from elements of the chemical name.

IC ▶ **abbreviation for** ■ integrated circuit. ■ internal-combustion: *the IC engine*.

i/c ▶ **abbreviation for** ■ (especially in military contexts) in charge of: *the Quartermaster General is i/c rations*. ■ in command: *2 i/c = second in command*.

-ic ▶ **suffix 1** forming adjectives such as *Islamic*, *terrific*.
2 forming nouns such as *lyric*, *mechanic*.
3 denoting a particular form or instance of a noun ending in *-ics*: *aesthetic* | *dietetic* | *tactic*.
4 Chemistry denoting an element in a higher valency: *ferric* | *sulphuric*. Compare with **-OUS**.
– ORIGIN from French *-ique*, Latin *-icus*, or Greek *-ikos*.

-ical ▶ **suffix** forming adjectives: **1** corresponding to nouns or adjectives usually ending in *-ic* (such as *comical* corresponding to *comic*).
2 corresponding to nouns ending in *-y* (such as *pathological* corresponding to *pathology*).

-ically ▶ **suffix** forming adverbs corresponding to adjectives ending in *-ic* or *-ical* (such as *tactically* corresponding to *tactical*).

ICAO ▶ **abbreviation for** International Civil Aviation Organization.

Icarus /ˈɪkərəs/ Greek Mythology the son of Daedalus, who escaped from Crete using wings made by his father but was killed when he flew too near the sun and the wax attaching his wings melted.
– DERIVATIVES **Icarian** adjective.

ICBM ▶ **abbreviation for** intercontinental ballistic missile.

ICC ▶ **abbreviation for** ■ International Chamber of Commerce. ■ International Cricket Council. ■ (in the US) Interstate Commerce Commission.

ICE ▶ **abbreviation for** ■ (in the UK) Institution of Civil Engineers. ■ internal-combustion engine.

ice ▶ **noun** [mass noun] frozen water, a brittle transparent crystalline solid: *the pipes were blocked with ice*.
■ [count noun] chiefly Brit. an ice cream, ice lolly, or portion of water ice. ■ informal diamonds. ■ figurative complete absence of friendliness or affection in manner or expression: *the ice in his voice was only to hide the pain*.
▶ **verb** [with obj.] **1** decorate (a cake) with icing.
2 N. Amer. informal clinch (something such as a victory or deal).
3 N. Amer. informal kill: *a man had been iced by the police*.
– PHRASES **break the ice** do or say something to relieve tension or get conversation going at the start of a party or when people meet for the first time. **ice the puck** Ice Hockey shoot the puck from one's own half of the rink to the other end without it hitting the goal or being touched by a teammate, for which a face-off is awarded in one's own end. **on ice 1** (of wine or food) kept chilled by being surrounded by ice. ■ figurative (especially of a plan or proposal) held in reserve for future consideration: *the recommendation was put on ice*. **2** (of an entertainment) performed by skaters: *Dick Whittington on Ice*. **on thin ice** in a precarious or risky situation: *you're skating on thin ice*.
– ORIGIN Old English *īs*, of Germanic origin; related to Dutch *ijs* and German *Eis*.
▶ **ice over** (of water or an object) become completely covered with ice.
ice up (of an object) become coated with or blocked by ice.

-ice ▶ **suffix** forming nouns such as *service*, *police*, and abstract nouns such as *avarice*, *justice*.
– ORIGIN from Old French *-ice*, from Latin *-itia*, *-itius*, *-itium*, or from other sources by assimilation.

ice age ▶ **noun** a glacial episode during a past geological period. See **GLACIAL PERIOD**.
■ (**the Ice Age**) the series of glacial episodes during the Pleistocene period.

ice axe ▶ **noun** an axe used by climbers for cutting footholds in ice, having a head with one pointed and one flattened end, and a spike at the foot.

ice bag ▶ **noun** a bag filled with ice and applied to the body to reduce swelling or lower temperature.

ice beer ▶ **noun** [mass noun] a type of strong lager brewed at sub-zero temperatures so that ice crystals form. These are then strained off to remove impurities and excess water.

iceberg ▶ **noun** a large floating mass of ice detached from a glacier or ice sheet and carried out to sea.
– PHRASES **the tip of an** (or **the**) **iceberg** the small perceptible part of a much larger situation or problem that remains hidden: *detected fraud is only the tip of the iceberg*.
– ORIGIN late 18th cent.: from Dutch *ijsberg*, from *ijs* 'ice' + *berg* 'hill'.

iceberg lettuce ▶ **noun** a lettuce of a variety having a dense round head of crisp pale leaves.

iceblink ▶ **noun** a bright appearance of the sky caused by reflection from a distant ice sheet.

iceblock ▶ **noun** Austral./NZ a block of flavoured ice on a stick.

ice blue ▶ **noun** [mass noun] a very pale blue colour.

iceboat ▶ **noun 1** a light, wind-driven vehicle with sails and runners, used for travelling on ice.
2 a boat used for breaking ice on a waterway.

ice-bound ▶ **adjective** completely surrounded or covered by ice: *the lake was ice-bound*.

icebox ▶ **noun** a chilled box or cupboard for keeping something cold, especially food.
■ Brit. a compartment in a refrigerator for making and storing ice. ■ US dated a refrigerator.

ice-breaker ▶ **noun** a ship designed for breaking a channel through ice.
■ a thing that serves to relieve inhibitions or tension between people, or start a conversation.

ice bucket ▶ **noun** a cylindrical container holding chunks of ice, either ready to serve in drinks or for chilling a bottle of wine in.

ice cap ▶ **noun** a covering of ice over a large area, especially on the polar region of a planet.

ice chest ▶ **noun** a chilled box for keeping something cold, especially food.

ice climbing ▶ **noun** [mass noun] the sport or activity of climbing glaciers.
– DERIVATIVES **ice climber** noun.

ice-cold ▶ **adjective** (especially of a liquid) very cold; as cold as ice: *there is plenty of ice-cold beer*.
■ figurative unemotional or dispassionate; unfeeling: *he is the epitome of ice-cold judgement*.

ice cream ▶ **noun** [mass noun] a soft frozen food made with sweetened and flavoured milk fat.
■ [count noun] a serving of this, typically in a tub or a wafer cone or on a stick.
– ORIGIN mid 18th cent.: alteration of *iced cream*.

ice cube ▶ **noun** a small block of ice made in a freezer, especially for adding to drinks.

iced ▶ **adjective** [attrib.] **1** (of a drink or other liquid) cooled in or mixed with pieces of ice: *jugs of iced water*.
■ (of a surface or object) covered or coated with ice: *I've played ice hockey on rivers, ponds, and iced barnyards*.
2 (of a cake or biscuit) decorated with icing.

ice dancing ▶ **noun** [mass noun] a form of ice skating incorporating choreographed dance moves, typically performed by skaters in pairs.
– DERIVATIVES **ice dance** noun, **ice dancer** noun.

iced lolly ▶ **noun** variant spelling of **ICE LOLLY**.

iced tea (also **ice tea**) ▶ **noun** [mass noun] a chilled drink of sweetened tea, typically flavoured with lemon.

icefall ▶ **noun 1** a steep part of a glacier like a frozen waterfall.
2 a fall of loose ice; an avalanche of ice.

ice field ▶ **noun** an expanse of ice, especially in polar regions.

icefish ▶ **noun** (pl. same or **-fishes**) **1** another term for **CAPELIN**.
2 a scaleless Antarctic fish of pallid appearance with spiny gill covers and a snout shaped like a duck's bill.
• *Chaenocephalus aceratus*, family Chaenichthyidae.
▶ **verb** (**ice-fish**) [no obj.] [usu. as noun **ice-fishing**] fish through holes in the ice on a lake or river.

ice floe ▶ **noun** see **FLOE**.

ice fog ▶ **noun** [mass noun] N. Amer. fog formed of minute ice crystals.

ice front ▶ **noun** the lower edge of a glacier.

ice hockey ▶ **noun** [mass noun] a fast contact sport played on an ice rink between two teams of six skaters, who attempt to drive a small rubber disc or puck into the opposing goal with hooked or angled sticks. It developed from field hockey in Canada in the second half of the 19th century.

ice house ▶ **noun** a building for storing ice, typically one situated partly or wholly underground.

Iceland an island country in the North Atlantic; pop. 300,000 (est. 1990); official language, Icelandic; capital, Reykjavik. Icelandic name **ISLAND**.

Iceland lies just south of the Arctic Circle, and only about 20 per cent of the land area is habitable. Situated at the north end of the Mid-Atlantic Ridge, it is volcanically active. First settled by Norse colonists in the 9th century, Iceland was under Norwegian rule from 1262 to 1380, when it passed to Denmark. Granted internal self-government in 1874, it became a fully fledged independent republic in 1944.

– DERIVATIVES **Icelander** noun.

Icelandic /ʌɪsˈlandɪk/ ▶ **adjective** of or relating to Iceland or its language.
▶ **noun** [mass noun] the language of Iceland. It is a Scandinavian language which has remained closely similar to Old Norse, due partly to the geographical isolation of Iceland and partly to a policy of avoiding loanwords.

Iceland moss (also **Iceland lichen**) ▶ **noun** a brown branching lichen with stiff spines along the

margins of the fronds, growing in mountain and moorland habitats. It can be boiled to produce an edible jelly.
● *Cetraria islandica*, order Parmeliales.

Iceland poppy ▶ noun a tall poppy which is widely cultivated for its colourful flowers and suitability for cutting, native to arctic and north temperate regions.
● *Papaver nudicaule*, family Papaveraceae.

Iceland spar ▶ noun [mass noun] a transparent variety of calcite, showing strong double refraction.

ice lolly (also **iced lolly**) ▶ noun Brit. a piece of flavoured ice or ice cream on a stick.

iceman ▶ noun (pl. **-men**) chiefly N. Amer. a man who sells or delivers ice.

ice milk ▶ noun [mass noun] N. Amer. a sweet frozen food similar to ice cream but containing less butterfat.

Iceni /ʌɪˈsiːni, -nʌɪ/ ▶ plural noun a tribe of ancient Britons inhabiting an area of SE England in present-day Norfolk and Suffolk. Their queen, Boudicca, led an unsuccessful rebellion against the Romans in AD 60.

ice pack ▶ noun 1 another term for **ICE BAG**.
2 see **PACK**[1] (sense 2).

ice pick ▶ noun 1 a small pick used by climbers to traverse ice-covered slopes.
2 a sharp, straight, pointed implement with a handle, used to break ice into small pieces for chilling food and drinks.

ice plant ▶ noun 1 either of two succulent plants which are widely cultivated for their flowers:
● a South African plant which has leaves covered with glistening fluid-filled hairs that resemble ice crystals (genera *Mesembryanthemum* and *Dorotheanthus*, family Aizoaceae, in particular *M. crystallinum*). ● an Asian stonecrop which bears domed heads of tiny pink flowers (*Sedum spectabile*, family Crassulaceae).
2 a machine or installation for making ice artificially.

ice rink ▶ noun see **RINK**.

ice shelf ▶ noun a floating sheet of ice permanently attached to a land mass.

ice show ▶ noun an entertainment performed by ice skaters.

ice skate ▶ noun a boot with a blade attached to the sole, used for skating on ice.
▶ verb (**ice-skate**) [no obj.] skate on ice as a sport or pastime.
– DERIVATIVES **ice skater** noun.

ice skating ▶ noun [mass noun] skating on ice as a sport or pastime. Ice skating became a recognized sport in 1876. Skaters are marked for technical and artistic excellence in performing a series of prescribed patterns (**figure skating**) or a choreographed series of dance moves (**ice dancing**).

ice storm ▶ noun chiefly N. Amer. a storm of freezing rain that leaves a coating of ice.

ice tea ▶ noun another term for **ICED TEA**.

ice water ▶ noun [mass noun] water melted from ice or with ice added to cool it.

ice yacht ▶ noun another term for **ICEBOAT** (in sense 1).

ICFTU ▶ abbreviation for International Confederation of Free Trade Unions.

I.Chem.E. ▶ abbreviation for (in the UK) Institution of Chemical Engineers.

I Ching /iː ˈtʃɪŋ/ ▶ noun an ancient Chinese manual of divination based on eight symbolic trigrams and sixty-four hexagrams, interpreted in terms of the principles of yin and yang. It was included as one of the 'five classics' of Confucianism. English name **BOOK OF CHANGES**.
– ORIGIN from Chinese *yijing* 'book of changes'.

ichneumon /ɪkˈnjuːmən/ ▶ noun 1 (also **ichneumon wasp** or **ichneumon fly**) a slender parasitic wasp with long antennae, which deposits its eggs in, on, or near the larvae of other insects.
● Family Ichneumonidae, order Hymenoptera: numerous genera and species.
2 another term for **EGYPTIAN MONGOOSE**.
– ORIGIN late 15th cent. (in sense 2): via Latin from Greek *ikhneumōn* 'tracker', from *ikhneuein* 'to track', from *ikhnos* 'track, footstep'.

ichnography /ɪkˈnɒɡrəfi/ ▶ noun (pl. **-ies**) a ground plan of a building or map of a region.
– ORIGIN late 16th cent.: from French *ichnographie*, or

via Latin from Greek *ikhnographia*, from *ikhnos* 'track' + *-graphia* (see **-GRAPHY**).

ichor /ˈʌɪkɔː/ ▶ noun [mass noun] Greek Mythology the fluid which flows like blood in the veins of the gods.
■ poetic/literary any blood-like fluid: *tomatoes drooled ichor from their broken skins*. ■ archaic a watery fetid discharge from a wound.
– DERIVATIVES **ichorous** /ˈʌɪk(ə)rəs/ adjective.
– ORIGIN mid 17th cent.: from Greek *ikhōr*.

ichthyic /ˈɪkθɪk/ ▶ adjective archaic fishlike.
– ORIGIN mid 19th cent.: from Greek *ikhthuïkos* 'fishy', from *ikhthus* 'fish'.

ichthyo- /ˈɪkθɪəʊ/ ▶ combining form relating to fish; fishlike: *ichthyosaur*.
– ORIGIN from Greek *ikhthus* 'fish'.

ichthyolite /ˈɪkθɪəlʌɪt/ ▶ noun Palaeontology a fossil fish.
– ORIGIN early 19th cent.: from **ICHTHYO-** 'fish' + Latin *oleum* 'oil' + *lithos* 'stone'.

ichthyology /ˌɪkθɪˈɒlədʒi/ ▶ noun [mass noun] the branch of zoology that deals with fishes.
– DERIVATIVES **ichthyological** adjective, **ichthyologist** noun.

ichthyophagous /ˌɪkθɪˈɒfəɡəs/ ▶ adjective formal fish-eating: *Americans are more ichthyophagous than ever*.
– DERIVATIVES **ichthyophagy** noun.

ichthyornis /ˌɪkθɪˈɔːnɪs/ ▶ noun a fossil gull-like fish-eating bird of the Upper Cretaceous period, with large toothed jaws.
● Genus *Ichthyornis*, order Ichthyornithiformes.
– ORIGIN modern Latin, from **ICHTHYO-** + Greek *ornis* 'bird'.

ichthyosaur /ˈɪkθɪəsɔː/ (also **ichthyosaurus** /ˌɪkθɪəˈsɔːrəs/) ▶ noun a fossil marine reptile of the Mesozoic era, resembling a dolphin with a long pointed head, four flippers, and a vertical tail.
● Order Ichthyosauria, subclass Diapsida: numerous genera, including *Ichthyosaurus*.
– ORIGIN mid 19th cent.: from **ICHTHYO-** 'fish' + Greek *sauros* 'lizard'.

ichthyosis /ˌɪkθɪˈəʊsɪs/ ▶ noun [mass noun] Medicine a congenital skin condition which causes the epidermis to become dry and horny like fish scales.
– DERIVATIVES **ichthyotic** adjective.

I-chun /iːˈtʃʊn/ variant of **YICHUN**.

ICI ▶ abbreviation for Imperial Chemical Industries (Limited).

-ician ▶ suffix (forming nouns) denoting a person skilled in or concerned with a field or subject (often corresponding to a noun ending in *-ic* or *-ics*): *politician | statistician*.
– ORIGIN from French *-icien*.

icicle ▶ noun a hanging, tapering piece of ice formed by the freezing of dripping water.
– ORIGIN Middle English: from **ICE** + dialect *ickle* 'icicle' (from Old English *gicel*).

icing ▶ noun [mass noun] 1 a mixture of sugar with liquid or fat, typically flavoured and coloured, and used as a coating for cakes or biscuits.
2 the formation of ice on an aircraft, ship, or other vehicle, or in an engine.
– PHRASES **the icing** (N. Amer. also **frosting**) **on the cake** an attractive but inessential addition or enhancement: *more goals would have been the icing on the cake*.

icing sugar ▶ noun [mass noun] chiefly Brit. finely powdered sugar used to make icing.

-icist ▶ suffix equivalent to **-ICIAN**.
– ORIGIN based on forms ending in **-IC**, + **-IST**.

-icity ▶ suffix forming abstract nouns especially from adjectives ending in *-ic* (such as *authenticity* from *authentic*).
– ORIGIN based on forms ending in **-IC**, + **-ITY**.

ick ▶ noun [mass noun] informal, chiefly N. Amer. a sticky or congealed substance, typically regarded with disgust: *she scrubbed the ick off the back of the stove* | [as exclamation] *oatmeal—ick!*
– ORIGIN 1940s: probably imitative.

-ick ▶ suffix archaic variant spelling of **-IC**.

Icknield Way /ˈɪkniːld/ an ancient pre-Roman track which crosses England in a wide curve from Wiltshire to Norfolk.

icky ▶ adjective (**-ier**, **-iest**) informal sticky, especially unpleasantly so.
■ distastefully sentimental: *a romantic sub-plot that is just plain icky*. ■ nasty or repulsive (used as a general

term of disapproval): *icky boys with all their macho strutting*.
– DERIVATIVES **ickiness** noun.
– ORIGIN 1930s: perhaps related to **SICK**[1] or to the child's word *ickle* 'little'.

-icle ▶ suffix forming nouns which were originally diminutives: *article | particle*.
– ORIGIN see **-CULE**.

icon /ˈʌɪkɒn, -k(ə)n/ (also **ikon**) ▶ noun a painting of Christ or another holy figure, typically in a traditional style on wood, venerated and used as an aid to devotion in the Byzantine and other Eastern Churches.
■ a person or thing regarded as a representative symbol of something: *this iron-jawed icon of American manhood*. ■ Computing a symbol or graphic representation on a VDU screen of a program, option, or window, especially one of several for selection. ■ Linguistics a sign which has a characteristic in common with the thing it signifies, for example the word *snarl* pronounced in a snarling way.
– ORIGIN mid 16th cent. (in the sense 'simile'): via Latin from Greek *eikōn* 'likeness, image'. Current senses date from the mid 19th cent. onwards.

iconic ▶ adjective of, relating to, or of the nature of an icon: *language is not in general an iconic sign system*.
■ (of a classical Greek statue) depicting a victorious athlete in a conventional style.
– DERIVATIVES **iconically** adverb, **iconicity** noun (especially in linguistics).
– ORIGIN late 17th cent.: from Latin *iconicus*, from Greek *eikonikos*, from *eikōn* 'likeness, image'.

iconify ▶ verb (**-ies**, **-ied**) [with obj.] Computing reduce (a window on a VDU screen) to a small symbol or graphic representation of itself so as to make room on the screen for other windows.

icono- ▶ combining form 1 of an image or likeness: *iconology*.
2 relating to icons: *iconodule*.
– ORIGIN from Greek *eikōn* 'likeness'.

iconoclasm /ʌɪˈkɒnəklaz(ə)m/ ▶ noun [mass noun] 1 the action of attacking or assertively rejecting cherished beliefs and institutions or established values and practices.
2 the rejection or destruction of religious images as heretical; the doctrine of iconoclasts.
– ORIGIN late 18th cent.: from **ICONOCLAST**, on the pattern of pairs such as *enthusiast, enthusiasm*.

iconoclast /ʌɪˈkɒnəklast/ ▶ noun 1 a person who attacks cherished beliefs or institutions.
2 a destroyer of images used in religious worship, in particular:
■ historical a supporter of the 8th- and 9th-century movement in the Byzantine Church which sought to abolish the veneration of icons and other religious images. ■ historical a Puritan of the 16th or 17th century.
– DERIVATIVES **iconoclastic** adjective, **iconoclastically** adverb.
– ORIGIN mid 17th cent. (in sense 2): via medieval Latin from ecclesiastical Greek *eikonoklastēs*, from *eikōn* 'likeness' + *klan* 'to break'.

iconodule /ʌɪˈkɒnə(ʊ)djuːl/ ▶ noun a person who favours the veneration of religious icons (especially as contrasted historically with an iconoclast).
– DERIVATIVES **iconodulist** noun.

iconography /ˌʌɪkəˈnɒɡrəfi/ ▶ noun (pl. **-ies**) 1 [mass noun] the use or study of images or symbols in visual arts.
■ the visual images, symbols, or modes of representation collectively associated with a person, cult, or movement: *the iconography of pop culture*.
2 the illustration of a subject by drawings or figures.
■ [count noun] a collection of illustrations or portraits.
– DERIVATIVES **iconographer** noun, **iconographic** adjective, **iconographical** adjective, **iconographically** adverb.
– ORIGIN early 17th cent. (denoting a drawing or plan): from Greek *eikonographia* 'sketch, description', from *eikōn* 'likeness' + *-graphia* 'writing'.

iconolatry /ˌʌɪkəˈnɒlətri/ ▶ noun [mass noun] chiefly derogatory the worship of icons.
– ORIGIN early 17th cent.: from ecclesiastical Greek *eikonolatreia*, from *eikōn* 'likeness' + *-latria* 'worship'.

iconology /ˌʌɪkəˈnɒlədʒi/ ▶ noun [mass noun] the study of visual imagery and its symbolism and interpretation, especially in social or political terms.

■symbolism: *the iconology of a work of art.*
– DERIVATIVES **iconological** adjective.

iconostasis /ˌʌɪkəˈnɒstəsɪs/ ▶ noun (pl. **iconostases** /-siːz/) a screen bearing icons, separating the sanctuary of many Eastern churches from the nave.
– ORIGIN mid 19th cent.: from modern Greek *eikonostasis*, from *eikōn* 'likeness' + *stasis* 'standing, stopping'.

icosahedron /ˌʌɪkɒsəˈhiːdrən, -ˈhɛd-/ ▶ noun (pl. **icosahedra** or **icosahedrons**) a solid figure with twenty plane faces, especially equilateral triangular ones.
– DERIVATIVES **icosahedral** adjective.
– ORIGIN late 16th cent.: via late Latin from Greek *eikosaedron*, neuter (used as a noun) of *eikosaedros* 'twenty-faced'.

-ics ▶ suffix (forming nouns) denoting arts or sciences, branches of study or action: *classics* | *politics.*
– ORIGIN from French *-iques*, Latin *-ica*, or Greek *-ika*, plural forms.

USAGE A noun ending in **-ics** meaning 'a subject of study or branch of knowledge' will usually take a singular rather than a plural verb, e.g. *politics is* a blood sport; *classics is* hardly studied at all these days. However, the same word may take a plural verb in cases where the sense is plural: *many of the classics were* formerly regarded with disdain.

ictal /ˈɪktəl/ ▶ adjective Medicine of or relating to a seizure.
– ORIGIN 1950s: from **ICTUS** + **-AL**.

icterine warbler /ˈɪkt(ə)rʌɪn/ ▶ noun a Eurasian warbler with bright yellow underparts.
● *Hippolais icterina,* family Sylviidae.
– ORIGIN mid 19th cent.: *icterine* from **ICTERUS** + **-INE**[1].

icterus /ˈɪkt(ə)rəs/ ▶ noun Medicine technical term for **JAUNDICE**.
– DERIVATIVES **icteric** /ɪkˈtɛrɪk/ adjective.
– ORIGIN early 18th cent.: via Latin from Greek *ikteros*. The Latin term denoted jaundice, also a yellowish-green bird (the sight of which was thought to cure jaundice).

Ictinus /ɪkˈtʌɪnəs/ (5th century BC), Greek architect. He is said to have designed the Parthenon in Athens with the architect Callicrates and the sculptor Phidias between 448 and 437 BC.

ictus /ˈɪktəs/ ▶ noun (pl. same or **ictuses**) 1 Prosody a rhythmical or metrical stress.
2 Medicine a stroke or seizure; a fit.
– ORIGIN early 18th cent. (denoting the beat of the pulse): from Latin, literally 'blow', from *icere* 'to strike'.

ICU ▶ abbreviation for intensive-care unit.

icy ▶ adjective (**icier, iciest**) covered with or consisting of ice: *there were icy patches on the roads.*
■very cold: *an icy wind.* ■ figurative (of a person's tone or manner) very unfriendly; hostile: *her voice was icy.*
– DERIVATIVES **icily** adverb, **iciness** noun.

ID ▶ abbreviation for ■ Idaho (in official postal use).
■ identification or identity: *they weren't carrying any ID* | [as modifier] *an ID card.*

Id ▶ noun variant spelling of **EID**.

I'd ▶ contraction of ■ I had: *I'd agreed to go.* ■ I should or I would: *I'd like a bath.*

id /ɪd/ ▶ noun Psychoanalysis the part of the mind in which innate instinctive impulses and primary processes are manifest. Compare with **EGO** and **SUPEREGO**.
– ORIGIN 1920s: from Latin, literally 'that', translating German *es*. The term was first used in this sense by Freud, following use in a similar sense by his contemporary, Georg Groddeck.

id. ▶ abbreviation for idem.

-id[1] ▶ suffix forming adjectives such as *putrid, torrid.*
– ORIGIN from French *-ide* from Latin *-idus.*

-id[2] ▶ suffix 1 forming nouns such as *chrysalid, pyramid.*
2 Biology forming names of structural constituents: *plastid.*
3 Botany forming names of plants belonging to a family with a name ending in *-idaceae: orchid.*
– ORIGIN from or suggested by French *-ide*, via Latin *-idis* from Greek *-is, -id-.*

-id[3] ▶ suffix forming nouns: 1 Zoology denoting an animal belonging to a family with a name ending in *-idae* or to a class with a name ending in *-ida: carabid | arachnid.*
2 denoting a member of a specified dynasty or family.
3 Astronomy denoting a meteor in a shower radiating from a specified constellation: *Geminids.*
■denoting a star of a class like one in a specified constellation: *cepheid.*
– ORIGIN from or suggested by Latin *-ides* (plural *-idae, -ida*), from Greek.

IDA ▶ abbreviation for International Development Association.

Ida /ˈʌɪdə/ 1 a mountain in central Crete, associated in classical times with the god Zeus. Rising to 2,456 m (8,058 ft), it is the highest peak in the island.
2 Astronomy asteroid 243, which is 52 km long and has a tiny moon (Dactyl), which is about 1.5 km across.

Idaho /ˈʌɪdəhəʊ/ a state of the north-western US, bordering on British Columbia to the north and containing part of the Rocky Mountains; pop. 1,007,750 (1990); capital, Boise. It became the 43rd state of the US in 1890.
– DERIVATIVES **Idahoan** noun & adjective.

IDB S. African ▶ abbreviation for illicit diamond buyer (or buying), an illegal trader (or illegal trading) in uncut diamonds.

iddingsite /ˈɪdɪŋzʌɪt/ ▶ noun [mass noun] a brownish mineral deposit consisting of a mixture of silicates, formed by alteration of olivine.
– ORIGIN late 19th cent.: from the name of Joseph P. Iddings (1857–1920), American geologist, + **-ITE**[1].

IDE Computing ▶ abbreviation for Integrated Drive Electronics, a standard for interfacing computers and their peripherals.

ide /ʌɪd/ ▶ noun another term for **ORFE**.
– ORIGIN mid 19th cent.: from modern Latin *idus*, from Swedish *id*.

-ide ▶ suffix Chemistry forming nouns: denoting binary compounds of a non-metallic or more electronegative element or group: *cyanide | sodium chloride.*
■denoting various other compounds: *peptide | saccharide.* ■ denoting elements of a series in the periodic table: *lanthanide.*
– ORIGIN originally used in *oxide.*

idea ▶ noun 1 a thought or suggestion as to a possible course of action: *they don't think it's a very good idea.*
■[in sing.] a concept or mental impression: *our menu list will give you some idea of how interesting a low-fat diet can be.* ■ an opinion or belief: *nineteenth-century ideas about drinking.* ■ [in sing.] a feeling that something is probable or possible: *he had an idea that she must feel the same.*
2 (**the idea**) the aim or purpose: *I took a job with the idea of getting some money together.*
3 Philosophy (in Platonic thought) an eternally existing pattern of which individual things in any class are imperfect copies.
■(in Kantian thought) a concept of pure reason, not empirically based in experience.
– PHRASES **get** (or **give someone**) **ideas** informal become (or make someone) ambitious, big-headed, or tempted to do something against someone else's will, especially make a sexual advance: *MacDougall began to get ideas above his station.* **have** (**got**) **no idea** informal not know at all: *she had no idea where she was going.* **not someone's idea of** informal not what someone regards as: *it's not my idea of a happy ending.* **put ideas into someone's head** suggest ambitions or thoughts that a person would not otherwise have had. **that's an idea** informal that suggestion or proposal is worth considering. **that's the idea** informal used to confirm to someone that they have understood something or they are doing something correctly: *'A sort of bodyguard?' 'That's the idea.'* **the very idea!** informal an exclamation of disapproval or disagreement.
– ORIGIN late Middle English (in sense 3): via Latin from Greek *idea* 'form, pattern', from the base of *idein* 'to see'.

ideal ▶ adjective 1 satisfying one's conception of what is perfect; most suitable: *the swimming pool is ideal for a quick dip | this is an ideal opportunity to save money.*
2 [attrib.] existing only in the imagination; desirable or perfect but not likely to become a reality: *in an ideal world, we might have made a different decision.*
■representing an abstract or hypothetical optimum: *mathematical modelling can determine theoretically ideal conditions.*
▶ noun a person or thing regarded as perfect: *you're my ideal of how a man should be.*
■a standard of perfection; a principle to be aimed at: *tolerance and freedom, the liberal ideals.*
– DERIVATIVES **ideally** adverb.
– ORIGIN late Middle English (as a term in Platonic philosophy, in the sense 'existing as an archetype'): from late Latin *idealis*, from Latin *idea* (see **IDEA**).

ideal gas ▶ noun Chemistry a hypothetical gas whose molecules occupy negligible space and have no interactions, and which consequently obeys the gas laws exactly.

idealism ▶ noun [mass noun] 1 the practice of forming or pursuing ideals, especially unrealistically: *the idealism of youth.* Compare with **REALISM**.
■(in art or literature) the representation of things in ideal or idealized form. Often contrasted with **REALISM** (in sense 2).
2 Philosophy any of various systems of thought in which the objects of knowledge are held to be in some way dependent on the activity of mind. Often contrasted with **REALISM** (in sense 3).
– DERIVATIVES **idealist** noun, **idealistic** adjective, **idealistically** adverb.
– ORIGIN late 18th cent. (in sense 2): from French *idéalisme* or German *Idealismus*, from late Latin *idealis* (see **IDEAL**).

ideality /ˌʌɪdɪˈalɪti/ ▶ noun (pl. **-ies**) [mass noun] formal the state or quality of being ideal: *the ideality of the island of Aran.*
■the quality of expressing or being characterized by ideals: *the loftiness and ideality of the Gettysburg Address.* ■ [count noun] archaic an ideal or idealized thing: *they commenced their married life with idealities about love.*

idealize (also **-ise**) ▶ verb [with obj.] [often as adj. **idealized**] regard or represent as perfect or better than in reality: *Helen's idealized accounts of their life together.*
– DERIVATIVES **idealization** noun, **idealizer** noun.

ideate /ˈʌɪdɪeɪt/ ▶ verb [with obj.] [often as adj. **ideated**] form an idea of; imagine or conceive: *the arc whose ideated centre is a nodal point in the composition.*
■[no obj.] form ideas; think.
– ORIGIN late 17th cent.: from medieval Latin *ideat-* 'formed as an idea', from the verb *ideare*, from Latin *idea* (see **IDEA**).

ideation ▶ noun [mass noun] the formation of ideas or concepts.
– DERIVATIVES **ideational** adjective, **ideationally** adverb.

idée fixe /ˌiːdeɪ ˈfiːks/ ▶ noun (pl. **idées fixes** pronunc. same) an idea or desire that dominates the mind; an obsession.
– ORIGIN French, literally 'fixed idea'.

idée reçue /ˌiːdeɪ rəˈs(j)uː/ ▶ noun (pl. **idées reçues** pronunc. same) a generally accepted concept or idea.
– ORIGIN French, literally 'received idea'.

idem /ˈʌɪdɛm, ˈɪdɛm/ ▶ adverb used in citations to indicate an author or word that has just been mentioned: *Marianne Elliott*, Partners in Revolution, *1982; idem*, Wolfe Tone, *1989.*
– ORIGIN Latin, 'the same'.

idempotent /ˌʌɪdɛmˈpəʊt(ə)nt, ˌʌɪˈdɛmpət(ə)nt/ Mathematics ▶ adjective denoting an element of a set which is unchanged in value when multiplied or otherwise operated on by itself.
▶ noun an element of this type.
– ORIGIN late 19th cent.: from Latin *idem* 'same' + **POTENT**[1].

ident /ˈʌɪdɛnt, ˈʌɪdənt/ ▶ noun short for **IDENTIFICATION**, especially in informal or technical use.

identical ▶ adjective 1 similar in every detail; exactly alike: *four girls in identical green outfits | the passage on the second floor was identical to the one below.*
■(of twins) developed from a single fertilized ovum, and therefore of the same sex and usually very similar in appearance. Compare with **FRATERNAL** (in sense 2). ■ [attrib.] (of something encountered on separate occasions) the same: *she stole a suitcase from the identical station at which she had been arrested before.*
2 Logic & Mathematics expressing an identity: *an identical proposition.*
– DERIVATIVES **identically** adverb.
– ORIGIN late 16th cent. (in sense 2): from medieval

Latin *identicus*, from late Latin *identitas* (see **IDENTITY**).

identification ▶ **noun** [mass noun] the action or process of identifying someone or something or the fact of being identified: *each child was tagged with a number for identification* | [count noun] *it may be impossible for relatives to make positive identifications.*
■ a means of proving a person's identity, especially in the form of official papers: *I asked to see his identification.* ■ a person's sense of identity with someone or something: *children's identification with story characters.* ■ the association or linking of one thing with another: *the growing identification of anti-slavery with political liberalism.*
– ORIGIN mid 17th cent.: originally from medieval Latin *identificat-* 'identified', from the verb *identificare*; later from **IDENTIFY**.

identification parade ▶ **noun** Brit. another term for **IDENTITY PARADE**.

identifier ▶ **noun** a person or thing that identifies something: *the new NHS number is to be known as the 'unique patient identifier'.*
■ a person who identifies with something or someone: *Labour identifiers and left-wingers.* ■ Computing a sequence of characters used to identify or refer to a program or an element, such as a variable or a set of data, within it.

identify ▶ **verb** (**-ies**, **-ied**) [with obj.] **1** (often **be identified**) establish or indicate who or what (someone or something) is: *the judge ordered that the girl should not be identified* | *the contact would* ***identify himself simply as*** *Cobra.*
■ recognize or distinguish (especially something considered worthy of attention): *a system that ensures that the pupil's real needs are identified.*
2 (**identify someone/thing with**) associate someone or something closely with; regard as having strong links with: *he was equivocal about being identified too closely with the peace movement.*
■ equate (someone or something) with: *because of my country accent, people identified me with a homely farmer's wife.* ■ [no obj.] (**identify with**) regard oneself as sharing the same characteristics or thinking as someone else: *I liked Fromm and identified with him.*
– DERIVATIVES **identifiable** adjective, **identifiably** adverb.
– ORIGIN mid 17th cent. (in the sense 'treat as being identical with'): from medieval Latin *identificare*, from late Latin *identitas* (see **IDENTITY**) + Latin *-ficare* (from *facere* 'make').

identikit /ʌɪˈdɛntɪkɪt/ ▶ **noun** trademark a picture of a person, especially one sought by the police, reconstructed from typical facial features according to witnesses' descriptions: [as modifier] *an identikit photograph.*
▶ **adjective** [attrib.] often derogatory having typical features and few unique ones; formulaic; standardized: *the pub was transformed by identikit 'Victoriana'.*
– ORIGIN 1960s: blend of **IDENTITY** and **KIT**[1].

identity ▶ **noun** (pl. **-ies**) **1** the fact of being who or what a person or thing is: *he knows the identity of the bombers* | [mass noun] *she believes she is the victim of mistaken identity.*
■ the characteristics determining this: *he wanted to develop a more distinctive Scottish Tory identity.* ■ [as modifier] (of an object) serving to establish who the holder, owner, or wearer is by bearing their name and often other details such as a signature or photograph: *an identity card.*
2 a close similarity or affinity: *the initiative created an identity between the City and the governing elite.*
3 Mathematics (also **identity operation**) a transformation that leaves an object unchanged.
■ (also **identity element**) an element of a set which, if combined with another element by a specified binary operation, leaves that element unchanged.
4 Mathematics the equality of two expressions for all values of the quantities expressed by letters, or an equation expressing this, e.g. $(x + 1)^2 = x^2 + 2x + 1$.
– ORIGIN late 16th cent. (in the sense 'quality of being identical'): from late Latin *identitas*, from Latin *idem* 'same'.

identity crisis ▶ **noun** Psychiatry a period of uncertainty and confusion in which a person's sense of identity becomes insecure, typically due to a change in their expected aims or role in society.

identity matrix ▶ **noun** Mathematics a square matrix in which all the elements of the principal diagonal are ones and all other elements are zeros. The effect of multiplying a given matrix by an identity matrix is to leave the given matrix unchanged.

identity parade ▶ **noun** Brit. a group of people including a suspect for a crime assembled for the purpose of having an eyewitness identify the suspect from among them.

ideogram /ˈɪdɪə(ʊ)gram, ˈʌɪd-/ ▶ **noun** a character symbolizing the idea of a thing without indicating the sounds used to say it. Examples include numerals and Chinese characters.
– ORIGIN mid 19th cent.: from Greek *idea* 'form' + **-GRAM**[1].

ideograph /ˈɪdɪə(ʊ)grɑːf, ˈʌɪd-/ ▶ **noun** another term for **IDEOGRAM**.
– DERIVATIVES **ideographic** adjective, **ideography** noun.
– ORIGIN mid 19th cent.: from Greek *idea* 'form' + **-GRAPH**.

ideologue /ˈʌɪdɪəlɒg, ˈɪd-/ ▶ **noun** an adherent of an ideology, especially one who is uncompromising and dogmatic: *a Nazi ideologue.*
– ORIGIN early 19th cent.: from French *idéologue*; see also **IDEOLOGY**.

ideology /ˌʌɪdɪˈɒlədʒi, ɪd-/ ▶ **noun 1** (pl. **-ies**) a system of ideas and ideals, especially one which forms the basis of economic or political theory and policy: *the ideology of republicanism.*
■ the ideas and manner of thinking characteristic of a group, social class, or individual: *a critique of bourgeois ideology.* ■ [mass noun] archaic visionary speculation, especially of an unrealistic or idealistic nature.
2 [mass noun] archaic the science of ideas; the study of their origin and nature.
– DERIVATIVES **ideological** adjective, **ideologically** adverb, **ideologist** noun.
– ORIGIN late 18th cent. (in sense 2): from French *idéologie*, from Greek *idea* 'form, pattern' + *-logos* (denoting discourse or compilation).

ides /ʌɪdz/ ▶ **plural noun** (in the ancient Roman calendar) a day falling roughly in the middle of each month (the 15th day of March, May, July, and October, and the 13th of other months) from which other dates were calculated. Compare with **NONES**, **CALENDS**.
– ORIGIN late Old English: from Old French, from Latin *idus* (plural), of unknown origin.

idigbo /ɪˈdɪgbəʊ/ ▶ **noun** a West African tree which has a distinctive pagodalike shape and yields weather-resistant timber.
• *Terminalia ivorensis*, family Combretaceae.
– ORIGIN a local name.

idio- /ˈɪdɪəʊ/ ▶ **combining form** personal; own: *idiotype.*
– ORIGIN from Greek *idios* 'own, distinct'.

idiocy ▶ **noun** (pl. **-ies**) [mass noun] extremely stupid behaviour: *the idiocy of decimating yew forests* | [count noun] *every aspect of public administration throws up its own idiocies.*
– ORIGIN early 16th cent. (originally denoting low intelligence): from **IDIOT**, probably on the pattern of pairs such as *lunatic, lunacy.*

idiographic ▶ **adjective** of or relating to the study or discovery of particular scientific facts and processes, as distinct from general laws. Often contrasted with **NOMOTHETIC**.

idiolect /ˈɪdɪəlɛkt/ ▶ **noun** the speech habits peculiar to a particular person.
– ORIGIN 1940s: from **IDIO-** 'own, personal' + *-lect* as in *dialect.*

idiom ▶ **noun 1** a group of words established by usage as having a meaning not deducible from those of the individual words (e.g. *over the moon, see the light*).
■ [mass noun] a form of expression natural to a language, person, or group of people: *he had a feeling for phrase and idiom.* ■ the dialect of a people or part of a country.
2 a characteristic mode of expression in music or art: *they were both working in a neo-Impressionist idiom.*
– ORIGIN late 16th cent.: from French *idiome*, or via late Latin from Greek *idiōma* 'private property, peculiar phraseology', from *idiousthai* 'make one's own', from *idios* 'own, private'.

idiomatic ▶ **adjective 1** using, containing, or denoting expressions that are natural to a native speaker: *the commercial uses distinctive idiomatic dialogue.*
2 appropriate to the style of art or music associated with a particular period, individual, or group: *a short Bach piece containing lots of idiomatic motifs.*
– DERIVATIVES **idiomatically** adverb.
– ORIGIN early 18th cent.: from Greek *idiōmatikos* 'peculiar, characteristic', from *idiōma* (see **IDIOM**).

idiopathic /ˌɪdɪə(ʊ)ˈpaθɪk/ ▶ **adjective** Medicine relating to or denoting any disease or condition which arises spontaneously or for which the cause is unknown.

idiopathy /ˌɪdɪˈɒpəθi/ ▶ **noun** (pl. **-ies**) Medicine a disease or condition which arises spontaneously or for which the cause is unknown.
– ORIGIN late 17th cent.: from modern Latin *idiopathia*, from Greek *idiopatheia*, from *idios* 'own, private' + *-patheia* 'suffering'.

idiophone /ˈɪdɪə(ʊ)fəʊn/ ▶ **noun** Music, technical an instrument the whole of which vibrates to produce a sound when struck, shaken, or scraped, such as a bell, gong, or rattle. Compare with **MEMBRANOPHONE**.

idiosyncrasy /ˌɪdɪə(ʊ)ˈsɪŋkrəsi/ ▶ **noun** (pl. **-ies**) (usu. **idiosyncrasies**) a mode of behaviour or way of thought peculiar to an individual: *one of his little idiosyncrasies was always preferring to be in the car first.*
■ a distinctive or peculiar feature or characteristic of a place or thing: *the idiosyncrasies of the prison system.* ■ Medicine an abnormal physical reaction by an individual to a food or drug.
– ORIGIN early 17th cent. (originally in the sense 'physical constitution peculiar to an individual'): from Greek *idiosunkrasia*, from *idios* 'own, private' + *sun* 'with' + *krasis* 'mixture'.

idiosyncratic /ˌɪdɪə(ʊ)sɪŋˈkratɪk/ ▶ **adjective** of or relating to idiosyncrasy; peculiar or individual: *she emerged as one of the great, idiosyncratic talents of the Nineties.*
– DERIVATIVES **idiosyncratically** adverb.
– ORIGIN late 18th cent.: from **IDIOSYNCRASY**, on the pattern of Greek *sunkratikos* 'mixed together'.

idiot ▶ **noun** informal a stupid person.
■ Medicine, archaic a mentally handicapped person.
– DERIVATIVES **idiotic** adjective, **idiotically** adverb.
– ORIGIN Middle English (denoting a person of low intelligence): via Old French from Latin *idiota* 'ignorant person', from Greek *idiōtēs* 'private person, layman, ignorant person', from *idios* 'own, private'.

idiot board (also **idiot card**) ▶ **noun** informal a board displaying a television script to a speaker as an aid to memory.

idiot box ▶ **noun** N. Amer. informal a television set.

idiot light ▶ **noun** N. Amer. informal a warning light that goes on when a fault occurs in a device.

idiot savant /ˌiːdjəʊ saˈvɒ̃, ˌɪdɪəʊ/ ▶ **noun** (pl. **idiot savants** or **idiots savants** pronunc. same) a person who is considered to be mentally handicapped but displays brilliance in a specific area, especially one involving memory.
■ a person who is extremely unworldly but displays natural wisdom and insight.
– ORIGIN French, literally 'knowledgeable idiot'.

idiotype /ˈɪdɪə(ʊ)tʌɪp/ ▶ **noun** Biology the set of genetic determinants of an individual.
■ Immunology a set of antigen-binding sites which characterizes the antibodies produced by a particular clone of antibody-producing cells.

idle ▶ **adjective** (**idler**, **idlest**) **1** (of a person) avoiding work; lazy.
■ (of a person) not working; unemployed. ■ (especially of a machine or factory) not active or in use: *assembly-lines* ***standing idle*** *for want of spare parts.* ■ [attrib.] (of time) characterized by inaction or absence of significant activity: *at no time in the day must there be an idle moment.* ■ (of money) held in cash or in accounts paying no interest.
2 without purpose or effect; pointless: *he did not want to waste valuable time in idle chatter.*
■ (especially of a threat or boast) without foundation: *I knew Ellen did not make idle threats.*
▶ **verb** [no obj.] (of a person) spend time doing nothing; be idle: *four men were idling outside the shop.*
■ [no obj., with adverbial of direction] move aimlessly or lazily: *Robert idled along the pavement.* ■ (of an engine) run slowly while disconnected from a load or out of gear: *the car is noisily idling in the street.* ■ [with obj.] cause (an engine) to idle. ■ [with obj.] N. Amer. take out of use or employment: *he will close the newspaper, idling 2,200 workers.*
– DERIVATIVES **idleness** noun.
– ORIGIN Old English *īdel* 'empty, useless', of West Germanic origin; related to Dutch *ijdel* 'vain, frivolous, useless' and German *eitel* 'bare, worthless'.

▶**idle something away** spend one's time doing nothing or very little.

idler ▶noun **1** a habitually lazy person.
▪a person who is doing nothing in particular, typically while waiting for something.
2 a pulley that transmits no power but guides or tensions a belt or rope.
▪an idle wheel.

idle wheel ▶noun an intermediate wheel between two geared wheels, especially when its purpose is to allow them to rotate in the same direction.

idli /ˈɪdliː/ ▶noun (pl. same or **idlis**) a south Indian steamed cake of rice, usually served with sambhar.
– ORIGIN from Malayalam and Kannada *iḍḍali*.

idly ▶adverb with no particular purpose, reason, or foundation: *'How was the race?' Kate asked idly.*
▪in an inactive or lazy way: *I can no longer stand idly by and let him take the blame.*

Ido /ˈiːdəʊ/ ▶noun [mass noun] an artificial universal language developed from Esperanto.
– ORIGIN early 19th cent.: Ido, literally 'offspring'.

idocrase /ˈʌɪdə(ʊ)kreɪz, -s/ ▶noun [mass noun] a mineral consisting of a silicate of calcium, magnesium, and aluminium, occurring typically as dark-green to brown prisms in metamorphosed limestone.
– ORIGIN early 19th cent.: from Greek *eidos* 'form' + *krasis* 'mixture'.

idol ▶noun an image or representation of a god used as an object of worship.
▪a person or thing that is greatly admired, loved, or revered: *a soccer idol.*
– ORIGIN Middle English: from Old French *idole*, from Latin *idolum* 'image, form' (used in ecclesiastical Latin in the sense 'idol'), from Greek *eidōlon*, from *eidos* 'form, shape'.

idolater /ʌɪˈdɒlətə/ ▶noun a person who worships an idol or idols.
– ORIGIN late Middle English: from Old French *idolatre*, based on Greek *eidōlolatrēs*, from *eidōlon* (see **IDOL**) + *-latrēs* 'worshipper'.

idolatrous ▶adjective worshipping idols: *the idolatrous peasantry.*
▪treating someone or something as an idol: *America's idolatrous worship of the auto.*

idolatry ▶noun [mass noun] worship of idols.
▪extreme admiration, love, or reverence for something or someone: *we must not allow our idolatry of art to obscure issues of political significance.*
– ORIGIN Middle English: from Old French *idolatrie*, based on Greek *eidōlolatreia*, from *eidōlon* (see **IDOL**) + *-latreia* 'worship'.

idolize (also **-ise**) ▶verb [with obj.] admire, revere, or love greatly or excessively: *he idolized his mother.*
– DERIVATIVES **idolization** noun, **idolizer** noun.

Idomeneus /ʌɪˌdɒmɪˈniːəs/ Greek Mythology king of Crete, son of Deucalion and descendant of Minos. He was forced to kill his son after vowing to sacrifice the first living thing that he met on his return from the Trojan war.

Id ul-Adha see **EID**.

Id ul-Fitr see **EID**.

idyll /ˈɪdɪl/ (also **idyl**) ▶noun an extremely happy, peaceful, or picturesque episode or scene, typically an idealized or unsustainable one: *the rural idyll remains strongly evocative in most industrialized societies.*
▪a short description in verse or prose of a picturesque scene or incident, especially in rustic life.
– ORIGIN late 16th cent. (in the Latin form): from Latin *idyllium*, from Greek *eidullion*, diminutive of *eidos* 'form, picture'.

idyllic ▶adjective (especially of a time or place) like an idyll; extremely happy, peaceful, or picturesque: *an attractive hotel in an idyllic setting.*
– DERIVATIVES **idyllically** adverb.

i.e. ▶abbreviation that is to say (used to add explanatory information or to state something in different words): *a walking boot which is synthetic, i.e. not leather or suede.*
– ORIGIN from Latin *id est* 'that is'.

-ie ▶suffix **1** variant spelling of **-Y**[2] (as in *auntie*).
2 archaic variant spelling of **-Y**[1], **-Y**[3].
– ORIGIN earlier form of *-y*.

IEA ▶abbreviation for International Energy Agency.

IEE ▶abbreviation for (in the UK) Institution of Electrical Engineers.

IEEE ▶abbreviation for (in the US) Institute of Electrical and Electronics Engineers.

Ieper /ˈiːpər/ Flemish name for **YPRES**.

-ier ▶suffix forming personal nouns denoting an occupation or interest: **1** pronounced with stress on the preceding element: *grazier.* [ORIGIN: Middle English: variant of **-ER**[1].]
2 pronounced with stress on the final element: *brigadier | cashier.* [ORIGIN: from French *-ier*, from Latin *-arius*.]

IF ▶abbreviation for intermediate frequency.

if ▶conjunction **1** introducing a conditional clause:
▪on the condition or supposition that; in the event that: *if you have a complaint, write to the director | if you like I'll put in a word for you.* ▪(with past tense) introducing a hypothetical situation: *if you had stayed, this would never have happened.* ▪whenever; every time: *if I go out she gets nasty.*
2 despite the possibility that; no matter whether: *if it takes me seven years, I shall do it.*
3 (often used in indirect questions) whether: *he asked if we would like some coffee | see if you can track it down.*
4 [with modal] expressing a polite request: *if I could trouble you for your names? | if you wouldn't mind giving him a message?*
5 expressing an opinion: *that's a jolly long walk, if you don't mind my saying so | if you ask me, he's in love.*
6 expressing surprise or regret: *well,* **if** *it* **isn't** *Frank! | if I could just be left alone.*
7 with implied reservation:
▪and perhaps not: *the new leaders have little if any control.* ▪used to admit something as being possible but regarded as relatively insignificant: *if there was any weakness, it was naivety | so what if he did?* ▪despite being (used before an adjective or adverb to introduce a contrast): *she was honest, if a little brutal.*
▶noun a condition or supposition: *there are so many* **ifs and buts** *in the policy.*
– PHRASES **if and only if** used to introduce a condition which is necessary as well as sufficient: *witches are real if and only if there are criteria for identifying witches.* **if and when** at a future time (should it arise): *if and when the film gets the green light, be sure you've read the book first.* **if anything** used to suggest tentatively that something may be the case (often the opposite of something previously implied): *I haven't made much of this—if anything, I've played it down.* **if I were you** used to accompany a piece of advice: *I would go to see him if I were you.* **if not** perhaps even (used to introduce a more extreme term than one first mentioned): *hundreds if not thousands of germs.* **if only 1** even if for no other reason than: *Willy would have to tell George more, if only to stop him pestering.* **2** used to express a wish, especially regretfully: *if only I had listened to you.* **if so** if that is the case.
– ORIGIN Old English *gif*, of Germanic origin; related to Dutch *of* and German *ob*.

> **USAGE** **If** and **whether** are more or less interchangeable in sentences like *I'll see* **if** *he left an address* and *I'll see* **whether** *he left an address*, although **whether** is generally regarded as more formal and suitable for written use.

IFAD ▶abbreviation for International Fund for Agricultural Development.

IFC ▶abbreviation for International Finance Corporation.

Ife /ˈiːfeɪ/ an industrial city in SW Nigeria; pop. 240,600 (1981). It was a major centre of the Yoruba kingdom from the 14th to the 17th centuries.

-iferous ▶combining form common form of **-FEROUS**.

iff ▶conjunction Logic & Mathematics if and only if.
– ORIGIN 1950s: arbitrary extension of *if*.

iffy ▶adjective (**iffier**, **iffiest**) informal full of uncertainty; doubtful: *the prospect for classes resuming next Wednesday seems iffy.*
▪of doubtful quality or legality: *a good wine merchant will change the iffy bottles for sound ones.*

-ific ▶suffix common form of **-FIC**.

-ification ▶suffix common form of **-FICATION**.

Ifni /ˈɪfni/ a former overseas province of Spain, on the SW coast of Morocco, ceded to Morocco in 1969.

-iform ▶combining form common form of **-FORM**.

IFP ▶abbreviation for Inkatha Freedom Party. See **INKATHA**.

IFR ▶abbreviation for instrument flight rules, used to regulate the flying and navigating of an aircraft using instruments alone.

Iftar /ˈɪftɑː/ ▶noun the meal eaten by Muslims after sunset during Ramadan.

Ig Biochemistry ▶abbreviation for immunoglobulin.

Igbo /ˈiːbəʊ/ (also **Ibo**) ▶noun (pl. same or **-os**) **1** a member of a people of SE Nigeria.
2 [mass noun] the language of this people, belonging to the Kwa group. It has some 12 million speakers.
▶adjective of or relating to this people or their language.
– ORIGIN a local name.

Iglesias /ɪˈgleɪzɪəs/, Julio (b.1943), Spanish singer. He has recorded more than sixty albums and is famous for love songs and ballads.

igloo ▶noun a dome-shaped Eskimo house, typically built from blocks of solid snow.
– ORIGIN mid 19th cent.: from Inuit *iglu* 'house'.

Ignatius Loyola, St /ɪgˌneɪʃəs ˈlɔɪələ, lɔɪˈəʊlə/ (1491–1556), Spanish theologian and founder of the Society of Jesus. His *Spiritual Exercises* (1548), an ordered scheme of meditations, is still used in the training of Jesuits. Feast day, 31 July.

igneous /ˈɪgnɪəs/ ▶adjective Geology (of rock) having solidified from lava or magma.
▪relating to or involving volcanic or plutonic processes: *igneous activity.* ▪rare of fire; fiery.
– ORIGIN mid 17th cent.: from Latin *igneus* (from *ignis* 'fire') + **-OUS**.

ignimbrite /ˈɪgnɪmbrʌɪt/ ▶noun [mass noun] Geology a volcanic rock consisting essentially of pumice fragments, formed by the consolidation of material deposited by pyroclastic flows.
– ORIGIN 1930s: from Latin *ignis* 'fire' + *imber, imbr-* 'shower of rain, storm cloud' + **-ITE**[1].

ignis fatuus /ˌɪgnɪs ˈfatjʊəs/ ▶noun (pl. **ignes fatui** /ˌigniːz ˈfatjʊʌɪ, ˌɪgneɪz, ˈfatjʊiː/) a will-o'-the-wisp.
– ORIGIN mid 16th cent.: modern Latin, literally 'foolish fire' (because of its erratic movement).

ignite /ɪgˈnʌɪt/ ▶verb catch fire or cause to catch fire: [no obj.] *furniture can give off lethal fumes when it ignites |* [with obj.] *he lit a cigarette which ignited the petrol fumes.*
▪[with obj.] figurative arouse (an emotion): *the words ignited new fury in him.* ▪[with obj.] figurative inflame or instigate (a situation): *they were about to ignite the European socialist revolution.*
– DERIVATIVES **ignitability** noun, **ignitable** adjective.
– ORIGIN mid 17th cent. (in the sense 'make intensely hot'): from Latin *ignire* 'set on fire', from *ignis* 'fire'.

igniter ▶noun **1** a device for igniting a fuel mixture in an engine.
2 a device for causing an electric arc.

ignition ▶noun [mass noun] the action of setting something on fire or starting to burn: *three minutes after ignition, the flames were still growing.*
▪the process of starting the combustion of fuel in the cylinders of an internal-combustion engine. ▪[count noun] (usu. **the ignition**) the mechanism for bringing this about, typically activated by a key or switch: *he put the key in the ignition.*
– ORIGIN early 17th cent. (denoting the heating of a substance to the point of combustion or chemical change): from medieval Latin *ignitio(n-)*, from the verb *ignire* 'set on fire' (see **IGNITE**).

ignitron /ɪgˈnʌɪtrɒn/ ▶noun a kind of rectifier with a mercury cathode, able to carry large electric currents.
– ORIGIN 1930s: from **IGNITE** or **IGNITION** + **-TRON**.

ignoble ▶adjective (**ignobler**, **ignoblest**) **1** not honourable in character or purpose: *ignoble feelings of intense jealousy.*
2 of humble origin or social status: *ignoble savages.*
– DERIVATIVES **ignobility** noun, **ignobly** adverb.
– ORIGIN late Middle English (in sense 2): from French, or from Latin *ignobilis*, from *in-* 'not' + *gnobilis*, older form of *nobilis* 'noble'.

ignominious /ˌɪgnəˈmɪnɪəs/ ▶adjective deserving or causing public disgrace or shame: *no other party risked ignominious defeat.*
– DERIVATIVES **ignominiously** adverb, **ignominiousness** noun.
– ORIGIN late Middle English: from French *ignominieux*, or Latin *ignominiosus*, from *ignominia* (see **IGNOMINY**).

ignominy /ˈɪgnəmɪni/ ▶noun [mass noun] public shame or disgrace: *the ignominy of being imprisoned.*

– ORIGIN mid 16th cent.: from French *ignominie* or Latin *ignominia*, from *in-* 'not' + a variant of *nomen* 'name'.

ignoramus /ˌɪɡnəˈreɪməs/ ▶ **noun** (pl. **ignoramuses**) an ignorant or stupid person.
– ORIGIN late 16th cent. (as the endorsement made by a grand jury on an indictment considered backed by insufficient evidence to bring before a petty jury): Latin, literally 'we do not know' (in legal use 'we take no notice of it'), from *ignorare* (see **IGNORE**). The modern sense may derive from the name of a character in George Ruggle's *Ignoramus* (1615), a satirical comedy exposing lawyers' ignorance.

ignorance ▶ **noun** [mass noun] lack of knowledge or information: *he acted in* ***ignorance of*** *basic procedures.*
– ORIGIN Middle English: via Old French from Latin *ignorantia*, from *ignorant-* 'not knowing' (see **IGNORANT**).

ignorant ▶ **adjective** lacking knowledge or awareness in general; uneducated or unsophisticated: *he was told constantly that he was ignorant and stupid.*
■ [predic.] lacking knowledge, information, or awareness about something in particular: *they were* ***ignorant of*** *astronomy.* ■ informal discourteous or rude: *this ignorant, pin-brained receptionist.* ■ black English easily angered: *I is an ignorant man—even police don't meddle with me.*
– DERIVATIVES **ignorantly** adverb.
– ORIGIN late Middle English: via Old French from Latin *ignorant-* 'not knowing', from the verb *ignorare* (see **IGNORE**).

ignoratio elenchi /ˌɪɡnəˈreɪʃɪəʊ ɪˈlɛŋkʌɪ/ ▶ **noun** (pl. **ignorationes elenchi** /-ˈəʊniːz/) Philosophy a logical fallacy which consists in apparently refuting an opponent while actually disproving something not asserted.
– ORIGIN Latin, literally 'ignorance of the elenchus'.

ignore ▶ **verb** [with obj.] refuse to take notice of or acknowledge; disregard intentionally: *he ignored her outraged question.*
■ fail to consider (something significant): *the rules ignore one important principle of cricket.*
– DERIVATIVES **ignorable** adjective, **ignorer** noun.
– ORIGIN late 15th cent. (in the sense 'be ignorant of'): from French *ignorer* or Latin *ignorare* 'not know, ignore', from *in-* 'not' + *gno-*, a base meaning 'know'. Current senses date from the early 19th cent.

ignotum per ignotius /ɪɡˌnəʊtəm pər ɪɡˈnəʊtɪəs/ ▶ **noun** [mass noun] the action of offering an explanation which is harder to understand than the thing it is meant to explain.
– ORIGIN late Latin, literally 'the unknown through something more unknown'.

Iguaçu /ˌɪɡwəˈsuː/ a river of southern Brazil. It rises in the Serra do Mar in SE Brazil and flows westwards for 1,300 km (800 miles) to the Paraná River, which it joins shortly below the Iguaçu Falls, a spectacular series of waterfalls. Spanish name **IGUAZÚ**.

iguana /ɪˈɡwɑːnə/ ▶ **noun** a large arboreal tropical American lizard with a spiny crest along the back and greenish coloration, occasionally kept as a pet.
• Genus *Iguana*, family Iguanidae: two species, in particular the common **green iguana** (*I. iguana*).
■ any iguanid lizard.
– ORIGIN mid 16th cent.: from Spanish, from Arawak *iwana*.

iguanid /ɪˈɡwɑːnɪd/ ▶ **noun** Zoology a lizard of the iguana family (Iguanidae). Iguanids are found mainly in the New World but also occur in Madagascar and on some Pacific islands.
– ORIGIN late 19th cent.: from modern Latin *Iguanidae* (plural), from the genus name *Iguana* (see **IGUANA**).

iguanodon /ɪˈɡwɑːnədɒn/ ▶ **noun** a large partly bipedal herbivorous dinosaur of the early to mid Cretaceous period, with a broad stiff tail and the thumb developed into a spike.
• Genus *Iguanodon*, infraorder Ornithopoda, order Ornithischia.
– ORIGIN modern Latin, from **IGUANA** + Greek *odous, odont-* 'tooth' (because its teeth resemble those of the iguana).

i.h.p. ▶ **abbreviation for** indicated horsepower.

IHS ▶ **abbreviation** Jesus.
– ORIGIN Middle English: from late Latin, representing Greek *ΙΗΣ* as an abbreviation of *Iēsous* 'Jesus' used in manuscripts and also as a symbolic or ornamental monogram, but later often taken as an abbreviation of various Latin phrases, notably *Iesus Hominum Salvator* 'Jesus Saviour of Men', *In Hoc Signo (vinces)* 'in this sign (thou shalt conquer)', and *In Hac Salus* 'in this (cross) is salvation'.

iiwi /ɪˈiːwi/ ▶ **noun** (pl. same or **iiwis**) a Hawaiian honeycreeper with a long downcurved bill and mainly bright red plumage.
• *Vestiaria coccinea*, family Drepanididae (or Fringillidae).
– ORIGIN late 18th cent.: from Hawaiian.

Ijo /ˈiːdʒəʊ/ (also **Ijaw**) ▶ **noun** (pl. same or **-os**) **1** a member of a people inhabiting the Niger delta in southern Nigeria.
2 [mass noun] the language of this people, an isolated member of the Niger–Congo family with several highly distinct dialects.
▶ **adjective** of or relating to this people or their language.

IJssel /ˈʌɪs(ə)l/ a river in the Netherlands. In part it is a distributary of the Rhine, which it leaves at Arnhem, joining the Oude IJssel ('Old IJssel') a few kilometres downstream, and flowing 115 km (72 miles) northwards through the eastern Netherlands to the IJsselmeer.

IJsselmeer /ˈʌɪs(ə)lmɛː, -mɪə/ a shallow lake in the NW Netherlands, created in 1932 by the building of a dam across the entrance to the old Zuider Zee. Large areas have since been reclaimed as polders.

ikat /ˈiːkat, ɪˈkat/ ▶ **noun** [mass noun] fabric made using an Indonesian decorative technique in which warp or weft threads, or both, are tie-dyed before weaving.
– ORIGIN 1930s: Malay, literally 'fasten, tie'.

ikebana /ˌɪkɪˈbɑːnə/ ▶ **noun** [mass noun] the art of Japanese flower arrangement, with formal display according to strict rules.
– ORIGIN Japanese, literally 'living flowers', from *ikeru* 'keep alive' + *hana* 'flower'.

Ikhnaton /ɪkˈnɑːt(ə)n/ variant form of **AKHENATEN**.

ikky ▶ **adjective** variant spelling of **ICKY**.

ikon ▶ **noun** variant spelling of **ICON**.

IL ▶ **abbreviation for** ■ Illinois (in official postal use). ■ Israel (international vehicle registration).

il- ▶ **prefix** variant spelling of **IN-**[1], **IN-**[2] assimilated before *l* (as in *illustrate, illuminate*).

-il ▶ **suffix** forming adjectives and nouns such as *civil* and *fossil*.
– ORIGIN from Old French, from Latin *-ilis*.

ilang-ilang ▶ **noun** variant spelling of **YLANG-YLANG**.

-ile ▶ **suffix** forming adjectives and nouns such as *agile* and *juvenile*.
■ Statistics forming nouns denoting a value of a variate which divides a population into the indicated number of equal-sized groups, or one of the groups itself: *decile* | *percentile*.
– ORIGIN variant of **-IL** especially in adoptions from French.

ilea plural form of **ILEUM**.

Île-de-France /ˌiːldəˈfrɑːns, French ildəfʀɑ̃s/ a region of north central France, incorporating the city of Paris.

ileitis /ˌɪlɪˈʌɪtɪs/ ▶ **noun** [mass noun] Medicine inflammation of the ileum.

ileostomy /ˌɪlɪˈɒstəmi/ ▶ **noun** (pl. **-ies**) a surgical operation in which a damaged part is removed from the ileum and the cut end diverted to an artificial opening in the abdominal wall.
■ an opening so formed.
– ORIGIN late 19th cent.: from **ILEUM** + Greek *stoma* 'mouth'.

Ilesha /ɪˈleɪʃə/ a city in SW Nigeria; pop. 342,400 (1991).

ileum /ˈɪlɪəm/ ▶ **noun** (pl. **ilea**) Anatomy the third portion of the small intestine, between the jejunum and the caecum.
– DERIVATIVES **ileac** adjective, **ileal** adjective.
– ORIGIN late 17th cent.: from medieval Latin, variant of **ILIUM**.

ileus /ˈɪlɪəs/ ▶ **noun** [mass noun or in sing.] Medicine a painful obstruction of the ileum or other part of the intestine.
– ORIGIN late 17th cent.: from Latin, from Greek *eileos, ilios* 'colic', apparently from *eilein* 'to roll'.

ilex /ˈʌɪlɛks/ ▶ **noun 1** the holm oak.
2 a tree or shrub of a genus that includes holly and its relatives.
• Genus *Ilex*, family Aquifoliaceae.
– ORIGIN late Middle English: from Latin, 'holm oak'.

ilia plural form of **ILIUM**.

iliac /ˈɪlɪak/ ▶ **adjective** of or relating to the ilium or the nearby regions of the lower body: *the iliac artery.*
– ORIGIN early 16th cent.: from late Latin *iliacus*, from *ilia* 'entrails'.

iliacus /ɪˈlʌɪəkəs/ (also **iliacus muscle**) ▶ **noun** Anatomy a triangular muscle which passes from the pelvis through the groin on either side and, together with the psoas, flexes the hip.
– ORIGIN early 17th cent.: from late Latin.

Iliad /ˈɪlɪəd/ a Greek hexameter epic poem in twenty-four books, traditionally ascribed to Homer, telling how Achilles killed Hector at the climax of the Trojan War.

Ilium /ˈɪlɪəm/ the alternative name for **TROY**, especially the 7th-century BC Greek city.

ilium /ˈɪlɪəm/ ▶ **noun** (pl. **ilia**) the large broad bone forming the upper part of each half of the pelvis.
– ORIGIN late Middle English (originally in the Greek form *ilion*, and denoting the ileum): from Latin, singular of *ilia* 'flanks, entrails'. Current senses date from the late 16th cent.

ilk ▶ **noun** [in sing.] a type of people or things similar to those already referred to: *the veiled suggestions that reporters* ***of his ilk*** *seem to be so good at* | *fascists, racists, and others of that ilk.*
■ (**of that ilk**) Scottish, chiefly archaic of the place or estate of the same name: *Sir Iain Moncreiffe of that Ilk.*
– ORIGIN Old English *ilca* 'same', of Germanic origin; related to **ALIKE**.

USAGE In modern use, **ilk** is used in phrases such as ***of his ilk, of that ilk***, to mean 'type' or 'sort'. The use arose out of a misunderstanding of the earlier, Scottish use in the phrase **of that ilk**, where it means 'of the same name or place'. For this reason, some traditionalists regard the modern use as incorrect. It is, however, the only common current use and is now part of standard English.

Ill. ▶ **abbreviation for** Illinois.

I'll ▶ **contraction of** I shall; I will: *I'll arrange it.*

ill ▶ **adjective 1** not in full health; sick: *her daughter is seriously ill* | [with submodifier] *a terminally ill patient.*
2 [attrib.] poor in quality: *ill judgement dogs the unsuccessful.*
■ harmful: *she had a cup of the same wine and suffered no ill effects.* ■ hostile: *I bear you no ill will.* ■ (especially of fortune) not favourable: *no one less deserved such ill fortune than McStay.*
▶ **adverb 1** [usu. in combination] badly, wrongly, or imperfectly: *some of his premises seem ill-chosen* | *it ill becomes one so beautiful to be gloomy.*
■ unfavourably or unpropitiously: *something which boded ill for unwary golfers.*
2 only with difficulty; hardly: *she could ill afford the cost of new curtains.*
▶ **noun 1** [as plural noun **the ill**] people who are ill: *a day centre for the mentally ill.*
2 (usu. **ills**) a problem or misfortune: *a lengthy work on the ills of society.*
■ [mass noun] evil; harm: *how could I wish him ill?*
– PHRASES **ill at ease** uncomfortable or embarrassed. **speak** (or **think**) **ill of** say (or think) something critical about.
– ORIGIN Middle English (in the senses 'wicked', 'malevolent', 'harmful', and 'difficult'): from Old Norse *illr* 'evil, difficult', of unknown origin.

ill-advised ▶ **adjective** (of a person) unwise or imprudent: *you would be ill-advised to go on your own.*
■ badly thought out: *ill-advised financial ventures.*
– DERIVATIVES **ill-advisedly** adverb.

ill-affected ▶ **adjective** archaic not inclined to be friendly or sympathetic.

ill-assorted ▶ **adjective** not well matched: *ill-assorted furniture.*

illation /ɪˈleɪʃ(ə)n/ ▶ **noun** [mass noun] archaic the action of inferring or drawing a conclusion.
■ [count noun] an inference.
– ORIGIN mid 16th cent.: from Latin *illatio(n-)*, from *illat-* 'brought in', from the verb *inferre* (see **INFER**).

illative /ɪˈleɪtɪv/ ▶ **adjective 1** of the nature of or stating an inference.
■ proceeding by inference.
2 Grammar relating to or denoting a case of nouns in some languages used to express motion into something.
▶ **noun** the illative case, or a word in this case.

– DERIVATIVES **illatively** adverb.
– ORIGIN late 16th cent.: from Latin *illativus*, from *illat-* 'brought in' (see **ILLATION**).

Illawarra /ˌɪləˈwɒrə/ ▶ noun (also **Illawarra shorthorn**) an animal of an Australian breed of red or roan dairy cattle.
– ORIGIN early 20th cent.: from the name of a coastal district south of Sydney, where the breed was developed.

ill-bred ▶ adjective badly brought up or rude.
– DERIVATIVES **ill breeding** noun.

ill-conceived ▶ adjective not carefully planned or considered: *ill-conceived schemes.*

ill-considered ▶ adjective badly thought out: *an ill-considered remark.*

ill-disposed ▶ adjective unfriendly or unsympathetic: *this fact was ignored by ill-disposed critics.*

illegal ▶ adjective contrary to or forbidden by law, especially criminal law: *illegal drugs.*
▶ noun chiefly N. Amer. an illegal immigrant.
– DERIVATIVES **illegality** noun (pl. **-ies**), **illegally** adverb.
– ORIGIN early 17th cent.: from French *illégal* or medieval Latin *illegalis*, from Latin *in-* 'not' + *legalis* 'according to the law'.

illegible /ɪˈlɛdʒɪb(ə)l/ ▶ adjective not clear enough to be read: *his handwriting is totally illegible.*
– DERIVATIVES **illegibility** noun, **illegibly** adverb.

illegitimate /ˌɪlɪˈdʒɪtɪmət/ ▶ adjective not authorized by the law; not in accordance with accepted standards or rules: *defending workers against illegitimate managerial practices.*
■ (of a child) born of parents not lawfully married to each other.
▶ noun a person who is illegitimate by birth.
– DERIVATIVES **illegitimacy** noun, **illegitimately** adverb.
– ORIGIN mid 16th cent.: from late Latin *illegitimus* (from *in-* 'not' + *legitimus* 'lawful'), suggested by **LEGITIMATE**.

ill fame ▶ noun [mass noun] dated disrepute.

ill-fated ▶ adjective destined to fail or have bad luck: *an ill-fated expedition.*

ill-favoured (US **ill-favored**) ▶ adjective unattractive or offensive: *a crotchety, ill-favoured human being.*

ill-founded ▶ adjective (especially of an idea or belief) not based on fact or reliable evidence: *ill-founded criticism | her fear may be ill-founded.*

ill-gotten ▶ adjective acquired by illegal or unfair means: *the mafiosi launder their **ill-gotten gains**.*

ill health ▶ noun [mass noun] poor physical or mental condition: *the president was absent due to ill health.*

ill humour ▶ noun [mass noun] irritability or bad temper.
– DERIVATIVES **ill-humoured** adjective.

illiberal ▶ adjective **1** opposed to liberal principles; restricting freedom of thought or behaviour: *illiberal and anti-democratic policies.*
2 rare uncultured or unrefined.
3 rare not generous; mean.
– DERIVATIVES **illiberality** noun, **illiberally** adverb.
– ORIGIN mid 16th cent. (in the sense 'vulgar, ill-bred'): from French *illibéral*, from Latin *illiberalis* 'mean, sordid', from *in-* 'not' + *liberalis* (see **LIBERAL**).

Illich /ˈɪlɪtʃ/, Ivan (b.1926), Austrian-born American educationist and writer. He advocated the deinstitutionalization of education, religion, and medicine. Notable works: *Deschooling Society* (1971) and *Limits to Medicine* (1978).

illicit ▶ adjective forbidden by law, rules, or custom: *illicit drugs | illicit sex.*
– DERIVATIVES **illicitly** adverb, **illicitness** noun.
– ORIGIN early 16th cent.: from French, or from Latin *illicitus*, from *in-* 'not' + *licitus* (see **LICIT**).

illimitable ▶ adjective without limits or an end: *the illimitable human capacity for evil.*
– DERIVATIVES **illimitability** noun, **illimitably** adverb.

Illinoian /ˌɪlɪˈnɔɪ(j)ən/ ▶ adjective Geology of, relating to, or denoting a Pleistocene glaciation in North America, preceding the Wisconsin and approximating to the Saale of northern Europe.
■ [as noun **the Illinoian**] the Illinoian glaciation or the system of deposits laid down during it.
– ORIGIN mid 19th cent.: from **ILLINOIS** + **-AN**.

Illinois /ˌɪlɪˈnɔɪ/ a state in the Middle West of the US; pop. 11,430,600 (1990); capital, Springfield. It was colonized by the French but was ceded to Britain in 1763. It was acquired by the US in 1783 and became the 21st state in 1818.
– DERIVATIVES **Illinoisan** noun & adjective.

illiquid /ɪˈlɪkwɪd/ ▶ adjective (of assets) not easily converted into cash: *illiquid investments.*
■ (of a market) with few participants and a low volume of activity.
– DERIVATIVES **illiquidity** noun.

illite /ˈɪlʌɪt/ ▶ noun [mass noun] a clay mineral of a group resembling micas, with a lattice structure which does not expand on absorption of water.
– ORIGIN 1930s: from **ILLINOIS** + **-ITE**[1].

illiterate /ɪˈlɪt(ə)rət/ ▶ adjective unable to read or write: *his parents were illiterate.*
■ [with submodifier] ignorant in a particular subject or activity: *the extent to which voters are politically illiterate.* ■ uncultured or poorly educated: *the ignorant, illiterate Town Council.* ■ (especially of a piece of writing) showing a lack of education, especially an inability to read or write well.
▶ noun a person who is unable to read or write.
– PHRASES **functionally illiterate** lacking the literacy necessary for coping with most jobs and many everyday situations.
– DERIVATIVES **illiteracy** noun, **illiterately** adverb, **illiterateness** noun.
– ORIGIN late Middle English: from Latin *illitteratus*, from *in-* 'not' + *litteratus* (see **LITERATE**).

ill-judged ▶ adjective lacking careful consideration; unwise: *an ill-judged decision.*

ill nature ▶ noun [mass noun] dated meanness and irritability.
– DERIVATIVES **ill-natured** adjective, **ill-naturedly** adverb.

illness ▶ noun a disease or period of sickness affecting the body or mind: *he died after a long illness* | [mass noun] *I've never missed a day's work through illness.*

illocution /ˌɪləˈkjuːʃ(ə)n/ ▶ noun an action performed by saying or writing something, e.g. ordering, warning, or promising.
– DERIVATIVES **illocutionary** adjective.

illogic ▶ noun [mass noun] reasoning or thought which is not logical.

illogical ▶ adjective lacking sense or clear, sound reasoning: *an illogical fear of the supernatural.*
– DERIVATIVES **illogicality** noun (pl. **-ies**), **illogically** adverb.

ill-omened ▶ adjective attended by bad omens: *ill-omened birds of prey.*

ill-starred ▶ adjective destined to fail or have many difficulties; unlucky: *an ill-starred expedition.*

ill temper ▶ noun [mass noun] irritability; anger.
– DERIVATIVES **ill-tempered** adjective.

ill-treat ▶ verb [with obj.] act cruelly towards (a person or animal).
– DERIVATIVES **ill-treatment** noun.

illude /ɪˈl(j)uːd/ ▶ verb [with obj.] poetic/literary trick; delude: *he had allowed his imagination to illude him.*
– ORIGIN late Middle English: from Latin *illudere* 'to mock'.

illume /ɪˈl(j)uːm/ ▶ verb [with obj.] poetic/literary light up; illuminate: *sparks from candles illume our faces.*
– ORIGIN late Middle English: abbreviation of **ILLUMINE**.

illuminance /ɪˈl(j)uːmɪnəns/ ▶ noun Physics the amount of luminous flux per unit area.

illuminant ▶ noun technical a means of lighting or source of light: *until 1880, oil was the only illuminant in use.*
▶ adjective giving off light.
– ORIGIN mid 17th cent.: from Latin *illuminant-* 'illuminating', from the verb *illuminare* (see **ILLUMINATE**).

illuminate /ɪˈl(j)uːmɪneɪt/ ▶ verb [with obj.] light up: *a flash of lightning illuminated the house* | figurative *his face was illuminated by a smile.*
■ decorate (a building or structure) with lights for a special occasion. ■ [often as adj. **illuminated**] decorate (a page or initial letter in a manuscript) with gold, silver, or coloured designs. ■ figurative [usu. as adj. **illuminating**] help to clarify or explain (a subject or matter): *a most illuminating discussion.* ■ enlighten (someone) spiritually or intellectually.
– DERIVATIVES **illuminatingly** adverb, **illuminative** adjective, **illuminator** noun.
– ORIGIN late Middle English: from Latin *illuminat-* 'illuminated', from the verb *illuminare*, from *in-* 'upon' + *lumen, lumin-* 'light'.

illuminati /ɪˌl(j)uːmɪˈnɑːtiː/ ▶ plural noun people claiming to possess special enlightenment or knowledge of something: *some mysterious standard known only to the illuminati of the organization.*
■ (**Illuminati**) a sect of 16th-century Spanish heretics who claimed special religious enlightenment. ■ (**Illuminati**) a Bavarian secret society founded in 1776, organized like the Freemasons.
– DERIVATIVES **illuminism** noun, **illuminist** noun.
– ORIGIN late 16th cent.: plural of Italian *illuminato* or Latin *illuminatus* 'enlightened', past participle of *illuminare* (see **ILLUMINATE**).

illumination ▶ noun [mass noun] lighting or light: *higher levels of illumination are needed for reading.*
■ (**illuminations**) lights used in decorating a building or other structure. ■ figurative spiritual or intellectual enlightenment. ■ figurative clarification: *these books form the most sustained analysis and illumination of the subject.* ■ the art of illuminating a manuscript. ■ [count noun] an illuminated design in a manuscript.
– ORIGIN Middle English: via Old French from late Latin *illuminatio(n-)*, from the verb *illuminare* (see **ILLUMINATE**).

illumine ▶ verb [with obj.] poetic/literary light up; brighten: *he moved her lamp so that her face was illumined.*
■ enlighten (someone) spiritually or intellectually: *he assures himself that he is illumined and not deluded.*
– ORIGIN Middle English: from Old French *illuminer*, from Latin *illuminare* (see **ILLUMINATE**).

ill-use ▶ verb [with obj.] (usu. **be ill-used**) ill-treat (someone).
▶ noun (**ill use**) [mass noun] ill-treatment.

illusion /ɪˈl(j)uːʒ(ə)n/ ▶ noun a false idea or belief: *he had no illusions about the trouble she was in.*
■ a deceptive appearance or impression: *the illusion of family togetherness* | [mass noun] *the tension between illusion and reality.* ■ a thing which is or is likely to be wrongly perceived or interpreted by the senses: *Zollner's illusion makes parallel lines seem to diverge by placing them on a zigzag-striped background.*
– PHRASES **be under the illusion that** believe mistakenly that: *the world is under the illusion that the original painting still hangs in the Winter Palace.* **be under no illusion** (or **illusions**) be fully aware of the true state of affairs.
– DERIVATIVES **illusional** adjective.
– ORIGIN Middle English (in the sense 'deceiving, deception'): via Old French from Latin *illusio(n-)*, from *illudere* 'to mock', from *in-* 'against' + *ludere* 'play'.

illusionism ▶ noun [mass noun] the principle or technique by which artistic representations are made to resemble real objects or to give an appearance of space by the use of perspective.
– DERIVATIVES **illusionistic** adjective.

illusionist ▶ noun a person who performs tricks that deceive the eye; a magician.

illusive /ɪˈl(j)uːsɪv/ ▶ adjective chiefly poetic/literary deceptive; illusory: *an illusive haven.*
– ORIGIN early 17th cent.: from medieval Latin *illusivus*, from Latin *illus-* 'mocked', from the verb *illudere* (see **ILLUSION**).

illusory /ɪˈl(j)uːs(ə)ri/ ▶ adjective based on illusion; not real: *she knew the safety of her room was illusory.*
– DERIVATIVES **illusorily** adverb, **illusoriness** noun.

illustrate ▶ verb [with obj.] provide (a book, newspaper, etc.) with pictures: *the guide is illustrated with full-colour photographs.*
■ explain or make (something) clear by using examples, charts, pictures, etc.: *the results are illustrated in Figure 7.* ■ serve as an example of: *the World Cup illustrated what high standards our players must achieve.*
– ORIGIN early 16th cent. (in the sense 'illuminate, shed light on'): from Latin *illustrat-* 'lit up', from the verb *illustrare*, from *in-* 'upon' + *lustrare* 'illuminate'.

illustration ▶ noun a picture illustrating a book, newspaper, etc.: *an illustration of a yacht.*
■ an example serving to clarify or prove something: *this accident is a graphic illustration of the disaster that's waiting to happen.* ■ [mass noun] the action or fact of illustrating something, either pictorially or by exemplification: *by way of illustration, I refer to the following case.*

– DERIVATIVES **illustrational** adjective.
– ORIGIN late Middle English (in the sense 'illumination; spiritual or intellectual enlightenment'): via Old French from Latin *illustratio(n-)*, from the verb *illustrare* (see **ILLUSTRATE**).

illustrative ▶ adjective serving as an example or explanation: *this timetable is provided for illustrative purposes only.*
– DERIVATIVES **illustratively** adverb.

illustrator ▶ noun a person who draws or creates pictures for magazines, books, advertising, etc.

illustrious /ɪˈlʌstrɪəs/ ▶ adjective well known, respected, and admired for past achievements: *his illustrious predecessor | an illustrious career.*
– DERIVATIVES **illustriously** adverb, **illustriousness** noun.
– ORIGIN mid 16th cent.: from Latin *illustris* 'clear, bright' + **-OUS**.

illuviation /ɪˌl(j)uːvɪˈeɪʃ(ə)n/ ▶ noun [mass noun] Soil Science the introduction of salts or colloids into one soil horizon from another by percolating water.
– DERIVATIVES **illuvial** adjective, **illuviated** adjective.
– ORIGIN early 20th cent.: from **IL-** 'in' + *-luvial* (on the pattern of *alluvial*) + **-ATION**.

ill will ▶ noun [mass noun] animosity or bitterness: *he didn't bear his estranged wife any ill will.*

Illyria /ɪˈlɪrɪə/ an ancient region along the east coast of the Adriatic Sea, including Dalmatia and what is now Montenegro and northern Albania.

Illyrian ▶ adjective of or relating to the ancient region of Illyria: *Illyrian tribes.*
■ of or denoting the branch of Indo-European languages represented by modern Albanian.
▶ noun a native or inhabitant of ancient Illyria.
■ [mass noun] the branch of the Indo-European family of languages represented by modern Albanian.

illywhacker /ˈɪlɪˌwakə/ ▶ noun Austral. informal a small-time confidence trickster.
– ORIGIN 1940s: of unknown origin.

ilmenite /ˈɪlmənʌɪt/ ▶ noun [mass noun] a black mineral consisting of oxides of iron and titanium, of which it is the main ore.
– ORIGIN early 19th cent.: named after the *Ilmen* mountains in the Urals + **-ITE**[1].

ILO ▶ abbreviation for International Labour Organization.

Ilocano /ˌɪləˈkɑːnəʊ/ ▶ noun (pl. same or **-os**) **1** a member of a people inhabiting NW Luzon in the Philippines.
2 [mass noun] the Austronesian language of this people, with over 5 million speakers. Also called **ILOKO**.
▶ adjective of or relating to this people or their language.
– ORIGIN Philippine Spanish, from *Ilocos*, the name of two provinces in the Philippines.

Iloilo /ˌiːləʊˈiːləʊ/ a port on the south coast of the island of Panay in the Philippines; pop. 309,500 (1990).

Ilonggo /ɪˈlɒŋgəʊ/ ▶ noun another term for **HILIGAYNON**.
– ORIGIN a local name.

Ilorin /ɪˈlɒrɪn/ a city in western Nigeria; pop. 390,000 (1986). In the 18th century it was the capital of a Yoruba kingdom that was eventually absorbed into a Fulani state in the early 19th century.

ILP ▶ abbreviation for Independent Labour Party.

ILR ▶ abbreviation for Independent Local Radio.

ILS ▶ abbreviation for instrument landing system, a system in which an aircraft's instruments interact with ground-based electronics to enable the pilot to land the aircraft safely in poor visibility.

ilvaite /ˈɪlvəʌɪt/ ▶ noun [mass noun] a mineral consisting of a basic silicate of calcium and iron, typically occurring as black prisms.
– ORIGIN early 19th cent.: from Latin *Ilva* 'Elba' + **-ITE**[1].

-ily ▶ suffix forming adverbs corresponding to adjectives ending in *-y* (such as *happily* corresponding to *happy*).
– ORIGIN see **-Y**[1], **-LY**[2].

I'm ▶ contraction of I am: *I'm a busy woman.*

im- ▶ prefix variant spelling of **IN-**[1], **IN-**[2] assimilated before *b, m, p* (as in *imbibe, immure, impart*).

image ▶ noun a representation of the external form of a person or thing in sculpture, painting, etc.
■ a visible impression obtained by a camera, telescope, microscope, or other device, or displayed on a video screen. ■ an optical appearance or counterpart produced by light or other radiation from an object reflected in a mirror or refracted through a lens. ■ Mathematics a point or set formed by mapping from another point or set. ■ a mental representation or idea: *he had an image of Uncle Walter throwing his crutches away.* ■ a simile or metaphor: *he uses the image of a hole to describe emotional emptiness.* ■ the general impression that a person, organization, or product presents to the public: *she strives to project an image of youth.* ■ [in sing.] a person or thing that closely resembles another: *he's the image of his father.* ■ [in sing.] semblance or likeness: *made in the image of God.* ■ (in biblical use) an idol.
▶ verb [with obj.] make a representation of the external form of: *artworks which imaged women's bodies.*
■ (usu. **be imaged**) make a visual representation of (something) by scanning it with a detector or electromagnetic beam: [as noun **imaging**] *medical imaging.* ■ form a mental picture or idea of: *it is possible for us to image a society in which no one committed crime.*
– DERIVATIVES **imageless** adjective.
– ORIGIN Middle English: from Old French, from Latin *imago*; related to **IMITATE**.

image intensifier ▶ noun a device used to make a brighter version of an image on a photoelectric screen.

image-maker ▶ noun a person employed to identify and create a favourable public image for a person, organization, or product.

image processing ▶ noun [mass noun] the analysis and manipulation of a digitized image, especially in order to improve its quality.
– DERIVATIVES **image processor** noun.

imager ▶ noun an electronic or other device which records images of something: *a thermal imager.*

imagery ▶ noun [mass noun] visually descriptive or figurative language, especially in a literary work: *Tennyson uses imagery to create a lyrical emotion.*
■ visual images collectively: *the impact of computer-generated imagery on contemporary art.* ■ visual symbolism: *the film's religious imagery.*
– ORIGIN Middle English (in the senses 'statuary, carved images collectively'): from Old French *imagerie*, from *imager* 'make an image', from *image* (see **IMAGE**).

imagesetter ▶ noun Computing a very high-quality type of colour printer used to print glossy magazines, newsletters, or other documents.

imaginable ▶ adjective possible to be thought of or believed: *the most spectacular views imaginable.*
– DERIVATIVES **imaginably** adverb.
– ORIGIN late Middle English: from late Latin *imaginabilis*, from Latin *imaginare* 'form an image of, represent', from *imago, imagin-* 'image'.

imaginal /ɪˈmadʒɪn(ə)l/ ▶ adjective **1** of or relating to an image: *imaginal education methods.*
2 Entomology of or relating to an adult insect or imago.
– ORIGIN late 19th cent.: from Latin *imago, imagin-* 'image' + **-AL**.

imaginal disc ▶ noun Entomology a thickening of the epidermis of an insect larva which, on pupation, develops into a particular organ of the adult insect.

imaginary ▶ adjective **1** existing only in the imagination: *Chris had imaginary conversations with her.*
2 Mathematics (of a number or quantity) expressed in terms of the square root of a negative number (usually the square root of −1, represented by *i* or *j*). See also **COMPLEX**.
– DERIVATIVES **imaginarily** adverb.
– ORIGIN late Middle English: from Latin *imaginarius*, from *imago, imagin-* 'image'.

imagination ▶ noun the faculty or action of forming new ideas, or images or concepts of external objects not present to the senses: *she'd never been blessed with a vivid imagination.*
■ [mass noun] the ability of the mind to be creative or resourceful: *technology gives workers the chance to use their imagination.* ■ the part of the mind that imagines things: *a girl who existed only in my imagination.*
– ORIGIN Middle English: via Old French from Latin *imaginatio(n-)*, from the verb *imaginari* 'picture to oneself', from *imago, imagin-* 'image'.

imaginative ▶ adjective having or showing creativity or inventiveness: *making imaginative use of computer software | he was imaginative beyond all other architects.*
– DERIVATIVES **imaginatively** adverb, **imaginativeness** noun.

imagine ▶ verb [with obj.] **1** form a mental image or concept of: *imagine a car journey from Edinburgh to London |* [with clause] *I couldn't imagine what she expected to tell them.*
■ [often as adj. **imagined**] believe (something unreal or untrue) to exist or be so: *they suffered from ill health, real or imagined, throughout their lives.*
2 [with clause] suppose or assume: *after Ned died, everyone imagined that Mabel would move away.*
■ [as exclamation] just suppose: *imagine! to outwit Heydrich!*
– DERIVATIVES **imaginer** noun.
– ORIGIN Middle English: from Old French *imaginer*, from Latin *imaginare* 'form an image of, represent' and *imaginari* 'picture to oneself', both from *imago, imagin-* 'image'.

imagineer /ɪˌmadʒɪˈnɪə/ ▶ noun a person who devises and implements a new or highly imaginative concept or technology, in particular one who devises the attractions in Walt Disney theme parks.
▶ verb [with obj.] [often as noun **imagineering**] devise and implement (such a concept or technology): *theme parks are benefiting from a new era of imagineering.*
– ORIGIN 1940s: from **IMAGINE**, on the pattern of *engineer*.

imagines plural form of **IMAGO**.

imaginings ▶ plural noun thoughts or fantasies: *this was quite beyond his worst imaginings.*

imagism /ˈɪmɪdʒɪz(ə)m/ ▶ noun [mass noun] a movement in early 20th-century English and American poetry which sought clarity of expression through the use of precise images. The movement derived in part from the aesthetic philosophy of T. E. Hulme and involved Ezra Pound, James Joyce, Amy Lowell, and others.
– DERIVATIVES **imagist** noun, **imagistic** adjective.

imago /ɪˈmeɪgəʊ/ ▶ noun (pl. **imagos** or **imagines** /ɪˈmeɪdʒɪniːz/) **1** Entomology the final and fully developed adult stage of an insect, typically winged.
2 Psychoanalysis an unconscious idealized mental image of someone, especially a parent, which influences a person's behaviour.
– ORIGIN late 18th cent. (in sense 1): modern Latin use of Latin *imago* 'image'. Sense 2 dates from the early 20th cent.

imam /ɪˈmɑːm/ ▶ noun the person who leads prayers in a mosque.
■ (**Imam**) a title of various Muslim leaders, especially of one succeeding Muhammad as leader of Shiite Islam: *Imam Khomeini.*
– DERIVATIVES **imamate** noun.
– ORIGIN from Arabic *'imām* 'leader', from *'amma* 'lead the way'.

Imam Bayildi /ɪˌmɑːm ˈbɑːjɪldi/ ▶ noun [mass noun] a Turkish dish consisting of aubergines stuffed with a garlic-flavoured onion and tomato mixture and baked.
– ORIGIN Turkish, literally 'the imam fainted' (from enjoyment or the cost of the dish).

Imari /ɪˈmɑːri/ ▶ noun [usu. as modifier] a type of richly decorated Japanese porcelain: *an Imari vase.*
– ORIGIN late 19th cent.: from the name of a port in NW Kyushu, Japan, from which it was shipped.

IMAX /ˈʌɪmaks/ ▶ noun [mass noun] trademark a technique of widescreen cinematography which produces an image approximately ten times larger than that from standard 35 mm film: [as modifier] *IMAX cinemas.*
– ORIGIN 1960s: from *i-* (probably representing a pronunciation of **EYE**) + *max* (short for **MAXIMUM**).

imbalance ▶ noun [mass noun] lack of proportion or relation between corresponding things: *tension is generated by the imbalance of power |* [count noun] *the condition is caused by a hormonal imbalance.*

imbecile /ˈɪmbɪsiːl/ ▶ noun informal a stupid person.
▶ adjective [attrib.] stupid; idiotic: *try not to make imbecile remarks.*
– DERIVATIVES **imbecilic** adjective, **imbecility** noun (pl. **-ies**).
– ORIGIN mid 16th cent. (as an adjective in the sense 'physically weak'): via French from Latin *imbecillus*, literally 'without a supporting staff', from *in-* (expressing negation) + *baculum* 'stick, staff'. The current sense dates from the early 19th cent.

imbed ▶ verb variant spelling of **EMBED**.

imbibe /ɪmˈbʌɪb/ ▶ verb [with obj.] formal, often humorous drink (alcohol): *they were imbibing far too many pitchers of beer* | [no obj.] *having imbibed too freely, he fell over.*
■ figurative absorb or assimilate (ideas or knowledge): *the Bolshevist propaganda which you imbibed in your youth.* ■ chiefly Botany (especially of seeds) absorb (water) into ultramicroscopic spaces or pores. ■ Botany place (seeds) in water in order to absorb it.
– DERIVATIVES **imbiber** noun, **imbibition** /ɪmbɪˈbɪʃ(ə)n/ noun (chiefly Botany).
– ORIGIN late Middle English (in the senses 'absorb or cause to absorb moisture' and 'take into solution'): from Latin *imbibere*, from *in-* 'in' + *bibere* 'to drink'.

imbizo /ɪmˈbiːzəʊ/ ▶ noun (pl. **-os**) S. African a gathering of the Zulu people called by a traditional leader.
– ORIGIN from Zulu *biza* 'summon, call'.

Imbolc /ˈɪmbɒlk/ ▶ noun an ancient Celtic festival celebrated on the second day of February.
– ORIGIN a Celtic word, literally 'in the belly or womb', the festival being dedicated to women and fertility.

imbongi /ɪmˈbɔːŋgi/ ▶ noun (pl. **izimbongi** or **iimbongi** or **imbongis**) S. African (in traditional African society) a poet employed to compose poems praising a chief.
– ORIGIN from Xhosa (plural *iim-*) and Zulu (plural *izim-*).

imbricate chiefly Zoology & Botany ▶ verb /ˈɪmbrɪkeɪt/ [with obj.] [usu. as adj. **imbricated**] arrange (scales, sepals, plates, etc.) so that they overlap like roof tiles: *these moulds have spherical bodies composed of imbricated triangular plates.*
■ [no obj.] [usu. as adj. **imbricating**] overlap: *a coating of imbricating scales.*
▶ adjective /ˈɪmbrɪkət/ (of scales, sepals, plates, etc.) having adjacent edges overlapping. Compare with **VALVATE**.
– DERIVATIVES **imbrication** noun.
– ORIGIN early 17th cent. (in the sense 'shaped like a pantile'): from Latin *imbricat-*, 'covered with roof tiles', from the verb *imbricare*, from *imbrex, imbric-* 'roof tile' (from *imber* 'shower of rain').

imbroglio /ɪmˈbrəʊlɪəʊ/ ▶ noun (pl. **-os**) an extremely confused, complicated, or embarrassing situation: *the Abdication imbroglio of 1936.*
■ archaic a confused heap.
– ORIGIN mid 18th cent.: Italian, from *imbrogliare* 'confuse'; related to **EMBROIL**.

Imbros /ˈɪmbrɒs/ a Turkish island in the NE Aegean Sea, near the entrance to the Dardanelles. Turkish name **IMROZ**.

imbrue /ɪmˈbruː/ ▶ verb (**imbrues, imbrued, imbruing**) [with obj.] archaic or poetic/literary stain (something, especially one's hands or sword): *they were unwilling to imbrue their hands in his blood.*
– ORIGIN late Middle English: from Old French *embruer* 'bedaub, bedabble', ultimately of Germanic origin and related to **BROTH**.

imbue /ɪmˈbjuː/ ▶ verb (**imbues, imbued, imbuing**) [with obj.] (often **be imbued with**) inspire or permeate with a feeling or quality: *he was imbued with a deep Christian piety.*
– ORIGIN late Middle English (in the sense 'saturate'): from French *imbu* 'moistened', from Latin *imbutus*, past participle of *imbuere* 'moisten'.

I.Mech.E. ▶ abbreviation for (in the UK) Institution of Mechanical Engineers.

IMF ▶ abbreviation for International Monetary Fund.

IMHO ▶ abbreviation for in my humble opinion (used especially in electronic mail).

Imhotep /ɪmˈhəʊtɛp/ (*fl.* 27th century BC), Egyptian architect and scholar, later deified. He probably designed the step pyramid built at Saqqara for the 3rd-dynasty pharaoh Djoser.

imidazole /ˌɪmɪˈdeɪzəʊl, ɪˈmɪdəzəʊl/ ▶ noun [mass noun] Chemistry a colourless crystalline compound with mildly basic properties, present as a substituent in the amino acid histidine.
● a heterocyclic compound; chem. formula: $C_3H_4N_2$.
– ORIGIN late 19th cent.: from **IMIDE** + **AZO-** + **-OLE**.

imide /ˈɪmʌɪd/ ▶ noun [mass noun] Chemistry an organic compound containing the group —CONHCO—, related to ammonia by replacement of two hydrogen atoms by acyl groups.
– ORIGIN mid 19th cent.: from French, arbitrary alteration of **AMIDE**.

I.Min.E. ▶ abbreviation for (in the UK) Institution of Mining Engineers.

imine /ˈɪmiːn/ ▶ noun [mass noun] Chemistry an organic compound containing the group —C=NH or —C=NR where R is an alkyl or other group.
– ORIGIN late 19th cent.: from **AMINE**, on the pattern of the pair *amide, imide.*

imipramine /ɪˈmɪprəmiːn/ ▶ noun [mass noun] a synthetic compound used to treat depression.
● A tricyclic amine; chem. formula: $C_{19}H_{24}N_2$.
– ORIGIN 1950s: from *imi(ne)* + *pr(opyl)* + **AMINE**.

imitate ▶ verb [with obj.] (often **be imitated**) take or follow as a model: *his style was imitated by many other writers.*
■ copy (a person's speech or mannerisms), especially for comic effect: *she imitated my Scots accent.* ■ copy or simulate: *synthetic fabrics can now imitate everything from silk to rubber.*
– DERIVATIVES **imitable** adjective, **imitator** noun.
– ORIGIN mid 16th cent.: from Latin *imitat-* 'copied', from the verb *imitari*; related to *imago* 'image'.

imitation ▶ noun a thing intended to simulate or copy something else: [as modifier] *an imitation sub-machine gun.*
■ [mass noun] the action of using someone or something as a model: *a child learns to speak by imitation.* ■ an act of imitating a person's speech or mannerisms, especially for comic effect: *he attempted an atrocious imitation of my English accent.* ■ Music the repetition of a phrase or melody in another part or voice, usually at a different pitch.
– PHRASES **imitation is the sincerest form of flattery** proverb copying someone or something is an implicit way of paying them a compliment.
– ORIGIN late Middle English: from Latin *imitatio(n-)*, from the verb *imitari* (see **IMITATE**).

imitative /ˈɪmɪtətɪv/ ▶ adjective 1 copying or following a model or example: *the derring-do of our film heroes inspired us to imitative feats.*
■ following a model or example without any attempt at originality: *an ill-conceived and imitative addition to the museum.*
2 (of a word) reproducing a natural sound (e.g. *fizz*) or pronounced in a way that is thought to correspond to the appearance or character of the object or action described (e.g. *blob*).
– DERIVATIVES **imitatively** adverb, **imitativeness** noun.

imli /ˈɪmliː/ ▶ noun Indian term for **TAMARIND**.
– ORIGIN via Hindi from Sanskrit *amlikā*.

immaculate ▶ adjective (especially of a person or their clothes) perfectly clean, neat, or tidy: *an immaculate white suit.*
■ free from flaws or mistakes; perfect: *an immaculate safety record.* ■ Catholic Theology free from sin. ■ Botany & Zoology uniformly coloured without spots or other marks.
– DERIVATIVES **immaculacy** noun, **immaculately** adverb, **immaculateness** noun.
– ORIGIN late Middle English (in the sense 'free from moral stain'): from Latin *immaculatus*, from *in-* 'not' + *maculatus* 'stained' (from *macula* 'spot').

Immaculate Conception ▶ noun the doctrine that God preserved the Virgin Mary from the taint of original sin from the moment she was conceived; it was defined as a dogma of the Roman Catholic Church in 1854.
■ the feast commemorating the Immaculate Conception on December 8th.

immanent /ˈɪmənənt/ ▶ adjective existing or operating within; inherent: *the protection of liberties is immanent in constitutional arrangements.*
■ (of God) permanently pervading and sustaining the universe. Often contrasted with **TRANSCENDENT**.
– DERIVATIVES **immanence** noun, **immanency** noun, **immanentism** noun, **immanentist** noun.
– ORIGIN mid 16th cent.: from late Latin *immanent-* 'remaining within', from *in-* 'in' + *manere* 'remain'.

Immanuel variant spelling of **EMMANUEL**.

immaterial ▶ adjective 1 unimportant under the circumstances; irrelevant: *so long as the band kept the beat, what they played was immaterial.*
2 Philosophy spiritual, rather than physical: *we have immaterial souls.*
– DERIVATIVES **immateriality** noun, **immaterially** adverb.
– ORIGIN late Middle English (in sense 2): from late Latin *immaterialis*, from *in-* 'not' + *materialis* 'relating to matter'.

immaterialism ▶ noun [mass noun] the belief that matter has no objective existence.
– DERIVATIVES **immaterialist** noun.

immature ▶ adjective not fully developed: *many of the fish caught are immature* | *immature fruit.*
■ (of a person or their behaviour) having or showing emotional or intellectual development appropriate to someone younger: *his immature sense of humour.*
– DERIVATIVES **immaturely** adverb, **immaturity** noun.
– ORIGIN mid 16th cent. (in the sense 'premature', referring to death): from Latin *immaturus* 'untimely, unripe', from *in-* 'not' + *maturus* 'ripe' (see **MATURE**).

immeasurable ▶ adjective too large, extensive, or extreme to measure: *immeasurable suffering.*
– DERIVATIVES **immeasurability** noun, **immeasurably** adverb.

immediacy /ɪˈmiːdɪəsi/ ▶ noun [mass noun] the quality of bringing one into direct and instant involvement with something, giving rise to a sense of urgency or excitement: *electronic mail works because it has the immediacy of a scribbled memo.*

immediate ▶ adjective 1 occurring or done at once; instant: *the authorities took no immediate action* | *the book's success was immediate.*
■ relating to or existing at the present time: *the immediate concern was how to avoid taxes.*
2 nearest in time, relationship, or rank: *a funeral with only the immediate family in attendance.*
■ nearest or next to in space: *roads in the immediate vicinity of the port.* ■ (of a relation or action) without an intervening medium or agency; direct: *coronary thrombosis was the immediate cause of death.*
3 Philosophy (of knowledge or reaction) gained or shown without reasoning; intuitive.
– DERIVATIVES **immediateness** noun.
– ORIGIN late Middle English (in the sense 'nearest in space or order'): from Old French *immediat*, or from late Latin *immediatus*, from *in-* 'not' + *mediatus* 'intervening', past participle of *mediare* (see **MEDIATE**).

immediate constituent ▶ noun Linguistics each of the constituents of a syntactic unit at the next level down in the hierarchy.

immediately ▶ adverb 1 at once; instantly: *I rang immediately for an ambulance.*
2 without any intervening time or space: *she was sitting immediately behind me.*
■ in direct or very close relation: *they would be the states most immediately affected by any such action.*
▶ conjunction chiefly Brit. as soon as: *let me know immediately she arrives.*

immedicable /ɪˈmɛdɪkəb(ə)l/ ▶ adjective archaic unable to be healed or treated; incurable.
– ORIGIN mid 16th cent.: from Latin *immedicabilis*, from *in-* 'not' + *medicabilis* (see **MEDICABLE**).

Immelmann /ˈɪm(ə)lmən/ (also **Immelmann turn**) ▶ noun an aerobatic manoeuvre consisting of a half loop followed by a half roll, resulting in reversal of direction and increased height.
– ORIGIN early 20th cent.: named after Max Immelmann (1890–1916), German fighter pilot.

immemorial ▶ adjective originating in the distant past; very old: *an immemorial custom.*
– DERIVATIVES **immemorially** adverb.
– ORIGIN early 17th cent.: from medieval Latin *immemorialis*, from *in-* 'not' + *memorialis* 'relating to the memory'.

immense ▶ adjective extremely large or great, especially in scale or degree: *the cost of restoration has been immense* | *an immense apartment building.*
– DERIVATIVES **immensity** noun.
– ORIGIN late Middle English: via French from Latin *immensus* 'immeasurable', from *in-* 'not' + *mensus* 'measured' (past participle of *metiri*).

immensely ▶ adverb to a great extent; extremely: [as submodifier] *the president was immensely popular.*

immerse ▶ verb 1 [with obj.] dip or submerge in a liquid: *immerse the paper in water for twenty minutes.*
■ baptize (someone) by immersion in water.
2 (**immerse oneself** or **be immersed**) figurative involve oneself deeply in a particular activity or interest: *she immersed herself in her work* | *she was still immersed in her thoughts.*
– ORIGIN early 17th cent.: from Latin *immers-* 'dipped into', from the verb *immergere*, from *in-* 'in' + *mergere* 'to dip'.

immersion ▶ noun [mass noun] the action of immersing someone or something in a liquid: *his back was still raw from immersion in the icy Atlantic sea.*

■deep mental involvement: *his total immersion in Marxism*. ■ chiefly N. Amer. a method of teaching a foreign language by the exclusive use of that language, usually at a special school. ■ baptism by immersing a person bodily (but not necessarily completely) in water. ■ Astronomy the disappearance of a celestial body in the shadow of or behind another.
– ORIGIN late 15th cent.: from late Latin *immersio(n-)*, from *immergere* 'dip into' (see IMMERSE).

immersion heater ▶ noun an electric heating element that is positioned in the liquid to be heated, typically in a domestic hot-water tank.

immersive ▶ adjective (of a computer display or system) generating a three-dimensional image which appears to surround the user.

immigrant ▶ noun a person who comes to live permanently in a foreign country.
– ORIGIN late 18th cent.: from Latin *immigrant-* 'immigrating', from the verb *immigrare*, on the pattern of *emigrant*.

immigrate ▶ verb [no obj.] come to live permanently in a foreign country: *an Australian who immigrated to Britain in 1982.*
– ORIGIN early 17th cent.: from Latin *immigrat-* 'immigrated', from the verb *immigrare*, from *in-* 'into' + *migrare* 'migrate'.

immigration ▶ noun [mass noun] the action of coming to live permanently in a foreign country: *a barrier to control illegal immigration from Mexico.*
■the place at an airport or country's border where government officials check the documents of people entering that country.

imminent ▶ adjective **1** about to happen: *they were in imminent danger of being swept away.*
2 archaic overhanging.
– DERIVATIVES **imminence** noun, **imminently** adverb.
– ORIGIN late Middle English: from Latin *imminent-* 'overhanging, impending', from the verb *imminere*, from *in-* 'upon, towards' + *minere* 'to project'.

immiscible /ɪˈmɪsɪb(ə)l/ ▶ adjective (of liquids) not forming a homogeneous mixture when added together: *benzene is immiscible with water.*
– DERIVATIVES **immiscibility** noun, **immiscibly** adverb.
– ORIGIN late 17th cent.: from late Latin *immiscibilis*, from *in-* 'not' + *miscibilis* (see MISCIBLE).

immiseration /ɪˌmɪzəˈreɪʃ(ə)n/ ▶ noun [mass noun] economic impoverishment.
– DERIVATIVES **immiserate** verb.
– ORIGIN 1940s: translating German *Verelendung*.

immiserization /ɪˌmɪzərʌɪˈzeɪʃ(ə)n/ ▶ noun another term for IMMISERATION.
– DERIVATIVES **immiserize** verb.

immitigable /ɪˈmɪtɪɡəb(ə)l/ ▶ adjective archaic unable to be made less severe or serious: *the pain was immitigable.*
– DERIVATIVES **immitigably** adverb.
– ORIGIN late 16th cent.: from late Latin *immitigabilis*, from *in-* 'not' + *mitigabilis* 'able to be mitigated'.

immittance /ɪˈmɪt(ə)ns/ ▶ noun Physics admittance and impedance (as a combined concept).
– ORIGIN 1950s: blend of IMPEDANCE and ADMITTANCE.

immixture ▶ noun [mass noun] archaic the process of mixing or being involved with something.

immobile ▶ adjective not moving; motionless: *she sat immobile for a long time.*
■incapable of moving or being moved: *an immobile workforce.*
– DERIVATIVES **immobility** noun.
– ORIGIN Middle English: from Old French, from Latin *immobilis*, from *in-* 'not' + *mobilis* (see MOBILE).

immobilism ▶ noun [mass noun] deep-seated resistance to political change.

immobilize (also **-ise**) ▶ verb [with obj.] prevent (something or someone) from moving or operating as normal: *I want you to immobilize their vehicle | fear had immobilized her.*
■restrict the movements of (a limb or patient) to allow healing: *other children in the ward were immobilized in traction.*
– DERIVATIVES **immobilization** noun.
– ORIGIN late 19th cent.: from French *immobiliser*, from *immobile* (see IMMOBILE).

immobilizer (also **-iser**) ▶ noun a device for immobilizing a motor vehicle in order to prevent theft.

immoderate ▶ adjective not sensible or restrained; excessive: *immoderate drinking.*

– DERIVATIVES **immoderately** adverb, **immoderation** noun.
– ORIGIN late Middle English: from Latin *immoderatus*, from *in-* 'not' + *moderatus* 'reduced, controlled' (past participle of *moderare*).

immodest ▶ adjective lacking humility or decency: *his immodest personality.*
– DERIVATIVES **immodestly** adverb, **immodesty** noun.
– ORIGIN late 16th cent.: from French *immodeste* or Latin *immodestus*, from *in-* 'not' + *modestus* (see MODEST).

immolate /ˈɪməleɪt/ ▶ verb [with obj.] kill or offer as a sacrifice, especially by burning.
– DERIVATIVES **immolation** noun, **immolator** noun.
– ORIGIN mid 16th cent.: from Latin *immolat-* 'sprinkled with sacrificial meal', from the verb *immolare*, from *in-* 'upon' + *mola* 'meal'.

immoral ▶ adjective not conforming to accepted standards of morality: *an immoral and unwinnable war.*
– DERIVATIVES **immorality** noun (pl. **-ies**), **immorally** adverb.

USAGE The words **immoral** and **amoral** are different in meaning: see usage at AMORAL.

immoral earnings ▶ plural noun earnings from prostitution.

immoralism ▶ noun [mass noun] a system of thought or behaviour that does not accept moral principles.
– DERIVATIVES **immoralist** noun.
– ORIGIN early 20th cent.: suggested by German *Immoralismus*.

immortal /ɪˈmɔːt(ə)l/ ▶ adjective living forever; never dying or decaying: *our mortal bodies are inhabited by immortal souls.*
■deserving to be remembered forever: *the immortal children's classic, 'The Wind in the Willows'.*
▶ noun an immortal being, especially a god of ancient Greece or Rome.
■a person of enduring fame: *he will always be one of the immortals of soccer.* ■ (**Immortals**) historical the royal bodyguard of ancient Persia. ■ (**Immortal**) a member of the French Academy.
– DERIVATIVES **immortality** /ɪmɔːˈtalɪti/ noun, **immortally** adverb.
– ORIGIN late Middle English: from Latin *immortalis*, from *in-* 'not' + *mortalis* (see MORTAL).

immortalize (also **-ise**) ▶ verb [with obj.] (usu. be **immortalized in**) confer enduring fame upon: *he will be forever immortalized in the history books.*
– DERIVATIVES **immortalization** noun.

immortelle /ɪmɔːˈtɛl/ ▶ noun **1** another term for EVERLASTING (in sense 2).
2 W. Indian a Caribbean tree of the pea family, with a spiny trunk and clusters of red, orange, or pinkish flowers.
● Genus *Erythrina*, family Leguminosae: two species.
– ORIGIN French (feminine adjective), literally 'everlasting'.

immotile /ɪˈməʊtʌɪl/ ▶ adjective Biology not motile.

immovable (also **immoveable**) ▶ adjective not able to be moved: *all immovable objects have graffiti sprayed on them.*
■(of a person) not yielding to argument or pressure. ■ (especially of a principle) fixed or unchangeable: *an immovable article of faith.* ■ Law (of property) consisting of land, buildings, or other permanent items.
▶ noun (**immovables**) Law immovable property.
– DERIVATIVES **immovability** noun, **immovably** adverb.

immune ▶ adjective resistant to a particular infection or toxin owing to the presence of specific antibodies or sensitized white blood cells: *they were naturally immune to hepatitis B.*
■protected or exempt, especially from an obligation or the effects of something: *they are immune from legal action.* ■ [predic.] not affected or influenced by something: *no one is immune to his immense charm.* ■ [attrib.] Biology of or relating to immunity: *the body's immune system.*
– ORIGIN late Middle English (in the sense 'free from (a liability)'): from Latin *immunis* 'exempt from public service or charge', from *in-* 'not' + *munis* 'ready for service'. Senses relating to physiological resistance date from the late 19th cent.

immune deficiency ▶ noun [mass noun] failure of the immune system to protect the body adequately from infection, due to the absence or insufficiency of some component process or substance.

immune response ▶ noun the reaction of the

cells and fluids of the body to the presence of a substance which is not recognized as a constituent of the body itself.

immunity ▶ noun (pl. **-ies**) [mass noun] the ability of an organism to resist a particular infection or toxin by the action of specific antibodies or sensitized white blood cells: *immunity to typhoid seems to have increased spontaneously.*
■protection or exemption from something, especially an obligation or penalty: *the rebels were given immunity from prosecution.* ■ Law officially granted exemption from legal proceedings. ■ (**immunity to**) lack of susceptibility, especially to something unwelcome or harmful: *products must have an adequate level of immunity to interference | [count noun] exercises designed to build an immunity to fatigue.*
– ORIGIN late Middle English: in the sense 'exemption (from a liability)': from Latin *immunitas*, from *immunis* (see IMMUNE).

immunize (also **-ise**) ▶ verb [with obj.] make (a person or animal) immune to infection, typically by inoculation: *the vaccine is used to immunize children against measles.*
– DERIVATIVES **immunization** noun, **immunizer** noun.

immuno- /ˈɪmjʊnəʊ, ɪˈmjuːnəʊ/ ▶ combining form Medicine representing IMMUNE, IMMUNITY, or IMMUNOLOGY.

immunoassay /ˌɪmjʊnəʊˈaseɪ, ɪˌmjuːnəʊ-/ ▶ noun Biochemistry a procedure for detecting or measuring specific proteins or other substances through their properties as antigens or antibodies: *these general principles can be applied to all immunoassays | [mass noun] the uses of immunoassay in industry.*

immunochemistry ▶ noun [mass noun] the branch of biochemistry concerned with immune responses and systems.

immunocompetent /ˌɪmjʊnəʊˈkɒmpɪtənt, ɪˌmjuːnəʊ-/ ▶ adjective Medicine having a normal immune response.
– DERIVATIVES **immunocompetence** noun.

immunocompromised ▶ adjective Medicine having an impaired immune system.

immunocytochemistry /ˌɪmjʊnəʊˌsʌɪtəʊˈkɛmɪstri, ɪˌmjuːnəʊ-/ ▶ noun [mass noun] the range of microscopical techniques used in the study of the immune system.
– DERIVATIVES **immunocytochemical** adjective.

immunodeficiency ▶ noun another term for IMMUNE DEFICIENCY.

immunodiffusion ▶ noun [mass noun] Biochemistry a technique for detecting or measuring antibodies and antigens by their precipitation when diffused together through a gel or other medium.

immunoelectrophoresis /ˌɪmjʊnəʊɪˌlɛktrə(ʊ)fəˈriːsɪs, ɪˌmjuːnəʊ-/ ▶ noun [mass noun] Biochemistry a technique for the identification of proteins in serum or other fluid by electrophoresis and subsequent immunodiffusion.

immunofluorescence /ˌɪmjʊnəʊˌflʊəˈrɛs(ə)ns, ɪˌmjuːnəʊ-, -flɔː-/ ▶ noun [mass noun] Biochemistry a technique for determining the location of an antigen (or antibody) in tissues by reaction with an antibody (or antigen) labelled with a fluorescent dye.
– DERIVATIVES **immunofluorescent** adjective.

immunogenic /ˌɪmjʊnəʊ(ʊ)ˈdʒɛnɪk, ɪˌmjuːnə(ʊ)-/ ▶ adjective relating to or denoting substances able to produce an immune response.
– DERIVATIVES **immunogenicity** noun.

immunoglobulin /ˌɪmjʊnəʊˈɡlɒbjʊlɪn, ɪˌmjuːnəʊ-/ ▶ noun [mass noun] Biochemistry any of a class of proteins present in the serum and cells of the immune system, which function as antibodies.

immunology ▶ noun [mass noun] the branch of medicine and biology concerned with immunity.
– DERIVATIVES **immunologic** adjective, **immunological** adjective, **immunologically** adverb, **immunologist** noun.

immunosorbent ▶ adjective Biochemistry relating to or denoting techniques making use of the absorption of antibodies by insoluble preparations of antigens.

immunosuppression ▶ noun [mass noun] Medicine the partial or complete suppression of the immune response of an individual. It is induced to help the survival of an organ after a transplant operation.
– DERIVATIVES **immunosuppressant** noun, **immunosuppressed** adjective.

immunosuppressive ▶ adjective Medicine (chiefly of drugs) partially or completely suppressing the immune response of an individual.
▶ noun a drug of this kind.

immunotherapy ▶ noun [mass noun] Medicine the prevention or treatment of disease with substances that stimulate the immune response.

immure /ɪˈmjʊə/ ▶ verb [with obj.] (usu. **be immured**) enclose or confine (someone) against their will: *her brother was immured in a lunatic asylum.*
– DERIVATIVES **immurement** noun.
– ORIGIN late 16th cent.: from French *emmurer* or medieval Latin *immurare*, from *in-* 'in' + *murus* 'wall'.

immutable /ɪˈmjuːtəb(ə)l/ ▶ adjective unchanging over time or unable to be changed: *an immutable fact.*
– DERIVATIVES **immutability** noun, **immutably** adverb.
– ORIGIN late Middle English: from Latin *immutabilis*, from *in-* 'not' + *mutabilis* (see **MUTABLE**).

IMO ▶ abbreviation for International Maritime Organization.

IMP Bridge ▶ abbreviation for International Match Point.

imp ▶ noun a mischievous child: *a cheeky young imp.*
■ a small, mischievous devil or sprite.
▶ verb [with obj.] repair a damaged feather in (the wing or tail of a trained hawk) by attaching part of a new feather.
– ORIGIN Old English *impa*, *impe* 'young shoot, scion', *impian* 'to graft', based on Greek *emphuein* 'to implant'. In late Middle English, the noun denoted a descendant, especially of a noble family, and later a child of the devil or a person regarded as such; hence a 'little devil' or mischievous child (early 17th cent.).

impact ▶ noun /ˈɪmpakt/ the action of one object coming forcibly into contact with another: *there was the sound of a third impact* | [mass noun] *bullets which expand and cause devastating injury on impact.*
■ the effect or influence of one person, thing, or action, on another: *our regional measures have had a significant impact on unemployment.*
▶ verb /ɪmˈpakt/ **1** [no obj.] come into forcible contact with another object: *the shell impacted twenty yards away.*
■ [with obj.] chiefly N. Amer. come into forcible contact with: *an asteroid impacted the earth some 60 million years ago.* ■ have a strong effect: *high interest rates have impacted on retail spending* | [with obj.] *the move is not expected to impact the company's employees.*
2 [with obj.] press firmly: *the animals' feet do not impact and damage the soil as cows' hooves do.*
– ORIGIN early 17th cent. (as a verb in the sense 'press closely, fix firmly'): from Latin *impact-* 'driven in', from the verb *impingere* (see **IMPINGE**).

> **USAGE** The phrasal verb impact on, as in *when produce is lost, it always impacts on the bottom line*, has been in the language since the 1960s. Many people disapprove of it, despite its relative frequency, saying that **make an impact on** or other equivalent wordings should be used instead. This may be partly because, in general, new formations of verbs from nouns (as in the case of impact) are regarded as somehow inferior; in addition, since the use of **impact** is associated with business and commercial writing, it has the unenviable status of 'jargon', which makes it doubly disliked.

impact crater ▶ noun a crater on a planet or satellite caused by the impact of a meteorite or other object, typically circular with a raised rim.

impacted ▶ adjective **1** chiefly Medicine pressed firmly together, in particular:
■ (of a tooth) wedged between another tooth and the jaw. ■ (of a fractured bone) having the parts crushed together. ■ (of faeces) lodged in the intestine.
2 strongly affected by something: *grandiose planning projects have had deleterious effects on impacted social groups.*

impaction ▶ noun [mass noun] Medicine the condition of being or process of becoming impacted, especially of faeces in the intestine.

impactive ▶ adjective having a strong effect or influence; making an impression: *impactive colour radiates from the sculptures.*

impactor ▶ noun chiefly Astronomy an object (such as a meteorite) which collides with another body.

impair ▶ verb [with obj.] weaken or damage (especially a human faculty or function): *a noisy job could permanently impair their hearing.*

– ORIGIN Middle English *enpeire*, from Old French *empeirier*, based on late Latin *pejorare* (from Latin *pejor* 'worse'). The current spelling is due to association with words derived from Latin beginning with *im-*.

impaired ▶ adjective having a disability of a specified kind: [in combination] *hearing-impaired children.*

impairment ▶ noun [mass noun] the state or fact of being impaired, especially in a specified faculty: *a degree of physical or mental impairment* | [count noun] *a speech impairment.*

impala /ɪmˈpɑːlə, -ˈpalə/ ▶ noun (pl. same) a graceful antelope often seen in large herds in open woodland in southern and East Africa.
● *Aepyceros melampus*, family Bovidae.
– ORIGIN late 19th cent.: from Zulu *i-mpala*.

impale ▶ verb [with obj.] **1** transfix or pierce with a sharp instrument: *his head was impaled on a pike and exhibited for all to see.*
2 Heraldry display (a coat of arms) side by side with another on the same shield, separated by a vertical line: [as adj. **impaled**] *the impaled arms of her husband and her father.*
■ (of a coat of arms) adjoin (another coat of arms) in this way.
– DERIVATIVES **impalement** noun, **impaler** noun.
– ORIGIN mid 16th cent. (in the sense 'enclose with stakes or pales'): from French *empaler* or medieval Latin *impalare*, from Latin *in-* 'in' + *palus* 'a stake'.

impalpable ▶ adjective unable to be felt by touch: *an impalpable ghost.*
■ not easily comprehended: *how would anyone come to a decision about something so impalpable as personhood?*
– DERIVATIVES **impalpability** noun, **impalpably** adverb.
– ORIGIN early 16th cent.: from French, or from late Latin *impalpabilis*, from *in-* 'not' + *palpabilis* (see **PALPABLE**).

impanation /ˌɪmpəˈneɪʃ(ə)n/ ▶ noun [mass noun] Theology the medieval and Reformation doctrine that the body of Christ is present within the Eucharistic bread and does not replace it. Compare with **CONSUBSTANTIATION**.
– DERIVATIVES **impanate** /ɪmˈpeɪnət/ adjective.
– ORIGIN mid 16th cent.: from medieval Latin *impanatio(n-)*, from *impanare* 'embody in bread', from *in-* 'in' + *panis* 'bread'.

impanel (also **empanel**) ▶ verb (**impanelled**, **impanelling**; US **impaneled**, **impaneling**) [with obj.] enlist or enrol (a jury).
■ enrol (someone) on to a jury: *several of her friends have been impanelled.*
– DERIVATIVES **impanelment** noun.
– ORIGIN late Middle English (originally as *empanel*): from Anglo-Norman French *empaneller*, from *em-* 'in' + Old French *panel* 'panel'.

impark ▶ verb [with obj.] historical enclose (animals) in a park.
■ enclose (land) to make it into a park.
– ORIGIN late Middle English: from Old French *emparquer*, from *em-* 'within' + *parc* 'park'.

impart ▶ verb [with obj.] make (information) known; communicate: *the teachers imparted a great deal of knowledge to their pupils.*
■ bestow (a quality): *its main use has been to impart a high surface gloss to finished articles.*
– DERIVATIVES **impartation** noun.
– ORIGIN late Middle English (in the sense 'give a share of'): from Old French *impartir*, from Latin *impartire*, from *in-* 'in' + *pars, part-* 'part'.

impartial ▶ adjective treating all rivals or disputants equally: *the minister cannot be impartial in the way that a judge would be.*
– DERIVATIVES **impartiality** noun, **impartially** adverb.

impassable ▶ adjective impossible to travel along or over: *the narrow channels are impassable to ocean-going ships.*
– DERIVATIVES **impassability** noun, **impassableness** noun, **impassably** adverb.

impasse /amˈpɑːs, ˈampɑːs/ ▶ noun a situation in which no progress is possible, especially because of disagreement; a deadlock: *the current political impasse.*
– ORIGIN mid 19th cent.: from French, from *im-* (expressing negation) + the stem of *passer* 'to pass'.

impassible /ɪmˈpasɪb(ə)l/ ▶ adjective chiefly Theology incapable of suffering or feeling pain: *belief in an impassible God.*

– DERIVATIVES **impassibility** noun, **impassibly** adverb.
– ORIGIN Middle English: via Old French from ecclesiastical Latin *impassibilis*, from Latin *in-* 'not' + *passibilis* (see **PASSIBLE**).

impassion ▶ verb [with obj.] make passionate: *her body had once pleased and impassioned him.*
– ORIGIN late 16th cent.: from Italian *impassionnare*, from *im-* (expressing intensive force) + *passione* 'passion', from Christian Latin *passio* (see **PASSION**).

impassioned ▶ adjective filled with or showing great emotion: *she made an impassioned plea for help.*

impassive ▶ adjective not feeling or showing emotion: *impassive passers-by ignore the performers.*
– DERIVATIVES **impassively** adverb, **impassiveness** noun, **impassivity** noun.

impasto /ɪmˈpastəʊ/ ▶ noun [mass noun] Art the process or technique of laying on paint or pigment thickly so that it stands out from a surface.
■ paint applied thickly.
– ORIGIN late 18th cent.: from Italian, from *impastare*, from *im-* 'upon' + *pasta* 'a paste', from late Latin.

impatiens /ɪmˈpatɪɛnz/ ▶ noun a plant of a genus that includes busy Lizzie and its many hybrids.
● Genus *Impatiens*, family Balsaminaceae.
– ORIGIN modern Latin , from Latin, literally 'impatient' (because the capsules of the plant readily burst open when touched).

impatient ▶ adjective **1** having or showing a tendency to be quickly irritated or provoked: *an impatient motorist blaring his horn* | *she was impatient with any restriction.*
■ [predic.] (**impatient of**) intolerant of: *a man impatient of bureaucracy.*
2 restlessly eager: *they are impatient for change* | [with infinitive] *he was impatient to be on his way.*
– DERIVATIVES **impatience** noun, **impatiently** adverb.
– ORIGIN late Middle English (in the senses 'lacking patience' and 'unbearable'): via Old French from Latin *impatient-* 'not bearing, impatient', from *in-* 'not' + *pati* 'suffer, bear' .

impeach ▶ verb [with obj.] call into question the integrity or validity of (a practice): *there is no desire to impeach the privileges of the House of Commons.*
■ Brit. charge with treason or another crime against the state. ■ chiefly US charge (the holder of a public office) with misconduct.
– DERIVATIVES **impeachable** adjective, **impeachment** noun.
– ORIGIN late Middle English (also in the sense 'hinder, prevent'; earlier as *empeche*): from Old French *empecher* 'impede', from late Latin *impedicare* 'catch, entangle' (based on *pedica* 'a fetter', from *pes, ped-* 'foot'). Compare with **IMPEDE**.

impeccable /ɪmˈpɛkəb(ə)l/ ▶ adjective (of behaviour, performance, or appearance) in accordance with the highest standards of propriety; faultless: *a man of impeccable character.*
■ Theology, rare not liable to sin.
– DERIVATIVES **impeccability** noun, **impeccably** adverb.
– ORIGIN mid 16th cent. (in the theological sense): from Latin *impeccabilis*, from *in-* 'not' + *peccare* 'to sin'.

impecunious /ˌɪmpɪˈkjuːnɪəs/ ▶ adjective having little or no money: *a titled but impecunious family.*
– DERIVATIVES **impecuniosity** noun, **impecuniousness** noun.
– ORIGIN late 16th cent.: from **IN-**¹ 'not' + obsolete *pecunious* 'having money, wealthy' (from Latin *pecuniosus*, from *pecunia* 'money').

impedance /ɪmˈpiːd(ə)ns/ ▶ noun the effective resistance of an electric circuit or component to alternating current, arising from the combined effects of ohmic resistance and reactance. See also **ACOUSTIC IMPEDANCE**.
● Impedance is usually expressed as a complex quantity $Z = R + jX$, where R is resistance, X is reactance, and j is the imaginary square root of -1.

impede /ɪmˈpiːd/ ▶ verb [with obj.] delay or prevent (someone or something) by obstructing them; hinder: *the sap causes swelling which can impede breathing.*
– ORIGIN late 16th cent.: from Latin *impedire* 'shackle the feet of', based on *pes, ped-* 'foot'. Compare with **IMPEACH**.

impediment /ɪmˈpɛdɪm(ə)nt/ ▶ noun a hindrance or

obstruction in doing something: *a serious impediment to scientific progress.*
■(also **speech impediment**) a defect in a person's speech, such as a lisp or stammer.
– DERIVATIVES **impedimental** adjective.
– ORIGIN late Middle English: from Latin *impedimentum*, from *impedire* (see **IMPEDE**).

impedimenta /ɪmˌpɛdɪˈmɛntə/ ▶ **plural noun** equipment for an activity or expedition, especially when considered as bulky or an encumbrance.
– ORIGIN early 17th cent.: from Latin, plural of *impedimentum* 'impediment', from *impedire* (see **IMPEDE**).

impel /ɪmˈpɛl/ ▶ **verb** (**impelled**, **impelling**) [with obj.] drive, force, or urge (someone) to do something: *financial difficulties* ***impelled*** *him* ***to*** *desperate measures* | [with obj. and infinitive] *a lack of equality impelled the oppressed to fight.*
■drive forward; propel: *vital energies impel him in unforeseen directions.*
– ORIGIN late Middle English (in the sense 'propel'): from Latin *impellere*, from *in-* 'towards' + *pellere* 'to drive'.

impeller (also **impellor**) ▶ **noun** the rotating part of a centrifugal pump, compressor, or other machine designed to move a fluid by rotation.
■a similar device turned by the flow of water past a ship's hull, used to measure speed or distance travelled.

impend /ɪmˈpɛnd/ ▶ **verb** [no obj.] [usu. as adj. **impending**] be about to happen: *my impending departure.*
■(of something bad) loom: *a negative feeling of bother* ***impended over*** *her.*
– ORIGIN late 16th cent.: from Latin *impendere*, from *in-* 'towards, upon' + *pendere* 'hang'.

impenetrable /ɪmˈpɛnɪtrəb(ə)l/ ▶ **adjective** **1** impossible to pass through or enter: *a dark, impenetrable forest.*
■(of a club or group) secretive and exclusive: *an impenetrable clique.* ■ impervious to new ideas or influences: *his career shows just how impenetrable European assumptions were.* ■ Physics (of matter) incapable of occupying the same space as other matter at the same time.
2 impossible to understand: *impenetrable interviews with French intellectuals.*
– DERIVATIVES **impenetrability** noun, **impenetrably** adverb.
– ORIGIN late Middle English: via French from Latin *impenetrabilis*, from *in-* 'not' + *penetrabilis* 'able to be pierced', from the verb *penetrare* (see **PENETRATE**).

impenitent ▶ **adjective** not feeling shame or regret about one's actions or attitudes.
– DERIVATIVES **impenitence** noun, **impenitency** noun, **impenitently** adverb.
– ORIGIN late Middle English: from ecclesiastical Latin *impaenitent-* 'not repenting', from Latin *in-* 'not' + *paenitere* 'repent'.

imperative ▶ **adjective** **1** of vital importance; crucial: *immediate action was imperative* | [with clause] *it is imperative that standards are maintained.*
2 giving an authoritative command; peremptory: *the bell pealed again, a final imperative call.*
■Grammar denoting the mood of a verb that expresses a command or exhortation, as in *come here!*
▶ **noun** **1** an essential or urgent thing: *free movement of labour was an economic imperative.*
■a factor or influence making something necessary: *the change came about through a financial imperative.* ■ a thing felt as an obligation: *the moral imperative of aiding Third World development.*
2 Grammar a verb or phrase in the imperative mood.
■(**the imperative**) the imperative mood.
– DERIVATIVES **imperatival** /ɪmˌpɛrəˈtʌɪv(ə)l/ adjective, **imperatively** adverb, **imperativeness** noun.
– ORIGIN late Middle English (as a grammatical term): from late Latin *imperativus* (literally 'specially ordered', translating Greek *prostatikē enklisis* 'imperative mood'), from *imperare* 'to command', from *in-* 'towards' + *parare* 'make ready'.

imperator /ˌɪmpəˈrɑːtɔː/ ▶ **noun** Roman History commander (a title conferred under the Republic on a victorious general and under the Empire on the emperor).
– DERIVATIVES **imperatorial** /ˌɪmpɛrəˈtɔːrɪəl, ɪmˌpɛrə-/ adjective.
– ORIGIN Latin, from *imperare* 'to order, command'.

imperceptible ▶ **adjective** impossible to perceive: *his head moved in an almost imperceptible nod.*
– DERIVATIVES **imperceptibility** /-ˈbɪlɪti/ noun, **imperceptibly** adverb.
– ORIGIN late Middle English: from French, or from medieval Latin *imperceptibilis*, from *in-* 'not' + *perceptibilis*, from the verb *percipere* (see **PERCEIVE**).

imperceptive ▶ **adjective** lacking in perception or insight: *he dismissed the remark as juvenile and imperceptive.*

impercipient ▶ **adjective** failing to perceive something.
– DERIVATIVES **impercipience** noun.

imperfect ▶ **adjective** **1** not perfect; faulty: *an imperfect grasp of English.*
■not fully formed or done; incomplete: *imperfect census records* | *smoke due to imperfect combustion.*
2 Grammar (of a tense) denoting a past action in progress but not completed at the time in question.
3 Music (of a cadence) ending on the dominant chord.
4 Law (of a gift, title, etc.) transferred without all the necessary conditions or requirements being met.
▶ **noun** (**the imperfect**) Grammar the imperfect tense.
– DERIVATIVES **imperfectly** adverb.
– ORIGIN Middle English *imparfit*, *imperfet*, from Old French *imparfait*, from Latin *imperfectus*, from *in-* 'not' + *perfectus* (see **PERFECT**). The spelling change in the 16th cent. was due to association with the Latin form.

imperfect competition ▶ **noun** [mass noun] the situation prevailing in a market in which elements of monopoly allow individual producers or consumers to exercise some control over market prices.

imperfection ▶ **noun** a fault, blemish, or undesirable feature: *the imperfections and injustices in our political system.*
■[mass noun] the state of being faulty or incomplete: *he accepted me without question, in all my imperfection.*
– ORIGIN late Middle English: via Old French from late Latin *imperfectio(n-)*, from *imperfectus* (see **IMPERFECT**).

imperfective Grammar ▶ **adjective** relating to or denoting an aspect of verbs in Slavic languages that expresses action without reference to its completion. The opposite of **PERFECTIVE**.
▶ **noun** the imperfective aspect, or an imperfective form of a verb.

imperfect rhyme ▶ **noun** a rhyme that only partly satisfies the usual criteria (e.g. *love* and *move*).

imperforate /ɪmˈpəːf(ə)rət/ ▶ **adjective** not perforated, in particular:
■Anatomy & Zoology lacking the normal opening: *unicellular spores of these parasites have an imperforate wall.* ■ (of a postage stamp or a block or sheet of stamps) lacking perforations, especially as an error.

imperial ▶ **adjective** **1** of or relating to an empire: *Britain's imperial era.*
■of or relating to an emperor: *the imperial family.* ■ majestic; magnificent: *the bedroom is huge and very imperial.* ■ imperious or domineering: *the party and its autocratic—many would say imperial—ways.*
2 of, relating to, or denoting the system of non-metric weights and measures (the ounce, pound, stone, inch, foot, yard, mile, acre, pint, gallon, etc.) formerly used for all measures in the UK, and still used for some.
3 chiefly historical (of a size of paper) measuring (in the UK) 762 × 559 mm (30 × 22 inches).
▶ **noun** a small pointed beard growing below the lower lip (associated with Napoleon III of France).
– DERIVATIVES **imperially** adverb.
– ORIGIN late Middle English: via Old French from Latin *imperialis*, from *imperium* 'command, authority, empire'; related to *imperare* 'to command'. Compare with **EMPEROR**, **EMPIRE**, also with **IMPERIOUS**.

imperial gallon ▶ **noun** see **GALLON** (sense 1).

imperialism ▶ **noun** [mass noun] a policy of extending a country's power and influence through colonization, use of military force, or other means: *the struggle against imperialism* | figurative *French ministers protested at US cultural imperialism.*
■chiefly historical rule by an emperor.
– DERIVATIVES **imperialistic** adjective, **imperialistically** adverb.

imperialist ▶ **adjective** of, relating to, supporting, or practising imperialism: *an imperialist regime.*
▶ **noun** chiefly derogatory a person who supports or practises imperialism.

imperialize (also **-ise**) ▶ **verb** [with obj.] [usu. as adj. **imperialized**] subject to imperial rule or influence: *people of an imperialized culture.*

imperial pigeon ▶ **noun** a tropical fruit-eating pigeon that typically has a pale greyish head and breast and a dark back, occurring in Australasia, Indonesia, and South Asia.
• Genus *Ducula*, family Columbidae.

imperial preference ▶ **noun** [mass noun] historical a system of tariff concessions granted by members of the British Empire or Commonwealth to one another.

imperil ▶ **verb** (**imperilled**, **imperilling**; US **imperiled**, **imperiling**) [with obj.] put at risk of being harmed, injured, or destroyed.
– ORIGIN late Middle English: from **PERIL**, probably on the pattern of *endanger*.

imperious /ɪmˈpɪərɪəs/ ▶ **adjective** assuming power or authority without justification; arrogant and domineering: *his imperious demands.*
– DERIVATIVES **imperiously** adverb, **imperiousness** noun.
– ORIGIN mid 16th cent.: from Latin *imperiosus*, from *imperium* 'command, authority, empire'; related to *imperare* 'to command'. Compare with **IMPERIAL**.

imperishable ▶ **adjective** enduring forever: *imperishable truths.*
– DERIVATIVES **imperishability** /-ˈbɪlɪti/ noun, **imperishableness** noun, **imperishably** adverb.

imperium /ɪmˈpɪərɪəm/ ▶ **noun** [mass noun] absolute power.
– ORIGIN mid 17th cent.: from Latin, 'command, authority, empire'; related to *imperare* 'to command'.

impermanent ▶ **adjective** not permanent.
– DERIVATIVES **impermanence** noun, **impermanency** noun, **impermanently** adverb.

impermeable /ɪmˈpəːmɪəb(ə)l/ ▶ **adjective** not allowing fluid to pass through: *an impermeable membrane.*
■not liable to be affected by pain or distress; insusceptible or imperturbable: *women who appear* ***impermeable to*** *pain.*
– DERIVATIVES **impermeability** noun.
– ORIGIN late 17th cent.: from French *imperméable*, or from late Latin *impermeabilis*, from *in-* 'not' + *permeabilis* (see **PERMEABLE**).

impermissible ▶ **adjective** not permitted or allowed: *forcing a woman to continue a pregnancy that will almost certainly kill her is impermissible.*
– DERIVATIVES **impermissibility** noun.

impersonal ▶ **adjective** **1** not influenced by, showing, or involving personal feelings: *the impersonal power of a government.*
■(of a place or organization) large, featureless, and anonymous: *an impersonal tower block.* ■ not betraying any personal information about the user or subject: *the room was bare, cramped, and impersonal.*
2 not existing as a person; having no personality: *he gradually came to believe in an impersonal God.*
3 Grammar (of a verb) used only with a formal subject (in English usually *it*) and expressing an action not attributable to a definite subject (as in *it is snowing*).
– DERIVATIVES **impersonality** noun, **impersonally** adverb.
– ORIGIN late Middle English (in sense 3): from late Latin *impersonalis*, from Latin *in-* 'not' + *personalis* (see **PERSONAL**).

impersonal pronoun ▶ **noun** the pronoun *it* when used without definite reference or antecedent, as in *it was snowing* and *it seems hard to believe.*

impersonate ▶ **verb** [with obj.] pretend to be (another person) as entertainment or in order to deceive someone: *it's a very serious offence to impersonate a police officer.*
– DERIVATIVES **impersonation** noun, **impersonator** noun.
– ORIGIN early 17th cent. (in the sense 'personify'): from **IN-**[2] 'into' + Latin *persona* 'person', on the pattern of *incorporate*.

impertinent ▶ **adjective** **1** not showing proper respect; rude: *an impertinent question.*
2 formal not pertinent to a particular matter; irrelevant: *talk of 'rhetoric' and 'strategy' is* ***impertinent to*** *this process.*

– DERIVATIVES **impertinence** noun, **impertinently** adverb.
– ORIGIN late Middle English (in sense 2): from Old French, or from late Latin *impertinent-* 'not having reference to', from Latin *in-* 'not' + *pertinere* 'pertain'.

imperturbable /ˌɪmpəˈtəːbəb(ə)l/ ▶ **adjective** unable to be upset or excited; calm: *an imperturbable tranquillity.*
– DERIVATIVES **imperturbability** noun, **imperturbably** adverb.
– ORIGIN late Middle English: from late Latin *imperturbabilis*, from *in-* 'not' + *perturbare* (see **PERTURB**).

impervious /ɪmˈpəːvɪəs/ ▶ **adjective** not allowing fluid to pass through: *an impervious layer of basaltic clay.*
■[predic.] (**impervious to**) unable to be affected by: *he worked, apparently impervious to the heat.*
– DERIVATIVES **imperviously** adverb, **imperviousness** noun.
– ORIGIN mid 17th cent.: from Latin *impervius* (from *in-* 'not' + *pervius* 'pervious') + **-OUS**.

impetigo /ˌɪmpɪˈtʌɪɡəʊ/ ▶ **noun** [mass noun] a contagious bacterial skin infection forming pustules and yellow crusty sores.
• This disease is caused by the bacteria *Streptococcus pyogenes* or *S. aureus*.
– ORIGIN late Middle English: from Latin, from *impetere* 'to assail, attack'.

impetrate /ˈɪmpətreɪt/ ▶ **verb** [with obj.] archaic beseech or beg for: *a slight testimonial which I thought fit to impetrate from that worthy nobleman.*
– ORIGIN late 15th cent.: from Latin *impetrat-* 'brought to pass', from the verb *impetrare* (based on *patrare* 'bring to pass').

impetuous ▶ **adjective** acting or done quickly and without thought or care: *her friend was headstrong and impetuous.*
■moving forcefully or rapidly: *an impetuous but controlled flow of water.*
– DERIVATIVES **impetuosity** noun, **impetuously** adverb, **impetuousness** noun.
– ORIGIN late Middle English: from Old French *impetueux*, from late Latin *impetuosus*, from *impetere* 'to assail, attack'.

impetus ▶ **noun** [mass noun] the force or energy with which a body moves: *hit the booster coil before the flywheel loses all its impetus.*
■the force that makes something happen or happen more quickly: *the crisis of the 1860s provided the original* **impetus for** *the settlements.*
– ORIGIN mid 17th cent.: from Latin, 'assault, force', from *impetere* 'assail', from *in-* 'towards' + *petere* 'seek'.

Imphal /ˈɪmfəl, ɪmˈfɑːl/ the capital of the state of Manipur in the far north-east of India, lying close to the border with Burma (Myanmar); pop. 156,620 (1991). It was the scene of an important victory in 1944 by Anglo-Indian forces over the Japanese.

impi /ˈɪmpi/ ▶ **noun** (pl. **impis**) a body of Zulu warriors.
■an armed band of Zulus involved in urban or rural conflict.
– ORIGIN Zulu, 'regiment, armed band'.

impiety /ɪmˈpʌɪɪti/ ▶ **noun** (pl. **-ies**) [mass noun] lack of piety or reverence, especially for a god: *he blamed the fall of the city on the impiety of the people* | [count noun] *one impiety will cost me my eternity in Paradise.*
– ORIGIN Middle English: from Old French *impiete* or Latin *impietas*, from *impius* 'impious'.

impinge ▶ **verb** (**impinging**) [no obj.] have an effect or impact, especially a damaging or negative one: *Nora was determined that the tragedy would* **impinge** *as little as possible* **on** *Constance's life.*
■advance over an area belonging to someone or something else; encroach: *the proposed fencing would* **impinge on** *a public bridleway.* ■ (**impinge on/upon**) Physics strike: *the gases impinge on the surface of the liquid.*
– DERIVATIVES **impingement** noun, **impinger** noun.
– ORIGIN mid 16th cent.: from Latin *impingere* 'drive something in or at', from *in-* 'into' + *pangere* 'fix, drive'. The word originally meant 'thrust at forcibly', then 'come into forcible contact'; hence 'encroach on' (mid 18th cent.).

impious /ˈɪmpɪəs, ɪmˈpʌɪəs/ ▶ **adjective** not showing respect or reverence, especially for a god: *the emperor's impious attacks on the Church.*
■(of a person or act) wicked: *impious villains.*
– DERIVATIVES **impiously** adverb, **impiousness** noun.
– ORIGIN mid 16th cent.: from Latin *impius* (from *in-* 'not' + *pius*: see **PIOUS**) + **-OUS**.

impish ▶ **adjective** inclined to do slightly naughty things for fun; mischievous: *he had an impish look about him.*
– DERIVATIVES **impishly** adverb, **impishness** noun.

implacable ▶ **adjective** unable to be placated: *he was an implacable enemy of Ted's.*
■relentless; unstoppable: *the implacable advance of the enemy.*
– DERIVATIVES **implacability** noun, **implacably** adverb.
– ORIGIN late Middle English: from Latin *implacabilis*, from *in-* 'not' + *placabilis* (see **PLACABLE**).

implant ▶ **verb** [usu. with obj.] /ɪmˈplɑːnt/ insert or fix (tissue or an artificial object) in a person's body, especially by surgery: *electrodes had been* **implanted in** *his brain.*
■(**implant someone/thing with**) provide someone or something with (something) by such action. ■ [no obj.] (of a fertilized egg) become attached to the wall of the uterus. ■ figurative establish or fix (an idea) in a person's mind.
▶**noun** /ˈɪmplɑːnt/ a thing implanted in something else, especially a piece of tissue, prosthetic device, or other object implanted in the body: *a silicone breast implant.*
– ORIGIN late Middle English: from late Latin *implantare* 'engraft', from Latin *in-* 'into' + *plantare* 'to plant'.

implantation ▶ **noun** [mass noun] the action of implanting or state of being implanted.
■Zoology & Medicine (in a mammal) the attachment of the fertilized egg or blastocyst to the wall of the womb at the start of pregnancy, often delayed in some mammals by several months. Also called **NIDATION**.
– ORIGIN late 16th cent.: from French, from *implanter* 'to implant'.

implausible ▶ **adjective** (of an argument or statement) not seeming reasonable or probable; failing to convince: *this is a blatantly implausible claim.*
– DERIVATIVES **implausibility** noun, **implausibly** adverb.

implement ▶ **noun** /ˈɪmplɪm(ə)nt/ **1** a tool, utensil, or other piece of equipment, especially as used for a particular purpose: *agricultural implements.*
2 [mass noun] Scots Law performance of an obligation.
▶**verb** /ˈɪmplɪmɛnt/ [with obj.] put (a decision, plan, agreement, etc.) into effect: *the scheme to implement student loans.*
– DERIVATIVES **implementation** noun, **implementer** noun.
– ORIGIN late Middle English (in the sense 'article of furniture, equipment, or dress'): partly from medieval Latin *implementa* (plural), partly from late Latin *implementum* 'filling up, fulfilment', both from Latin *implere* 'fill up' (later 'employ'), from *in-* 'in' + Latin *plere* 'fill'. The verb dates from the early 18th cent.

implicate ▶ **verb** /ˈɪmplɪkeɪt/ [with obj.] **1** show (someone) to be involved in a crime: *police claims* **implicated** *him* **in** *many more killings.*
■(**be implicated in**) bear some of the responsibility for (an action or process, especially a criminal or harmful one): *the team believe he is heavily implicated in the bombing* | *a chemical implicated in ozone depletion.*
2 [with clause] convey (a meaning or intention) indirectly through what one says, rather than stating it explicitly: *by saying that coffee would keep her awake, Mary implicated that she didn't want any.*
▶**noun** /ˈɪmplɪkət/ chiefly Logic a thing implied.
– DERIVATIVES **implicative** /ɪmˈplɪkətɪv/ adjective, **implicatively** adverb.
– ORIGIN late Middle English: from Latin *implicatus* 'folded in', past participle of *implicare* (see **IMPLY**). The original sense was 'entwine, entangle'; compare with **EMPLOY** and **IMPLY**. The earliest modern sense (sense 2), dates from the early 17th cent., but appears earlier in **IMPLICATION**.

implication ▶ **noun 1** the conclusion that can be drawn from something although it is not explicitly stated: *the implication is that no one person at the bank is responsible.*
■a likely consequence of something: *a victory which had important political implications.*
2 [mass noun] the action or state of being involved in something: *our implication in the problems.*
– PHRASES **by implication** by what is implied or suggested rather than by formal expression: *he criticized her and, by implication, her country.*
– DERIVATIVES **implicational** adjective.
– ORIGIN late Middle English (in the sense 'entwining, being entwined'): from Latin *implicatio(n-)*, from the verb *implicare* (see **IMPLICATE**).

implicature /ˈɪmplɪˌkətʃə, -ˌkeɪtʃə/ ▶ **noun** [mass noun] the action of implying a meaning beyond the literal sense of what is explicitly stated, for example saying *the frame is nice* and implying *I don't like the picture in it.*
■[count noun] a meaning so implied.

implicit /ɪmˈplɪsɪt/ ▶ **adjective 1** implied though not plainly expressed: *comments seen as implicit criticism of the policies.*
■[predic.] (**implicit in**) essentially or very closely connected with; always to be found in: *the values implicit in the school ethos.*
2 with no qualification or question; absolute: *an implicit faith in God.*
3 Mathematics (of a function) not expressed directly in terms of independent variables.
– DERIVATIVES **implicitly** adverb, **implicitness** noun.
– ORIGIN late 16th cent.: from French *implicite* or Latin *implicitus*, later form of *implicatus* 'entwined', past participle of *implicare* (see **IMPLY**).

implode /ɪmˈpləʊd/ ▶ **verb** collapse or cause to collapse violently inwards: [no obj.] *the windows on both sides of the room had imploded* | [with obj.] *these forces would implode the pellet to a density 100 times higher than that of lead.*
■[no obj.] figurative suffer sudden economic or political collapse: *can any amount of aid save the republics from imploding?*
– DERIVATIVES **implosion** noun, **implosive** adjective.
– ORIGIN late 19th cent.: from **IN-**[2] 'within' + Latin *plodere, plaudere* 'to clap', on the pattern of *explode.*

implore ▶ **verb** [reporting verb] beg someone earnestly or desperately to do something: [with obj. and infinitive] *he implored her to change her mind* | [with direct speech] *'Please don't talk that way,' Ellen implored.*
■[with obj.] archaic beg earnestly for: *I implore mercy.*
– DERIVATIVES **imploringly** adverb.
– ORIGIN early 16th cent.: from French *implorer* or Latin *implorare* 'invoke with tears'.

implosive ▶ **adjective** formed by implosion; tending to implode.
■Phonetics denoting a type of consonant produced in the glottis with an ingressive air flow.

impluvium /ɪmˈpluːvɪəm/ ▶ **noun** (pl. **impluvia** /-vɪə/) the square basin in the centre of the atrium of an ancient Roman house, which received rainwater from an opening in the roof.
– ORIGIN Latin, from *impluere* 'rain into'.

imply ▶ **verb** (**-ies, -ied**) [with obj.] strongly suggest the truth or existence of (something not expressly stated): *salesmen who use jargon to imply superior knowledge* | [with clause] *the report implies that two million jobs might be lost.*
■(of a fact or occurrence) suggest (something) as a logical consequence: *the forecasted traffic increase implied more roads and more air pollution.*
– DERIVATIVES **impliedly** adverb.
– ORIGIN late Middle English: from Old French *emplier*, from Latin *implicare*, from *in-* 'in' + *plicare* 'to fold'. The original sense was 'entwine, entangle'; in the 16th and 17th cents the word also meant 'employ'. Compare with **EMPLOY** and **IMPLICATE**.

USAGE Imply and infer do not mean the same thing and should not be used interchangeably: see **usage** at **INFER**.

impolder (also **empolder**) ▶ **verb** [with obj.] make (an area of the seabed) into a polder by reclaiming it from the sea.
– ORIGIN late 19th cent.: from Dutch *impolderen.*

impolite ▶ **adjective** not having or showing good manners; rude: *it would have been impolite to refuse.*
– DERIVATIVES **impolitely** adverb, **impoliteness** noun.
– ORIGIN early 17th cent. (in the sense 'unpolished'): from Latin *impolitus*, from *in-* 'not' + *politus* (see **POLITE**).

impolitic /ɪmˈpɒlɪtɪk/ ▶ **adjective** failing to possess or display prudence; unwise: *it was impolitic to pay the slightest tribute to the enemy.*
– DERIVATIVES **impoliticly** adverb.

imponderable ▶ **noun** a factor that is difficult or impossible to estimate or assess: *there are too many imponderables for an overall prediction.*
▶ **adjective 1** difficult or impossible to estimate, assess, or answer: *an imponderable problem of metaphysics.*

2 archaic or poetic/literary very light.
– DERIVATIVES **imponderability** /-ˈbɪlɪti/ noun, **imponderably** adverb.

import ▶ **verb** [with obj.] **1** bring (goods or services) into a country from abroad for sale: *most iron ore had to be imported from Spain* | [no obj.] *Caribbean countries import from the UK.*
■ introduce (an idea) from a different place or context: *new beliefs were often imported by sailors.* ■ Computing transfer (data) into a file or document.
2 archaic indicate or signify: *having thus seen, what is imported in a Man's trusting his Heart.*
■ express or make known: [with clause] *they passed a resolution importing that they relied on His Majesty's gracious promise.*
▶ **noun 1** (usu. **imports**) a commodity, article, or service brought in from abroad for sale.
■ (**imports**) sales of goods or services brought in from abroad, or the revenue from such sales: *this surplus pushes up the yen, which ought to boost imports.* ■ [mass noun] the action or process of importing goods or services: *the import of live cattle from Canada.*
2 [in sing.] the meaning or significance of something, especially when not directly stated: *the import of her message is clear.*
■ [mass noun] great significance; importance: *pronouncements of world-shaking import.*
– DERIVATIVES **importable** adjective, **importation** noun, **importer** noun.
– ORIGIN late Middle English (in the sense 'signify'): from Latin *importare* 'bring in' (in medieval Latin 'imply, mean, be of consequence'), from *in-* 'in' + *portare* 'carry'.

importance ▶ **noun** [mass noun] the state or fact of being of great significance or value: *the importance of democracy* | [count noun] *the relative importances of the external and internal causes.*
– PHRASES **full of one's own importance** having a very high opinion of oneself; self-important.
– ORIGIN early 16th cent.: from French, from medieval Latin *importantia*, from *important-* 'being of consequence', from the verb *importare* (see **IMPORT**).

important ▶ **adjective** of great significance or value; likely to have a profound effect on success, survival, or well-being: *important habitats for wildlife* | *it is important to avoid monosyllabic answers* | [sentence adverb] *the speech had passion and, more important, compassion.*
■ (of a person) having high rank or status. ■ (of an artist or artistic work) significantly original and influential.
– ORIGIN late Middle English: from medieval Latin *important-* 'being of consequence', from the verb *importare* (see **IMPORT**).

importantly ▶ **adverb 1** [sentence adverb] used to emphasize a significant point or matter: *a non-drinking, non-smoking, and, importantly, non-political sportsman.*
2 in a manner designed to draw attention to one's importance: *Kruger strutted forward importantly.*

importunate /ɪmˈpɔːtjʊnət/ ▶ **adjective** persistent, especially to the point of annoyance or intrusion: *importunate creditors.*
– DERIVATIVES **importunately** adverb, **importunity** noun (pl. **-ies**).
– ORIGIN early 16th cent.: from Latin *importunus* 'inconvenient, unseasonable', based on *Portunus*, the name of the god who protected harbours (from *portus* 'harbour'); compare with **OPPORTUNE**.

importune /ˌɪmpɔːˈtjuːn/ ▶ **verb** [with obj.] ask (someone) pressingly and persistently for or to do something: *if the £190,000 had never been paid, he would have been importuned by his creditors.*
■ [usu. as noun **importuning**] approach (someone) to offer one's services as a prostitute.
– ORIGIN mid 16th cent.: from French *importuner* or medieval Latin *importunari*, from Latin *importunus* 'inconvenient, unseasonable' (see **IMPORTUNATE**).

impose ▶ **verb 1** [with obj.] force (something unwelcome or unfamiliar) to be accepted or put in place: *the decision was theirs and was not* ***imposed on*** *them by others.*
■ put (a restriction) in place: *sanctions imposed on South Africa.* ■ require (a duty, charge, or penalty) to be undertaken or paid. ■ (**impose oneself**) exert firm control over something: *the director was unable to* ***impose himself on*** *the production.*
2 [no obj.] take advantage of someone by demanding their attention or commitment: *she realized that she had* ***imposed on*** *Miss Hatherby's kindness.*
3 [with obj.] Printing arrange (pages of type) so that they will be in the correct order after printing and folding.
– ORIGIN late 15th cent. (in the sense 'impute'): from French *imposer*, from Latin *imponere* 'inflict, deceive' (from *in-* 'in, upon' + *ponere* 'put'), but influenced by *impositus* 'inflicted' and Old French *poser* 'to place'.

imposing ▶ **adjective** grand and impressive in appearance: *an imposing 17th-century manor house.*
– DERIVATIVES **imposingly** adverb.

imposition ▶ **noun 1** [mass noun] the action or process of imposing something or of being imposed: *the imposition of martial law.*
2 a thing that is imposed, in particular:
■ an unfair or resented demand or burden. ■ a tax or duty. ■ an unsuitable addition to an artistic work or similar.
3 [mass noun] Printing the imposing of pages of type.
■ [count noun] a particular arrangement of imposed pages: *some samples of 16-page impositions.*
– ORIGIN late Middle English: from Latin *impositio(n-)*, from the verb *imponere* (see **IMPOSE**).

impossibilism ▶ **noun** [mass noun] belief in ideas or policy, especially on social reform, that are held to be unrealizable or impractical.
– DERIVATIVES **impossibilist** noun.

impossibility ▶ **noun** (pl. **-ies**) [mass noun] the state or fact of being impossible: *these sequences demonstrate the impossibility of turning comics into movies.*
■ [count noun] an impossible thing or situation: *they believe that a world at peace is an impossibility.*
– ORIGIN late Middle English: from French *impossibilite* or Latin *impossibilitas*, from *impossibilis*, from *in-* 'not' + *possibilis* (see **POSSIBLE**).

impossible ▶ **adjective** not able to occur, exist, or be done: *a seemingly impossible task* | [with infinitive] *it was almost impossible to keep up with him.*
■ very difficult to deal with: *she was in an impossible situation.* ■ informal (of a person) very unreasonable: *'Impossible woman!' the doctor complained.*
– ORIGIN Middle English: from Old French, or from Latin *impossibilis*, from *in-* 'not' + *possibilis* (see **POSSIBLE**).

impossibly ▶ **adverb** [sentence adverb] used to describe an event or action that is so difficult or unlikely one would not expect it to be possible: *he held her and, impossibly, she fell asleep.*
■ [as submodifier] so as to be impossible: *every task suddenly seemed impossibly difficult.* ■ [as submodifier] possessing the specified quality to an unbelievably high degree: *impossibly blonde hair.*

impost[1] /ˈɪmpəʊst/ ▶ **noun** a tax or similar compulsory payment.
■ Horse Racing the weight carried by a horse as a handicap.
– ORIGIN mid 16th cent.: from French (earlier form of *impôt*), from medieval Latin *impostus*, from Latin *impositus*, past participle of *imponere* (see **IMPOSE**).

impost[2] /ˈɪmpəʊst/ ▶ **noun** Architecture the top course of a pillar that supports an arch.
– ORIGIN late 15th cent.: from Italian *imposta*, feminine past participle of *imporre*, from Latin *imponere* (see **IMPOSE**).

impostor (also **imposter**) ▶ **noun** a person who pretends to be someone else in order to deceive others, especially for fraudulent gain.
– ORIGIN late 16th cent. (in early use spelled *imposture*, and sometimes confused with **IMPOSTURE** in meaning): from French *imposteur*, from late Latin *impostor*, contraction of *impositor*, from Latin *imponere* (see **IMPOSE**).

imposture ▶ **noun** an instance of pretending to be someone else in order to deceive others.
– ORIGIN mid 16th cent.: via French from late Latin *impostura*, from Latin *imposit-* 'imposed upon', from the verb *imponere* (see **IMPOSE**).

impotent /ˈɪmpət(ə)nt/ ▶ **adjective 1** unable to take effective action; helpless or powerless: *he was seized with an impotent anger.*
2 (of a man) abnormally unable to achieve an erection or orgasm.
■ (of a male animal) unable to copulate.
– DERIVATIVES **impotence** noun, **impotency** noun, **impotently** adverb.
– ORIGIN late Middle English: via Old French from Latin *impotent-* 'powerless', from *in-* 'not' + *potent-* (see **POTENT**[1]).

impound ▶ **verb** [with obj.] **1** seize and take legal custody of (something, especially a vehicle, goods, or documents) because of an infringement of a law or regulation: *vehicles parked where they cause an obstruction will be impounded.*
2 shut up (domestic animals) in a pound or enclosure.
■ lock up (someone). ■ (of a dam) hold back or confine (water).
– DERIVATIVES **impoundable** adjective, **impounder** noun, **impoundment** noun.

impoverish ▶ **verb** [with obj.] make (a person or area) poor: [as adj. **impoverished**] *impoverished peasant farmers.*
■ exhaust the strength, vitality, or natural fertility of: *the soil was impoverished by annual burning* | [as adj. **impoverished**] figurative *an impoverished and debased language.*
– DERIVATIVES **impoverishment** noun.
– ORIGIN late Middle English (formerly also as *empoverish*): from Old French *empoveriss-*, lengthened stem of *empoverir*, based on *povre* 'poor'.

impracticable ▶ **adjective** (of a course of action) impossible in practice to do or carry out: *it was impracticable to widen the road here.*
– DERIVATIVES **impracticability** noun, **impracticably** adverb.

USAGE Although there is considerable overlap, **impracticable** and **impractical** are not used in exactly the same way. **Impracticable** means 'impossible to carry out' and is normally used of a specific procedure or course of action, as in *poor visibility made the task difficult, even* ***impracticable***. **Impractical**, on the other hand, tends to be used in more general senses, often to mean simply 'unrealistic' or 'not sensible', as in *in windy weather an umbrella is* ***impractical***.

impractical ▶ **adjective 1** (of an object or course of action) not adapted for use or action; not sensible or realistic: *impractical high heels* | *his impractical romanticism.*
■ (of a person) not skilled or interested in doing practical work.
2 chiefly US impossible to do; impracticable.
– DERIVATIVES **impracticality** noun, **impractically** adverb.

imprecate /ˈɪmprɪkeɪt/ ▶ **verb** [with obj.] archaic utter (a curse) or invoke (evil) against someone or something.
– ORIGIN early 17th cent.: from Latin *imprecat-* 'invoked', from the verb *imprecari.*

imprecation ▶ **noun** formal a spoken curse: *she hurled her imprecations at anyone who might be listening.*
– DERIVATIVES **imprecatory** adjective.
– ORIGIN late Middle English: from Latin *imprecatio(n-)*, from *imprecari* 'invoke (evil)', from *in-* 'towards' + *precari* 'pray'.

imprecise ▶ **adjective** lacking exactness and accuracy of expression or detail: *the witness could give only vague and imprecise descriptions.*
– DERIVATIVES **imprecisely** adverb, **impreciseness** noun, **imprecision** noun.

impregnable ▶ **adjective** (of a fortified position) unable to be captured or broken into: *an impregnable wall of solid sandstone* | figurative *the seat I was offered appeared to be an impregnable Tory stronghold.*
■ unable to be defeated or destroyed; unassailable: *Liverpool should have used their good fortune to forge an impregnable half-time lead.*
– DERIVATIVES **impregnability** noun, **impregnably** adverb.
– ORIGIN late Middle English: from Old French *imprenable*, from *in-* 'not' + *prendre* 'take' (from Latin *prehendere*). The current spelling arose in the 16th cent., perhaps influenced by Old French variants.

impregnate /ˈɪmprɛɡneɪt/ ▶ **verb** [with obj.] **1** (usu. **be impregnated with**) soak or saturate (something) with a substance: *wood which had been impregnated with preservative.*
■ imbue with feelings or qualities: *an atmosphere impregnated with tension.*
2 make (a woman or female animal) pregnant.
■ Biology fertilize (a female reproductive cell or ovum).
– DERIVATIVES **impregnation** noun.
– ORIGIN early 17th cent. (in the sense 'fill'): from late Latin *impregnat-* 'made pregnant', from the verb *impregnare.*

impresario /ˌɪmprɪˈsɑːrɪəʊ/ ▶ **noun** (pl. **-os**) a person who organizes and often finances concerts, plays, or operas.

■chiefly historical the manager of a musical, theatrical, or operatic company.

– ORIGIN mid 18th cent.: from Italian, from *impresa* 'undertaking'.

imprescriptible /ˌɪmprɪˈskrɪptɪb(ə)l/ ▶**adjective** Law (of rights) unable to be taken away by prescription or by lapse of time.

– ORIGIN late 16th cent.: from medieval Latin *imprescriptibilis*, from *in-* 'not' + Latin *praescript-* (from *praescribere* 'prescribe').

impress[1] ▶**verb** [with obj.] **1** make (someone) feel admiration and respect: *they immediately impressed the judges* | [no obj.] *he has to put on an act to impress.*
2 make a mark or design on (an object) using a stamp or seal: *the Railway Company should impress the cards with a stamp.*
■apply (a mark) to something with pressure: *a revenue stamp was embossed or* ***impressed on*** *the instrument.* ■ figurative (**impress something on**) fix an idea in the mind of (someone): *nobody impressed on me the need to save.*
3 apply (an electric current or potential) from an external source.
▶**noun** [in sing.] an act of making an impression or mark: *bluish marks made by the impress of his fingers.*
■a mark made by a seal or stamp. ■ figurative the characteristic mark or quality of a person or attribute: *his desire to put his own impress on the films he made.*

– DERIVATIVES **impressible** adjective.

– ORIGIN late Middle English (in the sense 'apply with pressure'): from Old French *empresser*, from *em-* 'in' + *presser* 'to press', influenced by Latin *imprimere* (see **IMPRINT**). Sense 1 dates from the mid 18th cent.

impress[2] ▶**verb** [with obj.] historical force (someone) to serve in an army or navy: *a number of Poles, impressed into the German army.*
■commandeer (goods or equipment) for public service.

– DERIVATIVES **impressment** noun.

– ORIGIN late 16th cent.: from **IN-**[2] 'into' + **PRESS**[2].

impression ▶**noun 1** an idea, feeling, or opinion about something or someone, especially one formed without conscious thought or on the basis of little evidence: *his first impressions of Manchester were very positive* | *they give the impression that all is sweetness and light.*
■an effect produced on someone: *her courtesy and quick wit had made a good impression.* ■ [mass noun] a difference made by the action or presence of someone or something: *the floor was too dirty for the mop to make much impression.*
2 an imitation of a person or thing, especially one done to entertain: *he did an impression of Shirley Bassey.*
■a graphic or pictorial representation of someone or something: *the police have issued an artist's impression of the attacker.*
3 a mark impressed on a surface by something: *the impression of his body on the leaves.*
■Dentistry a negative copy of the teeth or mouth made by pressing them into a soft substance.
4 the printing of a number of copies of a book, periodical, or picture for issue at one time.
■[usu. with modifier] chiefly Brit. a particular printed version of a book or other publication, especially one reprinted from existing type, plates, or film with no or only minor alteration. Compare with **EDITION**. ■ a print taken from an engraving.

– PHRASES **under the impression that** believing, mistakenly or on the basis of little evidence, that something is the case: *he was under the impression that they had become friends.*

– DERIVATIVES **impressional** adjective.

– ORIGIN late Middle English: via Old French from Latin *impressio(n-)*, from *impress-* 'pressed in', from the verb *imprimere* (see **IMPRINT**).

impressionable ▶**adjective** easily influenced because of a lack of critical ability: *a girl of eighteen is highly impressionable.*

– DERIVATIVES **impressionability** noun, **impressionably** adverb.

– ORIGIN mid 19th cent.: from French, from *impressionner*, from Latin *impressio(n-)*, from the verb *imprimere* 'press into' (see **IMPRINT**).

Impressionism ▶**noun** [mass noun] a style or movement in painting originating in France in the 1860s, characterized by a concern with depicting the visual impression of the moment, especially in terms of the shifting effect of light and colour.
■a literary or artistic style that seeks to capture a feeling or experience rather than to achieve accurate depiction. ■ Music a style of composition (associated especially with Debussy) in which clarity of structure and theme is subordinate to harmonic effects, characteristically using the whole-tone scale.

> The Impressionist painters repudiated both the precise academic style and the emotional concerns of Romanticism, and their interest in objective representation, especially of landscape, was influenced by early photography. Impressionism met at first with suspicion and scorn, but soon became deeply influential. Its chief exponents included Monet, Renoir, Pissarro, Cézanne, Degas, and Sisley.

– ORIGIN from French *impressionnisme*, from *impressionniste*, originally applied unfavourably with reference to Monet's painting *Impression: Soleil levant* (1872).

Impressionist ▶**noun** a painter, writer, or composer who is an exponent of Impressionism.
▶**adjective** of or relating to Impressionism or its exponents.

impressionist ▶**noun** an entertainer who impersonates famous people.

impressionistic ▶**adjective 1** based on subjective reactions presented unsystematically: *a personal and impressionistic view of the war.*
2 (**Impressionistic**) in the style of Impressionism: *an Impressionistic portrait.*

– DERIVATIVES **impressionistically** adverb.

impressive ▶**adjective** evoking admiration through size, quality, or skill: grand, imposing, or awesome: *an impressive view of the mountains* | *impressive achievements in science.*

– DERIVATIVES **impressively** adverb, **impressiveness** noun.

imprest ▶**noun** a fund used by a business for small items of expenditure and restored to a fixed amount periodically.
■a sum of money advanced to a person for a particular purpose.

– ORIGIN mid 16th cent.: from the earlier phrase *in prest* 'as a loan', influenced by Italian or medieval Latin *imprestare* 'lend'.

imprimatur /ˌɪmprɪˈmeɪtə, -ˈmɑːtə, -ˈmɑːtʊə/ ▶**noun** an official licence issued by the Roman Catholic Church to print an ecclesiastical or religious book.
■[in sing.] a person's acceptance or guarantee that something is of a good standard: *the original LP enjoyed the imprimatur of the composer.*

– ORIGIN mid 17th cent.: from Latin, 'let it be printed', from the verb *imprimere* (see **IMPRINT**).

imprint ▶**verb 1** [with obj.] (usu. **be imprinted**) impress or stamp (a mark or outline) on a surface or body: *tyre marks were* ***imprinted in*** *the snow.*
■make an impression or mark on (something): *clothes* ***imprinted with*** *the logos of sports teams.* ■ figurative fix (an idea) firmly in someone's mind: *he'd always have this ghastly image* ***imprinted on*** *his mind.*
2 [no obj.] (**imprint on**) Zoology (of a young animal) come to recognize (another animal, person, or thing) as a parent or other object of habitual trust.
▶**noun 1** a mark made by pressing something on to a softer substance so that its outline is reproduced: *he made imprints of the keys in bars of soap.*
■figurative a lasting impression or effect: *years in the colonies had left their imprint.*
2 a printer's or publisher's name, address, and other details in a book or other printed item.
■a brand name under which books are published, typically the name of a former publishing house that is now part of a larger group.

– ORIGIN late Middle English (originally as *emprint*): from Old French *empreinter*, based on Latin *imprimere*, from *in-* 'into' + *premere* 'to press'.

imprison ▶**verb** [with obj.] (usu. **be imprisoned**) put or keep in prison or a place like a prison: *he was imprisoned three times for his activities.*

– DERIVATIVES **imprisonment** noun.

– ORIGIN Middle English *emprison*, from Old French *emprisoner*, from *em-* 'in' + *prison*.

impro ▶**noun** (pl. **-os**) [mass noun] informal improvisation, especially as a theatrical technique.

– ORIGIN 1970s: abbreviation.

improbable ▶**adjective** not likely to be true or to happen: *this account of events was seen by the jury as most improbable.*
■unexpected and apparently inauthentic: *the characters have improbable names.*

– DERIVATIVES **improbability** noun (pl. **-ies**), **improbably** adverb.

– ORIGIN late 16th cent.: from French, or from Latin *improbabilis* 'hard to prove', from *in-* 'not' + *probabilis* (see **PROBABLE**).

improbity /ɪmˈprəʊbɪti, -ˈprɒb-/ ▶**noun** [mass noun] formal wickedness or dishonesty.

– ORIGIN late 16th cent.: from Latin *improbitas*, from *improbus* 'wicked', from *in-* 'not' + *probus* 'good'. Compare with **PROBITY**.

impromptu /ɪmˈprɒm(p)tjuː/ ▶**adjective** & **adverb** done without being planned, organized, or rehearsed: [as adj.] *an impromptu press conference* | [as adv.] *he spoke impromptu.*
▶**noun** (pl. **impromptus**) a short piece of instrumental music, especially a solo, that is reminiscent of an improvisation.

– ORIGIN mid 17th cent. (as an adverb): from French, from Latin *in promptu* 'in readiness', from *promptus* (see **PROMPT**).

improper ▶**adjective** not in accordance with accepted rules or standards, especially of morality or honesty: *he was accused of improper behaviour in his business dealings* | *it is improper to end a sentence with a preposition.*
■lacking in modesty or decency: *it was thought improper for elderly women to wear bright colours.*

– DERIVATIVES **improperly** adverb.

– ORIGIN late Middle English: from French *impropre* or Latin *improprius*, from *in-* 'not' + *proprius* 'one's own, proper'.

improper fraction ▶**noun** a fraction in which the numerator is greater than the denominator, such as 5/4.

impropriate /ɪmˈprəʊprɪeɪt/ ▶**verb** [with obj.] [usu. as adj. **impropriated**] grant (an ecclesiastical benefice) to a corporation or person as their property.
■place (tithes or ecclesiastical property) in lay hands.

– DERIVATIVES **impropriation** noun.

– ORIGIN early 16th cent.: from Anglo-Latin *impropriat-* 'appropriated', from the verb *impropriare*, based on Latin *proprius* 'one's own, proper'.

impropriator ▶**noun** a person to whom a benefice is granted as their property.

impropriety /ˌɪmprəˈprʌɪəti/ ▶**noun** (pl. **-ies**) [mass noun] a failure to observe standards or show due honesty or modesty; improper behaviour or character: *she was scandalized at the impropriety of the question* | [count noun] *there are no demonstrable legal improprieties.*

– ORIGIN early 17th cent. (also in the sense 'inaccuracy, incorrectness'): from French *impropriété* or Latin *improprietas*, from *improprius* (see **IMPROPER**).

improv ▶**noun** another term for **IMPRO**.

improve ▶**verb** make or become better: [with obj.] *efforts to improve relations with China and Pakistan* | [as adj. **improved**] *improved road and rail links* | [no obj.] *his condition improved after glass was removed from his arm.*
■[with obj.] develop or increase in mental capacity by education or experience: *I subscribed to two magazines to improve my mind.* ■ [no obj.] (**improve on/upon**) achieve or produce something better than: *they are trying to improve on the tired old style.*

– DERIVATIVES **improvability** noun, **improvable** adjective, **improver** noun.

– ORIGIN early 16th cent. (as *emprowe* or *improwe*): from Anglo-Norman French *emprower* (based on Old French *prou* 'profit', ultimately from Latin *prodest* 'is of advantage'); *-owe* was changed to *-ove* under the influence of **PROVE**. The original sense was 'make a profit, increase the value of'; subsequently 'make greater in amount or degree'.

improvement ▶**noun** an example or instance of improving or being improved: *an improvement in East–West relations.*
■[mass noun] the action of improving or being improved: *there's still* ***room for improvement.*** ■ a thing that makes something better or is better than something else: *home improvements* | *it's an* ***improvement on*** *the last cake I made.*

– ORIGIN late Middle English *emprowement* (in the sense 'profitable management or use; profit'), from Anglo-Norman French, from *emprower* (see **IMPROVE**).

improvident ▶**adjective** not having or showing foresight; spendthrift or thoughtless: *improvident and undisciplined behaviour.*

– DERIVATIVES **improvidence** noun, **improvidently** adverb.

improving ▶ **adjective** giving moral or intellectual benefit: *a large, improving picture hung opposite.*

improvise ▶ **verb** [with obj.] create and perform (music, drama, or verse) spontaneously or without preparation: *the ability to improvise operatic arias in any given style* | [no obj.] *he was improvising to a backing of guitar chords* | [as adj. **improvised**] *improvised humour.*
■ produce or make (something) from whatever is available: *I improvised a costume for myself out of an old blue dress* | [as adj. **improvised**] *we camped out, sleeping on improvised beds.*
– DERIVATIVES **improvisation** noun, **improvisational** adjective, **improvisatorial** adjective, **improvisatory** adjective, **improviser** noun.
– ORIGIN early 19th cent.: from French *improviser* or its source, Italian *improvvisare*, from *improvviso* 'extempore', from Latin *improvisus* 'unforeseen', based on *provisus*, past participle of *providere* 'make preparation for'.

imprudent ▶ **adjective** not showing care for the consequences of an action; rash: *it would be imprudent to leave her winter coat behind.*
– DERIVATIVES **imprudence** noun, **imprudently** adverb.
– ORIGIN late Middle English: from Latin *imprudent-* 'not foreseeing', from *in-* 'not' + *prudent-* (see **PRUDENT**).

impudent /ˈɪmpjʊd(ə)nt/ ▶ **adjective** not showing due respect for another person; impertinent: *he could have strangled this impudent upstart.*
– DERIVATIVES **impudence** noun, **impudently** adverb.
– ORIGIN late Middle English (in the sense 'immodest, indelicate'): from Latin *impudent-*, from *in-* 'not' + *pudent-* 'ashamed, modest' (from *pudere* 'be ashamed').

impudicity /ˌɪmpjʊˈdɪsɪti/ ▶ **noun** [mass noun] formal lack of modesty.
– ORIGIN early 16th cent.: from French *impudicité*, from Latin *impudicitia*, from *impudicus* 'shameless', from *in-* 'not' + *pudere* 'be ashamed'.

impugn /ɪmˈpjuːn/ ▶ **verb** [with obj.] dispute the truth, validity, or honesty of (a statement or motive); call into question: *the father does not impugn her capacity as a good mother.*
– DERIVATIVES **impugnable** adjective, **impugnment** noun.
– ORIGIN late Middle English (also in the sense 'assault, attack physically'): from Latin *impugnare* 'assail', from *in-* 'towards' + *pugnare* 'fight'.

impuissant /ɪmˈpjuːɪs(ə)nt, -ˈpwiː-, -ˈpwɪs-/ ▶ **adjective** poetic/literary unable to take effective action; powerless.
– DERIVATIVES **impuissance** noun.
– ORIGIN early 17th cent.: French, from *im-* 'not' + *puissant* 'powerful'.

impulse ▶ **noun 1** a sudden strong and unreflective urge or desire to act: *I had an almost irresistible impulse to giggle* | [as modifier] *impulse buying.*
■ [mass noun] the tendency to act in this way: *he was a man of impulse, not premeditation.*
2 a driving or motivating force; an impetus: *an added impulse to this process of renewal.*
3 a pulse of electrical energy; a brief current: *nerve impulses* | *a spiral is used to convert radio waves into electrical impulses.*
4 Physics a force acting briefly on a body and producing a finite change of momentum.
■ a change of momentum so produced, equivalent to the average value of the force multiplied by the time during which it acts.
– PHRASES **on impulse** (or **on an impulse**) suddenly and without forethought; impulsively.
– ORIGIN early 17th cent. (as a verb in the sense 'give an impulse to'): the verb from Latin *impuls-* 'driven on', the noun from *impulsus* 'impulsion, outward pressure', both from the verb *impellere* (see **IMPEL**).

impulsion ▶ **noun** a strong urge to do something: *the impulsion of the singers to govern the pace.*
■ [mass noun] the force or motive behind an action or process: *attitudes changed under the impulsion of humanitarian considerations.*
– ORIGIN late Middle English (in the sense 'the act or an instance of impelling'): via Old French from Latin *impulsio(n-)*, from the verb *impellere* (see **IMPEL**).

impulsive ▶ **adjective 1** acting or done without forethought: *they had married as young impulsive teenagers* | *perhaps he's regretting his impulsive offer.*
2 Physics acting as an impulse.
– DERIVATIVES **impulsively** adverb, **impulsiveness** noun, **impulsivity** noun.
– ORIGIN late Middle English (in the sense 'tending to impel'): from French *impulsif, -ive* or late Latin *impulsivus*, from Latin *impuls-* 'driven onwards' (see **IMPULSE**). Sense 1 dates from the mid 18th cent.

impunity /ɪmˈpjuːnɪti/ ▶ **noun** [mass noun] exemption from punishment or freedom from the injurious consequences of an action: *the impunity enjoyed by military officers implicated in civilian killings* | *protestors burned flags on the streets* ***with impunity.***
– ORIGIN mid 16th cent.: from Latin *impunitas*, from *impunis* 'unpunished', from *in-* 'not' + *poena* 'penalty' or *punire* 'punish'.

impure ▶ **adjective 1** mixed with foreign matter; adulterated: *an impure form of heroin.*
■ dirty: *a parasite that thrives in impure water.* ■ (of a colour) mixed with another colour.
2 morally wrong, especially in sexual matters: *citizens suspected of harbouring impure thoughts.*
■ defiled or contaminated according to ritual prescriptions: *the perception of woman as impure.*
– DERIVATIVES **impurely** adverb, **impureness** noun.
– ORIGIN late Middle English (in the sense 'dirty, containing offensive matter'): from Latin *impurus*, from *in-* 'not' + *purus* 'pure'.

impurity ▶ **noun** (pl. **-ies**) [mass noun] the quality or condition of being impure.
■ [count noun] a thing or constituent which impairs the purity of something: *aluminium and lead are impurities frequently found in tap water.* ■ [count noun] Electronics a trace element deliberately added to a semiconductor; a dopant.
– ORIGIN late Middle English: from French *impurite* or Latin *impuritas*, from *impurus* (see **IMPURE**).

impute /ɪmˈpjuːt/ ▶ **verb** [with obj.] represent (something, especially something undesirable) as being done, caused, or possessed by someone; attribute: *the crimes* ***imputed to*** *Richard.*
■ Finance assign (a value) to something by inference from the value of the products or processes to which it contributes: [as adj. **imputed**] *recovering the initial outlay plus imputed interest.* ■ Theology ascribe (righteousness, guilt, etc.) to someone by virtue of a similar quality in another: *Christ's righteousness has been imputed to us.*
– DERIVATIVES **imputable** adjective, **imputation** noun.
– ORIGIN late Middle English: from Old French *imputer*, from Latin *imputare* 'enter in the account', from *in-* 'in, towards' + *putare* 'reckon'.

Imroz /ɪmˈrɔz/ Turkish name for **IMBROS**.

imshi /ˈɪmʃiː/ ▶ **exclamation** military slang, chiefly Austral. go away; be off.
– ORIGIN from colloquial Arabic *'mšī* 'go!', imperative of *mišī*.

I.Mun.E. ▶ **abbreviation for** (in the UK) Institution of Municipal Engineers.

IN ▶ **abbreviation for** Indiana (in official postal use).

In ▶ **symbol for** the chemical element indium.

in ▶ **preposition 1** expressing the situation of something that is or appears to be enclosed or surrounded by something else: *living in London* | *dressed in their Sunday best* | *soak it in warm soapy water* | *she saw it in the rear-view mirror.*
■ expressing motion with the result that something ends up within or surrounded by something else: *don't put coal in the bath* | *he got in his car and drove off.*
2 expressing a period of time during which an event takes place or a situation remains the case: *they met in 1885* | *at one o'clock in the morning* | *I hadn't seen him in years.*
3 expressing the length of time before a future event is expected to take place: *I'll see you in fifteen minutes.*
4 (often followed by a noun without a determiner) expressing a state or condition: *to be in love* | *I've got to put my affairs in order* | *a woman in her thirties* | *laid out in a straight line.*
■ indicating the quality or aspect with respect to which a judgement is made: *no discernible difference in quality.*
5 expressing inclusion or involvement: *I read it in a book* | *acting in a film.*
6 indicating someone's occupation or profession: *she works in publishing.*
7 indicating the language or medium used: *say it in French* | *put it in writing.*
■ indicating the key in which a piece of music is written: *Mozart's Piano Concerto in E flat.*
8 [with verbal noun] as an integral part of (an activity): *in planning public expenditure it is better to be prudent.*
9 expressing a value as a proportion of (a whole): *a local income tax running at six pence in the pound.*
▶ **adverb 1** expressing movement with the result that someone or something becomes enclosed or surrounded by something else: *come in* | *bring it in* | *presently the admiral breezed in.*
2 expressing the situation of being enclosed or surrounded by something: *we were locked in.*
3 expressing arrival at a destination: *the train got in very late.*
4 (of the tide) rising or at its highest level.
▶ **adjective 1** [predic.] (of a person) present at one's home or office: *we knocked at the door but there was no one in.*
2 informal fashionable: *pastels and light colours are in this year* | *the in thing to do.*
3 [predic.] (of the ball in tennis and similar games) landing within the designated playing area.
4 [predic.] Cricket batting: *which side is in?*
– PHRASES **be in for** have good reason to expect (typically something unpleasant): *it looks as if we're in for a storm.* ■ (**be in for it**) have good reason to expect trouble or retribution. **in all** see **ALL**. **in and out of** being a frequent visitor to (a house) or frequent inmate of (an institution): *he was in and out of jail for most of his twenties.* **in on** privy to (a secret). **in so far as** see **FAR**. **in that** for the reason that (used to specify the respect in which a statement is true): *I was fortunate in that I had friends.* **in with** informal enjoying friendly relations with: *the Krays were in with a couple of well-known MPs.* **the ins and outs** informal all the details (of something).
– ORIGIN Old English *in* (preposition), *inn, inne* (adverb), of Germanic origin; related to Dutch and German *in* (preposition), German *ein* (adverb), from an Indo-European root shared by Latin *in* and Greek *en*.

in. ▶ **abbreviation for** inch(es).

in-[1] ▶ **prefix 1** (added to adjectives) not: *infertile* | *inapt.*
2 (added to nouns) without; a lack of: *inappreciation.*
– ORIGIN from Latin.

USAGE In- is also found assimilated in the following forms: **il-** before **l**; **im-** before **b, m, p**; **ir-** before **r**.

in-[2] ▶ **prefix** in; into; towards; within: *induce* | *influx* | *inborn.*
– ORIGIN representing **IN** or the Latin preposition *in*.

USAGE In- is also found assimilated in the following forms: **il-** before **l**; **im-** before **b, m, p**; **ir-** before **r**.

-in[1] ▶ **suffix** Chemistry forming names of organic compounds, pharmaceutical products, proteins, etc.: *insulin* | *penicillin* | *dioxin.*
– ORIGIN alteration of **-INE**[4].

-in[2] ▶ **combining form** denoting a gathering of people having a common purpose, typically as a form of protest: *sit-in* | *sleep-in* | *love-in.*

-ina ▶ **suffix 1** denoting feminine names and titles: *tsarina.*
2 denoting names of musical instruments: *concertina.*
3 denoting names of plant and animal groups: *globigerina.*
– ORIGIN from Italian, Spanish, or Latin.

inability ▶ **noun** [with infinitive] the state of being unable to do something: *his inability to accept new ideas.*

in absentia /ˌɪn abˈsɛntɪə/ ▶ **adverb** while not present at the event being referred to: *two foreign suspects will be tried in absentia.*
– ORIGIN Latin, 'in absence'.

inaccessible ▶ **adjective** unable to be reached: *a remote and inaccessible cave* | *the city centre is* ***inaccessible to*** *traffic in most places.*
■ (of language or an artistic work) difficult to understand or appreciate. ■ unable to be seen or used: *such costs would make litigation inaccessible to private individuals.* ■ (of a person) not open to advances or influence; unapproachable.
– DERIVATIVES **inaccessibility** noun, **inaccessibly** adverb.
– ORIGIN late Middle English: from French, or from late Latin *inaccessibilis*, from *in-* 'not' + *accessibilis* (see **ACCESSIBLE**).

inaccuracy ▶ **noun** (pl. **-ies**) [mass noun] the quality or state of not being accurate: *a weapon of notorious inaccuracy.*

■[count noun] a feature or aspect of something that is not accurate: *reference works full of inaccuracies.*

inaccurate ▶ adjective not accurate: *false or inaccurate descriptions of goods | Khmer Rouge artillery was known to be inaccurate.*
– DERIVATIVES **inaccurately** adverb.

inaction ▶ noun [mass noun] lack of action where some is expected or appropriate.

inactivate ▶ verb [with obj.] make inactive or inoperative: *household bleach does not inactivate the virus* | [as adj. **inactivated**] *inactivated polio vaccine.*
– DERIVATIVES **inactivation** noun, **inactivator** noun.

inactive ▶ adjective not engaging in or involving any or much physical activity: *he might lose condition if he remained inactive | an inactive lifestyle.*
■not working; inoperative: *the device remains inactive while the computer is started up.* ■not engaging in an occupation or in political or other activity: *an inactive Russian spy.* ■ having no chemical or biological effect on something: *the inactive X chromosome.* ■(of a disease) not exhibiting symptoms.
– DERIVATIVES **inactively** adverb, **inactivity** noun.

inadequate ▶ adjective lacking the quality or quantity required; insufficient for a purpose: *these labels prove to be wholly inadequate | inadequate funding.*
■(of a person) unable to deal with a situation or with life: *a sad, solitary, inadequate man | I felt like a fraud, inadequate to the task.*
– DERIVATIVES **inadequacy** noun (pl. **-ies**), **inadequately** adverb.

inadmissible ▶ adjective 1 (especially of evidence in court) not accepted as valid.
2 not to be allowed or tolerated: *an inadmissible interference in the affairs of the Church.*
– DERIVATIVES **inadmissibility** noun, **inadmissibly** adverb.

inadvertent ▶ adjective not resulting from or achieved through deliberate planning: *he was pardoned for inadvertent manslaughter.*
■(of a mistake) made through lack of care.
– DERIVATIVES **inadvertence** noun, **inadvertency** noun, **inadvertently** adverb.
– ORIGIN mid 17th cent.: from **IN-**¹ 'not' + Latin *advertent-* 'turning the mind to' (from the verb *advertere*). The noun *inadvertence* dates from late Middle English.

inadvisable ▶ adjective likely to have unfortunate consequences; unwise: [with infinitive] *it would be inadvisable to involve more than one architect.*
– DERIVATIVES **inadvisability** noun.

inalienable ▶ adjective unable to be taken away from or given away by the possessor: *the shareholders have the inalienable right to dismiss directors.*
– DERIVATIVES **inalienability** noun, **inalienably** adverb.

inalterable ▶ adjective unable to be changed.
– DERIVATIVES **inalterability** noun, **inalterably** adverb.

inamorata /ɪˌnaməˈrɑːtə/ ▶ noun a person's female lover.
– ORIGIN mid 17th cent.: Italian, literally 'enamoured', feminine of *inamorato* (see **INAMORATO**).

inamorato /ɪˌnaməˈrɑːtəʊ/ ▶ noun (pl. **-os**) a person's male lover.
– ORIGIN late 16th cent.: Italian, literally 'enamoured', past partiple of the verb *inamorare*, based on Latin *amor* 'love'.

in-and-out ▶ adjective informal 1 involving inward and outward movement, especially rapid entrance and exit: *smuggling drugs was a quick in-and-out operation.*
2 inconsistent and unreliable: *this horse is a notoriously in-and-out performer.*

inane ▶ adjective silly; stupid: *don't constantly badger people with inane questions.*
– DERIVATIVES **inanely** adverb, **inaneness** noun, **inanity** noun (pl. **-ies**).
– ORIGIN mid 16th cent.: from Latin *inanis* 'empty, vain'.

inanga /ˈiːnaŋə/ ▶ noun NZ a small edible Australasian fish which spends its first year in the sea, thereafter living mainly in fresh water. The young are caught as whitebait. Also called **JOLLYTAIL**.
● *Galaxias maculatus*, family Galaxiidae.
– ORIGIN Maori.

inanimate ▶ adjective not alive, especially not in the manner of animals and humans: *inanimate objects like stones.*
■showing no sign of life; lifeless: *he was completely inanimate and it was difficult to see if he was breathing.*
– DERIVATIVES **inanimately** adverb.
– ORIGIN late Middle English: from late Latin *inanimatus* 'lifeless', from *in-* 'not' + *animatus* (see **ANIMATE**).

inanition /ˌɪnəˈnɪʃ(ə)n/ ▶ noun [mass noun] lack of mental or spiritual vigour and enthusiasm: *she was thinking that old age bred inanition.*
■exhaustion caused by lack of nourishment.
– ORIGIN late Middle English: from late Latin *inanitio(n-)*, from Latin *inanire* 'make empty', from *inanis* 'empty, vain'.

inapparent ▶ adjective Medicine causing no noticeable signs or symptoms: *many worm infections are clinically inapparent.*

inappetence ▶ noun [mass noun] chiefly Veterinary Medicine lack of appetite.
– DERIVATIVES **inappetent** adjective.

inapplicable ▶ adjective not relevant or appropriate: *the details are likely to be inapplicable to other designs.*
– DERIVATIVES **inapplicability** noun, **inapplicably** adverb.

inapposite /ɪnˈapəzɪt/ ▶ adjective out of place; inappropriate: *the Shakespearean allusions are inapposite.*
– DERIVATIVES **inappositely** adverb, **inappositeness** noun.

inappreciable ▶ adjective 1 too small or insignificant to be valued or perceived.
2 archaic too valuable to be properly estimated.
– DERIVATIVES **inappreciably** adverb.

inappreciative ▶ adjective another term for **UNAPPRECIATIVE**.
– DERIVATIVES **inappreciation** noun.

inappropriate ▶ adjective not suitable or proper in the circumstances: *there are penalties for inappropriate behaviour | it would be inappropriate for me to comment.*
– DERIVATIVES **inappropriately** adverb, **inappropriateness** noun.

inapt ▶ adjective unsuitable or inappropriate in the circumstances: *a more inapt name I cannot imagine.*
– DERIVATIVES **inaptitude** noun, **inaptly** adverb.

inarch ▶ verb [with obj.] Horticulture graft (a plant) by connecting a growing branch without separating it from its parent stock.
– ORIGIN early 17th cent. (formerly also as *enarch*): from **EN-**¹, **IN-**² 'into' + the verb **ARCH**¹.

inarguable ▶ adjective another term for **UNARGUABLE**.
– DERIVATIVES **inarguably** adverb.

inarticulate /ˌɪnɑːˈtɪkjʊlət/ ▶ adjective 1 unable to speak distinctly or express oneself clearly: *he was inarticulate with abashment and regret.*
■not clearly expressed or pronounced: *inarticulate complaints of inadequate remuneration.* ■ having no distinct meaning; unintelligible: *lurching up and down uttering inarticulate cries.* ■ not expressed; unspoken: *mention of her mother filled her with inarticulate irritation.*
2 without joints or articulations.
■Zoology denoting a brachiopod in which the valves of the shell have no hinge and are held together by muscles.
– DERIVATIVES **inarticulacy** noun, **inarticulately** adverb, **inarticulateness** noun.
– ORIGIN early 17th cent.: from **IN-**¹ 'not' + the adjective **ARTICULATE**; the sense 'not clearly pronounced' corresponds to that of late Latin *inarticulatus*.

inartistic ▶ adjective having or showing a lack of skill or talent in art.
– DERIVATIVES **inartistically** adverb.

inasmuch ▶ adverb (**inasmuch as**) to the extent that; in so far as: *these provisions apply only inasmuch as trade balance between Member States is affected.*
■considering that; since (used to specify the respect in which a statement is true): *a most unusual astronomer inasmuch as he was deaf and dumb.*
– ORIGIN Middle English: originally as *in as much*, translating Old French *en tant (que)* 'in so much (as)'.

inattentive ▶ adjective not paying attention to something: *a particularly dull and inattentive pupil.*

■failing to attend to the comfort or wishes of others: *I was disappointed by the food and the inattentive service.*
– DERIVATIVES **inattention** noun, **inattentively** adverb, **inattentiveness** noun.

inaudible ▶ adjective unable to be heard: *inaudible pulses of high-frequency sound.*
– DERIVATIVES **inaudibility** noun, **inaudibly** adverb.
– ORIGIN late Middle English: from late Latin *inaudibilis*, from *in-* 'not' + *audibilis* (see **AUDIBLE**).

inaugural /ɪˈnɔːɡjʊr(ə)l/ ▶ adjective [attrib.] marking the beginning of an institution, activity, or period of office: *his inaugural concert as Music Director.*
▶ noun an inaugural speech, especially one made by an incoming US president.
– ORIGIN late 17th cent.: from French (from *inaugurer* 'inaugurate', from Latin *inaugurare*) + **-AL**.

inaugurate /ɪˈnɔːɡjʊreɪt/ ▶ verb [with obj.] begin or introduce (a system, policy, or period): *he inaugurated a new policy of trade and exploration.*
■admit (someone) formally to office. ■ mark the beginning or first public use of (an organization or project): *the museum was inaugurated on September 12.*
– DERIVATIVES **inauguration** noun, **inaugurator** noun, **inauguratory** adjective.
– ORIGIN late 16th cent.: from Latin *inaugurat-* 'interpreted as omens (from the flight of birds)', based on *augurare* 'to augur'.

inauspicious ▶ adjective not conducive to success; unpromising: *in spite of an inauspicious beginning, Laura and Bernard succeeded within a few years.*
– DERIVATIVES **inauspiciously** adverb, **inauspiciousness** noun.

inauthentic ▶ noun not in fact what it is said to be: *the Holy Shroud of Turin is thought to have been proved inauthentic by radiocarbon dating.*
■not genuinely belonging to a style or period: *baroque harpsichord pieces played on the decidedly inauthentic modern Steinway.* ■ lacking full reality or sincerity: *people close to death could not waste time being inauthentic.*
– DERIVATIVES **inauthentically** adverb, **inauthenticity** noun.

in-between informal ▶ adjective situated somewhere between two extremes or recognized categories; intermediate: *I am not unconscious, but in some in-between state.*
▶ noun an intermediate thing: *successes, failures and in-betweens.*
– DERIVATIVES **in-betweener** noun.

inboard ▶ adverb & adjective within a ship, aircraft, or vehicle: [as adv.] *the spray was coming inboard now* | [as adj.] *the uncovered inboard engine.*
■towards the centre of a ship, aircraft, or vehicle: [as adv.] *move the clew inboard along the boom* | [as adj.] *the inboard ailerons on the wings were dead.*
▶ noun a boat's engine housed inside its hull.
■a boat with such an engine.

inborn ▶ adjective existing from birth: *an inborn defect in the formation of collagen.*
■natural to a person or animal: *people think doctors have inborn compassion.*

inbound ▶ adjective & adverb travelling towards a particular place, especially when returning to the original point of departure: [as adj.] *inbound traffic* | [as adv.] *we have three enemy planes inbound on bearing two ninety.*
▶ verb [with obj.] Basketball throw (the ball) from out of bounds, putting it into play.

inbounds ▶ adjective Basketball denoting or relating to a throw which puts the ball into play from out of bounds: *an inbounds pass.*

inbreathe ▶ verb [with obj.] poetic/literary breathe in or absorb: *he felt himself inbreathing power from on high.*

inbred ▶ adjective 1 produced by inbreeding: *a classic inbred Englishman.*
2 existing in a person or animal from birth; congenital: *inbred disease resistance in crops.*

inbreed ▶ verb (past and past participle **inbred**) [no obj.] [often as noun **inbreeding**] breed from closely related people or animals, especially over many generations.

inbuilt ▶ adjective existing as an original or essential part of something or someone: *the body's inbuilt ability to heal itself.*

in-bye (also **in-by**) chiefly Scottish & N. English ▶ adjective (of farmland or farming) situated or carried out near to the farm buildings.
▶ adverb near to the farm buildings.

Inc. N. Amer. ▶ **abbreviation for** Incorporated: *Northeast Airlines Inc.*

Inca ▶ **noun 1** a member of a South American Indian people living in the central Andes before the Spanish conquest.

When the Spanish invaded in the early 1530s, the Inca empire covered most of modern Ecuador and Peru, much of Bolivia, and parts of Argentina and Chile. Inca technology and architecture were highly developed despite a lack of wheeled vehicles and of writing. Their descendants, speaking Quechua, still make up about half of Peru's population.

2 the supreme ruler of this people.
– DERIVATIVES **Incaic** /ɪŋˈkeɪɪk/ adjective, **Incan** adjective.
– ORIGIN the name in Quechua, literally 'lord, royal person'.

inca ▶ **noun** a South American hummingbird having mainly blackish or bronze-coloured plumage with one or two white breast patches.
• Genus *Coeligena*, family Trochilidae: four species.

incalculable ▶ **adjective 1** too great to be calculated or estimated: *an archive of incalculable value.*
2 not able to be calculated or estimated: *the cost is incalculable but colossal.*
■ (of a person or their character) unpredictable: *under the pressure of anxiety his temper became incalculable.*
– DERIVATIVES **incalculability** noun, **incalculably** adverb.

in camera ▶ **adverb** see **CAMERA**[2].

incandesce /ˌɪnkanˈdɛs/ ▶ **verb** [no obj.] glow with heat: *the lights of the town lay incandescing across the prairie.*
– ORIGIN late 19th cent.: back-formation from **INCANDESCENT**.

incandescent ▶ **adjective** emitting light as a result of being heated: *plumes of incandescent liquid rock.*
■ (of an electric light) containing a filament which glows white-hot when heated by a current passed through it. ■ extremely angry: *I am incandescent at the way the OFT has acted.* ■ of outstanding and exciting quality; brilliant: *Mravinsky's incandescent performance of Siegfried's Funeral March.*
– DERIVATIVES **incandescence** noun, **incandescently** adverb.
– ORIGIN late 18th cent.: from French, from Latin *incandescent-* 'glowing', from the verb *incandescere*, from *in-* (expressing intensive force) + *candescere* 'become white' (from *candidus* 'white').

incant /ɪnˈkant/ ▶ **verb** [with obj.] chant or intone: *priests were incanting psalms round her body.*
– ORIGIN mid 16th cent. (in the sense 'use enchantment on'): from Latin *incantare* 'to chant, charm', from *in-* (expressing intensive force) + *cantare* 'sing'. The current sense dates from the mid 20th cent.

incantation ▶ **noun** a series of words said as a magic spell or charm: *an incantation to raise the dead.*
■ [mass noun] the use of such words: *there was no magic in such incantation* | [count noun] *incantations of old slogans.*
– DERIVATIVES **incantatory** adjective.
– ORIGIN late Middle English: via Old French from late Latin *incantatio(n-)*, from *incantare* 'chant, bewitch' (see **INCANT**).

incapable ▶ **adjective 1** [predic.] (**incapable of**) unable to do or achieve (something): *Wilson blushed and was incapable of speech.*
■ not able to be treated in a certain way; not admitting of something being done: *with the battery removed it was incapable of being driven at all.* ■ (of a person) too honest or moral to do a certain thing: *a man incapable of any kind of prejudice.*
2 unable to behave rationally or manage one's own affairs: *the pilot may become incapable from the lack of oxygen.*
– DERIVATIVES **incapability** noun, **incapably** adverb.
– ORIGIN late 16th cent.: from French, or from late Latin *incapabilis*, from *in-* 'not' + *capabilis* (see **CAPABLE**).

incapacitant ▶ **noun** a substance capable of temporarily incapacitating a person without wounding or killing them.
– ORIGIN 1960s: from **INCAPACITATE** + **-ANT**.

incapacitate /ˌɪnkəˈpasɪteɪt/ ▶ **verb** [with obj.] prevent from functioning in a normal way: *he was incapacitated by a heart attack.*
■ Law deprive (someone) of their legal capacity.
– DERIVATIVES **incapacitant** noun, **incapacitation** noun.
– ORIGIN mid 17th cent.: from **INCAPACITY** + **-ATE**[3].

incapacity ▶ **noun** (pl. **-ies**) [mass noun] physical or mental inability to do something or to manage one's affairs: *they can be sacked only for incapacity or misbehaviour.*
■ legal disqualification: *they are not subject to any legal incapacity.*
– ORIGIN early 17th cent.: from French *incapacité* or late Latin *incapacitas*, from *in-* (expressing negation) + *capacitas* (see **CAPACITY**).

incapacity benefit ▶ **noun** [mass noun] (in the UK) a state benefit paid to people who are unable to work due to illness or disability for a period of more than twenty-eight consecutive weeks.

in-car ▶ **adjective** [attrib.] occurring, situated, or carried in a car: *an in-car navigation system.*

incarcerate /ɪnˈkɑːsəreɪt/ ▶ **verb** [with obj.] (usu. **be incarcerated**) imprison: *many are incarcerated for property offences.*
■ [with obj. and adverbial of place] confine (someone) in a particular place: *he spent a long evening incarcerated below decks.*
– DERIVATIVES **incarceration** noun, **incarcerator** noun.
– ORIGIN mid 16th cent.: from medieval Latin *incarcerat-* 'imprisoned', from the verb *incarcerare*, from *in-* 'into' + Latin *carcer* 'prison'.

incarnadine /ɪnˈkɑːnədʌɪn/ poetic/literary ▶ **noun** [mass noun] a bright crimson or pinkish-red colour.
▶ **adjective** of a crimson or pinkish-red colour.
▶ **verb** [with obj.] colour (something) a bright crimson or pinkish-red.
– ORIGIN late 16th cent.: from French *incarnadin(e)*, from Italian *incarnadino*, variant of *incarnatino* 'flesh colour', based on Latin *incarnare* (see **INCARNATE**).

incarnate ▶ **adjective** /ɪnˈkɑːnət/ [often postpositive] (especially of a deity or spirit) embodied in flesh; in human form: *God incarnate* | *he chose to be incarnate as a man.*
■ [postpositive] represented in the ultimate or most extreme form: *here is capitalism incarnate.*
▶ **verb** /ˈɪnkɑːneɪt, -ˈkɑːneɪt/ [with obj.] embody or represent (a deity or spirit) in human form: *the idea that God incarnates himself in man.*
■ put (an idea or other abstract concept) into concrete form: *a desire to make things which will incarnate their personality.* ■ (of a person) be the living embodiment of (a quality): *the man who incarnates the suffering which has affected every single Mozambican.*
– ORIGIN late Middle English: from ecclesiastical Latin *incarnat-* 'made flesh', from the verb *incarnare*, from *in-* 'into' + *caro, carn-* 'flesh'.

incarnation ▶ **noun 1** a person who embodies in the flesh a deity, spirit, or abstract quality: *Rama was Vishnu's incarnation on earth.*
■ (**the Incarnation**) (in Christian theology) the embodiment of God the Son in human flesh as Jesus Christ.
2 (with reference to reincarnation) one of a series of lifetimes which a person spends on earth: *in my next incarnation, I'd like to be the Minister Of Fun.*
■ the form in which a person spends such a lifetime.
– ORIGIN Middle English (as a term in Christian theology): via Old French from ecclesiastical Latin *incarnatio(n-)*, from the verb *incarnare* (see **INCARNATE**).

incase ▶ **verb** variant spelling of **ENCASE**.

incautious ▶ **adjective** (of a person or an action) heedless of potential problems or risks: *he blames incautious borrowing during the boom.*
– DERIVATIVES **incaution** noun, **incautiously** adverb, **incautiousness** noun.
– ORIGIN mid 17th cent.: on the pattern of Latin *incautus*.

incendiary /ɪnˈsɛndɪəri/ ▶ **adjective 1** (of a device or attack) designed to cause fires: *incendiary bombs.*
2 tending to stir up conflict: *incendiary rhetoric* | *an incendiary slogan.*
■ very exciting: *an incendiary live performer.*
▶ **noun** (pl. **-ies**) an incendiary bomb or device.
■ a person who starts fires, especially in a military context. ■ a person who stirs up conflict.
– DERIVATIVES **incendiarism** noun.
– ORIGIN late Middle English: from Latin *incendiarius*, from *incendium* 'conflagration', from *incendere* 'set fire to'.

incense[1] /ˈɪnsɛns/ ▶ **noun** [mass noun] a gum, spice, or other substance that is burned for the sweet smell it produces.
■ the smoke or perfume of such a substance.
▶ **verb** [with obj.] perfume with incense or a similar fragrance: *the aroma of cannabis incensed the air.*
– DERIVATIVES **incensation** noun.
– ORIGIN Middle English (originally as *encense*): from Old French *encens* (noun), *encenser* (verb), from ecclesiastical Latin *incensum* 'something burnt, incense', neuter past participle of *incendere* 'set fire to', from *in-* 'in' + the base of *candere* 'to glow'.

incense[2] /ɪnˈsɛns/ ▶ **verb** [with obj.] (usu. **be incensed**) make very angry: *locals are incensed at the suggestion.*
– ORIGIN late Middle English (in the general sense 'inflame or excite someone with a strong feeling'): from Old French *incenser*, from Latin *incendere* 'set fire to'.

incense cedar ▶ **noun** a columnar North American cedar with scale-like leaves that smell of turpentine when crushed, grown as an ornamental in Europe.
• *Calocedrus decurrens*, family Cupressaceae.

incensory /ˈɪnsɛns(ə)ri/ ▶ **noun** (pl. **-ies**) another term for **CENSER**.
– ORIGIN early 17th cent. (denoting a burnt offering, or an altar for it): from medieval Latin *incensorium*, from *incensum* (see **INCENSE**[1]).

incentive ▶ **noun** a thing that motivates or encourages one to do something: *give farmers an incentive to improve their land.*
■ a payment or concession to stimulate greater output or investment: *tax incentives for investing in depressed areas* | [as modifier] *incentive payments.*
– ORIGIN late Middle English: from Latin *incentivum* 'something that sets the tune or incites', from *incantare* 'to chant or charm'.

incentivize (also **-ise**) ▶ **verb** [with obj.] provide (someone) with an incentive for doing something: *this is likely to incentivize management to find savings.*

incentre (US **incenter**) ▶ **noun** Geometry the centre of the incircle of a triangle or other figure.

incept /ɪnˈsɛpt/ ▶ **verb** [no obj.] Brit. historical graduate from a university with an academic degree.
– DERIVATIVES **inceptor** noun.
– ORIGIN mid 16th cent. (in the sense 'undertake, begin'): from Latin *incept-* 'begun', from the verb *incipere*. The current sense dates from the mid 19th cent.

inception ▶ **noun** [in sing.] the establishment or starting point of an institution or activity: *she has been on the board since its inception two years ago.*
– ORIGIN late Middle English: from Latin *inceptio(n-)*, from *incipere* 'begin'.

inceptisol /ɪnˈsɛptɪsɒl/ ▶ **noun** Soil Science a soil of an order comprising freely draining soils in which the formation of distinct horizons is not far advanced, such as brown earth.
– ORIGIN 1960s: from Latin *inceptum* 'beginning' (from the verb *incipere*) + **-SOL**.

inceptive ▶ **adjective** relating to or marking the beginning of something; initial.
■ Grammar (of a verb) expressing the beginning of an action.
▶ **noun** Grammar an inceptive verb.
– ORIGIN early 17th cent. (as a noun): from late Latin *inceptivus*, from *incept-* 'begun', from the verb *incipere*.

incertitude ▶ **noun** [mass noun] a state of uncertainty or hesitation: *some schools broke down under the stresses of policy incertitude.*
– ORIGIN late Middle English: from Old French, or from late Latin *incertitudo*, from *in-* (expressing negation) + *certitudo* (see **CERTITUDE**).

incessant ▶ **adjective** (of something regarded as unpleasant) continuing without pause or interruption: *the incessant beat of the music.*
– DERIVATIVES **incessancy** noun, **incessantly** adverb, **incessantness** noun.
– ORIGIN late Middle English: via Old French from late Latin *incessant-*, from *in-* 'not' + Latin *cessant-* 'ceasing' (from the verb *cessare*).

incest ▶ **noun** [mass noun] sexual relations between people classed as being too closely related to marry each other.
■ the crime of having sexual intercourse with a parent, child, sibling, or grandchild.
– ORIGIN Middle English: from Latin *incestus, incestum* 'unchastity, incest', from *in-* 'not' + *castus* 'chaste'.

incestuous /ɪnˈsɛstjʊəs/ ▶ **adjective 1** involving or guilty of incest: *the child of an incestuous relationship.*
2 (of human relations generally) excessively close

and resistant to outside influence: *the incestuous nature of literary journalism.*
 – DERIVATIVES **incestuously** adverb, **incestuousness** noun.
 – ORIGIN early 16th cent.: from late Latin *incestuosus,* from Latin *incestus* (see **INCEST**).

inch¹ ▶ noun **1** a unit of linear measure equal to one twelfth of a foot (2.54 cm): *the toy train is four inches long | eighteen inches of thread.*
 ■ (**inches**) informal a person's height or waist measurement: *my only reservation is the goalkeeper's lack of inches.* ■ [often with negative] a very small amount or distance: *I had no intention of budging an inch.*
 2 a unit used to express other quantities, in particular:
 ■ (as a unit of rainfall) a quantity that would cover a horizontal surface to a depth of one inch. ■ (also **inch of mercury**) (as a unit of atmospheric pressure) an amount that would support a column of mercury one-inch high in a barometer (equal to 33.86 millibars, 29.5 inches being equal to one bar). ■ (as a unit of map scale) so many inches representing one mile on the ground: [in combination] *one-inch maps of the east Midland counties.*
 ▶ verb [no obj., with adverbial of direction] move slowly and carefully in a specified direction: *inching along a motorway during the rush hour* | figurative *Spain's conservatives are inching ahead.*
 ■ [with obj. and adverbial of direction] cause (something) to move in this manner: *he inched the car forward.*
 – PHRASES **by inches 1** only just: *the shot missed her by inches.* **2** very slowly and gradually; bit by bit: *you can't let him die by inches like this.* **every inch 1** the whole surface, distance, or area: *between them they know every inch of the country.* **2** entirely; very much so: *he's every inch the gentleman.* **give someone an inch and he (or she) will take a mile** proverb once concessions have been made to someone they will demand a great deal. **inch by inch** gradually; bit by bit: *inch by inch he crept along the wall.* **within an inch of** very close to: *her mouth was within an inch of his chin.* (**to**) **within an inch of one's life** almost to the point of death: *he was beaten within an inch of his life.*
 – ORIGIN late Old English *ynce,* from Latin *uncia* 'twelfth part', from *unus* 'one' (probably denoting a unit). Compare with **OUNCE¹**.

inch² ▶ noun [in place names] chiefly Scottish a small island or a small area of high land: *Inchkeith.*
 – ORIGIN Middle English: from Scottish Gaelic *innis.*

-in-chief ▶ combining form supreme: *commander-in-chief.*

inchmeal ▶ adverb by inches; little by little.
 – ORIGIN mid 16th cent.: from **INCH¹** + -*meal* from Old English *mǣlum,* in the sense 'measure, quantity taken at one time'.

inchoate ▶ adjective /ɪnˈkəʊeɪt, ˈɪnk-, -ət/ just begun and so not fully formed or developed; rudimentary: *a still inchoate democracy.*
 ■ confused or incoherent: *inchoate proletarian protest.* ■ Law (of an offence, such as incitement or conspiracy) anticipating a further criminal act.
 – DERIVATIVES **inchoately** adverb, **inchoateness** noun.
 – ORIGIN mid 16th cent.: from Latin *inchoatus,* past participle of *inchoare,* variant of *incohare* 'begin'.

inchoative /ɪnˈkəʊətɪv/ ▶ adjective Grammar denoting an aspect of a verb expressing the beginning of an action, typically one occurring of its own accord. In many English verbs, inchoative uses alternate systematically with causative uses. Compare with **ERGATIVE**.
 ▶ noun an inchoative verb.

Inchon /ɪnˈtʃɒn/ a port on the west coast of South Korea, on the Yellow Sea near Seoul; pop. 1,818,300 (1990).

inchworm ▶ noun North American term for **LOOPER**.

incidence ▶ noun **1** the occurrence, rate, or frequency of a disease, crime, or something else undesirable: *an increased incidence of cancer.*
 ■ the way in which the burden of a tax falls upon the population: *the entire incidence falls on the workers.*
 2 [mass noun] Physics the intersection of a line, or something moving in a straight line, such as a beam of light, with a surface.
 – ORIGIN late Middle English (denoting a casual or subordinate event or circumstance): from Old French, or from medieval Latin *incidentia,* from Latin *incidere* 'fall upon, happen to' (see **INCIDENT**). Sense 1 dates from the early 19th cent.

incident ▶ noun **1** an event or occurrence: *several amusing incidents.*
 ■ a violent event, such as a fracas or assault: *one person was stabbed in the incident.* ■ a hostile clash between forces of rival countries. ■ (**incident of**) a case or instance of something happening: *there was not one incident of teasing from the 90 pupils.* ■ [mass noun] the occurrence of dangerous or exciting things: *my period in Egypt wasn't without incident.* ■ a distinct piece of action in a play or a poem.
 2 Law a privilege, burden, or right attaching to an office, estate, or other holding.
 ▶ adjective **1** [predic.] (**incident to**) liable to happen because of; resulting from: *the changes incident to economic development.*
 ■ Law attaching to: *the costs properly incident to a suit for foreclosure or redemption.*
 2 (especially of light or other radiation) falling on or striking something: *when an ion beam is incident on a surface.*
 ■ of or relating to incidence: *the incident angle.*
 – ORIGIN late Middle English: via Old French from Latin *incident-* 'falling upon, happening to', from the verb *incidere,* from *in-* 'upon' + *cadere* 'to fall'.

incidental ▶ adjective **1** accompanying but not a major part of something: *for the fieldworker who deals with real problems, paperwork is incidental* | *incidental expenses.*
 ■ occurring by chance in connection with something else: *the incidental catch of dolphins in the pursuit of tuna.*
 2 [predic.] (**incidental to**) liable to happen as a consequence of (an activity): *the ordinary risks incidental to a fireman's job.*
 ▶ noun (usu. **incidentals**) an incidental detail, expense, event, etc.: *an allowance to cover meals, taxis, and other incidentals.*
 – ORIGIN early 17th cent.: originally from medieval Latin *incidentalis,* from Latin *incident-* 'falling upon, happening to' (from the verb *incidere*).

incidentally ▶ adverb **1** [sentence adverb] used when a person has something more to say, or is about to add a remark unconnected to the current subject; by the way: *incidentally, it was many months before the whole truth was discovered.*
 2 in an incidental manner; as a chance occurrence: *the infection was discovered only incidentally at post-mortem examination.*

incidental music ▶ noun [mass noun] music used in a film or play as a background to create or enhance a particular atmosphere.

incident room ▶ noun a centre set up by the police to coordinate operations connected with a particular crime, accident, or other incident.

incinerate /ɪnˈsɪnəreɪt/ ▶ verb [with obj.] (often be **incinerated**) destroy (something, especially waste material) by burning: *waste packaging is to be incinerated rather than buried in landfills.*
 – DERIVATIVES **incineration** noun.
 – ORIGIN late 15th cent.: from medieval Latin *incinerat-* 'burnt to ashes', from the verb *incinerare,* from *in-* 'into, towards' + *cinis, ciner-* 'ashes'.

incinerator ▶ noun an apparatus for burning waste material, especially industrial waste, at high temperatures until it is reduced to ash.

incipient /ɪnˈsɪpɪənt/ ▶ adjective in an initial stage; beginning to happen or develop: *he could feel incipient anger building up* | *an incipient black eye.*
 ■ (of a person) developing into a specified type or role: *we seemed more like friends than incipient lovers.*
 – DERIVATIVES **incipience** noun, **incipiency** noun, **incipiently** adverb.
 – ORIGIN late 16th cent. (as a noun denoting a beginner): from Latin *incipient-* 'undertaking, beginning', from the verb *incipere,* from *in-* 'into, towards' + *capere* 'take'.

incipit /ˈɪnsɪpɪt/ ▶ noun the opening of a manuscript, early printed book, or chanted liturgical text. Compare with **EXPLICIT**.
 – ORIGIN Latin, literally '(here) begins'.

incircle ▶ noun Geometry a circle inscribed in a triangle or other figure so as to touch (but not cross) each side.

incise ▶ verb [with obj.] (usu. **be incised**) mark or decorate (an object or surface) with a cut or a series of cuts: *a button incised with a skull.*
 ■ cut (a mark or decoration) into a surface: *figures incised on upright stones.* ■ cut (skin or flesh) with a surgical instrument: *the wound was incised and drained.*
 – ORIGIN mid 16th cent.: from French *inciser,* from

Latin *incis-* 'cut into, engraved', from the verb *incidere,* from *in-* 'into' + *caedere* 'to cut'.

incised meander ▶ noun Geology a river meander which has been cut abnormally deeply into the landscape because uplift of the land has led to renewed downward erosion by the river.

incision ▶ noun a surgical cut made in skin or flesh: *an abdominal incision.*
 ■ a mark or decoration cut into a surface: *a block of marble delicately decorated with incisions.* ■ [mass noun] the action or process of cutting into something: *the method is associated with less blood loss during incision.*
 – DERIVATIVES **incisional** adjective.
 – ORIGIN late Middle English: from late Latin *incisio(n-),* from Latin *incidere* 'cut into' (see **INCISE**).

incisive ▶ adjective (of a person or mental process) intelligently analytical and clear-thinking: *she was an incisive critic.*
 ■ (of an account) accurate and sharply focused: *the songs offer incisive pictures of American ways.* ■ (of an action) quick and direct: *the most incisive move of a tight match.*
 – DERIVATIVES **incisively** adverb, **incisiveness** noun.
 – ORIGIN late Middle English (in the sense 'cutting, penetrating'): from medieval Latin *incisivus,* from Latin *incidere* 'cut into' (see **INCISE**).

incisor ▶ noun (also **incisor tooth**) a narrow-edged tooth at the front of the mouth, adapted for cutting. In humans there are four incisors in each jaw.
 – ORIGIN late 17th cent.: from medieval Latin, literally 'cutter', from Latin *incis-* (see **INCISE**).

incisure /ɪnˈsɪʒə/ (also **incisura** /ˌɪnsɪˈʒʊərə/) ▶ noun (pl. **incisures** or **incisurae** /-riː/) Anatomy a deep indentation or notch in an edge or surface.

incite ▶ verb [with obj.] encourage or stir up (violent or unlawful behaviour): *the offence of inciting racial hatred.*
 ■ urge or persuade (someone) to act in a violent or unlawful way: *he incited loyal subjects to rebellion.*
 – DERIVATIVES **incitation** noun, **incitement** noun, **inciter** noun.
 – ORIGIN late 15th cent.: from French *inciter,* from Latin *incitare,* from *in-* 'towards' + *citare* 'rouse'.

inciteful ▶ adjective (of words, actions, etc.) offering incitement.

incivility ▶ noun (pl. **-ies**) [mass noun] rude or unsociable speech or behaviour; lack of politeness.
 ■ [count noun] (often **incivilities**) an impolite or offensive comment.
 – ORIGIN mid 16th cent.: from French *incivilité* or late Latin *incivilitas,* from Latin *incivilis,* from *in-* 'not' + *civilis* 'of a citizen' (see **CIVIL**).

incl. ▶ abbreviation for including.

inclement /ɪnˈklɛm(ə)nt/ ▶ adjective (of the weather) unpleasantly cold or wet.
 – DERIVATIVES **inclemency** noun (pl. **-ies**).
 – ORIGIN early 17th cent.: from French *inclément* or Latin *inclement-,* from *in-* 'not' + *clement-* 'clement'.

inclination ▶ noun [mass noun] **1** a person's natural tendency or urge to act or feel in a particular way; a disposition or propensity: *John was a scientist by training and inclination* | [count noun] *he was free to follow his inclinations.*
 ■ (**inclination for/to/towards**) an interest in or liking for (something): *unpleasant stuff towards which I have no inclination.*
 2 a slope or slant: *changes in inclination of the line on the graph.*
 ■ a bending of the body or head in a bow: *the questioner's inclination of his head.* ■ the dip of a magnetic needle.
 3 the angle at which a straight line or plane is inclined to another.
 ■ Astronomy the angle between the orbital plane of a planet, comet, etc. and the ecliptic, or between the orbital plane of a satellite and the equatorial plane of its primary.
 – ORIGIN late Middle English: from Latin *inclinatio(n-),* from *inclinare* 'bend towards' (see **INCLINE**).

incline ▶ verb **1** (**be inclined to/towards/to do something**) feel willing or favourably disposed towards (an action, belief, or attitude): *he was inclined to accept the offer* | *Lucy was inclined to a belief in original sin.*
 ■ [with infinitive] (especially as a polite formula) tend towards holding a specified opinion: *I'm inclined to agree with you.* ■ [with obj.] make (someone) willing or disposed to do something: *his prejudice inclines him to*

overlook obvious facts. ■ [no obj.] feel favourably disposed to someone or something: *I incline to the view that this conclusion is untenable.*

2 (**be inclined to/to do something**) have a tendency to do something: *she's inclined to gossip with complete strangers.*
■ [with adverbial] have a specified disposition or talent: *some people are very mathematically inclined.*

3 [no obj., usu. with adverbial of direction] lean or turn away from a given plane or direction, especially the vertical or horizontal: *the bunker doors incline outwards* | [as adj. **inclined**] *an inclined ramp.*
■ [with obj.] bend (one's head) forwards and downwards.
▶ **noun** an inclined surface or slope, especially on a road, path, or railway: *the road climbs a long incline through a forest.*
■ an inclined plane: *the Hay Incline was built to raise boats from one canal level to another.*
– DERIVATIVES **inclinable** adjective, **incliner** noun.
– ORIGIN Middle English (originally in the sense 'bend (the head, the body, or oneself) towards something'; formerly also as *encline*): from Old French *encliner,* from Latin *inclinare,* from *in-* 'towards' + *clinare* 'to bend'.

inclined plane ▶ **noun** a plane inclined at an angle to the horizontal.
■ a sloping ramp up which heavy loads can be raised by ropes or chains.

inclinometer /ˌɪnklɪˈnɒmɪtə/ ▶ **noun** a device for measuring the angle of inclination of something, especially from the horizontal.
– ORIGIN mid 19th cent.: from Latin *inclinare* 'to incline' + -METER.

inclose ▶ verb variant spelling of ENCLOSE.

inclosure ▶ noun variant spelling of ENCLOSURE.

include ▶ verb [with obj.] **1** comprise or contain as part of a whole: *the price includes dinner, bed, and breakfast* | *other changes included the abolition of the death penalty.*
2 make part of a whole or set: *we have included some hints for beginners in this section.*
■ allow (someone) to share in an activity or privilege: *there were doubts as to whether she was included in the invitation.*
– ORIGIN late Middle English (also in the sense 'shut in'): from Latin *includere,* from *in-* 'into' + *claudere* 'to shut'.

USAGE **Include** has a broader meaning than **comprise**. In the sentence *the accommodation comprises 2 bedrooms, bathroom, kitchen, and living room,* the word **comprise** implies that there is no accommodation other than that listed. **Include** can be used in this way too, but it is also used in a non-restrictive way, implying that there may be other things not specifically mentioned that are part of the same category, as in *the price includes a special welcome pack.*

▶ **include someone/thing out** informal specifically exclude someone or something from a group or activity.

included ▶ adjective [postpositive] contained as part of a whole being considered: *all of Europe (Britain included)* | *service tax included.*

including ▶ preposition containing as part of the whole being considered: *languages including Welsh and Gaelic* | *weapons were recovered from the house, including a shotgun.*

inclusion ▶ noun **1** [mass noun] the action or state of including or of being included within a group or structure: *criticism of the new cabinet focused upon its inclusion of two non-elected members.*
■ [count noun] a person or thing that is included within a larger group or structure: *the exhibition features such inclusions as the study of the little girl.*
2 chiefly Geology a body or particle of distinct composition embedded in a rock or other material.
– ORIGIN early 17th cent.: from Latin *inclusio(n-),* from *includere* 'shut in'.

inclusive ▶ adjective including or covering all the services, facilities, or items normally expected or required: *the price is inclusive, with few incidentals.*
■ [predic.] (**inclusive of**) containing (a specified element) as part of a whole: *the package is inclusive of return flight* | *all prices are inclusive of VAT.* ■ [postpositive] with the inclusion of the extreme limits stated: *between the ages of 55 and 59 inclusive.* ■ not excluding any section of society or any party involved in something: *only an inclusive peace process will end the conflict.* ■ (of language) deliberately non-sexist, especially avoiding

the use of masculine pronouns to cover both men and women.
– DERIVATIVES **inclusively** adverb, **inclusiveness** noun.
– ORIGIN late 16th cent.: from medieval Latin *inclusivus,* from Latin *includere* (see INCLUDE).

inclusive fitness ▶ **noun** [mass noun] Genetics the ability of an individual organism to pass on its genes to the next generation, taking into account the shared genes passed on by the organism's close relatives.

inclusivism ▶ **noun** [mass noun] the practice of trying to incorporate diverse or unreconciled elements into a single system.
– DERIVATIVES **inclusivist** noun & adjective.

incog ▶ adjective, adverb, & noun informal, dated short for INCOGNITO.

incognito /ˌɪnkɒɡˈniːtəʊ, ɪnˈkɒɡnɪtəʊ/ ▶ **adjective & adverb** (of a person) having one's true identity concealed: [as adj.] *in order to observe you have to be incognito* | [as adv.] *he is now operating incognito.*
▶ **noun** (pl. **-os**) an assumed or false identity.
– ORIGIN mid 17th cent.: from Italian, literally 'unknown', from Latin *incognitus,* from *in-* 'not' + *cognitus* (past participle of *cognoscere* 'know').

incognizant (also **incognisant**) ▶ adjective formal lacking knowledge or awareness.
– DERIVATIVES **incognizance** noun.

incoherent ▶ adjective **1** (of spoken or written language) expressed in an incomprehensible or confusing way; unclear: *he screamed some incoherent threat.*
■ (of a person) unable to speak intelligibly: *he was incoherent with sentiment.* ■ (of an ideology, policy, or system) internally inconsistent; illogical: *the film is ideologically incoherent.*
2 Physics (of waves) having no definite or stable phase relationship.
– DERIVATIVES **incoherence** noun, **incoherency** noun (pl. **-ies**), **incoherently** adverb.

incohesion ▶ noun [mass noun] lack of social cohesion: *anxiety about national decline and incohesion.*

incombustible ▶ adjective (especially of a building material or component) consisting or made of material that does not burn if exposed to fire.
– DERIVATIVES **incombustibility** noun.
– ORIGIN late 15th cent.: from medieval Latin *incombustibilis,* from *in-* 'not' + *combustibilis* (see COMBUSTIBLE).

income ▶ noun money received, especially on a regular basis, for work or through investments: *he has a nice home and an adequate income* | [mass noun] *figures showed an overall increase in income this year.*
– ORIGIN Middle English (in the sense 'entrance, arrival', now only Scots): in early use from Old Norse *innkoma,* later from IN + COME. The current sense dates from the late 16th cent.

income group ▶ noun a section of the population classified according to their level of income.

incomer ▶ noun chiefly Brit. a person who has come to live in an area in which they have not grown up, especially in a close-knit rural or island community: *an English incomer to Orkney.*

-incomer /ˈɪnkʌmə/ ▶ **combining form** Brit. denoting a person with a specified level of income: *middle-incomer.*

income support ▶ noun [mass noun] (in the UK and Canada) payment made by the state in particular circumstances to people who are on a low income.

income tax ▶ noun [mass noun] tax levied directly on personal income.

incoming ▶ adjective in the process of coming in: *incoming passengers* | *the incoming tide.*
■ (of a message or communication) being received rather than sent: *an incoming call.* ■ (of an official or administration) having just been elected or appointed to succeed another: *the incoming Labour government.* ■ Brit. coming to settle in a country; immigrant: *incoming Indonesian settlers.*
▶ **noun** (**incomings**) revenue; income: *keep an account of your incomings and outgoings.*

incommensurable /ˌɪnkəˈmɛnʃ(ə)rəb(ə)l, -sjə-/ ▶ **adjective 1** not able to be judged by the same standard as something; having no common standard of measurement: *the two types of science.are incommensurable.*
2 Mathematics (of numbers) in a ratio that cannot be expressed as a ratio of integers.

■ irrational.
▶ **noun** (usu. **incommensurables**) an incommensurable quantity.
– DERIVATIVES **incommensurability** noun, **incommensurably** adverb.
– ORIGIN mid 16th cent. (in the mathematical sense): from late Latin *incommensurabilis,* from *in-* 'not' + *commensurabilis* (see COMMENSURABLE).

incommensurate /ˌɪnkəˈmɛnʃ(ə)rət, -sjə-/ ▶ **adjective 1** [predic.] (**incommensurate with**) out of keeping or proportion with: *man's influence on the earth's surface seems incommensurate with his scale.*
2 another term for INCOMMENSURABLE (in sense 1).
– DERIVATIVES **incommensurately** adverb, **incommensurateness** noun.

incommode ▶ verb [with obj.] formal inconvenience (someone): *they are incommoded by the traffic.*
– ORIGIN late 16th cent.: from French *incommoder* or Latin *incommodare,* from *in-* 'not' + *commodus* 'convenient'.

incommodious ▶ adjective formal or dated causing inconvenience or discomfort.
– DERIVATIVES **incommodiously** adverb, **incommodiousness** noun.

incommunicable ▶ adjective not able to be communicated to others: *the pain of separation took the form of an incommunicable depression.*
– DERIVATIVES **incommunicability** noun, **incommunicableness** noun, **incommunicably** adverb.
– ORIGIN mid 16th cent. (in the sense 'incommunicative'): from late Latin *incommunicabilis* 'not to be imparted', from *in-* 'not' + *communicabilis* (see COMMUNICABLE).

incommunicado /ˌɪnkəmjuːnɪˈkɑːdəʊ/ ▶ **adjective** not able, wanting, or allowed to communicate with other people: *they were separated and detained incommunicado.*
– ORIGIN mid 19th cent.: from Spanish *incomunicado,* past participle of *incomunicar* 'deprive of communication'.

incommunicative ▶ adjective another term for UNCOMMUNICATIVE.
– DERIVATIVES **incommunicatively** adverb, **incommunicativeness** noun.

incommutable ▶ adjective not capable of being changed or exchanged.
– DERIVATIVES **incommutably** adverb.
– ORIGIN late Middle English: from Latin *incommutabilis,* from *in-* 'not' + *commutabilis* (see COMMUTABLE).

in-company ▶ adjective occurring or existing within a company: *in-company training programmes.*

incomparable /ɪnˈkɒmp(ə)rəb(ə)l/ ▶ **adjective 1** without an equal in quality or extent; matchless: *the incomparable beauty of Venice.*
2 unable to be compared; totally different in nature or extent: *censorship still exists, but now it's absolutely incomparable with what it was.*
– DERIVATIVES **incomparability** noun, **incomparably** adverb.
– ORIGIN late Middle English: via Old French from Latin *incomparabilis,* from *in-* 'not' + *comparabilis* (see COMPARABLE).

incompatible ▶ adjective (of two things) so opposed in character as to be incapable of existing together: *cleverness and femininity were seen as incompatible.*
■ (of two people) unable to live together harmoniously. ■ [predic.] (**incompatible with**) (of one thing or person) not consistent or able to coexist with (another): *long hours are simply incompatible with family life.* ■ (of equipment, machinery, computer programs, etc.) not capable of being used in combination: *all four prototype camcorders used special tapes and were incompatible with each other.*
– DERIVATIVES **incompatibility** noun, **incompatibly** adverb.
– ORIGIN late Middle English: from medieval Latin *incompatibilis,* from *in-* 'not' + *compatibilis* (see COMPATIBLE).

incompetent ▶ adjective not having or showing the necessary skills to do something successfully: *a forgetful and utterly incompetent assistant.*
■ Law not qualified to act in a particular capacity: *the patient is deemed legally incompetent.* ■ Medicine (especially of a valve or sphincter) not able to perform its function.
▶ **noun** an incompetent person.
– DERIVATIVES **incompetence** noun, **incompetency** noun, **incompetently** adverb.

– ORIGIN late 16th cent. (in the sense 'not legally competent'): from French, or from late Latin *incompetent-*, from *in-* 'not' + Latin *competent-* 'being fit or proper' (see **COMPETENT**).

incompletable ▶ adjective rare unable to be completed.
– DERIVATIVES **incompletability** noun.

incomplete ▶ adjective not having all the necessary or appropriate parts: *the records are patchy and incomplete.*
■ not full or finished: *the analysis remains incomplete.*
– DERIVATIVES **incompletely** adverb, **incompleteness** noun.
– ORIGIN late Middle English: from late Latin *incompletus*, from Latin *in-* 'not' + *completus* 'filled, finished' (see **COMPLETE**).

incompleteness theorem (also **Gödel's incompleteness theorem**) ▶ noun Logic the theorem that in any sufficiently powerful, logically consistent formulation of logic or mathematics there must be true formulas which are neither provable nor disprovable. The theorem entails the corollary that the consistency of a logical system cannot be proved within that system.

incompletion ▶ noun [mass noun] the state of lacking something or of having failed to complete something: *humans with their profound sense of incompletion.*

incomprehensible ▶ adjective not able to be understood; not intelligible: *a language which is incomprehensible to anyone outside the office.*
– DERIVATIVES **incomprehensibility** noun, **incomprehensibleness** noun, **incomprehensibly** adverb.
– ORIGIN late Middle English (earlier than *comprehensible*): from Latin *incomprehensibilis*, from *in-* 'not' + *comprehensibilis* (see **COMPREHENSIBLE**).

incomprehension ▶ noun [mass noun] failure to understand something: *they gave him a look of complete incomprehension.*

incompressible ▶ adjective not able to be compressed.
– DERIVATIVES **incompressibility** noun.

incomputable ▶ adjective rare unable to be calculated or estimated: *incomputable riches.*
– ORIGIN early 17th cent.: from **IN-**¹ 'not' + Latin *computabilis* 'able to be counted' (see **COMPUTE**).

inconceivable ▶ adjective not capable of being imagined or grasped mentally; unbelievable: [with clause] *it seemed inconceivable that the president had been unaware of what was going on | they behaved with inconceivable cruelty.*
– DERIVATIVES **inconceivability** noun, **inconceivableness** noun, **inconceivably** adverb [as submodifier] *a crisis of inconceivably devastating proportions.*

inconclusive ▶ adjective not leading to a firm conclusion; not ending doubt or dispute: *the medical evidence is inconclusive.*
■ (of a victory) not achieved easily or by a large margin.
– DERIVATIVES **inconclusively** adverb, **inconclusiveness** noun.

Inconel /ˈɪnkənɛl/ ▶ noun [mass noun] trademark an alloy of nickel containing chromium and iron, resistant to corrosion at high temperatures.
– ORIGIN 1930s: apparently from I(nternational) N(ickel) Co(mpany), on the pattern of *nickel.*

incongruent /ɪnˈkɒŋɡrʊənt/ ▶ adjective incongruous; incompatible.
■ Chemistry (of melting, dissolution, or other process) affecting the components of an alloy or other substance differently.
– DERIVATIVES **incongruence** noun, **incongruently** adverb.
– ORIGIN late Middle English: from Latin *incongruent-*, from *in-* 'not' + *congruent-* 'meeting together' (see **CONGRUENT**).

incongruous /ɪnˈkɒŋɡrʊəs/ ▶ adjective not in harmony or keeping with the surroundings or other aspects of something: *the duffel coat looked incongruous with the black dress she wore underneath.*
– DERIVATIVES **incongruity** noun (pl. **-ies**), **incongruously** adverb.
– ORIGIN early 17th cent.: from Latin *incongruus* (from *in-* 'not' + *congruus* 'agreeing, suitable', from the verb *congruere*) + **-OUS**.

inconnu /ˈãkɒnuː, ˌãkɒnˈ(j)uː/ ▶ noun **1** an unknown person or thing.
2 (pl. same) an edible predatory freshwater whitefish that is related to the salmon. It lives in Eurasian and North American lakes close to the Arctic Circle.
● *Stenodus leucichthys,* family Salmonidae.
– ORIGIN early 19th cent.: French, literally 'unknown'.

inconsecutive ▶ adjective not in order or following continuously.
– DERIVATIVES **inconsecutively** adverb.

inconsequent ▶ adjective not connected or following logically; irrelevant: *people say the most stupid, inconsequent things when surprised.*
■ another term for **INCONSEQUENTIAL**.
– DERIVATIVES **inconsequence** noun, **inconsequently** adverb.
– ORIGIN late 16th cent.: from Latin *inconsequent-*, from *in-* 'not' + *consequent-* 'overtaking, following closely' (see **CONSEQUENT**).

inconsequential ▶ adjective not important or significant: *they talked about inconsequential things.*
– DERIVATIVES **inconsequentiality** noun (pl. **-ies**), **inconsequentially** adverb, **inconsequentialness** noun.

inconsiderable ▶ adjective [usu. with negative] of small size, amount, or extent: *a not inconsiderable amount of money.*
■ unimportant or insignificant: *a not inconsiderable artist.*
– ORIGIN late 16th cent. (in the sense 'impossible to imagine'): from French, or from Latin *inconsiderabilis,* from *in-* 'not' + *considerabilis* 'worthy of consideration' (see **CONSIDERABLE**).

inconsiderate ▶ adjective thoughtlessly causing hurt or inconvenience to others: *it's inconsiderate of her to go away without telling us.*
– DERIVATIVES **inconsiderately** adverb, **inconsiderateness** noun, **inconsideration** noun.
– ORIGIN late Middle English (originally in the sense 'not properly considered'): from Latin *inconsideratus,* from *in-* 'not' + *consideratus* 'examined, considered' (see **CONSIDERATE**).

inconsistency ▶ noun (pl. **-ies**) [mass noun] the fact or state of being inconsistent: *inconsistency between his expressed attitudes and his actual behaviour.*
■ [count noun] an inconsistent element or an instance of being inconsistent: *the single glaring inconsistency in the argument.*
– ORIGIN mid 17th cent.: from **INCONSISTENT**, on the pattern of *consistency.*

inconsistent ▶ adjective not staying the same throughout; having self-contradictory elements: *police interpretation of the law was often inconsistent.*
■ acting at variance with one's own principles or former conduct: *parents can become inconsistent and lacking in control over their children.* ■ (**inconsistent with**) not compatible or in keeping with: *he had done nothing inconsistent with his morality.* ■ erratic in behaviour or action: *we're too inconsistent to win the league.*
– DERIVATIVES **inconsistently** adverb.

inconsolable ▶ adjective (of a person or their grief) not able to be comforted or alleviated: *his widow, Jane, was inconsolable.*
– DERIVATIVES **inconsolability** noun, **inconsolably** adverb.
– ORIGIN late 16th cent.: from French, or from Latin *inconsolabilis,* from *in-* 'not' + *consolabilis* 'able to be consoled', from the verb *consolari* (see **CONSOLE**¹).

inconsonant ▶ adjective rare not in agreement or harmony; not compatible.
– DERIVATIVES **inconsonance** noun, **inconsonantly** adverb.

inconspicuous ▶ adjective not clearly visible or attracting attention; not conspicuous: *an inconspicuous red-brick building.*
– DERIVATIVES **inconspicuously** adverb, **inconspicuousness** noun.
– ORIGIN early 17th cent. (in the sense 'invisible, indiscernible'): from Latin *inconspicuus* (from *in-* 'not' + *conspicuus* 'clearly visible') + **-OUS**.

inconstant ▶ adjective frequently changing; variable or irregular: *their exact dimensions aren't easily measured since they are inconstant.*
■ (of a person or their behaviour) not faithful and dependable.
– DERIVATIVES **inconstancy** noun (pl. **-ies**), **inconstantly** adverb.

– ORIGIN late Middle English: via Old French from Latin *inconstant-*, from *in-* 'not' + *constant-* 'standing firm' (see **CONSTANT**).

incontestable ▶ adjective not able to be disputed.
– DERIVATIVES **incontestability** noun, **incontestably** adverb.
– ORIGIN late 17th cent.: from French, or from medieval Latin *incontestabilis,* from *in-* 'not' + *contestabilis* 'able to be called upon in witness', from the verb *contestari* (see **CONTEST**).

incontinent ▶ adjective **1** having no or insufficient voluntary control over urination or defecation.
2 lacking self-restraint; uncontrolled: *the incontinent hysteria of the massed pop fans.*
– DERIVATIVES **incontinence** noun, **incontinently** adverb.
– ORIGIN late Middle English (in sense 2): from Old French, or from Latin *incontinent-*, from *in-* 'not' + *continent-* 'holding together' (see **CONTINENT**²). Sense 1 dates from the early 19th cent.

incontrovertible ▶ adjective not able to be denied or disputed: *incontrovertible proof.*
– DERIVATIVES **incontrovertibility** noun, **incontrovertibly** adverb.

inconvenience ▶ noun [mass noun] trouble or difficulty caused to one's personal requirements or comfort: *the inconvenience of having to change trains.*
■ [count noun] a cause or instance of such trouble: *the inconveniences of life in a remote city.*
▶ verb [with obj.] cause such trouble or difficulty to: *noise and fumes from traffic would inconvenience residents.*
– ORIGIN late Middle English (originally in the sense 'incongruity, inconsistency', also in the general sense 'unsuitability'): via Old French from late Latin *inconvenientia* 'incongruity, inconsistency', from *in-* 'not' + Latin *convenient-* 'agreeing, fitting' (see **CONVENIENT**).

inconvenient ▶ adjective causing trouble, difficulties, or discomfort: *she telephoned frequently, usually at inconvenient times.*
– DERIVATIVES **inconveniently** adverb.
– ORIGIN late Middle English (originally in the sense 'incongruous' or 'unsuitable'): via Old French from Latin *inconvenient-*, from *in-* 'not' + *convenient-* 'agreeing, fitting' (see **CONVENIENT**). Current senses date from the mid 17th cent.

inconvertible ▶ adjective not able to be changed in form, function, or character.
■ (of currency) not able to be converted into another form on demand.
– DERIVATIVES **inconvertibility** noun, **inconvertibly** adverb.
– ORIGIN mid 17th cent.: from French, or from late Latin *inconvertibilis,* from *in-* 'not' + *convertibilis* (see **CONVERTIBLE**).

incoordination ▶ noun [mass noun] technical lack of coordination, especially the inability to use different parts of the body together smoothly and efficiently.

incorporate ▶ verb [with obj.] **1** put or take in (something) as part of a whole; include: *he has incorporated in his proposals a large number of measures | territories that had been incorporated into the Japanese Empire.*
■ contain or include (something) as part of a whole: *some schemes incorporated all these variations.* ■ combine (ingredients) into one substance: *add the cheeses and butter and process briefly to incorporate them.*
2 (often **be incorporated**) constitute (a company, city, or other organization) as a legal corporation.
▶ adjective **1** another term for **INCORPORATED**.
2 poetic/literary having a bodily form; embodied.
– DERIVATIVES **incorporation** noun, **incorporator** noun.
– ORIGIN late Middle English: from late Latin *incorporat-* 'embodied', from the verb *incorporare,* from *in-* 'into' + Latin *corporare* 'form into a body' (from *corpus, corpor-* 'body').

incorporated ▶ adjective (of a company or other organization) formed into a legal corporation: *the Incorporated Society of Musicians | [postpositive] Adobe Systems Incorporated.*

incorporative ▶ adjective tending to incorporate or include things.

incorporeal /ˌɪnkɔːˈpɔːrɪəl/ ▶ adjective not composed of matter; having no material existence: *millions believe in a supreme but incorporeal being they call God.*
■ Law having no physical existence.

– DERIVATIVES **incorporeality** noun, **incorporeally** adverb, **incorporeity** noun.
– ORIGIN late Middle English: from Latin *incorporeus*, from *in-* 'not' + *corporeus* (from *corpus*, *corpor-* 'body') + **-AL**.

incorrect ▶ adjective **1** not in accordance with fact; wrong: *the doctor gave you incorrect advice.*
2 not in accordance with a particular set of standards: *strictly speaking, the form of address was incorrect | this is grammatically incorrect.*
– DERIVATIVES **incorrectly** adverb, **incorrectness** noun.
– ORIGIN late Middle English: from Latin *incorrectus*, from *in-* 'not' + *correctus* 'made straight, amended' (see **CORRECT**). Originally in the general sense 'uncorrected', the word was later applied specifically to a book containing many errors because it had not been corrected for the press; hence sense 2 (late 17th cent.).

incorrigible ▶ adjective (of a person or their tendencies) not able to be corrected, improved, or reformed: *she's an incorrigible flirt.*
▶ noun a person of this type.
– DERIVATIVES **incorrigibility** noun, **incorrigibly** adverb [as submodifier] *the incorrigibly macho character of news-gathering operations.*
– ORIGIN Middle English: from Old French, or from Latin *incorrigibilis*, from *in-* 'not' + *corrigibilis* (see **CORRIGIBLE**).

incorrupt ▶ adjective rare (especially of a human body) not having undergone decomposition.
– ORIGIN late Middle English: from Latin *incorruptus*, from *in-* 'not' + *corruptus* 'destroyed, marred' (see **CORRUPT**).

incorruptible ▶ adjective **1** not susceptible to corruption, especially by bribery.
2 not subject to death or decay; everlasting.
– DERIVATIVES **incorruptibility** noun, **incorruptibly** adverb.
– ORIGIN Middle English: from Old French, or from ecclesiastical Latin *incorruptibilis*, from *in-* 'not' + *corruptibilis* 'corruptible, liable to decay'.

in-country ▶ adjective & adverb in a country rather than operating from outside but in relation to it: [as adv.] *selection for the posts takes place in London, or occasionally in-country.*

incrassate /ɪnˈkraseɪt/ ▶ adjective rare thickened in form or consistency.
– DERIVATIVES **incrassated** /ɪnˈkraseɪtɪd/ adjective.
– ORIGIN late 15th cent.: from late Latin *incrassatus* 'made thick', past participle of *incrassare*.

increase ▶ verb become or make greater in size, amount, intensity, or degree: [no obj.] *car use is increasing at an alarming rate* | [with obj.] *we are aiming to increase awareness of social issues* | [as adj. **increasing**] *the increasing numbers of students.*
▶ noun an instance of growing or making greater: *an increase from sixteen to eighteen clubs* | [mass noun] *some increase in inflation.*
– PHRASES **on the increase** becoming greater, more common, or more frequent.
– DERIVATIVES **increasable** adjective, **increasingly** adverb [sentence adverb] *increasingly, attention is paid to health and lifestyle* | [as submodifier] *an increasingly difficult situation.*
– ORIGIN Middle English (formerly also as *encrease*): from Old French *encreistre*, from Latin *increscere*, from *in-* 'into' + *crescere* 'grow'.

increate /ˌɪnkriːˈeɪt/ ▶ adjective poetic/literary not yet created.
– ORIGIN late Middle English: from ecclesiastical Latin *increatus*, from Latin *in-* 'not' + *creatus* (past participle of *creare* 'create').

incredible ▶ adjective **1** impossible to believe: *an almost incredible tale of triumph and tragedy.*
2 difficult to believe; extraordinary: *the noise from the crowd was incredible.*
■ informal amazingly good or beautiful: *I was mesmerized: she looked so incredible.*
– DERIVATIVES **incredibility** noun.
– ORIGIN late Middle English: from Latin *incredibilis*, from *in-* 'not'+ *credibilis* (see **CREDIBLE**).

incredibly ▶ adverb **1** [as submodifier] to a great degree; extremely or unusually: *Michele was incredibly brave.*
2 [sentence adverb] used to introduce a statement that is hard to believe; strangely: *incredibly, he was still alive.*

incredulity ▶ noun [mass noun] the state of being unwilling or unable to believe something: *he stared down the street in incredulity.*

incredulous ▶ adjective (of a person or their manner) unwilling or unable to believe something: *an incredulous gasp.*
– DERIVATIVES **incredulously** adverb, **incredulousness** noun.
– ORIGIN 16th cent.: from Latin *incredulus* (from *in-* 'not' + *credulus* 'believing, trusting', from *credere* 'believe') + **-OUS**.

increment /ˈɪŋkrɪm(ə)nt/ ▶ noun an increase or addition, especially one of a series on a fixed scale: *all sizes from 4–30 mm in 1 mm increments.*
■ a regular increase in salary on such a scale: *your first increment will be payable six months from your date of commencement.* ■ Mathematics a small positive or negative change in a variable quantity or function.
– DERIVATIVES **incremental** adjective, **incrementally** adverb.
– ORIGIN late Middle English: from Latin *incrementum*, from the stem of *increscere* 'grow' (see **INCREASE**).

incremental back-up ▶ noun Computing a security copy which contains only those files which have been altered since the last full back-up.

incrementalism ▶ noun [mass noun] belief in or advocacy of change by degrees; gradualism.
– DERIVATIVES **incrementalist** noun & adjective.

incriminate /ɪnˈkrɪmɪneɪt/ ▶ verb [with obj.] make (someone) appear guilty of a crime or wrongdoing; strongly imply the guilt of (someone): *he refused to answer questions in order not to incriminate himself* | [as adj. **incriminating**] *incriminating evidence.*
– DERIVATIVES **incrimination** noun, **incriminatory** adjective.
– ORIGIN mid 18th cent.: from late Latin *incriminat-* 'accused', from the verb *incriminare*, from *in-* 'into, towards' + Latin *crimen* 'crime'.

in-crowd ▶ noun (**the in-crowd**) informal a small group of people perceived by others to be particularly fashionable, informed, or popular.

incrust ▶ verb variant spelling of **ENCRUST**.

incrustation ▶ noun variant spelling of **ENCRUSTATION**.

incubate /ˈɪŋkjʊbeɪt/ ▶ verb [with obj.] (of a bird) sit on (eggs) in order to keep them warm and bring them to hatching.
■ (especially in a laboratory) keep (eggs, cells, bacteria, embryos, etc.) at a suitable temperature so that they develop: *the samples were incubated at 80°C for 3 minutes.* ■ (**be incubating something**) have an infectious disease developing inside one before symptoms appear: *the possibility that she was incubating early syphilis.* ■ [no obj.] develop slowly without outward or perceptible signs: *unfortunately the BSE bug incubates for around three years.*
– ORIGIN mid 17th cent.: from Latin *incubat-* 'lain on', from the verb *incubare*, from *in-* 'upon' + *cubare* 'to lie'.

incubation ▶ noun [mass noun] the process of incubating eggs, cells, bacteria, a disease, etc.: *the chick hatches after a month's incubation.*
– DERIVATIVES **incubative** adjective, **incubatory** /ˈɪŋkjʊbeɪt(ə)ri/ adjective.
– ORIGIN early 17th cent.: from Latin *incubatio(n-)* 'brooding', from the verb *incubare* (see **INCUBATE**).

incubation period ▶ noun the period over which eggs, cells, etc. are incubated.
■ the period between exposure to an infection and the appearance of the first symptoms.

incubator ▶ noun an enclosed apparatus providing a controlled and protective environment for the care of premature or unusually small babies.
■ an apparatus used to hatch eggs or grow micro-organisms under controlled conditions. ■ N. Amer. a place, especially with support staff and equipment, made available at low rent to new small businesses.

incubous /ˈɪŋkjʊbəs/ ▶ adjective Botany (of a liverwort) having leaves which point forward so that their upper edges overlap the lower edges of the leaves above. Often contrasted with **SUCCUBOUS**.
– ORIGIN mid 19th cent.: from Latin *incubare* 'lie on' + **-OUS**.

incubus /ˈɪŋkjʊbəs/ ▶ noun (pl. **incubi** /-bʌɪ/) a male demon believed to have sexual intercourse with sleeping women.
■ figurative a cause of distress or anxiety: *debt is a big incubus in developing countries.* ■ archaic a nightmare.
– ORIGIN Middle English: late Latin form of Latin *incubo* 'nightmare', from *incubare* 'lie on' (see **INCUBATE**).

incudes plural form of **INCUS**.

inculcate /ˈɪnkʌlkeɪt/ ▶ verb [with obj.] instil (an attitude, idea, or habit) by persistent instruction: *I tried to inculcate in my pupils an attitude of enquiry.*
■ teach (someone) an attitude, idea, or habit by such instruction: *they will try to inculcate you with a respect for culture.*
– DERIVATIVES **inculcation** noun, **inculcator** noun.
– ORIGIN mid 16th cent.: from Latin *inculcat-* 'pressed in', from the verb *inculcare*, from *in-* 'into' + *calcare* 'to tread' (from *calx*, *calc-* 'heel').

inculpate /ˈɪnkʌlpeɪt/ ▶ verb [with obj.] archaic accuse or blame.
■ incriminate: *someone placed the pistol in your room in order to inculpate you.*
– DERIVATIVES **inculpation** noun, **inculpatory** adjective.
– ORIGIN late 18th cent.: from late Latin *inculpat-* 'made culpable', from the verb *inculpare*, from *in-* 'upon, towards' + *culpare* 'to blame' (from *culpa* 'fault').

inculturation /ɪnˌkʌltʃəˈreɪʃ(ə)n/ (also **enculturation**) ▶ noun [mass noun] the gradual acquisition of the characteristics and norms of a culture or group by a person, another culture, etc.
■ the adaptation of Christian liturgy to a non-Christian cultural background.

incumbency ▶ noun (pl. **-ies**) the holding of an office or the period during which one is held.

incumbent /ɪnˈkʌmb(ə)nt/ ▶ adjective **1** [predic.] (**incumbent on/upon**) necessary for (someone) as a duty or responsibility: *it is incumbent on all decent people to concentrate on destroying this evil.*
2 [attrib.] (of an official or regime) currently holding office: *the incumbent President had been defeated.*
■ denoting a company having a sizeable share of a market: *powerful incumbent airlines.*
▶ noun the holder of an office or post.
– ORIGIN late Middle English (as a noun): from Anglo-Latin *incumbens*, *incumbent-*, from Latin *incumbere* 'lie or lean on', from *in-* 'upon' + a verb related to *cubare* 'lie'.

incunabulum /ˌɪnkjʊˈnabjʊləm/ (also **incunable** /ɪnˈkjuːnəb(ə)l/) ▶ noun (pl. **incunabula**) an early printed book, especially one printed before 1501.
■ (**incunabula**) archaic the early stages of the development of something.
– ORIGIN early 19th cent.: from Latin *incunabula* (neuter plural) 'swaddling clothes, cradle', from *in-* 'into' + *cunae* 'cradle'.

incur ▶ verb (**incurred**, **incurring**) [with obj.] become subject to (something unwelcome or unpleasant) as a result of one's own behaviour or actions: *I will pay any expenses incurred.*
– DERIVATIVES **incurrence** noun.
– ORIGIN late Middle English: from Latin *incurrere*, from *in-* 'towards' + *currere* 'run'.

incurable ▶ adjective (of a sick person or a disease) not able to be cured.
▶ noun a person who cannot be cured.
– DERIVATIVES **incurability** noun, **incurably** adverb [as submodifier] *incurably ill patients.*
– ORIGIN Middle English: from Old French, or from late Latin *incurabilis*, from *in-* 'not' + *curabilis* (see **CURABLE**).

incurious ▶ adjective (of a person or their manner) not eager to know something; lacking curiosity.
– DERIVATIVES **incuriosity** noun, **incuriously** adverb, **incuriousness** noun.
– ORIGIN late 16th cent. (in the sense 'careless'): partly from Latin *incuriosus* 'careless, indifferent', from *in-* 'not' + Latin *curiosus* 'careful' (see **CURIOUS**); partly from **IN-**[1] 'not' + **CURIOUS**.

incurrent ▶ adjective chiefly Zoology (of a vessel or opening) conveying fluid inwards. The opposite of **EXCURRENT**.
– ORIGIN late 16th cent. (in the sense 'falling within (a period)'): from Latin *incurrent-* 'running in', from the verb *incurrere* (see **INCUR**).

incursion /ɪnˈkəːʃ(ə)n/ ▶ noun an invasion or attack, especially a sudden or brief one.
– DERIVATIVES **incursive** adjective.
– ORIGIN late Middle English (formerly also as *encursion*): from Latin *incursio(n-)*, from the verb *incurrere* (see **INCUR**).

incurvate ▶ verb /ˈɪnkəˌveɪt/ [no obj.] [usu. as adj. **incurvated**] curve inwards.
▶ adjective /ɪnˈkəːvət/ curved inwards.
– DERIVATIVES **incurvation** noun.
– ORIGIN late Middle English (as an adjective): from Latin *incurvat-* 'bent into a curve', from the verb *incurvare*.

incurve ▶ verb [no obj.] [usu. as adj. **incurved**] curve inwards: *incurved horns.*
– ORIGIN late Middle English: from Latin *incurvare*, from *in-* 'in, towards' + *curvare* 'to curve'.

incus /ˈɪŋkəs/ ▶ noun (pl. **incudes** /ˈɪŋkjʊdiːz, ɪnˈkjuːdiːz/) Anatomy a small anvil-shaped bone in the middle ear, transmitting vibrations between the malleus and stapes.
– ORIGIN mid 17th cent.: from Latin, literally 'anvil'.

incuse /ɪnˈkjuːz/ ▶ noun an impression hammered or stamped on a coin.
▶ verb [with obj.] mark (a coin) with a figure by impressing it with a stamp.
– ORIGIN early 19th cent.: from Latin *incusus* 'forged with a hammer', past participle of *incudere*, from *in-* 'into' + *cudere* 'to forge'.

IND ▶ abbreviation for India (international vehicle registration).

Ind. ▶ abbreviation for ■ Independent. ■ India. ■ Indian. ■ Indiana.

indaba /ɪnˈdɑːbə/ ▶ noun S. African **1** a conference between members of southern African native peoples. **2** informal one's own problem or concern: *this country is our indaba and no one else's.*
– ORIGIN Xhosa and Zulu, 'discussion'.

indebted ▶ adjective owing money: *heavily indebted countries.*
■ owing gratitude for a service or favour: *I am indebted to her for her help in indexing my book.*
– DERIVATIVES **indebtedness** noun.
– ORIGIN Middle English *endetted*, from Old French *endette* 'involved in debt', past participle of *endetter*. The spelling change in the 16th cent. was due to association with medieval Latin *indebitare* (based on Latin *debitum* 'debt').

indecency ▶ noun (pl. **-ies**) [mass noun] indecent behaviour: *seven offences of rape and indecency.*
■ [count noun] an indecent act, gesture, or expression.

indecent ▶ adjective not conforming with generally accepted standards of behaviour or propriety; obscene: *the film was grossly indecent.*
■ not appropriate or fitting: *they leaped on the suggestion with indecent haste.*
– DERIVATIVES **indecently** adverb.
– ORIGIN late 16th cent.: from French *indécent* or Latin *indecent-*, from *in-* 'not' + *decent-* 'being fitting' (see **DECENT**).

indecent assault ▶ noun [mass noun] sexual attack that does not involve rape.

indecent exposure ▶ noun [mass noun] the crime of intentionally showing one's sexual organs in public.
■ the act of outraging public decency by being naked in a public place.

indecipherable /ˌɪndɪˈsʌɪf(ə)rəb(ə)l/ ▶ adjective not able to be read or understood.

indecision ▶ noun [mass noun] the inability to make a decision quickly.
– ORIGIN mid 18th cent.: from French *indécision*, from *in-* (expressing negation) + *décision*, from Latin *decisio(n-)*, from the verb *decidere* (see **DECIDE**).

indecisive ▶ adjective **1** not settling an issue: *these experimental results are indecisive.* **2** (of a person) not having or showing the ability to make decisions quickly and effectively.
– DERIVATIVES **indecisively** adverb, **indecisiveness** noun.

indeclinable /ˌɪndɪˈklʌɪnəb(ə)l/ ▶ adjective Grammar (of a noun, pronoun, or adjective in a highly inflected language) having no inflections.
– ORIGIN late Middle English: via French from Latin *indeclinabilis*, from *in-* 'not' + *declinabilis* 'able to be inflected' (see **DECLINE**).

indecomposable /ˌɪndiːkəmˈpəʊzəb(ə)l/ ▶ adjective Mathematics unable to be expressed as a product of factors or otherwise decomposed into simpler elements.

indecorous ▶ adjective not in keeping with good taste and propriety; improper.
– DERIVATIVES **indecorously** adverb, **indecorousness** noun.
– ORIGIN late 17th cent.: from Latin *indecorus* (from *in-* 'not' + *decorus* 'seemly') + **-OUS**.

indecorum /ˌɪndɪˈkɔːrəm/ ▶ noun [mass noun] failure to conform to good taste, propriety, or etiquette.
– ORIGIN late 16th cent. (denoting an indecorous act): from Latin, neuter of *indecorus* (see **INDECOROUS**).

indeed ▶ adverb **1** used to emphasize a statement or response confirming something already suggested: *it was not expected to last long, and indeed it took less than three weeks* | *'She should have no trouble hearing him.' 'No indeed.'*
■ used to emphasize a description, typically of a quality or condition: *it was a very good buy indeed* | *thank you very much indeed.* **2** used to introduce a further and stronger or more surprising point: *the idea is attractive to many men and indeed to many women.* **3** used in a response to express interest, incredulity, or contempt: *'His neck was broken.' 'Indeed?'* | *Nice boys, indeed—they were going to smash his head in!*
■ expressing interest of an ironical kind with repetition of a question just asked: *'Who'd believe it?' 'Who indeed?'*
– ORIGIN Middle English: originally as *in deed.*

indeedy ▶ adverb N. Amer. informal term for **INDEED** (in sense 1): *Yes, indeedy! That was a good question.*

indefatigable /ˌɪndɪˈfatɪɡəb(ə)l/ ▶ adjective (of a person or their efforts) persisting tirelessly: *an indefatigable defender of human rights.*
– DERIVATIVES **indefatigability** noun, **indefatigably** adverb.
– ORIGIN early 17th cent.: from French, or from Latin *indefatigabilis*, from *in-* 'not' + *de-* 'away, completely' + *fatigare* 'wear out'.

indefeasible /ˌɪndɪˈfiːzɪb(ə)l/ ▶ adjective chiefly Law & Philosophy not able to be lost, annulled, or overturned: *an indefeasible right.*
– DERIVATIVES **indefeasibility** noun, **indefeasibly** adverb.

indefectible /ˌɪndɪˈfɛktɪb(ə)l/ ▶ adjective rare not liable to fail, end, or decay.
■ perfect; faultless.

indefensible ▶ adjective **1** not justifiable by argument: *the policy of apartheid was morally indefensible.* **2** not able to be protected against attack: *the towns were tactically indefensible.*
– DERIVATIVES **indefensibility** noun, **indefensibly** adverb.

indefinable ▶ adjective not able to be defined or described exactly: *she reminds me, in some indefinable way, of my grandmother.*
– DERIVATIVES **indefinably** adverb.

indefinite ▶ adjective lasting for an unknown or unstated length of time: *they may face indefinite detention.*
■ not clearly expressed or defined; vague: *their status remains indefinite.* ■ Grammar (of a word, inflection, or phrase) not determining the person, thing, time, etc., referred to.
– DERIVATIVES **indefiniteness** noun.
– ORIGIN mid 16th cent.: from Latin *indefinitus*, from *in-* 'not' + *definitus* 'defined, set within limits' (see **DEFINITE**).

indefinite article ▶ noun Grammar a determiner (*a* and *an* in English) that introduces a noun phrase and implies that the thing referred to is non-specific (as in *she bought me a book; government is an art; he went to a public school*). Typically, the indefinite article is used to introduce new concepts into a discourse. Compare with **DEFINITE ARTICLE**.

indefinite integral ▶ noun Mathematics an integral expressed without limits, and so containing an arbitrary constant.

indefinitely ▶ adverb for an unlimited or unspecified period of time: *talks cannot go on indefinitely.*
■ [as submodifier] to an unlimited or unspecified degree or extent: *an indefinitely large number of channels.*

indefinite pronoun ▶ noun Grammar a pronoun that does not refer to any person, amount, or thing in particular, e.g. *anything, something, anyone, everyone.*

indehiscent /ˌɪndɪˈhɪs(ə)nt/ ▶ adjective Botany (of a pod or fruit) not splitting open to release the seeds when ripe.
– DERIVATIVES **indehiscence** noun.

indelible /ɪnˈdɛlɪb(ə)l/ ▶ adjective (of ink or a pen) making marks that cannot be removed.
■ not able to be forgotten or removed: *the story made an indelible impression on me.*
– DERIVATIVES **indelibility** noun, **indelibly** adverb.
– ORIGIN late 15th cent. (as *indeleble*): from French, or from Latin *indelebilis*, from *in-* 'not' + *delebilis* (from *delere* 'efface, delete'). The ending was altered under the influence of **-IBLE**.

indelicate ▶ adjective having or showing a lack of sensitive understanding or tact: *forgive me asking an indelicate question, but how are you off for money?*
■ slightly indecent: *an earthy, often indelicate sense of humour.*
– DERIVATIVES **indelicacy** noun (pl. **-ies**), **indelicately** adverb.

indemnify /ɪnˈdɛmnɪfʌɪ/ ▶ verb (**-ies, -ied**) [with obj.] compensate (someone) in respect of harm or loss: *you can be indemnified against breach of contract.*
■ secure (someone) against legal responsibility for their actions: *the servant would be indemnified for any damage caused by his negligence.*
– DERIVATIVES **indemnification** noun, **indemnifier** noun.
– ORIGIN early 17th cent.: from Latin *indemnis* 'unhurt, free from loss or damage', from *in-* (expressing negation) + *damnum* 'loss, damage'.

indemnity /ɪnˈdɛmnɪti/ ▶ noun (pl. **-ies**) [mass noun] security or protection against a loss or other financial burden: *no indemnity will be given for loss of cash.*
■ security against or exemption from legal responsibility for one's actions: *a deed of indemnity* | [count noun] *even warranties and indemnities do not provide complete protection.* ■ [count noun] a sum of money paid as compensation, especially a sum exacted by a victor in war as one condition of peace.
– ORIGIN late Middle English: from French *indemnite*, from late Latin *indemnitas*, from *indemnis* 'unhurt, free from loss'.

indemonstrable /ˌɪndɪˈmɒnstrəb(ə)l, ɪnˈdɛmən-/ ▶ adjective not able to be proved or demonstrated.
■ Philosophy (of a truth) axiomatic and hence unprovable.

indene /ˈɪndiːn/ ▶ noun [mass noun] Chemistry a colourless liquid hydrocarbon, obtained from coal tar and used in making synthetic resins.
● A bicyclic aromatic compound; chem. formula: C_9H_8.
– ORIGIN late 19th cent.: from **INDOLE** + **-ENE**.

indent¹ ▶ verb /ɪnˈdɛnt/ [with obj.] **1** start (a line of text) or position (a block of text, table, etc.) further from the margin than the main part of the text. **2** (usu. **be indented**) form deep recesses in (a line or surface): *a coastline indented by many fjords.* ■ make tooth-like notches in: *it has rounded leaves indented at the tip.* **3** [no obj.] make a requisition or written order for something. **4** historical divide (a document drawn up in duplicate) into its two copies with a zigzag line, thus ensuring identification. ■ draw up (a legal document) in exact duplicate.
▶ noun /ˈɪndɛnt/ **1** Brit. an official order or requisition for specified goods or stores. **2** a space left by indenting a line or block of text. **3** an indentation: *every indent in the coastline.* **4** an indenture.
– DERIVATIVES **indentor** noun.
– ORIGIN late Middle English (as a verb in the sense 'give a zigzag outline to, divide by a zigzag line'): from Anglo-Norman French *endenter* or medieval Latin *indentare*, from *en-, in-* 'into' + Latin *dens, dent-* 'tooth'.

indent² /ɪnˈdɛnt/ ▶ verb [with obj.] make a dent or depression in (something): *his chin was firm and slightly indented.*
■ impress (a mark) on something.

indentation ▶ noun **1** [mass noun] the action of indenting or the state of being indented: *paragraphs are marked off by indentation* | [count noun] *an indentation for each change of speaker.* **2** a deep recess in a surface or coastline: *the indentation between the upper lip and the nose.* ■ a tooth-like notch: *the leaves are covered in indentations.*

indentation test ▶ noun a test for determining the hardness of a solid by making an indentation in a sample under standard conditions and measuring the size of the indentation or the distance moved by the indenter.

indented ▶ adjective Heraldry divided or edged with a zigzag line.

indenter ▶ noun a small hard object used for producing an indentation in a solid in an indentation test.

indention ▶ noun archaic term for **INDENTATION**.

indenture /ɪnˈdɛntʃə/ ▶ noun a formal legal agreement, contract, or document, in particular:
■historical a deed of contract of which copies were made for the contracting parties with the edges indented for identification. ■a formal list, certificate, or inventory. ■an agreement binding an apprentice to a master: *the 30 apprentices have received their indentures on completion of their training.* ■[mass noun] the fact of being bound to service by such an agreement: *men in their first year after **indenture to** the Company of Watermen and Lightermen.* ■historical a contract by which a person agreed to work for a set period for a landowner in a British colony in exchange for passage to the colony.
▶verb [with obj.] (usu. **be indentured to**) chiefly historical bind (someone) by an indenture as an apprentice or labourer.
– DERIVATIVES **indentureship** noun.
– ORIGIN late Middle English *endenture*, via Anglo-Norman French from medieval Latin *indentura*, from *indentatus*, past participle of *indentare* (see **INDENT**[1]).

independence ▶ noun [mass noun] the fact or state of being independent: *Argentina gained independence from Spain in 1816 | I've always valued my independence.*
– ORIGIN mid 17th cent.: from **INDEPENDENT**, partly on the pattern of French *indépendance*.

Independence Day ▶ noun a day celebrating the anniversary of national independence.
■another term for **FOURTH OF JULY**.

Independence Hall a building in Philadelphia where the US Declaration of Independence was proclaimed and outside which the Liberty Bell is kept.

independency ▶ noun (pl. **-ies**) **1** rare an independent or self-governing state.
2 archaic term for **INDEPENDENCE**.

independent ▶ adjective **1** free from outside control; not depending on another's authority: *the study is totally **independent of** central government | Britain's largest independent advertising agency.*
■(of a country) self-governing: *India became independent in 1947.* ■not belonging to or supported by a political party: *the independent candidate.* ■(of broadcasting, a school, etc.) not supported by public funds. ■not influenced or affected by others; impartial: *a thorough and independent investigation of the case.* ■(**Independent**) historical Congregational.
2 not depending on another for livelihood or subsistence: *I wanted to remain independent in old age.*
■capable of thinking or acting for oneself: *advice for independent travellers.* ■(of income or resources) making it unnecessary to earn one's living: *a woman of independent means.*
3 not connected with another or with each other; separate: *we need two independent witnesses to testify | the legislature and the judicature are **independent of** one another.*
■not depending on something else for strength or effectiveness; free-standing: *an independent electric shower.* ■Mathematics (of one of a set of axioms, equations, or quantities) incapable of being expressed in terms of, or derived or deduced from, the others.
▶noun an independent person or body.
■an independent political candidate, councillor, etc. ■(**Independent**) historical a Congregationalist.
– DERIVATIVES **independently** adverb.
– ORIGIN early 17th cent. (as an adjective): partly on the pattern of French *indépendant*.

Independent Broadcasting Authority (abbrev.: **IBA**) (in the UK) the body responsible for regulating commercial television and radio, until its replacement in 1991 by the Independent Television Commission and the Radio Authority.

Independent Labour Party (abbrev.: **ILP**) a British socialist political party formed in 1893 under the leadership of Keir Hardie. It was instrumental in the formation of the Labour Party in 1906, but tension between the two parties grew in the 1930s over the questions of pacifism and support for communism, and by the early 1950s the Independent Labour Party had lost all its parliamentary representation.

independent suspension ▶ noun [mass noun] a form of vehicle suspension in which each wheel is supported independently of the others.

Independent Television Commission (abbrev.: **ITC**) (in the UK) an organization responsible for licensing and regulating commercial television. It replaced the Independent Broadcasting Authority in 1991.

independent variable ▶ noun Mathematics a variable (often denoted by *x*) whose variation does not depend on that of another.

in-depth ▶ adjective comprehensive and thorough: *in-depth analysis of the figures.*

indescribable ▶ adjective too unusual, extreme, or indefinite to be adequately described: *most prisoners suffered indescribable hardship.*
– DERIVATIVES **indescribability** noun, **indescribably** adverb.

indestructible ▶ adjective not able to be destroyed: *indestructible plastic containers.*
– DERIVATIVES **indestructibility** noun, **indestructibly** adverb.

indeterminable ▶ adjective not able to be definitely ascertained, calculated, or identified: *a woman of indeterminable age.*
■(of a dispute or difficulty) not able to be resolved.
– DERIVATIVES **indeterminably** adverb.
– ORIGIN late 15th cent. (in the sense 'unable to be limited'): from late Latin *indeterminabilis*, from *in-* 'not' + *determinabilis* (see **DETERMINABLE**).

indeterminacy principle ▶ noun another term for **UNCERTAINTY PRINCIPLE**.

indeterminate /ˌɪndɪˈtəːmɪnət/ ▶ adjective not certain, known, or established: *the date of manufacture is indeterminate.*
■left doubtful; vague: *many felt that the ending rendered the story incomplete, or at least indeterminate.* ■(of a judicial sentence) such that the convicted person's conduct determines the date of release. ■Mathematics (of a quantity) having no definite or definable value. ■Medicine (of a condition) from which a diagnosis of the underlying cause cannot be made: *indeterminate colitis.* ■Botany (of a plant shoot) not having all the axes terminating in a flower bud and so producing a shoot of indefinite length.
– DERIVATIVES **indeterminacy** noun, **indeterminately** adverb, **indeterminateness** noun.
– ORIGIN early 17th cent.: from late Latin *indeterminatus*, from *in-* 'not' + Latin *determinatus* 'limited, determined' (see **DETERMINATE**).

indeterminate vowel ▶ noun Phonetics the vowel /ə/ heard in '*a* moment ago'; a schwa.

indetermination ▶ noun [mass noun] the state of being uncertain or undecided.

indeterminism ▶ noun [mass noun] **1** Philosophy the doctrine that not all events are wholly determined by antecedent causes.
2 the state of being uncertain or undecided.
– DERIVATIVES **indeterminist** noun, **indeterministic** adjective.

index /ˈɪndɛks/ ▶ noun (pl. **indexes** or especially in technical use **indices** /ˈɪndɪsiːz/) **1** an alphabetical list of names, subjects, etc., with references to the places where they occur, typically found at the end of a book.
■an alphabetical list by title, subject, author, or other category of a collection of books or documents, for example in a library. ■Computing a set of items each of which specifies one of the records of a file and contains information about its address.
2 an indicator, sign, or measure of something: *exam results may serve as an **index of** the teacher's effectiveness.*
■a figure in a system or scale representing the average value of specified prices, shares, or other items as compared with some reference figure: *the hundred-shares index closed down 9.3.* ■a pointer on an instrument, showing a quantity, a position on a scale, etc. ■[with modifier] a number giving the magnitude of a physical property or other measured phenomenon in terms of a standard: *the oral hygiene index was calculated as the sum of the debris and calculus indices.*
3 Mathematics an exponent or other superscript or subscript number appended to a quantity.
4 Printing a symbol shaped like a pointing hand, typically used to draw attention to a note.
5 (**the Index**) short for **INDEX LIBRORUM PROHIBITORUM**.
▶verb [with obj.] **1** record (names, subjects, etc.) in an index: *the list indexes theses under regional headings.*
■provide an index to.
2 link the value of (prices, wages, or other payments) automatically to the value of a price index.
3 [no obj.] [often as noun **indexing**] (of a machine or part of one) rotate or otherwise move from one predetermined position to another in order to carry out a sequence of operations.
– DERIVATIVES **indexable** adjective, **indexation** noun, **indexer** noun, **indexible** adjective.
– ORIGIN late Middle English: from Latin *index*, *indic-* 'forefinger, informer, sign', from *in-* 'towards' + a second element related to *dicere* 'say' or *dicare* 'make known'; compare with **INDICATE**. The original sense 'index finger' (with which one points), came to mean 'pointer' (late 16th cent.), and figuratively something that serves to point to a fact or conclusion; hence a list of topics in a book ('pointing' to their location).

index case ▶ noun Medicine the first identified case in a group of related cases of a particular communicable or heritable disease.

index finger ▶ noun the finger next to the thumb; the forefinger.

index fossil ▶ noun Geology a fossil that is useful for dating and correlating the strata in which it is found.

index futures ▶ plural noun contracts to buy a range of shares at an agreed price but delivered and paid for later.

indexical /ɪnˈdɛksɪk(ə)l/ Linguistics ▶ adjective (of a word or expression, or its meaning) relating directly to something in the context in which it is used, as for example the pronouns *I* and *you*. Also called **DEICTIC**.
▶noun an indexical word or expression.
– ORIGIN early 20th cent.: coined in this sense by the American philosopher C. S. Peirce.

Index Librorum Prohibitorum /ˌɪndɛks lɪˌbrɔːrʊm prəʊˌhɪbɪˈtɔːrʊm/ an official list of books which Roman Catholics were forbidden to read or which were to be read only in expurgated editions, as contrary to Catholic faith or morals. The first Index was issued in 1557; it was revised at intervals until abolished in 1966.
– ORIGIN Latin, 'index of forbidden books'.

index-linked ▶ adjective Brit. adjusted according to the value of a retail price index: *an index-linked pension.*
– DERIVATIVES **index-linking** noun.

India a country in southern Asia occupying the greater part of the Indian subcontinent; pop. 859,200,000 (est. 1991); official languages, Hindi and English (fourteen other languages are recognized as official in certain regions; of these, Bengali, Gujarati, Marathi, Tamil, Telugu, and Urdu have most first-language speakers); capital, New Delhi. Hindi name **BHARAT**.
■a code word representing the letter I, used in radio communication.

> Much of India was united under a Muslim sultanate based around Delhi from the 12th century until incorporated in the Mogul empire in the 16th century. Colonial intervention began in the late 17th century, particularly by the British; in 1765 the East India Company acquired the right to administer Bengal. In 1858, after the Indian Mutiny, the Crown took over the Company's authority, and in 1876 Queen Victoria was proclaimed Empress of India. Independence was won in 1947, at which time India was partitioned, Pakistan being created from mainly Muslim territories in the north-east (now Bangladesh) and the north-west. A member of the Commonwealth, India is the second most populous country in the world.

– ORIGIN via Latin from Greek *India*, from *Indos*, the name of the River Indus, from Persian *Hind*, from Sanskrit *sindhu* 'river', specifically 'the Indus', also 'the region around the Indus' (compare with **SINDHI**). Both the Greeks and the Persians extended the name to include all the country east of the Indus. Compare with **HINDI** and **HINDU**.

India ink ▶ noun North American term for **INDIAN INK**.

Indiaman ▶ noun (pl. **-men**) historical a ship engaged in trade with India or the East or West Indies, especially an East Indiaman.
– ORIGIN early 18th cent.: from **INDIA** + *-man* from **MAN-OF-WAR**.

Indian ▶ adjective **1** of or relating to India or to the

subcontinent comprising India, Pakistan, and Bangladesh.
2 of or relating to the indigenous peoples of America.
▶noun **1** a native or national of India, or a person of Indian descent.
2 an American Indian.
3 Brit. informal an Indian meal or restaurant.
– DERIVATIVES **Indianization** noun, **Indianize** (also **-ise**) verb, **Indianness** noun.

USAGE The native peoples of America came to be described as **Indian** as a result of Christopher Columbus and other voyagers in the 15th–16th centuries believing that, when they reached the east coast of America, they had reached part of India by a new route. The terms **Indian** and **Red Indian** are today regarded as old-fashioned and inappropriate, recalling, as they do, the stereotypical portraits of the Wild West. **American Indian**, however, is well established, although the preference where possible is to make reference to specific peoples, as **Apache**, **Delaware**, and so on. See also usage at **AMERICAN INDIAN** and **NATIVE AMERICAN**.

Indiana /ˌɪndɪˈanə/ a state in the Middle West of the US; pop. 5,544,160 (1990); capital, Indianapolis. It was colonized by the French in the 18th century and ceded to Britain in 1763. It passed to the US in 1783 and became the 19th state in 1816.
– DERIVATIVES **Indianan** noun & adjective.

Indianapolis /ˌɪndɪəˈnapəlɪs/ the state capital of Indiana; pop. 741,950 (1990). The city hosts an annual 500-mile (804.5-km) motor race, known as the Indy 500.

Indian bean tree ▶noun a North American catalpa which is widely planted in urban parks in Europe.
● *Catalpa bignonioides*, family Bignoniaceae.

Indian bison ▶noun another term for GAUR.

Indian club ▶noun each of a pair of bottle-shaped clubs swung to exercise the arms in gymnastics.

Indian cobra ▶noun another term for SPECTACLED COBRA.

Indian corn ▶noun another term for MAIZE.

Indian defence ▶noun [usu. with modifier] Chess a defence in which Black responds to White's advance of the queen's pawn by moving the king's knight to square *f6*, usually following with a fianchetto.

Indian elephant ▶noun the elephant of southern Asia, which is smaller than the African elephant, with smaller ears and only one lip to the trunk. It is often tamed as a beast of burden in India. Also called ASIAN ELEPHANT.
● *Elephas maximus*, family Elephantidae.

Indian file ▶noun another term for SINGLE FILE.

Indian hemp ▶noun see HEMP.

Indian ink (also N. Amer. **India ink**) ▶noun [mass noun] deep black ink containing dispersed carbon particles, used especially in drawing and technical graphics.
– ORIGIN mid 17th cent.: originally applied to Chinese and Japanese pigments prepared in solid blocks and imported to Europe via India.

Indianism ▶noun **1** [mass noun] devotion to or adoption of the customs and culture of North American Indians.
2 a word or idiom characteristic of Indian English or North American Indians.

Indian meal ▶noun [mass noun] N. Amer. meal ground from maize.

Indian Mutiny a revolt of Indians against British rule, 1857–8. Also called SEPOY MUTINY.

Discontent with British administration resulted in widespread mutinies in British garrison towns, with accompanying massacres of white soldiers and inhabitants. After a series of sieges (most notably that of Lucknow) and battles, the revolt was put down; it was followed by the institution of direct rule by the British Crown in place of the East India Company administration.

Indian National Congress a broad-based political party in India, founded in 1885 and the principal party in government since independence in 1947. Following splits in the party the Indian National Congress (I), formed by Indira Gandhi as a breakaway group, was confirmed in 1981 as the official Congress party.

Indian Ocean the ocean to the south of India,

extending from the east coast of Africa to the East Indies and Australia.

Indian paintbrush ▶noun see PAINTBRUSH (sense 2).

Indian pipe ▶noun a plant with a yellowish stem and a single drooping flower, native to North America and NE Asia. It lacks chlorophyll and obtains nourishment via symbiotic fungi in its roots.
● *Monotropa uniflora*, family Monotropaceae.

Indian poke ▶noun see POKE³ (sense 2).

Indian red ▶noun [mass noun] a red ferric oxide pigment made typically by roasting ferrous salts.

Indian rhinoceros ▶noun a large one-horned rhinoceros with prominent skin folds and a prehensile upper lip, found in NE India and Nepal.
● *Rhinoceros unicornis*, family Rhinocerotidae.

Indian rope-trick ▶noun the supposed feat, performed in the Indian subcontinent, of climbing an upright, unsupported length of rope.

Indian runner ▶noun a duck of a slender upright breed, typically with white or fawn plumage, kept for egg laying.

Indian shot ▶noun see CANNA.

Indian sign ▶noun dated a magic spell or curse.

Indian subcontinent the part of Asia south of the Himalayas which forms a peninsula extending into the Indian Ocean, between the Arabian Sea and the Bay of Bengal. Historically forming the whole territory of greater India, the region is now divided between India, Pakistan, and Bangladesh.

Indian summer ▶noun a period of unusually dry, warm weather occurring in late autumn.
■ a period of happiness or success occurring late in life.

Indian yellow ▶noun [mass noun] an orange-yellow pigment originally obtained from the urine of cows fed on mango leaves.

India paper ▶noun [mass noun] soft, absorbent paper, originally imported from China and used for proofs of engravings.
■ very thin, tough, opaque printing paper, used especially for Bibles.

India rubber ▶noun [mass noun] natural rubber.

India rubber tree ▶noun another term for RUBBER PLANT (in sense 2).

Indic /ˈɪndɪk/ ▶adjective relating to or denoting the group of Indo-European languages comprising Sanskrit and the modern Indian languages which are its descendants.
▶noun [mass noun] this language group.
– ORIGIN via Latin from Greek *Indikos*, from *India* (see INDIA).

indican /ˈɪndɪkan/ ▶noun [mass noun] Biochemistry a potassium salt present in urine, in which it occurs as a product of the metabolism of indole.
■ Alternative name: **potassium indoxylsulphate**; chem. formula $C_8H_6NOSO_2OH$.
– ORIGIN mid 19th cent.: from Latin *indicum* 'indigo' (because of its early use denoting an indoxyl glucoside occurring in the leaves of indigo plants) + -AN.

indicant ▶noun a thing which indicates something.
– ORIGIN early 17th cent.: from Latin *indicant-* 'pointing out', from the verb *indicare* (see INDICATE).

indicate [with obj.] ▶verb **1** point out; show: *dotted lines indicate the text's margins.*
■ be a sign or symptom of; strongly imply: *sales indicate a growing market for such art* | [with clause] *his tone indicated that he didn't hold out much hope.* ■ admit to or state briefly: *the president analysed his willingness to use force against the rebels.* ■ (of a person) direct attention to (someone or something) by means of a gesture: *he indicated Cindy with a brief nod of the head.* ■ (of a gauge or meter) register a reading of (a quantity, dimension, etc.). ■ [no obj.] chiefly Brit. (of a driver or motor vehicle) signal an intention to turn in a specified direction using an indicator.
2 (usu. **be indicated**) suggest as a desirable or necessary course of action: *the treatment is likely to be indicated in severely depressed patients.*
– ORIGIN early 17th cent.: from Latin *indicat-* 'pointed out', from the verb *indicare*, from *in-* 'towards' + *dicare* 'make known'.

indicated horsepower ▶noun [mass noun] the power produced in a reciprocating engine by the working of the cylinders.

indication ▶noun a sign or piece of information that indicates something: *the visit was an indication of the improvement in relations between the countries.*
■ a reading given by a gauge or meter. ■ a symptom that suggests certain medical treatment is necessary: *heavy bleeding is a common indication for hysterectomy.*

indicative /ɪnˈdɪkətɪv/ ▶adjective **1** serving as a sign or indication of something: *having recurrent dreams is not necessarily indicative of any psychological problem.*
2 Grammar denoting a mood of verbs expressing simple statement of a fact. Compare with SUBJUNCTIVE.
▶noun Grammar a verb in the indicative mood.
■ (the indicative) the indicative mood.
– DERIVATIVES **indicatively** adverb.

indicator ▶noun **1** a thing, especially a trend or fact, that indicates the state or level of something: *car ownership is frequently used as an indicator of affluence.*
2 a device providing specific information on the state or condition of something, in particular:
■ [usu. with modifier] a gauge or meter of a specified kind: *a speed indicator.* ■ Brit. a board or screen in a railway station, airport, etc. giving current information. ■ a flashing light or (formerly) other device on a vehicle to show that it is about to change lanes or turn.
3 Chemistry a compound which changes colour at a specific pH value or in the presence of a particular substance, and can be used to monitor acidity, alkalinity, or the progress of a reaction.
4 (also **indicator species**) an animal or plant species which can be used to infer conditions in a particular habitat.

indicator diagram ▶noun a diagram of the variation of pressure and volume within a cylinder of a reciprocating engine.

indicatory /ɪnˈdɪkət(ə)ri, ˌɪndɪˈkeɪt(ə)ri/ ▶adjective rare term for INDICATIVE.

indicatrix /ˌɪndɪˈkeɪtrɪks, ɪnˈdɪkətrɪks/ (also **optical indicatrix**) ▶noun (pl. **indicatrices** /-trɪsiːz/) Crystallography an imaginary ellipsoidal surface whose axes represent the refractive indices of a crystal for light following different directions with respect to the crystal axes.
– ORIGIN late 19th cent.: modern Latin, feminine of Latin *indicator* 'something that points out'.

indices plural form of INDEX.

indicia /ɪnˈdɪʃɪə, -sɪə/ ▶plural noun formal signs, indications, or distinguishing marks: *the indicia of predictive child abuse.*
– ORIGIN early 17th cent.: plural of Latin *indicium*, from *index, indic-* 'informer, sign'.

indicolite /ɪnˈdɪkəlʌɪt/ ▶noun [mass noun] an indigo-blue gem variety of tourmaline.
– ORIGIN early 19th cent.: from Latin *indicum* 'indigo' + -LITE.

indict /ɪnˈdʌɪt/ ▶verb [with obj.] (usu. **be indicted**) formally accuse or charge (someone) with a serious crime: *his former manager was indicted for fraud.*
– DERIVATIVES **indictee** noun, **indicter** noun.
– ORIGIN Middle English *endite*, *indite*, from Anglo-Norman French *enditer*, based on Latin *indicere* 'proclaim, appoint', from *in-* 'towards' + *dicere* 'pronounce, utter'.

indictable ▶adjective (of an offence) rendering the person who commits it liable to be charged with a serious crime that warrants a trial by jury.
■ (of a person) liable to be charged with a crime.

indiction /ɪnˈdɪkʃ(ə)n/ ▶noun historical a fiscal period of fifteen years used as a means of dating events and transactions in the Roman Empire and in the papal and some royal courts. The system was instituted by the Emperor Constantine in AD 313 and was used until the 16th century in some places.
■ [with numeral] a particular year in such a period.
– ORIGIN from Latin *indictio(n-)*, from the verb *indicere* (see INDICT).

indictment /ɪnˈdʌɪtm(ə)nt/ ▶noun **1** Law a formal charge or accusation of a serious crime: *an indictment for conspiracy.*
■ [mass noun] the action of indicting or being indicted: *the indictment of twelve people who had imported cocaine.*
2 a thing that serves to illustrate that a system or situation is bad and deserves to be condemned: *these rapidly escalating crime figures are an indictment of our society.*
– ORIGIN Middle English *enditement*, *inditement*, from

Anglo-Norman French *enditement*, from *enditer* (see **INDICT**).

indie informal ▶ **adjective** (of a pop group or record label) not belonging or affiliated to a major record company.
■ characteristic of the deliberately unpolished or uncommercialized style of such groups.
▶ **noun** a pop group or record label of this type.
■ an independent film company.
– ORIGIN 1920s (first used with reference to film production): abbreviation of **INDEPENDENT**.

Indies archaic another term for **EAST INDIES** (in sense 2).
– ORIGIN plural of *Indy*, an obsolete variant of **INDIA**.

indifference ▶ **noun** [mass noun] **1** lack of interest, concern, or sympathy: *she shrugged, feigning indifference.*
■ unimportance: *it cannot be regarded as a matter of indifference.*
2 mediocrity: *the indifference of Chelsea's midfield.*
– ORIGIN late Middle English (in the sense 'being neither good nor bad'): from Latin *indifferentia*, from *in-* 'not' + *different-* 'differing, deferring' (from the verb *differre*).

indifference curve ▶ **noun** Economics a curve on a graph (the axes of which represent quantities of two commodities) linking those combinations of quantities which the consumer regards as of equal value.

indifferent ▶ **adjective** **1** having no particular interest or sympathy; unconcerned: *she seemed indifferent rather than angry | most workers were* ***indifferent to*** *foreign affairs.*
2 neither good nor bad; mediocre: *attempts to distinguish between good, bad, and indifferent work.*
■ not especially good; fairly bad: *a pair of indifferent watercolours.*
– DERIVATIVES **indifferently** adverb.
– ORIGIN late Middle English (in the sense 'having no partiality for or against'): via Old French from Latin *indifferent-* 'not making any difference', from *in-* 'not' + *different-* 'differing' (see **DIFFERENT**).

indifferentism ▶ **noun** [mass noun] the belief that differences of religious belief are of no importance.
– DERIVATIVES **indifferentist** noun.

indigene /ˈɪndɪdʒiːn/ ▶ **noun** an indigenous person.
– ORIGIN late 16th cent.: from French *indigène*, from Latin *indigena*, from *indi-* (strengthened form of *in-* 'into') + an element related to *gignere* 'beget'.

indigenize /ɪnˈdɪdʒɪnʌɪz/ (also **-ise**) ▶ **verb** [with obj.] bring (something) under the control, dominance, or influence of native people: *English has been indigenized in different parts of the world.*
– DERIVATIVES **indigenization** noun.

indigenous ▶ **adjective** originating or occurring naturally in a particular place; native: *the indigenous peoples of Siberia | coriander is* ***indigenous to*** *southern Europe.*
– DERIVATIVES **indigenously** adverb, **indigenousness** noun.
– ORIGIN mid 17th cent.: from Latin *indigena* 'a native' (see **INDIGENE**) + **-OUS**.

indigent /ˈɪndɪdʒ(ə)nt/ ▶ **adjective** poor; needy.
▶ **noun** a needy person.
– DERIVATIVES **indigence** noun.
– ORIGIN late Middle English: via Old French from late Latin *indigent-* 'lacking', from the verb *indigere*, from *indi-* (strengthened form of *in-* 'into') + *egere* 'to need'.

indigested ▶ **adjective** archaic term for **UNDIGESTED**.

indigestible ▶ **adjective** (of food) difficult or impossible to digest.
■ figurative too complex or awkward to read or understand easily: *a turgid and indigestible book.*
– DERIVATIVES **indigestibility** noun, **indigestibly** adverb.
– ORIGIN late 15th cent.: via French from late Latin *indigestibilis*, from *in-* 'not' + *digestibilis* (see **DIGESTIBLE**).

indigestion ▶ **noun** [mass noun] pain or discomfort in the stomach associated with difficulty in digesting food.
– DERIVATIVES **indigestive** adjective.
– ORIGIN late Middle English: from late Latin *indigestio(n-)*, from *in-* (expressing negation) + *digestio* (see **DIGESTION**).

Indigirka /ˌɪndɪˈgɪəkə/ a river of far eastern Siberia, which flows northwards for 1,779 km (1,112 miles) to the Arctic Ocean, where it forms a wide delta.

indignant ▶ **adjective** feeling or showing anger or annoyance at what is perceived as unfair treatment: *he was indignant at being the object of suspicion.*
– DERIVATIVES **indignantly** adverb.
– ORIGIN late 16th cent.: from Latin *indignant-* 'regarding as unworthy', from the verb *indignari*, from *in-* 'not' + *dignus* 'worthy'.

indignation ▶ **noun** [mass noun] anger or annoyance provoked by what is perceived as unfair treatment: *the letter filled Lucy with indignation.*
– ORIGIN late Middle English (also in the sense 'disdain, contempt'): from Latin *indignatio(n-)*, from *indignari* 'regard as unworthy'.

indignity ▶ **noun** (pl. **-ies**) [mass noun] treatment or circumstances that cause one to feel shame or to lose one's dignity: *the indignity of needing financial help* | [count noun] *he was subjected to all manner of indignities.*
– ORIGIN late 16th cent.: from French *indignité* or Latin *indignitas*, from *indignari* 'regard as unworthy'.

indigo /ˈɪndɪgəʊ/ ▶ **noun** (pl. **-os** or **-oes**) **1** a tropical plant of the pea family, which was formerly widely cultivated as a source of dark blue dye.
• Genus *Indigofera*, family Leguminosae: several species, in particular *I. tinctoria*.
2 [mass noun] the dark blue dye obtained from this plant.
■ a colour between blue and violet in the spectrum: [as modifier] *he dived into the indigo water.*
– ORIGIN mid 16th cent.: from Portuguese *índigo*, via Latin from Greek *indikon*, from *indikos* 'Indian (dye)' (see **INDIC**).

indigobird (also **indigo finch**) ▶ **noun** an African weaver related to the whydahs, the male having black plumage with blue or purple iridescence.
• Genus *Vidua*, family Ploceidae: four species.

indigoid /ˈɪndɪgɔɪd/ ▶ **adjective** (of a dye) related to indigotin in molecular structure.

indigo snake ▶ **noun** a large harmless American snake that typically has bluish-black skin which may be patterned. Also called **CRIBO**.
• *Drymarchon corais*, family Colubridae. Alternative name: **blue gopher snake**.

indigotin /ɪnˈdɪgətɪn, ˌɪndɪˈgəʊtɪn/ ▶ **noun** [mass noun] Chemistry a dark blue crystalline compound which is the main constituent of the dye indigo.
• Chem. formula: $(C_8H_6NO)_2$.
– ORIGIN mid 19th cent.: from **INDIGO** + *-t-* (for ease of pronunciation) + **-IN**[1].

Indio /ˈɪndɪəʊ/ ▶ **noun** (pl. **-os**) a member of any of the indigenous peoples of America or east Asia in areas formerly subject to Spain or Portugal.
– ORIGIN mid 19th cent.: from Spanish and Portuguese, literally 'Indian'.

Indira Gandhi Canal /ɪnˌdɪərə, ˌɪndərə/ a massive canal in NW India, bringing water to the Thar Desert of Rajasthan from the Harike Barrage on the Sutlej River. The canal, which is 650 km (406 miles) long, was completed in 1986. Former name **RAJASTHAN CANAL**.

indirect ▶ **adjective** **1** not directly caused by or resulting from something: *full employment would have an indirect effect on wage levels.*
■ not done directly; conducted through intermediaries: *local government under the indirect control of the British.* ■ (of costs) deriving from overhead charges or subsidiary work. ■ (of taxation) levied on goods and services rather than income or profits.
2 (of a route) not straight; not following the shortest way.
■ (of lighting) from a concealed source and diffusely reflected. ■ Soccer denoting a free kick from which a goal may not be scored directly.
3 avoiding direct mention or exposition of a subject: *an indirect attack on the Archbishop.*
– DERIVATIVES **indirectly** adverb, **indirectness** noun.
– ORIGIN late Middle English (in the sense 'not in full grammatical concord'): from medieval Latin *indirectus*, from *in-* 'not' + *directus* (see **DIRECT**).

indirection ▶ **noun** [mass noun] indirectness or lack of straightforwardness in action, speech, or progression: *his love of intrigue and sly indirection.*
– ORIGIN late 16th cent.: from **INDIRECT**, on the pattern of *direction*.

indirect object ▶ **noun** Grammar a noun phrase referring to someone or something that is affected by the action of a transitive verb (typically as a recipient), but is not the primary object (e.g. *him* in *give him the book*). Compare with **DIRECT OBJECT**.

indirect question ▶ **noun** Grammar a question in reported speech (e.g. *they asked who I was*).

indirect rule ▶ **noun** [mass noun] a system of government of one nation by another in which the governed people retain certain administrative, legal, and other powers.

indirect speech ▶ **noun** another term for **REPORTED SPEECH**.

indiscernible /ˌɪndɪˈsəːnɪb(ə)l/ ▶ **adjective** impossible to see or clearly distinguish.
– DERIVATIVES **indiscernibility** noun, **indiscernibly** adverb.

indiscipline ▶ **noun** [mass noun] lack of discipline.

indiscreet ▶ **adjective** having, showing, or proceeding from too great a readiness to reveal things that should remain secret or private.
– DERIVATIVES **indiscreetly** adverb.
– ORIGIN late Middle English (originally as *indiscrete* in the sense 'lacking discernment or judgement'): from late Latin *indiscretus* 'not separate or distinguishable' (in medieval Latin 'careless, indiscreet'), from *in-* 'not' + *discretus* 'separate' (see **DISCREET**). Compare with **INDISCRETE**.

indiscrete ▶ **adjective** rare not divided into distinct parts.
– ORIGIN early 17th cent. (in the sense 'not separate or distinguishable'; originally as *indiscreet*): from Latin *indiscretus*, from *in-* 'not' + *discretus* 'separate' (see **DISCREET**). Compare with **INDISCREET**.

indiscretion ▶ **noun** [mass noun] behaviour or speech that is indiscreet or displays a lack of good judgement: *he knew himself all too prone to indiscretion* | [count noun] *sexual indiscretions.*
– ORIGIN Middle English: from late Latin *indiscretio(n-)*, from *in-* (expressing negation) + *discretio* 'separation' (in late Latin 'discernment'), from *discernere* 'separate out, discern'.

indiscriminate /ˌɪndɪˈskrɪmɪnət/ ▶ **adjective** done at random or without careful judgement: *terrorist gunmen engaged in indiscriminate killing.*
■ (of a person) not using or exercising discrimination: *she was indiscriminate with her affections.*
– DERIVATIVES **indiscriminately** adverb, **indiscriminateness** noun, **indiscrimination** noun.
– ORIGIN late 16th cent. (in the sense 'haphazard, not selective'): from **IN-**[1] 'not' + Latin *discriminatus*, past participle of *discriminare* (see **DISCRIMINATE**).

indiscriminating ▶ **adjective** making no distinctions; indiscriminate.

indispensable ▶ **adjective** absolutely necessary: *he made himself* ***indispensable to*** *the parish priest.*
– DERIVATIVES **indispensability** noun, **indispensableness** noun, **indispensably** adverb.
– ORIGIN mid 16th cent. (in the sense 'not to be allowed or provided for by ecclesiastical dispensation'): from medieval Latin *indispensabilis*, from *in-* 'not' + *dispensabilis* (see **DISPENSABLE**).

indispose ▶ **verb** [with obj.] archaic **1** make (someone) unfit for or unable to do something.
2 make (someone) averse to something: *the miseries of the revolution had totally indisposed the people towards any interference with politics.*

indisposed ▶ **adjective** **1** slightly unwell: *my mother is indisposed.*
2 averse; unwilling: *the potential audience seemed* ***indisposed to*** *attend.*
– DERIVATIVES **indisposition** noun.
– ORIGIN late Middle English: from **IN-**[1] 'not' + **DISPOSED**, or past participle of *indispose* 'make unwell or unwilling'.

indisputable ▶ **adjective** unable to be challenged or denied: *a far from indisputable fact.*
– DERIVATIVES **indisputability** noun, **indisputably** adverb.
– ORIGIN mid 16th cent.: from late Latin *indisputabilis*, from *in-* 'not' + *disputabilis* (see **DISPUTABLE**).

indissociable ▶ **adjective** unable to be dissociated.

indissoluble /ˌɪndɪˈsɒljʊb(ə)l/ ▶ **adjective** unable to be destroyed; lasting: *an indissoluble friendship.*
– DERIVATIVES **indissolubility** noun, **indissolubly** adverb.
– ORIGIN late 15th cent.: from Latin *indissolubilis*, from *in-* 'not' + *dissolubilis* (see **DISSOLUBLE**).

indistinct ▶ adjective not clear or sharply defined: *his speech was slurred and indistinct.*
– DERIVATIVES **indistinctly** adverb, **indistinctness** noun.
– ORIGIN mid 16th cent.: from Latin *indistinctus*, from *in-* 'not' + *distinctus* 'separated, distinguished' (see **DISTINCT**).

indistinguishable ▶ adjective not able to be identified as different or distinct: *the counterfeit bills were virtually indistinguishable from the real thing.*
– DERIVATIVES **indistinguishably** adverb.

indite /ɪnˈdʌɪt/ ▶ verb [with obj.] archaic write; compose: *he indites the wondrous tale of Our Lord.*
– ORIGIN Middle English *endite*, from Old French *enditier*, based on Latin *indicere* (see **INDICT**).

indium /ˈɪndɪəm/ ▶ noun [mass noun] the chemical element of atomic number 49, a soft, silvery-white metal occurring naturally in association with zinc and some other metals. (Symbol: **In**)
– ORIGIN mid 19th cent.: from **INDIGO** (because there are two characteristic indigo lines in its spectrum) + **-IUM**.

individual ▶ adjective 1 [attrib.] single; separate: *individual tiny flowers.*
2 of or for a particular person: *the individual needs of the children.*
■designed for use by one person: *individual serving dishes.* ■ characteristic of a particular person or thing: *individual traits of style.* ■ having a striking or unusual character; original: *she creates her own, highly individual, landscapes.*
▶ noun a single human being as distinct from a group, class, or family: *boat trips for parties and individuals.*
■a single member of a class: *they live in a group or as individuals, depending on the species.* ■ [with adj.] informal a person of a specified kind: *the most selfish, egotistical individual I have ever met.* ■ a distinctive or original person.
– ORIGIN late Middle English (in the sense 'indivisible'): from medieval Latin *individualis*, from Latin *individuus*, from *in-* 'not' + *dividuus* 'divisible' (from *dividere* 'to divide').

individualism ▶ noun [mass noun] 1 the habit or principle of being independent and self-reliant.
■self-centred feeling or conduct; egoism.
2 a social theory favouring freedom of action for individuals over collective or state control.
– DERIVATIVES **individualist** noun & adjective, **individualistic** adjective, **individualistically** adverb.

individuality ▶ noun [mass noun] 1 the quality or character of a particular person or thing that distinguishes them from others of the same kind, especially when strongly marked: *clothes with real style and individuality.*
■(**individualities**) individual characteristics.
2 separate existence: *anything but individuality, anything but aloneness.*
– ORIGIN early 17th cent.: in early use from medieval Latin *individualitas.*

individualize (also **-ise**) ▶ verb [with obj.] give an individual character to: *have your shirt individualized with your own club name.*
■[usu. as adj. **individualized**] tailor (something) to suit the individual: *an individualized learning programme.*
– DERIVATIVES **individualization** noun.

individually ▶ adverb 1 one by one; singly; separately: *individually wrapped cheeses.*
■in a distinctive manner: *Dublin people dress more individually than people in London.*
2 personally; in an individual capacity: *partnerships and individually owned firms.*

individuate ▶ verb [with obj.] distinguish from others of the same kind; single out: *it is easy to individuate and enumerate the significant elements.*
– DERIVATIVES **individuation** noun.
– ORIGIN early 17th cent.: from medieval Latin *individuat-* 'singled out', from the verb *individuare*, from Latin *individuus*, from *in-* 'into' + *dividuus* 'divisible' (from *dividere* 'to divide').

indivisible ▶ adjective unable to be divided or separated: *privilege was indivisible from responsibility.*
■(of a number) unable to be divided by another number exactly without leaving a remainder.
– DERIVATIVES **indivisibility** noun, **indivisibly** adverb.
– ORIGIN late Middle English: from late Latin *indivisibilis*, from *in-* 'not' + *divisibilis* (see **DIVISIBLE**).

Indo- /ˈɪndəʊ/ ▶ combining form (used commonly in linguistic and ethnological terms) Indian; Indian and …: *Indo-Iranian.*
■relating to India.

– ORIGIN from Latin *Indus*, from Greek *Indos* 'Indian'.

Indo-Aryan ▶ adjective 1 relating to or denoting an Indo-European people who invaded NW India in the 2nd millennium BC. See **ARYAN**.
2 another term for **INDIC**.

Indo-China the peninsula of SE Asia containing Burma (Myanmar), Thailand, Malaya, Laos, Cambodia, and Vietnam; especially, the part of this area consisting of Laos, Cambodia, and Vietnam, which was a French dependency (**French Indo-China**) from 1862 to 1954.
– DERIVATIVES **Indo-Chinese** adjective & noun.

indochinite /ˌɪndəʊˈtʃʌɪnʌɪt/ ▶ noun Geology a tektite from the strewn field in Indo-China.
– ORIGIN 1940s: from **INDO-CHINA** + **-ITE**[1].

indocile ▶ adjective difficult to teach or discipline; not submissive.
– DERIVATIVES **indocility** noun.
– ORIGIN early 17th cent.: from French, or from Latin *indocilis*, from *in-* 'not' + *docilis* (see **DOCILE**).

indoctrinate /ɪnˈdɒktrɪneɪt/ ▶ verb [with obj.] teach (a person or group) to accept a set of beliefs uncritically: *broadcasting was a vehicle for indoctrinating the masses.*
■archaic teach or instruct (someone): *he indoctrinated them in systematic theology.*
– DERIVATIVES **indoctrination** noun, **indoctrinator** noun, **indoctrinatory** adjective.
– ORIGIN early 17th cent.: formerly also as *endoctrinate*): from **EN-**[1], **IN-**[2] 'into' + **DOCTRINE** + **-ATE**[3], or from obsolete *indoctrine* (verb), from French *endoctriner*, based on *doctrine* 'doctrine'.

Indo-European ▶ adjective of or relating to the family of languages spoken over the greater part of Europe and Asia as far as northern India.
■another term for **PROTO-INDO-EUROPEAN**.

The Indo-European languages have a history of over 3,000 years. Their unattested, reconstructed ancestor, Proto-Indo-European, is believed to have been spoken well before 4000 BC in a region somewhere to the north or south of the Black Sea. The family comprises twelve branches: Indic (including Sanskrit and its descendants), Iranian, Anatolian (including Hittite and other extinct languages), Armenian, Hellenic (Greek), Albanian (or Illyrian), Italic (including Latin and the Romance languages), Celtic, Tocharian (an extinct group from central Asia), Germanic (including English, German, Dutch, and the Scandinavian languages), Baltic, and Slavic (including Russian, Czech, Bulgarian, and Serbo-Croat).

▶ noun 1 [mass noun] the ancestral Proto-Indo-European language.
■the Indo-European family of languages.
2 a speaker of an Indo-European language, especially Proto-Indo-European.

Indo-Germanic ▶ adjective & noun former term for **INDO-EUROPEAN**.

Indo-Iranian ▶ adjective relating to or denoting a subfamily of Indo-European languages spoken in northern India and Iran.
▶ noun [mass noun] the Indo-Iranian subfamily of languages, divided into the Indic group and the Iranian group. Also called **ARYAN**.

indole /ˈɪndəʊl/ ▶ noun [mass noun] Chemistry a crystalline organic compound with an unpleasant odour, present in coal tar and in faeces.
● A heteroaromatic compound with fused benzene and pyrrole rings; chem. formula: C_8H_7N.
– ORIGIN mid 19th cent.: blend of **INDIGO** (because obtained artificially from indigo blue) and Latin *oleum* 'oil'.

indoleacetic acid /ˌɪndəʊləˈsiːtɪk, -ˈsɛtɪk/ ▶ noun [mass noun] Biochemistry a compound which is an acetic acid derivative of indole, especially one found as a natural growth hormone (auxin) in plants.
● Chem. formula: $C_8H_6(CH_3COOH)N$; seven isomers; auxin is **indole-3-acetic acid**.

indolent /ˈɪnd(ə)l(ə)nt/ ▶ adjective 1 wanting to avoid activity or exertion; lazy.
2 Medicine (of a disease condition) causing little or no pain.
■(especially of an ulcer) slow to develop, progress, or heal; persistent.
– DERIVATIVES **indolence** noun, **indolently** adverb.
– ORIGIN mid 17th cent.: from late Latin *indolent-*, from *in-* 'not' + *dolere* 'suffer or give pain'. The sense 'idle' arose in the early 18th cent.

Indology /ɪnˈdɒlədʒi/ ▶ noun [mass noun] the study of Indian history, literature, philosophy, and culture.
– DERIVATIVES **Indologist** noun.

Indo-Malaysian (also **Indo-Malayan**) ▶ adjective of or relating to both India and Malaya, in particular:

■denoting an ethnological region comprising Sri Lanka, the Malay peninsula, and the Malaysian islands. ■ (also **Indo-Malesian**) Biology denoting a major biogeographical region comprising the Indian subcontinent, Malesia, and East and SE Asia.

indomethacin /ˌɪndəʊˈmɛθəsɪn/ ▶ noun [mass noun] Medicine a compound with anti-inflammatory, antipyretic, and analgesic properties, used chiefly to treat rheumatoid arthritis and gout.
● Chem. formula: $C_{19}H_{16}NO_4Cl$.
– ORIGIN 1960s: from *indo(le)* + *meth(yl)* + *ac(etic)* + **-IN**[1].

indomitable /ɪnˈdɒmɪtəb(ə)l/ ▶ adjective impossible to subdue or defeat: *a woman of indomitable spirit.*
– DERIVATIVES **indomitability** noun, **indomitableness** noun, **indomitably** adverb.
– ORIGIN mid 17th cent. (in the sense 'untameable'): from late Latin *indomitabilis*, from *in-* 'not' + Latin *domitare* 'to tame'.

Indonesia /ˌɪndəˈniːzɪə, -ˈniːʒə, -ˈniːʃə/ a SE Asian country consisting of many islands in the Malay Archipelago; pop. 184,300,000 (est. 1990); languages, Indonesian (official), Malay, Balinese, Chinese, Javanese, and others; capital, Djakarta (on Java). Former name (until 1949) **DUTCH EAST INDIES**.

Indonesia consists of the territories of the former Dutch East Indies, of which the largest are Java, Sumatra, southern Borneo, western New Guinea, the Moluccas, and Sulawesi. The Dutch established control over the area in the 17th century. Independence was won in 1949, although Irian Jaya was not handed over until 1963; East Timor was annexed in 1976. An attempted communist coup was crushed by the army in 1965; General Suharto (b.1921) was President 1967–98.

– ORIGIN from **INDO-** + Greek *nēsos* 'island'.

Indonesian ▶ adjective of or relating to Indonesia, Indonesians, or their languages.
▶ noun 1 a native or national of Indonesia, or a person of Indonesian descent.
2 [mass noun] the group of Austronesian languages, closely related to Malay, which are spoken in Indonesia and neighbouring islands.
■another term for **BAHASA INDONESIA**.

indoor ▶ adjective [attrib.] situated, conducted, or used within a building or under cover: *indoor sports.*
■of or relating to sports played indoors: *the national indoor champion.*
– ORIGIN early 18th cent. (superseding earlier *within-door*): from **IN** (as a preposition) + **DOOR**. Compare with **INDOORS**.

indoors ▶ adverb into or within a building: *they went indoors and explored the house.*
▶ noun the area or space inside a building: *the rain makes indoors feel so warm and safe.*
– ORIGIN late 18th cent. (superseding earlier *within doors*): from **INDOOR**.

Indo-Pacific ▶ adjective of or relating to the Indian Ocean and the adjacent parts of the Pacific.
■another term for **AUSTRONESIAN**.
▶ noun [mass noun] the Indo-Pacific seas or ocean.

Indore /ɪnˈdɔː/ a manufacturing city of Madhya Pradesh in central India; pop. 1,087,000 (1991).

indorse ▶ verb US spelling of **ENDORSE**.

indorsement ▶ noun chiefly US variant spelling of **ENDORSEMENT**.

indoxyl /ɪnˈdɒksʌɪl, -sɪl/ ▶ noun [as modifier] Chemistry of or denoting the radical —ONC_8H_6—, derived from a hydroxy derivative of indole and present in indigotin.

Indra /ˈɪndrə/ Hinduism the warrior king of the heavens, god of war and storm, to whom many of the prayers in the Rig Veda are addressed.

indraught /ˈɪndrɑːft/ (US **indraft**) ▶ noun [mass noun] the drawing in of something.
■[count noun] an inward flow or current, especially of air.

indrawn ▶ adjective 1 [attrib.] (of breath) taken in.
2 (of a person) shy and introspective.

indri /ˈɪndri/ ▶ noun (pl. **indris**) a large, short-tailed Madagascan lemur which jumps from tree to tree in an upright position and rarely comes to the ground.
● *Indri indri*, family Indriidae.
– ORIGIN mid 19th cent.: from Malagasy *indry!* 'behold!' or *indry izy!* 'there he is!', mistaken for its name. The Malagasy name is *babakoto.*

indubitable /ɪnˈdjuːbɪtəb(ə)l/ ▶ adjective impossible to doubt; unquestionable: *an indubitable truth.*
– DERIVATIVES **indubitably** adverb [sentence adverb] *indubitably, liberalism parades under many guises.*

– ORIGIN late Middle English: from Latin *indubitabilis*, from *in-* 'not' + *dubitabilis* (see **DUBITABLE**).

induce /ɪnˈdjuːs/ ▶ **verb** [with obj.] **1** [with obj. and infinitive] succeed in persuading or influencing (someone) to do something: *the pickets induced many workers to stay away.*
2 bring about or give rise to: *none of these measures induced a change of policy.*
■ produce (an electric charge or current or a magnetic state) by induction. ■ [usu. as adj. **induced**] Physics cause (radioactivity) by bombardment with radiation.
3 Medicine bring on (childbirth or abortion) artificially, typically by the use of drugs.
■ bring on childbirth in (a pregnant woman) in this way. ■ bring on the birth of (a baby) in this way.
4 Logic derive by inductive reasoning.
– DERIVATIVES **inducer** noun, **inducible** adjective.
– ORIGIN late Middle English (formerly also as *enduce*): from Latin *inducere* 'lead in', from *in-* 'into' + *ducere* 'to lead', or from French *enduire*. Compare with **ENDUE**.

induced drag ▶ **noun** [mass noun] Aeronautics that part of the drag on an aerofoil which arises from the development of lift.

inducement ▶ **noun** a thing that persuades or influences someone to do something: *companies were prepared to build only in return for massive inducements* | [mass noun] [with infinitive] *there is no inducement to wait for payment.*
■ a bribe.

induct /ɪnˈdʌkt/ ▶ **verb** [with obj.] **1** admit (someone) formally to a post or organization: *new junior ministers were* **inducted into** *the government.*
■ formally introduce (a member of the clergy) into possession of a benefice. ■ US enlist (someone) for military service. ■ (**induct someone in/into**) introduce someone to (a difficult or obscure subject): *my master inducted me into the skills of magic.*
2 archaic install in a seat or room.
– DERIVATIVES **inductee** noun.
– ORIGIN late Middle English: from Latin *induct-* 'led into', from the verb *inducere* (see **INDUCE**).

inductance ▶ **noun** Physics the property of an electric conductor or circuit that causes an electromotive force to be generated by a change in the current flowing: [mass noun] *the inductance of the winding* | [count noun] *an inductance of 40 mH.*
■ [count noun] a component with this property.
– ORIGIN late 19th cent.: from **INDUCTION** + **-ANCE**.

induction ▶ **noun** [mass noun] **1** the action or process of inducting someone to a post or organization: **induction into** *membership of a masonic brotherhood.*
■ [usu. as modifier] a formal introduction to a new job or position: *an induction course.* ■ US enlistment into military service.
2 the process or action of bringing about or giving rise to something: *isolation, starvation, and other forms of stress induction.*
■ Medicine the process of bringing on childbirth or abortion by artificial means, typically by the use of drugs.
3 Logic the inference of a general law from particular instances. Often contrasted with **DEDUCTION**.
■ (**induction of**) the production of (facts) to prove a general statement. ■ (also **mathematical induction**) Mathematics a means of proving a theorem by showing that if it is true of any particular case it is true of the next case in a series, and then showing that it is indeed true in one particular case.
4 the production of an electric or magnetic state by the proximity (without contact) of an electrified or magnetized body. See also **MAGNETIC INDUCTION**.
■ the production of an electric current in a conductor by varying the magnetic field applied to the conductor.
5 the stage of the working cycle of an internal-combustion engine in which the fuel mixture is drawn into the cylinders.
– ORIGIN late Middle English: from Latin *inductio(n-)*, from the verb *inducere* 'lead into' (see **INDUCE**).

induction coil ▶ **noun** a coil for generating intermittent high voltage from a direct current.

induction hardening ▶ **noun** [mass noun] Metallurgy a process for hardening steel surfaces by induction heating followed by quenching.

induction heating ▶ **noun** [mass noun] heating of a material by inducing an electric current within it.

induction loop ▶ **noun** a sound system in which a loop of wire around an area in a building, such as a cinema or theatre, produces an electromagnetic signal received directly by hearing aids used by the partially deaf.

inductive ▶ **adjective** **1** characterized by the inference of general laws from particular instances: *instinct rather than inductive reasoning marked her approach to life.*
2 of, relating to, or caused by electric or magnetic induction.
■ possessing inductance.
– DERIVATIVES **inductively** adverb, **inductiveness** noun.
– ORIGIN late Middle English (in the sense 'leading to'): from Old French *inductif, -ive* or late Latin *inductivus* 'hypothetical' (later 'inducing, leading to'), from Latin *inducere* (see **INDUCE**). Sense 1 dates from the mid 18th cent.

inductivism ▶ **noun** [mass noun] the use of or preference for inductive methods of reasoning, especially in science.
– DERIVATIVES **inductivist** noun & adjective.

inductor ▶ **noun** **1** a component in an electric or electronic circuit which possesses inductance.
2 a substance that promotes an equilibrium reaction by reacting with one of the substances produced.
– ORIGIN mid 17th cent. (in the sense 'a person who inducts or initiates'): from late Latin, from Latin *inducere* (see **INDUCE**), or from **INDUCT** + **-OR**[1]. Current senses date from the early 20th cent.

indue ▶ **verb** variant spelling of **ENDUE**.

indulge ▶ **verb** [no obj.] (**indulge in**) allow oneself to enjoy the pleasure of: *we indulged in a cream tea.*
■ become involved in (an activity, typically one that is undesirable or disapproved of): *I don't indulge in idle gossip.* ■ informal allow oneself to enjoy a particular pleasure, especially that of alcohol: *I only indulge on special occasions.* ■ [with obj.] satisfy or yield freely to (a desire or interest): *she was able to indulge a growing passion for literature.* ■ [with obj.] allow (someone) to enjoy a desired pleasure: *I spent time indulging myself with secret feasts.*
– DERIVATIVES **indulger** noun.
– ORIGIN early 17th cent. (in the sense 'treat with excessive kindness'): from Latin *indulgere* 'give free rein to'.

indulgence ▶ **noun** **1** [mass noun] the action or fact of indulging: *indulgence in self-pity.*
■ the state or attitude of being indulgent or tolerant: *she regarded his affairs with a casual, slightly amused indulgence.* ■ [count noun] a thing that is indulged in; a luxury: *Claire collects shoes—it is her indulgence.*
2 chiefly historical (in the Roman Catholic Church) a grant by the Pope of remission of the temporal punishment in purgatory still due for sins after absolution. The unrestricted sale of indulgences by pardoners was a widespread abuse during the later Middle Ages.
3 an extension of the time in which a bill or debt has to be paid.
– ORIGIN late Middle English: via Old French from Latin *indulgentia*, from the verb *indulgere* (see **INDULGE**).

indulgent ▶ **adjective** having or indicating a readiness or over-readiness to be generous to or lenient with someone: *indulgent parents.*
■ self-indulgent: *a slightly adolescent, indulgent account of a love affair.*
– DERIVATIVES **indulgently** adverb.
– ORIGIN early 16th cent.: from French, or from Latin *indulgent-* 'giving free rein to', from the verb *indulgere.*

induline /ˈɪndjʊliːn/ ▶ **noun** any of a group of insoluble blue azine dyes.
– ORIGIN late 19th cent.: from *indo-* (denoting indigo) + **-ULE** + **-INE**[4].

indult /ɪnˈdʌlt/ ▶ **noun** (in the Roman Catholic Church) a licence granted by the Pope authorizing an act that the common law of the Church does not sanction.
– ORIGIN late 15th cent.: from French, from late Latin *indultum* 'grant, concession', neuter past participle of Latin *indulgere* 'indulge'.

indumentum /ˌɪndjʊˈmɛntəm/ ▶ **noun** (pl. **indumenta**) Botany & Zoology a covering of hairs (or feathers) on an animal or plant.
– ORIGIN mid 19th cent.: from Latin, literally 'garment', from *induere* 'put on, don'.

induna /ɪnˈduːnə/ ▶ **noun** S. African a tribal councillor or headman.
■ an African foreman. ■ a person in authority; a leader in a particular field.
– ORIGIN Xhosa and Zulu, from the nominal prefix *in-* + *duna* 'captain, councillor'.

Indurain /ˈɪndjʊraɪn/, Miguel (b.1964), Spanish cyclist, the first person to win the Tour de France five consecutive times, from 1991 onwards.

indurate /ˈɪndjʊreɪt/ ▶ **verb** [with obj.] [usu. as adj. **indurated**] harden: *a bed of indurated clay.*
– DERIVATIVES **induration** noun, **indurative** adjective.
– ORIGIN mid 16th cent.: from Latin *indurat-* 'made hard', from the verb *indurare* (based on *durus* 'hard').

Indus[1] /ˈɪndəs/ a river of southern Asia, about 2,900 km (1,800 miles) in length, flowing from Tibet through Kashmir and Pakistan to the Arabian Sea. Along its valley an early civilization flourished from *c.*2600 to 1760 BC, whose economic wealth was derived from well-attested sea and land trade with the rest of the Indian subcontinent.

Indus[2] /ˈɪndəs/ Astronomy an inconspicuous southern constellation (the Indian), between Capricornus and Pavo.
■ [as genitive **Indi** /ˈɪndʌɪ/] used with preceding letter or numeral to designate a star in this constellation: *the star Alpha Indi.*
– ORIGIN Latin.

indusium /ɪnˈdjuːzɪəm/ ▶ **noun** (pl. **indusia**) chiefly Botany a thin membranous covering, especially a shield covering a sorus on a fern frond.
– ORIGIN early 18th cent.: from Latin, literally 'tunic', from *induere* 'put on, don'.

industrial ▶ **adjective** of, relating to, or characterized by industry: *a small industrial town.*
■ having highly developed industries: *the major industrial nations.* ■ designed or suitable for use in industry: *industrial heating oil.* ■ (of a disease or injury) contracted or sustained in the course of employment, especially in a factory. ■ relating to or denoting a type of harsh, uncompromising rock music incorporating sounds resembling those produced by industrial machinery.
▶ **noun** (**industrials**) shares in industrial companies.
– DERIVATIVES **industrially** adverb.
– ORIGIN late 15th cent.: from **INDUSTRY** + **-AL**; in later use influenced by French *industriel.*

industrial action ▶ **noun** [mass noun] Brit. action taken by employees of a company as a protest, especially striking or working to rule.

industrial archaeology ▶ **noun** [mass noun] the study of equipment and buildings formerly used in industry.

industrial democracy ▶ **noun** [mass noun] the involvement of employees in the running of an industry, factory, company, etc.

industrial diamond ▶ **noun** a small diamond, not of gem quality, used in abrasives and in cutting and drilling tools.

industrial dispute ▶ **noun** a dispute between employers and employees.

industrial espionage ▶ **noun** [mass noun] spying directed towards discovering the secrets of a rival manufacturer or other industrial company.

industrial estate ▶ **noun** chiefly Brit. an area of land developed as a site for factories and other industrial businesses.

industrialism ▶ **noun** [mass noun] a social or economic system in which manufacturing industries are prevalent.

industrialist ▶ **noun** a person involved in the ownership and management of industry.

industrialize (also **-ise**) ▶ **verb** [with obj.] [often as adj. **industrialized**] develop industries in (a country or region) on a wide scale: *the industrialized nations.*
■ [no obj.] (of a country or region) build up a system of industries.
– DERIVATIVES **industrialization** noun.

industrial melanism ▶ **noun** [mass noun] Zoology the prevalence of dark-coloured varieties of animals (especially moths) in industrial areas where they are better camouflaged against predators than paler forms.

industrial park ▶ **noun** North American term for **INDUSTRIAL ESTATE**.

industrial relations ▶ **plural noun** the relations between management and workers in industry.

i

Industrial Revolution the rapid development of industry that occurred in Britain in the late 18th and 19th centuries, brought about by the introduction of machinery. It was characterized by the use of steam power, the growth of factories, and the mass production of manufactured goods.

industrial-strength ▸ adjective very strong or powerful: *an industrial-strength cleaner.*

Industrial Workers of the World (abbrev.: **IWW**) a radical US labour movement, founded in 1905 and, as part of the syndicalist movement, dedicated to the overthrow of capitalism. Its popularity declined after the First World War and by 1925 its membership was insignificant. Also called the **WOBBLIES**.

industrious ▸ adjective diligent and hard-working.
– DERIVATIVES **industriously** adverb, **industriousness** noun.
– ORIGIN late 15th cent. (in the sense 'skilful, clever, ingenious'): from French *industrieux* or late Latin *industriosus*, from Latin *industria* 'diligence'.

industry ▸ noun (pl. **-ies**) **1** [mass noun] economic activity concerned with the processing of raw materials and manufacture of goods in factories: *new investment incentives for British industry.*
■ [count noun] [with adj. or noun modifier] a particular form or branch of economic or commercial activity: *the car industry* | *the tourist industry.* ■ [count noun] [with adj. or noun modifier] informal an activity or domain in which a great deal of time or effort is expended: *the Shakespeare industry.*
2 [mass noun] hard work: *the kitchen became a hive of industry.*
– ORIGIN late Middle English (in sense 2): from French *industrie* or Latin *industria* 'diligence'.

indwell ▸ verb (past and past participle **indwelt**) **1** [with obj.] be permanently present in (someone's soul or mind); possess spiritually.
2 [as adj. **indwelling**] Medicine (of a catheter, needle, etc.) fixed in a person's body for a long period of time.
– DERIVATIVES **indweller** noun.
– ORIGIN late Middle English: originally translating Latin *inhabitare.*

Indy ▸ noun [mass noun] a form of motor racing in which cars are driven round a banked, regular oval circuit which allows for racing at exceptionally high speeds. It takes place chiefly in the US.
– ORIGIN 1950s: named after **INDIANAPOLIS**, where the principal Indy race is held.

Indycar ▸ noun a type of car used in Indy racing. ▸ adjective of or relating to Indy or Indycars.

-ine¹ /ʌɪn, ɪn, iːn/ ▸ suffix **1** (forming adjectives) belonging to; resembling in nature: *Alpine* | *asinine* | *canine.*
2 forming adjectives from the names of genera (such as *bovine* from the genus *Bos*) or from the names of subfamilies (such as *colubrine* from the subfamily *Colubrinae*).
– ORIGIN from French *-in, -ine,* or from Latin *-inus.*

-ine² /ʌɪn/ ▸ suffix forming adjectives from the names of minerals, plants, etc.: *crystalline* | *hyacinthine.*
– ORIGIN from Latin *-inus,* from Greek *-inos.*

-ine³ /ɪn, iːn/ ▸ suffix forming feminine nouns such as *heroine, margravine.*
– ORIGIN from French, via Latin *-ina* from Greek *-inē,* or from German *-in.*

-ine⁴ /iːn, ɪn/ ▸ suffix **1** forming chiefly abstract nouns and diminutives such as *doctrine, medicine, figurine.*
2 Chemistry forming names of alkaloids, halogens, amines, amino acids, and other substances: *cocaine* | *chlorine* | *thymine.*
– ORIGIN from French, from the Latin feminine form *-ina.*

inebriate formal or humorous ▸ verb /ɪˈniːbrɪeɪt/ [with obj.] [often as adj. **inebriated**] make drunk; intoxicate. ▸ noun /ɪˈniːbrɪət/ a drunkard. ▸ adjective /ɪˈniːbrɪət/ drunk; intoxicated.
– DERIVATIVES **inebriation** noun, **inebriety** noun.
– ORIGIN late Middle English (as an adjective): from Latin *inebriatus,* past participle of *inebriare* 'intoxicate' (based on *ebrius* 'drunk').

inedible ▸ adjective not fit or suitable for eating: *most of the meals were cold and inedible.*
– DERIVATIVES **inedibility** noun.

inedited ▸ adjective not edited or published.
■ published without editorial emendation.

ineducable /ɪnˈɛdjʊkəb(ə)l/ ▸ adjective considered incapable of being educated, especially (formerly) as a result of mental handicap.
– DERIVATIVES **ineducability** noun.

ineffable /ɪnˈɛfəb(ə)l/ ▸ adjective too great or extreme to be expressed or described in words: *the ineffable natural beauty of the Everglades.*
■ not to be uttered: *the ineffable Hebrew name that gentiles write as Jehovah.*
– DERIVATIVES **ineffability** noun, **ineffably** adverb.
– ORIGIN late Middle English: from Old French, or from Latin *ineffabilis,* from *in-* 'not' + *effabilis* (see **EFFABLE**).

ineffaceable /ɪnɪˈfeɪsəb(ə)l/ ▸ adjective unable to be erased or forgotten.
– DERIVATIVES **ineffaceability** noun, **ineffaceably** adverb.

ineffective ▸ adjective not producing any or the desired effect: *the legal sanctions against oil spills are virtually ineffective* | *a weak and ineffective president.*
– DERIVATIVES **ineffectively** adverb, **ineffectiveness** noun.

ineffectual ▸ adjective not producing any or the desired effect: *an ineffectual campaign.*
■ (of a person) lacking the ability or qualities to cope with a role or situation: *she was neglectful and ineffectual as a parent.*
– DERIVATIVES **ineffectuality** noun, **ineffectually** adverb, **ineffectualness** noun.
– ORIGIN late Middle English: from medieval Latin *ineffectualis,* from *in-* 'not' + *effectualis,* from Latin *effectus* (see **EFFECT**); in later use from **IN-**¹ 'not' + **EFFECTUAL**.

inefficacious /ˌɪnɛfɪˈkeɪʃəs/ ▸ adjective not producing the desired effect.
– DERIVATIVES **inefficacy** noun.

inefficient ▸ adjective not achieving maximum productivity; wasting or failing to make the best use of time or resources: *inefficient transport systems* | *the government was both inefficient and corrupt.*
– DERIVATIVES **inefficiency** noun, **inefficiently** adverb.

inegalitarian /ˌɪnɪɡalɪˈtɛːrɪən/ ▸ adjective characterized by or promoting inequality between people.

inelastic ▸ adjective **1** (of a substance or material) not elastic.
■ Economics (of demand or supply) insensitive to changes in price or income.
2 Physics (of a collision) involving an overall loss of translational kinetic energy.
– DERIVATIVES **inelastically** adverb, **inelasticity** noun.

inelegant ▸ adjective having or showing a lack of physical grace, elegance, or refinement: *he came skidding to an inelegant halt* | *an inelegant bellow of laughter.*
■ unappealing through being overly complicated: *an inelegant and complex piece of legislation.*
– DERIVATIVES **inelegance** noun, **inelegantly** adverb.
– ORIGIN early 16th cent.: from French *inélégant,* from Latin *inelegant-,* from *in-* 'not' + Latin *elegant-* 'fastidious, refined' (see **ELEGANT**).

ineligible ▸ adjective legally or officially unable to be considered for a position or benefit: *they were ineligible for jury service.*
■ dated not suitable or desirable, especially as a marriage partner: *as a son-in-law he was quite ineligible.*
– DERIVATIVES **ineligibility** noun, **ineligibly** adverb.

ineluctable /ˌɪnɪˈlʌktəb(ə)l/ ▸ adjective unable to be resisted or avoided; inescapable: *the ineluctable facts of history.*
– DERIVATIVES **ineluctability** /-ˈbɪlɪti/ noun, **ineluctably** adverb.
– ORIGIN early 17th cent.: from Latin *ineluctabilis,* from *in-* 'not' + *eluctari* 'struggle out'.

ineludible /ˌɪnɪˈl(j)uːdɪb(ə)l/ ▸ adjective rare unavoidable; inescapable.

inept ▸ adjective having or showing no skill; clumsy: *the referee's inept handling of the match.*
– DERIVATIVES **ineptitude** noun, **ineptly** adverb, **ineptness** noun.
– ORIGIN mid 16th cent. (in the sense 'not apt, unsuitable'): from Latin *ineptus,* from *in-* 'not' + *aptus* (see **APT**).

inequality ▸ noun (pl. **-ies**) [mass noun] difference in size, degree, circumstances, etc.; lack of equality:

social inequality | [count noun] *the widening inequalities in income.*
■ archaic lack of smoothness or regularity in a surface: *the inequality of the ground hindered their footing.* ■ Mathematics the relation between two expressions that are not equal, employing a sign such as ≠ 'not equal to', > 'greater than', or < 'less than'. ■ [count noun] Mathematics a symbolic expression of the fact that two quantities are not equal.
– ORIGIN late Middle English: from Old French *inequalite,* or from Latin *inaequalitas,* from *in-* 'not' + *aequalis* (see **EQUAL**).

inequitable ▸ adjective unfair; unjust: *the present taxes are inequitable.*
– DERIVATIVES **inequitably** adverb.

inequity ▸ noun (pl. **-ies**) [mass noun] lack of fairness or justice: *policies aimed at redressing racial inequity* | [count noun] *inequities in school financing.*

inequivalve /ɪnˈiːkwɪvalv/ ▸ adjective Zoology (of a bivalve shell) having the valves of different sizes.

ineradicable /ˌɪnɪˈradɪkəb(ə)l/ ▸ adjective unable to be destroyed or removed: *ineradicable hostility.*
– DERIVATIVES **ineradicably** adverb.

inerrant ▸ adjective incapable of being wrong.
– DERIVATIVES **inerrancy** noun, **inerrantist** noun.
– ORIGIN mid 19th cent.: from Latin *inerrant-* 'fixed', from *in-* 'not' + *errant-* 'erring' (see **ERRANT**).

inert ▸ adjective lacking the ability or strength to move: *she lay inert in her bed.*
■ lacking vigour: *an inert political system.* ■ chemically inactive.
– DERIVATIVES **inertly** adverb, **inertness** noun.
– ORIGIN mid 17th cent.: from Latin *iners, inert-* 'unskilled, inactive', from *in-* (expressing negation) + *ars, art-* 'skill, art'.

inert gas ▸ noun another term for **NOBLE GAS**.

inertia /ɪˈnəːʃə/ ▸ noun [mass noun] **1** a tendency to do nothing or to remain unchanged: *the bureaucratic inertia of the various tiers of government.*
2 Physics a property of matter by which it continues in its existing state of rest or uniform motion in a straight line, unless that state is changed by an external force. See also **MOMENT OF INERTIA**.
■ [with modifier] resistance to change in some other physical property: *the thermal inertia of the oceans will delay the full rise in temperature for a few decades.*
– DERIVATIVES **inertialess** adjective.
– ORIGIN early 18th cent. (in sense 2): from Latin, from *iners, inert-* (see **INERT**).

inertial ▸ adjective chiefly Physics of, relating to, or arising from inertia.
■ (of navigation or guidance) depending on internal instruments which measure a craft's acceleration and compare the calculated position with stored data. ■ (of a frame of reference) in which bodies continue at rest or in uniform straight motion unless acted on by a force.

inertia reel ▸ noun a reel device which allows a vehicle seat belt to unwind freely but which locks under force of impact or rapid deceleration.

inertia selling ▸ noun [mass noun] Brit. the sending of unsolicited goods to potential customers in the hope of making a sale.

inescapable ▸ adjective unable to be avoided or denied.
– DERIVATIVES **inescapability** noun, **inescapably** adverb.

inescutcheon /ˌɪnɪˈskʌtʃ(ə)n, ˌɪnɛ-/ ▸ noun Heraldry a small shield placed within a larger one.

-iness ▸ suffix forming nouns corresponding to adjectives ending in *-y* (such as *clumsiness* corresponding to *clumsy*).
– ORIGIN see **-Y¹**, **-NESS**.

in esse /ɪn ˈɛsi, ˈɛseɪ/ ▸ adverb in actual existence.
– ORIGIN Latin.

inessential ▸ adjective not absolutely necessary. ▸ noun (usu. **inessentials**) a thing that is not absolutely necessary.

inestimable ▸ adjective too great to calculate: *a treasure of inestimable value.*
– DERIVATIVES **inestimably** adverb.
– ORIGIN late Middle English: via Old French from Latin *inaestimabilis,* from *in-* 'not' + *aestimabilis* (see **ESTIMABLE**).

inevitable ▸ adjective certain to happen; unavoidable: *war was inevitable.*
■ informal so frequently experienced or seen that it is completely predictable: *the inevitable letter from the bank.*

▶**noun** (**the inevitable**) a situation that is unavoidable.
– DERIVATIVES **inevitability** noun, **inevitably** adverb [sentence adverb] *inevitably, policy failures were attributed to the government.*
– ORIGIN late Middle English: from Latin *inevitabilis*, from *in-* 'not' + *evitabilis* 'avoidable' (from *evitare* 'avoid').

inexact ▶**adjective** not quite accurate or correct: *an inexact description.*
– DERIVATIVES **inexactitude** noun, **inexactly** adverb, **inexactness** noun.

inexcusable ▶**adjective** too bad to be justified or tolerated: *Matt's behaviour was inexcusable.*
– DERIVATIVES **inexcusably** adverb.
– ORIGIN late Middle English: from Latin *inexcusabilis*, from *in-* 'not' + *excusabilis* 'able to be excused' (see **EXCUSE**).

inexhaustible ▶**adjective** (of an amount or supply of something) unable to be used up because existing in abundance: *his inexhaustible energy.*
– DERIVATIVES **inexhaustibility** noun, **inexhaustibly** adverb.

inexistent ▶**adjective** rare non-existent.

inexorable /ɪnˈɛks(ə)rəb(ə)l/ ▶**adjective** impossible to stop or prevent: *the seemingly inexorable march of new technology.*
■(of a person) impossible to persuade by request or entreaty: *the doctors were inexorable, and there was nothing to be done.*
– DERIVATIVES **inexorability** noun, **inexorably** adverb.
– ORIGIN mid 16th cent.: from French, or from Latin *inexorabilis*, from *in-* 'not' + *exorabilis* (from *exorare* 'entreat').

inexpedient ▶**adjective** not practical, suitable, or advisable.
– DERIVATIVES **inexpediency** noun.

inexpensive ▶**adjective** not costing a great deal; cheap.
– DERIVATIVES **inexpensively** adverb, **inexpensiveness** noun.

inexperience ▶**noun** [mass noun] lack of experience.
– DERIVATIVES **inexperienced** adjective.
– ORIGIN late 16th cent.: from French *inexpérience*, from late Latin *inexperientia*, from *in-* (expressing negation) + *experientia* 'experience'.

inexpert ▶**adjective** having or showing a lack of skill or knowledge: *an inexpert transcription from the real music.*
– DERIVATIVES **inexpertly** adverb.
– ORIGIN late Middle English (in the sense 'inexperienced'): via Old French from Latin *inexpertus*, from *in-* 'not' + *expertus* (see **EXPERT**).

inexpertise ▶**noun** [mass noun] lack of expertise.

inexpiable /ɪnˈɛkspɪəb(ə)l/ ▶**adjective** (of an offence or feeling) so bad as to be impossible to expiate.
– DERIVATIVES **inexpiably** adverb.
– ORIGIN late Middle English: from Latin *inexpiabilis*, from *in-* 'not' + *expiabilis* 'able to be appeased' (from *expiare* 'expiate').

inexplicable /ˌɪnɪkˈsplɪkəb(ə)l/, ˌɪnɛk-, ɪnˈɛksplɪ-/ ▶**adjective** unable to be explained or accounted for: *for some inexplicable reason her mind went completely blank.*
– DERIVATIVES **inexplicability** noun, **inexplicably** adverb [sentence adverb] *inexplicably, the pumps started to malfunction.*
– ORIGIN late Middle English: from French, or from Latin *inexplicabilis* 'that cannot be unfolded', from *in-* 'not' + *explicabilis* (see **EXPLICABLE**).

inexplicit ▶**adjective** not definitely or clearly expressed or explained.

inexpressible ▶**adjective** (of a feeling) too strong to be described or conveyed in words.
– DERIVATIVES **inexpressibly** adverb.

inexpressive ▶**adjective** showing no expression: *an inexpressive face.*
– DERIVATIVES **inexpressively** adverb, **inexpressiveness** noun.

inexpugnable /ˌɪnɪkˈspʌɡnəb(ə)l/, ˌɪnɛk-/ ▶**adjective** archaic term for **IMPREGNABLE**.
– ORIGIN late Middle English: via Old French from Latin *inexpugnabilis*, from *in-* 'not' + *expugnabilis* 'able to be taken by assault'.

inextensible /ˌɪnɪkˈstɛnsɪb(ə)l/, ˌɪnɛk-/ ▶**adjective** unable to be stretched or drawn out in length.

in extenso /ˌɪn ɛkˈstɛnsəʊ/ ▶**adverb** in full; at length: *the paper covered their speeches in extenso.*
– ORIGIN Latin, from *in* 'in' + *extensus*, past participle of *extendere* 'stretch out'.

inextinguishable ▶**adjective** unable to be extinguished or quenched: *a small inextinguishable candle* | figurative *an inextinguishable loquacity.*

in extremis /ˌɪn ɛkˈstriːmɪs/ ▶**adverb** in an extremely difficult situation.
■at the point of death.
– ORIGIN Latin, from *in* 'in' + *extremis*, ablative plural of *extremus* 'outermost'.

inextricable /ɪnˈɛkstrɪkəb(ə)l/, ˌɪnɪkˈstrɪk-, ˌɪnɛk-/ ▶**adjective** impossible to disentangle or separate: *the past and the present are inextricable.*
■impossible to escape from.
– DERIVATIVES **inextricability** noun, **inextricably** adverb.
– ORIGIN mid 16th cent.: from Latin *inextricabilis*, from *in-* 'not' + *extricare* 'unravel' (see **EXTRICATE**).

INF ▶**abbreviation for** intermediate-range nuclear force(s).

infall ▶**noun** [mass noun] Astronomy the falling of small objects or other matter on to or into a larger body.

infallibility ▶**noun** [mass noun] the quality of being infallible; the inability to be wrong: *his judgement became impaired by faith in his own infallibility.*
■(also **papal infallibility**) (in the Roman Catholic Church) the doctrine that in specified circumstances the Pope is incapable of error in pronouncing dogma.
– ORIGIN early 17th cent.: from obsolete French *infallibilité* or medieval Latin *infallibilitas* (based on Latin *fallere* 'deceive').

infallible /ɪnˈfalɪb(ə)l/ ▶**adjective** incapable of making mistakes or being wrong: *doctors are not infallible.*
■never failing; always effective: *infallible cures.* ■ (in the Roman Catholic Church) credited with papal infallibility: *for an encyclical to be infallible the Pope must speak ex cathedra.*
– DERIVATIVES **infallibly** adverb.
– ORIGIN late 15th cent.: from French *infaillible* or late Latin *infallibilis*, from *in-* 'not' + Latin *fallere* 'deceive'.

infamous ▶**adjective** well known for some bad quality or deed: *an infamous war criminal.*
■wicked; abominable: *the medical council disqualified him for infamous misconduct.* ■ Law, historical (of a person) deprived of all or some citizens' rights as a consequence of conviction for a serious crime.
– DERIVATIVES **infamously** adverb, **infamy** noun (pl. **-ies**).
– ORIGIN late Middle English: from medieval Latin *infamosus*, from Latin *infamis* (based on *fama* 'fame').

infancy ▶**noun** [mass noun] the state or period of early childhood or babyhood: *a son who died in infancy.*
■the early stage in the development or growth of something: *opinion polls were in their infancy.* ■ Law the condition of being a minor.
– ORIGIN late Middle English: from Latin *infantia* 'childhood, inability to speak', from *infans, infant-* (see **INFANT**).

infangthief /ˈɪnfaŋˌθiːf/ ▶**noun** [mass noun] historical the right of the lord of a manor to try and to punish a thief caught within the limits of his demesne.
– ORIGIN Old English *infangenthēof* 'thief seized within'.

infant ▶**noun** a very young child or baby.
■Brit. a schoolchild between the ages of five and seven: [as modifier] *their first year at infant school.* ■ [as modifier] denoting something in an early stage of its development: *the infant Labour Party.* ■ Law a person who has not attained legal majority.
– ORIGIN late Middle English: from Old French *enfant*, from Latin *infant-* 'unable to speak', from *in-* 'not' + *fant-* 'speaking' (from the verb *fari*).

infanta /ɪnˈfantə/ ▶**noun** historical a daughter of the ruling monarch of Spain or Portugal, especially the eldest daughter who was not heir to the throne.
– ORIGIN late 16th cent.: Spanish and Portuguese, feminine of **INFANTE**.

infante /ɪnˈfanteɪ/ ▶**noun** historical the second son of the ruling monarch of Spain or Portugal.
– ORIGIN mid 16th cent.: Spanish and Portuguese, from Latin *infans, infant-* (see **INFANT**).

infanteer /ˌɪnf(ə)nˈtɪə/ ▶**noun** military slang an infantryman.

infanticide /ɪnˈfantɪsʌɪd/ ▶**noun 1** [mass noun] the crime of a mother killing her child within a year of birth.
■the practice in some societies of killing unwanted children soon after birth.
2 a person who kills an infant, especially their own child.
– DERIVATIVES **infanticidal** adjective.
– ORIGIN mid 17th cent.: via French from late Latin *infanticidium*, from Latin *infant-* (see **INFANT**) + *-cidium* (see **-CIDE**).

infantile /ˈɪnf(ə)ntʌɪl/ ▶**adjective** of or occurring among babies or very young children: *infantile colic.*
■derogatory childish: *infantile jokes.*
– DERIVATIVES **infantility** noun (pl. **-ies**).
– ORIGIN late Middle English: from French, or from Latin *infantilis*, from *infans, infant-* (see **INFANT**).

infantile paralysis ▶**noun** [mass noun] dated poliomyelitis.

infantilism /ɪnˈfantɪlɪz(ə)m/ ▶**noun** [mass noun] childish behaviour.
■Psychology the persistence of infantile characteristics or behaviour in adult life.

infantilize /ɪnˈfantɪlʌɪz/ (also **-ise**) ▶**verb** [with obj.] treat (someone) as a child or in a way which denies their maturity in age or experience.
– DERIVATIVES **infantilization** noun.

infantine /ˈɪnf(ə)ntʌɪn/ ▶**adjective** archaic term for **INFANTILE**.
– ORIGIN early 17th cent.: from obsolete French *infantin*, variant of Old French *enfantin*, from *infans, infant-* (see **INFANT**).

infant mortality ▶**noun** [mass noun] the death of children under the age of one year.

infantry ▶**noun** [mass noun] soldiers marching or fighting on foot; foot soldiers collectively.
– ORIGIN late 16th cent.: from French *infanterie*, from Italian *infanteria*, from *infante* 'youth, infantryman', from *infant-* (see **INFANT**).

infantryman ▶**noun** (pl. **-men**) a soldier belonging to an infantry regiment.

infarct /ˈɪnfɑːkt, ɪnˈfɑːkt/ ▶**noun** Medicine a small localized area of dead tissue resulting from failure of blood supply.
– ORIGIN late 19th cent.: from modern Latin *infarctus*, from *infarcire* 'stuff into or with', from *in-* 'into' + Latin *farcire* 'to stuff'.

infarction /ɪnˈfɑːkʃ(ə)n/ ▶**noun** [mass noun] the obstruction of the blood supply to an organ or region of tissue, typically by a thrombus or embolus, causing local death of the tissue.

infatuate ▶**verb** (**be infatuated with**) be inspired with an intense but short-lived passion or admiration for: *she is infatuated with a handsome police chief.*
– DERIVATIVES **infatuation** noun.
– ORIGIN mid 16th cent.: from Latin *infatuat-* 'made foolish', from the verb *infatuare*, from *in-* 'into' + *fatuus* 'foolish'.

infauna /ˈɪnfɔːnə/ ▶**noun** [mass noun] Ecology the animals living in the sediments of the ocean floor or river or lake beds. Compare with **EPIFAUNA**.
– DERIVATIVES **infaunal** adjective.

infeasible ▶**adjective** not possible to do easily or conveniently; impracticable.
– DERIVATIVES **infeasibility** noun.

infect ▶**verb** [with obj.] affect (a person, organism, cell, etc.) with a disease-causing organism: *the chance that a child may have been infected with HIV.*
■contaminate (air, water, etc.) with harmful organisms. ■ Computing affect with a virus. ■ figurative (of a negative feeling or idea) take hold of or be communicated to (someone): *the panic in his voice infected her.*
– DERIVATIVES **infector** noun.
– ORIGIN late Middle English: from Latin *infect-* 'tainted', from the verb *inficere*, from *in-* 'into' + *facere* 'put, do'.

infection ▶**noun** [mass noun] the process of infecting or the state of being infected: *strict hygiene will limit the risk of infection.*
■[count noun] an infectious disease: *a chest infection.* ■ Computing the presence of a virus in, or its introduction into, a computer system.
– ORIGIN late Middle English: from late Latin *infectio(n-)*, from Latin *inficere* 'dip in, taint' (see **INFECT**).

infectious ▶**adjective** (of a disease or disease-

causing organism) liable to be transmitted to people, organisms, etc. through the environment.
- ■ liable to spread infection: *the dogs mays still be infectious.* ■ likely to spread or influence others in a rapid manner: *her enthusiasm is infectious.*
- DERIVATIVES **infectiously** adverb, **infectiousness** noun.

USAGE On the differences in meaning between **infectious** and **contagious**, see usage at **CONTAGIOUS**.

infective ▶ adjective capable of causing infection.
- ■ dated infectious: *infective hepatitis.*
- DERIVATIVES **infectiveness** noun.
- ORIGIN late Middle English: from Latin *infectivus*, from *inficere* 'to taint' (see **INFECT**).

infecund ▶ adjective Medicine & Zoology (of a woman or female animal) having low or zero fecundity; unable to bear children or young.
- DERIVATIVES **infecundity** noun.
- ORIGIN late Middle English: from Latin *infecundus*, from *in-* 'not' + *fecundus* 'fecund'.

infeed ▶ noun [mass noun] the action or process of supplying material to a machine.
- ■ [count noun] a mechanism which does this.

infelicitous ▶ adjective unfortunate; inappropriate: *his illustration is singularly infelicitous.*
- DERIVATIVES **infelicitously** adverb.

infelicity ▶ noun (pl. **-ies**) a thing that is inappropriate, especially a remark or expression: *she winced at their infelicities and at the clumsy way they talked.*
- ■ [mass noun] archaic unhappiness; misfortune.
- ORIGIN late Middle English (in the sense 'unhappiness'): from Latin *infelicitas*, from *infelix*, *infelic-* 'unhappy', from *in-* 'not' + *felix* 'happy'.

infer ▶ verb (**inferred**, **inferring**) [with obj.] deduce or conclude (information) from evidence and reasoning rather than from explicit statements: [with clause] *from these facts we can infer that crime has been increasing.*
- DERIVATIVES **inferable** (also **inferrable**) adjective.
- ORIGIN late 15th cent. (in the sense 'bring about, inflict'): from Latin *inferre* 'bring in, bring about' (in medieval Latin 'deduce'), from *in-* 'into' + *ferre* 'bring'.

USAGE There is a distinction in meaning between **infer** and **imply**. In the sentence *the speaker implied that the General had been a traitor,* **implied** means that something in the speaker's words **suggested** that this man was a traitor (though nothing so explicit was actually stated). However, in *we inferred from his words that the General had been a traitor,* **inferred** means that something in the speaker's words enabled the listeners to **deduce** that the man was a traitor. The two words **infer** and **imply** can describe the same event, but from different angles. Mistakes occur when **infer** is used to mean **imply**, as in *are you inferring that I'm a liar?* (instead of *are you implying that I'm a liar?*). The error is common enough for some dictionaries to record it as a more or less standard use: over 20 per cent of citations for **infer** in the British National Corpus are erroneous for **imply**.

inference /ˈɪnf(ə)r(ə)ns/ ▶ noun a conclusion reached on the basis of evidence and reasoning.
- ■ [mass noun] the process of reaching such a conclusion: *his emphasis on order and health, and by inference cleanliness.*
- DERIVATIVES **inferential** adjective, **inferentially** adverb.
- ORIGIN late 16th cent.: from medieval Latin *inferentia*, from *inferent-* 'bringing in', from the verb *inferre* (see **INFER**).

inferior ▶ adjective **1** lower in rank, status, or quality: *schooling in inner-city areas was inferior to that in the rest of the country.*
- ■ of low standard or quality: *inferior goods.* ■ Law (of a court or tribunal) able to have its decisions overturned by a higher court. ■ Economics denoting goods or services which are in greater demand during a recession than in a boom, for example second-hand clothes.
- **2** chiefly Anatomy low or lower in position: *ulcers located in the inferior and posterior wall of the duodenum.*
- ■ (of a letter, figure, or symbol) written or printed below the line. ■ Botany (of the ovary of a flower) situated below the sepals and enclosed in the receptacle.
- ▶ noun **1** a person lower than another in rank, status, or ability: *her social and intellectual inferiors.*

2 Printing an inferior letter, figure, or symbol.
- DERIVATIVES **inferiorly** adverb (only in sense 2 of the adjective).
- ORIGIN late Middle English (in sense 2): from Latin, comparative of *inferus* 'low'.

inferior conjunction ▶ noun Astronomy a conjunction of Mercury or Venus with the sun, in which the planet and the earth are on the same side of the sun.

inferiority ▶ noun [mass noun] the condition of being lower in status or quality than another or others.
- ORIGIN late 16th cent.: probably from medieval Latin *inferioritas*, from Latin *inferior* 'lower'.

inferiority complex ▶ noun an unrealistic feeling of general inadequacy caused by actual or supposed inferiority in one sphere, sometimes marked by aggressive behaviour in compensation.

inferior planet ▶ noun Astronomy either of the two planets Mercury and Venus, whose orbits are closer to the sun than the earth's.

infernal ▶ adjective **1** of, relating to, or characteristic of hell or the underworld: *the infernal regions | the infernal heat of the forge.*
- **2** [attrib.] informal irritating and tiresome (used for emphasis): *you're an infernal nuisance.*
- DERIVATIVES **infernally** adverb.
- ORIGIN late Middle English: from Old French, from Christian Latin *infernalis*, from Latin *infernus* 'below, underground', used by Christians to mean 'hell', on the pattern of *inferni* (masculine plural) 'the shades' and *inferna* (neuter plural) 'the lower regions'.

inferno ▶ noun (pl. **-os**) **1** a large fire that is dangerously out of control.
- **2** (usu. **Inferno**) hell (with reference to Dante's *Divine Comedy*).
- ■ figurative a place or situation that is too hot, chaotic, or noisy: *the inferno of the Friday evening rush hour.*
- ORIGIN mid 19th cent.: from Italian, from Christian Latin *infernus* (see **INFERNAL**).

infertile ▶ adjective (of a person, animal, or plant) unable to reproduce.
- ■ (of land) unable to sustain crops or vegetation.
- DERIVATIVES **infertility** noun.
- ORIGIN late 16th cent.: from French, or from late Latin *infertilis*, from *in-* 'not' + *fertilis* (see **FERTILE**).

infest ▶ verb [with obj.] (usu. **be infested**) (of insects or animals) be present (in a place or site) in large numbers, typically so as to cause damage or disease: *the house is infested with cockroaches | [as adj., in combination **-infested**] shark-infested waters.*
- DERIVATIVES **infestation** noun.
- ORIGIN late Middle English (in the sense 'torment, harass'): from French *infester* or Latin *infestare* 'assail', from *infestus* 'hostile'. The current sense dates from the mid 16th cent.

infeudation /ˌɪnfjuːˈdeɪʃ(ə)n/ ▶ noun [mass noun] historical under the feudal system, the action of putting someone into possession of a fee or fief.
- ORIGIN late 15th cent.: from medieval Latin *infeudatio(n-)*, from *infeudare* 'enfeoff' (based on *feudum* 'fee').

infibulate /ɪnˈfɪbjʊleɪt/ ▶ verb [with obj.] [usu. as adj. **infibulated**] perform infibulation on (a girl or woman).
- ORIGIN early 17th cent.: from Latin *infibulat-* 'fastened with a clasp', from the verb *infibulare*, from *in-* 'into' + *fibula* 'brooch'.

infibulation ▶ noun [mass noun] the practice of excising the clitoris and labia of a girl or woman and stitching together the edges of the vulva to prevent sexual intercourse. It is traditional in some NE African cultures but is highly controversial.

infidel /ˈɪnfɪd(ə)l/ chiefly archaic ▶ noun a person who does not believe in religion or who adheres to a religion other than that of the majority: [as plural noun **the infidel**] *they wanted to secure the Holy Places from the infidel.*
- ▶ adjective adhering to a religion other than that of the majority: *the infidel foe.*
- ORIGIN late 15th cent.: from French *infidèle* or Latin *infidelis*, from *in-* 'not' + *fidelis* 'faithful' (from *fides* 'faith', related to *fidere* 'to trust'). The word originally denoted a person of a religion other than one's own, specifically a Muslim (to a Christian), a Christian (to a Muslim), or a Gentile (to a Jew).

infidelity ▶ noun (pl. **-ies**) [mass noun] **1** the action or state of being unfaithful to a spouse or other sexual partner: *her infidelity continued after her marriage | [count noun] I ought not to have tolerated his infidelities.*
- **2** disbelief in a particular religion, especially Christianity.
- ORIGIN late Middle English (in the senses 'lack of faith' and 'disloyalty'): from Old French *infidelite* or Latin *infidelitas*, from *infidelis* 'not faithful' (see **INFIDEL**).

infield ▶ noun **1** the inner part of the field of play in various sports, in particular:
- ■ Cricket the part of the field closer to the wicket. ■ Baseball the area within and near the four bases. ■ the players stationed in the infield, collectively.
- **2** the land around or near a farmstead, especially arable land.
- ▶ adverb into or towards the inner part of the field of play.
- DERIVATIVES **infielder** noun (in sense 1).

infighting ▶ noun [mass noun] hidden conflict or competitiveness within an organization.
- ■ boxing closer to an opponent than at arm's length.
- DERIVATIVES **infighter** noun.

infill ▶ noun [mass noun] (also **infilling**) material that fills or is used to fill a space or hole.
- ■ buildings constructed to occupy the space between existing ones.
- ▶ verb [with obj.] (often **be infilled**) fill or block up (a space or hole).
- ■ construct new buildings between (existing structures).

infiltrate /ˈɪnfɪltreɪt/ ▶ verb [with obj.] **1** enter or gain access to (an organization, place, etc.) surreptitiously and gradually, especially in order to acquire secret information: *other areas of the establishment were infiltrated by fascists.*
- ■ introduce (someone) into an organization, place, etc. in this way. ■ figurative permeate or become a part of (something) in this way: *computing has infiltrated most professions now.* ■ Medicine (of a tumour, cells, etc.) spread into or invade (a tissue or organ).
- **2** (of a liquid) permeate (something) by filtration: *virtually no water infiltrates deserts such as the Sahara.*
- ■ introduce (a liquid) into something in this way: *lignocaine was infiltrated into the wound.*
- ▶ noun Medicine an infiltrating substance or a number of infiltrating cells.
- DERIVATIVES **infiltration** noun, **infiltrator** noun.

infimum /ɪnˈfʌɪməm/ ▶ noun Mathematics the largest quantity that is less than or equal to each of a given set or subset of quantities. The opposite of **SUPREMUM**.
- ORIGIN 1940s: from Latin, literally 'lowest part', neuter (used as a noun) of *infimus* 'lowest'.

in fine /ɪn ˈfʌɪni, ˈfiːneɪ/ ▶ adverb finally; in short; to sum up.
- ORIGIN Latin.

infinite /ˈɪnfɪnɪt/ ▶ adjective **1** limitless or endless in space, extent, or size; impossible to measure or calculate: *the infinite mercy of God | the infinite number of stars in the universe.*
- ■ very great in amount or degree: *he bathed the wound with infinite care.* ■ Mathematics greater than any assignable quantity or countable number. ■ Mathematics (of a series) able to be continued indefinitely.
- **2** Grammar another term for **NON-FINITE**.
- ▶ noun (**the infinite**) a space or quantity that is infinite.
- ■ (the Infinite) God.
- DERIVATIVES **infinitely** adverb [as submodifier] *the pay is infinitely better,* **infiniteness** noun.
- ORIGIN late Middle English: from Latin *infinitus*, from *in-* 'not' + *finitus* 'finished, finite' (see **FINITE**).

infinite regress ▶ noun chiefly Logic a sequence of reasoning or justification which can never come to an end.

infinitesimal /ˌɪnfɪnɪˈtɛsɪm(ə)l/ ▶ adjective extremely small: *an infinitesimal pause.*
- ▶ noun Mathematics an indefinitely small quantity; a value approaching zero.
- DERIVATIVES **infinitesimally** adverb.
- ORIGIN mid 17th cent.: from modern Latin *infinitesimus*, from Latin *infinitus* (see **INFINITE**), on the pattern of *centesimal*.

infinitesimal calculus ▶ noun see **CALCULUS** (sense 1).

infinitive /ɪnˈfɪnɪtɪv/ ▶ noun the basic form of a verb, without an inflection binding it to a particular subject or tense (e.g. *see* in *we came to see, let him see*).
- ▶ adjective having or involving such a form.

– DERIVATIVES **infinitival** /-ˈtʌɪv(ə)l/ adjective, **infinitivally** adverb.
– ORIGIN late Middle English (as an adjective): from Latin *infinitivus*, from *infinitus* (see **INFINITE**). The noun dates from the mid 16th cent.

infinitude /ɪnˈfɪnɪtjuːd/ ▶ **noun** [mass noun] the state or quality of being infinite or having no limit: *the infinitude of the universe.*
– ORIGIN mid 17th cent.: from Latin *infinitus* (see **INFINITE**), on the pattern of *magnitude*.

infinity ▶ **noun** (pl. **-ies**) [mass noun] the state or quality of being infinite: *the infinity of space.*
■[count noun] an infinite or very great number or amount: *an infinity of combinations.* ■ Mathematics a number greater than any assignable quantity or countable number (symbol ∞). ■ a point in space or time that is or seems infinitely distant: *the lawns stretched into infinity.*
– ORIGIN late Middle English: from Old French *infinite* or Latin *infinitas*, from *infinitus* (see **INFINITE**).

infirm ▶ **adjective** not physically or mentally strong, especially through age or illness.
■archaic (of a person or their judgement) weak; irresolute: *he was infirm of purpose.*
– DERIVATIVES **infirmly** adverb.
– ORIGIN late Middle English (in the general sense 'weak, frail'): from Latin *infirmus*, from *in-* 'not' + *firmus* 'firm'.

infirmarer /ɪnˈfəːm(ə)rə/ ▶ **noun** historical a person in charge of the infirmary in a medieval monastery.
– ORIGIN late Middle English: from Old French *enfermerier*, from *enfermerie* 'infirmary', based on Latin *infirmus* (see **INFIRM**).

infirmary ▶ **noun** (pl. **-ies**) a hospital.
■a place in a large institution for the care of those who are ill: *the prison infirmary.*
– ORIGIN late Middle English: from medieval Latin *infirmaria*, from Latin *infirmus* (see **INFIRM**).

infirmity ▶ **noun** (pl. **-ies**) [mass noun] physical or mental weakness: *old age and infirmity come to men and women alike* | [count noun] *the infirmities of old age.*

infix ▶ **verb** /ɪnˈfɪks/ [with obj.] **1** implant or insert firmly in something.
2 Grammar insert (a formative element) into the body of a word.
▶ **noun** /ˈɪnfɪks/ Grammar a formative element inserted in a word.
– DERIVATIVES **infixation** noun (only in sense 2 of the verb).
– ORIGIN early 16th cent.: from Latin *infix-* 'fixed in', from the verb *infigere*, from *in-* 'into' + *figere* 'fasten', reinforced by **IN-**² 'into' + **FIX**. The noun is on the pattern of *prefix* and *suffix*.

in flagrante delicto /ɪn fləˌɡranteɪ dɪˈlɪktəʊ, fləˌɡranti/ (also informal **in flagrante**) ▶ **adverb** in the very act of wrongdoing, especially in an act of sexual misconduct: *he had been **caught in flagrante** with the wife of the Association's Treasurer.*
– ORIGIN Latin, 'in the heat of the crime' (literally 'in blazing crime').

inflame ▶ **verb** [with obj.] **1** provoke or intensify (strong feelings, especially anger) in someone: *high fines further inflamed public feelings.*
■provoke (someone) to strong feelings: *her sister was inflamed with jealousy.* ■ make (a situation) worse.
2 (usu. **be inflamed**) cause inflammation in (a part of the body): *the finger joints were inflamed with rheumatoid arthritis.*
3 poetic/literary light up with or as if with flames: *the torches inflame the night to the eastward.*
– DERIVATIVES **inflamer** noun.
– ORIGIN Middle English *enflaume*, *inflaume*, from Old French *enflammer*, from Latin *inflammare*, from *in-* 'into' + *flamma* 'flame'.

inflammable ▶ **adjective** easily set on fire: *inflammable materials.*
■figurative likely to provoke strong feelings: *the most inflammable issue in US politics today.*
▶ **noun** (usu. **inflammables**) a substance which is easily set on fire.
– DERIVATIVES **inflammability** noun, **inflammableness** noun, **inflammably** adverb.
– ORIGIN early 17th cent.: from French, or from Latin *inflammare* (see **INFLAME**).

USAGE The words **inflammable** and **flammable** both have the same meaning 'easily set on fire'. This might seem surprising, given that the prefix **in-** normally has the function of negation, as in words like **indirect** and **insufficient**. It might be expected, therefore, that **inflammable** would mean the opposite of **flammable**, i.e. 'not easily set on fire'. In fact, **inflammable** is formed using a different Latin prefix **in-**, which has the meaning 'into' and here has the effect of intensifying the meaning of the word in English. The opposite of **inflammable** and **flammable** is either **non-inflammable** or **non-flammable**.

inflammation ▶ **noun** [mass noun] a localized physical condition in which part of the body becomes reddened, swollen, hot, and often painful, especially as a reaction to injury or infection: *chronic inflammation of the nasal cavities.*
– ORIGIN late Middle English: from Latin *inflammatio(n-)*, from the verb *inflammare* (see **INFLAME**).

inflammatory ▶ **adjective 1** relating to or causing inflammation of a part of the body.
2 (especially of speech or writing) arousing or intended to arouse angry or violent feelings.

inflatable ▶ **adjective** capable of being filled with air: *an inflatable mattress.*
▶ **noun** a plastic or rubber object that must be filled with air before use: *three sailors manned the inflatable.*

inflate ▶ **verb** [usu. with obj.] **1** fill (a balloon, tyre, or other expandable structure) with air or gas so that it becomes distended.
■[no obj.] become distended in this way.
2 increase (something) by a large or excessive amount: *objectives should be clearly set out so as not to duplicate work and inflate costs.*
■[usu. as adj. **inflated**] exaggerate: *you have a very inflated opinion of your worth.* ■ bring about inflation of (a currency) or in (an economy).
– DERIVATIVES **inflatedly** adverb, **inflater** (also **inflator**) noun.
– ORIGIN late Middle English: from Latin *inflat-* 'blown into', from the verb *inflare*, from *in-* 'into' + *flare* 'to blow'.

inflation ▶ **noun** [mass noun] **1** the action of inflating something or the condition of being inflated: *the inflation of a balloon* | *the gross inflation of salaries.*
■Astronomy (in some theories of cosmology) a very brief exponential expansion of the universe postulated to have interrupted the standard linear expansion shortly after the big bang.
2 Economics a general increase in prices and fall in the purchasing value of money: *policies aimed at controlling inflation* | [as modifier] *high inflation rates.*
– DERIVATIVES **inflationism** noun, **inflationist** noun & adjective.
– ORIGIN Middle English (in the sense 'the condition of being inflated with a gas'): from Latin *inflatio(n-)*, from *inflare* 'blow in to' (see **INFLATE**). Sense 2 dates from the mid 19th cent.

inflationary ▶ **adjective 1** of, characterized by, or tending to cause monetary inflation.
2 Astronomy of, relating to, or involving inflation.

inflect ▶ **verb** [with obj.] (often **be inflected**) **1** Grammar change the form of (a word) to express a particular grammatical function or attribute, typically tense, mood, person, number, and gender.
■[no obj.] (of a word or a language containing such words) undergo such change.
2 vary the intonation or pitch of (the voice), especially to express mood or feeling.
■influence or colour (music or writing) in tone or style. ■ vary the pitch of (a musical note).
3 technical bend or deflect (something), especially inwards.
– DERIVATIVES **inflective** adjective.
– ORIGIN late Middle English (in sense 3): from Latin *inflectere*, from *in-* 'into' + *flectere* 'to bend'.

inflection (chiefly Brit. also **inflexion**) ▶ **noun 1** Grammar a change in the form of a word (typically the ending) to express a grammatical function or attribute such as tense, mood, person, number, case, and gender.
■[mass noun] the process or practice of inflecting words.
2 [mass noun] the modulation of intonation or pitch in the voice: *she spoke slowly and without inflection* | [count noun] *the variety of his vocal inflections.*
■the variation of the pitch of a musical note.
3 chiefly Mathematics a change of curvature from convex to concave at a particular point on a curve.
– DERIVATIVES **inflectional** adjective, **inflectionally** adverb, **inflectionless** adjective.
– ORIGIN late Middle English (in the sense 'the action of bending inwards'): from Latin *inflexio(n-)*, from the verb *inflectere* 'bend in, curve' (see **INFLECT**).

inflexed ▶ **adjective** technical bent or curved inwards.

inflexible ▶ **adjective 1** unwilling to change or compromise: *once she had made up her mind, she was inflexible.*
■not able to be changed or adapted to particular circumstances: *inflexible rules.*
2 not able to be bent; stiff: *the heavy inflexible armour of the beetles.*
– DERIVATIVES **inflexibility** noun, **inflexibly** adverb.
– ORIGIN late Middle English: from Latin *inflexibilis*, from *in-* 'not' + *flexibilis* 'flexible'.

inflict ▶ **verb** [with obj.] cause (something unpleasant or painful) to be suffered by someone or something: *they **inflicted** serious injuries **on** three other men.*
■(**inflict something on**) impose something unwelcome on: *she is wrong to inflict her beliefs on everyone else.*
– DERIVATIVES **inflictable** adjective, **inflicter** noun.
– ORIGIN mid 16th cent. (in the sense 'afflict, trouble'): from Latin *inflict-* 'struck against', from the verb *infligere*, from *in-* 'into' + *fligere* 'to strike'.

infliction ▶ **noun** [mass noun] the action of inflicting something unpleasant or painful on someone or something: *the repeated infliction of pain.*
■[count noun] informal, dated a nuisance: *what an infliction he must be!*

in-flight ▶ **adjective** occurring or provided during an aircraft flight: *in-flight catering.*

inflorescence /ˌɪnflɔːˈrɛs(ə)ns, -flə-/ ▶ **noun** Botany the complete flower head of a plant including stems, stalks, bracts, and flowers.
■the arrangement of the flowers on a plant. ■ [mass noun] the process of flowering.
– ORIGIN mid 18th cent. (denoting the arrangement of a plant's flowers): from modern Latin *inflorescentia*, from late Latin *inflorescere* 'come into flower', from Latin *in-* 'into' + *florescere* 'begin to flower'.

inflow ▶ **noun** a large amount of money, people, or water, that moves or is transferred into a place: *some enclosed seas are subject to large inflows of fresh water* | [mass noun] *the firm experienced two years of cash inflow.*
– DERIVATIVES **inflowing** noun & adjective.

influence ▶ **noun** [mass noun] the capacity to have an effect on the character, development, or behaviour of someone or something, or the effect itself: *the influence of television violence* | *I was still **under the influence of** my parents* | [count noun] *their friends are having a bad **influence on** them.*
■the power to shape policy or ensure favourable treatment from someone, especially through status, contacts, or wealth: *the institute has considerable influence with teachers.* ■ [count noun] a person or thing with such a capacity or power: *Fiona was a good **influence on** her.* ■ Physics, archaic electrical or magnetic induction.
▶ **verb** [with obj.] have an influence on: *social forces influencing criminal behaviour.*
– PHRASES **under the influence** informal affected by alcoholic drink; drunk: *he was charged with driving under the influence.*
– DERIVATIVES **influenceable** adjective, **influencer** noun.
– ORIGIN late Middle English: from Old French, or from medieval Latin *influentia* 'inflow', from Latin *influere*, from *in-* 'into' + *fluere* 'to flow'. The word originally had the general sense 'an influx, flowing matter', also specifically (in astrology) 'the flowing in of ethereal fluid (affecting human destiny)'. The sense 'imperceptible or indirect action exerted to cause changes' was established in Scholastic Latin by the 13th cent., but not recorded in English until the late 16th cent.

influence peddling ▶ **noun** [mass noun] N. Amer. the use of position or political influence on someone's behalf in exchange for money or favours.
– DERIVATIVES **influence peddler** noun.

influent /ˈɪnflʊənt/ ▶ **adjective** flowing in: *Loch Leven's influent streams.*
▶ **noun** a stream, especially a tributary, which flows into another stream or lake.
– ORIGIN late Middle English (as an adjective): from

Latin *influent-* 'flowing in', from *influere* (see **INFLUENCE**). The noun is recorded from the mid 19th cent.

influential ▶ adjective having great influence on someone or something: *her work is influential in feminist psychology.*
▶ noun (usu. **influentials**) an influential person.
− DERIVATIVES **influentially** adverb.
− ORIGIN late 16th cent. (referring to astral influence): from medieval Latin *influentia* (see **INFLUENCE**).

influenza ▶ noun [mass noun] a highly contagious viral infection of the respiratory passages causing fever, severe aching, and catarrh, and often occurring in epidemics.
− DERIVATIVES **influenzal** adjective.
− ORIGIN mid 18th cent.: from Italian, literally 'influence', from medieval Latin *influentia* (see **INFLUENCE**). The Italian word also has the sense 'an outbreak of an epidemic', hence 'epidemic'. It was applied specifically to an influenza epidemic which began in Italy in 1743, later adopted in English as the name of the disease.

influx /'ɪnflʌks/ ▶ noun **1** an arrival or entry of large numbers of people or things: *a massive influx of refugees from front-line areas.*
2 an inflow of water into a river, lake, or the sea.
− ORIGIN late 16th cent. (denoting an inflow of liquid, gas, or light): from late Latin *influxus*, from *influere* 'flow in' (see **INFLUENCE**).

influx control ▶ noun [mass noun] (in South Africa during the apartheid era) the rigid limitation and control imposed upon the movement of black people into urban areas.

info ▶ noun [mass noun] informal information.
− ORIGIN early 20th cent.: abbreviation.

infobahn /'ɪnfəʊbɑːn/ ▶ noun informal a high speed computer network, especially the Internet.
− ORIGIN 1990s: blend of **INFORMATION** and **AUTOBAHN**.

infolded ▶ adjective technical turned or folded inwards.

infolding ▶ noun technical a turning or folding inwards; an inward fold.

infomercial /,ɪnfə(ʊ)'mɜː.ʃ(ə)l/ ▶ noun chiefly US an advertising film which promotes a product in an informative and supposedly objective style.
− ORIGIN 1980s: blend of **INFORMATION** and **COMMERCIAL**.

inform ▶ verb **1** [reporting verb] give (someone) facts or information; tell: [with obj.] *he wrote to her, informing her of the situation* | [with obj. and direct speech] *'That's nothing new,' she informed him* | [with obj. and clause] *they were informed that no risk was involved.*
■ [no obj.] give incriminating information about someone to the police or other authority: *surrendered terrorists began to inform on their former comrades.*
2 [with obj.] give an essential or formative principle or quality to: *the relationship of the citizen to the state is informed by the democratic ideal.*
− ORIGIN Middle English *enforme, informe* 'give form or shape to', also 'form the mind of, teach', from Old French *enfourmer*, from Latin *informare* 'shape, fashion, describe', from *in-* 'into' + *forma* 'a form'.

informal ▶ adjective having a relaxed, friendly, or unofficial style, manner, or nature: *an informal atmosphere* | *an informal agreement between the two companies.*
■ of or denoting a style of writing or conversational speech characterized by simpler grammatical structures, more familiar vocabulary, and greater use of idioms and metaphors. ■ (of dress) casual; suitable for everyday wear. ■ (of economic activity) carried on by self-employed or independent people on a small scale, especially unofficially or illegally.
− DERIVATIVES **informality** noun, **informally** adverb.

informal vote ▶ noun Austral./NZ an invalid vote or voting paper.

informant ▶ noun a person who gives information to another.
■ another term for **INFORMER**. ■ a person from whom a linguist or anthropologist obtains information about language, dialect, or culture.

informatics /,ɪnfə'matɪks/ ▶ plural noun [treated as sing.] Computing the science of processing data for storage and retrieval; information science.
− ORIGIN 1960s: from **INFORMATION** + **-ICS**, translating Russian *informatika.*

information ▶ noun [mass noun] **1** facts provided or

learned about something or someone: *a vital piece of information.*
■ [count noun] Law a charge lodged with a magistrates' court: *the tenant may lay an information against his landlord alleging the existence of a statutory nuisance.*
2 what is conveyed or represented by a particular arrangement or sequence of things: *genetically transmitted information.*
■ (in information theory) a mathematical quantity expressing the probability of occurrence of a particular sequence of symbols, impulses, etc., as against that of alternative sequences.
− DERIVATIVES **informational** adjective, **informationally** adverb.
− ORIGIN late Middle English (also in the sense 'formation of the mind, teaching'), via Old French from Latin *informatio(n-)*, from the verb *informare* (see **INFORM**).

information retrieval ▶ noun [mass noun] Computing the tracing and recovery of specific information from stored data.

information revolution ▶ noun the proliferation of the availability of information and the accompanying changes in its storage and dissemination owing to the use of computers.

information science ▶ noun [mass noun] Computing the study of processes for storing and retrieving information, especially scientific or technical information.

information superhighway ▶ noun see **SUPERHIGHWAY**.

information technology ▶ noun [mass noun] the study or use of systems (especially computers and telecommunications) for storing, retrieving, and sending information.

information theory ▶ noun [mass noun] the mathematical study of the coding of information in the form of sequences of symbols, impulses, etc. and of how rapidly such information can be transmitted, for example through computer circuits or telecommunications channels.

informative ▶ adjective providing useful or interesting information: *a thought-provoking, informative article.*
− DERIVATIVES **informatively** adverb, **informativeness** noun.
− ORIGIN late Middle English (in the sense 'formative, giving life or shape'): from medieval Latin *informativus*, from Latin *informare* 'give form to, instruct' (see **INFORM**).

informatory /ɪn'fɔːmət(ə)ri/ ▶ adjective giving information; informative.
■ Bridge (of a double) intended to convey information to one's partner rather than to score a penalty.
− ORIGIN late Middle English (but rare before the late 19th cent.): from Latin *informat-* 'shaped, described' (from the verb *informare*) + **-ORY²**.

informed ▶ adjective having or showing knowledge of a particular subject or situation: *an informed readership.*
■ (of a decision or judgement) based on an understanding of the facts of the situation.
− DERIVATIVES **informedly** /ɪn'fɔːmɪdli/ adverb, **informedness** /ɪn'fɔːmɪdnɪs/ noun.

informer ▶ noun a person who informs on another person to the police or other authority.

infotainment ▶ noun [mass noun] broadcast material which is intended both to entertain and to inform.
− ORIGIN 1980s (originally US): blend of **INFORMATION** and **ENTERTAINMENT**.

infotech ▶ noun short for **INFORMATION TECHNOLOGY**.

infra ▶ adverb (in a written document) below; further on: *see note, infra.*
− ORIGIN Latin, 'below'.

infra- /'ɪnfrə/ ▶ prefix below: *infraorder* | *infrasonic.*
■ Anatomy below or under a part of the body: *infrarenal.*
− ORIGIN from Latin *infra* 'below'.

infraclass ▶ noun Biology a taxonomic category that ranks below a subclass.

infraction ▶ noun chiefly Law a violation or infringement of a law or agreement.
− DERIVATIVES **infractor** noun.
− ORIGIN late Middle English: from Latin *infractio(n-)*, from the verb *infringere* (see **INFRINGE**).

infradian /ɪn'freɪdɪən/ ▶ adjective Physiology (of a rhythm or cycle) having a period of recurrence

longer than a day; occurring less than once a day. Compare with **ULTRADIAN**.
− ORIGIN mid 20th cent.: from **INFRA-** 'below' (i.e. expressing a lower frequency), on the pattern of *circadian.*

infra dig /,ɪnfrə 'dɪg/ ▶ adjective [predic.] informal beneath one; demeaning: *she regarded playing for the Pony Club as deeply infra dig.*
− ORIGIN early 19th cent.: abbreviation of Latin *infra dignitatem* 'beneath (one's) dignity'.

infralapsarian /,ɪnfrəlap'sɛːrɪən/ Theology ▶ noun a Calvinist holding the view that God's election of only some to everlasting life was not originally part of the divine plan, but a consequence of the Fall of Man.
▶ adjective of or relating to the infralapsarians or their doctrine.
− ORIGIN mid 18th cent.: from **INFRA-** 'below' + Latin *lapsus* 'fall' + **-ARIAN**.

infrangible /ɪn'fran(d)ʒɪb(ə)l/ ▶ adjective formal unbreakable; inviolable.
− DERIVATIVES **infrangibility** noun, **infrangibly** adverb.
− ORIGIN late 16th cent.: from French, or from medieval Latin *infrangibilis*, from *in-* 'not' + *frangibilis* (see **FRANGIBLE**).

infraorder ▶ noun Biology a taxonomic category that ranks below a suborder.

infrared ▶ adjective (of electromagnetic radiation) having a wavelength just greater than that of the red end of the visible light spectrum but less than that of microwaves. Infrared radiation has a wavelength from about 800 nm to 1 mm, and is emitted particularly by heated objects.
■ (of equipment or techniques) using or concerned with this radiation: *infrared cameras.*
▶ noun [mass noun] the infrared region of the spectrum; infrared radiation.

infrarenal ▶ adjective Anatomy below the kidney.

infrasonic ▶ adjective relating to or denoting sound waves with a frequency below the lower limit of human audibility.

infrasound ▶ noun [mass noun] sound waves with frequencies below the lower limit of human audibility.

infraspecific ▶ adjective Biology at a taxonomic level below that of species, e.g. subspecies, variety, cultivar, or form. In botany, Latin names at this level usually require the addition of a term denoting the rank.
■ occurring within a species: *infraspecific variation.*

infrastructure ▶ noun the basic physical and organizational structures and facilities (e.g. buildings, roads, power supplies) needed for the operation of a society or enterprise.
− DERIVATIVES **infrastructural** adjective.
− ORIGIN early 20th cent.: from French (see **INFRA-, STRUCTURE**).

infrequent ▶ adjective not occurring often; rare: *her visits were so infrequent.*
− DERIVATIVES **infrequency** noun, **infrequently** adverb.
− ORIGIN mid 16th cent. (in the sense 'little used, seldom done, uncommon'): from Latin *infrequent-* from *in-* 'not' + *frequent-* 'frequent'.

infringe ▶ verb [with obj.] actively break the terms of (a law, agreement, etc.).
■ act so as to limit or undermine (something); encroach on: *his legal rights were being infringed* | [no obj.] *I wouldn't infringe on his privacy.*
− DERIVATIVES **infringement** noun, **infringer** noun.
− ORIGIN mid 16th cent.: from Latin *infringere*, from *in-* 'into' + *frangere* 'to break'.

infructescence /,ɪnfrʌk'tɛs(ə)ns/ ▶ noun Botany an aggregate fruit.
− ORIGIN late 19th cent.: from **IN-²** 'in' + Latin *fructus* 'fruit', on the pattern of *inflorescence.*

infula /'ɪnfjʊlə/ ▶ noun (pl. **infulae** /-liː/) (in the Christian Church) either of the two ribbons on a bishop's mitre.
− ORIGIN early 17th cent.: from Latin, denoting a woollen fillet worn by a priest or placed on the head of a sacrificial victim.

infundibulum /,ɪnfʌn'dɪbjʊləm/ ▶ noun (pl. **infundibula** /-'dɪbjʊlə/) Anatomy & Zoology a funnel-shaped cavity or structure.
■ the hollow stalk which connects the hypothalamus and the posterior pituitary gland.
− DERIVATIVES **infundibular** adjective.

– ORIGIN mid 16th cent.: from Latin, 'funnel', from *infundere* 'pour in'.

infuriate ▶ verb /ɪnˈfjʊərɪeɪt/ [with obj.] make (someone) extremely angry and impatient: *I was infuriated by your article* | [as adj. **infuriating**] *that infuriating half-smile on his face.*
– DERIVATIVES **infuriatingly** adverb.
– ORIGIN mid 17th cent.: from medieval Latin *infuriat-* 'made angry', from the verb *infuriare*, from *in-* 'into' + Latin *furia* 'fury'.

infuse ▶ verb [with obj.] **1** fill; pervade: *her work is infused with an anger born of pain and oppression.*
■ instil (a quality) in someone or something: *he did his best to infuse good humour into his voice.* ■ Medicine allow (a liquid) to flow into a patient, vein, etc.: *saline was infused into the aorta.*
2 soak (tea, herbs, etc.) in liquid to extract the flavour or healing properties.
■ [no obj.] (of tea, herbs, etc.) be soaked in this way.
– DERIVATIVES **infuser** noun.
– ORIGIN late Middle English: from Latin *infus-* 'poured in', from the verb *infundere*, from *in-* 'into' + *fundere* 'pour'.

infusible ▶ adjective (of a substance) not able to be melted or fused.
– DERIVATIVES **infusibility** noun.

infusion ▶ noun **1** a drink, remedy, or extract prepared by soaking the leaves of a plant or herb in liquid.
■ [mass noun] the process of preparing such a drink, remedy, or extract.
2 [mass noun] the introduction of a new element or quality into something: *the infusion of $6.3 million for improvements* | [count noun] *an infusion of youthful talent.*
■ Medicine the slow injection of a substance into a vein or tissue.
– ORIGIN late Middle English (denoting the pouring in of a liquid): from Latin *infusio(n-)*, from the verb *infundere* (see **INFUSE**).

infusoria /ˌɪnfjʊˈzɔːrɪə, -ˈsɔːrɪə/ ▶ plural noun Zoology, dated single-celled organisms of the former group Infusoria, which consisted mainly of ciliate protozoans.
– ORIGIN modern Latin, from Latin *infundere* (see **INFUSE**); so named because they were originally found in infusions of decaying organic matter.

-ing[1] ▶ suffix **1** denoting a verbal action, an instance of this, or its result: *fighting* | *outing* | *building.*
■ denoting a verbal action relating to an occupation, skill, etc.: *banking* | *ice skating* | *welding.*
2 denoting material used for or associated with a process etc.: *cladding* | *piping.*
■ denoting something involved in an action or process but with no corresponding verb: *sacking.*
3 forming the gerund of verbs (such as *painting* as in *I love painting*).
– ORIGIN Old English *-ung, -ing,* of Germanic origin.

-ing[2] ▶ suffix **1** forming the present participle of verbs: *doing* | *calling.*
■ forming present participles used as adjectives: *charming.*
2 forming adjectives from nouns: *hulking.*
– ORIGIN Middle English: alteration of earlier *-ende*, later *-inde.*

-ing[3] ▶ suffix (used especially in names of coins and fractional parts) a thing belonging to or having the quality of: *farthing* | *riding.*
– ORIGIN Old English, of Germanic origin.

ingather ▶ verb [with obj.] formal gather (something) in or together: *it may not be possible to ingather that information within the time.*

ingeminate /ɪnˈdʒɛmɪneɪt/ ▶ verb [with obj.] archaic repeat or reiterate (a word or statement), typically for emphasis.
– PHRASES **ingeminate peace** call repeatedly for peace.
– ORIGIN late 16th cent. (originally as *engeminate*): from Latin *ingeminat-* 'redoubled', from the verb *ingeminare*, from *in-* (expressing intensive force) + *geminare* (see **GEMINATE**).

Ingenhousz /ˈɪŋən,huːs/, Jan (1730–99), Dutch scientist. He is best known for his work on photosynthesis, in which he discovered that sunlit green plants take in carbon dioxide, fix the carbon, and 'restore' the air (oxygen).

ingenious /ɪnˈdʒiːnɪəs/ ▶ adjective (of a person) clever, original, and inventive: *he was ingenious enough to overcome the limited budget.*

■ (of a machine or idea) cleverly and originally devised and well suited to its purpose.
– DERIVATIVES **ingeniously** adverb, **ingeniousness** noun.
– ORIGIN late Middle English: from French *ingénieux* or Latin *ingeniosus*, from *ingenium* 'mind, intellect'; compare with **ENGINE**.

ingénue /ˈaʒɔn(j)uː/ ▶ noun an innocent or unsophisticated young woman.
■ a part of this type in a play. ■ an actress who plays such a part.
– ORIGIN French, feminine of *ingénu* 'ingenuous', from Latin *ingenuus* (see **INGENUOUS**).

ingenuity /ˌɪndʒɪˈnjuːɪti/ ▶ noun [mass noun] the quality of being clever, original, and inventive.
– ORIGIN late 16th cent. (also in the senses 'nobility' and 'ingenuousness'): from Latin *ingenuitas* 'ingenuousness', from *ingenuus* 'inborn'. The current meaning arose by confusion of **INGENUOUS** with **INGENIOUS**.

ingenuous /ɪnˈdʒɛnjʊəs/ ▶ adjective (of a person or action) innocent and unsuspecting.
– DERIVATIVES **ingenuously** adverb, **ingenuousness** noun.
– ORIGIN late 16th cent.: from Latin *ingenuus* literally 'native, inborn', from *in-* 'into' + an element related to *gignere* 'beget'. The original sense was 'noble, generous', giving rise to 'honourably straightforward, frank', hence 'innocently frank' (late 17th cent.).

ingest ▶ verb [with obj.] take (food, drink, or another substance) into the body by swallowing and absorbing it.
■ figurative absorb (information): *he spent his days ingesting the contents of the library.*
– DERIVATIVES **ingestion** noun, **ingestive** adjective.
– ORIGIN early 17th cent.: from Latin *ingest-* 'brought in', from the verb *ingerere*, from *in-* 'into' + *gerere* 'carry'.

ingesta /ɪnˈdʒɛstə/ ▶ plural noun Medicine & Zoology substances taken into the body as nourishment; food and drink.
– ORIGIN early 18th cent.: from Latin, 'things brought in', neuter plural of *ingestus*, past participle of *ingerere*.

-ing form ▶ noun Grammar the form of English verbs ending in *-ing*, which can function as a noun, an adjective, and in the formation of continuous tenses. See also **PARTICIPLE, GERUND**.

ingle ▶ noun chiefly dialect a domestic fire or fireplace.
■ an inglenook.
– ORIGIN early 16th cent. (originally Scots): perhaps from Scottish Gaelic *aingeal* 'light, fire', Irish *aingeal* 'live ember'.

inglenook ▶ noun a space on either side of a large fireplace.
– ORIGIN late 18th cent.: from Scots **INGLE** + **NOOK**.

inglorious ▶ adjective (of an action or situation) causing shame or a loss of honour: *an inglorious episode in British imperial history.*
■ not famous or renowned.
– DERIVATIVES **ingloriously** adverb, **ingloriousness** noun.
– ORIGIN mid 16th cent.: from Latin *inglorius* (from *in-* (expressing negation) + *gloria* 'glory') + **-OUS**.

-ingly ▶ suffix forming adverbs denoting manner, nature, or condition: *startlingly* | *unwittingly.*

in-goal area ▶ noun Rugby the area between the goal line and the dead-ball line.

ingoing ▶ adjective [attrib.] going into or towards a particular place: *the paths of ingoing and outgoing rays.*

ingot /ˈɪŋɡət/ ▶ noun a block of steel, gold, silver, or other metal, typically oblong in shape.
– ORIGIN late Middle English (denoting a mould in which metal is cast): perhaps from **IN** + Old English *goten*, past participle of *geotan* 'pour, cast'.

ingraft ▶ verb variant spelling of **ENGRAFT**.

ingrain ▶ verb (also **engrain**) [with obj.] firmly fix or establish (a habit, belief, or attitude) in a person.
▶ adjective (of a textile) composed of fibres which have been dyed different colours before being woven.
– ORIGIN late Middle English (originally as *engrain* in the sense 'dye with cochineal or in fast colours'): from **EN-**[1], **IN-**[2] (as an intensifier) + the verb **GRAIN**. The adjective is from *in grain* 'fast-dyed', from the old use of *grain* meaning 'kermes, cochineal'.

ingrain carpet ▶ noun a reversible carpet in which the pattern appears on both sides.

ingrained ▶ adjective (also **engrained**) **1** (of a habit, belief, or attitude) firmly fixed or established; difficult to change: *his deeply ingrained Catholic convictions.*
2 (of dirt or a stain) deeply embedded and thus difficult to remove: *the ingrained dirt on the flaking paintwork.*

ingrate /ˈɪŋɡreɪt, ɪnˈɡreɪt/ formal or poetic/literary ▶ noun an ungrateful person.
▶ adjective ungrateful.
– ORIGIN late Middle English (as an adjective): from Latin *ingratus*, from *in-* 'not' + *gratus* 'grateful'.

ingratiate /ɪnˈɡreɪʃɪeɪt/ ▶ verb (**ingratiate oneself**) bring oneself into favour with someone by flattering or trying to please them: *a sycophantic attempt to ingratiate herself with the local aristocracy.*
– DERIVATIVES **ingratiation** noun.
– ORIGIN early 17th cent.: from Latin *in gratiam* 'into favour', on the pattern of obsolete Italian *ingratiare*, earlier form of *ingraziare*.

ingratiating ▶ adjective intended to gain approval or favour; sycophantic: *an ingratiating manner.*
– DERIVATIVES **ingratiatingly** adverb.

ingratitude ▶ noun [mass noun] a discreditable lack of gratitude: *he returned his daughter's care with ingratitude and unkindness.*
– ORIGIN Middle English: from Old French, or from late Latin *ingratitudo*, from Latin *ingratus* 'ungrateful' (see **INGRATE**).

ingravescent /ˌɪŋɡrəˈvɛs(ə)nt/ ▶ adjective Medicine (of a condition or symptom) gradually increasing in severity.
– DERIVATIVES **ingravescence** noun.
– ORIGIN early 19th cent.: from Latin *ingravescent-* 'growing heavy or worse', from the verb *ingravescere* (based on *gravis* 'heavy').

ingredient ▶ noun any of the foods or substances that are combined to make a particular dish.
■ a component part or element of something: *the affair contains all the ingredients of an insoluble mystery.*
– ORIGIN late Middle English: from Latin *ingredient-* 'entering', from the verb *ingredi*, from *in-* 'into' + *gradi* 'walk'.

Ingres /ˈaŋɡrə, French ɛ̃ɡr/, Jean Auguste Dominique (1780–1867), French painter. A pupil of Jacques-Louis David, he vigorously upheld neoclassicism in opposition to Delacroix's romanticism. Notable works: *Ambassadors of Agamemnon* (1801) and *The Bather* (1808).

ingress /ˈɪŋɡrɛs/ ▶ noun **1** a place or means of access; an entrance.
■ [mass noun] the action or fact of going in or entering; the capacity or right of entrance. ■ [mass noun] the unwanted introduction of water, foreign bodies, contaminants, etc.
2 Astronomy & Astrology the arrival of the sun, moon, or a planet in a specified constellation or part of the sky.
■ the beginning of a transit.
– DERIVATIVES **ingression** noun.
– ORIGIN late Middle English (in the sense 'an entrance or beginning'): from Latin *ingressus*, from the verb *ingredi* 'enter'.

ingressive ▶ adjective **1** of or relating to ingress; having the quality or character of entering.
2 Phonetics (of a speech sound) made with an intake of air rather than an exhalation. Compare with **EGRESSIVE**.
■ (of an airflow) inward.
▶ noun an ingressive sound, e.g. a click.

in-group ▶ noun an exclusive, typically small, group of people with a shared interest or identity.

ingrowing ▶ adjective growing inwards or within something, especially (of a toenail) growing abnormally so as to press into the flesh.

ingrown ▶ adjective growing or having grown within a thing; innate: *as Greek instinct or ingrown habit would have dictated.*
■ (of a toenail) having grown into the flesh. ■ preoccupied with oneself; inward-looking: *direct mail is a clubby, ingrown world in which everybody knows everybody.* ■ Geology (of an incised meander) asymmetric in cross section due to lateral erosion.

ingrowth ▶ noun a thing which has grown inwards or within something.
■ [mass noun] the action of growing inwards: *blocked by tumour ingrowth.*

inguinal /ˈɪŋgwɪn(ə)l/ ▶ **adjective** [attrib.] Anatomy of the groin: *inguinal lymph nodes.*
– DERIVATIVES **inguinally** adverb.
– ORIGIN late Middle English: from Latin *inguinalis*, from *inguen*, *inguin-* 'groin'.

ingulf ▶ **verb** archaic spelling of **ENGULF**.

ingurgitate /ɪnˈgəːdʒɪteɪt/ ▶ **verb** [with obj.] poetic/literary swallow (something) greedily.
– DERIVATIVES **ingurgitation** noun.
– ORIGIN late 16th cent.: from Latin *ingurgitat-* 'poured in, drenched', from the verb *ingurgitare*, from *in-* 'into' + *gurges*, *gurgit-* 'whirlpool, gulf'.

Ingush /ˈɪŋgʊʃ/ ▶ **noun** (pl. same or **Ingushes**) **1** a member of a people living mainly in the Ingush republic in the central Caucasus, between Chechnya and North Ossetia.
2 [mass noun] the North Caucasian language of this people.
▶ **adjective** of or relating to the Ingush or their language.
– ORIGIN Russian.

inhabit ▶ **verb** (**inhabited**, **inhabiting**) [with obj.] (of a person, animal, or group) live in or occupy (a place or environment): *a bird that inhabits North America* | *the region was inhabited by Indians.*
– DERIVATIVES **inhabitability** /-təˈbɪlɪti/ noun, **inhabitable** adjective, **inhabitation** noun.
– ORIGIN late Middle English *inhabite*, *enhabite*, from Old French *enhabiter* or Latin *inhabitare*, from *in-* 'in' + *habitare* 'dwell' (from *habere* 'have').

inhabitancy (also **inhabitance**) ▶ **noun** [mass noun] archaic living in a certain place as an inhabitant, especially during a specified period so as to acquire certain rights.

inhabitant ▶ **noun** a person or animal that lives in or occupies a place.
■ US a person who fulfils the residential or legal requirements for being a member of a state or parish.
– ORIGIN late Middle English: from Old French, from Latin *inhabitare* 'inhabit'.

inhalant ▶ **noun** a medicinal preparation for inhaling.
■ a solvent or other material producing vapour that is inhaled by drug abusers.
▶ **adjective** [attrib.] chiefly Zoology serving for inhalation: *an inhalant siphon.*

inhalation ▶ **noun** the action of inhaling or breathing in: [mass noun] *the inhalation of airborne particles* | [count noun] *with every inhalation air passes over the vocal cords.*
■ Medicine the inhaling of medicines or anaesthetics in the form of a gas or vapour. ■ [count noun] Medicine a preparation to be inhaled in the form of a vapour or spray.
– ORIGIN early 17th cent.: from medieval Latin *inhalatio(n-)*, from *inhalare* 'inhale'.

inhalator /ˈɪnhəˌleɪtə/ ▶ **noun** a device for inhaling something, especially oxygen; a respirator; an inhaler.

inhale /ɪnˈheɪl/ ▶ **verb** breathe in (air, gas, smoke, etc.): [with obj.] *he longed to inhale fresh air* | [no obj.] *they can continue to exhale while inhaling through the nose.*
■ [with obj.] N. Amer. informal eat (food) greedily or rapidly.
– ORIGIN early 18th cent.: from Latin *inhalare* 'breathe in', from *in-* 'in' + *halare* 'breathe'.

inhaler ▶ **noun** a portable device for administering a drug which is to be breathed in, used for relieving asthma and other bronchial or nasal congestion.

inharmonic ▶ **adjective** chiefly Music not harmonic.
– DERIVATIVES **inharmonicity** noun.

inharmonious ▶ **adjective** not forming or contributing to a pleasing whole; discordant: *an inharmonious, negative state of mind.*
– DERIVATIVES **inharmoniously** adverb.

inhaul ▶ **noun** Sailing a rope used to haul in the clew of a sail.

inhere /ɪnˈhɪə/ ▶ **verb** [no obj.] (**inhere in/within**) formal exist essentially or permanently in: *the potential for change that inheres within the adult education world.*
■ Law (of rights, powers, etc.) be vested in a person or group or attached to the ownership of a property: *the rights inhering in the property they owned.*
– ORIGIN mid 16th cent. (in the sense 'stick, cling to'): from Latin *inhaerere* 'stick to'.

inherent /ɪnˈhɪər(ə)nt, -ˈhɛr(ə)nt/ ▶ **adjective** existing in something as a permanent, essential, or characteristic attribute: *any form of mountaineering has its inherent dangers* | *the symbolism inherent in all folk tales.*
■ Law vested in (someone) as a right or privilege. ■ Linguistics (of an adjective) having the same meaning in both attributive and predicative uses. Contrasted with **NON-INHERENT**.
– DERIVATIVES **inherence** noun, **inherently** adverb.
– ORIGIN late 16th cent.: from Latin *inhaerent-* 'sticking to', from the verb *inhaerere*, from *in-* 'in, towards' + *haerere* 'to stick'.

inherit ▶ **verb** (**inherited**, **inheriting**) [with obj.] receive (money, property, or a title) as an heir at the death of the previous holder: *she inherited a fortune from her father.*
■ derive (a quality, characteristic, or predisposition) genetically from one's parents or ancestors: *she had inherited the beauty of her grandmother.* ■ receive or be left with (a situation, object, etc.) from a predecessor or former owner: *spending commitments inherited from previous governments.* ■ N. Amer. come into possession of (belongings) from someone else: *she inherits all her clothes from her older sisters.* ■ archaic come into possession of (something) as a right (especially in biblical translations and allusions): *master, what must I do to inherit eternal life?*
– DERIVATIVES **inheritor** noun.
– ORIGIN Middle English *enherite* 'receive as a right', from Old French *enheriter*, from late Latin *inhereditare* 'appoint as heir', from Latin *in-* 'in' + *heres*, *hered-* 'heir'.

inheritable ▶ **adjective** capable of being inherited: *these characteristics are inheritable* | *inheritable property.*
– DERIVATIVES **inheritability** noun.
– ORIGIN late Middle English (formerly also as *enheritable*): from Anglo-Norman French *enheritable* 'able to be made heir', from Old French *enheriter* (see **INHERIT**).

inheritance ▶ **noun** a thing that is inherited.
■ [mass noun] the action of inheriting: *the inheritance of traits.*
– ORIGIN late Middle English (formerly also as *enheritance*): from Anglo-Norman French *enheritaunce* 'being admitted as heir', from Old French *enheriter* (see **INHERIT**).

inheritance tax ▶ **noun** [mass noun] (in the UK) tax levied on property and money acquired by gift or inheritance (introduced in 1986 to replace capital transfer tax).

inhesion /ɪnˈhiːʒ(ə)n/ ▶ **noun** formal the action or state of inhering in something.
– ORIGIN mid 17th cent.: from late Latin *inhaesio(n-)*, from Latin *inhaerere* 'stick to'.

inhibin /ɪnˈhɪbɪn/ ▶ **noun** [mass noun] Biochemistry a gonadal hormone which inhibits the secretion of follicle-stimulating hormone, under consideration as a potential male contraceptive.
– ORIGIN 1930s: from Latin *inhibere* 'hinder' + **-IN**[1].

inhibit ▶ **verb** (**inhibited**, **inhibiting**) [with obj.] hinder, restrain, or prevent (an action or process): *cold inhibits plant growth.*
■ (**inhibit someone from doing something**) prevent or prohibit someone from doing something: *the earnings rule inhibited some retired people from working.* ■ make (someone) self-conscious and unable to act in a relaxed and natural way: *his mother's strictures would always inhibit him.* ■ chiefly Physiology & Biochemistry (chiefly of a drug or other substance) slow down or prevent (a process, reaction, or function) or reduce the activity of (an enzyme or other agent). ■ (in ecclesiastical law) forbid (a member of the clergy) to exercise clerical functions.
– DERIVATIVES **inhibitive** adjective.
– ORIGIN late Middle English (in the sense 'forbid (a person) to do something'): from Latin *inhibere* 'hinder', from *in-* 'in' + *habere* 'hold'.

inhibited ▶ **adjective** unable to act in a relaxed and natural way because of self-consciousness or mental restraint: *I could never appear nude, I'm far too inhibited.*

inhibition ▶ **noun 1** a feeling that makes one self-conscious and unable to act in a relaxed and natural way: *the children, at first shy, soon lost their inhibitions* | [mass noun] *she showed an enthusiasm for sex and a lack of inhibition which was entirely alien to him.*
■ Psychology a restraint on the direct expression of an instinct. ■ [mass noun] the action of inhibiting, restricting, or hindering a process. ■ [mass noun] the slowing or prevention of a process, reaction, or function by a particular substance.
2 Law, Brit. an order or writ of prohibition, especially against dealing with a specified piece of land or property.
– ORIGIN late Middle English (in the sense 'forbidding, a prohibition'): from Latin *inhibitio(n-)*, from the verb *inhibere* (see **INHIBIT**).

inhibitor ▶ **noun** a thing which inhibits someone or something.
■ a substance which slows down or prevents a particular chemical reaction or other process or which reduces the activity of a particular reactant, catalyst, or enzyme. ■ Genetics a gene whose presence prevents the expression of some other gene at a different locus. ■ Scots Law a person who takes out an inhibition.
– DERIVATIVES **inhibitory** adjective.

in-home ▶ **adjective** [attrib.] (of a service or activity) provided or taking place within a person's home: *in-home haircuts for children.*

inhomogeneous /ˌɪnhɒmə(ʊ)ˈdʒiːnɪəs, -ˈdʒɛn-, ˌɪnhəʊm-/ ▶ **adjective** not uniform in character or content; diverse.
■ Mathematics consisting of terms that are not all of the same degree or dimensions.
– DERIVATIVES **inhomogeneity** noun.

inhospitable /ˌɪnhɒˈspɪtəb(ə)l, ɪnˈhɒspɪt-/ ▶ **adjective** (of an environment) harsh and difficult to live in: *the inhospitable landscape.*
■ (of a person) unfriendly and unwelcoming towards people.
– DERIVATIVES **inhospitableness** noun, **inhospitably** adverb, **inhospitality** noun.
– ORIGIN late 16th cent.: French, from *in-* 'not' + *hospitable* (see **HOSPITABLE**).

in-house ▶ **adjective** /ˈɪnhaʊs/ [attrib.] done or existing within an organization: *in-house publications.*
▶ **adverb** /ɪnˈhaʊs/ without assistance from outside an organization; internally: *services previously provided in-house are being contracted out.*

inhuman ▶ **adjective 1** lacking human qualities of compassion and mercy; cruel and barbaric.
2 not human in nature or character: *the inhuman scale of the dinosaurs.*
– DERIVATIVES **inhumanly** adverb.
– ORIGIN late Middle English (originally as *inhumane*): from Latin *inhumanus*, from *in-* 'not' + *humanus* (see **HUMAN**).

inhumane ▶ **adjective** without compassion for misery or suffering; cruel.
– DERIVATIVES **inhumanely** adverb.
– ORIGIN late Middle English (in the sense 'inhuman, brutal'): originally a variant of **INHUMAN** (rare after 1700); in modern use from **IN-**[1] 'not' + **HUMANE** (the current sense dating from the early 19th cent.).

inhumanity ▶ **noun** (pl. **-ies**) [mass noun] extremely cruel and brutal behaviour: *man's inhumanity to man* | [count noun] *an elaborate review of man's inhumanities.*
– ORIGIN late 15th cent.: from Old French *inhumanite* or Latin *inhumanitas*, from *inhumanus* 'inhuman'.

inhumation /ˌɪnhjʊˈmeɪʃ(ə)n/ ▶ **noun** [mass noun] chiefly Archaeology the action or practice of burying the dead; the fact of being buried.
■ [count noun] a burial or buried corpse: *more than thirty human inhumations from various sites.*

inhume /ɪnˈhjuːm/ ▶ **verb** [with obj.] poetic/literary bury: *no hand his bones shall gather or inhume.*
– ORIGIN early 17th cent.: from Latin *inhumare*, from *in-* 'into' + *humus* 'ground'.

inimical /ɪˈnɪmɪk(ə)l/ ▶ **adjective** tending to obstruct or harm: *the policy was* ***inimical to*** *Britain's real interests.*
■ unfriendly; hostile: *an inimical alien power.*
– DERIVATIVES **inimically** adverb.
– ORIGIN early 16th cent.: from late Latin *inimicalis*, from Latin *inimicus* (see **ENEMY**).

inimitable /ɪˈnɪmɪtəb(ə)l/ ▶ **adjective** so good or unusual as to be impossible to copy; unique: *they took the charts by storm with their inimitable style.*
– DERIVATIVES **inimitability** noun, **inimitably** adverb.
– ORIGIN late 15th cent.: from French, or from Latin *inimitabilis*, from *in-* 'not' + *imitabilis* (from *imitari* 'imitate').

inion /ˈɪnɪɒn/ ▶ **noun** Anatomy the projecting part of the occipital bone at the base of the skull.
– ORIGIN early 19th cent.: from Greek, literally 'nape of the neck'.

iniquity /ɪˈnɪkwɪti/ ▶ **noun** (pl. **-ies**) [mass noun] immoral or grossly unfair behaviour: *a den of iniquity* | [count noun] *the iniquities of British taxation.*

– DERIVATIVES **iniquitous** adjective, **iniquitously** adverb, **iniquitousness** noun.
– ORIGIN Middle English: from Old French *iniquite*, from Latin *iniquitas*, from *iniquus*, from *in-* 'not' + *aequus* 'equal, just'.

initial ▶ **adjective** [attrib.] existing or occurring at the beginning: *our initial impression was favourable.*
■ (of a letter) at the beginning of a word.
▶ **noun** (usu. **initials**) the first letter of a name or word, typically a person's given name or a word forming part of a phrase: *the initials VAT stand for value added tax.*
▶ **verb** (**initialled**, **initialling**; N. Amer. **initialed**, **initialing**) [with obj.] mark or sign (a document) with one's initials, especially in order to authorize or validate it.
■ agree to or ratify (a treaty or contract) by signing it.
– ORIGIN early 16th cent.: from Latin *initialis*, from *initium* 'beginning', from *inire* 'go in', from *in-* 'into' + *ire* 'go'.

initialese /ɪˌnɪʃəˈliːz/ ▶ **noun** [mass noun] informal the use of abbreviations formed by using initial letters.

initialism ▶ **noun** an abbreviation consisting of initial letters pronounced separately (e.g. *BBC*).

initialize (also **-ise**) ▶ **verb** [with obj.] Computing **1** (often **be initialized to**) set to the value or put in the condition appropriate to the start of an operation: *the counter is initialized to one.*
2 format (a computer disk).
– DERIVATIVES **initialization** noun.

initially ▶ **adverb** [usu. sentence adverb] at first: *initially, he thought the new concept was nonsense.*

initial public offering ▶ **noun** chiefly US a company's flotation on the stock exchange.

initial teaching alphabet ▶ **noun** a 44-letter phonetic alphabet used to help those beginning to read and write English. It was used in many British primary schools in the 1960s but is now rarely seen.

initiand /ɪˈnɪʃɪand/ ▶ **noun** a person about to be initiated.
– ORIGIN early 20th cent.: from Latin *initiandus*, from *initiare* 'to initiate'.

initiate ▶ **verb** /ɪˈnɪʃɪeɪt/ [with obj.] **1** cause (a process or action) to begin: *he proposes to initiate discussions on planning procedures.*
2 admit (someone) into a secret or obscure society or group, typically with a ritual: *she had been formally* ***initiated into*** *the movement.*
■ [as plural noun **the initiated**] figurative a small group of people who share obscure knowledge: *boots known as DMs to the initiated.* ■ (**initiate someone in/into**) introduce someone to a particular activity or skill, especially a difficult or obscure one: *they were initiated into the mysteries of mathematics.*
▶ **noun** /ɪˈnɪʃɪət/ a person who has been initiated into an organization or activity, typically recently: *initiates of the Shiva cult* | [as modifier] *the initiate Marines.*
– DERIVATIVES **initiation** noun, **initiatory** adjective.
– ORIGIN mid 16th cent. (in sense 2): from Latin *initiat-* 'begun', from the verb *initiare*, from *initium* 'beginning'.

initiative ▶ **noun 1** [mass noun] the ability to assess and initiate things independently: *use your initiative, imagination, and common sense.*
2 [in sing.] the power or opportunity to act or take charge before others do: *we have lost the initiative and allowed our opponents to dictate the subject.*
3 an act or strategy intended to resolve a difficulty or improve a situation; a fresh approach to something: *a new initiative against car crime.*
■ a proposal made by one nation to another in an attempt to improve relations: *China welcomed the Soviet initiative.*
4 (**the initiative**) (especially in Switzerland and some US states) the right of citizens outside the legislature to originate legislation.
– PHRASES **on one's own initiative** without being prompted by others. **take** (or **seize**) **the initiative** be the first to take action in a particular situation: *anti-hunting groups have seized the initiative in the dispute.*
– ORIGIN late 18th cent.: from French, from Latin *initiare*, from *initium* 'beginning'.

initiator ▶ **noun** a person or thing that initiates someone or something.
■ Chemistry a substance which starts a chain reaction. ■ an explosive or device used to detonate a larger one.

inject ▶ **verb** [with obj.] **1** drive or force (a liquid, especially a drug or vaccine) into a person or animal's body with a syringe or similar device: *the doctor injected a painkilling drug.*
■ administer a drug or medicine to (a person or animal) in this way: *he* ***injected*** *himself* ***with*** *a drug overdose.* ■ [no obj.] inject oneself with a narcotic drug, especially habitually: *people who want to stop injecting.* ■ introduce (something) into a passage, cavity, or solid material under pressure: *inject the foam and allow it to expand.* ■ Physics introduce or feed (a current, beam of particles, etc.) into a substance or device. ■ place (a spacecraft or other object) into an orbit or trajectory: *many meteoroids are* ***injected into*** *hyperbolic orbits.*
2 introduce (a new or different element) into something, especially as a boost or interruption: *she tried to* ***inject*** *scorn* ***into*** *her tone.*
■ (**inject something with**) imbue something with (a new element): *he injected his voice with a confidence he didn't feel.*
– DERIVATIVES **injectable** adjective & noun.
– ORIGIN late 16th cent. (in the sense 'throw or cast on something'): from Latin *inject-* 'thrown in', from the verb *inicere*, from *in-* 'into' + *jacere* 'throw'.

injection ▶ **noun 1** an instance of injecting or being injected: *painkilling injections* | *an injection of capital was needed.*
■ a thing that is injected: *a morphine injection.* ■ [mass noun] the action of injecting: *the walls have been damp-proofed by injection.* ■ short for **FUEL INJECTION**. ■ Mathematics a one-to-one mapping.
2 [mass noun] the entry or placing of a spacecraft or other object into an orbit or trajectory.
– ORIGIN late Middle English: from Latin *injectio(n-)*, from the verb *inicere* (see **INJECT**).

injection moulding ▶ **noun** [mass noun] the shaping of rubber or plastic articles by injecting heated material into a mould.
– DERIVATIVES **injection-moulded** adjective.

injective ▶ **adjective** Mathematics of the nature of or relating to an injection or one-to-one mapping.

injector ▶ **noun** a person or thing that injects something.
■ (also **fuel injector**) (in an internal-combustion engine) the nozzle and valve through which fuel is sprayed into a combustion chamber. ■ (in a steam engine) a system of nozzles that uses steam to inject water into a pressurized boiler.

injera /ˈɪndʒiːrə/ ▶ **noun** [mass noun] a white leavened Ethiopian bread made from teff flour, similar to a crêpe.
– ORIGIN Amharic.

in-joke ▶ **noun** a joke that is shared exclusively by a small group of people.

injudicious ▶ **adjective** showing very poor judgement; unwise: *I took a few injudicious swigs of potent cider.*
– DERIVATIVES **injudiciously** adverb, **injudiciousness** noun.

Injun /ˈɪndʒ(ə)n/ ▶ **noun** US informal, offensive an American Indian.
– PHRASES **honest Injun** dated honestly; really: *I won't run away, honest Injun.*
– ORIGIN late 17th cent.: alteration of **INDIAN**.

injunct /ɪnˈdʒʌŋ(k)t/ ▶ **verb** [with obj.] issue a legal injunction against.
– ORIGIN late 19th cent.: from Latin *injunct-* 'imposed', from the verb *injungere* (see **ENJOIN**).

injunction ▶ **noun** an authoritative warning or order.
■ Law a judicial order restraining a person from beginning or continuing an action threatening or invading the legal right of another, or compelling a person to carry out a certain act, e.g. to make restitution to an injured party.
– DERIVATIVES **injunctive** adjective.
– ORIGIN late Middle English: from late Latin *injunctio(n-)*, from Latin *injungere* 'enjoin impose'.

injure ▶ **verb** [with obj.] do physical harm or damage to (someone): *the explosion injured several people.*
■ suffer physical harm or damage to (a part of one's body). ■ harm or impair (something): *a libel calculated to injure the company's reputation.* ■ archaic do injustice or wrong to (someone).
– DERIVATIVES **injurer** noun.
– ORIGIN late Middle English: back-formation from **INJURY**.

injured ▶ **adjective 1** harmed, damaged, or impaired: *a road accident left him severely injured.*
2 offended: *his injured pride.*

injurious /ɪnˈdʒʊərɪəs/ ▶ **adjective** causing or likely to cause damage or harm: *food which is* ***injurious to*** *health.*
■ (of language) maliciously insulting; libellous.
– DERIVATIVES **injuriously** adverb, **injuriousness** noun.
– ORIGIN late Middle English: from French *injurieux* or Latin *injuriosus*, from *injuria* 'a wrong' (see **INJURY**).

injury ▶ **noun** (pl. **-ies**) an instance of being injured: *she suffered an injury to her back* | *an ankle injury.*
■ [mass noun] the fact of being injured; harm or damage: *all escaped without serious injury.* ■ (**injury to**) offence to: *injury to his feelings.*
– PHRASES **do oneself an injury** informal suffer physical harm or damage.
– ORIGIN late Middle English: from Anglo-Norman French *injurie*, from Latin *injuria* 'a wrong', from *in-* (expressing negation) + *jus, jur-* 'right'.

injury time ▶ **noun** [mass noun] Brit. (in soccer and other sports) extra playing time allowed by a referee to compensate for time lost in dealing with injuries.

injustice ▶ **noun** [mass noun] lack of fairness or justice: *the injustice of the death penalty.*
■ [count noun] an unjust act or occurrence: *brooding over life's injustices.*
– PHRASES **do someone an injustice** judge a person unfairly.
– ORIGIN late Middle English: from Old French, from Latin *injustitia*, from *in-* 'not' + *justus* 'just, right'.

ink ▶ **noun** [mass noun] a coloured fluid or paste used for writing, drawing, printing, or duplicating: *the names are written in ink* | [count noun] *a picture executed in coloured inks.*
■ Zoology a black liquid ejected by a cuttlefish, octopus, or squid to confuse a predator.
▶ **verb 1** [with obj.] mark (words or a design) with ink: *the cork has the name of the château inked on to the side.*
■ cover (type or a stamp) with ink before printing: *a raised image is inked to produce an impression.* ■ (**ink something in**) fill in writing or a design with ink: *she inked in a cloud of dust.* ■ (**ink something out**) obliterate something, especially writing, with ink: *he carefully inked out each word.*
2 informal, chiefly N. Amer. sign (a contract).
■ secure the services of (someone) with a contract.
– DERIVATIVES **inker** noun.
– ORIGIN Middle English *enke, inke*, from Old French *enque*, via late Latin from Greek *enkauston*, denoting the purple ink used by Roman emperors for signatures, from *enkaiein* 'burn in'.

Inkatha /ɪnˈkɑːtə/ (in full **Inkatha Freedom Party**) (abbrev.: **IFP**) a mainly Zulu political party and organization in South Africa, founded in 1928 and revived in 1975 by Chief Buthelezi. It has a professed aim of racial equality and universal franchise in South Africa, but progress towards political reform was obstructed by violent clashes between Inkatha factions and members of the rival ANC.
– ORIGIN from Zulu *inkhata* 'crown of woven grass', a tribal emblem symbolizing the force unifying the Zulu nation.

inkberry ▶ **noun** (pl. **-ies**) a low-growing North American holly with black berries and nearly spineless leaves.
● *Ilex glabra*, family Aquifoliaceae.

ink-blot test ▶ **noun** another term for **RORSCHACH TEST**.

ink cap ▶ **noun** a widely distributed mushroom with a tall, narrow cap and slender white stem, turning into a black liquid after the spores are shed.
● Genus *Coprinus*, family Coprinaceae, class Hymenomycetes: several species, including the **common ink cap** (*C. atramentarius*). See also **SHAGGY INK CAP**.

inkhorn ▶ **noun** historical a small portable container for ink.
■ [as modifier] denoting words or expressions used only in academic writing: *I will avoid many of the inkhorn terms coined by the narratologists.*

ink-jet printer ▶ **noun** a printer in which the characters are formed by minute jets of ink.

inkle /ˈɪŋk(ə)l/ ▶ **noun** [mass noun] a kind of linen tape formerly used to make laces, or the linen yarn from which this is manufactured.
– ORIGIN mid 16th cent.: of unknown origin.

inkling ▶ **noun** a slight knowledge or suspicion; a

hint: *the records give us an inkling of how people saw the world.*
– ORIGIN late Middle English (in the sense 'a mention in an undertone, a hint'): from the rare verb *inkle* 'utter in an undertone', of unknown origin.

ink-pad ▶ noun an ink-soaked pad in a shallow box, used for inking a rubber stamp or taking fingerprints.

inkstand ▶ noun a stand for one or more ink bottles, typically incorporating a pen tray.

inkwell ▶ noun a pot for ink typically housed in a hole in a desk.

inky ▶ adjective (**inkier**, **inkiest**) **1** as dark as ink: *the cold inky blackness of a Mexican cave.*
2 stained with ink: *bureaucrats with inky fingers.*
– DERIVATIVES **inkiness** noun.

INLA ▶ abbreviation for Irish National Liberation Army.

inlaid past and past participle of **INLAY**.

inland /ˈɪnlənd, -land/ ▶ adjective situated in the interior of a country rather than on the coast: *the inland port of Gloucester.*
■ [attrib.] chiefly Brit. carried on within the limits of a country; domestic: *a network of waterways that allowed inland trade.*
▶ adverb /also ɪnˈland/ in or towards the interior of a country: *the path turned inland and met the road | the hills inland from Brighton.*
▶ noun (**the inland**) the parts of a country remote from the sea or frontiers; the interior.
– DERIVATIVES **inlander** noun.

inland navigation ▶ noun [mass noun] transportation by canals and rivers.

inland revenue ▶ noun [mass noun] Brit. public revenue consisting of income tax and some other direct taxes.
■ (**Inland Revenue**) (in the UK) the government department responsible for assessing and collecting such revenue.

Inland Sea an almost landlocked arm of the Pacific Ocean, surrounded by the Japanese islands of Honshu, Shikoku, and Kyushu. Its chief port is Hiroshima.

inland sea ▶ noun an entirely landlocked large body of salt or fresh water.

in-law ▶ noun a relative by marriage.

inlay ▶ verb /ɪnˈleɪ/ (past and past participle **inlaid**) [with obj.] (usu. **be inlaid**) ornament (an object) by embedding pieces of a different material in it, flush with its surface: *mahogany panelling inlaid with rosewood.*
■ embed (something) in an object in this way: *a small silver crown was inlaid in the wood.*
▶ noun /ˈɪnleɪ/ **1** a design, pattern, or piece of material inlaid in something: *ivory inlays that decorated wooden furnishings.*
■ a material or substance that is inlaid. ■ [mass noun] inlaid work: *the cathedral was decorated with mosaic and inlay.* ■ [mass noun] the technique of inlaying material.
2 a filling shaped to fit a tooth cavity.
3 a printed card or paper insert supplied with a CD, video, etc.: [as modifier] *an inlay card.*
– DERIVATIVES **inlayer** noun.
– ORIGIN mid 16th cent. (in the sense 'lay something in a place in order to hide or preserve it'): from **IN-**² 'into' + **LAY**¹.

inlet ▶ noun **1** a small arm of the sea, a lake, or a river.
2 a place or means of entry: *an air inlet.*
3 (chiefly in tailoring and dressmaking) an inserted piece of material.
– ORIGIN Middle English (denoting admission): from **IN** + the verb **LET**¹.

inlier /ˈɪnlʌɪə/ ▶ noun Geology an older rock formation isolated among newer rocks.
– ORIGIN mid 19th cent.: from **IN**, on the pattern of *outlier.*

in-line ▶ adjective **1** having parts arranged in a line: *a 20-valve in-line 5-cylinder engine.*
2 constituting an integral part of a continuous sequence of operations or machines: *a two-stream in-line fuel-oil blender.*
■ constituting an integral part of a computer program: *the parameters can be set up as in-line code.*

in-liner ▶ noun an in-line skater.
■ an in-line skate.

in-line skates ▶ plural noun a pair of roller skates in which the wheels on each boot are fixed in a single line along its sole.

– DERIVATIVES **in-line skater** noun, **in-line skating** noun.

in loco parentis /ɪn ˌləʊkəʊ pəˈrɛntɪs/ ▶ adverb & adjective (of a teacher or other adult responsible for children) in the place of a parent: [as adv.] *he was used to acting in loco parentis* | [as adj.] *they adhered to an in loco parentis approach when dealing with students.*
– ORIGIN Latin.

inly /ˈɪnli/ ▶ adverb poetic/literary inwardly: *inly stung with anger and disdain.*
– ORIGIN Old English *innlīce* (see **IN**, **-LY**²).

inlying /ˈɪnlʌɪɪŋ/ ▶ adjective [attrib.] situated within or near a centre.

Inmarsat /ˈɪnmɑːsat/ an international organization founded in 1978 that provides telecommunication services, as well as distress and safety communication services, to the world's shipping, aviation, and offshore industries.
– ORIGIN from initials of *International Maritime Satellite Organization.*

inmate ▶ noun a person living in an institution such as a prison or hospital.
■ archaic one of several occupants of a house.
– ORIGIN late 16th cent. (denoting a person who shared a house, specifically a lodger or subtenant): probably originally from **INN** + **MATE**¹, later associated with **IN**.

in medias res /ɪn ˌmiːdɪas ˈreɪz/ ▶ adverb into the middle of a narrative; without preamble: *having begun his story in medias res.*
■ into the midst of things.
– ORIGIN Latin.

in memoriam /ˌɪn mɪˈmɔːrɪam/ ▶ noun [often as modifier] an article written in memory of a dead person; an obituary: *in memoriam notices in the paper.*
▶ preposition in memory of (a dead person): *an openly revolutionary work in memoriam Che Guevara.*
– ORIGIN Latin.

inmost ▶ adjective poetic/literary innermost.
– ORIGIN Old English *innemest* (see **IN**, **-MOST**).

inn ▶ noun [usu. in names] a public house, typically one in the country, in some cases providing accommodation: *the Swan Inn.*
■ historical a house providing accommodation, food, and drink, especially for travellers.
– ORIGIN Old English (in the sense 'dwelling place, lodging'): of Germanic origin; related to **IN**. In Middle English the word was used to translate Latin *hospitium* (see **HOSPICE**), denoting a house of residence for students: this sense is preserved in the names of some buildings formerly used for this purpose, notably *Gray's Inn* and *Lincoln's Inn*, two of the **INNS OF COURT**. The current sense dates from late Middle English.

innards ▶ plural noun informal entrails.
■ internal workings (of a device or machine).
– ORIGIN early 19th cent.: representing a dialect pronunciation of **INWARDS**, used as a noun.

innate /ɪˈneɪt, ˈɪneɪt/ ▶ adjective inborn; natural: *her innate capacity for organization.*
■ Philosophy originating in the mind.
– DERIVATIVES **innately** adverb, **innateness** noun.
– ORIGIN late Middle English: from Latin *innatus*, past participle of *innasci*, from *in-* 'into' + *nasci* 'be born'.

inner ▶ adjective [attrib.] **1** situated inside or further in; internal: *an inner courtyard* | *the inner thigh.*
■ close to the centre: *inner London.* ■ close to the centre of power: *the inner cabinet.*
2 mental or spiritual: *a test of inner strength.*
■ (of thoughts or feelings) private and not expressed or discernible.
▶ noun the inner part of something: *using his rock shoes as inners for his double boots.*
■ (in archery and shooting) a division of the target next to the bullseye. ■ a shot that strikes this.
– DERIVATIVES **innerly** adverb (poetic/literary), **innerness** noun (poetic/literary).
– ORIGIN Old English *innera, innra*, comparative of **IN**.

inner bar ▶ noun (in the UK) Queen's or King's Counsel collectively.

inner child ▶ noun a person's supposed original or true self, especially when regarded as damaged or concealed by negative childhood experiences.

inner circle ▶ noun an exclusive group close to the centre of power of an organization or movement, regarded as elitist and secretive.

inner city ▶ noun [usu. as modifier] the area near the centre of a city, especially when associated with social and economic problems: *inner-city areas.*

inner ear ▶ noun the semicircular canals and cochlea, which form the organs of balance and hearing and are embedded in the temporal bone.

Inner Hebrides see **HEBRIDES**.

Inner House (in full **the Inner House of the Court of Session**) (in Scotland) either of two law courts that correspond to the Court of Appeal in England and Wales, each presided over by three judges.

inner light ▶ noun [in sing.] personal spiritual revelation; a source of enlightenment within oneself.
– ORIGIN mid 19th cent.: originally in Quaker doctrine.

inner man ▶ noun [in sing.] a man's soul or mind: *the complexities of the inner man.*
■ humorous a man's stomach: *the inner man was well catered for with pizza.*

Inner Mongolia an autonomous region of northern China, on the border with Mongolia; capital, Hohhot.

innermost ▶ adjective [attrib.] **1** (of thoughts or feelings) most private and deeply felt: *innermost beliefs and convictions.*
2 furthest in; closest to the centre: *the innermost layer.*

inner planet ▶ noun a planet whose orbit lies within the asteroid belt, i.e. Mercury, Venus, Earth, or Mars.

inner sanctum ▶ noun the most sacred place in a temple or church.
■ figurative a private or secret place to which few other people are admitted: *he walked into the inner sanctum of the editor's office.*

inner space ▶ noun **1** the region between the earth and outer space, or below the surface of the sea.
2 the part of the mind not normally accessible to consciousness.

inner speech ▶ noun [mass noun] the silent expression of conscious thought to oneself in a coherent linguistic form.

inner-spring ▶ adjective North American term for **INTERIOR-SPRUNG**.

Inner Temple one of the two Inns of Court on the site of the Temple in London. Compare with **MIDDLE TEMPLE**.

inner tube ▶ noun a separate inflatable tube inside a pneumatic tyre.

innervate /ˈɪnəveɪt, ɪˈnɜːveɪt/ ▶ verb [with obj.] Anatomy & Zoology supply (an organ or other body part) with nerves.
– DERIVATIVES **innervation** noun.
– ORIGIN late 19th cent.: from **IN**-² 'into' + **NERVE** + **-ATE**³.

inner woman ▶ noun [in sing.] a woman's soul or mind: *to behave as her inner woman prompts.*
■ humorous a woman's stomach: *after refreshing the inner woman, I was all for trying again.*

inning ▶ noun Baseball each division of a game during which both sides have a turn at batting.
– ORIGIN Old English *innung* 'a putting or getting in', related to **IN**. The current sense dates from the mid 19th cent.

innings ▶ noun (pl. same or informal **inningses**) **1** Cricket each of two or four divisions of a game during which one side has a turn at batting: *the highlight of the Surrey innings.*
■ a player's turn at batting: *he had played his greatest innings.* ■ the score achieved during this: *a solid innings of 78 by Marsh.*
2 a period during which a person or group is active or effective: *Brewer stepped up to the commission and had his innings too.*
– PHRASES **someone had a good innings** Brit. informal someone had a long and fulfilling life or career (said at or before their death or retirement).

innit informal ▶ contraction of isn't it.

innkeeper ▶ noun chiefly archaic a person who runs an inn.

innocence ▶ noun [mass noun] the state, quality, or fact of being innocent of a crime or offence: *they must prove their innocence.*
■ lack of guile or corruption; purity: *the healthy bloom in*

her cheeks gave her an aura of innocence. ■ used euphemistically to refer to a person's virginity: *they'd avenge assaults on her innocence by others.*
– PHRASES **in all innocence** without knowledge of something's significance or possible consequences: *she knew the gift had been chosen in all innocence.*
– DERIVATIVES **innocency** noun (archaic).
– ORIGIN Middle English: from Old French, from Latin *innocentia*, from *innocent-* 'not harming' (based on *nocere* 'injure').

innocent ▶ adjective **1** not guilty of a crime or offence: *they left an innocent man dead | the innocent party | he is innocent of Sir Thomas's death.*
■ [predic.] (**innocent of**) without; lacking: *a street quite innocent of bookshops.* ■ [predic.] (**innocent of**) without experience or knowledge of: *a man innocent of war's cruelties.*
2 [attrib.] not responsible for or directly involved in an event yet suffering its consequences: *an innocent bystander.*
3 free from moral wrong; not corrupted: *an innocent child.*
■ simple; naive: *she is a poor, innocent young creature.*
4 not involving or intended to cause harm or offence; harmless: *an innocent mistake.*
▶ noun an innocent person, in particular:
■ a pure, guileless, or naive person: *she was an innocent compared with this man.* ■ a person involved by chance in a situation, especially a victim of crime or war: *they are prepared to kill or maim innocents in pursuit of a cause.* ■ (**the Innocents**) the young children killed by Herod after the birth of Jesus (Matt. 2:16).
– DERIVATIVES **innocently** adverb.
– ORIGIN Middle English: from Old French, or from Latin *innocent-* 'not harming', from *in-* 'not' + *nocere* 'to hurt'.

Innocents' Day (also **Holy Innocents' Day**) ▶ noun a Christian festival commemorating the massacre of the Innocents, 28 December.

innocuous /ɪˈnɒkjʊəs/ ▶ adjective not harmful or offensive: *it was an innocuous question.*
– DERIVATIVES **innocuously** adverb, **innocuousness** noun.
– ORIGIN late 16th cent.: from Latin *innocuus*, from *in-* 'not' + *nocuus* 'injurious' (see **NOCUOUS**).

Inn of Court ▶ noun (in the UK) each of the four legal societies having the exclusive right of admitting people to the English bar.
■ any of the sets of buildings in London occupied by these societies.

innominate /ɪˈnɒmɪnət/ ▶ adjective not named or classified.
– ORIGIN mid 17th cent.: from late Latin *innominatus*, from *in-* 'not' + *nominatus* 'named' (past participle of *nominare*).

innominate artery ▶ noun Anatomy a large artery which branches from the aortic arch and divides into the right common carotid and right subclavian arteries.

innominate bone ▶ noun Anatomy the bone formed from the fusion of the ilium, ischium, and pubis; the hip bone.

innominate vein ▶ noun Anatomy either of two large veins of the neck formed by the junction of the external jugular and subclavian veins.

innovate /ˈɪnəveɪt/ ▶ verb [no obj.] make changes in something established, especially by introducing new methods, ideas, or products: *the company's failure to diversify and innovate competitively.*
■ [with obj.] introduce (something new, especially a product).
– DERIVATIVES **innovator** noun, **innovatory** adjective.
– ORIGIN mid 16th cent.: from Latin *innovat-* 'renewed, altered', from the verb *innovare*, from *in-* 'into' + *novare* 'make new' (from *novus* 'new').

innovation ▶ noun [mass noun] the action or process of innovating.
■ [count noun] a new method, idea, product, etc.: *technological innovations designed to save energy.*
– DERIVATIVES **innovational** adjective.
– ORIGIN late Middle English: from Latin *innovatio(n-)*, from the verb *innovare* (see **INNOVATE**).

innovative /ˈɪnəvətɪv/ ▶ adjective (of a product, idea, etc.) featuring new methods; advanced and original: *innovative designs | innovative ways to help unemployed people.*
■ (of a person) introducing new ideas; original and creative in thinking: *an innovative thinker.*

Innsbruck /ˈɪnzbrʊk, ˈɪns-/ a city in western Austria, capital of Tyrol; pop. 115,000 (1991).

Inns of Chancery ▶ plural noun historical (in the UK) the buildings in London formerly used as hostels for law students.

Inns of Court ▶ plural noun see **INN OF COURT**.

innuendo /ˌɪnjʊˈɛndəʊ/ ▶ noun (pl. **-oes** or **-os**) an allusive or oblique remark or hint, typically a suggestive or disparaging one: *she's always making sly innuendoes* | [mass noun] *a constant torrent of innuendo, gossip, lies, and half-truths.*
– ORIGIN mid 16th cent. (as an adverb in the sense 'that is to say, to wit', used in legal documents to introduce an explanation): Latin, 'by nodding at, by pointing to', ablative gerund of *innuere*, from *in-* 'towards' + *nuere* 'to nod'. The noun dates from the late 17th cent.

innumerable ▶ adjective too many to be counted (often used hyperbolically): *innumerable flags of all colours.*
– DERIVATIVES **innumerability** noun, **innumerably** adverb.
– ORIGIN Middle English: from Latin *innumerabilis*, from *in-* 'not' + *numerabilis* (see **NUMERABLE**).

innumerate ▶ adjective without a basic knowledge of mathematics and arithmetic.
▶ noun a person lacking such knowledge.
– DERIVATIVES **innumeracy** noun.

innutrition ▶ noun [mass noun] rare lack of nourishment.

innutritious ▶ adjective (of food) lacking in nutrients; not nourishing.

inobservance ▶ noun [mass noun] dated failure to observe or notice; inattention.
■ failure to keep or observe a law, custom, promise, etc.
– ORIGIN early 17th cent.: from French, or from Latin *inobservantia*, from *in-* (expressing negation) + *observantia* 'observance' (from *observare* 'observe').

inoculant ▶ noun a substance suitable for inoculating.

inoculate /ɪˈnɒkjʊleɪt/ ▶ verb [with obj.] treat (a person or animal) with a vaccine to produce immunity against a disease: *he* **inoculated** *his tenants* **against** *smallpox.* Compare with **VACCINATE**.
■ introduce (an infective agent) into an organism: *it can be* **inoculated into** *laboratory animals.* ■ introduce (cells or organisms) into a culture medium.
– DERIVATIVES **inoculable** adjective, **inoculation** noun, **inoculator** noun.
– ORIGIN late Middle English (in the sense 'graft a bud or shoot into a plant of a different type'): from Latin *inoculat-* 'engrafted', from the verb *inoculare*, from *in-* 'into' + *oculus* 'eye, bud'. The sense 'vaccinate' dates from the early 18th cent.

inoculum /ɪˈnɒkjʊləm/ ▶ noun (pl. **inocula**) Medicine a substance used for inoculation.
– ORIGIN early 20th cent.: modern Latin, from Latin *inoculare* (see **INOCULATE**), on the pattern of the pair *coagulate, coagulum.*

inodorous ▶ adjective having no smell; odourless.
– ORIGIN mid 17th cent.: from Latin *inodorus*, from *in-* 'not' + *odorus* 'odorous', or from **IN-**[1] 'not' + **ODOROUS**.

in-off ▶ noun Billiards & Snooker the pocketing of the cue ball (a scoring stroke in billiards, a foul in snooker) by bouncing it off another ball: *he attempted a very difficult in-off* | [as adv.] *going in-off on the penultimate red.*

inoffensive ▶ adjective not objectionable or harmful: *a shy, inoffensive, and sensitive girl.*
– DERIVATIVES **inoffensively** adverb, **inoffensiveness** noun.

inoperable ▶ adjective **1** Medicine not able to be suitably operated on: *inoperable cancer of the pancreas.*
2 not able to be operated: *the airfield was bombed and made inoperable.*
3 impractical; unworkable: *the procedures were inoperable.*
– DERIVATIVES **inoperability** noun, **inoperably** adverb.

inoperative ▶ adjective not working or taking effect: *the Act may be rendered inoperative.*

inopportune ▶ adjective occurring at an inconvenient time; not appropriate: *a storm blew up at an inopportune moment.*
– DERIVATIVES **inopportunely** adverb, **inopportuneness** noun.
– ORIGIN early 16th cent.: from Latin *inopportunus*, from *in-* 'not' + *opportunus* (see **OPPORTUNE**).

inordinate /ɪˈnɔːdɪnət/ ▶ adjective unusually or disproportionately large; excessive: *a case which had taken up an inordinate amount of time.*
■ archaic (of a person) unrestrained in feelings or behaviour; disorderly.
– DERIVATIVES **inordinately** adverb [as submodifier] *an inordinately expensive business.*
– ORIGIN late Middle English: from Latin *inordinatus*, from *in-* 'not' + *ordinatus* 'arranged, set in order' (past participle of *ordinare*).

inorganic ▶ adjective not arising from natural growth.
■ Chemistry of, relating to, or denoting compounds which are not organic (broadly, compounds not containing carbon). Compare with **ORGANIC**. ■ without organized physical structure. ■ Linguistics not explainable by the normal processes of etymology.
– DERIVATIVES **inorganically** adverb.

inosculate /ɪˈnɒskjʊleɪt/ ▶ verb [no obj.] formal join by intertwining or fitting closely together.
– DERIVATIVES **inosculation** noun.
– ORIGIN late 17th cent.: from **IN-**[2] 'into' + Latin *osculare* 'provide with a mouth or outlet' (from *osculum*, diminutive of *os* 'mouth'), on the pattern of Greek *anastomoun*, in the same sense.

inosine /ˈɪnə(ʊ)siːn/ ▶ noun [mass noun] Biochemistry a compound which is an intermediate in the metabolism of purine and is used in kidney transplantation to provide a temporary source of sugar. It is a nucleoside consisting of hypoxanthine linked to ribose.
– ORIGIN early 20th cent.: from Greek *is, in-* 'fibre, muscle' + **-OSE**[2] + **-INE**[4].

inositol /ʌɪˈnəʊsɪtɒl/ ▶ noun [mass noun] Biochemistry a simple carbohydrate which occurs in animal and plant tissue and is a vitamin of the B group.
• Alternative name: **hexahydroxycyclohexane**; chem. formula: $C_6H_{12}O_6$.
– ORIGIN late 19th cent.: from the earlier name *inosite* + **-OL**.

inotropic /ˌɪnə(ʊ)ˈtrəʊpɪk, -ˈtrɒpɪk/ ▶ adjective Physiology modifying the force or speed of contraction of muscles.

inpatient ▶ noun a patient who lives in hospital while under treatment.

in personam /ˌɪn pəˈsəʊnam/ ▶ adjective & adverb Law made or availing against or affecting a specific person only; imposing a personal liability: [as postpositive adj.] *rights and duties in personam* | [as adv.] *the view that trusts operate in personam.* Compare with **IN REM**.
– ORIGIN Latin, 'against a person'.

in-phase ▶ adjective of or relating to electrical signals that are in phase.

in potentia /ˌɪn pəˈtɛnʃɪə/ ▶ adverb as a possibility; potentially.
– ORIGIN Latin, 'in potentiality'.

inpouring ▶ noun [mass noun] the action of pouring something in; an infusion: *vast inpouring of public money.*

in propria persona /ɪn ˌprəʊprɪə pəːˈsəʊnə/ ▶ adverb in his or her own person.
– ORIGIN Latin.

input ▶ noun [mass noun] **1** what is put in, taken in, or operated on by any process or system: *there is little input from other professional members of the team.*
■ [count noun] a contribution of work, information, or material: *her input on issues was appreciated.* ■ energy supplied to a device or system; an electrical signal: *the input is a low-frequency signal.* ■ the action or process of putting or feeding something in: *the input of data to the system.* ■ the information fed into a computer or computer program: *pen-based computers take input from a stylus.*
2 Electronics a place where, or a device through which, energy or information enters a system: *the signal being fed through the main input.*
▶ verb (**inputting**; past and past participle **input** or **inputted**) [with obj.] put (data) into a computer.
– DERIVATIVES **inputter** noun.

input-output ▶ adjective [attrib.] Electronics of, relating to, or for both input and output.

inquest ▶ noun **1** Law a judicial inquiry to ascertain the facts relating to an incident.
■ Brit. an inquiry by a coroner's court into the cause of a death. ■ Brit. a coroner's jury.
2 informal a discussion analysing the outcome of a game, election, etc.

– ORIGIN Middle English from Old French *enqueste*, based on Latin *inquirere* (see **ENQUIRE**).

inquietude /ɪnˈkwʌɪətjuːd/ ▶ **noun** [mass noun] physical or mental restlessness or disturbance.
– ORIGIN late Middle English (in the sense 'disturbance of one's quietness or rest'): from Old French, or from late Latin *inquietudo*, from Latin *inquietus*, from *in-* 'not' + *quietus* 'quiet'.

inquiline /ˈɪnkwɪlʌɪn/ ▶ **noun** Zoology an animal exploiting the living space of another, e.g. an insect that lays its eggs in a gall produced by another.
– ORIGIN mid 17th cent.: from Latin *inquilinus* 'temporary resident', from *in-* 'into' + *colere* 'dwell'.

inquire ▶ **verb** another term for **ENQUIRE**.
– DERIVATIVES **inquirer** noun.
– ORIGIN Middle English *enquere* (later *inquere*), from Old French *enquerre*, from a variant of Latin *inquirere*, based on *quaerere* 'seek'. The spelling with *in-*, influenced by Latin, dates from the 15th cent.

USAGE On the difference between **inquire** and **enquire**, see usage at **ENQUIRE**.

inquiring ▶ **adjective** another term for **ENQUIRING**.

inquiry ▶ **noun** (pl. **-ies**) another term for **ENQUIRY**.

inquisition ▶ **noun 1** a period of prolonged and intensive questioning or investigation: *she relented in her determined inquisition and offered help.*
■ historical a judicial or official inquiry. ■ the verdict of a coroner's jury.
2 (**the Inquisition**) an ecclesiastical tribunal established by Pope Gregory IX *c.*1232 for the suppression of heresy. It was active chiefly in northern Italy and southern France, becoming notorious for the use of torture. In 1542 the papal Inquisition was reinstituted to combat Protestantism, eventually becoming an organ of papal government. See also **SPANISH INQUISITION**.
– DERIVATIVES **inquisitional** adjective.
– ORIGIN late Middle English (denoting a searching examination): via Old French from Latin *inquisitio(n-)* 'examination', from the verb *inquirere* (see **ENQUIRE**).

inquisitive ▶ **adjective** curious or inquiring: *he was very chatty and inquisitive about everything.*
■ unduly curious about the affairs of others; prying: *I didn't like to seem inquisitive.*
– DERIVATIVES **inquisitively** adverb, **inquisitiveness** noun.
– ORIGIN late Middle English: from Old French *inquisitif, -ive*, from late Latin *inquisitivus*, from the verb *inquirere* (see **ENQUIRE**).

inquisitor /ɪnˈkwɪzɪtə/ ▶ **noun** a person making an inquiry, especially one seen to be excessively harsh or searching: *the professional inquisitors of the press.*
■ historical an officer of the Inquisition.
– ORIGIN late Middle English: from French *inquisiteur*, from Latin *inquisitor*, from the verb *inquirere* (see **ENQUIRE**).

Inquisitor General ▶ **noun** the head of the Spanish Inquisition.

inquisitorial ▶ **adjective** of or like an inquisitor.
■ offensively prying. ■ Law (of a trial or legal procedure) in which the judge has an examining or enquiring role: *administration is accompanied by a form of inquisitorial justice.* Compare with **ACCUSATORIAL**, **ADVERSARIAL**.
– DERIVATIVES **inquisitorially** adverb.
– ORIGIN mid 18th cent.: from medieval Latin *inquisitorius* (from Latin *inquisitor*, from *inquirere* 'inquire') + **-AL**.

inquorate /ɪnˈkwɔːrət, -eɪt/ ▶ **adjective** Brit. (of an assembly) unable to proceed effectively because not enough members are present to make up a quorum: *they had boycotted the debate, leaving the house inquorate.*

in re /ɪn ˈriː, ˈreɪ/ ▶ **preposition** in the legal case of; with regard to: *the decision of the Court of Appeal in re Midland Railway Co's Agreement.*
– ORIGIN Latin, 'in the matter of'.

in rem /ɪn ˈrɛm/ ▶ **adjective** [often postpositive] Law made or availing against or affecting a thing, and therefore other people generally; imposing a general liability: *it confers a right in rem.* Compare with **IN PERSONAM**.
– ORIGIN Latin, 'against a thing'.

INRI ▶ **abbreviation** Jesus of Nazareth, King of the Jews (a traditional representation in art of the inscription over Christ's head at the Crucifixion).
– ORIGIN from the initials of Latin *Iesus Nazarenus Rex Iudaeorum.*

inro /ˈɪnrəʊ/ ▶ **noun** (pl. same or **-os**) an ornamental box with compartments for items such as seals and medicines, worn suspended from a girdle as part of traditional Japanese dress.
– ORIGIN early 17th cent.: from Japanese *inrō*, from *in* 'seal' + *rō* 'basket'.

inroad ▶ **noun 1** (usu. **make inroads in/into/on**) an instance of something being affected, encroached on, or destroyed by something else: *the firm is beginning to make inroads into the UK market | serious inroads had now been made into my pitiful cash reserves.*
2 a hostile attack; a raid: *the inroads and cross-border raiding of the Grahams.*
– ORIGIN mid 16th cent. (in sense 2): from **IN** + **ROAD** (from an early use in the sense 'riding').

inrush ▶ **noun** [in sing.] the sudden arrival or entry of something: *a great inrush of water occurred.*
– DERIVATIVES **inrushing** adjective & noun.

INS ▶ **abbreviation** for Immigration and Naturalization Service, a US government agency.

insalubrious /ˌɪnsəˈluːbrɪəs/ ▶ **adjective** (of a place) seedy and run-down; unwholesome.
– DERIVATIVES **insalubrity** noun.
– ORIGIN mid 17th cent.: from Latin *insalubris* (from *in-* 'not' + *salubris* 'salubrious') + **-OUS**.

insane ▶ **adjective** in a state of mind which prevents normal perception, behaviour, or social interaction; seriously mentally ill: *certifying patients as clinically insane | he had gone insane.*
■ (of an action or quality) characterized or caused by madness: *charging headlong in an insane frenzy | his eyes glowing with insane fury.* ■ in a state of extreme annoyance or distraction: *a fly whose buzzing had been driving me insane.* ■ (of an action or policy) extremely foolish; irrational or illogical: *she had an insane desire to giggle.*
– DERIVATIVES **insanely** adverb.
– ORIGIN mid 16th cent.: from Latin *insanus*, from *in-* 'not' + *sanus* 'healthy'.

insanitary ▶ **adjective** so dirty or germ-ridden as to be a danger to health: *insanitary conditions.*

insanity ▶ **noun** [mass noun] the state of being seriously mentally ill; madness: *he suffered from bouts of insanity* | [as complement] *he attempted to plead insanity.*
■ extreme foolishness or irrationality: *it might be pure insanity to take this loan* | [count noun] *the insanities of our time.*
– ORIGIN late 16th cent.: from Latin *insanitas*, from *insanus* (see **INSANE**).

insatiable /ɪnˈseɪʃəb(ə)l/ ▶ **adjective** (of an appetite or desire) impossible to satisfy: *an insatiable hunger for success.*
■ (of a person) having an insatiable appetite or desire for something, especially sex.
– DERIVATIVES **insatiability** noun, **insatiably** adverb.
– ORIGIN late Middle English: from Old French *insaciable* or Latin *insatiabilis*, from *in-* 'not' + *satiare* 'fill, satisfy' (see **SATIATE**).

insatiate /ɪnˈseɪʃɪət/ ▶ **adjective** poetic/literary never satisfied: *your strong desire is insatiate.*
– ORIGIN late Middle English: from Latin *insatiatus*, from *in-* 'not' + *satiatus* 'filled, satisfied', past participle of *satiare* (see **SATIATE**).

inscape ▶ **noun** poetic/literary the unique inner nature of a person or object as shown in a work of art, especially a poem.
– ORIGIN mid 19th cent. (originally in the poetic theory of Gerard Manley Hopkins): perhaps from **IN-**[2] 'within' + **-SCAPE**.

in-school ▶ **adjective** [attrib.] denoting an activity or process that takes place during school hours or on school premises: *an in-school method of assessment.*

inscribe ▶ **verb** [with obj.] (usu. **be inscribed**) **1** write or carve (words or symbols) on something, especially as a formal or permanent record: *his name was inscribed on the new silver trophy.*
■ mark (a tablet, metal sheet, or other object) with characters: *the memorial is* **inscribed with** *ten names* | [as adj. **inscribed**] *an inscribed watch.* ■ write an informal dedication to someone in or on (a book). ■ archaic enter the name of (someone) on a list or in a book; enrol. ■ [usu. as adj. **inscribed**] Brit. issue (loan stock) in the form of shares whose holders are listed in a register rather than issued with certificates.
2 Geometry draw (a figure) within another so that their boundaries touch but do not intersect: *a regular polygon inscribed in a circle.* Compare with **CIRCUMSCRIBE**.
– DERIVATIVES **inscribable** adjective, **inscriber** noun.
– ORIGIN late Middle English: from Latin *inscribere*, from *in-* 'into' + *scribere* 'write'.

inscription ▶ **noun** a thing inscribed, as on a monument or in a book: *the inscription on her headstone.*
■ [mass noun] the action of inscribing something: *the inscription of memorable utterances on durable materials.*
– DERIVATIVES **inscriptional** adjective, **inscriptive** adjective.
– ORIGIN late Middle English (denoting a short descriptive or dedicatory passage at the beginning of a book): from Latin *inscriptio(n-)*, from the verb *inscribere* (see **INSCRIBE**).

inscrutable /ɪnˈskruːtəb(ə)l/ ▶ **adjective** impossible to understand or interpret: *Guy looked blankly inscrutable.*
– DERIVATIVES **inscrutability** noun, **inscrutably** adverb.
– ORIGIN late Middle English: from ecclesiastical Latin *inscrutabilis*, from *in-* 'not' + *scrutari* 'to search' (see **SCRUTINY**).

inseam ▶ **noun** N. Amer. another term for **INSIDE LEG**.

insect ▶ **noun** an arthropod animal that is typically small, having six legs and generally one or two pairs of wings: [as modifier] *insect pests.*
■ informal any small invertebrate animal, especially one with several pairs of legs.

Insects are usually placed in the class Insecta (see also **HEXAPODA**). The body of a typical adult insect is divided into head, thorax (bearing the legs and wings), and abdomen. The class includes many familiar forms, such as flies, bees, wasps, moths, beetles, grasshoppers, and cockroaches. Insects are the most numerous animals in both numbers of individuals and of different kinds, with more than a million species in all habitats except the sea, and they are of enormous economic importance as pests and carriers of disease, and also as pollinators.

– ORIGIN early 17th cent. (originally denoting any small cold-blooded creature with a segmented body): from Latin (*animal*) *insectum* 'segmented (animal)' (translating Greek *zōion entomon*), from *insecare* 'cut up or into', from *in-* 'into' + *secare* 'to cut'.

insectan ▶ **adjective** [attrib.] Zoology of or relating to insects: *the insectan orders.*

insectarium /ˌɪnsɛkˈtɛːrɪəm/ (also **insectary** /ɪnˈsɛktəri/) ▶ **noun** (pl. **insectariums** or **insectaries**) a place where insects are kept, exhibited, and studied.

insecticide ▶ **noun** a substance used for killing insects.
– DERIVATIVES **insecticidal** adjective.

insectile ▶ **adjective** resembling or reminiscent of an insect or insects: *his insectile hands.*

Insectivora /ˌɪnsɛkˈtɪvərə/ Zoology an order of small mammals that comprises the shrews, moles, hedgehogs, tenrecs, moonrats, and solenodons. They are distinguished by mainly terrestrial habits and an insectivorous diet.

insectivore /ɪnˈsɛktɪvɔː/ ▶ **noun** an animal that feeds on insects, worms, and other invertebrates.
■ Zoology a mammal of the order Insectivora.
– ORIGIN mid 19th cent.: from modern Latin *insectivorus*, from *insectum* (see **INSECT**) + *-vorus* 'devouring', on the pattern of Latin *carnivorus* 'carnivorous'.

insectivorous /ˌɪnsɛkˈtɪv(ə)rəs/ ▶ **adjective** (of an animal) feeding on insects, worms, and other invertebrates.
■ (of a plant such as the sundew) able to capture and digest insects.

insecure ▶ **adjective 1** (of a person) not confident or assured; uncertain and anxious: *a top model who is notoriously insecure about her looks | a rather gauche, insecure young man.*
2 (of a thing) not firm or fixed; unsafe.
■ (of a job or position) from which removal or expulsion is always possible. ■ not firmly fixed; liable to give way or break: *an insecure footbridge.* ■ able to be broken into or illicitly accessed: *an insecure computer system.*
– DERIVATIVES **insecurely** adverb, **insecurity** noun.
– ORIGIN mid 17th cent.: from medieval Latin *insecurus* 'unsafe', from *in-* 'not' + Latin *securus* 'free from care', or from **IN-**[1] 'not' + **SECURE**.

inselberg /ˈɪns(ə)lbəːg, -z-/ ▶ **noun** Geology an isolated hill or mountain rising abruptly from a plain.

– ORIGIN early 20th cent.: from German, from *Insel* 'island' + *Berg* 'mountain'.

inseminate /ɪnˈsɛmɪneɪt/ ▶ **verb** [with obj.] (often **be inseminated**) introduce semen into (a woman or a female animal) by natural or artificial means.
– DERIVATIVES **insemination** noun.
– ORIGIN early 17th cent.: from Latin *inseminat-* 'sown', from the verb *inseminare*, from *in-* 'into' + *seminare* 'plant, sow' (from *semen, semin-* 'seed, semen').

inseminator ▶ **noun** a man or male animal inseminating a female.
▪ a person who performs artificial insemination of farm animals.

insensate ▶ **adjective** lacking physical sensation: *a patient who was permanently unconscious and insensate.*
▪ lacking sympathy or compassion; unfeeling: *a positively insensate hatred.* ▪ completely lacking sense or reason: *insensate jabbering.*
– DERIVATIVES **insensately** adverb.
– ORIGIN late 15th cent.: from ecclesiastical Latin *insensatus*, from *in-* 'not' + *sensatus* 'having senses' (see **SENSATE**).

insensibility ▶ **noun** [mass noun] unconsciousness: *I flogged him into insensibility.*
▪ inability to feel something, especially to be moved emotionally. ▪ lack of awareness or concern; indifference: *your* **insensibility to** *the extreme importance of the mission we are on.*
– ORIGIN late Middle English: partly from Old French *insensibilite* or late Latin *insensibilitas* (from *in-* 'not' + Latin *sensibilis* 'sensible', from *sensus* 'sense'), partly from **IN-**[1] 'without, lacking' + **SENSIBILITY**.

insensible ▶ **adjective 1** [usu. as complement] without one's mental faculties, typically a result of violence or intoxication; unconscious: *they knocked each other insensible with their fists | insensible with drink.*
▪ (especially of a body or bodily extremity) numb; without feeling: *the horny and insensible tip of the beak.*
2 [predic.] (**insensible of/to**) unaware of; indifferent to: *they slept on, insensible to the headlight beams.*
▪ without emotion; callous.
3 too small or gradual to be perceived; inappreciable: *varying by insensible degrees.*
– DERIVATIVES **insensibly** adverb.
– ORIGIN late Middle English (also in the senses 'unable to be perceived' and 'incapable of physical sensation'): partly from Old French *insensible* (from Latin *insensibilis*, from *in-* 'not' + *sensibilis*, from *sensus* 'sense'), partly from **IN-**[1] 'not' + **SENSIBLE**.

insensitive ▶ **adjective** showing or feeling no concern for others' feelings: *an insensitive remark.*
▪ not sensitive to a physical sensation: *she was remarkably* **insensitive to** *pain.* ▪ not aware of or able to respond to something: *both were in many ways* **insensitive to** *painting.*
– DERIVATIVES **insensitively** adverb, **insensitiveness** noun, **insensitivity** noun.

insentient ▶ **adjective** incapable of feeling or understanding things; inanimate: *it's arrogant to presume animals to be insentient.*
– DERIVATIVES **insentience** noun.

inseparable ▶ **adjective** unable to be separated or treated separately: *research and higher education seem inseparable.*
▪ (of one or more people) unwilling to be separated; usually seen together: *they met 18 months ago and have been inseparable ever since.* ▪ Grammar (of a prefix) not used as a separate word or (in German) not separated from the base verb when inflected. ▪ Grammar (of a German verb) consisting of a prefix and a base verb which are not separated when inflected, for example *wiederholen.*
▶ **noun** a person or thing inseparable from another.
– DERIVATIVES **inseparability** noun, **inseparably** adverb.
– ORIGIN late Middle English: from Latin *inseparabilis*, from *in-* 'not' + *separabilis* (see **SEPARABLE**).

insert ▶ **verb** /ɪnˈsəːt/ [with obj.] **1** place, fit, or thrust (something) into another thing, especially with care: *Claudia* **inserted** *her key* **in** *the lock.*
▪ include (text) in a piece of writing: *he immediately inserted a clause into later contracts | a notice has been inserted in the Journal.* ▪ place (a spacecraft or satellite) into an orbit or trajectory. ▪ (usu. **be inserted**) Biology incorporate (a piece of genetic material) into a chromosome.
2 (**be inserted**) Anatomy & Zoology (of a muscle or other organ) be attached to a part, especially that which is moved: *the muscle that raises the wing is* **inserted on** *the dorsal surface of the humerus.*
▶ **noun** /ˈɪnsəːt/ a thing that has been inserted, in particular:
▪ a loose page or section, typically one carrying an advertisement, in a magazine or other publication. ▪ an ornamental section of cloth or needlework inserted into the plain material of a garment. ▪ a shot inserted in a film or video.
– DERIVATIVES **insertable** adjective, **inserter** noun.
– ORIGIN late 15th cent. (in the sense 'include (text) in a piece of writing'): from Latin *insert-* 'put in', from the verb *inserere*, from *in-* 'into' + *serere* 'to join'.

insertion ▶ **noun 1** [mass noun] the action of inserting something: *the insertion of a line or two into the script.*
▪ the placing of a spacecraft or satellite into an orbit or trajectory.
2 a thing that is inserted, in particular:
▪ an amendment or addition inserted in a text. ▪ each appearance of an advertisement in a newspaper or periodical. ▪ an ornamental section of cloth or needlework inserted into the plain material of a garment.
3 Anatomy & Zoology the manner or place of attachment of an organ: *close to the point of leaf insertion.*
▪ the manner or place of attachment of a muscle to the part which it moves: *the names of the muscles and their* **insertions on** *the eyeball.*
4 [mass noun] Biology the addition of extra DNA or RNA into a section of genetic material.
– ORIGIN mid 16th cent. (in sense 2): from late Latin *insertio(n-)*, from Latin *inserere* (see **INSERT**).

in-service ▶ **adjective** (of training) intended for those actively engaged in the profession or activity concerned: *in-service training of library staff.*

INSET /ˈɪnsɛt/ ▶ **noun** [mass noun] training during term time for teachers in British state schools.
– ORIGIN 1970s: acronym from *in-service education and training.*

inset ▶ **noun** /ˈɪnsɛt/ a thing that is put in or inserted: *a pair of doors with their original stained-glass insets.*
▪ a small picture or map inserted within the border of a larger one. ▪ a section of fabric or needlework inserted into the material of a garment: *elastic insets in the waistband.* ▪ an insert in a magazine or similar publication.
▶ **verb** /ɪnˈsɛt/ (**insetting**; past and past participle **inset** or **insetted**) (usu. **be inset**) put in (something, especially a small picture or map) as an inset: *type in the text to be inset.*
▪ decorate with an inset: *tables inset with ceramic tiles.*
– DERIVATIVES **insetter** noun.

inshallah /ɪnˈʃalə/ ▶ **exclamation** if Allah wills it.
– ORIGIN from Arabic *in šā' Allāh.*

inshore ▶ **adjective** at sea but close to the shore: *inshore waters around Shetland.*
▪ used at sea but close to the shore: *an inshore lifeboat.*
▶ **adverb** towards or closer to the shore: *birds heading inshore to their breeding sites.*
– PHRASES **inshore of** nearer to shore than.

inside ▶ **noun** /ɪnˈsʌɪd/ **1** [usu. in sing.] the inner side or surface of a thing: *wipe the inside of the windscreen.*
▪ the part of a path nearer to a wall or further from a road. ▪ the lane or part of a road furthest from the centre: *overtaking* **on the inside.** ▪ the side of a bend or curve where the edge or surface is shorter: *the inside of the bend.*
2 the inner part; the interior: *the inside of the car was like an oven | pipes should be smooth* **on the inside.**
▪ (usu. **insides**) informal the stomach and bowels: *my insides are out of order.* ▪ Brit. dated the lower passenger section of a double-decker bus.
3 (**the inside**) informal a position affording private information: *will you be my spy on the inside?*
▶ **adjective** /ˈɪnsʌɪd/ [attrib.] situated on or in, or derived from, the inside: *an inside pocket.*
▪ (in hockey, soccer, and other sports) denoting positions nearer to the centre of the field: [in combination] *feeding the ball to an inside-forward.*
▶ **preposition** & **adverb** /ɪnˈsʌɪd/ **1** situated within the confines of (something): [as prep.] *a radio was playing inside the flat | he fitted a light inside the cupboard |* [as adv.] *Mr Jackson is waiting for you inside.*
▪ moving so as to end up within (something): [as prep.] *Anatoly reached inside his shirt and brought out a map |* [as adv.] *we walked inside.* ▪ within (the body or mind of a person), typically with reference to sensations of self-awareness: [as prep.] *she felt a stirring of life inside her | I just roll the phrases round inside my head |* [as adv.] *I was screaming inside.* ▪ informal in prison: *sentenced to three years inside.* ▪ (in soccer, rugby, and other sports) closer to the centre of the field than (another player): [as prep.] *he went inside Graves and scored near the post |* [as adv.] *Bennett cut inside and passed to Ventham.*
2 [prep.] in less than (the period of time specified): *the oven will have paid for itself inside 18 months.*
– PHRASES **inside of** N. Amer. informal within: *something inside of me wanted to believe him.* ▪ in less than (the period of time specified): *re-rigging a ship for a voyage inside of a week.*
– ORIGIN late Middle English (denoting the interior of the body): from **IN** + **SIDE**.

inside information ▶ **noun** [mass noun] information only available to those within an organization.

inside job ▶ **noun** informal a crime committed by or with the assistance of a person living or working on the premises where it occurred.

inside leg ▶ **noun** the length of a person's leg from crotch to ankle, or of the equivalent part of a pair of trousers.

inside money ▶ **noun** [mass noun] Economics money held in a form such as bank deposits which is an asset to the holder but also represents a liability for someone else.

inside out ▶ **adverb** with the inner surface turned outwards: *we had a very quick change and her dress was put on inside out.*
▶ **adjective** in such a condition: *inside-out clothes.*
– PHRASES **know someone/thing inside out** know someone or something very thoroughly. **turn something inside out** turn the inner surface of something outwards: *she played with her leather gloves, turning each finger inside out.* ▪ change something utterly: *it is not so easy to turn your whole life inside out.* ▪ informal cause utter confusion in; defeat totally: *he turned the defender inside out.*

insider ▶ **noun** a person within a group or organization, especially someone privy to information unavailable to others: *political insiders.*

insider dealing (also **insider trading**) ▶ **noun** [mass noun] the illegal practice of trading on the stock exchange to one's own advantage through having access to confidential information.

inside track ▶ **noun** the inner, shorter side of a racecourse.
▪ figurative a position of advantage: *he always had the inside track for the starring role.*

insidious /ɪnˈsɪdɪəs/ ▶ **adjective** proceeding in a gradual, subtle way, but with very harmful effects: *sexual harassment is a serious and insidious problem.*
– DERIVATIVES **insidiously** adverb, **insidiousness** noun.
– ORIGIN mid 16th cent.: from Latin *insidiosus* 'cunning', from *insidiae* 'an ambush or trick', from *insidere* 'lie in wait for', from *in-* 'on' + *sedere* 'sit'.

insight ▶ **noun** [mass noun] the capacity to gain an accurate and deep intuitive understanding of a person or thing: *this paper is alive with sympathetic* **insight into** *Shakespeare.*
▪ [count noun] an understanding of this kind. ▪ [mass noun] Psychiatry awareness by a mentally ill person that their mental experiences are abnormal symptoms not based in external reality.
– DERIVATIVES **insightful** adjective, **insightfully** adverb.
– ORIGIN Middle English (in the sense 'inner sight, mental vision, wisdom'): probably of Scandinavian and Low German origin and related to Swedish *insikt*, Danish *indsigt*, Dutch *inzicht*, and German *Einsicht.*

insignia /ɪnˈsɪɡnɪə/ ▶ **noun** (pl. same or **insignias**) a badge or distinguishing mark of military rank, office, or membership of an organization; an official emblem: *the royal insignia of Scotland.*
▪ chiefly poetic/literary a distinguishing mark or token of something: *they left eternally inert blooms, the insignia of melancholy.*
– ORIGIN mid 17th cent.: from Latin, plural of *insigne* 'sign, badge of office', neuter of *insignis* 'distinguished (as if by a mark)', from *in-* 'towards' + *signum* 'sign'.

USAGE **Insignia** is, in origin, a plural noun; its singular form is **insigne** but this is rarely used. In modern use, **insignia** takes the plural **insignia** or, occasionally, **insignias**: both are acceptable.

insignificant ▶ **adjective** too small or unimportant

to be worth consideration: *the sum required was insignificant compared with military spending.*
■(of a person) without power or influence. ■ meaningless: *insignificant yet enchanting phrases.*
– DERIVATIVES **insignificance** noun, **insignificancy** noun, **insignificantly** adverb.

insincere ▶ **adjective** not expressing genuine feelings: *she flashed him an insincere smile.*
– DERIVATIVES **insincerely** adverb, **insincerity** noun (pl. **-ies**).
– ORIGIN mid 17th cent.: from Latin *insincerus*, from *in-* 'not' + *sincerus* 'sincere'.

insinuate /ɪnˈsɪnjʊeɪt/ ▶ **verb** [with obj.] **1** suggest or hint (something bad or reprehensible) in an indirect and unpleasant way: [with clause] *he was insinuating that she slept her way to the top.*
2 (**insinuate oneself into**) manoeuvre oneself into (a position of favour or office) by subtle manipulation: *he insinuated himself into the king's confidence.*
■[with obj. and adverbial of direction] slide (oneself or a thing) slowly and smoothly into a position: *I insinuated my shoulder in the gap.*
– DERIVATIVES **insinuatingly** adverb, **insinuator** noun.
– ORIGIN early 16th cent. (used in legal contexts in the sense 'enter (a document) on the official register'): from Latin *insinuat-* 'introduced tortuously', from the verb *insinuare*, from *in-* 'in' + *sinuare* 'to curve'.

insinuation ▶ **noun** an unpleasant hint or suggestion of something bad: *I've done nothing to deserve all your vicious insinuations* | [mass noun] *a piece of filthy insinuation.*
– ORIGIN mid 16th cent.: from Latin *insinuatio(n-)*, from *insinuare* (see **INSINUATE**).

insinuendo /ɪnˌsɪnjʊˈɛndəʊ/ ▶ **noun** (pl. **-os**) chiefly humorous informal term for **INSINUATION**.
– ORIGIN late 19th cent.: blend of **INSINUATION** and **INNUENDO**.

insipid /ɪnˈsɪpɪd/ ▶ **adjective** lacking flavour: *mugs of insipid coffee.*
■lacking vigour or interest: *many artists continued to churn out insipid, shallow works.*
– DERIVATIVES **insipidity** noun, **insipidly** adverb, **insipidness** noun.
– ORIGIN early 17th cent.: from French *insipide* or late Latin *insipidus*, from *in-* 'not' + *sapidus* (see **SAPID**).

insist ▶ **verb** [no obj.] demand something forcefully, not accepting refusal: *she* **insisted on** *carrying her own bag* | [with clause] *he insisted that she came.*
■(**insist on**) demand forcefully to have something: *he insisted on answers to his allegations.* ■ (**insist on**) persist in doing something even though it is annoying or odd: *the heavy studded boots she insisted on wearing.* ■ [reporting verb] maintain or put forward a statement positively and assertively: [with clause] *the chairman insisted that all was not doom and gloom* | [with direct speech] *'I really am all right now,' Isabel insisted.*
– ORIGIN late 16th cent. (in the sense 'persist, persevere'): from Latin *insistere* 'persist', from *in-* 'upon' + *sistere* 'stand'.

insistence ▶ **noun** [mass noun] the fact or quality of insisting that something is the case or should be done: *Alison's insistence on doing the washing-up straight after the meal.*
– DERIVATIVES **insistency** noun.

insistent ▶ **adjective** insisting or demanding something; not allowing refusal: *Tony's soft, insistent questioning* | [with clause] *she was very insistent that I call her.*
■regular and repeated, and demanding attention: *a telephone started ringing, loud and insistent.*
– DERIVATIVES **insistently** adverb.

in situ /ɪn ˈsɪtjuː/ ▶ **adverb** & **adjective** in its original place: [as adv.] *mosaics and frescoes have been left in situ* | [as adj.] *a collection of in situ pumping engines.*
■in position: [as adv.] *her guests were all in situ.*
– ORIGIN Latin.

insobriety ▶ **noun** [mass noun] drunkenness.

insofar ▶ **adverb** variant spelling of ***in so far*** (see **FAR**).

insolation /ˌɪnsəˈleɪʃ(ə)n/ ▶ **noun** [mass noun] technical exposure to the sun's rays.
■the amount of solar radiation reaching a given area.
– ORIGIN early 17th cent.: from Latin *insolatio(n-)*, from the verb *insolare*, from *in-* 'towards' + *sol* 'sun'.

insole ▶ **noun** a removable sole worn in a shoe for warmth, as a deodorizer, or to improve the fit.
■the fixed inner sole of a boot or shoe.

insolent ▶ **adjective** showing a rude and arrogant lack of respect: *she hated the insolent tone of his voice.*
– DERIVATIVES **insolence** noun, **insolently** adverb.
– ORIGIN late Middle English (also in the sense 'extravagant, going beyond acceptable limits'): from Latin *insolent-* 'immoderate, unaccustomed, arrogant', from *in-* 'not' + *solent-* 'being accustomed' (from the verb *solere*).

insoluble ▶ **adjective 1** impossible to solve: *the problem is not insoluble.*
2 (of a substance) incapable of being dissolved: *once dry, the paints become* **insoluble in** *water.*
– DERIVATIVES **insolubility** noun, **insolubilize** (also **-ise**) verb, **insolubly** adverb.
– ORIGIN late Middle English: from Old French, or from Latin *insolubilis*, from *in-* 'not' + *solubilis* (see **SOLUBLE**).

insolvable ▶ **adjective** rare term for **INSOLUBLE**.

insolvent ▶ **adjective** unable to pay debts owed: *the company became insolvent.*
■relating to insolvency: *insolvent liquidation.*
▶ **noun** an insolvent person.
– DERIVATIVES **insolvency** noun.

insomnia ▶ **noun** [mass noun] habitual sleeplessness; inability to sleep.
– DERIVATIVES **insomniac** noun & adjective.
– ORIGIN early 17th cent.: from Latin, from *insomnis* 'sleepless', from *in-* (expressing negation) + *somnus* 'sleep'.

insomuch ▶ **adverb 1** (**insomuch that**) to such an extent that: *self is the source of evil insomuch that the purity of the soul increases as it loses selfhood.*
2 (**insomuch as**) inasmuch as: *the artist touches on the Kurds only insomuch as they impact on his primary focus.*
– ORIGIN late Middle English: originally as *in so much*, translating French *en tant (que)* 'in so much (as)'.

insouciance /ɪnˈsuːsɪəns/ ▶ **noun** [mass noun] casual lack of concern; indifference: *an impression of boyish insouciance.*
– DERIVATIVES **insouciant** adjective, **insouciantly** adverb.
– ORIGIN late 18th cent.: French, from *insouciant*, from *in-* 'not' + *souciant* 'worrying' (present participle of *soucier*).

inspan /ɪnˈspan/ ▶ **verb** (**inspanned, inspanning**) [with obj.] S. African yoke (draught animals, typically oxen) in a team to a vehicle.
■harness an animal or animals to (a vehicle). ■ figurative utilize (people or resources) for a particular purpose: *it awaited only the courage of the pioneers to inspan these natural resources in the service of civilization.*
– ORIGIN early 19th cent.: from Dutch *inspannen* 'to stretch', from *in-* 'in' + *spannen* 'to span'.

inspect ▶ **verb** [with obj.] look at (someone or something) closely, typically to assess their condition or to discover any shortcomings: *they were inspecting my outside paintwork for cracks and flaws.*
■examine (someone or something) to ensure that they reach an official standard: *customs officers came aboard to inspect our documents.*
– DERIVATIVES **inspection** noun.
– ORIGIN early 17th cent.: from Latin *inspect-* 'looked into, examined', from the verb *inspicere* (from *in-* 'in' + *specere* 'look at'), or from its frequentative, *inspectare*.

inspection chamber ▶ **noun** a manhole sited at a junction or bend in a drain to allow clearance of blockages.

inspector ▶ **noun 1** an official employed to ensure that official regulations are obeyed, especially in public services: *a prison inspector.*
■Brit. an official who examines bus or train tickets to check that they are valid.
2 a police officer ranking below a chief inspector: [as title] *Inspector Simmons.*
– DERIVATIVES **inspectorial** adjective, **inspectorship** noun.

inspectorate ▶ **noun** a body that ensures that the official regulations applying to a particular type of institution or activity are obeyed: *the factory inspectorate.*

inspector general ▶ **noun** the head of an inspectorate.
■Military a staff officer responsible for conducting inspections and investigations.

inspector of taxes (also **tax inspector**) ▶ **noun** (in the UK) an official of the Inland Revenue responsible for assessing and collecting income tax and some other taxes.

inspiration ▶ **noun** [mass noun] **1** the process of being mentally stimulated to do or feel something, especially to do something creative: *Helen had one of her flashes of inspiration* | *the Malvern Hills have provided inspiration for many artists.*
■the quality of having been so stimulated, especially when evident in something: *a rare moment of inspiration in an otherwise dull display.* ■ [count noun] a person or thing that stimulates in this way: *he is an inspiration to everyone.* ■ [count noun] a sudden brilliant, creative, or timely idea: *then I had an inspiration.* ■ the divine influence supposed to have led to the writing of the Bible.
2 [mass noun] the drawing in of breath; inhalation.
■[count noun] an act of breathing in; an inhalation.
– ORIGIN Middle English (in the sense 'divine guidance'): via Old French from late Latin *inspiratio(n-)*, from the verb *inspirare* (see **INSPIRE**).

inspirational ▶ **adjective** providing or showing creative or spiritual inspiration: *the team's inspirational captain.*

inspiratory /ɪnˈspʌɪrət(ə)ri/ ▶ **adjective** Physiology relating to the act of breathing in.

inspire ▶ **verb** [with obj.] **1** fill (someone) with the urge or ability to do or feel something, especially to do something creative: [with obj. and infinitive] *his passion for romantic literature inspired him to begin writing* | [as adj. **inspiring**] *so far, the scenery is not very inspiring.*
■create (a feeling, especially a positive one) in a person: *their past record does not inspire confidence.* ■ (**inspire someone with**) animate someone with (such a feeling): *he inspired his students with a vision of freedom.* ■ give rise to: *the film was successful enough to inspire a sequel.*
2 breathe in (air); inhale.
– DERIVATIVES **inspirer** noun, **inspiringly** adverb.
– ORIGIN Middle English *enspire*, from Old French *inspirer*, from Latin *inspirare* 'breathe or blow into' from *in-* 'into' + *spirare* 'breathe'. The word was originally used of a divine or supernatural being, in the sense 'impart a truth or idea to someone'.

inspired ▶ **adjective 1** of extraordinary quality, as if arising from some external creative impulse: *they had to thank the goalkeeper for some inspired saves.*
■(of a person) exhibiting such a creative impulse in the activity specified: *she was an inspired gardener.*
2 (of air or another substance) that is breathed in: *inspired air must be humidified.*
– DERIVATIVES **inspiredly** adverb.

inspirit ▶ **verb** (**inspirited, inspiriting**) [with obj.] [usu. as adj. **inspiriting**] encourage and enliven (someone): *the inspiriting beauty of Gothic architecture.*
– DERIVATIVES **inspiritingly** adverb.

inspissate /ɪnˈspɪseɪt/ ▶ **verb** [with obj.] [usu. as adj. **inspissated**] thicken or congeal: *inspissated secretions.*
– DERIVATIVES **inspissation** noun.
– ORIGIN early 17th cent.: from late Latin *inspissat-* 'made thick', from the verb *inspissare* (based on Latin *spissus* 'thick, dense').

inspissator /ˈɪnspɪˌseɪtə/ ▶ **noun** a heating device for thickening or congealing a liquid.

inst. ▶ **abbreviation for** ■ dated (in business letters) instant: *we are pleased to acknowledge receipt of your letter of 14 inst.* ■ institute; institution: *the Southwest Research Inst.*

instability ▶ **noun** (pl. **-ies**) [mass noun] lack of stability; the state of being unstable: *political and economic instability.*
■tendency to unpredictable behaviour or erratic changes of mood.
– ORIGIN late Middle English: from French *instabilité*, from Latin *instabilitas*, from *instabilis*, from *in-* 'not' + *stabilis* (see **STABLE**[1]).

install (also **instal**) ▶ **verb** (**installed, installing**) [with obj.] **1** place or fix (equipment or machinery) in position ready for use: *we're planning to install a new shower.*
2 place (someone) in a new position of authority, especially with ceremony: *he was installed as Prime Minister in 1966.*
■establish (someone) in a new place, condition, or role: *Ashley installed herself behind her table.*
– DERIVATIVES **installer** noun.
– ORIGIN late Middle English (in sense 2): from medieval Latin *installare*, from *in-* 'into' + *stallum* 'place, stall'. Sense 1 dates from the mid 19th cent.

installation ▶ **noun** **1** [mass noun] the action or process of installing someone or something, or of being installed: *the installation of a central heating system* | [count noun] *the use of the system could be followed by installations on other vehicles.*
2 a thing installed, in particular:
■ a large piece of equipment installed for use: *computer installations.* ■ a military or industrial establishment: *nuclear installations.* ■ an art exhibit constructed within a gallery: *a video installation.*

instalment (US also **installment**) ▶ **noun** **1** a sum of money due as one of several equal payments for something, spread over an agreed period of time: *the first instalment of a grant for housing* | *the purchase price is paid **in instalments**.*
2 any of several parts of something which are published, broadcast, or made public in sequence at intervals: *filming the final instalment in his Vietnam trilogy.*
3 [mass noun] the process of installing something; installation: *instalment will begin early next year.*
– ORIGIN mid 18th cent. (denoting the arrangement of payment by instalments): alteration of obsolete *estalment* (probably by association with **INSTALLATION**), from Anglo-Norman French *estalement*, from Old French *estaler* 'to fix'.

instalment credit ▶ **noun** [mass noun] credit for a fixed sum to be repaid in instalments, e.g. for hire purchase.

instalment plan ▶ **noun** an arrangement for payment by instalments.

instance ▶ **noun** an example or single occurrence of something: *a serious instance of corruption* | *the search finds every instance where the word appears.*
■ a particular case: *in this instance it mattered little.*
▶ **verb** [with obj.] cite (a fact, case, etc.) as an instance or example: *I instanced Bob as someone whose commitment had certainly got things done.*
– PHRASES **at first instance** Law at the first court hearing concerning a case. See also **COURT OF FIRST INSTANCE**. **at the instance of** formal at the request or instigation of: *prosecution at the instance of the police.* **for instance** as an example: *take Canada, for instance.* **in the first** (or **second** etc.) **instance** in the first (or second etc.) place; at the first (or second etc.) stage of a proceeding: *the appointment will be for three years in the first instance.*
– ORIGIN Middle English: via Old French from Latin *instantia* 'presence, urgency', from *instare* 'be present, press upon', from *in-* 'upon' + *stare* 'to stand'. The original sense was 'urgency, urgent entreaty', surviving in *at the instance of*. In the late 16th cent. the word denoted a particular case cited to disprove a general assertion, derived from medieval Latin *instantia* 'example to the contrary' (translating Greek *enstasis* 'objection'); hence the meaning 'single occurrence'.

instance court ▶ **noun** old-fashioned term for **COURT OF FIRST INSTANCE**.
■ (**Instance Court**) (in the UK) a branch of the former Admiralty Court dealing with private maritime matters.

instancy ▶ **noun** [mass noun] archaic urgency: *he told his servants to press the message with greater instancy.*
– ORIGIN early 16th cent.: from Latin *instantia* (see **INSTANCE**).

instant ▶ **adjective** **1** happening or coming immediately: *the offence justified instant dismissal.*
■ (of food) processed to allow very quick preparation: *instant coffee.* ■ (of a person) becoming a specified thing immediately or very suddenly: *become an instant millionaire.* ■ prepared very quickly and with little effort: *we can't promise instant solutions.*
2 urgent; pressing: *an instant desire to blame others when things go wrong.*
3 [postpositive] dated (in business letters) of the current month: *your letter of the 6th instant.*
4 archaic of the present moment.
▶ **noun** **1** a precise moment of time: *come here this instant!* | *at that instant the sun came out.*
2 a very short space of time; a moment: *for an instant the moon disappeared.*
■ (**Instants**) trademark lottery tickets that may be scratched or opened to reveal immediately whether a prize has been won.
3 [mass noun] informal instant coffee.
– ORIGIN late Middle English (in senses 2, 3, and 4 of the adjective): via Old French from Latin *instant-* 'being at hand', from the verb *instare*, from *in-* 'in, at' + *stare* 'to stand'.

instantaneous /ˌɪnst(ə)nˈteɪnɪəs/ ▶ **adjective** **1** occurring or done in an instant or instantly: *her reaction was almost instantaneous.*
■ operating or providing something instantly: *modern methods of instantaneous communication.*
2 Physics existing or measured at a particular instant: *measurement of the instantaneous velocity.*
– DERIVATIVES **instantaneity** noun, **instantaneously** adverb, **instantaneousness** noun.
– ORIGIN mid 17th cent.: from medieval Latin *instantaneus*, from Latin *instant-* 'being at hand' (from the verb *instare*), on the pattern of ecclesiastical Latin *momentaneus*.

instant camera ▶ **noun** a camera of a type with internal processing which produces a finished print rapidly after each exposure.

instanter /ɪnˈstantə/ ▶ **adverb** archaic or humorous at once; immediately: *we sealed the bargain instanter.*
– ORIGIN Latin.

instantiate /ɪnˈstanʃɪeɪt/ ▶ **verb** [with obj.] represent as or by an instance: *a study of two groups who seemed to instantiate productive aspects of this.*
■ (**be instantiated**) Philosophy (of a universal or abstract concept) have an instance; be represented by an actual example.
– DERIVATIVES **instantiation** noun.
– ORIGIN 1940s: from Latin *instantia* (see **INSTANCE**) + **-ATE**[3].

instantly ▶ **adverb** **1** at once; immediately: *she fell asleep almost instantly.*
2 archaic urgently or persistently.

instant replay ▶ **noun** an immediate playback of part of a television broadcast, typically one in slow motion showing an incident in a sporting event.

instar /ˈɪnstɑː/ ▶ **noun** Zoology a phase between two periods of moulting in the development of an insect larva or other invertebrate animal.
– ORIGIN late 19th cent.: from Latin, literally 'form, likeness'.

instate ▶ **verb** [with obj.] (usu. **be instated**) set up in position; install or establish: *many of the troops had only joined up when the new regime was instated.*
– ORIGIN early 17th cent. (formerly also as *enstate*): from **EN-**[1], **IN-**[2] 'into' + the noun **STATE**. Compare with earlier **REINSTATE**.

in statu pupillari /ɪn ˌstatjuː ˌpjuːpɪˈlɑːri/ ▶ **adjective** [often postpositive] **1** under guardianship, especially as a pupil: *we are not children in statu pupillari, but adults.*
2 in a junior position at university; not having a master's degree.
– ORIGIN Latin.

instauration /ˌɪnstɔːˈreɪʃ(ə)n/ ▶ **noun** [mass noun] formal the action of restoring or renewing something.
– DERIVATIVES **instaurator** /ˈɪnstɔːreɪtə/ noun.
– ORIGIN early 17th cent.: from Latin *instauratio(n-)*, from *instaurare* 'renew', from *in-* 'in, towards' + *staur-* (a stem also found in *restaurare* 'restore').

instead ▶ **adverb** as an alternative or substitute: *do not use lotions, but put on a clean dressing instead* | *she never married, preferring instead to remain single.*
■ (**instead of**) as a substitute or alternative to; in place of: *walk to work instead of going by car.*
– ORIGIN Middle English (originally as two words): from **IN** + **STEAD**.

instep ▶ **noun** the part of a person's foot between the ball and the ankle.
■ the part of a shoe which fits over or under this part of a foot. ■ a thing shaped like the inner arch of a foot.
– ORIGIN late Middle English: of unknown origin; compare with West Frisian *ynstap* 'opening in a shoe for insertion of the foot'.

instigate /ˈɪnstɪgeɪt/ ▶ **verb** [with obj.] bring about or initiate (an action or event): *they instigated a reign of terror* | *instigating legal proceedings.*
■ (**instigate someone to/to do something**) incite someone to do something, especially something bad: *instigating men to refuse allegiance to the civil powers.*
– DERIVATIVES **instigator** noun.
– ORIGIN mid 16th cent. (in the sense 'urge on'): from Latin *instigat-* 'urged, incited', from the verb *instigare*, from *in-* 'towards' + *stigare* 'prick, incite'.

instigation ▶ **noun** [mass noun] the action or process of instigating an action or event: *the Domesday Survey was compiled **at the instigation of** William I.*
– ORIGIN late Middle English (in the sense 'incitement'): from Old French, or from Latin *instigatio(n-)*, from the verb *instigare* (see **INSTIGATION**).

instil /ɪnˈstɪl/ (also **instill**) ▶ **verb** (**instilled**, **instilling**) [with obj.] **1** gradually but firmly establish (an idea or attitude, especially a desirable one) in a person's mind: *the standards her parents had **instilled into** her.*
2 put (a substance) into something in the form of liquid drops: *she was told how to instil eye drops.*
– DERIVATIVES **instillation** noun, **instilment** noun.
– ORIGIN late Middle English (in sense 2): from Latin *instillare*, from *in-* 'into' + *stillare* 'to drop' (from *stilla* 'a drop').

instinct ▶ **noun** an innate, typically fixed pattern of behaviour in animals in response to certain stimuli: *bream have strong predatory instincts.*
■ a natural or intuitive way of acting or thinking: *they retain their old authoritarian instincts.* ■ a natural propensity or skill of a specified kind: *his **instinct for** making the most of his chances.* ■ [mass noun] the fact or quality of possessing innate behaviour patterns: *instinct told her not to ask the question.*
▶ **adjective** [predic.] (**instinct with**) formal imbued or filled with (a quality, especially a desirable one): *these canvases are instinct with passion.*
– DERIVATIVES **instinctual** adjective, **instinctually** adverb.
– ORIGIN late Middle English (also in the sense 'instigation, impulse'): from Latin *instinctus* 'impulse', from the verb *instinguere*, from *in-* 'towards' + *stinguere* 'to prick'.

instinctive ▶ **adjective** relating to or prompted by instinct; apparently unconscious or automatic: *an instinctive distaste for conflict.*
■ (of a person) doing or being a specified thing apparently naturally or automatically: *an instinctive writer.*
– DERIVATIVES **instinctively** adverb.

institute ▶ **noun** [usu. in names] **1** a society or organization having a particular object or common factor, especially a scientific, educational, or social one: *the Institute of Architects* | *a research institute.*
2 (usu. **institutes**) archaic a commentary, treatise, or summary of principles, especially concerning law.
▶ **verb** [with obj.] **1** set in motion or establish (something, especially a programme, system, or inquiry): *the state instituted a national lottery* | *the award was instituted in 1900.*
■ begin (legal proceedings) in a court.
2 (often **be instituted**) appoint (someone) to a position, especially as a cleric: *his sons were **instituted to** the priesthood* | [with complement] *a testator who has instituted his daughter heir.*
– ORIGIN Middle English (in sense 2 of the verb): from Latin *institut-* 'established', from the verb *instituere*, from *in-* 'in, towards' + *statuere* 'set up'. The noun is from Latin *institutum* 'something designed, precept', neuter past participle of *instituere*; sense 1 dates from the early 19th cent.

institution ▶ **noun** **1** a society or organization founded for a religious, educational, social, or similar purpose: *a certificate from a professional institution.*
■ an organization providing residential care for people with special needs: *an institution for the severely handicapped.* ■ an established official organization having an important role in the life of a country, such as a bank, Church, or parliament: *the institutions of democratic government.* ■ a large company or other organization involved in financial trading: *City institutions.*
2 an established law, practice, or custom: ***the institution of** marriage.*
■ informal a well-established and familiar person, custom, or object: *he soon became something of a national institution.*
3 [mass noun] the action of instituting something: *a delay in the institution of proceedings.*
– ORIGIN late Middle English (in senses 2 and 3): via Old French from Latin *institutio(n-)*, from the verb *instituere* (see **INSTITUTE**). Sense 1 dates from the early 18th cent.

institutional ▶ **adjective** of, in, or like an institution or institutions: *institutional care* | *an institutional investor.*
■ unappealing or unimaginative: *the rooms are rather drab and institutional.* ■ expressed or organized in the form of institutions: *institutional religion.* ■ (of advertising) intended to create prestige rather than immediate sales.
– DERIVATIVES **institutionalism** noun, **institutionally** adverb.

institutionalize (also **-ise**) ▶ **verb** [with obj.] **1** establish (something, typically a practice or activity) as a convention or norm in an organization or culture: *a system which institutionalizes bad behaviour.*
2 (usu. **be institutionalized**) place or keep (someone) in a residential institution.
– DERIVATIVES **institutionalization** noun.

institutionalized (also **-ised**) ▶ **adjective** **1** established in practice or custom: *institutionalized religion | the danger of discrimination becoming institutionalized.*
2 (of a person, especially a long-term patient or prisoner) made apathetic and dependent after a long period in an institution.

in-store ▶ **adjective** & **adverb** within a store (shop): [as adj.] *an in-store bakery* | [as adv.] *the goods are promoted in-store.*

Inst.P. ▶ **abbreviation for** (in the UK) Institute of Physics.

INSTRAW International Research and Training Institute for the Advancement of Women, a United Nations agency.

instruct ▶ **verb** **1** [reporting verb] direct or command someone to do something, especially as an official order: [with obj. and infinitive] *she instructed him to wait* | [with direct speech] *'Look at me,' he instructed* | [with clause] *I instructed that she should be given hot, sweet tea.*
2 [with obj.] teach (someone) a subject or skill: *he* ***instructed*** *them* ***in*** *the use of firearms* | [with obj. and clause] *instructing electors how to record their votes.*
3 [with obj.] Law give a person direction, information, or authorization, in particular:
■ chiefly Brit. (of a client) employ or authorize (a solicitor or barrister) to act or speak on one's behalf: *he must indicate which of the firms he wishes to instruct.* ■ chiefly Brit. (of a solicitor) give directions or information to (a barrister) regarding a court case. ■ inform (someone) of a fact or situation: [with clause] *the bank was instructed that the money from the deposit account was now held by the company.*
– ORIGIN late Middle English (in sense 2): from Latin *instruct-* 'constructed, equipped, taught', from the verb *instruere*, from *in-* 'upon, towards' + *struere* 'pile up'.

instruction ▶ **noun** **1** (often **instructions**) a direction or order: *he issued instructions to the sheriff* | *he was acting on my instructions.*
■ (**instructions**) Law directions to a solicitor or counsel, or to a jury. ■ Computing a code or sequence in a computer program which defines an operation and puts it into effect.
2 (**instructions**) detailed information telling how something should be done, operated, or assembled: *always study the instructions supplied.*
3 [mass noun] teaching; education: *instruction in the Roman Catholic faith.*
– DERIVATIVES **instructional** adjective.
– ORIGIN late Middle English: via Old French from late Latin *instructio(n-)*, from the verb *instruere* (see **INSTRUCT**).

instruction set ▶ **noun** Computing the complete set of all the instructions in machine code that can be recognized and executed by a central processing unit.

instructive ▶ **adjective** useful and informative: *it is instructive to compare the two projects.*
– DERIVATIVES **instructively** adverb, **instructiveness** noun.

instructor ▶ **noun** a person who teaches something: *a driving instructor.*
■ N. Amer. a university teacher ranking below assistant professor.
– DERIVATIVES **instructorship** noun.

instructress ▶ **noun** a woman who teaches something: *a riding instructress.*

instrument ▶ **noun** **1** a tool or implement, especially one for delicate or scientific work: *a surgical instrument | instruments of torture | writing instruments.*
■ a thing used in pursuing an aim or policy; a means: *drama as an* ***instrument of*** *learning.* ■ a person who is exploited or made use of: *he was a mere instrument acting under coercion.*
2 a measuring device used to gauge the level, position, speed, etc. of something, especially a motor vehicle or aircraft.
3 (also **musical instrument**) an object or device for producing musical sounds: *a percussion instrument.*
4 a formal document, especially a legal one: *execution involves signature and unconditional delivery of the instrument.*
▶ **verb** [with obj.] equip (something) with measuring instruments.
– ORIGIN Middle English: from Old French, or from Latin *instrumentum* 'equipment, implement', from the verb *instruere* 'construct, equip'.

instrumental ▶ **adjective** **1** serving as an instrument or means in pursuing an aim or policy: *the Society was* ***instrumental in*** *bringing about legislation.*
■ relating to something's function as an instrument or means to an end: *a very instrumental view of education and how it relates to their needs.*
2 (of music) performed on instruments, not sung: *a largely instrumental piece.*
■ relating to musical instruments: *brilliance of instrumental colour.*
3 of or relating to an implement or measuring device: *instrumental error | instrumental delivery of a baby.*
4 Grammar denoting or relating to a case of nouns and pronouns (and words in grammatical agreement with them) indicating a means or instrument.
▶ **noun** **1** a piece of (usually non-classical) music performed solely by instruments, with no vocals.
2 (**the instrumental**) Grammar the instrumental case.
■ a noun in the instrumental case.
– DERIVATIVES **instrumentally** adverb.

instrumental conditioning ▶ **noun** [mass noun] Psychology a learning process in which behaviour is modified by the reinforcing or inhibiting effect of its consequence.

instrumentalism ▶ **noun** [mass noun] **1** a pragmatic philosophical approach which regards an activity (such as science, law, or education) chiefly as an instrument or tool for some practical purpose, rather than in more absolute or ideal terms, in particular:
■ Philosophy the pragmatic philosophy of John Dewey which supposes that thought is an instrument for solving practical problems, and that truth is not fixed but changes as the problems change. ■ (especially in Marxist theory) the view that the state and social organizations are tools which are exploited by the ruling class or by individuals in their own interests.
2 Music, rare instrumental technique.

instrumentalist ▶ **noun** **1** a player of a musical instrument.
2 an adherent of instrumentalism.
▶ **adjective** of or in terms of instrumentalism.

instrumentality ▶ **noun** (pl. **-ies**) [mass noun] the fact or quality of serving as an instrument or means to an end; agency: *a corporate body can act only through the instrumentality of human beings.*
■ [count noun] a thing which serves as an instrument or means to an end.

instrumentation ▶ **noun** [mass noun] **1** the particular instruments used in a piece of music; the manner in which a piece is arranged for instruments: *Telemann's specified instrumentation of flute, violin, and continuo.*
■ the arrangement or composition of a piece of music for particular musical instruments: *an experiment in instrumentation.*
2 measuring instruments regarded collectively: *the controls and instrumentation of an aircraft.*
■ the design, provision, or use of measuring instruments.

instrument panel (also **instrument board**) ▶ **noun** a surface in front of a driver's or pilot's seat, on which the vehicle's or aircraft's instruments are situated.

insubordinate ▶ **adjective** defiant of authority; disobedient to orders: *an insubordinate attitude.*
– DERIVATIVES **insubordinately** adverb, **insubordination** noun.

insubstantial ▶ **adjective** lacking strength and solidity: *the huts are relatively few and insubstantial | insubstantial evidence.*
■ not solid or real; imaginary: *the flickering light made her face seem insubstantial.*
– DERIVATIVES **insubstantiality** noun, **insubstantially** adverb.
– ORIGIN early 17th cent.: from late Latin *insubstantialis*, from *in-* 'not' + *substantialis* (see **SUBSTANTIAL**).

insufferable ▶ **adjective** too extreme to bear; intolerable: *the heat would be insufferable by July.*
■ having or showing unbearable arrogance or conceit: *an insufferable bully | insufferable male chauvinism.*
– DERIVATIVES **insufferableness** noun, **insufferably** adverb.
– ORIGIN late Middle English: perhaps via French (now dialect) *insouffrable*, based on Latin *sufferre* 'endure' (see **SUFFER**).

insufficiency ▶ **noun** [mass noun] the condition of being insufficient: *insufficiency of adequate housing* | [count noun] *there have been demands to redress such insufficiencies.*
■ Medicine the inability of an organ to perform its normal function: *renal insufficiency.*
– ORIGIN early 16th cent. (in the sense 'incompetence, inability'): from late Latin *insufficientia*, from *in-* 'not' + Latin *sufficere* 'be sufficient'.

insufficient ▶ **adjective** not enough; inadequate: *there was insufficient evidence to convict him.*
– DERIVATIVES **insufficiently** adverb.
– ORIGIN late Middle English (in the sense 'incapable, incompetent'): via Old French from late Latin *insufficient-* 'not sufficing', from *in-* 'not' + Latin *sufficere* (see **SUFFICE**).

insufflate /ˈɪnsəfleɪt/ ▶ **verb** [with obj.] **1** Medicine blow (air, gas, or powder) into a cavity of the body.
■ blow something into (a part of the body) in this way.
2 Theology blow or breathe on (someone) to symbolize spiritual influence.
– DERIVATIVES **insufflation** noun.
– ORIGIN late 17th cent.: from late Latin *insufflat-* 'blown into', from the verb *insufflare*, from *in-* 'into' + *sufflare* 'blow' (from *sub-* 'from below' + *flare* 'to blow'). Sense 2 dates from the early 20th cent.

insufflator ▶ **noun** **1** a device for blowing powder on to a surface in order to make fingerprints visible.
2 an instrument for medical insufflation.

insula /ˈɪnsjʊlə/ ▶ **noun** (pl. **insulae** /-liː/) **1** a tenement or apartment block in an ancient Roman city.
2 Anatomy a region of the brain deep in the cerebral cortex.
– ORIGIN Latin, literally 'island'.

insulant ▶ **noun** an insulating material.

insular ▶ **adjective** **1** ignorant of or uninterested in cultures, ideas, or peoples outside one's own experience: *a stubbornly insular farming people.*
■ lacking contact with other people: *people living restricted and sometimes insular existences.*
2 of, relating to, or from an island: *the movement of goods of insular origin | an insular product.*
■ of or relating to the art and craftwork of Britain and Ireland in the early Middle Ages, especially a form of Latin handwriting: *insular illumination of the 6th century.* ■ (of climate) equable because of the influence of the sea.
3 Anatomy of or relating to the insula of the brain.
– DERIVATIVES **insularity** noun, **insularly** adverb.
– ORIGIN mid 16th cent. (as a noun denoting an islander): from late Latin *insularis*, from *insula* 'island'.

insulate ▶ **verb** [with obj.] (often **be insulated**) **1** protect (something) by interposing material that prevents the loss of heat or the intrusion of sound: *the room was heavily* ***insulated against*** *all outside noise.*
■ prevent the passage of electricity to or from (something) by covering it in non-conducting material: *the case is carefully insulated to prevent short circuits.* ■ figurative protect from the unpleasant effects or elements of something: *he claims that the service is complacent and* ***insulated from*** *outside pressures.*
2 archaic make (land) into an island: *the village was insulated by every flood of the river.*
– ORIGIN mid 16th cent. (in sense 2): from Latin *insula* 'island' + **-ATE**³.

insulating tape ▶ **noun** [mass noun] adhesive tape used chiefly to cover exposed electric wires.

insulation ▶ **noun** [mass noun] the action of insulating something or someone: *keep your home warmer through insulation | heat insulation.*
■ the state of being insulated: *his comparative insulation from the world.* ■ material used to insulate something, especially a building: *fit insulation to all exposed pipes.*

insulator ▶ **noun** a thing or substance used for insulation, in particular:
■ a substance which does not readily allow the passage of heat or sound: *cotton is a poor insulator.* ■ a

substance or device which does not readily conduct electricity. ■ a block of material, typically glass or ceramic, enclosing a wire carrying an electric current where it crosses a support.

insulin ▶ **noun** [mass noun] Biochemistry a hormone produced in the pancreas by the islets of Langerhans, which regulates the amount of glucose in the blood. The lack of insulin causes a form of diabetes.
– ORIGIN early 20th cent.: from Latin *insula* 'island' + **-IN**[1].

insulin shock ▶ **noun** [mass noun] Medicine an acute physiological condition resulting from excess insulin in the blood, involving low blood sugar, weakness, convulsions, and potentially coma.

insulitis /ˌɪnsjʊˈlʌɪtɪs/ ▶ **noun** [mass noun] Medicine disease of the pancreas caused by the infiltration of lymphocytes.

insult ▶ **verb** /ɪnˈsʌlt/ [with obj.] speak to or treat with disrespect or scornful abuse: *you're insulting the woman I love* | [as adj. **insulting**] *their language is crude and* ***insulting to*** *women.*
▶ **noun** /ˈɪnsʌlt/ **1** a disrespectful or scornfully abusive remark or action: *he hurled insults at us* | *he saw the book as a deliberate* ***insult to*** *the Church.*
■ a thing so worthless or contemptible as to be offensive: *the present offer is an absolute insult.*
2 Medicine an event or occurrence which causes damage to a tissue or organ: *the movement of the bone causes a severe tissue insult.*
– PHRASES **add insult to injury** act in a way that makes a bad or displeasing situation worse.
– DERIVATIVES **insulter** noun, **insultingly** adverb.
– ORIGIN mid 16th cent. (as a verb in the sense 'exult, act arrogantly'): from Latin *insultare* 'jump or trample on', from *in-* 'on' + *saltare*, from *salire* 'to leap'. The noun (in the early 17th cent. denoting an attack) is from French *insulte* or ecclesiastical Latin *insultus*. The main current senses date from the 17th cent., the medical use dating from the early 20th cent.

insuperable /ɪnˈs(j)uːp(ə)rəb(ə)l/ ▶ **adjective** (of a difficulty or obstacle) impossible to overcome: *insuperable financial problems.*
– DERIVATIVES **insuperability** noun, **insuperably** adverb.
– ORIGIN Middle English (in the general sense 'invincible'): from Old French, or from Latin *insuperabilis*, from *in-* 'not' + *superabilis* (from *superare* 'overcome').

insupportable ▶ **adjective** **1** unable to be supported or justified: *he had arrived at a wholly insupportable conclusion.*
2 unable to be endured; intolerable: *the heat was insupportable.*
– DERIVATIVES **insupportably** adverb.
– ORIGIN mid 16th cent.: from French, from *in-* 'not' + *supportable* (from *supporter* 'to support').

insurance ▶ **noun** [mass noun] **1** a practice or arrangement by which a company or the state undertakes to provide a guarantee of compensation for specified loss, damage, illness, or death in return for payment of a specified premium: *many new borrowers take out* ***insurance against*** *unemployment or sickness.*
■ the business of providing such an arrangement: *Howard is in insurance.* ■ money paid for this: *my insurance has gone up.* ■ money paid out as compensation under such an arrangement: *when will I be able to collect the insurance?* ■ [count noun] an insurance policy.
2 a thing providing protection against a possible eventuality: *seeking closer ties with other oil-supplying nations as* ***insurance against*** *disruption of Middle East supplies* | [count noun] *a marquee was hired as an* ***insurance against*** *the weather.*
– ORIGIN late Middle English (originally as *ensurance* in the sense 'ensuring, assurance, a guarantee'): from Old French *enseurance*, from *enseurer* (see **ENSURE**). Sense 1 dates from the mid 17th cent.

> **USAGE** There is a technical distinction between **insurance** and **assurance** in the context of life insurance: see **usage** at **ASSURANCE**.

insurance broker ▶ **noun** a person or company registered as an adviser on matters of insurance and as an arranger of insurance cover with an insurer on behalf of a client.

insurance carrier ▶ **noun** N. Amer. an insurer; an insurance company.

insurance policy ▶ **noun** a document detailing the terms and conditions of a contract of insurance.

insurance stamp ▶ **noun** Brit. a stamp which certifies that a weekly payment has been made towards National Insurance.

insure /ɪnˈʃʊə/ ▶ **verb** [with obj.] arrange for compensation in the event of damage to or loss of (property), or injury to or the death of (someone), in exchange for regular advance payments to a company or to the state: *the table should be* ***insured for*** *£2,500* | *the company had* ***insured itself against*** *a fall of the dollar* | [no obj.] *businesses can* ***insure against*** *exchange rate fluctuations.*
■ secure the payment of (an amount in compensation) in this way: *your new sum insured is shown on your renewal notice.* ■ provide insurance cover in respect of: *subsidiaries set up to insure the risks of a group of companies.* ■ figurative (**insure someone against**) secure or protect someone against (a possible contingency): *by appeasing Celia they might insure themselves against further misfortune* | [no obj.] *such changes could insure against further violence and unrest.*
– DERIVATIVES **insurability** noun, **insurable** adjective.
– ORIGIN late Middle English (in the sense 'assure someone of something'): alteration of **ENSURE**.

> **USAGE** There is considerable overlap between the meaning and use of **insure** and **ensure**. In both British and US English the primary meaning of **insure** is the commercial sense of providing financial compensation in the event of damage to property; **ensure** is not used at all in this sense. For the more general senses, **ensure** is more likely to be used, but **insure** and **ensure** are often interchangeable, particularly in US English, e.g. *bail is posted to* ***insure*** *that the defendant appears for trial; the system is run to* ***ensure*** *that a good quality of service is maintained.*

insured ▶ **adjective** covered by insurance: *the insured car* | *a privately insured patient* | *an insured risk.*
▶ **noun** (**the insured**) (pl. same) a person or organization covered by insurance.

insurer ▶ **noun** a person or company that underwrites an insurance risk; the party in an insurance contract undertaking to pay compensation.

insurgent /ɪnˈsəːdʒ(ə)nt/ ▶ **adjective** [attrib.] rising in active revolt: *alleged links with insurgent groups.*
■ of or relating to rebels: *a series of insurgent attacks.*
▶ **noun** (usu. **insurgents**) a rebel or revolutionary: *an attack by armed insurgents.*
– DERIVATIVES **insurgence** noun, **insurgency** noun (pl. **-ies**).
– ORIGIN mid 18th cent. (as a noun): via French from Latin *insurgent-* 'arising', from the verb *insurgere*, from *in-* 'into, towards' + *surgere* 'to rise'.

insurmountable /ˌɪnsəˈmaʊntəb(ə)l/ ▶ **adjective** too great to be overcome: *an insurmountable problem.*
– DERIVATIVES **insurmountably** adverb.

insurrection /ˌɪnsəˈrɛkʃ(ə)n/ ▶ **noun** a violent uprising against an authority or government: *the insurrection was savagely put down* | [mass noun] *opposition to the new regime led to armed insurrection.*
– DERIVATIVES **insurrectionary** adjective, **insurrectionist** noun & adjective.
– ORIGIN late Middle English: via Old French from late Latin *insurrectio(n-)*, from *insurgere* 'rise up'.

insusceptible ▶ **adjective** not likely to be affected: *the larvae are* ***insusceptible to*** *most treatments.*
– DERIVATIVES **insusceptibility** noun.

inswinger ▶ **noun** Cricket a ball bowled with a swerve or swing from the off to the leg side.
– DERIVATIVES **inswing** noun, **inswinging** adjective.

int. ▶ **abbreviation** for ■ interior. ■ internal. ■ international.

intact ▶ **adjective** [often as complement] not damaged or impaired in any way; complete: *the church was almost in ruins but its tower remained intact.*
– DERIVATIVES **intactness** noun.
– ORIGIN late Middle English: from Latin *intactus*, from *in-* 'not' + *tactus* (past participle of *tangere* 'touch').

intagliated /ɪnˈtalɪeɪtɪd/ ▶ **adjective** archaic carved or engraved on the surface.
– ORIGIN late 18th cent.: from Italian *intagliato* 'engraved', past participle of *intagliare*, from *in-* 'into' + *tagliare* 'to cut'.

intaglio /ɪnˈtalɪəʊ, -ˈtɑːl-/ ▶ **noun** (pl. **-os**) a design incised or engraved into a material: *the dies bore a design* ***in intaglio.***
■ a gem with an incised design. ■ any printing process in which the type or design is etched or engraved, such as photogravure or dry point.
▶ **verb** (**-oes, -oed**) [with obj.] [usu. as adj. **intaglioed**] engrave or represent by an engraving: *a carved box with little intaglioed pineapples on it.*
– ORIGIN mid 17th cent.: Italian, from *intagliare* 'engrave'.

intake ▶ **noun** **1** an amount of food, air, or another substance taken into the body: *your daily intake of calories* | *his alcohol intake.*
■ an act of taking something into the body: *she heard his* ***sharp intake of breath*** | [mass noun] *a protective factor is the* ***intake of*** *cereal fibre.*
2 [treated as sing. or pl.] the people taken into an organization or institution at a particular time: *the new intake of MPs* | *the student intake.*
■ the number of such people: *the provincial Bar controls its intake.* ■ an act of taking in such people: *the first intake of women was in 1915.*
3 a location or structure through which something is taken in, e.g. water into a channel or pipe from a river, fuel or air into an engine or machine, commodities into a place, etc.: *cut rectangular holes for the air intake.*
■ [mass noun] the action of taking something in: *facilities for the intake of grain by road.*
4 [mass noun] N. English land reclaimed from a moor or common.
– ORIGIN Middle English (originally Scots and northern English): from **IN** + **TAKE**.

intangible ▶ **adjective** unable to be touched or grasped; not having physical presence: *the moonlight made things seem intangible.*
■ difficult or impossible to define or understand; vague and abstract: *the rose symbolized something intangible about their relationship.* ■ (of an asset or benefit) not constituting or represented by a physical object and of a value not precisely measurable: *intangible business property like trademarks and patents.*
▶ **noun** (usu. **intangibles**) an intangible thing: *intangibles like self-confidence and responsibility.*
– DERIVATIVES **intangibility** noun, **intangibly** adverb.
– ORIGIN early 17th cent. (as an adjective): from French, or from medieval Latin *intangibilis*, from *in-* 'not' + late Latin *tangibilis* (see **TANGIBLE**).

intarsia /ɪnˈtɑːsɪə/ ▶ **noun** [mass noun] [often as modifier] **1** a method of knitting with a number of colours, in which a separate length or ball of yarn is used for each area of colour (as opposed to different yarns being carried at the back of the work): *an intarsia design.*
2 an elaborate form of marquetry using inlays in wood, especially as practised in 15th-century Italy.
■ similar inlaid work in stone, metal, or glass.
– ORIGIN from Italian *intarsio*; in sense 2 superseding earlier *tarsia* (from Italian, 'marquetry'); the knitting term dates from the mid 19th cent.

integer /ˈɪntɪdʒə/ ▶ **noun** **1** a whole number; a number which is not a fraction.
2 a thing complete in itself.
– ORIGIN early 16th cent. (as an adjective meaning 'entire, whole'): from Latin, 'intact, whole', from *in-* (expressing negation) + the root of *tangere* 'to touch'. Compare with **ENTIRE**, also with **INTEGRAL**, **INTEGRATE**, and **INTEGRITY**.

integral ▶ **adjective** /ˈɪntɪgr(ə)l, ɪnˈtɛgr(ə)l/ **1** necessary to make a whole complete; essential or fundamental: *games are an integral part of the school's curriculum* | *systematic training should be* ***integral to*** *library management.*
■ [attrib.] included as part of the whole rather than supplied separately: *the unit comes complete with integral pump and heater.* ■ [attrib.] having or containing all parts that are necessary to be complete: *an authentic and integral announcement of the Christian faith.*
2 Mathematics of or denoted by an integer.
■ involving only integers, especially as coefficients of a function.
▶ **noun** /ˈɪntɪgr(ə)l/ Mathematics a function of which a given function is the derivative, i.e. which yields that function when differentiated, and which may express the area under the curve of a graph of the function. See also **DEFINITE INTEGRAL**, **INDEFINITE INTEGRAL**.
■ a function satisfying a given differential equation.
– DERIVATIVES **integrality** noun, **integrally** adverb.
– ORIGIN mid 16th cent.: from late Latin *integralis*, from *integer* 'whole' (see **INTEGER**). Compare with **INTEGRATE** and **INTEGRITY**.

USAGE There are two possible pronunciations for **integral** as an adjective: one with the stress on the **in-** and the other with the stress on the **-teg-**. In British English, the second pronunciation is sometimes frowned on, but both are acceptable as standard.

integral calculus ▶ **noun** [mass noun] a branch of mathematics concerned with the determination, properties, and application of integrals. Compare with **DIFFERENTIAL CALCULUS**.

integrand /ˈɪntɪgrand/ ▶ **noun** Mathematics a function that is to be integrated.
– ORIGIN late 19th cent.: from Latin *integrandus*, gerundive of *integrare* (see **INTEGRATE**).

integrant /ˈɪntɪgr(ə)nt/ ▶ **adjective** (of parts) making up or contributing to a whole; constituent.
▶ **noun** a component.
– ORIGIN mid 17th cent. (as an adjective): from French *intégrant*, from the verb *intégrer*, from Latin *integrare* (see **INTEGRATE**).

integrate ▶ **verb** /ˈɪntɪgreɪt/ [with obj.] **1** combine (one thing) with another so that they become a whole: *transport planning should be* ***integrated with*** *energy policy | public schools should be progressively* ***integrated into*** *the state system.*
■ combine (two things) so that they become a whole: *the problem of integrating the two approaches.* ■ [no obj.] (of a thing) combine with another to form a whole: *the stone will blend with the environment and* ***integrate into*** *the landscape.*
2 bring into equal participation in or membership of society or an institution or body: ***integrating*** *children with special needs* ***into*** *ordinary schools.*
■ [no obj.] come into equal participation in or membership of society or an institution or body: *she was anxious to* ***integrate*** *well* ***into*** *her husband's family.*
3 Mathematics find the integral of.
– DERIVATIVES **integrability** /ˌɪntɪgrəˈbɪlɪti/ noun, **integrable** /ˈɪntɪgrəb(ə)l/ adjective, **integrative** /ˈɪntɪgrətɪv/ adjective.
– ORIGIN mid 17th cent.: from Latin *integrat-* 'made whole', from the verb *integrare*, from *integer* 'whole' (see **INTEGER**). Compare with **INTEGRAL** and **INTEGRITY**.

integrated ▶ **adjective** having been integrated, in particular:
■ (of an institution, body, etc.) desegregated, especially racially: *integrated education.* ■ with various parts or aspects linked or coordinated: *an integrated and high-quality public transport system.* ■ chiefly Physics indicating the mean value or total sum of (temperature, an area, etc.): *integrated electron density along the line of sight.*

integrated circuit ▶ **noun** an electronic circuit formed on a small piece of semiconducting material, which performs the same function as a larger circuit made from discrete components.

integrated services digital network (abbrev.: **ISDN**) ▶ **noun** a telecommunications network through which sound, images, and data can be transmitted as digitized signals.

integrating ▶ **adjective** (of an instrument) indicating the mean value or total sum of a measured quantity.

integration ▶ **noun** [mass noun] **1** the action or process of integrating: *economic and political integration |* ***integration*** *of individual countries* ***into*** *trading blocs.*
■ the intermixing of people or groups previously segregated: *integration is the best hope for both black and white Americans.*
2 Mathematics the finding of an integral or integrals: *integration of an ordinary differential equation |* [count noun] *mathematical integrations.*
3 Psychology the coordination of processes in the nervous system, including diverse sensory information and motor impulses: *visuomotor integration.*
■ Psychoanalysis the process by which a well-balanced psyche becomes whole as the developing ego organizes the id, and the state which results or which treatment seeks to create or restore by countering the fragmenting effect of defence mechanisms.
– DERIVATIVES **integrationist** noun.

integrator ▶ **noun** a person or thing that integrates, in particular:
■ (also **system integrator** or **systems integrator**) Computing a company which markets commercial integrated software and hardware systems.
■ Electronics a computer chip or circuit which performs mathematical integration. ■ an instrument for indicating or registering the total amount or mean value of some physical quality such as area or temperature.

integrity /ɪnˈtɛgrɪti/ ▶ **noun** [mass noun] **1** the quality of being honest and having strong moral principles; moral uprightness: *a gentleman of complete integrity.*
2 the state of being whole and undivided: *upholding territorial integrity and national sovereignty.*
■ the condition of being unified, unimpaired, or sound in construction: *the structural integrity of the novel.* ■ internal consistency or lack of corruption in electronic data: [as modifier] *integrity checking.*
– ORIGIN late Middle English (in sense 2): from French *intégrité* or Latin *integritas*, from *integer* 'intact' (see **INTEGER**). Compare with **ENTIRETY**, **INTEGRAL**, and **INTEGRATE**.

integument /ɪnˈtɛgjʊm(ə)nt/ ▶ **noun** a tough outer protective layer, especially that of an animal or plant.
– DERIVATIVES **integumental** adjective, **integumentary** adjective.
– ORIGIN early 17th cent. (denoting a covering or coating): from Latin *integumentum*, from the verb *integere*, from *in-* 'in' + *tegere* 'to cover'.

intellect ▶ **noun** [mass noun] the faculty of reasoning and understanding objectively, especially with regard to abstract or academic matters: *he was a man of action rather than of intellect.*
■ [count noun] the understanding or mental powers of a particular person: *his keen intellect.* ■ [count noun] a clever or intellectual person: *sapping our country of some of its brightest intellects.*
– ORIGIN late Middle English: from Latin *intellectus* 'understanding', from *intellegere* 'understand' (see **INTELLIGENT**).

intellection ▶ **noun** [mass noun] the action or process of understanding, as opposed to imagination.
– DERIVATIVES **intellective** adjective.

intellectual /ˌɪntəˈlɛktʃʊəl, -tjʊəl/ ▶ **adjective** of or relating to the intellect: *children need intellectual stimulation.*
■ appealing to or requiring use of the intellect: *the film wasn't very intellectual, but it caught the mood of the times.* ■ possessing a highly developed intellect: *you are an intellectual girl, like your mother.*
▶ **noun** a person possessing a highly developed intellect.
– DERIVATIVES **intellectuality** noun, **intellectually** adverb.
– ORIGIN late Middle English: from Latin *intellectualis*, from *intellectus* 'understanding', from *intellegere* 'understand' (see **INTELLIGENT**).

intellectualism ▶ **noun** [mass noun] the exercise of the intellect at the expense of the emotions.
■ Philosophy the theory that knowledge is wholly or mainly derived from pure reason; rationalism.
– DERIVATIVES **intellectualist** noun.
– ORIGIN early 19th cent. (as a term in philosophy): from **INTELLECTUAL**, on the pattern of German *Intellektualismus*.

intellectualize (also **-ise**) ▶ **verb** [with obj.] **1** give an intellectual character to: *belief was a gut feeling—it couldn't be intellectualized.*
2 [no obj.] talk, write, or think intellectually: *people who* ***intellectualize about*** *fashion.*

intellectual property ▶ **noun** [mass noun] Law intangible property that is the result of creativity, such as patents, copyrights, etc.

intelligence ▶ **noun** [mass noun] **1** the ability to acquire and apply knowledge and skills: *an eminent man of great intelligence | they underestimated her intelligence.*
■ [count noun] a person or being with this ability: *extraterrestrial intelligences.*
2 the collection of information of military or political value: *the chief of military intelligence |* [as modifier] *the intelligence department.*
■ people employed in this, regarded collectively: *British intelligence has been able to secure numerous local informers.* ■ information collected in this way: *the gathering of intelligence.* ■ archaic information in general; news.
– DERIVATIVES **intelligential** adjective (archaic).
– ORIGIN late Middle English: via Old French from Latin *intelligentia*, from *intelligere* 'understand' (see **INTELLIGENT**).

intelligence quotient (abbrev.: **IQ**) ▶ **noun** a number representing a person's reasoning ability (measured using problem-solving tests) as compared to the statistical norm or average for their age, taken as 100.

intelligencer ▶ **noun** archaic a person who gathers intelligence, especially an informer, spy, or secret agent.

intelligent ▶ **adjective** having or showing intelligence, especially of a high level: *Annabelle is intelligent and hard-working | an intelligent guess.*
■ (of a device, machine, or building) able to vary its state or action in response to varying situations and requirements, and past experience. ■ (especially of a computer terminal) incorporating a microprocessor and having its own processing capability. Often contrasted with **DUMB**.
– DERIVATIVES **intelligently** adverb.
– ORIGIN early 16th cent.: from Latin *intelligent-* 'understanding', from the verb *intelligere*, variant of *intellegere* 'understand', from *inter* 'between' + *legere* 'choose'.

intelligentsia /ɪnˌtɛlɪˈdʒɛntsɪə/ ▶ **noun** (usu. **the intelligentsia**) [treated as sing. or pl.] intellectuals or highly educated people as a group, especially when regarded as possessing culture and political influence.
– ORIGIN early 20th cent.: from Russian *intelligentsiya*, from Polish *inteligencja*, from Latin *intelligentia* (see **INTELLIGENCE**).

intelligible /ɪnˈtɛlɪdʒɪb(ə)l/ ▶ **adjective** able to be understood; comprehensible: *this would make the system more intelligible to the general public.*
■ Philosophy able to be understood only by the intellect, not by the senses.
– DERIVATIVES **intelligibility** noun, **intelligibly** adverb.
– ORIGIN late Middle English (also in the sense 'capable of understanding'): from Latin *intelligibilis*, from *intelligere* 'understand' (see **INTELLIGENT**).

Intelsat /ˈɪntɛlsat/ an international organization of more than 100 countries, formed in 1964, which owns and operates the worldwide commercial communications satellite system.
– ORIGIN from *In(ternational) Tel(ecommunications) Sat(ellite Consortium).*

intemperate ▶ **adjective** having or showing a lack of self-control; immoderate: *intemperate outbursts concerning global conspiracies.*
■ given to or characterized by excessive indulgence, especially in alcohol: *an intemperate social occasion.*
– DERIVATIVES **intemperance** noun, **intemperately** adverb, **intemperateness** noun.
– ORIGIN late Middle English (in the sense 'inclement'): from Latin *intemperatus*, from *in-* 'not' + *temperatus* (see **TEMPERATE**).

intend ▶ **verb** [with obj.] **1** have (a course of action) as one's purpose or intention; plan: [with infinitive] *the company intends to cut about 4,500 jobs |* [with clause] *it was not intended that colleges should have to revise their current schemes.*
■ (**intend something as/to do something**) plan that something should be or do something: *a series of questions intended as a checklist.* ■ plan that speech should have (a particular meaning): *no offence was intended, I assure you.*
2 (**intend someone/thing for/to do something**) design or destine someone or something for a particular purpose or end: *pigs intended for human consumption | a one-roomed cottage intended to accommodate a family.*
■ (**be intended for**) be meant or designed for (a particular person or group) to have or use: *this benefit is intended for people incapable of work.*
– DERIVATIVES **intender** noun.
– ORIGIN Middle English *entend* (in the sense 'direct the attention to'), from Old French *entendre*, from Latin *intendere* 'intend, extend, direct', from *in-* 'towards' + *tendere* 'stretch, tend'.

intendant ▶ **noun 1** the administrator of an opera house or theatre.
2 chiefly historical a title given to a high-ranking official or administrator, especially in France, Spain, Portugal, or one of their colonies.
– DERIVATIVES **intendancy** noun.
– ORIGIN mid 17th cent.: from French, from Latin *intendere* 'to direct' (see **INTEND**).

intended ▶ **adjective** [attrib.] planned or meant: *the intended victim escaped.*
▶ **noun** (**one's intended**) informal the person one intends to marry; one's fiancé or fiancée.
– DERIVATIVES **intendedly** adverb.

intending ▶ **adjective** [attrib.] (of a person) planning or meaning to do or be the specified thing: *an intending client.*

intendment ▶ noun [mass noun] Law the sense in which the law understands or interprets something, such as the true intention of an Act.
– ORIGIN late Middle English (denoting an intended meaning): from Old French *entendement*, from *entendre* 'intend'.

intense ▶ adjective (**intenser**, **intensest**) **1** (of a condition, quality, feeling, etc.) existing in a high degree; very forceful or extreme: *the job demands intense concentration | the heat was intense.*
■ (of an action) highly concentrated: *a phase of intense activity.* ■ (of a colour) very strong or deep: *an intense blue.*
2 (of a person) feeling, or apt to feel, strong emotion; extremely earnest or serious: *an intense young woman, passionate about her art.*
■ expressing or marked by strong emotion: *a low, intense mutter.*
– DERIVATIVES **intensely** adverb, **intenseness** noun.
– ORIGIN late Middle English: from Old French, or from Latin *intensus* 'stretched tightly, strained', past participle of *intendere* (see **INTEND**).

USAGE **Intense** and **intensive** are clearly similar in meaning, but they differ in emphasis. **Intense** tends to relate to subjective responses—emotions and how we feel—while **intensive** tends to relate to objective descriptions. Thus, *an **intensive** course* simply describes the type of course: one that is designed to cover a lot of ground in a short time, e.g. by being full-time rather than part-time. On the other hand, in *the course was **intense***, **intense** describes how someone felt about the course.

intensifier ▶ noun a person or thing that intensifies, in particular:
■ Photography a chemical used to intensify a negative.
■ Grammar an adverb used to give force or emphasis, for example *really* in *my feet are really cold.* ■ short for **IMAGE INTENSIFIER**.

intensify ▶ verb (**-ies**, **-ied**) **1** become or make more intense: [no obj.] *the dispute began to intensify* | [with obj.] *they had intensified their military campaign.*
2 [with obj.] Photography increase the opacity of (a negative) using a chemical: *the negative may be intensified with bichloride.*
– DERIVATIVES **intensification** noun.
– ORIGIN early 19th cent.: coined by Coleridge.

intension ▶ noun **1** Logic the internal content of a concept. Often contrasted with **EXTENSION**.
2 [mass noun] archaic resolution or determination.
– DERIVATIVES **intensional** adjective, **intensionally** adverb.
– ORIGIN early 17th cent. (also in the sense 'straining, stretching'): from Latin *intensio(n-)*, from *intendere* (see **INTEND**). Sense 1 dates from the mid 19th cent.

intensity ▶ noun (pl. **-ies**) [mass noun] **1** the quality of being intense: *gazing into her face with disconcerting intensity | the pain grew in intensity.*
■ [count noun] an instance or degree of this: *an intensity that frightened her.*
2 chiefly Physics the measurable amount of a property, such as force, brightness, or a magnetic field: *hydrothermal processes of low intensity* | [count noun] *different light intensities.*

intensive ▶ adjective **1** concentrated on a single area or subject or into a short time; very thorough or vigorous: *she undertook an intensive Arabic course | eight days of intensive arms talks.*
■ (of agriculture) aiming to achieve the highest possible level of production within a limited area, especially by using chemical and technological aids: *intensive farming.* Often contrasted with **EXTENSIVE** (in sense 2). ■ [usu. in combination] (typically in business and economics) concentrating on or making much use of a specified thing: *computer-intensive methods.*
2 Grammar (of an adjective, adverb, or particle) expressing intensity; giving force or emphasis.
3 denoting a property which is measured in terms of intensity (e.g. concentration) rather than of extent (e.g. volume), and so is not simply increased by addition of one thing to another.
▶ noun Grammar an intensive adjective, adverb, or particle; an intensifier.
– DERIVATIVES **intensively** adverb, **intensiveness** noun.
– ORIGIN late Middle English (in the sense 'vehement, intense'): from French *intensif, -ive* or medieval Latin *intensivus*, from *intendere* (see **INTEND**).

USAGE On the difference between **intensive** and **intense**, see usage at **INTENSE**.

intensive care ▶ noun [mass noun] special medical treatment of a dangerously ill patient, with constant monitoring.

intent ▶ noun [mass noun] intention or purpose: *with alarm she realized his intent* | [count noun] *a real intent to cut back on social programmes.*
▶ adjective **1** [predic.] (**intent on/upon**) resolved or determined to do (something): *the government was intent on achieving greater efficiency.*
■ attentively occupied with: *Gill was intent on her gardening magazine.*
2 (especially of a look) showing earnest and eager attention: *a curiously intent look on her face.*
– PHRASES **to all intents and purposes** in all important respects: *a man who was to all intents and purposes illiterate.* **with intent** Law with the intention of committing a crime: *he denied arson with intent to endanger life | charges of wounding with intent.*
– DERIVATIVES **intently** adverb, **intentness** noun.
– ORIGIN Middle English: from Old French *entent, entente*, based on Latin *intendere* (see **INTEND**). The adjective is from Latin *intentus*, past participle of *intendere*.

intention ▶ noun **1** a thing intended; an aim or plan: *she was full of good intentions* | [with infinitive] *he announced his intention to stand for re-election.*
■ [mass noun] the action or fact of intending: *intention is just one of the factors that will be considered.* ■ (**one's intentions**) a person's designs, especially a man's, in respect to marriage: *if his intentions aren't honourable, I never want to see him again.*
2 Medicine the healing process of a wound. See **FIRST INTENTION**, **SECOND INTENTION**.
3 (**intentions**) Logic conceptions formed by directing the mind towards an object. See **FIRST INTENTIONS**, **SECOND INTENTIONS**.
– DERIVATIVES **intentioned** adjective [in combination] *a well-intentioned remark.*
– ORIGIN late Middle English: from Old French *entencion*, from Latin *intentio(n-)* 'stretching, purpose', from *intendere* (see **INTEND**).

intentional ▶ adjective done on purpose; deliberate: *intentional wrongdoing and harm.*
– DERIVATIVES **intentionally** adverb.
– ORIGIN mid 16th cent. (in the sense 'existing only in intention'): from French *intentionnel* or medieval Latin *intentionalis*, from Latin *intentio(n-)*, from *intendere* (see **INTEND**).

intentional fallacy ▶ noun (**the intentional fallacy**) (in literary theory) the fallacy of basing an assessment of a work on the author's intention rather than on one's response to the actual work.

intentionalism ▶ noun [mass noun] the theory that a literary work should be judged in terms of the author's intentions.

intentionality ▶ noun [mass noun] the fact of being deliberate or purposive.
■ Philosophy the quality of mental states (e.g. thoughts, beliefs, desires, hopes) which consists in their being directed towards some object or state of affairs.

intention tremor ▶ noun a trembling of a part of the body when attempting a precise movement, associated especially with disease of the cerebellum.

inter /ɪnˈtəː/ ▶ verb (**interred**, **interring**) [with obj.] (usu. **be interred**) place (a corpse) in a grave or tomb, typically with funeral rites.
– ORIGIN Middle English: from Old French *enterrer*, based on Latin *in-* 'into' + *terra* 'earth'.

inter. ▶ abbreviation for intermediate.

inter- ▶ prefix **1** between; among: *inter-agency | interblend.*
2 mutually; reciprocally: *interactive.*
– ORIGIN from Old French *entre-* or Latin *inter* 'between, among'.

interact ▶ verb [no obj.] act in such a way as to have an effect on each other: *all the stages in the process interact | the user **interacts** directly **with** the library.*
– DERIVATIVES **interactant** adjective & noun.

interaction ▶ noun [mass noun] reciprocal action or influence: *ongoing **interaction between** the two languages.*
■ Physics a particular way in which matter, fields, and atomic and subatomic particles affect one another, e.g. through gravitation or electromagnetism.
– DERIVATIVES **interactional** adjective.

interactionism ▶ noun [mass noun] Philosophy the theory that there are two entities, mind and body, each of which can have an effect on the other.
– DERIVATIVES **interactionist** noun & adjective.

interactive ▶ adjective (of two people or things) influencing or having an effect on each other: *fully sighted children in interactive play with others with defective vision.*
■ (of a computer or other electronic device) allowing a two-way flow of information between it and a user, responding to the user's input: *interactive video.*
– DERIVATIVES **interactively** adverb, **interactivity** noun.
– ORIGIN mid 19th cent.: from **INTERACT**, on the pattern of *active*.

inter-agency ▶ adjective occurring between different agencies: *inter-agency cooperation.*
■ constituted from more than one agency: *inter-agency groups.*

inter alia /ˌɪntər ˈeɪlɪə, ˈalɪə/ ▶ adverb among other things: *the study includes, inter alia, computers, aircraft, and pharmaceuticals.*
– ORIGIN Latin.

inter alios /ˌɪntər ˈeɪlɪəʊs, ˈalɪəʊs/ ▶ adverb among other people: *tuition to be given to them by, inter alios, a volunteer retired teacher.*
– ORIGIN Latin.

inter-allied ▶ adjective [attrib.] of or relating to two or more states formally cooperating for military purposes.

interarticular /ˌɪntərɑːˈtɪkjʊlə/ ▶ adjective Anatomy existing or acting between the adjacent surfaces of a joint.

interatomic ▶ adjective Physics existing or acting between atoms.

interbed ▶ verb (**-bedded**, **-bedding**) (**be interbedded**) Geology (of a stratum) be embedded among or between others.

interbreed ▶ verb (past and past participle **-bred**) [no obj.] (of an animal) breed with another of a different race or species: *wolves and dogs can interbreed.*
■ (of an animal) inbreed: [as noun **interbreeding**] *their energy and physique had been sapped by interbreeding.* ■ [with obj.] cause (an animal) to breed with another of a different race or species to produce a hybrid.

intercalary /ɪnˈtəːkəl(ə)ri, ˌɪntəˈkal(ə)ri/ ▶ adjective **1** (of a day or a month) inserted in the calendar to harmonize it with the solar year, e.g. 29 February in leap years.
■ (of an academic year or period) additional to the standard course and taken at a different institution. ■ of the nature of an insertion: *elaborate intercalary notes and footnotes.*
2 Botany (of the meristem of a plant) located between its daughter cells, especially (in a grass) at or near the base of a leaf.
– ORIGIN early 17th cent.: from Latin *intercalarius*, from *intercalare* (see **INTERCALATE**).

intercalate /ɪnˈtəːkəleɪt/ ▶ verb [with obj.] **1** interpolate (an intercalary period) in a calendar.
2 (usu. **be intercalated**) insert (something) between layers in a crystal lattice, geological formation, or other structure.
– DERIVATIVES **intercalation** noun.
– ORIGIN early 17th cent.: from Latin *intercalat-* 'proclaimed as inserted in the calendar', from the verb *intercalare*, from *inter-* 'between' + *calare* 'proclaim solemnly'.

intercede /ˌɪntəˈsiːd/ [no obj.] ▶ verb intervene on behalf of another: *I prayed that she would intercede for us.*
– DERIVATIVES **interceder** noun.
– ORIGIN late 16th cent.: from French *intercéder* or Latin *intercedere* 'intervene', from *inter-* 'between' + *cedere* 'go'.

intercellular ▶ adjective Biology located or occurring between cells: *intercellular spaces.*

intercensal /ˌɪntəˈsɛns(ə)l/ ▶ adjective of or relating to the interval between two censuses.

intercept ▶ verb /ˌɪntəˈsɛpt/ [with obj.] obstruct (someone or something) so as to prevent them from continuing to a destination: *intelligence agencies intercepted a series of telephone calls | I intercepted Edward on his way to work.*
■ chiefly Physics cut off or deflect (light or other electromagnetic radiation). ■ Mathematics (of a line or surface) mark or cut off (part of a space, line, or surface).

▶**noun** /ˈɪntəsɛpt/ an act or instance of intercepting something: *he read the file of radio intercepts.*
▪Mathematics the point at which a given line cuts a coordinate axis; the value of the coordinate at that point.
– DERIVATIVES **interception** noun, **interceptive** adjective.
– ORIGIN late Middle English (in the senses 'contain between limits' and 'halt (an effect)'): from Latin *intercept-* 'caught between', from the verb *intercipere*, from *inter-* 'between' + *capere* 'take'.

interceptor ▶**noun** a person or thing that stops or catches (someone or something) going from one place to another.
▪a fast aircraft for stopping or repelling hostile aircraft.

intercession /ˌɪntəˈsɛʃ(ə)n/ ▶**noun** [mass noun] the action of intervening on behalf of another: *appeals for intercession.*
▪the action of saying a prayer on behalf of another person: *prayers of intercession.*
– DERIVATIVES **intercessor** noun, **intercessory** adjective.
– ORIGIN late Middle English: from Latin *intercessio(n-)*, from the verb *intercedere* (see **INTERCEDE**).

interchange ▶**verb** /ɪntəˈtʃeɪn(d)ʒ/ [with obj.] (of two or more people) exchange (things) with each other: *superior and subordinates freely interchange ideas and information.*
▪put each of (two things) in the other's place: *the terms are often interchanged.* ▪ [no obj.] (of a thing) be able to be exchanged with another: *diesel units will* **interchange with** *the petrol ones.*
▶**noun** /ˈɪntətʃeɪn(d)ʒ/ **1** [mass noun] the action of interchanging things, especially information: *the interchange of ideas* | [count noun] *a free-market interchange of goods and services.*
▪[count noun] an exchange of words: *listening in shock to this venomous interchange.*
2 [mass noun] alternation: *the interchange of woods and meadows.*
3 a road junction designed on several levels so that traffic streams do not intersect.
▪a station where passengers may change from one railway line, bus service, etc. to another.
– DERIVATIVES **interchangeability** noun, **interchangeable** adjective, **interchangeableness** noun, **interchangeably** adverb.
– ORIGIN late Middle English: from Old French *entrechangier*, from *entre-* 'between' + *changier* 'to change'.

intercity ▶**adjective** [attrib.] existing or travelling between cities.
▪(also trademark **InterCity**) denoting express passenger rail services in the UK.

inter-class ▶**adjective** existing or conducted between different social classes.

intercollegiate ▶**adjective** existing or conducted between colleges or universities: *intercollegiate sports.*

intercolonial ▶**adjective** existing or conducted between colonies: *an intercolonial railway.*

intercolumniation /ˌɪntəkəlʌmnɪˈeɪʃ(ə)n/ ▶**noun** [mass noun] Architecture the distance between two adjacent columns.
▪the spacing of the columns of a building.
– DERIVATIVES **intercolumnar** adjective.

intercom ▶**noun** an electrical device allowing one-way or two-way communication.
– ORIGIN Second World War: abbreviation of **INTERCOMMUNICATION**.

intercommunicate ▶**verb** [no obj.] **1** engage in two-way communication: *Dr Haber gazed at this while* **intercommunicating with** *his receptionist.*
2 (of two rooms) have a common connecting door: *there were two apartments on the next floor, intercommunicating.*
– ORIGIN late 16th cent.: from Anglo-Latin *intercommunicat-* 'mutually communicated', from the verb *intercommunicare*.

intercommunication ▶**noun** [mass noun] the action of engaging in two-way communication.

intercommunion ▶**noun** [mass noun] participation in Holy Communion or other services by members of different religious denominations.

intercommunity ▶**adjective** [attrib.] existing or conducted between communities: *intercommunity relations.*

interconnect ▶**verb** [no obj.] connect with each other: *the way human activities* **interconnect with** *the environment* | [with obj.] *a high-speed data service can interconnect the hundreds of thousands of host computers and workstations.*
▶**noun** a device which is used to connect two things together.
– DERIVATIVES **interconnection** noun.

intercontinental ▶**adjective** relating to or travelling between continents: *an intercontinental flight* | *intercontinental ballistic missiles.*
– DERIVATIVES **intercontinentally** adverb.

interconvert ▶**verb** [with obj.] (usu. **be interconverted**) cause (two things) to be converted into each other: *oestrogens and androgens are easily interconverted in the laboratory.*
– DERIVATIVES **interconversion** noun, **interconvertible** adjective.

intercooler ▶**noun** an apparatus for cooling gas between successive compressions, especially in a supercharged vehicle engine.
– DERIVATIVES **intercool** verb.

intercorrelation /ˌɪntəkɒrəˈleɪʃ(ə)n/ ▶**noun** a mutual relationship or connection between two or more things: *analyses showing intercorrelations between sets of variables.*
– DERIVATIVES **intercorrelate** verb.

intercostal /ˌɪntəˈkɒst(ə)l/ Anatomy ▶**adjective** situated between the ribs: *the fifth left intercostal space.*
▶**noun** a muscle in this position.
– DERIVATIVES **intercostally** adverb.

intercourse ▶**noun** [mass noun] communication or dealings between individuals or groups: *the vital intercourse between the two halves of the empire.*
▪short for **SEXUAL INTERCOURSE**.
– ORIGIN late Middle English (denoting communication or dealings): from Old French *entrecours* 'exchange, commerce', from Latin *intercursus*, from *intercurrere* 'intervene', from *inter-* 'between' + *currere* 'run'. The specifically sexual use arose in the late 18th cent.

intercrop ▶**verb** (**-cropped**, **-cropping**) [with obj.] [often as noun **intercropping**] grow (a crop) among plants of a different kind, usually in the space between rows: *lettuce is particularly good for intercropping among young Brussels sprouts.*
▶**noun** a crop grown in such a way.

intercross ▶**verb** [no obj.] (of animals or plants of different breeds or varieties) interbreed.
▪[with obj.] cause to do this.
▶**noun** an instance of intercrossing of animals or plants.
▪an animal or plant resulting from this.

intercrural /ˌɪntəˈkrʊər(ə)l/ ▶**adjective** between the legs.

intercurrent ▶**adjective** **1** Medicine (of a disease) occurring during the progress of another disease: *complicated by intercurrent infection with other microbes.*
2 rare (of a time or event) intervening.
– ORIGIN early 17th cent.: from Latin *intercurrent-* 'intervening', from the verb *intercurrere*.

intercut ▶**verb** (**-cutting**; past and past participle **-cut**) [with obj.] alternate (scenes or shots) with contrasting scenes or shots to make one composite scene in a film: *pieces of archive film are* **intercut with** *brief interviews* | [no obj.] *the action intercuts between the time periods.*

interdenominational /ˌɪntədɪnɒmɪˈneɪʃ(ə)n(ə)l/ ▶**adjective** of or relating to more than one religious denomination: *an interdenominational service.*
– DERIVATIVES **interdenominationally** adverb.

interdepartmental ▶**adjective** of or relating to more than one department.
– DERIVATIVES **interdepartmentally** adverb.

interdependent ▶**adjective** (of two or more people or things) dependent on each other: *we in Europe are all increasingly interdependent.*
– DERIVATIVES **interdepend** verb, **interdependence** noun, **interdependency** noun.

interdict ▶**noun** /ˈɪntədɪkt/ an authoritative prohibition, in particular:
▪Law, chiefly Scottish a court order forbidding an act; a negative injunction. ▪(in the Roman Catholic Church) a sentence debarring a person, or especially a place, from ecclesiastical functions and privileges: *a papal interdict.*
▶**verb** /ˌɪntəˈdɪkt/ [with obj.] chiefly N. Amer. **1** prohibit or forbid (something): *society will never interdict sex.*
▪(**interdict someone from**) prohibit someone from (doing something): *I have not been interdicted from consuming or holding alcoholic beverages.*
2 intercept and prevent the movement of (a prohibited commodity or person): *the police established roadblocks throughout the country for interdicting drugs.*
▪Military impede (an enemy force), especially by aerial bombing of lines of communication or supply.
– DERIVATIVES **interdiction** noun.
– ORIGIN Middle English *entredite* (in the ecclesiastical sense), from Old French *entredit*, from Latin *interdictum*, past participle of *interdicere* 'interpose, forbid by decree', from *inter-* 'between' + *dicere* 'say'. The spelling change in the 16th cent. was due to association with the Latin form.

interdictor /ˌɪntəˈdɪktə/ ▶**noun** Military an aircraft designed to interrupt enemy supply operations by aerial bombing.

interdigital ▶**adjective** between the fingers or toes.

interdigitate /ˌɪntəˈdɪdʒɪteɪt/ ▶**verb** [no obj.] (of two or more things) interlock like the fingers of two clasped hands: [as adj. **interdigitating**] *interdigitating metal bars.*
– ORIGIN mid 19th cent.: from **INTER-** 'between' + **DIGIT** + **-ATE**[3].

interdisciplinary ▶**adjective** of or relating to more than one branch of knowledge: *an interdisciplinary research programme.*

interest ▶**noun** **1** [mass noun] the state of wanting to know or learn about something or someone: *she looked about her with interest.*
▪(**an interest in**) a feeling of wanting to know or learn about (something): *he developed an interest in art.* ▪ the quality of exciting curiosity or holding the attention: *a tale full of interest.* ▪ [count noun] a subject about which one is concerned or enthusiastic: *my particular interest is twentieth-century poetry.*
2 [mass noun] money paid regularly at a particular rate for the use of money lent, or for delaying the repayment of a debt: *the monthly rate of interest* | [as modifier] *interest payments.*
3 the advantage or benefit of a person or group: *the merger is not contrary to the public interest* | *we are acting in the best interests of our customers* | *the national interest.*
▪archaic the selfish pursuit of one's own welfare; self-interest.
4 a stake, share, or involvement in an undertaking, especially a financial one: *holders of voting rights must disclose their interests* | *he must have no personal* **interest in** *the outcome of the case.*
▪a legal concern, title, or right in property.
5 (usu. **interests**) a group or organization having a specified common concern, especially in politics or business: *food interests in Scotland must continue to invest.*
▶**verb** [with obj.] excite the curiosity or attention of (someone): *I thought the book might interest Eliot.*
▪(**interest someone in**) cause someone to undertake or acquire (something): *efforts were made to interest her in a purchase.*
– PHRASES **at interest** (of money borrowed) on the condition that interest is payable. **declare an** (or **one's**) **interest** make known one's financial interests in an undertaking before it is discussed. **in the interests** (or **interest**) **of something** for the benefit of: *in the interests of security we are keeping the information confidential.* **of interest** interesting: *much of it is of interest to historians.* **with interest** with interest charged or paid: *loans that must be paid back with interest.* ▪ (of an action) reciprocated with more force or vigour than the original one: *she returned his look with interest.*
– ORIGIN late Middle English (originally as *interess*): from Anglo-Norman French *interesse*, from Latin *interesse* 'differ, be important', from *inter-* 'between' + *esse* 'be'. The *-t* was added partly by association with Old French *interest* 'damage, loss', apparently from Latin *interest* 'it is important'. The original sense was 'the possession of a share in or a right to something'; hence sense 4. Sense 1 and the verb arose in the 18th cent. Sense 2 was influenced by medieval Latin *interesse* 'compensation for a debtor's defaulting'.

interested ▶**adjective** **1** showing curiosity or concern about something or someone; having a feeling of interest: *I had always been* **interested in** *history.*

2 [attrib.] having an interest or involvement; not impartial or disinterested: *seeking views from all interested parties.*
– DERIVATIVES **interestedly** adverb, **interestedness** noun.

interest-free ▶ **adjective** & **adverb** with no interest charged on money that has been borrowed: [as adj.] *interest-free credit* | [as adv.] *he lent the money interest-free.*

interesting ▶ **adjective** arousing curiosity or interest; holding or catching the attention: *an interesting debate* | *it will be very interesting to see what they come up with.*
– PHRASES **in an interesting condition** archaic used euphemistically to describe a woman as being pregnant.
– DERIVATIVES **interestingly** adverb *he talked interestingly and learnedly* | [sentence adverb] *interestingly, the researchers did notice a link*, **interestingness** noun.

interface ▶ **noun 1** a point where two systems, subjects, organizations, etc. meet and interact: *the **interface between** accountancy and the law.*
■ chiefly Physics a surface forming a common boundary between two portions of matter or space, for example between two immiscible liquids: *the surface tension of a liquid at its air/liquid interface.*
2 Computing a device or program enabling a user to communicate with a computer.
■ a device or program for connecting two items of hardware or software so that they can be operated jointly or communicate with each other.
▶ **verb** [no obj.] (**interface with**) **1** interact with (another system, person, organization, etc.): *his goal is to get people interfacing with each other.*
2 Computing connect with (another computer or piece of equipment) by an interface.

> **USAGE** The word **interface** is a relatively new word, having been in the language (as a noun) since the 1880s. However, in the 1960s it became widespread in computer use and, by analogy, began to enjoy a vogue as both a noun and a verb in all sorts of other spheres. Traditionalists object to it on the grounds that there are plenty of other words that could be used instead. Nevertheless it is now well established as a part of standard English.

interfacial ▶ **adjective 1** included between two faces of a crystal or other solid.
2 of, relating to, or forming a common boundary between two portions of matter or space.

interfacing ▶ **noun** [mass noun] a stiffish material, especially buckram, typically used between two layers of fabric in collars.

interfaith ▶ **adjective** [attrib.] of, relating to, or between different religions or members of different religions: *action to encourage interfaith dialogue.*

interfere ▶ **verb** [no obj.] **1** (**interfere with**) prevent (a process or activity) continuing or being carried out properly: *a holiday job would interfere with his studies.*
■ (of a thing) strike against (something) when working; get in the way of: *the rotors are widely separated and do not interfere with one another.* ■ handle or adjust (something) without permission, especially so as to cause damage: *he admitted interfering with a van.* ■ Law attempt to bribe or intimidate (a witness).
2 take part or intervene in an activity without invitation or necessity: *she tried not to **interfere in** her children's lives* | [as adj. **interfering**] *interfering busybodies.*
3 (**interfere with**) Brit. sexually molest or assault (someone, especially a child or young person) (used euphemistically).
4 Physics (of light or other electromagnetic waveforms) mutually act upon each other and produce interference: *light pulses interfere constructively in a fibre to emit a pulse.*
■ cause interference to a broadcasted radio signal.
5 (of a horse) knock one foot against the fetlock of another leg.
– DERIVATIVES **interferer** noun, **interferingly** adverb.
– ORIGIN late Middle English: from Old French *s'entreferir* 'strike each other', from *entre-* 'between' + *ferir* (from Latin *ferire* 'to strike').

interference ▶ **noun** [mass noun] **1** the action of interfering or the process of being interfered with: *he denied that there had been any **interference** in the country's internal affairs* | [count noun] *an unwarranted **interference with** personal liberty.*
■ American Football the legal blocking of an opponent to clear a way for the ball-carrier. ■ (in ice hockey and other sports) the illegal hindering of an opponent not in possession of the puck or ball.
2 Physics the combination of two or more electromagnetic waveforms to form a resultant wave in which the displacement is either reinforced or cancelled.
■ the fading or disturbance of received radio signals caused by unwanted signals from other sources, such as unshielded electrical equipment, or broadcasts from other stations or channels.
– PHRASES **run interference** American Football move in such a way as to cause interference (see sense 1 above). ■ N. Amer. informal intervene on someone's behalf, typically so as to protect them from distraction or annoyance: *Elizabeth was quick to run interference and said that the Professor would be very busy.*
– DERIVATIVES **interferential** adjective.
– ORIGIN mid 18th cent.: from **INTERFERE**, on the pattern of words such as *difference.*

interference fit ▶ **noun** a fit between two parts in which the external dimension of one part slightly exceeds the internal dimension of the part into which it has to fit.

interferogram /ˌɪntəˈfɪərə(ʊ)gram/ (also **interferogramme**) ▶ **noun** Physics a pattern formed by wave interference, especially one represented in a photograph or diagram.

interferometer /ˌɪntəfəˈrɒmɪtə/ ▶ **noun** Physics an instrument in which wave interference is employed to make precise measurements of length of displacement in terms of the wavelength.
– DERIVATIVES **interferometric** adjective, **interferometrically** adverb, **interferometry** noun.

interferon /ˌɪntəˈfɪərɒn/ ▶ **noun** [mass noun] Biochemistry a protein released by animal cells, usually in response to the entry of a virus, which has the property of inhibiting virus replication.
– ORIGIN 1950s: from **INTERFERE** + **-ON**.

interfile ▶ **verb** [with obj.] file (two or more sequences) together.
■ file (one or more items) into an existing sequence: *this index is **interfiled with** the main card catalogue.*

interflow ▶ **verb** [no obj.] poetic/literary mix or mingle: *the thousand varying shades interflowing like a lighted water.*

interfluve /ˈɪntəfluːv/ ▶ **noun** Geology a region between the valleys of adjacent watercourses, especially in a dissected upland.
– DERIVATIVES **interfluvial** adjective.
– ORIGIN early 20th cent.: back-formation from *interfluvial.*

interfuse ▶ **verb** [with obj.] poetic/literary join or mix (two or more things) together: *nowhere do art and life seem so interfused.*
– DERIVATIVES **interfusion** noun.
– ORIGIN late 16th cent.: from Latin *interfus-* 'poured among', from the verb *interfundere*, from *inter-* 'between' + *fundere* 'pour'.

intergalactic ▶ **adjective** of, relating to, or situated between two or more galaxies: *intergalactic gas.*
– DERIVATIVES **intergalactically** adverb.

intergeneric /ˌɪntədʒɪˈnɛrɪk/ ▶ **adjective** Biology existing between or obtained from different genera: *intergeneric differences* | *an intergeneric hybrid.*

interglacial Geology ▶ **adjective** of or relating to a period of milder climate between two glacial periods. Compare with **INTERSTADIAL**.
▶ **noun** an interglacial period.

intergovernmental /ˌɪntəgʌv(ə)nˈmɛnt(ə)l, -gʌv(ə)ˈmɛnt(ə)l/ ▶ **adjective** of, relating to, or conducted between two or more governments: *an intergovernmental conference.*
– DERIVATIVES **intergovernmentally** adverb.

intergrade ▶ **verb** [no obj.] Biology pass into another form by a series of intervening forms: *they have several forms which intergrade with each other.*
▶ **noun** an intervening form of this kind.
– DERIVATIVES **intergradation** noun.

intergrow ▶ **verb** (past **-grew**; past participle **-grown**) [no obj.] [usu. as adj. **intergrown**] (chiefly of crystals) grow into each other: *finely intergrown siderite.*

intergrowth ▶ **noun** a thing produced by intergrowing, especially of mineral crystals in rock.

interim /ˈɪnt(ə)rɪm/ ▶ **noun** the intervening time: ***in the interim** I'll just keep my fingers crossed.*
■ (usu. **interims**) chiefly Brit. an interim dividend, profit, result, etc.
▶ **adjective** in or for the intervening period; provisional or temporary: *an interim arrangement.*
■ chiefly Brit. relating to less than a full year's business activity: *an interim dividend* | *interim profit.*
▶ **adverb** archaic meanwhile.
– ORIGIN mid 16th cent. (denoting a temporary or provisional arrangement, originally for the adjustment of religious differences between the German Protestants and the Roman Catholic Church): from Latin, 'meanwhile'.

interior ▶ **adjective 1** situated within or inside; relating to the inside; inner: *the interior lighting is not adequate.*
■ [predic.] (**interior to**) chiefly technical situated further in or within: *the layer immediately interior to the epidermis.* ■ drawn, photographed, etc. within a building: *a light which is ideal for every interior shot.*
2 [attrib.] remote from the coast or frontier; inland: *the interior jungle regions.*
■ relating to internal or domestic affairs: *the interior minister.*
3 existing or taking place in the mind or soul; mental: *an interior monologue* | *driven by interior forces.*
▶ **noun** (usu. **the interior**) **1** the inner or indoor part of something, especially a building; the inside: *the interior has been much restored.*
■ an artistic representation of the inside of a building or room: *a few still lifes, interiors, and landscapes.*
2 the inland part of a country or region: *the plains of the interior.*
■ the internal affairs of a country: *the Minister of the Interior.*
– DERIVATIVES **interiorize** (also **-ise**) verb, **interiorly** adverb.
– ORIGIN late 15th cent.: from Latin, 'inner', comparative adjective from *inter* 'within'.

interior angle ▶ **noun** the angle between adjacent sides of a rectilinear figure.

interior decoration ▶ **noun** [mass noun] the decoration of the interior of a building or room, especially with regard for colour combination and artistic effect.
– DERIVATIVES **interior decorator** noun.

interior design ▶ **noun** [mass noun] the art or process of designing the interior decoration of a room or building.
– DERIVATIVES **interior designer** noun.

interiority ▶ **noun** [mass noun] the quality of being interior or inward.
■ inner character or nature; subjectivity: *the profound interiority of faith.*
– ORIGIN early 18th cent.: from medieval Latin *interioritas*, from Latin *interior* 'inner'.

interior monologue ▶ **noun** a piece of writing expressing a character's inner thoughts.

interior-sprung ▶ **adjective** Brit. (of a mattress) having coiled springs inside.

interject /ˌɪntəˈdʒɛkt/ ▶ **verb** [with obj.] say (something) abruptly, especially as an aside or interruption: *she interjected the odd question here and there* | [no obj.] *Christina felt bound to interject before there was open warfare.*
– DERIVATIVES **interjectory** adjective.
– ORIGIN late 16th cent.: from Latin *interject-* 'interposed', from the verb *interjicere*, from *inter-* 'between' + *jacere* 'to throw'.

interjection ▶ **noun** an abrupt remark, made especially as an aside or interruption.
■ an exclamation, especially as a part of speech (e.g. *ah!, dear me!*).
– DERIVATIVES **interjectional** adjective.
– ORIGIN late Middle English: via Old French from Latin *interjectio(n-)*, from the verb *interjicere* (see **INTERJECT**).

interlace ▶ **verb** [with obj.] bind intricately together; interweave: *the trees interlaced their branches so that only tiny patches of sky were visible.*
■ (**interlace something with**) mingle or intersperse something with: *discussion interlaced with esoteric mathematics.* ■ [no obj.] (of two or more things) cross each other intricately: [as adj. **interlacing**] *closely interlacing branches.* ■ Electronics scan (a video image) in such a way that alternate lines form one sequence which is followed by the other lines in a second sequence: [as adj. **interlaced**] *interlaced displays.*
– DERIVATIVES **interlacement** noun.
– ORIGIN late Middle English: from Old French *entrelacier*, from *entre-* 'between' + *lacier* 'to lace'.

Interlaken /ˈɪntəˌlɑːk(ə)n, German ˈɪntɐˌlakn/ the chief town of the Bernese Alps in central Switzerland, situated on the River Aare between Lake Brienz and Lake Thun; pop. 4,852 (1980).

interlanguage ▶ noun a language or form of language having features of two others, typically a pidgin or a version produced by a foreign learner.

interlard ▶ verb [with obj.] (**interlard something with**) intersperse or embellish speech or writing with different material: *a compendium of advertisements and reviews, interlarded with gossip.*
– ORIGIN late Middle English (in the sense 'mix with alternate layers of fat'): from French *entrelarder*, from *entre-* 'between' + *larder* 'to lard'.

interlay ▶ verb (past and past participle **-laid**) [with obj.] lay between or among; interpose: *strips of granite are* ***interlaid with*** *creamy Sardinian sardo.*
▶ noun [mass noun] an inserted layer: *remember to use interlay under foam-backed carpets.*
■ [count noun] Printing a sheet or piece of paper placed between a letterpress printing plate and its base to give increased pressure on certain areas.

interlayer ▶ noun a layer sandwiched between two others.
▶ adjective [attrib.] situated or occurring between two layers.

interleaf ▶ noun (pl. **-leaves**) an extra page, typically a blank one, between the leaves of a book.

interleave ▶ verb [with obj.] insert pages, typically blank ones, between the pages of (a book): *books of maps* ***interleaved with*** *tracing paper.*
■ place something between the layers of (something): *pasta interleaved with strips of courgette and carrot.* ■ Telecommunications mix (two or more digital signals) by alternating between them. ■ Computing divide (memory or processing power) between a number of tasks by allocating successive segments of it to each task in turn.

interleukin /ˌɪntəˈluːkɪn/ ▶ noun Biochemistry any of a class of glycoproteins produced by leucocytes for regulating immune responses.
– ORIGIN 1970s: from **INTER-** 'occurring between' + *leukocyte* (variant of **LEUCOCYTE**) + **-IN**[1].

interlibrary ▶ adjective [attrib.] between libraries.

interline[1] ▶ verb [with obj.] insert words between the lines of (a document or other text): *the writing was overwritten and interlined by many hands.*
■ insert (words) in this way.
– ORIGIN late Middle English: from medieval Latin *interlineare*, from *inter-* 'between' + Latin *linea* 'line'.

interline[2] ▶ verb [with obj.] put an extra lining between the ordinary lining and the fabric of (a garment, curtain, etc.), typically to provide extra strength.

interlinear ▶ adjective written or printed between the lines of a text: *interlinear glosses.*
■ (of a book) having the same text in different languages printed on alternate lines.
– ORIGIN late Middle English: from medieval Latin *interlinearis*, from *inter-* 'between' + Latin *linearis* (from *linea* 'line').

interlineate /ˌɪntəˈlɪnɪeɪt/ ▶ verb another term for **INTERLINE**[1].
– DERIVATIVES **interlineation** noun.
– ORIGIN late 17th cent.: from medieval Latin *interlineat-* 'interlined', from the verb *interlineare*.

interlingua /ˌɪntəˈlɪŋgwə/ ▶ noun an artificial language, devised for machine translation, that makes explicit the distinctions necessary for successful translation into a target language, even where they are not present in the source language.
■ (**Interlingua**) [mass noun] an artificial international language formed of elements common to the Romance languages, designed primarily for scientific and technical use.
– ORIGIN early 20th cent.: from **INTER-** 'between' + Latin *lingua* 'tongue'.

interlingual ▶ adjective between or relating to two languages: *interlingual dictionaries.*
■ of or relating to an interlingua or artificial interlanguage.

interlining ▶ noun [mass noun] material used as an extra lining between the ordinary lining and the fabric of a garment, curtain, etc.

interlink ▶ verb [with obj.] join or connect (two or more things) together: *the department's postgraduate work is closely* ***interlinked with*** *the MSc programme.*
– DERIVATIVES **interlinkage** noun.

interlobular /ˌɪntəˈlɒbjʊlə/ ▶ adjective Anatomy situated between lobes (e.g. of the kidney or liver).

interlock ▶ verb [no obj.] (of two or more things) engage with each other by overlapping or by the fitting together of projections and recesses: *their fingers interlocked.*
▶ noun **1** a device or mechanism for connecting or coordinating the function of different components.
2 (also **interlock fabric**) [mass noun] a fabric knitted with closely interlocking stitches allowing it to stretch, typically used in underwear.
– DERIVATIVES **interlocker** noun.

interlocutor /ˌɪntəˈlɒkjʊtə/ ▶ noun formal a person who takes part in a dialogue or conversation.
– DERIVATIVES **interlocution** noun.
– ORIGIN early 16th cent.: modern Latin, from Latin *interlocut-* 'interrupted (by speech)', from the verb *interloqui*, from *inter-* 'between' + *loqui* 'speak'.

interlocutory /ˌɪntəˈlɒkjʊt(ə)ri/ ▶ adjective **1** Law (of a decree or judgement) given provisionally during the course of a legal action.
2 rare of or relating to dialogue or conversation.
– ORIGIN late 15th cent.: from medieval Latin *interlocutorius*, from Latin *interloqui* 'interrupt' (see **INTERLOCUTOR**).

interloper /ˈɪntələʊpə/ ▶ noun a person who becomes involved in a place or situation where they are not wanted or are considered not to belong.
– DERIVATIVES **interlope** verb.
– ORIGIN late 16th cent. (denoting an unauthorized trader trespassing on the rights of a trade monopoly): from **INTER-** 'amid' + *-loper* as in archaic *landloper* 'vagabond' (from Middle Dutch *landlooper*).

interlude ▶ noun **1** an intervening period of time; an interval: *enjoying a lunchtime interlude.*
■ a pause between the acts of a play.
2 a thing occurring or done during an interval.
■ something performed during a theatre interval: *an orchestral interlude.* ■ a piece of music played between other pieces or between the verses of a hymn. ■ a temporary amusement or source of entertainment that contrasts with what goes before or after: *the romantic interlude withered rapidly once he was back in town.*
– ORIGIN Middle English (originally denoting a light dramatic entertainment): from medieval Latin *interludium*, from *inter-* 'between' + *ludus* 'play'.

intermarriage ▶ noun [mass noun] marriage between people of different races, castes, or religions: *intermarriage between Scots and English borderers was officially forbidden during many periods* | [count noun] *intermarriages with Muslim immigrants.*
■ marriage between close relations.

intermarry ▶ verb (**-ies**, **-ied**) [no obj.] (of people belonging to different races, castes, or religions) become connected by marriage: *over the centuries the Greeks* ***intermarried with*** *the natives.*
■ (of close relations) marry each other.

intermediary /ˌɪntəˈmiːdɪəri/ ▶ noun (pl. **-ies**) a person who acts as a link between people in order to try and bring about an agreement or reconciliation; a mediator: ***intermediaries between*** *lenders and borrowers.*
▶ adjective intermediate: *an intermediary stage.*
– ORIGIN late 18th cent.: from French *intermédiaire*, from Italian *intermediario*, from Latin *intermedius* (see **INTERMEDIATE**).

intermediate /ˌɪntəˈmiːdɪət/ ▶ adjective coming between two things in time, place, order, character, etc.: *an intermediate stage of development* | *a cooled liquid* ***intermediate between*** *liquid and solid.*
■ having more than a basic knowledge or level of skill but not yet advanced: *intermediate skiers.* ■ suitable for people of such a level: *an intermediate course.*
▶ noun an intermediate thing.
■ a person at an intermediate level of knowledge or skill. ■ a chemical compound formed by one reaction and then taking part in another, especially during synthesis.
▶ verb /ˌɪntəˈmiːdɪeɪt/ [no obj.] act as intermediary; mediate: *groups which* ***intermediated between*** *the individual and the state.*
– DERIVATIVES **intermediacy** noun, **intermediately** adverb, **intermediateness** noun, **intermediation** noun, **intermediator** noun.
– ORIGIN late Middle English: from medieval Latin *intermediatus*, from Latin *intermedius*, from *inter-* 'between' + *medius* 'middle'.

intermediate frequency ▶ noun the frequency to which a radio signal is converted during heterodyne reception.

intermediate host ▶ noun Biology an organism that supports the immature or non-reproductive forms of a parasite. Compare with **DEFINITIVE HOST**.

intermediate technology ▶ noun [mass noun] technology suitable for use in developing countries, typically making use of locally available resources.

intermedin /ˌɪntəˈmiːdɪn/ ▶ noun [mass noun] Physiology another term for **MELANOCYTE-STIMULATING HORMONE**.
– ORIGIN 1930s: from modern Latin (*pars*) *intermedia* 'intermediate part (of the pituitary)' + **-IN**[1].

intermedium /ˌɪntəˈmiːdɪəm/ ▶ noun (pl. **intermedia** /-ˈmiːdɪə/) Zoology (in tetrapods) a carpal in the centre of the wrist joint, or a tarsal in the centre of the ankle joint.
– ORIGIN late 16th cent. (denoting an intervening action or performance): from late Latin, neuter (used as a noun) of Latin *intermedius* 'intermediate'.

interment /ɪnˈtəːm(ə)nt/ ▶ noun [mass noun] the burial of a corpse in a grave or tomb, typically with funeral rites: *the day of interment* | [count noun] *interments took place in the churchyard.*

intermesh ▶ verb [no obj.] (of two or more things) mesh with one another.

intermezzo /ˌɪntəˈmɛtsəʊ/ ▶ noun (pl. **intermezzi** /-ˈmɛtsi/ or **intermezzos**) a short connecting instrumental movement in an opera or other musical work.
■ a similar piece performed independently. ■ a short piece for a solo instrument. ■ a light dramatic, musical, or other performance inserted between the acts of a play.
– ORIGIN late 18th cent.: from Italian, from Latin *intermedium* 'interval', neuter of *intermedius* (see **INTERMEDIATE**).

interminable ▶ adjective endless (often used hyperbolically): *we got bogged down in interminable discussions.*
– DERIVATIVES **interminableness** noun, **interminably** adverb.
– ORIGIN late Middle English: from Old French, or from late Latin *interminabilis*, from *in-* 'not' + *terminare* (see **TERMINATE**).

intermingle ▶ verb mix or mingle together: [no obj.] *daisies* ***intermingled with*** *huge expanses of gorse and foxgloves* | [with obj.] *Riesling grapes were always intermingled with other varieties.*

intermission ▶ noun a pause or break: *he was granted an intermission in his studies* | [mass noun] *the daily work goes on without intermission.*
■ an interval between parts of a play, film, or concert.
– ORIGIN late Middle English: from Latin *intermissio(n-)*, from the verb *intermittere* (see **INTERMIT**).

intermit /ˌɪntəˈmɪt/ ▶ verb (**intermitted**, **intermitting**) [with obj.] suspend or discontinue (an action or practice) for a time: *he was urged to intermit his application.*
■ [no obj.] (especially of a fever or pulse) cease or stop for a time.
– ORIGIN mid 16th cent.: from Latin *intermittere*, from *inter-* 'between' + *mittere* 'let go'.

intermittent ▶ adjective occurring at irregular intervals; not continuous or steady: *intermittent rain.*
– DERIVATIVES **intermittence** noun, **intermittency** noun, **intermittently** adverb.
– ORIGIN mid 16th cent.: from Latin *intermittent-* 'ceasing', from the verb *intermittere* (see **INTERMIT**).

intermittent claudication ▶ noun see **CLAUDICATION**.

intermix ▶ verb mix together: [with obj.] *the ore had to be handled so that it was not inadvertently* ***intermixed with*** *other material* | [no obj.] *along its southern edge low trees* ***intermix with*** *the shrubs.*
– DERIVATIVES **intermixable** adjective, **intermixture** noun.
– ORIGIN mid 16th cent. (originally as the past participle *intermixt*): from Latin *intermixtus*, past participle of *intermiscere* 'mix together', from *inter-* 'between' + *miscere* 'to mix'.

intermodal ▶ adjective involving two or more different modes of transport in conveying goods.

intermolecular ▶ adjective existing or taking place between molecules.

intern ▶ noun /ˈɪntəːn/ (also **interne**) chiefly N. Amer. a recent medical graduate receiving supervised training in a hospital and acting as an assistant physician or surgeon. Compare with **HOUSE OFFICER**.
■ a student or trainee who works, sometimes without pay, at a trade or occupation in order to gain work experience or satisfy requirements for a qualification.
▶ verb **1** /ɪnˈtəːn/ [with obj.] confine (someone) as a prisoner, especially for political or military reasons.
2 /ˈɪntəːn/ [no obj.] chiefly N. Amer. serve as an intern.
– DERIVATIVES **internment** noun (only in sense 1 of the verb), **internship** noun (only in the sense of the noun).
– ORIGIN early 16th cent. (as an adjective in the sense 'internal'): from French *interne* (adjective), *interner* (verb), from Latin *internus* 'inward, internal'. Current senses date from the 19th cent.

internal ▶ adjective **1** of or situated on the inside: *the tube had an internal diameter of 1.1 mm.*
■ inside the body: *internal bleeding.* ■ existing or occurring within an organization: *an internal telephone system.* ■ relating to affairs and activities within a country rather than with other countries; domestic: *the government's internal policies* | *internal flights.* ■ experienced in one's mind; inner rather than expressed: *internal feelings.* ■ of the inner nature of a thing; intrinsic: *he creates a dialogue internal to his work.*
2 Brit. (of a student) attending a university as well as taking its examinations.
▶ plural noun (**internals**) inner parts or features: *all the weapon's internals are well finished and highly polished.*
– DERIVATIVES **internality** noun, **internally** adverb.
– ORIGIN early 16th cent. (in the sense 'intrinsic'): from modern Latin *internalis*, from Latin *internus* 'inward, internal'.

internal clock ▶ noun a person's innate sense of time.
■ another term for **BIOLOGICAL CLOCK**.

internal-combustion engine ▶ noun an engine which generates motive power by the burning of petrol, oil, or other fuel with air inside the engine, the hot gases produced being used to drive a piston or do other work as they expand.

internal energy ▶ noun [mass noun] Physics the energy in a system arising from the relative positions and interactions of its parts.

internal evidence ▶ noun [mass noun] evidence derived from the contents of the thing discussed.

internal exile ▶ noun [mass noun] penal banishment from a part of one's own country.

internalize (also **-ise**) ▶ verb [with obj.] **1** Psychology make (attitudes or behaviour) part of one's nature by learning or unconscious assimilation.
■ acquire knowledge of (the rules of a language).
2 Economics incorporate (costs) as part of a pricing structure, especially social costs resulting from the manufacture and use of a product.
– DERIVATIVES **internalization** noun.

internal market ▶ noun **1** another term for **SINGLE MARKET**.
2 (in the UK) a system of decentralized funding in the National Health Service whereby hospital departments purchase each other's services contractually.

internal rhyme ▶ noun a rhyme involving a word in the middle of a line and another at the end of the line or in the middle of the next.

international ▶ adjective existing, occurring, or carried on between two or more nations: *international trade.*
■ agreed on by all or many nations: *a violation of international law.* ■ used by people of many nations: *large international hotels.*
▶ noun **1** Brit. a game or contest between teams representing different countries in a sport.
■ a player who has taken part in such a game or contest.
2 (**International**) any of four associations founded (1864–1936) to promote socialist or communist action.
■ a member of any of these.

The First International was formed by Karl Marx in London in 1864 as an international working men's association. The Second International was formed in Paris in 1889 to celebrate the 100th anniversary of the French Revolution and still survives as a loose association of social democrats. The Third International, also known as the Comintern, was formed by the Bolsheviks in 1919 to further the cause of world revolution. It was abolished in 1943. The Fourth International, a body of Trotskyist organizations, was formed in 1938 in opposition to the policies of the Stalin-dominated Third International.

– DERIVATIVES **internationality** noun, **internationally** adverb.

International Atomic Energy Agency (abbrev.: **IAEA**) an international organization set up in 1957 to promote research into and the development of atomic energy for peaceful purposes.

International Baccalaureate (abbrev.: **IB**) ▶ noun a set of examinations intended to qualify successful candidates for higher education in any of several countries.

International Bank for Reconstruction and Development (abbrev.: **IBRD**) an agency of the United Nations which constitutes the main part of the World Bank. It was established in 1945 and its headquarters are in Washington DC.

International Brigade a group of volunteers which was raised internationally by foreign communist parties and which fought on the Republican side in the Spanish Civil War.

international candle ▶ noun see **CANDLE**.

International Civil Aviation Organization an agency of the United Nations, founded in 1947 to study problems of international civil aviation and establish standards and regulations.

International Confederation of Free Trade Unions (abbrev.: **ICFTU**) an association formed in 1949 to promote free trade unionism worldwide. Its headquarters are in Brussels.

International Court of Justice a judicial court of the United Nations which replaced the Cour Permanente de Justice in 1945 and meets at The Hague.

International Date Line ▶ noun see **DATE LINE**.

International Development Association (abbrev.: **IDA**) an affiliate of the International Bank for Reconstruction and Development (World Bank) established in 1960 to provide assistance primarily in the poorer developing countries.

Internationale /ˌɪntənaʃəˈnɑːl/ **1** (**the Internationale**) a revolutionary song composed in France in the late 19th century. It was adopted by French socialists and subsequently by others, and was the official anthem of the USSR until 1944.
2 variant spelling of **INTERNATIONAL** (in sense 2 of the noun).
– ORIGIN French, feminine of *international* 'international'.

International Energy Agency (abbrev.: **IEA**) an agency founded in 1974, within the framework of the OECD, to coordinate energy supply and demand worldwide. Its headquarters are in Paris.

International Finance Corporation (abbrev: **IFC**) an affiliate of the International Bank for Reconstruction and Development (World Bank) established in 1956 to assist developing member countries by promoting the growth of the private sector of their economies.

International Fund for Agricultural Development (abbrev.: **IFAD**) an agency of the United Nations whose purpose is to mobilize additional funds for agricultural and rural development in developing countries through programmes that directly benefit the poorest rural populations. It began operations in 1977.

internationalism ▶ noun [mass noun] **1** the state or process of being international: *the internationalism of popular music.*
■ the advocacy of cooperation and understanding between nations.
2 (**Internationalism**) the principles of any of the four Internationals.
– DERIVATIVES **internationalist** noun.

internationalize (also **-ise**) ▶ verb [with obj.] **1** make (something) international.
2 bring (a place) under the protection or control of two or more nations: [as adj. **internationalized**] *an internationalized city.*

– DERIVATIVES **internationalization** noun.

International Labour Organization (abbrev.: **ILO**) an organization established in 1919 whose aim is to promote lasting peace through social justice, awarded the Nobel Peace Prize in 1969.

international law ▶ noun [mass noun] a body of rules established by custom or treaty and recognized by nations as binding in their relations with one another.

International Maritime Association an agency of the United Nations established in 1958 for cooperation and exchange of information among governments on matters relating to international shipping. Its headquarters are in London.

International Monetary Fund (abbrev.: **IMF**) an international organization established in 1945 which aims to promote international trade and monetary cooperation and the stabilization of exchange rates. Member countries contribute in gold and in their own currencies to provide a reserve on which they may draw to meet foreign obligations during periods of deficit in their international balance of payments. Payments are usually made on the basis of the country's acceptance of stipulated measures for economic correction, which often entail cuts in public expenditure and an increased cost of living, and have frequently caused controversy. It is affiliated to the UN, with headquarters in Washington DC.

International Organization for Standardization an organization founded in 1946 to standardize measurements for international industrial, commercial, and scientific purposes.

International Phonetic Alphabet (abbrev.: **IPA**) an internationally recognized set of phonetic symbols developed in the late 19th century, based on the principle of strict one-to-one correspondence between sounds and symbols.

International Society for Krishna Consciousness see **HARE KRISHNA**.

international style ▶ noun [mass noun] a functional style of 20th-century architecture, so called because it crossed national and cultural barriers. It is characterized by the use of steel and reinforced concrete, wide windows, uninterrupted interior spaces, simple lines, and strict geometric forms.

international system of units ▶ noun a system of physical units (**SI Units**) based on the metre, kilogram, second, ampere, kelvin, candela, and mole, together with a set of prefixes to indicate multiplication or division by a power of ten.
– ORIGIN translating French *Système International d'Unités*.

International Telecommunication Union (abbrev.: **ITU**) an organization whose purpose is to promote international cooperation in the use and improvement of telecommunications of all kinds. Founded in Paris in 1865 as the International Telegraph Union, it became an agency of the United Nations in 1947.

international unit ▶ noun a unit of activity or potency for vitamins, hormones, or other substances, defined individually for each substance in terms of the activity of a standard quantity or preparation.

internaut /ˈɪntənɔːt/ ▶ noun a user of the Internet, especially a habitual or skilled one.
– ORIGIN 1990s: blend of **INTERNET** and **ASTRONAUT**.

interne ▶ noun variant spelling of **INTERN**.

internecine /ɪntəˈniːsʌɪn/ ▶ adjective destructive to both sides in a conflict: *the region's history of savage internecine warfare.*
■ of or relating to conflict within a group or organization.
– ORIGIN mid 17th cent. (in the sense 'deadly, characterized by great slaughter'): from Latin *internecinus*, based on *inter-* 'among' + *necare* 'to kill'.

internee /ˌɪntəˈniː/ ▶ noun a person who is confined as a prisoner, especially for political or military reasons.

internegative ▶ noun Photography a second negative of an image made from the original negative.

Internet an international computer network providing electronic mail and information from

computers in educational institutions, government agencies, and industry, accessible to the general public via modem links.
– ORIGIN late 20th cent.: from **INTER-** 'reciprocal, mutual' + **NETWORK**.

interneuron /ˌɪntəˈnjʊərɒn/ (also **interneurone** /-rəʊn/) ▶ **noun** Physiology a neuron which transmits impulses between other neurons, especially as part of a reflex arc.
– DERIVATIVES **interneuronal** adjective.
– ORIGIN 1930s: from **INTERNUNCIAL** + **NEURON**.

internist ▶ **noun** Medicine, chiefly N. Amer. a specialist in internal diseases.
– ORIGIN early 20th cent.: from **INTERNAL** + **-IST**.

internode /ˈɪntənəʊd/ ▶ **noun** a slender part between two nodes or joints, in particular:
■ Botany a part of a plant stem between two of the nodes from which leaves emerge. ■ Anatomy a stretch of a nerve cell axon sheathed in myelin, between two nodes of Ranvier.
– ORIGIN mid 17th cent.: from Latin *internodium*, from *inter-* 'between' + *nodus* 'knot'.

internuclear ▶ **adjective** between nuclei (especially of atoms).

internuncial /ˌɪntəˈnʌnʃ(ə)l/ ▶ **adjective** [attrib.] Physiology (of neurons) forming connections between other neurons in the central nervous system.
– ORIGIN mid 19th cent.: from Latin *internuntius* (from *inter-* 'between' + *nuntius* 'messenger') + **-AL**.

interoceanic ▶ **adjective** between or connecting two oceans.

interoceptive /ˌɪntərəʊˈsɛptɪv/ ▶ **adjective** Physiology relating to stimuli produced within an organism, especially in the gut and other internal organs. Compare with **EXTEROCEPTIVE**.
– ORIGIN early 20th cent.: from **INTERIOR** + **RECEPTIVE**.

interoceptor /ˌɪntərəʊˈsɛptə/ ▶ **noun** Physiology a sensory receptor which receives stimuli from within the body, especially from the gut and other internal organs. Compare with **EXTEROCEPTOR**.

interoperable ▶ **adjective** (of computer systems or software) able to exchange and make use of information.
– DERIVATIVES **interoperability** noun.

interosseous /ˌɪntərˈɒsɪəs/ ▶ **adjective** situated between bones, in particular:
■ of or denoting certain muscles of the hand and foot. ■ of or denoting certain arteries of the forearm.

interpellate /ɪnˈtəːpɪleɪt/ ▶ **verb** [with obj.] **1** (in a parliament) interrupt the order of the day by demanding an explanation from (the minister concerned).
2 Philosophy (of an ideology or discourse) bring into being or give identity to (an individual or category). [ORIGIN: from the works of Althusser.]
– DERIVATIVES **interpellation** noun, **interpellator** noun.
– ORIGIN late 16th cent. (in the sense 'interrupt'): from Latin *interpellat-* 'interrupted (by speech)', from the verb *interpellare*, from *inter-* 'between' + *pellere* 'to drive'. Sense 1 dates from the late 19th cent.

interpenetrate ▶ **verb** mix or merge together: [no obj.] *the two concepts interpenetrate in interesting ways* | [with obj.] *fibres of meaning interpenetrate every strand of sound.*
– DERIVATIVES **interpenetration** noun, **interpenetrative** adjective.

interpersonal ▶ **adjective** [attrib.] of or relating to relationships or communication between people: *you will need good interpersonal skills.*
– DERIVATIVES **interpersonally** adverb.

interphase ▶ **noun** [mass noun] Biology the resting phase between successive mitotic divisions of a cell, or between the first and second divisions of meiosis.

interplanetary ▶ **adjective** situated or travelling between planets: *interplanetary missions.*

interplant ▶ **verb** [with obj.] (usu. **be interplanted**) plant (a crop or plant) together with another crop or plant.
■ plant (land) with a mixture of crops or plants.

interplay ▶ **noun** [mass noun] the way in which two or more things have an effect on each other: *the* ***interplay between*** *inheritance and learning.*

interpleader ▶ **noun** Law a suit pleaded between two parties to determine a matter of claim or right to property held by a third party.
– ORIGIN mid 16th cent.: from Anglo-Norman French *enterpleder*, from *enter-* 'between' + *pleder* 'to plead'.

Interpol /ˈɪntəpɒl/ an organization based in France that coordinates investigations made by the police forces of member countries into crimes with an international dimension.
– ORIGIN originally as the telegraphic address of the International Criminal Police Commission, founded in 1923; from *Inter(national) pol(ice)*.

interpolate /ɪnˈtəːpəleɪt/ ▶ **verb** [with obj.] insert (something) between fixed points: *illustrations were interpolated in the text.*
■ insert (words) in a book or other text, especially in order to give a false impression as to its date. ■ make such insertions in (a book or text). ■ interject (a remark) in a conversation: [with direct speech] *'I dare say,' interpolated her employer.* ■ Mathematics insert (an intermediate value or term) into a series by estimating or calculating it from surrounding known values.
– DERIVATIVES **interpolation** noun, **interpolative** adjective.
– ORIGIN early 17th cent.: from Latin *interpolat-* 'refurbished, altered', from the verb *interpolare*, from *inter-* 'between' + *-polare* (related to *polire* 'to polish').

interpolator ▶ **noun** a person who interpolates something.
■ a device or apparatus which guides a tool through a smooth curve when provided with a set of points defining the curve.

interpole ▶ **noun** an auxiliary pole of a commutator placed between the main poles to increase its efficiency.

interpose ▶ **verb 1** [with obj.] place or insert between one thing and another: *he* ***interposed*** *himself* ***between*** *her and the top of the stairs.*
2 [no obj.] intervene between parties: [with infinitive] *the legislature interposed to suppress these amusements.*
■ [with obj.] say (words) as an interruption: *if I might interpose a personal remark here.* ■ [with obj.] exercise or advance (a veto or objection) so as to interfere: *the memo interposes no objection to issuing a discharge.*
– ORIGIN late 16th cent.: from French *interposer*, from Latin *interponere* 'put in' (from *inter-* 'between' + *ponere* 'put'), but influenced by *interpositus* 'inserted' and Old French *poser* 'to place'.

interposition ▶ **noun** [mass noun] the action of interposing someone or something: *the interposition of members between tiers of management.*
■ interference: *prevented by the interposition of your wife.*
– ORIGIN late Middle English: from Latin *interpositio(n-)*, from the verb *interponere* (see **INTERPOSE**).

interpret ▶ **verb** (**interpreted**, **interpreting**) [with obj.] **1** explain the meaning of (information, words, or actions): *the evidence is difficult to interpret* | [no obj.] *interpreting for the deaf.*
■ [no obj.] translate orally the words of another person speaking a different language: *I agreed to interpret for Jean-Claude.* ■ perform (a dramatic role or piece of music) in a particular way that conveys one's understanding of the creator's ideas.
2 understand (an action, mood, or way of behaving) as having a particular meaning or significance: *she made a gesture which he chose to* ***interpret as*** *an invitation.*
– DERIVATIVES **interpretability** noun, **interpretable** adjective, **interpretative** adjective, **interpretatively** adverb, **interpretive** adjective, **interpretively** adverb.
– ORIGIN late Middle English: from Old French *interpreter* or Latin *interpretari* 'explain, translate', from *interpres*, *interpret-* 'agent, translator, interpreter'.

interpretation ▶ **noun** [mass noun] the action of explaining the meaning of something: *the interpretation of data.*
■ [count noun] an explanation or way of explaining: *this action is open to a number of interpretations.* ■ [count noun] a stylistic representation of a creative work or dramatic role: *two differing interpretations, both bearing the distinctive hallmarks of each writer's perspective.*
– DERIVATIVES **interpretational** adjective.
– ORIGIN late Middle English: from Old French *interpretation* or Latin *interpretatio(n-)*, from the verb *interpretari* (see **INTERPRET**).

interpreter ▶ **noun** a person who interprets, especially one who translates speech orally.
■ Computing a program that can analyse and execute a program line by line.
– ORIGIN late Middle English: from Old French *interpreteur*, from late Latin *interpretator*, from Latin *interpretari* (see **INTERPRET**).

interprovincial ▶ **adjective** existing or carried on between provinces of the same country.
▶ **noun** (usu. **interprovincials**) a sports tournament between different provinces of the same country.
■ a member of a team competing in such a tournament.

interquartile /ˌɪntəˈkwɔːtʌɪl/ ▶ **adjective** Statistics situated between the first and third quartiles of a distribution.

interracial ▶ **adjective** existing between or involving different races: *interracial conflict.*
– DERIVATIVES **interracially** adverb.

interregnum /ˌɪntəˈrɛgnəm/ ▶ **noun** (pl. **interregnums** or **interregna** /-nə/) a period when normal government is suspended, especially between successive reigns or regimes.
■ (**the Interregnum**) the period in English history from the execution of Charles I in 1649 to the Restoration of Charles II in 1660. ■ an interval between the periods of office of two incumbents in a parish.
– ORIGIN late 16th cent. (denoting temporary rule between reigns or during suspension of normal government): from Latin, from *inter-* 'between' + *regnum* 'reign'.

interrelate ▶ **verb** relate or connect to one other: [no obj.] *each component* ***interrelates with*** *all the others* | [with obj.] *shared values and mechanisms that interrelate peoples in all corners of the world.*
– DERIVATIVES **interrelatedness** noun.

interrelationship ▶ **noun** the way in which each of two or more things is related to the other or others: *the* ***interrelationship between*** *the comprehension and production of early vocabulary.*
– DERIVATIVES **interrelation** noun.

interrogate ▶ **verb** [with obj.] ask questions of (someone, especially a suspect or a prisoner) closely, aggressively, or formally.
■ Computing obtain data from (a computer file, database, storage device, or terminal). ■ (of an electronic device) transmit a signal to (another device, especially one on a vehicle) to obtain a response giving information about identity, condition, etc.
– DERIVATIVES **interrogator** noun.
– ORIGIN late 15th cent.: from Latin *interrogat-* 'questioned', from the verb *interrogare*, from *inter-* 'between' + *rogare* 'ask'.

interrogation ▶ **noun** [mass noun] the action of interrogating or the process of being interrogated: *would he keep his mouth shut* ***under interrogation?*** | [count noun] *he had conducted hundreds of criminal interrogations.*
– DERIVATIVES **interrogational** adjective.

interrogation point (also **interrogation mark**) ▶ **noun** another term for **QUESTION MARK**.

interrogative /ˌɪntəˈrɒgətɪv/ ▶ **adjective** having or conveying the force of a question: *a hard, interrogative stare.*
■ Grammar used in questions: *an interrogative adverb.* Contrasted with **AFFIRMATIVE** and **NEGATIVE**.
▶ **noun** a word used in questions, such as *how* or *what*.
■ a construction that has the force of a question.
– DERIVATIVES **interrogatively** adverb.
– ORIGIN early 16th cent.: from late Latin *interrogativus*, from Latin *interrogare* (see **INTERROGATE**).

interrogatory /ˌɪntəˈrɒgət(ə)ri/ ▶ **adjective** conveying the force of a question; questioning: *the guard moves away with an interrogatory stare.*
▶ **noun** (pl. **-ies**) Law a written question which is formally put to one party in a case by another party and which must be answered.
– ORIGIN mid 16th cent.: the noun from medieval Latin *interrogatoria*, plural of *interrogatorium*; the adjective from late Latin *interrogatorius*, based on Latin *interrogare* (see **INTERROGATE**).

interrupt ▶ **verb** [with obj.] **1** stop the continuous progress of (an activity or process): *the buzzer interrupted his thoughts.*
■ stop (someone speaking) by saying or doing something: *'Of course …' Shepherd began, but his son interrupted him* | [with direct speech] *'Hold on,' he interrupted.*
2 break the continuity of (a line or surface): *the coastal plain is interrupted by chains of large lagoons.*

▪obstruct (something, especially a view).
– DERIVATIVES **interruptible** adjective, **interruption** noun, **interruptive** adjective.
– ORIGIN late Middle English: from Latin *interrupt-* 'broken, interrupted', from the verb *interrumpere*, from *inter-* 'between' + *rumpere* 'to break'.

interrupted ▶ adjective **1** Botany (of a compound leaf, inflorescence, or other plant organ) made discontinuous by smaller interposed leaflets or intervals of bare stem.
2 Music (of a cadence) having a penultimate dominant chord that is followed not by the expected chord of the tonic but by another, usually that of the submediant.

interrupter (also **interruptor**) ▶ noun a person or thing that interrupts.
▪a device that automatically breaks an electric circuit if a fault develops.

inter se /ˌɪntə ˈseɪ/ ▶ adverb between or among themselves: *covenants entered into by all the shareholders inter se.*
– ORIGIN Latin.

intersect ▶ verb [with obj.] divide (something) by passing or lying across it: *occasionally the water table intersects the earth's surface, forming streams and lakes* | *the area is intersected only by minor roads.*
▪[no obj.] (of two or more things) pass or lie across each other: *lines of latitude and longitude intersect at right angles.*
– ORIGIN early 17th cent.: from Latin *intersect-* 'cut, intersected', from the verb *intersecare*, from *inter-* 'between' + *secare* 'to cut'.

intersection ▶ noun a point or line common to lines or surfaces that intersect: *the intersection of a plane and a cone.*
▪a point at which two or more things intersect, especially a road junction: *a red light at the intersection with Brompton Road.* ▪ an action of intersecting: *his course is on a direct intersection with ours.*
– DERIVATIVES **intersectional** adjective.
– ORIGIN mid 16th cent.: from Latin *intersectio(n-)*, from *intersecare* (see **INTERSECT**).

intersegmental /ˌɪntəsɛɡˈmɛnt(ə)l/ ▶ adjective chiefly Zoology situated or occurring between segments.
– DERIVATIVES **intersegmentally** adverb.

interseptal /ɪntəˈsɛpt(ə)l/ ▶ adjective Anatomy & Zoology situated between septa or partitions.

intersex ▶ noun [mass noun] the abnormal condition of being intermediate between male and female; hermaphroditism.
▪[count noun] an individual in this condition; a hermaphrodite.

intersexual ▶ adjective **1** existing or occurring between the sexes: *intersexual selection, or mate choice, was, to Darwin, the job of females.*
2 relating to or having the condition of being intermediate between male and female.
– DERIVATIVES **intersexuality** noun.

interspace ▶ noun a space between objects: *masks of Neptune occupy the interspaces between the roundels.*
▶ verb [with obj.] (usu. **be interspaced**) put or occupy a space between: *the great four-storey houses were **interspaced with** the ramshackle cottages of the workmen.*

interspecific /ˌɪntəspəˈsɪfɪk/ ▶ adjective Biology existing or occurring between different species: *interspecific differences.*
– DERIVATIVES **interspecifically** adverb.

intersperse ▶ verb [with obj.] (often **be interspersed**) scatter among or between other things; place here and there: ***interspersed between** tragic stories are a few songs supplying comic relief.*
▪diversify (a thing or things) with other things at intervals: *a patchwork of open fields **interspersed with** copses of pine.*
– DERIVATIVES **interspersion** noun.
– ORIGIN mid 16th cent. (in the sense 'diversify (something) by introducing other things at intervals'): from Latin *interspers-* 'scattered between', from *interspergere*, from *inter-* 'between' + *spargere* 'scatter'.

interspinal ▶ adjective Anatomy situated between the spines or spinose protuberances of the vertebrae.
– DERIVATIVES **interspinous** adjective.

interstadial /ˌɪntəˈsteɪdɪəl/ Geology ▶ adjective of or relating to a minor period of less cold climate during a glacial period. Compare with **INTERGLACIAL**.
▶ noun an interstadial period.
– ORIGIN early 20th cent.: from **INTER-** 'between' + *stadial* from Latin *stadialis*, from *stadium* 'stage'.

interstate ▶ adjective [attrib.] existing or carried on between states, especially of the US: *interstate travel.*
▪US in a different state from one referred to or understood: *their interstate rivals.*
▶ noun (also **interstate highway**) one of a system of motorways running between US states.
▶ adverb Austral. from one state to another: *House for sale. Owner moving interstate.*

interstellar /ˌɪntəˈstɛlə/ ▶ adjective occurring or situated between stars: *interstellar travel.*

interstice /ɪnˈtəːstɪs/ ▶ noun (usu. **interstices**) an intervening space, especially a very small one: *sunshine filtered through the interstices of the arching trees.*
– ORIGIN late Middle English: from Latin *interstitium*, from *intersistere* 'stand between', from *inter-* 'between' + *sistere* 'to stand'.

interstitial /ˌɪntəˈstɪʃ(ə)l/ ▶ adjective of, forming, or occupying interstices: *the interstitial space.*
▪Ecology (of minute animals) living in the spaces between individual sand grains in the soil or aquatic sediments: *the interstitial fauna of marine sands.*
– DERIVATIVES **interstitially** adverb.

intersubjective ▶ adjective Philosophy existing between conscious minds; shared by more than one conscious mind.
– DERIVATIVES **intersubjectively** adverb, **intersubjectivity** noun.

intertextuality /ˌɪntətɛkstjʊˈalɪti/ ▶ noun [mass noun] the relationship between texts, especially literary ones: *every text is a product of intertextuality.*
– DERIVATIVES **intertextual** adjective, **intertextually** adverb.

intertidal ▶ adjective Ecology of or denoting the area of a seashore which is covered at high tide and uncovered at low tide.

intertrack ▶ adjective [attrib.] (of betting, especially on horse races) involving bets placed at racecourses other than the one at which the race betted on is being run.

intertribal ▶ adjective existing or occurring between different tribes: *intertribal conflict.*
▪involving members of more than one tribe: *an intertribal group.*

intertrigo /ˌɪntəˈtrʌɪɡəʊ/ ▶ noun [mass noun] Medicine inflammation caused by the rubbing of one area of skin on another.
– ORIGIN early 18th cent.: from Latin, 'a sore place caused by rubbing', from *interterere* 'rub against each other'.

intertropical convergence zone ▶ noun a narrow zone near the equator where northern and southern air masses converge, typically producing low atmospheric pressure.

intertwine ▶ verb twist or twine together: [with obj.] *a net made of cotton **intertwined with** other natural fibres* | [no obj.] *the coils **intertwine with** one another like strands of spaghetti.*
▪[with obj.] figurative connect or link (two or more things) closely: *Dickens has been very clever to intertwine all these aspects and ideas.*
– DERIVATIVES **intertwinement** noun.

interval ▶ noun **1** an intervening time or space: *after his departure, there was an interval of many years without any meetings* | *the intervals between meals were very short.*
2 a pause; a break in activity: *an interval of mourning.*
▪Brit. a period of time separating parts of a theatrical or musical performance. ▪ a break between the parts of a sports match: *leading 3–0 at the interval.*
3 a space between two things; a gap.
▪the difference in pitch between two sounds.
– PHRASES **at intervals 1** with time between, not continuously: *the light flashed at intervals.* **2** with spaces between: *the path is marked with rocks at intervals.*
– DERIVATIVES **intervallic** adjective.
– ORIGIN Middle English: from Old French *entrevalle*, based on Latin *intervallum* 'space between ramparts, interval', from *inter-* 'between' + *vallum* 'rampart'.

interval estimate ▶ noun Statistics an interval within which the value of a parameter of a population has a stated probability of occurring. Compare with **POINT ESTIMATE**.

intervalometer /ˌɪntəvəˈlɒmɪtə/ ▶ noun Photography an attachment or facility on a camera that operates the shutter regularly at set intervals over a period. On a cine camera the device is used for time-lapse photography.

interval training ▶ noun [mass noun] training in which a runner alternates between running and jogging over set distances.

intervene ▶ verb [no obj.] **1** come between so as to prevent or alter a result or course of events: *he acted outside his authority when he **intervened in** the dispute* | [with infinitive] *their forces intervened to halt the attack.*
▪(of an event or circumstance) occur as a delay or obstacle to something being done: *Christmas intervened and the investigation was suspended.* ▪ interrupt verbally: [with direct speech] *'It's true!' he intervened.* ▪ Law interpose in a lawsuit as a third party.
2 [usu. as adj. **intervening**] occur in time between events: *to occupy the intervening months she took a job in a hospital.*
▪be situated between things: *they heard the sound of distant gunfire, muffled by the intervening trees.*
– DERIVATIVES **intervener** noun, **intervenient** adjective, **intervenor** noun.
– ORIGIN late 16th cent. (in the sense 'come in as an extraneous factor or thing'): from Latin *intervenire*, from *inter-* 'between' + *venire* 'come'.

intervention ▶ noun [mass noun] the action or process of intervening: *a high degree of state intervention in the economy* | [count noun] *any intervention by her in the debate on immigration would be unhelpful.*
▪interference by a state in another's affairs: *the government was reported to be considering military intervention.* ▪ action taken to improve a situation, especially a medical disorder: *two patients were referred for surgical intervention.*
– DERIVATIVES **interventional** adjective (chiefly in the medical sense).
– ORIGIN late Middle English: from Latin *interventio(n-)*, from the verb *intervenire* (see **INTERVENE**).

interventionist ▶ adjective favouring intervention, especially by a government in its domestic economy or by one state in the affairs of another.
▶ noun a person who favours intervention of this kind.
– DERIVATIVES **interventionism** noun.

intervertebral /ˌɪntəˈvəːtɪbr(ə)l/ ▶ adjective [attrib.] situated between vertebrae: *intervertebral joints.*

intervertebral disc ▶ noun see **DISC** (sense 3).

interview ▶ noun a meeting of people face to face, especially for consultation.
▪a conversation between a journalist or radio or television presenter and a person of public interest, used as the basis of a broadcast or publication. ▪ an oral examination of an applicant for a job, college place, etc.: *I am pleased to advise you that you have been selected for interview.* ▪ a session of formal questioning of a person by the police.
▶ verb [with obj.] (often **be interviewed**) hold an interview with (someone): *he arrived to be interviewed by a local TV station about the level of unemployment.*
▪question (someone) to discover their opinions or experience: *in a survey more than half the women interviewed hated the label 'housewife'.* ▪ orally examine (an applicant for a job, college place, etc.): *he came to be interviewed for a top job.* ▪ (of the police) question formally. ▪ [no obj., with adverbial] perform (well or badly) at an interview.
– DERIVATIVES **interviewee** noun, **interviewer** noun.
– ORIGIN early 16th cent. (formerly also as *enterview*): from French *entrevue*, from *s'entrevoir* 'see each other', from *voir* 'to see', on the pattern of *vue* 'a view'.

inter vivos /ˌɪntə ˈviːvəʊs/ ▶ adverb & adjective (especially of a gift as opposed to a legacy) between living people: [as adv.] *gifts made inter vivos* | [as postpositive adj.] *a gift inter vivos.*
– ORIGIN Latin.

intervocalic /ˌɪntəvə(ʊ)ˈkalɪk/ ▶ adjective Phonetics occurring between vowels: *in intervocalic position.*
– DERIVATIVES **intervocalically** adverb.

interwar ▶ adjective [attrib.] existing in the period between two wars, especially the two world wars (i.e. between 1918 and 1939).

interweave ▶ verb (past **-wove**; past participle **-woven**) weave or become woven together: [with obj.] *the rugs are made by tightly interweaving the warp and weft strands* | [no obj.] *the branches met and interwove above his head.*
▪[with obj.] figurative blend closely: *Wordsworth's political*

ideas are often ***interwoven with*** *his philosophical and religious beliefs.*

interwind /ˌɪntəˈwʌɪnd/ ▶ **verb** (past and past participle **-wound**) [with obj.] [usu. as adj. **interwound**] wind together: *a transformer consists of two interwound coils.*

interwork ▶ **verb** [no obj.] Computing (of items of hardware or software) be able to connect, communicate, or exchange data: *servers running new and old versions of the software will interwork.*

intestate /ɪnˈtɛsteɪt/ ▶ **adjective** [predic.] not having made a will before one dies: *he died intestate* | [postpositive] *in the event of his death intestate.*
■[attrib.] of or relating to a person who dies without having made a will: *his brother's posthumous children are admissible as intestate heirs.*
▶ **noun** a person who has died without having made a will.
– DERIVATIVES **intestacy** /-təsi/ noun.
– ORIGIN late Middle English: from Latin *intestatus*, from *in-* 'not' + *testatus* 'testified, witness' (see **TESTATE**).

intestinal flora ▶ **plural noun** [usu. treated as sing.] the symbiotic bacteria occurring naturally in the gut.

intestine (also **intestines**) ▶ **noun** (in vertebrates) the lower part of the alimentary canal from the end of the stomach to the anus: *the contents of the intestine* | [mass noun] *loops of intestine.* See also **LARGE INTESTINE, SMALL INTESTINE.**
■(especially in invertebrates) the whole alimentary canal from the mouth downward.
– DERIVATIVES **intestinal** adjective.
– ORIGIN late Middle English: from Latin *intestinum*, neuter of *intestinus*, from *intus* 'within'.

intichiuma /ˌɪntɪtʃɪˈuːmə/ ▶ **plural noun** sacred ceremonies performed by some Central Australian Aboriginals with the purpose of increasing the number of totemic plants or animals and thus ensuring a good food supply: *the intichiuma of rain.*
– ORIGIN Aranda.

intifada /ˌɪntɪˈfɑːdə/ ▶ **noun** the Palestinian uprising against Israeli occupation of the West Bank and Gaza Strip, beginning in 1987.
– ORIGIN from Arabic *intifāḍa* 'an uprising' (literally 'a jumping up as a reaction to something'), from *intifaḍa* 'be shaken, shake oneself'.

intima /ˈɪntɪmə/ ▶ **noun** (pl. **intimae** /-miː/) Anatomy & Zoology the innermost coating or membrane of a part or organ, especially of a vein or artery.
– DERIVATIVES **intimal** adjective.
– ORIGIN late 19th cent.: shortening of modern Latin *tunica intima* 'innermost sheath'.

intimacy ▶ **noun** (pl. **-ies**) [mass noun] close familiarity or friendship; closeness: *the* ***intimacy between*** *a husband and wife.*
■a private cosy atmosphere: *the room had a peaceful sense of intimacy about it.* ■ [count noun] an intimate act, especially sexual intercourse. ■ [count noun] an intimate remark: *here she was sitting swapping intimacies with a stranger.* ■ [in sing.] closeness of observation or knowledge of a subject: *he acquired an* ***intimacy with*** *Swahili literature.*

intimate[1] /ˈɪntɪmət/ ▶ **adjective 1** closely acquainted; familiar, close: *intimate friends* | *they are on intimate terms.*
■(of a place or setting) having or creating an informal friendly atmosphere: *an intimate little Italian restaurant.* ■ [predic.] used euphemistically to indicate that a couple are having a sexual relationship: *he was sickened by the thought of others having been* ***intimate with*** *her.* ■ involving very close connection: *their intimate involvement with their community.*
2 private and personal: *going into intimate details of his sexual encounters* | *intimate correspondence.*
3 (of knowledge) detailed; thorough: *an intimate knowledge of the software.*
▶ **noun** a very close friend: *his circle of intimates.*
– DERIVATIVES **intimately** adverb.
– ORIGIN early 17th cent. (as a noun): from late Latin *intimatus*, past participle of Latin *intimare* 'impress, make familiar', from *intimus* 'inmost'.

intimate[2] /ˈɪntɪmeɪt/ ▶ **verb** [with obj.] state or make known: *Mr Hutchison has intimated his decision to retire.*
■[with clause] imply or hint: *he had already intimated that he might not be able to continue.*
– DERIVATIVES **intimation** noun.
– ORIGIN early 16th cent.: from late Latin *intimat-* 'made known', from the verb *intimare* (see **INTIMATE**[1]). The noun *intimation* dates from late Middle English.

intimidate ▶ **verb** frighten or overawe (someone), especially in order to make them do what one wants: *the forts are designed to intimidate the nationalist population* | [as adj. **intimidating**] *the intimidating defence barrister.*
– DERIVATIVES **intimidatingly** adverb, **intimidation** noun, **intimidator** noun, **intimidatory** adjective.
– ORIGIN mid 17th cent.: from medieval Latin *intimidat-* 'made timid', from the verb *intimidare* (based on *timidus* 'timid').

intimism /ˈɪntɪmɪz(ə)m/ ▶ **noun** [mass noun] a style of painting showing intimate views of domestic interiors using Impressionist techniques, used by artists such as Bonnard in the early 20th century.
– DERIVATIVES **intimist** adjective & noun.
– ORIGIN early 20th cent.: from French *intimisme*, from Latin *intimus* 'innermost'.

intinction /ɪnˈtɪŋ(k)ʃ(ə)n/ ▶ **noun** [mass noun] the action of dipping the bread in the wine at a Eucharist so that a communicant receives both together.
– ORIGIN mid 16th cent.: from late Latin *intinctio(n-)*, from Latin *intingere*, from *in-* 'into' + *tingere* 'dip'. The word originally denoted the general action of dipping, especially into something coloured; compare with **TINGE**. The current sense dates from the late 19th cent.

intitule /ɪnˈtɪtjuːl/ ▶ **verb** [with obj.] Brit. give a specified title to (an Act of Parliament).
– ORIGIN late 15th cent. (formerly also as *entitule*): from Old French *entituler, intituler* (see **ENTITLE**).

into ▶ **preposition 1** expressing movement or action with the result that someone or something becomes enclosed or surrounded by something else: *cover the bowl and put it into the fridge* | *Sara got into her car and shut the door* | figurative *he walked into a trap sprung by the opposition.*
2 expressing movement or action with the result that someone or something makes physical contact with something else: *he crashed into a parked car.*
3 indicating a route by which someone or something may arrive at a particular destination: *the narrow road which led down into the village.*
4 indicating the direction towards which someone or something is turned when confronting something else: *with the wind blowing into your face* | *sobbing into her skirt.*
5 indicating an object of attention or interest: *a clearer insight into what is involved* | *an inquiry into the squad's practices.*
6 expressing a change of state: *a peaceful protest which turned into a violent confrontation* | *the fruit can be made into jam.*
7 expressing the result of an action: *they forced the club into a humiliating and expensive special general meeting.*
8 expressing division: *three into twelve goes four.*
9 informal (of a person) taking a lively and active interest in (something): *he's into surfing and jet-skiing.*
– ORIGIN Old English *intō* (see **IN, TO**).

intolerable ▶ **adjective** unable to be endured: *the intolerable pressures of his work.*
– DERIVATIVES **intolerably** adverb.
– ORIGIN late Middle English: from Old French, or from Latin *intolerabilis*, from *in-* 'not' + *tolerabilis* (see **TOLERABLE**).

intolerant ▶ **adjective** not tolerant of others' views, beliefs, or behaviour that differ from one's own: *he was* ***intolerant of*** *ignorance.*
■unable to be given (a medicine or other treatment) or to eat (a food) without adverse effects. ■ (of a plant or animal) unable to survive exposure to (physical influence).
– DERIVATIVES **intolerance** noun, **intolerantly** adverb.
– ORIGIN mid 18th cent.: from Latin *intolerant-*, from *in-* 'not' + *tolerant-* 'enduring' (see **TOLERANT**).

intonation ▶ **noun** [mass noun] **1** the rise and fall of the voice in speaking: *she spoke English with a German intonation.*
■the action of intoning or reciting in a singing voice.
2 accuracy of pitch in playing or singing: *poor woodwind intonation at the opening.*
3 the opening phrase of a plainsong melody.
– DERIVATIVES **intonational** adjective.
– ORIGIN early 17th cent. (in sense 3): from medieval Latin *intonatio(n-)*, from *intonare* (see **INTONE**).

intone /ɪnˈtəʊn/ ▶ **verb** [with obj.] say or recite with little rise and fall of the pitch of the voice: *he intoned a short Latin prayer* | [with direct speech] *'All rise,' intoned the usher.*
– DERIVATIVES **intoner** noun.
– ORIGIN late 15th cent. (originally as *entone*): from Old French *entoner* or medieval Latin *intonare*, from *in-* 'into' + Latin *tonus* 'tone'.

in toto /ɪn ˈtəʊtəʊ/ ▶ **adverb** as a whole: *such proposals should be subjected to specific criticism rather than rejected in toto.*
■[sentence adverb] in all; overall: *there was, in toto, an increase in legal regulation and public surveillance.*
– ORIGIN Latin.

intoxicant ▶ **noun** an intoxicating substance.

intoxicate ▶ **verb** [with obj.] [usu. as adj. **intoxicated**] (of alcoholic drink or a drug) cause (someone) to lose control of their faculties or behaviour.
■poison. ■ figurative excite or exhilarate: *he was intoxicated by cinema.*
– DERIVATIVES **intoxication** noun.
– ORIGIN late Middle English (in the sense 'poison'): from medieval Latin *intoxicare*, from *in-* 'into' + *toxicare* 'to poison', from Latin *toxicum* (see **TOXIC**).

intoxicating ▶ **adjective** (of alcoholic drink or a drug) liable to cause intoxication.
■figurative exhilarating or exciting: *the intoxicating touch of freedom.*
– DERIVATIVES **intoxicatingly** adverb.

intoximeter /ɪnˈtɒksɪmiːtə/ ▶ **noun** a non-portable instrument for measuring the alcohol content of a person's breath, especially in cases of suspected drunken driving, usually sited at a police station.
– ORIGIN 1950s: from *intoxication* (see **INTOXICATE**) + **-METER**.

intra- /ˈɪntrə/ ▶ **prefix** (added to adjectives) on the inside; within: *intramural* | *intrauterine.*
– ORIGIN from Latin *intra* 'inside'.

intracellular ▶ **adjective** Biology located or occurring within a cell or cells: *an increase in intracellular calcium.*
– DERIVATIVES **intracellularly** adverb.

intracranial ▶ **adjective** within the skull: *intracranial haemorrhage.*
– DERIVATIVES **intracranially** adverb.

intractable /ɪnˈtraktəb(ə)l/ ▶ **adjective** hard to control or deal with: *intractable economic problems* | *intractable pain.*
■(of a person) difficult; stubborn.
– DERIVATIVES **intractability** noun, **intractableness** noun, **intractably** adverb.
– ORIGIN late 15th cent.: from Latin *intractabilis*, from *in-* 'not' + *tractabilis* (see **TRACTABLE**).

intraday ▶ **adjective** [attrib.] Stock Exchange, N. Amer. occurring within one day: *the dollar slipped from an intraday high of 104.*

intrados /ɪnˈtreɪdɒs/ ▶ **noun** Architecture the lower or inner curve of an arch. Often contrasted with **EXTRADOS**.
– ORIGIN late 18th cent.: from French, from *intra-* 'on the inside' + *dos* 'the back' (from Latin *dorsum*).

intramolecular ▶ **adjective** existing or taking place within a molecule.
– DERIVATIVES **intramolecularly** adverb.

intramural /ˌɪntrəˈmjʊər(ə)l/ ▶ **adjective** situated or done within the walls of a building: *both intramural and churchyard graves.*
■chiefly N. Amer. taking place within a single educational institution: *recreational intramural games.* ■ forming part of normal university or college studies. ■ Medicine & Biology situated within the wall of a hollow organ or a cell: *an intramural haematoma.* ■ situated or done within a community: *an intramural social symbol within the tribe.*
– DERIVATIVES **intramurally** adverb.
– ORIGIN mid 19th cent.: from **INTRA-** 'within' + Latin *murus* 'wall' + **-AL**.

intramuscular ▶ **adjective** situated or taking place within, or administered into, a muscle: *an intramuscular injection.*
– DERIVATIVES **intramuscularly** adverb.

Intranet /ˈɪntrənɛt/ ▶ **noun** Computing a local or restricted communications network, especially a private network created using World Wide Web software.

intransigent /ɪnˈtransɪdʒ(ə)nt, -ˈtrɑː-, -nz-/ ▶ **adjective** unwilling or refusing to change one's views or to agree about something.
▶ **noun** an intransigent person.
– DERIVATIVES **intransigence** noun, **intransigency** noun, **intransigently** adverb.
– ORIGIN late 19th cent.: from French *intransigeant*, from Spanish *los intransigentes* (a name adopted by the extreme republicans in the Cortes, 1873–4);

based on Latin *in-* 'not' + *transigere* 'come to an understanding'.

intransitive /ɪnˈtransɪtɪv, -ˈtrɑː-, -nz-/ ▶ adjective (of a verb or a sense or use of a verb) not taking a direct object, e.g. *look* in *look at the sky*. The opposite of **TRANSITIVE**.
– DERIVATIVES **intransitively** adverb, **intransitivity** noun.
– ORIGIN early 17th cent.: from late Latin *intransitivus* 'not passing over', from *in-* 'not' + *transitivus* (see **TRANSITIVE**).

intrapreneur /ˌɪntrəprəˈnəː/ ▶ noun a manager within a company who promotes innovative product development and marketing.
– ORIGIN 1970s (originally US): from **INTRA-** 'within' + a shortened form of **ENTREPRENEUR**.

intraspecific ▶ adjective Biology produced, occurring, or existing within a species or between individuals of a single species: *intraspecific competition.*

intrathecal /ˌɪntrəˈθiːk(ə)l/ ▶ adjective Medicine occurring within or administered into the spinal theca: *intrathecal injection.*
– DERIVATIVES **intrathecally** adverb.

intrauterine /ˌɪntrəˈjuːtərʌɪn, -rɪn/ ▶ adjective within the uterus.

intrauterine device (abbrev.: **IUD**) ▶ noun a contraceptive device fitted inside the uterus and physically preventing the implantation of fertilized ova.

intravascular /ˌɪntrəˈvaskjʊlə/ ▶ adjective Medicine & Biology situated or occurring within a vessel or vessels of an animal or plant, especially within a blood vessel or blood vascular system.
– DERIVATIVES **intravascularly** adverb.

intravenous /ˌɪntrəˈviːnəs/ (abbrev.: **IV**) ▶ adjective existing or taking place within, or administered into, a vein or veins: *an intravenous drip.*
– DERIVATIVES **intravenously** adverb.

in tray ▶ noun chiefly Brit. a tray on someone's desk for letters addressed to them and other documents that they have to deal with.

intrazonal ▶ adjective Soil Science (of a soil) having a well-developed structure different from that expected for its climatic and vegetational zone owing to the overriding influence of relief, parent material, or some other local factor.

intrench ▶ verb variant spelling of **ENTRENCH**.

intrepid ▶ adjective fearless; adventurous (often used for rhetorical or humorous effect): *our intrepid reporter.*
– DERIVATIVES **intrepidity** noun, **intrepidly** adverb.
– ORIGIN late 17th cent.: from French *intrépide* or Latin *intrepidus*, from *in-* 'not' + *trepidus* 'alarmed'.

intricacy /ˈɪntrɪkəsi/ ▶ noun (pl. **-ies**) [mass noun] the quality of being intricate: *the exquisite intricacy of Indian silverwork.*
■ [count noun] (**intricacies**) details, especially of an involved or perplexing subject: *the intricacies of economic policy-making.*

intricate ▶ adjective very complicated or detailed: *an intricate network of canals.*
– DERIVATIVES **intricately** adverb.
– ORIGIN late Middle English: from Latin *intricat-* 'entangled', from the verb *intricare*, from *in-* 'into' + *tricae* 'tricks, perplexities'.

intrigant /ˈɪntrɪg(ə)nt/ ▶ noun a person who makes secret plans to do something illicit or detrimental to someone else.
– ORIGIN late 18th cent.: variant of French *intriguant*, from *intriguer* 'to intrigue'.

intrigue ▶ verb /ɪnˈtriːg/ (**intrigues**, **intrigued**, **intriguing**) **1** [with obj.] arouse the curiosity or interest of; fascinate: *I was intrigued by your question* | [as adj.] (**intriguing**) *the food is an intriguing combination of German and French.*
2 [no obj.] make secret plans to do something illicit or detrimental to someone: *the ministers were intriguing for their own gains.*
▶ noun /ɪnˈtriːg, ˈɪn-/ [mass noun] **1** the secret planning of something illicit or detrimental to someone: *the cabinet was a nest of intrigue* | [count noun] *the intrigues of local government officials.*
■ [count noun] a secret love affair.
2 a mysterious or fascinating quality: *within the region's borders is a wealth of interest and intrigue.*
– DERIVATIVES **intriguer** noun, **intriguingly** adverb *the album is intriguingly titled 'The Revenge Of The Goldfish'.*

– ORIGIN early 17th cent. (in the sense 'deceive, cheat'): from French *intrigue* 'plot', *intriguer* 'to tangle, to plot', via Italian from Latin *intricare* (see **INTRICATE**). Sense 1 of the verb, which was influenced by a later French sense 'to puzzle, make curious', arose in the late 19th cent.

intrinsic /ɪnˈtrɪnsɪk/ ▶ adjective belonging naturally; essential: *access to the arts is intrinsic to a high quality of life.*
– DERIVATIVES **intrinsically** adverb.
– ORIGIN late 15th cent. (in the general sense 'interior, inner'): from French *intrinsèque*, from late Latin *intrinsecus*, from the earlier adverb *intrinsecus* 'inwardly, inwards'.

intrinsic factor ▶ noun [mass noun] Biochemistry a substance secreted by the stomach which enables the body to absorb vitamin B_{12}. It is a glycoprotein.

intro ▶ noun (pl. **-os**) informal an introduction.
– ORIGIN early 19th cent.: abbreviation.

intro- ▶ prefix into; inwards: *introgression* | *introvert.*
– ORIGIN from Latin *intro* 'to the inside'.

introduce ▶ verb [with obj.] **1** (often **be introduced**) bring (something, especially a product, measure, or concept) into use or operation for the first time: *various new taxes were introduced* | [with obj. and infinitive] *measures were introduced to help families with children.*
■ (**introduce something to**) bring a subject to the attention of (someone) for the first time: *the programme is a bid to introduce opera to the masses.* ■ present (a new piece of legislation) for debate in a legislative assembly. ■ bring (a new plant, animal, or disease) to a place and establish it there: *he introduced the mangel-wurzel to Britain as a fodder crop.*
2 make (someone) known by name to another in person, especially formally: *I hope to introduce Jenny to them very soon.*
3 insert or bring into something: *a device which introduces chlorine into the pool automatically.*
4 occur at the start of; open: *a longer, more lyrical opening which introduces a courting song.*
■ (of a person) provide an opening explanation or announcement for (a television or radio programme, book, etc.).
– DERIVATIVES **introducer** noun.
– ORIGIN late Middle English (in the sense 'bring (a person) into a place or group'): from Latin *introducere*, from *intro-* 'to the inside' + *ducere* 'to lead'.

introduction ▶ noun **1** [mass noun] the bringing of a product, measure, concept, etc. into use or operation for the first time: *issues arising from the introduction of new technology.*
■ [mass noun] the action of bringing a new plant, animal, or disease to a place: *the introduction of muskrats into central Europe.* ■ [count noun] a thing, such as a product, measure, plant, etc. newly brought in: *newer introductions such as the cut-leaf Chinese vine.*
2 (often **introductions**) a formal presentation of one person to another, in which each is told the other's name: *he returned to his desk, leaving Michael to make the introductions* | [mass noun] *a letter of introduction.*
3 a thing preliminary to something else: *your talk will need an introduction which states clearly what you are talking about and why.*
■ an explanatory section at the beginning of a book, report, etc. ■ a preliminary section in a piece of music, often thematically different from the main section. ■ a book or course of study intended to introduce a subject to a person: *a good general introduction to the subject is A Social History of England.* ■ [in sing.] a person's first experience of a subject or thing: *my introduction to drama was through an amateur dramatic society.*
– ORIGIN late Middle English: from Latin *introductio(n-)*, from the verb *introducere* (see **INTRODUCE**).

introductory ▶ adjective serving as an introduction to a subject or topic; basic or preliminary: *an introductory course in Russian.*
■ intended to persuade someone to purchase something for the first time: *we are making a special introductory offer of a reduced subscription.*
– ORIGIN late Middle English (as a noun denoting an introductory text): from late Latin *introductorius*, from Latin *introducere* (see **INTRODUCE**).

introgression /ˌɪntrə(ʊ)ˈgrɛʃ(ə)n/ ▶ noun [mass noun] Biology the transfer of genetic information from one species to another as a result of hybridization between them and repeated backcrossing.
– DERIVATIVES **introgressive** adjective.

– ORIGIN mid 17th cent.: from Latin *introgredi* 'step in', from *intro-* 'to the inside' + *gradi* 'proceed, walk', on the pattern of *egression*, *ingression.*

introit /ˈɪntrɔɪt, ɪnˈtrəʊɪt/ ▶ noun a psalm or antiphon sung or said while the priest approaches the altar for the Eucharist.
– ORIGIN late Middle English (denoting an entrance or the action of going in): via Old French from Latin *introitus*, from *introire* 'enter', from *intro-* 'to the inside' + *ire* 'go'.

introjection /ˌɪntrə(ʊ)ˈdʒɛkʃ(ə)n/ ▶ noun [mass noun] Psychoanalysis the unconscious adoption of the ideas or attitudes of others.
– DERIVATIVES **introject** verb.
– ORIGIN mid 19th cent.: from **INTRO-** 'into', on the pattern of *projection.*

intromission ▶ noun the action or process of inserting the penis into the vagina in sexual intercourse.

intromittent organ /ˌɪntrə(ʊ)ˈmɪt(ə)nt/ ▶ noun Zoology the male copulatory organ of an animal.
– ORIGIN mid 19th cent.: *intromittent* from Latin *intromittent-* 'introducing', from the verb *intromittere*, from *intro-* 'to the inside' + *mittere* 'send'.

intron /ˈɪntrɒn/ ▶ noun Biochemistry a segment of a DNA or RNA molecule which does not code for proteins and interrupts the sequence of genes. Compare with **EXON**[1].
– DERIVATIVES **intronic** adjective.
– ORIGIN 1970s: from **INTRA-** 'within' + **-GENIC** + **-ON**.

introrse /ɪnˈtrɔːs/ ▶ adjective Botany & Zoology turned inwards. The opposite of **EXTRORSE**.
■ (of anthers) releasing their pollen towards the centre of the flower.
– ORIGIN mid 19th cent.: from Latin *introrsus*, from *introversus* 'turned inwards'.

introspect /ˌɪntrə(ʊ)ˈspɛkt/ ▶ verb [no obj.] examine one's own thoughts or feelings: *what they don't do is introspect much about the reasons for their plight.*
– ORIGIN late 17th cent.: from Latin *introspect-* 'looked into', from the verb *introspicere*, or from *introspectare* 'keep looking into'.

introspection ▶ noun [mass noun] the examination or observation of one's own mental and emotional processes: *quiet introspection can be extremely valuable.*
– DERIVATIVES **introspective** adjective, **introspectively** adverb, **introspectiveness** noun.

introvert ▶ noun a shy, reticent, and typically self-centred person.
■ Psychology a person predominantly concerned with their own thoughts and feelings rather than with external things. Compare with **EXTROVERT**.
▶ adjective another term for **INTROVERTED**.
– DERIVATIVES **introversion** noun, **introversive** /-ˈvəːsɪv/ adjective.
– ORIGIN mid 17th cent. (as a verb in the general sense 'turn one's thoughts inwards (in spiritual contemplation)'): from modern Latin *introvertere*, from *intro-* 'to the inside' + *vertere* 'to turn'. Its use as a term in psychology dates from the early 20th cent.

introverted ▶ adjective **1** of, denoting, or typical of an introvert.
■ (of a community, company, or other group) concerned principally with its own affairs; inward-looking or parochial.
2 Anatomy & Zoology (of an organ or other body part) turned or pushed inward on itself.

intrude ▶ verb **1** [no obj.] put oneself deliberately into a place or situation where one is unwelcome or uninvited: *he had no right to intrude into their lives* | *she felt awkward at intruding on private grief.*
■ enter with disruptive or adverse effect: *politics quickly intrude into the booklet.* ■ [with obj.] introduce into a situation with disruptive or adverse effect: *to intrude political criteria into military decisions risks reducing efficiency.*
2 [with obj.] Geology (of igneous rock) be forced or thrust into (a pre-existing formation): *the granite may have intruded these rock layers.*
■ (usu. **be intruded**) force or thrust (igneous rock) into a pre-existing formation.
– ORIGIN mid 16th cent. (in the sense 'usurp an office or right'; originally as *entrude*): from Latin *intrudere*, from *in-* 'into' + *trudere* 'to thrust'.

intruder ▶ noun a person who intrudes, especially into a building with criminal intent.

intrusion ▶ noun [mass noun] **1** the action of

intruding: *he was furious about this intrusion into his private life* | [count noun] *unacceptable intrusions of privacy.*
■[count noun] a thing that intrudes: *television can no longer be considered an intrusion into football.*
2 Geology the action or process of forcing a body of igneous rock between or through existing formations, without reaching the surface.
■[count noun] a body of igneous rock which has intruded the surrounding strata.
– ORIGIN late Middle English (in the sense 'invasion, usurpation'): from medieval Latin *intrusio(n-)*, from Latin *intrudere* 'thrust in' (see **INTRUDE**).

intrusive ▶ **adjective** **1** making an unwelcome manifestation with disruptive or adverse effect: *that was an intrusive question* | *tourist attractions that are environmentally intrusive.*
■(of a person) disturbing another by one's uninvited or unwelcome presence: *giving people information about their health without being too intrusive.*
2 Phonetics (of a sound) pronounced between words or syllables to facilitate pronunciation, such as an *r* in *saw a film.*
3 Geology of, relating to, or formed by intrusion.
– DERIVATIVES **intrusively** adverb, **intrusiveness** noun.

intrust ▶ **verb** archaic spelling of **ENTRUST**.

intubate /ˈɪntjʊbeɪt/ ▶ **verb** [with obj.] Medicine insert a tube into (a person or a body part, especially the trachea for ventilation).
– DERIVATIVES **intubation** noun.
– ORIGIN late 19th cent.: from **IN-**[2] 'into' + Latin *tuba* 'tube' + **-ATE**[3].

intuit /ɪnˈtjuːɪt/ ▶ **verb** [with obj.] understand or work out by instinct: *I intuited his real identity.*
– DERIVATIVES **intuitable** adjective.
– ORIGIN late 18th cent. (in the sense 'instruct, teach'): from Latin *intuit-* 'contemplated', from the verb *intueri*, from *in-* 'upon' + *tueri* 'to look'.

intuition ▶ **noun** [mass noun] the ability to understand something immediately, without the need for conscious reasoning: *we shall allow our intuition to guide us.*
■[count noun] a thing that one knows or considers likely from instinctive feeling rather than conscious reasoning: *your insights and intuitions as a native speaker are positively sought.*
– DERIVATIVES **intuitional** adjective.
– ORIGIN late Middle English (denoting spiritual insight or immediate spiritual communication): from late Latin *intuitio(n-)*, from Latin *intueri* 'consider' (see **INTUIT**).

intuitionism (also **intuitionalism**) ▶ **noun** [mass noun] Philosophy the theory that primary truths and principles (especially those of ethics and metaphysics) are known directly by intuition.
■the theory that mathematical knowledge is based on intuition and mental construction, rejecting certain modes of reasoning and the notion of independent mathematical objects.
– DERIVATIVES **intuitionist** noun & adjective.

intuitive ▶ **adjective** using or based on what one feels to be true even without conscious reasoning; instinctive: *I had an intuitive conviction that there was something unsound in him.*
■(chiefly of computer software) easy to use and understand.
– DERIVATIVES **intuitively** adverb, **intuitiveness** noun.
– ORIGIN late 15th cent. (originally used of sight, in the sense 'accurate, unerring'): from medieval Latin *intuitivus*, from Latin *intueri* (see **INTUIT**).

intumesce /ˌɪntjʊˈmɛs/ ▶ **verb** [no obj.] rare swell up.
– DERIVATIVES **intumescence** noun.
– ORIGIN late 18th cent.: from Latin *intumescere*, from *in-* 'into' + *tumescere* 'begin to swell' (from *tumere* 'swell').

intumescent ▶ **adjective** (of a coating or sealant) swelling up when heated, thus protecting the material underneath or sealing a gap in the event of a fire: *intumescent fire-retardant paints.*

intussusception /ˌɪntəsəˈsɛpʃ(ə)n/ ▶ **noun** **1** Medicine the inversion of one portion of the intestine within another.
2 [mass noun] Botany the growth of a cell wall by the deposition of cellulose: *the area of the surface increases uniformly by intussusception.*
– ORIGIN early 18th cent. (in the sense 'absorption'): from modern Latin *intussusceptio(n-)*, from Latin *intus* 'within' + *susceptio(n-)* (from *suscipere* 'take up').

intwine ▶ **verb** archaic spelling of **ENTWINE**.

Inuit /ˈɪnjʊɪt, ˈɪnʊɪt/ ▶ **noun** **1** [as plural noun] the members of an indigenous people of northern Canada and parts of Greenland and Alaska.
2 [mass noun] the language of this people, one of the three branches of the Eskimo-Aleut language family, with about 60,000 speakers. It is also known as **Inupiaq** or (especially to its speakers) as **Inuktitut**.
▶ **adjective** of or relating to the Inuit or their language.
– ORIGIN Inuit, plural of *inuk* 'person'.

USAGE The peoples inhabiting the regions from NW Canada to western Greenland prefer to be called **Inuit** rather than **Eskimo**, and this term now has official status in Canada. By analogy, the term **Inuit** is also used, usually in an attempt to be politically correct, as a synonym for **Eskimo** in general. However, this latter use, in including people from Siberia who are not Inupiaq-speakers, is, strictly speaking, not accurate. See also usage at **ESKIMO**.

Inuk /ˈɪnʊk/ ▶ **noun** (pl. **Inuit**) a member of the Inuit people: [as modifier] *drawings by an Inuk artist.*
– ORIGIN Inuit, literally 'person'.

Inuktitut /ɪˈnʊktɪtʊt/ (also **Inuktituk** /-tʊk/) ▶ **noun** [mass noun] the Inuit language.
– ORIGIN Inuit, literally 'the Inuk way', used as the title of a periodical.

inulin /ˈɪnjʊlɪn/ ▶ **noun** [mass noun] Biochemistry a complex of sugar present in the roots of various plants and used medically to test kidney function. It is a polysaccharide based on fructose.
– ORIGIN early 19th cent.: from Latin *inula* (identified by medieval herbalists with elecampane) + **-IN**[1].

inunction /ɪˈnʌŋ(k)ʃ(ə)n/ ▶ **noun** [mass noun] chiefly Medicine the rubbing of ointment or oil into the skin.
– ORIGIN late 15th cent.: from Latin *inunctio(n-)*, from *inunguere* 'smear on'.

inundate /ˈɪnʌndeɪt/ ▶ **verb** [with obj.] (usu. **be inundated**) flood: *the islands may be the first to be inundated as sea levels rise.*
■figurative overwhelm (someone) with things or people to be dealt with: *we've been **inundated with** complaints from listeners.*
– DERIVATIVES **inundation** noun.
– ORIGIN late 16th cent.: from Latin *inundat-* 'flooded', from the verb *inundare*, from *in-* 'into, upon' + *undare* 'to flow' (from *unda* 'a wave').

Inupiaq /ɪˈnuːpɪak/ (also **Inupiat** /-pɪat/, **Inupik** /-pɪk/) ▶ **noun** (pl. same) **1** a member of a group of Inuit people inhabiting northern Alaska.
2 [mass noun] the Inuit language.
▶ **adjective** of or relating to this people or their language.
– ORIGIN Inuit, from *inuk* 'person' + *piaq* 'genuine'.

inure /ɪˈnjʊə/ ▶ **verb** [with obj.] (usu. **be inured to**) accustom (someone) to something, especially something unpleasant: *these children have been inured to violence.*
■Law variant spelling of **ENURE** (in sense 1).
– DERIVATIVES **inurement** noun.
– ORIGIN late Middle English *inure, enure*, from an Anglo-Norman French phrase meaning 'in use or practice', from *en* 'in' + Old French *euvre* 'work' (from Latin *opera*).

inurn (also **enurn**) ▶ **verb** [with obj.] place or bury (something, especially ashes after cremation) in an urn.

in utero /ɪn ˈjuːtərəʊ/ ▶ **adverb** & **adjective** in a woman's uterus; before birth: [as adv.] *this damage may occur in utero* | [as adj.] *the in utero development of the gastrointestinal tract.*
– ORIGIN Latin.

inutile /ɪnˈjuːtɪl/ ▶ **adjective** useless; pointless.
– DERIVATIVES **inutility** noun.
– ORIGIN late Middle English: from Old French, from Latin *inutilis*, from *in-* 'not' + *utilis* 'useful'.

in vacuo /ɪn ˈvakjʊəʊ/ ▶ **adverb** in a vacuum: *the hydrochloric acid was removed by evaporation in vacuo.*
■away from or without the normal context or environment: *instead of dealing with individual aspects of lifestyle in vacuo, social factors are taken in account.*
– ORIGIN Latin.

invade ▶ **verb** [with obj.] (of an armed force or its commander) enter (a country or region) so as to subjugate or occupy it: *he decided to invade England and landed his troops at Hastings.*
■enter (a place, situation, or sphere of activity) in large numbers, especially with intrusive effect: *demonstrators invaded the Presidential Palace.* ■(of a parasite or disease) spread into (an organism or bodily part). ■(of a person or emotion) encroach or intrude on: *he felt his privacy was being invaded.*
– DERIVATIVES **invader** noun.
– ORIGIN late Middle English (in the sense 'attack or assault (a person)'): from Latin *invadere*, from *in-* 'into' + *vadere* 'go'.

invaginate /ɪnˈvadʒɪneɪt/ ▶ **verb** (**be invaginated**) chiefly Anatomy & Biology be turned inside out or folded back on itself to form a cavity or pouch.
– ORIGIN mid 17th cent.: back-formation from **INVAGINATION**.

invagination ▶ **noun** [mass noun] chiefly Anatomy & Biology the action or process of being turned inside out or folded back on itself to form a cavity or pouch.
■[count noun] a cavity or pouch so formed.
– ORIGIN mid 17th cent.: from modern Latin *invaginatio(n-)*, based on **IN-**[2] 'into' + Latin *vagina* 'sheath'.

invalid[1] /ˈɪnvəliːd, -lɪd/ ▶ **noun** a person made weak or disabled by illness or injury.
▶ **verb** (**invalided**, **invaliding**) [with obj.] (usu. **be invalided**) remove (someone) from active service in the armed forces because of injury or illness: *he was badly wounded and **invalided out** of the infantry.*
■disable (someone) by injury or illness.
– DERIVATIVES **invalidism** noun.
– ORIGIN mid 17th cent. (as an adjective in the sense 'infirm or disabled'): a special sense of **INVALID**[2], with a change of pronunciation.

invalid[2] /ɪnˈvalɪd/ ▶ **adjective** not valid, in particular:
■(especially of an official document or procedure) not legally recognized and therefore void because contravening a regulation or law: *the vote was declared invalid due to a technicality.* ■(especially of an argument, statement, or theory) not true because based on erroneous information or unsound reasoning: *a comparison is invalid if we are not comparing like with like.* ■(of computer instructions, data, etc.) not conforming to the correct format or specifications.
– DERIVATIVES **invalidly** adverb.
– ORIGIN mid 16th cent. (earlier than *valid*): from Latin *invalidus*, from *in-* 'not' + *validus* 'strong' (see **VALID**).

invalidate ▶ **verb** [with obj.] **1** make (an argument, statement, or theory) unsound or erroneous.
2 deprive (an official document or procedure) of legal efficacy because of contravention of a regulation or law: *a technical flaw in her papers invalidated her nomination.*
– DERIVATIVES **invalidation** noun.
– ORIGIN mid 17th cent.: from medieval Latin *invalidat-* 'annulled', from the verb *invalidare* (based on Latin *validus* 'strong').

invalidity ▶ **noun** [mass noun] **1** Brit. the condition of being an invalid.
2 the fact of not being valid: *the resolution on the invalidity of their independence declaration.*

invaluable ▶ **adjective** extremely useful; indispensable: *an invaluable source of information.*
– DERIVATIVES **invaluably** adverb.

Invar /ˈɪnvɑː/ ▶ **noun** [mass noun] trademark an alloy of iron and nickel with a negligible coefficient of expansion, used in the making of clocks and scientific instruments.
– ORIGIN early 20th cent.: abbreviation of **INVARIABLE**.

invariable ▶ **adjective** never changing: *disillusion was the almost invariable result.*
■(of a noun in an inflected language) having the same form in both the singular and the plural, as does *relais* in French. ■Mathematics (of a quantity) constant.
– DERIVATIVES **invariability** noun, **invariableness** noun.
– ORIGIN late Middle English: from French, or from late Latin *invariabilis*, from *in-* 'not' + *variabilis* (see **VARIABLE**).

invariably ▶ **adverb** in every case or on every occasion; always: *ranch meals are invariably big and hearty.*

invariant ▶ **adjective** never changing: *the pattern of cell divisions was found to be invariant.*
▶ **noun** Mathematics a function, quantity, or property which remains unchanged when a specified transformation is applied.
– DERIVATIVES **invariance** noun.

invasion ▶ **noun** an instance of invading a country or region with an armed force: *the Soviet invasion of*

Czechoslovakia | [mass noun] *in 1546 England had to be defended from invasion.*
■an incursion by a large number of people or things into a place or sphere of activity: *there was a brief pitch invasion when Sunderland scored.* ■an unwelcome intrusion into another's domain: *random drug testing of employees is an unwarranted invasion of privacy.*
– ORIGIN late Middle English: from late Latin *invasio(n-)*, from the verb *invadere* (see **INVADE**).

invasive ▶ **adjective** (especially of plants or a disease) tending to spread prolifically and undesirably or harmfully.
■(especially of an action or sensation) tending to intrude on a person's thoughts or privacy: *the sound of the piano was invasive.* ■(of medical procedures) involving the introduction of instruments or other objects into the body or body cavities: *minimally invasive surgery.*
– ORIGIN late Middle English: from obsolete French *invasif, -ive* or medieval Latin *invasivus*, from Latin *invadere* (see **INVADE**).

invected ▶ **adjective** [usu. postpositive] Heraldry having convex semicircular projections along the edge. Compare with **ENGRAILED**.

invective ▶ **noun** [mass noun] insulting, abusive, or highly critical language: *he let out a stream of invective.*
– ORIGIN late Middle English (originally as an adjective meaning 'reviling, abusive'): from Old French *invectif, -ive*, from late Latin *invectivus* 'attacking', from *invehere* (see **INVEIGH**). The noun is from late Latin *invectiva (oratio)* 'abusive or censorious (language)'.

inveigh /ɪnˈveɪ/ ▶ **verb** [no obj.] (**inveigh against**) speak or write about (something) with great hostility: *Marx inveighed against the evils of the property-owning classes.*
– ORIGIN late 15th cent. (in the sense 'carry in, introduce'; formerly also as *enveigh*): from Latin *invehere* 'carry in', *invehi* 'be carried into, assail', from *in-* 'into' + *vehere* 'carry'.

inveigle /ɪnˈviːɡ(ə)l, ɪnˈveɪɡ(ə)l/ ▶ **verb** [with obj. and adverbial] persuade (someone) to do something by means of deception or flattery: *we cannot inveigle him into putting pen to paper.*
■(**inveigle oneself** or **one's way into**) gain entrance to (a place) by using such methods.
– DERIVATIVES **inveiglement** noun.
– ORIGIN late 15th cent. (in the sense 'beguile, deceive'; formerly also as *enveigle*): from Anglo-Norman French *envegler*, alteration of Old French *aveugler* 'to blind', from *aveugle* 'blind'.

invent ▶ **verb** [with obj.] create or design (something that has not existed before); be the originator of: *he invented an improved form of the steam engine.*
■make up (an idea, name, story, etc.), especially so as to deceive: *I did not have to invent any tales about my past.*
– ORIGIN late 15th cent. (in the sense 'find out, discover'): from Latin *invent-* 'contrived, discovered', from the verb *invenire*, from *in-* 'into' + *venire* 'come'.

invention ▶ **noun** [mass noun] the action of inventing something, typically a process or device: *the invention of printing in the 15th century.*
■[count noun] something, typically a process or device, that has been invented: *medieval inventions included spectacles for reading and the spinning wheel.* ■creative ability: *his powers of invention were rather limited.* ■[count noun] something fabricated or made up: *you know my story is an invention.* ■used as a title for a short piece of music: *Bach's two-part Inventions.*
– ORIGIN Middle English (in the sense 'finding out, discovery'): from Latin *inventio(n-)*, from *invenire* 'discover' (see **INVENT**).

Invention of the Cross ▶ **noun** a festival, held on 3 May (Holy Rood Day), commemorating the reputed finding of the Cross of Christ by Helena, mother of the emperor Constantine, in AD 326.

inventive ▶ **adjective** (of a person) having the ability to create or design new things or to think originally: *she is the most inventive painter around.*
■(of a product, process, action, etc.) showing creativity or original thought: *methods of communication during the war were diverse and inventive.*
– DERIVATIVES **inventively** adverb, **inventiveness** noun.
– ORIGIN late Middle English: from French *inventif, -ive* or medieval Latin *inventivus*, from Latin *invenire* 'discover' (see **INVENT**).

inventor ▶ **noun** a person who invented a particular process or device or who invents things as an occupation.

inventory /ˈɪnv(ə)nt(ə)ri/ ▶ **noun** (pl. **-ies**) a complete list of items such as property, goods in stock, or the contents of a building.
■a quantity of goods held in stock: *in our warehouse you'll find a large inventory of new and used bicycles.* ■(in accounting) the entire stock of a business, including materials, components, work in progress, and finished product.
▶ **verb (-ies, -ied)** [with obj.] make a complete list of.
■enter in a list: *about forty possible sites were inventoried.*
– ORIGIN late Middle English: from medieval Latin *inventorium*, alteration of late Latin *inventarium*, literally 'a list of what is found', from Latin *invenire* 'come upon'.

inventress ▶ **noun** a female inventor.

inveracity /ˌɪnvəˈrasɪti/ ▶ **noun** (pl. **-ies**) a lie.
■[mass noun] untruthfulness.

Invercargill /ˌɪnvəˈkɑːɡɪl/ a city in New Zealand, capital of Southland region, South Island; pop. 51,980 (1991).

Inverness /ˌɪnvəˈnɛs/ a city in Scotland, administrative centre of Highland region, situated at the mouth of the River Ness; pop. 41,230 (1991).

inverse /ˈɪnvəːs, ɪnˈvəːs/ ▶ **adjective** [attrib.] opposite or contrary in position, direction, order, or effect: *the well-observed inverse relationship between disability and social contact.*
■chiefly Mathematics produced from or related to something else by a process of inversion.
▶ **noun** [usu. in sing.] something that is the opposite or reverse of something else: *his approach is the inverse of most research on ethnic and racial groups.*
■Mathematics a reciprocal quantity, mathematical expression, geometric figure, etc. which is the result of inversion. ■Mathematics an element which, when combined with a given element in an operation, produces the identity element for that operation.
– DERIVATIVES **inversely** adverb.
– ORIGIN late Middle English: from Latin *inversus*, past participle of *invertere* (see **INVERT**[1]).

inverse proportion (also **inverse ratio**) ▶ **noun** a relation between two quantities such that one increases in proportion as the other decreases.

inverse square law ▶ **noun** Physics a law stating that the intensity of an effect such as illumination or gravitational force changes in inverse proportion to the square of the distance from the source.

inversion ▶ **noun 1** [mass noun] the action of inverting something or the state of being inverted: *the inversion of the normal domestic arrangement* | [count noun] *an inversion of traditional customer–supplier relationships.*
■reversal of the normal order of words, typically for rhetorical effect but also found in the regular formation of questions in English. ■Music the process of inverting an interval, chord, or phrase. ■[count noun] Music an inverted interval, chord, or phrase. ■Physics (also **population inversion**) a transposition in the relative numbers of atoms, molecules, etc. occupying particular energy levels. ■Chemistry a reaction causing a change from one optically active configuration to the opposite configuration, especially the hydrolysis of dextrose to give a laevorotatory solution of fructose and glucose.
2 (also **temperature** or **thermal inversion**) a reversal of the normal decrease of air temperature with altitude, or of water temperature with depth.
■(also **inversion layer**) a layer of the atmosphere in which temperature increases with height.
3 [mass noun] Mathematics the process of finding a quantity, function, etc. from a given one such that the product of the two under a particular operation is the identity.
■the interchanging of numerator and denominator of a fraction, or antecedent and consequent of a ratio. ■the process of finding the expression which gives a given expression under a given transformation. ■[count noun] Geometry a transformation in which each point of a given figure is replaced by another point on the same straight line from a fixed point, especially in such a way that the product of the distances of the two points from the centre of inversion is constant.
4 (also **sexual inversion**) Psychology, dated the adoption of behaviour typical of the opposite sex; homosexuality.
– DERIVATIVES **inversive** adjective.
– ORIGIN mid 16th cent. (as a term in rhetoric, denoting the turning of an argument against the person who put it forward): from Latin *inversio(n-)*, from the verb *invertere* (see **INVERT**[1]).

inversion temperature ▶ **noun** Physics the temperature at which the Joule–Thomson effect for a given gas changes sign, so that the gas is neither heated nor cooled when allowed to expand without expending energy.

invert[1] ▶ **verb** /ɪnˈvəːt/ [with obj.] put upside down or in the opposite position, order, or arrangement: *invert the mousse on to a serving plate.*
■Music modify (a phrase) by reversing the direction of pitch changes. ■Music alter (an interval or triad) by changing the relative position of the notes in it. ■chiefly Mathematics subject to inversion; transform into its inverse.
▶ **noun** /ˈɪnvəːt/ **1** an arch constructed in an upside-down position to provide lateral support, e.g. in a tunnel.
■the concave lower surface of a sewer or drain.
2 Psychology, dated a person showing sexual inversion; a homosexual.
3 Philately a postage stamp printed with an error such that all or part of its design is upside down.
– DERIVATIVES **invertibility** noun, **invertible** adjective.
– ORIGIN mid 16th cent. (in the sense 'turn back to front'): from Latin *invertere*, literally 'turn inside out', from *in-* 'into' + *vertere* 'to turn'.

invert[2] /ˈɪnvəːt/ ▶ **noun** informal short for **INVERTEBRATE**.

invertase /ˈɪnvəːteɪz, ɪnˈvəːt-/ ▶ **noun** [mass noun] Biochemistry an enzyme produced by yeast which catalyses the hydrolysis of sucrose, forming invert sugar.

invertebrate /ɪnˈvəːtɪbrət/ ▶ **noun** an animal lacking a backbone, such as an arthropod, mollusc, annelid, coelenterate, etc. The invertebrates constitute an artificial division of the animal kingdom, comprising 95 per cent of animal species and about thirty different phyla. Compare with **VERTEBRATE**.
▶ **adjective** of, relating to, or belonging to this division of animals.
■humorous irresolute; spineless: *so invertebrate is today's Congress regarding foreign policy responsibilities.*
– ORIGIN early 19th cent. (as a noun): from modern Latin *invertebrata* (plural) 'the invertebrates' (former taxonomic group), from French *invertébrés*, from *in-* 'without' + Latin *vertebra* (see **VERTEBRA**).

inverted comma ▶ **noun** chiefly Brit. another term for **QUOTATION MARK**.

inverted snobbery ▶ **noun** [mass noun] derogatory the attitude of seeming to despise anything associated with wealth or social status, while at the same time elevating those things associated with lack of wealth and social position.
– DERIVATIVES **inverted snob** noun.

inverter ▶ **noun 1** an apparatus which converts direct current into alternating current.
2 Electronics a device that converts either of the two binary digits or signals into the other.

invert sugar ▶ **noun** [mass noun] a mixture of glucose and fructose obtained by the hydrolysis of sucrose.
– ORIGIN late 19th cent.: *invert* from *inverted*, because of the reversal of optical activity involved in its formation (see the chemical sense of **INVERSION**).

invest ▶ **verb 1** [no obj.] expend money with the expectation of achieving a profit or material result by putting it into financial schemes, shares, or property, or by using it to develop a commercial venture: *getting workers to* **invest in** *private pension funds* | [with obj.] *the company is to* **invest** *£12 m* **in** *its manufacturing site at Linlithglow.*
■[with obj.] devote (one's time, effort, or energy) to a particular undertaking with the expectation of a worthwhile result: *politicians who have* **invested** *so much time* **in** *the Constitution would be crestfallen.* ■[no obj.] (**invest in**) informal buy (something) whose usefulness will repay the cost.
2 [with obj.] (**invest someone/thing with**) provide or endow someone or something with (a particular quality or attribute): *the passage of time has invested the words with an unintended humour.*
■endow someone with (a rank or office). ■(**invest something in**) establish a right or power in.
3 [with obj.] archaic clothe or cover with a garment: *he stands before you* **invested in** *the full canonicals of his calling.*
4 [with obj.] archaic surround (a place) in order to besiege or blockade it: *Fort Pulaski was invested and captured.*

– DERIVATIVES **investable** adjective, **investible** adjective, **investor** noun.
– ORIGIN mid 16th cent. (in the senses 'clothe', 'clothe with the insignia of a rank', and 'endow with authority'): from French *investir* or Latin *investire*, from *in-* 'into, upon' + *vestire* 'clothe' (from *vestis* 'clothing'). Sense 1 (early 17th cent.) is influenced by Italian *investire*.

investigable ▶ adjective open to investigation, inquiry, or research.
– ORIGIN late 16th cent.: from late Latin *investigabilis*, from *investigare* (see **INVESTIGATE**).

investigate ▶ verb [with obj.] carry out a systematic or formal inquiry to discover and examine the facts of (an incident, allegation, etc.) so as to establish the truth: *police are today investigating a claim that the man was beaten unconscious by a gang.*
■ carry out research or study into (a subject, typically one in a scientific or academic field) so as to discover facts or information: [with clause] *future studies will investigate whether long-term use of the drugs could prevent cancer.* ■ make inquiries as to the character, activities, or background of (someone): *everyone with a possible interest in your brother's death must be thoroughly investigated.* ■ [no obj.] make a check to find out something: *when you didn't turn up I thought I'd better come back to investigate.*
– DERIVATIVES **investigator** noun, **investigatory** adjective.
– ORIGIN early 16th cent.: from Latin *investigat-* 'traced out', from the verb *investigare*, from *in-* 'into' + *vestigare* 'track, trace out'.

investigation ▶ noun [mass noun] the action of investigating something or someone; formal or systematic examination or research: *he is **under investigation** for receiving illicit funds.*
■ [count noun] a formal inquiry or systematic study: *an **investigation** has been launched **into** the potential impact of the oil spill.*
– DERIVATIVES **investigational** adjective.
– ORIGIN late Middle English: from Latin *investigatio(n-)*, from the verb *investigare* (see **INVESTIGATE**).

investigative /ɪnˈvɛstɪɡətɪv, -ɡeɪtɪv/ ▶ adjective of or concerned with investigating something: *a special investigative committee to look into the strikers' demands.*
■ (of journalism or a journalist) inquiring intensively into and seeking to expose malpractice, the miscarriage of justice, or other controversial issues.

investiture /ɪnˈvɛstɪtjə, -tʃə/ ▶ noun [mass noun] the action of formally investing a person with honours or rank: *the investiture of bishops.*
■ [count noun] a ceremony at which honours or rank are formally conferred on a particular person.
– ORIGIN late Middle English: from medieval Latin *investitura*, from *investire* (see **INVEST**).

investment ▶ noun [mass noun] **1** the action or process of investing money for profit or material result: *a debate over private **investment in** road-building* | [count noun] *the wealth generated allowed investments to be made in many new industries* | *a total investment of £50,000.*
■ [count noun] a thing that is worth buying because it may be profitable or useful in the future: *freezers really are a good investment for the elderly.* ■ [count noun] an act of devoting time, effort, or energy to a particular undertaking with the expectation of a worthwhile result: *the time spent in attending a one-day seminar is an investment in our professional futures.*
2 archaic the surrounding of a place by a hostile force in order to besiege or blockade it.

investment bank ▶ noun (in the US) a bank (similar to a UK merchant bank) that purchases large holdings of newly issued shares and resells them to investors.

investment bond ▶ noun (in the UK) a single-premium life insurance policy linked to a unit trust for long-term investment.

investment casting ▶ noun [mass noun] technical a technique for making small, accurate castings in refractory alloys using a mould formed around a pattern of wax or similar material which is then removed by melting.

investment grade ▶ noun [mass noun] a level of credit rating for stocks regarded as carrying a minimal risk to investors.

investment trust ▶ noun a limited company whose business is the investment of shareholders' funds, the shares being traded like those of any other public company.

inveterate /ɪnˈvɛt(ə)rət/ ▶ adjective [attrib.] having a particular habit, activity, or interest that is long-established and unlikely to change: *he was an inveterate gambler.*
■ (of a feeling or habit) long-established and unlikely to change.
– DERIVATIVES **inveteracy** noun, **inveterately** adverb.
– ORIGIN late Middle English (referring to disease, in the sense 'of long standing, chronic'): from Latin *inveteratus* 'made old', past participle of *inveterare* (based on *vetus, veter-* 'old').

inviable ▶ adjective not viable.
– DERIVATIVES **inviability** noun.

invidious /ɪnˈvɪdɪəs/ ▶ adjective (of an action or situation) likely to arouse or incur resentment or anger in others: *she'd put herself in an invidious position.*
■ (of a comparison or distinction) unfairly discriminating; unjust: *it seems invidious to make special mention of one aspect of his work.*
– DERIVATIVES **invidiously** adverb, **invidiousness** noun.
– ORIGIN early 17th cent.: from Latin *invidiosus*, from *invidia* (see **ENVY**).

invigilate /ɪnˈvɪdʒɪleɪt/ ▶ verb [no obj.] Brit. supervise candidates during an examination.
– DERIVATIVES **invigilation** noun, **invigilator** noun.
– ORIGIN mid 16th cent. (in the general sense 'watch over, keep watch'): from Latin *invigilat-* 'watched over', from the verb *invigilare*, from *in-* 'upon, towards' + *vigilare* 'watch' (from *vigil* 'watchful').

invigorate /ɪnˈvɪɡəreɪt/ ▶ verb [with obj.] give strength or energy to: *the shower had invigorated her* | [as adj. **invigorating**] *a brisk, invigorating walk.*
– DERIVATIVES **invigoratingly** adverb, **invigoration** noun, **invigorator** noun.
– ORIGIN mid 17th cent.: from medieval Latin *invigorat-* 'made strong', from the verb *invigorare*, from *in-* 'towards' + Latin *vigorare* 'make strong' (from *vigor* 'vigour').

invincible /ɪnˈvɪnsɪb(ə)l/ ▶ adjective too powerful to be defeated or overcome: *an invincible warrior.*
– DERIVATIVES **invincibility** noun, **invincibly** adverb.
– ORIGIN late Middle English (earlier than *vincible*): via Old French from Latin *invincibilis*, from *in-* 'not' + *vincibilis* (see **VINCIBLE**).

in vino veritas /ɪn ˌviːnəʊ ˈvɛrɪtɑːs/ ▶ exclamation under the influence of alcohol, a person tells the truth.
– ORIGIN Latin, literally 'truth in wine'.

inviolable /ɪnˈvʌɪələb(ə)l/ ▶ adjective never to be broken, infringed, or dishonoured: *an inviolable rule of chastity* | *the Polish–German border was inviolable.*
– DERIVATIVES **inviolability** noun, **inviolably** adverb.
– ORIGIN late Middle English: from French, or from Latin *inviolabilis*, from *in-* 'not' + *violabilis* 'able to be violated' (from the verb *violare*).

inviolate /ɪnˈvʌɪələt/ ▶ adjective free or safe from injury or violation: *an international memorial which must remain inviolate.*
– DERIVATIVES **inviolacy** noun, **inviolately** adverb.
– ORIGIN late Middle English: from Latin *inviolatus*, from *in-* 'not' + *violare* 'violate'.

inviscid /ɪnˈvɪsɪd/ ▶ adjective Physics having no or negligible viscosity.

invisible ▶ adjective unable to be seen; not visible to the eye: *this invisible gas is present to some extent in every home.*
■ concealed from sight; hidden: *he lounged in a doorway, invisible in the dark.* ■ figurative (of a person) treated as if unable to be seen; ignored or not taken into consideration: *before 1971, women artists were pretty well invisible.* ■ Economics relating to or denoting earnings which a country makes from the sale of services or other items not constituting tangible commodities: *invisible exports.*
▶ noun (**invisibles**) invisible exports and imports.
– DERIVATIVES **invisibility** noun, **invisibly** adverb.
– ORIGIN Middle English: from Old French, or from Latin *invisibilis*, from *in-* 'not' + *visibilis* (see **VISIBLE**).

invisible ink ▶ noun [mass noun] a type of ink used to produce writing that cannot be seen until the paper is heated or otherwise treated.

invitation ▶ noun a written or verbal request inviting someone to go somewhere or to do something: *a wedding invitation.*
■ [mass noun] the action of inviting someone to go somewhere or to do something: *a club with membership by invitation only* | *a herb garden where guests can only go **at the invitation of** the chef.* ■ [in sing.] a situation or action that tempts someone to do something or makes a particular outcome likely: *tactics like those of the colonel would have been an invitation to disaster.*
– ORIGIN late Middle English: from French, or from Latin *invitatio(n-)*, from *invitare* (see **INVITE**).

invitational N. Amer. ▶ adjective (especially of a competition) open only to those invited.
▶ noun a competition of such a type.

invitatory /ɪnˈvʌɪtət(ə)ri/ ▶ adjective containing or conveying an invitation.
■ (in the Christian Church) denoting a psalm or versicle acting as an invitation to worshippers, especially Psalm 95 (the Venite).
– ORIGIN Middle English: from late Latin *invitatorius*, from Latin *invitare* (see **INVITE**).

invite ▶ verb [with obj.] make a polite, formal, or friendly request to (someone) to go somewhere or to do something: *we were **invited to** a dinner at the Embassy* | [with obj. and infinitive] *she invited Patrick to sit down.*
■ make a formal or polite request for (something, especially an application for a job or opinions on a particular topic) from someone. ■ (of an action or situation) tend to elicit (a particular reaction or response) or to tempt (someone) to do something: *his use of the word did little but invite criticism.*
▶ noun informal an invitation.
– DERIVATIVES **invitee** noun, **inviter** noun.
– ORIGIN mid 16th cent.: from Old French *inviter*, or from Latin *invitare*.

inviting ▶ adjective offering the promise of an attractive or enjoyable experience: *the sea down there looks so inviting.*
– DERIVATIVES **invitingly** adverb.

in vitro /ɪn ˈviːtrəʊ/ ▶ adjective & adverb Biology (of processes or reactions) taking place in a test tube, culture dish, or elsewhere outside a living organism: [as adj.] *in vitro fertilization.* The opposite of **IN VIVO**.
– ORIGIN Latin, literally 'in glass'.

in vivo /ɪn ˈviːvəʊ/ ▶ adverb & adjective Biology (of processes) taking place in a living organism. The opposite of **IN VITRO**.
– ORIGIN Latin, 'in a living thing'.

invocation ▶ noun [mass noun] the action of invoking something or someone for assistance or as an authority: *the invocation of new disciplines and methodologies.*
■ the summoning of a deity or the supernatural: *his invocation of the ancient powers of Callanish.* ■ [count noun] an incantation used for this. ■ [count noun] (in the Christian Church) a form of words such as 'In the name of the Father' introducing a prayer, sermon, etc.
– DERIVATIVES **invocatory** /ɪnˈvɒkət(ə)ri/ adjective.
– ORIGIN late Middle English: via Old French from Latin *invocatio(n-)*, from the verb *invocare* (see **INVOKE**).

invoice ▶ noun a list of goods sent or services provided, with a statement of the sum due for these; a bill.
▶ verb [with obj.] send an invoice to (someone).
■ send an invoice for (goods or services provided).
– ORIGIN mid 16th cent.: originally the plural of obsolete *invoy*, from obsolete French *envoy* from *envoyer* 'send' (see **ENVOY**[1]).

invoke /ɪnˈvəʊk/ ▶ verb [with obj.] cite or appeal to (someone or something) as an authority for an action or in support of an argument: *the antiquated defence of insanity is rarely invoked in England.*
■ call on (a deity or spirit) in prayer, as a witness, or for inspiration. ■ call earnestly for: *she invoked his help against this attack.* ■ summon (a spirit) by charms or incantation. ■ give rise to; evoke: *how could she explain how the accident happened without invoking his wrath?* ■ Computing cause (a procedure) to be carried out.
– DERIVATIVES **invoker** noun.
– ORIGIN late 15th cent.: from French *invoquer*, from Latin *invocare*, from *in-* 'upon' + *vocare* 'to call'.

involatile ▶ adjective not volatile; unable to be vaporized.

involucre /ˈɪnvəl(j)uːkə/ ▶ noun **1** Anatomy a membranous envelope.
2 Botany a whorl or rosette of bracts surrounding an inflorescence (especially a capitulum) or at the base of an umbel.
– ORIGIN late 16th cent.: from French, or from Latin *involucrum*, from *involvere* 'roll in, envelop' (see **INVOLVE**).

involuntary ▶ adjective **1** done without conscious control: *she gave an involuntary shudder.*
■ (especially of muscles or nerves) concerned in bodily processes that are not under the control of the will. **2** done against someone's will; compulsory: *a policy of involuntary repatriation.*
– DERIVATIVES **involuntarily** adverb, **involuntariness** noun.

involute /ˈɪnvəl(j)uːt/ ▶ adjective **1** formal involved; intricate: *the art novel has grown increasingly involute.* **2** technical curled spirally.
■ Zoology (of a shell) having the whorls wound closely round the axis. ■ Botany (of a leaf or the cap of a fungus) rolled inwards at the edges.
▶ noun Geometry the locus of a point considered as the end of a taut string being unwound from a given curve in the plane of that curve. Compare with **EVOLUTE**.
– ORIGIN mid 17th cent.: from Latin *involutus*, past participle of *involvere* (see **INVOLVE**).

involuted ▶ adjective complicated; abstruse: *his involuted prose.*

involution ▶ noun **1** [mass noun] Physiology the shrinkage of an organ in old age or when inactive, e.g. of the womb after childbirth. **2** Mathematics a function, transformation, or operator that is equal to its inverse, i.e. which gives the identity when applied to itself. **3** [mass noun] formal the process of involving or complicating, or the state of being involved or complicated: *periods of artistic involution.*
– DERIVATIVES **involutional** adjective.
– ORIGIN late Middle English (in the sense '(part) curling inwards'): from Latin *involutio(n-)*, from *involvere* (see **INVOLVE**).

involve ▶ verb [with obj.] (of a situation or event) include (something) as a necessary part or result: *his transfer to another school would involve a lengthy assessment procedure.*
■ cause (a person or group) to experience or participate in an activity or situation: *what kind of organizations will be involved in setting up these projects?*
– ORIGIN late Middle English (in the senses 'enfold' and 'entangle'; formerly also as *envolve*): from Latin *involvere*, from *in-* 'into' + *volvere* 'to roll'.

involved ▶ adjective **1** [predic.] connected or concerned with someone or something, typically on an emotional or personal level: *Angela told me that she was involved with someone else.* **2** difficult to comprehend; complicated: *a long, involved conversation.*

involvement ▶ noun [mass noun] the fact or condition of being involved with or participating in something: *he was imprisoned for his involvement in a plot to overthrow the government.*
■ emotional or personal association with someone.

invulnerable ▶ adjective impossible to harm or damage.
– DERIVATIVES **invulnerability** noun, **invulnerably** adverb.
– ORIGIN late 16th cent. (earlier than *vulnerable*): from Latin *invulnerabilis*, from *in-* 'not' + *vulnerabilis* (see **VULNERABLE**).

-in-waiting ▶ combining form **1** denoting a position as attendant to a royal personage: *lady-in-waiting.* **2** awaiting a turn, confirmation of a process, etc.: *a political administration-in-waiting.*
■ about to happen: *an explosion-in-waiting.*

inwale /ˈɪnweɪl/ ▶ noun a longitudinal structural piece on the inside of a boat; an internal gunwale.

inward ▶ adjective [attrib.] directed or proceeding towards the inside; coming in from outside: *inward mail | a graceful inward movement of her wrist.*
■ existing within the mind, soul, or spirit, and often not expressed: *she felt an inward sense of release.*
▶ adverb variant of **INWARDS**.
– ORIGIN Old English *inweard*, *inneweard*, *innanweard* (see **IN**, **-WARD**).

inward investment ▶ noun [mass noun] investment made within a country from outside.

inward-looking ▶ adjective not interested in or taking account of other people or groups.

inwardly ▶ adverb (of a particular thought, feeling, or action) registered or existing in the mind but not expressed to others: *inwardly seething, he did as he was told.*
– ORIGIN Old English *inweardlíce* (see **INWARD**, **-LY**[2]).

inwardness ▶ noun [mass noun] preoccupation with one's inner self; concern with spiritual or philosophical matters rather than externalities.

inwards (also **inward**) ▶ adverb towards the inside: *the door began to swing inwards.*
■ into or towards the mind, spirit, or soul: *people must look inwards to gain insight into their own stress.*

inwrap ▶ verb variant spelling of **ENWRAP**.

inwreathe ▶ verb variant spelling of **ENWREATHE**.

inwrought /ɪnˈrɔːt, ˈɪnrɔːt/ ▶ adjective poetic/literary (of a fabric or garment) intricately embroidered with a particular pattern or decoration: *robes inwrought with gold.*

inyanga /ɪnˈjaŋgə, ɪnˈjɑːŋgə/ ▶ noun (pl. **inyangas** or **izinyanga**) S. African a traditional healer or diviner, especially one specializing in herbalism.
– ORIGIN Zulu, 'doctor, herbalist'.

in-your-face ▶ adjective informal blatantly aggressive or provocative; impossible to ignore or avoid: *hard-boiled, in-your-face action thrillers.*
– ORIGIN 1970s: from *in your face*, used as a derisive insult.

I/O Electronics ▶ abbreviation for input-output.

Io /ˈʌɪəʊ/ **1** Greek Mythology a priestess of Hera who was loved by Zeus. Trying to protect her from the jealousy of Hera, Zeus turned Io into a heifer. Hera sent a gadfly to torture the heifer, which then fled across the world and finally reached Egypt, where Zeus turned her back into human form. **2** Astronomy one of the Galilean moons of Jupiter, the fifth closest satellite to the planet, being actively volcanic and coloured red and yellow with sulphur compounds (diameter 3,630 km).

IOC ▶ abbreviation for International Olympic Committee.

iod- ▶ combining form variant spelling of **IODO-** shortened before a vowel (as in *iodic*).

iodic acid /ʌɪˈɒdɪk/ ▶ noun [mass noun] Chemistry a crystalline acid with strong oxidizing properties, made by oxidation of iodine.
● Chem. formula: HIO_3.
– DERIVATIVES **iodate** noun.

iodide /ˈʌɪədʌɪd/ ▶ noun [mass noun] Chemistry a compound of iodine with another element or group, especially a salt of the anion I^-.

iodinate /ˈʌɪədɪneɪt, ʌɪˈɒdɪneɪt/ ▶ verb [with obj.] [usu. as adj. **iodinated**] Chemistry introduce iodine into (a compound).
– DERIVATIVES **iodination** noun.

iodine /ˈʌɪədiːn, -ʌɪn, -ɪn/ ▶ noun [mass noun] the chemical element of atomic number 53, a non-metallic element forming black crystals and a violet vapour. (Symbol: **I**)
■ a solution of this in alcohol, used as a mild antiseptic.

> A member of the halogen group, iodine occurs chiefly as salts in seawater and brines. As a constituent of thyroid hormones it is required in small amounts in the body, and deficiency can lead to goitre.

– ORIGIN early 19th cent.: from French *iode* (from Greek *iōdēs* 'violet-coloured', from *ion* 'violet' + *-eidēs* 'like') + **-INE**[4].

iodism /ˈʌɪədɪz(ə)m/ ▶ noun [mass noun] Medicine iodine poisoning, causing thirst, diarrhoea, weakness, and convulsions.

iodo- (usu. **iod-** before a vowel) ▶ combining form Chemistry representing **IODINE**.

iodoform /ʌɪˈəʊdə(ʊ)fɔːm, ˈʌɪədə(ʊ)-, ʌɪˈɒdə(ʊ)-/ ▶ noun [mass noun] a volatile pale yellow sweet-smelling crystalline organic compound of iodine, with antiseptic properties.
● Alternative name: **triiodomethane**; chem. formula: CHI_3.
– ORIGIN mid 19th cent.: from **IODINE**, on the pattern of *chloroform*.

iodometry /ʌɪəˈdɒmɪtri/ ▶ noun [mass noun] Chemistry the quantitative analysis of a solution of an oxidizing agent by adding an iodide which reacts to form iodine, which is then titrated.
– DERIVATIVES **iodometric** adjective.

iodophor /ʌɪˈəʊdə(ʊ)fɔː, ˈʌɪəd-/ ▶ noun any of a group of disinfectants containing iodine in combination with a surfactant.

IOM ▶ abbreviation for Isle of Man.

io moth /ˈʌɪəʊ/ ▶ noun a large, mainly yellow North American moth of the silk moth family, with prominent eyespots on the hindwings.
● *Automeris io*, family Saturniidae.

– ORIGIN late 19th cent.: named after the Greek priestess **Io**.

ion /ˈʌɪən/ ▶ noun an atom or molecule with a net electric charge due to the loss or gain of one or more electrons. See also **CATION**, **ANION**.
– ORIGIN mid 19th cent.: from Greek, neuter present participle of *ienai* 'go'.

-ion ▶ suffix **1** forming nouns denoting verbal action: *communion.*
■ denoting an instance of this: *a rebellion.* ■ denoting a resulting state or product: *oblivion | opinion.*
– ORIGIN via French from Latin *-ion-*.

> USAGE The suffix **-ion** is usually found preceded by **s** (**-sion**), **t** (**-tion**), or **x** (**-xion**).

Iona /ʌɪˈəʊnə/ a small island in the Inner Hebrides, off the west coast of Mull. It is the site of a monastery founded by St Columba in about 563.

Ionesco /ˌiːəˈnɛskəʊ/, Eugène (1912–94), Romanian-born French dramatist, a leading exponent of the Theatre of the Absurd. Notable plays: *The Bald Prima Donna* (1950), *Rhinoceros* (1960).

ion exchange ▶ noun [mass noun] the exchange of ions of the same charge between an insoluble solid and a solution in contact with it, used in water-softening and other purification and separation processes.

ion exchanger ▶ noun a solid used in ion exchange, typically a special cross-linked synthetic resin or a zeolite.

Ionia /ʌɪˈəʊnɪə/ in classical times, the central part of the west coast of Asia Minor, which had long been inhabited by Hellenic people (the Ionians) and was again colonized by Greeks from the mainland from about the 8th century BC.

Ionian ▶ noun a member of an ancient Hellenic people inhabiting Attica, parts of western Asia Minor, and the Aegean islands in pre-classical times. They were apparently displaced from some areas by the Dorians in the 11th or 12th century BC but retained their settlements in Attica, especially Athens, where they were responsible for some of the greatest achievements of classical Greece. They also colonized the islands that became known as the Ionian Islands.
■ a native or inhabitant of the Ionian Islands.
▶ adjective of or relating to the Ionians, Ionia, or the Ionian Islands.

Ionian Islands a chain of about forty Greek islands off the western coast of mainland Greece, in the Ionian Sea, including Corfu, Cephalonia, Ithaca, and Zakinthos.

Ionian mode ▶ noun Music the mode represented by the natural diatonic scale C–C (the major scale).

Ionian Sea the part of the Mediterranean Sea between western Greece and southern Italy, at the mouth of the Adriatic.
– ORIGIN named, according to legend, after the priestess **Io**.

Ionic /ʌɪˈɒnɪk/ ▶ adjective **1** relating to or denoting a classical order of architecture characterized by a column with scroll shapes (volutes) on either side of the capital. **2** another term for **IONIAN**.
▶ noun [mass noun] **1** the Ionic order of architecture. **2** the ancient Greek dialect used in Ionia.
– ORIGIN late 16th cent.: via Latin from Greek *Iōnikos*, from *Iōnia* (see **IONIA**).

ionic /ʌɪˈɒnɪk/ ▶ adjective of, relating to, or using ions.
■ (of a chemical bond) formed by the electrostatic attraction of oppositely charged ions. Often contrasted with **COVALENT**.
– DERIVATIVES **ionically** adverb.

ionic strength ▶ noun Chemistry a quantity representing the strength of the electric field in a solution, equal to the sum of the molalities of each type of ion present multiplied by the square of their charges.

ionization chamber ▶ noun an instrument for detecting ionizing radiation.

ionize /ˈʌɪənʌɪz/ (also **-ise**) ▶ verb [with obj.] (usu. be **ionized**) convert (an atom, molecule, or substance) into an ion or ions, typically by removing one or more electrons.
■ [no obj.] become converted into an ion or ions in this way.
– DERIVATIVES **ionizable** adjective, **ionization** noun.

ionizer ▶ noun a device which produces ionization,

especially one used to improve the quality of the air in a room.

ionizing radiation ▶ noun [mass noun] radiation consisting of particles, X-rays, or gamma rays with sufficient energy to cause ionization in the medium through which it passes.

ionomer /aɪˈɒnəmə/ ▶ noun any of a class of polymer materials consisting of thermoplastic resins stabilized by ionic cross-linkages, used to make dental cement and sealants.

ionopause /aɪˈɒnə(ʊ)pɔːz/ ▶ noun Astronomy the upper boundary of the ionosphere of a planet, comet, or other celestial object.

ionophore /aɪˈɒnə(ʊ)fɔː/ ▶ noun Biochemistry a substance which is able to transport particular ions across a lipid membrane in a cell.

ionosphere /aɪˈɒnəsfɪə/ ▶ noun the layer of the earth's atmosphere which contains a high concentration of ions and free electrons and is able to reflect radio waves. It lies above the mesosphere and extends from about 80 to 1,000 km above the earth's surface.
  ■ a similar region above the surface of another planet.
– DERIVATIVES **ionospheric** adjective.

iontophoresis /aɪˌɒntə(ʊ)fəˈriːsɪs/ ▶ noun [mass noun] Medicine a technique of introducing ionic medicinal compounds into the body through the skin by applying a local electric current.
– ORIGIN early 20th cent.: from ION, on the pattern of *electrophoresis*.

-ior ▶ suffix forming adjectives of comparison: *anterior* | *senior*.
– ORIGIN from Latin.

iora /aɪˈɔːrə/ ▶ noun a small insectivorous Asian songbird with greenish back and yellow underparts.
  ● Genus *Aegithina*, family Irenidae (or Chloropseidae): four species.
– ORIGIN of obscure origin.

iota /aɪˈəʊtə/ ▶ noun **1** the ninth letter of the Greek alphabet (Ι, ι), transliterated as 'i'.
  ■ (**Iota**) [followed by Latin genitive] Astronomy the ninth star in a constellation: *Iota Piscium*.
  2 [in sing.] [usu. with negative] an extremely small amount: *nothing she said seemed to make an iota of difference*. [ORIGIN: *iota* being the smallest letter of the Greek alphabet.]
– ORIGIN from Greek *iōta*. Compare with JOT.

iota subscript ▶ noun (in Greek) a small iota written beneath a long vowel, forming the second element of a diphthong but not pronounced and not always represented in transliteration.

IOU ▶ noun a signed document acknowledging a debt.
– ORIGIN late 18th cent.: representing the pronunciation of *I owe you.*

-ious ▶ suffix (forming adjectives) characterized by; full of: *cautious* | *vivacious*.
– ORIGIN from French *-ieux*, from Latin *-iosus*.

IOW ▶ abbreviation for Isle of Wight.

Iowa /ˈaɪəwə/ a state in the Middle West of the US, acquired as part of the Louisiana Purchase in 1803; pop. 2,776,770 (1990); capital, Des Moines. It became the 29th state of the US in 1846.
– DERIVATIVES **Iowan** adjective & noun.

Iowa City a city in eastern Iowa; pop. 59,740 (1990). Founded in 1838, it was the state capital until replaced by Des Moines in 1858.

IPA ▶ abbreviation for ■ India pale ale, a type of light-coloured beer similar to bitter. [ORIGIN: said to have been brewed originally for the British colonies.] ■ International Phonetic Alphabet.

IP address ▶ noun Computing a unique string of numbers separated by full stops that identifies each computer attached to the Internet. It also usually has a version containing words separated by full stops.

Ipatieff /ɪˈpatɪɛf/, Vladimir Nikolaievich (1867–1952), Russian-born American chemist. He worked mainly on the catalysis of hydrocarbons, developing high octane fuels and techniques important to the petrochemical industry.

ipecac /ˈɪpɪkak/ ▶ noun short for IPECACUANHA.

ipecacuanha /ˌɪpɪkakjʊˈanə/ ▶ noun [mass noun] **1** the dried rhizome of a South American shrub, or a drug prepared from this, used as an emetic and expectorant.

2 the shrub that produces this rhizome, native to Brazil and cultivated elsewhere.
  ● *Cephaelis ipecacuanha*, family Rubiaceae.
  ■ used in names of other plants with similar uses, e.g. **American ipecacuanha**.
– ORIGIN early 17th cent.: from Portuguese, from Tupi-Guarani *ipekaaguéne* 'emetic creeper', from *ipe* 'small' + *kaa* 'leaves' + *guéne* 'vomit'.

Iphigenia /ˌɪfɪdʒɪˈnaɪə/ Greek Mythology the daughter of Agamemnon, who was obliged to offer her as a sacrifice to Artemis when the Greek fleet was becalmed on its way to the Trojan War. However, Artemis saved her life and took her to Tauris in the Crimea, where she became a priestess until rescued by her brother Orestes.

Ipiros /ˈɪpɪrɒs/ Greek name for EPIRUS.

IPMS ▶ abbreviation for (in the UK) Institution of Professionals, Managers, and Specialists.

IPO chiefly US ▶ abbreviation for initial public offering.

Ipoh /ˈiːpəʊ/ the capital of the state of Perak in western Malaysia; pop. 382,630 (1991). It replaced Taiping as state capital in 1937.

ipomoea /ˌɪpəˈmiːə/ ▶ noun a plant of the genus *Ipomoea* in the convolvulus family, especially (in gardening) a morning glory.
– ORIGIN modern Latin, from Greek *ips* 'worm' + *homoios* 'like'.

ippon /ˈɪpɒn/ ▶ noun a full point scored in judo, karate, and other martial sports.
– ORIGIN Japanese.

IPR ▶ abbreviation for intellectual property rights.

iproniazid /ˌɪprə(ʊ)ˈnaɪəzɪd/ ▶ noun [mass noun] Medicine a synthetic compound used as a drug to treat depression.
  ● A derivative of isoniazid; chem. formula: $(CH_3)_2CHNHNHCOC_5H_4N$.
– ORIGIN mid 20th cent.: from *i(so)pro(pyl)* + *(iso)niazid*.

ipse dixit /ˌɪpseɪ ˈdɪksɪt, ˌɪpsiː-/ ▶ noun a dogmatic and unproven statement.
– ORIGIN Latin, literally 'he himself said it', translating Greek *autos epha*, a phrase used of Pythagoras by his followers.

ipsilateral /ˌɪpsɪˈlat(ə)r(ə)l/ ▶ adjective belonging to or occurring on the same side of the body.
– ORIGIN early 20th cent.: formed irregularly from Latin *ipse* 'self' + LATERAL.

ipsissima verba /ɪpˌsɪsɪmə ˈvəːbə/ ▶ plural noun the precise words.
– ORIGIN Latin.

ipso facto /ˌɪpsəʊ ˈfaktəʊ/ ▶ adverb by that very fact or act: *the enemy of one's enemy may be ipso facto a friend*.
– ORIGIN Latin.

Ipswich /ˈɪpswɪtʃ/ the county town of Suffolk, a port and industrial town on the estuary of the River Orwell; pop. 115,500 (1991).

Ipswichian /ɪpˈswɪtʃɪən/ ▶ adjective of, relating to, or denoting the most recent interglacial period of the Pleistocene in Britain, preceding the Devensian glaciation and identified with the Eemian of northern Europe.
  ■ [as noun **the Ipswichian**] the Ipswichian interglacial or the system of deposits laid down during it.

IQ ▶ abbreviation for intelligence quotient.

Iqbal /ˈɪkbal/, Sir Muhammad (1875–1938), Indian poet and philosopher, generally regarded as the father of Pakistan. As president of the Muslim League in 1930, he advocated the creation of a separate Muslim state in NW India; the demands of the League led ultimately to the establishment of Pakistan in 1947.

-ique ▶ suffix archaic spelling of -IC.

Iquitos /ɪˈkiːtɒs/ a city in NE Peru, a river port on the west bank of the Amazon; pop. 274,700 (1992).

IR ▶ abbreviation for ■ infrared. ■ Iran (international vehicle registration).

Ir ▶ symbol for the chemical element iridium.

ir- ▶ prefix variant spelling of IN-¹, IN-² assimilated before r (as in *irradiate*, *irrelative*).

IRA ▶ abbreviation for ■ (in the US) Individual Retirement Account. ■ Irish Republican Army.

irade /ɪˈrɑːdi/ ▶ noun historical a written decree of the sultan of Turkey.
– ORIGIN Turkish, from Arabic *'irāda* 'will, decree', from *'arāda* 'intend'.

Iráklion /ɪˈrɑːklɪɒn/ Greek name for HERAKLION.

Iran /ɪˈrɑːn, ɪˈran/ a country in the Middle East, between the Caspian Sea and the Persian Gulf; pop. 54,600,000 (est. 1990); languages, Farsi (Persian) (official), Azerbaijani, Kurdish, Arabic, and others; capital, Tehran.

Previously known as Persia, the country adopted the name Iran in 1935. Iran was a monarchy until 1979, when the shah was overthrown in a popular uprising, headed by Ayatollah Khomeini, which led soon after to the establishment of an Islamic republic. From 1980 to 1988 Iran was at war with its neighbour Iraq. See also PERSIA.

Irangate /ɪˈrɑːngeɪt, ɪˈran-/ a US political scandal of 1987 involving the covert sale by the US of arms to Iran. The proceeds of the arms sales were used by officials to give arms to the anti-communist Contras in Nicaragua, despite Congressional prohibition. Also called IRAN–CONTRA AFFAIR.

Iranian ▶ adjective relating to Iran or its people.
  ■ relating to or denoting the group of Indo-European languages that includes Persian (Farsi), Pashto, Avestan, and Kurdish.
  ▶ noun a native or national of Iran, or a person of Iranian descent.

Iran–Iraq War the war of 1980–8 between Iran and Iraq in the general area of the Persian Gulf. It ended inconclusively after great hardship and loss of life on both sides. Also called GULF WAR.

Iraq /ɪˈrɑːk, ɪˈrak/ a country in the Middle East, on the Persian Gulf; pop. 17,583,450 (est. 1988); official language, Arabic; capital, Baghdad.

Iraq is traversed by the Tigris and Euphrates Rivers, whose valley was the site of the ancient civilizations of Mesopotamia. It was conquered by Arabia in the 7th century and from 1534 formed part of the Ottoman Empire. After the First World War a kingdom was established, although the country was under British administration until 1932. Saddam Hussein came to power as President in 1979. From 1980 to 1988 the country was at war with its eastern neighbour Iran. In 1990 Iraq invaded Kuwait; it was repelled by an international coalition of forces in the Gulf War of 1991. In 1998 the country was bombed by US and UK aircraft in response to its refusal to cooperate with UN weapons inspectors.

Iraqi ▶ adjective of or relating to Iraq, its people, or their language.
  ▶ noun (pl. **Iraqis**) **1** a native or national of Iraq, or a person of Iraqi descent.
  2 [mass noun] the form of Arabic spoken in Iraq.

IRAS a satellite launched in 1983 to map the distribution of infrared radiation in the sky.
– ORIGIN abbreviation of *Infrared Astronomical Satellite*.

irascible /ɪˈrasɪb(ə)l/ ▶ adjective (of a person) easily made angry.
  ■ characterized by or arising from anger.
– DERIVATIVES **irascibility** noun, **irascibly** adverb.
– ORIGIN late Middle English: via French from late Latin *irascibilis*, from Latin *irasci* 'grow angry', from *ira* 'anger'.

irate /aɪˈreɪt/ ▶ adjective feeling or characterized by great anger: *a barrage of irate letters*.
– DERIVATIVES **irately** adverb, **irateness** noun.
– ORIGIN mid 19th cent.: from Latin *iratus*, from *ira* 'anger'.

IRBM ▶ abbreviation for intermediate-range ballistic missile.

IRC ▶ abbreviation for Internet Relay Chat, an area of the network where users can communicate interactively with each other.

ire /ˈaɪə/ ▶ noun [mass noun] anger: *the plans provoked the ire of conservationists*.
– DERIVATIVES **ireful** adjective.
– ORIGIN Middle English: via Old French from Latin *ira*.

Ireland an island of the British Isles, lying west of Great Britain. Approximately four fifths of the area of Ireland forms the Republic of Ireland, with the remaining one fifth forming Northern Ireland.

Ireland was inhabited by Celts from about the 6th century BC. English invasions began in the 12th century under Henry II, although the whole of the island was not conquered until the time of the Tudors. Revolts against English rule led to English and Scottish families being settled on confiscated land; in parts of Ulster the descendants of Protestant settlers form a majority. After an unsuccessful rebellion in 1798, union of Britain and Ireland followed in 1801. In 1921 Ireland was partitioned by the Anglo-Irish Treaty.

Ireland, Republic of a country comprising approximately four fifths of Ireland; pop. 3,523,400

(1991); languages, Irish (official), English; capital, Dublin. Also called **IRISH REPUBLIC**.

The Anglo-Irish Treaty by which Ireland was partitioned in 1921 gave southern Ireland dominion status as the Irish Free State. The treaty was followed by civil war between the Free State government and republicans, led by Eamon de Valera, who rejected partition. The war ended in victory for the government in 1923. A new constitution as a sovereign state (Eire) was adopted in 1937. Eire remained neutral during the Second World War; in 1949 it left the Commonwealth and became fully independent as the Republic of Ireland. The Republic of Ireland joined the EC in 1973.

Irenaeus, St /ˌʌɪrɪˈniːəs/ (*c.*130–*c.*200 AD), Greek theologian, the author of *Against Heresies* (*c.*180), a detailed attack on Gnosticism. Feast day (in the Eastern Church) 23 August; (in the Western Church) 28 June.

irenic /ʌɪˈrɛnɪk, -ˈriː-/ (also **eirenic**) ▶ **adjective** formal aiming or aimed at peace.
▶ **noun** (**irenics**) a part of Christian theology concerned with reconciling different denominations and sects.
– DERIVATIVES **irenical** adjective.
– ORIGIN mid 19th cent.: from Greek *eirēnikos*, from *eirēnē* 'peace'. Compare with **EIRENICON**.

irenicon ▶ **noun** variant spelling of **EIRENICON**.

Irgun /ɪəˈɡʊn/ a right-wing Zionist organization founded in 1931. During the period when it was active (1937–48) it carried out violent attacks on Arabs and Britons in its campaign to establish a Jewish state; it was disbanded after the creation of Israel in 1948.
– ORIGIN from modern Hebrew *'irgūn (sĕḇā'ī lĕ'ummī)* '(national military) organization'.

Irian Jaya /ˌɪrɪən ˈdʒʌɪə/ a province of eastern Indonesia comprising the western half of the island of New Guinea together with the adjacent small islands; capital, Jayapura. Until its incorporation into Indonesia in 1963 it was known as Dutch New Guinea. Also called **WEST IRIAN**.

iridaceous /ˌʌɪrɪˈdeɪʃəs, ˌɪrɪ-/ ▶ **adjective** Botany of, relating to, or denoting plants of the iris family (Iridaceae), which grow from bulbs, corms, or rhizomes.
– ORIGIN mid 19th cent.: from modern Latin *Iridaceae* (plural), based on Greek *iris, irid-* 'rainbow', + **-OUS**.

iridectomy /ˌʌɪrɪˈdɛktəmi, ˌɪrɪ-/ ▶ **noun** (pl. **-ies**) a surgical procedure to remove part of the iris.

iridescent /ˌɪrɪˈdɛs(ə)nt/ ▶ **adjective** showing luminous colours that seem to change when seen from different angles.
– DERIVATIVES **iridescence** noun, **iridescently** adverb.
– ORIGIN late 18th cent.: from Latin *iris, irid-* 'rainbow' + **-ESCENT**.

iridium /ɪˈrɪdɪəm, ʌɪ-/ ▶ **noun** [mass noun] the chemical element of atomic number 77, a hard, dense silvery-white metal. (Symbol: **Ir**)
– ORIGIN early 19th cent.: modern Latin, from Latin *iris, irid-* 'rainbow' (so named because it forms compounds of various colours).

iridology /ˌʌɪrɪˈdɒlədʒi, ˌɪrɪ-/ ▶ **noun** [mass noun] (in alternative medicine) diagnosis by examination of the iris of the eye.
– DERIVATIVES **iridologist** noun.
– ORIGIN early 20th cent.: from Greek *iris, irid-* 'iris' + **-LOGY**.

irie /ˈʌɪriː/ black English ▶ **adjective** nice, good, or pleasing (used as a general term of approval): *the place is jumping with irie vibes | I feeling irie.*
▶ **exclamation** used by Rastafarians as a friendly greeting.
– ORIGIN perhaps representing a pronunciation of *all right*.

Iris Greek Mythology the goddess of the rainbow, who acted as a messenger of the gods.

iris ▶ **noun 1** a flat, coloured, ring-shaped membrane behind the cornea of the eye, with an adjustable circular opening (pupil) in the centre.
■ (also **iris diaphragm**) an adjustable diaphragm of thin overlapping plates for regulating the size of a central hole, especially for the admission of light to a lens.
2 a plant with showy flowers, typically of purple or yellow, and sword-shaped leaves. They are native to both Eurasia and North America and widely cultivated as ornamentals.
• Genus *Iris*, family Iridaceae (the **iris family**): many species and numerous hybrids. The iris family also includes the gladioli, crocuses, and freesias.
▶ **verb** [no obj., with adverbial of direction] (of an aperture, typically that of a lens) open or close in the manner of an iris or iris diaphragm.
– ORIGIN modern Latin, via Latin from Greek *iris* 'rainbow, iris'.

irised ▶ **adjective** poetic/literary coloured like a rainbow; iridescent.

Irish ▶ **adjective** of or relating to Ireland, its people, or the Celtic language traditionally and historically spoken there.
■ offensive (of a statement or action) paradoxical; illogical or apparently so.
▶ **noun** [mass noun] **1** (also **Irish Gaelic**) the Celtic language of Ireland.
2 [as plural noun **the Irish**] the people of Ireland; Irish people collectively.

Irish is now spoken regularly only in a few isolated areas in the west of Ireland, having elsewhere been displaced by English. It is, however, the first official language of the Republic of Ireland and is taught in all state schools. Scottish Gaelic was descended from it.

– DERIVATIVES **Irishness** noun.
– ORIGIN Middle English: from Old English *Īr-* (stem of *Īras* 'the Irish' and *Īrland* 'Ireland', obscurely related to **HIBERNIAN**) + **-ISH**[1].

Irish coffee ▶ **noun** [mass noun] coffee mixed with a dash of Irish whiskey and served with cream on top.

Irish elk ▶ **noun** an extinct giant European and North African deer of the Pleistocene epoch, with massive antlers up to 3 m (10 ft) across. Also called **GIANT DEER**.
• *Megaloceros giganteus*, family Cervidae.

Irish Free State the name for southern Ireland from 1921 until 1937 (see **IRELAND, REPUBLIC OF**).

Irishman ▶ **noun** (pl. **-men**) a male native or national of Ireland, or a man of Irish descent.

Irish moss ▶ **noun** another term for **CARRAGEEN**.

Irish National Liberation Army (abbrev.: **INLA**) a small paramilitary organization seeking union between Northern Ireland and the Republic of Ireland. It was formed in the early 1970s, probably as an offshoot of the Provisional IRA.

Irish Republic see **IRELAND, REPUBLIC OF**.

Irish Republican Army (abbrev.: **IRA**) the military arm of Sinn Fein, aiming for union between the Republic of Ireland and Northern Ireland.

The IRA was formed during the struggle for independence from Britain in 1916–21; in 1969 it split into Official and Provisional wings. The Official IRA became virtually inactive, while the Provisional IRA stepped up the level of violence against military and civilian targets in Northern Ireland, Britain, and Europe. The IRA declared a ceasefire in 1994 and another in 1997.

Irish Republican Brotherhood see **FENIAN**.

Irish Sea the sea separating Ireland from England and Wales.

Irish setter ▶ **noun** a dog of a breed of setter with a long, silky dark red coat and a long feathered tail.

Irish stew ▶ **noun** [mass noun] a stew made with mutton, potatoes, and onions.

Irish Sweepstake (also **Irish Sweep**) a sweepstake on the results of certain major horse races, authorized since 1930 by the government of the Republic of Ireland in order to benefit Irish hospitals. It is the largest international lottery.

Irish terrier ▶ **noun** a terrier of a rough-haired light reddish-brown breed.

Irish wolfhound ▶ **noun** a large, typically greyish hound of a rough-coated breed.

Irishwoman ▶ **noun** (pl. **-women**) a female native or national or Ireland, or a woman of Irish descent.

iritis /ʌɪˈrʌɪtɪs/ ▶ **noun** [mass noun] Medicine inflammation of the iris of the eye.

irk /əːk/ ▶ **verb** [with obj.] irritate; annoy: *it irks her to think of the runaround she received.*
– ORIGIN Middle English (in the sense 'be annoyed or disgusted'): perhaps from Old Norse *yrkja* 'to work'.

irksome ▶ **adjective** irritating; annoying.
– DERIVATIVES **irksomely** adverb, **irksomeness** noun.

Irkutsk /ɪəˈkʊtsk/ the chief city of Siberia, situated on the western shore of Lake Baikal in eastern Russia; pop. 635,000 (1990).

IRL ▶ **abbreviation** for the Republic of Ireland (international vehicle registration).

IRO ▶ **abbreviation** for ■ (in the UK) Inland Revenue Office. ■ International Refugee Organization.

iroko /ɪˈrəʊkəʊ, iː-/ ▶ **noun** (pl. **-os**) a tropical African tree which yields pale timber that is sometimes used as an oak or teak substitute.
• Genus *Chlorophora*, family Moraceae: several species, in particular *C. excelsa*.
– ORIGIN late 19th cent.: from Yoruba.

iron ▶ **noun 1** [mass noun] a strong, hard magnetic silvery-grey metal, the chemical element of atomic number 26, much used as a material for construction and manufacturing, especially in the form of steel. (Symbol: **Fe**)
■ used figuratively as a symbol or type of firmness, strength, or resistance: *her father had a will of iron* | [as modifier] *the iron grip of religion on minority cultures.*

Iron is widely distributed as ores such as haematite, magnetite, and siderite, and the earth's core is believed to consist largely of metallic iron and nickel. Besides steel, other important forms of the metal are cast iron and wrought iron. Chemically a transition element, iron is a constituent of some biological molecules, notably haemoglobin.

2 a tool or implement now or originally made of iron: *a caulking iron.*
■ (**irons**) fetters or handcuffs. ■ (**irons**) metal supports for a malformed leg. ■ (**irons**) informal stirrups.
3 a hand-held implement with a flat steel base which is heated (typically with electricity) to smooth clothes, sheets, etc.
4 a golf club with a metal head (typically with a numeral indicating the degree to which the head is angled in order to loft the ball).
■ a shot made with such a club.
5 Astronomy a meteorite containing a high proportion of iron.
▶ **verb** [with obj.] smooth (clothes, sheets, etc.) with an iron.
– PHRASES **have many** (or **other**) **irons in the fire** have many (or a range of) options or courses of action available or be involved in many activities or commitments at the same time. **in irons 1** having the feet or hands fettered. **2** (of a sailing vessel) stalled head to wind and unable to come about or tack either way. **iron hand** (or **fist**) used to refer to firmness or ruthlessness of attitude or behaviour: *Fascism's iron hand.* **an iron hand** (or **fist**) **in a velvet glove** firmness or ruthlessness cloaked in outward gentleness.
– DERIVATIVES **ironer** noun, **iron-like** adjective.
– ORIGIN Old English *īren, īsen, īsern*, of Germanic origin; related to Dutch *ijzer* and German *Eisen*, and probably ultimately from Celtic.
▶ **iron something out** remove creases from clothes, sheets, etc. by ironing. ■ figurative solve or settle difficulties or problems: *they had ironed out their differences.*

Iron Age a prehistoric period that followed the Bronze Age, when weapons and tools came to be made of iron.

The Iron Age is conventionally taken as beginning in the early 1st millennium BC, but iron-working began with the Hittites in Anatolia in *c.*1400 BC. Its arrival in Britain was associated with the first Celtic immigrants in about the 6th century BC. In much of Europe it ended at the Roman period, but outside the Roman Empire it continued to the 4th–6th centuries AD.

ironbark ▶ **noun** an Australian eucalyptus tree with thick, solid bark and hard, dense, durable timber.
• Genus *Eucalyptus*, family Myrtaceae: several species, including the **grey ironbark** (*E. paniculata*).

iron-bound ▶ **adjective** bound with iron: *an old iron-bound chest.*
■ rigorous; inflexible: *the iron-bound rules concerning the release of classified information.* ■ archaic (of a coast) faced or enclosed with rocks.

Iron Chancellor see **BISMARCK**[2].

ironclad ▶ **adjective** covered or protected with iron.
■ impossible to contradict, weaken, or change: *an ironclad guarantee.*
▶ **noun** historical a 19th-century warship with armour plating.

Iron Cross ▶ **noun** the highest German military decoration for bravery, instituted in 1813.

Iron Curtain ▶ **noun** (**the Iron Curtain**) a notional barrier separating the former Soviet bloc and the West prior to the decline of communism that followed the political events in eastern Europe in 1989.

Iron Duke see **WELLINGTON**[2].

Iron Gate a gorge through which a section of the River Danube flows, forming part of the boundary between Romania and Serbia. Navigation was improved by means of a ship canal constructed through it in 1896. Romanian name **PORȚILE DE FIER**, Serbo-Croat name **GVOZDENA VRATA**.

iron grey ▶ noun [mass noun] a dark grey colour.
■ [count noun] a horse of this colour.

Iron Guard a fascist Romanian political party that was founded in 1927 and ceased to exist after the Second World War.

iron horse ▶ noun poetic/literary a steam railway locomotive.

ironic /ʌɪˈrɒnɪk/ ▶ adjective using or characterized by irony: *his mouth curved into an ironic smile.*
■ happening in the opposite way to what is expected, and typically causing wry amusement because of this: [with clause] *it was ironic that now everybody had plenty of money for food they couldn't obtain it because everything was rationed.*
– DERIVATIVES **ironical** adjective.
– ORIGIN mid 17th cent.: from French *ironique* or late Latin *ironicus*, from Greek *eirōnikos* 'dissembling, feigning ignorance', from *eirōneia* (see **IRONY**[1]).

ironically ▶ adverb in an ironic manner.
■ used to denote a paradoxical, unexpected, or coincidental situation: [sentence adverb] *ironically, the rescue craft which saved her was the boat she was helping to pay for.*

ironing ▶ noun [mass noun] the task of ironing clothes, sheets, etc.
■ clothes, sheets, etc. that need to be or have just been ironed.

ironing board ▶ noun a long, narrow board covered with soft material and having folding legs, on which clothes, sheets, etc. are ironed.

ironist /ˈʌɪr(ə)nɪst/ ▶ noun a person who uses irony.
– ORIGIN early 18th cent.: from Greek *eirōn* 'dissembler' + **-IST**.

ironize /ˈʌɪr(ə)nʌɪz/ (also **-ise**) ▶ verb [with obj.] use ironically: *this novel also follows and yet ironizes many of the conventions of the picaresque narrative.*

Iron Lady the nickname of Margaret Thatcher while she was British Prime Minister.

iron lung ▶ noun a rigid case fitted over a patient's body, used for administering prolonged artificial respiration by means of mechanical pumps.

iron maiden ▶ noun (in historical contexts) an instrument of torture consisting of a coffin-shaped box lined with iron spikes.

iron man ▶ noun (especially in sporting contexts) an exceptionally strong or robust man.
■ [often as modifier] a multi-event sporting contest demanding stamina, in particular a consecutive triathlon of swimming, cycling, and running.

ironmaster ▶ noun a manufacturer of iron, especially (in former times) the proprietor of an ironworks.

ironmonger ▶ noun Brit. a person or shop selling hardware such as tools and household implements.
– DERIVATIVES **ironmongery** noun (pl. **-ies**).

iron mould (US **iron mold**) ▶ noun a spot caused by rust or an ink stain, especially on fabric.

iron-on ▶ adjective [attrib.] able to be fixed to the surface of a fabric by ironing.

iron ore ▶ noun [mass noun] a rock or mineral from which iron can be profitably extracted.

iron pan ▶ noun a hardpan in which iron oxides are the chief cementing agents.

iron pyrites ▶ noun see **PYRITES**.

iron rations ▶ plural noun a small emergency supply of food.

Ironsides a nickname for Oliver Cromwell.
■ [as plural noun] (in the English Civil War) Cromwell's cavalry troopers, so called by their Royalist opponents in allusion to their hardiness in battle.

ironstone ▶ noun [mass noun] **1** sedimentary rock containing a substantial proportion of iron compounds.
2 [usu. as modifier] a kind of dense, opaque stoneware.

ironware ▶ noun [mass noun] articles made of iron, typically domestic implements.

ironwood ▶ noun any of a number of trees that produce very hard timber, in particular:
● a southern African tree of the olive family (*Olea laurifolia*, family Oleaceae). ● a North American tree related to the hornbeam (*Ostrya virginiana*, family Betulaceae).

ironwork ▶ noun [mass noun] things or parts made of iron.

ironworks ▶ noun [treated as sing. or pl.] a place where iron is smelted or iron goods are made.

irony[1] /ˈʌɪrəni/ ▶ noun (pl. **-ies**) [mass noun] the expression of one's meaning by using language that normally signifies the opposite, typically for humorous or emphatic effect: *'Don't go overboard with the gratitude,' he rejoined with heavy irony.*
■ a state of affairs or an event that seems deliberately contrary to what one expects and is often amusing as a result: [with clause] *the irony is that I thought he could help me.* ■ (also **dramatic** or **tragic irony**) a literary technique, originally used in Greek tragedy, by which the full significance of a character's words or actions are clear to the audience or reader although unknown to the character.
– ORIGIN early 16th cent. (also denoting Socratic irony): via Latin from Greek *eirōneia* 'simulated ignorance', from *eirōn* 'dissembler'.

irony[2] /ˈʌɪəni/ ▶ adjective of or like iron: *an irony grey colour.*

Iroquoian ▶ noun [mass noun] a language family of eastern North America, including Cherokee and Mohawk. With the exception of Cherokee, all its members are extinct or nearly so.
▶ adjective of or relating to the Iroquois people or the Iroquoian language family.

Iroquois /ˈɪrəkwɔɪ, -kɔɪ/ ▶ noun (pl. same) **1** a member of a former confederacy of six American Indian peoples (Mohawk, Oneida, Seneca, Onondaga, Cayuga, and Tuscarora) who lived mainly in southern Ontario and Quebec and northern New York State.
2 [mass noun] any of the Iroquoian languages of these peoples.
▶ adjective of or relating to the Iroquois or their languages.
– ORIGIN French, from an Algonquian language.

IRQ ▶ abbreviation for Iraq (international vehicle registration).

irradiance ▶ noun [mass noun] **1** Physics the flux of radiant energy per unit area (normal to the direction of flow of radiant energy through a medium).
2 poetic/literary the fact of shining brightly.

irradiant ▶ adjective poetic/literary shining brightly.
– ORIGIN early 16th cent.: from Latin *irradiant-* 'shining upon', from the verb *irradiare* (based on *radius* 'ray').

irradiate ▶ verb [with obj.] **1** (often **be irradiated**) expose to radiation.
■ expose (food) to gamma rays to kill microorganisms.
2 illuminate (something) by or as if by shining light on it: *sunlight streamed down through stained glass, irradiating the faces of family and friends.*
– ORIGIN late 16th cent. (in the sense 'emit rays, shine upon'): from Latin *irradiat-* 'shone upon', from the verb *irradiare*, from *in-* 'upon' + *radiare* 'to shine' (from *radius* 'ray').

irradiation ▶ noun [mass noun] **1** the process or fact of irradiating or being irradiated.
2 Optics the apparent extension of the edges of an illuminated object seen against a dark background.

irrational ▶ adjective **1** not logical or reasonable.
■ not endowed with the power of reason.
2 Mathematics (of a number, quantity, or expression) not expressible as a ratio of two integers, and having an infinite and non-recurring expansion when expressed as a decimal. Examples of irrational numbers are the number π and the square root of 2.
– DERIVATIVES **irrationality** noun, **irrationalize** (also **-ise**) verb, **irrationally** adverb.
– ORIGIN late Middle English: from Latin *irrationalis*, from *in-* 'not' + *rationalis* (see **RATIONAL**).

irrationalism ▶ noun [mass noun] a system of belief or action that disregards or contradicts rational principles.
– DERIVATIVES **irrationalist** noun & adjective.

Irrawaddy /ˌɪrəˈwɒdi/ the principal river of Burma (Myanmar), 2,090 km (1,300 miles) long. It flows in a large delta into the eastern part of the Bay of Bengal.

irrebuttable /ˌɪrɪˈbʌtəb(ə)l/ ▶ adjective unable to be rebutted.

irreclaimable ▶ adjective not able to be reclaimed or reformed.

– DERIVATIVES **irreclaimably** adverb.

irreconcilable ▶ adjective (of ideas, facts, or statements) representing findings or points of view that are so different from each other that they cannot be made compatible: *these two views of the early medieval economy are irreconcilable.*
■ (of people) implacably hostile to each other.
▶ noun (usu. **irreconcilables**) any of two or more ideas, facts, or statements that cannot be made compatible.
– DERIVATIVES **irreconcilability** noun, **irreconcilably** adverb.

irrecoverable ▶ adjective not able to be recovered, regained, or remedied: *his liquid assets had to be written off as irrecoverable.*
– DERIVATIVES **irrecoverably** adverb.

irrecusable /ˌɪrɪˈkjuːzəb(ə)l/ ▶ adjective rare (of evidence or a statement) not able to be challenged or rejected.
– ORIGIN late 18th cent.: via French from late Latin *irrecusabilis*, from *in-* 'not' + *recusabilis* 'that should be refused' (from the verb *recusare*).

irredeemable ▶ adjective **1** not able to be saved, improved, or corrected: *so many irredeemable mistakes have been made.*
2 (of securities) on which no date is given for repayment of the capital sum.
– DERIVATIVES **irredeemability** /-ˈbɪlɪti/ noun, **irredeemably** adverb.

irredentist /ˌɪrɪˈdɛntɪst/ ▶ noun [usu. as modifier] a person advocating the restoration to their country of any territory formerly belonging to it.
■ historical (in 19th-century Italian politics) an advocate of the return to Italy of all Italian-speaking districts subject to other countries.
– DERIVATIVES **irredentism** noun.
– ORIGIN from Italian *irredentista*, from (*Italia*) *irredenta* 'unredeemed (Italy)'.

irreducible ▶ adjective not able to be reduced or simplified.
■ not able to be brought to a certain form or condition: *the imagery remains irreducible to textual structures.*
– DERIVATIVES **irreducibility** noun, **irreducibly** adverb.

irreflexive /ˌɪrɪˈflɛksɪv/ ▶ adjective Logic denoting a relation which never holds between a term and itself.

irreformable ▶ adjective (chiefly of religious dogma) unable to be revised or altered.

irrefragable /ɪˈrɛfrəɡəb(ə)l/ ▶ adjective not able to be refuted or disproved; indisputable.
– DERIVATIVES **irrefragably** adverb.
– ORIGIN mid 16th cent.: from late Latin *irrefragabilis*, from *in-* 'not' + *refragari* 'oppose'.

irrefutable /ɪˈrɛfjʊtəb(ə)l, ˌɪrɪˈfjuː-/ ▶ adjective impossible to deny or disprove: *irrefutable evidence.*
– DERIVATIVES **irrefutability** noun, **irrefutably** adverb.
– ORIGIN early 17th cent.: from late Latin *irrefutabilis*, from *in-* 'not' + *refutabilis* (from *refutare* 'repel, rebut').

irregardless ▶ adjective & adverb informal regardless.
– ORIGIN early 20th cent.: probably a blend of **IRRESPECTIVE** and **REGARDLESS**.

irregular ▶ adjective **1** not even or balanced in shape or arrangement: *her features were too irregular.*
■ occurring at uneven or varying rates or intervals: *an irregular heartbeat.* ■ Botany (of a flower) having the petals differing in size and shape; zygomorphic.
2 contrary to the rules or to that which is normal or established: *they were questioned about their involvement in irregular financial dealings.*
■ [attrib.] (of troops) not belonging to regular or established army units. ■ Grammar (of a verb or other word) having inflections that do not conform to the usual rules.
▶ noun (usu. **irregulars**) **1** a member of an irregular military force.
2 chiefly US an imperfect piece of merchandise sold at a reduced price.
– DERIVATIVES **irregularly** adverb.
– ORIGIN late Middle English (in the sense 'not conforming to rule (especially of the Church)'): via Old French from medieval Latin *irregularis*, from *in-* 'not' + *regularis* (see **REGULAR**).

irregularity ▶ noun (pl. **-ies**) [mass noun] the state or quality of being irregular: *there is evidence that fraud and irregularity continue on a large scale.*

■[count noun] (usu. **irregularities**) a thing that is irregular in form or nature: *irregularities of the heartbeat* | *financial irregularities*.
– ORIGIN Middle English: from Old French *irregularite*, from late Latin *irregularitas*, from *irregularis* (see **IRREGULAR**).

irrelative ▶ adjective rare unconnected; unrelated.
■irrelevant.
– DERIVATIVES **irrelatively** adverb.

irrelevant ▶ adjective not connected with or relevant to something.
– DERIVATIVES **irrelevance** noun, **irrelevancy** noun (pl. **-ies**), **irrelevantly** adverb.

irreligious ▶ adjective indifferent or hostile to religion: *an irreligious world.*
– DERIVATIVES **irreligion** noun, **irreligiously** adverb, **irreligiousness** noun.
– ORIGIN late Middle English: from Latin *irreligiosus*, from *in-* 'not' + *religiosus* (see **RELIGIOUS**).

irremediable /ˌɪrɪˈmiːdɪəb(ə)l/ ▶ adjective impossible to cure or put right.
– DERIVATIVES **irremediably** adverb.
– ORIGIN late Middle English: from Latin *irremediabilis*, from *in-* 'not' + *remediabilis* 'curable' (from *remedium* 'remedy').

irremissible ▶ adjective **1** (of a crime) unpardonable.
2 (of an obligation or duty) binding.
– ORIGIN late Middle English: from Old French, or from ecclesiastical Latin *irremissibilis*, from *in-* 'not' + *remissibilis* (from *remittere* 'remit').

irremovable ▶ adjective incapable of being removed: *the irremovable taint of corruption.*
■(of an official) unable to be displaced from office.
– DERIVATIVES **irremovability** noun, **irremovably** adverb.

irreparable /ɪˈrɛp(ə)rəb(ə)l/ ▶ adjective (of an injury or loss) impossible to rectify or repair: *they were doing irreparable damage to my heart and lungs.*
– DERIVATIVES **irreparability** /-ˈbɪlɪti/ noun, **irreparably** adverb.
– ORIGIN late Middle English: via Old French from Latin *irreparabilis*, from *in-* 'not' + *reparabilis* (see **REPARABLE**).

irreplaceable ▶ adjective impossible to replace if lost or damaged.
– DERIVATIVES **irreplaceably** adverb.

irrepressible ▶ adjective not able to be controlled or restrained: *a great shout of irrepressible laughter.*
– DERIVATIVES **irrepressibility** noun, **irrepressibly** adverb.

irreproachable ▶ adjective beyond criticism; faultless: *his private life was irreproachable.*
– DERIVATIVES **irreproachability** noun, **irreproachably** adverb.
– ORIGIN mid 17th cent.: from French *irreprochable*, from *in-* 'not' + *reprochable* (from *reprocher* 'to reproach').

irreproducible ▶ adjective not reproducible.

irresistible ▶ adjective too attractive and tempting to be resisted: *he found the delicious-looking cakes irresistible.*
■too powerful or convincing to be resisted: *she felt an irresistible urge to object.*
– DERIVATIVES **irresistibility** noun, **irresistibly** adverb.
– ORIGIN late 16th cent.: from medieval Latin *irresistibilis*, from *in-* 'not' + *resistibilis* (from *resistere* 'resist').

irresoluble /ˌɪrɪˈzɒljʊb(ə)l/ ▶ adjective unable to be resolved.
– ORIGIN mid 17th cent.: from Latin *irresolubilis* 'indissoluble'.

irresolute ▶ adjective showing or feeling hesitancy; uncertain: *she stood irresolute outside his door.*
– DERIVATIVES **irresolutely** adverb, **irresoluteness** noun, **irresolution** noun.
– ORIGIN late 16th cent.: from Latin *irresolutus* 'not loosened', or from **IN-**[1] 'not' + **RESOLUTE**.

irresolvable ▶ adjective (of a problem or dilemma) impossible to solve or settle.

irrespective ▶ adjective [predic.] (**irrespective of**) not taking (something) into account; regardless of: *child benefit is paid irrespective of income levels.*
– DERIVATIVES **irrespectively** adverb.

irresponsible ▶ adjective (of a person, attitude, or action) not showing a proper sense of

responsibility: [with infinitive] *it would have been irresponsible just to drive on.*
– DERIVATIVES **irresponsibility** noun, **irresponsibly** adverb.

irresponsive ▶ adjective not responsive to someone or something.
– DERIVATIVES **irresponsiveness** noun.

irretrievable ▶ adjective not able to be retrieved or put right: *the irretrievable breakdown of their marriage.*
– DERIVATIVES **irretrievability** noun, **irretrievably** adverb.

irreverent /ɪˈrɛv(ə)r(ə)nt/ ▶ adjective showing a lack of respect for people or things that are generally taken seriously: *she is irreverent about the whole business of politics.*
– DERIVATIVES **irreverence** noun, **irreverential** adjective, **irreverently** adverb.
– ORIGIN late Middle English: from Latin *irreverent-* 'not revering', from *in-* 'not' + *reverent-* 'revering' (see **REVERENT**).

irreversible ▶ adjective not able to be undone or altered: *she suffered irreversible damage to her health.*
– DERIVATIVES **irreversibility** noun, **irreversibly** adverb.

irreversible binomial ▶ noun Grammar a noun phrase consisting of two nouns joined by a conjunction, in which the conventional order is fixed. Examples include *bread and butter* and *kith and kin.*

irrevocable /ɪˈrɛvəkəb(ə)l/ ▶ adjective not able to be changed, reversed, or recovered; final: *an irrevocable step.*
– DERIVATIVES **irrevocability** noun, **irrevocably** adverb.
– ORIGIN late Middle English: from Old French, or from Latin *irrevocabilis*, from *in-* 'not' + *revocabilis* 'able to be revoked' (from the verb *revocare*).

irrigate /ˈɪrɪgeɪt/ ▶ verb [with obj.] supply water to (land or crops) to help growth, typically by means of channels.
■(of a river or stream) supply (land) with water. **■** figurative refresh or make fruitful: *wine irrigated the vast areas of his knowledge.* **■** Medicine apply a continuous flow of water or medication to (an organ or wound).
– DERIVATIVES **irrigable** adjective, **irrigation** noun, **irrigator** noun.
– ORIGIN early 17th cent.: from Latin *irrigat-* 'moistened', from the verb *irrigare*, from *in-* 'into' + *rigare* 'moisten, wet'.

irritable ▶ adjective having or showing a tendency to be easily annoyed or made angry: *she was tired and irritable.*
■Medicine (of a bodily part or organ) abnormally sensitive. **■** Medicine (of a condition) caused by such sensitivity. **■** Biology (of a living organism) having the property of responding actively to physical stimuli.
– DERIVATIVES **irritability** noun, **irritably** adverb.
– ORIGIN mid 17th cent.: from Latin *irritabilis*, from the verb *irritare* (see **IRRITATE**).

irritable bowel syndrome (abbrev.: **IBS**) ▶ noun [mass noun] a widespread condition involving recurrent abdominal pain and diarrhoea or constipation, often associated with stress, depression, anxiety, or previous intestinal infection.

irritant ▶ noun a substance that causes slight inflammation or other discomfort to the body.
■figurative a thing that is continually annoying or distracting: *in 1966 Vietnam was becoming an irritant to the government.*
▶ adjective causing slight inflammation or other discomfort to the body.
– DERIVATIVES **irritancy** noun.

irritate ▶ verb [with obj.] make (someone) annoyed, impatient, or angry: *his tone irritated her* | [as adj.] **irritating** *highly irritating remarks.*
■cause inflammation or other discomfort in (a part of the body). **■** Biology stimulate (an organism, cell, or organ) to produce an active response.
– DERIVATIVES **irritatedly** adverb, **irritatingly** adverb, **irritative** adjective, **irritator** noun.
– ORIGIN mid 16th cent. (in the sense 'excite, provoke'): from Latin *irritat-* 'irritated', from the verb *irritare.*

irritation ▶ noun [mass noun] the state of feeling annoyed, impatient, or angry.
■[count noun] a cause of this: *the minor irritations of life.* **■** the production of inflammation or other discomfort in a bodily part or organ. **■** Biology the

stimulation of an organism, cell, or organ to produce an active response.
– ORIGIN late Middle English: from Latin *irritatio(n-)*, from the verb *irritare* (see **IRRITATE**).

irrotational /ˌɪrəʊˈteɪʃ(ə)n(ə)l/ ▶ adjective Physics (especially of fluid motion) not rotational; having no rotation.

irrupt /ɪˈrʌpt/ ▶ verb [no obj.] enter forcibly or suddenly: *the spectre of social revolution once again irrupted into a confident capitalist world.*
■(of a bird or other animal) migrate into an area in abnormally large numbers.
– DERIVATIVES **irruption** noun, **irruptive** adjective.
– ORIGIN mid 19th cent.: from Latin *irrupt-* 'broken into', from the verb *irrumpere*, from *in-* 'into' + *rumpere* 'break'.

IRS ▶ abbreviation for (in the US) Internal Revenue Service.

Irtysh /ɪəˈtɪʃ/ a river of central Asia, which rises in the Altai Mountains in northern China and flows westwards into NE Kazakhstan, where it turns north-west into Russia, joining the River Ob near its mouth. Its length is 4,248 km (2,655 miles).

Irving[1] /ˈəːvɪŋ/, Sir Henry (1838–1905), English actor-manager; born *John Henry Brodribb*. He managed the Lyceum Theatre from 1878 to 1902, during which period he entered into a celebrated acting partnership with Ellen Terry.

Irving[2] /ˈəːvɪŋ/, Washington (1783–1859), American writer. He is best known for *The Sketch Book of Geoffrey Crayon, Gent* (1819–20), which contains such tales as 'Rip Van Winkle' and 'The Legend of Sleepy Hollow'.

Irvingite ▶ noun a member of the Catholic Apostolic Church, which followed the teachings of Edward Irving (1792–1834), who was originally a minister of the Church of Scotland.

IS ▶ abbreviation for Iceland (international vehicle registration).
– ORIGIN from Icelandic *Ísland.*

Is. ▶ abbreviation for **■** (also **Isa.**) Isaiah (in biblical references). **■** Island(s). **■** Isle(s).

is third person singular present of **BE**.

ISA ▶ abbreviation for **■** (in the UK) individual savings account, a scheme allowing individuals to hold shares, unit trusts, and cash free of tax on dividends, interest, and capital gains; in 1999 it replaced both personal equity plans (PEPs) and tax-exempt special savings accounts (TESSAs). **■** Computing industry standard architecture, a standard for connecting computers and their peripherals: [as modifier] *an ISA expansion slot.*

Isaac /ˈʌɪzək/ (in the Bible) a Hebrew patriarch, son of Abraham and Sarah and father of Jacob and Esau.

Isabella I (1451–1504), queen of Castile 1474–1504 and of Aragon 1479–1504. Her marriage in 1469 to Ferdinand of Aragon helped to join together the Christian kingdoms of Castile and Aragon, marking the beginning of the unification of Spain. They instituted the Spanish Inquisition (1478) and supported Columbus's famous expedition of 1492.

Isabella of France (1292–1358), daughter of Philip IV of France and wife of Edward II of England (1308–27). After returning to France in 1325, she organized an invasion of England in 1326 with her lover Roger de Mortimer, murdering Edward and replacing him with her son, Edward III. Edward took control in 1330, executing Mortimer and sending Isabella into retirement.

isagogics /ˌʌɪsəˈɡɒdʒɪks/ ▶ plural noun [treated as sing.] introductory study, especially of the literary and external history of the Bible prior to exegesis.
– DERIVATIVES **isagogic** adjective.
– ORIGIN mid 19th cent.: plural of *isagogic*, via Latin from Greek *eisagōgikos*, from *eisagōgē* 'introduction', from *eis* 'into' + *agein* 'to lead'.

Isaiah /ʌɪˈzʌɪə/ a major Hebrew prophet of Judah in the 8th century BC, who taught the supremacy of the God of Israel and emphasized the moral demands on worshippers.
■a book of the Bible containing his prophecies (and, it is generally thought, those of at least one later prophet: see **DEUTERO-ISAIAH**).

isallobar /ʌɪˈsaləʊbaː/ ▶ noun Meteorology a line on a map connecting points at which the barometric pressure has changed by an equal amount during a specified time.

– DERIVATIVES **isallobaric** adjective.
– ORIGIN early 20th cent.: from **ISO-** 'equal' + **ALLO-** 'other' + **BAR**[2].

isangoma /ˌɪsaŋˈɡɔːmɑː/ ▶ **noun** (pl. same or **isangomas**) variant spelling of **SANGOMA**.

isatin /ˈʌɪsətɪn/ ▶ **noun** [mass noun] Chemistry a red crystalline compound used in the manufacture of dyes.
• An indole derivative; chem. formula: $C_8H_5NO_2$.
– ORIGIN mid 19th cent.: from Latin *isatis* 'woad' (from Greek) + **-IN**[1].

ISBN ▶ **abbreviation for** international standard book number, a ten-digit number assigned to every book before publication, recording such details as language, provenance, and publisher.

ischaemia /ɪˈskiːmɪə/ (US **ischemia**) ▶ **noun** [mass noun] Medicine an inadequate blood supply to an organ or part of the body, especially the heart muscles.
– DERIVATIVES **ischaemic** adjective.
– ORIGIN late 19th cent. (denoting the stanching of bleeding): modern Latin, from Greek *iskhaimos* 'stopping blood', from *iskhein* 'keep back' + *haima* 'blood'.

Ischia /ˈɪskɪə/ an island in the Tyrrhenian Sea off the west coast of Italy, about 26 km (16 miles) west of Naples.

ischiorrhogic /ˌɪskɪə(ʊ)ˈrɒdʒɪk/ ▶ **adjective** Prosody (of an iambic line) having a spondee as its second, fourth, or sixth foot.
– ORIGIN mid 19th cent.: from Greek *iskhiorrhōgikos*, literally 'having broken hips, limping', from *iskhion* 'hip joint' + *rhōx, rhōg-* 'broken'.

ischium /ˈɪskɪəm/ ▶ **noun** (pl. **ischia** /-kɪə/) the curved bone forming the base of each half of the pelvis.
– DERIVATIVES **ischial** adjective.
– ORIGIN early 17th cent.: from Latin, from Greek *iskhion* 'hip joint', later 'ischium'.

ISDN ▶ **abbreviation for** integrated services digital network.

Ise /ˈiːseɪ/ a city in central Honshu island, Japan, on Ise Bay; pop. 104,000 (1990). Former name (until 1956) **UJIYAMADA**.

-ise[1] ▶ **suffix** variant spelling of **-IZE**.

> **USAGE** There are some verbs which must be spelled **-ise** and are not variants of the **-ize** ending. Most reflect a French influence; they include **advertise**, **televise**, **compromise**, **enterprise**, and **improvise**. For more details, see **usage** at **-IZE**.

-ise[2] ▶ **suffix** forming nouns of quality, state, or function: *expertise* | *franchise* | *merchandise*.
– ORIGIN from Old French *-ise*, from Latin *-itia*, *-itium*.

isentropic /ˌʌɪsɛnˈtrɒpɪk/ ▶ **adjective** Physics having equal entropy.

isethionic acid /ʌɪˌsiːθɪˈɒnɪk/ ▶ **noun** Chemistry a synthetic crystalline acid with detergent and surfactant properties.
• Alternative name: **2-hydroxyethanesulphonic acid**; chem. formula: $HOCH_2CH_2SO_3H$.
– DERIVATIVES **isethionate** noun.
– ORIGIN mid 19th cent.: *isethionic*, from **ISO-** 'equal' + *eth(er)* + Greek *theion* 'sulphur' + **-IC**.

Iseult /ɪˈzuːlt, ɪˈsuːlt/ a princess in medieval legend. According to one account, she was the sister or daughter of the king of Ireland, the wife of King Mark of Cornwall, and loved by Tristram. In another account, she was the daughter of the king of Brittany and wife of Tristram. Also called **ISOLDE**.

Isfahan /ˌɪsfəˈhɑːn/ (also **Esfahan**, **Ispahan**) an industrial city in central Iran, the country's third largest city; pop. 1,127,000 (1991). It was the capital of Persia from 1598 until 1722.

-ish[1] ▶ **suffix** forming adjectives: **1** (from nouns) having the qualities or characteristics of: *apish* | *girlish*.
▪ of the nationality of: *Swedish*.
2 (from adjectives) somewhat: *yellowish*.
▪ informal denoting an approximate age or time of day: *sixish*.
– ORIGIN Old English *-isc*, of Germanic origin; related to Old Norse *-iskr*, German and Dutch *-isch*, also to Greek *-iskos* (suffix forming diminutive nouns).

-ish[2] ▶ **suffix** forming verbs such as *abolish*, *establish*.
– ORIGIN from French *-iss-* (from stems of verbs ending in *-ir*), from Latin *-isc-* (suffix forming inceptive verbs); compare with **-ISH**[1].

Isherwood /ˈɪʃəwʊd/, Christopher (William Bradshaw) (1904–86), British-born American novelist. Notable novels: *Mr Norris Changes Trains* (1935), *Goodbye to Berlin* (1939; filmed as *Cabaret*, 1972).

Ishiguro /ˌɪʃɪˈɡʊərəʊ/, Kazuo (b.1954), Japanese-born British novelist. Notable novels: *The Remains of the Day* (1989).

Ishihara test /ɪʃɪˈhɑːrə/ ▶ **noun** a test for colour blindness in which the subject is asked to distinguish numbers or pathways printed in coloured spots on a background of spots of a different colour or colours.
– ORIGIN early 20th cent.: named after Shinobu *Ishihara* (1879–1963), Japanese ophthalmologist.

Ishmael /ˈɪʃmeɪəl/ (in the Bible) a son of Abraham and Hagar, his wife Sarah's maid, driven away with his mother after the birth of Isaac (Gen. 16:12). Ishmael (or Ismail) is also important in Islamic belief as the traditional ancestor of Muhammad and of the Arab peoples.
– DERIVATIVES **Ishmaelite** /ˈɪʃməˌlʌɪt/ noun.

Ishtar /ˈɪʃtɑː/ Near Eastern Mythology a Babylonian and Assyrian goddess of love and war whose name and functions correspond to those of the Phoenician goddess Astarte.

Isidore of Seville, St /ˈɪzɪdɔː/ (c.560–636), Spanish archbishop and Doctor of the Church; also called *Isidorus Hispalensis*. He is noted for his *Etymologies*, an encyclopedic work used by many medieval authors. Feast day, 4 April.

isinglass /ˈʌɪzɪŋˌɡlɑːs/ ▶ **noun** [mass noun] a kind of gelatin obtained from fish, especially sturgeon, and used in making jellies, glue, etc. and for fining real ale.
▪ chiefly US mica or a similar material in thin transparent sheets.
– ORIGIN mid 16th cent.: alteration (by association with **GLASS**) of obsolete Dutch *huysenblas* 'sturgeon's bladder', from *huysen* 'sturgeon' + *blas* 'bladder'.

Isis /ˈʌɪsɪs/ Egyptian Mythology a goddess of fertility, wife of Osiris and mother of Horus. Her worship spread to western Asia, Greece, and Rome, where she was identified with various local goddesses.

Iskenderun /ɪsˈkɛndəruːn/ a port and naval base in southern Turkey, on the Mediterranean coast; pop. 158,930 (1990). Formerly named Alexandretta, it lies on or near the site of Alexandria ad Issum, founded by Alexander the Great in 333 BC.

Islam /ˈɪzlɑːm, ɪzˈlɑːm, -lam/ ▶ **noun** [mass noun] the religion of the Muslims, a monotheistic faith regarded as revealed through Muhammad as the Prophet of Allah.
▪ the Muslim world: *the most enormous complex of fortifications in all Islam*.

> Founded in the Arabian peninsula in the 7th century AD, Islam is now the professed faith of nearly a billion people worldwide, particularly in North Africa, the Middle East, and parts of Asia. The ritual observances and moral code of Islam were said to have been given to Muhammad as a series of revelations, which were codified in the Koran. Islam is regarded by its adherents as the last of the revealed religions, and Muhammad is seen as the last of the prophets, building on and perfecting the examples and teachings of Abraham, Moses, and Jesus. There are two major branches in Islam, Sunni and Shia.

– DERIVATIVES **Islamism** noun, **Islamist** noun, **Islamization** noun, **Islamize** verb (also **-ise**).
– ORIGIN from Arabic *'islām* 'submission', from *'aslama* 'submit (to God)'.

Islamabad /ɪzˈlɑːməbad/ the capital of Pakistan, a modern planned city in the north of the country, which replaced Rawalpindi as capital in 1967; pop. 201,000 (1981).

Islamic /ɪzˈlamɪk, ɪzˈlɑːmɪk/ ▶ **adjective** of or relating to Islam: *the Islamic world* | *Islamic fundamentalism*.
– DERIVATIVES **Islamicization** noun, **Islamicize** (also **-ise**) verb.

Islamic Jihad /dʒɪˈhad, -ˈhɑːd/ (also **Jehad**) a Muslim fundamentalist terrorist group within the Shiite Hezbollah association.

Island /ˈiːsland/ Icelandic name for **ICELAND**.

island ▶ **noun** a piece of land surrounded by water.
▪ figurative a thing resembling an island, especially in being isolated, detached, or surrounded in some way: *the university is the last island of democracy in this country*. ▪ a free-standing kitchen cupboard unit with a worktop, allowing access from all sides. ▪ Anatomy a detached portion of tissue or group of cells. Compare with **ISLET**.
– ORIGIN Old English *īegland*, from *īeg* 'island' (from a base meaning 'watery, watered') + **LAND**. The change in the spelling of the first syllable in the 16th cent. was due to association with the unrelated word **ISLE**.

island arc ▶ **noun** Geology a curved chain of volcanic islands located at a tectonic plate margin, typically with a deep ocean trench on the convex side.

island area ▶ **noun** each of three administrative areas in Scotland (Orkney, Shetland, Western Isles), consisting of groups of islands.

Island Carib ▶ **noun** see **CARIB** (sense 3).

islander ▶ **noun** a native or inhabitant of an island.

island-hop ▶ **verb** [no obj.] [usu. as noun **island-hopping**] travel from one island to another, especially as a tourist in an area of small islands.

Islands of the Blessed (in classical mythology) a land, traditionally located near the place where the sun sets, to which the souls of the good were taken to enjoy a life of eternal bliss.

Islay /ˈʌɪleɪ/ a large island which is the southernmost of the Inner Hebrides, south of Jura.

isle ▶ **noun** chiefly poetic/literary an island or peninsula, especially a small one: *Crusoe's fabled isle* | [in place names] *the British Isles*.
– ORIGIN Middle English *ile*, from Old French, from Latin *insula*. The spelling with *s* (also in 15th-cent. French) is influenced by Latin.

Isle of Man an island in the Irish Sea which is a British Crown possession having home rule, with its own legislature (the Tynwald) and judicial system; pop. 69,790 (1991); capital, Douglas. The island was part of the Norse kingdom of the Hebrides in the Middle Ages, passing into Scottish hands in 1266 for a time, until the English gained control in the early 15th century. Its ancient language, Manx, is still occasionally used for ceremonial purposes.

Isle of Wight /wʌɪt/ an island off the south coast of England, a county since 1974; pop. 126,600 (1991); administrative centre, Newport. It lies at the entrance to Southampton Water and is separated from the mainland by the Solent and Spithead.

Isle of Wight disease ▶ **noun** [mass noun] a disease of bees that is caused by a parasitic mite.
• The mite is *Acarapis woodi*, order (or subclass) Acari.
– ORIGIN so named because it was first observed in the Isle of Wight in 1904.

islesman ▶ **noun** (pl. **-men**) a male native or inhabitant of a group of islands, especially the Hebrides, the Orkneys, or Shetland.

Isles of Scilly another name for the **SCILLY ISLES**.

islet /ˈʌɪlɪt/ ▶ **noun** **1** a small island.
2 Anatomy a portion of tissue structurally distinct from surrounding tissues.
▪ (**islets**) short for **ISLETS OF LANGERHANS**.
– ORIGIN mid 16th cent.: from Old French, diminutive of *isle* (see **ISLE**).

islets of Langerhans /ˈlaŋəhanz/ ▶ **plural noun** groups of pancreatic cells secreting insulin and glucagon.
– ORIGIN late 19th cent.: named after Paul *Langerhans* (1847–88), the German anatomist who first described them.

ism /ˈɪz(ə)m/ ▶ **noun** informal, chiefly derogatory a distinctive practice, system, or philosophy, typically a political ideology or an artistic movement: *of all the isms, fascism is the most repressive*.
– DERIVATIVES **ist** noun.
– ORIGIN late 17th cent.: independent usage of **-ISM**.

-ism ▶ **suffix** forming nouns: **1** denoting an action or its result: *baptism* | *exorcism*.
▪ denoting a state or quality: *barbarism*.
2 denoting a system, principle, or ideological movement: *Anglicanism* | *feminism* | *hedonism*.
▪ denoting a basis for prejudice or discrimination: *racism*.
3 denoting a peculiarity in language: *colloquialism* | *Americanism*.
4 denoting a pathological condition: *alcoholism*.
– ORIGIN from French *-isme*, via Latin from Greek *-ismos*, *-isma*.

Ismail Arabic spelling of **ISHMAEL**.

Ismaili /ˌɪsmʌɪˈiːli, ˌɪsmɑː-/ ▶ **noun** (pl. **Ismailis**) a member of a branch of Shiite Muslims that seceded from the main group in the 8th century because of their belief that Ismail, the son of the sixth Shiite imam, should have become the seventh imam.

isn't ▶ contraction of is not.

ISO[1] International Organization for Standardization.
– ORIGIN from Greek *isos* 'equal'; the term is often erroneously thought to be an abbreviation.

ISO[2] historical ▶ abbreviation for (in the UK) Imperial Service Order, awarded to British and commonwealth civil servants (discontinued in 1993).

iso- ▶ combining form equal: *isochron* | *isosceles*.
■ Chemistry (chiefly of hydrocarbons) isomeric: *isooctane*.
– ORIGIN from Greek *isos* 'equal'.

isoagglutination /ˌʌɪsəʊəˌgluːtɪˈneɪʃ(ə)n/ ▶ noun [mass noun] Physiology agglutination of sperms, erythrocytes, or other cells of an individual caused by a substance from another individual of the same species.

isobar /ˈʌɪsə(ʊ)bɑː/ ▶ noun 1 Meteorology a line on a map connecting points having the same atmospheric pressure at a given time or on average over a given period.
■ Physics a curve or formula representing a physical system at constant pressure.
2 Physics each of two or more isotopes of different elements, with the same atomic weight.
– DERIVATIVES **isobaric** adjective.
– ORIGIN mid 19th cent.: from Greek *isobaros* 'of equal weight', from *isos* 'equal' + *baros* 'weight'.

isobutane /ˌʌɪsəʊˈbjuːteɪn/ ▶ noun [mass noun] Chemistry a gaseous hydrocarbon isomeric with butane.
● Chem. formula: $CH_3CH(CH_3)_2$.

isobutyl /ˌʌɪsə(ʊ)ˈbjuːtʌɪl, -tɪl/ ▶ noun [as modifier] Chemistry of or denoting the alkyl radical —$CH_2CH(CH_3)_2$, derived from isobutane.

isocheim /ˈʌɪsə(ʊ)kʌɪm/ ▶ noun Meteorology a line on a map connecting points having the same average temperature in winter.
– ORIGIN mid 19th cent.: from **ISO-** 'equal' + Greek *kheima* 'winter weather'.

isochromatic /ˌʌɪsə(ʊ)krə'matɪk/ ▶ adjective of a single colour.

isochron /ˈʌɪsə(ʊ)krɒn/ ▶ noun chiefly Geology a line on a diagram or map connecting points relating to the same time or equal times.
– ORIGIN late 17th cent. (as an adjective in the sense 'isochronous'): from Greek *isokhronos*, from *isos* 'equal' + *khronos* 'time'.

isochronous /ʌɪˈsɒkrənəs/ ▶ adjective occurring at the same time.
■ occupying equal time.
– DERIVATIVES **isochronously** adverb.
– ORIGIN early 18th cent. (in the sense 'equal in duration or in frequency'): from modern Latin *isochronus* (from Greek *isokhronos*, from *isos* 'equal' + *khronos* 'time') + **-OUS**.

isoclinal /ˌʌɪsə(ʊ)ˈklʌɪn(ə)l/ ▶ adjective Geology denoting a fold in which the two limbs are parallel.
– ORIGIN mid 19th cent. (denoting 'equal magnetic inclination'): from **ISO-** 'equal' + Greek *klinein* 'to lean, slope' + **-AL**.

isocline /ˈʌɪsə(ʊ)klʌɪn/ ▶ noun a line on a diagram or map connecting points of equal gradient or inclination.
– DERIVATIVES **isoclinic** adjective.
– ORIGIN late 19th cent. (denoting an isoclinal line or fold): from Greek *isoklinēs* 'equally balanced', from *klinein* 'to lean, slope'.

isoclinic line ▶ noun a line on a map connecting points where the dip of the earth's magnetic field is the same.

Isocrates /ʌɪˈsɒkrətiːz/ (436–338 BC), Athenian orator whose written speeches are among the earliest political pamphlets.

isocratic /ˌʌɪsə(ʊ)ˈkratɪk/ ▶ adjective Chemistry (of a chromatographic method) involving a mobile phase whose composition is kept constant and uniform.
– ORIGIN early 19th cent.: from Greek *isokratia* 'equality of power' (from *isos* 'equal' + *kratos* 'strength') + **-IC**.

isocyanic acid /ˌʌɪsə(ʊ)sʌɪˈanɪk/ ▶ noun [mass noun] Chemistry a volatile pungent liquid, isomeric with cyanic acid.
● Chem. formula: HNCO. See also **FULMINIC ACID**.
– DERIVATIVES **isocyanate** noun.

isocyanide ▶ noun Chemistry an organic compound containing the group —NC bonded to an alkyl group. Such compounds are typically toxic, malodorous liquids.

isodiametric /ˌʌɪsə(ʊ)dʌɪə'metrɪk/ ▶ adjective chiefly Botany (of a cell, spore, etc.) roughly spherical or polyhedral.

isodynamic ▶ adjective Geography indicating or connecting points on the earth's surface at which the intensity of the magnetic force is the same.

isoelectric ▶ adjective having or involving no net electric charge or difference in electrical potential.

isoelectric focusing ▶ noun [mass noun] Biochemistry a technique of electrophoresis in which the resolution is improved by maintaining a pH gradient between the electrodes.

isoelectronic ▶ adjective Chemistry having the same numbers of electrons or the same electronic structure.

isoenzyme ▶ noun Biochemistry each of two or more enzymes with identical function but different structure.

isogamy /ʌɪˈsɒgəmi/ ▶ noun [mass noun] Biology sexual reproduction by the fusion of similar gametes. Compare with **ANISOGAMY**.
– DERIVATIVES **isogamete** noun, **isogamous** adjective.
– ORIGIN late 19th cent.: from **ISO-** 'equal' + Greek *-gamia* (from *gamos* 'marriage').

isogenic /ˌʌɪsə(ʊ)ˈdʒɛnɪk/ ▶ adjective Biology (of organisms) having the same or closely similar genotypes.

isogeotherm /ˌʌɪsə(ʊ)ˈdʒiːəθəːm/ ▶ noun Geography a line or plane on a diagram connecting points representing those in the interior of the earth having the same temperature.
– DERIVATIVES **isogeothermal** adjective.
– ORIGIN mid 19th cent.: from **ISO-** 'equal' + **GEO-** 'earth' + Greek *thermē* 'heat'.

isogloss /ˈʌɪsə(ʊ)glɒs/ ▶ noun Linguistics a line on a map marking an area having a distinct linguistic feature.
– ORIGIN early 20th cent.: from **ISO-** 'equal' + Greek *glōssa* 'tongue, word'.

isogonic /ˌʌɪsə(ʊ)ˈgɒnɪk/ ▶ adjective Geography indicating or connecting points of the earth's surface at which the magnetic declination is the same.
– ORIGIN mid 19th cent.: from Greek *isogōnios* 'equiangular' + **-IC**.

isohel /ˈʌɪsə(ʊ)hɛl/ ▶ noun Meteorology a line on a map connecting points having the same duration of sunshine.
– ORIGIN early 20th cent.: from **ISO-** 'equal' + Greek *hēlios* 'sun'.

isohyet /ˌʌɪsə(ʊ)ˈhʌɪɪt/ ▶ noun Meteorology a line on a map connecting points having the same amount of rainfall in a given period.
– ORIGIN late 19th cent.: from **ISO-** 'equal' + Greek *huetos* 'rain'.

isokinetic /ˌʌɪsə(ʊ)kɪˈnɛtɪk/ ▶ adjective characterized by or producing a constant speed.
■ Physiology of or relating to muscular action with a constant rate of movement.

isolate ▶ verb [with obj.] cause (a person or place) to be or remain alone or apart from others: *a country which is isolated from the rest of the world.*
■ identify (something) and examine or deal with it separately: *you can't isolate stress from the management context.* ■ Chemistry & Biology obtain or extract (a compound, micro-organism, etc.) in a pure form. ■ cut off the electrical or other connection to (something, especially a part of a supply network). ■ place (a person or animal) in quarantine as a precaution against infectious or contagious disease.
▶ noun a person or thing which has been or become isolated: *social isolates often become careless of their own welfare.*
■ Biology a culture of micro-organisms isolated for study.
– DERIVATIVES **isolable** adjective, **isolatable** adjective, **isolator** noun.
– ORIGIN early 19th cent. (as a verb): back-formation from **ISOLATED**.

isolated ▶ adjective far away from other places, buildings, or people; remote: *isolated farms and villages.*
■ having minimal contact or little in common with others: *he lived a very isolated existence.* ■ single; exceptional: *they were isolated incidents.*

– ORIGIN mid 18th cent.: from French *isolé*, from Italian *isolato*, from late Latin *insulatus* 'made into an island', from Latin *insula* 'island'.

isolating ▶ adjective (of a language) tending to have each element as an independent word without inflections.

isolation ▶ noun [mass noun] the process or fact of isolating or being isolated: *the isolation of older people.*
■ [count noun] an instance of isolating something, especially a compound or micro-organism. ■ [as modifier] denoting a hospital or ward for patients with contagious or infectious diseases.
– PHRASES **in isolation** without relation to other people or things; separately: *environmental problems must not be seen in isolation from social ones.*
– ORIGIN mid 19th cent.: from **ISOLATE**, partly on the pattern of French *isolation*.

isolationism ▶ noun [mass noun] a policy of remaining apart from the affairs or interests of other groups, especially the political affairs of other countries.
– DERIVATIVES **isolationist** noun.

Isolde /ɪˈzɒld, ɪˈzəʊldə/ another name for **ISEULT**.

isoleucine /ˌʌɪsə(ʊ)ˈluːsiːn/ ▶ noun [mass noun] Biochemistry a hydrophobic amino acid that is a constituent of most proteins. It is an essential nutrient in the diet of vertebrates.
● Chem. formula: $CH_3CH_2CH(CH_3)CH(NH_2)COOH$.

isoline /ˈʌɪsə(ʊ)lʌɪn/ ▶ noun another term for **ISOPLETH**.

isomer /ˈʌɪsəmə/ ▶ noun 1 Chemistry each of two or more compounds with the same formula but a different arrangement of atoms in the molecule and different properties.
2 Physics each of two or more atomic nuclei that have the same atomic number and the same mass number but different energy states.
– DERIVATIVES **isomeric** adjective, **isomerism** noun, **isomerize** (also **-ise**) verb.
– ORIGIN mid 19th cent.: from Greek *isomerēs* 'sharing equally', from *isos* 'equal' + *meros* 'a share'.

isomerase /ʌɪˈsɒməreɪz/ ▶ noun Biochemistry an enzyme which catalyses the conversion of a specified compound to an isomer.

isomerous /ʌɪˈsɒm(ə)rəs/ ▶ adjective Biology having or composed of parts that are similar in number or position.
– ORIGIN mid 19th cent.: from Greek *isomerēs* (see **ISOMER**) + **-OUS**.

isometric ▶ adjective 1 of or having equal dimensions.
2 Physiology of, relating to, or denoting muscular action in which tension is developed without contraction of the muscle.
3 (in technical or architectural drawing) incorporating a method of showing projection or perspective in which the three principal dimensions are represented by three axes 120° apart.
4 Mathematics (of a transformation) without change of shape or size.
– DERIVATIVES **isometrically** adverb, **isometry** noun (in sense 4).
– ORIGIN mid 19th cent.: from Greek *isometria* 'equality of measure' (from *isos* 'equal' + *-metria* 'measuring') + **-IC**.

isometrics ▶ plural noun a system of physical exercises in which muscles are caused to act against each other or against a fixed object.

isomorphic /ˌʌɪsə(ʊ)ˈmɔːfɪk/ ▶ adjective corresponding or similar in form and relations.
■ having the same crystalline form.
– DERIVATIVES **isomorphism** noun, **isomorphous** adjective.

-ison ▶ suffix (forming nouns) equivalent to **-ATION** (as in *comparison*, *jettison*).
– ORIGIN from Old French *-aison*, *-eison*, etc., from Latin *-atio(n)-*.

isoniazid /ˌʌɪsə(ʊ)ˈnʌɪəzɪd/ ▶ noun [mass noun] Medicine a synthetic compound used as a bacteriostatic drug, chiefly to treat tuberculosis.
● A derivative of nicotinic acid and hydrazine; chem. formula: $C_5H_5NCONHNH_2$.
– ORIGIN 1950s: from **ISO-** 'equal' + *ni(cotinic)* + *(hydr)azine* + **-IDE**.

isonitrile /ˌʌɪsə(ʊ)ˈnʌɪtrʌɪl/ ▶ noun Chemistry another term for **ISOCYANIDE**.

isooctane /ˌʌɪsəʊˈɒkteɪn/ ▶ noun [mass noun] Chemistry a liquid hydrocarbon present in petroleum. It serves as a standard in the system of octane numbers.
● Chem. formula: $(CH_3)_3CCH_2CH(CH_3)CH_3$.

isopach /ˈʌɪsə(ʊ)pak/ ▶ noun Geology a line on a map or diagram connecting points beneath which a particular stratum or group of strata has the same thickness.
− ORIGIN early 20th cent.: from ISO- 'equal' + Greek *pakhus* 'thick'.

isophote /ˈʌɪsə(ʊ)fəʊt/ ▶ noun a line in a diagram connecting points where the intensity of light is the same.
− ORIGIN early 20th cent.: from ISO- 'equal' + Greek *phōs*, *phōt-* 'light'.

isopleth /ˈʌɪsə(ʊ)plɛθ/ ▶ noun Meteorology a line on a map connecting points having equal incidence of a specified meteorological feature.
− ORIGIN early 20th cent.: from Greek *isoplēthēs* 'equal in quantity', from Greek *isos* 'equal' + *plēthos* 'multitude, quantity'.

Isopoda /ˌʌɪsəˈpəʊdə/ Zoology an order of mainly aquatic crustaceans that includes the woodlice and sea slaters. They have a flattened segmented body with seven similar pairs of legs, and many kinds are marine.
− DERIVATIVES **isopod** noun.
− ORIGIN modern Latin (plural), from Greek *isos* 'equal' + *pous*, *pod-* 'foot'.

isoprenaline /ˌʌɪsə(ʊ)ˈprɛnəliːn/ ▶ noun [mass noun] Medicine a synthetic derivative of adrenalin, used for the relief of bronchial asthma and pulmonary emphysema.
− ORIGIN 1950s: from elements of the systematic name *N-isopropylnoradrenaline*.

isoprene /ˈʌɪsə(ʊ)priːn/ ▶ noun [mass noun] Chemistry a volatile liquid hydrocarbon obtained from petroleum, whose molecule forms the basic structural unit of natural and synthetic rubbers.
● Chem. formula: $CH_2=C(CH_3)CH=CH_2$.
− ORIGIN mid 19th cent.: apparently from ISO- 'equal' + pr(opyl)ene.

isopropanol /ˌʌɪsə(ʊ)ˈprəʊpənɒl/ ▶ noun [mass noun] Chemistry a liquid alcohol, used as a solvent and in the industrial production of acetone.
● Chem. formula: $CH_3CHOHCH_3$.

isopropyl /ˌʌɪsəʊˈprəʊpʌɪl, -pɪl/ ▶ noun [as modifier] Chemistry of or denoting the alkyl radical —$CH(CH_3)_2$, derived from propane by removal of a hydrogen atom from the middle carbon atom.

isopropyl alcohol ▶ noun [mass noun] Chemistry another term for ISOPROPANOL.

isoproterenol /ˌʌɪsə(ʊ)prəʊtəˈriːnɒl/ ▶ noun another term for ISOPRENALINE.
− ORIGIN 1950s: from elements of the semi-systematic name *N-isopropylarterenol*.

Isoptera /ʌɪˈsɒptərə/ Entomology an order of insects that comprises the termites.
− DERIVATIVES **isopteran** noun & adjective.
− ORIGIN modern Latin (plural), from Greek *isos* 'equal' + *pteron* 'wing'.

isopycnal /ˌʌɪsə(ʊ)ˈpɪkn(ə)l/ ▶ adjective Oceanography (especially of an imaginary line or surface on a map or chart) connecting points in the ocean where the water has the same density.
− ORIGIN early 20th cent.: from ISO- 'equal' + Greek *puknos* 'dense' + -AL.

isopycnic /ˌʌɪsə(ʊ)ˈpɪknɪk/ ▶ adjective Biochemistry of or denoting ultracentrifugal separation techniques making use of differences in density between the components of a mixture.
− ORIGIN late 19th cent.: from ISO- 'equal' + Greek *puknos* 'dense' + -IC.

isorhythmic ▶ adjective Music (of a composition or part) in which the rhythm is often repeated but the pitch of the notes is varied each time.

isosbestic point /ˌʌɪsəʊsˈbɛstɪk/ ▶ noun Chemistry a wavelength at which the absorption of light by a mixed solution remains constant as the equilibrium between the components in the solution changes.
− ORIGIN early 20th cent.: *isosbestic* from ISO- 'equal' + Greek *sbestos* 'extinguished' (from *sbennunai* 'quench') + -IC.

isosceles /ʌɪˈsɒsɪliːz/ ▶ adjective (of a triangle) having two sides of equal length.
− ORIGIN mid 16th cent.: via late Latin from Greek *isoskelēs*, from *isos* 'equal' + *skelos* 'leg'.

isoseismal /ˌʌɪsə(ʊ)ˈsʌɪzm(ə)l/ ▶ adjective Geology relating to or denoting lines on a map connecting places where an earthquake was experienced with equal strength.
− DERIVATIVES **isoseismic** adjective.

isosmotic /ˌʌɪsɒzˈmɒtɪk/ ▶ adjective Biology having the same osmotic pressure.

isospin /ˈʌɪsə(ʊ)spɪn/ ▶ noun [mass noun] Physics a vector quantity or quantum number assigned to subatomic particles and atomic nuclei and having values such that similar particles differing only in charge-related properties (independent of the strong interaction between particles) can be treated as different states of a single particle.
− ORIGIN 1960s: contraction of *isotopic spin*, *isobaric spin*.

isostasy /ʌɪˈsɒstəsi/ ▶ noun [mass noun] Geology the equilibrium that exists between parts of the earth's crust, which behaves as if it consists of blocks floating on the underlying mantle, rising if material (such as an ice cap) is removed and sinking if material is deposited.
− DERIVATIVES **isostatic** adjective.
− ORIGIN late 19th cent.: from ISO- 'equal' + Greek *stasis* 'station'.

isotactic /ˌʌɪsə(ʊ)ˈtaktɪk/ ▶ adjective Chemistry (of a polymer) in which all the repeating units have the same stereochemical configuration.
− ORIGIN 1950s: from ISO- 'equal' + Greek *taktos* 'arranged' + -IC.

isothere /ˈʌɪsə(ʊ)θɪə/ ▶ noun Meteorology a line on a map connecting points having the same average temperature in summer.
− ORIGIN mid 19th cent.: from French *isothère*, from Greek *isos* 'equal' + *theros* 'summer'.

isotherm /ˈʌɪsə(ʊ)θəːm/ ▶ noun a line on a map connecting points having the same temperature at a given time or on average over a given period.
■ Physics a curve on a diagram joining points representing states or conditions of equal temperature.
− DERIVATIVES **isothermal** adjective & noun, **isothermally** adverb.
− ORIGIN mid 19th cent.: from French *isotherme*, from Greek *isos* 'equal' + *thermē* 'heat'.

isotonic /ˌʌɪsə(ʊ)ˈtɒnɪk/ ▶ adjective **1** Physiology (of muscle action) taking place with normal contraction.
2 Physiology denoting or relating to a solution having the same osmotic pressure as some other solution, especially one in a cell or a body fluid.
■ (of a drink) containing essential salts and minerals in the same concentration as in the body and intended to replace those lost as a result of sweating during vigorous exercise.
− DERIVATIVES **isotonically** adverb, **isotonicity** noun.
− ORIGIN early 19th cent. (as a musical term designating a system of tuning, characterized by equal intervals): from Greek *isotonos*, from *isos* 'equal' + *tonos* 'tone'.

isotope /ˈʌɪsətəʊp/ ▶ noun Chemistry each of two or more forms of the same element that contain equal numbers of protons but different numbers of neutrons in their nuclei, and hence differ in relative atomic mass but not in chemical properties; in particular, a radioactive form of an element.
− DERIVATIVES **isotopic** adjective, **isotopically** adverb, **isotopy** noun.
− ORIGIN 1913: coined by F. Soddy, from ISO- 'equal' + Greek *topos* 'place' (because the isotopes occupy the same place in the periodic table of elements).

isotropic /ˌʌɪsə(ʊ)ˈtrɒpɪk/ ▶ adjective Physics (of an object or substance) having a physical property which has the same value when measured in different directions. Often contrasted with ANISOTROPIC.
■ (of a property or phenomenon) not varying in magnitude according to the direction of measurement.
− DERIVATIVES **isotropically** adverb, **isotropy** /ʌɪˈsɒtrəpi/ noun.
− ORIGIN mid 19th cent.: from ISO- 'equal' + Greek *tropos* 'a turn' + -IC.

isozyme /ˈʌɪsə(ʊ)zʌɪm/ ▶ noun Biochemistry another term for ISOENZYME.

ispaghul /ˈɪspəɡuːl/ (also **ispaghula** /ˌɪspəˈɡuːlə/) ▶ noun [mass noun] the dried seeds of a southern Asian plantain, chiefly used medicinally in the treatment of dysentery.
● The plantain is *Plantago ovata*, family Plantaginaceae.
− ORIGIN early 19th cent.: from Persian and Urdu *ispaġol*, from *asp* 'horse' + *ġol* 'ear' (because of the shape of the leaves).

Ispahan /ˌɪspəˈhɑːn/ variant spelling of ISFAHAN.

I spy ▶ noun [mass noun] a children's game in which one player specifies the first letter of an object they can see, the other players then having to guess the identity of this object.

Israel[1] /ˈɪzreɪl/ **1** (also **children of Israel**) the Hebrew nation or people. According to tradition they are descended from the patriarch Jacob (also named Israel), whose twelve sons became founders of the twelve tribes.
2 the northern kingdom of the Hebrews (c.930–721 BC), formed after the reign of Solomon, whose inhabitants were carried away to captivity in Babylon. See also JUDAH (sense 2).
− ORIGIN from Hebrew *Yiśrā'ēl* 'he that strives with God' (see Gen. 32:28).

Israel[2] /ˈɪzreɪl/ a country in the Middle East, on the Mediterranean Sea; pop. 4,500,000 (est. 1990); languages, Hebrew (official), English, Arabic; capital (not recognized as such by the UN), Jerusalem.

The modern state of Israel was established as a Jewish homeland in 1948, on land that was at that time part of the British mandated territory of Palestine. Israel was immediately attacked by the surrounding Arab states, which it defeated. The continuing conflict with the neighbouring Arabs, mainly over the rights of the Palestinian Arabs displaced from their homes or living under Israeli rule, has caused continual tension and intermittent terrorist and military activity. Further wars occurred in 1956, 1967, and 1973, which resulted in Israeli occupation of eastern Jerusalem, the West Bank, the Gaza Strip, and the Golan Heights. In 1993 Israel and the Palestine Liberation Organization signed an agreement for limited Palestinian autonomy in the West Bank and the Gaza Strip. See also PALESTINE.

Israeli /ɪzˈreɪli/ ▶ adjective of or relating to the modern country of Israel.
▶ noun (pl. **Israelis**) a native or national of Israel, or a person of Israeli descent.

Israelite /ˈɪzrəlʌɪt/ ▶ noun a member of the ancient Hebrew nation, especially in the period from the Exodus to the Babylonian Captivity (c.12th to 6th centuries BC).
■ old-fashioned and sometimes offensive term for JEW.
▶ adjective of or relating to the Israelites.
− ORIGIN via late Latin from Greek *Israēlitēs*.

Israfel /ˈɪzrəfɛl/ (in Muslim tradition) the angel of music, who will sound the trumpet on the Day of Judgement.

Issa /ˈiːsɑː/ ▶ noun (pl. same or **Issas**) a member of a Somali people living in the Republic of Djibouti.
▶ adjective of or relating to the Issa.
− ORIGIN the name in Somali.

Issachar /ˈɪsəkə/ (in the Bible) a Hebrew patriarch, son of Jacob and Leah (Gen. 30:18).
■ the tribe of Israel traditionally descended from him.

issei /ˈiːseɪ/ ▶ noun (pl. same) N. Amer. a Japanese immigrant to North America. Compare with NISEI and SANSEI.
− ORIGIN Japanese, literally 'generation'.

Issigonis /ˌɪsɪˈɡəʊnɪs/, Sir Alec (Arnold Constantine) (1906–88), Turkish-born British car designer. His most famous designs were the Morris Minor (1948) and the Mini (1959).

ISSN ▶ abbreviation for international standard serial number, an eight-digit number assigned to many serial publications such as newspapers, magazines, annuals, and series of books.

issuant /ˈɪʃ(j)ʊənt, ˈɪsjʊ-/ ▶ adjective [predic.] Heraldry (of the upper part of an animal) shown rising up or out from another bearing, especially from the bottom of a chief or from behind a fess.
− ORIGIN early 17th cent.: from ISSUE + -ANT (on the pattern of French present participles ending in -ant).

issue /ˈɪʃ(j)uː, ˈɪsjuː/ ▶ noun **1** an important topic or problem for debate or discussion: *the issue of global warming* | *money is not an issue*.
2 [mass noun] the action of supplying or distributing an item for use, sale, or official purposes: *the issue of notes by the Bank of England*.
■ [count noun] each of a regular series of publications: *the December issue of the magazine*. ■ [count noun] a number

or set of items distributed at one time: *a share issue has been launched.*

3 [mass noun] formal or Law children of one's own: *the earl died without male issue.*

4 [mass noun] the action of flowing or coming out: *a point of issue* | [count noun] *an issue of blood.*

5 dated a result or outcome of something: *the chance of carrying such a scheme to a successful issue was small.*

▶**verb** (**issues, issued, issuing**) **1** [with obj.] supply or distribute (something): *licences were issued indiscriminately to any company.*

■(**issue someone with**) supply someone with (something). ■ formally send out or make known: *the minister issued a statement.* ■ put (something) on sale or into general use: *Christmas stamps to be issued in November.*

2 [no obj.] (**issue from**) come, go, or flow out from: *exotic smells issued from a nearby building.*

■result or be derived from: *the struggles of history issue from the divided heart of humanity.*

– PHRASES **at issue** under discussion; in dispute. **make an issue of** treat too seriously or as a problem. **take issue with** disagree with; challenge: *she takes issue with the notion of crime as unique to contemporary society.*

– DERIVATIVES **issuable** adjective, **issuance** noun, **issueless** adjective, **issuer** noun.

– ORIGIN Middle English (in the sense 'outflowing'): from Old French, based on Latin *exitus*, past participle of *exire* 'go out'.

issue of fact ▶**noun** Law a dispute in court in which the significance of a fact or facts is denied.

issue of law ▶**noun** Law a dispute in court in which the application of the law is contested.

-ist ▶**suffix** forming personal nouns and some related adjectives: **1** denoting an adherent of a system of beliefs, principles, etc. expressed by nouns ending in *-ism*: *hedonist* | *Marxist.* See **-ISM** 2.

■denoting a person who subscribes to a prejudice or practises discrimination: *sexist.*

2 denoting a member of a profession or business activity: *dentist* | *dramatist* | *florist.*

■denoting a person who uses a thing: *flautist* | *motorist.* ■ denoting a person who does something expressed by a verb ending in *-ize*: *plagiarist.*

– ORIGIN from Old French *-iste*, Latin *-ista*, from Greek *-istēs*.

Istanbul /ˌɪstanˈbʊl/ a port in Turkey on the Bosporus, lying partly in Europe, partly in Asia; pop. 7,309,190 (1990). Formerly the Roman city of Constantinople (330–1453), it was built on the site of the ancient Greek city of Byzantium. It was captured by the Ottoman Turks in 1453 and was the capital of Turkey from that time until 1923.

– ORIGIN Turkish, from Greek *eis tēn polin* 'into the city'.

isthmian /ˈɪsθmɪən, ˈɪstm-, ˈɪsm-/ ▶**adjective** of or relating to an isthmus.

■(**Isthmian**) of or relating to the Isthmus of Corinth in southern Greece.

Isthmian games games held by the ancient Greeks every other year near the Isthmus of Corinth.

isthmus /ˈɪsθməs, ˈɪstməs, ˈɪsməs/ ▶**noun** (pl. **isthmuses**) a narrow strip of land with sea on either side, forming a link between two larger areas of land.

■(pl. **isthmi**) Anatomy a narrow organ, passage, or piece of tissue connecting two larger parts.

– ORIGIN mid 16th cent.: via Latin from Greek *isthmos*.

istle /ˈɪstli/ ▶**noun** variant spelling of **IXTLE**.

IT ▶**abbreviation for** information technology.

it[1] ▶**pronoun** [third person singular] **1** used to refer to a thing previously mentioned or easily identified: *a room with two beds in it* | *this approach is refreshing because it breaks down barriers.*

■referring to an animal or child of unspecified sex: *she was holding the baby, cradling it and smiling into its face.* ■ referring to a fact or situation previously mentioned, known, or happening: *stop it, you're hurting me.*

2 used to identify a person: *it's me* | *it's a boy!*

3 used in the normal subject position in statements about time, distance, or weather: *it's half past five* | *it was two miles to the island* | *it is raining.*

4 used in the normal subject or object position when a more specific subject or object is given later in the sentence: *it is impossible to assess the problem* | *she found it interesting to learn about their strategy.*

5 [with clause] used to emphasize a following part of a sentence: *it is the child who is the victim.*

6 the situation or circumstances; things in general: *no one can stay here—it's too dangerous now* | *he would like to see you straight away if it's convenient.*

7 exactly what is needed or desired: *they thought they were it* | *you've either got it or you haven't.*

8 (usu. **'it'**) informal sexual intercourse or sex appeal: *the only thing I knew nothing about was 'it'.*

9 (usu. **'it'**) (in children's games) the player who has to catch the others.

– PHRASES **at it** see **AT**[1]. **that's it 1** that is the main point or difficulty: *'Is she going?' 'That's just it—she can't make up her mind.'* **2** that is enough or the end: *okay, that's it, you've cried long enough.* **this is it 1** the expected event is about to happen: *this is it—the big sale.* **2** this is enough or the end: *this is it, I'm going.* **3** this is the main point or difficulty.

– ORIGIN Old English *hit*, neuter of **HE**, of Germanic origin; related to Dutch *het*.

it[2] ▶**noun** [mass noun] Brit. informal, dated Italian vermouth: *he poured a gin and it.*

– ORIGIN 1930s: abbreviation.

ITA ▶**abbreviation for** initial teaching alphabet.

Itaipu /iːˈtʌɪpuː/ a dam on the Paraná River in SW Brazil, one of the world's largest hydroelectric installations, formally opened in 1982.

ital /ˈɪtal/ ▶**noun** [mass noun] (in Rastafarian culture) organically grown vegetarian food, cooked without salt.

– ORIGIN from *I* (used by Rastafarians to signify value) + **VITAL** or **VITTLE**.

ital. ▶**abbreviation for** italic (used as an instruction for a typesetter).

Italia /iˈtalja/ Italian name for **ITALY**.

Italian ▶**adjective** of or relating to Italy, its people, or their language.

▶**noun 1** a native or national of Italy, or a person of Italian descent.

2 [mass noun] the Romance language of Italy, descended from Latin. It is also one of the official languages of Switzerland, and there are roughly 60 million speakers worldwide.

– DERIVATIVES **Italianize** (also **-ise**) verb.

– ORIGIN late Middle English: from Italian *italiano*, from *Italia* 'Italy'.

Italianate ▶**adjective** Italian in character or appearance: *an Italianate staircase with triple loggia.*

– ORIGIN late 16th cent.: from Italian *italianato*, from *Italia* 'Italy'.

Italian garden ▶**noun** a type of garden characterized by clipped trees, box-edged beds of flowers, paved paths, statues, fountains, etc., and often arranged in terraces.

Italianism ▶**noun 1** an Italian characteristic, expression, or custom.

2 [mass noun] attachment to Italy or Italian ideas or practices.

Italianist ▶**noun** an expert in or student of the Italian language or Italian culture.

Italian parsley ▶**noun** another term for **FLAT-LEAVED PARSLEY**.

Italian vermouth ▶**noun** [mass noun] a type of bitter-sweet vermouth made in Italy.

Italic /ɪˈtalɪk/ ▶**adjective** relating to or denoting the branch of Indo-European languages that includes Latin, Oscan, Umbrian, and the Romance languages.

▶**noun** [mass noun] the Italic group of languages.

– ORIGIN late 19th cent.: via Latin from Greek *Italikos*, from *Italia* 'Italy'.

italic /ɪˈtalɪk/ ▶**adjective** Printing of the sloping kind of typeface used especially for emphasis or distinction and in foreign words.

■(of handwriting) modelled on 16th-century Italian handwriting, typically cursive and sloping and with elliptical or pointed letters.

▶**noun** (also **italics**) [mass noun] an italic typeface or letter: *the key words are in italics.*

– ORIGIN late Middle English (in the general sense 'Italian'): via Latin from Greek *Italikos*, from *Italia* 'Italy'. Senses relating to writing date from the early 17th cent.

italicize /ɪˈtalɪsʌɪz/ (also **-ise**) ▶**verb** [with obj.] print (text) in italics.

– DERIVATIVES **italicization** noun.

Italiot /ɪˈtalɪət/ ▶**noun** an inhabitant of any of the Greek colonies in ancient Italy.

▶**adjective** of or relating to these people.

– ORIGIN from Greek *Italiōtēs*, from *Italia* 'Italy'.

Italo- /ˈɪtələʊ, ɪˈtaləʊ/ ▶**combining form** Italian; Italian and ...: *Italophile* | *Italo-Grecian.*

■relating to Italy.

Italy a country in southern Europe; pop. 57,746,160 (est. 1990); official language, Italian; capital, Rome. Italian name **ITALIA**.

Italy was united under Rome from the 2nd century BC to the collapse of the empire in AD 476. In the Middle Ages it was dominated by several city states and the papacy and was the centre of the Renaissance. Modern Italy was created in the mid 19th century by a movement led by Garibaldi; the Sardinian monarch, Victor Emmanuel II, became king of Italy in 1861. Italy entered the First World War on the Allied side in 1915. In 1922 the country was taken over by the Fascist dictator Mussolini; participation in support of Germany during the Second World War resulted in defeat and Mussolini's downfall. Italy was a founder member of the EEC.

Itanagar /ˌiːtəˈnʌɡə/ a city in the far north-east of India, north of the Brahmaputra River, capital of the state of Arunachal Pradesh; pop. 17,300 (1991).

ITAR-Tass /ˈʌɪtɑː/ the official news agency of Russia, founded in 1925 in Leningrad as Tass, and renamed in 1992.

– ORIGIN from the initials of Russian *Informatsionnoe telegrafnoe agentstvo Rossii* 'Information Telegraph Agency of Russia', + **TASS**.

ITC ▶**abbreviation for** Independent Television Commission.

itch ▶**noun** [usu. in sing.] an uncomfortable sensation on the skin that causes a desire to scratch.

■informal a restless or strong desire: [with infinitive] *the itch to write fiction.* ■ [mass noun] [with modifier] a skin disease or condition of which itching is a symptom. ■ (**the itch**) informal scabies.

▶**verb** [no obj.] be the site of or cause an itch: *the bite itched like crazy.*

■(of a person) experience an itch. ■ informal feel a restless or strong desire to do something: [with infinitive] *your hands fairly itch to take the wheel.*

– PHRASES **an itching palm** figurative an avaricious nature.

– ORIGIN Old English *gycce* (noun), *gyccan* (verb), of West Germanic origin; related to Dutch *jeuk* (noun) and Dutch *jeuken*, German *jucken* (verb).

itching powder ▶**noun** a powder used to make someone's skin itch, typically as a practical joke.

itch mite ▶**noun** a parasitic mite which burrows under the skin, causing scabies in humans and sarcoptic mange in animals.

● *Sarcoptes scabiei*, family Sarcoptidae.

itchy ▶**adjective** (**itchier, itchiest**) having or causing an itch: *dry, itchy skin* | *an itchy rash.*

– PHRASES **get** (or **have**) **itchy feet** informal have or develop a strong urge to travel or move from place to place.

– DERIVATIVES **itchiness** noun.

it'd ▶**contraction of** ■ it had: *it'd been there for years.* ■ it would: *it'd be great to see you.*

-ite[1] ▶**suffix 1** forming names denoting natives of a country: *Israelite.*

■often derogatory denoting followers of a movement, doctrine, etc.: *Luddite* | *Trotskyite.*

2 used in scientific and technical terms:

■forming names of fossil organisms: *ammonite.* ■ forming names of minerals: *graphite.* ■ forming names of constituent parts of a body or organ: *somite.* ■ forming names of explosives and other commercial products: *dynamite* | *vulcanite.* ■ Chemistry forming names of salts or esters of acids ending in *-ous*: *sulphite.*

– ORIGIN from French *-ite*, via Latin *-ita* from Greek *itēs*.

-ite[2] ▶**suffix 1** forming adjectives such as *composite, erudite.*

2 forming nouns such as *appetite.*

3 forming verbs such as *unite.*

– ORIGIN from Latin *-itus*, past participle of verbs ending in *-ere* and *-ire*.

item ▶**noun** an individual article or unit, especially one that is part of a list, collection, or set: *the items on the agenda* | *an item of clothing.*

■a piece of news or information. ■ an entry in an account.

▶**adverb** archaic used to introduce each item in a list: *item two statute books ... item two drums.*

– PHRASES **be an item** informal (of a couple) be

involved in an established romantic or sexual relationship.

– ORIGIN late Middle English (as an adverb): from Latin, 'in like manner, also'. The noun sense arose (late 16th cent.) from the use of the adverb to introduce each statement in a list.

itemize (also **-ise**) ▶ **verb** [with obj.] present as a list of individual items: *I have itemized the morning's tasks.*
■ break down (a whole) into its constituent parts: [as adj. **itemized**] *an itemized bill.* ■ specify (an individual item or items).
– DERIVATIVES **itemization** /-ˈzeɪʃ(ə)n/ noun, **itemizer** noun.

iterate /ˈɪtəreɪt/ ▶ **verb** [with obj.] perform or utter repeatedly.
■ [no obj.] make repeated use of a mathematical or computational procedure, applying it each time to the result of the previous application; perform iteration.
▶ **noun** Mathematics a quantity arrived at by iteration.
– ORIGIN mid 16th cent.: from Latin *iterat-* 'repeated', from the verb *iterare*, from *iterum* 'again'.

iteration ▶ **noun** [mass noun] the repetition of a process or utterance.
■ repetition of a mathematical or computational procedure applied to the result of a previous application, typically as a means of obtaining successively closer approximations to the solution of a problem. ■ [count noun] a new version of a piece of computer hardware or software.
– ORIGIN late Middle English: from Latin *iteratio(n-)*, from the verb *iterare* (see **ITERATE**).

iterative ▶ **adjective** relating to or involving iteration, especially of a mathematical or computational process.
■ Linguistics denoting a grammatical rule that can be applied repeatedly. ■ Grammar another term for **FREQUENTATIVE**.
– DERIVATIVES **iteratively** adverb.
– ORIGIN late 15th cent.: from French *itératif, -ive*, from Latin *iterare* 'to repeat'; the grammar term is from late Latin *iterativus*.

Ithaca /ˈɪθəkə/ an island off the western coast of Greece in the Ionian Sea, the legendary home of Odysseus.

ithyphallic /ˌɪθɪˈfalɪk/ ▶ **adjective** (especially of a statue of a deity or other carved figure) having an erect penis.
– ORIGIN early 17th cent. (as a noun denoting a sexually explicit poem): via late Latin from Greek *ithuphallikos*, from *ithus* 'straight' + *phallos* 'phallus'.

Iti ▶ **noun** (pl. **Ities**) & **adjective** variant spelling of **EYETIE**.

-itic ▶ **suffix** forming adjectives and nouns corresponding to nouns ending in *-ite* (such as *Semitic* corresponding to *Semite*).
■ corresponding to nouns ending in *-itis* (such as *arthritic* corresponding to *arthritis*). ■ from other bases: *syphilitic*.
– ORIGIN from French *-itique*, via Latin *-iticus* from Greek *-itikos*.

itinerant /ɪˈtɪn(ə)r(ə)nt, ʌɪ-/ ▶ **adjective** travelling from place to place: *itinerant traders.*
▶ **noun** a person who travels from place to place.
– DERIVATIVES **itineracy** noun, **itinerancy** noun.
– ORIGIN late 16th cent. (used to describe a judge travelling on a circuit): from late Latin *itinerant-* 'travelling', from the verb *itinerari*, from Latin *iter, itiner-* 'journey, road'.

itinerary /ʌɪˈtɪn(ə)(rə)ri, ɪ-/ ▶ **noun** (pl. **-ies**) a planned route or journey.
■ a travel document recording these.
– ORIGIN late Middle English: from late Latin *itinerarium*, neuter of *itinerarius* 'of a journey or roads', from Latin *iter, itiner-* 'journey, road'.

itinerate /ɪˈtɪnəreɪt, ʌɪ-/ ▶ **verb** [no obj.] (especially of a church minister or a magistrate) travel from place to place to perform one's professional duty.
– DERIVATIVES **itineration** noun.
– ORIGIN early 17th cent.: from late Latin *itinerat-* 'travelled', from the verb *itinerari* (see **ITINERANT**).

-ition ▶ **suffix** (forming nouns) equivalent to **-ATION** (as in *audition, rendition*).
– ORIGIN from French, or from Latin *-itio(n)-*.

-itious[1] ▶ **suffix** forming adjectives corresponding to nouns ending in *-ition* (such as *ambitious* corresponding to *ambition*).
– ORIGIN from Latin *-itiosus*.

-itious[2] ▶ **suffix** (forming adjectives) related to; having the nature of: *fictitious* | *suppositious*.
– ORIGIN from late Latin *-itius*, alteration of Latin *-icius*.

-itis ▶ **suffix** forming names of inflammatory diseases: *cystitis* | *hepatitis*.
■ informal used with reference to a tendency or state of mind that is compared to a disease: *creditcarditis*.
– ORIGIN from Greek feminine form of adjectives ending in *-itēs* (combined with *nosos* 'disease' implied).

-itive ▶ **suffix** (forming adjectives) equivalent to **-ATIVE** (as in *genitive, positive*).
– ORIGIN from French *-itif, -itive* or Latin *-itivus* (from past participial stems ending in *-it*).

it'll ▶ **contraction of** it shall; it will.

ITN ▶ **abbreviation for** (in the UK) Independent Television News.

Ito /ˈiːtəʊ/, Prince Hirobumi (1841–1909), Japanese statesman, Premier four times between 1884 and 1901. He was prominent in drafting the Japanese constitution (1889) and helped to establish a bicameral national diet (1890). He was assassinated by a member of the Korean independence movement.

-itous ▶ **suffix** forming adjectives corresponding to nouns ending in *-ity* (such as *calamitous* corresponding to *calamity*).
– ORIGIN from French *-iteux*, from Latin *-itosus*.

its ▶ **possessive determiner** belonging to or associated with a thing previously mentioned or easily identified: *turn the camera on its side* | *he chose the area for its atmosphere.*
■ belonging to or associated with a child or animal of unspecified sex: *a baby in its mother's womb.*

USAGE A common error in writing is to confuse the possessive **its** (as in *turn the camera on **its** side*) with the contraction **it's** (short for either **it is** or **it has**, as in ***it's** my fault; **it's** been a hot day*). The confusion is at least partly understandable since other possessive forms (singular nouns) do take an apostrophe + **-s**, as in *the **girl's** bike; the **President's** smile.*

it's ▶ **contraction of** ■ it is: *it's my fault.* ■ it has: *it's been a hot day.*

itself ▶ **pronoun** [third person singular] **1** [reflexive] used as the object of a verb or preposition to refer to a thing or animal previously mentioned as the subject of the clause: *his horse hurt itself* | *wisteria was tumbling over itself.*
2 [emphatic] used to emphasize a particular thing or animal mentioned: *the roots are several inches long, though the plant itself is only a foot tall.*
■ used after a quality to emphasize what a perfect example of that quality someone or something is: *Mrs Vincent was kindness itself.*
– PHRASES **by itself** see ***by oneself*** at **BY**. **in itself** viewed in its essential qualities; considered separately from other things: *some would say bringing up a family was a full-time job in itself.*
– ORIGIN Old English (see **IT**[1], **SELF**).

itsy-bitsy (also **itty-bitty**) ▶ **adjective** informal very small; tiny.
– ORIGIN 1930s: from a child's form of **LITTLE** + *bitsy* (from **BIT**[1] + **-SY**).

ITU ▶ **abbreviation for** International Telecommunication Union.

ITV ▶ **abbreviation for** (in the UK) Independent Television.

-ity ▶ **suffix** forming nouns denoting quality or condition: *humility* | *probity*.
■ denoting an instance or degree of this: *a profanity.*
– ORIGIN from French *-ité*, from Latin *-itas, -itatis*.

IU ▶ **abbreviation for** international unit.

IUCN ▶ **abbreviation for** International Union for the Conservation of Nature.

IUD ▶ **abbreviation for** ■ intrauterine death (of the fetus before birth). ■ intrauterine device.

-ium ▶ **suffix** **1** forming nouns adopted unchanged from Latin (such as *alluvium*) or based on Latin or Greek words (such as *euphonium*).
2 (also **-um**) forming names of metallic elements: *cadmium* | *magnesium*.
3 denoting a region of the body: *pericardium*.
4 denoting a biological structure: *mycelium*.
– ORIGIN modern Latin in senses 2, 3, and 4, via Latin from Greek *-ion*.

IUPAC ▶ **abbreviation for** International Union of Pure and Applied Chemistry.

IV ▶ **abbreviation for** intravenous or intravenously.

Ivan[1] /ˈʌɪv(ə)n/ the name of six rulers of Russia:
■ Ivan I (*c.*1304–41), grand duke of Muscovy 1328–40. He strengthened and enlarged the duchy, making Moscow the ecclesiastical capital in 1326.
■ Ivan II (1326–59), grand duke of Muscovy 1353–9; known as **Ivan the Red**.
■ Ivan III (1440–1505), grand duke of Muscovy 1462–1505; known as **Ivan the Great**. He consolidated and enlarged his territory, defending it against a Tartar invasion in 1480 and adopting the title 'Ruler of all Russia' in 1472.
■ Ivan IV (1530–84), grand duke of Muscovy 1533–47 and first tsar of Russia 1547–84; known as **Ivan the Terrible**. He captured Kazan, Astrakhan, and Siberia, but the Tartar siege of Moscow and the Polish victory in the Livonian War (1558–82) left Russia weak and divided. In 1581 he killed his eldest son Ivan in a fit of rage, the succession passing to his mentally handicapped second son Fyodor.
■ Ivan V (1666–96), nominal tsar of Russia 1682–96.
■ Ivan VI (1740–64), infant tsar of Russia 1740–1.

Ivan[2] /ˈʌɪv(ə)n/ ▶ **noun** informal a Russian man, especially a Russian soldier.

I've ▶ **contraction of** I have.

-ive ▶ **suffix** (forming adjectives, also nouns derived from them) tending to; having the nature of: *active* | *corrosive* | *palliative*.
– DERIVATIVES **-ively** suffix forming corresponding adverbs, **-iveness** suffix forming corresponding nouns.
– ORIGIN from French *-if, -ive*, from Latin *-ivus*.

ivermectin /ˌʌɪvəˈmɛktɪn/ ▶ **noun** [mass noun] a compound of the avermectin group, used as an anthelmintic in veterinary medicine and as a treatment for river blindness.

Ives /ʌɪvz/, Charles (Edward) (1874–1954), American composer, noted for his use of polyrhythms, polytonality, quarter-tones, and aleatoric techniques. Notable works: *The Unanswered Question* (chamber work, 1906) and *Three Places in New England* (for orchestra, 1903–14).

IVF ▶ **abbreviation for** in vitro fertilization.

ivied ▶ **adjective** covered in ivy: *the ivied rectory.*
■ US of or relating to the academic institutions of the Ivy League.

ivorine /ˈʌɪvəriːn, -ʌɪn/ ▶ **noun** [mass noun] trademark an artificial product resembling ivory in colour or texture.

Ivory, James (b.1928), American film director. He has made a number of films in partnership with the producer Ismail Merchant, including *Heat and Dust* (1983) and *Howard's End* (1992).

ivory ▶ **noun** (pl. **-ies**) [mass noun] **1** a hard creamy-white substance composing the main part of the tusks of an elephant, walrus, or narwhal, often (especially formerly) used to make ornaments and other articles.
■ [count noun] an object made of ivory. ■ (**the ivories**) informal the keys of a piano: *Derek **tinkled the ivories** for us.* ■ (**ivories**) informal a person's teeth.
2 a creamy-white colour.
– DERIVATIVES **ivoried** adjective.
– ORIGIN Middle English: from Anglo-Norman French *ivurie*, based on Latin *ebur*.

ivory black ▶ **noun** [mass noun] a black carbon pigment made from charred ivory or (now usually) bone, used in drawing and painting.

Ivory Coast a country in West Africa, on the Gulf of Guinea; pop. 12,000,000 (est. 1990); languages, French (official), West African languages; capital, Yamoussoukro. French name **CÔTE D'IVOIRE**.

The area was explored by the Portuguese in the late 15th century. Subsequently it was disputed by traders from various European countries, who mainly sought ivory and slaves. It was made a French protectorate in 1842 and became a fully independent republic in 1960.

ivory nut ▶ **noun** the seed of a tropical American palm, which, when hardened, is a source of vegetable ivory. Also called **TAGUA NUT**.
• The palm is *Phytelephas macrocarpa*, family Palmae.

ivory tower ▶ **noun** a state of privileged seclusion or separation from the facts and practicalities of the real world: *the ivory tower of academia.*
– ORIGIN early 20th cent.: translating French *tour d'ivoire*, used by the writer Sainte-Beuve.

ivy ▶ **noun** [mass noun] a woody evergreen Eurasian

climbing plant, typically having shiny, dark green five-pointed leaves.
● Genus *Hedera*, family Araliaceae: several species, in particular the common *H. helix*, which is often seen climbing on tree trunks and walls.
■ used in names of similar climbing plants, e.g. **poison ivy**, **Boston ivy**.
– ORIGIN Old English *īfig*, of Germanic origin; related to the first elements of Dutch *eiloof* and German *Efeu*.

Ivy League ▶ noun a group of long-established universities in the eastern US having high academic and social prestige. It includes Harvard, Yale, Princeton, and Columbia.
– ORIGIN with reference to the ivy traditionally growing over the walls of these establishments.

IWC ▶ abbreviation for International Whaling Commission.

iwi /ˈiːwi/ ▶ noun (pl. same) NZ a community or people.
– ORIGIN Maori.

Iwo Jima /ˌiːwəʊ ˈdʒiːmə/ a small volcanic island, the largest of the Volcano Islands in the western Pacific, 1,222 km (760 miles) south of Tokyo. During the Second World War it was the heavily fortified site of a Japanese airbase, and its attack and capture in 1944–5 was one of the severest US campaigns. It was returned to Japan in 1968.

IWW ▶ abbreviation for Industrial Workers of the World.

ixia /ˈɪksɪə/ ▶ noun a South African plant of the iris family, which bears showy six-petalled starlike flowers on tall wiry stems and has sword-shaped leaves.
● Genus *Ixia*, family Iridaceae: many cultivars.
– ORIGIN modern Latin, from Latin, denoting a kind of thistle, from Greek.

Ixion /ɪkˈsʌɪən/ Greek Mythology a king punished by Zeus for attempting to seduce Hera by being pinned to a fiery wheel that revolved unceasingly through the underworld.

ixtle /ˈɪkstli/ (also **istle**) ▶ noun [mass noun] (in Mexico and Central America) a plant fibre used for cordage, nets, and carpets.
● This fibre is obtained chiefly from *Agave* species (family Agavaceae), in particular *A. funkiana* and *A. lechuguilla*.
– ORIGIN late 19th cent.: via American Spanish from Nahuatl *ixtli*.

Iyyar /ˈiːjɑː/ ▶ noun (in the Jewish calendar) the eighth month of the civil and second of the religious year, usually coinciding with parts of April and May.
– ORIGIN from Hebrew *'iyyār*.

izard /ˈɪzəd/ ▶ noun (in the Pyrenees) a chamois.
– ORIGIN late 18th cent.: from French *isard* or Gascon *isart*, of unknown origin.

-ize (also **-ise**) ▶ suffix forming verbs meaning:
1 make or become: *fossilize* | *privatize*.
■ cause to resemble: *Americanize*.
2 treat in a specified way: *pasteurize*.
■ treat or cause to combine with a specified substance: *carbonize* | *oxidize*.
3 follow a specified practice: *agonize* | *theorize*.
■ subject to a practice: *hospitalize*.
– DERIVATIVES **-ization** suffix forming corresponding nouns, **-izer** suffix forming agent nouns.
– ORIGIN from French *-iser*, via late Latin *-izare* from Greek verbs ending in *-izein*.

USAGE **1** The form **-ize** has been in use in English since the 16th century; although it is widely used in American English, it is not an Americanism. The alternative spelling **-ise** (reflecting a French influence) is in common use, especially in British English. It is obligatory in certain cases: first, where it forms part of a larger word element, such as **-mise** (= sending) in **compromise**, and **-prise** (= taking) in **surprise**; and second, in verbs corresponding to nouns with **-s-** in the stem, such as **advertise** and **televise**.
2 Adding **-ize** to a noun or adjective has been a standard way of forming new verbs for centuries, and verbs such as **characterize**, **terrorize**, and **sterilize** were all formed in this way hundreds of years ago. For some reason, people object to recent formations of this type: during the 20th century, there have been objections raised against **prioritize**, **finalize**, and **hospitalize**, among others. There doesn't seem to be any coherent reason for this, except that verbs formed from nouns tend, inexplicably, to be criticized as vulgar formations. Despite objections, it is clear that **-ize** forms are an accepted part of the standard language.

Izhevsk /ɪˈʒɛfsk/ an industrial city in central Russia, capital of the republic of Udmurtia; pop. 642,000 (1990). Former name (1984–87) **USTINOV**.

Izmir /ɪzˈmɪə/ a seaport and naval base in western Turkey, on an inlet of the Aegean Sea; pop. 1,757,410 (1990). It is the third largest city in Turkey. Former name **SMYRNA**.

Izmit /ˈɪzmɪt/ a city in NW Turkey, situated on the Gulf of Izmit, an inlet of the Sea of Marmara; pop. 256,880 (1990).

Iznik /ˈɪznɪk/ (also **Isnik**) ▶ adjective [attrib.] denoting colourful pottery and ceramic tiles produced during the 16th and 17th centuries in Iznik (ancient Nicaea), a town in NW Turkey.

Izod test /ˈʌɪzɒd/ ▶ noun a material strength test in which a notched specimen is broken by a blow from a pendulum, the energy absorbed being determined from the decrease in the swing of the pendulum.
– ORIGIN early 20th cent.: named after Edwin G. *Izod* (born 1876), the British engineer who devised the test.

Izvestia /ɪzˈvɛstɪə/ (also **Izvestiya**) a Russian daily newspaper founded in 1917 as the official organ of the Soviet government. It has continued to be published independently since the collapse of communist rule and the break-up of the Soviet Union.
– ORIGIN from Russian *izvestiya* 'news'.

izzat /ˈɪzʌt/ ▶ noun [mass noun] Indian honour, reputation, or prestige: *the izzat of the household was at stake*.
– ORIGIN Persian and Urdu, from Arabic *'izza* 'glory'.

Jj

J¹ (also **j**) ▶ **noun** (pl. **Js** or **J's**) **1** the tenth letter of the alphabet.
- ▪denoting the next after I (or H if I is omitted) in a set of items, categories, etc.
2 (**J**) a shape like that of a capital J (without a crosspiece).
3 archaic used instead of I as the Roman numeral for one in final position: *between ij and iij of the clock.*

J² ▶ **abbreviation for** ▪ jack (used in describing play in card games). ▪ Japan (international vehicle registration). ▪ Physics joule(s). ▪ (in titles) Journal (of): *J. Biol. Chem.*

j ▶ **symbol for** (*j*) (in electrical engineering and electronics) the imaginary quantity equal to the square root of minus one. Compare with **ı**.

ja /jɑː/ ▶ **exclamation** informal South African term for **YES**: *'Let's go swimming.' 'Ja!'* | *ja, this is the life!*
- PHRASES **ja well** used as an expression of embarrassment, apology, or world-weariness. **ja well no fine** used to express a non-committal, resigned, or ironical attitude.
- ORIGIN Dutch.

jab ▶ **verb** (**jabbed**, **jabbing**) [with obj. and adverbial] poke (someone or something) roughly or quickly, especially with something sharp or pointed: *she jabbed him in his ribs* | [no obj.] *he jabbed at the air with his finger.*
- ▪poke someone or something roughly or quickly with (a sharp or pointed object or a part of the body): *she jabbed the fork into the earth.*
▶ **noun** a quick, sharp blow, especially with the fist: *fast jabs to the face.*
- ▪informal a hypodermic injection, especially a vaccination: *an anti-tetanus jab.* ▪ a sharp, painful sensation or feeling: *the jabs of pain up my spine* | *a jab of envy.*
- ORIGIN early 19th cent. (originally Scots): variant of **JOB²**.

Jabalpur /ˌdʒʌb(ə)l'pʊə/ an industrial city and military post in Madhya Pradesh, central India; pop. 760,000 (1991).

jabber ▶ **verb** [no obj.] talk rapidly and excitedly but with little sense: *he jabbered away to his friends.*
▶ **noun** [mass noun] fast, excited talk that makes little sense: *stop your jabber.*
- ORIGIN late 15th cent.: imitative.

jabberwocky /'dʒabəˌwɒki/ ▶ **noun** (pl. **-ies**) [mass noun] invented or meaningless language; nonsense.
- ORIGIN early 20th cent.: from the title of a nonsense poem in Lewis Carroll's *Through the Looking Glass* (1871).

jabiru /'dʒabɪruː/ ▶ **noun** a large Central and South American stork with a black neck, mainly white plumage, and a large black upturned bill.
- ●*Ephippiorhynchus mycteria*, family Ciconiidae.
- ▪either of two related storks found in Asia, Australasia, and Africa.
- ORIGIN late 18th cent.: from Tupi-Guarani *jabirú*, from *j* 'that which has' + *abirú* 'swollen' (suggested by the bird's large neck).

jab jab ▶ **noun** W. Indian a devil, in particular as represented in a carnival masquerade.
- ORIGIN French Creole, from French *diable diable* 'devil devil'.

jaborandi /ˌdʒabə'randi/ ▶ **noun** **1** [mass noun] a drug made from the dried leaves of certain South American plants, which contain the alkaloid pilocarpine and promote salivation when chewed. **2** any of the plants that yield this drug.
- ●Several genera and species, in particular *Pilocarpus jaborandi* (family Rutaceae).
- ORIGIN early 17th cent.: from Tupi-Guarani *jaburandi*, literally 'a person who spits'.

jabot /'ʒabəʊ/ ▶ **noun** an ornamental frill or ruffle on the front of a shirt or blouse, typically made of lace.
- ORIGIN early 19th cent. (denoting a frill on a man's shirt): French, originally 'crop of a bird'.

jacal /hə'kɑːl/ ▶ **noun** (pl. **jacales** /hə'kɑːleɪz/) (in Mexico and the south-western US) a thatched wattle-and-daub hut.
- ORIGIN Mexican Spanish, from Nahuatl *xacalli*, contraction of *xamitl calli* 'adobe house'.

jacamar /'dʒakəmɑː/ ▶ **noun** an insectivorous bird of tropical American forests, with a long pointed bill, a long tail, and plumage that is typically iridescent green above.
- ●Family Galbulidae: several genera and species.
- ORIGIN early 19th cent.: from French, apparently from Tupi.

jacana /'dʒakənə/ (also **jaçana** /ˌdʒasə'nɑː/) ▶ **noun** a small tropical wading bird with greatly elongated toes and claws that enable it to walk on floating vegetation. Also called **LILY-TROTTER**.
- ●Family Jacanidae: several genera and species.
- ORIGIN mid 18th cent.: from Portuguese *jaçana*, from Tupi-Guarani *jasanã.*

jacaranda /ˌdʒakə'randə/ ▶ **noun** a tropical American tree which has blue trumpet-shaped flowers, fern-like leaves, and fragrant timber.
- ●Genus *Jacaranda*, family Bignoniaceae.
- ORIGIN mid 18th cent.: from Portuguese, from Tupi-Guarani *jakara'nda.*

jacinth /'dʒasɪnθ, 'dʒeɪ-/ ▶ **noun** [mass noun] a reddish-orange gem variety of zircon.
- ORIGIN Middle English: from Old French *iacinte* or medieval Latin *iacintus*, alteration of Latin *hyacinthus* (see **HYACINTH**).

jack¹ ▶ **noun** **1** a device for lifting heavy objects, especially one for raising the axle of a motor vehicle off the ground so that a wheel can be changed or the underside inspected.
2 a playing card bearing a representation of a soldier, page, or knave, normally ranking next below a queen.
3 (also **jack socket**) a socket with two or more pairs of terminals designed to receive a jack plug.
4 a small white ball in bowls, at which the players aim.
5 (also **jackstone**) a small round pebble or star-shaped piece of metal or plastic used in tossing and catching games.
- ▪(**jacks**) a game played by tossing and catching such pebbles or pieces of metal.
6 (**Jack**) used to typify an ordinary man: *he had that world-weary look of the working Jack who'd seen everything.* [ORIGIN: familiar form of the given name *John*.]
- ▪informal, chiefly US used as a form of address to a man whose name is not known. ▪ N. Amer. informal a lumberjack. ▪ informal a detective or police officer.
- ▪ archaic a steeplejack. ▪ the figure of a man striking the bell on a clock.
7 a small version of a national flag flown at the bow of a vessel in harbour to indicate its nationality.
8 [mass noun] US informal money.
9 a device for turning a spit.
10 a part of the mechanism in a spinet or harpsichord that connects a key to its corresponding string and causes the string to be plucked when the key is pressed down.
11 a marine fish that is typically laterally compressed with a row of large spiky scales along each side. Jacks are important in many places as food or game fish. Also called **POMPANO**, **SCAD**. [ORIGIN: originally a West Indian term.]
- ●Family Carangidae (the **jack family**): many genera and numerous species. The jack family also includes the horse mackerel, pilotfish, kingfishes, and trevallies.
12 the male of various animals, especially a merlin or (US) an ass.
13 used in names of animals that are smaller than similar kinds, e.g. **jack snipe**.
14 US informal short for **JACKSHIT**.
- PHRASES **before one can say Jack Robinson** informal very quickly or suddenly. **every man jack** informal each and every person (used for emphasis): *they're spies, every man jack of them.* **I'm all right, Jack** informal used to express selfish complacency. **jack of all trades (and master of none)** a person who can do many different types of work but who is not necessarily very competent at any of them. **on one's jack** (or **Jack Jones**) Brit. rhyming slang on one's own.
- ORIGIN late Middle English: from *Jack*, pet form of the given name *John*. The term was used originally to denote an ordinary man (sense 6), also a youth (mid 16th cent.), hence the 'knave' in cards and 'male animal'. The word also denoted various devices saving human labour, as though one had a helper (senses 1, 3, 9, and 10), and in compounds such as **JACKHAMMER** and **JACKKNIFE**); the general sense 'labourer' arose in the early 18th cent. and survives in **CHEAPJACK**, **LUMBERJACK**, **STEEPLE-JACK**, etc. Since the mid 16th cent. a notion of 'smallness' has arisen, hence senses 4, 5, 7, and 13.
▶**jack someone around** N. Amer. informal cause someone inconvenience or problems, especially by acting unfairly or indecisively.
jack in (or **into**) informal log into or connect up (a computer or electronic device).
jack something in Brit. informal give up or leave off from doing something, especially a job.
jack off vulgar slang masturbate.
jack up 1 informal inject oneself with a narcotic drug. **2** Austral. give up or refuse to participate in something.
jack something up raise something, especially a vehicle, with a jack. ▪ informal increase something by a considerable amount: *France jacked up its key bank interest rate.*

jack² ▶ **noun** historical **1** another term for **BLACKJACK** (in sense 5).
2 a sleeveless padded tunic worn by foot soldiers.
[ORIGIN: late Middle English: from Old French *jaque*; origin uncertain, perhaps based on Arabic.]

jack³ ▶ **adjective** [predic.] Austral./NZ tired of or bored

with someone or something: *people are getting jack of strikes.*
– ORIGIN late 19th cent.: from *jack up* 'give up'.

jackal /ˈdʒakəl, -kɔːl/ ▶ noun a slender long-legged wild dog that feeds on carrion, game, and fruit and often hunts cooperatively, found in Africa and southern Asia.
● Genus *Canis*, family Canidae: four species. See also **GOLDEN JACKAL**.
– ORIGIN early 17th cent.: from Turkish *çakal*, from Persian *šagāl*. The change in the first syllable was due to association with **JACK**[1].

jackanapes /ˈdʒakəneɪps/ ▶ noun **1** dated an impertinent person.
2 archaic a tame monkey.
– ORIGIN early 16th cent. (originally as *Jack Napes*): perhaps from a playful name for a tame ape, the initial *n-* by elision of *an ape* (compare with **NEWT**), and the final *-s* as in surnames such as *Hobbes*: hence applied to a person whose behaviour resembled that of an ape.

Jack and Jill party ▶ noun N. Amer. a party held for a couple soon to be married, to which both men and women are invited.

jack arch ▶ noun a small arch only one brick in thickness, especially as used in numbers to support a floor.

jackaroo /ˌdʒakəˈruː/ (also **jackeroo**) Austral. informal ▶ noun a young man working on a sheep or cattle station to gain experience.
▶ verb [no obj.] work as a jackaroo.
– ORIGIN late 19th cent.: alteration of an Aboriginal (Queensland) term *dhugai-iu* 'wandering white man', by blending **JACK**[1] and **KANGAROO**.

jackass ▶ noun **1** a stupid person.
2 a male ass or donkey.
3 Austral. short for **LAUGHING JACKASS**.

jack bean ▶ noun a tropical American climbing plant of the pea family, which yields an edible bean and pod and is widely grown for fodder in tropical countries.
● Genus *Canavalia*, family Leguminosae: in particular *C. ensiformis*.
■ the seed of this plant.

jackboot ▶ noun a large leather military boot reaching to the knee.
■ [in sing.] used as a symbol of cruel or authoritarian behaviour or rule: *a country under the jackboot of colonialism.*
– DERIVATIVES **jackbooted** adjective.

Jack-by-the-hedge ▶ noun a white-flowered European plant of the cabbage family, which grows typically in hedgerows and has leaves that smell of garlic when crushed. Also called **HEDGE GARLIC**.
● *Alliaria petiolata*, family Cruciferae.

jack chain ▶ noun a chain of unwelded links each consisting of a double loop of wire resembling a figure of 8, but with the loops in planes at right angles to each other.

Jack cheese ▶ noun North American term for **MONTEREY JACK**.

jackdaw ▶ noun a small grey-headed crow that typically nests in tall buildings and chimneys, noted for its inquisitiveness.
● Genus *Corvus*, family Corvidae: two species, in particular the Eurasian *C. monedula*.

jackeen /dʒaˈkiːn/ ▶ noun Irish, chiefly derogatory a city-dweller, especially a Dubliner.
– ORIGIN mid 19th cent.: diminutive of the pet name *Jack* (see **JACK**[1], **-EEN**).

jackeroo ▶ noun & verb variant spelling of **JACKAROO**.

jacket ▶ noun an outer garment extending either to the waist or the hips, typically having sleeves and a fastening down the front.
■ an outer covering, especially one placed round a tank or pipe to insulate it. ■ the skin of a potato: *potatoes cooked in their jackets.* ■ informal a jacket potato. ■ the dust jacket of a book. ■ a record sleeve. ■ a steel frame fixed to the seabed, forming the support structure of an oil production platform.
▶ verb (**jacketed**, **jacketing**) [with obj.] cover with a jacket.
– ORIGIN late Middle English: from Old French *jaquet*, diminutive of *jaque* (see **JACK**[2]).

jacket potato ▶ noun Brit. a baked potato served with the skin on.

jackfish ▶ noun (pl. same or **-fishes**) chiefly N. Amer. a pike or sauger, especially the northern pike.

Jack Frost ▶ noun a personification of frost: *the seedlings battled with Jack Frost.*

jackfruit ▶ noun a fast-growing tropical Asian tree related to the breadfruit.
● *Artocarpus heterophyllus*, family Moraceae.
■ the very large edible fruit of this tree, resembling a breadfruit and important as food in the tropics.
– ORIGIN late 16th cent.: from Portuguese *jaca* (from Malayalam *chakka*) + **FRUIT**.

jackhammer chiefly N. Amer. ▶ noun a portable pneumatic hammer or drill.
▶ verb [with obj.] beat or hammer heavily or loudly and repeatedly.

jackie hangman ▶ noun South African term for **FISCAL** (in sense 2).
– ORIGIN early 20th cent.: apparently so named because of the bird's habit of impaling its prey on long sharp thorns.

jack-in-office ▶ noun Brit. a self-important minor official.

jack-in-the-box ▶ noun a toy consisting of a box containing a figure on a spring which pops up when the lid is opened.

Jack-in-the-pulpit ▶ noun either of two small plants of the arum family:
● another term for **CUCKOO PINT**. ● a North American arum with a green or purple-brown spathe (*Arisaema triphyllum*, family Araceae).
– ORIGIN mid 19th cent.: so named because the erect spadix overarched by the spathe resembles a person in a pulpit.

jackknife ▶ noun (pl. **-knives**) **1** a large knife with a folding blade.
2 a dive in which the body is first bent at the waist and then straightened.
3 Statistics a method of assessing the variability of data by repeating a calculation on the sets of data obtained by removing one value from the complete set.
▶ verb (**-knifed**, **-knifing**) [with obj.] move (one's body) into a bent or doubled-up position: *the Major jackknifed his thin body at the waist* | [no obj.] *she jackknifed into a sitting position.*
■ [no obj.] (of an articulated vehicle) bend into a V-shape in an uncontrolled skidding movement. ■ [no obj.] (of a diver) perform a jackknife.

jackknife clam ▶ noun North American term for **RAZOR SHELL**.

jackknife fish ▶ noun a strikingly marked fish with a long upright dorsal fin, which lives among rocks and corals in the warm waters of the western Atlantic.
● *Equetus lanceolatus*, family Sciaenidae.

jackleg ▶ noun US informal an incompetent, unskilful, or dishonest person: [as modifier] *a jackleg carpenter.*

jack light ▶ noun N. Amer. a portable light, especially one used for fishing at night.

Jacklin, Tony (b.1944), English golfer; full name *Antony Jacklin*. He won the British Open in 1969 and in 1970 became the first British player to win the US Open for fifty years.

jack mackerel ▶ noun a game fish of the jack family, occurring in the eastern Pacific.
● *Trachurus symmetricus*, family Carangidae.

jack-o'-lantern ▶ noun **1** a lantern made from a hollowed-out pumpkin or turnip in which holes are cut to represent facial features, typically made at Halloween.
2 archaic a will-o'-the wisp.

jack pine ▶ noun a small, hardy North American pine with short needles.
● *Pinus banksiana*, family Pinaceae.

jack plane ▶ noun a medium-sized plane for use in rough joinery.

jack plug ▶ noun a plug consisting of a single shaft used to make a connection which transmits a signal, typically used in sound equipment.

jackpot ▶ noun a large cash prize in a game or lottery, especially one that accumulates until it is won.
– PHRASES **hit the jackpot** informal **1** win a jackpot. **2** have great or unexpected success, especially in making a lot of money quickly: *the theatre hit the jackpot with its first musical.*
– ORIGIN late 19th cent.: from **JACK**[1] + **POT**[1]. The term was originally used in a form of poker, where the pool or pot accumulated until a player could open the bidding with two jacks or better.

---

jackrabbit ▶ noun a hare found on the prairies and steppes of North America.
● Genus *Lepus*, family Leporidae: several species.
– ORIGIN mid 19th cent.: abbreviation of *jackass-rabbit*, because of its long ears.

Jack Russell (also **Jack Russell terrier**) ▶ noun a terrier of a small working breed with short legs.
– ORIGIN early 20th cent.: named after the Revd John (Jack) *Russell* (1795–1883), an English clergyman famed in fox-hunting circles as a breeder of such terriers.

jack screw ▶ noun a screw which can be turned to adjust the position of an object into which it fits.
■ another term for **SCREW JACK**.

jack shaft ▶ noun a small auxiliary or intermediate shaft in machinery.

jackshit ▶ noun [mass noun] [usu. with negative] US vulgar slang anything at all.

jacksie (also **jacksy**) ▶ noun Brit. informal a person's bottom.
– ORIGIN late 19th cent.: diminutive of **JACK**[1].

jack snipe ▶ noun a small dark Eurasian snipe.
● *Lymnocryptes minima*, family Scolopacidae.
■ N. Amer. any similar wader, e.g. the pectoral sandpiper or the common snipe.

jack socket ▶ noun see **JACK**[1] (sense 3).

Jackson[1] the state capital of Mississippi; pop. 196,640 (1990).
– ORIGIN originally known as *Le Fleur's Bluff*, it was later named after President Andrew *Jackson*.

Jackson[2], Andrew (1767–1845), American general and Democratic statesman, 7th President of the US 1829–37; known as **Old Hickory**. As President he replaced an estimated 20 per cent of those in public office with Democrat supporters, a practice that became known as the spoils system.

Jackson[3], Glenda (b.1936), English actress and politician. After a film career in which she won Oscars for her performances in *Women in Love* (1969) and *A Touch of Class* (1973), she became Labour MP for Hampstead and Highgate in 1992.

Jackson[4], Michael (Joe) (b.1958), American singer and songwriter. Having started singing with his four brothers, as the Jackson Five, he became the most commercially successful American star of the 1980s with the albums *Thriller* (1982) and *Bad* (1987).

Jackson[5], Thomas Jonathan (1824–63), American Confederate general; known as **Stonewall Jackson**. During the American Civil War he made his mark as a commander at the first battle of Bull Run in 1861 and later became the deputy of Robert E. Lee.

Jacksonian /dʒakˈsəʊnɪən/ ▶ adjective Medicine relating to or denoting a form of epilepsy in which seizures begin at one site (typically a digit or the angle of the mouth).
– ORIGIN late 19th cent.: from the name of John H. *Jackson* (1835–1911), English physician and neurologist, + **-IAN**.

Jacksonville an industrial city and port in NE Florida; pop. 672,970 (1990).
– ORIGIN named in honour of President Andrew Jackson.

jackstaff ▶ noun a short staff at a ship's bow, on which a jack is hoisted.

jackstay ▶ noun Nautical a rope, bar, or batten placed along a ship's yard to bend the head of a square sail to.
■ a line secured at both ends to serve as a support, e.g. for an awning.

jackstone ▶ noun see **JACK**[1] (sense 5).

jackstraw ▶ noun another term for **SPILLIKIN**.

jacksy ▶ noun (pl. **-ies**) variant spelling of **JACKSIE**.

Jack tar ▶ noun Brit. informal, dated a sailor.

Jack the Lad ▶ noun informal a brash, cocky young man.
– ORIGIN nickname of *Jack Sheppard*, an 18th-cent. thief.

Jack the Ripper an unidentified 19th-century English murderer. In 1888 at least six prostitutes were brutally killed in the East End of London, the bodies being mutilated in a way that indicated a knowledge of anatomy. The authorities received taunting notes from a person calling himself Jack the Ripper and claiming to be the murderer, but the cases remain unsolved.

jack-up (also **jack-up rig**) ▶ noun an offshore

---

b **b**ut | d **d**og | f **f**ew | g **g**et | h **h**e | j **y**es | k **c**at | l **l**eg | m **m**an | n **n**o | p **p**en | r **r**ed | s **s**it | t **t**op | v **v**oice | w **w**e | z **z**oo | ʃ **sh**e | ʒ deci**si**on | θ **th**in | ð **th**is | ŋ ri**ng** | x lo**ch** | tʃ **ch**ip | dʒ **j**ar

drilling rig the legs of which are lowered to the seabed from the operating platform.

Jacky (also **Jacky Jacky**) ▶ noun (pl. **-ies**) Austral., offensive an aboriginal.
– ORIGIN mid 19th cent.: diminutive of the pet name *Jack* (see JACK¹).

Jacky lizard ▶ noun a brownish SE Australian lizard which becomes paler as the temperature rises. When threatened it puffs itself up and opens its orange mouth.
● *Amphibolus muricatus*, family Agamidae.

Jacky Winter ▶ noun an Australasian flycatcher which has a grey-brown back and whitish underside and constantly wags its white-edged tail.
● *Microeca leucophaea*, family Eopsaltridae (or Muscicapidae). Alternative name: **Australian brown flycatcher**.
– ORIGIN late 19th cent.: diminutive form of the pet name *Jack* (see JACK¹) + *Winter* (imitative of the bird's cry).

Jacob /ˈdʒeɪkəb/ (in the Bible) a Hebrew patriarch, the younger of the twin sons of Isaac and Rebecca, who persuaded his brother Esau to sell him his birthright and tricked him out of his father's blessing (Gen. 25, 27). His twelve sons became the founders of the twelve tribes of ancient Israel.
– ORIGIN from Hebrew *yaʿaqōb* 'following after, supplanter'.

Jacobean /ˌdʒakəˈbiːən/ ▶ adjective of or relating to the reign of James I of England: *a Jacobean mansion.*
■ (of furniture) in the style prevalent during the reign of James I, especially being the colour of dark oak.
▶ noun a person who lived during this period.
– ORIGIN mid 19th cent. (in use earlier with reference to St James): from modern Latin *Jacobaeus* (from ecclesiastical Latin *Jacobus* 'James', from Greek *Iakōbos* 'Jacob') + -AN.

Jacobethan /ˌdʒakəˈbiːθ(ə)n/ ▶ adjective (especially of architecture) displaying a combination of Elizabethan and Jacobean styles.
– ORIGIN mid 20th cent.: blend of JACOBEAN and ELIZABETHAN.

Jacobi /dʒaˈkəʊbi/, Karl Gustav Jacob (1804–51), German mathematician. He worked on the theory of elliptic functions, in competition with Niels Abel.

Jacobian /dʒɔˈkəʊbiən/ Mathematics ▶ adjective of or relating to the work of the mathematician K. G. J. Jacobi.
▶ noun a determinant whose constituents are the derivatives of a number of functions (u, v, w, …) with respect to each of the same number of variables (x, y, z, …).

Jacobin /ˈdʒakəbɪn/ ▶ noun 1 historical a member of a democratic club established in Paris in 1789. The Jacobins were the most radical and ruthless of the political groups formed in the wake of the French Revolution, and in association with Robespierre they instituted the Terror of 1793–4.
■ an extreme political radical.
2 chiefly historical a Dominican friar.
3 (**jacobin**) a pigeon of a breed with reversed feathers on the back of its neck like a cowl.
4 (**jacobin**) a mainly green Central and South American hummingbird, with blue feathers on the head.
● *Florisuga mellivora* and *Melanotrichus fuscus*, family Trochilidae.
– DERIVATIVES **Jacobinic** adjective, **Jacobinical** adjective, **Jacobinism** noun.
– ORIGIN Middle English (in sense 2): from Old French, from medieval Latin *Jacobinus*, from ecclesiastical Latin *Jacobus* 'James'. The term was applied to the Dominicans in Old French from their church in Paris, St Jacques, near which they built their first convent; the latter eventually became the headquarters of the French revolutionary group.

Jacobite¹ /ˈdʒakəbʌɪt/ ▶ noun a supporter of the deposed James II and· his descendants in their claim to the British throne after the Revolution of 1688. Drawing most of their support from Catholic clans of the Scottish Highlands, Jacobites made attempts to regain the throne in 1689–90, 1715, 1719, and 1745–6, finally being defeated at the Battle of Culloden.
– DERIVATIVES **Jacobitical** adjective, **Jacobitism** noun.
– ORIGIN from Latin *Jacobus* 'James' (see JACOBEAN) + -ITE¹.

Jacobite² /ˈdʒakəbʌɪt/ ▶ noun a member of the Syrian Orthodox Church (Monophysite).
– ORIGIN early 15th cent.: from medieval Latin *Jacobita*, from the name of *Jacobus* Baradaeus, a 6th-cent. Syrian monk.

Jacobs, W. W. (1863–1943), English short-story writer; full name *William Wymark Jacobs*. He is noted for tales of the macabre such as 'The Monkey's Paw' (1902).

Jacob sheep ▶ noun a four-horned sheep of a piebald breed, kept as an ornamental animal or for its wool.

Jacob's ladder ▶ noun 1 a herbaceous Eurasian plant with blue or white flowers and slender pointed leaves, rows of which are said to resemble a ladder.
● *Polemonium caeruleum*, family Polemoniaceae.
2 a rope ladder with wooden rungs.
– ORIGIN mid 18th cent.: with biblical allusion to Jacob's dream of a ladder reaching to heaven (Gen. 28:12).

Jacobson's organ ▶ noun Zoology a scent organ consisting of a pair of sacs or tubes typically in the roof of the mouth. Such organs are present in many vertebrates, notably snakes and lizards.
– ORIGIN mid 19th cent.: named after Ludwig L. *Jacobson* (1783–1843), Dutch anatomist.

Jacob's staff ▶ noun a rod with a sliding cursor formerly used for measuring distances and heights.
– ORIGIN mid 16th cent. (denoting a pilgrim's staff): alluding to St. James (*Jacobus* in ecclesiastical Latin), whose symbols are a pilgrim's staff and a scallop shell.

jaconet /ˈdʒakənɪt/ ▶ noun [mass noun] a lightweight cotton cloth with a smooth and slightly stiff finish.
– ORIGIN mid 18th cent.: from Hindi *Jagannāth(purī)* (now *Puri*) in India, its place of origin; see also JUGGERNAUT.

Jacopo della Quercia see DELLA QUERCIA.

jacquard /ˈdʒakɑːd, -kəd/ ▶ noun an apparatus with perforated cards, fitted to a loom to facilitate the weaving of figured and brocaded fabrics.
■ [mass noun] a fabric made on a loom with such a device, with an intricate variegated pattern.
– ORIGIN early 19th cent.: named after Joseph M. *Jacquard* (1787–1834), French weaver and inventor.

jacquerie /ˈdʒeɪk(ə)ri/ ▶ noun a communal uprising or revolt.
– ORIGIN early 16th cent. (referring to the 1357 peasants' revolt against the nobles in northern France): from Old French, literally 'villeins', from *Jacques*, a given name used in the sense 'peasant'.

jactitation¹ /ˌdʒaktɪˈteɪʃ(ə)n/ ▶ noun [mass noun] Medicine the restless tossing of the body in illness.
■ the twitching of a limb or muscle.
– ORIGIN mid 17th cent.: expressive extension of earlier *jactation* 'restless tossing', from Latin *jactare* 'to throw'.

jactitation² ▶ noun (in phrase **jactitation of marriage**) archaic false declaration that one is married to a specified person.
– ORIGIN late 17th cent.: from medieval Latin *jactitatio(n-)* 'false declaration', from Latin *jactitare* 'to boast'.

jacuzzi /dʒəˈkuːzi/ ▶ noun (pl. **jacuzzis**) trademark a large bath with a system of underwater jets of water to massage the body.
– ORIGIN 1960s: named after Candido *Jacuzzi* (c.1903–86), Italian-born American inventor.

jade¹ ▶ noun [mass noun] a hard, typically green stone used for ornaments and implements and consisting of the minerals jadeite or nephrite.
■ [count noun] an ornament made of this. ■ a light bluish-green: [as modifier] *a baggy jade T-shirt.*
– ORIGIN late 16th cent.: from French *le jade* (earlier *l'ejade*), from Spanish *piedra de ijada* 'stone of the flank' (i.e. stone for colic, which it was believed to cure).

jade² ▶ noun archaic 1 a bad-tempered or disreputable woman.
2 an inferior or worn-out horse.
– ORIGIN late Middle English: of unknown origin.

jaded ▶ adjective tired, bored, or lacking enthusiasm, typically after having had too much of something: *meals to tempt the most jaded appetites.*
– DERIVATIVES **jadedly** adverb, **jadedness** noun.
– ORIGIN late 16th cent. (in the sense 'disreputable'): from JADE².

jadeite /ˈdʒeɪdʌɪt/ ▶ noun [mass noun] a green, blue, or white mineral which is one of the forms of jade. It is a silicate of sodium, aluminium, and iron and belongs to the pyroxene group.

j'adoube /ʒaˈduːb/ ▶ exclamation Chess a declaration by a player intending to adjust the placing of a chessman without making a move with it.
– ORIGIN French, literally 'I adjust'.

jaeger /ˈdʒeɪgə/ ▶ noun N. Amer. any of the smaller kinds of Arctic-breeding skuas.
● Genus *Stercorarius*, family Stercorariidae: three species, e.g. the **parasitic jaeger** or Arctic skua (*S. parasiticus*).
– ORIGIN mid 19th cent. (applied to any predatory seabird): from German *Jäger* 'hunter', from *jagen* 'to hunt'.

Jaffa¹ /ˈdʒafə/ a city and port on the Mediterranean coast of Israel, forming a southern suburb of the Tel Aviv conurbation and since 1949 united with Tel Aviv; pop. (with Tel Aviv) 355,200 (1994). Inhabited since prehistoric times, Jaffa was a Byzantine bishopric until captured by the Arabs in 636; later, it was a stronghold of the Crusaders. Hebrew name YAFO; biblical name JOPPA.

Jaffa² /ˈdʒafə/ (also **Jaffa orange**) ▶ noun Brit. a large oval orange of a thick-skinned variety.

Jaffna /ˈdʒafnə/ a city and port on the Jaffna peninsula at the northern tip of Sri Lanka; pop. 129,000 (1990).

Jag ▶ noun informal a Jaguar car: *an E-type Jag.*
– ORIGIN 1950s: abbreviation.

jag¹ ▶ noun a sharp projection.
■ chiefly Scottish a prick with something sharp, especially an injection.
▶ verb (**jagged, jagging**) [with obj.] stab, pierce, or prick: *she jagged herself in the mouth.*
– DERIVATIVES **jagger** noun.
– ORIGIN late Middle English (in the sense 'stab, pierce'): perhaps symbolic of sudden movement or unevenness (compare with JAM¹ and RAG¹).

jag² ▶ noun informal, chiefly N. Amer. 1 a bout of unrestrained activity or emotion, especially drinking, crying, or laughing: *an incredible crying jag.*
2 dialect a bundle: *a jag of hay.*
– ORIGIN late 16th cent. (in sense 2): of unknown origin. In the late 18th cent. the sense was 'portion, quantity', later 'as much alcohol as one can hold', hence 'a binge'. Sense 1 dates from the early 20th cent.

Jagannatha /ˌdʒagəˈnɑːθə/ another name for JUGGERNAUT.

jagged /ˈdʒagɪd/ ▶ adjective with rough, sharp points protruding: *the jagged edges gashed their fingers* | figurative *soothing her jagged nerves.*
– DERIVATIVES **jaggedly** adverb, **jaggedness** noun.
– ORIGIN late Middle English: from JAG¹.

Jagger, Mick (b.1943), English rock singer and songwriter; full name *Michael Philip Jagger*. He formed the Rolling Stones *c.*1962 with guitarist Keith Richards (b.1943), a childhood friend.

jaggery /ˈdʒag(ə)ri/ ▶ noun [mass noun] a coarse dark brown sugar made in India by evaporation of the sap of palm trees.
– ORIGIN late 16th cent.: from Portuguese *xagara*, *jag(a)ra*, from Malayalam *cakkarā*, from Sanskrit *śarkarā* 'sugar'.

jaggy ▶ adjective (**jaggier, jaggiest**) jagged.
■ (also **jaggie**) Scottish prickly: *a jaggy nettle.*

jagir /ˈdʒɑːgɪə/ ▶ noun (in parts of the Indian subcontinent) a district in which a grant of public revenues or produce has been made to an individual or group.
– ORIGIN from Persian and Urdu *jāgīr*, from Persian *jā* 'place' + *gīr* 'holding'.

jaguar /ˈdʒagjʊə/ ▶ noun a large heavily built cat that has a yellowish-brown coat with black spots, found mainly in the dense forests of Central and South America.
● *Panthera onca*, family Felidae.
– ORIGIN early 17th cent.: from Portuguese, from Tupi-Guarani *yaguára*.

jaguarundi /ˌdʒagwəˈrʌndi/ ▶ noun (pl. **jaguarundis**) a small American wild cat with a uniform red or grey coat, slender body, and short legs, found from Arizona to Argentina.
● *Felis yagouaroundi*, family Felidae.
– ORIGIN mid 19th cent.: from Portuguese, from Tupi-Guarani *yaguára* 'jaguar' + *undi* 'dark'.

Jah /dʒɑː, jɑː/ ▶ **noun** the Rastafarian name of God.
– ORIGIN representing Hebrew *Yāh*, abbreviation of **YAHWEH**. The current use was popularized in the mid 20th cent.

Jai /dʒʌɪ/ ▶ **exclamation** Indian victory! (used as an expression of praise or support, especially in political slogans).
– ORIGIN Hindi, literally 'long live!'

jai alai /ˌhʌɪ əˈlʌɪ/ ▶ **noun** [mass noun] a game like pelota played with large curved wicker baskets.
– ORIGIN Spanish, from Basque *jai* 'festival' + *alai* 'merry'.

jail (Brit. also **gaol**) ▶ **noun** a place for the confinement of people accused or convicted of a crime: *he spent 15 years* ***in jail*** | [as modifier] *a jail sentence.*
■ [mass noun] confinement in a jail: *she was sentenced to three months' jail.*
▶ **verb** [with obj.] (usu. **be jailed**) put (someone) in jail: *the driver was jailed for two years.*
– ORIGIN Middle English: based on Latin *cavea* (see **CAGE**). The word came into English in two forms, *jaiole* from Old French and *gayole* from Anglo-Norman French *gaole* (surviving in the spelling *gaol*), originally pronounced with a hard g, as in *goat*.

jailbait ▶ **noun** [mass noun] [treated as sing. or pl.] informal a young woman, or young women collectively, considered in sexual terms but under the age of consent.

jailbird ▶ **noun** informal a person who is or has been in prison, especially a criminal who has been jailed repeatedly.

jailbreak ▶ **noun** an escape from jail.

jailer (Brit. also **gaoler**) ▶ **noun** a person in charge of a jail or of the prisoners in it.

jailhouse ▶ **noun** chiefly N. Amer. a prison.

Jain /dʒeɪn/ ▶ **noun** an adherent of Jainism.
▶ **adjective** of or relating to Jainism.
– ORIGIN via Hindi from Sanskrit *jaina* 'of or concerning a *Jina*' (a great Jain teacher or holy man, literally 'victor'), from *ji-* 'conquer' or *jyā-* 'overcome'.

Jainism ▶ **noun** [mass noun] a non-theistic religion founded in India in the 6th century BC by the Jina Vardhamana Mahavira as a reaction against the teachings of orthodox Brahmanism, and still practised there. The Jain religion teaches salvation by perfection through successive lives, and non-injury to living creatures, and is noted for its ascetics. See also **SVETAMBARA** and **DIGAMBARA**.
– DERIVATIVES **Jainist** noun.

Jaipur /dʒʌɪˈpʊə/ a city in western India, the capital of Rajasthan; pop. 1,455,000 (1991).

Jakarta variant spelling of **DJAKARTA**.

jake /dʒeɪk/ ▶ **adjective** [predic.] N. Amer. & Austral./NZ informal all right; satisfactory: *everything was jake again.*
– ORIGIN early 20th cent.: of unknown origin.

jakes /dʒeɪks/ ▶ **noun** a toilet, especially an outdoor one.
– ORIGIN mid 16th cent.: perhaps from the given name *Jacques*, or as the genitive of the pet name *Jack* (see **JACK**[1]).

Jakobson /ˈjakəbs(ə)n/, Roman (Osipovich) (1896–1982), Russian-born American linguist. His most influential work described universals in phonology.

Jalalabad /dʒəˈlələbad/ a city in eastern Afghanistan, situated east of Kabul, near the border with Pakistan; pop. 61,000 (est. 1984).

Jalal ad-Din ar-Rumi /dʒəˌlal adˌdɪn ɑːˈruːmi/ (1207–73), Persian poet and Sufi mystic, founder of the order of whirling dervishes; also called *Mawlana*.

Jalandhar variant spelling of **JULLUNDUR**.

jalap /ˈdʒaləp, ˈdʒɒləp/ ▶ **noun** [mass noun] a purgative drug obtained chiefly from the tuberous roots of a Mexican climbing plant.
• This drug is obtained from *Ipomoea purga*, family Convolvulaceae.
– ORIGIN mid 17th cent.: from French, from Spanish (*purga de*) *Jalapa* (see **JALAPA**).

Jalapa /həˈlɑːpə, Spanish xaˈlapa/ a city in east central Mexico, capital of the state of Veracruz; pop. 288,330 (1990). Full name **JALAPA ENRÍQUEZ** /ɛnˈriːkɛz, Spanish enˈrrikes, -keθ/.

jalapeño /ˌhaləˈpeɪnjəʊ, -ˈpiːnəʊ/ (also **jalapeño pepper**) ▶ **noun** (pl. **-os**) a very hot green chilli pepper, used especially in Mexican-style cooking.
– ORIGIN 1940s (originally US): from Mexican Spanish (*chile*) *jalapeño*.

jalebi /dʒəˈleɪbi/ ▶ **noun** (pl. **jalebis**) an Indian sweet made of a coil of batter fried and steeped in syrup.
– ORIGIN from Hindi *jalebī*.

jaleo /haˈleɪəʊ, Spanish xaˈleo/ ▶ **noun** (pl. **-os**) a lively dance of Andalusian origin, or the music or handclapping which accompanies it.
■ a fast instrumental chorus in merengue music.
– ORIGIN mid 19th cent.: Spanish, literally 'hallo'.

Jalisco /həˈliːskəʊ/ a state of west central Mexico, on the Pacific coast; capital, Guadalajara.

jalopy /dʒəˈlɒpi/ ▶ **noun** (pl. **-ies**) informal an old car in a dilapidated condition.
– ORIGIN 1920s (originally US): of unknown origin.

jalousie /ˈʒaluziː/ ▶ **noun** a blind or shutter made of a row of angled slats.
– ORIGIN mid 18th cent.: French, literally 'jealousy', from Italian *geloso* 'jealous', also (by extension) 'screen', associated with the screening of women from view in the Middle East.

Jam. ▶ **abbreviation for** ■ Jamaica. ■ James (in biblical references).

jam[1] ▶ **verb** (**jammed**, **jamming**) **1** [with obj. and adverbial] squeeze or pack (someone or something) tightly into a specified space: *four of us were jammed in one compartment* | *people jammed their belongings into cars.*
■ push (something) roughly and forcibly into position or a space: *he jammed his hat on.* ■ [with obj.] crowd on to (a road) so as to block it: *the roads were jammed with traffic.* ■ [with obj.] cause (telephone lines) to be continuously engaged with a large number of calls: *listeners jammed a radio station's switchboard with calls.* ■ [no obj., with adverbial of direction] push or crowd into an area or space: *75,000 refugees jammed into a stadium today to denounce the accord.*
2 become or make unable to move or work due to a part seizing or becoming stuck: [no obj.] *the photocopier jammed* | [with obj.] *the doors were jammed open.*
■ [with obj.] make (a radio transmission) unintelligible by causing interference.
3 [no obj.] informal improvise with other musicians, especially in jazz or blues: *the opportunity to jam with Atlanta blues musicians.*
▶ **noun 1** an instance of a machine or thing seizing or becoming stuck: *paper jams.*
■ informal an awkward situation or predicament: *I'm* ***in a jam.*** ■ short for **TRAFFIC JAM**. ■ [often with modifier] Climbing a handhold obtained by stuffing a part of the body such as a hand or foot into a crack in the rock.
2 (also **jam session**) an informal gathering of musicians improvising together, especially in jazz or blues.
– PHRASES **jam on the brakes** operate the brakes of a vehicle suddenly and forcibly, typically in response to an emergency.
– ORIGIN early 18th cent.: probably symbolic; compare with **JAG**[1] and **CRAM**.

jam[2] ▶ **noun** [mass noun] chiefly Brit. a sweet spread or conserve made from fruit and sugar boiled to a thick consistency.
■ Brit. used in reference to something easy or pleasant: *they want it all, both ways and with jam on the top.*
▶ **verb** (**jammed**, **jamming**) [with obj.] make (fruit) into jam.
– PHRASES **jam tomorrow** Brit. a pleasant thing which is often promised but rarely materializes: *a promise of jam tomorrow wasn't enough to satisfy them.* [ORIGIN: phrase from Lewis Carroll's *Through the Looking Glass* (1871).]
– ORIGIN mid 18th cent.: perhaps from **JAM**[1].

jamadar /ˈdʒʌməˌdɑː/ (also **jemadar**) ▶ **noun** Indian **1** a minor official or junior officer.
■ historical an Indian officer in a sepoy regiment.
2 a person who sweeps homes or offices as a job.
– ORIGIN from Urdu *jam(a)'dār*, from Persian, from Arabic *jama'*, *jamā'a(t)* 'muster' + *-dār* 'holder'.

Jamaica /dʒəˈmeɪkə/ an island country in the Caribbean Sea, south-east of Cuba; pop. 2,314,480; official language, English; capital, Kingston.

> Visited by Columbus in 1494, Jamaica was colonized by the Spanish, who enslaved or killed the native people. Both the Spanish and the British, who took the island by force in 1655, imported slaves, mainly to work on sugar plantations. Self-government was achieved in 1944, and in 1962 Jamaica became an independent Commonwealth state.

– DERIVATIVES **Jamaican** adjective & noun.

Jamaica pepper ▶ **noun** another term for **ALLSPICE** (in senses 1 and 2).

jamb /dʒam/ ▶ **noun** a side post or surface of a doorway, window, or fireplace.
– ORIGIN Middle English: from Old French *jambe* 'leg, vertical support', based on Greek *kampē* 'joint'.

jambalaya /ˌdʒambəˈlʌɪə/ ▶ **noun** [mass noun] a Cajun dish of rice with shrimps, chicken, and vegetables.
– ORIGIN Louisiana French, from Provençal *jambalaia*.

jambeau /ˈʒambəʊ/ ▶ **noun** (pl. **jambeaux** pronunc. same or **jambeaus**) historical a piece of armour for the leg.
– ORIGIN late Middle English: apparently an Anglo-Norman French derivative of French *jambe* 'leg'.

jamboree /ˌdʒambəˈriː/ ▶ **noun** a large celebration or party, typically a lavish and boisterous one: *the film industry's annual jamboree in Cannes.*
■ a large rally of Scouts or Guides.
– ORIGIN mid 19th cent. (originally US slang): of unknown origin.

James[1] the name of seven Stuart kings of Scotland:
■ James I (1394–1437), son of Robert III, reigned 1406–37. A captive of the English until 1424, he returned to a country divided by baronial feuds, but managed to restore some measure of royal authority.
■ James II (1430–60), son of James I, reigned 1437–60. He considerably strengthened the position of the Crown by crushing the powerful Douglas family (1452–5).
■ James III (1451–88), son of James II, reigned 1460–88. His nobles raised an army against him in 1488, using his son, the future James IV, as a figurehead. The king was defeated and killed in battle.
■ James IV (1473–1513), son of James III, reigned 1488–1513. He forged a dynastic link with England through his marriage to Margaret Tudor, the daughter of Henry VII, and revitalized the traditional pact with France. When England and France went to war in 1513 he invaded England, but died in defeat at Flodden.
■ James V (1512–42), son of James IV, reigned 1513–42. During his reign Scotland was dominated by French interests. Relations with England deteriorated in the later years, culminating in an invasion by Henry VIII's army.
■ James VI (1566–1625), James I of England (see **JAMES**[2]).
■ James VII (1633–1701), James II of England (see **JAMES**[2]).

James[2] the name of two kings of England, Ireland, and Scotland:
■ James I (1566–1625), son of Mary, Queen of Scots, king of Scotland (as James VI) 1567–1625, and of England and Ireland 1603–25. He inherited the throne of England from Elizabeth I, as great-grandson of Margaret Tudor, daughter of Henry VII. His declaration of the divine right of kings and his intended alliance with Spain made him unpopular with Parliament.
■ James II (1633–1701), son of Charles I, king of England, Ireland, and (as James VII) Scotland 1685–8. His Catholic beliefs led to the rebellion of the Duke of Monmouth in 1685 and to James' later deposition in favour of William of Orange and Mary II. Attempts to regain the throne resulted in James's defeat at the Battle of the Boyne in 1690.

James[3], C. L. R. (1901–89), Trinidadian historian, journalist, political theorist, and novelist; full name *Cyril Lionel Robert James*. After working as a cricket columnist he established a reputation as a historian with his study of the Haitian revolution, *Black Jacobins* (1938).

James[4], Henry (1843–1916), American-born British novelist and critic. His early novels, notably *The Portrait of a Lady* (1881), deal with the relationship between European civilization and American life, while later works such as *What Maisie Knew* (1897) depict English life. He was the brother of William James.
– DERIVATIVES **Jamesian** adjective.

James[5], Jesse (Woodson) (1847–82), American outlaw. He joined with his brother **Frank** (1843–1915) and others to form a notorious band of outlaws which specialized in bank and train robberies and inspired many westerns.

James[6], Dame P. D. (b.1920), English writer of detective fiction; full name *Phyllis Dorothy James*. She is noted for her novels featuring the poet-detective Adam Dalgleish, including *A Taste for Death* (1986).

James[7], William (1842–1910), American philosopher and psychologist. A leading exponent of pragmatism, he sought a functional definition of truth, and in psychology he is credited with introducing the concept of the stream of consciousness. He was the brother of Henry James.

James, St¹, an Apostle, son of Zebedee and brother of John; known as **St James the Great**. He was put to death by Herod Agrippa I; afterwards, according to a Spanish tradition, his body was taken to Santiago de Compostela. Feast day, 25 July.

James, St², an Apostle; known as **St James the Less**. Feast day (in the Eastern Church) 9 October; (in the Western Church) 1 May.

James, St³, leader of the early Christian Church at Jerusalem; known as **St James the Just** or **the Lord's brother**. He was put to death by the Sanhedrin. Feast day, 1 May.

■ the epistle of the New Testament traditionally ascribed to St James.

James Bay a shallow southern arm of Hudson Bay, Canada.

– ORIGIN named after Captain Thomas *James* (*c*.1593–*c*.1635), who explored the region in 1631.

Jameson Raid /ˈdʒeɪmɪs(ə)n/ an abortive raid into Boer territory made in 1895–6 by pro-British extremists led by Dr L. S. Jameson (1853–1917) in an attempt to incite an uprising among recent, non-Boer immigrants. The raid contributed to the eventual outbreak of the Second Boer War.

Jamestown 1 a British settlement established in Virginia in 1607, abandoned when the state capital of Virginia was moved to Williamsburg at the end of the 17th century.
2 the capital and chief port of the island of St Helena; pop. 1,500 (1992).

jam jar ▶ noun Brit. rhyming slang a car.

jammer ▶ noun a transmitter used for jamming signals.

Jammu /ˈdʒʌmuː/ a town in NW India; pop. 206,000 (1991). It is the winter capital of the state of Jammu and Kashmir.

Jammu and Kashmir a mountainous state of NW India at the western end of the Himalayas, formerly part of Kashmir; capitals, Srinagar (in summer) and Jammu (in winter).

jammy¹ ▶ adjective (**jammier**, **jammiest**) covered with, filled with, or resembling jam: *a jammy doughnut.*
■ Brit. informal lucky: *they were jammy to win it.*

jammy² ▶ noun (pl. **-ies**) S. African informal a car, typically an old and well-worn one.
– ORIGIN perhaps an abbreviation of British rhyming slang JAM JAR.

Jamnagar /dʒʌmˈnʌɡə/ a port and walled city in the state of Gujarat, western India; pop. 325,000 (1991).

jam-packed ▶ adjective informal extremely crowded or full to capacity: *trains were jam-packed with holidaymakers.*

jamrool /dʒamˈruːl/ ▶ noun Indian term for ROSEAPPLE.

jam session ▶ noun see JAM¹ (sense 2).

Jamshedpur /ˌdʒʌmˈʃɛdˈpʊə/ an industrial city in the state of Bihar, NE India; pop. 461,000 (1991).

Jamshid /dʒamˈʃiːd/ a legendary early king of Persia, reputed inventor of the arts of medicine, navigation, and iron-working.

jamun /ˈdʒamʌn/ (also **jamun tree**) ▶ noun a large evergreen Asian tree of the myrtle family, which yields edible fruit, tanbark, and fuelwood.
● *Syzygium cumini*, family Myrtaceae.
■ the purplish edible berry of this tree.
– ORIGIN early 19th cent.: from Hindi *jāmun.*

Jan. ▶ abbreviation for January.

Janáček /ˈjanəˌtʃɛk/, Leoš (1854–1928), Czech composer. His works, much influenced by Moravian folk songs, include the opera *The Cunning Little Vixen* (1924) and the *Glagolitic Mass* (1927).

jane ▶ noun informal, chiefly US a woman.
– PHRASES **plain Jane** an unattractive girl or woman.
– ORIGIN early 20th cent.: from the given name *Jane.*

jangle ▶ verb make or cause to make a ringing metallic sound, typically a discordant one: [no obj.] *a bell jangled loudly* | [with obj.] *Ryan stood on the terrace jangling his keys.*
■ (with reference to nerves) be set or set on edge: [no obj.] *now it's over my nerves are jangling.*
▶ noun [in sing.] a ringing metallic sound: *the shrill jangle of the door bell.*

– DERIVATIVES **jangly** adjective.
– ORIGIN Middle English (in the sense 'talk excessively or noisily, squabble'): from Old French *jangler*, of unknown origin.

Janglish /ˈdʒaŋglɪʃ/ ▶ noun another name for JAPLISH.
– ORIGIN late 20th cent.: blend of JAPANESE and ENGLISH.

janissary /ˈdʒanɪs(ə)ri/ (also **janizary** /-z(ə)ri/) ▶ noun (pl. **-ies**) historical a member of the Turkish infantry forming the Sultan's guard between the 14th and 19th centuries.
■ a devoted follower or supporter.
– ORIGIN early 16th cent.: from French *janissaire*, based on Turkish *yeniçeri*, from *yeni* 'new' + *çeri* 'troops'.

janitor /ˈdʒanɪtə/ ▶ noun chiefly N. Amer. a caretaker or doorkeeper of a building.
– DERIVATIVES **janitorial** adjective.
– ORIGIN mid 16th cent.: from Latin, from *janua* 'door'.

jankers /ˈdʒaŋkəz/ ▶ noun [mass noun] Brit. military slang punishment for those who have committed a military offence: *the sergeant put me on jankers.*
– ORIGIN early 20th cent.: of unknown origin.

Jan Mayen /jan ˈmʌɪən/ a barren and virtually uninhabited island in the Arctic Ocean between Greenland and Norway, annexed by Norway in 1929.
– ORIGIN named after Jan *May*, the Dutch sea captain who claimed the island for his company and his country in 1614.

Jansen /ˈdʒans(ə)n/, Cornelius Otto (1585–1638), Flemish Roman Catholic theologian and founder of Jansenism. A strong opponent of the Jesuits, he proposed a reform of Christianity through a return to St Augustine.

Jansenism ▶ noun a Christian movement of the 17th and 18th centuries, based on Jansen's writings and characterized by moral rigour and asceticism.
– DERIVATIVES **Jansenist** noun.

Jansens /ˈdʒans(ə)nz/ (also **Janssen van Ceulen** /ˌdʒans(ə)n van ˈkɔːlən/) variant spelling of JOHNSON³.

January /ˈdʒanjʊ(ə)ri/ ▶ noun (pl. **-ies**) the first month of the year, in the northern hemisphere usually considered the second month of winter: *Sophie was two in January* | *last January my grandmother died.*
– ORIGIN Old English, from Latin *Januarius* (*mensis*) '(month) of *Janus*' (see JANUS), the Roman god who presided over doors and beginnings.

Janus /ˈdʒeɪnəs/ Roman Mythology an ancient Italian deity, guardian of doorways and gates and protector of the state in time of war. He is usually represented with two faces, so that he looks both forwards and backwards.

Jap ▶ noun & adjective informal, offensive short for JAPANESE.

Japan a country in east Asia, occupying a festoon of islands in the Pacific roughly parallel with the east coast of the Asiatic mainland; pop. 122,626,000 (est. 1988); official language, Japanese; capital, Tokyo. Japanese name NIPPON.

From the late 19th century Japan began a modernizing process which eventually made it into a major world power. It fought wars against China (1894–5) and Russia (1904–5), and after the First World War occupied Manchuria (1931) and invaded China (1937). Japan entered the Second World War on the Axis side with a surprise attack on Pearl Harbor in 1941. The country surrendered in 1945 after the dropping of atom bombs by the US on Hiroshima and Nagasaki. Japan is now the most highly industrialized country and the leading economic power in the region.

– ORIGIN rendering of Chinese *Rìben*.

japan ▶ noun [mass noun] a hard, dark, enamel-like varnish containing asphalt, used to give a black gloss to metal objects.
■ a kind of varnish in which pigments are ground, typically used to imitate lacquer on wood. ■ articles made in a Japanese style, especially when decorated with lacquer or enamel-like varnish.
▶ verb (**japanned**, **japanning**) [with obj.] cover (something) with a hard black varnish: [as adj. **japanned**] *a japanned tin tray.*
– ORIGIN late 17th cent.: from JAPAN.

Japan, Sea of the sea between Japan and the mainland of Asia.

Japan Current another name for KUROSHIO.

Japanese ▶ adjective of or relating to Japan or its language, culture, or people.
▶ noun (pl. same) **1** a native or national of Japan, or a person of Japanese descent.
2 [mass noun] the language of Japan, spoken by almost all of its population.

Japanese is probably related to Korean. It has many Chinese loan-words, and is usually written in vertical columns using Chinese characters (kanji) supplemented by two sets of syllabic characters (kana).

Japanese anemone ▶ noun an autumn-flowering anemone with large pink or white flowers. It is native to China and naturalized in Japan, and several cultivars have been developed.
● *Anemone hupehensis* var. *japonica*, family Ranunculaceae.

Japanese beetle ▶ noun a metallic green and copper chafer which is a pest of fruit and foliage as an adult and of grass roots as a larva. It is native to Japan but has spread elsewhere.
● *Popillia japonica*, family Scarabaeidae.

Japanese cedar ▶ noun see CRYPTOMERIA.

Japanese Current another name for KUROSHIO.

Japanese knotweed ▶ noun [mass noun] a tall fast-growing Japanese plant of the dock family, with bamboo-like stems and small white flowers. It has been grown as an ornamental but tends to become an aggressive weed.
● *Reynoutria japonica*, family Polygonaceae.

Japanese lantern ▶ noun another term for CHINESE LANTERN (in sense 1).

Japanese paper ▶ noun [mass noun] paper of a kind traditionally handmade in Japan, typically from vegetable fibres such as mulberry bark and without being sized, used for art and craft work.

Japanese quince ▶ noun another term for JAPONICA.

Japanese wax tree ▶ noun see WAX TREE.

Japanimation /dʒəˌpanɪˈmeɪʃ(ə)n/ ▶ noun another term for ANIME.
– ORIGIN 1980s: blend of JAPAN and ANIMATION.

jape ▶ noun a practical joke: *the childish jape of depositing a stink bomb in her locker.*
▶ verb [no obj.] say or do something in jest or mockery.
– DERIVATIVES **japery** noun.
– ORIGIN Middle English: apparently combining the form of Old French *japer* 'to yelp, yap' with the sense of Old French *gaber* 'to mock'.

Japheth /ˈdʒeɪfɛθ/ (in the Bible) a son of Noah (Gen. 10:1), traditional ancestor of the peoples living round the Mediterranean.

Japlish /ˈdʒaplɪʃ/ ▶ noun [mass noun] informal a blend of Japanese and English, either Japanese speech that makes liberal use of English expressions or unidiomatic English spoken by a Japanese.

japonica /dʒəˈpɒnɪkə/ ▶ noun an Asian shrub of the rose family, with bright red flowers followed by round white, green, or yellow edible fruits. Also called JAPANESE QUINCE.
● Genus *Chaenomeles*, family Rosaceae: several species, in particular *C. speciosa*, which is grown as an ornamental.
– ORIGIN early 19th cent.: modern Latin, feminine of *japonicus* 'Japanese'.

Jaques-Dalcroze /ˌʒakdalˈkrəʊz/, Émile (1865–1950), Austrian-born Swiss music teacher and composer. He evolved the eurhythmics method of teaching music and dance, establishing a school for eurhythmics instruction in 1910.

jar¹ ▶ noun a wide-mouthed cylindrical container made of glass or pottery, especially one used for storing food.
■ the contents of such a container: *we got through jars of mustard.* ■ Brit. informal a glass of beer: *let's have a jar.*
– DERIVATIVES **jarful** noun (pl. **-fuls**).
– ORIGIN late 16th cent.: from French *jarre*, from Arabic *jarra*.

jar² ▶ verb (**jarred**, **jarring**) **1** [with obj.] send a painful or damaging shock through (something, especially a part of the body): *he jarred the knee in training.*
■ [no obj.] strike against something with an unpleasant vibration or jolt: *the stick jarred on the bottom of the pond.*
2 [no obj.] have an unpleasant, annoying, or disturbing effect: *a laugh which jarred on the ears* | *the difference in their background began to jar.*
■ be incongruous in a striking or shocking way: *the play's symbolism jarred with the realism of its setting* | [as

adj. **jarring**| *the only jarring note was the modern appearance of the customers.*
▶ noun a physical shock or jolt.
■[mass noun] archaic discord; disagreement.
– ORIGIN late 15th cent. (as a noun in the sense 'disagreement, dispute'): probably imitative.

jar³ ▶ noun (in phrase **on the jar**) informal or dialect ajar.
– ORIGIN late 17th cent.: later form of obsolete *char* 'turn' (see also **AJAR**¹ and **CHARWOMAN**).

jardinière /ˌʒɑːdɪnˈjɛː/ ▶ noun **1** an ornamental pot or stand for the display of growing plants.
2 a garnish of mixed vegetables.
– ORIGIN mid 19th cent.: French, literally 'female gardener'.

jargon¹ /ˈdʒɑːɡ(ə)n/ ▶ noun [mass noun] special words or expressions used by a particular profession or group that are difficult for others to understand: *legal jargon.*
■[count noun] a form of language regarded as barbarous, debased, or hybrid.
– DERIVATIVES **jargonistic** adjective, **jargonize** verb (also **-ise**)
– ORIGIN late Middle English (originally in the sense 'twittering, chattering', later 'gibberish'): from Old French *jargoun*, of unknown origin. The main modern sense dates from the mid 17th cent.

jargon² /ˈdʒɑːɡ(ə)n/ (also **jargoon** /dʒɑːˈɡuːn/) ▶ noun [mass noun] a translucent, colourless, or smoky gem variety of zircon.
– ORIGIN mid 18th cent.: from French, from Italian *giargone*; probably ultimately related to **ZIRCON**.

Jargonelle /ˌdʒɑːɡəˈnɛl/ ▶ noun Brit. a pear of an early ripening variety.
– ORIGIN late 17th cent.: from French, diminutive of **JARGON**² (with reference to the colour).

jarl /jɑːl/ ▶ noun historical a Norse or Danish chief.
– ORIGIN Old Norse, literally 'man of noble birth'; related to **EARL**.

Jarlsberg /ˈjɑːlzbɔːɡ/ ▶ noun [mass noun] a kind of hard yellow Norwegian cheese with many small holes and a mild, nutty flavour.
– ORIGIN named after the town of *Jarlsberg*, Norway.

Jarman, Derek (1942–94), English film director and painter. His controversial films, informed by gay sensibilities, include *Jubilee* (1977), *Caravaggio* (1986), and *Edward II* (1991).

jarrah /ˈdʒɑrə/ ▶ noun a eucalyptus tree native to western Australia, yielding durable timber.
● *Eucalyptus marginata*, family Myrtaceae.
– ORIGIN mid 19th cent.: from Nyungar *djarryl*, *jerrhyl*.

Jarrow a town in NE England, on the Tyne estuary; pop. 31,310 (1981). From the 7th century until the Viking invasions its monastery was a centre of Northumbrian Christian culture. Its name is associated with a series of hunger marches to London by the unemployed during the Depression of the 1930s.

Jarry /ˈdʒari, French ʒaʁi/, Alfred (1873–1907), French dramatist. His satirical farce *Ubu Roi* (1896) anticipated surrealism and the Theatre of the Absurd.

jarul /ˈdʒɔːruːl/ (also **jarool**) ▶ noun a tropical Asian tree which bears large clusters of purple or white flowers.
● *Lagerstroemia speciosa*, family Lythraceae.
– ORIGIN mid 19th cent.: from Hindi.

Jaruzelski /jaruˈzɛlski/, Wojciech (b.1923), Polish general and statesman, Prime Minister 1981–5, head of state 1985–9, and President 1989–90. He responded to the rise of Solidarity by imposing martial law and banning trade union operation, but following the victory of Solidarity in the 1989 elections he supervised Poland's transition to a democracy.

Jas. ▶ abbreviation for James (in biblical references and generally).

jasmine /ˈdʒazmɪn, ˈdʒas-/ (also **jessamine**) ▶ noun an Old World shrub or climbing plant which bears fragrant flowers that are used in perfumery or tea and is popular as an ornamental.
● Genus *Jasminum*, family Oleaceae: many species, including the **winter jasmine**.
■used in names of other shrubs or climbers with fragrant flowers, e.g. **Cape jasmine**, **yellow jasmine**.
– ORIGIN mid 16th cent.: from French *jasmin* and obsolete French *jessemin*, from Arabic *yāsamīn*, from Persian *yāsamīn*.

jasmine tea ▶ noun [mass noun] a tea perfumed with dried jasmine blossom.

Jason Greek Mythology the son of the king of Iolcos in Thessaly, and leader of the Argonauts in the quest for the Golden Fleece.

jaspé /ˈdʒaspeɪ/ ▶ adjective randomly mottled or variegated, like jasper.
– ORIGIN mid 19th cent.: French, past participle of *jasper* 'to marble', from *jaspe* (see **JASPER**).

jasper ▶ noun [mass noun] an opaque reddish-brown variety of chalcedony.
– ORIGIN Middle English (originally denoting any bright-coloured chalcedony other than carnelian): from Old French *jasp(r)e*, from Latin *iaspis*, from Greek, of oriental origin.

Jassy /ˈjasi/ German name for **IAŞI**.

Jat /dʒɑːt/ ▶ noun a member of a people widely scattered throughout the north-west of the Indian subcontinent.
– ORIGIN from Hindi *Jāṭ*.

Jataka /ˈdʒʌtəkə/ ▶ noun any of the various stories of the former lives of the Buddha found in Buddhist literature.
– ORIGIN from Sanskrit *jātaka* 'born under'.

jatha /ˈdʒɑːtə/ ▶ noun Indian an armed parade, especially of Sikhs.
– ORIGIN from Punjabi, from Hindi *jāthā*.

jati /ˈdʒɑːti/ ▶ noun (pl. same or **jatis**) Indian a caste or subcaste.
– ORIGIN via Hindi from Sanskrit *jāti* 'birth'.

jato /ˈdʒeɪtəʊ/ ▶ noun (pl. **-os**) [mass noun] Aeronautics jet-assisted take-off.
■[count noun] an auxiliary power unit providing extra thrust at take-off.
– ORIGIN Second World War (originally US): acronym.

jaundice /ˈdʒɔːndɪs/ ▶ noun [mass noun] a medical condition with yellowing of the skin or whites of the eyes, arising from excess of the pigment bilirubin and typically caused by obstruction of the bile duct, by liver disease, or by excessive breakdown of red blood cells.
■bitterness, resentment, or envy.
– ORIGIN Middle English *jaunes*, from Old French *jaunice* 'yellowness', from *jaune* 'yellow'.

jaundiced ▶ adjective having or affected by jaundice, in particular unnaturally yellow in complexion.
■affected by bitterness, resentment, or envy: *they looked on politicians with a jaundiced eye.*

jaunt ▶ noun a short excursion or journey for pleasure: *her little jaunt in France was over.*
▶ verb [no obj.] make such an excursion or journey: *they went jaunting through Ireland.*
– ORIGIN late 16th cent.: of unknown origin. Originally depreciatory, early senses included 'tire a horse out by riding it up and down', 'traipse about', and (as a noun) 'troublesome journey'. The current positive sense dates from the mid 17th cent.

jaunting car ▶ noun historical a light two-wheeled horse-drawn vehicle formerly used in Ireland.

jaunty ▶ adjective (**-ier**, **-iest**) having or expressing a lively, cheerful, and self-confident manner: *there was no mistaking that jaunty walk.*
– DERIVATIVES **jauntily** adverb, **jauntiness** noun.
– ORIGIN mid 17th cent. (in the sense 'well-bred, genteel'): from French *gentil* (see **GENTLE**¹, **GENTEEL**).

Java¹ /ˈdʒɑːvə/ a large island in the Malay Archipelago, forming part of Indonesia; pop. 112,158,200 (1993) (with Madura).
– DERIVATIVES **Javan** noun & adjective.

Java² /ˈdʒɑːvə/ ▶ noun [mass noun] trademark a general-purpose computer programming language designed to produce programs that will run on any computer system.

java /ˈdʒɑːvə/ ▶ noun [mass noun] N. Amer. informal coffee.

Java man ▶ noun a fossil hominid of the Middle Pleistocene period, whose remains were found in Java in 1891.
● An early form of *Homo erectus* (formerly *Pithecanthropus*), family Hominidae.

Javanese ▶ noun (pl. same) **1** a native or inhabitant of Java, or a person of Javanese descent.
2 [mass noun] the Indonesian language of central Java, spoken by about 70 million people.

▶ adjective of or relating to Java, its people, or their language.

Javan rhinoceros ▶ noun a rare one-horned rhinoceros that is now confined to the lowland rainforests of Java.
● *Rhinoceros sondaicus*, family Rhinocerotidae.

Java Sea a sea in the Malay Archipelago of SE Asia, surrounded by the islands of Borneo, Java, and Sumatra.

Java sparrow ▶ noun a waxbill with a large red bill and black-and-white head, native to Java and Bali but introduced widely elsewhere and popular as a cage bird.
● *Padda oryzivora*, family Estrildidae.

javelin /ˈdʒav(ə)lɪn/ ▶ noun a light spear thrown in a competitive sport or as a weapon.
■(the javelin) the athletic event or sport of throwing the javelin: *his nearest rival in the javelin.*
– ORIGIN late Middle English: from Old French *javeline*, of Celtic origin.

javelina /ˌhavəˈliːnə/ ▶ noun North American term for **PECCARY**.
– ORIGIN early 19th cent.: from Spanish *jabalina*, from the feminine form of *jabalí* 'wild boar', from Arabic *jabali* 'mountaineer'.

jaw ▶ noun each of the upper and lower bony structures in vertebrates forming the framework of the mouth and containing the teeth.
■the lower movable bone of such a structure or the part of the face containing it: *she suffered a broken jaw.*
■(**jaws**) the mouth with its bones and teeth. ■(**jaws**) the grasping, biting, or crushing mouthparts of an invertebrate. ■(**jaws**) used to suggest the notion of being in danger from something such as death or defeat: *victory was snatched from the jaws of defeat.* ■(usu. **jaws**) the gripping parts of a tool or machine, such as a wrench or vice. ■(**jaws**) an opening likened to a mouth: *a passenger stepping from the jaws of a car ferry.* ■[mass noun] informal talk or gossip, especially when lengthy or tedious: *committee work is just endless jaw* | [count noun] *we ought to have a jaw.*
▶ verb [no obj.] informal talk at length; chatter: *he could still hear men jawing away about the vacuum cleaners.*
– DERIVATIVES **jawed** adjective [in combination] *square-jawed young men*, **jawless** adjective.
– ORIGIN late Middle English: from Old French *joe* 'cheek, jaw', of unknown origin.

jawan /dʒɔːˈwɑːn/ ▶ noun Indian a male police constable or private soldier.
– ORIGIN from Urdu *jawān* 'young man', from Persian; ultimately related to **YOUNG**.

jawbone ▶ noun a bone of the jaw, especially that of the lower jaw (the mandible), or either half of this.

jawbreaker ▶ noun **1** informal a word that is very long or hard to pronounce.
2 chiefly N. Amer. a large gobstopper.

jaw-dropping ▶ adjective informal amazing: *the jaw-dropping experience of taking the desert road.*
– DERIVATIVES **jaw-droppingly** adverb.

jawfish ▶ noun (pl. same or **-fishes**) a small fish with very large jaws which lives in shallow tropical seas. It often inhabits a burrow in the sand, the walls of which are lined with pieces of shell and stone.
● Family Opistognathidae: several genera and species.

jaw-jaw informal ▶ noun [mass noun] talking, especially lengthy and pointless discussion.
▶ verb talk, especially at length.
– ORIGIN mid 19th cent.: reduplication of **JAW**.

jawline ▶ noun the contour of the lower edge of a person's jaw: *he had a dark, unshaven jawline.*

Jaws of Life ▶ noun N. Amer. trademark a hydraulic apparatus used to pry apart the wreckage of crashed vehicles in order to free people trapped inside.

jay ▶ noun **1** a bird of the crow family with boldly patterned plumage, typically having blue feathers in the wings or tail.
● Family Corvidae: several genera and numerous species, in particular the Eurasian *Garrulus glandarius*, with a crest, mainly pinkish-brown plumage, and a harsh screech.
2 archaic a person who chatters impertinently.
– ORIGIN late 15th cent.: via Old French from late Latin *gaius*, *gaia*, perhaps from the Latin given name *Gaius*.

Jaycee /ˈdʒeɪsiː/ ▶ noun N. Amer. informal a member of a Junior Chamber of Commerce, a civic organization for business and community leaders.

– ORIGIN 1940s: representing the initials of *Junior Chamber*.

jaywalk ▶ **verb** [no obj., with adverbial of direction] chiefly N. Amer. cross or walk in the street or road unlawfully or without regard for approaching traffic.
– DERIVATIVES **jaywalker** noun.
– ORIGIN early 20th cent.: from **JAY** in the colloquial sense 'silly person' + **WALK**.

jazz ▶ **noun** [mass noun] a type of music of black American origin characterized by improvisation, syncopation, and usually a regular or forceful rhythm, emerging at the beginning of the 20th century. Brass and woodwind instruments and piano are particularly associated with jazz, although guitar and occasionally violin are also used; styles include Dixieland, swing, bebop, and free jazz.
▶ **verb** [no obj.] dated play or dance to jazz music.
– PHRASES **and all that jazz** informal and such similar things: *oh, love, life, and all that jazz.*
– DERIVATIVES **jazzer** noun.
– ORIGIN early 20th cent.: of unknown origin.
▶ **jazz something up** make something more lively or cheerful: *jazz up an all-white kitchen with red tiles.*

jazz age ▶ **noun** the 1920s in the US characterized as a period of carefree hedonism, wealth, freedom, and youthful exuberance, reflected in the novels of writers such as F. Scott Fitzgerald.

jazzbo ▶ **noun** (pl. **-os**) informal **1** a jazz musician or jazz enthusiast.
2 US archaic a person, especially a black man.
– ORIGIN early 20th cent.: of unknown origin.

jazzercise ▶ **noun** (trademark in the US) a type of fitness training combining aerobic exercise and jazz dancing.
– ORIGIN 1970s: blend of **JAZZ** and **EXERCISE**.

jazzman ▶ **noun** (pl. **-men**) a male jazz musician.

jazzy ▶ **adjective** (**jazzier, jazziest**) of, resembling, or in the style of jazz: *a jazzy piano solo.*
■ bright, colourful, and showy: *jazzy ties.*
– DERIVATIVES **jazzily** adverb, **jazziness** noun.

JCB ▶ **noun** Brit. trademark a type of mechanical excavator with a shovel at the front and a digging arm at the rear.
– ORIGIN 1960s: the initials of *J. C. Bamford*, the makers.

JCL Computing ▶ **abbreviation for** job control language.

J-cloth ▶ **noun** (trademark in the UK) a type of cloth used for household cleaning.
– ORIGIN late 20th cent.: *J* from Johnson and Johnson, the original makers.

JCR Brit. ▶ **abbreviation for** Junior Common (or Combination) Room.

JCS ▶ **abbreviation for** Joint Chiefs of Staff, the chief military advisory body to the President of the United States.

jealous ▶ **adjective** feeling or showing envy of or resentment at someone or at their achievements or perceived advantages: *she was always* **jealous of** *me.*
■ feeling or showing suspicion or resentment that someone one is in an emotional relationship with is attracted to or involved with someone else. ■ fiercely protective or vigilant of one's rights or possessions: *Howard is still a little* **jealous of** *his authority | they kept a jealous eye over their interests.* ■ (of God) demanding faithfulness and exclusive worship.
– DERIVATIVES **jealously** adverb.
– ORIGIN Middle English: from Old French *gelos*, from medieval Latin *zelosus* (see **ZEALOUS**).

jealousy ▶ **noun** (pl. **-ies**) [mass noun] the state or feeling of being jealous: *a sharp pang of jealousy |* [count noun] *resentments and jealousies festered.*
– ORIGIN Middle English: from Old French *gelosie*, from *gelos* (see **JEALOUS**).

jean ▶ **noun** [mass noun] heavy twilled cotton cloth, especially denim: [as modifier] *a jean jacket.*
■ [count noun] (in commercial use) a pair of jeans: *a button-fly jean.*
– ORIGIN late 15th cent. (as an adjective): from Old French *Janne* (now *Gênes*), from medieval Latin *Janua* 'Genoa', the place of original production. The noun sense comes from *jean fustian*, literally 'fustian from Genoa', used in the 16th cent. to denote a heavy twilled cotton cloth.

Jean Paul /ʒɒn 'pɔːl/ (1763–1825), German novelist; pseudonym of *Johann Paul Friedrich Richter.* He is noted for his romantic novels, including *Hesperus* (1795), and for comic works such as *Titan* (1800–3).

Jeans, Sir James Hopwood (1877–1946), English physicist and astronomer. Jeans proposed a theory for the formation of the solar system and was the first to propose that matter is continuously created throughout the universe, one of the tenets of the steady state theory.

jeans ▶ **plural noun** hard-wearing trousers made of denim or other cotton fabric, for informal wear.
– ORIGIN mid 19th cent.: plural of **JEAN**.

jebel /'dʒɛbɛl/ (also **djebel**) ▶ **noun** (in the Middle East and North Africa) a mountain or hill, or a range of hills.
– ORIGIN colloquial Arabic form of *jabal* 'mountain'.

Jedburgh /'dʒɛdb(ə)rə/ a town in southern Scotland near the English border, in Scottish Borders region.

Jeddah /'dʒɛdə/ variant spelling of **JIDDAH**.

jeep ▶ **noun** trademark a small, sturdy motor vehicle with four-wheel drive, especially one used by the military.
– ORIGIN Second World War (originally US): from the initials *GP*, standing for *general purpose*, influenced by 'Eugene the Jeep', a creature of great resourcefulness and power represented in the *Popeye* comic strip.

jeepers (also **jeepers creepers**) ▶ **exclamation** informal, chiefly US used to express surprise or alarm: *Jeepers! Do you think she saw?*
– ORIGIN 1920s: alteration of **JESUS**.

jeer ▶ **verb** [no obj.] make rude and mocking remarks, typically in a loud voice: *some of the younger men jeered at him |* [as adj. **jeering**] *the jeering crowds.*
■ [with obj.] shout such remarks at (someone): *councillors were jeered and heckled.*
▶ **noun** a rude and mocking remark.
– DERIVATIVES **jeeringly** adverb.
– ORIGIN mid 16th cent.: of unknown origin.

jeera /'dʒiːrə/ (also **zeera**) ▶ **noun** Indian term for **CUMIN**.
– ORIGIN from Hindi *jīrā*.

Jeeves the resourceful and influential valet of Bertie Wooster in the novels of P. G. Wodehouse.

Jeez (also **Jeeze, Geez**) ▶ **exclamation** informal a mild expression used to show surprise or annoyance.
– ORIGIN 1920s: abbreviation of **JESUS**.

Jefferies, (John) Richard (1848–87), English writer and naturalist renowned for his observation of English rural life. Notable works *Bevis* (novel, 1882) and *The Story of my Heart* (autobiography, 1883).

Jefferson, Thomas (1743–1826), American Democratic Republican statesman, 3rd President of the US 1801–9. He played a key role in the American leadership during the War of Independence and was the principal drafter of the Declaration of Independence (1776).
– DERIVATIVES **Jeffersonian** adjective & noun.

Jefferson City the state capital of Missouri; pop. 35,480 (1990).

Jeffreys, George, 1st Baron (*c.*1645–89), Welsh judge. Chief Justice of the King's Bench from 1683, he took part in the Popish Plot prosecutions and later became infamous for his brutal sentencing at the Bloody Assizes.

jehad ▶ **noun** variant spelling of **JIHAD**.

Jehoshaphat /dʒɪ'hɒʃəfat/ (also **Jehosaphat**) a king of Judah in the mid 9th century BC.
■ [as exclamation] (also **jumping Jehoshaphat**) a mild expletive: *Jehoshaphat! That would be ghastly.* [ORIGIN: probably a euphemism for **JESUS**.]

Jehovah /dʒɪ'həʊvə/ ▶ **noun** a form of the Hebrew name of God used in some translations of the Bible.
– ORIGIN from medieval Latin *Iehouah, Iehoua*, from Hebrew *YHWH* or *JHVH*, the consonants of the name of God, with the inclusion of vowels taken from *'ăḏōnāy* 'my lord'; see also **YAHWEH**.

Jehovah's Witness ▶ **noun** a member of a fundamentalist Christian sect (the Watch Tower Bible and Tract Society) founded in the US by Charles Taze Russell (1852–1916), denying many traditional Christian doctrines (including the divinity of Christ) but preaching the Second Coming of Christ, and refusing military service and blood transfusion on religious grounds.

Jehovist /dʒɪ'həʊvɪst/ ▶ **noun** another name for **YAHWIST**.

Jehu /'dʒiːhjuː/ (842–815 BC), king of Israel. He was famous for driving his chariot furiously (2 Kings 9).

jejune /dʒɪ'dʒuːn/ ▶ **adjective 1** naive, simplistic, and superficial: *their entirely predictable and usually jejune opinions.*
2 (of ideas or writings) dry and uninteresting: *the poem seems to me rather jejune.*
– DERIVATIVES **jejunely** adverb, **jejuneness** noun.
– ORIGIN early 17th cent.: from Latin *jejunus* 'fasting, barren'. The original sense was 'without food', hence 'not intellectually nourishing'.

jejunoileal /dʒɪˌdʒuːnəʊ'ɪlɪəl/ ▶ **adjective** Medicine of or involving the jejunum and the ileum, usually with reference to a bypass operation in which they are connected.

jejunum /dʒɪ'dʒuːnəm/ ▶ **noun** [in sing.] Anatomy the part of the small intestine between the duodenum and ileum.
– DERIVATIVES **jejunal** adjective.
– ORIGIN mid 16th cent.: from medieval Latin, neuter of *jejunus* 'fasting' (because it is usually found to be empty after death).

Jekyll[1] /'dʒɛk(ə)l/ , Dr, the central character of Robert Louis Stevenson's story *The Strange Case of Dr Jekyll and Mr Hyde* (1886). He discovers a drug which creates a separate personality (appearing in the character of Mr Hyde) into which Jekyll's evil impulses are channelled.
– PHRASES **a Jekyll and Hyde** a person alternately displaying opposing good and evil personalities.

Jekyll[2] /'dʒiːk(ə)l/, Gertrude (1843–1932), English horticulturalist and garden designer. She designed over 300 gardens for buildings designed by Edwin Lutyens, promoting colour design in garden planning and 'wild' gardens.

j

jell ▶ **verb** variant spelling of **GEL**[2].
– ORIGIN mid 18th cent.: back-formation from **JELLY**.

jellaba ▶ **noun** variant spelling of **DJELLABA**.

Jellicoe /'dʒɛlɪkəʊ/, John Rushworth, 1st Earl (1859–1935), British admiral, commander of the Grand Fleet at the Battle of Jutland.

jello (also trademark **Jell-O**) ▶ **noun** [mass noun] N. Amer. a fruit-flavoured gelatin dessert made up from a commercially prepared powder.

jelly ▶ **noun** (pl. **-ies**) **1** [mass noun] chiefly Brit. a sweet dessert, typically fruit-flavoured, made by warming and then cooling a liquid containing gelatin or a similar setting agent in a mould or dish so that it sets into a soft, firm, somewhat elastic mass.
■ used figuratively and in similes to refer to sensations of fear or strong emotion: *her legs felt like jelly.* ■ a similar clear preparation made with fruit or other ingredients as a condiment: *roast pheasant with redcurrant jelly.* ■ a similar savoury preparation made by boiling meat and bones. ■ any substance of a similar consistency: *frogs lay eggs coated in jelly.* ■ [count noun] a small sweet made with gelatin. ■ US term for **JAM**[2]. ■ (**jellies**) jelly shoes. ■ [count noun] Brit. informal a tablet of the drug Temazepam.
2 Brit. informal term for **GELIGNITE**.
▶ **verb** (**-ies, -ied**) [with obj.] [usu. as adj. **jellied**] set (food) as or in a jelly: *jellied cranberry sauce | jellied eels.*
– DERIVATIVES **jellification** noun, **jellify** verb, **jelly-like** adjective.
– ORIGIN late Middle English: from Old French *gelee* 'frost, jelly', from Latin *gelata* 'frozen', from *gelare* 'freeze', from *gelu* 'frost'.

jelly baby ▶ **noun** Brit. a jelly-like sweet in the stylized shape of a baby.

jelly bag ▶ **noun** a fine mesh bag used for straining the juice from cooked fruit, especially so that this liquid can be made into jelly.

jelly bean ▶ **noun** a bean-shaped sweet with a jelly-like centre and a firm sugar coating.

jellyfish ▶ **noun** (pl. same or **-fishes**) **1** a free-swimming marine coelenterate with a jelly-like bell- or saucer-shaped body that is typically transparent and has stinging tentacles around the edge.
• Classes Scyphozoa and Cubozoa.
2 informal a feeble person.

jelly roll ▶ **noun** N. Amer. a Swiss roll.

jelly shoe (also **jelly sandal**) ▶ **noun** a sandal made from brightly coloured or translucent moulded plastic.

jelutong /dʒɛ'luːtɒŋ/ ▶ **noun** a Malaysian tree with pale lightweight timber.
• Genus *Dyera*, family Apocynaceae: several species, in particular *D. costulata*, from which a latex is obtained.
– ORIGIN mid 19th cent.: from Malay.

jemadar /ˈdʒɛməˌdɑː/ ▶ **noun** variant spelling of **JAMADAR**.

jemmy (US **jimmy**) ▶ **noun** (pl. **-ies**) a short crowbar used by a burglar to force open a window or door.
▶ **verb** (**-ies**, **-ied**) [with obj.] informal force open (a window or door) with a jemmy.
– ORIGIN early 19th cent.: pet form of the given name *James* (compare with **JACK**[1]).

Jena /ˈjeɪnə, German ˈjeːna/ a university town in central Germany, in Thuringia; pop. 100,970 (1991). It is noted as a manufacturing centre for optical and precision instruments.

je ne sais quoi /ˌʒə nə seɪ ˈkwɑː, French ʒən sɛ kwa/ ▶ **noun** a quality that cannot be described or named easily: *that je ne sais quoi which makes a professional.*
– ORIGIN French, literally 'I do not know what'.

Jenkins, Roy (Harris), Baron Jenkins of Hillhead (b.1920), English Labour and Social Democrat MP and scholar. A Labour MP between 1948 and 1976, he co-founded the Social Democratic Party in 1981 and represented Glasgow Hillhead 1982–87. He then became Chancellor of Oxford University.

Jenkins's Ear, War of a war between England and Spain (1739). It was precipitated by a British sea captain, Robert Jenkins, who appeared before Parliament to produce what he claimed was his ear, cut off by the Spanish while they were carrying out a search of his ship in the Caribbean.

Jenner /ˈdʒɛnə/, Edward (1749–1823), English physician, the pioneer of vaccination. Jenner deliberately infected people with small amounts of cowpox as he believed it would protect them from catching smallpox. The practice was eventually accepted throughout the world, leading to the widespread use of vaccination for other diseases and eventually to the eradication of smallpox in the late 20th century.

jennet /ˈdʒɛnɪt/ ▶ **noun** a small Spanish horse.
– ORIGIN late Middle English: via French from Spanish *jinete* 'light horseman', from Spanish Arabic *Zenāta*, the name of a Berber people famous for horsemanship.

jenny ▶ **noun** (pl. **-ies**) **1** a female donkey or ass.
2 short for **SPINNING JENNY**.
– ORIGIN early 17th cent. (used to denote a female mammal or bird): pet form of the given name *Janet* (compare with **JACK**[1]).

jenny wren ▶ **noun** Brit. informal a wren.

jeon /dʒʌn/ ▶ **noun** (pl. same) a monetary unit of South Korea, equal to one hundredth of a won.
– ORIGIN Korean.

jeopardize /ˈdʒɛpədʌɪz/ (also **-ise**) ▶ **verb** [with obj.] put (someone or something) into a situation in which there is a danger of loss, harm, or failure: *a devaluation of the dollar would jeopardize New York's position as a financial centre.*

jeopardy /ˈdʒɛpədi/ ▶ **noun** [mass noun] danger of loss, harm, or failure: *the whole peace process is* **in jeopardy**.
■ Law danger arising from being on trial for a criminal offence.
– ORIGIN Middle English *iuparti*, from Old French *ieu parti* '(evenly) divided game'. The term was originally used in chess and other games to denote a problem, or a position in which the chances of winning or losing were evenly balanced, hence 'a dangerous situation'.

Jephthah /ˈdʒɛfθə/ (in the Bible) a judge of Israel who sacrificed his daughter in consequence of a vow that if victorious in battle he would sacrifice the first living thing that met him on his return (Judges 11, 12).

Jer. ▶ **abbreviation for** Jeremiah (in biblical references).

Jerba variant spelling of **DJERBA**.

jerboa /dʒəːˈbəʊə, ˈdʒəːbəʊə/ ▶ **noun** a desert-dwelling rodent with very long hind legs that enable it to walk upright and perform long jumps, found from North Africa to central Asia.
• Family Dipodidae: several genera and species.
– ORIGIN mid 17th cent.: modern Latin, from Arabic *yarbū'*.

jeremiad /ˌdʒɛrɪˈmʌɪad/ ▶ **noun** a long, mournful complaint or lamentation; a list of woes.
– ORIGIN late 18th cent.: from French *jérémiade*, from *Jérémie* 'Jeremiah', from ecclesiastical Latin *Jeremias*, with reference to the Lamentations of Jeremiah in the Old Testament.

Jeremiah /ˌdʒɛrɪˈmʌɪə/ (*c.*650–*c.*585 BC) a Hebrew major prophet who foresaw the fall of Assyria, the conquest of his country by Egypt and Babylon, and the destruction of Jerusalem. The biblical Lamentations are traditionally ascribed to him.
■ a book of the Bible containing his prophecies. ■ [as noun **a Jeremiah**] a person who complains continually or foretells disaster.

jerepigo /ˌdʒɛrɪˈpiːɡəʊ/ ▶ **noun** [mass noun] S. African a heavy, sweet, fortified dessert wine.
– ORIGIN alteration of *geropiga* (from Portuguese, *jeropiga*), a grape juice mixture added during the port-making process.

Jerez /hɛˈrɛθ, Spanish xeˈreθ, -ˈres/ a town in Andalusia, Spain; pop. 184,020 (1991). It is the centre of the sherry-making industry. Full name **JEREZ DE LA FRONTERA** /deɪ la frɒnˈtɛːrə, Spanish de la fronˈtera/.

Jericho /ˈdʒɛrɪkəʊ/ a town in Palestine, in the West Bank north of the Dead Sea.

According to the Bible, Jericho was a Canaanite city destroyed by the Israelites after they crossed the Jordan into the Promised Land; its walls were flattened by the shout of the army and the blast of the trumpets. Occupied by the Israelis since the Six Day War of 1967, in 1994 Jericho was the first area given partial autonomy under the PLO–Israeli peace accord.

jerk[1] ▶ **noun** **1** a quick, sharp, sudden movement: *he gave a sudden jerk of his head.*
■ a spasmodic muscular twitch. ■ [in sing.] Weightlifting the raising of a barbell above the head from shoulder level by an abrupt straightening of the arms and legs, typically as the second part of a clean and jerk.
2 informal, chiefly N. Amer. a contemptibly foolish person.
▶ **verb** [with obj. and adverbial] make (something) move with a jerk: *she jerked her chin up.*
■ [no obj., with adverbial of direction] move with a jerk: *his head jerked round | the van jerked forward.* ■ suddenly rouse or jolt (someone): *the thud jerked her back to reality.* ■ [with obj.] Weightlifting raise (a weight) from shoulder level to above the head.
– DERIVATIVES **jerker** noun.
– ORIGIN mid 16th cent. (denoting a stroke with a whip): probably imitative.
▶ **jerk someone around** N. Amer. informal deal with someone dishonestly or unfairly.
jerk off vulgar slang, chiefly N. Amer. masturbate.

jerk[2] ▶ **verb** [with obj.] [usu. as adj. **jerked**] prepare (pork or chicken) by marinating it in spices and barbecuing it over a wood fire.
▶ **noun** [mass noun] pork or chicken cooked in this way: *fiery Jamaican jerk* | [as modifier] *jerk chicken.*
– ORIGIN early 18th cent.: from Latin American Spanish *charquear*, from *charqui*, from Quechua *echarqui* 'dried flesh'.

jerkin ▶ **noun** a sleeveless jacket.
■ historical a man's close-fitting jacket, typically made of leather.
– ORIGIN early 16th cent.: of unknown origin.

jerkin head ▶ **noun** Architecture the end of a roof that is hipped for only part of its height, leaving a truncated gable.
– ORIGIN mid 19th cent.: perhaps from an alteration of *jerking* (from the verb **JERK**[1]) + **HEAD**; compare also with earlier *kirkin-head* (apparently arbitrarily formed from **KIRK**) in the same sense.

jerkwater ▶ **adjective** [attrib.] US informal of or associated with small, remote, and insignificant rural settlements: *some jerkwater town.*
– ORIGIN mid 19th cent.: from **JERK**[1] + **WATER**, from the need for early railway engines to be supplied with water in remote areas, by dipping a bucket into a stream and 'jerking' it out by rope.

jerky[1] ▶ **adjective** (**jerkier**, **jerkiest**) characterized by abrupt stops and starts: *the coach drew to a jerky halt.*
– DERIVATIVES **jerkily** adverb, **jerkiness** noun.

jerky[2] ▶ **noun** [mass noun] meat that has been cured by being cut into long, thin strips and dried: *beef jerky.*
– ORIGIN mid 19th cent.: from American Spanish *charqui*, from Quechua.

jeroboam /ˌdʒɛrəˈbəʊəm/ ▶ **noun** a wine bottle with a capacity four times larger than that of an ordinary bottle.
– ORIGIN early 19th cent.: named after *Jeroboam*, a king of Israel, 'who made Israel to sin' (1 Kings 11:28, 14:16).

Jerome /dʒəˈrəʊm/, Jerome K. (1859–1927), English novelist and dramatist; full name *Jerome Klapka Jerome.* He is chiefly remembered for his humorous novel *Three Men in a Boat* (1889).

Jerome, St (*c.*342–420), Doctor of the Church. He is chiefly known for his compilation of the Vulgate. Feast day, 30 September.

Jerry ▶ **noun** (pl. **-ies**) Brit. informal, dated a German (especially in military contexts).
■ [in sing.] the Germans collectively: *Jerry has some 200 dive-bombers at Spitzbergen.*
– ORIGIN First World War: probably an alteration of **GERMAN**.

jerry ▶ **noun** (pl. **-ies**) Brit. informal, dated a chamber pot.
– ORIGIN mid 19th cent.: probably a diminutive of **JEROBOAM**.

jerry-built ▶ **adjective** badly or hastily built with materials of poor quality.
– DERIVATIVES **jerry-builder** noun, **jerry-building** noun.
– ORIGIN mid 19th cent.: origin unknown; sometimes said to be from the name of a firm of builders in Liverpool, or to allude to the walls of Jericho, which fell down at the sound of Joshua's trumpets (Josh. 6:20).

jerrycan (also **jerrican**) ▶ **noun** a large flat-sided metal container for storing or transporting liquids, typically petrol or water.
– ORIGIN Second World War: from **JERRY** + **CAN**[2], because such containers were first used in Germany.

jerrymander ▶ **verb** Brit. variant spelling of **GERRYMANDER**.

Jersey the largest of the Channel Islands; pop. 82,810 (1990); capital, St Helier.

jersey ▶ **noun** (pl. **-eys**) **1** a knitted garment with long sleeves, worn over the upper body.
■ a distinctive shirt worn by a player or competitor in certain sports. ■ [mass noun] a soft, fine knitted fabric.
2 (**Jersey**) an animal of a breed of light brown dairy cattle from Jersey.
– ORIGIN late 16th cent. (denoting woollen worsted fabric made in Jersey): from **JERSEY**.

Jersey City an industrial city in NE New Jersey, on the Hudson River opposite New York City; pop. 228,540 (1990).

Jerusalem /dʒəˈruːsələm/ the holy city of the Jews, sacred also to Christians and Muslims, lying in the Judaean hills about 30 km (20 miles) from the River Jordan; pop. 561,900 (est. 1993).

The city was captured from the Canaanites by King David of the Israelites (*c.*1000 BC), who made it his capital. As the site of the Temple, built by Solomon (957 BC), it became also the centre of the Jewish religion. Since then it has shared the troubled history of the area—destroyed by the Babylonians in 586 BC and by the Romans in AD 70, and fought over by Saracens and Crusaders in the Middle Ages. From 1947 the city was divided between the states of Israel and Jordan until the Israelis occupied the whole city in June 1967 and proclaimed it the capital of Israel. It is revered by Christians as the place of Christ's death and resurrection, and by Muslims as the site of the Dome of the Rock.

Jerusalem artichoke ▶ **noun** **1** a knobbly edible tuber with white flesh, eaten as a vegetable.
2 the tall North American plant, closely related to the sunflower, which produces this tuber.
• *Helianthus tuberosus*, family Compositae.
– ORIGIN early 17th cent.: *Jerusalem*, alteration of Italian *girasole* 'sunflower'.

Jerusalem Bible ▶ **noun** a modern English translation of the Bible by mainly Roman Catholic scholars, published in 1966 and revised (as the **New Jerusalem Bible**) in 1985.

Jerusalem cross ▶ **noun** a cross with arms of equal length each ending in a bar; a cross potent.

Jerusalem thorn ▶ **noun** a thorny tropical American tree of the pea family, which is grown as an ornamental.
• *Parkinsonia aculeata*, family Leguminosae.

Jervis /ˈdʒɑːvɪs/, John, Earl St Vincent (1735–1823), British admiral. In 1797, as commander of the British fleet, he defeated a Spanish fleet off Cape St Vincent, for which he was created Earl St Vincent.

Jervis Bay Territory a territory on Jervis Bay on the SE coast of Australia. Incorporated in 1915 as a sea outlet for the Australian Capital Territory, it separated from the Capital Territory in 1988.

Jespersen /ˈjɛspəs(ə)n/ (Jens) Otto (Harry) (1860–1943), Danish philologist, grammarian, and educationist. He promoted the use of the 'direct method' in language teaching with the publication of his theoretical work *How to Teach a Foreign*

Language (1904). Other notable works: *Modern English Grammar* (1909–49).

jess Falconry ▶ **noun** (usu. **jesses**) a short leather strap that is fastened round each leg of a hawk, usually also having a ring or swivel to which a leash may be attached.
▶ **verb** [with obj.] put such straps on (a hawk).
– ORIGIN Middle English: from Old French *ges*, based on Latin *jactus* 'a throw', from *jacere* 'to throw'.

jessamine /ˈdʒɛsəmɪn/ ▶ **noun** variant spelling of **JASMINE**.

Jesse /ˈdʒɛsi/ (in the Bible) the father of David (1 Sam. 16), represented as the first in the genealogy of Jesus Christ.

Jesse tree ▶ **noun** a representation in carving or stained glass of the genealogy of Jesus as a tree with Jesse at the base and intermediate descendants on branching scrolls of foliage.

Jesse window ▶ **noun** a church window showing Jesus' descent from Jesse, typically in the form of a Jesse tree.

jessie (also **jessy**) ▶ **noun** (pl. **-ies**) Brit. derogatory an effeminate or homosexual man.
– ORIGIN 1920s: from the female given name *Jessie*.

jest ▶ **noun** a thing said or done for amusement; a joke: *there are jests about administrative gaffes* | [mass noun] *it was said **in jest**.*
■ archaic an object of derision: *lowly virtue is the jest of fools.*
▶ **verb** [no obj.] speak or act in a joking manner: *you jest, surely?* | [with direct speech] *'I don't know about maturing,' jests William.*
– ORIGIN late Middle English: from earlier *gest*, from Old French *geste*, from Latin *gesta* 'actions, exploits', from *gerere* 'do'. The original sense was 'exploit, heroic deed', hence 'a narrative of such deeds' (originally in verse); later the term denoted an idle tale, hence a joke (mid 16th cent.).

jester ▶ **noun** historical a professional joker or 'fool' at a medieval court, typically wearing a cap with bells on it and carrying a mock sceptre.
■ a person who habitually plays the fool.

Jesu /ˈdʒiːzjuː/ archaic form of **JESUS**.
– ORIGIN Middle English: from Old French. *Jesus* became the usual spelling in the 16th cent., but *Jesu* was often retained in translations of the Bible, reflecting Latin vocative use.

Jesuit /ˈdʒɛz(j)ʊɪt/ ▶ **noun** a member of the Society of Jesus, a Roman Catholic order of priests founded by St Ignatius Loyola, St Francis Xavier, and others in 1534, to do missionary work. The order was zealous in opposing the Reformation. Despite periodic persecution it has retained an important influence in Catholic thought and education.
– ORIGIN from French *jésuite* or modern Latin *Jesuita*, from Christian Latin *Iesus* (see **JESUS**).

Jesuitical ▶ **adjective** of or concerning the Jesuits.
■ dissembling or equivocating, in the manner once associated with Jesuits.
– DERIVATIVES **Jesuitically** adverb.

Jesuits' bark ▶ **noun** [mass noun] archaic cinchona bark.

Jesus (also **Jesus Christ** or **Jesus of Nazareth**), the central figure of the Christian religion.

> Jesus conducted a mission of preaching and healing (with reported miracles) in Palestine in about AD 28–30, which is described in the Gospels, as are his arrest, death by crucifixion, and Resurrection from the dead. His followers considered him to be the Christ or Messiah and the Son of God, and belief in his Resurrection became a central tenet of Christianity.

■ [as exclamation] an oath used to express irritation, dismay, or surprise.
– ORIGIN from Christian Latin *Iesus*, from Greek *Iēsous*, from a late Hebrew or Aramaic analogous formation based on *Yĕhōšūa'* 'Joshua'.

Jesus freak ▶ **noun** informal, chiefly derogatory a fervent evangelical Christian, especially one who adopts a lifestyle like that of a hippy.

JET ▶ **abbreviation for** Joint European Torus, a machine for conducting experiments in nuclear fusion, at Culham in Oxfordshire.

jet^1 ▶ **noun 1** a rapid stream of liquid or gas forced out of a small opening: *the firm unblocks your drain with high-pressure jets.*
■ a nozzle or narrow opening for sending out such a stream: *Agnes turned up the gas jet.*
2 an aircraft powered by one or more jet engines: *a private jet* | [as modifier] *a jet plane.*
■ a jet engine.
▶ **verb** (**jetted**, **jetting**) [no obj., with adverbial of direction] **1** travel by jet aircraft: *the newly-weds jetted off for a honeymoon in New York.*
2 spurt out in jets: *blood jetted from his nostrils.*
– ORIGIN late 16th cent. (as a verb meaning 'jut out'): from French *jeter* 'to throw', based on Latin *jactare*, frequentative of *jacere* 'to throw'.

jet^2 ▶ **noun** [mass noun] a hard black semi-precious variety of lignite, capable of being carved and highly polished.
■ a glossy black colour: [as modifier] *the gloss of her jet hair* | *jet black.*
– ORIGIN Middle English: from Old French *jaiet*, from Latin *Gagates*, from Greek *gagatēs* 'from *Gagai*', a town in Asia Minor.

jeté /ˈʒɛteɪ, ʒəˈteɪ/ ▶ **noun** Ballet a jump in which a dancer springs from one foot to land on the other with one leg extended outwards from the body while in the air. See also **GRAND JETÉ**, **PETIT JETÉ**.
– ORIGIN French, past participle of *jeter* 'to throw'.

jet engine ▶ **noun** an engine using jet propulsion for forward thrust, mainly used for aircraft.

jetfoil ▶ **noun** a type of passenger-carrying hydrofoil.
– ORIGIN 1970s: blend of **JET**^{1} and **HYDROFOIL**.

jet lag ▶ **noun** [mass noun] extreme tiredness and other physical effects felt by a person after a long flight across different time zones.
– DERIVATIVES **jet-lagged** adjective.

jetliner ▶ **noun** a large jet aircraft carrying passengers.
– ORIGIN 1940s: blend of **JET**^{1} and **AIRLINER**.

jet pipe ▶ **noun** the exhaust duct of a jet engine.

jet-propelled ▶ **adjective** moved by jet propulsion.

jet propulsion ▶ **noun** [mass noun] propulsion by the backward ejection of a high-speed jet of gas or liquid.

jetsam /ˈdʒɛts(ə)m/ ▶ **noun** [mass noun] unwanted material or goods that have been thrown overboard from a ship and washed ashore, especially material that has been discarded to lighten the vessel. Compare with **FLOTSAM**.
– ORIGIN late 16th cent. (as *jetson*): contraction of **JETTISON**.

jet set ▶ **noun** (**the jet set**) informal wealthy and fashionable people who travel widely and frequently for pleasure: [as modifier] *the jet-set lifestyle.*
– DERIVATIVES **jet-setter** noun, **jet-setting** adjective.

jet ski ▶ **noun** trademark a small jet-propelled vehicle which skims across the surface of water and is ridden in a similar way to a motorcycle.
▶ **verb** (**jet-ski**) [no obj.] [often as noun **jet-skiing**] ride on such a vehicle.
– DERIVATIVES **jet-skier** noun.

jet stream ▶ **noun 1** a narrow variable band of very strong predominantly westerly air currents encircling the globe several miles above the earth. There are typically two or three jet streams in each of the northern and southern hemispheres.
2 a flow of exhaust gases from a jet engine.

jettison /ˈdʒɛtɪs(ə)n, -z(ə)n/ ▶ **verb** [with obj.] throw or drop (something) from an aircraft or ship: *six aircraft jettisoned their loads in the sea.*
■ abandon or discard (someone or something that is no longer wanted): *the scheme was jettisoned.*
▶ **noun** [mass noun] the action of jettisoning something.
– ORIGIN late Middle English (as a noun denoting the throwing of goods overboard to lighten a ship in distress): from Old French *getaison*, from Latin *jactatio(n-)*, from *jactare* 'to throw' (see **JET**^{1}). The verb dates from the mid 19th cent.

jetton /ˈdʒɛt(ə)n/ ▶ **noun** a counter or token used as a gambling chip or to operate slot machines.
– ORIGIN mid 18th cent.: from French *jeton*, from *jeter* 'throw, add up accounts' (see **JET**^{1}); so named because the term was formerly used in accounting.

jetty ▶ **noun** (pl. **-ies**) a landing stage or small pier at which boats can dock or be moored.
■ a bridge or staircase used by passengers boarding an aircraft. ■ a breakwater constructed to protect or defend a harbour, stretch of coast, or riverbank.
– ORIGIN late Middle English: from Old French *jetee*, feminine past participle of *jeter* 'to throw' (see **JET**^{1}).

jetway ▶ **noun** (trademark in the UK) another term for **AIR BRIDGE**.

jeu d'esprit /ʒəː dɛˈspriː, French ʒø dɛspri/ ▶ **noun** (pl. **jeux d'esprit** pronunc. same) a light-hearted display of wit and cleverness, especially in a work of literature.
– ORIGIN French, literally 'game of the mind'.

jeunesse dorée /ʒəːˌnɛs ˈdɔːreɪ, French ʒœnɛs dɔre/ ▶ **noun** French term for **GILDED YOUTH**.

Jew ▶ **noun** a member of the people and cultural community whose traditional religion is Judaism and who trace their origins to the ancient Hebrew people of Israel.
– ORIGIN Middle English: from Old French *juiu*, via Latin from Greek *Ioudaios*, via Aramaic from Hebrew *yĕhūḏī*, from *yĕhūḏāh* 'Judah' (see **JUDAH**).

jewel ▶ **noun** a precious stone, typically a single crystal or piece of a hard lustrous or translucent mineral cut into shape with flat facets or smoothed and polished for use as an ornament.
■ (usu. **jewels**) an ornament or piece of jewellery containing such a stone or stones. ■ a hard precious stone used as a bearing in a watch, compass, or other device. ■ a very pleasing or valued person or thing; a very fine example: *she was a jewel of a nurse.*
– PHRASES **the jewel in the** (or **one's**) **crown** the most valuable or successful part of something: *quality education was once the jewel in Britain's crown.*
– ORIGIN Middle English: from Old French *joel*, from *jeu* 'game, play', from Latin *jocus* 'jest'.

jewel beetle ▶ **noun** a chiefly tropical beetle that has bold metallic colours and patterns. The larvae are mainly wood-borers and may be serious pests of timber.
● Family Buprestidae: numerous genera.

jewel box ▶ **noun 1** a bivalve mollusc which has a robust shell with a rough or spiny surface. It lives in warm seas, attached to rock or coral.
● Family Chamidae: *Chama* and other genera.
2 (also **jewel case**) a storage box for a compact disc.

jewelfish ▶ **noun** (pl. same or **-fishes**) a scarlet and green tropical freshwater cichlid.
● *Hemichromis bimaculatus*, family Cichlidae.

jewelled (US **jeweled**) ▶ **adjective** adorned, set with, or made from jewels: *a jewelled dagger.*

jeweller (US **jeweler**) ▶ **noun** a person or company that makes or sells jewels or jewellery.
– ORIGIN Middle English: from Old French *juelier*, from *joel* (see **JEWEL**).

jeweller's rouge ▶ **noun** [mass noun] finely ground ferric oxide, used as a polish for metal and optical glass.

jewellery (US also **jewelry**) ▶ **noun** [mass noun] personal ornaments, such as necklaces, rings, or bracelets, that are typically made from or contain jewels and precious metal.
– ORIGIN late Middle English: from Old French *juelerie*, from *juelier* 'jeweller', from *joel* (see **JEWEL**).

Jewess ▶ **noun** often offensive a Jewish woman or girl.

jewfish ▶ **noun** (pl. same or **-fishes**) a large sporting or food fish of warm coastal waters:
● a fish of the Atlantic and Pacific coasts of North America (*Epinephelus itajara*, family Serranidae). ● a fish of the Indo-Pacific (family Sciaenidae: several species), in particular the mulloway.

Jewish ▶ **adjective** relating to, associated with, or denoting Jews or Judaism: *the Jewish people.*
– DERIVATIVES **Jewishly** adverb, **Jewishness** noun.

Jewish calendar ▶ **noun** a complex ancient calendar in use among Jewish people.

> It is a lunar calendar adapted to the solar year, normally consisting of twelve months but having thirteen months in leap years, which occur seven times in every cycle of nineteen years. The years are reckoned from the Creation (which is placed at 3761 BC); the months are Nisan, Iyyar, Sivan, Thammuz, Ab, Elul, Tishri, Hesvan, Kislev, Tebet, Sebat, and Adar, with an intercalary month (First Adar) being added in leap years. The religious year begins with Nisan and ends with Adar, while the civil year begins with Tishri and ends with Elul.

Jewish New Year ▶ **noun** another term for **ROSH HASHANA**.

Jewison /ˈdʒuːɪs(ə)n/, Norman (b.1926), Canadian film director and producer. He is known particularly for the drama *In the Heat of the Night* (1967), which won five Oscars, the musical *Fiddler on the Roof* (1971), and the romantic comedy *Moonstruck* (1987).

Jewry /ˈdʒʊəri/ ▶ **noun** (pl. **-ies**) **1** [mass noun] Jews collectively.
2 historical a Jewish quarter in a town or city.
– ORIGIN Middle English: from Old French *juierie*, from *juiu* (see **JEW**).

Jew's ear ▶ noun a common fungus with a brown rubbery cup-shaped fruiting body, growing on dead or dying trees in both Eurasia and North America.
● *Auricularia auricula-judae*, family Auriculariaceae, class Hymenomycetes.
– ORIGIN mid 16th cent.: a mistranslation of medieval Latin *auricula Judae* 'Judas's ear', from its shape, and because it grows on the elder, which was said to be the tree from which Judas Iscariot hanged himself.

Jew's harp ▶ noun a small lyre-shaped musical instrument held between the teeth and struck with a finger. It can produce only one note, but harmonics are sounded by the player altering the shape of the mouth cavity.

Jezebel /ˈdʒɛzəbɛl/ (*fl.* 9th century BC), a Phoenician princess, traditionally the great-aunt of Dido and in the Bible the wife of Ahab king of Israel. She was denounced by Elijah for introducing the worship of Baal into Israel (1 Kings 16:31, 21:5–15, 2 Kings 9:30–7). Her use of make-up shocked Puritan England.
■ [as noun a **Jezebel**] a shameless or immoral woman.

Jhansi /ˈdʒɑːnsi/ a city in the state of Uttar Pradesh, northern India; pop. 301,000 (1991).

Jhelum /ˈdʒiːləm/ a river which rises in the Himalayas and flows through the Vale of Kashmir into Punjab, where it meets the Chenab River. It is one of the five rivers that gave Punjab its name. In ancient times it was called the Hydaspes.

jhuggi /ˈdʒʌɡi/ ▶ noun (pl. **jhuggis**) Indian a slum dwelling typically made of mud and corrugated iron.
– ORIGIN Hindi.

jhuggi jhopri /ˈdʒəʊpri/ ▶ noun (pl. **jhuggi jhopris**) Indian a slum; a cluster of jhuggis.
– ORIGIN Hindi.

-ji /dʒi/ ▶ combining form Indian used with names and titles to show respect: *Lalitaji* | *guruji*.
– ORIGIN via Hindi from Sanskrit *jaya* 'conquering'.

Jiang Jie Shi /ˌdʒjaŋ dʒiː ˈʃi/ variant form of CHIANG KAI-SHEK.

Jiangsu /ˌdʒjaŋˈsuː/ (also **Kiangsu**) a province of eastern China; capital, Nanjing. It includes much of the Yangtze delta.

Jiangxi /ˌdʒjaŋˈʃi/ (also **Kiangsi**) a province of SE China; capital, Nanchang.

jiao /dʒaʊ/ ▶ noun (pl. same) a monetary unit of China, equal to one tenth of a yuan.
– ORIGIN from Chinese *jiǎo*.

jib¹ ▶ noun **1** Sailing a triangular staysail set forward of the mast.
2 the projecting arm of a crane.
– ORIGIN mid 17th cent.: of unknown origin.

jib² ▶ verb (**jibbed**, **jibbing**) [no obj.] (of an animal, especially a horse) stop and refuse to go on: *he jibbed at the final fence.*
■ (of a person) be unwilling to do or accept something: *he jibs at paying large bills.*
– DERIVATIVES **jibber** noun.
– ORIGIN early 19th cent.: perhaps related to French *regimber* (earlier *regiber*) 'to buck, rear'; compare with JIBE¹.

jibba /ˈdʒɪbə/ (also **jibbah**, **djibba**, or **djibbah**) ▶ noun a long coat worn by Muslim men.
– ORIGIN mid 19th cent.: Egyptian variant of Arabic *jubba*.

jib boom ▶ noun Sailing a spar run out forward as an extension of the bowsprit.

jibe¹ (also **gibe**) ▶ noun an insulting or mocking remark; a taunt: *a jibe at his old rivals.*
▶ verb [no obj.] make insulting or mocking remarks; jeer: *some cynics in the media might jibe.*
– ORIGIN mid 16th cent. (as a verb): perhaps from Old French *giber* 'handle roughly' (in modern dialect 'kick'); compare with JIB².

jibe² ▶ verb & noun US variant of GYBE.

jibe³ ▶ verb [no obj.] N. Amer. informal be in accord; agree: *the verdict does not jibe with the medical evidence.*
– ORIGIN early 19th cent.: of unknown origin.

jib sheet ▶ noun Sailing a rope by which a jib is trimmed.

Jibuti variant spelling of DJIBOUTI.

jicama /ˈhiːkəmə/ ▶ noun [mass noun] the crisp white-fleshed edible tuber of the yam bean, used especially in Mexican cookery.
– ORIGIN early 17th cent.: from Mexican Spanish *jícama*, from Nahuatl *xícama*.

Jiddah /ˈdʒɪdə/ (also **Jeddah**) a seaport on the Red Sea coast of Saudi Arabia, near Mecca; pop. 1,400,000 (est. 1986).

jiffy (also **jiff**) ▶ noun [in sing.] informal a moment: *we'll be back in a jiffy.*
– ORIGIN late 18th cent.: of unknown origin.

Jiffy bag ▶ noun trademark a padded envelope for protecting fragile items in the post.

jig ▶ noun **1** a lively dance with leaping movements.
■ a piece of music for such a dance, typically in compound time.
2 a device that holds a piece of work and guides the tools operating on it.
3 Fishing a type of artificial bait that is jerked up and down through the water.
▶ verb (**jigged**, **jigging**) **1** [no obj.] dance a jig.
■ [with adverbial] move up and down with a quick jerky motion: *we were jigging about in our seats.*
2 [with obj.] equip (a factory or workshop) with a jig or jigs.
3 [no obj.] fish with a jig: *a man jigged for squid.*
– PHRASES **in jig time** N. Amer. informal extremely quickly; in a very short time. **the jig is up** N. Amer. informal the scheme or deception is revealed or foiled.
– ORIGIN mid 16th cent.: of unknown origin.

jigaboo /ˈdʒɪɡəbuː/ ▶ noun N. Amer. offensive a black person.
– ORIGIN early 20th cent.: related to slang *jig* (in the same sense); compare with the pair *bug*, *bugaboo*.

jigger¹ ▶ noun **1** a machine or vehicle with a part that rocks or moves to and fro, e.g. a jigsaw.
2 a person who dances a jig.
3 a small sail set at the stern of a ship.
■ a small tackle consisting of a double and single block with a rope.
4 a measure or small glass of spirits or wine.
5 informal a rest for a billiard cue.
6 Golf, dated a metal golf club with a narrow face.
7 Canadian & NZ a small hand- or power-operated railway vehicle used by railway workers.
▶ verb [with obj.] informal rearrange or tamper with.
– ORIGIN mid 16th cent. (originally a slang word for a door): from the verb JIG (the relationship with which is obscure in certain senses).

jigger² ▶ noun variant spelling of CHIGGER.

jiggered ▶ adjective Brit. informal damaged; broken: *the lens is totally jiggered.*
■ (of a person) exhausted.
– PHRASES **well, I'll be** (or **I'm**) **jiggered** used to express one's astonishment.
– ORIGIN mid 19th cent.: from JIGGER¹; its use to mean 'exhausted' is probably euphemistic for *buggered.*

jiggery-pokery ▶ noun [mass noun] informal, chiefly Brit. deceitful or dishonest behaviour.
– ORIGIN late 19th cent.: probably a variant of Scots *joukery-pawkery*, from *jouk* 'dodge, skulk', of unknown origin.

jiggle ▶ verb [no obj.] move about lightly and quickly from side to side or up and down: *the car jiggled on its springs.*
■ [with obj.] shake (something) lightly up and down or from side to side: *he was jiggling his car keys in his hand.*
▶ noun [in sing.] a quick light shake: *give that rack a jiggle.*
– DERIVATIVES **jiggly** adjective.
– ORIGIN mid 19th cent.: partly an alteration of JOGGLE¹, reinforced by JIG.

jigsaw ▶ noun **1** (also **jigsaw puzzle**) a puzzle consisting of a picture printed on cardboard or wood and cut into various pieces of different shapes that have to be fitted together.
■ figurative a puzzle that can only be resolved by assembling various pieces of information: *help the police put all the pieces of the jigsaw together.*
2 a machine saw with a fine blade enabling it to cut curved lines in a sheet of wood, metal, or plastic.

jihad /dʒɪˈhɑːd, -ˈhad/ ▶ noun a holy war undertaken by Muslims against unbelievers.
■ informal a single-minded or obsessive campaign: *the quest for greater sales became a jihad.*
– ORIGIN from Arabic *jihād*, literally 'effort', expressing, in Muslim thought, struggle on behalf of God and Islam.

Jilin /dʒiːˈlɪn/ (also **Kirin**) a province of NE China; capital, Changchun.
■ an industrial city in Jilin province; pop. 2,251,800 (1990).

jill ▶ noun variant spelling of GILL⁴.

jillaroo /ˌdʒɪləˈruː/ ▶ noun Austral. informal a female novice on a cattle station or sheep station.
– ORIGIN 1940s: from the given name *Jill*, on the pattern of *jackaroo*.

jillion /ˈdʒɪljən/ ▶ cardinal number informal, chiefly N. Amer. an extremely large number: *they ran jillions of ads.*
– ORIGIN 1940s: fanciful formation on the pattern of *billion* and *million*.

jilt ▶ verb [with obj.] (often be **jilted**) dated suddenly reject or abandon (a lover): *she died of a broken heart after being jilted by her lover.*
▶ noun archaic a person, especially a woman, who capriciously rejects a lover.
– ORIGIN mid 17th cent.: (in the sense 'deceive, trick'): of unknown origin.

Jim Crow ▶ noun US **1** [mass noun] the former practice of segregating black people in the US: [as modifier] *Jim Crow laws.*
■ [count noun] offensive a black person.
2 an implement for straightening iron bars or bending rails by screw pressure.
– DERIVATIVES **Jim Crowism** noun.
– ORIGIN mid 19th cent.: the name of a black character in a 19th-cent. plantation song.

jim-dandy N. Amer. informal ▶ adjective fine, outstanding, or excellent.
▶ noun an excellent or notable person or thing.
– ORIGIN late 19th cent.: from the given name *Jim* (pet form of *James*) + DANDY.

Jiménez de Cisneros /hiˌmɛnɛz deɪ sisˈnɛːrɒs, Spanish xiˌmeneθ de θisˈneros, xiˈmenes, sisˈneros/ (also **Ximenes de Cisneros**), Francisco (1436–1517), Spanish cardinal and statesman, regent of Spain 1516–17. He was Grand Inquisitor for Castile and Léon from 1507 to 1517, during which time he undertook a massive campaign against heresy, having some 2,500 alleged heretics put to death.

Jiminy /ˈdʒɪmɪni/ ▶ exclamation used in phrases as an expression of surprise: *by Jiminy, she was right | Jiminy Cricket!*
– ORIGIN early 19th cent.: alteration of GEMINI used as a mild oath in the mid 17th cent., a euphemistic form of *Jesus (Christ).*

jim-jams¹ ▶ plural noun informal a fit of depression or nervousness: *pre-race jim-jams.*
– ORIGIN mid 16th cent. (originally denoting a small article or knick-knack): fanciful reduplication. The current sense dates from the late 19th cent.

jim-jams² ▶ plural noun Brit. informal pyjamas.
– ORIGIN mid 20th cent.: abbreviation of *pie-jim-jams*, alteration of PYJAMAS.

Jimmu /ˈdʒɪmuː/ the legendary first emperor of Japan (660 BC), descendant of the sun goddess Amaterasu and founder of the imperial dynasty.

Jimmy ▶ noun Brit. informal **1** an act of urination. [ORIGIN 1930s: from *Jimmy Riddle*, rhyming slang for 'piddle'.]
2 chiefly Scottish used as a term of address to a male stranger.

jimmy ▶ noun & verb US spelling of JEMMY.

jimmygrant /ˈdʒɪmɪɡrənt/ ▶ noun Austral. rhyming slang an immigrant.

Jimmy Woodser /ˈwʊdzə/ ▶ noun Austral. informal a person who drinks alone or a drink taken on one's own.
– ORIGIN late 19th cent.: from a line in the poem *Jimmy Wood* (1892) by Barcroft Boake: 'Who drinks alone, drinks toast to Jimmy Wood, sir'.

jimson weed /ˈdʒɪms(ə)n/ (also **jimpson weed**) ▶ noun [mass noun] North American term for THORN APPLE.
– ORIGIN late 17th cent. (originally as *Jamestown weed*): named after JAMESTOWN in Virginia.

Jin /dʒɪn/ (also **Chin**) **1** a dynasty that ruled China AD 265–420, commonly divided into **Western Jin** (265–317) and **Eastern Jin** (317–420).
2 a dynasty that ruled Manchuria and northern China AD 1115–1234.

Jina /ˈdʒɪnə/ ▶ noun (in Jainism) a great teacher who has attained liberation from karma.
– ORIGIN from Sanskrit (see also JAIN).

Jinan /dʒiːˈnan/ (also **Tsinan**) a city in eastern China, the capital of Shandong province; pop. 2,290,000 (1990).

jing /dʒɪŋ/ ▶ **exclamation** variant of **JINGS**.

jingbang ▶ **noun** (in phrase **the whole jingbang**) informal the whole lot.
– ORIGIN mid 19th cent.: of unknown origin.

jingle ▶ **noun 1** [in sing.] a light ringing sound such as that made by metal objects being shaken together.
2 a short slogan, verse, or tune designed to be easily remembered, especially as used in advertising.
3 (also **jingle shell**) a bivalve mollusc with a fragile, slightly translucent shell, the lower valve of which has a hole through which pass byssus threads for anchorage.
• Family Anomidae: *Anomia* and other genera.
▶ **verb** make or cause to make a light metallic ringing sound: [no obj.] *her bracelets were jingling* | [with obj.] *he jingled the coins in his purse.*
■ [no obj.] (of writing) be full of alliteration or rhymes.
– DERIVATIVES **jingler** noun, **jingly** adjective.
– ORIGIN late Middle English: imitative.

jingo /ˈdʒɪŋgəʊ/ ▶ **noun** (pl. **-oes**) dated, chiefly derogatory a vociferous supporter of policy favouring war, especially in the name of patriotism.
– PHRASES **by jingo!** an exclamation of surprise.
– ORIGIN late 17th cent. (originally a conjuror's word): *by jingo* (and the noun sense) come from a popular song adopted by those supporting the sending of a British fleet into Turkish waters to resist Russia in 1878. The chorus ran: 'We don't want to fight, yet by Jingo! if we do, We've got the ships, we've got the men, and got the money too'.

jingoism ▶ **noun** [mass noun] chiefly derogatory extreme patriotism, especially in the form of aggressive or warlike foreign policy.
– DERIVATIVES **jingoist** noun, **jingoistic** adjective.

jings /dʒɪŋz/ (also **jing**) ▶ **exclamation** (often **by jings**) chiefly Scottish used to express surprise.
– ORIGIN late 18th cent.: alteration of **JINGO**.

jink /dʒɪŋk/ ▶ **verb** [no obj.] change direction suddenly and nimbly, as when dodging a pursuer: *she was too quick for him and jinked away every time.*
▶ **noun** a sudden quick change of direction.
– ORIGIN late 17th cent. (originally Scots as *high jinks*, denoting antics at drinking parties): probably symbolic of nimble motion. Current senses date from the 18th cent.

jinker /ˈdʒɪŋkə/ Austral. ▶ **noun** a wheeled conveyance for moving heavy logs.
■ a light two-wheeled cart.
▶ **verb** [with obj. and adverbial of direction] convey in a jinker.
– ORIGIN late 19th cent.: variant of early 19th-cent. Scots *janker*, a long pole on wheels for carrying logs.

jinn /dʒɪn/ (also **djinn**) ▶ **noun** (pl. same or **jinns**) (in Arabian and Muslim mythology) an intelligent spirit of lower rank than the angels, able to appear in human and animal forms and to possess humans. Compare with **GENIE**.
– ORIGIN from Arabic *jinnī*, plural *jinn*.

Jinnah /ˈdʒɪnə, ˈdʒɪnɑː/, Muhammad Ali (1876–1948), Indian statesman and founder of Pakistan. He headed the Muslim League in its struggle with the Hindu-oriented Indian National Congress over Indian independence, and in 1947 he became the first Governor General and President of Pakistan.

jinricksha /dʒɪnˈrɪkʃə/ (also **jinrikisha** /dʒɪnˈrɪkɪʃə/) ▶ **noun** another term for **RICKSHAW**.
– ORIGIN Japanese, from *jin* 'man' + *riki* 'strength' + *sha* 'vehicle'.

jinx ▶ **noun** a person or thing that brings bad luck.
▶ **verb** [with obj.] (usu. **be jinxed**) bring bad luck to; cast an evil spell on: *the play is jinxed.*
– ORIGIN early 20th cent. (originally US): probably a variant of *jynx* 'wryneck' (because the bird was used in witchcraft).

jird /dʒəːd/ ▶ **noun** a long-tailed burrowing rodent related to the gerbils, found in deserts and steppes from North Africa to China.
• Genus *Meriones*, family Muridae: several species.
– ORIGIN from Berber *(a)gherda*.

jism /ˈdʒɪz(ə)m/ (also **jissom** /ˈdʒɪsəm/, **jizz**) ▶ **noun** [mass noun] vulgar slang semen.
– ORIGIN mid 19th cent.: of unknown origin.

JIT ▶ **abbreviation for** (of manufacturing systems) just-in-time.

jit /dʒɪt/ (also **jit jive**) ▶ **noun** [mass noun] a style of dance music popular in Zimbabwe.
– ORIGIN Shona, from *jit* 'to dance'.

jitney /ˈdʒɪtni/ ▶ **noun** (pl. **-eys**) N. Amer. informal a bus or other vehicle carrying passengers for a low fare.
– ORIGIN early 20th cent. (originally denoting a five-cent piece): of unknown origin.

jitter informal ▶ **noun 1** (**jitters**) feelings of extreme nervousness: *a bout of the jitters.*
2 [mass noun] slight irregular movement, variation, or unsteadiness, especially in an electrical signal or electronic device.
▶ **verb** [no obj.] act nervously: *an anxious student who jittered at any provocation.*
■ (of a signal or device) suffer from jitter.
– DERIVATIVES **jitteriness** noun, **jittery** adjective.
– ORIGIN 1920s: of unknown origin.

jitterbug ▶ **noun 1** a fast dance popular in the 1940s, performed chiefly to swing music.
■ dated a person fond of dancing such a dance.
2 informal, dated a nervous person.
▶ **verb** (**-bugged**, **-bugging**) [no obj.] dance the jitterbug.
– ORIGIN 1930s (originally US): from the verb **JITTER** + **BUG**.

jiu-jitsu ▶ **noun** variant spelling of **JU-JITSU**.

Jivaro /ˈhiːvərəʊ/ ▶ **noun** (pl. same or **-os**) **1** a member of an indigenous people living widely scattered throughout the Amazon jungle.
2 [mass noun] any of the group of languages spoken by this people.
▶ **adjective** of or relating to this people or their language.
– DERIVATIVES **Jivaroan** adjective & noun.
– ORIGIN from Spanish *jíbaro*, probably from the local name *Shuara*, *Shiwora*.

jive ▶ **noun 1** a lively style of dance popular especially in the 1940s and 1950s, performed to swing music or rock and roll.
■ [mass noun] swing music. ■ [mass noun] a style of dance music popular in South Africa: *township jive.*
2 (also **jive talk**) [mass noun] a form of slang associated with black American jazz musicians.
■ informal, chiefly N. Amer. a thing, especially talk, which is deceptive or worthless: *a single image says more than any amount of blather and jive.*
▶ **verb** informal **1** [no obj.] perform the jive or a similar dance to popular music: *people were jiving in the aisles.*
2 [with obj.] N. Amer. informal taunt or sneer at: *Willy kept jiving him until Jimmy left.*
■ [no obj.] talk nonsense: *he wasn't jiving about that bartender.*
▶ **adjective** N. Amer. informal deceitful or worthless.
– DERIVATIVES **jiver** noun, **jivey** adjective.
– ORIGIN 1920s (originally US denoting meaningless or misleading speech): of unknown origin; the later musical sense 'jazz' gave rise to 'dance performed to jazz' (1940s).

jizz[1] ▶ **noun** informal (among birdwatchers and naturalists) the characteristic impression given by a particular species of animal or plant.
– ORIGIN 1920s: of unknown origin.

jizz[2] ▶ **noun** vulgar slang variant of **JISM**.

Jn ▶ **abbreviation for** ■ (with preceding numeral) an Epistle of John (in biblical references). ■ the Gospel of John.

Jnr ▶ **abbreviation for** Junior (in names).

jo ▶ **noun** (pl. **-oes**) Scottish archaic a sweetheart.
– ORIGIN early 16th cent.: variant of **JOY**.

Joachim, St /ˈdʒəʊəkɪm/ (in Christian tradition) the husband of St Anne and father of the Virgin Mary. He is first mentioned in an apocryphal work of the 2nd century, and then rarely referred to until much later times.

joanna ▶ **noun** Brit. rhyming slang a piano.

Joan of Arc, St (*c.*1412–31), French national heroine; known as **the Maid of Orleans**. She led the French armies against the English in the Hundred Years War, relieving besieged Orleans (1429) and ensuring that Charles VII could be crowned in previously occupied Reims. Captured by the Burgundians in 1430, she was handed over to the English, convicted of heresy, and burnt at the stake. She was canonized in 1920. Feast day, 30 May.

João Pessoa /ˌʒwaʊ pɛˈsəʊə/ a city in NE Brazil, on the Atlantic coast, capital of the state of Paraíba; pop. 484,290 (1990).

Job /dʒəʊb/ (in the Bible) a prosperous man whose patience and piety were tried by undeserved misfortunes, and who, in spite of his bitter lamentations, remained confident in the goodness and justice of God.
■ a book of the Bible telling of Job.

job[1] ▶ **noun 1** a paid position of regular employment: *the scheme could create 200 jobs* | *a part-time job.*
2 a task or piece of work, especially one that is paid: *she wants to be left alone to get on with the job* | *you did a good job of explaining.*
■ a responsibility or duty: *it's our job to find things out.* ■ [in sing.] informal a difficult task: *we thought you'd have a job getting there.* ■ [with modifier] informal a procedure to improve the appearance of something, especially an operation involving plastic surgery: *she's had a nose job* | *someone had done a skilful paint job.* ■ [with modifier] informal a thing of a specified nature: *the car was a blue malevolent-looking job.* ■ informal a crime, especially a robbery: *a series of daring bank jobs.* ■ Computing an operation or group of operations treated as a single and distinct unit.
▶ **verb** (**jobbed**, **jobbing**) **1** [no obj.] [usu. as adj. **jobbing**] do casual or occasional work: *a jobbing builder.*
2 [with obj.] buy and sell (stocks) as a broker-dealer, especially on a small scale.
3 [with obj.] N. Amer. informal cheat; betray.
4 [no obj.] archaic turn a public office or a position of trust to private advantage.
– PHRASES **big jobs** Brit. informal a euphemistic way of referring to faeces or defecation. **do the job** informal achieve the required result: *a piece of board will do the job.* **give something up as a bad job** informal decide that it is futile to devote further time or energy to something. **a good job** informal, chiefly Brit. a fortunate fact or circumstance: *it was a good job she hadn't brought the car.* **jobs for the boys** Brit. derogatory used in reference to the practice of giving paid employment to one's friends, supporters, or relations. **just the job** Brit. informal exactly what is needed. **make the best of a bad job** see **BEST**. **on the job** while working; at work. ■ Brit. informal engaged in sexual intercourse. **out of a job** unemployed; redundant.
– ORIGIN mid 16th cent. (in sense 2 of the noun): of unknown origin.

job[2] archaic ▶ **verb** (**jobbed**, **jobbing**) [with obj.] prod or stab: *he prepared to job the huge brute.*
■ thrust (something pointed) at or into something.
▶ **noun** an act of prodding, thrusting, or wrenching.
– ORIGIN late Middle English: apparently symbolic of a brief forceful action (compare with **JAB**).

job analyst ▶ **noun** a person employed to assess the essential factors of particular jobs and the qualifications needed to carry them out.

jobber ▶ **noun 1** historical (in the UK) a principal or wholesaler who dealt only on the Stock Exchange with brokers, not directly with the public.
2 N. Amer. a wholesaler.
3 a person who does casual or occasional work.
– ORIGIN late 17th cent. (in the sense 'broker, middleman', originally not derogatory): from **JOB**[1].

USAGE On the UK Stock Exchange the term **jobber** was officially replaced by **broker-dealer** in 1986, broker-dealers being entitled to act as both agents and principals in share dealings.

jobbery ▶ **noun** [mass noun] the practice of using a public office or position of trust for one's own gain or advantage.

jobbie ▶ **noun** informal **1** [with adj. or noun modifier] an object or product of a specified kind: *I just got the hang of these computer jobbies.*
2 Brit. a lump of excrement.

jobcentre ▶ **noun** (in the UK) a government office in a town displaying information and giving advice about available jobs and being involved in the administration of benefits to unemployed people.

job club ▶ **noun** (in the UK) an organization providing support and practical help for the long-term unemployed in seeking work.

job control language ▶ **noun** Computing a language enabling the user to define the tasks to be undertaken by the operating system.

job description ▶ **noun** a formal account of an employee's responsibilities.

job-hunt ▶ **verb** [no obj.] [usu. as noun **job-hunting**] informal seek employment.
– DERIVATIVES **job-hunter** noun.

jobless ▶ **adjective** unemployed.

– DERIVATIVES **joblessness** noun.

job lot ▶ noun a miscellaneous group of articles, especially when sold or bought together: *a job lot of stuff I bought from a demolition firm.*

job reservation ▶ noun [mass noun] (in South Africa during the apartheid era) the setting aside by law of certain skilled grades of employment for certain ethnic groups, particularly whites.

job rotation ▶ noun [mass noun] the practice of moving employees between different tasks to promote experience and variety.

Jobs /dʒɒbz/, Steven (Paul) (b.1955), American computer entrepreneur. Jobs set up the Apple computer company in 1976 with Steve Wozniak (b.1950), remaining chairman of the company until 1985.

Job's comforter /dʒəʊbz/ ▶ noun a person who aggravates distress under the guise of giving comfort.
– ORIGIN mid 18th cent.: alluding to the biblical story (Job 16:2) of the patriarch **JOB**.

job-share ▶ verb [no obj.] (of two part-time employees) jointly do a full-time job, sharing the remuneration.
▶ noun an arrangement of such a kind.
– DERIVATIVES **job-sharer** noun.

Job's tears /dʒəʊbz/ ▶ plural noun a SE Asian grass which bears its seeds inside hollow pear-shaped receptacles, which are grey and shiny and sometimes used as beads.
● *Coix lacryma-jobi*, family Gramineae.
– ORIGIN late 16th cent.: named after the patriarch **JOB**.

jobsworth ▶ noun Brit. informal an official who upholds petty rules even at the expense of humanity or common sense.
– ORIGIN 1970s: from 'it's more than my *job's worth* (not) to'.

Joburg /'dʒəʊbɜːg/ informal name for **JOHANNESBURG**.

Jocasta /dʒɒ'kastə/ Greek Mythology a Theban woman, the wife of Laius and mother and later wife of Oedipus.

Jock ▶ noun informal, often offensive a Scotsman (often as a form of address).
– ORIGIN early 16th cent.: Scots form of the given name *Jack*, originally as a name for an ordinary man (compare with **JACK**¹). The current sense dates from the late 18th cent.

jock¹ ▶ noun informal **1** a disc jockey.
2 N. Amer. an enthusiast or participant in a specified activity: *a computer jock.*
– ORIGIN late 18th cent.: abbreviation.

jock² ▶ noun N. Amer. informal another term for **JOCKSTRAP**.
■ an enthusiastic male athlete or sports fan, especially one with few other interests.
– DERIVATIVES **jockish** adjective.

jock³ ▶ noun US informal a pilot or astronaut.
– ORIGIN late 20th cent.: probably an abbreviation of **JOCKEY**, from its informal use in combinations such as *jet jockey*, *plow jockey*, where 'operation' or 'control' of equipment is involved.

jockey ▶ noun (pl. **-eys**) a person who rides in horse races, especially as a profession.
▶ verb (**-eys**, **-eyed**) [no obj.] struggle by every available means to gain or achieve something: *both men will be jockeying for the two top jobs.*
■ [with obj. and adverbial] handle or manipulate (someone or something) in a skilful manner: *he jockeyed his machine into a dive.*
– DERIVATIVES **jockeyship** noun.
– ORIGIN late 16th cent.: diminutive of **JOCK**. Originally the name for an ordinary man, lad, or underling, the word came to mean 'mounted courier', hence the current sense (late 17th cent.). Another early use 'horse-dealer' (long a byword for dishonesty) probably gave rise to the verb sense 'manipulate', whereas the main verb sense probably relates to the behaviour of jockeys manoeuvring for an advantageous position during a race.

jockey cap ▶ noun a strengthened cap with a long peak of a kind worn by jockeys.

Jockey Club an organization whose stewards are the central authority for the administration of horse racing in Britain. It was founded in 1750.

jock itch ▶ noun [mass noun] N. Amer. informal a fungal infection of the groin area.
– ORIGIN 1970s: *jock* from **JOCKSTRAP**.

jockstrap ▶ noun a support or protection for the male genitals, worn especially by sportsmen.
– ORIGIN late 19th cent.: from slang *jock* 'genitals' (of unknown origin) + **STRAP**.

jocose /dʒə'kəʊs/ ▶ adjective formal playful or humorous: *a jocose allusion.*
– DERIVATIVES **jocosely** adverb, **jocoseness** noun, **jocosity** /-'kɒsɪti/ noun (pl. **-ies**).
– ORIGIN late 17th cent.: from Latin *jocosus*, from *jocus* (see **JOKE**).

jocular /'dʒɒkjʊlə/ ▶ adjective fond of or characterized by joking; humorous or playful: *she sounded in a jocular mood | his voice was jocular.*
– DERIVATIVES **jocularity** noun, **jocularly** adverb.
– ORIGIN early 17th cent.: from Latin *jocularis*, from *joculus*, diminutive of *jocus* (see **JOKE**).

jocund /'dʒɒk(ə)nd, 'dʒəʊk-/ ▶ adjective formal cheerful and light-hearted: *a jocund wedding party.*
– DERIVATIVES **jocundity** noun (pl. **-ies**), **jocundly** adverb.
– ORIGIN late Middle English: via Old French from Latin *jocundus*, variant (influenced by *jocus* 'joke') of *jucundus* 'pleasant, agreeable', from *juvare* 'to delight'.

Jodhpur /'dʒɒdpʊə/ **1** a city in western India, in Rajasthan; pop. 649,000 (1991).
2 a former princely state of India, now part of Rajasthan.

jodhpurs /'dʒɒdpəz/ ▶ plural noun full-length trousers worn for horse riding, which are close-fitting below the knee and have reinforced patches on the inside of the leg.
– ORIGIN late 19th cent.: named after **JODHPUR**, where similar garments are worn by Indian men as part of everyday dress.

Jodrell Bank /'dʒɒdrəl/ the site in Cheshire of one of the world's largest radio telescopes, with a fully steerable dish 76 m (250 ft) in diameter.

joe ▶ noun N. Amer. informal **1** [mass noun] coffee. [ORIGIN: 1940s: of unknown origin.]
2 an ordinary man: *the average joe.* [ORIGIN: mid 19th cent.: pet form of the given name *Joseph*; compare with **JOE BLOGGS**.]

Joe Blake ▶ noun Austral. rhyming slang **1** a snake.
2 (**Joe Blakes**) the shakes; delirium tremens.

Joe Bloggs ▶ noun Brit. informal a name for a hypothetical average man.

Joe Blow ▶ noun North American term for **JOE BLOGGS**.

joe job ▶ noun Canadian informal a menial or monotonous task.

Joel /'dʒəʊəl/ a Hebrew minor prophet of the 5th or possibly 9th century BC.
■ a book of the Bible containing his prophecies.

Joe Public ▶ noun Brit. informal a name for a hypothetical representative member of the general public, or the general public personified.

joe-pye weed ▶ noun [mass noun] N. Amer. a tall perennial plant of the daisy family, which bears clusters of small purple flowers.
● *Eupatorium purpureum* and *E. maculatum*, family Compositae.
– ORIGIN early 19th cent.: of unknown origin.

Joe Sixpack ▶ noun chiefly US a name for a hypothetical ordinary working man.
– ORIGIN 1970s: from *Joe*, familiar abbreviation of the given name *Joseph*, used to denote any ordinary man; see also **SIX-PACK**.

joey¹ ▶ noun (pl. **-eys**) Austral. a young kangaroo, wallaby, or possum.
■ informal a baby or young child.
– ORIGIN from Aboriginal *joè*.

joey² ▶ noun historical a silver threepenny bit.
– ORIGIN 1930s: diminutive of the pet name *Joe*: the derivation remains unknown. The term (originally London slang) denoted a fourpenny piece in the 19th cent.

Joffre /ʒɒfrə, French ʒɔfʀ/, Joseph Jacques Césaire (1852–1931), French Marshal, Commander-in-Chief of the French army on the Western Front during the First World War.

jog ▶ verb (**jogged**, **jogging**) **1** [no obj.] run at a steady gentle pace, especially on a regular basis as a form of physical exercise: *he began to jog along the road |* [as noun **jogging**] *try cycling or gentle jogging.*
■ (of a horse) move at a slow trot. ■ move in an unsteady way, typically slowly: *the bus jogged and jolted.* ■ (**jog along/on**) continue in a steady, uneventful way: *our marriage worked and we jogged along.*
2 [with obj.] nudge or knock slightly: *a hand jogged his elbow.*
▶ noun **1** a spell of jogging: *his morning jog.*
■ [in sing.] a gentle running pace: *he set off along the bank at a jog.*
2 a slight push or nudge.
– PHRASES **jog someone's memory** cause someone to remember something suddenly.
– ORIGIN late Middle English (in the sense 'stab, pierce'): variant of **JAG**¹.

jogger ▶ noun a person who jogs as a form of physical exercise.
■ (**joggers**) loose trousers made of a stretchy fabric and typically elasticated at the waist and ankles, worn especially for jogging.

joggle¹ ▶ verb move or cause to move with repeated small bobs or jerks: [no obj.] *helium balloons were joggling above the crowds.*
▶ noun a bobbing or jerking movement.
– ORIGIN early 16th cent.: frequentative of **JOG**.

joggle² ▶ noun a joint between two pieces of stone, concrete, or timber consisting of a projection in one of the pieces fitting into a notch in the other or a small piece let in between the two.
▶ verb [with obj.] join (pieces of stone, concrete, or timber) in such a way.
– ORIGIN early 18th cent.: perhaps related to **JAG**¹.

Jogjakarta /,dʒɒgdʒə'kɑːtə/ variant spelling of **YOGYAKARTA**.

jog-shuttle ▶ noun [mass noun] a facility on some video recorders which allows the speed at which the tape is played to be varied.

jogtrot ▶ noun a slow trot.

Johannesburg /dʒəʊ'hanɪsbɜːg/ a city in South Africa, the capital of the province of Gauteng; pop. 1,916,000 (1991).

Johannine /dʒəʊ'hanaɪn/ ▶ adjective relating to the Apostle St John the Evangelist, or to the Gospel or Epistles of John in the New Testament.
– ORIGIN mid 19th cent.: from the medieval Latin given name *Johannes* 'John' + **-INE**¹.

Johannisberg /dʒəʊ'hanɪsbɜːg/ (also **Johannisberg Riesling**) ▶ noun the chief variety of the Riesling wine grape, originating in Germany and widely grown in California and elsewhere.
■ [mass noun] a white wine made from this grape.
– ORIGIN from the name of a castle and village on the Rhine, Germany, where it was originally produced.

Johannisberger /dʒə'hanɪsˌbɜːgə/ ▶ noun variant of **JOHANNISBERG**.

John¹ (1165–1216), son of Henry II, king of England 1199–1216; known as **John Lackland**. He lost most of his French possessions, including Normandy, to Phillip II of France. In 1209 he was excommunicated for refusing to accept Stephen Langton as Archbishop of Canterbury. Forced to sign Magna Carta by his barons (1215), he ignored its provisions and civil war broke out.

John² the name of six kings of Portugal:
■ **John I** (1357–1433), reigned 1385–1433; known as **John the Great**. Reinforced by an English army, he defeated the Castilians at Aljubarrota (1385), winning independence for Portugal.
■ **John II** (1455–95), reigned 1481–95.
■ **John III** (1502–57), reigned 1521–57.
■ **John IV** (1604–56), reigned 1640–56; known as **John the Fortunate**. The founder of the Braganza dynasty, he expelled a Spanish usurper and proclaimed himself king.
■ **John V** (1689–1750), reigned 1706–50.
■ **John VI** (1767–1826), reigned 1816–26.

John³, Augustus (Edwin) (1878–1961), Welsh painter. Frequent subjects of his work are the gypsies of Wales; he was also noted for his portraits of the wealthy and famous, particularly prominent writers. He was the brother of Gwen John.

John⁴, Barry (b.1945), Welsh rugby union player. During his international career (1966–72) he played at halfback and scored a record ninety points for his country.

John⁵, Sir Elton (Hercules) (b.1947), English pop and

rock singer, pianist, and songwriter; born *Reginald Kenneth Dwight*. His many hit songs include 'Your Song' (1970) and 'Nikita' (1985). His tribute to Diana, Princess of Wales, 'Candle in the Wind' (1997), became the highest-selling single in history.

John[6], Gwen (1876–1939), Welsh painter. The sister of Augustus John, she settled in France. In 1913 she converted to Catholicism; her paintings, noted for their grey tonality, often depict nuns or girls in interior settings.

john ▶ **noun** informal **1** chiefly N. Amer. a toilet.
2 a prostitute's client.
– ORIGIN early 20th cent. (in sense 2): from the given name *John*, used from late Middle English as a form of address to a man, or to denote various occupations, including that of priest (late Middle English) and policeman (mid 17th cent.).

John III (1624–96), king of Poland 1674–96; known as **John Sobieski**. In 1683 he relieved Vienna when it was besieged by the Turks, thereby becoming the hero of the Christian world.

John, St an Apostle, son of Zebedee and brother of James; known as **St John the Evangelist** or **St John the Divine**. He has traditionally been credited with the authorship of the fourth Gospel, Revelation, and three epistles of the New Testament. Feast day, 27 December.
■ the fourth Gospel (see **GOSPEL** sense 2). ■ any of the three epistles of the New Testament attributed to St John.

John Barleycorn ▶ **noun** a personification of barley, or of malt liquor.

johnboat ▶ **noun** N. Amer. a small flat-bottomed boat with square ends, used chiefly on inland waterways.

John Bull ▶ **noun** a personification of England or the typical Englishman, represented as a stout red-faced farmer in a top hat and high boots.
– ORIGIN late 18th cent.: from the name of a character representing the English nation in John Arbuthnot's satire *Law is a Bottomless Pit; or, the History of John Bull* (1712).

John Chrysostom, St see **CHRYSOSTOM, ST JOHN**.

John Citizen ▶ **noun** a hypothetical ordinary man.

John Crow ▶ **noun** West Indian term for **TURKEY VULTURE**.
– ORIGIN early 19th cent.: alteration of **CARRION CROW**.

John Doe ▶ **noun** Law, chiefly US an anonymous party, typically the plaintiff, in a legal action.
■ N. Amer. informal a hypothetical average man.
– ORIGIN mid 18th cent.: originally in legal use as a name of a fictitious plaintiff, corresponding to *Richard Roe*, used to represent the defendant.

John Dory ▶ **noun** (pl. **-ies**) an edible dory (fish) of the eastern Atlantic and Mediterranean, with a black oval mark on each side.
● *Zeus faber*, family Zeidae.

Johne's disease /ˈjəʊnəz/ ▶ **noun** [mass noun] a form of chronic enteritis in cattle and sheep, caused by a mycobacterium.
– ORIGIN early 20th cent.: named after Heinrich A. *Johne* (1839–1910), German veterinary surgeon.

John Innes /ˈɪnɪz/ (also **John Innes compost**) ▶ **noun** [mass noun] any of a group of composts prepared according to formulae developed at the John Innes Horticultural Institution in the late 1930s.

johnny ▶ **noun** (pl. **-ies**) Brit. informal **1** used as a name for an unknown man, often suggesting that he is unimportant or insignificant: *the security johnny insists that you sign the visitors' book.*
2 a condom.
– ORIGIN late 17th cent. (in sense 1): pet form of the given name *John*; sense 2 dates from the 1960s.

johnnycake ▶ **noun 1** [mass noun] N. Amer. maize flour bread typically baked or fried on a griddle.
2 (**johnny cake**) Austral./NZ a small, thin unleavened wheat loaf baked in wood ashes.
– ORIGIN early 18th cent.: also referred to as *journey cake*, which may be the original form.

johnny-come-lately ▶ **noun** informal a newcomer to or late starter at a particular place or sphere of activity.

Johnny-on-the-spot ▶ **noun** N. Amer. informal, dated a person who is at hand whenever needed.

Johnny Reb ▶ **noun** another term for **REB**[2].

John of Damascus, St (*c.*675–*c.*749), Syrian theologian and Doctor of the Church. A champion of image worship against the iconoclasts, he wrote the influential encyclopedic work on Christian theology *The Fount of Wisdom*. Feast day, 4 December.

John of Gaunt (1340–99), son of Edward III. John of Gaunt was effective ruler of England during the final years of his father's reign and the minority of Richard II. His son Henry Bolingbroke later became King Henry IV.

John of the Cross, St (1542–91), Spanish mystic and poet; born *Juan de Yepis y Alvarez*. A Carmelite monk and priest, he joined with St Teresa of Ávila in founding the 'discalced' Carmelite order in 1568. Feast day, 14 December.

John o'Groats /əˈɡrəʊts/ a village at the extreme NE point of the Scottish mainland.
– ORIGIN said to be named after *John de Groat* and his two brothers, who came from Holland with a royal letter of protection and built a house on the site in the 16th cent.

John Paul II (b.1920), Polish cleric, pope since 1978; born *Karol Jozef Wojtyla*. The first non-Italian pope since 1522, he upheld the Roman Catholic Church's traditional oppositions to artificial means of contraception and abortion, homosexuality, the ordination of women, and the relaxation of the rule of celibacy for priests.

John Q. Public ▶ **noun** North American term for **JOE PUBLIC**.

Johns, Jasper (b.1930), American painter, sculptor, and printmaker. A key figure in the development of pop art, he depicted commonplace and universally recognized images.

Johnson[1], Amy (1903–41), English aviator. In 1930 she became the first woman to fly solo to Australia. She later set records with her solo flights to Tokyo (1931) and to Cape Town (1932).

Johnson[2], Andrew (1808–75), American Democratic statesman, 17th President of the US 1865–9. His lenient policy towards the Southern states after the American Civil War led him to be impeached by the Republican majority in Congress; he was acquitted by a single vote.

Johnson[3] (also **Jansens** or **Janssen van Ceulen**), Cornelius (1593–*c.*1661), English-born Dutch portrait painter. He painted for the court of Charles I; after the outbreak of the English Civil War he emigrated to Holland (1643).

Johnson[4], Earvin (b.1959), American basketball player; known as **Magic Johnson**. He played for the Los Angeles Lakers from 1979 to 1991. After being diagnosed HIV-positive he won an Olympic gold medal in 1992 and then returned to the Lakers.

Johnson[5], Jack (1878–1946), American boxer. He was the first black world heavyweight champion (1908–15).

Johnson[6], Lyndon Baines (1908–73), American Democratic statesman, 36th President of the US 1963–9; known as **LBJ**. He continued the programme of reforming initiated by John F. Kennedy, but the increasing involvement of the US in the Vietnam War undermined his popularity.

Johnson[7], Robert (1911–38), American blues singer and guitarist. Despite his mysterious early death, he was very influential on the 1960s blues movement. Notable songs: 'I Was Standing at the Crossroads'.

Johnson[8], Samuel (1709–84), English lexicographer, writer, critic, and conversationalist; known as **Dr Johnson**. A leading figure in the literary London of his day, he is noted particularly for his *Dictionary of the English Language* (1755), edition of Shakespeare (1765), and *The Lives of the English Poets* (1777). James Boswell's biography of Johnson records details of his life and conversation.
– DERIVATIVES **Johnsonian** adjective.

John the Baptist, St, Jewish preacher and prophet, a contemporary of Jesus. In *c.*27 AD he preached and baptized on the banks of the River Jordan. Among those whom he baptized was Christ. He was beheaded by Herod Antipas after denouncing the latter's marriage to Herodias, the wife of Herod's brother Philip (Matt. 14:1–12). Feast day, 24 June.

John the Evangelist, St (also **John the Divine**) see **JOHN, ST**.

John the Fortunate, John IV of Portugal (see **JOHN**[2]).

John the Great, John I of Portugal (see **JOHN**[2]).

Johor /dʒəʊˈhɔː/ (also **Johore**) a state of Malaysia, at the southernmost point of mainland Asia, joined to Singapore by a causeway; capital, Johor Baharu.

Johor Baharu /bəˈhɑːruː/ the capital of the state of Johor in Malaysia; pop. 328,650 (1991).

joie de vivre /ˌʒwɑː də ˈviːvr(ə), French ʒwad vivʀ/ ▶ **noun** [mass noun] exuberant enjoyment of life.
– ORIGIN French, literally 'joy of living'.

join ▶ **verb** [with obj.] link; connect: *the tap was **joined** to a pipe* | *join the paragraphs **together**.*
■ become linked or connected to: *where the River Drave joins the Danube.* ■ connect (points) with a line: *join up the points in a different colour.* ■ [no obj., with adverbial] unite to form one entity or group: *they **joined up with** local environmentalists* | *countries **join together** to abolish restrictions on trade.* ■ become a member or employee of: *she joined the department last year.* ■ take part in: *I joined the demonstration* | [no obj.] *I **joined in** and sang along.* ■ [no obj.] (**join up**) become a member of the armed forces: *her brothers joined up in 1914.* ■ come into the company of: *after the show we were joined by Jessica's sister.* ■ support (someone) in an activity: *I am sure you will **join** me **in** wishing him every success.*
▶ **noun** a place or line where two or more things are connected or fastened together.
– PHRASES **join battle** formal begin fighting. **join the club** see **CLUB**[1]. **join forces** combine efforts. **join hands** hold each other's hands. ■ figurative work together: *education has been shy to join hands with business.*
– DERIVATIVES **joinable** adjective.
– ORIGIN Middle English: from Old French *joindre*, from Latin *jungere* 'to join'.

joinder /ˈdʒɔɪndə/ ▶ **noun** [mass noun] Law the action of bringing parties together; union.
– ORIGIN late Middle English: from Anglo-Norman French, from Old French *joindre* 'to join'.

joiner ▶ **noun 1** a person who constructs the wooden components of a building, such as stairs, doors, and door and window frames.
2 informal a person who readily joins groups or campaigns: *a compulsive joiner of revolutionary movements.*
– ORIGIN Middle English: from Old French *joigneor*, from *joindre* 'to join'.

joinery ▶ **noun** [mass noun] the wooden components of a building, such as stairs, doors, and door and window frames, viewed collectively.

joint ▶ **noun 1** a point at which parts of an artificial structure are joined.
■ Geology a break or fracture in a mass of rock, with no relative displacement of the parts. ■ a piece of flexible material forming the hinge of a book cover.
2 a structure in the human or animal body at which two parts of the skeleton are fitted together.
■ each of the distinct sections of a body or limb between the places at which they are connected: *the top two joints of his index finger.* ■ Brit. a large piece of meat cooked whole or ready for cooking: *a joint of ham.* ■ the part of a stem of a plant from which a leaf or branch grows. ■ a section of a plant stem between such parts; an internode.
3 informal an establishment of a specified kind, especially one where people meet for eating, drinking, or entertainment: *a burger joint.*
■ (**the joint**) N. Amer. prison.
4 informal a cannabis cigarette: *he rolled a joint.*
▶ **adjective** [attrib.] shared, held, or made by two or more people together: *a joint statement.*
■ sharing in a position, achievement, or activity: *a joint winner.* ■ Law applied or regarded together. Often contrasted with **SEVERAL**.
▶ **verb** [with obj.] **1** provide or fasten (something) with joints: [as adj. **jointed**] *jointed lever arms.*
■ fill up the joints of (masonry or brickwork) with mortar; point. ■ prepare (a board) for being joined to another by planing its edge.
2 cut (the body of an animal) into joints.
– PHRASES **out of joint** (of a joint of the body) out of position; dislocated: *he put his hip out of joint.* ■ in a state of disorder or disorientation: *time was thrown completely out of joint.*
– DERIVATIVES **jointless** adjective, **jointly** adverb.
– ORIGIN Middle English: from Old French, past participle of *joindre* 'to join' (see **JOIN**).

joint account ▶ **noun** a bank account held by more than one person, each individual having the right to deposit and withdraw funds.

j

joint and several ▶ **adjective** (of a legal obligation) undertaken by two or more people, each individual having liability for the whole.

jointer ▶ **noun 1** a plane used for preparing a wooden edge for fixing or joining to another.
■ a tool used for pointing masonry and brickwork.
2 a worker employed in jointing pipes or wires.

jointing ▶ **noun** [mass noun] **1** the action of providing with, connecting by, or preparing for a joint.
2 an arrangement of joints.

jointress ▶ **noun** Law, dated a widow who holds a jointure.
– ORIGIN early 17th cent.: feminine of obsolete *jointer* 'joint-owner'.

joint-stock company ▶ **noun** Finance a company whose stock is owned jointly by the shareholders.

joint tenancy ▶ **noun** the holding of an estate or property jointly by two or more parties, the share of each passing to the other or others on death.
– DERIVATIVES **joint tenant** noun.

jointure /ˈdʒɔɪntʃə/ ▶ **noun** Law an estate settled on a wife for the period during which she survives her husband, in lien of a dower.
– ORIGIN Middle English (in the sense 'junction, joint'): from Old French, from Latin *junctura* (see **JUNCTURE**). In late Middle English the term denoted the joint holding of property by a husband and wife for life, whence the current sense.

joint venture ▶ **noun** a commercial enterprise undertaken jointly by two or more parties which otherwise retain their distinct identities.

joist /dʒɔɪst/ ▶ **noun** a length of timber or steel supporting part of the structure of a building, typically arranged in parallel series to support a floor or ceiling.
– DERIVATIVES **joisted** adjective.
– ORIGIN late Middle English *giste*, from Old French, 'beam supporting a bridge', based on Latin *jacere* 'lie down'.

jojoba /həˈhəʊbə, həʊ-/ ▶ **noun 1** (also **jojoba oil**) [mass noun] an oil extracted from the seeds of an American shrub, widely used in cosmetics.
2 the leathery-leaved evergreen shrub or small tree that produces these seeds, native to south-western North America.
• *Simmondsia chinensis*, the only member of the family Simmondsiaceae.
– ORIGIN early 20th cent.: from Mexican Spanish.

joke ▶ **noun** a thing that someone says to cause amusement or laughter, especially a story with a funny punchline: *she was in a mood to tell jokes.*
■ a trick played on someone for fun. ■ [in sing.] informal a person or thing that is ridiculously inadequate: *public transport is a joke.*
▶ **verb** [no obj.] make jokes; talk humorously or flippantly: *she could laugh and* ***joke with*** *her colleagues* | [with direct speech] *'It's OK, we're not related,' she joked.*
■ [with obj.] archaic poke fun at: *he was pretending to joke his daughter.*
– PHRASES **be no joke** informal be a serious matter or difficult undertaking: *trying to shop with three children in tow is no joke.* **get** (or **be**) **beyond a joke** informal become (or be) something that is serious or worrying: *this rain's getting beyond a joke.* **make a joke of** laugh or be humorous about (something that is not funny in itself).
– DERIVATIVES **jokey** (also **joky**) adjective, **jokily** adverb, **jokiness** noun, **jokingly** adverb.
– ORIGIN late 17th cent. (originally slang): perhaps from Latin *jocus* 'jest, wordplay'.

joker ▶ **noun 1** a person who is fond of joking.
■ informal a foolish or inept person: *a bunch of jokers.*
2 a playing card, typically bearing the figure of a jester, used in some games as a wild card.
3 US a clause unobtrusively inserted in a bill or document and affecting its operation in a way not immediately apparent.
– PHRASES **the joker in the pack** a person or factor likely to have an unpredictable effect on events.

jol /dʒɔːl/ S. African informal ▶ **noun** an occasion of celebration and enjoyment; a good time.
▶ **verb** (**jolled**, **jolling**) [no obj.] **1** [with adverbial of direction] set off; go: *you could jol to the lake on a Sunday.*
2 have a good time; celebrate in a lively way: *everyone goes to clubs and jols till late.*
■ engage in a flirtation or a casual love affair.
– DERIVATIVES **joller** noun.
– ORIGIN Afrikaans, literally 'party'.

jolie laide /ˌʒɒlɪ ˈlɛd/ ▶ **noun** (pl. **jolies laides** pronunc. same) a woman whose face is attractive despite having ugly features.
– ORIGIN French, from *jolie* 'pretty' and *laide* 'ugly', feminine adjectives.

Joliot /ˈʒɒlɪəʊ, French ʒɔljo/, Jean-Frédéric (1900–58), French nuclear physicist. As Marie Curie's assistant at the Radium Institute he worked with her daughter **Irène** (1897–1956), whom he married (taking the name Joliot-Curie); together they discovered artificial radioactivity. Nobel Prize for Chemistry (1935, shared with his wife).

joliotium /ˌdʒɒlɪˈəʊtɪəm/ ▶ **noun** [mass noun] the name proposed by IUPAC for the chemical element of atomic number 105, now called **dubnium**.
– ORIGIN late 20th cent.: modern Latin, from the name of J-F **JOLIOT**.

jollification ▶ **noun** [mass noun] lively celebration with others; merrymaking.

jollity ▶ **noun** (pl. **-ies**) [mass noun] lively and cheerful activity or celebration: *a night of riotous jollity.*
■ the quality of being cheerful: *he was full of false jollity.*
– ORIGIN Middle English: from Old French *jolite*, from *joli* (see **JOLLY**[1]).

jollo /ˈdʒɒləʊ/ ▶ **noun** (pl. **-os**) Austral. informal a lively celebration or party.
– ORIGIN early 20th cent.: from **JOLLITY** + **-O**.

jollof rice /ˈdʒɒlɒf/ ▶ **noun** a West African stew made with rice, chilli peppers, and meat or fish.
– ORIGIN *jollof*, variant of **WOLOF**.

jolly[1] ▶ **adjective** (**jollier**, **jolliest**) happy and cheerful: *he was a jolly man full of jokes.*
■ informal, dated lively and entertaining: *we had a very jolly time.*
▶ **verb** (**-ies**, **-ied**) [with obj. and adverbial] informal encourage (someone) in a friendly way: *he* ***jollied*** *people* ***along*** | *they were trying to jolly her out of her torpor.*
■ (**jolly someone/thing up**) make someone or something more lively or cheerful: *ideas to jolly up a winter's party.*
▶ **adverb** [as submodifier] Brit. informal very; extremely: *that's a jolly good idea.*
▶ **noun** (pl. **-ies**) Brit. informal a party or celebration.
– PHRASES **get one's jollies** informal have fun or find pleasure. **jolly well** Brit. informal used for emphasis, especially when one is angry or irritated: *I'm going to keep on eating as much sugar as I jolly well like.*
– DERIVATIVES **jollily** adverb, **jolliness** noun.
– ORIGIN Middle English: from Old French *jolif*, an earlier form of *joli* 'pretty', perhaps from Old Norse *jól* (see **YULE**).

jolly[2] (also **jolly boat**) ▶ **noun** (pl. **-ies**) a clinker-built ship's boat that is smaller than a cutter, typically hoisted at the stern of the ship.
– ORIGIN early 18th cent.: perhaps related to **YAWL**.

Jolly Roger ▶ **noun** a pirate's flag with a white skull and crossbones on a black background.
– ORIGIN late 18th cent.: of unknown origin.

jollytail ▶ **noun** another term for **INANGA**.

Jolson /ˈdʒəʊls(ə)n/, Al (1886–1950), Russian-born American singer, film actor, and comedian; born *Asa Yoelson*. He made the Gershwin song 'Swanee' his trademark, and appeared in the first full-length talking film, *The Jazz Singer* (1927).

jolt /dʒəʊlt, dʒɒlt/ ▶ **verb** [with obj.] push or shake (someone or something) abruptly and roughly: *a surge in the crowd behind him jolted him forwards.*
■ figurative give a surprise or shock to (someone) in order to make them act or change: *she tried to* ***jolt*** *him* ***out of*** *his depression.* ■ [no obj., with adverbial] move with sudden lurches: *the train jolted into motion.*
▶ **noun** an abrupt rough or violent movement.
■ a surprise or shock, especially of an unpleasant kind and often manifested physically: *that information gave her a severe jolt.*
– DERIVATIVES **jolty** adjective.
– ORIGIN late 16th cent.: of unknown origin.

Jomon /ˈdʒəʊmən/ ▶ **noun** [usu. as modifier] Archaeology an early Mesolithic-type culture in Japan (*c.*10,000–300 BC), preceding the Yayoi period. It is characterized by pottery decorated with a distinctive cord pattern.
– ORIGIN from Japanese *jōmon* 'cord pattern'.

Jon. ▶ **abbreviation for** ■ Jonah (in biblical references). ■ Jonathan.

Jonagold /ˈdʒɒnəˌgəʊld/ ▶ **noun** a dessert apple of a variety with greenish-gold skin and crisp flesh.
– ORIGIN 1960s: blend of **JONATHAN**[2] and **GOLDEN DELICIOUS**.

Jonah /ˈdʒəʊnə/ (in the Bible) a Hebrew minor prophet. He was called by God to preach in Nineveh, but disobeyed and attempted to escape by sea; in a storm he was thrown overboard as a bringer of bad luck and swallowed by a great fish, only to be saved and finally succeed in his mission.
■ a book of the Bible telling of Jonah.

Jonathan[1] (in the Bible) a son of Saul, noted for his friendship with David (1 Sam. 18–20, 2 Sam. 1) and killed at the battle of Mount Gilboa (1 Sam. 31).

Jonathan[2] ▶ **noun** a cooking apple of a red-skinned variety first grown in the US.
– ORIGIN mid 19th cent.: named after *Jonathan* Hasbrouk (died 1846), American lawyer.

Jones[1], Daniel (1881–1967), British phonetician. He developed the International Phonetic Alphabet from 1907 and went on to invent the system of cardinal vowels. Notable works: *English Pronouncing Dictionary* (1917).

Jones[2], Inigo (1573–1652), English architect and stage designer. He introduced the Palladian style to England; notable buildings include the Queen's House at Greenwich (1616) and the Banqueting Hall at Whitehall (1619).

Jones[3], John Paul (1747–92), Scottish-born American admiral; born *John Paul*. He became famous for his raids off the northern coasts of Britain during the War of American Independence.

Jones[4], Bobby (1902–71), American golfer; full name *Robert Tyre Jones*. In a short competitive career (1923–30), and as an amateur, he won thirteen major competitions, including four American and three British open championships.

Jones[5], Tom (b.1940), Welsh pop singer; born *Thomas Jones Woodward*. Hits include 'It's Not Unusual' (1965), 'The Green, Green Grass of Home' (1966), and 'Delilah' (1968).

jones US, chiefly black slang ▶ **noun** a fixation on or compulsive desire for someone or something, typically a drug; an addiction: *a two-year amphetamine jones.*
▶ **verb** [no obj.] (**jones on/for**) have a fixation on; be addicted to: *Palmer was jonesing for some coke again.*
– ORIGIN 1960s: said to come from *Jones* Alley, in Manhattan, associated with drug addicts.

Joneses (usu. **the Joneses**) ▶ **noun** a person's neighbours or social equals.
– PHRASES **keep up with the Joneses** try to emulate or not be outdone by one's neighbours.
– ORIGIN late 19th cent.: from *Jones*, a commonly found British surname.

jong /jɒŋ/ S. African ▶ **noun** chiefly historical a young black male servant.
■ offensive a black man. ■ informal used as a form of address to both men and women, expressing affection or exasperation: *there are sharks out there, jong.* ■ a boyfriend or lover.
▶ **exclamation** used to express surprise, pleasure, or anger, or to add emphasis to a statement.
– ORIGIN Afrikaans, from earlier South African Dutch *jongen* 'lad'.

jongleur /ʒɒ̃ˈgləː/ ▶ **noun** historical an itinerant minstrel.
– ORIGIN French, variant of *jougleur* 'juggler', earlier *jogleor* 'pleasant, smiling', from Latin *joculator* 'joker'.

Jönköping /ˈjəːnˌtʃəːpɪŋ/ an industrial city in southern Sweden, at the south end of Lake Vättern; pop. 111,500 (1990).

jonquil /ˈdʒʌŋkwɪl, ˈdʒɒn-/ ▶ **noun** a narcissus with clusters of small fragrant yellow flowers and cylindrical leaves, native to southern Europe and NE Africa.
• *Narcissus jonquilla*, family Liliaceae (or Amaryllidaceae).
– ORIGIN early 17th cent.: from modern Latin *jonquilla* or French *jonquille*, from Spanish *junquillo*, diminutive of *junco*, from Latin *juncus* 'rush, reed'.

Jonson, Ben (1572–1637), English dramatist and poet; full name *Benjamin Jonson*. With his play *Every Man in his Humour* (1598) he established his 'comedy of humours', whereby each character is dominated by a particular obsession. He became the first Poet Laureate in the modern sense. Other notable works: *Volpone* (1606) and *Bartholomew Fair* (1614).
– DERIVATIVES **Jonsonian** adjective.

Joplin[1] /ˈdʒɒplɪn/, Janis (1943–70), American singer. She died from a heroin overdose just before her most successful album, *Pearl*, and her number-one single 'Me and Bobby McGee' were released.

Joplin[2] /ˈdʒɒplɪn/, Scott (1868–1917), American pianist and composer. He was the first of the creators of ragtime to write down his compositions. Notable compositions: 'Maple Leaf Rag' (1899), 'The Entertainer' (1902), and 'Gladiolus Rag' (1907).

Joppa /ˈdʒɒpə/ biblical name for **JAFFA**[1].

Jordaens /jɔːˈdɑːns/, Jacob (1593–1678), Flemish painter. Influenced by Rubens, he is noted for his boisterous peasant scenes painted in warm colours. Notable works: *The King Drinks* (1638).

Jordan[1] **1** a country in the Middle East east of the River Jordan; pop. 4,000,000 (est. 1990); official language, Arabic; capital, Amman. Official name **HASHEMITE KINGDOM OF JORDAN**.

Romans, Arabs, Crusaders, and Turks dominated the area successively until it was made a British protectorate in 1916 and achieved independence in 1946. During the war of 1948–9 that followed the establishment of the state of Israel, Jordan took over the area of the West Bank; this was recovered by Israel in Six Day War of 1967, after which many Palestinian refugees entered the country. A peace treaty with Israel was signed in 1994, ending an official state of war between the two countries.

2 a river flowing southward for 320 km (200 miles) from the Anti-Lebanon Mountains through the Sea of Galilee into the Dead Sea. John the Baptist baptized Christ in the River Jordan. It is regarded as sacred not only by Christians but also by Jews and Muslims.
– DERIVATIVES **Jordanian** /dʒɔːˈdeɪnɪən/ adjective & noun.

Jordan[2], Michael (Jeffrey) (b.1963), American basketball player. Playing for the Chicago Bulls from 1984, he was the National Basketball Association's Most Valuable Player five times.

jordan almond ▶ **noun** a high-quality almond of a variety grown chiefly in SE Spain.
– ORIGIN late Middle English: *jordan* apparently from French or Spanish *jardin* 'garden'.

jorum /ˈdʒɔːrəm/ ▶ **noun** historical a large bowl or jug used for serving drinks such as tea or punch.
– ORIGIN early 18th cent.: perhaps from *Joram* (2 Sam. 8:10), who 'brought with him vessels of silver, and vessels of gold' to King David.

Jorvik /ˈjɔːvɪk/ (also **Yorvik**) Viking name for **YORK**.

Jos. ▶ **abbreviation for** ■ Joseph. ■ Joshua (in biblical references).

Joseph (in the Bible) a Hebrew patriarch, son of Jacob. He was given a coat of many colours by his father, but was then sold by his jealous brothers into captivity in Egypt, where he attained high office (Gen. 30–50).

Joseph, St, husband of the Virgin Mary. A carpenter of Nazareth, he was betrothed to Mary at the time of the Annunciation. Feast day, 19 March.

Josephine (1763–1814), Empress of France 1804–9; full name *Marie Joséphine Rose Tascher de la Pagerie*. She married Napoleon in 1796. Their marriage proved childless and she was divorced by Napoleon in 1809.

Joseph of Arimathea /ˌarɪməˈθɪə/ a member of the council at Jerusalem who, after the Crucifixion, asked Pilate for Christ's body, which he buried. He is also known from the medieval story that he came to England with the Holy Grail and built the first church at Glastonbury.

Josephson junction ▶ **noun** Physics an electrical device in which two superconducting metals are separated by a thin layer of insulator, across which an electric current may flow in the absence of a potential difference. The current may be made to oscillate in proportion to an applied potential difference.
– ORIGIN 1960s: named after Brian D. *Josephson* (born 1940), British physicist.

Josephus /dʒəʊˈsiːfəs/, Flavius (*c.*37–*c.*100), Jewish historian, general, and Pharisee; born *Joseph ben Matthias*. His *Jewish War* gives an eyewitness account of the events leading up to the Jewish revolt against the Romans in 66, in which he was a leader.

Josh. ▶ **abbreviation for** Joshua (in biblical references).

josh informal ▶ **verb** [with obj.] tease (someone) in a playful way: *he loved to josh people.*
■ [no obj.] engage in joking or playful talk with others.
▶ **noun** [mass noun] N. Amer. good-natured banter.
– DERIVATIVES **josher** noun.
– ORIGIN mid 19th cent. (as a verb): of unknown origin.

Joshua /ˈdʒɒʃʊə/ (*fl. c.*13th century BC), the Israelite leader who succeeded Moses and led his people into the Promised Land.
■ the sixth book of the Bible, telling of the conquest of Canaan and its division among the twelve tribes of Israel.

Joshua tree ▶ **noun** a yucca which grows as a tree and has clusters of spiky leaves, native to arid regions of south-western North America.
• *Yucca brevifolia*, family Agavaceae.
– ORIGIN mid 19th cent.: apparently from **JOSHUA** (Josh. 8:18), the plant being likened to a man brandishing a spear.

Josquin des Prez see **DES PREZ**.

joss[1] ▶ **noun** a Chinese religious statue or idol.
– ORIGIN early 18th cent.: from Javanese *dejos*, from obsolete Portuguese *deos*, from Latin *deus* 'god'.

joss[2] ▶ **noun** informal, chiefly Austral./NZ a person of influence or importance.
– ORIGIN mid 19th cent.: from dialect *joss* 'foreman', of unknown origin.

josser ▶ **noun** informal **1** Brit. a man, typically an old man or one regarded with some contempt: *an old josser.*
2 Austral. a clergyman.
– ORIGIN late 19th cent.: from **JOSS**[1] + **-ER**[1].

joss house ▶ **noun** a Chinese temple.

joss stick ▶ **noun** a thin stick consisting of a substance that burns slowly and with a fragrant smell, used as incense.

jostle ▶ **verb** [with obj.] push, elbow, or bump against (someone) roughly, typically in a crowd: *he was jostled by passengers rushing for the gates* | [no obj.] *people* ***jostled against*** *us.*
■ [no obj.] (**jostle for**) struggle or compete forcefully for: *a jumble of images jostled for attention.*
▶ **noun** [mass noun] the action of jostling.
– ORIGIN late Middle English *justle*, from *just*, an earlier form of **JOUST**. The original sense was 'have sexual intercourse with'; current senses date from the mid 16th cent.

jot ▶ **verb** (**jotted, jotting**) [with obj.] write (something) quickly: *when you've found the answers,* ***jot them down.***
▶ **noun** [usu. with negative] a very small amount: *you didn't care a jot* | *I have yet to see* ***one jot of*** *evidence.*
– ORIGIN late 15th cent. (as a noun): via Latin from Greek *iōta*, the smallest letter of the Greek alphabet (see **IOTA**).

jota /ˈxəʊtə/ ▶ **noun** a folk dance from northern Spain, danced in couples in fast triple time.
– ORIGIN Spanish.

jotter ▶ **noun** Brit. a small pad or notebook used for notes or jottings.

jotting ▶ **noun** (usu. **jottings**) a brief note.

Jotun /ˈjəʊtʊn/ ▶ **noun** Scandinavian Mythology a member of the race of giants, enemies of the gods.
– ORIGIN from Old Norse *jǫtunn*, related to Old English *eoten*, of Germanic origin.

Jotunheim /ˈjəʊtʊnˌhʌɪm/ **1** Scandinavian Mythology a region of the universe, inhabited by giants.
2 a mountain range in south central Norway.

joual /ʒwal, ʒuːˈɑːl/ ▶ **noun** [mass noun] a non-standard form of popular Canadian French, influenced by English vocabulary and grammar.
– ORIGIN Canadian French dialect, from French *cheval* 'horse', apparently from the way *cheval* is pronounced in rural areas of Quebec.

jougs /dʒuːgz/ ▶ **plural noun** historical a hinged iron collar chained to a wall or post, used in medieval Scotland as an instrument of punishment.
– ORIGIN late 16th cent.: from French *joug* or Latin *jugum* 'yoke'.

jouissance /ˈʒwiːsɒ̃s, French ʒwisɑ̃s/ ▶ **noun** [mass noun] formal physical or intellectual pleasure, delight, or ecstasy.
– ORIGIN French, from *jouir* 'enjoy'.

jouk /dʒuːk/ ▶ **verb** [no obj., with adverbial of direction] Scottish & N. English turn or bend quickly, typically to avoid someone or something: *I jouked around the corner.*
– ORIGIN early 16th cent.: perhaps related to the verb **DUCK**[2].

Joule /dʒuːl/, James Prescott (1818–89), English physicist. Joule established that all forms of energy were basically the same and interchangeable—the first law of thermodynamics. The Joule–Thomson effect, discovered with William Thomson, later Lord Kelvin, in 1852, led to the development of the refrigerator and to the science of cryogenics. Joule also measured and described the heating effects of an electric current passing through a resistance.

joule /dʒuːl/ (abbrev.: **J**) ▶ **noun** the SI unit of work or energy, equal to the work done by a force of one newton when its point of application moves one metre in the direction of action of the force, equivalent to one 3600th of a watt-hour.
– ORIGIN late 19th cent.: named after J. P. **JOULE**.

Joule effect ▶ **noun** [mass noun] Physics the heating that occurs when an electric current flows through a resistance.

Joule's law Physics a law stating that the heat produced by an electric current i flowing through a resistance R for a time t is proportional to i^2Rt.

Joule–Thomson effect ▶ **noun** [mass noun] Physics the change of temperature of a gas when it is allowed to expand without doing any external work. The gas becomes cooler if it was initially below a certain temperature (the **inversion temperature**), or hotter if initially above it.

jounce /dʒaʊns/ ▶ **verb** jolt or bounce: [no obj.] *the car jounced wildly* | [with obj.] *the pilot jounced the ship through turbulence.*
– ORIGIN late Middle English: probably symbolic; compare with **BOUNCE**.

journal /ˈdʒəːn(ə)l/ ▶ **noun** **1** a newspaper or magazine that deals with a particular subject or professional activity: *medical journals* | [in names] *the* Wall Street Journal.
2 a daily record of news and events of a personal nature; a diary.
■ Nautical a logbook. ■ (**the Journals**) a record of the daily proceedings in the Houses of Parliament. ■ (in bookkeeping) a daily record of business transactions with a statement of the accounts to which each is to be debited and credited.
3 the part of a shaft or axle that rests on bearings.
– ORIGIN late Middle English (originally denoting a book containing the appointed times of daily prayers): from Old French *jurnal*, from late Latin *diurnalis* (see **DIURNAL**).

journalese ▶ **noun** [mass noun] informal a hackneyed style of writing supposedly characteristic of that in newspapers and magazines.

journalism ▶ **noun** [mass noun] the activity or profession of writing for newspapers or magazines or of broadcasting news on radio or television.
■ the product of such activity: *a collection of journalism.*

journalist ▶ **noun** a person who writes for newspapers or magazines or prepares news to be broadcast on radio or television.
– DERIVATIVES **journalistic** adjective, **journalistically** adverb.

journalize (also **-ise**) ▶ **verb** [with obj.] dated enter (notes or information) in a journal or account book: *I would gladly journalize some of my proceedings.*

journey ▶ **noun** (pl. **-eys**) an act of travelling from one place to another: *she went on a long journey* | figurative *your journey through life.*
▶ **verb** (**-eys, -eyed**) [no obj., with adverbial of direction] travel somewhere: *they journeyed south.*
– DERIVATIVES **journeyer** noun.
– ORIGIN Middle English: from Old French *jornee* 'day, a day's travel, a day's work' (the earliest senses in English), based on Latin *diurnum* 'daily portion', from *diurnus* (see **DIURNAL**).

journeyman ▶ **noun** (pl. **-men**) a trained worker who is employed by someone else.
■ a worker or sports player who is reliable but not outstanding: [as modifier] *a solid journeyman professional.*
– ORIGIN late Middle English: from **JOURNEY** (in the obsolete sense 'day's work') + **MAN**; so named because the journeyman was no longer bound by indentures but was paid by the day.

journo ▶ **noun** (pl. **-os**) informal a journalist.
– ORIGIN 1960s (originally an Australian usage): abbreviation.

joust /dʒaʊst/ ▶ **verb** [no obj.] [often as noun **jousting**] historical (of a medieval knight) engage in a sporting contest in which two opponents on horseback fight with lances.
■ figurative compete closely for superiority: *the guerrillas* ***jousted for*** *supremacy.*
▶ **noun** a medieval sporting contest in which two opponents on horseback fought with lances.
– DERIVATIVES **jouster** noun.
– ORIGIN Middle English (originally in the sense

'join battle, engage'): from Old French *jouster* 'bring together', based on Latin *juxta* 'near'.

J'Ouvert /dʒuːˈveɪ/ ▶ **noun** (in the Caribbean) the official start of carnival, at dawn on the Monday preceding Lent.
– ORIGIN French Creole, from French *jour ouvert* 'day opened'.

Jove /ˈdʒəʊv/ another name for **JUPITER**.
– PHRASES **by Jove** dated an exclamation indicating surprise or used for emphasis: *by Jove, yes, it's been warm all right.*
– ORIGIN from Latin *Jov-*, stem of Old Latin *Jovis*, replaced later by *Jupiter*. The exclamation *by Jove* dates from the late 16th cent.

jovial /ˈdʒəʊvɪəl, -vj(ə)l/ ▶ **adjective** cheerful and friendly: *she was in a jovial mood.*
– DERIVATIVES **joviality** noun, **jovially** adverb.
– ORIGIN late 16th cent.: from French, from late Latin *jovialis* 'of Jupiter' (see **JOVE**), with reference to the supposed influence of the planet Jupiter on those born under it.

Jovian /ˈdʒəʊvɪən/ ▶ **adjective** **1** (in Roman mythology) of or like the god Jove (or Jupiter).
2 of or relating to the planet Jupiter or the class of giant planets to which Jupiter belongs.
▶ **noun** a hypothetical or fictional inhabitant of the planet Jupiter.

jowar /dʒaʊˈɑː/ ▶ **noun** another term for **DURRA**.
– ORIGIN from Hindi *jauār*.

jowl ▶ **noun** (often **jowls**) the lower part of a person's or animal's cheek, especially when it is fleshy or drooping: *she had a large nose and heavy jowls.*
■ N. Amer. the cheek of a pig used as meat. ■ the loose fleshy part of the neck of certain animals, such as the dewlap of cattle or the wattle of birds.
– DERIVATIVES **jowled** adjective [in combination] *ruddy-jowled*, **jowly** adjective.
– ORIGIN Old English *ceole* (related to German *Kehle* 'throat, gullet'), partly merged with Old English *ceafl* 'jaw' (related to Dutch *kevels* 'cheekbones').

joy ▶ **noun** [mass noun] a feeling of great pleasure and happiness: *tears of joy | the joy of being alive.*
■ [count noun] a thing that causes joy: *the joys of country living.* ■ [usu. with negative] Brit. informal success or satisfaction: *you'll get no joy out of her.*
▶ **verb** [no obj.] poetic/literary rejoice: *I felt shame that I had ever joyed in his discomfiture or pain.*
– PHRASES **be full of the joys of spring** be lively and cheerful. **wish someone joy** Brit., chiefly ironic congratulate someone on something: *I wish you joy of your marriage.*
– DERIVATIVES **joyless** adjective, **joylessly** adverb.
– ORIGIN Middle English: from Old French *joie*, based on Latin *gaudium*, from *gaudere* 'rejoice'.

Joyce, James (Augustine Aloysius) (1882–1941), Irish writer. One of the most important writers of the modernist movement, he made his name with *Dubliners* (short stories, 1914). His novel *Ulysses* (1922) revolutionized the structure of the modern novel and developed the stream-of-consciousness technique. Other notable novels: *A Portrait of the Artist as a Young Man* (1914–15) and *Finnegans Wake* (1939).
– DERIVATIVES **Joycean** adjective & noun.

joyful ▶ **adjective** feeling, expressing, or causing great pleasure and happiness: *joyful music.*
– DERIVATIVES **joyfully** adverb, **joyfulness** noun.

joyous ▶ **adjective** chiefly poetic/literary full of happiness and joy: *scenes of joyous celebration.*
– DERIVATIVES **joyously** adverb, **joyousness** noun.

joypad ▶ **noun** an input device for a computer games console which uses buttons to control the motion of an image on the screen.
– ORIGIN late 20th cent.: blend of **JOYSTICK** and **KEYPAD**.

joyride ▶ **noun** informal a fast and dangerous ride in a stolen vehicle: *they went for a joyride.*
■ a ride for enjoyment in a vehicle or aircraft.

joyriding ▶ **noun** [mass noun] the action or practice of driving fast and dangerously in a stolen car for enjoyment.
– DERIVATIVES **joyrider** noun.

joystick ▶ **noun** informal the control column of an aircraft.
■ a lever that can be moved in several directions to control the movement of an image on a computer or similar display screen.

JP ▶ **abbreviation for** (in the UK) Justice of the Peace.

JPEG /ˈdʒeɪpɛɡ/ ▶ **noun** [mass noun] Computing a format for compressing images: [as modifier] *a JPEG image.*
– ORIGIN 1990s: abbreviation of *Joint Photographic Experts Group.*

Jr ▶ **abbreviation for** junior (in names): *John Smith Jr.*

Juan Carlos /hwɑːn ˈkɑːlɒs/ (b.1938), grandson of Alfonso XIII, king of Spain since 1975; full name *Juan Carlos Victor María de Borbón y Borbón.* Franco's chosen successor, he became king after Franco's death. His reign has seen Spain's increasing liberalization and its entry into NATO and the European Community.

Juan Fernandez Islands /ˌhwɑːn fəˈnandɛz/ a group of three almost uninhabited islands in the Pacific Ocean 640 km (400 miles) west of Chile.

Juárez /ˈhwɑːrɛz/, Benito Pablo (1806–72), Mexican statesman, President 1861–4 and 1867–72. Between 1864 and 1867 he was replaced as emperor by Maximilian, who was supported by the French.

Juba /ˈdʒuːbə/ the capital of the southern region of Sudan, on the White Nile; pop. 100,000 (est. 1990).

juba /ˈdʒuːbə/ ▶ **noun** [mass noun] a dance originating among plantation slaves in the southern US, featuring rhythmic handclapping and slapping of the thighs.
– ORIGIN late 19th cent.: of unknown origin.

Jubba /ˈdʒʊbə, ˈdʒuːbə/ a river in East Africa, rising in the highlands of central Ethiopia and flowing southwards for about 1,600 km (1,000 miles) through Somalia to the Indian Ocean.

jube ▶ **noun** Austral./NZ a jujube lozenge.
– ORIGIN 1930s: shortened form.

jubilant ▶ **adjective** feeling or expressing great happiness and triumph.
– DERIVATIVES **jubilance** noun, **jubilantly** adverb.
– ORIGIN mid 17th cent. (originally in the sense 'making a joyful noise'): from Latin *jubilant-* 'calling, hallooing', from the verb *jubilare* (see **JUBILATE**).

Jubilate /ˌdʒuːbɪˈlɑːteɪ/ ▶ **noun** [in sing.] Psalm 100, beginning *Jubilate deo* 'rejoice in God', especially as used as a canticle in the Anglican service of matins.
■ a musical setting of this.
– ORIGIN Latin, 'shout for joy!', imperative of *jubilare* (see **JUBILATE**).

jubilate /ˈdʒuːbɪleɪt/ ▶ **verb** [no obj.] archaic show great happiness; rejoice: *sing and jubilate aloud before God.*
– ORIGIN mid 17th cent.: from Latin *jubilat-* 'called out', from the verb *jubilare*, used by Christian writers to mean 'shout for joy'.

jubilation ▶ **noun** [mass noun] a feeling of great happiness and triumph.

jubilee ▶ **noun** a special anniversary of an event, especially one celebrating twenty-five or fifty years of a reign or activity: [as modifier] *jubilee celebrations.*
■ Jewish History a year of emancipation and restoration, kept every fifty years. ■ a period of remission from the penal consequences of sin, granted by the Roman Catholic Church under certain conditions for a year, usually at intervals of twenty-five years.
– ORIGIN late Middle English: from Old French *jubile*, from late Latin *jubilaeus (annus)* '(year) of jubilee', based on Hebrew *yōḇēl*, originally 'ram's-horn trumpet', with which the jubilee year was proclaimed.

Jubilee clip ▶ **noun** trademark a type of adjustable steel band secured with a screw.

Jubran /jʊˈbrɑːn/ variant form of **GIBRAN**.

Jud. ▶ **abbreviation for** ■ Judges (in biblical references). ■ Judith (Apocrypha) (in biblical references).

Judaea /dʒuːˈdiːə/ the southern part of ancient Palestine, corresponding to the former kingdom of Judah.
– DERIVATIVES **Judaean** adjective.

Judaeo- /dʒuːˈdiːəʊ/ (US **Judeo-**) ▶ **combining form** Jewish; Jewish and ...: *Judaeo-Christian.*
■ relating to Judaea.
– ORIGIN from Latin *Judaeus* 'Jewish'.

Judah /ˈdʒuːdə/ **1** (in the Bible) a Hebrew patriarch, the fourth son of Jacob.
■ the tribe of Israel traditionally descended from him, the most powerful of the twelve tribes of Israel.
2 the southern part of ancient Palestine, occupied by the tribe of Judah. After the reign of Solomon (*c.*930 BC) it formed a separate kingdom from Israel. Later known as **JUDAEA**.

Judaic /dʒuːˈdeɪɪk/ ▶ **adjective** of or relating to Judaism or the ancient Jews: *tenets of Judaic law.*
– ORIGIN early 17th cent.: from Latin *Judaicus*, from Greek *Ioudaïkos*, from *Ioudaios* (see **JEW**).

Judaism /ˈdʒuːdeɪɪz(ə)m/ ▶ **noun** [mass noun] the monotheistic religion of the Jews.
■ the Jews collectively.

> For its origins Judaism looks to the biblical covenant made by God with Abraham, and to the laws revealed to Moses and recorded in the Torah (supplemented by the rabbinical Talmud), which established the Jewish people's special relationship with God. Since the destruction of the Temple in Jerusalem in AD 70, the rituals of Judaism have centred on the home and the synagogue, the chief day of worship being the Sabbath (sunset on Friday to sunset on Saturday), and the annual observances including Yom Kippur and Passover.

– DERIVATIVES **Judaist** noun.
– ORIGIN from late Latin *Judaismus*, from Greek *Ioudaïsmos*, from *Ioudaios* (see **JEW**).

Judaize /ˈdʒuːdeɪʌɪz/ (also **-ise**) ▶ **verb** [with obj.] make Jewish; convert to Judaism.
■ [no obj.] follow Jewish customs or religious rites.
– DERIVATIVES **Judaization** noun.
– ORIGIN late 16th cent.: from Christian Latin *judaizare*, from Greek *ioudaizein*, from *Ioudaios* (see **JEW**).

Judas[1] /ˈdʒuːdəs/ an Apostle; full name **Judas Iscariot**. He betrayed Christ to the Jewish authorities in return for thirty pieces of silver; the Gospels leave his motives uncertain. Overcome with remorse, he later committed suicide.
■ [as noun] (usu. **a Judas**) a person who betrays a friend or comrade.

Judas[2] see **JUDE, ST**.

judas (also **judas hole**) ▶ **noun** a peephole in a door.
– ORIGIN mid 19th cent.: from *Judas* Iscariot (see **JUDAS**[1]), because of his association with betrayal.

Judas kiss ▶ **noun** an act of betrayal, especially one disguised as a gesture of friendship.
– ORIGIN early 15th cent.: with biblical allusion (Matt. 26:48) to the betrayal of Christ by Judas Iscariot.

Judas Maccabaeus /ˌmakəˈbiːəs/ (died *c.*161 BC), Jewish leader. Leading a Jewish revolt in Judaea against Antiochus IV Epiphanes from around 167, he recovered Jerusalem and dedicated the Temple anew. He is the hero of the two books of the Maccabees in the Apocrypha.

Judas tree ▶ **noun** a Mediterranean tree of the pea family, with purple flowers that typically appear before the rounded leaves.
• *Cercis siliquastrum*, family Leguminosae.

judder ▶ **verb** [no obj.] chiefly Brit. (especially of something mechanical) shake and vibrate rapidly and with force: *the steering wheel juddered in his hand.*
▶ **noun** an instance of rapid and forceful shaking and vibration: *the car gave a judder.*
– DERIVATIVES **juddery** adjective.
– ORIGIN 1930s: imitative; compare with **SHUDDER**.

Jude, St /dʒuːd/ an Apostle, supposed brother of James; also known as **Judas**. Thaddaeus is traditionally identified with him. According to tradition, he was martyred in Persia with St Simon. Feast day (with St Simon), 28 October.
■ the last epistle of the New Testament, ascribed to St Jude.

Judenrat /ˈjuːd(ə)nrɑːt, German ˈjuːdnraːt/ ▶ **noun** (pl. **Judenrate**) a council representing a Jewish community, especially in German-occupied territory during the Second World War.
– ORIGIN German, 'Jewish council'.

judenrein /ˈjuːd(ə)nrʌɪn/ ▶ **adjective** from which Jews are excluded (originally with reference to organizations in Nazi Germany).
– ORIGIN German, 'free of Jews'.

Judeo- ▶ **combining form** US spelling of **JUDAEO-**.

Judezmo /dʒuːˈdɛzməʊ/ ▶ **noun** another term for **LADINO**.

Judg. ▶ **abbreviation for** Judges (in biblical references).

judge ▶ **noun** a public officer appointed to decide cases in a law court.
■ a person who decides the results of a competition. ■ a person able or qualified to give an opinion on something: *she was a* **good judge of** *character.* ■ a leader having temporary authority in ancient Israel in the period between Joshua and the kings. See also **JUDGES**.
▶ **verb** [with obj.] form an opinion or conclusion about: *a production can be judged according to the canons of*

aesthetic criticism | [with clause] *it is hard to judge whether such opposition is justified* | [no obj.] ***judging from** his letters home, Monty was in good spirits.*
■decide (a case) in a law court: *other cases were judged by tribunal.* ■[with obj. and complement] give a verdict on (someone) in a law court: *she was judged innocent of murder.* ■decide the results of (a competition).
– DERIVATIVES **judgeship** noun.
– ORIGIN Middle English: from Old French *juge* (noun), *juger* (verb), from Latin *judex, judic-*, from *jus* 'law' + *dicere* 'to say'.

judge advocate ▶noun Law a barrister who advises a court martial on points of law and sums up the case.

Judge Advocate General ▶noun an officer in supreme control of the courts martial in the armed forces, excluding (in the UK) the navy.

judge-made ▶adjective Law constituted by judicial decisions rather than explicit legislation.

judgement (also **judgment**) ▶noun **1** [mass noun] the ability to make considered decisions or come to sensible conclusions: *an error of judgement* | *that is not, **in my judgement**, the end of the matter.*
■[count noun] an opinion or conclusion: *they make subjective judgements about children's skills.* ■[count noun] a decision of a law court or judge.
2 formal or humorous a misfortune or calamity viewed as a divine punishment: *the crash had been a **judgement on** the parents for wickedness.*
– PHRASES **against one's better judgement** contrary to what one feels to be wise or sensible. **pass judgement** (of a law court or judge) give a decision concerning a defendant or legal matter: *he **passed judgement on** the accused.* ■criticize or condemn someone from a position of assumed moral superiority. **reserve judgement** delay the process of judging or giving one's opinion. **sit in judgement** assume the right to judge someone, especially in a critical manner.
– ORIGIN Middle English: from Old French *jugement*, from *juger* 'to judge'.

USAGE In British English the normal spelling in general contexts is **judgement**. However, the spelling **judgment** is conventional in legal contexts, and in North American English.

judgemental (also **judgmental**) ▶adjective of or concerning the use of judgement: *judgemental decisions about the likelihood of company survival.*
■having or displaying an excessively critical point of view: *I don't like to sound judgemental, but it was a big mistake.*
– DERIVATIVES **judgementally** adverb.

Judgement Day ▶noun the time of the Last Judgement; the end of the world.

judgement in default ▶noun [mass noun] Law judgement awarded to the plaintiff on the defendant's failure to plead.

Judgement of Solomon (in the Bible) the arbitration of King Solomon over a baby claimed by two women (1 Kings 3:16–28). He proposed cutting the baby in half, and then gave it to the woman who showed concern for its life.

Judges the seventh book of the Bible, describing the conquest of Canaan under the leaders called 'judges' in an account that is parallel to that of the Book of Joshua and is probably more accurate historically. The book includes the stories of Deborah, Jael, Gideon, Jephthah, and Samson.

Judges' Rules ▶plural noun English Law rules regarding the admissibility of an accused's statements as evidence.

judgment ▶noun variant spelling of **JUDGEMENT**.

judgmental ▶adjective variant spelling of **JUDGEMENTAL**.

judicature /ˈdʒuːdɪkəˌtʃə, dʒuːˈdɪk-/ ▶noun [mass noun] the administration of justice.
■(**the judicature**) judges collectively; the judiciary.
– DERIVATIVES **judicatory** adjective.
– ORIGIN mid 16th cent.: from medieval Latin *judicatura*, from Latin *judicare* 'to judge'.

judicial /dʒuːˈdɪʃ(ə)l/ ▶adjective of, by, or appropriate to a law court or judge: *a judicial inquiry into the allegations* | *a judicial system.*
– DERIVATIVES **judicially** adverb.
– ORIGIN late Middle English: from Latin *judicialis*, from *judicium* 'judgement', from *judex* (see **JUDGE**).

Judicial Committee of the Privy Council (in the UK) a court made up of members of the House of Lords and others, which considers appeals made to the Sovereign in Council concerning decisions of some Commonwealth courts outside the UK.

judicial factor ▶noun Scots Law an agent legally appointed to administer a person's estate.

judicial review ▶noun [mass noun] (in the UK) a procedure by which a court can review an administrative action by a public body and (in England) secure a declaration, order, or award.
■(in the US) review by the Supreme Court of the constitutional validity of a legislative act.

judicial separation ▶noun another term for **LEGAL SEPARATION** (in sense 1).

judiciary /dʒʊˈdɪʃ(ə)ri/ ▶noun (pl. **-ies**) (usu. **the judiciary**) the judicial authorities of a country; judges collectively.
– ORIGIN early 19th cent.: from Latin *judiciarius*, from *judicium* 'judgement'.

judicious /dʒʊˈdɪʃəs/ ▶adjective having, showing, or done with good judgement or sense: *the judicious use of public investment.*
– DERIVATIVES **judiciously** adverb, **judiciousness** noun.
– ORIGIN late 16th cent.: from French *judicieux*, from Latin *judicium* 'judgement' (see **JUDICIAL**).

Judith (in the Apocrypha) a rich Israelite widow who saved the town of Bethulia from Nebuchadnezzar's army by seducing the besieging general Holofernes and cutting off his head while he slept.
■a book of the Apocrypha recounting the story of Judith.

judo ▶noun [mass noun] a sport of unarmed combat derived from ju-jitsu and intended to train the body and mind. It involves using holds and leverage to unbalance the opponent.
– DERIVATIVES **judoist** noun.
– ORIGIN late 19th cent.: Japanese, from *jū* 'gentle' + *dō* 'way'.

judoka /ˈdʒuːdəʊˌkə/ ▶noun a person who practises or is an expert in judo.
– ORIGIN Japanese, from **JUDO** + *-ka* 'person, profession'.

Judy ▶noun (pl. **-ies**) the wife of Punch in the Punch and Judy show.
■Brit. informal, dated a woman.
– ORIGIN early 19th cent.: pet form of the given name *Judith*.

jug ▶noun **1** Brit. a small or medium-sized cylindrical container with a handle and a lip, used for holding and pouring liquids.
■N. Amer. a large container for liquids, with a narrow mouth and typically a stopper or cap. ■the contents of such a container: *she gave us a big **jug of** water.*
2 (**the jug**) informal prison: *three months **in the jug**.*
3 (**jugs**) vulgar slang a woman's breasts.
4 (also **jug handle**) Climbing a secure hold that is cut into rock for climbing.
▶verb (**jugged, jugging**) [with obj.] **1** [usu. as adj. **jugged**] stew or boil (a hare or rabbit) in a covered container: *jugged hare.*
2 informal, chiefly US prosecute and imprison (someone).
– DERIVATIVES **jugful** noun (pl. **-fuls**).
– ORIGIN mid 16th cent.: perhaps from *Jug*, pet form of the given names *Joan, Joanna*, and *Jenny*.

jugal /ˈdʒuːg(ə)l/ ▶adjective **1** Anatomy of or relating to the zygoma (the bony arch of the cheek).
2 Entomology of or relating to the jugum of an insect's forewing.
– ORIGIN late 16th cent.: from Latin *jugalis*, from *jugum* 'yoke'.

jug band ▶noun a group of jazz, blues, or folk musicians using simple or improvised instruments such as jugs and washboards.

Jugendstil /ˈjuːgəndˌʃtiːl, German ˈjuːgntˌʃtil/ ▶noun German term for **ART NOUVEAU**.
– ORIGIN German, from *Jugend* 'youth' + *Stil* 'style'.

Juggernaut /ˈdʒʌgənɔːt/ Hinduism the form of Krishna worshipped in Puri, Orissa, where in the annual festival his image is dragged through the streets on a heavy chariot; devotees are said formerly to have thrown themselves under its wheels. Also called **JAGANNATHA**.
– ORIGIN via Hindi from Sanskrit *Jagannātha* 'Lord of the world'.

juggernaut /ˈdʒʌgənɔːt/ ▶noun Brit. a large heavy vehicle, especially an articulated lorry.
■a huge, powerful, and overwhelming force or institution: *the juggernaut of public expenditure.*
– ORIGIN mid 19th cent.: extension of **JUGGERNAUT**.

juggins ▶noun Brit. informal, dated a simple-minded or gullible person: *you silly juggins.*
– ORIGIN late 19th cent.: perhaps from the surname *Juggins*, from *Jug* (see **JUG**); compare with **MUGGINS**.

juggle ▶verb [with obj.] continuously toss into the air and catch (a number of objects) so as to keep at least one in the air while handling the others, typically for the entertainment of others.
■cope with by adroitly balancing: *she works full time, **juggling** her career **with** raising children.* ■misrepresent (something) so as to deceive or cheat someone: *defence chiefs juggled the figures on bomb tests.*
▶noun [in sing.] an act of juggling.
– DERIVATIVES **juggler** noun, **jugglery** noun.
– ORIGIN late Middle English (in the sense 'entertain with jesting, tricks, etc.'): back-formation from *juggler*, or from Old French *jogler*, from Latin *joculari* 'to jest', from *joculus*, diminutive of *jocus* 'jest'. Current senses date from the late 19th cent.

jug kettle ▶noun Brit. a tall, narrow electric kettle like a jug with a lid.

Jugoslav ▶noun & adjective old-fashioned variant spelling of **YUGOSLAV**.

Jugoslavia ▶noun old-fashioned variant spelling of **YUGOSLAVIA**.

jugular /ˈdʒʌgjʊlə/ ▶adjective **1** of the neck or throat.
2 Zoology (of fish's pelvic fins) located in front of the pectoral fins.
▶noun short for **JUGULAR VEIN**.
– PHRASES **go for the jugular** be aggressive or unrestrained in making an attack.
– ORIGIN late 16th cent.: from late Latin *jugularis*, from Latin *jugulum* 'collarbone, throat', diminutive of *jugum* 'yoke'.

jugular vein ▶noun any of several large veins in the neck, carrying blood from the head and face.

jugulate /ˈdʒʌgjʊleɪt/ ▶verb [with obj.] archaic kill (someone) by cutting the throat.
– ORIGIN early 17th cent.: from Latin *jugulat-* 'slain by a cut to the throat', from the verb *jugulare*, from *jugulum* 'throat' (see **JUGULAR**).

jugum /ˈdʒuːgəm/ ▶noun (pl. **juga**) chiefly Zoology a connecting ridge or projection.
■Entomology a lobe on the forewing of some moths which interlocks with the hindwing in flight.
– ORIGIN mid 19th cent.: from Latin, literally 'yoke'.

Jugurtha /dʒəˈgəːθə/ (d.104 BC), joint king of Numidia *c.*118–104. His attacks on his royal partners prompted intervention by Rome and led to the outbreak of the Jugurthine War (112–105). He was eventually captured by the Roman general Marius and executed in Rome.
– DERIVATIVES **Jugurthine** /-θʌɪn/ adjective.

juice ▶noun [mass noun] the liquid obtained from or present in fruit or vegetables: *add the juice of a lemon.*
■a drink made from such a liquid: *a carton of orange juice.* ■(**juices**) fluid secreted by the body, especially in the stomach to help digest food. ■(**juices**) the liquid that comes from meat or other food when cooked. ■informal electrical energy: *the batteries have run out of juice.* ■informal petrol: *he ran out of juice on the last lap.* ■N. Amer. informal alcoholic drink. ■(**juices**) a person's vitality or creative faculties: *it saps the creative juices.*
▶verb [with obj.] **1** extract the juice from (fruit or vegetables): *juice one orange at a time.*
2 (**juice something up**) informal, chiefly US liven something up: *they juiced it up with some love interest.*
3 [as adj. **juiced**] N. Amer. informal drunk.
– DERIVATIVES **juiceless** adjective.
– ORIGIN Middle English: via Old French from Latin *jus* 'broth, vegetable juice'.

juicer ▶noun an appliance for extracting juice from fruit and vegetables.

juicy ▶adjective (**juicier, juiciest**) (of food) full of juice; succulent: *a juicy apple* | *a juicy steak.*
■informal interestingly scandalous: *juicy gossip.* ■informal temptingly appealing: *the promise of juicy returns.*
– DERIVATIVES **juicily** adverb, **juiciness** noun.

ju-jitsu /dʒuːˈdʒɪtsuː/ (also **jiu-jitsu** or **ju-jutsu** /-ˈdʒʌtsuː/) ▶noun [mass noun] a Japanese system of

j

unarmed combat and physical training. Compare with **JUDO**.
– ORIGIN Japanese *jūjutsu*, from *jū* 'gentle' + *jutsu* 'skill'.

juju[1] /ˈdʒuːdʒuː/ ▶ **noun** [mass noun] a style of music popular among the Yoruba in Nigeria and characterized by the use of guitars and variable-pitch drums.
– ORIGIN perhaps from Yoruba *jo jo* 'dance'.

juju[2] /ˈdʒuːdʒuː/ ▶ **noun** a charm or fetish, especially of a type used by some West African peoples.
■ [mass noun] supernatural power attributed to such a charm or fetish: *juju and witchcraft*.
– ORIGIN early 17th cent.: of West African origin, perhaps from French *joujou* 'toy'.

jujube /ˈdʒuːdʒuːb/ ▶ **noun** **1** the edible berry-like fruit of a Eurasian plant, formerly taken as a cough cure.
■ chiefly N. Amer. a jujube-flavoured lozenge or sweet.
2 (also **jujube bush**) the shrub or small tree that produces this fruit, native to the warmer regions of Eurasia.
• *Ziziphus jujuba*, family Rhamnaceae.
– ORIGIN late Middle English: from French, or from medieval Latin *jujuba*, based on Greek *zizuphos*.

jukebox ▶ **noun** a machine that automatically plays a selected musical recording when a coin is inserted.
■ Computing a device which stores several computer disks in such a way that data can be read from any of them.
– ORIGIN 1930s: from Gullah *juke* 'disorderly' + **BOX**[1].

j

jukskei /ˈjəkskeɪ/ ▶ **noun** [mass noun] S. African a game in which a peg is thrown at a stake.
– ORIGIN South African Dutch, from Dutch *juk* 'yoke' + *skei* 'pin'; the game was originally played with sticks from an animal's yoke.

juku /ˈdʒʊkuː/ ▶ **noun** (pl. same) (in Japan) a private school or college attended in addition to an ordinary educational institution.
– ORIGIN Japanese.

Jul. ▶ **abbreviation for** July.

julep /ˈdʒuːlɛp/ ▶ **noun** a sweet flavoured drink made from a sugar syrup, sometimes containing alcohol or medication.
■ short for **MINT JULEP**.
– ORIGIN late Middle English: from Old French, from medieval Latin *julapium*, via Arabic from Persian *gulāb*, from *gul* 'rose' + *āb* 'water'.

julia /ˈdʒuːlɪə/ ▶ **noun** an orange and black American butterfly with long narrow forewings, found chiefly in tropical regions.
• *Dryas julia*, subfamily Heliconiinae, family Nymphalidae.

Julian[1] /ˈdʒuːlɪən/ ▶ **adjective** of or associated with Julius Caesar.
– ORIGIN from Latin *Julianus*, from the given name *Julius*.

Julian[2] /ˈdʒuːlɪən/ (*c*.331–63 AD), Roman emperor 360–3, nephew of Constantine; full name *Flavius Claudius Julianus*; known as **the Apostate**. He restored paganism as the state cult in place of Christianity, but this move was reversed after his death on campaign against the Persians.

Julian Alps an Alpine range in western Slovenia and NE Italy, rising to a height of 2,863 m (9,395 ft) at Triglav.

Julian calendar ▶ **noun** a calendar introduced by the authority of Julius Caesar in 46 BC, in which the year consisted of 365 days, every fourth year having 366 days. It was superseded by the Gregorian calendar, though it is still used by some Orthodox Churches. Dates in the Julian calendar are sometimes designated 'Old Style'.

Julian of Norwich (*c*.1342–*c*.1413), English mystic. She is said to have lived as a recluse outside St Julian's Church, Norwich. She is chiefly associated with the *Revelations of Divine Love* (*c*.1393), a description of a series of visions she had in which she depicts the Holy Trinity as Father, Mother, and Lord.

Julia set /ˈdʒuːlɪə/ ▶ **noun** Mathematics a set of complex numbers which do not converge to any limit when a given mapping is repeatedly applied to them. In some cases the result is a connected fractal set.
– ORIGIN 1970s: named after Gaston M. *Julia* (born 1893), Algerian-born French mathematician.

julienne /ˌdʒuːlɪˈɛn/ ▶ **noun** a portion of food cut into short, thin strips: *a julienne of vegetables* | [as modifier] *julienne leeks*.
▶ **verb** [with obj.] cut (food) into short, thin strips.
– ORIGIN early 18th cent. (originally as an adjective designating soup made of chopped vegetables, especially carrots): French, from the male given names *Jules* or *Julien*, of obscure development.

Juliet /ˈdʒuːlɪɛt/ ▶ **noun** a code word representing the letter J, used in radio communication.

Juliet cap ▶ **noun** a type of women's small ornamental cap, typically made of lace or net and often worn by brides.
– ORIGIN early 20th cent.: so named because it forms part of the usual costume of the heroine of Shakespeare's *Romeo and Juliet*.

Julius Caesar /ˌdʒuːlɪəs/, Gaius (100–44 BC), Roman general and statesman.

He established the First Triumvirate with Pompey and Crassus (60), and became consul in 59. Between 58 and 51 he fought the Gallic Wars, invaded Britain (55–54), and acquired immense power. After civil war with Pompey, which ended in Pompey's defeat at Pharsalus (48), Caesar became dictator of the Roman Empire; he was murdered on the Ides (15th) of March in a conspiracy led by Brutus and Cassius.

Jullundur /ˈdʒʌləndə/ (also **Jalandhar**) a city in Punjab, NW India; pop. 520,000 (1991).

July ▶ **noun** (pl. **Julys**) the seventh month of the year, in the northern hemisphere usually considered the second month of summer: *I had a letter from him in July* | *a festival held every July*.
– ORIGIN Middle English: from Latin *Julius* (*mensis*) '(month) of July', named after Julius Caesar.

jumar /ˈdʒuːmə/ Climbing ▶ **noun** a clamp that is attached to a fixed rope and automatically tightens when weight is applied and relaxes when it is removed.
▶ **verb** (**jumared**, **jumaring**) [no obj.] climb with the aid of such a clamp.
– ORIGIN 1960s: originally in Swiss use, of unknown origin.

jumbie /ˈdʒʌmbi/ ▶ **noun** W. Indian a spirit of a dead person, typically an evil one.
– ORIGIN from Kikongo *zumbi* 'fetish'.

jumbie bird ▶ **noun** W. Indian a bird of ill omen, especially a pygmy owl.
• *Glaucidium brasilianum*, family Strigidae. Alternative name: **ferruginous pygmy owl**.

jumble ▶ **noun** an untidy collection or pile of things: *the books were in a chaotic jumble*.
■ [mass noun] Brit. articles collected for a jumble sale.
▶ **verb** [with obj.] mix up in a confused or untidy way: *a drawer full of letters **jumbled together***.
– ORIGIN early 16th cent.: probably symbolic.

jumble sale ▶ **noun** Brit. a sale of miscellaneous second-hand articles, typically held in order to raise money for a charity or a special event.

jumbo informal ▶ **noun** (pl. **-os**) a very large person or thing.
■ (also **jumbo jet**) a very large airliner (originally and specifically a Boeing 747).
▶ **adjective** [attrib.] very large: *a jumbo pad*.
– ORIGIN early 19th cent. (originally of a person): probably the second element of **MUMBO-JUMBO**. Originally denoting a large and clumsy person, the term was popularized as the name of an elephant at London Zoo, sold in 1882 to the Barnum and Bailey circus.

jumbuck /ˈdʒʌmbʌk/ ▶ **noun** Austral. informal a sheep.
– ORIGIN early 19th cent.: of unknown origin, possibly Australian pidgin for *jump up*.

Jumna /ˈdʒʌmnə/ a river of northern India, which rises in the Himalayas and flows in a large arc southwards and south-eastwards, through Delhi, joining the Ganges below Allahabad. Its source (Yamunotri) and its confluence with the Ganges are both Hindu holy places. Hindi name **YAMUNA**.

jump ▶ **verb** **1** [no obj., usu. with adverbial of direction] push oneself off a surface and into the air by using the muscles in one's legs and feet: *the cat jumped off his lap* | *he jumped twenty-five feet to the ground*.
■ [with obj.] pass over (an obstacle or barrier) in such a way. ■ [with adverbial] (of an athlete or horse) perform in a competition involving such action: *his horse jumped well and won by five lengths*. ■ (especially of prices or figures) rise suddenly and by a large amount: *pre-tax profits jumped from £51,000 to £1.03 million*. ■ informal (of a place) be full of lively activity: *the bar is jumping on Fridays and Saturdays*. ■ [with obj.] informal (of driver or a vehicle) fail to stop at (a red traffic light). ■ [with obj.] get on or off (a train or other vehicle) quickly, typically illegally or dangerously. ■ [with obj.] N. Amer. take summary possession of (a mining concession or other piece of land) after alleged abandonment or forfeiture by the former occupant.
2 [no obj., usu. with adverbial] (of a person) move suddenly and quickly in a specified way: *Juliet **jumped to her feet*** | *they jumped back into the car and drove off*.
■ (of a person) make a sudden involuntary movement in reaction to something that causes surprise or shock: *an owl hooted nearby, making her jump*. ■ pass quickly or abruptly from one idea, subject, or state to another: *she jumped backwards and forwards in her narrative*. ■ [with obj.] omit or skip over (part of something) and pass on to a further point or stage. ■ (of a machine or device) move or jerk suddenly and abruptly: *the vibration can cause the needle to jump*. ■ (of a person) make a sudden, impulsive rush to do something: *Gordon jumped to my defence*. ■ Bridge make a bid that is higher than necessary, in order to signal a strong hand: *East jumped to four spades*. ■ [with obj.] informal attack (someone) suddenly and unexpectedly. ■ vulgar slang, chiefly N. Amer. have sexual intercourse with (someone).
3 [with obj.] N. Amer. informal start (a vehicle) using jump leads: *I jumped his saloon from my car's battery*.
▶ **noun** **1** an act of jumping from a surface by pushing upwards with one's legs and feet: *in making the short jump across the gully he lost his balance*.
■ an obstacle to be jumped, especially by a horse and rider in an equestrian competition. ■ an act of descending from an aircraft by parachute. ■ a sudden dramatic rise in amount, price, or value: *a 51 per cent jump in annual profits*. ■ a large or sudden transition or change: *the jump from county to Test cricket*. ■ Bridge a bid that is higher than necessary, signalling strength. ■ vulgar slang, chiefly N. Amer. an act of sexual intercourse.
2 a sudden involuntary movement caused by shock or surprise: *I woke up with a jump*.
■ (**the jumps**) informal extreme nervousness or anxiety.
– PHRASES **be jumping up and down** informal be very angry, upset, or excited. **get** (or **have**) **the jump on someone** informal, chiefly N. Amer. get (or have) an advantage over someone as a result of one's prompt action. **jump bail** see **BAIL**[1]. **jump someone's bones** N. Amer. vulgar slang have sexual intercourse with someone. **jump down someone's throat** informal respond to what someone has said in a sudden and angrily critical way. **jump for joy** be ecstatically happy: *I'm not exactly jumping for joy at the prospect*. **jump the gun** see **GUN**. **jump into bed with** informal engage readily in sexual intercourse with. **jump on the bandwagon** see **BANDWAGON**. **jump out of one's skin** informal be extremely startled. **jump the queue** (or US **jump in line**) push into a queue of people in order to be served or dealt with before one's turn. ■ figurative take unfair precedence over others: *the old boy networks were one way of jumping the promotion queue*. **jump the rails** (or **track**) (of a train) become dislodged from the track. **jump rope** N. Amer. skip using a rope. **jump ship** (of a sailor) leave the ship on which one is serving without having obtained permission to do so: *he jumped ship in Cape Town* | figurative *three producers jumped ship two weeks after the show's debut*. **jump through hoops** go through an elaborate or complicated procedure in order to achieve an objective. **jump** (or **leap**) **to conclusions** (or **the conclusion**) form an opinion hastily, before one has learned or considered all the facts. **jump to it!** informal used to exhort someone to prompt or immediate action. **one jump ahead** one step or stage ahead of someone else and so having the advantage over them: *the Americans were **one jump ahead of** the British in this*.
– DERIVATIVES **jumpable** adjective.
– ORIGIN early 16th cent. (in the sense 'be moved or thrown with a sudden jerk'): probably imitative of the sound of feet coming into contact with the ground.
▶ **jump at** accept (an opportunity or offer) with great eagerness: *I'd **jump at the chance** of a career in football*.
jump on informal attack or take hold of (someone) suddenly. ■ criticize (someone) suddenly and severely. ■ seize on (something) eagerly; give sudden (typically critical) attention to: *the paper jumped on the inconsistencies of his stories*.
jump out have a strong visual or mental impact; be very striking: *advertising posters that really **jump out at you***.

jump ball ▶ **noun** Basketball a ball put in play by the referee, who throws it up between two opposing players.

jump blues ▸ noun [mass noun] a style of popular music combining elements of swing and blues.

jumpcut ▸ noun (in film or television) an abrupt transition from one scene to another.
▸ verb (**jump-cut**) [no obj.] make such a transition.

jumped-up ▸ adjective informal denoting someone who considers themselves to be more important than they really are, or who has suddenly and undeservedly risen in status: *she's not really a journalist, more a jumped-up PR woman.*

jumper¹ ▸ noun 1 Brit. a knitted garment typically with long sleeves, worn over the upper body.
2 historical a loose outer jacket worn by sailors.
3 N. Amer. a pinafore dress.
– ORIGIN mid 19th cent. (in sense 2): probably from dialect *jump* 'short coat', perhaps from Scots *jupe* 'a man's (later also a woman's) loose jacket or tunic', via Old French from Arabic *jubba*. Compare with JIBBA.

jumper² ▸ noun 1 a person or animal that jumps.
2 (also **jumper wire**) a short wire used to shorten an electric circuit or close it temporarily.
3 Nautical a rope made fast to keep a yard or mast from jumping.
4 a heavy chisel-ended iron bar for drilling blast holes.
5 a mushroom-shaped brass part in a tap which supports the washer.

jumper cable ▸ noun North American term for JUMP LEAD.

jumping bean ▸ noun a plant seed that jumps as a result of the movement of a moth larva which is developing inside it.
■ Affected seeds are found in several plants of the family Euphorbiaceae, in particular the Mexican plant *Sebastiana pavoniana*, the seeds of which can contain larvae of the moth *Cydia saltitans*.

jumping gene ▸ noun informal term for TRANSPOSON.

jumping jack ▸ noun 1 a jump done from a standing position with the arms and legs pointing outwards.
2 Brit. dated a small firework producing repeated explosions.
3 a toy figure of a man, with movable limbs.

jumping Jehoshaphat ▸ exclamation see JEHOSHAPHAT.

jumping mouse ▸ noun a mouse-like rodent that has long back feet and typically moves in short hops, found in North America and China.
● Family Zapodidae: three genera, in particular *Zapus*, and several species.

jumping-off place (also **jumping-off point**) ▸ noun the point from which something is begun.

jumping plant louse ▸ noun a minute hopping bug with wings, resembling a miniature cicada. Many kinds are pests of cultivated plants.
● Family Psyllidae, suborder Homoptera.

jumping spider ▸ noun a large-eyed spider which hunts prey by stalking and pouncing on it.
● Family Salticidae, order Araneae.

jump instruction ▸ noun Computing an instruction in a computer program that causes processing to move to a different place in the program sequence.

jump jet ▸ noun a jet aircraft that can take off and land vertically, without need of a runway.

jump lead ▸ noun Brit. each of a pair of thick electric cables fitted with clips at either end, used for recharging a battery in a motor vehicle by connecting it to the battery in another.

jump-off ▸ noun a deciding round in a showjumping competition.

jump ring ▸ noun a wire ring made by bringing the two ends together without soldering or welding.

jump rope ▸ noun N. Amer. a skipping rope.

jump seat ▸ noun chiefly N. Amer. an extra seat in a car or taxi that folds back when not in use.

jump shift ▸ noun Bridge a bid that is both in a different suit from that bid by oneself or one's partner and at a higher level than necessary, indicating a strong hand.

jump shot ▸ noun 1 Basketball a shot made while jumping.
2 Billiards & Snooker a shot in which the cue ball is made to jump over another ball.

jump-start ▸ verb [with obj.] start (a car with a flat battery) with jump leads or by a sudden release of the clutch while it is being pushed.
■ figurative give an added impetus to (something that is proceeding slowly or is at a standstill): *she suggests ways to jump-start the sluggish educational system.*
▸ noun an act of starting a car in such a way.
■ figurative an added impetus.

jumpsuit ▸ noun a garment incorporating trousers and a sleeved top in one piece, worn as a fashion item, protective garment, or uniform.
– ORIGIN 1940s (originally US): so named because it was first used to denote a parachutist's garment.

jump-up ▸ noun 1 a jump in an upward direction.
■ an informal Caribbean dance or celebration.
2 Austral. informal an escarpment.

jumpy ▸ adjective (**jumpier**, **jumpiest**) informal (of a person) anxious and uneasy: *he was tired and jumpy.*
■ characterized by abrupt stops and starts or an irregular course: *a jumpy pulse.*
– DERIVATIVES **jumpily** adverb, **jumpiness** noun.

Jun. ▸ abbreviation for ■ June. ■ junior (in names): *John Smith Jun.*

jun /dʒʌn/ ▸ noun (pl. same) a monetary unit of North Korea, equal to one hundredth of a won.
– ORIGIN Korean.

junco /ˈdʒʌŋkəʊ/ ▸ noun (pl. **-os** or **-oes**) a North American songbird related to the buntings, with mainly grey and brown plumage.
● Genus *Junco*, family Emberizidae (subfamily Emberizinae): three or four species.
– ORIGIN early 18th cent. (originally 'reed bunting'): from Spanish, from Latin *juncus* 'rush, reed'.

junction ▸ noun 1 a point where two or more things are joined: *the junction of the two rivers.*
■ a place where two or more roads or railway lines meet.
2 Electronics a region of transition in a semiconductor between a part where conduction is mainly by electrons and a part where it is mainly by holes.
3 [mass noun] the action or fact of joining or being joined.
– ORIGIN early 18th cent. (in sense 3): from Latin *junctio(n-)*, from *jungere* 'to join'.

junction box ▸ noun a box containing a junction of electric wires or cables.

juncture /ˈdʒʌŋ(k)tʃə/ ▸ noun a particular point in events or time: *it is difficult to say at this juncture whether this upturn can be sustained.*
■ a place where things join: *the plane crashed at the juncture of two mountains.* ■ Phonetics the set of features in speech that enable a hearer to detect a word or phrase boundary (e.g. distinguishing *I scream* from *ice cream*).
– ORIGIN late Middle English (in the sense 'act of joining'): from Latin *junctura*, 'joint', from *jungere* 'to join'.

June ▸ noun the sixth month of the year, in the northern hemisphere usually considered the first month of summer: *the roses flower in June* | *each June the group meet for an informal reunion.*
– ORIGIN Middle English: from Old French *juin*, from Latin *Junius (mensis)* '(month) of June', variant of *Junonius* 'sacred to Juno'.

Juneau /ˈdʒuːnəʊ/ the state capital of Alaska, a seaport on an inlet of the Pacific Ocean in the south of the state; pop. 26,750 (1990).
– ORIGIN named after Joseph *Juneau* who discovered gold there in 1880.

juneberry ▸ noun (pl. **-ies**) a North American shrub of the rose family, some kinds of which are grown for their showy white flowers and bright autumn colours.
● Genus *Amelanchier*, family Rosaceae: many species, including *A. laevis*, which has naturalized in England.
■ the edible berry of this plant.

June bug ▸ noun another term for GARDEN CHAFER.

June War Arab name for SIX DAY WAR.

Jung /jʊŋ/, Carl (Gustav) (1875–1961), Swiss psychologist.

Jung originated the concept of introvert and extrovert personality, and of the four psychological functions of sensation, intuition, thinking, and feeling. He collaborated with Sigmund Freud in developing the psychoanalytic theory of personality, but later disassociated himself from Freud's preoccupation with sexuality as the determinant of personality, preferring to emphasize a mystical or religious factor in the unconscious.

– DERIVATIVES **Jungian** adjective & noun.

Jungfrau /ˈjʊŋfraʊ/ a mountain in the Swiss Alps, 4,158 m (13,642 ft) high.

jungle ▸ noun 1 an area of land overgrown with dense forest and tangled vegetation, typically in the tropics: *we set off into the jungle* | [mass noun] *the lakes are hidden in dense jungle.*
■ a wild tangled mass of vegetation or other things: *the garden was a jungle of bluebells.* ■ a situation or place of bewildering complexity or brutal competitiveness: *it's a jungle out there.*
2 (also **jungle music**) [mass noun] a style of dance music incorporating elements of ragga, hip hop, and hard core and consisting almost exclusively of very fast electronic drum tracks and slower synthesized bass lines, originating in Britain in the early 1990s. Compare with DRUM AND BASS.
– PHRASES **the law of the jungle** the principle that those who are strong and apply ruthless self-interest will be most successful.
– DERIVATIVES **jungled** adjective, **junglist** noun & adjective (only in sense 2), **jungly** adjective.
– ORIGIN late 18th cent.: via Hindi from Sanskrit *jāṅgala* 'rough and arid (terrain)'.

jungle cat ▸ noun a small wild cat that has a yellowish or greyish coat with dark markings on the legs and tail, living in dry forests from Egypt to SE Asia.
● *Felis chaus*, family Felidae.

jungle fever ▸ noun [mass noun] a severe form of malaria.

junglefowl ▸ noun (pl. same) a southern Asian game bird related to the domestic fowl, typically frequenting forested country.
● Genus *Gallus*, family Phasianidae: four species, in particular the **red junglefowl** (*G. gallus*), which is the ancestor of the domestic fowl.

jungle gym ▸ noun N. Amer. a climbing frame for children.
– ORIGIN 1920s: formerly a US trademark.

jungle juice ▸ noun [mass noun] informal powerful or roughly prepared alcoholic liquor.

jungle telegraph ▸ noun another term for BUSH TELEGRAPH.

jungli /ˈdʒʌŋɡli/ ▸ adjective Indian uncultured; wild.
– ORIGIN from JUNGLE + the suffix *-i* (as in Hindi); compare with Hindi *jaṅgli*.

junior ▸ adjective 1 of, for, or denoting young or younger people: *junior tennis.*
■ Brit. of, for, or denoting schoolchildren between the ages of 7 and 11. ■ N. Amer. of or for students in the third year of a course lasting four years at college or high school: *his junior year in college.* ■ (often **Junior**) [postpositive] [in names] denoting the younger of two who have the same name in a family, especially a son as distinct from his father: *John F. Kennedy Junior.*
2 low or lower in rank or status: *a junior minister* | *part of my function is to supervise those junior to me.*
▸ noun 1 a person who is a specified number of years younger than someone else: *he's five years my junior.*
■ Brit. a child attending a junior school. ■ N. Amer. a student in the third year at college or high school. ■ (in sport) a young competitor, typically under sixteen or eighteen. ■ N. Amer. informal used as a nickname or form of address for one's son.
2 a person with low rank or status compared with others: *an office junior.*
– DERIVATIVES **juniority** /-ˈprɪti/ noun.
– ORIGIN Middle English (as an adjective following a family name): from Latin, comparative of *juvenis* 'young'.

junior barrister ▸ noun (in the UK) a barrister who has not taken silk, i.e. is not a Queen's (or King's) Counsel.

junior college ▸ noun (in the US) a college offering courses for two years beyond high school, either as a complete training or in preparation for completion at a senior college.

junior combination room ▸ noun term used in Cambridge University for JUNIOR COMMON ROOM.

junior common room ▸ noun Brit. a room used for social purposes by the undergraduates of a college.
■ [treated as sing. or pl.] the undergraduates of a college regarded collectively.

junior high school ▸ noun (in the US and Canada) a school intermediate between an elementary school and a high school, generally for children in the seventh, eighth, and ninth grades.

junior lightweight ▶ **noun** [mass noun] a weight in professional boxing of 57.1–59 kilograms.
■[count noun] a professional boxer of this weight.

junior middleweight ▶ **noun** [mass noun] a weight in professional boxing of 66.7–69.8 kilograms.
■[count noun] a professional boxer of this weight.

junior school ▶ **noun** a school for young or younger children, in particular (in England and Wales) a school for children aged between 7 and 11.

junior technician ▶ **noun** a rank in the RAF, above senior aircraftman or senior aircraftwoman and below corporal.

junior welterweight ▶ **noun** [mass noun] a weight in professional boxing of 61.2–63.5 kilograms.
■[count noun] a professional boxer of this weight.

juniper /ˈdʒuːnɪpə/ ▶ **noun** an evergreen shrub or small tree which bears berry-like cones, widely distributed throughout Eurasia and North America. Many kinds have aromatic cones or foliage.
• Genus *Juniperus*, family Cupressaceae: many species, including the **common juniper** (*J. communis*), the berries of which are used for flavouring gin.
– ORIGIN late Middle English: from Latin *juniperus*.

junk¹ ▶ **noun** [mass noun] **1** informal old or discarded articles that are considered useless or of little value.
■worthless writing, talk, or ideas: *I can't write this kind of junk.* ■ Finance junk bonds.
2 informal heroin.
3 the lump of oily fibrous tissue in a sperm whale's head, containing spermaceti.
▶ **verb** [with obj.] informal discard or abandon unceremoniously: *sort out what could be sold off and junk the rest.*
– ORIGIN late Middle English (denoting an old or inferior rope): of unknown origin. Sense 1 dates from the mid 19th cent.

junk² ▶ **noun** a flat-bottomed sailing vessel of a kind typical of China and the East Indies, with a prominent stem and lugsails.
– ORIGIN mid 16th cent.: from obsolete French *juncque* or Portuguese *junco*, from Malay *jong*, reinforced by Dutch *jonk*.

Junkanoo /ˈdʒʌŋkaˌnuː, ˈdʒɒnkaˌnuː/ ▶ **noun** (chiefly in Jamaica, Belize, and the Bahamas) a masquerade held at Christmas, consisting of a street procession of characters in traditional costumes and dancing to drums, bells, and whistles.

junk bond ▶ **noun** a high-yielding high-risk security, typically issued by a company seeking to raise capital quickly in order to finance a takeover.

Junker /ˈjʊŋkə/ ▶ **noun** historical a German nobleman or aristocrat, especially a member of the Prussian aristocracy.
– DERIVATIVES **junkerdom** noun, **junkerism** noun.
– ORIGIN German, earlier *Junkher*, from Middle High German *junc* 'young' + *herre* 'lord'.

junket /ˈdʒʌŋkɪt/ ▶ **noun 1** [mass noun] a dish of sweetened and flavoured curds of milk, often served with fruit.
2 informal an extravagant trip or celebration, in particular one enjoyed by a government official at public expense.
▶ **verb** (**junketed**, **junketing**) [no obj.] [often as noun **junketing**] informal attend or go on such a trip or celebration.
– ORIGIN late Middle English: from Old French *jonquette* 'rush basket', from *jonc* 'rush', from Latin *juncus*. Originally denoting a rush basket, especially one for fish (remaining in dialect use), the term also denoted a cream cheese, formerly made in a rush basket or served on a rush mat. A later extended sense, 'feast, merrymaking', gave rise to sense 2.

junk food ▶ **noun** [mass noun] food that has low nutritional value, typically produced in the form of packaged snacks needing little or no preparation.

junkie (also **junky**) ▶ **noun** informal a drug addict.
■[with modifier] a person with a compulsive habit or obsessive dependency on something: *power junkies.*
– ORIGIN 1920s (originally US): from **JUNK¹**.

junk mail ▶ **noun** [mass noun] informal unsolicited advertising or promotional material received through the post.

junk shop ▶ **noun** informal a shop selling second-hand goods or inexpensive antiques.

junky informal ▶ **adjective** regarded as useless or of little value.
▶ **noun** (pl. **-ies**) variant spelling of **JUNKIE**.

junkyard ▶ **noun** US term for **SCRAPYARD**.

Juno /ˈdʒuːnəʊ/ **1** Roman Mythology the most important goddess of the Roman state, wife of Jupiter. She was originally an ancient Italian goddess. Greek equivalent **HERA**.
2 Astronomy asteroid 3, discovered in 1804 (diameter 244 km).

Junoesque /ˌdʒuːnəʊˈɛsk/ ▶ **adjective** (of a woman) imposingly tall and shapely.
– ORIGIN mid 19th cent.: from **JUNO** + **-ESQUE**.

Junr ▶ **abbreviation for** Junior (in names).

junta /ˈdʒʌntə, ˈhʊ-/ ▶ **noun 1** a military or political group that rules a country after taking power by force: *the country's ruling military junta.*
2 historical a deliberative or administrative council in Spain or Portugal.
– ORIGIN early 17th cent. (in sense 2): from Spanish and Portuguese, from Latin *juncta*, feminine past participle of *jungere* 'to join'.

junto /ˈdʒʌntəʊ/ ▶ **noun** (pl. **-os**) historical a political grouping or faction, especially in 17th- and 18th-century Britain.
– ORIGIN alteration of **JUNTA**, on the pattern of Spanish nouns ending in *-o*.

Jupiter /ˈdʒuːpɪtə/ **1** Roman Mythology the chief god of the Roman state religion, originally a sky god associated with thunder and lightning. His wife was Juno. Also called **JOVE**. Greek equivalent **ZEUS**. [ORIGIN: Latin, from *Jovis pater*, literally 'Father Jove'.]
2 Astronomy the largest planet in the solar system, a gas giant which is the fifth in order from the sun and one of the brightest objects in the night sky.

> Jupiter orbits between Mars and Saturn at an average distance of 778 million km from the sun. Although it has an equatorial diameter of 142,800 km the planet rotates in less than ten hours. Its upper atmosphere consists mainly of hydrogen with swirling clouds of ammonia and methane, with a circulation system that results in a number of distinct latitudinal bands. There are at least sixteen satellites, four of which (the Galilean moons) are visible through binoculars, and a faint ring system.

Jura¹ /ˈʒʊərə, French ʒyʀa/ a system of mountain ranges on the border of France and Switzerland.

Jura² /ˈdʒʊərə/ an island of the Inner Hebrides, north of Islay and south of Mull, separated from the west coast of Scotland by the Sound of Jura.

jural /ˈdʒʊər(ə)l/ ▶ **adjective** formal of or relating to the law.
■Philosophy of or relating to rights and obligations.
– ORIGIN mid 17th cent.: from Latin *jus, jur-* 'law, right' + **-AL**.

Jurassic /dʒʊˈrasɪk/ ▶ **adjective** Geology of, relating to, or denoting the second period of the Mesozoic era, between the Triassic and Cretaceous periods.
■[as noun **the Jurassic**] the Jurassic period or the system of rocks deposited during it.

> The Jurassic lasted from about 208 to 146 million years ago. Large reptiles, including the largest known dinosaurs, were dominant on both land and sea. Ammonites were abundant, and the first birds (including Archaeopteryx) appeared.

– ORIGIN mid 19th cent.: from French *jurassique*; named after the *Jura* Mountains (see **JURA¹**).

jurat /ˈdʒʊərat/ ▶ **noun** Law **1** chiefly historical a person who has taken an oath or who performs a duty on oath, e.g. a juror.
■(in the Channel Islands) a magistrate or other public official.
2 a statement on an affidavit of when, where, and before whom it was sworn.
– ORIGIN late Middle English: based on Latin *juratus* 'sworn', past participle of Latin *jurare*.

juridical /dʒʊˈrɪdɪk(ə)l/ ▶ **adjective** Law of or relating to judicial proceedings and the administration of the law.
– DERIVATIVES **juridically** adverb.
– ORIGIN early 16th cent.: from Latin *juridicus* (from *jus, jur-* 'law' + *dicere* 'say') + **-AL**.

jurisconsult /ˌdʒʊərɪskənˈsʌlt/ ▶ **noun** Law, chiefly historical an expert on law.
– ORIGIN early 17th cent.: from Latin *jurisconsultus*, from *jus, jur-* 'law' + *consultus* 'skilled' (from *consulere* 'take counsel').

jurisdiction /ˌdʒʊərɪsˈdɪkʃ(ə)n/ ▶ **noun** [mass noun] the official power to make legal decisions and judgements: *the English court had no **jurisdiction over** the defendants | he refused to acknowledge the **jurisdiction of** the bishop of Rome.*
■the extent of this power: *the claim will be **within the jurisdiction** of the industrial tribunal.* ■[count noun] a system of law courts; a judicature. ■[count noun] the territory or sphere of activity over which the legal authority of a court or other institution extends.
– DERIVATIVES **jurisdictional** adjective.
– ORIGIN Middle English: from Old French *jurediction*, from Latin *jurisdictio(n-)*, from *jus, jur-* 'law' + *dictio* 'saying' (from *dicere* 'say').

jurisprudence /ˌdʒʊərɪsˈpruːd(ə)ns/ ▶ **noun** [mass noun] the theory or philosophy of law.
■a legal system: *American jurisprudence.*
– DERIVATIVES **jurisprudent** adjective & noun, **jurisprudential** adjective.
– ORIGIN early 17th cent.: from late Latin *jurisprudentia*, from Latin *jus, jur-* 'law' + *prudentia* 'knowledge'.

jurist /ˈdʒʊərɪst/ ▶ **noun** an expert in or writer on law.
■N. Amer. a lawyer or a judge.
– DERIVATIVES **juristic** adjective.
– ORIGIN late 15th cent. (in the sense 'lawyer'): from French *juriste*, medieval Latin *jurista*, from *jus, jur-* 'law'.

juror ▶ **noun** a member of a jury.
■historical a person taking an oath, especially one of allegiance. Compare with **NONJUROR**.
– ORIGIN late Middle English: from Old French *jureor*, from Latin *jurator*, from *jurare* 'swear', from *jus, jur-* 'law'.

jury¹ ▶ **noun** (pl. **-ies**) a body of people (typically twelve in number) sworn to give a verdict in a legal case on the basis of evidence submitted to them in court: *the jury returned unanimous guilty verdicts.*
■a body of people selected to judge a competition.
▶ **verb** (**-ies, -ied**) [with obj.] (usu. **be juried**) chiefly N. Amer. judge (an art or craft exhibition or exhibit).
– PHRASES **the jury is out** a decision has not yet been reached on a controversial subject: *the jury is still out on whether self-regulation by doctors is adequate.*
– ORIGIN late Middle English: from Old French *juree* 'oath, inquiry', from Latin *jurata*, feminine past participle of *jurare* 'swear' (see **JUROR**).

jury² ▶ **adjective** [attrib.] Nautical (of a mast or other fitting) improvised or temporary: *we need to get that jury rudder fixed.*
– ORIGIN early 19th cent.: independent usage of the first element of early 17th-cent. *jury-mast* 'temporary mast', of uncertain origin (compare with **JURY-RIGGED**).

jury box ▶ **noun** a segregated area in which the jury sits in a court of law.

jury-rigged ▶ **adjective** (of a ship) having temporary makeshift rigging.
■chiefly US makeshift; improvised: *jury-rigged classrooms in gymnasiums.*
– ORIGIN late 18th cent.: *jury* perhaps based on Old French *ajurie* 'aid'.

jus /ʒuː, French ʒy/ ▶ **noun** (especially in French cuisine) a sauce: *chicken with a rich game jus.*
– ORIGIN French.

jus cogens /ˌdʒʌs ˈkəʊdʒɛnz/ ▶ **noun** [mass noun] Law the principles which form the norms of international law that cannot be set aside.
– ORIGIN Latin, literally 'compelling law'.

jus gentium /ˌdʒʌs ˈdʒɛntɪəm, -ʃɪəm, ˈgɛntɪəm/ ▶ **noun** [mass noun] Law international law.
– ORIGIN Latin, literally 'law of nations'.

Jussieu /ʒuːˈsjəː, French ʒusjœ/, Antoine Laurent de (1748–1836), French botanist. Jussieu grouped plants into families on the basis of common essential properties and, in *Genera Plantarum* (1789), developed the system on which modern plant classification is based.

jussive /ˈdʒʌsɪv/ ▶ **adjective** Grammar (of a form of a verb) expressing a command.
– ORIGIN mid 19th cent.: from Latin *juss-* 'commanded' (from the verb *jubere*) + **-IVE**.

just ▶ **adjective** based on or behaving according to what is morally right and fair: *a just and democratic society | fighting for a just cause.*
■(of treatment) deserved or appropriate in the circumstances: *we all get our just deserts.* ■(of an opinion or appraisal) well founded; justifiable: *these simplistic approaches have been the subject of just criticism.*
▶ **adverb 1** exactly: *that's just what I need | you're a human being, just like everyone else | conditions were **just as** bad | you can have it, but **not just yet**.*
■exactly or almost exactly at this or that moment: *she's just coming | we were just finishing breakfast.*

2 very recently; in the immediate past: *I've just seen the local paper.*
3 barely; by a little: *I got here just after nine* | *inflation fell to just over 4 per cent* | *I only just caught the train.*
4 simply; only; no more than: *they were just interested in making money.*
■ really; absolutely (used for emphasis): *they're just great.* ■ used as a polite formula for giving permission or making a request: *just help yourselves.* ■ [with modal] possibly (used to indicate a slight chance of something happening or being true): *it might just help.*
5 expressing agreement: *'Simon really messed things up.' 'Didn't he just?'*
– PHRASES **just about** informal almost exactly; nearly: *he can do just about anything.* **just as well** a good or fortunate thing: *it was just as well I didn't know at the time.* **just in case** as a precaution. **just a minute** (or **moment**, or **second**, etc.) used to ask someone to wait or pause for a short time. ■ used to interrupt someone, especially in protest or disagreement. **just now 1** at this moment: *it's pretty hectic just now.* **2** a little time ago: *she was talking to me just now.* **3** S. African in a little while; very soon: *I'll come just now but I want breakfast first.* **just on** (with reference to time and numbers) exactly: *it was just on midnight.* **just so 1** arranged or done very neatly and carefully: *polishing the furniture and making everything just so.* **2** formal used to express agreement.
– DERIVATIVES **justly** adverb, **justness** noun.
– ORIGIN late Middle English: via Old French from Latin *justus*, from *jus* 'law, right'.

juste milieu /ˌʒuːst miːˈljəː, French ʒystə miljø/ ▶ noun the happy medium; judicious moderation.
– ORIGIN French, literally 'correct mean'.

justice ▶ noun **1** [mass noun] just behaviour or treatment: *a concern for justice, peace, and genuine respect for people.*
■ the quality of being fair and reasonable: *the justice of his case.* ■ the administration of the law or authority in maintaining this: *a tragic miscarriage of justice.*
2 a judge or magistrate, in particular a judge of the Supreme Court of a country or state.
– PHRASES **bring someone to justice** arrest someone for a crime and ensure that they are tried in court. **do oneself justice** perform as well as one is able to. **do someone/thing justice** do, treat, or represent with due fairness or appreciation: *the brief menu does not do justice to the food.* **in justice to** out of fairness to: *I say this in justice to both of you.* **Mr** (or **Mrs**) **Justice** Brit. a form of address or reference to a judge of the supreme court (e.g. a High Court judge). **rough justice** see **ROUGH**.
– DERIVATIVES **justiceship** noun (in sense 2).
– ORIGIN late Old English *iustise* 'administration of the law', via Old French from Latin *justitia*, from *justus* (see **JUST**).

Justice of the Peace ▶ noun (in the UK) a lay magistrate appointed to hear minor cases, grant licences, etc., in a town, county, or other local district.

justiciable /dʒʌˈstɪʃəb(ə)l/ ▶ adjective Law (of a state or action) subject to trial in a court of law.
– ORIGIN late Middle English: from Old French, from *justicier* 'bring to trial', from medieval Latin *justitiare*, from Latin *justitia* 'equity', from *justus* (see **JUST**).

justiciar /dʒʌˈstɪʃə/ ▶ noun historical an administrator of justice, in particular:
■ a regent and deputy presiding over the court of a Norman or early Plantagenet king of England. ■ either of two supreme judges in medieval Scotland.
– ORIGIN late 15th cent.: from medieval Latin *justitiarius* (see **JUSTICIARY**).

justiciary /dʒʌˈstɪʃ(ə)ri/ ▶ noun (pl. **-ies**) chiefly Scottish an administrator of justice.
■ [mass noun] the administration of justice: [as modifier] *justiciary cases.*
– ORIGIN mid 16th cent.: from medieval Latin *justitiarius*, from *justitia*, from *justus* (see **JUST**).

justifiable ▶ adjective able to be shown to be right or reasonable; defensible: *it is not financially justifiable* | *their justifiable fears.*
– DERIVATIVES **justifiability** noun, **justifiableness** noun, **justifiably** adverb *he was justifiably angry.*
– ORIGIN early 16th cent. (in the sense 'justiciable'): from French, from *justifier* 'to justify'.

justifiable homicide ▶ noun [mass noun] the killing of a person in circumstances which allow the act to be regarded in law as without criminal guilt.

justified ▶ adjective **1** having, done for, or marked by a good or legitimate reason: *the doctors were justified in treating her.*
2 Theology declared or made righteous in the sight of God.
3 Printing having been adjusted so that the print fills a space evenly or forms a straight line at the margin: [in combination] *the output is left-justified.*

justify /ˈdʒʌstɪfʌɪ/ ▶ verb (**-ies, -ied**) [with obj.] **1** show or prove to be right or reasonable: *the person appointed has fully justified our confidence.*
■ be a good reason for: *the situation was grave enough to justify further investigation.*
2 Theology declare or make righteous in the sight of God.
3 Printing adjust (a line of type or piece of text) so that the print fills a space evenly or forms a straight edge at the margin.
– DERIVATIVES **justification** noun, **justificatory** adjective, **justifier** noun.
– ORIGIN Middle English (in the senses 'administer justice to' and 'inflict a judicial penalty on'): from Old French *justifier*, from Christian Latin *justificare* 'do justice to', from Latin *justus* (see **JUST**).

Justin, St (c.100–165), Christian philosopher; known as **St Justin the Martyr**. According to tradition he was martyred in Rome together with some of his followers. He is remembered for his *Apologia* (c.150). Feast day, 1 June.

Justinian /dʒʌˈstɪnɪən/ (483–565), Byzantine emperor 527–65; Latin name *Flavius Petrus Sabbatius Justinianus*. Through his general Belisarius he regained North Africa and Spain. He codified Roman law (529) and carried out a building programme throughout the Empire, of which St Sophia at Constantinople (532) was a part.

just-in-time ▶ adjective [attrib.] denoting a manufacturing system in which materials or components are delivered immediately before they are required in order to minimize storage costs.

jut ▶ verb (**jutted, jutting**) [no obj., with adverbial] extend out, over, or beyond the main body or line of something: *a rock jutted out from the side of the bank.*
■ [with obj.] cause (something, such as one's chin) to protrude: *she put up her head and jutted out her chin with determination.*
▶ noun a point that sticks out.
– ORIGIN mid 16th cent.: variant of **JET**[1].

Jute /dʒuːt/ ▶ noun a member of a Germanic people that (according to Bede) joined the Angles and Saxons in invading Britain in the 5th century, settling in a region including Kent and the Isle of Wight. They may have come from Jutland.
– DERIVATIVES **Jutish** adjective.
– ORIGIN Old English *Eotas, Iotas*, influenced later in spelling by medieval Latin *Jutae, Juti.*

jute /dʒuːt/ ▶ noun [mass noun] **1** rough fibre made from the stems of a tropical Old World plant, used for making twine and rope or woven into sacking or matting.
2 the herbaceous plant which is cultivated for this fibre, with edible young shoots.
● Genus *Corchorus*, family Tiliaceae: several species, in particular *C. capsularis* of China and *C. olitorius* of India.
■ used in names of other plants that yield fibre, e.g. **Chinese jute.**
– ORIGIN mid 18th cent.: from Bengali *jhūṭo*, from Prakrit *jūṭi.*

Jutland /ˈdʒʌtlənd/ a peninsula of NW Europe, forming the mainland of Denmark together with

the north German state of Schleswig-Holstein. Danish name **JYLLAND**.

Jutland, Battle of a major naval battle in the First World War, fought between the British Grand Fleet under Admiral Jellicoe and the German High Seas Fleet in the North Sea west of Jutland on 31 May 1916. Although the battle was indecisive the German fleet never again sought a full-scale engagement, and the Allies retained control of the North Sea.

Juvenal /ˈdʒuːvɪn(ə)l/ (c.60–c.140), Roman satirist; Latin name *Decimus Junius Juvenalis*. His sixteen verse satires present a savage attack on the vice and folly of Roman society, chiefly in the reign of the emperor Domitian.

juvenescence /ˌdʒuːvəˈnɛs(ə)ns/ ▶ noun [mass noun] formal the state or period of being young.
– DERIVATIVES **juvenescent** adjective.
– ORIGIN early 19th cent.: from Latin *juvenescent-* 'reaching the age of youth', from the verb *juvenescere*, from *juvenis* 'young'.

juvenile /ˈdʒuːvənʌɪl/ ▶ adjective of, for, or relating to young people: *juvenile crime.*
■ childish; immature: *she's bored with my juvenile conversation.* ■ of or denoting a theatrical or film role representing a young person: *the romantic juvenile lead.* ■ of or relating to young birds or other animals.
▶ noun a young person.
■ Law a person below the age at which ordinary criminal prosecution is possible (18 in most countries). ■ a young bird or other animal. ■ an actor who plays juvenile roles.
– DERIVATIVES **juvenility** /-ˈnɪlɪti/ noun.
– ORIGIN early 17th cent.: from Latin *juvenilis*, from *juvenis* 'young, a young person'.

juvenile court ▶ noun a court of law responsible for the trial or legal supervision of children under a specified age (18 in most countries). Compare with **YOUTH COURT**.

juvenile delinquency ▶ noun [mass noun] the habitual committing of criminal acts or offences by a young person, especially one below the age at which ordinary criminal prosecution is possible.
– DERIVATIVES **juvenile deliquent** noun.

juvenile hormone ▶ noun Entomology any of a number of hormones regulating larval development in insects and inhibiting metamorphosis.

juvenile offender ▶ noun a person below a specific age (18 in most countries) who has committed a crime.

juvenilia /ˌdʒuːvəˈnɪlɪə/ ▶ plural noun works produced by an author or artist while still young.
– ORIGIN early 17th cent.: from Latin, neuter plural of *juvenilis* (see **JUVENILE**).

juvenilize /ˈdʒuːvənɪlʌɪz/ (also **-ise**) ▶ verb [with obj.] make or keep young or youthful; arrest the development of.
■ [as adj. **juvenilized**] Entomology (of an insect or part of one) having a juvenile appearance or physiology; showing arrested or reversed development.

juvie /ˈdʒuːvi/ ▶ noun (pl. **-ies**) informal a youth, especially a juvenile delinquent.
– ORIGIN 1940s: abbreviation of **JUVENILE**.

juxtaglomerular /ˌdʒʌkstəɡlɒˈmɛrʊlə/ ▶ adjective Anatomy denoting a group of structures secreting regulatory hormones into the arteriole which leads into a glomerulus in the kidney.
– ORIGIN 1930s: from Latin *juxta* 'near to' + *glomerular* (see **GLOMERULUS**).

juxtapose /ˌdʒʌkstəˈpəʊz/ ▶ verb [with obj.] place or deal with close together for contrasting effect: *black-and-white photos of slums were starkly juxtaposed with colour images.*
– DERIVATIVES **juxtaposition** noun, **juxtapositional** adjective.
– ORIGIN mid 19th cent.: from French *juxtaposer*, from Latin *juxta* 'next' + French *poser* 'to place'.

Jylland /ˈjylan/ Danish name for **JUTLAND**.
Jyväskylä /ˈjuːvaskʊlə/ a city in central Finland; pop. 66,530 (1990).

Kk

K¹ (also **k**) ▸ noun (pl. **Ks** or **K's**) the eleventh letter of the alphabet.
■ denoting the next after J in a set of items, categories, etc.

K² ▸ abbreviation for ■ Cambodia (international vehicle registration). [ORIGIN: from *Kampuchea*.] ■ kelvin(s). ■ Computing kilobyte(s). ■ kilometre(s). ■ N. Amer. kindergarten. ■ king (used especially in describing play in card games and recording moves in chess): *declarer overruffed with* ♦*K and led another spade* | *18.Ke2*. ■ knit (as an instruction in knitting patterns): *K 42 rows*. ■ Köchel (catalogue of Mozart's works): *the Sinfonia Concertante, K364*. ■ informal thousand (used chiefly in expressing salaries or other sums of money). [ORIGIN: from **KILO-** 'thousand'.]
▸ symbol for the chemical element potassium. [ORIGIN: from modern Latin *kalium*.]

k ▸ abbreviation for [in combination] (in units of measurement) kilo-: *a distance of 700 kpc*.
▸ symbol for a constant in a formula or equation.
■ Chemistry Boltzmann's constant.

K2 the highest mountain in the Karakoram range, on the border between Pakistan and China. It is the second highest peak in the world, rising to 8,611 m (28,250 ft). It was discovered in 1856 and named K2 because it was the second peak to be surveyed in the Karakoram range. It was also formerly known as Mount Godwin-Austen after Col. H. H. Godwin-Austen, who first surveyed it. Also called **DAPSANG**.

ka /kɑː/ ▸ noun (in ancient Egypt) the supposed spiritual part of an individual human being or god, which survived (with the soul) after death and could reside in a statue of the person. See also **BA**.

Kaaba /'kɑːəbə/ (also **Caaba**) a square stone building in the centre of the Great Mosque at Mecca, the site most holy to Muslims and towards which they must face when praying. It stands on the site of a pre-Islamic shrine said to have been built by Abraham, and a sacred Black Stone is set in its south-eastern corner.
– ORIGIN from Arabic (*al-*)*ka'ba*, literally '(the) square house'.

Kaapenaar /'kɑːpəˌnɑː/ ▸ noun S. African **1** an inhabitant of Cape Town or the Cape Peninsula.
2 (**kaapenaar**) a small silvery edible marine fish common around the Cape.
● *Argyrozona argyrozona*, family Sparidae.
– ORIGIN Afrikaans, from *kaap* 'Cape' + the personal suffix *-enaar*.

kabaddi /'kʌbədi/ ▸ noun [mass noun] a sport of Indian origin played by teams of seven on a circular sand court. The players attempt to tag or capture opponents and must hold their breath while running, repeating the word 'kabaddi' to show that they are doing so.
– ORIGIN of uncertain origin; compare with Kannada *kabalisu* 'to gulp' and Hindi *kabaḍḍī* 'shout "kabaddi"'.

kabaka /kə'bɑːkə/ ▸ noun the traditional ruler of the Baganda people of Uganda.
– ORIGIN a local title.

Kabalega Falls /ˌkabə'leɪɡə/ a waterfall on the lower Victoria Nile near Lake Albert, in NW Uganda. Former name **MURCHISON FALLS**.

Kabardian /kə'bɑːdɪən/ ▸ adjective of or relating to an indigenous people of the NW Caucasus.
▸ noun **1** a member of this people.
2 [mass noun] the North Caucasian language of this people, with about 350,000 speakers.
– ORIGIN from Russian *Kabarda* place name + **-IAN**.

Kabardino-Balkaria /ˌkabə'diːnəʊ balˈkɑːrɪə/ an autonomous republic of SW Russia, on the border with Georgia; pop. 768,000 (1990); capital, Nalchik. Also called **KABARDA-BALKAR REPUBLIC** /ˌkabədə bal'kɑː/.

Kabbalah /kə'bɑːlə, 'kabələ/ (also **Kabbala**, **Cabbala**, **Cabala**, or **Qabalah**) ▸ noun the ancient Jewish tradition of mystical interpretation of the Bible, first transmitted orally and using esoteric methods (including ciphers). It reached the height of its influence in the later Middle Ages and remains significant in Hasidism.
– DERIVATIVES **Kabbalism** noun, **Kabbalist** noun, **Kabbalistic** adjective.
– ORIGIN from medieval Latin *cabala, cabbala*, from Rabbinical Hebrew *qabbālāh* 'tradition', from *qibbēl* 'receive, accept'.

kabeljou /ˌkab(ə)l'jəʊ/ (also **kabeljauw**) ▸ noun (pl. same) S. African a large predatory marine fish of the drum family, found in the Mediterranean, East Atlantic, and SW Indian Ocean. It is an important food fish in southern Africa.
● *Argyrosomus hololepidotus*, family Sciaenidae.
– ORIGIN early 18th cent.: from Afrikaans, from Dutch, 'cod'.

Kabila /ka'biːlə/, Laurent-Désiré (1939–2001), African statesman, President of the Democratic Republic of Congo (formerly Zaire) 1997–2001. Kabila's forces overthrew President Mobutu in 1997. On taking power Kabila changed the name of the country to Democratic Republic of Congo.

Kabinett /ˌkabɪ'nɛt, German ˌkabɪ'nɛt/ ▸ noun a wine of German origin or style of superior or reserve quality, especially one made from a specified quality of grape must, without added sugar.
– ORIGIN from German *Kabinettwein*, literally 'chamber wine'.

kabloona /kə'bluːnə/ ▸ noun (pl. **kabloonas**, **kabloonat** /-nat/) Canadian (among Inuit people) a person who is not a member of the Inuit; a white person.
– ORIGIN from Inuit *kabluna* 'big eyebrow'.

kabob /kə'bɒb/ ▸ noun US spelling of **KEBAB**.

kaboodle /kə'buːd(ə)l/ ▸ noun variant spelling of **CABOODLE**.

kaboom /kə'buːm/ ▸ exclamation used to represent the sound of a loud explosion.

kabuki /kə'buːki/ ▸ noun [mass noun] a form of traditional Japanese drama with highly stylized song, mime, and dance, now performed only by male actors, using exaggerated gestures and body movements to express emotions, and including historical plays, domestic dramas, and dance pieces.
– ORIGIN Japanese, originally as a verb meaning 'act dissolutely', later interpreted as if from *ka* 'song' + *bu* 'dance' + *ki* 'art'.

Kabul /'kɑːbɒl/ the capital of Afghanistan; pop.

700,000 (est. 1993). It is situated in the north-east of the country, with a strategic position commanding the mountain passes through the Hindu Kush, especially the Khyber Pass. It was capital of the Mogul empire 1504–1738 and in 1773 replaced Kandahar as capital of an independent Afghanistan.

Kabwe /'kabweɪ/ a town in central Zambia, situated to the north of Lusaka; pop. 167,000 (1990). It is the site of a cave which has yielded human fossils associated with the Upper Pleistocene period. Former name (1904–65) **BROKEN HILL**.

Kabyle /kə'baɪl/ ▸ noun **1** a member of a Berber people inhabiting northern Algeria.
2 [mass noun] the Berber dialect of this people.
▸ adjective of or relating to this people or their language.
– ORIGIN probably from Arabic *kabā'il*, plural of *kabīla* 'tribe'.

kachha ▸ noun variant spelling of **KUCCHA**.

Kachin /'katʃɪn/ ▸ noun **1** a member of an indigenous people living in northern Burma (Myanmar) and adjacent parts of China and India.
2 [mass noun] the Tibeto-Burman language of this people, with about 500,000 speakers.
▸ adjective of or relating to this people or their language.

kachina /kə'tʃiːnə/ (also **katsina**) ▸ noun (pl. **kachinas**) a deified ancestral spirit in the mythology of Pueblo Indians.
■ (also **kachina dancer**) a person who represents such a spirit in ceremonial dances. ■ (also **kachina doll**) a small carved figure representing such a spirit.
– ORIGIN from Hopi *kacina* 'supernatural', of Keres origin.

kadai /kʌ'dʌɪ/ ▸ noun variant spelling of **KARAHI**.

kadaitcha ▸ noun variant spelling of **KURDAITCHA**.

Kádár /'kɑːdɑː/, János (1912–89), Hungarian statesman, First Secretary of the Hungarian Socialist Workers' Party 1956–88 and Prime Minister 1956–8 and 1961–5. After crushing the Hungarian uprising of 1956, Kádár consistently supported the Soviet Union. His policy of 'consumer socialism' made Hungary the most affluent state in eastern Europe.

Kaddish /'kadɪʃ/ ▸ noun an ancient Jewish prayer sequence regularly recited in the synagogue service, including thanksgiving and praise and concluding with a prayer for universal peace.
■ a form of this prayer sequence recited for the dead.
– ORIGIN from Aramaic *qaddīš* 'holy'.

kadi ▸ noun (pl. **kadis**) variant spelling of **CADI**.

Kadiköy /kɑ'dikœj/ Turkish name for **CHALCEDON**.

kaffeeklatsch /'kafeɪˌklatʃ/ ▸ noun an informal social gathering at which coffee is served.
■ [mass noun] talking or gossip at such gatherings.
– ORIGIN German, from *Kaffee* 'coffee' + *Klatsch* 'gossip'.

Kaffir /'kafə/ ▸ noun offensive, chiefly S. African an insulting and contemptuous term for a black African.
– ORIGIN from Arabic *kāfir* 'infidel', from *kafara* 'not believe'.

USAGE The word **Kaffir** is first recorded in the 16th century (as **Caffre**) and was originally simply a descriptive term for a particular ethnic group. Now it is always a racially abusive and offensive term when used of people, and in South Africa its use is actionable.

Kaffir lily ▶ noun either of two South African plants with strap-like leaves and stems bearing a number of red, pink, or orange flowers.
● a plant with star-shaped flowers (*Schizostylis coccinea*, family Iridaceae). ● another term for **CLIVIA**.

kaffiyeh ▶ noun variant spelling of **KEFFIYEH**.

Kafir /ˈkafə/ ▶ noun a member of a people of the Hindu Kush mountains of NE Afghanistan.
– DERIVATIVES **Kafiri** adjective & noun.
– ORIGIN from Arabic *kāfir* (see **KAFFIR**).

kafir /ˈkafə/ ▶ noun a person who is not a Muslim (used chiefly by Muslims).
– ORIGIN from Arabic *kāfir* 'infidel, unbeliever'. Compare with **KAFFIR**.

Kafka /ˈkafkə/, Franz (1883–1924), Czech novelist, who wrote in German. His work is characterized by its portrayal of an enigmatic and nightmarish reality where the individual is perceived as lonely, perplexed, and threatened. Notable works: *The Metamorphosis* (1917) and *The Trial* (1925).
– DERIVATIVES **Kafkaesque** /ˌkafkəˈɛsk/ adjective.

kaftan /ˈkaftan/ (also **caftan**) ▶ noun a man's long belted tunic, worn in countries of the Near East.
■ a woman's long loose dress. ■ a loose shirt or top.
– ORIGIN late 16th cent.: from Turkish, from Persian *kaftān*, partly influenced by French *cafetan*.

Kagoshima /ˌkaɡəˈʃiːmə/ a city and port in Japan; pop. 537,000 (1990). Situated on the southern coast of Kyushu island, on the Satsuma Peninsula, it is noted for its porcelain (Satsuma ware).

kagoul (also **kagoule**) ▶ noun variant spelling of **CAGOULE**.

kagu /ˈkɑːɡuː/ ▶ noun a crested, almost flightless bluish-grey bird related to the rails, which is found only on the Pacific island of New Caledonia, and is now endangered.
● *Rhynochetos jubatus*, the only member of the family Rhynochetidae.
– ORIGIN mid 19th cent.: from Melanesian.

kahawai /ˈkɑːwʌɪ/ ▶ noun (pl. same) New Zealand term for *Australian salmon* (see **SALMON** (sense 2)).
– ORIGIN Maori.

kahikatea /ˌkɑːkɪkəˈtiːə/ ▶ noun a tall coniferous New Zealand tree which is used for its timber and resin. Its seeds, which are borne on conspicuous red stems, were formerly eaten by the Maoris.
● *Podocarpus* (or *Dacrycarpus*) *dacrydioides*, family Podocarpaceae.
– ORIGIN early 19th cent.: from Maori.

kahuna /kəˈhuːnə/ ▶ noun (in Hawaii) a wise man or shaman.
■ N. Amer. informal an important person; the person in charge: *one big kahuna runs the whole show*. ■ N. Amer. informal (in surfing) a very large wave.
– ORIGIN Hawaiian.

kai /kʌɪ/ (also **kaikai** /ˈkʌɪkʌɪ/) ▶ noun [mass noun] NZ informal food.
– ORIGIN Maori.

Kaifeng /kʌɪˈfɛŋ/ a city in Henan province, eastern China, on the Yellow River; pop. 693,100 (1990). Established in the 4th century BC, it is one of the oldest cities in China.

kainga /ˈkɑːɪŋə/ ▶ noun NZ a Maori village or settlement.
– ORIGIN Maori.

kainic acid /ˈkʌɪnɪk/ ▶ noun [mass noun] Medicine an organic acid extracted from a red alga, used to kill intestinal worms.
● Chem. formula: $C_{10}H_{15}NO_4$.
– ORIGIN mid 20th cent.: from Japanese *kainin* (from *kainin-sō*, name of the alga *Digenea simplex* from which it is extracted) + **-IC**.

kainite /ˈkʌɪnʌɪt, ˈkeɪnʌɪt/ ▶ noun [mass noun] a white mineral consisting of a double salt of hydrated magnesium sulphate and potassium chloride.
– ORIGIN mid 19th cent.: from German *Kainit*, from Greek *kainos* 'new, recent', because of the mineral's recent formation.

kairomone /ˈkʌɪrəməʊn/ ▶ noun Biology a chemical substance emitted by an organism and detected by another of a different species which gains advantage from this, e.g. a parasite seeking a host.
– ORIGIN late 20th cent.: from Greek *kairos*

'advantage, opportunity', on the pattern of *pheromone* .

kairos /ˈkʌɪrɒs/ ▶ noun [in sing.] chiefly Theology a propitious moment for decision or action.
– ORIGIN mid 20th cent.: Greek, literally 'opportunity'.

Kairouan /ˌkʌɪruːˈɑːn/ a city in NE Tunisia; pop. 72,250 (1984). It is a Muslim holy city and a place of pilgrimage.

Kaiser /ˈkʌɪzə/, German *kaɪzɐ/, Georg (1878–1945), German dramatist. He is best known for his expressionist plays *The Burghers of Calais* (1914), and *Gas I* (1918) and *Gas II* (1920); the last two provide a gruesome vision of futuristic science, ending with the extinction of all life by poisonous gas.

kaiser /ˈkʌɪzə/ ▶ noun **1** historical the German Emperor, the Emperor of Austria, or the head of the Holy Roman Empire: [as title] *Kaiser Wilhelm*.
2 (also **kaiser roll**) N. Amer. a round, crisp bread roll made by folding the corners of a square of dough into the centre, resulting in a pinwheel shape when baked.
– PHRASES **the Kaiser's War** dated the First World War.
– DERIVATIVES **kaisership** noun.
– ORIGIN Middle English *cayser*, from Old Norse *keisari*, based on Latin *Caesar* (see **CAESAR**), and later reinforced by Middle Dutch *keiser*. The modern English form (early 19th cent.) derives from German *Kaiser*.

Kaiserslautern /ˌkʌɪzəsˈlaʊt(ə)n, German ˌkaɪzɐsˈlaʊtɐn/ a city in western Germany, in Rhineland-Palatinate; pop. 100,540 (1991).

Kaiser Wilhelm, Wilhelm II of Germany (see **WILHELM II**).

kaizen /ˈkʌɪzɛn/ ▶ noun [mass noun] a Japanese business philosophy of continuous improvement of working practices, personal efficiency, etc.
– ORIGIN Japanese, literally 'improvement'.

kajal /ˈkʌdʒəl/ ▶ noun [mass noun] a black powder, typically lampblack, used in the Indian subcontinent as a cosmetic for women and children, either around the eyes or as a mark on the forehead.
– ORIGIN from Hindi *kājal*.

kaka /ˈkɑːkɑː/ ▶ noun a large New Zealand parrot with olive-brown and dull green upper parts and reddish underparts.
● *Nestor meridionalis*, family Psittacidae.
– ORIGIN late 18th cent.: from Maori.

kaka-beak (also **kaka-bill**) ▶ noun New Zealand term for **CLIANTHUS**.

kakapo /ˈkɑːkəpəʊ/ ▶ noun (pl. **-os**) a large flightless New Zealand parrot with greenish plumage, which is nocturnal, ground-dwelling, and now endangered. Also called **OWL PARROT**.
● *Strigops habroptilus*, family Psittacidae.
– ORIGIN mid 19th cent.: from Maori, literally 'night kaka'.

kakemono /ˌkɑːkɪˈməʊnəʊ, ˌkaki-/ ▶ noun (pl. **-os**) a Japanese unframed painting made on paper or silk and displayed as a wall hanging.
– ORIGIN late 19th cent.: Japanese, from *kake-* 'hang, suspend' + *mono* 'thing'.

kaki /ˈkɑːki/ ▶ noun the Japanese persimmon.
– ORIGIN early 18th cent.: from Japanese.

Kakiemon /kəˈkiːəmɒn/ ▶ adjective [attrib.] of or relating to a style of Japanese porcelain with sparse asymmetrical designs on a white ground, developed in the early 17th century.
– ORIGIN named after Sakaida Kakiemon (1596–1666), the first Japanese potter to work in this style.

Kalaallit Nunaat /kɑːˌlɑːlɪt nəˈnɑːt/ Inuit name for **GREENLAND**.

kala-azar /ˌkɑːləˈɑːzɑː/ ▶ noun [mass noun] a form of the disease leishmaniasis marked by emaciation, anaemia, fever, and enlargement of the liver and spleen.
● This is caused by *Leishmania donovani*, phylum Kinetoplastida, kingdom Protista.
– ORIGIN late 19th cent.: from Assamese, from *kālā* 'black' + *āzār* 'disease' (because of the bronzing of the skin often associated with it).

Kalahari Desert /ˌkaləˈhɑːri/ a high, vast, arid plateau in southern Africa north of the Orange River. It comprises most of Botswana with parts in Namibia and South Africa.

kalamkari /ˌkʌləmˈkɑːri/ ▶ noun [mass noun] a type of

cotton cloth printed by hand, originally made in southern India.
– ORIGIN from Hindi *kalamkārī*, literally 'painting'.

kalanchoe /ˌkalənˈkəʊi/ ▶ noun a tropical succulent plant with clusters of tubular flowers, sometimes producing miniature plants along the edges of the leaves and grown as an indoor or greenhouse plant.
● Genus *Kalanchoe*, family Crassulaceae.
– ORIGIN mid 19th cent.: modern Latin, from French, based on Chinese *gāláncài*.

Kalashnikov /kəˈlaʃnɪkɒf, -ˈlaʃ-/ ▶ noun a type of rifle or sub-machine gun made in Russia.
– ORIGIN 1970s: named after Mikhail T. *Kalashnikov* (born 1919), the Russian designer of the weapons.

kale /keɪl/ ▶ noun [mass noun] **1** a hardy cabbage of a variety which produces erect stems with large leaves and no compact head. See also **CURLY KALE**.
2 N. Amer. informal, dated money.
– ORIGIN Middle English: northern English form of **COLE**.

kaleidoscope /kəˈlʌɪdəskəʊp/ ▶ noun a toy consisting of a tube containing mirrors and pieces of coloured glass or paper, whose reflections produce changing patterns when the tube is rotated.
■ [in sing.] a constantly changing pattern or sequence of objects or elements: *the dancers moved in a kaleidoscope of colour*.
– DERIVATIVES **kaleidoscopic** adjective, **kaleidoscopically** adverb.
– ORIGIN early 19th cent.: from Greek *kalos* 'beautiful' + *eidos* 'form' + **-SCOPE**.

kalends ▶ plural noun variant spelling of **CALENDS**.

Kalevala /ˈkɑːlɛˌvɑːlə/ a collection of Finnish legends transmitted orally until published in the 19th century, and now regarded as the Finnish national epic.
– ORIGIN of Karelian origin.

Kaleyard School a group of late 19th-century fiction writers, including J. M. Barrie, who described local town life in Scotland in a romantic vein and with much use of the vernacular.
– ORIGIN from Scots *kaleyard*, literally 'kitchen garden'.

Kalgan /kɑːlˈɡɑːn/ Mongolian name for **ZHANGJIAKOU**.

Kalgoorlie /kalˈɡʊəli/ a gold-mining town in Western Australia; pop. 11,100 (est. 1987). Gold was discovered there in 1887, leading to a gold rush in the 1890s.

Kali /ˈkɑːli/ Hinduism the most terrifying goddess, wife of Shiva, often identified with Durga, and in her benevolent aspect with Parvati. She is typically depicted as black, naked, old, and hideous.
– ORIGIN from Sanskrit *Kālī* 'black'.

kali /ˈkeɪlʌɪ, ˈkali/ ▶ noun old-fashioned term for **SALTWORT**.
– ORIGIN late 16th cent.: from colloquial Arabic *ḳalī* 'calcined ashes of Salsola (and similar plants)'; compare with **ALKALI**.

Kalidasa /ˌkɑːlɪˈdɑːsə/ (probably fl. 5th century AD), Indian poet and dramatist. He is best known for his drama *Sakuntala*, the love story of King Dushyanta and the maiden Sakuntala.

Kalimantan /ˌkalɪˈmantan/ a region of Indonesia, comprising the southern part of the island of Borneo.

kalimba /kəˈlɪmbə/ ▶ noun a type of African thumb piano.
– ORIGIN 1950s: a local word; related to **MARIMBA**.

Kalinin[1] /kəˈliːnɪn/ former name (1931–91) for **TVER**.

Kalinin[2] /kəˈliːnɪn/, Mikhail (Ivanovich) (1875–1946), Soviet statesman, head of state of the USSR 1919–46. He founded the newspaper *Pravda* (1912).

Kaliningrad /kəˈliːnɪnɡrad/ **1** a port on the Baltic coast of eastern Europe, capital of the Russian region of Kaliningrad; pop. 406,000 (1990). It was known by its German name of Königsberg until 1946, when it was ceded to the Soviet Union under the Potsdam Agreement and renamed in honour of Kalinin. Its port is ice-free all the year round and is a significant naval base for the Russian fleet.
2 a region of Russia, an enclave situated on the Baltic coast of eastern Europe; capital, Kaliningrad. It shares its borders with Lithuania and Poland and is separated from Russia by the intervening countries of Lithuania, Latvia, and Belarus.

Kalisz /'kɑːlɪʃ/ a city in central Poland; pop. 106,150 (1990).

kalkoentjie /kal'kʊɪŋki/ ▶ noun (pl. **-ies**) **1** South African term for **LONGCLAW**.
2 S. African a plant of the iris family with a flower that resembles a turkey's wattle.
● Genera *Gladiolus* and *Tritonia*, family Iridaceae: several species.
– ORIGIN Afrikaans, from *kalkoen* 'turkey' + the diminutive suffix *-tjie*.

Kalmar /'kalmɑː/ a port in SE Sweden, on the Kalmar Sound opposite Öland; pop. 56,200 (1990).

Kalmar Sound a narrow strait between the mainland of SE Sweden and the island of Öland, in the Baltic Sea.

Kalmar, Union of the treaty which joined together the Crowns of Denmark, Sweden, and Norway in 1397, dissolved in 1523.

kalmia /'kalmɪə/ ▶ noun an evergreen leathery-leaved shrub of the heather family, bearing large clusters of pink or red flowers. It is native to North America and Cuba and widely grown as an ornamental.
● Genus *Kalmia*, family Ericaceae.
– ORIGIN modern Latin, named after Pehr *Kalm* (1716–1779), Swedish botanist.

Kalmyk /'kalmʌk/ (also **Kalmuck**) ▶ noun (pl. same or **Kalmyks** or **Kalmucks**) **1** a member of a mainly Buddhist people of Mongolian origin living chiefly in Kalmykia.
2 [mass noun] the Altaic language of this people.
▶ adjective of or relating to this people or their language.
– ORIGIN from Russian *kalmyk*.

Kalmykia /kal'mɪkɪə/ an autonomous republic in SW Russia, on the Caspian Sea; pop. 325,000 (1990); capital, Elista. Official name **REPUBLIC OF KALMYKIA-KHALMG TANGCH**.

kalong /'kɑːlɒŋ/ ▶ noun a flying fox found in SE Asia and Indonesia.
● Genus *Pteropus*, family Pteropodidae, in particular the large flying fox (*P. vampyrus*).
– ORIGIN early 19th cent.: from Javanese.

kalpa /'kalpə/ ▶ noun (in Hindu and Buddhist tradition) an immense period of time, reckoned as 4,320 million human years, and considered to be the length of a single cycle of the cosmos (or 'day of Brahma') from creation to dissolution.
– ORIGIN Sanskrit.

kalsomine /'kalsəmʌɪn/ (also **calcimine**) ▶ noun [mass noun] a kind of white or pale blue wash for walls and ceilings.
▶ verb [with obj.] whitewash with kalsomine.
– ORIGIN mid 19th cent.: of unknown origin.

Kaluga /kə'luːgə/ an industrial city and river port in European Russia, on the River Oka south-west of Moscow; pop. 314,000 (1990).

Kalyan /kʌl'jɑːn/ a city on the west coast of India, in the state of Maharashtra, north-east of Bombay; pop. 1,014,000 (1991).

Kama /'kɑːmə/ Hinduism the god of love, typically represented as a youth with a bowl of sugar cane, a bowstring of bees, and arrows of flowers.

kamacite /'kaməsʌɪt/ ▶ noun [mass noun] an alloy of iron and nickel occurring in some meteorites.
– ORIGIN late 19th cent.: from Greek *kamax, kamak-* 'vine pole' (because of the occurrence of the alloy in bar-shaped masses) + **-ITE**[1].

kamahi /'kɑːməhi/ ▶ noun a tall New Zealand forest tree with small cream-coloured flowers and dark timber.
● *Weinmannia racemosa*, family Cunoniaceae.
– ORIGIN mid 19th cent.: from Maori.

Kama Sutra /ˌkɑːmə 'suːtrə/ an ancient Sanskrit treatise on the art of love and sexual technique.
– ORIGIN Sanskrit, from *kāma* 'love' + *sūtra* 'thread'.

Kamba /'kambə/ ▶ noun (pl. same, **Kambas**, or **Wakamba**) **1** a member of a people of central Kenya, ethnically related to the Kikuyu.
2 [mass noun] the Bantu language of this people, with around 2.5 million speakers.
▶ adjective of or relating to this people or their language.
– ORIGIN a local name.

Kamchatka /kam'tʃatkə/ a vast mountainous peninsula of the NE coast of Siberian Russia, separating the Sea of Okhotsk from the Bering Sea; chief port, Petropavlovsk.

kame /keɪm/ ▶ noun Geology a steep-sided mound of sand and gravel deposited by a melting ice sheet.
– ORIGIN late 18th cent.: Scots form of **COMB**.

kameez /kə'miːz/ ▶ noun (pl. same or **kameezes**) a long tunic worn by many people from the Indian subcontinent, typically with a salwar or churidars.
– ORIGIN from Arabic *ḳamīṣ*, perhaps from late Latin *camisia* (see **CHEMISE**).

Kamenskoye /ka'mjɛnˌskɔɪjə/ former name (until 1936) for **DNIPRODZERZHINSK**.

Kamensk-Uralsky /ˌkaːmɪnskʊ'ralski/ an industrial city in central Russia, in the eastern foothills of the Urals; pop. 208,000 (1990).

Kamerlingh Onnes /ˌkaməlɪŋ 'ɒnɪs/, Heike (1853–1926), Dutch physicist. During his studies of cryogenic phenomena he achieved a temperature of less than one degree above absolute zero and succeeded in liquefying helium. Onnes discovered the phenomenon of superconductivity in 1911, and was awarded the Nobel Prize for Physics in 1913.

kami /'kɑːmi/ ▶ noun (pl. same) a divine being in the Shinto religion.
– ORIGIN Japanese.

kamikaze /ˌkamɪ'kɑːzi/ ▶ noun (in the Second World War) a Japanese aircraft loaded with explosives and making a deliberate suicidal crash on an enemy target.
■ the pilot of such an aircraft.
▶ adjective [attrib.] of or relating to such an attack or pilot.
■ reckless or potentially self-destructive: *he made a kamikaze run across three lanes of traffic.*
– ORIGIN Japanese, from *kami* 'divinity' + *kaze* 'wind', originally referring to the gale that, in Japanese tradition, destroyed the fleet of invading Mongols in 1281.

Kamilaroi /kə'mɪlərɔɪ/ ▶ noun (pl. same) **1** a member of a group of Australian Aboriginal peoples of north-eastern New South Wales.
2 [mass noun] the language of these peoples, now extinct.
▶ adjective of or relating to the Kamilaroi or their language.
– ORIGIN the name in Kamilaroi.

Kampala /kam'pɑːlə/ the capital of Uganda; pop. 773,460 (1991). It is situated on the northern shores of Lake Victoria and replaced Entebbe as capital when the country became independent in 1963.

kampong /kam'pɒŋ, 'kampɒŋ/ ▶ noun a Malaysian enclosure or village.
– ORIGIN Malay; compare with **COMPOUND**[2].

Kampuchea /ˌkampʊ'tʃiːə/ former name (1976–89) for **CAMBODIA**.
– DERIVATIVES **Kampuchean** noun & adjective.

Kan. ▶ abbreviation for Kansas.

kana /'kɑːnə/ ▶ noun [mass noun] the system of syllabic writing used for Japanese, having two forms, hiragana and katakana. Compare with **KANJI**.
– ORIGIN Japanese.

kanaka /kə'nakə, -'nɑːkə/ ▶ noun historical a Pacific Islander employed as an indentured labourer in Australia, especially in the sugar and cotton plantations of Queensland.
– ORIGIN Hawaiian, literally 'man'.

kanamycin /ˌkanə'mʌɪsɪn/ ▶ noun [mass noun] Medicine a broad-spectrum antibiotic obtained from a strain of bacteria.
– ORIGIN mid 20th cent.: from modern Latin *Streptomyces kanamyceticus*, the name of the source bacterium (see also **-MYCIN**).

Kanarese /ˌkanə'riːz/ (also **Canarese**) ▶ noun (pl. same) **1** a member of a people living mainly in Kanara, a district in SW India.
2 another term for **KANNADA**.
▶ adjective of or relating to Kanara, its people, or their language.

kanban /'kanban/ ▶ noun (also **kanban system**) [mass noun] a Japanese manufacturing system in which the supply of components is regulated through the use of a card displaying a sequence of specifications and instructions, sent along the production line.
■ [count noun] a card of this type.
– ORIGIN late 20th cent.: Japanese, literally 'billboard, sign'.

Kanchenjunga /ˌkantʃɛn'dʒʌŋgə/ (also **Kangchenjunga** or **Kinchinjunga**) a mountain in the Himalayas, on the border between Nepal and Sikkim. Rising to a height of 8,598 m (28,209 ft), it is the world's third highest mountain.
– ORIGIN Tibetan, literally 'the five treasures of the snows', referring to the five separate peaks of the summit.

Kandahar /ˌkandə'hɑː/ a city in southern Afghanistan; pop. 225,500 (est. 1988). From 1748 it was Afghanistan's first capital after independence, until being replaced by Kabul in 1773.

Kandinsky /kan'dɪnski/, Wassily (1866–1944), Russian painter and theorist. A pioneer of abstract art, he urged the expression of inner and essential feelings in art, rather than the representation of surface appearances. In 1911 he co-founded the Munich-based *Blaue Reiter* group of artists.

Kandy /'kandi/ a city in Sri Lanka; pop. 104,000 (1990). It was the capital (1480–1815) of the former independent kingdom of Kandy and contains one of the most sacred Buddhist shrines, the Dalada Maligava (Temple of the Tooth).
– DERIVATIVES **Kandyan** adjective.

kanga[1] ▶ noun Austral. informal **1** a kangaroo. [ORIGIN: abbreviation.]
2 a prison warder. [ORIGIN: from rhyming slang *kangaroo* 'screw'.]

kanga[2] ▶ noun variant spelling of **KHANGA**.

Kangar /'kaŋgɑː/ the capital of the state of Perlis in northern Malaysia, near the west coast of the Malay Peninsula; pop. 12,950 (1980).

kangaroo ▶ noun a large plant-eating marsupial with a long powerful tail and strongly developed hindlimbs that enable it to travel by leaping, found only in Australia and New Guinea.
● Genus *Macropus*, family Macropodidae: several species.
– PHRASES **have kangaroos in the** (or **one's**) **top paddock** Austral. informal be mad or eccentric.
– ORIGIN late 18th cent.: the name of a specific kind of kangaroo in an extinct Aboriginal language of North Queensland.

kangaroo court ▶ noun an unofficial court held by a group of people in order to try someone regarded, especially without good evidence, as guilty of a crime or misdemeanour.

kangaroo dog ▶ noun a dog of a large type bred to hunt kangaroos.

kangaroo grass ▶ noun [mass noun] a fodder grass which grows in very tall tussocks.
● Genus *Themeda*, family Gramineae: several species, in particular *T. australis*.

kangaroo mouse ▶ noun a small seed-eating hopping rodent with large cheek pouches and long hind legs, found in North America.
● Genus *Microdipodops*, family Heteromyidae: two species.

kangaroo paw ▶ noun an Australian plant which has long strap-like leaves and tubular flowers with woolly outer surfaces.
● Genera *Anigozanthos* and *Macropidia*, family Haemodoraceae: several species, in particular **Mangles' kangaroo paw** (*A. manglesii*), which is the floral emblem of Western Australia.

kangaroo rat ▶ noun a seed-eating hopping rodent with large cheek pouches and long hind legs, found from Canada to Mexico.
● Genus *Dipodomys*, family Heteromyidae: several species.

kangaroo vine ▶ noun an Australian evergreen climbing plant of the vine family, grown as a house plant.
● *Cissus antarctica*, family Vitaceae.

Kangchenjunga /ˌkaŋtʃɛn'dʒʌŋgə/ variant spelling of **KANCHENJUNGA**.

kangha /'kʌŋhə/ ▶ noun a comb worn in the hair as one of the five distinguishing signs of the Sikh Khalsa.
– ORIGIN from Punjabi *kaṅghā*.

Kango /'kaŋgəʊ/ ▶ noun (pl. **-oes**) trademark a heavy electrically powered hammer.
– ORIGIN mid 20th cent.: of unknown origin.

kangri /'kaŋgri/ ▶ noun Indian a small pot filled with lighted charcoal, used to transport fire or (in Kashmir) carried close to the body as a means of keeping warm.
– ORIGIN from Hindi *kāṅgrī*.

KaNgwane /ˌkɑːəŋ'gwɑːneɪ/ a former homeland established in South Africa for the Swazi people, now part of the province of Mpumalanga.

kanji /'kandʒi, 'kɑːn-/ ▶ noun [mass noun] a system of Japanese writing using Chinese characters, used primarily for content words. Compare with **KANA**.

– ORIGIN Japanese, from *kan* 'Chinese' + *ji* 'character'.

Kannada /ˈkanədə/ ▶ noun [mass noun] a Dravidian language related to Telugu and using a similar script. It is spoken by about 24 million people, mainly in Kanara and Karnataka in SW India. Also called **KANARESE**.
▶ adjective of or relating to this language.
– ORIGIN the name in Kannada.

Kano /ˈkɑːnəʊ/ a city in northern Nigeria; pop. 553,000 (est. 1986).

Kanpur /kɑːnˈpʊə/ (also **Cawnpore**) a city in Uttar Pradesh, northern India, on the River Ganges; pop. 2,100,000 (1991). It was the site of a massacre of British soldiers and European families in July 1857, during the Indian Mutiny.

Kans. ▶ abbreviation for Kansas.

Kansas /ˈkanzəs/ a state in the central US; pop. 2,477,570 (est. 1990); capital, Topeka. Acquired as part of the Louisiana Purchase in 1803, it became the 34th state of the US in 1861.
– DERIVATIVES **Kansan** adjective & noun.

Kansas City each of two adjacent cities in the US, situated at the junction of the Missouri and Kansas Rivers, one in NE Kansas (pop. 149,770 (1990)) and the other in NW Missouri (pop. 435,150 (1990)).

Kansu /kanˈsuː/ variant of **GANSU**.

Kant /kant/, Immanuel (1724–1804), German philosopher. In the *Critique of Pure Reason* (1781) he countered Hume's sceptical empiricism by arguing that any affirmation or denial regarding the ultimate nature of reality ('noumenon') makes no sense. All we can know are the objects of experience ('phenomena'), interpreted by space and time and ordered according to twelve key concepts. Kant's *Critique of Practical Reason* (1788) affirms the existence of an absolute moral law—the categorical imperative.
– DERIVATIVES **Kantian** adjective & noun, **Kantianism** noun.

Kanto /kanˈtəʊ/ a region of Japan, on the island of Honshu; capital, Tokyo.

KANU /ˈkɑːnuː/ ▶ abbreviation for Kenya African National Union.

kanuka /ˈkɑːnʊkə/ ▶ noun a small evergreen New Zealand tree with white flowers, yielding useful timber and products used in herbal medicine.
● *Leptospermum ericoides*, family Myrtaceae.
– ORIGIN early 20th cent.: from Maori.

kanzu /kanzuː/ ▶ noun a long white cotton or linen robe worn by East African men.
– ORIGIN early 20th cent.: from Kiswahili.

Kaohsiung /kaʊˈʃjʊŋ/ the chief port of Taiwan, on the SW coast; pop. 1,390,000 (1990).

kaoliang /ˈkeɪəʊˌljaŋ/ ▶ noun [mass noun] sorghum of a variety grown in China and used to make dough and alcoholic drinks.
● *Sorghum bicolor* var. *nervosum*, family Gramineae.
– ORIGIN early 20th cent.: from Chinese *gāoliang*, from *gāo* 'high' + *liáng* 'fine grain'.

kaolin /ˈkeɪəlɪn/ ▶ noun [mass noun] a fine soft white clay, resulting from the natural decomposition of other clays or feldspar. It is used for making porcelain and china, as a filler in paper and textiles, and in medicinal absorbents. Also called **CHINA CLAY**.
– DERIVATIVES **kaolinize** (also **-ise**) verb.
– ORIGIN early 18th cent.: from French, from Chinese *gāolǐng*, literally 'high hill', the name of a mountain in Jiangxi province where the clay is found.

kaolinite /ˈkeɪəlɪnʌɪt/ ▶ noun [mass noun] a white or grey clay mineral which is the chief constituent of kaolin.

kaon /ˈkeɪɒn/ ▶ noun Physics a meson having a mass several times that of a pion.
– ORIGIN 1950s: from *ka* representing the letter *K* (as a symbol for the particle) + **-ON**.

Kaonde /kaˈɒndeɪ/ ▶ noun (pl. same) **1** a member of a people living mainly in north-western Zambia. **2** [mass noun] the Bantu language of this people, with around 200,000 speakers.
▶ adjective of or relating to this people or their language.

Kapachira Falls /ˌkapəˈtʃɪərə/ a waterfall on the Shire River in southern Malawi. Former name **MURCHISON RAPIDS**.

kapellmeister /kəˈpɛlˌmʌɪstə/ ▶ noun the leader or conductor of an orchestra or choir.
■ historical a leader of a chamber ensemble or orchestra attached to a German court.
– ORIGIN mid 19th cent.: German, from *Kapelle* 'court orchestra' (from medieval Latin *capella* 'chapel') + *Meister* 'master'.

Kap Farvel /ˌkab farˈvɛl/ Danish name for Cape Farewell (see **FAREWELL, CAPE**, sense 1).

Kapil Dev /ˌkapɪl ˈdɛv/ (b.1959), Indian cricketer; full name *Kapil Dev Nikhanj*. Originally a medium-pace bowler, he soon developed into an all-rounder. As captain (1983–4) he led India to victory in the 1983 World Cup. In 1994 he set a new record of 432 test match wickets.

kapok /ˈkeɪpɒk/ ▶ noun [mass noun] a fine, fibrous cotton-like substance which grows around the seeds of the ceiba tree, used as stuffing for cushions, soft toys, etc.
■ (also **kapok tree**) another term for **CEIBA**.
– ORIGIN mid 18th cent.: from Malay *kapuk*.

Kapoor /kaˈpʊə/, (Prithvi) Raj (1924–88), Indian actor and film-maker. In 1944 he founded the Prithvi Theatres in Bombay, a company notable for the realism it brought to Hindi drama. Notable films include *Awara* (*The Vagabond*) (1951), which he directed and in which he took the title role.

Kaposi's sarcoma /kəˈpəʊsɪz/ ▶ noun [mass noun] Medicine a form of cancer involving multiple tumours of the lymph nodes or skin, occurring chiefly in people with depressed immune systems, e.g. as a result of Aids.
– ORIGIN late 19th cent.: named after Moritz K. *Kaposi* (1837–1902), Hungarian dermatologist.

kappa /ˈkapə/ ▶ noun the tenth letter of the Greek alphabet (Κ, κ), transliterated as 'k'.
■ (**Kappa**) [followed by Latin genitive] Astronomy the tenth star in a constellation: *Kappa Orionis*. ■ [as modifier] Biochemistry denoting one of the two types of light polypeptide chain present in all immunoglobulin molecules (the other being lambda).
– ORIGIN Greek.

kapu /ˈkapuː/ ▶ noun [mass noun] (in Hawaiian traditional culture and religion) a set of rules and prohibitions for everyday life.
– ORIGIN Hawaiian.

kapur /ˈkapə/ ▶ noun a large tropical Old World tree which yields light brown timber, edible fruit, and camphor.
● Genus *Dryobalanops*, family Dipterocarpaceae.
– ORIGIN mid 20th cent.: from Malay.

kaput /kəˈpʊt/ ▶ adjective [predic.] informal broken and useless; no longer working or effective.
– ORIGIN late 19th cent.: from German *kaputt*, from French (*être*) *capot* '(be) without tricks in a card game'; compare with **CAPOT**.

kara /ˈkɑːrə/ ▶ noun a steel bangle worn on the right wrist as one of the five distinguishing signs of the Sikh Khalsa.
– ORIGIN from Punjabi *karā*.

karabiner /ˌkarəˈbiːnə/ (also **carabiner**) ▶ noun a coupling link with a safety closure, used by rock climbers.
– ORIGIN 1930s: shortened from German *Karabinerhaken* 'spring hook'.

Karachai-Cherkessia /ˌkaratʃʌɪˌtʃɛːˈkɛsɪə/ an autonomous republic in the northern Caucasus, SW Russia; pop. 436,000 (1995); capital, Cherkessk. Official name **KARACHAI-CHERKESS REPUBLIC**.

Karachay /ˌkarəˈtʃʌɪ/ (also **Karachai**) ▶ noun **1** a member of an indigenous people living in Karachai-Cherkessia. **2** (also **Karachay-Balkar**) [mass noun] the Turkic language of this people, with under 200,000 speakers.
▶ adjective of or relating to this people or their language.

Karachi /kəˈrɑːtʃi/ a major city and port in Pakistan, capital of Sind province; pop. 6,700,000 (est. 1991). Situated on the Arabian Sea, it was the capital of Pakistan 1947–59 before being replaced by Rawalpindi.

Karafuto /ˌkarəˈfuːtəʊ/ the Japanese name for the southern part of the island of Sakhalin.

Karaganda /karəɡanˈda/ Russian name for **QARAGHANDY**.

karahi /ˈkʌrʌɪ/ (also **kadai** or **karai**) ▶ noun (pl. **karahis**) a small, bowl-shaped frying pan with two handles used in Indian cookery, chiefly for preparing balti dishes.
– ORIGIN from Hindi *karāhī*.

Karaite /ˈkɛːrʌɪt/ ▶ noun a member of a Jewish sect founded in the 8th century and located chiefly in the Crimea and nearby areas, and in Israel, which rejects rabbinical interpretation in favour of a literal interpretation of the scriptures.
– ORIGIN early 18th cent.: from Hebrew *Qārā'īm* 'Scripturalists' (from *qārā'* 'read') + **-ITE**[1].

Karaj /kaˈrɑːdʒ/ a city in northern Iran, to the west of Tehran; pop. 442,000 (1991).

Karajan /ˈkarəjan/, Herbert von (1908–89), Austrian conductor, chiefly remembered as the principal conductor of the Berlin Philharmonic Orchestra (1955–89).

karaka /kəˈrɑːkə/ ▶ noun a New Zealand tree with orange berries containing seeds which are poisonous unless roasted.
● *Corynocarpus laevigata*, family Corynocarpaceae
– ORIGIN mid 19th cent.: from Maori.

Karakalpak /ˌkarəˈkalpak/ ▶ noun **1** a member of an indigenous people living in the Karakalpak autonomous republic of Russia, south of the Aral Sea. **2** [mass noun] the Turkic language of this people, with about 300,000 speakers.
▶ adjective of or relating to this people or their language.

Karakoram /ˌkarəˈkɔːrəm/ a great mountain system of central Asia, extending over 480 km (300 miles) south-eastwards from NE Afghanistan to Kashmir and forming part of the borders of India and Pakistan with China. One of the highest mountain systems in the world, it consists of a group of parallel ranges, forming a westwards continuation of the Himalayas, with many peaks over 7,900 m (26,000 ft), the highest being K2.

Karakorum /ˌkarəˈkɔːrəm/ an ancient city in central Mongolia, now ruined, which was the capital of the Mongol empire, established by Genghis Khan in 1220. The capital was moved to Khanbaliq (modern Beijing) in 1267, and Karakorum was destroyed by Chinese forces in 1388.

karakul /ˈkarəkʊl/ (also **caracul**) ▶ noun a sheep of an Asian breed with a dark curled fleece when young.
■ [mass noun] cloth or fur made from or resembling the fleece of such a sheep.
– ORIGIN mid 19th cent.: from Russian, from the name of an oasis in Uzbekistan and of two lakes in Tadjikistan, based on Turkic.

Kara Kum /ˌkarə ˈkuːm/ a desert in central Asia, to the east of the Caspian Sea, covering much of Turkmenistan. Russian name **KARAKUMY** /ˌkarəˈkumij/.

karanga /kəˈraŋə/ ▶ noun NZ a Maori ritual chant of welcome.

karaoke /ˌkarəˈəʊki, ˌkarɪ-/ ▶ noun [mass noun] a form of entertainment, offered typically by bars and clubs, in which people take turns to sing popular songs into a microphone over pre-recorded backing tracks.
– ORIGIN 1970s: from Japanese, literally 'empty orchestra'.

Kara Sea /ˈkɑːrə/ an arm of the Arctic Ocean off the northern coast of Russia, bounded to the east by the islands of Severnaya Zemlya and to the west by Novaya Zemlya.

karat ▶ noun US spelling of **CARAT** (in sense 2).

karate /kəˈrɑːti/ ▶ noun [mass noun] an oriental system of unarmed combat using the hands and feet to deliver and block blows, widely practised as a sport. It was formalized in Okinawa in the 17th century, and popularized via Japan after about 1920. Karate is performed barefoot in loose padded clothing, with a coloured belt indicating the level of skill, and involves mental as well as physical training.
– ORIGIN Japanese, from *kara* 'empty' + *te* 'hand'.

karate-chop ▶ verb [with obj.] strike sharply with the side of the hand.

karateka /kəˈrɑːtɪkɑː/ ▶ noun (pl. same or **karatekas**) a practitioner of karate.

Karbala /ˈkɑːbələ/ a city in southern Iraq; pop. 184,600 (est. 1985). A holy city for Shiite Muslims, it is the site of the tomb of Husayn, grandson of Muhammad, who was killed there in AD 680.

karee ▶ **noun** variant spelling of **KARREE**.

Karelia /kəˈreɪlɪə, -ˈriːlɪə/ a region of NE Europe on the border between Russia and Finland. Following Finland's declaration of independence in 1917, part of Karelia became a region of Finland and part an autonomous republic of the Soviet Union. After the Russo-Finnish war of 1939–40 the greater part of Finnish Karelia was ceded to the Soviet Union. The remaining part of Karelia constitutes a province of eastern Finland.
– DERIVATIVES **Karelian** adjective & noun.

Karen /kəˈrɛn/ ▶ **noun** (pl. same or **Karens**) **1** a member of an indigenous people of eastern Burma (Myanmar) and western Thailand.
2 [mass noun] the language of this people, which probably belongs to the Sino-Tibetan family. Its highly distinct dialects have over 5 million speakers altogether.
▶ **adjective** of or relating to this people or their language.
– ORIGIN from Burmese *ka-reng* 'wild unclean man'.

Karen State a state in SE Burma (Myanmar), on the border with Thailand; capital, Pa-an. Inaugurated in 1954 as an autonomous state of Burma, the state was given the traditional Karen name of Kawthoolay in 1964, but reverted to Karen after the 1974 constitution limited its autonomy. The people are engaged in armed conflict with the Burmese government in an attempt to gain independence. Also called **KAWTHOOLAY**, **KAWTHULEI**.

karez /ˈkɑːrɛz/ ▶ **noun** (pl. same) (in parts of central southern Asia) a qanat.
– ORIGIN Pashto, from Persian.

karezza /kəˈrɛtsə/ ▶ **noun** [mass noun] sexual intercourse in which ejaculation is avoided.
– ORIGIN late 19th cent.: from Italian *carezza* 'a caress'.

Kariba, Lake /kəˈriːbə/ a large, man-made lake on the Zambia–Zimbabwe border in central Africa. It was created by the damming of the Zambezi River by the Kariba Dam, and it is the chief source of hydroelectric power for Zimbabwe and Zambia.

Kariba Dam a concrete arch dam on the Zambezi River, 385 km (240 miles) downstream from the Victoria Falls. It was built in 1955–9, creating Lake Kariba and providing a bridge over the Zambezi between Zambia and Zimbabwe.

Karitane /ˌkarɪˈtɑːni/ ▶ **adjective** [attrib.] NZ trained or administered according to the principles of child care and nutrition advocated by the Royal New Zealand Society for the Health of Women and Children (the Plunket Society): *a Karitane hospital.*
– ORIGIN early 20th cent.: from the name of a township in South Island, New Zealand.

Karl XII /kɑːl/ variant spelling of **CHARLES XII**.

Karl-Marx-Stadt /kɑːlˈmɑːksˌʃtat, German karlˈmarksˌʃtat/ former name (1953–90) for **CHEMNITZ**.

Karloff /ˈkɑːlɒf/, Boris (1887–1969), British-born American actor; born *William Henry Pratt*. His name is chiefly linked with horror films, such as *Frankenstein* (1931) and *The Body Snatcher* (1945).

Karlovy Vary /ˌkɑːləvɪ ˈvɑːri/ a spa town in the western Czech Republic; pop. 56,290 (1991). It is famous for its alkaline thermal springs. German name **KARLSBAD** /ˈkarlsbaːt/.

Karlsruhe /ˈkɑːlzˌruːə, German ˈkarlsˌruːə/ an industrial town and port on the Rhine in western Germany; pop. 278,580 (1991).

karma /ˈkɑːmə, ˈkəːmə/ ▶ **noun** [mass noun] (in Hinduism and Buddhism) the sum of a person's actions in this and previous states of existence, viewed as deciding their fate in future existences.
■ informal destiny or fate, following as effect from cause.
– DERIVATIVES **karmic** adjective, **karmically** adverb.
– ORIGIN from Sanskrit *karman* 'action, effect, fate'.

karma yoga ▶ **noun** [mass noun] Hinduism the discipline of selfless action as a way to perfection.

Karnak /ˈkɑːnak/ a village in Egypt on the Nile, now largely amalgamated with Luxor. It is the site of the northern complex of monuments of ancient Thebes, including the great temple of Amun.

Karnataka /kəˈnɑːtəkə/ a state in SW India; capital, Bangalore. Former name (until 1973) **MYSORE**.

Karnaugh map /ˈkɑːnɔː/ (also **Karnaugh diagram**) ▶ **noun** Mathematics & Electronics a diagram consisting of a rectangular array of squares each representing a different combination of the variables of a Boolean function.
– DERIVATIVES **Karnaugh mapping** noun.
– ORIGIN mid 20th cent.: named after Maurice *Karnaugh* (born 1924), American physicist.

Kärnten /ˈkɛrntn̩/ German name for **CARINTHIA**.

karo /ˈkɑːrəʊ/ ▶ **noun** an ornamental evergreen shrub or small tree with leathery leaves and clusters of small, dark red flowers, native to New Zealand and naturalized in parts of Europe.
• *Pittosporum crassifolium*, family Pittosporaceae.
– ORIGIN mid 19th cent.: from Maori.

Karoo /kəˈruː/ (also **Karroo**) an elevated semi-desert plateau in South Africa.
■ [as noun **a karoo**] S. African a tract of semi-desert land.
– ORIGIN from Khoikhoi, literally 'hard, dry'.

karoshi /kaˈrəʊʃi/ ▶ **noun** [mass noun] (in Japan) death caused by overwork or job-related exhaustion.
– ORIGIN Japanese, from *ka* 'excess' + *rō* 'labour' + *shi* 'death'.

kaross /kəˈrɒs/ ▶ **noun** S. African a rug or blanket of sewn animal skins, formerly worn as a garment by African people, now used as a bed or floor covering.
– ORIGIN South African Dutch, from Khoikhoi *karos*.

Karpov /ˈkɑːpɒf/, Anatoli (Yevgenevich) (b.1951), Russian chess player. He was world champion from 1975 until defeated by Gary Kasparov in 1985.

karree /kəˈriː/ (also **karee**) ▶ **noun** S. African an evergreen African tree related to sumac, which has willow-like foliage and yields useful timber.
• Genus *Rhus*, family Anacardiaceae, in particular *R. lancea*.
– ORIGIN early 19th cent.: from Afrikaans, from Nama *karib*.

karren /ˈkarən/ ▶ **plural noun** Geology grooves and fissures, typically separated by sharp ridges, produced in a hard limestone surface by water erosion.
– ORIGIN late 19th cent.: from German *Karren*.

karri /ˈkari/ ▶ **noun** (pl. **karris**) a tall Australian eucalyptus with hard red wood.
• *Eucalyptus diversicolor*, family Myrtaceae.
– ORIGIN late 19th cent.: from Nyungar.

Karroo variant spelling of **KAROO**.

Kars /kɑːs/ a city and province in NE Turkey; pop. 78,455 (1990).

karst /kɑːst/ ▶ **noun** [mass noun] Geology landscape underlain by limestone which has been eroded by dissolution, producing ridges, towers, fissures, sinkholes and other characteristic landforms: [as modifier] *karst topography* | [count noun] *it was strange country, broken into hummocks and karsts and mesas.*
– DERIVATIVES **karstic** adjective, **karstification** noun, **karstify** verb (**-ies**, **ied**).
– ORIGIN late 19th cent.: from German *der Karst*, the name of a limestone region in Slovenia.

kart ▶ **noun** a small unsprung motor-racing vehicle typically having four wheels and consisting of a tubular frame with a rear-mounted engine.
– DERIVATIVES **karting** noun.
– ORIGIN mid 20th cent.: shortening of **GO-KART**.

Kartvelian /kɑːtˈviːlɪən/ ▶ **adjective** & **noun** another term for ***South Caucasian*** (see **CAUCASIAN** sense 3).
– ORIGIN from Georgian *Kartvelebi* 'Georgians' + **-IAN**.

karyo- ▶ **combining form** Biology denoting the nucleus of a cell: *karyotype.*
– ORIGIN from Greek *karuon* 'kernel'.

karyokinesis /ˌkarɪəʊkɪˈniːsɪs, -kʌɪ-/ ▶ **noun** [mass noun] Biology division of a cell nucleus during mitosis.
– ORIGIN late 19th cent.: from **KARYO-** 'cell nucleus' + Greek *kinēsis* 'movement' (from *kinein* 'to move').

karyolysis /ˌkarɪˈɒlɪsɪs/ ▶ **noun** [mass noun] Biology dissolution of a cell nucleus, especially during mitosis.

karyotype /ˈkarɪə(ʊ)tʌɪp/ ▶ **noun** Biology & Medicine the number and visual appearance of the chromosomes in the cell nuclei of an organism or species.
– DERIVATIVES **karyotypic** adjective.

karyotyping ▶ **noun** [mass noun] Biology & Medicine the determination of a karyotype, e.g. to detect chromosomal abnormalities.

karzy ▶ **noun** variant spelling of **KHAZI**.

kasbah /ˈkazbɑː/ (also **casbah**) ▶ **noun** the citadel of a North African city.
■ (**the kasbah**) the area surrounding such a citadel, typically the old part of a city.
– ORIGIN mid 18th cent.: from French *casbah*, from Arabic *ḳaṣaba* 'citadel'.

Kasha /ˈkaʃə/ ▶ **noun** [mass noun] trademark a soft, napped fabric of wool and hair.
■ a kind of cotton flannel used as a lining material.
– ORIGIN early 20th cent.: of unknown origin.

kasha /ˈkaʃə/ ▶ **noun** [mass noun] porridge made from cooked buckwheat or similar grain, typical of Russian and Polish cookery.
■ uncooked buckwheat groats.
– ORIGIN Russian.

Kashmir /kaʃˈmɪə/ a region on the northern border of India and NE Pakistan. Formerly a state of India, it has been disputed between India and Pakistan since partition in 1947, with sporadic outbreaks of fighting. The north-western part is controlled by Pakistan, most of it forming the state of Azad Kashmir, while the remainder is incorporated into the Indian state of Jammu and Kashmir.

Kashmir goat ▶ **noun** a goat of a Himalayan breed yielding fine, soft wool, which is used to make cashmere.

Kashmiri /kaʃˈmɪəri/ ▶ **adjective** of or relating to Kashmir, its people, or their language.
▶ **noun 1** a native or inhabitant of Kashmir.
2 [mass noun] the Indic language of Kashmir, spoken by over 3 million people and written in both Devanagari and Arabic script.

kashrut /kaʃˈruːt/ (also **kashruth**) ▶ **noun** [mass noun] the body of Jewish religious laws concerning the suitability of food, the use of ritual objects, etc.
■ the observance of these laws.
– ORIGIN Hebrew, literally 'legitimacy (in religion)'; see also **KOSHER**.

Kashubian /kəˈʃuːbɪən/ ▶ **noun 1** a native or inhabitant of Kashubia, a region of Poland west and north-west of Gdansk.
2 [mass noun] the Western Slavic vernacular language spoken by about 200,000 people in Kashubia. It is closely related to Polish.
▶ **adjective** of or relating to Kashubia, its people, or their language.

Kasparov /ˈkaspərɒf/, Garry (b.1963), Azerbaijani chess player of Armenian-Jewish descent; born *Garry Weinstein*. At the age of 22 he became the youngest-ever world champion, defeating Anatoli Karpov in 1985; he held the title until 2000. In 1997 he was beaten in a match with the IBM computer Deeper Blue.

Kassel /ˈkas(ə)l/ a city in central Germany, in Hesse; pop. 196,830 (1991). It was the capital of the kingdom of Westphalia (1807–13) and of the Prussian province of Hesse-Nassau (1866–1944).

Kasur /kəˈsʊə/ a city in Punjab province, NE Pakistan; pop. 155,000 (1981).

kata /ˈkɑːtɑː/ ▶ **noun** [mass noun] a system of individual training exercises for practitioners of karate and other martial arts.
■ [count noun] (pl. same or **katas**) an individual exercise of this kind.
– ORIGIN Japanese.

katabatic /ˌkatəˈbatɪk/ ▶ **adjective** Meteorology (of a wind) caused by local downward motion of cool air.
– ORIGIN late 19th cent.: from Greek *katabatikos*, from *katabainein* 'go down'.

katabolism ▶ **noun** variant spelling of **CATABOLISM**.

katakana /ˌkatəˈkɑːnə/ ▶ **noun** [mass noun] the more angular form of kana (syllabic writing) used in Japanese, primarily used for words of foreign origin. Compare with **HIRAGANA**.
– ORIGIN early 18th cent.: Japanese, literally 'side kana'.

katana /kəˈtɑːnə/ ▶ **noun** a long, single-edged sword used by Japanese samurai.
– ORIGIN early 17th cent.: Japanese.

Katanga /kəˈtaŋgə/ former name (until 1972) for **SHABA**.

Katangese /ˌkataŋˈgiːz/ ▶ **noun** (pl. same) a native or inhabitant of Shaba (before 1972 called Katanga).
▶ **adjective** of or relating to the Katangese.

Kathak /ˈkʌtək/ ▶ **noun 1** [mass noun] a type of northern Indian classical dance, with alternating passages of mime and dancing.
2 (pl. same or **kathaks**) a member of a northern Indian caste of storytellers and musicians.
– ORIGIN from Sanskrit *kathaka* 'professional storyteller', from *kathā* 'story'.

b **b**ut | d **d**og | f **f**ew | g **g**et | h **h**e | j **y**es | k **c**at | l **l**eg | m **m**an | n **n**o | p **p**en | r **r**ed | s **s**it | t **t**op | v **v**oice | w **w**e | z **z**oo | ʃ **sh**e | ʒ deci**s**ion | θ **th**in | ð **th**is | ŋ ri**ng** | x lo**ch** | tʃ **ch**ip | dʒ **j**ar

Kathakali /ˌkɑːtəˈkɑːli, ˌkʌtəˈkʌli/ ▶ noun [mass noun] a form of dramatic dance of southern India, based on Hindu literature and characterized by masks, stylized costume and make-up, and frequent use of mime.
– ORIGIN from Malayalam, from Sanskrit *kathā* 'story' + Malayalam *kaḷi* 'play'.

katharevousa /ˌkaθəˈrɛvuːsə/ ▶ noun [mass noun] a heavily archaized form of modern Greek used in traditional literary writing, as opposed to the form which is spoken and used in everyday writing (called demotic).
– ORIGIN early 20th cent.: modern Greek, literally 'purified', feminine of *kathareuōn*, present participle of Greek *kathareuein* 'be pure', from *katharos* 'pure'.

katharometer /ˌkaθəˈrɒmɪtə/ ▶ noun an instrument for detecting a gas or measuring its concentration in a mixture, by measuring changes in thermal conductivity.
– ORIGIN early 20th cent.: from Greek *katharos* 'pure' + -METER.

Kathiawar /ˌkatɪəˈwɑː/ a peninsula on the western coast of India, in the state of Gujarat, separating the Gulf of Kutch from the Gulf of Cambay.

Kathmandu /ˌkatmanˈduː/ the capital of Nepal; pop. 419,000 (1991). It is situated in the Himalayas at an altitude of 1,370 m (4,450 ft).

kathode ▶ noun archaic spelling of CATHODE.

katipo /ˈkatɪpəʊ/ ▶ noun (pl. -os) a highly venomous New Zealand spider which is black with a red spot on the back, closely related to the American black widow.
● *Latrodectus mactans katipo*, family Theridiidae.
– ORIGIN mid 19th cent.: from Maori.

Katowice /ˌkatəˈviːtsə/ a city in SW Poland; pop. 349,360 (1990). It is the industrial centre of the Silesian coal-mining region.

katsina ▶ noun (pl. **katsinam**) variant of KACHINA.

katsuobushi /ˌkatswəʊˈbʊʃi/ ▶ noun [mass noun] dried fish prepared in hard blocks from the skipjack tuna and used in Japanese cookery.
– ORIGIN Japanese.

katsura /katˈsʊərə/ ▶ noun **1** an ornamental East Asian tree which has leaves that resemble those of the Judas tree and light, fine-grained timber.
● *Cercidiphyllum japonicum*, the only member of the family Cercidiphyllaceae.
2 a type of Japanese wig worn mainly by women.
– ORIGIN early 20th cent.: from Japanese.

Kattegat /ˈkatɪgat/ a strait, 225 km (140 miles) in length, between Sweden and Denmark. It is linked to the North Sea by the Skagerrak and to the Baltic Sea by the Øresund.

katydid /ˈkeɪtɪdɪd/ ▶ noun a large, typically green, bush cricket that is native to North America. The male makes a characteristic sound which resembles the name.
● *Microcentrum* and other genera, family Tettigoniidae.

katzenjammer /ˈkatsənˌdʒamə/ ▶ noun [mass noun] US informal, dated confusion; uproar.
■ [count noun] a hangover; a severe headache resulting from a hangover.
– ORIGIN mid 19th cent.: from German *Katzen* (combining form of *Katze* 'cat') + *Jammer* 'distress'; popularized by the cartoon *Katzenjammer Kids*, drawn by Rudolf Dirks in 1897 for the *New York Journal*, featuring two incorrigible children.

Kauai /kaʊˈwɑːi/ an island in the state of Hawaii, separated from Oahu by the Kauai Channel; chief town, Lihue.

Kauffmann /ˈkaʊfman/ (also **Kauffman**), (Maria Anna Catherina) Angelica (1740–1807), Swiss painter. In London from 1766, she became well known for her neoclassical and allegorical paintings. She was a founder member of the Royal Academy of Arts (1768).

kaumatua /kaʊˈmɑːtʊə/ ▶ noun NZ a Maori elder.
– ORIGIN Maori.

Kaunas /ˈkaʊnəs/ an industrial city and river port in southern Lithuania, at the confluence of the Viliya and Neman Rivers; pop. 430,000 (1991).

Kaunda /kɑːˈʊndə/, Kenneth (David) (b.1924), Zambian statesman, President 1964–91. He led the United National Independence Party to electoral victory in 1964, becoming Prime Minister and the first President of independent Zambia.

kaupapa /ˈkaʊpɒpɒ/ ▶ noun NZ a principle or policy.
– ORIGIN Maori.

kauri /ˈkaʊri/ ▶ noun (pl. **kauris**) (also **kauri pine**) a tall coniferous forest tree with broad leathery leaves, which produces valuable timber and dammar resin. It grows in warm countries from Malaysia to New Zealand.
● Genus *Agathis*, family Araucariaceae: several species, in particular *A. australis* of New Zealand.
– ORIGIN early 19th cent.: from Maori.

kauri gum (also **kauri resin**) ▶ noun [mass noun] the resin of the kauri tree, used as a varnish, and often also found in fossilized form where the tree formerly grew.

kava /ˈkɑːvə/ ▶ noun [mass noun] **1** a narcotic sedative drink made in Polynesia from the crushed roots of a plant of the pepper family.
2 the Polynesian shrub from which this root is obtained.
● *Piper methysticum*, family Piperaceae.
– ORIGIN late 18th cent.: from Tongan.

Kaválla /kəˈvalə/ a port on the Aegean coast of NE Greece; pop. 56,520 (1991). Originally a Byzantine city and fortress, it was Turkish until 1912, when it was ceded to Greece.

Kaveri variant spelling of CAUVERY.

Kawabata /ˌkɑːwəˈbɑːtə/, Yasunari (1899–1972), Japanese novelist. Known as an experimental writer in the 1920s, he reverted to traditional Japanese novel forms in the mid 1930s. He was the first Japanese writer to win the Nobel Prize for Literature (1968).

kawa-kawa /ˈkɑːwəˌkɑːwə/ ▶ noun a New Zealand shrub of the pepper family with aromatic leaves, cultivated as an ornamental. Also called PEPPER TREE.
● *Macropiper excelsum*, family Piperaceae.
– ORIGIN mid 19th cent.: from Maori.

Kawasaki /ˌkɑːwəˈsɑːki/ an industrial city on the SE coast of the island of Honshu, Japan; pop. 1,174,000 (1990).

Kawasaki disease ▶ noun [mass noun] a disease in young children with an unknown cause, giving rise to a rash, glandular swelling and sometimes damage to the heart.
– ORIGIN 1960s: named after Tomisaku *Kawasaki*, Japanese physician.

Kawthoolay /ˌkɔːθuːˈleɪ/ (also **Kawthulei**) former name (1964–74) for KAREN STATE.

kayak /ˈkʌɪak/ ▶ noun a canoe of a type used originally by the Inuit, made of a light frame with a watertight covering having a small opening in the top to sit in.
▶ verb (**kayaks**, **kayaked**, **kayaking**) [no obj.] [usu. as noun **kayaking**] travel in or use a kayak.
– ORIGIN mid 18th cent.: from Inuit *qayaq*.

kayakeet /ˈkʌɪkiːt, ˌkaja-/ ▶ noun W. Indian the common lantana, a scrambling shrub with prickly stems and flowers that turn from yellow to orange and finally to pinkish-red.
● *Lantana camara*, family Verbenaceae.
– ORIGIN French Creole, from Latin American Spanish *cariaquito*.

Kaye, Danny (1913–87), American actor and comedian; born *David Daniel Kominski*. He was known for his mimicry, comic songs, and slapstick humour. Notable films: *The Secret Life of Walter Mitty* (1947), *Hans Christian Andersen* (1952).

kayo /keɪˈəʊ/ Boxing, informal ▶ noun (pl. -os) a knockout.
▶ verb (-oes, -oed) [with obj.] knock (someone) out.
– ORIGIN 1920s: representing the pronunciation of KO.

Kayseri /ˈkʌɪsəri/ a city in central Turkey, capital of a province of the same name; pop. 421,360 (1990). Known as Kayseri since the 11th century, it was formerly called Caesarea Mazaca and was the capital of Cappadocia.

kazachoc /ˌkazəˈtʃɒk/ ▶ noun a Slavic dance with a fast and typically quickening tempo, featuring a step in which a squatting dancer kicks out each leg alternately to the front.
– ORIGIN early 20th cent.: Russian, diminutive of *kazak* 'Cossack'.

Kazakh /kəˈzak, ˈkazak/ ▶ noun **1** a member of a people living chiefly in Kazakhstan. Traditionally nomadic, Kazakhs are predominantly Sunni Muslims.
2 [mass noun] the Turkic language of this people, with over 7 million speakers.

▶ adjective of or relating to this people or their language.
– ORIGIN Russian, from Turkic; see COSSACK.

Kazakhstan /ˌkazəkˈstɑːn, -ˈstan/ a republic in central Asia, on the southern border of Russia, extending from the Caspian Sea eastwards to the Altai Mountains and China; population 16,899,000 (est. 1991); languages, Kazakh (official), Russian; capital, Astana.

The Turkic tribes of Kazakhstan were overrun by the Mongols in the 13th century, and the region was eventually absorbed into the Russian empire. Kazakhstan formed a constituent republic of the Soviet Union, becoming an independent republic within the Commonwealth of Independent States in 1991.

Kazan¹ /kəˈzan, -ˈzɑːn/ a port situated on the River Volga to the east of Nizhni Novgorod in Russia, capital of the autonomous republic of Tatarstan; pop. 1,103,000 (1990).

Kazan² /kəˈzan/, Elia (b.1909), Turkish-born American film and theatre director; born *Elia Kazanjoglous*. In 1947 he co-founded the Actors' Studio, one of the leading centres of method acting. Kazan directed *A Streetcar Named Desire* on stage (1947) and then on film (1953). Other notable films: *On the Waterfront* (1954) and *East of Eden* (1955).

kazillion /kəˈzɪljən/ ▶ cardinal number another term for GAZILLION.

kazoo /kəˈzuː/ ▶ noun a small, simple musical instrument consisting of a hollow pipe with a hole in it, over which is a thin covering that vibrates and adds a buzzing sound when the player sings or hums into the pipe.
– ORIGIN late 19th cent.: apparently imitative of the sound produced.

KB ▶ abbreviation for ■ (also **Kb**) kilobyte(s). ■ (in the UK) King's Bench.

kb Biochemistry ▶ abbreviation for kilobase(s).

KBE ▶ abbreviation for (in the UK) Knight Commander of the Order of the British Empire.

Kbps ▶ abbreviation for kilobits per second.

kbyte ▶ abbreviation for kilobyte(s).

KC ▶ abbreviation for King's Counsel.

kc ▶ abbreviation for kilocycle(s).

kcal ▶ abbreviation for kilocalorie(s).

KCB ▶ abbreviation for (in the UK) Knight Commander of the Order of the Bath.

KCMG ▶ abbreviation for (in the UK) Knight Commander of the Order of St Michael and St George.

kc/s ▶ abbreviation for kilocycles per second.

KCVO ▶ abbreviation for (in the UK) Knight Commander of the Royal Victorian Order.

KE ▶ abbreviation for kinetic energy.

kea /ˈkiːə/ ▶ noun a New Zealand mountain parrot with a long, narrow bill and mainly olive-green plumage, sometimes feeding on carrion.
● *Nestor notabilis*, family Psittacidae.
– ORIGIN mid 19th cent.: from Maori, imitative of its call.

keaki /keɪˈɑːki, keɪˈaki/ ▶ noun a Japanese tree of the elm family, which is cultivated as an ornamental, for its timber, and as a bonsai tree.
● *Zelkova serrata*, family Ulmaceae.
– ORIGIN Japanese.

Kean, Edmund (1787–1833), English actor, renowned for his interpretations of Shakespearean tragic roles, notably those of Macbeth and Iago.

Keating, Paul (John) (b.1944), Australian Labor statesman, Prime Minister 1991–96. He resigned from parliament in 1996, having been defeated in the general election by the Liberal-National coalition.

Keaton, Buster (1895–1966), American actor and director; born *Joseph Francis Keaton*. His deadpan face and acrobatic skills made him one of the biggest comedy stars of the silent-film era. He starred in and directed films including *The Navigator* (1924), and *The General* (1926).

Keats, John (1795–1821), English poet. A principal figure of the romantic movement, he wrote all of his most famous poems, including 'La Belle Dame sans Merci', 'Ode to a Nightingale', and 'Ode on a Grecian Urn', in 1818 (published in 1820).
– DERIVATIVES **Keatsian** adjective.

kebab /kɪˈbab, kəˈbɑːb/ (N. Amer. also **kabob**) ▶ noun a

dish of pieces of meat roasted or grilled on a skewer or spit.
■ [usu. with modifier] a dish of any kind of food cooked in pieces in this way: *swordfish kebabs*.
– ORIGIN late 17th cent.: from Arabic *kabāb*, partly via Urdu, Persian, and Turkish.

Keble /ˈkiːb(ə)l/, John (1792–1866), English churchman. His sermon on national apostasy (1833) is generally held to mark the beginning of the Oxford Movement, which he founded with John Henry Newman and Edward Pusey.

Kebnekaise /ˌkɛbnəˈkʌɪsə/ the highest peak in Sweden, in the north of the country, rising to a height of 2,117 m (6,962 ft).

keck[1] ▶ **verb** [no obj.] informal feel as if one is about to vomit; retch.
– ORIGIN early 17th cent.: imitative.

keck[2] ▶ **noun** dialect cow parsley or a similar plant.
– ORIGIN early 17th cent.: from earlier dialect *kex* (perhaps of Celtic origin), interpreted as plural.

kecks ▶ **plural noun** Brit. informal trousers, knickers, or underpants.
– ORIGIN 1960s: phonetic respelling of obsolete *kicks* 'trousers'.

ked ▶ **noun** a wingless louse fly, especially one that parasitizes sheep.
• Several species in the family Hippoboscidae, in particular the **sheep ked** (*Melophagus ovinus*).
– ORIGIN late 16th cent.: of unknown origin.

Kedah /ˈkɛdə/ a state of NW Malaysia, on the west coast of the Malay Peninsula; capital, Alor Setar.

keddah ▶ **noun** variant spelling of **KHEDA**.

kedge /kɛdʒ/ ▶ **verb** [with obj.] move (a ship or boat) by hauling in a hawser attached to a small anchor dropped at some distance.
■ [no obj.] (of a ship or boat) move in such a way.
▶ **noun** (also **kedge anchor**) a small anchor used for such a purpose.
– ORIGIN late 15th cent.: perhaps a specific use of dialect *cadge* 'bind, tie'.

kedgeree /ˈkɛdʒəriː/ ▶ **noun** [mass noun] **1** (also **khichri**) an Indian dish consisting chiefly of rice, split pulses, onions, and eggs.
2 a European dish consisting chiefly of fish, rice, and hard-boiled eggs.
– ORIGIN from Hindi *khichṛī*, from Sanskrit *khiccā*, a dish of rice and sesame.

Keegan /ˈkiːg(ə)n/, (Joseph) Kevin (b.1951), English footballer and manager. He played as an attacker for clubs including Liverpool and Hamburg, and played for England 1972–82. He has managed Newcastle United and Fulham, and was England coach 1999–2000.

keek Scottish ▶ **verb** [no obj., with adverbial of direction] peep surreptitiously: *he keeked through the window*.
▶ **noun** [in sing.] a surreptitious glance.
– ORIGIN late Middle English: perhaps related to Dutch *kijken* 'have a look'.

keel[1] ▶ **noun** the lengthwise timber or steel structure along the base of a ship, on which the framework of the whole is built up, in some vessels extended downwards as a blade or ridge to increase stability.
■ Zoology a ridge along the breastbone of many birds to which the flight muscles are attached; the carina. ■ Botany a prow-shaped pair of petals present in flowers of the pea family. ■ poetic/literary a ship.
▶ **verb** [no obj.] (**keel over**) (of a boat or ship) turn over on its side; capsize.
■ informal (of a person or thing) fall over; collapse.
– DERIVATIVES **keeled** adjective, **keelless** adjective.
– ORIGIN Middle English: from Old Norse *kjǫlr*, of Germanic origin.

keel[2] ▶ **noun** Brit. a flat-bottomed boat of a kind formerly used on the Rivers Tyne and Wear for loading colliers.
– ORIGIN Middle English: from Middle Low German *kēl*, Middle Dutch *kiel* 'ship, boat'.

keelage ▶ **noun** [mass noun] rare a toll or due payable by a ship on entering or anchoring in a harbour.

keelback ▶ **noun** a harmless Australian snake which lives close to water, where it feeds exclusively on frogs and the cane toad, whose venom it is immune to.
• *Amphiesma mairii*, family Colubridae.
– ORIGIN so named because each scale on the back has a keel.

keelboat ▶ **noun** **1** a yacht built with a permanent keel rather than a centreboard.
2 a large, flat freight boat used on American rivers.

Keeler, Christine (b.1942), English model and showgirl. She achieved notoriety with her affair with the Conservative cabinet minister John Profumo in 1963 when she was also mistress of a Soviet attaché. Profumo resigned and Keeler was imprisoned on related charges.

keeler ▶ **noun** [often in combination] a boat having a keel, especially one of a specified type: *a long-keeler*.

keelhaul ▶ **verb** [with obj.] historical punish (someone) by dragging them through the water under the keel of a ship, either across the width or from bow to stern.
■ often humorous punish or reprimand severely.
– ORIGIN mid 17th cent.: from Dutch *kielhalen*.

keelie[1] /ˈkiːli/ ▶ **noun** (pl. **-ies**) Scottish & N. English a disreputable inhabitant of a town or city, especially one from Glasgow.
– ORIGIN early 19th cent.: perhaps related to **GILLIE**.

keelie[2] /ˈkiːli/ ▶ **noun** (pl. **-ies**) Scottish & N. English a small hawk or falcon, such as the sparrowhawk or kestrel.
– ORIGIN early 19th cent.: perhaps imitative of its call.

Keeling Islands /ˈkiːlɪŋ/ another name for **COCOS ISLANDS**.

keelson /ˈkiːls(ə)n/ (also **kelson**) ▶ **noun** a structure running the length of a ship and fastening the timbers or plates of the floor to its keel.
– ORIGIN Middle English *kelswayn*, related to Low German *kielswīn*, from *kiel* 'keel of a ship' + *swīn* 'swine' (used as the name of a timber).

keema /ˈkiːmə/ ▶ **noun** [mass noun] Indian minced meat.
– ORIGIN from Hindi *kīmā*.

Keemun /ˈkiːmuːn/ ▶ **noun** [mass noun] a black tea grown in Keemun, China.

keen[1] ▶ **adjective** **1** having or showing eagerness or enthusiasm: *a keen gardener* | *a keen desire to learn*.
■ [predic.] (**keen on**) interested in or attracted by (someone or something): *Bob makes it obvious he's keen on her*.
2 sharp or penetrating, in particular:
■ (of a sense) highly developed: *I have keen eyesight*. ■ (of mental faculties) quick to understand or function: *her keen intellect*. ■ (of the air or wind) extremely cold; biting. ■ (of the edge or point of a blade) sharp. ■ poetic/literary (of a smell, light, or sound) penetrating; clear.
3 Brit. (of prices) very low; competitive.
4 [predic.] N. Amer. informal, dated excellent: *I would soon fly to distant stars—how keen!*
– PHRASES (**as**) **keen as mustard** Brit. informal extremely eager or enthusiastic.
– DERIVATIVES **keenly** adverb, **keenness** noun.
– ORIGIN Old English *cēne* 'wise, clever', also 'brave, daring', of Germanic origin; related to Dutch *koen* and German *kühn* 'bold, brave'. Current senses date from Middle English.

keen[2] ▶ **verb** [no obj.] wail in grief for a dead person; sing a keen.
■ [usu. as noun **keening**] make an eerie wailing sound: *the keening of the cold night wind*.
▶ **noun** an Irish funeral song accompanied with wailing in lamentation for the dead.
– DERIVATIVES **keener** noun.
– ORIGIN mid 19th cent.: from Irish *caoinim* 'I wail'.

Keene, Charles Samuel (1823–91), English illustrator and caricaturist. He is remembered for his work in the weekly journal *Punch* from 1851.

keep ▶ **verb** (past and past participle **kept** /kɛpt/) [with obj.] **1** have or retain possession of: *my father would keep the best for himself* | *she had trouble keeping her balance*.
■ retain or reserve for use in the future: *return one copy to me, keeping the other for your files*. ■ put or store in a regular place: *the stand where her umbrella was kept*. ■ retain one's place in or on (a seat or saddle, the ground, etc.) against opposition or difficulty: *can you keep your saddle, or shall I carry you on a pillion?* ■ delay or detain; cause to be late: *I won't keep you, I know you've got a busy evening*.
2 continue or cause to continue in a specified condition, position, course, etc.: [no obj., with complement] *she could have had some boyfriend she kept quiet about* | *keep left along the wall* | [with obj. and complement] *she might be kept alive artificially by machinery*.
■ [no obj., with present participle] continue doing or do repeatedly or habitually: *he keeps going on about the murder*. ■ [no obj.] (of a perishable commodity) remain in good condition. ■ [no obj., with adverbial] Brit. be in a specified state of health: *he had not been keeping well for the past three months*. ■ [with obj. and present participle] make (someone) do something for a period of time: *I have kept her waiting too long*. ■ archaic continue to follow (a way, path, or course): *the friars and soldiers removed, keeping their course towards Jericho*.
3 provide for the sustenance of (someone): *he had to keep his large family in the manner he had chosen*.
■ provide (someone) with a regular supply of a commodity: *the money should* **keep him in** *cigarettes for a week*. ■ own and look after (an animal) for pleasure or profit. ■ own and manage (a shop or business). ■ guard; protect: *his only thought is to* **keep** *the boy* **from** *harm*. ■ support (someone, especially a woman) financially in return for sexual favours. ■ [no obj.] act as a goalkeeper or wicketkeeper.
4 honour or fulfil (a commitment or undertaking): *I'll keep my promise, naturally*.
■ observe (a religious occasion) in the prescribed manner: *today's consumers do not keep the Sabbath*. ■ pay due regard to (a law or custom).
5 make written entries in (a diary) on a regular basis: *the master kept a weekly journal*.
■ write down as (a record): *keep a note of the whereabouts of each item*.
▶ **noun** **1** [mass noun] food, clothes, and other essentials for living: *the Society are paying for your keep*.
■ the cost of such items.
2 [mass noun] archaic charge; control: *if from shepherd's keep a lamb strayed far*.
3 the strongest or central tower of a castle, acting as a final refuge.
– PHRASES **you can't keep a good man** (or **woman**) **down** informal a competent person will always recover well from setbacks or problems. **for keeps** informal permanently; indefinitely. **keep one's feet** manage not to fall. **keep goal** chiefly Soccer act as a goalkeeper. **keep going** make an effort to live normally when in a difficult situation. **keep open house** provide general hospitality. **keep to oneself** avoid contact with others. **keep something to oneself** refuse to disclose or share something. **keep up with the Joneses** try to maintain the same social and material standards as one's friends or neighbours. **keep wicket** Cricket act as a wicketkeeper.
– DERIVATIVES **keepable** adjective.
– ORIGIN late Old English *cēpan* 'seize, take in', also 'care for, attend to', of unknown origin.
▶ **keep someone after** US make a pupil stay at school after normal hours as a punishment.
keep at (or **keep someone at**) persist (or force someone to persist) with: *it was the best part of a day's work but I kept at it*.
keep away (or **keep someone away**) stay away (or make someone stay away): *keep away from the edge of the cliff*.
keep back (or **keep someone/thing back**) remain (or cause someone or something to remain) at a distance: *he had kept back from the river when he could*.
keep someone back make a pupil repeat a year at school because of poor marks. ■ Brit. make a pupil stay at school after normal hours as a punishment.
keep something back retain or withhold something: *the father kept back £5 for himself*. ■ decline to disclose something. ■ prevent tears from flowing.
keep down stay hidden by crouching or lying down: *Keep down! There's someone coming*.
keep someone down **1** make a pupil repeat a year at school because of poor marks. **2** hold someone in subjection.
keep something down **1** cause something to remain at a low level: *the population of aphids is normally kept down by other animals*. **2** retain food or drink in one's stomach without vomiting.
keep from (or **keep someone from**) avoid (or cause someone to avoid) doing something: *Dinah bit her lips to keep from screaming* | *he could hardly* **keep himself from** *laughing*.
keep something from **1** cause something to remain a secret from (someone). **2** cause something to stay out of: *she could not keep the dismay from her voice*.
keep in with remain on good terms with (someone).
keep someone in confine someone indoors or in a particular place: *he should be kept in overnight for a second operation*.
keep something in restrain oneself from

expressing a feeling: *he wanted to make me mad, but I kept it all in.*
keep off 1 avoid encroaching on or touching. ■ avoid consuming or smoking: *the first thing was to keep off alcohol.* ■ avoid (a subject). **2** (of bad weather) fail to occur.
keep someone/thing off prevent someone or something from encroaching on or touching: *keep your hands off me.*
keep someone off prevent someone from attending (school).
keep on continue to do something: *they would have preferred to keep on working.*
keep on about speak about (something) repeatedly.
keep on at annoy (someone) by making frequent requests: *he'd kept on at her, wanting her to go out with him.*
keep someone/thing on continue to use or employ someone or something.
keep out (or **keep someone/thing out**) remain (or cause someone or something to remain) outside: *cover with cheesecloth to keep out flies.*
keep to avoid leaving (a path, road, or place). ■ adhere to (a schedule). ■ observe (a promise). ■ confine or restrict oneself to: *nothing is more irritating than people who do not keep to the point.*
keep someone under hold a person or group in subjection: *the local people are kept under by the army.*
keep up move or progress at the same rate as someone or something else: *often they had to pause to allow him to keep up.* ■ meet a commitment to pay or do something regularly: *if you do not* **keep up with** *the payments, the loan company can make you sell your home.*
keep up with learn about or be aware of (current events or developments). ■ continue to be in contact with (someone).
keep someone up prevent someone from going to bed or to sleep.
keep something up maintain or preserve something in the existing state; continue a course of action: *keep up the good work.* ■ keep something in an efficient or proper state: *the rector could not afford to keep up the grounds.* ■ make something remain at a high level: *he was whistling to keep up his spirits.*

keeper ▶ **noun 1** a person who manages or looks after something or someone, in particular:
■ Brit. a custodian of a museum or gallery collection. ■ short for **GOALKEEPER** or **WICKETKEEPER**. ■ an animal attendant employed in a zoo. Compare with **ZOOKEEPER**. ■ short for **GAMEKEEPER**. ■ a person who is regarded as being in charge of someone else: *I would not stop him—I'm his wife, not his keeper.*
2 [with adj.] a food or drink that remains in a specified condition if stored: *hazelnuts are good keepers.*
3 informal a thing worth keeping: *they were deciding which measurements are questionable and which are keepers.*
■ N. Amer. a fish large enough to be kept when caught.
4 an object which keeps another in place, or protects something more fragile or valuable, in particular:
■ a plain ring to preserve a hole in a pierced ear lobe; a sleeper. ■ a ring worn to keep a more valuable one on the finger. ■ a bar of soft iron placed across the poles of a horseshoe magnet to maintain its strength.
5 American Football a play in which the quarterback receives the ball from the centre and runs with it.
– DERIVATIVES **keepership** noun.

keep-fit ▶ **noun** [mass noun] chiefly Brit. regular exercises to improve personal fitness and health.

keeping ▶ **noun** [mass noun] the action of owning, maintaining, or protecting something: *the keeping of dogs* | [in combination] *careful record-keeping is needed.*
– PHRASES **in someone's keeping** in someone's care or custody. **in** (or **out of**) **keeping with** in (or out of) harmony or conformity with: *the cuisine is in keeping with the hotel's Edwardian character.*

keepnet ▶ **noun** Fishing a net for keeping fish alive until they are returned to the water.

keepsake ▶ **noun** a small item kept in memory of the person who gave it or originally owned it.

keeshond /ˈkeɪshɒnd/ ▶ **noun** a dog of a Dutch breed with long thick grey hair resembling a large Pomeranian.
– ORIGIN 1920s: Dutch, from *Kees* (pet form of the given name *Cornelius*) + *hond* 'dog'.

keester /ˈkiːstə/ ▶ **noun** variant spelling of **KEISTER**.

kef /kɛf/ ▶ **noun** & **adjective** variant spelling of **KIF**.

Kefallinía /ˌkɛfaliˈnia/ Greek name for **CEPHALONIA**.

keffiyeh /kəˈfiː(j)ə/ (also **kaffiyeh**) ▶ **noun** a Bedouin Arab's kerchief worn as a headdress.
– ORIGIN early 19th cent.: from Arabic *keffiyya, kūfiyya*.

Keflavik /ˈkɛfləvɪk/ a fishing port in SW Iceland; pop. 7,525 (1990). Iceland's international airport is located nearby.

keftedes /kɛfˈtɛðiːz/ ▶ **plural noun** (in Greek cookery) small meatballs made with herbs and onions.
– ORIGIN from Greek *kephtedes*, plural of *kephtes*, via Turkish from Persian *koftah* (see **KOFTA**).

keg ▶ **noun** a small barrel, especially one of less than 10 gallons or (in the US) 30 gallons.
■ short for **KEG BEER**.
– ORIGIN early 17th cent.: variant of Scots and US dialect *cag*, from Old Norse *kaggi*.

keg beer ▶ **noun** [mass noun] Brit. beer supplied in a keg, to which carbon dioxide has been added.

kegger ▶ **noun** US informal a party at which beer is served, typically from kegs.
■ a keg of beer.

keiretsu /keɪˈrɛtsuː/ ▶ **noun** (pl. same) (in Japan) a conglomeration of businesses linked together by cross-shareholdings to form a robust corporate structure.
– ORIGIN Japanese, from *kei* 'systems' + *retsu* 'tier'.

keister /ˈkiːstə/ (also **keester**) ▶ **noun** N. Amer. informal **1** a person's buttocks.
2 dated a suitcase, bag, or box for carrying possessions or merchandise.
– ORIGIN late 19th cent. (in sense 2): of unknown origin.

Kejia /keɪˈdʒjaː/ ▶ **noun** another term for **HAKKA**.

Kekulé /ˈkɛkjʊleɪ, German ˈkeːkule/, Friedrich August, (1829–96), German chemist; full name *Friedrich August Kekulé von Stradonitz*. One of the founders of structural organic chemistry, he is best known for discovering the ring structure of benzene.

Kelantan /kəˈlantən/ a state of northern Malaysia, on the east coast of the Malay Peninsula; capital, Kota Baharu.

kelim ▶ **noun** variant spelling of **KILIM**.

Keller /ˈkɛlə/, Helen (Adams) (1880–1968), American writer, social reformer, and academic. Blind and deaf from the age of nineteen months, she learned how to read, type, and speak with the help of a tutor. She went on to champion the cause of blind and deaf people throughout the world.

Kellogg /ˈkɛlɒg/, Will Keith (1860–1951), American food manufacturer. He collaborated with his brother, a doctor, to develop a breakfast cereal for sanatorium patients, of crisp flakes of rolled and toasted wheat and corn. He established the W. K. Kellogg company in 1906, eventually leading to a revolution in Western eating habits.

Kellogg Pact (also **Kellogg–Briand Pact**) a treaty renouncing war as an instrument of national policy, signed in Paris in 1928 by representatives of fifteen nations. It grew out of a proposal made by the French Premier Aristide Briand (1862–1932) to Frank B. Kellogg (1856–1937), US Secretary of State.

Kells, Book of /kɛlz/ an illuminated manuscript of the Gospels, perhaps made by Irish monks in Iona in the 8th or early 9th century, now kept at Trinity College, Dublin.
– ORIGIN *Kells*, the name of a town in County Meath, Ireland, where the manuscript was formerly kept.

Kelly[1], Ned (1855–80), Australian outlaw; full name *Edward Kelly*. Leader of a band of horse and cattle thieves and bank raiders operating in Victoria, he was eventually hanged in Melbourne.

Kelly[2], Gene (1912–96), American dancer and choreographer; full name *Eugene Curran Kelly*. He performed in and choreographed many film musicals, including *An American in Paris* (1951) and *Singin' in the Rain* (1952).

Kelly[3], Grace (Patricia) (1928–82), American film actress; also called (from 1956) **Princess Grace of Monaco**. She starred in *High Noon* (1952) and also made three Hitchcock films, including *Rear Window* (1954), before retiring from films in 1956 on her marriage to Prince Rainier III of Monaco. She died in a road accident.

Kelly[4], Petra (Karin) (1947–92), German political leader. In 1979 she co-founded the German Green Party, becoming the Party's leading spokesperson and, in 1983, one of seventeen Green Party members of the West German Parliament. The cause of her death remains a subject of controversy.

keloid /ˈkiːlɔɪd/ ▶ **noun** Medicine an area of irregular fibrous tissue formed at the site of a scar or injury.
– ORIGIN mid 19th cent.: via French from Greek *khēlē* 'crab's claw' + **-OID**.

kelp ▶ **noun** [mass noun] a large brown seaweed that typically has a long, tough stalk with a broad frond divided into strips. Some kinds grow to a very large size and form underwater 'forests' that support a large population of animals.
• Family Laminariaceae, class Phaeophyceae, including the genera *Laminaria* (used in some areas as manure) and *Macrocystis* (harvested in the US as a source of algin).
■ the calcined ashes of seaweed, used as a source of various salts.
– ORIGIN late Middle English: of unknown origin.

kelpfish ▶ **noun** (pl. same or **-fishes**) any of a number of fish that live among kelp or other marine algae, in particular:
• a small fish with the dorsal fin running the length of the body, of the Pacific coast of North America (*Gibbonsia* and other genera, family Clinidae). • an Australian fish which lives among seagrass and algae (family Chironemidae: several genera).

kelpie /ˈkɛlpi/ ▶ **noun 1** a water spirit of Scottish folklore, typically taking the form of a horse, reputed to delight in the drowning of travellers.
2 a sheepdog of an Australian breed with a smooth coat, originally bred from a Scottish collie.
– ORIGIN late 17th cent.: perhaps from Scottish Gaelic *cailpeach, colpach* 'bullock, colt'. Sense 2 apparently comes from the name of a particular bitch, *King's Kelpie* (c.1879).

kelson /ˈkɛls(ə)n/ ▶ **noun** variant spelling of **KEELSON**.

kelt ▶ **noun** a salmon or sea trout after spawning and before returning to the sea.
– ORIGIN Middle English: of unknown origin.

Kelvin, William Thomson, 1st Baron (1824–1907), British physicist and natural philosopher. He is best known for introducing the absolute scale of temperature. He also restated the second law of thermodynamics and was involved in the laying of the first Atlantic cable, for which he invented several instruments.

kelvin (abbrev.: **K**) ▶ **noun** the SI base unit of thermodynamic temperature, equal in magnitude to the degree Celsius.
– ORIGIN late 19th cent.: named after Lord **KELVIN**.

Kelvin scale ▶ **noun** a scale of temperature with absolute zero as zero, and the triple point of water as exactly 273.16 degrees.

Kemal Pasha /kɛˈmɑːl ˌpɑːʃə/ see **ATATÜRK**.

Kemble[1] /ˈkɛmb(ə)l/, Fanny (1809–93), English actress; full name *Frances Anne Kemble*. The daughter of Charles Kemble and the niece of Sarah Siddons, she was a success in both Shakespearean comedy and tragedy.

Kemble[2] /ˈkɛmb(ə)l/, John Philip (1757–1823), English actor-manager, brother of Sarah Siddons. Noted for his performances in Shakespearean tragedy, he was manager of Drury Lane (1788–1803) and Covent Garden (1803–17) theatres. His younger brother **Charles Kemble** (1775–1854) was also a successful actor-manager.

Kemerovo /ˈkɛmɪrəvə/ an industrial city in south central Russia, to the east of Novosibirsk; pop. 521,000 (1990).

kemp ▶ **noun** a coarse hair or fibre in wool.
– DERIVATIVES **kempy** adjective.
– ORIGIN late Middle English (originally denoting a coarse human hair): from Old Norse *kampr* 'beard, whisker'.

Kempe, Margery (c.1373–c.1440), English mystic. From about 1432 to 1436 she dictated one of the first autobiographies in English, *The Book of Margery Kempe*. It gives an account of her series of pilgrimages, as well as details of her mystic self-transcendent visions.

Kempis, Thomas à, see **THOMAS À KEMPIS**.

kempt ▶ **adjective** (of a person or a place)

maintained in a neat and clean condition; well cared for: *she was looking as thoroughly kempt as ever*.
– ORIGIN Old English *cemd-*, past participle of *cemban* 'to comb', of Germanic origin; related to **COMB**. The Middle English form *kemb* survives in dialect.

ken ▶ noun [in sing.] one's range of knowledge or sight: *such determination is beyond my ken*.
▶ verb (**kenning**; past and past participle **kenned** or **kent**) [with obj.] Scottish & N. English know: *d'ye ken anyone who can boast of that?*
■ recognize; identify: *that's him—d'ye ken him?*
– ORIGIN Old English *cennan* 'tell, make known', of Germanic origin; related to Dutch and German *kennen* 'know, be acquainted with', from an Indo-European root shared by **CAN**[1] and **KNOW**. Current senses of the verb date from Middle English; the noun from the mid 16th cent.

kenaf /kəˈnaf/ ▶ noun [mass noun] a brown plant fibre similar to jute, used to make ropes and coarse cloth.
– ORIGIN late 19th cent.: from Persian, variant of *kanab* 'hemp'.

Kendal /ˈkɛnd(ə)l/ a town in Cumbria, NW England; pop. 24,200 (1981).

Kendal Green ▶ noun [mass noun] a kind of rough green woollen cloth.
■ the green colour of this cloth.

Kendall /ˈkɛnd(ə)l/, Edward Calvin (1886–1972), American biochemist. He isolated crystalline thyroxine from the thyroid gland, and from the adrenal cortex he obtained a number of steroid hormones, one of which was later named cortisone. Nobel Prize for Physiology or Medicine (1950).

Kendal mint cake ▶ noun [mass noun] a hard peppermint-flavoured sweet which is sold in flat rectangular blocks and is popular with ramblers and hill climbers.

kendo /ˈkɛndəʊ/ ▶ noun [mass noun] a Japanese form of fencing with two-handed bamboo swords, originally developed as a safe form of sword training for samurai.
– DERIVATIVES **kendoist** noun.
– ORIGIN Japanese, from *ken* 'sword' + *dō* 'way'.

Keneally /kəˈnali, -ˈniːli/, Thomas (Michael) (b.1935), Australian novelist. He first gained recognition for *The Chant of Jimmie Blacksmith* (1972), but is probably best known for his Booker Prize-winning novel *Schindler's Ark* (1982), filmed by Steven Spielberg in 1993 as *Schindler's List*.

Kennedy the name of a family of US politicians:
■ John F. (1917–63), 35th President of the US 1961–3; in full *John Fitzgerald Kennedy*; known as *JFK*. The youngest man ever to be elected US President (at 43), he was a popular advocate of civil rights. In foreign affairs he recovered from the Bay of Pigs fiasco to demand successfully the withdrawal of Soviet missiles from Cuba (the Cuban Missile Crisis). Kennedy was assassinated while riding in a motorcade through Dallas, Texas.
■ Robert (1925–68), US Attorney General 1961–4; full name *Robert Francis Kennedy*. He closely assisted his brother John in domestic policy, and was also a champion of the civil rights movement. He was assassinated during his campaign as a prospective presidential candidate.
■ Teddy (b.1932), brother of John and Robert, US Senator since 1962; full name *Edward Moore Kennedy*. His political career has been overshadowed by his involvement in a car accident at Chappaquiddick Island (1969), in which his assistant Mary Jo Kopechne drowned.

Kennedy, Cape former name (1963–73) for **CANAVERAL, CAPE**.

kennel ▶ noun a small shelter for a dog.
■ (usu. **kennels**) [treated as sing. or pl.] a boarding or breeding establishment for dogs. ■ figurative a small or sordid dwelling.
▶ verb (**kennelled**, **kennelling**; US **kenneled**, **kenneling**) [with obj.] put (a dog) in a kennel.
– ORIGIN Middle English: from an Old Northern French variant of Old French *chenil*, from Latin *canis* 'dog'.

Kennelly /ˈkɛnəli/, Arthur Edwin (1861–1939), American electrical engineer. His principal work was on the theory of alternating currents. Independently of O. Heaviside, he also discovered the layer in the atmosphere responsible for reflecting radio waves back to the earth.

Kennelly layer (also **Kennelly–Heaviside layer**) ▶ noun another name for **E-LAYER**.

kennelmaid ▶ noun a woman who works in a kennels.

kennelman ▶ noun (pl. **-men**) a man who works in a kennels, especially for a hunt.

Kenneth I (d.858), king of Scotland *c.*844–58; known as **Kenneth MacAlpin**. He is traditionally viewed as the founder of the kingdom of Scotland, which was established following his defeat of the Picts in about 844.

kenning ▶ noun a compound expression in Old English and Old Norse poetry with metaphorical meaning, e.g. *oar-steed* = ship.
– ORIGIN late 19th cent.: from Old Norse, from *kenna* 'know, perceive'; related to **KEN**.

keno /ˈkiːnəʊ/ ▶ noun [mass noun] a game of chance similar to bingo, based on the drawing of numbers and covering of corresponding numbers on cards.
– ORIGIN early 19th cent.: from French *kine*, denoting a set of five winning lottery numbers.

kenosis /kɪˈnəʊsɪs/ ▶ noun [mass noun] (in Christian theology) the renunciation of the divine nature, at least in part, by Christ in the Incarnation.
– DERIVATIVES **kenotic** adjective.
– ORIGIN late 19th cent.: from Greek *kenōsis* 'an emptying', from *kenoein* 'to empty', from *kenos* 'empty', with biblical allusion (Phil. 2:7) to Greek *heauton ekenōse*, literally 'emptied himself'.

Kensington /ˈkɛnzɪŋtən/ a fashionable residential district in central London. Part of the borough of Kensington and Chelsea, it contains Kensington Palace, Kensington Gardens, and the Victoria and Albert Museum, Natural History Museum, and Science Museum.

kenspeckle /ˈkɛnˌspɛk(ə)l/ ▶ adjective Scottish easily recognizable; conspicuous.
– ORIGIN mid 16th cent.: of Scandinavian origin, probably based on Old Norse *kenna* 'know, perceive' and *spak-*, *spek-* 'wise or wisdom'.

Kent[1] a county on the SE coast of England; county town, Maidstone.
– DERIVATIVES **Kentish** adjective.
– ORIGIN from Latin *Cantium*, of Celtic origin.

Kent[2], William (*c.*1685–1748), English architect and landscape gardener. Chiefly remembered for his landscape gardens at Stowe House in Buckinghamshire (*c.*1730), he also promoted the Palladian style of architecture in England.

kent past and past participle of **KEN**.

kente /ˈkɛntɛ/ ▶ noun [mass noun] a brightly coloured, banded material made in Ghana.
■ [count noun] a long garment made from this material, worn loosely around the shoulders and waist.
– ORIGIN mid 20th cent.: from Twi, 'cloth'.

kentia palm /ˈkɛntɪə/ (also **kentia**) ▶ noun an Australasian palm tree which is popular as a house plant while it is young.
● *Howeia* (or *Howea*, formerly *Kentia*) *forsteriana*, family Palmae.
– ORIGIN late 19th cent.: modern Latin, named after William Kent (died 1828), botanical collector.

Kentish glory ▶ noun a large European moth with orange-brown and white markings, occurring chiefly on moorland and in open woodland.
● *Endromis versicolora*, the only member of the family Endromidae.

Kentish plover ▶ noun a small white-breasted plover related to the ringed plover, found on most continents.
● *Charadrius alexandrinus*, family Charadriidae; American races are sometimes treated as a different species. North American name: **snowy plover**.
– ORIGIN early 19th cent.: so named because of its first discovery in Kent, but now extinct in Britain.

Kentish ragstone (also **Kentish rag**) ▶ noun [mass noun] a hard, compact limestone found in Kent, used for paving and building.

Kenton, Stan (1912–79), American bandleader, composer, and arranger; born *Stanley Newcomb*. He formed his own orchestra in 1940 and is particularly associated with the big-band jazz style of the 1950s.

Kentucky /kɛnˈtʌki/ a state in the south-eastern US; pop. 3,685,300 (1990); capital, Frankfort. Ceded by the French to the British in 1763, Kentucky entered the Union as the 15th state in 1792.
– DERIVATIVES **Kentuckian** adjective.

Kentucky Derby ▶ noun an annual horse race for three-year-olds at Louisville, Kentucky. First held in 1875, it is the oldest horse race in the US.

Kenya /ˈkɛnjə/ an equatorial country in East Africa, on the Indian Ocean; pop. 25,016,000 (est. 1991); languages, Swahili (official), English (official), Kikuyu; capital, Nairobi.

Populated largely by Bantu-speaking peoples, Kenya became a British Crown Colony in 1920. The demands made on land by European settlers led to the Mau Mau rebellion of the 1950s. Kenya became an independent state within the Commonwealth in 1963, and a republic was established the following year.

– DERIVATIVES **Kenyan** adjective & noun.

Kenya, Mount a mountain in central Kenya, just south of the equator, rising to a height of 5,200 m (17,058 ft). The second highest mountain in Africa, it gave its name to the country Kenya.

Kenya African National Union (abbrev.: **KANU**) a Kenyan political party formed in 1960 and led first by Jomo Kenyatta. KANU won the first Kenyan elections and took the country into independence in 1963; it has since dominated Kenyan politics, ruling as the sole legal party 1982–91.

Kenyatta /kɛnˈjatə/, Jomo (*c.*1891–1978), Kenyan statesman, Prime Minister of Kenya 1963 and President 1964–78. Imprisoned for alleged complicity in the Mau Mau uprising (1952–61), on his release he was elected president of the Kenya African National Union and led Kenya to independence in 1963, subsequently serving as its first President.

kep /kɛp/ ▶ verb (**kepped**, **kepping**) [with obj.] Scottish & N. English catch.
– ORIGIN late Middle English (originally in the sense 'meet, receive the force of (a blow)'): differentiated form of the verb **KEEP**.

kepi /ˈkɛpi, ˈkeɪpi/ ▶ noun (pl. **kepis**) a French military cap with a horizontal peak.
– ORIGIN mid 19th cent.: from French *képi*, from Swiss German *Käppi*, diminutive of *Kappe* 'cap'.

Kepler /ˈkɛplə/, Johannes (1571–1630), German astronomer. His analysis of Tycho Brahe's planetary observations led him to discover the three laws governing orbital motion.
– DERIVATIVES **Keplerian** adjective.

Kepler's laws three theorems describing orbital motion. The first law states that planets move in elliptical orbits with the sun at one focus. The second states that the radius vector of a planet sweeps out equal areas in equal times. The third law relates the distances of the planets from the sun to their orbital periods.

kept past and past participle of **KEEP**.

Kerala /ˈkɛrələ/ a state on the coast of SW India; capital, Trivandrum. It was created in 1956 from the former state of Travancore-Cochin and part of Madras.
– DERIVATIVES **Keralite** adjective & noun.

kerat- ▶ combining form variant spelling of **KERATO-** shortened before a vowel (as in *keratectomy*).

keratectomy /ˌkɛrəˈtɛktəmi/ ▶ noun [mass noun] surgical removal of a section or layer of the cornea, usually performed using a laser to correct myopia.

keratin /ˈkɛrətɪn/ ▶ noun [mass noun] a fibrous protein forming the main structural constituent of hair, feathers, hoofs, claws, horns, etc.
– ORIGIN mid 19th cent.: from Greek *keras*, *kerat-* 'horn' + **-IN**[1].

keratinize /ˈkɛrətɪnʌɪz, kəˈrat-/ (also **-ise**) ▶ verb Biology change or become changed into a form containing keratin: [with obj.] *the products of the epidermal line are ultimately keratinized* | [no obj.] *the cells keratinize under oestrogenic action*.
– DERIVATIVES **keratinization** noun.
– ORIGIN late 19th cent.: from Greek *keratinos* 'horny' + **-IZE**.

keratinocyte /ˌkɛrəˈtɪnə(ʊ)sʌɪt/ ▶ noun Biology an epidermal cell which produces keratin.

keratinous /kəˈratɪnəs/ ▶ adjective Biology containing or made from keratin.

keratitis /ˌkɛrəˈtʌɪtɪs/ ▶ noun [mass noun] Medicine inflammation of the cornea of the eye.

kerato- ▶ combining form (also **kerat-**) **1** relating to keratin or horny tissue.
2 relating to the cornea.
– ORIGIN from Greek *keras*, *kerat-* 'horn'.

keratoplasty /ˈkɛrətə(ʊ),plasti/ ▶ noun [mass noun] surgery carried out on the cornea, especially corneal transplantation.

keratosis /ˌkɛrəˈtəʊsɪs/ ▶ noun (pl. **keratoses**) Medicine a horny growth, especially on the skin.

keratotomy /ˌkɛrəˈtɒtəmi/ ▶ noun [mass noun] a surgical operation involving cutting into the cornea of the eye. The most common form is **radial keratotomy**, performed to correct myopia.

kerb (US **curb**) ▶ noun a stone edging to a pavement or raised path.
– ORIGIN mid 17th cent. (denoting a raised border or frame): variant of **CURB**.

kerb-crawling ▶ noun [mass noun] Brit. the action of driving slowly along the edge of the road in search of sex from a prostitute or female passer-by.
– DERIVATIVES **kerb-crawler** noun.

kerb drill ▶ noun Brit. a set of precautions, especially looking to right and left, taken before crossing the road and typically taught to children.

kerbing ▶ noun [mass noun] **1** the stones collectively forming a kerb.
2 the action of hitting a kerb with a car, leading to possible damage to the tyres or suspension.

kerb market ▶ noun a market for selling shares not dealt with on the normal stock exchange, or for dealing after hours.

kerbside (US **curbside**) ▶ noun the side of a road or pavement that is nearer to the kerb.

kerbstone (US **curbstone**) ▶ noun a long, narrow stone or concrete block, laid end to end with others to form a kerb.

kerb weight ▶ noun the weight of a motor car without occupants or baggage.

Kerch /kəːtʃ/ a city in southern Ukraine, the chief port and industrial centre of the Crimea, at the eastern end of the Kerch peninsula; pop. 176,000 (1990).

kerchief /ˈkəːtʃɪf/ ▶ noun a piece of fabric used to cover the head.
■ poetic/literary a handkerchief.
– DERIVATIVES **kerchiefed** adjective.
– ORIGIN Middle English *kerchef*, from Old French *cuevrechief*, from *couvrir* 'to cover' + *chief* 'head'.

kereru /ˈkɛrəru/ ▶ noun NZ a New Zealand pigeon which has mainly greenish metallic plumage with white underparts and a purplish-crimson bill and feet.
● *Hemiphaga novaeseelandiae*, family Columbidae. Alternative name: **New Zealand pigeon**.
– ORIGIN late 19th cent.: from Maori.

Keres /ˈkɛrɛs/ ▶ noun (pl. same) **1** a member of a Pueblo Indian people inhabiting parts of New Mexico.
2 [mass noun] the language of this people, of unknown affinity, with fewer than 8,000 speakers.
▶ adjective of or relating to this people or their language.
– ORIGIN from American Spanish *Queres*, from American Indian.

kerf /kəːf/ ▶ noun **1** a slit made by cutting, especially with a saw.
2 the cut end of a felled tree.
– DERIVATIVES **kerfed** adjective.
– ORIGIN Old English *cyrf* 'cutting, a cut', of West Germanic origin; related to **CARVE**.

kerfuffle /kəˈfʌf(ə)l/ ▶ noun [in sing.] informal, chiefly Brit. a commotion or fuss, especially one caused by conflicting views: *there was a kerfuffle over the chairmanship.*
– ORIGIN early 19th cent.: perhaps from Scots *curfuffle* (probably from Scottish Gaelic *car* 'twist, bend' + imitative Scots *fuffle* 'to disorder'), or related to Irish *cior thual* 'confusion, disorder'.

Kerguelen Islands /ˈkəːgɪlɪn, kəːˈɡeɪlən/ a group of islands in the southern Indian Ocean, comprising the island of Kerguelen and some 300 small islets, forming part of French Southern and Antarctic Territories.
– ORIGIN named after the Breton navigator Yves-Joseph de *Kerguélen*-Trémarec, who discovered the islands in 1772.

Kérkira /ˈkɛrkɪrə/ modern Greek name for **CORFU**.

Kerkrade /ˈkəːkrɑːdə/ a mining town in the southern Netherlands, on the German border; pop. 53,280 (1991). An international music competition is held there every four years.

Kermadec Islands /kəːˈmadək/ a group of uninhabited islands in the western South Pacific, north of New Zealand, administered by New Zealand since 1887.

kermes /ˈkəːmɪz/ ▶ noun **1** [mass noun] a red dye used, especially formerly, for colouring fabrics and manuscripts.
■ the dried bodies of a female scale insect, which are crushed to yield this dye.
2 (**oak kermes**) the scale insect that is used for this dye, forming berry-like galls on the kermes oak.
● *Kermes ilicis*, family Eriococcidae, suborder Homoptera.
– ORIGIN late 16th cent. (denoting the kermes oak): from French *kermès*, from Arabic *ḳirmiz*; related to **CRIMSON**.

kermes oak ▶ noun a very small evergreen Mediterranean oak which sometimes remains as a shrub. It has prickly holly-like leaves and was formerly prized as a host plant for kermes insects.
● *Quercus coccifera*, family Fagaceae.

kermis /ˈkəːmɪs/ ▶ noun a summer fair held in towns and villages in the Netherlands.
■ US a fair or carnival, especially one held to raise money for a charity.
– ORIGIN late 16th cent.: Dutch, originally denoting a mass on the anniversary of the dedication of a church, when a fair was held, from *kerk* 'church' + *mis* 'Mass'.

Kern, Jerome (David) (1885–1945), American composer. A major influence in the development of the musical, he wrote several musical comedies, including *Showboat* (1927).

kern[1] Printing ▶ verb [with obj.] **1** [usu. as noun **kerning**] adjust the spacing between (letters or characters) in a piece of text to be printed.
■ make (letters) overlap.
2 design (metal type) with a projecting part beyond the body or shank.
▶ noun the part of a metal type projecting beyond its body or shank.
– ORIGIN late 17th cent.: perhaps from French *carne* 'corner', from Latin *cardo, cardin-* 'hinge'.

kern[2] (also **kerne**) ▶ noun **1** historical a light-armed Irish foot soldier.
2 archaic a peasant; a rustic.
– ORIGIN late Middle English: from Irish *ceithearn*, from Old Irish *ceithern* 'band of foot soldiers'.

kernel /ˈkəːn(ə)l/ ▶ noun a softer, usually edible part of a nut, seed, or fruit stone contained within its hard shell.
■ the seed and hard husk of a cereal, especially wheat.
■ [in sing.] the central or most important part of something: *this is the kernel of the argument*. ■ the most basic level or core of an operating system of a computer, responsible for resource allocation, file management, and security. ■ [as modifier] Linguistics denoting a basic unmarked linguistic string.
– ORIGIN Old English *cyrnel*, diminutive of **CORN**[1].

kernite /ˈkəːnʌɪt/ ▶ noun [mass noun] a transparent crystalline mineral which consists of hydrated sodium borate and is a major source of borax.
– ORIGIN early 20th cent.: from *Kern* (the name of the Californian county where it was discovered) + **-ITE**[1].

kero /ˈkɛrəʊ/ ▶ noun [mass noun] Austral./NZ informal kerosene.
– ORIGIN 1930s: abbreviation.

kerogen /ˈkɛrədʒ(ə)n/ ▶ noun [mass noun] a complex fossilized organic material, found in oil shale and other sedimentary rock, which is insoluble in common organic solvents and yields petroleum products on distillation.
– ORIGIN early 20th cent.: from Greek *kēros* 'wax' + **-GEN**.

kerosene /ˈkɛrəsiːn/ (also **kerosine**) ▶ noun [mass noun] a light fuel oil obtained by distilling petroleum, used especially in jet engines and domestic heating boilers; paraffin oil.
– ORIGIN mid 19th cent.: from Greek *kēros* 'wax' (because the solid form of paraffin is wax-like) + **-ENE**.

Kerouac /ˈkɛruak/, Jack (1922–69), American novelist and poet, of French-Canadian descent; born *Jean-Louis Lebris de Kérouac*. A leading figure of the beat generation, he is best known for his semi-autobiographical novel *On the Road* (1957).

Kerr effect /kəː/ ▶ noun [mass noun] Physics **1** the rotation of the plane of polarization of light when reflected from a magnetized surface.

2 the production of double refraction in a substance by an electric field.
– ORIGIN early 20th cent.: named after John *Kerr* (1824–1907), the Scottish physicist who studied these effects.

kerria /ˈkɛrɪə/ ▶ noun an East Asian shrub of the rose family, which is cultivated for its yellow flowers, especially as the double-flowered variety.
● *Kerria japonica*, family Rosaceae.
– ORIGIN early 19th cent.: modern Latin, named after William *Ker(r)* (died 1814), English botanical collector.

Kerry[1] a county of the Republic of Ireland, on the SW coast in the province of Munster; county town, Tralee.

Kerry[2] ▶ noun (pl. **-ies**) an animal of a breed of small black dairy cattle.

Kerry blue ▶ noun a terrier of a breed with a silky blue-grey coat.

Kerry Hill ▶ noun a sheep of a breed having a thick fleece and black markings near the muzzle and feet.
– ORIGIN early 20th cent.: from *Kerry*, the name of a town and neighbouring hill range in Powys, Wales.

kersey /ˈkəːzi/ ▶ noun [mass noun] a kind of coarse, ribbed cloth with a short nap, woven from short-stapled wool.
– ORIGIN late Middle English: probably from *Kersey*, a town in Suffolk where woollen cloth was made.

kerseymere /ˈkəːzɪmɪə/ ▶ noun [mass noun] a fine twilled woollen cloth.
– ORIGIN late 18th cent.: alteration of *cassimere*, variant of **CASHMERE**, changed by association with **KERSEY**.

keruing /ˈkɛrɔɪŋ/ ▶ noun a timber tree related to the gurjun, growing in Malaysia, Sabah, and Indonesia.
● Genus *Dipterocarpus*, family Dipterocarpaceae: several species.
– ORIGIN early 20th cent.: from Malay.

Kesey /ˈkiːzi/, Ken (Elton) (b.1935), American novelist. His best-known novel, *One Flew over the Cuckoo's Nest* (1962), is based on his experiences as a ward attendant in a mental hospital.

kesh /keɪʃ/ (also **kes**) ▶ noun [mass noun] the uncut hair and beard worn as one of the five distinguishing signs of the Sikh Khalsa.
– ORIGIN from Punjabi *keś*.

keskidee /ˌkɛskɪˈdiː/ ▶ noun variant spelling of **KISKADEE**.

kestrel ▶ noun a small falcon that hovers with rapidly beating wings while searching for prey on the ground.
● Genus *Falco*, family Falconidae: several species, in particular the **common kestrel** (*F. tinnunculus*) of Eurasia and Africa, and the **American kestrel** (*F. sparverius*).
– ORIGIN late Middle English *castrel*, perhaps from *casserelle*, dialect variant of Old French *crecerelle*, perhaps imitative of its call.

Keswick /ˈkɛzɪk/ a market town and tourist centre on the northern shores of Derwent Water in Cumbria, NW England; pop. 5,645 (1981).

ketamine /ˈkiːtəmiːn/ ▶ noun [mass noun] a synthetic compound used as an anaesthetic and analgesic drug and also (illicitly) as a hallucinogen.
● Chem. formula: $C_{13}H_{16}NOCl$.
– ORIGIN mid 20th cent.: blend of **KETONE** and **AMINE**.

ketch ▶ noun a two-masted, fore-and-aft rigged sailing boat with a mizzenmast stepped forward of the rudder and smaller than its foremast.
– ORIGIN mid 17th cent.: later form of obsolete *catch*, probably from **CATCH**.

ketchup /ˈkɛtʃəp, -ʌp/ (also **catchup**, US also **catsup**) ▶ noun [mass noun] a spicy sauce made chiefly from tomatoes and vinegar, used as a relish.
– ORIGIN late 17th cent.: perhaps from Chinese (Cantonese dialect) *k'ē chap* 'tomato juice'.

ketene /ˈkiːtiːn/ ▶ noun Chemistry a pungent colourless reactive gas, used as an intermediate in chemical synthesis.
● Chem. formula: $CH_2=C=O$.
■ [count noun] any substituted derivative of this.
– ORIGIN early 20th cent.: from **KETONE** + **-ENE**.

keto acid /ˈkiːtəʊ/ ▶ noun Chemistry a compound whose molecule contains both a carboxyl group (—COOH) and a ketone group (—CO—).

ketonaemia /ˌkiːtəˈniːmɪə/ (US **ketonemia**) ▶ noun [mass noun] Medicine the presence of an abnormally high concentration of ketone bodies in the blood.

ketone /ˈkiːtəʊn/ ▶ **noun** Chemistry an organic compound containing a carbonyl group =C=O bonded to two alkyl groups, made by oxidizing secondary alcohols. The simplest such compound is acetone.
– DERIVATIVES **ketonic** /kɪˈtɒnɪk/ adjective.
– ORIGIN mid 19th cent.: from German *Keton*, alteration of *Aketon* 'acetone'.

ketone bodies ▶ **plural noun** Biochemistry three related compounds (one of which is acetone) produced during the metabolism of fats.

ketonuria /ˌkiːtə(ʊ)ˈnjʊərɪə/ ▶ **noun** [mass noun] Medicine the excretion of abnormally large amounts of ketone bodies in the urine, characteristic of diabetes mellitus, starvation, or other medical conditions.

ketosis /kɪˈtəʊsɪs/ ▶ **noun** [mass noun] Medicine a condition characterized by raised levels of ketone bodies in the body, associated with abnormal fat metabolism and diabetes mellitus.
– DERIVATIVES **ketotic** adjective.

Kettering, Charles Franklin (1876–1958), American automobile engineer. His first significant development was the electric starter (1912). As head of research at General Motors he discovered tetraethyl lead as an anti-knock agent and defined the octane rating of fuels; he also did important work on diesel engines, synchromesh gearboxes, automatic transmissions, and power steering.

kettie ▶ **noun** variant of **CATTY**[2].

kettle ▶ **noun** a metal or plastic container with a lid, spout, and handle, used for boiling water.
– PHRASES **a different kettle of fish** informal a completely different type of person or thing from the one previously mentioned: *he's certainly a different kettle of fish from old Rowell.* **the pot calling the kettle black** see **POT**[1]. **a pretty** (or **fine**) **kettle of fish** informal an awkward state of affairs.
– DERIVATIVES **kettleful** noun (pl. **-fuls**).
– ORIGIN Old English *cetel, cietel*, of Germanic origin, based on Latin *catillus*, diminutive of *catinus* 'deep container for cooking or serving food'. In Middle English the word's form was influenced by Old Norse *ketill*.

kettledrum ▶ **noun** a large drum shaped like a bowl, with a membrane adjustable for tension (and so pitch) stretched across. Also collectively called **TIMPANI**.
– DERIVATIVES **kettledrummer** noun.

kettle hole ▶ **noun** Geology a hollow, typically filled by a lake, resulting from the melting of a mass of ice trapped in glacial deposits.

Keuper /ˈkɔɪpə/ ▶ **noun** [mass noun] Geology a European series of sedimentary rocks of Upper Triassic age, represented in England chiefly by marls and sandstones: [as modifier] *the red Keuper marls.*
– ORIGIN mid 19th cent. (originally a miners' term): German.

keurboom /ˈkɪəbʊəm/ ▶ **noun** S. African a small southern African tree which typically bears drooping clusters of scented mauve flowers.
• Genus *Virgilia*, family Leguminosae.
– ORIGIN early 18th cent.: from Afrikaans, from *keur* 'choice' + *boom* 'tree'.

keV ▶ **abbreviation for** kilo-electronvolt(s).

kevel /ˈkɛv(ə)l/ ▶ **noun** a large cleat fitted to the gunwale of a ship and used in belaying ropes.
– ORIGIN Middle English: of unknown origin.

Kevlar /ˈkɛvlɑː/ ▶ **noun** [mass noun] trademark a synthetic fibre of high tensile strength used especially as a reinforcing agent in the manufacture of tyres and other rubber products.

Kew Gardens the Royal Botanic Gardens at Kew, in Richmond, London. Developed by the mother of George III with the aid of Sir Joseph Banks, the gardens are now an important botanical institution.

kewpie /ˈkjuːpi/ (also **kewpie doll**) ▶ **noun** (trademark in the US) a type of doll characterized by a large head, big eyes, chubby cheeks, and a curl or topknot on top of its head.
– ORIGIN early 20th cent. (originally US): from **CUPID** + **-IE**.

key[1] ▶ **noun** (pl. **-eys**) **1** a small piece of shaped metal with incisions cut to fit the wards of a particular lock, and which is placed into a lock and turned to open or close it.
■ a similar implement for operating a switch in the form of a lock, especially one operating the ignition of a motor vehicle. ■ an instrument for grasping and turning a screw, peg, or nut, especially one for winding a clock or turning a valve. ■ a pin, bolt, or wedge inserted between other pieces, or fitting into a hole or space designed for it, so as to lock parts together.
2 one of several buttons on a panel for operating a typewriter, word processor, or computer terminal.
■ a lever depressed by the finger in playing an instrument such as the organ, piano, flute, or concertina. ■ a lever operating a mechanical device for making or breaking an electric circuit, for example in telegraphy.
3 a thing that provides a means of gaining access to or understanding something: *the* **key** *to Derek's behaviour may lie submerged in his unhappy past.*
■ an explanatory list of symbols used in a map, table, etc. ■ a set of answers to exercises or problems. ■ a word or system for solving a cipher or code. ■ the first move in the solution of a chess problem. ■ Computing a field in a record which is used to identify that record uniquely.
4 Music a group of notes based on a particular note and comprising a scale, regarded as forming the tonal basis of a piece or passage of music: *the key of E minor.*
■ the tone or pitch of someone's voice: *his voice had changed to a lower key.* ■ figurative the prevailing tone or tenor of a piece of writing, situation, etc.: *it was like the sixties all over again, in a new, more austerely intellectual key.* ■ the prevailing range of tones or intensities in a painting: *these mauves, lime greens, and saffron yellows recall the high key of El Greco's palette.*
5 the dry winged fruit of an ash, maple, or sycamore, typically growing in bunches; a samara.
6 the part of a first coat of wall plaster that passes between the laths and so secures the rest.
■ [in sing.] the roughness of a surface, helping the adhesion of plaster or other material.
7 Basketball the keyhole-shaped area marked on the court near each basket.
▶ **adjective** of paramount or crucial importance: *she became a key figure in the suffragette movement.*
▶ **verb** (**-eys**, **-eyed**) [with obj.] **1** enter or operate on (data) by means of a computer keyboard: *she* **keyed in** *a series of commands* | [no obj.] *a hacker caused considerable disruption after* **keying into** *a vital database.*
2 [with obj. and adverbial] (usu. **be keyed**) fasten (something) in position with a pin, wedge, or bolt: *the coils may be keyed into the slots by fibre wedges.*
■ (**key something to**) make something fit in with or be linked to: *this optimism is keyed to the possibility that the US might lead in the research field.* ■ (**key someone/thing into/in with**) cause someone or something to be in harmony with: *to those who are keyed into his lunatic sense of humour, the arrival of any Bergman movie is a major comic event.*
3 roughen (a surface) to help the adhesion of plaster or other material.
4 word (an advertisement in a particular periodical), typically by varying the form of the address given, so as to identify the publication generating particular responses.
5 N. Amer. informal be the crucial factor in achieving: *Ewing keyed a 73–35 advantage on the boards with twenty rebounds.*
– PHRASES **in** (or **out of**) **key** in (or out of) harmony: *this vaguely uplifting conclusion is out of key with the body of his book.* **under lock and key** see **LOCK**[1].
– DERIVATIVES **keyed** adjective, **keyer** noun, **keyless** adjective.
– ORIGIN Old English *cǣg, cǣge*, of unknown origin.
▶ **key someone up** (usu. **be keyed up**) make someone nervous, tense, or excited, especially before an important event.

key[2] ▶ **noun** a low-lying island or reef, especially in the Caribbean. Compare with **CAY**.
– ORIGIN late 17th cent.: from Spanish *cayo* 'shoal, reef', influenced by **QUAY**.

keyboard ▶ **noun 1** a panel of keys that operate a computer or typewriter.
2 a set of keys on a piano or similar musical instrument.
■ an electronic musical instrument with keys arranged as on a piano: *she plays keyboard and guitar.*
▶ **verb** [with obj.] enter (data) by means of a keyboard.
– DERIVATIVES **keyboarder** noun, **keyboardist** noun (in sense 2 of the noun).

key card (also **card key**) ▶ **noun** a small plastic card, sometimes used instead of a door key in hotels, bearing magnetically encoded data that can be read and processed by an electronic device.

key grip ▶ **noun** the person in a film crew who is in charge of the camera equipment.

keyholder ▶ **noun** a person who is entrusted with keeping a key to commercial or industrial premises.

keyhole ▶ **noun** a hole in a lock into which the key is inserted.
■ a circle cut out of a garment as a decorative effect, typically at the front or back neckline of a dress.

keyhole limpet ▶ **noun** a limpet which has an aperture at the apex of the shell, sometimes extending to the margin.
• Family Fissurellidae, class Gastropoda.

keyhole saw ▶ **noun** a saw with a long, narrow blade for cutting small holes such as keyholes.

keyhole surgery ▶ **noun** [mass noun] Brit. informal minimally invasive surgery carried out through a very small incision, with special instruments and techniques including fibre optics.

key industry ▶ **noun** an industry that is essential to the functioning of others, such as the manufacture of machine tools.

Key Largo a resort island off the south coast of Florida, the northernmost and the longest of the Florida Keys.

key light ▶ **noun** the main source of light in a photograph or film.

Key lime ▶ **noun** a small yellowish lime with a sharp flavour.
– ORIGIN named after the Florida *Keys*.

key map ▶ **noun** a map in bare outline, to simplify the use of a full map.

key money ▶ **noun** [mass noun] informal money paid to a landlord as an inducement, by a person wishing to rent a property.
■ Brit. a payment required from a new tenant of rented accommodation in exchange for the provision of a key to the premises.

Keynes /keɪnz/, John Maynard, 1st Baron (1883–1946), English economist. He laid the foundations of modern macroeconomics with *The General Theory of Employment, Interest and Money* (1936), in which he argued that full employment is determined by effective demand and requires government spending on public works to stimulate this.
– DERIVATIVES **Keynesian** adjective & noun, **Keynesianism** noun.

keynote ▶ **noun 1** a prevailing tone or central theme, typically one set or introduced at the start of a conference: *individuality is the keynote of the Nineties* | [as modifier] *he delivered the keynote address at the launch.*
2 Music the note on which a key is based.

keynoter ▶ **noun** a person who delivers a speech setting out or introducing the central theme of a conference.

keypad ▶ **noun** a miniature keyboard or set of buttons for operating a portable electronic device, telephone, or other equipment.

keypunch ▶ **noun** a device for transferring data by means of punched holes or notches on a series of cards or paper tape.
▶ **verb** [with obj.] put into the form of punched cards or paper tape by means of such a device.
– DERIVATIVES **keypuncher** noun.

key ring ▶ **noun** a metal ring on to which keys may be threaded in order to keep them together.

key signature ▶ **noun** Music any of several combinations of sharps or flats after the clef at the beginning of each stave indicating the key of a composition.

Key Stage ▶ **noun** (in the UK) any of the four fixed stages into which the national curriculum is divided, each having its own prescribed course of study. At the end of each stage, pupils are required to complete standard assessment tasks.

Keystone a US film company formed in 1912, remembered for its silent slapstick comedy films, many featuring the bumbling Keystone Kops police characters.

keystone ▶ **noun** a central stone at the summit of an arch, locking the whole together.
■ [usu. in sing.] the central principle or part of a policy,

system, etc., on which all else depends: *cooperation remains the keystone of the government's security policy.*

Keystone State informal name for **PENNSYLVANIA**.

keystroke ▶ noun a single depression of a key on a keyboard, especially as a measure of work.

keyway ▶ noun a slot cut in a part of a machine or an electrical connector, to ensure correct orientation with another part which is fitted with a key.

Key West a city in southern Florida, at the southern tip of the Florida Keys; pop. 24,800 (1990). It is the southernmost city in continental US.

keyword ▶ noun a word or concept of great significance: *homes and jobs are the keywords in the campaign.*
■ a word which acts as the key to a cipher or code. ■ an informative word used in an information retrieval system to indicate the content of a document. ■ a significant word mentioned in an index.

KG ▶ abbreviation for (in the UK) Knight of the Order of the Garter.

kg ▶ abbreviation for kilogram(s).

KGB the state security police (1954–91) of the former USSR with responsibility for external espionage, internal counter-intelligence, and internal 'crimes against the state'.
– ORIGIN Russian, abbreviation of *Komitet gosudarstvennoĭ bezopasnosti* 'Committee of State Security'.

Kgs ▶ abbreviation for Kings (in biblical references).

Khabarovsk /kə'bɑːrɒfsk/ a krai (administrative territory) on the east coast of Siberian Russia.
■ its capital, a city on the Amur River, on the Chinese border; pop. 608,000 (1990).

Khachaturian /ˌkatʃəˈtʊəriən/, Aram (Ilich) (1903–78), Soviet composer, born in Georgia. His music is richly romantic and reflects his lifelong interest in the folk music of Armenia, Georgia, and Russia. Notable works include *Gayane* (ballet, 1942), his Second Symphony (1943), and *Spartacus* (ballet, 1954).

khadi /'kɑːdə/ (also **khaddar**) ▶ noun [mass noun] an Indian homespun cotton cloth.
– ORIGIN from Punjabi, from Hindi *khādī.*

Khakassia /kɑːˈkasɪə/ an autonomous republic in south central Russia; pop. 569,000 (est. 1990); capital, Abakan.

khaki /'kɑːki/ ▶ noun (pl. **khakis**) [mass noun] a textile fabric of a dull brownish-yellow colour, in particular a strong cotton fabric used in military clothing.
■ a dull brownish-yellow colour: [as modifier] *the pale khaki sand.* ■ (**khakis**) trousers or clothing of this fabric and colour.
– ORIGIN mid 19th cent.: from Urdu *kākī* 'dust-coloured', from *kāk* 'dust', from Persian.

Khaki Campbell ▶ noun a duck of a light brown breed, kept for egg laying.

khalasi /kə'lasi/ ▶ noun (pl. **khalasis**) (in the Indian subcontinent) a manual worker, especially a docker, porter, or sailor.
– ORIGIN from Urdu *kalāsī, kalāšī.*

Khalistan /'kalɪstɑːn, -stan/ the name given by Sikh nationalists to a proposed independent Sikh state.
– ORIGIN compare with Arabic *khālsa* 'pure, real, proper'.

Khalkha /'kɑːlkə/ ▶ noun 1 a member of a section of the Mongolian people, constituting the bulk of the population of Mongolia.
2 [mass noun] the language of these people, a demotic form of Mongolian adopted as the official language of Mongolia.
▶ adjective of or relating to this people or their language.
– ORIGIN of unknown origin.

Khalkís /xal'kis/ Greek name for **CHALCIS**.

Khalsa /'kʌlsə/ ▶ noun the body or company of fully initiated Sikhs, to which devout orthodox Sikhs are ritually admitted at puberty. The Khalsa was founded in 1699 by the last Guru (Gobind Singh). Members show their allegiance by five signs (called the five Ks): kangha (comb), kara (steel bangle), kesh (uncut hair, covered by a turban, and beard), kirpan (short sword) and kuccha (short trousers, originally for riding).
– ORIGIN via Urdu from Persian, from the feminine form of Arabic *kāliṣ* 'pure, belonging to'.

Khama /'kɑːmə/, Sir Seretse (1921–80), Botswanan statesman, Prime Minister of Bechuanaland 1965 and first President of Botswana 1966–80.

Khambat, Gulf of /kɑːmˈbɑːt/ another name for **CAMBAY, GULF OF**.

khamsin /'kamsɪn/ ▶ noun an oppressive, hot southerly or south-easterly wind blowing in Egypt in spring.
– ORIGIN late 17th cent.: from Arabic *ḳamsīn*, from *ḳamsūn* 'fifty' (being the approximate duration in days).

Khan¹, Ayub, see **AYUB KHAN**.

Khan² /kɑːn/, Imran (b.1952), Pakistani cricketer; full name *Imran Ahmad Khan Niazi.* An all-rounder, he served as Pakistan's captain in four periods between 1982 and 1992. After retiring from cricket in 1992, he entered politics in Pakistan.

Khan³ /kɑːn/, Jahangir (b.1963), Pakistani squash player. In 1979 he became world amateur champion at the age of 15; after turning professional he was world squash champion five consecutive times (1981–5), and again in 1988.

khan¹ /kɑːn, kan/ ▶ noun a title given to rulers and officials in central Asia, Afghanistan, and certain other Muslim countries.
■ any of the successors of Genghis Khan, supreme rulers of the Turkish, Tartar, and Mongol peoples and emperors of China in the Middle Ages.
– DERIVATIVES **khanate** noun.
– ORIGIN late Middle English: from Old French *chan*, medieval Latin *canus, caanus*, from Turkic *ḳān* 'lord, prince'.

khan² /kɑːn, kan/ ▶ noun (in the Middle East) an inn for travellers, built around a central courtyard.
– ORIGIN from Persian *kān.*

khana /'kɑːnə/ ▶ noun [mass noun] Indian food.
■ [count noun] a meal.
– ORIGIN via Hindi from the Sanskrit root *khād-* 'eat'.

khanga /'kaŋɡə/ (also **kanga**) ▶ noun [mass noun] a light East African cotton fabric printed with coloured designs, used mainly for women's clothing.
– ORIGIN mid 20th cent.: from Kiswahili.

Khaniá /xa'nja/ Greek name for **CHANIA**.

khansama /'kɑːnsəˌmɑː/ ▶ noun Indian a male cook, who often also assumes the role of house steward.
– ORIGIN from Urdu and Persian *kānsāmān*, from *kān* 'master' + *sāmān* 'household goods'.

khapra beetle /'kaprə/ ▶ noun a small dark brown beetle, the larva of which is a serious pest of stored grain and cereal products.
● *Trogoderma granarium*, family Dermestidae.
– ORIGIN late 19th cent.: from Hindi *khaprā*, from Sanskrit *kharpara* 'thief'.

Kharg Island /kɑːɡ/ a small island at the head of the Persian Gulf, site of Iran's principal deep-water oil terminal.

kharif /ka'riːf/ ▶ noun [mass noun] (in the Indian subcontinent) the autumn crop sown at the beginning of the summer rains.
– ORIGIN Persian and Urdu, from Arabic *karīf* 'autumn, autumnal rain'.

Kharkiv /'hɑːkɪv/ an industrial city in NE Ukraine, in the Donets basin; pop. 1,618,000 (1990). Russian name **KHARKOV** /'xarʲkɒf/.

Khartoum /kɑːˈtuːm/ the capital of Sudan, situated at the junction of the Blue Nile and the White Nile; pop. 924,500 (1993).

> In 1885 a British and Egyptian force under the command of General Gordon was besieged in Khartoum for ten months by the Mahdists, who eventually stormed the garrison, killing most of the defenders. It remained under the control of the Mahdists until they were defeated by the British in 1898 and the city was recaptured by General Kitchener.

khat /kɑːt/ ▶ noun [mass noun] 1 the leaves of an Arabian shrub, which are chewed (or drunk as an infusion) as a stimulant.
2 the shrub that produces these leaves, growing in mountainous regions and often cultivated.
● *Catha edulis*, family Celastraceae.
– ORIGIN mid 19th cent.: from Arabic *ḳāt.*

khayal /kɑːˈjaːl/ (also **khyal**) ▶ noun a traditional type of song from the northern part of the Indian subcontinent, with instrumental accompaniment and typically having two main themes.
– ORIGIN from Hindi *khayāl.*

Khaylitsa /kaɪˈlɪtsə/ a township 40 km (25 miles) south-east of Cape Town, South Africa; pop. 189,600

(1991). Designed to accommodate 250,000 people, it was built in 1983 for black Africans from the squatter camps of Crossroads, Langa, and KTC.

Khazar /kə'zɑː/ ▶ noun a member of a Turkic people who occupied a large part of southern Russia from the 6th to the 11th centuries and who converted to Judaism in the 8th century.
▶ adjective of or relating to the Khazars.
– ORIGIN of unknown origin.

khazi /'kɑːzi/ (also **karzy**) ▶ noun (pl. **khazies**) Brit. informal a toilet.
– ORIGIN 1960s: from Italian *casa* 'house'.

kheda /'keɪdə/ (also **keddah** or **kheddah**) ▶ noun (in the Indian subcontinent) an enclosure for the capture of wild elephants.
– ORIGIN from Assamese and Bengali *khedā.*

Khedive /kɪˈdiːv/ ▶ noun the title of the viceroy of Egypt under Turkish rule 1867–1914.
– DERIVATIVES **Khedival** adjective, **Khedivial** adjective.
– ORIGIN via French from Ottoman Turkish *ḳediv*, from Persian *ḳadiw* 'prince' (variant of *ḳudaiw* 'minor god', from *ḳuda* 'god').

Kherson /kɪə'sɒn/ a port on the south coast of Ukraine, on the Dnieper estuary; pop. 361,000 (1990).

khichri /'kɪtʃri/ ▶ noun variant of **KEDGEREE** (in sense 1).

Khios /'xiɒs/ Greek name for **CHIOS**.

khir /'kɪə/ ▶ noun [mass noun] an Indian dish of sweet rice pudding.
– ORIGIN from Hindi *khīr.*

Khitai /kɪ'tʌɪ/ variant of **CATHAY**.

Khmer /kmɛː/ ▶ noun 1 an ancient kingdom in SE Asia which reached the peak of its power in the 11th century, when it ruled over the entire Mekong valley from the capital at Angkor. It was destroyed by Siamese conquests in the 12th and 14th centuries.
2 a native or inhabitant of the ancient Khmer kingdom.
3 a native or inhabitant of Cambodia.
4 [mass noun] the language of the Khmers, belonging to the Mon-Khmer family. It is the official language of Cambodia, spoken by about 7 million people. Also called **CAMBODIAN**.
▶ adjective of, relating to, or denoting the Khmers or their language.
– ORIGIN the name in Khmer.

Khmer Republic former official name (1970–5) for **CAMBODIA**.

Khmer Rouge /ruːʒ/ a communist guerrilla organization which opposed the Cambodian government in the 1960s and waged a civil war from 1970, taking power in 1975.

> Under Pol Pot the Khmer Rouge undertook a forced reconstruction of Cambodian society, involving mass deportations from the towns to the countryside and mass executions. More than two million died before the regime was overthrown by the Vietnamese in 1979. Khmer Rouge forces have continued a programme of guerrilla warfare from bases in Thailand.

– ORIGIN from **KHMER** + French *rouge* 'red'.

Khoikhoi /'kɔɪkɔɪ/ (also **Khoi-khoin** /-kɔɪn/, **Khoi**) ▶ noun (pl. same) a member of a group of indigenous peoples of South Africa and Namibia, traditionally nomadic hunter-gatherers, including the Nama people and the ancestors of the Griquas.
▶ adjective of or relating to this people or their languages.
– ORIGIN Nama, literally 'men of men'.

> **USAGE** Khoikhoi should be used in preference to Hottentot, since the latter is likely to cause offence: see usage at **HOTTENTOT**.

Khoisan /'kɔɪsɑːn/ ▶ noun 1 [usu. treated as pl.] a collective term for the Khoikhoi (Hottentot) and San (Bushmen) peoples of southern Africa.
2 [mass noun] a language family of southern Africa, including the languages of the Khoikhoi and San, now having fewer than a million speakers altogether, and notable for the use of clicks (made by suction with the tongue) as additional consonants.
▶ adjective of or relating to these languages or their speakers.
– ORIGIN blend of **KHOIKHOI** and **SAN**.

Khoja /'kəʊdʒə/ ▶ noun a member of a Muslim sect found mainly in western India.
– ORIGIN early 17th cent. (in the sense 'Muslim

scribe or teacher'): from Turkish *hoca*, from Persian.

kho-kho /ˈkəʊkəʊ/ ▶ **noun** [mass noun] an Indian game of tag with two teams of twelve people.
– ORIGIN from Marathi *khō-khō*.

Khomeini /xɒˈmeɪni/, Ruhollah (1900–89), Iranian Shiite Muslim leader; known as **Ayatollah Khomeini**. He returned from exile in 1979 to lead an Islamic revolution which overthrew the shah. He established Iran as a fundamentalist Islamic republic and relentlessly pursued the Iran–Iraq War 1980–8.

Khonsu /ˈkɒnsuː/ Egyptian Mythology a moon god worshipped especially at Thebes, a member of a triad as the divine son of Amun and Mut.

Khorramshahr /ˌxɔːrəmˈʃɑː/ an oil port on the Shatt al-Arab waterway in western Iran. It was almost totally destroyed during the Iran–Iraq War of 1980–8. Former name (until 1924) **MOHAMMERAH**.

khoum /kuːm/ ▶ **noun** a monetary unit of Mauritania, equal to one fifth of an ouguiya.
– ORIGIN from Arabic *ḵums* 'one fifth'.

Khrushchev /ˈkrʊʃtʃɒf, ˌkrʊsˈtʃɒf/, Nikita (Sergeevich) (1894–1971), Soviet statesman, Premier of the USSR 1958–64. He was First Secretary of the Communist Party of the USSR 1953–64 after the death of Stalin, whom he denounced in 1956. He came close to war with the US over the Cuban Missile Crisis in 1962 and also clashed with China, which led to his being ousted by Brezhnev and Kosygin.
– DERIVATIVES **Khrushchevian** adjective.

Khufu /ˈkuːfuː/ see **CHEOPS**.

Khulna /ˈkʊlnɑː/ an industrial city in southern Bangladesh, on the Ganges delta; pop. 601,050 (1991).

Khunjerab Pass /ˈkʌnjərɑːb/ a high-altitude pass through the Himalayas, on the Karakoram highway at a height of 4,900 m (16,088 ft), linking China and Pakistan.

khus-khus /ˈkʌskʌs/ ▶ **noun** another term for **VETIVER**.
– ORIGIN early 19th cent.: from Urdu and Persian *ḵasḵas*.

khyal /kɪˈɑːl/ ▶ **noun** variant spelling of **KHAYAL**.

Khyber Pass /ˈkʌɪbə/ a mountain pass in the Hindu Kush, on the border between Pakistan and Afghanistan at a height of 1,067 m (3,520 ft). The pass was for long of great commercial and strategic importance, the route by which successive invaders entered India, and was garrisoned by the British intermittently between 1839 and 1947.

kHz ▶ **abbreviation for** kilohertz.

ki ▶ **noun** variant spelling of **CHI**[2].

kiaat /kɪˈɑːt/ ▶ **noun** a tree with fragrant yellow flowers and useful timber that resembles teak, native to tropical and southern Africa.
• *Pterocarpus angolensis*, family Leguminosae.
– ORIGIN mid 19th cent.: via Dutch from Malay *kayu jati* 'teak wood'.

kiang /kɪˈaŋ/ ▶ **noun** an animal of a large race of the Asian wild ass with a thick furry coat, native to the Tibetan plateau.
• *Equus hemionus kiang*, family Equidae; sometimes treated as a separate species. Compare with **ONAGER**, **KULAN**.
– ORIGIN mid 19th cent.: from Tibetan *kyang*.

Kiangsi /kjaŋˈsiː/ variant of **JIANGXI**.

Kiangsu /kjaŋˈsuː/ variant of **JIANGSU**.

kia ora /ˌkɪə ˈɔːrə/ ▶ **exclamation** (in New Zealand) a greeting wishing good health.
– ORIGIN Maori.

kibble[1] /ˈkɪb(ə)l/ ▶ **verb** [with obj.] [usu. as adj. **kibbled**] grind or chop (beans, grain, etc.) coarsely.
▶ **noun** [mass noun] N. Amer. ground meal shaped into pellets, especially for pet food.
– ORIGIN late 18th cent.: of unknown origin.

kibble[2] /ˈkɪb(ə)l/ ▶ **noun** Brit. an iron hoisting bucket used in mines.
– ORIGIN late Middle English: from Middle High German *kübel*, from medieval Latin *cupellus* 'corn-measure', diminutive of *cuppa* 'cup'.

kibbutz /kɪˈbʊts/ ▶ **noun** (pl. **kibbutzim** /-ˈtsiːm/) a communal settlement in Israel, typically a farm.
– ORIGIN 1930s: from modern Hebrew *qibbūṣ* 'gathering'.

kibbutznik /kɪˈbʊtsnɪk/ ▶ **noun** a member of a kibbutz.

kibe /kʌɪb/ ▶ **noun** an ulcerated chilblain, especially one on the heel.
– ORIGIN late Middle English: of unknown origin.

kibitka /kɪˈbɪtkə/ ▶ **noun 1** a type of Russian hooded sledge.
2 a circular tent, covered with felt, formerly used by Tartars.
– ORIGIN late 18th cent.: Russian, from Tartar and Kyrgyz *kibit* (from Arabic *qubbat* 'dome') + the Russian suffix *-ka*.

kibitz /ˈkɪbɪts/ ▶ **verb** [no obj.] informal, chiefly N. Amer. look on and offer unwelcome advice, especially at a card game.
■ speak informally; chat: *she **kibitzed with** friends.*
– DERIVATIVES **kibitzer** noun.
– ORIGIN 1920s: Yiddish, from colloquial German, from German *Kiebitz* 'interfering onlooker' (literally 'lapwing').

kiblah /ˈkɪblə/ (also **qibla**) ▶ **noun** [in sing.] the direction of the Kaaba (the sacred building at Mecca), to which Muslims turn at prayer.
– ORIGIN mid 17th cent.: from Arabic *ḳibla* 'that which is opposite'.

kibosh /ˈkʌɪbɒʃ/ (also **kybosh**) ▶ **noun** (in phrase **put the kibosh on**) informal put an end to; dispose of decisively: *he put the kibosh on the deal.*
– ORIGIN mid 19th cent.: of unknown origin.

kick[1] ▶ **verb 1** [with obj. and adverbial] strike or propel forcibly with the foot: *police **kicked down** the door of a flat* | [with obj. and complement] *he kicked the door open.*
■ [no obj.] strike out or flail with the foot or feet: *she **kicked out at** him* | [with obj.] *he kicked his feet free of a vine.* ■ (**kick oneself**) be annoyed with oneself for doing something foolish or missing an opportunity. ■ (chiefly in rugby) score (a goal) by a kick. ■ [no obj.] (of a gun) recoil when fired.
2 [with obj.] informal succeed in giving up (a habit or addiction).
▶ **noun 1** a blow or forceful thrust with the foot: *a kick in the head.*
■ (in sport) an instance of striking the ball with the foot: *Ball blasted the kick wide.* ■ Brit. (chiefly in rugby) a player of specified kicking ability. ■ the recoil of a gun when discharged. ■ a sudden forceful jolt: *the shuttle accelerated with a kick.* ■ Billiards & Snooker an irregular movement of the ball caused by dust.
2 [in sing.] informal the sharp stimulant effect of something, especially alcohol.
■ a thrill of pleasurable, often reckless excitement: *rich kids turning to crime just **for kicks** | I **get** such **a kick out of** driving a racing car.* ■ [with modifier] a specified temporary interest or enthusiasm: *the jogging kick.*
– PHRASES **kick against the pricks** see **PRICK**. **kick (some) ass** (or **butt**) N. Amer. vulgar slang act in a forceful or aggressive manner. **kick someone's ass** (or **butt**) N. Amer. vulgar slang beat, dominate, or defeat someone. **a kick at the can** (or **cat**) Canadian informal an opportunity to achieve something. **kick the bucket** informal die. **kick one's heels** see **HEEL**[1]. **a kick in the pants** (or **up the backside**) informal an unwelcome surprise that prompts or forces fresh effort: *the competition will be healthy, but we needed a kick in the pants.* **a kick in the teeth** informal a grave setback or disappointment: *this broken promise is a kick in the teeth for football.* **kick someone in the teeth** informal cause someone a grave setback or disappointment. **kick something into touch** Brit. informal reject something firmly. [ORIGIN: with reference to rugby, the ball in touch being out of play.] **kick someone when they are down** cause further misfortune to someone who is already in a difficult situation. **kick over the traces** see **TRACE**[2]. **kick up a fuss** (or **a stink**) informal object loudly or publicly to something. **kick up one's heels** see **HEEL**[1]. **kick someone upstairs** informal remove someone from an influential position in a business by giving them an ostensible promotion.
– DERIVATIVES **kickable** adjective.
– ORIGIN late Middle English: of unknown origin.
▶ **kick against** express resentment at or frustration with (an institution or restriction).
kick around (or **about**) (of a thing) lie unwanted or unexploited: *the idea has been kicking around for more than a year now.* ■ (of a person) drift idly from place to place: *I kicked around picking up odd jobs.*
kick someone around (or **about**) treat someone roughly or without respect.
kick something around (or **about**) discuss an idea casually or idly.
kick back N. Amer. informal be at leisure; relax.
kick down chiefly Brit. change quickly into a lower gear in a car with an automatic transmission by a sudden full depression of the accelerator.
kick in (especially of a device or drug) become activated; come into effect.
kick something in N. Amer. informal contribute something, especially money: *if you subscribe now we'll kick in a bonus.*
kick off (of a football match) be started or resumed by a player kicking the ball from the centre spot. ■ (of a team or player) begin or resume a match in this way. ■ informal (of an event) begin.
kick something off 1 remove something, especially shoes, by striking out vigorously with the foot or feet. **2** informal begin something: *the presidential primary kicks off the political year.*
kick someone out informal expel or dismiss someone.

kick[2] ▶ **noun** archaic an indentation in the bottom of a glass bottle, diminishing the internal capacity.
– ORIGIN mid 19th cent.: of unknown origin.

kick-and-rush ▶ **adjective** denoting soccer played vigorously but with little skill.

Kickapoo /ˈkɪkəpuː/ ▶ **noun** (pl. same or **Kickapoos**) **1** a member of an American Indian people formerly living in Wisconsin, and now in Kansas, Oklahoma, and northern central Mexico.
2 [mass noun] the Algonquian language of this people, now nearly extinct.
▶ **adjective** of or relating to this people or their language.
– ORIGIN from Kickapoo *kiikaapoa*.

kick-ass ▶ **adjective** [attrib.] informal, chiefly N. Amer. forceful, vigorous, and aggressive.

kickback ▶ **noun 1** a sudden forceful recoil: *the kickback from the gun punches your shoulder.*
2 informal a payment made to someone who has facilitated a transaction or appointment, especially illicitly.

kickball ▶ **noun** [mass noun] N. Amer. an informal game combining elements of baseball and soccer, in which a soccer ball is thrown to a person who kicks it and proceeds to run the bases.

kick-boxing ▶ **noun** [mass noun] a form of martial art which combines boxing with elements of karate, in particular kicking with bare feet.
– DERIVATIVES **kick-boxer** noun.

kick-down ▶ **noun** Brit. a device for changing gear in a motor vehicle with automatic transmission by full depression of the accelerator.

kick drum ▶ **noun** informal a bass drum played using a pedal.

kicker ▶ **noun 1** a person or animal that kicks.
■ the player in a team who scores by kicking or who kicks to gain positional advantage.
2 N. Amer. informal an unexpected and often unpleasant discovery or turn of events: *the kicker was you couldn't get a permit.*
■ an extra clause in a contract: *Hale added a kicker to the mortgage.*
3 informal a small outboard motor.
4 (in poker) a high third card retained in the hand with a pair at the draw.

kicking ▶ **noun** [mass noun] the action of striking or propelling someone or something with the foot: *Fox's kicking is vital to the All Blacks' game.*
■ [usu. in sing.] a punishment or assault in which the victim is kicked repeatedly: *they gave him a good kicking.*
▶ **adjective** informal (especially of music) lively and exciting: *their seriously kicking debut, 'Paradise'.*

kicking strap ▶ **noun 1** a strap used to prevent a horse from kicking.
2 Sailing a rope lanyard fixed to a boom to prevent it from rising.

kick-off ▶ **noun** the start or resumption of a football match, in which a player kicks the ball from the centre of the field: *three minutes before kick-off.*
■ informal a start of an event or activity.

kick plate ▶ **noun** a metal plate at the base of a door or panel to protect it from damage or wear.

kick-pleat ▶ **noun** an inverted pleat in a narrow skirt to allow freedom of movement.

kickshaw ▶ **noun** archaic a fancy but insubstantial cooked dish, especially one of foreign origin.
■ chiefly N. Amer. an elegant but insubstantial trinket.
– ORIGIN late 16th cent.: from French *quelque chose* 'something'. The French spelling was common in

the 17th cent.; the present form results from interpretation of *quelque chose* as plural.

kicksorter ▶ **noun** informal a device for analysing electrical pulses according to amplitude.

kickstand ▶ **noun** a metal rod attached to a bicycle or motorcycle, lying horizontally when not in use, that may be kicked into a vertical position to support the vehicle when it is stationary.

kick-start ▶ **verb** [with obj.] start (an engine on a motorcycle) with a downward thrust of a pedal.
■ figurative provide the initial impetus to: *they need to kick-start the economy.*
▶ **noun** a device to start an engine by the downward thrust of a pedal, as in older motorcycles.
■ [in sing.] an act of starting an engine in this way. ■ [in sing.] figurative an impetus given to get a process or thing started or restarted: *new investment will provide the kick-start needed to escape from recession.*

kick-turn ▶ **noun** Skiing a turn carried out while stationary by lifting first one and then the other ski through 180°.
■ (in skateboarding) a turn performed with the front wheels lifted off the ground.

kicky ▶ **adjective** N. Amer. informal exciting or fashionable.

kid[1] ▶ **noun 1** informal a child or young person.
■ used as an informal form of address: *we'll be seeing ya, kid!*
2 a young goat.
■ [mass noun] leather made from a young goat's skin: [as modifier] *white kid gloves.*
▶ **verb** (**kidded**, **kidding**) [no obj.] (of a goat) give birth.
– PHRASES **handle** (or **treat**) **someone or something with kid gloves** deal with someone or something very carefully or tactfully. **kids' stuff** informal a thing regarded as childishly simple or naive: *all this was kids' stuff though compared to the directing.* **our kid** Brit. informal one's younger brother or sister (often used as a form of address): *come here, our kid.*
– ORIGIN Middle English (in sense 2): from Old Norse *kith*, of Germanic origin; related to German *Kitze*.

kid[2] ▶ **verb** (**kidded**, **kidding**) [with obj.] informal deceive (someone) in a playful or teasing way: *you're kidding me!* | [no obj.] *we were just **kidding around**.*
■ [with obj. and clause] deceive or fool (someone): *he likes to kid everyone he's the big macho tough guy* | *they **kid themselves** that it's still the same.*
– PHRASES **no kidding** used to emphasize the truth of a statement: *no kidding, she's gone.*
– DERIVATIVES **kidder** noun, **kiddingly** adverb.
– ORIGIN early 19th cent.: perhaps from **KID**[1], expressing the notion 'make a child or goat of'.

kid[3] ▶ **noun** archaic a small wooden tub, especially a sailor's mess tub for grog or rations.
– ORIGIN mid 18th cent.: perhaps a variant of **KIT**[1].

kid brother ▶ **noun** informal a younger brother.

Kidd, William (1645–1701), Scottish pirate; known as **Captain Kidd**. Sent to the Indian Ocean in 1695 in command of an anti-pirate expedition, Kidd became a pirate himself. In 1699 he went to Boston in the hope of obtaining a pardon, but was arrested and later hanged in London.

Kidderminster /ˈkɪdəˌmɪnstə/ a town in west central England, in Worcestershire, on the River Stour; pop. 50,750 (1981).

Kidderminster carpet ▶ **noun** a reversible carpet made of two cloths of different colours woven together.
– ORIGIN late 17th cent.: named after **KIDDERMINSTER**, a centre of carpet-making.

kiddie (also **kiddy**) ▶ **noun** (pl. **-ies**) informal a young child.

kiddiewink ▶ **noun** Brit. humorous a small child.
– ORIGIN 1950s: a familiar extension of **KIDDIE**.

kiddle /ˈkɪd(ə)l/ ▶ **noun** a dam or other barrier in a river, with an opening fitted with nets to catch fish.
■ an arrangement of fishing nets hung on stakes along the seashore for the same purpose.
– ORIGIN Middle English: from Old French *quidel*.

kiddo ▶ **noun** (pl. **-os** or **-oes**) informal a friendly or slightly condescending form of address.

kiddush /ˈkɪdʊʃ/ ▶ **noun** [in sing.] a ceremony of prayer and blessing over wine, performed by the head of a Jewish household at the meal ushering in the Sabbath (on a Friday night) or a holy day, or at the lunch preceding it.
– ORIGIN mid 18th cent.: from Hebrew *qiddūš* 'sanctification'.

kiddy ▶ **noun** variant spelling of **KIDDIE**.

kideo ▶ **noun** (pl. **-os**) a television programme, video, or video game made specifically for children.
– ORIGIN late 20th cent.: from **KID**[1], on the pattern of *video*.

kidnap ▶ **verb** (**kidnapped**, **kidnapping**; US also **kidnaped**, **kidnaping**) [with obj.] take (someone) away illegally by force, typically to obtain a ransom.
▶ **noun** [mass noun] the action of kidnapping someone: *they were arrested for robbery and kidnap.*
– DERIVATIVES **kidnapper** noun.
– ORIGIN late 17th cent.: back-formation from *kidnapper*, from **KID**[1] + slang *nap* 'nab, seize'.

kidney ▶ **noun** (pl. **-eys**) each of a pair of organs in the abdominal cavity of mammals, birds, and reptiles, excreting urine.
■ [mass noun] the kidney of a sheep, ox, or pig as food. ■ [mass noun] temperament, nature, or kind: *I hoped that he would not prove of similar kidney.*

> The kidneys' main function is to purify the blood by removing nitrogenous waste products and excreting them in the urine. They also control the fluid and ion levels in the body, by excreting any excesses. The kidneys were anciently thought to control disposition and temperament.

– ORIGIN Middle English: of obscure origin.

kidney bean ▶ **noun** a kidney-shaped bean, especially a dark red one from a dwarf French bean plant.

kidney dialysis ▶ **noun** see **DIALYSIS**.

kidney dish ▶ **noun** a kidney-shaped dish used as a receptacle in an operating theatre or doctor's surgery.

kidney machine ▶ **noun** an apparatus that performs the functions of the human kidney (outside the body), when one or both organs are damaged; an artificial kidney or dialysis machine.

kidney ore ▶ **noun** [mass noun] haematite occurring in rounded, kidney-shaped masses.

kidney punch ▶ **noun** a punch to the kidney area (illegal in boxing).

kidney-shaped ▶ **adjective** shaped like a kidney, with one side concave and the other convex and with rounded ends.

kidney stone ▶ **noun** a hard mass formed in the kidneys, typically consisting of insoluble calcium compounds; a renal calculus.

kidney tubule ▶ **noun** Anatomy each of the long, fine, convoluted tubules conveying urine from the glomeruli to the renal pelvis in the vertebrate kidney. Water and salts are reabsorbed into the blood along their length. Also called **RENAL TUBULE**, **URINIFEROUS TUBULE**.

kidney vetch ▶ **noun** a yellow- or orange-flowered grassland plant of the pea family. Native to Europe and the Mediterranean, it is sometimes grown as a fodder crop. Also called **LADY'S FINGER**.
• *Anthyllis vulneraria*, family Leguminosae.

kidney worm ▶ **noun** a parasitic nematode worm which infests the kidneys of mammals.
• Several species in the class Phasmida, in particular *Stephanurus dentatus* (in pigs) and the large *Dioctophyma renale* (in humans and other mammals).

kidology /kɪˈdɒlədʒi/ ▶ **noun** [mass noun] informal, chiefly Brit. the art or practice of deliberately deceiving or teasing people.
– ORIGIN mid 20th cent.: formed irregularly from the verb **KID**[2] + **-LOGY**.

kid sister ▶ **noun** informal a younger sister.

kidskin ▶ **noun** another term for **KID**[1] (in sense 2).

kidstakes /ˈkɪdsteɪkz/ ▶ **plural noun** Austral./NZ informal nonsense; pretence.
– ORIGIN early 20th cent.: probably a humorous formation based on slang *kid* 'humbug'.

kidult ▶ **noun** [often as modifier] informal a television programme, film, video, or game intended to appeal to both children and adults: *high-tech kidult entertainment.*
– ORIGIN mid 20th cent.: blend of **KID**[1] and **ADULT**.

kidvid ▶ **noun** [mass noun] informal children's television or video entertainment.
■ [count noun] a children's programme or videotape.
– ORIGIN late 20th cent.: from *kids' video*.

kiekie /ˈkiːkiː/ ▶ **noun** a New Zealand climbing plant with edible bracts, and leaves which are used for basket-making and weaving.
• *Freycinetia banksii*, family Pandanaceae.
– ORIGIN mid 19th cent.: from Maori.

Kiel /kiːl/ a naval port in northern Germany, capital of Schleswig-Holstein, on the Baltic Sea coast at the eastern end of the Kiel Canal; pop. 247,100 (1991).

kielbasa /kiːlˈbasə/ ▶ **noun** [mass noun] a type of highly seasoned Polish sausage, typically containing garlic.
– ORIGIN Polish, literally 'sausage'.

Kiel Canal a man-made waterway, 98 km (61 miles) in length, in NW Germany, running westwards from Kiel to Brunsbüttel at the mouth of the Elbe. It connects the North Sea with the Baltic and was constructed in 1895 to provide the German navy with a shorter route between these two seas.

Kielce /ˈkjɛltsə/ an industrial city in southern Poland; pop. 214,200 (1990).

kier /kɪə/ ▶ **noun** a vat.
– ORIGIN late 16th cent.: from Old Norse *ker* 'container, tub'.

kierie /ˈkɪri/ ▶ **noun** (pl. **-ies**) S. African a short, thick stick with a knobbed head, traditionally used as a club or missile by the indigenous peoples of South Africa.
– ORIGIN from Khoikhoi *kirri* 'walking stick'.

Kierkegaard /ˈkɪəkəˌgɑːd/, Søren (Aabye) (1813–55), Danish philosopher. A founder of existentialism, he affirmed the importance of individual experience and choice and believed one could know God only through a 'leap of faith', and not through doctrine. Notable works: *Either-Or* (1843) and *The Sickness unto Death* (1849).
– DERIVATIVES **Kierkegaardian** adjective.

kieselguhr /ˈkiːz(ə)lˌgʊə/ ▶ **noun** [mass noun] a form of diatomaceous earth used in various manufacturing and laboratory processes, chiefly as a filter, filler, or insulator.
– ORIGIN late 19th cent.: from German, from *Kiesel* 'gravel' + dialect *Guhr* (literally 'yeast') used to denote a loose earthy deposit, found in the cavities of rocks.

kieserite /ˈkiːzərʌɪt/ ▶ **noun** [mass noun] a fine-grained white mineral consisting of hydrated magnesium sulphate, occurring often in salt mines.
– ORIGIN mid 19th cent.: from the name of Dietrich G. *Kieser* (1779–1862), German physician, + **-ITE**[1].

Kieslowski /kɪˈslɒfski/, Krzysztof (1941–96), Polish film director. Noted for their mannered style and their artistic, philosophical nature, his films include the series *Dekalog* (1988), each film being a visual interpretation of one of the Ten Commandments, and the trilogy *Three Colours* (1993–4).

Kiev /ˈkiːɛf/ the capital of Ukraine, an industrial city and port on the River Dnieper; pop. 2,616,000 (1990). Founded in the 8th century, it became capital of the Ukrainian Soviet Socialist Republic in 1934. In 1991 it became capital of independent Ukraine.

kif /kɪf/ (also **kef**) ▶ **noun** [mass noun] a substance, especially cannabis, smoked to produce a drowsy state.
▶ **adjective** S. African informal very good (used as a general term of approval): *that T-shirt's kif.*
– ORIGIN early 19th cent.: from Arabic *kayf* 'enjoyment, well-being'.

Kigali /kɪˈgɑːli/ the capital of Rwanda; pop. 234,500 (1993).

kike /kʌɪk/ ▶ **noun** N. Amer. informal an offensive term for a Jewish person.
– ORIGIN early 20th cent.: of unknown origin.

Kikládhes /kiˈklaðɛs/ Greek name for **CYCLADES**.

kikoi /kɪˈkɔɪ/ ▶ **noun** (pl. **kikois**) [mass noun] a distinctive East African striped cloth with an end fringe.
■ [count noun] a garment made of this cloth, worn around the waist.
– ORIGIN mid 20th cent.: from Kiswahili.

Kikongo /kɪˈkɒŋgəʊ/ ▶ **noun** [mass noun] either of two similar Bantu languages spoken in the Congo, the Democratic Republic of Congo (Zaire), and adjacent areas. They have around 4.7 million speakers altogether.
▶ **adjective** of or relating to this language.
– ORIGIN the name in Kikongo.

Kikuyu /kɪˈkuːjuː/ ▶ **noun** (pl. same or **Kikuyus**) **1** a member of a people forming the largest ethnic group in Kenya.
2 [mass noun] the Bantu language of this people, with over 5 million speakers.

k

3 (**kikuyu**, **kikuyu grass**) a creeping perennial grass which is native to Kenya and cultivated elsewhere as a lawn and fodder grass.
● *Pennisetum clandestinum*, family Gramineae.
▶**adjective** of or relating to this people or their language.
– ORIGIN a local name.

Kilauea /ˌkiːlaʊˈeɪə/ a volcano with a crater roughly 8 km (5 miles) long by 5 km (3 miles) broad on the island of Hawaii, situated on the eastern flanks of Mauna Loa at an altitude of 1,247 m (4,090 ft).

Kildare /kɪlˈdɛː/ a county of the Republic of Ireland, in the east, in the province of Leinster; county town, Naas.

kilderkin /ˈkɪldəkɪn/ ▶**noun** a cask for liquids or other substances, holding 16 or 18 gallons.
■this amount as a unit of measurement.
– ORIGIN late Middle English: from Middle Dutch *kinderkin*, variant of *kinerkijn*, diminutive of *kintal* (see **QUINTAL**).

kilim /kɪˈliːm, ˈkiːlɪm/ (also **kelim**) ▶**noun** a flat-woven carpet or rug made in Turkey, Kurdistan, and neighbouring areas.
– ORIGIN late 19th cent.: via Turkish from Persian *gelīm*.

Kilimanjaro, Mount /ˌkɪlɪmənˈdʒɑːrəʊ/ an extinct volcano in northern Tanzania. It has twin peaks, the higher of which, Kibo (5,895 m, 19,340 ft), is the highest mountain in Africa.

Kilkenny /kɪlˈkɛni/ a county of the Republic of Ireland, in the south-east, in the province of Leinster.
■its county town; pop. 8,510 (1991).

Kilkenny cats two cats which, according to legend, fought until only their tails remained.

kill ▶**verb** [with obj.] **1** cause the death of (a person, animal, or other living thing): *her father was killed in a car crash* | [no obj.] *a robber armed with a shotgun who kills in cold blood.*
■put an end to or cause the failure or defeat of (something): *the Stock Exchange voted to kill the project.* ■ stop (a computer programme or process). ■ informal switch off (a light or engine). ■ informal delete (a line, paragraph, or file) from a document or computer. ■ (in soccer or other ball games) make (the ball) stop: *after killing the ball with his chest and his thigh, he brushed past Reeves.* ■ Tennis hit (the ball) so that it cannot be returned. ■ neutralize or subdue (an effect or quality): *the sauce would kill the taste of the herbs.* ■ informal consume the entire contents of (a bottle containing an alcoholic drink).
2 informal overwhelm (someone) with an emotion: *the suspense is killing me.*
■(**kill oneself**) overexert oneself: *I killed myself carrying those things home.* ■ used hyperbolically to indicate that someone is extremely angry with another person: *my Mum and Dad will kill me if they catch me out here.* ■ cause pain or anguish to: *my feet are killing me.*
3 pass (time, or a specified amount of it), typically while waiting for a particular event: *when he reached the station he found he actually had an hour to kill.*
▶**noun** [usu. in sing.] an act of killing, especially of one animal by another: *a lion has made a kill.*
■an animal or animals killed, either by a hunter or another animal: *the vulture is able to survey the land and locate a fresh kill.* ■ informal an act of destroying or disabling an enemy aircraft, submarine, etc.
– PHRASES **be in at the kill** be present at or benefit from the successful conclusion of an enterprise. **go** (or **move in** or **close in**) **for the kill** take decisive action to turn a situation to one's advantage. **if it kills one** informal whatever the problems or difficulties involved: *we are going to smile and be pleasant if it kills us.* **kill oneself laughing** informal be overcome with laughter. **kill or cure** Brit. (of a remedy for a problem) likely to either work well or fail catastrophically, with no possibility of partial success: *the spring Budget will be kill or cure.* **kill two birds with one stone** proverb achieve two aims at once. **kill with** (or **by**) **kindness** spoil with overindulgence.
– ORIGIN Middle English (in the sense 'strike, beat', also 'put to death'): probably of Germanic origin and related to **QUELL**. The noun originally denoted a stroke or blow.
▶**kill someone/thing off** get rid of or destroy completely, especially in large numbers: *there is every possibility all river life would be killed off for generations.* ■(of a writer) bring about the 'death' of a fictional character.

kill out (of an animal) yield (a specified amount of meat) when slaughtered.

Killarney /kɪˈlɑːni/ a town in the south-west of the Republic of Ireland, in County Kerry, famous for the beauty of the nearby lakes and mountains; pop. 7,250 (1991).

Killarney fern ▶**noun** a rare bristle fern which grows on rocks by streams in a few parts of western Europe.
● *Trichomanes speciosum*, family Hymenophyllaceae.

killas /ˈkɪləs/ ▶**noun** [mass noun] argillaceous slate or phyllite occurring in Cornwall in contact with granite.
– ORIGIN late 17th cent.: probably from Cornish.

killdeer /ˈkɪldɪə/ (also **killdeer plover**) ▶**noun** a widespread American plover with a plaintive call that resembles its name.
● *Charadrius vociferus*, family Charadriidae.
– ORIGIN mid 18th cent.: imitative of its call.

killer ▶**noun 1** a person, animal, or thing that kills: [as modifier] *a killer virus.*
■informal a formidable or excellent person or thing: *that wind's a killer.* ■ a hilarious joke.
2 Austral./NZ informal an animal that has been selected for slaughter.

killer bee ▶**noun** informal, chiefly US an Africanized honeybee. See **AFRICANIZE** (sense 2).

killer cell ▶**noun** Physiology a white blood cell (a type of lymphocyte) which destroys infected or cancerous cells.

killer instinct ▶**noun** a ruthless determination to succeed or win.

killer whale ▶**noun** a large toothed whale with distinctive black-and-white markings and a prominent dorsal fin. It lives in groups that hunt fish, seals, and penguins cooperatively. Also called **ORCA**.
● *Orcinus orca*, family Delphinidae.

killick /ˈkɪlɪk/ ▶**noun 1** a heavy stone used by small craft as an anchor.
■a small anchor.
2 Brit. Nautical slang a leading seaman. [ORIGIN: so named because the leading seaman's badge bore the symbol of an anchor.]
– ORIGIN mid 17th cent.: of unknown origin.

killifish /ˈkɪlɪfɪʃ/ ▶**noun** (pl. same or **-fishes**) a small toothcarp of fresh or brackish water, typically brightly coloured. They are mainly native to America and include many popular aquarium fishes.
● Families Cyprinodontidae (or Fundulidae), which includes numerous genera of egg-laying killifishes, and Poeciliidae, which includes a few live-bearing species.
– ORIGIN early 19th cent.: apparently from **KILL** and **FISH**[1].

killing ▶**noun** an act of causing death, especially deliberately.
▶**adjective** causing death: [in combination] *weed-killing.*
■informal exhausting; unbearable: *the suspense will be killing.* ■ dated overwhelmingly funny.
– PHRASES **make a killing** have a great financial success: *they're a safe investment, you can make a killing overnight.*
– DERIVATIVES **killingly** adverb.

killing bottle ▶**noun** Entomology a bottle containing poisonous vapour in which insects collected as specimens are killed.

killing field ▶**noun** (usu. **killing fields**) a place where a heavy loss of life has occurred, typically as the result of massacre or genocide during a time of warfare or violent civil unrest.

killing zone (also **kill zone**) ▶**noun 1** the area of a military engagement with a high concentration of fatalities.
2 the area of the human body where entry of a projectile would kill, especially as indicated on a target for shooting practice.

killjoy ▶**noun** a person who deliberately spoils the enjoyment of others through resentful or overly sober behaviour.

kill ratio ▶**noun** the proportion of casualties on each side in a military action.

Kilmarnock /kɪlˈmɑːnək/ a town in west central Scotland, administrative centre of East Ayrshire; pop. 44,300 (1991).

kiln ▶**noun** a furnace or oven for burning, baking, or drying, especially one for calcining lime or firing pottery.
– ORIGIN Old English *cylene*, from Latin *culina* 'kitchen, cooking stove'.

kiln-dry ▶**verb** [with obj.] [usu. as noun **kiln-drying**] dry (a material such as wood or sand) in a kiln.

Kilner jar /ˈkɪlnə/ ▶**noun** trademark a glass preserving jar with a metal lid which forms an airtight seal, used to bottle fruit and vegetables.
– ORIGIN mid 20th cent.: from the name of the manufacturing company.

kilo ▶**noun** (pl. **-os**) **1** a kilogram.
2 rare a kilometre.
3 a code word representing the letter K, used in radio communication.
– ORIGIN late 19th cent.: from French, abbreviation of *kilogramme*, *kilomètre*.

kilo- /ˈkɪləʊ, ˈkiːləʊ/ ▶**combining form** (used commonly in units of measurement) denoting a factor of 1,000: *kilojoule* | *kilolitre.*
– ORIGIN via French from Greek *khilioi* 'thousand'.

kilobase (abbrev.: **kb**) ▶**noun** Biochemistry (in expressing the lengths of nucleic acid molecules) one thousand bases.

kilobit ▶**noun** a unit of computer memory or data equal to 1,024 bits.

kilobyte (abbrev.: **Kb** or **KB**.) ▶**noun** Computing a unit of memory or data equal to 1,024 bytes.

kilocalorie ▶**noun** a unit of energy of one thousand calories (equal to one large calorie).

kilocycle (abbrev.: **kc**) ▶**noun** a former measure of frequency, equivalent to 1 kilohertz.

kilogram (also **kilogramme**) (abbrev.: **kg**) ▶**noun** the SI unit of mass, equivalent to the international standard kept at Sèvres near Paris (approximately 2.205 lb).
– ORIGIN late 18th cent.: from French *kilogramme* (see **KILO-**, **GRAM**[1]).

kilohertz (abbrev.: **kHz**) ▶**noun** a measure of frequency equivalent to 1,000 cycles per second.

kilojoule (abbrev.: **kJ**) ▶**noun** 1,000 joules, especially as a measure of the energy value of foods.

kilolitre (US **kiloliter**) (abbrev.: **kl**) ▶**noun** 1,000 litres (equivalent to 220 imperial gallons).

kilometre /ˈkɪləˌmiːtə, kɪˈlɒmɪtə/ (US **kilometer**) (abbrev.: **km**) ▶**noun** a metric unit of measurement equal to 1,000 metres (approximately 0.62 miles).
– DERIVATIVES **kilometric** adjective.
– ORIGIN late 18th cent.: from French *kilomètre* (see **KILO-**, **METRE**[1]).

USAGE There are two possible pronunciations for **kilometre**: one with the stress on the **ki-** and the other with the stress on the **-lo-**. The first is traditionally considered correct, with a stress pattern similar to other units of measurement such as **centimetre**. The second pronunciation, which originated in US English and is now also very common in British English, is still regarded as incorrect by some people, especially in British English.

kiloton (also **kilotonne**) ▶**noun** a unit of explosive power equivalent to 1,000 tons of TNT.

kilovolt (abbrev.: **kV**) ▶**noun** 1,000 volts.

kilowatt (abbrev.: **kW**) ▶**noun** a measure of one thousand watts of electrical power.

kilowatt-hour (abbrev.: **kWh**) ▶**noun** a measure of electrical energy equivalent to a power consumption of one thousand watts for one hour.

Kilroy a mythical person, popularized by American servicemen in the Second World War, who left such inscriptions as 'Kilroy was here' on walls all over the world.
– ORIGIN of the many unverifiable accounts of the source of the term, one claims that James J. *Kilroy* of Halifax, Massachusetts, a shipyard employee, wrote 'Kilroy was here' on sections of warships after inspection; the phrase is said to have been reproduced by shipyard workers who entered the armed services.

kilt ▶**noun** a knee-length skirt of pleated tartan cloth, traditionally worn by men as part of Scottish Highland dress and now also worn by women and girls.
▶**verb** [with obj.] gather (a garment or material) in vertical pleats: [as adj. **kilted**] *kilted skirts.*
■(**kilt something up**) tuck up skirts around the body.
– DERIVATIVES **kilted** adjective.
– ORIGIN Middle English (as a verb in the sense 'tuck up around the body'): of Scandinavian origin;

compare with Danish *kilte (op)* 'tuck (up)' and Old Norse *kilting* 'a skirt'. The noun dates from the mid 18th cent.

kilter ▶ **noun** (in phrase **out of kilter**) out of harmony or balance: *daylight saving throws everybody's body clock out of kilter.*
– ORIGIN early 17th cent.: of unknown origin.

kiltie /ˈkɪlti/ (also **kilty**) ▶ **noun** informal a person who wears a kilt (often used as a humorous or slightly derogatory term for a Scot).

Kimberley /ˈkɪmbəli/ **1** a city in South Africa, in the province of Northern Cape; pop. 167,060 (1991). It has been a diamond-mining centre since the early 1870s. [ORIGIN: named after the 1st Earl of *Kimberley*, a British Colonial Secretary.]
2 (also **the Kimberleys**) a plateau region in the far north of Western Australia. A mining and cattle-rearing region, it was the scene of a gold rush in 1885.

kimberlite /ˈkɪmbəlʌɪt/ ▶ **noun** [mass noun] Geology a rare, blue-tinged, coarse-grained intrusive igneous rock sometimes containing diamonds, found in South Africa and Siberia. Also called **BLUE GROUND**.
– ORIGIN late 19th cent.: from **KIMBERLEY**, + **-ITE**[1].

Kimbundu see **MBUNDU**.

kimchi /ˈkɪmtʃi/ ▶ **noun** [mass noun] spicy pickled cabbage, the national dish of Korea.
– ORIGIN Korean.

Kim Il Sung /ˌkɪm ɪl ˈsʊŋ/ (1912–94), Korean communist statesman, first Premier of North Korea 1948–72 and President 1972–94; born *Kim Song Ju*. He precipitated the Korean War (1950–3), and remained committed to the reunification of the country. He maintained a one-party state and created a personality cult around himself and his family; on his death he was quickly replaced in power by his son **Kim Jong Il** (b.1942).

kimono /kɪˈməʊnəʊ/ ▶ **noun** (pl. **-os**) a long, loose robe with wide sleeves and tied with a sash, originally worn as a formal garment in Japan and now also used elsewhere as a dressing gown.
– DERIVATIVES **kimonoed** adjective.
– ORIGIN mid 17th cent.: Japanese, from *ki* 'wearing' + *mono* 'thing'.

kin ▶ **noun** [in sing.] [treated as pl.] one's family and relations: *his kin are entrepreneurs.*
▶ **adjective** [predic.] (of a person) related: *he was* **kin to** *the brothers.* See also **AKIN**.
– DERIVATIVES **kinless** adjective.
– ORIGIN Old English *cynn*, of Germanic origin; related to Dutch *kunne*, from an Indo-European root meaning 'give birth to', shared by Greek *genos* and Latin *genus* 'race'.

-kin ▶ **suffix** forming diminutive nouns such as *bumpkin, catkin.*
– ORIGIN from Middle Dutch *-kijn, -ken*, Middle Low German *-kīn*.

kina[1] /ˈkiːnə/ ▶ **noun** (pl. same) the basic monetary unit of Papua New Guinea, equal to 100 toea.
– ORIGIN Papuan.

kina[2] /ˈkiːnə/ ▶ **noun** (pl. same) an edible sea urchin occurring on New Zealand coasts.
• *Evechinus chloroticus*, class Echinoidea.
– ORIGIN mid 20th cent.: from Maori.

Kinabalu, Mount /ˌkɪnəbəˈluː/ a mountain in the state of Sabah in eastern Malaysia, on the north coast of Borneo. Rising to 4,094 m (13,431 ft), it is the highest peak of Borneo and of SE Asia.

kinaesthesia /ˌkɪnɪsˈθiːzɪə, ˌkʌɪn-/ (US **kinesthesia**) ▶ **noun** [mass noun] awareness of the position and movement of the parts of the body by means of sensory organs (proprioceptors) in the muscles and joints.
– DERIVATIVES **kinaesthetic** adjective.
– ORIGIN late 19th cent.: from Greek *kinein* 'to move' + *aisthēsis* 'sensation'.

kinase /ˈkʌɪneɪz/ ▶ **noun** [usu. with modifier] Biochemistry an enzyme that catalyses the transfer of a phosphate group from ATP to a specified molecule.
– ORIGIN early 20th cent.: from Greek *kinein* 'to move' + **-ASE**.

Kincardineshire /kɪnˈkɑːdɪnʃɪə, -ʃə/ a former county of eastern Scotland. In 1975 it became part of Grampian region and in 1996 part of Aberdeenshire.

Kinchinjunga /ˌkɪntʃɪnˈdʒʌŋgə/ variant of **KANCHENJUNGA**.

kincob /ˈkɪŋkɒb/ ▶ **noun** [mass noun] a rich Indian fabric brocaded with gold or silver.
– ORIGIN early 18th cent.: from Urdu and Persian *kamḵāb*, alteration of *kamḵā* 'damask silk', from Chinese.

kind[1] ▶ **noun** a group of people or things having similar characteristics: *all kinds of music | a new kind of education | more data of this kind would be valuable.*
■ [mass noun] character; nature: *the trials were different in* **kind** *from any that preceded them | true* **to kind**. ■ each of the elements (bread and wine) of the Eucharist: *communion* **in both kinds**.
– PHRASES **in kind** in the same way; with something similar: *if he responded positively, they would respond in kind.* ■ (of payment) in goods or services as opposed to money. **one's (own) kind** people with whom one has a great deal in common: *we stick with our own kind.* **someone's kind** used to express disapproval of a certain type of person: *I don't apologize to her kind ever.* **kind of** informal rather; to some extent (often expressing vagueness or used as a meaningless filler): *it got kind of cosy.* **a kind of** something resembling (used to express vagueness or moderate a statement): *teaching based on a kind of inspired guesswork.* **nothing of the kind** not at all like the thing in question: *my son had done nothing of the kind before.* ■ used to express an emphatic denial: *'He made you do that?' 'He did nothing of the kind.'* **of its kind** within the limitations of its class: *this new building was no doubt excellent of its kind.* **of a kind** used to indicate that something is not as good as it might be expected to be: *there is tribute, of a kind, in such popularity.* **one of a kind** unique. **something of the kind** something like the thing in question: *they had always suspected something of the kind.* **two** (or **three, four**, etc.) **of a kind** the same or very similar: *she and her sister were two of a kind.* ■ (of cards) having the same face value but of a different suit.
– ORIGIN Old English *cynd(e), gecynd(e)*, of Germanic origin; related to **KIN**. The original sense was 'nature, the natural order', also 'innate character, form, or condition' (compare with **KIND**[2]); hence 'a class or race distinguished by innate characteristics'.

USAGE In standard use, **kind** is used as a normal noun with a singular or a plural, as in the following examples: ***these kinds of** questions **are** not relevant; **this kind of** question **is** not relevant.* However, in the following example, **kind** does not become plural even though it is used with the plural determiner **these**: ***these kind of** questions **are** not relevant.* The ungrammatical *these kind* (rather than *these kinds*) has been recorded since the 14th century and arose because the plural noun (here, **questions**) is treated as the head of the noun phrase, **kind of** being regarded almost as if it were a one-word adjective. In English, adjectives are invariable, i.e. they do not agree in number; by analogy **kind of** is also taken to be invariable. In the British National Corpus, the use *these kind* is found in 20 per cent of citations for this sense. See also **usage** at **LOT**.

kind[2] ▶ **adjective** having or showing a friendly, generous, and considerate nature: *she was a good, kind woman | he was very* **kind to** *me.*
■ [predic.] used in a polite request: *would you be kind enough to repeat what you said?* ■ [predic.] (**kind to**) (of a consumer product) gentle on (a part of the body): *look for rollers that are kind to hair.* ■ archaic affectionate; loving.
– ORIGIN Old English *gecynde* 'natural, native'; in Middle English the earliest sense is 'well-born or well-bred', whence 'well-disposed by nature, courteous, gentle, benevolent'.

kinda informal ▶ **contraction of** kind of: *I think it's kinda funny.*
– ORIGIN early 20th cent. (originally US): alteration.

kinder /ˈkɪndə/ ▶ **noun** Austral. informal short for **KINDERGARTEN**.

kindergarten /ˈkɪndəˌgɑːt(ə)n/ ▶ **noun** an establishment where children below the age of compulsory education play and learn; a nursery school.
– DERIVATIVES **kindergartener** noun.
– ORIGIN mid 19th cent.: from German, literally 'children's garden'.

kind-hearted ▶ **adjective** having a kind and sympathetic nature.
– DERIVATIVES **kind-heartedly** adverb, **kind-heartedness** noun.

kindie ▶ **noun** (pl. **-ies**) variant spelling of **KINDY**.

kindle[1] /ˈkɪnd(ə)l/ ▶ **verb** [with obj.] light or set on fire.
■ arouse or inspire (an emotion or feeling): *a love of art was kindled in me.* ■ [no obj.] (of an emotion) be aroused: *she hesitated, suspicion kindling within her.* ■ [no obj.] become impassioned or excited: *they greeted him with an immense crusading acclaim, kindling to the daring of it.*
– DERIVATIVES **kindler** noun.
– ORIGIN Middle English: based on Old Norse *kynda*, influenced by Old Norse *kindill* 'candle, torch'.

kindle[2] /ˈkɪnd(ə)l/ ▶ **verb** [no obj.] (of a hare or rabbit) give birth.
– ORIGIN Middle English: apparently a frequentative of **KIND**[1].

kindling ▶ **noun** [mass noun] **1** small sticks or twigs used for lighting fires.
2 (in neurology) a process by which a seizure or other brain event is both initiated and its recurrence made more likely.

kindly[1] ▶ **adverb** in a kind manner: *'Never mind,' she said kindly.*
■ please (used in a polite request or demand, often ironically): *will you kindly sign the enclosed copy of this letter.*
– PHRASES **look kindly on** regard (someone or something) sympathetically. **not take kindly to** not welcome or be pleased by (someone or something). **take something kindly** like or be pleased by something. **thank someone kindly** thank someone very much.
– ORIGIN Old English *gecyndelīce* 'naturally, characteristically' (see **KIND**[2], **-LY**[2]).

kindly[2] ▶ **adjective** (**kindlier, kindliest**) **1** kind; warm-hearted; gentle: *he was a quiet, kindly man.*
2 archaic native-born.
– DERIVATIVES **kindliness** noun.

kindness ▶ **noun** [mass noun] the quality of being friendly, generous, and considerate.
■ [count noun] a kind act: *it is a kindness I shall never forget.*

kindred /ˈkɪndrɪd/ ▶ **noun** [in sing.] [treated as pl.] one's family and relations.
■ [mass noun] relationship by blood: *ties of kindred.*
▶ **adjective** [attrib.] similar in kind; related: *books on kindred subjects.*
– ORIGIN Middle English: from **KIN** + *-red* (from Old English *rǣden* 'condition'), with insertion of *-d-* in the modern spelling through phonetic development (as in *thunder*).

kindred spirit ▶ **noun** a person whose interests or attitudes are similar to one's own.

kindy /ˈkɪndi/ ▶ **noun** (pl. **-ies**) Austral./NZ informal short for **KINDERGARTEN**.

kine /kʌɪn/ ▶ **plural noun** archaic cows collectively.

kinematics /ˌkɪnɪˈmatɪks, ˌkʌɪn-/ ▶ **plural noun** [usu. treated as sing.] the branch of mechanics concerned with the motion of objects without reference to the forces which cause the motion. Compare with **DYNAMICS**.
■ [usu. treated as pl.] the features or properties of motion in an object, regarded in such a way.
– DERIVATIVES **kinematic** adjective, **kinematically** adverb.
– ORIGIN mid 19th cent.: from Greek *kinēma, kinēmat-* 'motion' (from *kinein* 'to move') + **-ICS**.

kinematic viscosity ▶ **noun** Mechanics a quantity measuring the dynamic viscosity of a fluid per unit density.

kinematograph /ˌkɪnɪˈmatəgrɑːf/ ▶ **noun** variant spelling of **CINEMATOGRAPH**.

kinescope /ˈkɪnɪskəʊp/ ▶ **noun** US a television tube.
■ a film recording of a television broadcast.
– ORIGIN mid 20th cent.: originally a proprietary name, from Greek *kinēsis* 'movement' + **-SCOPE**.

kinesics /kɪˈniːsɪks, kʌɪ-/ ▶ **plural noun** [usu. treated as sing.] the study of the way in which certain body movements and gestures serve as a form of non-verbal communication.
■ [usu. treated as pl.] certain body movements and gestures regarded in such a way.
– ORIGIN 1950s: from Greek *kinēsis* 'motion' (from *kinein* 'to move') + **-ICS**.

kinesiology /kɪˌniːsɪˈɒlədʒi, kʌɪ-/ ▶ **noun** [mass noun] the study of the mechanics of body movements.
– DERIVATIVES **kinesiological** adjective, **kinesiologist** noun.
– ORIGIN late 19th cent.: from Greek *kinēsis* 'movement' (from *kinein* 'to move') + **-LOGY**.

kinesis /kɪˈniːsɪs, kʌɪ-/ ▶ **noun** (pl. **kineses**) [mass noun] movement; motion.

■[count noun] Biology an undirected movement of a cell, organism, or part in response to an external stimulus. Compare with TAXIS. ■ Zoology mobility of the bones of the skull, as in some birds and reptiles.
– ORIGIN early 17th cent.: from Greek *kinēsis* 'movement', from *kinein* 'to move'.

kinesthesia ▶ noun US spelling of KINAESTHESIA.

kinetic /kɪˈnɛtɪk, kʌɪ-/ ▶ adjective of, relating to, or resulting from motion.
■(of a work of art) depending on movement for its effect.
– DERIVATIVES **kinetically** adverb.
– ORIGIN mid 19th cent.: from Greek *kinētikos*, from *kinein* 'to move'.

kinetic art ▶ noun [mass noun] a form of art that depends on movement for its effect. The term was coined by Naum Gabo and Antoine Pevsner in 1920 and is associated with the work of Alexander Calder.

kinetic energy ▶ noun [mass noun] Physics energy which a body possesses by virtue of being in motion. Compare with POTENTIAL ENERGY.

kinetics /kɪˈnɛtɪks, kʌɪ-/ ▶ plural noun [usu. treated as sing.] the branch of chemistry or biochemistry concerned with measuring and studying the rates of reactions.
■[usu. treated as pl.] the rates of chemical or biochemical reaction. ■ Physics another term for DYNAMICS (in sense 1).

kinetic theory ▶ noun [mass noun] the body of theory which explains the physical properties of matter in terms of the motions of its constituent particles.

kinetin /ˈkʌɪnɪtɪn/ ▶ noun [mass noun] a synthetic compound similar to kinin, used to stimulate cell division in plants.
– ORIGIN 1950s: from Greek *kinetos* 'movable' (from *kinein* 'to move') + -IN[1].

kineto- ▶ combining form relating to movement.
– ORIGIN from Greek *kinētos* 'movable'.

kinetochore /kɪˈniːtəkɔː, kʌɪ-/ ▶ noun another term for CENTROMERE.
– ORIGIN mid 20th cent.: from KINETO- 'of movement' + Greek *khōros* 'place'.

kinetoplast /kɪˈniːtəplast, -plɑːst, kʌɪ-/ ▶ noun Biology a mass of mitochondrial DNA lying close to the nucleus in some flagellate protozoa.

kinetoscope /kɪˈniːtəskəʊp, kʌɪ-/ ▶ noun an early motion-picture device in which the images were viewed through a peephole.

kinfolk ▶ plural noun another term for KINSFOLK.

King[1], B. B. (b.1925), American blues singer and guitarist; born *Riley B King*. An established blues performer, he came to the notice of a wider audience in the late 1960s, when his style of guitar playing was imitated by rock musicians.

King[2], Billie Jean (b.1943), American tennis player. She won a record twenty Wimbledon titles, including six singles titles (1966–8; 1972–3; 1975), ten doubles titles, and four mixed doubles titles.

King[3], Martin Luther (1929–68), American Baptist minister and civil rights leader. He opposed discrimination against blacks by organizing non-violent resistance and peaceful mass demonstrations and was a notable orator. He was assassinated in Memphis. Nobel Peace Prize (1964).

King[4], William Lyon Mackenzie (1874–1950), Canadian Liberal statesman, Prime Minister 1921–6, 1926–30, and 1935–48. The grandson of William Lyon Mackenzie, he played an important role in establishing the status of the self-governing nations of the Commonwealth.

king ▶ noun 1 the male ruler of an independent state, especially one who inherits the position by right of birth: [as title] *King Henry VIII.*
■a person or thing regarded as the finest or most important in its sphere or group: *a country where football is king* | *the king of rock.* ■ [attrib.] used in names of animals and plants that are particularly large, e.g. **king cobra.** ■ (**the King**) (in the UK) the national anthem when there is a male sovereign.
2 the most important chess piece, of which each player has one, which the opponent has to checkmate in order to win. The king can move in any direction, including diagonally, to any adjacent square that is not attacked by an opponent's piece or pawn.
■a piece in draughts with extra capacity for moving, made by crowning an ordinary piece that has

reached the opponent's baseline. ■ a playing card bearing a representation of a king, normally ranking next below an ace.
▶ verb [with obj.] archaic make (someone) king.
■(**king it**) dated act in an unpleasantly superior and domineering manner: *he kings it over the natives on his atoll.*
– PHRASES **a king's ransom** see RANSOM. **live like a king** (or **queen**) live in great comfort and luxury.
– DERIVATIVES **kinghood** noun, **kingless** adjective, **kinglike** adjective, **kingliness** noun, **kingly** adjective, **kingship** noun.
– ORIGIN Old English *cyning*, *cyng*, of Germanic origin; related to Dutch *koning* and German *König*, also to KIN.

King Alfred's cakes ▶ plural noun another term for CRAMP BALLS.

kingbird ▶ noun a large American tyrant flycatcher, typically with a grey head and back and yellowish or white underparts.
● Genus *Tyrannus*, family Tyrannidae: several species.

kingbolt ▶ noun a kingpin in a mechanical structure.

King Charles spaniel ▶ noun a spaniel of a small breed, typically with a white, black, and tan coat.

king cobra ▶ noun a brownish cobra with an orange-cream throat patch, native to the Indian subcontinent. It is the largest of all venomous snakes. Also called HAMADRYAD.
● *Ophiophagus hannah*, family Elapidae.

king crab ▶ noun 1 another term for HORSESHOE CRAB.
2 N. Amer. an edible crab of the North Pacific, resembling a spider crab.
● Genus *Paralithodes*, family Lithodidae.

kingcraft ▶ noun [mass noun] archaic the art of ruling as a king, especially with reference to the use of clever or crafty diplomacy in dealing with subjects.

kingcup ▶ noun British term for MARSH MARIGOLD.

kingdom ▶ noun 1 a country, state, or territory ruled by a king or queen:
■a realm associated with or regarded as being under the control of a particular person or thing: *the kingdom of dreams.*
2 the spiritual reign or authority of God.
■the rule of God or Christ in a future age. ■ heaven as the abode of God and of the faithful after death.
3 each of the three traditional divisions (animal, vegetable, and mineral) in which natural objects have conventionally been classified.
■Biology the highest category in taxonomic classification.
– PHRASES **come into** (or **to**) **one's kingdom** achieve recognition or supremacy. **till** (or **until**) **kingdom come** informal forever. **to kingdom come** informal into the next world: *the truck was blown to kingdom come.*
– ORIGIN Old English *cyningdōm* 'kingship' (see KING, -DOM).

King Edward ▶ noun an oval potato of a variety with a white skin mottled with red.
– ORIGIN 1920s: named after *King Edward* VII.

king eider ▶ noun an Arctic eider duck, the male of which has a red bill and colourful plumage on the head.
● *Somateria spectabilis*, family Anatidae.

kingfish ▶ noun (pl. same or **-fishes**) any of a number of large sporting fish, many of which are edible:
● a fish of the jack family (Carangidae), including the **yellowtail kingfish** (*Seriola grandis*) of the South Pacific.
● (**northern kingfish**) a fish of the drum family (*Menticirrhus saxatilis*, family Sciaenidae), of the east coast of North America. ● a western Atlantic fish of the mackerel family (*Scomberomorus cavalla*, family Scombridae).

kingfisher ▶ noun an often brightly coloured bird with a large head and long sharp beak, typically diving for fish from a perch. Many of the tropical kinds live in forests and feed on terrestrial prey such as insects and lizards.
● Family Alcedinidae: many genera and numerous species, e.g. the small **river kingfisher** (*Alcedo atthis*), with bright blue and orange plumage, found from Europe to Australasia.

kingfisher blue ▶ noun [mass noun] a brilliant blue colour.

king-hit Austral. informal ▶ noun a knockout blow, especially an unfair one.
▶ verb [with obj.] punch (someone) suddenly and hard, often unfairly.

King in Council ▶ noun (in the UK) the Privy

Council as issuing Orders in Council or receiving petitions when the reigning monarch is a king.

King James Bible (also **King James Version**) ▶ noun another name for AUTHORIZED VERSION.

kingklip /ˈkɪŋklɪp/ ▶ noun a cusk-eel of South African waters, which is an important commercial food fish.
● *Genypterus capensis*, family Ophidiidae.
– ORIGIN early 19th cent.: abbreviation of *kingklipfish*, partly translating Afrikaans *koningklipvis* 'king rock fish'.

King Kong a huge ape-like monster featured in the film *King Kong* (1933).

kinglet ▶ noun 1 chiefly derogatory a minor king.
2 chiefly N. Amer. a very small warbler of a group that includes the goldcrest, having an orange or yellow crown.
● Genus *Regulus*, family Sylviidae: several species, e.g. the American **golden-crowned kinglet** (*R. satrapa*).

King Log ▶ noun a ruler or leader noted for extreme laxity. It derives from a classical fable in which the frogs wanted a king, and Jupiter gave them a log of wood; when they complained, he sent them a stork, which promptly gobbled them up. See also KING STORK.

kingmaker ▶ noun a person who brings leaders to power through the exercise of political influence.
– ORIGIN used originally with reference to the Earl of Warwick (see WARWICK[2]).

King of Arms ▶ noun Heraldry (in the UK) a chief herald. Those now at the College of Arms are the Garter, Clarenceux, and Norroy and Ulster Kings of Arms; the Lyon King of Arms has jurisdiction in Scotland.

king of beasts ▶ noun chiefly poetic/literary the lion (used in reference to the animal's perceived grandeur).

king of birds ▶ noun chiefly poetic/literary the eagle (used in reference to the bird's perceived grandeur).

King of Kings ▶ noun (in the Christian Church) used as a name or form of address for God.
■a title assumed by certain kings who rule over lesser kings.

King of the Castle ▶ noun [mass noun] Brit. a children's game in which the object is to beat one's rivals to an elevated position at the top of a mound or other high place.

king of the herrings ▶ noun another term for ALLIS SHAD and OARFISH.

king penguin ▶ noun a large penguin native to the Falklands and other Antarctic islands.
● *Aptenodytes patagonica*, family Spheniscidae.

kingpin ▶ noun a main or large bolt in a central position.
■a vertical bolt used as a pivot. ■ a person or thing that is essential to the success of an organization or operation: *the kingpins of the television industry.*

king post ▶ noun an upright post in the centre of a roof truss, extending from the tie beam to the apex of the truss.

king prawn ▶ noun a large edible prawn which is of great commercial value.
● Genus *Penaeus*, class Malacostraca.

kin group ▶ noun a group of people related by blood or marriage.

Kings the name of two books of the Bible, recording the history of Israel from the accession of Solomon to the destruction of the Temple in 586 BC.

King's Bench ▶ noun (in the UK) in the reign of a king, the term for QUEEN'S BENCH.

king's bishop ▶ noun Chess each player's bishop on the king's side of the board at the start of a game.

King's bounty ▶ noun historical (in the UK) a sum of money given from royal funds to a mother who had had a multiple birth of three or more.

Kings Canyon National Park a national park in the Sierra Nevada, California, to the north of Sequoia National Park. Established in 1940, it preserves groves of ancient sequoia trees, including some of the largest in the world.

King's Champion ▶ noun another term for CHAMPION OF ENGLAND.

King's Counsel (abbrev.: **KC**) ▶ noun (in the UK) in the reign of a king, the term for QUEEN'S COUNSEL.

King's English ▶ noun another term for **QUEEN'S ENGLISH**.

King's evidence ▶ noun in the reign of a king, the term for **QUEEN'S EVIDENCE**.

king's evil ▶ noun [mass noun] (usu. **the king's evil**) historical scrofula, formerly held to be curable by the royal touch.

kingside ▶ noun Chess the half of the board on which both kings stand at the start of a game (the right-hand side for White, left for Black).

king-sized (also **king-size**) ▶ adjective (especially of a commercial product) of a larger size than the standard; very large: *a king-sized bed.*

king's knight ▶ noun Chess each player's knight on the king's side of the board at the start of a game.

Kingsley /ˈkɪŋzli/, Charles (1819–75), English novelist and clergyman. He is remembered for his historical novel *Westward Ho!* (1855) and for his classic children's story *The Water-Babies* (1863).

kingsnake ▶ noun a large, smooth-scaled North American constrictor which typically has shiny dark brown or black skin with lighter markings.
● Genus *Lampropeltis*, family Colubridae: several species, in particular *L. getulus*. Compare with **MILK SNAKE**.

king's pawn ▶ noun Chess the pawn occupying the square immediately in front of each player's king at the start of a game.

king's rook ▶ noun Chess each player's rook on the king's side of the board at the start of a game.

king's shilling ▶ noun a shilling formerly given to a recruit when enlisting in the army during the reign of a king.
– PHRASES **take the King's shilling** archaic enlist.

King's speech ▶ noun (in the UK) in the reign of a king, the term for **QUEEN'S SPEECH**.

Kingston 1 the capital and chief port of Jamaica; pop. 538,140 (1991). Founded in 1693, it became capital in 1870.
2 a port in SE Canada, on Lake Ontario, at the head of the St Lawrence River; pop. 56,600 (1991); metropolitan area pop. 94,710.

Kingston-upon-Hull official name for **HULL**.

King Stork ▶ noun a tyrannical ruler or leader noted for extremes of oppression. See **KING LOG**.

Kingstown the capital and chief port of St Vincent in the Caribbean; pop. 26,220 (1991).

kinin /ˈkʌɪnɪn/ ▶ noun **1** Biochemistry any of a group of substances formed in body tissue in response to injury. They are polypeptides and cause vasodilation and smooth muscle contraction.
2 Botany a compound that promotes cell division and inhibits ageing in plants. Also called **CYTOKININ**.
– ORIGIN 1950s: from Greek *kinein* 'to move' + **-IN**[1].

kink ▶ noun a sharp twist or curve in something that is otherwise straight: *a kink in the road.*
■ figurative a flaw or obstacle in a plan, operation, etc.: *though the system is making some headway, there are still some kinks to iron out.* ■ figurative a quirk of character or behaviour. ■ informal a person with unusual sexual preferences.
▶ verb form or cause to form a sharp twist or curve: [no obj.] *the river kinks violently in a right angle* | [with obj.] *when the spine gets kinked, the muscles react with pain.*
– ORIGIN late 17th cent.: from Middle Low German *kinke*, probably from Dutch *kinken* 'to kink'.

kinkajou /ˈkɪŋkəˌdʒuː/ ▶ noun an arboreal nocturnal fruit-eating mammal with a prehensile tail and a long tongue, found in the tropical forests of Central and South America.
● *Potos flavus*, family Procyonidae.
– ORIGIN late 18th cent.: from French *quincajou*, alteration of **CARCAJOU**.

Kinki /ˈkiːŋkiː/ a region of Japan, on the island of Honshu; capital, Osaka.

kinky ▶ adjective (**kinkier**, **kinkiest**) **1** informal involving or given to unusual sexual behaviour.
■ (of clothing) sexually provocative in an unusual way: *kinky underwear.*
2 having kinks or twists: *long and kinky hair.*
– DERIVATIVES **kinkily** adverb, **kinkiness** noun.
– ORIGIN mid 19th cent. (in sense 2): from **KINK** + **-Y**[1].

Kinneret, Lake /ˈkɪnərɛt/ another name for Sea of Galilee (see **GALILEE, SEA OF**).

kinnikinnick /ˌkɪnɪkɪˈnɪk/ (also **-nic** or **-nik**) ▶ noun [mass noun] a smoking mixture used by North American Indians as a substitute for tobacco or for mixing with it, typically consisting of dried sumac leaves and the inner bark of willow or dogwood.
■ [count noun] N. Amer. the bearberry, which was also sometimes used in this mixture.
– ORIGIN late 18th cent.: from a Delaware (Unami) word meaning 'admixture'.

kino /ˈkiːnəʊ/ ▶ noun [mass noun] a gum obtained from certain tropical trees by tapping, used locally as an astringent in medicine and in tanning.
● The trees belong to genera in various families, in particular *Pterocarpus* and *Butea* (family Leguminosae).
– ORIGIN late 18th cent.: apparently from a West African language.

Kinorhyncha /ˌkʌɪnə(ʊ)ˈrɪŋkə/ Zoology a small phylum of minute marine invertebrates that have a spiny body and burrow in sand or mud.
– DERIVATIVES **kinorhynch** /ˈkʌɪnə(ʊ)rɪŋk/ noun.
– ORIGIN modern Latin (plural), from Greek *kinein* 'set in motion' + *rhunkos* 'snout'.

Kinross-shire /kɪnˈrɒsʃɪə, -ʃə/ a former county of east central Scotland.

-kins ▶ suffix equivalent to **-KIN**, often expressing endearment.

kin selection ▶ noun [mass noun] Zoology natural selection in favour of behaviour by individuals which may decrease their chance of survival but increases that of their kin (who share a proportion of their genes).

Kinsey /ˈkɪnzi/, Alfred Charles (1894–1956), American zoologist and sex researcher. He carried out pioneering studies into sexual behaviour by interviewing large numbers of people. His best-known work, *Sexual Behaviour in the Human Male* (1948, also known as the *Kinsey Report*), was controversial but highly influential.

kinsfolk (also **kinfolk**) ▶ plural noun (in anthropological or formal use) a person's blood relations, regarded collectively.
■ a group of people related by blood: *a set of kinsfolk.*

Kinshasa /kɪnˈʃɑːsə, -ˈʃɑːzə/ the capital of Zaire (Democratic Republic of Congo), a port on the River Congo, in the south-west; pop. 3,804,000 (1991). Founded in 1881 by the explorer Sir Henry Morton Stanley, it became capital of the Republic of Zaire in 1960. Former name (until 1966) **LÉOPOLDVILLE**.

kinship ▶ noun [mass noun] blood relationship.
■ [count noun] a sharing of characteristics or origins: *they felt a kinship with architects.*

kinship group ▶ noun Anthropology a family, clan, or other group based on kinship.

kinsman ▶ noun (pl. **-men**) (in anthropological or formal use) one of a person's male blood relations.

kinswoman ▶ noun (pl. **-women**) (in anthropological or formal use) one of a person's female blood relations.

Kintyre /kɪnˈtʌɪə/ a peninsula on the west coast of Scotland, to the west of Arran, extending southwards for 64 km (40 miles) into the North Channel and separating the Firth of Clyde from the Atlantic Ocean. Its southern tip is the Mull of Kintyre.

kiosk /ˈkiːɒsk/ ▶ noun a small open-fronted hut or cubicle, from which newspapers, refreshments, tickets, etc. are sold.
■ (usu. **telephone kiosk**) Brit. a public telephone booth. ■ archaic (in Turkey and Iran) a light open pavilion or summer house.
– ORIGIN early 17th cent. (in the sense 'pavilion'): from French *kiosque*, from Turkish *köşk* 'pavilion', from Persian *kuš*.

kip[1] informal ▶ noun **1** Brit. a sleep; a nap: *I might have a little kip* | [mass noun] *he was trying to get some kip.*
■ chiefly Scottish a bed.
2 Irish a place that is considered to be unpleasant, typically because it is dirty or sordid: *he couldn't get a start in this kip of a city.*
▶ verb (**kipped**, **kipping**) [no obj., with adverbial] Brit. sleep: *they kipped down for the night.*
– ORIGIN mid 18th cent. (in the sense 'brothel'): perhaps related to Danish *kippe* 'hovel, tavern'.

kip[2] ▶ noun (in leather-making) the hide of a young or small animal.
■ a set or bundle of such hides.
– ORIGIN late Middle English: perhaps related to Middle Dutch *kip*, *kijp* 'bundle (of hides)'.

kip[3] ▶ noun (pl. same or **kips**) the basic monetary unit of Laos, equal to 100 ats.
– ORIGIN Thai.

kip[4] ▶ noun (in Australia) a small piece of wood from which coins are spun in the game of two-up.
– ORIGIN late 19th cent.: perhaps related to Irish *cipin* 'small stick, dibble'.

Kipling, (Joseph) Rudyard (1865–1936), British novelist, short-story writer, and poet. Born in India, he is known for his poems, such as 'If' and 'Gunga Din', and his children's tales, notably *The Jungle Book* (1894) and the *Just So Stories* (1902). Nobel Prize for Literature (1907).
– DERIVATIVES **Kiplingesque** adjective.

kippa /kɪˈpɑː/ (also **kipa**, **kipah**, or **kippah**) ▶ noun a skullcap worn by Orthodox male Jews.
– ORIGIN mid 20th cent.: from modern Hebrew *kippāh*.

kipper[1] ▶ noun **1** a kippered fish, especially a herring.
■ Austral. informal, derogatory an English person. [ORIGIN: from the popular association of a liking for *kippers* with the English.]
2 a male salmon in the spawning season.
▶ verb [with obj.] [usu. as adj. **kippered**] cure (a herring or other fish) by splitting it open and salting and drying it in the open air or in smoke.
– ORIGIN Old English *cypera* (in sense 2), of Germanic origin; related to Old Saxon *kupiro*, perhaps also to **COPPER**[1].

kipper[2] ▶ noun Austral. an Aboriginal male who has been initiated into manhood.
– ORIGIN from Dharuk *gibara*, from *giba* 'a stone' (because of its use in the ceremonial extraction of teeth).

kipper tie ▶ noun a brightly coloured and very wide tie.

kipsie /ˈkɪpsi/ (also **kipsy**) ▶ noun (pl. **-ies**) Austral. informal an improvised dwelling or shelter.
– ORIGIN early 20th cent.: perhaps from **KIP**[1].

Kir /kɪə/ ▶ noun [mass noun] trademark a drink made from dry white wine and crème de cassis.
– ORIGIN 1960s: named after Canon Félix *Kir* (1876–1968), a mayor of Dijon who is said to have invented the recipe.

kirby grip /ˈkəːbi/ (also trademark **Kirbigrip**) ▶ noun Brit. a type of hairgrip consisting of a thin folded and sprung metal strip or wire.
– ORIGIN 1920s: named after *Kirby*, Beard & Co. Ltd, of Birmingham, England, the original manufacturers.

Kirchhoff /ˈkɪəxhɒf, German ˈkɪrçhɔf/, Gustav Robert (1824–87), German physicist, a pioneer in spectroscopy. Working with Bunsen, he developed a spectroscope and discovered that solar absorption lines are specific to certain elements. He also developed the concept of black-body radiation and discovered the elements caesium and rubidium.

Kirchhoff's laws Physics two laws concerning electric networks in which steady currents are flowing. The first law states that the algebraic sum of the currents in all the conductors that meet in a point is zero. The second law states that the algebraic sum of the products of current and resistance in each part of any closed path in a network is equal to the algebraic sum of the electromotive forces in the path.
– ORIGIN mid 19th cent.: named after G. R. **KIRCHHOFF**.

Kirchner /ˈkɪəxnə, German ˈkɪrçnɐ/, Ernst Ludwig (1880–1938), German expressionist painter. In 1905 he was a founder of the first group of German expressionists. His paintings are characterized by the use of bright, contrasting colours and angular outlines, and often depict claustrophobic street scenes.

Kirghiz ▶ noun & adjective variant spelling of **KYRGYZ**.

Kirghizia /kɪəˈgɪzɪə/ another name for **KYRGYZSTAN**.

Kiribati /ˌkɪrɪˈbas, ˈkɪrɪbəts/ a country in the SW Pacific including the Gilbert Islands, the Line Islands, the Phoenix Islands, and Banaba (Ocean Island); pop. 71,000 (est. 1991); official languages, English and I-Kiribati (local Austronesian language); capital, Bairiki (on Tarawa).

Inhabited by Micronesian people, the islands were sighted by the Spaniards in the mid 16th century. Britain declared a protectorate over the Gilbert and Ellice Islands in 1892, and they became a colony in 1915. British links with the Ellice Islands (now Tuvalu) ended in 1975, and in 1979 Kiribati became an independent republic within the Commonwealth.

Kirin /kiːˈrɪn/ variant of **JILIN**.

Kiritimati /kɪˈrɪsɪməs, ˌkɪrɪtɪˈmɑːti/ an island in the Pacific Ocean, one of the Line Islands of Kiribati; pop. 2,530 (1990). The largest atoll in the world, it was discovered by Captain James Cook on Christmas Eve 1777 and was British until it became part of an independent Kiribati in 1979. Former name (until 1981) **CHRISTMAS ISLAND**.

kirk /kəːk/ ▶ **noun** Scottish & N. English **1** a church.
2 (**the Kirk** or **the Kirk of Scotland**) the Church of Scotland as distinct from the Church of England or from the Episcopal Church in Scotland.
– ORIGIN Middle English: from Old Norse *kirkja*, from Old English *cirice* (see **CHURCH**).

Kirkcaldy /kəːˈkɒdi/ an industrial town and port in Fife, SE Scotland, on the north shore of the Firth of Forth; pop. 47,150 (1991).

Kirkcudbright /kəːˈkuːbri/ a town in Dumfries and Galloway, SW Scotland, on the River Dee; pop. 3,400 (1981).

Kirkcudbrightshire /kəːˈkuːbrɪʃɪə, -ʃə/ a former county of SW Scotland. It became part of the region of Dumfries and Galloway in 1975.

kirkman /ˈkəːkmən/ ▶ **noun** (pl. **-men**) Scottish a clergyman or member of the Church of Scotland.

Kirk session ▶ **noun** the lowest court in the Church of Scotland, composed of the minister and elders of the parish.
■ historical a court of this type in other Presbyterian Churches.

Kirkuk /kəːˈkʊk/ an industrial city in northern Iraq, centre of the oil industry in that region; pop. 208,000 (1985).

Kirkwall /ˈkəːkwɔːl/ a port in the Orkney Islands; pop. 6,000 (1981). Situated on Mainland, it is the chief town of the islands.

kirkyard ▶ **noun** Scottish a churchyard.

Kirlian photography /ˈkəːlɪən/ ▶ **noun** [mass noun] a technique for recording photographic images of corona discharges and hence, supposedly, the auras of living creatures.
– ORIGIN late 20th cent.: from the name of Semyon D. and Valentina K. *Kirlian*, Russian electricians.

Kirman /kɪəˈmɑːn/ ▶ **noun** a carpet of a kind typically having soft, delicate colouring and naturalistic designs.
– ORIGIN late 19th cent.: from *Kirman*, the name of a province and town in SE Iran.

Kirov /ˈkɪərɒf/ former name (1934–92) for **VYATKA**.

Kirovabad /ˌkɪərəvəˈbad/ former name (1935–89) for **GÄNCÄ**.

kirpan /kəːˈpɑːn/ ▶ **noun** a short sword or knife with a curved blade, worn (sometimes in miniature form) as one of the five distinguishing signs of the Sikh Khalsa.
– ORIGIN from Punjabi and Hindi *kirpān*, from Sanskrit *kṛpāṇa* 'sword'.

kirsch /kɪəʃ/ (also **kirschwasser** /ˈkɪəʃvasə/) ▶ **noun** [mass noun] brandy distilled from the fermented juice of cherries.
– ORIGIN German, abbreviation of *Kirschenwasser*, from *Kirsche* 'cherry' + *Wasser* 'water'.

kirtan /ˈkɪətʌn/ ▶ **noun** Hinduism a devotional song, typically about the life of Krishna, in which a group repeats lines sung by a leader.
– ORIGIN from Sanskrit *kīrtana*.

kirtle /ˈkəːt(ə)l/ ▶ **noun** archaic a woman's gown or outer petticoat.
■ a man's tunic or coat.
– ORIGIN Old English *cyrtel*, of Germanic origin, probably based on Latin *curtus* 'short'.

Kiruna /ˈkɪərʊnə/ the northernmost town of Sweden, situated in the Lapland iron-mining region; pop. 26,150 (1990).

Kisangani /ˌkɪsaŋˈgɑːni/ a city in northern Zaire (Democratic Republic of Congo), on the River Congo; pop. 373,400 (1991). Former name (until 1966) **STANLEYVILLE**.

kish /kɪʃ/ ▶ **noun** [mass noun] a scum of impure graphite, formed on molten iron during smelting.
– ORIGIN early 19th cent.: of uncertain origin; compare with French dialect *quiasse* 'scum on metal' (French *chiasse* 'insect excrement').

Kishinyov /kʲiʃiˈnof/ Russian name for **CHIŞINĂU**.

kishke /ˈkɪʃkə/ ▶ **noun** a beef intestine stuffed with a savoury filling.
■ (usu. **kishkes**) US informal a person's guts.
– ORIGIN mid 20th cent.: Yiddish, from Polish *kiszka* or Ukrainian *kishka*.

kiskadee /ˌkɪskəˈdiː/ (also **keskidee**) ▶ **noun** a large tyrant flycatcher with a black-and-white-striped head and bright yellow breast, found mainly in tropical America.
• The **greater kiskadee** (*Pitangus sulphuratus*) and the **lesser kiskadee** (*Philohydor lictor*), family Tyrannidae.
– ORIGIN late 19th cent.: imitative of its call.

Kislev /ˈkɪslɛf/ (also **Kislew**) ▶ **noun** (in the Jewish calendar) the third month of the civil and ninth of the religious year, usually coinciding with parts of November and December.
– ORIGIN from Hebrew *kislēw*.

kismet /ˈkɪzmɛt, -mɪt, -s-/ ▶ **noun** [mass noun] destiny; fate: *what chance did I stand against kismet?*
– ORIGIN early 19th cent.: from Turkish, from Arabic *ḳismat* 'division, portion, lot', from *ḳasama* 'to divide'.

kiss ▶ **verb** [with obj.] touch with the lips as a sign of love, sexual desire, reverence, or greeting: *he kissed her on the lips* | [with obj. and complement] *she kissed the children goodnight* | [no obj.] *we started kissing.*
■ Billiards & Snooker (of a ball) lightly touch (another ball) in passing.
▶ **noun 1** a touch with the lips in kissing.
■ Billiards & Snooker a slight touch of a ball against another ball. ■ used to express affection at the end of a letter (conventionally represented by the letter X): *she sent lots of love and a whole line of kisses.*
2 N. Amer. a small cake or biscuit, typically a meringue.
■ a small sweet, especially one made of chocolate.
– PHRASES **kiss and make up** become reconciled. **kiss and tell** chiefly derogatory recount one's sexual exploits, especially to the media concerning a famous person: [as modifier] *this isn't a kiss-and-tell book.* **kiss someone's arse** (or N. Amer. **ass**) vulgar slang behave obsequiously towards someone. **kiss ass** N. Amer. vulgar slang behave in an obsequious or sycophantic way. **kiss something better** informal comfort a sick or injured person, especially a child, by kissing the sore or injured part of their body as a gesture of removing pain. **kiss something goodbye** (or **kiss goodbye to something**) informal accept the certain loss of something: *I could kiss my career goodbye.* **kiss of death** an action or event that causes certain failure for an enterprise: *it would be the kiss of death for the company if it could be proved that the food was unsafe.* **kiss of life** mouth-to-mouth resuscitation. ■ figurative an action or event that revives a failing enterprise: *good ratings gave the programme the kiss of life.* **kiss of peace** a ceremonial kiss given or exchanged as a sign of unity, especially the kiss of the consecrated elements during the Christian Eucharist. **kiss the rod** accept punishment submissively.
– DERIVATIVES **kissable** adjective.
– ORIGIN Old English *cyssan* (verb), of Germanic origin; related to Dutch *kussen* and German *küssen*.
▶ **kiss someone/thing off** N. Amer. informal dismiss someone rudely; end a relationship abruptly.
kiss up to N. Amer. informal behave sycophantically or obsequiously towards (someone) in order to obtain something.

kiss-ass ▶ **adjective** N. Amer. vulgar slang having or showing an obsequious or sycophantic eagerness to please.

kiss-curl ▶ **noun** a small curl of hair trained to lie flat on the forehead, at the nape of the neck, or in front of the ear.

kissel /ˈkɪs(ə)l/ ▶ **noun** [mass noun] a dessert made from fruit juice or purée boiled with sugar and water and thickened with potato or cornflour.
– ORIGIN from Russian *kisel'*, from a base shared by *kislyĭ* 'sour'.

kisser ▶ **noun 1** [usu. with adj.] a person who kisses someone: *he's a good kisser.* [ORIGIN: mid 16th cent.: from the verb **KISS** + **-ER**[1].]
2 informal a person's mouth: *I belted him one, right on the kisser.* [ORIGIN: mid 19th cent.: originally boxing slang.]

kissing bug ▶ **noun** a bloodsucking North American assassin bug which can inflict a painful bite on humans and often attacks the face.
• *Melanolestes picipes*, family Reduviidae, suborder Heteroptera.

kissing cousin ▶ **noun** a relative known well enough to be given a kiss in greeting.

kissing disease ▶ **noun** informal a disease transmitted by contact with infected saliva, especially mononucleosis.

Kissinger /ˈkɪsɪndʒə/, Henry (Alfred) (b.1923), German-born American statesman and diplomat, Secretary of State 1973–7. In 1973 he helped negotiate the withdrawal of US troops from South Vietnam, for which he shared the Nobel Peace Prize. He later restored US diplomatic relations with Egypt in the wake of the Yom Kippur War.

kissing gate ▶ **noun** Brit. a small gate hung in a U- or V-shaped enclosure, letting one person through at a time.

kissing gourami ▶ **noun** an edible SE Asian freshwater fish which is widely kept in aquaria. Individuals sometimes press their fleshy lips together, probably as a threat display.
• *Helostoma temminckii*, family Helostomatidae.

kiss-off ▶ **noun** informal, chiefly N. Amer. a rude or abrupt dismissal, especially from a job or romantic relationship.

kissogram ▶ **noun** a novelty greeting or message delivered by a man or woman who accompanies it with a kiss, pre-arranged as a humorous surprise for the recipient.

kissy ▶ **adjective** informal characterized by or given to kissing; amorous: *Dean and I were just getting kissy.*

kissy-face ▶ **noun** [mass noun] N. Amer. informal a puckering of the lips as if to kiss someone: *she made kissy-face when she saw me.*
– PHRASES **play kissy-face** (or **kissy-kissy**) engage in kissing or petting, especially in public. ■ behave in an excessively friendly way in order to gain favour.

kist ▶ **noun 1** variant spelling of **CIST**[1].
2 S. African a chest used for storing clothes and linen. [ORIGIN: South African Dutch, from Dutch.]

Kiswahili /ˌkiːswəˈhiːli, ˌkɪswɑː-/ ▶ **noun** another term for **SWAHILI** (in sense 1).
– ORIGIN from the Bantu prefix *ki-* (used in names of languages) + **SWAHILI**.

kit[1] ▶ **noun 1** a set of articles or equipment needed for a specific purpose: *a first-aid kit.*
■ [mass noun] Brit. the clothing and other items belonging to a soldier or used in an activity such as sport: *boys in football kit.* ■ a set of all the parts needed to assemble something: *an aircraft kit.*
2 Brit. a large basket, box, or other container, especially for fish.
▶ **verb** [with obj.] (**kit someone/thing out/up**) (usu. **be kitted out/up**) chiefly Brit. provide someone or something with the appropriate clothing or equipment: *we were all kitted out in life jackets.*
– PHRASES **get one's kit off** Brit. informal take off all one's clothes.
– ORIGIN Middle English: from Middle Dutch *kitte* 'wooden vessel', of unknown origin. The original sense 'wooden tub' was later applied to other containers; the use denoting a soldier's equipment (late 18th cent.) probably arose from the idea of a set of articles packed in a container.

kit[2] ▶ **noun** the young of certain animals, such as the beaver, ferret, and mink.
■ informal term for **KITTEN**.

kit[3] ▶ **noun** historical a small violin, especially one used by a dancing master.
– ORIGIN early 16th cent.: perhaps from Latin *cithara* (see **CITTERN**).

Kitakyushu /ˌkiːtəˈkjuːʃuː/ a port in southern Japan, on the north coast of Kyushu island; pop. 1,026,470 (1990).

kitbag ▶ **noun** a long, cylindrical canvas bag, used especially for carrying a soldier's clothes and personal possessions.

kit car ▶ **noun** a car sold in kit form and designed to be assembled by the purchaser.

kit-cat ▶ **noun** a canvas of a standard size (typically 36 × 28 in., 91.5 × 71 cm), especially as used for a life-size portrait (**kit-cat portrait**) showing the sitter's head, shoulders, and one or both hands.
– ORIGIN mid 18th cent.: named after a series of portraits of the members of the **KIT-CAT CLUB**.

Kit-Cat Club an association of prominent Whigs and literary figures founded in the early part of the 18th century. According to Alexander Pope its members included Richard Steele, Joseph Addison, William Congreve, and John Vanbrugh.
– ORIGIN named after *Kit* (= Christopher) *Cat* or *Catling*, who kept the pie house in Shire Lane, by

Temple Bar, the original meeting place of the club.

kitchen ▶noun **1** a room or area where food is prepared and cooked. ■a set of fitments and units that are sold together and fixed in place in such a room or area: *a fully fitted kitchen at a bargain price.* ■ [mass noun] cuisine: *the dried shrimp pastes of the Thai kitchen.* **2** informal the percussion section of an orchestra. **3** [as modifier] (of a language) in an uneducated or domestic form: *kitchen Swahili.*
– PHRASES **everything but the kitchen sink** informal, humorous everything imaginable.
– ORIGIN Old English *cycene*, of West Germanic origin; related to Dutch *keuken* and German *Küche*, based on Latin *coquere* 'to cook'.

kitchen cabinet ▶noun a group of unofficial advisers to the holder of an elected office who are considered to be unduly influential.

kitchen-diner ▶noun a room used as both a kitchen and a dining room.

Kitchener[1] /ˈkɪtʃɪnə/ a city in Ontario, southern Canada; pop. 168,300 (1991); metropolitan area pop. 356,420. Settled by German Mennonites in 1806, as Dutch Sand Hills, it was renamed Berlin in 1830 and Kitchener in 1916, in honour of Field Marshal Kitchener.

Kitchener[2] /ˈkɪtʃɪnə/, (Horatio) Herbert, 1st Earl Kitchener of Khartoum (1850–1916), British soldier and statesman. At the outbreak of the First World War he was made Secretary of State for War. He had previously defeated the Mahdist forces at Omdurman in 1898, served as Chief of Staff in the Second Boer War, and been Commander-in-Chief (1902–9) in India.

kitchener ▶noun historical a range fitted with various appliances such as ovens, plate-warmers, water heaters, etc.

kitchenette ▶noun a small kitchen or part of a room equipped as a kitchen.

kitchen garden ▶noun a garden or area where vegetables, fruit, or herbs are grown for domestic use.

kitchen midden ▶noun a prehistoric refuse heap which marks an ancient settlement, chiefly containing bones, shells, and stone implements.

kitchen paper ▶noun [mass noun] absorbent paper used for drying and cleaning purposes in a kitchen or elsewhere, typically sold as a roll.

kitchen police (abbrev.: **KP**) ▶noun [usu. treated as pl.] US military slang enlisted men detailed to help the cook by washing dishes, peeling vegetables, and other kitchen duties.

kitchen porter ▶noun a person employed to wash dishes and carry out other menial duties in the kitchen of a restaurant or hotel.

kitchen roll ▶noun [mass noun] Brit. kitchen paper.

kitchen-sink ▶adjective [attrib.] (in art forms) characterized by great realism in the depiction of drab or sordid subjects. The term is most used of post-war British drama, such as John Osborne's *Look Back in Anger* (1956) and Arnold Wesker's *Roots* (1959), which uses working-class domestic settings rather than the drawing rooms of conventional middle-class drama, and of a short-lived school of British social realist painters.

kitchen tea ▶noun Austral./NZ a party held before a wedding to which female guests bring items of kitchen equipment as presents for the bride-to-be.

kitchenware ▶noun [mass noun] the utensils used in a kitchen.

kite ▶noun **1** a toy consisting of a light frame with thin material stretched over it, flown in the wind at the end of a long string. ■Brit. informal, dated an aircraft. ■ Sailing, informal a spinnaker or other high, light sail. **2** a medium to large long-winged bird of prey which typically has a forked tail and frequently soars on updraughts of air. ●*Milvus* and other genera, family Accipitridae: many species, in particular the **red kite** and **black kite**. **3** informal a fraudulent cheque, bill, or receipt. ■an illicit or surreptitious letter or note. ■ archaic a person who exploits or preys on others. **4** Geometry a quadrilateral figure having two pairs of equal adjacent sides, symmetrical only about its diagonals.
▶verb **1** [no obj.] [usu. as noun **kiting**] fly a kite.

■[with adverbial of direction] fly; move quickly: *he kited into England on Concorde.* **2** [with obj.] informal, chiefly N. Amer. write or use (a cheque, bill, or receipt) fraudulently.
– PHRASES **(as) high as a kite** informal intoxicated with drugs or alcohol.
– ORIGIN Old English *cȳta* (as a noun in sense 2); probably of imitative origin and related to German *Kauz* 'screech owl'. The toy was so named because it hovers in the air like the bird.

kite-flying ▶noun [mass noun] the action of flying a kite on a string. ■the action of trying something out to test public opinion. ■ informal the fraudulent writing or using of a cheque, bill, or receipt.

Kitemark ▶noun trademark (in the UK) an official kite-shaped mark on goods approved by the British Standards Institution.

kitenge /kɪˈtɛŋɡi/ ▶noun [mass noun] an East African cotton fabric printed in various colours and designs with distinctive borders, used especially for women's clothing.
– ORIGIN mid 20th cent.: from Kiswahili *kitengele*.

kit fox ▶noun a small nocturnal fox with a yellowish-grey back and large, close-set ears, found in the deserts and steppes of the south-western US. ●*Vulpes macrotis*, family Canidae.
– ORIGIN early 19th cent.: *kit* probably from KIT[2] (because of its small size).

kith /kɪθ/ ▶noun (in phrase **kith and kin** or **kith or kin**) one's relations: *a widow without kith or kin.*
– ORIGIN Old English *cȳthth*, of Germanic origin; related to COUTH. The original senses were 'knowledge', 'one's native land', and 'friends and neighbours'. The phrase *kith and kin* originally denoted one's country and relatives; later one's friends and relatives.

kitke /ˈkɪtkə/ ▶noun South African term for CHALLAH.
– ORIGIN perhaps from Hebrew *kikkār* 'loaf'.

kitsch /kɪtʃ/ ▶noun [mass noun] art, objects, or design considered to be in poor taste because of excessive garishness or sentimentality, but sometimes appreciated in an ironic or knowing way: *the lava lamp is a bizarre example of sixties kitsch* | [as modifier] *a kitsch cottage atmosphere.*
– DERIVATIVES **kitschiness** noun, **kitschy** adjective.
– ORIGIN 1920s: German.

kitten ▶noun **1** a young cat. ■the young of several other animals, such as the rabbit and beaver. **2** a stout furry grey and white moth, the caterpillar of which resembles that of the puss moth. ●Genus *Furcula*, family Notodontidae.
▶verb [no obj.] (of a cat or certain other animals) give birth.
– PHRASES **have kittens** Brit. informal be extremely nervous or upset.
– ORIGIN late Middle English *kitoun*, *ketoun*, from an Anglo-Norman French variant of Old French *chitoun*, diminutive of *chat* 'cat'.

kittenish ▶adjective playful, lively, or flirtatious: *her voice had that kittenish quality.*
– DERIVATIVES **kittenishly** adverb, **kittenishness** noun.

kittiwake /ˈkɪtɪweɪk/ ▶noun a small gull that nests in colonies on sea cliffs, having a loud call that resembles its name. ●Genus *Rissa*, family Laridae: two species, in particular the black-legged *Rissa tridactyla* of the North Atlantic and North Pacific.
– ORIGIN early 17th cent. (originally Scots): imitative of its call.

kittle /ˈkɪt(ə)l/ (also **kittle-cattle** /ˈkɪt(ə)lkat(ə)l/) ▶adjective archaic difficult to deal with; prone to erratic behaviour.
– ORIGIN mid 16th cent.: from *kittle* 'to tickle' (now Scots and dialect), probably from Old Norse *kitla*.

kitty[1] ▶noun (pl. **-ies**) **1** a fund of money for communal use, made up of contributions from a group of people. ■a pool of money in some gambling card games. **2** (in bowls) the jack.
– ORIGIN early 19th cent. (denoting a jail): of unknown origin.

kitty[2] ▶noun (pl. **-ies**) a pet name or a child's name for a kitten or cat.

kitty-corner ▶adjective & adverb N. Amer. another term for CATER-CORNERED.

Kitty Hawk a town on a narrow sand peninsula on the Atlantic coast of North Carolina. It was there that, in 1903, the Wright brothers made the first powered aeroplane flight.

Kitwe /ˈkɪtweɪ/ a city in the Copperbelt mining region of northern Zambia; pop. 338,000 (1990).

Kitzbühel /ˈkɪtsˌbjʊəl, German ˈkɪtsˌbyːəl/ a town in the Tyrol, western Austria; pop. 7,840 (1981). It is a popular resort centre for winter sports.

kiva /ˈkiːvə/ ▶noun a chamber, built wholly or partly underground, used by male Pueblo Indians for religious rites.
– ORIGIN late 19th cent.: from Hopi *kíva*.

Kivu, Lake /ˈkiːvuː/ a lake in central Africa, on the Zaire (Democratic Republic of Congo)–Rwanda frontier.

Kiwanis /kɪˈwɑːnɪs/ (in full **Kiwanis Club**) ▶noun a North American society of business and professional people formed to maintain commercial ethics and as a social and charitable organization.
– DERIVATIVES **Kiwanian** noun & adjective.
– ORIGIN early 20th cent.: of unknown origin.

kiwi ▶noun (pl. **kiwis**) **1** a flightless New Zealand bird with hair-like feathers, having a long downcurved bill with sensitive nostrils at the tip. ●Family Apterygidae and genus *Apteryx*: three species. **2** (**Kiwi**) informal a New Zealander, especially a soldier or member of a national sports team.
– ORIGIN mid 19th cent.: from Maori.

kiwi fruit ▶noun (pl. same) a fruit with a thin hairy skin, green flesh, and black seeds. Formerly called CHINESE GOOSEBERRY. ● This fruit is obtained from the East Asian climbing plant *Actinidia chinensis* (family Actinidiaceae).

kJ ▶abbreviation for kilojoule(s).

KKK ▶abbreviation for Ku Klux Klan.

KL informal ▶abbreviation for Kuala Lumpur.

kl ▶abbreviation for kilolitre(s).

Klagenfurt /ˈklɑːɡənˌfʊət, German ˈklɑːɡnˌfʊrt/ a city in southern Austria, capital of Carinthia; pop. 89,500 (1991).

Klaipeda /ˈklʌɪpədə/ a city and port in Lithuania, on the Baltic Sea; pop. 206,000 (1991). Former name (1918–23 and 1941–4, when under German control) MEMEL.

Klamath /ˈklaməθ/ ▶noun (pl. same or **Klamaths**) **1** a member of an American Indian people of the Oregon–California border. **2** [mass noun] the Penutian language of this people, now extinct or very nearly so.
▶adjective of or relating to this people or their language.
– ORIGIN from Chinook.

Klan ▶noun the Ku Klux Klan or a large organization within it.

Klansman ▶noun (pl. **-men**) a member of the Ku Klux Klan.

Klanswoman ▶noun (pl. **-women**) a female member of the Ku Klux Klan.

Klaproth /ˈklaprəʊt/, Martin Heinrich (1743–1817), German chemist, one of the founders of analytical chemistry. He discovered three new elements (zirconium, uranium, and titanium) in certain minerals, and contributed to the identification of others. A follower of Lavoisier, he helped to introduce the latter's new system of chemistry into Germany.

klatch /klatʃ/ ▶noun N. Amer. a social gathering, especially a coffee party.
– ORIGIN mid 20th cent.: from German *Klatsch* 'gossip'.

Klausenburg /ˈklaʊz(ə)nˌbɔːɡ, German ˈklaʊznˌbʊrk/ German name for CLUJ-NAPOCA.

klaxon /ˈklaks(ə)n/ ▶noun trademark an electric horn or warning hooter.
– ORIGIN early 20th cent.: from the name of the manufacturing company.

klebsiella /ˌklɛbzɪˈɛlə/ ▶noun [mass noun] a bacterium which causes respiratory, urinary, and wound infections. ●Genus *Klebsiella*; non-motile Gram-negative rods.
– ORIGIN modern Latin, from the name *Klebs* (see KLEBS–LÖFFLER BACILLUS).

Klebs–Löffler bacillus /ˌklɛbzˈlɜːflə/ ▶noun (pl. **bacilli**) a bacterium that causes diphtheria in humans and similar diseases in other animals.

● *Corynebacterium diphtheriae*; non-motile Gram-positive rods.
– ORIGIN late 19th cent.: named after Theodore A. E. *Klebs* (1834–1913), and Friedrich A. J. *Löffler* (1852–1915), German bacteriologists.

Klee /kleɪ/, Paul (1879–1940), Swiss painter, resident in Germany from 1906. He joined Kandinsky's *Blaue Reiter* group in 1912 and later taught at the Bauhaus (1920–33). His work is characterized by his sense of colour and moves freely between abstraction and figuration. Although some of his paintings have a childlike quality, his later work became increasingly sombre.

Kleenex ▶ noun (pl. same or **Kleenexes**) trademark an absorbent disposable paper tissue.

Klein¹ /klaɪn/, Calvin (Richard) (b.1942), American fashion designer, known for his understated fashions for both men and women.

Klein² /klaɪn/, Melanie (1882–1960), Austrian-born psychoanalyst. Klein was the first psychologist to specialize in the psychoanalysis of small children. Her discoveries led to an understanding of the more severe mental disorders found in children.

Klein bottle ▶ noun Mathematics a closed surface with only one side, formed by passing one end of a tube through the side of the tube and joining it to the other end.
– ORIGIN 1940s: named after Felix *Klein* (1849–1925), the German mathematician who first described it.

Klemperer /ˈklɛmpərə, German ˈklɛmpərə/, Otto (1885–1973), German-born conductor and composer. While conductor at the Kroll Theatre in Berlin (1927–31), he was noted as a champion of new work. He became an American citizen in 1937 and subsequently became known for his interpretations of Beethoven, Brahms, and Mahler.

klepht /klɛft/ ▶ noun **1** a Greek independence fighter, especially one who fought the Turks in the 15th century or during the war of independence (1821–8).
2 a Greek brigand or bandit.
– ORIGIN from modern Greek *klephtēs*, from Greek *kleptēs* 'thief' The original klephts led an outlaw existence in the mountains; those who maintained this after the war of independence became mere bandits.

kleptomania /ˌklɛptə(ʊ)ˈmeɪnɪə/ ▶ noun [mass noun] a recurrent urge to steal, typically without regard for need or profit.
– DERIVATIVES **kleptomaniac** noun & adjective.
– ORIGIN mid 19th cent.: from Greek *kleptēs* 'thief' + -MANIA.

kleptoparasite ▶ noun Zoology a bird, insect, or other animal which habitually robs animals of other species of food.
– DERIVATIVES **kleptoparasitic** adjective, **kleptoparasitism** noun.
– ORIGIN late 20th cent.: from Greek *kleptēs* 'thief' + PARASITE.

Klerk, F. W. de, see DE KLERK.

Klerksdorp /ˈklɛːksdɔːp/ a city in South Africa, in North-West Province, south-west of Johannesburg; pop. 238,865 (1980).

kletterschuh /ˈklɛtəʃuː/ ▶ noun (pl. **kletterschuhe**) a light boot with a cloth or felt sole, worn especially for rock climbing.
– ORIGIN early 20th cent.: from German *Kletterschuh* 'climbing shoe'.

klezmer /ˈklɛzmə/ ▶ noun (pl. **klezmorim** /-rɪm/) [mass noun] (also **klezmer music**) traditional eastern European Jewish music.
■ [count noun] a musician who plays this kind of music.
– ORIGIN mid 20th cent.: Yiddish, contraction of Hebrew *kēlē zemer* 'musical instruments'.

klick (also **klik**) ▶ noun informal a kilometre.
– ORIGIN mid 20th cent.: of unknown origin; the term was originally used in the Vietnam War.

klieg /kliːg/ (also **klieg light**) ▶ noun a powerful electric lamp used in filming.
– ORIGIN 1920s: named after the American brothers, Anton T. *Kliegl* (1872–1927) and John H. *Kliegl* (1869–1959), who invented it.

Klimt /klɪmt/, Gustav (1862–1918), Austrian painter and designer. Co-founder of the Vienna Secession (1897), he is known for his decorative and allegorical paintings and his portraits of women. Notable works: *The Kiss* (1908).

Klinefelter's syndrome /ˈklaɪnˌfɛltəz/ ▶ noun [mass noun] Medicine a syndrome affecting males in which the cells have an extra X chromosome (in addition to the normal XY), characterized by a tall thin physique, small infertile testes, and enlarged breasts.
– ORIGIN mid 20th cent.: named after Harry F. *Klinefelter* (born 1912), American physician.

klipfish /ˈklɪpfɪʃ, ˈkləp-/ ▶ noun a small bottom-dwelling fish, typically found in shallow water or rock pools.
● *Clinus* and other genera, family Clinidae: several species, in particular the brightly coloured *C. superciliosus*.
– ORIGIN late 18th cent.: partial translation of Dutch *klipvis* or Danish *klipfisk* 'rock fish'.

klipspringer /ˈklɪpˌsprɪŋə/ ▶ noun a small rock-dwelling antelope with a yellowish-grey coat, an arched back, and a stiff bouncing gait, native to southern Africa.
● *Oreotragus oreotragus*, family Bovidae.
– ORIGIN late 18th cent.: from Afrikaans, from Dutch *klip* 'rock' + *springer* 'jumper'.

Klondike /ˈklɒndʌɪk/ a tributary of the Yukon River, in Yukon Territory, NW Canada, which rises in the Ogilvie mountains and flows 160 km (100 miles) westwards to join the Yukon at Dawson. It gave its name to the surrounding region, which became famous when gold was found in nearby Bonanza Creek in 1896. In the ensuing gold rush of 1897–8 thousands settled in the area to mine gold.
■ [as noun] figurative a source of valuable material. ■ [as noun] chiefly N. Amer. a form of the card game patience or solitaire.

klong /klɒŋ/ ▶ noun (in Thailand) a canal.
– ORIGIN Thai.

kloof /kluːf/ ▶ noun S. African a steep-sided, wooded ravine or valley.
– ORIGIN Afrikaans, from Middle Dutch *clove* 'cleft'.

Klosters /ˈklɒʊstəz, German ˈkloːstɐs/ an Alpine winter-sports resort in eastern Switzerland, near the Austrian border.

kludge /klʌdʒ, kluːdʒ/ informal ▶ noun an ill-assorted collection of parts assembled to fulfil a particular purpose.
■ Computing a machine, system, or program that has been badly put together.
▶ verb [with obj.] use ill-assorted parts to make (something): *Hugh had to kludge something together.*
– ORIGIN 1960s: invented word, perhaps influenced by BODGE and FUDGE.

klutz /klʌts/ ▶ noun informal, chiefly N. Amer. a clumsy, awkward, or foolish person.
– DERIVATIVES **klutziness** noun, **klutzy** adjective.
– ORIGIN 1960s: from Yiddish *klots* 'wooden block'.

Kluxer /ˈklʌksə/ ▶ noun a member of the Ku Klux Klan.

klystron /ˈklʌɪstrɒn/ ▶ noun Physics an electron tube that generates or amplifies microwaves by velocity modulation.
– ORIGIN 1930s: from Greek *kluzein*, *klus*- 'wash over' + -TRON.

km ▶ abbreviation for kilometre(s).

K-meson ▶ noun another term for KAON.
– ORIGIN 1950s: from *K* (for KAON) + MESON.

kn. ▶ abbreviation for knot(s).

knack ▶ noun [in sing.] an acquired or natural skill at performing a task: *she got the knack of it in the end.*
■ a tendency to do something: *the band have a knack of warping classic soul songs.*
– ORIGIN late Middle English (originally denoting a clever or deceitful trick): probably related to obsolete *knack* 'sharp blow or sound', of imitative origin (compare with Dutch *knak* 'crack, snap').

knacker Brit. ▶ noun **1** a person whose business is the disposal of dead or unwanted animals, especially those whose flesh is not fit for human consumption.
2 (**knackers**) vulgar slang testicles.
▶ verb [with obj.] [often as adj. **knackered**] Brit. informal tire (someone) out; exhaust: *you look absolutely knackered.*
■ damage severely.
– ORIGIN late 16th cent. (originally denoting a harness-maker, then a slaughterer of horses): possibly from obsolete *knack* 'trinket'. The word also had the sense 'old worn-out horse' (late 18th cent.). Sense 2 may be from dialect *knacker* 'castanet', from obsolete *knack* 'make a sharp abrupt noise', of imitative origin. It is unclear whether the verb represents a figurative use of 'slaughter', from sense 1, or of 'castrate', from sense 2.

knacker's yard ▶ noun Brit. a place where old or injured animals are taken to be slaughtered.

knackwurst /ˈnakwɔːst/ (also **knockwurst**) ▶ noun [mass noun] a type of short, fat, highly seasoned German sausage.
– ORIGIN mid 20th cent.: from German *Knackwurst*, from *knacken* 'make a cracking noise' + *Wurst* 'sausage'.

knag /nag/ ▶ noun a short projection from the trunk or branch of a tree, such as a dead branch.
■ a knot in wood.
– ORIGIN late Middle English: from Low German *knagge*.

knaidel /ˈkneɪd(ə)l/ (also **kneidel**) ▶ noun (pl. **knaidlach** /ˈkneɪdlax/) (usu. **knaidels**) a type of dumpling eaten especially in Jewish households during Passover.
– ORIGIN from Yiddish *kneydel*.

knap¹ /nap/ ▶ noun archaic the crest of a hill.
– ORIGIN Old English *cnæpp, cnæp*.

knap² /nap/ ▶ verb (**knapped, knapping**) [with obj.] Architecture & Archaeology shape (a piece of stone, typically flint) by striking it so as to make stone tools or weapons or to give a flat-faced stone for building walls: [as adj. **knapped**] *buildings made of knapped flint.*
■ archaic strike with a hard short sound; knock.
– DERIVATIVES **knapper** noun.
– ORIGIN late Middle English (in the sense 'to knock, rap'): imitative; compare with Dutch and German *knappen* 'crack, crackle'.

knapsack ▶ noun a soldier's or hiker's bag with shoulder straps, carried on the back, and typically made of canvas or other weatherproof material.
– ORIGIN early 17th cent.: from Middle Low German, from Dutch *knapzack*, probably from German *knappen* 'to bite' + *zak* 'sack'.

knapsack sprayer ▶ noun a sprayer consisting of a hand-held nozzle supplied from a pressurized reservoir that is carried on the back like a knapsack.

knapweed ▶ noun [mass noun] a tough-stemmed Eurasian plant that typically has purple thistle-like flower heads, occurring chiefly in grassland and on roadsides.
● Genus *Centaurea*, family Compositae: several species, including the widespread **common** (or **lesser**) **knapweed** (*C. nigra*) (also called **HARDHEADS**).
– ORIGIN late Middle English (originally as *knopweed*): from KNOP (because of its hard rounded involucre or 'head') + WEED.

knar /nɑː/ ▶ noun archaic a knot or protuberance on a tree trunk or root.
– ORIGIN Middle English *knarre* (denoting a rugged rock or stone); related to Middle Low German *knarre* 'knobbly protuberance'; compare with KNUR.

knave ▶ noun archaic a dishonest or unscrupulous man.
■ another term for JACK in cards.
– DERIVATIVES **knavery** noun (pl. **-ies**), **knavish** adjective, **knavishly** adverb, **knavishness** noun.
– ORIGIN Old English *cnafa* 'boy, servant', of West Germanic origin; related to German *Knabe* 'boy'.

knawel /ˈnɔːɪl/ ▶ noun a low-growing inconspicuous plant of the pink family, which grows in temperate regions of the northern hemisphere.
● Genus *Scleranthus*, family Caryophyllaceae.
– ORIGIN late 16th cent.: from German *Knauel, Knäuel* 'knotgrass'.

knead ▶ verb [with obj.] work (moistened flour or clay) into dough or paste with the hands.
■ make (bread or pottery) by such a process. ■ massage or squeeze with the hands: *she kneaded his back.*
– DERIVATIVES **kneadable** adjective, **kneader** noun.
– ORIGIN Old English *cnedan*, of Germanic origin; related to Dutch *kneden* and German *kneten*.

knee ▶ noun the joint between the thigh and the lower leg in humans.
■ the corresponding or analogous joint in other animals. ■ the upper surface of someone's thigh when they are sitting; a person's lap: *they were eating their suppers on their knees.* ■ the part of a garment covering the knee. ■ an angled piece of wood or metal frame used to connect and support the beams and timbers of a wooden ship. ■ an abrupt obtuse or approximately right-angled bend in a graph between parts where the slope varies smoothly.
▶ verb (**knees, kneed, kneeing**) [with obj.] hit (someone) with one's knee: *she kneed him in the groin.*
– PHRASES **at one's mother's** (or **father's**) **knee** at

an early age. **bend** (or **bow**) **the** (or **one's**) **knee** (**to**) kneel in submission; submit. **bring someone/thing to their/its knees** reduce someone or something to a state of weakness or submission. **fall** (or **drop**, or **sink**, etc.) **to one's knees** assume a kneeling position. **on bended knee(s)** kneeling, especially in entreaty or worship: *did your guy propose on bended knee?* **on one's knees** in a kneeling position. ■ figurative on the verge of collapse: *when they took over, the newspaper was on its knees.* **weak at the knees** overcome by a strong feeling, typically desire.
– ORIGIN Old English *cnēow, cnēo*, of Germanic origin; related to Dutch *knie* and German *Knie*, from an Indo-European root shared by Latin *genu* and Greek *gonu*.

knee bend ▶ **noun** an act of bending the knee, especially as a physical exercise in which the body is raised and lowered without the use of the hands.

kneeboard ▶ **noun 1** a board placed across the lap to be used as a table.
2 a short board for surfing or waterskiing in a kneeling position.
– DERIVATIVES **kneeboarder** noun, **kneeboarding** noun.

knee breeches ▶ **plural noun** archaic short trousers worn by men and fastened at or just below the knee.

kneecap ▶ **noun** the convex bone in front of the knee joint; the patella.
▶ **verb** (**-capped**, **-capping**) [with obj.] shoot (someone) in the knee or leg as a form of punishment: [as noun **kneecapping**] *petty crimes are punished by kneecapping.*

knee-deep ▶ **adjective** immersed up to the knees: *children running through a field were knee-deep in mist.*
■ having more than one needs or wants of something: *we shall soon be knee-deep in conflicting legal views.* ■ so deep as to reach the knees: *the snow was almost knee-deep.*
▶ **adverb** so as to be immersed up to the knees: *his leg plunged knee-deep into the water.*

knee-high ▶ **adjective** & **adverb** so high as to reach the knees: [as adj.] *knee-high boots* | [as adv.] *they were wading knee-high in the water.*
▶ **noun** (usu. **knee-highs**) a nylon stocking with an elasticated top that reaches to a person's knee.
– PHRASES **knee-high to a grasshopper** informal very small or very young.

kneehole ▶ **noun** a space for the knees, especially one under a desk: [as modifier] *a kneehole desk.*

knee-jerk ▶ **noun** a sudden involuntary reflex kick caused by a blow on the tendon just below the knee.
▶ **adjective** [attrib.] (of a response) automatic and unthinking: *a knee-jerk reaction.*
■ (of a person) responding in this way: *knee-jerk radicals.*

kneel ▶ **verb** (past and past participle **knelt** or chiefly N. Amer. also **kneeled**) [no obj.] (of a person) be in or assume a position in which the body is supported by a knee or the knees, typically as a sign of reverence or submission: *they* **knelt down** *and prayed.*
– ORIGIN Old English *cnēowlian*, from *cnēow* (see **KNEE**).

knee-length ▶ **adjective** (especially of an article of clothing) reaching up to or down to the knees: *knee-length boots.*

kneeler ▶ **noun** a person who kneels, especially in prayer.
■ a cushion or bench for kneeling on.

knee-pan ▶ **noun** old-fashioned term for **KNEECAP**.

knee-slapper ▶ **noun** N. Amer. informal an uproariously funny joke.
– DERIVATIVES **knee-slapping** adjective.

knees-up ▶ **noun** [in sing.] Brit. informal a lively party or gathering: *we had a bit of a knees-up last night.*

knee-trembler ▶ **noun** informal an act of sexual intercourse between people in a standing position.

kneidel ▶ **noun** (pl. **kneidlach**) variant spelling of **KNAIDEL**.

knell /nɛl/ poetic/literary ▶ **noun** [in sing.] the sound of a bell, especially when rung solemnly for a death or funeral.
■ figurative used with reference to an announcement, event, or sound that is regarded as a solemn warning of the end of something: *the decision will probably toll the knell for the facility.*
▶ **verb** [no obj.] (of a bell) ring solemnly, especially for a death or funeral.
■ [with obj.] proclaim (something) by or as if by a knell.
– ORIGIN Old English *cnyll* (noun), *cnyllan* (verb), of West Germanic origin; related to Dutch *knal* (noun), *knallen* (verb) 'bang, pop, crack'. The current spelling (dating from the 16th cent.) is perhaps influenced by **BELL**[1].

knelt past and past participle of **KNEEL**.

Knesset /ˈknɛsɛt/ the parliament of modern Israel, established in 1949. It consists of 120 members elected every four years.
– ORIGIN Hebrew, literally 'gathering'.

knew past of **KNOW**.

knickerbocker ▶ **noun 1** (**knickerbockers**) loose-fitting breeches gathered at the knee or calf.
2 (**Knickerbocker**) a New Yorker.
■ a descendant of the original Dutch settlers in New York.
– DERIVATIVES **knickerbockered** adjective.
– ORIGIN mid 19th cent. (originally in sense 2): named after Diedrich *Knickerbocker*, pretended author of W. Irving's *History of New York* (1809). Sense 1 is said to have arisen from the resemblance of knickerbockers to the knee breeches worn by Dutch men in Cruikshank's illustrations in Irving's book.

Knickerbocker Glory ▶ **noun** Brit. a dessert consisting of ice cream served with fruit, cream, and other sweet ingredients in a tall glass.

knickers ▶ **plural noun** Brit. a woman's or girl's undergarment, covering the body from the waist or hips to the top of the thighs and having two holes for the legs.
■ N. Amer. knickerbockers. ■ [as exclamation] Brit. informal expressing contempt or annoyance: *oh, knickers to the lot of them!*
– PHRASES **get one's knickers in a twist** Brit. informal become upset or angry.
– DERIVATIVES **knickered** adjective, **knickerless** adjective.
– ORIGIN late 19th cent. (in the sense 'short trousers'): abbreviation of *knickerbockers* (see **KNICKERBOCKER**).

knick-knack (also **nick-nack**) ▶ **noun** (usu. **knick-knacks**) small worthless objects, especially household ornaments.
– DERIVATIVES **knick-knackery** noun.
– ORIGIN late 16th cent. (in the sense 'a petty trick'): reduplication of **KNACK**.

knick point /ˈnɪk/ (also **nick point**) ▶ **noun** Geology an abrupt change of gradient in the profile of a stream or river, typically due to a change in the rate of erosion.
– ORIGIN early 20th cent.: partial translation of German *Knickpunkt*, from *Knick* 'bend' + *Punkt* 'point'.

knicks ▶ **plural noun** Brit. informal short for **KNICKERS**.

knife ▶ **noun** (pl. **knives**) a cutting instrument composed of a blade and a handle into which it is fixed, either rigidly or with a joint.
■ an instrument such as this used as a weapon. ■ a cutting blade forming part of a machine.
▶ **verb** [with obj.] stab (someone) with a knife.
■ [no obj., with adverbial] cut like a knife: *a shard of steel knifed through the mainsail.*
– PHRASES **before you can say knife** informal very quickly; almost instantaneously. **(that) one could cut with a knife** (of an accent or atmosphere) very obvious. **get** (or **stick**) **the knife into** (or **in**) **someone** informal do something hostile or aggressive to someone. **go** (or **be**) **under the knife** informal have surgery. **the knives are out (for someone)** informal there is open hostility (towards someone). **like a (hot) knife through butter** very easily; without any resistance or difficulty: *anti-aircraft fire would slice through the car like a hot knife through butter.* **twist** (or **turn**) **the knife (in the wound)** deliberately make someone's sufferings worse.
– DERIVATIVES **knife-like** adjective, **knifer** noun.
– ORIGIN late Old English *cnīf*, from Old Norse *knífr*, of Germanic origin.

knife block ▶ **noun** a block of wood or other solid material, containing long hollow grooves in which kitchen knives of various sizes can be inserted up to the handle.

knife-edge ▶ **noun** the edge of a knife.
■ [as modifier] (of creases or pleats in a garment) very fine. ■ [in sing.] a tense situation, especially one finely balanced between success and failure: *they have been living on a knife-edge since his libel action.* ■ a steel wedge on which a pendulum or other device oscillates or is balanced. ■ a narrow, sharp ridge; an arête.

knifefish ▶ **noun** (pl. same or **-fishes**) a semi-nocturnal freshwater fish with a reduced or absent dorsal fin and a long anal fin which reaches from the belly to the tail:
• a New World fish with a narrow eel-like body (families Rhamphichthyidae and Gymnotidae: several genera).
• another term for **FEATHERBACK**.

knifeman ▶ **noun** (pl. **-men**) a man who uses a knife to commit a crime.

knife pleat ▶ **noun** a sharp, narrow pleat on a skirt made in one direction and typically overlapping another.

knifepoint ▶ **noun** the pointed end of a knife.
– PHRASES **at knifepoint** under threat of injury from a knife: *she was raped at knifepoint.*

knife rest ▶ **noun** a metal or glass support for a carving knife or carving fork at table.

knife-throwing ▶ **noun** [mass noun] a circus act or other entertainment in which knives are thrown at a target.
– DERIVATIVES **knife-thrower** noun.

knight ▶ **noun 1** (in the Middle Ages) a man who served his sovereign or lord as a mounted soldier in armour.
■ (in the Middle Ages) a man raised by a sovereign to honourable military rank after service as a page and squire. ■ (also **knight of the shire**) historical a gentleman representing a shire or county in Parliament. [ORIGIN: originally parliamentary members chosen from those holding the rank of knight.] ■ poetic/literary a man devoted to the service of a woman or a cause: *in all your quarrels I will be your knight.* ■ dated (in ancient Rome) a member of the class of equites. ■ (in ancient Greece) a citizen of the second class in Athens, called *hippeus* in Greek.
2 (in the UK) a man awarded a non-hereditary title by the sovereign in recognition of merit or service and entitled to use the honorific 'Sir' in front of his name.
3 a chess piece, typically with its top shaped like a horse's head, that moves by jumping to the opposite corner of a rectangle two squares by three. Each player starts the game with two knights.
▶ **verb** [with obj.] (usu. **be knighted**) invest (someone) with the title of knight.
– PHRASES **knight in shining armour** (or **knight on a white charger**) an idealized or chivalrous man who comes to the rescue of a woman in a difficult situation. **knight of the road** informal a man who frequents the roads, for example a travelling sales representative, tramp, or (formerly) a highwayman.
– DERIVATIVES **knightliness** noun, **knightly** adjective & (poetic/literary) adverb.
– ORIGIN Old English *cniht* 'boy, youth, servant', of West Germanic origin; related to Dutch *knecht* and German *Knecht*. Sense 2 dates from the mid 16th cent.; the uses relating to Greek and Roman history derive from comparison with medieval knights.

knightage ▶ **noun** rare a list and account of knights.

knight bachelor ▶ **noun** (pl. **knights bachelor**) a knight not belonging to any particular order.

knight commander ▶ **noun** a very high class in some orders of knighthood.

knight errant ▶ **noun** a medieval knight wandering in search of chivalrous adventures.
– DERIVATIVES **knight-errantry** noun.

knighthood ▶ **noun** the title, rank, or status of a knight: *he received a knighthood in the Birthday Honours* | [mass noun] *the basis of feudal knighthood.*

knight marshal ▶ **noun** historical an officer of the royal household with judicial functions.

knight of the shire ▶ **noun** see **KNIGHT** (sense 1).

Knightsbridge a district in the West End of London, to the south of Hyde Park, noted for its fashionable and expensive shops.

knight service ▶ **noun** [mass noun] (in the Middle Ages) the tenure of land by a knight on condition of performing military service.

Knights Hospitallers a military and religious order founded as the Knights of the Order of the Hospital of St John of Jerusalem in the 11th century.

k

Originally protectors of pilgrims, they also undertook the care of the sick. During the Middle Ages they became a powerful and wealthy military force, with foundations in various European countries. In England, the order was revived in 1831 and was responsible for the foundation of the St John Ambulance Brigade in 1888.

Knights Templars (also **Knights Templar**) a religious and military order for the protection of pilgrims to the Holy Land, founded as the Poor Knights of Christ and of the Temple of Solomon in 1118.

The order became powerful and wealthy, but its members' arrogance towards rulers, together with their wealth and their rivalry with the Knights Hospitallers, led to their downfall; the order was suppressed in 1312, many of its possessions being given to the Hospitallers.

kniphofia /nɪˈfəʊfɪə, nʌɪ-, nɪpˈhəʊfɪə/ ▶**noun** a plant of a genus that comprises the red-hot pokers.
• Genus *Kniphofia*, family Liliaceae (or Aloaceae).
– ORIGIN modern Latin; named after Johann H. *Kniphof* (1704–1763), German botanist.

knish /knɪʃ/ ▶**noun** a dumpling of flaky dough with a savoury filling that is baked or fried.
– ORIGIN Yiddish, from Russian *knish*, *knysh*, denoting a kind of bun or dumpling.

knit ▶**verb** (**knitting**; past and past participle **knitted** or (especially in sense 2) **knit**) **1** [with obj.] make (a garment, blanket, etc.) by interlocking loops of wool or other yarn with knitting needles or on a machine.
■ make (a stitch or row of stitches) in such a way. ■ make (a plain stitch) in knitting: *knit one, purl one.*
2 [no obj.] become united: *disparate regions had begun to* **knit together** *under the king* | [as adj., with submodifier] (**knit**) *a closely knit family.*
■ (of parts of a broken bone) become joined. ■ [with obj.] cause to unite or combine: *he* **knitted together** *a squad of players other clubs had disregarded.*
3 [with obj.] tighten (one's eyebrows) in a frown of concentration, disapproval, or anxiety.
■ [no obj.] (of someone's eyebrows) tighten in such a frown: *Kate's heavy brows* **knitted together**.
▶**noun** (**knits**) knitted garments.
– DERIVATIVES **knitter** noun.
– ORIGIN Old English *cnyttan*, of West Germanic origin; related to German dialect *knütten*, also to **KNOT**[1]. The original sense was 'tie in or with a knot', hence 'join, unite' (sense 2); an obsolete Middle English sense 'knot string to make a net' gave rise to sense 1.

knitbone ▶**noun** another term for **COMFREY**.

knitting ▶**noun** [mass noun] the craft or action of knitting.
■ material which is in the process of being knitted: *I put down my knitting.*
– PHRASES **stick to the** (or **one's**) **knitting** informal (of an organization) concentrate on a familiar area of activity rather than diversify.

knitting machine ▶**noun** a machine with a bank of needles on which garments can be knitted.

knitting needle ▶**noun** a long, thin, pointed rod used as part of a pair for knitting by hand.

knitwear ▶**noun** [mass noun] knitted garments.

knives plural form of **KNIFE**.

knob ▶**noun** a rounded lump or ball, especially at the end or on the surface of something.
■ a handle on a door or drawer shaped like a ball. ■ a rounded button for adjusting or controlling a machine. ■ a small lump of a substance: *add a* **knob** *of butter or margarine.* ■ chiefly N. Amer. a prominent round hill. ■ vulgar slang a man's penis.
▶**verb** (**knobbed, knobbing**) [with obj.] Brit. vulgar slang (of a man) have sexual intercourse with (someone).
– PHRASES **with** (**brass**) **knobs on** Brit. informal and something more: *it is the rock 'n' roll statement with knobs on.* ■ used for returning and strengthening an insult: *'Lazy tyke!' 'Lazy yourself with brass knobs on!* [ORIGIN: with allusion to the addition of decorative knobs to an object as an embellishment.]
– DERIVATIVES **knobbed** adjective, **knobby** adjective, **knob-like** adjective.
– ORIGIN late Middle English: from Middle Low German *knobbe* 'knot, knob, bud'.

knobble ▶**noun** Brit. a small knob or lump on something.
– ORIGIN late Middle English: diminutive of **KNOB**.

knobbly ▶**adjective** (**-ier, -iest**) having lumps which give a misshapen appearance: *knobbly knees* | *knobbly potatoes.*

knobkerrie /ˈnɒbˌkɛri/ (also **knobkierie**) ▶**noun** a short stick with a knobbed head, traditionally used as a weapon by the indigenous peoples of South Africa.
▶**verb** [with obj.] beat with such a stick.
– ORIGIN mid 19th cent.: from **KNOB** + *-kerrie* (from Nama *kieri* 'knobkerrie'), suggested by Afrikaans *knopkierie*.

knobstick ▶**noun** **1** another term for **KNOBKERRIE**.
2 archaic term for **BLACKLEG**.

knock ▶**verb** **1** [no obj.] strike a surface noisily to attract attention, especially when waiting to be let in through a door: *he strolled over and* **knocked on** *a door marked Enquiries.*
■ strike or thump together or against something: *my knees were knocking and my lips quivering.* ■ (of a motor or other engine) make a regular thumping or rattling noise, e.g. through pinking.
2 [with obj.] collide with (someone or something), giving them a hard blow: *he deliberately ran against her, knocking her shoulder* | [no obj.] *he* **knocked into** *an elderly man with a walking stick.*
■ [with obj. and adverbial of direction] force to move or fall with a deliberate or accidental blow or collision: *he'd* **knocked over** *a glass of water.* ■ injure or damage by striking: *she knocked her knee painfully on the table* | figurative *you have had a setback that has knocked your self-esteem.* ■ make (a hole or a dent) in something by striking it forcefully: *he suggests we knock a hole through the wall into the broom cupboard.* ■ demolish the barriers between (rooms or buildings): *two of the downstairs rooms had been* **knocked into one**. ■ informal talk disparagingly about; criticize.
3 [with obj.] informal approach (a specified age): *he's younger than his brother—knocking seventy.*
▶**noun** **1** a sudden short sound caused by a blow, especially on a door to attract attention or gain entry.
■ [mass noun] a continual thumping or rattling sound made by an engine.
2 a blow or collision: *the casing is tough enough to withstand knocks.*
■ an injury caused by a blow or collision. ■ a discouraging experience; a setback: *the region's industries have taken a severe knock.* ■ informal a critical comment.
3 Cricket, informal an innings, especially of an individual batsman: *a splendid knock of 117 against Somerset.*
– PHRASES **knock someone's block off** informal hit someone very hard in anger. **knock the bottom out of** see **BOTTOM**. **knock someone dead** informal greatly impress someone. **knock someone for six** see **SIX**. **knock people's heads together** see *bang people's heads together* at **BANG**[1]. **knock something into a cocked hat** see **COCKED HAT**. **knock someone into the middle of next week** informal hit someone very hard. **knock someone** (or **something**) **into shape** see **SHAPE**. **knock it off** informal used to tell someone to stop doing something that one finds annoying or foolish. **knock someone/thing on the head** stun or kill someone by a blow on the head. ■ Brit. informal prevent an idea, plan, or proposal from being developed or carried out. **knock on wood** see *touch wood* at **WOOD**. **knock someone's socks off** see **SOCK**. **knock spots off** Brit. informal easily outdo. **the school of hard knocks** painful or difficult experiences that are seen to be useful in teaching someone about life. **you could have knocked me** (or **her**, **him**, etc.) **down with a feather** informal used to express great surprise.
– ORIGIN Old English *cnocian*, of imitative origin.
▶**knock about** (or **around**) informal travel without a specific purpose: *for a couple of years she and I knocked around the Mediterranean.* ■ happen to be present: *it gets confusing when there are too many people knocking about.* ■ chiefly Brit. spend time with someone: *she* **knocked around with** *artists.*
knock someone/thing about (or **around**) injure or damage by rough treatment.
knock someone back Brit. informal **1** reject or discourage a person or their request or suggestion. **2** cost someone a specified, typically large, amount of money: *buying that house must have knocked them back a bit.*
knock something back **1** informal consume a drink quickly and entirely. **2** work risen dough by vigorous kneading to expel air before baking.
knock someone down (of a person or vehicle) strike or collide with someone so as to cause them to fall to the ground.
knock something down **1** demolish a building. ■ take machinery or furniture to pieces for transportation. **2** (at an auction) confirm the sale of an article to a bidder by a knock with a hammer. ■ informal reduce the price of an article. **3** US informal earn a specified sum as a wage. **4** Austral./NZ informal spend a pay cheque freely. [ORIGIN: with reference to spending money on alcohol (compare with *knock back*).]
knock off informal stop work.
knock someone off **1** informal kill someone. **2** Brit. vulgar slang have sexual intercourse with a woman.
knock something off **1** informal produce a piece of work quickly and easily, especially to order. **2** informal deduct an amount from a total: *when the bill came they knocked off £600 because of a little scratch.* **3** Brit. informal steal something. ■ N. Amer. informal rob a shop or similar establishment. ■ N. Amer. informal make an illegal copy of a product. **4** Cricket score the total needed for victory: *there was plenty of time for the Middlesbrough batsmen to knock off the runs.*
knock on **1** informal grow old: *don't you think you're knocking on a bit for this?* **2** (also **knock the ball on**) Rugby illegally drive the ball with the hand or arm towards the opponents' goal line.
knock someone out make a person unconscious, typically with a blow to the head. ■ knock down (a boxer) for a count of ten, thereby winning the contest. ■ defeat a competitor in a knockout competition: *England had been* **knocked out of** *the World Cup.* ■ (**knock oneself out**) informal work so hard that one is exhausted. ■ informal astonish or greatly impress someone.
knock something out **1** destroy a machine or damage it so that it stops working. ■ destroy or disable enemy installations or equipment. **2** informal produce work at a steady fast rate: *if you knock out a thousand words a day you'll soon have finished.* **3** empty a tobacco pipe by tapping it against a surface. **4** Austral./NZ informal earn a specified sum of money.
knock someone over another way of saying **knock someone down**.
knock something over N. Amer. informal rob a shop or similar establishment.
knock someone sideways informal astonish someone.
knock something together assemble something in a hasty and makeshift way.
knock up Brit. informal (in a racket game) practise before formal play begins.
knock someone up **1** Brit. wake or attract the attention of someone by knocking at their door. **2** informal, chiefly US make a woman pregnant.
knock something up **1** Brit. make something in a hurry. **2** Cricket score runs rapidly.

knockabout ▶**adjective** **1** denoting a rough, slapstick comic performance.
2 (of clothes) suitable for rough use.
▶**noun** **1** a rough, slapstick comic performance.
2 US & Austral. a tramp.
■ Austral. a farm or station handyman.
3 N. Amer. a small yacht or dinghy.

knock-back ▶**noun** informal a refusal, rejection, or setback: *don't despair if you have a few knockbacks.*

knock-down ▶**adjective** [attrib.] **1** informal (of a price) very low. [ORIGIN: used earlier to refer to reserve prices set at an auction.]
2 capable of knocking down or overwhelming someone or something: *repeated knock-down blows.*
■ (of furniture) easily dismantled and reassembled.
▶**noun** **1** Boxing an act of knocking an opponent down.
■ Sailing an instance of a boat toppling over owing to the force of the wind.
2 Austral./NZ informal an introduction to someone. [ORIGIN: antonym of *pickup*.]

knock-down-drag-out ▶**noun** informal a free-for-all fight: [as modifier] *knock-down-drag-out fights.*

knocker ▶**noun** **1** a metal or wooden instrument hinged to a door and rapped by visitors to attract attention and gain entry.
■ informal a person who buys or sells from door to door, especially with intent to deceive.
2 informal a person who continually finds fault.
3 (**knockers**) informal a woman's breasts.
– PHRASES **on the knocker** informal **1** Brit. going from door to door canvassing, buying, or selling. **2** Austral./NZ (of payment) immediately; on demand: *he has to pay cash on the knocker.*

knocker-up ▶**noun** (pl. **knockers-up**) Brit. historical a person employed to rouse workers by knocking at their doors or windows.

knock-for-knock agreement ▶ **noun** Brit. an agreement between insurance companies by which each pays its own policyholders regardless of liability.

knocking copy ▶ **noun** [mass noun] advertising or publicity that discredits a competitor's product.

knocking shop ▶ **noun** Brit. informal a brothel.

knock knees ▶ **plural noun** a condition in which the legs curve inwards so that the feet are apart when the knees are touching.
– DERIVATIVES **knock-kneed** adjective.

knock-off ▶ **noun** informal a copy or imitation, especially of an expensive or designer product: [as modifier] *knock-off merchandise.*

knock-on ▶ **noun 1** [usu. as modifier] chiefly Brit. a secondary, indirect, or cumulative effect: *movements in oil prices have **knock-on effects** on other fuels.*
2 Rugby an act of knocking on, for which a penalty or scrum is awarded to the opposition.

knockout ▶ **noun** an act of knocking someone out, especially in boxing: [as modifier] *a knockout blow.*
■ Brit. a tournament in which the loser in each round is eliminated. ■ [in sing.] informal an extremely attractive or impressive person or thing: *he must have been a knockout when he was young.*

knockout drops ▶ **plural noun** a drug in liquid form added to a drink to cause unconsciousness.

knockout mouse ▶ **noun** Genetics a mouse whose DNA has been genetically engineered so that it does not express particular proteins.

knock-up ▶ **noun** [usu. in sing.] Brit. (in tennis or other racket sports) a period of practice play, especially before formal play begins.

knockwurst /ˈnɒkwəːst/ ▶ **noun** variant spelling of **KNACKWURST**.

Knole sofa /nəʊl/ ▶ **noun** a sofa with adjustable sides allowing conversion into a bed.
– ORIGIN mid 20th cent.: named after *Knole* Park, Kent, site of the original sofa (*c.*1605–20) from which others were designed.

knoll[1] /nəʊl/ ▶ **noun** a small hill or mound.
– ORIGIN Old English *cnoll* 'hilltop', of Germanic origin; related to German *Knolle* 'clod, lump, tuber' and Dutch *knol* 'tuber, turnip'.

knoll[2] /nəʊl/ ▶ **verb** & **noun** archaic form of **KNELL**.
– ORIGIN Middle English: probably an imitative alteration of **KNELL**.

knop /nɒp/ ▶ **noun** a knob, especially an ornamental one, for example in the stem of a wine glass.
■ an ornamental loop or tuft in yarn.
– ORIGIN Middle English: from Middle Low German and Middle Dutch *knoppe*.

knopper gall /ˈnɒpə/ ▶ **noun** a hard, irregular umbrella-like gall which forms on an oak acorn in response to the developing larva of a gall wasp.
• The wasp is *Andricus quercuscalicis*, family Cynipidae.
– ORIGIN late 19th cent.: *knopper* from German *Knopper* 'gallnut'.

Knossos /ˈknɒsəs, ˈnɒs-/ the principal city of Minoan Crete, the remains of which are situated on the north coast of Crete. The city site was occupied from Neolithic times until *c.*1200 BC. Excavations by Sir Arthur Evans from 1899 onwards revealed the remains of a luxurious palace, which he called the Palace of Minos.

knot[1] ▶ **noun 1** a fastening made by tying a piece of string, rope, or something similar.
■ a particular method of tying a knot: *you need to master two knots, the clove hitch and the sheet bend.* ■ a tangled mass in something such as hair. ■ an ornamental ribbon.
2 a knob, protuberance, or node in a stem, branch, or root.
■ a hard mass formed in a tree trunk at the intersection with a branch, resulting in a round cross-grained piece in timber when cut through. ■ a hard lump of tissue in an animal or human body. ■ a tense constricted feeling in the body: *the knot of tension at the back of her neck.* ■ a small tightly packed group of people: *the little **knot of** people clustered around the doorway.*
3 a unit of speed equivalent to one nautical mile per hour, used especially of ships, aircraft, or winds.
■ chiefly historical a length marked by knots on a log line, as a measure of speed: *some days the vessel **logged** 12 **knots**.*
▶ **verb** (**knotted**, **knotting**) [with obj.] **1** fasten with a knot: *the scarves were knotted loosely around their throats.*
■ make (a carpet or other decorative item) with knots. ■ make (something, especially hair) tangled.
2 cause (a muscle) to become tense and hard.
■ [no obj.] (of the stomach) tighten as a result of nervousness or tension.
– PHRASES **at a rate of knots** Brit. informal very fast. **get knotted** Brit. informal used to express contemptuous rejection of someone. **tie someone (up) in knots** informal make someone completely confused: *they **tied themselves in knots** over what to call the country.* **tie the knot** informal get married.
– DERIVATIVES **knotless** adjective, **knotter** noun.
– ORIGIN Old English *cnotta*, of West Germanic origin; related to Dutch *knot*.

knot[2] ▶ **noun** (pl. same or **knots**) a small, relatively short-billed sandpiper, with a reddish-brown or blackish breast in the breeding season.
• Genus *Calidris*, family Scolopacidae: two species, in particular the **red knot** (*C. canutus*), which breeds in the Arctic and winters in the southern hemisphere.
– ORIGIN late Middle English: of unknown origin.

knot garden ▶ **noun** a formal garden laid out in an intricate design.

knotgrass ▶ **noun** [mass noun] a common Eurasian plant of the dock family, with jointed creeping stems and small pink flowers. It is a serious weed in some areas.
• Genus *Polygonum*, family Polygonaceae: several species, in particular *P. aviculare*.
■ any of a number of other plants, especially grasses, with jointed stems.

knothole ▶ **noun** a hole in a piece of timber where a knot has fallen out, or in a tree trunk where a branch has decayed.

knotted wrack ▶ **noun** [mass noun] a dark olive-green seaweed with flat branching fronds which bear air bladders, occurring on rocky seashores.
• *Ascophyllum nodosum*, class Phaeophyceae.

knotting ▶ **noun** [mass noun] **1** the action or craft of tying knots in yarn to make carpets or other decorative items.
■ the knots tied in a carpet or other item.
2 a preparation applied to knots in wooden boards prior to painting to prevent resin from oozing through, typically consisting of shellac dissolved in methylated spirits.

knotty ▶ **adjective** (**knottier**, **knottiest**) full of knots: *panelling in knotty pine.*
■ (of a problem or matter) extremely difficult or intricate.
– DERIVATIVES **knottily** adverb, **knottiness** noun.

knotweed ▶ **noun** [mass noun] a plant of the dock family, which typically has sheaths where the leaves join the stems and is often an invasive weed.
• *Polygonum* and other genera, family Polygonaceae: several species, in particular **Japanese knotweed**.
■ knotgrass.

knotwork ▶ **noun** [mass noun] ornamental work consisting of or representing intertwined and knotted cords.

knout /naʊt/ ▶ **noun** (in imperial Russia) a whip used to inflict punishment, often causing death.
▶ **verb** [with obj.] flog (someone) with such a whip.
– ORIGIN mid 17th cent.: via French from Russian *knut*, from Old Norse *knútr*; related to **KNOT**[1].

know ▶ **verb** (past **knew**; past participle **known**) **1** [with clause] be aware of through observation, inquiry, or information: *most people know that CFCs can damage the ozone layer | I know what I'm doing.*
■ [with obj.] have knowledge or information concerning: *I would write to him if I knew his address* | [no obj.] *I **know of** one local who shot himself.* ■ be absolutely certain or sure about something: *I just knew it was something I wanted to do* | [with obj.] *I knew it!*
2 [with obj.] have developed a relationship with (someone) through meeting and spending time with them; be familiar or friendly with: *he knew and respected Laura.*
■ have a good command of (a subject or language). ■ recognize (someone or something): *Isabel couldn't hear the words clearly but she knew the voice.* ■ be familiar or acquainted with (something): *a little restaurant she knew near Leicester Square.* ■ have personal experience of (an emotion or situation): *a man who had known better times.* ■ (usu. **be known as**) regard or perceive as having a specified characteristic: *he is also known as an amateur painter.* ■ (usu. **be known as**) give (someone or something) a particular name or title: *the doctor was universally known as 'Hubert'.* ■ (**know someone/thing from**) be able to distinguish one person or thing from (another): *you are convinced you know your own baby from any other in the world.*
3 [with obj.] archaic have sexual intercourse with (someone). [ORIGIN: a Hebraism which has passed into modern languages; compare with German *erkennen*, French *connaître*.]
– PHRASES **all one knows** used to emphasize the limited nature of one's knowledge concerning something: *all I knew was that she was a schoolteacher.* ■ used to emphasize the importance or significance of the following fact or facts: *all she knew was that she was cold and hungry and thirsty.* **and one knows it** said to emphasize that someone is well aware of a fact although they might pretend otherwise: *the Right Honourable Gentleman's priorities do not add up and he knows it.* **—— as we know it** as is familiar or customary in the present: *apocalyptic expectations, envisaging **the end of the world as we know it**.* **before one knows where one is** (or **before one knows it**) informal with baffling speed. **be in the know** be aware of something known only to a few people: *he had a tip from a friend in the know: the horse was a cert.* **be not to know** have no way of being aware of: *you weren't to know he was about to die.* **don't I know it!** informal used as an expression of rueful assent or agreement. **don't you know** informal, dated used to emphasize what one has just said or is about to say: *I was, don't you know, a great motoring enthusiast in those days.* **for all someone knows** used to express the limited scope or extent of one's information: *she could be dead for all I know.* **God** (or **goodness** or **heaven**) **knows 1** used to emphasize that one does not know something: *God knows what else they might find.* **2** used to emphasize the truth of a statement: *God knows, we deserve a spot of bubbly after all these years.* **I know 1** I agree: *'It's not the same without Rosie.' 'I know.'* **2** (also **I know what**) I have a new idea or suggestion: *I know what, let's do it now.* **know best** have better knowledge or more appropriate skills. **know better than** be wise or polite enough to avoid doing a particular thing: *you ought to know better than to ask that.* **know someone by sight** recognize someone by their appearance without knowing their name or being so well acquainted as to talk to them. **know different** (or **otherwise**) be aware of information or evidence to the contrary. **know something for a fact** be aware of something that is irrefutable or beyond doubt: *I know for a fact that he can't speak a word of Japanese.* **know someone in the biblical sense** informal, humorous have sexual intercourse with someone. **know no bounds** have no limits: *their courage knows no bounds.* **know one's own mind** be decisive and certain. **know one's way around** be familiar with (an area, procedure, or subject). **know the ropes** have experience of the appropriate procedures. [ORIGIN: with reference to ropes used in sailing.] **know what's what** informal be experienced and competent in a particular area. **know who's who** be aware of the identity and status of each person. **let it be** (or **make something**) **known** ensure that people are informed about something, especially via a third party: [with clause] *the Minister let it be known that he was not seeking reappointment.* **not know from nothing** N. Amer. informal be totally ignorant, either generally or concerning something in particular: *she shakes her head while you talk, as if to say you don't know from nothing.* **not know the first thing about** have not the slightest idea about (something). **not know that** informal used to express one's doubts about one's ability to do something: *I don't know that I can sum up my meaning on paper.* **not know what to do with oneself** be at a loss as to know what to do, typically through boredom, embarrassment, or anxiety. **not know where** (or **which way**) **to look** feel great embarrassment and not know how to react. **not want to know** informal refuse to react or take notice: *they just didn't want to know when I gave my side of the story.* **what does —— know?** informal used to indicate that someone knows nothing about the subject in question: *what does he know about football, anyway?* **what do you know (about that)?** informal, chiefly N. Amer. used as an expression of surprise. **wouldn't you like to know?** informal used to express the speaker's firm intention not to reveal something in spite of a questioner's curiosity: *'You're loaded, aren't you, Bella?' 'Wouldn't you like to know?'* **you know** informal used to imply that what is

being referred to is known to or understood by the listener: *when in Rome, you know.* ■ used as a gap-filler in conversation: *oh well, you know, I was wondering if you had any jobs for me.* **you know something** (or **what**)? informal used to indicate that one is going to say something interesting or surprising: *you know what? I believed her.* **you never know** informal you can never be certain.
- DERIVATIVES **knowable** adjective, **knower** noun.
- ORIGIN Old English *cnāwan* (earlier *gecnāwan*) 'recognize, identify', of Germanic origin; from an Indo-European root shared by Latin (g)*noscere*, Greek *gignōskein*, also by CAN[1] and KEN.

know-all ▶ noun informal, chiefly Brit. a person who behaves as if they know everything.

knowbot /ˈnəʊbɒt/ ▶ noun Computing a program on a network (especially the Internet) which operates independently and has reasoning and decision-making capabilities.
- ORIGIN late 20th cent.: from *knowledgeable robot*.

know-how ▶ noun [mass noun] practical knowledge or skill; expertise: *technical know-how.*

knowing ▶ adjective showing or suggesting that one has knowledge or awareness that is secret or known to only a few people: *a knowing smile.*
■ chiefly derogatory experienced or shrewd, especially excessively or prematurely so: *today's society is too knowing, too corrupt.* ■ done in full awareness or consciousness: *a knowing breach of the order by the appellants.*
▶ noun [mass noun] the state of being aware or informed.
- PHRASES **there is no knowing** no one can tell.
- DERIVATIVES **knowingly** adverb, **knowingness** noun.

know-it-all ▶ noun chiefly N. Amer. another term for KNOW-ALL.

knowledge ▶ noun [mass noun] **1** facts, information, and skills acquired by a person through experience or education; the theoretical or practical understanding of a subject: *a thirst for knowledge | her considerable knowledge of antiques.*
■ what is known in a particular field or in total; facts and information: *the transmission of knowledge.* ■ Philosophy true, justified belief; certain understanding, as opposed to opinion.
2 awareness or familiarity gained by experience of a fact or situation: *the programme had been developed without his knowledge | he denied all knowledge of the overnight incidents.*
- PHRASES **come to one's knowledge** become known to one. **to (the best of) my knowledge 1** so far as I know. **2** as I know for certain.
- ORIGIN Middle English (originally as a verb in the sense 'acknowledge, recognize', later as a noun): from an Old English compound based on *cnāwan* (see KNOW).

knowledgeable (also **knowledgable**) ▶ adjective intelligent and well informed: *she is very knowledgeable about livestock and pedigrees.*
- DERIVATIVES **knowledgeability** noun, **knowledgeably** adverb.

known past participle of KNOW. ▶ adjective recognized, familiar, or within the scope of knowledge: *plants little known to western science | the known world.*
■ [attrib.] publicly acknowledged to be: *a known criminal.* ■ Mathematics (of a quantity or variable) having a value that can be stated.

know-nothing ▶ noun **1** an ignorant person.
2 (**Know-Nothing**) US historical a member of a political party in the US, prominent from 1853 to 1856, which was antagonistic towards Roman Catholics and recent immigrants, and whose members preserved its secrecy by denying its existence.
- DERIVATIVES **know-nothingism** noun.

Knox /nɒks/, John (c.1505–72), Scottish Protestant reformer. Knox played a central part in the establishment of the Church of Scotland within a Scottish Protestant state, and led opposition to the Catholic Mary, Queen of Scots when she returned to rule in her own right in 1561.

Knoxville /ˈnɒksvɪl/ a port on the Tennessee River, in eastern Tennessee; pop. 165,120 (1990).

Knt ▶ abbreviation for Knight.

knuckle ▶ noun a part of a finger at a joint where the bone is near the surface, especially where the finger joins the hand: *Charlotte rapped on the window with her knuckles.*
■ a projection of the carpal or tarsal joint of a quadruped. ■ a joint of meat consisting of such a projection together with the adjoining parts: *a knuckle of pork.*
▶ verb [with obj.] rub or press (something, especially the eyes) with the knuckles.
- PHRASES **go the knuckle** Austral. informal fight with fists. **near the knuckle** Brit. informal verging on the indecent or offensive.
- DERIVATIVES **knuckly** adjective.
- ORIGIN Middle English *knokel* (originally denoting the rounded shape when a joint such as the elbow or knee is bent), from Middle Low German, Middle Dutch *knökel*, diminutive of *knoke* 'bone'. In the mid 18th cent. the verb *knuckle* (*down*) expressed setting the knuckles down to shoot the taw in a game of marbles, hence the notion of applying oneself with concentration.

knuckle down 1 apply oneself seriously to a task. **2** (also **knuckle under**) give in; submit.

knuckleball ▶ noun Baseball a slow pitch which moves erratically, made by releasing the ball from the knuckles of the first joints of the index and middle finger.
- DERIVATIVES **knuckleballer** noun.

knuckle bone ▶ noun **1** a bone forming or corresponding to a knuckle.
■ a knuckle of meat.
2 (**knuckle bones**) animal knuckle bones used in the game of jacks.
■ the game of jacks.

knuckleduster ▶ noun a metal guard worn over the knuckles in fighting to increase the effect of blows.

knucklehead ▶ noun informal a stupid person.

knuckle joint ▶ noun a joint connecting two parts of a mechanism, in which a projection in one fits into a recess in the other.

knuckle sandwich ▶ noun informal a punch in the mouth.

knur /nɜː/ ▶ noun a small wooden or porcelain ball used in a game (**knur and spell**) resembling trapball, played in northern England.
- ORIGIN late Middle English *knorre*, variant of *knarre* (see KNAR).

knurl /nɜːl/ ▶ noun a small projecting knob or ridge, especially in a series around the edge of something.
- DERIVATIVES **knurled** adjective.
- ORIGIN early 17th cent.: apparently a derivative of KNUR.

Knut variant spelling of CANUTE.

KO[1] ▶ abbreviation for kick-off.

KO[2] Boxing ▶ noun a knockout in a boxing match. See also KAYO.
▶ verb (**KO's**, **KO'd**, **KO'ing**) [with obj.] knock (an opponent) out in a boxing match.
- ORIGIN 1920s: abbreviation.

koa /ˈkəʊə/ ▶ noun a large Hawaiian forest tree which yields dark red timber.
● *Acacia koa*, family Leguminosae.
- ORIGIN early 19th cent.: from Hawaiian.

koala /kəʊˈɑːlə/ ▶ noun a bear-like arboreal Australian marsupial that has thick grey fur and feeds on eucalyptus leaves. Also called NATIVE BEAR in Australia.
● *Phascolarctos cinereus*, the only member of the family Phascolarctidae.
- ORIGIN early 19th cent.: from Dharuk.

> **USAGE** In general use, **koala bear** (as opposed to **koala**) is widely used. Zoologists, however, regard this form as incorrect on the grounds that, despite appearances, koalas are completely unrelated to bears.

koan /ˈkəʊɑːn, ˈkəʊan/ ▶ noun a paradoxical anecdote or riddle without a solution, used in Zen Buddhism to demonstrate the inadequacy of logical reasoning and provoke enlightenment.
- ORIGIN Japanese, literally 'matter for public thought', from Chinese *gōngàn* 'official business'.

kob[1] ▶ noun (pl. same) an antelope with a reddish coat and lyre-shaped horns, found on the savannah of southern Africa.
● *Kobus kob*, family Bovidae.
- ORIGIN late 18th cent.: from Wolof *kooba.*

kob[2] (also **cob**) ▶ noun (pl. same) S. African a fish of the drum family, especially the kabeljou.

- ORIGIN early 20th cent.: abbreviation of KABELJOU, with anglicization of the vowel.

Kobe /ˈkəʊbi/ a port in central Japan, on the island of Honshu; pop. 1,477,420 (1990). The city was severely damaged by an earthquake in 1995.

København /ˌkøbənˈhaʊn/ Danish name for COPENHAGEN.

kobo /ˈkəʊbəʊ/ ▶ noun (pl. same) a monetary unit of Nigeria, equal to one hundredth of a naira.
- ORIGIN corruption of COPPER.

kobold /ˈkəʊbɒld/ ▶ noun (in Germanic mythology) a spirit who haunts houses or lives underground in caves or mines.
- ORIGIN from German *Kobold.*

Koch /kɒx/, Robert (1843–1910), German bacteriologist, who identified the organisms causing anthrax, tuberculosis, and cholera. Nobel Prize for Physiology or Medicine (1905).

Köchel number /ˈkɜːx(ə)l/ ▶ noun Music a number given to each of Mozart's compositions in the complete catalogue of his works compiled by the Austrian scientist L. von Köchel (1800–77) and his successors.

kochia /ˈkəʊkɪə, ˈkɒtʃɪə/ ▶ noun a shrubby Eurasian plant of the goosefoot family, grown for its decorative foliage which turns deep fiery red in the autumn. Also called BURNING BUSH, SUMMER CYPRESS.
● *Bassia* (formerly *Kochia*) *scoparia*, family Chenopodiaceae.
- ORIGIN late 19th cent.: named after Wilhelm D. J. Koch (1771–1849), German botanist.

Kodály /ˈkəʊdaɪ/, Zoltán (1882–1967), Hungarian composer. His main source of inspiration was his native land; he was also involved in the collection and publication of Hungarian folk songs. Notable works: *Psalmus Hungaricus* (choral, 1923) and *Háry János* (opera, 1925–7).

Kodiak bear /ˈkəʊdɪak/ ▶ noun an animal of a large race of the North American brown bear or grizzly, found on islands to the south of Alaska.
● *Ursus arctos middendorffi*, family Ursidae.
- ORIGIN late 19th cent.: named after *Kodiak* Island, Alaska.

koeksister /ˈkʊksɪstə/ (also **koesister** /ˈkuːsɪstə/) ▶ noun S. African a plaited doughnut dipped in syrup.
- ORIGIN from Afrikaans *koe(k)sister*, perhaps from *koek* 'cake' + *sissen* 'to sizzle'.

koel /ˈkəʊəl/ ▶ noun an Asian and Australasian cuckoo with a call that resembles its name, the male typically having all-black plumage.
● Genus *Eudynamys*, family Cuculidae: one or two species, in particular *E. scolopacea.*
- ORIGIN early 19th cent.: from Hindi *koël*, from Sanskrit *kokila* in the same sense.

Koestler /ˈkɜːstlə/, Arthur (1905–83), Hungarian-born British novelist and essayist. His best-known novel, *Darkness at Noon* (1940), exposed the Stalinist purges of the 1930s. He left money in his will to found a university chair in parapsychology.

kofta /ˈkɒftə, ˈkəʊftə/ ▶ noun (pl. same or **koftas**) (in Middle Eastern and Indian cookery) a savoury ball made with minced meat, paneer, or vegetables.
- ORIGIN from Urdu and Persian *koftah* 'pounded meat'.

koftgari /ˈkəʊftɡəˌriː/ ▶ noun [mass noun] a kind of damascene work of the Indian subcontinent, in which a pattern traced on steel is inlaid with gold.
- ORIGIN late 19th cent.: from Urdu and Persian *kuftgarī* 'beaten work'.

kohanga reo /kəˌhaŋə ˈreɪəʊ/ ▶ noun NZ a kindergarten where lessons are conducted in Maori.
- ORIGIN Maori, literally 'language nest'.

kohen /ˈkɒhɛn, kɔɪn/ (also **cohen**) ▶ noun (pl. **kohanim** /-nɪm/ or **cohens**) Judaism a member of the priestly caste, having certain rights and duties in the synagogue.
- ORIGIN from Hebrew, literally 'priest'.

Kohima /kəʊˈhiːmə/ a city in the far north-east of India, capital of the state of Nagaland; pop. 53,000 (1991).

Koh-i-noor /ˈkəʊɪˌnʊə/ a famous Indian diamond which has a history going back to the 14th century. It passed into British possession on the annexation of Punjab in 1849, and was set in the queen's state crown for the coronation of George VI (1937).
- ORIGIN from Persian *kōh-i nūr* 'mountain of light'.

Kohl /kəʊl/, Helmut (b.1930), German statesman,

Chancellor of the Federal Republic of Germany 1982–90, and of Germany 1990–98. As Chancellor he showed a strong commitment to NATO and to closer European union within the EU.

kohl /kəʊl/ ▶ noun [mass noun] a black powder, usually antimony sulphide or lead sulphide, used as eye make-up especially in Eastern countries.
– ORIGIN late 18th cent.: from Arabic *kuḥl*.

kohlrabi /kəʊl'rɑːbi/ ▶ noun (pl. **kohlrabies**) a cabbage of a variety with an edible turnip-like swollen stem.
– ORIGIN early 19th cent.: via German from Italian *cavoli rape*, plural of *cavola rapa*, from medieval Latin *caulorapa*, from Latin *caulis* (see COLE) + *rapum*, *rapa* 'turnip'; compare with French *chou-rave*.

koi /kɔɪ/ (also **koi carp**) ▶ noun (pl. same) a common carp of a large ornamental variety, originally bred in Japan.
– ORIGIN early 18th cent.: from Japanese, 'carp'.

Koil /kɔɪl/ see ALIGARH.

koine /'kɔɪniː/ ▶ noun [mass noun] the common language of the Greeks from the close of the classical period to the Byzantine era.
■ [count noun] a common language shared by various peoples; a lingua franca.
– ORIGIN late 19th cent.: from Greek *koinē* (*dialektos*) 'common (language)'.

koinonia /kɔɪ'nəʊnɪə/ ▶ noun [mass noun] Theology Christian fellowship or communion, with God or, more commonly, with fellow Christians.
– ORIGIN early 20th cent.: from Greek *koinōnia* 'fellowship'.

kokako /'kɔːkəkəʊ/ ▶ noun a large New Zealand wattlebird with dark blue-grey plumage, a black downcurved bill, and two blue or orange wattles.
● *Callaeas cinerea*, family Callaeidae.
– ORIGIN late 19th cent.: from Maori.

kokanee /'kəʊkani/ ▶ noun (pl. same or **kokanees**) a sockeye salmon of a dwarf variety which lives in landlocked lakes in western North America.
– ORIGIN late 19th cent.: from Shuswap (a Salish language).

kokowai /'kɔːkɔːˌwʌɪ/ ▶ noun NZ red ochre (burnt red clay) used to decorate wood or other materials.
– ORIGIN Maori.

kola ▶ noun variant spelling of COLA (in sense 2).

Kola Peninsula /'kəʊlə/ a peninsula on the NW coast of Russia, separating the White Sea from the Barents Sea. The port of Murmansk lies on its northern coast.

Kolhapur /ˌkəʊlhɑː'pʊə/ an industrial city in the state of Maharashtra, western India; pop. 405,000 (1991).

kolinsky /kə'lɪnski/ ▶ noun (pl. **-ies**) a dark brown weasel with a bushy tail, found from Siberia to Japan.
● *Mustela sibirica*, family Mustelidae. Alternative name: **Siberian weasel**.
■ [mass noun] the fur of this animal.
– ORIGIN mid 19th cent.: from the place name *Kola*, a port in NW Russia, + the pseudo-Russian ending *-insky*.

Kolkata /kɒl'kɑːtə/ official name (from 2000) for CALCUTTA.

Kolkhis /'kɒlxɪs/ Greek name for COLCHIS.

kolkhoz /'kɒlkɒz, kʌlk'hɔːz/ ▶ noun (pl. same or **kolkhozes** or **kolkhozy**) a collective farm in the former USSR.
– ORIGIN 1920s: Russian, from *kol(lektivnoe) khoz(yaĭstvo)* 'collective farm'.

Köln /kœln/ German name for COLOGNE.

Kol Nidre /kɒl 'niːdreɪ/ ▶ noun an Aramaic prayer annulling vows made before God, sung by Jews at the opening of the Day of Atonement service on the eve of Yom Kippur.
– ORIGIN from Aramaic *kol niḏrē* 'all the vows' (the opening words of the prayer).

kolo /'kəʊləʊ/ ▶ noun (pl. **-os**) a Slavic dance performed in a circle.
– ORIGIN late 18th cent.: Serbo-Croat, literally 'wheel'.

Kolozsvár /'kɒlɒʒvɑːr/ Hungarian name for CLUJ-NAPOCA.

Kolyma /ˌkɒlɪ'mɑː/ a river of far eastern Siberia, which flows approximately 2,415 km (1,500 miles) northwards to the Arctic Ocean.

komatiite /kə'matɪʌɪt/ ▶ noun [mass noun] Geology a magnesium-rich extrusive rock, typically with a characteristic texture of criss-crossing olivine crystals.
– DERIVATIVES **komatiitic** adjective.
– ORIGIN mid 20th cent.: from *Komati* (the name of a river in southern Africa) + -ITE[1].

komatik /'kɒmatɪk/ ▶ noun a sledge drawn by dogs, used by the people of Labrador.
– ORIGIN early 19th cent.: from Inuit *qamutik*.

kombi /'kɒmbi, 'kʊmbi/ (also **combi**) ▶ noun (pl. **kombis**) S. African a minibus, especially one used to transport passengers commercially.
– ORIGIN from a proprietary name, abbreviation of German *Kombiwagen* 'combination car'.

kombu /'kɒmbuː/ ▶ noun [mass noun] a brown seaweed used in Japanese cooking, especially as a base for stock.
● Genus *Laminaria*, class Phaeophyceae.
– ORIGIN late 19th cent.: Japanese.

Komi[1] /'kɔːmi/ an autonomous republic of NW Russia; pop. 1,265,000 (1990); capital, Syktyvkar.

Komi[2] /'kɔːmi/ ▶ noun 1 a member of an indigenous people of northern Russia west of the Urals.
2 [mass noun] the Finno-Ugric language of this people, with about 350,000 speakers. Formerly called ZYRIAN.
▶ adjective of or relating to this people or their language.
– ORIGIN the name in Komi.

Komodo /kə'məʊdəʊ/ a small island in Indonesia, in the Lesser Sunda Islands, situated between the islands of Sumbawa and Flores.

Komodo dragon ▶ noun a monitor lizard which captures large prey such as pigs by ambush. Occurring only on Komodo and neighbouring Indonesian islands, it is the largest living lizard.
● *Varanus komodoensis*, family Varanidae.

Komondor /'kɒmənˌdɔː/ ▶ noun a powerful sheepdog of a white breed with a dense coat.
– ORIGIN Hungarian.

Komsomol /'kɒmsəmɒl/ historical an organization for communist youth in the former Soviet Union.
– ORIGIN Russian, from *Kommunisticheskiĭ Soyuz Molodëzhi* 'Communist League of Youth'.

Komsomolsk /ˌkɒmsə'mɒlsk/ an industrial city in the far east of Russia, on the Amur River; pop. 318,000 (1990). It was built in 1932 by members of the Komsomol on the site of the village of Permskoe. Also called KOMSOMOLSK-ON-AMUR /-ˌɒnə'mʊə/.

Kondratiev /kɒn'drɑːtjɛf/ ▶ noun [usu. as modifier] Economics each of a series of cycles or waves of economic contraction and expansion lasting about fifty years, postulated by Kondratiev in the 1920s.
– ORIGIN mid 20th cent.: named after Nikolai D. Kondratiev (1892–c.1935), Russian economist.

koneke /'kɒnɛki/ ▶ noun NZ a farm or logging wagon, usually with runners at the front and wheels at the back.
– ORIGIN from Maori *kōneke*.

Kongo /'kɒŋɡəʊ/ ▶ noun (pl. same or **-os**) 1 a member of an indigenous people inhabiting the region of the River Congo in west central Africa.
2 [mass noun] Kikongo, the Bantu language of this people.
▶ adjective of or relating to this people or their language.
– ORIGIN the name in Kikongo.

kongoni /kɒŋ'ɡəʊni/ ▶ noun (pl. same) a hartebeest, in particular one of a pale yellowish-brown race found in Kenya and Tanzania.
● *Alcelaphus buselaphus cokii*, family Bovidae.
– ORIGIN early 20th cent.: from Kiswahili.

Königgrätz /'køːnɪçˌɡrɛts/ German name for HRADEC KRÁLOVÉ.

Königsberg /'køːnɪçsbɛrk/ German name for KALININGRAD.

konimeter /kə'nɪmɪtə/ ▶ noun an instrument for collecting dust samples which directs a measured volume of air on to a greased slide to which any dust present will stick.
– ORIGIN early 20th cent.: from Greek *konis* 'dust' + -METER.

Konkani /'kəʊŋkəni/ ▶ noun [mass noun] an Indic language that is the main language of Goa and adjacent parts of Maharashtra. It has about 5 million speakers. Also called GOANESE.

▶ adjective of or relating to this language.
– ORIGIN from Marathi and Hindi *konkanī*, from Sanskrit *koṅkaṇa* 'Konkan' (a coastal region of western India).

Kon-Tiki /kɒn'tiːki/ the raft made of balsa logs in which Thor Heyerdahl sailed from the western coast of Peru to the islands of Polynesia in 1947.
– ORIGIN named after an Inca god.

Konya /'kɒnjə/ a city in SW central Turkey; pop. 513,350 (1990). An ancient Phrygian settlement, it became the capital of the Seljuk sultans towards the end of the 11th century.

kook ▶ noun N. Amer. informal a mad or eccentric person.
– ORIGIN 1960s: probably from CUCKOO.

kookaburra /'kʊkəˌbʌrə/ ▶ noun a very large Australasian kingfisher that feeds on terrestrial prey such as reptiles and birds.
● Genus *Dacelo*, family Alcedinidae: two species, in particular the **laughing kookaburra** or laughing jackass (*D. novaeguineae*), which has a loud cackling call.
– ORIGIN late 19th cent.: from Wiradhuri *gugubarra*.

kooky ▶ adjective (**kookier**, **kookiest**) informal strange or eccentric: *I like kooky foreign films.*
– DERIVATIVES **kookily** adverb, **kookiness** noun.

Kooning, Willem de, see DE KOONING.

koori /'kʊəri/ ▶ noun (pl. **koories**) Austral. an Aboriginal.
– ORIGIN from Awabakal (an Aboriginal language), literally 'man'.

kop ▶ noun 1 (usu. **the Kop**) Brit. a high bank of terracing at certain soccer grounds where spectators formerly stood, notably at Liverpool Football Club. [ORIGIN: from *Spioen Kop*, site of a Boer War battle in which troops from Lancashire led the assault (Liverpool then being part of Lancashire).]
2 S. African informal the head: *he's got cuts in his kop.*
■ [mass noun] intelligence: *this puzzle takes a bit of kop.* [ORIGIN: Afrikaans, from Dutch, literally 'head' (compare with COP[2]).]

kopek /'kəʊpɛk, 'kɒpɛk/ (also **copeck** or **kopeck**) ▶ noun a monetary unit of Russia and some other countries of the former USSR, equal to one hundredth of a rouble.
– ORIGIN from Russian *kopeĭka*, diminutive of *kop'ē* 'lance' (from the figure on the coin (1535) of Tsar Ivan IV, bearing a lance instead of a sword).

koppie /'kɒpi/ (also **kopje**) ▶ noun S. African a small hill in a generally flat area.
– ORIGIN Afrikaans, from Dutch *kopje*, diminutive of *kop* 'head'.

kora /'kɔːrə/ ▶ noun a West African musical instrument shaped like a lute, with 21 strings passing over a high bridge, and played like a harp.
– ORIGIN late 18th cent.: a local word.

koradji /'kɒrədʒi, kɒ'radʒi/ ▶ noun Austral. (pl. **koradjis**) an Aboriginal medicine man.
– ORIGIN from Dharuk *garraaji* 'doctor'.

Koran /kɔː'rɑːn, kə-/ (also **Quran** or **Qur'an** /kʊ-/) ▶ noun the Islamic sacred book, believed to be the word of God as dictated to Muhammad by the archangel Gabriel and written down in Arabic. The Koran consists of 114 units of varying lengths, known as *suras*; the first sura is said as part of the ritual prayer. These touch upon all aspects of human existence, including matters of doctrine, social organization, and legislation.
– DERIVATIVES **Koranic** /-'ranɪk, -'rɑːnɪk/ adjective.
– ORIGIN from Arabic *ḳur'ān* 'recitation', from *ḳara'a* 'read, recite'.

Korbut /'kɔːbət/, Olga (b.1955), Soviet gymnast, born in Belarus. She won two individual gold medals at the 1972 Olympic Games.

Korchnoi /'kɔːtʃnɔɪ/, Viktor (Lvovich) (b.1931), Russian chess player. He ranked third (c.1967–75) and then second (c.1975–80) in the world.

Korda /'kɔːdə/, Sir Alexander (1893–1956), Hungarian-born British film producer and director; born *Sándor Kellner*. Notable productions: *The Third Man* (1949).

Kordofan /ˌkɔːdə'fɑːn/ a region of central Sudan.

kore /'kɔːreɪ/ ▶ noun (pl. **korai**) an archaic Greek statue of a young woman, standing and clothed in long loose robes.
– ORIGIN from Greek *korē* 'maiden'.

Korea /kə'rɪə/ a region of east Asia forming a peninsula between the Sea of Japan and the Yellow

Sea, now divided into the countries of North Korea and South Korea.

Ruled from the 14th century by the Korean Yi dynasty but more recently dominated by the Chinese and Japanese in turn, Korea was annexed by Japan in 1910. Following the Japanese surrender at the end of the Second World War, Korea was partitioned along the 38th parallel in 1948.

Korea, Democratic People's Republic of official name for **NORTH KOREA**.

Korea, Republic of official name for **SOUTH KOREA**.

Korean ▶ adjective of or relating to North or South Korea or its people or language.
▶ noun **1** a native or national of North or South Korea, or a person of Korean descent.
2 [mass noun] the language of Korea, which has roughly 68 million speakers worldwide. It has its own writing system, and is now generally regarded as distantly related to Japanese.

Korean War the war of 1950–3 between North and South Korea.

UN troops, dominated by US forces, countered the invasion of South Korea by North Korean forces by invading North Korea, while China intervened on the side of the North. Peace negotiations were begun in 1951, and the war ended two years later with the restoration of previous boundaries.

korero /'kɒːrərəʊ/ ▶ noun (pl. **-os**) [mass noun] NZ talk, conversation, or discussion.
■ [count noun] a conference.
– ORIGIN Maori.

korfball /'kɔːfbɔːl/ ▶ noun [mass noun] a game similar to basketball, played by teams each consisting of six men and six women.
– ORIGIN early 20th cent.: from Dutch *korfbal*, from *korf* 'basket' + *bal* 'ball'.

korhaan /kɔːˈhɑːn, kəˈrɑːn/ ▶ noun S. African a small crested bustard, which is typically boldly marked and has penetrating repetitive calls.
● Genus *Eupodotis*, family Otididae: several species.
– ORIGIN mid 18th cent.: Afrikaans, from the imitative base *kor-*, *knor-* (compare with Dutch *korren* 'coo') + *haan* 'cock'.

kori /'kɔːri/ (also **kori bustard**) ▶ noun a very large bustard with a crested head, native to sub-Saharan Africa.
● *Ardeotis kori*, family Otididae.
– ORIGIN early 19th cent.: from Setswana *kgori*.

Kórinthos /'kɒrinθɒs/ Greek name for **CORINTH**.

korma /'kɔːmə/ ▶ noun a mildly spiced Indian curry dish of meat or fish marinated in yogurt or curds.
– ORIGIN from Urdu *ḳormā*, from Turkish *kavurma*.

Korsakoff's syndrome /'kɔːsəkɒfs/ (also **Korsakoff's psychosis**) ▶ noun [mass noun] a serious mental illness, typically the result of chronic alcoholism, characterized by disorientation and a tendency to invent explanations to cover a loss of memory of recent events.
– ORIGIN early 20th cent.: named after Sergei S. *Korsakoff* (1854–1900), Russian psychiatrist.

Kortrijk /'kɔːtrʌɪk/ a city in western Belgium, in West Flanders; pop. 76,140 (1991). French name **COURTRAI**.

koru /'kɔːru/ ▶ noun a stylized fern-leaf motif in Maori carving and tattooing.
– ORIGIN mid 20th cent.: Maori.

koruna /'kɒrʊnə, kəˈruːnə/ ▶ noun the basic monetary unit of Bohemia, Moravia, and Slovakia, equal to 100 haleru.
– ORIGIN Czech, literally 'crown'.

Korup National Park /'kɒrəp/ a national park in western Cameroon, on the border with Nigeria. It was established in 1961 to protect a large area of tropical rainforest.

Koryak /'kɒrjak/ ▶ noun (pl. same or **Koryaks**) **1** a member of an indigenous people of the northern Kamchatka peninsula.
2 [mass noun] the language of this people, which has about 5,000 speakers and is related to Chukchi.
▶ adjective of or relating to the Koryaks or their language.
– ORIGIN from Russian *koryaki* (plural).

Kos /kɒs/ (also **Cos**) a Greek island in the SE Aegean, one of the Dodecanese group.

Kosciusko /ˌkɒʃˈtʃʊskəʊ/, Thaddeus (1746–1817), Polish soldier and patriot; full Polish name *Tadeusz Andrzej Bonawentura Kościuszko*. After fighting for the Americans during the War of American

Independence, he led a nationalist uprising against Russia in Poland in 1794.

Kosciusko, Mount /ˌkɒzɪˈʌskəʊ/ a mountain in SE Australia, in the Great Dividing Range in SE New South Wales. Rising to a height of 2,228 m (7,234 ft), it is the highest mountain in Australia.
– ORIGIN named by the explorer Sir Paul Edmund de Strzelecki (1797–1873), in honour of T. **KOSCIUSKO**.

kosher /'kəʊʃə/ ▶ adjective (of food, or premises in which food is sold, cooked, or eaten) satisfying the requirements of Jewish law: *a kosher kitchen*.
■ (of a person) observing Jewish food laws. ■ figurative genuine and legitimate: *when he buys a record abroad, it is impossible to know whether it's kosher.*

Restrictions on the foods suitable for Jews are derived from rules in the books of Leviticus and Deuteronomy. Animals must be slaughtered and prepared in the prescribed way, in which the blood is drained from the body, while certain creatures, notably pigs and shellfish, are forbidden altogether. Meat and milk must not be cooked or consumed together, and separate utensils must be kept for each. Strict observance of these rules is today confined mainly to Orthodox Jews.

▶ verb [with obj.] prepare (food) according to the requirements of Jewish law.
■ figurative give (something) the appearance of being legitimate: *see them scramble to kosher illegal evidence.*
– PHRASES **keep** (or **eat**) **kosher** observe the Jewish food regulations (kashrut).
– ORIGIN mid 19th cent.: from Hebrew *kāšēr* 'proper'.

Košice /'kɒʃɪtsə/ an industrial city in southern Slovakia; pop. 234,840 (1991).

Kosovo /'kɒsəvə/ an autonomous province of Serbia; capital, Priština. It borders on Albania and the majority of the people are of Albanian descent. In 1998 Kosovo was attacked by Serbian forces intent on expelling the Albanian population; the aggression was halted by NATO bombing in 1999, and Kosovo was put under UN administration.

Kossuth /'kɒsuːθ, 'kɒʃuːt/, Lajos (1802–94), Hungarian statesman and patriot. He led the 1848 insurrection against the Hapsburgs, but after brief success the uprising was crushed and he began a lifelong period of exile.

Kostroma /ˌkɒstrəˈmɑː/ an industrial city in European Russia, situated on the River Volga; pop. 280,000 (1990).

Kosygin /kɒˈsiːgɪn/, Aleksei (Nikolaevich) (1904–80), Soviet statesman, Premier of the USSR 1964–80. He devoted most of his attention to internal economic affairs, being gradually eased out of the leadership by Brezhnev.

Kota /'kəʊtə/ an industrial city in Rajasthan state, in NW India, on the Chambal River; pop. 536,000 (1991).

Kota Baharu /ˌkəʊtə bəˈhɑːruː/ a city in Malaysia, on the east coast of the Malay Peninsula, the capital of the state of Kelantan; pop. 219,200 (1991).

Kota Kinabalu /ˌkɪnəbəˈluː/ a port in Malaysia, on the north coast of Borneo, capital of the state of Sabah; pop. 56,000 (1980).

Kotka /'kɒtkə/ a port on the south coast of Finland; pop. 56,630 (1990).

koto /'kəʊtəʊ/ ▶ noun (pl. **-os**) a Japanese zither about six feet long, with thirteen silk strings passed over small movable bridges.
– ORIGIN late 18th cent.: Japanese.

kotwal /'kɒtwʌl/ ▶ noun Indian a police officer.
– ORIGIN via Hindi from Sanskrit *koṭṭapāla*.

kotwali /kɒtˈwɑːli/ ▶ noun Indian a police station.

Kotzebue /'kɒtsɪb(j)uː/, August von (1761–1819), German dramatist. His many plays were popular in both Germany and England. He was a political informant to Tsar Alexander I and was assassinated by the Germans.

koulibiac ▶ noun variant spelling of **COULIBIAC**.

koumiss /'kuːmɪs/ (also **kumiss** or **kumis**) ▶ noun [mass noun] a fermented liquor prepared from mare's milk, used as a drink and medicine by Asian nomads.
– ORIGIN late 16th cent.: based on Tartar *kumiz*.

kouprey /'kuːpreɪ/ ▶ noun a very rare grey ox found in the forests of SE Asia.
● *Bos sauveli*, family Bovidae.
– ORIGIN 1940s: from Khmer.

kourbash /'kʊəbaʃ/ ▶ noun variant spelling of **KURBASH**.

kouros /'kuːrɒs/ ▶ noun (pl. **kouroi** /-rɔɪ/) an archaic

Greek statue of a young man, standing and often naked.
– ORIGIN Greek, Ionic form of *koros* 'boy'.

Kourou /kuˈruː/ a town on the north coast of French Guiana; pop. 11,200 (1990). Nearby is a satellite-launching station of the European Space Agency, established in 1967.

kowari /kəˈwɑːri/ ▶ noun (pl. **kowaris**) a small carnivorous marsupial with a pointed snout, large eyes, and a black bushy tip to the tail, found in central Australia.
● *Dasycercus byrnei*, family Dasyuridae.
– ORIGIN from Diyari and Ngamini (Aboriginal languages) *kariri*.

kowhai /'kəʊwʌɪ, 'kɔːfʌɪ/ ▶ noun a tree of the pea family, which bears hanging clusters of yellow flowers. It is native to New Zealand and Chile and yields useful timber.
● *Sophora tetraptera*, family Leguminosae.
– ORIGIN mid 19th cent.: from Maori.

Kowloon /kaʊˈluːn/ a densely populated peninsula on the SE coast of China, forming part of Hong Kong. It is separated from Hong Kong Island by Victoria Harbour.

kowtow /kaʊˈtaʊ/ ▶ verb [no obj.] historical kneel and touch the ground with the forehead in worship or submission as part of Chinese custom.
■ figurative act in an excessively subservient manner: *she didn't have to kowtow to a boss.*
▶ noun historical an act of kneeling and touching the ground with the forehead in such a way.
– DERIVATIVES **kowtower** noun.
– ORIGIN early 19th cent.: from Chinese *kētóu*, from *kē* 'knock' + *tóu* 'head'.

Kozhikode /'kəʊʒəˌkəʊd/ another name for **CALICUT**.

KP ▶ abbreviation for kitchen police.

kph ▶ abbreviation for kilometres per hour.

Kr ▶ symbol for the chemical element krypton.

Kra, Isthmus of /krɑː/ the narrowest part of the Malay Peninsula, forming part of southern Thailand.

kraal /krɑːl/ S. African ▶ noun a traditional African village of huts, typically enclosed by a fence.
■ another term for **HOMESTEAD** (in sense 3). ■ an enclosure for cattle or sheep.
▶ verb [with obj.] drive (cattle or sheep) into an enclosure: *they kraal their sheep every night.*
■ figurative restrict or separate (people) to a particular area or into groups.
– ORIGIN Dutch, from Portuguese *curral* (see **CORRAL**).

Krafft-Ebing /kraft'ɛbɪŋ/, Richard von (1840–1902), German physician and psychologist. He established the relationship between syphilis and general paralysis and pioneered the systematic study of aberrant sexual behaviour.

kraft /krɑːft/ (also **kraft paper**) ▶ noun [mass noun] a kind of strong, smooth brown wrapping paper.
– ORIGIN early 20th cent.: from Swedish, literally 'strength', used to form the term *kraftpapper* 'kraft paper'.

Kragujevac /'kraɡʊjəˌvats/ a city in central Serbia; pop. 147,300 (1991). It was the capital of Serbia 1818–39.

krai /krʌɪ/ (also **kray**) ▶ noun (pl. **krais**) an administrative territory of Russia. In pre-revolutionary times krais were each made up of a number of provinces, becoming in 1924 large administrative units in the Soviet territorial system. By the time of the break-up of the USSR in 1991 there were six krais.
– ORIGIN from Russian *krai* 'edge, border'.

krait /krʌɪt/ ▶ noun a highly venomous Asian snake of the cobra family.
● Genus *Bungarus*, family Elapidae: several species, including the black and yellow **banded krait** (*B. fasciatus*). See also **SEA KRAIT**.
– ORIGIN late 19th cent.: from Hindi *karait*.

Krakatoa /ˌkrakəˈtəʊə/ a small volcanic island in Indonesia, lying between Java and Sumatra, scene of a great eruption in 1883 which destroyed most of the island.

kraken /'krɑːk(ə)n/ ▶ noun an enormous mythical sea monster said to appear off the coast of Norway.
– ORIGIN Norwegian.

Kraków /'krakʊf/ Polish name for **CRACOW**.

krantz /krɑːns/ (also **krans**) ▶ noun S. African a precipitous or overhanging wall of rocks.
– ORIGIN South African Dutch, from Dutch *krans*, literally 'coronet'.

Krasnodar /ˌkrasnəˈdɑː/ a krai (administrative territory) in the northern Caucasus, on the Black Sea in southern Russia.
■ its capital, a port on the lower Kuban River; pop. 627,000 (1990). It was known until 1922 as Yekaterinodar (Ekaterinodar).

Krasnoyarsk /ˌkrasnəˈjɑːsk/ a krai (administrative territory) in central Siberian Russia.
■ its capital, a port on the Yenisei River; pop. 922,000 (1990).

Kraut /kraʊt/ ▶ noun informal, offensive a German.
– ORIGIN First World War: shortening of SAUERKRAUT.

kray ▶ noun variant spelling of KRAI.

Krebs cycle /krɛbz/ ▶ noun Biochemistry the sequence of reactions by which most living cells generate energy during the process of aerobic respiration. It takes place in the mitochondria, using up oxygen and producing carbon dioxide and water as waste products, and ADP is converted to energy-rich ATP.
– ORIGIN 1940s: named after Sir Hans A. *Krebs* (1900–81), German-born British biochemist.

kreef /kriːf/ ▶ noun S. African a spiny lobster of southern Africa.
● *Jasus lalandii*, family Palinuridae.
– ORIGIN mid 19th cent.: from Afrikaans, from Dutch *kreeft* 'lobster'.

Krefeld /ˈkreɪfɛlt/ an industrial town and port on the Rhine in western Germany, in North Rhine-Westphalia; pop. 245,770 (1991).

Kreisler /ˈkraɪslə/, German /ˈkraɪslɐ/, Fritz (1875–1962), Austrian-born American violinist and composer. A noted virtuoso, in 1910 he gave the first performance of Elgar's violin concerto, which was dedicated to him.

Kremenchuk /ˌkrɛmənˈtʃuːk, ˌkrɪmɪn-/ an industrial city in east central Ukraine, on the River Dnieper; pop. 238,000 (1990). Russian name KREMENCHUG.

kremlin /ˈkrɛmlɪn/ ▶ noun a citadel within a Russian town.
■ (the Kremlin) the citadel in Moscow. ■ the Russian or (formerly) USSR government housed within this citadel.
– ORIGIN mid 17th cent.: via French from Russian *kreml'* 'citadel'.

Kremlinology /ˌkrɛmlɪˈnɒlədʒi/ ▶ noun [mass noun] the study and analysis of Soviet or Russian policies.
– DERIVATIVES **Kremlinologist** noun.

kreplach /ˈkrɛplɑːx/ ▶ plural noun (in Jewish cookery) triangular noodles filled with chopped meat or cheese and served with soup.
– ORIGIN from Yiddish *kreplekh*, plural of *krepel*, from German dialect *Kräppel* 'fritter'.

kriegspiel /ˈkriːɡspiːl/ ▶ noun [mass noun] a war game in which blocks representing armies or other military units are moved about on maps.
■ a form of chess in which each player has a separate board and can only infer the position of the opponent's forces from limited information given by an umpire who disallows illegal moves.
– ORIGIN late 19th cent.: from German, from *Krieg* 'war' + *Spiel* 'game'.

Kriemhild /ˈkriːmhɪlt/ (in the Nibelungenlied) a Burgundian princess, wife of Siegfried and later of Etzel (Attila the Hun), whom she marries in order to be revenged on her brothers for Siegfried's murder.

krill ▶ noun (pl. same) a small shrimp-like planktonic crustacean of the open seas. It is eaten by a number of larger animals, notably the baleen whales.
● *Meganyctiphanes norvegica*, class Malacostraca.
– ORIGIN early 20th cent.: from Norwegian *kril* 'small fish fry'.

krimmer /ˈkrɪmə/ ▶ noun [mass noun] tightly curled grey or black fur made from the wool of young Crimean lambs.
– ORIGIN mid 19th cent.: from German, from *Krim* 'Crimea'.

Krio /ˈkriːəʊ/ ▶ noun [mass noun] an English-based creole language of Sierra Leone. It is the first language of about 350,000 people and is used as a lingua franca by over 3 million.
▶ adjective of or relating to this language.

– ORIGIN probably an alteration of CREOLE.

kris /kriːs/ (also archaic **creese**) ▶ noun a Malay or Indonesian dagger with a wavy-edged blade.
– ORIGIN late 16th cent.: based on Malay *keris*.

Krishna /ˈkrɪʃnə/ Hinduism one of the most popular gods, the eighth and most important avatar or incarnation of Vishnu.

He is worshipped in several forms: as the child god whose miracles and pranks are extolled in the Puranas; as the divine cowherd whose erotic exploits, especially with his favourite, Radha, have produced both romantic and religious literature; and as the divine charioteer who preaches to Arjuna on the battlefield in the Bhagavadgita.

– ORIGIN from Sanskrit *Kṛṣṇa*, literally 'black'.

Krishnaism /ˈkrɪʃnʌɪz(ə)m/ ▶ noun [mass noun] Hinduism the worship of the god Krishna as an incarnation of Vishnu.

Krishnamurti /ˌkrɪʃnəˈmʊəti/, Jiddu (1895–1986), Indian spiritual leader. His spiritual philosophy is based on a rejection of organized religion and the attainment of self-realization by introspection.

Krishna River a river which rises in the Western Ghats of southern India and flows generally eastwards for 1,288 km (805 miles) to the Bay of Bengal.

Kristallnacht /ˈkrɪst(ə)l,nɑːxt, German krɪsˈtalnaxt/ the occasion of concerted violence by Nazis throughout Germany and Austria against Jews and their property on the night of 9–10 November 1938.
– ORIGIN German, literally 'night of crystal', referring to the broken glass produced by the smashing of shop windows.

Kristiania variant spelling of CHRISTIANIA.

Kristiansand /ˈkrɪstʃən,sand/ a ferry port on the south coast of Norway, in the Skagerrak; pop. 65,690 (1991).

Kriti /ˈkriːti/ Greek name for CRETE.

Krivoi Rog /krɪˌvoi ˈrok/ Russian name for KRYVY RIH.

kromesky /krə(ʊ)ˈmɛski, ˈkrɒmɛski/ ▶ noun (pl. **-ies**) a croquette of minced meat or fish, rolled in bacon and fried.
– ORIGIN from Polish *kromeczka* 'small slice'.

krona /ˈkrəʊnə/ ▶ noun **1** (pl. **kronor** pronunc. same) the basic monetary unit of Sweden, equal to 100 öre. [ORIGIN: Swedish, 'crown'.]
2 (pl. **kronur** pronunc. same) the basic monetary unit of Iceland, equal to 100 aurar. [ORIGIN: from Icelandic *króna*, 'crown'.]

krone /ˈkrəʊnə/ ▶ noun (pl. **kroner** pronunc. same) the basic monetary unit of Denmark and Norway, equal to 100 øre.
– ORIGIN Danish and Norwegian, literally 'crown'.

Kronos variant spelling of CRONUS.

Kronstadt /ˈkrɒnʃtat/ German name for BRAŞOV.

kroon /kruːn/ ▶ noun (pl. **kroons** or **krooni**) the basic monetary unit of Estonia, equal to 100 sents.
– ORIGIN Estonian, literally 'crown'; compare with KRONA, KRONE.

Kropotkin /krəˈpɒtkɪn/, Prince Peter (1842–1921), Russian anarchist. Imprisoned in 1874, he escaped abroad in 1876 and did not return to Russia until after the Revolution. His works include *Modern Science and Anarchism* (1903).

Kru /kruː/ ▶ noun (pl. same) **1** a member of a seafaring people of the coast of Liberia and Ivory Coast.
2 [mass noun] the Niger–Congo language of this people, consisting of a large number of highly differentiated dialects.
▶ adjective of or relating to the Kru or their language.
– ORIGIN from a West African language.

Kru Coast a section of the coast of Liberia to the north-west of Cape Palmas, inhabited by the Kru people.

Kruger /ˈkruːɡə/, Stephanus Johannes Paulus (1825–1904), South African soldier and statesman, President of Transvaal (1883–99). He led the Afrikaners to victory in the First Boer War in 1881. His refusal to allow equal rights to non-Boer immigrants was one of the causes of the Second Boer War.

Kruger National Park a national park in South Africa, in eastern Transvaal on the Mozambique border. It was originally a game reserve established in 1898 by President Kruger.

krugerrand /ˈkruːɡərand/ (also **Kruger**) ▶ noun a

South African gold coin with a portrait of President Kruger on the obverse.
– ORIGIN 1967: from the name of S. J. P. KRUGER + RAND[1].

krummholz /ˈkrʌmhɒlts/ ▶ noun [mass noun] stunted wind-blown trees growing near the tree line on mountains.
– ORIGIN early 20th cent.: from German, literally 'crooked wood'.

krummhorn /ˈkrʌmhɔːn, ˈkrʊm-/ (also **crumhorn**) ▶ noun a medieval wind instrument with an enclosed double reed and an upward-curving end, producing an even, nasal sound.
– ORIGIN from German, from *krumm* 'crooked' + *Horn* 'horn'.

Krupp /krʊp/, Alfred (1812–87), German arms manufacturer. His company played a pre-eminent part in German arms production from the 1840s through to the end of the Second World War.

krypton /ˈkrɪptɒn/ ▶ noun [mass noun] the chemical element of atomic number 36, a member of the noble gas series. It is obtained by distillation of liquid air, and is used in some kinds of electric light. (Symbol: **Kr**)
– ORIGIN late 19th cent.: from Greek *krupton*, neuter of *kruptos* 'hidden'.

krytron /ˈkrʌɪtrɒn/ ▶ noun Physics a high-speed solid-state switching device which is triggered by a pulse of coherent light and is used in the triggers of nuclear devices.
– ORIGIN late 20th cent.: first element of obscure derivation + -TRON.

Kryvy Rih /krɪˌviː ˈrɪx/ an industrial city in southern Ukraine, at the centre of an iron-ore mining region; pop. 717,000 (1990). Russian name KRIVOI ROG.

KS ▶ abbreviation for ■ Kansas (in official postal use). ■ Kaposi's sarcoma. ■ (in the UK) King's Scholar.

Kshatriya /ˈkʃatrɪə/ ▶ noun a member of the second of the four great Hindu castes, the military caste. The traditional function of the Kshatriyas is to protect society by fighting in wartime and governing in peacetime.
– ORIGIN late 18th cent.: from Sanskrit *kṣatriya*, from *kshatra* 'rule, authority'.

KStJ ▶ abbreviation for Knight of the Order of St John, an international organization of Christian people which undertakes charitable work.

KT ▶ abbreviation for ■ (in the UK) Knight of the Order of the Thistle. ■ Knight Templar.

Kt ▶ abbreviation for Knight.

kt ▶ abbreviation for knot(s): *a cruising speed of 240 kt.*

K/T boundary short for CRETACEOUS–TERTIARY BOUNDARY.
– ORIGIN late 20th cent.: *K/T*, from the symbols for *Cretaceous* and *Tertiary*.

Kuala Lumpur /ˌkwɑːlə ˈlʊmpʊə/ the capital of Malaysia, in the south-west of the Malay Peninsula; pop. 1,145,000 (1991).

Kuala Trengganu /trəŋˈɡanuː/ (also **Kuala Terengganu**) the capital of the state of Trengganu in Malaysia, on the east coast of the Malay Peninsula at the mouth of the Trengganu River; pop. 228,650 (1991).

Kuantan /kwɑːnˈtɑːn/ the capital of the state of Pahang in Malaysia, on the east coast of the Malay Peninsula; pop. 198,950 (1991).

Kuan Yin /ˌkwɑːn ˈjɪn/ (in Chinese Buddhism) the goddess of compassion.

Kublai Khan /ˌkuːblʌɪ ˈkɑːn/ (1216–94), Mongol emperor of China, grandson of Genghis Khan. With his brother Mangu (then Mongol Khan) he conquered southern China (1252–9). After Mangu's death in 1259 he completed the conquest of China, founded the Yuan dynasty, and established his capital on the site of the modern Beijing.

Kubrick /ˈkjuːbrɪk/, Stanley (1928–99), American film director, producer, and writer. Notable films: *2001: A Space Odyssey* (1968) and *A Clockwork Orange* (1971).

kuccha /ˈkʌtʃʌ/ (also **kachha**) ▶ plural noun short trousers ending above the knee, worn as one of the five distinguishing signs of the Sikh Khalsa.
– ORIGIN Punjabi.

kuchen /ˈkuːx(ə)n/ ▶ noun (pl. same) a cake, especially one eaten with coffee.
– ORIGIN from German *Kuchen*.

Kuching /ˈkuːtʃɪŋ/ a port in Malaysia, on the

Sarawak River near the NW coast of Borneo, capital of the state of Sarawak; pop. 148,000 (1991).

kudos /'kju:dɒs/ ▶ noun [mass noun] praise and honour received for an achievement.
– ORIGIN late 18th cent.: Greek.

> USAGE **Kudos** comes from Greek and means 'praise'. Despite appearances, it is not a plural form. This means that there is no singular form **kudo** and that use as a plural, as in the following sentence, is incorrect: *he received **many kudos** for his work* (correct use is *he received **a lot of kudos*** …).

kudu /'ku:du:, 'kʊdʊ/ ▶ noun (pl. same or **kudus**) an African antelope that has a greyish or brownish coat with white vertical stripes, and a short bushy tail. The male has long spirally curved horns.
● Genus *Tragelaphus*, family Bovidae: the **greater kudu** (*T. strepsiceros*) and the **lesser kudu** (*T. imberbis*).
– ORIGIN late 18th cent.: from Afrikaans *koedoe*, from Xhosa *i-qudu*.

kudzu /'kʊdzu:/ (also **kudzu vine**) ▶ noun a quick-growing East Asian climbing plant with reddish-purple flowers, used as a fodder crop and for erosion control.
● *Pueraria lobata*, family Leguminosae.
– ORIGIN late 19th cent.: from Japanese *kuzu*.

Kufic /'kju:fɪk/ ▶ noun [mass noun] an early angular form of the Arabic alphabet found chiefly in decorative inscriptions.
▶ adjective of or in this type of script.
– ORIGIN early 18th cent.: from the name *Kufa*, a city south of Baghdad, Iraq (because it was attributed to the city's scholars), + -IC.

kugel /'ku:g(ə)l/ ▶ noun **1** [mass noun] (in Jewish cookery) a kind of savoury pudding of potatoes or other vegetables.
2 S. African derogatory a spoilt and materialistic young Jewish woman with a distinctive nasal accent.
– ORIGIN Yiddish, literally 'ball'; sense 2 is an extended use.

Kuibyshev /'ku:ɪbɪˌʃef/ former name (1935–91) for SAMARA.

Ku Klux Klan /ˌku: klʌks 'klan/ (abbrev.: **KKK**) an extremist right-wing secret society in the US.

> The Ku Klux Klan was originally founded in the southern states after the Civil War to oppose social change and black emancipation by violence and terrorism. Although disbanded twice, it re-emerged in the 1950s and 1960s and continues at a local level. Members disguise themselves in white robes and hoods, and often use a burning cross as a symbol of their organization.

– DERIVATIVES **Ku Kluxer** noun, **Ku Klux Klansman** noun (pl. **-men**).
– ORIGIN perhaps from Greek *kuklos* 'circle' and CLAN.

kukri /'kʊkri/ ▶ noun (pl. **kukris**) a curved knife broadening towards the point, used by Gurkhas.
– ORIGIN early 19th cent.: from Nepalese *khukuri*.

kuku /'ku:ku:/ ▶ noun NZ another term for KERERU.

kula /'ku:lə/ ▶ noun [mass noun] (in some Pacific communities) an inter-island system of ceremonial gift exchange as a prelude to or at the same time as regular trading.
– ORIGIN Melanesian.

kulak /'ku:lak/ ▶ noun historical a peasant in Russia wealthy enough to own a farm and hire labour. Emerging after the emancipation of serfs in the 19th century the kulaks resisted Stalin's forced collectivization, but millions were arrested, exiled, or killed.
– ORIGIN Russian, literally 'fist, tight-fisted person', from Turkic *kol* 'hand'.

kulan /'ku:lən/ ▶ noun an animal of a race of the Asian wild ass, native to the central Asian steppes.
● *Equus hemionus kulan*, family Equidae. Compare with ONAGER, KIANG.
– ORIGIN late 18th cent.: from Turkic.

kulcha /'kʊltʃə/ ▶ noun a small, round Indian bread made from flour, milk, and butter, typically stuffed with meat or vegetables.
– ORIGIN from Persian *kulīca*.

kulfi /'kʊlfi/ ▶ noun [mass noun] a type of Indian ice cream, typically served in the shape of a cone.
– ORIGIN from Hindi *kulfī*.

kultarr /'kʊltɑ:/ ▶ noun a nocturnal carnivorous marsupial mouse with long hindlimbs and a plumed tail, found in arid regions of Australia.
● *Antechinomys laniger*, family Dasyuridae.

– ORIGIN probably from Yitha-yitha (an Aboriginal language).

Kultur /kʊl'tʊə, German kʊl'tu:ɐ/ ▶ noun [mass noun] German civilization and culture (sometimes used derogatorily to suggest elements of racism, authoritarianism, or militarism).
– ORIGIN German, from Latin *cultura* or French *culture* (see CULTURE).

Kulturkampf /kʊl'tʊəkampf, German kʊl'tu:ɐ-kampf/ a conflict from 1872 to 1887 between the German government (headed by Bismarck) and the papacy for the control of schools and Church appointments, in which Bismarck was forced to concede to the Catholic Church.
– ORIGIN German, from KULTUR + *Kampf* 'struggle'.

Kum variant spelling of QOM.

Kumamoto /ˌku:mə'məʊtəʊ/ a city in southern Japan, on the west coast of Kyushu island; pop. 579,300 (1990).

kumara /'ku:mərə/ ▶ noun (pl. same) NZ a sweet potato.
– ORIGIN late 18th cent.: from Maori.

Kumasi /ku'masi/ a city in southern Ghana; pop. 376,250 (1984). It is the capital of the Ashanti region.

Kumayri /ku'majri/ Russian name for GYUMRI.

Kumbh Mela /kʊm 'meɪlə/ ▶ noun a Hindu festival and assembly, held once every twelve years at four locations in India, at which pilgrims bathe in the waters of the Ganges and Jumna Rivers.
– ORIGIN from Sanskrit, literally 'pitcher festival', from *kumbh* 'pitcher' + *melā* 'assembly'.

kumis (also **kumiss**) ▶ noun variant spelling of KOUMISS.

kumite /'ku:mɪteɪ/ ▶ noun [mass noun] (in martial arts) freestyle fighting.
– ORIGIN Japanese, literally 'sparring'.

kumkum /'kʊmkʊm/ ▶ noun [mass noun] a red powder used ceremonially, especially by Hindu women to make a small distinctive mark on the forehead.
– ORIGIN mid 20th cent.: from Sanskrit *kuṅkuma* 'saffron'.

kümmel /'kʊm(ə)l/ ▶ noun [mass noun] a sweet liqueur flavoured with caraway and cumin seeds.
– ORIGIN from German, from Old High German *kumil*, variant of *kumīn* (see CUMIN).

kumquat /'kʌmkwɒt/ (also **cumquat**) ▶ noun **1** an orange-like fruit related to the citruses, with an edible sweet rind and acid pulp. It is eaten raw or used in preserves.
2 The East Asian shrub or small tree which yields this fruit, and which hybridizes with citrus trees.
● Genus *Fortunella*, family Rutaceae.
– ORIGIN late 17th cent.: from Chinese (Cantonese dialect) *kam kwat* 'little orange'.

Kuna /'ku:nə/ (also **Cuna**) ▶ noun (pl. same or **Kunas**)
1 a member of an American Indian people of the isthmus of Panama.
2 [mass noun] the Chibchan language of this people, with about 35,000 speakers.
▶ adjective of or relating to the Kunas or their language.
– ORIGIN the name in Kuna.

kuna /'ku:nə/ ▶ noun (pl. **kune**) the basic monetary unit of Croatia, equal to 100 lipa.

kundalini /ˌkʊndə'li:ni/ ▶ noun [mass noun] (in yoga) latent female energy believed to lie coiled at the base of the spine.
■ (also **kundalini yoga**) a system of meditation directed towards the release of such energy.
– ORIGIN Sanskrit, literally 'snake'.

Kundera /'kʊndərə/, Milan (b.1929), Czech novelist. He emigrated to France in 1975 after his books were proscribed in Czechoslovakia following the Soviet military invasion of 1968. Notable works: *The Book of Laughter and Forgetting* (1979) and *The Unbearable Lightness of Being* (1984).

Kung /kʊŋ/ ▶ noun **1** (pl. same) a member of a San (Bushman) people of the Kalahari Desert in southern Africa.
2 [mass noun] the Khoisan language of this people, with about 10,000 speakers.
▶ adjective of or relating to the Kung or their language.
– ORIGIN Khoikhoi *!Kung*, literally 'people'.

kung fu /kʊŋ 'fu:, kʌŋ/ ▶ noun [mass noun] a primarily unarmed Chinese martial art resembling karate.

– ORIGIN from Chinese *gongfu*, from *gong* 'merit' + *fu* 'master'.

K'ung Fu-tzu /ˌkʊŋ fu:'tsu:/ see CONFUCIUS.

Kunlun Shan /ˌkʊnlʊn 'ʃɑ:n/ a range of mountains in western China, on the northern edge of the Tibetan plateau, extending eastwards for over 1,600 km (1,000 miles) from the Pamir Mountains. Its highest peak is Muztag, which rises to 7,723 m (25,338 ft).

Kunming /kʊn'mɪŋ/ a city in SW China, capital of Yunnan province; pop. 1,611,900 (1990).

kunzite /'kʌntsʌɪt, 'kʌnzʌɪt/ ▶ noun [mass noun] a lilac-coloured gem variety of spodumene which fluoresces or changes colour when irradiated.
– ORIGIN early 20th cent.: from the name of George F. *Kunz* (1856–1932), American gemmologist, + -ITE[1].

Kuomintang /ˌkwəʊmɪn'taŋ/ (also **Guomindang**) a nationalist party founded in China under Sun Yat-sen in 1912, and led by Chiang Kai-shek from 1925. It held power from 1928 until the Communist Party took power in October 1949 and subsequently formed the central administration of Taiwan.
– ORIGIN from Chinese, 'national people's party'.

Kuopio /kʊ'əʊpɪəʊ/ a city in southern Finland, capital of a province of the same name; pop. 80,610 (1990).

Kupffer cell /'kʊpfə/ ▶ noun Anatomy a phagocytic cell which forms the lining of the sinusoids of the liver and is involved in the breakdown of red blood cells.
– ORIGIN early 20th cent.: named after Karl Wilhelm von *Kupffer* (1829–1902), Bavarian anatomist.

kurbash /'kʊəbaʃ/ (also **kourbash**) ▶ noun a whip, typically of hippopotamus hide, used as an instrument of punishment in Turkey and Egypt.
– ORIGIN early 19th cent.: from Arabic *kurbāj*, from Turkish *kırbaç* 'whip'.

kurchatovium /ˌkə:tʃə'təʊvɪəm/ ▶ noun [mass noun] historical a name proposed in the former USSR for the artificial radioactive element of atomic number 104, now called **rutherfordium**.
– ORIGIN 1960s: named after Igor V. *Kurchatov* (1903–60), Russian nuclear physicist.

Kurd /kə:d/ ▶ noun a member of a mainly pastoral Islamic people living in Kurdistan.
– ORIGIN the name in Kurdish.

kurdaitcha /kə'dʌɪtʃə/ (also **kadaitcha**) ▶ noun [mass noun] Austral. the use among Aboriginals of a bone in spells intended to cause sickness or death.
■ [count noun] a man empowered to point the bone at a victim.
– ORIGIN probably from Aranda.

Kurdish /'kə:dɪʃ/ ▶ adjective of or relating to the Kurds or their language.
▶ noun [mass noun] the language of the Kurds, which belongs to the Iranian group and is spoken by about 10 million people.

Kurdistan /ˌkə:dɪ'stɑ:n, -'stan/ an extensive region in the Middle East south of the Caucasus, the traditional home of the Kurdish people.

> The area includes large parts of eastern Turkey, northern Iraq, western Iran, eastern Syria, Armenia, and Azerbaijan. The creation of a separate state of Kurdistan, proposed by the Allies after the First World War, is opposed by Iraq, Iran, Syria, and Turkey. Following persecution of the Kurds by Iraq in the aftermath of the Gulf War of 1991, certain areas designated safe havens were established for the Kurds in northern Iraq, although these havens are not officially recognized as a state.

Kure /kʊ'reɪ/ a city in southern Japan, on the south coast of the island of Honshu, near Hiroshima; pop. 216,720 (1990).

Kurgan /kʊə'gɑ:n/ a city in central Russia, commercial centre for an agricultural region; pop. 360,000 (1990).

kurgan /kʊə'gɑ:n/ ▶ noun Archaeology a prehistoric burial mound or barrow of a type found in southern Russia and the Ukraine.
■ (**Kurgan**) a member of the ancient people who built such burial mounds.
▶ adjective of or relating to the ancient Kurgans.
– ORIGIN Russian, of Turkic origin; compare with Turkish *kurgan* 'castle'.

kuri /'kʊri/ ▶ noun (pl. **kuris**) NZ a dog, especially a mongrel.
■ informal an unpleasant or disliked person.
– ORIGIN Maori, 'dog'.

Kurile Islands /kʊə'ri:l/ (also **Kuril Islands** or the **Kurils**) a chain of 56 islands between the Sea of

Okhotsk and the North Pacific, stretching from the southern tip of the Kamchatka peninsula to the north-eastern corner of the Japanese island of Hokkaido. They are the subject of dispute between Russia and Japan.

Kurosawa /ˌkʊrəˈsɑːwə/, Akira (1910–98), Japanese film director. Notable films: *Rashomon* (1950) and *Ran* (1985), a Japanese version of Shakespeare's *King Lear*.

Kuroshio /ˌkʊrəˈʃiːəʊ/ a warm current flowing in the Pacific Ocean north-eastwards past Japan and towards Alaska. Also called **JAPANESE CURRENT**, **JAPAN CURRENT**.
– ORIGIN late 19th cent.: Japanese, from *kuro* 'black' + *shio* 'tide'.

kurrajong /ˈkʌrədʒɒŋ/ (also **currajong**) ▶ noun an Australian plant which produces useful tough fibre.
● Several species, in particular a small tree with shiny pointed leaves and boat-shaped leathery seed cases (*Brachychiton populneus*, family Sterculiaceae).
– ORIGIN early 19th cent.: from Dharuk *garrajung* 'fibre fishing line'.

kursaal /ˈkʊəsɑːl, -z-/ ▶ noun a building provided for the entertainment of visitors at a German spa.
– ORIGIN mid 19th cent.: from German, from *Kur* 'cure' + *Saal* 'room'.

Kursk /kʊəsk/ an industrial city in SW Russia; pop. 430,000 (1990). It was the scene of an important Soviet victory in the Second World War.

kurta /ˈkəːtə/ (also **kurtha**) ▶ noun a loose collarless shirt worn by people from the Indian subcontinent, usually with a salwar, churidars, or pyjama.
– ORIGIN from Urdu and Persian *kurtah*.

kurtosis /kəːˈtəʊsɪs/ ▶ noun [mass noun] Statistics the sharpness of the peak of a frequency-distribution curve.
– ORIGIN early 20th cent.: from Greek *kurtōsis* 'a bulging', from *kurtos* 'bulging, convex'.

kuru /ˈkʊruː/ ▶ noun [mass noun] Medicine a fatal disease of the brain occurring in some peoples in New Guinea and thought to be caused by a virus-like agent such as a prion.
– ORIGIN 1950s: a local word.

kurus /kəˈruːʃ/ ▶ noun (pl. same) a monetary unit of Turkey, equal to one hundredth of a Turkish lira.
– ORIGIN from Turkish *kuruş*.

Kuşadasi /ˈkʊʃəˌdəsɪ/ a resort town on the Aegean coast of western Turkey; pop. 31,910 (1990).

Kushan /ˈkʊʃɑːn/ ▶ noun (pl. same or **Kushans**) a member of an Iranian dynasty which invaded the Indian subcontinent and established a powerful empire in the north-west between the 1st and 3rd centuries AD.
▶ adjective of or relating to this people or their dynasty.
– ORIGIN from Prakrit *kuṣāṇa* (adjective), from Iranian.

kusimanse ▶ noun variant spelling of **CUSIMANSE**.

kusti /ˈkʊsti:/ ▶ noun (pl. **kustis**) a cord worn round the waist by Parsees, consisting of seventy-two threads to represent the chapters of one of the portions of the Zend-Avesta.
– ORIGIN mid 19th cent.: from Persian and Gujarati.

Kutaisi /ˌkʊtaˈiːsi/ an industrial city in central Georgia; pop. 236,100 (1990). One of the oldest cities in Transcaucasia, it has been the capital of various kingdoms, including Colchis and Abkhazia.

Kutani /kʊˈtɑːni/ ▶ noun [mass noun] (also **Kutani ware**) a kind of richly decorated Japanese porcelain, especially that of the 17th century, or of a 19th-century red and gold style.
– ORIGIN late 19th cent.: from *Kutani-mura*, the name of a Japanese village in the former province of Kaga.

Kutch, Gulf of /kʌtʃ, kʊtʃ/ an inlet of the Arabian Sea on the west coast of India.

Kutch, Rann of /kʌtʃ, kʊtʃ, ran/ a vast salt marsh in the north-west of the Indian subcontinent, on the shores of the Arabian Sea, extending over the boundary between SE Pakistan and the state of Gujarat in NW India.

Kuwait /kʊˈweɪt/ a country on the NW coast of the Persian Gulf; pop. 1,200,000 (est. 1991); official language, Arabic; capital, Kuwait City.

Kuwait has been an autonomous Arab sheikhdom, under the rule of an amir, from the 18th century, although the British established a protectorate from 1897 until 1961. One of the world's leading oil-producing countries, Kuwait was invaded by Iraq in August 1990, the occupying forces being expelled in the Gulf War of 1991.

– DERIVATIVES **Kuwaiti** adjective & noun.

Kuwait City a port on the Persian Gulf, the capital city of Kuwait; pop. 44,335 (1985).

Kuzbass /kʊzˈbas/ another name for **KUZNETS BASIN**.

Kuznets Basin /kʊzˈnjɛts/ (also **Kuznetsk** /-ˈnjɛtsk/) an industrial region of southern Russia, situated in the valley of the Tom River, between Tomsk and Novokuznetsk. The region is rich in iron and coal deposits. Also called **KUZBASS**.

kV ▶ abbreviation for kilovolt(s).

kvass /kvɑːs/ ▶ noun [mass noun] (especially in Russia) a fermented drink, low in alcohol, made from rye flour or bread with malt.
– ORIGIN from Russian *kvas*.

kvell /kvɛl/ ▶ verb [no obj.] N. Amer. informal feel happy and proud.
– ORIGIN 1960s: from Yiddish *kveln*, from Middle High German, literally 'well up'.

kvetch /kvɛtʃ/ N. Amer. informal ▶ noun a person who complains a great deal.
▶ a complaint.
▶ verb [no obj.] complain.
– ORIGIN 1960s: from Yiddish *kvetsh* (noun), *kvetshn* (verb), from Middle High German *quetschen*, literally 'crush'.

kW ▶ abbreviation for kilowatt(s).

Kwa /kwɑː/ ▶ noun [mass noun] a major branch of the Niger–Congo family of languages, spoken from the Ivory Coast to Nigeria and including Igbo and Yoruba.
▶ adjective of or relating to this group of languages.
– ORIGIN the name in Kwa.

kwacha /ˈkwɑːtʃə/ ▶ noun the basic monetary unit of Zambia and Malawi, equal to 100 ngwee in Zambia and 100 tambala in Malawi.
– ORIGIN previously used as a Zambian nationalist slogan calling for a new 'dawn' of freedom, later applied to the currency of the newly independent state.

Kwakiutl /ˈkwɑːˌkjʊt(ə)l/ ▶ noun (pl. same or **Kwakiutls**) 1 a member of an American Indian people of the NW Pacific coast, living mainly on Vancouver Island.
2 [mass noun] the Wakashan language of this people, now virtually extinct.
▶ adjective of or relating to the Kwakiutl or their language.
– ORIGIN the name in Kwakiutl.

KwaNdebele /ˌkwɑː(ə)ndəˈbiːli/ a former homeland established in South Africa for the Ndebele people, now part of the province of Mpumalanga.

Kwangchow /kwaŋˈtʃaʊ/ variant of **GUANGZHOU**.

Kwangju /kwaŋˈdʒuː/ a city in SW South Korea; pop. 1,144,700 (1990).

Kwangsi Chuang /ˌkwaŋsiː ˈtʃwaŋ/ variant of **GUANGXI ZHUANG**.

Kwangtung /kwaŋˈtʊŋ/ variant of **GUANGDONG**.

kwanza /ˈkwanzə/ ▶ noun (pl. same or **kwanzas**) the basic monetary unit of Angola, equal to 100 lwei.
– ORIGIN perhaps from a Kiswahili word meaning 'first'.

Kwanzaa /ˈkwanzɑː/ ▶ noun N. Amer. a secular festival observed by many African Americans from 26 December to 1 January as a celebration of their cultural heritage and traditional values.
– ORIGIN from Kiswahili *matunda ya kwanza*, literally 'first fruits (of the harvest)', from *kwanza* 'first'.

kwashiorkor /ˌkwɒʃɪˈɔːkɔː, ˌkwa-/ ▶ noun [mass noun] a form of malnutrition caused by protein deficiency in the diet, typically affecting young children in the tropics.
– ORIGIN 1930s: a local word in Ghana.

KwaZulu /kwaˈzuːluː/ a former homeland established in South Africa for the Zulu people, now part of the province of KwaZulu/Natal. The general area was formerly known as Zululand.

KwaZulu/Natal a province of eastern South Africa, on the Indian Ocean; capital, Pietermaritzburg. Formerly called Natal, it became

one of the new provinces of South Africa following the democratic elections of 1994. See also **NATAL**.

Kweichow /kweɪˈtʃaʊ/ variant of **GUIZHOU**.

Kweilin /kweɪˈlɪn/ variant of **GUILIN**.

Kweiyang /kweɪˈjaŋ/ variant of **GUIYANG**.

kwela /ˈkweɪlə/ ▶ noun [mass noun] a style of rhythmical, repetitive popular music of central and southern Africa, resembling jazz, in which the lead part is usually played on the penny whistle.
■ [count noun] a type of dance done to this music.
– ORIGIN mid 20th cent.: Afrikaans, perhaps from Zulu *khwela* 'mount, climb'.

Kwesui /kweɪˈsweɪ/ former name (until 1954) for **HOHHOT**.

kWh ▶ abbreviation for kilowatt-hour(s).

KWIC ▶ noun [mass noun] [as modifier] Computing denoting a database search in which the keyword is shown highlighted in the middle of the display, with the text forming its context on either side.
– ORIGIN 1950s: abbreviation.

KWT ▶ abbreviation for Kuwait (international vehicle registration).

KY ▶ abbreviation for Kentucky (in official postal use).

Ky ▶ abbreviation for Kentucky.

kyanite /ˈkaɪənaɪt/ ▶ noun [mass noun] a blue or green crystalline mineral consisting of aluminium silicate, used in heat-resistant ceramics.
– DERIVATIVES **kyanitic** adjective.
– ORIGIN late 18th cent.: from Greek *kuanos*, *kuaneos* 'dark blue' + -ITE[1].

kyanize /ˈkaɪənaɪz/ (also -ise) ▶ verb [with obj.] treat (wood) with a solution of mercuric chloride to prevent decay.
– ORIGIN mid 19th cent.: named after John H. *Kyan* (1774–1850), the Irish inventor who patented the process in 1832.

kyat /kiːˈɑːt/ ▶ noun (pl. same or **kyats**) the basic monetary unit of Burma (Myanmar), equal to 100 pyas.
– ORIGIN Burmese.

kybosh ▶ noun variant spelling of **KIBOSH**.

Kyd, Thomas (1558–94), English dramatist. His anonymously published *The Spanish Tragedy* (1592), an early example of revenge tragedy, was very popular on the Elizabethan stage.

kyle /kʌɪl/ ▶ noun Scottish a narrow sea channel.
– ORIGIN mid 16th cent.: from Scottish Gaelic *caol* 'strait', (as an adjective) 'narrow'.

kylie /ˈkaɪli/ ▶ noun Austral. a boomerang.
– ORIGIN from Nyungar (and other Aboriginal languages) *garli*.

kylin /ˈkiːlɪn/ ▶ noun a mythical composite animal, often figured on Chinese and Japanese ceramics.
– ORIGIN mid 19th cent.: from Chinese *qilin*, from *qi* 'male' + *lin* 'female'.

kylix /ˈkaɪlɪks, ˈkɪl-/ ▶ noun (pl. **kylikes** or **kylixes**) an ancient Greek cup with a shallow bowl and a tall stem.
– ORIGIN from Greek *kulix*.

kyloe /ˈkaɪləʊ/ ▶ noun Scottish name for **HIGHLAND CATTLE**.
– ORIGIN early 19th cent.: from Scottish Gaelic *gaidhealach* 'Gaelic, Highland'.

kymograph /ˈkaɪmə(ʊ)grɑːf/ ▶ noun an instrument for recording variations in pressure, e.g. in sound waves or in blood within blood vessels, by the trace of a stylus on a rotating cylinder.
– DERIVATIVES **kymographic** adjective.
– ORIGIN mid 19th cent.: from Greek *kuma* 'wave' + -GRAPH.

Kyoto /kɪˈəʊtəʊ/ an industrial city in central Japan, on the island of Honshu; pop. 1,461,140 (1990). Founded in the 8th century, it was the imperial capital from 794 until 1868.

kype /kʌɪp/ ▶ noun a hook formed on the lower jaw of adult male salmon and trout during the breeding season.
– ORIGIN mid 20th cent.: variant of Scots *kip*, perhaps influenced by PIKE[1].

kyphosis /kʌɪˈfəʊsɪs/ ▶ noun [mass noun] Medicine excessive outward curvature of the spine, causing hunching of the back. Compare with **LORDOSIS**.
– DERIVATIVES **kyphotic** adjective.

– ORIGIN mid 19th cent.: from Greek *kuphōsis*, from *kuphos* 'bent, hunchbacked'.

Kyrgyz /kɪəˈgiːz, ˈkəːgɪz/ (also **Kirghiz**) ▸ noun (pl. same) **1** a member of an indigenous people of central Asia, living chiefly in Kyrgyzstan. **2** [mass noun] the Turkic language of this people, with approximately 2 million speakers. ▸ adjective of or relating to this people or their language. – ORIGIN the name in Kyrgyz.

Kyrgyzstan /ˌkɪəgɪˈstɑːn, -ˈstan/ a mountainous country in central Asia, on the north-western border of China; population 4,448,000 (est. 1991); official language, Kyrgyz; capital, Bishkek. Also called **KIRGHIZIA**; **KYRGYZ REPUBLIC**.

The region was annexed by Russia in 1864, and became a constituent republic of the Soviet Union. On the break-up of the USSR in 1991 Kyrgyzstan became an independent republic within the Commonwealth of Independent States.

Kyrie /ˈkɪrɪeɪ/ (also **Kyrie eleison** /ɪˈleɪɪzɒn, -sɒn, ɛˈleɪ-/) ▸ noun a short repeated invocation (in Greek or in translation) used in many Christian liturgies, especially at the beginning of the Eucharist or as a response in a litany. – ORIGIN from Greek *Kurie eleēson* 'Lord, have mercy'.

kyte /kʌɪt/ ▸ noun Scottish a person's belly or stomach. – ORIGIN mid 16th cent.: of unknown origin.

kyu /kjuː/ (also **kyu grade**) ▸ noun a numbered grade of the less advanced level of proficiency in judo, karate, and other martial arts. Compare with **DAN**[1].

■ a person who has achieved such a grade. – ORIGIN from Japanese *kyū* 'class'.

Kyushu /kɪˈuːʃuː/ the most southerly of the four main islands of Japan, constituting an administrative region; pop. 13,296,000 (1990); capital, Fukuoka.

Kyzyl /kəˈzɪl/ a city in south central Russia, on the Yenisei River, capital of the republic of Tuva; pop. 80,000 (1989).

Kyzyl Kum /kəˌzɪl ˈkuːm/ an arid desert region in central Asia, extending eastwards from the Aral Sea to the Pamir Mountains and covering part of Uzbekistan and southern Kazakhstan.

k

Ll

L¹ (also **l**) ▶ **noun** (pl. **Ls** or **L's**) **1** the twelfth letter of the alphabet.
■ denoting the next after K in a set of items, categories, etc.
2 (**L**) a shape like that of a capital L: [in combination] *a four-storey L-shaped building.*
■ (usu. **ell**) chiefly N. Amer. an extension of a building or room that is at right angles to the main part. ■ (usu. **ell**) chiefly N. Amer. a bend or joint for connecting two pipes at right angles.
3 the Roman numeral for 50. [ORIGIN: originally a symbol identified with the letter *L*, because of coincidence of form. In ancient Roman notation, *L* with a stroke above denoted 50.000.]

L² ▶ **abbreviation for** ■ (in tables of sports results) games lost. ■ Chemistry laevorotatory: *L-tryptophan.* ■ (**L.**) Lake, Loch, or Lough (chiefly on maps): *L. Ontario.* ■ large (as a clothes size). ■ Brit. (on a motor vehicle) learner driver. See also **L-DRIVER, L-PLATE.** ■ (**L.**) Linnaeus (as the source of names of animal and plant species): *Swallowtail Butterfly* Papilio machaon (*L., 1758*). ■ lire. ■ Luxembourg (international vehicle registration).
▶ **symbol for** ■ Chemistry Avogadro's constant. ■ Physics inductance.

l ▶ **abbreviation for** ■ (giving position or direction) left: *l to r: Gordon, Anthony, Jerry, and Mark.* ■ (chiefly in horse racing) length(s): *distances 5 l, 3 l.* ■ (**l.**) (in textual references) line: *l. 648.* ■ Chemistry liquid. ■ litre(s). ■ (**l.**) archaic pound(s): *a salary of 4l. a week.*
▶ **symbol for** (in mathematical formulae) length.

£ ▶ **abbreviation** (preceding a numeral) pound or pounds (of money).
– ORIGIN the initial letter of Latin *libra* 'pound, balance', written in copperplate with one or two crossbars: crossbars were formerly used to indicate an abbreviation.

LA ▶ **abbreviation for** ■ Library Association. ■ Los Angeles. ■ Louisiana (in official postal use).

La ▶ **abbreviation for** ■ (**La.**) Louisiana.
▶ **symbol for** ■ the chemical element lanthanum.

la ▶ **noun** Music variant spelling of **LAH.**

laager /ˈlɑːɡə/ S. African ▶ **noun** historical a camp or encampment formed by a circle of wagons.
■ figurative an entrenched position or viewpoint that is defended against opponents: *an educational laager, isolated from the outside world.*
▶ **verb** [with obj.] historical form (vehicles) into a laager.
■ [no obj.] make camp.
– ORIGIN South African Dutch, from Dutch *leger, lager* 'camp'. Compare with **LAGER, LAIR¹,** and **LEAGUER².**

laaitie ▶ **noun** variant spelling of **LIGHTY.**

Laayoune variant spelling of **LAʼYOUN.**

Lab ▶ **abbreviation for** ■ Brit. (following a politician's name) Labour. ■ a Labrador dog.

lab ▶ **noun** informal a laboratory: *a science lab.*
– ORIGIN late 19th cent.: abbreviation.

Laban /ˈlɑːb(ə)n/, Rudolf von (1879–1958), Hungarian choreographer and dancer. A pioneer of the central European school of modern dance, in 1920 he published the first of several volumes outlining his system of dance notation.

la Barca, Pedro Calderón de see **CALDERÓN DE LA BARCA.**

labarum /ˈlabərəm/ ▶ **noun** rare a banner or flag bearing symbolic motifs.
■ historical Constantine the Great's imperial standard, which bore Christian symbolic imagery fused with the military symbols of the Roman Empire.
– ORIGIN early 17th cent.: from late Latin, of unknown origin.

labdanum /ˈlabdənəm/ ▶ **noun** variant spelling of **LADANUM.**

labefaction /ˌlabɪˈfakʃ(ə)n/ ▶ **noun** [mass noun] archaic deterioration or downfall.
– ORIGIN early 17th cent.: from Latin *labefactio(n-),* from *labefacere* 'weaken', from *labi* 'to fall' + *facere* 'make'.

label ▶ **noun 1** a small piece of paper, fabric, plastic, or similar material attached to an object and giving information about it.
■ a piece of fabric sewn inside a garment and bearing the brand name, size, or instructions for care. ■ the piece of paper in the centre of a gramophone record giving the artist and title. ■ a company that produces recorded music: *independent labels.* ■ the name or trademark of a fashion company: *she plans to launch her own designer clothes label.* ■ a classifying phrase or name applied to a person or thing, especially one that is inaccurate or restrictive: *my reluctance to stick a label on myself politically.* ■ (in a dictionary entry) a word or words used to specify the subject area, register, or geographical origin of the word being defined. ■ Computing a string of characters used to refer to a particular instruction in a program. ■ Biology & Chemistry a radioactive isotope, fluorescent dye, or enzyme used to make something identifiable for study.
2 Heraldry a narrow horizontal strip, typically with three downward projections, that is superimposed on a coat of arms by an eldest son during the life of his father.
3 Architecture another term for **DRIPSTONE.**
▶ **verb** (**labelled, labelling;** US **labeled, labeling**) [with obj.] attach a label to (something): *she labelled the parcels neatly, writing the addresses in capital letters.*
■ assign to a category, especially inaccurately or restrictively: *people who were labelled as 'mentally handicapped'* | [with obj. and complement] *the critics labelled him a loser.* ■ Biology & Chemistry make (a substance, molecule, or cell) identifiable or traceable by replacing an atom with one of a distinctive radioactive isotope, or by attaching a fluorescent dye, enzyme, or other molecule.
– DERIVATIVES **labeller** noun.
– ORIGIN Middle English (denoting a narrow strip or band): from Old French, 'ribbon', probably of Germanic origin and related to **LAP¹.**

La Belle Province /la ˌbɛl prɒˈvɑ̃s, French la bɛl prɔvɛ̃s/ informal name for **QUEBEC.**
– ORIGIN French, literally 'the Beautiful Province'.

labellum /ləˈbɛləm/ ▶ **noun** (pl. **labella**) **1** Entomology each of a pair of lobes at the tip of the proboscis in some insects.
2 Botany a central petal at the base of an orchid flower, typically larger than the other petals and of a different shape.
– ORIGIN early 19th cent.: from Latin, diminutive of *labrum* 'lip'.

labia /ˈleɪbɪə/ ▶ **plural noun 1** Anatomy the inner and outer folds of the vulva, at either side of the vagina.

2 plural form of **LABIUM.**

labial /ˈleɪbɪəl/ ▶ **adjective 1** chiefly Anatomy of or relating to the lips.
■ Dentistry (of the surface of a tooth) adjacent to the lips. ■ Zoology of, resembling, or serving as a lip, lip-like part, or labium.
2 Phonetics (of a consonant) requiring partial or complete closure of the lips (e.g. *p, b, f, v, m, w*), or (of a vowel) requiring rounded lips (e.g. *oo* in m**oo**n).
▶ **noun** Phonetics a labial sound.
– DERIVATIVES **labialize** (also **-ise**) verb (only in sense 2), **labially** adverb.
– ORIGIN late 16th cent.: from medieval Latin *labialis,* from Latin *labium* 'lip'.

labia majora /məˈdʒɔːrə/ ▶ **plural noun** Anatomy the larger outer folds of the vulva.

labia minora /mɪˈnɔːrə/ ▶ **plural noun** Anatomy the smaller inner folds of the vulva.

labiate /ˈleɪbɪət/ ▶ **noun** Botany a plant of the mint family (Labiatae), with a distinctive two-lobed flower.
▶ **adjective 1** Botany of, relating to, or denoting plants of the mint family.
2 Botany & Zoology resembling or possessing a lip or labium.
– ORIGIN early 18th cent. (as an adjective in the sense 'two-lipped', describing a corolla or calyx): from modern Latin *labiatus,* from *labium* 'lip'.

labile /ˈleɪbɪl, -ʌɪl/ ▶ **adjective** technical liable to change; easily altered.
■ of or characterized by emotions which are easily aroused, freely expressed, and tend to alter quickly and spontaneously; emotionally unstable. ■ Chemistry easily broken down or displaced.
– DERIVATIVES **lability** /ləˈbɪlɪti/ noun.
– ORIGIN late Middle English (in the sense 'liable to err or sin'): from late Latin *labilis,* from *labi* 'to fall'.

labio- /ˈleɪbɪəʊ/ ▶ **combining form** of or relating to the lips: *labiodental.*
– ORIGIN from Latin *labium* 'lip'.

labiodental ▶ **adjective** Phonetics (of a sound) made with the lips and teeth, for example *f* and *v*.

labiovelar ▶ **adjective** Phonetics (of a sound) made with the lips and soft palate, for example *w*.

labium /ˈleɪbɪəm/ ▶ **noun** (pl. **labia** /-bɪə/) **1** Entomology a fused mouthpart which forms the floor of the mouth of an insect.
2 Botany the lower lip of the flower of a plant of the mint family.
– ORIGIN late 16th cent. (in the general sense 'lip, lip-like structure'): from Latin, 'lip'; related to **LABRUM.**

lablab /ˈlablab/ ▶ **noun** [mass noun] an Asian plant of the pea family, which is widely grown in the tropics for its edible seeds and pods and as a fodder crop.
● *Lablab purpureus,* family Leguminosae.
– ORIGIN early 19th cent.: from Arabic *lablāb.*

labor etc. ▶ **noun** US and Australian spelling of **LABOUR** etc.

laboratory /ləˈbɒrə.t(ə)ri, ˈlab(ə)rə.t(ə)ri/ ▶ **noun** (pl. **-ies**) a room or building fitted out for scientific experiments, research, or teaching, or for the

manufacture of drugs or chemicals: [as modifier] *laboratory tests.*
■[as modifier] (of an animal) bred for or used in experiments in laboratories: *studies on laboratory rats.*
– ORIGIN early 17th cent.: from medieval Latin *laboratorium*, from Latin *laborare* 'to labour'.

labored ▶ **adjective** US spelling of **LABOURED**.

laborer ▶ **noun** US spelling of **LABOURER**.

laborious /ləˈbɔːrɪəs/ ▶ **adjective** (especially of a task, process, or journey) requiring considerable effort and time: *years of laborious training | the work is very slow and laborious.*
■(especially of speech or writing style) showing obvious signs of effort and lacking in fluency: *his slow laborious style.*
– DERIVATIVES **laboriously** adverb, **laboriousness** noun.
– ORIGIN late Middle English (also in the sense 'industrious, assiduous'): from Old French *laborieux*, from Latin *laboriosus*, from *labor* 'labour'.

laborism ▶ **noun** US spelling of **LABOURISM**.

Laborite ▶ **noun** US spelling of **LABOURITE**.

Labor Party, Australian see **AUSTRALIAN LABOR PARTY**.

labour (US, Austral. **labor**) ▶ **noun** [mass noun] **1** work, especially hard physical work: *the price of repairs includes labour, parts, and VAT | manual labour.*
■workers, especially manual workers, considered collectively: *non-union casual labour.* ■such workers considered as a social class or political force: [as modifier] *the labour movement.* ■[as modifier] (**Labour**) a department of government concerned with a nation's workforce: *the post of Labour Secretary.*
2 (**Labour**) [treated as sing. or pl.] the Labour Party.
3 the process of childbirth, especially the period from the start of uterine contractions to delivery: *a woman **in labour**.*
▶**adjective** (**Labour**) of, relating to, or supporting the Labour Party: *the Labour leader.*
▶**verb** [no obj.] work hard; make great effort: *they laboured from dawn to dusk in two shifts | it now looks as if the reformers had laboured in vain.*
■work at an unskilled manual occupation: *he was eking out an existence by labouring |* [as adj. **labouring**] *the labouring classes.* ■[with obj.] archaic till (the ground): *the land belonged to him who laboured it.* ■have difficulty in doing something despite working hard: *Coleraine laboured against confident opponents.* ■(of an engine) work noisily and with difficulty: *the wheels churned, the engine labouring.* ■[with adverbial of direction] move or proceed with trouble or difficulty: *they **laboured up** a steep, tortuous track.* ■(of a ship) roll or pitch heavily.
– PHRASES **a labour of Hercules** see **HERCULES**. **a labour of love** a task done for pleasure, not reward. **labour the point** explain or discuss something at excessive or unnecessary length.
– ORIGIN Middle English: from Old French *labour* (noun), *labourer* (verb), both from Latin *labor* 'toil, trouble'.
▶**labour under 1** carry (a very heavy load or object) with difficulty. **2** be deceived or misled by (a mistaken belief): *you've been labouring under a bit of a misapprehension.*

labour brigade ▶ **noun** a unit or group of workers, especially one organized by the state or a local authority.

labour camp ▶ **noun** a prison camp in which a regime of hard labour is enforced.

Labour Day ▶ **noun** a public holiday or day of festivities held in honour of working people, in many countries on 1 May, in the US and Canada on the first Monday in September.

laboured (US **labored**) ▶ **adjective** done with great effort and difficulty: *his breathing was becoming less laboured.*
■(especially of humour or a performance) not spontaneous or fluent: *one of Adolf's laboured jokes.*

labourer (US **laborer**) ▶ **noun** a person doing unskilled manual work for wages: *a farm labourer.*

labour exchange ▶ **noun** former term for **JOBCENTRE**.

labour force ▶ **noun** all the members of a particular organization or population who are able to work, viewed collectively.

labour-intensive ▶ **adjective** (of a form of work) needing a large workforce or a large amount of work in relation to output.

labourism (US **laborism**) ▶ **noun** the principles of a Labour Party or the labour movement.
– DERIVATIVES **labourist** noun & adjective.

Labourite (US **Laborite**) ▶ **noun** a member or supporter of a Labour Party.

labour-only ▶ **adjective** [attrib.] (of a subcontractor) supplying only the labour for a particular piece of work.

Labour Party ▶ **noun** a left-of-centre political party formed to represent the interests of ordinary working people, in particular a major British party that since the Second World War has been in power 1945–51, 1964–70, 1974–9, and since 1997. Arising from the trade union movement at the end of the 19th century, it replaced the Liberals as the country's second party after the First World War.

labour-saving ▶ **adjective** [attrib.] (of an appliance) designed to reduce the amount of work needed to do something.

labour theory of value ▶ **noun** [mass noun] the Marxist theory that the value of a commodity should be determined by the amount of human labour used in its production.

labour union ▶ **noun** chiefly N. Amer. a trade union.

labour ward ▶ **noun** a room in a hospital set aside for childbirth.

Labour Weekend ▶ **noun** NZ the weekend including Labour Day.

labra plural form of **LABRUM**.

Labrador[1] /ˈlabrədɔː/ a coastal region of eastern Canada, which forms the mainland part of the province of Newfoundland and Labrador.

Labrador[2] /ˈlabrədɔː/ (also **Labrador dog** or **retriever**) ▶ **noun** a retriever of a breed that most typically has a black or yellow coat, widely used as a gun dog or as a guide for a blind person.
– ORIGIN early 20th cent.: named after the **LABRADOR PENINSULA**, where the breed was developed. The name *Labrador dog* had been applied in the 19th cent. to a much larger breed, similar to the Newfoundland.

Labrador Current a cold ocean current which flows southwards from the Arctic Ocean along the NE coast of North America. It meets the warm Gulf Stream in an area off the coast of Newfoundland which is noted for its dense fogs.

labradorescence /ˌlabrədɔːˈrɛs(ə)ns/ ▶ **noun** [mass noun] Mineralogy the brilliant iridescence exhibited by some specimens of labradorite and other feldspars.
– DERIVATIVES **labradorescent** adjective.

labradorite /ˌlabrəˈdɔːrʌɪt/ ▶ **noun** [mass noun] a mineral of the plagioclase feldspar group, found in many igneous rocks.
– ORIGIN early 19th cent.: from **LABRADOR PENINSULA**, where it was found, + **-ITE**[1].

Labrador Peninsula a broad peninsula of eastern Canada, between Hudson Bay, the Atlantic, and the Gulf of St Lawrence. Consisting of the Ungava Peninsula and Labrador, it contains most of Quebec and the mainland part of the province of Newfoundland and Labrador. Also called **LABRADOR-UNGAVA** /ʊŋˈgeɪvə, -ˈgɑːvə/.

Labrador tea ▶ **noun** a low-growing northern shrub of the heather family, with fragrant leathery evergreen leaves which are sometimes used locally in Canada as a tea substitute.
● Genus *Ledum*, family Ericaceae.

labret /ˈleɪbrɪt/ ▶ **noun** an object such as a small piece of shell, bone, or stone inserted into the lip as an ornament in some cultures.
– ORIGIN mid 19th cent.: diminutive of **LABRUM**.

labrish /ˈlabrɪʃ/ ▶ **noun** [mass noun] W. Indian gossip.
– ORIGIN probably a corruption of the verb **BLABBER**.

labrum /ˈleɪbrəm/ ▶ **noun** (pl. **labra** /-brə/) Zoology a structure corresponding to a lip, especially the upper border of the mouthparts of a crustacean or insect.
– DERIVATIVES **labral** adjective.
– ORIGIN early 18th cent.: from Latin, literally 'lip'; related to **LABIUM**.

Labrusca /ləˈbrʊskə/ ▶ **noun** [mass noun] a variety of grape obtained from a wild vine native to the eastern US.
● *Vitis labrusca*, family Vitaceae.
■a wine made from this grape.
– ORIGIN from Latin *labrusca*, denoting a wild vine.

La Bruyère /ˌla bruːˈjɛː, French la bʀyjɛʀ/, Jean de (1645–96), French writer and moralist. He is known for his *Caractères* (1688), based on a translation of the *Characters* of Theophrastus and exposing the vanity and corruption of human behaviour by satirizing Parisian society.

Labuan /ləˈbuːən/ a small Malaysian island off the north coast of Borneo; pop. 26,410 (1980); capital, Victoria.

laburnum /ləˈbəːnəm/ ▶ **noun** a small European tree which has hanging clusters of yellow flowers followed by slender pods containing poisonous seeds. The hard timber is sometimes used as an ebony substitute.
● Genus *Laburnum*, family Leguminosae.
– ORIGIN modern Latin, from Latin.

labyrinth /ˈlab(ə)rɪnθ/ ▶ **noun 1** a complicated irregular network of passages or paths in which it is difficult to find one's way; a maze: ***a labyrinth of** passages and secret chambers.*
■figurative an intricate and confusing arrangement: *a **labyrinth of** conflicting laws and regulations.*
2 Anatomy a complex structure in the inner ear which contains the organs of hearing and balance. It consists of bony cavities (the **bony labyrinth**) filled with fluid and lined with sensitive membranes (the **membranous labyrinth**).
■Zoology an organ of intricate structure, in particular the accessory respiratory organs of certain fishes.
– DERIVATIVES **labyrinthian** adjective.
– ORIGIN late Middle English (referring to the maze constructed by Daedalus to house the Minotaur): from French *labyrinthe* or Latin *labyrinthus*, from Greek *laburinthos*.

labyrinth fish ▶ **noun** a freshwater fish with poorly developed gills and a labyrinthine accessory breathing organ, native to Africa and Asia.
● Suborder Anabantoidei: Belontiidae and related families, with many species, including such popular aquarium fishes as the gouramis and the fighting fish.

labyrinthine /ˌlabəˈrɪnθʌɪn/ ▶ **adjective** (of a network or layout) like a labyrinth; irregular and twisting: *labyrinthine streets and alleys.*
■(of a system) intricate and confusing: *a world of labyrinthine plots and counterplots | labyrinthine tax laws.*

labyrinthitis /ˌlab(ə)rɪnˈθʌɪtɪs/ ▶ **noun** [mass noun] Medicine inflammation of the labyrinth or inner ear.

labyrinthodont /ˌlabəˈrɪnθədɒnt/ ▶ **adjective** Zoology (of teeth) having the enamel deeply folded to form a labyrinthine structure.
■Palaeontology of or relating to a group of large fossil amphibians of the late Devonian to early Triassic periods having such teeth.
▶**noun** a labyrinthodont amphibian.
● Former subclass Labyrinthodontia: several families, but no longer considered to be a single group.
– ORIGIN mid 19th cent.: from modern Latin *Labyrinthodontia*, from Greek *laburinthos* 'labyrinth' + *odous, odont-* 'tooth'.

LAC ▶ **abbreviation for** Leading Aircraftman.

lac[1] ▶ **noun** [mass noun] a resinous substance secreted as a protective covering by the lac insect, used to make varnish, shellac, sealing wax, dyes, etc.
– ORIGIN late Middle English: from medieval Latin *lac, lac(c)a*, from Portuguese *laca*, based on Hindi *lākh* or Persian *lāk*.

lac[2] ▶ **adjective** [attrib.] Biology denoting the ability of normal strains of the bacterium *E. coli* to metabolize lactose, or the genetic factors involved in this ability (which is lost in some mutant strains): *the lac operon.*
– ORIGIN 1940s: abbreviation of **LACTOSE**.

lac[3] ▶ **noun** variant spelling of **LAKH**.

Lacan /laˈkɒ̃, French lakɑ̃/, Jacques (1901–81), French psychoanalyst and writer. A notable post-structuralist, he reinterpreted Freudian psychoanalysis, especially the theory of the unconscious, in the light of structural linguistics and anthropology.
– DERIVATIVES **Lacanian** /laˈkeɪnɪən/ adjective & noun, **Lacanianism** noun.

Laccadive Islands /ˈlakədɪv/ one of the groups of islands forming the Indian territory of Lakshadweep in the Indian Ocean.

laccase /ˈlakeɪz/ ▶ **noun** [mass noun] Biochemistry a copper-containing enzyme which oxidizes hydroquinones to quinones, involved in the setting of lac.
– ORIGIN late 19th cent.: from medieval Latin *lacca* (see **LAC**[1]) + **-ASE**.

laccolith /ˈlakəlɪθ/ ▶ **noun** Geology a mass of igneous rock, typically lens-shaped, that has been intruded between rock strata causing uplift in the shape of a dome.
– ORIGIN late 19th cent.: from Greek *lakkos* 'reservoir' + **-LITH**.

lace ▶ **noun 1** [mass noun] a fine open fabric, typically one of cotton or silk, made by looping, twisting, or knitting thread in patterns and used especially for trimming garments.
■ braid used for trimming, especially on military dress uniforms.
2 (usu. **laces**) a cord or leather strip passed through eyelets or hooks on opposite sides of a shoe or garment and then pulled tight and fastened.
▶ **verb** [with obj.] **1** fasten or tighten (a shoe or garment) by tying its laces: *he put the shoes on and* ***laced*** *them* ***up***.
■ compress the waist of (someone) with a laced corset: *Rosina* ***laced*** *her* ***up*** *tight to show off her neat pretty waist.* ■ (**lace someone into**) fasten someone into (a garment) by tightening the laces: *she couldn't breathe, laced into this frock.* ■ [no obj.] (of a garment or shoe) be fastened by means of laces: *the shoes laced at the front.*
2 [with obj. and adverbial] entwine or tangle (things, especially fingers) together: *he* ***laced*** *his fingers* ***together*** *and sat back.*
■ (**lace something through**) pass a lace or cord through (a hole).
3 (often **be laced with**) add an ingredient, especially alcohol, to (a drink or dish) to enhance its flavour or strength: *he gave us coffee laced with brandy* | figurative *his voice was laced with derision.*
– ORIGIN Middle English: from Old French *laz, las* (noun), *lacier* (verb), based on Latin *laqueus* 'noose' (also an early sense in English). Compare with **LASSO**.
▶ **lace into** informal assail or tackle (something): *Marion laced into the gin and tonic as if it was going out of fashion.*

lacebark ▶ **noun** any of a number of trees or shrubs which possess a lacy bark or inner bark, in particular:
• an evergreen Caribbean shrub with a lacy inner bark that is used ornamentally (*Lagetta lagetto*, family Thymelaeaceae).
• a small ornamental New Zealand tree (genus *Hoheria*, family Malvaceae).

lace bug ▶ **noun** a small plant-eating bug that has a raised net-like pattern on the wings and upper surface.
• Family Tingidae, suborder Heteroptera: several genera.

lacecap ▶ **noun** a hydrangea of a group of varieties that have flat flower heads with fertile florets in the centre surrounded by sterile florets. Compare with **HORTENSIA**.
• *Hydrangea macrophylla* vars., family Hydrangeaceae.

laced ▶ **adjective** trimmed or fitted with lace or laces: *heavy laced boots.*

Lacedaemonian /ˌlasɪdɪˈməʊnɪən/ ▶ **noun** a native or inhabitant of Lacedaemon, an area of ancient Greece comprising the city of Sparta and its surroundings.
▶ **adjective** of Lacedaemon or its inhabitants; Spartan.

lace glass ▶ **noun** [mass noun] a type of Venetian glass, having designs resembling lace.

La Ceiba /la ˈseɪbə/ a seaport on the Caribbean coast of Honduras; pop. 68,200 (1988).

lacemaking ▶ **noun** [mass noun] the activity of making lace.
– DERIVATIVES **lacemaker** noun.

lace pillow ▶ **noun** a cushion placed on the lap to provide support in lacemaking.

lacerate /ˈlasəreɪt/ ▶ **verb** [with obj.] tear or deeply cut (something, especially flesh or skin): *the point had lacerated his neck* | [as adj. **lacerated**] *his badly lacerated hands and knees.*
– DERIVATIVES **laceration** noun.
– ORIGIN late Middle English: from Latin *lacerat-* 'mangled', from the verb *lacerare*, from *lacer* 'mangled, torn'.

Lacerta /ləˈsəːtə/ Astronomy a small and inconspicuous northern constellation (the Lizard), on the edge of the Milky Way between Cygnus and Andromeda.
■ [as genitive **Lacertae** /-tiː/] used with preceding letter or numeral to designate a star in this constellation: *the star Alpha Lacertae.*
– ORIGIN Latin.

lacertid /ləˈsəːtɪd/ ▶ **noun** Zoology a typical lizard of a large family (Lacertidae) to which most European lizards belong.
– ORIGIN late 19th cent.: from modern Latin *Lacertidae* (plural), from Latin *lacerta* 'lizard'.

Lacertilia /ˌlasəˈtɪlɪə/ Zoology a group of reptiles that comprises the lizards. Also called **SAURIA**.
• Suborder Lacertilia (or Sauria), order Squamata.
– DERIVATIVES **lacertilian** noun & adjective.
– ORIGIN modern Latin (plural), from Latin *lacerta* 'lizard'.

lace-up ▶ **adjective** (of a shoe or garment) fastened with laces: *flat lace-up shoes.*
▶ **noun** chiefly Brit. a shoe or boot that is fastened with laces: *brown leather lace-ups.*

lacewing ▶ **noun** a slender delicate insect with large clear membranous wings. Both the adults and larvae are typically predators of aphids.
• Several families in the order Neuroptera, in particular Chrysopidae (the **green lacewings**).

lacewood ▶ **noun** [mass noun] the timber of the plane tree.

lacework ▶ **noun** [mass noun] lace fabric and other items made of lace viewed collectively.
■ the process of making lace.

lachenalia /ˌlaʃəˈneɪlɪə/ ▶ **noun** a plant of a genus which comprises the Cape cowslips.
• Genus *Lachenalia*, family Liliaceae.
– ORIGIN modern Latin, named after Werner de *la Chenal* (1736–1800), Swiss botanist.

laches /ˈlatʃɪz, ˈleɪ-/ ▶ **noun** [mass noun] Law unreasonable delay in making an assertion or claim, such as asserting a right, claiming a privilege, or making an application for redress, which may result in refusal.
– ORIGIN late Middle English (in the sense 'slackness, negligence'): from Old French *laschesse*, from *lasche* 'loose, lax', based on Latin *laxus*. The current sense dates from the late 16th cent.

Lachesis /ˈlakɪsɪs/ Greek Mythology one of the three Fates.
– ORIGIN Greek, literally 'getting by lot'.

Lachlan /ˈlaklən/ a river of New South Wales, Australia, which rises in the Great Dividing Range and flows some 1,472 km (920 miles) north-west then south-west to join the Murrumbidgee River near the border with Victoria.
– ORIGIN named after *Lachlan* Macquarie, the governor of New South Wales from 1810 to 1821.

lachrymal /ˈlakrɪm(ə)l/ (also **lacrimal** or **lacrymal**) ▶ **adjective 1** formal or poetic/literary connected with weeping or tears.
2 (usu. **lacrimal**) Physiology & Anatomy concerned with the secretion of tears: *lacrimal cells.*
▶ **noun 1** (usu. **lacrimal** or **lacrimal bone**) Anatomy a small bone forming part of the eye socket.
2 short for **LACHRYMAL VASE**.
– ORIGIN late Middle English (in sense 2 of the adjective): from medieval Latin *lachrymalis*, from Latin *lacrima* 'tear'.

lachrymal vase ▶ **noun** historical a phial holding the tears of mourners at a funeral.

lachrymation /ˌlakrɪˈmeɪʃ(ə)n/ (also **lacrimation** or **lacrymation**) ▶ **noun** [mass noun] poetic/literary or Medicine the flow of tears.
– ORIGIN late 16th cent.: from Latin *lacrimatio(n-)*, from *lacrimare* 'weep', from *lacrima* 'tear'.

lachrymator /ˈlakrɪˌmeɪtə/ (also **lacrimator**) ▶ **noun** chiefly Medicine a substance that irritates the eyes and causes tears to flow.

lachrymatory /ˈlakrɪməˌt(ə)ri/ (also **lacrimatory**) ▶ **adjective** technical or poetic/literary relating to, tending to cause, or containing tears: *a lachrymatory secretion.*
▶ **noun** (pl. **-ies**) a phial of a kind found in ancient Roman tombs and thought to be a lachrymal vase.
– ORIGIN mid 17th cent. (as a noun denoting a phial): from Latin *lacrima*, on the pattern of *chrismatory.*

lachrymose /ˈlakrɪməʊs, -z/ ▶ **adjective** formal or poetic/literary tearful or given to weeping: *she was pink-eyed and lachrymose.*
■ inducing tears; sad: *a lachrymose children's classic.*
– DERIVATIVES **lachrymosely** adverb, **lachrymosity** noun.
– ORIGIN mid 17th cent. (in the sense 'like tears; liable to exude in drops'): from Latin *lacrimosus*, from *lacrima* 'tear'.

lacing ▶ **noun 1** [mass noun] the laced fastening of a shoe or garment.
■ lace trimming, especially on a uniform.
2 a dash of spirits added to a drink: *coffee to which he added* ***a*** *liberal* ***lacing of*** *brandy.*

lacing course ▶ **noun** a strengthening course of bricks built into an arch or wall.

laciniate /ləˈsɪnɪət/ (also **laciniated** /-eɪtɪd/) ▶ **adjective** Botany & Zoology divided into deep narrow irregular segments.
– ORIGIN mid 18th cent.: from Latin *lacinia* 'fringe, hem, flap of a garment' + **-ATE**[2].

lac insect ▶ **noun** an Asian scale insect which lives on croton trees and produces secretions that are used in the production of shellac.
• *Laccifer lacca*, family Lacciferidae, suborder Homoptera.

lack ▶ **noun** [mass noun] the state of being without or not having enough of something: *the case was dismissed* ***for lack of*** *evidence* | *there is* ***no lack of*** *entertainment aboard ship* | [in sing.] *there is a lack of parking space in the town.*
▶ **verb** [with obj.] be without or deficient in: *the novel lacks imagination* | [no obj.] *she* ***lacks in*** *patience* | *Sam did not* ***lack for*** *friends.*
– ORIGIN Middle English: corresponding to, and perhaps partly from, Middle Dutch and Middle Low German *lak* 'deficiency', Middle Dutch *laken* 'lack, blame'.

lackadaisical /ˌlakəˈdeɪzɪk(ə)l/ ▶ **adjective** lacking enthusiasm and determination; carelessly lazy: *a lackadaisical defence left Spurs adrift in the second half.*
– DERIVATIVES **lackadaisically** adverb.
– ORIGIN mid 18th cent. (also in the sense 'feebly sentimental'): from the archaic interjection *lackaday, lackadaisy* (see **ALACK**) + **-ICAL**.

lackaday ▶ **exclamation** archaic an expression of surprise, regret, or grief.
– ORIGIN late 17th cent.: shortening of *alack-a-day.*

lackey ▶ **noun** (pl. **-eys**) **1** a servant, especially a liveried footman or manservant.
■ derogatory a person who is obsequiously willing to obey or serve another person or group of people.
2 (also **lackey moth**) a brownish European moth of woods and hedgerows, the caterpillars of which live communally in a silken tent on the food tree. [ORIGIN: mid 19th cent.: from the resemblance of the coloured stripes of its caterpillars to a footman's livery.]
• *Malacosoma neustria*, family Lasiocampidae.
▶ **verb** (also **lacquey**) (**-eys, -eyed**) [with obj.] archaic behave servilely to; wait upon as a lackey.
– ORIGIN early 16th cent.: from French *laquais*, perhaps from Catalan *alacay*, from Arabic *al-ḳā'id* 'the chief'.

lacking ▶ **adjective** [predic.] not available or in short supply: *adequate resources and funds are both sadly lacking at present.*
■ (of a quality) missing or absent: *there was something lacking in our marriage.* ■ deficient or inadequate: *the students are not* ***lacking in*** *intellectual ability* | *workers were asked in what way they* ***found*** *their managers* ***lacking.***

lacklustre (US **lackluster**) ▶ **adjective** lacking in vitality, force, or conviction; uninspired or uninspiring: *no excuses were made for the team's lacklustre performance.*
■ (of the hair or the eyes) not shining; dull.

Lac Léman /lak lemɑ̃/ French name for Lake Geneva (see **GENEVA, LAKE**).

Laclos /laˈkləʊ, French laklo/, Pierre Choderlos de (1741–1803), French novelist; full name *Pierre-Ambroise-François Choderlos de Laclos*. He is chiefly remembered for his epistolary novel *Les Liaisons dangereuses* (1782).

Laconia /ləˈkəʊnɪə/ (also **Lakonia**) a modern department and ancient region of Greece, in the SE Peloponnese. Throughout the classical period the region was dominated by its capital, Sparta.
– DERIVATIVES **Laconian** adjective & noun.

laconic /ləˈkɒnɪk/ ▶ **adjective** (of a person, speech, or style of writing) using very few words: *his laconic reply suggested a lack of interest in the topic.*
– DERIVATIVES **laconically** adverb, **laconicism** noun, **laconism** noun.
– ORIGIN mid 16th cent. (in the sense 'Laconian'): via Latin from Greek *Lakōnikos*, from *Lakōn* 'Laconia, Sparta', the Spartans being known for their terse speech.

a cat | ɑː arm | ɛ bed | ɛː hair | ə ago | əː her | ɪ sit | i cosy | iː see | ɒ hot | ɔː saw | ʌ run | ʊ put | uː too | ʌɪ my | aʊ how | eɪ day | əʊ no | ɪə near | ɔɪ boy | ʊə poor | ʌɪə fire | aʊə sour

laconicum /ləˈkɒnɪkəm/ ▶ noun (pl. **laconica**) the sweating-room in a Roman bath.
– ORIGIN Latin, neuter of *Laconicus* 'Laconic', this type of room being first used by the Spartans.

La Coruña /la koˈruɲa/ Spanish name for **CORUNNA**.

lacquer /ˈlakə/ ▶ noun [mass noun] **1** a liquid made of shellac dissolved in alcohol, or of synthetic substances, that dries to form a hard protective coating for wood, metal, etc.
■(also **hair lacquer**) Brit. a chemical substance sprayed on hair to keep it in place.
2 the sap of the lacquer tree used to varnish wood or other materials.
■decorative ware made of wood coated with lacquer: [as modifier] *a small lacquer box.*
▶ verb [with obj.] [often as adj. **lacquered**] coat with lacquer: *the lacquered Chinese table.*
– DERIVATIVES **lacquerer** noun.
– ORIGIN late 16th cent. (denoting lac): from obsolete French *lacre* 'sealing wax', from Portuguese *laca* (see **LAC**[1]).

lacquer tree ▶ noun an East Asian tree with white sap that turns dark on exposure to air, producing a hard-wearing varnish traditionally used in lacquerwork.
●*Rhus verniciflua*, family Anacardiaceae.

lacquerware ▶ noun [mass noun] articles that have a decorative lacquer coating, viewed collectively.

lacquerwork ▶ noun [mass noun] lacquerware.
■the design, construction, or finish of lacquerware.

lacquey ▶ noun & verb archaic spelling of **LACKEY**.

lacrimal ▶ adjective & noun variant spelling of **LACHRYMAL**.

lacrimation ▶ noun variant spelling of **LACHRYMATION**.

lacrimator ▶ noun variant spelling of **LACHRYMATOR**.

lacrimatory ▶ adjective variant spelling of **LACHRYMATORY**.

lacrosse /ləˈkrɒs/ ▶ noun [mass noun] a team game, originally played by North American Indians, in which the ball is thrown, carried, and caught with a long-handled stick having a curved L-shaped or triangular frame at one end with a piece of shallow netting in the angle.
– ORIGIN mid 19th cent.: from French (*le jeu de*) *la crosse* '(the game of) the hooked stick'. Compare with **CROSSE**.

lacrymal ▶ adjective & noun variant spelling of **LACHRYMAL**.

lacrymation ▶ noun variant spelling of **LACHRYMATION**.

lactalbumin /lakˈtalbjʊmɪn/ ▶ noun [mass noun] Biochemistry a protein or mixture of similar proteins occurring in milk, obtained after the removal of casein and soluble in a salt solution.
– ORIGIN late 19th cent.: from **LACTO-** 'of milk' + **ALBUMIN**.

lactam /ˈlaktam/ ▶ noun Chemistry an organic compound containing an amide group —NHCO— as part of a ring.
– ORIGIN late 19th cent.: blend of **LACTONE** and **AMIDE**.

lactarium /lakˈtɛːrɪəm/ ▶ noun (pl. **lactaria**) rare a dairy.
– ORIGIN early 19th cent.: modern Latin, neuter (used as a noun) of Latin *lactarius* 'relating to milk'.

lactase /ˈlakteɪz/ ▶ noun [mass noun] Biochemistry an enzyme which catalyses the hydrolysis of lactose to glucose and galactose.
– ORIGIN late 19th cent.: from **LACTOSE** + **-ASE**.

lactate[1] /lakˈteɪt/ ▶ verb [no obj.] (of a female mammal) secrete milk.
– ORIGIN late 19th cent.: back-formation from **LACTATION**.

lactate[2] /ˈlakteɪt/ ▶ noun [mass noun] Chemistry a salt or ester of lactic acid.
– ORIGIN late 18th cent.: from **LACTIC** + **-ATE**[1].

lactation ▶ noun [mass noun] the secretion of milk by the mammary glands.
■the suckling of young.
– DERIVATIVES **lactational** adjective.
– ORIGIN mid 17th cent.: from Latin *lactatio(n-)*, from *lactare* 'suckle', from *lac*, *lact-* 'milk'.

lacteal /ˈlaktɪəl/ ▶ adjective of milk.

■Anatomy (of a vessel) conveying chyle or other milky fluid.
▶ plural noun (**lacteals**) Anatomy the lymphatic vessels of the small intestine which absorb digested fats.
– ORIGIN mid 17th cent.: from Latin *lacteus* (from *lac*, *lact-* 'milk') + **-AL**.

lactescent /lakˈtɛs(ə)nt/ ▶ adjective milky in appearance.
■Botany yielding a milky latex.
– ORIGIN mid 17th cent.: from Latin *lactescent-* 'being milky', from the verb *lactere*, from *lac*, *lact-* 'milk'.

lactic /ˈlaktɪk/ ▶ adjective of, relating to, or obtained from milk.
– ORIGIN late 18th cent.: from Latin *lac*, *lact-* 'milk' + **-IC**.

lactic acid ▶ noun [mass noun] Biochemistry a colourless syrupy organic acid formed in sour milk, and produced in the muscle tissues during strenuous exercise.
●Chem. formula: $CH_3CH(OH)COOH$.

lactiferous /lakˈtɪf(ə)rəs/ ▶ adjective chiefly Anatomy forming or conveying milk or milky fluid: *lactiferous ducts.*
– ORIGIN late 17th cent.: from Latin *lac*, *lact-* 'milk' + **-FEROUS**.

lacto- ▶ combining form **1** of or relating to milk: *lactoscope.*
2 from or relating to lactic acid or lactose: *lactobacillus.*
– ORIGIN from Latin *lac*, *lact-* 'milk'.

lactobacillus /ˌlaktəʊbəˈsɪləs/ ▶ noun (pl. **lactobacilli** /-lʌɪ/) Biology a rod-shaped bacterium which produces lactic acid from the fermentation of carbohydrates.
●Genus *Lactobacillus*; non-motile Gram-positive bacteria.

lactoferrin /ˌlaktəʊˈfɛrɪn/ ▶ noun [mass noun] Biochemistry a protein present in milk and other secretions, with bactericidal and iron-binding properties.

lactoflavin /ˌlaktəʊˈfleɪvɪn/ ▶ noun another term for **RIBOFLAVIN**.

lactogenic /ˌlaktə(ʊ)ˈdʒɛnɪk/ ▶ adjective Physiology (of a hormone or other substance) inducing the secretion of milk.

lactoglobulin /ˌlaktə(ʊ)ˈglɒbjʊlɪn/ ▶ noun [mass noun] Biochemistry a protein or mixture of similar proteins occurring in milk, obtained after the removal of casein and precipitated in a salt solution.

lactometer /lakˈtɒmɪtə/ ▶ noun an instrument for measuring the density of milk.

lactone /ˈlaktəʊn/ ▶ noun Chemistry an organic compound containing an ester group —OCO— as part of a ring.

lacto-ovo-vegetarian ▶ noun a person who eats vegetables, eggs, and dairy products but who does not eat meat.

lactoprotein ▶ noun [mass noun] the protein component of milk.

lactoscope ▶ noun an instrument for measuring the quality of milk from its translucence.

lactose /ˈlaktəʊz, -s/ ▶ noun [mass noun] Chemistry a sugar present in milk. It is a disaccharide containing glucose and galactose units.

lactosuria /ˌlaktə(ʊ)ˈsjʊərɪə/ ▶ noun [mass noun] the presence of lactose in the urine.

lacto-vegetarian ▶ noun a person who abstains from eating meat and eggs.

lactulose /ˈlaktjʊləʊz/ ▶ noun [mass noun] Chemistry a synthetic sugar with laxative properties. It is a disaccharide consisting of glucose and fructose units.
– ORIGIN 1930s: from **LACTO-** 'of milk', perhaps on the pattern of *cellulose.*

lacuna /ləˈkjuːnə/ ▶ noun (pl. **lacunae** /-niː/ or **lacunas**) an unfilled space or interval; a gap: *the journal has filled a lacuna in Middle Eastern studies.*
■a missing portion in a book or manuscript. ■Anatomy a cavity or depression, especially in bone.
– DERIVATIVES **lacunal** adjective, **lacunary** adjective, **lacunate** adjective, **lacunose** adjective.
– ORIGIN mid 17th cent.: from Latin, 'pool', from *lacus* 'lake'.

lacunar[1] /ləˈkjuːnə/ ▶ adjective of or relating to a lacuna.

lacunar[2] /ləˈkjuːnə/ ▶ noun a vault or ceiling consisting of recessed panels.
■a panel in such a vault or ceiling.

lacustrine /ləˈkʌstrʌɪn, -trɪn/ ▶ adjective technical or poetic/literary of, relating to, or associated with lakes.
– ORIGIN early 19th cent.: from Latin *lacus* 'lake' (the stem *lacustr-* influenced by Latin *palustris* 'marshy') + **-INE**[1].

LACW ▶ abbreviation for Leading Aircraftwoman.

lacy ▶ adjective (**lacier**, **laciest**) made of, resembling, or trimmed with lace: *a lacy petticoat.*
– DERIVATIVES **lacily** adverb, **laciness** noun.

lad ▶ noun **1** informal a boy or young man (often as a form of address): *I read that book when I was a lad* | *come in, lad, and shut the door.*
■(**lads**) chiefly Brit. a group of men sharing recreational, working, or other interests: *she wouldn't let him go out with the lads any more* | *a furious row ensued between the referee and our lads.* ■Brit. a man who is boisterously macho in his behaviour or actions, especially one who is very interested in sexual conquest: *Tony was a bit of a lad—always had an eye for the women.*
2 Brit. a stable worker (regardless of age or sex).
– ORIGIN Middle English: of unknown origin.

Ladakh /ləˈdɑːk/ a high-altitude region of NW India, Pakistan, and China, containing the Ladakh and Karakoram mountain ranges and the upper Indus valley; chief town, Leh (in India).

Ladakhi /ləˈdɑːki/ ▶ noun (pl. **Ladakhis**) **1** a native or inhabitant of Ladakh.
2 [mass noun] the language of Ladakh, a dialect of Tibetan.
▶ adjective of or relating to Ladakh, the Ladakhis, or their language.
– ORIGIN the name in Ladakhi.

ladanum /ˈlad(ə)nəm/ (also **labdanum**) ▶ noun [mass noun] a gum resin obtained from the twigs of a southern European rock rose, used in perfumery and for fumigation.
●The rock rose is usually *Cistus ladanifer*, family Cistaceae.
– ORIGIN mid 16th cent.: via Latin from Greek *ladanon*, *lēdanon*, from *lēdon* 'mastic'.

ladder ▶ noun a structure consisting of a series of bars or steps between two upright lengths of wood, metal, or rope, used for climbing up or down something.
■figurative a series of ascending stages by which someone or something may advance or progress: *employees on their way up the career ladder.* ■Brit. a vertical strip of unravelled fabric in tights or stockings.
▶ verb [with obj.] Brit. cause (tights or stockings) to develop a ladder: [as adj. **laddered**] *her dress was crumpled and her tights were laddered.*
■[no obj.] (of tights or stockings) develop a ladder.
– ORIGIN Old English *hlæd(d)er*, of West Germanic origin; related to Dutch *leer* and German *Leiter*.

ladder-back (also **ladder-back chair**) ▶ noun an upright chair with a back resembling a ladder.

ladder stitch ▶ noun [mass noun] a stitch in embroidery consisting of transverse bars.

ladder tournament ▶ noun a sporting contest in which the participants are listed in ranking order and can move up by defeating the one above.

laddertron /ˈladətrɒn/ ▶ noun a device used to carry charge to the terminals of some electrostatic accelerators, consisting of a series of metal bars joined at each end by non-conducting links to form a closed loop.
– ORIGIN 1970s: from **LADDER** + **-TRON**.

laddie ▶ noun informal, chiefly Scottish a boy or young man (often as a form of address): *he's just a wee laddie.*

laddish ▶ adjective characteristic of a young man who behaves in a boisterously macho manner.
– DERIVATIVES **laddishness** noun.

laddu /ˈlʌduː/ (also **laddoo** or **ladoo**) ▶ noun (pl. **laddus**) an Indian sweet, typically made from flour, sugar, and shortening, which is prepared by frying and then shaping into a ball.
– ORIGIN from Hindi *laḍḍū*.

lade /leɪd/ ▶ verb (past participle **laden**) [with obj.] archaic put cargo on board (a ship).
■ship (goods) as cargo: *the surplus products must be laden on board the vessels.* ■[no obj.] (of a ship) take on cargo.
– ORIGIN Old English *hladan*, of West Germanic origin; related to Dutch and German *laden* 'to load', also to **LADLE** and perhaps to **LATHE**.

laden ▶ adjective heavily loaded or weighed down: *a tree laden with apples* | [in combination] *the moisture-laden air.*
– ORIGIN late 16th cent.: past participle of **LADE**.

la-di-da (also **lah-di-dah**) informal ▶ **adjective** pretentious or snobbish, especially in manner or speech: *do I really look or sound like a la-di-da society lawyer?*
▶ **exclamation** expressing derision at someone's pretentious manner or speech: *'La-di-da!' snapped Alison, as her sister sank into a curtsy.*
– ORIGIN late 19th cent.: imitative of an affected manner of speech.

ladies plural form of **LADY**.

ladies' chain ▶ **noun** a figure in a quadrille or other dance.

ladies' fingers ▶ **plural noun** Brit. another term for **OKRA**.

ladies' man (also **lady's man**) ▶ **noun** [in sing.] informal a man who enjoys spending time and flirting with women.

ladies' night ▶ **noun** a function at a men's institution or club to which women are invited.
▪ a session at a nightclub to which women are admitted free of charge or at a reduced rate.

ladies' room ▶ **noun** chiefly N. Amer. a toilet for women in a public or institutional building.

ladies' tresses ▶ **noun** US spelling of **LADY'S TRESSES**.

ladified ▶ **adjective** variant spelling of **LADYFIED**.

ladify ▶ **verb** variant spelling of **LADYFY**.

Ladin /lə'diːn/ ▶ **noun** [mass noun] the Rhaeto-Romance dialect of the Engadine in Switzerland.
– ORIGIN mid 19th cent.: from Latin *Latinus* (see **LATIN**).

lading /'leɪdɪŋ/ ▶ **noun** [mass noun] archaic the action or process of loading a ship with cargo.
▪ [count noun] a cargo.

Ladino /lə'diːnəʊ/ ▶ **noun** (pl. **-os**) **1** [mass noun] the language of some Sephardic Jews, especially formerly in Mediterranean countries. It is based on medieval Spanish, with an admixture of Hebrew, Greek, and Turkish words, and is written in modified Hebrew characters. Also called **JUDEZMO**.
2 a mestizo or Spanish-speaking white person in Central America.
– ORIGIN Spanish, from Latin *Latinus* (see **LATIN**).

ladino /lə'diːnəʊ/ ▶ **noun** (pl. **-os**) a white (or Dutch) clover of a large variety native to Italy and cultivated for fodder in North America.
– ORIGIN 1920s: from Italian.

Ladislaus I /'ladɪsˌlɔːs/ (*c.*1040–95), king of Hungary 1077–95; canonized as **St Ladislaus**. He extended Hungarian power and advanced the spread of Christianity. Feast day, 27 June.

Ladislaus II /'ladɪsˌlaʊs/ (*c.*1351–1434), king of Poland 1386–1434; Polish name **Władysław**. As grand duke of Lithuania, he acceded to the Polish throne on his marriage to the Polish monarch, Queen Jadwiga, thus uniting Lithuania and Poland.

ladle ▶ **noun** a large long-handled spoon with a cup-shaped bowl, used for serving soup, stew, or sauce.
▪ a vessel for transporting molten metal in a foundry.
▶ **verb** [with obj. and adverbial] serve (soup, stew, or sauce) with a ladle: *she* **ladled out** *onion soup* | figurative *he was* **ladling out** *his personal philosophy of life.*
▪ transfer (liquid) from one receptacle to another: *he ladled the water into an empty bucket.*
– DERIVATIVES **ladleful** noun (pl. **-fuls**), **ladler** noun.
– ORIGIN Old English *hlædel*, from *hladan* (see **LADE**).

Ladoga, Lake /'lɑːdəɡə/ a large lake in NW Russia, north-east of St Petersburg, near the border with Finland. It is the largest lake in Europe, with an area of 17,700 sq. km (6,837 sq. miles).

ladoo ▶ **noun** variant spelling of **LADDU**.

lad's love ▶ **noun** another term for **SOUTHERNWOOD**.

lady ▶ **noun** (pl. **-ies**) **1** a woman (used as a polite or old-fashioned form of reference): *I spoke to the lady at the travel agency* | [as modifier] *a lady doctor.*
▪ (**the Ladies**) Brit. a women's public toilet. ▪ chiefly N. Amer. an informal, often brusque, form of address to a woman: *I'm sorry, lady, but you have the wrong number.* ▪ used as a courteous designation for a female fellow member of the House of Commons: *the Right Honourable Lady has promised me her full support.*
2 a woman of superior social position, especially one of noble birth.
▪ a courteous, decorous, or genteel woman: *his wife was a real lady, with such nice manners.* ▪ (**Lady**) a title used by peeresses, female relatives of peers, the wives and widows of knights, etc.: *Lady Caroline Lamb.* ▪ a woman at the head of a household: *he always asked the lady of the house the shade of paint she would like.*
3 (**one's lady**) dated a man's wife: *welcoming the vice-president and his lady* | [as modifier] *my lady wife.*
▪ (also **lady friend**) a woman with whom a man is romantically or sexually involved. ▪ historical a woman to whom a man, especially a knight, is chivalrously devoted.
– PHRASES **find the lady** another term for **THREE-CARD TRICK**. **it isn't over till the fat lady sings** used to convey that there is still time for a situation to change. [ORIGIN: by association with the final aria in tragic opera.] **ladies who lunch** informal, often derogatory women with both the means and free time to meet each other socially for lunch in expensive restaurants. **Lady Bountiful** a woman who engages in ostentatious acts of charity, more to impress others than out of a sense of concern for those in need. [ORIGIN: early 19th cent.: from the name of a character in Farquhar's *The Beaux' Stratagem* (1707).] **Lady Luck** chance personified as a controlling power in human affairs: *it seemed Lady Luck was still smiling on them.* **Lady Muck** Brit. informal a haughty or pretentious woman (often as a mocking form of address): *it's that woman, Lady Muck herself—who does she think she is?* **My Lady** a polite form of address to female judges and certain noblewomen.
– DERIVATIVES **ladyhood** noun.
– ORIGIN Old English *hlǣfdīge* (denoting a woman to whom homage or obedience is due, such as the wife of a lord or the mistress of a household, also specifically the Virgin Mary), from *hlāf* 'loaf' + a Germanic base meaning 'knead', related to **DOUGH**; compare with **LORD**. In **LADY DAY** and other compounds where it signifies possession, it represents the Old English genitive *hlǣfdīgan* '(Our) Lady's'.

Lady altar ▶ **noun** the altar in a Lady chapel.

ladybird ▶ **noun** a small beetle with a domed back which is typically red or yellow with black spots. Both the adults and larvae are important predators of aphids. Also called **LADYBUG** in North America.
● Family Coccinellidae: several genera and species, including the common European **seven-spot ladybird** (*Coccinella septempunctata*).

ladybug ▶ **noun** North American term for **LADYBIRD**.

Lady chapel ▶ **noun** a chapel in a church or cathedral, typically to the east of the high altar in a cathedral, to the south in a church, dedicated to the Virgin Mary.

Lady Day ▶ **noun** 25 March (the feast of the Annunciation), a quarter day in England, Wales, and Ireland.
– ORIGIN with reference to *Our Lady*, the Virgin Mary.

lady fern ▶ **noun** a tall, graceful fern of worldwide distribution which favours moist shady habitats.
● *Athyrium* and other genera, family Woodsiaceae: several species, in particular *A. filix-femina*.

ladyfied (also **ladified**) ▶ **adjective** having the manner of a socially superior woman; pretentiously refined.

ladyfinger ▶ **noun** North American term for **LADY'S FINGER** (in sense 2).

ladyfish ▶ **noun** (pl. same or **-fishes**) any of a number of marine fishes of warm coastal waters, several of which are popular with anglers, notably:
▪ a tenpounder. ▪ a bonefish.

ladyfy (also **ladify**) ▶ **verb** (**-ies**, **-ied**) [with obj.] archaic give (a woman) the title of Lady.

lady-in-waiting ▶ **noun** (pl. **ladies-in-waiting**) a woman who attends a queen or princess.

ladykiller ▶ **noun** informal an attractive, charming man who habitually seduces women.

ladylike ▶ **adjective** behaving or dressing in a way considered appropriate for or typical of a well-bred, decorous woman or girl.
▪ (of an activity or occupation) considered suitable for such a woman or girl: *it wasn't ladylike to be too interested in men.*
– DERIVATIVES **ladylikeness** noun.

lady-love ▶ **noun** dated a female lover or sweetheart: *he was delivering chocolates to his lady-love.*

Lady Mayoress ▶ **noun** the title of the wife of a Lord Mayor.

lady of the bedchamber ▶ **noun** (in the UK) a female attendant to the queen or queen mother, ranking in the royal household above woman of the bedchamber.

lady of the night ▶ **noun** used euphemistically to refer to a prostitute.

lady's bedstraw ▶ **noun** a yellow-flowered Eurasian bedstraw which smells of hay when dried and was formerly used to make a mattress for sleeping on.
● *Galium verum*, family Rubiaceae.

lady's companion ▶ **noun** Brit. a small case or bag containing needlework items.

lady's finger ▶ **noun** Brit. **1** another term for **KIDNEY VETCH**.
2 a finger-shaped sponge cake with a crunchy sugar topping.

ladyship ▶ **noun** (**Her/Your Ladyship**) a respectful form of reference or address to a woman who has a title: *the car is outside, Your Ladyship.*
▪ ironic a form of reference or address to a woman thought to be acting in a pretentious or snobbish way: *bow everyone, Her Ladyship's actually gracing us with her presence!*

lady's maid ▶ **noun** chiefly historical a maid who attended to the personal needs of her mistress.

lady's man ▶ **noun** variant spelling of **LADIES' MAN**.

lady's mantle ▶ **noun** a herbaceous European plant of the rose family, with lobed rounded leaves and inconspicuous greenish flowers, and formerly valued in herbal medicine.
● *Alchemilla vulgaris*, family Rosaceae.

Ladysmith /'leɪdɪˌsmɪθ/ a town in eastern South Africa, in KwaZulu/Natal. It was subjected to a four-month siege by Boer forces during the Second Boer War.
– ORIGIN named after the wife of the governor of Natal, Sir Harry *Smith* (1787–1860).

lady's slipper ▶ **noun** an orchid of north temperate regions, the flower of which has a conspicuous pouch- or slipper-shaped lip. Also called **SLIPPER ORCHID**.
● Genus *Cypripedium*, family Orchidaceae.

lady's smock ▶ **noun** another term for **CUCKOOFLOWER**.

lady's tresses (US also **ladies' tresses**) ▶ **plural noun** [usu. treated as sing.] a short orchid with small white flowers, growing chiefly in north temperate regions.
● Genus *Spiranthes* (and *Goodyera*), family Orchidaceae.

Lady Superior ▶ **noun** the head of a convent or nunnery in certain orders.

lady's waist ▶ **noun** Austral. informal a small gracefully shaped glass.

Lae /'lɑːeɪ/ an industrial seaport on the east coast of Papua New Guinea, the country's second largest city; pop. 80,655 (1990).

Laennec's cirrhosis /la'ɛnɛks/ ▶ **noun** [mass noun] Medicine a type of cirrhosis of the liver characterized by a nodular appearance of the liver surface, associated with alcoholism.
– ORIGIN early 19th cent.: named after René T. H. *Laënnec* (1781–1826), the French physician who described the condition.

Laetrile /'leɪtrʌɪl/ ▶ **noun** [mass noun] trademark a compound extracted from peach stones, formerly used controversially to treat cancer.
– ORIGIN 1950s: from a blend of **LAEVOROTATORY** and **NITRILE**.

laevo- /'liːvəʊ/ (also **levo-**) ▶ **combining form** on or to the left: *laevorotatory.*
– ORIGIN from Latin *laevus* 'left'.

laevorotatory /ˌliːvəʊ'rəʊtət(ə)ri/ (US **levorotatory**) ▶ **adjective** Chemistry (of a compound) having the property of rotating the plane of a polarized light ray to the left, i.e. anticlockwise facing the oncoming radiation. The opposite of **DEXTROROTATORY**.
– DERIVATIVES **laevorotation** noun.

laevulose /'liːvjʊləʊz, -s/ (US **levulose**) ▶ **noun** Chemistry another term for **FRUCTOSE**.

Lafayette /ˌlafʌɪ'(j)ɛt/ (also **La Fayette**), Marie Joseph Paul Yves Roch Gilbert du Motier, Marquis de (1757–1834), French soldier and statesman. He fought alongside the American colonists in the War of Independence and commanded the National Guard (1789–91) in the French Revolution.

Laffer curve /'lafə/ ▶ **noun** Economics a supposed relationship between economic activity and the rate of taxation which suggests that there is an optimum tax rate which maximizes tax revenue.

– ORIGIN 1970s: named after Arthur *Laffer* (born 1942), American economist.

La Fontaine /ˌla fɒnˈtɛn, -teɪn, French la fɔ̃tɛn/, Jean de (1621–95), French poet. He is chiefly remembered for his *Fables* (1668–94), drawn from oriental, classical, and contemporary sources.

lag[1] ▶ verb (**lagged**, **lagging**) [no obj.] **1** fall behind in movement, progress, or development; not keep pace with another or others: *they stopped to wait for one of the children who was lagging behind.*
2 N. Amer. another term for **STRING** (in sense 6).
▶ noun **1** (also **time lag**) a period of time between one event or phenomenon and another: *there was a time lag between the commission of the crime and its reporting to the police.*
2 Physics a retardation in an electric current or movement.
– DERIVATIVES **lagger** noun.
– ORIGIN early 16th cent. (as a noun in the sense 'hindmost person (in a game, race, etc.)', also 'dregs'): related to the dialect adjective *lag* (perhaps from a fanciful distortion of **LAST**[1], or of Scandinavian origin: compare with Norwegian dialect *lagga* 'go slowly').

lag[2] ▶ verb (**lagged**, **lagging**) [with obj.] (usu. **be lagged**) enclose or cover (a boiler, pipes, etc.) with material that provides heat insulation: [as adj. **lagged**] *a lagged hot-water tank.*
– DERIVATIVES **lagger** noun.
– ORIGIN late 19th cent.: from earlier *lag* 'piece of insulating cover'.

lag[3] Brit. informal ▶ noun a person who has been frequently convicted and sent to prison: *both old lags were sentenced to ten years' imprisonment.*
▶ verb (**lagged**, **lagging**) [with obj.] archaic arrest or send to prison.
– ORIGIN late 16th cent. (as a verb in the sense 'carry off, steal'): of unknown origin. Current senses date from the 19th century.

lagan /ˈlag(ə)n/ ▶ noun [mass noun] archaic (in legal contexts) goods or wreckage lying on the bed of the sea.
– ORIGIN mid 16th cent.: from Old French, perhaps of Scandinavian origin and related to **LAY**[1].

lagar /laˈɡɑː/ ▶ noun (pl. **lagares**) (in Spain and Portugal) a large, typically stone trough in which grapes are trodden.
– ORIGIN Spanish, from Latin *lacus*, denoting a vat for freshly pressed wine.

Lag b'Omer /lɑːɡ ˈbəʊmə/ ▶ noun a Jewish festival held on the 33rd day of the Omer (the period between Passover and Pentecost), traditionally regarded as celebrating the end of a plague in the 2nd century.
– ORIGIN from Hebrew *lāg* (pronunciation of the letters L (*lamed*) and G (*gimel*) symbolizing 33) + *bā* 'in the' + *ʿōmer* (see **OMER**).

lagena /ləˈdʒiːnə/ ▶ noun (pl. **lagenae** /-niː/) Zoology an extension of the saccule of the ear in some vertebrates, corresponding to the cochlear duct in mammals.
– ORIGIN late 19th cent.: from Latin, literally 'flagon', from Greek *lagunos*.

lager ▶ noun [mass noun] a kind of beer, effervescent and light in colour and body.
– ORIGIN mid 19th cent.: from German *Lagerbier* 'beer brewed for keeping', from *Lager* 'storehouse'. Compare with **LAAGER**, **LAIR**[1], and **LEAGUER**[2].

Lagerlöf /ˈlɑːɡələːf/, Selma (Ottiliana Lovisa) (1858–1940), Swedish novelist. She made her name with *Gösta Berlings Saga* (1891), and was the first woman to be the sole winner of a Nobel Prize (Literature, 1909).

lager lout ▶ noun Brit. informal a young man who regularly behaves in an offensive way, typically as a result of excessive drinking.

laggard /ˈlaɡəd/ ▶ noun a person who makes slow progress and falls behind others: *staff were under enormous pressure and there was no time for laggards.*
▶ adjective slower than desired or expected: *a bell to summon laggard children to school.*
– DERIVATIVES **laggardly** adjective & adverb, **laggardness** noun.
– ORIGIN early 18th cent. (as an adjective): from **LAG**[1].

lagged ▶ adjective Economics showing a delayed effect: *a lagged measure of unemployment.*

lagging ▶ noun [mass noun] material providing heat insulation for a boiler, pipes, etc.

– ORIGIN mid 19th cent.: from **LAG**[2].

La Gioconda /ˌla dʒɪəˈkɒndə/ another name for **MONA LISA**.

lagniappe /laˈnjap/ ▶ noun N. Amer. something given as a bonus or gratuity.
– ORIGIN Louisiana French, from Spanish *la ñapa*.

Lagomorpha /ˈlaɡəˌmɔːfə/ Zoology an order of mammals that comprises the hares, rabbits, and pikas. They are distinguished by the possession of double incisor teeth, and were formerly placed with the rodents.
– DERIVATIVES **lagomorph** noun & adjective.
– ORIGIN modern Latin (plural), from Greek *lagōs* 'hare' + *morphē* 'form'.

lagoon ▶ noun a stretch of salt water separated from the sea by a low sandbank or coral reef.
■the enclosed water of an atoll. ■ N. Amer. & Austral./NZ a small freshwater lake near a larger lake or river. ■ an artificial pool for the treatment of effluent or to accommodate an overspill from surface drains during heavy rain.
– DERIVATIVES **lagoonal** adjective.
– ORIGIN early 17th cent.: from Italian and Spanish *laguna*, from Latin *lacuna* (see **LACUNA**).

Lagos /ˈleɪɡɒs/ the chief city of Nigeria, a port on the Gulf of Guinea; pop. 1,347,000 (1992). Originally a centre of the slave trade, it became capital of the newly independent Nigeria in 1960. It was replaced as capital by Abuja in 1991.

Lagrange /laˈɡrɒ̃ʒ, French laɡrɑ̃ʒ/, Joseph Louis, Comte de (1736–1813), Italian-born French mathematician. He is remembered for his proof that every positive integer can be expressed as a sum of at most four squares, and for his work on mechanics and its application to the description of planetary and lunar motion.

Lagrangian point /ləˈɡrɒ̃ʒɪən/ ▶ noun one of five points in the plane of orbit of one body around another (e.g. the moon around the earth) at which a small third body can remain stationary with respect to both.

lah (also **la**) ▶ noun Music (in tonic sol-fa) the sixth note of a major scale.
■the note A in the fixed-doh system.
– ORIGIN Middle English: representing (as an arbitrary name for the note) the first syllable of Latin *labii*, taken from a Latin hymn (see **SOLMIZATION**).

La Habana /la aˈβana/ Spanish name for **HAVANA**[1].

lahar /ˈlɑːhɑː/ ▶ noun Geology a destructive mudflow on the slopes of a volcano.
– ORIGIN 1920s: from Javanese.

lah-di-dah ▶ noun & exclamation variant spelling of **LA-DI-DA**.

Lahnda /ˈlɑːndə/ ▶ noun [mass noun] an Indic language of the western Punjab and adjacent areas of Pakistan, with some 58 million speakers. It is sometimes classified as a dialect of Punjabi.
▶ adjective of or relating to this language.
– ORIGIN early 20th cent.: from Punjabi *lahandā*, literally 'western'.

Lahore /ləˈhɔː/ the capital of Punjab province and second largest city of Pakistan, situated near the border with India; pop. 3,200,000 (est. 1991).

Lahu /lɑːˈhuː/ ▶ noun (pl. same or **Lahus**) **1** a member of an indigenous people of SW China and Laos.
2 [mass noun] the Tibeto-Burman language of this people.
▶ adjective of or relating to the Lahu or their language.
– ORIGIN the name in Lahu.

Laibach /ˈlaɪbax/ German name for **LJUBLJANA**.

laic /ˈleɪɪk/ formal ▶ adjective non-clerical; lay.
▶ noun a layperson; a non-cleric.
– DERIVATIVES **laical** adjective, **laically** adverb.
– ORIGIN mid 16th cent.: from late Latin *laicus* (see **LAY**[2]).

laicity /leɪˈɪsɪti/ ▶ noun [mass noun] formal the status or influence of the laity.

laicize /ˈleɪɪsʌɪz/ (also **-ise**) ▶ verb [with obj.] formal withdraw clerical character, control, or status from (someone or something): *when his priestly vocation no longer satisfied him he had asked to be laicized.*
– DERIVATIVES **laicism** noun, **laicization** noun.

laid past and past participle of **LAY**[1].

laid-back ▶ adjective informal relaxed and easy-going: *he was being very laid-back about it all.*

laid paper ▶ noun [mass noun] paper that has a finely ribbed appearance. Compare with **WOVE PAPER**.

lain past participle of **LIE**[1].

Laing /laŋ/, R. D. (1927–89), Scottish psychiatrist; full name *Ronald David Laing*. He became famous for his controversial views on madness and in particular on schizophrenia, linking what society calls insanity with politics and family structure.

lair[1] ▶ noun a wild animal's resting place, especially one which is well hidden.
■a secret or private place in which a person seeks concealment or seclusion.
– ORIGIN Old English *leger* 'resting-place, bed', of Germanic origin; related to Dutch *leger* 'bed, camp' and German *Lager* 'storehouse', also to **LIE**[1]. Compare with **LAAGER**, **LAGER**, and **LEAGUER**[2].

lair[2] Austral./NZ informal ▶ noun a flashily dressed man who enjoys showing off.
▶ verb [no obj.] dress or behave in a flashy manner: *some of us laired up in Assam silk suits.*
– DERIVATIVES **lairy** adjective.
– ORIGIN 1930s: back-formation from *lairy* (earlier as Cockney slang in the sense 'knowing, conceited'), alteration of **LEERY**.

lairage /ˈlɛːrɪdʒ/ ▶ noun a place where cattle or sheep may be rested on the way to market or slaughter.

laird /lɛːd/ ▶ noun (in Scotland) a person who owns a large estate.
– DERIVATIVES **lairdship** noun.
– ORIGIN late Middle English: Scots form of **LORD**.

laissez-aller /ˌlɛseɪˈaleɪ, French leseale/ ▶ noun [mass noun] absence of restraint; unconstrained freedom.
– ORIGIN French, literally 'allow to go'.

laissez-faire /ˌlɛseɪˈfɛː, French lɛsefɛʀ/ ▶ noun [mass noun] a policy or attitude of leaving things to take their own course, without interfering.
■Economics abstention by governments from interfering in the workings of the free market: [as modifier] *laissez-faire capitalism.*
– DERIVATIVES **laisser-faireism** noun.
– ORIGIN French, literally 'allow to do'.

laissez-passer /ˌlɛseɪˈpaseɪ, French lɛsepase/ ▶ noun a document allowing the holder to pass; a permit.
– ORIGIN French, literally 'allow to pass'.

laissez vibrer /ˌlɛse ˈviːbreɪ, French lɛse vibʀe/ ▶ imperative verb a musical instruction used to indicate that a note made by striking or plucking should be allowed to fade away without damping.
– ORIGIN French, literally 'allow to vibrate'.

laity /ˈleɪɪti/ ▶ noun [usu. treated as pl.] (**the laity**) lay people, as distinct from the clergy.
■ordinary people, as distinct from professionals or experts.
– ORIGIN late Middle English: from **LAY**[2] + **-ITY**.

Laius /ˈlaɪəs/ Greek Mythology a king of Thebes, the father of Oedipus and husband of Jocasta.

lake[1] ▶ noun a large area of water surrounded by land: *boys were swimming in the lake* | [in names] *Lake Victoria.*
■a pool of liquid: *the fish was served in a bright lake of spicy carrot sauce.* ■ [with modifier] figurative a large surplus of a liquid commodity: *the EU wine lake.* ■ (**the Lakes**) another name for the **LAKE DISTRICT**.
– DERIVATIVES **lakelet** noun.
– ORIGIN late Old English (denoting a pond or pool), from Old French *lac*, from Latin *lacus* 'basin, pool, lake'.

lake[2] ▶ noun [often with modifier] an insoluble pigment made by combining a soluble organic dye and an insoluble mordant.
■[mass noun] a purplish-red pigment of this kind, originally one made with lac.
– ORIGIN early 17th cent.: variant of **LAC**[1].

Lake Albert, Lake Baikal, etc. see **ALBERT, LAKE; BAIKAL, LAKE,** etc.

Lake District a region of lakes and mountains in Cumbria.

lake dwelling ▶ noun a prehistoric hut built on piles driven into the bed or shore of a lake.
– DERIVATIVES **lake-dweller** noun.

Lakeland another term for **LAKE DISTRICT**.

Lakeland terrier ▶ noun a terrier of a small stocky breed originating in the Lake District.

Lake of the Woods a lake on the border between Canada and the US, to the west of the Great Lakes.

Lake Poets (also **Lake School**) the poets Samuel Taylor Coleridge, Robert Southey, and William Wordsworth, who lived in and were inspired by the Lake District.

laker ▶ noun N. Amer. informal **1** a lake trout.
2 a ship constructed for sailing on the Great Lakes.

lakeside ▶ noun the land adjacent to a lake.

lake trout ▶ noun any of a number of fishes of the salmon family, which live in large lakes and are highly prized as a game fish and as food:
● a European brown trout of a large race. ● a North American charr (*Salvelinus namaycush*, family Salmonidae).

lakh /lak, lɑːk/ ▶ noun (also **lac**) Indian a hundred thousand: *they fixed the price at five lakhs of rupees.*
– ORIGIN via Hindi from Sanskrit *laksa*.

Lakonia variant spelling of **LACONIA**.

Lakota /ləˈkəʊtə/ ▶ noun (pl. same or **Lakotas**) **1** a member of an American Indian people of western South Dakota (also called **Teton Sioux**).
2 [mass noun] the Siouan language of this people, with about 6,000 speakers.
▶ adjective of or relating to this people or their language.
– ORIGIN the name in Lakota, related to the word **DAKOTA**[1].

laksa /ˈlɑːksə/ ▶ noun [mass noun] a Malaysian dish of Chinese origin, consisting of rice noodles served in a curry sauce or hot soup.
– ORIGIN Malay.

Lakshadweep /lakˈʃadwiːp, ˌlʌkʃədˈwiːp/ a group of islands off the Malabar Coast of SW India, constituting a Union Territory in India; pop. 51,680 (1991); capital, Kavaratti. The group consists of the Laccadive, Minicoy, and Amindivi Islands.

Lakshmi /ˈlʌkʃmi/ Hinduism the goddess of prosperity, consort of Vishnu. She assumes different forms (e.g. Radha, Sita) in order to accompany her husband in his various incarnations.

la-la land ▶ noun [mass noun] N. Amer. informal Los Angeles or Hollywood, especially with regard to the lifestyle and attitudes of those living there or associated with it.
■ a fanciful state or dreamworld.
– ORIGIN *la-la*, reduplication of LA (i.e. Los Angeles).

lalapalooza ▶ noun variant spelling of **LOLLAPALOOZA**.

laldy /ˈlaldi/ ▶ noun [mass noun] Scottish a beating.
– PHRASES **give it laldy** do something with vigour or enthusiasm.
– ORIGIN late 19th cent.: perhaps imitative, or from Old English *lǽl* 'whip, weal'.

Lalique /laˈliːk/, René (1860–1945), French jeweller, famous for his art nouveau brooches and combs and his decorative glassware.

Lallans /ˈlalənz/ ▶ noun [mass noun] a distinctive Scottish literary form of English, based on standard older Scots.
▶ adjective of, in, or relating to this language.
– ORIGIN early 18th cent. (also, as an adjective, *Lallan*): Scots variant of *Lowlands*, with reference to a central Lowlands dialect.

lallation /laˈleɪʃ(ə)n/ ▶ noun [mass noun] imperfect speech, especially the repetition of meaningless sounds by babies.
■ the pronunciation of *r* as *l*.
– ORIGIN mid 17th cent.: from Latin *lallatio(n)-*, from *lallare* 'sing a lullaby'.

lallygag /ˈlaligag/ ▶ verb variant spelling of **LOLLYGAG**.

La Louvière /ˌla luːˈvɪɛː, French la luvjɛʁ/ an industrial city in SW Belgium, in the province of Hainaut west of Charleroi; pop. 76,430 (1991).

Lam. ▶ abbreviation for Lamentations (in biblical references).

lam[1] ▶ verb (**lammed**, **lamming**) [with obj.] informal hit (someone) hard: *I'll come over and lam you in the mouth in a minute.*
■ [no obj.] (**lam into**) attack: *they surged up and down in their riot gear, lamming into anyone in their path.*
– ORIGIN late 16th cent.: perhaps of Scandinavian origin and related to Norwegian and Danish *lamme* 'paralyse'.

lam[2] N. Amer. informal ▶ noun (in phrase **on the lam**) in flight, especially from the police: *he went on the lam and is living under a false name.*
▶ verb (**lammed**, **lamming**) [no obj.] escape; flee.

– ORIGIN late 19th cent.: from **LAM**[1].

lama /ˈlɑːmə/ ▶ noun **1** an honorific title applied to a spiritual leader in Tibetan Buddhism, whether a reincarnate lama (such as the Dalai Lama) or one who has earned the title in life.
2 a Tibetan or Mongolian Buddhist monk.
– ORIGIN mid 17th cent.: from Tibetan *bla-ma* (the initial *b* being silent), literally 'superior one'.

Lamaism /ˈlɑːməˌɪz(ə)m/ ▶ noun [mass noun] the system of doctrine and observances inculcated and maintained by lamas; Tibetan Buddhism.
– DERIVATIVES **Lamaist** noun & adjective.

Lamarck /laˈmɑːk, French lamaʁk/, Jean Baptiste de (1744–1829), French naturalist. He was an early proponent of organic evolution, although his theory is not widely accepted today. He suggested that species could have evolved from each other by small changes in their structure, and that the mechanism of such change (not now generally considered possible) was that characteristics acquired in order to survive could be passed on to offspring.
– DERIVATIVES **Lamarckian** noun & adjective, **Lamarckism** noun.

Lamartine /ˌlamɑːˈtiːn, French lamaʁtin/, Alphonse Marie Louis de (1790–1869), French poet, statesman, and historian. He was Minister of Foreign Affairs in the provisional government following the Revolution of 1848. Notable works: *Méditations poétiques* (1820).

lamasery /ˈlɑːməs(ə)ri, ləˈmɑːs(ə)ri/ ▶ noun (pl. **-ies**) a monastery of lamas.

Lamaze /ləˈmɑːz, laˈmaz/ ▶ adjective [attrib.] relating to a method of childbirth involving exercises and breathing control to give pain relief without drugs.
– ORIGIN 1950s: from the name of Fernand *Lamaze* (1891–1957), French physician.

Lamb, Charles (1775–1834), English essayist and critic. Together with his sister Mary he wrote *Tales from Shakespeare* (1807). Other notable works: *Essays of Elia* (1823).

lamb ▶ noun a young sheep.
■ [mass noun] the flesh of such young sheep as food.
■ figurative used as the epitome of meekness, gentleness, or innocence: *to her amazement, he accepted her decision like a lamb.* ■ used to describe or address someone regarded with affection or pity, especially a young child: *the poor lamb is very upset.* ■ (**the Lamb**) short for LAMB OF GOD.
▶ verb [no obj.] (of a ewe) give birth to lambs.
■ [with obj.] tend (ewes) at lambing time.
– PHRASES **in lamb** (of a ewe) pregnant. **like a lamb to the slaughter** as a helpless victim.
– DERIVATIVES **lamber** noun, **lamblike** adjective.
– ORIGIN Old English, of Germanic origin; related to Dutch *lam* and German *Lamm*.
▶ **lamb someone/thing down** Austral. **1** tend (ewes) at lambing time. **2** informal encourage (someone) to squander their money, especially on alcohol: *Pitt had been lambed down at the Pig and Whistle.* ■ squander (money) in such a way.

lambada /lamˈbɑːdə/ ▶ noun a fast erotic Brazilian dance which couples perform with their stomachs touching.
– ORIGIN 1980s: Portuguese, literally 'a beating', from *lambar* 'to beat'.

lambaste /lamˈbeɪst/ (also **lambast** /-ˈbast/) ▶ verb [with obj.] criticize (someone or something) harshly: *they lambasted the report as a gross distortion of the truth.*
– ORIGIN mid 17th cent. (in the sense 'beat, thrash'): from **LAM**[1] + **BASTE**[3]. The current sense dates from the late 19th cent.

lambda /ˈlamdə/ ▶ noun the eleventh letter of the Greek alphabet (Λ, λ), transliterated as 'l'.
■ (**Lambda**) [followed by Latin genitive] Astronomy the eleventh star in a constellation: *Lambda Tauri.* ■ Biology a type of bacteriophage virus used in genetic research: [as modifier] *lambda phage.* ■ Anatomy the point at the back of the skull where the parietal bones and the occipital bone meet. ■ (λ) Biochemistry denoting one of the two types of light polypeptide chain present in all immunoglobulin molecules (the other being kappa).
▶ symbol for ■ (λ) wavelength. ■ (λ) Astronomy celestial longitude.
– ORIGIN Greek.

lambdoid /ˈlamdɔɪd/ ▶ adjective resembling the Greek letter lambda in form.
■ Anatomy of or denoting the suture near the back of the skull, which connects the parietal bones with the occipital.
– DERIVATIVES **lambdoidal** adjective.

lambent /ˈlamb(ə)nt/ ▶ adjective poetic/literary (of light or fire) glowing, gleaming, or flickering with a soft radiance: *the magical, lambent light of the north.*
– DERIVATIVES **lambency** noun, **lambently** adverb.
– ORIGIN mid 17th cent.: from Latin *lambent-* 'licking', from the verb *lambere*.

Lambert, (Leonard) Constant (1905–51), English composer, conductor, and critic. He wrote the music for the ballet *Romeo and Juliet* (1926) and the jazz work *The Rio Grande* (1929), later becoming musical director of Sadler's Wells (1930–47).

lambert /ˈlambət/ ▶ noun a former unit of luminance, equal to the emission or reflection of one lumen per square centimetre.
– ORIGIN early 20th cent.: named after Johann H. *Lambert* (1728–77), German physicist.

Lambeth a borough of inner London, on the south bank of the Thames; pop. 220,100 (1991).

Lambeth Conference ▶ noun an assembly of bishops from the Anglican Communion, usually held every ten years (since 1867) at Lambeth Palace and presided over by the Archbishop of Canterbury.

Lambeth Palace a palace in the London borough of Lambeth, the residence of the Archbishop of Canterbury since 1197.

Lambeth Walk ▶ noun a social dance with a walking step, popular in the late 1930s.
– ORIGIN created for the revue *Me and My Girl* and named after a street in Lambeth.

lambing ▶ noun [mass noun] the birth of lambs on a farm: *lambing begins in mid January.*

lambkin ▶ noun a small or young lamb.
■ used as a term of endearment for a young child.

Lamb of God ▶ noun a title of Jesus Christ (see John 1:29). Compare with **AGNUS DEI**.

lambrequin /ˈlambrɪkɪn/ ▶ noun **1** N. Amer. a short piece of decorative drapery hung over the top of a door or window or draped from a shelf or mantelpiece.
2 a cloth covering the back of a medieval knight's helmet, represented in heraldry as the mantling.
– ORIGIN early 18th cent. (in sense 2): from French, from the Dutch diminutive of *lamper* 'veil'.

Lambrusco /lamˈbruskəʊ/ ▶ noun [mass noun] a variety of wine grape grown in the Emilia-Romagna region of North Italy.
■ a sparkling red wine made from this grape. ■ a red or white wine of a similar kind produced elsewhere.
– ORIGIN Italian, literally 'grape of the wild vine'.

lamb's ears ▶ plural noun [usu. treated as sing.] a SW Asian plant of the mint family, which has grey-green woolly leaves and is cultivated as an ornamental, particularly for ground cover.
● *Stachys byzantina*, family Labiatae.

lamb's fry ▶ noun [mass noun] lamb's offal as food, in particular:
■ Brit. lamb's testicles. ■ Austral. lamb's liver.

lambskin ▶ noun [mass noun] prepared skin from a lamb with the wool on or as leather: [as modifier] *lambskin gloves.*

lamb's lettuce ▶ noun [mass noun] a small blue-flowered herbaceous plant of dry soils, native to Europe and the Mediterranean and sometimes used in salad. Also called **CORN SALAD**.
● *Valerianella locusta*, family Valerianaceae.

lamb's quarter (also **lamb's quarters**) ▶ noun North American term for **FAT HEN**.

lamb's-tails ▶ plural noun Brit. catkins from the hazel tree.

lamb's tongue ▶ noun another term for **LAMB'S EARS**.

lambswool ▶ noun [mass noun] fine wool from a young sheep, used to make knitted garments, blankets, etc. with a soft handle.

lame ▶ adjective **1** (of a person or animal) unable to walk without difficulty as the result of an injury or illness affecting the leg or foot: *his horse went lame.*
■ (of a leg or foot) affected in this way.
2 (of an explanation or excuse) unconvincingly feeble: *the TV licensing teams hear a lot of lame excuses.*
■ (of something intended to be entertaining) uninspiring and dull. ■ (of a person) naive or inept, especially socially: *anyone who doesn't know that is*

obviously lame. ■(of verse or metrical feet) halting; metrically defective.
▶**verb** [with obj.] make (a person or animal) lame: *he was badly lamed during the expedition.*
– DERIVATIVES **lamely** adverb, **lameness** noun.
– ORIGIN Old English *lama*, of Germanic origin, related to Dutch *lam* and German *lahm*.

lamé /ˈlɑːmeɪ/ ▶**noun** [mass noun] fabric with interwoven gold or silver threads.
▶**adjective** (of fabric or a garment) having such threads.
– ORIGIN 1920s: French, from Latin *lamina* (see **LAMINA**).

lamebrain ▶**noun** informal a stupid person.
– DERIVATIVES **lamebrained** adjective.

lame dog ▶**noun** a person who is in need or who is the object of charity.

lame duck ▶**noun** an ineffectual or unsuccessful person or thing: *the British crew are no longer the lame ducks of the Olympic team.*
■N. Amer. an official (especially the President) in the final period of office, after the election of a successor: [as modifier] *a lame-duck administration.*

lamella /ləˈmɛlə/ ▶**noun** (pl. **lamellae** /-liː/) a thin layer, membrane, scale, or plate-like tissue or part, especially in bone tissue.
■Botany a membranous fold in a chloroplast.
– DERIVATIVES **lamellar** adjective, **lamellate** adjective, **lamelliform** adjective, **lamellose** adjective.
– ORIGIN late 17th cent.: from Latin, diminutive of *lamina* 'thin plate'.

lamellibranch /ləˈmɛlɪbraŋk/ ▶**noun** another term for **BIVALVE**.
– ORIGIN mid 19th cent.: from modern Latin *Lamellibranchia* (former class name), from Latin *lamella* (diminutive of *lamina* 'thin plate') + Greek *brankhia* 'gills'.

lamellicorn /ləˈmɛlɪkɔːn/ ▶**noun** former term for **SCARABAEOID**.
– ORIGIN mid 19th cent.: from modern Latin *Lamellicornia* (former taxonomic name), from Latin *lamella* 'thin plate' + *cornu* 'horn'.

lamellipodium /ləˌmɛlɪˈpəʊdɪəm/ ▶**noun** (pl. **lamellipodia**) Zoology a flattened extension of a cell, by which it moves over or adheres to a surface.
– DERIVATIVES **lamellipodial** adjective.
– ORIGIN 1970s: from **LAMELLA**, on the pattern of *pseudopodium*.

lament ▶**noun** a passionate expression of grief or sorrow: *his mother's night-long laments for his father* | [mass noun] *a song full of lament and sorrow.*
■a song, piece of music, or poem expressing such emotions: *the piper played a lament.* ■ an expression of regret or disappointment; a complaint: *there were constant laments about the conditions of employment.*
▶**verb** [with obj.] mourn (a person's loss or death): *he was lamenting the death of his infant daughter.*
■[no obj.] (**lament for/over**) express one's grief passionately about: *the women wept and lamented over him.* ■ [reporting verb] express regret or disappointment over something considered unsatisfactory, unreasonable, or unfair: [with obj.] *she lamented the lack of shops in the town* | [with direct speech] *'We could have won,' lamented the England captain.*
– DERIVATIVES **lamentation** noun, **lamenter** noun.
– ORIGIN late Middle English (as a verb): from French *lamenter* or Latin *lamentari*, from *lamenta* (plural) 'weeping, wailing'.

lamentable /ˈlaməntəb(ə)l/ ▶**adjective** **1** (of circumstances or conditions) deplorably bad or unsatisfactory: *the facilities provided were lamentable, not merely basic but squalid.*
■(of an event, action, or attitude) unfortunate; regrettable: *her open prejudice showed lamentable immaturity.*
2 archaic full of or expressing sorrow or grief.
– DERIVATIVES **lamentably** adverb [as submodifier] *she was lamentably ignorant.*
– ORIGIN late Middle English (in the sense 'mournful', also 'pitiable, regrettable'): from Old French, or from Latin *lamentabilis*, from the verb *lamentari* (see **LAMENT**).

Lamentations (in full **the Lamentations of Jeremiah**) a book of the Bible telling of the desolation of Judah after the fall of Jerusalem in 586 BC.

lamented ▶**adjective** (often **the late lamented**) a conventional way of describing someone who has died or something that has been lost or ceased to exist: *the late and much lamented Leonard Bernstein.*

lamergeier ▶**noun** variant spelling of **LAMMERGEIER**.

lamia /ˈleɪmɪə/ ▶**noun** (pl. **lamias** or **lamiae** /-ɪiː/) a mythical monster supposed to have the body of a woman, and to prey on human beings and suck the blood of children.
– ORIGIN via Latin from Greek, denoting a carnivorous fish or mythical monster.

lamina /ˈlamɪnə/ ▶**noun** (pl. **laminae** /-niː/) technical a thin layer, plate, or scale of sedimentary rock, organic tissue, or other material.
– DERIVATIVES **laminose** adjective.
– ORIGIN mid 17th cent.: from Latin.

laminal /ˈlamɪn(ə)l/ ▶**adjective** Phonetics (of a consonant) formed with the blade of the tongue touching the alveolar ridge.
– ORIGIN 1950s: from **LAMINA** + **-AL**.

laminar /ˈlamɪnə/ ▶**adjective** **1** consisting of laminae.
2 Physics (of a flow) taking place along constant streamlines, not turbulent.

laminate ▶**verb** /ˈlamɪneɪt/ [with obj.] [often as adj. **laminated**] overlay (a flat surface) with a layer of plastic or some other protective material.
■manufacture by placing layer on layer. ■ split into layers or leaves. ■ beat or roll (metal) into thin plates.
▶**noun** /ˈlamɪnət/ a laminated structure or material, especially one made of layers fixed together to form a hard, flat, or flexible material.
■a small badge made of laminated plastic bearing the wearer's name and used for identification purposes.
▶**adjective** in the form of a lamina or laminae.
– DERIVATIVES **laminable** adjective, **lamination** noun, **laminator** noun.
– ORIGIN mid 17th cent.: from **LAMINA** + **-ATE**[2].

laminectomy /ˌlamɪˈnɛktəmi/ ▶**noun** (pl. **-ies**) a surgical operation to remove the back of one or more vertebrae, usually to give access to the spinal cord or to relieve pressure on nerves.

lamington /ˈlamɪŋtən/ ▶**noun** Austral./NZ a square of sponge cake dipped in melted chocolate and grated coconut.
– ORIGIN apparently from the name of Lord *Lamington*, Governor of Queensland (1895–1901).

laminin /ˈlamɪnɪn/ ▶**noun** [mass noun] Biochemistry a fibrous protein present in the basal lamina of the epithelia.

laminitis /ˌlamɪˈnʌɪtɪs/ ▶**noun** [mass noun] inflammation of sensitive layers of tissue (laminae) inside the hoof in horses and other animals. It is particularly prevalent in ponies feeding on rich spring grass and can cause extreme lameness.

lamium /ˈleɪmɪəm/ ▶**noun** (pl. **lamiums**) a plant of a genus which comprises the dead-nettles.
● Genus *Lamium*, family Labiatae.
– ORIGIN modern Latin, from Latin, from Greek *lamia* 'gaping mouth' (because of the shape of the flowers).

Lammas /ˈlaməs/ (also **Lammas Day**) ▶**noun** the first day of August, formerly observed as harvest festival.
– ORIGIN Old English *hlāfmæsse* (see **LOAF**[1], **MASS**), later interpreted as if it were from **LAMB** + **MASS**.

lammergeier /ˈlaməˌgʌɪə/ (also **lamergeier** or **lammergeyer**) ▶**noun** a large Old World vulture of mountainous country, with a wingspan of 3 m (10 ft) and dark beard-like feathers, noted for its habit of dropping bones from a height to break them. Also called **BEARDED VULTURE**.
● *Gypaetus barbatus*, family Accipitridae.
– ORIGIN early 19th cent.: from German *Lämmergeier*, from *Lämmer* (plural of *Lamm* 'lamb') + *Geier* 'vulture'.

lamp ▶**noun** a device for giving light, either one consisting of an electric bulb together with its holder and shade or cover, or one burning gas or a liquid fuel and consisting of a wick or mantle and a glass shade: *a table lamp.*
■an electrical device producing ultraviolet, infrared, or other radiation, used for therapeutic purposes. ■ poetic/literary a source of spiritual or intellectual inspiration.
▶**verb** **1** [with obj.] supply with lamps; illuminate: *inspectors can lamp the lines between the manholes for routine maintenance observations.*
■[no obj.] poetic/literary shine: *an evil fire out of their eyes came lamping.*
2 [no obj.] [often as noun **lamping**] hunt at night using lamps, especially for rabbits.
– DERIVATIVES **lamper** noun, **lampless** adjective.
– ORIGIN Middle English: via Old French from late Latin *lampada*, from Latin *lampas*, *lampad-* 'torch', from Greek.

lampas[1] /ˈlampəs/ ▶**noun** [mass noun] a condition of horses, in which there is swelling of the fleshy lining of the roof of the mouth behind the front teeth.
– ORIGIN early 16th cent.: from French, probably via French dialect from the Germanic base of the verb **LAP**[3].

lampas[2] /ˈlampəs/ ▶**noun** [mass noun] a patterned drapery and upholstery fabric similar to brocade, made of silk, cotton, or rayon, originally imitating Indian painted and resist-dyed textiles and later imported from China, Iran, and France.
– ORIGIN mid 19th cent.: from French *lampas*, *lampasse*, of unknown origin.

lampblack ▶**noun** [mass noun] a black pigment made from soot.

lamp chimney ▶**noun** a glass cylinder positioned over the wick of an oil lamp to encircle and provide a draught for the flame.

Lampedusa /ˌlampɪˈduːzə/, Giuseppe Tomasi de (1896–1957), Italian novelist. His only novel *Il Gattopardo* (*The Leopard*) was originally rejected by publishers but won worldwide acclaim on its posthumous publication in 1958.

lampern /ˈlampən/ ▶**noun** a lamprey of rivers and coastal waters in NW Europe.
● *Lampetra fluviatilis*, family Petromyzonidae.
– ORIGIN Middle English: from Old French *lampreion*, diminutive of *lampreie* 'lamprey'.

lamplight ▶**noun** [mass noun] the light cast from a lamp: *he was working in the stables by lamplight.*
– DERIVATIVES **lamplit** adjective.

lamplighter ▶**noun** historical a person employed to light street gaslights by hand.

lampoon /lamˈpuːn/ ▶**verb** [with obj.] publicly criticize (someone or something) by using ridicule, irony, or sarcasm: *the actor was lampooned by the British press.*
▶**noun** a speech or text criticizing someone or something in this way.
– DERIVATIVES **lampooner** noun, **lampoonist** noun.
– ORIGIN mid 17th cent.: from French *lampon*, said to be from *lampons* 'let us drink' (used as a refrain), from *lamper* 'gulp down', nasalized form of *laper* 'to lap (liquid)'.

lamp post ▶**noun** a tall pole with a light at the top; a street light.

lamprey /ˈlampri/ ▶**noun** (pl. **-eys**) an eel-like aquatic jawless vertebrate that has a sucker mouth with horny teeth and a rasping tongue. The adult is often parasitic, attaching itself to other fish and sucking their blood.
● Family Petromyzonidae: several genera and species.
– ORIGIN Middle English: from Old French *lampreie*, from medieval Latin *lampreda*, probably from Latin *lambere* 'to lick' + *petra* 'stone' (because the lamprey attaches itself to stones by its mouth).

lamprophyre /ˈlamprəˌfʌɪə/ ▶**noun** [mass noun] Geology a porphyritic igneous rock consisting of a fine-grained feldspathic groundmass with phenocrysts chiefly of biotite.
– ORIGIN late 19th cent.: from Greek *lampros* 'bright, shining' + *porphureos* 'purple'.

lampshade ▶**noun** a cover for a lamp, used to soften or direct its light.

lamp shell ▶**noun** a marine invertebrate which superficially resembles a bivalve mollusc but has two or more arms of ciliated tentacles (lophophore) that are extended for filter-feeding. Lamp shells are common as fossils. Also called ***brachiopod***.
● Phylum Brachiopoda: numerous groups in the Palaeozoic era but few surviving to the present day.
– ORIGIN mid 19th cent.: from its resemblance to an ancient oil lamp.

lamp standard ▶**noun** another term for **LAMP POST**.

LAN ▶**abbreviation for** local area network.

lanai /ləˈnʌɪ/ ▶**noun** (pl. **lanais**) a porch or veranda.
– ORIGIN Hawaiian.

Lanarkshire /ˈlanəkʃɪə, -ʃə/ a former county of SW central Scotland, now divided into the administrative regions of **North Lanarkshire** and **South Lanarkshire**.

Lancashire[1] /ˈlaŋkəʃɪə, -ʃə/ a county of NW

England, on the Irish Sea; administrative centre, Preston.

Lancashire² /ˈlaŋkəʃə/ ▶**noun** [mass noun] a mild white cheese with a crumbly texture.

Lancashire hotpot ▶**noun** a stew of meat, onion, and potato, typically covered with a layer of sliced potato.

Lancaster¹ /ˈlaŋkəstə/ a city in Lancashire, on the estuary of the River Lune; pop. 44,450 (1981). It was the county town and administrative centre of Lancashire until 1974.

Lancaster² /ˈlaŋkəstə/, Burt (1913–94), American film actor; full name *Burton Stephen Lancaster*. He starred in films such as *From Here to Eternity* (1953), *Elmer Gantry* (1960), for which he won an Oscar, and *Field of Dreams* (1989).

Lancaster, Duchy of an estate vested in the Crown, consisting of properties in Lancashire and elsewhere in England.

Lancaster, House of the English royal house descended from John of Gaunt, Duke of Lancaster, that ruled England from 1399 (Henry IV) until 1461 (the deposition of Henry VI) and again on Henry's brief restoration in 1470–1. With the red rose as its emblem it fought the Wars of the Roses with the House of York; Lancaster's descendants, the Tudors, eventually prevailed through Henry VII's accession to the throne in 1485.

Lancaster House Agreement an agreement which brought about the establishment of the independent state of Zimbabwe, reached in September 1979 at Lancaster House in London.

Lancastrian /laŋˈkastrɪən/ ▶**noun** **1** a native of Lancashire or Lancaster.
2 historical a follower of the House of Lancaster.
▶**adjective** of or relating to Lancashire or Lancaster, or the House of Lancaster.

lance ▶**noun** historical a long weapon with a wooden shaft and a pointed steel head, used by a horseman in charging.
■a similar weapon used in hunting fish or whales. ■ another term for **LANCER** (in sense 1). ■ [usu. with modifier] a metal pipe supplying a jet of oxygen to a furnace or to make a very hot flame for cutting. ■ a rigid tube at the end of a hose for pumping or spraying liquid.
▶**verb** [with obj.] Medicine prick or cut open with a lancet or other sharp instrument: figurative *the prime minister made it one of his priorities to* **lance the boil** *of corruption.*
■pierce with or as if with a lance: *the teenager had been lanced by a wooden splinter* | [no obj.] figurative *his eyes lanced right through her.* ■ [no obj., with adverbial of direction] move suddenly and quickly: *he lanced through Harlequins' midfield to score Swansea's lone try* | *pain lanced through her.* ■ [with obj. and adverbial of direction] poetic/literary fling; launch: *he affirms to have lanced darts at the sun.*
– ORIGIN Middle English: from Old French *lance* (noun), *lancier* (verb), from Latin *lancea* (noun).

lance bombardier ▶**noun** a rank of non-commissioned officer in an artillery regiment of the British army, corresponding to that of a lance corporal in the infantry.

lance corporal ▶**noun** a rank of non-commissioned officer in the British army, above private and below corporal.
– ORIGIN late 18th cent.: on the analogy of obsolete *lancepesade*, the lowest grade of non-commissioned officer, based on Italian *lancia spezzata* 'broken lance'.

lancejack ▶**noun** Brit. military slang a lance corporal or lance bombardier.

lancelet /ˈlɑːnslɪt/ ▶**noun** a small elongated marine invertebrate that resembles a fish but lacks jaws and obvious sense organs. Lancelets possess a notochord and are among the most primitive chordates.
• Subphylum Cephalochordata, phylum Chordata: several species, including amphioxus.
– ORIGIN mid 19th cent.: from the noun **LANCE** (because of its long narrow form) + **-LET**.

Lancelot /ˈlɑːnsələt, -lɒt/ (also **Launcelot** /ˈlɔːn-/) (in Arthurian legend) the most famous of Arthur's knights, lover of Queen Guinevere and father of Galahad.

lanceolate /ˈlɑːnsɪələt/ ▶**adjective** technical shaped like a lance head; of a narrow oval shape tapering to a point at each end: *the leaves are lanceolate.*
– ORIGIN mid 18th cent.: from late Latin *lanceolatus*, from Latin *lanceola*, diminutive of *lancea* 'a lance'.

lancer ▶**noun** **1** historical a soldier of a cavalry regiment armed with lances.
■(**Lancer**) a soldier belonging to a regiment that still retains this title: *the Queen's Royal Lancers.*
2 (**lancers**) [treated as sing.] a quadrille for eight or sixteen pairs.
– ORIGIN late 16th cent.: from French *lancier*, from *lance* 'a lance'.

lance sergeant ▶**noun** a rank in the Foot Guards equivalent to corporal.

lancet /ˈlɑːnsɪt/ ▶**noun** **1** a small, broad two-edged surgical knife or blade with a sharp point.
2 a lancet arch or window.
■[as modifier] shaped like a lancet arch: *a lancet clock.*
– DERIVATIVES **lanceted** adjective.
– ORIGIN late Middle English (also denoting a small lance): from Old French *lancette*, diminutive of *lance* 'a lance'.

lancet arch ▶**noun** an arch with an acutely pointed head.

lancetfish ▶**noun** (pl. same or **-fishes**) a long slender predatory fish with a large sail-like dorsal fin, living in the deeper waters of open oceans.
• Family Alepisauridae and genus *Alepisaurus*: two or three species.

lancet window ▶**noun** a high and narrow window with an acutely pointed head.

lancewood ▶**noun** any of a number of hardwood trees with tough elastic timber, in particular:
• a Caribbean tree (*Oxandra lanceolata*, family Annonaceae).
• a New Zealand tree (*Pseudopanax crassifolius*, family Araliaceae).

Lanchow /lanˈtʃaʊ/ variant of **LANZHOU**.

Lancs. ▶**abbreviation for** Lancashire.

Land /land, German lant/ ▶**noun** (pl. **Länder** /ˈlɛndə, German ˈlɛndɐ/) a province of Germany or Austria.
– ORIGIN German, literally 'land'.

land ▶**noun** **1** [mass noun] the part of the earth's surface that is not covered by water, as opposed to the sea or the air: *the reptiles lay their eggs on land* | *after four weeks at sea we sighted land.*
■[as modifier] living or travelling on land rather than in water or the air: *a land force.* ■ an expanse of land; an area of ground, especially in terms of its ownership or use: *the land north of the village* | *waste land* | (**lands**) *the Indians were wiped out as gold prospectors invaded their lands.* ■ (**the land**) ground or soil used as a basis for agriculture: *my family had worked the land for many years.* ■ [count noun] S. African an area of ground fenced off for cultivation; a field. [ORIGIN: from Dutch *land* 'piece of ground'.]
2 a country or state: *the valley is one of the most beautiful in the land* | *the lands of the Middle East* | *America, the land of political equality.*
■figurative a realm or domain: *you are living in a fantasy land.*
3 the space between the rifling-grooves in a gun.
▶**verb** **1** [with obj.] put ashore: *he landed his troops at Hastings.*
■[no obj.] go ashore; disembark: *the marines landed at a small fishing jetty.* ■ unload (goods) from a ship: *the fishing boats landed their catch at the port.* ■ bring (a fish) to land, especially with a net or hook. ■ informal succeed in obtaining or achieving (something desirable), especially in the face of strong competition: *she landed the starring role in a new film.* ■ (of a rugby player) succeed in scoring (a penalty, goal, etc.): *Walters landed a second penalty in the opening minute of the second half.*
2 [no obj.] come down through the air and alight on the ground: *we will be landing at Gatwick Airport in a few moments.*
■[with obj.] bring (an aircraft or spacecraft) to the ground or the surface of water, especially in a controlled way: *the co-pilot landed the plane.* ■ reach the ground after falling or jumping: *he leapt over the fence and landed nimbly on his feet.* ■ [with adverbial of place] (of an object) come to rest after falling or being thrown: *the plate landed in her lap.* ■ informal (of something unpleasant or unexpected) arrive suddenly: *there seemed to be more problems than ever landing on her desk this week.*
3 [with obj.] (**land someone in**) informal cause someone to be in (a difficult or unwelcome situation): *his exploits always landed him in trouble.*
■(**land someone with**) inflict (an unwelcome task or a difficult situation) on someone: *the mistake landed the company with a massive bill.*
4 [with obj.] informal inflict (a blow) on someone: *I won the fight without landing a single punch* | [with two objs] *I landed him one.*
– PHRASES **how the land lies** what the state of affairs is: *let's keep it to ourselves until we see how the land lies.* **in the land of the living** humorous alive or awake. **the land of Nod** humorous a state of sleep. [ORIGIN: punningly, with biblical allusion to the place name *Nod* (Gen. 4:16).] **land** (or **fall**) **on one's feet** have good luck or success: *after some ups and downs he has finally landed on his feet.* **live off the land** live on whatever food one can obtain by hunting, gathering, or subsistence farming.
– ORIGIN Old English, of Germanic origin; related to Dutch *land* and German *Land*.
▶**land up** **1** reach a place or destination: *the ship landed up on the south coast of Devon* | *I landed up in prison* **2** (**land up with**) end up with (a certain, usually unwelcome, situation): *I landed up with three broken ribs.*

Land Acts a series of British parliamentary acts concerning land tenure in Ireland, passed in 1870, 1881, 1903, and 1909, intended to give tenants greater security and further rights.

land agent ▶**noun** Brit. **1** a person employed to manage an estate on behalf of its owners.
2 a person who deals with the sale of land.
– DERIVATIVES **land agency** noun.

Landau /ˈlandɔː/, Lev (Davidovich) (1908–68), Soviet theoretical physicist, born in Russia. Active in many fields, Landau was awarded the Nobel Prize for Physics in 1962 for his work on the superfluidity and thermal conductivity of liquid helium.

landau /ˈlandɔː, -aʊ/ ▶**noun** a horse-drawn four-wheeled enclosed carriage with a removable front cover and a back cover that can be raised and lowered.
– ORIGIN mid 18th cent.: named after *Landau*, near Karlsruhe in Germany, where it was first made.

landaulet /ˌlandɔːˈlɛt, -də-/ ▶**noun** a small landau.
■chiefly historical a car with a folding hood over the rear seats.

land bank ▶**noun** **1** a large body of land held by a public or private organization for future development or disposal.
2 a bank whose main function is to provide loans for land purchase, especially by farmers.

land breeze ▶**noun** a breeze blowing towards the sea from the land, especially at night owing to the relative warmth of the sea. Compare with **SEA BREEZE**.

land bridge ▶**noun** a connection between two land masses, especially a prehistoric one that allowed humans and animals to colonize new territory before being cut off by the sea, as across the Bering Strait and the English Channel.

land crab ▶**noun** a crab that lives in burrows inland and migrates in large numbers to the sea to breed.
• Family Gecarcinidae: *Cardisoma* and other genera.

land drain ▶**noun** a drain made of porous or perforated piping and placed in a gravel-filled trench, used for subsoil drainage.

landed ▶**adjective** [attrib.] owning much land, especially through inheritance: *the landed aristocracy.*
■consisting of, including, or relating to such land: *the decline of landed estates* | *landed income.*

Länder plural form of **LAND**.

lander ▶**noun** a spacecraft designed to land on the surface of a planet or moon: *a lunar lander.* Compare with **ORBITER**.

landfall ▶**noun** **1** an arrival at land on a sea or air journey.
2 a collapse of a mass of land, especially one which blocks a route.

landfill ▶**noun** [mass noun] the disposal of refuse and other waste material by burying it and covering it over with soil, especially as a method of filling in and reclaiming excavated pits: [as modifier] *landfill sites.*
■waste material used to reclaim ground in this way. ■ [count noun] an area filled in by this process.

landform ▶**noun** a natural feature of the earth's surface.

land girl ▶**noun** historical (in the UK) a woman doing farm work, especially during the Second World War.

land grant ▶**noun** N. Amer. a grant of public land,

especially to an institution or to American Indians: [as modifier] *land grant colleges.*

landgrave /ˈlan(d)ɡreɪv/ ▶ noun historical a count having jurisdiction over a territory.
■ the title of certain German princes.
– ORIGIN late Middle English: from Middle Low German, from *land* 'land' + *grave* 'count' (used as a title).

landholder ▶ noun a person who owns land, especially one who either makes their living from it or rents it out to others.

landholding ▶ noun a piece of land owned or rented.
■ [mass noun] possession or rental of land.

landing ▶ noun 1 an instance of coming or bringing something to land, either from the air or from water: *we made a perfect landing at the airstrip.*
■ [mass noun] the action or process of doing this: *the landing of men on the moon.* ■ an act of unloading troops in enemy territory as part of a military operation: *the D-Day landings.* ■ (also **landing place**) a place where people and goods can be landed from a boat or ship: *the ferry landing.*
2 a level area at the top of a staircase or between one flight of stairs and another.

landing craft ▶ noun a boat specially designed for putting troops and military equipment ashore on a beach.

landing gear ▶ noun the undercarriage of an aircraft.

landing light ▶ noun (usu. **landing lights**) a bright lamp on an aircraft that is switched on prior to landing.
■ a light of a kind that is arranged in rows along each side of an aircraft runway.

landing net ▶ noun a net for landing a large fish which has been hooked.

landing pad ▶ noun a small area designed for helicopters to land on and take off from.

landing stage ▶ noun a platform, typically a floating one, on to which passengers from a boat disembark or cargo is unloaded.

landing strip ▶ noun an airstrip.

landlady ▶ noun (pl. **-ies**) a woman who lets land, a building, or an apartment to a tenant.
■ a woman who keeps lodgings, a boarding house, or (Brit.) a public house.

land law ▶ noun [mass noun] (also **land laws**) the law governing landed property.

Land League an Irish organization formed in 1879 to campaign for tenants' rights. Its techniques included the use of the boycott against anyone taking on a farm from which the tenant had been evicted. The Land Act of 1881 met many of the League's demands.

ländler /ˈlɛndlə/ ▶ noun an Austrian folk dance in triple time, a precursor of the waltz.
– ORIGIN late 19th cent.: German, from *Landl* 'Upper Austria'.

landless ▶ adjective (especially of an agricultural worker) owning no land.
– DERIVATIVES **landlessness** noun.

landline ▶ noun a conventional telecommunications connection by cable laid across land, typically either on poles or buried underground.

landlocked ▶ adjective (especially of a state) almost or entirely surrounded by land; having no coastline or seaport: *a midget state landlocked in the mountains.*
■ (of a lake) enclosed by land and having no navigable route to the sea. ■ (of a fish, especially a North American salmon) cut off from the sea in the past and now confined to fresh water.

landlord ▶ noun a man (in legal use also a woman) who lets land, a building, or an apartment to a tenant.
■ a man who keeps lodgings, a boarding house, or (Brit.) a public house.

landlordism ▶ noun [mass noun] the system whereby land (or property) is owned by landlords to whom tenants pay a fixed rent.

landlubber ▶ noun informal a person unfamiliar with the sea or sailing.

landmark ▶ noun 1 an object or feature of a landscape or town that is easily seen and recognized from a distance, especially one that

enables someone to establish their location: *the spire was once a landmark for ships sailing up the river.*
■ historical the boundary of an area of land, or an object marking this.
2 an event, discovery, or change marking an important stage or turning point in something: *the birth of a child is an important landmark in the lives of all concerned* | [as modifier] *a landmark decision.*

land mass ▶ noun a continent or other large body of land.

landmine ▶ noun an explosive mine laid on or just under the surface of the ground.

land mullet ▶ noun a large burrowing lizard of the skink family, with shiny fishlike scales, native to the coastal regions of eastern Australia.
● *Egernia major*, family Scincidae.

Land of Enchantment informal name for **NEW MEXICO**.

land office ▶ noun chiefly N. Amer. a government office recording dealings in public land.
– PHRASES **do a land-office business** N. Amer. informal do a lot of successful trading.

Land of Opportunity informal name for **ARKANSAS**.

Landor /ˈlandɔː/, Walter Savage (1775–1864), English poet and essayist. His works include the oriental epic poem *Gebir* (1798), and *Imaginary Conversations of Literary Men and Statesmen* (prose, 1824–8).

landowner ▶ noun a person who owns land, especially a large amount of land.
– DERIVATIVES **landownership** noun, **landowning** adjective & noun.

landplane ▶ noun an aircraft which can only operate from or alight on land.

landrace ▶ noun a pig of a large white breed, originally developed in Denmark.
– ORIGIN 1930s: from Danish.

landrail ▶ noun another term for **CORNCRAKE**.

land reform ▶ noun [mass noun] the statutory division of agricultural land and its re-allocation to landless people.

Land Registry a government department with which titles to or charges upon land must be registered.

Landsat a series of artificial satellites that monitor the earth's resources by photographing the surface at different wavelengths. The resulting images provide information about agriculture, geology, ecological changes, etc.

landscape ▶ noun 1 all the visible features of an area of countryside or land, often considered in terms of their aesthetic appeal: *the soft colours of the Northumbrian landscape* | *a bleak urban landscape.*
■ a picture representing an area of countryside: [as modifier] *a landscape painter.* ■ [mass noun] the genre of landscape painting. ■ figurative the distinctive features of a particular situation or intellectual activity: *the event transformed the political landscape.*
2 [as modifier] (of a page, book, or illustration, or the manner in which it is set or printed) wider than it is high. Compare with **PORTRAIT** (sense 2).
▶ verb [with obj.] (usu. **be landscaped**) improve the aesthetic appearance of (a piece of land) by changing its contours, adding ornamental features, or planting trees and shrubs: *the site has been tastefully landscaped* | [as mass noun **landscaping**] *the company spent £15,000 on landscaping.*
– DERIVATIVES **landscapist** noun.
– ORIGIN late 16th cent. (denoting a picture of natural scenery): from Middle Dutch *lantscap*, from *land* 'land' + *scap* (equivalent of **-SHIP**).

landscape architecture ▶ noun [mass noun] the art and practice of designing the outdoor environment, especially designing parks or gardens together with buildings and roads to harmonize with each other.
– DERIVATIVES **landscape architect** noun.

landscape gardening ▶ noun [mass noun] the art and practice of laying out grounds in a way which is ornamental or which imitates natural scenery.
– DERIVATIVES **landscape gardener** noun.

landscape history ▶ noun [mass noun] the history of the rural landscape, as determined from visible features, ecological and archaeological evidence, and documentary records.

land scrip ▶ noun see **SCRIP**¹ (sense 2).

Landseer /ˈlandsɪə/, Sir Edwin Henry (1802–73), English painter and sculptor. He is best known for

his animal subjects such as *The Monarch of the Glen* (1851). As a sculptor he is chiefly remembered for the bronze lions in Trafalgar Square (1867).

Land's End a rocky promontory in SW Cornwall, which forms the westernmost point of England. The approximate distance by road from Land's End to John o'Groats is 1,400 km (876 miles).

landside ▶ noun the side of an airport terminal to which the general public has unrestricted access.

landsknecht /ˈlan(d)sknɛkt/ ▶ noun historical a member of a class of mercenary soldiers in the German and other continental armies in the 16th and 17th centuries.
– ORIGIN from German *Landsknecht*, literally 'soldier of the land'.

landslide ▶ noun 1 the sliding down of a mass of earth or rock from a mountain or cliff.
2 an overwhelming majority of votes for one party in an election: *winning the election by a landslide.*

landslip ▶ noun chiefly Brit. another term for **LANDSLIDE** (in sense 1).

Landsmål /ˈlantsmɔːl/ ▶ noun another term for **NYNORSK**.
– ORIGIN Norwegian, literally 'language of the land'.

landsman ▶ noun (pl. **-men**) a person unfamiliar with the sea or sailing.

Landsteiner /ˈlandstʌɪnə/, Karl (1868–1943), Austrian-born American physician. In 1930 Landsteiner was awarded a Nobel Prize for devising the ABO system of classifying blood. He was also the first to describe the rhesus factor in blood.

land tax ▶ noun [mass noun] tax levied on landed property.

landtie ▶ noun a beam or piece of masonry supporting a wall or other vertical structure by connecting it with the ground.

landward ▶ adverb (also **landwards**) towards land: *the ship turned landward.*
▶ adjective facing towards land as opposed to sea: *the landward side of the road.*

land yacht ▶ noun a wind-powered wheeled vehicle with sails, used for recreation and sport.

lane ▶ noun 1 a narrow road, especially in a rural area: *she drove along the winding lane.*
■ [in place names] a street in an urban area: *Drury Lane.* ■ Astronomy a dark streak or band which shows up against a bright background, especially in a spiral galaxy.
2 a division of a road marked off with painted lines and intended to separate single lines of traffic according to speed or direction: *the car accelerated and moved into the outside lane* | *a bus lane.*
■ each of a number of parallel strips of track or water for runners, rowers, or swimmers in a race: *she went into the final in lane three.* ■ a path or course prescribed for or regularly followed by ships or aircraft: *the shipping lanes of the South Atlantic.* ■ (in tenpin bowling) a long narrow strip of floor down which the ball is bowled. ■ Biochemistry each of a number of notional parallel strips in the gel of an electrophoresis plate, occupied by a single sample.
– PHRASES **it's a long lane that has no turning** proverb nothing goes on forever; change is inevitable.
– ORIGIN Old English, related to Dutch *laan*; of unknown ultimate origin.

Lang, Fritz (1890–1976), Austrian-born film director, resident in the US from 1933. He directed the silent dystopian film *Metropolis* (1927), making the transition to sound in 1931 with the thriller M. His later work included *The Big Heat* (1953).

Langland /ˈlaŋlənd/, William (*c.*1330–*c.*1400), English poet. He is best known for *Piers Plowman* (*c.*1367–70), a long allegorical poem which takes the form of a spiritual pilgrimage.

langlauf /ˈlaŋlaʊf/ ▶ noun [mass noun] cross-country skiing: [as modifier] *langlauf skiers.*
– ORIGIN 1920s: from German, literally 'long run'.

Langley, Samuel Pierpoint (1834–1906), American astronomer and aviation pioneer. He invented the bolometer (1879–81) and contributed to the design of early aircraft.

Langmuir /ˈlaŋmjʊə/, Irving (1881–1957), American chemist and physicist. His principal work was in surface chemistry, especially applied to catalysis. He also worked on high-temperature electrical discharges in gases and studied atomic structure.

Langmuir–Blodgett film /ˈblɒdʒɪt/ ▶ noun Chemistry a monomolecular layer of an organic

material which can be used to build extremely small electronic devices.
– ORIGIN named after **LANGMUIR**, and Katherine B. *Blodgett* (1898–1979), American physicist and chemist.

langosta /laŋˈɡɒstə/ ▶ noun chiefly US another term for **LANGOUSTE**.
– ORIGIN Spanish.

langouste /ˈlɒŋɡuːst/ ▶ noun a spiny lobster, especially when prepared and cooked.
– ORIGIN French, from Old Provençal *lagosta*, based on Latin *locusta* 'locust, crustacean'.

langoustine /ˈlɒŋɡustiːn/ ▶ noun another term for **NORWAY LOBSTER**, especially when prepared and cooked.
– ORIGIN French, from *langouste* (see **LANGOUSTE**).

langra /ˈlɑːŋɡrə, ˈlaŋɡrə/ ▶ noun a mango of a variety which has pale green skin when ripe.
– ORIGIN from Hindi *lāngra*.

lang syne /laŋ ˈsʌɪn/ Scottish archaic ▶ adverb in the distant past; long ago: *we talked of races run lang syne.*
▶ noun [mass noun] times gone by; the old days.
– ORIGIN early 16th cent.: from *lang*, Scots variant of **LONG**[1] + **SYNE**.

Langton, Stephen (*c.*1150–1228), English prelate, Archbishop of Canterbury 1207–15; 1218–28. A champion of the English Church, he was involved in the negotiations leading to the signing of Magna Carta.

Langtry /ˈlaŋtri/, Lillie (1853–1929), British actress; born *Emilie Charlotte le Breton*. She made her stage debut in 1881 and later became the mistress of the Prince of Wales, later Edward VII.

language ▶ noun 1 [mass noun] the method of human communication, either spoken or written, consisting of the use of words in a structured and conventional way: *a study of the way children learn language* | [as modifier] *language development.*
■ any non-verbal method of expression or communication: *body language.*
2 the system of communication used by a particular community or country: *the book was translated into twenty-five languages.*
■ Computing a system of symbols and rules for writing programs or algorithms.
3 [mass noun] the manner or style of a piece of writing or speech: *he explained the procedure in simple, everyday language.*
■ the phraseology and vocabulary of a certain profession, domain, or group of people: *legal language.* ■ (usu. as **bad/foul/strong language**) coarse, crude, or offensive language: *strong language.*
– PHRASES **speak the same language** understand one another as a result of shared opinions or values.
– ORIGIN Middle English: from Old French *langage*, based on Latin *lingua* 'tongue'.

language area ▶ noun 1 Physiology the area of the cerebral cortex thought to be particularly involved in the processing of language: *the language areas of the left cerebral hemisphere.*
2 a region where a particular language is spoken.
3 an aspect of a language or its grammar or vocabulary: *language areas with which students are already familiar.*

language engineering ▶ noun [mass noun] any of a variety of computing procedures that use tools such as machine-readable dictionaries and sentence parsers in order to process natural languages for industrial applications such as speech recognition and speech synthesis.

language laboratory ▶ noun a room equipped with audio and visual equipment, such as tape and video recorders, for learning a foreign language.

language of flowers ▶ noun [mass noun] a set of symbolic meanings attached to different flowers when they are given or arranged.

langue /lɒ̃ɡ/ ▶ noun (pl. pronounced same) Linguistics a language viewed as an abstract system used by a speech community, in contrast to the actual linguistic behaviour of individuals. Contrasted with **PAROLE**.
– ORIGIN 1920s: French, from Latin *lingua* 'language, tongue'.

langued /ˈlaŋd/ ▶ adjective Heraldry having the tongue of a specified tincture.
– ORIGIN late Middle English: from French *langué* 'tongued' + **-ED**[2].

langue de chat /ˌlɒ̃ɡ də ˈʃɑː/ ▶ noun a very thin finger-shaped crisp biscuit or piece of chocolate.
– ORIGIN French, literally 'cat's tongue'.

Languedoc /ˌlɒ̃ɡ(ə)ˈdɒk, French lɑ̃ɡdɔk/ a former province of southern France, which extended from the Rhône valley to the northern foothills of the eastern Pyrenees.

langue d'oc /lɒ̃ɡ ˈdɒk, French lɑ̃ɡ dɔk/ ▶ noun [mass noun] the form of medieval French spoken south of the Loire, generally characterized by the use of *oc* to mean 'yes', and forming the basis of modern Provençal. Compare with **OCCITAN**.
– ORIGIN from Old French *langue* 'language' (from Latin *lingua* 'tongue'), *d'* (from *de* 'of'), and *oc* (from Latin *hoc*) 'yes'. Compare with **LANGUE D'OÏL**.

Languedoc-Roussillon /ˌruːsiːˈjɔ̃, French ʁusijɔ̃/ a region of southern France, on the Mediterranean coast, extending from the Rhône delta to the border with Spain.

langue d'oïl /lɒ̃ɡ ˈdɔɪl, French lɑ̃ɡ dɔjl/ ▶ noun [mass noun] the form of medieval French spoken north of the Loire, generally characterized by the use of *oïl* to mean 'yes', and forming the basis of modern French.
– ORIGIN from Old French *langue* 'language' (from Latin *lingua* 'tongue'), *d'* (from *de* 'of'), and *oïl* (from Latin *hoc ille*) 'yes'. Compare with **LANGUE D'OC**.

languid ▶ adjective 1 (of a person, manner, or gesture) displaying or having a disinclination for physical exertion or effort; very slow and relaxed: *his languid demeanour irritated her.*
■ (of an occasion or period of time) pleasantly lazy and peaceful: *the terrace was perfect for languid days in the Italian sun.*
2 weak or faint from illness or fatigue: *she was pale, languid, and weak, as if she had delivered a child.*
– DERIVATIVES **languidly** adverb, **languidness** noun.
– ORIGIN late 16th cent. (in sense 2): from French *languide* or Latin *languidus*, from *languere* (see **LANGUISH**).

languish ▶ verb [no obj.] 1 (of a person or other living thing) lose or lack vitality; grow weak or feeble: *plants may appear to be languishing simply because they are dormant.*
■ fail to make progress or be successful: *Kelso languish near the bottom of the Scottish First Division.* ■ archaic pine with love or grief: *she still languished after Richard.* ■ archaic assume or display a sentimentally tender or melancholy expression or tone: *when a visitor comes in, she smiles and languishes.*
2 be forced to remain in an unpleasant place or situation: *he has been languishing in a Mexican jail since 1974.*
– DERIVATIVES **languisher** noun, **languishingly** adverb, **languishment** noun (archaic).
– ORIGIN Middle English (in the sense 'become faint, feeble, or ill'): from Old French *languiss-*, lengthened stem of *languir* 'languish', from a variant of Latin *languere*, related to *laxus* 'loose, lax'.

languor /ˈlaŋɡə/ ▶ noun [mass noun] 1 the state or feeling, often pleasant, of tiredness or inertia: *he remembered the languor and warm happiness of those golden afternoons.*
2 an oppressive stillness of the air: *the afternoon was hot, quiet, and heavy with languor.*
– DERIVATIVES **languorous** adjective, **languorously** adverb.
– ORIGIN Middle English: via Old French from Latin, from *languere* (see **LANGUISH**). The original sense was 'illness, disease, distress', later 'faintness, lassitude'; current senses date from the 18th cent., when such lassitude became associated with a sometimes rather self-indulgent romantic yearning.

langur /ˈlaŋɡə, lanˈɡʊə/ ▶ noun a long-tailed arboreal Asian monkey with a characteristic loud call.
● *Presbytis* and other genera, family Cercopithecidae: several species. Compare with **LEAF MONKEY**.
– ORIGIN early 19th cent.: via Hindi from Sanskrit *lāṅgūla*.

lani ▶ noun variant spelling of **LARNEY**.

lank ▶ adjective 1 (of hair) long, limp, and straight.
■ (of a person) lanky.
2 S. African informal very numerous or plentiful: *come and share our braai—we've got lank meat.* [ORIGIN: perhaps from Afrikaans *geld lank* 'money galore'.]
■ very good; fantastic: *my dad's got a lank new car.* [ORIGIN: perhaps related to Afrikaans *lank nie sleg nie* 'not at all bad'.]

– DERIVATIVES **lankly** adverb (only in sense 1), **lankness** noun.
– ORIGIN Old English *hlanc* 'thin, not filled out', of Germanic origin; related to High German *lenken* 'to bend, turn', also to **FLINCH**[1] and **LINK**[1].

lanky ▶ adjective (**lankier**, **lankiest**) (of a person) ungracefully thin and tall.
– DERIVATIVES **lankily** adverb, **lankiness** noun.

lanner /ˈlanə/ (also **lanner falcon**) ▶ noun a falcon with a dark brown back and buff cap, found in SE Europe, the Middle East, and Africa.
● *Falco biarmicus*, family Falconidae.
■ Falconry the female of this bird.
– ORIGIN late Middle English: from Old French *lanier*, perhaps a noun use of *lanier* 'cowardly', from a derogatory use of *lanier* 'wool merchant', from Latin *lana* 'wool'.

lanneret /ˈlanərɪt/ ▶ noun Falconry a male lanner, which is smaller than the female.
– ORIGIN late Middle English: from Old French *laneret*, diminutive of *lanier* (see **LANNER**).

lanolin ▶ noun [mass noun] a fatty substance found naturally on sheep's wool. It is extracted as a yellowish viscous mixture of esters and used as a base for ointments.
– ORIGIN late 19th cent.: coined in German from Latin *lana* 'wool' + *oleum* 'oil' + **-IN**[1].

Lansing /ˈlansɪŋ/ the state capital of Michigan; pop. 127,320 (1990).

lansquenet /ˈlɑːnskənɛt, ˈlans-/ ▶ noun 1 [mass noun] historical a gambling game of German origin involving betting on cards turned up by the dealer.
2 archaic variant of **LANDSKNECHT**.
– ORIGIN early 17th cent. (in sense 2): via French from German *Landsknecht* (see **LANDSKNECHT**).

lantana /lanˈtɑːnə, -ˈteɪnə/ ▶ noun a tropical evergreen shrub of the verbena family, several kinds of which are cultivated as ornamentals.
● Genus *Lantana*, family Verbenaceae: many species, in particular the South American scrambler *L. camara*, grown as an ornamental and sometimes becoming a serious weed.
– ORIGIN modern Latin, from the specific name of the wayfaring tree *Viburnum lantana*, which it resembles superficially.

Lantau /lanˈtaʊ/ an island of Hong Kong, situated to the west of Hong Kong Island and forming part of the New Territories. Chinese name **TAI YUE SHAN**.

lantern ▶ noun 1 a lamp with a transparent case protecting the flame or electric bulb, and typically having a handle by which it can be carried or hung: *a paper lantern.*
■ the light chamber at the top of a lighthouse.
2 a square, curved, or polygonal structure on the top of a dome or a room, with the sides glazed or open so as to admit light.
– ORIGIN Middle English: from Old French *lanterne*, from Latin *lanterna*, from Greek *lamptēr* 'torch, lamp', from *lampein* 'to shine'.

Lantern Festival ▶ noun another name for **BON**.

lanternfish ▶ noun (pl. same or **-fishes**) a deep-sea fish that has light organs on its body, seen chiefly when it rises to the surface at night.
● Family Myctophidae: several genera and species.

lantern fly ▶ noun a chiefly tropical bug which is typically brightly coloured and may have a large bizarrely shaped head. It was formerly thought to be luminescent.
● Family Fulgoridae, suborder Homoptera.

lantern jaw ▶ noun a long, thin jaw and prominent chin.
– DERIVATIVES **lantern-jawed** adjective.

lantern slide ▶ noun historical a mounted photographic transparency for projection by a magic lantern.

lantern wheel ▶ noun a cylindrical gearwheel.

lanthanide /ˈlanθənʌɪd/ ▶ noun Chemistry any of the series of fifteen metallic elements from lanthanum to lutetium in the periodic table. See also **RARE EARTH**.
– ORIGIN 1920s: from **LANTHANUM** + **-IDE**.

lanthanum /ˈlanθənəm/ ▶ noun [mass noun] the chemical element of atomic number 57, a silvery-white rare earth metal. (Symbol: **La**)
– ORIGIN mid 19th cent.: from Greek *lanthanein* 'escape notice' (because it was long undetected in cerium oxide) + **-UM**.

lanugo /ləˈnjuːɡəʊ/ ▶ noun [mass noun] fine, soft hair,

especially that which covers the body and limbs of a human fetus.
– ORIGIN late 17th cent.: from Latin, 'down', from *lana* 'wool'.

lanyard /ˈlanjəd/ ▶ **noun** a rope used to secure or raise and lower something such as the shrouds and sails of a sailing ship or a flag on a flagpole.
■ a cord passed round the neck, shoulder, or wrist for holding a knife, whistle, or similar object.
– ORIGIN late Middle English *lanyer*, in the general sense 'a short length of rope or line for securing something', from Old French *laniere*. The change in the ending in the 17th cent. was due to association with **YARD**[1].

Lanzarote /ˌlanzəˈrɒti, Spanish lanθaˈrote, lansa-/ one of the Canary Islands, the most easterly island of the group; chief town, Arrecife. A series of volcanic eruptions in about 1730 dramatically altered the island's landscape, creating an area of volcanic cones in the south-west known as the 'Mountains of Fire'.

Lanzhou /lanˈdʒəʊ/ (also **Lanchow**) a city in northern China, on the upper Yellow River, capital of Gansu province; pop. 1,480,000 (1990).

LAO ▶ **abbreviation for** Laos (international vehicle registration).

Lao /laʊ/ ▶ **noun** (pl. same or **Laos**) **1** a member of an indigenous people of Laos and NE Thailand.
2 [mass noun] the language of this people, closely related to Thai, with about 3 million speakers. Also called ***Laotian***.
▶ **adjective** of or relating to the Lao or their language.
– ORIGIN the name in Lao.

Laocoon /leɪˈɒkəʊɒn/ Greek Mythology a Trojan priest who, with his two sons, was crushed to death by two great sea serpents as a penalty for warning the Trojans against drawing the wooden horse of the Greeks into Troy.

Laodicean /ˌleɪə(ʊ)dɪˈsiːən/ archaic ▶ **adjective** lukewarm or half-hearted, especially with respect to religion or politics.
▶ **noun** a person with such an attitude.
– ORIGIN early 17th cent.: from Latin *Laodicea* in Asia Minor, with reference to the early Christians there (Rev. 3:16), + **-AN**.

laogai /laʊˈgʌɪ/ ▶ **noun** (**the laogai**) (in China) a system of labour camps, many of whose inmates are political dissidents.
– ORIGIN Chinese, 'reform through labour'.

Laois /liːʃ/ (also **Laoighis**, **Leix**) a county of the Republic of Ireland, in the province of Leinster; county town, Portlaoise. Former name **QUEEN'S COUNTY**.

Laos /laʊs, ˈlɑːɒs/ a landlocked country in SE Asia; pop. 4,279,000 (est. 1991); official language, Laotian; capital, Vientiane.

Part of French Indo-China, Laos became independent in 1949, but for most of the next twenty-five years was torn by civil strife between the communist Pathet Lao movement and government supporters. In 1975 the Pathet Lao achieved total control and a communist republic was established.

– DERIVATIVES **Laotian** adjective & noun.

Lao-tzu /laʊˈtsuː/ (also **Laoze** /-ˈtseɪ/) (*fl.* 6th century BC), Chinese philosopher traditionally regarded as the founder of Taoism and author of the Tao-te-Ching, its most sacred scripture.
– ORIGIN Chinese, literally 'Lao the Master'.

lap[1] ▶ **noun 1** (usu. **one's lap**) the flat area between the waist and knees of a seated person: *come and sit on my lap.*
■ the part of an item of clothing, especially a skirt or dress, covering the lap.
2 archaic a hanging flap on a garment or a saddle.
– PHRASES **fall** (or **drop**) **into someone's lap** (of something pleasant or desirable) come someone's way without any effort having been made: *women fall at his feet, power falls into his lap.* **in someone's lap** as someone's responsibility: *she **dumped** the problem **in my lap**.* **in the lap of the gods** (of the success of a plan or event) open to chance; depending on factors that one cannot control. **in the lap of luxury** in conditions of great comfort and wealth.
– DERIVATIVES **lapful** noun (pl. **-fuls**).
– ORIGIN Old English *læppa*, of Germanic origin; related to Dutch *lap*, German *Lappen* 'piece of cloth'. The word originally denoted a fold or flap of a garment (compare with **LAPEL**), later specifically one that could be used as a pocket or pouch, or the front of a skirt when held up to catch or carry something (Middle English), hence the area between the waist and knees as a place where a child could be nursed or an object held.

lap[2] ▶ **noun 1** one circuit of a track or racetrack.
■ a stage in a swim consisting of two lengths of a pool.
■ a section of a journey or other endeavour: *we caught a cab for the last lap of our journey.*
2 an overlapping or projecting part.
■ [mass noun] the amount by which one thing overlaps or covers a part of another. ■ Metallurgy a defect formed in rolling when a projecting part is accidentally folded over and pressed against the surface of the metal. ■ (in a steam engine) the distance by which the valve overlaps the steam port (or the exhaust port).
3 a single turn of rope, thread, or cable round a drum or reel.
■ a layer or sheet, typically wound on a roller, into which cotton or wool is formed during its manufacture.
4 (in a lapping machine) a rotating disc with a coating of fine abrasive for polishing.
■ a polishing tool of a special shape, coated or impregnated with an abrasive.
▶ **verb** (**lapped**, **lapping**) [with obj.] **1** overtake (a competitor in a race) to become one or more laps ahead: *she lapped all of her rivals in the 3,000 metres.*
■ [no obj.] (of a competitor or vehicle in a race) complete a lap, especially in a specified time: *Mansell lapped two tenths of a second faster than anyone else.*
2 (**lap someone/thing in**) poetic/literary enfold or swathe a person or thing, especially a part of the body, in (something soft): *he was lapped in blankets* | figurative *I was accustomed to being lapped in luxury.*
3 [no obj.] project beyond or overlap something: *the blanket of snow **lapped over** the roofs of the house.*
4 polish (a gem, or a metal or glass surface) with a lapping machine.
– ORIGIN Middle English (as a verb in the sense 'coil, fold, or wrap'): from **LAP**[1]. Sense 1 of the noun and verb date from the mid 19th cent.

lap[3] ▶ **verb** (**lapped**, **lapping**) [with obj.] **1** (of an animal) take up (liquid) with the tongue in order to drink: *the cat was **lapping up** a saucer of milk.*
■ (**lap something up**) accept something eagerly and with obvious pleasure: *she's lapping up the attention.*
2 (of water) wash against (something) with a gentle rippling sound: *the waves lapped the shore* | [no obj.] *the sound of the river lapping against the banks.*
▶ **noun** [in sing.] the action of water washing gently against something: *listening to the comfortable lap of the waves against the shore.*
– ORIGIN Old English *lapian*, of Germanic origin; related to Middle Low German and Middle Dutch *lapen*.

lapa /ˈlɑːpə/ (also **lappa**) ▶ **noun** S. African a courtyard or similar enclosure, especially the first of two courtyards in a traditional Sotho homestead.
– ORIGIN from Sotho *lelapa*.

La Palma /lɑː ˈpɑːlmə, ˈpɑːmə/ one of the Canary Islands, the most north-westerly in the group. It is the site of an astronomical observatory.

laparoscopy /ˌlapəˈrɒskəpi/ ▶ **noun** (pl. **-ies**) a surgical procedure in which a fibre optic instrument is inserted through the abdominal wall to view the organs in the abdomen or permit small-scale surgery.
– DERIVATIVES **laparoscope** noun, **laparoscopic** adjective, **laparoscopically** adverb.
– ORIGIN mid 19th cent.: from Greek *lapara* 'flank' + **-SCOPY**.

laparotomy /ˌlapəˈrɒtəmi/ ▶ **noun** (pl. **-ies**) a surgical incision into the abdominal cavity, for diagnosis or in preparation for major surgery.
– ORIGIN mid 19th cent.: from Greek *lapara* 'flank' + **-TOMY**.

La Paz /la ˈpaz, lɑː ˈpɑːz/ **1** the capital of Bolivia, in the north-west of the country near the border with Peru; pop. 711,040 (1992). (The judicial capital is Sucre.) Situated in the Andes at an altitude of 3,660 m (12,000 ft), La Paz is the highest capital city in the world.
2 a city in Mexico, near the southern tip of the Baja California peninsula, capital of the state of Baja California Sur; pop. 1,050,000 (est. 1991).

lap belt ▶ **noun** a safety belt worn across the lap.

lap dance ▶ **noun** chiefly N. Amer. an erotic dance or striptease performed close to, or sitting on the lap of, a paying customer.
– DERIVATIVES **lap dancer** noun, **lap dancing** noun.

lap desk ▶ **noun** a portable writing case or surface, especially one for use on the lap.

lap dissolve ▶ **noun** a fade-out of a scene in a film that overlaps with a fade-in of a new scene, so that one appears to dissolve into the other.

lapdog ▶ **noun** a small dog kept as a pet.
■ figurative a person or organization which is influenced or controlled by another: *the government and its media lapdogs.*

lapel ▶ **noun** the part on each side of a coat or jacket immediately below the collar which is folded back on either side of the front opening.
– DERIVATIVES **lapelled** adjective [in combination] *a narrow-lapelled suit.*
– ORIGIN mid 17th cent.: diminutive of **LAP**[1].

lapidary /ˈlapɪd(ə)ri/ ▶ **adjective** (of language) engraved on or suitable for engraving on stone and therefore elegant and concise: *a lapidary statement.*
■ of or relating to stone and gems and the work involved in engraving, cutting, or polishing.
▶ **noun** (pl. **-ies**) a person who cuts, polishes, or engraves gems.
– ORIGIN Middle English (as a noun): from Latin *lapidarius* (in late Latin 'stonecutter'), from *lapis*, *lapid-* 'stone'. The adjective dates from the early 18th cent.

lapilli /ləˈpɪlʌɪ/ ▶ **plural noun** Geology rock fragments ejected from a volcano.
– ORIGIN mid 18th cent. (in the general sense 'stones, pebbles'): via Italian from Latin, plural of *lapillus*, diminutive of *lapis* 'stone'.

lapis lazuli /ˌlapɪs ˈlazjʊlʌɪ, -li/ (also **lapis**) ▶ **noun** [mass noun] a bright blue metamorphic rock consisting largely of lazurite, used for decoration and in jewellery.
■ a bright blue pigment formerly made by crushing this, being the original ultramarine. ■ the colour ultramarine.
– ORIGIN late Middle English: from Latin *lapis* 'stone' and medieval Latin *lazuli*, genitive of *lazulum*, from Persian *lāžward* 'lapis lazuli'. Compare with **AZURE**.

Lapita /laˈpiːtə/ ▶ **noun** [usu. as modifier] Archaeology a prehistoric Oceanic culture centred on Melanesia, dated to about *c.*1500–500 BC. It is characterized by pottery distinctively stamped with a toothed instrument.
– ORIGIN mid 20th cent.: from the name of a site in New Caledonia.

Lapith /ˈlapɪθ/ ▶ **noun** Greek Mythology a member of a Thessalian people who fought and defeated the centaurs.
– ORIGIN via Latin from Greek *Lapithai* (plural).

lap joint ▶ **noun** a joint made by halving the thickness of each member at the joint and fitting them together.

Laplace /laˈplɑːs, French laplas/, Pierre Simon, Marquis de (1749–1827), French applied mathematician and theoretical physicist. His treatise *Mécanique céleste* (1799–1825) is an extensive mathematical analysis of geophysical matters and of planetary and lunar motion.

Lapland /ˈlapland/ a region of northern Europe which extends from the Norwegian Sea to the White Sea and lies mainly within the Arctic Circle. It consists of the northern parts of Norway, Sweden, and Finland, and the Kola Peninsula of Russia.
– DERIVATIVES **Laplander** noun.
– ORIGIN late 16th cent.: from Swedish *Lappland*, from *Lapp* (see **LAPP**) + *land* 'land'.

La Plata /lɑː ˈplɑːtə/ a port in Argentina, on the River Plate (Río de la Plata) south-east of Buenos Aires; pop. 640,000 (1991).

lap of honour ▶ **noun** Brit. a celebratory circuit of a sports field, track, or court by the person or team that has won a contest.

Lapp ▶ **noun 1** a member of an indigenous people of the extreme north of Scandinavia, traditionally associated with the herding of reindeer.
2 [mass noun] the Finno-Ugric language of this people, with nine distinct dialects spoken by around 25,000 people altogether.
▶ **adjective** of or relating to the Lapps or their language.
– ORIGIN Swedish, perhaps originally a term of contempt and related to Middle High German *lappe* 'simpleton'.

b **but** | d **dog** | f **few** | g **get** | h **he** | j **yes** | k **cat** | l **leg** | m **man** | n **no** | p **pen** | r **red** | s **sit** | t **top** | v **voice** | w **we** | z **zoo** | ʃ **she** | ʒ **decision** | θ **thin** | ð **this** | ŋ **ring** | x **loch** | tʃ **chip** | dʒ **jar**

USAGE Although the term **Lapp** is still widely used and is the most familiar term to many people, the people themselves prefer to be called **Sami**.

lappa ▶ **noun** variant spelling of **LAPA**.

lappet /ˈlapɪt/ ▶ **noun** **1** a small flap or fold, in particular:
▪a fold or hanging piece of flesh in some animals. ▪ a loose or overlapping part of a garment.
2 (also **lappet moth**) a brownish moth, the hairy caterpillars of which have fleshy lappets along each side of the body.
• Several species in the family Lasiocampidae: including the common Eurasian *Gastropacha quercifilia*.
– DERIVATIVES **lappeted** adjective.
– ORIGIN late Middle English (denoting a lobe of the ear, liver, etc.): diminutive of **LAP**[1].

lapping machine ▶ **noun** a machine with a rotating abrasive disc for polishing gems, metal, and optical glass.

Lappish ▶ **adjective** of or relating to the Lapps (Sami) or their language.
▶ **noun** [mass noun] the Lapp language.

lap robe ▶ **noun** N. Amer. a travelling rug.

lapsang souchong /ˈlapsaŋ/ ▶ **noun** [mass noun] a variety of souchong tea with a smoky flavour.
– ORIGIN late 19th cent.: from an invented first element + **SOUCHONG**.

lapse ▶ **noun** **1** a brief or temporary failure of concentration, memory, or judgement: *a **lapse of** concentration in the second set cost her the match.*
▪a weak or careless decline from previously high standards: *tracing his **lapse into** petty crime.* ▪ Law the termination of a right or privilege through disuse or failure to follow appropriate procedures.
2 an interval or passage of time: *there was a considerable **lapse of** time between the two events.*
▶ **verb** [no obj.] **1** (of a right, privilege, or agreement) become invalid because it is not used, claimed, or renewed; expire: *he let his membership of CND lapse.*
▪(of a state or activity) fail to be maintained; come to an end: *if your diet has lapsed it's time you revived it.* ▪ (of an adherent of a particular religion or doctrine) cease to follow the rules and practices of that religion or doctrine: [as adj. **lapsed**] *a lapsed Catholic.*
2 (**lapse into**) pass gradually into (an inferior state or condition): *the country has lapsed into chaos.*
▪revert to (a previous or more familiar style of speaking or behaviour): *the girls lapsed into French.*
– ORIGIN late Middle English: from Latin *lapsus*, from *labi* 'to glide, slip, or fall'; the verb reinforced by Latin *lapsare* 'to slip or stumble'.

lapse rate ▶ **noun** the rate at which air temperature falls with increasing altitude.

lapstone ▶ **noun** a shoemaker's stone held in the lap and used to beat leather on.

lapstrake chiefly N. Amer. ▶ **noun** a clinker-built boat.
▶ **adjective** (also **lapstraked**) clinker-built.

lapsus calami /ˌlapsəs ˈkaləmʌɪ/ ▶ **noun** (pl. same) formal a slip of the pen.
– ORIGIN Latin.

lapsus linguae /ˌlapsəs ˈlɪŋgwʌɪ/ ▶ **noun** (pl. same) formal a slip of the tongue.
– ORIGIN Latin.

Laptev Sea /ˈlaptɛf/ a part of the Arctic Ocean, which lies to the north of Russia between the Taimyr Peninsula and the New Siberian Islands.

laptop (also **laptop computer**) ▶ **noun** a microcomputer that is portable and suitable for use while travelling.

lap-weld ▶ **verb** [with obj.] weld (something) with the edges overlapping.
▶ **noun** (**lap weld**) a weld made in this way.

lapwing ▶ **noun** a large plover, typically having a black-and-white head and underparts and a loud call.
• Genus *Vanellus*, family Charadriidae: several species, in particular the (**northern**) **lapwing** (*V. vanellus*) of Eurasia (also called the **GREEN PLOVER** or **PEEWIT**), which has a dark green back and a crest.
– ORIGIN Old English *hlēapewince*, from *hlēapan* 'to leap' and a base meaning 'move from side to side' (whence also **WINK**); so named because of the way it flies. The spelling was changed in Middle English by association with **LAP**[2] and **WING**.

L'Aquila /ˈlakwila/ Italian name for **AQUILA**[2].

LAR ▶ **abbreviation for** Libya (international vehicle registration).
– ORIGIN from *Libyan Arab Republic*.

lar (also **lar gibbon**) ▶ **noun** the common gibbon, which has white hands and feet and is found in Thailand and Malaysia.
• *Hylobates lar*, family Hylobatidae.
– ORIGIN early 19th cent.: from Latin, literally 'household god'.

Lara /ˈlɑːrə/, Brian (Charles) (b.1969), West Indian cricketer. He scored 375 against England in Antigua (1994), breaking the record test score, and 501 not out, a world record in first-class cricket, for Warwickshire against Durham (1994).

Laramie /ˈlarəmi/ a city in SE Wyoming; pop. 26,690 (1990). It was first settled in 1868, during the construction of the Union Pacific Railroad.

larboard /ˈlɑːbɔːd, -bəd/ ▶ **noun** Nautical archaic term for **PORT**[3].
– ORIGIN Middle English *ladebord* (see **LADE**, **BOARD**), referring to the side on which cargo was put aboard. The change to *lar-* in the 16th cent. was due to association with **STARBOARD**.

larceny /ˈlɑːs(ə)ni/ ▶ **noun** (pl. **-ies**) [mass noun] theft of personal property. In English law larceny was replaced as a statutory crime by theft in 1968. See also **GRAND LARCENY**, **PETTY LARCENY**.
– DERIVATIVES **larcener** noun (archaic), **larcenist** noun, **larcenous** adjective.
– ORIGIN late 15th cent.: from Old French *larcin*, from Latin *latrocinium*, from *latro(n-)* 'robber', earlier 'mercenary soldier', from Greek *latreus*.

larch ▶ **noun** a coniferous tree with bunches of deciduous bright green needles, found in cool regions of the northern hemisphere. It is grown for its tough timber and its resin (which yields turpentine).
• Genus *Larix*, family Pinaceae: several species, including the **common** (or **European**) **larch** (*L. decidua*).
– ORIGIN mid 16th cent.: from Middle High German *larche*, based on Latin *larix*.

lard ▶ **noun** [mass noun] fat from the abdomen of a pig that is rendered and clarified for use in cooking.
▪informal excess human fat that is seen as unhealthy and unattractive.
▶ **verb** [with obj.] **1** insert strips of fat or bacon in (meat) before cooking.
▪smear or cover (a foodstuff) with lard or fat, typically to prevent it drying out during storage.
2 (usu. **be larded with**) embellish (talk or writing) with an excessive number of esoteric or technical expressions: *his conversation is larded with quotations from Coleridge.*
▪cover or fill thickly or excessively: *the pages were larded with corrections and crossings-out.*
– DERIVATIVES **lardy** adjective.
– ORIGIN Middle English (also denoting fat bacon or pork): from Old French 'bacon', from Latin *lardum*, *laridum*, related to Greek *larinos* 'fat'.

lardass /ˈlɑːdɑːs, ˈlɑːdas/ ▶ **noun** N. Amer. informal, derogatory a fat person, especially one with large buttocks or who is regarded as lazy.

larder ▶ **noun** a room or large cupboard for storing food.
– ORIGIN Middle English (denoting a store of meat): from Old French *lardier*, from medieval Latin *lardarium*, from *laridum* (see **LARD**).

larder beetle ▶ **noun** a brownish scavenging beetle which is a pest of stored products, especially meat and hides.
• *Dermestes lardarius*, family Dermestidae.

lardon /ˈlɑːdən/ (also **lardoon** /-ˈduːn/) ▶ **noun** a chunk or cube of bacon used to lard meat.
– ORIGIN late Middle English: from French, from *lard* 'bacon' (see **LARD**).

lardy cake ▶ **noun** Brit. a cake made with bread dough, lard, and currants.

lares /ˈlɑːriːz/ ▶ **plural noun** gods of the household worshipped in ancient Rome. See also **PENATES**.
– PHRASES **lares and penates** the home.
– ORIGIN Latin.

Largactil /lɑːˈgaktɪl/ ▶ **noun** trademark for **CHLORPROMAZINE**.
– ORIGIN mid 20th cent.: of unknown origin.

large ▶ **adjective** **1** of considerable or relatively great size, extent, or capacity: *add a large clove of garlic | the concert attracted large crowds.*
▪of greater size than the ordinary, especially with reference to a size of clothing or to the size of a packaged commodity: *the jumper comes in small, medium, and large sizes.* ▪ pursuing an occupation or commercial activity on a significant scale: *many large investors are likely to take a different view.*
2 of wide range or scope: *we can afford to take a larger view of the situation.*
– PHRASES **at large** **1** (especially of a criminal or dangerous animal) at liberty; escaped or not yet captured: *the fugitive was still at large.* **2** as a whole; in general: *there has been a loss of community values in society at large.* **3** US in a general way; without particularizing: *he served as an ambassador at large in the Reagan Administration.* **4** dated at length; in great detail: *writing at large on the policies he wished to pursue.* **in large measure** (or **part**) to a great extent: *the success of the conference was due in large part to its organizers.* (**as**) **large as life** see **LIFE**. **larger than life** see **LIFE**.
– DERIVATIVES **largeness** noun, **largish** adjective (usu. in sense 1).
– ORIGIN Middle English (in the sense 'liberal in giving, lavish, ample in quantity'): via Old French from Latin *larga*, feminine of *largus* 'copious'.

large calorie ▶ **noun** see **CALORIE**.

large-hearted ▶ **adjective** sympathetic and generous.

large intestine ▶ **noun** Anatomy the caecum, colon, and rectum collectively.

largely ▶ **adverb** [sentence adverb] to a great extent; on the whole; mostly: *he was soon arrested, largely through the efforts of Tom Poole.*

large-minded ▶ **adjective** open to and tolerant of other people's ideas; liberal.

largemouth ▶ **noun** N. Amer. the largemouth bass (see **BLACK BASS**).

large-scale ▶ **adjective** **1** involving large numbers or a large area; extensive: *large-scale commercial farming.*
2 (of a map or model) made to a scale large enough to show certain features in detail.

largesse /lɑːˈ(d)ʒɛs/ (also **largess**) ▶ **noun** [mass noun] generosity in bestowing money or gifts upon others: *dispensing his money with such largesse.*
▪money or gifts given generously: *the distribution of largesse to the local population.*
– ORIGIN Middle English: from Old French, from Latin *largus* 'copious'.

larghetto /lɑːˈgɛtəʊ/ Music ▶ **adverb** & **adjective** (especially as a direction) in a fairly slow tempo.
▶ **noun** (pl. **-os**) a passage or movement marked to be performed in this way.
– ORIGIN Italian, diminutive of *largo* 'broad'.

largo /ˈlɑːgəʊ/ Music ▶ **adverb** & **adjective** (especially as a direction) in a slow tempo and dignified in style.
▶ **noun** (pl. **-os**) a passage, movement, or composition marked to be performed in this way.
– ORIGIN Italian, from Latin *largus* 'copious, abundant'.

lari /ˈlɑːriː/ ▶ **noun** (pl. same or **laris**) a monetary unit of the Maldives, equal to one hundredth of a rufiyaa.
– ORIGIN from Persian.

Lariam /ˈlarɪəm/ ▶ **noun** trademark for **MEFLOQUINE**.
– ORIGIN 1980s: probably from partial rearrangement of **MALARIA**.

lariat /ˈlarɪət/ ▶ **noun** a rope used as a lasso or for tethering.
– ORIGIN mid 19th cent.: from Spanish *la reata* from *la* 'the' and *reatar* 'tie again' (based on Latin *aptare* 'adjust', from *aptus* 'apt, fitting').

La Rioja /ˌlɑː rɪˈɒhə/ an autonomous region of northern Spain, in the wine-producing valley of the River Ebro; capital, Logroño.

Larissa /ləˈrɪsə/ a city in Greece, the chief town of Thessaly; pop. 113,000 (1991). Greek name **LÁRISA** /ˈlarisa/.

lark[1] ▶ **noun** a small ground-dwelling songbird with elongated hind claws and a song that is delivered on the wing, typically crested and with brown streaky plumage.
• Family Alaudidae: many genera and numerous species, e.g. the **skylark** and **shorelark**.
▪used in names of similar birds of other families, e.g. **meadowlark**. ▪ informal a person who habitually gets up early, and who feels at their most productive early in the day. Often contrasted with **OWL**.
– PHRASES **be up with the lark** get out of bed very early in the morning.
– ORIGIN Old English *lāferce*, *lǣwerce*; related to Dutch *leeuwerik* and German *Lerche*; of unknown ultimate origin.

lark² informal ▶ **noun** something done for fun, especially something mischievous or daring; an amusing adventure or escapade: *I only went along for a lark.*
■ [usu. with modifier] Brit. used to suggest that an activity is foolish or a waste of time: *he's serious about this music lark.*
▶ **verb** [no obj.] enjoy oneself by behaving in a playful and mischievous way: *he's always joking and larking about in the office.*
– DERIVATIVES **larkiness** noun, **larky** adjective.
– ORIGIN early 19th cent.: perhaps from dialect *lake* 'play', from Old Norse *leika*, but compare with **SKYLARK** in the same sense, which is recorded earlier.

Larkin, Philip (Arthur) (1922–85), English poet. His poetry is characterized by an air of melancholy and bitterness, and by stoic wit. Notable works: *The Whitsun Weddings* (1964) and *High Windows* (1974).

larkspur ▶ **noun** an annual Mediterranean plant of the buttercup family, which bears spikes of spurred flowers. It is closely related to the delphiniums, with which it has been bred to produce a number of cultivated hybrids.
• Genus *Consolida* (formerly *Delphinium*), family Ranunculaceae.

larn ▶ **verb** dialect form of **LEARN**.

larney /lɑːni/ (also **larnie**, **lani**,or **lorny**) S. African informal ▶ **noun** (pl. **-eys** or **-ies**) derogatory a white man.
■ an employer or a member of the upper classes.
▶ **adjective** suggesting wealth and high status; smart and elegant.
– ORIGIN from Isicamtho (a South African urban argot) *lani(e)* 'white man', of unknown ultimate origin; perhaps related to Malay *rani* 'rich'.

La Rochefoucauld /la ˈrɒʃfuːkəʊ, French la rɔʃfuko/, François de Marsillac, Duc de (1613–80), French writer and moralist. Notable works: *Réflexions, ou sentences et maximes morales* (1665).

La Rochelle /ˌla rɒˈʃɛl, French la rɔʃɛl/ a port on the Atlantic coast of western France; pop. 73,740 (1990).

Larousse /laˈruːs, French larus/, Pierre (1817–75), French lexicographer and encyclopedist. He edited the fifteen-volume *Grand dictionnaire universel du XIXᵉ siècle* (1866–76), which aimed to treat every area of human knowledge. In 1852 he co-founded the publishing house of Larousse.

larrikin /ˈlarɪkɪn/ ▶ **noun** Austral. a boisterous, often badly behaved young man.
■ a person with apparent disregard for convention; a maverick: [as modifier] *the larrikin trade union leader.*
– ORIGIN mid 19th cent.: from English dialect, perhaps from the given name *Larry* (pet form of *Lawrence*) + **-KIN**.

larrup /ˈlarəp/ ▶ **verb** (**larruped**, **larruping**) [with obj.] informal thrash or whip (someone).
– ORIGIN early 19th cent. (originally dialect): perhaps related to **LATHER** or **LEATHER**.

larva /ˈlɑːvə/ ▶ **noun** (pl. **larvae** /-viː/) the active immature form of an insect, especially one that differs greatly from the adult and forms the stage between egg and pupa, e.g. a caterpillar or grub. Compare with **NYMPH** (in sense 2).
■ an immature form of other animals that undergo some metamorphosis, e.g. a tadpole.
– DERIVATIVES **larval** adjective, **larvicide** noun.
– ORIGIN mid 17th cent. (denoting a disembodied spirit or ghost): from Latin, literally 'ghost, mask'.

Larvacea /lɑːˈveɪʃə/ Zoology a class of minute transparent planktonic animals related to the sea squirts. They have a tadpole-like body which is typically enclosed in a gelatinous 'house' that is regularly shed and replaced.
– DERIVATIVES **larvacean** adjective & noun.
– ORIGIN modern Latin (plural), from **LARVA**.

Larwood, Harold (1904–95), English cricketer. A fearsome fast bowler for Nottinghamshire, in the 1932–3 MCC tour of Australia he bowled fast short-pitched 'bodyline' deliveries, and was involved in controversy when several of the home batsmen were badly injured.

laryngeal /ləˈrɪn(d)ʒɪəl/ ▶ **adjective** of or relating to the larynx: *the laryngeal artery.*
■ Phonetics (of a speech sound) made in the larynx with the vocal cords partly closed and partly vibrating (producing, in English, the so-called 'creaky voice' sound): *laryngeal consonants.*
– ORIGIN late 18th cent.: from modern Latin *laryngeus* 'relating to the larynx' + **-AL**.

laryngitis /ˌlarɪnˈdʒʌɪtɪs/ ▶ **noun** [mass noun] inflammation of the larynx, typically resulting in huskiness or loss of the voice, harsh breathing, and a painful cough.
– DERIVATIVES **laryngitic** /-ˈdʒɪtɪk/ adjective.

laryngology /ˌlarɪŋˈɡɒlədʒi/ ▶ **noun** [mass noun] the branch of medicine that deals with the larynx and its diseases.
– DERIVATIVES **laryngologist** noun.

laryngoscope /ləˈrɪŋɡəskəʊp/ ▶ **noun** an instrument for examining the larynx, or for inserting a tube through it.
– DERIVATIVES **laryngoscopy** noun.

laryngotomy /ˌlarɪŋˈɡɒtəmi/ ▶ **noun** [mass noun] surgical incision into the larynx, typically to provide an air passage when breathing is obstructed.

larynx /ˈlarɪŋks/ ▶ **noun** (pl. **larynges** /ləˈrɪn(d)ʒiːz/) Anatomy the hollow muscular organ forming an air passage to the lungs and holding the vocal cords in humans and other mammals; the voice box.
– ORIGIN late 16th cent.: modern Latin, from Greek *larunx*.

lasagne /ləˈzanjə, -ˈsan-, -ˈsɑːn-, -ˈzɑːn-/ ▶ **noun** [mass noun] pasta in the form of sheets or wide strips.
■ an Italian dish consisting of this cooked and served with meat or vegetables and a cheese sauce.
– ORIGIN Italian, plural of *lasagna*, based on Latin *lasanum* 'chamber pot', perhaps also 'cooking pot'.

La Salle /la ˈsal/, René-Robert Cavelier, Sieur de (1643–87), French explorer. He sailed down the Ohio and Mississippi Rivers to the sea from Canada in 1682, naming the Mississippi basin Louisiana in honour of Louis XIV.

La Scala /la ˈskɑːlə/ an opera house in Milan built 1776–8 on the site of the church of Santa Maria della Scala.

Lascar /ˈlaskə/ ▶ **noun** dated a sailor from India or SE Asia.
– ORIGIN early 17th cent.: from Portuguese *lascari*, from Urdu and Persian *laškarī* 'soldier', from *laškar* 'army'.

Lascaux /laˈskəʊ, French lasko/ the site of a cave in the Dordogne, France, which is richly decorated with Palaeolithic wall paintings of animals dated to the Magdalenian period.

lascivious /ləˈsɪvɪəs/ ▶ **adjective** (of a person, manner, or gesture) feeling or revealing an overt and often offensive sexual desire: *he gave her a lascivious wink.*
– DERIVATIVES **lasciviously** adverb, **lasciviousness** noun.
– ORIGIN late Middle English: from late Latin *lasciviosus*, from Latin *lascivia* 'lustfulness', from *lascivus* 'lustful, wanton'.

lase /leɪz/ ▶ **verb** [no obj.] (of a substance, especially a gas or crystal) undergo the physical processes employed in a laser; function as or in a laser.
– ORIGIN 1960s: back-formation from **LASER**, interpreted as an agent noun.

laser ▶ **noun** a device that generates an intense beam of coherent monochromatic light (or other electromagnetic radiation) by stimulated emission of photons from excited atoms or molecules. Lasers are used in drilling and cutting, alignment and guidance, and in surgery; the optical properties are exploited in holography, reading bar codes, and in recording and playing compact discs.
– ORIGIN 1960s: acronym from *light amplification by stimulated emission of radiation*, on the pattern of *maser*.

laserdisc ▶ **noun** a disc which resembles a compact disc and functions in a similar manner, but is the size of a long-playing record. It is used mainly for high-quality video and for interactive multimedia on computer.

laser gun ▶ **noun** a hand-held device incorporating a laser beam, used typically for reading a bar code, or for determining the distance or speed of an object.
■ (in science fiction) a weapon that uses a powerful laser beam.

laser printer ▶ **noun** a printer linked to a computer producing good-quality printed material by using a laser to form a pattern of electrostatically charged dots on a light-sensitive drum, which attract toner (or dry ink powder). The toner is transferred to a piece of paper and fixed by a heating process.

LaserVision ▶ **noun** [mass noun] trademark a system for the reproduction of video signals recorded on a laserdisc.
– ORIGIN 1980s: from **LASER** + **VISION**, on the pattern of *television*.

lash ▶ **verb** [with obj.] **1** strike (someone) with a whip or stick: *they lashed him repeatedly about the head.*
■ beat forcefully against (something): *waves lashed the coast* | [no obj.] *torrential rain was lashing down.* ■ [no obj.] (**lash out**) hit or kick out at someone or something: *the woman had lashed out in fear* | figurative *in his speech, he lashed out at his enemies.* ■ (**lash someone into**) drive someone into (a particular state or condition): *fear lashed him into a frenzy.*
2 [with obj. and adverbial of direction] (of an animal) move (a part of the body, especially the tail) quickly and violently: *the cat was lashing its tail back and forth.*
■ [no obj., with adverbial of direction] (of a part of the body) move in this way.
3 [with obj. and adverbial] fasten (something) securely with a cord or rope: *the hatch was securely lashed down* | *he lashed the flag to the mast.*
▶ **noun 1** a sharp blow or stroke with a whip or rope, typically given as a form of punishment: *he was sentenced to fifty lashes for his crime* | figurative *she felt the lash of my tongue.*
■ the flexible leather part of a whip, used for administering such blows. ■ (**the lash**) punishment in the form of a beating with a whip or rope: *they were living under the threat of the lash.*
2 (usu. **lashes**) an eyelash: *she fluttered her long dark lashes.*
– DERIVATIVES **lashed** adjective [in combination] *long-lashed eyes*, **lasher** noun, **lashless** adjective.
– ORIGIN Middle English (in the sense 'make a sudden movement'): probably imitative.
▶ **lash out** Brit. spend money extravagantly: *I decided to lash out and treat myself* | *let's lash out on a taxi.*

lashing ▶ **noun 1** an act or instance of whipping: *I threatened to give him a good lashing!* | figurative *he was on the receiving end of a verbal lashing yesterday.*
2 (usu. **lashings**) a cord used to fasten something securely.

lashings ▶ **plural noun** Brit. informal a copious amount of something, especially food or drink: *chocolate cake with lashings of cream.*

lash-up ▶ **noun** chiefly Brit. a makeshift, improvised structure or arrangement.

Las Palmas /laːs ˈpɑːməs, ˈpɑːlməs/ a port and resort on the north coast of the island of Gran Canaria, capital of the Canary Islands; pop. 372,270 (1991). Full name **LAS PALMAS DE GRAN CANARIA** /də ˌɡran kəˈnɛːrɪə/.

La Spezia /la ˈspɛtsɪə/ an industrial port in NW Italy; pop. 103,000 (1990). Since 1861 it has been Italy's chief naval station.

lasque /lɑːsk/ (also **lasque diamond**) ▶ **noun** a flat, ill-formed, or veiny diamond.
– ORIGIN late 17th cent.: perhaps from Persian *lašk* 'piece'.

lass ▶ **noun** chiefly Scottish & N. English a girl or young woman: *he married a lass from Yorkshire* | *village lasses.*
– ORIGIN Middle English: based on Old Norse *laskura* (feminine adjective) 'unmarried'.

Lassa fever /ˈlasə/ ▶ **noun** [mass noun] an acute and often fatal viral disease, with fever, occurring chiefly in West Africa. It is usually acquired from infected rats.
– ORIGIN 1970s: named after the village of *Lassa*, in NW Nigeria, where it was first reported.

lassi /ˈlasi/ ▶ **noun** [mass noun] a sweet or savoury Indian drink made from a yogurt or buttermilk base with water.
– ORIGIN from Hindi *lassī*.

lassie ▶ **noun** chiefly Scottish & N. English another term for **LASS**.

lassitude /ˈlasɪtjuːd/ ▶ **noun** [mass noun] a state of physical or mental weariness; lack of energy: *she was overcome by lassitude and retired to bed* | *a patient complaining of lassitude and inability to concentrate.*
– ORIGIN late Middle English: from French, from Latin *lassitudo*, from *lassus* 'tired'.

lasso /ləˈsuː, ˈlasəʊ/ ▶ **noun** (pl. **-os** or **-oes**) a rope with a noose at one end, used especially in North America for catching cattle.
▶ **verb** (**-oes**, **-oed**) [with obj.] catch (an animal) with a lasso: *at last his father lassoed the horse.*

– DERIVATIVES **lassoer** noun.
– ORIGIN mid 18th cent.: representing an American Spanish pronunciation of Spanish *lazo*, based on Latin *laqueus* 'noose'. Compare with **LACE**.

Lassus /ˈlasəs/, Orlande de (*c.*1532–94), Flemish composer; Italian name *Orlando di Lasso*. A notable composer of polyphonic music, he wrote over 2,000 secular and sacred works.

last[1] ▶ **adjective** [attrib.] **1** coming after all others in time or order; final: *they caught the last bus.* ■ met with or encountered after any others: *the last house in the village.* ■ the lowest in importance or rank: *finishing in last place* | [as complement] *he* **came last** *in the race.* ■ (**the last**) the least likely or suitable: *addicts are often the last people to face up to their problems* | **the last thing she needed** *was a husband.*
2 most recent in time; latest: *last year* | [postpositive] *your letter of Sunday last.* ■ immediately preceding in order; previous in a sequence: *their last album.* ■ most recently mentioned or enumerated: *this last point is critical.*
3 only remaining: *it's our last hope.*
▶ **adverb 1** on the last occasion before the present; previously: *a woman last heard of in Cornwall.*
2 [in combination] after all others in order or sequence: *the last-named film.*
3 (especially in enumerating points) lastly: *and last, I'd like to thank you all for coming.*
▶ **noun** (pl. same) the last person or thing; the one occurring, mentioned, or acting after all others: *the last of their guests had gone* | *eating as if every mouthful were his last.* ■ (**the last of**) the only part of something that remains: *they drank the last of the wine.* ■ [in sing.] last position in a race, contest, or ranking: *Lion Cavern came from last in a slowly run race.* ■ (**the last**) the last round in a boxing match or similar: *on the ropes for a spell in the last.* ■ (**the last**) the end or last moment, especially death: *he was dead, having refused morphia* **to the last**. ■ (**the last**) the last mention or sight of someone or something: *that was* **the last we saw of** *her.*
– PHRASES **at last** (or **at long last**) in the end; after much delay: *you've come back to me at last!* **in the** (or **as a**) **last resort** see **RESORT**. **—— one's last** do something for the last time: *the dying embers sparked their last.* **last but not least** last in order of mention or occurrence but not of importance. **last ditch** used to denote a final, often desperate, act to achieve something in the face of difficulty: [as modifier] *a last-ditch attempt to acquire some proper qualifications.* **one's** (or **the**) **last gasp** see **GASP**. **last orders** (in a bar or public house) an expression used to inform customers that closing time is approaching and that any further drinks should be purchased immediately: *last orders, gentlemen, please.* **the last straw** see **STRAW**. **last thing** late in the evening, especially as a final act before going to bed: *I think having that cup of tea* **last thing at night** *really helps.* **on one's last legs** see **LEG**.
– ORIGIN Old English *latost* (adverb) 'after all others in a series', of Germanic origin; related to Dutch *laatst*, *lest* and German *letzt*, also to **LATE**.

last[2] ▶ **verb** [no obj.] **1** [with adverbial] (of a process, activity, or state of things) continue for a specified period of time: *the guitar solo lasted for twenty minutes* | *childhood seems to last forever.*
2 continue to function well or to be in good condition for a considerable or specified length of time: *the car is built to last* | *a lip pencil lasts longer than lipstick.* ■ (of a person) manage to continue in a post or course of action: *how long does he reckon he'll last as manager?* ■ survive or endure: *she managed to* **last out** *until the end of the programme* | *his condition is so serious that he won't last the night.* ■ [with obj.] (of provisions or resources) be adequate or sufficient for (someone), especially for a specified length of time: *he filled the freezer with enough food to last him for three months.*
– ORIGIN Old English *lǣstan*, of Germanic origin, related to German *leisten* 'afford, yield', also to **LAST**[3].

last[3] ▶ **noun** a shoemaker's model for shaping or repairing a shoe or boot.
– ORIGIN Old English *lǣste*, of Germanic origin, from a base meaning 'follow'; related to Dutch *leest* and German *Leisten*.

last-gasp ▶ **adjective** [attrib.] informal done at the last possible moment, typically in desperation: *Wilson levelled with a last-gasp try.*

last hurrah ▶ **noun** chiefly US a final act, performance, or effort, especially in politics: *Arthur's last hurrah in Washington.*

lasting ▶ **adjective** enduring or able to endure over a long period of time: *they left a lasting impression* | *a lasting, happy marriage.*
– DERIVATIVES **lastingly** adverb, **lastingness** noun.

Last Judgement ▶ **noun** the judgement of humankind expected in some religious traditions to take place at the end of the world.

lastly ▶ **adverb** in the last place (used to introduce the last of a series of points or actions): *lastly, I would like to thank my parents.*

last minute (also **last moment**) ▶ **noun** the latest possible time before an event: *the visit was cancelled* **at the last minute** | [as modifier] *a last-minute change of plans.*

last name ▶ **noun** one's surname.

last number redial ▶ **noun** see **REDIAL**.

last offices ▶ **plural noun** the preparation of a corpse for burial; laying out.

last post ▶ **noun** (in the British armed forces) the second of two bugle calls giving notice of the hour of retiring at night, played also at military funerals and acts of remembrance.

last rites ▶ **plural noun** (in the Christian Church) rites administered to a person who is about to die.

Last Supper the supper eaten by Jesus and his disciples on the night before the Crucifixion, as recorded in the New Testament and commemorated by Christians in the Eucharist.

last trump ▶ **noun** the trumpet blast that in some religious beliefs is thought will wake the dead on Judgement Day.

last word ▶ **noun 1** a final or definitive pronouncement on or decision about a subject: *he's always determined to* **have the last word**.
2 the finest or most modern, fashionable, or advanced example of something: *the new flat* **is the last word in** *luxury.*

Las Vegas /las ˈveɪgəs/ a city in southern Nevada; pop. 258,295 (1990). It is noted for its casinos and nightclubs.

lat[1] /lat/ ▶ **noun** (pl. **lati** /ˈlati/ or **lats**) the basic monetary unit of Latvia, equal to 100 santims.
– ORIGIN from the first syllable of *Latvija* 'Latvia'.

lat[2] /lat/ ▶ **noun** (usu. **lats**) informal (in bodybuilding) a latissimus muscle.
– ORIGIN mid 20th cent.: abbreviation.

lat. ▶ **abbreviation for** latitude: *between approximately 40° and 50° S. lat.*

Latakia /ˌlatəˈkiːə/ a seaport on the coast of western Syria, opposite the north-eastern tip of Cyprus; pop. 293,000 (1993).

latch ▶ **noun** a metal bar with a catch and lever used for fastening a door or gate. ■ a spring lock for an outer door, which catches when the door is closed and can only be opened from the outside with a key. ■ Electronics a circuit which retains whatever output state results from a momentary input signal until reset by another signal. ■ the part of a knitting machine needle which closes or opens to hold or release the wool.
▶ **verb** [with obj.] fasten (a door or gate) with a latch: *she latched the door carefully.* ■ [no obj.] Electronics (of a device) become fixed in a particular state.
– PHRASES **on the latch** (of a door or gate) closed but not locked: *let yourself in, the door's on the latch.*
– ORIGIN Old English *læccan* 'take hold of, grasp (physically or mentally)', of Germanic origin.
▶ **latch on** (of a breastfeeding baby) manage to get its mouth into the correct position around the nipple.
latch on to informal **1** attach oneself to (someone) as a constant and usually unwelcome companion: *he spent the whole evening trying to latch on to my friends.* ■ take up (an idea or trend) enthusiastically: *the newspapers latched on to the idea of healthy eating.* ■ Brit. (of a football or rugby player) take advantage of (another player's move), typically in order to score a goal or try: *Nevin latched on to a miscued header to smash home the winning goal.* ■ (of one substance) cohere with (another). **2** understand the meaning of (something): [with clause] *she'll soon latch on to what is happening.*

latchet /ˈlatʃɪt/ ▶ **noun** archaic a narrow thong or lace for fastening a shoe or sandal.
– ORIGIN late Middle English: from Old French *lachet*, variant of *lacet*, from *laz* 'lace'.

latchkey ▶ **noun** (pl. **-eys**) a key of an outer door of a house.

latchkey child ▶ **noun** a child who is at home without adult supervision for some part of the day, especially after school until a parent returns from work.

late ▶ **adjective 1** doing something or taking place after the expected, proper, or usual time: *his late arrival* | *she was half an hour* **late for** *her lunch appointment.*
2 belonging or taking place far on in a particular time or period: *they won the game with a late goal.* ■ [attrib.] denoting the advanced stage of a period: *the late 1960s* | *arriving in the late afternoon.* ■ far on in the day or night: *I'm sorry the call is so late* | *it's* **too late for** *sherry.* ■ originating at a point far on in an artistic period or artist's life: *his highly abstracted late landscapes* | *late Gothic style.* ■ flowering or ripening towards the end of the season: *the last late chrysanthemums.*
3 (**the/one's late**) (of a specified person) no longer alive: *the late Francis Bacon* | *her late husband's grave.* ■ no longer having the specified status; former: *a late colleague of mine.*
4 (**latest**) of recent date: *the latest news.*
▶ **adverb 1** after the expected, proper, or usual time: *she arrived late.*
2 far on in time; towards the end of a period: *it happened* **late in** *1984.* ■ at or until a time far on in the day or night: *now I'm old enough to stay up late.* ■ (**later**) at a time in the near future; afterwards: *I'll see you later* | **later on** *it will be easier.*
3 (**late of**) formerly but not now living or working in a specified place or institution: *Mrs Halford, late of the County Records Office.*
▶ **noun** (**the latest**) the most recent news or fashion: *have you heard the latest?*
– PHRASES **at the latest** no later than the time specified: *all new cars will be required to meet this standard by 1997 at the latest.* **late in the day** (or N. Amer. **game**) at a late stage in proceedings, especially too late to be useful: *you've realized it a little late in the day.* **of late** recently: *she'd been drinking too much of late.*
– DERIVATIVES **lateness** noun.
– ORIGIN Old English *læt* (adjective; also in the sense 'slow, tardy'), *late* (adverb), of Germanic origin; related to German *lass*, from an Indo-European root shared by Latin *lassus* 'weary', **LET**[1], and **LET**[2].

latecomer ▶ **noun** a person who arrives late: *latecomers were not admitted before the interval.*

late cut Cricket ▶ **noun** a cut made with a delayed action so as to send the ball to the off side behind the wicket.
▶ **verb** (**late-cut**) [with obj.] hit (the ball) with such a stroke; hit a ball delivered by (the bowler) with such a stroke.

lateen /ləˈtiːn/ ▶ **noun** (also **lateen sail**) a triangular sail on a long yard at an angle of 45° to the mast. ■ a ship rigged with such a sail.
– ORIGIN mid 16th cent.: from French (*voile*) *Latine* 'Latin (sail)', so named because it was common in the Mediterranean.

late-glacial ▶ **adjective** Geology of or relating to the later stages of the final (Weichsel or Devensian) glaciation, from the beginning of the rise in temperature about 15,000 years ago to the beginning of the Flandrian about 10,000 years ago. Compare with **POSTGLACIAL**.

late Latin ▶ **noun** [mass noun] Latin of about AD 200–600.

lately ▶ **adverb** recently; not long ago: *she hasn't been looking too well lately.*
– ORIGIN Old English *lætlīce* 'slowly, tardily' (see **LATE**, **-LY**[2]).

late-model ▶ **adjective** chiefly N. Amer. (especially of a car) recently made or of a recent design.

La Tène /la ˈtɛn/ ▶ **noun** [usu. as modifier] Archaeology the second cultural phase of the European Iron Age, following the Hallstatt period (*c.*480 BC) and lasting until the coming of the Romans. This culture represents the height of Celtic power, being characterized by hill forts, rich and elaborate burials, and distinctively crafted artefacts.
– ORIGIN late 19th cent.: named after a district in Switzerland, where remains of the culture were first identified.

latent ▶ **adjective** (of a quality or state) existing but

not yet developed or manifest; hidden, concealed: *discovering her latent talent for diplomacy.*
■ Biology (of a bud, resting stage, etc.) lying dormant or hidden until circumstances are suitable for development or manifestation. ■ (of a disease) in which the usual symptoms are not yet manifest. ■ (of a micro-organism, especially a virus) present in the body without causing disease, but capable of doing so at a later stage, or when transmitted to another body.
– DERIVATIVES **latency** noun, **latently** adverb.
– ORIGIN late Middle English: from Latin *latent-* 'being hidden', from the verb *latere*.

latent heat ▶ **noun** [mass noun] Physics the heat required to convert a solid into a liquid or vapour, or a liquid into a vapour, without change of temperature.

latent image ▶ **noun** Photography an image on an exposed film or print that has not yet been made visible by developing.

latent period ▶ **noun 1** Medicine the period between infection with a virus or other micro-organism and the onset of symptoms, or between exposure to radiation and the appearance of a cancer.
2 Physiology the delay between the receipt of a stimulus by a sensory nerve and the response to it.

later (also **laters**) ▶ **exclamation** informal, chiefly US goodbye for the present; see you later.

-later ▶ **combining form** denoting a person who worships a specified thing: *idolater.*
– ORIGIN from Greek *-latrēs* 'worshipper'.

lateral ▶ **adjective** of, at, towards, or from the side or sides: *the plant takes up water through its lateral roots.*
■ Anatomy & Zoology situated on one side or other of the body or of an organ, especially in the region furthest from the median plane. The opposite of **MEDIAL**. ■ Medicine (of a disease or condition) affecting the side or sides of the body, or confined to one side of the body. ■ Physics acting or placed at right angles to the line of motion or of strain. ■ Phonetics (of a consonant, especially the English clear *l*, or its articulation) formed by or involving partial closure of the air passage by the tongue, which is so placed as to allow the breath to flow on one or both sides of the point of contact.
▶ **noun 1** a side part of something, especially a shoot or branch growing out from the side of a stem.
2 Phonetics a lateral consonant.
3 American Football a pass thrown either sideways or back from the direction of the forward progress of the ball-carrier.
– DERIVATIVES **laterally** adverb.
– ORIGIN late Middle English: from Latin *lateralis*, from *latus, later-* 'side'.

laterality ▶ **noun** [mass noun] dominance of one side of the brain in controlling particular activities or functions, or of one of a pair of organs such as the eyes or hands.

lateralize ▶ **verb** (**be lateralized**) (of the brain) show laterality.
■ [with adverbial] (of an organ, function, or activity) be largely under the control of one or other side of the brain: *this is a function which is usually lateralized on the right.* ■ [with adverbial] Medicine (of a lesion or pathological process) be diagnosed as localized to one or other side of the brain.
– DERIVATIVES **lateralization** noun.

lateral line ▶ **noun** Zoology a visible line along the side of a fish consisting of a series of sense organs which detect pressure and vibration.

lateral thinking ▶ **noun** [mass noun] chiefly Brit. the solving of problems by an indirect and creative approach, typically through viewing the problem in a new and unusual light.

lateral ventricle ▶ **noun** Anatomy each of the first and second ventricles in the centre of each cerebral hemisphere of the brain.

Lateran /ˈlatərən/ the site in Rome containing the cathedral church of Rome (a basilica dedicated to St John the Baptist and St John the Evangelist) and the Lateran Palace, where the popes resided until the 14th century.

Lateran Council any of five general councils of the Western Church held in the Lateran Palace in 1123, 1139, 1179, 1215, and 1512–17. The council of 1215 condemned the Albigenses as heretical and clarified the Church doctrine on transubstantiation, the Trinity, and the Incarnation.

Lateran Treaty a concordat signed in 1929 in the Lateran Palace between the kingdom of Italy (represented by Mussolini) and the Holy See (represented by Pope Pius XI), which recognized as fully sovereign and independent the papal state under the name Vatican City.

laterite /ˈlatərʌɪt/ ▶ **noun** [mass noun] a reddish clayey material, hard when dry, forming a topsoil in some tropical or subtropical regions and sometimes used for building.
■ Geology a clayey soil horizon rich in iron and aluminium oxides, formed by weathering of igneous rocks in moist warm climates.
– DERIVATIVES **lateritic** adjective.
– ORIGIN early 19th cent.: from Latin *later* 'brick' + **-ITE**[1].

latex /ˈleɪtɛks/ ▶ **noun** (pl. **latexes** or **latices** /-tɪsiːz/) [mass noun] a milky fluid found in many plants, such as poppies and spurges, which exudes when the plant is cut and coagulates on exposure to the air. The latex of the rubber tree is the chief source of natural rubber.
■ a synthetic product resembling this consisting of a dispersion in water of polymer particles, used to make paints, coatings, and other products.
– ORIGIN mid 17th cent. (denoting various bodily fluids, especially the watery part of blood): from Latin, literally 'liquid, fluid'.

lath /lɑːθ, laθ/ ▶ **noun** (pl. **laths** /lɑːθs, lɑːðz, laθs/) a thin flat strip of wood, especially one of a series forming a foundation for the plaster of a wall or the tiles of a roof or made into a trellis or fence.
■ [mass noun] laths collectively as a building material, especially as a foundation for supporting plaster.
▶ **verb** [with obj.] cover (a wall or ceiling) with laths.
– ORIGIN Old English *lætt*, of Germanic origin; related to Dutch *lat* and German *Latte*, also to **LATTICE**.

lathe /leɪð/ ▶ **noun** a machine for shaping wood, metal, or other material by means of a rotating drive which turns the piece being worked on against changeable cutting tools.
▶ **verb** [with obj.] shape with a lathe.
– ORIGIN Middle English: probably from Old Danish *lad* 'structure, frame', perhaps from Old Norse *hlath* 'pile, heap', related to *hlatha* (see **LADE**).

lather /ˈlɑːðə, ˈlaðə/ ▶ **noun** [mass noun] a frothy white mass of bubbles produced by soap, washing powder, or similar cleansing substance when mixed with water.
■ heavy sweat visible on a horse's coat as a white foam. ■ (**a lather**) informal a state of agitation or nervous excitement: *Dad had* **got into a right lather** *by the time I got home.*
▶ **verb** [with obj.] **1** cause (soap) to form a frothy white mass of bubbles when mixed with water.
■ [no obj.] (of soap, washing powder, or a similar cleansing substance) form a frothy white mass of bubbles in such a way: *soap will not lather in hard water.* ■ rub soap on to (a part of the body) until a lather is produced: *she was lathering herself languidly beneath the shower* | [no obj.] *he lathered and started to shave.* ■ cause (a horse) to become covered with sweat: *his horse was* **lathered up** *by the end of the day.* ■ (**lather something with**) cover something liberally with (a substance): *she lathered a slice of toast with butter.* ■ (**lather something on**) spread a substance liberally on: *we lathered the cream on our scones.*
2 informal thrash (someone).
– DERIVATIVES **lathery** adjective.
– ORIGIN Old English *lēathor* (denoting washing soda or its froth), *lēthran* (verb), of Germanic origin; related to Old Norse *lauthr* (noun), from an Indo-European root shared by Greek *loutron* 'bath'.

lathi /ˈlɑːtiː/ ▶ **noun** (pl. **lathis**) (in the Indian subcontinent) a long, heavy iron-bound bamboo stick used as a weapon, especially by police.
– ORIGIN from Hindi *lāṭhī*.

lathyrism /ˈlaθɪrɪz(ə)m/ ▶ **noun** [mass noun] a tropical disease marked by tremors, muscular weakness, and paraplegia, especially prevalent in the Indian subcontinent. It is commonly attributed to continued consumption of the seeds of the grass pea.
– ORIGIN late 19th cent.: from modern Latin *Lathyrus* (genus name of various leguminous plants) + **-ISM**.

latices plural form of **LATEX**.

laticifer /laˈtɪsɪfə/ ▶ **noun** Botany a cell, tissue, or vessel that contains or conducts latex.
– DERIVATIVES **laticiferous** /latɪˈsɪf(ə)rəs/ adjective.
– ORIGIN mid 19th cent.: from Latin *latex, latic-* 'fluid' + *-fer* 'bearing'.

latifundium /ˌlɑːtɪˈfʌndɪəm, ˌlatɪ-/ ▶ **noun** (pl. **latifundia**) a large landed estate or ranch in ancient Rome or more recently in Spain or Latin America, typically worked by slaves.
– ORIGIN mid 17th cent.: from Latin, from *latus* 'broad' + *fundus* 'landed estate', partly via Spanish.

Latimer /ˈlatɪmə/, Hugh (*c.*1485–1555), English Protestant prelate and martyr. One of Henry VIII's chief advisers when the king broke with the papacy, under Mary I he was condemned for heresy and burnt at the stake at Oxford with Nicholas Ridley.

Latin ▶ **noun 1** [mass noun] the language of ancient Rome and its empire, widely used historically as a language of scholarship and administration.

Latin is a member of the Italic branch of the Indo-European family of languages. After the decline of the Roman Empire it continued to be a medium of communication among educated people throughout the Middle Ages in Europe and elsewhere, and remained the liturgical language of the Roman Catholic Church until the reforms of the second Vatican Council (1962–5); it is still used for scientific names in biology and astronomy. The Romance languages are derived from it.

2 a native or inhabitant of a country whose language developed from Latin, especially a Latin American.
■ [mass noun] music of a kind originating in Latin America, characterized by dance rhythms and extensive use of indigenous percussion instruments.
▶ **adjective** of, relating to, or in the Latin language: *Latin poetry.*
■ of or relating to the countries or peoples using languages, such as French and Spanish, that developed from Latin. ■ of, relating to, or characteristic of Latin American music or dance: *snapping his fingers to a Latin beat.* ■ of or relating to the Western or Roman Catholic Church (as historically using Latin for its rites): *the Latin patriarch of Antioch.* ■ historical of or relating to ancient Latium or its inhabitants.
– DERIVATIVES **Latinism** noun, **Latinist** noun.
– ORIGIN from Latin *Latinus* 'of Latium' (see **LATIUM**).

Latina /ləˈtiːnə/ chiefly US ▶ **noun** a female Latin American inhabitant of the United States.
▶ **adjective** of or relating to these inhabitants.
– ORIGIN Latin American Spanish, feminine of *Latino* (see **LATINO**).

Latin America the parts of the American continent where Spanish or Portuguese is the main national language (i.e. Mexico and, in effect, the whole of Central and South America including many of the Caribbean islands).
– DERIVATIVES **Latin American** noun & adjective.

Latinate /ˈlatɪneɪt/ ▶ **adjective** (of language) having the character of Latin: *Latinate oaths.*

Latin Church the Christian Church which originated in the Western Roman Empire, giving allegiance to the Pope of Rome, and historically using Latin for the liturgy; the Roman Catholic Church as distinguished from Orthodox and Uniate Churches.

Latin cross ▶ **noun** a plain cross in which the vertical part below the horizontal is longer than the other three parts.

Latinity ▶ **noun** [mass noun] the use of Latin style or words of Latin origin.

Latinize (also **-ise**) ▶ **verb** [with obj.] **1** give a Latin or Latinate form to (a word): *his name was Latinized into Confucius.*
■ archaic translate into Latin. ■ [no obj.] archaic use Latin forms or idiom.
2 make (a people or culture) conform to the ideas and customs of the ancient Romans, the Latin peoples, or the Latin Church.
– DERIVATIVES **Latinization** noun, **Latinizer** noun.
– ORIGIN late 16th cent.: from late Latin *Latinizare*, from Latin *Latinus* (see **LATIN**).

Latin lover ▶ **noun** a Latin male popularly characterized as having a romantic, passionate temperament and great sexual prowess.

Latino /ləˈtiːnəʊ/ chiefly US ▶ **noun** (pl. **-os**) a Latin American inhabitant of the United States.
▶ **adjective** of or relating to these inhabitants.
– ORIGIN Latin American Spanish, probably a special use of Spanish *latino* (see **LATIN**).

Latin square ▶ **noun** an arrangement of letters or symbols that each occur *n* times, in a square array of n^2 compartments so that no letter appears twice in the same row or column.

▪such an arrangement used as the basis of experimental procedures in which it is desired to control or allow for two sources of variability while investigating a third.

latissimus /lɑːˈtɪsɪməs/ (also **latissimus dorsi** /ˈdɔːsʌɪ, -siː/) ▶ **noun** (pl. **latissimi** /lɑːˈtɪsɪmʌɪ, -miː/) Anatomy either of a pair of large, roughly triangular muscles covering the lower part of the back, extending from the sacral, lumbar, and lower thoracic vertebrae to the armpits.
– ORIGIN early 17th cent.: modern Latin, from *musculus latissimus dorsi*, literally 'broadest muscle of the back'.

latitude /ˈlatɪtjuːd/ ▶ **noun 1** the angular distance of a place north or south of the earth's equator, or of the equator of a celestial object, usually expressed in degrees and minutes: *at a latitude of 51° N* | [mass noun] *lines of latitude.*
▪(**latitudes**) regions, especially with reference to their temperature and distance from the equator: *temperate latitudes* | *northern latitudes.* ▪ Astronomy see **CELESTIAL LATITUDE.**
2 [mass noun] scope for freedom of action or thought: *journalists have considerable latitude in criticizing public figures.*
▪Photography the range of exposures for which an emulsion or printing paper will give acceptable contrast: *a film with a latitude which is outstanding.*
– DERIVATIVES **latitudinal** adjective, **latitudinally** adverb.
– ORIGIN late Middle English: from Latin *latitudo* 'breadth', from *latus* 'broad'.

latitudinarian /ˌlatɪtjuːdɪˈnɛːrɪən/ ▶ **adjective** allowing latitude in religion; showing no preference among varying creeds and forms of worship.
▶ **noun** a person with a latitudinarian attitude.
– DERIVATIVES **latitudinarianism** noun.
– ORIGIN mid 17th cent.: from Latin *latitudo* 'breadth' (see **LATITUDE**) + **-ARIAN.**

Latium /ˈleɪʃɪəm/ an ancient region of west central Italy, west of the Apennines and south of the River Tiber. Settled during the early part of the 1st millennium BC by a branch of the Indo-European people known as the Latini, it had become dominated by Rome by the end of the 4th century BC; it is now part of the modern region of Lazio.

latke /ˈlʌtkə/ ▶ **noun** (in Jewish cookery) a pancake, especially one made with grated potato.
– ORIGIN Yiddish.

Latona /ləˈtəʊnə/ Roman Mythology Roman name for **LETO.**

La Tour /la ˈtʊə, French la tuʀ/, Georges de (1593–1652), French painter. He is best known for his nocturnal religious scenes and his subtle portrayal of candlelight. Notable works: *St Joseph the Carpenter* (1645) and *The Denial of St Peter* (1650).

latria /ləˈtrʌɪə, ˈlatrɪə/ ▶ **noun** [mass noun] (in the Roman Catholic Church) supreme worship allowed to God alone. Compare with **DULIA.**
– ORIGIN early 16th cent.: from late Latin, from Greek *latreia* 'worship', from *latreuein* 'serve'.

latrine /ləˈtriːn/ ▶ **noun** (often **latrines**) a toilet, especially a communal one in a camp or barracks.
– ORIGIN Middle English (rare before the mid 19th cent.): via French from Latin *latrina*, contraction of *lavatrina*, from *lavare* 'to wash'.

-latry ▶ **combining form** denoting worship of a specified thing: *idolatry.*
– ORIGIN from Greek *-latria* 'worship'.

latte /ˈlɑːteɪ, ˈlateɪ/ ▶ **noun** short for **CAFFÈ LATTE.**

latten /ˈlat(ə)n/ ▶ **noun** [mass noun] historical an alloy of copper and zinc resembling brass, hammered into thin sheets and used to make monumental brasses and church ornaments.
– ORIGIN Middle English: from Old French *laton*, of unknown origin.

latter ▶ **adjective** [attrib.] **1** situated or occurring nearer to the end of something than to the beginning: *the latter half of 1989.*
▪belonging to the final stages of something, especially of a person's life: *heart disease dogged his latter years.* ▪ recent: *the project has had low cash flows in latter years.*
2 (**the latter**) denoting the second or second mentioned of two people or things: *the Russians could advance into either Germany or Austria—they chose the latter option* | [as noun] *the President appoints the Prime Minister and, on the latter's advice, the rest of the government.*
– ORIGIN Old English *lætra* 'slower', comparative of *læt* (see **LATE**).

USAGE It is not considered good writing style to use **latter** to refer to more than two things. For an explanation, see **usage** at **FORMER**[1].

latter-day ▶ **adjective** [attrib.] modern or contemporary, especially when mirroring some person or thing of the past: *the book is built round the story of the Flood and a latter-day Noah.*

Latter-Day Saints (abbrev.: **LDS**) ▶ **plural noun** the Mormons' name for themselves.

latterly ▶ **adverb** recently: *latterly, his painting has shown a new freedom of expression.*
▪in the later stages of a period of time, especially of a person's life: *he worked on the paper for fifty years, latterly as its political editor.*

lattice ▶ **noun** a structure consisting of strips of wood or metal crossed and fastened together with square or diamond-shaped spaces left between, used typically as a screen or fence or as a support for climbing plants.
▪an interlaced structure or pattern resembling this: *the lattice of branches above her.* ▪ Physics a regular repeated three-dimensional arrangement of atoms, ions, or molecules in a metal or other crystalline solid.
– ORIGIN Middle English: from Old French *lattis*, from *latte* 'lath', of Germanic origin.

latticed ▶ **adjective** decorated with or in the form of a lattice: *a latticed screen.*

lattice energy ▶ **noun** Chemistry a measure of the energy contained in the crystal lattice of a compound, equal to the energy that would be released if the component ions were brought together from infinity.

lattice frame (also **lattice girder**) ▶ **noun** an iron or steel structure consisting of two horizontal beams connected by diagonal struts.

lattice window ▶ **noun** a window with small panes set in diagonally crossing strips of lead.

latticework ▶ **noun** [mass noun] interlacing strips of wood, metal, or other material forming a lattice.

latticinio /ˌlatɪˈtʃiːnjəʊ/ (also **latticino** /-nəʊ/) ▶ **noun** [mass noun] an opaque white glass used in threads to decorate clear Venetian glass.
– ORIGIN Italian, literally 'dairy produce', from medieval Latin *lacticinium.*

Latvia /ˈlatvɪə/ a country on the eastern shore of the Baltic Sea, between Estonia and Lithuania; pop. 2,693,000 (est. 1991); official language, Latvian; capital, Riga.

Latvia was annexed by Russia in the 18th century after periods of Polish and Swedish rule. It was proclaimed an independent republic in 1918, but in 1940 was annexed by the Soviet Union as a constituent republic. In 1991, on the break-up of the USSR, Latvia became an independent republic once again.

Latvian ▶ **adjective** of or relating to Latvia, its people, or its language.
▶ **noun 1** a native or citizen of Latvia, or a person of Latvian descent.
2 [mass noun] the language of Latvia, which belongs to the Baltic branch of the Indo-European family and has about 1.5 million speakers.

Laud /lɔːd/, William (1573–1645), English prelate, Archbishop of Canterbury 1633–45. His attempts to restore some pre-Reformation practices in England and Scotland aroused great hostility and were a contributory cause of the English Civil War. He was executed for treason.

laud /lɔːd/ ▶ **verb** [with obj.] formal praise (a person or their achievements) highly, especially in a public context: *the obituary lauded him as a great statesman and soldier* | [as adj., with submodifier] (**lauded**) *her much lauded rendering of Lady Macbeth.*
▶ **noun** [mass noun] archaic praise: *all glory, laud, and honour to Thee Redeemer King.*
– ORIGIN late Middle English: the noun from Old French *laude*, the verb from Latin *laudare*, both from Latin *laus, laud-* 'praise' (see also **LAUDS**).

Lauda /ˈlaʊdə/, Niki (b.1949), Austrian motor-racing driver; full name *Nikolaus Andreas Lauda.* World champion in 1975, he suffered severe injuries in the 1976 German Grand Prix, but won two more championships (1977 and 1984). He retired in 1985.

laudable ▶ **adjective** (of an action, idea, or aim) deserving praise and commendation: *laudable though the aim might be, the results have been criticized.*
– DERIVATIVES **laudability** noun, **laudably** adverb.
– ORIGIN late Middle English: from Latin *laudabilis*, from *laus, laud-* 'praise'.

laudanum /ˈlɔːd(ə)nəm, ˈlɒ-/ ▶ **noun** [mass noun] an alcoholic solution containing morphine, prepared from opium and formerly used as a narcotic painkiller.
– ORIGIN mid 16th cent. (applied to various preparations containing opium): modern Latin, the name given by Paracelsus to a costly medicament of which opium was believed to be the active ingredient; perhaps a variant of Latin *ladanum* (see **LADANUM**).

laudation /lɔːˈdeɪʃ(ə)n/ ▶ **noun** [mass noun] formal praise; commendation.
– ORIGIN late Middle English: from Latin *laudatio(n-)*, from the verb *laudare* (see **LAUD**).

laudatory /ˈlɔːdət(ə)ri/ ▶ **adjective** (of speech or writing) expressing praise and commendation.
– ORIGIN mid 16th cent.: from late Latin *laudatorius*, from *laudat-* 'praised', from the verb *laudare* (see **LAUD**).

Lauder /ˈlɔːdə/, Sir Harry (1870–1950), Scottish music-hall comedian; born *Hugh MacLennan Lauder.* He became highly popular singing songs such as 'Roamin' in the Gloamin'', and entertained troops at home and abroad in both world wars.

lauds /lɔːdz/ ▶ **noun** a service of morning prayer in the Divine Office of the Western Christian Church, traditionally said or chanted at daybreak, though historically it was often held with matins on the previous night.
– ORIGIN Middle English: from the frequent use, in Psalms 148–150, of the Latin imperative *laudate!* 'praise ye!' (see also **LAUD**).

laugh ▶ **verb** [no obj.] make the spontaneous sounds and movements of the face and body that are the instinctive expressions of lively amusement and sometimes also of contempt or derision: *she couldn't help laughing at his jokes* | *he* ***laughed out loud.***
▪(**laugh at**) ridicule; scorn. ▪ (**laugh something off**) dismiss something embarrassing, unfortunate, or potentially serious by treating it in a light-hearted way or making a joke of it. ▪ (**be laughing**) informal be in a fortunate or successful position: *if next year's model is as successful, Ford will be laughing.*
▶ **noun 1** an act of laughing: *she gave a loud, silly laugh.*
2 (**a laugh**) informal a thing that causes laughter or derision: *that's a laugh, the idea of you cooking a meal!*
▪a person who is good fun or amusing company: *I like Peter—he's* ***a good laugh.*** ▪ a source of fun or amusement: *she decided to play along with him* ***for a laugh*** | *he knew his performance was* ***good for a laugh.***
– PHRASES **be laughing all the way to the bank** informal be making a great deal of money very easily. **have the last laugh** be finally vindicated, thus confounding earlier scepticism. **he who laughs last laughs longest** proverb don't rejoice too soon, in case your delight at your own good fortune is premature. **laugh one's head off** laugh heartily or uncontrollably. **laugh in someone's face** show open contempt for someone by laughing rudely at them in their presence: figurative *vandals and muggers who laugh in the face of the law.* **the laugh is on me** (or **you**, **him**, etc.) the tables are turned and now the other person is the one who appears ridiculous: *all the critics had laughed at him—well, the laugh was on them now.* **laugh like a drain** Brit. informal laugh raucously. **a laugh a minute** very funny: *it's a laugh a minute when Lois gets together with her dad.* **laugh on the other side of one's face** (or N. Amer. **out of the other side of one's mouth**) be discomfited after feeling satisfaction or confidence about something. **laugh someone/thing out of court** dismiss with contempt as being obviously ridiculous. **laugh oneself silly** (or **sick**) laugh uncontrollably or for a long time. **laugh something to scorn** dated ridicule something. **laugh up one's sleeve** be secretly or inwardly amused. **no laughing matter** something serious that should not be joked about: *heavy snoring is no laughing matter.* **play something for laughs** (of a performer) try to arouse laughter in an audience, especially in inappropriate circumstances.
– ORIGIN Old English *hlæhhan, hliehhan*, of Germanic origin; related to Dutch and German *lachen*, also to **LAUGHTER.**

l

laughable ▶ adjective so ludicrous as to be amusing: *if it didn't make me so angry it would be laughable.*
– DERIVATIVES **laughably** adverb [as submodifier] *his antics were laughably pretentious.*

laugher ▶ noun **1** a person who laughs.
2 N. Amer. informal a sporting match or competition which is so easily won by one team or competitor that it seems absurd.

laughing gas ▶ noun non-technical term for **NITROUS OXIDE**.

laughing hyena ▶ noun another term for **SPOTTED HYENA**.

laughing jackass ▶ noun Austral. the laughing kookaburra. See **KOOKABURRA**.

laughingly ▶ adverb with amused ridicule or ludicrous inappropriateness: *we finally reached what we laughingly called civilization.*
■ in an amused way; with laughter.

laughing stock ▶ noun [in sing.] a person subjected to general mockery or ridicule.

laughing-thrush ▶ noun a gregarious thrush-like babbler of South and SE Asia, typically with dark grey or brown plumage and a boldly marked head, and a cackling call.
● Genus *Garrulax*, family Timaliidae: many species.

laughter ▶ noun [mass noun] the action or sound of laughing: *he roared with laughter.*
– ORIGIN Old English *hleahtor*, of Germanic origin; related to German *Gelächter*, also to **LAUGH**.

Laughton /ˈlɔːt(ə)n/, Charles (1899–1962), British-born American actor. He is remembered for character roles such as Henry VIII (*The Private Life of Henry VIII*, 1933); he also played Quasimodo in *The Hunchback of Notre Dame* (1939).

launce /lɑːns, lans/ ▶ noun another term for **SAND EEL**.
– ORIGIN early 17th cent.: early variant of **LANCE** (because of its shape).

Launcelot variant spelling of **LANCELOT**.

Launceston /ˈlɔːns(ə)stən/ a city in northern Tasmania, on the Tamar estuary, the second largest city of the island; pop. 66,750 (1991).

launch¹ ▶ verb [with obj.] **1** set (a boat) in motion by pushing it or allowing it to roll into the water: *the town's lifeboat was launched to rescue the fishermen.*
■ set (a newly built ship or boat) afloat for the first time, typically as part of an official ceremony: *the ship was launched in 1843 by Prince Albert.* ■ send (a missile, satellite, or spacecraft) on its course or into orbit: *they launched two Scud missiles.* ■ [with obj. and adverbial of direction] hurl (something) forcefully: *a chair was launched at him.* ■ [with adverbial of direction] (**launch oneself**) (of a person) make a sudden energetic movement: *I launched myself out of bed.* ■ utter (criticism or a threat) vehemently: *he launched a biting attack on BBC chiefs.*
2 start or set in motion (an activity or enterprise): *the government is to launch a £1.25 million publicity campaign.*
■ introduce (a new product or publication) to the public for the first time: *two new Ford models are to be launched in the US next year.*
▶ noun an act or an instance of launching something: *the launch of a new campaign against drinking and driving.*
■ an occasion at which a new product or publication is introduced to the public: *a book launch.*
– ORIGIN Middle English (in the sense 'hurl a missile, discharge with force'): from Anglo-Norman French *launcher*, variant of Old French *lancier* (see **LANCE**).
▶ **launch into** begin (something) energetically and enthusiastically: *he launched into a two-hour sales pitch.*
launch out make a start on a new and challenging enterprise: *she wasn't brave enough to launch out by herself.*

launch² ▶ noun a large motor boat, used especially for short trips.
■ historical the largest boat carried on a man-of-war.
– ORIGIN late 17th cent. (denoting the longboat of a man-of-war): from Spanish *lancha* 'pinnace', perhaps from Malay *lancharan*, from *lanchar* 'swift, nimble'.

launcher ▶ noun a structure that holds a rocket or missile during launching.
■ a rocket that is used to convey a satellite or spacecraft into orbit.

launch pad (also **launching pad**) ▶ noun the area on which a rocket stands for launching, typically consisting of a platform with a supporting structure.

launch vehicle ▶ noun a rocket-powered vehicle used to send artificial satellites or spacecraft into space.

launder ▶ verb [with obj.] wash and iron (clothes or linen): *he wasn't used to laundering his own bed linen* | [as adj., with submodifier] (**laundered**) *freshly laundered sheets.*
■ conceal the origins of (money obtained illegally) by transfers involving foreign banks or legitimate businesses. ■ alter (information) to make it appear more acceptable: *we began to notice attempts to launder the data retrospectively.*
▶ noun a trough for holding or conveying water, especially (in mining) one used for washing ore.
■ a channel for conveying molten metal from a furnace or container to a ladle or mould.
– DERIVATIVES **launderer** noun.
– ORIGIN Middle English (as a noun denoting a person who washes linen): contraction of *lavender*, from Old French *lavandier*, based on Latin *lavanda* 'things to be washed', from *lavare* 'to wash'.

launderette (also **laundrette**) ▶ noun an establishment with coin-operated washing machines and driers for public use.

laundress ▶ noun a woman who is employed to launder clothes and linen.

laundromat ▶ noun chiefly N. Amer. (trademark in the US) a launderette.
– ORIGIN 1940s (originally US, as the proprietary name of a washing machine): blend of **LAUNDER** and **AUTOMATIC**.

laundry ▶ noun (pl. **-ies**) **1** [mass noun] clothes and linen that need to be washed or that have been newly washed: *piles of dirty laundry.*
■ the action or process of washing such items: *cooking and laundry were undertaken by domestic staff.*
2 a room in a house, hotel, or institution where clothes and linen can be washed and ironed.
■ a firm washing and ironing clothes and linen commercially.
– ORIGIN early 16th cent.: contraction of Middle English *lavendry*, from Old French *lavanderie*, from *lavandier* 'person who washes linen' (see **LAUNDER**).

laundry list ▶ noun a long or exhaustive list of people or things: *a laundry list of people and organizations that would have to be won over.*

laundryman ▶ noun (pl. **-men**) a man who is employed to launder clothes and linen.

Laurasia /lɔːˈreɪzɪə, -ʃə/ a vast continental area believed to have existed in the northern hemisphere and to have resulted from the break-up of Pangaea in Mesozoic times. It comprised the present North America, Greenland, Europe, and most of Asia north of the Himalayas.

laureate /ˈlɒrɪət, ˈlɔː-/ ▶ noun a person who is honoured with an award for outstanding creative or intellectual achievement: *a Nobel laureate.*
■ short for **POET LAUREATE**.
▶ adjective poetic/literary wreathed with laurel as a mark of honour.
■ (of a crown or wreath) consisting of laurel.
– DERIVATIVES **laureateship** noun.
– ORIGIN late Middle English (as an adjective): from Latin *laureatus*, from *laurea* 'laurel wreath', from *laurus* 'laurel'.

laurel ▶ noun **1** any of a number of shrubs and other plants with dark green glossy leaves, in particular:
● short for **CHERRY LAUREL**. ● historical the bay tree. See **BAY²**.
2 an aromatic evergreen shrub related to the bay tree, several kinds of which form forests in tropical and warm countries.
● Family Lauraceae: many genera and species.
3 (usu. **laurels**) the foliage of the bay tree woven into a wreath or crown and worn on the head as an emblem of victory or mark of honour in classical times.
■ figurative honour: *she has rightly won laurels for this brilliantly perceptive first novel.*
▶ verb (**laurelled, laurelling**; US **laureled, laureling**) [with obj.] adorn with or as if with a laurel: *they banish our anger forever when they laurel the graves of our dead.*
– PHRASES **look to one's laurels** be careful not to lose one's superior position to a rival. **rest on one's laurels** be so satisfied with what one has already done or achieved that one makes no further effort.

– ORIGIN Middle English *lorer*, from Old French *lorier*, from Provençal *laurier*, from earlier *laur*, from Latin *laurus*.

Laurel and Hardy an American comedy duo consisting of **Stan Laurel** (born *Arthur Stanley Jefferson*) (1890–1965) and **Oliver Hardy** (1892–1957). British-born Stan Laurel played the scatterbrained and often tearful innocent, Oliver Hardy his pompous, overbearing, and frequently exasperated friend. They brought their distinctive slapstick comedy to many films from 1927 onwards.

Laurence, (Jean) Margaret (1926–87), Canadian novelist. Her life in Somalia and Ghana (1950–7) influenced her early work, including *This Side Jordan* (1960). Other notable works: *The Stone Angel* (1964).

Laurentian Plateau /lɒˈrɛnʃ(ə)n/ another name for **CANADIAN SHIELD**.
– ORIGIN *Laurentian* from Latin *Laurentius* 'Lawrence' (from St *Lawrence* River) + **-AN**.

Laurier /ˈlɔːrɪeɪ/, Sir Wilfrid (1841–1919), Canadian Liberal statesman, Prime Minister 1896–1911. He was Canada's first French-Canadian and Roman Catholic Prime Minister.

laurustinus /ˌlɒrəˈstaɪnəs, ˌlɔː-/ ▶ noun an evergreen winter-flowering viburnum with dense glossy green leaves and white or pink flowers, native to the Mediterranean area.
● *Viburnum tinus*, family Caprifoliaceae.
– ORIGIN early 17th cent.: modern Latin, from Latin *laurus* 'laurel' + *tinus* 'wild laurel'.

Lausanne /ləʊˈzan/ a town in SW Switzerland, on the north shore of Lake Geneva; pop. 122,600 (1990).

Lausitzer Neisse /ˌlaʊzɪtsə ˈnaɪsɪ/ German name for **NEISSE** (in sense 1).

lav ▶ noun informal a lavatory.
– ORIGIN early 20th cent.: abbreviation.

lava ▶ noun [mass noun] hot molten or semi-fluid rock erupted from a volcano or fissure, or solid rock resulting from cooling of this.
– ORIGIN mid 18th cent.: from Italian (Neapolitan dialect), denoting the lava stream from Vesuvius, but originally denoting a stream caused by sudden rain, from *lavare* 'to wash', from Latin.

lavabo /ləˈveɪbəʊ, ləˈvɑː-/ ▶ noun (pl. **-os**) (in the Roman Catholic Church) a towel or basin used for the ritual washing of the celebrant's hands at the offertory of the Mass.
■ [mass noun] ritual washing of this type. ■ dated a washbasin. ■ /ˈlavəbəʊ/ a monastery washing trough.
– ORIGIN mid 18th cent.: from Latin, literally 'I will wash', in *Lavabo inter innocentes manus meas* 'I will wash my hands in innocence' (Ps. 26:6), which was recited at the washing of hands in the Roman rite.

lava dome ▶ noun a mound of viscous lava which has been extruded from a volcanic vent.

lava flow ▶ noun a mass of flowing or solidified lava.

lavage /ˈlavɪdʒ, laˈvɑːʒ/ ▶ noun Medicine washing out of a body cavity, such as the colon or stomach, with water or a medicated solution.
– ORIGIN late 18th cent. (in the general sense 'washing, a wash'): from French, from *laver* 'to wash'.

lava lamp ▶ noun a transparent electric lamp containing a viscous liquid in which a brightly coloured waxy substance is suspended, rising and falling in irregular and constantly changing shapes.

lavatera /ˌlavəˈtɛːrə/ ▶ noun a plant of a genus that includes the tree mallow.
● Genus *Lavatera*, family Malvaceae.
– ORIGIN modern Latin, named after the brothers *Lavater*, 17th- and 18th-cent. Swiss naturalists.

lavatorial ▶ adjective of or relating to lavatories, in particular:
■ (of conversation or humour) characterized by undue reference to toilets and their use: *the comic's lavatorial schoolboy humour appealed to many people.* ■ resembling the style or architecture supposed to typify public lavatories: *the lavatorial utility that was a feature of subway design.*

lavatory ▶ noun (pl. **-ies**) a toilet.
– ORIGIN late Middle English: from late Latin *lavatorium* 'place for washing', from Latin *lavare* 'to wash'. The word originally denoted something in which to wash, such as a bath or piscina, later (mid

17th cent.) a room with washing facilities; the current sense dates from the 19th cent.

lavatory paper ▶ noun Brit. toilet paper.

lava tube ▶ noun a natural tunnel within a solidified lava flow, formerly occupied by flowing molten lava.

lave /leɪv/ ▶ verb [with obj.] poetic/literary wash: *she ran cold water in the basin, laving her face and hands.*
■ (of water) wash against or over (something): *the sea below laved the shore with small, agitated waves.*
– DERIVATIVES **lavation** noun.
– ORIGIN Old English *lafian*, from Latin *lavare* 'to wash'; reinforced in Middle English by Old French *laver.*

lavender ▶ noun [mass noun] **1** a small aromatic evergreen shrub of the mint family, with narrow leaves and bluish-purple flowers. Lavender has been widely used in perfumery and medicine since ancient times.
● Genus *Lavandula*, family Labiatae.
■ the flowers and stalks of such a shrub dried and used to give a pleasant smell to clothes and bed linen. ■ (also **lavender oil**) a scented oil distilled from lavender flowers. ■ used in names of similar plants, e.g. **cotton lavender**, **sea lavender**. ■ informal used in reference to effeminacy or homosexuality: *Rick is so hard-boiled that any touch of lavender is wiped away.* ■ dated used in reference to refinement or gentility: [as modifier] *she had a certain lavender charm.*
2 a pale blue colour with a trace of mauve.
▶ verb [with obj.] perfume with lavender.
– ORIGIN Middle English: from Anglo-Norman French *lavendre*, based on medieval Latin *lavandula.*

lavender cotton ▶ noun another term for COTTON LAVENDER.

lavender water ▶ noun [mass noun] a perfume made from distilled lavender, alcohol, and ambergris.

Laver /ˈleɪvə/, Rod (b.1938), Australian tennis player; full name *Rodney George Laver*. In 1962 he became the second man (after Don Budge in 1938) to win the four major singles championships (British, American, French, and Australian) in one year; in 1969 he was the first to repeat this.

laver¹ /ˈlɑːvə, ˈleɪvə/ (also **purple laver**) ▶ noun [mass noun] an edible seaweed with thin sheet-like fronds of a reddish-purple and green colour which becomes black when dry. Laver typically grows on exposed shores, but in Japan it is cultivated in estuaries.
● *Porphyra umbilicaulis*, division Rhodophyta.
– ORIGIN late Old English (as the name of a water plant mentioned by Pliny), from Latin. The current sense dates from the early 17th cent.

laver² /ˈleɪvə/ ▶ noun archaic or poetic/literary a basin or similar container used for washing oneself.
■ (in biblical use) a large brass bowl for Jewish priests' ritual ablutions.
– ORIGIN Middle English: from Old French *laveoir*, from late Latin *lavatorium* 'place for washing' (see LAVATORY).

laver bread ▶ noun [mass noun] a Welsh dish of laver which is boiled, dipped in oatmeal, and fried.
– ORIGIN early 18th cent.: *laver* from LAVER¹.

lavish ▶ adjective sumptuously rich, elaborate, or luxurious: *a lavish banquet.*
■ (of a person) very generous or extravagant: *he was lavish with his hospitality.* ■ spent or given in profusion: *lavish praise.*
▶ verb [with obj.] (**lavish something on**) bestow something in generous or extravagant quantities upon: *the media couldn't lavish enough praise on the film.*
■ (**lavish something with**) cover something thickly or liberally with: *she lavished our son with kisses.*
– DERIVATIVES **lavishly** adverb, **lavishness** noun.
– ORIGIN late Middle English (as a noun denoting profusion): from Old French *lavasse* 'deluge of rain', from *laver* 'to wash', from Latin *lavare.*

Lavoisier /laˈvwʌzɪeɪ, French lavwazje/, Antoine Laurent (1743–94), French scientist, regarded as the father of modern chemistry. He caused a revolution in chemistry by his description of combustion as the combination of substances with air, or more specifically the gas oxygen.

Law¹, (Andrew) Bonar (1858–1923), Canadian-born British Conservative statesman, Prime Minister 1922–3. He was leader of the Conservative Party 1911–21. He retired in 1921, but returned in 1922, following Lloyd George's resignation, to become Prime Minister for six months.

Law², Denis (b.1940), Scottish footballer. He made his international debut in 1958 and went on to win forty caps for Scotland. He had his greatest success with Manchester United.

law ▶ noun **1** [mass noun] (often **the law**) the system of rules which a particular country or community recognizes as regulating the actions of its members and which it may enforce by the imposition of penalties: *they were taken to court for breaking the law* | *a licence is required by law* | [as modifier] *law enforcement.*
■ [count noun] an individual rule as part of such a system: *an initiative to tighten up the laws on pornography.* ■ such systems as a subject of study or as the basis of the legal profession: *he was still practising law* | [as modifier] *a law firm.* Compare with JURISPRUDENCE. ■ a thing regarded as having the binding force or effect of a formal system of rules: *he had supreme control—what he said was law.* ■ (**the law**) informal the police: *he'd never been in trouble with the law in his life.* ■ statute law and the common law. Compare with EQUITY. ■ [count noun] a rule defining correct procedure or behaviour in a sport: *the laws of the game.*
2 a statement of fact, deduced from observation, to the effect that a particular natural or scientific phenomenon always occurs if certain conditions are present: *the second law of thermodynamics.*
■ a generalization based on a fact or event perceived to be recurrent: *the first law of American corporate life is that dead wood floats.*
3 [mass noun] the body of divine commandments as expressed in the Bible or other religious texts.
■ (**the Law**) the Pentateuch as distinct from the other parts of the Hebrew Bible (the Prophets and the Writings). ■ (also **the Law of Moses**) the precepts of the Pentateuch. Compare with TORAH.
– PHRASES **at** (or **in**) **law** according to or concerned with the laws of a country: *an agreement enforceable at law* | *a barrister-at-law.* **be a law unto oneself** behave in a manner that is not conventional or predictable. **go to law** resort to legal action in order to settle a matter. **law and order** a situation characterized by respect for and obedience to the rules of a society. **the law of the jungle** see JUNGLE. **lay down the law** issue instructions to other people in an authoritative or dogmatic way. **take the law into one's own hands** punish someone for an offence according to one's own ideas of justice, especially in an illegal or violent way. **take someone to law** initiate legal proceedings against someone. **there's no law against it** informal used in spoken English to assert that one is doing nothing wrong, especially in response to an actual or implied criticism: *I can laugh, can't I? There's no law against it.*
– ORIGIN Old English *lagu*, from Old Norse *lag* 'something laid down or fixed', of Germanic origin and related to LAY¹.

law-abiding ▶ adjective obedient to the laws of society: *a law-abiding citizen.*
– DERIVATIVES **law-abidingness** noun.

law agent ▶ noun (in Scotland) a solicitor.

lawbreaker ▶ noun a person who breaks the law.
– DERIVATIVES **lawbreaking** noun & adjective.

law centre ▶ noun (in the UK) an independent publicly funded advisory service on legal matters.

Law Commission (in the UK) a body of legal advisers responsible for systematically reviewing the law of England and Wales, or of Scotland, which recommends changes and the removal of obsolete legislation.

law court ▶ noun a court of law.

lawful ▶ adjective conforming to, permitted by, or recognized by law or rules: *it is an offence to carry a weapon in public without lawful authority.*
■ dated (of a child) born within a lawful marriage.
– DERIVATIVES **lawfully** adverb, **lawfulness** noun.

lawgiver ▶ noun a person who draws up and enacts laws.

lawks ▶ exclamation dated (especially among cockneys) expressing surprise, awe, or consternation: *'Lawks, girl, where've you sprung from?'*
– ORIGIN mid 18th cent.: alteration of LORD.

lawless ▶ adjective not governed by or obedient to laws; characterized by a lack of civic order: *it was a lawless, anarchic city.*
– DERIVATIVES **lawlessly** adverb, **lawlessness** noun.

law lord ▶ noun (in the UK) a member of the House of Lords qualified to perform its legal work.

lawmaker ▶ noun a legislator.

– DERIVATIVES **law-making** adjective & noun.

lawman ▶ noun (pl. **-men**) (in the US) a law-enforcement officer, especially a sheriff.

lawn¹ ▶ noun an area of short, regularly mown grass in the garden of a house or park.
– DERIVATIVES **lawned** adjective.
– ORIGIN mid 16th cent.: alteration of dialect *laund* 'glade, pasture', from Old French *launde* 'wooded district, heath', of Celtic origin. The current sense dates from the mid 18th cent.

lawn² ▶ noun [mass noun] a fine linen or cotton fabric used for making clothes.
– DERIVATIVES **lawny** adjective.
– ORIGIN Middle English: probably from *Laon*, the name of a city in France important for linen manufacture.

lawn bowling ▶ noun North American term for BOWLS.

lawn chair ▶ noun N. Amer. a folding chair for use out of doors.

lawnmower ▶ noun a machine for cutting the grass on a lawn.

lawn party ▶ noun N. Amer. a garden party.

lawn tennis ▶ noun [mass noun] dated or formal the usual form of tennis, played with a soft ball on an open court.

law of averages ▶ noun the supposed principle that future events are likely to turn out so that they balance any past deviation from a presumed average.

law office ▶ noun N. Amer. a lawyer's office.

Law Officer (in full **Law Officer of the Crown**) ▶ noun (in England and Wales) the Attorney General or the Solicitor General, or (in Scotland) the Lord Advocate or the Solicitor General for Scotland.

law of mass action Chemistry ▶ noun the principle that the rate of a chemical reaction is proportional to the masses of the reacting substances.

law of nations ▶ noun [mass noun] Law international law.

law of nature ▶ noun **1** another term for NATURAL LAW (in senses 1 and 2).
2 informal a regularly occurring or apparently inevitable phenomenon observable in human society.

law of parsimony ▶ noun see PARSIMONY.

law of succession ▶ noun the law regulating the inheritance of property.
■ (**Law of Succession**) the law regulating the appointment of a new monarch or head of state.

Lawrence¹, D. H. (1885–1930), English novelist, poet, and essayist; full name *David Herbert Lawrence*. His work is characterized by its condemnation of industrial society and by its frank exploration of sexual relationships, as in *Lady Chatterley's·Lover*, originally published in Italy in 1928, but not available in England in unexpurgated form until 1960. Other notable works: *Sons and Lovers* (1913).

Lawrence², Ernest Orlando (1901–58), American physicist. He developed the first circular particle accelerator, later called a cyclotron, and opened the way for high-energy physics. He also worked on providing fissionable material for the atom bomb. Nobel Prize for Physics (1939).

Lawrence³, Sir Thomas (1769–1830), English painter. He achieved success with his full-length portrait (1789) of Queen Charlotte, the wife of King George III, and by 1810 he was recognized as the leading portrait painter of his time.

Lawrence⁴, T. E. (1888–1935), British soldier and writer; full name *Thomas Edward Lawrence*; known as **Lawrence of Arabia**. From 1916 onwards he helped to organize the Arab revolt against the Turks in the Middle East, contributing to General Allenby's eventual victory in Palestine in 1918. Lawrence described this period in *The Seven Pillars of Wisdom* (1926).

Lawrence, St (d.258), Roman martyr and deacon of Rome; Latin name *Laurentius*. According to tradition, Lawrence was ordered by the prefect of Rome to deliver up the treasure of the Church; when in response to this order he presented the poor people of Rome to the prefect, he was roasted to death on a gridiron. Feast day, 10 August.

lawrencium /lɒˈrɛnsɪəm/ ▶ noun [mass noun] the chemical element of atomic number 103, a radioactive metal of the actinide series.

Lawrencium does not occur naturally and was first made by bombarding californium with boron nuclei. (Symbol: **Lr**)

– ORIGIN 1960s: modern Latin, named after E. O. *Lawrence* (see **LAWRENCE**[2]), who founded the laboratory in which it was produced.

Law Society the professional body responsible for regulating solicitors in England and Wales, established in 1825.

laws of war ▶ plural noun the rules and conventions, recognized by civilized nations, which limit belligerents' action.

Lawson's cypress ▶ noun a slender North American conifer with dense foliage and lower branches arising at ground level. It is widely grown for timber and as an ornamental with many cultivars.
• *Chamaecyparis lawsoniana*, family Cupressaceae.

– ORIGIN mid 19th cent.: named after Peter Lawson (died 1820) and his son Charles (1794–1873), the Scottish nurserymen who first cultivated it.

lawsuit ▶ noun a claim or dispute brought to a law court for adjudication: *his lawyer **filed a lawsuit** against Los Angeles city.*

law term ▶ noun Brit. a period appointed for the sitting of law courts.

lawyer ▶ noun a person who practises or studies law, especially (in the UK) a solicitor or a barrister or (in the US) an attorney.

– DERIVATIVES **lawyerly** adjective.

lawyer's wig ▶ noun another term for **SHAGGY INK CAP**.

lawyer vine (also **lawyer cane**) ▶ noun an Australian climbing palm which is thickly covered in sharp spines and recurved hooks. It grows in rainforest, where groups may form dense tangled thickets.
• Genus *Calamus*, family Palmae.

– ORIGIN early 20th cent.: probably so named by humorous analogy with 'tortuous' legal arguments.

lax ▶ adjective **1** not sufficiently strict or severe: *lax security arrangements at the airport | he'd been a bit lax about discipline in school lately.*
▪ careless: *a mixture of demanding bowling and lax batsmanship saw four wickets fall after lunch.*
2 (of the limbs or muscles) relaxed.
▪ (of the bowels) loose. ▪ Phonetics (of a speech sound, especially a vowel) pronounced with the vocal muscles relaxed. The opposite of **TENSE**[1].

– DERIVATIVES **laxity** noun, **laxly** adverb, **laxness** noun.

– ORIGIN late Middle English (in the sense 'loose', said of the bowels): from Latin *laxus*.

laxative ▶ adjective (chiefly of a drug or medicine) tending to stimulate or facilitate evacuation of the bowels.
▶ noun a medicine which has such an effect.

– ORIGIN late Middle English: via Old French *laxatif, -ive* or late Latin *laxativus*, from Latin *laxare* 'loosen' (from *laxus* 'loose').

lay[1] ▶ verb (past and past participle **laid**) **1** [with obj. and adverbial of place] put down, especially gently or carefully: *she laid the baby in his cot.*
▪ [with obj.] prevent (something) from rising off the ground: *there may have been the odd light shower just to lay the dust.*
2 [with obj.] put down and set in position for use: *it is advisable to have your carpet laid by a professional |* figurative *the groundwork for change had been laid.*
▪ set cutlery, crockery, and mats on (a table) in preparation for a meal: *she laid the table for the evening meal.* ▪ (often **be laid with**) cover (a surface) with objects or a substance: *the floor was laid with mattresses.* ▪ make ready (a trap) for someone: *she wouldn't put it past him to lay a trap for her.* ▪ put the material for (a fire) in place and arrange it. ▪ work out (an idea or suggestion) in detail ready for use or presentation: *I'd like more time to lay my plans.* ▪ (**lay something before**) present information or suggestions to be considered and acted upon by (someone): *he laid before Parliament proposals for the establishment of the committee.* ▪ (usu. **be laid**) locate (an episode in a play, novel, etc.) in a certain place: *no one who knew the area could be in doubt where the scene was laid.* ▪ Nautical follow (a specified course). ▪ [with obj.] stake (an amount of money) in a wager: *she suspected he was pulling her leg, but she wouldn't have laid money on it.* ▪ [with obj.] trim (a hedge) back, cutting the branches half through, bending them down, and interweaving them.
3 [with obj.] used with an abstract noun so that the phrase formed has the same meaning as the verb related to the noun used, e.g. 'lay the blame on' means 'to blame': *she **laid** great **stress** on little courtesies.*
▪ (**lay something on**) require (someone) to endure or deal with a responsibility or difficulty: *this is an absurdly heavy guilt trip to lay on anyone.*
4 [with obj.] (of a female bird, insect, reptile, or amphibian) produce (an egg) from inside the body: *flamingos lay only one egg |* [no obj.] *the hens were laying at the same rate as usual.*
5 [with obj.] vulgar slang have sexual intercourse with.
▶ noun **1** [in sing.] the general appearance of an area of land, including the direction of streams, hills, and similar features: *the lay of the surrounding countryside.*
▪ the position or direction in which something lies: *roll the carpet against the lay of the nap.* ▪ the direction or amount of twist in rope strands.
2 vulgar slang an act of sexual intercourse.
▪ [with adj.] a person with a particular ability or availability as a sexual partner.
3 [mass noun] the laying of eggs or the period during which they are laid.

– PHRASES **in lay** (of a hen) laying eggs regularly. **lay something at someone's door** see **DOOR**. **lay something bare** bring something out of concealment; expose something: *the sad tale of failure was laid bare.* **lay a charge** make an accusation: *we could lay a charge of gross negligence.* **lay claim to something** assert that one has a right to something: *four men laid claim to the leadership.* ▪ assert that one possesses a skill or quality: *she has never laid claim to medical knowledge.* **lay down the law** see **LAW**. **lay eyes on** see **EYE**. **lay a** (or **the**) **ghost** get rid of a distressing, frightening, or worrying memory or thought: *we need to lay the ghost of the past and condemn Nazism.* **lay hands on 1** find and take possession of: *they huddled trying to keep warm under anything they could lay hands on.* **2** place one's hands on or over, especially in confirmation, ordination, or spiritual healing. **lay** (or **put**) **one's hands on** find and acquire: *I would read every book I could lay my hands on.* **lay hold of** (or **on**) catch at with one's hands: *he was afraid she might vanish if he did not lay hold of her.* ▪ gain possession of: *the gun was the only one he had been able to lay hold of.* **lay it on the line** see **LINE**[1]. **lay someone low** (of an illness) reduce someone to inactivity. ▪ bring to an end the high position or good fortune formerly enjoyed by someone: *she reflected on how quickly fate can lay a person low.* **lay something on the table** see **TABLE**. **lay something on thick** (or **with a trowel**) informal grossly exaggerate or overemphasize something. **lay someone open to** expose someone to the risk of (something): *his position could lay him open to accusations of favouritism.* **lay oneself out to do something** chiefly Brit. make a special effort to do something: *she's laying herself out to be pleasant.* **lay siege to** see **SIEGE**. **lay store by** see **STORE**. **lay someone/thing to rest** bury a body in a grave. ▪ soothe and dispel fear, anxiety, grief, or a similar unpleasant emotion: *suspicion will be laid to rest by fact rather than hearsay.* **lay something (to) waste** see **WASTE**.

– ORIGIN Old English *lecgan*, of Germanic origin; related to Dutch *leggen* and German *legen*, also to **LIE**[1].

USAGE The verb **lay** means, broadly, 'put something down', as in *they are going to **lay** the carpet.* The past tense and the past participle of this verb is **laid**, as in *they **laid** the groundwork or she had **laid** careful plans.* The verb **lie**, on the other hand, means 'be in a horizontal position to rest', as in *why don't you **lie** on the floor?* The past tense of this verb is **lay** (*he **lay** on the floor*) and the past participle is **lain** (*she had **lain** on the bed for hours*). Thus, in correct use, **lay** can be either the past tense of **lie** or the base form of **lay**. In practice many speakers make the mistake of using **lay, laying,** and **laid** as if they meant **lie, lying, lay,** and **lain**. Examples of incorrect use: *why don't you **lay** on the bed* (correct form is **lie**); *she was **laying** on the bed* (correct form is **lying**); *he had **laid** on the floor for hours* (correct form is **lain**).

▶ **lay about** beat or attack (someone) violently: *they weren't against laying about you with sticks and stones.* ▪ (**lay about one**) strike out wildly on all sides: *the mare laid about her with her front legs and teeth.*
lay something aside put something to one side: *he laid aside his book.* ▪ keep business to deal with later. ▪ reserve money for the future or for a particular cause: *he begged them to lay something aside towards the cause.* ▪ give up a practice or attitude: *the situation gave them a good reason to lay aside their differences.*
lay something down 1 put something that one has been holding on the ground or another surface: *she finished her eclair and laid down her fork.* ▪ give up the use or enjoyment of something: *they renounced violence and laid down their arms.* ▪ sacrifice one's life in a noble cause: *he laid down his life for his country.* **2** formulate and enforce or insist on a rule or principle: *stringent criteria have been laid down.* **3** set something in position for use on the ground or a surface: *the floors were constructed by laying down precast concrete blocks.* ▪ establish something in or on the ground: *the ancient grid of streets was laid down by Roman planners.* ▪ begin to construct a ship or railway. ▪ (usu. **be laid down**) build up a deposit of a substance: *these cells lay down new bone tissue.* **4** store wine in a cellar. **5** pay or wager money. **6** informal record a piece of music: *he was invited to the studio to lay down some backing vocals.*
lay something in/up build up a stock of something in case of need.
lay into informal attack violently with words or blows: *three youths laid into him.*
lay off informal give up: *I laid off smoking for seven years.* ▪ [usu. in imperative] used to advise someone to stop doing something: *lay off—he's not going to tell you.*
lay someone off discharge a worker temporarily or permanently because of a shortage of work; make someone redundant.
lay something off 1 chiefly Soccer pass the ball to a teammate who can make progress with it. **2** paint the final layer on a wall or other surface, so as to give a smooth finish. **3** (of a bookmaker) insure against a loss resulting from a large bet by placing a similar bet with another bookmaker.
lay something on chiefly Brit. provide a service or amenity: *the council provides a grant to lay on a bus.*
lay someone out 1 prepare someone for burial after death. **2** informal knock someone unconscious: *he was lucky that the punch didn't lay him out.*
lay something out 1 spread something out to its full extent, especially so that it can be seen: *the police were insisting that suitcases should be opened and their contents laid out.* **2** construct or arrange buildings or gardens according to a plan: *they proceeded to lay out a new town.* ▪ arrange and present material for printing and publication: *the brochure is beautifully laid out.* ▪ explain something clearly and carefully: *we need a paper laying out our priorities.* **3** informal spend a sum of money: *look at the money I had to lay out for your uniform.*
lay up Golf hit the ball deliberately to a lesser distance than possible, typically in order to avoid a hazard.
lay someone up put someone out of action through illness or injury: *he was laid up with his familiar fever.*
lay something up 1 see ***lay something in***. **2** take a ship or other vehicle out of service: *our boats were laid up during the winter months.* **3** assemble plies or layers in the arrangement required for the manufacture of plywood or other laminated material.

lay[2] ▶ adjective [attrib.] **1** not ordained into or belonging to the clergy: *a lay preacher.*
2 not having professional qualifications or expert knowledge, especially in law or medicine: *a lay member of the Health Authority.*

– ORIGIN Middle English: from Old French *lai*, via late Latin from Greek *laïkos*, from *laos* 'people'. Compare with **LAIC**.

lay[3] ▶ noun a short lyric or narrative poem meant to be sung.
▪ poetic/literary a song: *on his lips there died the cheery lay.*

– ORIGIN Middle English: from Old French *lai*, corresponding to Provençal *lais*, of unknown origin.

lay[4] past of **LIE**[1].

layabout ▶ noun derogatory a person who habitually does little or no work.

Layamon /ˈlʌɪəmən/ (late 12th century), English poet and priest. He wrote the verse chronicle known as the *Brut*, a history of England which introduces for the first time in English the story of King Arthur.

layaway ▶ noun **1** [mass noun] N. Amer. a system of

paying a deposit to secure an article for later purchase: *she picked up a coat she had on layaway.*
2 Climbing a handhold that is used to best effect by leaning out to the side of it.

layback ▶ noun [mass noun] Climbing a method of climbing a crack in rock by leaning back and pulling with the hands on one face, with the feet against the other face.

lay brother ▶ noun a man who has taken the vows of a religious order but is not ordained or obliged to take part in the full cycle of liturgy and is employed in ancillary or manual work.

lay-by ▶ noun (pl. **lay-bys**) **1** an area at the side of a road where vehicles may pull off the road and stop.
■ a similar arrangement on a canal.
2 [mass noun] Austral./NZ & S. African a system of paying a deposit to secure an article for later purchase: *you could secure it by lay-by.*

layer ▶ noun **1** a sheet, quantity, or thickness of material, typically one of several, covering a surface or body: *arrange a layer of aubergines in a dish* | figurative *the structure of deception takes on another layer.*
■ a level of seniority in the hierarchy of an organization: *a managerial layer.*
2 [in combination] a person or thing that lays something: *the worms are prolific egg-layers.*
■ a hen that lays eggs.
3 a shoot fastened down to take root while attached to the parent plant.
▶ verb [with obj.] [often as adj. **layered**] **1** arrange in a layer or layers: *the current trend for layered clothes.*
■ cut (hair) in overlapping layers: *her layered, shoulder-length hair.*
2 propagate (a plant) as a layer: *a layered shoot.*
– ORIGIN Middle English (denoting a mason): from **LAY**[1] + **-ER**[1]. The sense 'stratum of material covering a surface' (early 17th cent.) may represent a respelling of an obsolete agricultural use of **LAIR**[1] denoting quality of soil.

layer cake ▶ noun chiefly US a cake of two or more layers with jam, cream, or icing between.

layering ▶ noun [mass noun] **1** the action of arranging something in layers.
■ Geology the presence or formation of layers in sedimentary or igneous rock.
2 the method or activity of propagating a plant by producing layers.

layer-out ▶ noun (pl. **layers-out**) dated a person who prepares a corpse for burial.

layette ▶ noun a set of clothing, bedclothes, and sometimes toiletries for a newborn child.
– ORIGIN mid 19th cent.: from French, diminutive of Old French *laie* 'drawer', from Middle Dutch *laege.*

lay figure ▶ noun a dummy or jointed manikin of a human body used by artists, especially for arranging drapery on.
– ORIGIN late 18th cent.: from obsolete *layman*, from Dutch *leeman*, from obsolete *led*, earlier form of *lid* 'joint'.

layman ▶ noun (pl. **-men**) **1** a non-ordained member of a Church.
2 a person without professional or specialized knowledge in a particular subject: *the book seems well-suited to the interested layman.*

lay-off ▶ noun **1** a temporary or permanent discharge of a worker or workers.
2 a period during which someone is unable to take part in a sport or other activity due to injury or illness.

La'youn /laˈjuːn/ (also **Laayoune**) the capital of Western Sahara; pop. 96,800 (1982). Arabic name **EL AAIÚN**.

layout ▶ noun the way in which the parts of something are arranged or laid out: *the road layout.*
■ the way in which text or pictures are set out on a page: *the layout is uncluttered and the illustrations are helpful.* ■ [mass noun] the process of setting out material on a page or in a work: *doing layout for newspapers and magazines.* ■ a thing arranged or set out in a particular way: *a model railway layout.*

layover ▶ noun chiefly N. Amer. a period of rest or waiting before a further stage in a journey.

layperson ▶ noun a non-ordained member of a Church.
■ a person without professional or specialized knowledge in a particular subject.

lay reader ▶ noun (in the Anglican Church) a layperson licensed to preach and to conduct some

religious services, but not licensed to celebrate the Eucharist.

layshaft ▶ noun Brit. a second or intermediate transmission shaft in a machine.

lay sister ▶ noun a woman who has taken the vows of a religious order but is not obliged to take part in the full cycle of liturgy and is employed in ancillary or manual work.

lay-up ▶ noun **1** [mass noun] the state or action of something, especially a ship, being laid up.
2 Basketball a one-handed shot made from near the basket, especially one that rebounds off the backboard.

laywoman ▶ noun (pl. **-women**) a non-ordained female member of a Church.

lazar /ˈleɪzə, ˈlazə/ ▶ noun archaic a poor and diseased person, especially one afflicted by an unpleasant disease such as leprosy.
– ORIGIN Middle English: from medieval Latin *lazarus*, with biblical allusion to *Lazarus*, the name of a beggar covered in sores (Luke 16:20).

lazarette /ˌlazəˈrɛt/ (also **lazaret**) ▶ noun **1** the after part of a ship's hold, used for stores.
2 a lazaretto.
– ORIGIN early 17th cent. (denoting an isolation hospital): from French *lazaret*, from Italian *lazaretto* (see **LAZARETTO**).

lazaretto /ˌlazəˈrɛtəʊ/ ▶ noun (pl. **-os**) chiefly historical an isolation hospital for people with infectious diseases, especially leprosy or plague.
■ a building (or ship) used for quarantine. ■ a military or prison hospital.
– ORIGIN mid 16th cent.: from Italian, diminutive of *lazzaro* 'beggar', from medieval Latin *lazarus* (see **LAZAR**).

Lazarist /ˈlazərɪst/ ▶ noun a member of the Congregation of the Mission, a Catholic organization founded at the priory of St Lazare in Paris by St Vincent de Paul to preach to the rural poor and train candidates for the priesthood. Also called **VINCENTIAN**.
– ORIGIN from French *Lazariste*, from the biblical name *Lazarus* (see **LAZAR**).

laze ▶ verb [no obj.] spend time in a relaxed, lazy manner: *she spent the day at home, reading the papers and generally lazing around.*
■ [with obj.] (**laze something away**) pass time in such a way: *laze away a long summer day.*
▶ noun [in sing.] a spell of acting in such a way.
– ORIGIN late 16th cent.: back-formation from **LAZY**.

Lazio /ˈlatsɪəʊ/ an administrative region of west central Italy, on the Tyrrhenian Sea, including the ancient region of Latium; capital, Rome.

lazuli /ˈlazjʊlʌɪ, -li/ ▶ noun short for **LAPIS LAZULI**.

lazurite /ˈlazjʊrʌɪt/ ▶ noun [mass noun] a bright blue mineral which is the chief constituent of lapis lazuli and consists chiefly of a silicate and sulphate of sodium and aluminium.

lazy ▶ adjective (**lazier**, **laziest**) unwilling to work or use energy: *I'm very lazy by nature* | *he was too lazy to cook.*
■ characterized by lack of effort or activity: *they were enjoying a really lazy holiday.* ■ showing a lack of effort or care: *lazy writing.* ■ (of a river) slow-moving.
– DERIVATIVES **lazily** adverb, **laziness** noun.
– ORIGIN mid 16th cent.: perhaps related to Low German *lasich* 'languid, idle'.

lazybones ▶ noun (pl. same) informal a lazy person (often as a form of address).

lazy daisy stitch ▶ noun [mass noun] an embroidery stitch in the form of a flower petal.

lazy eye ▶ noun an eye with poor vision that is mainly caused by underuse, especially the unused eye in squint.

lazy jack ▶ noun Sailing a small rope extending vertically from the topping lifts to the boom for holding a fore-and-aft sail when taking it in.

lazy locking ▶ noun a car safety feature involving the automatic closing of its electric windows when the car is locked.

lazy Susan ▶ noun a revolving stand or tray on a table, used especially for holding condiments.

lazy tongs ▶ noun a set of extending tongs for grasping objects at a distance, with several connected pairs of levers pivoted like scissors.

LB ▶ abbreviation for Liberia (international vehicle registration).

lb ▶ abbreviation for ■ pound(s) (in weight). [ORIGIN: from Latin *libra.*] ■ Cricket leg bye(s).

LBC ▶ abbreviation for (in the UK) London Broadcasting Company.

LBDR ▶ abbreviation for Lance Bombardier.

LBO ▶ abbreviation for leveraged buyout.

lbw Cricket ▶ abbreviation for leg before wicket.

l.c. ▶ abbreviation for ■ in the passage cited. [ORIGIN: from Latin *loco citato.*] ■ letter of credit. ■ lower case.

LCC historical ▶ abbreviation for London County Council.

LCD ▶ abbreviation for ■ Electronics & Computing liquid crystal display. ■ Mathematics lowest (or least) common denominator.

LCM Mathematics ▶ abbreviation for lowest (or least) common multiple.

LCPL ▶ abbreviation for Lance Corporal.

LD ▶ abbreviation for lethal dose (of a toxic compound, drug, or pathogen). It is usually written with a following numeral indicating the percentage of a group of animals or cultured cells or micro-organisms killed by such a dose, typically standardized at 50 per cent (**LD$_{50}$**).

Ld ▶ abbreviation for Lord: *Ld Lothian.*

LDC ▶ abbreviation for less-developed country.

Ldg ▶ abbreviation for Leading (in navy ranks).

LDL Biochemistry ▶ abbreviation for low-density lipoprotein.

l-dopa ▶ noun [mass noun] Biochemistry the laevorotatory form of dopa, used to treat Parkinson's disease. Also called **LEVODOPA**.

L-driver ▶ noun Brit. a learner driver.

LDS ▶ abbreviation for ■ Latter-Day Saints. ■ Licentiate in Dental Surgery.

LE ▶ abbreviation for language engineering.

-le[1] ▶ suffix **1** forming names of appliances or instruments: *bridle* | *thimble.*
2 forming names of animals and plants: *beetle.*
– ORIGIN Old English, of Germanic origin.

-le[2] (also **-el**) ▶ suffix forming nouns having or originally having a diminutive sense: *mantle* | *battle* | *castle.*
– ORIGIN Middle English *-el*, *-elle*, partly from Old English and partly from Old French (based on Latin forms).

-le[3] ▶ suffix (forming adjectives from an original verb) apt to; liable to: *brittle* | *nimble.*
– ORIGIN Middle English: from earlier *-el*, of Germanic origin.

-le[4] ▶ suffix forming verbs, chiefly those expressing repeated action or movement (as in *babble*, *dazzle*), or having diminutive sense (as in *nestle*).
– ORIGIN Old English *-lian*, of Germanic origin.

LEA ▶ abbreviation for (in the UK) Local Education Authority.

lea ▶ noun poetic/literary an open area of grassy or arable land: *the lowing herd winds slowly o'er the lea.*
– ORIGIN Old English *lēa(h)*, of Germanic origin; related to Old High German *loh* 'grove', from an Indo-European root shared by Sanskrit *lokás* 'open space', Latin *lucus* 'grove', and perhaps also **LIGHT**[1].

Leach, Bernard (Howell) (1887–1979), British potter, born in Hong Kong. In 1920 he founded his pottery at St Ives in Cornwall with the Japanese potter Shoji Hamada.

leach ▶ verb [with obj. and adverbial of direction] make (a soluble chemical or mineral) drain away from soil, ash, or similar material by the action of percolating liquid, especially rainwater: *the nutrient is quickly leached away.*
■ [no obj., with adverbial of direction] (of a soluble chemical or mineral) drain away from soil, ash, etc. in this way: *coats of varnish prevent the dye leaching out.* ■ [with obj.] subject (soil, ash, etc.) to this process.
– ORIGIN Old English *leccan* 'to water', of West Germanic origin. The current sense dates from the mid 19th cent.

leachate ▶ noun [mass noun] technical water that has percolated through a solid and leached out some of the constituents.

Leacock, Stephen (Butler) (1869–1949), Canadian humorist and economist. He is chiefly remembered for his many humorous short stories, parodies, and essays. Notable works: *Sunshine Sketches of a Little Town* (1912).

lead[1] /liːd/ ▶ verb (past and past participle **led** /lɛd/) [with

obj.] **1** cause (a person or animal) to go with one by holding them by the hand, a halter, a rope, etc. while moving forward: *she emerged leading a bay horse.*
■ [with obj. and adverbial of direction] show (someone or something) the way to a destination by going in front of or beside them: *she stood up and led her friend to the door.* ■ be a reason or motive for (someone): *nothing that I have read about the case leads me to the conclusion that anything untoward happened* | [with obj. and infinitive] *a fascination for art led him to start a collection of paintings.* ■ [no obj., with adverbial of direction] be a route or means of access to a particular place or in a particular direction: *a door leading to a better-lit corridor.* ■ [no obj.] (**lead to**) culminate in (a particular event): *closing the plant will lead to 300 job losses.* ■ [no obj.] (**lead on to**) form a stage in a process which leads probably or inevitably to (a particular end): *his work on digestion led on to study of proteins and fats.* ■ (**lead something through**) cause a liquid or easily moving matter to pass through (a channel).
2 be in charge or command of: *a military delegation was led by the Chief of Staff.*
■ organize and direct: *the conference included sessions led by people with personal knowledge of the area.* ■ set (a process) in motion: *they are waiting for an expansion of world trade to lead a recovery.* ■ be the principal player of (a group of musicians): *since the forties he has led his own big bands.* ■ [no obj.] (**lead with**) assign the most important position to (a particular news item): *the radio news led with the murder.*
3 be superior to (competitors or colleagues): *there will be specific areas or skills in which other nations lead the world.*
■ have the first place in (a competition); be ahead of (competitors): *the Wantage jockey was leading the field.* ■ [no obj.] have the advantage in a race or game: [with complement] *he followed up with a break of 105 to lead 3–0.*
4 have or experience (a particular way of life): *she's led a completely sheltered life.*
5 initiate (action in a game or contest), in particular:
■ (in card games) play (the first card) in a trick or round of play. ■ [no obj.] (**lead with**) Boxing make an attack with (a particular punch or fist): *Adam led with a left.*
▶ *noun* **1** the initiative in an action; an example for others to follow: *Britain is now taking the environmental lead.*
■ a clue to be followed in the resolution of a problem: *detectives investigating the murder are chasing new leads.* ■ (in card games) an act or right of playing first in a trick or round of play: *it's your lead.* ■ the card played first in a trick or round.
2 (**the lead**) a position of advantage in a contest; first place: *they were beaten 5–3 after twice being in the lead.*
■ an amount by which a competitor is ahead of the others: *the team held a slender one-goal lead.*
3 the chief part in a play or film: *she had the lead in a new film* | [as modifier] *the lead role.*
■ the person playing the chief part: *he still looked like a romantic lead.* ■ [usu. as modifier] the chief performer or instrument of a specified type: *that girl will be your lead dancer.* ■ [often as modifier] the item of news given the greatest prominence in a newspaper or magazine: *the lead story.*
4 Brit. a strap or cord for restraining and guiding a dog or other domestic animal.
5 a wire that conveys electric current from a source to an appliance, or that connects two points of a circuit together.
6 the distance advanced by a screw in one turn.
7 a channel, in particular:
■ an artificial watercourse leading to a mill. ■ a channel of water in an ice field.
− PHRASES **lead someone astray** cause someone to act or think foolishly or wrongly. **lead someone by the nose** informal control someone totally, especially by deceiving them. **lead someone a dance** see DANCE. **lead from the front** take an active role in what one is urging and directing others to do. **lead someone up** (or N. Amer. **down**) **the garden path** informal give someone misleading clues or signals. **lead the way** see WAY. **lead with one's chin** informal (of a boxer) leave one's chin unprotected. ■ figurative behave or speak incautiously.
− ORIGIN Old English *lǣdan*, of Germanic origin; related to Dutch *leiden* and German *leiten*, also to LOAD and LODE.
▶ **lead off 1** start: *the newsletter leads off with a report on tax bills.* ■ Baseball bat first in a game or inning. ■ Baseball (of a base-runner) be in a position to run from a base while standing off the base. **2** (of a

door, room, or path) provide access away from a central space: *a farm track led off to the left.*
lead someone on mislead or deceive someone, especially into believing that one is in love with or attracted to them.
lead up to immediately precede: *the weeks leading up to the elections.* ■ result in: *fashioning a policy appropriate to the situation entails understanding the forces that led up to it.*

lead² /lɛd/ ▶ *noun* **1** [mass noun] a heavy bluish-grey soft ductile metal, the chemical element of atomic number 82. It has been used in roofing, plumbing, ammunition, storage batteries, radiation shields, etc., and its compounds have been used in crystal glass, as an anti-knock agent in petrol, and (formerly) in paints. (Symbol: **Pb**)
2 an item or implement made of lead, in particular:
■ (**leads**) Brit. sheets or strips of lead covering a roof. ■ Brit. a piece of lead-covered roof. ■ (**leads**) lead frames holding the glass of a lattice or stained-glass window. ■ Nautical a lump of lead suspended on a line to determine the depth of water.
3 [mass noun] graphite used as the part of a pencil that makes a mark.
4 Printing a blank space between lines of print. [ORIGIN: originally with reference to the metal strip used to create this space.]
− PHRASES **get the lead out** informal, chiefly N. Amer. move or work more quickly. **lead in one's pencil** informal vigour or energy, especially sexual energy in a man.
− ORIGIN Old English *lēad*, of West Germanic origin; related to Dutch *lood* 'lead' and German *Lot* 'plummet, solder'.

lead-acid ▶ *adjective* denoting a secondary cell or battery in which the electrodes are plates or grids of lead (or lead alloy) immersed in dilute sulphuric acid. The anode is coated with lead dioxide and the cathode with spongy lead.

lead article ▶ *noun* chiefly N. Amer. the principal article in a newspaper or magazine.

lead balloon
− PHRASES **go down** (or N. Amer. **over**) **like a lead balloon** (of a speech, proposal, or joke) be poorly received: *the idea would go down like a lead balloon.*

Leadbeater's possum /ˈlɛdbɛtəz/ ▶ *noun* a small grey and white Australian possum, living only in high-altitude eucalyptus forests in eastern Victoria, where it feeds on gum.
● *Gymnobelidus leadbeateri,* family Petauridae.
− ORIGIN mid 20th cent.: named after John Leadbeater (*c.*1832–88), Australian taxidermist.

lead crystal ▶ *noun* another term for LEAD GLASS.

leaded ▶ *adjective* **1** (of windowpanes or a roof) framed, covered, or weighted with lead: *Georgian-style leaded windows.*
2 (of petrol) containing tetraethyl lead: *leaded fuel.*
3 (of type) having the lines separated by leads.

leaded light ▶ *noun* a window consisting of a lattice of small panes held within lead cames.

leaden ▶ *adjective* dull, heavy, or slow: *his eyelids were leaden with sleep.*
■ of the colour of lead; dull grey: *the snow fell from a leaden sky.* ■ archaic made of lead: *a leaden coffin.*
− DERIVATIVES **leadenly** adverb, **leadenness** noun.
− ORIGIN Old English *lēaden* (see LEAD², -EN²).

leaden seal ▶ *noun* chiefly historical a seal made of lead, used especially for papal documents.

leader ▶ *noun* **1** the person who leads or commands a group, organization, or country: *the leader of a protest group.*
■ a person followed by others: *he is a leader among his classmates.* ■ (also **Leader of the House**) Brit. a member of the government officially responsible for initiating business in Parliament. ■ the person or team that is winning a sporting competition at a particular time: *Nora was up among the leaders.* ■ an organization or company that is the most advanced or successful in a particular area: *a leader in the use of video conferencing.* ■ the horse placed at the front in a team or pair.
2 the principal player in a music group.
■ Brit. the principal first violinist in an orchestra. ■ N. Amer. a conductor of a small musical group.
3 Brit. a leading article in a newspaper.
4 a short strip of non-functioning material at each end of a reel of film or recording tape for connection to the spool.
■ a length of filament attached to the end of a fishing line to carry the hook or fly.

5 a shoot of a plant at the apex of a stem or main branch.
6 (**leaders**) Printing a series of dots or dashes across the page to guide the eye, especially in tabulated material.
− DERIVATIVES **leaderless** adjective.

leader board ▶ *noun* a scoreboard showing the names and current scores of the leading competitors, especially in a golf match.

leaderene /ˌliːdəˈriːn/ ▶ *noun* Brit. humorous a female leader, especially an autocratic one.
− ORIGIN 1980s (originally a humorous or ironic name for Margaret Thatcher): from LEADER + *-ene,* on the pattern of female given names such as *Marlene.*

leadership ▶ *noun* [mass noun] the action of leading a group of people or an organization: *different styles of leadership.*
■ the state or position of being a leader: *the leadership of the party.* ■ [treated as sing. or pl.] the leaders of an organization, country, etc.: *a change of leadership had become desirable.*

lead-footed ▶ *adjective* N. Amer. informal **1** slow; clumsy: *the most lead-footed guy can try aerobic moves.*
2 tending to drive too quickly.

lead-free ▶ *adjective* (of petrol) without added tetraethyl lead.

lead glass ▶ *noun* [mass noun] glass containing a substantial proportion of lead oxide, making it more refractive. Also called LEAD CRYSTAL.

lead-in ▶ *noun* **1** an introduction or preamble which allows one to move smoothly on to the next part of something: [as modifier] *the lead-in note.*
2 a wire leading in from outside, especially from an aerial to a receiver or transmitter.

leading¹ /ˈliːdɪŋ/ ▶ *adjective* [attrib.] most important: *a number of leading politicians.*
▶ *noun* [mass noun] guidance or leadership, especially in a spiritual context.
■ [count noun] an instance of such guidance: *the leadings of the Holy Spirit.*

leading² /ˈlɛdɪŋ/ ▶ *noun* [mass noun] the amount of blank space between lines of print.

leading aircraftman ▶ *noun* a male rank in the RAF, above aircraftman and below senior aircraftman.

leading aircraftwoman ▶ *noun* a female rank in the RAF, above aircraftwoman and below senior aircraftwoman.

leading article ▶ *noun* Brit. a newspaper article giving the editorial opinion.

leading counsel ▶ *noun* the senior barrister of the team which represents either party in a legal case.

leading dog ▶ *noun* Austral./NZ a sheepdog trained to run ahead of a flock of sheep to control its speed.

leading edge ▶ *noun* the front edge of something, in particular:
■ Aeronautics the foremost edge of an aerofoil, especially a wing or propeller blade. ■ Electronics the part of a pulse in which the amplitude increases. ■ the forefront or vanguard, especially of technological development: [as modifier] *leading-edge research.*

leading lady ▶ *noun* the actress playing the principal female part in a film or play.

leading light ▶ *noun* a person who is prominent or influential in a particular field or organization: *Lesley is a leading light in a local netball team.*

leading man ▶ *noun* the actor playing the principal male part in a play, film, or television show.

leading note ▶ *noun* Music another term for SUBTONIC.

leading question ▶ *noun* a question that prompts or encourages the answer wanted.

leading rein ▶ *noun* a rein used to lead a horse along, especially when ridden by an inexperienced rider.

leading seaman ▶ *noun* a rank in the Royal Navy, above able seaman and below petty officer.

leading tone ▶ *noun* Music North American term for SUBTONIC.

lead-off ▶ *adjective* (of an action) beginning a series or a process: *the album's lead-off track.*
■ Baseball denoting the first batter in a line-up or of an inning.

lead pencil ▶ noun a pencil of graphite enclosed in wood.

lead poisoning ▶ noun [mass noun] acute or chronic poisoning due to the absorption of lead into the body. Also called **PLUMBISM**.

lead shot ▶ noun another term for **SHOT**[1] (in sense 3).

lead tetraethyl ▶ noun Chemistry another term for **TETRAETHYL LEAD**.

lead time ▶ noun the time between the initiation and completion of a production process.

lead-up ▶ noun [in sing.] an event, point, or sequence that leads up to something else: *the lead-up to the elections*.

leadwort /ˈlɛdwəːt/ ▶ noun another term for **PLUMBAGO** (in sense 2).

leaf ▶ noun (pl. **leaves**) **1** a flattened structure of a higher plant, typically green and blade-like, that is attached to a stem directly or via a stalk. Leaves are the main organs of photosynthesis and transpiration.
■any of a number of similar plant structures, e.g. bracts, sepals, and petals. ■[mass noun] foliage regarded collectively. ■[mass noun] the state of having leaves: *the trees are still* ***in leaf***. ■[mass noun] the leaves of tobacco or tea: [as modifier] *leaf tea*.
2 a thing that resembles a leaf in being flat and thin, typically something that is one of two or more similar items forming a set or stack.
■a single thickness of paper, especially in a book with each side forming a page. ■[mass noun] [with modifier] gold, silver, or other specified metal in the form of very thin foil. ■the hinged part or flap of a door, shutter, or table. ■an extra section inserted to extend a table. ■the inner or outer part of a cavity wall or double-glazed window.
▶verb [no obj.] **1** (of a plant, especially a deciduous one in spring) put out new leaves.
2 (**leaf through**) turn over (the pages of a book or the papers in a pile), reading them quickly or casually: *he leafed through the stack of notes*.
– PHRASES **shake** (or **tremble**) **like a leaf** (of a person) tremble greatly, especially from fear.
– DERIVATIVES **leafage** noun, **leafed** adjective [in combination] *purple-leafed dahlias*, **leafless** adjective, **leaf-like** adjective.
– ORIGIN Old English *lēaf*, of Germanic origin; related to Dutch *loof* and German *Laub*.

leaf beetle ▶ noun a small beetle that feeds chiefly on leaves and typically has bright metallic colouring. Some kinds are serious crop pests.
• Family Chrysomelidae: numerous species.

leafbird ▶ noun a tree-dwelling songbird of South and SE Asia with mainly green plumage and a black bill, the male typically having a black throat.
• Genus *Chloropsis*, family Irenidae (or Chloropseidae): several species.

leaf curl ▶ noun [mass noun] a plant condition distinguished by the presence of curling leaves, caused by environmental stress or disease.

leafcutter ant ▶ noun a tropical ant which cuts pieces from leaves and carries them back to the nest for use as a culture medium for growing food fungi.
• Genus *Atta*, family Formicidae.

leafcutter bee ▶ noun a solitary bee which cuts pieces from leaves, typically of roses, and uses them to construct cells in its nest.
• Genus *Megachile*, family Megachilidae.

leaf-fall ▶ noun [mass noun] the shedding of leaves by a plant.

leaf fat ▶ noun [mass noun] dense fat occurring in layers around the kidneys of some animals, especially pigs.

leaf fish ▶ noun a small deep-bodied predatory freshwater fish, with mottled brownish-green coloration which gives it a leaf-like appearance.
• Two species in the family Nandidae: *Monocirrhus polyacanthus* of South America, and *Polycentropsis abbreviata* of Africa.

leaf green ▶ noun [mass noun] a bright, deep green colour.

leafhopper ▶ noun a small plant bug which is typically brightly coloured and leaps when disturbed. It can be a serious crop pest in warm regions.
• Family Cicadellidae, suborder Homoptera: numerous genera.

leaf insect ▶ noun a large slow-moving tropical insect related to the stick insects, with a flattened body that is leaf-like in shape and colour.
• Family Phylliidae, order Phasmida: *Phyllium* and other genera.

leaflet ▶ noun **1** a printed sheet of paper, sometimes folded, containing information or advertising and usually distributed free.
2 Botany each of the leaflike structures that together make up a compound leaf, such as in the ash and horse chestnut.
■(in general use) a young leaf.
▶verb (**leafleted**, **leafleting**) [with obj.] distribute leaflets to (people or an area): *tourists visiting the area are being leafleted* | [no obj.] *they were leafleting in Victoria Square*.

leaf litter ▶ noun see **LITTER** (sense 3).

leaflove ▶ noun an African bulbul that frequents dense thickets, with mainly drab brown plumage and a loud bubbling call.
• The **leaflove** (*Phyllastrephus scandens*) and the **yellow-throated leaflove** (*Chlorocichla flavicollis*), family Pycnonotidae.

leaf miner ▶ noun a small fly, moth, or sawfly whose larvae burrow between the two surfaces of a leaf.

leaf monkey ▶ noun a leaf-eating arboreal Asian monkey that is related to the langurs.
• Genus *Presbytis*, family Cercopithecidae: several species.

leaf mould ▶ noun [mass noun] **1** soil consisting chiefly of decayed leaves.
2 a fungal disease of tomatoes in which mould develops on the leaves.
• The fungus is *Fulvia fulva* (formerly *Cladosporium fulvum*), subdivision Deuteromycotina.

leaf-nosed bat ▶ noun a bat with a leaf-like appendage on the snout.
• Families Hipposideridae (Old World) and Phyllostomatidae (New World): numerous species.

leaf roll ▶ noun [mass noun] a virus disease of potatoes marked by upward curling of the leaves.

leaf roller ▶ noun an insect, especially a small moth, whose larvae roll up the leaves of plants which they feed upon.

leaf spot ▶ noun [mass noun] [usu. with modifier] any of a large number of fungal, bacterial, or viral plant diseases which cause leaves to develop discoloured spots.

leaf spring ▶ noun a spring made of a number of strips of metal curved slightly upwards and clamped together one above the other.

leaf-tailed gecko ▶ noun a gecko with a wide flat leaf-shaped tail and cryptic skin colour.
• Genus *Phyllurus* (four Australian species), family Pygopodidae, and *Uroplatus* (several Madagascan species), family Gekkonidae.

leaf trace ▶ noun Botany a strand of conducting vessels extending from the stem to the base of a leaf.

leaf warbler ▶ noun a small, slender Old World songbird with a brown or greenish back and whitish or yellowish underparts.
• Genus *Phylloscopus*, family Sylviidae: many species, including the chiffchaff and willow warbler.

leafy ▶ adjective (**leafier**, **leafiest**) (of a plant) having many leaves.
■having or characterized by much foliage because of an abundance of trees or bushes: *a remote, leafy glade*. ■(of a plant) producing or grown for its broad-bladed leaves: *green leafy vegetables*. ■resembling a leaf or leaves: *a three-pointed leafy bract*.
– DERIVATIVES **leafiness** noun.

league[1] ▶ noun **1** a collection of people, countries, or groups that combine for a particular purpose, typically mutual protection or cooperation: *the League of Nations*.
■an agreement to combine in this way.
2 a group of sports clubs which play each other over a period for a championship.
■the contest for the championship of such a league: *the year we won the league*. ■[mass noun] short for **RUGBY LEAGUE**.
3 a class or category of quality or excellence: *the two men were* ***not in the same league*** | *Austin's* ***in a league of his own***.
▶verb (**leagues**, **leagued**, **leaguing**) [no obj.] join in a league or alliance: *Oscar had* ***leagued with*** *other construction firms*.
– PHRASES **in league** conspiring with another or others: *he is* ***in league with*** *the devil*.
– ORIGIN late Middle English (denoting a compact for mutual protection or advantage): via French from Italian *lega*, from *legare* 'to bind', from Latin *ligare*.

league[2] ▶ noun a former measure of distance by land, usually about three miles.
– ORIGIN late Middle English: from late Latin *leuga*, *leuca*, late Greek *leugē*, or from Provençal *lega* (modern French *lieue*).

league football ▶ noun [mass noun] Austral. rugby league or Australian Rules football played in leagues.

League of Arab States an organization of Arab states, founded in 1945 in Cairo, whose purpose is to ensure cooperation among its member states and protect their independence and sovereignty. Also called **ARAB LEAGUE**.

League of Nations an association of countries established in 1919 by the Treaty of Versailles to promote international cooperation and achieve international peace and security. It was powerless to stop Italian, German, and Japanese expansionism leading to the Second World War, and was replaced by the United Nations in 1945.

leaguer[1] ▶ noun [with adj. or noun modifier] chiefly N. Amer. a member of a particular league, especially a sports player: *an assembly of minor leaguers in spring training*.

leaguer[2] ▶ noun & verb variant of **LAAGER**.
– ORIGIN late 16th cent.: from Dutch *leger* 'camp'. Compare with **LAAGER**, **LAGER**, and **LAIR**[1].

league table ▶ noun Brit. a list of the competitors in a league, showing their ranking according to performance in a particular season.
■a comparison of achievement or merit in a competitive area: *a national league table of school results*.

leak ▶ verb [no obj.] (of a container or covering) accidentally lose or admit contents, especially liquid or gas, through a hole or crack: *the roof leaked* | [as adj. **leaking**] *a leaking gutter* | [with obj.] *the drums were leaking an unidentified liquid*.
■[with adverbial of direction] (of liquid, gas, etc.) pass in or out through a hole or crack in such a way: *water kept leaking in*. ■figurative (of secret information) become known: *worrying stories* ***leaked out***. ■[with obj.] intentionally disclose (secret information): *a report was leaked to the press* | [as adj. **leaked**] *a leaked government document*.
▶noun a hole in a container or covering through which contents, especially liquid or gas, may accidentally pass: *I checked all of the pipework for leaks*.
■[mass noun] the action of leaking in such a way: *the leak of fluid may occur* | [count noun] *a gas leak*. ■a similar escape of electric charge or current. ■an intentional disclosure of secret information: *one of the employees was responsible for the leak*.
– PHRASES **have** (or **take**) **a leak** informal urinate.
– DERIVATIVES **leaker** noun.
– ORIGIN late Middle English: probably of Low German or Dutch origin and related to **LACK**.

leakage ▶ noun [mass noun] the accidental admission or escape of a fluid or gas through a hole or crack: *we're saving water by reducing leakage* | [count noun] *there have been no leakages of radioactive material*.
■Physics the gradual escape of an electric charge or current, or magnetic flux. ■deliberate disclosure of confidential information.

Leakey a family of eminent Kenyan archaeologists and anthropologists. **Louis (Seymour Bazett)** (1903–72) pioneered the investigation of human origins in East Africa. He began excavations at Olduvai Gorge and together with Mary discovered the remains of early hominids and their implements, including *Australopithecus* (or *Zinjanthropus*) *boisei* in 1959. His British-born wife **Mary (Douglas)** (1913–96) discovered *Homo habilis* and *Homo erectus* at Olduvai in 1960. Their son **Richard (Erskine)** (b.1944) was appointed director of the new Kenya Wildlife Service in 1989, but resigned in 1994 following a controversial political campaign to remove him.

leaky ▶ adjective (**leakier**, **leakiest**) having a leak or leaks: *a leaky roof*.
■given to disclosing secrets: *leaky sources at the company*.
– DERIVATIVES **leakiness** noun.

leal /liːl/ ▶ adjective Scottish archaic loyal and honest: *his leal duty to the King*.
– ORIGIN Middle English: from Old French *leel*, earlier form of *loial* (see **LOYAL**).

Leamington Spa /ˈlɛmɪŋtən/ a town in central England, in Warwickshire, south-east of

Birmingham; pop. 57,350 (1981). Noted for its saline springs, it was granted the status of royal spa after a visit by Queen Victoria in 1838. Official name **ROYAL LEAMINGTON SPA**.

Lean, Sir David (1908–91), English film director. He made many notable films, including *Lawrence of Arabia* (1962), *Doctor Zhivago* (1965), and *A Passage to India* (1984).

lean[1] ▶ **verb** (past and past participle **leaned** or chiefly Brit. **leant**) [no obj., with adverbial] be in or move into a sloping position: *he leaned back in his chair.*
■(**lean against/on**) incline from the perpendicular and rest for support on or against (something): *a man was leaning against the wall.* ■[with obj.] (**lean something against/on**) cause something to rest on or against: *he leaned his elbows on the table.*
▶**noun** a deviation from the perpendicular; an inclination: *the vehicle has a definite lean to the left.*
– PHRASES **lean over backwards** see **BACKWARDS**.
– ORIGIN Old English *hleonian*, *hlinian*, of Germanic origin; related to Dutch *leunen* and German *lehnen*, from an Indo-European root shared by Latin *inclinare* and Greek *klinein*.
▶**lean on 1** rely on or derive support from: *they have learned to lean on each other for support.* **2** put pressure on (someone) to act in a certain way: *a determination not to allow the majority to lean on the minority.*
lean to/towards incline or be partial to (a view or position): *I now lean towards sabotage as the cause of the crash.*

lean[2] ▶ **adjective 1** (of a person or animal) thin, especially healthily so; having no superfluous fat: *his lean, muscular body.*
■(of meat) containing little fat: *lean bacon.* ■(of an industry or company) efficient and with no wastage: *staff were pruned, ostensibly to produce a leaner and fitter organization.*
2 (of an activity or a period of time) offering little reward, substance, or nourishment; meagre: *the lean winter months | keep a small reserve to tide you over **the lean years**.*
3 (of a vaporized fuel mixture) having a high proportion of air: *lean air-to-fuel ratios.*
▶**noun** [mass noun] the lean part of meat.
– DERIVATIVES **leanly** adverb, **leanness** noun.
– ORIGIN Old English *hlǣne*, of Germanic origin.

lean-burn ▶ **adjective** of or relating to an internal-combustion engine designed to run on a lean mixture to reduce pollution: *lean-burn technology.*

Leander /lɪ'andə/ **1** Greek Mythology a young man, the lover of the priestess Hero. He was drowned swimming across the Hellespont to visit her.
2 (also **Leander Club**) the oldest amateur rowing club in the world, founded early in the 19th century, now based in Henley-on-Thames. Membership is a mark of distinction in the rowing world.

leaning ▶ **noun** (often **leanings**) a tendency or partiality of a particular kind: *his early leanings towards socialism.*

lean-to ▶ **noun** (pl. **-os**) a building sharing one wall with a larger building, and having a roof that leans against that wall: [as modifier] *a lean-to garage.*
■a temporary shelter, either supported or free-standing.

leap ▶ **verb** (past or past participle **leaped** or **leapt**) [no obj., with adverbial] jump or spring a long way, to a great height, or with great force: *he leapt on to the parapet* | figurative *Fabia's heart leapt excitedly.*
■move quickly and suddenly: *Polly leapt to her feet.* ■[with obj.] jump across: *Peter leapt the last few stairs.* ■make a sudden rush to do something; act eagerly and suddenly: *everybody leapt into action.* ■(**leap at**) accept (an opportunity) eagerly: *they leapt at the opportunity to combine fun with fund-raising.* ■(of a price or figure) increase dramatically: *sales leapt by a third last year.* ■(**leap out**) (especially of writing) be conspicuous; stand out: *amid the notes, a couple of items leap out.*
▶**noun** a forceful jump or quick movement: *she came downstairs in a series of flying leaps.*
■a dramatic increase in price, amount, etc.: *a leap of 75 per cent in two years.* ■a sudden abrupt change or transition: *a leap of faith.* ■[in place names] a thing to be leaped over or from: *Lover's Leap.*
– PHRASES **a leap in the dark** a daring step or enterprise whose consequences are unpredictable. **by** (or **in**) **leaps and bounds** with startlingly rapid progress: *productivity improved in leaps and bounds.* **leap to the eye** (especially of writing) be immediately apparent.
– DERIVATIVES **leaper** noun.
– ORIGIN Old English *hlēapan* (verb), *hlȳp* (noun), of Germanic origin; related to Dutch *lopen*, German *laufen* (verb), and Dutch *loop*, German *Lauf* (noun), all meaning 'run', also to **LOPE**.

leap day ▶ **noun** the intercalary day in a leap year; 29 February.

leapfrog ▶ **noun** [mass noun] a game in which players in turn vault with parted legs over others who are bending down.
▶**verb** (**-frogged**, **-frogging**) [no obj.] perform such a vault: *they leapfrogged around the courtyard.*
■[no obj., with adverbial] (of a person or group) surpass or overtake another to move into a leading or dominant position: *she leapfrogged into a sales position.* ■[with obj.] pass over (a stage or obstacle): *attempts to leapfrog the barriers of class.*

leap second ▶ **noun** a second which is occasionally inserted into the atomic scale of reckoning time in order to bring it into line with solar time. It is indicated by an additional bleep in the time signal at the end of some years.

leap year ▶ **noun** a year, occurring once every four years, which has 366 days including 29 February as an intercalary day.
– ORIGIN late Middle English: probably from the fact that feast days after February in such a year fell two days later than in the previous year, rather than one day later as in other years, and could be said to have 'leaped' a day.

Lear[1] /lɪə/ a legendary early king of Britain, the central figure in Shakespeare's tragedy *King Lear*. He is mentioned by the chronicler Geoffrey of Monmouth.

Lear[2] /lɪə/, Edward (1812–88), English humorist and illustrator. He wrote *A Book of Nonsense* (1845) and *Laughable Lyrics* (1877). He also published illustrations of birds and of his travels around the Mediterranean.

learn ▶ **verb** (past and past participle **learned** or chiefly Brit. **learnt**) [with obj.] **1** gain or acquire knowledge of or skill in (something) by study, experience, or being taught: *they'd started learning French* | [with infinitive] *she is learning to play the piano* | [no obj.] *we learn from experience.*
■commit to memory: *I'd learned too many grim poems in school.* ■become aware of (something) by information or from observation: [with clause] *I learned that they had eaten already* | [no obj.] *the trading standards office **learned of** the illegal network.*
2 archaic or informal teach (someone): *'That'll learn you,' he chuckled* | [with obj. and infinitive] *we'll have to learn you to milk cows.*
– PHRASES **learn one's lesson** see **LESSON**.
– DERIVATIVES **learnability** noun, **learnable** adjective.
– ORIGIN Old English *leornian* 'learn' (in Middle English also 'teach'), of West Germanic origin; related to German *lernen*, also to **LORE**[1].

> **USAGE** In modern standard English, it is incorrect to use **learn** to mean **teach**, as in *that'll **learn** you* (correct use is *that'll **teach** you*). This incorrect use has been recorded since the 13th century but for a long time was not considered incorrect. Over the centuries it has, for example, been used by writers such as Spenser, Bunyan, and Samuel Johnson. The use did not fall into disfavour until the early 19th century. It is now only found in non-standard and dialect use.

learned /'lə:nɪd/ ▶ **adjective** (of a person) having much knowledge acquired by study.
■showing, requiring, or characterized by learning; scholarly: *an article in a learned journal.* ■Brit. used as a courteous description of a lawyer in certain formal contexts: *my learned friend.*
– DERIVATIVES **learnedly** adverb, **learnedness** noun.
– ORIGIN Middle English: from **LEARN**, in the sense 'teach'.

learned helplessness ▶ **noun** [mass noun] Psychiatry a condition in which a person suffers from a sense of powerlessness, arising from a traumatic event or persistent failure to succeed. It is thought to be one of the underlying causes of depression.

learner ▶ **noun** a person who is learning a subject or skill: *a fast learner.*
■(also **learner driver**) a person who is learning to drive a motor vehicle and has not yet passed a driving test.

learner's dictionary ▶ **noun** a simple dictionary designed for the use of foreign students.

learning ▶ **noun** [mass noun] the acquisition of knowledge or skills through experience, practice, study, or by being taught: *these children experienced difficulties in learning* | [as modifier] *an important learning process.*
■knowledge acquired in this way: *I liked to parade my learning in front of my sisters.*
– ORIGIN Old English *leornung* (see **LEARN**, **-ING**[1]).

learning curve ▶ **noun** the rate of a person's progress in gaining experience or new skills: *the latest software packages have a steep learning curve.*

learning difficulties ▶ **plural noun** difficulties in acquiring knowledge and skills to the normal level expected of those of the same age, especially because of mental handicap or cognitive disorder.

> **USAGE** The phrase **learning difficulties** became prominent in the 1980s. It is broad in scope, covering general conditions such as Down's syndrome as well as more specific cognitive or neurological conditions such as dyslexia and attention deficit disorder. In emphasizing the difficulty experienced rather than any perceived 'deficiency', it is considered less discriminatory and more positive than other terms such as **mentally handicapped**, and is now the standard accepted term in official contexts, especially in Britain.

learning disability ▶ **noun** a condition giving rise to learning difficulties, especially when not associated with physical handicap.

Leary, Timothy (Francis) (1920–96), American psychologist and drug pioneer. After experimenting with consciousness-altering drugs including LSD, he was dismissed from his teaching post at Harvard University in 1963 and became a figurehead for the hippy drug culture.

lease ▶ **noun** a contract by which one party conveys land, property, services, etc. to another for a specified time, usually in return for a periodic payment.
▶**verb** [with obj.] grant (property) on lease; let: *she leased the site **to** a local company.*
■take (property) on lease; rent: *land was **leased from** the Duchy of Cornwall.*
– PHRASES **a new lease of** (or N. Amer. **on**) **life** a substantially improved prospect of life or use after rejuvenation or repair.
– DERIVATIVES **leasable** adjective.
– ORIGIN late Middle English: from Old French *lais*, *leis*, from *lesser*, *laissier* 'let, leave', from Latin *laxare* 'make loose', from *laxus* 'loose, lax'.

leaseback ▶ **noun** [often as modifier] the leasing of a property back to the vendor: *leaseback agreements.*

leasehold ▶ **noun** [mass noun] the holding of property by lease: *a form of leasehold* | [as modifier] *leasehold premises.* Often contrasted with **FREEHOLD**.
■[count noun] a property held by lease.
– DERIVATIVES **leaseholder** noun.
– ORIGIN early 18th cent.: from **LEASE**, on the pattern of *freehold*.

Lease-Lend historical another term for **LEND-LEASE**.

leash ▶ **noun** a dog's lead.
■Falconry a thong or string attached to the jesses of a hawk, used for tying it to a perch or a creance.
■figurative a restraint: *her bristling temper was kept on a leash.*
▶**verb** [with obj.] put a leash on (a dog).
■figurative restrain: *his violence was barely leashed.*
– PHRASES **strain at the leash** figurative be eager to begin or do something.
– ORIGIN Middle English: from Old French *lesse*, *laisse*, from *laissier* in the specific sense 'let run on a slack lead' (see **LEASE**).

least ▶ **determiner** & **pronoun** (usu. **the least**) smallest in amount, extent, or significance: [as determiner] *who has the least money?* | *he never had the least idea what to do about it* | [as pronoun] *how others see me is **the least of** my worries* | *it's the least I can do.*
▶**adjective** used in names of very small animals and plants, e.g. **least shrew**.
▶**adverb** to the smallest extent or degree: *my best menu was the one I had practised **the least** | turning up when he was least expected | only the least expensive lot sold | I never hid the truth, **least of all** from you.*
– PHRASES **at least 1** not less than; at the minimum: *clean the windows at least once a week.* **2** if nothing else (used to add a positive comment about a generally negative situation): *the options aren't*

complete, but at least they're a start. **3** anyway (used to modify something just stated): *they seldom complained—officially at least.* **at the least** (or **very least**) **1** (used after amounts) not less than; at the minimum: *stay ten days at the least.* **2** taking the most pessimistic or unfavourable view: *a programme which is, at the very least, excellent PR for the hospital.* **least said, soonest mended** proverb a difficult situation will be resolved more quickly if there is no more discussion of it. **not in the least** not in the smallest degree; not at all: *he was not in the least taken aback.* **not least** in particular; notably: *there is a great deal at stake, not least in relation to the environment.* **to say the least** (**of it**) used as an understatement (implying the reality is more extreme, usually worse): *his performance was disappointing to say the least.*
– ORIGIN Old English *lǣst*, *lǣsest*, of Germanic origin; related to **LESS**.

least common denominator ▶ **noun** another term for **LOWEST COMMON DENOMINATOR**.

least common multiple ▶ **noun** another term for **LOWEST COMMON MULTIPLE**.

least significant bit (abbrev.: **LSB**) ▶ **noun** Computing the bit in a binary number which is of the lowest numerical value.

least squares ▶ **noun** [mass noun] a method of estimating a quantity or fitting a graph to data so as to minimize the sum of the squares of the differences between the observed values and the estimated values.

leastways (also **leastwise**) ▶ **adverb** dialect or informal at least: *I don't hold with foreigners, leastways not here in King's Magnum Parva.*

leat /liːt/ ▶ **noun** Brit. an open watercourse conducting water to a mill.
– ORIGIN late 16th cent.: from Old English *-gelǣt* (recorded in *wætergelǣt* 'water channel'), related to *lǣtan* 'to let'.

leather ▶ **noun 1** [mass noun] a material made from the skin of an animal by tanning or a similar process: [as modifier] *a leather jacket.*
■ Brit., dated material of this type when used to make a cricket ball or football: *the sound of leather on willow.*
2 a thing made of leather, in particular:
■ a piece of leather as a polishing cloth. ■ short for **STIRRUP LEATHER**. ■ (**leathers**) leather clothes, especially those worn by a motorcyclist.
▶ **verb** [with obj.] **1** [usu. as adj. **leathered**] cover with leather: *his leathered foot.*
2 beat or thrash (someone): *he caught me and leathered me black and blue* | [as noun **leathering**] *go, before you get a leathering.*
– ORIGIN Old English *lether*, of Germanic origin; related to Dutch *leer* and German *Leder*, from an Indo-European root shared by Irish *leathar* and Welsh *lledr*.

leatherback (also **leatherback turtle**) ▶ **noun** a very large black turtle with a thick leathery shell, living chiefly in tropical seas.
• *Dermochelys coriacea*, the only member of the family Dermochelyidae.

leather-bound ▶ **adjective** (especially of a book) strengthened by being covered in leather.

leather carp ▶ **noun** a carp of a variety which lacks scales.

leathercloth ▶ **noun** [mass noun] strong, coated fabric embossed to resemble leather.

leatherette ▶ **noun** [mass noun] imitation leather.

leather-hard ▶ **adjective** (of unfired pottery) dried and hardened enough to be trimmed or decorated with slip but not enough to be fired.

leatherjacket ▶ **noun 1** Brit. the tough-skinned larva of a large crane fly. It lives in the soil, where it feeds on plant matter and can seriously damage the roots of grasses and crops.
• Genus *Tipula*, family Tipulidae.
2 any of a number of tough-skinned marine fishes, in particular:
• a fish of the jack family (Carangidae), in particular a slender fish of American coastal waters, with a greenish back and a bright yellow tail (*Oligoplites saurus*). • a filefish or triggerfish (family Balistidae).

leatherleaf ▶ **noun** a low-growing evergreen shrub of the heather family, found in north temperate regions.
• *Chamaedaphne calyculata*, family Ericaceae.

leathern ▶ **adjective** [attrib.] archaic made of leather.

leatherneck ▶ **noun** US informal a marine.
– ORIGIN late 19th cent.: with allusion to the leather lining inside the collar of a marine's uniform.

leatherwear ▶ **noun** [mass noun] articles of clothing made of leather.

leatherwood ▶ **noun 1** an evergreen American shrub or small tree with tough flexible bark. It is valued as a source of nectar by bee-keepers in North America.
• *Cyrilla racemiflora*, family Cyrillaceae.
2 a Tasmanian eucryphia tree which bears fragrant white flowers and yields tough pinkish timber.
• *Eucryphia lucida*, family Eucryphiaceae.

leathery ▶ **adjective** having a tough, hard texture like leather: *brown, leathery skin.*
– DERIVATIVES **leatheriness** noun.

leathery turtle ▶ **noun** another term for **LEATHERBACK**.

leave[1] ▶ **verb** (past and past participle **left**) **1** [with obj.] go away from: *she left London on June 6* | [no obj.] *we were almost the last to leave* | *the England team* **left for** *Pakistan on Monday.*
■ depart from permanently: *at the age of sixteen he left home.* ■ cease attending (a school or college) or working for (an organization): *she is leaving the BBC after 20 years.*
2 [with obj.] allow to remain: *the parts he disliked he would alter and the parts he didn't dislike he'd leave.*
■ (**be left**) remain to be used or dealt with: *we've even got one of the Christmas puddings* **left over** *from last year* | [with infinitive] *a retired person with no mortgage left to pay.* ■ [with obj. and adverbial of place] go away from a place without taking (someone or something): *we had not* **left** *any of our belongings* **behind** | figurative *women had been* **left behind** *in the struggle for pay equality.* ■ abandon (a spouse or partner): *her boyfriend* **left** *her* **for** *another woman.* ■ have as (a surviving relative) after one's death: *he leaves a wife and three children.* ■ bequeath: *he left £500 to the National Asthma Campaign* | [with two objs] *Cornelius had left her fifty pounds a year for life.*
3 [with obj. and adverbial or complement] cause (someone or something) to be in a particular state or position: *he'll leave you in no doubt about what he thinks* | *I'll leave the door open* | *the children were* **left with** *feelings of loss.*
■ [with obj. and infinitive] let (someone) do or deal with something without offering help or assistance: *infected people are often rejected by family and friends, leaving them to face this chronic condition alone.* ■ [with obj.] cause to remain as a trace or record: *dark fruit that would leave purple stains on the table napkins* | figurative *they leave the impression that they can be bullied.* ■ [with obj.] deposit or entrust to be kept, collected, or attended to: *she left a note for me.* ■ [with obj.] (**leave something to**) entrust a decision, choice, or action to (someone else, especially someone considered better qualified): *the choice of which link to take is generally* **left up to** *the reader.*
▶ **noun** (in snooker, croquet, and other games) the position in which a player leaves the balls for the next player.
– PHRASES **be left at the post** be beaten from the start of a race or competition. **be left for dead** be abandoned as being almost dead or certain to die. **be left to oneself** be allowed to do what one wants: *women, left to themselves, would make the world a beautiful place to live in.* ■ be in the position of being alone or solitary: *left to himself he removed his shirt and tie.* **leave someone/thing alone** see **ALONE**. **leave someone be** informal refrain from disturbing or interfering with someone. **leave someone cold** fail to interest someone: *the Romantic poets left him cold.* **leave go** informal remove one's hold or grip: *leave go of me!* **leave hold of** cease holding. **leave it at that** abstain from further comment or action: *if you are not sure of the answers, say so, and leave it at that.* **leave much** (or **a lot**) **to be desired** be highly unsatisfactory.
– DERIVATIVES **leaver** noun.
– ORIGIN Old English *lǣfan* 'bequeath', also 'allow to remain, leave in place' of Germanic origin; related to German *bleiben* 'remain'.
▶ **leave off** discontinue (an activity): *the dog left off chasing the sheep.* ■ come to an end: *he resumed the other story at the point where the previous author had left off.*
leave something off omit to put on: *a bolt may have been left off the plane's forward door during production.*
leave someone/thing out fail to include: *it seemed unkind to leave Daisy out, so she was invited too* | [as adj. **left out**] *Olivia was feeling rather left out.* ■ [usu. in imperative] (**leave it out**) Brit. informal stop it: *'Leave it out,' I said sternly, pushing him off.*

leave[2] ▶ **noun** [mass noun] **1** (also **leave of absence**) time when one has permission to be absent from work or from duty in the armed forces: *Joe was home* **on leave** | [count noun] *he requested a leave without pay.*
2 [often with infinitive] permission: *leave from the court to commence an action.*
– PHRASES **by** (or **with**) **your leave 1** with your permission: *with your leave, I will send him your address.* **2** an apology for rude or unwelcome behaviour: *she came in without so much as a by your leave.* **take one's leave** formal say goodbye: *he went to* **take his leave of** *his hostess.* **take leave of one's senses** see **SENSE**. **take leave to do something** formal venture or presume to do something: *whether this amounts to much, one may take leave to doubt.*
– ORIGIN Old English *lēaf* 'permission', of West Germanic origin; related to **LIEF** and **LOVE**.

leaved ▶ **adjective** [in combination] having a leaf or leaves of a particular kind or number: *ivy-leaved toadflax.*

leaven /ˈlɛv(ə)n/ ▶ **noun** [mass noun] a substance, typically yeast, that is added to dough to make it ferment and rise.
■ dough that is reserved from an earlier batch in order to start a later one fermenting. ■ figurative a pervasive influence that modifies something or transforms it for the better: *they acted as an intellectual leaven to the warriors who dominated the city.*
▶ **verb** [with obj.] **1** [usu. as adj. **leavened**] cause (dough or bread) to ferment and rise by adding leaven: *leavened breads are forbidden during Passover.*
2 permeate and modify or transform (something) for the better: *the proceedings should be leavened by humour* | [as noun **leavening**] *companies of Territorial Army volunteers with a leavening of regular soldiers.*
– ORIGIN Middle English: from Old French *levain*, based on Latin *levamen* 'relief' (literally 'means of raising'), from *levare* 'to lift'.

leaves plural form of **LEAF**.

leave-taking ▶ **noun** an act of saying goodbye: *the leave-taking was formal, with none of her earlier displays of emotion.*

leavings ▶ **plural noun** things that have been left as worthless: *she dropped her lunch leavings into a bin.*

Leavis /ˈliːvɪs/, F. R. (1895–1978), English literary critic; full name *Frank Raymond Leavis*. Founder and editor of the quarterly *Scrutiny* (1932–53), he emphasized the value of critical study of English literature to preserving cultural continuity. Notable works: *The Great Tradition* (1948).
– DERIVATIVES **Leavisite** noun & adjective.

Lebanon /ˈlɛbənən/ a country in the Middle East with a coastline on the Mediterranean Sea; pop. 2,700,000 (est. 1990); official language, Arabic; capital, Beirut.

Part of the Ottoman Empire from the early 16th century, Lebanon became a French mandate after the First World War and achieved independence in 1943. Until the mid 1970s the country prospered, but conflict between the Christian and Muslim communities, the influx of Palestinian refugees, and repeated Middle Eastern wars chronically destabilized the country. The first general elections for twenty years were held in 1992.

– DERIVATIVES **Lebanese** adjective & noun.

Lebanon Mountains a range of mountains in Lebanon. Running parallel to the Mediterranean coast, it rises to a height of 3,087 m (10,022 ft) at Qornet es Saouda. It is separated from the Anti-Lebanon Mountains, on the border with Syria, by the Bekaa valley.

Lebensraum /ˈleɪb(ə)nzˌraʊm, German ˈleːbnsˌraʊm/ ▶ **noun** [mass noun] the territory which a state or nation believes is needed for its natural development.
– ORIGIN German, literally 'living space' (originally with reference to Germany).

Leblanc /ləˈblɒ̃(k), French ləblɑ̃/, Nicolas (1742–1806), French surgeon and chemist. He developed a process for making soda ash (sodium carbonate) from common salt, enabling the large-scale manufacture of glass, soap, paper, and other chemicals.

Lebowa /ləˈbəʊə/ a former homeland established in South Africa for the North Sotho people, now part of the province of Northern Transvaal.

Lebrun /ləˈbrəːn, French ləbrœ̃/, Charles (1619–90), French painter, designer, and decorator. He was prominent in the development and institutionalization of French art and was a leading exponent of French classicism. In 1648 he helped to found the Royal Academy of Painting and Sculpture.

Le Carré /lə ˈkareɪ/, John (b.1931), English novelist; pseudonym of *David John Moore Cornwell*. He is known for his unromanticized and thoughtful spy novels, which often feature the British agent George Smiley and include *The Spy Who Came in from the Cold* (1963) and *Tinker, Tailor, Soldier, Spy* (1974).

leccy /ˈlɛki/ ▶ noun [mass noun] Brit. informal electricity.

lech /lɛtʃ/ informal, derogatory ▶ noun a lecher.
■ a lecherous urge or desire: *I think he has a kind of lech for you*.
▶ verb [no obj.] act in a lecherous or lustful manner: *businessmen leching after bimbos*.
– ORIGIN late 18th cent. (denoting a strong desire, particularly sexually): back-formation from **LECHER**.

Le Chatelier's principle /ˌlə ʃaˈtɛljeɪ/ Chemistry a principle stating that if a constraint (such as a change in pressure, temperature, or concentration of a reactant) is applied to a system in equilibrium, the equilibrium will shift so as to tend to counteract the effect of the constraint.
– ORIGIN early 20th cent.: named after Henry *le Chatelier* (1850–1936), French chemist.

lecher /ˈlɛtʃə/ ▶ noun a lecherous man.
– ORIGIN Middle English: from Old French *lichiere, lecheor*, from *lechier* 'live in debauchery or gluttony', ultimately of West Germanic origin and related to **LICK**.

lecherous ▶ adjective having or showing excessive or offensive sexual desire: *she ignored his lecherous gaze*.
– DERIVATIVES **lecherously** adverb, **lecherousness** noun.
– ORIGIN Middle English: from Old French *lecheros*, from *lecheor* (see **LECHER**).

lechery ▶ noun [mass noun] excessive or offensive sexual desire; lustfulness.
– ORIGIN Middle English: from Old French *lecherie*, from *lecheor* (see **LECHER**).

lechwe /ˈlɛːtʃwi/ ▶ noun (pl. same) a rough-coated grazing antelope with pointed hooves and long horns, found in swampy grassland in southern Africa and the Sudan.
● Genus *Kobus*, family Bovidae: two species, in particular *K. leche*.
– ORIGIN mid 19th cent.: from Setswana.

lecithin /ˈlɛsɪθɪn/ ▶ noun Biochemistry another term for **PHOSPHATIDYLCHOLINE**.
– ORIGIN mid 19th cent.: from Greek *lekithos* 'egg yolk' + **-IN**[1].

lecithinase /ˈlɛsɪθɪˌneɪz/ ▶ noun Biochemistry another term for **PHOSPHOLIPASE**.

lecker ▶ adjective variant spelling of **LEKKER**.

Leclanché cell /ləˈklɒʃeɪ/ ▶ noun a primary electrochemical cell having a zinc cathode in contact with zinc chloride, ammonium chloride (as a solution or a paste) as the electrolyte, and a carbon anode in contact with a mixture of manganese dioxide and carbon powder.
– ORIGIN late 19th cent.: named after Georges *Leclanché* (1839–82), French chemist.

Leconte de Lisle /lə kɒnt də ˈliːl, French ləkɔ̃t də lil/, Charles Marie René (1818–94), French poet and leader of the Parnassians. His poetry often draws inspiration from mythology, biblical history, and exotic Eastern landscape. Notable works: *Poèmes antiques* (1852).

Le Corbusier /lə kɔːˈbjuːzɪeɪ, French lə kɔrbyzje/ (1887–1965), French architect and town planner, born in Switzerland; born *Charles Édouard Jeanneret*. A pioneer of the international style, he developed theories on functionalism, the use of new materials and industrial techniques, and the Modulor, a modular system of standard-sized units.

lectern /ˈlɛktə(r)n, -tə:n/ ▶ noun a tall stand with a sloping top to hold a book or notes, and from which someone, typically a preacher or lecturer, can read while standing up.
– ORIGIN Middle English: from Old French *letrun*, from medieval Latin *lectrum*, from *legere* 'to read'.

lectin ▶ noun Biochemistry any of a class of proteins, chiefly of plant origin, which bind specifically to

certain sugars and so cause agglutination of particular cell types.
– ORIGIN 1950s: from Latin *lect-* 'chosen' (from the verb *legere*) + **-IN**[1].

lection /ˈlɛkʃ(ə)n/ ▶ noun archaic a reading of a text found in a particular copy or edition.
– ORIGIN Middle English (in the sense 'election'): from Latin *lectio(n-)* 'choosing, reading', from the verb *legere*. The current sense dates from the mid 17th cent.

lectionary /ˈlɛkʃ(ə)n(ə)ri/ ▶ noun (pl. **-ies**) a list or book of portions of the Bible appointed to be read at divine service.
– ORIGIN late 18th cent.: from medieval Latin *lectionarium*, from *lect-* 'chosen, read', from the verb *legere*.

lector /ˈlɛktɔː/ ▶ noun 1 a reader, especially someone who reads lessons in a church service.
2 a lecturer, especially one employed in a foreign university to teach in their native language.
– ORIGIN late Middle English: from Latin, from *lect-* 'read, chosen', from the verb *legere*.

lectrice /lɛkˈtriːs/ ▶ noun a female lector in a university.
– ORIGIN late 19th cent.: from French, literally 'female reader'.

lecture ▶ noun an educational talk to an audience, especially one of students in a university.
■ a long serious speech, especially one given as a scolding or reprimand: *the usual lecture on table manners*.
▶ verb [no obj.] deliver an educational lecture or lectures: *he was lecturing at the University of Birmingham*.
■ [with obj.] give a lecture to (a class or other audience): *he was lecturing future generations of health-service professionals.* ■ [with obj.] talk seriously or reprovingly to (someone): *I do not wish to be lectured about smoking*.
– ORIGIN late Middle English (in the sense 'reading, a text to read'): from Old French, or from medieval Latin *lectura*, from Latin *lect-* 'read, chosen', from the verb *legere*.

lecturer ▶ noun a person who gives lectures, especially as an occupation at a university or college of higher education.

lectureship ▶ noun a post as a lecturer: *a three-year lectureship in English Literature*.

lecture theatre ▶ noun see **THEATRE**.

lecythus /ˈlɛsɪθəs/ ▶ noun (pl. **lecythi** /-θʌɪ/) a thin narrow-necked vase or flask from ancient Greece.
– ORIGIN via late Latin from Greek *lēkuthos*.

LED ▶ abbreviation for light-emitting diode, a semiconductor diode which glows when a voltage is applied.

led past and past participle of **LEAD**[1].

Leda /ˈliːdə/ Greek Mythology the wife of Tyndareus king of Sparta. She was loved by Zeus, who visited her in the form of a swan; among her children were the Dioscuri, Helen, and Clytemnestra.

lederhosen /ˈleɪdəˌhəʊz(ə)n/ ▶ plural noun leather shorts with H-shaped braces, traditionally worn by men in Alpine regions such as Bavaria.
– ORIGIN from German, from *Leder* 'leather' + *Hosen* 'trousers'.

ledge ▶ noun 1 a narrow horizontal surface projecting from a wall, cliff, or other surface: *he heaved himself up over a ledge*.
■ a window ledge.
2 an underwater ridge, especially of rocks beneath the sea near the shore: *a reef ledge*.
3 Mining a stratum of metal- or ore-bearing rock; a vein of quartz or other mineral.
– DERIVATIVES **ledged** adjective, **ledgy** adjective.
– ORIGIN Middle English (denoting a strip of wood or other material fixed across a door, gate, etc.): perhaps from an early form of **LAY**[1]. Sense 1 dates from the mid 16th cent.

ledger ▶ noun 1 a book or other collection of financial accounts of a particular type: *the total balance of the purchases ledger*.
2 a flat stone slab covering a grave.
3 a horizontal scaffolding pole, parallel to the face of the building.
4 a weight used on a fishing line without a float, to anchor the bait in a particular place: [as modifier] *ledger tackle*.
▶ verb [no obj.] fish using a ledger.
– ORIGIN late Middle English *legger, ligger* (denoting a large bible or breviary), probably from variants of

LAY[1] and **LIE**[1], influenced by Dutch *legger* and *ligger*. Current senses date from the 16th cent., except the fishing senses, known from the 17th cent.

ledger line ▶ noun Music variant spelling of **LEGER LINE**.

Lee[1], Bruce (1941–73), American actor; born *Lee Yuen Kam*. An expert in kung fu, he starred in a number of martial arts films, such as *Enter the Dragon* (1973).

Lee[2], Christopher (Frank Carandini) (b.1922), English actor. His reputation is chiefly based on the horror films that he made for the British film company Hammer, which include *Dracula* (1958).

Lee[3], Gypsy Rose (1914–70), American striptease artist; born *Rose Louise Hovick*. In the 1930s she became famous on Broadway for her sophisticated striptease act.

Lee[4], (Nelle) Harper (b.1926), American novelist. She won a Pulitzer Prize with her only novel, *To Kill a Mockingbird* (1960), about the sensational trial of a black man falsely charged with raping a white woman.

Lee[5], Laurie (1914–97), English writer. He is best known for his autobiographical novels *Cider With Rosie* (1959) and *As I Walked Out One Midsummer Morning* (1969), evocative accounts of his childhood in rural Gloucestershire and his travelling experiences in pre-war Europe.

Lee[6], Robert E. (1807–70), American general; full name *Robert Edward Lee*. He was the commander of the Confederate army of Northern Virginia for most of the American Civil War. His invasion of the North was repulsed at the Battle of Gettysburg (1863) and he surrendered in 1865.

Lee[7], Spike (b.1957), American film director; born *Shelton Jackson Lee*. Lee's declared intention is to express the richness of black American culture; films such as *Do the Right Thing* (1989) and *Malcolm X* (1992) sparked controversy with their treatment of racism.

lee ▶ noun [mass noun] shelter from wind or weather given by a neighbouring object: *he went round the front of the cab to be out of the wind and lit a cigarette in its lee*.
■ (also **lee side**) the sheltered side; the side away from the wind: *ducks were taking shelter on the lee of the island*. Contrasted with **WEATHER**.
– ORIGIN Old English *hlēo, hlēow* 'shelter', of Germanic origin; probably related to *luke-* in **LUKEWARM**.

leeboard ▶ noun a plank frame fixed to the side of a flat-bottomed boat and let down into the water to reduce drifting to the leeward side.

leech[1] ▶ noun 1 an aquatic or terrestrial annelid worm with suckers at both ends. Many species are bloodsucking parasites, especially of vertebrates, and others are predators.
● Class Hirudinea: many species. See also **MEDICINAL LEECH**.
2 a person who extorts profit from or sponges on others: *they are leeches feeding off the hard-working majority*.
▶ verb [no obj.] (**leech on/off**) habitually exploit or rely on: *he's leeching off the abilities of others*.
– PHRASES **like a leech** persistently or clingingly present: *he's been hanging around Caroline like a leech*.
– ORIGIN Old English *lǣce, lȳce*; related to Middle Dutch *lake, lieke*.

leech[2] ▶ noun archaic a doctor or healer.
– ORIGIN Old English *lǣce*, of Germanic origin.

leech[3] ▶ noun Sailing the after or leeward edge of a fore-and-aft sail, the leeward edge of a spinnaker, or a vertical edge of a square sail.
– ORIGIN late 15th cent.: probably of Scandinavian origin and related to Swedish *lik*, Danish *lig*, denoting a rope sewn round the edge of a sail to stop the canvas tearing.

leechcraft ▶ noun [mass noun] archaic the art of healing.
– ORIGIN Old English *lǣcecrǣft* (see **LEECH**[2], **CRAFT**).

Leeds an industrial city in northern England, a unitary council formerly in Yorkshire; pop. 674,400 (1991). It developed as a wool town in the Middle Ages, becoming a centre of the clothing trade in the Industrial Revolution.

Lee–Enfield (also **Lee–Enfield rifle**) ▶ noun a bolt-action rifle of a type formerly used by the British army.

lee gage ▶ noun see **GAUGE** (sense 3).

lee helm ▶ **noun** [mass noun] Sailing the tendency of a ship to turn its bow to the leeward side.

lee ho ▶ **exclamation** Sailing a command or warning given by a helmsman to indicate the moment of going about.

leek ▶ **noun** a plant related to the onion, with flat overlapping leaves forming an elongated cylindrical bulb which together with the leaf bases is eaten as a vegetable. It is used as a Welsh national emblem.
• *Allium porrum*, family Liliaceae (or Alliaceae).
– ORIGIN Old English *lēac*, of Germanic origin; related to Dutch *look* and German *Lauch*.

leer[1] ▶ **verb** [no obj.] look or gaze in an unpleasant, malign, or lascivious way: *bystanders were leering at the nude painting* | [as adj. **leering**] *every leering eye in the room was on her.*
▶ **noun** an unpleasant, malign, or lascivious look.
– DERIVATIVES **leeringly** adverb.
– ORIGIN mid 16th cent. (in the general sense 'look sideways or askance'): perhaps from obsolete *leer* 'cheek', from Old English *hlēor*, as though the sense were 'to glance over one's cheek'.

leer[2] ▶ **noun** variant spelling of **LEHR**.

leervis /ˈlɪərfəs/ ▶ **noun** (pl. same) S. African a large greyish marine fish with small scales which give the skin a leathery appearance. It lives in the Mediterranean and around the western and southern coasts of Africa, where it is a popular game fish.
• *Lichia amia*, family Carangidae.
– ORIGIN mid 19th cent.: from Afrikaans, from Dutch *leer* 'leather' + *vis* 'fish'.

leery ▶ **adjective** (**leerier**, **leeriest**) cautious or wary due to realistic suspicions: *a city* **leery of** *gang violence.*
– DERIVATIVES **leeriness** noun.
– ORIGIN late 17th cent.: from obsolete *leer* 'looking askance', from **LEER**[1] + **-Y**[1].

lees ▶ **plural noun** the sediment of wine in the barrel.
■ figurative dregs; refuse: *the lees of the Venetian underworld.*
– ORIGIN late Middle English: plural of obsolete *lee* in the same sense, from Old French *lie*, from medieval Latin *liae* (plural), of Gaulish origin.

lee shore ▶ **noun** a shore lying on the leeward side of a ship (and on to which a ship could be blown in foul weather).

lee side ▶ **noun** see **LEE**.

leet[1] (also **court leet**) ▶ **noun** historical a yearly or half-yearly court of record that the lords of certain manors held.
■ the jurisdiction of such a court.
– ORIGIN Middle English: from Anglo-Norman French *lete* or Anglo-Latin *leta*, of unknown origin.

leet[2] ▶ **noun** Scottish a list of candidates selected for a post.
– ORIGIN late Middle English: probably from Old French *lit(t)e*, variant of *liste* 'list'.

Leeuwenhoek /ˈleɪv(ə)nhuːk/, Antoni van (1632–1723), Dutch naturalist. He developed a lens for scientific purposes and was the first to observe bacteria, protozoa, and yeast. He accurately described red blood cells, capillaries, striated muscle fibres, spermatozoa, and the crystalline lens of the eye.

leeward /ˈliːwəd, ˈluːəd/ ▶ **adjective** & **adverb** on or towards the side sheltered from the wind or towards which the wind is blowing; downwind: [as adj.] *the leeward side of the house* | [as adv.] *we pitched our tents* **leeward of** *a hill.* Contrasted with **WINDWARD**.
▶ **noun** [mass noun] the side sheltered or away from the wind: *the ship was drifting* **to leeward**.

Leeward Islands /ˈliːwəd/ a group of islands in the Caribbean, constituting the northern part of the Lesser Antilles. The group includes Guadeloupe, Antigua, St Kitts, and Montserrat.
– ORIGIN *Leeward* with reference to the islands' situation further downwind (in terms of the prevailing south-easterly winds) than the Windward Islands.

lee wave ▶ **noun** a standing wave generated on the sheltered side of a mountain by an air current passing over or around it, and often made visible by the formation of clouds.

leeway ▶ **noun** [mass noun] **1** the amount of freedom to move or act that is available: *the government had several months' leeway to introduce reforms.*
■ margin of safety: *there is little leeway if anything goes wrong.*
2 the sideways drift of a ship to leeward of the desired course: *the leeway is only about 2°.*
– PHRASES **make up (the) leeway** Brit. struggle out of a bad position, especially by recovering lost time.

Le Fanu /ˈlɛfənjuː, lə ˈfɑːnuː/, Joseph Sheridan (1814–73), Irish novelist. He is best known for his stories of mystery, suspense, and the supernatural such as *The House by the Churchyard* (1861) and *Uncle Silas* (1864).

left[1] ▶ **adjective 1** on, towards, or relating to the side of a human body or of a thing which is to the west when the person or thing is facing north: *her left eye* | *the left side of the road.*
■ denoting the side of something which is in an analogous position: *the left edge of the text.* ■ on this side from the point of view of a spectator.
2 of or relating to a person or group favouring radical, reforming, or socialist views: *Left politics.* [ORIGIN: see **LEFT WING**.]
▶ **adverb** on or to the left side: *turn left here* | *keep left.*
▶ **noun 1** (**the left**) the left-hand part, side, or direction: *turn to the left* | (**one's left**) *the general sat to his left.*
■ (in football or a similar sport) the left-hand half of the field when facing the opponents' goal: *a free kick from the left.* ■ the left wing of an army: *a token attack on the Russian left.*
2 (often **the Left**) [treated as sing. or pl.] a group or party favouring radical, reforming, or socialist views: *the Left is preparing to fight presidential elections.*
■ the section of a party or group holding such views more strongly: *he is on the left of the party.*
3 [count noun] a thing on the left-hand side or done with the left hand, in particular:
■ a left turn: *take a left here.* ■ a road, entrance, etc. on the left: *my road's the first left.* ■ a person's left fist, especially a boxer's: *a dazzler with the left.* ■ a blow given with this: *a left to the body.*
– PHRASES **have two left feet** be clumsy or awkward. **left, right, and centre** (also **left and right** or **right and left**) on all sides: *deals were being done left, right, and centre.*
– DERIVATIVES **leftish** adjective.
– ORIGIN Old English *lyft*, *left* 'weak' (the left-hand side being regarded as the weaker side of the body), of West Germanic origin.

left[2] past and past participle of **LEAVE**[1].

left back ▶ **noun** a defender in soccer or field hockey who plays primarily in a position on the left of the field.

Left Bank a district of the city of Paris, situated on the left bank of the River Seine, to the south of the river. It is an area noted for its intellectual and artistic life.

left bank ▶ **noun** the bank of a river, on the left as one faces downstream.

left brain ▶ **noun** the left-hand side of the human brain, which is believed to be associated with linear and analytical thought.

left field ▶ **noun** Baseball the part of the outfield to the left of the batter when facing the pitcher: *a high fly* **to left field**.
■ figurative a position or direction that is surprising or unconventional: *seldom do so many witty touches come* **out of left field**. ■ figurative a position of ignorance, error, or confusion: *he's way* **over in left field** *on these issues.*
▶ **adjective** (of artistic work) radical or experimental: *left-field guitar-based music.* [ORIGIN: first applied to jazz.]
– DERIVATIVES **left fielder** noun.

left-footed ▶ **adjective** (of a person) using one's left foot more naturally and effectively than the right.
■ (especially of a kick) done with a person's left foot: *he drove a left-footed shot into the net.*

left hand ▶ **noun** the hand of a person's left side.
■ the region or direction on the left side of a person or thing: *there was a vast forest on the left hand.*
▶ **adjective** [attrib.] on or towards the left side of a person or thing: *his left-hand pocket.*
■ done with or using the left hand: *an excellent left-hand catch by Smith.*
– PHRASES **marry with the left hand** Brit. marry morganatically. [ORIGIN: from a German custom by which the bridegroom gave the bride his left hand in such marriages.]

left-hand drive ▶ **noun** [mass noun] a motor-vehicle steering system with the steering wheel and other controls fitted on the left side, designed for use in countries where vehicles drive on the right-hand side of the road.
■ [count noun] a vehicle with steering of this type.

left-handed ▶ **adjective 1** (of a person) using the left hand more naturally than the right: *a left-handed batsman.*
■ (of a tool or item of equipment) made to be used with the left hand: *left-handed golf clubs.* ■ made or performed with the left hand: *my left-handed scrawl.*
2 turning to the left; towards the left, in particular:
■ (of a screw) advanced by turning anticlockwise. ■ Biology (of a spiral shell or helix) sinistral. ■ (of a racecourse) turning anticlockwise.
3 perverse: *we take a left-handed pleasure in our errors.*
■ (especially of a compliment) ambiguous.
▶ **adverb** with the left hand: *a significant number play the game left-handed.*
– DERIVATIVES **left-handedly** adverb, **left-handedness** noun.

left-hander ▶ **noun 1** a left-handed person.
■ a blow struck with a person's left hand.
2 a corner on a road or racing circuit that bends to the left.

leftie ▶ **noun** variant spelling of **LEFTY**.

leftism ▶ **noun** [mass noun] the political views or policies of the left.
– DERIVATIVES **leftist** noun & adjective.

left-leaning ▶ **adjective** sympathetic to or tending towards the left in politics: *a left-leaning professor.*

left luggage ▶ **noun** [mass noun] Brit. travellers' luggage left in temporary storage at a railway station, bus station, or airport.
■ (also **left-luggage office**) a room where such luggage may be stored temporarily for a small charge: *I picked up my parcel from left luggage.*

leftmost ▶ **adjective** [attrib.] furthest to the left: *the leftmost edge of the screen.*

leftover ▶ **noun** (usu. **leftovers**) something, especially food, remaining after the rest has been used.
▶ **adjective** [attrib.] remaining; surplus: *yesterday's leftover bread.*

left turn ▶ **noun** a turn that brings a person's front to face the way their left side did before: *take a left turn into Cumberland Road.*

leftward ▶ **adverb** (also **leftwards**) towards the left.
▶ **adjective** going towards or facing the left: *they moved their eyes in a leftward direction.*

left wing ▶ **noun** (**the left wing**) **1** the radical, reforming, or socialist section of a political party or system. [ORIGIN: with reference to the National Assembly in France (1789–91), where the nobles sat to the president's right and the commons to the left.]
2 the left side of a team on the field in soccer, rugby, and field hockey: *his usual position on the left wing.*
■ the left side of an army: *the Allied left wing.*
▶ **adjective** radical, reforming, or socialist: *left-wing activists.*
– DERIVATIVES **left-winger** noun.

lefty (also **leftie**) ▶ **noun** (pl. **-ies**) informal **1** a person who supports or is involved in left-wing politics.
2 a left-handed person.

leg ▶ **noun 1** each of the limbs on which a person or animal walks and stands: *Adams broke his leg* | *he was off* **as fast as his legs would carry him** | [as modifier] *a leg injury.*
■ a leg of an animal or bird as food: *a roast leg of lamb.* ■ a part of a garment covering a leg or part of a leg: *his trouser leg.* ■ (**legs**) N. Amer. informal used to refer to the sustained popularity or success of a product or idea: *some books have legs, others don't.*
2 each of the supports of a chair, table, or other piece of furniture: *table legs.*
■ a long, thin support or prop: *the house was set on legs.*
3 a section or stage of a journey or process: *the return leg of his journey.*
■ Sailing a run made on a single tack. ■ (in soccer and other sports) each of two games constituting a round of a competition. ■ a section of a relay or other race done in stages: *one leg of its race round the globe.* ■ a single game in a darts match.
4 a branch of a forked object.
5 (also **leg side**) Cricket the half of the field (as divided lengthways through the pitch) away from which the batsman's feet are pointed when standing to receive the ball. The opposite of **OFF**.

6 archaic an obeisance made by drawing back one leg and bending it while keeping the front leg straight.
▶**verb** (**legged, legging**) [with obj.] **1** (**leg it**) informal travel by foot; walk.
■run away: *he legged it after someone shouted at him.*
2 chiefly historical propel (a boat) through a tunnel on a canal by pushing with one's legs against the tunnel roof or sides.
– PHRASES **feel** (or **find**) **one's legs** become able to stand or walk. **get one's leg over** vulgar slang (of a man) have sexual intercourse. **have the legs of** Brit. be able to go faster or further than (a rival). **not have the legs** (of a ball, especially in golf) not have insufficient momentum to reach the desired point. **not have a leg to stand on** have no facts or sound reasons to support one's argument or justify one's actions. **on one's hind legs** Brit. informal standing up to make a speech: *he wasn't afraid to get up on his hind legs at a social gathering and talk.* **on one's last legs** near the end of life, usefulness, or existence: *the foundry business was on its last legs.*
– DERIVATIVES **legged** adjective [in combination] *a four-legged animal*, **legger** noun [in combination] *a three-legger.*
– ORIGIN Middle English (superseding **SHANK**): from Old Norse *leggr* (compare with Danish *læg* 'calf (of the leg)'), of Germanic origin.

legacy ▶**noun** (pl. **-ies**) an amount of money or property left to someone in a will.
■a thing handed down by a predecessor: *the legacy of centuries of neglect.*
▶**adjective** Computing denoting software or hardware that has been superseded but is difficult to replace because of its wide use.
– ORIGIN late Middle English (also denoting the function or office of a deputy, especially a papal legate): from Old French *legacie*, from medieval Latin *legatia* 'legateship', from *legatus* 'person delegated' (see **LEGATE**).

legal ▶**adjective 1** [attrib.] of, based on, or concerned with the law: *the European legal system.*
■appointed or required by the law: *a legal requirement.* ■of or relating to theological legalism. ■Law recognized by common or statute law, as distinct from equity.
2 permitted by law: *he claimed that it had all been legal.*
– DERIVATIVES **legally** adverb [sentence adverb] *legally, we're still very much married.*
– ORIGIN late Middle English (in the sense 'to do with Mosaic law'): from French, or from Latin *legalis*, from *lex, leg-* 'law'. Compare with **LOYAL**.

legal aid ▶**noun** [mass noun] payment from public funds allowed, in cases of need, to help pay for legal advice or proceedings.

legal capacity ▶**noun** [mass noun] a person's authority under law to engage in a particular undertaking or maintain a particular status.

legal clinic ▶**noun** N. Amer. a place where one can obtain legal advice and assistance, paid for by legal aid.

legal eagle (also **legal beagle**) ▶**noun** informal a lawyer, especially one who is keen and astute.

legalese /ˌliːɡəˈliːz/ ▶**noun** [mass noun] informal the formal and technical language of legal documents.

legal fiction ▶**noun** an assertion accepted as true, though probably fictitious, to achieve a useful purpose in legal matters.

legal holiday ▶**noun** N. Amer. a public holiday established by law.

legalism ▶**noun** [mass noun] excessive adherence to law or formula.
■Theology adherence to moral law rather than to personal religious faith.
– DERIVATIVES **legalist** noun & adjective, **legalistic** adjective, **legalistically** adverb.

legality ▶**noun** (pl. **-ies**) [mass noun] the quality or state of being in accordance with the law: *documentation testifying to the legality of the arms sale.*
■(**legalities**) obligations imposed by law.
– ORIGIN late Middle English: from French *légalité* or medieval Latin *legalitas* 'relating to the law', from Latin *legalis* (see **LEGAL**).

legalize (also **-ise**) ▶**verb** [with obj.] make (something that was previously illegal) permissible by law: *homosexuality and abortion have been legalized.*
– DERIVATIVES **legalization** noun.

legal person ▶**noun** Law an individual, company, or other entity which has legal rights and is subject to obligations.

legal separation ▶**noun 1** an arrangement by which a husband or wife remain married but live apart, following a court order. Also called **JUDICIAL SEPARATION**.
2 an arrangement by which a child lives apart from a natural parent and with another natural or foster-parent of their choice, following a court decree.

legal tender ▶**noun** [mass noun] coins or banknotes that must be accepted if offered in payment of a debt.

legate /ˈlɛɡət/ ▶**noun 1** a member of the clergy, especially a cardinal, representing the Pope.
■archaic an ambassador or messenger.
2 a general or governor of an ancient Roman province, or their deputy: *the Roman legate of Syria.*
– DERIVATIVES **legateship** noun, **legatine** /-tɪn/ adjective.
– ORIGIN late Old English, from Old French *legat*, from Latin *legatus*, past participle of *legare* 'depute, delegate, bequeath'.

legate a latere /ˌlɛɡət ɑː ˈlatəreɪ, -ri/ ▶**noun** a papal legate of the highest class, with full powers.
– ORIGIN early 16th cent.: from **LEGATE** + Latin *a latere* 'by a third party'.

legatee /ˌlɛɡəˈtiː/ ▶**noun** a person who receives a legacy.
– ORIGIN late 17th cent.: from 15th-cent. *legate* 'bequeath' (from Latin *legare* 'delegate, bequeath') + **-EE**.

legation ▶**noun 1** a diplomatic minister, especially one below the rank of ambassador, and their staff.
■the official residence of a diplomatic minister.
2 archaic the position or office of legate; a legateship.
■[mass noun] the sending of a legate, especially a papal legate, on a mission.
– ORIGIN late Middle English (denoting the sending of a papal legate; also the mission itself): from Latin *legatio(n-)*, from *legare* 'depute, delegate, bequeath'.

legato /lɪˈɡɑːtəʊ/ ▶**adverb** & **adjective** Music in a smooth flowing manner, without breaks between notes. Compare with **STACCATO**.
▶**noun** [mass noun] performance in this manner.
– ORIGIN Italian, literally 'bound'.

legator /lɪˈɡeɪtə/ ▶**noun** rare a testator, especially one who leaves a legacy.
– ORIGIN mid 17th cent.: from Latin, from *legat-* 'deputed, delegated, bequeathed', from the verb *legare*.

leg before wicket (also **leg before**) (abbrev.: **lbw**) Cricket ▶**adverb** & **adjective** [predic.] (of a batsman) adjudged by the umpire to be out through obstructing the ball with the leg (or other part of the body) rather than the bat, when the ball would otherwise have hit the wicket.

leg break ▶**noun** Cricket a ball which deviates from the leg side towards the off side after pitching.

leg bye ▶**noun** Cricket a run scored from a ball that has touched part of the batsman's body (apart from the hand) without touching the bat, the batsman having made an attempt to hit it.

leg-cutter ▶**noun** Cricket a fast leg break.

legend ▶**noun 1** a traditional story sometimes popularly regarded as historical but not authenticated: *the legend of King Arthur* | [mass noun] *according to legend he banished all the snakes from Ireland.*
2 an extremely famous or notorious person, especially in a particular field: *the man was **a living legend** | a screen legend.*
3 an inscription, especially on a coin or medal.
■a caption: *a picture of a tiger with the legend 'Go ahead make my day'.* ■the wording on a map or diagram explaining the symbols used: *see legend to Fig. 1.*
4 historical the story of a saint's life: *the mosaics illustrate the Legends of the Saints.*
▶**adjective** [predic.] very well known: *his speed and ferocity in attack were legend.*
– ORIGIN Middle English (in sense 4): from Old French *legende*, from medieval Latin *legenda* 'things to be read', from Latin *legere* 'read'. Sense 1 dates from the early 17th cent.

legendary ▶**adjective 1** of, described in, or based on legends: *a legendary British king of the 4th century.*
2 remarkable enough to be famous; very well known: *her wisdom in matters of childbirth was legendary.*
– DERIVATIVES **legendarily** adverb.
– ORIGIN early 16th cent. (as a noun denoting a collection of legends, especially of saints' lives): from medieval Latin *legendarius*, from *legenda* 'things to be read' (see **LEGEND**).

Léger /ˈleɪʒeɪ, French leʒe/, Fernand (1881–1955), French painter. From about 1909 he was associated with the cubist movement, but then developed a style inspired by machinery and modern technology; works include the *Contrast of Forms* series (1913).

legerdemain /ˌlɛdʒədɪˈmeɪn/ ▶**noun** [mass noun] skilful use of one's hands when performing conjuring tricks.
■deception; trickery.
– ORIGIN late Middle English: from French *léger de main* 'dexterous', literally 'light of hand'.

leger line /ˈlɛdʒə/ ▶**noun** Music a short line added for notes above or below the range of a stave.
– ORIGIN late 19th cent.: *leger*, variant of **LEDGER**.

leggings ▶**plural noun 1** tight-fitting stretch trousers worn by women and children.
2 stout protective overgarments for the legs.

leggy ▶**adjective** (**leggier, leggiest**) **1** (of a woman) having attractively long legs: *a leggy redhead.*
■long-legged: *a leggy type of collie.*
2 (of a plant) having an excessively long and straggly stem: *tulips may grow tall and leggy.*
– DERIVATIVES **legginess** noun.

Leghari /lɛɡˈhɑːri/, Farooq Ahmed (b.1940), Pakistani statesman, President 1993–7.

leghold trap ▶**noun** a type of trap with a mechanism that catches and holds an animal by one of its legs.

Leghorn /ˈlɛɡhɔːn/ another name for **LIVORNO**.

leghorn /lɛˈɡɔːn, ˈlɛɡhɔːn/ ▶**noun 1** [mass noun] fine plaited straw.
■(also **leghorn hat**) [count noun] a hat made of this.
2 (**Leghorn**) a chicken of a small hardy breed.
– ORIGIN mid 18th cent.: Anglicized from the Italian name *Leghorno* (now **LIVORNO**), from where the straw and fowls were imported.

legible ▶**adjective** (of handwriting or print) clear enough to read: *the original typescript is scarcely legible.*
– DERIVATIVES **legibility** noun, **legibly** adverb.
– ORIGIN late Middle English: from late Latin *legibilis*, from *legere* 'to read'.

legion ▶**noun 1** a division of 3,000–6,000 men, including a complement of cavalry, in the ancient Roman army.
■(**the Legion**) the Foreign Legion. ■(**the Legion**) any of the national associations of former servicemen and servicewomen instituted after the First World War, such as the Royal British Legion or the American Legion.
2 (**a legion/legions of**) a vast host, multitude, or number of people or things: *legions of photographers and TV cameras.*
▶**adjective** [predic.] great in number: *her fans are legion.*
– ORIGIN Middle English: via Old French from Latin *legio(n-)*, from *legere* 'choose, levy'. The adjective dates from the late 17th cent., in early use often in the phrase *my, their, etc. name is legion*, i.e. 'we, they, etc. are many' (Mark 5:9).

legionary ▶**noun** (pl. **-ies**) a soldier in a Roman legion.
▶**adjective** [attrib.] of an ancient Roman legion: *the legionary fortress of Isca.*
– ORIGIN late Middle English: from Latin *legionarius*, from *legio(n-)* (see **LEGION**).

legioned ▶**adjective** poetic/literary arrayed in legions.

legionella /ˌliːdʒəˈnɛlə/ ▶**noun** (pl. **legionellae** /-liː/) [mass noun] the bacterium which causes legionnaires' disease, flourishing in air conditioning and central heating systems.
• *Legionella pneumophila*, a motile aerobic rod-shaped (or filamentous) Gram-negative bacterium.
■informal legionnaires' disease.
– ORIGIN late 20th cent.: modern Latin, from **LEGION** + the diminutive suffix *-ella*.

legionnaire /ˌliːdʒəˈnɛː/ ▶**noun** a member of a legion, in particular an ancient Roman legion or the French Foreign Legion.
– ORIGIN early 19th cent.: from French *légionnaire*, from *légion* 'legion', from Latin *legio* (see **LEGION**).

legionnaires' disease ▶ noun [mass noun] a form of bacterial pneumonia first identified after an outbreak at an American Legion meeting in 1976. It is spread chiefly by water droplets through air conditioning and similar systems. See also **LEGIONELLA**.

Legion of Honour a French order of distinction founded in 1802.
– ORIGIN translation of French *Légion d'honneur*.

leg-iron ▶ noun (usu. **leg-irons**) a metal band or chain placed around a prisoner's ankle as a restraint.

legislate /ˈlɛdʒɪsleɪt/ ▶ verb [no obj.] make or enact laws: *they legislated against discrimination in the workplace.*
■ (**legislate for/against**) figurative make provision or preparation for (a situation or occurrence): *you cannot legislate for bad luck like that.* ■ [with obj.] cover, effect, or create by making or enacting laws: *constitutional changes will be legislated.*
– ORIGIN early 18th cent.: back-formation from **LEGISLATION**.

legislation ▶ noun [mass noun] laws, considered collectively: *housing legislation.*
– ORIGIN mid 17th cent. (denoting the enactment of laws): from late Latin *legis latio(n-)*, literally 'proposing of a law', from *lex* 'law' and *latus* 'raised' (past participle of *tollere*).

legislative /ˈlɛdʒɪslətɪv/ ▶ adjective having the power to make laws: *the country's supreme legislative body.*
■ of or relating to laws or the making of them: *legislative proposals.* Often contrasted with **EXECUTIVE**. ■ of or relating to a legislature: *legislative elections.*
– DERIVATIVES **legislatively** adverb.

legislator ▶ noun a person who makes laws; a member of a legislative body.
– ORIGIN late 15th cent.: from Latin *legis lator*, literally 'proposer of a law', from *lex* 'law' and *lator* 'proposer, mover' (see also **LEGISLATION**).

legislature /ˈlɛdʒɪslətʃə/ ▶ noun the legislative body of a country or state.
– ORIGIN late 17th cent.: from **LEGISLATION**, on the pattern of *judicature*.

legit /lɪˈdʒɪt/ ▶ adjective informal legal; conforming to the rules: *is this car legit?*
■ (of a person) not engaging in illegal activity or attempting to deceive; honest: *to see if he's legit, I call up the business to ask some questions.*
– PHRASES **go legit** begin to behave honestly after a period of illegal activity.
– ORIGIN early 20th cent.: abbreviation of **LEGITIMATE**.

legitimate ▶ adjective /lɪˈdʒɪtɪmət/ conforming to the law or to rules: *his claims to legitimate authority.*
■ able to be defended with logic or justification: *a legitimate excuse for being late.* ■ (of a child) born of parents lawfully married to each other. ■ (of a sovereign) having a title based on strict hereditary right: *the last legitimate Anglo-Saxon king.* ■ constituting or relating to serious drama as distinct from musical comedy, revue, etc.: *the legitimate theatre.*
▶ verb [with obj.] make legitimate; justify or make lawful: *the regime was not legitimated by popular support.*
– DERIVATIVES **legitimacy** noun, **legitimately** adverb, **legitimation** noun, **legitimatization** noun, **legitimatize** (also **-ise**) verb.
– ORIGIN late Middle English (in the sense 'born of parents lawfully married to each other'): from medieval Latin *legitimatus* 'made legal', from the verb *legitimare*, from Latin *legitimus* 'lawful', from *lex, leg-* 'law'.

legitimism ▶ noun [mass noun] support for a sovereign or pretender whose claim to a throne is based on direct descent.
– DERIVATIVES **legitimist** noun & adjective.
– ORIGIN late 19th cent.: from French *légitimisme*, from *légitime*, from Latin *legitimus* (see **LEGITIMATE**).

legitimize (also **-ise**) ▶ verb [with obj.] make legitimate: *voters legitimize the government through the election of public officials.*
– DERIVATIVES **legitimization** noun.

legless ▶ adjective **1** having no legs.
2 Brit. informal extremely drunk, especially to the point of not being able to stand up.

legless lizard ▶ noun a lizard which lacks legs and has a snake-like or worm-like appearance, in particular:

● an Australian lizard of a group that includes the scalyfoots (several genera in the family Pygopodidae). ● a North American lizard of California and Baja California (genus *Anniella* and family Anniellidae).

legman ▶ noun (pl. **-men**) a person employed to do simple tasks such as running errands or collecting information from outside their workplace.
■ N. Amer. a reporter whose job it is to gather information about news stories at the scene of the event or from an original source.

Lego ▶ noun [mass noun] trademark a construction toy consisting of interlocking plastic building blocks.
– ORIGIN 1950s: from Danish *leg godt* 'play well', from *lege* 'to play'.

leg-of-mutton sleeve ▶ noun a sleeve which is full and loose on the upper arm but close-fitting on the forearm and wrist.

leg-over ▶ noun vulgar slang an instance of sexual intercourse.

leg-pull ▶ noun informal a trick or practical joke.
– DERIVATIVES **leg-pulling** noun.

leg rest ▶ noun a support for a seated person's leg.

legroom ▶ noun [mass noun] space in which a seated person can put their legs.

leg-rope ▶ noun Austral./NZ a noosed rope used to secure an animal by one hind leg.

leg-show ▶ noun informal, dated a theatrical production in which dancing girls display their legs.

leg side ▶ noun see LEG (sense 5).

leg slip ▶ noun Cricket a fielding position just behind the batsman on the leg side.
■ a fielder at this position.

leg spin ▶ noun [mass noun] Cricket a type of spin bowling which causes the ball to deviate from the leg side towards the off side after pitching; leg breaks.
– DERIVATIVES **leg-spinner** noun.

leg stump ▶ noun Cricket the stump on the leg side of a wicket.

leg trap ▶ noun Cricket a group of fielders close to the wicket on the leg side.

leguan /ˈlɛgjʊən/ (also **leguaan** or **likkewaan**) ▶ noun S. African a large African monitor lizard.
● Genus *Varanus*, family Varanidae: the **water leguan** or Nile monitor, and *V. exanthematicus*, which lives in burrows in savannah and semi-desert habitats.
– ORIGIN late 18th cent.: from Dutch, probably from French *l'iguane* 'the iguana'. The variant *likkewaan* is from Afrikaans.

legume /ˈlɛgjuːm/ ▶ noun a leguminous plant, especially one grown as a crop.
■ a seed, pod, or other edible part of a leguminous plant used as food. ■ Botany the long seed pod of a leguminous plant.
– ORIGIN mid 17th cent. (denoting the edible portion of the plant): from French *légume*, from Latin *legumen*, from *legere* 'to pick' (because the fruit may be picked by hand).

leguminous /lɪˈgjuːmɪnəs/ ▶ adjective Botany of, relating to, or denoting plants of the pea family (Leguminosae). These have seeds in pods, distinctive flowers, and typically root nodules containing symbiotic bacteria able to fix nitrogen. Compare with **PAPILIONACEOUS**.
– ORIGIN late Middle English (in the sense 'relating to pulses'): from medieval Latin *leguminosus*, from *legumen* (see **LEGUME**).

leg-up ▶ noun [in sing.] help to mount a horse or high object: *give me a leg-up over the wall.*
■ help to improve one's position: *the council is to provide a financial leg-up for the club.*

leg warmer ▶ noun one of a pair of tubular knitted garments designed to cover the leg from ankle to knee or thigh, typically worn by dancers during rehearsal.

legwork ▶ noun work that involves much travelling about to collect information, especially when such work is difficult but boring.

Leh /leɪ/ a town in Jammu and Kashmir, northern India, to the east of Srinagar near the Indus River; pop. 9,000 (est. 1991). It is the chief town of the Himalayan region of Ladakh, and the administrative centre of Ladakh district.

Lehár /ˈleɪhɑː/, Franz (Ferencz) (1870–1948), Hungarian composer. He is chiefly known for his operettas, of which the most famous is *The Merry Widow* (1905).

Le Havre /lə ˈhɑːvr(ə)/, French /lə ˈɑːvr/ a port in northern France, on the English Channel at the mouth of the Seine; pop. 197,220 (1990).

lehr /lɪə/ (also **leer**) ▶ noun a furnace used for the annealing of glass.
– ORIGIN mid 17th cent.: of unknown origin.

lei[1] /leɪ, ˈleɪi/ ▶ noun a Polynesian garland of flowers.
– ORIGIN Hawaiian.

lei[2] plural form of **LEU**.

Leibniz /ˈlaɪbnɪts/, Gottfried Wilhelm (1646–1716), German rationalist philosopher, mathematician, and logician. He argued that the world is composed of single units (monads), each of which is self-contained but acts in harmony with every other, as ordained by God, and so this world is the best of all possible worlds. Leibniz also made the important distinction between necessary and contingent truths and devised a method of calculus independently of Newton.
– DERIVATIVES **Leibnizian** adjective & noun.

Leibovitz /ˈliːbəvɪts/, Annie (b.1950), American photographer. She was chief photographer of *Rolling Stone* magazine (1973–83) before moving to *Vanity Fair*, and has produced portraits of many celebrities.

Leicester[1] /ˈlɛstə/ a city in central England, on the River Soar, the county town of Leicestershire; pop. 270,600. It was founded as a Roman settlement where the Fosse Way crosses the Soar (AD 50–100).

Leicester[2] /ˈlɛstə/, Earl of, see **DUDLEY**[2].

Leicester[3] /ˈlɛstə/ ▶ noun **1** (also **Red Leicester**) [mass noun] a kind of mild firm cheese, typically orange-coloured and originally made in Leicestershire.
2 (also **Border Leicester**) a sheep of a breed often crossed with other breeds to produce lambs for the meat industry.
3 (also **Blue-faced Leicester**) a sheep of a breed similar to the Border Leicester, but with finer wool and a darker face.

Leicestershire /ˈlɛstəʃɪə, -ʃə/ a county of central England; county town, Leicester.

Leichhardt /ˈlaɪkhɑːt/, (Friedrich Wilhelm) Ludwig (1813–48), Australian explorer, born in Prussia. After emigrating to Australia in 1841, he began a series of geological surveys; he disappeared during an attempt at a transcontinental crossing.

Leics. ▶ abbreviation for Leicestershire.

Leiden /ˈlaɪd(ə)n/ (also **Leyden**) a city in the west Netherlands, 15 km (9 miles) north-east of The Hague; pop. 111,950 (1991). It is the site of the country's oldest university, founded in 1575.

Leif Ericsson see **ERICSSON**[2].

Leigh /liː/, Vivien (1913–67), British actress, born in India; born *Vivian Mary Hartley*. She won Oscars for her performances in *Gone with the Wind* (1939) and *A Streetcar Named Desire* (1951). She was married to Laurence Olivier from 1940 to 1961.

Leighton /ˈleɪt(ə)n/, Frederic, 1st Baron Leighton of Stretton (1830–96), English painter and sculptor. He was a leading exponent of Victorian neoclassicism and chiefly painted large-scale mythological and genre scenes. Notable works: *Flaming June* (painting, *c.*1895).

Leinster /ˈlɛnstə/ a province of the Republic of Ireland, in the south-east of the country, centred on Dublin.

leiothrix /ˈlaɪə(ʊ)θrɪks/ (also **red-billed leiothrix**) ▶ noun an Asian bird of the babbler family, with orange-yellow underparts and a melodious song, popular as a cage bird. Also called **PEKIN ROBIN**.
● *Leiothrix lutea*, family Timaliidae.
– ORIGIN modern Latin, from Greek *leios* 'smooth' + *thrix* 'hair'.

Leipzig /ˈlaɪpsɪg, German ˈlaɪptsɪç/ an industrial city in east central Germany; pop. 503,190 (1991).

leishmania /liːʃˈmeɪnɪə/ ▶ noun (pl. same or **leishmanias** or **leishmaniae** /-ˈmeɪnɪaɪ/) a single-celled parasitic protozoan which spends part of its life cycle in the gut of a sandfly and part in the blood and other tissues of a vertebrate.
● Genus *Leishmania*, phylum Kinetoplastida, kingdom Protista.
– ORIGIN modern Latin, from the name of William B. *Leishman* (1856–1926), British pathologist.

leishmaniasis /ˌliːʃməˈnaɪəsɪs/ ▶ noun [mass noun] a tropical and subtropical disease caused by leishmania and transmitted by the bite of sandflies. It affects either the skin or the internal organs.

Leisler's bat /ˈlʌɪzləz/ ▶ **noun** a small blackish bat related to the noctule, found from Europe and North Africa to central Asia.
• *Nyctalus leisleri*, family Vespertilionidae.
– ORIGIN early 20th cent.: named after T. P *Leisler*, 19th-cent. German zoologist.

leister /ˈliːstə/ ▶ **noun** a pronged spear used for catching salmon.
▶ **verb** [with obj.] spear (a fish) with a leister.
– ORIGIN mid 16th cent.: from Old Norse *ljóstr*, from *ljósta* 'to strike'.

leisure /ˈlɛʒə/ ▶ **noun** [mass noun] free time.
■ use of free time for enjoyment: *increased opportunities for leisure* | [as modifier] *leisure activities*. ■ (**leisure for/to do something**) opportunity afforded by free time to do something: *writers with enough leisure to practise their art*.
– PHRASES **at leisure 1** not occupied; free: *the rest of the day can be spent at leisure*. **2** in an unhurried manner: *the poems were left for others to read at leisure*. **at one's leisure** at one's ease or convenience. **lady** (or **man** or **gentleman**) **of leisure** a woman or man of independent means or whose time is free from obligations to others.
– ORIGIN Middle English: from Old French *leisir*, based on Latin *licere* 'be allowed'.

leisure centre ▶ **noun** a large public building with many different sports and exercise facilities.

leisure complex ▶ **noun** a large establishment (or group of establishments) that provides facilities for a wide range of entertainment, exercise, and sport.

leisured ▶ **adjective** having ample leisure, especially through being rich: *the leisured classes*.
■ leisurely: *the leisured life of his college*.

leisurely ▶ **adjective** acting or done at leisure; unhurried or relaxed: *a leisurely breakfast at our hotel*.
▶ **adverb** without hurry: *couples strolled leisurely along*.
– DERIVATIVES **leisureliness** noun.

leisurewear ▶ **noun** [mass noun] casual clothes designed to be worn for leisure activities, particularly tracksuits and other sportswear.

leitmotif /ˈlʌɪtməʊˌtiːf/ (also **leitmotiv**) ▶ **noun** a recurrent theme throughout a musical or literary composition, associated with a particular person, idea, or situation.
– ORIGIN late 19th cent.: from German *Leitmotiv*, from *leit-* 'leading' (from *leiten* 'to lead') + *Motiv* 'motive'.

Leitrim /ˈliːtrɪm/ a county of the Republic of Ireland, in the province of Connacht; county town, Carrick-on-Shannon.

Leix variant spelling of **LAOIS**.

lek[1] /lɛk/ ▶ **noun** the basic monetary unit of Albania, equal to 100 qintars.
– ORIGIN Albanian.

lek[2] /lɛk/ ▶ **noun** a patch of ground used for communal display in the breeding season by the males of certain birds and mammals, especially black grouse. Each male defends a small territory in order to attract females for mating.
▶ **verb** [no obj.] [usu. as adj. **lekking**] take part in such a display: *antelopes mate in lekking grounds*.
– ORIGIN late 19th cent.: perhaps from Swedish *leka* 'to play'.

lekker /ˈlɛkə, ˈlʌkə/ (also **lecker, leke**) S. African informal ▶ **adjective** good; pleasant: *it wasn't a lekker experience seeing ourselves as others see us*.
■ slightly intoxicated. ■ (of water) safe or good to drink.
▶ **adverb 1** well: *we got on lekker*.
2 [as submodifier] extremely: *he was lekker drunk*.
– ORIGIN Afrikaans, from Dutch, literally 'delicious'.

lekkergoed /ˈlɛkə(r)xʊt, -xuːt/ ▶ **noun** [mass noun] S. African sweet food; sweets.
– ORIGIN Afrikaans, literally 'delicious stuff'.

lekker lewe /ˈlɛkə ˌlɪəvə/ ▶ **noun** (**the lekker lewe**) S. African informal the good life.
– ORIGIN Afrikaans, literally 'delicious life'.

lekker ou /ˈlɛkər əʊ/ ▶ **noun** (pl. **lekker ous**) S. African informal a man who is liked, approved of, and trusted.
– ORIGIN Afrikaans, literally 'fine fellow'.

Lely /ˈliːli/, Sir Peter (1618–80), Dutch portrait painter, resident in England from 1641; Dutch name *Pieter van der Faes*. He became principal court painter to Charles II. Notable works include *Windsor Beauties*, a series painted during the 1660s.

LEM ▶ **abbreviation for** lunar excursion module.

leman /ˈlɛmən, ˈliː-/ ▶ **noun** (pl. **lemans**) archaic a lover or sweetheart.
■ an illicit lover, especially a mistress.
– ORIGIN Middle English *lēofman*, from *lēof* (see **LIEF**) + **MAN**.

Le Mans /lə ˈmɒ̃/ an industrial town in NW France; pop. 148,465 (1990). It is the site of a motor-racing circuit, on which a 24-hour endurance race (established in 1923) is held each summer.

Lemberg /ˈlɛmbɛrk/ German name for **LVIV**.

lemma[1] /ˈlɛmə/ ▶ **noun** (pl. **lemmas** or **lemmata** /-mətə/) **1** a subsidiary or intermediate theorem in an argument or proof.
2 a heading indicating the subject or argument of a literary composition, an annotation, or a dictionary entry.
– ORIGIN late 16th cent.: via Latin from Greek *lēmma* 'something assumed'; related to *lambanein* 'take'.

lemma[2] /ˈlɛmə/ ▶ **noun** (pl. **lemmas** or **lemmata** /-mətə/) Botany the lower bract of the floret of a grass. Compare with **PALEA**.
– ORIGIN mid 18th cent. (denoting the husk or shell of a fruit): from Greek, from *lepein* 'to peel'.

lemmatize (also **-ise**) ▶ **verb** [with obj.] sort so as to group together inflected or variant forms of the same word.
– DERIVATIVES **lemmatization** noun.

lemme informal ▶ **contraction of** let me: *lemme ask you something*.

lemming ▶ **noun** a small, short-tailed, thickset rodent related to the voles, found in the Arctic tundra.
• *Lemmus*, *Dicrostonyx*, and other genera, family Muridae: several species, in particular the **Norway lemming** (*L. lemmus*), which is noted for its fluctuating populations and periodic mass migrations.
■ a person who unthinkingly joins a mass movement, especially a headlong rush to destruction: *a seething herd of lemmings on the road*.
– ORIGIN early 18th cent.: from Norwegian and Danish; related to Old Norse *lómundr*.

Lemmon, Jack (b.1925), American actor; born *John Uhler*. He made his name in comedy films, such as *Some Like It Hot* (1959), later playing serious dramatic parts and winning an Oscar for *Save the Tiger* (1973).

Lemnos /ˈlɛmnɒs/ a Greek island in the northern Aegean Sea; chief town, Kástron. Greek name **LÍMNOS**.

lemon ▶ **noun 1** a pale yellow oval citrus fruit with thick skin and fragrant, acidic juice.
■ [mass noun] a drink made from or flavoured with lemon juice: *a port and lemon* | [as modifier] *lemon tea*.
2 (also **lemon tree**) the evergreen citrus tree which produces this fruit, widely cultivated in warm climates.
• *Citrus limon*, family Rutaceae.
3 [mass noun] a pale yellow colour: [as modifier] *lemon yellow* | *a lemon T-shirt*.
4 informal a person or thing regarded as unsatisfactory, disappointing, or feeble.
– DERIVATIVES **lemony** adjective.
– ORIGIN Middle English: via Old French *limon* (in modern French denoting a lime) from Arabic *līmūn* (a collective term for fruits of this kind); compare with **LIME**[2].

lemonade ▶ **noun** [mass noun] a drink made from lemon juice and water sweetened with sugar.
■ Brit. a sweet colourless carbonated drink containing lemon flavouring.
– ORIGIN mid 17th cent.: from French *limonade*, from *limon* 'lemon'.

lemon balm ▶ **noun** see **BALM** (sense 3).

lemon curd (Brit. also **lemon cheese**) ▶ **noun** [mass noun] a conserve with a thick consistency made from lemons, butter, eggs, and sugar.

lemon drop ▶ **noun** a yellow, lemon-flavoured boiled sweet.

lemon geranium ▶ **noun** a pelargonium which contains an aromatic oil that smells of lemon.
• *Pelargonium crispum*, family Geraniaceae.

lemon grass ▶ **noun** [mass noun] a fragrant tropical grass which yields an oil that smells of lemon. It is widely used in Asian cooking and in perfumery and medicine.
• *Cymbopogon citratus*, family Gramineae.

lemon sole ▶ **noun** a common European flatfish of the plaice family. It is an important food fish.
• *Microstomus kitt*, family Pleuronectidae.
– ORIGIN mid 19th cent.: *lemon* from French *limande*, of unknown origin.

lemon-squeezer ▶ **noun** a small kitchen device for extracting the juice from lemons.

lemon thyme ▶ **noun** thyme of a hybrid variety having lemon-scented leaves.
• *Thymus × citriodorus*, family Labiatae.

lemon verbena ▶ **noun** a South American shrub of the verbena family, with lemon-scented leaves that are used as flavouring and to make a sedative tea.
• *Aloysia triphylla*, family Verbenaceae.

lemonwood ▶ **noun** a small evergreen New Zealand tree whose leaves produce a lemon-like smell when crushed. Also called **TARATA** in New Zealand.
• *Pittosporum eugenoides*, family Pittosporaceae.

lempira /lɛmˈpɪərə/ ▶ **noun** the basic monetary unit of Honduras, equal to 100 centavos.
– ORIGIN named after *Lempira*, a 16th-cent. Indian chieftain who opposed the Spanish conquest of Honduras.

lemur /ˈliːmə/ ▶ **noun** an arboreal primate with a pointed snout and typically a long tail, found only in Madagascar. Compare with **FLYING LEMUR**.
• Lemuridae and other families, suborder Prosimii; includes also the sifaka, indri, and aye-aye.
– ORIGIN late 18th cent.: modern Latin, from Latin *lemures* (plural) 'spirits of the dead' (from its spectre-like face).

Lena /ˈleɪnə/ a river in Siberia, which rises in the mountains on the western shore of Lake Baikal and flows for 4,400 km (2,750 miles) into the Laptev Sea. It is famous for the goldfields in its basin.

Lenclos /lɒ̃ˈkləʊ, French lɑ̃klo/, Ninon de (1620–1705), French courtesan; born *Anne de Lenclos*. She was a famous wit and beauty who advocated a form of Epicureanism in her book *La Coquette vengée* (1659), and later presided over one of the most distinguished literary salons of the age.

lend ▶ **verb** (past and past participle **lent**) [with two objs] **1** grant to (someone) the use of (something) on the understanding that it shall be returned: *Stewart asked me to lend him my car* | *the pictures were lent to each museum in turn*.
■ allow (a person or organization) the use of (a sum of money) under an agreement to pay it back later, typically with interest: *no one would lend him the money* | [no obj.] *banks lend only to their current account customers* | [as noun **lending**] *balance sheets weakened by unwise lending*.
2 contribute or add (something, especially a quality) to: *the smile lent his face a boyish charm*.
3 (**lend oneself to**) accommodate or adapt oneself to: *John stiffly lent himself to her aromatic embraces*.
■ (**lend itself to**) (of a thing) be suitable for: *bay windows lend themselves to blinds*.
– PHRASES **lend an ear** (or **one's ears**) listen sympathetically or attentively: *the Samaritans lend their ears to those in crisis*. **lend a hand** (or **a helping hand**) see ***give a hand*** at **HAND**. **lend one's name to** allow oneself to be publicly associated with: *he lent his name and prestige to the organizers of the project*.
– DERIVATIVES **lendable** adjective.
– ORIGIN Old English *lǣnan*, of Germanic origin; related to Dutch *lenen*, also to **LOAN**[1]. The addition of the final *-d* in late Middle English was due to association with verbs such as *bend* and *send*.

USAGE **1** Reciprocal pairs of words such as **lend** and **borrow** (or **teach** and **learn**) are often confused. Common uses in informal speech in a number of British dialects include *can I **lend** your pen?* (correct standard use is *can I **borrow** your pen?*).
2 There is no noun **lend** in standard English, where **loan** is the correct word to use. However, it is used informally in a number of dialects and varieties, including Scottish, Northern Irish, and northern English, as in, for example, *can I have a **lend** of your pen?*

lender ▶ **noun** an organization or person that lends money: *a mortgage lender*.

lending library ▶ **noun** a public library from which books may be borrowed and taken away for a short time.

Lendl /ˈlɛnd(ə)l/, Ivan (b.1960), Czech-born tennis player. He won many singles titles in the 1980s and early 1990s, including the US, Australian, and the French Open championships. He became an American citizen in 1992.

Lend-Lease historical an arrangement made in 1941 whereby the US supplied military equipment and armaments to the UK and its allies, originally as a loan in return for the use of British-owned military bases. Also called **LEASE-LEND**.

length /lɛŋθ, lɛŋkθ/ ▶ **noun 1** [mass noun] the measurement or extent of something from end to end; the greater of two or the greatest of three dimensions of a body: *it can reach over two feet* ***in length*** | *the length of the coast track.*
■ the amount of time occupied by something: *delivery must be within a reasonable length of time.* ■ the quality of being long: *the length of the waiting list.* ■ the full distance that a thing extends for: *the muscles running* ***the length of*** *my spine.* ■ the extent of a garment in a vertical direction when worn: *the length of her skirt.* ■ Prosody & Phonetics the metrical quantity or duration of a vowel or syllable.
2 the extent of something, especially as a unit of measurement:
■ the length of a swimming pool as a measure of the distance swum: *fifty lengths of the pool.* ■ the length of a horse, boat, etc., as a measure of the lead in a race: *the mare won the race last year by seven lengths.* ■ (**one's length**) the full extent of one's body: *he awkwardly lowered his length into the small car.* ■ (in bridge or whist) the number of cards of a suit held in one's hand, especially when five or more.
3 a stretch or piece of something: ***a stout length of*** *wood.*
4 a degree or extreme to which a course of action is taken: *they* ***go to great lengths to*** *avoid the press.*
5 Cricket the distance from the batsman at which the ball pitches, especially a ball that is well bowled: *Lewis tended to bowl short of a length.*
– PHRASES **at length 1** in detail; fully: *these aspects have been discussed at length.* **2** after a long time: *at length she laid down the pencil.* **the length and breadth of** the whole extent of: *women from the length and breadth of Russia.*
– ORIGIN Old English *lengthu*, of Germanic origin; related to Dutch *lengte*, also to **LONG**[1].

-length ▶ **combining form** reaching up to or down to the place specified: *knee-length.*
■ of the size, duration, or extent specified: *full-length* | *medium-length* | *feature-length.*

lengthen ▶ **verb** make or become longer: [with obj.] *she lengthened her stride to catch him up* | [no obj.] *in the spring when the days are lengthening* | [as adj. **lengthening**] *the lengthening shadows.*
■ [with obj.] Prosody & Phonetics make (a vowel or syllable) long.

lengthman ▶ **noun** (pl. **-men**) Brit. archaic a person employed to maintain a section of road or railway.

lengthways ▶ **adverb** in a direction parallel with a thing's length: *cut the courgettes in half lengthways.*

lengthwise ▶ **adverb** lengthways: *halve the potatoes lengthwise.*
▶ **adjective** [attrib.] lying or moving lengthways.

lengthy ▶ **adjective** (**lengthier**, **lengthiest**) (especially in reference to time) of considerable or unusual length, especially so as to be tedious: *lengthy delays.*
– DERIVATIVES **lengthily** adverb, **lengthiness** noun.

lenient /ˈliːnɪənt/ ▶ **adjective 1** (of punishment or a person in authority) merciful or tolerant: *judges were far too lenient with petty criminals.*
2 archaic emollient.
– DERIVATIVES **lenience** noun, **leniency** noun, **leniently** adverb.
– ORIGIN mid 17th cent. (in sense 2): from Latin *lenient-* 'soothing', from the verb *lenire*, from *lenis* 'mild, gentle'.

Lenin /ˈlɛnɪn/, Vladimir Ilich (1870–1924), the principal figure in the Russian Revolution and first Premier of the Soviet Union 1918–24; born *Vladimir Ilich Ulyanov.*

Lenin was the first political leader to attempt to put Marxist principles into practice. In 1917 he established Bolshevik control after the overthrow of the tsar, and in 1918 became head of state (Chairman of the Council of People's Commissars). With Trotsky he defeated counter-revolutionary forces in the Russian Civil War, but was forced to moderate his policies to allow the country to recover from the effects of war and revolution.

Leninakan /ˌlɛnɪnəˈkɑːn/ former name (1924–91) for **GYUMRI**.

Leningrad /ˈlɛnɪngrad/ former name (1924–91) for **ST PETERSBURG**.

Leninism ▶ **noun** [mass noun] Marxism as interpreted and applied by Lenin.
– DERIVATIVES **Leninist** noun & adjective, **Leninite** noun & adjective.
– ORIGIN early 20th cent.: named after **LENIN**.

lenis /ˈlɛnɪs, ˈleɪnɪs, ˈliːnɪs/ Phonetics ▶ **adjective** (of a consonant) weakly articulated, especially denoting the less or least strongly articulated of two or more similar consonants. Voiced consonants are normally lenis. The opposite of **FORTIS**.
▶ **noun** (pl. **lenes**) a consonant of this type.
– ORIGIN early 20th cent.: from Latin, literally 'mild, gentle'.

lenite /ˈliːnʌɪt, lɪˈnʌɪt/ ▶ **verb** (**be lenited**) (of a consonant in a Celtic language) be pronounced with palatalization.
– ORIGIN early 20th cent.: back-formation from **LENITION**.

lenition /lɪˈnɪʃ(ə)n/ ▶ **noun** [mass noun] (in Celtic languages) the process or result of palatalizing a consonant.
– ORIGIN early 20th cent.: from Latin *lenis* 'soft' + **-ITION**, suggested by German *Lenierung.*

lenitive /ˈlɛnɪtɪv/ Medicine, archaic ▶ **adjective** (of a medicine) laxative.
▶ **noun** a medicine of this type.
– ORIGIN late Middle English: from medieval Latin *lenitivus*, from *lenit-* 'softened', from the verb *lenire.*

lenity /ˈlɛnɪti/ ▶ **noun** [mass noun] poetic/literary kindness; gentleness.
– ORIGIN late Middle English: from Old French *lenite*. or from Latin *lenitas*, from *lenis* 'gentle'.

Lennon, John (1940–80), English pop and rock singer, guitarist, and songwriter. A founder member of the Beatles, he wrote most of their songs in collaboration with Paul McCartney. He was assassinated outside his home in New York.

leno /ˈliːnəʊ/ ▶ **noun** (pl. **-os**) [mass noun] an openwork fabric with the warp threads twisted in pairs before weaving.
– ORIGIN late 18th cent.: from French *linon*, from *lin* 'flax', from Latin *linum*. Compare with **LINEN**.

Le Nôtre /lə ˈnəʊtr(ə), French lə notʀ/, André (1613–1700), French landscape gardener. He designed many formal gardens, including the parks of Vaux-le-Vicomte and Versailles. These incorporated his ideas on geometric formality and equilibrium.

lens ▶ **noun** a piece of glass or other transparent substance with curved sides for concentrating or dispersing light rays, used singly (as in a magnifying glass) or with other lenses (as in a telescope).
■ the light-gathering device of a camera, typically containing a group of compound lenses. ■ Physics an object or device which focuses or otherwise modifies the direction of movement of light, sound, electrons, etc. ■ Anatomy short for **CRYSTALLINE LENS**. ■ short for **CONTACT LENS**.
– DERIVATIVES **lensed** adjective, **lensless** adjective.
– ORIGIN late 17th cent.: from Latin, 'lentil' (because of the similarity in shape).

lens hood ▶ **noun** a tube or ring attached to the front of a camera lens to prevent unwanted light from reaching the film.

lensman ▶ **noun** (pl. **-men**) a professional photographer or cameraman.

Lent ▶ **noun** the period preceding Easter which in the Christian Church is devoted to fasting, abstinence, and penitence in commemoration of Christ's fasting in the wilderness. In the Western Church it runs from Ash Wednesday to Holy Saturday, and so includes forty weekdays.
■ (**Lents**) the boat races held at Cambridge University in the Lent term.
– ORIGIN Middle English: abbreviation of **LENTEN**.

lent past and past participle of **LEND**.

-lent ▶ **suffix** forming adjectives such as *pestilent, violent*. Compare with **-ULENT**.

Lenten ▶ **adjective** [attrib.] of, in, or appropriate to Lent: *Lenten food.*
– ORIGIN Old English *lencten* 'spring, Lent', of Germanic origin, related to **LONG**[1] (perhaps with reference to the lengthening of the day in spring); now interpreted as being from **LENT** + **-EN**[2].

Lenten fare ▶ **noun** [mass noun] chiefly archaic food appropriate to Lent, especially that without meat.

Lenten rose ▶ **noun** a hellebore that is cultivated for its flowers which appear in late winter or early spring.
● *Helleborus orientalis*, family Ranunculaceae.

lentic /ˈlɛntɪk/ ▶ **adjective** Ecology (of organisms or habitats) inhabiting or situated in still fresh water. Compare with **LOTIC**.
– ORIGIN mid 20th cent.: from Latin *lentus* 'calm, slow' + **-IC**.

lenticel /ˈlɛntɪsɛl/ ▶ **noun** Botany one of many raised pores in the stem of a woody plant that allows gas exchange between the atmosphere and the internal tissues.
– ORIGIN mid 19th cent.: from modern Latin *lenticella*, diminutive of Latin *lens, lent-* 'lentil'.

lenticular /lɛnˈtɪkjʊlə/ ▶ **adjective 1** shaped like a lentil, especially by being biconvex: *lenticular lenses.*
2 of or relating to the lens of the eye.
– ORIGIN late Middle English: from Latin *lenticularis*, from *lenticula*, diminutive of *lens, lent-* 'lentil'.

lentiform nucleus ▶ **noun** Anatomy the lower of the two grey nuclei of the corpus striatum.
– ORIGIN early 18th cent.: *lentiform* from Latin *lens, lent-* 'lentil' + **-IFORM**.

lentigo /lɛnˈtʌɪgəʊ/ ▶ **noun** (pl. **lentigines** /-ˈtɪdʒɪniːz/) [mass noun] a condition marked by small brown patches on the skin, typically in elderly people.
– ORIGIN late Middle English (denoting a freckle or pimple): from Latin, from *lens, lent-* 'lentil'.

lentil ▶ **noun 1** a high-protein pulse which is dried and then soaked and cooked prior to eating. There are several varieties of lentils, including green ones and smaller orange ones, which are typically sold split.
2 the plant which yields this pulse, native to the Mediterranean and Africa and grown also for fodder.
● *Lens culinaris*, family Leguminosae.
– ORIGIN Middle English: from Old French *lentille*, from Latin *lenticula*, diminutive of *lens, lent-* 'lentil'.

lentisc /lɛnˈtɪsk/ ▶ **noun** the mastic tree.
– ORIGIN late Middle English: from Latin *lentiscus.*

lentivirus /ˈlɛntɪˌvʌɪrəs/ ▶ **noun** Medicine any of a group of retroviruses producing illnesses characterized by a delay in the onset of symptoms after infection.
– ORIGIN 1970s: from Latin *lentus* 'slow' + **VIRUS**.

lent lily ▶ **noun** Brit. the European wild daffodil, which typically has pale creamy-white outer petals.
● *Narcissus pseudonarcissus*, family Liliaceae (or Amaryllidaceae).

lento /ˈlɛntəʊ/ ▶ **adverb & adjective** Music (especially as a direction) slow or slowly.
▶ **noun** (pl. **-os**) a passage or movement marked to be performed in this way.
– ORIGIN Italian.

lentoid /ˈlɛntɔɪd/ ▶ **adjective** another term for **LENTICULAR** (in sense 1).
– ORIGIN late 19th cent.: from Latin *lens, lent-* 'lentil' + **-OID**.

Lent term ▶ **noun** Brit. the university term in which Lent falls.

Lenz's law /ˈlɛntsɪz, ˈlɛnzɪz/ Physics a law stating that the direction of an induced current is always such as to oppose the change in the circuit or the magnetic field that produces it.
– ORIGIN mid 19th cent.: named after Heinrich F. E. *Lenz* (1804–65), German physicist.

Leo[1] the name of thirteen popes, notably:
■ Leo I (d.461), pope from 440 and Doctor of the Church; known as **Leo the Great**; canonized as St Leo I. He defined the doctrine of the Incarnation at the Council of Chalcedon (451) and extended the power of the Roman see to Africa, Spain, and Gaul. Feast day (in the Eastern Church) 18 February; (in the Western Church) 11 April.
■ Leo X (1475–1521), pope from 1513; born *Giovanni de' Medici*. He excommunicated Martin Luther and bestowed on Henry VIII of England the title of Defender of the Faith. He was a noted patron of learning and the arts.

Leo[2] **1** Astronomy a large constellation (the Lion), said to represent the lion slain by Hercules. It contains the bright stars Regulus and Denebola and numerous galaxies.
■ [as genitive **Leonis** /liːˈəʊniːs/] used with preceding letter or numeral to designate a star in this constellation: *the star Omicron Leonis.*

2 Astrology the fifth sign of the zodiac, which the sun enters about 23 July.

■ **(a Leo)** (pl. **-os**) a person born when the sun is in this sign.
– DERIVATIVES **Leonian** noun & adjective (only in sense 2).
– ORIGIN Latin.

Leo III (c.680–741), Byzantine emperor 717–41. He repulsed several Muslim invasions and carried out an extensive series of reforms. In 726 he banned icons and other religious images; the resulting iconoclastic controversy led to over a century of political and religious turmoil.

Leo Minor /ˈliːəʊ ˈmaɪnə/ Astronomy a small and inconspicuous northern constellation (the Little Lion), immediately north of Leo.
■ [as genitive **Leonis Minoris** /liːˌəʊnɪs mɪˈnɔːrɪs/] used with preceding letter or numeral to designate a star in this constellation: *the star Alpha Leonis Minoris*.
– ORIGIN Latin.

León /leɪˈɒn/ **1** a city in northern Spain; pop. 146,270 (1991). It is the capital of the province and former kingdom of León, now part of Castilla-León region.
2 an industrial city in central Mexico; pop. 872,450 (1990).
3 a city in western Nicaragua, the second largest city in the country; pop. 158,577 (1991).

Leonard, Elmore (John) (b.1925), American thriller writer. After working as an advertising copywriter, in 1967 he turned to writing screenplays and novels. Notable works: *Freaky Deaky* (1988) and *Get Shorty* (1990).

Leonardo da Vinci /ˌliːəˈnɑːdəʊ də ˈvɪntʃi/ (1452–1519), Italian painter, scientist, and engineer.

> His paintings are notable for their use of the technique of *sfumato* and include *The Virgin of the Rocks* (1483–5), *The Last Supper* (1498), and the enigmatic *Mona Lisa* (1504–5). He devoted himself to a wide range of other subjects, from anatomy and biology to mechanics and hydraulics: his nineteen notebooks include studies of the human circulatory system and plans for a type of aircraft and a submarine.

Leonberg /ˈliːənbəːg/ ▶ noun a large dog of a breed typically having a golden coat, produced by crossing a St Bernard and a Newfoundland.
– ORIGIN early 20th cent.: named after a town in SW Germany.

leone /liːˈəʊn/ ▶ noun the basic monetary unit of Sierra Leone, equal to 100 cents.

Leonids /ˈliːənɪdz/ Astronomy an annual meteor shower with a radiant in the constellation Leo, reaching a peak about 17 November.
– ORIGIN late 19th cent.: from Latin *leo*, *leon-* (see **LEO**²) + **-ID**³.

Leonine /ˈliːənaɪn/ ▶ adjective **1** of or relating to one of the popes named Leo, especially the part of Rome fortified by Leo IV.
2 Prosody (of medieval Latin verse) in hexameter or elegiac metre with internal rhyme.
▶ (of English verse) with internal rhyme.
▶ plural noun **(Leonines)** Prosody verse of this type.
– ORIGIN late Middle English: from the name *Leo*, from Latin *leo* 'lion'. Sense 2 may be from the name of a medieval poet, but his identity is not known.

leonine /ˈliːənaɪn/ ▶ adjective of or resembling a lion or lions: *a handsome, leonine profile*.
– ORIGIN late Middle English: from Old French, or from Latin *leoninus*, from *leo*, *leon-* 'lion'.

Leonine City the part of Rome in which the Vatican stands, walled and fortified by Pope Leo IV.

leopard ▶ noun a large solitary cat that has a fawn or brown coat with black spots and usually hunts at night, widespread in the forests of Africa and southern Asia. Also called **PANTHER**.
● *Panthera pardus*, family Felidae. See also **BLACK PANTHER**.
■ Heraldry the spotted leopard as a heraldic device; also, a lion passant guardant as in the arms of England.
■ [as modifier] spotted like a leopard: *a leopard-print outfit*.
– PHRASES **a leopard can't change his spots** proverb people can't change their basic nature.
– ORIGIN Middle English: via Old French from late Latin *leopardus*, from late Greek *leopardos*, from *leōn* 'lion' + *pardos* (see **PARD**).

leopard cat ▶ noun a small East Asian wild cat that has a yellowish-brown coat with black spots and often lives near water.
● *Felis bengalensis*, family Felidae.

leopardess ▶ noun a female leopard.

leopard frog ▶ noun a common greenish-brown North American frog which has dark leopard-like spots with a pale border.
● *Rana pipiens*, family Ranidae.

leopard moth ▶ noun a large white European moth with black spots, the larvae of which tunnel into trees and can cause damage.
● *Zeuzera pyrina*, family Cossidae.

leopard's bane ▶ noun a herbaceous Eurasian plant of the daisy family, with large yellow flowers which typically bloom early in the spring.
● Genus *Doronicum*, family Compositae.

leopard seal ▶ noun a large grey Antarctic seal which has leopard-like spots and preys on penguins and other seals.
● *Hydrurga leptonyx*, family Phocidae.

leopard-skin ▶ adjective (of a garment) made of a fabric resembling the spotted skin of a leopard: *leopard-skin pedal pushers*.

Leopold I /ˈliːəpəʊld/ (1790–1865), first king of Belgium 1831–65. The fourth son of the Duke of Saxe-Coburg-Saalfield, Leopold was an uncle of Queen Victoria. In 1830 he refused the throne of Greece, but a year later accepted that of the newly independent Belgium.

Léopoldville /ˈliːəpəʊldˌvɪl/ former name (until 1966) for **KINSHASA**.

leotard /ˈliːətɑːd/ ▶ noun a close-fitting one-piece garment, made of a stretchy fabric, which covers a person's body from the shoulders to the top of the thighs and typically the arms, worn by dancers or people exercising indoors.
– ORIGIN early 20th cent.: named after Jules *Léotard* (1839–70), French trapeze artist.

Leo the Great Pope Leo I (see **LEO**¹).

Lepanto, Battle of /lɪˈpantəʊ/ a naval battle fought in 1571 close to the port of Lepanto at the entrance to the Gulf of Corinth. The Christian forces of Rome, Venice, and Spain defeated a large Turkish fleet, ending for the time being Turkish naval domination in the eastern Mediterranean.

Lepanto, Gulf of another name for the Gulf of Corinth (see **CORINTH, GULF OF**).

Lepcha /ˈlɛptʃə/ ▶ noun **1** a member of a people living mainly in mountain valleys in Sikkim, western Bhutan, and parts of Nepal and West Bengal.
2 [mass noun] the Tibeto-Burman language of this people, with over 50,000 speakers.
▶ adjective of or relating to the Lepchas or their language.
– ORIGIN from Nepali *lāpche*.

leper ▶ noun a person suffering from leprosy.
■ a person who is avoided or rejected by others for moral or social reasons: *the story made her out to be a social leper*.
– ORIGIN late Middle English: probably from an attributive use of *leper* 'leprosy', from Old French *lepre*, via Latin from Greek *lepra*, feminine of *lepros* 'scaly', from *lepas*, *lepis* 'scale'.

lepidocrocite /ˌlɛpɪdəʊˈkrəʊsʌɪt/ ▶ noun [mass noun] a red to reddish-brown mineral consisting of ferric hydroxide, typically occurring as scaly or fibrous crystals.

lepidolite /ˈlɛpɪdəlʌɪt, lɪˈpɪdəlʌɪt/ ▶ noun [mass noun] a mineral of the mica group containing lithium, typically grey or lilac in colour.
– ORIGIN late 18th cent.: from Greek *lepis*, *lepid-* 'scale' + **-LITE**.

Lepidoptera /ˌlɛpɪˈdɒpt(ə)rə/ Entomology an order of insects that comprises the butterflies and moths. They have four large scale-covered wings that bear distinctive markings, and larvae that are caterpillars.
■ **(lepidoptera)** [as plural noun] insects of this order.
– DERIVATIVES **lepidopteran** adjective & noun, **lepidopterous** adjective.
– ORIGIN modern Latin (plural), from Greek *lepis*, *lepid-* 'scale' + *pteron* 'wing'.

lepidopterist /ˌlɛpɪˈdɒpt(ə)rɪst/ ▶ noun a person who studies or collects butterflies and moths.

Lepidus /ˈlɛpɪdəs/, Marcus Aemilius (died c.13 BC), Roman statesman and triumvir. A supporter of Julius Caesar in the civil war against Pompey, he was elected consul in 46, and appointed one of the Second Triumvirate with Octavian and Antony in 43.

leporine /ˈlɛpərʌɪn/ ▶ adjective of or resembling a hare or hares.
– ORIGIN mid 17th cent.: from Latin *leporinus*, from *lepus*, *lepor-* 'hare'.

lepospondyl /ˌlɛpə(ʊ)ˈspɒndɪl/ ▶ noun an early fossil amphibian of the Carboniferous and Permian periods, distinguished by vertebrae shaped liked hourglasses.
● Microsauria and related orders, formerly placed in the subclass Lepospondyli.
– ORIGIN 1930s: from modern Latin *Lepospondyli* (plural), from Greek *lepos* 'husk' + *spondulos* 'vertebra'.

leprechaun /ˈlɛprəkɔːn/ ▶ noun (in Irish folklore) a small, mischievous sprite.
– ORIGIN early 17th cent.: from Irish *leipreachán*, based on Old Irish *luchorpán*, from *lu* 'small' + *corp* 'body'.

lepromatous /lɛˈprəʊmətəs/ ▶ adjective Medicine relating to or denoting the more severe of the two principal forms of leprosy, marked by thickening of the skin and nerves, the formation of lumps on the skin, and often severe loss of feeling and paralysis leading to disfigurement. Compare with **TUBERCULOID**.

leprosarium /ˌlɛprəˈsɛːrɪəm/ ▶ noun a hospital for people with leprosy.
– ORIGIN mid 19th cent.: from late Latin *leprosus* 'leprous' + **-ARIUM**.

leprosy ▶ noun [mass noun] **1** a contagious disease that affects the skin, mucous membranes, and nerves, causing discoloration and lumps on the skin and, in severe cases, disfigurement and deformities. Leprosy is now mainly confined to tropical Africa and Asia. Also called **HANSEN'S DISEASE**.
● Leprosy is caused by the bacterium *Mycobacterium leprae*, which is Gram-positive, non-motile, and acid-fast.
2 moral corruption or contagion.
– ORIGIN mid 16th cent. (superseding Middle English *lepry*): from **LEPROUS** + **-Y**³.

leprous ▶ adjective suffering from leprosy.
■ relating to or resembling leprosy: *leprous growths*.
– ORIGIN Middle English: via Old French from late Latin *leprosus*, from Latin *lepra* 'scaly' (see **LEPER**).

lepta plural form of **LEPTON**¹.

leptin ▶ noun [mass noun] Biochemistry a protein produced by fatty tissue which is believed to regulate fat storage in the body.
– ORIGIN 1990s: from Greek *leptos* 'fine, thin' + **-IN**¹.

Leptis Magna /ˌlɛptɪs ˈmagnə/ an ancient seaport and trading centre on the Mediterranean coast of North Africa, near present-day Al Khums in Libya. Founded by the Phoenicians, it became one of the three chief cities of Tripolitania and was later a Roman colony under Trajan.

lepto- ▶ combining form small; narrow: *leptocephalic*.
– ORIGIN from Greek *leptos* 'fine, thin, delicate'.

leptocephalic /ˌlɛptə(ʊ)sɪˈfalɪk, -kɛˈfalɪk-/ (also **leptocephalous** /-ˈsɛf(ə)ləs, -ˈkɛf-/) ▶ adjective narrow-skulled.

leptokurtic /ˌlɛptə(ʊ)ˈkəːtɪk/ ▶ adjective Statistics (of a frequency distribution or its graphical representation) having greater kurtosis than the normal distribution; more concentrated about the mean. Compare with **PLATYKURTIC, MESOKURTIC**.
– DERIVATIVES **leptokurtosis** noun.
– ORIGIN early 20th cent.: from **LEPTO-** 'narrow' + Greek *kurtos* 'bulging' + **-IC**.

leptomeninges /ˌlɛptəʊmɪˈnɪndʒiːz/ ▶ plural noun Anatomy the inner two meninges, the arachnoid and the pia mater, between which circulates the cerebrospinal fluid.
– DERIVATIVES **leptomeningeal** adjective.

lepton¹ /ˈlɛptɒn/ ▶ noun (pl. **lepta**) a former monetary unit of Greece used only in calculations, worth one hundredth of a drachma.
– ORIGIN from Greek *lepton*, neuter of *leptos* 'small'.

lepton² /ˈlɛptɒn/ ▶ noun Physics a subatomic particle, such as an electron, muon, or neutrino, which does not take part in the strong interaction.
– DERIVATIVES **leptonic** adjective.
– ORIGIN 1940s: from Greek *leptos* 'small' + **-ON**.

lepton number ▶ noun Physics a quantum number assigned to subatomic particles that is ±1 for leptons and 0 for other particles and is conserved in all known interactions.

leptospirosis /ˌlɛptə(ʊ)spʌɪˈrəʊsɪs/ ▶ noun [mass noun]

an infectious bacterial disease occurring in rodents, dogs, and other mammals, which can be transmitted to humans. See also **WEIL'S DISEASE**.

• The bacterium is a spirochaete of the genus *Leptospira*.

– ORIGIN 1920s: from **LEPTO-** 'narrow' + Greek *speira* 'coil' + **-OSIS**.

leptotene /ˈlɛptə(ʊ)tiːn/ ▶ **noun** [mass noun] Biology the first stage of the prophase of meiosis, during which each chromosome becomes visible as two fine threads (chromatids).

– ORIGIN early 20th cent.: from **LEPTO-** 'narrow, fine' + Greek *tainia* 'band, ribbon'.

Lepus /ˈliːpəs/ Astronomy a small constellation (the Hare) at the foot of Orion, said to represent the hare pursued by him.

■ [as genitive **Leporis** /liːˈpɔːrɪs/] used with preceding letter or numeral to designate a star in this constellation: *the star R Leporis.*

– ORIGIN Latin.

Lerner /ˈləːnə/, Alan J. (1918–1986), American lyricist and dramatist; full name *Alan Jay Lerner*. He wrote a series of musicals with composer Frederick Loewe (1904–88) which were also filmed, including *My Fair Lady* (1956; filmed 1964). He won Oscars for the films *An American in Paris* (1951) and *Gigi* (1958).

Lerwick /ˈləːwɪk/ the capital of the Shetland Islands, on the island of Mainland; pop. 7,220 (1991). The most northerly town in the British Isles, it is a fishing centre and a service port for the oil industry.

les (also **lez**) ▶ **noun** informal a lesbian.

Lesage /ləˈsɑːʒ, French ləsaʒ/, Alain-René (1668–1747), French novelist and dramatist. He is best known for the picaresque novel *Gil Blas* (1715–35).

Lesbian ▶ **adjective** from or relating to the island of Lesbos.

lesbian ▶ **noun** a homosexual woman.

▶ **adjective** of or relating to homosexual women or to homosexuality in women: *a lesbian relationship.*

– DERIVATIVES **lesbianism** noun.

– ORIGIN late 19th cent.: via Latin from Greek *Lesbios*, from **LESBOS**, home of Sappho, who expressed affection for women in her poetry, + **-IAN**.

lesbo ▶ **noun** (pl. **-os**) informal a lesbian.

– ORIGIN 1940s: abbreviation.

Lesbos /ˈlɛzbɒs/ a Greek island in the eastern Aegean, off the coast of NW Turkey; chief town, Mytilene. Its artistic golden age of the late 7th and early 6th centuries BC produced the poets Alcaeus and Sappho. Greek name **LÉSVOS**.

Lesch–Nyhan syndrome /lɛʃˈnʌɪhən/ ▶ **noun** [mass noun] a rare hereditary disease which affects young boys, usually causing early death. It is marked by compulsive self-mutilation of the head and hands, together with mental handicap and involuntary muscular movements.

– ORIGIN 1960s: named after Michael *Lesch* (born 1939) and William L. *Nyhan* (born 1926), American physicians.

lese-majesty /liːzˈmadʒɪsti/ ▶ **noun** [mass noun] the insulting of a monarch or other ruler; treason.

– ORIGIN late Middle English: from French *lèse-majesté*, from Latin *laesa majestas* 'injured sovereignty'.

lesion /ˈliːʒ(ə)n/ ▶ **noun** chiefly Medicine a region in an organ or tissue which has suffered damage through injury or disease, such as a wound, ulcer, abscess, tumour, etc.

– ORIGIN late Middle English: via Old French from Latin *laesio(n-)*, from *laedere* 'injure'.

Lesotho /ləˈsuːtuː/ a landlocked mountainous country forming an enclave in South Africa; pop. 1,816,000 (est. 1991); official languages, Sesotho and English; capital, Maseru.

The region was settled by the Sotho people in the 16th century, coming under British rule (as Basutoland) in 1868. The country became an independent kingdom within the Commonwealth in 1966, changing its name to Lesotho.

less ▶ **determiner & pronoun** a smaller amount of; not as much: [as determiner] *the less time spent there, the better* | [as pronoun] *storage is* **less of** *a problem than it used to be* | *ready in* **less than** *an hour.*

■ fewer in number: [as determiner] *short hair presented less problems than long hair* | [as pronoun] *a population of* **less than** *200,000.*

▶ **adjective** archaic of lower rank or importance: *James the Less.*

▶ **adverb** to a smaller extent; not so much: *he listened less to the answer than to Kate's voice* | *that this is a positive stereotype makes it* **no less a** *stereotype.*

■ **(less than)** far from; certainly not: *Mitch looked less than happy* | *the data was less than ideal.*

▶ **preposition** before subtracting (something); minus: *£900,000 less tax.*

– PHRASES **in less than no time** informal very quickly or soon. **less and less** at a continually decreasing rate. **much** (or **still**) **less** used to introduce something as being even less likely or suitable than something else already mentioned: *what woman would consider a date with him, much less a marriage?* **no less** used to suggest, often ironically, that something is surprising or impressive: *Peter cooked dinner—fillet steak and champagne, no less.* ■ **(no less than)** used to emphasize a surprisingly large amount.

– ORIGIN Old English *lǣssa*, of Germanic origin; related to Old Frisian *lēssa*, from an Indo-European root shared by Greek *loisthos* 'last'.

USAGE In standard English **less** should only be used with uncountable things (***less** money*, ***less** time*). With countable things it is incorrect to use **less** (***less** people* and ***less** words*); strictly speaking, correct use is ***fewer** people* and ***fewer** words*. See also **usage** at **FEW**.

-less ▶ **suffix** forming adjectives and adverbs:

1 (from nouns) not having; without; free from: *flavourless* | *skinless.*

2 (from verbs) not affected by or not carrying out the action of the verb: *fathomless* | *tireless.*

– DERIVATIVES **-lessly** suffix forming corresponding adverbs, **-lessness** suffix forming corresponding nouns.

– ORIGIN Old English *-lēas*, from *lēas* 'devoid of'.

less-developed country ▶ **noun** a non-industrialized or Third World country.

lessee /lɛˈsiː/ ▶ **noun** a person who holds the lease of a property; a tenant.

– DERIVATIVES **lesseeship** noun.

– ORIGIN late 15th cent.: from Old French *lesse*, past participle of *lesser* 'to let, leave', + **-EE**.

lessen ▶ **verb** make or become less; diminish: [with obj.] *the years have lessened the gap in age between us* | [no obj.] *the warmth of the afternoon lessened.*

Lesseps /ˈlɛsəps, French lesɛp/, Ferdinand Marie, Vicomte de (1805–94), French diplomat. From 1854 onwards, while in the consular service in Egypt, he devoted himself to the project of the Suez Canal. In 1881 he embarked on the building of the Panama Canal, but the project was abandoned in 1889.

lesser ▶ **adjective** [attrib.] not so great or important as the other or the rest: *he was convicted of a lesser assault charge* | *they nest mostly in Alaska and* **to a lesser extent** *in Siberia.*

■ lower in terms of rank or quality: *the lesser aristocracy* | *you're looking down your nose at us lesser mortals.* ■ used in names of animals and plants which are smaller than similar kinds, e.g. **lesser spotted woodpecker**, **lesser celandine**.

– PHRASES **the lesser evil** (or **the lesser of two evils**) the less harmful or unpleasant of two bad choices or possibilities: *authoritarianism may seem a lesser evil than abject poverty.*

– ORIGIN Middle English: a double comparative, from **LESS** + **-ER**[2].

Lesser Antilles see **ANTILLES**.

Lesser Bairam ▶ **noun** an annual Muslim festival at the end of Ramadan.

lesser celandine ▶ **noun** see **CELANDINE**.

lesser-known ▶ **adjective** not as well or widely known as others of the same kind.

lesser noctule ▶ **noun** another term for **LEISLER'S BAT**.

lesser panda ▶ **noun** another term for **RED PANDA**.

Lesser Sunda Islands see **SUNDA ISLANDS**.

lesser water boatman ▶ **noun** see **WATER BOATMAN**.

Lessing[1], Doris (May) (b.1919), British novelist and short-story writer, brought up in Rhodesia. An active communist in her youth, she frequently deals with social and political conflicts in her fiction, especially as they affect women. Notable novels: *The Grass is Singing* (1950).

Lessing[2], Gotthold Ephraim (1729–81), German dramatist and critic. In his critical works, such as *Laokoon* (1766), he suggested that German writers look to English literature rather than the French classical school. He also wrote both tragedy and comedy.

Les Six /leɪ ˈsiːs, French le sis/ (also **the Six**) a group of six Parisian composers (Louis Durey, Arthur Honegger, Darius Milhaud, Germaine Tailleferre, Georges Auric, and Francis Poulenc) formed after the First World War, whose music represents a reaction against romanticism and Impressionism.

– ORIGIN French, literally 'the Six'.

lesson ▶ **noun 1** an amount of teaching given at one time; a period of learning or teaching: *an advanced lesson in maths* | *a driving lesson.*

■ a thing learned or to be learned by a pupil. ■ a thing learned by experience: *lessons should have been learned from two similar collisions.* ■ an occurrence, example, or punishment that serves or should serve to warn or encourage: *let that be a lesson to you!*

2 a passage from the Bible read aloud during a church service, especially either of two readings at morning and evening prayer in the Anglican Church.

▶ **verb** [with obj.] archaic instruct or teach (someone).

■ admonish or rebuke (someone).

– PHRASES **learn one's lesson** acquire a greater understanding of the world through a particular unpleasant or stressful experience. **teach someone a lesson** punish or hurt someone as a deterrent: *they were teaching me a lesson for daring to complain.*

– ORIGIN Middle English: from Old French *leçon*, from Latin *lectio* (see **LECTION**).

lessor /lɛˈsɔː, ˈlɛsɔː/ ▶ **noun** a person who leases or lets a property to another; a landlord.

– ORIGIN late Middle English: from Anglo-Norman French, from Old French *lesser* 'let, leave'.

lest ▶ **conjunction** formal with the intention of preventing (something undesirable); to avoid the risk of: *he spent whole days in his room, headphones on lest he disturb anyone.*

■ (after a clause indicating fear) because of the possibility of something undesirable happening; in case: *she sat up late worrying lest he be murdered on the way home.*

– ORIGIN Old English *thȳ lǣs the* 'whereby less that', later *the lǣste*.

USAGE There are very few contexts in English where the subjunctive mood is, strictly speaking, required: **lest** remains one of them. Thus the standard use is *she was worrying **lest** he **be** attacked* (not ***lest** he **was** …*) or *she is using headphones **lest** she **disturb** anyone* (not *… **lest** she **disturbs** anyone*). See also **SUBJUNCTIVE**.

Lésvos /ˈlezvɔs/ Greek name for **LESBOS**.

let[1] ▶ **verb** (**letting**; past and past participle **let**) **1** [with obj. and infinitive] not prevent or forbid; allow: *my boss let me leave early* | *you mustn't let yourself get so involved.*

■ [with obj. and adverbial of direction] allow to pass in a particular direction: *could you let the dog out?* | *a tiny window that let in hardly any light.*

2 [with obj. and infinitive] used in the imperative to formulate various expressions:

■ **(let us** or **let's)** used as a polite way of making or responding to a suggestion, giving an instruction, or introducing a remark: *let's have a drink* | *'Shall we go?' 'Yes, let's'.* ■ **(let me** or **let us)** used to make a polite offer of help: *'Here, let me,' offered Bruce.* ■ used to express one's strong desire for something to happen or be the case: *'Dear God,' Jessica prayed, 'let him be all right.'* ■ used as a way of expressing defiance or challenge: *if he wants to walk out, well let him!* ■ used to express an assumption upon which a theory or calculation is to be based: *let A and B stand for X and Y respectively.*

3 [with obj.] allow someone to have the use of (a room or property) in return for regular payments: *homeowners will be able to let rooms to lodgers without having to pay tax* | *they've* **let out** *their flat.*

■ award (a contract for a particular project) to an applicant: *preliminary contracts were let and tunnelling work started.*

▶ **noun** Brit. a period during which a room or property is rented to someone: *I've taken a month's let on the flat.*

■ a property available for rent: *an unfurnished let.*

– PHRASES **let alone** used to indicate that something is far less likely, possible, or suitable than something else already mentioned: *he was incapable of leading a bowling team, let alone a country.* **let someone/thing alone** see **ALONE**. **let someone/thing be** stop disturbing or interfering with: *let him be—he knows what he wants.* **let someone down gently** seek to give someone bad

l

news in a way that avoids causing them too much distress or humiliation. **let something drop** (or **fall**) casually reveal a piece of information: *from the things he let drop I think there was a woman in his life.* **let fall** Geometry draw (a perpendicular) from an outside point to a line. **let fly** attack, either physically or verbally: *the troops let fly with shells loaded with chemical weapons.* **let oneself go 1** act in an unrestrained or uninhibited way: *you need to unwind and let yourself go.* **2** become careless or untidy in one's habits or appearance: *he's really let himself go since my mother died.* **let someone/thing go 1** allow someone or something to escape or go free: *they let the hostages go.* ■ dismiss an employee. **2** (also **let go** or **let go of**) relinquish one's grip on someone or something: *Adam let go of the reins* | figurative *you must let the past go.* **let someone have it** informal attack someone physically or verbally: *I really let him have it for worrying me so much.* **let in** (or **out**) **the clutch** engage (or release) the clutch of a vehicle by releasing pressure on (or applying it to) the clutch pedal. **let it drop** (or **rest**) say or do no more about a matter or problem. **let it go** (or **pass**) choose not to react to an action or remark: *the decision worried us, but we let it go.* **let someone know** inform someone: *let me know what you think of him.* **let someone/thing loose** release someone or something: *let the dog loose for a minute.* ■ allow someone freedom of action in a particular place or situation: *people are only* **let loose on** *the system once they have received sufficient training.* ■ suddenly utter a sound or remark: *he let loose a stream of abuse.* **let me see** (or **think**) used when one is pausing, trying to remember something, or considering one's next words: *now let me see, where did I put it?* **let me tell you** used to emphasize a statement: *let me tell you, I was very scared!* **let off steam** see **STEAM**. **let rip** see **RIP**[1]. **let's face it** (or **let's be honest**) informal used to convey that one must be realistic about an unwelcome fact or situation: *let's be honest, your taste in men is famously bad.* **let slip** see **SLIP**[1]. **let's pretend** a game or set of circumstances in which one behaves as though a fictional or unreal situation is a real one. **let's say** (or **let us say**) used as a way of introducing a hypothetical or possible situation: *let's say we agreed to go our separate ways.* **to let** (of a room or property) available for rent.

– ORIGIN Old English *lǣtan* 'leave behind, leave out', of Germanic origin; related to Dutch *laten* and German *lassen*, also to **LATE**.

▶ **let down** (of an aircraft or a pilot) descend prior to making a landing.

let someone down fail to support or help someone as they had hoped or expected. ■ (**let someone/thing down**) have a detrimental effect on the overall quality or success of someone or something: *the whole machine is let down by the tacky keyboard.*

let something down 1 lower something slowly or in stages: *they let down a basket on a chain.* **2** make a garment longer by lowering the hem. **3** Brit. deflate a tyre.

let oneself in for informal involve oneself in (something likely to be difficult or unpleasant): *I didn't know what I was letting myself in for.*

let someone in on/into allow someone to know or share (something secret or confidential): *I'll let you into a secret.*

let something into set something back into (the surface to which it is fixed), so that it does not project from it: *the basin is partly let into the wall.*

let someone off 1 punish someone lightly or not at all for a misdemeanour or offence: *he was let off with a caution.* **2** excuse someone from a task or obligation: *he let me off work for the day.*

let something off cause a gun, firework, or bomb to fire or explode.

let on informal **1** reveal or divulge information to someone: *she knows a lot more than she lets on* | [with clause] *I never let on that he made me feel anxious.* **2** pretend: [with clause] *they all let on they didn't hear me.*

let out N. Amer. (of lessons at school, a meeting, or an entertainment) finish, so that those attending are able to leave: *his classes let out at noon.*

let someone out release someone from obligation or suspicion: *they've started looking for motives—that lets me out.*

let something out 1 utter a sound or cry: *he let out a sigh of happiness.* **2** make a garment looser or larger, typically by adjusting a seam. **3** reveal a piece of information: [with clause] *she let out that he'd given her a lift home.*

let up informal (of something undesirable) become less intense or severe: *the rain's letting up—it'll be clear soon.* ■ relax one's efforts: *she was so far ahead that she could afford to let up a bit.* ■ (**let up on**) informal treat or deal with in a more lenient manner: *she didn't let up on Cunningham.*

let[2] ▶ **noun** (in racket sports) a circumstance under which a service is nullified and has to be taken again, especially (in tennis) when the ball clips the top of the net and falls within bounds.

▶ **verb** (**letting**; past and past participle **letted** or **let**) [with obj.] archaic hinder: *pray you let us not; we fain would greet our mother.*

– PHRASES **let or hindrance** formal obstruction or impediment: *the passport opened frontiers to the traveller* **without let or hindrance**. **play a let** (in tennis, squash, etc.) play a point again because the ball or one of the players has been obstructed.

– ORIGIN Old English *lettan* 'hinder', of Germanic origin; related to Dutch *letten*, also to **LATE**.

-let ▶ **suffix 1** (forming nouns) denoting a smaller or lesser kind: *booklet* | *starlet.*
2 denoting articles of ornament or dress: *anklet* | *necklet.*

– ORIGIN originally corresponding to French *-ette* added to nouns ending in *-el.*

let-down ▶ **noun 1** a disappointment: *the election was a bit of a let-down.*
2 [mass noun] the release of milk in a nursing mother or lactating animal as a reflex response to suckling or massage.
3 Aeronautics the descent of an aircraft or spacecraft prior to landing.

lethal ▶ **adjective** sufficient to cause death: *a lethal cocktail of drink and pills.*
■ harmful or destructive: *the Krakatoa eruption was the most lethal on record.* ■ (especially of a footballer or his shooting) very accurate: *the most lethal striker in the league.*

– DERIVATIVES **lethality** noun, **lethally** adverb.

– ORIGIN late 16th cent. (in the sense 'causing spiritual death'): from Latin *lethalis*, from *lethum*, a variant (influenced by Greek *lēthē* 'forgetfulness'), of *letum* 'death'.

lethal chamber ▶ **noun** an enclosed space in which animals may be killed painlessly with gas.

lethal injection ▶ **noun** an injection administered for the purposes of euthanasia or as a means of capital punishment.

lethargic /lɪˈθɑːdʒɪk/ ▶ **adjective** affected by lethargy; sluggish and apathetic: *I felt tired and a little lethargic.*

– DERIVATIVES **lethargically** adverb.

– ORIGIN late Middle English: via Latin from Greek *lēthargikos*, from *lēthargos* 'forgetful'.

lethargy /ˈlɛθədʒi/ ▶ **noun** [mass noun] a lack of energy and enthusiasm: *there was an air of lethargy about him* | [in sing.] *she might have sunk into a lethargy.*
■ Medicine a pathological state of sleepiness or deep unresponsiveness and inactivity.

– ORIGIN late Middle English: via Old French from late Latin *lethargia*, from Greek *lēthargia*, from *lēthargos* 'forgetful', from the base of *lanthanesthai* 'forget'.

Lethe /ˈliːθi/ Greek Mythology a river in Hades whose water when drunk made the souls of the dead forget their life on earth.

– DERIVATIVES **Lethean** /liːˈθiːən/ adjective.

– ORIGIN via Latin from Greek *lēthē* 'forgetfulness', from the base of *lanthanesthai* 'forget'.

Leticia /ləˈtiːsɪə, Spanish leˈtisja, -ˈtiθja/ a town and river port at the southern tip of Colombia, on the upper reaches of the Amazon on the border with Brazil and Peru; pop. 24,090 (1985).

Leto /ˈliːtəʊ/ Greek Mythology the daughter of a Titan, mother (by Zeus) of Artemis and Apollo. Roman name **LATONA**.

let-off ▶ **noun** informal a chance to escape or avoid something, especially defeat: *the team had two let-offs as shots rebounded to strike the defenders' legs.*

let-out ▶ **noun** Brit. informal an opportunity to escape from or avoid a difficult situation.

let-out clause ▶ **noun** informal a clause specifying a circumstance in which the terms of an agreement or contract shall not apply.

let's ▶ **contraction** of let us: *let's meet for a drink sometime.*

Lett ▶ **noun** old-fashioned term for **LATVIAN**.

– DERIVATIVES **Lettish** adjective.

– ORIGIN from German *Lette*, from Latvian *Latvi*.

letter ▶ **noun 1** a character representing one or more of the sounds used in speech; any of the symbols of an alphabet: *a capital letter.*
■ (**letters**) Brit. informal the initials of a degree or other qualification: *your personality and style matter far more than letters after your name.* ■ US a school or college initial as a mark of proficiency, especially in sport: [as modifier] *a letter jacket.*
2 a written, typed, or printed communication, especially one sent in an envelope by post or messenger: *he sent a letter to Mrs Falconer.*
■ (**letters**) a legal or formal document of this kind.
3 the precise terms of a statement or requirement; the strict verbal interpretation: *we must be seen to keep the spirit of the law as well as the letter.*
4 (**letters**) literature: *the world of letters.*
■ archaic scholarly knowledge; erudition.
5 [mass noun] Printing a style of typeface.

▶ **verb 1** [with obj.] inscribe letters or writing on: *her name was lettered in gold.*
■ classify with letters: *he numbered and lettered the paragraphs.*
2 [no obj.] US informal be given a school or college initial as a mark of proficiency in sport.

– PHRASES **to the letter** with adherence to every detail: *the method was followed to the letter.*

– ORIGIN Middle English: from Old French *lettre*, from Latin *litera*, *littera* 'letter of the alphabet', (plural) 'epistle, literature, culture'.

letter bomb ▶ **noun** an explosive device hidden in a small package and sent to someone with the intention of harming or killing them.

letter box ▶ **noun** chiefly Brit. a box attached to an outside wall, or a slot in the door of a house or other building, into which mail is delivered.
■ (**letterbox**) [usu. as modifier] a format for presenting widescreen films on a standard television screen in which the image is displayed in approximately its original proportions across the middle of the screen, leaving horizontal black bands above and below: *this uncut version is presented in letterbox format.*
▶ **verb** (**letterbox**) [with obj.] record (a widescreen film) on to video in letterbox format.

letter-card ▶ **noun** Brit. a card that can be posted without an envelope by folding it in half to seal its gummed edges.

letter-carrier ▶ **noun** N. Amer. a postman or postwoman.

lettered ▶ **adjective** dated formally educated: *though not lettered, he read widely.*

letterform ▶ **noun** the graphic form of a letter of the alphabet, either as written or in a particular type font.

letterhead ▶ **noun** a printed heading on stationery, stating a person or organization's name and address.

letter-heading ▶ **noun** another term for **LETTERHEAD**.

lettering ▶ **noun** [mass noun] the process of inscribing letters.
■ the letters inscribed on something, especially decorative ones.

letter missive (also **letters missive**) ▶ **noun** a letter from the monarch to a dean and chapter nominating a person to be elected bishop.

letter of comfort ▶ **noun** an assurance about a debt, short of a legal guarantee, given to a bank by a third party.

letter of credence ▶ **noun** a letter of introduction or recommendation, especially of an ambassador.

letter of credit ▶ **noun** a letter issued by a bank to another bank (especially one in a different country) to serve as a guarantee for payments made to a specified person under specified conditions.

letter of intent ▶ **noun** a document containing a declaration of the intentions of the writer.

letter of marque ▶ **noun** (usu. **letters of marque**) historical a licence to fit out an armed vessel and use it in the capture of enemy merchant shipping and to commit acts which would otherwise have constituted piracy.
■ a ship carrying such a licence.

– ORIGIN late Middle English: Law French *marque*, from Old French *marque* 'right of reprisal'.

letter-perfect ▶ **adjective** another term for **WORD-PERFECT**.

letterpress ▶ **noun** [mass noun] **1** printing from a hard, raised image under pressure, using viscous ink.
2 Brit. printed text as opposed to illustrations.

letter-quality ▶ **adjective** (of a printer attached to a computer) producing print of a quality suitable for business letters.
■ (of a document) printed to such a standard.

letterset ▶ **noun** [mass noun] a method of printing in which ink is transferred from a raised surface to a blanket wrapped round a cylinder and from that to the paper.
– ORIGIN 1960s: blend of **LETTERPRESS** and **OFFSET**.

letters missive ▶ **noun** variant of **LETTER MISSIVE**.

letters of administration ▶ **plural noun** Law authority to administer the estate of someone who has died without making a will.

letters patent ▶ **plural noun** an open document issued by a monarch or government conferring a patent or other right.
– ORIGIN late Middle English: from medieval Latin *litterae patentes*, literally 'letters lying open'.

letters rogatory /ˈrəʊɡət(ə)ri/ ▶ **plural noun** Law documents making a request through a foreign court for the obtaining of information or evidence from a specified person within the jurisdiction of that court.
– ORIGIN mid 19th cent.: *rogatory* from medieval Latin *rogatorius* 'interrogatory'.

letting ▶ **noun** [mass noun] the action of renting out a property: *the premises were safe at the time of the letting* | [count noun] *she introduced prospective tenants and arranged lettings.*
■ [count noun] a property that is let or available to be let.

lettuce ▶ **noun** a cultivated plant of the daisy family, with edible leaves that are a usual ingredient of salads. Many varieties of lettuce have been developed with a range of form, texture, and colour.
● *Lactuca sativa*, family Compositae.
■ used in names of other plants with edible green leaves, e.g. **lamb's lettuce**, **sea lettuce**.
– ORIGIN Middle English: from Old French *letues*, *laitues*, plural of *laitue*, from Latin *lactuca*, from *lac*, *lact-* 'milk' (because of its milky juice).

let-up ▶ **noun** [in sing.] informal a pause or reduction in the intensity of something dangerous, difficult, or tiring: *there had been no* **let-up in** *the eruption.*

Letzeburgesch /ˌlɛts(ə)bəːˈɡɛʃ, ˈlɛts(ə)ˌbəːɡɪʃ/ (also **Letzebuergesch**) ▶ **noun** & **adjective** another term for **LUXEMBURGISH**.
– ORIGIN from a local name for **LUXEMBOURG** + *-esch* (equivalent of **-ISH**[1]).

leu /ˈleɪuː/ ▶ **noun** (pl. **lei** /leɪ/) the basic monetary unit of Romania, equal to 100 bani.
– ORIGIN Romanian, literally 'lion'.

leucine /ˈluːsiːn/ ▶ **noun** [mass noun] Biochemistry a hydrophobic amino acid which is a constituent of most proteins. It is an essential nutrient in the diet of vertebrates.
● Chem. formula: $(CH_3)_2CHCH_2CH(NH_2)COOH$.
– ORIGIN early 19th cent.: coined in French from Greek *leukos* 'white' + **-INE**[4].

leucistic /luːˈsɪstɪk/ ▶ **adjective** Zoology (of an animal) having whitish fur, plumage, or skin due to a lack of pigment.
– ORIGIN from **LEUCO-** 'white' + the adjectival suffix *-istic*.

leuco- (also **leuko-**) ▶ **combining form 1** white: *leucoma*.
2 representing **LEUCOCYTE**.
– ORIGIN from Greek *leukos* 'white'.

leucocyte /ˈluːkə(ʊ)sʌɪt/ (also **leukocyte**) ▶ **noun** Physiology a colourless cell which circulates in the blood and body fluids and is involved in counteracting foreign substances and disease; a white (blood) cell. There are several types, all amoeboid cells with a nucleus, including lymphocytes, granulocytes, monocytes, and macrophages.
– DERIVATIVES **leucocytic** adjective.

leucocytosis /ˌluːkə(ʊ)sʌɪˈtəʊsɪs/ (also **leukocytosis**) ▶ **noun** [mass noun] Medicine an increase in the number of white cells in the blood, especially during an infection.
– DERIVATIVES **leucocytotic** adjective.

leucoderma /ˌluːkə(ʊ)ˈdəːmə/ ▶ **noun** another term for **VITILIGO**.

leucoma /luːˈkəʊmə/ ▶ **noun** Medicine a white opacity in the cornea of the eye.
– ORIGIN early 18th cent.: modern Latin, from Greek *leukōma*.

leucon /ˈluːkɒn/ ▶ **noun** Zoology a sponge of a grade of structure of the most complex type, composed of a mass of flagellated chambers and water canals. Compare with **ASCON** and **SYCON**.
– DERIVATIVES **leuconoid** adjective.

leucopenia /ˌluːkə(ʊ)ˈpiːnɪə/ (also **leukopenia**) ▶ **noun** [mass noun] Medicine a reduction in the number of white cells in the blood, typical of various diseases.
– DERIVATIVES **leucopenic** adjective.
– ORIGIN late 19th cent.: from Greek *leukos* 'white' + *penia* 'poverty'.

leucoplast /ˈluːkə(ʊ)plast, -plɑːst/ ▶ **noun** Botany a colourless organelle found in plant cells, used for the storage of starch or oil.

leucorrhoea /ˌluːkəˈriːə/ (US **leucorrhea**, **leukorrhea**) ▶ **noun** [mass noun] a whitish or yellowish discharge of mucus from the vagina.

leucosis /luːˈkəʊsɪs/ (also **leukosis**) ▶ **noun** [mass noun] a leukaemic disease of animals, especially one of a group of malignant viral diseases of poultry or cattle.
– DERIVATIVES **leucotic** adjective.

leucotomy /luːˈkɒtəmi/ ▶ **noun** (pl. **-ies**) [mass noun] the surgical cutting of white nerve fibres within the brain, especially prefrontal lobotomy, formerly used to treat mental illness.

leucotriene /ˌluːkə(ʊ)ˈtrʌɪiːn/ (also **leukotriene**) ▶ **noun** Biochemistry any of a group of biologically active compounds, originally isolated from leucocytes. They are metabolites of arachidonic acid, containing three conjugated double bonds.

leukaemia /luːˈkiːmɪə/ (US **leukemia**) ▶ **noun** [mass noun] a malignant progressive disease in which the bone marrow and other blood-forming organs produce increased numbers of immature or abnormal leucocytes. These suppress the production of normal blood cells, leading to anaemia and other symptoms.
– DERIVATIVES **leukaemic** adjective.
– ORIGIN mid 19th cent.: coined in German from Greek *leukos* 'white' + *haima* 'blood'.

leukaemogenic /luːˌkiːmə(ʊ)ˈdʒɛnɪk/ (US **leukemogenic**) ▶ **adjective** Medicine relating to or promoting the development of leukaemia.
– DERIVATIVES **leukaemogen** /luːˈkiːmədʒən/ noun, **leukaemogenesis** noun.

leuko- ▶ **combining form** variant spelling of **LEUCO-**.

Leuven /ˈləːv(ə)n/ a town in Belgium, east of Brussels; pop. 85,020 (1991). French name **LOUVAIN**.

Lev. ▶ **abbreviation** for Leviticus (in biblical references).

lev /lɛv, lɛf/ (also **leva** /ˈlɛvə/) ▶ **noun** (pl. **leva** or **levas** or **levs**) the basic monetary unit of Bulgaria, equal to 100 stotinki.
– ORIGIN Bulgarian, variant of *lăv* 'lion'.

levade /ləˈvɑːd/ ▶ **noun** a movement performed in classical riding, in which the horse lifts its forelegs from the ground and balances on its deeply bent hind legs, with the body forming an angle of 30° to the ground.
– ORIGIN 1940s: from French, from *lever* 'raise'.

Levallois /ləˈvalwɑː/ ▶ **noun** [usu. as modifier] Archaeology a flint-working technique associated with the Mousterian culture of the Neanderthals, in which a flint is trimmed so that a flake of predetermined size and shape can be struck from it.
– DERIVATIVES **Levalloisean** /ˌlɛvəˈlɔɪzɪən/ adjective.
– ORIGIN early 20th cent.: named after a suburb of northern Paris.

levamisole /lɪˈvamɪsəʊl/ ▶ **noun** [mass noun] Medicine a synthetic compound used as an anthelmintic drug (especially in animals) and in cancer chemotherapy.
● A polycyclic imidazole derivative; chem. formula: $C_{11}H_{12}N_2S$.
– ORIGIN 1960s: from **LEVO-** (it being a laevorotatory isomer) + *(tetra)misole*, the name of an anthelmintic drug.

Levant /lɪˈvant/ archaic the eastern part of the Mediterranean with its islands and neighbouring countries.
– ORIGIN late 15th cent.: from French, literally 'rising', present participle of *lever* 'to lift' used as a noun in the sense 'point of sunrise, east'.

levant /lɪˈvant/ ▶ **verb** [no obj.] Brit. archaic run away, typically leaving unpaid debts.
– ORIGIN early 17th cent.: perhaps from **LEVANT**: compare with French *faire voile en Levant* 'be stolen or spirited away', literally 'set sail for the Levant'.

levanter[1] /lɪˈvantə/ ▶ **noun** a strong easterly wind in the Mediterranean region.

levanter[2] /lɪˈvantə/ ▶ **noun** archaic a person who runs away leaving unpaid debts.

Levantine /lɪˈvantʌɪn, ˈlɛv(ə)n-, -tɪn/ chiefly archaic ▶ **adjective** of or trading to the Levant: *the Levantine coast.*
▶ **noun** a person who lives in or comes from the Levant.

Levant morocco ▶ **noun** [mass noun] high-grade large-grained morocco leather.

Levant storax ▶ **noun** see **STORAX** (sense 1).

Levant wormseed ▶ **noun** see **WORMSEED**.

levator /lɪˈveɪtə/ (also **levator muscle**) ▶ **noun** Anatomy a muscle whose contraction causes the raising of a part of the body.
– ORIGIN early 17th cent.: from Latin, literally 'a person who lifts', from *levare* 'raise, lift'.

levee[1] /ˈlɛvi, ˈlɛveɪ/ ▶ **noun** a reception or assembly of people, in particular:
■ archaic or N. Amer. a formal reception of visitors or guests. ■ historical an afternoon assembly for men held by the British monarch or their representative. ■ archaic a reception of visitors just after rising from bed.
– ORIGIN late 17th cent. (denoting a reception of visitors after rising from bed) : from French *levé*, variant of *lever* 'rising', from the verb *lever*.

levee[2] /ˈlɛvi, lɪˈviː/ ▶ **noun** an embankment built to prevent the overflow of a river.
■ a ridge of sediment deposited naturally alongside a river by overflowing water. ■ chiefly US a landing place; a quay.
– ORIGIN early 18th cent. (originally US): from French *levée*, feminine past participle of *lever* 'to lift'.

level ▶ **noun 1** a position on a real or imaginary scale of amount, quantity, extent, or quality: *a high level of unemployment* | *debt rose to unprecedented levels.*
■ a social, moral, or intellectual standard: *at six he could play chess at an advanced level* | [mass noun] *women do better at degree level.* ■ a position in a real or notional hierarchy: *a fairly junior level of management.*
2 a height or distance from the ground or another stated or understood base: *storms caused river levels to rise.*
3 an instrument giving a line parallel to the plane of the horizon for testing whether things are horizontal.
■ Surveying an instrument for giving a horizontal line of sight.
4 a flat tract of land: *flooded levels* | [in place names] *the Somerset Levels.*
▶ **adjective 1** having a flat and even surface without slopes or bumps: *we had reached level ground.*
■ horizontal: *a large paved double courtyard which was level, despite the steep gradient of the hill.* ■ at the same height as someone or something else: *his eyes were* **level with** *hers.* ■ having the same relative position; not in front of or behind: *the car braked suddenly, then backed rapidly until it was* **level with** *me.* ■ (of a quantity of a dry substance) with the contents not rising above the brim of the measure: *a level teaspoon of salt.* ■ unchanged; not having risen or fallen: *earnings were level at 17.5p a share.* ■ chiefly Brit. having the same position or score in a race or contest: *the two teams finished level on points at the end of the series.*
2 calm and steady: *'Adrian,' she said in a level voice that surprised her.*
▶ **verb** (**levelled**, **levelling**; US **leveled**, **leveling**) **1** [with obj.] give a flat and even surface to: *contractors started levelling the ground for the new power station.*
■ Surveying ascertain differences in the height of (land). ■ demolish (a building or town): *bulldozers are now waiting to level their home.*
2 [no obj.] (**level off/out**) begin to fly horizontally after climbing or diving.
■ (of a path, road, or incline) cease to slope upwards or downwards: *the track levelled out and there below us was the bay.* ■ cease to fall or rise in number, amount, or quantity: *inflation has levelled out at an acceptable rate.*

■ [with obj.] (**level something up/down**) increase or reduce the amount, number, or quantity of something in order to remove a disparity.
3 [with obj.] aim (a weapon): *he* **levelled** *a long-barrelled pistol* **at** *us.*
■ direct (a criticism or accusation): *accusations of corruption had been* **levelled against** *him.*
4 [no obj.] (**level with**) informal be frank or honest with (someone): *when are you going to level with me?*
– PHRASES **do one's level best** do one's utmost; make all possible efforts. **find its (own) level** (of a liquid) reach the same height in containers which are interconnected. ■ reach a stable level, value, or position without interference. **find one's (own) level** (of a person) reach a position that seems appropriate and natural in relation to one's associates. **level of attainment** Brit. a rating of the ability of a school pupil, on a scale of 1 to 10. **be level pegging** Brit. be in a position of having equal scores or achievements during a contest: *the two were level pegging after three heats.* **a level playing field** a situation in which everyone has a fair and equal chance of succeeding. **on the level** informal honest; truthful: *Eddie said my story was on the level.* **on a level with** in the same horizontal plane as. ■ equal with: *they were treated as menials, on a level with cooks.*
– DERIVATIVES **levelly** adverb (only in sense 2 of the adjective), **levelness** noun.
– ORIGIN Middle English (denoting an instrument to determine whether a surface is horizontal): from Old French *livel*, based on Latin *libella*, diminutive of *libra* 'scales, balance'.

level crossing ▶ **noun** Brit. a place where a railway and a road, or two railway lines, cross at the same level.

level-headed ▶ **adjective** calm and sensible.
– DERIVATIVES **level-headedly** adverb, **level-headedness** noun.

leveller (US **leveler**) ▶ **noun 1** a person who advocates the abolition of social distinctions.
■ (**Leveller**) an extreme radical dissenter in the English Civil War (1642–9), calling for the abolition of the monarchy, social and agrarian reforms, and religious freedom.
2 a person or thing that levels something.

levelling screw ▶ **noun** a screw, typically one of three, for adjusting part of a machine or instrument to a precise level.

lever /ˈliːvə/ ▶ **noun** a rigid bar resting on a pivot, used to help move a heavy or firmly fixed load with one end when pressure is applied to the other.
■ a projecting arm or handle that is moved to operate a mechanism: *she pulled a lever at the base of the cage.* ■ figurative a means of exerting pressure on someone to act in a particular way: *rich countries increasingly use foreign aid as a lever to promote political pluralism.*
▶ **verb** [with obj. and adverbial] lift or move with a lever: *she levered the lid off the pot with a screwdriver.*
■ move (someone or something) with a concerted physical effort: *she levered herself up against the pillows.* ■ [no obj.] use a lever: *the men got hold of the coffin and levered at it with crowbars.* ■ figurative exert pressure on (someone) to do something: *the Inspector made another attempt to lever a concrete fact from them.*
– ORIGIN Middle English: from Old French *levier, leveor*, from *lever* 'to lift'.

leverage ▶ **noun** [mass noun] **1** the exertion of force by means of a lever or an object used in the manner of a lever: *my spade hit something solid that wouldn't respond to leverage.*
■ mechanical advantage gained in this way: *use a metal bar to increase the leverage.* ■ figurative the power to influence a person or situation to achieve a particular outcome: *the right wing had lost much of its political leverage in the Assembly.*
2 Finance another term for **GEARING** (in sense 2).
▶ **verb** [with obj.] [usu. as adj. **leveraged**] use borrowed capital for (an investment), expecting the profits made to be greater than the interest payable: *a leveraged takeover bid.*

leveraged buyout ▶ **noun** the purchase of a controlling share in a company by its management using outside capital.

lever escapement ▶ **noun** a mechanism in a watch connecting the escape wheel and the balance wheel using two levers.

leveret /ˈlɛv(ə)rɪt/ ▶ **noun** a young hare in its first year.
– ORIGIN late Middle English: from Anglo-Norman French, diminutive of *levre*, from Latin *lepus, lepor-* 'hare'.

Leverhulme /ˈliːvəhjuːm/, 1st Viscount (1851–1925), English industrialist and philanthropist; born *William Hesketh Lever.* He and his brother manufactured soap under the trade name Sunlight; their company, Lever Bros., came to form the basis of the international corporation Unilever. Leverhulme founded the model village Port Sunlight for his company's workers.

Leverkusen /ˈleɪvəˌkuːz(ə)n, German ˈleːvɐˌkuːzn/ an industrial city in western Germany, in North Rhine-Westphalia, on the River Rhine north of Cologne; pop. 161,150 (1991).

Le Verrier /lə ˈvɛrɪeɪ, French lə vɛrje/, Urbain (1811–77), French mathematician. His analysis of the motions of the planets suggested that an unknown body was disrupting the orbit of Uranus. Le Verrier prompted the German astronomer **Johann Galle** (1812–1910) to investigate, and the planet Neptune was discovered in 1846.

lever watch ▶ **noun** a watch with a lever escapement.

Levi[1] /ˈliːvʌɪ/ (in the Bible) a Hebrew patriarch, son of Jacob and Leah (Gen. 29:34).
■ the tribe of Israel traditionally descended from him.

Levi[2] /ˈleɪvi/, Primo (1919–87), Italian novelist and poet, of Jewish descent. His experiences as a survivor of Auschwitz are recounted in his first book *If This is a Man* (1947).

leviathan /lɪˈvʌɪəθ(ə)n/ ▶ **noun** (in biblical use) a sea monster, identified in different passages with the whale and the crocodile (e.g. Job 41, Ps. 74:14), and with the Devil (after Isa. 27:1).
■ a very large aquatic creature, especially a whale: *the great leviathans of the deep.* ■ a thing that is very large or powerful, especially a ship. ■ an autocratic monarch or state. [ORIGIN: with allusion to Hobbes' *Leviathan* (1651).]
– ORIGIN via late Latin from Hebrew *liwyāṯān*.

levigate /ˈlɛvɪgeɪt/ ▶ **verb** [with obj.] archaic reduce (a substance) to a fine powder or smooth paste.
– DERIVATIVES **levigation** noun.
– ORIGIN mid 16th cent.: from Latin *levigat-* 'made smooth, polished', from the verb *levigare*, from *levis* 'smooth'.

levin /ˈlɛvɪn/ ▶ **noun** [mass noun] archaic lightning; thunderbolts.
– ORIGIN Middle English: probably of Scandinavian origin.

levirate /ˈliːvɪrət, ˈlɛv-/ ▶ **noun** (usu. **the levirate**) a custom of the ancient Hebrews and some other peoples by which a man may be obliged to marry his brother's widow: [as modifier] *levirate marriages.*
– ORIGIN early 18th cent.: from Latin *levir* 'brother-in-law' + **-ATE**[1].

Lévi-Strauss /ˌlɛvɪˈstraʊs, French levistros/, Claude (b.1908), French social anthropologist. A pioneer in the use of a structuralist analysis to study cultural systems, he regarded language as an essential common denominator underlying cultural phenomena.

levitate /ˈlɛvɪteɪt/ ▶ **verb** [no obj.] rise and hover in the air, typically by means of supposed magical powers: *he seems to levitate about three inches off the ground.*
■ [with obj.] cause (something) to rise and hover in such a way.
– DERIVATIVES **levitation** noun, **levitator** noun.
– ORIGIN late 17th cent.: from Latin *levis* 'light', on the pattern of *gravitate.*

Levite /ˈliːvʌɪt/ ▶ **noun** a member of the Hebrew tribe of Levi, especially of that part of it which provided assistants to the priests in the worship in the Jewish temple.
– ORIGIN Middle English: from late Latin *levita*, from Greek *leuitēs*, from Hebrew *Lēwī* 'Levi'.

Levitical /lɪˈvɪtɪk(ə)l/ ▶ **adjective 1** of or relating to the Levites or the tribe of Levi: *a Levitical priest.*
2 Judaism (of rules concerning codes of conduct, temple rituals, etc.) derived from the biblical Book of Leviticus: *a Levitical edict.*
– ORIGIN mid 16th cent.: via late Latin from Greek *levitikos*, from *Levi* (see **LEVITE**), + **-AL**.

Leviticus /lɪˈvɪtɪkəs/ the third book of the Bible, containing details of law and ritual.

levity /ˈlɛvɪti/ ▶ **noun** [mass noun] the treatment of a serious matter with humour or in a manner lacking due respect: *as an attempt to introduce a note of levity, the words were a disastrous flop.*
– ORIGIN mid 16th cent.: from Latin *levitas*, from *levis* 'light'.

levo- ▶ **combining form** US spelling of **LAEVO-**.

levodopa /ˌliːvə(ʊ)ˈdəʊpə/ ▶ **noun** another term for **L-DOPA**.

levonorgestrel /ˌliːvəʊnɔːˈdʒɛstr(ə)l/ ▶ **noun** [mass noun] Biochemistry a synthetic steroid hormone which has a similar effect to progesterone and is used in some contraceptive pills.
– ORIGIN 1970s: from **LEVO-** (it being a laevorotatory isomer) + *norgestrel*, a synthetic steroid hormone.

levulose ▶ **noun** US spelling of **LAEVULOSE**.

levy /ˈlɛvi/ ▶ **verb** (**-ies, -ied**) [with obj.] **1** (often **be levied**) impose (a tax, fee, or fine): *a new tax could be* **levied on** *industry to pay for cleaning up contaminated land.*
■ impose a tax, fee, or fine on: *there will be powers to levy the owner.* ■ [no obj.] (**levy on/upon**) seize (property) to satisfy a legal judgement: *there were no goods to levy upon.*
2 archaic enlist (someone) for military service: *he sought to levy one man from each vill for service.*
■ begin to wage (war).
▶ **noun** (pl. **-ies**) **1** an act of levying a tax, fee, or fine: *police forces receive 49 per cent of their funding from local government via a* **levy on** *the rates.*
■ a tax so raised. ■ a sum collected for a specific purpose, especially as a supplement to an existing subscription: *the trade-union political levy.* ■ an item or set of items of property seized to satisfy a legal judgement.
2 historical an act of enlisting troops.
■ (usu. **levies**) a body of troops that have been enlisted: *lightly armed local levies.*
– DERIVATIVES **leviable** adjective.
– ORIGIN Middle English (as a noun): from Old French *levee*, feminine past participle of *lever* 'raise', from Latin *levare*, from *levis* 'light'.

lewd ▶ **adjective** crude and offensive in a sexual way: *she began to gyrate to the music and sing a lewd song.*
– DERIVATIVES **lewdly** adverb, **lewdness** noun.
– ORIGIN Old English *lǣwede*, of unknown origin. The original sense was 'belonging to the laity'; in Middle English, 'belonging to the common people, vulgar', and later 'worthless, vile, evil', leading to the current sense.

Lewes /ˈluːɪs/ a town in southern England on the River Ouse eight miles north-east of Brighton, the county town of East Sussex; pop. 14,970 (1981). It was the site in 1264 of a battle in which the younger Simon de Montfort defeated Henry III.

Lewis[1] the northern part of the island of Lewis and Harris in the Outer Hebrides.

Lewis[2], Cecil Day, see **DAY LEWIS**.

Lewis[3], C. S. (1898–1963), British novelist, religious writer, and literary scholar; full name *Clive Staples Lewis.* He broadcast and wrote on religious and moral issues, and created the imaginary land of Narnia for a series of children's books. Notable works: *The Lion, the Witch, and the Wardrobe* (1950).

Lewis[4], Carl (b.1961), American athlete; full name *Frederick Carleton Lewis.* He won Olympic gold medals in 1984, 1988, 1992, and 1996 (his ninth) for sprinting and the long jump, and has broken the world record for the 100 metres on several occasions.

Lewis[5], Jerry Lee (b.1935), American rock-and-roll singer and pianist. In 1957 he had hits with 'Whole Lotta Shakin' Going On' and 'Great Balls of Fire'. His career was interrupted when his marriage to his fourteen-year-old cousin caused a public outcry.

Lewis[6], (Harry) Sinclair (1885–1951), American novelist, known for satirical works such as *Main Street* (1920), *Babbitt* (1922), and *Elmer Gantry* (1927). He was the first American writer to receive the Nobel Prize for Literature (1930).

Lewis[7], Meriwether (1774–1809), American explorer. Together with William Clark he led an expedition to explore the newly acquired Louisiana Purchase (1804–6). They travelled from St Louis to the Pacific Coast and back.

Lewis[8], (Percy) Wyndham (1882–1957), British novelist, critic, and painter, born in Canada. He was a leader of the vorticist movement, and with Ezra Pound edited the magazine *Blast* (1914–15). Notable novels: *The Apes of God* (1930).

lewis ▶ **noun** a steel device for gripping heavy blocks

of stone or concrete for lifting, consisting of three pieces arranged to form a dovetail, the outside pieces being fixed in a dovetail mortise by the insertion of the middle piece.
– ORIGIN late Middle English: probably from Old French *lous*, plural of *lou(p)* 'wolf', the name of a kind of siege engine.

Lewis acid ▶ noun Chemistry a compound or ionic species which can accept an electron pair from a donor compound.
– ORIGIN 1940s: named after Gilbert N. *Lewis* (1875–1946), American chemist.

Lewis and Harris (also **Lewis with Harris**) the largest and northernmost island of the Outer Hebrides in Scotland; chief town, Stornoway. The island, which is separated from the mainland by the Minch, consists of a northern part, Lewis, and a smaller and more mountainous southern part, Harris.

Lewis base ▶ noun Chemistry a compound or ionic species which can donate an electron pair to an acceptor compound.
– ORIGIN 1960s: named after G. N. *Lewis* (see **LEWIS ACID**).

Lewis gun ▶ noun chiefly historical a light air-cooled machine gun with a magazine operated by gas from its own firing, used mainly in the First World War.
– ORIGIN early 20th cent.: named after its inventor, Isaac N. *Lewis* (1858–1931), a colonel in the US army.

Lewisian /luːˈɪsɪən/ ▶ adjective Geology of, relating to, or denoting the earlier stage of the Proterozoic aeon in NW Scotland, from about 2500 to 1100 million years ago, when the oldest rocks in Britain were deposited.
■ [as noun **the Lewisian**] the Lewisian stage or the system of rocks deposited during it.
– ORIGIN mid 19th cent.: from the name of the Island of *Lewis* in the Outer Hebrides (where the chief outcrops of these rocks are found) + **-IAN**.

lewisite /ˈluːɪsʌɪt/ ▶ noun [mass noun] a dark oily liquid producing an irritant gas that causes blisters, developed for use in chemical warfare.
● An organic compound of arsenic; chem. formula: $ClCH=CHAsCl_2$.
– ORIGIN 1920s: named after Winford L. *Lewis* (1878–1943), American chemist.

Lewis with Harris another name for **LEWIS AND HARRIS**.

Lexan /ˈlɛksan/ ▶ noun [mass noun] trademark a transparent plastic (polycarbonate) of high impact strength, used for cockpit canopies, bulletproof screens, etc.
– ORIGIN 1950s: an invented name.

lexeme /ˈlɛksiːm/ ▶ noun Linguistics a basic lexical unit of a language consisting of one word or several words, the elements of which do not separately convey the meaning of the whole.
– ORIGIN 1940s: from **LEXICON** + **-EME**.

lex fori /lɛks ˈfɔːrʌɪ/ ▶ noun [mass noun] Law the law of the country in which an action is brought.
– ORIGIN Latin, 'law of the court'.

lexical /ˈlɛksɪk(ə)l/ ▶ adjective of or relating to the words or vocabulary of a language: *lexical analysis.*
■ relating to or of the nature of a lexicon or dictionary: *a lexical entry.*
– DERIVATIVES **lexically** adverb.
– ORIGIN mid 19th cent.: from Greek *lexikos* 'of words' (from *lexis* 'word') + **-AL**.

lexical meaning ▶ noun the meaning of a word considered in isolation from the sentence containing it, and regardless of its grammatical context, e.g. of *love* in or as represented by *loves, loved, loving,* etc.

lexicographer ▶ noun a person who compiles dictionaries.

lexicography /ˌlɛksɪˈkɒɡrəfi/ ▶ noun [mass noun] the practice of compiling dictionaries.
– DERIVATIVES **lexicographic** adjective, **lexico-graphical** adjective, **lexicographically** adverb.

lexicology ▶ noun [mass noun] the study of the form, meaning, and behaviour of words.
– DERIVATIVES **lexicological** adjective, **lexico-logically** adverb.

lexicon /ˈlɛksɪk(ə)n/ ▶ noun the vocabulary of a person, language, or branch of knowledge: *the size of the English lexicon.*

■ a dictionary, especially of Greek, Hebrew, Syriac, or Arabic: *a Greek-Latin lexicon.*
– ORIGIN early 17th cent.: modern Latin, from Greek *lexikon (biblion)* '(book) of words', from *lexis* 'word', from *legein* 'speak'.

lexigram /ˈlɛksɪɡram/ ▶ noun a symbol representing a word, especially one used in learning a language.

Lexington 1 a city in central Kentucky; pop. 225,270 (with Fayette). It is a noted horse-breeding centre.
2 a residential town north-west of Boston, Massachusetts; pop. 28,970 (1990). It was the scene in 1775 of the first battle in the War of American Independence.

lexis /ˈlɛksɪs/ ▶ noun [mass noun] the total stock of words in a language: *a notable loss of English lexis.*
■ the level of language consisting of vocabulary, as opposed to grammar or syntax.
– ORIGIN 1950s (denoting the wording, as opposed to other elements, in a piece of writing): from Greek, literally 'word' (see **LEXICON**).

lex loci /lɛks ˈləʊsʌɪ/ ▶ noun [mass noun] Law the law of the country in which a transaction is performed, a tort is committed, or a property is situated.
– ORIGIN Latin, 'law of the place'.

lex talionis /lɛks ˌtaliˈəʊnɪs/ ▶ noun [mass noun] the law of retaliation, whereby a punishment resembles the offence committed in kind and degree.
– ORIGIN Latin, from *lex* 'law' and *talio(n-)* 'retaliation' from *talis* 'such').

ley[1] /leɪ/ (also **temporary ley**) ▶ noun a piece of land put down to grass, clover, etc., for a single season or a limited number of years, in contrast to permanent pasture.
– ORIGIN Old English *lǣge* 'fallow' (recorded in *lǣghrycg* 'ridge left at the edge of a ploughed field'); related to **LAY**[1] and **LIE**[1].

ley[2] /leɪ, liː/ (also **ley line**) ▶ noun a supposed straight line connecting three or more prehistoric or ancient sites, sometimes regarded as the line of a former track and associated by some with lines of energy and other paranormal phenomena.
– ORIGIN 1920s: variant of **LEA**.

Leyden variant spelling of **LEIDEN**.

Leyden jar /ˈlʌɪd(ə)n/ ▶ noun an early form of capacitor consisting of a glass jar with layers of metal foil on the outside and inside.
– ORIGIN mid 18th cent.: named after *Leyden* (see **LEIDEN**), where it was invented (1745).

ley farming ▶ noun [mass noun] chiefly Brit. the alternate growing of crops and grass.

Leyland cypress /ˈleɪlənd/ ▶ noun a fast-growing hybrid conifer which is narrowly conical with a dense growth of shoots bearing scale-like leaves, widely grown as a screening plant or for shelter. Also called **LEYLANDII**.
● × *Cupressocyparis leylandii*, family Cupressaceae; a hybrid between the Nootka cypress and the Monterey cypress (macrocarpa).
– ORIGIN 1930s: named after Christopher J. *Leyland* (1849–1926), British horticulturist.

leylandii /leɪˈlandɪʌɪ/ ▶ noun (pl. same) a Leyland cypress.
– ORIGIN from the modern Latin taxonomic name.

Leyte /ˈleɪti/ an island in the central Philippines; pop. 1,362,050 (1990); chief town, Tacloban.

lez ▶ noun variant spelling of **LES**.

lezzy ▶ noun (pl. **-ies**) informal a lesbian.

LF ▶ abbreviation for low frequency.

LGV Brit. ▶ abbreviation for large goods vehicle.

LH Biochemistry ▶ abbreviation for luteinizing hormone.

l.h. ▶ abbreviation for left hand.

Lhasa /ˈlɑːsə/ the capital of Tibet; pop. 139,800 (1996). It is situated in the northern Himalayas at an altitude of 3,600 m (c.11,800 ft), on a tributary of the Brahmaputra.

> Its inaccessibility and the hostility of the Tibetan Buddhist priests to foreign visitors—to whom Lhasa was closed until the 20th century—earned it the title of the Forbidden City. The spiritual centre of Tibetan Buddhism, Lhasa was the seat of the Dalai Lama until 1959, when direct Chinese administration was imposed on the city.

Lhasa apso /ˈapsəʊ/ ▶ noun (pl. **-os**) a dog of a small long-coated breed, typically gold or grey and white, originating at Lhasa.
– ORIGIN mid 20th cent.: from **LHASA** + Tibetan *a-sob.*

LHD ▶ abbreviation for left-hand drive.

LI ▶ abbreviation for ■ Light Infantry. ■ (in the US) Long Island.

Li ▶ symbol for the chemical element lithium.

li /liː/ ▶ noun (pl. same) a Chinese unit of distance, equal to about 0.6 km (0.4 mile).

liability ▶ noun (pl. **-ies**) **1** [mass noun] the state of being responsible for something, especially by law: *once you contact the card protection scheme your liability for any loss ends.*
■ [count noun] (usu. **liabilities**) a thing for which someone is responsible, especially a debt or financial obligation: *valuing the company's liabilities and assets.*
2 [usu. in sing.] a person or thing whose presence or behaviour is likely to cause embarrassment or put one at a disadvantage: *he was unfit and a liability in the match.*

liable ▶ adjective [predic.] **1** responsible by law; legally answerable: *the supplier of goods or services can become liable for breach of contract in a variety of ways.*
■ (**liable to**) subject by law to: *non-resident trustees are liable to the basic rate of tax.*
2 [with infinitive] likely to do or to be something: *patients were liable to faint if they stood up too suddenly.*
■ (**liable to**) likely to experience (something undesirable): *areas liable to flooding.*
– ORIGIN late Middle English: perhaps from Anglo-Norman French, from French *lier* 'to bind', from Latin *ligare*.

liaise /lɪˈeɪz/ ▶ verb [no obj.] establish a working relationship, typically in order to cooperate on a matter of mutual concern: *she will liaise with teachers across the country.*
■ (**liaise between**) act as a link to assist communication between (two or more people or groups): *civil servants who liaise between the prime minister and departmental ministers.*
– ORIGIN 1920s (originally military slang): back-formation from **LIAISON**.

liaison ▶ noun [mass noun] **1** communication or cooperation which facilitates a close working relationship between people or organizations: *the head porter works in close liaison with the reception office.*
■ [count noun] a person who acts as a link to assist communication or cooperation between groups of people: *he's our liaison with a number of interested parties.* ■ [count noun] a sexual relationship, especially one that is secret and involves unfaithfulness to a partner.
2 the binding or thickening agent of a sauce, often based on egg yolks.
3 Phonetics (in French and other languages) the sounding of a consonant that is normally silent at the end of a word, because the next word begins with a vowel.
■ introduction of a consonant between a word that ends in a vowel and another that begins with a vowel, as in English *law and order.*
– ORIGIN mid 17th cent. (as a cookery term): from French, from *lier* 'to bind'.

liaison officer ▶ noun a person who is employed to form a working relationship between two organizations to their mutual benefit.

liana /lɪˈɑːnə/ (also **liane** /-ˈɑːn/) ▶ noun a woody climbing plant that hangs from trees, especially in tropical rainforests.
■ the free-hanging stem of such a plant.
– ORIGIN late 18th cent.: from French *liane* 'clematis, liana', of unknown origin.

Liao[1] /ljaʊ/ a river of NE China, which rises in Inner Mongolia and flows about 1,450 km (900 miles) east and south to the Gulf of Liaodong at the head of the gulf of Bo Hai.

Liao[2] /ljaʊ/ a dynasty which ruled much of Manchuria and part of NE China AD 947–1125.

Liaodong Peninsula /ˌljaʊˈdʊŋ/ a peninsula in NE China, which extends southwards into the Yellow Sea between Bo Hai and Korea Bay.

Liaoning /ˌljaʊˈnɪŋ/ a province of NE China, bordered on the east by North Korea; capital, Shenyang.

liar ▶ noun a person who tells lies.
– ORIGIN Old English *lēogere* (see **LIE**[2], **-AR**[4]).

liard /ˈljɑː, ljɑːd/ ▶ noun historical a small coin formerly current in France, worth three deniers or a quarter of a sou.
– ORIGIN French, of unknown origin.

liar dice ▶ noun [mass noun] a gambling game

resembling poker dice, in which the thrower conceals the dice thrown and sometimes declares a false score.

lias /ˈlʌɪəs/ ▶ **noun** (**the Lias**) Geology the earliest epoch of the Jurassic period, lasting from about 208 to 178 million years ago.
■the system of rocks deposited during this epoch, consisting of shales and limestones rich in fossils. ■(also **blue lias**) [mass noun] a blue-grey clayey limestone derived from marl deposited in the Lower Jurassic, found chiefly in SW England.
– DERIVATIVES **liassic** adjective.
– ORIGIN late Middle English (denoting blue lias): from Old French *liais* 'hard limestone', probably from *lie* (see **LEES**).

liatris /lʌɪˈatrɪs/ ▶ **noun** (pl. same) a plant of a genus which includes the blazing stars of the daisy family.
• Genus *Liatris*, family Compositae.
– ORIGIN modern Latin, of unknown origin.

Lib. ▶ **abbreviation for** Liberal.

lib ▶ **noun** [mass noun] informal (in the names of political movements) liberation: *I'm all for* **women's lib**.
– ORIGIN 1970s: abbreviation.

libation /lʌɪˈbeɪʃ(ə)n/ ▶ **noun** a drink poured out as an offering to a deity.
■[mass noun] the pouring out of such a drink-offering: *gin was poured in libation*. ■humorous a drink: *they steadily worked their way through free food and the occasional libation.*
– ORIGIN late Middle English: from Latin *libatio(n-)*, from *libare* 'pour as an offering'.

libber ▶ **noun** [usu. with modifier] informal a member or advocate of a movement calling for the liberation of people or animals: *a women's libber.*

Lib Dem ▶ **noun** informal (in the UK) Liberal Democrat: *I'm voting Lib Dem.*

libeccio /lɪˈbɛtʃɪəʊ, Italian liˈbettʃo/ ▶ **noun** a strong south-westerly wind blowing on the sea to the west of Italy.
– ORIGIN Italian.

libel ▶ **noun 1** Law a published false statement that is damaging to a person's reputation; a written defamation. Compare with **SLANDER**.
■[mass noun] the action or crime of publishing such a statement: *a councillor who sued two national newspapers for libel* | [as modifier] *a libel action*. ■a false and typically malicious statement about a person. ■a thing or circumstance that brings undeserved discredit on a person by misrepresentation.
2 (in admiralty and ecclesiastical law) a plaintiff's written declaration.
▶ **verb** (**libelled**, **libelling**; US **libeled**, **libeling**) [with obj.]
1 Law defame (someone) by publishing a libel: *the jury found that he was libelled by a newspaper.*
■make a false and typically malicious statement about.
2 (in admiralty and ecclesiastical law) bring a suit against (someone).
– DERIVATIVES **libeller** noun.
– ORIGIN Middle English (in the general sense 'a document, a written statement'): via Old French from Latin *libellus*, diminutive of *liber* 'book'.

libellous /ˈlʌɪb(ə)ləs/ (US also **libelous**) ▶ **adjective** containing or constituting a libel: *a libellous newspaper story.*
– DERIVATIVES **libellously** adverb.

Liberace /ˌlɪbəˈrɑːtʃi/ (1919–87), American pianist and entertainer; full name *Wladziu Valentino Liberace*. He was known for his romantic arrangements of popular piano classics and for his flamboyant costumes.

liberal ▶ **adjective 1** willing to respect or accept behaviour or opinions different from one's own; open to new ideas: *they have more liberal views towards marriage and divorce than some people.*
■favourable to or respectful of individual rights and freedoms: *liberal citizenship laws.* ■(in a political context) favouring individual liberty, free trade, and moderate political and social reform: *a liberal democratic state.* ■(**Liberal**) of or characteristic of Liberals or a Liberal Party. ■(**Liberal**) (in the UK) of or relating to the Liberal Democrat party: *the Liberal leader.* ■Theology regarding many traditional beliefs as dispensable, invalidated by modern thought, or liable to change.
2 [attrib.] (of education) concerned mainly with broadening a person's general knowledge and experience, rather than with technical or professional training.
3 (especially of an interpretation of a law) broadly construed or understood; not strictly literal or exact: *they could have given the 1968 Act a more liberal interpretation.*
4 given, used, or occurring in generous amounts: *liberal amounts of wine had been consumed.*
■(of a person) giving generously: *Sam was too* **liberal** *with the wine.*
▶ **noun** a person of liberal views.
■(**Liberal**) a supporter or member of a Liberal Party. ■(**Liberal**) (in the UK) a Liberal Democrat.
– DERIVATIVES **liberalism** noun, **liberalist** noun, **liberalistic** adjective, **liberally** adverb, **liberalness** noun.
– ORIGIN Middle English: via Old French from Latin *liberalis*, from *liber* 'free (man)'. The original sense was 'suitable for a free man', hence 'suitable for a gentleman' (one not tied to a trade), surviving in *liberal arts*. Another early sense 'generous' (compare with sense 4) gave rise to an obsolete meaning 'free from restraint', leading to sense 1 (late 18th cent.).

liberal arts ▶ **plural noun** chiefly N. Amer. arts subjects such as literature and history, as distinct from science and technology.
■historical the medieval trivium and quadrivium.
– ORIGIN *liberal*, as distinct from *servile* or *mechanical* (i.e. involving manual labour) and originally referring to arts and sciences considered 'worthy of a free man'; later the word related to general intellectual development rather than vocational training.

Liberal Democrat ▶ **noun** (in the UK) a member of a party (formerly the Social and Liberal Democrats) formed from the Liberal Party and members of the Social Democratic Party.

liberality ▶ **noun** [mass noun] **1** the quality of giving or spending freely.
2 the quality of being open to new ideas and free from prejudice: *liberality towards bisexuality.*
– ORIGIN Middle English: from Old French *liberalite*, or from Latin *liberalitas*, from *liberalis* (see **LIBERAL**).

liberalize (also **-ise**) ▶ **verb** [with obj.] remove or loosen restrictions on (something, typically an economic or political system): *several agreements to liberalize trade were signed.*
– DERIVATIVES **liberalization** noun, **liberalizer** noun.

Liberal Party ▶ **noun** a political party advocating liberal policies, in particular a British party that emerged in the 1860s from the old Whig Party and until the First World War was one of the two major parties in Britain. The name was discontinued in official use in 1988, when the party regrouped with elements of the Social Democratic Party to form the Social and Liberal Democrats, now known as the Liberal Democrats.

Liberal Party of Australia an Australian political party established in its modern form by Robert Menzies in 1944, in opposition to the Australian Labor Party. It first gained power in 1949.

Liberal Party of Canada a Canadian political party generally taking a moderate, left-of-centre position. The party emerged in the mid 19th century, and held power for most of the period 1963–84.

liberal studies ▶ **plural noun** [usu. treated as sing.] Brit. an additional course in arts subjects taken by students studying for a qualification in science, technology, or the humanities.

Liberal Unionist ▶ **noun** a member of a group of British Liberal MPs who left the party in 1886 because of Gladstone's support for Irish Home Rule. Led by Joseph Chamberlain from 1891, they formed an alliance with the Conservative Party in Parliament, and merged officially with them in 1909 as the Conservative and Unionist Party.

liberate ▶ **verb** [with obj.] (often **be liberated**) set (someone) free from a situation, especially imprisonment or slavery, in which their liberty is severely restricted: *the serfs had been liberated.*
■free (a country, city, or people) from enemy occupation: *twelve months earlier Paris had been liberated.* ■release (someone) from a state or situation which limits freedom of thought or behaviour: *the use of computers can* **liberate** *pupils* **from** *the constraints of disabilities* | [as adj. **liberating**] *the arts can have a liberating effect on people.* ■free (someone) from rigid social conventions, especially those concerned with accepted sexual roles: *ways of working politically that liberate women.* ■informal steal (something): *the drummer's wearing a beret he's liberated from Lord knows where.* ■Chemistry & Physics release (gas, energy, etc.) as a result of chemical reaction or physical decomposition: *energy liberated by the annihilation of matter.*
– DERIVATIVES **liberation** noun, **liberationist** noun, **liberator** noun.
– ORIGIN late 16th cent.: from Latin *liberat-* 'freed', from the verb *liberare*, from *liber* 'free'.

liberated ▶ **adjective 1** (of a person) showing freedom from social conventions or traditional ideas, especially with regard to sexual roles: *the modern image of the independent, liberated woman.*
2 (of a place or people) freed from enemy occupation: *liberated areas of the country.*

liberation theology ▶ **noun** [mass noun] a movement in Christian theology, developed mainly by Latin American Roman Catholics, which attempts to address the problems of poverty and social injustice as well as spiritual matters.

Liberation Tigers of Tamil Eelam another name for **TAMIL TIGERS**.

Liberia /lʌɪˈbɪərɪə/ a country on the Atlantic coast of West Africa; pop. 2,639,000 (est. 1991); languages, English (official), English-based pidgin; capital, Monrovia.

Liberia was founded in 1822 as a settlement for freed slaves from the US, and was proclaimed independent in 1847. Indigenous peoples, however, form the majority of the population. In 1980 a coup overthrew the predominant Liberian–American elite, and a civil war began in 1990, ending with a ceasefire in 1996.

– DERIVATIVES **Liberian** adjective & noun.
– ORIGIN from Latin *liber* 'free'.

libero /ˈliːbərəʊ/ ▶ **noun** (pl. **-os**) Soccer another term for **SWEEPER** (in sense 2).
– ORIGIN 1960s: from Italian, abbreviation of *battitore libero* 'free defender', literally 'free beater'.

libertarian /ˌlɪbəˈtɛːrɪən/ ▶ **noun 1** an adherent of libertarianism: [as modifier] *libertarian philosophy.*
■a person who advocates civil liberty.
2 a person who believes in free will.
– ORIGIN late 18th cent. (in sense 2): from **LIBERTY**, on the pattern of words such as *unitarian*.

libertarianism ▶ **noun** [mass noun] an extreme laissez-faire political philosophy advocating only minimal state intervention in the lives of citizens.

Its adherents believe that private morality is not the state's affair, and that therefore activities such as drug use and prostitution that arguably harm no one but the participants should not be illegal. Libertarianism shares elements with anarchism, although it is generally associated more with the political right (chiefly in the US); it lacks the concern of traditional liberalism with social justice.

libertine /ˈlɪbətiːn, -tɪn, -tʌɪn/ ▶ **noun 1** a person, especially a man, who behaves without moral principles or a sense of responsibility, especially in sexual matters.
2 a freethinker in matters of religion.
▶ **adjective 1** characterized by a disregard of morality, especially in sexual matters: *his more libertine impulses.*
2 freethinking.
– DERIVATIVES **libertinage** noun, **libertinism** noun.
– ORIGIN late Middle English (denoting a freed slave or the son of one): from Latin *libertinus* 'freedman', from *liber* 'free'. In the mid 16th cent., imitating French *libertin*, the term denoted a member of any of various antinomian sects in France; hence sense 2.

liberty ▶ **noun** (pl. **-ies**) [mass noun] **1** the state of being free within society from oppressive restrictions imposed by authority on one's way of life, behaviour, or political views: *compulsory retirement would interfere with individual liberty.*
■[count noun] (usu. **liberties**) an instance of this; a right or privilege, especially a statutory one: *the Bill of Rights was intended to secure basic civil liberties.* ■the state of not being imprisoned or enslaved: *people who attacked phone boxes would lose their liberty.* ■(**Liberty**) the personification of liberty as a female figure.
2 the power or scope to act as one pleases: *individuals should enjoy the liberty to pursue their own interests and preferences.*
■Philosophy a person's freedom from control by fate or necessity. ■[count noun] informal a presumptuous remark or action: *how did he know what she was thinking?—it was a liberty!* ■Nautical shore leave granted to a sailor.
– PHRASES **at liberty 1** not imprisoned: *he was at liberty for three months before he was recaptured.*
2 allowed or entitled to do something: *competent*

adults are generally **at liberty** *to refuse medical treatment.* **take liberties 1** behave in an unduly familiar manner towards a person: *you've* **taken** *too many* **liberties with** *me.* **2** treat something freely, without strict faithfulness to the facts or to an original: *the scriptwriter has* **taken few liberties with** *the original narrative.* **take the liberty** venture to do something without first asking permission: *I have* **taken the liberty of** *submitting an idea to several of their research departments.*

– ORIGIN late Middle English: from Old French *liberte,* from Latin *libertas,* from *liber* 'free'.

Liberty, Statue of a statue at the entrance to New York harbour, a symbol of welcome to immigrants, representing a draped female figure carrying a book of laws in her left hand and holding aloft a torch in her right. Dedicated in 1886, it was designed by Frédéric-Auguste Bartholdi and was the gift of the French, commemorating the alliance of France and the US during the War of American Independence.

Liberty Bell a bell in Philadelphia first rung on 8 July 1776 to celebrate the first public reading of the Declaration of Independence. It bears the legend 'Proclaim liberty throughout all the land unto all the inhabitants thereof' (Leviticus 25:10).

liberty boat ▸ noun Brit. a boat carrying sailors who have leave to go on shore.

liberty bodice ▸ noun Brit. trademark a girl's or woman's close-fitting sleeveless undergarment made from thick cotton and covering the upper body.

liberty cap ▸ noun **1** a common small European toadstool which has a greyish-brown cap with a distinct boss and a long thin stem, containing the hallucinogen psilocybin. See also MAGIC MUSHROOM.
● *Psilocybe semilanceata,* family Strophariaceae, class Hymenomycetes.
2 another term for CAP OF LIBERTY.

Liberty Hall ▸ noun a place where one may do as one likes.

liberty horse ▸ noun a horse that performs in a circus without a rider.

liberty man ▸ noun Brit. a sailor with leave to go ashore.

liberty of the subject ▸ noun [in sing.] chiefly Brit. the rights of a subject under constitutional rule.

Liberty ship ▸ noun historical a prefabricated US-built freighter of the Second World War.

libidinous /lɪˈbɪdɪnəs/ ▸ adjective showing excessive sexual drive; lustful.
– DERIVATIVES **libidinously** adverb, **libidinousness** noun.
– ORIGIN late Middle English: from Latin *libidinosus,* from *libido* 'desire, lust'.

libido /lɪˈbiːdəʊ, lɪˈbʌɪdəʊ/ ▸ noun (pl. **-os**) [mass noun] sexual desire: *loss of libido* | [count noun] *a deficient libido.*
■ Psychoanalysis the energy of the sexual drive as a component of the life instinct.
– DERIVATIVES **libidinal** adjective, **libidinally** adverb.
– ORIGIN early 20th cent.: from Latin, literally 'desire, lust'.

Li Bo /liː ˈbəʊ/ variant of LI PO.

LIBOR /ˈlʌɪbɔː/ ▸ abbreviation for London interbank offered rate, the basic rate of interest used in lending between banks on the London interbank market.

Libra /ˈliːbrə, ˈlɪb-, ˈlʌɪb-/ **1** Astronomy a small constellation (the Scales or Balance), said to represent the pair of scales which is the symbol of justice. It contains no bright stars.
■ [as genitive **Librae** /ˈliːbriː, ˈlɪb-, ˈlʌɪb-/] used with preceding letter or numeral to designate a star in this constellation: *the star Alpha Librae.*
2 Astrology the seventh sign of the zodiac, which the sun enters at the northern autumnal equinox (about 23 September).
■ (**a Libra**) a person born when the sun is in this sign.
– DERIVATIVES **Libran** noun & adjective (only in sense 2).
– ORIGIN Latin.

libra /ˈlʌɪbrə/ ▸ noun (pl. **librae** /ˈlʌɪbriː/) (in ancient Rome) a unit of weight, equivalent to 12 ounces (0.34 kg). It was the forerunner of the pound.
– ORIGIN Latin, 'pound, balance'.

librarian ▸ noun a person in charge of or assisting in a library.

– DERIVATIVES **librarianship** noun.
– ORIGIN late 17th cent. (denoting a scribe or copyist): from Latin *librarius* 'relating to books', (used as a noun) 'bookseller, scribe', + -AN.

library ▸ noun (pl. **-ies**) a building or room containing collections of books, periodicals, and sometimes films and recorded music for people to read, borrow, or refer to: *a school library* | [as modifier] *a library book.*
■ a collection of books and periodicals held in such a building or room: *the Institute houses an outstanding library of 35,000 volumes on the fine arts.* ■ a collection of films, recorded music, genetic material, etc., organized systematically and kept for research or borrowing: *a record library.* ■ a series of books, recordings, etc., issued by the same company and similar in appearance. ■ a room in a private house where books are kept. ■ (also **software library**) Computing a collection of programs and software packages made generally available, often loaded and stored on disk for immediate use.
– ORIGIN late Middle English: via Old French from Latin *libraria* 'bookshop', feminine (used as a noun) of *librarius* 'relating to books', from *liber, libr-* 'book'.

library edition ▸ noun an edition which is of large size and has good-quality print and binding, especially the standard edition of a writer's works.

Library of Congress the US national library, in Washington DC.

library school ▸ noun a college or a department in a university or polytechnic teaching librarianship.

library science ▸ noun [mass noun] the study of librarianship.

libration /lʌɪˈbreɪʃ(ə)n/ ▸ noun Astronomy an apparent or real oscillation of the moon, by which parts near the edge of the disc that are often not visible from the earth sometimes come into view.
– DERIVATIVES **librate** verb.
– ORIGIN early 17th cent. (denoting an oscillating motion, or equilibrium): from Latin *libratio(n-),* from the verb *librare,* from *libra* 'a balance'.

libretto /lɪˈbrɛtəʊ/ ▸ noun (pl. **libretti** /-ti/ or **librettos**) the text of an opera or other long vocal work.
– DERIVATIVES **librettist** noun.
– ORIGIN mid 18th cent.: from Italian, diminutive of *libro* 'book', from Latin *liber.*

Libreville /ˈliːbrəvɪl/ the capital of Gabon, a port on the Atlantic coast at the mouth of the Gabon river; pop. 352,000 (1992).

Librium /ˈlɪbrɪəm/ ▸ noun trademark for CHLORDIAZEPOXIDE.
– ORIGIN 1960s: of unknown origin.

Libya /ˈlɪbɪə/ a country in North Africa; pop. 4,714,000 (est. 1991); official language, Arabic; capital, Tripoli.
■ancient North Africa west of Egypt.

Much of Libya forms part of the Sahara Desert, with a narrow coastal plain bordering the Mediterranean; the country has major oil deposits. The area came under Turkish domination in the 16th century, was annexed by Italy in 1912, and became an independent kingdom in 1951.

– DERIVATIVES **Libyan** adjective & noun.

lice plural form of LOUSE.

licence (US **license**) ▸ noun a permit from an authority to own or use something, do a particular thing, or carry on a trade (especially in alcoholic liquor): *a gun licence* | [as modifier] *a television licence fee.*
■ [mass noun] formal or official permission to do something: *a subsidiary company continued to manufacture cranes under licence from a Norwegian firm.* ■ [mass noun] a writer's or artist's freedom to deviate from fact, or from conventions such as grammar, metre, or perspective, for effect: *artistic licence.* ■ [mass noun] freedom to behave as one wishes, especially in a way which results in excessive or unacceptable behaviour: *the government was criticized for giving the army too much licence.* ■ (**a licence to do something**) a reason or excuse to do something wrong or excessive: *police say that the lenient sentence is a licence to assault.*
– PHRASES **licence to print money** a very lucrative commercial activity, typically one perceived as requiring little effort.
– ORIGIN late Middle English: via Old French from Latin *licentia* 'freedom, licentiousness' (in medieval Latin 'authority, permission'), from *licere* 'be lawful or permitted'.

license (also **licence**) ▸ verb [with obj.] (often **be**

licensed) grant a licence to (someone or something) to permit the use of something or to allow an activity to take place: *all caravan sites had to be licensed before they could start operating* | [with obj. and infinitive] *he ought not to have been licensed to fly a plane* | [as adj. **licensing**] *a licensing authority*
■authorize the use, performance, or release of (something): *the company expect that the drug will be licensed for use in the USA within the next year* | *he was required to delete certain scenes before the film could be licensed for showing.* ■ dated give permission to ' (someone) to do something: [with obj. and infinitive] *he was licensed to do no more than send a message.*
– DERIVATIVES **licensable** adjective, **licenser** noun, **licensor** noun.
– ORIGIN late Middle English: from LICENCE. The spelling *-se* arose by analogy with pairs such as *practice, practise.*

licensed (also **licenced**) ▸ adjective having an official licence: *a licensed taxi operator.*
■(of premises) having a licence for the sale of alcoholic liquor: *a licensed restaurant.*

licensed victualler ▸ noun see VICTUALLER (sense 1).

licensee ▸ noun the holder of a licence, especially to sell alcoholic drinks.

license plate ▸ noun North American term for NUMBER PLATE.

licentiate /lʌɪˈsɛnʃɪət/ ▸ noun **1** the holder of a certificate of competence to practise a certain profession.
■(in certain universities, especially abroad) a degree between that of bachelor and master or doctor. ■ the holder of such a degree.
2 a licensed preacher not yet having an appointment, especially in a Presbyterian Church.
– DERIVATIVES **licentiateship** noun.
– ORIGIN late 15th cent.: from medieval Latin, noun use of *licentiatus* 'having freedom', based on *licentia* 'freedom'.

licentious /lʌɪˈsɛnʃəs/ ▸ adjective **1** promiscuous and unprincipled in sexual matters.
2 archaic disregarding accepted rules or conventions, especially in grammar or literary style.
– DERIVATIVES **licentiously** adverb, **licentiousness** noun.
– ORIGIN late Middle English: from Latin *licentiosus,* from *licentia* 'freedom'.

lichee ▸ noun variant spelling of LYCHEE.

lichen /ˈlʌɪk(ə)n, ˈlɪtʃ(ə)n/ ▸ noun **1** a simple slow-growing plant which typically forms a low crust-like, leaf-like, or branching growth on rocks, walls, and trees.

Lichens are composite plants consisting of a fungus that contains photosynthetic algal cells. Their classification is based upon that of the fungal partner, which in most cases belongs to the subdivision Ascomycotina, and the algal partners are either green algae or cyanobacteria. Lichens obtain their water and nutrients from the atmosphere and can be sensitive indicators of atmospheric pollution.

2 [mass noun] [usu. with modifier] a skin disease in which small round hard lesions occur close together.
– DERIVATIVES **lichened** adjective (in sense 1), **lichenology** noun (in sense 1), **lichenous** adjective (in sense 2).
– ORIGIN early 17th cent.: via Latin from Greek *leikhēn.*

Lichfield /ˈlɪtʃfiːld/ a town in central England, in Staffordshire north of Birmingham; pop. 25,740 (1981). It was the birthplace of Samuel Johnson.

licht /lɪxt/ ▸ noun, adjective, & verb Scottish variant of LIGHT[1], LIGHT[2].

Lichtenstein /ˈlɪktənˌstʌɪn/, Roy (1923–97), American painter and sculptor. A leading exponent of pop art, he became known for paintings inspired by comic strips. Notable works: *Whaam!* (1963).

licit /ˈlɪsɪt/ ▸ adjective not forbidden; lawful: *usage patterns differ between licit and illicit drugs.*
– DERIVATIVES **licitly** adverb.
– ORIGIN late 15th cent.: from Latin *licitus* 'allowed', from the verb *licere.*

lick ▸ verb [with obj.] **1** pass the tongue over (something), typically in order to taste, moisten, or clean it: *he licked the stamp and stuck it on the envelope* | [no obj.] *he licked at his damaged hand with his tongue.*
■[no obj., with adverbial of direction] figurative (of a flame, wave, or breeze) move lightly and quickly like a tongue: *the flames licked around the wood.*

2 informal defeat (someone) comprehensively: *all right Mary, I know when I'm licked.*
■ thrash: *she stands tall and could lick any man in the place.*
■ (**lick someone/thing down**) W. Indian cut or knock someone or something down.
▶ **noun 1** an act of licking something with the tongue: *Sammy gave his fingers a long lick.*
■ figurative a movement of flame, water, etc. resembling this.
2 informal a small amount or quick application of something, especially paint: *all she'd need to do to the kitchen was give it **a lick of** paint.*
3 (often **licks**) informal a short phrase or solo in jazz or popular music: *cool guitar licks.*
4 informal a smart blow: *his mother gave him several licks for daring to blaspheme.*
– PHRASES **at a lick** informal at a fast pace; with considerable speed. **a lick and a promise** informal a hasty performance of a task, especially of cleaning something. **lick someone's boots** (or vulgar slang **arse**) be excessively obsequious towards someone, especially to gain favour from them. **lick someone/thing into shape** see **SHAPE**. **lick one's lips** (or **chops**) look forward to something with eager anticipation. **lick one's wounds** retire to recover one's strength or confidence after a defeat or humiliating experience: *the political organization he worked for was licking its wounds after electoral defeat.*
– DERIVATIVES **licker** noun [usu. in combination].
– ORIGIN Old English *liccian*, of West Germanic origin; related to Dutch *likken* and German *lecken*, from an Indo-European root shared by Greek *leikhein* and Latin *lingere*.

lickerish /ˈlɪkərɪʃ/ ▶ **adjective 1** lecherous: *a barrage of lickerish grins and dirty jokes.*
2 W. Indian or archaic fond of eating; greedy.
– DERIVATIVES **lickerishly** adverb.
– ORIGIN late 15th cent.: alteration of obsolete *lickerous*, in the same sense, from an Anglo-Norman French variant of Old French *lecheros* (see **LECHEROUS**).

lickety-split ▶ **adverb** N. Amer. informal as quickly as possible; immediately: *I took off lickety-split across the lawn.*
– ORIGIN early 19th cent. (in the phrase *as fast as lickety* 'at full speed'): from a fanciful extension of **LICK** + the verb **SPLIT**.

lick hole ▶ **noun** Austral. a salt lick, or a place where a block of salt is placed for stock to lick.

licking ▶ **noun** informal a heavy defeat or beating.

lickspittle ▶ **noun** a person who behaves obsequiously to those in power.

licorice ▶ **noun** US spelling of **LIQUORICE**.

lictor /ˈlɪktə/ ▶ **noun** (in ancient Rome) an officer attending the consul or other magistrate, bearing the fasces, and executing sentence on offenders.
– ORIGIN Latin, perhaps related to *ligare* 'to bind'.

lid ▶ **noun** a removable or hinged cover for the top of a container: *a large frying pan with a lid | a dustbin lid.*
■ (usu. **lids**) an eyelid: *eyes now hooded beneath heavy lids.* ■ the top crust of a pie. ■ Botany the operculum of a moss capsule. ■ informal a hat, especially a motorcyclist's crash helmet.
– PHRASES **keep a** (or **the**) **lid on** informal keep (an emotion or process) from going out of control: *she was no longer able to keep the lid on her simmering anger.* ■ keep secret: *she keeps a very tight lid on her own private life.* **put a** (or **the**) **lid on** informal put a stop to or be the culmination of: *it's time to put the lid on all the talk.* **take** (or **lift**) **the lid off** (or **lift the lid on**) informal reveal unwelcome secrets about.
– DERIVATIVES **lidded** adjective, **lidless** adjective.
– ORIGIN Old English *hlid*, of Germanic origin, from a base meaning 'cover'; related to Dutch *lid*.

lidar /ˈlʌɪdɑː/ ▶ **noun** [mass noun] a detection system which works on the principle of radar, but uses light from a laser.
– ORIGIN 1960s: blend of **LIGHT**[1] and **RADAR**.

Liddell /ˈlɪd(ə)l/, Eric (Henry) (1902–45), British athlete and missionary, born in China. In the 1924 Olympic Games he won the 400 metres in a world record time. His exploits were celebrated in the film *Chariots of Fire* (1981).

Liddell Hart /ˌlɪd(ə)l ˈhɑːt/, Sir Basil Henry (1895–1970), British military historian and theorist. He developed principles of mobile warfare, which were adopted by both sides in the Second World War.

Lidingö /ˈliːdɪŋəː/ an island suburb of Stockholm in Sweden, in the north-east of the city; pop. 38,400 (1990).

Lido /ˈliːdəʊ/ **1** an island reef off the coast of NE Italy, in the northern Adriatic. It separates the Lagoon of Venice from the Gulf of Venice. Full name **LIDO DI MALAMOCCO** /dɪ ˌmaləˈmɒkəʊ/.
2 (also **the Lido**) a town and beach resort in NE Italy, on the Lido reef opposite Venice; pop. 20,950 (1980).

lido /ˈliːdəʊ, ˈlʌɪ-/ ▶ **noun** (pl. **-os**) a public open-air swimming pool or bathing beach.
– ORIGIN late 17th cent.: from Italian *Lido*, the name of a bathing beach near Venice, from *lido* 'shore', from Latin *litus*.

lidocaine /ˈlɪdə(ʊ)keɪn/ ▶ **noun** chiefly N. Amer. another term for **LIGNOCAINE**.
– ORIGIN 1940s: from (*acetani*)*lid*(*e*) + *-caine* (from **COCAINE**).

Lie /liː/, Trygve Halvdan (1896–1968), Norwegian Labour politician, first Secretary General of the United Nations 1946–53.

lie[1] ▶ **verb** (**lying**; past **lay**; past participle **lain**) [no obj., with adverbial] **1** (of a person or animal) be in or assume a horizontal or resting position on a supporting surface: *the body of a man lay face downwards on the grass | I had to **lie down** for two hours because I was groggy | Lily lay back on the pillows and watched him.*
■ (of a thing) rest flat on a surface: *a book lay open on the table.* ■ (of a dead person) be buried in a particular place.
2 be, remain, or be kept in a specified state: *the abbey lies in ruins today | putting homeless families into private houses that would otherwise lie empty.*
■ (of something abstract) reside or be found: *the solution lies in a return to 'traditional family values'.*
3 (of a place) be situated in a specified position or direction: *the small village of Kexby lies about five miles due east of York.*
■ (of a competitor or team) be in a specified position during a competition or within a group: *United, currently lying in fifth place, have recovered after a shaky start.* ■ (of a scene) extend from the observer's viewpoint in a specified direction: *stand here, and all of Amsterdam lies before you.*
4 Law (of an action, charge, or claim) be admissible or sustainable.
▶ **noun** (usu. **the lie**) the way, direction, or position in which something lies: *he was familiarizing himself with **the lie of** the streets.*
■ Golf the position in which a golf ball comes to rest, especially as regards the ease of the next shot. ■ the lair or place of cover of an animal or a bird.
– PHRASES **let something lie** take no action regarding a controversial or problematic matter. **lie heavy on one** cause one to feel troubled or uncomfortable. **lie in state** (of the corpse of a person of national importance) be laid in a public place of honour before burial. **lie in wait** conceal oneself, waiting to surprise, attack, or catch someone. **lie low** (especially of a criminal) keep out of sight; avoid detection or attention: *at the time of the murder he appears to have been lying low in a barn.* **the lie** (N. Amer. **lay**) **of the land** the way in which an area's features or characteristics present themselves. ■ figurative the current situation or state of affairs: *she was beginning to see the lie of the land with her in-laws.* **take something lying down** [usu. with negative] accept an insult, setback, rebuke, etc. without reacting or protesting.
– ORIGIN Old English *licgan*, of Germanic origin; related to Dutch *liggen* and German *liegen*, from an Indo-European root shared by Greek *lektron*, *lekhos* and Latin *lectus* 'bed'.

USAGE The verb **lie** is often confused with the verb **lay**, giving rise to incorrect uses such as *he is **laying** on the bed* (correct use is *he is **lying** on the bed*) or *why don't you **lie** it on the bed?* (correct use is *why don't you **lay** it on the bed?*). See **usage** at **LAY**[1].

▶ **lie ahead** be going to happen; be in store: *I'm excited by what lies ahead.*
lie around/about (of an object) be left carelessly out of place: *I became irritated at the pills and potions lying around in every corner of the house.* ■ (of a person) pass the time lazily or aimlessly: *you all just lay around all day on your backsides, didn't you?*
lie behind be the real, often hidden, reason for (something): *a subtle strategy lies behind such silly claims.*
lie in Brit. remain in bed after the normal time for getting up. ■ archaic (of a pregnant woman) go to bed to give birth.
lie off Nautical (of a ship) stand some distance from shore or from another ship.
lie over US break one's journey: *Steven and I will lie over in New York, then fly to London.*
lie to Nautical (of a ship) come almost to a stop with its head towards the wind.
lie up (of a ship) go into dock or be out of commission. ■ (**lie something up**) put a boat in dock or out of commission.
lie with 1 (of a responsibility or problem) be attributable to (someone): *the ultimate responsibility for the violence lies with the country's president.* **2** archaic have sexual intercourse with.

lie[2] ▶ **noun** an intentionally false statement: *Mungo felt a pang of shame at **telling** Alice **a lie** | the whole thing is **a pack of lies**.*
■ used with reference to a situation involving deception or founded on a mistaken impression: *all their married life she had been **living a lie**.*
▶ **verb** (**lies**, **lied**, **lying**) [no obj.] tell a lie or lies: *why had Ashenden lied about his visit to London? |* [with direct speech] *'I am sixty-five,' she lied.*
■ (**lie one's way into/out of**) get oneself into or out of a situation by lying: *you lied your way on to this voyage by implying you were an experienced crew.* ■ (of a thing) present a false impression; be deceptive: *the camera cannot lie.*
– PHRASES **give the lie to** serve to show that (something seemingly apparent or previously stated or believed) is not true: *these figures give the lie to the notion that Britain is excessively strike-ridden.* **I tell a lie** (or **that's a lie**) informal an expression used to correct oneself immediately when one realizes that one has made an incorrect remark: *I never used to dream—I tell a lie, I did dream when I was little.* **lie through one's teeth** informal tell an outright lie without remorse.
– ORIGIN Old English *lyge* (noun), *lēogan* (verb), of Germanic origin; related to Dutch *liegen* and German *lügen*.

Liebchen /ˈliːbtʃ(ə)n, German ˈliːpçən/ ▶ **noun** a person who is very dear to another (often used as a term of endearment).
– ORIGIN German, diminutive of *lieb* 'dear'.

Liebfraumilch /ˈliːbfraʊˌmɪlʃ, German ˈliːpfraʊˌmɪlç/ ▶ **noun** [mass noun] a light white wine from the Rhine region.
– ORIGIN German, from *lieb* 'dear' + *Frau* 'lady' (referring to the Virgin Mary, patroness of the convent where it was first made) + *Milch* 'milk'.

Liebig /ˈliːbɪx, German ˈliːbɪç/, Justus von, Baron (1803–73), German chemist and teacher. With Friedrich Wöhler he discovered the benzoyl radical, and demonstrated that such radicals were groups of atoms that remained unchanged in many chemical reactions.

Liechtenstein /ˈlɪktənˌstʌɪn, German ˈlɪçtnˌʃtaɪn/ a small independent principality in the Alps, between Switzerland and Austria; pop. 28,880 (1990); official language, German; capital, Vaduz.

The principality was created in 1719 within the Holy Roman Empire, becoming independent of the German confederation in 1866. Liechtenstein is economically integrated with Switzerland.

– DERIVATIVES **Liechtensteiner** noun.

lied /liːd, -t/ ▶ **noun** (pl. **lieder** /ˈliːdə/) a type of German song, especially of the Romantic period, typically for solo voice with piano accompaniment.
– ORIGIN from German *Lied*.

lie detector ▶ **noun** an instrument for determining whether a person is telling the truth by testing for physiological changes considered to be associated with lying, but generally not accepted for judicial purposes. Compare with **POLYGRAPH**.

lie-down ▶ **noun** chiefly Brit. a short rest in which one lies down on a bed, sofa, etc.: *he felt badly in need of a lie-down.*

lief /liːf/ ▶ **adverb** (**as lief**) archaic as happily; as gladly: *he would just as lief eat a pincushion.*
– ORIGIN Old English *lēof* 'dear, pleasant', of Germanic origin: related to **LEAVE**[2] and **LOVE**.

Liège /lɪˈɛʒ, French ljɛʒ/ a province of eastern Belgium. Formerly ruled by independent prince-bishops, it became a part of the Netherlands in 1815 and of Belgium in 1830. Flemish name **LUIK**.
■ its capital city; pop. 194,600 (1991).

liege /liːdʒ/ historical ▶ **adjective** [attrib.] concerned with or relating to the relationship between a feudal superior and a vassal: *an oath of fealty and **liege** homage.*

▶ **noun** (also **liege lord**) a feudal superior or sovereign. ■ a vassal or subject: *the king's lieges.*

– ORIGIN Middle English: via Old French *lige, liege* from medieval Latin *laeticus*, probably of Germanic origin.

liegeman ▶ **noun** (pl. **-men**) historical a vassal who owes feudal service or allegiance to a nobleman.

lie-in ▶ **noun** chiefly Brit. a prolonged stay in bed in the morning.

lien /liːn, ˈliːən, ˈlʌɪən/ ▶ **noun** Law a right to keep possession of property belonging to another person until a debt owed by that person is discharged.

– ORIGIN mid 16th cent.: from French, via Old French *loien* from Latin *ligamen* 'bond', from *ligare* 'to bind'.

lierne /lɪˈəːn/ ▶ **noun** [usu. as modifier] Architecture (in vaulting) a short rib connecting the bosses and intersections of the principal ribs: *a fine lierne vault.*

– ORIGIN late Middle English: from French, perhaps a transferred use of dialect *lierne* (standard French *liane*) 'clematis'.

lieu /ljuː, luː/ ▶ **noun** (in phrase **in lieu**) instead: *the company issued additional shares to shareholders **in lieu** of a cash dividend.*

– ORIGIN Middle English: via French from Latin *locus* 'place'.

Lieut. ▶ **abbreviation for** Lieutenant.

lieutenant /lɛfˈtɛnənt/ ▶ **noun** a deputy or substitute acting for a superior: *two of Lenin's leading lieutenants.*

■ a rank of officer in the British army, above second lieutenant and below captain. ■ a rank of officer in the navy, above sub lieutenant and below lieutenant commander. ■ (in the US) a police officer next in rank below captain. ■ informal the adult assistant leader of a company of Guides, officially termed **Assistant Guide Guider** since 1968.

– DERIVATIVES **lieutenancy** noun (pl. **-ies**).

– ORIGIN late Middle English: from Old French (see **LIEU, TENANT**).

> **USAGE** In the normal British pronunciation of **lieutenant** the first syllable sounds like **lef-**. In the standard US pronunciation the first syllable, in contrast, rhymes with **do**. It is difficult to explain where the **f** in the British pronunciation comes from. Probably, at some point before the 19th century, the **u** at the end of Old French **lieu** was read and pronounced as a **v**, and the **v** later became an **f**.

lieutenant colonel ▶ **noun** a rank of officer in the army and the US air force, above major and below colonel.

lieutenant commander ▶ **noun** a rank of officer in the navy, above lieutenant and below commander.

lieutenant general ▶ **noun** a high rank of officer in the army, above major general and below general.

lieutenant governor ▶ **noun** the acting or deputy governor of a state or province, under a governor or Governor General.

– DERIVATIVES **lieutenant governorship** noun.

Lieutenant of the Tower ▶ **noun** (in the UK) the acting commandant of the Tower of London.

life ▶ **noun** (pl. **lives**) **1** [mass noun] the condition that distinguishes animals and plants from inorganic matter, including the capacity for growth, reproduction, functional activity, and continual change preceding death: *the origins of life.*

■ living things and their activity: *some sort of life existed on Mars | lower forms of life | the ice-cream vendors were the only signs of life.* ■ the state of being alive as a human being: *she didn't want to die; she loved life | a superficial world where life revolved around the minutiae of outward appearance.* ■ [with adj. or noun modifier] a particular type or aspect of people's existence: *an experienced teacher will help you settle into school life | revelations about his private life.* ■ vitality, vigour, or energy: *she was beautiful and full of life.*

2 the existence of an individual human being or animal: *a disaster that claimed the lives of 266 Americans.*

■ [often with adj. or noun modifier] a way of living: *his father decided to start a new life in California.* ■ a biography: *a life of Shelley.* ■ either of the two states of a person's existence separated by death (as in Christianity and some other religious traditions): *too much happiness in this life could reduce the chances of salvation in the next.* ■ any of a number of successive existences in which a soul is held to be reincarnated (as in Hinduism and some other religious traditions). ■ a chance to live after narrowly escaping death (especially with reference to the nine lives traditionally attributed to cats). ■ (in various games, especially card games) one of a specified number of chances each player has before being put out.

3 (usu. **one's life**) the period between the birth and death of a living thing, especially a human being: *she has lived all her life in the country | I want to be with you for the rest of my life | they became friends **for life**.*

■ the period during which something inanimate or abstract continues to exist, function, or be valid: *underlay helps to prolong the life of a carpet.* ■ [mass noun] informal a sentence of imprisonment for life.

4 [mass noun] (in art) the depiction of a subject from a real model, rather than from an artist's imagination: *the pose and clothing were sketched **from life** | [as modifier] life drawing.* See also **STILL LIFE**.

– PHRASES **bring** (or **come**) **to life** regain or cause to regain consciousness or return as if from death: *all this was of great interest to her, as if she were coming to life after a long sleep.* ■ (with reference to a fictional character or inanimate object) cause or seem to be alive or real: *he brings the character of MacDonald to life with power and precision | all the puppets came to life again.* ■ make or become active, lively, or interesting: *soon, with the return of the peasants and fishermen, the village comes to life again | you can bring any room to life with these coordinating cushions.* **do anything for a quiet life** make any concession to avoid being disturbed. **for dear** (or **one's**) **life** as if or in order to escape death: *I clung on to the tree for dear life | Sue struggled free and ran for her life.* **for the life of me** [with modal and negative] informal however hard I try; even if my life depended on it: *I can't for the life of me understand what it is you see in that place.* **frighten the life out of** terrify. **get a life** [often in imperative] informal start living a fuller or more interesting existence: *if he's a waster then get yourself out of there and get a life.* **give one's life for** die for. **(as) large as life** informal used to emphasize that a person is conspicuously present: *he was standing nearby, large as life.* **larger than life** (of a person) attracting special attention because of unusual and flamboyant appearance or behaviour. ■ (of a thing) seeming disproportionately important: *your problems seem larger than life at that time of night.* **life and limb** see **LIMB**[1]. **the life and soul of the party** a vivacious and sociable person. **life in the fast lane** informal an exciting and eventful lifestyle, especially one bringing wealth and success. **one's life's work** the work (especially that of an academic or artistic nature) accomplished in or pursued throughout someone's lifetime. **lose one's life** be killed: *he lost his life in a car accident.* **a matter of life and death** a matter of vital importance. **not on your life** informal said to emphasize one's refusal to comply with a request: *'I want to see Clare alone'. 'Not on your life,' said Buzz.* **save someone's** (or **one's own**) **life** prevent someone's (or one's own) death: *the driver of the train managed to save his life by leaping out of the cab.* ■ informal provide much-needed relief from boredom or a difficult situation. **see life** gain a wide experience of the world, especially its more pleasurable aspects. **take one's life in one's hands** risk being killed. **take someone's** (or **one's own**) **life** kill someone (or oneself). **that's life** an expression of one's acceptance of a situation, however difficult: *we'll miss each other, but still, that's life.* **this is the life** an expression of contentment with one's present circumstances: *Ice cubes clinked in crystal glasses. 'This is the life,' she said.* **to the life** exactly like the original: *there he was, Nathan to the life, sitting at a table.* **to save one's life** [with modal and negative] even if one's life were to depend on it: *she couldn't stop crying now to save her life.*

– ORIGIN Old English *līf*, of Germanic origin; related to Dutch *lijf*, German *Leib* 'body', also to **LIVE**[1].

life-and-death ▶ **adjective** deciding whether someone lives or dies; vitally important.

life assurance ▶ **noun** chiefly Brit. another term for **LIFE INSURANCE**.

> **USAGE** There is a technical distinction between **life assurance** and **life insurance**: see **usage** at **ASSURANCE**.

lifebelt ▶ **noun** chiefly Brit. a ring of buoyant or inflatable material used to help a person who has fallen into water to stay afloat.

lifeblood ▶ **noun** [mass noun] poetic/literary the blood, as being necessary to life.

■ figurative the indispensable factor or influence that gives something its strength and vitality: *the movement of coal was the lifeblood of British railways.*

lifeboat ▶ **noun** a specially constructed boat launched from land to rescue people in distress at sea.

■ a small boat kept on a ship for use in emergency, typically one of a number on deck or suspended from davits.

– DERIVATIVES **lifeboatman** noun (pl. **-men**).

lifebuoy ▶ **noun** chiefly Brit. a buoyant support such as a lifebelt for keeping a person afloat in water.

life cycle ▶ **noun** the series of changes in the life of an organism including reproduction.

life expectancy ▶ **noun** the average period that a person may expect to live.

life force ▶ **noun** [mass noun] the force or influence that gives something its vitality or strength: *the passionate life force of the symphony.*

■ the spirit or energy which animates living creatures; the soul.

life form ▶ **noun** any living thing.

life-giving ▶ **adjective** sustaining or revitalizing life: *the life-giving water of baptism.*

lifeguard ▶ **noun** an expert swimmer employed to rescue bathers who get into difficulty at a beach or swimming pool.

Life Guards ▶ **plural noun** (in the UK) a regiment of the Household Cavalry.

life history ▶ **noun** the series of changes undergone by an organism during its lifetime.

■ the story of a person's life, especially when told at tedious length.

life imprisonment ▶ **noun** [mass noun] a long term of imprisonment, which (in the UK) is now the only sentence for murder and the maximum for any crime. It is indeterminate in length, and in practice is rarely for the whole of a criminal's remaining life.

life instinct ▶ **noun** Psychoanalysis an innate desire for self-preservation, manifest in hunger, self-defensive aggression, and the sexual instincts. Compare with **DEATH INSTINCT**.

life insurance ▶ **noun** [mass noun] insurance that pays out a sum of money either on the death of the insured person or after a set period.

> **USAGE** There is a technical distinction between **life insurance** and **life assurance**: see **usage** at **ASSURANCE**.

life interest ▶ **noun** [mass noun] Law a right to property that a person holds for life but cannot dispose of further.

life jacket ▶ **noun** a sleeveless buoyant or inflatable jacket for keeping a person afloat in water.

lifeless ▶ **adjective** dead or apparently dead: *his lifeless body was taken from the river.*

■ lacking vigour, vitality, or excitement: *my hair always seems to look lank and lifeless.* ■ devoid of living things.

– DERIVATIVES **lifelessly** adverb, **lifelessness** noun.

– ORIGIN Old English *līflēas* (see **LIFE, -LESS**).

lifelike ▶ **adjective** very similar to the person or thing represented: *the artist had etched a lifelike horse.*

– DERIVATIVES **lifelikeness** noun.

lifeline ▶ **noun 1** a rope or line used for life-saving, typically one thrown to rescue someone in difficulties in water or one used by sailors to secure themselves to a boat.

■ a line used by a diver for sending signals to the surface. ■ figurative a thing which is essential for the continued existence of someone or something or which provides a means of escape from a difficult situation: *fertility treatment can seem like a lifeline to childless couples.* ■ Brit. an emergency telephone counselling service.

2 (in palmistry) a line on the palm of a person's hand, regarded as indicating how long they will live.

– PHRASES **throw a lifeline to** (or **throw someone a lifeline**) provide (someone) with a means of escaping from a difficult situation.

life list ▶ **noun** Ornithology a list of all the kinds of birds observed by a person during his or her life.

lifelong ▶ **adjective** lasting or remaining in a particular state throughout a person's life: *the two* *men were to remain lifelong friends | a lifelong Conservative.*

life member ▶ **noun** a person who has lifelong membership of a society.
– DERIVATIVES **life membership** noun.

life office ▶ **noun** an office or company dealing in life insurance.

life peer ▶ **noun** (in the UK) a peer whose title cannot be inherited.
– DERIVATIVES **life peerage** noun.

life peeress ▶ **noun** a woman holding a life peerage.

life policy ▶ **noun** a life insurance policy.

life preserver ▶ **noun 1** Brit. a short truncheon with a heavily loaded end.
2 N. Amer. a buoyant apparatus such as a lifebelt or life jacket to keep someone afloat in water.

lifer ▶ **noun 1** informal a person serving a life sentence.
2 N. Amer. a person who spends their life in a particular career, especially in one of the armed forces.

life raft ▶ **noun** a raft, typically inflatable, for use in an emergency at sea.

life ring ▶ **noun** another term for **LIFEBELT**.

lifesaver ▶ **noun 1** informal a thing that saves one from serious difficulty: *a microwave oven could be a lifesaver this Christmas.*
2 (also **surf lifesaver**) Austral./NZ a lifeguard working on a beach.

life sciences ▶ **plural noun** the sciences concerned with the study of living organisms, including biology, botany, zoology, microbiology, physiology, biochemistry, and related subjects. Often contrasted with **PHYSICAL SCIENCES**.
– DERIVATIVES **life scientist** noun.

life sentence ▶ **noun** a punishment of life imprisonment or of imprisonment for a specified long period, e.g. (in Canada) 25 years. A judge may recommend the minimum period before a prisoner may be considered for parole.

life-size (also **life-sized**) ▶ **adjective** of the same size as the person or thing represented: *a life-size model of a discus-thrower.*

lifespan ▶ **noun** the length of time for which a person or animal lives or a thing functions: *the human lifespan.*

lifestyle ▶ **noun** the way in which a person or group lives: *the benefits of a healthy lifestyle.*
■ [as modifier] denoting advertising or products designed to appeal to a consumer by association with a desirable lifestyle.

life support ▶ **noun** [mass noun] Medicine maintenance of vital functions following disablement or in an adverse environment: [as modifier] *a life-support machine.*
■ informal equipment in a hospital used for this: *a patient on life support.*

life table ▶ **noun** a table of statistics relating to life expectancy and mortality for a given category of people.
■ Zoology a similar table for a population of animals divided into cohorts of given age.

life-threatening ▶ **adjective** (especially of an illness or injury) potentially fatal.

lifetime ▶ **noun** the duration of a person's life: *a reward for a lifetime's work.*
■ the duration of a thing's existence or usefulness: *it may well take the lifetime of a Parliament to put things right.* ■ informal used to express the view that a period is very long: *five weeks was a lifetime, anything could have happened.*
– PHRASES **of a lifetime** (of a chance or experience) such as does not occur more than once in a person's life: *because of Frankie she had rejected the opportunity of a lifetime.*

lifeworld ▶ **noun** Philosophy all the immediate experiences, activities, and contacts that make up the world of an individual or corporate life.
– ORIGIN 1940s: translating German *Lebenswelt*.

Liffey /ˈlɪfi/ a river of eastern Ireland, which flows for 80 km (50 miles) from the Wicklow Mountains to Dublin Bay. The city of Dublin is situated at its mouth.

Lifford /ˈlɪfəd/ the county town of Donegal, in the Republic of Ireland; pop. 1,460 (1986).

LIFO /ˈlʌɪfəʊ/ ▶ **abbreviation for** last in, first out (chiefly with reference to methods of stock valuation and data storage). Compare with **FIFO**.

lift ▶ **verb 1** [with obj.] raise to a higher position or level: *he lifted his trophy over his head.*
■ move (one's eyes or face) to face upwards and look at someone or something: *he lifted his eyes for an instant.* ■ increase the volume or pitch of (one's voice): *Willie sang boldly, **lifting up** his voice.* ■ increase (a price or amount): *the building society lifted its interest rates by 0.75 of a point.* ■ [with obj. and adverbial] transport by air: *a helicopter lifted 11 crew to safety from the ship.* ■ [no obj.] move upwards; be raised: *Thomas's eyelids drowsily lifted | their voices lifted in wails and cries.* ■ [no obj.] (of a cloud, fog, etc.) move upwards or away: *the factory smoke hung low, never lifted | the grey weather lifted on the following Wednesday.* ■ perform cosmetic surgery on (especially the face or breasts) to reduce sagging: *surgeons lift and remove excess skin from the face and neck.* ■ dig up (something, especially root vegetables at harvest).
2 [with obj. and adverbial of direction] pick up and move to a different position: *he lifted her down from the pony's back.*
■ figurative enable (someone or something) to escape from a particular state of mind or situation, especially an unpleasant one: *two billion barrels of oil that could **lift** this nation **out of** chronic poverty.* ■ improve the rank or position of (a person or team): *this victory lifted United into third place.* ■ carry off or win (a prize or event): *she staged a magnificent comeback to lift the British Open title.*
3 [with obj.] raise (a person's spirits or confidence); encourage or cheer: *we heard inspiring talks which lifted our spirits.*
■ [no obj.] (of a person's mood) become happier: *suddenly his heart lifted and he could have wept with relief.*
4 [with obj.] formally remove or end (a legal restriction, decision, or ban): *the European Community lifted its oil embargo against South Africa.*
5 [with obj.] informal steal (something, especially a minor item of property): *the shirt she had lifted from a supermarket.*
■ use (a person's work or ideas) without permission or acknowledgement: *this is a hackneyed adventure lifted straight from a vintage Lassie episode.* ■ arrest: *that night the army came and lifted Buckley.*
▶ **noun 1** something that is used for lifting, in particular:
■ Brit. a platform or compartment housed in a shaft for raising and lowering people or things to different floors or levels. ■ a device incorporating a moving cable for carrying people, typically skiers, up or down a mountain. ■ a built-up heel or device worn in a boot or shoe to make the wearer appear taller or to correct shortening of a leg.
2 an act of lifting: *weightlifters attempting a particularly heavy lift.*
■ a rise in price or amount: *the company has already produced a 10 per cent lift in profits.* ■ an increase in volume or pitch of a person's speaking voice. ■ informal an instance of stealing or plagiarizing something. ■ [mass noun] upward force that counteracts the force of gravity, produced by changing the direction and speed of a moving stream of air: *it had separate engines to provide lift and generate forward speed.* ■ the maximum weight that an aircraft can raise. ■ [mass noun] Cricket the tendency of a ball bowled to rise sharply on bouncing.
3 a free ride in another person's vehicle: *Miss Green is giving me a lift back to school.*
4 [in sing.] a feeling of encouragement or increased cheerfulness: *winning this match has **given** everyone at the club **a lift**.*
– PHRASES **lift a finger** (or **hand**) [usu. with negative] make the slightest effort to do something, especially to help someone: *he never once lifted a finger to get Jimmy released from prison.* **lift his** (or **its**) **leg** informal (of a male dog) urinate.
– DERIVATIVES **liftable** adjective, **lifter** noun.
– ORIGIN Middle English: from Old Norse *lypta*, of Germanic origin; related to **LOFT**.
▶ **lift off** (of an aircraft, spacecraft, or rocket) rise from the ground or a launch pad, especially vertically.

lift-off ▶ **noun** take-off, especially the vertical take-off of a spacecraft, rocket, or helicopter.

lift pump ▶ **noun** a simple pump consisting of a piston moving in a cylinder, both parts incorporating a valve.

lig Brit. informal ▶ **verb** (**ligged**, **ligging**) [no obj.] take advantage of free parties, travel, or other benefits offered by companies for publicity purposes.
▶ **noun** a free party or show provided for publicity.
– DERIVATIVES **ligger** noun.
– ORIGIN 1960s: from a dialect variant of **LIE**[1], literally 'lie about, loaf', whence 'freeload'.

ligament /ˈlɪɡəm(ə)nt/ ▶ **noun** Anatomy a short band of tough, flexible fibrous connective tissue which connects two bones or cartilages or holds together a joint.
■ a membranous fold that supports an organ and keeps it in position. ■ any similar connecting or binding structure. ■ archaic a bond of union.
– DERIVATIVES **ligamental** adjective, **ligamentary** adjective, **ligamentous** adjective.
– ORIGIN late Middle English: from Latin *ligamentum* 'bond', from *ligare* 'to bind'.

ligand /ˈlɪɡ(ə)nd/ ▶ **noun** Chemistry an ion or molecule attached to a metal atom by coordinate bonding.
■ Biochemistry a molecule that binds to another (usually larger) molecule.
– ORIGIN 1950s: from Latin *ligandus* 'that can be tied', gerundive of *ligare* 'to bind'.

ligase /ˈlɪɡeɪz/ ▶ **noun** Biochemistry an enzyme which brings about ligation of DNA or another substance.
– ORIGIN 1960s: from Latin *ligare* 'to bind' + **-ASE**.

ligate /lɪˈɡeɪt/ ▶ **verb** [with obj.] (usu. **be ligated**) Surgery tie up (an artery or vessel).
– ORIGIN late 16th cent.: from Latin *ligat-* 'tied', from the verb *ligare*.

ligation ▶ **noun** [mass noun] **1** the surgical procedure of tying a ligature tightly around a blood vessel or other duct or tube in the body.
2 Biochemistry the joining of two DNA strands or other molecules by a phosphate ester linkage.
– ORIGIN late Middle English: from late Latin *ligatio(n-)*, from the verb *ligare* (see **LIGATE**).

ligature /ˈlɪɡətʃə/ ▶ **noun 1** a thing used for tying or binding something tightly.
■ a cord or thread used in surgery, especially to tie up a bleeding artery.
2 Music a slur or tie.
3 Printing a character consisting of two or more joined letters, e.g. *æ*, *fl*.
■ a stroke that joins adjacent letters in writing or printing.
▶ **verb** [with obj.] bind or connect with a ligature.
– ORIGIN Middle English: via late Latin *ligatura* from Latin *ligat-* 'bound', from the verb *ligare*.

liger /ˈlʌɪɡə/ ▶ **noun** the hybrid offspring of a male lion and a tigress. Compare with **TIGON**.
– ORIGIN 1930s: blend of **LION** and **TIGER**.

Ligeti /ˈlɪɡəti/, György Sándor (b.1923), Hungarian composer. His orchestral works *Apparitions* (1958–9) and *Atmosphères* (1961) dispense with the formal elements of melody, harmony, and rhythm.

light[1] ▶ **noun 1** [mass noun] the natural agent that stimulates sight and makes things visible: *the light of the sun | [in sing.] the lamps in the street shed a faint light into the room.*
■ [count noun] a source of illumination, especially an electric lamp: *a light came on in his room.* ■ (**lights**) decorative illuminations: *Christmas lights.* ■ [count noun] (usu. **lights**) a traffic light: *turn right at the lights.* ■ [in sing.] an expression in someone's eyes indicating a particular emotion or mood: *a shrewd light entered his eyes.* ■ the amount or quality of light in a place: *the plant requires good light | [count noun] in some lights she could look beautiful.* ■ Law the light falling on the windows of a house. See **ANCIENT LIGHTS**.

Visible light is electromagnetic radiation whose wavelength falls within the range to which the human retina responds, i.e. between about 390 nm (violet light) and 740 nm (red). White light consists of a roughly equal mixture of all visible wavelengths, which can be separated to yield the colours of the spectrum, as was first demonstrated conclusively by Newton. In the 20th century it has become apparent that light consists of energy quanta called photons which behave partly like waves and partly like particles. The velocity of light in a vacuum is 299,792 km per second.

2 [mass noun] understanding of a problem or mystery; enlightenment: *she saw light dawn on the woman's face.*
■ spiritual illumination by divine truth. ■ (**lights**) a person's opinions, standards, and abilities: *leaving the police to do the job **according to their lights**.*
3 an area of something that is brighter or paler than its surroundings: *sunshine will brighten the natural lights in your hair.*
4 a device used to produce a flame or spark: *he asked me for a light.*
5 a window or opening in a wall to let light in.
■ any of the perpendicular divisions of a mullioned window. ■ any of the panes of glass forming the roof or side of a greenhouse or the top of a cold frame.

b **but** | d **dog** | f **few** | g **get** | h **he** | j **yes** | k **cat** | l **leg** | m **man** | n **no** | p **pen** | r **red** | s **sit** | t **top** | v **voice** | w **we** | z **zoo** | ʃ **she** | ʒ deci**sion** | θ **thin** | ð **this** | ŋ ri**ng** | x lo**ch** | tʃ **chip** | dʒ **jar**

6 a person notable or eminent in a particular sphere of activity or place: *such lights of Liberalism as the historian Goldwin Smith.*
7 Brit. (in a crossword puzzle) a blank space to be filled by a letter.
▶**verb** (past **lit**; past participle **lit** or **lighted**) [with obj.] **1** provide with light or lighting; illuminate: *the room was lit by a number of small lamps | lightning suddenly* **lit up** *the house.*
▪switch on (an electric light): *only one of the table lamps was lit.* ▪[with obj. and adverbial] provide a light for (someone) so that they can see where they are going: *I'll light you down to the gate.* ▪[no obj.] (**light up**) become illuminated: *the sign to fasten seat belts lit up.*
2 make (something) start burning; ignite: *Alan gathered sticks and lit a fire |* [as adj. **lighted** or **lit**] *a lit cigarette.*
▪[no obj.] begin to burn; be ignited: *the gas wouldn't light properly.* ▪(**light something up**) ignite a cigarette, cigar, or pipe and begin to smoke it: *she lit up a cigarette and puffed on it serenely |* [no obj.] *workers who light up in prohibited areas face dismissal.*
▶**adjective 1** having a considerable or sufficient amount of natural light; not dark: *the bedrooms are light and airy | it was almost light outside.*
2 (of a colour) pale: *her eyes were light blue.*
– PHRASES **bring** (or **come**) **to light** make (or become) widely known or evident: *an investigation to bring to light examples of extravagant expenditure.* **go out like a light** informal fall asleep or lose consciousness suddenly. **in a —— light** in the way specified; so as to give a specified impression: *the audit portrayed the company in a very favourable light.* **in the light of** (or N. Amer. **in light of**) drawing knowledge or information from; taking (something) into consideration: *the exorbitant prices are explainable in the light of the facts.* **light a fire under someone** see **FIRE**. **light and shade** the contrast between lighter and darker areas in a painting. ▪the contrast between more and less intense emphatic treatment of something: *the sinfonietta players bring ample light and shade to the music.* **light at the end of the tunnel** a long-awaited indication that a period of hardship or adversity is nearing an end. **light the fuse** see **FUSE**[2]. **the light of day** daylight. ▪general public attention: *bringing old family secrets into the light of day.* **the light of someone's life** a much loved person. **lights out** bedtime in a school dormitory, military barracks, or other institution, when lights should be switched off. ▪a bell, bugle call, or other signal announcing this. **lit up** informal, dated drunk. **see the light** understand or realize something after prolonged thought or doubt. ▪undergo religious conversion. **see the light of day** be born. ▪figurative come into existence; be made public, visible, or available: *this software first saw the light of day back in 1993.* **throw** (or **cast** or **shed**) **light on** help to explain (something) by providing further information about it.
– DERIVATIVES **lightish** adjective, **lightless** adjective, **lightness** noun.
– ORIGIN Old English *lēoht*, *līht* (noun and adjective), *līhtan* (verb), of Germanic origin; related to Dutch *licht* and German *Licht*, from an Indo-European root shared by Greek *leukos* 'white' and Latin *lux* 'light'.
▶**light up** (or **light something up**) (with reference to a person's face or eyes) suddenly become or cause to be animated with liveliness or joy: *his eyes lit up and he smiled | a smile of delight lit up her face.*

light[2] ▶**adjective 1** of little weight; easy to lift: *they are very light and portable | you're* **as light as a feather**.
▪deficient in weight, especially by a specified amount: *the sack of potatoes is 5 kilos light.* ▪not strongly or heavily built or constructed; small of its kind: *light, impractical clothes | light armour.* ▪carrying or suitable for small loads: *light commercial vehicles.* ▪carrying only light armaments: *light infantry.* ▪(of a vehicle, ship, or aircraft) travelling unladen or with less than a full load. ▪(of food or a meal) small in quantity and easy to digest: *a light supper.* ▪(of a foodstuff) low in fat, cholesterol, sugar, or other rich ingredients: *stick to a light diet.* ▪(of drink) not heavy on the stomach or strongly alcoholic: *a glass of light Hungarian wine.* ▪(of food, especially pastry or sponge cake) fluffy or well aerated during cooking. ▪(of soil) friable, porous, and workable. ▪(of an isotope) having not more than the usual mass; (of a compound) containing such an isotope.
2 relatively low in density, amount, or intensity: *passenger traffic was light | light autumn rains | trading was light for most of the day.*
▪(of sleep or a sleeper) easily disturbed. ▪easily borne or done: *he received a relatively light sentence | some light housework.*
3 gentle or delicate: *she planted a light kiss on his cheek | my breathing was steady and light.*
▪(of a building) having an appearance suggestive of lightness: *the building is lofty and light in its tall nave and choir.* ▪(of type) having thin strokes; not bold.
4 (of entertainment) requiring little mental effort; not profound or serious: *pop is thought of as light entertainment | some light reading.*
▪not serious or solemn: *his tone was light.* ▪free from worry or unhappiness; cheerful: *I left the island with a light heart.*
5 archaic (of a woman) unchaste; promiscuous.
– PHRASES **be light on** be rather short of: *we're light on fuel.* **be light on one's feet** (of a person) be quick or nimble. **a** (or **someone's**) **light touch** the ability to deal with something delicately, tactfully, or in an understated way: *a novel which handles its tricky subject with a light touch.* **make light of** treat as unimportant: *I didn't mean to make light of your problems.* **make light work of** accomplish (a task) quickly and easily. **travel light** travel with a minimum load or minimum luggage.
– DERIVATIVES **lightish** adjective, **lightly** adverb, **lightness** noun.
– ORIGIN Old English *lēocht*, *līht* (noun), *lēohte* (adverb), of Germanic origin; related to Dutch *licht* and German *leicht*, from an Indo-European root shared by **LUNG**.

light[3] ▶**verb** (past and past participle **lit** or **lighted**) [no obj.] **1** (**light on/upon**) come upon or discover by chance: *he lit on a possible solution.*
2 archaic descend: *from the horse he lit down.*
▪(**light on**) fall and settle or land on (a surface): *a feather just lighted on the ground.*
– ORIGIN Old English *līhtan* (in sense 2; also 'lessen the weight of'), from **LIGHT**[2]; compare with **ALIGHT**[1].
▶**light into** N. Amer. informal criticize severely; attack: *he lit into him for his indiscretion.*
light out N. Amer. informal depart hurriedly.

light air ▶**noun** a very light movement of the air.
▪a wind of force 1 on the Beaufort scale (1–3 knots or 1–6 kph).

light box ▶**noun** a flat box with a side of translucent glass or plastic and containing an electric light, so as to provide an evenly lighted flat surface or even illumination, such as in a studio.

light breeze ▶**noun** a wind of force 2 on the Beaufort scale (4–6 knots or 7–12 kph).

Light Brigade, Charge of the see **CHARGE OF THE LIGHT BRIGADE**.

light bulb ▶**noun** a glass bulb inserted into a lamp or a socket in a ceiling, which provides light by passing an electric current through a pocket of inert gas.

light cone ▶**noun** Physics a surface in space–time, represented as a cone in three dimensions, comprising all the points from which a light signal would reach a given point (at the apex) simultaneously, and which therefore appear simultaneous to an observer at the apex.

light curve ▶**noun** Astronomy a graph showing the variation in the light received over a period of time from a variable star or other varying celestial object.

light-emitting diode ▶**noun** see **LED**.

lighten[1] ▶**verb** make or become lighter in weight, pressure, or severity: [with obj.] *efforts to lighten the burden of regulation |* [no obj.] *the strain had lightened.*
▪make or become more cheerful or less serious: [with obj.] *she attempted a joke to lighten the atmosphere |* [no obj.] *Robbie felt her spirits lighten a little.*

lighten[2] ▶**verb 1** make or become lighter or brighter: [no obj.] *the sky began to lighten in the east |* [with obj.] *she had lightened her hair*
▪[with obj.] archaic enlighten spiritually: *now the Lord lighten thee, thou art a great fool.*
2 [no obj.] (**it lightens, it is lightening**, etc.) rare emit flashes of lightning; flash with lightning: *it thundered and lightened.*

light engine ▶**noun** a railway locomotive running with no vehicles attached.
▶**adverb** (of a locomotive) running with no vehicles attached: *75069 returned light engine.*

lightening ▶**noun** a drop in the level of the womb during the last weeks of pregnancy as the head of the fetus engages in the pelvis.

lighter[1] ▶**noun** a device that produces a small flame, typically used to light cigarettes.

lighter[2] ▶**noun** a flat-bottomed barge or other unpowered boat used to transfer goods to and from ships in harbour.
– DERIVATIVES **lighterman** noun (pl. **-men**).
– ORIGIN late Middle English: from **LIGHT**[2] (in the sense 'unload'), or from Middle Low German *luchter*.

lighterage ▶**noun** [mass noun] the transference of cargo by means of a lighter.

lighter-than-air ▶**adjective** [attrib.] relating to or denoting a balloon or other aircraft weighing less than the air it displaces, and so flying as a result of its own buoyancy.

lightfast ▶**adjective** (of a dye or pigment) not prone to discolour when exposed to light.
– DERIVATIVES **lightfastness** noun.

light-fingered ▶**adjective 1** prone to steal: *light-fingered shoplifters.*
2 having or showing delicate skill with the hands: *it is played with an irresistibly light-fingered spontaneity.*

light flyweight ▶**noun** [mass noun] the lowest weight in amateur boxing, ranging up to 48 kg.
▪[count noun] an amateur boxer of this weight.

light-footed ▶**adjective** fast, nimble, or stealthy on one's feet: *a light-footed leap.*
– DERIVATIVES **light-footedly** adverb.

light gun ▶**noun** Computing a hand-held gunlike photosensitive device used chiefly in computer games, held to the display screen for passing information to the computer.

light-headed ▶**adjective** dizzy and slightly faint: *she felt light-headed with relief.*
– DERIVATIVES **light-headedly** adverb, **light-headedness** noun.

light-hearted ▶**adjective** frivolously amusing and entertaining: *a light-hearted speech.*
– DERIVATIVES **light-heartedly** adverb, **light-heartedness** noun.

light heavyweight ▶**noun** [mass noun] a weight in boxing and other sports intermediate between middleweight and heavyweight. In the amateur boxing scale it ranges from 75 to 81 kg. Also called **CRUISERWEIGHT**.
▪[count noun] a boxer or other competitor of this weight.

lighthouse ▶**noun** a tower or other structure containing a beacon light to warn or guide ships at sea.

light industry ▶**noun** [mass noun] the manufacture of small or light articles.

lighting ▶**noun** [mass noun] equipment in a room, studio, theatre, or street for producing light: *fluorescent bulbs for street lighting.*
▪the arrangement or effect of lights: *the lighting was very flat.*

lighting cameraman ▶**noun** (in films) a person in charge of the lighting of sets being filmed.

lighting-up time ▶**noun** Brit. the time at which motorists are required by law to switch their vehicles' lights on.

light meter ▶**noun** an instrument for measuring the intensity of light, used chiefly to show the correct exposure when taking a photograph.

light middleweight ▶**noun** [mass noun] a weight in amateur boxing ranging from 67 to 71 kg.
▪an amateur boxer of this weight.

light music ▶**noun** [mass noun] popular music for light entertainment, especially as broadcast on the radio or played as background music.

lightning ▶**noun** [mass noun] the occurrence of a natural electrical discharge of very short duration and high voltage between a cloud and the ground or within a cloud, accompanied by a bright flash and typically also thunder: *a tremendous flash of lightning.*
▪[count noun] poetic/literary a flash or discharge of this kind: *the sky was a mass of black cloud out of which lightnings flashed.*
▶**adjective** [attrib.] very quick: *a lightning cure for his hangover | galloping across the country at lightning speed.*
– PHRASES **lightning never strikes twice in the same place** proverb an unusual situation or event is unlikely to happen again in exactly the same circumstances or to the same person. **like (greased) lightning** very quickly.
– ORIGIN Middle English: special use of *lightening* (verbal noun from **LIGHTEN**[2]).

USAGE The form **lightning** is historically a contracted form of **lightening** (it was at one time spelled **light'ning**) but the two forms are now two distinct words. In the sense *thunder and* **lightning** and **lightning** *speed*, the spelling is always **lightning**, while in the sense 'make or become lighter' the spelling is always **lightening**. More than 15 per cent of citations for **lightening** in the British National Corpus are in fact misspellings of **lightning**.

lightning bug ▶ noun North American term for **FIREFLY**.

lightning chess ▶ noun [mass noun] a form of chess in which moves must be made at very short intervals.

lightning conductor (also chiefly N. Amer. **lightning rod**) ▶ noun Brit. a metal rod or wire fixed to an exposed part of a building or other tall structure to divert lightning harmlessly into the ground.
■ figurative a person or thing that attracts a lot of criticism, especially in order to divert attention from more serious issues or allow a more important public figure to appear blameless.

lightning strike ▶ noun Brit. a strike by workers after little or no warning, especially without official union backing.

light opera ▶ noun another term for **OPERETTA**.

light pen ▶ noun **1** Computing a hand-held pen-like photosensitive device held to the display screen of a computer terminal for passing information to the computer.
2 a hand-held light-emitting device used for reading bar codes.

light pollution ▶ noun [mass noun] brightening of the night sky that inhibits the observation of stars and planets, caused by street lights and other man-made sources.

lightproof ▶ adjective able to block out light completely.

light railway ▶ noun a railway constructed for light traffic.

light reaction ▶ noun **1** [mass noun] the reaction of something, especially the iris of the eye, to different intensities of light.
2 (**the light reaction**) Biochemistry the reaction which occurs as the first phase of photosynthesis, in which energy in the form of light is absorbed and converted to chemical energy in the form of ATP.

lights ▶ plural noun the lungs of sheep, pigs, or bullocks, used as food, especially for pets.
– PHRASES **punch someone's lights out** beat someone up.
– ORIGIN Middle English: use of **LIGHT**[2] as a noun (so named because of their lightness). Compare with **LUNG**.

light-sensitive ▶ adjective (of a surface or substance) changing physically or chemically when exposed to light.
■ Biology (of a cell, organ, or tissue) able to detect the presence or intensity of light.

lightship ▶ noun a moored or anchored boat with a beacon light to warn or guide ships at sea.

light show ▶ noun a spectacle of coloured lights that move and change, especially at a pop concert.

lightsome ▶ adjective chiefly poetic/literary **1** merry and carefree.
2 gracefully nimble: *lightsome, high-flying dancers.*
– DERIVATIVES **lightsomely** adverb, **lightsomeness** noun.

light table ▶ noun a horizontal or tilted surface of translucent glass or plastic with a light behind it, used as a light box for viewing transparencies or negatives.

light trap ▶ noun **1** Zoology an illuminated trap for attracting and catching nocturnal animals, especially moths and other flying insects.
2 Photography a device for excluding light from a darkroom without preventing entry into it.

light vessel ▶ noun another term for **LIGHTSHIP**.

light water ▶ noun [mass noun] **1** water containing the normal proportion (or less) of deuterium oxide, i.e. about 0.02 per cent, especially to distinguish it from heavy water.
2 foam formed by water and a fluorocarbon surfactant, which floats on flammable liquids lighter than water and is used in firefighting.

lightweight ▶ noun **1** [mass noun] a weight in boxing and other sports intermediate between featherweight and welterweight. In the amateur boxing scale it ranges from 57 to 60 kg.
■ [count noun] a boxer or other competitor of this weight.
2 a person or thing that is lightly built or constructed.
■ a person of little importance or influence, especially in a particular sphere: *he was regarded as a political lightweight.*
▶ adjective **1** of thin material or build and weighing less than average: *a lightweight grey suit.*
2 containing little serious matter: *the newspaper is lightweight and trivial.*
■ (of a person) having little importance or influence: *he is too lightweight to become Chancellor.*

light well ▶ noun an open area or vertical shaft in the centre of a building, typically roofed with glass, bringing natural light to the lower floors or basement.

light welterweight ▶ noun [mass noun] a weight in amateur boxing ranging from 60 to 63.5 kg.
■ [count noun] an amateur boxer of this weight.

lightwood ▶ noun **1** chiefly Austral. a tree yielding timber that is pale in colour or light in weight.
• Several species, in particular the hickory wattle (*Acacia implexa*, family Leguminosae).
2 [mass noun] US firewood that burns easily and with a bright flame; kindling.

lighty /ˈlʌɪti/ (also **laaitie, litie**) ▶ noun (pl. **-ies**) S. African informal a male child, adolescent, or young adult.
■ a young convict; a junior gang member. ■ used as a term of address, often to someone to whom the speaker feels superior: *don't underestimate us,* **my** ***lighty.***
– ORIGIN apparently from the adjective **LIGHT**[2] from *light of heart* + **-Y**[2]; the variant *laaitie* shows Afrikaans influence.

light year ▶ noun Astronomy a unit of astronomical distance equivalent to the distance that light travels in one year, which is 9.4607×10^{12} km (nearly 6 million million miles).
■ (**light years**) informal a long distance or great amount: *the new range puts them* ***light years ahead*** *of the competition.*

ligneous /ˈlɪɡnɪəs/ ▶ adjective made, consisting of, or resembling wood; woody.
– ORIGIN early 17th cent.: from Latin *ligneus* 'relating to wood' + **-OUS**.

ligni- ▶ combining form relating to wood: *lignify.*
– ORIGIN from Latin *lignum* 'wood'.

lignify /ˈlɪɡnɪfʌɪ/ ▶ verb (**-ies, -ied**) [with obj.] [usu. as adj. **lignified**] Botany make rigid and woody by the deposition of lignin in cell walls.
– DERIVATIVES **lignification** noun.

lignin /ˈlɪɡnɪn/ ▶ noun [mass noun] Botany a complex organic polymer deposited in the cell walls of many plants, making them rigid and woody.
– ORIGIN early 19th cent.: from **LIGNI-** 'of wood' + **-IN**[1].

lignite /ˈlɪɡnʌɪt/ ▶ noun [mass noun] a soft brownish coal showing traces of plant structure, intermediate between bituminous coal and peat.
– DERIVATIVES **lignitic** adjective.
– ORIGIN early 19th cent.: coined in French from Latin *lignum* 'wood' + **-ITE**[1].

ligno- ▶ combining form relating to wood: *lignotuber.*
■ representing **LIGNIN**: *lignocellulose.*
– ORIGIN from Latin *lignum* 'wood'.

lignocaine /ˈlɪɡnə(ʊ)keɪn/ ▶ noun [mass noun] Medicine a synthetic compound used as a local anaesthetic, e.g. for dental surgery, and in treating abnormal heart rhythms.
• An aromatic amide; chem. formula: $C_{14}H_{22}N_2O$.
– ORIGIN 1950s: from **LIGNO-** (Latin equivalent of **XYLO-**, used in the earlier name *xylocaine* and reflecting chemical similarity to **XYLENE**) + *-caine* (from **COCAINE**).

lignocellulose /ˌlɪɡnə(ʊ)ˈsɛljʊləʊz, -s/ ▶ noun [mass noun] Botany a complex of lignin and cellulose present in the cell walls of woody plants.

lignotuber /ˈlɪɡnəʊˌtjuːbə/ ▶ noun Botany a rounded woody growth at or below ground level on some shrubs and trees that grow in areas subject to fire or drought, containing a mass of buds and food reserves.

lignum vitae /ˌlɪɡnəm ˈvʌɪtiː, ˈviːtʌɪ/ ▶ noun another term for **GUAIACUM**.
– ORIGIN Latin, wood of life.

ligroin /ˈlɪɡrəʊɪn/ ▶ noun [mass noun] Chemistry a volatile hydrocarbon mixture obtained from petroleum, used as a solvent.
– ORIGIN late 19th cent.: of unknown origin.

ligula /ˈlɪɡjʊlə/ ▶ noun (pl. **ligulae** /-liː/) Entomology the strap-shaped terminal part of an insect's labium, typically lobed.
– DERIVATIVES **ligular** adjective.
– ORIGIN mid 18th cent.: from Latin 'strap'.

ligulate /ˈlɪɡjʊlət/ ▶ adjective chiefly Botany strap-shaped, such as the ray florets of plants of the daisy family.
■ (of a plant) having ray florets or ligules.

ligule /ˈlɪɡjuːl/ ▶ noun Botany a narrow strap-shaped part of a plant, especially a membranous scale on the inner side of the leaf sheath at its junction with the blade in most grasses and sedges.
– ORIGIN early 19th cent.: from Latin *ligula* 'strap'.

Liguria /lɪˈɡ(j)ʊərɪə/ a coastal region of NW Italy, which extends along the Mediterranean coast from Tuscany to the border with France; capital, Genoa. In ancient times Liguria extended as far as the Atlantic seaboard.
– DERIVATIVES **Ligurian** adjective & noun.
– ORIGIN from Latin *Ligur* 'Ligurian', from Greek *Ligus.*

Ligurian Sea a part of the northern Mediterranean, between Corsica and the NW coast of Italy.

ligustrum /lɪˈɡʌstrəm/ ▶ noun a plant of a genus that comprises the privets.
• Genus *Ligustrum*, family Oleaceae.
– ORIGIN mid 17th cent.: from Latin.

likable ▶ adjective variant spelling of **LIKEABLE**.

like[1] ▶ preposition **1** having the same characteristics or qualities as; similar to: *there were other suits like mine in the shop | they were like brothers | she looked nothing like Audrey Hepburn.*
■ in the manner of; in the same way or to the same degree as: *he was screaming like a banshee | you must run like the wind.* ■ in a way appropriate to: *students were angry at being treated like children.* ■ such as one might expect from; characteristic of: *just like you to put a damper on people's enjoyment.* ■ used in questions to ask about the characteristics or nature of someone or something: *What is it like to be a tuna fisherman? | What's she like?*
2 used to draw attention to the nature of an action or event: *I apologize for coming over unannounced like this | why are you talking about me like that?*
3 such as; for example: *the cautionary vision of works like* Animal Farm *and* 1984.
▶ conjunction informal **1** in the same way that; as: *people who change countries like they change clothes.*
2 as though; as if: *I felt like I'd been kicked by a camel.*
▶ noun used with reference to a person or thing of the same kind as another: *the quotations could be arranged to put* ***like with like*** *| I know him—him and his like.*
■ (**the like**) a thing or things of the same kind (often used to express surprise or for emphasis): *did you ever hear the like? | a church interior* ***the like of which*** *he had never seen before.*
▶ adjective [attrib.] (of a person or thing) having similar qualities or characteristics to another person or thing: *I responded in like manner | the grouping of children of like ability together.*
■ [predic.] (of a portrait or other image) having a faithful resemblance to the original: *'Who painted the dog's picture? It's very like'.*
▶ adverb **1** informal used in speech as a meaningless filler or to signify the speaker's uncertainty about an expression just used: *there was this funny smell—sort of dusty like.*
2 (**like as/to**) archaic in the manner of: *like as a ship with dreadful storm long tossed.*
– PHRASES **and the like** and similar things; et cetera. **like anything** informal to a great degree: *they would probably worry like anything.* **(as) like as not** probably: *she would be in bed by now, like as not.* **like enough** (or **most like**) archaic probably: *he'll have lost a deal of blood, I dare say, and like enough he's still losing it.* **like ——, like ——** as —— is, so is ——: *like father, like son.* **like so** informal in this manner: *the votive candles are arranged like so.* **the likes of** informal used of someone or something regarded as a type: *she didn't want to associate with the likes of me.* **more like** informal nearer to (a specified number or description) than one previously given: *he believes the figure should be more like £10 million.* ■ (**more like it**) nearer to what is required or expected; more satisfactory. **of**

(**a**) **like mind** (of a person) sharing the same opinions or tastes.
– ORIGIN Middle English: from Old Norse *líkr*; related to **ALIKE**.

USAGE In the sentence *he's behaving* **like** *he owns the place*, **like** is a conjunction meaning 'as if', a usage regarded as incorrect in standard English. Although **like** has been used as a conjunction in this way since the 15th century by many respected writers, it is still frowned upon and considered unacceptable in formal English, where **as if** should be used instead.

like[2] ▶ **verb** [with obj.] **1** find agreeable, enjoyable, or satisfactory: *I like all Angela Carter's stories* | [with present participle] *people who don't like reading books* | [with infinitive] *I like to be the centre of attention.*
2 wish for; want: *would you like a cup of coffee?* | [with infinitive] *I'd like to hire a car* | [with obj. and infinitive] *I'd like you to stay* | [no obj.] N. Amer. *we would* **like for** *you to work for us.*
■(**would like to do something**) used as a polite formula: *we would like to apologize for the late running of this service.* ■ (**not like doing/to do something**) feel reluctant to do something: *I don't like leaving her on her own too long.* ■ choose to have (something); prefer: *how do you like your coffee?* ■ [in questions] feel about or regard (something): *how would you like it if it happened to you?*
▶ **noun** (**likes**) the things one likes or prefers: *a wide variety of likes, dislikes, tastes, and income levels.*
– PHRASES **if you like 1** if it suits or pleases you: *we could go riding if you like.* **2** used when expressing something in a new or unusual way: *it's a whole new branch of chemistry, a new science if you like.* **I like that!** used as an exclamation expressing affront. **like it or not** informal used to indicate that someone has no choice in a matter: *you're celebrating with us, like it or not.* **not like the look** (or **sound**) **of** find worrying or alarming: *I don't like the look of that head injury.*
– ORIGIN Old English *līcian* 'be pleasing', of Germanic origin; related to Dutch *lijken*.

-like ▶ **combining form** (added to nouns) similar to; characteristic of: *pealike* | *crust-like.*

likeable (also **likable**) ▶ **adjective** (especially of a person) pleasant, friendly, and easy to like.
– DERIVATIVES **likeability** noun, **likeableness** noun, **likeably** adverb.

likelihood ▶ **noun** [mass noun] the state or fact of something's being likely; probability: *young people who can see no* **likelihood of** *finding employment* | [in sing.] *situations where there is* **a likelihood of** *violence.*
– PHRASES **in all likelihood** very probably.

likely ▶ **adjective** (**likelier**, **likeliest**) **1** such as well might happen or be true; probable: *speculation on the likely effect of opting out* | [with clause] **it was likely that** *he would make a televised statement* | [with infinitive] *sales are likely to drop further.*
2 apparently suitable; promising: *a likely-looking spot.*
■appearing to have vigour or ability: *likely lads.*
▶ **adverb** probably: *we will most likely go to a bar.*
– PHRASES **a likely story** used to express disbelief of an account or excuse: *'She's your lodger? A likely story!'* **as likely as not** probably: *I won't take their pills, because as likely as not they'd poison me.* **not likely!** informal certainly not; I refuse: *'Are you going home?' 'Not likely!'*
– DERIVATIVES **likeliness** noun.
– ORIGIN Middle English: from Old Norse *líkligr*, from *líkr* (see **LIKE**[1]).

USAGE In standard British English the adverb **likely** must be preceded by a submodifier such as **very**, **most**, or **more**, as in *we will* **most likely** *see him later.* In informal US English, use without a submodifier is very common and not regarded as incorrect, as in *we will* **likely** *see him later.*

like-minded ▶ **adjective** having similar tastes or opinions: *a radio ham with like-minded friends all over the world.*
– DERIVATIVES **like-mindedness** noun.

liken ▶ **verb** [with obj.] (**liken someone/thing to**) point out the resemblance of someone or something to: *racism is likened to a contagious disease.*
– ORIGIN Middle English: from **LIKE**[1] + **-EN**[1].

likeness ▶ **noun** [mass noun] the fact or quality of being alike; resemblance: *her* **likeness to** *him was astonishing* | [count noun] *a family likeness can be seen among all the boys.*
■the semblance, guise, or outward appearance of: *humans are described as being made in God's likeness.* ■ [count noun] a portrait or representation: *the only known likeness of Dorothy as a young woman.*
– ORIGIN Old English *gelīcnes* (see **ALIKE**, **-NESS**).

Likert scale /ˈlʌɪkət/ ▶ **noun** Psychology a scale used to represent people's attitudes to a topic.
– ORIGIN mid 20th cent.: named after Rensis *Likert* (1903–81), American psychologist.

likewise ▶ **adverb 1** in the same way; also: *the programmes of study will apply from five years of age, likewise the attainment targets.*
■[sentence adverb] used to introduce a point similar or related to one just made: *The banks advise against sending cash. Likewise, sending British cheques may cause problems.*
2 in a like manner; similarly: *I stuck out my tongue and Frankie* **did likewise**.
– ORIGIN late Middle English: from the phrase *in like wise.*

liking ▶ **noun** [in sing.] a feeling of regard or fondness: *Mrs Parsons had* **a liking for** *gin and tonic* | *she'd* **taken an** *instant* **liking to** *Arnie's new girlfriend.*
– PHRASES **for one's liking** to suit one's taste or wishes: *he is a little too showy for my liking.* **to one's liking** to one's taste; pleasing: *his coffee was just to his liking.*
– ORIGIN Old English *līcung* (see **LIKE**[2], **-ING**[1]).

likkewaan /ˈlɪkəvɑːn/ ▶ **noun** variant spelling of **LEGUAN**.

Likud /lɪˈkuːd/ a coalition of right-wing Israeli political parties, formed in 1973. Likud returned to power in 1996 under Benjamin Netanyahu.
– ORIGIN Hebrew, literally 'consolidation, unity'.

likuta /lɪˈkuːtə/ ▶ **noun** (pl. **makuta** /məˈkuːtə/) a monetary unit of Zaire (Democratic Republic of Congo), equal to one hundredth of a zaire.
– ORIGIN Kikongo.

lilac ▶ **noun** a Eurasian shrub or small tree of the olive family, which has fragrant violet, pink, or white blossom and is a popular garden ornamental.
● Genus *Syringa*, family Oleaceae; several species, in particular the **common lilac** (*S. vulgaris*), with many cultivars.
■[mass noun] a pale pinkish-violet colour.
▶ **adjective** of a pale pinkish-violet colour.
– ORIGIN early 17th cent.: from obsolete French, via Spanish and Arabic from Persian *līlak*, variant of *nīlak* 'bluish', from *nīl* 'blue'.

lilangeni /ˌliːlaŋˈgeɪni/ ▶ **noun** (pl. **emalangeni** /ɪˌmalaŋˈgeɪni/) the basic monetary unit of Swaziland, equal to 100 cents.
– ORIGIN from the Bantu prefix *li-* (used to denote a singular) + *-langeni* 'member of a royal family'.

liliaceous /ˌlɪlɪˈeɪʃəs/ ▶ **adjective** Botany of, relating to, or denoting plants of the lily family (Liliaceae). These have elongated leaves which grow from a corm, bulb, or rhizome.
– ORIGIN mid 18th cent.: from modern Latin *Liliaceae* (plural), based on Latin *lilium* 'lily', + **-OUS**.

Lilienthal /ˈliːlɪəntɑːl/, Otto (1848–96), German pioneer in the design and flying of gliders. Working with his brother, he made over 2,000 flights in various gliders before being killed in a crash.

Lilith /ˈlɪlɪθ/ a female demon of Jewish folklore, who tries to kill newborn children. In the Talmud she is the first wife of Adam, dispossessed by Eve.

Lille /liːl/ an industrial city in northern France, near the border with Belgium; pop. 178,300 (1990).

Lillee /ˈlɪli/, Dennis (Keith) (b.1949), Australian cricketer. A fast bowler, he took 355 wickets in seventy matches during his career in test cricket (1971–84).

Lilliburlero /ˌlɪlɪbəˈlɛːrəʊ/ a song ridiculing the Irish, popular at the end of the 17th century. With different words the song has remained associated with the Orange Party, as 'Protestant Boys'.

Lilliputian /ˌlɪlɪˈpjuːʃ(ə)n/ ▶ **adjective** trivial or very small: *America's banks look Lilliputian in comparison with Japan's.*
▶ **noun** a trivial or very small person or thing.
– ORIGIN early 18th cent.: from the imaginary country of *Lilliput* in Swift's *Gulliver's Travels*, inhabited by people 6 inches (15 cm) high, + **-IAN**.

lilly-pilly ▶ **noun** (pl. **-ies**) an Australian evergreen tree of the myrtle family, with edible pink, purple, or white berries.
● *Acmena smithii*, family Myrtaceae.
– ORIGIN mid 19th cent.: of unknown origin.

lilo /ˈlʌɪləʊ/ (also trademark **Li-lo**) ▶ **noun** (pl. **-os**) a type of inflatable mattress which is used as a bed or for floating on water.
– ORIGIN 1930s: alteration of *lie low.*

Lilongwe /lɪˈlɒŋweɪ/ the capital of Malawi; pop. 233,970 (1987).

lilt ▶ **noun** a characteristic rising and falling of the voice when speaking; a pleasant gentle accent: *he spoke with a faint but recognizable Irish lilt.*
■a pleasant, gently swinging rhythm in a song or tune: *the lilt of the Hawaiian music.* ■ archaic, chiefly Scottish a cheerful tune.
▶ **verb** [no obj.] [often as adj. **lilting**] speak, sing, or sound with a lilt: *a lilting Irish accent.*
– ORIGIN late Middle English *lulte* (in the senses 'sound (an alarm)' or 'lift up (the voice)'), of unknown origin.

lily ▶ **noun 1** a bulbous plant with large trumpet-shaped, typically fragrant, flowers on a tall, slender stem. Lilies have long been cultivated, some kinds being of symbolic importance and some used in perfumery.
● Genus *Lilium*, family Liliaceae (the **lily family**). This family includes many flowering bulbs, such as bluebells, hyacinths, and tulips. Several plants are often placed in different families, especially the Alliaceae (onions and their relatives), Aloaceae (aloes), and Amaryllidaceae (amaryllis, daffodils, jonquil), and as many as 38 families are sometimes recognized.
■short for **WATER LILY**. ■ used in names of other plants with similar flowers or leaves, e.g. **arum lily**.
2 a heraldic fleur-de-lis.
– DERIVATIVES **lilied** adjective.
– ORIGIN Old English *lilie*, from Latin *lilium*, from Greek *leirion*.

lily-livered ▶ **adjective** weak and cowardly.

lily of the valley ▶ **noun** a European plant of the lily family, with broad leaves and arching stems of fragrant white bell-shaped flowers.
● Genus *Convallaria*, family Liliaceae.

lily pad ▶ **noun** a round floating leaf of a water lily.

lily-trotter ▶ **noun** (especially in Africa) a jacana.

lily-white ▶ **adjective** pure or ideally white.
■without fault or corruption; totally innocent or immaculate: *they want me to conform, to be lily-white.*

Lima /ˈliːmə/ the capital of Peru; pop. 5,706,130 (1993). Founded in 1535 by Francisco Pizarro, it was the capital of the Spanish colonies in South America until the 19th century.
■a code word representing the letter L, used in radio communication.

lima bean /ˈliːmə/ ▶ **noun 1** an edible flat whitish bean. See also **BUTTER BEAN**.
2 the tropical American plant which yields this bean.
● *Phaseolus lunatus* (or *limensis*), family Leguminosae.
– ORIGIN mid 18th cent.: *lima* from the name of the Peruvian capital **LIMA**.

Limassol /ˈlɪməsɒl/ a port on the south coast of Cyprus, on Akrotiri Bay; pop. 143,400 (est. 1993).

limb[1] ▶ **noun** an arm or leg of a person or four-legged animal, or a bird's wing.
■a large branch of a tree. ■ a projecting landform such as a spur of a mountain range, or each of two or more such projections as in a forked peninsula or archipelago. ■ a projecting section of a building. ■ a branch of a cross. ■ each half of an archery bow.
– PHRASES **life and limb** life and all bodily faculties: *a reckless disregard for life and limb.* **out on a limb 1** isolated: *Aberdeen is rather out on a limb.* **2** in or into a position where one is not joined or supported by anyone else: *going out on a limb to support unglamorous causes.* **tear someone limb from limb** violently dismember someone.
– DERIVATIVES **limbed** adjective [in combination] *long-limbed*, **limbless** adjective.
– ORIGIN Old English *lim* (also in the sense 'organ or part of the body'), of Germanic origin.

limb[2] ▶ **noun 1** Astronomy the edge of the disc of a celestial object, especially the sun or moon.
2 Botany the blade or broad part of a leaf or petal.
■the spreading upper part of a tube-shaped flower.
3 the graduated arc of a quadrant or other scientific instrument, used for measuring angles.
– ORIGIN late Middle English: from French *limbe* or Latin *limbus* 'hem, border'.

Limba /ˈlɪmbə/ ▶ **noun** (pl. same or **Limbas**) **1** a member of a West African people of Sierra Leone and Guinea.
2 [mass noun] the Niger–Congo language of this people, with about 300,000 speakers.

▶**adjective** of or relating to the Limbas or their language.
– ORIGIN the name in Limba.

limba ▶**noun** another term for **AFARA**.
– ORIGIN 1930s: from *limbo*, the name used in Gabon.

limber[1] /ˈlɪmbə/ ▶**adjective** (of a person or body part) lithe; supple.
▪(of a thing) flexible: *limber graphite fishing rods.*
▶**verb** [no obj.] warm up in preparation for exercise or activity, especially sport or athletics: *the acrobats were* ***limbering up*** *for the big show.*
▪[with obj.] make (oneself or a body part) supple: *I limbered my fingers with a few practice bars.*
– DERIVATIVES **limberness** noun.
– ORIGIN mid 16th cent. (as an adjective): perhaps from **LIMBER**[2] in the dialect sense 'cart shaft', with allusion to the to-and-fro motion.

limber[2] /ˈlɪmbə/ ▶**noun** the detachable front part of a gun carriage, consisting of two wheels and an axle, a pole, and a frame holding one or more ammunition boxes.
▶**verb** [with obj.] attach a limber to (a gun).
– ORIGIN Middle English *lymour*, apparently related to medieval Latin *limonarius* from *limo*, *limon-* 'shaft'.

limberneck ▶**noun** [mass noun] a kind of botulism affecting poultry.

limber pine ▶**noun** a small pine tree with tough pliant branches, which is native to the Rocky mountains of North America.
• *Pinus flexilis*, family Pinaceae.

limbic system /ˈlɪmbɪk/ ▶**noun** a complex system of nerves and networks in the brain, involving several areas near the edge of the cortex concerned with instinct and mood. It controls the basic emotions (fear, pleasure, anger) and drives (hunger, sex, dominance, care of offspring).
– ORIGIN late 19th cent.: *limbic* from French *limbique*, from Latin *limbus* 'edge'.

limbo[1] ▶**noun** [mass noun] **1** (in some Christian beliefs) the supposed abode of the souls of unbaptized infants, and of the just who died before Christ's coming.
2 an uncertain period of awaiting a decision or resolution; an intermediate state or condition: ***in limbo****, waiting for people to decide what to do.*
▪[in sing.] a state of neglect or oblivion: *children left in an emotional limbo.*
– ORIGIN late Middle English: from the medieval Latin phrase *in limbo*, from *limbus* 'hem, border, limbo'.

limbo[2] ▶**noun** (pl. **-os**) a West Indian dance in which the dancer bends backwards to pass under a horizontal bar which is progressively lowered to a position just above the ground.
▶**verb** [no obj.] dance in such a way.
– ORIGIN 1950s: from **LIMBER**[1].

Limburg /ˈlɪmbəːɡ/ a former duchy of Lorraine, divided in 1839 between Belgium and the Netherlands. It now forms a province of NE Belgium (capital, Hasselt) and a province of the SE Netherlands (capital, Maastricht). French name **LIMBOURG** /lɛ̃buʀ/.

Limburger ▶**noun** [mass noun] a soft white cheese with a characteristic strong smell, originally made in Limburg.

limbus /ˈlɪmbəs/ ▶**noun** (pl. **limbi** /-bʌɪ/) Anatomy the border or margin of a structure, especially the junction of the cornea and sclera in the eye.
– ORIGIN late Middle English (denoting limbo): from Latin, 'edge, border'. The current sense dates from the late 17th cent.

lime[1] ▶**noun** (also **quicklime**) [mass noun] a white caustic alkaline substance consisting of calcium oxide, which is obtained by heating limestone and combines with water with the production of much heat.
▪(also **slaked lime**) a white alkaline substance consisting of calcium hydroxide, made by adding water to quicklime. ▪(in general use) any of a number of calcium compounds, especially calcium hydroxide, used as an additive to soil or water. ▪archaic birdlime.
▶**verb** [with obj.] **1** treat (soil or water) with lime to reduce acidity and improve fertility or oxygen levels.
▪[often as adj. **limed**] give (wood) a bleached appearance by treating it with lime: *limed oak dining furniture.*
2 archaic catch (a bird) with birdlime.
– DERIVATIVES **limy** adjective (**limier**, **limiest**).
– ORIGIN Old English *līm*, of Germanic origin; related to Dutch *lijm*, German *Leim*, also to **LOAM**.

lime[2] ▶**noun 1** a rounded citrus fruit similar to a lemon but greener, smaller, and with a distinctive acid flavour.
▪[mass noun] a drink made from or flavoured with lime juice: *lager and lime.*
2 (also **lime tree**) the evergreen citrus tree which produces this fruit, widely cultivated in warm climates.
• *Citrus aurantifolia*, family Rutaceae.
3 [mass noun] a bright light green colour like that of a lime: [as modifier] *dayglo orange, pink, or lime green.*
– ORIGIN mid 17th cent.: from French, from modern Provençal *limo*, Spanish *lima*, from Arabic *līma*; compare with **LEMON**.

lime[3] (also **lime tree**) ▶**noun** a deciduous tree with heart-shaped leaves and fragrant yellowish blossom, native to north temperate regions. The pale timber is used for carving and cheap furniture. Also called **LINDEN**.
• Genus *Tilia*, family Tiliaceae: many species, including the widely grown hybrid **common lime** (*T.* × *europaea*), and the **small-leaved lime** (*T. cordata*), which dominated the pre-Neolithic forests of much of lowland England.
– ORIGIN early 17th cent.: alteration of obsolete *line*, from Old English *lind* (see **LINDEN**).

lime[4] W. Indian ▶**verb** [no obj., with adverbial] sit or stand around talking with others: *boys and girls were liming along the roadside as if they didn't have anything to do.*
▶**noun** an informal social gathering characterized by semi-ritualized talking.
– ORIGIN origin uncertain; said to be from **LIMEY** (because of the number of British sailors present during the Second World War), or from *suck a lime*, expressing bitterness at not being invited to a gathering.

limeade ▶**noun** [mass noun] a drink made from lime juice sweetened with sugar.

limeburner ▶**noun** historical a person whose job was burning limestone in order to obtain lime.

limekiln ▶**noun** a kiln in which limestone is burnt or calcined to produce quicklime.

limelight ▶**noun** (**the limelight**) the focus of public attention: *the works that brought the artists into the limelight.*

limen /ˈlʌɪmɛn, ˈliː-/ ▶**noun** (pl. **limens** or **limina** /ˈlʌɪmɪnə, ˈliː-/) Psychology a threshold below which a stimulus is not perceived or is not distinguished from another.
– ORIGIN mid 17th cent.: from Latin 'threshold'.

limepit ▶**noun** historical a pit containing lime in which hides were placed to remove hair and fur.

Limerick /ˈlɪmərɪk/ a county of the Republic of Ireland, in the west of the province of Munster.
▪its county town, on the River Shannon; pop. 52,040 (est. 1991).

limerick /ˈlɪm(ə)rɪk/ ▶**noun** a humorous five-line poem with a rhyme scheme *aabba*.
– ORIGIN late 19th cent.: said to be from the chorus 'will you come up to Limerick?', sung between improvised verses at a gathering.

limestone ▶**noun** [mass noun] a hard sedimentary rock, composed mainly of calcium carbonate or dolomite, used as building material and in the making of cement.

limestone pavement ▶**noun** a horizontal or gently sloping expanse of bare limestone, consisting of large blocks (clints) separated by deep eroded fissures (grikes).

lime sulphur ▶**noun** [mass noun] an insecticide and fungicide containing calcium polysulphides, made by boiling lime and sulphur in water.

limewash ▶**noun** [mass noun] a mixture of lime and water used for coating walls.
▶**verb** [with obj.] apply such a mixture to: [as adj. **limewashed**] *limewashed cottages.*

lime water ▶**noun** [mass noun] Chemistry a solution of calcium hydroxide in water, which is alkaline and turns milky in the presence of carbon dioxide.

Limey ▶**noun** (pl. **-eys**) N. Amer. & Austral., chiefly derogatory a British person.
– ORIGIN late 19th cent.: from **LIME**[2] + **-Y**[1], because of the former enforced consumption of lime juice in the British navy.

liminal /ˈlɪmɪn(ə)l/ ▶**adjective** technical **1** of or relating to a transitional or initial stage of a process.
2 occupying a position at, or on both sides of, a boundary or threshold.
– DERIVATIVES **liminality** noun.
– ORIGIN late 19th cent.: from Latin *limen*, *limin-* 'threshold' + **-AL**.

limit ▶**noun 1** a point or level beyond which something does not or may not extend or pass: *the failure showed the* ***limits of*** *British power | the 10-minute* ***limit on*** *speeches | there was no* ***limit to*** *his imagination.*
▪(often **limits**) the terminal point or boundary of an area or movement: *the city limits | the upper limit of the tidal reaches.* ▪the furthest extent of one's physical or mental endurance: *Mary Ann tried everyone's patience* ***to the limit*** *| other horses were reaching their limit.*
2 a restriction on the size or amount of something permissible or possible: *an age limit | a weight limit.*
▪a speed limit: *a 30 mph limit.* ▪(also **legal limit**) the maximum concentration of alcohol in the blood that the law allows in the driver of a motor vehicle: *the risk of drinkers inadvertently going* ***over the limit****.*
3 Mathematics a point or value which a sequence, function, or sum of a series can be made to approach progressively, until they are as close to it as desired.
▶**verb** (**limited**, **limiting**) [with obj.] set or serve as a limit to: *try to limit the amount you drink | class sizes are* ***limited to*** *a maximum of 10 |* [as adj. **limiting**] *a limiting factor.*
– PHRASES **be the limit** informal be intolerably troublesome or irritating. **off limits** out of bounds: *they declared the site off limits |* figurative *there was no topic that was off limits for discussion.* **within limits** moderately; up to a point: **without limit** with no restriction.
– DERIVATIVES **limitative** adjective.
– ORIGIN late Middle English: from Latin *limes*, *limit-* 'boundary, frontier'. The verb is from Latin *limitare*, from *limes*.

limitary ▶**adjective** rare of, relating to, or subject to restriction.

limitation ▶**noun 1** (often **limitations**) a limiting rule or circumstance; a restriction: *severe* ***limitations on*** *water use.*
▪a condition of limited ability; a defect or failing: *she knew her limitations better than she knew her worth.* ▪[mass noun] the action of limiting something: *the limitation of local authorities' powers.*
2 (also **limitation period**) Law a legally specified period beyond which an action may be defeated or a property right is not to continue. See also **STATUTE OF LIMITATIONS**.
– ORIGIN late Middle English: from Latin *limitatio(n-)*, from the verb *limitare* (see **LIMIT**).

limit bid ▶**noun** Bridge a bid showing that the value of the bidder's hand is only just sufficient for a bid.

limited ▶**adjective** restricted in size, amount, or extent; few, small, or short: *a limited number of places are available | special offers available for a limited period | the legislation has had a limited effect.*
▪(of a monarchy or government) exercised under limitations of power prescribed by a constitution. ▪(of a person) not great in ability or talents: *I think he is a very limited man.* ▪(**Limited**) Brit. denoting a limited company (used after a company name): *Times Newspapers Limited.*
– DERIVATIVES **limitedness** noun.

limited company (also **limited liability company**) ▶**noun** Brit. a private company whose owners are legally responsible for its debts only to the extent of the amount of capital they invested. See also **PUBLIC LIMITED COMPANY**.

limited edition ▶**noun** an edition of a book, or reproduction of a print or object, limited to a specific number of copies.

limited liability ▶**noun** [mass noun] Brit. the condition by which shareholders are legally responsible for the debts of a trading company only to the extent of the nominal value of their shares.

limited partner ▶**noun** a partner in a company or venture whose liability towards its debts is legally limited to the extent of his or her investment.
– DERIVATIVES **limited partnership** noun.

limited war ▶**noun** a war in which the weapons used, the nations or territory involved, or the objectives pursued are restricted in some way, in particular one in which the use of nuclear weapons is avoided.

limiter ▶**noun** a person or thing that limits something, in particular:
▪Electronics a circuit whose output is restricted to a

certain range of values irrespective of the size of the input. Also called **CLIPPER**. ■ (also **speed limiter**) a device that prevents a vehicle from being driven above a specified speed.

limitless ▶ adjective without end, limit, or boundary: *our resources are not limitless.*
– DERIVATIVES **limitlessly** adverb, **limitlessness** noun.

limit point ▶ noun Mathematics a point for which every neighbourhood contains at least one point belonging to a given set.

limit switch ▶ noun a switch preventing the travel of an object in a mechanism past some predetermined point, mechanically operated by the motion of the object itself.

limn /lɪm/ ▶ verb [with obj.] poetic/literary depict or describe in painting or words.
■ suffuse or highlight (something) with a bright colour or light: *a crescent moon limned each shred with white gold.*
– ORIGIN late Middle English (in the sense 'illuminate a manuscript'): alteration of obsolete *lumine* 'illuminate', via Old French *luminer* from Latin *luminare* 'make light'.

limner /ˈlɪmnə/ ▶ noun chiefly historical a painter, especially of portraits or miniatures.

limnology /lɪmˈnɒlədʒi/ ▶ noun [mass noun] the study of the biological, chemical, and physical features of lakes and other bodies of fresh water.
– DERIVATIVES **limnological** adjective, **limnologist** noun.
– ORIGIN late 19th cent.: from Greek *limnē* 'lake' + **-LOGY**.

Límnos /ˈlimnɔs/ Greek name for **LEMNOS**.

limo ▶ noun (pl. **-os**) short for **LIMOUSINE**.

Limoges /lɪˈməʊʒ, French limɔʒ/ a city in west central France, the principal city of Limousin; pop. 136,400 (1990). Famous in the late Middle Ages for enamel work, it has been noted since the 18th century for the production of porcelain.

Limón /lɪˈmɒn/ a port on the Caribbean coast of Costa Rica; pop. 75,430 (est. 1995). Also called **PUERTO LIMÓN**.

limonene /ˈlɪməniːn/ ▶ noun [mass noun] Chemistry a colourless liquid hydrocarbon with a lemon-like scent, present in lemon oil, orange oil, and similar essential oils.
• A terpene; chem. formula: $C_{10}H_{16}$.

limonite /ˈlʌɪmənʌɪt/ ▶ noun [mass noun] an amorphous brownish secondary mineral consisting of a mixture of hydrous ferric oxides, important as an iron ore.
– DERIVATIVES **limonitic** adjective.
– ORIGIN early 19th cent.: from German *Limonit*, probably from Greek *leimōn* 'meadow' (suggested by the earlier German name *Wiesenerz*, literally 'meadow ore').

Limousin[1] /ˈlimuːzã, French limuzɛ̃/ a region and former province of central France, centred on Limoges.

Limousin[2] /ˈlɪmʊzã, French limuzɛ̃/ ▶ noun **1** a native or inhabitant of Limousin.
2 [mass noun] the French dialect of this region.
3 an animal of a French breed of beef cattle.
▶ adjective of or relating to this people or their dialect.

limousine /ˈlɪməziːn, ˌlɪməˈziːn/ ▶ noun a large, luxurious motor car, especially one driven by a chauffeur who is separated from the passengers by a partition.
■ chiefly N. Amer. a passenger vehicle carrying people to and from an airport.
– ORIGIN early 20th cent.: from French, feminine adjective meaning 'of Limousin', originally denoting a caped cloak worn in *Limousin* (see **LIMOUSIN**[1]): the car originally had a roof that protected the outside driving seat.

limousine liberal ▶ noun US derogatory a wealthy liberal.

limp[1] ▶ verb [no obj.] walk with difficulty, typically because of a damaged or stiff leg or foot: *he limped off during Saturday's game.*
■ [with adverbial of direction] (of a damaged ship, aircraft, or vehicle) proceed with difficulty: *the badly damaged aircraft limped back to Sicily.*
▶ noun a tendency to limp: a gait impeded by injury or stiffness: *he walked with a limp.*
– ORIGIN late Middle English (in the sense 'fall short of'): related to obsolete *limphalt* 'lame', and probably of Germanic origin.

limp[2] ▶ adjective lacking internal strength or structure; not stiff or firm: *she let her whole body go limp | the flags hung limp and still.*
■ having or denoting a book cover that is not stiffened with board. ■ without energy or will: *he was feeling too limp to argue | a limp handshake.*
– DERIVATIVES **limply** adverb, **limpness** noun.
– ORIGIN early 18th cent.: of unknown origin; perhaps related to **LIMP**[1], having the basic sense 'hanging loose'.

limpet ▶ noun a marine mollusc which has a shallow conical shell and a broad muscular foot, proverbial for the way it clings tightly to rocks.
• Patellidae, Fissurellidae (the keyhole limpets), and other families, class Gastropoda: numerous species, including the **common limpet** (*Patella vulgata*).
– ORIGIN Old English *lempedu*, from medieval Latin *lampreda* 'limpet, lamprey'.

limpet mine ▶ noun a mine designed to be attached magnetically to a ship's hull and set to explode after a certain time.

limpid ▶ adjective (of a liquid) free of anything that darkens; completely clear.
■ (of a person's eyes) unclouded; clear. ■ (especially of writing or music) clear and accessible or melodious: *the limpid notes of a recorder.*
– DERIVATIVES **limpidity** noun, **limpidly** adverb.
– ORIGIN late Middle English: from Latin *limpidus*; perhaps related to **LYMPH**.

limpkin ▶ noun a wading marshbird related to the rails, with long legs and a long bill, found in the south-eastern US and tropical America.
• *Aramus guarauna*, the only member of the family Aramidae.
– ORIGIN late 19th cent.: from **LIMP**[1] (with reference to the bird's limping gait) + **-KIN**.

Limpopo /lɪmˈpəʊpəʊ/ a river of SE Africa. Rising as the Crocodile River near Johannesburg, it flows 1,770 km (1,100 miles) in a sweeping curve to the north and east to meet the Indian Ocean in Mozambique, north of Maputo. For much of its course it forms South Africa's boundary with Botswana and Zimbabwe.

limp-wristed ▶ adjective informal, derogatory (of a man, especially a homosexual) effeminate.

limulus /ˈlɪmjʊləs/ ▶ noun (pl. **limuli**) an arthropod of a genus that comprises the North American horseshoe crab and its extinct relatives.
• Genus *Limulus*, class Merostomata.
– ORIGIN modern Latin, from Latin *limulus* 'somewhat oblique', from *limus* 'oblique'.

linac /ˈlɪnak/ ▶ noun short for **LINEAR ACCELERATOR**.

Linacre /ˈlɪnəkə/, Thomas (*c.*1460–1524), English physician and classical scholar. In 1518 he founded the College of Physicians in London, and became its first president. He translated Galen's Greek works on medicine and philosophy into Latin, reviving studies in anatomy, botany, and clinical medicine in Britain.

linage /ˈlʌɪnɪdʒ/ ▶ noun [mass noun] the number of lines in printed or written matter, especially when used to calculate payment.

Lin Biao /lɪn ˈbjaʊ/ (also **Lin Piao**) (1908–71), Chinese communist statesman and general. He was nominated to become Mao's successor in 1969. Having staged an unsuccessful coup in 1971, he was reported to have been killed in a plane crash while fleeing to the Soviet Union.

linchpin (also **lynchpin**) ▶ noun **1** a pin passed through the end of an axle to keep a wheel in position.
2 a person or thing vital to an enterprise or organization: *regular brushing is the linchpin of all good dental hygiene.*
– ORIGIN late Middle English: from Old English *lynis* (in the sense 'linchpin') + **PIN**.

Lincoln[1] /ˈlɪŋk(ə)n/ **1** a city in eastern England, the county town of Lincolnshire; pop. 81,900 (1991). It was founded by the Romans as Lindum Colonia.
2 the state capital of Nebraska; pop. 191,970 (1990). Founded as Lancaster in 1856, it was made state capital in 1867 and renamed in honour of Abraham Lincoln.

Lincoln[2] /ˈlɪŋk(ə)n/, Abraham (1809–65), American Republican statesman, 16th President of the US 1861–5. His election as President on an anti-slavery platform helped precipitate the American Civil War; he was assassinated shortly after the war ended. Lincoln was noted for his succinct, eloquent speeches, including the Gettysburg address of 1863.

Lincoln green ▶ noun [mass noun] historical bright green woollen cloth originally made at Lincoln.

Lincoln Memorial a monument in Washington DC to Abraham Lincoln, designed by Henry Bacon (1866–1924). Built in the form of a Greek temple, the monument houses a large statue of Lincoln.

Lincoln red ▶ noun an animal of a breed of red shorthorn cattle, producing both meat and milk.

Lincolnshire /ˈlɪŋkənʃɪə, -ʃə/ a county on the east coast of England; county town, Lincoln. The former northern part of the county, included in Humberside 1974–96, is now divided into the unitary councils of **North Lincolnshire** and **North East Lincolnshire**.

Lincoln's Inn one of the Inns of Court in London.

Lincrusta /lɪŋˈkrʌstə/ ▶ noun [mass noun] trademark a wallpaper covered with embossed linoleum.
– ORIGIN late 19th cent.: from Latin *linum* 'flax' + *crusta* 'bark', suggested by **LINOLEUM**.

Lincs. ▶ abbreviation for Lincolnshire.

linctus /ˈlɪŋktəs/ ▶ noun [mass noun] Brit. thick liquid medicine, especially cough mixture.
– ORIGIN late 17th cent.: from Latin, from *lingere* 'to lick'.

Lind[1], James (1716–94), Scottish physician. He laid the foundations for the discovery of vitamins by performing experiments on scurvy in sailors. After his death the Royal Navy officially adopted the practice of giving lime juice to sailors.

Lind[2], Jenny (1820–87), Swedish soprano; born *Johanna Maria Lind Goldschmidt*. She was known as 'the Swedish nightingale' for the purity and agility of her voice.

lindane /ˈlɪndeɪn/ ▶ noun [mass noun] a synthetic organochlorine insecticide, now generally restricted in use owing to its toxicity and persistence in the environment. Also called **GAMMA-HCH**.
• An isomer of benzene hexachloride; chem. formula: $C_6H_{12}Cl_6$.
– ORIGIN 1940s: named after Teunis van der *Linden*, 20th-cent. Dutch chemist.

Lindbergh /ˈlɪndbəːg/, Charles (Augustus) (1902–74), American aviator. In 1927 he made the first solo transatlantic flight in a single-engined monoplane, *Spirit of St Louis*. He moved to Europe with his wife to escape the publicity surrounding the kidnap and murder of his two-year-old son in 1932.

Lindemann /ˈlɪndəmən/, Frederick Alexander, see **CHERWELL**.

linden ▶ noun another term for the lime tree (**LIME**[3]), especially in North America.
– ORIGIN Old English (as an adjective in the sense 'made of wood from the lime tree'): from *lind* 'lime tree' (compare with **LIME**[3]) + **-EN**[3], reinforced by obsolete Dutch *lindenboom* and German *Lindenbaum*.

Lindisfarne /ˈlɪndɪsˌfɑːn/ a small island off the coast of Northumberland, north of the Farne Islands. Linked to the mainland by a causeway exposed only at low tide, it is the site of a church and monastery founded by St Aidan in 635. Also called **HOLY ISLAND**.

Lindsay /ˈlɪndzi/ a family of Australian artists. **Sir Lionel Lindsay** (1874–1961) was an art critic, watercolour painter, and graphic artist. His brother, **Norman Lindsay** (1874–1969), was a graphic artist, painter, critic, and novelist.

Lindum Colonia /ˌlɪndəm kəˈləʊnɪə/ Roman name for **LINCOLN**[1].

line[1] ▶ noun **1** a long, narrow mark or band: *a row of closely spaced dots will look like a continuous line | I can't draw a straight line.*
■ Mathematics a straight or curved continuous extent of length without breadth. ■ a positioning or movement of a thing or things that creates or appears to follow such a line: *her mouth set in an angry line | the ball rose in a straight line.* ■ a furrow or wrinkle in the skin of the face or hands. ■ a contour or outline considered as a feature of design or composition: *crisp architectural lines | [mass noun] the artist's use of clean line and colour.* ■ (on a map or graph) a curve connecting all points having a specified common property. ■ a line marking the starting or finishing point in a race. ■ a line painted on to a field or court that relates in various ways to the rules of a game or sport. ■ (**the Line**) the equator. ■ a notional limit or boundary: *the issue of peace cut*

across class lines | television blurs the line between news and entertainment. ■ each of the very narrow horizontal sections forming a television picture. ■ Physics a narrow range of the spectrum that is noticeably brighter or darker than the adjacent parts. ■ (**the line**) the level of the base of most letters, such as *h* and *x*, in printing and writing. ■ [as modifier] Printing & Computing denoting an illustration or graphic consisting of lines and solid areas, with no gradation of tone: *a line block | line art.* ■ each of (usually five) horizontal lines forming a stave in musical notation. ■ a sequence of notes or tones forming an instrumental or vocal melody: *a powerful melodic line.*

2 a length of cord, rope, wire, or other material serving a particular purpose: *wring the clothes and hang them on the line | a telephone line.*
■ a telephone connection: *she had a crank **on the line**.* ■ a railway track. ■ a branch or route of a railway system: *the Glasgow to London line.* ■ a company that provides ships, aircraft, or buses on particular routes on a regular basis: *a major shipping line.*

3 a horizontal row of written or printed words.
■ a part of a poem forming one such row: *each stanza has eight lines.* ■ (**lines**) the words of an actor's part in a play or film. ■ a particularly noteworthy written or spoken sentence: *his speech ended with a line about the failure of justice.* ■ (**lines**) an amount of text or number of repetitions of a sentence written out as a school punishment.

4 a row of people or things: *a line of altar boys proceeded down the aisle.*
■ N. Amer. a queue. ■ a connected series of people following one another in time (used especially of several generations of a family): *we follow the history of a family through the male line.* ■ a series of related things: *the bill is the latest in a long line of measures to protect society from criminals.* ■ a range of commercial goods: *the company intends to hire more people and expand its product line.*

5 an area or branch of activity: *the stresses unique to their **line of work**.*
■ a direction, course, or channel: *lines of communication | he opened another line of attack.* ■ (**lines**) a manner of doing or thinking about something: *you can't run a business **on these lines** | the superintendent was thinking **along the same lines**.* ■ an agreed approach; a policy: *the official line is that there were no chemical attacks on allied troops.* ■ informal a false or exaggerated account or story: *he feeds me a line about this operation.*

6 a connected series of military fieldworks or defences facing an enemy force: *raids behind enemy lines.*
■ an arrangement of soldiers or ships in a column or line formation; a line of battle. ■ (**the line**) regular army regiments (as opposed to auxiliary forces or household troops).

▶ **verb** [with obj.] **1** stand or be positioned at intervals along: *a processional route lined by people waving flags.*
2 [usu. as adj. **lined**] mark or cover with lines: *a thin woman with a lined face | lined paper.*

– PHRASES **above the line 1** Finance denoting or relating to money spent on items of current expenditure. **2** Bridge denoting bonus points and penalty points, which do not count towards the game. **all** (**the way**) **down** (or **along**) **the line** at every point or stage: *the mistakes were due to lack of care all down the line.* **along** (or **down**) **the line** at a further, later, or unspecified point: *I knew that somewhere down the line there would be an inquest.* **below the line 1** Finance denoting or relating to money spent on items of capital expenditure. **2** Bridge denoting points for tricks bid and won, which count towards the game. **bring someone/thing into line** cause someone or something to conform: *the change in the law will **bring** Britain **into line with** Europe.* **come down to the line** (of a race) be closely fought right until the end. **come into line** conform: *Britain has **come into line with** other Western democracies in giving the vote to its citizens living abroad.* **the end of the line** the point at which further effort is unproductive or one can go no further. **get a line on** informal learn something about. **in line 1** under control: *that threat **kept** a lot of people **in line**.* **2** chiefly N. Amer. in a queue: *I always peer at other people's baskets as we **stand in line**.* **in line for** likely to receive: *the club are in line for a windfall of three hundred thousand pounds.* **in the line of duty** while one is working (used mainly of police officers or soldiers). **in** (or **out of**) **line with** in (or not in) alignment or accordance with: *remuneration is in line with comparable international organizations.* **lay** (or **put**) **it on the line** speak frankly. (**draw**) **a line in the sand** (state that one has reached) a point beyond which one will not go. **line of communications** see COMMUNICATION. **line of credit** an amount of credit extended to a borrower. **line of fire** the expected path of gunfire or a missile: *residents within line of fire were evacuated from their homes.* **line of flight** the route taken through the air. **line of force** an imaginary line which represents the strength and direction of a magnetic, gravitational, or electric field at any point. **the line of least resistance** see RESISTANCE. **line of march** the route taken in marching. **line of scrimmage** American Football the imaginary line separating the teams at the beginning of a play. **line of sight** a straight line along which an observer has unobstructed vision: *a building which obstructs our line of sight.* **line of vision** the straight line along which an observer looks: *Jimmy moved forward into Len's line of vision.* **on the line 1** at serious risk: *their careers were on the line.* **2** (of a picture in an exhibition) hung with its centre about level with the spectator's eye. **out of line** informal behaving in a way that breaks the rules or is considered disreputable or inappropriate: *he had never **stepped out of line** with her before.*

– ORIGIN Old English *līne* 'rope, series', probably of Germanic origin, from Latin *linea* (*fibra*) 'flax (fibre)', from Latin *linum* 'flax', reinforced in Middle English by Old French *ligne*, based on Latin *linea*.

▶ **line out** Baseball be caught out after hitting a line drive.
line something out transplant seedlings from beds into nursery lines, where they are grown before being moved to their permanent position.
line someone/thing up 1 arrange a number of people or things in a straight row. ■ (**line up**) (of a number of people or things) be arranged in this way: *we would line up across the parade ground, shoulder to shoulder.* **2** have someone or something ready or prepared: *have you got any work lined up?*

line² ▶ **verb** [with obj.] cover the inside surface of (a container or garment) with a layer of different material: *a basket **lined with** polythene.*
■ form a layer on the inside surface of (an area); cover as if with a lining: *hundreds of telegrams lined the walls.* ■ informal fill (something, especially one's stomach): *Yorkshire pudding to line your stomach.*

– PHRASES **line one's pocket** make money, especially by dishonest means.

– ORIGIN late Middle English: from obsolete *line* 'flax', with reference to the common use of linen for linings.

lineage /ˈlɪnɪɪdʒ/ ▶ **noun 1** [mass noun] lineal descent from an ancestor; ancestry or pedigree.
■ [count noun] Anthropology a social group tracing its descent from a single ancestor.
2 [count noun] Biology a sequence of species each of which is considered to have evolved from its predecessor: *the chimpanzee and gorilla lineages.*
■ a sequence of cells in the body which developed from a common ancestral cell: *the myeloid lineage.*

– ORIGIN Middle English: from Old French *lignage*, from Latin *linea* 'a line' (see LINE¹).

lineal /ˈlɪnɪəl/ ▶ **adjective 1** in a direct line of descent or ancestry: *a lineal descendant.*
2 of, relating to, or consisting of lines; linear.

– DERIVATIVES **lineally** adverb.

– ORIGIN late Middle English: via Old French from late Latin *linealis*, from *linea* 'a line' (see LINE¹).

lineament /ˈlɪnɪəm(ə)nt/ ▶ **noun 1** (usu. **lineaments**) poetic/literary a distinctive feature or characteristic, especially of the face.
2 Geology a linear feature on the earth's surface, such as a fault.

– ORIGIN late Middle English: from Latin *lineamentum*, from *lineare* 'make straight', from *linea* 'a line' (see LINE¹).

linear /ˈlɪnɪə/ ▶ **adjective 1** arranged in or extending along a straight or nearly straight line: *linear arrangements | linear in shape | linear movement.*
■ consisting of or predominantly formed using lines or outlines: *simple linear designs.* ■ involving one dimension only: *linear elasticity.* ■ Mathematics able to be represented by a straight line on a graph; involving or exhibiting directly proportional change in two related quantities: *linear functions | linear relationship.*
2 progressing from one stage to another in a single series of steps; sequential: *a linear narrative.*

– DERIVATIVES **linearity** noun, **linearly** adverb.

– ORIGIN mid 17th cent.: from Latin *linearis*, from *linea* 'a line' (see LINE¹).

Linear A the earlier of two related forms of writing discovered at Knossos in Crete between 1894 and 1901, found on tablets and vases dating from *c.*1700 to 1450 BC and still largely unintelligible.

linear accelerator ▶ **noun** Physics an accelerator in which particles travel in straight lines, not in closed orbits.

Linear B a form of Bronze Age writing discovered on tablets in Crete, dating from *c.*1400 to 1200 BC. In 1952 it was shown to be a syllabic script composed of linear signs, derived from Linear A and older Minoan scripts, representing a form of Mycenaean Greek.

linear equation ▶ **noun** an equation between two variables that gives a straight line when plotted on a graph.

linearize (also **-ise**) ▶ **verb** [with obj.] technical make linear; represent in or transform into a linear form.

– DERIVATIVES **linearization** noun, **linearizer** noun.

linear motor ▶ **noun** an electric induction motor which produces straight-line motion (as opposed to rotary motion) by means of a linear stator and rotor placed in parallel. It has been used to drive trams and monorails, where one part of the motor is on the underside of the vehicle and the other is in the track.

linear perspective ▶ **noun** [mass noun] a type of perspective used by artists, in which the relative size, shape, and position of objects is determined by drawn or imagined lines converging at a point on the horizon.

linear programming ▶ **noun** [mass noun] a mathematical technique for maximizing or minimizing a linear function of several variables, such as output or cost.

lineation /ˌlɪnɪˈeɪʃ(ə)n/ ▶ **noun** [mass noun] the action or process of drawing lines or marking with lines.
■ [count noun] a line or linear marking; an arrangement or group of lines: *magnetic lineations.* ■ [count noun] a contour or outline. ■ the division of text into lines: *the punctuation and lineation are reproduced accurately.*

– ORIGIN late Middle English: from Latin *lineatio(n-)*, from *lineare* 'make straight'.

linebacker ▶ **noun** American Football a defensive player positioned just behind the line of scrimmage.

line breeding ▶ **noun** [mass noun] the selective breeding of animals for a desired feature by mating them within a closely related line.

line dancing ▶ **noun** [mass noun] a type of country and western dancing in which dancers line up in a row without partners and follow a choreographed pattern of steps to music.

– DERIVATIVES **line dance** noun, **line-dance** verb, **line dancer** noun.

line drawing ▶ **noun** a drawing done using only narrow lines, without blocks of shading.

line drive ▶ **noun** Baseball a powerfully struck shot that travels close to the ground.

line engraving ▶ **noun** [mass noun] the art or technique of engraving by lines incised on the plate, as distinguished from etching and mezzotint.
■ [count noun] an engraving executed in this manner.

– DERIVATIVES **line-engraved** adjective, **line engraver** noun.

linefeed ▶ **noun** [mass noun] the action of advancing paper in a printing machine by the space of one line.
■ Computing the analogous movement of text on a VDU screen.

linefish ▶ **noun** [mass noun] S. African fish of smaller species, caught from the shore or with lines from boats rather than by trawlers.

line integral ▶ **noun** Mathematics the integral, taken along a line, of any function that has a continuously varying value along that line.

Line Islands a group of eleven islands in the central Pacific, straddling the equator south of Hawaii. Eight of the islands, including Kiritimati (Christmas Island), form part of Kiribati; the remaining three are uninhabited dependencies of the US.

Lineker /ˈlɪnɪkə/, Gary (Winston) (b.1960), English footballer. A striker with Leicester City, Everton, Barcelona, and Tottenham Hotspur, Lineker scored forty-eight goals for England, one short of Bobby Charlton's record.

lineman ▸ noun (pl. **-men**) **1** a person employed in laying and maintaining railway track.
■ North American term for **LINESMAN** (in sense 2).
2 American Football a player positioned on the line of scrimmage.

line manager ▸ noun chiefly Brit. a person with direct managerial responsibility for a particular employee.
■ a manager involved in running the main business activities of a company.
– DERIVATIVES **line management** noun.

linen ▸ noun [mass noun] cloth woven from flax.
■ garments or other household articles such as sheets made, or originally made, of linen.
– ORIGIN Old English *līnen* (as an adjective in the sense 'made of flax'), of West Germanic origin; related to Dutch *linnen*, German *Leinen*, also to obsolete *line* 'flax'.

linen basket ▸ noun chiefly Brit. a receptacle with a lid, for holding soiled clothing.

linenfold ▸ noun [mass noun] carved or moulded ornaments, especially on a panel, representing folds or scrolls of linen.

line of battle ▸ noun a disposition of troops for action in battle.
■ historical a battle formation of warships in line ahead.

line-out ▸ noun Rugby Union a formation of parallel lines of opposing forwards at right angles to the touchline when the ball is thrown in.
■ an occasion when the ball is thrown in to such a formation.

line printer ▸ noun a machine that prints output from a computer a line at a time rather than character by character.

liner[1] ▸ noun **1** (also **ocean liner**) a large luxurious passenger ship of a type formerly used on a regular line.
2 a fine paintbrush used for painting thin lines and for outlining.
■ a cosmetic used for outlining or accentuating a facial feature, or a brush or pencil for applying this.
3 a boat engaged in sea fishing with lines as opposed to nets.
4 a ferret held on a leash or line while rabbiting, used to help recover another ferret lost underground.

liner[2] ▸ noun a lining in an appliance, device, or container, especially a removable one, in particular:
■ the lining of a garment. ■ (also **nappy liner**) a disposable lining for a baby's nappy. ■ (also **cylinder liner**) a replaceable metal sleeve placed within the cylinder of an engine, forming a durable surface to withstand wear from the piston.

-liner ▸ combining form informal denoting a text of a specified number of lines such as an advertisement or a spoken passage in a play, dialogue, etc.: *two-liner*.

liner note ▸ noun (usu. **liner notes**) the text printed on a paper insert issued as part of the packaging of a compact disc or on the sleeve of a gramophone record.

lineside ▸ adjective Brit. another term for **TRACKSIDE**.

linesman ▸ noun (pl. **-men**) **1** (in games played on a field or court) an official who assists the referee or umpire from the touchline, especially in deciding on whether the ball is out of play.
2 Brit. a person employed for the repair and maintenance of telephone or electricity power lines.

line spectrum ▸ noun Physics an emission spectrum consisting of separate isolated lines.
■ an emission (of light, sound, or other radiation) composed of a number of discrete frequencies or energies.

line squall ▸ noun Meteorology a violent local storm occurring as one of a number along a cold front.

line-up ▸ noun **1** a group of people or things brought together in a particular context, especially the members of a sports team or a group of musicians or other performers: *a talented batting line-up.*
2 chiefly N. Amer. a line or queue of people or things.
■ another term for **IDENTIFICATION PARADE**.

line work ▸ noun [mass noun] **1** drawings or designs carried out with a pen or pencil, as opposed to wash or similar techniques.

2 work on lines, especially as a linesman or a production-line worker.

ling[1] ▸ noun any of a number of long-bodied edible marine fishes:
● a large East Atlantic fish related to the cod (genus *Molva*, family Gadidae), in particular *M. molva*, which is of commercial importance. ● a related Australian fish (*Lotella callarias*, family Gadidae) ● a similar but unrelated Australian fish (*Genypterus blacodes*, family Ophidiidae).
– ORIGIN Middle English *lenge*, probably from Middle Dutch; related to **LONG**[1].

ling[2] ▸ noun the common heather of Eurasia.
– ORIGIN Middle English: from Old Norse *lyng*, of unknown origin.

-ling ▸ suffix **1** forming nouns from nouns (such as *hireling, sapling*).
2 forming nouns from adjectives and adverbs (such as *darling, sibling, underling*).
3 forming diminutive words: *gosling*.
■ often with depreciatory reference: *princeling*.
– ORIGIN Old English; sense 3 from Old Norse.

Lingala /lɪŋˈɡɑːlə/ ▸ noun [mass noun] a Bantu language used by over 8 million people as a lingua franca in northern parts of Congo and Zaire (Democratic Republic of Congo).
– ORIGIN a local name.

lingam /ˈlɪŋɡəm/ (also **linga** /ˈlɪŋɡə/) ▸ noun Hinduism a symbol of divine generative energy, especially a phallus or phallic object as a symbol of Shiva. Compare with **YONI**.
– ORIGIN from Sanskrit *liṅga*, literally 'mark, (sexual) characteristic'.

lingcod /ˈlɪŋkɒd/ ▸ noun (pl. same) a large slender greenling, which has large teeth and is greenish-brown with golden spots. It lives along the Pacific coast of North America, where it is a valuable commercial and sporting fish.
● *Ophiodon elongatus*, family Hexagrammidae.

linger ▸ verb [no obj.] stay in a place longer than necessary, typically because of a reluctance to leave: *she lingered in the yard, enjoying the warm sunshine | she let her eyes linger on him suggestively.*
■ (**linger over**) spend a long time over (something): *she lingered over her meal.* ■ be slow to disappear or die: *the tradition seems to linger on | we are thankful that she didn't linger on and suffer.*
– DERIVATIVES **lingerer** noun.
– ORIGIN Middle English (in the sense 'dwell, abide'): frequentative of obsolete *leng* 'prolong', of Germanic origin; related to German *längen* 'make long(er)', also to **LONG**[1].

lingerie /ˈlãʒ(ə)ri/ ▸ noun [mass noun] women's underwear and nightclothes.
– ORIGIN mid 19th cent.: from French, from *linge* 'linen'.

lingering ▸ adjective [attrib.] lasting for a long time or slow to end: *there are still some lingering doubts in my mind | a painful and lingering death.*
– DERIVATIVES **lingeringly** adverb.

lingo ▸ noun (pl. **-os** or **-oes**) informal, often humorous or derogatory a foreign language or local dialect: *they were unable to speak a word of the local lingo.*
■ the vocabulary or jargon of a particular subject or group of people.
– ORIGIN mid 17th cent.: probably via Portuguese *lingoa* from Latin *lingua* 'tongue'.

lingonberry /ˈlɪŋɡ(ə)nˌb(ə)ri, -ˌbɛri/ ▸ noun (pl. **-ies**) another term for the cowberry, especially in Scandinavia where the berries are much used in cookery.
■ an Arctic variety of this plant occurring in Russia and North America.
– ORIGIN 1950s: from Swedish *lingon* 'cowberry' + **BERRY**.

lingua franca /ˌlɪŋɡwə ˈfraŋkə/ ▸ noun (pl. **lingua francas**) a language that is adopted as a common language between speakers whose native languages are different.
■ [mass noun] historical a mixture of Italian with French, Greek, Arabic, and Spanish, formerly used in the Levant.
– ORIGIN late 17th cent.: from Italian, literally 'Frankish tongue'.

lingual /ˈlɪŋɡw(ə)l/ ▸ adjective technical **1** of or relating to the tongue.
■ (of a sound) formed by the tongue. ■ Anatomy near or on the side towards the tongue.
2 of or relating to speech or language: *his demonstrations of lingual dexterity.*
– DERIVATIVES **lingually** adverb.

– ORIGIN mid 17th cent.: from medieval Latin *lingualis*, from Latin *lingua* 'tongue, language'.

linguine /lɪŋˈɡwiːneɪ, -ni/ ▸ plural noun small pieces of pasta in the form of narrow ribbons.
– ORIGIN Italian, plural of *linguina*, diminutive of *lingua* 'tongue'.

linguist ▸ noun **1** a person skilled in foreign languages.
2 a person who studies linguistics.
– ORIGIN late 16th cent.: from Latin *lingua* 'language' + **-IST**.

linguistic ▸ adjective of or relating to language or linguistics.
– DERIVATIVES **linguistically** adverb.

linguistic competence ▸ noun see **COMPETENCE**.

linguistic performance ▸ noun see **PERFORMANCE** (sense 2).

linguistics /lɪŋˈɡwɪstɪks/ ▸ plural noun [treated as sing.] the scientific study of language and its structure, including the study of grammar, syntax, and phonetics. Specific branches of linguistics include sociolinguistics, dialectology, psycholinguistics, computational linguistics, comparative linguistics, and structural linguistics.
– DERIVATIVES **linguistician** /-ˈstɪʃ(ə)n/ noun.

lingulate /ˈlɪŋɡjʊleɪt/ ▸ adjective Botany & Zoology tongue-shaped.
■ Zoology denoting a type of burrowing brachiopod with an inarticulate shell and a long pedicle.
– ORIGIN mid 19th cent.: from Latin *lingulatus*, based on *lingua* 'tongue', from *lingere* 'to lick'.

linhay /ˈlɪni/ ▸ noun dialect a shed or other farm building open in front, typically with a lean-to roof.
– ORIGIN late 17th cent.: of unknown origin.

liniment /ˈlɪnɪm(ə)nt/ ▸ noun [mass noun] an embrocation for rubbing on the body to relieve pain, especially one made with oil.
– ORIGIN late Middle English: from late Latin *linimentum*, from Latin *linire* 'to smear'.

lining ▸ noun a layer of different material covering the inside surface of something: *self-clean oven linings | [as modifier] lining paper.*
■ an additional layer of different material attached to the inside of a garment or curtain to make it warmer or hang better: *leather gloves with fur linings.*

linish /ˈlɪnɪʃ/ ▸ verb [with obj.] technical polish or remove excess material from (something) by contact with an abrasive moving belt.
– DERIVATIVES **linisher** noun.
– ORIGIN 1970s (as a verb): blend of **LINEN** and **FINISH**.

link[1] ▸ noun **1** a relationship between two things or situations, especially where one thing affects the other: *a commission to investigate a link between pollution and forest decline.*
■ a social or professional connection between people or organizations: *he retained strong links with the media.* ■ something that enables communication between people: *sign language interpreters represent a vital link between the deaf and hearing communities.* ■ a means of contact by radio, telephone, or computer between two points: *they set up a satellite link with Tokyo.* ■ a means of travel or transport between two places: *a high-speed rail link to the channel tunnel.* ■ Computing a code or instruction which connects one part of a program or an element in a list to another.
2 a ring or loop in a chain.
■ a unit of measurement of length equal to one hundredth of a surveying chain (7.92 inches).
▸ verb make, form, or suggest a connection with or between: [with obj.] *rumours that linked his name with Judith | foreign and domestic policy are linked | [no obj.] she linked up with an artistic group.*
■ connect or join physically: [with obj.] *a network of routes linking towns and villages | the cows are linked up to milking machines | [no obj.] three different groups, each linking with the other.* ■ [with obj.] clasp; intertwine: *once outside he linked arms with her.*
– ORIGIN late Middle English (denoting a loop; also as a verb in the sense 'connect physically'): from Old Norse *hlekkr*, of Germanic origin; related to German *Gelenk* 'joint'.

link[2] ▸ noun historical a torch of pitch and tow for lighting the way in dark streets.
– ORIGIN early 16th cent.: perhaps from medieval Latin *li(n)chinus* 'wick', from Greek *lukhnos* 'light'.

linkage ▸ noun [mass noun] the action of linking or the state of being linked.

■[count noun] a system of links: *a complex linkage of nerves.* ■ the linking of different issues in political negotiations. ■ Genetics the tendency of groups of genes on the same chromosome to be inherited together.

linked list ▶ noun Computing an ordered set of data elements, each containing a link to its successor (and sometimes its predecessor).

linker ▶ noun a thing which links other things, in particular:
■ Computing a program used with a compiler or assembler to provide links to the libraries needed for an executable program. ■ an attachment on a knitting machine for linking two pieces of knitting.

linking ▶ adjective connecting or joining something to something else.
■ Phonetics denoting a consonant that is sounded at a boundary between two words or morphemes where two vowels would otherwise be adjacent, as in *law(r) and order.* See also LIAISON.

linkman ▶ noun (pl. **-men**) Brit. a person serving as a connection between groups of people.
■ a person providing continuity between items in a radio or television programme or between such programmes.

Linköping /ˈlɪnˌtʃɔːpɪŋ/ an industrial town in SE Sweden; pop. 122,270 (1990). It was a noted cultural and ecclesiastical centre in the Middle Ages.

links ▶ plural noun (also **golf links**) [treated as sing. or pl.] a golf course, especially one on grass-covered sandy ground near the sea.
■ another term for LINKSLAND.
– ORIGIN Old English *hlinc* 'rising ground', perhaps related to LEAN[1].

linksland ▶ noun [mass noun] Scottish level or undulating sandy ground covered by coarse grass and near the sea.
– ORIGIN 1920s: from Scots *links* 'rising ground' (see LINKS) + LAND.

linkspan ▶ noun a hinged bridge on the quay at a port or ferry terminal which can be connected with a ramp on a vessel to allow loading or unloading.

link-up ▶ noun an instance of two or more people or things connecting or joining.
■ a connection enabling two or more people or machines to communicate with each other: *a live satellite link-up.*

linkwork ▶ noun [mass noun] a kind of gearing which transmits motion by a series of links rather than by wheels or bands.

linn ▶ noun Scottish archaic a waterfall.
■ the pool below a waterfall. ■ a steep precipice.
– ORIGIN early 16th cent., from Scottish Gaelic *linne*, Irish *linn*, related to Welsh *llyn* 'lake'.

Linnaeus /lɪˈniːəs, -ˈneɪəs/, Carolus (1707–78), Swedish botanist, founder of modern systematic botany and zoology; Latinized name of *Carl von Linné.* He devised an authoritative classification system for flowering plants involving binomial Latin names (later superseded by that of Antoine Jussieu), and also a classification method for animals.
– DERIVATIVES **Linnaean** (also **Linnean**) adjective & noun.

linnet ▶ noun a mainly brown and grey finch with a reddish breast and forehead.
● Genus *Acanthis,* family Fringillidae: three species, in particular the Eurasian *A. cannabina.*
– ORIGIN early 16th cent.: from Old French *linette,* from *lin* 'flax' (because the bird feeds on flaxseeds).

lino ▶ noun (pl. **-os**) chiefly Brit. informal term for LINOLEUM.

linocut ▶ noun a design or form carved in relief on a block of linoleum.
■ a print made from such a block.

linocutting ▶ noun [mass noun] the action or technique of making a print from a linocut block.

linoleic acid /ˌlɪnə(ʊ)ˈliːɪk, -ˈleɪɪk/ ▶ noun [mass noun] Chemistry a polyunsaturated fatty acid present as a glyceride in linseed oil and other oils and essential in the human diet.
● Chem. formula: $C_{17}H_{31}COOH$.
– DERIVATIVES **linoleate** noun.
– ORIGIN mid 19th cent.: from Latin *linum* 'flax' + OLEIC ACID.

linolenic acid /ˌlɪnə(ʊ)ˈlɛnɪk, -ˈliːnɪk/ ▶ noun [mass noun] Chemistry a polyunsaturated fatty acid (with one more double bond than linoleic acid) present as a

glyceride in linseed and other oils and essential in the human diet.
● Chem. formula: $C_{17}H_{29}COOH$; several isomers, notably **gamma-linolenic acid,** present in evening primrose oil.
– DERIVATIVES **linolenate** noun.
– ORIGIN late 19th cent.: from German *Linolensäure,* from *Linolsäure* 'linoleic acid', with the insertion of *-en-* (from -ENE).

linoleum /lɪˈnəʊlɪəm/ ▶ noun [mass noun] a material consisting of a canvas backing thickly coated with a preparation of linseed oil and powdered cork, used especially as a floor covering.
– DERIVATIVES **linoleumed** adjective.
– ORIGIN late 19th cent.: from Latin *linum* 'flax' + *oleum* 'oil'.

Linotype /ˈlaɪnə(ʊ)tʌɪp/ ▶ noun Printing trademark a composing machine producing lines of words as single strips of metal, used chiefly for newspapers. It is now rarely used.
– ORIGIN late 19th cent.: alteration of the phrase *line o' type.*

Lin Piao /lɪn ˈpjaʊ/ variant of LIN BIAO.

linsang /ˈlɪnsaŋ/ ▶ noun a small secretive relation of the civet, with a spotted or banded coat and a long tail, found in the forests of SE Asia and West Africa.
● Family Viverridae: genera *Prionodon* (two Asian species) and *Poiana* (one African species).
– ORIGIN early 19th cent.: via Javanese from Malay.

linseed ▶ noun [mass noun] the seeds of the flax plant, which are the source of linseed oil and linseed cake.
■ the flax plant, especially when grown for linseed oil.
– ORIGIN Old English *līnsǣd,* from *līn* 'flax' + *sǣd* 'seed'.

linseed cake ▶ noun [mass noun] pressed linseed used as cattle food.

linseed oil ▶ noun [mass noun] a pale yellow oil extracted from linseed, used especially in paint and varnish.

linsey-woolsey /ˌlɪnzɪˈwʊlzɪ/ (also **linsey-wolsey**) ▶ noun [mass noun] a strong, coarse fabric with a linen or cotton warp and a woollen weft.
– ORIGIN late 15th cent.: from *linsey,* originally denoting a coarse linen fabric (probably from *Lindsey,* a village in Suffolk where the material was first made) + WOOL + *-sey* as a rhyming suffix.

linstock ▶ noun historical a long pole used to hold a match for firing a cannon.
– ORIGIN late 16th cent.: from earlier *lintstock,* from Dutch *lontstok,* from *lont* 'match' + *stok* 'stick'. The change in the first syllable was due to association with LINT.

lint ▶ noun [mass noun] short, fine fibres which separate from the surface of cloth or yarn during processing.
■ Brit. a fabric, originally of linen, with a raised nap on one side, used for dressing wounds. ■ the fibrous material of a cotton boll. ■ Scottish flax fibres prepared for spinning.
– DERIVATIVES **linty** adjective.
– ORIGIN late Middle English *lynnet* 'flax prepared for spinning', perhaps from Old French *linette* 'linseed', from *lin* 'flax'.

lintel ▶ noun a horizontal support of timber, stone, concrete, or steel across the top of a door or window.
– DERIVATIVES **lintelled** (US **linteled**) adjective.
– ORIGIN Middle English: from Old French, based on late Latin *liminare,* from Latin *limen* 'threshold'.

linter ▶ noun a machine for removing the short fibres from cotton seeds after ginning.
■ (**linters**) fibres of this kind.

lintie /ˈlɪntɪ/ ▶ noun (pl. **-ies**) Scottish term for LINNET.

liny ▶ adjective (**linier, liniest**) informal marked with lines; wrinkled.

Linz /lɪnts/ an industrial city in northern Austria, on the River Danube, capital of the state of Upper Austria; pop. 202,855 (1991).

lion ▶ noun a large tawny-coloured cat that lives in prides, found in Africa and NW India. The male has a flowing shaggy mane and takes little part in hunting, which is done cooperatively by the females.
● *Panthera leo,* family Felidae.
■ the lion as an emblem (e.g. of English or Scottish royalty) or as a charge in heraldry. ■ (**the Lion**) the zodiacal sign or constellation Leo. ■ figurative a brave, strong, or fiercely cruel person. ■ (**Lion**) (also **British Lion**) a member of a touring international rugby

union team representing the British Isles. ■ (**Lion**) a member of a Lions Club.
– PHRASES **the lion's den** a demanding, intimidating, or unpleasant place or situation: *he marched reluctantly into the lion's den to address the charity gala.* **the lion's share** the largest part of something. **throw someone to the lions** cause someone to be in an extremely dangerous or unpleasant situation. [ORIGIN: with reference to the throwing of Christians to the lions in Roman times.]
– DERIVATIVES **lion-like** adjective.
– ORIGIN Middle English: from Anglo-Norman French *liun,* from Latin *leo, leon-,* from Greek *leōn, leont-.*

lion dance ▶ noun a traditional Chinese dance in which the dancers are masked and costumed to resemble lions.

lioness ▶ noun a female lion.

lionhead ▶ noun a goldfish of a large-headed variety.

lionhearted ▶ adjective brave and determined.

lionize /ˈlaɪənaɪz/ (also **-ise**) ▶ verb [with obj.] give a lot of public attention and approval to (someone); treat as a celebrity: *modern sportsmen are lionized and fêted.*
– DERIVATIVES **lionization** noun, **lionizer** noun.

Lions Club ▶ noun a worldwide charitable society devoted to social and international service, taking its membership primarily from business and professional groups.

lion's paw ▶ noun a large Caribbean bivalve mollusc with a thick reddish fan-shaped shell that bears coarse radial ribs.
● *Chlamys nodosus,* family Pectinidae.

lion tamarin ▶ noun a rare tamarin with a golden or black and golden coat and an erect mane, found only in Brazil.
● Genus *Leontopithecus,* family Callitrichidae (or Callitrichidae): the **golden lion tamarin** (*L. rosalia*), and three other species that have been recently recognized or discovered.

lip ▶ noun **1** either of the two fleshy parts which form the upper and lower edges of the opening of the mouth: *he kissed her on the lips.*
■ (**lips**) used to refer to a person's speech or to current topics of conversation: *downsizing is on everyone's lips at the moment.* ■ another term for LABIUM (in senses 1 and 2).
2 the edge of a hollow container or an opening: *drawing her finger around the lip of the cup.*
■ a rounded, raised, or extended piece along an edge.
3 [mass noun] informal impudent talk: *don't give me any of your lip!*
▶ verb (**lipped, lipping**) [with obj.] (of water) lap against: *beaches lipped by the surf rimming the Pacific.*
■ Golf hit the rim of (a hole) but fail to go in.
– PHRASES **bite one's lip** repress an emotion; stifle laughter or a retort: *she bit her lip to stop the rush of bitter words.* **curl one's lip** raise a corner of one's upper lip to show contempt; sneer. **lick** (or **smack**) **one's lips** look forward to something with relish; show one's satisfaction. **my** (or **his** etc.) **lips are sealed** see SEAL[1]. **pass one's lips** be eaten, drunk, or spoken. **pay lip service to** express approval of or support for (something) without taking any significant action.
– DERIVATIVES **lipless** adjective, **lip-like** adjective, **lipped** adjective [in combination] *her pale-lipped mouth.*
– ORIGIN Old English *lippa,* of Germanic origin; related to Dutch *lip* and German *Lippe,* from an Indo-European root shared by Latin *labia, labra* 'lips'.

lipa /ˈliːpə/ ▶ noun (pl. same or **lipas**) a monetary unit of Croatia, equal to one hundredth of a kuna.

lipaemia /lɪˈpiːmɪə/ (US **lipemia**) ▶ noun [mass noun] Medicine the presence in the blood of an abnormally high concentration of emulsified fat.
– ORIGIN late 19th cent.: from Greek *lipos* 'fat' + -AEMIA.

Lipari Islands /ˈlɪpəri, Italian lipˈpari/ a group of seven volcanic islands in the Tyrrhenian Sea, off the NE coast of Sicily, and in Italian possession. Believed by the ancient Greeks to be the home of Aeolus, the islands were formerly known as the Aeolian Islands.

lipase /ˈlɪpeɪz, ˈlaɪp-/ ▶ noun [mass noun] Biochemistry a pancreatic enzyme that catalyses the breakdown of fats to fatty acids and glycerol or other alcohols.
– ORIGIN late 19th cent.: from Greek *lipos* 'fat' + -ASE.

lip brush ▶ noun a small brush designed for applying lipstick.

Lipchitz /ˈlɪpʃɪts/, Jacques (1891–1973), Lithuanian-born French sculptor; born *Chaim Jacob Lipchitz*. After producing cubist works such as *Sailor with a Guitar* (1914), he explored the interpenetration of solids and voids in his series of 'transparent' sculptures of the 1920s.

Lipetsk /ˈlɪpɪtsk/ an industrial city in SW Russia, on the Voronezh River; pop. 455,000 (1990).

lipgloss ▶ noun [mass noun] a cosmetic applied to the lips to provide a glossy finish and sometimes sheer colour.

lipid ▶ noun Chemistry any of a class of organic compounds that are fatty acids or their derivatives and are insoluble in water but soluble in organic solvents. They include many natural oils, waxes, and steroids.
– ORIGIN early 20th cent.: from French *lipide*, based on Greek *lipos* 'fat'.

lipidosis /ˌlɪpɪˈdəʊsɪs/ (also **lipoidosis**) ▶ noun (pl. **lipidoses** /-siːz/) Medicine a disorder of lipid metabolism in the body tissues.

Lipizzaner /ˌlɪpɪˈtsɑːnə, ˌlɪpɪˈzeɪnə/ (also **Lippizaner**) ▶ noun a horse of a fine white breed used especially in displays of dressage.
– ORIGIN early 20th cent.: from German, from *Lippiza*, site of the former Austrian Imperial stud near Trieste.

lipline ▶ noun the outline of a person's lips, especially with reference to the application of cosmetics.

lipliner ▶ noun [mass noun] a cosmetic applied to the outline of the lips, mainly to prevent the unwanted spreading of lipstick or lipgloss.

lip microphone ▶ noun a small microphone designed to be held or worn close to a person's mouth.

Li Po /liː ˈpəʊ/ (also **Li Bo** or **Li T'ai Po**) (AD 701–62), Chinese poet. Typical themes in his poetry are wine, women, and the beauties of nature.

lipo- /ˈlɪpəʊ, ˈlʌɪpəʊ/ ▶ combining form relating to fat or other lipids: *liposuction | lipoprotein*.
– ORIGIN from Greek *lipos* 'fat'.

lipogenesis /ˌlɪpə(ʊ)ˈdʒɛnɪsɪs, ˌlʌɪ-/ ▶ noun [mass noun] Physiology the metabolic formation of fat.
– DERIVATIVES **lipogenic** adjective.

lipogram ▶ noun a composition from which the writer systematically omits a certain letter or certain letters of the alphabet.
– DERIVATIVES **lipogrammatic** adjective.
– ORIGIN early 18th cent.: back-formation from Greek *lipogrammatos* 'lacking a letter', from *lip-* (stem of *leipein* 'to leave (out)') + *gramma* 'letter'.

lipoidosis /ˌlɪpɔɪˈdəʊsɪs/ ▶ noun variant spelling of **LIPIDOSIS**.

lipolysis /lɪˈpɒlɪsɪs/ ▶ noun [mass noun] Physiology the breakdown of fats and other lipids by hydrolysis to release fatty acids.
– DERIVATIVES **lipolytic** adjective.

lipoma /lɪˈpəʊmə/ ▶ noun (pl. **lipomas** or **lipomata** /-mətə/) Medicine a benign tumour of fatty tissue.

lipophilic /ˌlɪpə(ʊ)ˈfɪlɪk, ˌlʌɪ-/ ▶ adjective Biochemistry tending to combine with or dissolve in lipids or fats.

lipopolysaccharide /ˌlɪpəʊpɒlɪˈsakərʌɪd, ˌlʌɪ-/ ▶ noun Biochemistry a complex molecule containing both lipid and polysaccharide parts.

lipoprotein ▶ noun Biochemistry any of a group of soluble proteins that combine with and transport fat or other lipids in the blood plasma.

liposome /ˈlɪpəsəʊm, ˈlʌɪ-/ ▶ noun Biochemistry a minute spherical sac of phospholipid molecules enclosing a water droplet, especially as formed artificially to carry drugs or other substances into the tissues.

liposuction /ˈlɪpə(ʊ)ˌsʌkʃ(ə)n, ˈlʌɪ-/ ▶ noun [mass noun] a technique in cosmetic surgery for removing excess fat from under the skin by suction.

lipotropin /ˌlɪpəʊˈtrəʊpɪn, ˌlʌɪ-/ (also **lipotrophin** /-ˈtrəʊfɪn/) ▶ noun Biochemistry a hormone secreted by the anterior pituitary gland which promotes the release of fat reserves from the liver into the bloodstream.

Lippes loop /ˈlɪpɪz/ ▶ noun a type of intrauterine contraceptive device made of inert plastic in a double S-shape, which can be inserted for long periods.
– ORIGIN 1960s: named after Jack *Lippes* (born 1924), American obstetrician.

Lippi[1] /ˈlɪpi/, Filippino (c.1457–1504), Italian painter, son of Fra Filippo Lippi. Having trained with his father and Botticelli he completed a fresco cycle begun by Masaccio in the Brancacci Chapel, Florence; other works include the series of frescoes in the Carafa Chapel in Rome and the painting *The Vision of St Bernard* (c.1486).

Lippi[2] /ˈlɪpi/, Fra Filippo (c.1406–69), Italian painter. He was a pupil of Masaccio, whose influence can be seen in the fresco *The Relaxation of the Carmelite Rule* (c.1432); his later style is more decorative and less monumental than his early work.

Lippizaner ▶ noun variant spelling of **LIPIZZANER**.

Lippmann /ˈlɪpmən/, Gabriel Jonas (1845–1921), French physicist. He is best known today for his production of the first fully orthochromatic colour photograph in 1893.

lippy informal ▶ adjective (**lippier**, **lippiest**) insolent; impertinent.
▶ noun (also **lippie**) [mass noun] lipstick.

lip-read ▶ verb [no obj.] (of a deaf person) understand speech from observing a speaker's lip movements.
– DERIVATIVES **lip-reader** noun.

lipsalve ▶ noun [mass noun] Brit. a preparation, typically in stick form, to prevent or relieve sore lips.

lipstick ▶ noun [mass noun] coloured cosmetic applied to the lips from a small solid stick.

lip-sync (also **-synch**) ▶ verb [with obj.] (of an actor or singer) move the lips silently in synchronization with (a pre-recorded soundtrack).
▶ noun [mass noun] the action of using such a technique.
– DERIVATIVES **lip-syncer** noun.

liquate /lɪˈkweɪt/ ▶ verb [with obj.] Metallurgy separate or purify (a metal) by melting it.
– DERIVATIVES **liquation** noun.
– ORIGIN mid 19th cent.: from Latin *liquat-* 'made liquid', from the verb *liquare*; related to **LIQUOR**.

liquefied petroleum gas (abbrev.: **LPG**) ▶ noun [mass noun] a mixture of light gaseous hydrocarbons (ethane, propane, butane, etc.) made liquid by pressure and used as fuel.

liquefy /ˈlɪkwɪfʌɪ/ (also **liquify**) ▶ verb (**-ies**, **-ied**) make or become liquid: [with obj.] *the minimum pressure required to liquefy a gas* | [no obj.] *as the fungus ripens, the cap turns black and liquefies*.
– DERIVATIVES **liquefaction** noun, **liquefactive** adjective, **liquefiable** adjective, **liquefier** noun.
– ORIGIN late Middle English: from French *liquéfier* from Latin *liquefacere* 'make liquid', from *liquere* 'be liquid'.

liquescent /lɪˈkwɛs(ə)nt/ ▶ adjective poetic/literary becoming or apt to become liquid.
– ORIGIN early 18th cent.: from Latin *liquescent-* 'becoming liquid', from the verb *liquescere* (see **LIQUEFY**).

liqueur /lɪˈkjʊə/ ▶ noun a strong, sweet flavoured alcoholic spirit, usually drunk after a meal.
■ a chocolate with a liqueur filling: *a box of liqueurs*.
– ORIGIN mid 18th cent.: from French, 'liquor'.

liquid ▶ adjective 1 having a consistency like that of water or oil, i.e. flowing freely but of constant volume.
■ having the translucence of water; clear: *looking into those liquid dark eyes*. ■ [attrib.] denoting a substance normally a gas that has been liquefied by cold or pressure: *liquid oxygen*. ■ not fixed or stable; fluid.
2 (of a sound) clear, pure, and flowing; harmonious: *the liquid song of the birds*.
3 (of assets) held in cash or easily converted into cash.
■ having ready cash or liquid assets. ■ (of a market) having a high volume of activity.
▶ noun 1 a liquid substance: *drink plenty of liquids*.
2 a consonant produced by allowing the airstream to flow over the sides of the tongue, typically *l* and *r* (in British English pronunciation).
– DERIVATIVES **liquidly** adverb, **liquidness** noun.
– ORIGIN late Middle English: from Latin *liquidus*, from *liquere* 'be liquid'.

liquidambar /ˌlɪkwɪdˈambə/ ▶ noun a deciduous North American and Asian tree with maple-like leaves and bright autumn colours, yielding aromatic resinous balsam.
● Genus *Liquidambar*, family Hamamelidaceae: several species, including *L. orientalis* of Asia, which yields Levant storax, and the sweet gum of North America.
■ [mass noun] liquid balsam obtained chiefly from the Asian liquidambar tree, used medicinally and in perfume. Also called **STORAX**.
– ORIGIN late 16th cent.: modern Latin, apparently formed irregularly from Latin *liquidus* 'liquid' + medieval Latin *ambar* 'amber'.

liquidate ▶ verb [with obj.] 1 wind up the affairs of (a company or firm) by ascertaining liabilities and apportioning assets.
■ [no obj.] (of a company) undergo such a process. ■ convert (assets) into cash: *a plan to liquidate £1 billion worth of property over seven years*. ■ pay off (a debt).
2 eliminate, typically by violent means; kill.
– DERIVATIVES **liquidation** noun.
– ORIGIN mid 16th cent. (in the sense 'set out (accounts) clearly'): from medieval Latin *liquidat-* 'made clear', from the verb *liquidare*, from Latin 'liquidus' (see **LIQUID**). Sense 1 was influenced by Italian *liquidare* and French *liquider*, sense 2 by Russian *likvidirovat'*.

liquidator ▶ noun a person appointed to wind up the affairs of a company or firm.

liquid crystal ▶ noun a substance which flows like a liquid but has some degree of ordering in the arrangement of its molecules.

liquid crystal display ▶ noun a form of visual display used in electronic devices, in which a layer of a liquid crystal is sandwiched between two transparent electrodes. The application of an electric current to a small area of the layer alters the alignment of its molecules, which affects its reflectivity or its transmission of polarized light, and so makes it opaque.

liquidity /lɪˈkwɪdɪti/ ▶ noun [mass noun] Finance the availability of liquid assets to a market or company.
■ liquid assets; cash. ■ a high volume of activity in a market.
– ORIGIN early 17th cent.: from French *liquidité* or medieval Latin *liquiditas*, from Latin *liquidus* (see **LIQUID**).

liquidity preference ▶ noun [mass noun] Economics (in Keynesian theory) the preference of investors for holding liquid assets rather than securities or long-term interest-bearing investments.

liquidity ratio ▶ noun Finance the ratio between the liquid assets and the liabilities of a bank or other institution.

liquidize (also **-ise**) ▶ verb [with obj.] Brit. convert (solid food) into a liquid or purée, typically by using a liquidizer: *liquidize the soup until quite smooth*.

liquidizer (also **-iser**) ▶ noun Brit. a machine for liquidizing food or other material.

liquid lunch ▶ noun informal, humorous a drinking session at lunchtime taking the place of a meal.

liquid measure ▶ noun a unit for measuring the volume of liquids.

liquid paraffin ▶ noun [mass noun] chiefly Brit. a colourless, odourless oily liquid consisting of a mixture of hydrocarbons obtained from petroleum, used as a laxative.

liquid storax ▶ noun see **STORAX** (sense 1).

liquify ▶ verb variant spelling of **LIQUEFY**.

liquor /ˈlɪkə/ ▶ noun [mass noun] 1 alcoholic drink, especially distilled spirits.
2 a liquid produced or used in a process of some kind, in particular:
■ water used in brewing. ■ liquid in which something has been steeped or cooked. ■ liquid which drains from food during cooking. ■ the liquid from which a substance has been crystallized or extracted.
▶ verb [with obj.] 1 dress (leather) with grease or oil.
2 steep (something, especially malt) in water.
– ORIGIN Middle English (denoting liquid or something to drink): from Old French *lic(o)ur*, from Latin *liquor*; related to *liquare* 'liquefy', *liquere* 'be fluid'.

▶ **liquor up** (or **liquor someone up**) N. Amer. informal get (or make someone) drunk.

liquorice /ˈlɪk(ə)rɪs, -rɪʃ/ (US **licorice**) ▶ noun 1 [mass noun] a sweet, chewy, aromatic black substance made by evaporation from the juice of a root and used as a sweet and in medicine.
■ a sweet flavoured with such a substance.

2 the widely distributed plant of the pea family from which this product is obtained.
• Genus *Glycyrrhiza*, family Leguminosae; many species are used locally to obtain liquorice, the chief commercial source being the cultivated *G. glabra*.
– ORIGIN Middle English: from Old French *licoresse*, from late Latin *liquiritia*, from Greek *glukurrhiza*, from *glukus* 'sweet' + *rhiza* 'root'.

liquorish /ˈlɪkərɪʃ/ ▶ **adjective 1** archaic form of **LICKERISH**.
2 fond of or indicating a fondness for liquor. [ORIGIN: late 19th cent.: from **LIQUOR** + **-ISH**[1], by analogy with **LICKERISH**.]
– DERIVATIVES **liquorishness** noun.

lira /ˈlɪərə/ ▶ **noun** (pl. **lire** /ˈlɪərə, ˈlɪəreɪ, ˈlɪəri/) **1** (until the introduction of the euro in 2002) the basic monetary unit of Italy, notionally equal to 100 centesimos.
2 the basic monetary unit of Turkey, equal to 100 kurus.
– ORIGIN Italian, from Provençal *liura*, from Latin *libra* 'pound'.

liriodendron /ˌlɪrɪə(ʊ)ˈdɛndrɒn/ ▶ **noun** a tree of a small genus which includes the tulip tree.
• Genus *Liriodendron*, family Magnoliaceae.
– ORIGIN modern Latin, from Greek *leirion* 'lily' + *dendron* 'tree'.

liripipe /ˈlɪrɪpʌɪp/ ▶ **noun** a long tail hanging from the back of a hood, especially in medieval or academic dress.
– ORIGIN early 17th cent.: from medieval Latin *liripipium* 'tippet of a hood, cord', of unknown origin.

lis[1] /lɪs/ ▶ **noun** (pl. same or **lisses**) short for **FLEUR-DE-LIS**.

lis[2] /lɪs/ ▶ **noun** Law a lawsuit. See also **LIS PENDENS**.
– ORIGIN mid 18th cent.: from Latin *lis* 'dispute'.

lis alibi pendens /lɪs ˌalɪbʌɪ ˈpɛndɛnz/ ▶ **noun** Law a lawsuit pending elsewhere.
– ORIGIN Latin.

Lisbon /ˈlɪzbən/ the capital and chief port of Portugal, on the Atlantic coast at the mouth of the River Tagus; pop. 677,790 (1991). Portuguese name **LISBOA** /liʒˈboə/.

Lisburn /ˈlɪzbəːn/ a town in Northern Ireland, to the south-west of Belfast, on the border between Antrim and Down; pop. 40,390 (1981).

Lisdoonvarna /ˌlɪsduːnˈvɑːnə/ a spa town in the Republic of Ireland, in County Clare; pop. 607 (1981).

lisente plural form of **SENTE**.

lisle /lʌɪl/ (also **lisle thread**) ▶ **noun** [mass noun] a fine, smooth cotton thread used especially for stockings.
– ORIGIN mid 16th cent.: from *Lisle*, former spelling of **LILLE**, the original place of manufacture.

Lisp ▶ **noun** [mass noun] a high-level computer programming language devised for list processing.
– ORIGIN 1950s: from *lis(t) p(rocessor)*.

lisp ▶ **noun** a speech defect in which *s* is pronounced like *th* in *thick* and *z* is pronounced like *th* in *this*.
▶ **verb** [no obj.] speak with a lisp.
– DERIVATIVES **lisper** noun, **lispingly** adverb.
– ORIGIN Old English *wlispian* (recorded in *āwlyspian*), from *wlisp* (adjective) 'lisping', of imitative origin; compare with Dutch *lispen* and German *lispeln*.

lis pendens /lɪs ˈpɛndɛnz/ ▶ **noun** Law a pending legal action.
■ a formal notice of this.
– ORIGIN Latin.

Lissajous figure /ˈlɪsəʒuː/ ▶ **noun** Mathematics any of a number of characteristic looped or curved figures traced out by a point undergoing two independent simple harmonic motions at right angles with frequencies in a simple ratio.
– ORIGIN late 19th cent.: named after Jules A. *Lissajous* (1822–80), French physicist.

lissom (also **lissome**) ▶ **adjective** (of a person or their body) thin, supple, and graceful.
– DERIVATIVES **lissomness** noun.
– ORIGIN late 18th cent.: contraction, from **LITHE** + **-SOME**[1].

list[1] ▶ **noun 1** a number of connected items or names written or printed consecutively, typically one below the other: *consult the list of drugs on page 326 | writing a shopping list.*
■ a set of items considered as being in the same category or having a particular order of priority: *unemployment came top of the list of issues that the public thought the parties should be talking about.* ■ Computing a formal structure analogous to a list, by which items of data can be stored or processed in a definite order. [ORIGIN: late 16th cent.: from French *liste*, of Germanic origin.]
2 (**lists**) historical palisades enclosing an area for a tournament.
■ the scene of a contest or combat. [ORIGIN: late Middle English: from Old French *lisse*.]
3 a selvedge of a piece of fabric. [ORIGIN: Middle English, from Old English *liste* 'border', of Germanic origin; related to Dutch *lijst* and German *Leiste*.]
▶ **verb** [with obj.] **1** make a list of: *I have listed four reasons below.*
■ (often **be listed**) include or enter in a list: *93 men were still listed as missing.* ■ [no obj.] (**list at/for**) be on a list of products at (a specified price): *the bottom-of-the-line Mercedes lists for $52,050.*
2 archaic enlist for military service.
– PHRASES **enter the lists** issue or accept a challenge.
– DERIVATIVES **listable** adjective.

list[2] ▶ **verb** [no obj.] (of a ship) lean over to one side, typically because of a leak or unbalanced cargo. Compare with **HEEL**[2].
▶ **noun** an instance of a ship leaning over in such a way.
– ORIGIN early 17th cent.: of unknown origin.

list[3] archaic ▶ **verb** [no obj.] want; like: [with clause] *let them think what they list.*
▶ **noun** [mass noun] desire; inclination: *I have little list to write.*
– ORIGIN Old English *lystan* (verb), of Germanic origin, from a base meaning 'pleasure'.

list box ▶ **noun** Computing a box on the screen that contains a list of options, only one of which can be selected.

list broking ▶ **noun** [mass noun] trading in mailing lists for marketing or publicity by direct mail.
– DERIVATIVES **list broker** noun.

listed ▶ **adjective 1** (of a building in the UK) officially designated as being of historical importance and having protection from demolition or major alterations.
2 relating to or denoting companies whose shares are quoted on the main market of the London Stock Exchange: *listed securities.*

listel /ˈlɪstəl/ ▶ **noun** Architecture a narrow strip with a flat surface running between mouldings. Also called **FILLET**.
– ORIGIN late 16th cent.: from Italian *listello*, diminutive of *lista* 'strip, band'.

listen ▶ **verb** [no obj.] give one's attention to a sound: *evidently he was not listening | sit and* ***listen to*** *the radio.*
■ take notice of and act on what someone says; respond to advice or a request: *I told her over and over again, but she wouldn't listen.* ■ make an effort to hear something; be alert and ready to hear something: *they* ***listened for*** *sounds from the baby's room.* ■ [in imperative] used to urge someone to pay attention to what one is going to say: *listen, I've had an idea.*
▶ **noun** [in sing.] an act of listening to something.
– ORIGIN Old English *hlysnan* 'pay attention to', of Germanic origin.
▶ **listen in** listen to a private conversation, especially secretly. ■ use a radio receiving set to listen to a broadcast or conversation.

listenable ▶ **adjective** easy or pleasant to listen to.
– DERIVATIVES **listenability** noun.

listener ▶ **noun** a person who listens, especially someone who does so in an attentive manner.
■ a person listening to a radio station or programme.

listening post ▶ **noun** a station for intercepting electronic communications.
■ a point near an enemy's lines for detecting movements by sound.

Lister, Joseph, 1st Baron (1827–1912), English surgeon, inventor of antiseptic techniques in surgery. He realized the significance of Louis Pasteur's germ theory in connection with sepsis and in 1865 he used carbolic acid dressings on patients who had undergone surgery.

lister ▶ **noun** US a plough with a double mouldboard.
– ORIGIN late 19th cent.: from late 18th-cent. *list* 'prepare land for a crop' (see **LIST**[1], **-ER**[1]).

listeria /lɪˈstɪərɪə/ ▶ **noun** [mass noun] a type of bacterium which infects humans and other warm-blooded animals through contaminated food.
• *Listeria monocytogenes*; motile aerobic Gram-negative rods.
■ informal food poisoning or other disease caused by infection with listeria; listeriosis.
– ORIGIN 1940s: modern Latin, named after Joseph *Lister* (1827–1912), English surgeon.

listeriosis /lɪˌstɪərɪˈəʊsɪs/ ▶ **noun** [mass noun] disease caused by infection with listeria.

listing ▶ **noun 1** a list or catalogue.
■ [mass noun] the drawing up of a list. ■ an entry in a list or register. ■ an entry for a company in the Official List of Securities of the London Stock Exchange, for which certain requirements must be satisfied.
2 a selvedge of a piece of fabric.

listless ▶ **adjective** lacking energy or enthusiasm: *bouts of listless depression.*
– DERIVATIVES **listlessly** adverb, **listlessness** noun.
– ORIGIN Middle English: from obsolete *list* 'appetite, desire' + **-LESS**.

Liston /ˈlɪst(ə)n/, Sonny (1932–70), American boxer; born *Charles Liston*. In 1962 he became world heavyweight champion but in 1964 lost his title to Muhammad Ali (then Cassius Clay).

list price ▶ **noun** the price of an article as shown in a list issued by the manufacturer or by the general body of manufacturers of the particular class of goods.

list processing ▶ **noun** [mass noun] Computing the manipulation of data organized as lists.

LISTSERV ▶ **noun** [mass noun] trademark an electronic mailing list of people who wish to receive specified information from the Internet.
■ [count noun] (**listserv**) any similar application.

list system ▶ **noun** a system of voting (used in several European countries) in which votes are cast for a list of candidates rather than an individual, to allow a degree of proportional representation.

Liszt /lɪst/, Franz (1811–86), Hungarian composer and pianist. He was a key figure in the romantic movement; many of his piano compositions combine lyricism with great technical complexity, while his twelve symphonic poems (1848–58) created a new musical form.
– DERIVATIVES **Lisztian** adjective & noun.

lit past and past participle of **LIGHT**[1], **LIGHT**[3].

Li T'ai Po /ˌliː tʌɪ ˈpəʊ/ variant of **LI PO**.

litany /ˈlɪt(ə)ni/ ▶ **noun** (pl. **-ies**) a series of petitions for use in church services or processions, usually recited by the clergy and responded to in a recurring formula by the people.
■ (**the Litany**) such petitions and responses contained in the Book of Common Prayer. ■ a tedious recital or repetitive series: *a litany of complaints.*
– ORIGIN Middle English: from Old French *letanie*, via ecclesiastical Latin from Greek *litaneia* 'prayer', from *litē* 'supplication'.

litas /ˈliːtas/ ▶ **noun** (pl. same) the basic monetary unit of Lithuania, equal to 100 centas.

litchi ▶ **noun** variant spelling of **LYCHEE**.

lit crit ▶ **abbreviation for** literary criticism.

lite ▶ **adjective** of or relating to low-fat or low-sugar versions of manufactured food or drink products, especially to low-calorie light beer.
■ N. Amer. informal lacking in substance; facile.
▶ **noun 1** [mass noun] light beer with relatively few calories.
2 N. Amer. a courtesy light in a motor vehicle.
– ORIGIN 1950s: a deliberate respelling of **LIGHT**[1], **LIGHT**[2].

-lite ▶ **suffix** forming names of rocks, minerals, and fossils: *rhyolite | zeolite.*
– ORIGIN from French, from Greek *lithos* 'stone'.

liter ▶ **noun** US spelling of **LITRE**.

literacy ▶ **noun** [mass noun] the ability to read and write.
– ORIGIN late 19th cent.: from **LITERATE**, on the pattern of *illiteracy*.

literae humaniores /ˌlɪtərʌɪ hjuːˌmanɪˈɔːriːz/ ▶ **plural noun** [treated as sing.] the honours course in classics, philosophy, and ancient history at Oxford University.
– ORIGIN Latin, literally 'the more humane studies'.

literal ▶ **adjective 1** taking words in their usual or most basic sense without metaphor or allegory: *dreadful in its literal sense, full of dread.*
■ free from exaggeration or distortion: *you shouldn't take this as a literal record of events.* ■ informal absolute (used to emphasize that a strong expression is

deliberately chosen to convey one's feelings): *fifteen years of literal hell.*
2 (of a translation) representing the exact words of the original text.
▪(of a visual representation) exactly copied; realistic as opposed to abstract or impressionistic.
3 (also **literal-minded**) (of a person or performance) lacking imagination; prosaic.
4 of, in, or expressed by a letter or the letters of the alphabet: *literal mnemonics.*
▶**noun** Printing, Brit. a misprint of a letter.
– DERIVATIVES **literality** noun, **literalize** (also **-ise**) verb, **literalness** noun.
– ORIGIN late Middle English: from Old French, or from late Latin *litteralis*, from Latin *littera* (see **LETTER**).

literalism ▶**noun** [mass noun] the interpretation of words in their usual or most basic sense, without allowing for metaphor or exaggeration: *biblical literalism.*
– DERIVATIVES **literalist** noun, **literalistic** adjective.

literally ▶**adverb** in a literal manner or sense; exactly: *the driver* **took it literally** *when asked to go straight over the roundabout | Tiramisu, literally translated 'pull-me-up'.*
▪informal used to acknowledge that something is not literally true but is used for emphasis or to express strong feeling: *I have received literally thousands of letters.*

USAGE In its standard use **literally** means 'in a literal sense, as opposed to a non-literal or exaggerated sense', as for example in *I told him I never wanted to see him again, but I didn't expect him to take it* ***literally.*** In recent years an extended use of **literally** (and also **literal**) has become very common, where **literally** (or **literal**) is used deliberately in non-literal contexts, for added effect, as in *they bought the car and* ***literally*** *ran it into the ground.* This use can lead to unintentional humorous effects (*we were* ***literally*** *killing ourselves laughing*) and is not acceptable in standard English, though it accounts for more than 20 per cent of use in the British National Corpus.

literary ▶**adjective 1** [attrib.] concerning the writing, study, or content of literature, especially of the kind valued for quality of form: *the great literary works of the nineteenth century.*
▪concerned with literature as a profession: *literary editor of* Punch.
2 (of language) associated with literary works or other formal writing; having a marked style intended to create a particular emotional effect.
– DERIVATIVES **literarily** adverb, **literariness** noun.
– ORIGIN mid 17th cent. (in the sense 'relating to the letters of the alphabet'): from Latin *litterarius*, from *littera* (see **LETTER**).

literary agent ▶**noun** a professional agent who acts on behalf of an author in dealing with publishers and others involved in promoting the author's work.

literary criticism ▶**noun** [mass noun] the art or practice of judging and commenting on the qualities and character of literary works.

Modern critics tend to pass over the concerns of earlier centuries, such as formal categories or the place of moral or aesthetic value; some analyse texts as self-contained entities, in isolation from external factors, while others discuss them in terms of spheres such as biography, history, Marxism, or feminism. Since the 1950s the concepts of meaning and authorship have been explored or questioned by structuralism, post-structuralism, post-modernism, and deconstruction.

– DERIVATIVES **literary critic** noun.

literary executor ▶**noun** a person entrusted with a dead writer's papers and copyrighted and unpublished works.

literary history ▶**noun** [mass noun] the study of the literature of a particular style, region, or historical period.
▪the history of the treatment of, and references to, a particular subject in literature: *lesbian literary history.*
– DERIVATIVES **literary historian** noun.

literate ▶**adjective** (of a person) able to read and write.
▪having or showing education or knowledge, typically in a specified area: *we need people who are economically and politically literate.*
▶**noun** a literate person.
▪dated an Anglican cleric ordained without a university degree.
– DERIVATIVES **literately** adverb.
– ORIGIN late Middle English: from Latin *litteratus*, from *littera* (see **LETTER**).

literati /ˌlɪtəˈrɑːtiː/ ▶**plural noun** well-educated people who are interested in literature.
– ORIGIN early 17th cent.: from Latin, plural of *literatus* 'acquainted with letters', from *littera* (see **LETTER**).

literatim /ˌlɪtəˈrɑːtɪm, -ˈreɪtɪm/ ▶**adverb** formal (of the copying of a text) letter by letter.
– ORIGIN from medieval Latin.

literature ▶**noun** [mass noun] written works, especially those considered of superior or lasting artistic merit: *a great work of literature.*
▪books and writings published on a particular subject: *the* **literature** *on environmental epidemiology.*
▪leaflets and other printed matter used to advertise products or give advice.
– ORIGIN late Middle English (in the sense 'knowledge of books'): via French from Latin *litteratura*, from *littera* (see **LETTER**).

lith ▶**noun** [mass noun] photographic film with a very thin coat of emulsion, producing images of high contrast and density.
– ORIGIN mid 20th cent.: abbreviation of **LITHOGRAPHY, LITHOGRAPHIC**.

-lith ▶**suffix** denoting types of stone: *laccolith | monolith.*
– ORIGIN from Greek *lithos* 'stone'.

litharge /ˈlɪθɑːdʒ/ ▶**noun** [mass noun] lead monoxide, especially a red form used as a pigment and in glass and ceramics.
• Chem. formula: PbO.
– ORIGIN Middle English: from Old French *litarge*, via Latin from Greek *litharguros*, from *lithos* 'stone' + *arguros* 'silver'.

lithe ▶**adjective** (especially of a person's body) thin, supple, and graceful.
– DERIVATIVES **lithely** adverb, **litheness** noun.
– ORIGIN Old English *līthe* 'gentle, meek' also 'mellow', of Germanic origin; related to German *lind* 'soft, gentle'.

lithesome ▶**adjective** another term for **LITHE**.

lithia /ˈlɪθɪə/ ▶**noun** [mass noun] Chemistry lithium oxide, a white alkaline solid.
• Chem. formula: Li_2O.
– ORIGIN early 19th cent.: modern Latin, alteration of earlier *lithion*, from Greek, neuter of *litheios*, from *lithos* 'stone', on the pattern of words such as *soda*.

lithiasis /lɪˈθʌɪəsɪs/ ▶**noun** [mass noun] Medicine the formation of stony concretions (calculi) in the body, most often in the gall bladder or urinary system.
– ORIGIN mid 17th cent.: from medieval Latin, based on Greek *lithos* 'stone'.

lithic /ˈlɪθɪk/ ▶**adjective** chiefly Archaeology & Geology of the nature of or relating to stone.
▪Medicine, dated relating to calculi.
– ORIGIN late 18th cent.: from Greek *lithikos*, from *lithos* 'stone'.

lithify /ˈlɪθɪfʌɪ/ ▶**verb** (**-ies, -ied**) [with obj.] chiefly Geology transform (a sediment or other material) into stone.
– DERIVATIVES **lithification** noun.
– ORIGIN late 19th cent.: from Greek *lithos* 'stone' + **-FY**.

lithium /ˈlɪθɪəm/ ▶**noun** [mass noun] the chemical element of atomic number 3, a soft silver-white metal. It is the lightest of the alkali metals. (Symbol: **Li**)
▪lithium carbonate or another lithium salt, used as a mood-stabilizing drug.
– ORIGIN early 19th cent.: from **LITHIA** + **-IUM**.

litho /ˈlʌɪθəʊ, ˈlɪθ-/ informal ▶**noun** (pl. **-os**) short for **LITHOGRAPHY** or **LITHOGRAPH**.
▶**adjective** short for **LITHOGRAPHIC**.
▶**verb** (**-oes, -oed**) short for **LITHOGRAPH**.

litho- ▶**combining form 1** of or relating to stone: *lithosol.*
2 relating to a calculus: *lithotomy.*
– ORIGIN from Greek *lithos* 'stone'.

lithograph /ˈlɪθəɡrɑːf, ˈlʌɪ-/ ▶**noun** a lithographic print.
▶**verb** [with obj.] print by lithography: [as adj. **lithographed**] *a set of lithographed drawings.*
– ORIGIN early 19th cent.: back-formation from **LITHOGRAPHY**.

lithographic ▶**adjective** of, relating to, or produced by lithography: *lithographic prints.*
– DERIVATIVES **lithographically** adverb.

lithographic limestone ▶**noun** [mass noun] a compact fine-grained yellowish limestone used in lithography. It sometimes contains finely preserved Upper Jurassic fossils.

lithography /lɪˈθɒɡrəfi/ ▶**noun** [mass noun] the process of printing from a flat surface treated so as to repel the ink except where it is required for printing.
▪Electronics an analogous method for making printed circuits.

The earliest forms of lithography used greasy ink to form an image on a piece of limestone which was then etched with acid and treated with gum arabic. In a modern press, rollers transfer ink to a thin aluminium plate wrapped round a cylinder. In **offset lithography** the image is transferred to an intermediate rubber-covered cylinder before being printed.

– DERIVATIVES **lithographer** noun.
– ORIGIN early 19th cent.: from German *Lithographie* (see **LITHO-, -GRAPHY**).

lithology /lɪˈθɒlədʒi/ ▶**noun** [mass noun] the study of the general physical characteristics of rocks. Compare with **PETROLOGY**.
▪the general physical characteristics of a rock or the rocks in a particular area: *the lithology of South Wales.*
– DERIVATIVES **lithologic** adjective, **lithological** adjective, **lithologically** adverb.

lithophane /ˈlɪθəfeɪn, ˈlʌɪ-/ ▶**noun** [mass noun] a kind of ornamentation of porcelain visible when held to the light, produced by pressing designs into it when soft.
▪[count noun] an object with such a decoration.
– ORIGIN 1940s: from Greek *lithos* 'stone' + *-phanēs* 'appearing'.

lithophyte /ˈlɪθə(ʊ)fʌɪt, ˈlʌɪ-/ ▶**noun** Botany a plant that grows on bare rock or stone.

lithopone /ˈlɪθəpəʊn/ ▶**noun** [mass noun] a white pigment made from zinc sulphide and barium sulphate.
– ORIGIN late 19th cent.: from **LITHO-** 'stone, crystals' + Greek *ponos* '(thing) produced by work'.

lithosol /ˈlɪθəsɒl/ ▶**noun** Soil Science a thin soil consisting mainly of partially weathered rock fragments.

lithosphere /ˈlɪθəsfɪə/ ▶**noun** Geology the rigid outer part of the earth, consisting of the crust and upper mantle.
– DERIVATIVES **lithospheric** adjective.

lithotomy /lɪˈθɒtəmi/ ▶**noun** [mass noun] surgical removal of a calculus (stone) from the bladder, kidney, or urinary tract.
– DERIVATIVES **lithotomist** noun.
– ORIGIN mid 17th cent.: via late Latin from Greek *lithotomia* (see **LITHO-, -TOMY**).

lithotomy position ▶**noun** a supine position of the body with the legs separated, flexed, and supported in raised stirrups, originally used for lithotomy and later also for childbirth.

lithotomy stirrups ▶**plural noun** see **STIRRUP** (sense 2).

lithotripsy /ˈlɪθəˌtrɪpsi/ ▶**noun** [mass noun] Surgery a treatment, typically using ultrasound shock waves, by which a kidney stone or other calculus is broken into small particles that can be passed out by the body.
– DERIVATIVES **lithotripter** (also **lithotriptor**) noun, **lithotriptic** adjective.
– ORIGIN mid 19th cent.: from **LITHO-** 'of stone' + Greek *tripsis* 'rubbing', from *tribein* 'to rub'.

lithotrity /lɪˈθɒtrɪti/ ▶**noun** [mass noun] Surgery a surgical procedure involving the mechanical breaking down of gallstones or other calculi.
– DERIVATIVES **lithotrite** noun.
– ORIGIN early 19th cent.: from **LITHO-** 'of stone' + Latin *tritor* 'thing that rubs' + **-Y**[3].

Lithuania /ˌlɪθ(j)uːˈeɪnɪə/ a country on the SE shore of the Baltic sea; pop. 3,765,000 (est. 1991); languages, Lithuanian (official), Russian; capital, Vilnius.

Lithuania was absorbed into the Russian empire in 1795, having been united with Poland since 1386. It was declared an independent republic in 1918, but in 1940 was annexed by the Soviet Union as a constituent republic. In 1991, on the break-up of the USSR, Lithuania became an independent republic once again.

Lithuanian ▶**adjective** of or relating to Lithuania or its people or language.
▶**noun 1** a native or citizen of Lithuania, or a person of Lithuanian descent.

l

2 [mass noun] the language of Lithuania, which belongs to the Baltic branch of the Indo-European family and has about 3.5 million speakers.

litie ▶ **noun** variant spelling of **LIGHTY**.

litigant ▶ **noun** a person involved in a lawsuit.
▶ **adjective** [postpositive] archaic involved in a lawsuit: *the parties litigant.*
– ORIGIN mid 17th cent.: from French, from Latin *litigant-* 'carrying on a lawsuit', from the verb *litigare* (see **LITIGATE**).

litigate /ˈlɪtɪɡeɪt/ ▶ **verb** [no obj.] go to law; be a party to a lawsuit.
■ [with obj.] take (a claim or a dispute) to a law court.
– DERIVATIVES **litigation** noun, **litigator** noun.
– ORIGIN early 17th cent.: from Latin *litigat-* 'disputed in a lawsuit', from the verb *litigare*, from *lis, lit-* 'lawsuit'.

litigious /lɪˈtɪdʒəs/ ▶ **adjective** concerned with lawsuits or litigation.
■ unreasonably prone to go to law to settle disputes. ■ suitable to become the subject of a lawsuit.
– DERIVATIVES **litigiously** adverb, **litigiousness** noun.
– ORIGIN late Middle English: from Old French *litigieux* or Latin *litigiosus* from *litigium* 'litigation', from *lis, lit-* 'lawsuit'.

litmus /ˈlɪtməs/ ▶ **noun** [mass noun] a dye obtained from certain lichens that is red under acid conditions and blue under alkaline conditions.
– ORIGIN Middle English: from Old Norse *lit-mosi*, from *litr* 'dye' + *mosi* 'moss'.

litmus paper ▶ **noun** paper stained with litmus which is used to indicate the acidity or alkalinity of a substance.

litmus test ▶ **noun** Chemistry a test for acidity or alkalinity using litmus.
■ figurative a decisively indicative test: *effectiveness in these areas is often a good litmus test of overall quality.*

litoptern /lɪˈtɒptəːn/ ▶ **noun** an extinct South American hoofed mammal resembling a horse or camel, found from the Palaeocene to the Pleistocene epochs.
● Order Litopterna: several families.
– ORIGIN early 20th cent.: from modern Latin *Litopterna*, from Greek *litos* 'smooth' + *pternē* 'heel bone'.

litotes /lʌɪˈtəʊtiːz/ ▶ **noun** [mass noun] ironical understatement in which an affirmative is expressed by the negative of its contrary (e.g. *I shan't be sorry* for *I shall be glad*).
– ORIGIN late 16th cent.: via late Latin from Greek *litotēs*, from *litos* 'plain, meagre'.

litre (US **liter**) (abbrev.: **l**) ▶ **noun** a metric unit of capacity, formerly defined as the volume of one kilogram of water under standard conditions, now equal to 1,000 cubic centimetres (about 1.75 pints).
– DERIVATIVES **litreage** /ˈliːt(ə)rɪdʒ/ noun.
– ORIGIN late 18th cent.: from French, alteration of *litron* (an obsolete measure of capacity), via medieval Latin from Greek *litra*, a Sicilian monetary unit.

LittD ▶ **abbreviation for** Doctor of Letters.
– ORIGIN from Latin *Litterarum Doctor.*

litter ▶ **noun 1** [mass noun] rubbish, such as paper, tins, and bottles, that is left lying in an open or public place: *fines for dropping litter.*
■ [in sing.] an untidy collection of things lying about: *a litter of sleeping bags on the floor.*
2 a number of young animals born to an animal at one time: *a litter of five kittens.*
3 [mass noun] material forming a bedding or carpet, in particular:
■ (also **cat litter**) granular absorbent material lining a tray where a cat can urinate and defecate when indoors. ■ straw or other plant matter used as bedding for animals. ■ (also **leaf litter**) decomposing but recognizable leaves and other debris forming a layer on top of the soil, especially in forests.
4 historical a vehicle containing a bed or seat enclosed by curtains and carried on men's shoulders or by animals.
■ a framework with a couch for transporting the sick and wounded.
▶ **verb** [with obj.] **1** make (a place) untidy with rubbish or a large number of objects left lying about: *clothes and newspapers littered the floor.*
■ [with obj. and adverbial] (usu. **be littered**) leave (rubbish or a number of objects) lying untidily in a place: *there was broken glass littered about.* ■ (usu. **be littered with**) figurative fill (a text, history, etc.) with examples of something unpleasant: *news pages have been littered with doom and gloom about company collapses.*
2 archaic provide (a horse or other animal) with litter as bedding.
– ORIGIN Middle English (in sense 4 of the noun): from Old French *litiere*, from medieval Latin *lectaria*, from Latin *lectus* 'bed'. Sense 1 dates from the mid 18th cent.

littérateur /ˌlɪtərɑːˈtəː/ ▶ **noun** a person who is interested in and knowledgeable about literature.
– ORIGIN early 19th cent.: French.

litterbug (Brit. also **litter lout**) ▶ **noun** informal a person who carelessly drops litter in a public place.

little ▶ **adjective** small in size, amount, or degree (often used to convey an appealing diminutiveness or express an affectionate or condescending attitude): *the plants will grow into little bushes | a little puppy dog | a boring little man | he's a good little worker.*
■ (of a person) young or younger: *my little brother | when she was little she was always getting into scrapes.* ■ [attrib.] denoting something, especially a place, that is the smaller or smallest of those so named or is named after a similar larger one: *the village of Little Chesterton.* ■ [attrib.] used in names of animals and plants that are smaller than related kinds, e.g. **little grebe**. ■ [attrib.] of short distance or duration: *stay for a little while | we climbed up a little way.* ■ [attrib.] relatively unimportant; trivial (often used ironically): *we have a little problem | I can't remember every little detail.*
▶ **determiner** & **pronoun 1** (**a little**) a small amount of: [as determiner] *we got a little help from a training scheme* | [as pronoun] *you only see* ***a little of*** *what he can do.*
■ [pronoun] a short time or distance: *after a little, the rain stopped.*
2 used to emphasize how small an amount is: [as determiner] *I have little doubt of their identity | there was very little time to be lost* | [as pronoun] *he ate and drank very little | the rouble is worth so little these days.*
▶ **adverb** (**less**, **least**) **1** (**a little**) to a small extent: *he reminded me a little of my parents | I was always a little afraid of her.*
2 (used for emphasis) only to a small extent; not much or often: *he was little known in this country | he had slept little these past weeks.*
■ hardly or not at all: ***little did he know*** *what wheels he was putting into motion.*
– PHRASES **in little** archaic on a small scale; in miniature. **little by little** by degrees; gradually: *little by little the money dried up.* **little or nothing** hardly anything. **make little of** treat as unimportant: *they made little of their royal connection.* **no little** considerable: *a factor of no little importance.* **not a little** a great deal (of); much: *not a little consternation was caused.* ■ very: *it was not a little puzzling.* **quite a little** a fairly large amount of: *some spoke quite a little English.* ■ a considerable: *it turned out to be quite a little bonanza.* **quite the little ——** used when condescendingly or ironically recognizing that someone has a particular quality or accomplishment: *you've become quite the little horsewoman.*
– DERIVATIVES **littleness** noun.
– ORIGIN Old English *lȳtel*, of Germanic origin; related to Dutch *luttel*, German dialect *lützel*.

Little Ararat see **ARARAT, MOUNT**.

little auk ▶ **noun** a small, stubby short-billed auk with black plumage and white underparts, breeding in the Arctic.
● *Alle alle*, family Alcidae.

Little Bear the constellation Ursa Minor.

Little Bighorn, Battle of a battle in which General George Custer and his forces were defeated by Sioux warriors on 25 June 1876, popularly known as Custer's Last Stand. It took place in the valley of the Little Bighorn River in Montana.

little black dress ▶ **noun** informal a woman's short or medium-length black dress suitable for almost any social engagement.

Little Corporal a nickname for Napoleon.

little end ▶ **noun** (in a piston engine) the smaller end of the connecting rod, attached to the piston.

Little Englander ▶ **noun** a person who opposes an international role or policy for England (or, in practice, for Britain).

little finger ▶ **noun** the smallest finger, at the outer end of the hand, furthest from the thumb.
– PHRASES **twist** (or **wind** or **wrap**) **someone around one's little finger** have the ability to make someone do whatever one wants.

little grebe ▶ **noun** a small, dumpy Old World grebe with a short neck and bill and a trilling call.
● Genus *Tachybaptus*, family Podicipedidae: three species, in particular the widespread *T. ruficollis* (also called **DABCHICK**).

little green man ▶ **noun** informal an imaginary person from outer space.

little hours ▶ **plural noun** (in the Western Church) the offices of prime, terce, sext, and none.

little house ▶ **noun** Austral./NZ or dialect used as a euphemism for an outdoor toilet.

little ice age ▶ **noun** a comparatively cold period occurring between major glacial periods, in particular one such period which reached its peak during the 17th century.

Little League ▶ **noun** [mass noun] N. Amer. organized baseball played by children aged between 8 and 12.

Little Lord Fauntleroy see **FAUNTLEROY**.

little man ▶ **noun** a person who conducts business or life on a small or ordinary scale; an average person.
■ a local workman or craftsman: *they were forced to get a little man in to build them more shelves.* ■ dated used as a form of address to a young boy.

Little Masters a group of 16th-century Nuremberg engravers, followers of Dürer, who worked small-dimension plates with biblical, mythological, and genre scenes.
– ORIGIN mistranslation of German *Kleinmeister* 'masters in small (prints)'.

Little Minch see **MINCH**.

little ones ▶ **plural noun** young children.

Little Ouse another name for **OUSE** (in sense 4).

little owl ▶ **noun** a small owl with speckled plumage, native to Eurasia and Africa and introduced to Britain.
● *Athene noctua*, family Strigidae.

little people ▶ **plural noun 1** the ordinary people in a country, organization etc. who do not have much power.
2 small supernatural creatures such as fairies and leprechauns.

Little Rhody informal name for **RHODE ISLAND**.

Little Rock the state capital of Arkansas; pop. 175,800 (1990).

Little Russian ▶ **noun** & **adjective** former term for **UKRAINIAN**.

Little St Bernard Pass see **ST BERNARD PASS**.

little slam ▶ **noun** Bridge another term for **SMALL SLAM**.

little theatre ▶ **noun** a small independent theatre used for experimental or avant-garde drama, or for community, non-commercial productions.

Little Tibet another name for **BALTISTAN**.

little toe ▶ **noun** the smallest toe, on the outer side of the foot.

Littlewood, (Maud) Joan (b.1914), English theatre director. She co-founded the Theatre Workshop (1945), which set out to present established plays in radical productions and to stage contemporary working-class plays. She is particularly remembered for her production of the musical *Oh, What a Lovely War* (1963).

littoral /ˈlɪt(ə)r(ə)l/ ▶ **adjective** of, relating to, or situated on the shore of the sea or a lake: *the littoral states of the Indian Ocean.*
■ Ecology of, relating to, or denoting the zone of the seashore between high- and low-water marks, or the zone near a lake shore with rooted vegetation: *limpets and other littoral molluscs.*
▶ **noun** a region lying along a shore: *irrigated regions of the Mediterranean littoral.*
■ Ecology the littoral zone.
– ORIGIN mid 17th cent.: from Latin *littoralis*, from *litus, litor-* 'shore'.

Littré /ˈlɪtreɪ, French litʀe/, Émile (1801–81), French lexicographer and philosopher. He was the author of the major *Dictionnaire de la langue française* (1863–77). A follower of Auguste Comte, he became the leading exponent of positivism after Comte's death.

liturgical /lɪˈtəːdʒɪk(ə)l/ ▶ **adjective** of or related to liturgy or public worship.
– DERIVATIVES **liturgically** adverb, **liturgist** /ˈlɪtədʒɪst/ noun.
– ORIGIN mid 17th cent.: via medieval Latin from Greek *leitourgikos* (see **LITURGY**) + **-AL**.

liturgics /lɪˈtəːdʒɪks/ ▶ **plural noun** [treated as sing.] the study of liturgies.

liturgiology /lɪˌtəːdʒɪˈɒlədʒi/ ▶ **noun** [mass noun] another term for LITURGICS.
– DERIVATIVES **liturgiological** adjective, **liturgiologist** noun.

liturgy /ˈlɪtədʒi/ ▶ **noun** (pl. **-ies**) **1** a form or formulary according to which public religious worship, especially Christian worship, is conducted.
■ a religious service conducted according to such a form or formulary. ■ (**the Liturgy**) the Communion office of the Orthodox Church. ■ (**the Liturgy**) Brit. archaic the Book of Common Prayer.
2 (in ancient Greece) a public office or duty performed voluntarily by a rich Athenian.
– ORIGIN mid 16th cent.: via French or late Latin from Greek *leitourgia* 'public service, worship of the gods', from *leitourgos* 'minister', from *lēitos* 'public' + *-ergos* 'working'.

Litvak /ˈlɪtvak/ ▶ **noun** a Jew from the region of Lithuania.

Liuzhou /ljuːˈdʒəʊ/ (also **Liuchow** /-ˈtʃaʊ/) an industrial city in southern China, in Guangxi Zhuang province north-east of Nanning; pop. 740,000 (1990).

livable ▶ **adjective** variant spelling of LIVEABLE.

live[1] /lɪv/ ▶ **verb 1** [no obj.] remain alive: *the doctors said she had only six months to live | both cats lived to a ripe age.*
■ [with adverbial] be alive at a specified time: *he lived four centuries ago.* ■ [with adverbial] spend one's life in a particular way or under particular circumstances: *people are living in fear in the wake of the shootings.* ■ [with obj. and adverbial] lead (one's life) in a particular way: *he was living a life of luxury in Australia.* ■ supply oneself with the means of subsistence: *they* **live by** *hunting and fishing.* ■ survive in someone's mind; be remembered: *only the name* **lived on**. ■ have an exciting or fulfilling life: *he couldn't wait to get out of school and really start living.* ■ archaic (of a ship) escape destruction; remain afloat.
2 [no obj., with adverbial] make one's home in a particular place or with a particular person: *I've lived in the East End all my life | they lived with his grandparents.*
■ informal (of an object) be kept in a particular place: *I told her where the coffee lived and went back to sleep.*
– PHRASES **as I live and breathe** used, especially in spoken English, to express one's surprise at coming across someone or something: *good God, Jack Stone, as I live and breathe!* **be living on borrowed time** see BORROW. **live and breathe something** be extremely interested in or enthusiastic about a particular subject or activity and so devote a great deal of one's time to it: *they live and breathe Italy and all things Italian.* **live and let live** proverb you should tolerate the opinions and behaviour of others so that they will similarly tolerate your own. **live by one's wits** see WIT[1]. **live dangerously** do something risky, especially on a habitual basis. **live for the moment** see MOMENT. **live in hope** be or remain optimistic about something. **live in the past** have old-fashioned or outdated ideas and attitudes. ■ dwell on or reminisce at length about past events. **live in sin** see SIN[1]. **live it up** informal spend one's time in an extremely enjoyable way, typically by spending a great deal of money or engaging in an exciting social life. **live off** (or **on**) **the fat of the land** see FAT. **live off the land** see LAND. **live out of a suitcase** live or stay somewhere on a temporary basis and with only a limited selection of one's belongings, typically because one's occupation requires a great deal of travelling. **live one's own life** follow one's own plans and principles independent of others. **live rough** live and sleep outdoors as a consequence of having no proper home. **live to fight another day** survive a particular experience or ordeal. **live to regret something** come to wish that one had not done something: *those who put work before their family life often live to regret it.* **live to tell the tale** survive a dangerous experience and be able to tell others about it. **live with oneself** be able to retain one's self-respect as a consequence of one's actions: *taking money from children—how can you live with yourself?* **long live ——!** said to express loyalty or support for a specified person or thing: *long live the Queen!* **where one lives** N. Amer. informal at, to, or in the right, vital, or most vulnerable spot: *it gets me where I live.* **you haven't lived** used, especially in spoken English, as a way of enthusiastically recommending something to someone who has not experienced it. **you** (or **we**) **live and learn** used, especially in spoken English, to acknowledge that a fact is new to one.
– ORIGIN Old English *libban*, *lifian*, of Germanic origin; related to Dutch *leven* and German *leben*, also to LIFE and LEAVE[1].
▶ **live something down** [usu. with negative] succeed in making others forget something embarrassing that has happened.
live for regard as the purpose or most important aspect of one's life: *Tony lived for his painting.*
live in (of an employee or student) reside at the place where one works or studies.
live off (or **on**) depend on (someone or something) as a source of income or support: *if you think you're going to live off me for the rest of your life, you're mistaken.* ■ have (a particular amount of money) with which to buy food and other necessities. ■ subsist on (a particular type of food). ■ (of a person) eat, or seem to eat, only (a particular type of food): *she used to live on bacon and tomato sandwiches.*
live out (of an employee or student) reside away from the place where one works or studies.
live something out 1 do in reality that which one has thought or dreamed about: *your wedding day is the one time that you can live out your most romantic fantasies.* **2** spend the rest of one's life in a particular place or particular circumstances: *he lived out his days as a happy family man.*
live through survive (an unpleasant experience or period): *both men lived through the Depression.*
live together (especially of a couple not married to each other) share a home and have a sexual relationship.
live up to fulfil (expectations). ■ fulfil (an undertaking): *the president lived up to his promise to set America swiftly on a new path.*
live with 1 share a home and have a sexual relationship with (someone to whom one is not married). **2** accept or tolerate (something unpleasant): *our marriage was a failure—you have to learn to live with that fact.*

live[2] /lʌɪv/ ▶ **adjective 1** [attrib.] not dead or inanimate; living: *live animals | the number of live births and deaths.*
■ (of a vaccine) containing viruses or bacteria that are living but of a mild or attenuated strain. ■ (of yogurt) containing the living micro-organisms by which it is formed.
2 (of a musical performance) given in concert, not on a recording: *there is traditional live music played most nights.*
■ (of a broadcast) transmitted at the time of occurrence, not from a recording: *live coverage of the match.* ■ (of a musical recording) made during a concert, not in a studio: *a live album.*
3 (of a wire or device) connected to a source of electric current.
■ of, containing, or using undetonated explosive: *live ammunition.* ■ (of coals) burning; glowing. ■ (of a match) unused. ■ (of a wheel or axle in machinery) moving or imparting motion.
4 (of a question or subject) of current or continuing interest and importance: *the future organization of Europe has become a live issue.*
▶ **adverb** as or at an actual event or performance: *the match will be televised live.*
– PHRASES **go live** Computing (of a system) become operational.
– ORIGIN mid 16th cent.: shortening of ALIVE.

liveable (US also **livable**) ▶ **adjective** worth living: *fatherhood makes life more liveable.*
■ (of an environment or climate) fit to live in: *one of the most liveable cities in the world.* ■ [predic.] (**liveable with**) informal easy or bearable to live with.
– DERIVATIVES **liveability** noun.

live action ▶ **noun** [mass noun] action in films involving filming real people or animals, as contrasted with animation or computer-generated effects.

live bait ▶ **noun** [mass noun] small living fish or worms used to entice prey.

livebearer ▶ **noun** a small, chiefly freshwater, American toothcarp that has internal fertilization and gives birth to live young. Many livebearers, including the guppy, swordtail, mollies, platies, and gambusias, are very popular in aquaria.
• Family Poeciliidae: many genera and species.

live-bearing ▶ **adjective** (of an animal) bearing live young rather than laying eggs; viviparous or ovoviviparous.

live-born ▶ **adjective** born alive, not stillborn.

lived-in ▶ **adjective** (of a room or building) showing comforting signs of wear and habitation.
■ informal (of a person's face) marked by experience.

live-in ▶ **adjective** [attrib.] (of a domestic employee) resident in an employer's house: *a live-in housekeeper.*
■ (of a person) living with another in a sexual relationship: *a live-in lover.* ■ residential: *a live-in treatment program.*
▶ **noun** informal a person who shares another's living accommodation as a sexual partner or as an employee.

livelihood ▶ **noun** a means of securing the necessities of life: *people whose livelihoods depend on the rainforest.*
– ORIGIN Old English *līflād* 'way of life', from *līf* 'life' + *lād* 'course' (see LODE). The change in the word's form in the 16th cent. was due to association with LIVELY and -HOOD.

live load ▶ **noun** the weight of people or goods in a building or vehicle. Often contrasted with DEAD LOAD.

livelong[1] /ˈlɪvlɒŋ/ ▶ **adjective** [attrib.] poetic/literary (of a period of time) entire: *all this* **livelong day** *I lay in the sun.*
– ORIGIN late Middle English *leve longe* 'dear long' (see LIEF, LONG[1]). The change in spelling of the first word was due to association with LIVE[1].

livelong[2] /ˈlɪvlɒŋ/ ▶ **noun** a stonecrop, especially orpine.

lively ▶ **adjective** (**livelier**, **liveliest**) full of life and energy; active and outgoing: *she joined a lively team of reporters.*
■ (of a place or atmosphere) full of activity and excitement: *Barcelona's many lively bars.* ■ intellectually stimulating or perceptive: *a lively discussion | her lively mind.* ■ ironic, chiefly Brit. difficult; challenging: *a lively homeward passage dodging aircraft and E-boats.* ■ (of a boat) rising lightly to the waves.
– PHRASES **look lively** [usu. in imperative] informal move more quickly and energetically: *'Look lively, lads, keep in step,' Charlie shouted.*
– DERIVATIVES **livelily** adverb, **liveliness** noun.
– ORIGIN Old English *līflic* 'living, animate' (see LIFE, -LY[1]).

liven ▶ **verb** make or become more lively or interesting: [with obj.] *liven up bland foods with a touch of mustard* | [no obj.] *the match didn't* **liven up** *until the second half.*

live oak ▶ **noun** a large, spreading, evergreen North American oak, which typically supports a large quantity of Spanish moss and other epiphytes.
• *Quercus virginiana*, family Fagaceae.

liver[1] ▶ **noun** a large lobed glandular organ in the abdomen of vertebrates, involved in many metabolic processes.
■ a similar organ in other animals. ■ [mass noun] the flesh of an animal's liver as food: *slices of lamb's liver* | [as modifier] *liver pate* | [count noun] *chicken livers.* ■ (also **liver colour**) [mass noun] a dark reddish brown.

The liver's main role is in the processing of the products of digestion into substances useful to the body. It also neutralizes harmful substances in the blood, secretes bile for the digestion of fats, synthesizes plasma proteins, and stores glycogen and some minerals and vitamins. It was anciently supposed to be the seat of love and violent emotion.

– ORIGIN Old English *lifer*, of Germanic origin; related to German *Leber*, Dutch *lever*.

liver[2] ▶ **noun** [with adj. or noun modifier] a person who lives in a specified way: *a clean liver | high livers.*

liver chestnut ▶ **noun** a horse of a dark chestnut colour.

liver fluke ▶ **noun** a fluke which has a complex life cycle and is of medical and veterinary importance. The adult lives within the liver tissues of a vertebrate, and the larva within one or more secondary hosts such as a snail or fish.
• Many species in the subclass Digenea, class Trematoda, including the **Chinese liver fluke** (*Opisthorchis sinensis*), which infests humans, and *Fasciola hepatica*, which infests sheep and cattle.

liverish ▶ **adjective** slightly ill, as though having a disordered liver.
■ unhappy and bad-tempered. ■ resembling liver in colour: *a liverish red.*
– DERIVATIVES **liverishly** adverb, **liverishness** noun.

liver of sulphur ▶ **noun** [mass noun] archaic a liver-coloured mixture containing potassium sulphide, used in medicinal ointment.

Liverpool[1] /'lɪvəpuːl/ a city and seaport in NW England, situated at the east side of the mouth of the River Mersey; pop. 448,300 (1991). Liverpool developed as a port in the 17th century with the import of cotton from America and the export of textiles produced in Lancashire and Yorkshire, and in the 18th century became an important centre of shipbuilding and engineering.

Liverpool[2] /'lɪvəpuːl/, Robert Banks Jenkinson, 2nd Earl of (1770–1828), British Tory statesman, Prime Minister 1812–27.

Liverpudlian /ˌlɪvəˈpʌdlɪən/ ▶ noun a native of Liverpool.
- ■[mass noun] the dialect or accent of people from Liverpool.
▶ adjective of or relating to Liverpool.
- ORIGIN mid 19th cent.: humorous formation from **LIVERPOOL**[1] + **PUDDLE**.

liver rot ▶ noun [mass noun] disease of the liver, especially that caused in sheep by the liver fluke.

liver salts ▶ plural noun Brit. salts taken in water to relieve indigestion or nausea.

liver sausage ▶ noun [mass noun] chiefly Brit. a savoury meat paste in the form of a sausage containing cooked liver, or a mixture of liver and pork.

liver spot ▶ noun a small brown spot on the skin, especially as caused by a skin condition such as lentigo.
- DERIVATIVES **liver-spotted** adjective.

liverwort /'lɪvəwɔːt/ ▶ noun a small flowerless green plant with leaf-like stems or lobed leaves, occurring in moist habitats. They lack true roots and reproduce by means of spores released from capsules.
- ● Class Hepaticae, division Bryophyta.
- ORIGIN late Old English, from **LIVER**[1] + **WORT**, translating medieval Latin *hepatica*.

livery[1] ▶ noun (pl. **-ies**) **1** a special uniform worn by a servant, an official, or a member of a City Company.
- ■a special design and colour scheme used on the vehicles, aircraft, or products of a particular company.
2 N. Amer. short for **LIVERY STABLE**.
3 (in the UK) the members of a City livery company collectively.
4 historical a provision of food or clothing for servants.
5 (in full **livery of seisin**) Brit. historical the ceremonial procedure at common law of conveying freehold land to a grantee.
- PHRASES **at livery** (of a horse) kept for the owner and fed and cared for at a fixed charge.
- DERIVATIVES **liveried** adjective (only in sense 1).
- ORIGIN Middle English: from Old French *livree* 'delivered', feminine past participle of *livrer*, from Latin *liberare* 'liberate' (in medieval Latin 'hand over'). The original sense was 'the dispensing of food, provisions, or clothing to servants'; hence sense 4, also 'allowance of provender for horses', surviving in the phrase *at livery* and in **LIVERY STABLE**. Sense 1 arose because medieval nobles provided matching clothes to distinguish their servants from others'.

livery[2] ▶ adjective **1** resembling liver in colour or consistency: *he was short with livery lips*.
- ■informal liverish: *port always makes you livery*.
2 dialect (of soil) heavy.

livery company ▶ noun (in the UK) any of a number of Companies of the City of London descended from the medieval trade guilds. They are now largely social and charitable organizations.
- ORIGIN mid 18th cent.: so named because of the distinctive costume formerly used for special occasions.

liveryman ▶ noun (pl. **-men**) (in the UK) a member of a livery company.

livery stable (also **livery yard**) ▶ noun a stable where horses are kept at livery or let out for hire.

lives plural form of **LIFE**.

livestock ▶ noun [mass noun] farm animals regarded as an asset: *markets for the trading of livestock*.

liveware ▶ noun [mass noun] informal working personnel, especially computer personnel, as distinct from the inanimate or abstract things they work with.

live weight ▶ noun [mass noun] the weight of an

animal before it has been slaughtered and prepared as a carcass.

live wire ▶ noun informal an energetic and unpredictable person.

livid ▶ adjective **1** informal furiously angry: *he was livid at being left out.*
2 (of a colour or the skin) having a dark angry tinge: *livid bruises.*
- DERIVATIVES **lividity** noun, **lividly** adverb, **lividness** noun.
- ORIGIN late Middle English (in the sense 'of a bluish leaden colour'): from French *livide* or Latin *lividus*, from *livere* 'be bluish'. The sense 'furiously angry' dates from the early 20th cent.

living ▶ noun **1** [usu. in sing.] an income sufficient to live on or the means of earning it: *she was struggling to make a living as a dancer* | *what does he do for a living?*
- ■Brit. (in church use) a position as a vicar or rector with an income or property.
2 [mass noun] [with adj. or noun modifier] the pursuit of a lifestyle of the specified type: *the benefits of country living.*
▶ adjective alive: *living creatures* | [as plural noun **the living**] *flowers were for the living.*
- ■[attrib.] (of a place) used for living rather than working in: *the living quarters of the pub.* ■ (of a language) still spoken and used. ■ [attrib.] poetic/literary (of water) perennially flowing: *streams of living water.*
- PHRASES **be (the) living proof that** (or **of**) show by one's existence and qualities that something is the case: *she is living proof that hard work need not be ageing.* **in** (or **within**) **living memory** within or during a time that is remembered by people still alive: *the worst recession in living memory.* **the living image of** an exact copy or likeness of.

living death ▶ noun [in sing.] a state of existence that is as bad as being dead; a life of hopeless and unbroken misery.

living rock ▶ noun [mass noun] rock that is not detached but still forms part of the earth: *a chamber cut out of the living rock.*
- ■natural rock placed in an aquarium as a habitat for sessile organisms.

living room ▶ noun a room in a house for general and informal everyday use.

Livingstone[1] former name for **MARAMBA**.

Livingstone[2], David (1813–73), Scottish missionary and explorer. He went to Bechuanaland as a missionary in 1841. On extensive travels, he discovered Lake Ngami (1849), the Zambezi River (1851), and the Victoria Falls (1855). In 1866 he went in search of the source of the Nile, and was found in poor health by Sir Henry Morton Stanley in 1871.

living stone ▶ noun a small succulent southern African plant which resembles a pebble in appearance. It consists of two fleshy cushion-like leaves divided by a slit through which a daisy-like flower emerges.
- ● Genus *Lithops*, family Aizoaceae.

Livingstone daisy ▶ noun a low spreading succulent plant which bears glistening daisy-like flowers in many colours, native to southern Africa.
- ● *Dorotheanthus* (formerly *Mesembryanthemum*) *bellidiformis*, family Aizoaceae.
- ORIGIN 1930s: of unknown origin.

living wage ▶ noun [in sing.] a wage which is high enough to maintain a normal standard of living.

living will ▶ noun a written statement detailing a person's desires regarding their medical treatment in circumstances in which they are no longer able to express informed consent, especially an advance directive.

Livonia /lɪˈvəʊnɪə/ a region on the east coast of the Baltic Sea, north of Lithuania, comprising most of present-day Latvia and Estonia. German name **LIVLAND** /'liːflant/.
- DERIVATIVES **Livonian** adjective & noun.

Livorno /lɪˈvɔːnəʊ, Italian liˈvorno/ a port in NW Italy, in Tuscany, on the Ligurian Sea; pop. 171,265 (1990). It is the site of the Italian Naval Academy. Also called **LEGHORN**.

Livy /'lɪvi/ (59 BC–AD 17), Roman historian; Latin name *Titus Livius*. His history of Rome from its foundation to his own time contained 142 books, of which thirty-five survive (including the earliest history of the war with Hannibal).

lixiviate /lɪkˈsɪvɪeɪt/ ▶ verb [with obj.] Chemistry archaic

separate (a substance) into soluble and insoluble constituents by the percolation of liquid.
- DERIVATIVES **lixiviation** noun.
- ORIGIN mid 17th cent.: from modern Latin *lixiviat-* 'impregnated with lye', from the verb *lixiviare*, from *lixivius* 'made into lye', from *lix* 'lye'.

Lizard a promontory in SW England, in Cornwall. Its southern tip, Lizard Point, is the southernmost point of the British mainland.

lizard ▶ noun a reptile that typically has a long body and tail, four legs, movable eyelids, and a rough, scaly, or spiny skin.
- ● Suborder Lacertilia (or Sauria), order Squamata: many families.
- ORIGIN late Middle English: from Old French *lesard(e)*, from Latin *lacertus* 'lizard, sea fish', also 'muscle'.

lizardfish ▶ noun (pl. same or **-fishes**) a fish of lizardlike appearance with a broad bony head, pointed snout, and heavy shiny scales. It lives in warm shallow seas, where it often rests on the bottom propped up on its pelvic fins.
- ● Family Synodontidae: several genera and species, including the widespread *Trachinocephalus myops* (also called **SNAKEFISH**).

lizard orchid ▶ noun a tall orchid with greenish flowers that have a very long twisted lip and a goat-like smell. It has spread from the Mediterranean area to more northern parts of Europe.
- ● *Himantoglossum hircinum*, family Orchidaceae.

lizard's tail ▶ noun a North American bog plant with long tapering spikes of fragrant white flowers.
- ● *Saururus cernuus*, family Saururaceae.

LJ ▶ abbreviation for (pl. **L JJ**) (in the UK) Lord Justice.

Ljubljana /ljuːˈbljɑːnə/ the capital of Slovenia; pop. 267,000 (1991). The city was founded (as Emona) by the Romans in 34 BC. German name **LAIBACH**.

Lk. ▶ abbreviation for the Gospel of Luke (in biblical references).

ll. ▶ abbreviation for (in textual references) lines.

'll ▶ contraction of shall; will: *I'll get the food on.*

llama /'lɑːmə/ ▶ noun a domesticated pack animal of the camel family found in the Andes, valued for its soft woolly fleece.
- ● *Lama glama*, family Camelidae, probably descended from the wild guanaco.
- ■[mass noun] the wool of the llama. ■ [mass noun] cloth made from such wool.
- ORIGIN early 17th cent.: from Spanish, probably from Quechua.

Llandudno /lanˈdɪdnəʊ, hlan-/ a resort town in Conwy, northern Wales, on the Irish Sea; pop. 14,370 (1981).

llanero /lɑːˈnɛːrəʊ, lj-/ ▶ noun (pl. **-os**) (in South America) an inhabitant of a llano, in particular one who works as a cowboy.
- ORIGIN Spanish.

llano /'lɑːnəʊ, 'ljɑː-/ ▶ noun (pl. **-os**) (in South America) a treeless grassy plain.
- ORIGIN Spanish, from Latin *planum* 'plain'.

LLB ▶ abbreviation for Bachelor of Laws.
- ORIGIN from Latin *legum baccalaureus*.

LLD ▶ abbreviation for Doctor of Laws.
- ORIGIN from Latin *legum doctor*.

Llewelyn /luːˈɛlɪn, hluː-/ (d.1282), prince of Gwynedd in North Wales; also known as **Llywelyn ap Gruffydd**. Proclaiming himself prince of all Wales in 1258, he was recognized by Henry III in 1265. His refusal to pay homage to Edward I led the latter to invade and subjugate Wales (1277–84); Llewelyn died in an unsuccessful rebellion.

LLM ▶ abbreviation for Master of Laws.
- ORIGIN from Latin *legum magister*.

Llosa, Mario Vargas, see **VARGAS LLOSA**.

Lloyd[1] /lɔɪd/, Harold (Clayton) (1893–1971), American film comedian. Performing his own hair-raising stunts, he used physical danger as a source of comedy in silent movies such as *High and Dizzy* (1920), *Safety Last* (1923), and *The Freshman* (1925).

Lloyd[2] /lɔɪd/, Marie (1870–1922), English music-hall entertainer; born *Matilda Alice Victoria Wood*. She achieved fame for her risqué songs and extravagant costumes and took her act to the US, South Africa, and Australia.

Lloyd George, David, 1st Earl Lloyd George of Dwyfor (1863–1945), British Liberal statesman, Prime Minister 1916–22. As Chancellor of the Exchequer (1908–15), he introduced old-age pensions (1908) and national insurance (1911). His coalition government was threatened by economic problems and trouble in Ireland, and he resigned when the Conservatives withdrew their support in 1922.

Lloyd's an incorporated society of insurance underwriters in London, made up of private syndicates. Founded in 1871, Lloyd's originally dealt only in marine insurance.
■short for **LLOYD'S REGISTER**.
– ORIGIN named after the coffee house of Edward *Lloyd* (*fl.* 1688–1726), in which underwriters and merchants congregated and where *Lloyd's List* was started in 1734.

Lloyd's List ▶ **noun** a daily newsletter relating to shipping, published in London.

Lloyd's Register (in full **Lloyd's Register of Shipping**) a classified list of merchant ships over a certain tonnage, published annually in London.
■the corporation that produces this list and lays down the specifications for ships on which it is based.

Lloyd Webber, Sir Andrew, Baron Lloyd Webber of Sydmonton (b.1948), English composer. His many successful musicals, several of them written in collaboration with the lyricist Sir Tim Rice, include *Jesus Christ Superstar* (1970), *Cats* (1981), and *The Phantom of the Opera* (1986).

Llywelyn ap Gruffydd /luːˈɛlɪn ap ˈɡrɪfɪð, hluː-/ see **LLEWELYN**.

LM /ɛm/ ▶ **abbreviation for** ■long metre. ■lunar module.

lm ▶ **abbreviation for** lumen(s).

LMS ▶ **abbreviation for** (in the UK) local management of schools.

LMT ▶ **abbreviation for** Local Mean Time, the standard time in the relevant time zone.

ln Mathematics ▶ **abbreviation for** natural logarithm.
– ORIGIN from modern Latin *logarithmus naturalis*.

LNB ▶ **abbreviation for** low noise blocker, a circuit on a satellite dish which selects the required signal from the transmission.

LNG ▶ **abbreviation for** liquefied natural gas.

lo ▶ **exclamation** archaic used to draw attention to an interesting or amazing event: *and lo, the star, which they saw in the east, went before them.*
– PHRASES **lo and behold** used to present a new scene, situation, or turn of events, often with the suggestion that though surprising, it could in fact have been predicted: *you took me out and, lo and behold, I got home to find my house had been ransacked.*
– ORIGIN natural exclamation: first recorded as *lā* in Old English; reinforced in Middle English by a shortened form of *loke* 'look!', imperative of **LOOK**.

loa /ˈləʊə/ ▶ **noun** (pl. same or **loas**) a god in the voodoo cult of Haiti.
– ORIGIN Haitian Creole.

Loach /ləʊtʃ/, Ken (b.1936), English film director; full name *Kenneth Loach*. He has persistently explored social and political issues in works including the TV film *Cathy Come Home* (1966) and the feature film *Kes* (1969).

loach /ləʊtʃ/ ▶ **noun** a small elongated bottom-dwelling freshwater fish with several barbels near the mouth, found in Eurasia and NW Africa.
• Family Cobitidae and Homalopteridae (or Balitoridae): several genera and numerous species.
– ORIGIN Middle English: from Old French *loche*, of unknown origin.

load ▶ **noun 1** a heavy or bulky thing that is being carried or is about to be carried: *in addition to their own food, they must carry a load of up to eighty pounds.*
■the total number or amount that can be carried in something, especially a vehicle of a specified type: *a lorry **load of** soldiers.* ■the material carried along by a stream, glacier, ocean current, etc. ■an amount of items washed or to be washed in a washing machine or dishwasher at one time: *I do at least six **loads** of washing a week.*
2 a weight or source of pressure borne by someone or something: *the increased **load on** the heart caused by a raised arterial pressure | the arch has hollow spandrels to lighten the **load on** the foundations.*
■the amount of work to be done by a person or machine: *Arthur has a light teaching load.* ■a burden of responsibility, worry, or grief: *consumers will find it difficult to service their heavy load of debt.*
3 (**a load of**) informal a lot of (often used to express one's disapproval or dislike of something): *she was talking **a load of rubbish**.*
■(**a load/loads**) informal plenty: *she spends **loads of** money on clothes | there's loads to see here, even when it rains.*
4 the amount of power supplied by a source; the resistance of moving parts to be overcome by a motor.
■the amount of electricity supplied by a generating system at any given time. ■Electronics an impedance or circuit that receives or develops the output of a transistor or other device.
▶ **verb** [with obj.] **1** put a load or large amount of something on or in (a vehicle, ship, container, etc.): *they go to Calais to **load up** their transit vans with cheap beer.*
■[with obj. and adverbial] (often **be loaded**) place (a load or large quantity of something) on or in a vehicle, ship, container, etc.: *stolen property from a burglary was **loaded into** a taxi.* ■[no obj.] (of a ship or vehicle) take on a load: *when we came to the quay the ship was still loading.*
2 make (someone or something) carry or hold a large or excessive amount of heavy things: *Elaine was **loaded down with** bags full of shopping.*
■(**load someone/thing with**) figurative supply someone or something in overwhelming abundance or to excess with: *the King and Queen loaded Columbus with wealth and honours.* ■(**load someone with**) figurative burden someone with (worries, responsibilities, etc.). ■(usu. **be loaded**) bias towards a particular outcome: *the odds were loaded against them before the match.*
3 insert (something) into a device so that it will operate: *load the cassette into the camcorder.*
■insert something into (a device) so that it can be operated. ■charge (a firearm) with ammunition. ■Computing transfer (a program or data) into memory, or into the central processor from storage. ■Computing transfer programs into (a computer memory or processor).
– PHRASES **get a load of** informal used to draw attention to someone or something: *get a load of what we've just done.* **get** (or **have**) **a load on** informal, chiefly N. Amer. become drunk. **load the bases** Baseball have base-runners on all three bases. **load the dice against/in favour of someone** put someone at a disadvantage or advantage. **take a** (or **the**) **load off one's feet** sit or lie down. **take a load off someone's mind** bring someone relief from anxiety. **under load** subject to a mechanical or electrical load.
– ORIGIN Old English *lād* 'way, journey, conveyance', of Germanic origin: related to German *Leite*, also to **LEAD**[1]; compare with **LODE**. The verb dates from the late 15th cent.

loaded ▶ **adjective 1** carrying or bearing a load, especially a large one: *a heavily loaded freight train.*
■(of a firearm) charged with ammunition: *a loaded gun.* ■[predic.] (**loaded with**) containing in abundance or to excess: *your average chocolate bar is loaded with fat.* ■[predic.] informal having a lot of money; wealthy: *she doesn't really have to work—they're loaded.* ■[predic.] N. Amer. informal having had too much alcohol; drunk: *man, did I **get loaded** after I left his house.* ■N. Amer. informal (of a car) equipped with many optional extras; de luxe: *1989 Ford 250 LXT: low miles, loaded.*
2 weighted or biased towards a particular outcome: *a trick like the one with the loaded dice.*
■(of a word, statement, or question) charged with an underlying meaning or implication: *avoid politically loaded terms like 'nation' | 'Anything else?' It was a loaded question and Kelly knew it.*
– PHRASES **loaded for bear** see **BEAR**[2].

loader ▶ **noun 1** a machine or person that loads something.
■an attendant who loads guns at a shoot.
2 [in combination] a gun, machine, or lorry which is loaded in a specified way: *a front-loader.*

load factor ▶ **noun** the ratio of the average or actual amount of some quantity and the maximum possible or permissible.
■the ratio between the lift and the weight of an aircraft.

loading ▶ **noun** [mass noun] **1** the application of a mechanical load or force to something.
■the amount of electric current or power delivered to a device. ■the maximum electric current or power taken by an appliance. ■the provision of extra electrical inductance to improve the properties of a transmission wire or aerial.
2 the application of an extra amount of something to balance some other factor.
■[count noun] an increase in an insurance premium due to a factor increasing the risk involved. ■[count noun] Austral. an increment added to a basic wage for special skills or qualifications.
▶ **adjective** [in combination] (of a gun, machine, or lorry) loaded in a specified way: *a front-loading dishwasher.*

loading bay ▶ **noun** a bay or recess in a building where vehicles are loaded and unloaded.

loading coil ▶ **noun** a coil used to provide additional inductance in an electric circuit, in order to reduce distortion and attenuation of transmitted signals or to reduce the resonant frequency of an aerial.

loading dock ▶ **noun** see **DOCK**[1].

loading gauge ▶ **noun** the maximum permitted height and width for rolling stock on a railway.
■a frame suspended above a railway track to indicate these limits.

loading shovel ▶ **noun** a vehicle with a power-operated shovel for scooping up material and carrying it short distances.

load line ▶ **noun** another term for **PLIMSOLL LINE**.

loadmaster ▶ **noun** the member of an aircraft's crew responsible for the cargo.

loadsa ▶ **contraction of** loads of (in the sense 'lots' representing non-standard use): *Bond gets to shoot loadsa bad guys.*

load-shedding ▶ **noun** [mass noun] action to reduce the load on something, especially the interruption of an electricity supply to avoid excessive load on the generating plant.

loadspace ▶ **noun** the space in a motor vehicle for carrying a load.

loadstone ▶ **noun** variant spelling of **LODESTONE**.

loaf[1] ▶ **noun** (pl. **loaves**) a quantity of bread that is shaped and baked in one piece and usually sliced before being eaten: *a **loaf of bread** | a granary loaf.*
■[usu. with modifier] a quantity of other food formed into a particular shape, and often sliced into portions.
– PHRASES **half a loaf is better than no bread** proverb it is better to accept less than one wants or expects than to have nothing at all. **use one's loaf** Brit. informal use one's common sense. [ORIGIN: probably from *loaf of bread*, rhyming slang for 'head'.]
– ORIGIN Old English *hlāf*, of Germanic origin; related to German *Laib*.

loaf[2] ▶ **verb** [no obj.] idle one's time away, typically by aimless wandering or loitering: *don't let him see you **loafing about** with your hands in your pockets.*
– ORIGIN mid 19th cent.: probably a back-formation from **LOAFER**.

loafer ▶ **noun 1** a person who idles their time away.
2 trademark a leather shoe shaped like a moccasin, with a flat heel.
– ORIGIN mid 19th cent.: perhaps from German *Landläufer* 'tramp', from *Land* 'land' + *laufen* (dialect *lofen*) 'to run'.

loaf sugar ▶ **noun** [mass noun] sugar from or comprising a sugarloaf.

loam ▶ **noun** [mass noun] a fertile soil of clay and sand containing humus.
■Geology a soil with roughly equal proportions of sand, silt, and clay. ■a paste of clay and water with sand, chopped straw, etc., used in making bricks and plastering walls.
– DERIVATIVES **loaminess** noun, **loamy** adjective.
– ORIGIN Old English *lām* 'clay', of West Germanic origin: related to Dutch *leem* and German *Lehm*, also to **LIME**[1].

loan[1] ▶ **noun** a thing that is borrowed, especially a sum of money that is expected to be paid back with interest: *borrowers can **take out a loan** for £84,000.*
■an act of lending something to someone: *she offered to buy him dinner in return for the loan of the flat.* ■short for **LOANWORD**.
▶ **verb** [with obj.] (often **be loaned**) lend (a sum of money or item of property): *the word processor was loaned to us by the theatre | [with two objs] he knew Rab would not loan him money.*
– PHRASES **on loan** (of a thing) being borrowed: *the painting is at present **on loan to** the Tate Gallery.* ■(of a worker or sports player) on secondment to another organization or team, typically for an agreed fixed period.
– DERIVATIVES **loanable** adjective, **loanee** noun, **loaner** noun.
– ORIGIN Middle English (also denoting a gift from a superior): from Old Norse *lán*, of Germanic origin; related to Dutch *leen*, German *Lehn*, also to **LEND**.

loan[2] (also **loaning**) ▶ **noun** [usu. in place names] Scottish a

lane or narrow path, especially one leading to open ground: *Whitehouse Loan.*
■an open, uncultivated piece of land where cows are milked.
– ORIGIN late Middle English variant of **LANE**.

loan capital ▶ **noun** [mass noun] money required to run a business which is raised from loans rather than shares.

loan collection ▶ **noun** **1** a collection of works of art or other objects lent by various owners for an exhibition.
2 a collection of books, museum exhibits, etc. which are available for loan to members of the public.

loanholder ▶ **noun** a person or organization holding the securities for a loan; a mortgagee.

loaning (also **lonning**) ▶ **noun** another term for **LOAN**².

loan shark ▶ **noun** informal, derogatory a moneylender who charges extremely high rates of interest, typically under illegal conditions.

loan translation ▶ **noun** an expression adopted by one language from another in a more or less literally translated form. Also called **CALQUE**.

loanword ▶ **noun** a word adopted from a foreign language with little or no modification.

loath /ləʊθ/ (also **loth**) ▶ **adjective** [predic., with infinitive] reluctant; unwilling: *I was loath to leave.*
– ORIGIN Old English *lāth* 'hostile, spiteful', of Germanic origin; related to Dutch *leed*, German *Leid* 'sorrow'.

loathe /ləʊð/ ▶ **verb** [with obj.] feel intense dislike or disgust for: *she loathed him on sight* | [as noun **loathing**] *the thought filled him with loathing.*
– DERIVATIVES **loather** noun.
– ORIGIN Old English *lāthian*, of Germanic origin; related to **LOATH**.

loathsome ▶ **adjective** causing hatred or disgust; repulsive: *this loathsome little swine.*
– DERIVATIVES **loathsomely** adverb, **loathsomeness** noun.
– ORIGIN Middle English: from archaic *loath* 'disgust, loathing' + **-SOME**¹.

loaves plural form of **LOAF**¹.

lob ▶ **verb** (**lobbed**, **lobbing**) [with obj. and adverbial of direction] throw or hit (a ball or missile) in a high arc: *he lobbed the ball over their heads.*
■[with obj.] (in soccer or tennis) kick or hit the ball over (an opponent) in such a way: *he managed to lob the keeper.*
▶ **noun** (chiefly in soccer and tennis) a ball kicked or hit in a high arc over an opponent or a stroke producing this result.
■Cricket a ball bowled with a slow underarm action.
– ORIGIN late 16th cent. (in the senses 'cause or allow to hang heavily' and 'behave like a lout'): from the archaic noun *lob* 'lout', 'pendulous object', probably from Low German or Dutch (compare with modern Dutch *lubbe* 'hanging lip'). The current sense dates from the mid 19th cent.

Lobachevsky /ˌlɒbəˈtʃɛfski/, Nikolai Ivanovich (1792–1856), Russian mathematician. At about the same time as Gauss and **János Bolyai** (1802–60), he independently discovered non-Euclidean geometry. His work was not widely recognized until the non-Euclidean nature of space–time was revealed by the general theory of relativity.

lobar /ˈləʊbə/ ▶ **adjective** [attrib.] chiefly Anatomy & Medicine of, relating to, or affecting a lobe, especially a whole lobe of a lung.

lobate /ˈləʊbeɪt/ ▶ **adjective** Biology having a lobe or lobes: *lobate oak leaves.*
– DERIVATIVES **lobation** noun.

lobby ▶ **noun** (pl. **-ies**) **1** a room providing a space out of which one or more other rooms or corridors lead, typically one near the entrance of a public building.
2 (in the UK) any of several large halls in the Houses of Parliament in which MPs may meet members of the public.
■(in the UK) (also **division lobby**) each of two corridors in the Houses of Parliament to which MPs retire to vote. ■ (**the lobby**) informal (in the UK) the lobby correspondents collectively.
3 a group of people seeking to influence politicians or public officials on a particular issue: *members of the anti-abortion lobby* | [as modifier] *lobby groups.*
■[in sing.] an organized attempt by members of the public to influence politicians or public officials: *a recent lobby of Parliament by pensioners.*
▶ **verb** (**-ies**, **-ied**) [with obj.] seek to influence (a politician or public official) on an issue: *it is recommending that booksellers lobby their MPs* | [no obj.] *a region-wide group **lobbying for** better rail services.*
– DERIVATIVES **lobbyist** noun.
– ORIGIN mid 16th cent. (in the sense 'monastic cloister'): from medieval Latin *lobia*, *lobium* 'covered walk, portico'. The verb sense (originally US) derives from the practice of frequenting the lobby of a house of legislature to influence its members into supporting a cause.

lobby correspondent ▶ **noun** (in the UK) a senior political journalist of a group receiving direct but unattributable briefings from the government.

lobe ▶ **noun** a roundish and flattish part of something, typically each of two or more such parts divided by a fissure, and often projecting or hanging. See also **EAR LOBE**.
■each of the parts of the cerebrum of the brain.
– DERIVATIVES **lobed** adjective, **lobeless** adjective.
– ORIGIN late Middle English: via late Latin from Greek *lobos* 'lobe, pod'.

lobectomy ▶ **noun** (pl. **-ies**) [mass noun] surgical removal of a lobe of an organ such as the thyroid gland, lung, liver, or brain.

lobe-finned fish (also **lobefin**) ▶ **noun** a fish of a largely extinct group having fleshy lobed fins, including the probable ancestors of the amphibians. Compare with **RAY-FINNED FISH**.
● Subclass Crossopterygia (or Actinistia or Coelacanthimorpha): the only living representative is the coelacanth.

lobelia /ləˈbiːlɪə/ ▶ **noun** a chiefly tropical or subtropical plant of the bellflower family, in particular an annual widely grown as a bedding plant. Some kinds are aquatic, and some grow as thick-trunked shrubs or trees on African mountains.
● Genus *Lobelia*, family Campanulaceae: many species, including the popular blue-flowered *L. erinus*.
– ORIGIN modern Latin, named after Matthias de Lobel (1538–1616), Flemish botanist to James I.

Lobito /lʊˈbiːtəʊ/ a seaport and natural harbour on the Atlantic coast of Angola; pop. 150,000 (est. 1983).

loblolly /ˈlɒblɒli/ ▶ **noun** (pl. **-ies**) **1** (also **loblolly pine**) a North American pine tree with very long slender needles, which is an important source of timber.
● *Pinus taeda*, family Pinaceae.
2 (also **loblolly bay**) a small evergreen tree of the tea family, with bay-like leaves and white camellialike flowers, native to SE North America.
● *Gordonia lasianthus*, family Theaceae.
– ORIGIN late 16th cent. (denoting thick gruel): the reason for the application of the word to the two plants, and the word's origin, are unknown.

lobo /ˈləʊbəʊ/ ▶ **noun** (pl. **-os**) N. Amer. (in the south-western US and Mexico) a timber wolf.
– ORIGIN mid 19th cent.: from Spanish, from Latin *lupus* 'wolf'.

lobola /ləˈbəʊlə/ (also **lobolo** /ləˈbəʊləʊ/) ▶ **noun** (among southern African peoples) a bride price, especially one paid with cattle.
■[mass noun] the practice of making such a payment.
– ORIGIN Zulu and Xhosa.

lobopod /ˈləʊbə(ʊ)pɒd/ ▶ **noun** Zoology the lobopodium of an onychophoran.
■an onychophoran: [as modifier] *a lobopod animal.*

lobopodium /ˌləʊbə(ʊ)ˈpəʊdɪəm/ ▶ **noun** (pl. **lobopodia** /-ɪə/) Zoology a blunt limb or organ resembling a limb, in particular:
■the primitive leg of an onychophoran. ■ a lobe-like pseudopodium in an amoeba.
– DERIVATIVES **lobopodial** adjective.
– ORIGIN early 20th cent.: from modern Latin *lobosus* 'having many lobes, large lobed' + **PODIUM**.

lobotomize (also **-ise**) ▶ **verb** [with obj.] (often **be lobotomized**) Surgery perform a lobotomy on.
■informal reduce the mental or emotional capacity or ability to function of: *couples we knew who had been lobotomized by the birth of their children.*
– DERIVATIVES **lobotomization** noun.

lobotomy /ləˈbɒtəmi/ ▶ **noun** (pl. **-ies**) a surgical operation involving incision into the prefrontal lobe of the brain, formerly used to treat mental illness. Compare with **LEUCOTOMY**.

lobscouse /ˈlɒbskaʊs/ ▶ **noun** [mass noun] a stew formerly eaten by sailors, consisting of meat, vegetables, and ship's biscuit.
– ORIGIN early 18th cent.: of unknown origin; compare with Dutch *lapskous*, Danish and Norwegian *lapskaus*, and German *Lapskaus*.

lobster ▶ **noun** a large marine crustacean with a cylindrical body, stalked eyes, and the first of its five pairs of limbs modified as pincers.
● *Homarus* and other genera, class Malacostraca.
■[mass noun] the flesh of this animal as food. ■ [mass noun] a deep red colour typical of a cooked lobster. ■ Austral./NZ a freshwater crayfish, especially one whose claws are eaten as food.
▶ **verb** [no obj.] catch lobsters.
– ORIGIN Old English *lopustre*, alteration of Latin *locusta* 'crustacean, locust'.

lobster claw ▶ **noun** a tropical American plant with brightly coloured flowers which resemble a lobster claw, each being composed of boat-shaped bracts.
● *Heliconia bihai*, family Heliconiaceae.

lobster moth ▶ **noun** a brown woodland European moth with a caterpillar that has long legs and an upturned tail reminiscent of a lobster.
● *Stauropus fagi*, family Notodontidae.

lobster Newburg /ˈnjuːbəːg/ ▶ **noun** [mass noun] a dish of lobster cooked in a thick cream sauce containing sherry or brandy.
– ORIGIN probably named after *Newburgh*, New York.

lobster pot ▶ **noun** a basket-like trap in which lobsters are caught.

lobster thermidor /ˈθəːmɪdɔː/ ▶ **noun** [mass noun] a dish of lobster cooked in a cream sauce, returned to its shell, sprinkled with cheese, and browned under the grill.
– ORIGIN *thermidor* from **THERMIDOR**.

lobule /ˈlɒbjuːl/ ▶ **noun** chiefly Anatomy a small lobe.
– DERIVATIVES **lobular** adjective, **lobulate** /-lət/ adjective, **lobulated** adjective.
– ORIGIN late 17th cent.: from **LOBE**, on the pattern of words such as *globule*.

lobworm ▶ **noun** a large earthworm used as fishing bait.
– ORIGIN mid 17th cent.: from **LOB** in the obsolete sense 'pendulous object'.

local ▶ **adjective** belonging or relating to a particular area or neighbourhood, typically exclusively so: *researching local history* | *the local post office.*
■denoting a telephone call made to a nearby place and charged at a relatively low rate. ■ denoting a train or bus serving a particular district, with frequent stops: *the village has an excellent local bus service.* ■ (in technical use) relating to a particular region or part, or to each of any number of these: *a local infection* | *migration can regulate the local density of animals.* ■ Computing denoting a variable or other entity that is only available for use in one part of a program. ■ Computing denoting a device that can be accessed without the use of a network. Compare with **REMOTE**.
▶ **noun** a local person or thing, in particular:
■an inhabitant of a particular area or neighbourhood: *the street was full of locals and tourists.* ■ Brit. informal a pub convenient to a person's home: *a pint in the local.* ■ a local train or bus service: *catch the local into New Delhi.* ■ N. Amer. a local branch of an organization, especially a trade union. ■ short for **LOCAL ANAESTHETIC**. ■ Stock Exchange slang a floor trader who trades on their own account, rather than on behalf of other investors.
– DERIVATIVES **locally** adverb, **localness** noun.
– ORIGIN late Middle English: from late Latin *localis*, from Latin *locus* 'place'.

local anaesthetic ▶ **noun** [mass noun] an anaesthetic that affects a restricted area of the body. Compare with **GENERAL ANAESTHETIC**.

local area network (abbrev.: **LAN**) ▶ **noun** a computer network that links devices within a building or group of adjacent buildings, especially one with a radius of less than 1 km.

local authority ▶ **noun** Brit. an administrative body in local government.

local bus ▶ **noun** Computing a high-speed data connection directly linking peripheral devices to the processor and memory, allowing activities that require high data transmission rates such as video display.

local colour ▶ **noun** [mass noun] **1** the customs,

manner of speech, dress, or other typical features of a place or period that contribute to its particular character: *reporters in search of local colour and gossip.*
2 Art the actual colour of a thing in ordinary daylight, uninfluenced by the proximity of other colours.

local derby ▶ **noun** a sports match between two rival teams from the same area.

locale /ləʊˈkɑːl/ ▶ **noun** a place where something happens or is set, or that has particular events associated with it: *her summers were spent in a variety of exotic locales.*
– ORIGIN late 18th cent.: from French *local* (noun), respelled to indicate stress on the final syllable; compare with **MORALE**.

local government ▶ **noun** [mass noun] the administration of a particular county or district, with representatives elected by those who live there.

Local Group Astronomy the cluster of galaxies of which our Galaxy is a member.

localism ▶ **noun** [mass noun] preference for a locality, particularly to one's own area or region.
■ derogatory the limitation of ideas and interests resulting from this. ■ [count noun] a characteristic of a particular locality, such as a local idiom or custom.
– DERIVATIVES **localist** noun & adjective.

locality ▶ **noun** (pl. **-ies**) the position or site of something: *the rock's size and locality.*
■ an area or neighbourhood, especially as regarded as a place occupied by certain people or as the scene of particular activities: *the results of other schools in the locality | a working-class locality.*
– ORIGIN early 17th cent.: from French *localité* or late Latin *localitas*, from *localis* 'relating to a place' (see **LOCAL**).

localize (also **-ise**) ▶ **verb** [with obj.] [often as adj. **localized**] restrict (something) to a particular place: *symptoms include localized pain and numbness.*
■ make (something) local in character: *there'd now be a more localized news service.* ■ assign (something) to a particular place: *most vertebrates localize sounds by orienting movements.*
– DERIVATIVES **localizable** adjective, **localization** noun.

local option ▶ **noun** a choice available to a local administration to accept or reject national legislation (e.g. concerning the sale of alcoholic liquor).

local preacher ▶ **noun** a Methodist layperson authorized to conduct services in a particular circuit.

local time ▶ **noun** time as reckoned in a particular region or time zone.
■ time at a particular place as measured from the sun's transit over the meridian at that place, defined as noon.

Locarno /ləˈkɑːnəʊ, Italian loˈkarno/ a resort in southern Switzerland, at the northern end of Lake Maggiore; pop. 14,150 (1990).

Locarno Pact a series of agreements made in Locarno in 1925 between the UK, Germany, France, Belgium, Poland, and Czechoslovakia in an attempt to ensure the future peace of Europe. The Pact guaranteed the common borders of France, Germany, and Belgium and the demilitarization of the Rhineland, as specified by the Treaty of Versailles.

locate /lə(ʊ)ˈkeɪt/ ▶ **verb** [with obj.] discover the exact place or position of: *engineers were working to locate the fault.*
■ [with obj. and adverbial of place] (usu. **be located**) situate in a particular place: *these popular apartments are centrally located.* ■ [with obj. and adverbial] place within a particular context: *they locate their policies in terms of wealth creation.* ■ [no obj., with adverbial of place] N. Amer. establish oneself or one's business in a specified place: *his marketing strategy has been to locate in small towns.*
– DERIVATIVES **locatable** adjective.
– ORIGIN early 16th cent.: from Latin *locat-* 'placed', from the verb *locare*, from *locus* 'place'. The original sense was as a legal term meaning 'let out on hire', later (late 16th cent.) 'assign to a particular place', then (particularly in North American usage) 'establish in a place'. The sense 'discover the exact position of' dates from the late 19th cent.

location ▶ **noun 1** a particular place or position: *the property is set in a convenient location.*
■ an actual place or natural setting in which a film or broadcast is made, as distinct from a simulation in a studio: *the movie was filmed entirely **on location**.* ■ [mass noun] the action or process of placing someone or something in a particular position: *the location of new housing beyond the existing built-up areas.* ■ a position or address in computer memory.
2 S. African historical an area where black South Africans were obliged to live, usually on the outskirts of a town or city. The term was later replaced by *township*.
– DERIVATIVES **locational** adjective.
– ORIGIN late 16th cent.: from Latin *locatio(n-)*, from the verb *locare* (see **LOCATE**).

locative /ˈlɒkətɪv/ Grammar ▶ **adjective** relating to or denoting a case in some languages of nouns, pronouns, and adjectives, expressing location.
▶ **noun** (**the locative**) the locative case.
■ a word in the locative case.
– ORIGIN early 19th cent.: from **LOCATE**, on the pattern of *vocative*.

locator ▶ **noun** a device or system for locating something, typically by means of radio signals.

loc. cit. ▶ **abbreviation** in the passage already cited.
– ORIGIN from Latin *loco citato*.

loch /lɒk, lɒx/ ▶ **noun** Scottish a lake.
■ (also **sea loch**) an arm of the sea, especially when narrow or partially landlocked.
– ORIGIN late Middle English: from Scottish Gaelic.

lochan /ˈlɒk(ə)n, ˈlɒx(ə)n/ ▶ **noun** Scottish a small loch.
– ORIGIN late 17th cent.: from Scottish Gaelic, diminutive of *loch*.

lochia /ˈlɒkɪə, ˈləʊ-/ ▶ **noun** [mass noun] Medicine the normal discharge from the uterus after childbirth.
– DERIVATIVES **lochial** adjective.
– ORIGIN late 17th cent.: modern Latin, from Greek *lokhia*, neuter plural (used as a noun) of *lokhios* 'of childbirth'.

Loch Ness a deep lake in NW Scotland, in the Great Glen. Forming part of the Caledonian Canal, it is 38 km (24 miles) long, with a maximum depth of 230 m (755 ft).

Loch Ness monster a large creature alleged to live in the deep waters of Loch Ness. Reports of its existence date from the time of St Columba (6th century); despite recent scientific expeditions, there is still no proof of its existence.

loci plural form of **LOCUS**.

loci classici plural form of **LOCUS CLASSICUS**.

locie /ˈləʊki/ (also **lokey**) ▶ **noun** (pl. **-ies** or **-eys**) N. Amer. & NZ informal a locomotive.

lock[1] ▶ **noun 1** a mechanism for keeping a door, lid, etc. fastened, typically operated only by a key of a particular form: *the key turned firmly in the lock.*
■ a similar device used to prevent the operation or movement of a vehicle or other machine: *a steering lock | a bicycle lock.* ■ (in wrestling and martial arts) a hold that prevents an opponent from moving a limb. ■ [in sing.] archaic a number of interlocked or jammed items: *I have seen all Albermarle Street closed by a lock of carriages.*
2 a short confined section of a canal or other waterway where the water level can be changed by the use of gates and sluices, used for raising and lowering boats between two gates.
■ an airlock.
3 [mass noun] the turning of the front wheels of a vehicle to change its direction of motion.
■ (also **full lock**) the maximum extent of this.
4 (also **lock forward**) Rugby a player in the second row of a scrum.
5 (**a lock**) N. Amer. informal a person or thing that is certain to succeed; a certainty.
6 archaic a mechanism for exploding the charge of a gun.
▶ **verb 1** [with obj.] fasten or secure (something) with a lock: *she closed and locked her desk |* [as adj. **locked**] *behind locked doors.*
■ (**lock something up**) shut and secure something, especially a building, by fastening its doors with locks: *the diplomatic personnel locked up their building and walked off |* [no obj.] *you could lock up for me when you leave.* ■ [with obj. and adverbial] enclose or shut in by locking or fastening a door, lid, etc.: *the prisoners are locked in overnight | Phil locked away the takings every night.* ■ (**lock someone up/away**) imprison someone. ■ (**lock something up/away**) invest money in something so that it is not easily accessible: *vast sums of money locked up in pension funds.* ■ (**lock someone down**) N. Amer. confine a prisoner to their cell, especially so as to gain control. ■ [no obj.] (of a door, window, box, etc.) become or be able to be secured through activation of a lock: *the door will automatically lock behind you.*
2 make or become rigidly fixed or immovable: [with obj.] *he locked his hands behind her neck |* [no obj.] *their gaze locked for several long moments.*
■ [with obj.] (**lock someone/thing in**) engage or entangle in (an embrace or struggle): *they were locked in a legal battle.* ■ [with obj.] (**lock someone/thing into**) cause to become caught or involved in: *they were now locked into the system.* ■ [with obj.] (of land, hills, ice, etc.) enclose; surround: *the vessel was **locked in** ice.*
3 [no obj.] [with adverbial of direction] go through a lock on a canal: *we locked through at Moore Haven.*
– PHRASES **have a lock on** N. Amer. informal have an unbreakable hold on or total control over. **lock horns** engage in conflict. **lock, stock, and barrel** including everything; completely: *the place is owned lock, stock, and barrel by an oil company.* [ORIGIN: referring to the complete mechanism of a firearm.] **under lock and key** securely locked up.
– DERIVATIVES **lockable** adjective, **lockless** adjective.
– ORIGIN Old English *loc*, of Germanic origin; related to German *Loch* 'hole'.
▶ **lock on to** locate (a target) by radar or similar means and then track.
lock someone out 1 keep someone out of a room or building by locking the door. **2** (of an employer) subject employees to a lockout.
lock someone out of exclude someone from: *those now locked out of the job market.*

lock[2] ▶ **noun** a piece of a person's hair that coils or hangs together: *she pushed back **a lock of** hair.*
■ chiefly poetic/literary (**locks**) a person's hair: *flowing locks and a long white beard.* ■ a tuft of wool or cotton.
– DERIVATIVES **locked** adjective [in combination] *his curly-locked comrades.*
– ORIGIN Old English *locc*, of Germanic origin; related to Dutch *lok*, German *Locke*, possibly also to **LOCK**[1].

lockage ▶ **noun** [mass noun] the construction or use of locks on waterways.
■ the amount of rise and fall of water levels resulting from the use of locks. ■ money paid as a toll for the use of a lock.

lockdown ▶ **noun** N. Amer. the confining of prisoners to their cells, typically in order to regain control during a riot.

Locke[1], John (1632–1704), English philosopher, a founder of empiricism and political liberalism. His *Two Treatises of Government* (1690) argues that the authority of rulers has a human origin and is limited. In *An Essay concerning Human Understanding* (1690) he argued that all knowledge is derived from sense-experience.
– DERIVATIVES **Lockean** adjective.

Locke[2], Joseph (1805–60), English civil engineer. A pioneer in railways, he enjoyed a lifelong association with Thomas Brassey, building important lines in England, Scotland, and France.

locker ▶ **noun 1** a small lockable cupboard or compartment, typically as one of a number placed together for public or general use, e.g. in schools, sports changing rooms, or large railway stations.
■ a chest or compartment on a ship or boat for clothes, stores, equipment, or ammunition.
2 a device that locks something.
– ORIGIN late Middle English: probably related to Flemish *loker*.

Lockerbie /ˈlɒkəbi/ a town in SW Scotland, in Dumfries and Galloway; pop. 3,560 (1981). In 1988 the wreckage of an American airliner, destroyed by a terrorist bomb, crashed on the town, killing all those on board and eleven people on the ground.

locker room ▶ **noun** a room containing lockers for the storage of personal belongings, especially a sports changing room.
▶ **adjective** [attrib.] regarded as characteristic of or suited to a men's locker room, especially as being coarse or ribald: *locker-room humour.*

locket ▶ **noun 1** a small ornamental case, typically made of gold or silver, worn round a person's neck on a chain and used to hold things of sentimental value, such as a photograph or lock of hair.
2 a metal plate or band on a scabbard.
– ORIGIN late Middle English (in sense 2): from Old French *locquet*, diminutive of *loc* 'latch, lock', of Germanic origin; related to **LOCK**[1]. Sense 1 dates from the late 17th cent.

lockfast ▶ adjective Scottish secured with a lock: *lockfast areas in which to store equipment.*

lock forward ▶ noun another term for **LOCK**¹ (in sense 4).

lock-in ▶ noun 1 an arrangement according to which a person or company is obliged to negotiate or trade only with a specific company.
2 a period during which customers are locked into a bar or pub after closing time to continue drinking privately.

lockjaw ▶ noun non-technical term for **TRISMUS**.

lock-keeper ▶ noun a person who is employed to attend and maintain a lock on a river or canal.

lock-knit ▶ adjective [attrib.] (of a fabric) knitted with an interlocking stitch.

locknut ▶ noun a nut screwed down on another to keep it tight.
■ a nut designed so that, once tightened, it cannot be accidentally loosened.

lockout ▶ noun the exclusion of employees by their employer from their place of work until certain terms are agreed to.

locksmith ▶ noun a person who makes and repairs locks.

lockstep ▶ noun [mass noun] a way of marching with each person as close as possible to the one in front: *the trio marched in lockstep* | [as adv.] *hundreds of shaven-headed youths march lockstep into the stadium.*

lock stitch ▶ noun [mass noun] a stitch made by a sewing machine by firmly linking together two threads or stitches.

lock-up ▶ noun 1 a jail, especially a temporary one.
2 Brit. non-residential premises that can be locked up, typically a small shop or garage.
3 [mass noun] the locking up of premises for the night.
■ the time of doing this: *hurrying back to their houses before lock-up.*
4 [mass noun] the action of becoming fixed or immovable: *anti-lock braking helps prevent wheel lock-up.*
5 an investment in assets which cannot readily be realized or sold on in the short term.

Lockyer /ˈlɒkjə/, Sir (Joseph) Norman (1836–1920), English astronomer. His spectroscopic analysis of the sun led to his discovery of a new element, which he named *helium*. He founded both the Science Museum in London and the scientific journal *Nature*, which he edited for fifty years.

loco¹ ▶ noun (pl. **-os**) informal a locomotive.
– ORIGIN mid 19th cent.: abbreviation.

loco² ▶ adjective informal crazy.
– ORIGIN late 19th cent.: from Spanish, 'insane'.

locomotion ▶ noun [mass noun] movement or the ability to move from one place to another: *the muscles that are concerned with locomotion* | *he preferred walking to other forms of locomotion.*
– ORIGIN mid 17th cent.: from Latin *loco*, ablative of *locus* 'place' + *motio* (see **MOTION**).

locomotive ▶ noun a powered railway vehicle used for pulling trains: *a diesel locomotive.*
▶ adjective [attrib.] of, relating to, or effecting locomotion: *locomotive power.*
■ archaic (of a machine, vehicle, or animal) having the power of progressive motion: *locomotive bivalves have the strongest hinges.*
– ORIGIN early 17th cent. (as an adjective): from modern Latin *locomotivus*, from Latin *loco* (ablative of *locus* 'place') + late Latin *motivus* 'motive', suggested by medieval Latin *in loco moveri* 'move by change of position'.

locomotor ▶ adjective [attrib.] chiefly Biology of or relating to locomotion: *locomotor organs.*
– ORIGIN early 19th cent.: from **LOCOMOTION** + **MOTOR**.

locomotor ataxia ▶ noun [mass noun] Medicine loss of coordination of movement, especially as a result of syphilitic infection of the spinal cord. Also called **TABES DORSALIS**.

locomotory ▶ adjective chiefly Zoology relating to or having the power of locomotion: *locomotory cilia.*

locoweed ▶ noun [mass noun] 1 a widely distributed plant of the pea family, which, if eaten by livestock, can cause a brain disorder, the symptoms of which include unpredictable behaviour and loss of coordination.
● Genus *Astragalus* (and *Oxytropis*), family Leguminosae.

2 US informal cannabis.

Locrian mode /ˈlɒkrɪən/ ▶ noun Music the mode represented by the natural diatonic scale B–B (containing a minor 2nd, 3rd, 6th, and 7th, and a diminished 5th).
– ORIGIN late 19th cent.: *Locrian* from Greek *Locris*, a division of ancient Greece, + **-IAN**; named after an ancient Greek mode but not identifiable with it.

locule /ˈlɒkjuːl/ ▶ noun another term for **LOCULUS**.

loculus /ˈlɒkjʊləs/ ▶ noun (pl. **loculi** /-lʌɪ, -liː/) chiefly Botany each of a number of small separate cavities, especially in an ovary.
– DERIVATIVES **locular** adjective.
– ORIGIN mid 19th cent.: from Latin, 'compartment', diminutive of *locus* 'place'.

locum /ˈləʊkəm/ ▶ noun informal short for **LOCUM TENENS**.

locum tenens /ˌləʊkəm ˈtiːnɛnz, ˈtɛn-/ ▶ noun (pl. **locum tenentes** /tɪˈnɛntiːz, tɛ-/) a person who stands in temporarily for someone else of the same profession, especially a cleric or doctor.
– DERIVATIVES **locum tenency** noun.
– ORIGIN mid 17th cent.: from medieval Latin, literally 'one holding a place' (see **LOCUS, TENANT**).

locus /ˈləʊkəs/ ▶ noun (pl. **loci** /-sʌɪ, -kʌɪ, -kiː/)
1 technical a particular position, point, or place: *it is impossible to specify the exact locus in the brain of these neural events.*
■ the effective or perceived location of something abstract: *the real locus of power is the informal council.*
■ Genetics the position of a gene or mutation on a chromosome. ■ Law short for **LOCUS STANDI**.
2 Mathematics a curve or other figure formed by all the points satisfying a particular equation of the relation between coordinates, or by a point, line, or surface moving according to mathematically defined conditions.
– ORIGIN early 18th cent.: from Latin, 'place'.

locus classicus /ˌləʊkəs ˈklasɪkəs, ˌlɒkəs/ ▶ noun (pl. **loci classici** /ˌləʊsʌɪ ˈklasɪsʌɪ, ˌlɒkiː ˈklasɪkiː/) a passage considered to be the best known or most authoritative on a particular subject.
– ORIGIN Latin, literally 'classical place'.

locus standi /ˌləʊkəs ˈstandʌɪ, ˌlɒkəs/ ▶ noun (pl. **loci standi** /ˌləʊsʌɪ ˈstandʌɪ, ˌlɒkiː ˈstandiː/) Law the right or capacity to bring an action or to appear in a court.
– ORIGIN Latin, literally 'place of standing'.

locust ▶ noun 1 a large and mainly tropical grasshopper with strong powers of flight. It is usually solitary, but from time to time there is a population explosion and it migrates in vast swarms which cause extensive damage to crops.
● Several species in the family Acrididae, including the migratory locust (*Locusta migratoria*), which is sometimes seen in Europe.
■ (also **seventeen-year locust**) US the periodical cicada.
2 (also **locust bean**) the large edible pod of some plants of the pea family, in particular the carob bean, which is said to resemble a locust.
3 (also **locust tree**) any of a number of pod-bearing trees of the pea family, in particular the carob tree and the false acacia.
– ORIGIN Middle English: via Old French *locuste* from Latin *locusta* 'locust, crustacean'.

locust years ▶ plural noun years of hardship or poverty.

locution /ləˈkjuːʃ(ə)n/ ▶ noun 1 a word or phrase, especially with regard to style or idiom.
■ [mass noun] a person's style of speech: *his impeccable locution.*
2 an utterance regarded in terms of its intrinsic meaning or reference, as distinct from its function or purpose in context. Compare with **ILLOCUTION, PERLOCUTION**.
■ [mass noun] language regarded in terms of locutionary rather than illocutionary or perlocutionary acts.
– DERIVATIVES **locutionary** adjective.
– ORIGIN late Middle English: from Old French, or from Latin *locutio(n-)*, from *loqui* 'speak'.

lode /ləʊd/ ▶ noun a vein of metal ore in the earth.
■ [in sing.] figurative a rich source of something: *a rich lode of scandal and alleged crime.*
– ORIGIN Old English *lād* 'way, course', variant of **LOAD**. The term denoted a watercourse in late Middle English and a lodestone in the early 16th cent. The current sense dates from the early 17th cent.

loden /ˈləʊd(ə)n/ ▶ noun [mass noun] a thick waterproof woollen cloth.
■ the dark green colour in which such cloth is often made.
– ORIGIN early 20th cent.: from German *Loden*.

lodestar ▶ noun a star that is used to guide the course of a ship, especially the pole star.
– ORIGIN Middle English: from **LODE** in the obsolete sense 'way, course' + **STAR**.

lodestone (also **loadstone**) ▶ noun a piece of magnetite or other naturally magnetized mineral, able to be used as a magnet.
■ [mass noun] a mineral of this kind; magnetite.

Lodge¹, David (John) (b.1935), English novelist and academic. Honorary professor of Modern English Literature at the University of Birmingham since 1976, he often satirizes academia and literary criticism in his novels, which include *Changing Places* (1975) and *Small World* (1984).

Lodge², Sir Oliver (Joseph) (1851–1940), English physicist. He made important contributions to the study of electromagnetic radiation, and was a pioneer of radio-telegraphy.

lodge ▶ noun 1 a small house at the gates of a park or in the grounds of a large house, typically occupied by a gatekeeper, gardener, or other employee.
■ a small country house occupied in season for sports such as hunting, shooting, fishing, and skiing: *a hunting lodge.* ■ [in names] a large house or hotel: *Cumberland Lodge.* ■ a porter's quarters at the main entrance of a college or other large building. ■ the residence of a head of a college, especially at Cambridge. ■ an American Indian tent or wigwam. ■ a beaver's den.
2 a branch or meeting place of an organization such as the Freemasons.
▶ verb 1 [with obj.] present (a complaint, appeal, claim, etc.) formally to the proper authorities: *he has 28 days in which to lodge an appeal.*
■ (**lodge something in/with**) leave money or a valuable item in (a place) or with (someone) for safe keeping.
2 [with adverbial of place] make or become firmly fixed or embedded in a particular place: [with obj.] *they had to remove a bullet lodged near his spine* | [no obj.] figurative *the image had lodged in her mind.*
3 [no obj., with adverbial] stay or sleep in another person's house, paying money for one's accommodation: *the man who lodged in the room next door.*
■ [with obj. and adverbial] provide (someone) with a place to sleep or stay in return for payment.
4 [with obj.] (of wind or rain) flatten (a standing crop): [as adj. **lodged**] *rain that soaks standing or lodged crops.*
■ [no obj.] (of a crop) be flattened in such a way.
– ORIGIN Middle English *loge*, via Old French *loge* 'arbour, hut' from medieval Latin *laubia, lobia* (see **LOBBY**), of Germanic origin; related to German *Laube* 'arbour'.

lodgement ▶ noun 1 chiefly poetic/literary a place in which a person or thing is located, deposited, or lodged: *they found a lodgement for the hook in the crumbling parapet.*
2 [mass noun] the depositing of money in a particular bank, account, etc.
– ORIGIN late 16th cent.: from French *logement* 'dwelling', from Old French *loge* 'arbour' (see **LODGE**).

lodgepole pine ▶ noun a straight-trunked pine tree which grows in the mountains of western North America, widely grown for timber and traditionally used by some American Indians in the construction of lodges.
● *Pinus contorta* var. *latifolia*, family Pinaceae.

lodger ▶ noun a person who pays rent to live in a property with the owner.

lodging ▶ noun a place in which someone lives or stays temporarily: *they found a cheap lodging in a backstreet* | [mass noun] *a fee for board and lodging.*
■ (**lodgings**) a room or rooms rented out to someone, usually in the same residence as the owner: *he took lodgings at a tavern in Muswell Street.*

lodging house ▶ noun a private house in which rooms are rented for living or staying temporarily.

lodicule /ˈlɒdɪkjuːl/ ▶ noun Botany a small green or white scale below the ovary of a grass flower.
– ORIGIN mid 19th cent.: from Latin *lodicula*, diminutive of *lodix* 'coverlet'.

Łódź /wʊtʃ/ an industrial city in central Poland,

south-west of Warsaw, the second largest city in the country; pop. 848,260 (1990).

loerie ▶ **noun** (pl. **-ies**) variant spelling of **LOURIE**.

loess /ˈləʊɪs, lɜːs/ ▶ **noun** [mass noun] Geology a loosely compacted yellowish-grey deposit of wind-blown sediment of which extensive deposits occur e.g. in eastern China and the American Midwest.
– DERIVATIVES **loessial** adjective, **loessic** adjective.
– ORIGIN mid 19th cent.: from German *Löss*, from Swiss German *lösch* 'loose'.

Loewi /ˈləʊi/, Otto (1873–1961), American pharmacologist and physiologist, born in Germany. He was the first to show that a chemical neurotransmitter is produced at the junction between a parasympathetic nerve and a muscle. This he identified as the substance acetylcholine. Nobel Prize for Physiology or Medicine (1936, shared with Sir Henry Dale).

lo-fi (also **low-fi**) ▶ **adjective** of or employing sound reproduction of a lower quality than hi-fi: *defiantly lo-fi recording techniques.*
■ (of popular music) recorded and produced with basic equipment and thus having a raw and unsophisticated sound.
▶ **noun** [mass noun] sound reproduction or music of such a kind.
– ORIGIN 1950s: from an alteration of **LOW**[1] + *-fi* on the pattern of *hi-fi*.

Lofoten Islands /ləˈfəʊt(ə)n/ an island group off the NW coast of Norway. They are situated within the Arctic Circle, south-west of the Vesterålen group.

loft ▶ **noun 1** a room or space directly under the roof of a house or other building, which may be used for accommodation or storage.
■ a gallery in a church or hall: *a choir loft.* ■ short for **ORGAN LOFT**. ■ a large, open area over a shop, warehouse, or factory, especially when converted into living space. ■ a pigeon house.
2 [mass noun] Golf upward inclination given to the ball in a stroke.
■ backward slope of the head of a club, designed to give upward inclination to the ball.
3 [mass noun] the thickness of insulating matter in an object such as a sleeping bag or a padded coat.
▶ **verb** [with obj. and adverbial of direction] kick, hit, or throw (a ball or missile) high up: *he lofted the ball over the Everton goalkeeper.*
■ [with obj.] [usu. as adj. **lofted**] give backward slope to the head of (a golf club): *a lofted metal club.*
– ORIGIN late Old English, from Old Norse *lopt* 'air, sky, upper room', of Germanic origin; related to Dutch *lucht* and German *Luft*.

lofter ▶ **noun 1** a decoy placed in a tree to attract pigeons. [ORIGIN: 1970s: from the noun **LOFT**.]
2 Golf, dated a nine-iron or similar lofted club. [ORIGIN: late 19th cent.: from the verb **LOFT**.]

lofting ▶ **noun** [mass noun] the work carried out by a loftsman.

loftsman ▶ **noun** (pl. **-men**) a person who draws up full-size outlines from the drawing or plans for parts of a ship or aircraft.

lofty ▶ **adjective** (**loftier**, **loftiest**) **1** of imposing height: *the elegant square was shaded by lofty palms.*
■ of a noble or exalted nature: *an extraordinary mixture of harsh reality and lofty ideals.* ■ proud, aloof, or self-important: *lofty intellectual disdain.*
2 (of wool and other textiles) thick and resilient.
– DERIVATIVES **loftily** adverb, **loftiness** noun.
– ORIGIN Middle English: from **LOFT**, influenced by **ALOFT**.

log[1] ▶ **noun 1** a part of the trunk or a large branch of a tree that has fallen or been cut off.
2 (also **logbook**) an official record of events during the voyage of a ship or aircraft: *a ship's log.*
■ a regular or systematic record of incidents or observations: *keep a detailed log of your activities.*
3 an apparatus for determining the speed of a ship, originally one consisting of a float attached to a knotted line that is wound on a reel, the distance run out in a certain time being used as an estimate of the vessel's speed.
▶ **verb** (**logged**, **logging**) [with obj.] **1** enter (an incident or fact) in the log of a ship or aircraft or in another systematic record: *the incident has to be logged | the red book where we log our calls.*
■ (of a ship or aircraft) achieve (a certain distance or speed): *she had logged more than 12,000 miles since she had been launched.* ■ (of an aircraft pilot) attain (a certain amount of flying time).
2 cut down (an area of forest) in order to exploit the timber commercially.
– PHRASES (**as**) **easy as falling off a log** informal very easy.
– ORIGIN Middle English (in the sense 'bulky mass of wood'): of unknown origin; perhaps symbolic of the notion of heaviness. Sense 3 originally denoted a thin quadrant of wood loaded to float upright in the water, whence 'ship's journal' in which information from the log board was recorded.
▶ **log in** (or **on**) go through the procedures to begin use of a computer system, which includes establishing the identity of the user.
log off (or **out**) go through the procedures to conclude use of a computer system.

log[2] ▶ **noun** short for **LOGARITHM**: [as modifier] *log tables* | [prefixed to a number or algebraic symbol] *log x.*

log$_e$ ▶ **symbol for** natural logarithm.

-log ▶ **combining form** US spelling of **-LOGUE**.

logan /ˈlɒg(ə)n, ˈləʊg(ə)n/ (also **logan stone**) ▶ **noun** another term for **ROCKING STONE**.
– ORIGIN mid 18th cent.: from *logging* (from dialect *log* 'to rock').

Logan, Mount /ˈləʊg(ə)n/ a mountain in SW Yukon Territory, Canada, near the border with Alaska. Rising to 6,054 m (19,850 ft), it is the highest peak in Canada and the second-highest peak in North America.

loganberry /ˈləʊg(ə)nˌb(ə)ri, -ˌbɛri/ ▶ **noun 1** an edible dull-red soft fruit, considered to be a hybrid of a raspberry and an American dewberry.
2 the scrambling blackberry-like plant which bears this fruit.
● *Rubus loganobaccus*, family Rosaceae.
– ORIGIN late 19th cent.: from the name of John H. Logan (1841–1928), American horticulturalist, + **BERRY**.

logarithm /ˈlɒgərɪð(ə)m, -rɪθ-/ (abbrev.: **log**) ▶ **noun** a quantity representing the power to which a fixed number (the base) must be raised to produce a given number.

> Logarithms can be used to simplify calculations, as the addition and subtraction of logarithms is equivalent to multiplication and division, though the use of printed tables of logarithms for this has declined with the spread of electronic calculators. They also allow a geometric relationship to be represented conveniently by a straight line. The base of a **common logarithm** is 10, and that of a **natural logarithm** is the number *e* (2.71828 …).

– ORIGIN early 17th cent.: from modern Latin *logarithmus*, from Greek *logos* 'reckoning, ratio' + *arithmos* 'number'.

logarithmic ▶ **adjective** of, relating to, or expressed in terms of logarithms.
■ (of a scale) constructed so that successive points along an axis, or graduations which are an equal distance apart, represent values which are in an equal ratio. ■ (of a curve) forming a straight line when plotted on a logarithmic scale; exponential.
– DERIVATIVES **logarithmically** adverb.

logarithmic spiral ▶ **noun** another term for **EQUIANGULAR SPIRAL**.

logbook ▶ **noun** another term for **LOG**[1] (in sense 2).
■ Brit. another term for **REGISTRATION DOCUMENT**.

log cabin ▶ **noun** a hut built of whole or split logs.
■ [usu. as modifier] a pattern of squares used for patchwork quilts resembling the patterning of wood in a log cabin.

loge /ləʊʒ/ ▶ **noun** a private box or enclosure in a theatre.
– ORIGIN mid 18th cent.: from French.

-loger ▶ **combining form** equivalent to **-LOGIST**.
– ORIGIN on the pattern of words such as (*astro*)*loger*.

log flume ▶ **noun** a water chute ride at an amusement park.

logger ▶ **noun 1** a person who fells trees for timber; a lumberjack.
2 a device for making a systematic recording of events, observations, or measurements.

loggerhead ▶ **noun 1** (also **loggerhead turtle**) a reddish-brown turtle with a very large head, occurring chiefly in warm seas.
● *Caretta caretta*, family Cheloniidae.
2 (also **loggerhead shrike**) a widespread North American shrike, having mainly grey plumage with a black eyestripe, wings, and tail.
● *Lanius ludovicianus*, family Laniidae.
3 archaic a foolish person.
– PHRASES **at loggerheads** in violent dispute or disagreement: *councillors were* **at loggerheads with** *the government over the grant allocation.* [ORIGIN: possibly a use of *loggerhead* in the late 17th-cent. sense 'long-handled iron instrument for heating liquids and tar', perhaps wielded as a weapon.]
– ORIGIN late 16th cent. (in sense 3): from dialect *logger* 'block of wood for hobbling a horse' + **HEAD**.

loggia /ˈləʊdʒə, ˈlɒ-, -dʒɪə/ ▶ **noun** a gallery or room with one or more open sides, especially one that forms part of a house and has one side open to the garden.
■ an open-sided extension to a house.
– ORIGIN mid 18th cent.: from Italian, 'lodge'.

logging ▶ **noun** [mass noun] the activity or business of felling trees and cutting and preparing the timber.

logia plural form of **LOGION**.

logic ▶ **noun** [mass noun] **1** reasoning conducted or assessed according to strict principles of validity: *experience is a better guide to this than deductive logic | he explains his move with simple logic | the logic of the argument is faulty.*
■ a particular system or codification of the principles of proof and inference: *Aristotelian logic.* ■ the systematic use of symbolic and mathematical techniques to determine the forms of valid deductive argument. ■ the quality of being justifiable by reason: *there's no logic in telling her not to hit people when that's what you're doing.* ■ (**logic of**) the course of action or line of reasoning suggested or made necessary by: *if the logic of capital is allowed to determine events.*
2 a system or set of principles underlying the arrangements of elements in a computer or electronic device so as to perform a specified task.
■ logical operations collectively.
– DERIVATIVES **logician** noun.
– ORIGIN late Middle English: via Old French *logique* and late Latin *logica* from Greek *logikē* (*tekhnē*) '(art) of reason', from *logos* 'word, reason'.

-logic ▶ **combining form** equivalent to **-LOGICAL** (as in *pharmacologic*).
– ORIGIN from Greek *-logikos*.

logical ▶ **adjective** of or according to the rules of logic or formal argument: *a logical impossibility.*
■ characterized by clear, sound reasoning: *the information is displayed in a simple and logical fashion.* ■ (of an action, development, decision, etc.) natural or sensible given the circumstances: *it is a logical progression from the job before.* ■ capable of clear rational thinking: *her logical mind.*
– DERIVATIVES **logicality** /-ˈkalɪti/ noun, **logically** adverb [sentence adverb] *such a situation is logically impossible.*
– ORIGIN late Middle English: from medieval Latin *logicalis* from late Latin *logica* (see **LOGIC**).

-logical ▶ **combining form** in adjectives corresponding chiefly to nouns ending in *-logy* (such as *pharmacological* corresponding to *pharmacology*).

logical atomism ▶ **noun** [mass noun] Philosophy the theory that all propositions can be analysed into simple independent elements of meaning corresponding to elements making up facts about the world. It formed part of the early thought of Wittgenstein and Bertrand Russell.

logical empiricism ▶ **noun** see **LOGICAL POSITIVISM**.

logical form ▶ **noun** Logic the abstract form in which an argument or proposition may be expressed in logical terms, as distinct from its particular content.

logical necessity ▶ **noun** [mass noun] that state of things which obliges something to be as it is because no alternative is logically possible.
■ [count noun] a thing which logically must be so.

logical operation ▶ **noun** an operation of the kind used in logic, e.g. conjunction or negation.
■ Computing an operation that acts on binary numbers to produce a result according to the laws of Boolean logic (e.g. the AND, OR, and NOT functions).

logical positivism ▶ **noun** [mass noun] a form of positivism, developed by members of the Vienna Circle, which considers that the only meaningful philosophical problems are those which can be solved by logical analysis. Also called **LOGICAL EMPIRICISM**.

logic bomb ▶ **noun** Computing a set of instructions secretly incorporated into a program so that if a particular condition is satisfied they will be carried out, usually with harmful effects.

logic chopping ▸ noun [mass noun] the practice of engaging in excessively pedantic argument.

logic circuit ▸ noun Electronics a circuit for performing logical operations on input signals.

logicism /'lɒdʒɪsɪz(ə)m/ ▸ noun [mass noun] Philosophy the theory that all mathematics can ultimately be deduced from purely formal logical axioms, introduced by Frege and developed by Bertrand Russell.
– DERIVATIVES **logicist** noun.

login (also **logon**) ▸ noun an act of logging in to a computer system.

logion /'lɒgɪɒn, 'ləʊ-/ ▸ noun (pl. **logia** /-gɪə/) a saying attributed to Christ, especially one not recorded in the canonical Gospels.
– ORIGIN late 19th cent.: from Greek, 'oracle', from *logos* 'word'.

-logist ▸ combining form indicating a person skilled or involved in a branch of study denoted by a noun ending in -*logy* (such as *biologist* corresponding to *biology*).

logistic ▸ adjective of or relating to logistics: *logistic problems*.
– DERIVATIVES **logistical** adjective, **logistically** adverb.

logistic curve ▸ noun Statistics a sigmoid curve used in population studies which increases exponentially for small values of the variable, and approaches a constant value asymptotically for large values.

logistics /lə'dʒɪstɪks/ ▸ plural noun [treated as sing. or pl.] the detailed coordination of a complex operation involving many people, facilities, or supplies: *the logistics of a large-scale rock show demand certain necessities*.
– ORIGIN late 19th cent. (in the sense 'movement and supplying of troops and equipment'): from French *logistique*, from *loger* 'lodge'.

logjam ▸ noun a crowded mass of logs blocking a river.
■ a situation that seems irresolvable: *the president can use the power of the White House to break the logjam over this issue*. ■ a backlog: *keeping a diary may ease the logjam of work considerably*.

log line ▸ noun a line to which a ship's log is attached.

log-log ▸ adjective Mathematics denoting a graph or graph paper having or using a logarithmic scale along both axes.

log-normal ▸ adjective Statistics of or denoting a set of data in which the logarithm of the variate is distributed according to a normal distribution.
– DERIVATIVES **log-normality** noun, **log-normally** adverb.

logo /'lɒgəʊ, 'ləʊgəʊ/ ▸ noun (pl. **-os**) a symbol or other small design adopted by an organization to identify its products, uniform, vehicles, etc.: *the Olympic logo was emblazoned across the tracksuits*.
– ORIGIN 1930s: abbreviation of **LOGOGRAM** or **LOGOTYPE**.

logocentric ▸ adjective regarding words and language as a fundamental expression of an external reality (especially applied as a negative term to traditional Western thought by postmodernist critics).
– DERIVATIVES **logocentrism** noun.
– ORIGIN 1930s: from Greek *logos* 'word, reason' + **-CENTRIC**.

logoff ▸ noun another term for **LOGOUT**.

logogram ▸ noun a sign or character representing a word or phrase, such as those used in shorthand and some ancient writing systems.
– ORIGIN mid 19th cent.: from Greek *logos* 'word' + **-GRAM**[1].

logograph ▸ noun another term for **LOGOGRAM**.
– DERIVATIVES **logographic** adjective.

logomachy /lə'gɒməki/ ▸ noun (pl. **-ies**) rare an argument about words.
– ORIGIN mid 16th cent.: from Greek *logomakhia*, from *logos* 'word' + *-makhia* 'fighting'.

logon ▸ noun another term for **LOGIN**.

logophile /'lɒgə(ʊ)fʌɪl/ ▸ noun a lover of words.

logorrhoea /ˌlɒgə'rɪə/ (US **logorrhea**) ▸ noun [mass noun] a tendency to extreme loquacity.
– DERIVATIVES **logorrhoeic** adjective.

– ORIGIN early 20th cent.: from Greek *logos* 'word' + *rhoia* 'flow'.

Logos /'lɒgɒs/ ▸ noun Theology the Word of God, or principle of divine reason and creative order, identified in the Gospel of John with the second person of the Trinity incarnate in Jesus Christ.
■ [mass noun] (in Jungian psychology) the principle of reason and judgement, associated with the animus. Often contrasted with **EROS**.
– ORIGIN Greek, 'word, reason'.

logotype ▸ noun Printing a single piece of type that prints a word or group of separate letters.
■ a single piece of type that prints a logo or emblem. ■ a logo.
– ORIGIN early 19th cent.: from Greek *logos* 'word' + **TYPE**.

logout (also **logoff**) ▸ noun an act of logging out of a computer system.

logrolling ▸ noun [mass noun] N. Amer. **1** informal the practice of exchanging favours, especially in politics by reciprocal voting for each other's proposed legislation. [ORIGIN: from the phrase *you roll my log and I'll roll yours*.]
2 a sport in which two contestants stand on a floating log and try to knock each other off by spinning it with their feet.
– DERIVATIVES **logroller** noun.

Logroño /lɒ'grɒnjəʊ/ a market town in northern Spain, on the River Ebro, capital of La Rioja region; pop. 126,760 (1991).

logrunner ▸ noun a ground-dwelling Australasian songbird, having a blackish or mottled brown back and a spine-tipped tail. Also called **SPINETAIL**.
● Genus *Orthonyx*, family Orthonychidae (the **logrunner family**): two species; the logrunner family also includes whipbirds, quail-thrushes, and rail-babblers.

-logue (US also **-log**) ▸ combining form **1** denoting discourse of a specified type: *dialogue*.
2 denoting compilation: *catalogue*.
3 equivalent to **-LOGIST**.
– ORIGIN from French -*logue*, from Greek -*logos*, -*logon*.

logwood ▸ noun a spiny Caribbean tree of the pea family, the dark heartwood of which yields haematoxylin and other dyes.
■ *Haematoxylon campechianum*, family Leguminosae.

logy /'ləʊgi/ ▸ adjective (**logier**, **logiest**) N. Amer. dull and heavy in motion or thought; sluggish.
– ORIGIN mid 19th cent.: of uncertain origin; compare with Dutch *log* 'heavy, dull'.

-logy ▸ combining form **1** (usu. as **-ology**) denoting a subject of study or interest: *psychology*.
2 denoting a characteristic of speech or language: *eulogy*.
■ denoting a type of discourse: *trilogy*.
– ORIGIN from French -*logie* or medieval Latin -*logia*, from Greek.

Lohengrin /'ləʊən,grɪn, German 'lo:ən,gri:n/ (in medieval French and German romances) the son of Perceval (Parsifal). He was summoned from the temple of the Holy Grail and taken in a boat to Antwerp, where he consented to marry Elsa of Brabant on condition that she did not ask who he was. Elsa broke this condition and he was carried away again in the boat.

loiasis /ləʊ'ʌɪəsɪs/ ▸ noun [mass noun] a tropical African disease caused by infestation with eye worms, which cause transient subcutaneous swellings, often accompanied by pain or fever.
– ORIGIN early 20th cent.: modern Latin, from *loa* (a local Angolan word for the parasite) + **-IASIS**.

loin ▸ noun (usu. **loins**) the part of the body on both sides of the spine between the lowest (false) ribs and the hip bones.
■ (**loins**) chiefly poetic/literary the region of the sexual organs, especially when regarded as the source of erotic or procreative power: *he felt a stirring in his loins at the thought*. ■ (**loin**) a joint of meat that includes the vertebrae of the loins: *loin of pork with kidney*.
– ORIGIN Middle English: from Old French *loigne*, based on Latin *lumbus*.

loincloth ▸ noun a single piece of cloth wrapped round the hips, typically worn by men in some hot countries as their only garment.

Loire /lwɑː, French lwaʀ/ a river of west central France. France's longest river, it rises in the Massif Central and flows 1,015 km (630 miles) north and west to the Atlantic at St-Nazaire.

loiter ▸ verb [no obj., with adverbial of place] stand or wait

around idly or without apparent purpose: *she saw Mary loitering near the cloakrooms*.
■ [with adverbial of direction] travel indolently and with frequent pauses: *they loitered along in the sunshine, stopping at the least excuse*.
– PHRASES **loiter with intent** English Law, dated stand or wait around with the intention of committing an offence.
– DERIVATIVES **loiterer** noun.
– ORIGIN late Middle English: perhaps from Middle Dutch *loteren* 'wag about'.

lokey ▸ noun variant spelling of **LOCIE**.

Loki /'ləʊki/ Scandinavian Mythology a mischievous and sometimes evil god who contrived the death of Balder and was punished by being bound to a rock.

Lok Sabha /ˌləʊk sə'bɑː/ ▸ noun the lower house of the Indian Parliament. Compare with **RAJYA SABHA**.
– ORIGIN from Hindi *lok* 'the public' and *sabhā* 'assembly'.

LOL ▸ abbreviation for laughing (or laugh) out loud (used in e-mail).

Lolita /lə(ʊ)'liːtə/ ▸ noun a sexually precocious young girl.
– ORIGIN from the name of a character in the novel *Lolita* (1958) by Vladimir Nabokov (1899–1977).

loll ▸ verb [no obj., with adverbial] sit, lie, or stand in a lazy, relaxed way: *the two girls lolled in their chairs*.
■ hang loosely; droop: *he slumped against a tree trunk, his head lolling back* | *her tongue was lolling out between her teeth*. ■ [with obj.] stick out (one's tongue) so that it hangs loosely out of the mouth: *the boy lolled out his tongue*.
– ORIGIN late Middle English: probably symbolic of dangling.

Lolland /'lɒlaːn/ a Danish island in the Baltic Sea, to the south of Zealand and west of Falster.
– ORIGIN Danish, literally 'low land'.

lollapalooza /ˌlɒləpə'luːzə/ (also **lalapalooza** etc.) ▸ noun N. Amer. informal a person or thing that is particularly impressive or attractive: *it's a lollapalooza, just like your other books*.
– ORIGIN late 19th cent.: of fanciful formation.

Lollard /'lɒləd/ ▸ noun a follower of John Wyclif. The Lollards believed that the Church should aid people to live a life of evangelical poverty and imitate Christ. Their ideas influenced the thought of John Huss, who in turn influenced Martin Luther.
– DERIVATIVES **Lollardism** noun, **Lollardy** noun.
– ORIGIN originally a derogatory term, derived from a Dutch word meaning 'mumbler', based on *lollen* 'to mumble'.

lollipop ▸ noun a sweet on the end of a stick, typically a large, flat, rounded boiled sweet.
■ British term for **ICE LOLLY**. ■ figurative a treat or reward (handed out like a lollipop to a child). ■ informal a short, entertaining, but undemanding piece of classical music.
– ORIGIN late 18th cent.: perhaps from dialect *lolly* 'tongue' + **POP**[1].

lollipop lady (also **lollipop woman** or **man**) ▸ noun Brit. informal a woman (or man) who is employed to help children cross the road safely near a school by holding up a circular sign on a pole to stop the traffic.

lollop ▸ verb (**lolloped**, **lolloping**) [no obj., with adverbial of direction] move in an ungainly way in a series of clumsy paces or bounds: *the bear lolloped along the path*.
– ORIGIN mid 18th cent.: probably from **LOLL**, associated with **TROLLOP**.

lollo rosso /ˌlɒləʊ 'rɒsəʊ/ ▸ noun [mass noun] lettuce of a variety with deeply divided red-edged leaves.

lolly ▸ noun (pl. **-ies**) informal **1** chiefly Brit. a lollipop.
■ Austral./NZ a sweet, especially a boiled one.
2 [mass noun] Brit. money: *you've done brilliantly raising all that lovely lolly*.
– ORIGIN mid 19th cent.: abbreviation. Sense 2 dates from the 1940s.

lollygag (also **lallygag**) ▸ verb (**lollygagged**, **lollygagging**) [no obj.] N. Amer. informal spend time aimlessly; idle: *he sends her to Arizona every January to lollygag in the sun*.
■ [with adverbial of direction] dawdle: *we're lollygagging along*.
– ORIGIN mid 19th cent.: of unknown origin.

Lombard /'lɒmbəd, -bɑːd/ ▸ noun **1** a member of a Germanic people who invaded Italy in the 6th century.

2 a native of Lombardy in northern Italy.
3 [mass noun] the Italian dialect of Lombardy.
▶**adjective** of or relating to Lombardy, or to the Lombards or their language.
– DERIVATIVES **Lombardic** adjective (only in sense 1).
– ORIGIN from Italian *lombardo*, representing late Latin *Langobardus*, of Germanic origin, from the base of **LONG**[1] + the ethnic name *Bardi*.

Lombard Street a street in the City of London containing many of the principal London banks.
– ORIGIN so named because formerly occupied by bankers from *Lombardy*.

Lombardy /ˈlɒmbədi/ a region of central northern Italy, between the Alps and the River Po; capital, Milan. Italian name **LOMBARDIA** /ˌlombarˈdia/.

Lombardy poplar ▶**noun** a black poplar of a variety which has a distinctive tall, slender columnar form. It arose as a mutation in Italy and is widely cultivated.
• *Populus nigra* var. *italica*, family Salicaceae.

Lombok /ˈlɒmbɒk/ a volcanic island of the Lesser Sunda group in Indonesia, between Bali and Sumbawa; pop. 2,500,000 (1991); chief town, Mataram.

Lomé /ˈləʊmeɪ/ the capital and chief port of Togo, on the Gulf of Guinea; pop. 450,000 (1990).

Lomé Convention an agreement on trade and development aid, reached in Lomé in 1975, between the EC and forty-six African, Caribbean, and Pacific Ocean states, aiming for technical cooperation and the provision of development aid. Further agreements have been signed by a larger group.

loment /ˈləʊmɛnt/ (also **lomentum** /lə(ʊ)ˈmɛntəm/) ▶**noun** Botany the pod of some leguminous plants, breaking up when mature into one-seeded joints.
– ORIGIN mid 19th cent.: from Latin, literally 'bean-meal' (originally used as a cosmetic), from *lavare* 'to wash'.

Lomond, Loch /ˈləʊmənd/ a lake in west central Scotland, to the north-west of Glasgow. It is the largest freshwater lake in Scotland.

London[1] **1** the capital of the United Kingdom, situated in SE England on the River Thames; pop. 6,378,600 (1991).

> London was settled as a river port and trading centre, called Londinium, shortly after the Roman invasion of AD 43, and, since the Middle Ages, has been a flourishing centre. It is divided administratively into the City of London, which is the country's financial centre, and thirty-two boroughs.

2 an industrial city in SE Ontario, Canada, situated to the north of Lake Erie; pop. 310,585 (1991).
– DERIVATIVES **Londoner** noun.

London[2], Jack (1876–1916), American novelist; pseudonym of *John Griffith Chaney*. The Klondike gold rush of 1897 provided the material for his famous works depicting struggle for survival. Notable works: *The Call of the Wild* (1903) and *White Fang* (1906).

London broil ▶**noun** N. Amer. a grilled steak served cut diagonally in thin slices.

London clay ▶**noun** [mass noun] clay forming an extensive layer in SE England, dating from the lower Eocene period.

Londonderry /ˈlʌnd(ə)nˌdɛri/ one of the Six Counties of Northern Ireland, formerly an administrative area.
■ its chief town, a city and port on the River Foyle near its outlet on the north coast; pop. 62,700 (1981). It was formerly called Derry, a name still used by many. In 1613 it was granted to the City of London for colonization and became known as Londonderry.

Londoner ▶**noun** a person from London.

London gin ▶**noun** [mass noun] a variety of dry gin in which the flavouring substances are added during, not after, distillation.

London plane ▶**noun** a plane tree which is considered to be a hybrid between the American and the oriental planes. Its flaking bark renders it resistant to pollution and it is widely planted in towns.
• *Platanus* × *hispanica*, family Platanaceae.

London pride ▶**noun** a European saxifrage with rosettes of fleshy leaves and stems of pink starlike flowers.
• *Saxifraga* × *urbium*, family Saxifragaceae.

lone ▶**adjective** [attrib.] having no companions; solitary or single: *I approached a lone drinker across the bar* | *we sheltered under a lone tree.*
■ lacking the support of others; isolated: *I am by no means a lone voice.* ■ Brit. (of a parent) not having a partner to share the care of one's child or children: *poverty among lone mothers.* ■ poetic/literary (of a place) unfrequented and remote: *houses in lone rural settings.*
– ORIGIN late Middle English: shortening of **ALONE**.

lone hand ▶**noun** (in euchre or quadrille) a hand played against the rest, or a player playing such a hand.
– PHRASES **play a lone hand** act on one's own without help.

lonely ▶**adjective** (**lonelier**, **loneliest**) sad because one has no friends or company: *lonely old people whose families do not care for them.*
■ without companions; solitary: *passing long lonely hours looking on to the street.* ■ (of a place) unfrequented and remote: *a lonely stretch of country lane.*
– DERIVATIVES **loneliness** noun.

lonely heart ▶**noun** [usu. as modifier] a person looking for a lover or friend by advertising in a newspaper: *a lonely hearts column.*

lone pair ▶**noun** Chemistry a pair of electrons occupying an orbital in an atom or molecule and not directly involved in bonding.

loner ▶**noun** a person that prefers not to associate with others.

lonesome ▶**adjective** chiefly US solitary or lonely: *she felt lonesome and out of things.*
■ remote and unfrequented: *a lonesome, unfriendly place.*
– PHRASES **by** (or Brit. **on**) **one's lonesome** informal all alone.
– DERIVATIVES **lonesomeness** noun.

Lone Star State informal name for **TEXAS**.

lone wolf ▶**noun** a person who prefers to act alone.

long[1] ▶**adjective** (**longer**, **longest**) **1** measuring a great distance from end to end: *a long corridor* | *long black hair* | *the queue for tickets was long.*
■ (after a measurement and in questions) measuring a specified distance from end to end: *a boat 150 feet long* | *how long is the leash?* ■ (of a journey) covering a great distance: *I went for a long walk.* ■ (of a garment or sleeves on a garment) covering the whole of a person's legs or arms: *a sweater with long sleeves.* ■ of elongated shape: *shaped like a torpedo, long and thin.* ■ (of a ball in sport) travelling a great distance, or further than expected or intended: *he tried to head a long ball from Jones back to the keeper.* ■ informal (of a person) tall.
2 lasting or taking a great amount of time: *a long and distinguished career* | *she took a long time to dress.*
■ (after a noun of duration and in questions) lasting or taking a specified amount of time: *the debates will be 90 minutes long.* ■ [attrib.] seeming to last more time than is the case; lengthy or tedious: *serving long hours on the committee.* ■ (of a person's memory) retaining things for a great amount of time.
3 relatively great in extent: *write a long report* | *a long list of candidates.*
■ (after a noun of extent and in questions) having a specified extent: *the statement was three pages long.*
4 Phonetics (of a vowel) categorized as long with regard to quality and length (e.g. in standard British English the vowel /uː/ in *food* is long as distinct from the short vowel /ʊ/ in *good*).
■ Prosody (of a vowel or syllable) having the greater of the two recognized durations.
5 (of odds or a chance) reflecting or representing a low level of probability: *winning against long odds* | *you're taking a long chance.*
6 Finance (of shares, bonds, or other assets) bought in advance, with the expectation of a rise in price.
■ (of a broker or their position in the market) buying or based on long stocks. ■ (of a security) maturing at a distant date.
7 (of a drink) large in volume and typically of a cold refreshing liquid in which alcohol, if present, is not concentrated.
8 [predic.] (**long on**) informal well-supplied with: *an industry that seems long on ideas but short on cash.*
▶**noun 1** [mass noun] a long interval or period: *see you before long* | *it will not be for long.*
2 a long sound such as a long signal in Morse code or a long vowel or syllable: *two longs and a short.*
3 (**longs**) Finance long-dated securities, especially gilts.
■ assets held in a long position.
▶**adverb** (**longer**; **longest**) **1** for a long time: *we hadn't known them long* | *an experience they will long remember* | *his long-awaited Grand Prix debut.*
■ in questions about a period of time: *how long have you been working?* ■ at a time distant from a specified event or point of time: *it was abandoned long ago* | *the work was compiled long after his death.* ■ [comparative with negative] after an implied point of time: *he couldn't wait any longer.* ■ (after a noun of duration) throughout a specified period of time: *it rained all day long.*
2 (with reference to the ball in sport) at, to, or over a great distance: *the Cambridge side played the ball long.*
■ beyond the point aimed at; too far: *he threw the ball long.*
– PHRASES **as** (or **so**) **long as 1** during the whole time that: *they have been there as long as anyone can remember.* **2** provided that: *as long as you fed him, he would be cooperative.* **be long** take a long time to happen or arrive: *it won't be long before you're hooked* | *sit down, tea won't be long.* **in the long run** over or after a long period of time; eventually: *it saves money in the long run.* **the long and the short of it** all that can or need be said: *the long and short of it is, I must make something or be miserable.* **long in the tooth** rather old. [ORIGIN: originally said of horses, from the recession of the gums with age.] **long time no see** informal it's a long time since we last met (used as a greeting). [ORIGIN: in humorous imitation of broken English spoken by an American Indian.] **not by a long shot** by no means: *we're not there yet, not by a long shot.* **so long** S. African in the meanwhile. [ORIGIN: a loan translation of Afrikaans *solank* in the same sense.] **take the long view** think beyond the current situation; plan for the future.
– DERIVATIVES **longish** adjective.
– ORIGIN Old English *lang, long* (adjective), *lange, longe* (adverb), of Germanic origin; related to Dutch and German *lang*.

long[2] ▶**verb** [no obj.] have a strong wish or desire: *she longed for a little more excitement* | [with infinitive] *we are longing to see the new baby.*
– ORIGIN Old English *langian* 'grow long, prolong', also 'dwell in thought, yearn', of Germanic origin; related to Dutch *langen* 'present, offer' and German *langen* 'reach, extend'.

long. ▶**abbreviation for** longitude.

-long ▶**combining form** (added to nouns) for the duration of: *lifelong.*

longan /ˈlɒŋg(ə)n/ ▶**noun** an edible juicy fruit from a plant related to the lychee, cultivated in SE Asia.
• The plant is *Dimocarpus longan*, family Sapindaceae.
– ORIGIN mid 18th cent.: from Chinese *lóngyǎn*, literally 'dragon's eye'.

long-and-short work ▶**noun** [mass noun] Architecture alternating tall quoins and horizontal slabs forming a corner of a medieval church or other building.

Long Beach a port and resort in California, situated on the south side of the Los Angeles conurbation; pop. 429,430 (1990).

longbill ▶**noun** a small African warbler frequenting dense vegetation, with mainly olive-green plumage and a long thin bill.
• Genus *Macrosphenus*, family Sylviidae: five species.

longboard ▶**noun** a type of long surfboard.

longboat ▶**noun** a large boat which may be launched from a sailing ship.
■ another term for **LONGSHIP**.

longbow ▶**noun** a large bow drawn by hand and shooting a long feathered arrow. It was the chief weapon of English armies from the 14th century until the introduction of firearms.

long-case clock ▶**noun** another term for **GRANDFATHER CLOCK**.

longclaw ▶**noun** a large ground-dwelling African pipit, having bright yellow or red underparts marked with black, and long hind claws.
• Genus *Macronyx* family Motacillidae: several species.

long corner ▶**noun** (in field hockey) a penalty hit taken from the back line within 5 yards of the corner.

long-dated ▶**adjective** (of securities) not due for early payment or redemption.

long-day ▶**adjective** [attrib.] (of a plant) needing a long period of light each day to initiate flowering, which therefore happens naturally as the days lengthen in the spring.

long distance ▶**adjective** travelling or operating

between distant places: *a long-distance lorry driver* | *long-distance phone calls.*

▶ **adverb** between distant places: *travelling long distance.*

▶ **noun** [often as modifier] Athletics a race distance of 6 miles or 10,000 metres (6 miles 376 yds), or longer: *a long-distance runner.*

long division ▶ **noun** [mass noun] arithmetical division in which the divisor has two or more figures, and a series of workings is made as successive groups of digits of the dividend are divided by the divisor, to avoid excessive mental calculation.

longdog ▶ **noun** informal a greyhound or other hound of similar body shape.

long dozen ▶ **noun** (**a long dozen**) thirteen.

long-drawn (also **long-drawn-out**) ▶ **adjective** continuing for a long time, especially for longer than is necessary. *long-drawn-out negotiations.*

long drop ▶ **noun** S. African informal a pit toilet.

longe ▶ **noun** variant of **LUNGE**[2].

long-eared bat ▶ **noun** an insectivorous bat with ears that are very long in proportion to the body.
  ● *Plecotus* and other genera, family Vespertilionidae: several species, in particular the **common** (or **brown**) **long-eared bat** (*P. auritus*) of Eurasia.

longeron /ˈlɒn(d)ʒərɒn/ ▶ **noun** a longitudinal structural component of an aircraft's fuselage.
– ORIGIN early 20th cent.: from French, literally 'girder'.

longevity /lɒnˈdʒɛvɪti/ ▶ **noun** [mass noun] long life: *the greater longevity of women compared with men.*
– ORIGIN early 17th cent.: from late Latin *longaevitas*, from Latin *longus* 'long' + *aevum* 'age'.

long face ▶ **noun** an unhappy or disappointed expression.
– DERIVATIVES **long-faced** adjective.

Longfellow /ˈlɒŋfɛləʊ/, Henry Wadsworth (1807–82), American poet. He is known for 'The Wreck of the Hesperus' and 'The Village Blacksmith' (both 1841) and *The Song of Hiawatha* (1855).

long figure (also **long price**) ▶ **noun** archaic a high price.

Longford /ˈlɒŋfəd/ a county of the Republic of Ireland, in the province of Leinster.
  ■ its county town; pop. 6,390 (1991).

longhair ▶ **noun** 1 chiefly US a person with long hair or characteristics associated with it, such as a hippy or intellectual.
2 a cat of a long-haired breed.

longhand ▶ **noun** [mass noun] ordinary handwriting (as opposed to shorthand, typing, or printing): *he wrote out the reply in longhand* | [as modifier] *a longhand draft.*

long haul ▶ **noun** a long distance (in reference to the transport of goods or passengers): [as modifier] *a long-haul flight.*
  ■ a prolonged and difficult effort or task: *implementing the White Paper is likely to be a long haul.*
– PHRASES **over the long haul** chiefly N. Amer. over an extended period of time.

long-headed ▶ **adjective** dated having or showing foresight and good judgement.
– DERIVATIVES **long-headedness** noun.

long hop ▶ **noun** Cricket a short-pitched, easily hit ball.

longhorn ▶ **noun** 1 an animal of a breed of cattle with long horns.
2 (also **longhorn beetle**) an elongated beetle with long antennae, the larva of which typically bores in wood and can be a pest of timber.
  ● Family Cerambycidae (formerly in the superfamily Longicornia).

long-horned grasshopper ▶ **noun** former term for **BUSH CRICKET**.

longhouse ▶ **noun** a type of dwelling housing a family and animals under one roof.
  ■ historical the traditional dwelling of the Iroquois and other North American Indians. ■ a large communal village house in parts of Malaysia and Indonesia.

long hundredweight ▶ **noun** see **HUNDRED-WEIGHT**.

longicorn /ˈlɒn(d)ʒɪkɔːn/ ▶ **noun** former term for **LONGHORN** (in sense 2).
– ORIGIN mid 19th cent.: from modern Latin *longicornis*, from Latin *longus* 'long' + *cornu* 'horn'.

longing ▶ **noun** a yearning desire: *Miranda felt a*

wistful *longing for the old days* | [with infinitive] *a longing to be free* | [mass noun] *its tale of love and longing.*
▶ **adjective** [attrib.] having or showing such desire: *her longing eyes.*
– DERIVATIVES **longingly** adverb.

Longinus /lɒnˈdʒʌɪnəs/ (*fl.* 1st century AD), Greek scholar. He is the supposed author of a Greek literary treatise *On the Sublime*, concerned with the moral function of literature, which influenced Augustan writers such as Dryden and Pope.

Long Island an island on the coast of New York State. Its western tip, comprising the New York districts of Brooklyn and Queens, is separated from Manhattan and the Bronx by the East River and is linked to Manhattan by the Brooklyn Bridge.

Long Island iced tea ▶ **noun** a cocktail consisting of rum, vodka, gin, and other spirits mixed with cola and lemon juice.

longitude /ˈlɒŋ(d)ʒɪtjuːd, ˈlɒŋgɪ-/ ▶ **noun** the angular distance of a place east or west of the Greenwich meridian, or west of the standard meridian of a celestial object, usually expressed in degrees and minutes: *at a longitude of 2° W* | [mass noun] *lines of longitude.*
  ■ Astronomy see **CELESTIAL LONGITUDE**.
– ORIGIN late Middle English (also denoting length and tallness): from Latin *longitudo*, from *longus* 'long'.

longitudinal /ˌlɒndʒɪˈtjuːdɪn(ə)l, ˌlɒŋgɪ-/ ▶ **adjective** 1 running lengthwise rather than across: *longitudinal muscles* | *longitudinal stripes* | *longitudinal extent.*
  ■ (of research or data) involving information about an individual or group gathered over a long period of time.
2 of or relating to longitude; measured from east to west: *longitudinal positions.*
– DERIVATIVES **longitudinally** adverb.

longitudinal wave ▶ **noun** Physics a wave vibrating in the direction of propagation.

long johns ▶ **plural noun** informal underpants with closely fitted legs that extend to the wearer's ankles.

long jump ▶ **noun** (**the long jump**) an athletic event in which competitors jump as far as possible along the ground in one leap.
– DERIVATIVES **long jumper** noun.

longleaf pine ▶ **noun** a large North American pine tree with long needles and cones, which is an important source of turpentine. Also called **PITCH PINE**.
  ● *Pinus palustris*, family Pinaceae.

long leg ▶ **noun** Cricket a fielding position far behind the batsman on the leg side.
  ■ a fielder at this position.

long lens ▶ **noun** a lens with a long focal length, especially as a camera attachment for taking photographs from a great distance.

long-life ▶ **adjective** (of perishable goods) treated so as to stay fresh for longer than usual: *long-life milk.*

long line ▶ **noun** a deep-sea fishing line: [as modifier] *a long line fishing boat.*
– DERIVATIVES **long liner** noun chiefly N. Amer..

long-liner ▶ **noun** chiefly N. Amer. a fishing vessel which uses long-lines.

longlist ▶ **noun** a list of selected names or things from which a shortlist is to be compiled.
▶ **verb** [with obj.] (often **be longlisted**) place on such a list.

long-lived ▶ **adjective** living or lasting a long time.

long-lost ▶ **adjective** [attrib.] lost or absent for a long time: *a long-lost friend* | *his long-lost youth.*

Long March the epic withdrawal of the Chinese communists from SE to NW China in 1934–5, over a distance of 9,600 km (6,000 miles). 100,000 people, led by Mao Zedong, left the communist rural base after it was almost destroyed by the Kuomintang; 20,000 people survived the journey.

long mark ▶ **noun** informal term for **MACRON**.

long measure ▶ **noun** archaic a measure of length; a linear measure.

long metre (abbrev.: **LM**) ▶ **noun** 1 a metrical pattern for hymns in which the stanzas have four lines with eight syllables each.
2 Prosody a quatrain of iambic tetrameters with alternate lines rhyming.

longneck ▶ **noun** N. Amer. informal a beer bottle with a long, narrow neck and a capacity of 330 ml.

long off ▶ **noun** Cricket a fielding position far behind the bowler and towards the off side.
  ■ a fielder at this position.

long on ▶ **noun** Cricket a fielding position far behind the bowler and towards the on side.
  ■ a fielder at this position.

Long Parliament the English Parliament which sat from November 1640 to March 1653, was restored for a short time in 1659, and finally voted its own dissolution in 1660. It was summoned by Charles I and sat through the English Civil War and on into the interregnum which followed.

long pig ▶ **noun** a translation of a term formerly used in some Pacific Islands for human flesh as food.

long-playing ▶ **adjective** (of a gramophone record) about 30 cm in diameter and designed to rotate at 33⅓ revolutions per minute.
– DERIVATIVES **long-player** noun.

long-range ▶ **adjective** 1 (especially of vehicles or missiles) able to be used or be effective over long distances: *long-range bombers.*
2 relating to a period of time that extends far into the future: *long-range forecasts* | *long-range plans.*

long reins ▶ **plural noun** a pair of long reins used to school a horse from the ground.
▶ **verb** (**long-rein**) [no obj.] [usu. as noun **long-reining**] school a horse with such reins.

long-running ▶ **adjective** continuing for a long time: *a long-running dispute over EU subsidies.*

long s ▶ **noun** an obsolete form of lower-case s, written or printed as ʃ. It was used in initial and medial but not final position in a word, and was generally abandoned in English-language printing shortly before 1800.

Longshan /lɒnˈʃan/ ▶ **noun** [usu. as modifier] Archaeology a Neolithic civilization of the Yellow River valley in China (*c.*2500–1700 BC), between the Yangshao and Shang periods. It is characterized by pottery kiln-fired to a uniform black colour and by the establishment of towns.

longship ▶ **noun** a long, narrow warship, powered by both oar and sail with many rowers, used by the Vikings and other ancient northern European peoples.

longshore ▶ **adjective** [attrib.] existing on, frequenting, or moving along the seashore: *longshore currents.*
– ORIGIN early 19th cent.: from *along shore.*

longshore drift ▶ **noun** [mass noun] the movement of material along a coast by waves which approach at an angle to the shore but recede directly away from it.

longshoreman ▶ **noun** (pl. **-men**) N. Amer. a docker.

long shot ▶ **noun** a venture or guess that has only the slightest chance of succeeding or being accurate: *it's a long shot, but well worth trying.*
– PHRASES **(not) by a long shot** informal (not) by far or at all: *she had not told Rory everything, not by a long shot.*

long sight ▶ **noun** [mass noun] the inability to see things clearly, especially if they are relatively close to the eyes, owing to the focusing of rays of light by the eye at a point behind the retina. Also called **HYPERMETROPIA**.

long-sighted ▶ **adjective** having long sight.
  ■ figurative having imagination or foresight.
– DERIVATIVES **long-sightedly** adverb, **long-sightedness** noun.

long-sleever ▶ **noun** Austral. informal a large glass of beer.

longspur ▶ **noun** a mainly Canadian songbird related to the buntings, with brownish plumage and a boldly marked head in the male.
  ● Genus *Calcarius*, family Emberizidae (subfamily Emberizinae): three or four species.

long-standing ▶ **adjective** having existed or continued for a long time: *a long-standing tradition.*

long-stay ▶ **adjective** [attrib.] denoting or relating to people staying somewhere for a long time: *long-stay patients.*

longstop ▶ **noun** Cricket a fielding position (not normally used in the modern game) directly behind the wicketkeeper.
  ■ a fielder at this position.

long-suffering ▶ **adjective** having or showing patience in spite of troubles, especially those caused by other people: *his long-suffering wife.*
– DERIVATIVES **long-sufferingly** adverb.

long suit ▶ **noun** (in bridge or whist) a holding of several cards of one suit in a hand, typically 5 or more out of the 13.
■ [usu. with negative] an outstanding personal quality or achievement: *tact was not his long suit.*

longtail (also **green longtail**) ▶ **noun** a West African montane warbler with greenish plumage and a long tail.
● *Urolais epichlora*, family Sylviidae; sometimes also members of the genus *Prinia*.
■ informal any long-tailed bird, e.g. a pheasant.

long-tailed duck ▶ **noun** a marine diving duck that breeds in Arctic Eurasia and North America, the male having very long tail feathers and mainly white plumage in winter.
● *Clangula hyemalis*, family Anatidae. North American name: **oldsquaw**.

long-tailed tit ▶ **noun** a small Eurasian songbird that resembles a tit, having black, white, and pink plumage and a long slender tail, and building a domed nest.
● Genus *Aegithalos*, family Aegithalidae: several species, in particular *A. caudatus*.

long-term ▶ **adjective** occurring over or relating to a long period of time: *the long-term unemployed | the long-term effects of smoking.*

long-time ▶ **adjective** [attrib.] (especially of a person) having had a specified role or identity for a long time: *his long-time friend and colleague.*

long tom ▶ **noun** informal, historical **1** a large cannon with a long range.
2 a trough for washing gold-bearing deposits.

long ton ▶ **noun** see **TON**[1].

longueur /lɒ̃(ŋ)ˈɡəː/ ▶ **noun** a tedious passage in a book or other work: *its brilliant comedy passages do not cancel out the occasional longueurs.*
■ [mass noun] tedious periods of time: *the last act is sometimes marred by longueur.*
– ORIGIN French, literally 'length'.

long vacation ▶ **noun** Brit. the summer break of three months taken by universities and (formerly) law courts.

long waist ▶ **noun** a low waist on a dress or a person's body.
– DERIVATIVES **long-waisted** adjective.

longwall ▶ **adjective** [attrib.] Mining of or involving a single long face worked (usually mechanically) along its whole length.

long wave ▶ **noun** a radio wave of a wavelength above one kilometre (and a frequency below 300 kHz): [as modifier] *long-wave radio.*
■ [mass noun] broadcasting using radio waves of 1 to 10 km wavelength: *listening to BBC Radio 4* ***on long wave.***

longways (also **longwise**) ▶ **adverb** lengthways: *it has been sliced longways to show the internal structure.*

long-winded ▶ **adjective** (of speech or writing) continuing at length and in a tedious way: *his good wishes were long-winded but sincere.*
■ archaic capable of doing something for a long time without needing a rest.
– DERIVATIVES **long-windedly** adverb, **long-windedness** noun.

longwool ▶ **noun** a sheep of a breed with long wool.

lonicera /lɒˈnɪs(ə)rə/ ▶ **noun** a plant of a genus which comprises the honeysuckles.
● Genus *Lonicera*, family Caprifoliaceae.
– ORIGIN modern Latin, named after Adam *Lonitzer* (1528–86), German botanist.

lonning ▶ **noun** another term for **LOAN**[2].

Lonsdale belt ▶ **noun** Boxing an ornate belt awarded to a professional boxer winning a British title fight. A fighter winning three title fights in one weight division is given a belt to keep.
– ORIGIN early 20th cent.: named after the fifth Earl of Lonsdale, Hugh Cecil Lowther (1857–1944), who presented the first one.

loo[1] ▶ **noun** Brit. informal a toilet.
– ORIGIN 1940s: many theories have been put forward about the word's origin: one suggests the source is *Waterloo*, a trade name for iron cisterns in the early part of the century; the evidence remains inconclusive.

loo[2] ▶ **noun** [mass noun] a gambling card game, popular from the 17th to the 19th centuries, in which a player who fails to win a trick must pay a sum to a pool.
– ORIGIN late 17th cent.: abbreviation of obsolete *lanterloo* from French *lanturlu*, a meaningless song refrain.

looey (also **looie**) ▶ **noun** (pl. **-eys** or **-ies**) US military slang short for **LIEUTENANT**.

loofah /ˈluːfə/ ▶ **noun 1** a coarse, fibrous cylindrical object which is used like a bath sponge for washing. It consists of the dried fibrous matter of the fluid-transport system of a marrow-like fruit.
2 the tropical Old World climbing plant of the gourd family which produces these fruits, which are also edible.
● *Luffa cylindrica*, family Cucurbitaceae.
– ORIGIN late 19th cent.: from Egyptian Arabic *lūfa*, denoting the plant.

look ▶ **verb** [no obj.] **1** [no obj., usu. with adverbial of direction] direct one's gaze towards someone or something or in a specified direction: *people were* ***looking at*** *him | they looked up as he came quietly into the room.*
■ (of a building or room) have a view or outlook in a specified direction: *the principal rooms* ***look out over*** *Mylor Harbour.* ■ (**look through**) ignore (someone) by pretending not to see them: *he glanced up once but looked right through me.* ■ [with obj.] dated express or show (something) by one's gaze: *Poirot looked a question.* ■ (**look something over**) inspect something quickly with a view to establishing its merits: *they looked over a property in Great Marlborough Street.* ■ (**look through**) peruse (a book or other written material): *we looked through all the books and this was still the one we liked best.* ■ (**look round/around**) move round (a place or building) in order to view whatever it might contain that is of interest: *he spent the morning and afternoon looking round Edinburgh.* ■ (**look at/on**) think of or regard in a specified way: *I look at tennis differently from some coaches.* ■ (**look at**) examine (a matter, especially a problem) and consider what action to take: *a committee is looking at the financing of the BBC.* ■ (**look into**) investigate: *the police looked into his business dealings.* ■ (**look for**) attempt to find: *Howard has been looking for you.* ■ [with clause] ascertain with a quick glance: *people finishing work don't* ***look where*** *they're going.*
2 [with complement or adverbial] have the appearance or give the impression of being: *her father looked unhappy | the home* ***looked like*** *a prison* | [as adj., in combination **-looking**] *a funny-looking bloke.*
■ (**look like**) informal show a likelihood of: [with present participle] *Leeds didn't look like scoring from any of their corners* | [with clause] *it doesn't look like you'll be moving to Liverpool.* ■ (**look oneself**) appear one's normal, healthy self: *he just didn't look himself at all.*
3 (**look to**) rely on to do or provide something: *she will look to you for help.*
■ [with infinitive] hope or expect to do something: *universities are looking to expand their intakes.* ■ [with clause] archaic take care; make sure: *Look ye obey the masters of the craft.*
▶ **noun 1** an act of directing one's gaze in order to see someone or something: *let me get a closer look.*
■ an expression of a feeling or thought by such an act: *the orderly gave me a funny look.* ■ a scrutiny or examination: *the government should be* ***taking a look at*** *the amount of grant the council receives.*
2 the appearance of someone or something, especially as expressing a particular quality: *the bedraggled look of the village.*
■ (**looks**) a person's facial appearance considered aesthetically: *he had charm,* ***good looks****, and an amusing insouciance.* ■ a style or fashion: *Italian designers unveiled their latest look.*
▶ **exclamation** (also **look here!**) used to call attention to what one is going to say: *'Look, this is ridiculous.'*
– PHRASES **look one's age** appear to be as old as one really is. **look alive** see *look lively*. **look before you leap** proverb one shouldn't act without first considering the possible consequences or dangers. **look daggers at** see **DAGGER**. **look down one's nose at** another way of saying *look down on*. **look for trouble** see **TROUBLE**. **look someone in the eye** (or **face**) look directly at someone without showing embarrassment, fear, or shame. **look lively** (or dated **alive**) informal used to tell someone to be quick in doing something. **look the other way** deliberately ignore wrongdoing by others: *they do look the other way at corrupt practices here.* **look sharp** be quick. **look small** see **SMALL**. **look to the future** consider and plan for what is in the future, rather than worrying about the past or present. **look someone up and down** scrutinize someone carefully.
– ORIGIN Old English *lōcian* (verb), of West Germanic origin; related to German dialect *lugen*.
▶ **look after** take care of: *women who stay at home to look after children.*
look back 1 think of the past: *don't waste time* ***looking back on*** *things which have caused you distress.* **2** [with negative] suffer a setback or interrupted progress: *she launched her own company in 1981 and has never looked back.*
look down on regard (someone) with a feeling of superiority.
look forward to await eagerly: *we look forward to seeing you.*
look in make a short visit or call: *I will* ***look in on*** *you tomorrow.*
look on watch without getting involved: *Cameron was looking on and making no move to help.*
look out [usu. in imperative] be vigilant and take notice: *'Look out!' warned Billie, seeing a movement from the room beyond |* ***look out for*** *the early warning signals.*
look something out Brit. search for and produce something: *I've got a catalogue somewhere and I'll look it out if you're interested.*
look up (of a situation) improve: *things seemed to be looking up at last.*
look someone up informal make social contact with someone.
look something up search for and find a piece of information in a reference book.
look up to have a great deal of respect for (someone): *he needed a model, someone to look up to.*

look-ahead ▶ **noun** an act of judging or calculating possible or likely events or states in the (immediate) future.

lookalike ▶ **noun** a person or thing that closely resembles another, especially someone who looks very similar to a famous person: *an Elvis Presley lookalike.*

look-and-say ▶ **noun** [mass noun] [as modifier] denoting a method of teaching reading based on the visual recognition of words rather than the association of sounds and letters. Compare with **PHONIC**.

looker ▶ **noun** [with adj.] a person with a specified appearance: *a tough looker is not necessarily a tough fighter.*
■ informal a very attractive person, especially a woman: *he shook his head in admiration—she was some looker.*

looker-on ▶ **noun** (pl. **lookers-on**) a person who is a spectator rather than a participant in a situation.

look-in ▶ **noun** [in sing.] informal a chance to take part or succeed in something: *they didn't let the other side* ***get a look-in*** *in the semi-final.*

looking glass ▶ **noun** a mirror.
■ [as modifier] being or involving the opposite of what is normal or expected: *a looking-glass land | looking-glass logic.*

lookit N. Amer. informal ▶ **verb** [with obj., in imperative] look at: *Hey, lookit that!*
▶ **exclamation** used to draw attention to what one is about to say: *lookit, Pete, this is serious.*

lookout ▶ **noun** a place from which to keep watch or view landscape.
■ a person stationed to keep watch for danger or trouble: *they acted as lookouts at the post office.* ■ archaic a view over a landscape. ■ [in sing.] [with adj.] informal, chiefly Brit. used to indicate whether a likely outcome is good or bad: *'What if he gets fits?' 'It's a bad lookout in that case.'* ■ (**one's lookout**) Brit. informal a person's own concern: *if you can't take an interest in local affairs, that's your lookout.*
– PHRASES **be on the lookout** (or **keep a lookout**) **for** be alert to (danger or trouble): *he told them to be on the lookout for dangerous gas.* ■ keep searching for (something that is wanted): *we kept a sharp lookout for animals and saw several waterbuck.*

look-see ▶ **noun** informal a brief look or inspection: *we are just about to take a little look-see around the hotel.*
– ORIGIN late 19th cent.: from, or in imitation of, pidgin English.

looky ▶ **exclamation** informal used to draw attention to what one is about to say: *Looky there! You've gone and broken it.*

loom[1] ▶ **noun** an apparatus for making fabric by weaving yarn or thread.
– ORIGIN Old English *gelōma* 'tool', shortened to *lome* in Middle English.

loom[2] ▶ **verb** [no obj., with adverbial] appear as a shadowy form, especially one that is large or threatening: *vehicles loomed out of the darkness.*
■ [no obj.] (of an event regarded as ominous or

l

threatening) seem about to happen: *there is a crisis looming | dearer mortgages* ***loomed large*** *last night.*
▶**noun** [in sing.] a vague and often exaggerated first appearance of an object seen in darkness or fog, especially at sea: *the loom of the land.*
■the dim reflection by cloud or haze of a light which is not directly visible, e.g. from a lighthouse over the horizon.
– ORIGIN mid 16th cent.: probably from Low German or Dutch; compare with East Frisian *lōmen* 'move slowly', Middle High German *lüemen* 'be weary'.

loon[1] ▶**noun** informal a silly or foolish person.
– ORIGIN late 19th cent.: from **LOON**[2] (referring to the bird's actions when escaping from danger), perhaps influenced by **LOONY**.

loon[2] ▶**noun** North American term for **DIVER** (in sense 2).
– ORIGIN mid 17th cent.: probably by alteration of Shetland dialect *loom*, denoting especially a guillemot or a diver, from Old Norse.

loon[3] ▶**verb** [no obj., with adverbial] Brit. informal act in a foolish or desultory way: *he decided to loon around London.*
– ORIGIN 1960s: of unknown origin.

loonie ▶**noun** (pl. **-ies**) Canadian informal a Canadian one-dollar coin, introduced in 1987.

loons (also **loon pants**) ▶**plural noun** Brit. dated close-fitting casual trousers widely flared from the knees downwards.
– ORIGIN 1970s: from **LOON**[3].

loony informal ▶**noun** (pl. **-ies**) a mad or silly person: *she was working with a bunch of loonies.*
▶**adjective** (**loonier**, **looniest**) mad or silly: *loony drivers.*
– DERIVATIVES **looniness** noun.
– ORIGIN mid 19th cent.: abbreviation of **LUNATIC**.

loony bin ▶**noun** informal, offensive a home or hospital for people with mental illnesses.

loop ▶**noun 1** a shape produced by a curve that bends round and crosses itself.
■a length of thread, rope, or similar material, doubled or crossing itself, typically used as a fastening or handle. ■a curved stroke forming part of a letter (e.g. *b, p*). ■(also **loop line**) a length of railway track which is connected at either end to the main line and on to which trains can be diverted to allow others to pass. ■(also **loop road**) a stretch of road that diverges from a main road and joins it again. ■(also **loop-the-loop**) a manoeuvre in which an aircraft describes a vertical circle in the air. ■Skating a manoeuvre describing a curve that crosses itself, made on a single edge. ■dated a contraceptive coil. ■short for **INDUCTION LOOP**.
2 a structure, series, or process the end of which is connected to the beginning.
■an endless strip of tape or film allowing continuous repetition. ■a complete circuit for an electric current. ■Computing a programmed sequence of instructions that is repeated until or while a particular condition is satisfied.
▶**verb** [with obj. and adverbial] form (something) into a loop or loops; encircle: *she looped her arms around his neck.*
■[no obj., with adverbial] follow a course that forms a loop or loops: *the canal loops for two miles through the city.* ■put into or execute a loop of tape, film, or computing instructions. ■(also **loop the loop**) circle an aircraft vertically in the air.
– PHRASES **in** (or **out of**) **the loop** informal, chiefly US aware (or unaware) of information known to only a privileged few. **throw** (or **knock**) **someone for a loop** N. Amer. informal surprise or astonish someone; catch someone off guard.
– ORIGIN late Middle English: of unknown origin; compare with Scottish Gaelic *lùb* 'loop, bend'.

loop diuretic ▶**noun** Medicine a powerful diuretic which inhibits resorption of water and sodium from the loop of Henle.

looper ▶**noun 1** a caterpillar of a geometrid moth, which moves forward by arching itself into loops. Also called **MEASURING WORM** or (in North America) **INCHWORM**.
2 a device for making loops.

loophole ▶**noun 1** an ambiguity or inadequacy in the law or a set of rules: *they exploited tax loopholes.*
2 archaic an arrow slit in a wall.
▶**verb** [with obj.] make arrow slits in (a wall or building).
– ORIGIN late 16th cent. (denoting an arrow slit): from obsolete *loop* 'embrasure' + **HOLE**.

loop of Henle /'hɛnli/ ▶**noun** Anatomy the part of a kidney tubule which forms a long loop in the medulla of the kidney, from which water and salts are resorbed into the blood.
– ORIGIN mid 19th cent.: named after Friedrich G. J. Henle (1809–85), German anatomist.

loop pile ▶**noun** [mass noun] pile in a carpet or other textile which consists of uncut loops.

loop stitch ▶**noun** [mass noun] a method of sewing or knitting in which each stitch incorporates a free loop of thread, for ornament or to give a thick pile.
– DERIVATIVES **loop-stitched** adjective, **loop stitching** noun.

loopy ▶**adjective** (**loopier**, **loopiest**) **1** informal mad or silly: *the author comes across as a bit loopy.*
2 having many loops: *a big, loopy signature.*
– DERIVATIVES **loopiness** noun.

loose /luːs/ ▶**adjective 1** not firmly or tightly fixed in place; detached or able to be detached: *a loose tooth | the lorry's trailer came loose.*
■not held or tied together; not packaged or placed in a container: *wear your hair loose | pockets bulging with loose change.* ■(of a person or animal) free from confinement; not bound or tethered: *the bull was loose with cattle in the field | the tethered horses* ***broke loose.*** ■not strict or exact: *a loose interpretation.* ■not close or compact in structure: *a loose weave |* figurative *a loose federation of political and industrial groups.* ■typical of diarrhoea: *many patients report loose bowel movements.*
2 (of a garment) not fitting tightly or closely: *she slipped into a loose T-shirt and shorts.*
3 relaxed; physically slack: *she swung back into her easy, loose stride |* [in combination] *a loose-limbed walk.*
■careless and indiscreet in what is said: *there is too much loose talk about the situation.* ■dated promiscuous; immoral: *she ran the risk of being called a loose woman.* ■(of the ball in a game) in play but not in any player's possession. ■(of play, especially in rugby) with the players not close together. ■(of play in cricket) inaccurate or careless: *Lucas punished some loose bowling severely.*
▶**noun** (**the loose**) Rugby, Brit. loose play: *they gained the better of the encounters in the loose.*
▶**verb** [with obj.] set free; release: *the hounds have been loosed.*
■untie; unfasten: *the ropes were loosed.* ■relax (one's grip): *he loosed his grip suddenly.* ■discharge; fire: *he* ***loosed off*** *a shot through the back of the vehicle.*
– PHRASES **hang** (or **stay**) **loose** [often as imperative] informal, chiefly US be relaxed; refrain from taking anything too seriously: *hang loose, baby!* **on the loose** having escaped from confinement: *a serial killer is on the loose.*
– DERIVATIVES **loosely** adverb, **looseness** noun.
– ORIGIN Middle English *loos* 'free from bonds', from Old Norse *lauss*, of Germanic origin; related to Dutch and German *los*.

USAGE The words **loose** and **lose** are different and should not be confused: see **usage** at **LOSE**.

loose box ▶**noun** Brit. a stable, or an enclosed area in a stable building, in which a horse is kept and within which it does not need to be tied.

loose cannon ▶**noun** an unpredictable or uncontrolled person who is liable to cause unintentional damage.

loose cover ▶**noun** Brit. a removable fitted cloth cover for a chair or sofa.

loose end ▶**noun** a detail that is not yet settled or explained: *Mark arrived back at his office to tie up any loose ends.*
– PHRASES **be at a loose end** (or N. Amer. **at loose ends**) have nothing specific to do.

loose-footed ▶**adjective** (of a boat's sail) having no boom or not secured to a boom at the foot.

loose forward ▶**noun** Rugby a forward who plays at the back of the scrum.

loose head ▶**noun** Rugby the forward in the front row of a scrummage who is nearest to the scrum half as the ball is put in.

loose housing ▶**noun** [mass noun] partly covered barns or sheds for livestock with access to a feeding area (as distinct from individual pens or crates).
■the raising of livestock using such accommodation.

loose-knit ▶**adjective** knitted with large loose stitches: *she wears a large loose-knit sweater.*
■connected in a tenuous or ill-defined way; not closely linked: *a loose-knit grouping of independent states.*

loose-leaf ▶**adjective** (of a notebook or folder) having each sheet of paper separate and removable.

loosen ▶**verb** [with obj.] make (something tied, fastened, or fixed in place) less tight or firm: *loosen your collar and tie.*
■make more lax: *his main mistake was to loosen monetary policy |* [as noun **loosening**] *a loosening of the benefit rules.* ■relax (one's grip or muscles): *he loosened his hold so she could pull her arms free.* ■[no obj.] become relaxed or less tight: *the stiffness in his shoulders had loosened.* ■make (a connection or relationship) less strong: *he wanted to strengthen rather than loosen union links.* ■(with reference to the bowels) make or become relaxed prior to excretion: [no obj.] *his bowels loosened in terror.*
– PHRASES **loosen someone's tongue** make someone talk freely.
▶**loosen up** warm up in preparation for an activity: *arrive early to loosen up and hit some practice shots.* ■make or become relaxed: *they taught me to have fun at work and loosen up |* (**loosen someone up**) *the beer is loosening him up.*

loosener ▶**noun** a person or thing that loosens something.
■informal a relatively undemanding challenge early in a game or competition, before the participants are fully settled or warmed up.

loose rein ▶**noun** [in sing.] a manner of riding in which the reins are held slackly, so that the horse is able to relax and stretch: ***on a loose rein,*** *he ran better.*
■a lack of strict control in organizing something: *he ran foreign affairs* ***on a loose rein.***

loose scrum (also **loose scrummage**) ▶**noun** Rugby a scrum formed by the players round the ball during play, not ordered by the referee.

loosestrife /'luːs,strʌɪf/ ▶**noun** any of a number of tall plants which bear upright spikes of flowers and grow by water and in wet ground:
●several plants of the genus *Lythrum* (family Lythraceae), in particular the **purple loosestrife** (*L. salicaria*) of the Old World. ●several plants of the genus *Lysimachia* (family Primulaceae), in particular the **yellow loosestrife** (*L. vulgaris*) of Eurasia.
– ORIGIN mid 16th cent.: from **LOOSE** + **STRIFE**, taking the Greek name *lusimakheion* (actually from *Lusimakhos*, the name of its discoverer) to be directly from *luein* 'undo' + *makhē* 'battle'.

loot ▶**noun** [mass noun] goods, especially private property, taken from an enemy in war.
■stolen money or valuables: *two men wearing stocking masks, each swinging a bag of loot.* ■informal money; wealth: *ten thousand quid is a lot of loot.*
▶**verb** [with obj.] steal goods from (a place), typically during a war or riot: *police confronted the protestors who were looting shops.*
■steal (goods) in such circumstances: *tonnes of food aid awaiting distribution had been looted.* ■Indian steal (something) from someone: *a gang looted Rs. 1.5 lakh from a passenger.*
– DERIVATIVES **looter** noun.
– ORIGIN early 19th cent. (as a verb): from Hindi *lūṭ*, from Sanskrit *luṇṭh-* 'rob'.

loo table ▶**noun** a circular table for playing the card game loo on, or a table made in a similar style.

lop[1] ▶**verb** (**lopped**, **lopping**) [with obj.] cut off (a branch, limb, or other protrusion) from the main body of a tree: *they* ***lopped off*** *more branches to save the tree.*
■informal remove (something regarded as unnecessary or burdensome): *it lops an hour off journey times.* ■remove branches from (a tree).
▶**noun** [mass noun] branches and twigs lopped off trees.
– PHRASES **lop and top** parts lopped off a tree, such as branches and twigs.
– ORIGIN late Middle English (as a noun denoting branches and twigs of trees).

lop[2] ▶**verb** (**lopped**, **lopping**) [no obj.] N. Amer. or archaic **1** hang loosely or limply; droop: *a stomach that lopped over his belt.*
■[with adverbial of direction] move in a loping or slouching way: *he lopped towards the plane.* ■archaic dawdle; hang about.
– ORIGIN late 16th cent.: probably symbolic of limpness; compare with **LOB**.

lope ▶**verb** [no obj., with adverbial of direction] run or move with a long bounding stride: *the dog was loping along by his side |* [as adj. **loping**] *a loping stride.*
▶**noun** [in sing.] a long bounding stride: *they set off at a fast lope.*
– ORIGIN Middle English: variant of Scots *loup*, from Old Norse *hlaupa* 'leap'.

lop-ears ▶**plural noun** ears that droop down by the sides of an animal's head: *a dark pig with lop-ears.*

– DERIVATIVES **lop-eared** adjective.

loperamide /ləʊˈpɛrəmʌɪd/ ▶ **noun** [mass noun] Medicine a synthetic drug of the opiate class which inhibits peristalsis and is used to treat diarrhoea.
– ORIGIN 1970s: probably from (ch)lo(ro-) + (pi)per(idine) + AMIDE.

lopho- ▶ **combining form** Zoology crested: lophodont.
– ORIGIN from Greek lophos 'crest'.

lophodont /ˈləʊfə(ʊ)dɒnt, ˈlɒf-/ ▶ **adjective** Zoology (of molar teeth) having transverse ridges on the grinding surfaces, characteristic of some ungulates. ■(of an ungulate) having such teeth.
– ORIGIN late 19th cent.: from LOPHO- 'crest' + Greek odous, odont- 'tooth'.

lophophorate /ləˈfɒfəreɪt, ˌləʊfəˈfɔːreɪt/ Zoology ▶ **adjective** of or relating to small aquatic invertebrates belonging to a group of phyla characterized by the possession of lophophores. They include bryozoans, brachiopods, and horseshoe worms.
▶ **noun** a lophophorate animal.

lophophore /ˈləʊfəfɔː, ˈlɒf-/ ▶ **noun** Zoology a horseshoe-shaped structure bearing ciliated tentacles around the mouth in certain small marine invertebrates.

Lop Nor /lɒp ˈnɔː/ (also **Lop Nur** /ˈnʊə/) a dried-up salt lake in the arid basin of the Tarim River in NW China, used since 1964 for nuclear testing.

lopolith /ˈlɒpə(ʊ)lɪθ/ ▶ **noun** Geology a large saucer-shaped intrusion of igneous rock.
– ORIGIN early 20th cent.: from Greek lopas 'basin' + -LITH.

loppers ▶ **plural noun** a cutting tool, especially for pruning trees: a good pair of loppers.

loppy ▶ **noun** (pl. **-ies**) Austral./NZ another term for ROUSEABOUT.
– ORIGIN late 19th cent.: probably from English dialect lop 'hang about' or dialect loppy 'flea-ridden'.

lopsided ▶ **adjective** with one side lower or smaller than the other: a lopsided grin.
– DERIVATIVES **lopsidedly** adverb, **lopsidedness** noun.
– ORIGIN early 18th cent.: from LOP² + SIDE + -ED¹.

loquacious /lɒˈkweɪʃəs/ ▶ **adjective** talkative.
– DERIVATIVES **loquaciously** adverb, **loquaciousness** noun, **loquacity** noun.
– ORIGIN mid 17th cent.: from Latin loquax, loquac- (from loqui 'talk') + -IOUS.

loquat /ˈlɒkwɒt/ ▶ **noun** 1 a small yellow egg-shaped acidic fruit.
2 the evergreen East Asian tree of the rose family which bears this fruit, cultivated in subtropical regions for its fruit and as an ornamental. ● Eriobotrya japonica, family Rosaceae.
– ORIGIN early 19th cent.: from Chinese dialect luh kwat 'rush orange'.

loquitur /ˈlɒkwɪtə/ (abbrev.: **loq.**) ▶ **verb** (he or she) speaks (with the speaker's name following, as a stage direction or to inform the reader).
– ORIGIN Latin, from loqui 'talk, speak'.

lor ▶ **exclamation** Brit. informal used to indicate surprise or dismay: Lor, look at that! Isn't it horrible?
– ORIGIN mid 19th cent.: abbreviation of LORD.

Loran /ˈlɔːran, ˈlɒ-/ ▶ **noun** [mass noun] a system of long-distance navigation in which position is determined from the intervals between signal pulses received from widely spaced radio transmitters.
– ORIGIN 1940s: from lo(ng)-ra(nge) n(avigation).

loranthus /lɒˈranθəs/ ▶ **noun** a semi-parasitic Asian plant of the mistletoe family, which has orange or red flowers and oval berries. ● Family Loranthaceae; most species formerly in the genus Loranthus are now placed in other genera.
– ORIGIN modern Latin (genus name), from Latin lorum 'strap' + Greek anthos 'flower'.

lorazepam /lɔːˈreɪzɪpam, -ˈrazə-/ ▶ **noun** [mass noun] Medicine a drug of the benzodiazepine group, used especially to treat anxiety.
– ORIGIN 1960s: from (ch)lor(o-) ('chlorine') + -azepam, on the pattern of words such as diazepam.

Lorca /ˈlɔːkə/, Federico García (1898–1936), Spanish poet and dramatist. His works include Gypsy Ballads (verse, 1928) and intense, poetic tragedies evoking the passionate emotions of Spanish life, notably Blood Wedding (1933) and The House of Bernarda Alba (1945).

lord ▶ **noun** a peer of the realm; a man of noble rank or high office.
■(**Lord**) a title given formally to a baron, and less formally to a marquess, earl, or viscount (prefixed to a family or territorial name): Lord Derby. ■ (**the Lords**) the House of Lords, or its members collectively. ■ (**Lord**) a courtesy title given to a younger son of a duke or marquess (prefixed to a Christian name): Lord John Russell. ■ in compound titles of other people of authority: Lord High Executioner. ■ historical a feudal superior, especially the proprietor of a manor house. ■ a master or ruler: our lord the king. ■ (**Lord**) a name for God or Christ: give thanks to the Lord. ■ Astrology, dated the ruling planet of a sign, house, or chart.
▶ **exclamation** (**Lord**) used in exclamations expressing surprise or worry, or for emphasis: Lord, I'm cold!
▶ **verb** 1 [with obj.] archaic confer the title of Lord upon.
2 (**lord it over**) act in a superior and domineering manner towards (someone).
– PHRASES **live like a lord** live sumptuously. **Lord (God) of hosts** God as Lord over earthly or heavenly armies. **lord of the manor** the owner of a manor house (formerly the master of a feudal manor). **Lord of Misrule** historical a person presiding over Christmas games and revelry in a wealthy household. **the Lord's Day** Sunday. **the Lord's Prayer** the prayer taught by Christ to his disciples, beginning 'Our Father.' **the Lord's Supper** the Eucharist; Holy Communion (especially in Protestant use). **My Lord** a polite form of address to judges, bishops, and certain noblemen. **Our Lord** Christ.
– DERIVATIVES **lordless** adjective, **lord-like** adjective.
– ORIGIN Old English hláford, from hláfweard 'bread-keeper', from a Germanic base (see LOAF¹, WARD). Compare with LADY.

Lord Advocate ▶ **noun** the principal Law Officer of the Crown in Scotland.

Lord Bishop ▶ **noun** the formal title of a bishop, in particular of a diocesan bishop (as distinct from a suffragan).

Lord Chamberlain (also **Lord Chamberlain of the Household**) ▶ **noun** (in the UK) the official in charge of the royal household, formerly the licenser of plays.

Lord Chancellor ▶ **noun** (in the UK) the highest officer of the Crown, who presides in the House of Lords, the Chancery Division, or the Court of Appeal.
■ historical an officer of state acting as head of the judiciary and administrator of the royal household.

Lord Chief Justice ▶ **noun** (in the UK) the officer presiding over the Queen's Bench Division and the Court of Appeal (Criminal Division).

Lord Commissioner ▶ **noun** 1 the representative of the Crown at the General Assembly of the Church of Scotland.
2 (**Lords Commissioners**) (in the UK) the members of a board performing the duties of a high state office put in commission.

Lord Fauntleroy see FAUNTLEROY.

Lord Great Chamberlain of England ▶ **noun** the hereditary holder of a ceremonial office whose responsibilities include attendance on the monarch at a coronation.

Lord High Admiral a title of the British monarch, originally the title of an officer who governed the Royal Navy and had jurisdiction over maritime causes.

Lord High Chancellor ▶ **noun** another term for LORD CHANCELLOR.

Lord High Commissioner ▶ **noun** another term for LORD COMMISSIONER.

Lord High Treasurer ▶ **noun** see TREASURER.

Lord Howe Island a volcanic island in the SW Pacific off the east coast of Australia, administered as part of New South Wales; pop. 320 (1989).
– ORIGIN named after Admiral Lord Howe (1726–99), who was First Lord of the Admiralty when it was first visited.

Lord Justice (also **Lord Justice of Appeal**) ▶ **noun** (pl. **Lords Justices**) (in the UK) a judge in the Court of Appeal.

Lord Lieutenant ▶ **noun** (in the UK) the chief executive authority and head of magistrates in each county.
■ historical the viceroy of Ireland.

lordling ▶ **noun** archaic, chiefly derogatory a minor lord.

lordly ▶ **adjective** (**lordlier**, **lordliest**) of, character-

istic of, or suitable for a lord: lordly titles | they were putting on lordly airs.
– DERIVATIVES **lordliness** noun.
– ORIGIN Old English hláfordlic (see LORD, -LY¹).

Lord Lyon ▶ **noun** see LYON.

Lord Mayor ▶ **noun** the title of the mayor in London and some other large British cities.

Lord Muck ▶ **noun** Brit. informal a man who is socially pretentious or pompous and self-opinionated.

Lord of Appeal (in full **Lord of Appeal in Ordinary**) ▶ **noun** formal term for LAW LORD.

Lord Ordinary ▶ **noun** (in Scotland) any of the judges of the Outer House of the Court of Session.

lordosis /lɔːˈdəʊsɪs/ ▶ **noun** [mass noun] Medicine excessive inward curvature of the spine. Compare with KYPHOSIS.
– DERIVATIVES **lordotic** adjective.
– ORIGIN early 18th cent.: modern Latin, from Greek lordōsis, from lordos 'bent backwards'.

Lord President of the Council ▶ **noun** (in the UK) the cabinet minister presiding at the Privy Council.

Lord Privy Seal ▶ **noun** (in the UK) a senior cabinet minister without specified official duties.

Lord Protector of the Commonwealth ▶ **noun** see PROTECTOR (sense 3).

Lord Provost ▶ **noun** the head of a municipal corporation or borough in certain Scottish cities.

Lord's a cricket ground in St John's Wood, north London, headquarters since 1814 of the MCC.
– ORIGIN named after the cricketer Thomas Lord (1755–1832).

lords and ladies ▶ **noun** another term for CUCKOO PINT.

Lords Commissioners ▶ **plural noun** the members of a board performing the duties of a high state office put in commission.

lordship ▶ **noun** 1 [mass noun] supreme power or rule: his lordship over the other gods.
■ archaic the authority or state of being a lord. ■ [count noun] historical a piece of land or territory belonging to or under the jurisdiction of a lord: lands including the lordship of Denbigh.
2 (**His/Your** etc. **Lordship**) a respectful form of reference or address to a judge, a bishop, or a man with a title: if Your Lordship pleases.
■ ironic a form of address or reference to a man thought to give himself airs.
– ORIGIN Old English hláfordscipe (see LORD, -SHIP).

Lords of Session ▶ **plural noun** (in Scotland) the judges of the Court of Session.

Lords spiritual ▶ **plural noun** the bishops in the House of Lords.

Lords temporal ▶ **plural noun** the members of the House of Lords other than the bishops.

Lord Treasurer ▶ **noun** see TREASURER.

Lordy ▶ **exclamation** informal used to express surprise or dismay: Lordy! Whatever happened?

lore¹ ▶ **noun** [mass noun] a body of traditions and knowledge on a subject or held by a particular group, typically passed from person to person by word of mouth: the jinns of Arabian lore | baseball lore.
– ORIGIN Old English lár 'instruction', of Germanic origin: related to Dutch leer, German Lehre, also to LEARN.

lore² ▶ **noun** Zoology the surface on each side of a bird's head between the eye and the upper base of the beak, or between the eye and nostril in snakes.
– ORIGIN early 19th cent.: from Latin lorum 'strap'.

Lorelei /ˈlɒrəlʌɪ/ a rock on the bank of the Rhine, held by legend to be the home of a siren whose song lures boatmen to destruction.
■ the siren said to live on this rock.

Loren /lɒˈrɛn/, Sophia (b.1934), Italian actress; born Sofia Scicolone. She has starred in both Italian and American films, including the slapstick comedy The Millionairess (1960) and the wartime drama La Ciociara (1961), for which she won an Oscar.

Lorentz /ˈlɒrənts/, Hendrik Antoon (1853–1928), Dutch theoretical physicist. He worked on the forces affecting electrons and realized that electrons and cathode rays were the same thing. For their work on electromagnetic theory he and his pupil Pieter Zeeman (1865–1943) shared the 1902 Nobel Prize for Physics.

Lorentz contraction ▶ **noun** another term for **FITZGERALD CONTRACTION**.

Lorentz force ▶ **noun** Physics the force which is exerted by a magnetic field on a moving electric charge.

Lorentz transformation ▶ **noun** Physics the set of equations which in Einstein's special theory of relativity relate the space and time coordinates of one frame of reference to those of another.

Lorenz /'lɒrənts/, Konrad (Zacharias) (1903–89), Austrian zoologist. He pioneered the science of ethology, emphasizing innate rather than learned behaviour or conditioned reflexes. Lorenz extrapolated his studies in ornithology to human behaviour patterns, and compared the ill effects of the domestication of animals to human civilizing processes. He shared a Nobel Prize in 1973 with Karl von Frisch and Nikolaas Tinbergen.

Lorenz attractor ▶ **noun** Mathematics a strange attractor in the form of a two-lobed figure formed by a trajectory which spirals around the two lobes, passing randomly between them.
– ORIGIN 1970s: named after Edward N. *Lorenz* (born 1917), American meteorologist.

Lorenz curve ▶ **noun** Economics a graph on which the cumulative percentage of total national income (or some other variable) is plotted against the cumulative percentage of the corresponding population (ranked in increasing size of share). The extent to which the curve sags below a straight diagonal line indicates the degree of inequality of distribution.
– ORIGIN early 20th cent.: named after Max O. *Lorenz* (born 1876), the American statistician who devised the curve.

Lorenzo de' Medici /lə'rɛnzəʊ/ (1449–92), Italian statesman and scholar. A patron of the arts and humanist learning, he supported Botticelli, Leonardo da Vinci, and Michelangelo among others. He was also a noted poet and scholar in his own right.

lo-res (also **low-res**) ▶ **adjective** informal (of a display or an image) showing a small amount of detail.
– ORIGIN late 20th cent.: from *low-resolution*.

Loreto /lə'rɛtəʊ/ a town in eastern Italy, near the Adriatic coast to the south of Ancona; pop. 10,640 (1990). It is the site of the 'Holy House', said to be the home of the Virgin Mary and to have been brought from Nazareth by angels in 1295.

lorgnette /lɔː'njɛt/ (also **lorgnettes**) ▶ **noun** a pair of glasses or opera glasses held in front of a person's eyes by a long handle at one side.
– ORIGIN early 19th cent.: from French, from *lorgner* 'to squint'.

lorica /lə'rʌɪkə/ ▶ **noun** (pl. **loricae** /-kiː/ or **loricas**)
1 historical a Roman corselet or cuirass of leather.
2 Zoology the rigid case or shell of some rotifers and protozoans.
– ORIGIN Latin, literally 'breastplate'.

loricate /'lɒrɪkeɪt, -kət/ ▶ **adjective** Zoology (of an animal) having a protective covering of plates or scales.
■ having a lorica.
– ORIGIN early 19th cent.: from Latin *loricatus*, from *lorica* 'breastplate', from *lorum* 'strap'.

Loricifera /ˌlɒrɪ'sɪfərə/ Zoology a minor phylum of minute marine invertebrates (genus *Nanaloricus*), resembling rotifers and living in gravel.
– DERIVATIVES **loriciferan** noun & adjective.
– ORIGIN modern Latin (plural), from Latin *lorica* 'breastplate' + *ferre* 'to bear'.

Lorient /'lɒrɪɒ̃/ a port in NW France, on the south coast of Brittany; pop. 61,630 (1990).

lorikeet /'lɒrɪkiːt/ ▶ **noun** a small bird of the lory family, found chiefly in New Guinea.
• *Charmosyna* and other genera, family Loridae (or Psittacidae): several species.
■ Australian term for **LORY**.
– ORIGIN late 18th cent.: diminutive of **LORY**, on the pattern of *parakeet*.

lorilet /'lɒrɪlət, ˌlɒrɪ'lɛt/ ▶ **noun** Austral. another term for **FIG PARROT**.
– ORIGIN mid 20th cent.: from **LORY** + the diminutive suffix **-LET**.

loriner /'lɒrɪnə/ (also **lorimer**) ▶ **noun** archaic a maker of small iron objects, especially bits, spurs, stirrups, and mountings for horse's bridles.
– ORIGIN Middle English: from Old French *lorenier*, from *lorain* 'harness strap', from Latin *lorum* 'strap'.

loris /'lɔːrɪs/ ▶ **noun** (pl. **lorises**) a small, slow-moving nocturnal primate with a short or absent tail, living in dense vegetation in South Asia.
• Genera *Loris* and *Nycticebus*, family Lorisidae, suborder Prosimii: the **slender loris** (*L. tardigradus*) of South India and Sri Lanka, and the **slow loris** (genus *Nycticebus*, two species) of SE Asia.
– ORIGIN late 18th cent.: from French, perhaps from obsolete Dutch *loeris* 'clown'.

lorn ▶ **adjective** poetic/literary lonely and abandoned; forlorn.
– ORIGIN Middle English: past participle of obsolete *lese* from Old English *lēosan* 'lose'.

lorny ▶ **noun** variant spelling of **LARNEY**.

Lorraine /lə'reɪn, French lɔrɛn/ a region of NE France, between Champagne and the Vosges mountains. The modern region corresponds to the southern part of the medieval kingdom of Lorraine, which extended from the North Sea to Italy.
– ORIGIN from Latin *Lotharingia*, from *Lothair*, the name of a king (825–69).

Lorraine, Claude see **CLAUDE LORRAINE**.

Lorraine cross ▶ **noun** a cross with one vertical and two horizontal bars. It was the symbol of Joan of Arc, and in the Second World War was adopted by the Free French forces of General de Gaulle.

Lorre /'lɒri/, Peter (1904–64), Hungarian-born American actor; born *Laszlo Lowenstein*. He was known for the sinister roles he played, as in the German film *M* (1931), *The Maltese Falcon* (1941), and *The Raven* (1963).

lorry /'lɒri/ ▶ **noun** (pl. **-ies**) Brit. a large, heavy motor vehicle for transporting goods or troops; a truck.
– PHRASES **fall off of the back a lorry** (of goods) be acquired in dubious or unspecified circumstances.
– ORIGIN mid 19th cent.: perhaps from the given name *Laurie*.

lory /'lɔːri/ ▶ **noun** (pl. **-ies**) a small Australasian and SE Asian parrot with a brush-tipped tongue for feeding on nectar and pollen, having mainly green plumage with patches of bright colour. Called **LORIKEET** in Australia.
• Family Loridae (or Psittacidae): several genera and species, e.g. the brightly coloured **rainbow lory** or **rainbow lorikeet** (*Trichoglossus haematodus*).
– ORIGIN late 17th cent.: from Malay *lūrī*.

Los Alamos /lɒs 'aləmɒs/ a town in northern New Mexico; pop. 11,450 (1990). It has been a centre for nuclear research since the 1940s, when it was the site of the development of the first atomic and hydrogen bombs.

Los Angeleno ▶ **noun** variant of **ANGELENO**.

Los Angeles /lɒs 'andʒɪliːz, -lɪs/ a city on the Pacific coast of southern California, the second largest city in the US; pop. 3,485,400 (1990). It has become a major centre of industry, film-making, and television in the 20th century, its metropolitan area having expanded to include towns such as Beverly Hills, Hollywood, Santa Monica, and Pasadena.

lose /luːz/ ▶ **verb** (past and past participle **lost**) [with obj.]
1 be deprived of or cease to have or retain (something): *I've lost my appetite* | *Linda was very upset about losing her job* | *the company may find itself losing customers to cheaper rivals.*
■ [with two objs] cause (someone) to fail to gain or retain (something): *you lost me my appointment at London University.* ■ be deprived of (a close relative or friend) through their death or as a result of the breaking off of a relationship: *she lost her husband in the fire.* ■ (of a pregnant woman) miscarry (a baby) or suffer the death of (a baby) during childbirth. ■ (**be lost**) be destroyed or killed, especially through accident or as a result of military action: *a fishing disaster in which 129 local men were lost.* ■ decrease in (body weight); undergo a reduction of (a specified amount of weight): *she couldn't eat and began to lose weight.* ■ waste or fail to take advantage of (time or an opportunity): *he may have lost his chance of taking over as world No. 1* | *the government* ***lost no time in*** *holding fresh elections.* ■ (of a watch or clock) become slow by (a specified amount of time): *this clock will neither gain nor lose a second.* ■ (**lose it**) informal lose control of one's temper or emotions: *in the end I completely lost it—I was screaming at them.*
2 become unable to find (something or someone): *I've lost the car keys.*
■ cease or become unable to follow (the right route): *the clouds came down and we lost the path.* ■ evade or shake off (a pursuer): *he came after me waving his revolver, but I easily lost him.* ■ N. Amer. informal get rid of (an undesirable person or thing): *lose that creep!* ■ informal cause (someone) to be unable to follow an argument or explanation: *sorry, Tim, you've lost me there.* ■ (**lose oneself in**/**be lost in**) be or become deeply absorbed in (something): *he had been lost in thought.*
3 fail to win (a game or contest): *England lost eight out of the eleven one-day internationals* | [no obj.] *they lost by one vote* | [as adj. **losing**] *the losing side.*
■ [with two objs] cause (someone) to fail to win (a game or contest): *that shot lost him the championship.*
4 earn less (money) than one is spending or has spent: *the paper is losing £1.5 million a month* | [no obj.] *he lost heavily on box office flops.*
– PHRASES **have nothing to lose** be in a situation that is so bad that even if an action or undertaking is unsuccessful it cannot make it any worse. **lose face** come to be less highly respected: *he was trying to work out how he could go back home without losing face.* **lose heart** become discouraged. **lose one's heart to** see **HEART**. **lose height** (of an aircraft) descend to a lower level in flight. **lose one's mind** (or **one's marbles**) informal go insane. **lose sleep** [usu. with negative] worry about something: *no one is losing any sleep over what he thinks of us.* **lose one's** (or **the**) **way** become lost; fail to reach one's destination. ■ figurative no longer have a clear idea of one's purpose or motivation in an activity or business: *the company has lost its way and should pull out of general insurance.* **you can't lose** used to express the conviction that someone must inevitably profit from an action or undertaking: *we're offering them for only £2.50—you can't lose!*
– ORIGIN Old English *losian* 'perish, destroy', also 'become unable to find', from *los* 'loss'.

USAGE The verb **lose** is sometimes mistakenly written as **loose**, as in *this would cause them to **loose** 20 to 50 per cent* (correct form is … *to **lose** 20 to 50 per cent*). There is a word **loose**, but it is very different—normally an adjective, meaning 'untethered; not held in place; detached', as in ***loose** cobbles*; *the handle was **loose***; *set **loose***.

▶ **lose out** be deprived of an opportunity to do or obtain something; be disadvantaged: *youngsters who were* ***losing out on*** *regular schooling.* ■ be beaten in competition or replaced by: *they were disappointed at losing out to Berlin in the semi-finals.*

losel /'ləʊz(ə)l/ archaic or dialect ▶ **noun** a worthless person.
▶ **adjective** good-for-nothing; worthless.
– ORIGIN late Middle English: apparently from *los-*, stem of obsolete *lese* 'lose', + **-EL**.

loser ▶ **noun** a person or thing that loses or has lost something, especially a game or contest.
■ [with adj.] a person who accepts defeat with good or bad grace, as specified: *we won fair and square—they should concede that bravely and be good losers.* ■ a person or thing that is put at a disadvantage by a particular situation or course of action: *children are the losers when politicians keep fiddling around with education.* ■ informal a person who fails frequently or is generally unsuccessful in life: *a ragtag community of rejects and losers.* ■ Bridge a card that is expected to be part of a losing trick.
– PHRASES **be on** (or **on to**) **a loser** informal be involved in a course of action that is bound to fail.

losing battle ▶ **noun** [in sing.] a struggle that seems certain to end in failure: *the police force is fighting a losing battle against a rising tide of crime.*

loss ▶ **noun** [mass noun] the fact or process of losing something or someone: *avoiding loss of time* | [count noun] *funding cuts will lead to job losses* | [in combination] *loss-making industries.*
■ the state or feeling of grief when deprived of someone or something of value: *I feel a terrible sense of loss.* ■ [in sing.] a person who or thing that is badly missed when lost: *he will be a great* ***loss to*** *many people.*
– PHRASES **at a loss 1** puzzled or uncertain what to think, say, or do: [with infinitive] *she became popular, and was at a loss to know why* | *he was* ***at a loss for*** *words.* **2** making less money than is spent buying, operating, or producing something: *a railway running at a loss.*
– ORIGIN Old English *los* 'destruction', of Germanic origin; related to Old Norse *los* 'breaking up of the ranks of an army' and **LOOSE**; later probably a back-formation from *lost*, past participle of **LOSE**.

loss adjuster ▶ **noun** an insurance agent who assesses the amount of compensation that should be paid after a person has claimed on their insurance policy.

loss-leader ▶ **noun** a product sold at a loss to attract customers.

lossless ▶ **adjective** having or involving no dissipation of electrical or electromagnetic energy.
■Computing of or relating to data compression without loss of information.

lossy ▶ **adjective** having or involving the dissipation of electrical or electromagnetic energy.
■Computing of or relating to data compression in which unnecessary information is discarded.

lost past and past participle of **LOSE**. ▶ **adjective**
1 unable to find one's way; not knowing one's whereabouts: *Help! We're lost! | they* **got lost** *in the fog.*
■unable to be found: *he turned up with my lost golf clubs.* ■ [predic.] (of a person) very confused or insecure or in great difficulties: *she stood there clutching a drink, feeling completely lost | I'd* **be lost without** *her.*
2 denoting something that has been taken away or cannot be recovered: *if only one could recapture one's lost youth.*
■(of time or an opportunity) not used advantageously; wasted: *the decision meant a lost opportunity to create 200 jobs.* ■ having perished or been destroyed: *a memorial to the lost crewmen.*
3 (of a game or contest) in which a defeat has been sustained: *the lost election of 1979.*
– PHRASES **all is not lost** used to suggest that there is still some chance of success or recovery. **be lost for words** be so surprised, confused, or upset that one cannot think what to say. **be lost on** fail to influence or be noticed or appreciated by (someone): *the significance of his remarks was not lost on Scott.* **get lost** [often in imperative] informal go away (used as an expression of anger or impatience): *Why don't you leave me alone? Go on, get lost!* **give someone up for lost** stop expecting that a missing person will be found alive. **make up for lost time** do something faster or more often in order to compensate for not having done it quickly or often enough before.

lost cause ▶ **noun** a person or thing that can no longer hope to succeed or be changed for the better.

lost generation ▶ **noun** the generation reaching maturity during and just after the First World War, a high proportion of whose men were killed during those years.
■an unfulfilled generation coming to maturity during a period of instability.
– ORIGIN phrase applied by Gertrude Stein to disillusioned young American writers, such as Ernest Hemingway, Scott Fitzgerald, and Ezra Pound, who went to live in Paris in the 1920s.

lost labour ▶ **noun** [mass noun] archaic fruitless effort.

Lost Tribes (also **Ten Lost Tribes of Israel**) the ten tribes of Israel taken away *c.*720 BC by Sargon II to captivity in Assyria (2 Kings 17:6), from which they are believed never to have returned, while the tribes of Benjamin and Judah remained. See also **TRIBES OF ISRAEL**.

lost wax ▶ **noun** another term for **CIRE PERDUE**.

Lot[1] /lɒt, ləʊ/ a river of southern France, which rises in the Auvergne and flows 480 km (300 miles) west to meet the Garonne south-east of Bordeaux.

Lot[2] /lɒt/ (in the Bible) the nephew of Abraham, who was allowed to escape from the destruction of Sodom (Gen. 19). His wife, who disobeyed orders and looked back, was turned into a pillar of salt.

lot ▶ **pronoun** (**a lot** or **lots**) informal a large number or amount; a great deal: *there are* **a lot of** *actors in the cast | they took* **a lot of** *abuse | a lot can happen in eight months | we had* **lots of** *fun.*
■(**the lot** or **the whole lot**) chiefly Brit. the whole number or quantity that is involved or implied: *you might as well take the whole lot.*
▶ **adverb** (**a lot** or **lots**) informal a great deal; much: *he played tennis a lot last year | thanks a lot | I feel* **a whole lot** *better.*
▶ **noun 1** [treated as sing. or pl.] informal a particular group, collection, or set of people or things: *it's just one lot of rich people stealing from another lot |* **you lot** *think you're clever, don't you?*
■[with adj.] chiefly Brit. a group or person of a specified kind (generally used in a derogatory or dismissive way): *an inefficient lot, our Council | he was known as a ne'er-do-well and a bad lot.*
2 an article or set of articles for sale at an auction: *nineteen lots failed to sell | the picture is lot 16.*
3 [mass noun] the making of a decision by a method that involves random selection, in particular by the choosing of one from a number of pieces of folded paper or similar, one of which has a concealed mark: *officers were elected rather than selected* **by lot**.
■[in sing.] the choice resulting from such a process: *eventually the lot fell on the King's daughter.*
4 [in sing.] a person's luck or condition in life, especially as determined by fate or destiny: *schemes to improve the lot of the disadvantaged.*
5 chiefly N. Amer. a plot of land assigned for sale or for a particular use: *a vacant lot | a fenced-off back lot.*
■(also **parking lot**) a car park. ■ an area of land near a film studio where outside filming may be done. ■ the area at a car dealership where cars for sale are kept.
▶ **verb** (**lotted**, **lotting**) [with obj.] divide (items) into lots for sale at an auction: *the contents have already been lotted up, and the auction takes place on Monday.*
– PHRASES **all over the lot** US informal in a state of confusion or disorganization. **draw** (or **cast**) **lots** decide by lot: *we drew lots to decide the order.* **fall to someone's lot** become someone's task or responsibility. **throw in one's lot with** decide to ally oneself closely with and share the fate of (a person or group).
– ORIGIN Old English *hlot* (noun), of Germanic origin; related to Dutch *lot*, German *Los*. The original meanings were sense 3 and (by extension) the sense 'a portion assigned to someone'; the latter gave rise to the other noun senses. The pronoun and adverb uses date from the early 19th cent.

USAGE 1 The expressions **a lot of** and **lots of** are used before nouns to mean 'a large number or amount of'. In common with other words denoting quantities, **lot** itself does not normally function as a head noun, meaning that it does not itself determine whether the following verb is singular or plural. Thus, although **lot** is singular in *a lot of people*, the verb which follows is not singular. In this case the word **people** acts as the head noun and, being plural, ensures that the following verb is also plural: *a lot of people* **were** *assembled* (not *a lot of people* **was** *assembled*). See also **usage** at **NUMBER**.
2 A lot of and **lots of** are very common in speech and writing but they still have a distinctly informal feel and are generally not considered acceptable for formal English, where alternatives such as **many** or **a large number** are used instead.
3 Written as one word **alot** is incorrect, although not uncommon.

lota /ˈləʊtə/ ▶ **noun** Indian a round water pot, typically of polished brass.
– ORIGIN from Hindi *loṭā*.

lo-tech ▶ **adjective** & **noun** variant spelling of **LOW-TECH**.

loth ▶ **adjective** variant spelling of **LOATH**.

Lothario /ləˈθɛːrɪəʊ, -ˈθɑː-/ ▶ **noun** (pl. **-os**) a man who behaves selfishly and irresponsibly in his sexual relationships with women.
– ORIGIN from a character in Rowe's *Fair Penitent* (1703).

Lothian /ˈləʊðɪən/ a former local government region in central Scotland, now divided into **East Lothian**, **Midlothian**, and **West Lothian**.

Loti /lɒˈtiː/, Pierre (1850–1923), French novelist; pseudonym of *Louis Marie Julien Viaud*. His voyages as a naval officer provided the background for works such as *Pêcheur d'Islande* (1886) and *Matelot* (1893).

loti /ˈləʊti, ˈluːti/ ▶ **noun** (pl. **maloti** /məˈləʊti, -ˈluːti/) the basic monetary unit of Lesotho, equal to 100 lisente.
– ORIGIN Sesotho.

lotic /ˈləʊtɪk/ ▶ **adjective** Ecology (of organisms or habitats) inhabiting or situated in rapidly moving fresh water. Compare with **LENTIC**.
– ORIGIN early 20th cent.: from Latin *lotus* 'washing' + **-IC**.

lotion ▶ **noun** [mass noun] a thick, smooth liquid preparation designed to be applied to the skin for medicinal or cosmetic purposes.
– ORIGIN late Middle English: from Old French, or from Latin *lotio(n-)*, from *lot-* 'washed', from the verb *lavare*.

Lotka–Volterra /ˌlɒtkəvɒlˈtɛrə/ ▶ **adjective** [attrib.] Ecology of or relating to a mathematical model which uses coupled differential equations to describe and predict the variation of two interacting populations, especially a predator and a prey species.
– ORIGIN 1950s: from the names of Alfred J. *Lotka* (1880–1949), Austrian-born American statistician, and Vito *Volterra* (1860–1940), Italian mathematician.

lotta (also **lotsa**) informal ▶ **contraction of** lots of (representing non-standard use): *I saw a lotta courage out there, and a lotta hard work.*

lottery ▶ **noun** (pl. **-ies**) a means of raising money by selling numbered tickets and giving prizes to the holders of numbers drawn at random.
■[in sing.] a process or thing whose success or outcome is governed by chance: *the lottery of life.*
– ORIGIN mid 16th cent.: probably from Dutch *loterij*, from *lot* 'lot'.

Lotto /ˈlɒtəʊ/, Lorenzo (*c.*1480–1556), Italian painter. He chiefly painted religious subjects, though he also produced a number of notable portraits, such as *A Lady as Lucretia* (*c.*1533).

lotto ▶ **noun** [mass noun] a children's game similar to bingo, in which numbered or illustrated counters or cards are drawn by the players.
■chiefly N. Amer. a lottery.
– ORIGIN late 18th cent.: from Italian.

lotus ▶ **noun 1** either of two large water lilies:
• (also **sacred lotus**) a red-flowered Asian lily (*Nelumbo nucifera*, family Nelumbonaceae). • (also **Egyptian lotus**) a lily regarded as sacred in ancient Egypt (the white-flowered *Nymphaea lotus* and the blue-flowered *N. caerulea*, family Nymphaeaceae).
2 (in Greek mythology) a legendary plant whose fruit induces a dreamy forgetfulness and an unwillingness to depart.
■the flower of the sacred lotus as a symbol in Asian art and religion.
■short for **LOTUS POSITION**.
– ORIGIN late 15th cent. (denoting a type of clover or trefoil, described by Homer as food for horses): via Latin from Greek *lōtos*, of Semitic origin. The term was used by classical writers to denote various trees and plants; the legendary plant (sense 2) mentioned by Homer, was thought by later Greek writers to be *Ziziphus lotus*, a relative of the jujube.

lotusbird ▶ **noun** Austral. a jacana with a pink comb on the forehead, found in Australasia and Indonesia.
• *Irediparra gallinacea*, family Jacanidae. Alternative name: **comb-crested jacana**.

lotus-eater ▶ **noun** a person who spends their time indulging in pleasure and luxury rather than dealing with practical concerns.
– DERIVATIVES **lotus-eating** adjective.

lotus position (also **lotus posture**) ▶ **noun** a cross-legged position for meditation, with the feet resting on the thighs.

Lotus Sutra ▶ **noun** Buddhism one of the most important texts in Mahayana Buddhism, significant particularly in China and Japan and given special veneration by the Nichiren sect.

Louangphrabang variant spelling of **LUANG PRABANG**.

louche /luːʃ/ ▶ **adjective** disreputable or sordid in a rakish or appealing way: *the louche world of the theatre.*
– ORIGIN early 19th cent.: from French, literally 'squinting'.

loud ▶ **adjective** producing or capable of producing much noise; easily audible: *they were kept awake by loud music | she had a loud voice.*
■strong or emphatic in expression: *there were loud protests from the lumber barons.* ■ vulgarly obtrusive; flashy: *a man in a loud checked suit.*
▶ **adverb** with a great deal of volume: *they shouted as loud as they could.*
– PHRASES **out loud** aloud; audibly: *she laughed out loud.*
– DERIVATIVES **louden** verb, **loudly** adverb, **loudness** noun.
– ORIGIN Old English *hlūd*, of West Germanic origin; related to Dutch *luid*, German *laut*, from an Indo-European root meaning 'hear', shared by Greek *kluein* 'hear', *klutos* 'famous' and Latin *cluere* 'be famous'.

loudhailer ▶ **noun** chiefly Brit. an electronic device used to amplify the sound of a person's voice so that it can be heard at a distance; a megaphone.

loudmouth ▶ **noun** informal a person who tends to talk too much in an offensive or tactless way.
– DERIVATIVES **loud-mouthed** adjective.

loudspeaker ▶ **noun** an apparatus that converts electrical impulses into sound, typically as part of a public address system.

Lou Gehrig's disease ▶ **noun** [mass noun] a form of motor neuron disease; amyotrophic lateral sclerosis.
– ORIGIN 1940s: named after H. L. **GEHRIG**.

lough /lɒk, lɒx/ ▶ **noun** Anglo-Irish spelling of **LOCH**.
– ORIGIN Middle English: from Irish *loch*. The spelling *lough* survived in Ireland but the pronunciation was replaced by that of the Irish word.

Loughborough /ˈlʌfb(ə)rə/ a town in Leicestershire, on the River Soar north of Leicester; pop. 46,120 (1981).

Louis[1] /ˈluːi/ the name of eighteen kings of France:
■Louis I (778–840), son of Charlemagne, king of the West Franks and Holy Roman Emperor 814–40.
■Louis II (846–79), reigned 877–9.
■Louis III (863–82), son of Louis II, reigned 879–82.
■Louis IV (921–54), reigned 936–54.
■Louis V (967–87), reigned 979–87.
■Louis VI (1081–1137), reigned 1108–37.
■Louis VII (1120–80), reigned 1137–80.
■Louis VIII (1187–1226), reigned 1223–6.
■Louis IX (1214–70), son of Louis VIII, reigned 1226–70; canonized as **St Louis**. He conducted two unsuccessful crusades, dying of plague in Tunis during the second. Feast day, 25 August.
■Louis X (1289–1316), reigned 1314–16.
■Louis XI (1423–83), son of Charles VII, reigned 1461–83. He continued his father's work in laying the foundations of a united France ruled by an absolute monarchy.
■Louis XII (1462–1515), reigned 1498–1515.
■Louis XIII (1601–43), son of Henry IV of France, reigned 1610–43. During his minority the country was ruled by his mother Marie de Médicis. From 1624 he was heavily influenced in policy-making by his chief minister Cardinal Richelieu.
■Louis XIV (1638–1715), son of Louis XIII, reigned 1643–1715; known as **the Sun King**. His reign represented the high point of the Bourbon dynasty and of French power in Europe, and in this period French art and literature flourished. His almost constant wars of expansion united Europe against him, however, and gravely weakened France's financial position.
■Louis XV (1710–74), great-grandson and successor of Louis XIV, reigned 1715–74. He led France into the Seven Years War (1756–63).
■Louis XVI (1754–93), grandson and successor of Louis XV, reigned 1774–92. His minor concessions and reforms in the face of the emerging French Revolution proved disastrous. As the Revolution became more extreme, he was executed with his wife, Marie Antoinette, and the monarchy was abolished.
■Louis XVII (1785–95), son of Louis XVI, titular king who died in prison during the Revolution.
■Louis XVIII (1755–1824), brother of Louis XVI, reigned 1814–24. After his nephew Louis XVII's death he became titular king in exile until the fall of Napoleon in 1814, when he returned to Paris on the summons of Talleyrand and was officially restored to the throne.

Louis[2] /ˈluːɪs/, Joe (1914–81), American boxer; born *Joseph Louis Barrow*; known as the **Brown Bomber**. He was heavyweight champion of the world 1937–49, defending his title twenty-five times during that period.

louis /ˈluːi/ (also **louis d'or** /-ˈdɔː/) ▶ **noun** (pl. same /ˈluːɪz/) a gold coin issued in France between 1640 and 1793.
■another term for **NAPOLEON** (in sense 1).
– ORIGIN from *Louis*, the name of many kings of France.

Louis I (1326–82), king of Hungary 1342–82 and of Poland 1370–82; known as **Louis the Great**. Under his rule Hungary became a powerful state; he fought two successful wars against Venice (1357–8; 1378–81), and the rulers of Serbia, Wallachia, Moldavia, and Bulgaria became his vassals.

Louis, St, Louis IX of France (see **LOUIS**[1]).

Louisiana /luːˌiːzɪˈanə/ a state in the southern US, on the Gulf of Mexico; pop. 4,219,970 (1990); capital, Baton Rouge. Louisiana originally denoted the large region of the Mississippi basin claimed for France by the explorer La Salle in 1682. It was sold by the French and sold to the US in the Louisiana Purchase of 1803. The smaller area now known as Louisiana became the 18th state in 1812.
– DERIVATIVES **Louisianan** (also **Louisianian**) adjective & noun.
– ORIGIN named in honour of *Louis XIV*.

Louisiana Purchase the territory sold by France to the US in 1803, comprising the western part of the Mississippi valley and including the modern state of Louisiana.

Louis Philippe /ˌluːɪ fɪˈliːp/ (1773–1850), king of France 1830–48. After the restoration of the Bourbons he became the focus for liberal discontent and was made king, replacing Charles X. His regime was gradually undermined by radical discontent and eventually overthrown.

Louis the Great, Louis I of Hungary (see **LOUIS I**).

Louisville /ˈluːɪvɪl/ an industrial city and river port in northern Kentucky, on the Ohio River just south of the border with Indiana; pop. 269,060 (1990). It is the site of the annual Kentucky Derby.

lounge ▶ **verb** [no obj., with adverbial of place] lie, sit, or stand in a relaxed or lazy way: *several students were lounging about reading papers.*
▶ **noun 1** a public room in a hotel, theatre, or club in which to sit and relax.
■a spacious area in an airport with seats for waiting passengers: *the departure lounge.* ■ Brit. a sitting room in a house.
2 [in sing.] Brit. an act or spell of lounging.
– ORIGIN early 16th cent. (in the sense 'move indolently'): perhaps symbolic of slow movement. Sense 1 of the noun dates from the late 19th cent.

lounge bar ▶ **noun** Brit. the smarter and more lavishly furnished bar in a public house or hotel. Compare with **PUBLIC BAR**.

lounge lizard ▶ **noun** informal an idle man who spends his time in places frequented by rich and fashionable people.

lounger ▶ **noun** a comfortable piece of furniture for relaxing on, especially an outdoor chair that adjusts or extends, allowing a person to recline.
■a person spending their time lazily or in a relaxed way.

lounge suit ▶ **noun** Brit. a man's suit consisting of a matching jacket and trousers, worn during the day, especially in the workplace.

loup /laʊp/ ▶ **verb** & **noun** Scottish and northern English variant of **LEAP**.
– ORIGIN Middle English: from Old Norse *hlaupa* (verb), *hlaup* (noun).

loupe /luːp/ ▶ **noun** a small magnifying glass used by jewellers and watchmakers.
– ORIGIN late 19th cent.: from French.

louping-ill /ˈlaʊpɪŋɪl/ ▶ **noun** [mass noun] a viral disease attacking animals, especially sheep, which is transmitted by ticks and causes staggering and jumping.
– ORIGIN late Middle English: from **LOUP** (because of the symptom of spasmodic jumping) + the noun **ILL**.

lour /ˈlaʊə/ (also **lower**) ▶ **verb** [no obj.] look angry or sullen; frown: *the lofty statue lours at patients in the infirmary.*
■(of the sky, weather, or landscape) look dark and threatening: [as adj. **louring**] *a day of louring cloud.*
▶ **noun** a scowl.
■a dark and gloomy appearance of the sky, weather or landscape.
– DERIVATIVES **louringly** adverb, **loury** adjective.
– ORIGIN Middle English: of unknown origin.

lourdan /ˈlʊəd(ə)n/ ▶ **noun** & **adjective** variant spelling of **LURDAN**.

Lourdes /lʊəd, French luʀd/ a town in SW France, at the foot of the Pyrenees; pop. 16,580 (1990). It has been a major place of Roman Catholic pilgrimage since in 1858 a young peasant girl, Marie Bernarde Soubirous (St Bernadette), claimed to have had a series of visions of the Virgin Mary.

Lourenço Marques /ləˌrɛnsəʊ ˈmɑːks/ former name (until 1976) for **MAPUTO**.

lourie /ˈlaʊəri/ (also **loerie**) ▶ **noun** (pl. **-ies**) S. African another term for **TURACO** and **GO-AWAY BIRD**.
– ORIGIN Afrikaans, from Dutch *lori*. Compare with **LORY**.

louse ▶ **noun 1** (pl. **lice**) either of two small wingless parasitic insects that live on the skin of mammals and birds:
• (**sucking louse**) an insect with piercing mouthparts, found only on mammals (order Anoplura or Siphunculata). See also **BODY LOUSE**, **HEAD LOUSE**. • (**biting louse**) an insect with a large head and jaws, found chiefly on birds (order Mallophaga).
■used in names of small invertebrates that parasitize aquatic animals or infest plants, e.g. **fish louse**.
2 (pl. **louses**) informal a contemptible or unpleasant person.
▶ **verb** [with obj.] **1** (**louse something up**) informal spoil or ruin something: *he loused up my promotion chances.*
2 archaic remove lice from.
– ORIGIN Old English *lūs*, (plural) *lȳs*, of Germanic origin; related to Dutch *luis*, German *Laus*.

louse fly ▶ **noun** a flattened bloodsucking fly which may have reduced or absent wings and typically spends much of its life on one individual of the host species.
• Family Hippoboscidae: several genera.

louser ▶ **noun** informal, chiefly Irish a mean, unpleasant, or contemptible person.

lousewort ▶ **noun** a partially parasitic herbaceous plant of the figwort family, typically favouring damp habitats. It is native to both Eurasia and North America and was formerly reputed to harbour lice.
• Genus *Pedicularis*, family Scrophulariaceae: several species, including the red rattle.

lousy ▶ **adjective** (**lousier**, **lousiest**) **1** informal very poor or bad; disgusting: *the service is usually lousy* | *lousy weather.*
■[predic.] ill; in poor physical condition: *she felt lousy.*
2 infested with lice.
■[predic.] (**lousy with**) informal teeming with (something regarded as bad or undesirable): *the town is lousy with tourists.*
– DERIVATIVES **lousily** adverb, **lousiness** noun.

lout ▶ **noun** an uncouth or aggressive man or boy.
– DERIVATIVES **loutish** adjective, **loutishly** adverb, **loutishness** noun.
– ORIGIN mid 16th cent.: perhaps from archaic *lout* 'to bow down', of Germanic origin.

Louth /laʊθ/ a county of the Republic of Ireland, on the east coast in the province of Leinster; county town, Dundalk.

Louvain /luvɛ̃/ French name for **LEUVEN**.

louvar /ˈluːvɑː/ ▶ **noun** a large brightly coloured fish with a distinctive high forehead. It lives in warm open seas, feeding on jellyfishes and comb jellies.
• *Luvarus imperialis*, the only member of the family Luvaridae.

Louvre /ˈluːvr(ə)/, French luvʀ/ the principal museum and art gallery of France, in Paris, housed in the former royal palace built by Francis I. The Louvre holds the Mona Lisa and the Venus de Milo.

louvre /ˈluːvə/ (US also **louver**) ▶ **noun 1** each of a set of angled slats or flat strips fixed or hung at regular intervals in a door, shutter, or screen to allow air or light to pass through.
2 a domed structure on a roof, with side openings for ventilation.
– DERIVATIVES **louvred** adjective.
– ORIGIN Middle English (in sense 2): from Old French *lover*, *lovier* 'skylight', probably of Germanic origin and related to **LODGE**.

lovable (also **loveable**) ▶ **adjective** inspiring or deserving love or affection.
– DERIVATIVES **lovability** noun, **lovableness** noun, **lovably** adverb.

lovage /ˈlʌvɪdʒ/ ▶ **noun** a large edible white-flowered plant of the parsley family.
• Several species in the family Umbelliferae, in particular a Mediterranean herb (*Levisticum officinale*), which is chiefly used for flavouring liqueurs .
– ORIGIN Middle English *loveache*, alteration (as if from **LOVE** + obsolete *ache* 'parsley') of Old French *luvesche*, *levesche*, via late Latin *levisticum* from Latin *ligusticum*, neuter of *ligusticus* 'Ligurian'.

lovat /ˈlʌvət/ (also **lovat green**) ▶ **noun** [mass noun] a muted green colour used especially in tweed and woollen garments.
– ORIGIN early 20th cent.: from *Lovat*, a place name in Highland Scotland.

love ▶ **noun 1** [mass noun] an intense feeling of deep affection: *babies fill parents with intense feelings of love* | *their **love for** their country.*
■a deep romantic or sexual attachment to someone: *it was love at first sight* | *they were both **in love with** her* | *we were slowly **falling in love**.* ■ (**Love**) a personified figure of love, often represented as Cupid. ■ a great interest and pleasure in something: *his **love for** football* | *we share a **love of** music.* ■ affectionate greetings conveyed to someone on one's behalf. ■ a formula

for ending an affectionate letter: *take care, lots of love, Judy.*
2 a person or thing that one loves: *she was **the love of his life** | their two great loves are tobacco and whisky.*
■Brit. informal a friendly form of address: *it's all right, love.* ■**(a love)** informal used to express affectionate approval for someone: *don't fret, there's a love.*
3 [mass noun] (in tennis, squash, and some other sports) a score of zero; nil: *love fifteen | he was down two sets to love.* [ORIGIN: apparently from the phrase *play for love* (i.e. the love of the game, not for money); folk etymology has connected the word with French *l'oeuf* 'egg', from the resemblance in shape between an egg and a zero.]
▶**verb** [with obj.] feel a deep romantic or sexual attachment to (someone): *do you love me?*
■like very much; find pleasure in: *I'd love a cup of tea, thanks | I just love dancing |* [as adj., in combination **-loving**] *a fun-loving girl.*
– PHRASES **for love** for pleasure not profit: *he played **for the love of** the game.* **for the love of God** used to express annoyance, surprise, or urgent pleading: *for the love of God, get me out of here!* **for the love of Mike** Brit. informal used to accompany an exasperated request or to express dismay. **love me, love my dog** proverb if you love someone, you must accept everything about them, even their faults or weaknesses. **make love 1** have sexual intercourse. **2 (make love to)** dated pay amorous attention to (someone). **not for love or money** informal not for any inducement or in any circumstances: *they'll not return for love or money.* **there's no** (or **little** or **not much**) **love lost between** there is mutual dislike between (two or more people mentioned).
– DERIVATIVES **loveless** adjective, **lovelessly** adverb, **lovelessness** noun, **loveworthy** adjective.
– ORIGIN Old English *lufu*, of Germanic origin; from an Indo-European root shared by Sanskrit *lubhyati* 'desires', Latin *libet* 'it is pleasing', *libido* 'desire', also by LEAVE[2] and LIEF.

loveable ▶ **adjective** variant spelling of LOVABLE.

love affair ▶ **noun** a romantic or sexual relationship between two people, especially one that is outside marriage.
■an intense enthusiasm or liking for something: *he had a lifelong love affair with the cinema.*

love apple ▶ **noun** an old-fashioned term for a tomato.

lovebird ▶ **noun 1** a very small African and Madagascan parrot with mainly green plumage and typically a red or black face, noted for the affectionate behaviour of mated birds.
• Genus *Agapornis*, family Psittacidae: several species.
2 (lovebirds) informal an openly affectionate couple.

love bite ▶ **noun** a temporary red mark on a person's skin caused by a lover biting or sucking it as a sexual act.

love child ▶ **noun** a child born to parents who are not married to each other.

love feast ▶ **noun** historical a feast in token of fellowship among early Christians; an agape.
■a religious service or gathering imitating this, especially among early Methodists.

love game ▶ **noun 1** an episode of romantic intrigue or playful sexual contact.
2 (in tennis and similar sports) a game in which the loser makes no score.

love handles ▶ **plural noun** informal deposits of excess fat at a person's waistline.

love-hate ▶ **adjective** [attrib.] (of a relationship) characterized by ambivalent feelings of love and hate felt by one or each of two or more parties.

love-in ▶ **noun** informal, dated a gathering or party at which people are encouraged to express feelings of friendship and physical attraction, associated with the hippies of the 1960s.
– ORIGIN 1960s: originally with reference to Californian hippy gatherings.

love-in-a-mist ▶ **noun** a Mediterranean plant of the buttercup family, which bears blue flowers surrounded by delicate thread-like green bracts, giving a hazy appearance to the flowers.
• *Nigella damascena*, family Ranunculaceae.

love-in-idleness ▶ **noun** another term for HEARTSEASE.

love interest ▶ **noun** [mass noun] a theme or subsidiary plot in a story or film in which the main element is the affection of lovers.
■[count noun] an actor whose role is chiefly concerned with this.

Lovelace[1], Augusta Ada King, Countess of (1815–52), English mathematician. The daughter of Lord Byron, she became assistant to Charles Babbage and worked with him on his mechanical computer.

Lovelace[2], Richard (1618–57), English poet. A Royalist, he was imprisoned in 1642, when he probably wrote his famous poem 'To Althea, from Prison'.

love-lies-bleeding ▶ **noun** a South American plant with long drooping tassels of crimson flowers. Cultivated today as an ornamental, its seeds and leaves were formerly eaten in the Andes.
• *Amaranthus caudatus*, family Amaranthaceae.

love life ▶ **noun** the area of a person's life concerning their relationships with lovers.

Lovell /ˈlʌv(ə)l/, Sir (Alfred Charles) Bernard (b.1913), English astronomer and physicist, and pioneer of radio astronomy. He founded Manchester University's radio observatory at Jodrell Bank, where he directed the construction of the large radio telescope that is now named after him.

Lovelock, James (Ephraim) (b.1919), English scientist. He is best known for the **Gaia hypothesis**, first presented by him in 1972 and discussed in several popular books, including *Gaia* (1979).

lovelock ▶ **noun** archaic a curl of hair worn on the temple or forehead.

lovelorn ▶ **adjective** unhappy because of unrequited love.

lovely ▶ **adjective (lovelier, loveliest)** exquisitely beautiful: *you have lovely eyes | lovely views.*
■informal very pleasant or enjoyable; delightful: *we've had a lovely day | she's a lovely person.*
▶**noun** (pl. **-ies**) informal a glamorous woman or girl: *a bevy of rock lovelies.*
■used as an affectionate form of address: *don't worry, my lovely.*
– DERIVATIVES **lovelily** adverb, **loveliness** noun.
– ORIGIN Old English *luflic* (see LOVE, -LY[1]).

love match ▶ **noun** a marriage based on the mutual love of the couple rather than social or financial considerations.

love nest ▶ **noun** informal a place where two lovers spend time together, especially in secret.

lover ▶ **noun** a person having a sexual or romantic relationship with someone, especially outside marriage.
■a person who likes or enjoys something specified: *he was a great lover of cats | music lovers.*
– DERIVATIVES **loverless** adjective.

love seat ▶ **noun** a small sofa for two people, especially one designed in an S-shape so that the couple can face each other.

lovesick ▶ **adjective** in love, or missing the person one loves, so much that one is unable to act normally: *you're dripping around like some lovesick teenager.*
– DERIVATIVES **lovesickness** noun.

lovesome ▶ **adjective** poetic/literary lovely or lovable.

love vine ▶ **noun** [mass noun] N. Amer. & W. Indian the dodder, which is sometimes used medicinally and as a love charm.

lovey ▶ **noun** (pl. **-eys**) Brit. informal used as an affectionate form of address: *Ruth, lovey, are you there?*

lovey-dovey ▶ **adjective** informal very affectionate or romantic, especially excessively so: *a lovey-dovey couple.*

loving ▶ **adjective** feeling or showing love or great care: *a kind and loving father.*
▶**noun** [mass noun] the demonstration of love or great care.
– DERIVATIVES **lovingly** adverb, **lovingness** noun.

loving cup ▶ **noun** a large two-handled cup, passed round at banquets for each guest to drink from in turn.

loving kindness ▶ **noun** [mass noun] tenderness and consideration towards others.
– ORIGIN from usage in Coverdale's translation of the Psalms.

Low, Sir David (Alexander Cecil) (1891–1963), New Zealand-born British cartoonist famous for his political cartoons and for inventing the character Colonel Blimp.

low[1] ▶ **adjective 1** of less than average height from top to bottom or to the top from the ground: *the school is a long, low building | a low table.*
■situated not far above the ground, the horizon, or sea level: *the sun was low in the sky.* ■located at or near the bottom of something: *low back pain | he smashed a pane **low down** in the window.* ■(of a river or lake) below the usual water level; shallow. ■(of latitude) near the equator. ■(of women's clothing) cut so as to reveal the neck and the upper part of the breasts: *the low neckline of her blouse |* [in combination] *a low-cut black dress.* ■Phonetics (of a vowel) pronounced with the tongue held low in the mouth; open. ■(of a sound or note) deep: *his low, husky voice.*
2 below average in amount, extent, or intensity; small: *bringing up children on a low income | shops with low levels of staff and service | cook over low heat.*
■(of a substance or food) containing smaller quantities than usual of a specified ingredient: *vegetables are **low in** calories |* [in combination] *low-fat spreads.* ■(of a supply) small or reduced in quantity: *food and ammunition were **running low**.* ■having a small or reduced quantity of a supply: *they were **low on** fuel.* ■(of a sound) not loud: *they were told to keep the volume very low.*
3 ranking below other people or things in importance or class: *jobs with low status | training will be given low priority.*
■(of art or culture) considered to be inferior in quality and refinement: *the dual traditions of high and low art.* ■less good than is expected or desired; inferior: *the standard of living is low.* ■unscrupulous or dishonest: *practise a little low cunning | low tricks.* ■(of an opinion) unfavourable: *he had a low opinion of himself.*
4 [predic.] depressed or lacking in energy: *I was feeling low.*
▶**noun** a low point, level or figure: *his popularity ratings are at an all-time low.*
■a particularly bad or difficult moment: *the highs and lows of an actor's life.* ■informal a state of depression or low spirits. ■an area of low barometric pressure; a depression.
▶**adverb 1** in or into a low position or state: *she pressed on, bent low to protect her face.*
2 quietly: *we were talking low so we wouldn't wake Dean.*
■at or to a low pitch: *the sopranos have to sing rather low.*
– PHRASES **the lowest of the low** the people regarded as the most immoral or socially inferior of all.
– DERIVATIVES **lowish** adjective, **lowness** noun.
– ORIGIN Middle English: from Old Norse *lágr*, of Germanic origin; related to Dutch *laag*, also to LIE[1].

low[2] ▶ **verb** [no obj.] (of a cow) make a characteristic deep sound: [as noun **lowing**] *the lowing of cattle.*
▶**noun** a sound made by cattle; a moo.
– ORIGIN Old English *hlōwan*, of Germanic origin; related to Dutch *loeien*, from an Indo-European root shared by Latin *clamare* 'to shout'.

lowan ▶ **noun** Austral. another term for MALLEEFOWL.

lowball ▶ **noun** Baseball a ball pitched so as to pass over the plate below the level of the batter's knees.
■[as modifier] N. Amer. informal (of an estimate, bid, etc.) deceptively or unrealistically low.
– DERIVATIVES **lowballing** noun.

low-born ▶ **adjective** born to a family that has a low social status.

lowboy ▶ **noun** N. Amer. **1** a low chest or table with drawers and short legs. Compare with HIGHBOY.
2 (also **lowboy trailer**) a trailer with a low frame for transporting very tall or heavy loads.

lowbrow ▶ **adjective** not highly intellectual or cultured: *lowbrow tabloids.*
▶**noun** a person of such a type.

Low Church ▶ **adjective** of or adhering to a tradition within the Anglican Church (and some other denominations) which is Protestant in outlook and gives relatively little emphasis to ritual, sacraments, and the authority of the clergy. Compare with HIGH CHURCH, BROAD CHURCH.
▶**noun** [treated as sing. or pl.] the principles or adherents of this tradition.
– DERIVATIVES **Low Churchman** noun (pl. **-men**).

low-class ▶ **adjective** of a low or inferior standard, quality, or social class: *low-class places of amusement.*

low comedy ▶ **noun** [mass noun] comedy in which the subject and the treatment border on farce.

Low Countries the region of NW Europe comprising the Netherlands, Belgium, and Luxembourg.

low-density lipoprotein (abbrev.: **LDL**) ▶ **noun**

[mass noun] the form of lipoprotein in which cholesterol is transported in the blood.

low-down informal ▶ adjective mean and unfair: *dirty low-down tricks.*

▶ noun (**the low-down**) the true facts or relevant information about something: *get the low-down on the sit-in.*

Lowell[1] /ˈləʊəl/, Amy (Lawrence) (1874–1925), American poet. A leading imagist poet, she is known for her polyphonic prose and sensuous imagery.

Lowell[2] /ˈləʊəl/, James Russell (1819–91), American poet and critic. His works include the satirical *Biglow Papers* (1848 and 1867; prose and verse) and volumes of essays including *Among my Books* (1870).

Lowell[3] /ˈləʊəl/, Percival (1855–1916), American astronomer. Lowell inferred the existence of a ninth planet beyond Neptune, and when it was eventually discovered in 1930 it was given the name Pluto, with a symbol that also included his initials. He was the brother of Amy Lowell.

Lowell[4] /ˈləʊəl/, Robert (Traill Spence) (1917–77), American poet. His poetry, often describing his manic depression, is notable for its intense confessional nature and for its complex imagery.

low-end ▶ adjective denoting the cheaper products of a range, especially of audio or computer equipment.

lower[1] ▶ adjective comparative of **LOW**[1]. **1** less high: *the lower levels of the building | managers lower down the hierarchy.*

■ (in names of forms in schools) denoting the first of two conventionally numbered forms through which pupils pass in successive years: *he left school in the lower sixth.* ■ (of an animal or plant) showing relatively primitive or simple characteristics. ■ (often **Lower**) Geology & Archaeology denoting an older (and hence usually deeper) part of a stratigraphic division or archaeological deposit or the period in which it was formed or deposited: *Lower Cretaceous | Lower Palaeolithic.*

2 [in place names] situated to the south: *the union of Upper and Lower Egypt.*

▶ adverb in or into a lower position: *the sun sank lower.*

– DERIVATIVES **lowermost** adjective.

lower[2] ▶ verb [with obj.] move (someone or something) in a downward direction: *he watched the coffin being lowered into the ground.*

■ reduce the height, pitch, or elevation of: *she lowered her voice to a whisper.* ■ make or become less in amount, extent, or value: [with obj.] *traffic speeds must be lowered* | [no obj.] *temperatures lowered.* ■ direct (one's eyes) downwards. ■ (**lower oneself**) behave in a way that is perceived as unworthy or debased.

– PHRASES **lower the boom on** N. Amer. informal treat (someone) severely. ■ put a stop to (an activity): *let's lower the boom on high-level corruption.*

lower[3] ▶ verb & noun variant spelling of **LOUR**.

lower animals ▶ plural noun animals of relatively simple or primitive characteristics as contrasted with humans or with more advanced animals such as mammals or vertebrates.

Lower Austria a state of NE Austria; capital, St Pölten. German name **NIEDERÖSTERREICH**.

Lower California another name for **BAJA CALIFORNIA**.

Lower Canada the mainly French-speaking region of Canada around the lower St Lawrence River, in what is now southern Quebec.

lower case ▶ noun [mass noun] small letters as opposed to capital letters (upper case): *the name may be typed in lower case* | [as modifier] *lower-case letters.*

– ORIGIN referring originally to the lower of two cases of type positioned on an angled stand for use by a compositor (see **UPPER CASE**).

lower chamber ▶ noun another term for **LOWER HOUSE**.

lower class ▶ noun [treated as sing. or pl.] the social group that has the lowest status; the working class.

▶ adjective of, relating to, or characteristic of people belonging to such a group: *a lower-class area.*

lower court ▶ noun Law a court whose decisions may be overruled by another court on appeal.

lower criticism ▶ noun [mass noun] dated another term for **TEXTUAL CRITICISM** (especially as applied to the Bible, in contrast to **HIGHER CRITICISM**).

lower deck ▶ noun the deck of a ship situated immediately above the hold.

■ the petty officers and crew of a ship, collectively.

lower house ▶ noun the larger of two sections of a bicameral parliament or similar legislature, typically with elected members and having the primary responsibility for legislation.

■ (**the Lower House**) (in the UK) the House of Commons.

Lower Hutt /hʌt/ a city in New Zealand, near Wellington; pop. 63,860 (1986). It is the site of the Prime Minister's official residence, Vogel House.

lower orders ▶ plural noun dated the lower classes of society.

lower plants ▶ plural noun plants of relatively simple or primitive characteristics, especially those which are not vascular plants i.e. algae, mosses, liverworts, and sometimes fungi.

lower regions ▶ plural noun archaic hell or the underworld.

Lower Saxony a state of NW Germany; capital, Hanover. It corresponds to the north-western part of the former kingdom of Saxony. German name **NIEDERSACHSEN**.

lower school ▶ noun the section of a larger school which comprises or caters for the younger pupils, especially those below the fifth form.

lowest common denominator ▶ noun Mathematics the lowest common multiple of the denominators of several vulgar fractions.

■ figurative the broadest or most widely applicable requirement or circumstance. ■ derogatory the level of the least discriminating audience or consumer group.

lowest common multiple (abbrev.: **LCM**) ▶ noun Mathematics the lowest quantity that is a multiple of two or more given quantities (e.g. 12 is the lowest common multiple of 2, 3, and 4).

Lowestoft /ˈləʊɪstɒft/ a fishing port and resort town on the North Sea coast of eastern England, in NE Suffolk; pop. 59,875 (1981). It is the most easterly English town.

low-fi ▶ adjective variant spelling of **LO-FI**.

low frequency ▶ noun (in radio) 30–300 kilohertz.

low gear ▶ noun a gear that causes a wheeled vehicle to move slowly, due to a low ratio between the speed of the wheels and that of the mechanism driving them.

Low German ▶ noun [mass noun] a vernacular language spoken in much of northern Germany, more closely related to Dutch than to standard German. Also called **PLATTDEUTSCH**.

low-grade ▶ adjective of low quality or strength: *low-grade steel | low-grade fuels.*

■ at a low level in a salary or employment structure: *low-grade clerical jobs.* ■ (of a medical condition) of a less serious kind; minor: *a low-grade malignancy.*

low-impact ▶ adjective [attrib.] **1** denoting exercises, typically aerobics, designed to put little or no harmful stress on the body.

2 (of an activity, industry, or product) affecting or altering the environment as little as possible.

low-key ▶ adjective not elaborate, showy, or intensive; modest or restrained: *their marriage was a very quiet, low-key affair.*

■ Art & Photography having a predominance of dark or muted tones.

lowland /ˈləʊlənd/ ▶ noun [mass noun] (also **lowlands**) low-lying country: *economic power gravitated towards the lowlands* | [as modifier] *lowland farming.*

■ (**the Lowlands**) the region of Scotland lying south and east of the Highlands.

– DERIVATIVES **lowlander** (also **Lowlander**) noun.

Low Latin ▶ noun [mass noun] medieval and later forms of Latin.

low latitudes ▶ plural noun regions near the equator.

low-level ▶ adjective situated relatively near or below ground level: *low-level flying was banned.*

■ of or showing a small degree of some measurable quantity, for example radioactivity: *the dumping of low-level waste.* ■ of relatively little importance, scope, or prominence; basic: *opportunities to progress beyond low-level jobs.* ■ Computing of or relating to programming languages or operations which are relatively close to machine code in form.

low life ▶ noun [mass noun] people or activities characterized as being disreputable and often criminal: *crackheads, loafers, and general Nineties low life.*

■ (**lowlife**) [count noun] informal a person of such a kind.

– DERIVATIVES **low-lifer** noun.

lowlight ▶ noun **1** (**lowlights**) darker streaks in a person's hair produced by dyeing.

2 informal a particularly disappointing or dull event or feature.

– ORIGIN early 20th cent.: from **LOW**[1], suggested by **HIGHLIGHT**.

low-loader ▶ noun Brit. a lorry with a low floor and no sides, for transporting heavy loads.

lowly ▶ adjective (**lowlier**, **lowliest**) low in status or importance; humble: *she'd been too good for her lowly position.*

■ (of an organism) primitive or simple.

▶ adverb to a low degree; in a low manner: *lowly paid workers.*

– DERIVATIVES **lowlily** adverb, **lowliness** noun.

low-lying ▶ adjective at low altitude above sea level: *flooding problems in low-lying areas.*

Low Mass ▶ noun (in the Catholic Church) Mass with no music and a minimum of ceremony.

low-minded ▶ adjective vulgar or sordid in mind or character.

– DERIVATIVES **low-mindedness** noun.

low-pass ▶ adjective [attrib.] Electronics (of a filter) transmitting all frequencies below a certain value.

low-pitched ▶ adjective **1** (of a sound or voice) deep or relatively quiet.

2 (of a roof) having only a slight slope.

low profile ▶ noun [in sing.] a position of avoiding or not attracting much attention or publicity: *he's not the sort of politician to keep a low profile.*

▶ adjective **1** avoiding attention or publicity: *a low-profile campaign.*

2 (of an object) lower or slimmer than is usual for objects of its type.

■ (of a motor-vehicle tyre) of smaller diameter and greater width than usual, for high-performance use.

low relief ▶ noun see **RELIEF** (sense 4).

low-res ▶ adjective variant spelling of **LO-RES**.

low-residue ▶ adjective (of a meal or diet) designed to produce relatively little faeces and urine.

low-rider ▶ noun US a customized vehicle with hydraulic jacks that allow the chassis to be lowered nearly to the road.

– DERIVATIVES **low-riding** noun.

low-rise ▶ adjective (of a building) having few storeys: *low-rise apartment blocks.*

▶ noun a building having few storeys.

Lowry[1] /ˈlaʊəri/, (Clarence) Malcolm (1909–57), English novelist. His experiences living in Mexico in the 1930s provided the background for his symbolic semi-autobiographical novel *Under the Volcano* (1947).

Lowry[2] /ˈlaʊəri/, L. S. (1887–1976), English painter; full name *Laurence Stephen Lowry*. He painted small matchstick figures set against the iron and brick expanse of urban and industrial landscapes, settings provided by his life in Salford, near Manchester.

low season ▶ noun [in sing.] Brit. the least popular time of year at a resort, hotel, or tourist attraction, when prices are lowest:

low spirits ▶ plural noun a feeling of sadness and despondency: *he was in low spirits.*

– DERIVATIVES **low-spirited** adjective, **low-spiritedness** noun.

Low Sunday ▶ noun the Sunday after Easter.

– ORIGIN perhaps so named in contrast to the high days of Holy Week and Easter.

low-tech (also **lo-tech**) ▶ adjective involved in, employing, or requiring only low technology: *low-tech water-purifying and solar-heating systems.*

▶ noun (**low tech**) short for **LOW TECHNOLOGY**.

low technology ▶ noun [mass noun] less advanced or relatively unsophisticated technological development or equipment.

low tension (also **low voltage**) ▶ noun an electrical potential not large enough to cause injury or damage if diverted.

low tide ▶ noun the state of the tide when at its lowest level: *islets visible at low tide.*

■ figurative a low or bad point: *the larder had hit low tide.*

low water ▶ noun another term for **LOW TIDE**.

low-water mark ▶ noun the level reached by the

sea at low tide, or by a lake or river during a drought or dry season.
■ a minimum recorded level or value: *the market was approaching its low-water mark.*

Low Week ▶ noun the week that begins with Low Sunday.

low-yield ▶ adjective producing little; giving a low return: *low-yield investment.*
■ (of a nuclear weapon) having a relatively low explosive force.

lox[1] /lɒks/ ▶ noun [mass noun] liquid oxygen.
– ORIGIN early 20th cent.: acronym from *liquid oxygen explosive*, later interpreted as being from *liquid oxygen.*

lox[2] /lɒks/ ▶ noun [mass noun] N. Amer. smoked salmon.
– ORIGIN 1940s: from Yiddish *laks.*

loxodrome /'lɒksədrəʊm/ ▶ noun another term for RHUMB (in sense 1).
– DERIVATIVES **loxodromic** adjective.

loyal ▶ adjective giving or showing firm and constant support or allegiance to a person or institution: *he remained loyal to the government | loyal service.*
– DERIVATIVES **loyally** adverb.
– ORIGIN mid 16th cent.: from French, via Old French *loial* from Latin *legalis* (see LEGAL).

loyalist ▶ noun a person who remains loyal to the established ruler or government, especially in the face of a revolt.
■ (**Loyalist**) a supporter of union between Great Britain and Northern Ireland. ■ (**Loyalist**) a colonist of the American revolutionary period who supported the British cause.
– DERIVATIVES **loyalism** noun.

loyal toast ▶ noun a toast proposed and drunk to the sovereign of one's country.

loyalty ▶ noun (pl. **-ies**) [mass noun] the quality of being loyal to someone or something: *his extreme loyalty to the Crown.*
■ [count noun] (often **loyalties**) a strong feeling of support or allegiance: *rows with in-laws are distressing because they cause divided loyalties.*

loyalty card ▶ noun Brit. an identity card issued by a retailer to its customers as part of a consumer incentive scheme, whereby credits are accumulated for future discounts every time a transaction is recorded.

Loyalty Islands a group of islands in the SW Pacific, forming part of the French overseas territory of New Caledonia; pop. 17,910 (1989).

lozenge /'lɒzɪn(d)ʒ/ ▶ noun a rhombus or diamond shape.
■ a small medicinal tablet, originally of this shape, taken for sore throats and dissolved in the mouth: *throat lozenges.* ■ Heraldry a charge in the shape of a solid diamond, in particular one on which the arms of an unmarried or widowed woman are displayed.
– ORIGIN Middle English: from Old French *losenge*, probably derived from the base of Spanish *losa*, Portuguese *lousa* 'slab', late Latin *lausiae (lapides)* 'stone slabs'.

Lozi /'ləʊzi/ ▶ noun (pl. same or **Lozis**) **1** a member of an African people living mainly in western Zambia.
2 [mass noun] the Bantu language of this people, with about 450,000 speakers.
▶ adjective of or relating to the Lozi or their language.
– ORIGIN a local name.

LP ▶ abbreviation for ■ long-playing (gramophone record): *two LP records | a collection of LPs.* ■ low pressure.

l.p. ▶ abbreviation for low pressure.

LPG ▶ abbreviation for liquefied petroleum gas.

L-plate ▶ noun Brit. a sign bearing the letter L, attached to the front and rear of a motor vehicle to indicate that it is being driven by a learner.

LPN ▶ abbreviation for (in North America) Licensed Practical Nurse. See PRACTICAL NURSE.

LPO ▶ abbreviation for London Philharmonic Orchestra.

Lr ▶ symbol for the chemical element lawrencium.

LS ▶ abbreviation for Lesotho (international vehicle registration).

LSB Computing ▶ abbreviation for least significant bit.

LSD ▶ noun [mass noun] a synthetic crystalline compound, lysergic acid diethylamide, which is a powerful hallucinogenic drug.

● Chem. formula: $C_{20}H_{26}N_2O.$
– ORIGIN mid 20th cent.: abbreviation.

l.s.d. ▶ noun [mass noun] Brit. dated money.
– ORIGIN from Latin *librae* ('pounds'), *solidi*, *denarii* (both denoting Roman coins).

LSE ▶ abbreviation for London School of Economics.

LSO ▶ abbreviation for London Symphony Orchestra.

Lt ▶ abbreviation for ■ Lieutenant. ■ (also **lt**) Military light.

LTA ▶ abbreviation for Lawn Tennis Association.

Ltd Brit. ▶ abbreviation for (after a company name) Limited.

LTP ▶ abbreviation for long-term potentiation. See POTENTIATION.

Lu ▶ symbol for the chemical element lutetium.

Lualaba /ˌluːəˈlɑːbə/ a river of central Africa, which rises near the southern border of Zaire (Democratic Republic of Congo) and flows northwards for about 640 km (400 miles), joining the Lomami to form the River Congo.

Luanda /luːˈandə/ the capital of Angola, a port on the Atlantic coast; pop. 2,250,000 (est. 1995).

Luang Prabang /ˌluːˌaŋ prəˈbaŋ/ (also **Louangphrabang**) a city in NW Laos, on the Mekong River; pop. 44,240 (est. 1984). It was the royal residence and Buddhist religious centre of Laos until the end of the monarchy in 1975.

luau /'luːaʊ/ ▶ noun (pl. same or **luaus**) a Hawaiian party or feast, especially one accompanied by some form of entertainment.
– ORIGIN from Hawaiian *lu'au.*

Luba /'luːbə/ ▶ noun (pl. same or **Lubas**) **1** a member of a people living mainly in south-eastern Zaire (Democratic Republic of Congo).
2 [mass noun] the Bantu language of this people, with about 8 million speakers. Also called **CHILUBA**.
▶ adjective of or relating to the Luba or their language.
– ORIGIN a local name.

lubber ▶ noun **1** archaic or dialect a big, clumsy person.
2 short for **LANDLUBBER**.
– DERIVATIVES **lubberlike** adjective, **lubberly** adjective & adverb.
– ORIGIN late Middle English: perhaps via Old French *lobeor* 'swindler, parasite' from *lober* 'deceive'.

lubber line (also **lubber's line**) ▶ noun a line marked on the compass in a ship or aircraft, showing the direction straight ahead.

Lubbock /'lʌbək/ a city in NW Texas; pop. 186,200 (1990).

lube /luːb/ informal, chiefly N. Amer. & Austral. ▶ noun a lubricant.
▶ verb [with obj.] lubricate (something).
– ORIGIN 1930s: abbreviation.

Lübeck /'luːbɛk, German 'lyːbɛk/ a port in northern Germany, on the Baltic coast in Schleswig-Holstein, north-east of Hamburg; pop. 211,000 (1991). Between the 14th and 19th centuries it was an important city within the Hanseatic League.

Lubianka variant spelling of **LUBYANKA**.

Lublin /'lʊblɪn/ a manufacturing city in eastern Poland; pop. 351,350 (1990).

lubra /'luːbrə/ ▶ noun Austral. offensive an Aboriginal woman.
– ORIGIN mid 19th cent.: from Tasmanian *lubara.*

lubricant ▶ noun a substance used for lubricating an engine or component, such as oil or grease.
▶ adjective lubricating: *a thin lubricant film.*
– ORIGIN early 19th cent.: from Latin *lubricant-* 'making slippery', from the verb *lubricare* (see LUBRICATE).

lubricate /'luːbrɪkeɪt/ ▶ verb [with obj.] apply a substance such as oil or grease to (an engine or component) so as to minimize friction and allow smooth movement: *remove the nut and lubricate the thread* | [as adj. **lubricating**] *lubricating oils.*
■ make (something) slippery or smooth by applying an oily substance. ■ figurative make (a process) run smoothly: *the availability of credit lubricated the channels of trade.* ■ figurative make someone convivial, especially with alcohol: *men lubricated with alcohol speak their true feelings.*
– DERIVATIVES **lubrication** noun, **lubricator** noun.
– ORIGIN early 17th cent.: from Latin *lubricat-* 'made slippery', from the verb *lubricare*, from *lubricus* 'slippery'.

lubricious /luːˈbrɪʃəs/ (also **lubricous** /'luːbrɪkəs/)

▶ adjective **1** offensively displaying or intended to arouse sexual desire.
2 smooth and slippery with oil or a similar substance.
– DERIVATIVES **lubriciously** adverb, **lubricity** noun.
– ORIGIN late 16th cent.: from Latin *lubricus* 'slippery' + -IOUS.

Lubumbashi /ˌluːbʊmˈbaʃi/ a city in SE Zaire (Democratic Republic of Congo), near the border with Zambia, capital of the region of Shaba; pop. 739,100 (1991). Former name (until 1966) **ELISABETHVILLE**.

Lubyanka /luːˈbjaŋkə/ (also **Lubianka**) a building in Moscow used as a prison and as the headquarters of the KGB and other Russian secret police organizations since the Russian Revolution.

Lucan[1] /'luːk(ə)n/ (AD 39–65), Roman poet, born in Spain; Latin name *Marcus Annaeus Lucanus.* His major work is *Pharsalia*, a hexametric epic in ten books dealing with the civil war between Julius Caesar and Pompey.

Lucan[2] /'luːk(ə)n/ ▶ adjective of or relating to St Luke.
– ORIGIN via ecclesiastical Latin from Greek *Loukas* 'Luke' + -AN.

Lucas, George (Walton) (b.1944), American film director, producer, and screenwriter. He wrote and directed the science-fiction film *Star Wars* (1977), and wrote and produced Steven Spielberg's *Raiders of the Lost Ark* (1981) and the sequels of each film.

Lucas van Leyden /ˌluːkəs van ˈlʌɪd(ə)n/ (c.1494–1533), Dutch painter and engraver. He produced his most significant work as an engraver, including *Ecce Homo* (1510). His paintings include portraits, genre scenes, and religious subjects.

Lucca /'luːkə/ a city in northern Italy, in Tuscany to the west of Florence; pop. 86,440 (1990).

luce /luːs/ ▶ noun (pl. same) a pike (fish), especially when full-grown.
– ORIGIN late Middle English: via Old French *lus, luis* from late Latin *lucius.*

lucent /'luːs(ə)nt/ ▶ adjective poetic/literary glowing with or giving off light: *the moon was lucent in the background.*
– DERIVATIVES **lucency** noun.
– ORIGIN late Middle English: from Latin *lucent-* 'shining', from the verb *lucere* (see LUCID).

Lucerne /luːˈsɜːn, French lysɛʁn/ a resort on the western shore of Lake Lucerne, in central Switzerland; pop. 59,370 (1990). German name **LUZERN**.

lucerne /luːˈsɜːn/ ▶ noun another term for **ALFALFA**.
– ORIGIN mid 17th cent.: from French *luzerne*, from modern Provençal *luzerno* 'glow-worm' (with reference to its shiny seeds).

Lucerne, Lake a lake in central Switzerland, surrounded by the four cantons of Lucerne, Nidwalden, Uri, and Schwyz. Also called **LAKE OF THE FOUR CANTONS**; German name **VIERWALDSTÄTTERSEE**.

lucid /'luːsɪd/ ▶ adjective **1** expressed clearly; easy to understand: *a lucid account | write in a clear and lucid style.*
■ showing ability to think clearly, especially in the intervals between periods of confusion or insanity: *he has a few lucid moments every now and then.* ■ Psychology (of a dream) experienced with the dreamer feeling awake, aware of dreaming, and able to control events consciously.
2 poetic/literary bright or luminous: *birds dipped their wings in the lucid flow of air.*
– DERIVATIVES **lucidity** noun, **lucidly** adverb.
– ORIGIN late 16th cent. (in sense 2): from Latin *lucidus* (perhaps via French *lucide* or Italian *lucido*) from *lucere* 'shine', from *lux, luc-* 'light'.

Lucifer /'luːsɪfə/ ▶ noun **1** another name for **SATAN**. [ORIGIN: by association with the 'son of the morning' (Isa. 14:12), believed by Christian interpreters to be a reference to Satan.]
2 poetic/literary the planet Venus when it rises in the morning.
3 (**lucifer**) archaic a match struck by rubbing it on a rough surface.
– ORIGIN Old English, from Latin, 'light-bringing, morning star', from *lux, luc-* 'light' + *-fer* 'bearing'.

lucifugous /luːˈsɪfjʊgəs/ ▶ adjective chiefly Zoology shunning the light.

– ORIGIN mid 17th cent.: from Latin *lucifugus* (from *lux, luc-* 'light' + *fugere* 'to fly') + **-OUS**.

lucine /'lu:si:n/ ▶ **noun** a bivalve mollusc which typically has a rounded white shell with radial and concentric ridges, found in tropical and temperate seas.
• Family Lucinidae: *Lucina* and other genera.

lucite /'lu:sʌɪt/ ▶ **noun** [mass noun] trademark, chiefly US a solid transparent plastic made of polymethyl methacrylate (the same material as perspex or plexiglas).
– ORIGIN 1930s: from Latin *lux, luc-* 'light' + **-ITE**[1].

luck ▶ **noun** [mass noun] success or failure apparently brought by chance rather than through one's own actions: *it was just luck that the first kick went in* | *they're supposed to bring* ***good luck***.
■chance considered as a force that causes good or bad things to happen. ■ something regarded as bringing about or portending good or bad things: *I don't like Friday—it's* ***bad luck***.
▶ **verb** [no obj.] (**luck into/upon**) informal chance to find or acquire: *he lucked into a disc-jockey job.*
■(**luck out**) N. Amer. achieve success or advantage by good luck: *I lucked out and found a wonderful woman.*
– PHRASES **as luck would have it** used to indicate the fortuitousness of a situation: *as luck would have it, his route took him very near where they lived.* **bad** (or **tough** or **rotten**) **luck** informal used to express sympathy or commiserations. **be in** (or **out of**) **luck** be fortunate (or unfortunate). **for luck** to bring good fortune: *I wear this crystal under my costume for luck.* **good** (or **the best of**) **luck** used to express wishes for success: ***good luck*** *with your studies!* **one's luck is in** one is fortunate. **the luck of the draw** the outcome of chance rather than something one can control: *quality of care depends largely on the luck of the draw.* **no such luck** informal used to express disappointment that something has not happened or is unlikely to happen. **ride one's luck** let favourable events take their course without taking undue risks. **try one's luck** do something that involves risk or luck, hoping to succeed: *he thought he'd* ***try his luck*** *at farming in Canada.* **with** (**any** or **a bit of**) **luck** expressing the hope that something will happen in the way described: *with luck we should be there in time for breakfast.* **worse luck** informal used to express regret about something: *I have to go to secretarial school, worse luck.*
– ORIGIN late Middle English (as a verb): perhaps from Middle Low German or Middle Dutch *lucken*. The noun use (late 15th cent.) is from Middle Low German *lucke*, related to Dutch *geluk*, German *Glück*, of West Germanic origin and possibly related to **LOCK**[1].

luckily ▶ **adverb** [sentence adverb] it is fortunate that: *luckily they didn't recognize me* | ***luckily*** *for me it's worked out.*

luckless ▶ **adjective** having bad luck; unfortunate.
– DERIVATIVES **lucklessly** adverb, **lucklessness** noun.

Lucknow /'lʌknaʊ/ a city in northern India, capital of the state of Uttar Pradesh; pop. 1,592,000 (1991). In 1857, during the Indian Mutiny, its British residency was twice besieged by Indian insurgents.

lucky ▶ **adjective** (**luckier**, **luckiest**) having, bringing, or resulting from good luck: *you had a very lucky escape* | *three's my lucky number.*
– PHRASES **you** (or **he** etc.) **will be lucky** (or **should be so lucky**) used to imply in an ironic or resigned way that someone's wishes or expectations are unlikely to be fulfilled: *'A shirt would be nice.' 'You'll be lucky.'* **lucky devil** (or **lucky you**, **her**, etc.) used to express envy at someone else's good fortune.
– DERIVATIVES **luckiness** noun.

lucky bag ▶ **noun** Brit. another term for **GRAB BAG**.

lucky bean ▶ **noun** a plant of the pea family which produces poisonous shiny scarlet beans with a black eye, sometimes used as amulets.
• *Abrus* and other genera, family Leguminosae: several species, in particular *A. precatorius*.
■the beans of any of these plants.

lucky dip ▶ **noun** Brit. a game in which small prizes are concealed in a container and chosen at random by participants, usually in return for a small payment.
■a process of choosing or deciding something purely at random.

lucrative /'lu:krətɪv/ ▶ **adjective** producing a great deal of profit: *a lucrative career as a stand-up comedian.*
– DERIVATIVES **lucratively** adverb, **lucrativeness** noun.
– ORIGIN late Middle English: from Latin *lucrativus*, from *lucrat-* 'gained', from the verb *lucrari*, from *lucrum* (see **LUCRE**).

lucre /'lu:kə/ ▶ **noun** [mass noun] money, especially when regarded as sordid or distasteful or gained in a dishonourable way: *officials getting their hands grubby with* ***filthy lucre***.
– ORIGIN late Middle English: from French *lucre* or Latin *lucrum*; the phrase *filthy lucre* is with biblical allusion to Tit. 1:11.

Lucretia /lu:'kri:ʃə/ (in Roman legend) a woman who was raped by a son of Tarquinius Superbus and took her own life; this led to the expulsion of the Tarquins from Rome by a rebellion under Brutus.

Lucretius /lu:'kri:ʃəs/ (*c.*94–*c.*55 BC), Roman poet and philosopher; full name *Titus Lucretius Carus*. His didactic hexametric poem *On the Nature of Things* is an exposition of the materialist atomist physics of Epicurus, which aims to give peace of mind by showing that fear of the gods and of death is without foundation.

lucubrate /'lu:kjʊbreɪt/ ▶ **verb** [no obj.] archaic discourse learnedly in writing.
– DERIVATIVES **lucubrator** noun.
– ORIGIN early 17th cent.: from Latin *lucubrat-* '(having) worked by lamplight', from the verb *lucubrare*.

lucubration ▶ **noun** [mass noun] formal study; meditation: *after sixteen years' lucubration he produced this account.*
■[count noun] (usu. **lucubrations**) a piece of writing, typically a pedantic or over-elaborate one.
– ORIGIN late 16th cent.: from Latin *lucubratio(n-)*, from the verb *lucubrare* (see **LUCUBRATE**).

luculent /'lu:kjʊl(ə)nt/ ▶ **adjective** rare **1** (of writing or speech) clearly expressed.
2 brightly shining.
– DERIVATIVES **luculently** adverb.
– ORIGIN late Middle English (in sense 2): from Latin *luculentus*, from *lux, luc-* 'light'.

Lucullan /lu:'kʌlən, lʊ-/ ▶ **adjective** (especially of food) extremely luxurious: *a Lucullan repast for one.*
– ORIGIN mid 19th cent.: from the name of Licinius *Lucullus*, Roman general of the 1st cent. BC, famous for giving lavish banquets, + **-AN**.

Lucy the nickname of a partial female skeleton of a fossil hominid found in Ethiopia in 1974, about 3.2 million years old and 1.2 m (4 ft) in height.
• *Australopithecus afarensis*, family Hominidae. This species is regarded by many as the ancestor of all subsequent *Australopithecus* and *Homo* species.

lud ▶ **noun** (**m'lud** or **my lud**) Brit. used to address a judge in a court of law: *so it is alleged, m'lud.*
– ORIGIN early 18th cent.: alteration of **LORD**.

Luda /lu:'dɑ:/ an industrial conurbation and port in NE China, in the province of Liaoning at the south-eastern tip of the Liaodong Peninsula; pop. 1,630,000 (est. 1986). It comprises the cities of Lushun and Dalian.

Luddite /'lʌdʌɪt/ ▶ **noun** a member of any of the bands of English workers who destroyed machinery, especially in cotton and woollen mills, which they believed was threatening their jobs (1811–16).
■a person opposed to increased industrialization or new technology: *a small-minded Luddite resisting progress.*
– DERIVATIVES **Luddism** noun, **Ludditism** noun.
– ORIGIN perhaps named after Ned *Lud*, a participant in the destruction of machinery, + **-ITE**[1].

Ludendorff /'lu:d(ə)n,dɔ:f, German 'lu:dn,dɔrf/, Erich (1865–1937), German general, Chief of Staff to General von Hindenburg during the First World War and later a Nazi Party MP (1924–8).

luderick /'lu:d(ə)rɪk, 'lʌdrɪk/ ▶ **noun** (pl. same) an edible herbivorous fish of Australasian coastal waters and estuaries. Also called **BLACKFISH**.
• *Girella tricuspidata*, family Kyphosidae.
– ORIGIN late 19th cent.: from Ganay (an Aboriginal language) *ludarag*.

Ludhiana /,lʊdɪ'ɑ:nə/ a city in NW India, in Punjab south-east of Amritsar; pop. 1,012,000 (1991).

ludic /'lu:dɪk/ ▶ **adjective** formal showing spontaneous and undirected playfulness.
– ORIGIN 1940s: from French *ludique*, from Latin *ludere* 'to play', from *ludus* 'sport'.

ludicrous ▶ **adjective** so foolish, unreasonable, or out of place as to be amusing: *it's ludicrous that I have been fined* | *every night he wore a ludicrous outfit.*
– DERIVATIVES **ludicrously** adverb [as submodifier] *a ludicrously inadequate army*, **ludicrousness** noun.
– ORIGIN early 17th cent. (in the sense 'sportive, intended as a jest'): from Latin *ludicrus* (probably from *ludicrum* 'stage play') + **-OUS**.

ludo ▶ **noun** [mass noun] Brit. a simple game in which players move counters round a board according to throws of a dice.
– ORIGIN late 19th cent.: from Latin, 'I play'.

Ludwig /'lʊdvɪg, German 'lu:tvɪç/ the name of three kings of Bavaria:
■**Ludwig I** (1786–1868), reigned 1825–48. He became unpopular due to his reactionary policies, lavish expenditure, and his domination by the dancer Lola Montez, and he was forced to abdicate in favour of his son.
■**Ludwig II** (1845–86), reigned 1864–86. A patron of the arts, he became a recluse and built a series of elaborate castles. He was declared insane and deposed in 1886.
■**Ludwig III** (1845–1921), reigned 1913–8.

Ludwigshafen /'lʊdvɪgz,hɑ:f(ə)n, German 'lu:tvɪçs,ha:fn/ an industrial river port in west central Germany, south-west of Mannheim, on the River Rhine in the state of Rhineland-Palatinate; pop. 165,370 (1991).

lues /'l(j)u:i:z/ (also **lues venerea** /vɪ'nɪərɪə/) ▶ **noun** [mass noun] dated a serious infectious disease, particularly syphilis.
– DERIVATIVES **luetic** /l(j)u:'ɛtɪk/ adjective.
– ORIGIN mid 17th cent.: from Latin, literally 'plague'.

luff chiefly Sailing ▶ **noun** the edge of a fore-and-aft sail next to the mast or stay.
▶ **verb** [with obj.] **1** steer (a yacht) nearer the wind: *I came aft and luffed her for the open sea.*
■obstruct (an opponent in yacht racing) by sailing closer to the wind.
2 raise or lower (the jib of a crane or derrick).
– ORIGIN Middle English: from Old French *lof*, probably from Low German.

Luftwaffe /'lʊftwɑfə, German 'lʊftvafə/ the German air force.
– ORIGIN German, from *Luft* 'air' + *Waffe* 'weapon'.

lug[1] ▶ **verb** (**lugged**, **lugging**) [with obj. and adverbial of direction] carry or drag (a heavy or bulky object) with great effort: *she began to lug her suitcase down the stairs.*
■figurative be encumbered with: *he had lugged his poor wife round for so long.*
▶ **noun** a box or crate used for transporting fruit.
– ORIGIN late Middle English: probably of Scandinavian origin: compare with Swedish *lugga* 'pull a person's hair' (from *lugg* 'forelock').

lug[2] ▶ **noun 1** (usu. **lugs**) Scottish & N. English or informal a person's ear.
2 a projection on an object by which it may be carried or fixed in place.
3 informal, chiefly US a loutish man. [ORIGIN: contemptuous use, perhaps from the 19th-cent. term denoting the lowest grade of tobacco.]
– ORIGIN late 15th cent. (denoting the ear flap of a hat): probably of Scandinavian origin: compare with Swedish *lugg* 'forelock, nap of cloth'.

lug[3] ▶ **noun** short for **LUGWORM**.

Luganda /lu:'gandə/ ▶ **noun** [mass noun] the Bantu language of the Baganda people, widely used in Uganda and having over 2 million speakers.
▶ **adjective** of or relating to this language.

Lugano /lu:'gɑ:nəʊ/ a town in southern Switzerland, on the northern shore of Lake Lugano; pop. 26,010 (1990).

Lugansk /lu'gansk/ Russian name for **LUHANSK**.

Lugdunum /lʊg'du:nəm/ Roman name for **LYONS**.

luge /lu:ʒ/ ▶ **noun** a light toboggan for one or two people, ridden in a sitting or supine position.
■[mass noun] a sport in which competitors make a timed descent of a course riding such toboggans.
▶ **verb** [no obj.] ride on a luge.
– ORIGIN late 19th cent. (as a verb): from Swiss French.

Luger /'lu:gə/ ▶ **noun** (trademark in the US) a type of German automatic pistol.
– ORIGIN early 20th cent.: named after George *Luger* (1849–1923), German firearms expert.

luggable ▶ **adjective** (especially of computer equipment) portable but only with difficulty.

luggage ▶ **noun** [mass noun] suitcases or other bags in which to pack personal belongings for travelling.
■ figurative past experiences or long-held ideas and opinions perceived as burdensome encumbrances: *they carry some psychological luggage.*
– ORIGIN late 16th cent. (originally denoting inconveniently heavy baggage): from **LUG**[1] + **-AGE**.

lugger ▶ **noun** a small sailing ship with two or three masts and a lugsail on each.
– ORIGIN mid 18th cent.: from **LUGSAIL** + **-ER**[1].

lughole ▶ **noun** Brit. informal a person's ear.

Lugosi /lə'gəʊsi/, Bela (born Béla Ferenc Blasko) (1884–1956), Hungarian-born American actor famous for his roles in horror films such as *Dracula* (1931) and *The Wolf Man* (1940).

lugsail /'lʌgseɪl, -s(ə)l/ ▶ **noun** an asymmetrical four-sided sail which is bent on and hoisted from a steeply inclined yard.
– ORIGIN late 17th cent.: probably from **LUG**[2] + the noun **SAIL**.

lugubrious /lʊ'gu:brɪəs/ ▶ **adjective** looking or sounding sad and dismal.
– DERIVATIVES **lugubriously** adverb, **lugubriousness** noun.
– ORIGIN early 17th cent.: from Latin *lugubris* (from *lugere* 'mourn') + **-OUS**.

lugworm ▶ **noun** a bristle worm that lives in muddy sand, leaving characteristic worm casts on lower shores. It is widely used as bait by fishermen.
• *Arenicola marina*, class Polychaeta.
– ORIGIN early 19th cent.: from earlier *lug* 'lugworm' (of unknown origin) + **WORM**.

Luhansk /lu:'hansk/ an industrial city in eastern Ukraine, in the Donets Basin; pop. 501,000 (1990). Former name **VOROSHILOVGRAD** (1935–58 and 1970–91). Russian name **LUGANSK**.

Luik /lœyk/ Flemish name for **LIÈGE**.

Lukács /'lu:katʃ/, György (1885–1971), Hungarian philosopher, literary critic, and politician. His best-known work is *History and Class Consciousness* (1923), in which he stresses the central role of alienation in Marxist thought.

Luke, St an evangelist, closely associated with St Paul and traditionally the author of the third Gospel and the Acts of the Apostles. Feast day, 18 October.
■ the third Gospel (see **GOSPEL** sense 2).

lukewarm ▶ **adjective** (of liquid or food that should be hot) only moderately warm; tepid: *they drank bitter lukewarm coffee.*
■ (of a person, attitude, or action) unenthusiastic: *Britain is lukewarm about the proposal.*
– DERIVATIVES **lukewarmly** adverb, **lukewarmness** noun.
– ORIGIN late Middle English: from dialect *luke* (probably from dialect *lew* 'lukewarm' and related to **LEE**) + **WARM**.

lull ▶ **verb** [with obj.] calm or send to sleep, typically with soothing sounds or movements: *the rhythm of the boat lulled her to sleep.*
■ cause (someone) to feel deceptively secure or confident: *the rarity of earthquakes there has lulled people into a false sense of security.* ■ allay (a person's doubts, fears, or suspicions), typically by deception. ■ [no obj.] (of noise or a storm) abate or fall quiet: *conversation lulled for an hour.*
▶ **noun** a temporary interval of quiet or lack of activity: *for two days there had been a* ***lull in*** *the fighting.*
– PHRASES **the lull before the storm** see **STORM**.
– ORIGIN Middle English: imitative of sounds used to quieten a child; compare with Latin *lallare* 'sing to sleep', Swedish *lulla* 'hum a lullaby', and Dutch *lullen* 'talk nonsense'. The noun (first recorded in the sense 'soothing drink') dates from the mid 17th cent.

lullaby ▶ **noun** (pl. **-ies**) a quiet, gentle song sung to send a child to sleep.
▶ **verb** (**-ies**, **-ied**) [with obj.] rare sing to (someone) to get them to go to sleep: *she lullabied us, she fed us.*
– ORIGIN mid 16th cent.: from **LULL** + *bye-bye*, a sound used as a refrain in lullabies; compare with **BYE-BYES**.

Lully /'lʊli, French lyli/, Jean-Baptiste (1632–87), French composer, born in Italy; Italian name *Giovanni Battista Lulli*. His operas, which include *Alceste* (1674) and *Armide* (1686), mark the beginning of the French operatic tradition.

lulu ▶ **noun** informal an outstanding example of a particular type of person or thing: *as far as nightmares went, this one was a lulu.*
– ORIGIN late 19th cent.: perhaps from *Lulu*, pet form of the given name *Louise*.

lum /lʌm/ ▶ **noun** Scottish & N. English a chimney.
– ORIGIN early 16th cent.: perhaps from Old French *lum* 'light', from Latin *lumen*.

luma /'lu:ma/ ▶ **noun** (pl. same or **lumas**) a monetary unit of Armenia, equal to one hundredth of a dram.

lumbago /lʌm'beɪgəʊ/ ▶ **noun** [mass noun] pain in the muscles and joints of the lower back.
– ORIGIN late 17th cent.: from Latin, from *lumbus* 'loin'.

lumbar /'lʌmbə/ ▶ **adjective** [attrib.] relating to the lower part of the back: *backache in the lumbar region.*
– ORIGIN mid 17th cent.: from medieval Latin *lumbaris*, from Latin *lumbus* 'loin'.

lumbar puncture ▶ **noun** [mass noun] Medicine the procedure of taking fluid from the spine in the lower back through a hollow needle, usually done for diagnostic purposes.

lumber[1] ▶ **verb** [no obj., with adverbial of direction] move in a slow, heavy, awkward way: *a truck lumbered past* | [as adj. **lumbering**] *Bob was the big, lumbering, gentle sort* | figurative *a lumbering bureaucracy.*
– ORIGIN late Middle English *lomere*, perhaps symbolic of clumsy movement.

lumber[2] ▶ **noun** [mass noun] **1** chiefly Brit. articles of furniture or other household items that are no longer useful and inconveniently take up storage space.
2 chiefly N. Amer. timber sawn into rough planks or otherwise partly prepared.
▶ **verb 1** [with obj.] (usu. **be lumbered with**) Brit. informal burden (someone) with an unwanted responsibility, task, or set of circumstances: *the banks do not want to be lumbered with a building that they cannot sell.*
2 [no obj.] [usu. as noun **lumbering**] chiefly N. Amer. cut and prepare forest timber for transport and sale.
– ORIGIN mid 16th cent.: perhaps from **LUMBER**[1]; later associated with obsolete *lumber* 'pawnbroker's shop'.

lumber[3] Scottish informal ▶ **verb** [with obj.] casually strike up a relationship with (a prospective sexual partner).
▶ **noun** a person regarded as a prospective sexual partner.
– ORIGIN 1960s: of unknown origin.

lumberer ▶ **noun** chiefly N. Amer. a person engaged in the lumber trade, especially a lumberjack.

lumberjack (also **lumberman**) ▶ **noun** (especially in North America) a person who fells trees, cuts them into logs, or transports them to a sawmill.

lumberjacket ▶ **noun** a warm, thick jacket, typically in a bright colour with a check pattern, of the kind worn by lumberjacks.

lumber room ▶ **noun** Brit. a room where disused or bulky things are kept.

lumbersome ▶ **adjective** bulky and awkward to handle or use.
– DERIVATIVES **lumbersomeness** noun.

lumen[1] /'lu:mɛn/ (abbrev.: **lm**) ▶ **noun** Physics the SI unit of luminous flux, equal to the amount of light emitted per second in a unit solid angle of one steradian from a uniform source of one candela.
– ORIGIN late 19th cent.: from Latin, literally 'light'.

lumen[2] /'lu:mən/ ▶ **noun** (pl. **lumina** /-mɪnə/) Anatomy the central cavity of a tubular or other hollow structure in an organism or cell.
– DERIVATIVES **luminal** /'lu:mɪn(ə)l/ adjective.
– ORIGIN late 19th cent.: from Latin, literally 'opening'.

lum hat ▶ **noun** Scottish informal a top hat.

Lumière /'lu:mɪɛ:, French lymjɛʀ/, Auguste Marie Louis Nicholas (1862–1954) and Louis Jean (1864–1948), French inventors and pioneers of cinema. In 1895 the brothers patented their 'Cinématographe', a cine camera and projector in one. They also invented the improved 'autochrome' process of colour photography.

luminaire /'lu:mɪnɛ:, ˌlu:mɪ'nɛ:/ ▶ **noun** a complete electric light unit (used especially in technical contexts).
– ORIGIN early 20th cent. from French.

Luminal /'lu:mɪn(ə)l/ ▶ **noun** trademark for **PHENOBARBITONE**.
– ORIGIN early 20th cent.: probably from Latin *lumen* 'light' (rendering *phen-*, from Greek *phaino-* 'shining'), + **-AL**.

luminance /'lu:mɪn(ə)ns/ ▶ **noun** [mass noun] Physics the intensity of light emitted from a surface per unit area in a given direction.
■ the component of a television signal which carries information on the brightness of the image.
– ORIGIN late 19th cent. (as a general term meaning 'light, brightness'): from Latin *luminant-* 'illuminating' (from the verb *luminare*) + **-ANCE**.

luminary /'lu:mɪn(ə)ri/ ▶ **noun** (pl. **-ies**) **1** a person who inspires or influences others, especially one prominent in a particular sphere: *one of the luminaries of child psychiatry.*
2 an artificial light.
■ poetic/literary a natural light-giving body, especially the sun or moon.
– ORIGIN late Middle English: from Old French *luminarie* or late Latin *luminarium*, from Latin *lumen*, *lumin-* 'light'.

luminesce /ˌlu:mɪ'nɛs/ ▶ **verb** [no obj.] emit light by luminescence.
– ORIGIN late 19th cent.: back-formation from **LUMINESCENCE**.

luminescence /ˌlu:mɪ'nɛs(ə)ns/ ▶ **noun** [mass noun] the emission of light by a substance that has not been heated, as in fluorescence and phosphorescence.
– DERIVATIVES **luminescent** adjective.
– ORIGIN late 19th cent.: from Latin *lumen*, *lumin-* 'light' + *-escence* (denoting a state).

luminiferous /ˌlu:mɪ'nɪf(ə)rəs/ ▶ **adjective** chiefly archaic producing or transmitting light.

luminosity ▶ **noun** (pl. **-ies**) [mass noun] luminous quality: *acrylic colours retain freshness and luminosity.*
■ Astronomy the intrinsic brightness of a celestial object (as distinct from its apparent brightness diminished by distance). ■ Physics the rate of emission of radiation, visible or otherwise.

luminous /'lu:mɪnəs/ ▶ **adjective** full of or shedding light; bright or shining, especially in the dark: *the luminous dial on his watch* | *a luminous glow.*
■ (of a person's complexion or eyes) glowing with health, vigour, or a particular emotion: *her eyes were* ***luminous with*** *joy.* ■ (of a colour) very bright; harsh to the eye: *he wore luminous green socks.* ■ Physics relating to light as it is perceived by the eye, rather than in terms of its actual energy.
– DERIVATIVES **luminously** adverb, **luminousness** noun.
– ORIGIN late Middle English: from Old French *lumineux* or Latin *luminosus*, from *lumen*, *lumin-* 'light'.

lumme /'lʌmi/ ▶ **exclamation** Brit. informal, dated an expression of surprise or interest: *'Lumme!' said Quigley. 'She isn't half a size!'*
– ORIGIN late 19th cent.: from (*Lord*) *love me*.

lummox /'lʌməks/ ▶ **noun** informal, chiefly N. Amer. a clumsy, stupid person: *watch it, you great lummox!*
– ORIGIN early 19th cent.: of unknown origin.

lump[1] ▶ **noun 1** a compact mass of a substance, especially one without a definite or regular shape: *there was a* ***lump of*** *ice floating in the milk.*
■ a swelling under the skin, especially one caused by injury or disease: *he was unhurt apart from a huge lump on his head.* ■ informal a heavy, ungainly, or slow-witted person: *I wouldn't stand a chance against a big lump like you.*
2 (**the lump**) Brit. informal the state of being self-employed and paid without deduction of tax, especially in the building industry: *'Working?' 'Only on the lump, here and there'* | [as modifier] *lump labour.*
▶ **verb 1** [with obj. and adverbial] put in an indiscriminate mass or group; treat as alike without regard for particulars: *Hong Kong and Bangkok tend to* ***be lumped together*** *in holiday brochures* | *Nigel didn't like being* ***lumped in*** *with prisoners.*
■ [no obj.] (in taxonomy) classify plants or animals in relatively inclusive groups, disregarding minor variations.
2 [with obj. and adverbial of direction] Brit. carry (a heavy load) somewhere with difficulty: *the coalman had to lump one-hundredweight sacks right through the house.*
– PHRASES **a lump in the throat** a feeling of tightness or dryness in the throat caused by strong emotion, especially sadness: *there was a lump in her*

throat as she gazed down at her uncle's gaunt features.
take (or **get**) **one's lumps** informal, chiefly N. Amer. suffer punishment; be attacked or defeated.
– ORIGIN Middle English: perhaps from a Germanic base meaning 'shapeless piece'; compare with Danish *lump* 'lump', Norwegian and Swedish dialect *lump* 'block, log', and Dutch *lomp* 'rag'.

lump² ▶ verb (**lump it**) informal accept or tolerate a disagreeable situation whether one likes it or not: *you can like it or lump it but I've got to work.*
– ORIGIN late 16th cent. (in the sense 'look sulky'): symbolic of displeasure; compare with words such as *dump* and *grump*. The current sense dates from the early 19th cent.

lumpectomy ▶ noun (pl. **-ies**) a surgical operation in which a lump is removed from the breast, typically when cancer is present but has not spread.

lumpen ▶ adjective **1** lumpy and misshapen; ugly and ponderous: *her own body was lumpen and awkward.*
■boorish and stupid. ■ (in Marxist contexts) uninterested in revolutionary advancement.
▶ plural noun (**the lumpen**) the lumpenproletariat.
– ORIGIN mid 20th cent.: back-formation from **LUMPENPROLETARIAT**; the sense 'misshapen, ponderous' by association with **LUMPISH**.

lumpenproletariat /ˌlʌmpənprəʊlɪˈtɛːrɪət/ ▶ noun [treated as sing. or pl.] (especially in Marxist terminology) the unorganized and unpolitical lower orders of society who are not interested in revolutionary advancement.
– ORIGIN early 20th cent.: from German (a term originally used by Karl Marx), from *Lumpen* 'rag, rogue' + **PROLETARIAT**.

lumper ▶ noun **1** a docker, especially one who unloads cargoes from fishing boats.
2 a person (especially a taxonomist) who attaches more importance to similarities than to differences in classification. Contrasted with **SPLITTER**.

lumpfish ▶ noun (pl. same or **-fishes**) a North Atlantic lumpsucker, the roe of which is sometimes used as a substitute for caviar.
● *Cyclopterus lumpus*, family Cyclopteridae.
– ORIGIN early 17th cent.: from Middle Low German *lumpen*, Middle Dutch *lompe* + **FISH**[1].

lumpish ▶ adjective roughly or clumsily formed or shaped: *those large and lumpish hands could produce exquisitely fine work.*
■(of a person) stupid and lethargic.
– DERIVATIVES **lumpishly** adverb, **lumpishness** noun.

lumpsucker ▶ noun a globular fish of cooler northern waters, typically having a ventral sucker and spiny fins; a lumpfish.
● Family Cyclopteridae: several genera and species.

lump sugar ▶ noun [mass noun] sugar in the form of small cubes.

lump sum ▶ noun a single payment made at a particular time, as opposed to a number of smaller payments or instalments.

lumpy ▶ adjective (**lumpier**, **lumpiest**) full of or covered with lumps: *he lay on the lumpy mattress.*
■Nautical (of water) formed by the wind into small waves: *there's a lumpy sea running.*
– DERIVATIVES **lumpily** adverb, **lumpiness** noun.

lumpy jaw ▶ noun [mass noun] infection of the jaw with actinomycete bacteria, common in cattle.

Luna /ˈluːnə/ a series of Soviet moon probes launched in 1959–76. They made the first hard and soft landings on the moon (1959 and 1966).

lunacy ▶ noun (pl. **-ies**) [mass noun] the state of being a lunatic; insanity (not in technical use): *it has been suggested that originality demands a degree of lunacy.*
■extreme folly or eccentricity: *such an economic policy would be sheer lunacy.*
– ORIGIN mid 16th cent. (originally referring to insanity of an intermittent kind attributed to changes of the moon): from **LUNATIC** + **-ACY**.

luna moth ▶ noun a large North American moon moth which has pale green wings with long tails and transparent eyespots bearing crescent-shaped markings.
● *Actias luna*, family Saturniidae.
– ORIGIN late 19th cent.: *luna* from Latin *luna* 'moon' (from its markings).

lunar /ˈluːnə/ ▶ adjective of, determined by, or resembling the moon: *a lunar landscape.*

– ORIGIN late Middle English: from Latin *lunaris*, from *luna* 'moon'.

lunar caustic ▶ noun [mass noun] Chemistry, archaic silver nitrate, especially fused in the form of a stick.
– ORIGIN early 19th cent.: *lunar* in the sense 'containing silver'.

lunar cycle ▶ noun another term for **METONIC CYCLE**.

lunar day ▶ noun the interval of time between two successive crossings of the meridian by the moon (roughly 24 hours and 50 minutes).

lunar distance ▶ noun the angular distance of the moon from the sun, a planet, or a star, used in finding longitude at sea.

lunar eclipse ▶ noun an eclipse in which the moon appears darkened as it passes into the earth's shadow.

Lunarian /luːˈnɛːrɪən/ ▶ noun (in science fiction) an imagined inhabitant of the moon.

lunar module (abbrev.: **LM**) ▶ noun a small craft used for travelling the moon's surface and an orbiting spacecraft (formerly known as **lunar excursion module** or **LEM**).

lunar month ▶ noun a month measured between successive new moons (roughly 29½ days).
■(in general use) a period of four weeks.

lunar node ▶ noun Astronomy each of the two points at which the moon's orbit cuts the ecliptic.

lunar observation ▶ noun a measurement of the position of the moon in order to calculate longitude from lunar distance.

lunar roving vehicle (abbrev.: **LRV**) (also **lunar rover**) ▶ noun a vehicle designed for use by astronauts on the moon's surface, used on the last three missions of the *Apollo* project. Also called **MOON BUGGY**.

lunar year ▶ noun a period of twelve lunar months (approximately 354 days).

lunate /ˈluːneɪt/ ▶ adjective crescent-shaped.
▶ noun **1** Archaeology a crescent-shaped prehistoric stone implement.
2 (also **lunate bone**) Anatomy a crescent-shaped carpal bone situated in the centre of the wrist and articulating with the radius.
– ORIGIN late 18th cent.: from Latin *lunatus*, from *luna* 'moon'.

lunatic ▶ noun a person who is mentally ill (not in technical use).
■an extremely foolish or eccentric person: *this lunatic just accelerated out from the side of the road.*
▶ adjective [attrib.] mentally ill (not in technical use).
■extremely foolish, eccentric, or absurd: *he would be asked to acquiesce in some lunatic scheme.*
– ORIGIN Middle English: from Old French *lunatique*, from late Latin *lunaticus*, from Latin *luna* 'moon' (from the belief that changes of the moon caused intermittent insanity).

lunatic asylum ▶ noun dated a mental home or mental hospital.

lunatic fringe ▶ noun an extreme or eccentric minority within society or a group.

lunation /luːˈneɪʃ(ə)n/ ▶ noun Astronomy another term for **LUNAR MONTH**.
– ORIGIN late Middle English: from medieval Latin *lunatio(n-)*, from Latin *luna* 'moon'.

lunch ▶ noun a meal eaten in the middle of the day, typically one that is lighter or less formal than an evening meal: *a light lunch* | [mass noun] *do join us for lunch.*
▶ verb [no obj., with adverbial] eat lunch: *he told his wife he was lunching with a client.*
■[with obj.] take (someone) out for lunch: *public relations people lunch their clients there.*
– PHRASES **do lunch** informal, chiefly N. Amer. meet for lunch. **out to lunch** informal temporarily not in command of one's mental faculties. **there's no such thing as a free lunch** proverb it isn't possible to get something for nothing.
– DERIVATIVES **luncher** noun.
– ORIGIN early 19th cent.: abbreviation of **LUNCHEON**.

lunch box ▶ noun a container in which to carry a packed meal.
■a portable computer slightly larger than a laptop. ■ humorous a man's genitals.

luncheon ▶ noun a formal lunch or a formal word for lunch.

– ORIGIN late 16th cent. (in the sense 'thick piece, hunk'): possibly an extension of obsolete *lunch* 'thick piece, hunk', from Spanish *lonja* 'slice'.

luncheonette ▶ noun N. Amer. a small, informal restaurant serving light lunches.

luncheon meat ▶ noun [mass noun] finely minced cooked pork mixed with cereal, sold in a tin and typically eaten cold in slices.

luncheon voucher (abbrev.: **LV**) ▶ noun Brit. a document issued to employees by their employer as part of their pay and able to be exchanged for food at restaurants and shops.

lunch hour ▶ noun a period in the middle of the day (usually an hour), when people stop work to have lunch.

lunchroom ▶ noun N. Amer. a room or establishment in which lunch is served or in which it may be eaten; a school or office canteen.

lunchtime ▶ noun the time in the middle of day when lunch is eaten.

Lund /lʊnd/ a city in SW Sweden, just north-east of Malmö; pop. 87,680 (1991). Its university was founded in 1666.

Lunda /ˈlʊndə, ˈluːndə/ ▶ noun (pl. same or **Balunda** /baˈlʊndə, -luːndə/ or **Lundas**) **1** a member of any of several peoples living mainly in northern Zambia and adjoining parts of Zaire (Democratic Republic of Congo) and Angola. From the 16th to 19th centuries they ruled a substantial empire.
2 [mass noun] any of several Bantu languages of these peoples, especially one spoken by about 200,000 people mainly in NW Zambia.
▶ adjective of, relating to, or denoting this people or their language.
– ORIGIN a local name.

Lundy /ˈlʌndi/ **1** a granite island in the Bristol Channel, off the coast of north Devon.
2 a shipping forecast area covering the Bristol Channel and the eastern Celtic Sea.

lune /luːn/ ▶ noun a crescent-shaped figure formed on a sphere or plane by two arcs intersecting at two points.
– ORIGIN early 18th cent.: from French, from Latin *luna* 'moon'.

lunette /luːˈnɛt/ ▶ noun something crescent-shaped, in particular:
■an arched aperture or window, especially one in a domed ceiling. ■ a crescent-shaped or semicircular alcove containing something such as a painting or statue. ■ a fortification with two faces forming a projecting angle, and two flanks. ■ Christian Church a holder for the consecrated host in a monstrance. ■ a ring fixed to a vehicle, by which it can be towed.
– ORIGIN late 16th cent. (denoting a semicircular horseshoe): from French, diminutive of *lune* 'moon', from Latin *luna*.

lung ▶ noun each of the pair of organs situated within the ribcage, consisting of elastic sacs with branching passages into which air is drawn, so that oxygen can pass into the blood and carbon dioxide be removed. Lungs are characteristic of vertebrates other than fish, though similar structures are present in some other animal groups.
■(usu. **lungs**) figurative the open spaces in a town or city, where its inhabitants can get fresher air.
– DERIVATIVES **lunged** adjective [in combination] *strong-lunged*, **lungful** noun (pl. **-fuls**), **lungless** adjective.
– ORIGIN Old English *lungen*, of Germanic origin; related to Dutch *long* and German *Lunge*, from an Indo-European root shared by **LIGHT**[2]; compare with **LIGHTS**.

lunge¹ ▶ noun a sudden forward thrust of the body, typically with an arm outstretched to attack someone or seize something: *Lucy made a lunge for Gabriel's wrist* | *a crude lunge at United's goalscorer.*
■the basic attacking move in fencing, in which the leading foot is thrust forward close to the floor with the knee bent while the back leg remains straightened. ■ an exercise or gymnastic movement resembling the lunge of a fencer.
▶ verb (**lunging** or **lungeing**) [no obj., with adverbial of direction] make a lunge: *McCulloch raised his cudgel and lunged at him* | *John lunged forward and grabbed him by the throat.*
■[with obj. and adverbial of direction] make a sudden forward thrust with (a part of the body or a weapon): *Billy lunged his spear at the fish.*
– ORIGIN mid 18th cent.: from earlier *allonge*, from French *allonger* 'lengthen'.

lunge[2] (also **longe**) ▶ **noun** a long rein on which a horse is held and made to move in a circle round its trainer.
▶ **verb** (**lungeing**) [with obj.] exercise (a horse or rider) on a lunge.
– ORIGIN early 18th cent.: from French *longe*, from *allonge* 'lengthening out'.

lunge[3] ▶ **noun** N. Amer. short for **MUSKELLUNGE**.

lungfish ▶ **noun** (pl. same or **-fishes**) an elongated freshwater fish with one or two sacs which function as lungs, enabling it to breathe air. It lives in poorly oxygenated water and can aestivate in mud for long periods to survive drought.
● Subclass Dipnoi: families Ceratodontidae (one Australian species), Lepidosirenidae (one South American species), and Protopteridae (four African species).

lungi /ˈlʊŋgiː/ ▶ **noun** (pl. **lungis**) a length of cotton cloth worn as a loincloth in India or as a skirt in Burma (Myanmar), where it is the national dress for both sexes.
– ORIGIN Urdu.

lungless salamander ▶ **noun** a slender-bodied chiefly aquatic salamander native to America and southern Europe. Having neither lungs nor gills, it breathes through the skin and lining of the mouth.
● Family Plethodontidae: numerous genera, including *Plethodon* (the American woodland salamanders) and *Hydromantes* (two European species).

lungworm ▶ **noun** a parasitic nematode worm found in the lungs of mammals, especially farm and domestic animals.
● *Dictyocaulus* and other genera, class Phasmida.

lungwort ▶ **noun 1** a bristly herbaceous European plant of the borage family, typically having white-spotted leaves and pink flowers which turn blue as they age. [ORIGIN: so named because the leaves were said to have the appearance of a diseased lung.]
● Genus *Pulmonaria*, family Boraginaceae: several species, in particular *P. officinalis*.
2 (also **tree lungwort**) a large lichen which grows on trees, forming lobed fronds which are green or brown above and orange-brown below. [ORIGIN: so named because of its former use to treat lung disease, because of its apparent resemblance to lung tissue.]
● *Lobaria pulmonaria*, order Peltigerales.

lunisolar /ˌluːnɪˈsəʊlə/ ▶ **adjective** of or concerning the combined motions or effects of the sun and moon.
■ of or employing a calendar year divided according to the phases of the moon, but adjusted in average length to fit the length of the solar cycle. ■ of or denoting a 532-year period over which both the lunar months and the days of the week return to the same point in relation to the solar year.
– ORIGIN late 17th cent.: from Latin *luna* 'moon' + **SOLAR**[1].

lunitidal /ˌluːnɪˈtʌɪd(ə)l/ ▶ **adjective** denoting the interval between the time at which the moon crosses a meridian and the time of high tide at that meridian.

lunk ▶ **noun** short for **LUNKHEAD**.

lunker ▶ **noun** N. Amer. informal an exceptionally large specimen of something, in particular (among anglers) a fish.
– ORIGIN early 20th cent.: of unknown origin.

lunkhead ▶ **noun** informal a slow-witted person.
– ORIGIN mid 19th cent.: probably from an alteration of **LUMP**[1] + **HEAD**.

lunula /ˈluːnjʊlə/ ▶ **noun** (pl. **lunulae** /-liː/) a crescent-shaped object or mark, in particular:
■ the white area at the base of a fingernail. ■ a crescent-shaped Bronze Age ornament worn as a necklace.
– DERIVATIVES **lunular** adjective, **lunulate** adjective.
– ORIGIN late 16th cent. (denoting a crescent-shaped geometrical figure): from Latin, diminutive of *luna* 'moon'.

lunule /ˈluːnjuːl/ ▶ **noun** another term for **LUNULA**.

Luo /ˈluːəʊ/ ▶ **noun** (pl. same or **-os**) **1** a member of an East African people of Kenya and the upper Nile valley.
2 [mass noun] the Nilotic language of this people, with over 3 million speakers.
▶ **adjective** of or relating to the Luo or their language.
– ORIGIN the name in Luo.

Luoyang /ləʊˈjaŋ/ an industrial city in east central China, in Henan province on the Luo River; pop. 1,160,000 (1990). Between the 4th and 6th centuries AD the construction of cave temples to the south of the city made it an important Buddhist centre. Former name **HONAN**.

lupara /lʊˈpɑːrə/ ▶ **noun** a sawn-off shotgun, especially as used by the Mafia.
– ORIGIN Italian, slang term from *lupa* 'she-wolf'.

Lupercalia /ˌluːpəˈkeɪlɪə/ (also in sing. **Lupercal** /ˈluːpəkal/) ▶ **plural noun** [usu. treated as sing.] an ancient Roman festival of purification and fertility, held annually on 15 February.
– DERIVATIVES **Lupercalian** adjective.
– ORIGIN Latin, neuter plural of *lupercalis* 'relating to *Lupercus*', Roman equivalent of the Greek god Pan.

lupin /ˈluːpɪn/ (also **lupine** /-pɪn/) ▶ **noun** a plant of the pea family, with deeply divided leaves and tall colourful tapering spikes of flowers.
● Genus *Lupinus*, family Leguminosae: several species, in particular the popular cultivar **Russell lupin**.
– ORIGIN late Middle English: from Latin *lupinus*.

lupine /ˈluːpʌɪn/ ▶ **adjective** of, like, or relating to a wolf or wolves.
– ORIGIN mid 17th cent.: from Latin *lupinus*, from *lupus* 'wolf'.

lupulin /ˈluːpjʊlɪn/ ▶ **noun** [mass noun] a bitter yellowish powder found on glandular hairs beneath the scales of the flowers of the female hop plant.
– ORIGIN early 19th cent.: from the modern Latin use as an epithet of Latin *lupulus* (as in *Humulus lupulus*), a plant mentioned by Pliny and perhaps denoting 'wild hops', + **-IN**[1].

Lupus /ˈluːpəs/ Astronomy a southern constellation (the Wolf), lying partly in the Milky Way between Scorpius and Centaurus.
■ [as genitive **Lupi** /ˈluːpʌɪ/] used with preceding letter or numeral to designate a star in this constellation: *the star Delta Lupi*.
– ORIGIN Latin.

lupus /ˈluːpəs/ ▶ **noun** [mass noun] any of various ulcerous skin diseases, especially lupus vulgaris or lupus erythematosus.
– DERIVATIVES **lupoid** adjective, **lupous** adjective.
– ORIGIN late 16th cent.: from Latin, literally 'wolf'.

lupus erythematosus /ˌɛrɪθiːməˈtəʊsəs/ ▶ **noun** [mass noun] an inflammatory disease causing scaly red patches on the skin, especially on the face, and sometimes affecting connective tissue in the internal organs.
– ORIGIN from **LUPUS** + modern Latin *erythematosus*, from Greek *eruthēma* 'reddening'.

lupus vulgaris /vʌlˈgɑːrɪs, -ˈgɛːrɪs/ ▶ **noun** [mass noun] chronic direct infection of the skin with tuberculosis, causing dark red patches.
– ORIGIN 1940s: from **LUPUS** + Latin *vulgaris* 'common'.

lur /lʊə/ (also **lure**) ▶ **noun** a Scandinavian S-shaped bronze trumpet dating from the Bronze Age.
– ORIGIN Danish and Norwegian, originally denoting a wooden shepherd's horn.

lurch[1] ▶ **noun** [usu. in sing.] an abrupt uncontrolled movement, especially an unsteady tilt or roll: *the boat **gave a** violent **lurch** and he missed his footing.*
▶ **verb** [no obj., with adverbial] make an abrupt, unsteady, uncontrolled movement or series of movements; stagger: *the car lurched forward | Stuart lurched to his feet |* figurative *he was lurching from one crisis to the next.*
– ORIGIN late 17th cent. (as a noun denoting the sudden leaning of a ship to one side): of unknown origin.

lurch[2] ▶ **noun** (in phrase **leave someone in the lurch**) leave an associate or friend abruptly and without assistance or support when they are in a difficult situation.
– ORIGIN mid 16th cent. (denoting a state of discomfiture): from French *lourche*, the name of a game resembling backgammon, used in the phrase *demeurer lourche* 'be discomfited'.

lurcher ▶ **noun 1** Brit. a cross-bred dog, typically a retriever, collie, or sheepdog crossed with a greyhound, of a kind originally used for hunting and by poachers for catching rabbits.
2 archaic a prowler, swindler, or petty thief.
– ORIGIN early 16th cent. (in sense 2): from obsolete *lurch* 'remain in a place furtively', variant of **LURK**.

lurdan /ˈləːdən/ (also **lurdane** or **lourdan**) archaic ▶ **noun** an idle or incompetent person.
▶ **adjective** lazy; good-for-nothing.
– ORIGIN Middle English: from Old French *lourdin*, from *lourd* 'heavy', *lort* 'foolish', from Latin *luridus* 'lurid'.

lure[1] /l(j)ʊə/ ▶ **verb** [with obj. and adverbial] tempt (a person or an animal) to do something or to go somewhere, especially by offering some form of reward: *the child was lured into a car but managed to escape.*
▶ **noun** something that tempts or is used to tempt a person or animal to do something: *the film industry always has been a glamorous lure for young girls.*
■ the strongly attractive quality of a person or thing: *the lure of the exotic East.* ■ a type of bait used in fishing or hunting. ■ Falconry a bunch of feathers with a piece of meat attached to a long string, swung around the head of the falconer to recall a hawk.
– ORIGIN Middle English: from Old French *luere*, of Germanic origin; probably related to German *Luder* 'bait'.

lure[2] /lʊə/ ▶ **noun** variant spelling of **LUR**.

lurex /ˈl(j)ʊərɛks/ ▶ **noun** [mass noun] trademark a type of yarn or fabric which incorporates a glittering metallic thread.
– ORIGIN 1940s: of unknown origin.

lurgy /ˈləːgi/ ▶ **noun** (pl. **-ies**) Brit. humorous an unspecified or indeterminate illness: *I had caught **the dreaded lurgy**.*
– ORIGIN mid 20th cent.: of unknown origin; frequently used in the British radio series *The Goon Show*, of the 1950s and 1960s.

lurid /ˈl(j)ʊərɪd/ ▶ **adjective** very vivid in colour, especially so as to create an unpleasantly harsh or unnatural effect: *lurid food colourings | a pair of lurid shorts.*
■ (of a description) presented in vividly shocking or sensational terms, especially giving explicit details of crimes or sexual matters: *the more lurid details of the massacre were too frightening for the children.*
– DERIVATIVES **luridly** adverb, **luridness** noun.
– ORIGIN mid 17th cent. (in the sense 'pale and dismal in colour'): from Latin *luridus*; related to *luror* 'wan or yellow colour'.

lurk ▶ **verb** [no obj., with adverbial of place] (of a person or animal) be or remain hidden so as to wait in ambush for someone or something: *a ruthless killer still lurked in the darkness.*
■ (of an unpleasant quality) be present in a latent or barely discernible state, although still presenting a threat: *fear lurks beneath the surface |* [as adj. **lurking**] *he lives with a lurking fear of exposure as a fraud.* ■ [no obj.] read communications on an electronic network without making one's presence known.
▶ **noun** Austral. informal a profitable stratagem; a dodge or scheme: *you'll soon learn the lurks and perks.* [ORIGIN: from British English slang *lurk* 'method of fraud'.]
– DERIVATIVES **lurker** noun.
– ORIGIN Middle English: perhaps from **LOUR** + the frequentative suffix *-k* (as in *talk*).

lurve ▶ **noun** & **verb** non-standard spelling of **LOVE** (used in humorous reference to romantic infatuation).
– ORIGIN late 20th cent.: as a parody of the pronunciation of *love* in popular romantic songs.

Lusaka /luːˈsɑːkə/ the capital of Zambia; pop. 982,000 (1990).

Lusatian /luːˈseɪʃ(ə)n/ ▶ **adjective** & **noun** another term for **SORBIAN**.

luscious ▶ **adjective** (of food or wine) having a pleasingly rich, sweet taste: *a luscious and fragrant dessert wine.*
■ richly verdant or opulent. ■ (of a woman) very sexually attractive.
– DERIVATIVES **lusciously** adverb, **lusciousness** noun.
– ORIGIN late Middle English: perhaps an alteration of obsolete *licious*, shortened form of **DELICIOUS**.

lush[1] ▶ **adjective** (of vegetation, especially grass) growing luxuriantly: *lush greenery and cultivated fields.*
■ opulent and luxurious: *a hall of gleaming marble, as lush as a Byzantine church.* ■ (of colour or music) very rich and providing great sensory pleasure: *lush orchestrations.* ■ (of a woman) very sexually attractive: *Marianne, with her lush body and provocative green eyes.*
– DERIVATIVES **lushly** adverb, **lushness** noun.
– ORIGIN late Middle English: perhaps an alteration of obsolete *lash* 'soft, lax', from Old French *lasche* 'lax', by association with **LUSCIOUS**.

lush[2] informal, chiefly US ▶ **noun** a heavy drinker, especially a habitual one.
▶ **verb** [with obj.] dated make (someone) drunk: *Mr Hobart **got** so **lushed up** he was spilling drinks down his shirt.*

– ORIGIN late 18th cent.: perhaps a humorous use of **LUSH**[1].

Lushai /luːˈʃʌɪ/ ▶ noun another name for **MIZO** (in sense 2).

Lushun /luːˈʃʊn/ a port on the Liaodong Peninsula in NE China, now part of the urban complex of Luda. It was leased by Russia for use as a Pacific naval port from 1898 until 1905, when it was known as Port Arthur.

Lusitania[1] /ˌluːsɪˈteɪnɪə/ an ancient Roman province in the Iberian peninsula, corresponding to modern Portugal.
– DERIVATIVES **Lusitanian** adjective & noun.

Lusitania[2] /ˌluːsɪˈteɪnɪə/ a Cunard liner which was sunk by a German submarine in the Atlantic in May 1915 with the loss of over 1,000 lives.

lusophone /ˈluːsəfəʊn/ ▶ adjective Portuguese-speaking.
– ORIGIN 1970s: from luso- (representing **LUSITANIA**[1]) + **-PHONE**.

lust ▶ noun [mass noun] very strong sexual desire: *he knew that his lust for her had returned.*
■ [in sing.] a passionate desire for something: *a lust for power.* ■ (usu. **lusts**) chiefly Theology a sensuous appetite regarded as sinful: *lusts of the flesh.*
▶ verb [no obj.] have a very strong sexual desire for someone: *he really lusted after me in those days.*
■ feel a strong desire for something: *pregnant women lusting for pickles and ice cream.*
– DERIVATIVES **lustful** adjective, **lustfully** adverb, **lustfulness** noun.
– ORIGIN Old English (also in the sense 'pleasure, delight'), of Germanic origin; related to Dutch *lust* and German *Lust*.

luster ▶ noun US spelling of **LUSTRE**[1], **LUSTRE**[2].

lusterware ▶ noun US spelling of **LUSTREWARE**.

lustra plural form of **LUSTRUM**.

lustral /ˈlʌstr(ə)l/ ▶ adjective relating to or used in ceremonial purification.
– ORIGIN mid 16th cent.: from Latin *lustralis*, from *lustrum* (see **LUSTRUM**).

lustrate /ˈlʌstreɪt/ ▶ verb [with obj.] rare purify by expiatory sacrifice, ceremonial washing, or some other ritual action: *a soul lustrated in the baptismal waters.*
– DERIVATIVES **lustration** noun.
– ORIGIN early 17th cent.: from Latin *lustrat-* 'purified by lustral rites', from the verb *lustrare*, from *lustrum* (see **LUSTRUM**).

lustre[1] (US **luster**) ▶ noun [mass noun] **1** a gentle sheen or soft glow, especially that of a partly reflective surface: *the lustre of the Milky Way | she couldn't eat and her hair lost its lustre.*
■ figurative glory or distinction: *a celebrity player to add lustre to the line-up.* ■ the manner in which the surface of a mineral reflects light.
2 a substance imparting or having a shine or glow, in particular:
■ a thin coating containing unoxidized metal which gives an iridescent glaze to ceramics. ■ ceramics with such a glaze; lustreware: [as modifier] *lustre jugs.* ■ a type of finish on a photographic print, less reflective than a gloss finish. ■ a fabric or yarn with a sheen or gloss. ■ Brit. a thin dress material with a cotton warp, woollen weft, and a glossy surface.
3 [count noun] a prismatic glass pendant on a chandelier or other ornament.
■ a cut-glass chandelier or candelabra.
– DERIVATIVES **lustreless** adjective.
– ORIGIN early 16th cent.: from French, from Italian *lustro*, from the verb *lustrare*, from Latin *lustrare* 'illuminate'.

lustre[2] (US **luster**) ▶ noun another term for **LUSTRUM**.

lustred ▶ adjective (especially of ceramics) having an iridescent surface; shining.

lustreware (US **lusterware**) ▶ noun [mass noun] ceramic articles with an iridescent metallic glaze.

lustring (also **lustrine** /ˈlʌstriːn/ or **lutestring**) ▶ noun [mass noun] historical a glossy silk fabric, or a satin-weave fabric resembling it.
– ORIGIN late 17th cent.: from French *lustrine* or from Italian *lustrino*, from *lustro* 'lustre'.

lustrous ▶ adjective having lustre; shining: *large, lustrous eyes.*
– DERIVATIVES **lustrously** adverb, **lustrousness** noun.

lustrum /ˈlʌstrəm/ ▶ noun (pl. **lustra** /-trə/ or **lustrums**) chiefly poetic/literary or historical a period of five years.
– ORIGIN late 16th cent.: from Latin, originally denoting a purificatory sacrifice after a quinquennial census.

lusty ▶ adjective (**lustier**, **lustiest**) healthy and strong; full of vigour: *the other farmsteads had lusty young sons to work the land | lusty singing.*
– DERIVATIVES **lustily** adverb, **lustiness** noun.
– ORIGIN Middle English: from **LUST** (in the early sense 'vigour') + **-Y**[1].

lusus naturae /ˌluːsəs nəˈtjʊəriː, -rʌɪ/ ▶ noun (pl. same /-suːs/ or **lususes**) rare a freak of nature.
– ORIGIN Latin, literally 'a sport of nature'.

lutanist ▶ noun variant spelling of **LUTENIST**.

lutchet /ˈlʌtʃɪt/ ▶ noun a fitting on the deck of a barge or wherry to which the foot of the mast is fixed, allowing the mast to be lowered by pivoting when passing under bridges.
– ORIGIN early 19th cent.: perhaps from the northern English dialect verb *lutch* 'lift', or an alteration of **LATCHET**.

lute[1] ▶ noun a plucked stringed instrument with a long neck bearing frets and a rounded body with a flat front, rather like a halved egg in shape.
– ORIGIN Middle English: from Old French *lut, leut*, probably via Provençal from Arabic *al-ʿūd*.

lute[2] ▶ noun (also **luting**) [mass noun] liquid clay or cement used to seal a joint, coat a crucible, or protect a graft.
■ [count noun] a rubber seal for a jar.
▶ verb [with obj.] seal, join, or coat with lute.
– ORIGIN late Middle English: from Old French *lut* or medieval Latin *lutum*, a special use of Latin *lutum* 'potter's clay'.

luteal /ˈluːtɪəl/ ▶ adjective Anatomy of or relating to the corpus luteum.

lutein /ˈluːtɪɪn/ ▶ noun [mass noun] Biochemistry a deep yellow pigment of the xanthophyll class, found in the leaves of plants, in egg yolk, and in the corpus luteum.
– ORIGIN mid 19th cent.: from Latin *luteum* 'yolk of egg' (neuter of *luteus* 'yellow') + **-IN**[1].

luteinizing hormone /ˈluːtənʌɪzɪŋ/ (also **-ising**) ▶ noun [mass noun] Biochemistry a hormone secreted by the anterior pituitary gland that stimulates ovulation in females and the synthesis of androgen in males.

lutenist /ˈluːt(ə)nɪst/ (also **lutanist**) ▶ noun a lute player.
– ORIGIN early 17th cent.: from medieval Latin *lutanista*, from *lutana* 'lute'.

luteo- /ˈluːtɪəʊ/ ▶ combining form **1** orange-coloured: *luteofulvous.*
2 relating to the corpus luteum: *luteotrophic.*
– ORIGIN from Latin *luteus* (or neuter *luteum*) 'yellow'.

luteofulvous /ˌluːtɪəʊˈfʌlvəs/ ▶ adjective of an orange-tawny colour.

luteotrophic hormone /ˌluːtɪə(ʊ)ˈtrəʊfɪk, -ˈtrɒfɪk/ (also **luteotropic hormone** /-ˈtrəʊpɪk, -ˈtrɒpɪk/) ▶ noun another term for **PROLACTIN**.

luteous /ˈluːtɪəs, ˈljuː-/ ▶ adjective Biology of a deep orange-yellow or greenish yellow colour.
– ORIGIN mid 17th cent.: from Latin *luteus* 'yellow' + **-OUS**.

lutestring /ˈluːtstrɪŋ/ ▶ noun variant spelling of **LUSTRING**.

Lutetia /luːˈtiːʃə/ Roman name for **PARIS**[1].

lutetium /luːˈtiːʃɪəm, -sɪəm/ ▶ noun [mass noun] the chemical element of atomic number 71, a rare silvery-white metal of the lanthanide series. (Symbol: **Lu**)
– ORIGIN early 20th cent.: from French *lutécium*, from Latin *Lutetia*, the ancient name of Paris, the home of its discoverer.

Luther /ˈluːθə, German ˈlʊtɐ/, Martin (1483–1546), German Protestant theologian, the principal figure of the German Reformation. He preached the doctrine of justification by faith rather than by works and attacked the sale of indulgences (1517) and papal authority. In 1521 he was excommunicated at the Diet of Worms. His translation of the Bible into High German (1522–34) contributed significantly to the development of German literature in the vernacular.

Lutheran ▶ noun a follower of Martin Luther.
■ a member of the Lutheran Church.
▶ adjective of or characterized by the theology of Martin Luther.
■ of or relating to the Lutheran Church.
– DERIVATIVES **Lutheranism** noun, **Lutheranize** (also **-ise**) verb.

Lutheran Church the Protestant Church accepting the Augsburg Confession of 1530, with justification by faith alone as a cardinal doctrine. The Lutheran Church is the largest Protestant body, with substantial membership in Germany, Scandinavia, and the US.

luthern /ˈluːθən/ ▶ noun old-fashioned term for **DORMER**.
– ORIGIN mid 17th cent.: perhaps an alteration of earlier *lucarne* 'skylight', from Old French.

luthier /ˈluːtɪə/ ▶ noun a maker of stringed instruments such as violins or guitars.
– ORIGIN late 19th cent.: from French, from *luth* 'lute'.

Luthuli /luːˈtuːli/ (also **Lutuli**), Albert John (c.1898–1967), South African political leader. His presidency of the African National Congress (1952–60) was marked by a programme of civil disobedience for which he was awarded the Nobel Peace Prize (1960).

Lutine Bell /ˈluːtiːn/ a bell kept at Lloyd's in London and rung whenever there is an important announcement to be made to the underwriters. It was salvaged from HMS *Lutine*, which sank in 1799 with a large cargo of gold and bullion.

luting ▶ noun see **LUTE**[2].

lutino /luːˈtiːnəʊ/ ▶ noun (pl. **-os**) [often as modifier] a bird (especially a cage bird of the parrot family) with more yellow in the plumage than usual for the species.
– ORIGIN early 20th cent.: from Latin *luteus* 'yellow' + *-ino*, on the pattern of *albino*.

lutist ▶ noun a lute player.
■ a maker of lutes; a luthier.

Lutomer Riesling /ˈluːtəmə/ ▶ noun [mass noun] a Riesling wine produced in the Ljutomer region of northern Slovenia.

Luton an industrial town to the north-west of London, a unitary council formerly in Bedfordshire; pop. 167,300 (1991).

Lutosławski /ˌluːtəˈswafski/, Witold (1913–94), Polish composer, noted for his orchestral music. From the early 1960s his works have been characterized by a blend of notational composition and aleatoric sections.

Lutuli variant spelling of **LUTHULI**.

Lutyens[1] /ˈlʌtjənz/, (Agnes) Elizabeth (1906–83), English composer. She was one of the first English composers to use the twelve-note system, as in her *Chamber Concerto No. 1* (1939). She was the daughter of Sir Edwin Lutyens.

Lutyens[2] /ˈlʌtjənz/, Sir Edwin (Landseer) (1869–1944), English architect. He established his reputation designing country houses, but is particularly known for his plans for New Delhi (1912), where he introduced an open garden-city layout, and for the Cenotaph in London (1919–21).

lutz /lʊts/ ▶ noun a jump in skating from the backward outside edge of one skate to the backward outside edge of the other, with one or more full turns in the air.
– ORIGIN 1930s: named after the Austrian skater Alois Lutz (1899–1918).

luv ▶ noun & verb non-standard spelling of **LOVE** (representing informal or dialect use).

Luvale /loˈvɑːleɪ/ ▶ noun (pl. same) **1** a member of a people living mainly in eastern Angola and western Zaire (Democratic Republic of Congo).
2 [mass noun] the Bantu language of this people, with around 600,000 speakers. Also called **LWENA**.
▶ adjective of or relating to this people or their language.

luvvy (also **luvvie**) ▶ noun (pl. **-ies**) Brit. informal **1** often derogatory an actor or actress, especially one who is particularly effusive or affected.
2 (as a form of address) variant spelling of **LOVEY**.
– DERIVATIVES **luvviedom** noun.

Luwian /ˈluːwɪən/ (also **Luvian** /ˈluːvɪən/) ▶ noun [mass noun] an ancient Anatolian language of the 2nd millennium BC, related to Hittite. It is recorded in both cuneiform and hieroglyphic scripts, and may have been the language spoken in Troy at the time of the Homeric war.

– ORIGIN from *Luwia*, part of Asia Minor, + **-AN**.

lux /lʌks/ (abbrev.: **lx**) ▶ **noun** (pl. same) the SI unit of illuminance, equal to one lumen per square metre.
– ORIGIN late 19th cent.: from Latin, literally 'light'.

luxate /ˈlʌkseɪt/ ▶ **verb** [with obj.] Medicine dislocate.
– DERIVATIVES **luxation** noun.
– ORIGIN early 17th cent.: from Latin *luxat-* 'dislocated', from the verb *luxare*, from *luxus* 'out of joint'.

luxe /lʌks, lʊks/ ▶ **noun** [mass noun] luxury: [as modifier] *the luxe life*.
– ORIGIN mid 16th cent.: from French, from Latin *luxus* 'abundance'.

Luxembourg /ˈlʌksəmbəːg/ a country in western Europe, situated between Belgium, Germany, and France; pop. 378,000 (est. 1991); official languages, Luxemburgish, French, and German; capital, Luxembourg.
▪ the capital of the Grand Duchy of Luxembourg; pop. 75,620 (1991). It is the seat of the European Court of Justice. ▪ a province of SE Belgium, until 1839 a province of the Grand Duchy of Luxembourg; capital, Arlon.

Annexed by France in 1795, Luxembourg became an independent grand duchy as a result of the Treaty of Vienna in 1815. It formed a customs union with Belgium in 1922, extended in 1948 into the Benelux Customs Union with the Netherlands. It was a founder member of the EEC in 1957.

– DERIVATIVES **Luxembourger** noun.

Luxemburg /ˈlʌksəmbəːg/, Rosa (1871–1919), Polish-born German revolutionary leader. Together with the German socialist **Karl Liebknecht** (1871–1919) she founded the revolutionary group known as the Spartacus League in 1916 and the German Communist Party in 1918.

Luxemburgish /ˈlʌksəmˌbəːgɪʃ/ ▶ **noun** [mass noun] the local language of Luxembourg, a form of German with a strong admixture of French. Also called **LETZEBURGESCH**.

Luxor /ˈlʌksɔː/ a city in eastern Egypt, on the east bank of the Nile; pop. 142,000 (1991). It is the site of the southern part of ancient Thebes and contains the ruins of the temple built by Amenhotep III and of monuments erected by Ramses II. Arabic name **EL UQSUR**.
– ORIGIN from Arabic *al-uqṣur* 'the castles'.

luxuriant /lʌgˈʒʊərɪənt, lʌgˈzjʊə-, lʌkˈsjʊə-/ ▶ **adjective** (of vegetation) rich and profuse in growth; lush.
▪ (of hair) thick and healthy.
– DERIVATIVES **luxuriance** noun, **luxuriantly** adverb.
– ORIGIN mid 16th cent.: from Latin *luxuriant-* 'growing rankly', from the verb *luxuriare*, from *luxuria* 'luxury, rankness'.

luxuriate /lʌgˈʒʊərɪeɪt, lʌgˈzjʊə-, lʌkˈsjʊə-/ ▶ **verb** [no obj.] (**luxuriate in/over**) enjoy (something) as a luxury; take self-indulgent delight in: *she was luxuriating in a long bath*.
– ORIGIN early 17th cent.: from Latin *luxuriat-* 'grown in abundance', from the verb *luxuriare*.

luxurious ▶ **adjective** extremely comfortable, elegant, or enjoyable, especially in a way that involves great expense: *the bedrooms have luxurious marble bathrooms | many of the leadership led relatively luxurious lives*.
▪ giving self-indulgent or sensual pleasure: *a luxurious wallow in a scented bath*.
– DERIVATIVES **luxuriously** adverb, **luxuriousness** noun.
– ORIGIN Middle English (in the sense 'lascivious'): from Old French *luxurios*, from Latin *luxuriosus*, from *luxuria* 'luxury'.

luxury ▶ **noun** (pl. **-ies**) [mass noun] the state of great comfort and extravagant living: *he lived a life of luxury*.
▪ [count noun] an inessential, desirable item which is expensive or difficult to obtain: *luxuries like chocolate, scent, and fizzy wine | he considers bananas a luxury*.
▶ **adjective** [attrib.] luxurious or of the nature of a luxury: *a luxury yacht | luxury goods*.
– ORIGIN Middle English (denoting lechery): from Old French *luxurie*, *luxure*, from Latin *luxuria*, from *luxus* 'excess'. The earliest current sense dates from the mid 17th cent.

Luzern /luˈtsɛrn/ German name for **LUCERNE**.

Luzon /luːˈzɒn/ the most northerly and the largest island in the Philippines. Its chief towns are Quezon City and Manila, the country's capital.

LV ▶ **abbreviation for** (in the UK) luncheon voucher.

Lviv /lvɪv/ an industrial city in western Ukraine, near the border with Poland; pop. 798,000 (1990). Russian name **Lvov** /ljvɔf/; Polish name **Lwów**; German name **LEMBERG**.

LVO ▶ **abbreviation for** Lieutenant of the Royal Victorian Order.

LWB ▶ **abbreviation for** long wheelbase.

lwei /ləˈweɪ/ ▶ **noun** (pl. same) a monetary unit of Angola, equal to one hundredth of a kwanza.
– ORIGIN a local word.

Lwena ▶ **noun** another term for **LUVALE** (the language).

LWM ▶ **abbreviation for** low-water mark.

L-word ▶ **noun** informal, humorous used in place of the word 'liberal' in a political context where this word is regarded as having negative connotations.

Lwów /lvuf/ Polish name for **LVIV**.

lx Physics ▶ **abbreviation for** lux.

LXX ▶ **symbol for** Septuagint.
– ORIGIN special use of the Roman numeral for 70.

-ly[1] ▶ **suffix** forming adjectives meaning: **1** having the qualities of: *brotherly | rascally*.
2 recurring at intervals of: *hourly | quarterly*.
– ORIGIN Old English *-lic*, of Germanic origin; related to **LIKE**[1].

-ly[2] ▶ **suffix** forming adverbs from adjectives, chiefly denoting manner or degree: *greatly | happily | pointedly*.
– ORIGIN Old English *-līce*, of Germanic origin.

Lyallpur /ˌlʌɪəlˈpʊə/ former name (until 1979) for **FAISALABAD**.

lyase /ˈlʌɪeɪz/ ▶ **noun** Biochemistry an enzyme which catalyses the joining of specified molecules or groups by a double bond.

lycaenid /lʌɪˈsiːnɪd/ ▶ **noun** Entomology a small butterfly of a family (Lycaenidae) that includes the blues, coppers, hairstreaks, and arguses.
– ORIGIN late 19th cent.: from modern Latin *Lycaenidae* (plural), from the genus name *Lycaena*, apparently from Greek *lukaina* 'she-wolf'.

lycanthrope /ˈlʌɪk(ə)nˌθrəʊp/ ▶ **noun** a werewolf.
– ORIGIN early 17th cent.: from modern Latin *lycanthropus*, from Greek *lukanthrōpos* 'wolf man' (see **LYCANTHROPY**).

lycanthropy /lʌɪˈkanθrəpi/ ▶ **noun** [mass noun] the supernatural transformation of a person into a wolf, as recounted in folk tales.
▪ archaic a form of madness involving the delusion of being an animal, usually a wolf, with correspondingly altered behaviour.
– DERIVATIVES **lycanthropic** adjective.
– ORIGIN late 16th cent. (as a supposed form of madness): from modern Latin *lycanthropia*, from Greek *lukanthrōpia*, from *lukos* 'wolf' + *anthrōpos* 'man'.

lycée /ˈliːseɪ, French lise/ ▶ **noun** (pl. pronounced same) a secondary school in France that is funded by the state.
– ORIGIN French, from Latin *lyceum* (see **LYCEUM**).

Lyceum /lʌɪˈsiːəm/ the garden at Athens in which Aristotle taught philosophy.
▪ [as noun **the Lyceum**] Aristotelian philosophy and its followers. ▪ [as noun **a lyceum**] US archaic a literary institution, lecture hall, or teaching place.
– ORIGIN via Latin from Greek *Lukeion*, neuter of *Lukeios*, epithet of Apollo (from whose neighbouring temple the Lyceum was named).

lychee /ˈlʌɪtʃiː, ˈlɪ-/ (also **litchi** or **lichee**) ▶ **noun** **1** a small rounded fruit with sweet white scented flesh, a large central stone, and a thin rough skin.
2 the Chinese tree which bears this fruit.
• *Nephelium litchi* (or *Litchi chinensis*), family Sapindaceae.
– ORIGIN late 16th cent.: from Chinese *lìzhī*.

lychgate /ˈlɪtʃgeɪt/ (also **lichgate**) ▶ **noun** a roofed gateway to a churchyard, formerly used at burials for sheltering a coffin until the clergyman's arrival.
– ORIGIN late 15th cent.: from Old English *līc* 'body' + **GATE**[1].

lychnis /ˈlɪknɪs/ ▶ **noun** a plant of a genus which includes the campions, ragged robin, and a number of cultivated ornamental flowers.
• Genus *Lychnis*, family Caryophyllaceae.
– ORIGIN modern Latin, via Latin from Greek *lukhnis*, denoting a red flower, from *lukhnos* 'lamp'.

Lycia /ˈlɪsɪə/ an ancient region on the coast of SW Asia Minor, between Caria and Pamphylia.
– DERIVATIVES **Lycian** adjective & noun.

lycopene /ˈlʌɪkə(ʊ)piːn/ ▶ **noun** [mass noun] Biochemistry a red carotenoid pigment present in tomatoes and many berries and fruits.
– ORIGIN 1930s: from the variant *lycopin* (from modern Latin *Lycopersicon*, a genus name including the tomato) + **-ENE**.

lycopod /ˈlʌɪkə(ʊ)pɒd/ ▶ **noun** Botany a clubmoss, especially a lycopodium. Giant lycopods the size of trees were common in the Carboniferous period.
• Class Lycopsida: several families.
– ORIGIN mid 19th cent.: Anglicized form of **LYCOPODIUM**.

lycopodium /ˌlʌɪkə(ʊ)ˈpəʊdɪəm/ ▶ **noun** a plant of a genus that includes the common clubmosses.
• Genus *Lycopodium*, family Lycopodiaceae.
▪ (usu. **lycopodium powder** or **lycopodium seed**) [mass noun] a fine flammable powder consisting of clubmoss spores, formerly used as an absorbent in surgery, in experiments in the physical sciences, and in making fireworks.
– ORIGIN modern Latin, from Greek *lukos* 'wolf' + *pous*, *pod-* 'foot' (because of the claw-like shape of the root).

Lycopsida /lʌɪˈkɒpsɪdə/ Botany a class of pteridophyte plants that comprises the clubmosses and their extinct relatives.
– DERIVATIVES **lycopsid** noun & adjective.
– ORIGIN modern Latin (plural), from Greek *lukos* 'wolf' + *opsis* 'appearance'.

Lycra /ˈlʌɪkrə/ ▶ **noun** [mass noun] trademark an elastic polyurethane fibre or fabric used especially for close-fitting sports clothing.

Lycurgus /lʌɪˈkəːgəs/ (9th century BC), Spartan lawgiver. He is traditionally held to have been the founder of the constitution and military regime of ancient Sparta.

lyddite /ˈlɪdʌɪt/ ▶ **noun** [mass noun] chiefly historical a high explosive containing picric acid, used chiefly by the British during the First World War.
– ORIGIN late 19th cent.: named after *Lydd*, a town in Kent where the explosive was first tested, + **-ITE**[1].

Lydgate /ˈlɪdgeɪt/, John (*c*.1370–*c*.1450), English poet and monk. His copious output of verse, often in Chaucerian style, includes the poetical translations the *Troy Book* (1412–20) and *The Fall of Princes* (1431–8).

Lydia /ˈlɪdɪə/ an ancient region of western Asia Minor, south of Mysia and north of Caria. It became a powerful kingdom in the 7th century BC but in 546 its final king, Croesus, was defeated by Cyrus and it was absorbed into the Persian empire. Lydia was probably the first realm to use coined money.

Lydian ▶ **noun** **1** a native or inhabitant of Lydia.
2 [mass noun] the extinct language of the Lydians, an Anatolian language of which some inscriptions and other texts have survived, in a version of the Greek alphabet.
▶ **adjective** of or relating to the Lydians or their language.

Lydian mode ▶ **noun** Music the mode represented by the natural diatonic scale F–F (containing an augmented 4th).

lye ▶ **noun** [mass noun] a strongly alkaline solution, especially of potassium hydroxide, used for washing or cleansing.
– ORIGIN Old English *lēag*, of Germanic origin: related to Dutch *loog*, German *Lauge*, also to **LATHER**.

Lyell /ˈlʌɪəl/, Sir Charles (1797–1875), Scottish geologist. His textbook *Principles of Geology* (1830–3) influenced a generation of geologists and held that the earth's features were shaped over a long period of time by natural processes, thus clearing the way for Darwin's theory of evolution.

lying[1] present participle of **LIE**[1].

lying[2] present participle of **LIE**[2]. ▶ **adjective** [attrib.] not telling the truth: *he's a lying, cheating, snake in the grass*.
– DERIVATIVES **lyingly** adverb.

lying-in ▶ **noun** archaic seclusion before and after childbirth; confinement.

lying-in-state ▶ **noun** the display of the corpse of a public figure for public tribute before it is buried or cremated.

lyke wake /lʌɪk/ ▶ **noun** Brit. a night spent watching over a dead body, typically acting as a celebration to mark the passing of the person's soul.
– ORIGIN late Middle English: from *lyke* (from Old

English *lic* 'body': compare with **LYCHGATE**) and the noun **WAKE**[1].

Lyly /ˈlɪli/, John (c.1554–1606), English prose writer and dramatist. His prose romance in two parts, *Euphues, The Anatomy of Wit* (1578) and *Euphues and his England* (1580) was written in an elaborate style that became known as *euphuism*.

Lyman series /ˈlaɪmən/ Physics a series of lines in the ultraviolet spectrum of atomic hydrogen, between 122 and 91 nanometres.
– ORIGIN early 20th cent.: named after Theodore *Lyman* (1874–1954), American physicist.

Lyme disease /laɪm/ ▶ noun [mass noun] a form of arthritis caused by bacteria that are transmitted by ticks.
● Lyme disease is caused by the spirochaete *Borrelia burgdorferi.*
– ORIGIN 1970s: named after *Lyme*, a town in Connecticut, US, where an outbreak occurred.

lymph /lɪmf/ ▶ noun [mass noun] **1** Physiology a colourless fluid containing white blood cells, which bathes the tissues and drains through the lymphatic system into the bloodstream.
■ fluid exuding from a sore or inflamed tissue.
2 poetic/literary pure water.
– DERIVATIVES **lymphoid** adjective, **lymphous** adjective.
– ORIGIN late 16th cent. (in sense 2): from French *lymphe* or Latin *lympha*, *limpa* 'water'.

lymph- ▶ combining form variant spelling of **LYMPHO-** shortened before a vowel, as in *lymphangiography.*

lymphadenitis /ˌlɪmfadɪˈnaɪtɪs/ ▶ noun [mass noun] Medicine inflammation of the lymph nodes.

lymphadenopathy /ˌlɪmfadɪˈnɒpəθi/ ▶ noun [mass noun] Medicine a disease affecting the lymph nodes.

lymphangiography /ˌlɪmfandʒɪˈɒɡrəfi/ ▶ noun [mass noun] Medicine X-ray examination of the vessels of the lymphatic system after injection of a substance opaque to X-rays.
– DERIVATIVES **lymphangiogram** noun, **lymphangiographic** adjective.

lymphangitis /ˌlɪmfanˈdʒaɪtɪs/ ▶ noun [mass noun] Medicine inflammation of the walls of the lymphatic vessels.

lymphatic ▶ adjective **1** [attrib.] Physiology of or relating to lymph or its secretion: *lymphatic vessels | lymphatic drainage.*
2 archaic (of a person) pale, flabby, or sluggish.
▶ noun Anatomy a vein-like vessel conveying lymph in the body.
– ORIGIN mid 17th cent. (in the sense 'frenzied, mad'): from Latin *lymphaticus* 'mad', from Greek *numpholēptos* 'seized by nymphs'; now associated with **LYMPH**, on the pattern of words such as *spermatic.*

lymphatic system ▶ noun the network of vessels through which lymph drains from the tissues into the blood.

lymph gland ▶ noun less technical term for **LYMPH NODE**.

lymph node ▶ noun Physiology each of a number of small swellings in the lymphatic system where lymph is filtered and lymphocytes are formed.

lympho- (also **lymph-** before a vowel) ▶ combining form representing **LYMPH**: *lymphocyte.*

lymphoblast /ˈlɪmfə(ʊ)blast/ ▶ noun Medicine an abnormal cell resembling a large lymphocyte, produced in large numbers in a form of leukaemia.
– DERIVATIVES **lymphoblastic** adjective.

lymphocyte /ˈlɪmfə(ʊ)saɪt/ ▶ noun Physiology a form of small leucocyte (white blood cell) with a single round nucleus, occurring especially in the lymphatic system.
– DERIVATIVES **lymphocytic** adjective.

lymphoid /ˈlɪmfɔɪd/ ▶ adjective Anatomy & Medicine of, relating to, or denoting the tissue responsible for producing lymphocytes and antibodies. This tissue occurs in the lymph nodes, thymus, tonsils, and spleen, and dispersed elsewhere in the body.

lymphokine /ˈlɪmfə(ʊ)kʌɪn/ ▶ noun Physiology a substance of a type produced by lymphocytes and having an effect on other cells of the immune system.
– ORIGIN 1960s: from **LYMPHO-** + Greek *kinein* 'to move'.

lymphoma /lɪmˈfəʊmə/ ▶ noun (pl. **lymphomas** or **lymphomata** /-mətə/) [mass noun] Medicine cancer of the lymph nodes.

lymphoreticular /ˌlɪmfə(ʊ)rɪˈtɪkjʊlə/ ▶ adjective another term for **RETICULOENDOTHELIAL**.

lynch ▶ verb [with obj.] (of a group of people) kill (someone) for an alleged offence without a legal trial, especially by hanging.
– DERIVATIVES **lyncher** noun.
– ORIGIN mid 19th cent.: from *Lynch's law*, named after Capt. William *Lynch*, head of a self-constituted judicial tribunal in Virginia c.1780.

lynchet /ˈlɪn(t)ʃɪt/ ▶ noun a ridge or ledge formed along the downhill side of a plot by ploughing in ancient times.
– ORIGIN late 17th cent.: probably from dialect *linch* 'rising ground'; compare with **LINKS**.

lynch mob ▶ noun a band of people intent on lynching someone.

lynchpin ▶ noun variant spelling of **LINCHPIN**.

Lynn, Dame Vera (b.1917), English singer; born *Vera Margaret Lewis*. She is known chiefly for her rendering of such songs as 'We'll Meet Again' and 'White Cliffs of Dover', which she sang to the troops in the Second World War.

Lynx /lɪŋks/ Astronomy an inconspicuous northern constellation (the Lynx), between Ursa Major and Gemini.
■ [as genitive **Lyncis** /ˈlɪnsɪs/] used with preceding letter or numeral to designate a star in this constellation: *the star Alpha Lyncis.*
– ORIGIN via Latin from Greek *lunx.*

lynx ▶ noun a wild cat with yellowish-brown fur (sometimes spotted), a short tail, and tufted ears, found chiefly in the northern latitudes of North America and Eurasia.
● Genus *Lynx*, family Felidae: the **Eurasian lynx** (*L. lynx*) and the **Canadian lynx** (*L. canadensis* or *L. lynx*).
■ [mass noun] the fur of the lynx. ■ (**African lynx**) see **CARACAL**.
– ORIGIN Middle English: via Latin from Greek *lunx.*

lynx-eyed ▶ adjective keen-sighted.

Lyon (in full **Lord Lyon** or **Lyon King of Arms**) ▶ noun the chief herald of Scotland.
– ORIGIN late Middle English: archaic variant of **LION**, named from the lion on the royal shield.

Lyon Court ▶ noun the court over which the Lyon King of Arms presides.

lyonnaise /ˌliːəˈneɪz/ ▶ adjective (of food, especially sliced potatoes) cooked with onions or with a white wine and onion sauce.
– ORIGIN French, 'characteristic of the city of Lyons'.

Lyons /ˈliːɒ̃, French ljɔ̃/ an industrial city and river port in SE France, situated at the confluence of the Rhône and Saône Rivers; pop. 422,440 (1990). Founded by the Romans in AD 43 as Lugdunum, it was an important city of Roman Gaul. French name **LYON** /ljɔ̃/.

lyophilic /ˌlaɪə(ʊ)ˈfɪlɪk/ ▶ adjective Chemistry (of a colloid) readily dispersed by a solvent and not easily precipitated.
– ORIGIN early 20th cent.: from Greek *luein* 'loosen, dissolve' + *philos* 'loving'.

lyophilize /laɪˈɒfɪlaɪz/ (also **-ise**) ▶ verb [with obj.] technical freeze-dry (a substance).
– DERIVATIVES **lyophilization** noun.

lyophobic /ˌlaɪəˈfəʊbɪk/ ▶ adjective Chemistry (of a colloid) not lyophilic.

Lyotard /ˈljɒtɑː, French ljɔtar/, Jean-François (1924–98), French philosopher and literary critic. He outlined his 'philosophy of desire', based on the politics of Nietzsche, in *L'Économie libidinale* (1974). In later books he adopted a postmodern quasi-Wittgensteinian linguistic philosophy.

Lyra /ˈlaɪrə/ Astronomy a small northern constellation (the Lyre), said to represent the lyre invented by Hermes. It contains the bright star Vega.
■ [as genitive **Lyrae** /ˈlaɪriː/] used with preceding letter or numeral to designate a star in this constellation: *the star Beta Lyrae.*
– ORIGIN Latin.

lyrate /ˈlaɪreɪt/ ▶ adjective Biology lyre-shaped.
– ORIGIN mid 18th cent.: from Latin *lyra* 'lyre' + **-ATE**[2].

lyre ▶ noun a stringed instrument like a small U-shaped harp with strings fixed to a crossbar, used especially in ancient Greece. Modern instruments of this type are found mainly in East Africa.
– ORIGIN Middle English: via Old French *lire* and Latin *lyra* from Greek *lura.*

lyrebird ▶ noun a large Australian songbird, the male of which has a long lyre-shaped tail and is noted for his remarkable song and display.
● Family Menuridae and genus *Menura*: two species, in particular the **superb lyrebird** (*M. novaehollandiae*).

lyretail ▶ noun a small African killifish which is popular in aquaria. The colour pattern and shape of the tail, especially in the brightly coloured male, are suggestive of a lyre.
● Several genera and species, family Cyprinodontidae.

lyric ▶ adjective **1** (of poetry) expressing the writer's emotions, usually briefly and in stanzas or recognized forms.
■ (of a poet) writing in this manner.
2 (of a singing voice) using a light register: *a lyric soprano with a light, clear timbre.*
▶ noun (usu. **lyrics**) **1** a lyric poem or verse.
■ [mass noun] lyric poetry as a literary genre.
2 the words of a song: *she has published both music and lyrics for a number of songs.*
– ORIGIN late 16th cent.: from French *lyrique* or Latin *lyricus*, from Greek *lurikos*, from *lura* 'lyre'.

lyrical ▶ adjective **1** (of literature, art, or music) expressing the writer's emotions in an imaginative and beautiful way: *he gained a devoted following for his lyrical cricket writing.*
■ (of poetry or a poet) lyric: *Wordsworth's Lyrical Ballads.*
2 of or relating to the words of a popular song: *the lyrical content of his songs.*
– PHRASES **wax lyrical** talk in a highly enthusiastic and effusive way: *waxing lyrical about his splendid son-in-law.*
– DERIVATIVES **lyrically** adverb.

lyricism ▶ noun [mass noun] an artist's expression of emotion in an imaginative and beautiful way; the quality of being lyrical.

lyricist ▶ noun a person who writes the words to a popular song or musical.

lyrist ▶ noun **1** /ˈlaɪərɪst/ a person who plays the lyre. **2** /ˈlɪrɪst/ a lyric poet.
– ORIGIN mid 17th cent.: from Latin *lyrista*, from Greek *luristēs*, from *lura* 'lyre'.

Lysander /lʌɪˈsandə/ (d.395 BC), Spartan general. He defeated the Athenian navy in 405 and captured Athens in 404, so bringing the Peloponnesian War to an end.

lysate /ˈlaɪzeɪt/ ▶ noun Biology a preparation containing the products of lysis of cells.

lyse /lʌɪz/ ▶ verb Biology undergo or cause to undergo lysis.
– ORIGIN early 20th cent.: back-formation from **LYSIS**.

Lysenko /lɪˈsɛŋkəʊ/, Trofim Denisovich (1898–1976), Soviet biologist and geneticist. He was an adherent of Lamarck's theory of evolution by the inheritance of acquired characteristics. Since his ideas harmonized with Marxist ideology he was favoured by Stalin and dominated Soviet genetics for many years.

lysergic acid /lʌɪˈsəːdʒɪk/ (abbrev.: **LSD**) ▶ noun [mass noun] Chemistry a crystalline compound prepared from natural ergot alkaloids or synthetically, from which the drug LSD (**lysergic acid diethylamide**) can be made.
● A tetracyclic acid; chem. formula: $C_{16}H_{16}N_2O_2$.
– ORIGIN 1930s: *lysergic* from (*hydro*)*lys*(*is*) + *erg*(*ot*) + **-IC**.

lysin /ˈlaɪsɪn/ ▶ noun Biology an antibody or other substance able to cause lysis of cells (especially bacteria).
– ORIGIN early 20th cent.: from German *Lysine.*

lysine /ˈlaɪsiːn/ ▶ noun [mass noun] Biochemistry a basic amino acid which is a constituent of most proteins. It is an essential nutrient in the diet of vertebrates.
● Chem. formula: $NH_2(CH_2)_4CH(NH_2)COOH$.
– ORIGIN late 19th cent.: from German *Lysin*, based on **LYSIS**.

Lysippus /lʌɪˈsɪpəs/ (4th century BC), Greek sculptor. He is said to have introduced a naturalistic scheme of proportions for the human body into Greek sculpture.

lysis /ˈlaɪsɪs/ ▶ noun [mass noun] Biology the disintegration of a cell by rupture of the cell wall or membrane.
– ORIGIN early 19th cent.: from Latin, from Greek *lusis* 'loosening', from *luein* 'loosen'.

-lysis ▶ combining form denoting disintegration or decomposition: ■ in nouns specifying an agent: *hydrolysis.* ■ in nouns specifying a reactant:

haemolysis. ■ in nouns specifying the nature of the process: *autolysis.*
– ORIGIN via Latin from Greek *lusis* 'loosening'.

Lysol /ˈlʌɪsɒl/ ▶ noun [mass noun] trademark a disinfectant consisting of a mixture of cresols and soft soap.
– ORIGIN late 19th cent.: from LYSIS + -OL.

lysosome /ˈlʌɪsəsəʊm/ ▶ noun Biology an organelle in the cytoplasm of eukaryotic cells containing degradative enzymes enclosed in a membrane.
– DERIVATIVES **lysosomal** adjective.

lysozyme /ˈlʌɪsəzʌɪm/ ▶ noun [mass noun] Biochemistry an enzyme which catalyses the destruction of the cell walls of certain bacteria, and occurs notably in tears and egg white.
– ORIGIN early 20th cent.: from LYSIS + a shortened form of ENZYME.

lytic /ˈlɪtɪk/ ▶ adjective Biology of, relating to, or causing lysis: *the lytic activity of bile acids.*
– DERIVATIVES **lytically** adverb.

-lytic ▶ combining form in adjectives corresponding to nouns ending in *-lysis* (such as *hydrolytic* corresponding to *hydrolysis*).
– ORIGIN from Greek *-lutikos* 'able to loosen'.

Lytton /ˈlɪt(ə)n/, 1st Baron (1803–73), British novelist, dramatist, and statesman; born *Edward George Earle Bulwer-Lytton*. He achieved literary success with *Pelham* (1828), a novel of fashionable society, and also wrote historical romances (such as *The Last Days of Pompeii*, 1834) and plays. He became an MP in 1831 and later served in many diplomatic roles including Viceroy of India (1876–80).

Mm

M¹ (also **m**) ▶ noun (pl. **Ms** or **M's**) **1** the thirteenth letter of the alphabet.
■ denoting the next after L in a set of items, categories, etc.
2 (M) a shape like that of a capital M.
3 the Roman numeral for 1,000. [ORIGIN: from Latin *mille*.]

M² ▶ abbreviation for ■ Cricket (on scorecards) maiden over(s). ■ male. ■ Malta (international vehicle registration). ■ medium (as a clothes size). ■ [in combination] (in units of measurement) mega-: *8 Mbytes of memory*. ■ Astronomy Messier (catalogue of nebulae): *the galaxy M33*. ■ Chemistry (with reference to solutions) molar: *0.15 M NaCl solution*. ■ Monsieur: *M Chirac*. ■ (in UK road designations) motorway: *the M25*.
▶ symbol for Physics mutual inductance.

m ▶ abbreviation for ■ mare. ■ married: *m twice; two d*. ■ masculine. ■ (*m*-) [in combination] Chemistry meta-: *m-xylene*. ■ metre(s). ■ mile(s). ■ [in combination] (in units of measurement) milli-: *100 mA*. ■ million(s): *£5 m*. ■ minute(s).
▶ symbol for Physics mass: $E = mc^2$.

m' ▶ possessive determiner Brit. short for **MY** (representing the pronunciation used by lawyers in court to refer to or address the judge or a fellow barrister on the same side): *he can't hold the Bible, m'lud*.

'm¹ informal ▶ abbreviation for am: *I'm a doctor*.

'm² ▶ noun informal madam: *yes'm*.

MA ▶ abbreviation for ■ Massachusetts (in official postal use). ■ Master of Arts: *David Jones, MA*. ■ Morocco (international vehicle registration). [ORIGIN: from French *Maroc*.]

ma ▶ noun informal one's mother: *I want my ma*.
– ORIGIN early 19th cent.: abbreviation of **MAMA**.

ma'am ▶ noun a term of respectful or polite address used for:
■ Brit. female royalty. ■ a female police officer above the rank of sergeant who is senior to the speaker. ■ a female officer in the armed forces who is senior to the speaker. ■ N. Amer. or Brit. archaic any woman.
– ORIGIN mid 17th cent.: contraction of **MADAM**.

maar /mɑː/ ▶ noun Geology a broad, shallow crater, typically filled by a lake, formed by a volcanic explosion with little lava.
– ORIGIN early 19th cent.: from German dialect, originally denoting a kind of crater lake in the Eifel district of Germany.

Maas /mɑːs/ Dutch name for **MEUSE**.

maas /mɑːs/ ▶ noun [mass noun] S. African thick, naturally soured milk.
– ORIGIN Afrikaans, from Zulu *amasi* (plural), denoting curdled milk.

Maasai ▶ noun & adjective variant spelling of **MASAI**.

maasbanker /mɑːsˈbaŋkə/ ▶ noun (pl. same or **maasbankers**) South African term for **HORSE MACKEREL**.
– ORIGIN from Dutch *marsbanker*.

Maastricht /ˈmɑːstrɪxt/ an industrial city in the Netherlands, capital of the province of Limburg, situated on the River Maas near the Belgian and German borders; pop. 117,420 (1991).

Maastricht Treaty a treaty on European economic and monetary union, agreed by the heads of government of the twelve member states of the European Community at a summit meeting in Maastricht in December 1991. Ratification was completed in October 1993.

Maat /mɑːt/ Egyptian Mythology the goddess of truth, justice, and cosmic order, daughter of Ra. She is depicted as a young and beautiful woman, standing or seated, with a feather on her head.

mabela /məˈbiːlə/ (also **mabele**) ▶ noun [mass noun] S. African sorghum of a variety grown in southern Africa, used chiefly for making porridge and beer.
■ meal or porridge made from this.
– ORIGIN early 19th cent.: compare with Zulu and Xhosa *amabele*, plural of *ibele*.

Mabinogion /ˌmabɪˈnɒɡɪən, -ˈnəʊɡɪən/ a collection of Welsh prose tales of the 11th–13th centuries, dealing with Celtic legends and mythology.
– ORIGIN from Welsh *Mabinogi* 'instruction for young bards'.

Mabuse /məˈbjuːz/ Jan (*c.*1478–*c.*1533), Flemish painter; Flemish name *Jan Gossaert*. He was one of the first artists to disseminate the Italian style in the Netherlands.

Mac ▶ noun informal, chiefly N. Amer. a form of address for a man whose name is unknown to the speaker.
– ORIGIN early 17th cent. (originally a form of address to a Scotsman): from *Mac*-, a patronymic prefix in many Scots and Irish surnames.

mac (also **mack**) ▶ noun Brit. informal a mackintosh.
– ORIGIN early 20th cent.: abbreviation.

macabre /məˈkɑːbr(ə)/ ▶ adjective disturbing and horrifying because of involvement with or depiction of death and injury: *a macabre series of murders*.
– ORIGIN late 19th cent.: from French *macabre*, from *Danse Macabre* 'dance of death', from Old French, perhaps from *Macabé* 'a Maccabee', with reference to a miracle play depicting the slaughter of the Maccabees.

macadam /məˈkadəm/ ▶ noun [mass noun] broken stone of even size used in successively compacted layers for surfacing roads and paths, and typically bound with tar or bitumen.
– DERIVATIVES **macadamed** adjective.
– ORIGIN early 19th cent.: named after John L. McAdam (1756–1836), the British surveyor who advocated using this material.

macadamia /ˌmakəˈdeɪmɪə/ ▶ noun an Australian rainforest tree with slender, glossy evergreen leaves and globular edible nuts.
● Genus *Macadamia*, family Proteaceae: several species, especially *M. integrifolia* and *M. tetraphylla*, which are cultivated for their nuts.
■ (also **macadamia nut**) the edible nut of this tree.
– ORIGIN modern Latin, named after John Macadam (1827–65), Australian chemist.

macadamize ▶ verb [with obj.] make or cover with macadam: [as adj. **macadamized**] *macadamized roads*.

macajuel /ˈmakawɛl/ ▶ noun West Indian term for **BOA CONSTRICTOR**.
– ORIGIN from an American Indian word.

McAleese /ˌmakəˈliːs/, Mary (Patricia) (b.1951), Irish stateswoman, President since 1997.

MacAlpin /məˈkalpɪn/, Kenneth, see **KENNETH I**.

Macanese /ˌmakəˈniːz/ ▶ noun (pl. same) **1** a native or inhabitant of Macao, especially one of mixed Chinese and Portuguese descent.
2 [mass noun] a Portuguese creole formerly used in Macao.
▶ adjective of or relating to Macao or the Macanese.
– ORIGIN from **MACAO**, on the pattern of words such as *Japanese*.

Macao /məˈkaʊ/ a former Portuguese dependency on the SE coast of China, on the west side of the Pearl River estuary opposite Hong Kong; pop. 467,000 (est. 1991); official languages, Portuguese and Cantonese; capital, Macao City. Portuguese name **MACAU**.

> The area comprises the Macao peninsula and two nearby islands. Macao was developed by the Portuguese as a trading post, becoming in the 18th century the chief centre of trade between Europe and China. Under the terms of a 1987 agreement sovereignty passed to China in 1999.

– DERIVATIVES **Macanese** adjective & noun.

Macapá /ˌmakəˈpɑː/ a town in northern Brazil, on the Amazon delta, capital of the state of Amapá; pop. 166,750 (1990).

macaque /məˈkɑːk, -ˈkak/ ▶ noun a medium-sized, chiefly forest-dwelling Old World monkey which has a long face and cheek pouches for holding food.
● Genus *Macaca*, family Cercopithecidae: several species, including the rhesus monkey and the barbary ape.
– ORIGIN late 17th cent.: via French and Portuguese; based on the Bantu morpheme *ma* (denoting a plural) + *kaku* 'monkey'.

Macaronesia /ˌmakərə(ʊ)ˈniːzɪə/ Botany a phytogeographical region comprising the Azores, Madeira, Canary Islands, and Cape Verde Islands in the eastern North Atlantic.
– DERIVATIVES **Macaronesian** adjective.
– ORIGIN from Greek *makarōn nēsoi* 'islands of the Blessed' (mythical islands later associated with the Canaries).

macaroni /ˌmakəˈrəʊni/ ▶ noun (pl. **-ies**) **1** [mass noun] a variety of pasta formed in narrow tubes.
2 an 18th-century British dandy affecting Continental fashions.
– ORIGIN late 16th cent.: from Italian *maccaroni* (now usually spelled *maccheroni*), plural of *maccarone*, from late Greek *makaria* 'food made from barley'.

macaronic /ˌmakəˈrɒnɪk/ ▶ adjective denoting language, especially burlesque verse, containing words or inflections from one language introduced into the context of another.
▶ noun (usu. **macaronics**) macaronic verse, especially that which mixes the vernacular with Latin.
– ORIGIN early 17th cent. (in the sense 'characteristic of a jumble or medley'): from modern Latin *macaronicus*, from obsolete Italian *macaronico*, a humorous formation from *macaroni* (see **MACARONI**).

macaroni cheese ▶ noun [mass noun] a savoury dish of macaroni in a cheese sauce.

macaroni penguin ▶ noun a penguin with an orange crest, breeding on islands in the Antarctic.
● *Eudyptes chrysolophus*, family Spheniscidae.
– ORIGIN early 19th cent.: so named because the

---

b **b**ut | d **d**og | f **f**ew | g **g**et | h **h**e | j **y**es | k **c**at | l **l**eg | m **m**an | n **n**o | p **p**en | r **r**ed | s **s**it | t **t**op | v **v**oice | w **w**e | z **z**oo | ʃ **sh**e | ʒ deci**s**ion | θ **th**in | ð **th**is | ŋ ri**ng** | x lo**ch** | tʃ **ch**ip | dʒ **j**ar

orange crest was thought to resemble the hairstyle of dandies known as *macaronies* (see **MACARONI**).

macaroon /ˌmakəˈruːn/ ▶ noun a light biscuit made with egg white, sugar, and ground almonds or sometimes coconut.
– ORIGIN late 16th cent.: from French *macaron*, from Italian *maccarone* (see **MACARONI**).

MacArthur, Douglas (1880–1964), American general. Commander of US (later Allied) forces in the SW Pacific during the Second World War, he accepted Japan's surrender in 1945, and administered the ensuing Allied occupation.

Macassar /məˈkasə/ ▶ noun 1 (also **Macassar oil**) [mass noun] a kind of oil formerly used by men to make their hair shine and lie flat.
2 variant spelling of **MAKASSAR**.
– ORIGIN mid 17th cent.: earlier form of **MAKASSAR**. The oil was originally represented as consisting of ingredients from Makassar.

Macassarese ▶ noun & adjective archaic spelling of **MAKASARESE**.

Macau /məˈkau/ Portuguese name for **MACAO**.

Macaulay[1] /məˈkɔːli/, Dame (Emilie) Rose (1881–1958), English novelist and essayist. Notable novels: *Potterism* (1920), *The World My Wilderness* (1950), and *The Towers of Trebizond* (1956).

Macaulay[2] /məˈkɔːli/, Thomas Babington, 1st Baron (1800–59), English historian, essayist, and philanthropist. He was a civil servant in India, where he established a system of education and a new criminal code, before returning to Britain and devoting himself to literature and politics. Notable works: *The Lays of Ancient Rome* (1842) and *History of England* (1849–61).

macaw /məˈkɔː/ ▶ noun a large long-tailed parrot with brightly coloured plumage, native to Central and South America.
● *Ara* and related genera: family Psittacidae: several species.
– ORIGIN early 17th cent.: from Portuguese *macao*, of unknown origin.

Macbeth (c.1005–57), king of Scotland 1040–57. He came to the throne after killing his cousin Duncan I in battle, and was himself defeated and killed by Malcolm III. Shakespeare's tragedy *Macbeth* considerably embroiders the historical events.

McBurney's point ▶ noun Medicine a point on the surface of the abdomen which lies one third of the way along a line from the tip of the hip bone to the navel, and is the point of maximum tenderness in appendicitis.
– ORIGIN late 19th cent.: named after Charles McBurney (1845–1913), American surgeon.

Macc. ▶ abbreviation for Maccabees (Apocrypha) (in biblical references).

Maccabaeus, Judas, see **JUDAS MACCABAEUS**.

Maccabees /ˈmakəbiːz/ ▶ plural noun historical the members or followers of the family of the Jewish leader Judas Maccabaeus.
■ (in full **the Books of (the) Maccabees**) four books of Jewish history and theology, of which the first and second are in the Apocrypha and feature Judas Maccabaeus.
– DERIVATIVES **Maccabean** /ˌmakəˈbiːən/ adjective.
– ORIGIN late Middle English: from Latin *Maccabaeus*, an epithet applied to Judas, perhaps from Hebrew *maqqebet* 'hammer' (by association with the religious revolt led by Judas).

McCarthy[1], Joseph (Raymond) (1909–57), American Republican politician. Between 1950 and 1954 he was the instigator of widespread investigations into alleged communist infiltration in US public life.

McCarthy[2], Mary (Therese) (1912–89), American novelist and critic. Notable novels: *The Groves of Academe* (1952) and *The Group* (1963).

McCarthyism ▶ noun [mass noun] a vociferous campaign against alleged communists in the US government and other institutions carried out under Senator Joseph McCarthy in the period 1950–4. Many of the accused were blacklisted or lost their jobs, though most did not in fact belong to the Communist Party.
– DERIVATIVES **McCarthyist** adjective & noun, **McCarthyite** adjective & noun.

McCartney, Sir (James) Paul (b.1942), English pop and rock singer, songwriter, and bass guitarist. A founder member of the Beatles, he wrote most of their songs in collaboration with John Lennon.

After the group broke up in 1970 he formed the band Wings.

McCoy ▶ noun (in phrase **the real McCoy**) informal the real thing; the genuine article: *the apparent fake turned out to be the real McCoy*.

McCullers /məˈkʌləz/, (Lula) Carson (1917–67), American writer. Her work deals sensitively with loneliness and the plight of the eccentric. Notable works: *The Heart is a Lonely Hunter* (1940) and *The Ballad of The Sad Cafe* (1951).

MacDiarmid /məkˈdɜːmɪd/, Hugh (1892–1978), Scottish poet and nationalist; pseudonym of *Christopher Murray Grieve*. The language of his poems drew on the language of various regions of Scotland and historical periods. He was a founder member (1928) of the National Party of Scotland (later the Scottish National Party).

MacDonald[1], Flora (1722–90), Scottish Jacobite heroine. She aided Charles Edward Stuart's escape from English pursuit, after his defeat at Culloden, by smuggling him from Benbecula to Skye in a small boat, disguised as her maid.

Macdonald[2], Sir John Alexander (1815–91), Scottish-born Canadian statesman, Prime Minister 1867–73 and 1878–91. He played a leading role in the confederation of the Canadian provinces, and was appointed first Prime Minister of the Dominion of Canada.

MacDonald[3], (James) Ramsay (1866–1937), British Labour statesman, Prime Minister 1924, 1929–31, and 1931–5. He served as Britain's first Labour Prime Minister.

MacDonnell Ranges a series of mountain ranges extending westwards from Alice Springs in Northern Territory, Australia. The highest peak is Mount Liebig, which rises to a height of 1,524 m (4,948 ft).
– ORIGIN named after Sir Richard *MacDonnell*, governor of South Australia when John Mcdouall Stuart explored the ranges in 1860.

Mace ▶ noun [mass noun] trademark an irritant chemical used in an aerosol to disable attackers.
▶ verb (also **mace**) [with obj.] spray (someone) with Mace.
– ORIGIN 1960s (originally US): probably from **MACE**[1].

mace[1] ▶ noun 1 a staff of office, especially that which lies on the table in the House of Commons when the Speaker is in the chair, regarded as a symbol of the authority of the House.
2 historical a heavy club, typically having a metal head and spikes.
– ORIGIN Middle English: from Old French *masse* 'large hammer'.

mace[2] ▶ noun [mass noun] the reddish fleshy outer covering of the nutmeg, dried as a spice.
– ORIGIN Middle English *macis* (taken as plural), via Old French from Latin *macir*.

macédoine /ˈmasɪdwɑːn/ ▶ noun a mixture of vegetables or fruit cut into small pieces or in jelly.
– ORIGIN French, literally 'Macedonia', with reference to the mixture of peoples in the Macedonian Empire of Alexander the Great.

Macedonia /ˌmasɪˈdəʊnɪə/ 1 (also **Macedon** /ˈmasɪd(ə)n/) an ancient country in SE Europe, at the northern end of the Greek peninsula. In classical times it was a kingdom which under Philip II and Alexander the Great became a world power. The region is now divided between Greece, Bulgaria, and the republic of Macedonia.
2 a region in the north-east of modern Greece; capital, Thessaloníki.
3 a landlocked republic in the Balkans; pop. 2,038,000 (est. 1991); official language, Macedonian; capital, Skopje. Formerly a constituent republic of Yugoslavia, Macedonia became independent after a referendum in 1991.

Macedonian ▶ noun 1 a native or inhabitant of the republic of Macedonia.
■ a native of ancient Macedonia. ■ a native or inhabitant of the region of Macedonia in modern Greece.
2 [mass noun] the Southern Slavic language of the republic of Macedonia and adjacent parts of Bulgaria.
■ the language of ancient Macedonia, probably a dialect of Greek.
▶ adjective of or relating to Macedonia or Macedonian.

Macedonian Wars a series of four wars between Rome and Macedonia in the 3rd and 2nd centuries

BC, which ended in the defeat of Macedonia and its annexation as a Roman province (148 BC).

Maceió /ˌmasɛˈjɔː/ a port in eastern Brazil, on the Atlantic coast; pop. 699,760 (1990). It is the capital of the state of Alagoas.

McEnroe /ˈmakɪnrəʊ/, John (Patrick) (b.1959), American tennis player. He won seven Wimbledon titles (three for the singles: 1981, 1983–4) and four US Open singles championships (1979–84).

macer /ˈmeɪsə/ ▶ noun (in Scotland) an official who keeps order in a law court.
– ORIGIN Middle English: from Old French *massier*, from *masse* (see **MACE**[1]).

macerate /ˈmasəreɪt/ ▶ verb [with obj.] 1 soften or break up (something, especially food) by soaking in a liquid.
■ [no obj.] become softened or broken up by soaking.
2 archaic cause to grow thinner or waste away, especially by fasting.
– DERIVATIVES **maceration** noun, **macerator** noun.
– ORIGIN mid 16th cent.: from Latin *macerat-* 'made soft, soaked', from the verb *macerare*.

macfarlane /məkˈfɑːlən/ ▶ noun dated a type of overcoat with a shoulder cape and slits for access to pockets in clothing worn underneath.
– ORIGIN 1920s: probably from the name of the designer or original manufacturer of the coat, which was first popular in France.

Macgillicuddy's Reeks /məˌgɪlɪˈkʌdɪz ˈriːks/ a range of hills in County Kerry in SW Ireland.

McGonagall /məˈgɒnəg(ə)l/, William (1830–1902), Scottish poet. His poetry is naive yet entertaining doggerel which has won him a reputation as one of the worst poets in the world.

McGuffin ▶ noun an object or device in a film or a book which serves merely as a trigger for the plot.
– ORIGIN late 20th cent.: a Scottish surname, said to have been borrowed by the English film director, Alfred Hitchcock, from a humorous story involving such a pivotal factor.

Mach[1] /mɑːk, mak, German max/, Ernst (1838–1916), Austrian physicist and philosopher of science. He did important work on aerodynamics, while his writings inspired the logical positivist philosophers of the 1920s and influenced scientists such as Einstein and Niels Bohr.

Mach[2] /mɑːk, mak/ (also **Mach number**) ▶ noun the ratio of the speed of a body to the speed of sound in the surrounding medium. It is often used with a numeral (as **Mach 1**, **Mach 2**, etc.) to indicate the speed of sound, twice the speed of sound, etc.

machair /ˈmakə, ˈmaxə/ ▶ noun [mass noun] (in Scotland, especially the Western Isles) low-lying arable or grazing land formed near the coast by the deposition of sand and shell fragments by the wind.
– ORIGIN late 17th cent.: from Scottish Gaelic.

machan /mʌˈtʃɑːn/ ▶ noun Indian, chiefly historical an elevated platform used as a vantage for shooting tigers and other large animals.
– ORIGIN via Hindi from Sanskrit *mañcaka*.

mache /mɑːʃ/ ▶ noun another term for **LAMB'S LETTUCE**.
– ORIGIN late 17th cent. (originally as the Anglicized plural form *maches*): from French *mâche*.

macher /ˈmaxə/ ▶ noun US informal, chiefly derogatory an important or overbearing person.
– ORIGIN 1930s: from Yiddish *makher*, from Middle High German *Macher* 'doer, active person'.

machete /məˈtʃɛti, -ˈʃɛti/ ▶ noun a broad, heavy knife used as an implement or weapon, originating in Central America and the Caribbean.
– ORIGIN late 16th cent.: from Spanish, from *macho* 'hammer'.

Machiavel /ˈmakɪəvɛl/ ▶ noun archaic a person compared to Machiavelli for favouring expediency over morality.

Machiavelli /ˌmakɪəˈvɛli/, Niccolò di Bernardo dei (1469–1527), Italian statesman and political philosopher. His best-known work is *The Prince* (1532), which advises rulers that the acquisition and effective use of power may necessitate unethical methods.
■ [as noun **a Machiavelli**] a person perceived as prepared to use unethical means to gain an advantage.

Machiavellian /ˌmakɪəˈvɛlɪən/ ▶ adjective
1 cunning, scheming, and unscrupulous, especially in politics or in advancing one's career.

2 of or relating to Niccolò Machiavelli.
▶ noun a person who schemes in such a way.
– DERIVATIVES **machiavellianism** noun.

machicolate /məˈtʃɪkəleɪt/ ▶ verb [with obj.] [usu. as adj. **machicolated**] provide with machicolations: *a machicolated fortress.*
– ORIGIN late 18th cent.: from Anglo-Latin *machicollare,* based on Provençal *machacol,* from *macar* 'to crush' + *col* 'neck'.

machicolation ▶ noun (in medieval fortifications) an opening between the supporting corbels of a projecting parapet or the vault of a gate, through which stones or burning objects could be dropped on attackers.
■ a projecting structure containing a series of such openings.

machinable /məˈʃiːnəb(ə)l/ ▶ adjective (of a material) able to be worked by a machine tool.
– DERIVATIVES **machinability** noun.

machinate /ˈmakɪneɪt, ˈmaʃ-/ ▶ verb [no obj.] engage in plots and intrigues; scheme: *he often machinated against other English bishops.*
– DERIVATIVES **machination** noun, **machinator** noun.
– ORIGIN early 16th cent. (used transitively in the sense 'to plot (a malicious act)'): from Latin *machinat-* 'contrived', from the verb *machinari,* from *machina* (see **MACHINE**).

machine ▶ noun an apparatus using or applying mechanical power and having several parts, each with a definite function and together performing a particular task: *a fax machine | a shredding machine.*
■ [usu. with modifier] a coin-operated dispenser: *a cigarette machine.* ■ technical any device that transmits a force or directs its application. ■ figurative an efficient and well-organized group of powerful people: *his campaign illustrated the continuing strength of a powerful political machine.* ■ figurative a person who acts with the mechanical efficiency of a machine: *comedians are more than just laugh machines.*
▶ verb [with obj.] (especially in manufacturing) make or operate on with a machine: [as adj. **machined**] *a decoratively machined brass rod.*
■ Brit. sew or make with a sewing machine.
– ORIGIN mid 16th cent. (originally denoting a structure of any kind): from French, via Latin from Doric Greek *makhana* (Greek *mēkhanē,* from *mēkhos* 'contrivance').

machine code (also **machine language**) ▶ noun [mass noun] a computer programming language consisting of binary or hexadecimal instructions which a computer can respond to directly.

machine gun ▶ noun an automatic gun that fires bullets in rapid succession for as long as the trigger is pressed.
▶ verb (**machine-gun**) [with obj.] shoot with a machine gun.
– DERIVATIVES **machine-gunner** noun.

machine head ▶ noun each of the small pegs on the head of a guitar, used for tightening the strings.

machine instruction ▶ noun Computing an instruction in machine code.

machine-readable ▶ adjective (of data or text) in a form that a computer can process.

machinery ▶ noun [mass noun] machines collectively; the components of a machine: *farm machinery.*
■ the organization or structure of something or for doing something: *the machinery of the state.*

machine screw ▶ noun a fastening device similar to a bolt but having a socket in its head which allows it to be turned with a screwdriver.

machine tool ▶ noun a non-portable powered tool for cutting or shaping metal, wood, or other material, such as a lathe or milling machine.
– DERIVATIVES **machine-tooled** adjective.

machine translation (also **automatic translation**) ▶ noun [mass noun] translation carried out by a computer.

machine washable ▶ adjective (of clothes or other fabric articles) able to be washed in a washing machine without damage.

machinist ▶ noun a person who operates a machine, especially a machine tool.
■ Brit. a person who operates a sewing machine. ■ a person who makes machinery.

machismo /məˈtʃɪzməʊ, -ˈkɪz-/ ▶ noun [mass noun] strong or aggressive masculine pride.
– ORIGIN 1940s: from Mexican Spanish, from *macho* 'male', from Latin *masculus.*

Machmeter /ˈmɑːkmiːtə, ˈmak-/ ▶ noun an instrument in an aircraft indicating airspeed as a Mach number.

Mach number ▶ noun see **MACH²**.

MACHO ▶ noun Astronomy a compact object, such as a brown dwarf, a low-mass star, or a black hole, of a kind which it is thought may constitute part of the dark matter in galactic haloes.
– ORIGIN 1990s: acronym from *Massive (Astrophysical) Compact Halo Object.*

macho /ˈmatʃəʊ/ ▶ adjective showing aggressive pride in one's masculinity: *the big macho tough guy.*
▶ noun (pl. **-os**) a man who is aggressively proud of his masculinity.
■ [mass noun] machismo.
– ORIGIN 1920s: from Mexican Spanish, 'masculine or vigorous'.

Mach's principle Physics the hypothesis that a body's inertial mass results from its interaction with the rest of the matter in the universe.

Machtpolitik /ˈmɑːxtpɒliˌtiːk/ ▶ noun [mass noun] power politics.
– ORIGIN German.

Machu Picchu /ˌmɑːtʃu ˈpiːktʃuː/ a fortified Inca town in the Andes in Peru, which the invading Spaniards never found. It is famous for its dramatic position, perched high on a steep-sided ridge.

Macías Nguema /məˌsiːəs əŋˈgweɪmə/ former name (1973–9) for **BIOKO**.

macintosh ▶ noun variant spelling of **MACKINTOSH**.

McIntosh (also **McIntosh red**) ▶ noun a dessert apple of a Canadian variety with deep red skin.
– ORIGIN late 19th cent.: named after John *McIntosh* (1777–1845 or 1846), the American-born Canadian farmer on whose farm the apple was discovered as a wild variety.

McJob /məkˈdʒɒb/ ▶ noun a low-paid job with few prospects, typically one taken by an overqualified person.

mack ▶ noun variant spelling of **MAC**.

Mackay /məˈkaɪ/ a port in NE Australia, on the coast of Queensland; pop. 40,250 (est. 1991).
– ORIGIN named after Captain John *MacKay,* who explored the region in 1860.

Mackenzie¹ /məˈkɛnzi/, Sir Alexander (1764–1820), Scottish explorer of Canada. He discovered the Mackenzie River in 1789 and in 1793 became the first European to reach the Pacific Ocean by land along a northern route.

Mackenzie² /məˈkɛnzi/, Sir Compton (1883–1972), English novelist, essayist, and poet; full name *Edward Montague Compton Mackenzie.* He is best known for his novels, which include *Sinister Street* (1913–14) and *Whisky Galore* (1947).

Mackenzie³ /məˈkɛnzi/, William Lyon (1795–1861), Scottish-born Canadian politician and journalist, involved with the movement for political reform in Canada. In 1837 he led an unsuccessful rebellion in Toronto and fled to New York.

Mackenzie River the longest river in Canada, flowing 1,700 km (1,060 miles) north-westwards from the Great Slave Lake to the Beaufort Sea, a part of the Arctic Ocean.

mackerel ▶ noun (pl. same or **mackerels**) a migratory surface-dwelling predatory fish, commercially important as a food fish.
● *Scomber* and other genera, family Scombridae (the **mackerel family**): many species, in particular the **North Atlantic mackerel** (*S. scombrus*). The members of the mackerel family, which includes the tunas, are fast-moving marine predators and often popular as game fish.
– ORIGIN Middle English: from Old French *maquerel,* of unknown origin.

mackerel shark ▶ noun another term for **PORBEAGLE**.

mackerel sky ▶ noun a sky dappled with rows of small white fleecy (typically cirrocumulus) clouds, like the pattern on a mackerel's back.

mackinaw /ˈmakɪnɔː/ (also **mackinaw coat** or **jacket**) ▶ noun chiefly N. Amer. a short coat or jacket made of a thick, heavy woollen cloth, typically with a plaid design.
– ORIGIN early 19th cent.: named after *Mackinaw* City, Michigan, formerly an important trading post.

McKinlay /məˈkɪnli/, John (1819–72), Scottish-born explorer. He led an expedition (1861) to search for the missing explorers Burke and Wills. He found

only traces of their party, but carried out valuable exploratory work in the Australian interior.

McKinley /məˈkɪnli/, William (1843–1901), American Republican statesman, 25th President of the US 1897–1901. He was assassinated by an anarchist.

McKinley, Mount a mountain in south central Alaska. Rising to 6,194 m (20,110 ft), it is the highest mountain in North America. Also called **DENALI**.

Mackintosh, Charles Rennie (1868–1928), Scottish architect, designer, and painter. A leading exponent of art nouveau, he pioneered the new concept of functionalism in architecture and interior design. Notable among his designs is the Glasgow School of Art (1898–1909).

mackintosh (also **macintosh**) ▶ noun Brit. a full-length waterproof coat.
■ [mass noun] [usu. as modifier] cloth waterproofed with rubber.
– ORIGIN mid 19th cent.: named after Charles *Macintosh* (1766–1843), the Scottish inventor who originally patented the cloth.

mackle /ˈmak(ə)l/ ▶ noun a blurred impression in printing.
– ORIGIN late 16th cent.: from French *macule,* from Latin *macula* 'stain'.

macle /ˈmak(ə)l/ ▶ noun **1** a diamond or other crystal that is twinned.
2 another term for **CHIASTOLITE**.
– ORIGIN early 19th cent.: from French, from Anglo-Latin *mascula* 'mesh'.

Maclean¹ /məˈkleɪn/, Alistair (1922–87), Scottish novelist, writer of thrillers including *The Guns of Navarone* (1957) and *Where Eagles Dare* (1967).

Maclean² /məˈkleɪn/, Donald (Duart) (1913–83), British Foreign Office official and Soviet spy. After acting as a Soviet agent from the late 1930s he fled to the USSR with Guy Burgess in 1951.

Macleod /məˈklaʊd/, John James Rickard (1876–1935), Scottish physiologist. He directed the research on pancreatic extracts by F. G. Banting and C. H. Best which led to the discovery and isolation of insulin. Macleod shared a Nobel Prize for Physiology or Medicine with Banting in 1923.

McLuhan /məˈkluːən/, (Herbert) Marshall (1911–80), Canadian writer and thinker. He became famous in the 1960s for his phrase 'the medium is the message' and his argument that it is the characteristics of a particular medium rather than the information it disseminates which influence and control society.

Macmillan, (Maurice) Harold, 1st Earl of Stockton (1894–1986), British Conservative statesman, Prime Minister 1957–63. His term of office saw the signing of the Test-Ban Treaty (1963) with the US and the USSR. Macmillan resigned on grounds of ill health shortly after the scandal surrounding John Profumo.

McNaghten rules /məkˈnɔːt(ə)n/ (also **M'Naghten** or **McNaughten rules**) Brit. rules or criteria for judging criminal responsibility where there is a question of insanity.
– ORIGIN established by the House of Lords, following the case of *Regina v McNaghten* (1843).

MacNeice /məkˈniːs/, (Frederick) Louis (1907–63), Northern Irish poet. His work, such as *Collected Poems* (1966), is characterized by the use of assonance, internal rhymes, and ballad-like repetitions.

Macquarie /məˈkwɒri/, Lachlan (1762–1824), Scottish-born Australian colonial administrator, governor of New South Wales 1809–21.

Macquarie River a river in New South Wales, Australia, rising on the western slopes of the Great Dividing Range and flowing 960 km (600 miles) north-west to join the River Darling, of which it is a headwater.

macramé /məˈkrɑːmi/ ▶ noun [mass noun] the art of knotting cord or string in patterns to make decorative articles.
■ [usu. as modifier] fabric or articles made in this way.
– ORIGIN mid 19th cent.: French, from Turkish *makrama* 'tablecloth or towel', from Arabic *miḵrama* 'bedspread'.

macro ▶ noun (pl. **-os**) **1** (also **macro instruction**) Computing a single instruction that expands automatically into a set of instructions to perform a particular task.

2 Photography a macro lens.
▶ adjective **1** large-scale; overall: *the analysis of social events at the macro level.* Often contrasted with **MICRO**.
2 Photography relating to or used in macrophotography.
– ORIGIN independent usage of **MACRO-**.

macro- ▶ combining form **1** long; over a long period: *macroevolution.*
2 large; large-scale: *macromolecule | macronutrient.*
■(used in medical terms) large compared with the norm: *macrocephaly.*
– ORIGIN from Greek *makros* 'long, large'.

macrobiotic /ˌmakrə(ʊ)baɪˈɒtɪk/ ▶ adjective constituting, relating to, or following a diet of whole pure prepared foods which is based on Buddhist principles of the balance of yin and yang.
▶ plural noun (**macrobiotics**) [treated as sing.] the use or theory of such a diet.

macrocarpa /ˌmakrə(ʊ)ˈkɑːpə/ ▶ noun a cypress tree with a large spreading crown of horizontal branches and leaves that smell of lemon when crushed, native to a small area of California. Also called **MONTEREY CYPRESS**.
● *Cupressus macrocarpa*, family Cupressaceae.
– ORIGIN early 20th cent.: modern Latin, from **MACRO-** 'large' + Greek *karpos* 'fruit'.

macrocephalic /ˌmakrə(ʊ)sɪˈfalɪk, -kɛˈfalɪk-/ (also **macrocephalous**) ▶ adjective Anatomy having an unusually large head.
– DERIVATIVES **macrocephaly** noun.

macrocosm /ˈmakrə(ʊ)kɒz(ə)m/ ▶ noun the universe; the cosmos.
■the whole of a complex structure, especially as represented or epitomized in a small part of itself (a microcosm).
– DERIVATIVES **macrocosmic** adjective, **macrocosmically** adverb.

macrocyclic /ˌmakrə(ʊ)ˈsʌɪklɪk, -ˈsɪk-/ ▶ adjective Chemistry of, relating to, or denoting a ring composed of a relatively large number of atoms, such as occur in haem, chlorophyll, and several natural antibiotics.
– DERIVATIVES **macrocycle** noun.

macroeconomics ▶ plural noun [treated as sing.] the part of economics concerned with large-scale or general economic factors, such as interest rates and national productivity.
– DERIVATIVES **macroeconomic** adjective.

macroeconomy ▶ noun a large-scale economic system.

macroevolution ▶ noun [mass noun] Biology major evolutionary change. The term applies mainly to the evolution of whole taxonomic groups over long periods of time.
– DERIVATIVES **macroevolutionary** adjective.

macrogamete ▶ noun Biology (especially in protozoans) the larger of a pair of conjugating gametes, usually regarded as female.

macro lens ▶ noun Photography a lens suitable for taking photographs unusually close to the subject.

macrolepidoptera /ˌmakrəʊlɛpɪˈdɒpt(ə)rə/ ▶ plural noun Entomology the butterflies and (generally) larger moths, comprising those of interest to the general collector.
– ORIGIN modern Latin (plural), from **MACRO-** 'large' + **LEPIDOPTERA**.

macromolecule ▶ noun Chemistry a molecule containing a very large number of atoms, such as a protein, nucleic acid, or synthetic polymer.
– DERIVATIVES **macromolecular** adjective.

macron /ˈmakrɒn/ ▶ noun a written or printed mark (¯) used to indicate a long vowel in some languages and phonetic transcription systems, or a stressed vowel in verse.
– ORIGIN mid 19th cent.: from Greek *makron*, neuter of *makros* 'long'.

macronutrient ▶ noun Biology a substance required in relatively large amounts by living organisms, in particular:
■a type of food (e.g. fat, protein, carbohydrate) required in large amounts in the diet. ■a chemical element (e.g. potassium, magnesium, calcium) required in large amounts for plant growth and development.

macrophage /ˈmakrə(ʊ)feɪdʒ/ ▶ noun Physiology a large phagocytic cell found in stationary form in the tissues or as a mobile white blood cell, especially at sites of infection.

macrophotography ▶ noun [mass noun] photography producing photographs of small items larger than life size.

macrophyte /ˈmakrə(ʊ)fʌɪt/ ▶ noun Botany a plant, especially an aquatic plant, large enough to be seen by the naked eye.

macropod /ˈmakrə(ʊ)pɒd/ ▶ noun Zoology a plant-eating marsupial mammal of an Australasian family that comprises the kangaroos and wallabies.
● Family Macropodidae: several genera, in particular *Macropus*.
– ORIGIN late 19th cent.: from modern Latin *Macropodidae* (plural), from **MACRO-** 'large' + Greek *pous, pod-* 'foot'.

Macroscelidea /ˌmakrə(ʊ)skɪˈlɪdɪə/ Zoology a small order of mammals that comprises the elephant shrews.
– ORIGIN modern Latin (plural), from Greek *makros* 'large' + *skelos* 'leg'.

macroscopic /ˌmakrə(ʊ)ˈskɒpɪk/ ▶ adjective visible to the naked eye; not microscopic.
■of or relating to large-scale or general analysis.
– DERIVATIVES **macroscopically** adverb.

Macro-Siouan /ˌmakrəʊˈsuːən/ ▶ noun [mass noun] a proposed phylum of North American languages including the Siouan, Iroquoian, and Caddoan families and some others.
▶ adjective of or relating to this language phylum.

macrostructure ▶ noun the large-scale or overall structure of something, e.g. an organism, a mechanical construction, or a written text.
■a large-scale structure.
– DERIVATIVES **macrostructural** adjective.

macruran /məˈkrʊərən/ ▶ adjective Zoology of, relating to, or denoting those decapod crustaceans (such as lobsters and crayfish) which have a relatively long abdomen.
– DERIVATIVES **macrurous** adjective.
– ORIGIN mid 19th cent. (as a noun): from modern Latin *Macrura* (former suborder name), from Greek *makros* 'long' + *oura* 'tail', + **-AN**.

macula /ˈmakjʊlə/ ▶ noun (pl. **maculae** /-liː/) another term for **MACULE**.
■(also **macula lutea**) /ˈluːtɪə/ (pl. **maculae luteae** /-tiː/) Anatomy an oval yellowish area surrounding the fovea near the centre of the retina in the eye, which is the region of greatest visual acuity.
– ORIGIN late Middle English: from Latin, 'spot'.

macular ▶ adjective **1** relating to the macula of the eye.
2 of or consisting of a distinct spot or spots.

maculate /ˈmakjʊleɪt/ poetic/literary ▶ adjective spotted or stained.
▶ verb [with obj.] mark with a spot or spots; stain.
– DERIVATIVES **maculation** noun.
– ORIGIN late Middle English (as a verb): from Latin *maculat-* 'spotted', from the verb *maculare*, from *macula* 'spot'.

macule /ˈmakjuːl/ ▶ noun a distinct spot, such as a discoloured spot on the skin.
– ORIGIN late 15th cent.: from French, or from Latin *macula* 'spot'.

macumba /məˈkʊmbə/ ▶ noun [mass noun] a black religious cult practised in Brazil, using sorcery, ritual dance, and fetishes.
– ORIGIN Portuguese.

macushla /məˈkʊʃlə/ ▶ noun a fond Irish form of address.
– ORIGIN from Irish *mo* 'my' + *cuisle* 'pulse' (see also **ACUSHLA**).

mad ▶ adjective (**madder, maddest**) mentally ill; insane: *he felt as if he were going mad.*
■(of a person, conduct, or an idea) extremely foolish or ill-advised: *Antony's mother told him he was mad to be leaving Dublin.* ■in a frenzied mental or physical state: *she pictured loved ones mad with anxiety about her | it was a mad dash to get ready.* ■informal enthusiastic about someone or something: *I'm mad about jacket potatoes with lots of butter* | [postpositive, in combination] *Kenny was always football-mad.* ■informal very angry: *he must be pretty mad at her for not being at home when they arrived.* ■Brit. informal very exciting. ■(of a dog) rabid.
▶ verb (**madded, madding**) [with obj.] archaic make mad or insane.
– PHRASES **go mad** informal allow oneself to get carried away by enthusiasm or excitement: *let's go mad and splash out.* **like mad** informal with great intensity, energy, or enthusiasm: *I ran like mad.* (**as**) **mad as a hatter** informal completely crazy. [ORIGIN: with reference to Lewis Carroll's character the Mad Hatter in *Alice's Adventures in Wonderland* (1865), the allusion being to the effects of mercury poisoning from the use of mercurous nitrate in the manufacture of felt hats.] **mad keen** informal extremely enthusiastic: *some men are mad keen on football.*
– ORIGIN Old English *gemǣd(e)d* 'maddened', participial form related to *gemād* 'mad', of Germanic origin.

Madagascar /ˌmadəˈgaskə/ an island country in the Indian Ocean, off the east coast of Africa; pop. 12,016,000 (est. 1991); official languages, Malagasy and French; capital, Antananarivo.

Settled by peoples of mixed Indo-Melanesian and African descent, Madagascar was visited by the Portuguese in 1500 but resisted colonization until the French established control in 1896. It regained its independence as the Malagasy Republic in 1960, changing its name back to Madagascar in 1975. Madagascar is the fourth largest island in the world, and many of its plants and animals are not found elsewhere.

– DERIVATIVES **Madagascan** adjective & noun.

madam ▶ noun used to address or refer to a woman in a polite or respectful way: *Can I help you, madam?*
■(**Madam**) used to address a woman at the start of a formal or business letter: *Dear Madam, …* ■(**Madam**) used before a title or address or refer to a female holder of that position: *Madam President.* ■ Brit. informal a conceited or precocious girl or young woman: *she's a proper little madam.* ■ a female brothel-keeper.
– ORIGIN Middle English: from Old French *ma dame* 'my lady'.

Madame /məˈdɑːm, ˈmadəm, French madam/ ▶ noun (pl. **Mesdames**) a title or form of address used of or to a French-speaking woman: *Madame Bovary.*
■used as a title for women in artistic or exotic occupations, such as musicians or fortune tellers.
– ORIGIN French; compare with **MADAM**.

madarosis /ˌmadəˈrəʊsɪs/ ▶ noun [mass noun] Medicine absence or loss of the eyelashes (and sometimes the eyebrows), either as a congenital condition or as a result of an infection.
– ORIGIN late 17th cent.: modern Latin, from Greek, 'baldness', from *madaros* 'bald'.

madcap ▶ adjective amusingly eccentric: *a surreal, madcap novel.*
■done or thought up without considering the consequences; crazy or reckless: *madcap rail privatization plans.*
▶ noun an eccentric person.

mad cow disease ▶ noun informal term for **BSE**.

madden ▶ verb [with obj.] [often as adj. **maddened**] drive (someone) insane: *he fixed her in a maddened stare.*
■make (someone) extremely irritated or annoyed: *this is ridiculous, he told her, maddened by her reaction.*

maddening ▶ adjective extremely annoying; infuriating: *she put the coins back with maddening slowness.*
– DERIVATIVES **maddeningly** adverb.

madder ▶ noun a scrambling or prostrate Eurasian plant related to the bedstraws, with whorls of four to six leaves.
● Genera *Rubia* and *Sherardia*, family Rubiaceae: several species, in particular *R. tinctorum* of southern Europe and western Asia, formerly cultivated for its root which yields a red dye, and the Eurasian **wild madder** (*R. peregrina*).
■[mass noun] a red dye or pigment obtained from the root of this plant, or a synthetic dye resembling it.
– ORIGIN Old English *mædere*, of Germanic origin; obscurely related to Dutch *mede*, in the same sense.

madding ▶ adjective poetic/literary **1** acting madly; frenzied.
2 maddening.
– PHRASES **far from the madding crowd** secluded or removed from public notice. [ORIGIN: in allusion to use in Gray's *Elegy*, also to the title of one of Thomas Hardy's novels.]

made past and past participle of **MAKE**. ▶ adjective [usu. in combination] made or formed in a particular place or by a particular process: *a Japanese-made camera | handmade chocolates.*

Madeira[1] /məˈdɪərə/ **1** an island in the Atlantic Ocean off NW Africa, the largest of the Madeiras, a group of islands which constitutes an autonomous region of Portugal; pop. 269,500 (est. 1986); capital, Funchal. Encountered by the Portuguese in 1419,

the islands were occupied by the Spanish 1580–1640 and the British 1807–14.
2 a river in NW Brazil, which rises on the Bolivian border and flows about 1,450 km (900 miles) to meet the Amazon east of Manaus. It is navigable to large ocean-going vessels as far as Pôrto Velho.
– DERIVATIVES **Madeiran** adjective & noun.
– ORIGIN Portuguese, literally 'timber' (from Latin *materia* 'substance'), because of the island's dense woods.

Madeira² /mə'dɪərə/ (also **Madeira wine**) ▶ noun [mass noun] a fortified white wine from the island of Madeira.

Madeira cake (also **Madeira sponge**) ▶ noun [mass noun] Brit. a close-textured, rich kind of sponge cake.
– ORIGIN so named because it was eaten as an accompaniment to a glass of Madeira.

madeleine /'madlɛın, 'mad(ə)lɛn/ ▶ noun a small rich sponge cake, baked in a fluted tin or mould and typically decorated with coconut and jam.
– ORIGIN French, probably named after *Madeleine Paulmier*, 19th-cent. French pastry cook.

made man ▶ noun N. Amer. a man whose success in life is assured.

Mademoiselle /ˌmadəmwə'zɛl/, French madmwazɛl/ ▶ noun (pl. **Mesdemoiselles**) a title or form of address used of or to an unmarried French-speaking woman: *Mademoiselle Rossignol* | *thank you, Mademoiselle.*
■ (**mademoiselle**) a young Frenchwoman. ■ (**mademoiselle**) dated a French governess. ■ (**mademoiselle**) a female French teacher in an English-speaking school.
– ORIGIN French, from *ma* 'my' + *demoiselle* 'damsel'.

maderization /ˌmadəraɪ'zeɪʃ(ə)n/ (also **-isation**) ▶ noun [mass noun] a form of oxidation which gives white wine a brownish colour and caramelized flavour like that of Madeira.
– DERIVATIVES **maderized** adjective.
– ORIGIN 1950s: from French *madérisation*, from *madériser*, from *Madère* 'Madeira'.

made road ▶ noun Brit. a road surfaced with a material such as tarmac or concrete.

made to measure ▶ adjective chiefly Brit. (of clothes) specially made to fit a particular person.
■ figurative designed to fulfil a particular set of requirements: *amenities and attractions for a made-to-measure vacation.*

made to order ▶ adjective specially made according to a customer's specifications.
■ figurative ideally suited to certain requirements: *a formalism seemingly made to order for the problem at hand.*

made-up ▶ adjective **1** wearing make-up.
2 invented; not true: *a made-up story.*
3 (of a meal or drink) prepared in advance of sale.
4 (of a road) surfaced with a material such as tarmac.

madhouse ▶ noun historical a mental institution.
■ informal a psychiatric hospital. ■ [in sing.] a scene of extreme confusion or uproar: *this place is a madhouse.*

Madhya Pradesh /ˌmʌdjə prə'dɛʃ/ a large state in central India, formed in 1956; capital, Bhopal.

Madison¹ /'madɪs(ə)n/ the state capital of Wisconsin; pop. 191,260 (1990).
– ORIGIN named after President James *Madison* (see **MADISON²**).

Madison² /'madɪs(ə)n/, James (1751–1836), American Democratic Republican statesman, 4th President of the US 1809–17. He played a leading part in drawing up the US Constitution (1787) and proposed the Bill of Rights (1791).

Madison³ /'madɪs(ə)n/ ▶ noun an energetic group dance popular in the 1960s.
– ORIGIN of unknown origin.

madison /'madɪs(ə)n/ ▶ noun a cycle relay race for teams of two or more riders, typically held over several days.
– ORIGIN named after *Madison* Square Garden, New York, the site of the first such race in 1892.

Madison Avenue a street in New York City, centre of the American advertising business.

madly ▶ adverb in a manner suggesting or characteristic of insanity: *his eyes bulged madly.*
■ in a wild or uncontrolled manner: *her heart thudded madly against her ribs.* ■ informal with extreme intensity: *the boys are all madly in love with you.*

madman ▶ noun (pl. **-men**) a man who is mentally ill.
■ an extremely foolish or reckless person: *car got out of control—some madman going too fast.* ■ used in similes to refer to a person who does something very fast, intensely, or violently: *I was working like a madman.*

madness ▶ noun [mass noun] the state of being mentally ill, especially severely.
■ extremely foolish behaviour: *in this day and age it is madness to allow children to roam around after dark.* ■ a state of frenzied or chaotic activity: *from about midnight to three in the morning it's absolute madness in here.*

mado /'meɪdəʊ/ ▶ noun (pl. **-os**) a small yellowish marine fish with brown longitudinal streaks, occurring around eastern Australia and New Zealand.
● Genus *Atypichthys*, family Kyphosidae: two species.
– ORIGIN late 19th cent.: probably from an Aboriginal language of Queensland.

Madonna¹ ▶ noun (**the Madonna**) the Virgin Mary.
■ (usu. **madonna**) a picture, statue, or medallion of the Madonna, typically depicted seated and holding the infant Jesus. ■ an idealized virtuous and beautiful woman.
– ORIGIN late 16th cent. (as a respectful form of address to an Italian woman): Italian, from *ma* (old form of *mia* 'my') + *donna* 'lady' (from Latin *domina*).

Madonna² (b.1958), American pop singer and actress; born *Madonna Louise Ciccone*. Albums such as *Like a Virgin* (1984) and her image as a sex symbol brought her international stardom in the mid 1980s.

madonna lily ▶ noun a tall white-flowered lily with golden pollen. Native to Asia Minor, it is traditionally associated with purity and is often depicted in paintings of the Madonna.
● *Lilium candidum*, family Liliaceae.

Madras /mə'drɑːs, -'dras/ **1** a seaport on the east coast of India, capital of Tamil Nadu; pop. 3,795,000 (1991). Official name (since 1995) **CHENNAI**.
2 former name (until 1968) for the state of Tamil Nadu.

madras /mə'drɑːs, -'dras/ ▶ noun [mass noun] **1** a strong cotton fabric, typically patterned with colourful stripes or checks.
2 a hot spiced curry dish, typically made with meat.
– ORIGIN mid 19th cent.: by association with **MADRAS**.

madrasa /mə'drasə/ (also **madrasah** or **medrese**) ▶ noun a college for Islamic instruction.
– ORIGIN Arabic, from *darasa* 'to study'.

Madreporaria /ˌmadrɛpə'rɛːrɪə/ Zoology another term for **SCLERACTINIA**.
– DERIVATIVES **madreporarian** noun & adjective, **madrepore** noun (dated).
– ORIGIN modern Latin (plural), from *Madrepora* (genus name), from Italian, probably from *madre* 'mother', with reference to the prolific growth of the coral.

madreporite /ma'drɛpəraɪt, ˌmadrɪ'pɔːraɪt/ ▶ noun Zoology a perforated plate by which the entry of seawater into the vascular system of an echinoderm is controlled.
– ORIGIN early 19th cent.: from *madrepore* (see **MADREPORARIA**) + **-ITE¹**.

Madrid /mə'drɪd/ the capital of Spain; pop. 2,984,600 (1991). Situated on a high plateau in the centre of the country, it replaced Valladolid as capital in 1561.

madrigal /'madrɪɡ(ə)l/ ▶ noun a part-song for several voices, especially one of the Renaissance period, typically arranged in elaborate counterpoint and without instrumental accompaniment.
– DERIVATIVES **madrigalian** /-'ɡeɪlɪən/ adjective, **madrigalist** noun.
– ORIGIN from Italian *madrigale* (from medieval Latin *carmen matricale* 'simple song'), from *matricalis* 'maternal or primitive', from *matrix* 'womb'.

madrilene /ˌmadrɪ'liːn, -'lɛn/ ▶ noun [mass noun] a clear soup, usually served cold.
– ORIGIN from French (*consommé à la*) *madrilène*, literally 'soup in the Madrid style'.

Madrilenian /ˌmadrɪ'leɪnɪən/ ▶ adjective of or relating to Madrid.
▶ noun a native or inhabitant of Madrid.
– ORIGIN from **MADRILEÑO** + **-IAN**.

Madrileño /ˌmadrɪ'lɛnjəʊ/ ▶ noun (pl. **-os**) a native or inhabitant of Madrid.
– ORIGIN Spanish.

madroño /mə'drəʊnjəʊ/ (also **madroña** /-njə/) ▶ noun (pl. **-os**) an evergreen tree related to the strawberry tree, with white flowers, red berries, and glossy leaves, native to western North America.
● *Arbutus menziesii*, family Ericaceae.
– ORIGIN mid 19th cent.: from Spanish.

madtom ▶ noun a small North American freshwater catfish which has a venom gland at the base of the pectoral fin spines, with which it can inflict a painful wound.
● Genus *Noturus*, family Ictaluridae: numerous species, including the common **tadpole madtom** (*N. gyrinus*).

Madura /mə'dʊərə/ an island of Indonesia, off the NE coast of Java. Its chief town is Pamekasan.

Madurai /'madjʊraɪ/ a city in Tamil Nadu in southern India; pop. 952,000 (1991).

Madurese /ˌmadjʊ'riːz/ ▶ noun (pl. same) **1** a native or inhabitant of the island of Madura in Indonesia.
2 [mass noun] an Indonesian language spoken by over 12 million people in Madura and nearby parts of Java.
▶ adjective of or relating to the inhabitants of Madura or their language.

madwoman ▶ noun (pl. **-women**) a woman who is mentally ill.
■ used in similes to refer to a woman who does something very fast, intensely, or violently.

Maeander /mi:'andə/ ancient name for **MENDERES**.

Maecenas /mʌɪ'siːnəs/, Gaius (c.70–8 BC), Roman statesman. He was a trusted adviser of Augustus and a notable patron of poets such as Virgil and Horace.

maedi /'meɪdi/ ▶ noun [mass noun] a form of progressive pneumonia in sheep, caused by a lentivirus. See also **VISNA**.
– ORIGIN 1950s: from Icelandic, literally 'shortness of breath'.

maelstrom /'meɪlstrəm/ ▶ noun a powerful whirlpool in the sea or a river.
■ figurative a scene or state of confused and violent movement or upheaval: *the train station was a maelstrom of crowds* | *a maelstrom of violence and recrimination.*
– ORIGIN late 17th cent.: from early modern Dutch (denoting a mythical whirlpool supposed to exist in the Arctic Ocean, west of Norway), from *maalen* 'grind, whirl' + *stroom* 'stream'.

Maelzel's metronome /'mɛlts(ə)lz/ ▶ noun see **MM**.

maenad /'miːnad/ ▶ noun (in ancient Greece) a female follower of Bacchus, traditionally associated with divine possession and frenzied rites.
– DERIVATIVES **maenadic** adjective.
– ORIGIN late 16th cent.: via Latin from Greek *Mainas, Mainad-*, from *mainesthai* 'to rave'.

maestoso /mʌɪ'stəʊzəʊ, -səʊ/ Music ▶ adverb & adjective (especially as a direction) in a majestic manner.
▶ noun (pl. **-os**) a movement or passage performed or marked to be performed in this way.
– ORIGIN Italian, 'majestic', based on Latin *majestas* 'majesty'.

maestro /'mʌɪstrəʊ/ ▶ noun (pl. **maestri** /-stri/ or **maestros**) a distinguished musician, especially a conductor or performer of classical music.
■ a great or distinguished figure in any sphere: *a movie maestro.*
– ORIGIN early 18th cent.: Italian, 'master', from Latin *magister*.

Maeterlinck /'meɪtəlɪŋk/, Count Maurice (1862–1949), Belgian poet, dramatist, and essayist. His prose dramas *La Princesse Maleine* (1889) and *Pelléas et Mélisande* (1892) established him as a leading figure in the symbolist movement. Nobel Prize for Literature (1911).

Mae West ▶ noun informal, dated an inflatable life jacket, originally as issued to RAF personnel during the Second World War.
– ORIGIN 1940s: from the name of the American film actress *Mae West* (see **WEST²**), noted for her large bust.

Mafeking /'mafɪkɪŋ/ a town in South Africa, in North-West Province. In 1899–1900, during the Second Boer War, a small British force commanded by Lord Baden-Powell was besieged there for 215 days; its eventual relief was greeted in Britain with widespread celebration. Modern name (since 1980) **MAFIKENG**.

MAFF ▶ abbreviation for (in the UK) Ministry of Agriculture, Fisheries, and Food.

Mafia /ˈmafɪə/ ▶ noun (**the Mafia**) [treated as sing. or pl.] an organized international body of criminals, operating originally in Sicily and now especially in Italy and the US and having a complex and ruthless behavioural code.
■ (usu. **mafia**) any similar group using extortion and other criminal methods. ■ (usu. **mafia**) a group that is regarded as exerting a hidden sinister influence: *the British literary mafia*.
– ORIGIN Italian (Sicilian dialect), originally in the sense 'bragging'.

mafic /ˈmafɪk/ ▶ adjective Geology relating to, denoting, or containing a group of dark-coloured, mainly ferromagnesian minerals such as pyroxene and olivine. Often contrasted with **FELSIC**.
– ORIGIN early 20th cent.: blend of **MAGNESIUM** and a contracted form of **FERRIC**.

Mafikeng modern name for **MAFEKING**.

Mafioso /ˌmafɪˈəʊzəʊ, -səʊ/ ▶ noun (pl. **Mafiosi** /-zi, -si/) a member of the Mafia.
– ORIGIN Italian.

mag ▶ noun informal **1** a magazine (periodical).
2 a magazine (of ammunition).
3 [mass noun] magnesium or magnesium alloy.
4 a magneto.
5 magnitude (of stars or other celestial objects).

maga /ˈmɑːɡə/ (also **marga**) ▶ adjective W. Indian (of a person or part of the body) very thin.
– ORIGIN compare with Dutch *mager* 'lean', French *maigre* 'thin'.

Magadha /ˈmʌɡədə/ an ancient kingdom situated in the valley of the River Ganges in NE India (modern Bihar) which was the centre of several empires, notably those of the Mauryan and Gupta dynasties, between the 6th century BC and the 8th century AD.

Magadi, Lake /məˈɡɑːdi/ a salt lake in the Great Rift Valley, in southern Kenya, with extensive deposits of sodium carbonate and other minerals.

Magahi /ˈmʌɡəhi/ ▶ noun [mass noun] one of the Bihari group of languages, spoken by some 12 million people in central Bihar and West Bengal.
▶ adjective of or relating to this language.
– ORIGIN from Hindi *Magadhī* 'of Magadha'.

magalogue /ˈmaɡəlɒɡ/ ▶ noun a promotional catalogue or sales brochure designed to resemble a high-quality magazine.
– ORIGIN 1970s: blend of **MAGAZINE** and **CATALOGUE**.

magazine /ˌmaɡəˈziːn/ ▶ noun **1** a periodical publication containing articles and illustrations, typically covering a particular subject or area of interest: *a car magazine* | *a women's magazine*.
■ (also **magazine programme**) a regular television or radio programme comprising a variety of topical news or entertainment items.
2 a chamber for holding a supply of cartridges to be fed automatically to the breech of a gun.
■ a similar device feeding a camera, compact disc player, etc.
3 a store for arms, ammunition, explosives, and provisions for use in military operations.
– ORIGIN late 16th cent.: from French *magasin*, from Italian *magazzino*, from Arabic *maḵzin*, *maḵzan* 'storehouse', from *kazana* 'store up'. The term originally meant 'store' and was often used from the mid 17th cent. in the title of books providing information useful to particular groups of people, whence sense 1 (mid 18th cent.). Sense 3, a contemporary specialization of the original meaning, gave rise to sense 2 in the mid 18th cent.

magdalen /ˈmaɡdəlɪn/ ▶ noun (**the Magdalen** or **the Magdalene**) St Mary Magdalene.
■ archaic a reformed prostitute. ■ archaic a home for reformed prostitutes.
– ORIGIN late Middle English: via ecclesiastical Latin from Greek (*Maria hē*) *Magdalēnē* '(Mary of) *Magdala*' (to whom Jesus appeared after his resurrection; John 20:1–18), commonly identified (probably wrongly) with the sinner of Luke 7:37.

Magdalena /ˌmaɡdəˈleɪnə/ the principal river of Colombia, rising in the Andes and flowing northwards for about 1,600 km (1,000 miles) to enter the Caribbean at Barranquilla.

Magdalenian /ˌmaɡdəˈliːnɪən/ ▶ adjective Archaeology of, relating to, or denoting the final Palaeolithic culture in Europe, following the Solutrean and dated to about 17,000–11,500 years ago. It is characterized by a range of bone and horn tools, and by highly developed cave art.
■ [as noun **the Magdalenian**] the Magdalenian culture or period.
– ORIGIN late 19th cent.: from French *Magdalénien* 'from La Madeleine', a site in the Dordogne, France, where objects from this culture were found.

Magdeburg /ˈmaɡdəˌbɜːɡ, German ˈmakdəˌbʊrk/ an industrial city in Germany, the capital of Saxony-Anhalt, situated on the River Elbe and linked to the Rhine and Ruhr by the Mittelland Canal; pop. 290,000 (est. 1990).

Magdeburg hemispheres ▶ plural noun a pair of copper or brass hemispheres joined to form a hollow globe from which the air can be extracted to demonstrate the pressure of the atmosphere, which then prevents them from being pulled apart.
– ORIGIN early 19th cent.: named after the city of **MAGDEBURG**, home of the inventor, Otto von Guericke (1602–86).

mage /meɪdʒ/ ▶ noun archaic or poetic/literary a magician or learned person.
– ORIGIN late Middle English: Anglicized form of Latin *magus* (see **MAGUS**).

Magellan¹ /məˈɡelən/, Ferdinand (*c*.1480–1521), Portuguese explorer; Portuguese name *Fernão Magalhães*. In 1519 he sailed from Spain, rounding South America through the strait which now bears his name, and reached the Philippines in 1521. He was killed in a skirmish on Cebu; the survivors sailed back to Spain round Africa, completing the first circumnavigation of the globe (1522).

Magellan² /məˈɡelən/ an American space probe launched in 1989 to map the surface of Venus, using radar to penetrate the dense cloud cover. The probe was deliberately burned up in Venus's atmosphere in 1994.

Magellan, Strait of a passage separating Tierra del Fuego and other islands from mainland South America, connecting the Atlantic and Pacific Oceans.

Magellanic Clouds /ˌmadʒɪˈlanɪk/ Astronomy two diffuse luminous patches in the southern sky, now known to be small irregular galaxies that are the closest to our own. The **Large Magellanic Cloud** is about 169,000 light years away and the **Small Magellanic Cloud** is about 210,000 light years.
– ORIGIN named after the Portuguese explorer *Magellan* (see **MAGELLAN¹**).

Magen David /ˌmɑːɡɛn dɑːˈviːd/ ▶ noun a hexagram used as a symbol of Judaism.
– ORIGIN early 20th cent.: Hebrew, literally 'shield of David', with reference to David, King of Israel (see **DAVID¹**).

magenta /məˈdʒɛntə/ ▶ noun [mass noun] a light mauvish-crimson which is one of the primary subtractive colours, complementary to green.
■ the dye fuchsin.
– ORIGIN mid 19th cent.: named after *Magenta* in northern Italy, site of a battle (1859) fought shortly before the dye (of blood-like colour) was discovered.

Maggid /ˈmɑːɡɪd/ ▶ noun (pl. **Maggidim** /-ɪm/) an itinerant Jewish preacher.
– ORIGIN late 19th cent.: from Hebrew *maggīd* 'narrator'.

maggie ▶ noun (pl. **-ies**) **1** dialect term for **MAGPIE**.
2 Scottish term for **GUILLEMOT**.

Maggie's drawers ▶ noun US military slang a red flag used to indicate a miss in target practice.
– ORIGIN 1940s: said to be in reference to a song entitled *Those Old Red Flannel Drawers That Maggie Wore*.

Maggiore, Lake /maˈdʒɔːreɪ/ the second largest of the lakes of northern Italy, extending into southern Switzerland.

maggot /ˈmaɡət/ ▶ noun **1** a soft-bodied legless larva, especially that of a fly or other insect found in decaying matter.
■ figurative an agent of insidious decay: *must achievement always carry the maggot of guilt in it?* [mass noun] Fishing bait consisting of a maggot or maggots.
2 archaic a whimsical fancy.
– DERIVATIVES **maggoty** adjective.
– ORIGIN late Middle English: perhaps an alteration

of dialect *maddock*, from Old Norse *mathkr*, of Germanic origin.

Maghrib /ˈmaɡrɪb, ˈmʌɡrəb/ (also **Maghreb**) a region of North and NW Africa between the Atlantic Ocean and Egypt, comprising the coastal plain and Atlas Mountains of Morocco, together with Algeria, Tunisia, and sometimes also Tripolitania. Compare with **BARBARY**.

Magi /ˈmeɪdʒaɪ/ (**the Magi**) the 'wise men' from the East who brought gifts to the infant Jesus (Matt. 2:1), said in later tradition to be kings named Caspar, Melchior, and Balthasar who brought gifts of gold, frankincense, and myrrh.
– ORIGIN see **MAGUS**.

magi plural form of **MAGUS**.

Magian /ˈmeɪdʒɪən/ ▶ adjective of or relating to the magi of ancient Persia.
■ of or relating to the Magi who brought gifts to the infant Jesus.
▶ noun a magus or one of the Magi.

magic ▶ noun [mass noun] the power of apparently influencing the course of events by using mysterious or supernatural forces: *do you believe in magic?* | *suddenly, as if by magic, the doors start to open.*
■ mysterious tricks, such as making things disappear and appear again, performed as entertainment. ■ a quality that makes something seem removed from everyday life, especially in a way that gives delight: *the magic of the theatre.* ■ informal something which has such a quality: *the lovely town of Urbino is pure magic.* ■ informal exceptional skill or talent: *Everton became the latest side to get a taste of the Ian Wright magic.*
▶ adjective **1** used in magic or working by magic; having or apparently having supernatural powers: *a magic wand.*
■ [attrib.] very effective in producing results, especially desired ones: *confidence is the magic ingredient needed to spark recovery.*
2 informal wonderful; exciting: *it was a great time, magic.*
▶ verb (**magicked**, **magicking**) [with obj. and adverbial] move, change, or create by or as if by magic: *he must have been magicked out of the car at the precise second it exploded.*
– PHRASES **like magic** remarkably effectively or rapidly: *it repels rain like magic.*
– ORIGIN late Middle English (also in the sense 'a magical procedure'): from Old French *magique*, from Latin *magicus* (adjective), from Latin *magica* (noun), from Greek *magikē* (*tekhnē*) '(art of) a magus': magi were regarded as magicians.

magical ▶ adjective **1** relating to or using magic: *magical healing powers.*
■ resembling magic; produced or working as if by magic: *he had a gentle, magical touch with the child.*
2 beautiful or delightful in such a way as to seem removed from everyday life: *it was a magical evening of pure nostalgia.*
– DERIVATIVES **magically** adverb.

magical realism ▶ noun another term for **MAGIC REALISM**.

magic bullet ▶ noun informal a medicine or other remedy with wonderful or highly specific properties, especially one that has not yet been discovered.

magic carpet ▶ noun (especially in stories set in Arabia) a mythical carpet that is able to transport people through the air.

magic circle ▶ noun a small group of people privileged to receive confidential information or make important decisions.
■ (**Magic Circle**) (in the UK) a society of conjurors.

magic eye ▶ noun **1** informal a photoelectric cell or similar electrical device used for identification, detection, or measurement.
2 a small cathode ray tube in some radio receivers that displays a pattern which enables the radio to be accurately tuned.

magician ▶ noun a person with magical powers.
■ a conjuror. ■ informal a person with exceptional skill in a particular area.
– ORIGIN late Middle English: from Old French *magicien*, from late Latin *magica* (see **MAGIC**).

magick ▶ noun archaic spelling of **MAGIC**.
– DERIVATIVES **magickal** adjective.

magic lantern ▶ noun historical a simple form of image projector used for showing photographic slides.

Magic Marker ▶ noun trademark an indelible marker pen.

magic mushroom ▶ noun informal any toadstool with hallucinogenic properties, especially the liberty cap and its relatives.
● Genus *Psilocybe*, family Strophariaceae, class Hymenomycetes: several species, including *P. mexicana*, which is traditionally consumed by American Indians in Mexico.

magic number ▶ noun a figure regarded as significant or momentous in a particular context.
■ chiefly Baseball the number which, at a given stage in the season, signifies the combination of wins for the first-placed team and defeats for the second-placed team which will assure the former of championship victory.

magic realism (also **magical realism**) ▶ noun [mass noun] a literary or artistic genre in which realistic narrative and naturalistic technique are combined with surreal elements of dream or fantasy.
— DERIVATIVES **magic realist** noun.

magic square ▶ noun a square divided into smaller squares each containing a number, such that the figures in each vertical, horizontal, and diagonal row add up to the same value.

magilp ▶ noun variant spelling of **MEGILP**.

Maginot Line /ˈmaʒɪnəʊ/ a system of fortifications constructed by the French along their eastern border between 1929 and 1934, outflanked by German forces in 1940.
— ORIGIN named after André *Maginot* (1877–1932), a French minister of war.

magister /ˈmadʒɪstə, məˈdʒɪstə/ ▶ noun archaic a title or form of address given to scholars, especially those qualified to teach in a national university.
— ORIGIN late Middle English: from Latin, 'master'.

magisterial /ˌmadʒɪˈstɪərɪəl/ ▶ adjective **1** having or showing great authority: *a magisterial pronouncement*.
■ domineering; dictatorial: *he dropped his somewhat magisterial style of questioning.*
2 relating to or conducted by a magistrate.
■ (of a person) holding the office of a magistrate.
— DERIVATIVES **magisterially** adverb.
— ORIGIN early 17th cent.: from medieval Latin *magisterialis*, from late Latin *magisterius*, from Latin *magister* 'master'.

magisterium /ˌmadʒɪˈstɪərɪəm/ ▶ noun [mass noun] the teaching authority of the Roman Catholic Church, especially as exercised by bishops or the Pope.
■ the official and authoritative teaching of the Church.
— ORIGIN mid 19th cent.: Latin, 'the office of master', from *magister* (see **MAGISTER**).

magistracy /ˈmadʒɪstrəsi/ ▶ noun (pl. **-ies**) the office or authority of a magistrate.
■ (the magistracy) magistrates collectively.

magistral /ˈmadʒɪstr(ə)l, məˈdʒɪstr(ə)l/ ▶ adjective formal or archaic relating to a master or masters.
— ORIGIN late 16th cent.: from French, or from Latin *magistralis*, from *magister* 'master'.

magistrand /ˈmadʒɪstrand/ ▶ noun Scottish a final-year undergraduate (now only at the University of St Andrews).
— ORIGIN early 17th cent.: from medieval Latin *magistrandus* 'someone who is suitable to become a Master of Arts'.

magistrate /ˈmadʒɪstrət, -streɪt/ ▶ noun a civil officer or lay judge who administers the law, especially one who conducts a court that deals with minor offences and holds preliminary hearings for more serious ones.
— DERIVATIVES **magistrature** /-trətʃə/ noun.
— ORIGIN late Middle English: from Latin *magistratus* 'administrator', from *magister* 'master'.

Maglemosian /ˌmagləˈməʊsɪən, -z-/ ▶ adjective Archaeology of, relating to, or denoting a northern European Mesolithic culture, dated to about 9,500–7,700 years ago.
■ [as noun **the Maglemosian**] the Maglemosian culture or period.
— ORIGIN early 20th cent.: from *Maglemose*, the name of a town in Denmark where objects from this culture were found, + **-IAN**.

maglev /ˈmaɡlɛv/ ▶ noun [mass noun] [usu. as modifier] a transport system in which trains glide above a track, supported by magnetic repulsion and propelled by a linear motor: *maglev trains*.
— ORIGIN late 20th cent.: from *mag(netic) lev(itation)*.

magma /ˈmaɡmə/ ▶ noun **1** [mass noun] hot fluid or semi-fluid material below or within the earth's crust from which lava and other igneous rock is formed by cooling.
2 [count noun] dated, chiefly US a fluid medicinal suspension of a solid.
— DERIVATIVES **magmatic** adjective.
— ORIGIN late Middle English (in the sense 'residue of dregs after evaporation or pressing of a semi-liquid substance'): via Latin from Greek *magma* (from *massein* 'knead').

magma chamber ▶ noun a reservoir of magma within the earth's crust beneath a volcano.

magmatism ▶ noun [mass noun] Geology the motion or activity of magma.

Magna Carta /ˌmaɡnə ˈkɑːtə/ a charter of liberty and political rights obtained from King John of England by his rebellious barons at Runnymede in 1215, which came to be seen as the seminal document of English constitutional practice.
■ [as noun **a Magna Carta**] a similar document of rights.
— ORIGIN from medieval Latin, 'great charter'.

magna cum laude /ˌmaɡnə kʌm ˈlɔːdi, ˌmaɡnə kʊm ˈlaʊdeɪ/ ▶ adverb & adjective chiefly N. Amer. with great distinction (with reference to university degrees and diplomas).
— ORIGIN Latin, literally 'with great praise'.

Magna Graecia /ˌmaɡnə ˈɡriːsɪə, ˈɡriːʃə/ the ancient Greek cities of southern Italy, founded from c.750 BC onwards by colonists from Euboea, Sparta, and elsewhere in Greece.
— ORIGIN Latin, literally 'Great Greece'.

magnanimous /maɡˈnanɪməs/ ▶ adjective very generous or forgiving, especially towards a rival or someone less powerful than oneself: *she should be magnanimous in victory.*
— DERIVATIVES **magnanimity** /ˌmaɡnəˈnɪmɪti/ noun, **magnanimously** adverb.
— ORIGIN mid 16th cent.: from Latin *magnanimus* (from *magnus* 'great' + *animus* 'soul') + **-OUS**.

magnate /ˈmaɡneɪt/ ▶ noun a wealthy and influential person, especially in business.
— ORIGIN late Middle English: from late Latin *magnas, magnat-* 'great man', from Latin *magnus* 'great'.

magnesia /maɡˈniːʒə, -zɪə, -ʃə/ ▶ noun [mass noun] Chemistry magnesium oxide.
● Chem. formula: MgO.
■ hydrated magnesium carbonate used as an antacid and laxative.
— ORIGIN late Middle English (referring to a mineral said to be an ingredient of the philosopher's stone): via medieval Latin from Greek *Magnēsia*, denoting a mineral from Magnesia in Asia Minor.

magnesian /maɡˈniːzɪən, -ʒ(ə)n/ ▶ adjective (chiefly of rocks and minerals) containing or relatively rich in magnesium.

magnesite /ˈmaɡnɪsʌɪt/ ▶ noun [mass noun] a whitish mineral consisting of magnesium carbonate, used as a refractory lining in some furnaces.

magnesium /maɡˈniːzɪəm/ ▶ noun the chemical element of atomic number 12, a silver-white metal of the alkaline earth series. It is used to make strong lightweight alloys, especially for the aerospace industry, and is also used in flash bulbs and pyrotechnics, as it burns with a brilliant white flame. (Symbol: **Mg**)

magnesium flare (also **magnesium light**) ▶ noun a brilliant white flare containing metallic magnesium wire or ribbon.

magnet ▶ noun a piece of iron (or an ore, alloy, or other material) which has its component atoms so ordered that the material exhibits properties of magnetism, such as attracting other iron-containing objects or aligning itself in an external magnetic field.
■ archaic term for **LODESTONE**. ■ figurative a person or thing that has a powerful attraction: *the beautiful stretch of white sand is a magnet for sun worshippers.*
— ORIGIN late Middle English (denoting lodestone): from Latin *magnes, magnet-*, from Greek *magnēs lithos* 'lodestone', probably influenced by Anglo-Norman French *magnete* (from Latin *magnes, magnet-*).

magnetic ▶ adjective **1** having the properties of a magnet; exhibiting magnetism: *the clock has a magnetic back to stick to the fridge.*
■ capable of being attracted by or acquiring the properties of a magnet: *steel is magnetic.* ■ relating to or involving magnetism: *an airborne magnetic survey.*

■ (of a bearing in navigation) measured relative to magnetic north.
2 very attractive or alluring: *his magnetic personality.*
— DERIVATIVES **magnetically** adverb.
— ORIGIN early 17th cent.: from late Latin *magneticus*, from Latin *magneta* (see **MAGNET**).

magnetic compass ▶ noun another term for **COMPASS** (in sense 1).

magnetic disk ▶ noun see **DISC** (sense 1).

magnetic equator ▶ noun the irregular imaginary line, passing round the earth near the equator, on which a magnetic needle has no dip (see **DIP** sense 4).

magnetic field ▶ noun a region around a magnetic material or a moving electric charge within which the force of magnetism acts.

magnetic inclination ▶ noun another term for **DIP** (in sense 5).

magnetic induction ▶ noun [mass noun] **1** magnetic flux or flux density.
2 the process by which an object or material is magnetized by an external magnetic field.

magnetic mine ▶ noun a mine detonated by the proximity of a magnetized body such as a ship or tank.

magnetic moment ▶ noun Physics the property of a magnet that interacts with an applied field to give a mechanical moment.

magnetic needle ▶ noun a piece of magnetized steel used as an indicator on the dial of a compass and in magnetic and electrical apparatus.

magnetic north ▶ noun the direction in which the north end of a compass needle or other freely suspended magnet will point in response to the earth's magnetic field. It deviates from true north over time and from place to place because the earth's magnetic poles are not fixed in relation to its axis.

magnetic pole ▶ noun each of the points near the extremities of the axis of rotation of the earth or another celestial body where a magnetic needle dips vertically.
■ each of the two points or regions of an artificial or natural magnet to and from which the lines of magnetic force are directed.

magnetic resonance imaging (abbrev.: **MRI**) ▶ noun [mass noun] a form of medical imaging which measures the response of the atomic nuclei of body tissues to high-frequency radio waves when placed in a strong magnetic field, and produces images of the internal organs.

magnetic storm ▶ noun a disturbance of the magnetic field of the earth (or other celestial body).

magnetic tape ▶ noun [mass noun] tape used in recording sound, pictures, or computer data.

magnetic termite ▶ noun a North Australian termite which builds tall flattened mounds that are aligned north–south.
● *Amitermes meridionalis*, family Termitidae.

magnetic variation ▶ noun see **VARIATION** (sense 1).

magnetism ▶ noun [mass noun] a physical phenomenon produced by the motion of electric charge, which results in attractive and repulsive forces between objects.
■ the property of being magnetic. ■ figurative the ability to attract and charm people: *his personal magnetism attracted men to the brotherhood.*

All magnetism is due to circulating electric currents. In magnetic materials the magnetism is produced by electrons orbiting within the atoms; in most substances the magnetic effects of different electrons cancel each other out, but in some, such as iron, a net magnetic field can be induced by aligning the atoms.

— ORIGIN early 17th cent.: from modern Latin *magnetismus*, from Latin *magneta* (see **MAGNET**).

magnetite /ˈmaɡnɪtʌɪt/ ▶ noun [mass noun] a grey-black magnetic mineral which consists of an oxide of iron and is an important form of iron ore.
— ORIGIN mid 19th cent.: from **MAGNET** + **-ITE**[1].

magnetize (also **-ise**) ▶ verb [with obj.] give magnetic properties to; make magnetic.
■ figurative attract strongly as if by a magnet.
— DERIVATIVES **magnetizable** adjective, **magnetization** noun, **magnetizer** noun.

magneto ▶ noun (pl. **-os**) a small electric generator containing a permanent magnet and used to provided high-voltage pulses, especially (formerly)

in the ignition systems of internal-combustion engines.
– ORIGIN late 19th cent.: abbreviation of **MAGNETO-ELECTRIC**.

magneto- /mag'ni:təʊ/ ▶ **combining form** relating to a magnet or magnetism: *magneto-electric.*

magneto-electric ▶ **adjective** relating to the electric currents generated in a material by its motion in a magnetic field.
■ (of an electric generator) using permanent magnets.
– DERIVATIVES **magneto-electricity** noun.

magnetograph ▶ **noun** an instrument for recording measurements of magnetic forces.

magnetohydrodynamics /mag,ni:təʊ,haɪdrə(ʊ)daɪ'namɪks/ ▶ **plural noun** [treated as sing.] the branch of physics that studies the behaviour of an electrically conducting fluid such as a plasma or molten metal acted on by a magnetic field.
– DERIVATIVES **magnetohydrodynamic** adjective.

magnetometer /,magnɪ'tɒmɪtə/ ▶ **noun** an instrument used for measuring magnetic forces, especially the earth's magnetism.
– DERIVATIVES **magnetometry** noun.

magnetomotive force /mag,ni:tə(ʊ)'məʊtɪv/ ▶ **noun** Physics a quantity representing the line integral of the magnetic intensity around a closed line (e.g. the sum of the magnetizing forces along a circuit).

magneton /'magnɪtɒn/ ▶ **noun** a unit of magnetic moment in atomic and nuclear physics.
– ORIGIN early 20th cent.: from **MAGNETIC** + **-ON**.

magneto-optical ▶ **adjective** of, relating to, or employing both optical and magnetic phenomena or technology.

magnetopause ▶ **noun** the outer limit of a magnetosphere.

magnetoresistance ▶ **noun** Physics the dependence of the electrical resistance of a body on an external magnetic field.
– DERIVATIVES **magnetoresistive** adjective.

magnetosphere ▶ **noun** the region surrounding the earth or another astronomical body in which its magnetic field is the predominant effective magnetic field.
– DERIVATIVES **magnetospheric** adjective.

magnetotail ▶ **noun** Astronomy the broad elongated extension of the earth's magnetosphere on the side away from the sun.

magnetron /'magnɪtrɒn/ ▶ **noun** an electron tube for amplifying or generating microwaves, with the flow of electrons controlled by an external magnetic field.
– ORIGIN early 20th cent.: from **MAGNETIC** + -tron from **ELECTRON**.

Magnificat /mag'nɪfɪkat/ ▶ **noun** a canticle used in Christian liturgy, especially at vespers and evensong, the text being the hymn of the Virgin Mary (Luke 1:46–55).
– ORIGIN Middle English: Latin, literally 'magnifies' (from the opening words, which translate as 'my soul magnifies the Lord').

magnification ▶ **noun** [mass noun] the action or process of magnifying something or being magnified, especially visually: *visible under high magnification.*
■ [count noun] the degree to which something is or can be magnified: *at this magnification the pixels making up the image become visible.* ■ [count noun] the magnifying power of an instrument: *this microscope should give a magnification of about ×100.* ■ [count noun] a magnified reproduction of something.

magnificence ▶ **noun** [mass noun] the quality of being magnificent.
■ (**His/Your** etc. **Magnificence**) chiefly historical a title given to a monarch or other distinguished person, or used in addressing them.

magnificent ▶ **adjective 1** impressively beautiful, elaborate, or extravagant; striking: *a dramatic landscape of magnificent mountains* | *the interior layout is magnificent.*
2 very good; excellent: *she paid tribute to their magnificent efforts.*
– DERIVATIVES **magnificently** adverb.
– ORIGIN late Middle English: via Old French from Latin *magnificent-* 'making great, serving to magnify', based on *magnus* 'great'.

magnifico /mag'nɪfɪkəʊ/ ▶ **noun** (pl. **-oes**) informal an eminent, powerful, or illustrious person.

– ORIGIN late 16th cent.: Italian, 'magnificent', originally used to denote a Venetian magnate.

magnify ▶ **verb** (**-ies**, **-ied**) [with obj.] **1** make (something) appear larger than it is, especially with a lens or microscope: *the retinal image will be magnified.*
■ increase the volume of (a sound). ■ intensify: *the risk is magnified if there is any dirty material next to the skin.* ■ exaggerate the importance or effect of: *she tended to magnify the defects of those she disliked.*
2 archaic extol; glorify: *praise the Lord and magnify Him.*
– DERIVATIVES **magnifier** noun.
– ORIGIN late Middle English (in the senses 'show honour to (God)' and 'make greater in size or importance'): from Old French *magnifier* or Latin *magnificare*, based on Latin *magnus* 'great'. Sense 1 dates from the mid 17th cent.

magnifying glass ▶ **noun** a lens that produces an enlarged image, typically set in a frame with a handle and used to examine small or finely detailed things such as fingerprints, stamps, and fine print.

magniloquent /mag'nɪləkwənt/ ▶ **adjective** using high-flown or bombastic language.
– DERIVATIVES **magniloquence** noun, **magniloquently** adverb.
– ORIGIN mid 17th cent.: from Latin *magniloquus* (from *magnus* 'great' + *-loquus* '-speaking') + **-ENT**.

Magnitogorsk /,magni:tə'gɔ:sk/ an industrial city in southern Russia, on the Ural River close to the border with Kazakhstan; pop. 443,000 (1990).

magnitude /'magnɪtju:d/ ▶ **noun** [mass noun] **1** the great size or extent of something: *they may feel discouraged at the magnitude of the task before them.*
■ great importance: *events of tragic magnitude.*
2 size: *electorates of less than average magnitude.*
■ [count noun] a numerical quantity or value: *the magnitudes of all the economic variables could be determined.*
3 the degree of brightness of a star. The magnitude of an astronomical object is now reckoned as the negative logarithm of the brightness; a decrease of one magnitude represents an increase in brightness of 2.512 times.
■ [count noun] the class into which a star falls by virtue of its brightness. ■ [count noun] a difference of one on a scale of brightness, treated as a unit of measurement.
– ORIGIN late Middle English (also in the sense 'greatness of character'): from Latin *magnitudo*, from *magnus* 'great'.

magnolia /mag'nəʊliə/ ▶ **noun** a tree or shrub with large, typically creamy-pink, waxy flowers. Magnolias are widely grown as specimen trees.
● Genus *Magnolia*, family Magnoliaceae.
■ [mass noun] a pale creamy-white colour like that of magnolia blossom.
– ORIGIN modern Latin, named after Pierre *Magnol* (1638–1715), French botanist.

Magnolia State informal name for **MISSISSIPPI**.

magnox /'magnɒks/ ▶ **noun** [mass noun] a magnesium-based alloy used to enclose uranium fuel elements in some nuclear reactors.
■ (**Magnox**) [as modifier] denoting the first widely used British design of nuclear power station, which used fuel clad with this alloy.
– ORIGIN 1950s: from the phrase *mag(nesium) n(o) o(xidation)*.

magnum /'magnəm/ ▶ **noun** (pl. **magnums**) a thing of a type that is larger than normal, in particular:
■ a wine bottle of twice the standard size, normally 1½ litres. ■ (often as modifier) (trademark in the US) a gun designed to fire cartridges that are more powerful than its calibre would suggest.
– ORIGIN late 18th cent.: from Latin, neuter (used as a noun) of *magnus* 'great'.

magnum opus /,magnəm 'əʊpəs, 'ɒpəs/ ▶ **noun** (pl. **magnum opuses** or **magna opera** /,magnə 'əʊpərə, 'ɒpərə/) a large and important work of art, music, or literature, especially one regarded as the most important work of an artist or writer.
– ORIGIN late 18th cent.: from Latin, 'great work'.

Magnus effect /'magnəs/ ▶ **noun** [mass noun] Physics the force exerted on a rapidly spinning cylinder or sphere moving through air or another fluid in a direction at an angle to the axis of spin. This force is responsible for the swerving of balls when hit or thrown with spin.

– ORIGIN 1920s: named after Heinrich G. *Magnus* (1802–70), German scientist.

Magog see **GOG AND MAGOG**.

magpie ▶ **noun 1** a long-tailed crow with boldly marked (or green) plumage and a raucous voice.
● Family Corvidae: five genera and several species, in particular the black-and-white (**black-billed**) **magpie** (*Pica pica*) of Eurasia and North America.
2 (also **bell magpie**) chiefly Austral. any bird of the Australasian butcher-bird family, having black-and-white plumage and musical calls.
● Family Cracticidae: several species, in particular the **Australian** (or **black-backed**) **magpie** (*Gymnorhina tibicen*).
3 used in similes or comparisons to refer to a person who collects things, especially things of little use or value, or a person who chatters idly.
4 the division of a circular target next to the outer one; a shot which strikes this.
– ORIGIN late 16th cent.: probably shortening of dialect *maggot the pie*, *maggoty-pie*, from *Magot* (Middle English pet form of the given name *Marguerite*) + **PIE**[2].

magpie lark ▶ **noun** a common ground-dwelling Australian songbird with black-and-white plumage, long legs, and a loud piping call. Also called **PEEWEE**.
● *Grallina cyanoleuca*, family Grallinidae (which is sometimes taken to include the mud-nesters).

magpie moth ▶ **noun** a white moth with black and yellow spots, the caterpillars of which are similarly coloured and feed on fruit bushes, where they can be a pest.
● Genus *Abraxas*, family Geometridae: several species, in particular *A. grossulariata*.

Magritte /ma'gri:t, French magʀit/, René (François Ghislain) (1898–1967), Belgian surrealist painter. His paintings display startling or amusing juxtapositions of the ordinary, the strange, and the erotic, depicted in a realist manner.

magsman ▶ **noun** (pl. **-men**) Austral. informal a confidence trickster.
■ a person who likes telling stories; a raconteur.
– ORIGIN early 19th cent.: from English dialect *mag* 'prattle' + **MAN**.

maguey /'magweɪ/ ▶ **noun** an agave plant, especially one yielding pulque.
– ORIGIN mid 16th cent.: via Spanish from Taino.

magus /'meɪgəs/ ▶ **noun** (pl. **magi** /'meɪdʒaɪ/) a member of a priestly caste of ancient Persia.
■ a sorcerer.
– ORIGIN Middle English: via Latin and Greek from Old Persian *maguš*.

mag wheel ▶ **noun** N. Amer. a motor-vehicle wheel made from lightweight magnesium steel, typically having a pattern of holes or spokes around the hub.

Magyar /'magjɑ:/ ▶ **noun 1** a member of a people who originated in the Urals and migrated westwards to settle in what is now Hungary in the 9th century AD.
2 [mass noun] the Uralic language of this people; Hungarian.
▶ **adjective** of or relating to this people or language.
– ORIGIN the name in Hungarian.

Magyarország /'mɔ,ɔrɔr,sa:g/ Hungarian name for **HUNGARY**.

Mahabad /,mɑ:hə'bad/ a city in NW Iran, near the Iraqi border, with a chiefly Kurdish population; pop. 63,000 (1986). Between 1941 and 1946 it was the centre of a Soviet-supported Kurdish republic.

Mahabharata /,mɑ:hə'bɑ:rətə/ one of the two great Sanskrit epics of the Hindus, existing in its present form since *c*.400 AD. It describes the civil war waged between the five Pandava brothers and their one hundred stepbrothers at Kuruksetra near modern Delhi.
– ORIGIN Sanskrit, literally 'great Bharata', i.e. the great epic of the Bharata dynasty.

mahajan /mə'hɑːjɑːn/ ▶ **noun** Indian a moneylender.
– ORIGIN via Hindi from Sanskrit *mahājana* 'head of a tribe or caste', from *mahā* 'great' + *jána* 'man'.

Mahamad /'mahəmad/ ▶ **noun** the body of trustees ruling a Sephardic synagogue.
– ORIGIN Hebrew, *'amad* 'to stand'.

mahant /mə'hʌnt/ ▶ **noun** Hinduism a chief priest of a temple or the head of a monastery.
– ORIGIN Hindi.

maharaja /,mɑ:(h)ə'rɑ:dʒə, ,mɑhə-/ (also **maharajah**) ▶ **noun** historical an Indian prince.

maharani /ˌmɑː(h)əˈrɑːni, ˌmɑːhə-/ (also **maharanee**) ▶ noun a maharaja's wife or widow.
– ORIGIN from Hindi *mahārānī*, from Sanskrit *mahā* 'great' + *rājñī* 'ranee'.

Maharashtra /ˌmɑːhəˈraʃtrə, -ˈrɑːʃtrə/ a large state in western India bordering on the Arabian Sea, formed in 1960 from the SE part of the former Bombay State; capital, Bombay.
– DERIVATIVES **Maharashtrian** adjective & noun.

Maharishi /ˌmɑː(h)əˈrɪʃi/ ▶ noun a great Hindu sage or spiritual leader.
– ORIGIN alteration of Sanskrit *maharṣi*, from *mahā* 'great' + *ṛṣi* 'rishi'.

mahatma /məˈhatmə, məˈhɑː-/ ▶ noun (in the Indian subcontinent) a person regarded with reverence or loving respect; a holy person or sage.
■ (the Mahatma) Mahatma Gandhi. ■ (in some forms of theosophy) a person in India or Tibet said to have preternatural powers.
– ORIGIN from Sanskrit *mahātman*, from *mahā* 'great' + *ātman* 'soul'.

Mahaweli /ˌmɑːhəˈweɪli/ the largest river in Sri Lanka. Rising in the central highlands, it flows 330 km (206 miles) to the Bay of Bengal near Trincomalee.

Mahayana /ˌmɑː(h)əˈjɑːnə, ˌmɑːhə-/ (also **Mahayana Buddhism**) ▶ noun [mass noun] one of the two major traditions of Buddhism, now practised in a variety of forms especially in China, Tibet, Japan, and Korea. The tradition emerged around the 1st century AD and is typically concerned with personal spiritual practice and the ideal of the bodhisattva. Compare with **THERAVADA**.
– ORIGIN from Sanskrit, from *mahā* 'great' + *yāna* 'vehicle'.

Mahdi /ˈmɑːdi/ ▶ noun (pl. **Mahdis**) (in popular Muslim belief) a spiritual and temporal leader who will rule before the end of the world and restore religion and justice.
■ a person claiming to be this leader, notably Muhammad Ahmad of Dongola in Sudan (1843–85), whose revolutionary movement captured Khartoum and overthrew the Egyptian regime. ■ (in Shiite belief) the twelfth imam, who is expected to return and triumph over injustice.
– DERIVATIVES **Mahdism** noun, **Mahdist** noun & adjective.
– ORIGIN from Arabic (*al-*)*mahdī* 'he who is guided in the right way', passive participle of *hadā* 'to guide'.

Mahfouz /mɑːˈfuːz/, Naguib (b.1911), Egyptian novelist and short-story writer. He was the first writer in Arabic to be awarded the Nobel Prize for Literature (1988). Notable works: *Miramar* (novel, 1967).

Mahican /məˈhiːk(ə)n/ (also **Mohican**) ▶ noun 1 a member of an American Indian people formerly inhabiting the Upper Hudson Valley in New York State. Compare with **MOHEGAN**.
2 [mass noun] the extinct Algonquian language of this people.
▶ adjective of or relating to the Mahicans or their language.
– ORIGIN the name in Mahican, said to mean 'wolf'.

Mahilyow /ˌmɑːhɪlˈjɔə/ an industrial city and railway centre in eastern Belarus, on the River Dnieper; pop. 363,000 (1990). Russian name **MOGILYOV**.

mahimahi /ˈmɑːhɪˌmɑːhi/ ▶ noun Hawaiian term for **DORADO** (in sense 1).

mah-jong /mɑːˈdʒɒŋ/ (also **mah-jongg**) ▶ noun a Chinese game played, usually by four people, with 136 or 144 rectangular pieces called tiles.
– ORIGIN early 20th cent.: from Chinese dialect *ma-tsiang*, literally 'sparrows'.

Mahler /ˈmɑːlə/, German /ˈmaːlɐ/, Gustav (1860–1911), Austrian composer, conductor, and pianist. Forming a link between romanticism and the experimentalism of Schoenberg, his works include nine complete symphonies (1888–1910) and the symphonic song cycle *Das Lied von der Erde* (1908).
– DERIVATIVES **Mahlerian** /-ˈlɪərɪən/ adjective.

mahlstick /ˈmɔːlstɪk/ ▶ noun US spelling of **MAULSTICK**.

mahoe¹ /məˈhəʊi/ ▶ noun a small bushy New Zealand tree of the violet family, with whitish bark and clusters of small greenish flowers.
● *Melicytus ramiflorus*, family Violaceae.

mahoe² /məˈhəʊi/ ▶ noun W. Indian any of a number of tropical trees and shrubs yielding bast that is used to make cordage.
● Several species, especially of the genus *Hibiscus* (family Malvaceae), in particular the widespread *H. tiliaceus* and the Caribbean *H. elatus*.
– ORIGIN from Arawak *maho*.

mahogany /məˈhɒɡəni/ ▶ noun 1 [mass noun] hard reddish-brown timber from a tropical tree, used for quality furniture.
■ a rich reddish-brown colour like that of mahogany wood.
2 the tropical American tree which produces this timber, widely harvested from the wild.
● Genus *Swietenia*, family Meliaceae: three species, especially *S. mahogoni*.
■ used in names of trees which yield similar timber, e.g. **African mahogany**.
– ORIGIN mid 17th cent.: of unknown origin.

Mahon /məˈhɒn/ (also **Port Mahon**) the capital of the island of Minorca, a port on the SE coast; pop. 21,800 (1991). Spanish name **MAHÓN**.

mahonia /məˈhəʊnɪə/ ▶ noun an evergreen shrub of the barberry family, which produces clusters of small fragrant yellow flowers followed by purple or black berries, native to east Asia and North and Central America.
● Genus *Mahonia*, family Berberidaceae.
– ORIGIN modern Latin, named after Bernard McMahon (*c*.1775–1816), American botanist.

Mahore /məˈhɔː/ another name for **MAYOTTE**.

mahout /məˈhaʊt/ ▶ noun (in the Indian subcontinent and SE Asia) a person who works with, rides, and tends an elephant.
– ORIGIN from Hindi *mahāvat*.

Mahratta ▶ noun variant spelling of **MARATHA**.

Mahratti ▶ noun variant spelling of **MARATHI**.

mahseer /ˈmɑːsɪə/ ▶ noun a large edible freshwater fish of the carp family, native to northern India and the Himalayan region.
● Genus *Tor*, family Cyprinidae: several species, in particular the **Putitor mahseer** (*T. putitora*), which is a prized sporting fish.
– ORIGIN via Hindi from Sanskrit *mahā* 'great' + *śaphara* 'carp'.

mahua /ˈmɑːhʊə/ (also **mahwa** /ˈmɑːʊwə/) ▶ noun an Indian tree which has fleshy edible flowers and yields oil-rich seeds.
● *Madhuca latifolia*, family Sapotaceae.
■ [mass noun] an alcoholic drink produced from the nectar-rich flowers of this tree.
– ORIGIN late 17th cent.: via Hindi from Sanskrit *madhūka*, from *madhu* 'sweet'.

Maia¹ /ˈmaɪə/ Greek Mythology the daughter of Atlas and mother of Hermes.

Maia² /ˈmaɪə/ Roman Mythology a goddess associated with Vulcan and also (by confusion with **MAIA¹**) with Mercury (Hermes). She was worshipped on 1 May and 15 May; that month is named after her.

maid ▶ noun a female domestic servant.
■ archaic or poetic/literary a girl or young woman, especially an unmarried one. ■ archaic or poetic/literary a virgin.
– ORIGIN Middle English: abbreviation of **MAIDEN**.

maidan /maɪˈdɑːn/ ▶ noun (in the Indian subcontinent) an open space in or near a town, used as a parade ground or for events such as public meetings and polo matches.
– ORIGIN from Urdu and Persian *maidān*, from Arabic *maydān*.

maiden ▶ noun 1 archaic or poetic/literary a girl or young woman, especially an unmarried one.
■ a virgin.
2 (also **maiden over**) Cricket an over in which no runs are scored.
▶ adjective [attrib.] 1 (of a woman, especially an older one) unmarried: *a maiden aunt*.
■ (of a female animal) unmated.
2 being or involving the first attempt or act of its kind: *the Titanic's maiden voyage*.
■ denoting a horse that has never won a race or a race intended for such horses. ■ (of a tree or other fruiting plant) in its first year of growth.
– DERIVATIVES **maidenhood** noun, **maidenish** adjective, **maiden-like** adjective, **maidenly** adjective.
– ORIGIN Old English *mæġden*, from a Germanic diminutive meaning 'maid, virgin'; related to German *Mädchen*, diminutive of *Magd* 'maid', from

maidenhair (also **maidenhair fern**) ▶ noun a chiefly tropical fern of delicate appearance, having slender-stalked fronds with round or wedge-shaped divided lobes.
● Genus *Adiantum*, family Adiantaceae: several species, in particular *A. capillus-veneris* of Eurasia and North America.

maidenhair tree ▶ noun the ginkgo, whose leaves resemble those of the maidenhair fern.

Maidenhead a town in southern England to the west of London on the River Thames; pop. 60,460 (1981).

maidenhead ▶ noun [mass noun] virginity.
■ dated the hymen.

maiden name ▶ noun the surname that a married woman used before she was married and which she may still use when married, especially in her employment or as a pen name.

maiden over ▶ noun see **MAIDEN** (sense 2).

Maid Marian (in English folklore) the lover of Robin Hood.

maid of honour ▶ noun 1 an unmarried noblewoman attending a queen or princess.
■ N. Amer. a principal bridesmaid.
2 Brit. a small tart filled with flavoured milk curds.

maidservant ▶ noun dated a female domestic servant.

Maidstone a town in SE England, on the River Medway, the county town of Kent; pop. 133,200 (1991).

maieutic /meɪˈjuːtɪk/ ▶ adjective of or denoting the Socratic mode of enquiry, which aims to bring a person's latent ideas into clear consciousness.
▶ plural noun (**maieutics**) [treated as sing.] the maieutic method.
– ORIGIN mid 17th cent.: from Greek *maieutikos*, from *maieuesthai* 'act as a midwife', from *maia* 'midwife'.

maigre /ˈmeɪɡə/ ▶ adjective (in the Roman Catholic Church) denoting a day on which abstinence from meat is ordered.
■ (of food) suitable for eating on maigre days.
– ORIGIN late 17th cent.: from French, literally 'lean'.

Maikop /maɪˈkɒp/ a city in SW Russia, capital of the republic of Adygea; pop. 120,000 (1990).

mail¹ ▶ noun [mass noun] letters and parcels sent by post.
■ (N. Amer. & W. Indian also **the mails**) the postal system: *you can order by mail*. ■ [in sing.] a single delivery or collection of mail: *I had a notice in by this morning's mail*. ■ Computing electronic mail. ■ [count noun] dated a vehicle, such as a train, carrying mail. ■ [count noun] archaic a bag of letters to be sent by post. ■ [in names] used in titles of newspapers: *the Daily Mail*.
▶ verb [with obj.] send (a letter or parcel) by post: *three editions were mailed to our members*.
■ Computing send (someone) electronic mail.
– DERIVATIVES **mailable** adjective.
– ORIGIN Middle English (in the sense 'travelling bag'): from Old French *male* 'wallet', of West Germanic origin. The notion 'by post' dates from the mid 17th cent.

mail² ▶ noun [mass noun] historical armour made of metal rings or plates joined together flexibly.
■ the protective shell or scales of certain animals.
▶ verb [with obj.] clothe or cover with mail: [as adj. **mailed**] *a mailed gauntlet*.
– PHRASES **the mailed fist** the use of physical force to maintain control or impose one's will.
– ORIGIN Middle English (also denoting the individual metal elements composing mail armour): from Old French *maille*, from Latin *macula* 'spot or mesh'.

mailbag ▶ noun a large sack or bag for carrying mail.
■ the letters received by a person, especially a public figure such as a Member of Parliament or magazine columnist.

mailboat ▶ noun historical a ship or boat that carried mail.

mail bomb ▶ noun 1 US term for **LETTER BOMB**.
2 an overwhelmingly large quantity of e-mail messages sent to one e-mail address.
▶ verb (**mail-bomb**) [with obj.] send an overwhelmingly large quantity of e-mail messages to (someone).

mailbox ▶ noun chiefly N. Amer. a box into which mail is delivered, especially one mounted on a post at the entrance to a person's property.

■North American term for **POSTBOX**. ■ a computer file in which e-mail messages received by a particular user are stored.

mail carrier ▶ noun N. Amer. a person who delivers post.

mail cart ▶ noun Brit. historical a cart for carrying mail by road.
■ a light vehicle for carrying children.

mail drop ▶ noun 1 N. Amer. a receptacle for mail, especially one in which mail is kept until the addressee collects it.
2 Brit. a delivery of mail, advertising leaflets, or other material.

Mailer, Norman (b.1923), American novelist and essayist. Notable novels: *The Naked and the Dead* (1948) and *The Presidential Papers* (1963).

mailer ▶ noun 1 chiefly N. Amer. the sender of a letter or package by post.
■ a person employed to dispatch newspapers or periodicals by post. ■ a free advertising pamphlet, brochure, or catalogue sent out by post. ■ a container used for conveying items by post.
2 Computing a program that sends electronic mail messages.

mailing ▶ noun [mass noun] the action or process of sending something by mail.
■ [count noun] something sent by mail, especially a piece of mass advertising.

mailing list ▶ noun a list of the names and addresses of people to whom material such as advertising matter, information, or a magazine may be mailed, especially regularly.

maillot /ˈmaɪjəʊ/ ▶ noun (pl. pronounced same) 1 a pair of tights worn for dancing or gymnastics.
■ chiefly N. Amer. a woman's tight-fitting one-piece swimsuit.
2 a jersey or top, especially one worn in sports such as cycling.
– ORIGIN French.

mailman ▶ noun (pl. **-men**) N. Amer. a postman.

mail merge ▶ noun [mass noun] Computing the automatic addition of names and addresses from a database to letters and envelopes in order to facilitate sending mail, especially advertising, to many addresses.

mail order ▶ noun [mass noun] the selling of goods to customers by post, generally involving selection from a special catalogue.

mail-out ▶ noun an instance of sending out by post a number of items such as promotion brochures at one time.

mailshot Brit. ▶ noun a dispatch of mail, especially advertising and promotional material, to a large number of addresses.
■ an item sent in this way.
▶ verb [with obj.] send such material to (a large number of people).

maim ▶ verb [with obj.] wound or injure (someone) so that part of the body is permanently damaged: *100,000 soldiers were killed or maimed.*
– ORIGIN Middle English: from Old French *mahaignier*, of unknown origin.

Maimonides /maɪˈmɒnɪdiːz/ (1135–1204), Jewish philosopher and Rabbinic scholar, born in Spain; born *Moses ben Maimon*. His *Guide for the Perplexed* (1190) attempts to reconcile Talmudic scripture with the philosophy of Aristotle.

Main /maɪn/ a river of SW Germany which rises in northern Bavaria and flows 500 km (310 miles) westwards, through Frankfurt, to meet the Rhine at Mainz.

main¹ ▶ adjective [attrib.] chief in size or importance: *a main road | the main problem is one of resources.*
▶ noun 1 a principal pipe carrying water or gas to buildings, or taking sewage from them.
■ a principal cable carrying electricity. ■ **(the mains)** Brit. the source of public water, gas, or electricity supply through pipes or cables.
2 (the main) archaic or poetic/literary the open ocean.
3 Nautical short for **MAINSAIL** or **MAINMAST**.
– PHRASES **by main force** through sheer strength. **in the main** on the whole.
– ORIGIN Middle English: from Old English *mægen* 'physical force', reinforced by Old Norse *meginn*, *megn* 'strong, powerful', both from a Germanic base meaning 'have power'.

main² ▶ noun 1 (in the game of hazard) a number

(5, 6, 7, 8, or 9) called by a player before dice are thrown.
2 historical a match between fighting cocks.
– ORIGIN late 16th cent.: probably from the phrase *main chance*.

main beam ▶ noun 1 a principal beam which transmits a load directly to a column.
2 the undipped beam of the headlights of a motor vehicle.

main brace ▶ noun the brace attached to the main yard of a sailing ship.

main clause ▶ noun Grammar a clause that can form a complete sentence standing alone, having a subject and a predicate. Contrasted with **SUBORDINATE CLAUSE**.

main course ▶ noun 1 the most substantial course of a meal.
2 the mainsail of a square-rigged sailing ship.

maincrop ▶ adjective Brit. denoting a vegetable produced as a principal crop of the season.

main drag ▶ noun (usu. **the main drag**) informal, chiefly N. Amer. the main street of a town.

Maine a NE state of the US, on the Atlantic coast; pop. 1,227,930 (1990); capital, Augusta. Visited by John Cabot in 1498 and colonized from England in the 17th and 18th centuries, it became the 23rd state of the US in 1820.
– DERIVATIVES **Mainer** noun.

Maine Coon (also **Maine Coon cat**) ▶ noun a large, powerful cat of a long-haired breed, originally from America.
– ORIGIN 1970s: so named because of partial resemblance to the raccoon.

mainframe ▶ noun 1 a large high-speed computer, especially one supporting numerous workstations or peripherals.
2 the central processing unit and primary memory of a computer.

Mainland 1 the largest island in Orkney.
2 the largest island in Shetland.

mainland ▶ noun a large continuous extent of land that includes the greater part of a country or territory, as opposed to offshore islands and detached territories.
– DERIVATIVES **mainlander** noun.

main line ▶ noun a chief railway line: [as modifier] *a main-line station.*
■ a principal route, course, or connection: *the main line of evolution.* ■ N. Amer. a chief road or street. ■ informal a principal vein as a site for a drug injection.
▶ verb **(mainline)** [with obj.] informal inject (a drug) intravenously: *Mariella mainlines cocaine five to seven times a day | [no obj.] he started mainlining on heroin.*
– DERIVATIVES **mainliner** noun.

mainly ▶ adverb more than anything else: *he is mainly concerned with fiction.*
■ for the most part: *the west will be mainly dry.*

mainmast ▶ noun the principal mast of a ship, typically the second mast in a sailing ship of three or more masts.

mainplane ▶ noun a principal supporting surface of an aircraft (typically a wing), as opposed to a tailplane.

mainsail /ˈmeɪnseɪl, -s(ə)l/ ▶ noun the principal sail of a ship, especially the lowest sail on the mainmast in a square-rigged vessel.
■ the sail set on the after part of the mainmast in a fore-and-aft rigged vessel.

main sequence ▶ noun Astronomy a series of star types to which most stars belong, represented on a Hertzsprung–Russell diagram as a continuous band extending from the upper left (hot, bright stars) to the lower right (cool, dim stars).

mainsheet ▶ noun a sheet used for controlling and trimming the mainsail of a sailing boat.

mainspring ▶ noun the principal spring in a watch, clock, or other mechanism.
■ figurative something that plays a principal part in motivating or maintaining a movement, process, or activity: *the mainspring of anti-communism.*

mainstay ▶ noun a stay which extends from the maintop to the foot of the foremast of a sailing ship.
■ figurative a thing on which something else is based or depends: *whitefish are the mainstay of the local industry.*

mainstream ▶ noun **(the mainstream)** the ideas, attitudes, or activities that are regarded as normal or conventional; the dominant trend in opinion,

fashion, or the arts: *they are becoming integrated into the mainstream of British life.*
■ (also **mainstream jazz**) [mass noun] jazz that is neither traditional nor modern, based on the 1930s swing style and consisting especially of solo improvisation on chord sequences.
▶ adjective belonging to or characteristic of the mainstream: *mainstream politics | a mixture of mainstream and avant-garde artists.*
■ (of a school or class) for pupils without special needs.

main street ▶ noun the principal street of a town.
■ **(Main Street)** chiefly US used in reference to the materialism, mediocrity, or parochialism regarded as typical of small-town life. [ORIGIN: from the title of a novel (1920) by Sinclair Lewis.]

maintain ▶ verb [with obj.] 1 cause or enable (a condition or state of affairs) to continue: *the need to maintain close links between industry and schools.*
■ keep (something) at the same level or rate: *agricultural prices will have to be maintained.* ■ keep (a building, machine, or road) in good condition or in working order by checking or repairing it regularly.
2 provide with necessities for life or existence: *the allowance covers the basic costs of maintaining a child.*
■ keep (a military unit) supplied with equipment and other requirements. ■ archaic give one's support to; uphold: *the king swears he will maintain the laws of God.*
3 [reporting verb] state something strongly to be the case; assert: [with obj.] *he has always maintained his innocence* | [with clause] *he had persistently maintained that he would not stand against his old friend* | [with direct speech] *'It was not an ideology at all,' she maintained.*
– DERIVATIVES **maintainability** noun, **maintainable** adjective.
– ORIGIN Middle English (also in the sense 'practise (a good or bad action) habitually'): from Old French *maintenir*, from Latin *manu tenere* 'hold in the hand'.

maintained ▶ adjective Brit. (of a school) financed with public money.

maintainer ▶ noun a person or thing that maintains something, in particular computer software.
■ (also **maintainor**) Law, historical a person guilty of aiding a party in a legal action without lawful cause.

maintenance ▶ noun [mass noun] 1 the process of maintaining or preserving someone or something or the state of being maintained: *crucial conditions for the maintenance of democratic government.*
■ the process of keeping something in good condition: *car maintenance* | [as modifier] *essential maintenance work.*
2 the provision of financial support for a person's living expenses, or the support so provided.
■ (also **separate maintenance**) a husband's or wife's provision for a spouse after separation or divorce. ■ Law, historical the former offence of aiding a party in a legal action without lawful cause.
– ORIGIN Middle English (in the sense 'aiding a party in a legal action without lawful cause'): from Old French, from *maintenir* (see **MAINTAIN**).

maintenance order ▶ noun a court order directing payment of a regular fixed sum for maintenance to be paid to a spouse after separation or divorce.

Maintenon /ˈmãtənɔ̃, French mɛ̃tnɔ̃/, Françoise d'Aubigné, Marquise de (1635–1719), mistress and later second wife of the French king Louis XIV.

maintop ▶ noun a platform around the head of the lower section of a sailing ship's mainmast.

maintopmast /meɪnˈtɒpmɑːst/ ▶ noun the second section of a sailing ship's mainmast.

main verb ▶ noun Grammar 1 the verb in a main clause.
2 the head of a verb phrase, for example *eat* in *might have been going to eat it.*

Mainz /maɪnts/ a city in western Germany, capital of Rhineland-Palatinate, situated at the confluence of the Rhine and Main Rivers; pop. 182,870 (1991).

maiolica /məˈjɒlɪkə, maɪˈɒlɪkə/ ▶ noun [mass noun] fine earthenware with coloured decoration on an opaque white tin glaze, originating in Italy during the Renaissance.
– ORIGIN mid 16th cent.: Italian, from *Maiolica* 'Majorca'.

maisonette /ˌmeɪzəˈnɛt/ ▶ noun a set of rooms for living in, typically on two storeys of a larger building and with its own entrance from outside.
– ORIGIN late 18th cent.: from French *maisonnette*, diminutive of *maison* 'house'.

maistry /ˈmeɪstri/ ▶ noun (pl. **-ies**) (in the Indian subcontinent) a master workman; a foreman.

– ORIGIN from Portuguese *mestre* 'master'.

mai tai /ˈmʌɪ tʌɪ/ ▶ **noun** chiefly US a cocktail based on light rum, curaçao, and fruit juices.
– ORIGIN Polynesian.

Maithili /ˈmʌɪtɪli/ ▶ **noun** [mass noun] one of the Bihari group of languages, spoken by some 25 million people in northern Bihar, elsewhere in India, and in Nepal.
– ORIGIN Sanskrit (as an adjective), from *Mithilā*, a place in northern Bihar.

maître d'hôtel /ˌmeɪtrə dəʊˈtɛl, French mɛtʀ dotɛl/ (also **maître d'** /ˌmeɪtrə ˈdiː/) ▶ **noun** (pl. **maîtres d'hôtel** pronunc. same or **maître d's**) the head waiter of a restaurant.
■ the manager of a hotel.
– ORIGIN mid 16th cent.: French, literally 'master of (the) house'.

Maitreya /mʌɪˈtreɪjə/ Buddhism the Buddha who will appear in the future.
– ORIGIN Sanskrit, from *mitra* 'friend or friendship'.

maize ▶ **noun** [mass noun] a Central American cereal plant which yields large grains set in rows on a cob. It is familiar as cornflakes, popcorn, and corn on the cob, and the many varieties include some used for stockfeed and corn oil.
• *Zea mays*, family Gramineae; it was domesticated before 5000 BC, though the wild ancestor is unidentified.
– ORIGIN mid 16th cent.: from Spanish *maíz*, from Taino *mahiz*.

maizena /məˈziːnə, meɪ-/ ▶ **noun** [mass noun] S. African fine maize flour or corn flour, used as a thickener in cooking.
– ORIGIN mid 19th cent.: originally a brand name, based on **MAIZE**.

Maj. ▶ **abbreviation for** Major.

majestic ▶ **adjective** having or showing impressive beauty or dignity: *the majestic castle walls.*
– DERIVATIVES **majestically** adverb.

majesty ▶ **noun** (pl. **-ies**) **1** impressive stateliness, dignity, or beauty: *the majesty of Ben Nevis.*
2 royal power: *the majesty of the royal household.*
■ (**His**, **Your**, etc. **Majesty**) a title given to a sovereign or a sovereign's wife or widow: *Her Majesty the Queen.* ■ (**Her** or **His Majesty's**) Brit. used in the title of several state institutions: *Her Majesty's Inspectorate of Schools.*
– ORIGIN Middle English (in the sense 'greatness of God'): from Old French *majeste*, from Latin *majestas*, from a variant of *majus*, *major-* (see **MAJOR**).

majlis /ˈmadʒlɪs, madʒˈlɪs/ ▶ **noun** the parliament of various North African and Middle Eastern countries, especially Iran.
– ORIGIN Arabic, literally 'assembly'.

majolica /məˈjɒlɪkə, -ˈdʒɒl-/ ▶ **noun** [mass noun] a kind of earthenware made in imitation of Italian maiolica, especially in England during the 19th century.
– ORIGIN variant of **MAIOLICA**.

Major, John (b.1943), British Conservative statesman, Prime Minister 1990–7.
– DERIVATIVES **Majorism** noun.

major ▶ **adjective** **1** [attrib.] important, serious, or significant: *the use of drugs is a major problem.*
■ greater or more important; main: *he got the major share of the spoils.* ■ (of a surgical operation) serious or life-threatening: *he had to undergo major surgery.*
2 Music (of a scale) having intervals of a semitone between the third and fourth, and seventh and eighth degrees. Contrasted with **MINOR**.
■ (of an interval) equivalent to that between the tonic and another note of a major scale, and greater by a semitone than the corresponding minor interval. ■ [postpositive] (of a key) based on a major scale, tending to produce a bright or joyful effect: *Prelude in G Major.*
3 Brit. dated (appended to a surname in public schools) indicating the elder of two brothers.
4 Logic (of a term) occurring as the predicate in the conclusion of a categorical syllogism.
■ (of a premise) containing the major term in a categorical syllogism.
▶ **noun** **1** a rank of officer in the army and the US air force, above captain and below lieutenant colonel. [ORIGIN: Shortening of **SERGEANT MAJOR**, formerly a high rank.]
■ [with modifier] an officer in charge of a section of band instruments: *a trumpet major.*
2 Music a major key, interval, or scale.
■ Bell-ringing a system of change-ringing using eight bells.
3 a major world organization, company, or competition.
4 N. Amer. a student's principal subject or course.
■ [often with modifier] a student specializing in a specified subject: *a math major.*
5 Logic a major term or premise.
6 Bridge short for **MAJOR SUIT**.
▶ **verb** [no obj.] (**major in**) N. Amer. & Austral./NZ specialize in (a particular subject) at college or university: *I was trying to decide if I should major in drama or English.*
– ORIGIN Middle English: from Latin, comparative of *magnus* 'great'; perhaps influenced by French *majeur*.

major arcana ▶ **noun** see **ARCANA**.

major axis ▶ **noun** Geometry the longer axis of an ellipse, passing through its foci.

Majorca /məˈjɔːkə/ the largest of the Balearic Islands; pop. 614,000 (1990); capital, Palma. Spanish name **MALLORCA**.
– DERIVATIVES **Majorcan** adjective and noun.

major-domo /ˌmeɪdʒəˈdəʊməʊ/ ▶ **noun** (pl. **-os**) the chief steward of a large household.
– ORIGIN late 16th cent.: via Spanish and Italian from medieval Latin *major domus* 'highest official of the household'.

major general ▶ **noun** a rank of officer in the army and the US air force, above brigadier or brigadier general and below lieutenant general.
– ORIGIN mid 17th cent.: shortening of *sergeant major general*.

majoritarian /məˌdʒɒrɪˈtɛːrɪən/ ▶ **adjective** governed by or believing in decision by a majority.
▶ **noun** a person who is governed by or believes in decision by a majority.
– DERIVATIVES **majoritarianism** noun.

majority ▶ **noun** (pl. **-ies**) **1** the greater number: *in **the majority of** cases all will go smoothly* | [as modifier] *it was a majority decision.*
■ Brit. the number by which the votes cast for one party or candidate exceed those of the next in rank: *Labour retained the seat with a majority of 9,830.* ■ a party or group receiving the greater number of votes. ■ US the number by which votes for one candidate are more than those for all other candidates together.
2 [mass noun] the age when a person is legally considered a full adult, in most contexts either 18 or 21.
3 the rank or office of a major.
– PHRASES **be in the majority** belong to or constitute the larger group or number: *publishing houses where women are in the majority.*
– ORIGIN mid 16th cent. (denoting superiority): from French *majorité*, from medieval Latin *majoritas*, from Latin *major* (see **MAJOR**).

USAGE Strictly speaking, **majority** should be used with countable nouns to mean 'the greater number', as in *the majority of cases.* Use with uncountable nouns to mean 'the greatest part', as in *I spent the majority of the day reading* or *she ate the majority of the meal* is not considered good standard English, although it is common in informal contexts.

majority rule ▶ **noun** [mass noun] the principle that the greater number should exercise greater power.

majority verdict ▶ **noun** English Law a verdict agreed by all but one or two of the members of a jury.

major league ▶ **noun** N. Amer. the highest-ranking league in a particular professional sport, especially baseball.
– DERIVATIVES **major-leaguer** noun.

majorly ▶ **adverb** [as submodifier] informal very; extremely: *I'm majorly depressed.*

major piece ▶ **noun** Chess a rook or queen.

major planet ▶ **noun** any of the nine planets, as distinct from an asteroid or smaller body.

major prophet ▶ **noun** any of the prophets after whom the longer prophetic books of the Bible are named; Isaiah, Jeremiah, or Ezekiel.

major suit ▶ **noun** Bridge spades or hearts.
– ORIGIN early 20th cent.: so named because of their higher scoring value.

major tranquillizer ▶ **noun** a tranquillizer of the kind used to treat psychotic states.

majuscule /ˈmadʒəskjuːl/ ▶ **noun** [mass noun] large lettering, either capital or uncial, in which all the letters are usually the same height.
■ [count noun] a large letter.
– DERIVATIVES **majuscular** /məˈdʒʌskjʊlə/ adjective.
– ORIGIN early 18th cent.: from French, from Latin *majuscula (littera)* 'somewhat greater (letter)'.

Makarios III /məˈkɑːrɪɒs/ (1913–77), Greek Cypriot archbishop and statesman, first President of the republic of Cyprus 1960–77; born *Mikhail Christodolou Mouskos*. He reorganized the movement for enosis (union of Cyprus with Greece) and was exiled 1956–9 by the British for allegedly supporting the EOKA terrorist campaign.

Makasarese /məˌkasəˈriːz/ (also **Makassarese**) ▶ **noun** (pl. same) **1** a native or inhabitant of Makassar (now Ujung Pandang) in Indonesia.
2 [mass noun] the Indonesian language of this people, with around 1.6 million speakers.
▶ **adjective** of or relating to this people or their language.

Makassar /məˈkasə/ (also **Macassar** or **Makasar**) former name (until 1973) for **UJUNG PANDANG**.

Makassar Strait a stretch of water separating the islands of Borneo and Sulawesi and linking the Celebes Sea in the north with the Java Sea in the south.

make ▶ **verb** (past and past participle **made**) [with obj.]
1 form (something) by putting parts together or combining substances; construct; create: *my grandmother made a dress for me* | *the body is **made from** four pieces of maple* | *cricket bats are **made of** willow.*
■ (**make something into**) alter something so that it forms or constitutes (something else): *buffalo's milk can be made into cheese.* ■ compose, prepare, or draw up (something written or abstract): *she made her will.* ■ prepare (a dish, drink, or meal) for consumption: *she was making lunch for Lucy and Francis* | [with two objs] *I'll make us both a cup of tea.* ■ arrange bedclothes tidily on (a bed) ready for use. ■ arrange and light materials for (a fire). ■ (in sport, especially soccer) enable a teammate to score (a goal) by one's play. ■ Electronics complete or close (a circuit).
2 cause (something) to exist or come about; bring about: *the drips had made a pool on the floor.*
■ [with obj. and complement or infinitive] cause to become or seem: *decorative features make brickwork more interesting* | *the best way to disarm your critics is to make them laugh.* ■ carry out, perform, or produce (a specified action, movement, or sound): *Asquith made a speech of forty minutes* | *anyone can make a mistake.* ■ communicate or express (an idea, request, or requirement): *I tend to **make** heavy **demands on** people* | [with two objs] *make him an offer he can't refuse.* ■ undertake or agree to (an aim or purpose): *we made a deal.* ■ chiefly archaic enter into a contract of (marriage): *a marriage made in heaven.* ■ [with obj. and complement] appoint or designate (someone) to a position: *he was made a fellow of the Royal Institute.* ■ [with obj. and complement] represent or cause to appear in a specified way: *the issue price makes them good value.* ■ cause or ensure the success or advancement of: *the work which really made Wordsworth's reputation.*
3 [with obj. and infinitive] compel (someone) to do something: *she bought me a brandy and made me drink it.*
4 constitute; amount to: *they made an unusual duo.*
■ serve as or become through development or adaptation: *this fern makes a good house plant.* ■ consider to be; estimate as: *How many are there? I **make it** sixteen.* ■ agree or decide on (a specified arrangement), typically one concerning a time or place: *let's **make it** 7.30.*
5 gain or earn (money or profit): *he'd made a lot of money out of hardware.*
■ Cricket score (a specified number of runs): *he made a century.*
6 arrive at (a place) within a specified time or in time for (a train or other transport): *we've got a lot to do if you're going to make the shuttle* | *they didn't always **make it** on time.*
■ (**make it**) succeed in something; become successful: *he waited confidently for his band to make it.* ■ achieve a place in: *these dogs seldom make the news* | *they **made it to** the semi-final.* ■ chiefly N. Amer. achieve the rank of: *he wasn't going to make captain.*
7 [no obj., with adverbial of direction] go or prepare to go in a particular direction: *he struggled to his feet and **made towards** the car.*
■ [with infinitive] act as if one is about to perform an action: *she **made as if to** leave the room.*
8 informal, chiefly N. Amer. induce (someone) to have sexual intercourse with one: *he had been trying to make Cynthia for two years now* | *his alleged quest to **make it with** the world's most attractive women.*
9 (in bridge, whist, and similar games) win (a trick).
■ win a trick with (a card). ■ win the number of tricks

that fulfils (a contract). ■ shuffle (a pack of cards) for dealing.
10 [no obj.] (of the tide) begin to flow or ebb.
▶**noun 1** the manufacturer or trade name of a particular product: *the make, model, and year of his car.*
■the structure or composition of something.
2 the making of electrical contact.
■the position in which this is made.
– PHRASES **be made of money** [often with negative] informal be very rich. **be made up** N. English informal be very pleased; be delighted: *we're made up about the baby.* **have (got) it made** informal be in a position where success is certain: *because your dad's a manager, he's got it made.* **make a day** (or **night**) **of it** devote a whole day (or night) to an activity, especially an enjoyable one. **make someone's day** make an otherwise ordinary or dull day pleasingly memorable for someone. **make a House** Brit. secure the presence of enough members for a quorum or support in the House of Commons. **make do** manage with the limited or inadequate means available: *Dad would have to* **make do with** *an old car.* **make like** N. Amer. informal pretend to be; imitate: *tell the whole group to make like a bird by putting their arms out.* **make or break** be the factor which decides whether (something) will succeed or fail. **make sail** Sailing spread a sail or sails. ■ start a voyage. **make time 1** find an occasion when time is available to do something: *the nurse should make time to talk to the patient.* **2** N. Amer. informal make sexual advances to someone: *I couldn't* **make time with** *Marilyn because she was already a senior.* **make up one's mind** make a decision; decide: *he made up his mind to attend the meeting.* **make way 1** allow room for someone or something else: *the land is due to be concreted over to* **make way for** *a car park.* **2** chiefly Nautical make progress; travel. **on the make** informal intent on gain, typically in an unscrupulous way. ■ looking for a sexual partner. **put the make on** N. Amer. informal make sexual advances to (someone).
– DERIVATIVES **makable** (also **makeable**) adjective.
– ORIGIN Old English *macian*, of West Germanic origin, from a base meaning 'fitting'; related to **MATCH**[1].
▶**make after** archaic pursue (someone).
make away another way of saying ***make off***.
make away with another way of saying ***make off with***. ■ kill (someone) furtively and illicitly: *for all we know she could have been made away with.*
make for 1 move or head towards (a place): *I made for the life raft and hung on for dear life.* ■ approach (someone) to attack them. **2** tend to result in or be received as (a particular thing): *job descriptions never make for exciting reading.* **3** (**be made for**) be eminently suited for (a particular function): *a man made for action.* ■ form an ideal partnership; be ideally suited: *you two were just* **made for each other**.
make something of give or ascribe a specified amount of attention or importance to: *oddly, he makes little of America's low investment rates.* ■ understand or derive advantage from: *they stared at the stone but could* **make nothing of it**. ■ [with negative or in questions] conclude to be the meaning or character of: *he wasn't sure what to make of Russell.*
make off leave hurriedly, especially in order to avoid duty or punishment: *they made off without paying.*
make off with carry (something) away illicitly: *burglars made off with all their wedding presents.*
make out informal **1** make progress; fare: *how are you making out, now that the summer's over?* **2** N. Amer. informal engage in sexual activity: *Ernie was* **making out with** *Berenice.*
make someone/thing out 1 manage with some difficulty to see or hear something: *in the dim light it was difficult to make out the illustration.* ■ understand the character or motivation of: *I can't make her out—she's so inconsistent.* **2** [with infinitive or clause] assert; represent: *I'm not as bad as I'm* **made out to be**. ■ try to give a specified impression; pretend: *he made out he was leaving.* **3** draw up or write out a list or document, especially an official one: *advice about making out a will | send a cheque* **made out to** *Trinity College.*
make something over 1 transfer the possession of something to someone: *if he dies childless he is to make over his share of the estate to his brother.* **2** completely transform or remodel something, especially a person's hairstyle, make-up, or clothes.
make up be reconciled after a quarrel: *let's kiss and make up.*
make someone up apply cosmetics to oneself or another.
make something up 1 (also **make up for**) serve or act to compensate for something lost, missed, or deficient: *I'll make up the time tomorrow.* ■ (**make it up to**) compensate someone for negligent or unfair treatment: *I'll try to make it up to you in the future.* **2** (**make up**) (of parts) compose or constitute (a whole): *women make up 56 per cent of the student body | the team is made up of three women and two men.* ■ complete an amount or group: *he brought along a girl to make up a foursome.* **3** put together or prepare something from parts or ingredients: *make up the mortar to a consistency that can be moulded in the hands.* ■ get an amount or group together: *he was trying to make up a party to go dancing.* ■ prepare a bed for use with fresh sheets and bedclothes. ■ Printing arrange type and illustrations into pages or arrange the type and illustrations on a page. **4** concoct or invent a story, lie, or plan: *she enjoyed making up tall tales.*
make up to informal attempt to win the favour of (someone) by being pleasant: *you can't go on about morals when you're making up to Adam like that.*
make with US informal proceed to use or supply: *make with the feet, honey—you're embarrassing Jim.*

make-and-break ▶**adjective** denoting a switch or other device that alternately makes and breaks electrical contact.
▶**noun** a switch or other device in which electrical contact is automatically made and broken.

make-before-break ▶**adjective** denoting a switch or other device in which a new electrical connection is made before the existing one is broken.

make-believe ▶**noun** [mass noun] the action of pretending or imagining, typically that things are better than they really are: *she's living in a world of make-believe.*
▶**adjective** imitating something real; pretend: *he was firing a make-believe gun at the spy planes.*
▶**verb** [no obj.] pretend; imagine: [with clause] *Brenda rode along, make-believing she was a knight riding to the rescue.*

make-do ▶**adjective** [attrib.] makeshift, ad hoc, or temporary: *his make-do clothes.*

makeover ▶**noun** a complete transformation or remodelling of something, especially a person's hairstyle, make-up, or clothes.

maker ▶**noun 1** [usu. in combination] a person or thing that makes or produces something: *film-makers | a bread-maker.*
2 (**our, the**, etc. **Maker**) God; the Creator.
– PHRASES **meet one's Maker** chiefly humorous die.

makeready ▶**noun** [mass noun] (in letterpress printing) final adjustment of a forme for printing, with overlays and underlays to achieve the correct pressure over the whole printing area.

makeshift ▶**adjective** acting as an interim and temporary measure: *arranging a row of chairs to form a makeshift bed.*
▶**noun** a temporary substitute or device.

make-up ▶**noun** [mass noun] **1** cosmetics such as lipstick or powder applied to the face, used to enhance or alter the appearance.
2 the composition or constitution of something: *studying the make-up of ocean sediments.*
■the combination of qualities that form a person's temperament: *a curiously unexpected timidity in his make-up.*
3 Printing the arrangement of type, illustrations, etc. on a printed page: *page make-up.*
4 [count noun] N. Amer. a supplementary test or assignment given to a student who missed or failed the original one.

makeweight ▶**noun** something put on a scale to make up the required weight.
■an extra person or thing needed to complete something: *I had to tag him on to group deals as a makeweight.*

make-work chiefly N. Amer. ▶**adjective** denoting an activity that serves mainly to keep someone busy and is of little value in itself: *a make-work scheme for lawyers.*
▶**noun** [mass noun] work or activity of this kind.

Makgadikgadi Pans /ˌmagəˈdiːgədi/ an extensive area of salt pans in central Botswana.

Makhachkala /ˌmaxətʃkəˈlɑː/ a port in SW Russia, on the Caspian Sea, capital of the autonomous republic of Dagestan; pop. 327,000 (1990). Former name (until 1922) **PORT PETROVSK**.

making ▶**noun 1** [mass noun] the process of making or producing something: *the making of videos |* [in combination] *decision-making.*
2 (**makings**) informal money made; earnings or profit.
3 (**makings**) essential qualities or ingredients needed for something: *a film with all the makings of a cinematic success.*
■(**makings**) N. Amer. & Austral./NZ informal paper and tobacco for rolling a cigarette.
– PHRASES **be the making of someone** ensure someone's success or favourable development: *this place has been the making of me in many ways.* **in the making** in the process of developing or being made: *a campaign that's been two years in the making.* **of one's (own) making** (of a difficulty) caused by oneself.

Makkah /ˈmakɑː/ Arabic name for **MECCA**.

mako[1] /ˈmɑːkəʊ, ˈmeɪkəʊ/ (also **mako shark**) ▶**noun** (pl. **-os**) a large fast-moving oceanic shark with a deep blue back and white underparts.
• Genus *Isurus*, family Lamnidae: two species.
– ORIGIN mid 19th cent.: from Maori.

mako[2] /ˈmɑːkəʊ, ˈmakəʊ/ ▶**noun** (pl. **-os**) a small New Zealand tree which bears large clusters of pink flowers followed by dark red berries. Also called **WINEBERRY**.
• *Aristotelia racemosa*, family Elaeocarpaceae.
– ORIGIN mid 19th cent.: from Maori.

Makonde /məˈkɒndeɪ/ ▶**noun** (pl. same or **Makondes**) **1** a member of a people inhabiting southern Tanzania and NE Mozambique.
2 [mass noun] the Bantu language of this people, with about 1 million speakers.
▶**adjective** of or relating to this people or their language.
– ORIGIN the name in Makonde.

Maksutov telescope /makˈsuːtɒf, ˈmaksʊˌtɒf/ ▶**noun** a type of catadioptric telescope having a deeply curved meniscus lens. A secondary mirror on the back of the lens brings the light to a focus just behind a hole in the primary mirror.
– ORIGIN mid 20th cent.: named after Dmitri D. *Maksutov* (1896–1964), Soviet astronomer.

Makua /ˈmakuːə/ ▶**noun** (pl. same or **Makuas**) **1** a member of a people inhabiting the border regions of Mozambique, Malawi, and Tanzania.
2 [mass noun] the Bantu language of this people, with around 3.5 million speakers.
– ORIGIN a local name.

makuta plural form of **LIKUTA**.

makutu /məˈkuːtuː/ ▶**noun** [mass noun] NZ sorcery; witchcraft.
■[count noun] a magic spell.
– ORIGIN Maori.

MAL ▶**abbreviation for** Malaysia (international vehicle registration).

Mal. ▶**abbreviation for** Malachi (in biblical references).

mal- ▶**combining form 1** in an unpleasant degree: *malodorous.*
2 in a faulty manner: *malfunction.*
■in an improper manner: *malpractice.* ■ in an inadequate manner: *malnourishment.*
3 not: *maladroit.*
– ORIGIN from French *mal*, from Latin *male* 'badly'.

mala /ˈmɑːlɑː/ ▶**noun** Indian a garland of flowers, as given in welcome to a visiting dignitary.
– ORIGIN from Hindi *mālā*.

Malabar Christians a group of Christians of SW India who trace their foundation to a mission of St Thomas the Apostle and have historically used a Syriac liturgy. Many now form a Uniate (Catholic) Church; others have links to the Syrian Orthodox or the Anglican Church.

Malabar Coast /ˈmaləbɑː/ the southern part of the west coast of India, including the coastal region of Karnataka and most of the state of Kerala.
– ORIGIN *Malabar* from *Malabars*, the name of an ancient Dravidian people.

Malabo /məˈlɑːbəʊ/ the capital of Equatorial Guinea, on the island of Bioko; pop. 10,000 (est. 1986).

malabsorption ▶**noun** [mass noun] imperfect absorption of food material by the small intestine.

Malacca variant spelling of **MELAKA**.

malacca /məˈlakə/ ▶ noun [mass noun] brown cane that is widely used for walking sticks and umbrella handles.
● The cane is obtained from the stem of a Malaysian climbing palm (*Calamus scipionum*, family Palmae).
■ [count noun] a walking stick of malacca cane.
– ORIGIN mid 19th cent.: from the place name MALACCA.

Malacca, Strait of the channel between the Malay Peninsula and the Indonesian island of Sumatra, an important sea passage linking the Indian Ocean to the South China Sea. The ports of Melaka and Singapore lie on this strait.

Malachi /ˈmaləkʌɪ/ a book of the Bible belonging to a period before Ezra and Nehemiah.
– ORIGIN from Hebrew *mal'ākī*, literally 'my messenger'; *Malachi* is probably not a personal name, though often taken as such.

malachite /ˈmaləkʌɪt/ ▶ noun [mass noun] a bright green mineral consisting of hydrated basic copper carbonate. It typically occurs in masses and fibrous aggregates and is capable of taking a high polish.
– ORIGIN late Middle English: from Old French *melochite*, via Latin from Greek *molokhitis*, from *molokhē*, variant of *malakhē* 'mallow'.

malaco- /ˈmaləkəʊ/ ▶ combining form soft: *malacostracan*.
– ORIGIN from Greek *malakos* 'soft'.

malacology /ˌmaləˈkɒlədʒi/ ▶ noun [mass noun] the branch of zoology that deals with molluscs. Compare with CONCHOLOGY.
– DERIVATIVES **malacological** adjective, **malacologist** noun.

Malacostraca /ˌmaləˈkɒstrəkə/ Zoology a large class of crustaceans which includes crabs, shrimps, lobsters, isopods, and amphipods. They have compound eyes, which are typically on stalks.
– DERIVATIVES **malacostracan** adjective & noun.
– ORIGIN modern Latin (plural), from MALACO- 'soft' + Greek *ostrakon* 'shell'.

maladaptive ▶ adjective technical not providing adequate or appropriate adjustment to the environment or situation.
– DERIVATIVES **maladaptation** noun, **maladapted** adjective.

maladjusted ▶ adjective failing or unable to cope with the demands of a normal social environment: *maladjusted behaviour*.
– DERIVATIVES **maladjustment** noun.

maladminister ▶ verb [with obj.] formal manage or administer inefficiently, badly, or dishonestly.
– DERIVATIVES **maladministration** noun.

maladroit /ˌmaləˈdrɔɪt/ ▶ adjective inefficient or ineffective; clumsy.
– DERIVATIVES **maladroitly** adverb, **maladroitness** noun.
– ORIGIN late 17th cent.: French.

malady ▶ noun (pl. **-ies**) formal a disease or ailment: *an incurable malady* | figurative *the nation's maladies*.
– ORIGIN Middle English: from Old French *maladie*, from *malade* 'sick', based on Latin *male* 'ill' + *habitus* 'having (as a condition)'.

mala fide /ˌmeɪlə ˈfʌɪdiː, ˌmalə ˈfiːdeɪ/ ▶ adjective & adverb chiefly Law in bad faith; with intent to deceive: [as adj.] *a mala fide abuse of position*.
– ORIGIN Latin, ablative of MALA FIDES.

mala fides /ˈfʌɪdiːz, ˈfiːdeɪz/ ▶ noun chiefly Law bad faith; intent to deceive.
– ORIGIN Latin.

Malaga[1] /ˈmaləgə/ a seaport on the Andalusian coast of southern Spain; pop. 524,750 (1991). Spanish name MÁLAGA /ˈmalaɣa/.

Malaga[2] /ˈmaləgə/ ▶ noun [mass noun] a sweet fortified wine from Malaga.

Malagasy /ˌmaləˈgasi/ ▶ noun (pl. same or **-ies**) **1** a native or national of Madagascar.
2 [mass noun] the Austronesian language of Madagascar, a group of dialects spoken by some 10 million people.
▶ adjective of or relating to Madagascar or its people or language.
– ORIGIN variant of MADAGASCAR; earlier forms included *Malegass*, *Madegass*, because of dialect division between the sounds -l- and -d-.

Malagasy Republic former name (1960–75) for MADAGASCAR.

malagueña /ˌmaləˈgeɪnjə/ ▶ noun a Spanish dance similar to the fandango.

– ORIGIN mid 19th cent.: Spanish.

malaguetta /ˌmaləˈgɛtə/ (also **malagueta**) ▶ noun another term for GRAINS OF PARADISE.
– ORIGIN mid 16th cent.: probably from French *malaguette*, perhaps based on a diminutive of Italian *melica* 'millet'.

malaise /maˈleɪz/ ▶ noun a general feeling of discomfort, illness, or uneasiness whose exact cause is difficult to identify: *a society afflicted by a deep cultural malaise* | [mass noun] *a general air of malaise*.
– ORIGIN mid 18th cent.: from French, from Old French *mal* 'bad' (from Latin *malus*) + *aise* 'ease'.

Malamud /ˈmaləməd/, Bernard (1914–86), American novelist and short-story writer. Notable works: *The Fixer* (1967).

malamute /ˈmaləmjuːt/ (also **malemute**) ▶ noun a powerful dog of a breed with a thick, grey coat, bred by the Inuit and typically used to pull sledges.
– ORIGIN late 19th cent.: from Inuit *malimiut*, the name of a people of Kotzebue Sound, Alaska, who developed the breed.

malanga /məˈlaŋgə/ ▶ noun another term for TANNIA.
– ORIGIN early 20th cent.: from American Spanish, probably from Kikongo, plural of *elanga* 'water lily'.

malapert /ˈmaləpəːt/ archaic ▶ adjective boldly disrespectful to a person of higher standing.
▶ noun an impudent person.
– ORIGIN Middle English: from MAL- 'improperly' + archaic *apert* 'insolent'.

malapropism /ˈmaləprɒˌpɪz(ə)m/ (US also **malaprop**) ▶ noun the mistaken use of a word in place of a similar-sounding one, often with unintentionally amusing effect, as in, for example, 'dance a *flamingo*' (instead of *flamenco*).
– ORIGIN mid 19th cent.: from the name of the character Mrs *Malaprop* in Sheridan's play *The Rivals* (1775) + -ISM.

malapropos /ˌmaləprəˈpəʊ/ formal ▶ adverb inopportunely; inappropriately.
▶ adjective inopportune; inappropriate: *these terms applied to him seem to me malapropos*.
▶ noun (pl. same) something inappropriately said or done.
– ORIGIN mid 17th cent.: from French *mal à propos*, from *mal* 'ill' + *à* 'to' + *propos* 'purpose'.

malar /ˈmeɪlə/ ▶ adjective Anatomy & Medicine of or relating to the cheek: *a slight malar flush*.
▶ noun (also **malar bone**) another term for ZYGOMATIC BONE.
– ORIGIN late 18th cent.: from modern Latin *malaris*, from Latin *mala* 'jaw'.

Mälaren /ˈmɛlərɛn/ a lake in SE Sweden, extending inland from the Baltic Sea. The city of Stockholm is situated at its outlet.

malaria ▶ noun [mass noun] an intermittent and remittent fever caused by a protozoan parasite which invades the red blood cells and is transmitted by mosquitoes in many tropical and subtropical regions.
● The parasite belongs to the genus *Plasmodium* (phylum Sporozoa) and is transmitted by female mosquitoes of the genus *Anopheles*.
– DERIVATIVES **malarial** adjective, **malarian** adjective, **malarious** adjective.
– ORIGIN mid 18th cent.: from Italian, from *mal'aria*, contracted from *mala aria* 'bad air'. The term originally denoted the unwholesome atmosphere caused by the exhalations of marshes, to which the disease was formerly attributed.

malariology /məˌlɛːrɪˈɒlədʒi/ ▶ noun [mass noun] the scientific study of malaria.
– DERIVATIVES **malariological** adjective, **malariologist** noun.

malarkey /məˈlɑːki/ ▶ noun [mass noun] informal meaningless talk; nonsense: *don't give me that malarkey*.
– ORIGIN 1920s: of unknown origin.

malathion /ˌmaləˈθʌɪɒn/ ▶ noun [mass noun] a synthetic organophosphorus compound which is used as an insecticide and is relatively harmless to plants and other animals.
– ORIGIN 1950s: from (*diethyl*) *mal(eate)* (see MALEIC ACID) + THIO- + -ON.

Malawi /məˈlɑːwi/ a country of south central Africa, in the Great Rift Valley; pop. 8,796,000 (est. 1991);

official languages, English and Nyanja; capital, Lilongwe.

As Nyasaland Malawi was a British protectorate from 1891, and from 1953 to 1963 was a part of the Federation of Rhodesia and Nyasaland. It became an independent Commonwealth state under Hastings Banda in 1964 and a republic in 1966.

– DERIVATIVES **Malawian** adjective & noun.

Malawi, Lake another name for Lake Nyasa (see NYASA, LAKE).

Malay /məˈleɪ/ ▶ noun **1** a member of a people inhabiting Malaysia and Indonesia.
■ a person of Malay descent.
2 [mass noun] the Austronesian language of the Malays, closely related to Indonesian and spoken by about 20 million people. It is the official language of Malaysia, where it is the first language of about half the population.
▶ adjective of or relating to this people or language.
– ORIGIN from Malay *Malayu* (now *Melayu*).

Malaya a former country in SE Asia, consisting of the southern part of the Malay Peninsula and some adjacent islands (originally including Singapore), now forming the western part of the federation of Malaysia and known as West Malaysia.

The area was colonized by the Dutch, Portuguese, and the British, who eventually became dominant; the several Malay states federated under British control in 1896. The country became independent in 1957, the federation expanding into Malaysia in 1963.

Malayalam /ˌmaləˈjɑːləm/ ▶ noun [mass noun] the Dravidian language of the Indian state of Kerala, spoken by about 30 million people. It is closely related to Tamil.
▶ adjective of or relating to this language or its speakers.
– ORIGIN early 19th cent.: from Malayalam, from *mala* (Tamil *malai*) 'mountain' + *āl* 'man'.

Malayan ▶ noun another term for MALAY.
▶ adjective of or relating to Malays, the Malay language, or Malaya (now part of Malaysia).

Malayan sun bear ▶ noun see SUN BEAR.

Malayan zebra ▶ noun see ZEBRA (sense 2).

Malay Archipelago a very large group of islands, including Sumatra, Java, Borneo, the Philippines, and New Guinea, lying between SE Asia and Australia. They constitute the bulk of the area formerly known as the East Indies.

Malayo- ▶ combining form Malay; Malay and …: *Malayo-Polynesian*.

Malayo-Polynesian ▶ noun another term for AUSTRONESIAN.

Malay Peninsula a peninsula in SE Asia separating the Indian Ocean from the South China Sea. It extends approximately 1,100 km (700 miles) southwards from the Isthmus of Kra and comprises the southern part of Thailand and the whole of Malaya (West Malaysia).

Malaysia /məˈleɪzɪə, -ˈleɪʒə/ a country in SE Asia; pop. 18,294,000 (est. 1991); official language, Malay; capital, Kuala Lumpur.

Malaysia is a federation consisting of **East Malaysia** (the northern part of Borneo, including Sabah and Sarawak) and **West Malaysia** (the southern part of the Malay Peninsula, formerly Malaya). The two parts of Malaysia are separated from each other by 650 km (400 miles) of the South China Sea. Malaysia federated as an independent Commonwealth state in 1963; Singapore withdrew in 1965.

– DERIVATIVES **Malaysian** adjective & noun.

malcoha /ˈmalkəʊə/ (also **malkoha**) ▶ noun a long-tailed cuckoo found in South and SE Asia, with dark grey or brown plumage.
● *Rhopodytes* and other genera: family Cuculidae: several species.
– ORIGIN late 20th cent.: of unknown origin.

Malcolm the name of four kings of Scotland:
■ Malcolm I (d. 954), reigned 943–54.
■ Malcolm II (c.954–1034), reigned 1005–34.
■ Malcolm III (c.1031–93), son of Duncan I, reigned 1058–93; known as **Malcolm Canmore** (from Gaelic *Ceann-mor* great head). He came to the throne after killing Macbeth in battle (1057), and was responsible for helping to form Scotland into an organized kingdom.
■ Malcolm IV (1141–65), grandson of David I, reigned 1153–65; known as **Malcolm the Maiden**. His reign witnessed a progressive loss of power to Henry II of England; he died young and without an heir.

Malcolm X (1925–65), American political activist; born *Malcolm Little*. He joined the Nation of Islam in

1946 and became a vigorous campaigner for black rights, initially advocating the use of violence. In 1964 he converted to orthodox Islam and moderated his views on black separatism; he was assassinated the following year.

malcontent /ˈmalkəntɛnt/ ▶ noun a person who is dissatisfied and rebellious.
▶ adjective dissatisfied and complaining or making trouble.
– DERIVATIVES **malcontented** adjective.
– ORIGIN late 16th cent.: from French, from *mal* 'badly, ill' + *content* 'pleased'.

mal de mer /ˌmal də ˈmɛː, French mal də mɛʀ/ ▶ noun [mass noun] seasickness.
– ORIGIN French.

maldevelopment ▶ noun [mass noun] chiefly Medicine & Biology faulty or imperfect development.

maldistribution ▶ noun [mass noun] uneven distribution of something, especially when disadvantageous or unfair: *the maldistribution of wealth.*
– DERIVATIVES **maldistributed** adjective.

Maldives /ˈmɔːldʌɪvz, -diːv/ (also **Maldive Islands**) a country consisting of a chain of coral islands in the Indian Ocean south-west of Sri Lanka; pop. 221,000 (est. 1991); official language, Maldivian; capital, Male.

The islands were probably first settled from southern India and Sri Lanka, but later came under Arab influence. A British protectorate from 1887, the Maldives became independent within the Commonwealth under the rule of a sultan in 1965 and then a republic in 1968.

Maldivian /mɔːlˈdɪvɪən/ ▶ noun 1 a native or inhabitant of the Maldives.
2 [mass noun] the Indic language spoken in the Maldives, related to Sinhalese.
▶ adjective of or relating to the Maldives, their inhabitants, or their language.

mal du siècle /ˌmal d(j)uː ˈsjɛkl, French mal dy sjɛkl/ ▶ noun [mass noun] world-weariness.
– ORIGIN French, literally 'sickness of the century.'

Male /ˈmɑːleɪ/ the capital of the Maldives; pop. 55,130 (est. 1991).

male ▶ adjective of or denoting the sex that produces small, typically motile gametes, especially spermatozoa, with which a female may be fertilized or inseminated to produce offspring: *male children.*
■ relating to or characteristic of men or male animals; masculine: *male unemployment | a deep male voice.* ■ (of a plant or flower) bearing stamens but lacking functional pistils. ■ (of parts of machinery, fittings, etc.) designed to enter, fill, or fit inside a corresponding female part.
▶ noun a male person, plant, or animal: *the audience consisted of adult males | the male of the species.*
– DERIVATIVES **maleness** noun.
– ORIGIN late Middle English: from Old French *masle*, from Latin *masculus*, from *mas* 'a male'.

malediction /ˌmalɪˈdɪkʃ(ə)n/ ▶ noun a magical word or phrase uttered with the intention of bringing about evil or destruction; a curse.
– DERIVATIVES **maledictive** adjective, **maledictory** adjective.
– ORIGIN late Middle English: from Latin *maledictio(n-)*, from *maledicere* 'speak evil of'.

malefactor /ˈmalɪˌfaktə/ ▶ noun formal a person who commits a crime or some other wrong.
– DERIVATIVES **malefaction** noun.
– ORIGIN late Middle English: from Latin, from *malefact-* 'done wrong', from the verb *malefacere*, from *male* 'ill' + *facere* 'do'.

male fern ▶ noun a fern with brown scales on the stalks of the fronds, found in woodland in both North America and Eurasia.
● Genus *Dryopteris*, family Dryopteridaceae: several species, in particular *D. filix-mas*.

malefic /məˈlɛfɪk/ ▶ adjective poetic/literary causing or capable of causing harm or destruction, especially by supernatural means.
■ Astrology relating to the planets Saturn and Mars, traditionally considered to have an unfavourable influence.
– DERIVATIVES **maleficence** noun, **maleficent** adjective.
– ORIGIN mid 17th cent.: from Latin *maleficus*, from *male* 'ill' + *-ficus* 'doing'.

Malegaon /ˈmɑːləgaʊn/ a city in western India, in

Maharashtra north-east of Bombay; pop. 342,000 (1991).

maleic acid /məˈleɪk/ ▶ noun [mass noun] Chemistry a crystalline acid made by distilling malic acid and used in making synthetic resins.
● Alternative name: *cis*-**butenedioic acid**; chem. formula: HOOCCH═CHCOOH.
– DERIVATIVES **maleate** noun.
– ORIGIN mid 19th cent.: *maleic* from French *maléique*, alteration of *malique* (see **MALIC ACID**).

male menopause ▶ noun a stage in a middle-aged man's life supposedly corresponding to the menopause of a woman, associated with the loss of potency and a crisis of confidence and identity (not in technical use).

malemute ▶ noun variant spelling of **MALAMUTE**.

Malenkov /ˈmalɪnkɒf/, Georgi (Maksimilianovich) (1902–88), Soviet statesman, born in Russia. He became Prime Minister and First Secretary of the Soviet Communist Party in 1953, but was forced to resign in 1955 following internal party struggles.

maleo /ˈmalɪəʊ/ (also **maleo fowl**) ▶ noun (pl. **-os**) a megapode found in Sulawesi, with black upper parts and white underparts.
● *Macrocephalon maleo*, family Megapodiidae.
– ORIGIN mid 19th cent.: from the Moluccan dialect of Malay.

Malesia /məˈliːzɪə/ Botany a phytogeographical region comprising Malaysia, Indonesia, New Guinea, the Philippines, and Brunei.
– DERIVATIVES **Malesian** adjective.

Malevich /ˈmalɪvɪtʃ/, Kazimir (Severinovich) (1878–1935), Russian painter and designer, founder of the suprematist movement. In his abstract works he used only basic geometrical shapes and a severely restricted range of colour.

malevolent /məˈlɛv(ə)l(ə)nt/ ▶ adjective having or showing a wish to do evil to others: *the glint of dark, malevolent eyes | some malevolent force of nature.*
– DERIVATIVES **malevolence** noun, **malevolently** adverb.
– ORIGIN early 16th cent.: from Latin *malevolent-* 'wishing evil', from *male* 'ill' + *volent-* 'wishing' (from the verb *velle*).

malfeasance /malˈfiːz(ə)ns/ ▶ noun [mass noun] Law wrongdoing, especially (US) by a public official.
– DERIVATIVES **malfeasant** noun & adjective.
– ORIGIN late 17th cent.: from Anglo-Norman French *malfaisance*, from *mal-* 'evil' + Old French *faisance* 'activity'. Compare with **MISFEASANCE**.

malformation ▶ noun a deformity; an abnormally formed part of the body.
■ [mass noun] the condition of being abnormal in shape or form: *malformation of one or both ears.*
– DERIVATIVES **malformed** adjective.

malfunction ▶ verb [no obj.] (of a piece of equipment or machinery) fail to function normally or satisfactorily: *the unit is clearly malfunctioning.*
▶ noun a failure to function in a normal or satisfactory manner.

Malherbe /maˈlɛːb, French malɛʀb/ François de (1555–1628), French poet. An architect of classicism in poetic form and grammar, he criticized excess of emotion and ornamentation and the use of Latin and dialectal forms.

Mali /ˈmɑːli/ a landlocked country in West Africa, south of Algeria; pop. 8,706,000 (est. 1991); languages, French (official), other languages mainly of the Mande group; capital, Bamako. Former name (until 1958) **FRENCH SUDAN**.

Conquered by the French in the late 19th century, Mali became part of French West Africa. It became a partner with Senegal in the Federation of Mali in 1959 and achieved full independence a year later, on the withdrawal of Senegal.

– DERIVATIVES **Malian** adjective & noun.

mali /ˈmɑːli/ ▶ noun (pl. **malis**) Indian a gardener.
– ORIGIN via Hindi from Sanskrit, from *mālā* 'garland'.

Malibu[1] /ˈmalɪbuː/ a resort on the Pacific coast of southern California, immediately to the west of Los Angeles.

Malibu[2] /ˈmalɪbuː/ (also **Malibu board**) ▶ noun (pl. **Malibus**) a lightweight surfboard, typically relatively long with a rounded front end.
– ORIGIN 1960s: named after *Malibu* beach (see **MALIBU**[1]).

malic acid /ˈmalɪk/ ▶ noun [mass noun] Chemistry a

crystalline acid present in unripe apples and other fruits.
● Chem. formula: HOOCCH₂CH(OH)COOH.
– DERIVATIVES **malate** noun.
– ORIGIN late 18th cent.: *malic* from French *malique*, from Latin *malum* 'apple'.

malice ▶ noun [mass noun] the intention or desire to do evil; ill will: *I bear no malice towards anybody.*
■ Law wrongful intention, especially as increasing the guilt of certain offences.
– ORIGIN Middle English: via Old French from Latin *malitia*, from *malus* 'bad'.

malice aforethought ▶ noun [mass noun] Law the intention to kill or harm which is held to distinguish unlawful killing from murder.

malicious ▶ adjective characterized by malice; intending or intended to do harm: *malicious damage.*
– DERIVATIVES **maliciously** adverb, **maliciousness** noun.
– ORIGIN Middle English (also in the sense 'wicked'): from Old French *malicios*, from Latin *malitiosus*, from *malitia* (see **MALICE**).

malign /məˈlʌɪn/ ▶ adjective evil in nature or effect; malevolent: *she had a strong and malign influence.*
■ archaic (of a disease) malignant.
▶ verb [with obj.] speak about (someone) in a spitefully critical manner: *don't you dare malign her in my presence.*
– DERIVATIVES **maligner** noun, **malignity** /məˈlɪgnɪti/ noun, **malignly** adverb.
– ORIGIN Middle English: via Old French *maligne* (adjective), *malignier* (verb), based on Latin *malignus* 'tending to evil', from *malus* 'bad'.

malignancy /məˈlɪgnənsi/ ▶ noun (pl. **-ies**) [mass noun] 1 the state or presence of a malignant tumour; cancer: *after biopsy, evidence of malignancy was found.*
■ [count noun] a cancerous growth. ■ [count noun] a form of cancer: *diffuse malignancies such as leukaemia.*
2 the quality of being malign or malevolent: *her eyes sparkled with renewed malignancy.*

malignant ▶ adjective 1 (of a disease) very virulent or infectious.
■ (of a tumour) tending to invade normal tissue or to recur after removal; cancerous. Contrasted with **BENIGN**.
2 malevolent: *in the hands of malignant fate.*
– DERIVATIVES **malignantly** adverb.
– ORIGIN mid 16th cent. (also in the sense 'likely to rebel against God or authority'): from late Latin *malignant-* 'contriving maliciously', from the verb *malignare*. The term was used in its early sense to describe those sympathetic to the royalist cause during the English Civil War.

malignant pustule ▶ noun [mass noun] a form of anthrax causing severe skin ulceration.

malik /ˈmɑːlɪk/ ▶ noun (in parts of the Indian subcontinent and the Middle East) the chief of a village or community.
– ORIGIN from Arabic, active participle of *malaka* 'possess or rule'.

malimbe /məˈlɪmbi/ (also **malimbi**) ▶ noun a weaver bird found mainly in west and central Africa, having black plumage with red on the head or throat.
● Genus *Malimbus*, family Ploceidae.
– ORIGIN late 20th cent.: of unknown origin.

Malines /maˈliːn/ French name for **MECHELEN**.

malinger /məˈlɪŋgə/ ▶ verb [no obj.] exaggerate or feign illness in order to escape duty or work.
– DERIVATIVES **malingerer** noun.
– ORIGIN early 19th cent.: back-formation from *malingerer*, apparently from French *malingre*, perhaps formed as *mal-* 'wrongly, improperly' + *haingre* 'weak', probably of Germanic origin.

Malin Head /ˈmalɪn/ a point on the coast of County Donegal, the northernmost point of Ireland. The shipping forecast area **Malin** covers the Atlantic north of Ireland and west of the southern half of Scotland.

Malinke /məˈlɪŋkeɪ/ ▶ noun (pl. same or **Malinkes**) 1 a member of a West African people living mainly in Senegal, Mali, and Ivory Coast.
2 [mass noun] the Mande language of this people, with about 800,000 speakers.
▶ adjective of or relating to the Malinke or their language.
– ORIGIN the name in Malinke.

Malinowski /ˌmalɪˈnɒfski/, Bronisław Kaspar (1884–

1942), Polish anthropologist. He initiated the technique of 'participant observation' and developed the functionalist approach to anthropology.

malison /'malɪz(ə)n, -s-/ ▸ noun archaic a curse.
– ORIGIN Middle English: from Old French.

malkoha ▸ noun variant spelling of **MALCOHA**.

mall /mal, mɔːl, mɒl/ ▸ noun **1** (also **shopping mall**) a large enclosed shopping area from which traffic is excluded.
2 a sheltered walk or promenade.
3 historical another term for the game **PALL-MALL**.
■an alley used for this.
– ORIGIN mid 17th cent. (in sense 3): probably a shortening of **PALL-MALL**. Sense 2 derives from *The Mall*, a tree-bordered walk in St James's Park, London, so named because it was the site of a pall-mall alley. Sense 1 dates from the 1960s.

mallam /'maləm/ ▸ noun (in Nigeria and other parts of Africa) a learned man or scribe.
– ORIGIN from Hausa *mālam(i)*.

mallard ▸ noun (pl. same or **mallards**) the commonest duck of the northern hemisphere and the ancestor of most domestic ducks, the male having a dark green head and white collar.
● *Anas platyrhynchos*, family Anatidae.
– ORIGIN Middle English: from Old French 'wild drake', from *masle* 'male'.

Mallarmé /,malɑːˈmeɪ, French malaʀme/, Stéphane (1842–98), French poet. A symbolist, he experimented with rhythm and syntax by transposing words and omitting grammatical elements. Notable poems: 'Hérodiade' (*c*.1871) and 'L'Après-midi d'un faune' (1876).

Malle /mal/, Louis (1932–95), French film director. His films *Ascenseur pour l'échafaud* (1958) and *Les Amants* (1959) are seminal examples of the French *nouvelle vague*. Other notable films: *Pretty Baby* (1978) and *Au Revoir les enfants* (1987).

malleable /'malɪəb(ə)l/ ▸ adjective (of a metal or other material) able to be hammered or pressed permanently out of shape without breaking or cracking.
■figurative easily influenced; pliable: *younger actresses with more malleable identities*.
– DERIVATIVES **malleability** noun, **malleably** adverb.
– ORIGIN late Middle English (in the sense 'able to be hammered'): via Old French from medieval Latin *malleabilis*, from Latin *malleus* 'a hammer'.

mallee /'mali/ ▸ noun a low-growing bushy Australian eucalyptus which typically has several slender stems.
● Genus *Eucalyptus*, family Myrtaceae: several species, in particular *E. dumosa*.
■[mass noun] scrub which is dominated by mallee bushes, typical of some arid parts of Australia.
– ORIGIN mid 19th cent.: from Wuywurung (an Aboriginal language).

malleefowl (also **mallee bird** or **mallee hen**) ▸ noun (pl. same) a megapode found in the mallee scrub of southern Australia, with pale patterned plumage. Compare with **MALEO**.
● *Leipoa ocellata*, family Megapodiidae.

malleolus /ma'liːələs/ ▸ noun (pl. **malleoli** /-lʌɪ/) Anatomy a bony projection with a shape likened to a hammer head, especially each of those on either side of the ankle.
– ORIGIN late 17th cent.: from Latin, diminutive of *malleus* 'hammer'.

mallet ▸ noun a hammer with a large wooden head, used especially for hitting a chisel.
■a long-handled wooden stick with a head like a hammer, used for hitting a croquet or polo ball.
– ORIGIN late Middle English: from Old French *maillet*, from *mail* 'hammer', from Latin *malleus*.

malleus /'malɪəs/ ▸ noun (pl. **mallei** /'malɪʌɪ/) Anatomy a small bone in the middle ear which transmits vibrations of the eardrum to the incus.
– ORIGIN mid 17th cent.: from Latin, literally 'hammer'.

malling /'mɔːlɪŋ/ ▸ noun [mass noun] N. Amer. **1** the development of shopping malls.
2 the action or activity of passing time in a shopping mall: *Jessie had time to go malling*.

Mallophaga /mə'lɒfəgə/ Entomology an order of insects that comprises the biting lice. See also **PHTHIRAPTERA**.
– DERIVATIVES **mallophagan** noun & adjective.

– ORIGIN modern Latin (plural), from Greek *mallos* 'lock of wool' + -*phagos* 'eating'.

Mallorca /ma'jorka/ Spanish name for **MAJORCA**.

mallow ▸ noun a herbaceous plant with hairy stems, pink or purple flowers, and disc-shaped fruit. Several kinds are grown as ornamentals and some are edible.
● Genus *Malva*, family Malvaceae (the **mallow family**): many species. This family also includes the hollyhocks, hibiscus, and abutilon. See also **MARSH MALLOW, TREE MALLOW**.
– ORIGIN Old English *meal(u)we*, from Latin *malva*; related to Greek *malakhē*; compare with **MAUVE**.

malm /mɑːm/ ▸ noun [mass noun] a soft, crumbly chalky rock, or the fertile loamy soil produced as it weathers.
■(also **malm brick**) [count noun] a fine-quality brick made originally from malm, marl, or a similar chalky clay.
– ORIGIN Old English *mealm-*, of Germanic origin; related to **MEAL**².

Malmö /'mɑːlmə/ a port and fortified city in SW Sweden, situated on the Øresund opposite Copenhagen; pop. 233,900 (1990).

malmsey /'mɑːmzi/ ▸ noun [mass noun] a fortified Madeira wine of the sweetest type.
■historical a strong, sweet white wine imported from Greece and the eastern Mediterranean islands.
– ORIGIN late Middle English: from Middle Dutch *malemeseye*, via Old French from *Monemvasia*, the name of a port in SE mainland Greece. Compare with **MALVOISIE**.

malnourished ▸ adjective suffering from malnutrition.
– DERIVATIVES **malnourishment** noun.

malnutrition ▸ noun [mass noun] lack of proper nutrition, caused by not having enough to eat, not eating enough of the right things, or being unable to use the food that one does eat.

maloca /mə'ləʊkə/ ▸ noun (among the Yanomami and other South American peoples) a large communal hut.
– ORIGIN Brazilian Portuguese, 'large hut', earlier 'unexpected attack by American Indians': this type of hut sometimes served as an arsenal or place of protection.

malocclusion ▸ noun [mass noun] Dentistry imperfect positioning of the teeth when the jaws are closed.

malodorous ▸ adjective smelling very unpleasant.

malodour ▸ noun a very unpleasant smell.

malolactic /,malə(ʊ)'laktɪk/ ▸ adjective of or denoting bacterial fermentation which converts malic acid to lactic acid, especially as a secondary process used to reduce the acidity of some wines.
▸ noun [mass noun] fermentation of this kind.

malonic acid /mə'lɒnɪk/ ▸ noun [mass noun] Chemistry a crystalline acid obtained by the oxidation of malic acid.
● Alternative name: **propane-1,3-dioic acid**; chem. formula: $HOOCCH_2COOH$.
– DERIVATIVES **malonate** noun.
– ORIGIN mid 19th cent.: *malonic* from French *malonique*, alteration of *malique* 'malic'.

malope /'maləpi/ ▸ noun a plant of the mallow family, with wide trumpet-shaped flowers.
● Genus *Malope*, family Malvaceae.

Malory /'maləri/, Sir Thomas (d.1471), English writer. His major work, *Le Morte d'Arthur* (printed 1483), is a prose translation of a collection of the legends of King Arthur, selected from French and other sources.

maloti plural form of **LOTI**.

malperformance ▸ noun [mass noun] faulty or inadequate performance of a task.

Malpighi /mal'piːgi/, Marcello (*c*.1628–94), Italian microscopist. He discovered the alveoli and capillaries in the lungs and the fibres and red cells of clotted blood, and demonstrated the pathway of blood from arteries to veins.

Malpighian layer /mal'pɪgɪən/ ▸ noun Zoology & Anatomy a layer in the epidermis in which skin cells are continually formed by division.

Malpighian tubule ▸ noun Zoology a tubular excretory organ, numbers of which open into the gut in insects and some other arthropods.

Malplaquet, Battle of /,malpla'keɪ, 'malplə,keɪ/ a battle in 1709 during the War of the Spanish Succession, near the village of Malplaquet in northern France, on the border with Belgium. A force of allied British and Austrian troops under

the Duke of Marlborough won a victory over the French.

malpractice ▸ noun [mass noun] improper, illegal, or negligent professional activity or treatment, especially by a medical practitioner, lawyer, or public official: *victims of medical malpractice* | [count noun] *investigations into malpractices and abuses of power*.

malpresentation ▸ noun [mass noun] Medicine abnormal positioning of a fetus at the time of delivery.

Malraux /mal'rəʊ, French malʀo/, André (1901–76), French novelist, politician, and art critic. Involved in the Chinese communist uprising of 1927 and the Spanish Civil War, he was later appointed France's first Minister of Cultural Affairs (1959–69). Notable novels: *La Condition humaine* (1933).

malt /mɔːlt, mɒlt/ ▸ noun [mass noun] barley or other grain that has been steeped, germinated, and dried, used especially for brewing or distilling and vinegar-making.
■chiefly Brit. short for **MALT WHISKY**. ■ N. Amer. short for **MALTED MILK**.
▸ verb [with obj.] convert (grain) into malt: [as noun **malting**] *barley is grown for malting*.
■[no obj.] (of a seed) become malt when germination is checked by drought.
– DERIVATIVES **maltiness** noun, **malty** adjective.
– ORIGIN Old English *m(e)alt*, of Germanic origin; related to **MELT**.

Malta /'mɔːltə, 'mɒl-/ an island country in the central Mediterranean, about 100 km (60 miles) south of Sicily; pop. 356,000 (est. 1991); official languages, Maltese and English; capital, Valletta.

Historically of great strategic importance, the island has been held in turn by invaders including the Greeks, Arabs, Normans, and Knights Hospitallers. It was annexed by Britain in 1814 and was an important naval base until independence within the Commonwealth in 1964. Besides Malta itself, the country includes two other inhabited islands, Gozo and Comino.

Malta fever ▸ noun another term for **UNDULANT FEVER**.
– ORIGIN mid 19th cent.: named after **MALTA**, where it was once prevalent.

maltase /'mɒlteɪz, 'mɔːl-/ ▸ noun [mass noun] Biochemistry an enzyme, present in saliva and pancreatic juice, which catalyses the breakdown of maltose and similar sugars to form glucose.

malted ▸ adjective mixed with malt or a malt extract: *malted biscuits*.

malted milk ▸ noun [mass noun] a hot drink made from dried milk and a malt preparation.
■the powdered mixture from which this drink is made.

Maltese /mɒl'tiːz, mɔːl-/ ▸ noun (pl. same) **1** a native or national of Malta or a person of Maltese descent.
2 [mass noun] the national language of Malta, a Semitic language related to Arabic but much influenced by Italian, Spanish, and Norman French.
▸ adjective of or relating to Malta, its people, or their language.

Maltese cross ▸ noun a cross with arms of equal length which broaden from the centre and have their ends indented in a shallow V-shape.
– ORIGIN so named because the cross was formerly worn by the Knights of Malta, a religious order.

Maltese dog (also **Maltese terrier**) ▸ noun a dog of a very small long-haired breed, typically with white hair.

malthouse ▸ noun a building in which malt is prepared and stored.

Malthus /'malθəs/, Thomas Robert (1766–1834), English economist and clergyman. In *Essay on Population* (1798) he argued that without the practice of 'moral restraint' the population tends to increase at a greater rate than its means of subsistence, resulting in the population checks of war, famine, and epidemic.
– DERIVATIVES **Malthusian** /mal'θjuːzɪən/ adjective & noun, **Malthusianism** noun.

maltings ▸ noun Brit. a malthouse.

malt liquor ▸ noun [mass noun] alcoholic liquor made from malt by fermentation rather than distillation, for example beer.

maltodextrin ▶ **noun** [mass noun] dextrin containing maltose, used as a food additive.

maltose /ˈmɔːltəʊz, -s, mɒlt-/ ▶ **noun** [mass noun] Chemistry a sugar produced by the breakdown of starch, e.g. by enzymes found in malt and saliva. It is a disaccharide consisting of two linked glucose units.
– ORIGIN mid 19th cent.: from **MALT** + **-OSE**².

maltreat ▶ **verb** [with obj.] (often **be maltreated**) treat (a person or animal) cruelly or with violence: *children die from neglect or are maltreated by their carers.*
– DERIVATIVES **maltreater** noun, **maltreatment** noun.
– ORIGIN early 18th cent.: from French *maltraiter*.

maltster ▶ **noun** chiefly Brit. a person whose occupation is making malt.

malt whisky ▶ **noun** [mass noun] whisky made only from malted barley and not blended with grain whisky.

Maluku /məˈluːkuː/ Indonesian name for **MOLUCCA ISLANDS**.

malvaceous /malˈveɪʃəs/ ▶ **adjective** Botany of, relating to, or denoting plants of the mallow family (Malvaceae).
– ORIGIN late 17th cent.: from modern Latin *Malvaceae* (plural), based on Latin *malva* 'mallow', + **-OUS**.

Malvasia /ˌmalvəˈsiːə, -ˈziːə/ ▶ **noun** [mass noun] a variety of grape used to make white and red wines, especially in Italy.
– ORIGIN Italian form of the place name *Monemvasia*, in the Peloponnese (see **MALMSEY**).

Malvern Hills /ˈmɔːlv(ə)n/ (also **the Malverns**) a range of hills in western England, in Herefordshire and Worcestershire. The highest point is Worcestershire Beacon (425 m; 1,394 ft).

malversation /ˌmalvəˈseɪʃ(ə)n/ ▶ **noun** [mass noun] formal corrupt behaviour in a position of trust, especially in public office: *a charge of malversation.*
– ORIGIN mid 16th cent.: from French, from *malverser*, from Latin *male* 'badly' + *versari* 'behave'.

Malvinas, Islas /malˈviːnəs, ˈiːzlas, Spanish malˈβinas, ˈislas/ the name by which the Falkland Islands are known in Argentina.

malvoisie /ˈmalvɔɪzi, ˌmalvɔɪˈziː, French malvwazi/ ▶ **noun** [mass noun] (in French-speaking countries) any of several grape varieties used to make full-flavoured white wines.
– ORIGIN from Old French *malvesie*, from the French form of *Monemvasia* (see **MALMSEY**).

mam ▶ **noun** informal **1** chiefly Brit. one's mother: [as name] *it was better when Mam was alive.* [ORIGIN: late 16th cent.: perhaps imitative of a child's first syllables (see **MAMA**).]
2 chiefly US a term of respectful or polite address used for any woman: *'You all ride them horses down here?' 'Yes, mam.'* [ORIGIN: variant of **MA'AM**.]

mama /ˈmamə, məˈmɑː/ (also **mamma**) ▶ **noun** **1** chiefly dated or N. Amer. one's mother (especially as a child's term): [as name] *come along and meet Mama.*
2 US informal a mature woman: *the ultimate tough blues mama.*
– ORIGIN mid 16th cent.: imitative of a child's first syllables *ma, ma*.

mamaguy /ˈmaməgʌɪ/ ▶ **verb** [with obj.] W. Indian try to deceive (someone), especially with flattery or untruths: *don't try to mamaguy me at all!*
– ORIGIN from Spanish *mamar gallo* 'make a monkey of'.

mama-san /ˈmaməsan/ ▶ **noun** (in Japan and the Far East) a woman in a position of authority, especially one in charge of a geisha house or bar.
– ORIGIN Japanese, from *mama* 'mother' + *san*, an honorific title used as a mark of politeness.

mamba /ˈmambə/ ▶ **noun** **1** a large, agile, highly venomous African snake.
● Genus *Dendroaspis*, family Elapidae: three species. See also **BLACK MAMBA**.
2 S. African an unusually talented, skilful, or intelligent person.
3 [mass noun] S. African informal a home-brewed alcoholic drink.
– ORIGIN mid 19th cent.: from Zulu *imamba*.

mambo /ˈmambəʊ/ ▶ **noun** (pl. **-os**) **1** a Latin American dance similar in rhythm to the rumba.
2 a voodoo priestess.
▶ **verb** (**-oes, -oed**) [no obj.] dance the mambo.
– ORIGIN 1940s: from American Spanish, probably from Haitian Creole, from Yoruba, literally 'to talk'.

mamee ▶ **noun** variant spelling of **MAMMEE**.

mamelon /ˈmamılən/ ▶ **noun** Biology a small rounded structure, e.g. the central knob of a tubercle on a sea urchin.
– ORIGIN mid 19th cent.: from French, 'nipple', from *mamelle* 'breast', from Latin *mamilla* 'little breast'.

Mameluke /ˈmaməluːk/ ▶ **noun** a member of a regime that formerly ruled parts of the Middle East. Descended from slaves, they ruled Syria (1260–1516) and Egypt (1250–1517), and continued as a ruling military caste in Ottoman Egypt until massacred by the viceroy Muhammad Ali in 1811.
– ORIGIN from French *mameluk*, from Arabic *mamlūk* (passive participle used as a noun meaning 'slave'), from *malaka* 'possess'.

Mamet /ˈmamıt/, David (b.1947), American dramatist, director, and screenwriter. Notable plays: *Glengarry Glen Ross* (Pulitzer Prize, 1984) and *Oleanna* (1992).

mamey ▶ **noun** variant spelling of **MAMMEE**.

mamilla /maˈmılə/ (also **mammilla**) ▶ **noun** (pl. **mamillae** /-liː/) Anatomy the nipple of a woman's breast.
■ the corresponding organ in any mammal. ■ a nipple-shaped structure.
– ORIGIN late 17th cent.: from Latin, diminutive of *mamma* 'breast' (see **MAMMA**²).

mamillary /ˈmamıləri/ (also **mammillary**) ▶ **adjective** rounded like a breast or nipple, in particular:
■ (of minerals) having several smoothly rounded convex surfaces. ■ Anatomy denoting two rounded bodies in the floor of the hypothalamus in the brain.
– ORIGIN early 17th cent.: from modern Latin *mamillaris*, from *mamilla* (see **MAMILLA**). The spelling variant of *-mm-* was due to association with **MAMMARY**.

mamillated /ˈmamıleıtıd/ (also **mammillated**) ▶ **adjective** technical covered with rounded mounds or lumps.
■ (of minerals) mamillary.
– DERIVATIVES **mamillate** adjective.
– ORIGIN mid 18th cent.: from **MAMILLA** + the adjectival suffix *-ated*.

mamma¹ /ˈmamə, məˈmɑː/ ▶ **noun** variant spelling of **MAMA**.

mamma² /ˈmamə/ ▶ **noun** (pl. **mammae** /-miː/) a milk-secreting organ of female mammals (in humans, the breast).
■ a corresponding non-secretory structure in male mammals.
– DERIVATIVES **mammiform** adjective.
– ORIGIN Old English, from Latin, 'breast'.

mammal ▶ **noun** a warm-blooded vertebrate animal of a class that is distinguished by the possession of hair or fur, females that secrete milk for the nourishment of the young, and (typically) the birth of live young.

> The first small mammals evolved from reptiles about 200 million years ago, and the group diversified rapidly after the extinction of the dinosaurs to become the dominant form of land animal, with around 4,000 living species. Mammals belong to the class Mammalia, which contains the subclass Prototheria (monotremes) and the infraclasses Metatheria (marsupials) and Eutheria (placental mammals such as rodents, cats, whales, bats, and humans).

– DERIVATIVES **mammalian** adjective.
– ORIGIN early 19th cent.: Anglicized form (first used in the plural) of modern Latin *mammalia*, neuter plural of Latin *mammalis* (adjective), from *mamma* 'breast' (see **MAMMA**²).

mammaliferous /ˌmaməˈlıf(ə)rəs/ ▶ **adjective** Geology containing mammalian fossil remains.

mammal-like reptile ▶ **noun** another term for **SYNAPSID**.

mammalogy /maˈmalədʒi/ ▶ **noun** [mass noun] the branch of zoology concerned with mammals.
– DERIVATIVES **mammalogist** noun.

mammary /ˈmaməri/ ▶ **adjective** [attrib.] denoting or relating to the human female breasts or the milk-secreting organs of other mammals: *mammary tumour viruses.*
▶ **noun** (pl. **-ies**) informal a breast.
– ORIGIN late 17th cent.: from **MAMMA**² + **-ARY**¹.

mammary gland ▶ **noun** the milk-producing gland of women or other female mammals.

mammee /maˈmiː/ (also **mamee, mamey**) ▶ **noun** **1** (also **mammee apple**) a large tropical American tree having large edible red fruit with red rind and sweet yellow flesh.
● *Mammea americana*, family Guttiferae.
2 (also **mammee sapote**) a Central American tree having edible russet fruit with spicy red flesh. [ORIGIN: *sapote* from Spanish *zapote* 'sapodilla'.]
● *Pouteria sapota*, family Sapotaceae.
– ORIGIN late 16th cent.: from Spanish *mamei*, from Taino.

mammilla ▶ **noun** variant spelling of **MAMILLA**.

mammogram /ˈmaməgram/ ▶ **noun** an image obtained by mammography.

mammography /maˈmɒgrəfi/ ▶ **noun** [mass noun] Medicine a technique using X-rays to diagnose and locate tumours of the breasts.
– ORIGIN 1930s: from **MAMMA**² + **-GRAPHY**.

Mammon /ˈmamən/ ▶ **noun** [mass noun] wealth regarded as an evil influence or false object of worship and devotion. It was taken by medieval writers as the name of the devil of covetousness, and revived in this sense by Milton.
– DERIVATIVES **Mammonism** noun, **Mammonist** noun.
– ORIGIN late Middle English: via late Latin from New Testament Greek *mamōnas* (see Matt. 6:24, Luke 16:9–13), from Aramaic *māmōn* 'riches'.

mammoth ▶ **noun** a large extinct elephant of the Pleistocene epoch, typically hairy with a sloping back and long curved tusks.
● Genus *Mammuthus*, family Elephantidae: several species. See **WOOLLY MAMMOTH**.
▶ **adjective** huge: *a mammoth corporation.*
– ORIGIN early 18th cent.: from Russian *mamo(n)t*, probably of Siberian origin.

Mammoth Cave National Park a national park in west central Kentucky, site of the largest known cave system in the world. It consists of over 480 km (300 miles) of charted passageways and contains some spectacular rock formations.

mammy ▶ **noun** (pl. **-ies**) informal one's mother (especially as a child's word): *he was screaming for his mammy.*
■ offensive (formerly in the southern United States) a black nursemaid or nanny in charge of white children.
– ORIGIN early 16th cent.: from **MAM** + **-Y**²; compare with **MOMMY** and **MUMMY**¹.

Mamoutzu /maˈmuːtsuː/ the capital (since 1977) of Mayotte; pop. 12,120.

Mam'selle /mamˈzɛl/ ▶ **noun** short for **MADEMOISELLE**.

Man. ▶ **abbreviation for** Manitoba.

man ▶ **noun** (pl. **men**) **1** an adult human male.
■ a male worker or employee: *over 700 men were made redundant | the BBC's man in India.* ■ a male member of a sports team: *Johnson took the ball past three men and scored.* ■ (**men**) ordinary members of the armed forces as distinct from the officers: *he had a platoon of forty men to prepare for battle.* ■ a husband, boyfriend, or lover: *the two of them lived for a time as man and wife.* ■ [with modifier] a male person associated with a particular place, activity, or occupation: *a Cambridge man | I'm a solid Labour man.* ■ a male pursued or sought by another, especially in connection with a crime: *Inspector Bull was sure they would find their man.* ■ dated a manservant or valet: *get me a cocktail, my man.* ■ historical a vassal.
2 a human being of either sex; a person: *God cares for all races and all men.*
■ (also **Man**) [in sing.] human beings in general; the human race: *places untouched by the ravages of man.* ■ [in sing.] an individual; one: *a man could buy a lot with eighteen million dollars.* ■ a person with the good qualities typically associated with males, such as bravery, spirit, or toughness: *she was more of a man than any of them.* ■ [in sing.] [with adj. or noun modifier] a type of prehistoric human named after the place where the remains were found: *Cro-Magnon man.*
3 (usu. **the Man**) informal a group or person in a position of authority over others, such as a corporate employer or the police: *they've mastered their emotive grunge-pop without haggling with the Man.*
■ black slang white people collectively regarded as the controlling group in society: *he urged that black college athletes boycott the Man's Rose Bowl.*
4 a figure or token used in playing a board game.
▶ **verb** (**manned, manning**) [with obj.] **1** (often **be manned**) provide (something, especially a place or machine) with the personnel to run, operate, or defend it: *the firemen manned the pumps and fought the blaze.*

■provide someone to fill (a post or office): *the chaplaincy was formerly manned by the cathedral.*
2 archaic fortify the spirits or courage of: *he* ***manned himself*** *with dauntless air.*
▶**exclamation** informal, chiefly N. Amer. used, irrespective of the sex of the person addressed, to express surprise, admiration, delight, etc., or for emphasis: *wow, like cosmic, man.*
– PHRASES **as —— as the next man** as —— as the average person: *I'm as ambitious as the next man.* **as one man** with everyone acting together or in agreement: *the crowd rose to their feet as one man.* **be someone's** (or **the**) man be the person perfectly suited to a particular requirement or task: *for any colouring and perming services, David's your man.* **be man enough to do** (or **for**) be brave enough to do: *he has not been man enough to face up to his responsibilities.* **every man for himself and the devil take the hindmost** proverb everyone should (or does) look after their own interests rather than considering those of others: *in previous student flats she'd shared, it was every man for himself | full speed ahead and the devil take the hindmost.* [ORIGIN: with allusion to a chase by the Devil, in which the slowest will be caught.] **make a man out of someone** (of an experience or person) turn a young man into a mature adult: *I make men out of them and teach them never to let anyone outsmart them.* **man about town** a fashionable male socialite. **man and boy** dated throughout life from youth: *the time when families worked in the fields man and boy.* **the man in the moon** the imagined likeness of a face seen on the surface of a full moon. ■ figurative used, especially in comparisons, to refer to someone regarded as out of touch with real life: *a kid with no more idea of what a girl needed than the man in the moon.* **the man in** (or US **on**) **the street** an ordinary person, often with regard to their opinions, or as distinct from an expert: *he had been his eyes and ears in the community, voiced the opinions of the man in the street.* **man of action** see **ACTION**. **man of the cloth** a clergyman. **man of God** a clergyman.■ a holy man or saint. **man of honour** a man who adheres to what is right or to a high standard of conduct. **man of the house** the male head of a household. **man of letters** a male scholar or author. **man of the match** the team member who has given the most outstanding performance in a particular game. **man of the moment** a man of importance at a particular time. **man of straw** (also **straw man**) **1** a person compared to a straw image; a sham. ■ a sham argument set up to be defeated. **2** a person undertaking a financial commitment without adequate means. **man of the world** see **WORLD**. **the man on the Clapham omnibus** Brit. the average man, especially with regard to his opinions. **man's best friend** an affectionate or approving way of referring to the dog. **a man's man** a man whose personality is such that he is more popular and at ease with other men than with women. **man to man 1** in a direct and frank way between two men; openly and honestly: *he was able to talk man to man with the delegates | a man-to-man chat.* **2** denoting a defensive tactic in soccer or other sport in which each player is responsible for marking one opponent: *one of the best man-to-man markers in the English game | Washington's cornerbacks are fast enough to cover man-to-man.* **men in** (**grey**) **suits** powerful men within an organization who exercise their influence or authority anonymously. **men in white coats** humorous psychiatrists or psychiatric workers (used to imply that someone is mad or mentally unbalanced): *I wondered how much more stupid I could get before the men in white coats would lead me away.* **the men's** (or **the men's room**) a men's public toilet. **my** (or **my good** or **my dear**) **man** Brit. dated a patronizing form of address to a man. **separate** (or **sort out**) **the men from the boys** informal show or prove which people in a group are truly competent, brave, or mature. **to a man** without exception: *to a man, we have all taken a keen interest in the business.*
– DERIVATIVES **manless** adjective.
– ORIGIN Old English *man(n)*, (plural) *menn* (noun), *mannian* (verb), of Germanic origin; related to Dutch *man*, German *Mann*, and Sanskrit *manu* 'mankind'.

USAGE Traditionally the word **man** has been used to refer not only to adult males but also to human beings in general, regardless of sex. There is a historical explanation for this: in Old English the principal sense of **man** was 'a human being', and the words **wer** and **wif** were used to refer specifically to 'a male person' and 'a female person' respectively. Subsequently, **man** replaced **wer** as the normal term for 'a male person', but at the same time the older sense 'a human being' remained in use.
In the second half of the twentieth century the generic use of **man** to refer to 'human beings in general' (as in *reptiles were here long before man appeared on the earth*) became problematic; the use is now often regarded as sexist or at best old-fashioned. In some contexts, alternative terms such as **the human race** or **humankind** may be used. Fixed phrases and sayings such as *time and tide wait for no* ***man*** can be easily rephrased, e.g. *time and tide wait for* ***nobody***. However, in other cases, particularly in compound forms, alternatives have not yet become established: there are no standard accepted alternatives for **manpower** or the verb **man**, for example.

-man ▶**combining form** in nouns denoting:
■a male of a specified nationality or origin: *Frenchman | Yorkshireman.* ■ a man belonging to a distinct specified group: *layman.* ■ a person, especially a male, having a specified occupation or role: *exciseman | chairman | oarsman.* ■ a ship of a specified kind: *merchantman.*

USAGE Traditionally, the form **-man** was combined with other words to create a term denoting an occupation or role, as in **fireman**, **layman**, **chairman**, and **freshman**. As the role of women in society has changed, with the result that women are now more likely to be in roles previously held exclusively by men, many of these terms ending in **-man** have been challenged as sexist and out of date. As a result, there has been a gradual shift away from **-man** compounds except where referring to a specific male person. Alternative gender-neutral terms are used, for example **firefighter** and **fresher**, and new ones which only a few decades ago seemed odd or awkward today seem unexceptionable: **chair/chairperson**, **layperson**, and **sportsperson**.

Man, Isle of see **ISLE OF MAN**.

mana /ˈmɑːnə/ ▶**noun** [mass noun] (especially in Polynesian, Melanesian, and Maori belief) pervasive supernatural or magical power.
– ORIGIN Maori.

manacle /ˈmanək(ə)l/ ▶**noun** (usu. **manacles**) a metal band, chain, or shackle for fastening someone's hands or ankles: *the practice of keeping prisoners in manacles.*
▶**verb** [with obj.] (usu. **be manacled**) fetter (a person or part of the body) with manacles: *his hands were manacled behind his back.*
– ORIGIN Middle English: from Old French *manicle* 'handcuff', from Latin *manicula*, diminutive of *manus* 'hand'.

manage ▶**verb 1** [with obj.] be in charge of (a company, establishment, or undertaking); administer; run: *their elder son managed the farm.*
■administer and regulate (resources under one's control): *we manage our cash extremely well.* ■ have the position of supervising (staff) at work: *the skills needed to manage a young, dynamic team.* ■ be the manager of (a sports team or a performer): *he managed five or six bands in his career.* ■ maintain control or influence over (a person or animal): *she manages horses better than anyone I know.* ■ (often **be managed**) control the use or exploitation of (land): *the forest is managed to achieve maximum growth.*
2 [no obj.] succeed in surviving or in attaining one's aims, especially against heavy odds; cope: *Catherine* ***managed on*** *five hours' sleep a night.*
■[with obj.] succeed in doing, achieving, or producing (something, especially something difficult): *she managed a brave but unconvincing smile |* [with infinitive] *Blanche finally managed to hail a cab |* ironic *one fund managed to lose money.* ■ [with obj.] succeed in dealing with or withstanding (something): *there was more stress and anxiety than he could manage.* ■ [with obj.] be free to attend on (a certain day) or at (a certain time): *he could not manage 24 March after all.*
– ORIGIN mid 16th cent. (in the sense 'put (a horse) through the paces of the manège'): from Italian *maneggiare*, based on Latin *manus* 'hand'.

manageable ▶**adjective** able to be managed, controlled, or accomplished without great difficulty: *it leaves hair feeling soft and manageable.*
– DERIVATIVES **manageability** noun, **manageableness** noun, **manageably** adverb.

managed care ▶**noun** [mass noun] US a system of health care emphasizing preventative medicine and home treatment.

managed currency ▶**noun** a currency whose exchange rate is regulated or controlled by the government.

managed economy ▶**noun** an economy in which the framework and general policies are regulated or controlled by the government.

managed fund ▶**noun** an investment fund run on behalf of an investor by an agent (typically, an insurance company).

management ▶**noun** [mass noun] **1** the process of dealing with or controlling things or people: *the management of the British economy.*
■the responsibility for and control of a company or similar organization: *a successful career in management.* ■ [treated as sing. or pl.] the people in charge of running a company or organization, regarded collectively: *management were extremely cooperative.* ■ Medicine & Psychiatry the treatment or control of diseases, injuries, or disorders, or the care of patients who suffer them: *long-term management of patients with cirrhosis.*
2 archaic trickery; deceit: *if there has been any management in the business, it has been concealed from me.*

management accounting ▶**noun** [mass noun] the provision of financial data and advice to a company for use in the organization and development of its business.
– DERIVATIVES **management accountant** noun.

management company ▶**noun** a company which is set up to manage a group of properties, a unit trust, an investment fund, etc.

manager ▶**noun 1** a person responsible for controlling or administering all or part of a company or similar organization: *the manager of a bar.*
■a person who controls the activities, business dealings, and other aspects of the career of an entertainer, sports player, group of musicians, etc. ■ a person in charge of the activities, tactics, and training of a sports team. ■ [with modifier] Computing a program or system that controls or organizes a peripheral device or process: *a file manager.*
2 Brit. a member of either House of Parliament appointed with others for some duty in which both Houses are concerned.
– DERIVATIVES **managership** noun.

manageress ▶**noun** a female manager.

managerial ▶**adjective** relating to management or managers, especially of a company or similar organization: *managerial skills.*
– DERIVATIVES **managerially** adverb.

managerialism ▶**noun** [mass noun] belief in or reliance on the use of professional managers in administering or planning an activity.
– DERIVATIVES **managerialist** noun & adjective.

managing ▶**adjective** [attrib.] **1** chiefly Brit. having executive control or authority: *a managing editor.*
2 archaic economical: *a managing man.*

Managua /məˈnɑːgwə/ the capital of Nicaragua; pop 682,100 (1985). The city was almost completely destroyed by an earthquake in 1972.

manaia /məˈnʌɪə/ ▶**noun** a motif in Maori carving with a birdlike head and a human body.
– ORIGIN Maori.

manakin /ˈmanəkɪn/ ▶**noun** a small tropical American bird with a large head and small bill, the male of which is typically brightly coloured. Compare with **MANNIKIN**.
● Family Pipridae (or Cotingidae, Tyrannidae): several genera and many species.
– ORIGIN early 17th cent.: variant of **MANIKIN**.

Manama /məˈnɑːmə/ the capital of Bahrain; pop. 140,400 (est. 1991).

mañana /manˈjɑːnə/ ▶**adverb** in the indefinite future (used to indicate procrastination): *the exhibition will be ready mañana.*
– ORIGIN Spanish, literally 'tomorrow'.

Mana Pools National Park /ˈmɑːnə/ a national park in northern Zimbabwe, in the Zambezi valley north-east of Lake Kariba, established in 1963.

Manasseh /məˈnasi, -ˈnasə/ (in the Bible) a Hebrew patriarch, son of Jacob (Gen. 48:19).
■the tribe of Israel traditionally descended from him.

Manasses, Prayer of see **PRAYER OF MANASSES**.

manat /ˈmanat/ ▶**noun** (pl. same) the basic monetary unit of Azerbaijan and Turkmenistan, equal to 100 gopik in Azerbaijan and 100 tenge in Turkmenistan.

man-at-arms ▶ noun (pl. **men-at-arms**) archaic a soldier, especially one heavily armed and mounted on horseback.

manatee /ˌmanəˈtiː, ˈmanəti:/ ▶ noun a sea cow with a rounded tail flipper, living in shallow coastal waters and adjacent rivers of the tropical Atlantic.
● Family Trichechidae and genus *Trichechus*: three species.
– ORIGIN mid 16th cent.: from Spanish *manati*, from Carib *manáti*.

Manaus /məˈnaʊs/ a city in NW Brazil, capital of the state of Amazonas; pop. 1,011,600. It is the principal commercial centre of the upper Amazon region.

Manawatu /ˌmanəˈwɑːtuː/ a river of North Island, New Zealand, flowing into Cook Strait.

Manchester[1] an industrial city in NW England; pop. 397,400 (1991). Founded in Roman times, it developed in the 18th and 19th centuries as a centre of the English cotton industry.

Manchester[2] (also **Manchester goods** or **wares**) ▶ noun [mass noun] Austral./NZ cotton textiles; household linen.

Manchester Ship Canal a waterway in NW England, which links Manchester with the estuary of the River Mersey and the Irish Sea. Opened in 1894, it is 57 km (36 miles) long.

Manchester terrier ▶ noun a small terrier of a breed with a short black-and-tan coat.

Manchester warehouse ▶ noun Brit. archaic a cotton textile warehouse.

manchet /ˈmantʃɪt/ ▶ noun historical a loaf of the finest kind of wheaten bread.
– ORIGIN late Middle English: perhaps from obsolete *maine* 'flour of the finest quality' + obsolete *cheat*, denoting a kind of wheaten bread.

manchineel /ˌman(t)ʃɪˈniːl/ ▶ noun a Caribbean tree which has acrid apple-like fruit and poisonous milky sap which can cause temporary blindness.
● *Hippomane mancinella*, family Euphorbiaceae.
– ORIGIN late 17th cent.: from French *mancenille*, from Spanish *manzanilla*, diminutive of *manzana* 'apple', based on Latin *matiana* (*poma*) (neuter plural), denoting a kind of apple.

Manchu /manˈtʃuː/ ▶ noun 1 a member of a people originally living in Manchuria, who formed the last imperial dynasty of China (1644–1912).
2 [mass noun] the Tungusic language of the Manchus, still spoken by a few thousand people in Xinjiang, though most Manchus now speak Chinese.
▶ adjective of or relating to the Manchu people or their language.
– ORIGIN the name in Manchu, literally 'pure'.

Manchuria /manˈtʃʊəriə/ a mountainous region forming the NE portion of China, now comprising the provinces of Jilin, Liaoning, and Heilongjiang. In 1932 it was declared an independent state by Japan and renamed Manchukuo; it was restored to China in 1945.

manciple /ˈmansɪp(ə)l/ ▶ noun chiefly archaic an officer who buys provisions for a college, an Inn of Court, or a monastery.
– ORIGIN Middle English: via Anglo-Norman French and Old French from Latin *mancipium* 'purchase', from *manceps* 'buyer', from *manus* 'hand' + *capere* 'take'.

Mancunian /manˈkjuːnɪən/ ▶ noun a native or inhabitant of Manchester.
▶ adjective of or relating to Manchester.
– ORIGIN early 20th cent.: from *Mancunium*, the Latin name of Manchester, + -AN.

-mancy ▶ combining form divination by a specified means: *geomancy*.
– DERIVATIVES **-mantic** combining form in corresponding adjectives.
– ORIGIN from Old French *-mancie*, via late Latin *-mantia* from Greek *manteia* 'divination'.

Mandaean /manˈdiːən/ (also **Mandean**) ▶ noun 1 a member of a Gnostic sect surviving in Iraq and SW Iran, who regard John the Baptist as the Messiah. They stress salvation through knowledge of the divine origin of the soul.
2 [mass noun] the language of this sect, a form of Aramaic.
▶ adjective of or relating to the Mandaeans or their language.
– ORIGIN late 19th cent.: from Mandaean Aramaic

mandaia 'Gnostics, those who have knowledge' (from *manda* 'knowledge') + -AN.

mandala /ˈmandələ, ˈmʌn-/ ▶ noun a circular figure representing the universe in Hindu and Buddhist symbolism.
■ Psychoanalysis such a symbol in a dream, representing the dreamer's search for completeness and self-unity.
– DERIVATIVES **mandalic** adjective.
– ORIGIN from Sanskrit *maṇḍala* 'disc'.

Mandalay /ˌmandəˈleɪ/ a port on the Irrawaddy River in central Burma (Myanmar); pop. 533,000 (1983). Founded in 1857, it was the capital until 1885 of the Burmese kingdom. It is an important Buddhist religious centre.

mandamus /manˈdeɪməs/ ▶ noun [mass noun] Law a judicial writ issued as a command to an inferior court or ordering a person to perform a public or statutory duty: *an order of mandamus*.
– ORIGIN mid 16th cent.: from Latin, literally 'we command'.

Mandan /ˈmand(ə)n/ ▶ noun (pl. same or **Mandans**) 1 a member of an American Indian people formerly living along the northern reaches of the Missouri River.
2 [mass noun] the Siouan language of this people, now virtually extinct.
▶ adjective of or relating to this people or their language.
– ORIGIN from North American French *Mandane*, probably from Dakota Sioux *mawátāna*.

mandapam /ˈmʌndəpʌm/ (also **mandap** /ˈmʌndəp/) ▶ noun (in southern India) a temple porch.
■ a temporary platform set up for weddings and religious ceremonies.
– ORIGIN from Sanskrit *maṇḍapam*.

mandarin[1] /ˈmand(ə)rɪn/ ▶ noun 1 (**Mandarin**) [mass noun] the standard literary and official form of Chinese, spoken by over 730 million people: [as modifier] *Mandarin Chinese*.
2 an official in any of the nine top grades of the former imperial Chinese civil service.
■ [as modifier] (especially of clothing) characteristic or supposedly characteristic of such officials: *a red-buttoned mandarin cap*. ■ an ornament consisting of a nodding figure in traditional Chinese dress, typically made of porcelain. ■ [mass noun] porcelain decorated with Chinese figures dressed as mandarins. ■ a powerful official or senior bureaucrat, especially one perceived as reactionary and secretive: *a civil service mandarin*.
– DERIVATIVES **mandarinate** noun.
– ORIGIN late 16th cent. (denoting a Chinese official): from Portuguese *mandarim*, via Malay from Hindi *mantrī* 'counsellor'.

mandarin[2] /ˈmand(ə)rɪn/ (also **mandarine** /-riːn/, **mandarin orange**) ▶ noun 1 a small flattish citrus fruit with a loose skin, especially a variety with yellow-orange skin. Compare with TANGERINE.
2 the citrus tree that yields this fruit.
● *Citrus reticulata*, family Rutaceae.
– ORIGIN late 18th cent.: from French *mandarine*; perhaps related to MANDARIN[1], the colour of the fruit being likened to the official's yellow robes.

mandarin collar ▶ noun a small, close-fitting upright collar.

mandarin duck ▶ noun a small tree-nesting East Asian duck, the male of which has showy plumage with an orange ruff and orange sail-like feathers on each side of the body.
● *Aix galericulata*, family Anatidae.

mandarin jacket ▶ noun a plain jacket with a mandarin collar, typically of embroidered silk.

mandatary /ˈmandət(ə)ri/ ▶ noun (pl. **-ies**) historical a person or state receiving a mandate.
– ORIGIN late 15th cent. (denoting a person appointed by a papal mandate): from late Latin *mandatarius*, from *mandatum* (see MANDATE).

mandate ▶ noun /ˈmandeɪt/ 1 an official order or commission to do something: *a mandate to seek the release of political prisoners.*
■ Law a commission by which a party is entrusted to perform a service, especially without payment and with indemnity against loss by that party. ■ a written authority enabling someone to carry out transactions on another's bank account. ■ historical a commission from the League of Nations to a member state to administer a territory: *the British mandate in Palestine.*
2 the authority to carry out a policy or course of

action, regarded as given by the electorate to a party or candidate that is victorious in an election: *he called an election to seek a mandate for his policies.*
■ Canadian a period during which a government is in power.
▶ verb /manˈdeɪt/ [with obj.] 1 give (someone) authority to act in a certain way: *the rightful king was mandated and sanctioned by God* | [with obj. and infinitive] *the President mandated him to form a new government.*
■ require (something) to be done; make mandatory: *the government began mandating better car safety.*
2 historical assign (territory) under a mandate of the League of Nations: [as adj. **mandated**] *mandated territories.*
– ORIGIN early 16th cent.: from Latin *mandatum* 'something commanded', neuter past participle of *mandare*, from *manus* 'hand' + *dare* 'give'. Sense 2 of the noun has been influenced by French *mandat.*

mandatory /ˈmandət(ə)ri/ ▶ adjective required by law or rules; compulsory: *wearing helmets was made mandatory for pedal cyclists.*
■ of or conveying a command: *he did not want the guidelines to be mandatory.*
▶ noun (pl. **-ies**) variant spelling of MANDATARY.
– DERIVATIVES **mandatorily** adverb.
– ORIGIN late 15th cent.: from late Latin *mandatorius*, from Latin *mandatum* 'something commanded'.

man-day ▶ noun a day regarded in terms of the amount of work that can be done by one person within this period.

Mande /ˈmɑːndeɪ/ ▶ noun (pl. same or **Mandes**) 1 a member of any of a large group of peoples of West Africa.
2 [mass noun] the group of Niger–Congo languages spoken by these peoples, many of which are mutually intelligible. They include Malinke, Mende, and Bambara.
▶ adjective of or relating to these peoples or the Mande group of languages.
– ORIGIN the name in Mande.

Mandean ▶ noun & adjective variant spelling of MANDAEAN.

Mandela /manˈdɛlə/, Nelson (Rolihlahla) (b.1918), South African statesman, President 1994–9. He was sentenced to life imprisonment in 1964 as an activist for the African National Congress (ANC). Released in 1990, as leader of the ANC he engaged in talks on the introduction of majority rule with President F. W. de Klerk, with whom he shared the Nobel Peace Prize in 1993. He became the country's first democratically elected President in 1994.

Mandelbrot /ˈmand(ə)lbrɒt/, Benoit (b.1924), Polish-born French mathematician. Mandelbrot is known as the pioneer of fractal geometry.

Mandelbrot set ▶ noun Mathematics a particular set of complex numbers which has a highly convoluted fractal boundary when plotted.

Mandelstam /ˈmand(ə)lˌʃtam/ (also **Mandelshtam**), Osip (Emilevich) (1891–1938), Russian poet, a member of the Acmeist group. Sent into internal exile in 1934, he died in a prison camp. Notable works: *Stone* (1913) and *Tristia* (1922).

Mandeville /ˈmandəvɪl/, Sir John (14th century), English nobleman. He is remembered as the reputed author of a book of travels and travellers' tales which was actually compiled by an unknown hand from the works of several writers.

mandible /ˈmandɪb(ə)l/ ▶ noun Anatomy & Zoology the jaw or a jawbone, especially the lower jawbone in mammals and fishes.
■ either of the upper and lower parts of a bird's beak. ■ either half of the crushing organ in an arthropod's mouthparts.
– DERIVATIVES **mandibular** adjective, **mandibulate** adjective.
– ORIGIN late Middle English: from Old French, or from late Latin *mandibula*, from *mandere* 'to chew'.

Manding /ˈmandɪŋ/ (also **Mandingo** /manˈdɪŋɡəʊ/) ▶ noun & adjective another term for MANDE.

Mandinka /manˈdɪŋkə/ ▶ noun (pl. same or **Mandinkas**) 1 a member of a West African people living mainly in Senegal, Gambia, and Sierra Leone.
2 [mass noun] the Mande language of this people, with about 770,000 speakers.
▶ adjective of or relating to the Mandinkas or their language.
– ORIGIN the name in Mandinka.

mandir /ˈmandɪə/ ▶ noun chiefly Indian a Hindu temple.

– ORIGIN from Hindi and Sanskrit *mandira* 'dwelling place, temple'.

mandola /man'dəʊlə/ ▶ noun a large tenor or bass mandolin, used in ensembles and folk groups.
■ (also **mandora** /-'dɔːrə/) historical an early stringed instrument of the mandolin or cittern type.
– ORIGIN early 18th cent.: from Italian.

mandolin ▶ noun **1** a musical instrument resembling a lute, having paired metal strings plucked with a plectrum. It has a characteristic tremolo when sustaining long notes.
2 (also **mandoline**) a kitchen utensil consisting of a flat frame with adjustable cutting blades for slicing vegetables.
– DERIVATIVES **mandolinist** noun.
– ORIGIN early 18th cent.: from French *mandoline*, from Italian *mandolino*, diminutive of *mandola* (see **MANDOLA**).

mandorla /man'dɔːlə/ ▶ noun another term for **VESICA PISCIS**.
– ORIGIN late 19th cent.: from Italian, literally 'almond'.

mandragora /man'dragərə/ ▶ noun poetic/literary the mandrake, especially when used as a narcotic.
– ORIGIN Old English, via medieval Latin from Latin and Greek *mandragoras*.

mandrake ▶ noun a Mediterranean plant of the nightshade family, with white or purple flowers and large yellow berries. It has a forked fleshy root which supposedly resembles the human form and was formerly widely used in medicine and magic, allegedly shrieking when pulled from the ground.
● *Mandragora officinarum*, family Solanaceae.
– ORIGIN Middle English *mandrag(g)e*, from Middle Dutch *mandrag(r)e*, from medieval Latin *mandragora*; associated with **MAN** (because of the shape of its root) + *drake* in the Old English sense 'dragon'.

Mandrax /'mandraks/ ▶ noun [mass noun] trademark a sedative drug containing methaqualone and diphenhydramine hydrochloride.
– ORIGIN 1960s: of unknown origin.

mandrel /'mandr(ə)l/ ▶ noun **1** a shaft or spindle in a lathe to which work is fixed while being turned.
2 a cylindrical rod round which metal or other material is forged or shaped.
3 Brit. a miner's pick.
– ORIGIN early 16th cent. (in sense 3): of unknown origin.

mandrill /'mandrɪl/ ▶ noun a large West African baboon with a brightly coloured red and blue face, the male having a blue rump.
● *Mandrillus sphinx*, family Cercopithecidae.
– ORIGIN mid 18th cent.: probably from **MAN** + **DRILL**[3].

manducate /'mandjʊkeɪt/ ▶ verb [with obj.] formal chew or eat.
– DERIVATIVES **manducation** noun, **manducatory** adjective.
– ORIGIN early 17th cent.: from Latin *manducat-* 'chewed', from the verb *manducare*, from *manduco* 'guzzler', from *mandere* 'to chew'.

mane ▶ noun a growth of long hair on the neck of a horse, lion, or other animal.
■ a person's long hair: *he had a mane of white hair.*
– DERIVATIVES **maned** adjective [in combination] *a black-maned lion*, **maneless** adjective.
– ORIGIN Old English *manu*, of Germanic origin; related to Dutch *manen*.

maneater ▶ noun **1** an animal that has a propensity for killing and eating humans.
■ another term for **GREAT WHITE SHARK**.
2 informal a dominant woman who has many sexual partners.
– DERIVATIVES **man-eating** adjective.

maneb /'manɛb/ ▶ noun [mass noun] a white compound used as a fungicidal powder on vegetables and fruit.
● Alternative name: **manganese ethylene bisdithiocarbamate**; chem. formula: $C_4H_6N_2S_4Mn$.

maned wolf ▶ noun a tall long-legged wild dog that has a reddish coat with black hair across the shoulders and large erect ears, native to the grasslands of South America.
● *Chrysocyon brachyurus*, family Canidae.

manège /ma'nɛʒ/ ▶ noun an arena or enclosed area in which horses and riders are trained.
■ [mass noun] the movements of a trained horse. ■ [mass noun] horsemanship.

– ORIGIN mid 17th cent.: French, from Italian (see **MANAGE**).

manes /'mɑːneɪz, 'meɪniːz/ ▶ plural noun (in Roman mythology) the deified souls of dead ancestors.
– ORIGIN Latin.

Manet /'maneɪ/, Édouard (1832–83), French painter. He adopted a realist approach which greatly influenced the Impressionists, using pure colour to give a direct unsentimental effect. Notable works: *Déjeuner sur l'herbe* (1863), *Olympia* (1865), and *A Bar at the Folies-Bergère* (1882).

Manetho /ma'nɛθəʊ/ (3rd century BC), Egyptian priest. He wrote a history of Egypt from mythical times to 323, in which he arbitrarily divided the succession of rulers known to him into thirty dynasties, an arrangement which is still followed.

maneuver ▶ noun & verb US spelling of **MANOEUVRE**.

man Friday ▶ noun a male helper or follower.
– ORIGIN from *Man Friday*, the name of a character in Defoe's novel *Robinson Crusoe* (1719).

manful ▶ adjective resolute or brave, especially in the face of adversity: *a manful attempt to smile.*
– DERIVATIVES **manfully** adverb, **manfulness** noun.

manga /'maŋɡa/ ▶ noun [mass noun] a Japanese genre of cartoons, comic books, and animated films, typically having a science-fiction or fantasy theme and sometimes including violent or sexually explicit material. Compare with **ANIME**.
– ORIGIN Japanese, from *man* 'indiscriminate' + *ga* 'picture'.

mangabey /'maŋɡəbeɪ/ ▶ noun a medium-sized long-tailed monkey native to the forests of West and central Africa.
● Genus *Cercocebus*, family Cercopithecidae: several species.
– ORIGIN late 18th cent.: by erroneous association with *Mangabey*, a region of Madagascar.

manganate /'maŋɡənət, -neɪt/ ▶ noun Chemistry a salt in which the anion contains both manganese and oxygen, especially one of the anion MnO_4^{2-}.

manganese /'maŋɡəniːz/ ▶ noun [mass noun] the chemical element of atomic number 25, a hard grey metal of the transition series. Manganese is an important component of special steels and magnetic alloys. (Symbol: **Mn**)
■ the black dioxide of this as an industrial raw material or additive, especially in glass-making.
– ORIGIN late 17th cent.: via French from Italian *manganese*, unexplained alteration of medieval Latin *magnesia* (see **MAGNESIA**).

manganese bronze ▶ noun [mass noun] an alloy of copper and zinc with manganese.

manganese nodule ▶ noun a small concretion consisting of manganese and iron oxides, occurring in large numbers in ocean-floor sediment.

manganic /maŋ'ɡanɪk/ ▶ adjective Chemistry of manganese with a higher valency, usually three. Compare with **MANGANOUS**.

Manganin /'maŋɡənɪm/ ▶ noun [mass noun] Brit. trademark an alloy of copper, manganese, and nickel, used chiefly in electrical apparatus.
– ORIGIN 1920s: from **MANGANESE** + **-IN**[1].

manganite /'maŋɡənʌɪt/ ▶ noun [mass noun] a mineral consisting of basic manganese oxide, typically occurring as steel-grey or black prisms.

manganous /'maŋɡənəs/ ▶ adjective Chemistry of manganese with a valency of two. Compare with **MANGANIC**.

mange /meɪn(d)ʒ/ ▶ noun [mass noun] a skin disease of mammals caused by parasitic mites and occasionally communicable to humans. It typically causes severe itching, hair loss, and the formation of scabs and lesions. See also **DEMODECTIC MANGE**, **SARCOPTIC MANGE**.
– ORIGIN late Middle English: from Old French *mangeue*, from *mangier* 'eat', from Latin *manducare* 'to chew'.

mangel /'maŋɡ(ə)l/ (also **mangel-wurzel** /-ˌwɔːz(ə)l/) ▶ noun another term for **MANGOLD**.

manger ▶ noun a long open box or trough for horses or cattle to eat from.
– ORIGIN Middle English: from Old French *mangeure*, based on Latin *manducat-* 'chewed' (see **MANDUCATE**).

mangetout /'mɒ̃ʒtuː, -'tuː/ ▶ noun (pl. same or **mangetouts** pronunc. same) chiefly Brit. a pea of a

variety with an edible pod, eaten when the pod is young and flat. Compare with **SUGAR SNAP**.
– ORIGIN early 19th cent.: from French, literally 'eat all'.

mangey ▶ adjective variant spelling of **MANGY**.

mangle[1] ▶ noun chiefly Brit. a machine having two or more cylinders turned by a handle, between which wet laundry is squeezed (to remove excess moisture) and pressed.
■ US a large machine for ironing sheets or other fabrics, usually when they are damp, using heated rollers.
▶ verb [with obj.] press or squeeze with a mangle.
– ORIGIN late 17th cent.: from Dutch *mangel*, from *mangelen* 'to mangle', from medieval Latin *mango*, *manga*, from Greek *manganon* 'axis, engine'.

mangle[2] ▶ verb [with obj.] severely mutilate, disfigure, or damage by cutting, tearing, or crushing: *the car was mangled almost beyond recognition* | figurative *he was mangling Bach on the piano.*
– DERIVATIVES **mangler** noun.
– ORIGIN late Middle English: from Anglo-Norman French *mahangler*, apparently a frequentative of *mahaignier* 'maim'.

mango ▶ noun (pl. **-oes** or **-os**) **1** a fleshy yellowish-red tropical fruit which is eaten ripe or used green for pickles or chutneys.
2 (also **mango tree**) the evergreen Indian tree which bears this fruit, widely cultivated in the tropics.
● *Mangifera indica*, family Anacardiaceae; many local varieties.
3 a tropical American hummingbird that typically has green plumage with purple feathers on the wings, tail, or head.
● Genus *Anthracothorax*, family Trochilidae: several species, e.g. the **Jamaican mango** (*A. mango*), which has a dark bronze-green back, purple head, and black underside.
– ORIGIN late 16th cent.: from Portuguese *manga*, from a Dravidian language.

mangold /'maŋɡəʊld/ ▶ noun a beet of a variety with a large root, cultivated as stockfeed.
● *Beta vulgaris* subsp. *crassa*, family Chenopodiaceae.
– ORIGIN mid 19th cent.: from German *Mangoldwurzel*, from *Mangold* 'beet' + *Wurzel* 'root'.

mangonel /'maŋɡən(ə)l/ ▶ noun historical a military device for throwing stones and other missiles.
– ORIGIN Middle English: from Old French *mangonel(le)*, from medieval Latin *manganellus*, diminutive of late Latin *manganum*, from Greek *manganon* 'axis of a pulley'.

mangosteen /'maŋɡəstiːn/ ▶ noun **1** a tropical fruit with sweet juicy white segments of flesh inside a thick reddish-brown rind.
2 the slow-growing Malaysian tree which bears this fruit.
● *Garcinia mangostana*, family Guttiferae.
– ORIGIN late 16th cent.: from Malay *manggustan*, dialect variant of *manggis*.

mangrove ▶ noun a tree or shrub which grows in muddy, chiefly tropical coastal swamps which are inundated at high tide. Mangroves typically have numerous tangled roots above ground and form dense thickets.
● Genera in several families, in particular *Rhizophora* and related genera (family Rhizophoraceae), and *Avicennia* (family Verbenaceae or Avicenniaceae).
■ (also **mangrove swamp**) a tidal swamp which is dominated by mangroves and associated vegetation.
– ORIGIN early 17th cent.: probably from Portuguese *mangue*, Spanish *mangle*, from Taino. The change in the ending was due to association with **GROVE**.

mangy (also **mangey**) ▶ adjective (**mangier**, **mangiest**) having mange.
■ in poor condition; shabby: *a girl in a mangy fur coat.*
– DERIVATIVES **manginess** noun.

manhandle ▶ verb [with obj.] move (a heavy object) by hand with great effort: *men used to manhandle the piano down the stairs.*
■ handle (someone) roughly by dragging or pushing.

Manhattan an island near the mouth of the Hudson River forming part of the city of New York. The site of the original Dutch settlement of New Amsterdam, it is now a borough containing the commercial and cultural centre of New York City.
– ORIGIN named after the Algonquin tribe from whom the Dutch settlers claimed to have bought the island in 1626.

manhattan ▶ noun a cocktail made of vermouth and a spirit, typically whisky, sometimes with a dash of bitters.

Manhattan Project the code name for the American project set up in 1942 to develop an atom bomb. The project culminated in 1945 with the detonation of the first nuclear weapon, at White Sands in New Mexico.

manhole ▶ noun a small covered opening in a floor, pavement, or other surface to allow a person to enter, especially an opening in a pavement leading to a sewer.

manhood ▶ noun [mass noun] the state or period of being a man rather than a child: *boys in the process of growing to manhood.*
■ men, especially those of a country, regarded collectively: *Germany had lost the best of her young manhood.* ■ archaic the condition of being human: *the unity of Godhead and manhood in Christ.* ■ qualities traditionally associated with men, such as courage, strength, and sexual potency: *we drank to prove our manhood.* ■ (**one's manhood**) informal used euphemistically to refer to a man's penis.

man-hour ▶ noun an hour regarded in terms of the amount of work that can be done by one person within this period.

manhunt ▶ noun an organized search for a person, especially a criminal.

mania ▶ noun [mass noun] mental illness marked by periods of great excitement or euphoria, delusions, and overactivity.
■ [count noun] an excessive enthusiasm or desire; an obsession: *he had a mania for automobiles.*
– ORIGIN late Middle English: via late Latin from Greek, literally 'madness', from *mainesthai* 'be mad'.

-mania ▶ combining form Psychology denoting a specified type of mental abnormality or obsession: *kleptomania.*
■ denoting extreme enthusiasm or admiration: *Beatlemania.*
– DERIVATIVES **-maniac** combining form in corresponding nouns.

maniac /ˈmeɪnɪak/ ▶ noun a person exhibiting extreme symptoms of wild behaviour, especially when violent and dangerous: *a homicidal maniac.*
■ [with adj. or noun modifier] informal an obsessive enthusiast: *a religious maniac.* ■ Psychiatry, archaic a person suffering from mania.
– DERIVATIVES **maniacal** /məˈnʌɪək(ə)l/ adjective, **maniacally** /məˈnʌɪək(ə)li/ adverb.
– ORIGIN early 16th cent. (as an adjective): via late Latin from late Greek *maniakos*, from *mania* (see **MANIA**).

manic ▶ adjective showing wild and apparently deranged excitement and energy: *his manic enthusiasm* | *a manic grin.*
■ frenetically busy; frantic: *the pace is utterly manic.* ■ Psychiatry relating to or affected by mania: *the manic interludes in depression.*
– DERIVATIVES **manically** adverb.

Manicaland /məˈniːkələnd/ a gold-mining province of eastern Zimbabwe; capital, Mutare.

manic depression ▶ noun [mass noun] a mental disorder marked by alternating periods of elation and depression.
– DERIVATIVES **manic-depressive** adjective & noun.

Manichaean /ˌmanɪˈkiːən/ (also **Manichean**) ▶ adjective chiefly historical of or relating to Manichaeism.
■ of or characterized by dualistic contrast or conflict between opposites.
▶ noun an adherent of Manichaeism.
– DERIVATIVES **Manichaeanism** noun.

Manichaeism /ˌmanɪˈkiːɪz(ə)m/ (also **Manicheism**) ▶ noun [mass noun] a dualistic religious system with Christian, Gnostic, and pagan elements, founded in Persia in the 3rd century by Manes (*c.*216–*c.*276). The system was based on a supposed primeval conflict between light and darkness. It spread widely in the Roman Empire and in Asia, and survived in Chinese Turkestan until the 13th century.
■ religious or philosophical dualism.
– ORIGIN early 17th cent.: from late Latin *Manichaeus* (from the name *Manes*: see above) + **-ISM**.

Manichee /ˈmanɪkiː/ ▶ noun & adjective archaic term for **MANICHAEAN**.
– ORIGIN Middle English: from late Latin *Manichaei*, plural of *Manichaeus* (see **MANICHAEISM**).

manicotti /ˌmanɪˈkɒti/ ▶ plural noun large tubular pasta shapes.
– ORIGIN Italian, plural of *manicotto* 'muff'.

manicou /ˈmanɪkuː/ ▶ noun W. Indian an opossum.
● Several species in the family Didelphidae, especially in the genera *Didelphis* and *Marmosa*.
– ORIGIN from an American Indian word.

manicure ▶ noun a cosmetic treatment of the hands involving cutting, shaping, and often painting of the nails, removal of the cuticles, and softening of the skin.
▶ verb [with obj.] give a manicure to.
■ [usu. as adj. **manicured**] trim neatly: *manicured lawns.*
– ORIGIN late 19th cent.: from French, from Latin *manus* 'hand' + *cura* 'care'.

manicurist ▶ noun a person who performs manicures professionally.

manifest¹ ▶ adjective clear or obvious to the eye or mind: *her manifest charm and proven ability.*
▶ verb [with obj.] display or show (a quality or feeling) by one's acts or appearance; demonstrate: *Lizzy manifested signs of severe depression.*
■ (often **be manifested in**) be evidence of; prove: *bad industrial relations are often manifested in disputes and strikes.* ■ [no obj.] (of an ailment) become apparent through the appearance of symptoms: *a disorder that usually manifests in middle age.* ■ [no obj.] (of a ghost or spirit) appear: *one deity manifested in the form of a bird.*
– DERIVATIVES **manifestly** adverb.
– ORIGIN late Middle English: via Old French from Latin *manifestus.*

manifest² ▶ noun a document giving comprehensive details of a ship and her cargo and other contents, passengers, and crew for the use of customs officers.
■ a list of passengers or cargo in an aircraft. ■ a list of the wagons forming a freight train.
▶ verb [with obj.] record in such a document: *every passenger is manifested at the point of departure.*
– ORIGIN mid 16th cent. (denoting a manifestation): from Italian *manifesto* (see **MANIFESTO**). The current sense dates from the early 17th cent.

manifestation ▶ noun an event, action, or object that clearly shows or embodies something, especially a theory or an abstract idea: *the first obvious manifestations of global warming.*
■ [mass noun] the action or fact of showing something in such a way: *the manifestation of anxiety over disease.* ■ a symptom or sign of an ailment: *a characteristic manifestation of Wilson's disease.* ■ a version or incarnation of something or someone: *the butterfly was one of the many manifestations of the Goddess.* ■ an appearance of a ghost or spirit.
– ORIGIN late Middle English: from late Latin *manifestatio(n-)*, from the verb *manifestare* 'make public'.

manifest destiny ▶ noun [mass noun] the 19th-century doctrine or belief that the expansion of the United States throughout the American continents was both justified and inevitable.

manifesto ▶ noun (pl. **-os**) a public declaration of policy and aims, especially one issued before an election by a political party or candidate.
– ORIGIN mid 17th cent.: from Italian, from *manifestare*, from Latin, 'make public', from *manifestus* 'obvious' (see **MANIFEST¹**).

manifold /ˈmanɪfəʊld/ ▶ adjective formal or poetic/literary many and various: *the implications of this decision were manifold.*
■ having many different forms or elements: *the appeal of the crusade was manifold.*
▶ noun 1 [often with modifier] a pipe or chamber branching into several openings.
■ (in an internal-combustion engine) the part conveying air and fuel from the carburettor to the cylinders or that leading from the cylinders to the exhaust pipe: *the exhaust manifold.*
2 technical something with many different parts or forms, in particular:
■ Mathematics a collection of points forming a certain kind of set, such as those of a topologically closed surface or an analogue of this in three or more dimensions. ■ (in Kantian philosophy) the sum of the particulars furnished by sense before they have been unified by the synthesis of the understanding.
– DERIVATIVES **manifoldly** adverb, **manifoldness** noun.
– ORIGIN Old English *manigfeald*; current noun senses date from the mid 19th cent.

manifold pressure ▶ noun [mass noun] Aeronautics the pressure in the intake manifold of an internal-combustion engine.

manikin (also **mannikin**) ▶ noun 1 a person who is very small, especially one not otherwise abnormal or deformed.
2 a jointed model of the human body, used in anatomy or as an artist's lay figure.
– ORIGIN mid 16th cent.: from Dutch *manneken*, diminutive of *man* 'man'.

Manila¹ /məˈnɪlə/ the capital and chief port of the Philippines, on the island of Luzon; pop. 1,599,000 (1990).

Manila² /məˈnɪlə/ (also **Manilla**) ▶ noun 1 (also **Manila hemp**) [mass noun] the strong fibre of a Philippine plant, used for rope, matting, paper, etc.: [as modifier] *Manila rope.*
● The plant is *Musa textilis*, family Musaceae.
■ (also **Manila paper**) strong brown paper, originally made from Manila hemp.
2 [often as modifier] a cigar or cheroot made in Manila.
– ORIGIN late 17th cent. (as an adjective meaning 'from Manila'): from **MANILA¹**.

manilla /məˈnɪlə/ ▶ noun a metal bracelet used by some African peoples as a medium of exchange.
– ORIGIN mid 16th cent.: from Spanish, based on Latin *manicula* (see **MANACLE**).

manille /məˈnɪl/ ▶ noun (in the card games ombre and quadrille) the second-best trump or honour.
– ORIGIN late 17th cent.: from French (perhaps influenced by *main* 'hand'), from *malille*, also used as a term in card games, from Spanish *malilla*, diminutive of *mala* feminine of *malo* 'bad'. Although 'bad' because of its low value, the card acquires power when its suit is trumps.

manioc /ˈmanɪɒk/ ▶ noun another term for **CASSAVA**.
– ORIGIN mid 16th cent.: from French, from Tupi *manioca.*

maniple /ˈmanɪp(ə)l/ ▶ noun 1 a subdivision of a Roman legion, containing either 120 or 60 men.
2 (in church use) a vestment formerly worn by a priest celebrating the Eucharist, consisting of a strip hanging from the left arm.
– DERIVATIVES **manipular** adjective (only in sense 1).
– ORIGIN late Middle English (in sense 2): from Old French *maniple*, from Latin *manipulus* 'handful, troop', from *manus* 'hand' + the base of *plere* 'fill'.

manipulate /məˈnɪpjʊleɪt/ ▶ verb [with obj.] 1 handle or control (a tool, mechanism, etc.), typically in a skilful manner: *he manipulated the dials of the set.*
■ alter, edit, or move (text or data) on a computer. ■ examine or treat (a part of the body) by feeling or moving it with the hand: *a system of healing based on manipulating the ligaments of the spine.*
2 control or influence (a person or situation) cleverly, unfairly, or unscrupulously: *the masses were deceived and manipulated by a tiny group.*
■ alter (data) or present (statistics) so as to mislead.
– DERIVATIVES **manipulability** noun, **manipulable** adjective, **manipulatable** adjective, **manipulation** noun, **manipulator** noun, **manipulatory** adjective.
– ORIGIN early 19th cent.: back-formation from earlier *manipulation*, from Latin *manipulus* 'handful'.

manipulative ▶ adjective 1 characterized by unscrupulous control of a situation or person: *she was sly, selfish, and manipulative.*
2 of or relating to manipulation of an object or part of the body: *a manipulative skill.*
– DERIVATIVES **manipulatively** adverb, **manipulativeness** noun.

Manipur /ˌmʌnɪˈpʊə/ a small state in the far east of India, east of Assam, on the border with Burma (Myanmar); capital, Imphal.

Manipuri /ˌmʌnɪˈpʊəri/ ▶ noun (pl. same or **Manipuris**) 1 a native or inhabitant of Manipur.
2 [mass noun] the official language of Manipur, which belongs to the Tibeto-Burman family.
▶ adjective of or relating to the people of Manipur or their language.

Manit. ▶ abbreviation for Manitoba.

Manitoba /ˌmanɪˈtəʊbə/ a province of central Canada, with a coastline on Hudson Bay; pop. 1,093,200 (1991); capital, Winnipeg. The area was part of Rupert's Land from 1670 until it was transferred to Canada by the Hudson's Bay Company and became a province in 1870.
– DERIVATIVES **Manitoban** adjective & noun.

manitou /ˈmanɪtuː/ ▶ noun (among certain Algonquian North American Indians) a good or evil spirit as an object of reverence.

– ORIGIN late 17th cent.: via French from an Algonquian language.

mankind ▶ **noun** [mass noun] **1** human beings considered collectively; the human race: *research for the benefit of all mankind.*
2 archaic men, as distinct from women.

USAGE On the use of **mankind** versus that of **humankind** or **the human race**, see **usage** at **MAN**.

manky ▶ **adjective** (**mankier**, **mankiest**) Brit. informal **1** inferior; worthless: *he wanted recruits for his manky bee-keeping society.*
2 grimy; dirty: *the man in the manky mackintosh.*
– ORIGIN 1950s: probably from obsolete *mank* 'mutilated, defective', from Old French *manque*, from Latin *mancus* 'maimed'.

Manley, Michael (Norman) (1923–97), Jamaican statesman, Prime Minister 1972–80 and 1989–92.

manlike ▶ **adjective** **1** resembling a human being: *a manlike creature.*
2 (of a woman) having an appearance or qualities associated with men.

manly ▶ **adjective** (**manlier**, **manliest**) having or denoting those good qualities traditionally associated with men, such as courage, strength, and frankness: *an open and manly countenance.*
■ (of an activity) befitting a man: *honest, manly sports.*
– DERIVATIVES **manliness** noun.

man-made ▶ **adjective** made or caused by human beings (as opposed to occurring or being made naturally); artificial: *a man-made lake.*

Mann, Thomas (1875–1955), German novelist and essayist. The role and character of the artist in relation to society is a constant theme in his works. Notable works: *Buddenbrooks* (1901), *Death in Venice* (1912), and *Dr Faustus* (1947). Nobel Prize for Literature (1929).

manna ▶ **noun** [mass noun] (in the Bible) the substance miraculously supplied as food to the Israelites in the wilderness (Exod. 16).
■ an unexpected or gratuitous benefit: *the cakes were* ***manna from heaven*** | *a major aircraft accident is manna to lawyers.* ■ (in Christian contexts) spiritual nourishment, especially the Eucharist. ■ a sweet gum obtained from the manna ash or a similar plant, used as a mild laxative.
– ORIGIN Old English, via late Latin and Greek from Aramaic *mannā*, from Hebrew *mān*, corresponding to Arabic *mann*, denoting an exudation of the tamarisk *Tamarix mannifera*.

manna ash ▶ **noun** an ash tree which bears fragrant white flowers and exudes a sweet edible gum (manna) from its branches when they are damaged, native to southern Europe and south-west Asia.
● *Fraxinus ornus*, family Oleaceae.

Mannar /məˈnɑː/ an island off the NW coast of Sri Lanka, linked to India by the chain of coral islands and shoals known as Adam's Bridge.
■ a town on this island; pop. 14,000 (1981).

Mannar, Gulf of an inlet of the Indian Ocean lying between NW Sri Lanka and the southern tip of India. It lies to the south of Adam's Bridge, which separates it from the Palk Strait.

manned ▶ **adjective** (especially of an aircraft or spacecraft) having a human crew: *a manned mission to Mars.*

mannequin /ˈmanɪkɪn, -kwɪn/ ▶ **noun** a dummy used to display clothes in a shop window.
■ chiefly historical a young woman or man employed to show clothes to customers.
– ORIGIN mid 18th cent.: from French (see **MANIKIN**).

manner ▶ **noun** **1** a way in which a thing is done or happens: *taking notes in an unobtrusive manner.*
■ a style in literature or art: *a dramatic poem* ***in the manner of*** *Goethe.* ■ [mass noun] Grammar a semantic category of adverbs and adverbials which answer the question 'how?': *an adverb of manner.* ■ (**manner of**) chiefly poetic/literary a kind or sort: *what manner of man is he?*
2 a person's outward bearing or way of behaving towards others: *his arrogance and pompous manner* | *a shy and diffident manner.*
3 (**manners**) polite or well-bred social behaviour: *didn't your mother teach you any manners?*
■ social behaviour or habits: *Trevor apologized for his son's bad manners.* ■ the way a motor vehicle handles or performs.
– PHRASES **all manner of** many different kinds of: *they accuse me of all manner of evil things.* **by no manner of means** see **MEANS**. **in a manner of speaking** in some sense; so to speak. **to the manner born** naturally at ease in a specified job or situation: *she slipped into a more courtly role as if to the manner born.* [ORIGIN: with allusion to Shakespeare's *Hamlet* I. iv. 17.] ■ destined by birth to follow a custom or way of life.
– DERIVATIVES **mannerless** adjective.
– ORIGIN Middle English: from Old French *maniere*, based on Latin *manuarius* 'of the hand', from *manus* 'hand'.

mannered ▶ **adjective** **1** [in combination] behaving in a specified way: *bad-mannered* | *well-mannered.*
2 (of a writer, artist, or artistic style) marked by idiosyncratic mannerisms; artificial, stilted, and over-elaborate in delivery: *inane dialogue and mannered acting.*

mannerism ▶ **noun** **1** a habitual gesture or way of speaking or behaving; an idiosyncrasy: *learning the great man's speeches and studying his mannerisms.*
■ Psychiatry an ordinary gesture or expression that becomes abnormal through exaggeration or repetition.
2 [mass noun] excessive or self-conscious use of a distinctive style in art, literature, or music: *he seemed deliberately to be stripping his art of mannerism.*
3 (**Mannerism**) [mass noun] a style of 16th-century Italian art preceding the Baroque, characterized by unusual effects of scale, lighting, and perspective, and the use of bright, often lurid colours. It is particularly associated with the work of Pontormo, Vasari, and the later Michelangelo.
– DERIVATIVES **mannerist** noun & adjective, **manneristic** adjective.

mannerly ▶ **adjective** well-mannered; polite.
– DERIVATIVES **mannerliness** noun.

Mannheim /ˈmanhʌɪm/ an industrial port at the confluence of the Rhine and the Neckar in Baden-Württemberg, SW Germany; pop. 314,685 (1991).

mannie (also **manny**) ▶ **noun** (pl. **-ies**) informal, chiefly Scottish a boy.

mannikin ▶ **noun** **1** a small waxbill of the Old World tropics, typically having brown, black, and white plumage and popular as a cage bird. Compare with **MANAKIN**.
● Genus *Lonchura*, family Estrildidae: many species.
2 variant spelling of **MANIKIN**.

Manning, Olivia (Mary) (1908–80), English novelist. Her experiences in Bucharest, Athens, and Egypt between 1939 and 1946 formed the basis for her Balkan and Levant trilogies, written between 1960 and 1980.

mannish ▶ **adjective** derogatory (of a woman) having characteristics that are stereotypically associated with men and considered unbecoming in a woman: *a mannish, sadistic matron.*
– DERIVATIVES **mannishly** adverb, **mannishness** noun.
– ORIGIN Old English *mennisc* 'human' (see **MAN**, **-ISH**[1]). The current sense dates from late Middle English.

mannish water ▶ **noun** [mass noun] W. Indian a type of highly seasoned stew made from the head and other parts of a goat, served especially at festivals or other special occasions.
– ORIGIN traditionally served to a bridegroom on his wedding night and so named because of its association with potency.

mannitol /ˈmanɪtɒl/ ▶ **noun** [mass noun] Chemistry a colourless sweet-tasting crystalline compound which is found in many plants and is used in various foods and medical products.
● An alcohol; chem. formula: $CH_2OH(CHOH)_4CH_2OH$.
– ORIGIN late 19th cent.: from *mannite*, in the same sense, + **-OL**.

mannose /ˈmanəʊz, -s/ ▶ **noun** [mass noun] Chemistry a sugar of the hexose class which occurs as a component of many natural polysaccharides.
– ORIGIN late 19th cent.: from *mannite* 'mannitol' + **-OSE**[2].

Mann–Whitney U test (also **Mann–Whitney test**) ▶ **noun** Statistics a method of testing whether the difference between independent observations from two populations has zero median, and hence whether the populations are in fact the same.
– ORIGIN mid 20th cent.: named after Henry B. Mann (born 1905), Austrian-born American mathematician, and Donald R. Whitney (born 1915), American statistician.

manny ▶ **noun** variant spelling of **MANNIE**.

Mano /ˈmɑːnəʊ/ a river of West Africa. It rises in NW Liberia and flows to the Atlantic, forming for part of its length the boundary between Liberia and Sierra Leone.

mano-a-mano /ˌmɑːnəʊ ə ˈmɑːnəʊ, ˌmanəʊ a ˈmanəʊ/ US informal ▶ **adverb** & **adjective** hand-to-hand; man-to-man: [as adv.] *they want to settle this mano-a-mano* | [as adj.] *mano-a-mano games.*
▶ **noun** (pl. **-os**) an intense fight or contest between two adversaries; a duel: *a real courtroom mano-a-mano.*
– ORIGIN Spanish, 'hand-to-hand'.

manoeuvrable (US **maneuverable**) ▶ **adjective** (of a craft or vessel) able to be manoeuvred easily while in motion.
– DERIVATIVES **manoeuvrability** noun.

manoeuvre /məˈnuːvə/ (US **maneuver**) ▶ **noun** **1** a movement or series of moves requiring skill and care.
■ a carefully planned scheme or action, especially one involving deception: *shady financial manoeuvres.* ■ [mass noun] the fact or process of taking such action: *the economic policy provided no* ***room for manoeuvre.***
2 (**manoeuvres**) a large-scale military exercise of troops, warships, and other forces: *the Russian vessel was* ***on manoeuvres.***
▶ **verb** (**manoeuvred**, **manoeuvring**) **1** perform or cause to perform a movement or series of moves requiring skill and care: [no obj.] *the lorry was unable to manoeuvre comfortably in the narrow street* | [with obj. and adverbial of direction] *she tried to manoeuvre her trolley round people.*
2 [with obj. and adverbial] carefully guide or manipulate (someone or something) in order to achieve an end: *they were manoeuvring him into a betrayal of his countryman.*
■ [no obj.] carefully manipulate a situation to achieve an end: [as noun **manoeuvring**] *British manoeuvring for post-war influence.*
– DERIVATIVES **manoeuvrer** noun.
– ORIGIN mid 18th cent. (as a noun in the sense 'tactical movement'): from French *manœuvre* (noun), *manœuvrer* (verb), from medieval Latin *manuoperare* from Latin *manus* 'hand' + *operari* 'to work'.

man-of-war (also **man-o'-war**) ▶ **noun** (pl. **men-of-war** or **men-o'-war**) historical an armed sailing ship.
■ (also **man-of-war bird**) another term for **FRIGATE BIRD**. ■ short for **PORTUGUESE MAN-OF-WAR**.

man-of-war fish ▶ **noun** a fish of tropical oceans which is often found among the tentacles of the Portuguese man-of-war, where it sometimes browses on the host's body and tentacles.
● *Nomeus gronovii*, family Nomeidae.

manoir /ˈmanwɑː, French manwaʀ/ ▶ **noun** a large country house or manor house in France.
– ORIGIN French.

manometer /məˈnɒmɪtə/ ▶ **noun** an instrument for measuring the pressure acting on a column of fluid, especially one with a U-shaped tube of liquid in which a difference in the pressures acting in the two arms of the tube causes the liquid to reach different heights in the two arms.
– DERIVATIVES **manometric** adjective.
– ORIGIN mid 18th cent.: from French *manomètre*, from Greek *manos* 'thin' + *-mètre* '(instrument) measuring'.

ma non troppo ▶ **adverb** see **TROPPO**[1].

manor ▶ **noun** **1** (also **manor house**) a large country house with lands; the principal house of a landed estate.
■ chiefly historical (especially in England and Wales) a unit of land, originally a feudal lordship, consisting of a lord's demesne and lands rented to tenants. ■ historical (in North America) an estate held in fee farm, especially one granted by royal charter in a British colony or by the Dutch governors of what is now New York State.
2 (usu. **one's manor**) Brit. informal the district covered by a police station.
■ one's own neighbourhood or home territory: *they were the undisputed rulers of their manor.*
– DERIVATIVES **manorial** adjective.
– ORIGIN Middle English: from Anglo-Norman French *maner* 'dwelling', from Latin *manere* 'remain'.

man orchid ▶ **noun** a European orchid of calcareous grassland, the greenish-yellow flowers of which have a lip that resembles a dangling human figure.
● *Aceras anthropophorum*, family Orchidaceae.

man page ▶ noun Computing a document forming part of the online documentation of a computer system.
– ORIGIN short for *manual page*.

manpower ▶ noun [mass noun] the number of people working or available for work or service: *the police had only limited manpower.*

manqué /ˈmɒŋkeɪ/ ▶ adjective [postpositive] having failed to become what one might have been; unfulfilled: *an actor manqué.*
– ORIGIN late 18th cent.: French, past participle of *manquer* 'to lack'.

Man Ray see RAY[2].

manrope ▶ noun a rope on the side of a ship's gangway or ladder, for support in walking or climbing.

Mans, Le see LE MANS.

mansard /ˈmansɑːd, -səd/ ▶ noun (also **mansard roof**) a roof which has four sloping sides, each of which becomes steeper halfway down.
■ Brit. another term for GAMBREL. ■ a storey or apartment under a mansard roof.
– ORIGIN mid 18th cent.: from French *mansarde*, named after F. MANSART.

Mansart /ˈmɒsɑː, French mɑ̃saʁ/, François (1598–1666), French architect. He rebuilt part of the château of Blois, which incorporated the type of roof now named after him.

manse /mans/ ▶ noun the house occupied by a minister of a Scottish Presbyterian church.
– PHRASES **son** (or **daughter**) **of the manse** the child of a Scottish Presbyterian minister.
– ORIGIN late 15th cent. (denoting the principal house of an estate): from medieval Latin *mansus* 'house, dwelling', from *manere* 'remain'.

Mansell /ˈmans(ə)l/, Nigel (b.1954), English motor-racing driver. He won the Formula One world championship in 1992 and the Indycar championship in 1993.

manservant ▶ noun (pl. **menservants**) a male servant.

Mansfield, Katherine (1888–1923), New Zealand short-story writer; pseudonym of *Kathleen Mansfield Beauchamp*. Her stories range from extended impressionistic evocations of family life to short sketches.

-manship ▶ suffix (forming nouns) denoting skill in a subject or activity: *marksmanship.*

mansion ▶ noun a large, impressive house.
■ [in names] Brit. a large building or terrace divided into flats: *Carlyle Mansions.*
– ORIGIN late Middle English (denoting the chief residence of a lord): via Old French from Latin *mansio(n-)* 'place where someone stays', from *manere* 'remain'.

mansion house ▶ noun Brit. the house of a lord mayor or a landed proprietor.
■ **(the Mansion House)** the official residence of the Lord Mayor of London.

man-sized (also **man-size**) ▶ adjective of the size of a human being: *man-sized plants.*
■ big enough for a man: *chunky man-sized jumpers.*

manslaughter ▶ noun [mass noun] the crime of killing a human being without malice aforethought, or otherwise in circumstances not amounting to murder: *the defendant was convicted of manslaughter.*

Manson[1], Charles (b.1934), American cult leader. He founded a commune based on free love and complete subordination to him. In 1969 its members carried out a series of murders, including that of the American actress Sharon Tate, for which he and some followers received the death sentence (later commuted to life imprisonment).

Manson[2], Sir Patrick (1844–1922), Scottish physician, pioneer of tropical medicine. He discovered the organism responsible for elephantiasis and established that it was spread by the bite of a mosquito; he then suggested a similar role for the mosquito in spreading malaria.

mansuetude /ˈmanswɪtjuːd/ ▶ noun [mass noun] archaic meekness; gentleness.
– ORIGIN late Middle English: from Old French, or from Latin *mansuetudo*, from *mansuetus* 'gentle, tame', from *manus* 'hand' + *suetus* 'accustomed'.

manta /ˈmantə/ ▶ noun a devil ray that occurs in all tropical seas and may reach very great size. It is sometimes seen leaping high out of the water.
● *Manta birostris*, family Mobulidae.
– ORIGIN late 17th cent.: from Latin American Spanish, literally 'large blanket'.

manteau /ˈmantəʊ/ ▶ noun historical a loose gown or cloak worn by women.
– ORIGIN late 17th cent.: from French; compare with MANTUA.

Mantegna /manˈtɛnjə/, Andrea (1431–1506), Italian painter and engraver, noted especially for his frescoes.

mantel (also **mantle**) ▶ noun a mantelpiece or mantelshelf.
– ORIGIN mid 16th cent.: specialized use of MANTLE[1].

mantelet /ˈmant(ə)lɪt/ ▶ noun variant spelling of MANTLET.

Mantell /manˈtɛl/, Gideon Algernon (1790–1852), English geologist. Mantell is best known as the first person to recognize dinosaur remains as reptilian. In 1825 he published a description of the teeth of a 'giant fossil lizard' which he named *Iguanodon*.

mantelletta /ˌmantɪˈlɛtə/ ▶ noun (pl. **mantellettas** or **mantellette** /-teɪ/) a sleeveless vestment reaching to the knees, worn by cardinals, bishops, and other high-ranking Catholic ecclesiastics.
– ORIGIN mid 19th cent.: from Italian, from a diminutive of Latin *mantellum* 'mantle'.

mantelpiece (also **mantlepiece**) ▶ noun a structure of wood, marble, or stone above and around a fireplace.
■ a mantelshelf.

mantelshelf (also **mantleshelf**) ▶ noun a shelf above a fireplace.
■ Climbing a projecting shelf or ledge of rock. ■ Climbing a move for climbing on such a ledge from below by pressing down on it with the hands to raise the upper body, enabling a foot or knee to reach the ledge.
▶ verb [no obj.] Climbing perform a mantelshelf move.

manteltree ▶ noun a beam or arch across the opening of a fireplace, supporting the masonry above.

mantic /ˈmantɪk/ ▶ adjective formal of or relating to divination or prophecy.
– ORIGIN mid 19th cent.: from Greek *mantikos*, from *mantis* 'prophet'.

manticore /ˈmantɪkɔː/ ▶ noun a mythical beast typically depicted as having the body of a lion, the face of a man, and the sting of a scorpion.
– ORIGIN late Middle English: from Old French, via Latin from Greek *mantikhōras*, corrupt reading in Aristotle for *martikhoras*, from an Old Persian word meaning 'maneater'.

mantid ▶ noun another term for MANTIS.

mantilla /manˈtɪlə/ ▶ noun a lace or silk scarf worn by women over the hair and shoulders, especially in Spain.
– ORIGIN Spanish, diminutive of *manta* 'mantle'.

mantis /ˈmantɪs/ (also **praying mantis**) ▶ noun (pl. same or **mantises**) a slender predatory insect related to the cockroach. It waits motionless for prey with its large spiky forelegs folded like hands in prayer.
● Suborder Mantodea, order Dictyoptera: Mantidae and other families, and many species, including *Mantis religiosa* of southern Europe.
– ORIGIN mid 17th cent.: modern Latin, from Greek, literally 'prophet'.

mantissa /manˈtɪsə/ ▶ noun **1** Mathematics the part of a logarithm after the decimal point.
2 Computing the part of a floating-point number which represents the significant digits of that number, and which is multiplied by the base raised to the exponent to give the actual value of the number.
– ORIGIN mid 17th cent.: from Latin, literally 'makeweight', perhaps from Etruscan.

mantis shrimp ▶ noun a predatory marine crustacean with a pair of large spined front legs that resemble those of a mantis and are used for capturing prey.
● Order Stomatopoda: many species, including the European *Squilla desmaresti*.

mantle[1] ▶ noun **1** a loose sleeveless cloak or shawl, worn especially by women.
■ figurative a covering of a specified sort: *the houses were covered with a thick mantle of snow.* ■ (also **gas mantle**) a fragile mesh cover fixed round a gas jet to give an incandescent light when heated. ■ Ornithology a bird's back, scapulars, and wing coverts, especially when of a distinctive colour. ■ Zoology an outer or enclosing layer of tissue, especially (in molluscs, cirripedes, and brachiopods) a fold of skin enclosing the viscera and secreting the shell.
2 an important role or responsibility that passes from one person to another: *the second son has now assumed his father's mantle.* [ORIGIN: with allusion to the passing of Elijah's cloak (mantle) to Elisha (2 Kings 2:13).]
3 Geology the region of the earth's interior between the crust and the core, believed to consist of hot, dense silicate rocks (mainly peridotite).
■ the corresponding part of another planetary body: *the lunar mantle.*
▶ verb **1** [with obj.] poetic/literary clothe in or as if in a mantle; cloak or envelop: *heavy mists mantled the forested slopes.*
■ archaic (of blood) suffuse (the face): *a warm pink mounted to the girl's cheeks and mantled her brow.* ■ [no obj.] (of the face) glow with a blush: *her rich face mantling with emotion.* ■ [no obj.] archaic (of a liquid) become covered with a head or froth.
2 [no obj.] (of a bird of prey on the ground or on a perch) spread the wings and tail, especially so as to cover captured prey.
– ORIGIN Old English *mentel*, from Latin *mantellum* 'cloak'; reinforced in Middle English by Old French *mantel*.

mantle[2] ▶ noun variant spelling of MANTEL.

mantlepiece ▶ noun variant spelling of MANTELPIECE.

mantle plume ▶ noun see PLUME.

mantleshelf ▶ noun variant spelling of MANTELSHELF.

mantlet (also **mantelet**) ▶ noun **1** historical a woman's short, loose sleeveless cloak or shawl.
2 a bulletproof screen for a soldier.
– ORIGIN late Middle English: from Old French *mantelet*, diminutive of *mantel* 'mantle'.

mantling ▶ noun Heraldry a piece of ornamental drapery depicted issuing from a helmet and surrounding a shield. Compare with LAMBREQUIN (in sense 2).
■ [mass noun] drapery of this kind.
– ORIGIN late 16th cent.: from MANTLE[1] + -ING[1].

Mantoux test /ˈmɒtuː, ˈmantuː/ ▶ noun Medicine a test for immunity to tuberculosis using intradermal injection of tuberculin.
– ORIGIN 1930s: named after Charles *Mantoux* (1877–1947), French physician.

mantra /ˈmantrə/ ▶ noun (originally in Hinduism and Buddhism) a word or sound repeated to aid concentration in meditation.
■ a Vedic hymn. ■ a statement or slogan repeated frequently: *the environmental mantra that energy has for too long been too cheap.*
– DERIVATIVES **mantric** adjective.
– ORIGIN late 18th cent.: Sanskrit, literally 'instrument of thought', from *man* 'think'.

mantrap ▶ noun a trap for catching people, especially trespassers or poachers.

Mantua /ˈmantjʊə/ a town in Lombardy, northern Italy, on the River Mincio; pop. 54,230 (1990). Italian name MANTOVA /ˈmantovə/.
– DERIVATIVES **Mantuan** noun & adjective.

mantua /ˈmantjʊə/ ▶ noun a woman's loose gown of a kind fashionable during the 17th and 18th centuries.
– ORIGIN alteration of French *manteau*, influenced by MANTUA.

Manu /ˈmʌnuː/ the archetypal first man of Hindu mythology, survivor of the great flood and father of the human race. He is also the legendary author of one of the most famous codes of Hindu religious law, the *Manusmriti* (Laws of Manu), composed in Sanskrit and dating in its present form from the 1st century BC.

manual ▶ adjective of or done with the hands: *a manual occupation.*
■ (of a machine or device) worked by hand, not automatically or electronically: *a manual typewriter.* ■ [attrib.] using or working with the hands: *a manual labourer.*
▶ noun **1** a book of instructions, especially for operating a machine or learning a subject; a handbook: *a computer manual | a training manual.*
■ a small book: *a pocket-sized manual of the artist's*

aphorisms. ■ historical a book of the forms to be used by priests in the administration of the sacraments.
2 a thing operated or done by hand rather than automatically or electronically, in particular:
■ an organ keyboard played with the hands not the feet. ■ a vehicle with manual transmission.
– DERIVATIVES **manually** adverb.
– ORIGIN late Middle English: from Old French *manuel*, from (and later assimilated to) Latin *manualis*, from *manus* 'hand'.

manual alphabet ▶ **noun** another term for **FINGER ALPHABET**.

manubrium /məˈn(j)uːbrɪəm/ ▶ **noun** (pl. **manubria** or **manubriums**) Anatomy & Zoology a handle-shaped projection or part, in particular:
■ the broad upper part of the sternum of mammals, with which the clavicles and first ribs articulate. ■ the tube which bears the mouth of a coelenterate.
– DERIVATIVES **manubrial** adjective.
– ORIGIN mid 17th cent. (as a rare usage in the sense 'handle'): from Latin 'haft'.

manucode /ˈmanjʊkəʊd/ ▶ **noun** a bird of paradise of which the male and female have similar blue-black plumage and breed as stable pairs.
• Genus *Manucodia*, family Paradisaeidae: five species, in particular the **trumpet manucode** or trumpet bird (*M. keraudrenii*), the male of which has a loud trumpeting call.
– ORIGIN mid 19th cent.: from French, from modern Latin *manucodiata* (used in the same sense from the mid 16th to 18th cents), from Malay *manuk dewata* 'bird of the gods'.

Manueline /ˈmanjʊəlʌɪn/ ▶ **adjective** denoting a style of Portuguese architecture developed during the reign of Manuel I (1495–1521) and characterized by ornate elaborations of Gothic and Renaissance styles.

manufactory ▶ **noun** (pl. **-ies**) archaic a factory.
– ORIGIN early 17th cent. (denoting a manufactured article): from **MANUFACTURE**, on the pattern of *factory*.

manufacture ▶ **noun** [mass noun] the making of articles on a large scale using machinery: *the manufacture of armoured vehicles.*
■ [with modifier] a specified branch of industry: *the porcelain manufacture for which France became justly renowned.* ■ (**manufactures**) manufactured goods or articles: *exports and imports of manufactures.*
▶ **verb** [with obj.] **1** make (something) on a large scale using machinery: *firms who manufacture ball bearings* | [as adj. **manufacturing**] *a manufacturing company.*
■ (of a living thing) produce (a substance) naturally. ■ make or produce (something abstract) in a merely mechanical way: [as adj. **manufactured**] *manufactured love songs.*
2 invent or fabricate (evidence or a story): *claims that the entire row had been manufactured by the press.*
– DERIVATIVES **manufacturability** noun, **manufacturable** adjective, **manufacturer** noun.
– ORIGIN mid 16th cent. (denoting something made by hand): from French (re-formed by association with Latin *manu factum* 'made by hand'), from Italian *manifattura*. Sense 1 dates from the early 17th cent.

manuka /ˈmɑːnʊkə, maˈnuːkə/ ▶ **noun** a small tree with aromatic leaves which are sometimes used for tea, native to New Zealand and Tasmania.
• *Leptospermum scoparium*, family Myrtaceae.
– ORIGIN mid 19th cent.: from Maori.

manul /ˈmɑːnʊl/ ▶ **noun** another term for **PALLAS'S CAT**.
– ORIGIN late 18th cent.: apparently from Kyrgyz.

manumit /ˌmanjʊˈmɪt/ ▶ **verb** (**manumitted**, **manumitting**) [with obj.] historical release from slavery; set free.
– DERIVATIVES **manumission** noun, **manumitter** noun.
– ORIGIN late Middle English: from Latin *manumittere*, literally 'send forth from the hand', from *manus* 'hand' + *mittere* 'send'.

manure ▶ **noun** [mass noun] animal dung used for fertilizing land.
■ any compost or artificial fertilizer.
▶ **verb** [with obj.] (often **be manured**) apply manure to (land): *the ground should be well dug and manured.*
– ORIGIN late Middle English (as a verb in the sense 'cultivate (land)'): from Anglo-Norman French *mainoverer*, Old French *manouvrer* (see **MANOEUVRE**). The noun sense dates from the mid 16th cent.

manus /ˈmeɪnəs/ ▶ **noun** (pl. same) chiefly Zoology the terminal segment of a forelimb, corresponding to the hand and wrist in humans.
– ORIGIN early 19th cent.: from Latin, 'hand'.

manuscript ▶ **noun** a book, document, or piece of music written by hand rather than typed or printed: *an illuminated manuscript.*
■ an author's handwritten or typed text that has not yet been published: *several manuscripts in his own hand* | *her autobiography remained* **in manuscript**.
– ORIGIN late 16th cent.: from medieval Latin *manuscriptus*, from *manu* 'by hand' + *scriptus* 'written' (past participle of *scribere*).

manuscript paper ▶ **noun** [mass noun] paper printed with staves for writing music on.

Manutius, Aldus, see **ALDUS MANUTIUS**.

Manx ▶ **adjective** of or relating to the Isle of Man.
▶ **noun 1** [mass noun] the now extinct Celtic language formerly spoken in the Isle of Man, still used for some ceremonial purposes.
2 (**the Manx**) the Manx people collectively.
– DERIVATIVES **Manxman** noun (pl. **-men**), **Manxwoman** noun (pl. **-women**).
– ORIGIN from Old Norse, from Old Irish *Manu* 'Isle of Man' + *-skr* (equivalent of **-ISH**[1]).

Manx cat ▶ **noun** a cat of a breed having no tail or an extremely short one.

Manx Loghtan /ˈlɒxt(ə)n/ ▶ **noun** a sheep of a primitive breed with several pairs of horns and tawny red-brown wool.

Manx shearwater ▶ **noun** a dark-backed shearwater that nests on remote islands in the NE Atlantic, Mediterranean, and Hawaiian waters.
• *Puffinus puffinus*, family Procellariidae.

many ▶ **determiner, pronoun, & adjective** (**more**, **most**) a large number of: [as determiner] *many people agreed with her* | [as pronoun] *the solution to* **many of** *our problems* | *many think it is a new craze* | [as adj.] *one of my many errors.*
▶ **noun** [as plural noun **the many**] the majority of people: *music for the many.*
– PHRASES **as many** the same number of: *changing his mind for the third time in as many months.* **a good** (or **great**) **many** a large number: *a good many of us.* **have one too many** informal become slightly drunk. **how many** used to ask what a particular quantity is: *how many books did you sell?* **many a ——** a large number of: *many a good man has been destroyed by booze.* **many's the ——** used to indicate that something happens often: *many's the night he's been called out in the small hours.*
– ORIGIN Old English *manig*, of Germanic origin; related to Dutch *menig* and German *manch*.

manyatta /manˈjatə/ ▶ **noun** (among the Masai and some other African peoples) a group of huts forming a unit within a common fence.
– ORIGIN Masai.

manyfold ▶ **adverb** by many times: *the problems would be multiplied manyfold.*
▶ **adjective** involving multiplication by many times: *the manyfold increase in staffing levels.*

manyplies /ˈmɛnɪplʌɪz/ ▶ **noun** old-fashioned term for **OMASUM**.
– ORIGIN late 18th cent.: from **MANY** + *plies*, plural of **PLY**[1] (because of its many folds).

many-sided ▶ **adjective** having many sides or aspects: *the reasons for poor collaboration are complex and many-sided.*
– DERIVATIVES **many-sidedness** noun.

manzanilla /ˌmanzəˈnɪlə, -ˈniːljə/ ▶ **noun** [mass noun] a pale, very dry Spanish sherry.
– ORIGIN Spanish, literally 'chamomile' (because the flavour is said to be reminiscent of that of chamomile).

manzanita /ˌmanzəˈniːtə/ ▶ **noun** an evergreen dwarf shrub related to bearberry, native to California.
• Genus *Arctostaphylos*, family Ericaceae: several species, in particular *A. manzanita*.
– ORIGIN mid 19th cent.: from Spanish, diminutive of *manzana* 'apple'.

Manzoni /manˈzəʊni/, Alessandro (1785–1873), Italian novelist, dramatist, and poet. He is remembered chiefly as the author of the novel *I Promessi sposi* (1825–42), a historical reconstruction of 17th-century Lombardy.

Mao /maʊ/ ▶ **noun** [as modifier] denoting a jacket or suit of a plain style with a mandarin collar, associated with communist China.
– ORIGIN 1960s: by association with **MAO ZEDONG**.

Maoism ▶ **noun** [mass noun] the communist doctrines of Mao Zedong as formerly practised in China, having as a central idea permanent revolution and stressing the importance of the peasantry, of small-scale industry, and of agricultural collectivization.
– DERIVATIVES **Maoist** noun & adjective.

Maori /ˈmaʊri/ ▶ **noun** (pl. same or **Maoris**) **1** a member of the aboriginal people of New Zealand.
2 [mass noun] the Polynesian language of this people, with about 100,000 speakers.
▶ **adjective** of or relating to the Maoris or their language.

> The Maoris arrived in New Zealand as part of a series of waves of migration from Tahiti, probably from the 9th century onwards. They lost large amounts of land in the colonization of New Zealand by the British, in particular after the Maori Wars of the mid 19th century, and now number about 280,000.

– ORIGIN the name in Maori.

Maori bug ▶ **noun** NZ a large black wingless cockroach which emits an unpleasant smell when disturbed.
• *Platyzosteria novaeseelandiae*, suborder Blattodea.

Maori dog ▶ **noun** an extinct dog of Polynesian origin which was first introduced to New Zealand by the Maoris.

Maori hen ▶ **noun** New Zealand term for **WEKA**.

Maori oven ▶ **noun** NZ a traditional earthen oven in which food is cooked on heated stones.

Maoritanga /ˌmaʊrɪˈtaŋə/ ▶ **noun** [mass noun] Maori culture, traditions, and way of life.
– ORIGIN Maori.

Maori Wars a series of wars fought intermittently in 1845–8 and 1860–72 between Maoris and the colonial government of New Zealand over the enforced sale of Maori lands to Europeans, which was forbidden by the Treaty of Waitangi.

mao-tai /maʊˈtʌɪ/ ▶ **noun** [mass noun] a strong sorghum-based liquor distilled in SW China.
– ORIGIN named after a town in SW China.

Mao Zedong /ˌmaʊ dziːˈdʊŋ/ (also **Mao Tse-tung** /tseɪˈtʊŋ/) (1893–1976), Chinese statesman, chairman of the Communist Party of the Chinese People's Republic 1949–76 and head of state 1949–59.

> A co-founder of the Chinese Communist Party in 1921 and its effective leader from the time of the Long March (1934–5), he eventually defeated both the occupying Japanese and rival Kuomintang nationalist forces to create the People's Republic of China in 1949, becoming its first head of state. At first Mao followed the Soviet Communist model, but from 1956 he introduced his own measures, such as the brief period of freedom of expression known as Hundred Flowers and the economically disastrous Great Leap Forward (1958–60). Despite having resigned as head of state Mao instigated the Cultural Revolution (1966–8), during which he became the focus of a personality cult.

map ▶ **noun 1** a diagrammatic representation of an area of land or sea showing physical features, cities, roads, etc.: *a street map* | figurative *expansion of the service sector is reshaping the map of employment.*
■ a two-dimensional representation of the positions of stars or other astronomical objects. ■ a diagram or collection of data showing the spatial arrangement or distribution of something over an area: *an electron density map.* ■ Biology a representation of the sequence of genes on a chromosome or of bases in a DNA or RNA molecule. ■ Mathematics another term for **MAPPING**.
2 informal, dated a person's face.
▶ **verb** (**mapped**, **mapping**) [with obj.] represent (an area) on a map; make a map of: *inaccessible parts will be mapped from the air.*
■ record in detail the spatial distribution of (something): *the project to map the human genome.* ■ [with obj. and adverbial] associate (a group of elements or qualities) with an equivalent group, according to a particular formula or model: *the transformational rules map deep structures into surface structures.* ■ Mathematics associate each element of (a set) with an element of another set. ■ [no obj., with adverbial] be associated or linked to something: *it is not obvious that the subprocesses of language will map on to individual brain areas.*
– PHRASES **off the map** (of a place) very distant or remote: *just a hick town, right off the map.* **put something on the map** bring something to prominence: *the exhibition put Cubism on the map.* **wipe something off the map** obliterate something totally.
– DERIVATIVES **mapless** adjective, **mappable** adjective, **mapper** noun.

– ORIGIN early 16th cent.: from medieval Latin *mappa mundi*, literally 'sheet of the world', from Latin *mappa* 'sheet, napkin' + *mundi* 'of the world' (genitive of *mundus*).

▶ **map something out** plan a route or course of action in detail: *I mapped out a route over familiar country near home.*

map butterfly ▶ **noun** a butterfly that has boldly patterned wings of cream, brown, and sometimes orange-red, crossed by lines which are said to give it a map-like appearance.
● Genera *Cyrestis* and *Araschnia*, subfamily Nymphalinae, family Nymphalidae.

mapepire /'mapɛ,pii:, 'mapɪ,pɪə/ ▶ **noun** [usu. with modifier] W. Indian a snake.
– ORIGIN alteration of Carib *matapi*.

maple ▶ **noun** a tree or shrub with lobed leaves, winged fruits, and colourful autumn foliage, grown as an ornamental or for its timber or syrupy sap.
● Genus *Acer*, family Aceraceae: many species, including the common European **field maple** (*A. campestre*), the North American **sugar maple** (*A. saccharum*), and the **Japanese maple** (*A. palmatum*), which has many cultivars.
– ORIGIN Old English *mapel* (as the first element of *mapeltrēow*, *mapulder* 'maple tree'); used as an independent word from Middle English.

maple leaf ▶ **noun** the leaf of the maple, used as an emblem of Canada.

maple sugar ▶ **noun** [mass noun] N. Amer. sugar produced by evaporating the sap of certain maples, especially the sugar maple.

maple syrup ▶ **noun** [mass noun] syrup produced from the sap of certain maples, especially the sugar maple.

map-maker ▶ **noun** a cartographer.
– DERIVATIVES **map-making** noun.

Mappa Mundi /,mapə 'mʊndi/ a famous 13th-century map of the world, now in Hereford cathedral, England. The map is round and typical of similar maps of the time in that it depicts Jerusalem at its centre.
– ORIGIN from medieval Latin, literally 'sheet of the world'.

mappemonde /map'məʊnd/ ▶ **noun** a medieval map of the world.
– ORIGIN late Middle English: from Old French, from medieval Latin (see **MAPPA MUNDI**).

mapping ▶ **noun** Mathematics & Linguistics an operation that associates each element of a given set (the domain) with one or more elements of a second set (the range).

map projection ▶ **noun** see **PROJECTION** (sense 6).

map reference ▶ **noun** a set of numbers and letters specifying a location as represented on a map.

map turtle ▶ **noun** a small North American freshwater turtle with bold patterns on the shell and head.
● Genus *Graptemys*, family Emydidae: several species, in particular *G. geographica.*

Mapuche /ma'pʊtʃi/ ▶ **noun** (pl. same or **Mapuches**)
1 a member of an American Indian people of central Chile and adjacent parts of Argentina, noted for their resistance to colonial Spanish and later Chilean domination.
2 [mass noun] the Araucanian language of this people, with about 400,000 speakers.
▶ **adjective** relating to or denoting this people or their language.
– ORIGIN the name in Mapuche, from *mapu* 'land' + *che* 'people'.

Maputo /mə'puːtəʊ, -tu:/ the capital and chief port of Mozambique, on the Indian Ocean in the south of the country; pop. 1,098,000 (1991). Founded as a Portuguese fortress in the late 18th century, it became the capital of Mozambique in 1907. Former name (until 1976) **LOURENÇO MARQUES**.

maquette /ma'kɛt/ ▶ **noun** a sculptor's small preliminary model or sketch.
– ORIGIN early 20th cent.: from French, from Italian *machietta*, diminutive of *macchia* 'spot'.

maquila /mə'kiːlə/ ▶ **noun** another term for **MAQUILADORA.**

maquiladora /,makɪlə'dɔːrə/ ▶ **noun** a factory in Mexico run by a foreign company and exporting its products to the country of that company.
– ORIGIN Mexican Spanish, from *maquilar* 'assemble'.

maquillage /,makɪ'jɑːʒ/ ▶ **noun** [mass noun] make-up; cosmetics.
– ORIGIN French, from *maquiller* 'to make up', from Old French *masquiller* 'to stain'.

maquis /ma'kiː, French maki/ ▶ **noun** (pl. same)
1 (**the Maquis**) the French resistance movement during the German occupation (1940–5).
■ a member of this movement.
2 [mass noun] dense scrub vegetation consisting of hardy evergreen shrubs and small trees, characteristic of coastal regions in the Mediterranean.
– ORIGIN early 19th cent. (in sense 2): from French, 'brushwood', from Corsican Italian *macchia*.

maquisard /,makɪ'zɑː, French makizar/ ▶ **noun** a member of the Maquis.

Mar. ▶ **abbreviation for** March.

mar ▶ **verb** (**marred, marring**) [with obj.] impair the appearance of; disfigure: *no wrinkles marred her face.*
■ impair the quality of; spoil: *violence marred a number of New Year celebrations.*
– ORIGIN Old English *merran* 'hinder, damage', of Germanic origin; probably related to Dutch *marren* 'loiter'.

mara /'mɑːrə/ ▶ **noun** a burrowing hare-like cavy with long hindlimbs and greyish fur, native to South America.
● Genus *Dolichotis*, family Caviidae: two species.
– ORIGIN mid 19th cent.: from American Spanish *mará.*

marabou /'marəbuː/ ▶ **noun** (also **marabou stork**) a large African stork with a massive bill and large neck pouch, which feeds mainly by scavenging.
● *Leptoptilos crumeniferus*, family Ciconiidae.
■ [mass noun] down from the wing or tail of the marabou used as a trimming for hats or clothing.
– ORIGIN early 19th cent.: from French, from Arabic *murābiṭ* 'holy man' (see also **MARABOUT**), the stork being regarded as holy.

marabout /'marəbuːt/ ▶ **noun** a Muslim hermit or monk, especially in North Africa.
■ a shrine marking the burial place of a Muslim hermit or monk.
– ORIGIN early 17th cent.: via French and Portuguese from Arabic *murābiṭ* 'holy man'.

marabunta /,marə'bʌntə/ ▶ **noun** W. Indian a social wasp.
– ORIGIN late 19th cent.: a local word in Guyana.

maraca /mə'rakə/ ▶ **noun** a hollow club-like gourd or gourd-shaped container filled with beans, pebbles, or similar objects, shaken as a percussion instrument, usually in pairs, in Latin American music.
– ORIGIN early 17th cent.: from Portuguese *maracá*, from Tupi.

Maracaibo /,marə'kaɪbəʊ/ a city and port in NW Venezuela, situated on the channel linking the Gulf of Venezuela with Lake Maracaibo; pop. 1,400,640 (1991).

Maracaibo, Lake a large lake in NW Venezuela, linked by a narrow channel to the Gulf of Venezuela and the Caribbean Sea.

Maradona /,marə'dɒnə/, Diego (Armando) (b.1960), Argentinian footballer. He captained the Argentina team that won the World Cup in 1986, arousing controversy when his apparent handball scored a goal in the quarter-final match against England.

marae /mə'rʌɪ/ ▶ **noun** (pl. same) **1** the courtyard of a Maori meeting house, especially as a social or ceremonial forum.
2 historical a Polynesian sacrificial altar or sacred enclosure.
– ORIGIN of Polynesian origin.

maraging steel /'mɑːreɪdʒɪŋ/ ▶ **noun** [mass noun] a steel alloy, containing up to 25 per cent nickel and other metals, strengthened by a process of slow cooling and age hardening.
– ORIGIN 1960s: *maraging* from *mar-* (abbreviation of **MARTENSITE**, because the process involves conversion of austenite to martensite) + *aging* from the verb **AGE**.

Maramba /mə'rambə/ a city in southern Zambia, about 5 km (3 miles) from the Zambezi River and the Victoria Falls; pop. 94,640 (1987). Formerly called Livingstone in honour of the explorer David Livingstone, it was the capital of Northern Rhodesia from 1911 until Lusaka became capital in 1935.

Maranhão /,marə'njaʊ/ a state of NE Brazil, on the Atlantic coast; capital, São Luís.

Marañón /,marə'njɒn/ a river of northern Peru, which rises in the Andes and forms one of the principal headwaters of the Amazon.

maranta /mə'rantə/ ▶ **noun** a tropical American plant of a genus which includes the prayer plant and the arrowroot.
● Genus *Maranta*, family Marantaceae.
■ a calathea.
– ORIGIN modern Latin, named after Bartollomeo *Maranta*, 16th-cent. Italian herbalist.

marari /ma'rari/ ▶ **noun** NZ the butterfish of New Zealand (*Odax pullus*).
– ORIGIN from Maori.

maraschino /,marə'skiːnəʊ, -'ʃiːnəʊ/ ▶ **noun** (pl. **-os**) [mass noun] a strong, sweet liqueur made from small black Dalmatian cherries.
■ [count noun] a maraschino cherry.
– ORIGIN Italian, from *marasca* (the name of the cherry), from *amaro* 'bitter', from Latin *amarus.*

maraschino cherry ▶ **noun** a cherry preserved in maraschino or maraschino-flavoured syrup.

marasmus /mə'razməs/ ▶ **noun** [mass noun] Medicine undernourishment causing a child's weight to be significantly too low for their age (e.g. below 75 per cent or below 60 per cent of normal).
– DERIVATIVES **marasmic** adjective.
– ORIGIN mid 17th cent.: modern Latin, from Greek *marasmos* 'withering', from *marainein* 'wither'.

Marat /'mara:, French maʀa/, Jean Paul (1743–93), French revolutionary and journalist. A virulent critic of the moderate Girondists, he was instrumental (with Danton and Robespierre) in their fall from power in 1793.

Maratha /mə'rɑːtə, -'ratə/ (also **Mahratta**) ▶ **noun** a member of the princely and military castes of the former Hindu kingdom of Maharashtra in central India. The Marathas rose in rebellion against the Muslim Moguls and in 1674 established their own kingdom under the leadership of Shivaji. They came to dominate southern and central India but were later subdued by the British.
– ORIGIN via Hindi from Sanskrit *Mahārāṣṭra* 'great kingdom'.

Marathi /mə'rɑːti, -'rati/ (also **Mahratti**) ▶ **noun** [mass noun] the Indic language of the Marathas, spoken by about 60 million people in Maharashtra and elsewhere.

marathon ▶ **noun** a long-distance running race, strictly one of 26 miles 385 yards (42.195 km).
■ [usu. with modifier] a long-lasting or difficult task or operation of a specified kind: *the last leg of an interview marathon which began this summer.* ■ [as modifier] of great duration or distance; very long: *embarking on a marathon UK tour.*
– DERIVATIVES **marathoner** noun.
– ORIGIN late 19th cent.: from *Marathōn* in Greece, the scene of a victory over the Persians in 490 BC; the modern race is based on the tradition that a messenger ran from Marathon to Athens (22 miles) with the news. The original account by Herodotus told of the messenger Pheidippides running 150 miles from Athens to Sparta before the battle, seeking help.

maraud /mə'rɔːd/ ▶ **verb** [no obj.] [often as adj. **marauding**] go about in search of things to steal or people to attack: *marauding gangs of looters.*
■ [with obj.] raid and plunder (a place).
– DERIVATIVES **marauder** noun.
– ORIGIN late 17th cent.: from French *marauder*, from *maraud* 'rogue'.

maravedi /,marə'veɪdi/ ▶ **noun** (pl. **maravedis**) a medieval Spanish copper coin and monetary unit.
– ORIGIN Spanish, from Arabic *murābiṭīn* 'holy men', a name applied to the North African Berber rulers of Muslim Spain, from the late 11th cent. to 1145.

Marbella /maː'beɪjə/ a resort town on the Costa del Sol of southern Spain, in Andalusia; pop. 80,645 (1991).

marble ▶ **noun** **1** [mass noun] a hard crystalline metamorphic form of limestone, typically white with mottlings or streaks of colour, which is capable of taking a polish and is used in sculpture and architecture.
■ used in similes and comparisons with reference to the smoothness, hardness, or colour of marble: *her shoulders were as white as marble.* ■ [count noun] a marble sculpture.

m

2 a small ball of coloured glass or similar material used as a toy.
■**(marbles)** [treated as sing.] a game in which such balls are rolled along the ground.
3 (**one's marbles**) informal one's mental faculties: *I thought she'd lost her marbles, asking a question like that.*
▶ **verb** [with obj.] stain or streak (something) so that it looks like variegated marble: *the low stone walls were marbled with moss and lichen.*
– DERIVATIVES **marbler** noun, **marbly** adjective.
– ORIGIN Middle English: via Old French (variant of *marbre*), from Latin *marmor*, from Greek *marmaros* 'shining stone', associated with *marmairein* 'to shine'.

Marble Arch a large arch with three gateways at the NE corner of Hyde Park in London. Designed by John Nash, it was erected in 1827 in front of Buckingham Palace and moved in 1851 to its present site.

marble cake ▶ noun a cake with a mottled appearance, made of light and dark sponge.

marbled ▶ adjective (especially of paper or the edges of a book) having a streaked and patterned appearance like that of variegated marble.
■(of meat) streaked with alternating layers or swirls of lean and fat.

marbled polecat ▶ noun a Eurasian polecat which has a black coat with white or yellow markings.
● *Vormela peregusna*, family Mustelidae.

marbled white ▶ noun a white European butterfly with black markings which lives in rough grassland.
● Genus *Melanargia*, subfamily Satyrinae, family Nymphalidae: several species, including the common *M. galathea*.

marble gall ▶ noun a hard spherical gall which forms on the common oak in response to the developing larva of a gall wasp.
● The wasp is *Andricus kollari*, family Cynipidae.

marbleize (also **-ise**) ▶ verb [with obj.] give a marble-like variegated finish to (an object or material): [as adj. **marbleized**] *an old financial ledger with a marbleized cover.*

marbling ▶ noun [mass noun] colouring or marking that resembles marble, especially as a decorative finish for interior walls.
■streaks of fat in lean meat.

Marburg /ˈmɑːbɔːg, German ˈmaːrbʊrk/ **1** a city in the state of Hesse in west central Germany; pop. 71,358 (1989). It was the scene in 1529 of a debate between German and Swiss theologians, notably Martin Luther and Ulrich Zwingli, on the doctrine of consubstantiation.
2 German name for **MARIBOR**.

Marburg disease ▶ noun [mass noun] an acute, often fatal, form of haemorrhagic fever. It is caused by a filovirus (**Marburg virus**) which normally lives in African monkeys.

marc ▶ noun [mass noun] the refuse of grapes or other fruit that have been pressed for winemaking.
■an alcoholic spirit distilled from this.
– ORIGIN early 17th cent.: from French, from *marcher* in the early sense 'to tread or trample'.

Marcan /ˈmɑːk(ə)n/ ▶ adjective of or relating to St Mark or the Gospel ascribed to him.

marcasite /ˈmɑːkəsaɪt, -ziːt/ ▶ noun a semi-precious stone consisting of iron pyrites.
■[mass noun] a bronze-yellow mineral consisting of iron disulphide but differing from pyrite in typically forming aggregates of tabular crystals. ■ a piece of polished steel or a similar metal cut as a gem.
– ORIGIN late Middle English: from medieval Latin *marcasita*, from Arabic *marḳašīta*, from Persian.

marcato /mɑːˈkɑːtəʊ/ ▶ adverb & adjective Music (especially as a direction) played with emphasis.
– ORIGIN Italian, 'marked, accented', of Germanic origin.

Marceau /mɑːˈsəʊ, French marso/, Marcel (b.1923), French mime artist. He is known for appearing as the white-faced Bip, a character he developed from the French Pierrot character.

marcel /mɑːˈsɛl/ dated ▶ noun (also **marcel wave**) a deep artificial wave in the hair.
▶ verb (**marcelled**, **marcelling**) [with obj.] give such a wave to (hair).
– ORIGIN late 19th cent.: named after *Marcel* Grateau (1852–1936), the Parisian hairdresser who invented it.

marcescent /mɑːˈsɛs(ə)nt/ ▶ adjective Botany (of leaves or fronds) withering but remaining attached to the stem.
– DERIVATIVES **marcescence** noun.
– ORIGIN early 18th cent.: from Latin *marcescent-* 'beginning to wither', from *marcere* 'wither'.

March ▶ noun the third month of the year, in the northern hemisphere usually considered the first month of spring: *the work was completed in March* | [as modifier] *the March issue of the magazine.*
– ORIGIN Middle English: from an Old French dialect variant of *marz*, from Latin *Martius* (*mensis*) '(month) of Mars'.

march[1] ▶ verb [no obj., usu. with adverbial of direction] walk in a military manner with a regular measured tread: *members of the Royal British Legion marched past the Cenotaph.*
■walk or proceed quickly and with determination: *without a word she marched from the room.* ■ [with obj. and adverbial of direction] force (someone) to walk somewhere quickly: *she gripped Rachel's arm and marched her out through the doors.* ■ walk along public roads in an organized procession to protest about something: *unemployed shipyard workers marched from Jarrow to London* | *they planned to **march on** Baton Rouge.* ■ figurative (of something abstract) proceed or advance inexorably: *time marches on.*
▶ noun an act or instance of marching: *the relieving force was more than a day's march away.*
■a piece of music composed to accompany marching or with a rhythmic character suggestive of marching. ■ a procession as a protest or demonstration: *a protest march.* ■ [in sing.] figurative the progress or continuity of something abstract that is considered to be moving inexorably onwards: *Marx's theory of the inevitable march of history.*
– PHRASES **march to (the beat of) a different tune** (or **drummer**) informal consciously adopt a different approach or attitude to the majority of people; be unconventional. **on the march** marching: *the army was on the march at last.* ■ figurative making progress: *United are on the march again.*
– ORIGIN late Middle English: from French *marcher* 'to walk' (earlier 'to trample'), of uncertain origin.

march[2] ▶ noun (usu. **Marches**) a frontier or border area between two countries or territories, especially between England and Wales or (formerly) England and Scotland: *the Welsh Marches.*
■(**the Marches**) a region of east central Italy, between the Apennines and the Adriatic Sea; capital, Ancona. Italian name **MARCHE** /ˈmarke/.
▶ verb [no obj.] (**march with**) (of a country, territory, or estate) have a common frontier with.
– ORIGIN Middle English: from Old French *marche* (noun), *marchir* (verb), of Germanic origin; related to **MARK**[1].

marcher[1] ▶ noun a person taking part in a protest march.

marcher[2] ▶ noun chiefly historical an inhabitant of a frontier or border district.

marchesa /mɑːˈkeɪzə, Italian marˈkeza/ ▶ noun (pl. **marchese** /mɑːˈkeɪzɪ, Italian marˈkeze/) an Italian marchioness.
– ORIGIN Italian, feminine of **MARCHESE**.

marchese /mɑːˈkeɪzeɪ, Italian marˈkeze/ ▶ noun (pl. **marchesi** /mɑːˈkeɪzɪ, Italian marˈkezi/) an Italian marquis.
– ORIGIN Italian.

March hare ▶ noun informal a brown hare in the breeding season, noted for its leaping, boxing, and chasing in circles.
– PHRASES **(as) mad as a March hare** (of a person) completely mad or irrational; crazy.

marching order ▶ noun [mass noun] Military equipment for marching: *they stood before their Company Commander dressed in full marching order.*

marching orders ▶ plural noun instructions from a superior officer for troops to depart.
■informal a dismissal or sending off: *the ref called me over and gave me my marching orders.*

marchioness /ˌmɑːʃəˈnɛs, ˈmɑːʃ(ə)nɪs/ ▶ noun the wife or widow of a marquess.
■a woman holding the rank of marquess in her own right.
– ORIGIN late 16th cent.: from medieval Latin *marchionissa*, feminine of *marchio(n)-* 'ruler of a border territory', from *marcha* 'march' (see **MARCH**[2]).

marchpane /ˈmɑːtʃpeɪn/ ▶ noun archaic spelling of **MARZIPAN**.

march past ▶ noun chiefly Brit. a formal march by troops past a saluting point at a review.

Marciano /ˌmɑːsɪˈɑːnəʊ/, Rocky (1923–69), American boxer; born *Rocco Francis Marchegiano*. He became world heavyweight champion in 1952 and successfully defended his title six times until he retired, undefeated, in 1956.

Marconi /mɑːˈkəʊni, Italian marˈkoni/, Guglielmo (1874–1937), Italian electrical engineer, the father of radio. In 1912 Marconi produced a continuously oscillating wave, essential for the transmission of sound. He went on to develop short-wave transmission over long distances. Nobel Prize for Physics (1909).

Marco Polo /ˌmɑːkəʊ ˈpəʊləʊ/ (c.1254–c.1324), Italian traveller. With his father and uncle he travelled to China and the court of Kublai Khan via central Asia (1271–75). He eventually returned home (1292–5) via Sumatra, India, and Persia.

marcottage /ˌmɑːkɒˈtɑːʒ, mɑːˈkɒtɪdʒ/ ▶ noun [mass noun] a method of propagating plants in which an incision is made below a joint or node and covered with a thick layer of moss or other substance into which new roots grow.
– ORIGIN early 20th cent.: from French, literally 'layering', from the verb *marcotter*.

Marcus Aurelius see **AURELIUS**.

Marcuse /mɑːˈkuːzə/, Herbert (1898–1979), German-born American philosopher. A member of the Frankfurt School, in *Soviet Marxism* (1958) he argued that revolutionary change can come only from alienated elites such as students.

Mar del Plata /ˌmɑː dɛl ˈplɑːtə/ a fishing port and resort in Argentina, on the Atlantic coast south of Buenos Aires; pop. 520,000 (1991).

Mardi Gras /ˌmɑːdi ˈɡrɑː, French mardi ɡra/ ▶ noun a carnival held in some countries on Shrove Tuesday, most famously in New Orleans.
■Austral./NZ a carnival or fair held at any time.
– ORIGIN French, literally 'fat Tuesday', alluding to the last day of feasting before the fast and penitence of Lent.

Marduk /ˈmɑːdʊk/ Babylonian Mythology the chief god of Babylon, who became lord of the gods of heaven and earth after conquering Tiamat, the monster of primeval chaos.

mardy ▶ adjective (**-ier**, **-iest**) N. English sulky and whining.
– ORIGIN early 20th cent.: from dialect *mard* 'spoilt' (describing a child), alteration of *marred* (see **MAR**).

Mare, Walter de la, see **DE LA MARE**.

mare[1] /mɛː/ ▶ noun the female of a horse or other equine animal.
■Brit. informal, derogatory a woman.
– ORIGIN Old English *mearh* 'horse', *mere* 'mare', from a Germanic base with cognates in Celtic languages meaning 'stallion'. The sense 'male horse' died out at the end of the Middle English period.

mare[2] /ˈmɑːreɪ, -ri/ ▶ noun (pl. **maria** /ˈmɑːrɪə/) Astronomy a large, level basalt plain on the surface of the moon, appearing dark by contrast with highland areas: *Mare Imbrium.*
– ORIGIN mid 19th cent.: special use of Latin *mare* 'sea'; these areas were once thought to be seas.

mare clausum /ˌmɑːreɪ ˈklaʊsʊm, ˈklɔːzəm/ ▶ noun (pl. **maria clausa** /ˌmɑːrɪə ˈklaʊsə, ˈklɔːzə/) Law the sea under the jurisdiction of a particular country.
– ORIGIN Latin, 'closed sea'.

Marek's disease /ˈmɑːrɛks/ ▶ noun [mass noun] an infectious disease of poultry caused by a herpesvirus, which attacks nerves and causes paralysis or initiates widespread tumour formation.
– ORIGIN 1960s: named after Josef *Marek* (died 1952), Hungarian veterinary surgeon.

mare liberum /ˌmɑːreɪ ˈliːbərəm, ˈlʌɪbərəm/ ▶ noun (pl. **maria libera** /ˌmɑːrɪə ˈliːbərə, ˈlʌɪbərə/) Law the sea open to all nations.
– ORIGIN Latin, literally 'free sea'.

maremma /məˈrɛmə/ ▶ noun (pl. **maremme** /-mi/) (especially in Italy) an area of low, marshy land near a seashore.
– ORIGIN mid 19th cent.: Italian, from Latin *maritima*, feminine of *maritimus* (see **MARITIME**).

Marengo /məˈrɛŋɡəʊ/ ▶ adjective [postpositive] (of chicken or veal) sautéed in oil, served with a

tomato sauce, and traditionally garnished with eggs and crayfish: *chicken Marengo*.
– ORIGIN named after the village of Marengo in northern Italy, scene of the battle of Marengo, after which the dish is said to have been served to Napoleon.

Marengo, Battle of a decisive French victory of Napoleon's campaign in Italy in 1800, close to the village of Marengo, near Turin. Napoleon crossed the Alps to defeat and capture an Austrian army, a victory which led to Italy coming under French control again.

mare's nest ▶ noun **1** a complex and difficult situation; a muddle: *your desk's usually a mare's nest.* **2** an illusory discovery: *the mare's nest of perfect safety.*
– ORIGIN late 16th cent.: formerly in the phrase *to have found* (or *spied*) *a mare's nest* (i.e. something that does not exist), used in the sense 'to have discovered something amazing'.

mare's tail ▶ noun **1** a widely distributed water plant with whorls of narrow leaves around a tall stout stem.
● *Hippuris vulgaris*, family Haloragaceae.
2 (**mare's tails**) long straight streaks of cirrus cloud.

Mareva injunction /məˈreɪvə, məˈriːvə/ ▶ noun English Law a court order freezing a debtor's assets, usually in order to prevent them being taken abroad.
– ORIGIN named after *Mareva Compania Naveria S.A.*, the first plaintiff to be granted such an injunction (1975).

Marfan's syndrome /ˈmɑːfæz/ ▶ noun [mass noun] Medicine a hereditary disorder of connective tissue, resulting in abnormally long and thin digits and also frequently in optical and cardiovascular defects.
– ORIGIN 1930s: named after Antonin B. J. *Marfan* (1858–1942), French paediatrician.

marg /mɑːɡ/ ▶ noun [usu. in place names] Indian a road or street: *Mahatma Gandhi Marg.*
– ORIGIN via Hindi from Sanskrit *mārga* 'way, road'.

marga ▶ adjective variant spelling of **MAGA**.

Margaret, Princess, Margaret Rose (1930–2002), only sister of Elizabeth II. In 1960 she married Antony Armstrong-Jones, who was later created Earl of Snowdon; the marriage was dissolved in 1978. Their two children are David, Viscount Linley and Lady Sarah Chatto.

Margaret, St (*c*.1046–93), Scottish queen, wife of Malcolm III. She exerted a strong influence over royal policy during her husband's reign, and was instrumental in the reform of the Scottish Church. Feast day, 16 November.

margarine /ˌmɑːdʒəˈriːn, ˈmɑːɡəriːn/ ▶ noun [mass noun] a butter substitute made from vegetable oils or animal fats.
– ORIGIN late 19th cent.: from French, from Greek *margaron* 'pearl' (because of the lustre of the crystals of esters from which it was first made) + -INE⁴.

Margarita /ˌmɑːɡəˈriːtə/ an island in the Caribbean Sea, off the coast of Venezuela. Visited by Columbus in 1498, it was used as a base by Simón Bolívar in 1816 in the struggle for independence from Spanish rule.

margarita /ˌmɑːɡəˈriːtə/ ▶ noun a cocktail made with tequila and citrus fruit juice.
– ORIGIN from the Spanish given name equivalent to *Margaret*.

margate /ˈmɑːɡɪt/ ▶ noun a deep-bodied greyish fish which typically occurs in small groups in warm waters of the western Atlantic.
● Two species in the family Pomadasyidae: *Haemulon album*, a large grunt which is an important food fish, and the mainly nocturnal **black margate** (*Anisotremus surinamesis*).
– ORIGIN mid 18th cent.: of unknown origin.

margay /ˈmɑːɡeɪ/ ▶ noun a small South American wild cat with large eyes and a yellowish coat with black spots and stripes.
● *Felis wiedii*, family Felidae.
– ORIGIN late 18th cent.: via French from Tupi *marakaya*.

marge¹ ▶ noun [mass noun] Brit. informal margarine.
– ORIGIN 1920s: abbreviation.

marge² ▶ noun poetic/literary a margin or edge.

– ORIGIN mid 16th cent.: from French, from Latin *margo* 'margin'.

margin ▶ noun **1** the edge or border of something: *the eastern margin of the Indian Ocean* | figurative *they were forced to live on the margins of society.*
■the blank border on each side of the print on a page. ■ a line ruled on paper to mark off a margin.
2 an amount by which a thing is won or falls short: *they won by a convincing 17-point margin.*
■an amount of something included so as to be sure of success or safety: *there was no margin for error.* ■ the lower limit of possibility, success, etc.: *the lighting is considerably brighter than before but is still at the margins of acceptability.* ■ a profit margin. ■ Finance a sum deposited with a broker to cover the risk of loss on a transaction on account. ■ Austral./NZ an increment to a basic wage, paid for extra skill or responsibility.
▶verb (**margined, margining**) [with obj.] **1** provide with an edge or border: *its leaves are margined with yellow.*
■archaic annotate or summarize (a text) in the margins.
2 deposit an amount of money with a broker as security for (an account or transaction): [as adj. **margined**] *a margined transaction.*
– PHRASES **margin of error** an amount (usually small) that is allowed for in case of miscalculation or change of circumstances.
– DERIVATIVES **margined** adjective [in combination] *a wide-margined volume.*
– ORIGIN late Middle English: from Latin *margo*, *margin-* 'edge'.

marginal ▶ adjective of, relating to, or situated at the edge or margin of something.
■of secondary or minor importance; not central: *it seems likely to make only a marginal difference* | *a marginal criminal element.* ■(of a decision or distinction) very narrow: *a marginal offside decision.* ■ of or written in the margin of a page: *marginal notes.* ■ of or relating to water adjacent to the land's edge or coast: *water lilies and marginal aquatics.* ■ (chiefly of costs or benefits) relating to or resulting from small or unit changes. ■(of taxation) relating to increases in income. ■ chiefly Brit. (of a parliamentary seat) having a small majority and therefore at risk in an election. ■ close to the limit of profitability, especially through difficulty of exploitation: *marginal farmland.*
▶noun **1** chiefly Brit. a parliamentary seat that has a small majority and is therefore at risk in an election.
2 a plant that grows in water adjacent to the edge of land.
– DERIVATIVES **marginality** noun.
– ORIGIN late 16th cent.: from medieval Latin *marginalis*, from *margo*, *margin-* (see **MARGIN**).

marginal benefit ▶ noun Economics the additional benefit arising from a unit increase in a particular activity.

marginal cost ▶ noun Economics the cost added by producing one extra item of a product.

marginalia /ˌmɑːdʒɪˈneɪlɪə/ ▶ plural noun marginal notes.
– ORIGIN mid 19th cent.: from medieval Latin, neuter plural of *marginalis*, from *margo*, *margin-* (see **MARGIN**).

marginalize (also **-ise**) ▶ verb [with obj.] treat (a person, group, or concept) as insignificant or peripheral: *higher education continues to exclude and marginalize female students* | [as adj. **marginalized**] *members of marginalized cultural groups.*
– DERIVATIVES **marginalization** noun.

marginally ▶ adverb to only a limited extent; slightly: *inflation is predicted to drop marginally* | [as submodifier] *he's marginally worse than he was.*

marginate Biology ▶ verb /ˈmɑːdʒɪneɪt/ [with obj.] provide with a margin or border; form a border to.
▶adjective /ˈmɑːdʒɪnət/ having a distinct margin or border.
– DERIVATIVES **margination** noun.

margin call ▶ noun Finance a demand by a broker that an investor deposit further cash or securities to cover possible losses.

margin release ▶ noun a device on a typewriter allowing a word to be typed beyond the margin normally set.

margrave /ˈmɑːɡreɪv/ ▶ noun historical the hereditary title of some princes of the Holy Roman Empire.
– DERIVATIVES **margravate** /ˈmɑːɡrəvət/ noun.
– ORIGIN mid 16th cent., from Middle Dutch *markgrave* 'count of a border territory', from *marke* 'boundary' + *grave* 'count' (used as a title).

margravine /ˈmɑːɡrəviːn/ ▶ noun historical the wife of a margrave.
– ORIGIN late 17th cent.: from Dutch *markgravin*, feminine of *markgraaf*, earlier *markgrave* (see **MARGRAVE**).

marguerite /ˌmɑːɡəˈriːt/ ▶ noun another term for OX-EYE DAISY.
– ORIGIN early 17th cent.: French equivalent of the given name Margaret.

Mari¹ /ˈmɑːri/ an ancient city on the west bank of the Euphrates, in Syria. Its period of greatest importance was from the late 19th to the mid 18th centuries BC; the vast palace of the last king, Zimri-Lin, has yielded an archive of 25,000 cuneiform tablets, which are the principal source for the history of northern Syria and Mesopotamia at that time.

Mari² /ˈmɑːri/ ▶ noun (pl. same or **Maris**) **1** a member of a people of the central Volga valley in Russia.
2 [mass noun] the Uralic language of this people, which has two dialects with over 700,000 speakers altogether. Formerly called **CHEREMIS**.
▶adjective of or relating to this people or their language.
– ORIGIN the name in Mari.

maria plural form of **MARE**².

mariachi /ˌmɑːrɪˈɑːtʃi/ ▶ noun (pl. **mariachis**) [as modifier] denoting a type of traditional Mexican folk music, typically performed by a small group of strolling musicians dressed in native costume.
■a musician in such a group.
– ORIGIN from Mexican Spanish *mariache*, *mariachi* 'street singer'.

Maria de' Medici see **MARIE DE MÉDICIS**.

mariage blanc /ˌmɑːrɪɑːʒ ˈblɒ̃, French maʀjaʒ blɑ̃/ ▶ noun (pl. **mariages blancs** pronunc. same) an unconsummated marriage.
– ORIGIN French, literally 'white marriage'.

mariage de convenance /ˌmɑːrɪɑːʒ də ˌkɒvəˈnɒ̃s, French maʀjaʒ də kɔ̃vnɑ̃s/ ▶ noun (pl. **mariages de convenance** pronunc. same) French term for *marriage of convenience* (see **MARRIAGE**).

Marian /ˈmɛːrɪən/ ▶ adjective **1** of or relating to the Virgin Mary.
2 of or relating to Queen Mary I of England.

Mariana Islands /ˌmɑːrɪˈɑːnə/ (also **the Marianas**) a group of islands in the western Pacific, comprising Guam and the Northern Marianas.
– ORIGIN translating *Las Marianas*, the name given by Spanish colonists to the islands, in honour of *Maria Anna*, widow of Philip IV.

Mariana Trench an ocean trench to the south-east of the Mariana Islands in the western Pacific, with the greatest known ocean depth (11,034 m, 36,201 ft at the Challenger Deep).

Maria Theresa /məˈriːə təˈreɪzə/ (1717–80), Archduchess of Austria, queen of Hungary and Bohemia 1740–80. The daughter of the Emperor Charles VI, she succeeded to the Habsburg dominions in 1740 by virtue of the Pragmatic Sanction. Her accession triggered the War of the Austrian Succession, which in turn led to the Seven Years War.

Mari Autonomous Republic another name for **MARI EL**.

Maribor /ˈmaribɔː/ an industrial city in NE Slovenia, on the River Drava near the border with Austria; pop. 103,900 (1991). German name **MARBURG**.

mariculture /ˈmarɪˌkʌltʃə/ ▶ noun [mass noun] the cultivation of fish or other marine life for food.
– ORIGIN early 20th cent.: from *mare*, *mari-* 'sea' + CULTURE, on the pattern of words such as *agriculture*.

Marie Antoinette /ˌmari ˌɒtwəˈnɛt, French maʀi ɑ̃twanɛt/ (1755–93), French queen, wife of Louis XVI. A daughter of Maria Theresa, she married the future Louis XVI of France in 1770. Her extravagant lifestyle led to widespread unpopularity and, like her husband, she was executed during the French Revolution.

Marie Byrd Land /ˌmari ˈbəːd/ a region of Antarctica bordering the Pacific, between Ellsworth Land and the Ross Sea.
– ORIGIN named after the wife of Richard E. *Byrd*, the American naval commander who explored the region in 1929.

Marie Celeste variant spelling of **MARY CELESTE**.

Marie de Médicis /mə,riː də ˌmeɪdɪˈsiːs/ (1573–1642), queen of France; Italian name *Maria de' Medici*. The second wife of Henry IV of France, she ruled as regent during the minority of her son Louis XIII (1610–17) and retained her influence after her son came to power.

Mari El /ˌmɑːriː ˈɛl/ an autonomous republic in European Russia, north of the Volga; pop. 754,000 (1990); capital, Yoshkar-Ola. Also called **MARI AUTONOMOUS REPUBLIC**.

Marie Rose ▶noun a cold sauce made from mayonnaise and tomato purée and served with seafood, especially prawns.

marigold ▶noun a plant of the daisy family with yellow, orange, or copper-brown flowers, which is widely cultivated as an ornamental.
• Genera *Calendula* (the **common** (or **pot**) **marigold**) and *Tagetes* (the **French** and **African marigolds**), family Compositae.
■used in names of other plants with yellow flowers, e.g. **corn marigold**, **marsh marigold**.
– ORIGIN late Middle English: from the given name *Mary* (probably referring to the Virgin) + dialect *gold*, denoting the corn or garden marigold in Old English.

marijuana /ˌmarɪˈhwɑːnə/ (also **marihuana**) ▶noun [mass noun] cannabis, especially as smoked in cigarettes.
– ORIGIN late 19th cent.: from Latin American Spanish.

marimba /məˈrɪmbə/ ▶noun a deep-toned xylophone of African origin. The modern form was developed in the US *c.*1910.
– ORIGIN early 18th cent.: from Kimbundu, perhaps via Portuguese.

marina ▶noun a specially designed harbour with moorings for pleasure yachts and small boats.
– ORIGIN early 19th cent.: from Italian or Spanish, feminine of *marino*, from Latin *marinus* (see **MARINE**).

marinade /ˌmarɪˈneɪd/ ▶noun a sauce, typically made of oil, vinegar, spices, and herbs, in which meat, fish, or other food is soaked before cooking in order to flavour or soften it.
■[with modifier] a dish prepared using such a mixture: *a chicken marinade.*
▶verb /ˈmarɪneɪd/ another term for **MARINATE**.
– ORIGIN late 17th cent. (as a verb): from French, from Spanish *marinada*, via *marinar* 'pickle in brine' from *marino* (see **MARINA**).

marinara /ˌmɑːrɪˈnɑːrə, ˈmar-/ ▶noun [usu. as modifier] (in Italian cooking) a sauce made from tomatoes, onions, and herbs, served especially with pasta.
– ORIGIN from the Italian phrase *alla marinara* 'sailor-style'.

marinate /ˈmarɪneɪt/ ▶verb [with obj.] soak (meat, fish, or other food) in a marinade: *the beef was marinated in red wine vinegar.*
■[no obj.] (of food) undergo such a process.
– DERIVATIVES **marination** noun.
– ORIGIN mid 17th cent.: from Italian *marinare* 'pickle in brine', or from French *mariner* (from *marine* 'brine').

marine /məˈriːn/ ▶adjective of, found in, or produced by the sea: *marine plants | marine biology.*
■of or relating to shipping or naval matters: *marine insurance.* ■(of artists or painting) depicting scenes at sea: *marine painters.*
▶noun a member of a body of troops trained to serve on land or sea, in particular (in the UK) a member of the Royal Marines or (in the US) a member of the Marine Corps.
– PHRASES **tell that to the marines** a scornful expression of disbelief. [ORIGIN: from the saying *that will do for the marines but the sailors won't believe it*, referring to the *horse marines*, an imaginary corps of cavalrymen employed to serve as marines (thus out of their element).]
– ORIGIN Middle English (as a noun in the sense 'seashore'): from Old French *marin*, *marine*, from Latin *marinus*, from *mare* 'sea'.

marine iguana ▶noun a large lizard with webbed feet, which swims strongly and feeds on marine algae, native to the Galapagos Islands. It is the only marine lizard.
• *Amblyrhynchus cristatus*, family Iguanidae.

Mariner a series of American space probes launched in 1962–77 to investigate the planets Venus, Mars, and Mercury.

mariner ▶noun a sailor.
– ORIGIN Middle English: from Old French *marinier*, from medieval Latin *marinarius*, from Latin *marinus* (see **MARINE**).

mariner's compass ▶noun archaic term for **COMPASS** (in sense 1).

marine toad ▶noun another term for **CANE TOAD**.

Marinetti /ˌmarɪˈnɛti/, Filippo Tommaso (1876–1944), Italian poet and dramatist. He launched the futurist movement with a manifesto (1909) which exalted technology, glorified war, and demanded revolution in the arts.

marinize /məˈriːnʌɪz/ (also **-ise**) ▶verb [with obj.] modify, convert, or adapt for marine use: [as adj. **marinized**] *a three-cylinder marinized 26 hp diesel.*

Mariolatry /ˌmɛːrɪˈɒlətri/ ▶noun [mass noun] idolatrous worship of the Virgin Mary.
– ORIGIN early 17th cent.: from *Maria* (Latin equivalent of 'Mary') + **-LATRY**, on the pattern of *idolatry*.

Mariology /ˌmɛːrɪˈɒlədʒi/ ▶noun [mass noun] the part of Christian theology dealing with the Virgin Mary.
– DERIVATIVES **Mariological** adjective.

marionette /ˌmarɪəˈnɛt/ ▶noun a puppet worked by strings.
■figurative a person controlled by others: *the weaker ministers degenerated into marionettes.*
– ORIGIN early 17th cent.: from French *marionnette*, from *Marion*, diminutive of the given name *Marie*.

mariposa tulip /ˌmarɪˈpəʊsə/ (also **mariposa lily**) ▶noun a North American lily with large brightly coloured cup-shaped flowers.
• Genus *Calochortus*, family Liliaceae.
– ORIGIN mid 19th cent.: *mariposa* from Spanish, literally 'butterfly'.

Maris Piper /ˈmarɪs/ ▶noun a potato of a popular variety with creamy flesh and smooth oval tubers.
– ORIGIN 1970s: named after *Maris* Lane, original site of the Plant Breeding Institute; *Piper* was chosen arbitrarily as a word beginning with *p-* for *potato*.

Marist /ˈmɛːrɪst, ˈmarɪst/ ▶noun **1** (also **Marist Father**) a member of the Society of Mary, a Roman Catholic missionary and teaching order.
2 (also **Marist Brother**) a member of the Little Brothers of Mary, a Roman Catholic teaching order.
– ORIGIN late 19th cent.: from French *Mariste*, from the given name *Marie*, equivalent of *Mary*.

marital ▶adjective of or relating to marriage or the relations between husband and wife: *marital fidelity.*
– DERIVATIVES **maritally** adverb.
– ORIGIN early 16th cent.: from Latin *maritalis*, from *maritus* 'husband'.

marital status ▶noun a person's state of being single, married, separated, divorced, or widowed.

maritime ▶adjective connected with the sea, especially in relation to seafaring commercial or military activity: *a maritime museum | maritime law.*
■living or found in or near the sea: *dolphins and other maritime mammals.* ■bordering on the sea: *two species of Diptera occur in the maritime Antarctic.* ■denoting a climate that is moist and temperate owing to the influence of the sea.
– ORIGIN mid 16th cent.: from Latin *maritimus*, from *mare* 'sea'.

maritime pine ▶noun a pine tree with long thick needles and clustered cones, native to the coasts of the Mediterranean and Iberia. Also called **CLUSTER PINE**.
• *Pinus pinaster*, family Pinaceae.

Maritime Provinces (also **the Maritimes**) the Canadian provinces of New Brunswick, Nova Scotia, and Prince Edward Island, with coastlines on the Gulf of St Lawrence and the Atlantic. Compare with **ATLANTIC PROVINCES**.

Maritsa /məˈrɪtsə/ a river of southern Europe, which rises in the Rila Mountains of SW Bulgaria and flows 480 km (300 miles) south to the Aegean Sea. It forms the border between Bulgaria and Greece and that between Greece and Turkey. Its ancient name is the Hebros or Hebrus. Turkish name **MERIÇ**; Greek name **ÉVROS**.

Mariupol /ˌmarɪˈuːpɒl/ an industrial port on the south coast of Ukraine, on the Sea of Azov; pop. 517,000 (1989). Former name (1948–89) **ZHDANOV**.

Marius /ˈmarɪəs/, Gaius (*c.*157–86 BC), Roman general and politician. Elected consul in 107 BC, he defeated Jugurtha and invading Germanic tribes. After a power struggle with Sulla he was expelled from Italy, but returned to take Rome by force in 87 BC.

marjoram /ˈmɑːdʒ(ə)rəm/ ▶noun (also **sweet marjoram**) [mass noun] an aromatic southern European plant of the mint family, the leaves of which are used as a culinary herb.
• *Origanum majorana*, family Labiatae.
■(also **wild marjoram**) another term for **OREGANO**.
– ORIGIN late Middle English: from Old French *majorane*, from medieval Latin *majorana*, of unknown ultimate origin.

mark[1] ▶noun **1** a small area on a surface having a different colour from its surroundings, typically one caused by accident or damage: *the blow left a red mark down one side of her face.*
■a spot, area, or feature on a person's or animal's body by which they may be identified or recognized: *he was five feet nine, with no distinguishing marks.*
2 a line, figure, or symbol made as an indication or record of something.
■a written symbol made on a document in place of a signature by someone who cannot write. ■a level or stage that is considered significant: *unemployment had passed the two million mark.* ■a sign or indication of a quality or feeling: *the flag was at half mast as a mark of respect.* ■a characteristic property or feature: *it is the mark of a civilized society to treat its elderly members well.* ■a competitor's starting point in a race. ■Rugby Union the act of cleanly catching the ball direct from a kick, knock-on, or forward throw by an opponent, on or behind one's own 22-metre line, and exclaiming 'Mark', after which a free kick can be taken by the catcher. ■Australian Rules an act of catching a ball that has been kicked at least ten metres before it reaches the ground, or the spot from which the subsequent kick is taken. ■Nautical a piece of material or a knot used to indicate a depth on a sounding line. ■Telecommunications one of two possible states of a signal in certain systems. The opposite of **SPACE**. ■Brit. a particular temperature level in a gas oven: *preheat the oven to Gas Mark 5.*
3 a point awarded for a correct answer or for proficiency in an examination or competition: *many candidates lose marks because they don't read the questions carefully* | figurative *full marks to them for highlighting the threat to the rainforest.*
■a figure or letter representing the total of such points and signifying a person's score: *the highest mark was 98 per cent.* ■(also **handicap mark**) Horse Racing an official assessment of a horse's form, expressed as a figure between 0 and 140 and used as the basis for calculating the weight the horse has to carry in a race: *horses tend to run **off** a higher **mark** over fences than they would over hurdles.* ■(especially in athletics) a time or distance achieved by a competitor, especially one which represents a record or personal best.
4 (followed by a numeral) a particular model or type of a vehicle, machine, or device: *a Mark 10 Jaguar.*
5 a target: *few bullets could have missed their mark.*
■informal, chiefly US a person who is easily deceived or taken advantage of: *they figure I'm an easy mark.*
▶verb [with obj.] **1** make (a visible impression or stain) on: *he fingered the photograph gently, careful not to mark it.*
■[no obj.] become stained: *it is made from a sort of woven surface which doesn't mark or tear.*
2 write a word or symbol on (an object), typically for identification: *she marked all her possessions with her name* | [with obj. and complement] *an envelope marked 'private and confidential'.*
■write (a word or figure) on an object: *she **marked** the date **down** on a card.* ■(**mark something off**) put a line by or through something written or printed on paper to indicate that it has passed or been dealt with: *he marked off their names in a ledger.* ■Austral./NZ make a symbol on the ear of (a lamb).
3 show the position of: *the top of the pass marks the border between Alaska and the Yukon.*
■separate or delineate (a particular section or area of something): *you need to **mark out** the part of the garden where the sun lingers longest.* ■(of a particular quality or feature) separate or distinguish (someone or something) from other people or things: *his sword **marked** him **out** as an officer.* ■(**mark someone out for**) select or destine someone for (a particular role or condition): *the solicitor general marked him out for government office.* ■(**mark someone down as**) judge someone to be (a particular type or class of person): *she had marked him down as a dangerous liberal.* ■acknowledge, honour, or celebrate (an important event or occasion) with a particular action: *to mark*

its fiftieth birthday the charity held a fashion show. ■ be an indication of (a significant occasion, stage, or development): *a series of incidents which marked a new phase in the terrorist campaign.* ■ (usu. **be marked**) characterize as having a particular quality or feature: *the reaction to these developments has been marked by a note of hysteria.* ■ (of a clock or watch) show (a certain time): *his watch marked five past eight.*
4 (of a teacher or examiner) assess the standard of (a piece of written work) by assigning points for proficiency or correct answers: *the examiner may have hundreds of scripts to mark.*
■ (**mark someone/thing down**) reduce the number of marks awarded to a pupil, candidate, or their work.
5 notice or pay careful attention to: *he'll leave you, you mark my words!*
6 Brit. (of a player in a team game) stay close to (a particular opponent) in order to prevent them getting or passing the ball: *each central defender marks one attacker.*
■ Australian Rules catch (the ball) from a kick of at least ten metres.
– PHRASES **be quick** (or **slow**) **off the mark** be fast (or slow) in responding to a situation or understanding something. **get off the mark** get started. **leave** (or **make**) **its** (or **one's** or **a**) **mark** have a lasting or significant effect: *he left his mark on English football.* **make one's mark** attain recognition or distinction. **one's mark** Brit. something which is particularly typical of or suitable for someone: *'I took you out.' 'To a motel! That's just about your mark!'* **mark time** (of troops) march on the spot without moving forward. ■ figurative pass one's time in routine activities until a more favourable or interesting opportunity presents itself. **mark you** chiefly Brit. used to emphasize or draw attention to a statement: *I was persuaded, against my better judgement, mark you, to vote for him.* **near** (or **close**) **to the mark** almost accurate: *to say he was their legal adviser would be nearer the mark.* **off** (or **wide of**) **the mark** incorrect or inaccurate: *his solutions are completely off the mark.* **of mark** dated having importance or distinction: *he had been a man of mark.* **on the mark** correct; accurate. **on your marks** used to instruct competitors in a race to prepare themselves in the correct starting position: *on your marks, get set, go!* **up to the mark** of the required standard. ■ [usu. with negative] (of a person) as healthy or in as good spirits as usual: *Johnny's not feeling up to the mark at the moment.*
– ORIGIN Old English *mearc, gemerce* (noun), *mearcian* (verb), of Germanic origin; from an Indo-European root shared by Latin *margo* 'margin'.
▶ **mark something down** (of a retailer) reduce the indicated price of an item.
mark something up 1 (of a retailer) add a certain amount to the cost of goods to cover overheads and profit: *they mark up the price of imported wines by 66 per cent.* **2** annotate or correct text for printing, keying, or typesetting.

mark² ▶ noun **1** (until the introduction of the euro in 2002) the basic monetary unit of Germany, equal to 100 pfennig; a Deutschmark or, formerly, an Ostmark.
2 a former English and Scottish money of account, equal to thirteen shillings and four pence in the currency of the day.
■ a denomination of weight for gold and silver, formerly used throughout western Europe and typically equal to 8 ounces (226.8 grams).
– ORIGIN Old English *marc*, from Old Norse *mǫrk*; probably related to **MARK**¹.

Mark, St an Apostle, companion of St Peter and St Paul, traditional author of the second Gospel. Feast day, 25 April.
■ the second Gospel, the earliest in date (see **GOSPEL** sense 2).

Mark Antony see **ANTONY**.

markdown ▶ noun a reduction in price.

marked ▶ adjective **1** having a visible mark: *its short bill and heavily marked underparts.*
■ (of playing cards) having distinctive marks on their backs to assist cheating. ■ Linguistics (of words or forms) distinguished by a particular feature: *the word 'drake' is semantically marked as masculine; the unmarked form is 'duck'.*
2 clearly noticeable; evident: *a marked increase in UK sales.*
– DERIVATIVES **markedly** adverb (only in sense 2), **markedness** noun.

marked man ▶ noun a person who is singled out for special treatment, especially to be harmed or killed.

marker ▶ noun **1** an object used to indicate a position, place, or route: *they erected a granite marker at the crash site* | [as modifier] *a marker post.*
■ a thing serving as a standard of comparison or as an indication of what may be expected: *he has already* ***laid down a marker*** *by setting a fast time during practice.* ■ a radio beacon used to guide the pilot of an aircraft. ■ N. Amer. informal a promissory note; an IOU.
2 (also **marker pen**) a felt-tip pen with a broad tip.
3 a player in a team sport who stays close to a particular opponent to prevent them from getting or passing the ball.
4 a person who assesses the standard of a written test or examination.
■ a person who records the score in a game, especially in snooker or billiards.

market ▶ noun **1** a regular gathering of people for the purchase and sale of provisions, livestock, and other commodities: *farmers* ***going to market.***
■ an open space or covered building where vendors convene to sell their goods.
2 an area or arena in which commercial dealings are conducted: *the UK market remained in recession* | *the labour market.*
■ a demand for a particular commodity or service: *there is* ***a market for*** *ornamental daggers.* ■ the state of trade at a particular time or in a particular context: *the bottom's fallen out of the market.* ■ the free market; the operation of supply and demand: *future development cannot simply be left to the market* | [as modifier] *market forces.* ■ a stock market.
▶ verb (**marketed**, **marketing**) [with obj.] advertise or promote (something): *the product was marketed under the name 'aspirin'.*
■ offer for sale: *sheep farmers are still unable to market their lambs.* ■ [no obj.] dated buy or sell goods in a market: *then I have to go uptown and market.*
– PHRASES **be in the market for** wish to buy. **make a market** Finance take part in active dealing in particular shares or other assets. **on the market** available for sale: *he bought every new gadget as it* ***came on the market.***
– DERIVATIVES **marketer** noun.
– ORIGIN Middle English, via Anglo-Norman French from Latin *mercatus*, from *mercari* 'buy' (see also **MERCHANT**).

marketable ▶ adjective able or fit to be sold or marketed: *the fish are perfectly marketable.*
■ in demand: *marketable skills.*
– DERIVATIVES **marketability** noun.

market basket ▶ noun a large basket, typically one with a lid, used to carry provisions.
■ a selected list of food and household items chosen as a representative sample of common purchases and used to measure the cost of living.

market cross ▶ noun a stone cross situated in the marketplace of a British town, typically dating from the Middle Ages.
■ an arcaded building in a marketplace.

market day ▶ noun chiefly Brit. a day on which a market is regularly held: *Saturday is market day.*

marketeer ▶ noun a person who sells goods or services in a market: *a consumer-goods marketeer.*
■ [with modifier] a person who works in or advocates a particular type of market.

market garden ▶ noun chiefly Brit. a place where vegetables and fruit are grown for sale.
– DERIVATIVES **market gardener** noun, **market gardening** noun.

marketing ▶ noun [mass noun] the action or business of promoting and selling products or services, including market research and advertising.

marketing mix ▶ noun a combination of factors that can be controlled by a company to influence consumers to purchase its products.

marketization ▶ noun [mass noun] the exposure of an industry or service to market forces.
■ the conversion of a national economy from a planned to a market economy.
– DERIVATIVES **marketize** verb.

market leader ▶ noun the company selling the largest quantity of a particular type of product.
■ a product which outsells its competitors.

market-maker ▶ noun a dealer in securities or other assets who undertakes to buy or sell at specified prices at all times.

marketplace ▶ noun an open space where a market is or was formerly held in a town.
■ the arena of competitive or commercial dealings; the world of trade: *the changing demands of the global marketplace.*

market research ▶ noun [mass noun] the action or activity of gathering information about consumers' needs and preferences.
– DERIVATIVES **market researcher** noun.

market share ▶ noun the portion of a market controlled by a particular company or product.

market town ▶ noun (in the UK) a town of moderate size in a rural area, where a regular market is held.

market value ▶ noun the amount for which something can be sold on a given market. Often contrasted with **BOOK VALUE**.

markhor /ˈmɑːkɔː/ ▶ noun a large wild goat with very long twisted horns, native to central Asia.
● *Capra falconeri*, family Bovidae.
– ORIGIN mid 19th cent.: from Persian *mār-kwār*, from *mār* 'serpent' + *kwār* '-eating'.

marking ▶ noun (usu. **markings**) an identification mark, especially a symbol on an aircraft: *RAF camouflage and markings.*
■ a mark or pattern of marks on an animal's fur, feathers, or skin: *the distinctive black-and-white markings on its head.* ■ Music a word or symbol on a score indicating the correct tempo, dynamic, or other aspect of performance.

markka /ˈmɑːkɑː, -kə/ ▶ noun (until the introduction of the euro in 2002) the basic monetary unit of Finland, equal to 100 penniä.
– ORIGIN Finnish.

Markova /mɑːˈkəʊvə, ˈmɑːkəvə/, Dame Alicia (b.1910), English ballet dancer; born *Lilian Alicia Marks*. She founded the Markova–Dolin Ballet with Anton Dolin in 1935 and was prima ballerina with the London Festival Ballet 1950–2.

Markov model /ˈmɑːkɒf/ (also **Markov chain**) ▶ noun Statistics a stochastic model describing a sequence of possible events in which the probability of each event depends only on the state attained in the previous event.
– ORIGIN mid 20th cent.: named after Andrei A. *Markov* (1856–1922), Russian mathematician.

Marks, Simon, 1st Baron Marks of Broughton (1888–1964), English businessman. In 1907 he inherited the Marks and Spencer Penny Bazaars established by his father and Thomas Spencer. These formed the nucleus of the retail chain Marks & Spencer, created in 1926.

marksman ▶ noun (pl. **-men**) a person skilled in shooting: *a police marksman.*
■ informal a footballer skilled in scoring goals.
– DERIVATIVES **marksmanship** noun.

markswoman ▶ noun (pl. **-women**) a woman skilled in shooting, especially with a pistol or rifle.

mark-to-market ▶ adjective Finance denoting or relating to a system of valuing assets by the most recent market price.

mark-up ▶ noun **1** the amount added to the cost price of goods to cover overheads and profit.
2 [mass noun] the process or result of correcting text in preparation for printing.
3 [mass noun] Computing a set of tags assigned to elements of a text to indicate their structural or logical relation to the rest of the text.

marl¹ ▶ noun [mass noun] an unconsolidated sedimentary rock or soil consisting of clay and lime, formerly used typically as fertilizer.
▶ verb [with obj.] (often **be marled**) apply marl to.
– DERIVATIVES **marly** adjective.
– ORIGIN Middle English: from Old French *marle*, from medieval Latin *margila*, from Latin *marga*, of Celtic origin.

marl² ▶ noun [mass noun] [usu. as modifier] a mottled yarn of differently coloured threads, or fabric made from this yarn: *blue marl leggings.*
– ORIGIN late 19th cent.: shortening of **MARBLED**.

Marlborough /ˈmɔːlb(ə)rə/, John Churchill, 1st Duke of (1650–1722), British general. He was commander of British and Dutch troops in the War of the Spanish Succession and won a series of victories (notably at Blenheim in 1704) over the French armies of Louis XIV, ending Louis's attempts to dominate Europe.

marled ▶ adjective (chiefly of yarn or fabric) mottled or streaked.

m

– ORIGIN early 16th cent.: perhaps a shortening of **MARBLED**.

Marley, Bob (1945–81), Jamaican reggae singer, guitarist, and songwriter; full name *Robert Nesta Marley*. Having formed the trio the Wailers in 1965, in the 1970s he was instrumental in popularizing reggae. His lyrics often reflected his commitment to Rastafarianism.

marlin /ˈmɑːlɪn/ ▶ noun a large edible billfish of warm seas, which is a highly prized game fish and typically reaches a great weight.
● Genera *Makaira* and *Tetrapterus*, family Istiophoridae: several species.
– ORIGIN early 20th cent.: from **MARLINSPIKE** (with reference to its pointed snout).

marline /ˈmɑːlɪn/ ▶ noun [mass noun] Nautical light rope made of two strands.
– ORIGIN late Middle English: from Middle Low German *marling*, with the ending influenced by **LINE**[1].

marlinspike (also **marlinespike**) ▶ noun a pointed metal tool used by sailors to separate strands of rope or wire.
– ORIGIN early 17th cent. (originally as *marling spike*): from *marling*, present participle of *marl* 'fasten with marline' (from Dutch *marlen* 'keep binding') + **SPIKE**[1].

Marlowe, Christopher (1564–93), English dramatist and poet. As a dramatist he brought a new strength and vitality to blank verse; his work influenced Shakespeare's early historical plays. Notable plays: *Doctor Faustus* (c.1590) and *The Jew of Malta* (1592).
– DERIVATIVES **Marlovian** adjective & noun.

marm ▶ noun chiefly N. Amer. variant spelling of **MA'AM**.

marmalade ▶ noun [mass noun] a preserve made from citrus fruit, especially bitter oranges, prepared like jam.
– ORIGIN late 15th cent.: from Portuguese *marmelada* 'quince jam', from *marmelo* 'quince', based on Greek *melimēlon* (from *meli* 'honey' + *mēlon* 'apple').

marmalade cat ▶ noun a cat with orange fur and darker orange markings.

Marmara, Sea of /ˈmɑːmərə/ a small sea in NW Turkey. Connected by the Bosporus to the Black Sea and by the Dardanelles to the Aegean, it separates European Turkey from Asian Turkey. In ancient times it was known as the Propontis.

Marmite /ˈmɑːmʌɪt/ ▶ noun [mass noun] trademark a dark savoury paste made from yeast extract and vegetable extract, used in sandwiches and for flavouring.

marmite /ˈmɑːmʌɪt, mɑːˈmiːt/ ▶ noun an earthenware cooking container.
– ORIGIN early 19th cent.: French, from Old French *marmite* 'hypocritical', with reference to the hidden contents of the lidded pot, from *marmotter* 'to mutter' + *mite* 'cat'.

marmoreal /mɑːˈmɔːrɪəl/ ▶ adjective poetic/literary made of or likened to marble.
– DERIVATIVES **marmoreally** adverb.
– ORIGIN late 18th cent.: from Latin *marmoreus* (from *marmor* 'marble') + **-AL**.

marmoset /ˈmɑːməzɛt/ ▶ noun a small tropical American monkey with a silky coat and a long tail.
● Family Callitrichidae (or Callithricidae): genus *Callithrix* (three species), and the **pygmy marmoset** (*Cebuella pygmaea*).
– ORIGIN late Middle English (also in the sense 'grotesque figure'): from Old French *marmouset* 'grotesque image', of unknown ultimate origin.

marmot /ˈmɑːmət/ ▶ noun a heavily built gregarious burrowing rodent of both Eurasia and North America, typically living in mountainous country.
● Genus *Marmota*, family Sciuridae: several species.
– ORIGIN early 17th cent.: from French *marmotte*, probably via Romansch *murmont* from late Latin *mus montanus* 'mountain mouse'; compare with French *marmotter* 'mutter through the teeth'.

Marne /mɑːn, French marn/ a river of east central France, which rises in the Langres plateau north of Dijon and flows 525 km (328 miles) north and west to join the Seine near Paris. Its valley was the scene of two important battles in the First World War. The first battle (September 1914) halted and repelled the German advance on Paris; the second (July 1918) ended the final German offensive.

marocain /ˌmarəˈkeɪn/ ▶ noun [mass noun] a dress fabric of ribbed crêpe, made of silk or wool or both.

– ORIGIN 1920s: from French, literally 'Moroccan', from *Maroc* 'Morocco'.

Maronite /ˈmarənʌɪt/ ▶ noun a member of a Christian sect of Syrian origin, living chiefly in Lebanon and in communion with the Roman Catholic Church.
▶ adjective [attrib.] of or relating to the Maronites.
– ORIGIN early 16th cent.: from medieval Latin *Maronita*, from the name of John *Maro*, a 7th-cent. Syrian religious leader, who may have been the first Maronite patriarch.

Maroon ▶ noun a member of a group of black people living in the mountains and forests of Suriname and the West Indies, descended from runaway slaves.
– ORIGIN mid 17th cent.: from French *marron* meaning 'feral', from Spanish *cimarrón* 'wild', (as a noun) 'runaway slave'.

maroon[1] ▶ adjective of a brownish-crimson colour.
▶ noun 1 [mass noun] a brownish-crimson colour.
2 chiefly Brit. a firework that makes a loud bang, used mainly as a signal or warning. [ORIGIN: early 19th cent.: so named because the firework makes the noise of a chestnut (see below) bursting in the fire.]
– ORIGIN late 17th cent. (in the sense 'chestnut'): from French *marron* 'chestnut', via Italian from medieval Greek *maraon*. The sense relating to colour dates from the late 18th cent.

maroon[2] ▶ verb [with obj.] (often **be marooned**) leave (someone) trapped and isolated in an inaccessible place, especially an island: *a novel about schoolboys marooned on a desert island.*
– ORIGIN early 18th cent.: from **MAROON**, originally in the form *marooned* 'lost in the wilds'.

marque[1] /mɑːk/ ▶ noun a make of car, as distinct from a specific model.
– ORIGIN early 20th cent.: from French, back-formation from *marquer* 'to brand', of Scandinavian origin.

marque[2] /mɑːk/ ▶ noun see **LETTER OF MARQUE**.

marquee /mɑːˈkiː/ ▶ noun 1 chiefly Brit. a large tent used for social or commercial functions.
2 N. Amer. a roof-like projection over the entrance to a theatre, hotel, or other building.
■ [as modifier] leading; pre-eminent: *a marquee player.* [ORIGIN: with allusion to the practice of billing the name of an entertainer on the *marquee* (i.e. awning) over the entrance to a theatre.]
– ORIGIN late 17th cent.: from **MARQUISE**, taken as plural and assimilated to **-EE**.

marquesa /mɑːˈkeɪzə/ ▶ noun a Spanish marchioness.
– ORIGIN Spanish.

Marquesan /mɑːˈkeɪz(ə)n, -s(ə)n/ ▶ noun 1 a native or inhabitant of the Marquesas Islands, especially a member of the aboriginal Polynesian people of these islands.
2 [mass noun] the Polynesian language of this people.
▶ adjective of or relating to the Marquesans or their language.

Marquesas Islands /mɑːˈkeɪzəs, -səs/ a group of volcanic islands in the South Pacific, forming part of French Polynesia; pop. 7,540 (1988). The islands were annexed by France in 1842. The largest island is Hiva Oa, on which the French painter Paul Gauguin spent the last two years of his life.

marquess /ˈmɑːkwɪs/ ▶ noun a British nobleman ranking above an earl and below a duke. Compare with **MARQUIS**.
– ORIGIN early 16th cent.: variant of **MARQUIS**.

marquessate /ˈmɑːkwɪsət/ ▶ noun variant spelling of **MARQUISATE**.

marquetry /ˈmɑːkɪtri/ (also **marquetery** or **marqueterie**) ▶ noun [mass noun] inlaid work made from small pieces of variously coloured wood or other materials, used chiefly for the decoration of furniture.
– ORIGIN mid 16th cent.: from French *marqueterie*, from *marqueter* 'to variegate'.

Marquette /mɑːˈkɛt, French markɛt/, Jacques (1637–75), French Jesuit missionary and explorer. Arriving in North America in 1666, he played a prominent part in the attempt to Christianize the American Indians, and explored the Wisconsin and Mississippi rivers.

Márquez, Gabriel García, see **GARCÍA MÁRQUEZ**.

marquis /ˈmɑːkwɪs/ ▶ noun (in some European

countries) a nobleman ranking above a count and below a duke. Compare with **MARQUESS**.
■ another term for **MARQUESS**.
– ORIGIN Middle English: from Old French *marchis*, reinforced by Old French *marquis*, both from the base of **MARCH**[2].

marquisate /ˈmɑːkwɪsət/ (also **marquessate**) ▶ noun the rank or dignity of a marquess or marquis.
■ the territorial lordship or possessions of a marquis or margrave.
– ORIGIN early 16th cent.: from **MARQUIS**, on the pattern of words such as French *marquisat*, Italian *marchesato*.

Marquis de Sade see **SADE**.

marquise /mɑːˈkiːz/ ▶ noun 1 the wife or widow of a marquis. Compare with **MARCHIONESS**.
■ a woman holding the rank of marquis in her own right.
2 a finger ring set with a pointed oval gem or cluster of gems.
3 archaic term for **MARQUEE**.
4 a chilled dessert similar to a chocolate mousse.
– ORIGIN early 17th cent.: French, feminine of **MARQUIS**.

marquisette /ˌmɑːkɪˈzɛt/ ▶ noun [mass noun] a fine light cotton, rayon, or silk gauze fabric, now chiefly used for net curtains.
– ORIGIN early 20th cent.: from French, diminutive of **MARQUISE**.

Marrakesh /ˌmarəˈkɛʃ/ (also **Marrakech**) a city in western Morocco, in the foothills of the High Atlas Mountains; pop. 602,000 (1993). It was founded in 1062 as the capital of the Almoravids.

marram /ˈmarəm/ (also **marram grass**) ▶ noun a coarse European grass of coastal sand dunes, binding the loose sand with its tough rhizomes.
● *Ammophila arenaria*, family Gramineae.
– ORIGIN mid 17th cent.: from Old Norse *marálmr*, from *marr* 'sea' + *hálmr* 'haulm'.

Marrano /məˈrɑːnəʊ/ ▶ noun (pl. **-os**) (in medieval Spain) a christianized Jew or Moor, especially one who merely professed conversion in order to avoid persecution.
– ORIGIN Spanish, of unknown origin.

marri /ˈmari/ ▶ noun (pl. **marris**) an Australian eucalyptus tree with rough grey-brown bark and ornamental flowers.
● *Eucalyptus calophylla*, family Myrtaceae.
– ORIGIN mid 19th cent.: from Nyungar.

marriage ▶ noun 1 [mass noun] the formal union of a man and a woman, typically recognized by law, by which they become husband and wife.
■ [count noun] a relationship between married people or the period for which it lasts: *a happy marriage* | *the children from his first marriage.* ■ [count noun] figurative a combination or mixture of two or more elements: *a marriage of jazz, pop, blues, and gospel.*
2 (in bezique and other card games) a combination of a king and queen of the same suit.
– PHRASES **by marriage** as a result of a marriage: *the estate passed by marriage to the Burlingtons.* **in marriage** as husband or wife: *he asked my father for my hand in marriage.* **marriage of convenience** a marriage concluded to achieve a practical purpose.
– ORIGIN Middle English: from Old French *mariage*, from *marier* 'marry'.

marriageable ▶ adjective fit or suitable for marriage, especially in being wealthy or of the right age.
– DERIVATIVES **marriageability** noun.

marriage broker ▶ noun (in a culture where arranged marriages are customary) a person who arranges marriages for a fee.

marriage bureau ▶ noun an establishment which arranges introductions between people who want to get married.

marriage certificate ▶ noun a copy of the record of a legal marriage, with details of names, date, etc.

marriage guidance ▶ noun [mass noun] [often as modifier] (in the UK) counselling of married couples who have problems in their relationship.

marriage licence ▶ noun Brit. a licence which couples must obtain before getting married, except in civil marriage by certificate or church marriage authorized by the publication of banns.
■ chiefly US a marriage certificate.

marriage lines ▶ plural noun informal, chiefly Brit. a marriage certificate.

Marriage of the Adriatic a ceremony formerly held on Ascension Day in Venice to symbolize the city's sea power, during which the doge dropped a ring into the water from his official barge.

marriage portion ▶ noun see **PORTION**.

marriage settlement ▶ noun Brit. an arrangement by which property is given or secured when a couple get married.

married ▶ adjective (of two people) united in marriage: *a married couple.*
■(of one person) having a husband or wife: *a happily married man.* ■ of or relating to marriage: *married life.* ■ figurative closely combined or linked: *in the seventeenth century science was still* ***married to*** *religion.*
▶noun (usu. **marrieds**) a married person: *we were young* ***marrieds*** *during World War Two.*

marron /ˈmarən/ ▶ noun (pl. same or **marrons**) a large Australian freshwater crayfish which lives on the sandy bottoms of rivers and streams.
• *Cherax tenuimanus*, infraorder Astacidea.
– ORIGIN 1940s: from Nyungar *marran*.

marron glacé /ˌmarɒ̃ ˈglaseɪ/ ▶ noun (pl. **marrons glacés** pronunc. same) a chestnut preserved in and coated with sugar.
– ORIGIN French, 'iced chestnut'.

marrow ▶ noun **1** (also **vegetable marrow**) Brit. a long white-fleshed gourd with thin green skin, which is eaten as a vegetable.
2 the plant of the gourd family which produces this.
• *Cucurbita pepo*, family Cucurbitaceae.
3 (also **bone marrow**) [mass noun] a soft fatty substance in the cavities of bones, in which blood cells are produced (often taken as typifying strength and vitality).
– PHRASES **to the marrow** to one's innermost being: *a sight which chilled me to the marrow.*
– DERIVATIVES **marrowless** adjective, **marrowy** adjective.
– ORIGIN Old English *mearg, mærg* (in sense 3), of Germanic origin; related to Dutch *merg* and German *Mark*. Sense 1 dates from the early 19th cent.

marrowbone ▶ noun a bone containing edible marrow.

marrowfat pea ▶ noun a pea of a large variety which is processed and sold in cans.

marry[1] ▶ verb (**-ies**, **-ied**) [with obj.] **1** join in marriage: *I was married in church | the priest who married us | my sister* ***got married to*** *a Welshman.*
■take (someone) as one's wife or husband in marriage: *Eric asked me to marry him.* ■ [no obj.] enter into marriage: *they had no plans to marry.* ■ [no obj.] (**marry into**) become a member of (a family) by marriage. ■ (of a parent or guardian) give (a son or daughter) in marriage, especially for reasons of expediency: *her parents married her to a wealthy landowner.*
2 cause to meet or fit together; combine: *the two halves are trimmed and* ***married up*** *| the show* ***marries*** *poetry* ***with*** *art.*
■[no obj.] meet or blend with something: *most Chardonnays don't* ***marry*** *well* ***with*** *salmon.* ■ Nautical splice (rope ends) together without increasing their girth.
– PHRASES **marry in haste, repent at leisure** proverb those who rush impetuously into marriage may spend a long time regretting doing so. **marry money** informal marry a rich person.
– ORIGIN Middle English: from Old French *marier*, from Latin *maritare*, from *maritus*, literally 'married', (as a noun) 'husband'.

marry[2] ▶ exclamation archaic expressing surprise, indignation, or emphatic assertion.
– ORIGIN late Middle English: variant of **MARY**[1].

Marryat /ˈmarɪət/, Frederick (1792–1848), English novelist and naval officer; known as **Captain Marryat**. Notable works: *Peter Simple* (1833), *Mr Midshipman Easy* (1836), *The Children of the New Forest* (1847).

marrying ▶ adjective [attrib.] likely or inclined to marry: *I'm* ***not the marrying kind.***

Mars 1 Roman Mythology the god of war and the most important Roman god after Jupiter. The month of March is named after him. Greek equivalent **ARES**.
2 Astronomy a small reddish planet which is the fourth in order from the sun and is periodically visible to the naked eye.

> Mars orbits between earth and Jupiter at an average distance of 228 million km from the sun, and has an equatorial diameter of 6,787 km. Its characteristic red colour arises from the iron-rich minerals covering its surface. There is a tenuous atmosphere of carbon dioxide and the seasonal polar caps are mainly of frozen carbon dioxide. Unambiguous evidence of life has yet to be found. There are two small satellites, Phobos and Deimos.

Marsala /mɑːˈsɑːlə/ ▶ noun [mass noun] a dark, sweet fortified dessert wine that resembles sherry, produced in Sicily.
– ORIGIN named after *Marsala*, a town in Sicily where it was originally made.

Marseillaise /ˌmɑːseɪˈjɛz, -s(ə)ˈleɪz/ the national anthem of France, written by Rouget de Lisle in 1792 and first sung in Paris by Marseilles patriots.
– ORIGIN French, feminine of *Marseillais* 'of Marseilles'.

Marseilles /mɑːˈseɪ, -ˈseɪlz/ a city and port on the Mediterranean coast of southern France; pop. 807,725 (1990). French name **MARSEILLE** /marsɛj/.

Mars Global Surveyor see **GLOBAL SURVEYOR**.

Marsh, Dame Ngaio (Edith) (1899–1982), New Zealand writer of detective fiction. Her works include *Vintage Murder* (1937) and *Final Curtain* (1947).

marsh ▶ noun an area of low-lying land which is flooded in wet seasons or at high tide, and typically remains waterlogged at all times.
– DERIVATIVES **marshiness** noun, **marshy** adjective.
– ORIGIN Old English *mer(i)sc* (perhaps influenced by late Latin *mariscus* 'marsh'), of West Germanic origin.

marshal ▶ noun **1** an officer of the highest rank in the armed forces of some countries.
■chiefly historical a high-ranking officer of state.
2 US a federal or municipal law officer.
■the head of a police department. ■ N. Amer. the head of a fire department.
3 an official responsible for supervising public events, especially sports events or parades.
■(in the UK) an official accompanying a judge on circuit, with secretarial and social duties.
▶verb (**marshalled**, **marshalling**; US **marshaled**, **marshaling**) [with obj.] **1** arrange or assemble (a group of people, especially soldiers) in order: *the general marshalled his troops |* figurative *he paused for a moment, as if marshalling his thoughts.*
■[with obj. and adverbial of direction] guide or usher (someone) ceremoniously: *guests were marshalled into position.* ■ [with obj.] correctly position or arrange (rolling stock). ■ [with obj.] guide or direct the movement of (an aircraft) on the ground at an airport.
2 Heraldry combine (coats of arms), typically to indicate marriage, descent, or the bearing of office.
– DERIVATIVES **marshaller** noun, **marshalship** noun.
– ORIGIN Middle English (denoting a high-ranking officer of state): from Old French *mareschal* 'farrier, commander', from late Latin *mariscalcus*, from Germanic elements meaning 'horse' (compare with **MARE**[1]) and 'servant'.

Marshall, George C. (1880–1959), American general and statesman; full name *George Catlett Marshall*. As US Secretary of State (1947–9) he initiated the programme of economic aid to European countries known as the Marshall Plan. Nobel Peace Prize (1953).

Marshallese /ˌmɑːʃəˈliːz/ ▶ noun (pl. same) **1** a native or inhabitant of the Marshall Islands.
2 [mass noun] the Micronesian language of the Marshall Islands.
▶adjective of or relating to the Marshall Islands, their inhabitants, or their language.

marshalling yard ▶ noun a large railway yard in which freight wagons are sorted into trains and sent on their way.

Marshall Islands (also **the Marshalls**) a country consisting of two chains of islands in the NW Pacific; pop. 43,420 (1990); languages, English (official), local Austronesian languages; capital, Majuro.

> The islands were made a German protectorate in 1885. After being under Japanese mandate following the First World War they were administered by the US as part of the Pacific Islands Trust Territory from 1947 until 1986, when they became a republic in free association with the US.

– ORIGIN named after John Marshall, an English adventurer who visited the islands in 1788.

Marshall Plan a programme of financial aid and other initiatives, sponsored by the US, designed to boost the economies of western European countries after the Second World War. It was originally advocated by Secretary of State George C. Marshall and passed by Congress in 1948. Official name **EUROPEAN RECOVERY PROGRAM**.

Marshal of the Royal Air Force ▶ noun the highest rank of officer in the RAF.

marshalsea /ˈmɑːs(ə)lsiː/ ▶ noun (in England) a court formerly held before the steward and the knight marshal of the royal household. It was abolished in 1849.
■(**the Marshalsea**) a former prison in Southwark, London, under the control of the knight marshal.
– ORIGIN late Middle English (earlier *marchalcy*): from Anglo-Norman French *marschalcie*, from late Latin *mariscalcia*, from *mariscalcus* 'marshal'.

Marsh Arab ▶ noun a member of a semi-nomadic Arab people inhabiting marshland in southern Iraq, near the confluence of the Tigris and Euphrates rivers.

marshbird ▶ noun a bird that frequents marshes and reed beds, in particular:
• a brown streaked Australian warbler (genus *Megalurus*, family Sylviidae). Also called **GRASSBIRD**. • a South American bird of the American blackbird family (genus *Pseudoleistes*, family Icteridae).

marsh fern ▶ noun a tall, graceful fern that grows in fens and marshes in both Eurasia and North America.
• *Thelypteris palustris*, family Thelypteridaceae.

marsh fever ▶ noun [mass noun] malaria, so called in reference to the marshes where the mosquitoes that transmit it breed.

marsh frog ▶ noun a large, gregarious European frog with a pointed snout, warty skin, and a loud laughing call.
• *Rana ridibunda*, family Ranidae.

marsh gas ▶ noun [mass noun] methane, especially as generated by decaying matter in marshes.

marsh harrier ▶ noun a dark-backed Old World harrier that frequents marshes and reed beds.
• Genus *Circus*, family Accipitridae: several species, including the **western marsh harrier** (*C. aeruginosus*) of Eurasia and North Africa, the female of which has a cream-coloured crown.

marsh hawk ▶ noun North American term for **HEN HARRIER**.

marshland ▶ noun [mass noun] (also **marshlands**) land consisting of marshes.

marshmallow ▶ noun [mass noun] an item of confectionery made from a soft mixture of sugar, albumen, and gelatin.

marsh mallow ▶ noun a tall pink-flowered European plant which typically grows in brackish marshes. The roots were formerly used to make marshmallow, and it is sometimes cultivated for use in medicine.
• *Althaea officinalis*, family Malvaceae.

marsh marigold ▶ noun a plant of the buttercup family which has large yellow flowers and grows in damp ground and shallow water, native to north temperate regions. Also called **KINGCUP**.
• *Caltha palustris*, family Ranunculaceae.

marsh snail ▶ noun any of a number of snails which live in marshy habitats or ponds, in particular:
• a European freshwater snail (*Galba* (or *Limnaea*) *palustris*, family Limnaeidae). • an American salt-marsh snail (family Ellobiidae).

marsh tit ▶ noun a Eurasian woodland tit (songbird) with mainly grey-brown plumage, a shiny black cap, and white cheeks.
• *Parus palustris*, family Paridae.

marsh treader ▶ noun North American term for **WATER MEASURER**.

marshwort ▶ noun a white-flowered plant of the parsley family which grows beside streams and in boggy areas.
• Genus *Apium*, family Umbelliferae: several species, in particular *A. nodiflorum*.

Mars Pathfinder see **PATHFINDER**.

Marston Moor, Battle of a battle of the English Civil War, fought in 1644 on Marston Moor near York, in which the Royalist armies suffered a defeat which fatally weakened Charles I's cause.

marsupial /mɑːˈsuːpɪəl/ Zoology ▶ noun a mammal of an order whose members are born incompletely developed and are typically carried and suckled in a pouch on the mother's belly. Marsupials are

found mainly in Australia and New Guinea, though three families, including the opossums, live in America.
• Order Marsupialia and infraclass Metatheria, subclass Theria.
▶ **adjective** of or relating to this order.
– ORIGIN late 17th cent. (in the sense 'resembling a pouch'): from modern Latin *marsupialis*, via Latin from Greek *marsupion* 'pouch' (see **MARSUPIUM**).

marsupial cat ▶ **noun** a white-spotted catlike marsupial related to the quolls, native to New Guinea.
• *Dasyurus albopunctatus*, family Dasyuridae.

marsupial mole ▶ **noun** a mole-like burrowing Australian marsupial with yellow fur, stubby limbs, and a horny shield on the front of the head.
• *Notoryctes typhlops*, the only member of the family Notoryctidae.

marsupial mouse ▶ **noun** a carnivorous mouse-like marsupial native to Australia and New Guinea.
• Several genera and species, family Dasyuridae.

marsupium /mɑːˈsuːpɪəm/ ▶ **noun** (pl. **marsupia** /-pɪə/) Zoology a pouch that protects eggs, offspring, or reproductive structures, especially the pouch of a female marsupial mammal.
– ORIGIN mid 17th cent.: via Latin from Greek *marsupion*, diminutive of *marsipos* 'purse'.

Marsyas /ˈmɑːsɪəs/ Greek Mythology a satyr who challenged Apollo to a contest in flute playing and was flayed alive when he lost.

mart ▶ **noun** [usu. with modifier] a trade centre or market: *the cattle mart.*
– ORIGIN late Middle English: from Middle Dutch *mart*, variant of *marct* 'market'.

Martaban, Gulf of /ˌmɑːtəˈbɑːn/ an inlet of the Andaman Sea, a part of the Indian Ocean, on the coast of SE Burma (Myanmar) east of Rangoon.

martagon lily /ˈmɑːtəg(ə)n/ ▶ **noun** a Eurasian lily that typically has small purple flowers which are said to resemble turbans. Also called ***Turk's cap lily***.
• *Lilium martagon*, family Liliaceae.
– ORIGIN late Middle English (as *mortagon*): from medieval Latin *martagon*, of uncertain origin.

Martel, Charles, see **CHARLES MARTEL**.

Martello /mɑːˈtɛləʊ/ (also **Martello tower**) ▶ **noun** (pl. **-os**) any of numerous small circular forts that were erected for defence purposes along the SE coasts of England during the Napoleonic Wars.
– ORIGIN alteration (by association with Italian *martello* 'hammer') of Cape *Mortella* in Corsica, where such a tower proved difficult for the English to capture in 1794.

marten /ˈmɑːtɪn/ ▶ **noun** a semi-arboreal weasel-like mammal found in Eurasia and North America, hunted for its fur in many northern countries.
• Genus *Martes*, family Mustelidae: several species. See **PINE MARTEN, STONE MARTEN**.
– ORIGIN Middle English (frequently in the plural, denoting the fur): from Old French (*peau*) *martrine* 'marten (fur)', from *martre*, of West Germanic origin.

martenot ▶ **noun** see **ONDES MARTENOT**.

martensite /ˈmɑːtɪnzʌɪt/ ▶ **noun** [mass noun] Metallurgy a hard and very brittle solid solution of carbon in iron that is the main constituent of hardened steel.
– DERIVATIVES **martensitic** adjective.
– ORIGIN late 19th cent.: named after Adolf *Martens* (1850–1914), German metallurgist, + **-ITE**[1].

Martha (in the New Testament) the sister of Lazarus and Mary and friend of Jesus (Luke 10:40).
■ [as noun **a Martha**] a woman kept very busy, especially in domestic affairs.

Martha's Vineyard a resort island off the coast of Massachusetts, to the south of Cape Cod.

Martial /ˈmɑːʃ(ə)l/ (*c.*40–*c.*104 AD), Roman epigrammatist, born in Spain; Latin name *Marcus Valerius Martialis*. His fifteen books of epigrams, in a variety of metres, reflect all facets of Roman life.

martial /ˈmɑːʃ(ə)l/ ▶ **adjective** of or appropriate to war; warlike: *martial bravery.*
– DERIVATIVES **martially** adverb.
– ORIGIN late Middle English: from Old French, or from Latin *martialis*, from *Mars*, *Mart-* (see **MARS**).

martial arts ▶ **plural noun** various sports or skills, mainly of Japanese origin, which originated as forms of self-defence or attack, such as judo, karate, and kendo.
– DERIVATIVES **martial artist** noun.

martial eagle ▶ **noun** a brown eagle with a brown-spotted white belly, which is Africa's largest eagle.
• *Polmaetus bellicosus*, family Accipitridae.

martial law ▶ **noun** [mass noun] military government, involving the suspension of ordinary law.

Martian ▶ **adjective** of or relating to the planet Mars or its supposed inhabitants.
▶ **noun** a hypothetical or fictional inhabitant of Mars.
– ORIGIN late Middle English (in the senses 'subject to Mars's influence' and 'martial'): from Latin *Mars*, *Mart-* (see **MARS**) + **-IAN**.

Martin[1], Dean (1917–95), American singer and actor; born *Dino Paul Crocetti*. He joined with Frank Sinatra and Sammy Davis Jr (1925–90) in a number of films, including *Bells are Ringing* (1960), and had his own television show from 1965.

Martin[2], Sir George (Leonard) (b.1926), English record producer. He was involved with most of the Beatles' recordings, producing the revolutionary *Revolver* (1966) and *Sergeant Pepper's Lonely Hearts Club Band* (1967).

Martin[3], Steve (b.1945), American actor and comedian. He made his name with farcical film comedies such as *The Jerk* (1979) and went on to write, produce, and star in *Roxanne* (1987) and *LA Story* (1991).

martin ▶ **noun** a swift-flying insectivorous songbird of the swallow family, typically having a less strongly forked tail than a swallow.
• Family Hirundinidae: several genera and numerous species, e.g. the **house martin** and **sand martin**.
– ORIGIN late Middle English: probably a shortening of obsolete *martinet*, from French, probably from the name of St *Martin* of Tours, celebrated at **MARTINMAS**.

Martin, St (d.397), French bishop (Bishop of Tours from 371), a patron saint of France. When giving half his cloak to a beggar he received a vision of Christ, after which he was baptized. Feast day, 11 November.

Martineau /ˈmɑːtɪnəʊ/, Harriet (1802–76), English writer. She wrote mainly on social, economic, and historical subjects, and is known for her twenty-five-volume series *Illustrations of Political Economy* (1832–4) and her translation of Auguste Comte's *Philosophie positive* (1853).

martinet /ˌmɑːtɪˈnɛt/ ▶ **noun** a strict disciplinarian, especially in the armed forces.
– DERIVATIVES **martinettish** (also **martinetish**) adjective.
– ORIGIN late 17th cent. (denoting the system of drill invented by Martinet): named after Jean *Martinet*, 17th-cent. French drill master.

martingale /ˈmɑːtɪŋgeɪl/ ▶ **noun 1** a strap, or set of straps, attached at one end to the noseband (**standing martingale**) or reins (**running martingale**) of a horse and at the other end to the girth. It is used to prevent the horse from raising its head too high.
2 [mass noun] a gambling system of continually doubling the stakes in the hope of an eventual win that must yield a net profit.
– ORIGIN late 16th cent.: from French, from Spanish *almártaga*, from Arabic *al-marta'a* 'the fastening', influenced by *martingale*, from Occitan *martegal* 'inhabitant of Martigues (in Provence)'.

Martini[1] /mɑːˈtiːni, Italian marˈtini/, Simone (*c.*1284–1344), Italian painter. His work is characterized by strong outlines and the use of rich colour, as in *The Annunciation* (1333).

Martini[2] /mɑːˈtiːni/ ▶ **noun** [mass noun] trademark a type of vermouth produced in Italy.
■ [count noun] a cocktail made from gin and dry vermouth.
– ORIGIN named (as a trademark) after *Martini* and Rossi, an Italian firm selling vermouth.

Martinique /ˌmɑːtɪˈniːk, French martinik/ a French island in the Caribbean, in the Lesser Antilles group; pop. 359,570 (1990); capital, Fort-de-France.
– DERIVATIVES **Martiniquan** noun & adjective.

Martinist ▶ **noun** an adherent of a form of mystical pantheism developed by the French philosopher L. C. de Saint-Martin (1743–1803).
– DERIVATIVES **Martinism** noun.

Martinmas /ˈmɑːtɪnməs/ ▶ **noun** St Martin's Day, 11 November.

Martinware ▶ **noun** [mass noun] a type of brown salt-glazed pottery made by the Martin brothers in Southall, near London, in the late 19th and early 20th centuries.

martlet /ˈmɑːtlɪt/ ▶ **noun** Heraldry a bird like a swallow without feet, borne (typically with the wings closed) as a charge or a mark of cadency for a fourth son.
– ORIGIN late Middle English (denoting a swift): from Old French *merlet*, influenced by *martinet* (see **MARTIN**).

martyr ▶ **noun** a person who is killed because of their religious or other beliefs: *the first Christian martyr.*
■ a person who displays or exaggerates their discomfort or distress in order to obtain sympathy or admiration: *she wanted to play the martyr.* ■ (**martyr to**) a constant sufferer from (an ailment): *I'm a martyr to migraine!*
▶ **verb** [with obj.] (usu. **be martyred**) kill (someone) because of their beliefs: *she was martyred for her faith.*
■ cause great pain or distress to: *there was no need to martyr themselves again.*
– DERIVATIVES **martyrization** (also **-isation**) noun, **martyrize** (also **-ise**) verb.
– ORIGIN Old English *martir*, via ecclesiastical Latin from Greek *martur* 'witness' (in Christian use, 'martyr').

martyrdom ▶ **noun** [mass noun] the death or suffering of a martyr.
■ a display of feigned or exaggerated suffering to obtain sympathy or admiration.
– ORIGIN Old English *martyrdōm* (see **MARTYR, -DOM**).

martyred ▶ **adjective** (of a person) having been martyred: *a martyred saint.*
■ (of an attitude or manner) showing feigned or exaggerated suffering to obtain sympathy or admiration: *he got into the car with a martyred air.*

martyrology ▶ **noun** (pl. **-ies**) [mass noun] the branch of history or literature that deals with the lives of martyrs.
■ [count noun] a list or register of martyrs.
– DERIVATIVES **martyrological** adjective, **martyrologist** noun.
– ORIGIN late 16th cent.: via medieval Latin from ecclesiastical Greek *marturologion*, from *martur* 'martyr' + *logos* 'account'.

martyry ▶ **noun** (pl. **-ies**) a shrine or church erected in honour of a martyr.
– ORIGIN Middle English (denoting martyrdom): via medieval Latin from Greek *marturion* 'martyrdom'.

Maruts /ˈmʌrʊts/ Hinduism the sons of Rudra. In the Rig Veda they are the storm gods, Indra's helpers. Also called **RUDRAS**.

marvel ▶ **verb** (**marvelled**, **marvelling**; US **marveled**, **marveling**) [no obj.] be filled with wonder or astonishment: *she marvelled at Geoffrey's composure* | [with direct speech] *'It looks huge,' marvelled Clare.*
▶ **noun** a wonderful or astonishing person or thing: *the marvels of technology* | *Charlie, you're a marvel!*
– DERIVATIVES **marveller** noun.
– ORIGIN Middle English (as a noun): from Old French *merveille*, from late Latin *mirabilia*, neuter plural of Latin *mirabilis* 'wonderful', from *mirari* 'wonder at'.

Marvell /mɑːˈvɛl, ˈmɑːv(ə)l/, Andrew (1621–78), English metaphysical poet. He was best known during his lifetime for his verse satires and pamphlets attacking the corruption of Charles II and his ministers; most of his poetry was published posthumously and was not recognized until the 20th century. Notable poems: 'To his Coy Mistress' and 'Bermudas'.

marvellous (US **marvelous**) ▶ **adjective** causing great wonder; extraordinary: *these marvellous technological toys are fun to play with.*
■ extremely good or pleasing; splendid: *you have done a marvellous job* | *it's marvellous to see you.*
– DERIVATIVES **marvellously** adverb, **marvellousness** noun.
– ORIGIN Middle English: from Old French *merveillus*, from *merveille* (see **MARVEL**).

marvel of Peru ▶ **noun** a tropical American herbaceous plant with fragrant trumpet-shaped flowers which open late in the afternoon. Also called ***four o'clock plant***.
• *Mirabilis jalapa*, family Nyctaginaceae.

marvy ▶ **adjective** informal wonderful; marvellous.

Marwari /məˈwɑːri/ ▶ **noun** [mass noun] an Indic

m

language of Rajasthan in India, spoken by about 10 million people.
▶ **adjective** of or relating to this language.
– ORIGIN from Hindi *Mārvār*, from Sanskrit *maru* 'desert'.

Marx, Karl (Heinrich) (1818–83), German political philosopher and economist, resident in England from 1849. The founder of modern communism with Friedrich Engels, he collaborated with him in the writing of the *Communist Manifesto* (1848), and enlarged it into a series of books, most notably the three-volume *Das Kapital*.

Marx Brothers a family of American comedians, consisting of the brothers **Chico** (Leonard, 1886–1961), **Harpo** (Adolph Arthur, 1888–1964), **Groucho** (Julius Henry, 1890–1977), and **Zeppo** (Herbert, 1901–79). Their films, which are characterized by their anarchic humour, include *Duck Soup* (1933) and *A Night at the Opera* (1935).

Marxisant /ˌmɑːksɪˈzɒ̃/ ▶ **adjective** having Marxist leanings: *a Marxisant government.*
– ORIGIN 1960s: from French, from *Marxiste* 'Marxist'.

Marxism ▶ **noun** [mass noun] the political and economic theories of Karl Marx and Friedrich Engels, later developed by their followers to form the basis for the theory and practice of communism.

Central to Marxist theory is an explanation of social change in terms of economic factors, according to which the means of production provide the economic *base* which influences or determines the political and ideological *superstructure*. Marx and Engels predicted the revolutionary overthrow of capitalism by the proletariat and the eventual attainment of a classless communist society.

– DERIVATIVES **Marxist** noun & adjective.

Marxism–Leninism ▶ **noun** [mass noun] the doctrines of Marx as interpreted and put into effect by Lenin in the Soviet Union and (at first) by Mao Zedong in China.
– DERIVATIVES **Marxist–Leninist** noun & adjective.

Mary[1], mother of Jesus; known as **the** (**Blessed**) **Virgin Mary**, or **St Mary**, or **Our Lady**. According to the Gospels she was a virgin betrothed to Joseph and conceived Jesus by the power of the Holy Spirit. She has been venerated by Catholic and Orthodox Churches from the earliest Christian times. Feast days, 1 January (Roman Catholic Church), 25 March (Annunciation), 15 August (Assumption), 8 September (Immaculate Conception).

Mary[2] the name of two queens of England:
▪Mary I (1516–58), daughter of Henry VIII, reigned 1553–8; known as **Mary Tudor** or **Bloody Mary**. In an attempt to reverse the country's turn towards Protestantism she instigated the series of religious persecutions by which she earned her nickname.
▪Mary II (1662–94), daughter of James II, reigned 1689–94. Having been invited to replace her Catholic father on the throne after his deposition in 1689, she insisted that her husband, William of Orange, be crowned along with her.

Mary[3] ▶ **noun** (pl. **-ies**) (in Australian pidgin) an Aboriginal woman or girl.

Mary, Queen of Scots (1542–87), daughter of James V, queen of Scotland 1542–67; known as **Mary Stuart**. A devout Catholic, she was unable to control her Protestant lords, and fled to England in 1567. She became the focus of several Catholic plots against Elizabeth I and was eventually beheaded.

Mary, St see **MARY**[1].

Mary Celeste /sɪˈlɛst/ (also **Marie Celeste**) an American brig that was found in the North Atlantic in December 1872 in perfect condition but abandoned. The fate of the crew and the reason for the abandonment of the ship remain a mystery.

Maryland a state of the eastern US, on the Atlantic coast, surrounding Chesapeake Bay; pop. 4,781,470 (1990); capital, Annapolis. Colonized from England in the 17th century, it was one of the original thirteen states of the Union (1788).
– DERIVATIVES **Marylander** noun.
– ORIGIN named after Queen Henrietta *Maria*, wife of Charles I.

Mary Magdalene, St /ˈmagdəliːn/ (also **Magdalen**) (in the New Testament) a woman of Magdala in Galilee. She was a follower of Jesus, who cured her of evil spirits (Luke 8:2); she is also traditionally identified with the 'sinner' of Luke 7:37. Feast day, 22 July.

Mary Rose a heavily armed ship, built for Henry VIII, that in 1545 sank with the loss of nearly all her company when going out to engage the French fleet off Portsmouth. The hull was raised in 1982.

Mary Stuart see **MARY, QUEEN OF SCOTS**.

Mary Tudor, Mary I of England (see **MARY**[2]).

marzipan /ˈmɑːzɪpan, ˌmɑːzɪˈpan/ ▶ **noun** [mass noun] a sweet yellowish paste of ground almonds, sugar, and egg whites, used to make small cakes or sweets or to coat large cakes.
▪[count noun] a sweet or cake made of or based on marzipan.
▶ **verb** [with obj.] [usu. as adj. **marzipanned**] cover with marzipan: *a marzipanned cake.*
– ORIGIN late 15th cent. (as *marchpane*): from Italian *marzapane*, possibly from Arabic. The form *marchpane* (influenced by **MARCH** and obsolete *pain* 'bread') was more usual until the late 19th cent., when *marzipan* (influenced by German, which has the same spelling) displaced it.

mas /mɑːs/ ▶ **noun** W. Indian a festival or carnival.
– ORIGIN abbreviation of **MASQUERADE**.

masa /ˈmasa/ ▶ **noun** [mass noun] (in Latin American cuisine) dough made from maize flour and used to make tortillas, tamales, etc.
– ORIGIN Spanish.

Masaccio /maˈsatʃɪəʊ/, (1401–28), Italian painter; born *Tommaso Giovanni di Simone Guidi*. The first artist to apply the laws of perspective to painting, he is remembered particularly for his frescoes in the Brancacci Chapel in Florence (1424–7).

Masada /məˈsɑːdə/ the site of the ruins of a palace and fortification built by Herod the Great on the SW shore of the Dead Sea in the 1st century BC. It was a Jewish stronghold in the Zealots' revolt against the Romans (AD 66–73) and was the scene in AD 73 of mass suicide by the Jewish defenders when the Romans breached the citadel after a siege of nearly two years.

Masai /ˈmɑːsʌɪ, məˈsʌɪ, mɑːˈsʌɪ/ (also **Maasai**) ▶ **noun** (pl. same or **Masais**) **1** a member of a pastoral people living in Tanzania and Kenya.
2 [mass noun] the Nilotic language of the Masai, with about 700,000 speakers.
▶ **adjective** of or relating to the Masai or their language.

masala /məˈsɑːlə/ ▶ **noun** [mass noun] any of a number of spice mixtures ground into a paste or powder for use in Indian cookery.
▪a dish flavoured with this: *chicken masala.*
– ORIGIN from Urdu *maṣālaḥ*, based on Arabic *maṣāliḥ* 'ingredients, materials'.

Masaryk /ˈmasərɪk/, Tomáš (Garrigue) (1850–1937), Czechoslovak statesman, President 1918–35. He became Czechoslovakia's first President when the country achieved independence in 1918.

Masbate /masˈbɑːti/ an island in the central Philippines; pop. 599,355 (1990).

Mascagni /maˈskɑːnji/, Pietro (1863–1945), Italian composer and conductor. He is especially remembered for the opera *Cavalleria Rusticana* (1890).

mascara /maˈskɑːrə/ ▶ **noun** [mass noun] a cosmetic for darkening and thickening the eyelashes.
– DERIVATIVES **mascaraed** adjective.
– ORIGIN late 19th cent.: from Italian, literally 'mask', from Arabic *maskara* 'buffoon'.

Mascarene Islands /ˌmaskəˈriːn/ (also **the Mascarenes**) a group of three islands in the western Indian Ocean, east of Madagascar, comprising Réunion, Mauritius, and Rodrigues.
– ORIGIN named after the 16th-cent. Portuguese navigator Pedro de *Mascarenhas*.

mascarpone /ˌmaskəˈpəʊneɪ, -ˈpəʊni/ ▶ **noun** [mass noun] a soft, mild Italian cream cheese.

mascle /ˈmɑːsk(ə)l/ ▶ **noun** Heraldry a lozenge voided, i.e. with a central lozenge-shaped aperture.
– ORIGIN late Middle English: from Anglo-Norman French, from Anglo-Latin *mascula* 'mesh'.

mascon /ˈmaskɒn/ ▶ **noun** Astronomy a concentration of denser material below the surface of the moon or other body, causing a local increase in gravitational pull.
– ORIGIN 1960s: from *mas(s) con(centration)*.

mascot ▶ **noun** a person or thing that is supposed to bring good luck or that is used to symbolize a particular event or organization: *the squadron's mascot was a young lion cub.*
– ORIGIN late 19th cent.: from French *mascotte*, from modern Provençal *mascotto*, feminine diminutive of *masco* 'witch'.

masculine ▶ **adjective** **1** having qualities or appearance traditionally associated with men: *he is outstandingly handsome and robust, very masculine.*
▪of or relating to men; male: *a masculine voice.*
2 Grammar of or denoting a gender of nouns and adjectives, conventionally regarded as male.
▶ **noun** (**the masculine**) the male sex or gender.
▪Grammar a masculine word or form.
– DERIVATIVES **masculinely** adverb, **masculinity** noun.
– ORIGIN late Middle English (in grammatical use): via Old French from Latin *masculinus*, from *masculus* 'male'.

masculine rhyme ▶ **noun** Prosody a rhyme between final stressed syllables (e.g. *blow/flow, confess/redress*). Compare with **FEMININE RHYME**.

masculinist (also **masculist**) ▶ **adjective** characterized by or denoting attitudes or values held to be typical of men: *masculinist language.*
▪of or relating to the advocacy of the rights or needs of men.
▶ **noun** an advocate of the rights or needs of men.

masculinize (also **-ise**) ▶ **verb** [with obj.] induce male physiological characteristics in.
▪cause to appear or seem masculine: [as adj. **masculinized**] *a slightly masculinized swagger.*
– DERIVATIVES **masculinization** noun.

Masefield /ˈmeɪsfiːld/, John (Edward) (1878–1967), English poet and novelist. He was appointed Poet Laureate in 1930. Notable works: *Salt-Water Ballads* (1902).

maser /ˈmeɪzə/ ▶ **noun** a device using the stimulated emission of radiation by excited atoms to amplify or generate coherent monochromatic electromagnetic radiation in the microwave range. Compare with **LASER**.
– ORIGIN 1950s: acronym from *microwave amplification by the stimulated emission of radiation.*

Maseru /məˈsɛːruː/ the capital of Lesotho, situated on the Caledon River near the border with the province of Free State in South Africa; pop. 367,000 (est. 1992).

mash ▶ **noun** a uniform mass made by crushing a substance into a soft pulp, sometimes with the addition of liquid: *pound the garlic to a mash.*
▪[mass noun] bran mixed with hot water, given as a warm food to horses or other animals. ▪[mass noun] Brit. informal boiled and mashed potatoes, typically with milk and butter added. ▪[mass noun] (in brewing) a mixture of powdered malt and hot water, which is stood until the sugars dissolve to form the wort.
▶ **verb** [with obj.] **1** reduce (a food or other substance) to a uniform mass by crushing it: *mash the beans to a paste* | [as adj. **mashed**] *mashed potato.*
▪crush or smash (something) to a pulp: *he almost had his head mashed by a slamming door.* ▪[no obj.] US & W. Indian informal press forcefully on (something): *the worst thing you can do is mash the brake pedal.*
2 (in brewing) mix (powdered malt) with hot water to form wort.
3 Brit. informal infuse or brew (tea).
▪[no obj.] (of tea) draw; brew.
– ORIGIN Old English *māsc* (used as a brewing term), of West Germanic origin; perhaps ultimately related to **MIX**.

masher ▶ **noun** **1** a utensil for mashing food.
2 informal, dated a fashionable young man, especially of the Edwardian era; a dandy. [ORIGIN: late 19th cent.: probably a derivative of slang *mash* 'attract sexually', perhaps from Romany *masherava* 'allure'.]

Mashhad /maʃˈhad/ (also **Meshed**) a city in NE Iran, close to the border with Turkmenistan; pop. 1,463,500 (1986). The burial place in AD 809 of the Abbasid caliph Harun ar-Rashid and in 818 of the Shiite leader Ali ar-Rida, it is a holy city of the Shiite Muslims. It is the second largest city in Iran.

mashie /ˈmaʃi/ ▶ **noun** Golf, dated an iron used for lofting or for medium distances.
– ORIGIN late 19th cent.: perhaps from French *massue* 'club'.

mash note ▶ **noun** N. Amer. informal a letter which expresses infatuation with or gushing appreciation of someone.
– ORIGIN late 19th cent.: from slang *mash* 'infatuation' + **NOTE**.

Mashona /məˈʃəʊnə/ ▶ **noun** [mass noun] the Shona

people collectively, particularly those of Zimbabwe.
▶**adjective** of or relating to the Shona people.
– ORIGIN the name in Shona.

Mashonaland an area of northern Zimbabwe, occupied by the Shona people. A former province of Southern Rhodesia, it is now divided into the three provinces of Mashonaland East, West, and Central.

mash tun ▶**noun** (in brewing) a vat in which malt is mashed.

masjid /ˈmʌsdʒɪd, ˈmas-/ ▶**noun** Arabic word for a mosque.

mask ▶**noun 1** a covering for all or part of the face, in particular:
■a covering worn as a disguise, or to amuse or terrify other people. ■a covering made of fibre or gauze and fitting over the nose and mouth to protect against dust or air pollutants, or made of sterile gauze and worn to prevent infection of the wearer or (in surgery) of the patient. ■a protective covering fitting over the whole face, worn in fencing, ice hockey, and other sports. ■a respirator used to filter inhaled air or to supply gas for inhalation. ■a face pack. ■Entomology the enlarged labium of a dragonfly larva, which can be extended to seize prey.
2 a likeness of a person's face in clay or wax, especially one made by taking a mould from the face.
■a person's face regarded as having set into a particular expression: *his face was a mask of rage.* ■a hollow model of a human head worn by ancient Greek and Roman actors. ■the face or head of an animal, especially of a fox, as a hunting trophy.
■archaic a masked person.
3 figurative a disguise or pretence: *she let her mask of moderate respectability slip.*
4 Photography a piece of something such as card used to cover a part of an image that is not required when exposing a print.
■Electronics a patterned metal film used in the manufacture of microcircuits to allow selective modification of the underlying material.
▶**verb** [with obj.] cover (the face) with a mask.
■conceal (something) from view: *the poplars masked a factory.* ■disguise or hide (a sensation or quality): *brandy did not completely mask the bitter taste.* ■cover (an object or surface) so as to protect it from a process, especially painting: ***mask off*** *doors and cupboards with sheets of plastic.*
– DERIVATIVES **masked** adjective.
– ORIGIN mid 16th cent.: from French *masque*, from Italian *maschera*, *mascara*, probably from medieval Latin *masca* 'witch, spectre', but influenced by Arabic *maskara* 'buffoon'.

masked ball ▶**noun** a ball at which participants wear masks to conceal their faces.

masker ▶**noun 1** a thing that masks or conceals something else.
2 a person taking part in a masquerade or masked ball.

masking tape ▶**noun** [mass noun] adhesive tape used in painting to cover areas on which paint is not wanted.

maskinonge /ˈmaskɪnɒn(d)ʒ, -ˈnɒn(d)ʒi/ ▶**noun** another term for **MUSKELLUNGE**.

masochism /ˈmasəkɪz(ə)m/ ▶**noun** [mass noun] the tendency to derive pleasure, especially sexual gratification, from one's own pain or humiliation.
■(in general use) the enjoyment of what appears to be painful or tiresome: *isn't there some masochism involved in taking on this kind of project?*
– DERIVATIVES **masochist** noun, **masochistic** adjective, **masochistically** adverb.
– ORIGIN late 19th cent.: named after Leopold von Sacher-Masoch (1835–95), the Austrian novelist who described it, + **-ISM**.

Mason[1], A. E. W. (1865–1948), English novelist; full name *Alfred Edward Woodley Mason*. Notable works: *The Four Feathers* (adventure story, 1902) and *Musk and Amber* (historical novel, 1942).

Mason[2], James (Neville) (1909–84), English actor. He acted in more than a hundred films, notably *A Star is Born* (1954), *Lolita* (1962), and *Georgy Girl* (1966).

mason ▶**noun 1** a builder and worker in stone.
2 (**Mason**) a Freemason.
▶**verb** [with obj.] build from or strengthen with stone.
■cut, hew, or dress (stone).
– ORIGIN Middle English: from Old French *masson* (noun), *maçonner* (verb), probably of Germanic origin; perhaps related to **MAKE**.

mason bee ▶**noun** a solitary bee that nests in cavities within which it constructs cells of sand and other particles glued together with saliva.
• *Osmia* and other genera, family Apidae.

Mason–Dixon Line ▶**noun** (in the US) the boundary between Maryland and Pennsylvania, taken as the northern limit of the slave-owning states before the abolition of slavery.
– ORIGIN named after Charles *Mason* and Jeremiah *Dixon*, the 18th-cent. English astronomers who surveyed it in 1763–7.

Masonic /məˈsɒnɪk/ ▶**adjective** of or relating to Freemasons: *a Masonic lodge.*

Masonite ▶**noun** [mass noun] trademark, chiefly N. Amer. fibreboard made from wood fibre pulped under steam at high pressure.
– ORIGIN 1920s: from the name of the *Mason* Fibre Co., Laurel, Mississippi, US, + **-ITE**[1].

Mason jar ▶**noun** chiefly N. Amer. a wide-mouthed glass jar with an airtight screw top, used for preserving fruit and vegetables.
– ORIGIN late 19th cent.: named after John L. *Mason* (died 1902), American inventor.

masonry ▶**noun** [mass noun] **1** stonework.
■the work of a mason.
2 (**Masonry**) Freemasonry.

mason's mark ▶**noun** a distinctive device carved on stone by the mason who dressed it.

mason wasp ▶**noun** a solitary wasp that nests in a cavity or in a hole in the ground, sealing the nest with mud or similar material.
• Several genera in the family Eumenidae.

masoor /mʌˈsʊə/ (also **masoor dahl**) ▶**noun** a lentil of a small orange-red variety.
– ORIGIN from Hindi *masūr*.

Masorah /məˈsɔːrə/ (also **Massorah**) ▶**noun** (**the Masorah**) the collection of information and comment on the text of the traditional Hebrew Bible by the Masoretes.
■the Masoretic text of the Bible.
– ORIGIN from Hebrew *māsōrāh* based on *'āsar* 'to bind', later interpreted in the sense 'tradition' (as if from *māsar* 'hand down').

Masorete /ˈmasəriːt/ (also **Massorete**) ▶**noun** any of the Jewish scholars of the 6th to 10th centuries AD who contributed to the establishment of a recognized text of the Hebrew Bible, and to the compilation of the Masorah.
– DERIVATIVES **Masoretic** /-ˈrɛtɪk/ adjective.
– ORIGIN from French *Massoret* and modern Latin *Massoreta*, from Hebrew *māsōreṯ*; related to *māsōrāh* (see **MASORAH**).

masque /mɑːsk/ ▶**noun** a form of amateur dramatic entertainment, popular among the nobility in 16th- and 17th-century England, which consisted of dancing and acting performed by masked players.
– DERIVATIVES **masquer** noun.
– ORIGIN early 16th cent. (in the sense 'masquerade or masqued ball'): probably a back-formation (with spelling influenced by French *masque* 'mask') from *masker*, from Italian *mascar* 'person wearing a mask'.

masquerade /ˌmɑːskəˈreɪd, ˌmas-/ ▶**noun** a false show or pretence: *he had unwillingly gone along with the masquerade.*
■[mass noun] the wearing of disguise: *dressing up, role playing, and masquerade.* ■a masked ball.
▶**verb** [no obj.] pretend to be someone one is not: *a journalist* ***masquerading as*** *a man in distress.*
■be disguised or passed off as something else: *the idle gossip that* ***masquerades as*** *news in some local papers.*
– DERIVATIVES **masquerader** noun.
– ORIGIN late 16th cent.: from French *mascarade*, from Italian *mascherata*, from *maschera* 'mask'.

Mass ▶**noun** the Christian Eucharist or Holy Communion, especially in the Roman Catholic Church: *we went to Mass | the Latin Mass.*
■a celebration of this: *there was a Mass and the whole family was supposed to go.* ■a musical setting of parts of the liturgy used in the Mass.
– PHRASES **hear Mass** attend a celebration of the Mass without taking communion (especially as the former usual practice of lay Catholics).
– ORIGIN Old English *mæsse*, from ecclesiastical Latin *missa*, from Latin *miss-* 'dismissed', from *mittere*, perhaps from the last words of the service, *Ite, missa est* 'Go, it is the dismissal'.

Mass. ▶**abbreviation for** Massachusetts.

mass ▶**noun 1** a coherent, typically large body of matter with no definite shape: *a* ***mass of*** *curly hair | from here the trees were a dark mass.*
■a large number of people or objects crowded together: ***a mass of*** *cyclists.* ■a large amount of material: ***a mass of*** *conflicting evidence.* ■(**masses**) informal a large quantity or amount of something: *we get* ***masses of*** *homework.* ■any of the main portions in a painting or drawing that each have some unity in colour, lighting, or some other quality: *the masterly distribution of masses.*
2 (**the mass of**) the majority of: *the great mass of the population had little interest in the project.*
■(**the masses**) the ordinary people.
3 [mass noun] Physics the quantity of matter which a body contains, as measured by its acceleration under a given force or by the force exerted on it by a gravitational field.
■(in general use) weight.
▶**adjective** [attrib.] relating to, done by, or affecting large numbers of people or things: *the film has mass appeal | a mass exodus of refugees.*
▶**verb** assemble or cause to assemble into a mass or as one body: [with obj.] *both countries began massing troops in the region* | [no obj.] *clouds massed heavily on the horizon.*
– PHRASES **be a mass of** be completely covered with. **in mass** as a body. **in the mass** as a whole: *her genuine affection for humanity in the mass.*
– DERIVATIVES **massless** adjective.
– ORIGIN late Middle English: from Old French *masse*, from Latin *massa*, from Greek *maza* 'barley cake'; perhaps related to *massein* 'knead'.

massa /ˈmasə/ ▶**noun** (in representations of black speech) master: *'Massa, I have some news for you, sah.'*

Massachusetts /ˌmasəˈtʃuːsɪts/ a state in the north-eastern US, on the Atlantic coast; pop. 6,016,425 (1990); capital, Boston. Settled by the Pilgrim Fathers in 1620, it was a centre of resistance to the British before becoming one of the original thirteen states of the Union (1788).

Massachusetts Institute of Technology (abbrev.: **MIT**) a US institute of higher education, famous for scientific and technical research, founded in 1861 in Cambridge, Massachusetts.

massacre ▶**noun** an indiscriminate and brutal slaughter of people: *the attack was described as a cold-blooded massacre* | [mass noun] *she says he is an accomplice to massacre.*
■informal a heavy defeat of a sporting team or contestant.
▶**verb** [with obj.] deliberately and violently kill (a large number of people).
■informal inflict a heavy defeat on (a sporting team or contestant). ■informal perform (a piece of music, a play, etc.) very ineptly: *the choir was massacring 'In the Bleak Midwinter'.*
– ORIGIN late 16th cent.: from French, of unknown origin.

Massacre of St Bartholomew the massacre of Huguenots throughout France ordered by Charles IX at the instigation of his mother, Catherine de' Medici, and begun without warning on 24 August (the feast of St Bartholomew) 1572.

massage /ˈmasɑːʒ, məˈsɑːʒ, -dʒ/ ▶**noun** [mass noun] the rubbing and kneading of muscles and joints of the body with the hands, especially to relieve tension or pain: *massage can ease tiredness and jet lag* | [count noun] *a massage will help loosen you up.*
▶**verb** [with obj.] **1** rub and knead (a person or part of the body) with the hands.
■(**massage something in/into/on to**) rub a substance into (the skin or hair). ■flatter (someone's ego): *I chose a man who massaged my bruised ego.*
2 manipulate (figures) to give a more acceptable result: *the accounts had been massaged and adjusted to suit the government.*
– DERIVATIVES **massager** noun.
– ORIGIN late 19th cent.: from French, from *masser* 'knead, treat with massage', probably from Portuguese *amassar* 'knead', from *massa* 'dough'.

massage parlour ▶**noun** an establishment providing massage.
■used euphemistically to refer to a brothel.

massasauga /ˌmasəˈsɔːgə/ ▶**noun** a small North American rattlesnake of variable colour which favours damp habitats.
• *Sistrurus catenatus*, family Viperidae.
– ORIGIN mid 19th cent.: formed irregularly from **MISSISSAUGA**.

Massawa /məˈsɑːwə/ (also **Mitsiwa**) the chief port of Eritrea, on the Red Sea; pop. 27,500 (1984).

mass defect ▶ noun Physics the difference between the mass of an isotope and its mass number.

massé /'maseɪ/ ▶ noun [usu. as modifier] Billiards & Snooker a stroke made with an inclined cue, imparting swerve to the ball: *a massé shot.*
- ORIGIN late 19th cent.: French, past participle of *masser*, describing the action of making such a stroke.

mass energy ▶ noun [mass noun] Physics mass and energy regarded as interconvertible manifestations of the same phenomenon, according to the laws of relativity.
- ■ the mass of a body regarded relativistically as energy.

masseter /ma'siːtə/ (also **masseter muscle**) ▶ noun Anatomy a muscle which runs through the rear part of the cheek from the temporal bone to the lower jaw on each side and closes the jaw in chewing.
- ORIGIN late 16th cent.: from Greek *masētēr*, from *masasthai* 'to chew'.

masseur /ma'səː/ ▶ noun a person who provides massage professionally.
- ORIGIN French, from *masser* 'to massage'.

masseuse /ma'səːz/ ▶ noun a female masseur.
- ORIGIN French.

massicot /'masɪkɒt/ ▶ noun [mass noun] a yellow form of lead monoxide, used as a pigment.
- ORIGIN late 15th cent.: from French (influenced by Italian *marzacotto* 'unguent'), ultimately from Arabic *martak*.

massif /'masɪf, ma'siːf/ ▶ noun a compact group of mountains, especially one that is separate from other groups.
- ORIGIN early 16th cent. (denoting a large building): French adjective meaning 'massive', used as a noun. The current sense dates from the late 19th cent.

Massif Central /ˌmasiːf sɒ'trɑːl/, French *massif sãtral/* a mountainous plateau in south central France. Covering almost one sixth of the country, it rises to a height of 1,887 m (6,188 ft) at Puy de Sancy in the Auvergne.

Massine /ma'siːn/, Léonide Fédorovitch (1895–1979), Russian-born choreographer and ballet dancer, a French citizen from 1944; born *Leonid Fyodorovich Myasin.* He was the originator of the symphonic ballet, and danced in and choreographed the film *The Red Shoes* (1948).

Massinger /'masɪndʒə/, Philip (1583–1640), English dramatist. Notable works: *The Duke of Milan* (1621–2), *A New Way to Pay Old Debts* (1625–6), and *The City Madam* (1632).

massive ▶ adjective 1 large and heavy or solid: *a massive rampart of stone.*
- 2 exceptionally large: *massive crowds are expected.* ■ very intense or severe: *a massive heart attack.* ■ informal particularly successful or influential: *they're going to be massive.*
- 3 Geology (of rocks or beds) having no discernible form or structure.
- ■ (of a mineral) not visibly crystalline.
- ▶ noun Brit. informal a group of young people from a particular area with a common interest in hip-hop or jungle music: *the Bristol massive.*
- DERIVATIVES **massively** adverb [as submodifier] *a massively complicated network,* **massiveness** noun.
- ORIGIN late Middle English: from French *massif, -ive,* from Old French *massis,* based on Latin *massa* (see MASS).

mass market ▶ noun the market for goods that are produced in large quantities.
- ▶ verb (**mass-market**) [with obj.] market (a product) on a large scale.

mass media ▶ plural noun (usu. **the mass media**) [treated as sing. or pl.] the media.

mass noun ▶ noun Grammar 1 a noun denoting something which cannot be counted (e.g. a substance or quality), in English usually a noun which lacks a plural in ordinary usage and is not used with the indefinite article, e.g. *luggage, china, happiness.* Contrasted with COUNT NOUN.
- 2 a noun denoting something which normally cannot be counted but which may be countable when it refers to different units or types, e.g. *coffee, bread (drank some coffee, ordered two coffees; ate some bread, stocks several different breads).*

mass number ▶ noun Physics the total number of protons and neutrons in a nucleus.

mass observation ▶ noun [mass noun] Brit., chiefly

historical the study and recording of the social habits and opinions of ordinary people.

Masson /'masõ/, André (1896–1987), French painter and graphic artist. He joined the surrealists in the mid 1920s and pioneered 'automatic' drawing, a form of fluid, spontaneous composition intended to express images emerging from the unconscious.

Massorah ▶ noun variant spelling of MASORAH.

Massorete ▶ noun variant spelling of MASORETE.

mass-produce ▶ verb [with obj.] produce large quantities of (a standardized article) by an automated mechanical process: [as adj. **mass-produced**] *cheap mass-produced goods.*
- DERIVATIVES **mass-producer** noun, **mass production** noun.

mass spectrograph ▶ noun a mass spectrometer in which the particles are detected photographically.

mass spectrometer ▶ noun an apparatus for separating isotopes, molecules, and molecular fragments according to mass. The sample is vaporized and ionized, and the ions are accelerated in an electric field and deflected by a magnetic field into a curved trajectory that gives a distinctive mass spectrum.

mass spectrum ▶ noun a distribution of ions shown by the use of a mass spectrograph or mass spectrometer.

mass transit ▶ noun [mass noun] N. Amer. public transport, especially in an urban area.

massy ▶ adjective poetic/literary or archaic consisting of a large mass; bulky; massive: *a round massy table.*

mast¹ ▶ noun a tall upright post, spar, or other structure on a ship or boat, typically one of several and in sailing vessels generally carrying a sail or sails.
- ■ a similar structure on land, especially a flagpole or a television or radio transmitter.
- PHRASES **before the mast** historical serving as an ordinary seaman in a sailing ship (quartered in the forecastle). **nail** (or **pin**) **one's colours to the mast** declare openly and firmly what one believes or favours: *they nailed their colours to the mast of youth revolt.*
- DERIVATIVES **masted** adjective [in combination] *a single-masted fishing boat.*
- ORIGIN Old English *mæst,* of West Germanic origin; related to Dutch *mast* and German *Mast.*

mast² ▶ noun [mass noun] the fruit of beech, oak, chestnut, and other forest trees, especially as food for pigs and wild animals.
- ORIGIN Old English *mæst,* of West Germanic origin; probably related to MEAT.

mastaba /'mastəbə/ ▶ noun 1 Archaeology an ancient Egyptian tomb consisting of an underground burial chamber with rooms above it (at ground level) to store offerings.
- 2 (in Islamic countries) a bench, typically of stone, attached to a house.
- ORIGIN from Arabic *maṣṭaba.*

mast cell ▶ noun a cell filled with basophil granules, found in numbers in connective tissue and releasing histamine and other substances during inflammatory and allergic reactions.
- ORIGIN late 19th cent.: *mast* from German *Mast* 'fattening, feeding'.

mastectomy /ma'stɛktəmi/ ▶ noun (pl. **-ies**) a surgical operation to remove a breast.
- ORIGIN 1920s: from Greek *mastos* 'breast' + -ECTOMY.

master¹ ▶ noun 1 chiefly historical a man who has people working for him, especially servants or slaves: *he acceded to his master's wishes.*
- ■ a person who has dominance or control of something: *he was master of the situation.* ■ a machine or device directly controlling another: [as modifier] *a master cylinder.* Compare with SLAVE. ■ dated a male head of a household: *the master of the house.* ■ the male owner of a dog, horse, or other domesticated animal.
- 2 a skilled practitioner of a particular art or activity: *I'm a master of disguise.*
- ■ a great artist, especially one belonging to the accepted canon: *the work of the great masters is spread around the art galleries of the world.* ■ a very strong chess player, especially one who has qualified for the title at international tournaments: *a chess master.* See also GRAND MASTER. ■ (**Masters**) [treated as sing.] (in

some sports) a class for competitors over the usual age for the highest level of competition.
- 3 a person who holds a second or further degree from a university or other academic institution (only in titles and set expressions): *a master's degree* | *a Master of Arts.*
- 4 a man in charge of an organization or group, in particular:
- ■ chiefly Brit. a male schoolteacher, especially at a public or prep school: *the games master.* ■ the head of a college or school. ■ the presiding officer of a livery company or Masonic lodge. ■ the captain of a merchant ship. ■ the person in control of a pack of hounds. ■ (in England and Wales) an official of the Supreme Court.
- 5 used as a title prefixed to the name of a boy not old enough to be called 'Mr': *Master James Wishart.*
- ■ archaic a title for a man of high rank or learning. ■ the title of the heir apparent of a Scottish viscount or baron.
- 6 an original film, recording, or document from which copies can be made: [as modifier] *the master tape.*
- ▶ adjective [attrib.] 1 having or showing very great skill or proficiency: *a master painter.*
- ■ denoting a person skilled in a particular trade and able to teach others: *a master bricklayer.*
- 2 main; principal: *the master bedroom.*
- ▶ verb [with obj.] 1 acquire complete knowledge or skill in (an accomplishment, technique, or art): *I never mastered Latin.*
- 2 gain control of; overcome: *I managed to master my fears.*
- 3 make a master copy of (a film or record).
- PHRASES **be one's own master** be independent or free to do as one wishes. **make oneself master of** acquire a thorough knowledge of or facility in.
- DERIVATIVES **masterdom** noun, **masterhood** noun, **masterless** adjective, **mastership** noun.
- ORIGIN Old English *mæg(i)ster* (later reinforced by Old French *maistre*), from Latin *magister*; probably related to *magis* 'more' (i.e. 'more important').

master² ▶ noun [in combination] a ship or boat with a specified number of masts: *a three-master.*

Master Aircrew ▶ noun a generic RAF rank equivalent to warrant officer, only applied to members of an aircrew.

master-at-arms ▶ noun (pl. **masters-at-arms**) a warrant officer appointed to carry out or supervise police duties on board a ship.

master chief petty officer ▶ noun a rank in the US navy, above senior chief petty officer and below warrant officer.

masterclass ▶ noun a class, especially in music, given by an expert to highly talented students.

master corporal ▶ noun a rank in the Canadian army and air force, above corporal and below sergeant.

masterful ▶ adjective 1 powerful and able to control others: *he looked masculine and masterful.*
- 2 performed or performing very skilfully: *a masterful assessment of the difficulties.*
- DERIVATIVES **masterfully** adverb, **masterfulness** noun.

> USAGE Some writers maintain a distinction between **masterful** and **masterly**, using **masterful** to mean 'powerful and able to control others' (*a masterful tone of voice*) and **masterly** to mean 'with the skill of a master' (*a masterly performance*). In practice the two words overlap considerably in the second meaning: more than half the citations for **masterful** in the Oxford Reading Programme relate to the sense 'with the skill of a master'.

master gunnery sergeant ▶ noun a rank of non-commissioned officer in the US marines, above master sergeant and below sergeant major.

master key ▶ noun a key that opens several locks, each of which also has its own key.

masterly ▶ adjective performed or performing in a very skilful and accomplished way: *his masterly account of rural France.*

master mariner ▶ noun a seaman qualified to be a captain, especially of a merchant ship.

master mason ▶ noun 1 a skilled mason, especially one who employs other workers.
- 2 a fully qualified Freemason.

mastermind ▶ noun a person with an outstanding intellect: *an eminent musical mastermind.*
- ■ someone who plans and directs an ingenious and

complex scheme or enterprise: *the mastermind behind the project.*
▶**verb** [with obj.] plan and direct (an ingenious and complex scheme or enterprise).

master of ceremonies ▶**noun** a person in charge of procedure at a state or public occasion.
■a person who introduces speakers, players, or entertainers.

Master of the Rolls ▶**noun** (in England and Wales) the judge who presides over the Court of Appeal (Civil Division) and who was formerly in charge of the Public Record Office.

masterpiece ▶**noun** a work of outstanding artistry, skill, or workmanship: *a great literary masterpiece* | *the car was a masterpiece of space-age technology.*
■an artist's or craftsman's best piece of work: *Picasso's masterpiece* Guernica. ■ historical a piece of work by a craftsman accepted as qualification for membership of a guild as an acknowledged master.

master plan ▶**noun** a comprehensive or far-reaching plan of action.

master seaman ▶**noun** a rank in the Canadian navy, above leading seaman and below petty officer.

master sergeant ▶**noun** a high rank of non-commissioned officer in the US armed forces, in the army above sergeant first class and below sergeant major, in the air force above technical sergeant and below senior master sergeant, and in the marines above gunnery sergeant and below master gunnery sergeant.

mastersinger ▶**noun** another term for **MEISTERSINGER**.

Masters Tournament a prestigious US golf competition, held in Augusta, Georgia, in which golfers (chiefly professionals) compete only by invitation on the basis of their past achievements.

master stroke ▶**noun** an outstandingly skilful and opportune act; a very clever move.

master switch ▶**noun** a switch controlling the supply of electricity or fuel to an entire system.
■Biology a substance or gene that regulates gene expression or embryonic development, or initiates cancer.

master warrant officer ▶**noun** a rank in the Canadian army and air force, above warrant officer and below chief warrant officer.

masterwork ▶**noun** a masterpiece.

masterwort ▶**noun** a plant of the parsley family with white or pinkish flowers and lobed leaves, native to central and southern Europe.
• Two genera in the family Umbelliferae: *Peucedanum*, with loose flower heads, and *Astrantia*, with small compact starlike flower heads surrounded by prominent bracts.

mastery ▶**noun** [mass noun] **1** comprehensive knowledge or skill in a subject or accomplishment: *she played with some mastery.*
■the action or process of mastering a subject or accomplishment: *a child's mastery of language.*
2 control or superiority over someone or something: *man's* **mastery over** *nature.*
– ORIGIN Middle English: from Old French *maistrie*, from *maistre* 'master'.

masthead ▶**noun 1** the highest part of a ship's mast or of the lower section of a mast.
2 the title of a newspaper or magazine at the head of the front or editorial page.
■chiefly N. Amer. the listed details in a newspaper or magazine referring to ownership, advertising rates, etc.
▶**verb** [with obj.] **1** historical send (a sailor) to the masthead, especially as a punishment.
2 raise (a flag or sail) to the masthead.

mastic /ˈmastɪk/ ▶**noun 1** [mass noun] an aromatic gum or resin exuded from the bark of a Mediterranean tree, used in making varnish and chewing gum and as a flavouring.
2 (also **mastic tree**) the bushy evergreen Mediterranean tree which yields mastic and has aromatic leaves and fruit, closely related to the pistachio.
• *Pistacia lentiscus*, family Anacardiaceae.
■used in names of similar or related trees, e.g. **American mastic**.
3 [mass noun] a putty-like waterproof filler and sealant used in building.
– ORIGIN late Middle English: via Old French and Latin from Greek *mastikhē* (perhaps from *mastikhan* 'masticate').

masticate /ˈmastɪkeɪt/ ▶**verb** [with obj.] chew (food).
– DERIVATIVES **mastication** noun, **masticator** noun, **masticatory** adjective.
– ORIGIN mid 17th cent.: from late Latin *masticat-* 'chewed', from the verb *masticare*, from Greek *mastikhan* 'gnash the teeth' (related to *masasthai* 'to chew').

mastiff /ˈmastɪf, ˈmɑː-/ ▶**noun** a dog of a large, strong breed with drooping ears and pendulous lips.
– ORIGIN Middle English: obscurely representing Old French *mastin*, based on Latin *mansuetus* 'tame'.

mastiff bat ▶**noun** a heavily built free-tailed bat with a broad muzzle, found mainly in America and Australasia.
• *Eumops*, *Molossus*, and other genera, family Molossidae: several species.
■another term for **BULLDOG BAT**.

Mastigophora /ˌmastɪˈɡɒfərə/ Zoology a group of single-celled animals that includes the protozoal flagellates, which are now generally divided among several phyla of the kingdom Protista.
• Subphylum (or superclass) Mastigophora.
– DERIVATIVES **mastigophoran** noun & adjective.
– ORIGIN modern Latin (plural), from Greek *mastigophoros*, from *mastix*, *mastig-* 'whip' + *-phoros* 'bearing'.

mastitis /maˈstʌɪtɪs/ ▶**noun** [mass noun] inflammation of the mammary gland in the breast or udder, typically due to bacterial infection via a damaged nipple or teat.
– ORIGIN mid 19th cent.: from Greek *mastos* 'breast' + **-ITIS**.

mastodon /ˈmastədɒn/ ▶**noun** a large extinct elephant-like mammal of the Miocene to Pleistocene epochs, having teeth of a relatively primitive form and number.
• Mammutidae and other families, order Proboscidea: many species, including *Mammut americanus*, which possibly survived to historical times in North America.
– ORIGIN early 19th cent.: modern Latin, from Greek *mastos* 'breast' + *odous*, *odont-* 'tooth' (with reference to nipple-shaped tubercles on the crowns of its molar teeth).

mastoid /ˈmastɔɪd/ ▶**adjective** Anatomy of or relating to the mastoid process: *mastoid disease.*
▶**noun** Anatomy the mastoid process.
■(**mastoids**) [treated as sing.] informal mastoiditis.
– ORIGIN mid 18th cent.: via French and modern Latin from Greek *mastoeidēs* 'breast-shaped', from *mastos* 'breast'.

mastoiditis /ˌmastɔɪˈdʌɪtɪs/ ▶**noun** [mass noun] Medicine inflammation of the mastoid process.

mastoid process ▶**noun** a conical prominence of the temporal bone behind the ear, to which neck muscles are attached, and which has air spaces linked to the middle ear.

masturbate /ˈmastəbeɪt/ ▶**verb** [no obj.] stimulate one's genitals with one's hand for sexual pleasure.
■[with obj.] stimulate the genitals of (someone) to give them sexual pleasure.
– DERIVATIVES **masturbation** noun, **masturbator** noun, **masturbatory** adjective.
– ORIGIN mid 19th cent.: from Latin *masturbat-* 'masturbated', from the verb *masturbari*, of unknown ultimate origin.

Masuria /məˈsjʊərɪə/ a low-lying forested lakeland region of NE Poland. Formerly part of East Prussia, it was assigned to Poland after the Second World War. Also called **MASURIAN LAKES**.

mat¹ ▶**noun 1** a piece of protective material placed on a floor, in particular:
■a piece of coarse material placed on a floor for people to wipe their feet on. ■ a piece of resilient material for landing on in gymnastics, wrestling, or similar sports. ■ a small rug. ■ a piece of coarse material for lying on: *a beach mat.*
2 a small piece of cork, card, or similar material placed on a table or other surface to protect it from the heat or moisture of an object placed on it.
■(also **mouse mat**) a small piece of rigid or slightly resilient material on which a computer mouse is moved.
3 a thick, untidy layer of something hairy or woolly: *his chest was covered by a thick mat of soft fair hair.*
▶**verb** (**matted**, **matting**) [with obj.] tangle (something, especially hair) in a thick mass: *sweat matted his hair* | *the fur on its flank was matted with blood.*
■[no obj.] become tangled.
– PHRASES **go to the mat** informal vigorously engage in an argument or dispute, typically on behalf of a particular person or cause. **on the mat** informal being reprimanded by someone in authority. [ORIGIN: with military reference to the orderly room mat, where an accused would stand before the commanding officer.]
– ORIGIN Old English *m(e)att(e)*, of West Germanic origin; related to Dutch *mat* and German *Matte*, from late Latin *matta*, from Phoenician.

mat² ▶**noun** short for **MATRIX** (in sense 2).

mat³ ▶**noun** variant spelling of **MATT**.

Mata /ˈmɑːtəː/ ▶**noun** Indian a mother (often used as a respectful form of address for a woman).
– ORIGIN via Hindi from Sanskrit *mātā* 'mother'.

Matabele /ˌmatəˈbiːli/ ▶**noun** the Ndebele people collectively, particularly those of Zimbabwe.
– ORIGIN from Sotho *matebele*, singular *letebele*, the name given to this people.

Matabeleland a former province of Southern Rhodesia, lying between the Limpopo and Zambezi rivers and occupied by the Matabele people. It is now divided into the two Zimbabwean provinces of Matabeleland North and South.

matador /ˈmatədɔː/ ▶**noun 1** a bullfighter whose task is to kill the bull.
2 (in ombre, skat, and other card games) any of the highest trumps.
3 [mass noun] a domino game in which halves are matched so as to make a total of seven.
■[count noun] any of the dominoes which have seven spots altogether, together with the double blank.
– ORIGIN Spanish, literally 'killer', from *matar* 'to kill', from Persian *māt* 'dead'; senses relating to games are extended uses, expressing a notion of 'dominance, control'.

Mata Hari /ˌmɑːtə ˈhɑːri/ (1876–1917), Dutch dancer and secret agent; born *Margaretha Geertruida Zelle*. She probably worked for both French and German intelligence services before being executed by the French in 1917.
■[as noun **a Mata Hari**] a beautiful and seductive female spy.
– ORIGIN from Malay *mata* 'eye' and *hari* 'day', as a compound meaning 'sun'.

matai¹ /ˈmatʌɪ/ ▶**noun** (pl. **matais**) a coniferous New Zealand tree which yields pale timber.
• *Prumnopitys taxifolia*, family Podocarpaceae. Alternative name: **black pine**.
– ORIGIN mid 19th cent.: from Maori.

matai² /məˈtʌɪ/ ▶**noun** (pl. same) (in a Samoan extended family or clan) the person who is chosen to succeed to a chief's or orator's title and honoured as the head of the family.
– ORIGIN Samoan.

matamata /ˌmatəˈmatə/ ▶**noun** a grotesque South American freshwater turtle that has a broad flat head and neck with irregular projections of skin resembling waterweed.
• *Chelus fimbriatus*, family Chelidae.
– ORIGIN mid 19th cent.: of unknown origin; probably from a South American Indian language.

match¹ ▶**noun 1** a contest in which people or teams compete against each other in a particular sport: *a boxing match.*
2 a person or thing able to contend with another as an equal in quality or strength: *they were* **no match for** *the trained mercenaries.*
3 a person or thing that resembles or corresponds to another: *the child's identical twin would be a perfect match for organ donation.*
■Computing a string that fulfils the specified conditions of a computer search. ■ a pair that corresponds or is very similar: *the headdresses and bouquet were a perfect match.* ■ the fact or appearance of corresponding: *stones of a perfect match and colour.*
4 a person viewed in regard to their eligibility for marriage, especially as regards class or wealth: *he was an unsuitable match for any of their girls.*
■a marriage: *a dynastic match.*
▶**verb** [with obj.] **1** correspond or cause to correspond in some essential respect; make or be harmonious: [with obj.] *I thought we'd have primrose walls to match the bath* | *she* **matched** *her steps* **to** *his* | [no obj.] *the jacket and trousers do not match* | [as adj. **matching**] *a set of matching coffee cups.*
■[with obj.] team (someone or something) with someone or something else appropriate or harmonious: *they* **matched** *suitably qualified applicants* **with** *institutions*

which had vacancies | *she was trying to* ***match*** *the draperies* ***to*** *the couch.*

2 be equal to (something) in quality or strength: *his anger matched her own.*

▪succeed in reaching or equalling (a standard or quality): *he tried to match her nonchalance.* ▪ equalize (two coupled electrical impedances) so as to bring about the maximum transfer of power from one to the other.

3 place (a person or group) in contest or competition with another: *the big names were* ***matched against*** *nobodies* | [as adj., with submodifier] (**matched**) *evenly matched teams.*

– PHRASES **make a match** form a partnership, especially by getting married. **meet one's match** encounter one's equal in strength or ability. **to match** corresponding in some essential respect with something previously mentioned or chosen: *a new coat and a hat to match.*

– DERIVATIVES **matchable** adjective.

– ORIGIN Old English *gemæcca* 'mate, companion', of West Germanic origin; related to the base of **MAKE**.

▶**match up to** be as good as or equal to: *she matches up to the challenges of the job.*

match someone with archaic bring about the marriage of someone to: *try if you can to match her with a duke.*

match² ▶**noun** a short, thin piece of wood or cardboard used to light a fire, being tipped with a composition that ignites when rubbed against a rough surface.

▪historical a piece of wick or cord designed to burn at a uniform rate, used for firing a cannon or lighting gunpowder.

– PHRASES **put a match to** set fire to.

– ORIGIN late Middle English (in the sense 'wick of a candle'): from Old French *meche*, perhaps from Latin *myxa* 'spout of a lamp', later 'lamp wick'.

matchboard ▶**noun** [mass noun] interlocking boards joined together by a tongue cut along the edge of one board and fitting into a groove along the edge of another.

matchbook ▶**noun** N. Amer. a small cardboard folder of matches with a striking surface on the back.

matchbox ▶**noun** a small box in which matches are sold.

▪[usu. as modifier] something very small, especially a house, flat, or room: *her new thimble-sized matchbox apartment.*

matchless ▶**adjective** unable to be equalled; incomparable: *the Parthenon has a matchless beauty.*

– DERIVATIVES **matchlessly** adverb.

matchlock ▶**noun** historical a type of gun with a lock in which a piece of wick or cord was placed for igniting the powder.

▪a lock of this kind.

matchmaker ▶**noun** a person who enjoys arranging relationships and marriages between others.

▪a person who arranges marriages in Jewish or Asian communities. ▪ figurative a person or company that brings parties together for commercial purposes.

– DERIVATIVES **matchmaking** noun.

match play ▶**noun** [mass noun] play in golf in which the score is reckoned by counting the holes won by each side, as opposed to the number of strokes taken. Compare with **STROKE PLAY**.

match point ▶**noun 1** (in tennis and other sports) a point which if won by one of the players or sides will also win them the match.

2 (in duplicate bridge) a unit of scoring in matches and tournaments.

matchstick ▶**noun** the stem of a match.

▪something likened to a match in being long and thin: *cut the vegetables into matchsticks* | [as modifier] *matchstick limbs.* ▪ [as modifier] (of a figure) drawn with short, thin straight lines: *matchstick men.*

matchwood ▶**noun** [mass noun] very small pieces or splinters of wood: *the bomb reduced the flimsy huts to matchwood.*

▪light poor-quality wood.

mate¹ ▶**noun 1** Brit. informal a friend or companion: *I was with a mate* | *my best mate Steve.*

▪used as a friendly form of address between men or boys: *'See you then, mate.'* ▪ [in combination] a fellow member or joint occupant of a specified thing: *his table-mates.*

2 each of a pair of birds or other animals: *a male bird sings to court a mate.*

▪informal a person's husband, wife, or other sexual partner.

3 an assistant or deputy, in particular:

▪an assistant to a skilled worker: *a plumber's mate.* ▪ an officer on a merchant ship subordinate to the master. See also **FIRST MATE**.

▶**verb 1** [no obj.] (of animals or birds) come together for breeding; copulate: *successful males may* ***mate with*** *many females* | [as noun **mating**] *ovulation occurs only if mating has taken place.*

▪[with obj.] bring (animals or birds) together for breeding. ▪ humorous join in marriage or sexual partnership: *people tend to* ***mate with*** *others in their own social class.*

2 [with obj.] join or connect mechanically: *a four-cylinder engine* ***mated to*** *a five-speed gearbox.*

▪[no obj.] be connected or joined.

– DERIVATIVES **mateless** adjective.

– ORIGIN late Middle English: from Middle Low German *māt(e)* 'comrade', of West Germanic origin; related to **MEAT** (the underlying notion being that of eating together).

mate² ▶**noun & verb** Chess short for **CHECKMATE**.

– PHRASES **fool's mate** a game in which White is mated by Black's queen on the second move. **scholar's mate** a game in which White mates Black on the fourth move with the queen, supported by the king's bishop.

– ORIGIN Middle English: the noun from Anglo-Norman French *mat* (from the phrase *eschec mat* 'checkmate'); the verb from Anglo-Norman French *mater* 'to checkmate'.

maté /ˈmateɪ/ (also **yerba maté**) ▶**noun** [mass noun] **1** (also **maté tea**) an infusion of the leaves of a South American shrub, which is high in caffeine but rather bitter.

▪the leaves of this shrub.

2 the South American shrub of the holly family which produces these leaves.

● *Ilex paraguariensis*, family Aquifoliaceae.

– ORIGIN early 18th cent.: from Spanish *mate*, from Quechua *mati*.

matelassé /ˌmat(ə)ˈlaseɪ/ ▶**adjective** (of a silk or wool fabric) having a raised design like quilting.

▶**noun** [mass noun] fabric of this type.

– ORIGIN late 19th cent.: French, literally 'quilted', past participle of *matelasser*, from *matelas* 'mattress'.

matelot /ˈmatləʊ/ ▶**noun** Brit. informal a sailor.

– ORIGIN mid 19th cent. (nautical slang): from French, variant of *matenot*, from Middle Dutch *mattenoot* 'bed companion', because sailors had to share hammocks in twos.

matelote /ˈmat(ə)ləʊt/ ▶**noun** [mass noun] a dish of fish in a sauce of wine and onions.

– ORIGIN French, from *à la matelote*, literally 'mariner-style', from *matelot* 'sailor' (see **MATELOT**).

mater /ˈmeɪtə/ ▶**noun** Brit. informal, dated mother: *the mater has kept on the house in London.*

– ORIGIN Latin.

mater dolorosa /ˌmɑːtə ˌdɒləˈrəʊsə, ˌmeɪtə/ the Virgin Mary sorrowing for the death of Christ, especially as a representation in art.

– ORIGIN from medieval Latin, 'sorrowful mother'.

materfamilias /ˌmeɪtəfəˈmɪlɪas/ ▶**noun** (pl. **matresfamilias**) the female head of a family or household. Compare with **PATERFAMILIAS**.

– ORIGIN Latin, from *mater* 'mother' + *familias*, old genitive form of *familia* 'family'.

material ▶**noun** [mass noun] **1** the matter from which a thing is or can be made: *goats can eat more or less any plant material* | [count noun] *materials such as brass* | *highly flammable materials.*

▪(usu. **materials**) things needed for an activity: *cleaning materials.* ▪ [with adj. or noun modifier] a person of a specified quality or suitability: *he's not really Olympic material.*

2 facts, information, or ideas for use in creating a book or other work: *his colonial experiences gave him material.*

▪items, especially songs or jokes, comprising a performer's act: *a watchable band playing original material.*

3 cloth or fabric: *a piece of dark material* | [count noun] *dress materials.*

▶**adjective 1** [attrib.] denoting or consisting of physical objects rather than the mind or spirit: *the material world* | *moral and material support.*

▪concerned with physical needs or desires: *material living standards have risen.* ▪ concerned with the matter of reasoning, not its form: *political conflict lacks mathematical or material certitude.*

2 important; essential; relevant: *the insects did not do any material damage to the crop.*

▪chiefly Law (of evidence or a fact) significant, influential or relevant, especially to the extent of determining a cause or affecting a judgement: *information that could be* ***material to*** *a murder inquiry.*

– ORIGIN late Middle English (in the sense 'relating to matter'): from late Latin *materialis*, adjective from Latin *materia* 'matter'.

material cause ▶**noun** Philosophy (in Aristotelian thought) the matter or substance which constitutes a thing.

materialism ▶**noun** [mass noun] **1** a tendency to consider material possessions and physical comfort as more important than spiritual values.

2 Philosophy the doctrine that nothing exists except matter and its movements and modifications.

▪the doctrine that consciousness and will are wholly due to material agency. See also **DIALECTICAL MATERIALISM**.

– DERIVATIVES **materialist** noun & adjective, **materialistic** adjective, **materialistically** adverb.

materiality ▶**noun** (pl. **-ies**) [mass noun] the quality or character of being material or composed of matter.

▪chiefly Law the quality of being relevant or significant: *the applicant must establish materiality on the balance of probabilities.*

materialize (also **-ise**) ▶**verb** [no obj.] **1** (of a ghost, spirit, or similar entity) appear in bodily form.

▪[with obj.] cause to appear in bodily or physical form. ▪ [with obj.] rare represent or express in material form.

2 become actual fact; happen: *the forecast rate of increase did not materialize.*

▪appear or be present: *the train didn't materialize.*

– DERIVATIVES **materialization** noun.

materially ▶**adverb 1** [often as submodifier] substantially; considerably: *materially different circumstances.*

2 in terms of wealth or material possessions: *a materially and culturally rich area.*

materia medica /məˌtɪərɪə ˈmɛdɪkə/ ▶**noun** [mass noun] the body of remedial substances used in the practice of medicine.

▪the study of the origin and properties of these substances.

– ORIGIN late 17th cent.: modern Latin, translation of Greek *hulē iatrikē* 'healing material' (the title of a work by Dioscorides).

materia prima /məˌtɪərɪə ˈprʌɪmə/ ▶**noun** [mass noun] primeval matter; fundamental substance.

– ORIGIN Latin.

materiel /məˌtɪərɪˈɛl/ ▶**noun** [mass noun] military materials and equipment. Often contrasted with **PERSONNEL**.

– ORIGIN early 19th cent.: from French *matériel*, adjective (used as a noun).

maternal ▶**adjective** of or relating to a mother, especially during pregnancy or shortly after childbirth: *maternal age* | *maternal care.*

▪[attrib.] related through the mother's side of the family: *my maternal grandfather.* ▪ denoting feelings associated with or typical of a mother; motherly: *maternal instincts.*

– DERIVATIVES **maternalism** noun, **maternalist** adjective, **maternalistic** adjective, **maternally** adverb.

– ORIGIN late 15th cent.: from French *maternel*, from Latin *maternus*, from *mater* 'mother'.

maternity ▶**noun** [mass noun] motherhood.

▪[usu. as modifier] the period during pregnancy and shortly after childbirth: *maternity leave* | *maternity clothes.*

– ORIGIN early 17th cent.: from French *maternité*, from Latin *maternus*, from *mater* 'mother'.

mateship ▶**noun** [mass noun] Austral. informal companionship or friendship, especially between men.

matey (also **maty**) Brit. informal ▶**adjective** (**matier**, **matiest**) familiar and friendly; sociable: *a fixed, matey grin.*

▶**noun** used as a familiar and typically hostile form of address, especially to a stranger: *'Shove off, matey, she's mine.'*

– DERIVATIVES **mateyness** (also **matiness**) noun, **matily** adverb.

math ▶**noun** [mass noun] N. Amer. informal mathematics: *she teaches math and science.*

– ORIGIN mid 19th cent.: abbreviation.

mathematical ▶**adjective** of or relating to mathematics: *mathematical equations.*

■(of a proof or analysis) rigorously precise: *mathematical thinking* ▪ figurative *he arranged the meal with mathematical precision on a plate.*
– DERIVATIVES **mathematically** adverb.
– ORIGIN late Middle English: from Latin *mathematicalis*, from Greek *mathēmatikos*, from *mathēma*, *mathēmat-* 'science', from the base of *manthanein* 'learn'.

mathematical induction ▶ noun see **INDUCTION** (sense 3).

mathematical logic ▶ noun [mass noun] the part of mathematics concerned with the study of formal languages, formal reasoning, the nature of mathematical proof, provability of mathematical statements, computability, and other aspects of the foundations of mathematics.

mathematical tables ▶ plural noun tables of logarithms and trigonometric values.

mathematician ▶ noun an expert in or student of mathematics.
– ORIGIN late Middle English: from Old French *mathematicien*, from Latin *mathematicus* 'mathematical', from Greek *mathēmatikos* (see **MATHEMATICAL**).

mathematics ▶ plural noun [usu. treated as sing.] the abstract science of number, quantity, and space. Mathematics may be studied in its own right (**pure mathematics**), or as it is applied to other disciplines such as physics and engineering (**applied mathematics**).
■[often treated as pl.] the mathematical aspects of something: *the mathematics of general relativity.*
– ORIGIN late 16th cent.: plural of obsolete *mathematic* 'mathematics', from Old French *mathematique*, from Latin (*ars*) *mathematica* 'mathematical (art)', from Greek *mathēmatikē* (*tekhnē*), from the base of *manthanein* 'learn'.

mathematize (also **-ise**) ▶ verb [with obj.] regard or treat (a subject or problem) in mathematical terms.
– DERIVATIVES **mathematization** noun.

maths ▶ plural noun [treated as sing.] Brit. informal mathematics: [as modifier] *her mother was a maths teacher.*
– ORIGIN early 20th cent.: abbreviation.

Matilda¹ (1102–67), English princess, daughter of Henry I and mother of Henry II; known as **the Empress Maud**. Henry's only legitimate child, she was named his heir, but her cousin Stephen seized the throne on Henry's death in 1135. She waged an unsuccessful civil war against Stephen until 1148.

Matilda² ▶ noun Austral. informal a bushman's bundle.
– PHRASES **waltz** (or **walk**) **Matilda** carry such a bundle.
– ORIGIN late 19th cent.: from the given name *Matilda.*

matinal /'matɪn(ə)l/ ▶ adjective rare relating to or taking place in the morning.
– ORIGIN early 19th cent.: from French, from *matin* 'morning'.

matinee /'matɪneɪ/ ▶ noun an afternoon performance in a theatre or cinema.
– ORIGIN mid 19th cent.: from French *matinée*, literally 'morning (as a period of activity)', from *matin* 'morning': performances were formerly also in the morning.

matinee coat ▶ noun Brit. a baby's short coat.

matinee idol ▶ noun informal, dated a handsome actor admired chiefly by women.

matins (also **mattins**) ▶ noun a service of morning prayer in various Churches, especially the Anglican Church.
■ a service forming part of the traditional Divine Office of the Western Christian Church, originally said (or chanted) at or after midnight, but historically often held with lauds on the previous evening. ■ (also **matin**) poetic/literary the morning song of birds.
– ORIGIN Middle English: from Old French *matines*, plural (influenced by ecclesiastical Latin *matutinae* 'morning prayers') of *matin* 'morning', from Latin *matutinum*, neuter of *matutinus* 'early in the morning', from *Matuta*, the name of the dawn goddess.

Matisse /ma'ti:s/, Henri (Emile Benoît) (1869–1954), French painter and sculptor. His use of non-naturalistic colour led him to be regarded as a leader of the fauvists. His later painting and sculpture displays a trend towards formal simplification and abstraction, and includes large figure compositions and abstracts made from cut-out coloured paper.

Mato Grosso /,matu: 'grɒsəʊ/ a high plateau region of SW Brazil, forming a watershed between the Amazon and Plate river systems. The region is divided into two states, **Mato Grosso** (capital, Cuiabá) and **Mato Grosso do Sul** (capital, Campo Grande).
– ORIGIN Portuguese, literally 'dense forest'.

matriarch /'meɪtrɪɑ:k/ ▶ noun a woman who is the head of a family or tribe.
■ an older woman who is powerful within a family or organization: *a domineering matriarch.*
– DERIVATIVES **matriarchal** /-'ɑ:k(ə)l/ adjective, **matriarchate** noun.
– ORIGIN early 17th cent.: from Latin *mater* 'mother', on the false analogy of *patriarch.*

matriarchy ▶ noun (pl. **-ies**) a system of society or government ruled by a woman or women.
■ a form of social organization in which descent and other relationship are reckoned through the female line. ■ [mass noun] the state of being an older, powerful woman in a family or group: *she cherished a dream of matriarchy—catered to by grandchildren.*

matric /mə'trɪk/ ▶ noun [mass noun] Brit. informal, dated matriculation.
– ORIGIN late 19th cent.: abbreviation.

matrices plural form of **MATRIX**.

matricide /'matrɪsʌɪd, 'meɪtrɪ-/ ▶ noun [mass noun] the killing of one's mother: *a man suspected of matricide.*
■ [count noun] a person who kills their mother.
– DERIVATIVES **matricidal** adjective.
– ORIGIN late 16th cent.: from Latin *matricidium*, from *mater*, *matr-* 'mother' + -*cidium* (see **-CIDE**).

matriculate /mə'trɪkjʊleɪt/ ▶ verb **1** [no obj.] be enrolled at a college or university: *he matriculated at Edinburgh University for a degree in pure science.*
■ [with obj.] admit (a student) to membership of a college or university. ■ S. African pass the final school-leaving examination.
2 [with obj.] Heraldry, chiefly Scottish record (arms) in an official register.
– ORIGIN late 16th cent.: from medieval Latin *matriculat-* 'enrolled', from the verb *matriculare*, from late Latin *matricula* 'register', diminutive of Latin *matrix.*

matriculation ▶ noun [mass noun] **1** the action of matriculating at a college or university: [as modifier] *matriculation requirements.*
■ [count noun] historical an examination to qualify for enrolment at a college or university. ■ [count noun] (in South Africa) a school-leaving examination taken at the end of the twelfth year of schooling.
2 Heraldry, chiefly Scottish the registration of arms in an official register.

matrifocal ▶ adjective (of a society, culture, etc.) based on the mother as the head of the family or household.
– ORIGIN 1950s: from Latin *mater*, *matr-* 'mother' + **FOCAL**.

matrilineal ▶ adjective of or based on kinship with the mother or the female line.
– DERIVATIVES **matrilineally** adverb.
– ORIGIN early 20th cent.: from Latin *mater*, *matr-* 'mother' + **LINEAL**.

matrilocal ▶ adjective of or denoting a custom in marriage whereby the husband goes to live with the wife's community. Also called **UXORILOCAL**.
– DERIVATIVES **matrilocality** noun.
– ORIGIN early 20th cent.: from Latin *mater*, *matr-* 'mother' + **LOCAL**.

matrimonial ▶ adjective of or relating to marriage or married people: *the matrimonial home.*
– DERIVATIVES **matrimonially** adverb.
– ORIGIN late Middle English: via Old French from Latin *matrimonialis*, from *matrimonium* (see **MATRIMONY**).

matrimony /'matrɪməni/ ▶ noun [mass noun] the state or ceremony of being married; marriage: *a couple joined in matrimony* | *the sacrament of holy matrimony.*
– ORIGIN late Middle English: via Old French from Latin *matrimonium*, based on *mater*, *matr-* 'mother'.

matrioshka ▶ noun variant spelling of **MATRYOSHKA**.

matrix /'meɪtrɪks/ ▶ noun (pl. **matrices** /-si:z/ or **matrixes**) **1** an environment or material in which something develops; a surrounding medium or structure: *Oxbridge was the matrix of the ideology.*
■ a mass of fine-grained rock in which gems, crystals, or fossils are embedded. ■ Biology the substance between cells or in which structures are embedded.
■ fine material: *the matrix of gravel paths is hoed regularly.*
2 a mould in which something, such as a gramophone record or printing type, is cast or shaped.
3 Mathematics a rectangular array of quantities or expressions in rows and columns that is treated as a single entity and manipulated according to particular rules.
■ a grid-like array of elements, especially of data items; a lattice. ■ an organizational structure in which two or more lines of command, responsibility, or communication may run through the same individual.
– ORIGIN late Middle English (in the sense 'womb'): from Latin, 'breeding female', later 'womb', from *mater*, *matr-* 'mother'.

matrix isolation ▶ noun [mass noun] Chemistry a technique for preparing free radicals or other unstable species by trapping them in a very cold inert substrate (such as solid argon) so that they can be studied spectroscopically.

matrix printer ▶ noun another term for **DOT MATRIX PRINTER**.

matron ▶ noun **1** a woman in charge of domestic and medical arrangements at a boarding school or other establishment.
■ Brit. the woman in charge of the nursing in a hospital (the official term in Britain is now **senior nursing officer**). ■ chiefly US a female prison officer.
2 a married woman, especially a dignified and sober middle-aged one.
– DERIVATIVES **matronhood** noun.
– ORIGIN late Middle English (in sense 2): from Old French *matrone*, from Latin *matrona*, from *mater*, *matr-* 'mother'.

matronly ▶ adjective like or characteristic of a matron or married woman, especially in being dignified, staid, or rather fat: *she was beginning to look matronly.*

matron of honour ▶ noun a married woman attending the bride at a wedding.

matronymic /,matrə'nɪmɪk/ (also **metronymic**) ▶ noun a name derived from the name of a mother or female ancestor.
▶ adjective (of a name) so derived.
– ORIGIN late 18th cent.: from Latin *mater*, *matr-* 'mother', on the pattern of *patronymic.*

matryoshka /,matrɪ'ɒʃka/ (also **matryoshka doll** or **matrioshka**) ▶ noun (pl. **matryoshki** /-ki/) another term for **RUSSIAN DOLL**.
– ORIGIN 1940s: from Russian *matrëshka.*

matsuri /mat'su:ri/ ▶ noun a solemn festival celebrated periodically at Shinto shrines in Japan.
– ORIGIN Japanese.

Matsuyama /,matsu:'jɑ:mə/ a city in Japan, the capital and largest city of the island of Shikoku; pop. 443,320 (1990).

Matt. ▶ abbreviation for Matthew (especially in biblical references).

matt (also **matte** or **mat**) ▶ adjective (of a colour, paint, or surface) dull and flat, without a shine: *matt black.*
▶ noun **1** [mass noun] a matt colour, paint, or finish: *the varnishes are available in gloss, satin, and matt.*
2 a sheet of cardboard placed on the back of a picture, either as a mount or to form a border around the picture.
▶ verb (**matted**, **matting**) [with obj.] (often **be matted**) give a matt appearance to (something).
– ORIGIN early 17th cent. (as a verb): from French *mat.*

mattar /'mʌtə:/ ▶ noun Indian term for **PEA**.

matte¹ /mat/ ▶ noun [mass noun] an impure product of the smelting of sulphide ores, especially those of copper or nickel.
– ORIGIN mid 19th cent.: from French (in Old French meaning 'curds'), feminine of *mat* (adjective) 'matt', used as a noun.

matte² /mat/ ▶ noun a mask used to obscure part of an image in a film and allow another image to be substituted, combining the two.
– ORIGIN mid 19th cent.: from French, perhaps from *mat* (see **MATT**).

matte³ ▶ adjective, noun, & verb variant spelling of **MATT**.

matted ▶ adjective **1** (especially of hair or fur)

tangled into a thick mass: *a cardigan of matted grey wool.*
2 covered or furnished with mats: *the matted floor.*

matter ▶ **noun 1** [mass noun] physical substance in general, as distinct from mind and spirit; (in physics) that which occupies space and possesses rest mass, especially as distinct from energy: *the structure and properties of matter.*
■a substance or material: *organic matter | vegetable matter.* ■ a substance in or discharged from the body: *faecal matter | waste matter.* ■ written or printed material: *reading matter.*
2 an affair or situation under consideration; a topic: *a great deal of work was done on this matter | financial matters.*
■Law something which is to be tried or proved in court; a case. ■ (**matters**) the present situation or state of affairs: *we can do nothing to change matters.* ■ (**a matter for/of**) something that evokes a specified feeling: *it's a matter of complete indifference to me.* ■ (**a matter for**) something that is the concern of a specified person or agency: *the evidence is a matter for the courts.*
3 [usu. with negative or in questions] (**the matter**) the reason for distress or a problem: *what's the matter? | pretend that nothing's the matter.*
4 the substance or content of a text as distinct from its manner or form.
■Printing the body of a printed work, as distinct from titles, headings, etc. ■ Logic the particular content of a proposition, as distinct from its form.
▶ **verb** [no obj.] **1** [usu. with negative or in questions] be of importance; have significance: *it doesn't matter what the guests wear | what did it* **matter to** *them? | to him, animals mattered more than human beings.*
■(of a person) be important or influential: *she was trying to get known by the people who matter.*
2 rare (of a wound) secrete or discharge pus.
– PHRASES **for that matter** used to indicate that a subject or category, though mentioned second, is as relevant or important as the first: *I am not sure what value it adds to determining public, or for that matter private, policy.* **in the matter of** as regards: *the British are given pre-eminence in the matter of tea.* **it is only a matter of time** there will not be long to wait: *it's only a matter of time before the general is removed.* **a matter of 1** no more than (a specified period of time): *they were shown the door in a matter of minutes.* **2** a thing that involves or depends on: *it's a matter of working out how to get something done.* **a matter of course** the natural or expected thing: *the reports are published as a matter of course.* **a matter of form** a point of correct procedure: *they must as a matter of proper form check to see that there is no tax liability.* **a matter of record** see **RECORD**. **no matter 1** [with clause] regardless of: **no matter what** *the government calls them, they are cuts.* **2** it is of no importance: *'No matter, I'll go myself.'* **to make matters worse** with the result that a bad situation is made worse. **what matter?** Brit. dated why should that worry us?: *what matter if he was a Protestant or not?*
– ORIGIN Middle English: via Old French from Latin *materia* 'timber, substance', also 'subject of discourse', from *mater* 'mother'.

Matterhorn /ˈmatəhɔːn, German ˈmatɐˌhɔrn/ a mountain in the Alps, on the border between Switzerland and Italy. Rising to 4,477 m (14,688 ft), it was first climbed in 1865 by the English mountaineer Edward Whymper. French name **MONT CERVIN**; Italian name **MONTE CERVINO**.

matter of fact ▶ **noun** something that belongs to the sphere of fact as distinct from opinion or conjecture: *it's a matter of fact that they had a relationship.*
■Law the part of a judicial inquiry concerned with the truth of alleged facts. Often contrasted with **MATTER OF LAW**.
▶ **adjective** (**matter-of-fact**) unemotional and practical: *he was characteristically calm and matter-of-fact.*
■concerned only with factual content rather than style or expression: *the text is written in a breezy matter-of-fact manner.*
– PHRASES **as a matter of fact** in reality (used especially to correct a falsehood or misunderstanding): *as a matter of fact, I was talking to him this afternoon.*
– DERIVATIVES **matter-of-factly** adverb, **matter-of-factness** noun.

matter of law ▶ **noun** Law the part of a judicial inquiry concerned with the interpretation of the law. Often contrasted with **MATTER OF FACT**.

Matthew, St an Apostle, a tax-gatherer from Capernaum in Galilee, traditional author of the first Gospel. Feast day, 21 September.
■the first Gospel, written after AD 70 and based largely on that of St Mark.

Matthew Paris (*c.*1199–1259), English chronicler and Benedictine monk, noted for his *Chronica Majora*, a history of the world from the Creation to the mid 13th century.

Matthews, Sir Stanley (1915–2000), English footballer. A winger famous for his dribbling skill, he played for Stoke City, Blackpool, and England and remained a professional player until he was 50.

Matthias, St /məˈθʌɪəs/ an Apostle, chosen by lot after the Ascension to replace Judas. Feast day (in the Western Church) 14 May; (in the Eastern Church) 9 August.

matting ▶ **noun** [mass noun] **1** material used for mats, especially coarse fabric woven from a natural fibre: *rush matting.*
2 the process of becoming matted.

mattins ▶ **noun** variant spelling of **MATINS**.

mattock ▶ **noun** an agricultural tool shaped like a pickaxe, with an adze and a chisel edge as the ends of the head.
– ORIGIN Old English *mattuc*, of uncertain origin.

mattress ▶ **noun** a fabric case filled with deformable or resilient material, used for sleeping on.
■Engineering a flat structure of brushwood, concrete, or other material used as strengthening or support for foundations, embankments, etc.
– ORIGIN Middle English: via Old French and Italian from Arabic *maṭraḥ* 'carpet or cushion', from *ṭaraḥa* 'to throw'.

maturate /ˈmatjʊreɪt/ ▶ **verb** [no obj.] Medicine (of a boil, abscess, etc.) form pus.
– ORIGIN mid 16th cent.: from Latin *maturat-* 'ripened, hastened', from the verb *maturare*, from *maturus* (see **MATURE**).

maturation ▶ **noun** [mass noun] the action or process of maturing: *sexual maturation.*
■(of wine or other fermented drink) the process of becoming ready for drinking. ■ the ripening of fruit: *pod maturation.* ■ Medicine the development of functional ova or sperm cells. ■ the formation of pus in a boil, abscess, etc.
– DERIVATIVES **maturational** adjective, **maturative** adjective.
– ORIGIN late Middle English (denoting the formation of pus): from medieval Latin *maturatio(n-)*, from Latin *maturare* (see **MATURE**).

mature ▶ **adjective** (**maturer, maturest**) **1** fully developed physically; full-grown: *she was now a mature woman | owls are sexually mature at one year.*
■having reached an advanced stage of mental or emotional development characteristic of an adult: *a young man mature beyond his years.* ■ (of thought or planning) careful and thorough: *on mature reflection he decided they should not go.* ■ used euphemistically to describe someone as being middle-aged or old: *Miss Walker was a mature lady when she married.* ■ (of a style) fully developed: *Van Gogh's mature work.* ■ (of a plant or planted area) complete in natural development: *mature trees.* ■ (of certain foodstuffs or drinks) ready for consumption.
2 denoting an economy, industry, or market that has developed to a point where substantial expansion and investment no longer takes place.
3 (of a bill) due for payment.
▶ **verb** [no obj.] **1** (of a person or animal) become physically mature: *children mature at different ages | she* **matured into** *a woman.*
■develop fully: *the trees take at least thirty years to mature.* ■ (of a person) reach an advanced stage of mental or emotional development: *men mature as they grow older.* ■ (with reference to certain foodstuffs or drinks) become or cause to become ready for consumption: [no obj.] *leave the cheese to mature* | [with obj.] *the Scotch is matured for a minimum of three years.*
2 (of an insurance policy, security, etc.) reach the end of its term and hence become payable.
– DERIVATIVES **maturely** adverb.
– ORIGIN late Middle English: from Latin *maturus* 'timely, ripe'; perhaps related to **MATINS**.

mature student ▶ **noun** chiefly Brit. an adult student who is older than most other students, especially one who is over 25.

maturity ▶ **noun** [mass noun] the state, fact, or period of being mature: *their experience, maturity, and strong work ethic | the delicate style of his maturity.*
■the time when an insurance policy, security, etc. matures.
– ORIGIN late Middle English: from Latin *maturitas*, from *maturus* (see **MATURE**).

matutinal /ˌmatjʊˈtʌɪn(ə)l, məˈtjuːtɪn(ə)l/ ▶ **adjective** formal of or occurring in the morning.
– ORIGIN mid 16th cent.: from late Latin *matutinalis*, from Latin *matutinus* 'early'.

maty ▶ **adjective & noun** variant spelling of **MATEY**.

matzo /ˈmatsə, ˈmatsəʊ/ (also **matzoh** or **matzah**) ▶ **noun** (pl. **matzos, matzohs,** or **matzoth** /-əʊt/) a crisp biscuit of unleavened bread, traditionally eaten by Jews during Passover.
– ORIGIN Yiddish, from Hebrew *maṣṣāh*.

matzo ball ▶ **noun** a small dumpling made of seasoned matzo meal bound together with egg and chicken fat, typically served in chicken soup.

matzo meal ▶ **noun** [mass noun] meal made from ground matzos.

mauby /ˈməʊbi/ ▶ **noun** [mass noun] a West Indian drink made from the bark of trees of the buckthorn family.
– ORIGIN from Carib *mabi*, denoting a drink made from sweet potatoes.

maud /mɔːd/ ▶ **noun** a grey-striped plaid cloak, formerly worn by shepherds in Scotland.
– ORIGIN late 18th cent.: of unknown origin.

maudlin /ˈmɔːdlɪn/ ▶ **adjective** self-pityingly or tearfully sentimental, especially through drunkenness: *the drink made her maudlin | a maudlin ballad.*
– ORIGIN late Middle English (as a noun denoting Mary Magdalen): from Old French *Madeleine*, from ecclesiastical Latin *Magdalena* (see **MAGDALEN**). The sense of the adjective derives from allusion to pictures of Mary Magdalen weeping.

Maugham /mɔːm/, (William) Somerset (1874–1965), British novelist, short-story writer, and dramatist, born in France. Notable works: *Of Human Bondage* (novel, 1915), *The Moon and Sixpence* (novel, 1919), *East of Suez* (play, 1922), and *Cakes and Ale* (novel, 1930).

Maui /ˈmaʊi/ the second largest of the Hawaiian islands, lying to the north-west of the island of Hawaii.

maul ▶ **verb** [with obj.] (of an animal) wound (a person or animal) by scratching and tearing: *a man was mauled by a lion at London Zoo.*
■treat (something) roughly. ■ handle (someone) roughly, especially in pursuit of sexual gratification: *she hated being mauled around by macho chauvinist pigs.* ■ informal defeat heavily in a game or match: *the team were mauled 4–0 by Manchester City.* ■ subject to fierce or damaging criticism: [as noun **mauling**] *he faces a mauling at next week's conference.* ■ [no obj.] Rugby Union take part in a maul.
▶ **noun 1** Rugby Union a loose scrum formed around a player with the ball off the ground. Compare with **RUCK**[1].
2 another term for **BEETLE**[2] (in sense 1).
– ORIGIN Middle English (in the sense 'hammer or wooden club', also 'strike with a heavy weapon'): from Old French *mail*, from Latin *malleus* 'hammer'.

maulana /maʊˈlɑːnə/ ▶ **noun** [often as title] a Muslim man revered for his religious learning or piety.
– ORIGIN mid 19th cent.: from Arabic *mawlānā* 'our master'.

mauler ▶ **noun** (usu. **maulers**) informal a hand: *keep your rotten maulers off my things!*

maulstick /ˈmɔːlstɪk/ (US also **mahlstick**) ▶ **noun** a light stick with a padded leather ball at one end, held against work by a painter or signwriter to support and steady the brush hand.
– ORIGIN mid 17th cent.: from Dutch *maalstok*, from *malen* 'to paint' + *stok* 'stick'.

maulvi ▶ **noun** (pl. **maulvis**) variant spelling of **MOULVI**.

Mau Mau /ˈmaʊ maʊ/ an African secret society originating among the Kikuyu that in the 1950s used violence and terror to try to expel European settlers and end British rule in Kenya. The British eventually subdued the organization, but Kenya gained independence in 1963.
■(**mau-mau**) [as verb] [with obj.] US informal terrorize or threaten (someone).
– ORIGIN Kikuyu.

Mauna Kea /ˌmaʊnə ˈkeɪə/ an extinct volcano on the island of Hawaii, in the central Pacific. Rising to 4,205 m (13,796 ft), it is the highest peak in the Hawaiian islands. The summit area is the site of several large astronomical telescopes.

Mauna Loa /ˈləʊə/ an active volcano on the island of Hawaii, to the south of Mauna Kea, rising to 4,169 m (13,678 ft).

maund /mɔːnd/ ▶ **noun** Indian a woven basket with a handle or handles.
– ORIGIN Old English *mand*, reinforced by Old French *mande*, of Germanic origin; related to Dutch *mand*.

maunder /ˈmɔːndə/ ▶ **verb** [no obj.] talk in a rambling manner: *Dennis **maundered on** about the wine.*
■ [with adverbial] move or act in a dreamy or idle manner: *he maunders through the bank, composing his thoughts.*
– ORIGIN early 17th cent.: perhaps from obsolete *maunder* 'to beg'.

Maunder minimum /ˈmɔːndə/ a prolonged minimum in sunspot activity on the sun between about 1645 and 1715, which coincided with the Little Ice Age in the northern hemisphere.
– ORIGIN 1970s: named after Edward W. *Maunder* (1851–1928), English astronomer.

Maundy /ˈmɔːndi/ ▶ **noun** [mass noun] (in the UK) a public ceremony on the Thursday before Easter at which the monarch distributes Maundy money.
■ (also **Royal Maundy**) Maundy money: [as modifier] *a George I Maundy fourpence.*
– ORIGIN Middle English: from Old French *mande*, from Latin *mandatum* 'mandate, commandment', from *mandatum novum* 'new commandment' (see John 13:34).

Maundy money ▶ **noun** [mass noun] specially minted silver coins distributed by the British sovereign on Maundy Thursday. The number of recipients and the face value in pence of the amount they each receive traditionally correspond to the number of years in the sovereign's age.

Maundy Thursday ▶ **noun** the Thursday before Easter, observed in the Christian Church as a commemoration of the Last Supper.

Maupassant /ˈməʊpasɒ̃, French mopasɑ̃/, (Henri René Albert) Guy de (1850–93), French novelist and short-story writer. He wrote about 300 short stories and six novels in a simple, direct narrative style. Notable novels: *Une Vie* (1883) and *Bel-Ami* (1885).

Mauretania /ˌmɒrɪˈteɪnɪə/ an ancient region of North Africa, corresponding to the northern part of Morocco and western and central Algeria.
– DERIVATIVES **Mauretanian** adjective & noun.
– ORIGIN based on Latin *Mauri* 'Moors', by whom the region was originally occupied.

Mauriac /ˈmɒrɪak, French mɔrjak/, François (1885–1970), French novelist, dramatist, and critic. His stories show the conflicts of convention, religion, and human passions suffered by prosperous bourgeoisie. Notable works: *Thérèse Desqueyroux* (novel, 1927). Nobel Prize for Literature (1952).

Mauritania /ˌmɒrɪˈteɪnɪə/ a country in West Africa with a coastline on the Atlantic Ocean; pop. 2,023,000 (est. 1991); languages, Arabic (official), French; capital, Nouakchott.

Mauritania was a centre of Berber power in the 11th and 12th centuries, at which time Islam became established in the region. Later, nomadic Arab tribes became dominant, while on the coast European nations, especially France, established trading posts. A French protectorate from 1902 and a colony from 1920, Mauritania achieved full independence in 1961.

– DERIVATIVES **Mauritanian** adjective & noun.

Mauritius /məˈrɪʃəs/ an island country in the Indian Ocean, about 850 km (550 miles) east of Madagascar; pop. 1,105,740 (est. 1993); languages, English (official), French Creole, Indian languages; capital, Port Louis.

Previously uninhabited, Mauritius was discovered by the Portuguese in the early 16th century. It was held by the Dutch 1598–1710 and then by the French until 1810, when it was ceded to Britain. Mauritius became independent as a member of the Commonwealth in 1968.

– DERIVATIVES **Mauritian** adjective & noun.
– ORIGIN named by the Dutch in honour of Prince *Maurice* of Nassau, a stadtholder of the United Provinces.

Maury /ˈmɔːri/, Matthew Fontaine (1806–73), American oceanographer. He conducted the first systematic survey of oceanic winds and currents, and published charts of his findings.

Maurya /ˈmaʊrɪə/ a dynasty which ruled northern India 321–*c.*184 BC. It was founded by Chandragupta Maurya, who introduced a centralized government and uniform script. The oldest extant Indian art dates from this era.
– DERIVATIVES **Mauryan** adjective.

mausoleum /ˌmɔːsəˈliːəm, -z-/ ▶ **noun** (pl. **mausolea** /-ˈlɪə/ or **mausoleums**) a building, especially a large and stately one, housing a tomb or tombs.
– ORIGIN late 15th cent.: via Latin from Greek *Mausōleion*, from *Mausōlos*, the name of a king of Caria (4th cent. BC), to whose tomb in Halicarnassus the name was originally applied.

mauve /məʊv/ ▶ **adjective** of a pale purple colour.
▶ **noun** [mass noun] **1** a pale purple colour: *a few pale streaks of mauve were all that remained of the sunset* | [count noun] *glowing with soft pastel mauves and pinks.*
2 historical a bright but delicate pale purple aniline dye prepared by William H. Perkin in 1856. It was the first synthetic dyestuff.
– DERIVATIVES **mauvish** adjective.
– ORIGIN mid 19th cent.: from French, literally 'mallow', from Latin *malva*.

mauveine /ˈməʊviːn/ ▶ **noun** another term for **MAUVE** (in sense 2).

maven /ˈmeɪv(ə)n/ ▶ **noun** [often with modifier] N. Amer. informal an expert or connoisseur: *fashion mavens.*
– ORIGIN 1960s: Yiddish.

maverick ▶ **noun 1** an unorthodox or independent-minded person: *he was something of a maverick.*
■ a person who refuses to conform to a particular party or group: *a Tory back-bench maverick.*
2 N. Amer. an unbranded calf or yearling.
▶ **adjective** unorthodox: *a maverick detective.*
– ORIGIN mid 19th cent.: from the name of Samuel A. *Maverick* (1803–70), a Texas engineer and rancher who did not brand his cattle.

mavis /ˈmeɪvɪs/ ▶ **noun** poetic/literary a song thrush.
– ORIGIN late Middle English: from Old French *mauvis*, of unknown origin.

maw ▶ **noun** the jaws or throat of a voracious animal: *a gigantic wolfhound with a fearful, gaping maw.*
■ informal the mouth or gullet of a greedy person: *I was cramming large pieces of toast and cheese down my maw.*
– ORIGIN Old English *maga* (in the sense 'stomach'), of Germanic origin; related to Dutch *maag* and German *Magen* 'stomach'.

mawkish ▶ **adjective** sentimental in a feeble or sickly way: *a mawkish poem.*
■ archaic or dialect having a faint sickly flavour: *the mawkish smell of warm beer.*
– DERIVATIVES **mawkishly** adverb, **mawkishness** noun.
– ORIGIN mid 17th cent. (in the sense 'inclined to sickness'): from obsolete *mawk* 'maggot', from Old Norse *mathkr*, of Germanic origin.

Mawlana /mɔːˈlɑːnə/ another name for **JALAL AD-DIN AR-RUMI**.

max ▶ **abbreviation for** maximum.
▶ **noun** informal a maximum amount or setting: *the sound is distorted **to the max**.*
▶ **adverb** informal at the most: *the trip costs about 35p max.*
▶ **verb** N. Amer. informal reach or cause to reach the limit of capacity or ability: [no obj.] *job growth in high technology will **max out**.*

maxi ▶ **noun** (pl. **maxis**) a thing that is very large of its kind, in particular:
■ a skirt or coat reaching to the ankle. ■ (also **maxi yacht** or **maxi boat**) a racing yacht of between approximately 15 and 20 metres in length.
– ORIGIN 1960s: abbreviation of **MAXIMUM**, on the pattern of *mini*.

maxi- ▶ **combining form** very large or long: *a maxi-farm.*
– ORIGIN from **MAXIMUM**.

maxilla /makˈsɪlə/ ▶ **noun** (pl. **maxillae** /-liː/) Anatomy & Zoology the jaw or jawbone, specifically the upper jaw in most vertebrates. In humans it also forms part of the nose and eye socket.
■ (in many arthropods) each of a pair of mouthparts used in chewing.
– ORIGIN late Middle English: from Latin, 'jaw'.

maxillary ▶ **adjective** Anatomy & Zoology of or attached to a jaw or jawbone, especially the upper jaw: *a maxillary fracture* | *maxillary teeth.*
■ of or relating to the maxillae of an arthropod.
– ORIGIN early 17th cent.: from **MAXILLA**, probably suggested by Latin *maxillaris*.

maxilliped /makˈsɪlɪpɛd/ ▶ **noun** Zoology (in crustaceans) an appendage modified for feeding, situated in pairs behind the maxillae.
– ORIGIN mid 19th cent.: from **MAXILLA** + Latin *pes*, *ped-* 'foot'.

maxillofacial /makˌsɪlə(ʊ)ˈfeɪʃ(ə)l, ˌmaksɪlə(ʊ)-/ ▶ **adjective** Anatomy of or relating to the jaws and face: *maxillofacial surgery.*
– ORIGIN late 19th cent.: from *maxillo-* (combining form of Latin *maxilla* 'jaw') + **FACIAL**.

maxim ▶ **noun** a short, pithy statement expressing a general truth or rule of conduct: *the maxim that actions speak louder than words.*
– ORIGIN late Middle English (denoting an axiom): from French *maxime*, from medieval Latin (*propositio*) *maxima* 'largest or most important (proposition)'.

maxima plural form of **MAXIMUM**.

maximal ▶ **adjective** of or constituting a maximum; the highest or greatest possible: *the maximal speed.*
– DERIVATIVES **maximally** adverb.

maximalist ▶ **noun** (especially in politics) a person who holds extreme views and is not prepared to compromise.
▶ **adjective** of or denoting an extreme opinion: *the maximalist interpretation is more promising.*
– DERIVATIVES **maximalism** noun.
– ORIGIN early 20th cent.: from **MAXIMAL**, on the pattern of Russian *maksimalist*.

maximand /ˈmaksɪmand/ ▶ **noun** chiefly Economics a quantity or thing which is to be maximized.
– ORIGIN 1950s: from **MAXIMIZE** + **-AND**.

Maxim gun ▶ **noun** the first fully automatic water-cooled machine gun, designed in Britain in 1884 and used especially in the First World War.
– ORIGIN named after Sir Hiram S. *Maxim* (1840–1916), American-born British inventor.

Maximilian /ˌmaksɪˈmɪlɪən/ (1832–67), Austrian emperor of Mexico 1864–7; full name *Ferdinand Maximilian Joseph*. Brother of Franz Josef, Maximilian was established as emperor of Mexico under French auspices in 1864. He was executed by a popular uprising led by Benito Juárez.

maximin /ˈmaksɪmɪn/ ▶ **noun** Mathematics the largest of a series of minima. Compare with **MINIMAX**.
■ [as modifier] denoting a method or strategy in game theory that maximizes the smallest gain that can be relied on by a participant in a game or other situation of conflict.
– ORIGIN 1950s: blend of **MAXIMUM** and **MINIMUM**, on the pattern of *minimax*.

maximize (also **-ise**) ▶ **verb** [with obj.] make as large or great as possible: *the company was aiming to maximize profits.*
■ make the best use of: *a thriller that maximizes the potential of its locations.*
– DERIVATIVES **maximization** noun, **maximizer** noun.
– ORIGIN early 19th cent.: from Latin *maximus* (see **MAXIMUM**) + **-IZE**.

maximum ▶ **adjective** [attrib.] as great, high, or intense as possible or permitted: *the vehicle's maximum speed* | *a maximum penalty of ten years' imprisonment.*
■ denoting the greatest or highest point or amount attained: *the maximum depth of the pool is 2 metres.*
▶ **noun** (pl. **maxima** /-mə/ or **maximums**) the greatest or highest amount possible or attained: *the school takes a maximum of 32 pupils* | *production levels are near their maximum.*
■ a maximum permitted custodial sentence for an offence: *an offence which carries a maximum of 14 years.*
▶ **adverb** at the most: *it has a length of 4 feet maximum.*
– ORIGIN mid 17th cent. (as a noun): from modern Latin, neuter (used as a noun) of the Latin adjective *maximus*, superlative of *magnus* 'great'. The adjective use dates from the early 19th cent.

maximum sustainable yield (abbrev.: **MSY**) ▶ **noun** [mass noun] (especially in forestry and fisheries) the maximum level at which a natural resource can be routinely exploited without long-term depletion.
■ Ecology the size of a natural population at which it produces a maximum rate of increase, typically at half the carrying capacity.

maxixe /makˈsiːks, məˈʃiːʃə/ ▶ **noun** a Brazilian dance for couples, resembling the polka and the local tango.
– ORIGIN early 20th cent.: Portuguese.

Maxwell[1], James Clerk (1831–79), Scottish

physicist. He extended the ideas of Faraday and Kelvin in his equations of electromagnetism and succeeded in unifying electricity and magnetism, identifying the electromagnetic nature of light, and postulating the existence of other electromagnetic radiation.

Maxwell[2], (Ian) Robert (1923–91), Czech-born British publisher and media entrepreneur; born *Jan Ludvík Hoch*. He died in obscure circumstances while yachting off Tenerife; it subsequently emerged that he had misappropriated company pension funds.

maxwell (abbrev.: **Mx**) ▶ **noun** Physics a unit of magnetic flux in the c.g.s. system, equal to that induced through one square centimetre by a perpendicular magnetic field of one gauss.
– ORIGIN early 20th cent.: named after J. C. *Maxwell* (see **MAXWELL**[1]).

Maxwell–Boltzmann distribution Physics a formula describing the statistical distribution of particles in a system among different energy levels. The number of particles in a given energy level is proportional to $\exp(-E_{kT})$, where E is the energy of the level, k is Boltzmann's constant, and T is the absolute temperature.
– ORIGIN 1920s: named after J. C. *Maxwell* (see **MAXWELL**[1]) and L. **BOLTZMANN**.

Maxwell Davies, Sir Peter, see **DAVIES**[1].

Maxwell's demon Physics a hypothetical being imagined as controlling a hole in a partition dividing a gas-filled container into two parts, and allowing only fast-moving molecules to pass in one direction, and slow-moving molecules in the other. This would result in one side of the container becoming warmer and the other colder, in violation of the second law of thermodynamics.
– ORIGIN late 19th cent.: named after J. C. *Maxwell* (see **MAXWELL**[1]).

Maxwell's equations Physics a set of four linear partial differential equations which summarize the classical properties of the electromagnetic field.
– ORIGIN early 20th cent.: named after J. C. *Maxwell* (see **MAXWELL**[1]).

May ▶ **noun** the fifth month of the year, in the northern hemisphere usually considered the last month of spring: *the new model makes its showroom debut in May* | *Rovers were promoted last May.*
■ (usu. **one's May**) poetic/literary one's bloom or prime: *others murmured that their May was passing.*
– ORIGIN late Old English, from Old French *mai*, from Latin *Maius* (*mensis*) '(month) of the goddess *Maia*'.

may[1] ▶ **modal verb** (3rd sing. present **may**; past **might** /mʌɪt/) **1** expressing possibility: *that may be true* | *he may well win.*
■ used when admitting that something is so before making another, more important, point: *they may have been old-fashioned but they were excellent teachers.*
2 expressing permission: *you may use a sling if you wish* | *may I ask a few questions?*
3 expressing a wish or hope: *may she rest in peace.*
– PHRASES **be that as it may** despite that; nevertheless. **may as well** another way of saying *might as well* (see **MIGHT**[1]). **that is as may be** that may or may not be so (implying that this is not a significant consideration).
– ORIGIN Old English *mæg*, of Germanic origin, from a base meaning 'have power'; related to Dutch *mogen* and German *mögen*, also to **MAIN**[1] and **MIGHT**[2].

USAGE On the difference in use between **may** and **can**, see usage at **CAN**[1].

may[2] ▶ **noun** [mass noun] the hawthorn or its blossom.
– ORIGIN late Middle English: from **MAY**.

Maya /ˈmʌɪə, ˈmeɪjə/ ▶ **noun** (pl. same or **Mayas**) **1** a member of an American Indian people of Yucatán and elsewhere in Central America. **2** [mass noun] the language of this people, still spoken by about half a million people.
▶ **adjective** of or relating to this people or their language.

The Maya civilization developed over an extensive area of southern Mexico, Guatemala, and Belize from the 2nd millennium BC, reaching its peak *c.*300–*c.*900 AD. Its remains include stone temples built on pyramids and ornamented with sculptures. The Mayas had a cumbersome system of pictorial writing and an extremely accurate calendar system.

– ORIGIN the name in Maya.

maya /ˈmɑːjə/ ▶ **noun** [mass noun] Hinduism the supernatural power wielded by gods and demons.
■ Hinduism & Buddhism the power by which the universe becomes manifest; the illusion or appearance of the phenomenal world.
– ORIGIN from Sanskrit *māyā*, from *mā* 'create'.

Mayakovsky /ˌmʌɪəˈkɒfski/, Vladimir (Vladimirovich) (1893–1930), Soviet poet and dramatist, born in Georgia. A fervent futurist, he wrote in a declamatory, aggressive avant-garde style, which he altered to have a comic mass appeal after the Bolshevik revolution.

Mayan /ˈmʌɪjən, ˈmeɪjən/ ▶ **noun** [mass noun] a large family of American Indian languages spoken in Central America, of which the chief members are Maya, Quiché, and Tzeltal.
▶ **adjective 1** denoting, relating to, or belonging to this family of languages.
2 relating to or denoting the Maya people.

mayapple ▶ **noun** an American herbaceous plant of the barberry family, which bears a yellow egg-shaped fruit in May. The plant has long been used medicinally.
● *Podophyllum peltatum*, family Berberidaceae.

maybe ▶ **adverb** perhaps; possibly: *maybe I won't go back* | *maybe she'd been wrong to accept this job.*
▶ **noun** a mere possibility or probability: *no ifs, buts, or maybes.*
– PHRASES **that's as maybe** used to admit that a point in an argument is true before introducing another, more important point: *well, that's as maybe but it's not the way the BBC works.*
– ORIGIN late Middle English: from the phrase *it may be* (*that*).

May bug ▶ **noun** another term for **COCKCHAFER**.

May Day ▶ **noun** 1 May, celebrated in many countries as a traditional springtime festival or as an international day honouring workers.
■ (in the UK) a public holiday on the first Monday in May.

Mayday ▶ **exclamation** an international radio distress signal used by ships and aircraft.
▶ **noun** a distress signal using the word 'Mayday'.
– ORIGIN 1920s: representing a pronunciation of French *m'aider*, from *venez m'aider* 'come and help me'.

Mayer /ˈmeɪə/, Louis B. (1885–1957), Russian-born American film executive; full name *Louis Burt Mayer*; born *Eliezer Mayer*. In 1924 he formed Metro-Goldwyn-Mayer (MGM) with Samuel Goldwyn; he headed the company until 1951.

mayest /ˈmeɪɪst/ archaic second person singular present of **MAY**[1].

Mayfair a fashionable and opulent district in the West End of London.
– ORIGIN originally the site of a fair held annually in May in the 17th and 18th cents.

Mayflower the ship in which the Pilgrim Fathers sailed from England to America.

mayflower ▶ **noun** the trailing arbutus.

mayfly ▶ **noun** (pl. **-flies**) a short-lived slender insect with delicate transparent wings and two or three long filaments on the tail. It lives close to water, where the chiefly herbivorous aquatic larvae develop.
● Order Ephemeroptera: several families and many species.
■ an artificial fishing fly that imitates such an insect.

mayhap ▶ **adverb** archaic perhaps; possibly.
– ORIGIN mid 16th cent.: from *it may hap.*

mayhem ▶ **noun** [mass noun] violent or damaging disorder; chaos: *complete mayhem broke out.*
■ Law, chiefly historical the crime of maliciously injuring or maiming someone, originally so as to render the victim defenceless.
– ORIGIN early 16th cent.: from Old French *mayhem* (see **MAIM**). The sense 'disorder, chaos' (originally US) dates from the late 19th cent.

maying ▶ **noun** [mass noun] archaic celebration of May Day.

Maynooth /meɪˈnuːθ/ a village in County Kildare in the Republic of Ireland; pop. 1,300 (1981). It is the site of St Patrick's College, a Roman Catholic seminary founded in 1795.

mayn't ▶ **contraction of** may not.

Mayo a county in the Republic of Ireland, in the north-west in the province of Connacht; county town, Castlebar.

mayo ▶ **noun** informal short for **MAYONNAISE**.

mayonnaise ▶ **noun** [mass noun] a thick creamy dressing consisting of egg yolks beaten with oil and vinegar and seasoned.
■ [with modifier] Brit. a mixture of mayonnaise and a specified ingredient, especially as a sandwich filling: *egg mayonnaise.*
– ORIGIN French, probably from the feminine of *mahonnais* 'of or from Port *Mahon*', the capital of Minorca.

mayor ▶ **noun** the elected head of the municipal corporation of a city or borough.
– DERIVATIVES **mayoral** adjective, **mayorship** noun.
– ORIGIN Middle English: from Old French *maire*, from the Latin adjective *major* 'greater', used as a noun in late Latin.

mayoralty /ˈmɛːr(ə)lti/ ▶ **noun** (pl. **-ies**) the office of mayor: *the party failed to win the mayoralty.*
■ a mayor's period of office.
– ORIGIN late Middle English: from Old French *mairalte*, from *maire* (see **MAYOR**).

mayoress /ˈmɛːrɪs, ˌmɛːˈrɛs/ ▶ **noun 1** the wife of a mayor.
2 a woman holding the office of mayor.

Mayotte /mɑːˈjɒt/ an island to the east of the Comoros in the Indian Ocean; pop. 94,410 (1991); languages, French (official), local Swahili dialect; capital, Mamoutzu. When the Comoros became independent in 1974, Mayotte remained an overseas territory of France. Also called **MAHORE**.

maypole ▶ **noun** a pole painted and decorated with flowers, round which people traditionally dance on May Day holding long ribbons attached to the top.

maypop ▶ **noun** the yellow edible fruit of a North American passion flower.
● The plant is *Passiflora incarnata*, family Passifloraceae.

May queen ▶ **noun** a pretty girl chosen and crowned in traditional celebrations of May Day.

Mayr /ˈmʌɪə, ˈmeɪə/, Ernst Walter (b.1904), German-born American zoologist. He argued for a neo-Darwinian approach to evolution in his classic *Animal Species and Evolution* (1963).

mayst archaic second person singular present of **MAY**[1].

mayweed ▶ **noun** [mass noun] a plant of the daisy family which typically grows as a weed of fields and waste ground.
● Several species in the family Compositae, in particular **stinking mayweed** (*Anthemis cotula*) and **scentless mayweed** (*Tripleurospermum inodorum*).
– ORIGIN mid 16th cent.: from *maythe(n)*, an earlier name for this plant (in Old English *mægethe*, *magothe*) + **WEED**.

Mazar-e-Sharif /mɑˌzɑːriːˈʃɑːriːf/ a city in northern Afghanistan; pop. 130,600 (est. 1988). The city, whose name means 'tomb of the saint', is the reputed burial place of Ali, son-in-law of Muhammad.

Mazarin /ˈmazərɪn, -rɛ̃, French mazarɛ̃/, Jules (1602–61), Italian-born French statesman; Italian name *Giulio Mazzarino*. Sent to Paris as the Italian papal legate (1634), he became a naturalized Frenchman, and was made a cardinal in 1641 and then chief minister of France (1642).

mazarine blue /ˌmazəˈriːn, ˈmazəriːn/ ▶ **noun** a migratory blue butterfly of Eurasian meadows.
● *Cyaniris semiargus*, family Lycaenidae.
– ORIGIN late 17th cent. (denoting a rich deep blue colour): apparently from the name of Cardinal Jules **MAZARIN**, or of the Duchesse de *Mazarin* (died 1699), though the connection is unknown.

Mazatlán /ˌmazatˈlɑːn/ a seaport and resort in Mexico, on the Pacific coast in the state of Sinaloa; pop. 314,250 (1990). Founded in 1531, it developed as a centre of Spanish trade with the Philippines.

Mazdaism /ˈmazdəˌɪz(ə)m/ ▶ **noun** another term for **ZOROASTRIANISM**.
– DERIVATIVES **Mazdaist** noun & adjective.
– ORIGIN late 19th cent.: from Avestan *mazdā* (short for **AHURA MAZDA**) + **-ISM**.

mazdoor /mʌzˈdʊə/ ▶ **noun** Indian an unskilled labourer.
– ORIGIN from Hindi *mazdūr.*

maze ▶ **noun** a network of paths and hedges designed as a puzzle through which one has to find a way.
■ a complex network of paths or passages: *they were trapped in a menacing maze of corridors.* ■ a confusing mass of information: *a maze of petty regulations.*

▶**verb** (**be mazed**) archaic or dialect be dazed and confused: *she was still mazed with the drug she had taken.*
– ORIGIN Middle English (denoting delirium or delusion): probably from the base of **AMAZE**, of which the verb is a shortening.

mazel tov /ˈmaz(ə)l ˌtɔːv, ˌtɒf/ ▶**exclamation** a Jewish phrase expressing congratulations or wishing someone good luck.
– ORIGIN from modern Hebrew *mazzāl ṭōḇ*, literally 'good star'.

mazer /ˈmeɪzə/ ▶**noun** historical a hardwood drinking bowl.
– ORIGIN Middle English: from Old French *masere*, of Germanic origin.

mazuma /məˈzuːmə/ ▶**noun** [mass noun] informal, chiefly US money; cash.
– ORIGIN early 20th cent.: Yiddish, from Hebrew *mĕzummān*, from *zimmēn* 'prepare'.

mazurka /məˈzəːkə, məˈzʊəkə/ ▶**noun** a lively Polish dance in triple time.
– ORIGIN early 19th cent.: via German from Polish *mazurka*, denoting a woman of the province Mazovia.

mazy ▶**adjective** (**mazier**, **maziest**) **1** like a maze; labyrinthine: *the museum's mazy treasure house.* **2** N. English confused, giddy, or dizzy.

mazzard /ˈmazəd/ ▶**noun** another term for **GEAN**.

Mazzini /matˈsiːni/, Giuseppe (1805–72), Italian nationalist leader. He founded the patriotic movement Young Italy (1831) and was a leader of the Risorgimento. Following the country's unification as a monarchy in 1861, he continued to campaign for a republican Italy.

MB ▶**abbreviation for** ▪Bachelor of Medicine. [ORIGIN: from Latin *Medicinae Baccalaureus*.] ▪Manitoba (in official postal use). ▪(also **Mb**) Computing megabyte: *a 800 MB hard disk.*

MBA ▶**abbreviation for** Master of Business Administration.

Mbabane /ˌ(ə)mbɑːˈbɑːni/ the capital of Swaziland; pop. 38,300 (1986).

mbaqanga /ˌ(ə)mbɑːˈkɑːŋɡə/ ▶**noun** [mass noun] a rhythmical popular music style of southern Africa.
– ORIGIN from Zulu *umbaqanga*, literally 'steamed maize bread', used to express the combined notion of the homely cultural sustenance of the townships and the musicians' 'daily bread' (coined in this sense by trumpeter Michael Xaba).

MBE ▶**abbreviation for** (in the UK) Member of the Order of the British Empire.

Mbeki /(ə)mˈbekɪ/, Thabo (b.1942), South African statesman, President since 1999.

mbira /(ə)mˈbɪərə/ ▶**noun** (especially in southern Africa) another term for **THUMB PIANO**.
– ORIGIN late 19th cent.: from Shona, probably an alteration of *rimba* 'a note'.

MBO ▶**abbreviation for** management buyout.

Mbundu /(ə)mˈbʊnduː/ ▶**noun** (pl. same) **1** a member of either of two peoples of western Angola (sometimes distinguished as **Mbundu** and **Ovimbundu**). **2** [mass noun] either of the Bantu languages of these peoples, often distinguished as **Umbundu** (related to Herero and spoken by around 3 million people) and **Kimbundu** (related to Kikongo and spoken by nearly 2 million people).
▶**adjective** of or relating to these peoples or their languages.

Mbuti /(ə)mˈbuːti/ ▶**noun** (pl. same or **Mbutis**) a member of a pygmy people of western Uganda and adjacent areas of Zaire (Democratic Republic of Congo).
▶**adjective** of or relating to this people.
– ORIGIN the name in local languages.

Mbyte ▶**abbreviation for** megabyte(s).

MC ▶**abbreviation for** ▪Master of Ceremonies. ▪(in the US) Member of Congress. ▪(in an astrological chart) the midheaven. [ORIGIN: from Latin *Medium Coeli*.] ▪(in the UK) Military Cross. ▪Monaco (international vehicle registration). ▪music cassette (of pre-recorded audio tape).

Mc ▶**abbreviation for** megacycle(s), a unit of frequency equal to one million cycles.

MCB ▶**abbreviation for** miniature circuit-breaker.

MCC Marylebone Cricket Club, founded in 1787, which has its headquarters at Lord's Cricket Ground in London. The tacitly accepted governing body of cricket until 1969, it continues to have primary responsibility for the game's laws.

mcg ▶**abbreviation for** microgram.

MCh (also **M Chir**) ▶**abbreviation for** Master of Surgery.
– ORIGIN from Latin *Magister Chirurgiae*.

mCi ▶**abbreviation for** millicurie(s), a quantity of a radioactive substance having one thousandth of a curie of radioactivity: *15 mCi of the radionuclide.*

MCom ▶**abbreviation for** Master of Commerce.

MCP informal ▶**abbreviation for** male chauvinist pig.

MCpl ▶**abbreviation for** Master Corporal.

MCPO ▶**abbreviation for** Master Chief Petty Officer.

MCR Brit. ▶**abbreviation for** Middle Common Room.

Mc/s ▶**abbreviation for** megacycles per second, a unit of frequency equal to one million cycles per second.

MD ▶**abbreviation for** ▪Doctor of Medicine. [ORIGIN: from Latin *Medicinae Doctor*.] ▪Brit. Managing Director. ▪Maryland (in official postal use). ▪Medicine mentally deficient. ▪musical director.

Md ▶**symbol for** the chemical element mendelevium.

Md. ▶**abbreviation for** Maryland.

MDF ▶**abbreviation for** medium density fibreboard.

MDMA ▶**abbreviation for** methylenedioxy-methamphetamine, the drug Ecstasy.

MDT ▶**abbreviation for** Mountain Daylight Time (see **MOUNTAIN TIME**).

ME ▶**abbreviation for** ▪Maine (in official postal use). ▪Middle English. ▪Medicine myalgic encephalomyelitis (chronic fatigue syndrome).

Me ▶**abbreviation for** ▪Maine. ▪Maître (title of a French advocate).

me[1] ▶**pronoun** [first person singular] **1** used by a speaker to refer to himself or herself as the object of a verb or preposition: *do you understand me?* | *wait for me!* Compare with **I**[2]. ▪used after the verb 'to be' and after 'than' or 'as': *hi, it's me* | *you have more than me.* ▪N. Amer. informal to or for myself: *I've got me a job.* **2** informal used in exclamations: *dear me!* | *silly me!*
– PHRASES **me and mine** my relatives.
– ORIGIN Old English *mē*, accusative and dative of **I**[2], of Germanic origin; related to Dutch *mij*, German *mir* (dative), from an Indo-European root shared by Latin *me*, Greek *(e)me*, and Sanskrit *mā*.

USAGE **1** Traditional grammar teaches that it is correct to say *between you and me* and incorrect to say *between you and I*. For details, see usage at **BETWEEN**. **2** Which of the following is correct: *you have more than me* or *you have more than I*? See usage at **PERSONAL PRONOUN**.

me[2] (also **mi**) ▶**noun** Music (in tonic sol-fa) the third note of a major scale. ▪the note E in the fixed-doh system.
– ORIGIN late Middle English *mi*, representing (as an arbitrary name for the note) the first syllable of *mira*, taken from a Latin hymn (see **SOLMIZATION**).

mea culpa /ˌmeɪə ˈkʊlpə, ˌmiːə ˈkʌlpə/ ▶**noun** an acknowledgement of one's fault or error: [as exclamation] *'Well, whose fault was that?' 'Mea culpa!'* Frank said.
– ORIGIN Latin, 'by my fault'.

Mead, Margaret (1901–78), American anthropologist and social psychologist. She worked in Samoa and the New Guinea area and wrote a number of studies of primitive cultures.

mead[1] ▶**noun** [mass noun] chiefly historical an alcoholic drink of fermented honey and water.
– ORIGIN Old English *me(o)du*, of Germanic origin; related to Dutch *mee* and German *Met*, from an Indo-European root shared by Sanskrit *madhu* 'sweet drink, honey' and Greek *methu* 'wine'.

mead[2] ▶**noun** poetic/literary a meadow.
– ORIGIN Old English *mǣd*, of Germanic origin; related to **MOW**[1].

meadow ▶**noun** a piece of grassland, especially one used for hay. ▪a piece of low ground near a river.
– DERIVATIVES **meadowy** adjective.
– ORIGIN Old English *mǣdwe*, oblique case of *mǣd* (see **MEAD**[2]), from the Germanic base of **MOW**.

meadow brown ▶**noun** a common Eurasian butterfly that has brown and orange wings with small eyespots.
● *Maniola jurtina*, subfamily Satyrinae, family Nymphalidae.

meadow fescue ▶**noun** [mass noun] a tall Eurasian fescue which is a valuable pasture and hay grass.
● *Festuca pratensis*, family Gramineae.

meadow grass ▶**noun** [mass noun] a perennial creeping grass which is widely used for fodder and lawns, and for sowing roadside verges. Also called **BLUEGRASS** in North America.
● Genus *Poa*, family Gramineae: many species, in particular the **common meadow grass** (*P. pratensis*) of Eurasia.

meadowland ▶**noun** [mass noun] (also **meadowlands**) land used for the cultivation of grass, especially for hay.

meadowlark ▶**noun** a ground-dwelling songbird of the American blackbird family, with a brown streaky back and typically yellow and black underparts.
● Genus *Sturnella*, family Icteridae: five species, in particular the widespread yellow-breasted **eastern meadowlark** (*S. magna*).

meadow mouse ▶**noun** another term for **MEADOW VOLE**.

meadow mushroom ▶**noun** another term for **FIELD MUSHROOM**.

meadow pipit ▶**noun** a common streaky brown pipit of open country, found in Europe and the Middle East.
● *Anthus pratensis*, family Motacillidae.

meadow rue ▶**noun** a widely distributed plant of the buttercup family, which typically has divided leaves and heads of small fluffy yellow flowers.
● Genus *Thalictrum*, family Ranunculaceae: many species, including the European **common meadow rue** (*T. flavum*).

meadow saffron ▶**noun** a poisonous autumn crocus which produces lilac flowers in the autumn while leafless. Native to Europe and North Africa, it is a source of the drug colchicine. Also called **NAKED LADIES**.
● *Colchicum autumnale*, family Liliaceae.

meadowsweet ▶**noun** a tall Eurasian plant of the rose family, with heads of creamy-white sweet-smelling flowers, growing in damp meadows.
● *Filipendula ulmaria*, family Rosaceae.

meadow vole ▶**noun** a burrowing vole that occurs in grassland and open country in Eurasia and North America.
● Genus *Microtus*, family Muridae: numerous species, in particular *Microtus pennsylvanicus* of the northern US and Canada, and including the field vole.

meagre[1] (US **meager**) ▶**adjective** lacking in quantity or quality: *they were forced to supplement their meagre earnings.* ▪(of a person or animal) lean; thin. ▪(of ideas or writing) lacking fullness; unsatisfying: *a curriculum which is mean, meagre, and mechanical.*
– DERIVATIVES **meagrely** adverb, **meagreness** noun.
– ORIGIN Middle English (in the sense 'lean'): from Old French *maigre*, from Latin *macer*.

meagre[2] ▶**noun** Brit. another term for **KABELJOU**.
– ORIGIN mid 16th cent.: from French, noun use of *maigre* 'lean, thin'.

meal[1] ▶**noun** any of the regular occasions in a day when a reasonably large amount of food is eaten. ▪the food eaten on such an occasion: *a perfectly cooked meal.*
– PHRASES **make a meal of** Brit. informal treat (a task or occurrence) with more attention or care than necessary, especially for effect. **meals on wheels** meals delivered to old people or invalids who cannot cook for themselves.
– ORIGIN Old English *mǣl* (also in the sense 'measure', surviving in words such as *piecemeal* 'measure taken at one time'), of Germanic origin. The early sense of *meal* involved a notion of 'fixed time'; compare with Dutch *maal* 'meal, (portion of) time' and German *Mal* 'time', *Mahl* 'meal', from an Indo-European root meaning 'to measure'.

meal[2] ▶**noun** [mass noun] the edible part of any grain or pulse ground to powder. ▪Scottish oatmeal. ▪US maize flour. ▪any powdery substance made by grinding: *herring meal.*
– ORIGIN Old English *melu, meolo*, of Germanic origin; related to Dutch *meel* and German *Mehl*, from an Indo-European root shared by Latin *molere* 'to grind'.

meal beetle ▶**noun** a dark brown beetle which is a pest of stored grain and cereal products. Its larva is the mealworm.
● *Tenebrio molitor*, family Tenebrionidae.

mealie (also **mielie**) ▶ **noun** (usu. **mealies**) chiefly S. African a maize plant.
■[mass noun] maize kernels; sweetcorn: [as modifier] *mealie pudding.* ■ a corn cob.
– ORIGIN early 19th cent.: from Afrikaans *mielie*, from Portuguese *milho* 'maize, millet' from Latin *milium*.

mealie meal ▶ **noun** [mass noun] S. African maize meal, used especially for porridge.

mealiepap ▶ **noun** [mass noun] S. African porridge made of mealie meal.

mealie rice ▶ **noun** [mass noun] S. African crushed maize kernels, used as a substitute for rice.

meal moth ▶ **noun** a small moth which infests mills, granaries, and other places where grain is stored. The larvae spin silken webs.
• Several species in the family Pyralidae, in particular the **meal moth** (*Pyralis farinalis*) and the **Indian meal moth** (*Plodia interpunctella*).

meal ticket ▶ **noun** a person or thing that is exploited as a source of regular income: *the violin was going to be my meal ticket.*

mealtime ▶ **noun** the time at which a meal is eaten: *is there self-service **at mealtimes**? | it must be mealtime soon.*

mealworm ▶ **noun** the larva of the meal beetle, which is used as food for captive birds and other insectivorous animals.

mealy ▶ **adjective** (**mealier**, **mealiest**) of, like, or containing meal: *a mealy flavour | mealy puddings.*
■(of a person's complexion, an animal's muzzle, or a bird's plumage) pale. ■ (of part of a plant or fungus) covered with granules resembling meal.
– DERIVATIVES **mealiness** noun.

mealy bug ▶ **noun** a small sap-sucking scale insect which is coated with a white powdery wax that resembles meal. It forms large colonies and can be a serious pest, especially in greenhouses.
• Family Pseudococcidae, suborder Homoptera: *Pseudococcus* and other genera.

mealy-mouthed ▶ **adjective** afraid to speak frankly or straightforwardly: *mealy-mouthed excuses.*

mean[1] ▶ **verb** (past and past participle **meant**) [with obj.] **1** intend to convey, indicate, or refer to (a particular thing or notion); signify: *I don't know what you mean | he was asked to clarify what his remarks meant | I meant you, not Jones.*
■(of a word) have (something) as its signification in the same language or its equivalent in another language: *its name means 'painted rock' in Cherokee.* ■ genuinely intend to convey or express (something): *when she said that before she meant it.* ■ (**mean something to**) be of some specified importance to (someone), especially as a source of benefit or object of affection: *animals have always meant more to him than people.*
2 intend (something) to occur or be the case: *they mean no harm* | [with infinitive] *it was meant to be a secret.*
■(**be meant to do something**) be supposed or intended to do something: *we were meant to go over yesterday.* ■ (often **be meant for**) design or destine for a particular purpose: *the jacket was meant for a much larger person.* ■ (**mean something by**) have as a motive or excuse in explanation: *what do you mean by leaving me out here in the cold?* ■ (**be meant to be**) be generally considered to be: *this one's meant to be priceless.*
3 have as a consequence or result: *the proposals are likely to mean another hundred closures* | [with clause] *heavy rain meant that the pitch was waterlogged.*
■necessarily or usually entail or involve: *coal stoves mean a lot of smoke.*
– PHRASES **I mean** used to clarify or correct a statement or to introduce a justification or explanation: *I mean, it's not as if I owned property.* **mean business** be in earnest. **mean to say** [usu. in questions] really admit or intend to say: *do you mean to say you've uncovered something new?* **mean well** have good intentions, but not always the ability to carry them out.
– ORIGIN Old English *mænan*, of West Germanic origin; related to Dutch *meenen* and German *meinen*, from an Indo-European root shared by **MIND**.

mean[2] ▶ **adjective 1** unwilling to give or share things, especially money; not generous: *she felt mean not giving a tip | they're not **mean with** the garlic.*
2 unkind, spiteful, or unfair: *it was very **mean of** me | I was **mean to** them over the festive season.*
■N. Amer. vicious or aggressive in behaviour: *the dogs were considered mean, vicious, and a threat.*
3 (especially of a place) poor in quality and appearance; shabby: *her home was mean and small.*
■(of a person's mental capacity or understanding) inferior; poor: *it was obvious to even the meanest intelligence.* ■ dated of low birth or social class: *a muffler like that worn by the meanest of people.*
4 informal excellent; very skilful or effective: *he's a mean cook | she dances a mean Charleston.*
– PHRASES **mean streets** used in reference to a socially deprived area of a city, or one which is noted for violence and crime: *the mean streets of the South Bronx.* **no mean ——** denoting something very good of its kind: *it was no mean feat.*
– DERIVATIVES **meanly** adverb, **meanness** noun.
– ORIGIN Middle English, shortening of Old English *gemǣne*, of Germanic origin, from an Indo-European root shared by Latin *communis* 'common'. The original sense was 'common to two or more persons', later 'inferior in rank', leading to sense 3 and a sense 'ignoble, small-minded', from which senses 1 and 2 (which became common in the 19th cent.) arose.

mean[3] ▶ **noun 1** the quotient of the sum of several quantities and their number; an average: *acid output was calculated by taking the mean of all three samples.* See also **ARITHMETIC MEAN**, **GEOMETRIC MEAN**.
■the term or one of the terms midway between the first and last terms of a progression.
2 a condition, quality, or course of action equally removed from two opposite (usually unsatisfactory) extremes: *the measure expresses a mean between saving and splashing out.*
▶ **adjective** [attrib.] **1** (of a quantity) calculated as a mean; average: *by 1989 the mean age at marriage stood at 24.8 for women and 26.9 for men.*
2 equally far from two extremes: *hope is the mean virtue between despair and presumption.*
– ORIGIN Middle English: from Old French *meien*, from Latin *medianus* 'middle' (see **MEDIAN**).

mean anomaly ▶ **noun** Astronomy the angle in an imaginary circular orbit corresponding to a planet's eccentric anomaly.

meander /mɪˈandə, miː-/ ▶ **verb** [no obj., with adverbial of direction] (of a river or road) follow a winding course: *a river that meandered gently through a meadow* | [as adj. **meandering**] *a meandering lane.*
■(of a person) wander at random: *kids meandered in and out.* ■ [no obj.] (of a speaker or text) proceed aimlessly or with little purpose: *a stylish offbeat thriller which occasionally meanders.*
▶ **noun** (usu. **meanders**) a winding curve or bend of a river or road: *the river flows in sweeping meanders.*
■[in sing.] a circuitous journey, especially an aimless one: *a leisurely meander round the twisting coastline road.*
■ an ornamental pattern of winding or interlocking lines, e.g. in a mosaic.
– ORIGIN late 16th cent. (as a noun): from Latin *maeander*, from Greek *Maiandros*, the name of a river (see **MENDERES**).

mean free path ▶ **noun** Physics the average distance travelled by a gas molecule or other particle between collisions with other particles.

meanie (also **meany**) ▶ **noun** (pl. **-ies**) informal a mean or small-minded person.

meaning ▶ **noun** what is meant by a word, text, concept, or action: *the meaning of the word 'supermarket'* | [mass noun] *it was as if time had lost all meaning.*
■[mass noun] implied or explicit significance: *he gave me a look full of meaning.* ■ [mass noun] important or worthwhile quality; purpose: *this can lead to new meaning in the life of older people.*
▶ **adjective** [attrib.] intended to communicate something that is not directly expressed: *she gave Gabriel a meaning look.*
– PHRASES **not know the meaning of the word** informal behave as if unaware of the concept referred to or implied: *'Humanity? You don't know the meaning of the word!'*
– DERIVATIVES **meaningly** adverb.
– ORIGIN late Middle English: verbal noun from **MEAN**[1].

meaningful ▶ **adjective** having meaning: *meaningful elements in a language | words likely to be **meaningful to** pupils.*
■having a serious, important, or useful quality or purpose: *the new structure would bring meaningful savings.* ■ communicating something that is not directly expressed: *meaningful glances and repressed passion.* ■ Logic having a recognizable function in a logical language or other sign system.
– DERIVATIVES **meaningfully** adverb, **meaningfulness** noun.

meaningless ▶ **adjective** having no meaning or significance: *the paragraph was a jumble of meaningless words.*
■having no purpose or reason: *the Great War was an outstanding example of meaningless conflict | rules are **meaningless to** a child if they do not have a rationale.*
– DERIVATIVES **meaninglessly** adverb, **meaninglessness** noun.

means ▶ **plural noun 1** [usu. treated as sing.] (often **means of/to do something**) an action or system by which a result is brought about; a method: *technology seen as a means to bring about emancipation | resolving disputes by peaceful means.*
2 money; financial resources: *a woman of modest but independent means | prospective students without the means to attend Cornell.*
■resources; capability: *he has the means to kill every one of those people.* ■ wealth: *a man of means.*
– PHRASES **beyond** (or **within**) **one's means** beyond (or within) one's budget or income: *the government is living beyond its means.* **by all means** of course; certainly (granting a permission): *'May I make a suggestion?' 'By all means.'* **by any means** (following a negative) in any way; at all: *I'm not poor by any means.* **by means of** with the help or agency of: *supplying water to cities by means of aqueducts.* **by no means** (or **by no manner of means**) not at all; certainly not: *the outcome is by no means guaranteed.* **means of grace** Christian Theology the sacraments and other religious agencies viewed as the means by which divine grace is imparted to the soul, or by which growth in grace is promoted. **means of production** (especially in a political context) the facilities and resources for producing goods. **a means to an end** a thing that is not valued or important in itself but is useful in achieving an aim: *higher education was seen primarily as a means to an end.*
– ORIGIN late Middle English: plural of **MEAN**[3], the early sense being 'intermediary'.

mean sea level ▶ **noun** the sea level halfway between the mean levels of high and low water.

mean solar day ▶ **noun** Astronomy the time between successive passages of the mean sun across the meridian.

mean solar time ▶ **noun** [mass noun] Astronomy time as calculated by the motion of the mean sun. The time shown by an ordinary clock corresponds to mean solar time.

means test ▶ **noun** an official investigation into someone's financial circumstances to determine whether they are eligible for a welfare payment.
▶ **verb** (**means-test**) [with obj.] [usu. as adj. **means-tested**] make (a welfare payment) conditional on a means test: *means-tested benefits.*
■subject (someone) to a means test.

mean sun ▶ **noun** an imaginary sun conceived as moving through the sky throughout the year at a constant speed equal to the mean rate of the real sun, used in calculating solar time.

meant past and past participle of **MEAN**[1].

meantime ▶ **adverb** (also **in the meantime**) meanwhile: *in the meantime I'll make some enquiries of my own | Scotland, meantime, had her own monarchs.*
– ORIGIN Middle English (as a noun): from **MEAN**[3] + **TIME**.

mean time ▶ **noun** another term for **MEAN SOLAR TIME**. See also **GREENWICH MEAN TIME**.

meanwhile ▶ **adverb** (also **in the meanwhile**) in the intervening period of time: *meanwhile, I will give you a prescription for some pills.*
■at the same time: *steam for a further five minutes; meanwhile, make a white sauce.*
– ORIGIN late Middle English: from **MEAN**[3] + **WHILE**.

meany ▶ **noun** variant spelling of **MEANIE**.

measles ▶ **plural noun** (often **the measles**) [treated as sing.] an infectious viral disease causing fever and a red rash on the skin, typically occurring in childhood.
■a disease of pigs and other animals caused by the encysted larvae of the human tapeworm.
– ORIGIN Middle English *maseles*, probably from Middle Dutch *masel* 'pustule' (compare with modern Dutch *mazelen* 'measles'). The spelling

change was due to association with Middle English *mesel* 'leprous, leprosy'.

measly ▶ adjective (**measlier**, **measliest**) informal contemptibly small or few: *three measly votes.*

– ORIGIN late 16th cent. (describing a pig or pork infected with measles): from **MEASLES** + **-Y**[1]. The current sense dates from the mid 19th cent.

measurable ▶ adjective able to be measured: *objectives should be measurable and achievable.*
■ large enough to be measured; noticeable; definite: *a small but measurable improvement in behaviour.*

– DERIVATIVES **measurability** noun, **measurably** adverb [as submodifier] *the company's performance was measurably better.*

– ORIGIN Middle English (in the sense 'moderate'): from Old French *mesurable*, from late Latin *mensurabilis*, from Latin *mensurare* 'to measure'.

measure ▶ verb [with obj.] **1** ascertain the size, amount, or degree of (something) by using an instrument or device marked in standard units or by comparing it with an object of known size: *the amount of water collected is measured in pints | they will* ***measure up*** *the room and install the wardrobes.*
■ be of (a specified size or degree): *the fabric measures 137 cm wide.* ■ ascertain the size and proportions of (someone) in order to make or provide clothes for them: *he will be measured for his team blazer next week.* ■ (**measure something out**) take an exact quantity or fixed amount of something: *she helped to measure out the ingredients.* ■ estimate or assess the extent, quality, value, or effect of (something): *it is hard to measure teaching ability.* ■ (**measure someone/thing against**) judge someone or something by comparison with (a certain standard): *she did not need to measure herself against some ideal.* ■ [no obj.] (**measure up**) reach the required or expected standard; fulfil expectations: *I'm afraid we didn't* ***measure up to*** *the standards they set.* ■ scrutinize (someone) keenly in order to form an assessment of them: *the two shook hands and silently* ***measured*** *each other* ***up***.
2 consider (one's words or actions) carefully: *I had better measure my words so as not to embarrass anyone.*
3 archaic travel over (a certain distance or area): *we must measure twenty miles today.*
▶ noun **1** a plan or course of action taken to achieve a particular purpose: *cost-cutting measures | children were evacuated as a precautionary measure.*
■ a legislative bill: *the Senate passed the measure by a 48–30 vote.* ■ [mass noun] archaic punishment or retribution imposed or inflicted on someone: *her husband had dealt out* ***hard measure*** *to her.*
2 a standard unit used to express the size, amount, or degree of something: *a furlong is an obsolete measure of length | tables of weights and measures.*
■ [mass noun] a system or scale of such units: *the original dimensions were in imperial measure.* ■ a container of standard capacity used for taking fixed amounts of a substance. ■ a particular amount of something: ***a measure of*** *egg white.* ■ a standard official amount of an alcoholic drink as served in a licensed establishment. ■ a graduated rod or tape used for ascertaining the size of something. ■ Printing the width of a full line of type or print, typically expressed in picas. ■ Mathematics a quantity contained in another an exact number of times; a divisor.
3 a certain quantity or degree of something: *the states retain a large measure of independence.*
■ an indication or means of assessing the degree, extent, or quality of something: *it was a measure of the team's problems that they were still working after 2 a.m.*
4 the rhythm of a piece of poetry or a piece of music.
■ a particular metrical unit or group: *measures of two or three syllables are more frequent in English prose.* ■ N. Amer. a bar of music or the time of a piece of music. ■ archaic a dance, typically one that is grave or stately: *now tread we a measure!*
5 (**measures**) [with modifier] a group of rock strata.

– PHRASES **beyond measure** to a very great extent: *it irritates him beyond measure.* **for good measure** in addition to what has already been done, said, or given: *he added a couple of chillies for good measure.* **get** (or **take** or **have**) **the measure of** assess or have assessed the character, nature, or abilities of (someone or something): *he's got her measure—she won't fool him.* **in —— measure** to the degree specified: *his rapid promotion was due in some measure to his friendship with the king.* **measure one's length** dated (of a person) fall flat on the ground. **measure of capacity** a standard unit of volume used for containers, liquids, and substances such as grain.

– ORIGIN Middle English (as a noun in the senses 'moderation', 'instrument for measuring', 'unit of capacity'): from Old French *mesure*, from Latin *mensura*, from *mens-* 'measured', from the verb *metiri*.

measured ▶ adjective having a slow, regular rhythm: *she set off with measured tread.*
■ (of speech or writing) carefully considered; deliberate and restrained: *his measured prose.*

– DERIVATIVES **measuredly** adverb.

measureless ▶ adjective having no bounds or limits; unlimited: *Otto had measureless charm.*

measurement ▶ noun [mass noun] the action of measuring something: *accurate measurement is essential* | [count noun] *a telescope with which precise measurements can be made.*
■ [count noun] the size, length, or amount of something, as established by measuring: *his inside leg measurement.* ■ [count noun] a unit or system of measuring: *a hand is a measurement used for measuring horses.*

measuring jug (also **measuring cup**) ▶ noun a jug or cup marked up in graded amounts, used in cooking.

measuring tape ▶ noun another term for **TAPE MEASURE**.

measuring worm ▶ noun another term for **LOOPER**.

meat ▶ noun [mass noun] **1** the flesh of an animal (especially a mammal) as food: *rabbit meat* | [as modifier] *meat pies* | [count noun] *cold meats.*
■ the flesh of a person's body: *this'll put meat on your bones!* ■ chiefly US the edible part of fruits, nuts, or eggs. ■ (**the meat of**) the essence or chief part of something: *he did the meat of the climb on the first day.*
2 archaic food of any kind.

– PHRASES **be meat and drink to** Brit. **1** be a source of great pleasure to: *meat and drink to me, this life is!* **2** be a routine matter or task for: *he should be meat and drink to the English defence.* **easy meat** informal a person or animal that is easily overcome or outwitted. **meat and potatoes** ordinary but fundamental things; basic ingredients: *the club's meat and potatoes remains blues performers.* **one man's meat is another man's poison** proverb things liked or enjoyed by one person may be distasteful to another.

– DERIVATIVES **meatless** adjective.

– ORIGIN Old English *mete* 'food' or 'article of food' (as in *sweetmeat*), of Germanic origin.

meat ant ▶ noun a carnivorous Australian ant, especially a large reddish-purple kind that builds mounds.
• Genus *Iridomyrmex*, family Formicidae: several species, in particular *I. purpureus*.

meat axe ▶ noun a butcher's cleaver.

meatball ▶ noun a ball of minced or chopped meat.
■ N. Amer. informal a dull or stupid person.

Meath /miːθ/ a county in the eastern part of the Republic of Ireland, in the province of Leinster; county town, Navan.

meathead ▶ noun informal a stupid person.

meat hook ▶ noun a sharp metal hook of a kind used to hang meat carcasses and joints.
■ (**meat hooks**) informal a person's hands or arms: *get your big meat hooks out of those pies!*

meat loaf ▶ noun [mass noun] minced or chopped meat moulded into the shape of a loaf and baked.

meat market ▶ noun informal a meeting place such as a bar or disco for people seeking sexual encounters.

meat safe ▶ noun Brit. historical a cupboard or cover of wire gauze or a similar material, used for storing meat.

meatus /mɪˈeɪtəs/ ▶ noun (pl. same or **meatuses**) Anatomy a passage or opening leading to the interior of the body: *the urethral meatus.*
■ (also **external auditory meatus**) the passage leading into the ear.

– ORIGIN late Middle English: from Latin, 'passage' from *meare* 'to flow, run'.

meat wagon ▶ noun informal an ambulance or hearse.
■ a police van.

meaty ▶ adjective (**meatier**, **meatiest**) consisting of or full of meat: *a meaty flavour.*
■ fleshy; brawny: *the tall, meaty young man.* ■ full of substance or interest; satisfying: *the ballet has stayed the course because of the meaty roles it offers.*

– DERIVATIVES **meatily** adverb, **meatiness** noun.

mebos /ˈmiːbɒs/ ▶ noun [mass noun] S. African a confection made from apricots soaked in brine, stoned, pulped, sugared, and sun-dried.

– ORIGIN South African Dutch, probably from Japanese *umeboshi* 'plums pickled in salt and dried'.

Mecca a city in western Saudi Arabia, an oasis town in the Red Sea region of Hejaz, east of Jiddah, considered by Muslims to be the holiest city of Islam; pop. 618,000 (est. 1986). Arabic name **MAKKAH**.
■ [as noun **a Mecca**] a place which attracts people of a particular group or with a particular interest: *Holland is* ***a Mecca for*** *jazz enthusiasts.*

The birthplace in AD 570 of the prophet Muhammad, it was the scene of his early teachings before his emigration to Medina in 622 (the Hegira). On Muhammad's return to Mecca in 630 it became the centre of the new Muslim faith. It is the site of the Great Mosque and the Kaaba, and is a centre of Islamic ritual, including the haj pilgrimage which leads thousands of visitors to the city each year.

– DERIVATIVES **Meccan** adjective & noun.

Meccano /mɪˈkɑːnəʊ/ ▶ noun [mass noun] [often as modifier] trademark a children's construction set for making mechanical models, consisting chiefly of metal girders, brackets, and other components.

– ORIGIN early 20th cent.: an invented word suggested by *mechanic*.

mech ▶ noun informal **1** a mechanic.
2 the gear mechanism of a bicycle.

– ORIGIN mid 20th cent.: abbreviation.

mechanic ▶ noun **1** a skilled manual worker, especially one who repairs and maintains machinery: *a car mechanic.*
2 archaic a manual labourer or artisan: *the Mechanics' Institute.*

– ORIGIN late Middle English (as an adjective in the sense 'relating to manual labour'): via Old French or Latin from Greek *mēkhanikos*, from *mēkhanē* (see **MACHINE**).

mechanical ▶ adjective **1** working or produced by machines or machinery: *a mechanical device.*
■ of or relating to machines or machinery: *a mechanical genius | mechanical failure.*
2 (of a person or action) not having or showing thought or spontaneity; automatic: *she stopped the mechanical brushing of her hair.*
3 relating to physical forces or motion; physical: *the smoothness was the result of mechanical abrasion.*
■ (of a theory) explaining phenomena in terms only of physical processes. ■ of or relating to mechanics as a science.
▶ noun **1** (**mechanicals**) the working parts of a machine, especially a car.
2 (usu. **mechanicals**) archaic (especially with allusion to Shakespeare's *A Midsummer Night's Dream*) a manual worker: *rude mechanicals.*

– DERIVATIVES **mechanically** adverb, **mechanicalness** noun.

– ORIGIN late Middle English (describing an art or occupation concerned with the design or construction of machines): via Latin from Greek *mēkhanikos* (see **MECHANIC**) + **-AL**.

mechanical advantage ▶ noun the ratio of the force produced by a machine to the force applied to it, used in assessing the performance of a machine.

mechanical drawing ▶ noun a scale drawing of a mechanical or architectural structure done with precision instruments.
■ [mass noun] the action or process of making such drawings.

mechanical engineering ▶ noun [mass noun] the branch of engineering dealing with the design, construction, and use of machines.

– DERIVATIVES **mechanical engineer** noun.

mechanician ▶ noun a person skilled in the design or construction of machinery.

mechanics ▶ plural noun **1** [treated as sing.] the branch of applied mathematics dealing with motion and forces producing motion.
■ machinery as a subject; engineering.
2 the machinery or working parts of something: *he looks at the mechanics of a car before the bodywork.*
■ the way in which something is done or operated; the practicalities or details of something: *the mechanics of cello playing.*

mechanism ▶ noun **1** a system of parts working together in a machine; a piece of machinery: *the gunner injured his arm in the turret mechanism.*
2 a natural or established process by which

something takes place or is brought about: *we have no mechanism for assessing the success of forwarded enquiries* | *the mechanism by which genes build bodies.*
■a contrivance in the plot of a literary work: *Irma La Douce is a musical based on the farce mechanism.*
3 [mass noun] Philosophy the doctrine that all natural phenomena, including life and thought, allow mechanical explanation by physics and chemistry.
– ORIGIN mid 17th cent.: from modern Latin *mechanismus*, from Greek *mēkhanē* (see **MACHINE**).

mechanist /ˈmɛk(ə)nɪst/ ▸ noun **1** Philosophy a person who believes in the doctrine of mechanism.
2 a person skilled in the design or construction of machinery.

mechanistic ▸ adjective of or relating to theories which explain phenomena in purely physical or deterministic terms: *a mechanistic interpretation of nature.*
■determined by physical processes alone: *he insisted that animals were entirely mechanistic.*
– DERIVATIVES **mechanistically** adverb.

mechanize (also **-ise**) ▸ verb [with obj.] (often be **mechanized**) introduce machines or automatic devices into (a process, activity, or place): *the farm was mechanized in the 1950s.*
■equip (a military force) with modern weapons and vehicles: [as adj. **mechanized**] *the units comprised tanks and mechanized infantry.* ■give a mechanical character to: *public virtue cannot be mechanized or formulated.*
– DERIVATIVES **mechanization** noun, **mechanizer** noun.

mechano- /ˈmɛk(ə)nəʊ/ ▸ combining form mechanical; relating to a mechanical source: *mechanoreceptor.*
– ORIGIN from Greek *mēkhanē* 'machine'.

mechanoreceptor ▸ noun Zoology a sense organ or cell that responds to mechanical stimuli such as touch or sound.
– DERIVATIVES **mechanoreceptive** adjective.

mechatronics ▸ plural noun [treated as sing.] technology combining electronics and mechanical engineering.
– ORIGIN 1980s: blend of **MECHANICS** and **ELECTRONICS**.

Mechelen /ˈmɛxələn/ a city in northern Belgium, north of Brussels; pop. 75,310 (1991). It is noted for its cathedral, and for Mechlin lace. French name **MALINES**.

Mechlin /ˈmɛklɪn/ (also **Mechlin lace**) ▸ noun [mass noun] lace made at Mechelen (formerly known as Mechlin), characterized by patterns outlined in heavier thread.

Mecklenburg /ˈmɛklənbɔːɡ, German ˈmɛklənbʊrk/ a former state of NE Germany, on the Baltic coast, now part of Mecklenburg-West Pomerania.

Mecklenburg-West Pomerania a state of NE Germany, on the coast of the Baltic Sea; capital, Schwerin. It consists of the former state of Mecklenburg and the western part of Pomerania.

MEcon ▸ abbreviation for Master of Economics.

meconium /mɪˈkəʊnɪəm/ ▸ noun [mass noun] Medicine the dark green substance forming the first faeces of a newborn infant.
– ORIGIN early 18th cent.: from Latin, literally 'poppy juice', from Greek *mēkōnion*, from *mēkōn* 'poppy'.

meconopsis /ˌmiːkəˈnɒpsɪs, ˌmɛkə-/ ▸ noun (pl. same or **meconopses**) a Eurasian poppy which is sometimes grown as an ornamental.
● Genus *Meconopsis*, family Papaveraceae: several species, in particular the blue-flowered Tibetan or blue poppy (*M. betonicifolia*) and the Welsh poppy.
– ORIGIN modern Latin, from Greek *mēkōn* 'poppy' + *opsis* 'appearance'.

Mecoptera /məˈkɒptərə/ Entomology an order of insects that comprises the scorpion flies.
– DERIVATIVES **mecopteran** noun & adjective.
– ORIGIN modern Latin (plural), from Greek *mēkos* 'length' + *pteron* 'wing'.

MEd ▸ abbreviation for Master of Education.

Med ▸ noun (**the Med**) informal, chiefly Brit. the Mediterranean Sea.
– ORIGIN 1940s: abbreviation.

med. ▸ abbreviation for ■ informal, chiefly N. Amer. medical: *med. school.* ■ medium.

médaillon /ˌmeɪdʌɪˈjɒ̃/ ▸ noun (pl. pronounced same) a small flat round or oval cut of meat or fish: *veal médaillons.*

– ORIGIN French, literally 'medallion'.

medaka /məˈdɑːkə/ ▸ noun a small, slender freshwater fish with the dorsal fin set back near the tail, native to parts of SE Asia and Japan.
● Family Oryziatidae and genus *Oryzias*: several species.
– ORIGIN early 20th cent.: from Japanese *me(y)* 'eye' + *-daka* 'high'.

medal ▸ noun a metal disc with an inscription or design, made to commemorate an event or awarded as a distinction to someone such as a soldier, athlete, or scholar.
– DERIVATIVES **medallic** adjective.
– ORIGIN late 16th cent.: from French *médaille*, from Italian *medaglia*, from medieval Latin *medalia* 'half a denarius', from Latin *medialis* 'medial'.

medalled ▸ adjective honoured with a medal or medals: *the most medalled athlete in Britain.*

medallion ▸ noun a piece of jewellery in the shape of a medal, typically worn as a pendant.
■an oval or circular painting, panel, or design used to decorate a building or textile. ■ another term for **MÉDAILLON**.
– ORIGIN mid 17th cent.: from French *médaillon*, from Italian *medaglione*, augmentative of *medaglia* (see **MEDAL**).

medallist (US **medalist**) ▸ noun **1** an athlete or other person awarded a medal: *an Olympic gold medallist.*
2 an engraver or designer of medals.

medal play ▸ noun Golf another term for **STROKE PLAY**.

Medan /ˈmɛdɑːn/ a city in Indonesia, in NE Sumatra near the Strait of Malacca; pop. 1,730,000 (1990). It was established as a trading post by the Dutch in 1682 and became a leading commercial centre.

Medawar /ˈmɛdəwə/, Sir Peter (Brian) (1915–87), English immunologist. He studied the biology of tissue transplantation, and showed that the rejection of grafts was the result of an immune mechanism. Nobel Prize for Physiology or Medicine (1960).

meddle ▸ verb [no obj.] interfere in or busy oneself unduly with something that is not one's concern: *I don't want him meddling in our affairs* | [as noun **meddling**] *bureaucratic meddling.*
■(**meddle with**) touch or handle (something) without permission: *you have no right to come in here meddling with my things.*
– DERIVATIVES **meddler** noun.
– ORIGIN Middle English (in the sense 'mingle, mix'): from Old French *medler*, variant of *mesler*, based on Latin *miscere* 'to mix'.

meddlesome ▸ adjective fond of meddling; interfering: *heaven rid him of meddlesome politicians!*
– DERIVATIVES **meddlesomely** adverb, **meddlesomeness** noun.

Mede /miːd/ ▸ noun a member of an Indo-European people who inhabited ancient Media, establishing an extensive empire during the 7th century BC, which was conquered by Cyrus the Great of Persia in 550 BC.
– PHRASES **law of the Medes and Persians** informal something which cannot be altered. [ORIGIN: with biblical allusion to Dan. vi. 12.]
– ORIGIN from Latin *Medi*, Greek *Mēdoi*, plural forms.

Medea /mɪˈdiːə/ Greek Mythology a sorceress, daughter of Aeetes king of Colchis, who helped Jason to obtain the Golden Fleece and married him. When Jason deserted her for Creusa, the daughter of King Creon of Corinth, she took revenge by killing Creon, Creusa, and her own children, and fled to Athens.

Medellín /ˌmɛdeɪˈjiːn/ a city in eastern Colombia, the second largest city in the country; pop. 1,581,300 (1992). A major centre of coffee production, it has in recent years gained a reputation as the hub of the Colombian drug trade.

medevac /ˈmɛdɪvak/ (also **medivac**) N. Amer. ▸ noun [mass noun] the evacuation of military or other casualties to hospital in a helicopter or aeroplane.
▸ verb (**medevacked**, **medevacking**) [with obj. and adverbial of direction] transport (someone) in this way: *I was medevacked out of Freetown.*
– ORIGIN 1960s: blend of **MEDICAL** and **EVACUATION**.

medfly ▸ noun (pl. **-flies**) chiefly N. Amer. another term for **MEDITERRANEAN FRUIT FLY**.

Media /ˈmiːdɪə/ an ancient region of Asia to the south-west of the Caspian Sea, corresponding

approximately to present-day Azerbaijan, NW Iran, and NE Iraq. Originally inhabited by the Medes, the region was conquered in 550 BC by Cyrus the Great of Persia.
– DERIVATIVES **Median** adjective.

media[1] /ˈmiːdɪə/ ▸ noun **1** plural form of **MEDIUM**.
2 (usu. **the media**) [treated as sing. or pl.] the main means of mass communication (especially television, radio, and newspapers) regarded collectively: [as modifier] *the campaign won media attention.*

> **USAGE** The word **media** comes from the Latin plural of **medium**. The traditional view is that it should therefore be treated as a plural noun in all its senses in English and be used with a plural rather than a singular verb: *the media **have** not followed the reports* (rather than 'has'). In practice, in the sense 'television, radio, and the press collectively', it behaves as a collective noun (like **staff** or **clergy**, for example), which means that it is now acceptable in standard English for it to take either a singular or a plural verb.

media[2] /ˈmiːdɪə/ ▸ noun (pl. **mediae** /-dɪiː/) Anatomy an intermediate layer, especially in the wall of a blood vessel.
– ORIGIN late 19th cent.: shortening of modern Latin *tunica* (or *membrana*) *media* 'middle sheath (or layer)'.

mediacy ▸ noun [mass noun] **1** the quality of being mediate.
2 rare term for *mediation* (see **MEDIATE**).

mediaeval ▸ adjective variant spelling of **MEDIEVAL**.

media event ▸ noun an event intended primarily to attract publicity: *a staged media event.*

mediagenic /ˌmiːdɪəˈdʒɛnɪk/ ▸ adjective chiefly US tending to convey a favourable impression when reported by the media, especially by television.

medial ▸ adjective technical situated in the middle, in particular:
■Anatomy & Zoology situated near the median plane of the body or the midline of an organ. The opposite of **LATERAL**. ■ Phonetics (of a speech sound) in the middle of a word. ■ Phonetics (especially of a vowel) pronounced in the middle of the mouth; central.
– DERIVATIVES **medially** adverb.
– ORIGIN late 16th cent. (in the sense 'relating to the mean or average'): from late Latin *medialis*, from Latin *medius* 'middle'.

median /ˈmiːdɪən/ ▸ adjective [attrib.] **1** denoting or relating to a value or quantity lying at the mid point of a frequency distribution of observed values or quantities, such that there is an equal probability of falling above or below it: *the median duration of this treatment was four months.*
■denoting the middle term of a series arranged in order of magnitude, or (if there is no middle term) the mean of the middle two terms.
2 technical, chiefly Anatomy situated in the middle, especially of the body: *the median part of the sternum.*
▸ noun **1** the median value of a range of values: *acreages ranged from one to fifty-two with a median of twenty-four.*
2 (also **median strip**) North American term for **CENTRAL RESERVATION**.
3 Geometry a straight line drawn from any vertex of a triangle to the middle of the opposite side.
– DERIVATIVES **medianly** adverb.
– ORIGIN late Middle English (denoting a median vein or nerve): from medieval Latin *medianus*, from *medius* 'mid'.

mediant /ˈmiːdɪənt/ ▸ noun Music the third note of the diatonic scale of any key.
– ORIGIN mid 18th cent.: from French *médiante*, from Italian *mediante* 'coming between', present participle of obsolete *mediare* 'come between', from late Latin *mediare* 'be in the middle of'.

mediastinitis /ˌmiːdɪəstɪˈnʌɪtɪs/ ▸ noun [mass noun] Medicine inflammation of the mediastinum of the thorax.

mediastinum /ˌmiːdɪəˈstʌɪnəm/ ▸ noun (pl. **mediastina** /-nə/) Anatomy a membranous partition between two body cavities or two parts of an organ, especially that between the lungs.
– DERIVATIVES **mediastinal** adjective.
– ORIGIN late Middle English: neuter of medieval Latin *mediastinus* 'medial', based on Latin *medius* 'middle'.

media studies ▸ plural noun [usu. treated as sing.] the

study of the mass media, especially as an academic subject.

mediate ▶ **verb** /ˈmiːdɪeɪt/ **1** [no obj.] intervene between people in a dispute in order to bring about an agreement or reconciliation: *Wilson attempted to* ***mediate between*** *the powers to end the war.*
■ [with obj.] intervene in (a dispute) to bring about an agreement. ■ [with obj.] bring about (an agreement or solution) by intervening in a dispute: *efforts to mediate a peaceful resolution of the conflict.*
2 [with obj.] technical bring about (a result such as a physiological effect): *the right hemisphere plays an important role in mediating tactile perception of direction.*
■ be a means of conveying: *this important ministry of mediating the power of the word.* ■ form a connecting link between: *structures which mediate gender divisions.*
▶ **adjective** /ˈmiːdɪət/ connected indirectly through another person or thing; involving an intermediate agency: *public law institutions are a type of mediate state administration.*
– DERIVATIVES **mediately** adverb, **mediation** noun, **mediator** noun, **mediatory** /ˈmiːdɪət(ə)ri/ adjective.
– ORIGIN late Middle English (as an adjective in the sense 'interposed'): from late Latin *mediatus* 'placed in the middle', past participle of the verb *mediare*, from Latin *medius* 'middle'.

medic[1] /ˈmɛdɪk/ ▶ **noun** informal a medical practitioner or student.
– ORIGIN mid 17th cent.: from Latin *medicus* 'physician', from *mederi* 'heal'.

medic[2] /ˈmiːdɪk/ ▶ **noun** variant spelling of **MEDICK**.

medicable ▶ **adjective** rare able to be treated or cured medically.
– ORIGIN late 16th cent. (in the sense 'possessing medicinal properties'): from Latin *medicabilis*, from *medicari* 'administer remedies to' (see **MEDICATE**).

Medicaid (in the US) a federal system of health insurance for those requiring financial assistance.
– ORIGIN 1960s: from **MEDICAL** + **AID**.

medical ▶ **adjective** of or relating to the science of medicine, or to the treatment of illness and injuries: *a medical centre | the medical profession.*
■ of or relating to conditions requiring medical but not surgical treatment: *he was transferred for further treatment to a medical ward.*
▶ **noun** an examination to assess a person's state of physical health or fitness.
– DERIVATIVES **medically** adverb.
– ORIGIN mid 17th cent.: via French from medieval Latin *medicalis*, from Latin *medicus* 'physician'.

medical certificate ▶ **noun** a certificate from a doctor giving the state of someone's health.

medical examination ▶ **noun** an examination to determine someone's physical health.

medicalize (also **-ise**) ▶ **verb** [with obj.] view (something) in medical terms; treat as a medical problem, especially unwarrantedly: *doctors tend to medicalize manifestations of distress, prescribing drugs such as sleeping tablets.*
– DERIVATIVES **medicalization** noun.
– ORIGIN 1970s: from **MEDICAL** + **-IZE**.

medical jurisprudence ▶ **noun** [mass noun] the branch of law relating to medicine.
■ forensic medicine.

medical officer ▶ **noun 1** Brit. a doctor in charge of the health services of a local authority or other organization.
2 a qualified doctor serving in the armed forces.

medical practitioner ▶ **noun** a physician or surgeon.

medicament /mɪˈdɪkəm(ə)nt, ˈmɛdɪk-/ ▶ **noun** a substance used for medical treatment.
– ORIGIN late Middle English: via French from Latin *medicamentum*, from *medicari* (see **MEDICATE**).

Medicare (in the US) a federal system of health insurance for people over 65 years of age.
■ (in Canada and Australia) a national health-care scheme financed by taxation.
– ORIGIN 1960s: from **MEDICAL** + **CARE**.

medicate ▶ **verb** [with obj.] (often **be medicated**) administer medicine or a drug to (someone): *both infants were heavily medicated to alleviate their seizures.*
■ treat (a condition) using medicine or a drug. ■ add a medicinal substance to (a dressing or product): [as adj. **medicated**] *medicated shampoo.*
– DERIVATIVES **medicative** adjective.
– ORIGIN early 17th cent.: from Latin *medicat-* 'treated', from the verb *medicari* 'administer remedies to', from *medicus* (see **MEDIC**[1]).

medication ▶ **noun** [mass noun] a substance used for medical treatment, especially a medicine or drug: *he'd been taking medication for depression* | [count noun] *certain medications can cause dizziness.*
■ treatment using drugs: *chronic gastrointestinal symptoms which may require prolonged medication.*

Medicean /ˌmɛdɪˈtʃiːən, -ˈsiːən, mɛˈdiːtʃɪən/ ▶ **adjective** of or relating to the Medici family.

Medici /ˈmɛdɪtʃi, məˈdiːtʃi/ (also **de' Medici**) a powerful Italian family of bankers and merchants whose members effectively ruled Florence for much of the 15th century and from 1569 were grand dukes of Tuscany. **Cosimo** and **Lorenzo de' Medici** were notable rulers and patrons of the arts in Florence; the family also provided four popes (including **Leo X**) and two queens of France (**Catherine de' Medici** and **Marie de Médicis**).

medicinal ▶ **adjective** (of a substance or plant) having healing properties: *medicinal herbs* | humorous *a large medicinal Scotch.*
■ relating to or involving medicines or drugs.
▶ **noun** a medicinal substance.
– DERIVATIVES **medicinally** adverb.
– ORIGIN late Middle English: from Latin *medicinalis*, from *medicina* (see **MEDICINE**).

medicinal leech ▶ **noun** a large European leech which was formerly much used in medicine for bloodletting. After biting it secretes an anticoagulant to ensure the flow of blood.
• *Hirudo medicinalis*, family Hirudidae.

medicine ▶ **noun** [mass noun] **1** the science or practice of the diagnosis, treatment, and prevention of disease (in technical use often taken to exclude surgery).
2 a compound or preparation used for the treatment or prevention of disease, especially a drug or drugs taken by mouth: *give her some medicine* | [count noun] *your doctor will be able to prescribe medicines.*
■ such substances collectively: *an aid convoy loaded with food and medicine.*
3 (among North American Indians and some other peoples) a spell, charm, or fetish believed to have healing, protective, or other power: *Fleur was murdering him by use of* ***bad medicine.***
– PHRASES **give someone a dose** (or **taste**) **of their own medicine** give someone the same bad treatment that they have given to others: *tired of his humiliation of me, I decided to give him a taste of his own medicine.* **take one's medicine** submit to something disagreeable such as punishment.
– ORIGIN Middle English: via Old French from Latin *medicina*, from *medicus* 'physician'.

medicine ball ▶ **noun** a large, heavy solid ball thrown and caught for exercise.

medicine cabinet (also **medicine chest**) ▶ **noun** a box containing medicines and first-aid items.

medicine man ▶ **noun** (among North American Indians and some other peoples) a person believed to have magical powers of healing; a shaman.

medicine wheel ▶ **noun** a stone circle built by North American Indians, believed to have religious, astronomical, territorial, or calendrical significance.

Médicis, Marie de, see **MARIE DE MÉDICIS**.

medick /ˈmiːdɪk/ ▶ **noun** a Eurasian and African plant of the pea family related to alfalfa, some kinds of which are grown for fodder or green manure and some are troublesome weeds.
• Genus *Medicago*, family Leguminosae.
– ORIGIN late Middle English: from Latin *medica*, from Greek *Mēdikē (poa)* 'Median (grass)'.

medico ▶ **noun** (pl. **-os**) informal a medical practitioner or student.
– ORIGIN late 17th cent.: via Italian from Latin *medicus* 'physician'.

medico- ▶ **combining form** relating to the field of medicine: *medico-social.*
– ORIGIN from Latin *medicus* 'physician'.

medieval /ˌmɛdɪˈiːv(ə)l, mɪ:-/ (also **mediaeval**) ▶ **adjective** of or relating to the Middle Ages: *a medieval castle.*
■ informal, derogatory very old-fashioned or primitive: *the guerrillas' medieval behaviour has become an embarrassment to their supporters.*
– DERIVATIVES **medievalism** noun, **medievalist** noun, **medievalize** (also **-ise**) verb, **medievally** adverb.
– ORIGIN early 19th cent.: from modern Latin *medium aevum* 'middle age' + **-AL**.

medieval history ▶ **noun** [mass noun] the history of the 5th–15th centuries.

medieval Latin ▶ **noun** [mass noun] Latin of about AD 600–1500.

Medina /mɛˈdiːnə/ a city in western Saudi Arabia, around an oasis some 320 km (200 miles) north of Mecca; pop. 500,000 (est. 1981). Arabic name **AL MADINAH**.

Medina was the refuge of Muhammad's infant Muslim community from its removal from Mecca in AD 622 until its return there in 630. It is Muhammad's burial place and the site of the first Islamic mosque, constructed around his tomb. It is considered by Muslims to be the second most holy city after Mecca, and a visit to the prophet's tomb at Medina often forms a sequel to the formal pilgrimage to Mecca.

medina /mɛˈdiːnə/ ▶ **noun** the old Arab or non-European quarter of a North African town.
– ORIGIN Arabic, literally 'town'.

mediocracy ▶ **noun** (pl. **-ies**) a dominant class consisting of mediocre people, or a system in which mediocrity is rewarded.

mediocre /ˌmiːdɪˈəʊkə/ ▶ **adjective** of only moderate quality; not very good: *a mediocre actor.*
– DERIVATIVES **mediocrely** adverb.
– ORIGIN late 16th cent.: from French *médiocre*, from Latin *mediocris* 'of middle height or degree', literally 'somewhat rugged or mountainous', from *medius* 'middle' + *ocris* 'rugged mountain'.

mediocrity ▶ **noun** (pl. **-ies**) [mass noun] the quality or state of being mediocre: *the team suddenly came good after years of mediocrity.*
■ [count noun] a person of mediocre ability.

meditate ▶ **verb** [no obj.] think deeply or focus one's mind for a period of time, in silence or with the aid of chanting, for religious or spiritual purposes or as a method of relaxation.
■ (**meditate on/upon**) think deeply or carefully about (something): *he went off to meditate on the new idea.* ■ [with obj.] plan mentally; consider: *they had suffered severely, and they began to meditate retreat.*
– DERIVATIVES **meditator** noun.
– ORIGIN mid 16th cent.: from Latin *meditat-* 'contemplated', from the verb *meditari*, from a base meaning 'measure'; related to **METE**[1].

meditation ▶ **noun** [mass noun] the action or practice of meditating: *a life of meditation.*
■ [count noun] a written or spoken discourse expressing considered thoughts on a subject: *his later letters are intense* ***meditations on*** *man's exploitation of his fellows.*
– ORIGIN Middle English: from Old French, from Latin *meditatio(n-)*, from *meditari* (see **MEDITATE**).

meditative /ˈmɛdɪˌtətɪv, -ˌteɪtɪv/ ▶ **adjective** of, involving, or absorbed in meditation or considered thought: *meditative techniques.*
– DERIVATIVES **meditatively** adverb, **meditativeness** noun.
– ORIGIN early 17th cent.: from **MEDITATE** + **-IVE**, reinforced by French *méditatif, -ive*.

Mediterranean /ˌmɛdɪtəˈreɪnɪən/ ▶ **adjective** of or characteristic of the Mediterranean Sea, the countries bordering it, or their inhabitants: *a leisurely Mediterranean cruise | our temperatures are Mediterranean.*
■ (of a person's complexion) relatively dark, as is common in some Mediterranean countries.
▶ **noun 1** (**the Mediterranean**) the Mediterranean Sea or the countries bordering it.
2 a native of a country bordering on the Mediterranean.
– ORIGIN mid 16th cent.: from Latin *mediterraneus* 'inland' (from *medius* 'middle' + *terra* 'land') + **-AN**.

Mediterranean climate ▶ **noun** a climate distinguished by warm, wet winters under prevailing westerly winds and calm, hot, dry summers, as is characteristic of the Mediterranean region and parts of California, Chile, South Africa, and SW Australia.

Mediterranean fruit fly ▶ **noun** a fruit fly whose larvae can be a serious pest of citrus and other fruits. Native to the Mediterranean region, it has spread to other regions including the US. Also called **MEDFLY**, chiefly in North America.
• *Ceratitis capitata*, family Tephritidae.

Mediterranean Sea an almost landlocked sea between southern Europe, the north coast of Africa, and SW Asia. It is connected with the Atlantic by the Strait of Gibraltar, with the Red Sea by the Suez Canal, and with the Black Sea by the Dardanelles, the Sea of Marmara, and the Bosporus.

medium ▶ noun (pl. **media** or **mediums**) **1** an agency or means of doing something: *using the latest technology as* ***a medium for*** *job creation* | *their primitive valuables acted as* ***a medium of*** *exchange.*
■ a means by which something is communicated or expressed: *here the Welsh language is the medium of instruction.*
2 the intervening substance through which impressions are conveyed to the senses or a force acts on objects at a distance: *radio communication needs no physical medium between the two stations* | *the medium between the cylinders is a vacuum.*
■ the substance in which an organism lives or is cultured: *grow bacteria in a nutrient-rich medium.*
3 a liquid (e.g. oil or water) with which pigments are mixed to make paint.
■ the material or form used by an artist, composer, or writer: *oil paint is the most popular medium for glazing.*
4 (pl. **mediums**) a person claiming to be in contact with the spirits of the dead and to communicate between the dead and the living.
5 the middle quality or state between two extremes; a reasonable balance: *you have to* ***strike a happy medium between*** *looking like royalty and looking like a housewife.*
▶ adjective about halfway between two extremes of size or another quality; average: *John is six feet tall, of medium build* | *medium-length hair.*
■ Cricket (of bowling or a bowler) of a pace intermediate between fast and slow bowling.
– DERIVATIVES **mediumism** noun (only in sense 4), **mediumistic** adjective (only in sense 4), **mediumship** noun (only in sense 4).
– ORIGIN late 16th cent. (originally denoting something intermediate in nature or degree): from Latin, literally 'middle', neuter of *medius*.

medium frequency ▶ noun a radio frequency between 300 kHz and 3 MHz.

medium-pacer ▶ noun Cricket a seam bowler who bowls at a medium pace.
■ a ball bowled at medium pace.

medium-range ▶ adjective (of an aircraft or missile) able to travel or operate over a medium distance: *medium-range nuclear missiles.*

medium wave ▶ noun chiefly Brit. a radio wave of a frequency between 300 kHz and 3 MHz.
■ [mass noun] broadcasting using such radio waves: *you can no longer get Radio 2* ***on medium wave.***

medivac ▶ noun & verb variant spelling of **MEDEVAC**.

medlar ▶ noun a small bushy tree of the rose family, which bears small brown apple-like fruits.
● *Mespilus germanica*, family Rosaceae.
■ the fruit of this tree, which is only edible after it has begun to decay.
– ORIGIN late Middle English: from Old French *medler*, from *medle* 'medlar fruit', from Latin *mespila*, from Greek *mespilē*, *mespilon*.

medley ▶ noun (pl. **-eys**) a varied mixture of people or things; a miscellany: *an interesting medley of flavours.*
■ a collection of songs or other musical items performed as a continuous piece: *a medley of Beatles songs.* ■ a swimming race in which contestants swim sections in different strokes, either individually or in relay teams.
▶ adjective archaic mixed; motley: *a medley range of vague and variable impressions.*
▶ verb (past and past participle **-eyed** or **-ied**) [with obj.] archaic make a medley of; intermix.
– ORIGIN Middle English (denoting hand-to-hand combat, also cloth made of variegated wool): from Old French *medlee*, variant of *meslee* 'melee', based on medieval Latin *misculare* 'to mix'; compare with **MEDDLE**.

Médoc /meɪˈdɒk, French medɔk/ ▶ noun (pl. same) [mass noun] a red wine produced in Médoc, the area along the left bank of the Gironde estuary in SW France.

medrese /mɛˈdrɛseɪ/ ▶ noun variant spelling of **MADRASA**.

medulla /mɛˈdʌlə/ ▶ noun Anatomy the inner region of an organ or tissue, especially when it is distinguishable from the outer region or cortex (as in a kidney, an adrenal gland, or hair).
■ short for **MEDULLA OBLONGATA**. ■ [mass noun] Botany the soft internal tissue or pith of a plant.
– DERIVATIVES **medullary** adjective.
– ORIGIN late Middle English (in the sense 'bone marrow'): from Latin, 'pith or marrow'.

medulla oblongata /ˌɒblɒŋˈɡɑːtə/ ▶ noun the continuation of the spinal cord within the skull, forming the lowest part of the brainstem and containing control centres for the heart and lungs.
– ORIGIN late 17th cent.: modern Latin, literally 'elongated medulla'.

Medusa /mɪˈdjuːzə/ Greek Mythology the only mortal gorgon, whom Perseus killed by cutting off her head.

medusa /mɪˈdjuːzə, -sə/ ▶ noun (pl. **medusae** /-ziː, -siː/ or **medusas**) Zoology a free-swimming sexual form of a coelenterate such as a jellyfish, typically having an umbrella-shaped body with stinging tentacles around the edge. In some species, medusae are a phase in the life cycle which alternates with a polypoid phase. Compare with **POLYP**.
■ a jellyfish.
– ORIGIN mid 18th cent.: named by association with **MEDUSA**.

medusa fish ▶ noun a fish of the cool temperate waters of the North Pacific, the young of which typically accompany jellyfishes and may feed on their tentacles.
● *Icichthys lockingtoni*, family Centrolophidae.

medusoid /mɪˈdjuːsɔɪd/ Zoology ▶ adjective of, relating to, or resembling a medusa or jellyfish.
■ of, relating to, or denoting the medusa phase in the life cycle of a coelenterate. Compare with **POLYPOID** (in sense 1).
▶ noun a medusa or jellyfish.
■ a medusoid reproductive bud.

meed ▶ noun archaic a deserved share or reward: *he must extract from her some meed of approbation.*
– ORIGIN Old English *mēd*, of Germanic origin; from an Indo-European root shared by Greek *misthos* 'reward'.

meeja /ˈmiːdʒə/ (also **meejah**) ▶ plural noun non-standard spelling of **MEDIA**[1], used humorously in imitation of informal British speech.

meek ▶ adjective quiet, gentle, and easily imposed on; submissive: *I used to call her Miss Mouse because she was so meek and mild* | *the meek compliance of our domestic politicians.*
– DERIVATIVES **meekly** adverb, **meekness** noun.
– ORIGIN Middle English *me(o)c* (also in the sense 'courteous or indulgent'), from Old Norse *mjúkr* 'soft, gentle'.

meerkat /ˈmɪəkat/ ▶ noun a small southern African mongoose, especially the suricate.
● *Suricata* and other genera, family Herpestidae: three species.
■ S. African any of a number of mongooses or similar-sized mammals, e.g. the zorilla or a ground squirrel.
– ORIGIN early 18th cent.: from South African Dutch, from Dutch, 'long-tailed monkey', apparently from *meer* 'sea' + *kat* 'cat', but perhaps originally an alteration of an oriental word; compare with Hindi *markaṭ* 'ape'.

meerschaum /ˈmɪəʃɔːm, -ʃəm/ ▶ noun [mass noun] a soft white clay-like material consisting of hydrated magnesium silicate, found chiefly in Turkey.
■ (also **meerschaum pipe**) [count noun] a tobacco pipe with the bowl made from this.
– ORIGIN late 18th cent.: from German, literally 'sea-foam', from *Meer* 'sea' + *Schaum* 'foam', translation of Persian *kef-i-daryā* (alluding to the frothy appearance of the silicate).

Meerut /ˈmɪərət/ a city in northern India, in Uttar Pradesh north-east of Delhi; pop. 850,000 (1991). It was the scene in May 1857 of the first uprising against the British in the Indian Mutiny.

meet[1] ▶ verb (past and past participle **met**) [with obj.] **1** come into the presence or company of (someone) by chance or arrangement: *a week later I met him in the street* | [no obj.] *we met for lunch* | *they arranged to* ***meet up*** *that afternoon.*
■ make the acquaintance of (someone) for the first time: *she took Paul to meet her parents* | [no obj.] *we met at an office party.* ■ [no obj.] (of a group of people) assemble for a particular purpose: *the committee meets once a fortnight.* ■ [no obj.] (**meet with**) chiefly US have a meeting with (someone): *he met with the president on September 16.* ■ go to a place and wait there for (a person or their means of transport) to arrive: *Stuart* ***met*** *us* ***off*** *the boat.* ■ play or oppose in a contest: *in the final group match, England will meet the Australians* | [no obj.] *the teams will meet in the European Cup final at Wembley.* ■ touch; join: *Harry's lips met hers* | [no obj.] *the curtains failed to meet in the middle* | figurative *our eyes met across the table.* ■ encounter or be faced with (a particular fate, situation, attitude, or reaction): *he met his death in 1946* | [no obj.] *we* ***met with*** *a slight setback.* ■ (**meet something with**) have (a particular reaction) to: *the announcement was met with widespread protests.* ■ [no obj.] (**meet with**) receive (a particular reaction): *I'm sorry if it doesn't meet with your approval.*
2 fulfil or satisfy (a need, requirement, or condition): *this policy is doing nothing to meet the needs of women.*
■ deal with or respond to (a problem or challenge) satisfactorily: *they failed to meet the noon deadline.* ■ pay (a financial claim or obligation): *all your household expenses will still have to be met.*
▶ noun **1** a gathering of riders and hounds at a particular place before the hunt begins.
■ an organized event at which a number of races or other athletic or sporting contests are held.
2 informal a meeting or assignation, typically one with an illicit purpose: *the meet with Frank is on for 10 o'clock.*
– PHRASES **meet the case** Brit. be adequate. **meet someone's eye** (or **eyes** or **ear**) be visible (or audible): *the sight that met his eyes was truly amazing.* **meet someone's eye** (or **eyes** or **gaze**) look directly at someone: *for a moment, he refused to meet her eyes.* **meet someone halfway** make a compromise with someone: *I am prepared to meet him halfway by paying him a further £25,000.* **meet one's Maker** see **MAKER**. **meet one's match** see **MATCH**[1]. **there's more to someone/thing than meets the eye** a person or situation is more complex or interesting than they appear.
– ORIGIN Old English *mētan* 'come upon, come across', of Germanic origin; related to Dutch *moeten*, also to **MOOT**.

meet[2] ▶ adjective archaic suitable; fit; proper: *it was not* ***meet for*** *us to see the king's dishonour.*
– DERIVATIVES **meetly** adverb, **meetness** noun.
– ORIGIN Middle English (in the sense 'made to fit'): shortening of Old English *gemǣte*, of Germanic origin; related to **METE**[1].

meeting ▶ noun **1** an assembly of people, especially the members of a society or committee, for discussion or entertainment: *the Chief Constable held a meeting to talk about policing in Gloucestershire.*
■ a gathering of people, especially Quakers, for worship. ■ an organized event at which a number of races or other athletic or sporting contests are held: *an athletics meeting.* See also **RACE MEETING**.
2 a coming together of two or more people, by chance or arrangement: *he intrigued her on their first meeting.*
– PHRASES **a meeting of minds** an understanding or agreement between people.

meeting ground ▶ noun an area of knowledge or interest held in common by two or more people or disciplines.

meeting house ▶ noun a Quaker place of worship.
■ N. Amer. historical a Protestant place of worship.

mefloquine /ˈmɛfləkwiːn/ ▶ noun [mass noun] Medicine an antimalarial drug consisting of a fluorinated derivative of quinoline.
– ORIGIN 1970s: from *me(thyl)* + *fl(uor)o* + *quin(olin)e*.

meg ▶ noun short for **MEGABYTE**.

mega informal ▶ adjective **1** very large; huge: *he has signed a mega deal to make five movies.*
2 excellent: *it will be a mega film.*
▶ adverb [as submodifier] extremely: *they are mega rich.*
– ORIGIN 1980s: independent usage of **MEGA-**.

mega- ▶ combining form **1** large: *megalith*.
2 (in units of measurement) denoting a factor of one million (10^6): *megahertz* | *megadeath*.
3 Computing denoting a factor of 2^{20}.
– ORIGIN from Greek *megas* 'great'.

megabit ▶ noun Computing a unit of data size or (when expressed per second) network speed, equal to one million or (strictly) 1,048,576 bits.

megabuck ▶ noun (usu. **megabucks**) informal a million dollars.
■ a huge sum of money: *he has been earning megabucks for decades* | [as modifier] *megabuck salaries.*

megabyte (abbrev.: **Mb** or **MB**) ▶ noun Computing a unit of information equal to one million or (strictly) 1,048,576 bytes.

Megachiroptera /ˌmɛɡəkʌɪˈrɒpt(ə)rə/ Zoology a division of bats that comprises the fruit bats and flying foxes.
● Suborder Megachiroptera and family Pteropodidae, order Chiroptera.

– DERIVATIVES **megachiropteran** noun & adjective.
– ORIGIN modern Latin (plural), from **MEGA-** 'large' + **CHIROPTERA**.

megadeath ▶ noun a unit used in quantifying the casualties of nuclear war, equal to the deaths of one million people.

Megaera /mɪˈdʒɪərə/ Greek Mythology one of the Furies.

megafauna ▶ noun Zoology the large mammals of a particular region, habitat, or geological period.
■ Ecology animals that are large enough to be seen with the naked eye.
– DERIVATIVES **megafaunal** adjective.

megaflop[1] ▶ noun Computing a unit of computing speed equal to one million or (strictly) 1,048,576 floating-point operations per second.
– ORIGIN 1970s: back-formation from megaflops (see **MEGA-**, **-FLOP**).

megaflop[2] ▶ noun informal a thing that is a complete failure.
– ORIGIN late 20th cent.: a pun on **MEGAFLOP**[1].

megagamete ▶ noun another term for **MACROGAMETE**.

megahertz (abbrev.: **MHz**) ▶ noun (pl. same) one million hertz, especially as a measure of the frequency of radio transmissions or the clock speed of a computer.

megalith ▶ noun Archaeology a large stone that forms a prehistoric monument (e.g. a standing stone) or part of one (e.g. a stone circle or chambered tomb).
– ORIGIN mid 19th cent.: back-formation from **MEGALITHIC**.

megalithic ▶ adjective Archaeology of, relating to, or denoting prehistoric monuments made of or containing megaliths.
■ (often **Megalithic**) of, relating to, or denoting prehistoric cultures characterized by the erection of megalithic monuments. ■ figurative massive or monolithic: the weekly meetings were megalithic in proportion.
– ORIGIN mid 19th cent.: from **MEGA-** 'large' + Greek lithos 'stone' + **-IC**.

megalo- /ˈmɛɡələʊ/ ▶ combining form great: megaloblast.
– ORIGIN from Greek megas, megal- 'great'.

megaloblast /ˈmɛɡələ(ʊ)blɑːst/ ▶ noun Medicine a large, abnormally developed red blood cell typical of certain forms of anaemia, associated with a deficiency of folic acid or of vitamin B12.
– DERIVATIVES **megaloblastic** adjective.

megalomania ▶ noun [mass noun] obsession with the exercise of power, especially in the domination of others.
■ delusion about one's own power or importance (typically as a symptom of manic or paranoid disorder).
– DERIVATIVES **megalomanic** adjective.

megalomaniac ▶ noun a person who is obsessed with his or her own power.
■ a person who suffers delusions of his or her own power or importance.
▶ adjective exhibiting megalomania.
– DERIVATIVES **megalomaniacal** adjective.

megalopolis /ˌmɛɡəˈlɒp(ə)lɪs/ ▶ noun a very large, heavily populated city or urban complex.
– ORIGIN mid 19th cent.: from **MEGALO-** 'great' + Greek polis 'city'.

megalopolitan ▶ adjective of or denoting a very large city: megalopolitan traffic.
▶ noun an inhabitant of a very large city.
– ORIGIN mid 17th cent.: from **MEGALO-** 'great' + Greek politēs 'citizen' + **-AN**.

megalosaurus /ˌmɛɡ(ə)lə(ʊ)ˈsɔːrəs/ ▶ noun a large carnivorous bipedal dinosaur of the mid Jurassic period, whose remains have been found only in England.
● Genus Megalosaurus, suborder Theropoda, order Saurischia; the first dinosaur to be described and named (1824).
– ORIGIN modern Latin, from **MEGALO-** 'great' + Greek sauros 'lizard'.

megamouth (also **megamouth shark**) ▶ noun a shark with a very large wide mouth and tiny teeth, first captured in 1976 off the Hawaiian Islands.
● Megachasma pelagios, the only member of the family Megachasmidae.

megaphone ▶ noun a large funnel-shaped device for amplifying and directing the voice.
▶ verb [with obj.] utter through, or as if through, a megaphone: the director stood around megaphoning orders.

– DERIVATIVES **megaphonic** adjective.

megapode /ˈmɛɡəpəʊd/ ▶ noun a large ground-dwelling Australasian and SE Asian bird that builds a large mound of debris to incubate its eggs by the heat of decomposition. Also called **MOUND-BUILDER**.
● Family Megapodiidae (the **megapode family**), which comprises the scrubfowls, brush-turkeys, malleefowl, and maleo.
– ORIGIN mid 19th cent.: from modern Latin Megapodius (genus name), from **MEGA-** 'large' + Greek pous, pod- 'foot'.

megaron /ˈmɛɡər(ə)n/ ▶ noun Archaeology the central hall of a large Mycenaean house.
– ORIGIN Greek.

megaspore ▶ noun Botany the larger of the two kinds of spores produced by some ferns. Compare with **MICROSPORE**.

megastar ▶ noun informal a very famous person, especially in the world of entertainment.
– DERIVATIVES **megastardom** noun.

megastore ▶ noun a very large shop, typically one specializing in a particular type of product: a computer megastore.

megastructure ▶ noun a massive construction or structure, especially a complex of many buildings.

megatherium /ˌmɛɡəˈθɪərɪəm/ ▶ noun (pl. **megatheriums** or **megatheria**) an extinct giant ground sloth of the Pliocene and Pleistocene epochs in America, reaching a height of 5m (16 ft) when standing erect.
● Genus Megatherium, family Megatheriidae.
– ORIGIN modern Latin, from Greek mega thērion 'great animal'.

megaton (also **megatonne**) ▶ noun a unit of explosive power chiefly used for nuclear weapons, equivalent to one million imperial tons (or metric tons) of TNT: H-bombs of fifteen megatons each.

megavolt (abbrev.: **MV**) ▶ noun a unit of electromotive force equal to one million volts.

megawatt (abbrev.: **MW**) ▶ noun a unit of power equal to one million watts, especially as a measure of the output of a power station.

me generation ▶ noun a generation of people that are concerned chiefly with themselves, especially in being selfishly materialistic.

Megger /ˈmɛɡə/ ▶ noun trademark an instrument for measuring the resistance of electrical insulation.
– ORIGIN early 20th cent.: perhaps from **MEGOHM**.

Meghalaya /meɪˈɡɑːləjə/ a small state in the extreme north-east of India, on the northern border of Bangladesh; capital, Shillong. It was created in 1970 from part of Assam.

Megiddo /məˈɡɪdəʊ/ an ancient city of NW Palestine, situated to the south-east of Haifa in present-day Israel. Its commanding location made the city the scene of many early battles, and from its name the word Armageddon ('hill of Megiddo') is derived. It was the scene in 1918 of the defeat of Turkish forces by the British under General Allenby.

Megillah /məˈɡɪlə/ a book of the Hebrew scriptures (the Song of Solomon, Ruth, Lamentations, Ecclesiastes, and Esther) appointed to be read on certain Jewish notable days, especially the Book of Esther, read at the festival of Purim.
■ [as noun **the whole megillah**] N. Amer. informal something in its entirety, especially a complicated set of arrangements or a long-winded story.
– ORIGIN from Hebrew měgillāh, literally 'scroll'.

megilp /məˈɡɪlp/ (also **magilp**) ▶ noun [mass noun] a mixture of mastic resin and linseed oil added to oil paints, widely used in the 19th century.
– ORIGIN mid 18th cent.: of unknown origin.

megohm /ˈmɛɡəʊm/ ▶ noun a unit of electrical resistance equal to one million ohms.
– ORIGIN mid 19th cent.: from **MEGA-** (as a unit of measurement) + **OHM**.

megrim[1] /ˈmiːɡrɪm/ ▶ noun archaic **1** (**megrims**) depression; low spirits: fresh air and exercise, she generally found, could banish most megrims.
2 a whim or fancy.
– ORIGIN late Middle English: variant of **MIGRAINE**.

megrim[2] /ˈmiːɡrɪm/ ▶ noun a flatfish which occurs in deep water off the Atlantic coast of Europe, where it is fished commercially. Also called **SAIL-FLUKE**, **WHIFF**[2].
● Lepidorhombus whiffiagonis, family Scophthalmidae (or Bothidae).

■ another term for **SCALDFISH**.
– ORIGIN mid 19th cent.: of unknown origin.

meibomian /maɪˈbəʊmɪən/ ▶ adjective Anatomy relating to or denoting large sebaceous glands of the human eyelid, whose infection results in inflammation and swelling: meibomian cysts.
– ORIGIN early 19th cent.: from the name of Heinrich Meibom (1638–1700), German anatomist, + **-IAN**.

Meiji /ˈmeɪdʒi/ ▶ noun [usu. as modifier] the period when Japan was ruled by the emperor Meiji Tenno, marked by the modernization and westernization of the country.
– ORIGIN Japanese, literally 'enlightened government'.

Meiji Tenno /ˈtɛnəʊ/ (1852–1912), emperor of Japan 1868–1912; born Mutsuhito. He took the name Meiji Tenno when he became emperor. He encouraged Japan's rapid modernization and political reform.

meiofauna /ˈmʌɪəʊˌfɔːnə/ ▶ noun Ecology minute interstitial animals living in soil and aquatic sediments.
– ORIGIN 1960s: from Greek meiōn 'less or smaller' + **FAUNA**.

meiosis /maɪˈəʊsɪs/ ▶ noun (pl. **meioses** /-siːz/) [mass noun] **1** Biology a type of cell division that results in two daughter cells each with half the chromosome number of the parent cell, as in the production of gametes. Compare with **MITOSIS**.
2 another term for **LITOTES**.
– DERIVATIVES **meiotic** adjective, **meiotically** adverb.
– ORIGIN mid 16th cent. (in sense 2): modern Latin, from Greek meiōsis, from meioun 'lessen', from meiōn 'less'. Sense 1 dates from the early 20th cent.

Meir /meɪˈɪə/, Golda (1898–1978), Israeli stateswoman, Prime Minister 1969–74; born Goldie Mabovich. Born in Ukraine, she emigrated to the US in 1907 and in 1921 to Palestine. Following Israel's independence she served in ministerial posts from 1949 to 1966 before being elected Prime Minister.

Meissen[1] /ˈmʌɪs(ə)n/ a city in eastern Germany, in Saxony, on the River Elbe north-west of Dresden; pop. 39,280 (1981). It is famous for its porcelain.

Meissen[2] /ˈmʌɪs(ə)n/ ▶ noun [mass noun] fine hard-paste porcelain produced in Meissen since 1710, in Britain often called Dresden china.

Meissner effect /ˈmʌɪsnə/ ▶ noun [mass noun] Physics the expulsion of magnetic flux when a material becomes superconducting in a magnetic field. If the magnetic field is applied after the material has become superconducting, the flux cannot penetrate it.
– ORIGIN 1930s; named after Fritz W. Meissner (1882–1974), German physicist.

Meissner's corpuscle ▶ noun Anatomy a sensory nerve ending that is sensitive to mechanical stimuli, found in the dermis in various parts of the body.
– ORIGIN late 19th cent.: named after Georg Meissner (1829–1905), German anatomist.

-meister /ˈmʌɪstə/ ▶ combining form denoting a person regarded as skilled or prominent in a specified area of activity: funk-meister | gag-meister.
– ORIGIN from German Meister 'master'.

Meistersinger /ˈmʌɪstəsɪŋə/ ▶ noun (pl. same) a member of one of the guilds of German lyric poets and musicians which flourished from the 12th to 17th century. Their technique was elaborate and they were subject to rigid regulations.
– ORIGIN German, from Meister 'master' + Singer 'singer'.

Meitner /ˈmʌɪtnə/, Lise (1878–1968), Austrian-born Swedish physicist. She worked in the field of radiochemistry with Otto Hahn, discovering the element protactinium with him in 1917. She also formulated the concept of nuclear fission with her nephew Otto Frisch.

meitnerium /mʌɪtˈnɪərɪəm/ ▶ noun [mass noun] the chemical element of atomic number 109, a very unstable element made by high-energy atomic collisions. (Symbol: **Mt**)
– ORIGIN modern Latin, from the name of L. **MEITNER**.

Mekele /mɪˈkeɪli/ a city in northern Ethiopia, the capital of Tigray province; pop. 62,000 (est. 1984).

Meknès /mɛkˈnɛs/ a city in northern Morocco, in the Middle Atlas mountains west of Fez; pop.

119,700 (1994). In the 17th century it was the residence of the Moroccan sultan.

Mekong /miːˈkɒŋ/ a river of SE Asia, which rises in Tibet and flows south-east and south for 4,180 km (2,600 miles) through southern China, Laos, Cambodia, and Vietnam to its extensive delta on the South China Sea. It forms the boundary between Laos and its western neighbours Burma and Thailand.

mela /ˈmeɪlə/ ▶ noun Indian a fair or Hindu festival.
– ORIGIN from Sanskrit *melā* 'assembly'.

melaena /mɪˈliːnə/ (also **melena**) ▶ noun [mass noun] Medicine dark sticky faeces containing partly digested blood.
■ the production of such faeces, following internal bleeding or the swallowing of blood.
– ORIGIN early 19th cent.: modern Latin, from Greek *melaina*, feminine of *melas* 'black'.

Melaka /məˈlakə/ (also **Malacca**) a state of Malaysia, on the SW coast of the Malay Peninsula, on the Strait of Malacca.
■ its capital and chief port; pop. 88,070 (1980). It was conquered by the Portuguese in 1511 and played an important role in the development of trade between Europe and the East, especially China.

melaleuca /ˌmeləˈl(j)uːkə/ ▶ noun an Australian shrub or tree which bears spikes of bottlebrush-like flowers. Some kinds are a source of timber or medicinal oil.
● Genus *Melaleuca*, family Myrtaceae: many species, including the Australian paperbarks.
– ORIGIN modern Latin: from Greek *melas* 'black' + *leukos* 'white' (because of the fire-blackened white bark of some Asian species).

melamine /ˈmeləmiːn/ ▶ noun [mass noun] **1** Chemistry a white crystalline compound made by heating cyanamide and used in making plastics.
● A heterocyclic amine; chem. formula: $(CNH_2)_3N_3$.
2 (also **melamine resin**) a plastic used chiefly for laminated coatings, made by copolymerizing this compound with formaldehyde.
– ORIGIN mid 19th cent.: from German *melam* (an arbitrary formation), denoting an insoluble amorphous organic substance, + AMINE.

melancholia /ˌmelənˈkəʊlɪə/ ▶ noun [mass noun] deep sadness or gloom; melancholy: *rain slithered down the windows, encouraging a creeping melancholia.*
■ dated a mental condition marked by persistent depression and ill-founded fears.
– ORIGIN late Middle English (denoting black bile): from late Latin (see MELANCHOLY).

melancholy ▶ noun [mass noun] a deep, pensive, and long-lasting sadness.
■ another term for MELANCHOLIA (as a mental condition). ■ historical another term for BLACK BILE.
▶ adjective sad, gloomy, or depressed: *she felt a little melancholy* | *the dog has a melancholy expression.*
■ causing or expressing sadness; depressing: *the study makes melancholy if instructive reading.*
– DERIVATIVES **melancholic** adjective, **melancholically** adverb.
– ORIGIN Middle English: from Old French *melancolie*, via late Latin from Greek *melankholia*, from *melas*, *melan-* 'black' + *kholē* 'bile', an excess of which was formerly believed to cause depression.

Melanchthon /məˈlaŋkθɒn/, Philipp (1497–1560), German Protestant reformer; born *Philipp Schwarzerd*. He succeeded Luther as leader of the Reformation movement in Germany in 1521 and drew up the Augsburg Confession (1530).

Melanesia /ˌmeləˈniːzɪə, -ˈniːʒə/ a region of the western Pacific to the south of Micronesia and west of Polynesia. It contains the Bismarck Archipelago, the Solomon Islands, Vanuatu, New Caledonia, Fiji, and the intervening islands.
– ORIGIN from Greek *melas* 'black' + *nēsos* 'island'.

Melanesian /ˌmeləˈniːzɪ(ə)n, -ʒ(ə)n/ ▶ adjective of or relating to Melanesia, its peoples, or their languages.
▶ noun **1** a native or inhabitant of any of the islands of Melanesia.
2 [mass noun] any of the languages of Melanesia, mostly Austronesian languages related to Malay but also including Neo-Melanesian (or Tok Pisin), an English-based pidgin.

melange /meɪˈlɒ̃ʒ/ ▶ noun a mixture; a medley: *a melange of tender vegetables and herbs.*
– ORIGIN from French *mélange*, from *mêler* 'to mix'.

melanin /ˈmelənɪn/ ▶ noun [mass noun] a dark brown to

black pigment occurring in the hair, skin, and iris of the eye in people and animals. It is responsible for tanning of skin exposed to sunlight.
– ORIGIN mid 19th cent.: from Greek *melas*, *melan-* 'black' + -IN¹.

melanism /ˈmelənɪz(ə)m/ ▶ noun [mass noun] chiefly Zoology unusual darkening of body tissues caused by excessive production of melanin, especially as a form of colour variation in animals.
– DERIVATIVES **melanic** /mɪˈlanɪk/ adjective.

melanite /ˈmelənʌɪt/ ▶ noun [mass noun] a velvet-black variety of andradite (garnet).
– ORIGIN early 19th cent.: from Greek *melas*, *melan-* 'black' + -ITE¹.

melanocyte /ˈmelənə(ʊ)sʌɪt, mɪˈlanə(ʊ)-/ ▶ noun Physiology a mature melanin-forming cell, typically in the skin.

melanocyte-stimulating hormone ▶ noun [mass noun] Physiology a hormone secreted by the pituitary gland that is involved in pigmentation changes in some animals.

melanoid /ˈmelənɔɪd/ ▶ adjective **1** resembling melanin.
2 resembling melanosis.

melanoma /ˌmeləˈnəʊmə/ ▶ noun Medicine a tumour of melanin-forming cells, typically a malignant tumour associated with skin cancer: *melanomas can appear anywhere on the body* | [mass noun] *the incidence of melanoma is rising steadily.*
– ORIGIN mid 19th cent.: from Greek *melas*, *melan-* 'black' + -OMA.

melanosis /ˌmeləˈnəʊsɪs/ ▶ noun [mass noun] Medicine a condition of abnormal or excessive production of melanin in the skin or other tissue.
– DERIVATIVES **melanotic** adjective.
– ORIGIN early 19th cent.: modern Latin, from Greek *melas*, *melan-* 'black' + -OSIS.

melatonin /ˌmeləˈtəʊnɪn/ ▶ noun [mass noun] Biochemistry a hormone secreted by the pineal gland which inhibits melanin formation and is thought to be concerned with regulating the reproductive cycle.
– ORIGIN 1950s: from Greek *melas* 'black' + SEROTONIN.

Melba¹, Dame Nellie (1861–1931), Australian operatic soprano; born *Helen Porter Mitchell*. She was born near Melbourne, from which city she took her professional name. Melba gained worldwide fame with her coloratura singing.

Melba² ▶ noun (in phrase **do a Melba**) Austral. informal return from retirement, or make several farewell appearances.
– ORIGIN 1970s: from the name of the operatic soprano Dame Nellie *Melba* (see MELBA¹), who made repeated 'farewell' appearances.

Melba sauce ▶ noun [mass noun] a sauce made from puréed raspberries thickened with icing sugar.

Melba toast ▶ noun [mass noun] very thin crisp toast.

Melbourne¹ /ˈmelbən/ the capital of Victoria, SE Australia, on the Bass Strait opposite Tasmania; pop. 2,762,000 (1991). It became state capital in 1851 and was capital of Australia from 1901 until 1927. It is a major port and the second largest city in Australia.

Melbourne² /ˈmelbən, -bɔːn/, William Lamb, 2nd Viscount (1779–1848), British Whig statesman, Prime Minister 1834 and 1835–41. He became chief political adviser to Queen Victoria after her accession in 1837.

Melchior /ˈmelkɪɔː/ the traditional name of one of the Magi, represented as a king of Nubia.

Melchizedek /melˈkɪzɪdɛk/ (in the Bible) a priest and king of Salem (which is usually identified with Jerusalem). He was revered by Abraham, who paid tithes to him (Gen. 14:18).

meld¹ ▶ verb blend; combine: [with obj.] *Australia's winemakers have melded modern science with traditional art* | [no obj.] *the nylon bristles shrivel and meld together.*
▶ noun a thing formed by merging or blending: *a meld of many contributions.*
– ORIGIN 1930s: perhaps a blend of MELT and WELD¹.

meld² ▶ verb [with obj.] (in rummy, canasta, and other card games) lay down or declare (a combination of cards) in order to score points: *a player has melded four kings.*
▶ noun a completed set or run of cards in any of these games.
– ORIGIN late 19th cent. (originally US): from German *melden* 'announce'.

Meleager /ˌmelɪˈeɪgə/ (*fl.* 1st century BC), Greek poet, best known as the compiler of *Stephanos*, one of the first large anthologies of epigrams.

melee /ˈmeleɪ/ ▶ noun a confused fight, skirmish, or scuffle: *several people were hurt in the melee.*
■ a confused mass of people: *the melee of people that were always thronging the streets.*
– ORIGIN mid 17th cent.: from French *mêlée*, from an Old French variant of *meslee* (see MEDLEY).

melena ▶ noun variant spelling of MELAENA.

melic /ˈmelɪk/ ▶ adjective (of a poem, especially an ancient Greek lyric) meant to be sung.
– ORIGIN late 17th cent.: via Latin from Greek *melikos*, from *melos* 'song'.

melick (also **melic**, **melick grass**) ▶ noun a grass occurring in temperate regions, especially in woodland.
● Genus *Melica*, family Gramineae: many species, especially the European **wood melick** (*M. uniflora*).
– ORIGIN late 18th cent.: from modern Latin *melica*, perhaps from Italian *melica* 'sorghum'.

Melilla /meˈliːjə/ a Spanish enclave on the Mediterranean coast of Morocco; pop. (with Ceuta) 56,600 (1991). It was occupied by Spain in 1497.

melilot /ˈmelɪlɒt/ ▶ noun a fragrant herbaceous plant of the pea family, which is native to Eurasia and north Africa and is sometimes grown as forage or green manure.
● Genus *Melilotus*, family Leguminosae.
– ORIGIN Middle English: from Old French, via Latin from Greek *melilōtos* 'honey lotus'.

melioidosis /ˌmelɪɔɪˈdəʊsɪs/ ▶ noun [mass noun] an infectious disease of rodents, similar to glanders. It is occasionally transmitted to people, in whom it can cause pneumonia, multiple abscesses, and septicaemia, and is often fatal.
● The agent is the bacterium *Pseudomonas pseudomallei*.
– ORIGIN 1920s: from Greek *mēlis*, denoting a disease (probably glanders) affecting asses, + -OID + -OSIS.

meliorate /ˈmiːlɪəreɪt/ ▶ verb formal another term for AMELIORATE.
– DERIVATIVES **melioration** noun, **meliorative** adjective.
– ORIGIN mid 16th cent.: from late Latin *meliorat-* 'improved' from the verb *meliorare*, based on *melior* 'better'.

meliorism /ˈmiːlɪərɪz(ə)m/ ▶ noun [mass noun] Philosophy the belief that the world can be made better by human effort.
– DERIVATIVES **meliorist** noun & adjective, **melioristic** adjective.
– ORIGIN late 19th cent.: from Latin *melior* 'better' + -ISM.

melisma /mɪˈlɪzmə/ ▶ noun (pl. **melismas** or **melismata** /-mətə/) Music a group of notes sung to one syllable of text.
– DERIVATIVES **melismatic** adjective.
– ORIGIN late 19th cent.: from Greek, literally 'melody'.

Melkite /ˈmelkʌɪt/ ▶ noun an Orthodox or Uniate Christian belonging to the patriarchate of Antioch, Jerusalem, or Alexandria.
■ historical an Eastern Christian adhering to the Orthodox faith as defined by the councils of Ephesus (AD 431) and Chalcedon (AD 451) and as accepted by the Byzantine emperor.
– ORIGIN via ecclesiastical Latin from Byzantine Greek *Melkhitai*, plural representing Syriac *malkāyā* 'royalists' (i.e. expressing agreement with the Byzantine emperor), from *malkā* 'king'.

melliferous /meˈlɪf(ə)rəs/ ▶ adjective yielding or producing honey.
– ORIGIN mid 17th cent.: from Latin *mellifer* (from *mel* 'honey' + *-fer* 'bearing') + -OUS.

mellifluent /meˈlɪflʊənt/ ▶ adjective another term for MELLIFLUOUS.
– DERIVATIVES **mellifluence** noun.
– ORIGIN early 17th cent.: from late Latin *mellifluent-*, from Latin *mel*, *mell(i)-* 'honey' + *fluent-* 'flowing' (from the verb *fluere*).

mellifluous /meˈlɪfluəs/ ▶ adjective (of a voice or words) sweet or musical; pleasant to hear: *the voice was mellifluous and smooth.*
– DERIVATIVES **mellifluously** adverb, **mellifluousness** noun.
– ORIGIN late 15th cent.: from late Latin *mellifluus* (from *mel* 'honey' + *fluere* 'to flow') + -OUS.

Mellon /ˈmelən/, Andrew (William) (1855–1937), American financier and philanthropist. He donated his art collection to establish the National Gallery of Art in Washington DC in 1941.

mellophone /ˈmɛləfəʊn/ ▶ noun a brass instrument similar to the orchestral French horn, played mainly in military and concert bands.
– ORIGIN 1920s: from **MELLOW** + **-PHONE**.

mellotron /ˈmɛlətrɒn/ ▶ noun an electronic keyboard instrument in which each key controls the playback of a single pre-recorded musical sound.
– ORIGIN 1960s: from **MELLOW** + -tron, element of **ELECTRONIC**.

mellow ▶ adjective 1 (especially of sound, taste, and colour) pleasantly smooth or soft; free from harshness: she was hypnotized by the mellow tone of his voice | slow cooking gives the dish a sweet, mellow flavour.
■ archaic (of fruit) ripe, soft, sweet, and juicy: one dish of mellow apples. ■ (of wine) well-matured and smooth: delicious, mellow, ripe, fruity wines.
2 (of a person's character) softened or matured by age or experience: a more mellow personality.
■ relaxed and good-humoured: Jean-Claude was feeling mellow. ■ informal relaxed and cheerful through being slightly drunk: everybody got very mellow and slept well.
3 (of earth) rich and loamy.
▶ verb make or become mellow: with obj.] even a warm sun could not mellow the North Sea breeze | [no obj.] fuller-flavoured whiskies mellow with wood maturation | informal I need to mellow out, I need to calm down.
– DERIVATIVES **mellowly** adverb, **mellowness** noun.
– ORIGIN late Middle English (in the sense '(of fruit) ripe, soft, sweet, and juicy'): perhaps from attributive use of Old English melu, melw- (see **MEAL**²). The verb dates from the late 16th cent.

melodeon /mɪˈləʊdɪən/ (also **melodion**) ▶ noun 1 a small accordion of German origin, played especially by folk musicians. [ORIGIN: mid 19th cent.: probably from **MELODY**, on the pattern of accordion.]
2 a small organ popular in the 19th century, similar to the harmonium. [ORIGIN: alteration of earlier melodium.]

melodic ▶ adjective of, having, or producing melody: melodic and rhythmic patterns.
■ pleasant-sounding: his voice was deep and melodic.
– DERIVATIVES **melodically** adverb.
– ORIGIN early 19th cent.: from French mélodique, via late Latin from Greek melōidikos, from melōidia 'melody'.

melodica /mɪˈlɒdɪkə/ ▶ noun a wind instrument with a small keyboard controlling a row of reeds, and a mouthpiece at one end.
– ORIGIN 1960s: from **MELODY**, on the pattern of harmonica.

melodic minor ▶ noun Music a minor scale with the sixth and seventh degrees raised when ascending and lowered when descending.

melodious ▶ adjective of, producing, or having a pleasant tune; tuneful: the melodious chant of the monks.
■ pleasant-sounding: a melodious voice.
– DERIVATIVES **melodiously** adverb, **melodiousness** noun.
– ORIGIN late Middle English: from Old French melodieus, from melodie (see **MELODY**).

melodist ▶ noun a composer of melodies.
■ a singer.

melodize (also **-ise**) ▶ verb [no obj.] rare make or play music.

melodrama ▶ noun 1 a sensational dramatic piece with exaggerated characters and exciting events intended to appeal to the emotions.
■ [mass noun] the genre of drama of this type. ■ [mass noun] language, behaviour, or events that resemble drama of this kind: what little is known of his early life is cloaked in melodrama.
2 historical a play interspersed with songs and orchestral music accompanying the action.
– DERIVATIVES **melodramatist** noun, **melodramatize** (also **-ise**) verb.
– ORIGIN early 19th cent.: from French mélodrame, from Greek melos 'music' + French drame 'drama'.

melodramatic ▶ adjective of or relating to melodrama.
■ characteristic of melodrama, especially in being exaggerated, sensationalized, or overemotional: he flung the door open with a melodramatic flourish.
– DERIVATIVES **melodramatically** adverb.

melodramatics ▶ plural noun melodramatic behaviour, action, or writing.

melody ▶ noun (pl. **-ies**) a sequence of single notes that is musically satisfying: he picked out an intricate melody on his guitar.
■ [mass noun] such sequences of notes collectively: his great gift was for melody. ■ the principal part in harmonized music: we have the melody and bass of a song composed by Strozzi.
– ORIGIN Middle English (also in the sense 'sweet music'): from Old French melodie, via late Latin from Greek melōidia, from melos 'song'.

melon ▶ noun 1 the large round fruit of a plant of the gourd family, with sweet pulpy flesh and many seeds.
■ [mass noun] the edible flesh of such fruit: a slice of melon. ■ (usu. **melons**) informal a woman's breast.
2 the Old World plant which yields this fruit.
● Cucumis melo subsp. melo, family Cucurbitaceae: many varieties.
3 Zoology a mass of waxy material in the head of dolphins and other toothed whales, thought to focus acoustic signals.
– ORIGIN late Middle English: via Old French from late Latin melo, melon-, contraction of Latin melopepo, from Greek mēlopepōn, from mēlon 'apple' + pepōn 'gourd'.

melon hole ▶ noun Austral. another term for **GILGAI**.

Melos /ˈmiːlɒs/ a Greek island in the Aegean Sea, in the south-west of the Cyclades group. It was the centre of a flourishing civilization in the Bronze Age and is the site of the discovery in 1820 of a Hellenistic marble statue of Aphrodite, the Venus de Milo. Greek name **MILOS**.

Melpomene /mɛlˈpɒmɪni/ Greek & Roman Mythology the Muse of tragedy.
– ORIGIN Greek, literally 'singer'.

melt ▶ verb [no obj.] 1 become liquefied by heat: place under a hot grill until the cheese has melted | the icebergs were melting away.
■ [with obj.] change (something) to a liquid condition by heating it: the hot metal melted the wax | [as adj. **melted**] asparagus with melted butter. ■ [with obj.] (**melt something down**) melt something, especially a metal article, so that the material it is made of can be used again: beautiful objects are being melted down and sold for scrap. ■ dissolve in liquid: add 400g sugar and boil until the sugar melts.
2 become more tender or loving: she was so beautiful that I melted.
■ [with obj.] make (someone) more tender or loving: Richard gave her a smile which melted her heart.
3 [no obj., with adverbial] leave or disappear unobtrusively: the compromise was accepted and the opposition melted away | the figure melted into thin air.
■ (of a feeling or state) disappear: their original determination to exact vengeance melted away. ■ (**melt into**) change or merge imperceptibly into (another form or state): the cheers melted into gasps of admiration.
▶ noun an act of melting: the precipitation falls as snow and is released during the spring melt.
■ [mass noun] metal or other material in a melted condition. ■ an amount melted at any one time. ■ [with modifier] N. Amer. a sandwich, hamburger, or other dish containing or topped with melted cheese: a tuna melt.
– PHRASES **melt in the mouth** (of food) be deliciously light or tender and need little or no chewing.
– DERIVATIVES **meltable** adjective, **melter** noun, **meltingly** adverb.
– ORIGIN Old English meltan, mieltan, of Germanic origin; related to Old Norse melta 'to malt, digest', from an Indo-European root shared by Greek meldein 'to melt', Latin mollis 'soft', also by **MALT**.

meltdown ▶ noun an accident in a nuclear reactor in which the fuel overheats and melts the reactor core or shielding.
■ figurative a disastrous event, especially a rapid fall in share prices: the 1987 stock market meltdown.

meltemi /mɛlˈtɛmi/ (also **meltemi wind**) ▶ noun a dry north-westerly wind which blows during the summer in the eastern Mediterranean.
– ORIGIN from modern Greek meltémi, Turkish meltem.

melting point ▶ noun the temperature at which a given solid will melt.

melting pot ▶ noun a pot in which metals or other materials are melted and mixed.
■ figurative a place where different peoples, styles, theories, etc. are mixed together: a melting pot of

disparate rhythms and cultures. ■ a situation in which things are constantly changing and the outcome is uncertain: the future of the railway is still in the melting pot.

melton ▶ noun [mass noun] heavy woollen cloth with a close-cut nap, used for overcoats and jackets.
– ORIGIN early 19th cent.: named after Melton Mowbray, a town in central England, formerly a centre of manufacture.

meltwater ▶ noun [mass noun] (also **meltwaters**) water formed by the melting of snow and ice, especially from a glacier.

Melville, Herman (1819–91), American novelist and short-story writer. His experiences on a whaling ship formed the basis of several novels, notably Moby Dick (1851). Other notable works: Billy Budd (first published in 1924).

member ▶ noun 1 an individual belonging to a group such as a society or team: the first woman sculptor to be made a member of the Royal Academy | interest from members of the public.
■ (**Member**) a person formally elected to take part in the proceedings of certain organizations: Member of Parliament for Stretford. ■ a part or branch of a political body: [as modifier] member countries of the Central African Customs Union. ■ used in the title awarded to a person admitted to (usually the lowest grade of) certain honours: Member of the Order of the British Empire.
2 a constituent piece of a complex structure: the main member that joins the front and rear axles.
■ a part of a sentence, equation, group of figures, mathematical set, etc.
3 archaic a part or organ of the body, especially a limb.
■ (also **male member**) the penis. Compare with **MEMBRUM VIRILE**.
– DERIVATIVES **membered** adjective [in combination] (chiefly Chemistry) a six-membered oxygen-containing ring.
– ORIGIN Middle English: via Old French from Latin membrum 'limb'.

membership ▶ noun [mass noun] the fact of being a member of a group: countries seeking membership of the European Union | [as modifier] a membership card.
■ [in sing.] the number or body of members in a group: our membership has grown by 600,000 in the past 18 months.

membrane ▶ noun Anatomy & Zoology a pliable sheet-like structure acting as a boundary, lining, or partition in an organism.
■ a thin pliable sheet or skin of various kinds: the concrete should include a membrane to prevent rising damp. ■ Biology a microscopic double layer of lipids and proteins which bounds cells and organelles and forms structures within cells.
– DERIVATIVES **membranaceous** adjective, **membraneous** adjective, **membranous** adjective.
– ORIGIN late Middle English: from Latin membrana, from membrum 'limb'.

membranophone /mɛmˈbreɪnəfəʊn/ ▶ noun Music an instrument in which the sound is produced by a stretched membrane, such as a drum or kazoo.

membranous labyrinth ▶ noun see **LABYRINTH**.

membrum virile /ˌmɛmbrəm vɪˈrʌɪli, vɪˈriːli/ ▶ noun archaic the penis.
– ORIGIN Latin, literally 'male member'.

meme /miːm/ ▶ noun Biology an element of a culture or system of behaviour that may be considered to be passed from one individual to another by non-genetic means, especially imitation.
– DERIVATIVES **memetic** adjective.
– ORIGIN 1970s: from Greek mimēma 'that which is imitated', on the pattern of gene.

Memel /ˈmeɪm(ə)l/ 1 German name for **KLAIPEDA**.
■ a former district of East Prussia, centred on the city of Memel (Klaipeda). It became an autonomous region of Lithuania in 1924. In 1938 it was taken by Germany, but it was restored to Lithuania by the Soviet Union in 1945.
2 the River Neman in its lower course (see **NEMAN**).

memento /mɪˈmɛntəʊ/ ▶ noun (pl. **-os** or **-oes**) an object kept as a reminder or souvenir of a person or event: you can purchase a memento of your visit.
– ORIGIN late Middle English (denoting a prayer of commemoration): from Latin, literally 'remember!', imperative of meminisse.

memento mori /mɪˌmɛntəʊ ˈmɔːri, -rʌɪ/ ▶ noun (pl. same) an object serving as a warning or reminder of death, such as a skull.

– ORIGIN Latin, literally 'remember (that you have) to die'.

Memnon /ˈmɛmnɒn/ Greek Mythology an Ethiopian king who went to Troy to help Priam, his uncle, and was killed.

memo ▶ **noun** (pl. **-os**) informal a written message, especially in business.
– ORIGIN early 18th cent.: abbreviation of **MEMORANDUM**.

memoir ▶ **noun 1** a historical account or biography written from personal knowledge or special sources: *in 1924 she published a short memoir of her husband.*
■ (**memoirs**) an autobiography or a written account of one's memory of certain events or people.
2 an essay on a learned subject: *an important memoir on Carboniferous crustacea.*
■ (**memoirs**) the proceedings or transactions of a learned society: *Memoirs of the Royal Society.*
– DERIVATIVES **memoirist** noun.
– ORIGIN late 15th cent. (denoting a memorandum or record): from French *mémoire* (masculine), a special use of *mémoire* (feminine) 'memory'.

memorabilia /ˌmɛm(ə)rəˈbɪlɪə/ ▶ **plural noun** objects kept or collected because of their historical interest, especially those associated with memorable people or events: *railway memorabilia.*
■ archaic memorable or noteworthy things.
– ORIGIN late 18th cent.: from Latin, neuter plural of *memorabilis* 'memorable'.

memorable ▶ **adjective** worth remembering or easily remembered, especially because of being special or unusual: *this victory was one of the most memorable of his career.*
– DERIVATIVES **memorability** noun, **memorably** adverb.
– ORIGIN late 15th cent.: from Latin *memorabilis*, from *memorare* 'bring to mind', from *memor* 'mindful'.

memorandum ▶ **noun** (pl. **memoranda** or **memorandums**) a note or record made for future use: *the two countries signed a memorandum of understanding on economic cooperation.*
■ a written message, especially in business or diplomacy: *he told them of his decision in a memorandum.* ■ Law a document recording the terms of a contract or other legal details.
– ORIGIN late Middle English: from Latin, literally 'something to be brought to mind', gerundive of *memorare*. The original use was as an adjective, placed at the head of a note of something to be remembered or of a record made for future reference.

memorial ▶ **noun 1** something, especially a structure, established to remind people of a person or event: *the National Monument built as* ***a memorial to*** *those who fell in the Napoleonic wars.*
■ [as modifier] intended to commemorate someone or something: *a memorial service in the dead man's honour.*
2 chiefly historical a statement of facts, especially as the basis of a petition: *the Council sent a strongly worded memorial to the Chancellor of the Exchequer.*
■ a record or chronicle: *Mrs Carlyle's Letters and Memorials.* ■ an informal diplomatic paper.
– ORIGIN late Middle English: from late Latin *memoriale* 'record, memory, monument', from Latin *memorialis* 'serving as a reminder', from *memoria* 'memory'.

Memorial Day ▶ **noun** (in the US) a day on which those who died on active service are remembered, usually the last Monday in May.

memorialist ▶ **noun** a person who gives a memorial address or writes a memorial.

memorialize (also **-ise**) ▶ **verb** [with obj.] preserve the memory of; commemorate: *the novel memorialized their childhood summers.*

memorize (also **-ise**) ▶ **verb** [with obj.] commit to memory; learn by heart: *he memorized thousands of verses.*
– DERIVATIVES **memorizable** adjective, **memorization** noun, **memorizer** noun.

memory ▶ **noun** (pl. **-ies**) **1** a person's power to remember things: *I've a great* ***memory for*** *faces | my grandmother is losing her memory.*
■ [mass noun] the power of the mind to remember things: *the brain regions responsible for memory.* ■ the mind regarded as a store of things remembered: *he searched his memory frantically for an answer.*
2 something remembered from the past; a recollection: *one of my earliest memories is of sitting on his knee* | [mass noun] *the mind can bury all memory of traumatic abuse.*
■ [mass noun] the remembering or recollection of a dead person, especially one who was popular or respected: *clubs devoted to the memory of Sherlock Holmes.* ■ [mass noun] the length of time over which people continue to remember a person or event: *the worst slump in recent memory.*
3 the part of a computer in which data or program instructions can be stored for retrieval.
■ [mass noun] capacity for storing information in this way: *the module provides 16Mb of memory.*
– PHRASES **from memory** without reading or referring to notes: *each child was required to recite a verse from memory.* **in memory of** intended to remind people of, especially to honour a dead person. **take a trip** (or **walk**) **down memory lane** deliberately recall pleasant or sentimental memories.
– ORIGIN Middle English: from Old French *memorie*, from Latin *memoria*, from *memor* 'mindful, remembering'.

memory bank ▶ **noun** the memory device of a computer or other device.

memory board ▶ **noun** Computing a detachable board containing memory chips, which can be connected to a computer.

memory book ▶ **noun** US a scrapbook.

memory cell ▶ **noun** Physiology a long-lived lymphocyte capable of responding to a particular antigen on its reintroduction, long after the exposure that prompted its production.

memory jogger ▶ **noun** something that helps a person to remember something.

memory mapping ▶ **noun** [mass noun] a technique in which a computer treats peripheral devices as if they were located in the main memory.

memory span ▶ **noun** the length of time over which something can be remembered.
■ Psychology a measure of short-term memory equal to the maximum number of items that a person can recall in the correct order immediately after being presented with them once (typically about seven).

memory trace ▶ **noun** a hypothetical permanent change in the nervous system brought about by memorizing something; an engram.

Memphis /ˈmɛmfɪs/ **1** an ancient city of Egypt, whose ruins are situated on the Nile about 15 km (nearly 10 miles) south of Cairo. It is thought to have been founded as the capital of the Old Kingdom of Egypt *c.*3100 BC and is the site of the pyramids of Saqqara and Giza and the Sphinx.
2 a river port on the Mississippi in the extreme south-west of Tennessee; pop. 610,340 (1990). Founded in 1819, it was the home in the late 19th century of blues music, the scene in 1968 of the assassination of Martin Luther King, and the childhood home and burial place of Elvis Presley.

memsahib /ˈmɛmsʌˌhiːb, ˈmɛmsɑːb/ ▶ **noun** Indian dated a married white or upper-class woman (often used as a respectful form of address by non-whites).
– ORIGIN from *mem* (representing an Indian pronunciation of **MA'AM**) + **SAHIB**.

men plural form of **MAN**.

menace ▶ **noun** a person or thing that is likely to cause harm; a threat or danger: *a new initiative aimed at beating the menace of drugs | the snakes are* ***a menace to*** *farm animals.*
■ [mass noun] a threatening quality, tone, or atmosphere: *he spoke the words with a hint of menace.* ■ (**menaces**) threatening words or actions: *a demand of money* ***with menaces.***
▶ **verb** [with obj.] (often **be menaced**) threaten, especially in a malignant or hostile manner: *Africa's elephants are still menaced by poaching* | [as adj. **menacing**] *a menacing tone of voice.*
– DERIVATIVES **menacer** noun, **menacingly** adverb.
– ORIGIN Middle English: via Old French from late Latin *minacia*, from Latin *minax*, *minac-* 'threatening', from *minae* 'threats'.

menadione /ˌmɛnəˈdʌɪəʊn/ ▶ **noun** [mass noun] Medicine a synthetic yellow compound related to menaquinone, used to treat haemorrhage.
• Alternative name: **2-methyl-1,4-naphthoquinone**; chem. formula: $C_{11}H_8O_2$.
– ORIGIN 1940s: from *me(thyl)* + *na(phthalene)* + the suffix *-dione*, used in names of compounds containing two carbonyl groups.

ménage /meɪˈnɑːʒ/ ▶ **noun** the members of a household: *the Clelland ménage.*
– ORIGIN Middle English: from Old French *menage*, from *mainer* 'to stay', influenced by Old French *mesnie* 'household', both ultimately based on Latin *manere* 'remain'.

ménage à trois /meɪˌnɑːʒ ɑː ˈtrwʌ/ ▶ **noun** (pl. **ménages à trois** pronunc. same) an arrangement in which three people live or have a relationship together, typically a married couple and the lover of one of them.
– ORIGIN French, 'household of three'.

menagerie /məˈnadʒ(ə)ri/ ▶ **noun** a collection of wild animals kept in captivity for exhibition.
■ figurative a strange or diverse collection of people or things: *some other specimen in the television menagerie.*
– ORIGIN late 17th cent.: from French *ménagerie*, from *ménage* (see **MÉNAGE**).

Menai Strait /ˈmɛnʌɪ/ a channel separating Anglesey from the mainland of NW Wales. It is spanned by two bridges, a suspension bridge built by Thomas Telford 1819–26 and a second, built by Robert Stephenson 1846–50.

Menander /məˈnandə/ (*c.*342–292 BC), Greek dramatist. His comic plays deal with domestic situations and capture colloquial speech patterns. The sole complete extant play is *Dyskolos*.

Menapian /mɪˈnapɪən/ ▶ **adjective** Geology of, relating to, or denoting a Middle Pleistocene glaciation in northern Europe, possibly corresponding to the Günz of the Alps.
■ [as noun **the Menapian**] the Menapian glaciation or the system of deposits laid down during it.
– ORIGIN 1950s: from Latin *Menapii*, a people of northern Gaul in Roman times, + **-IAN**.

menaquinone /ˌmɛnəˈkwɪnəʊn/ ▶ **noun** [mass noun] Biochemistry one of the K vitamins, a compound produced by bacteria in the large intestine and essential for the blood-clotting process. It is an isoprenoid derivative of menadione. Also called ***vitamin*** K_2.
– ORIGIN 1940s: from the chemical name *me(thyl)-na(phtho)quinone*.

menarche /mɛˈnɑːki/ ▶ **noun** the first occurrence of menstruation.
– ORIGIN late 19th cent.: modern Latin, from Greek *mēn* 'month' + *arkhē* 'beginning'.

Mencius /ˈmɛnʃɪəs/ (*c.*371–*c.*289 BC), Chinese philosopher; Latinized name of *Meng-tzu* or *Mengzi* ('Meng the Master'). Noted for developing Confucianism, he believed that rulers should provide for the welfare of the people and that human nature is intrinsically good.
■ one of the Four Books of Confucianism, containing the teachings of Mencius.

Mencken /ˈmɛŋkən/, H. L. (1880–1956), American journalist and literary critic; full name *Henry Louis Mencken*. In his book *The American Language* (1919) he opposed the dominance of European culture in America.

mend ▶ **verb** [with obj.] **1** repair (something that is broken or damaged): *workmen were mending faulty cabling | a patch was used to mend the garment.*
■ [no obj.] return to health; heal: *foot injuries can take months to mend.* ■ improve (an unpleasant situation, especially a disagreement): *quarrels could be mended by talking.*
2 add fuel to (a fire).
▶ **noun** a repair in a material: *the mends were so perfect you could not even tell the board had been damaged.*
– PHRASES **mend (one's) fences** make peace with a person: *is it too late to mend fences with your ex-wife?* **mend one's manners** act more politely. **mend one's ways** improve one's habits or behaviour. **on the mend** improving in health or condition; recovering: *on the mend after a stomach operation | the economy is on the mend.*
– DERIVATIVES **mendable** adjective, **mender** noun.
– ORIGIN Middle English: shortening of **AMEND**.

mendacious /mɛnˈdeɪʃəs/ ▶ **adjective** not telling the truth; lying: *mendacious propaganda.*
– DERIVATIVES **mendaciously** adverb.
– ORIGIN early 17th cent.: from Latin *mendax*, *mendac-* 'lying' (related to *mendum* 'fault') + **-IOUS**.

mendacity ▶ **noun** [mass noun] untruthfulness: *people publicly castigated for past mendacity.*
– ORIGIN mid 17th cent.: from ecclesiastical Latin *mendacitas*, from *mendax*, *mendac-* 'lying' (see **MENDACIOUS**).

Mende /ˈmɛndi/ ▶ noun (pl. same) **1** a member of a people inhabiting Sierra Leone in West Africa. **2** [mass noun] the language of this people, belonging to the Mande group. It has over 1 million speakers.
▶ adjective relating to or denoting this people or their language.
– ORIGIN the name in Mende.

Mendel /ˈmɛnd(ə)l/, Gregor Johann (1822–84), Moravian monk, the father of genetics. From systematically breeding peas he demonstrated the transmission of characteristics in a predictable way by factors (genes) which remain intact and independent between generations and do not blend, though they may mask one another's effects.

Mendeleev /ˌmɛndəˈleɪɛf/, Dmitri (Ivanovich) (1834–1907), Russian chemist. He developed the periodic table and successfully predicted the discovery of several new elements.

mendelevium /ˌmɛndəˈliːvɪəm, -ˈleɪvɪəm/ ▶ noun [mass noun] the chemical element of atomic number 101, a radioactive metal of the actinide series. It does not occur naturally and was first made in 1955 by bombarding einsteinium with helium ions. (Symbol: **Md**)
– ORIGIN modern Latin, from the name of D. **MENDELEEV**.

Mendelian /mɛnˈdiːlɪən/ ▶ adjective Biology of or relating to Mendel's theory of heredity: *Mendelian genetics*.
▶ noun a person who accepts or advocates Mendel's theory of heredity.

Mendelism /ˈmɛnd(ə)lɪz(ə)m/ ▶ noun [mass noun] Biology the theory of heredity as formulated by Mendel.

Mendelssohn /ˈmɛnd(ə)ls(ə)n/, German /ˈmɛndlzoːn/, Felix (1809–47), German composer and pianist; full name *Jakob Ludwig Felix Mendelssohn-Bartholdy*. His romantic music is elegant, light, and melodically inventive. Notable works include the overture *Fingal's Cave* (1830–2), the oratorio *Elijah* (1846), and eight volumes of *Lieder ohne Worte* (*Songs Without Words*) for piano.

Menderes /ˌmɛndəˈrɛs/ a river of SW Turkey. Rising in the Anatolian plateau, it flows for some 384 km (240 miles), entering the Aegean Sea south of the Greek island of Samos. Known in ancient times as the Maeander, and noted for its winding course, it gave its name to the verb *meander*.

mendicant /ˈmɛndɪk(ə)nt/ ▶ adjective given to begging.
■ of or denoting one of the religious orders who originally relied solely on alms: *a mendicant friar*.
▶ noun a beggar.
■ a member of a mendicant order.
– DERIVATIVES **mendicancy** noun.
– ORIGIN late Middle English: from Latin *mendicant-* 'begging', from the verb *mendicare*, from *mendicus* 'beggar', from *mendum* 'fault'.

mendicity /mɛnˈdɪsɪti/ ▶ noun [mass noun] the condition or activities of a beggar.
– ORIGIN late Middle English: from Old French *mendicite*, from Latin *mendicitas*, from *mendicus* 'beggar'.

mending ▶ noun [mass noun] things to be repaired by sewing or darning: *a muddle of books and mending*.

Mendip Hills (also **the Mendips**) a range of limestone hills in SW England.

Mendoza[1] /mɛnˈdəʊzə, Spanish menˈdosa, -θa/ a city in western Argentina, situated in the foothills of the Andes at the centre of a wine-producing region; pop. 121,700 (1991).

Mendoza[2] /mɛnˈdəʊzə, Spanish menˈdoθa, -sa/, Antonio de (c.1490–1552), Spanish colonial administrator, the first viceroy of New Spain (1535–50).

Menelaus /ˌmɛnɪˈleɪəs/ Greek Mythology king of Sparta, husband of Helen and brother of Agamemnon. Helen was stolen from him by Paris, an event which provoked the Trojan War.

Menes /ˈmiːniːz/, Egyptian pharaoh, reigned c.3100 BC. He founded the first dynasty that ruled Egypt.

menfolk (US also **menfolks**) ▶ plural noun a group of men considered collectively, especially the men of a particular family or community: *the menfolk of the village watch the goings-on*.

Meng-tzu /ˈmʌŋˈtsuː/ (also **Mengzi** /ˈmɛŋˈziː/) Chinese name for **MENCIUS**.

menhaden /mɛnˈheɪd(ə)n/ ▶ noun a large deep-bodied fish of the herring family, which occurs along the east coast of North America. The oil-rich flesh is used to make fishmeal and fertilizer.
● Genus *Brevoortia*, family Clupeidae: several species, in particular *B. tyrannus*.
– ORIGIN late 18th cent.: from Algonquian.

menhir /ˈmɛnhɪə/ ▶ noun Archaeology a tall upright stone of a kind erected in prehistoric times in western Europe.
– ORIGIN mid 19th cent.: from Breton *men* 'stone' + *hir* 'long'.

menial /ˈmiːnɪəl/ ▶ adjective (of work) not requiring much skill and lacking prestige: *menial factory jobs*.
■ [attrib.] dated (of a servant) domestic.
▶ noun a person with a menial job.
■ dated a domestic servant.
– DERIVATIVES **menially** adverb.
– ORIGIN late Middle English (in the sense 'domestic'): from Old French, from *mesnee* 'household'.

Ménière's disease /mɛnˈjɛː/ (also **Ménière's syndrome**) ▶ noun [mass noun] a disease of unknown cause affecting the membranous labyrinth of the ear, causing progressive deafness and attacks of tinnitus and vertigo.
– ORIGIN late 19th cent.: named after Prosper *Ménière* (1799–1862), French physician.

meninges /mɪˈnɪndʒiːz/ ▶ plural noun (sing. **meninx**) Anatomy the three membranes (the dura mater, arachnoid, and pia mater) that line the skull and vertebral canal and enclose the brain and spinal cord.
– DERIVATIVES **meningeal** adjective.
– ORIGIN modern Latin, from Greek *mēninx*, *mēning-* 'membrane'.

meningioma /mɪˌnɪndʒɪˈəʊmə/ ▶ noun (pl. **meningiomas** or **meningiomata**) Medicine a tumour, usually benign, arising from meningeal tissue of the brain.

meningitis /ˌmɛnɪnˈdʒʌɪtɪs/ ▶ noun [mass noun] inflammation of the meninges caused by viral or bacterial infection and marked by intense headache and fever, sensitivity to light, and muscular rigidity, leading (in severe cases) to convulsions, delirium, and death.
– DERIVATIVES **meningitic** adjective.

meningocele /mɪˈnɪŋɡ(ə)siːl, -ˈnɪndʒ(ə)(ʊ)-/ ▶ noun Medicine a protrusion of the meninges through a gap in the spine due to a congenital defect.

meningococcus /mɪˌnɪŋɡəʊˈkɒkəs, -ˌnɪndʒəʊ-/ ▶ noun (pl. **meningococci** /-ˈkɒk(s)ʌɪ, -ˈkɒk(s)iː/) a bacterium involved in some forms of meningitis and cerebrospinal infection.
● *Neisseria meningitidis*, a non-motile spherical Gram-negative bacterium.
– DERIVATIVES **meningococcal** adjective.
– ORIGIN late 19th cent.: from **MENINGES** + **COCCUS**.

meningoencephalitis /mɪˈnɪŋɡəʊ̯enˌsefəˈlʌɪtɪs, -ˈnɪndʒəʊ-, -ˌkɛf-/ ▶ noun [mass noun] Medicine inflammation of the membranes of the brain and the adjoining cerebral tissue.

meninx /ˈmiːnɪŋks/ singular form of **MENINGES**.

meniscectomy /ˌmɛnɪˈsɛktəmi/ ▶ noun [mass noun] surgical removal of a meniscus, especially that of the knee.

meniscus /mɪˈnɪskəs/ ▶ noun (pl. **menisci** /-sʌɪ/) Physics the curved upper surface of a liquid in a tube.
■ [usu. as modifier] a lens that is convex on one side and concave on the other. ■ Anatomy a thin fibrous cartilage between the surfaces of some joints, e.g. the knee.
– ORIGIN late 17th cent.: modern Latin, from Greek *mēniskos* 'crescent', diminutive of *mēnē* 'moon'.

Mennonite /ˈmɛnənʌɪt/ ▶ noun (chiefly in the US and Canada) a member of a Protestant sect originating in Friesland in the 16th century, emphasizing adult baptism and rejecting Church organization, military service, and public office.
– ORIGIN from the name of its founder, *Menno* Simons (1496–1561), + **-ITE**[1].

meno /ˈmɛnəʊ/ ▶ adverb Music (in directions) less.
– ORIGIN Italian.

meno- ▶ combining form relating to menstruation: *menopause*.
– ORIGIN from Greek *mēn* 'month'.

menology /mɪˈnɒlədʒi/ ▶ noun (pl. **-ies**) a calendar of the Greek Orthodox Church containing biographies of the saints.

– ORIGIN early 17th cent.: via modern Latin from ecclesiastical Greek *mēnologion*, from *mēn* 'month' + *logos* 'account'.

Menominee /mɪˈnɒmɪni/ (also **Menomini**) ▶ noun (pl. same or **Menominees**) **1** a member of an American Indian people of NE Wisconsin. **2** [mass noun] the extinct Algonquian language of this people.
▶ adjective relating to or denoting this people or their language.
– ORIGIN from Ojibwa *manōmini*, literally 'wild-rice person'.

meno mosso /ˌmɛnəʊ ˈmɒsəʊ/ ▶ adverb & adjective Music (especially as a direction) less quickly.
– ORIGIN Italian.

menopause /ˈmɛnəpɔːz/ ▶ noun the ceasing of menstruation.
■ the period in a woman's life (typically between 45 and 50 years of age) when this occurs.
– DERIVATIVES **menopausal** adjective.
– ORIGIN late 19th cent.: from modern Latin *menopausis* (see **MENO-**, **PAUSE**).

menorah /mɪˈnɔːrə/ ▶ noun (**the Menorah**) a sacred candelabrum with seven branches used in the Temple in Jerusalem, originally that made by the craftsman Bezalel and placed in the sanctuary of the Tabernacle (Exod. 37:17 ff.).
■ a candelabrum used in Jewish worship, especially one with eight branches used at Hanukkah.
– ORIGIN Hebrew.

Menorca /meˈnorka/ Spanish name for **MINORCA**.

menorrhagia /ˌmɛnəˈreɪdʒɪə/ ▶ noun [mass noun] Medicine abnormally heavy bleeding at menstruation.
– ORIGIN late 18th cent.: modern Latin, from **MENO-** 'of menstruation' + *-rrhag-*, stem of Greek *rhēgnunai* 'to burst'.

menorrhoea /ˌmɛnəˈriːə/ ▶ noun [mass noun] Medicine the flow of blood at menstruation.
– ORIGIN mid 19th cent.: back-formation from **AMENORRHOEA**.

Mensa[1] /ˈmɛnsə/ Astronomy a small, faint southern constellation (the Table or Table Mountain), lying between Dorado and the south celestial pole. It contains part of the Large Magellanic Cloud.
■ [as genitive **Mensae** /ˈmɛnsiː/] used with preceding letter or numeral to designate a star in this constellation: *the star Alpha Mensae*.
– ORIGIN Latin.

Mensa[2] /ˈmɛnsə/ an international organization founded in England in 1945 whose members must achieve very high scores in IQ tests to be admitted.
– ORIGIN Latin, 'table', with allusion to a round table at which all members have equal status.

mensch /mɛnʃ/ (also **mensh**) ▶ noun N. Amer. informal a person of integrity and honour.
– ORIGIN 1930s: Yiddish *mensh*, from German *Mensch*, literally 'person'.

menses /ˈmɛnsiːz/ ▶ plural noun blood and other matter discharged from the uterus at menstruation.
■ [treated as sing.] the time of menstruation: *a late menses*.
– ORIGIN late 16th cent.: from Latin, plural of *mensis* 'month'.

Menshevik /ˈmɛnʃɪvɪk/ ▶ noun historical a member of the non-Leninist wing of the Russian Social Democratic Workers' Party, opposed to the Bolsheviks and defeated by them after the overthrow of the tsar in 1917.
– ORIGIN from Russian *Men'shevik* 'a member of the minority', from *men'she* 'less'. Lenin coined the name at a time when the party was (untypically) in the minority for a brief period.

men's movement ▶ noun (chiefly in the US) a movement aimed at liberating men from traditional views about their character and role in society.

mens rea /ˌmɛnz ˈriːə/ ▶ noun [mass noun] Law the intention or knowledge of wrongdoing that constitutes part of a crime, as opposed to the action or conduct of the accused. Compare with **ACTUS REUS**.
– ORIGIN Latin, literally 'guilty mind'.

men's room ▶ noun chiefly N. Amer. a men's toilet in a public or institutional building.

menstrual ▶ adjective of or relating to the menses or menstruation: *menstrual blood*.

– ORIGIN late Middle English: from Latin *menstrualis*, from *menstruum* 'menses', from *mensis* 'month'.

menstrual cycle ▶ noun the process of ovulation and menstruation in women and other female primates.

menstrual period ▶ noun see PERIOD (sense 3).

menstruate /ˈmɛnstrʊeɪt/ ▶ verb [no obj.] (of a woman) discharge blood and other material from the lining of the uterus as part of the menstrual cycle.
– ORIGIN mid 17th cent.: from late Latin *menstruat-* 'menstruated', from the verb *menstruare*, from Latin *menstrua* 'menses'.

menstruation ▶ noun [mass noun] the process in a woman of discharging blood and other materials from the lining of the uterus at intervals of about one lunar month from puberty until the menopause, except during pregnancy.

menstruous ▶ adjective of, relating to, or in the process of menstruation.
– ORIGIN late Middle English: from Old French *menstrueus*, from late Latin *menstruosus*, from *menstrua* 'menses'.

menstruum /ˈmɛnstrʊəm/ ▶ noun (pl. **menstrua** /-strʊə/) **1** [mass noun] menses.
2 archaic a solvent.
– ORIGIN late Middle English (in sense 1): from Latin, neuter of *menstruus* 'monthly', from *mensis* 'month'. Sense 2 is by alchemical analogy of the supposed agency of a solvent in the transmutation of metals into gold with the supposed action of menses on the ovum.

mensurable ▶ adjective able to be measured; having fixed limits.
■ Music another term for MENSURAL.
– ORIGIN late Middle English (in the sense 'moderate'): from late Latin *mensurabilis*, from *mensurare* 'to measure', from Latin *mensura* 'measure'.

mensural /ˈmɛnʃ(ə)r(ə)l, -sjə-/ ▶ adjective of or involving measuring: *mensural investigations*.
■ Music involving notes of definite duration and usually a regular metre.
– ORIGIN late 16th cent.: from Latin *mensuralis*, from *mensura* 'measure'.

mensuration ▶ noun [mass noun] measuring.
■ Mathematics the measuring of geometric magnitudes, lengths, areas, and volumes.
– ORIGIN late 16th cent. (denoting measurement in general): from late Latin *mensuratio(n-)*, from *mensurare* 'to measure'.

menswear ▶ noun [mass noun] clothes for men.

-ment ▶ suffix **1** forming nouns expressing the means or result of an action: *curtailment* | *excitement* | *treatment*.
2 forming nouns from adjectives (such as *merriment* from *merry*).
– ORIGIN from French, or from Latin *-mentum*.

mental ▶ adjective **1** of or relating to the mind: *mental faculties* | *mental phenomena*.
■ carried out by or taking place in the mind: *a quick mental calculation* | *I started my mental journey*.
2 of, relating to, or suffering from disorders or illnesses of the mind: *a mental hospital*.
■ [predic.] informal insane; crazy: *go mental to the sounds of DJ Steve McMahon*.
– DERIVATIVES **mentally** adverb.
– ORIGIN late Middle English: from late Latin *mentalis*, from Latin *mens, ment-* 'mind'.

USAGE The use of **mental** in compounds such as **mental hospital** and **mental patient** is first recorded at the end of the 19th century and was the normal accepted term in the first half of the 20th century. It is now, however, regarded as old-fashioned, sometimes even offensive, and has been largely replaced by the term **psychiatric** in both general and official use.

mental age ▶ noun a person's mental ability expressed as the age at which an average person reaches the same ability: *she was 65 but had a mental age of two*.

mental block ▶ noun an inability to recall some specific thing or perform some mental action.

mental cruelty ▶ noun [mass noun] conduct that makes another person suffer but does not involve physical assault.

mental defective ▶ noun dated a person with a mental handicap.

mental deficiency ▶ noun [mass noun] dated the condition of having a mental handicap.

mental handicap ▶ noun a condition in which the intellectual capacity of a person is permanently lowered or underdeveloped to an extent which prevents normal function in society.

USAGE The terms **mental handicap** and **mentally handicapped**, though widely used a few decades ago, have fallen out of favour in recent years and have been largely replaced in official contexts by newer terms such as **learning difficulties**. See usage at LEARNING DIFFICULTIES.

mentalism ▶ noun [mass noun] Philosophy the theory that physical and psychological phenomena are ultimately explicable only in terms of a creative and interpretative mind.
– DERIVATIVES **mentalist** noun & adjective, **mentalistic** adjective.

mentality ▶ noun (pl. **-ies**) **1** often derogatory the characteristic attitude of mind or way of thinking of a person or group: *the yuppie mentality of the eighties*.
2 [mass noun] the capacity for intelligent thought.
– ORIGIN late 17th cent. (in the sense 'mental process'): from the adjective MENTAL + -ITY. Current senses date from the mid 19th cent.

mentally handicapped ▶ adjective (of a person) having very limited intellectual functions.

mental set ▶ noun another term for MINDSET.

mentation ▶ noun [mass noun] technical mental activity.
– ORIGIN mid 19th cent.: from Latin *mens, ment-* 'mind' + -ATION.

menthol ▶ noun [mass noun] a crystalline compound with a cooling minty taste and odour, found in peppermint and other natural oils. It is used as a flavouring and in decongestants and analgesics.
● An alcohol, **2-isopropyl-5-methylcyclohexanol**; chem. formula: $C_{10}H_{19}OH$.
– ORIGIN late 19th cent.: from German, from Latin *mentha* 'mint' + -OL.

mentholated ▶ adjective treated with or containing menthol: *mentholated shaving creams*.

mention ▶ verb [with obj.] refer to something briefly and without going into detail: *I haven't mentioned it to William yet* | [with clause] *I mentioned that my father was meeting me later*.
■ [with obj.] (often **be mentioned**) make a reference to (someone) as being noteworthy, especially as a potential candidate for a post: *he is still regularly mentioned as a possible secretary of state*.
▶ noun a reference to someone or something: *their eyes light up at a mention of Sartre* | [mass noun] *she made no mention of her disastrous trip to Paris*.
■ a formal acknowledgement of something outstanding or noteworthy: *he received a special mention and a prize of £100* | [mass noun] *two other points are worthy of mention*. See also HONOURABLE MENTION.
■ (in full **mention in dispatches**) Brit. an instance of being mentioned in dispatches.
– PHRASES **be mentioned in dispatches** Brit. be commended for one's actions by name in an official military report. **don't mention it** a polite expression used to indicate that thanks or an apology are not necessary. **mention someone in one's will** leave a legacy to someone. **not to mention** used to introduce an additional fact or point which reinforces the point being made: *I'm amazed you find the time, not to mention the energy, to do any work at all*.
– DERIVATIVES **mentionable** adjective.
– ORIGIN Middle English (originally in *make mention of*): via Old French from Latin *mentio(n-)*; related to MIND.

mento ▶ noun (pl. **-os**) [mass noun] a style of Jamaican folk music based on a traditional dance rhythm in duple time.
– ORIGIN early 20th cent.: of unknown origin.

mentor ▶ noun an experienced and trusted adviser: *he was her friend and mentor until his death in 1915*.
■ an experienced person in a company, college, or school who trains and counsels new employees or students.
▶ verb [with obj.] to advise or train (someone, especially a younger colleague).
– ORIGIN mid 18th cent.: via French and Latin from Greek *Mentōr*, the name of the adviser of the young Telemachus in Homer's *Odyssey*.

mentum /ˈmɛntəm/ ▶ noun Entomology a part of the base of the labium in some insects.

– ORIGIN early 19th cent.: from Latin, literally 'chin'.

menu ▶ noun a list of dishes available in a restaurant: *the waiter handed her a menu* | figurative *politics and sport are on the menu tonight*.
■ the food available or to be served in a restaurant or at a meal: *a no-fuss dinner-party menu*. ■ Computing a list of commands or facilities, especially one displayed on screen.
– ORIGIN mid 19th cent.: from French, 'detailed list' (noun use of *menu* 'small, detailed'), from Latin *minutus* 'very small'.

menu bar ▶ noun Computing a horizontal bar, typically located at the top of the screen below the title bar, containing drop-down menus.

menudo /mɪˈnuːdəʊ/ ▶ noun (pl. **-os**) [mass noun] a spicy Mexican soup made from tripe.
– ORIGIN noun use of a Mexican Spanish adjective meaning 'small'.

menu-driven ▶ adjective (of a program or computer) used by making selections from menus.

Menuhin /ˈmɛnjʊɪn/, Sir Yehudi (1916–99), American-born British violinist. He founded a school of music, named after him, in Surrey in 1962.

Menzies /ˈmɛnzɪz/, Sir Robert Gordon (1894–1978), Australian Liberal statesman, Prime Minister 1939–41 and 1949–66. He is Australia's longest-serving Prime Minister.

Meo /miːˈəʊ/ ▶ noun (pl. same or **-os**) & adjective another term for HMONG.

meow ▶ noun & verb variant spelling of MIAOW.

MEP ▶ abbreviation for Member of the European Parliament.

mepacrine /ˈmɛpəkriːn, -ɪːn/ ▶ noun another term for QUINACRINE.
– ORIGIN 1940s: from *me(thoxy-* + *p(entane)* + *acr(id)ine*.

meperidine /məˈpɛrɪdiːn/ ▶ noun another term for PETHIDINE.
– ORIGIN 1940s: blend of METHYL and PIPERIDINE.

Mephistopheles /ˌmɛfɪˈstɒfɪliːz/ ▶ noun an evil spirit to whom Faust, in the German legend, sold his soul.
– DERIVATIVES **Mephistophelean** /-ˈfiːlɪən, -fɪˈliːən/ (also **Mephistophelian**) adjective.

mephitic /mɪˈfɪtɪk/ ▶ adjective (especially of a gas or vapour) foul-smelling; noxious.
– ORIGIN early 17th cent.: from late Latin *mephiticus*, from *mephitis* 'noxious exhalation'.

-mer ▶ combining form denoting polymers and related kinds of molecule: *elastomer*.
– ORIGIN from Greek *meros* 'part'.

meranti /məˈranti/ ▶ noun [mass noun] white, red, or yellow hardwood timber from Malaysia or Indonesia.
● This timber is obtained from trees of the genus *Shorea*, family Dipterocarpaceae.
– ORIGIN late 18th cent.: from Malay.

merbau /ˈmɜːbaʊ/ ▶ noun a tropical hardwood tree which yields valuable timber, native to Malaysia and Indonesia.
● Genus *Intsia*, family Leguminosae: three species, in particular *I. palembanica*.
– ORIGIN late 18th cent.: from Malay.

merbromin /mɜːˈbrəʊmɪn/ ▶ noun [mass noun] a greenish iridescent crystalline compound which dissolves in water to give a red solution used as an antiseptic. It is a fluorescein derivative containing bromine and mercury.
– ORIGIN 1940s: from MERCURIC + BROMO- + -IN[1].

Merc /mɜːk/ ▶ noun informal a Mercedes car.

merc /mɜːk/ ▶ noun informal a mercenary soldier.

mercado /mɜːˈkɑːdəʊ/ ▶ noun (pl. **-os**) (in Spain and Spanish-speaking countries) a market.
– ORIGIN Spanish, from Latin *mercatus* 'market'.

Mercalli scale /mɜːˈkali/ a twelve-point scale for expressing the local intensity of an earthquake, ranging from I (virtually imperceptible) to XII (total destruction).
– ORIGIN 1920s: named after Giuseppe *Mercalli* (1850–1914), Italian geologist.

mercantile /ˈmɜːk(ə)ntʌɪl/ ▶ adjective of or relating to trade or commerce; commercial: *the shift of wealth to the mercantile classes*.
■ of or relating to mercantilism.
– ORIGIN mid 17th cent.: from French, from Italian, from *mercante* 'merchant'.

mercantile marine ▶ noun another term for MERCHANT NAVY.

mercantilism /ˈməːk(ə)ntʌɪˌlɪz(ə)m/ ▶ **noun** [mass noun] belief in the benefits of profitable trading; commercialism.
■ chiefly historical the economic theory that trade generates wealth and is stimulated by the accumulation of profitable balances, which a government should encourage by means of protectionism.
– DERIVATIVES **mercantilist** noun & adjective.

mercaptan /məˈkapt(ə)n/ ▶ **noun** Chemistry another term for **THIOL**.
– ORIGIN mid 19th cent.: from modern Latin *mercurium captans*, literally 'capturing mercury'.

Mercator /məːˈkeɪtə/, Gerardus (1512–94), Flemish geographer and cartographer, resident in Germany from 1552; Latinized name of *Gerhard Kremer*. He invented the system of map projection that is named after him.

Mercator projection ▶ **noun** a projection of a map of the world on to a cylinder in such a way that all the parallels of latitude have the same length as the equator, used especially for marine charts and certain climatological maps.

mercenary /ˈməːsɪn(ə)ri/ ▶ **adjective** (of a person or their behaviour) primarily concerned with making money at the expense of ethics: *she's nothing but a mercenary little gold-digger.*
▶ **noun** (pl. **-ies**) a professional soldier hired to serve in a foreign army.
■ a person primarily concerned with material reward at the expense of ethics: *cricket's most infamous mercenary.*
– DERIVATIVES **mercenariness** noun.
– ORIGIN late Middle English (as a noun): from Latin *mercenarius* 'hireling', from *merces, merced-* 'reward'.

mercer ▶ **noun** Brit., chiefly historical a dealer in textile fabrics, especially silks, velvets, and other fine materials.
– DERIVATIVES **mercery** noun.
– ORIGIN Middle English: from Old French *mercier*, based on Latin *merx, merc-* 'goods'.

mercerize (also **-ise**) ▶ **verb** [with obj.] [often as adj. **mercerized**] treat (cotton fabric or thread) under tension with caustic alkali to increase its strength and give it a shiny, silky appearance.
– ORIGIN mid 19th cent.: from the name of John Mercer (died 1866), said to have invented the process, + **-IZE**.

merchandise ▶ **noun** /ˈməːtʃ(ə)ndʌɪs, -z/ [mass noun] goods to be bought and sold: *shops which offered an astonishing range of merchandise.*
■ products used to promote a particular film, pop group, etc., or linked to a particular fictional character; merchandising.
▶ **verb** /ˈməːtʃ(ə)ndʌɪz/ (also **-ize**) [with obj.] promote the sale of (goods), especially by their presentation in retail outlets: *a new breakfast food can easily be merchandised.*
■ advertise or publicize (an idea or person): *they are merchandising 'niceness' to children.* ■ archaic trade or traffic in (something), especially inappropriately. ■ [no obj.] archaic engage in the business of a merchant.
– DERIVATIVES **merchandisable** adjective, **merchandiser** noun.
– ORIGIN late Middle English: from Old French *marchandise*, from *marchand* 'merchant'.

merchandising ▶ **noun** [mass noun] the activity of promoting the sale of goods, especially by their presentation in retail outlets: *problems rooted in overexpansion and poor merchandising.*
■ products used to promote a particular film, pop group, etc., or linked to a particular fictional character: *the characters are still popular and found on a wide variety of merchandising.*

Merchant, Ismail (b.1936), Indian film producer. In 1961 he became a partner with James Ivory in Merchant Ivory Productions. Together they have made a number of films, such as *Howard's End* (1992).

merchant ▶ **noun 1** a person or company involved in wholesale trade, especially one dealing with foreign countries or supplying merchandise to a particular trade: *a builders' merchant* | *a tea merchant.*
■ chiefly N. Amer. a retail trader; a shopkeeper: *the credit cards are accepted by 10 million merchants worldwide.* ■ (especially in historical contexts) a person involved in trade or commerce: *prosperous merchants and clothiers had established a middle class.*
2 [usu. with modifier] informal, chiefly derogatory a person with a partiality or aptitude for a particular activity or viewpoint: *his driver was no speed merchant* | *a merchant of death.*
▶ **adjective** [attrib.] of or relating to merchants, trade, or commerce: *the growth of the merchant classes.*
■ (of ships, sailors, or shipping activity) involved with commerce rather than military activity: *a merchant seaman.*
– ORIGIN Middle English: from Old French *marchant*, based on Latin *mercari* 'to trade', from *merx, merc-* 'merchandise'.

merchantable ▶ **adjective** suitable for purchase or sale: *goods must be of merchantable quality.*
– ORIGIN late 15th cent.: from the verb *merchant* 'haggle, trade as a merchant', from Old French *marchander*, from *marchand* 'merchant'.

Merchant Adventurers an English trading guild which was involved in trade overseas, principally with the Netherlands during the 15th–18th centuries.

merchant bank ▶ **noun** chiefly Brit. a bank dealing in commercial loans and investment.
– DERIVATIVES **merchant banker** noun.

merchantman ▶ **noun** (pl. **-men**) another term for **MERCHANT SHIP**.

merchant marine ▶ **noun** chiefly US another term for **MERCHANT NAVY**.

merchant navy ▶ **noun** (often **the merchant navy**) chiefly Brit. a country's shipping which is involved in commerce and trade, as opposed to military activity.

merchant prince ▶ **noun** a person involved in trade whose wealth is sufficient to confer political influence.

Mercia /ˈməːʃɪə, ˈməːsɪə/ a former kingdom of central England. It was established by invading Angles in the 6th century AD in the border areas between the new Anglo-Saxon settlements in the east and the Celtic regions in the west.
■ used in names of modern organizations to refer to parts of the English midlands: *West Mercia Police.*
– DERIVATIVES **Mercian** adjective & noun.

merciful ▶ **adjective** showing or exercising mercy: *it was the will of a merciful God that all should be saved.*
■ (of an event) coming as a mercy; bringing someone relief from something unpleasant: *her death was a merciful release.*
– DERIVATIVES **mercifulness** noun.

mercifully ▶ **adverb 1** in a merciful manner.
2 to one's great relief; fortunately: [sentence adverb] *mercifully, I was able to complete all I had to do within a few days.*

merciless ▶ **adjective** showing no mercy or pity: *a merciless attack with a blunt instrument* | figurative *the merciless summer heat.*
– DERIVATIVES **mercilessly** adverb, **mercilessness** noun.

Merckx /məːks/, Eddy (b.1945), Belgian racing cyclist. During his professional career he won the Tour de France five times (1969–72 and 1974).

Mercouri /məːˈkʊəri/, Melina (1925–94), Greek actress and politician; born *Anna Amalia Mercouri*. Her films include *Never on Sunday* (1960). She was exiled for opposing the military junta who took power in Greece in 1967, but was elected to Parliament in the socialist government of 1978, becoming Minister of Culture in 1985.

mercurial /məːˈkjʊərɪəl/ ▶ **adjective 1** (of a person) subject to sudden or unpredictable changes of mood or mind: *his mercurial temperament.*
2 of or containing the element mercury.
3 (**Mercurial**) of the planet Mercury.
▶ **noun** (usu. **mercurials**) a drug or other compound containing mercury.
– DERIVATIVES **mercuriality** /-ˈalɪti/ noun, **mercurially** adverb.
– ORIGIN late Middle English (in sense 3): from Latin *mercurialis* 'relating to the god Mercury', from *Mercurius* 'Mercury'. Sense 1 dates from the mid 17th cent.

mercuric /məːˈkjʊərɪk/ ▶ **adjective** Chemistry of mercury with a valency of two; of mercury(II). Compare with **MERCUROUS**.

mercuric chloride ▶ **noun** [mass noun] a toxic white crystalline compound, used as a fungicide.
● Chem. formula: $HgCl_2$.

Mercurochrome /məːˈkjʊərəkrəʊm/ ▶ **noun** US trademark for **MERBROMIN**.
– ORIGIN early 20th cent.: from **MERCURY**[1] + Greek *khrōma* 'colour'.

mercurous /ˈməːkjʊrəs/ ▶ **adjective** Chemistry of mercury with a valency of one; of mercury(I): Compare with **MERCURIC**.

Mercury 1 Roman Mythology the Roman god of eloquence, skill, trading, and thieving, herald and messenger of the gods, who was identified with Hermes. [ORIGIN: from Latin *Mercurius*, from *merx, merc-* 'merchandise'.]
■ used in names of newspapers and journals: *the Leicester Mercury.*
2 Astronomy a small planet that is the closest to the sun in the solar system, sometimes visible to the naked eye just after sunset.

> Mercury orbits within the orbit of Venus at an average distance of 57.9 million km from the sun. With a diameter of 4,878 km it is only a third larger than earth's moon, which it resembles in having a heavily cratered surface. Its 'day' of 58.65 days is precisely two thirds the length of its 'year' of 87.97 days. Daytime temperatures average 170°C. There is no atmosphere and the planet has no satellites.

– DERIVATIVES **Mercurian** adjective.

mercury[1] ▶ **noun** [mass noun] the chemical element of atomic number 80, a heavy silvery-white metal which is liquid at ordinary temperatures. (Symbol: **Hg**) Also called **QUICKSILVER**.
■ the column of such metal in a thermometer or barometer, or its height as indicating atmospheric temperature or pressure: *the mercury rises, the skies steam, and the nights swelter.* ■ historical this metal or one of its compounds used medicinally, especially to treat syphilis.
– ORIGIN Middle English: from Latin *Mercurius* (see sense 1 of **MERCURY**).

mercury[2] ▶ **noun** a plant of a genus which includes dog's mercury.
● Genus *Mercurialis*, family Euphorbiaceae.
– ORIGIN mid 16th cent.: from the genus name, from Latin *mercurialis* 'of the god Mercury'.

mercury tilt switch ▶ **noun** an electric switch in which the circuit is made by mercury flowing into a gap when the device tilts.

mercury vapour lamp ▶ **noun** a lamp in which light is produced by an electrical discharge through mercury vapour.

mercy ▶ **noun** (pl. **-ies**) [mass noun] compassion or forgiveness shown towards someone whom it is within one's power to punish or harm: *the boy was screaming and begging for mercy* | [count noun] *the mercies of God.*
■ [count noun] an event to be grateful for, especially because its occurrence prevents something unpleasant or provides relief from suffering: *his death was in a way a mercy.* ■ [as modifier] (especially of a journey or mission) performed out of a desire to relieve suffering; motivated by compassion: *mercy missions to refugees caught up in the fighting.*
▶ **exclamation** archaic used in expressions of surprise or fear: *'Mercy me!' uttered Mrs Diggory.*
– PHRASES **at the mercy of** completely in the power or under the control of: *consumers were at the mercy of every rogue in the marketplace.* **be thankful** (or **grateful**) **for small mercies** be relieved that an unpleasant situation is alleviated by minor advantages. **have mercy on** (or **upon**) show compassion or forgiveness to: *may the Lord have mercy on her soul.* **leave someone/thing to the mercy of** expose someone or something to a situation of probable danger or harm: *the forest is left to the mercy of the loggers.* **throw oneself on someone's mercy** intentionally place oneself in someone's hands in the expectation that they will behave mercifully towards one.
– ORIGIN Middle English: from Old French *merci* 'pity' or 'thanks', from Latin *merces, merced-* 'reward', in Christian Latin 'pity, favour, heavenly reward'.

mercy killing ▶ **noun** [mass noun] the killing of a patient suffering from an incurable and painful disease, typically by the administration of large doses of painkilling drugs.

merde /mɛːd, French mɛrd/ ▶ **exclamation** a French word for 'shit', used as a mild, generally humorous exclamation in English: *Merde! What had she done!*

mere[1] /mɪə/ ▶ **adjective** [attrib.] that is solely or no more or better than what is specified: *they dismissed Bolton for a mere fourteen runs* | *questions that cannot be answered by mere mortals.*
■ (**the merest**) the smallest or slightest: *the merest hint of make-up.*

– ORIGIN late Middle English (in the senses 'pure' and 'sheer, downright'): from Latin *merus* 'undiluted'.

mere² /mɪə/ ▶ noun chiefly poetic/literary a lake or pond: [in place names] *Hornsea Mere*.

– ORIGIN Old English, of Germanic origin; related to Dutch *meer* 'lake' and German *Meer* 'sea', from an Indo-European root shared by Russian *more* and Latin *mare*.

mere³ /'mɛri/ ▶ noun a Maori war club, especially one made of greenstone.

– ORIGIN Maori.

Meredith /'mɛrədɪθ/, George (1828–1909), English novelist and poet. His semi-autobiographical verse collection *Modern Love* (1862) describes the disillusionment of married love. Other notable works: *The Egoist* (novel, 1871).

merely ▶ adverb just; only: *she seemed to him not merely an intelligent woman, but a kind of soulmate*.

merengue /mə'rɛŋgeɪ/ (also **meringue**) ▶ noun [mass noun] a Caribbean style of dance music typically in duple and triple time, chiefly associated with Dominica and Haiti.

■ a style of dancing associated with such music, with alternating long and short stiff-legged steps.

– ORIGIN late 19th cent.: probably American Spanish; compare perhaps with the sense 'upheaval, disorder', attested in Argentina, Paraguay, and Uruguay.

mereology /,mɛri'ɒlədʒi/ ▶ noun [mass noun] Philosophy the abstract study of the relations between parts and wholes.

– DERIVATIVES **mereological** adjective.

– ORIGIN 1940s: from French, formed irregularly from Greek *meros* 'part' + -LOGY.

mere right ▶ noun Law a right with no remedy.

meretricious /,mɛrɪ'trɪʃəs/ ▶ adjective 1 apparently attractive but having in reality no value or integrity: *meretricious souvenirs for the tourist trade*. 2 archaic of, relating to, or characteristic of a prostitute.

– DERIVATIVES **meretriciously** adverb, **meretriciousness** noun.

– ORIGIN early 17th cent.: from Latin *meretricius* (adjective from *meretrix*, *meretric*- 'prostitute', from *mereri* 'be hired') + -OUS.

merganser /mɜː'gansə, -sə/ ▶ noun a fish-eating diving duck with a long, thin serrated and hooked bill. Also called SAWBILL.

● Genus *Mergus*, family Anatidae: six species, including the **red-breasted merganser** (*M. serrator*), goosander, and smew.

– ORIGIN mid 17th cent.: modern Latin, from Latin *mergus* 'diver' (from *mergere* 'to dive') + *anser* 'goose'.

merge ▶ verb combine or cause to combine to form a single entity, especially a commercial organization: [no obj.] *the merchant-banking arm of the group merged with another broker in 1995* | [with obj.] *the company plans to merge its US oil production operations with those of a London-based organization*.

■ [no obj.] blend or fade gradually into something else so as to become indistinguishable from it: *he crouched low and endeavoured to merge into the darkness of the forest*. ■ [with obj.] cause to blend or fade into something else in such a way. ■ [with obj.] (usu. **merge something in**) Law absorb (a title or estate) in another.

– ORIGIN mid 17th cent. (in the sense 'immerse (oneself)'): from Latin *mergere* 'to dip, plunge'. The use in legal contexts is from Anglo-Norman French *merger*.

merger ▶ noun a combination of two things, especially companies, into one: *a merger between two supermarket chains* | [mass noun] *local companies ripe for merger or acquisition*.

■ [mass noun] Law the merging of one estate or title in another.

– ORIGIN early 18th cent.: from Anglo-Norman French *merger* (verb used as a noun): see MERGE.

Meriç /mə'riːtʃ/ Turkish name for MARITSA.

Mérida /'mɛridə/ 1 a city in western Spain, on the Guadiana River, capital of Extremadura region; pop. 49,830 (1991). 2 a city in SE Mexico, capital of the state of Yucatán; pop. 557,340 (1990).

meridian /mə'rɪdɪən/ ▶ noun 1 a circle of constant longitude passing through a given place on the earth's surface and the terrestrial poles.

■ Astronomy a circle passing through the celestial poles and the zenith of a given place on the earth's surface. 2 (in acupuncture and Chinese medicine) each of a set of pathways in the body along which vital energy is said to flow. There are twelve such pathways associated with specific organs.

▶ adjective [attrib.] relating to or situated at a meridian: *the meridian moon*.

– ORIGIN late Middle English: from Old French *meridien*, from Latin *meridianum* (neuter, used as a noun) 'noon', from *medius* 'middle' + *dies* 'day'. The use in astronomy is due to the fact that the sun crosses a meridian at noon.

meridian circle ▶ noun Astronomy a telescope mounted so as to move only on a North–South line, for observing the transit of celestial objects across the meridian.

meridional /mə'rɪdɪən(ə)l/ ▶ adjective 1 of or in the south; southern: *the meridional leg of the journey*.

■ relating to or characteristic of the inhabitants of southern Europe, especially the South of France: *she was meridional in temperament*. 2 of or relating to a meridian: *the meridional line of demarcation*.

■ Meteorology (chiefly of winds and air flow) aligned with lines of longitude.

▶ noun a native or inhabitant of the south, especially the south of France.

– ORIGIN late Middle English: via Old French from late Latin *meridionalis*, formed irregularly from Latin *meridies* 'midday, south'.

meringue¹ /mə'raŋ/ ▶ noun an item of sweet food made from a mixture of egg whites and sugar baked until crisp and typically decorated or filled with whipped cream: *chocolate meringues* | [mass noun] *cover the pudding with meringue*.

– ORIGIN from French, of unknown origin.

meringue² /mə'raŋ/ ▶ noun variant spelling of MERENGUE.

merino /mə'riːnəʊ/ ▶ noun (pl. **-os**) (also **merino sheep**) a sheep of a breed with long, fine wool.

■ [mass noun] a soft woollen or wool-and-cotton material resembling cashmere, originally of merino wool. ■ [mass noun] a fine woollen yarn. ■ chiefly W. Indian an undershirt, originally one made of such wool.

– ORIGIN late 18th cent.: from Spanish, of unknown origin.

Merionethshire /,mɛrɪ'ɒnɪθʃɪə, -ʃə/ a former county of NW Wales. It became a part of Gwynedd in 1974.

meristem /'mɛrɪstɛm/ ▶ noun Botany a region of plant tissue, found chiefly at the growing tips of roots and shoots and in the cambium, consisting of actively dividing cells forming new tissue.

– DERIVATIVES **meristematic** /-stə'matɪk/ adjective.

– ORIGIN late 19th cent.: formed irregularly from Greek *meristos* 'divisible', from *merizein* 'divide into parts', from *meros* 'part'. The suffix -*em* is on the pattern of words such as *xylem*.

merit ▶ noun [mass noun] the quality of being particularly good or worthy, especially so as to deserve praise or reward: *composers of outstanding merit*.

■ [count noun] a feature or fact that deserves praise or reward: *the relative merits of both approaches have to be considered*. ■ [count noun] a pass grade in an examination denoting above-average performance: *if you expect to pass, why not go for a merit or a distinction?* Compare with DISTINCTION. ■ (**merits**) chiefly Law the intrinsic rights and wrongs of a case, outside of any other considerations. ■ (**merits**) Theology good deeds regarded as entitling someone to a future reward from God.

▶ verb (**merited**, **meriting**) [with obj.] deserve or be worthy of (something, especially reward, punishment, or attention): *the results have been encouraging enough to merit further investigation*.

– PHRASES **judge** (or **consider**) **something on its merits** assess something solely with regard to its intrinsic quality rather than other external factors.

– ORIGIN Middle English (originally in the sense 'deserved reward or punishment'): via Old French from Latin *meritum* 'due reward', from *mereri* 'earn, deserve'.

merit good ▶ noun (Brit. usu. **merit goods**) a commodity or service, such as education, that is regarded by society or government as good.

meritocracy /,mɛrɪ'tɒkrəsi/ ▶ noun (pl. **-ies**) [mass noun] government or the holding of power by people selected on the basis of their ability.

■ [count noun] a society governed by such people or in which such people hold power. ■ [count noun] a ruling or influential class of educated or skilled people.

– DERIVATIVES **meritocratic** /-tə'kratɪk/ adjective.

Merit, Order of see ORDER OF MERIT.

meritorious /,mɛrɪ'tɔːrɪəs/ ▶ adjective deserving reward or praise: *a medal for meritorious conduct*.

■ Law, chiefly N. Amer. (of an action or claim) likely to succeed on the merits of the case.

– DERIVATIVES **meritoriously** adverb, **meritoriousness** noun.

– ORIGIN late Middle English (in the sense 'entitling a person to reward'): from late Latin *meritorius* (from *merit*- 'earned', from the verb *mereri*) + -OUS.

merkin /'mɜːkɪn/ ▶ noun an artificial covering of hair for the pubic area.

– ORIGIN early 17th cent.: apparently a variant of dialect *malkin*, diminutive of *Malde* (early form of the given name *Maud*).

merle /mɜːl/ ▶ noun Scottish or archaic a blackbird.

– ORIGIN late Middle English: via Old French from Latin *merula*.

Merlin (in Arthurian legend) a magician who aided and supported King Arthur.

merlin ▶ noun a small dark falcon that hunts small birds, found throughout most of Eurasia and North America.

● *Falco columbarius*, family Falconidae.

– ORIGIN late Middle English: from Anglo-Norman French *merilun*, from Old French *esmerillon*, augmentative of *esmeril*, of Germanic origin; related to German *Schmerl*.

merlon /'mɜːlən/ ▶ noun the solid part of an embattled parapet between two embrasures.

– ORIGIN early 18th cent.: from French, from Italian *merlone*, from *merlo* 'battlement'.

Merlot /'mɜːləʊ, -lɒt/ ▶ noun [mass noun] a variety of black wine grape originally from the Bordeaux region of France.

■ a red wine made from this grape.

– ORIGIN French.

mermaid ▶ noun a fictitious or mythical half-human sea creature with the head and trunk of a woman and the tail of a fish, conventionally depicted as beautiful and with long flowing golden hair.

– ORIGIN Middle English: from MERE² (in the obsolete sense 'sea') + MAID.

mermaid's purse ▶ noun the horny egg case of a skate, ray, or small shark.

merman ▶ noun (pl. **-men**) the male equivalent of a mermaid.

mero- ▶ combining form partly; partial: *meronym*. Often contrasted with HOMO-.

– ORIGIN from Greek *meros* 'part'.

Meroe /'mɛrəʊi/ an ancient city on the Nile, in present-day Sudan north-east of Khartoum. Founded in *c*.750 BC, it was the capital of the ancient kingdom of Cush from *c*.590 BC until it fell to the invading Aksumites in the early 4th century AD.

– DERIVATIVES **Meroitic** adjective & noun.

meronym /'mɛrənɪm/ ▶ noun Linguistics a term which denotes part of something but which is used to refer to the whole of it, e.g. *faces* when used to mean *people* in *I see several familiar faces present*.

– DERIVATIVES **meronymy** /mə'rɒnəmi/ noun.

– ORIGIN from Greek *meros* 'part' + *onuma* 'name'.

-merous ▶ combining form Biology having a specified number of parts: *pentamerous*.

– ORIGIN on the pattern of words such as (*di*)*merous* (see also -MER).

Merovingian /,mɛrə'vɪn(d)ʒɪən/ ▶ adjective of or relating to the Frankish dynasty founded by Clovis and reigning in Gaul and Germany *c*.500–750.

▶ noun a member of this dynasty.

– ORIGIN from French *mérovingien*, from medieval Latin *Merovingi* 'descendants of Merovich' (Clovis) grandfather, semi-legendary 5th-cent. Frankish leader).

merrily ▶ adverb 1 in a cheerful way.

■ in a brisk and lively way: *a fire burned merrily in the hearth*. 2 without consideration of possible problems or future implications: *no presidential candidate can denounce high public spending while merrily buying local votes with the taxpayers' money*.

merriment ▶ noun [mass noun] gaiety and fun: *her eyes sparkled with merriment*.

merry ▶ adjective (**merrier**, **merriest**) cheerful and lively: *the narrow streets were dense with merry throngs of students* | *a merry grin*.
■ (of an occasion or season) characterized by festivity and rejoicing: *he wished me a merry Christmas*. ■ [predic.] Brit. informal slightly and good-humouredly drunk: *after the third bottle of beer he began to feel quite merry*.
– PHRASES **go on one's merry way** informal carry on with a course of action regardless of the consequences. **make merry** enjoy oneself with others by dancing and drinking. **the more the merrier** the more people or things there are, the better a situation will be.
– DERIVATIVES **merriness** noun.
– ORIGIN Old English *myrige* 'pleasing, delightful', of Germanic origin; related to **MIRTH**.

merry andrew ▶ noun archaic a person who entertains others by means of comic antics; a clown.

merry-go-round ▶ noun a revolving machine with model horses or cars on which people ride for amusement.
■ figurative a continuous cycle of activities or events, especially when perceived as having no purpose or producing no result: *the football management merry-go-round*. ■ [as modifier] Brit. denoting freight trains which deliver bulk loads (typically coal from collieries to power stations) on a continuous cycle, loading and unloading automatically while moving.

merrymaking ▶ noun [mass noun] the process of enjoying oneself with others by dancing and drinking.
– DERIVATIVES **merrymaker** noun.

merrythought ▶ noun dated, chiefly Brit. the wishbone of a bird.

Mersa Matruh /ˌmɜːsə məˈtruː/ a town on the Mediterranean coast of Egypt, 250 km (156 miles) west of Alexandria; pop. 112,770 (1990).

Mersenne number /mɜːˈsɛn/ ▶ noun Mathematics a number of the form $2^p - 1$, where *p* is a prime number. Such a number which is itself prime is also called a **Mersenne prime**.
– ORIGIN late 19th cent.: named after Marin *Mersenne* (1588–1648), French mathematician.

Mersey /ˈmɜːzi/ a river in NW England, which rises in the Peak District of Derbyshire and flows 112 km (70 miles) to the Irish Sea near Liverpool.

Merseyside a metropolitan county of NW England.

Mersin /mɜːˈsiːn/ an industrial port in southern Turkey, on the Mediterranean south-west of Adana; pop. 422,360 (1990).

Merthyr Tydfil /ˌmɜːθə ˈtɪdvɪl/ a town in South Wales, traditionally a mining area; pop. 59,300 (1990).

Meru /ˈmɛruː/ ▶ noun (pl. same or **Merus**) **1** a member of a people of central Kenya.
2 [mass noun] the Bantu language of this people, with over 1 million speakers.
▶ adjective of or relating to this people or their language.
– ORIGIN from the name of a town and district in central Kenya.

merveille du jour /mɛːˌveɪ d(j)uː ˈʒʊə/ ▶ noun a European moth with greyish-green coloration that camouflages it when at rest on lichen-covered bark.
● *Dichonia aprilina*, family Noctuidae.
– ORIGIN late 19th cent.: from French, literally 'wonder of the day'.

mesa /ˈmeɪsə/ ▶ noun an isolated flat-topped hill with steep sides, found in landscapes with horizontal strata.
– ORIGIN mid 18th cent.: Spanish, literally 'table', from Latin *mensa*.

mésalliance /meˈzalɪəns/ ▶ noun a marriage with a person thought to be unsuitable or of a lower social position.
– ORIGIN French, from *més-* 'wrong, misdirected' + *alliance* (see **ALLIANCE**).

Mesa Verde /ˌmeɪsə ˈvɜːdi/ a high plateau in southern Colorado, with the remains of many prehistoric Pueblo Indian dwellings.
– ORIGIN Spanish, literally 'green table(land)'.

mescal /ˈmɛskal, mɛˈskal/ ▶ noun **1** another term for **MAGUEY**.
■ [mass noun] an intoxicating liquor distilled from the sap of an agave. Compare with **TEQUILA, PULQUE**.
2 another term for **PEYOTE**.

– ORIGIN early 18th cent.: from Spanish *mezcal*, from Nahuatl *mexcalli*.

mescal buttons ▶ plural noun another term for **PEYOTE BUTTONS**.

mescaline /ˈmɛskəlɪn, -liːn/ (also **mescalin** /-lɪn/) ▶ noun [mass noun] a hallucinogenic and intoxicating compound present in mescal buttons.
● Alternative name: **3,4,5-trimethoxyphenethylamine**; chem. formula: $(CH_3O)_3C_6H_2CH_2CH_2NH_2$.

mesclun /ˈmɛsklən/ ▶ noun [mass noun] a Provençal green salad made from a selection of lettuces with other edible leaves and flowers.
– ORIGIN Provençal, literally 'mixture', from *mesclar* 'mix thoroughly'.

Mesdames /meɪˈdɑːm, -ˈdam/ ▶ plural noun **1** plural form of **MADAME**.
2 formal used as a title to refer to more than one woman simultaneously: *prizes were won by Mesdames Carter, Roseby, and Barrington*.

Mesdemoiselles /meɪd-, French med-/ plural form of **MADEMOISELLE**.

meself ▶ pronoun non-standard spelling of **MYSELF**, used as a representation of informal speech.

mesembryanthemum /mɪˌzɛmbrɪˈanθɪməm/ ▶ noun a succulent South African plant of a genus that contains, or formerly contained, the ice plants, Livingstone daisy, Hottentot fig, and pigface.
● *Mesembryanthemum* and related genera, family Aizoaceae.
– ORIGIN modern Latin, based on Greek *mesēmbria* 'noon' + *anthemon* 'flower'.

mesencephalon /ˌmɛsɛnˈsɛf(ə)lɒn, ˌmiːz-, -ˈkɛf-/ ▶ noun Anatomy another term for **MIDBRAIN**.
– DERIVATIVES **mesencephalic** adjective.
– ORIGIN mid 19th cent.: from Greek *mesos* 'middle' + **ENCEPHALON**.

mesenchyme /ˈmɛsɛnkaɪm, ˈmiːz-/ ▶ noun [mass noun] Embryology a loosely organized, mainly mesodermal embryonic tissue which develops into connective and skeletal tissues, including blood and lymph.
– DERIVATIVES **mesenchymal** adjective.
– ORIGIN late 19th cent.: from Greek *mesos* 'middle' + *enkhuma* 'infusion'.

mesenteron /mɪˈsɛntərɒn/ ▶ noun Zoology the middle section of the intestine, especially in an embryo or in an arthropod.
– ORIGIN late 19th cent.: from Greek *mesos* 'middle' + *enteron* 'intestine'.

mesentery /ˈmɛs(ə)nt(ə)ri/ ▶ noun (pl. **-ies**) Anatomy a fold of the peritoneum which attaches the stomach, small intestine, pancreas, spleen, and other organs to the posterior wall of the abdomen.
– DERIVATIVES **mesenteric** adjective.
– ORIGIN late Middle English: via medieval Latin from Greek *mesenterion*, from *mesos* 'middle' + *enteron* 'intestine'.

mesh ▶ noun **1** [mass noun] material made of a network of wire or thread: *mesh for fishing nets* | [count noun] *finer wire meshes are used for smaller particles*.
■ the spacing of the strands of such material: *if the mesh is too big, small rabbits can squeeze through*.
2 an interlaced structure: *cell fragments which agglutinate and form intricate meshes*.
■ [in sing.] figurative used with reference to a complex or constricting situation: *the ravelled mesh of events and her own emotions*. ■ Computing a set of finite elements used to represent a geometric object for modelling or analysis. ■ Computing a computer network in which each computer or processor is connected to a number of others, especially as an n-dimensional lattice.
▶ verb **1** [no obj.] (of the teeth of a gearwheel) lock together or be engaged with another gearwheel: *one gear meshes with the input gear*.
■ make or become entangled or entwined: [no obj.] *their fingers meshed* | [with obj.] *I don't want to get meshed in the weeds*. ■ figurative be or bring into harmony: [no obj.] *her memory of events doesn't mesh with the world around her*.
2 [with obj.] represent a geometric object as a set of finite elements for computational analysis or modelling.
– PHRASES **in mesh** (of the teeth of gearwheels) engaged.
– DERIVATIVES **meshed** adjective.
– ORIGIN late Middle English: probably from an unrecorded Old English word related to (and perhaps reinforced in Middle English by) Middle Dutch *maesche*, of Germanic origin.

Meshed /məˈʃɛd/ variant of **MASHHAD**.

meshuga /mɪˈʃʊɡə/ (also **meshugga**) ▶ adjective informal, chiefly N. Amer. (of a person) mad; idiotic: *either a miracle is taking place, or we're all meshuga*.
– ORIGIN late 19th cent.: from Yiddish *meshuge*, from Hebrew.

meshugaas /mɪˈʃʊɡɑːs/ ▶ noun [mass noun] informal, chiefly N. Amer. mad or idiotic ideas or behaviour: *there's method in this man's meshugaas*.
– ORIGIN early 20th cent.: Yiddish, noun from **MESHUGA**.

meshuggener /mɪˈʃʊɡənə/ ▶ noun informal, chiefly N. Amer. a mad or idiotic person.
– ORIGIN early 20th cent.: variant of **MESHUGA**.

mesia /ˈmiːzɪə/ (also **silver-eared mesia**) ▶ noun a SE Asian bird of the babbler family, the male having red and yellow plumage with a black-and-white head.
● *Leiothrix argentauris*, family Timaliidae.
– ORIGIN modern Latin (former genus name).

mesial /ˈmiːzɪəl/ ▶ adjective Anatomy of, in, or directed towards the middle line of a body.
– DERIVATIVES **mesially** adverb.
– ORIGIN early 19th cent.: formed irregularly from Greek *mesos* 'middle' + **-IAL**.

mesic[1] /ˈmiːzɪk, ˈmɛzɪk/ ▶ adjective Ecology (of an environment or habitat) containing a moderate amount of moisture. Compare with **HYDRIC** and **XERIC**.
– ORIGIN 1920s: from Greek *mesos* 'middle' + **-IC**.

mesic[2] /ˈmiːzɪk, ˈmɛzɪk/ ▶ adjective Physics of or relating to a meson.
■ denoting a system analogous to an atom in which a meson takes the place of either an orbital electron or the nucleus.

mesite /ˈmɛzɪt/ ▶ noun a small endangered ground-dwelling bird found in Madagascar, resembling a thrush but related to the button-quails.
● Family Mesitornithidae: two genera, in particular *Mesitornis*, and three species.
– ORIGIN from French *mésite*, from a Malagasy word.

Mesmer /ˈmɛzmə/, Franz Anton (1734–1815), Austrian physician. Mesmer is chiefly remembered for introducing a therapeutic technique involving hypnotism; it was bound up with his ideas about 'animal magnetism', however, and steeped in sensationalism.

mesmeric /mɛzˈmɛrɪk/ ▶ adjective causing a person to become completely transfixed and unaware of anything else around them: *she found herself staring into his mesmeric gaze*.
■ archaic of, relating to, or produced by mesmerism.
– DERIVATIVES **mesmerically** adverb.

mesmerism ▶ noun [mass noun] historical the therapeutic system of F. A. Mesmer.
■ (in general use) hypnotism.
– DERIVATIVES **mesmerist** noun.
– ORIGIN late 18th cent.: named after F. A. **MESMER**.

mesmerize (also **-ise**) ▶ verb [with obj.] (often be **mesmerized**) hold the attention of (someone) to the exclusion of all else or so as to transfix them: *she was mesmerized by the blue eyes that stared so intently into her own* | [as adj. **mesmerizing**] *a mesmerizing stare*.
■ archaic hypnotize (someone).
– DERIVATIVES **mesmerization** noun, **mesmerizer** noun, **mesmerizingly** adverb.

mesne /miːn/ ▶ adjective Law intermediate.
– ORIGIN late Middle English (as adverb and noun): from Old French, variant of Anglo-Norman French *meen* 'middle' (see **MEAN**[3]).

mesne lord ▶ noun Brit. historical a lord holding an estate from a superior feudal lord.

mesne profits ▶ plural noun Law the profits of an estate received by a tenant in wrongful possession and recoverable by the landlord.

meso- /ˈmɛsəʊ, ˈmɛzəʊ, ˈmiːsəʊ, ˈmiːzəʊ/ ▶ combining form middle; intermediate: *mesoblast* | *mesomorph*.
– ORIGIN from Greek *mesos* 'middle'.

Meso-America the central region of America, from central Mexico to Nicaragua, especially as a region of ancient civilizations and native cultures before the arrival of the Spanish.
– DERIVATIVES **Meso-American** adjective & noun.

mesoblast /ˈmɛsə(ʊ)blast, ˈmɛz-, ˈmiːs-, ˈmiːz-/ ▶ noun Embryology the mesoderm of an embryo in its earliest stages.

mesocarp ▶ noun Botany the middle layer of the

pericarp of a fruit, between the endocarp and the exocarp.

mesocephalic /ˌmɛsə(ʊ)sɪˈfalɪk, ˌmɛz-, ˌmiːs-, ˌmiːz-, -kɛ-/ ▶ **adjective** Anatomy having a head of medium proportions, not markedly brachycephalic or dolichocephalic.

mesoderm ▶ **noun** [mass noun] Embryology the middle layer of an embryo in early development, between the endoderm and ectoderm.
– DERIVATIVES **mesodermal** adjective.
– ORIGIN late 19th cent.: from **MESO-** 'middle' + Greek *derma* 'skin'.

mesofauna ▶ **noun** [mass noun] Ecology soil animals of intermediate size, such as earthworms, arthropods, nematodes, and molluscs.

mesogastrium ▶ **noun** (pl. **mesogastria**) Anatomy the middle region of the abdomen between the epigastrium and the hypogastrium.
– DERIVATIVES **mesogastric** adjective.
– ORIGIN mid 19th cent.: modern Latin, from **MESO-** 'middle' + Greek *gastēr, gastr-* 'stomach'.

mesokurtic /ˌmɛsəʊˈkəːtɪk, ˌmɛz-, ˌmiːs-, ˌmiːz-/ ▶ **adjective** Statistics (of a frequency distribution or its graphical representation) having the same kurtosis as the normal distribution. Compare with **LEPTOKURTIC, PLATYKURTIC.**
– DERIVATIVES **mesokurtosis** noun.
– ORIGIN early 20th cent.: from **MESO-** 'middle' + Greek *kurtos* 'bulging' + **-IC**.

Mesolithic ▶ **adjective** Archaeology of, relating to, or denoting the middle part of the Stone Age, between the Palaeolithic and Neolithic.
■ [as noun **the Mesolithic**] the Mesolithic period. Also called **MIDDLE STONE AGE.**

In Europe, the Mesolithic falls between the end of the last glacial period (*c*.8500 BC) and the beginnings of agriculture. Mesolithic people lived by hunting, gathering, and fishing, and the period is characterized by the use of microliths and the first domestication of an animal (the dog).

– ORIGIN mid 19th cent.: from **MESO-** 'middle' + Greek *lithos* 'stone' + **-IC**.

Mesolóngion /ˌmɛsəˈlɒŋɡɪɒn/ Greek name for **MISSOLONGHI.**

mesomerism /mɪˈsɒmərɪz(ə)m, mɪˈzɒm-/ ▶ **noun** Chemistry old-fashioned term for **RESONANCE.**
– DERIVATIVES **mesomeric** adjective.

mesomorph ▶ **noun** Physiology a person whose build is compact and muscular. Compare with **ECTOMORPH** and **ENDOMORPH.**
– DERIVATIVES **mesomorphic** adjective.
– ORIGIN 1920s: *meso-* from *mesodermal* (being the layer of the embryo giving rise to physical characteristics which predominate) + **-MORPH**.

meson /ˈmiːzɒn, ˈmɛzɒn/ ▶ **noun** Physics a subatomic particle which is intermediate in mass between an electron and a proton and transmits the strong interaction that binds nucleons together in the atomic nucleus.
– DERIVATIVES **mesonic** /mɪˈzɒnɪk/ adjective.
– ORIGIN 1930s: from **MESO-** 'intermediate' + **-ON**.

mesopause ▶ **noun** the boundary in the earth's atmosphere between the mesosphere and the thermosphere, at which the temperature stops decreasing with increasing height and begins to increase.

mesopelagic /ˌmɛsə(ʊ)pɪˈladʒɪk, ˌmɛz-, ˌmiːs-, ˌmiːz-/ ▶ **adjective** Biology (of fish and other organisms) inhabiting the intermediate depths of the sea, between about 200 and 1,000 metres (approximately 650 and 3,300 ft) down.

mesophyll ▶ **noun** [mass noun] Botany the inner tissue (parenchyma) of a leaf, containing many chloroplasts.
– ORIGIN mid 19th cent.: from **MESO-** 'middle' + Greek *phullon* 'leaf'.

mesophyte ▶ **noun** Botany a plant needing only a moderate amount of water.
– DERIVATIVES **mesophytic** adjective.

Mesopotamia /ˌmɛsəpəˈteɪmɪə/ an ancient region of SW Asia in present-day Iraq, lying between the rivers Tigris and Euphrates. Its alluvial plains were the site of the civilizations of Akkad, Sumer, Babylonia, and Assyria.
– DERIVATIVES **Mesopotamian** adjective & noun.
– ORIGIN from Greek *mesos* 'middle' + *potamos* 'river'.

mesosaur ▶ **noun** an extinct small aquatic reptile of the early Permian period, with an elongated body, flattened tail, and a long narrow snout with numerous needle-like teeth.
● Genus *Mesosaurus*, order Mesosauria, subclass Anapsida.
– ORIGIN 1950s: modern Latin, from Greek *mesos* 'middle' + *sauros* 'lizard'.

mesoscale ▶ **noun** chiefly Meteorology an intermediate scale, especially that between the scales of weather systems and of microclimates, on which storms and other phenomena occur.

mesosphere ▶ **noun** the region of the earth's atmosphere above the stratosphere and below the thermosphere, between about 50 and 80 km in altitude.

mesothelioma /ˌmɛsə(ʊ)ˌθiːlɪˈəʊmə, ˌmɛz-, ˌmiːs-, ˌmiːz-/ ▶ **noun** [mass noun] Medicine a cancer of mesothelial tissue, associated especially with exposure to asbestos.

mesothelium /ˌmɛsə(ʊ)ˈθiːlɪəm, ˌmɛz-, ˌmiːs-, ˌmiːz-/ ▶ **noun** (pl. **mesothelia**) [mass noun] Anatomy the epithelium that lines the pleurae, peritoneum, and pericardium.
■ Embryology the surface layer of the embryonic mesoderm, from which this is derived.
– DERIVATIVES **mesothelial** adjective.
– ORIGIN late 19th cent.: from **MESO-** 'middle' + a shortened form of **EPITHELIUM.**

mesothorax ▶ **noun** Entomology the middle segment of the thorax of an insect, bearing the forewings or elytra.
– DERIVATIVES **mesothoracic** adjective.

mesozoan /ˌmɛsəˈzəʊən, ˌmiːz-/ ▶ **noun** Zoology a minute worm which is an internal parasite of marine invertebrates. It lacks any internal organs other than reproductive cells, and dissolved nutrients are absorbed directly from the host's tissues.
● Phyla Orthonectida and Rhombozoa; formerly placed together in the phylum Mesozoa, which was thought to be intermediate between protozoans and metazoans.
– ORIGIN early 20th cent.: from modern Latin *Mesozoa* (from *mesos* 'intermediate' + *zōion* 'animal') + **-AN**.

Mesozoic /ˌmɛsə(ʊ)ˈzəʊɪk, ˌmɛz-, ˌmiːs-, ˌmiːz-/ ▶ **adjective** Geology of, relating to, or denoting the era between the Palaeozoic and Cenozoic eras, comprising the Triassic, Jurassic, and Cretaceous periods.
■ [as noun **the Mesozoic**] the Mesozoic era or the system of rocks deposited during it.

The Mesozoic lasted from about 245 to 65 million years ago. Large reptiles were dominant on land and sea throughout this time, vegetation had become abundant, and the first mammals, birds, and flowering plants appeared.

– ORIGIN mid 19th cent.: from **MESO-** 'intermediate' + Greek *zōion* 'animal' (referring to the appearance of the first mammals) + **-IC**.

mespilus /ˈmɛspɪləs/ ▶ **noun** see **SNOWY MESPILUS.**

mesquite /ˈmɛskiːt, mɛˈskiːt/ ▶ **noun** a spiny tree or shrub of the pea family, native to arid regions of south-western US and Mexico. It yields useful timber, tanbark, medicinal products, and edible pods.
● Genus *Prosopis*, family Leguminosae: several species, in particular *P. glandulosa*.
– ORIGIN mid 18th cent.: from Mexican Spanish *mezquite*.

mesquite bean ▶ **noun** an edible pod from the mesquite, which can be eaten whole, used to produce flour, or fed to animals.

mess ▶ **noun** [usu. in sing.] **1** a dirty or untidy state of things or of a place: *she made a mess of the kitchen | my hair was a mess.*
■ a thing or collection of things causing such a state: *she replaced the jug and mopped up the mess.* ■ a person who is dirty or untidy: *I look a mess.* ■ a portion of semi-solid or pulpy food, especially one that looks unappetizing: *a mess of mashed black beans and rice.* ■ [with modifier] used euphemistically to refer to the excrement of a domestic animal: *dog mess.* ■ figurative a situation or state of affairs that is confused or full of difficulties: *the economy is still in a terrible mess.* ■ figurative a person whose life or affairs are confused or troubled: *he needs treatment of some kind—he's a real mess.*
2 a building or room in which members of the armed forces take their meals: *the sergeants' mess.*
▶ **verb 1** [with obj.] make untidy or dirty: *you've messed up my beautiful carpet.*
■ [no obj.] (of a domestic animal) defecate: *they had some problems with dogs messing in the store.* ■ make dirty by defecating: *he feared he would mess the bed.*
2 [no obj., with adverbial] take one's meals in a particular place or with a particular person, especially in an armed forces' mess: *I messed at first with Harry, who was to become a lifelong friend | they messed together.*
– PHRASES **mess with someone's head** US informal cause someone to feel frustrated, anxious, or upset.
– ORIGIN Middle English: from Old French *mes* 'portion of food', from late Latin *missum* 'something put on the table', past participle of *mittere* 'send, put'. The original sense was 'a serving of food', also 'a serving of liquid or pulpy food', later 'liquid food for an animal'; this gave rise (early 19th cent.) to the senses 'unappetizing concoction' and 'predicament', on which sense 1 is based. In late Middle English the term also denoted any of the small groups into which the company at a banquet was divided (who were served from the same dishes); hence, 'a group who regularly eat together' (recorded in military use from the mid 16th cent.).
▶ **mess about/around** behave in a silly or playful way, especially so as to cause irritation. ■ spend time doing something in a pleasantly desultory way, with no definite purpose or serious intent: *messing about in boats.*
mess about/around with interfere with: *the minister messed around with health, and look at the state we are in.* ■ informal engage in a sexual relationship with (someone, especially the partner of another person).
mess someone about/around Brit. informal cause someone inconvenience or problems, especially by acting unfairly or indecisively.
mess up informal mishandle a situation: *he singled out the pit closures fiasco as an example of how the government has messed up.*
mess someone up informal cause someone emotional or psychological problems: *I was unhappy and really messed up.* ■ chiefly US inflict violence or injury on someone: *the wreck messed him up so much that he can't walk.*
mess something up informal cause something to be spoiled by inept handling: *an error like that could easily mess up an entire day's work.*
mess with informal meddle or interfere with so as to spoil or cause trouble: *stop messing with things you don't understand.*

message ▶ **noun 1** a verbal, written, or recorded communication sent to or left for a recipient who cannot be contacted directly: *if I'm not there leave a message on the answerphone.*
■ (also **mail message**) an item of electronic mail. ■ an electronic communication generated automatically by a computer program and displayed on a VDU: *an error message.* ■ a significant point or central theme, especially one that has political, social, or moral importance: *a campaign to get the message about home security across.* ■ a divinely inspired communication from a prophet or preacher.
2 Scottish & Irish an errand: *he would run those interminable messages after school to the pub or the bookie.*
■ (**messages**) things bought on an errand; shopping.
– PHRASES **get the message** informal infer an implication from a remark or action. **send a message** make a significant statement, either implicitly or by one's actions: *the elections sent a message to political quarters that the party was riding a wave of popularity.*
– ORIGIN Middle English: from Old French, based on Latin *missus*, past participle of *mittere* 'send'.

message box ▶ **noun** Computing a small box that appears on a computer screen to inform the user of something, such as the occurrence of an error.

message stick ▶ **noun** (among Australian Aboriginals) a piece of wood carved with symbolic patterns which convey a message from one community to another, and which may also identify the bearer.

message switching ▶ **noun** [mass noun] Computing & Telecommunications a mode of data transmission in which a message is sent as a complete unit and routed via a number of intermediate nodes at which it is stored and then forwarded.

messaging ▶ **noun** [mass noun] the sending and processing of electronic mail by computer.

Messalina /ˌmɛsəˈliːnə/ (also **Messallina**), Valeria (*c*.22–48 AD), Roman empress, third wife of

Claudius. She became notorious in Rome for the murders she instigated in court and for her extramarital affairs, and was executed on Claudius' orders.

Messeigneurs plural form of **MONSEIGNEUR**.

messenger ▶ **noun** a person who carries a message or is employed to carry messages.
▪ Biochemistry a substance that conveys information or a stimulus within the body.
▶ **verb** [with obj. and adverbial of direction] chiefly US send (a document or package) by messenger: *could you have it messengered over to me?*
– PHRASES **shoot** (or **kill**) **the messenger** treat the bearer of bad news as if they were to blame for it.
– ORIGIN Middle English: from Old Northern French *messanger*, variant of Old French *messager*, from Latin *missus* (see **MESSAGE**).

messenger RNA (abbrev.: **mRNA**) ▶ **noun** [mass noun] the form of RNA in which genetic information transcribed from DNA as a sequence of bases is transferred to a ribosome.

Messerschmidt /ˈmɛsəˌʃmɪt, German ˈmɛsɐˌʃmɪt/, Willy (1898–1978), German aircraft designer and industrialist; full name *Wilhelm Emil Messerschmidt*. He designed and constructed his first glider in 1915 and set up a company in 1923. The Messerschmidt 109 became the standard fighter of the Luftwaffe during the Second World War.

mess hall ▶ **noun** chiefly N. Amer. a room or building where soldiers or other groups of people eat together.

Messiaen /ˈmɛsiã, French mɛsjɑ̃/, Olivier (Eugène Prosper Charles) (1908–92), French composer. His music was influenced by Greek and Hindu rhythms, birdsong, Stravinsky and Debussy, and the composer's Roman Catholic faith. Notable works: *Quartet for the End of Time* (1941).

messiah /mɪˈsʌɪə/ ▶ **noun** **1** (**the Messiah**) the promised deliverer of the Jewish nation prophesied in the Hebrew Bible.
▪ Jesus regarded by Christians as the Messiah of the Hebrew prophecies and the saviour of humankind.
2 a leader or saviour of a particular group or cause: *to Germany, Hitler was more a messiah than a political leader.*
– DERIVATIVES **messiahship** noun.
– ORIGIN Old English *Messias*: via late Latin and Greek from Hebrew *māšîaḥ* 'anointed'.

messianic /ˌmɛsɪˈanɪk/ ▶ **adjective** of or relating to the Messiah: *the messianic role of Jesus.*
▪ inspired by hope or belief in a messiah: *the messianic expectations of that time.* ▪ fervent or passionate: *an admirable messianic zeal.*
– DERIVATIVES **messianism** /mɪˈsʌɪənɪz(ə)m/ noun.
– ORIGIN mid 19th cent.: from French *messianique*, from *Messie* (see **MESSIAH**), on the pattern of *rabbinique* 'rabbinical'.

Messidor /ˈmɛsɪdɔː, French mɛsidɔʀ/ ▶ **noun** the tenth month of the French Republican calendar (1793–1805), originally running from 19 June to 18 July.
– ORIGIN French, from Latin *messis* 'harvest' + Greek *dōron* 'gift'.

Messier /ˈmɛsɪə, French mɛsje/, Charles (1730–1817), French astronomer. He discovered a number of nebulae, galaxies, and star clusters, which he designated by M numbers. Almost all of these designations, such as M1 (the Crab Nebula), are still in use today.

Messieurs plural form of **MONSIEUR**.

Messina /mɛˈsiːnə/ a city in NE Sicily; pop. 274,850 (1990). Founded in 730 BC by the Greeks, it is situated on the Strait of Messina.

Messina, Strait of a channel separating the island of Sicily from the 'toe' of Italy. It forms a link between the Tyrrhenian and Ionian seas. The strait, which is 32 km (20 miles) in length, is noted for the strength of its currents.

mess jacket ▶ **noun** a short jacket worn by a military officer on formal occasions in the mess.

mess kit ▶ **noun** **1** the uniform worn by a military officer on formal occasions in the mess.
2 a soldier's cooking and eating utensils.

messmate ▶ **noun** (in the navy) a person with whom one shares communal accommodation.

Messrs ▶ **plural noun** used as a title to refer formally to more than one man simultaneously, or in names of companies: *Messrs Sotheby.*
– ORIGIN late 18th cent.: abbreviation of **MESSIEURS**.

mess tin ▶ **noun** Brit. a rectangular metal dish with a folding handle, used by soldiers for cooking and for eating or drinking out of.

messuage /ˈmɛswɪdʒ/ ▶ **noun** Law a dwelling house with outbuildings and land assigned to its use.
– ORIGIN late Middle English: from Anglo-Norman French, based on Latin *manere* 'dwell'.

messy ▶ **adjective** (**messier**, **messiest**) **1** untidy or dirty: *his messy hair.*
▪ generating or involving mess or untidiness: *stripping wallpaper can be a messy, time-consuming job.*
2 (of a situation) confused and difficult to deal with: *a messy divorce.*
– DERIVATIVES **messily** adverb, **messiness** noun.

mestiza /mɛˈstiːzə, Spanish mesˈtisa, -ˈtiθa/ ▶ **noun** (in Latin America) a woman of mixed race, especially the offspring of a Spaniard and an American Indian.
– ORIGIN Spanish, feminine of *mestizo* (see **MESTIZO**).

mestizo /mɛˈstiːzəʊ, Spanish mesˈtiso, -ˈtiθo/ ▶ **noun** (pl. **-os**) (in Latin America) a man of mixed race, especially the offspring of a Spaniard and an American Indian.
– ORIGIN Spanish 'mixed', based on Latin *mixtus*.

Met informal ▶ **abbreviation for** ▪ meteorological: *a Met report.* ▪ (also **the Met Office**) the Meteorological Office in the UK. ▪ metropolitan: *the Met county abolition.* ▪ (**the Met**) [treated as sing. or pl.] the Metropolitan Police in London. ▪ (**the Met**) the Metropolitan Opera House in New York. ▪ (**the Met**) the Metropolitan Museum of Art in New York.

met past and past participle of **MEET**[1].

met- ▶ **combining form** variant spelling of **META-** shortened before a vowel or *h* (as in *metonym*).

meta- (also **met-** before a vowel or h) ▶ **combining form** **1** denoting a change of position or condition: *metamorphosis.*
2 denoting position behind, after, or beyond: *metacarpus.*
3 denoting something of a higher or second-order kind: *metalanguage* | *metonym.*
4 Chemistry denoting substitution at two carbon atoms separated by one other in a benzene ring, e.g. in 1,3 positions: *metadichlorobenzene.* Compare with **ORTHO-** and **PARA-**[1].
5 Chemistry denoting a compound formed by dehydration: *metaphosphoric acid.*
– ORIGIN from Greek *meta* 'with, across, or after'.

metabolic pathway ▶ **noun** see **PATHWAY**.

metabolism /mɪˈtabəlɪz(ə)m/ ▶ **noun** [mass noun] the chemical processes that occur within a living organism in order to maintain life.

> Two kinds of metabolism are often distinguished: **constructive metabolism**, the synthesis of the proteins, carbohydrates, and fats which form tissue and store energy, and **destructive metabolism**, the breakdown of complex substances and the consequent production of energy and waste matter.

– DERIVATIVES **metabolic** /ˌmɛtəˈbɒlɪk/ adjective, **metabolically** adverb.
– ORIGIN late 19th cent.: from Greek *metabolē* 'change' (from *metaballein* 'to change') + **-ISM**.

metabolite /mɪˈtabəlʌɪt/ ▶ **noun** Biochemistry a substance formed in or necessary for metabolism.

metabolize (also **-ise**) ▶ **verb** [with obj.] (of a body or organ) process (a substance) by metabolism.
▪ [no obj.] (of a substance) undergo processing by metabolism: *the refined foods soon metabolize.*
– DERIVATIVES **metabolizable** adjective, **metabolizer** noun.

metacarpal ▶ **noun** any of the five bones of the hand.
▪ any of the equivalent bones in an animal's forelimb.
▶ **adjective** of or relating to these bones.

metacarpus ▶ **noun** (pl. **metacarpi**) the group of five bones of the hand between the wrist (carpus) and the fingers.
▪ this part of the hand.
– ORIGIN late Middle English: modern Latin, alteration of Greek *metakarpion*.

metacentre (US **metacenter**) ▶ **noun** the point of intersection between a vertical line through the centre of buoyancy of a floating body such as a ship and a vertical line through the new centre of buoyancy when the body is tilted, which must be above the centre of gravity to ensure stability.
– DERIVATIVES **metacentric** adjective.
– ORIGIN late 18th cent.: from French *métacentre* (see **META-**, **CENTRE**).

metachromasia /ˌmɛtəkrə(ʊ)ˈmeɪzɪə/ (also **metachromasy** /-ˈkrəʊməsi/) ▶ **noun** [mass noun] Biology the property of certain biological materials of staining a different colour from that of the stain used.
▪ the property of certain stains of changing colour in the presence of certain biological materials.
– DERIVATIVES **metachromatic** adjective.
– ORIGIN early 20th cent.: modern Latin, from **META-** (expressing change) + Greek *khrōma* 'colour'.

metachrosis /ˌmɛtəˈkrəʊsɪs/ ▶ **noun** [mass noun] Zoology the ability of chameleons and some other animals to change colour.
– ORIGIN late 19th cent.: modern Latin, from **META-** (denoting a change of condition) + Greek *khrōsis* 'colouring'.

metacognition ▶ **noun** [mass noun] Psychology awareness and understanding of one's own thought processes.
– DERIVATIVES **metacognitive** adjective.

metafiction ▶ **noun** [mass noun] fiction in which the author self-consciously alludes to the artificiality or literariness of a work by parodying or departing from novelistic conventions (especially naturalism) and traditional narrative techniques.
– DERIVATIVES **metafictional** adjective.

metafile ▶ **noun** Computing a piece of graphical information stored in a format that can be exchanged between different systems or software.

metage /ˈmiːtɪdʒ/ ▶ **noun** [mass noun] the official weighing of loads of coal, grain, or other material.
▪ the duty paid for this.
– ORIGIN early 16th cent.: from **METE**[1] + **-AGE**.

metagenesis /ˌmɛtəˈdʒɛnɪsɪs/ ▶ **noun** [mass noun] Biology the alternation of generations between sexual and asexual reproduction.
– ORIGIN late 19th cent.: modern Latin.

metal ▶ **noun** [mass noun] **1** a solid material which is typically hard, shiny, malleable, fusible, and ductile, with good electrical and thermal conductivity (e.g. iron, gold, silver, copper, and aluminium, and alloys such as brass and steel): *vessels made of ceramics or metal* | [count noun] *being a metal, aluminium readily conducts heat.*
▪ (**metals**) the steel tracks of a railway. ▪ Heraldry gold and silver (as tinctures in blazoning).
2 (also **road metal**) broken stone for use in road-making.
3 molten glass before it is blown or cast.
4 heavy metal or similar rock music.
▶ **verb** (**metalled**, **metalling**; N. Amer. **metaled**, **metaling**) [with obj.] [usu. as adj. **metalled**] **1** make out of or coat with metal: *a range of metalled key rings.*
2 Brit. make or mend (a road) with road metal: *follow the metalled road for about 200 yards.*
– ORIGIN Middle English: from Old French *metal* or Latin *metallum*, from Greek *metallon* 'mine, quarry, or metal'.

metalanguage ▶ **noun** a form of language or set of terms used for the description or analysis of another language. Compare with **OBJECT LANGUAGE** (in sense 1).
▪ Logic a system of propositions about propositions.

metaldehyde /mɪˈtaldɪhʌɪd/ ▶ **noun** [mass noun] Chemistry a solid made by polymerizing acetaldehyde. It is used in slug pellets and as a fuel for portable stoves.
• Chem. formula: $C_4H_4O_4(CH_3)_4$.

metal detector ▶ **noun** an electronic device that gives an audible or other signal when it is close to metal, used for example to search for buried objects or to detect hidden weapons.

metalflake ▶ **noun** [mass noun] [usu. as modifier] trademark a metallized film added to paint to increase protection against rust.

metalinguistics ▶ **plural noun** [treated as sing.] the branch of linguistics that deals with metalanguages.
– DERIVATIVES **metalinguistic** adjective.

metallic ▶ **adjective** of, relating to, or resembling metal or metals: *metallic alloys* | *a curious metallic taste.*
▪ (of sound) resembling that produced by metal objects striking each other; sharp and ringing: *the terrifying, metallic clamour of the fire-engine bell.* ▪ (of a person's voice); emanating or as if emanating via an electronic medium: *a metallic voice rasped tinnily from*

a concealed speaker. ■ having the sheen or lustre of metal: *a beautiful metallic green sports car.*
▶ **noun** (usu. **metallics**) an article or substance made of or containing metal: *metallics can be recycled.* ■ a paint, fabric, or colour with a metallic sheen.
– DERIVATIVES **metallically** adverb.
– ORIGIN late Middle English: via Latin from Greek *metallikos*, from *metallon* (see **METAL**).

metallicity ▶ **noun** (pl. **-ies**) [mass noun] the property of being metallic. ■ Astronomy the proportion of the material of a star or other celestial object that is an element other than hydrogen or helium.

metalliferous ▶ **adjective** (chiefly of deposits of minerals) containing or producing metal.
– ORIGIN mid 17th cent.: from Latin *metallifer* 'metal-bearing' + **-OUS**.

metalline /ˈmɛtəlʌɪn/ ▶ **adjective** rare metallic.

metallize (also **-ise**, US also **metalize**) ▶ **verb** [with obj.] coat with a thin layer of metal. ■ make metallic in form or appearance.
– DERIVATIVES **metallization** noun.

metallogenic /mɪˌtalə(ʊ)ˈdʒɛnɪk, ˈmɛt(ə)lə(ʊ)-/ ▶ **adjective** Geology of or relating to the formation or occurrence of deposits of metals or their ores.

metallography /ˌmɛtəˈlɒɡrəfi/ ▶ **noun** [mass noun] the descriptive science of the structure and properties of metals.
– DERIVATIVES **metallographic** adjective, **metallographical** adjective, **metallographically** adverb.

metalloid ▶ **noun** another term for **SEMIMETAL**.

metallophone /mɪˈtalə(ʊ)fəʊn, ˈmɛt(ə)lə(ʊ)-/ ▶ **noun** a musical instrument in which the sound is produced by striking metal bars of varying pitches.

metallurgy /mɪˈtalədʒi, ˈmɛt(ə)ˌləːdʒi/ ▶ **noun** [mass noun] the branch of science and technology concerned with the properties of metals and their production and purification.
– DERIVATIVES **metallurgic** /ˌmɛtəˈləːdʒɪk/ adjective, **metallurgical** adjective, **metallurgically** adverb, **metallurgist** noun.
– ORIGIN early 18th cent.: from Greek *metallon* 'metal' + *-ourgia* 'working'.

metalmark ▶ **noun** a butterfly with brilliant metallic markings on the wings, found chiefly in tropical America.
• Family Riodinidae: several genera.

metalware ▶ **noun** [mass noun] (also **metalwares**) utensils or other articles made of metal.

metalwork ▶ **noun** [mass noun] the art of making things out of metal. ■ metal objects collectively: *a wealth of fine metalwork, including a sword.* ■ the metal part of a construction: *engineers spotted cracks in the metalwork.*
– DERIVATIVES **metalworker** noun, **metalworking** noun.

metamathematics ▶ **plural noun** [usu. treated as sing.] the field of study that deals with the structure and formal properties of mathematics and similar formal systems.
– DERIVATIVES **metamathematical** adjective, **metamathematically** adverb, **metamathematician** noun.

metamere /ˈmɛtəmɪə/ ▶ **noun** Zoology another term for **SOMITE**.
– ORIGIN late 19th cent.: from **META-** 'together with' + Greek *meros* 'part'.

metameric /ˌmɛtəˈmɛrɪk/ ▶ **adjective** **1** Zoology of, relating to, or consisting of several similar segments or somites.
2 Chemistry, dated having the same proportional composition and molecular weight, but different functional groups and chemical properties; isomeric.
– DERIVATIVES **metamer** /ˈmɛtəmə/ noun, **metamerically** adverb, **metamerism** noun.

metamessage ▶ **noun** an underlying meaning or implicit message, especially in advertising.

metamorphic ▶ **adjective** **1** Geology denoting rock that has undergone transformation by heat, pressure, or other natural agencies, e.g. in the folding of strata or the nearby intrusion of igneous rocks. ■ of or relating to such rocks or metamorphism.
2 of or marked by metamorphosis: *the supermodels' metamorphic ability to bend their looks.*
– ORIGIN early 19th cent.: from **META-** (denoting a change of condition) + Greek *morphē* 'form' + **-IC**.

metamorphism ▶ **noun** [mass noun] Geology alteration of the composition or structure of a rock by heat, pressure, or other natural agency.

metamorphose /ˌmɛtəˈmɔːfəʊz/ ▶ **verb** [no obj.] (of an insect or amphibian) undergo metamorphosis, especially into the adult form: *feed the larvae to your fish before they* ***metamorphose into*** *adults.* ■ change completely in form or nature: *a father seeing his daughter* ***metamorphosing from*** *girl* ***into*** *woman.* ■ [with obj.] cause (something) to change completely. ■ [with obj.] Geology subject (rock) to metamorphism: [as adj. **metamorphosed**] *a metamorphosed sandstone.*
– ORIGIN late 16th cent.: from French *métamorphoser*, from *métamorphose* (see **METAMORPHOSIS**).

metamorphosis /ˌmɛtəˈmɔːfəsɪs, ˌmɛtəmɔːˈfəʊsɪs/ ▶ **noun** (pl. **metamorphoses** /-siːz/) [mass noun] Zoology (in an insect or amphibian) the process of transformation from an immature form to an adult form in two or more distinct stages. ■ a change of the form or nature of a thing or person into a completely different one: *his metamorphosis from presidential candidate to talk-show host.*
– ORIGIN late Middle English: via Latin from Greek *metamorphōsis*, from *metamorphoun* 'transform, change shape'.

metanoia /ˌmɛtəˈnɔɪə/ ▶ **noun** [mass noun] change in one's way of life resulting from penitence or spiritual conversion.
– ORIGIN late 19th cent.: from Greek, from *metanoein* 'change one's mind'.

metaphase ▶ **noun** [mass noun] Biology the second stage of cell division, between prophase and anaphase, during which the chromosomes become attached to the spindle fibres.

metaphor ▶ **noun** a figure of speech in which a word or phrase is applied to an object or action to which it is not literally applicable: *'I had fallen through a trapdoor of depression,' said Mark, who was fond of theatrical metaphors* | [mass noun] *her poetry depends on suggestion and metaphor.* ■ a thing regarded as representative or symbolic of something else, especially something abstract: *the amounts of money being lost by the company were enough to make it a* ***metaphor for*** *an industry that was teetering.*
– DERIVATIVES **metaphoric** adjective, **metaphorical** adjective, **metaphorically** adverb.
– ORIGIN late 15th cent.: from French *métaphore*, via Latin from Greek *metaphora*, from *metapherein* 'to transfer'.

metaphosphoric acid ▶ **noun** [mass noun] Chemistry a glassy deliquescent solid obtained by heating orthophosphoric acid.
• A polymer; chem. formula $(HPO_3)_n$.
– DERIVATIVES **metaphosphate** noun.

metaphrase ▶ **noun** a literal, word-for-word translation, as opposed to a paraphrase.
▶ **verb** [with obj.] alter the phrasing or language of.
– DERIVATIVES **metaphrastic** adjective.
– ORIGIN early 17th cent. (denoting a metrical translation): from Greek *metaphrazein*, literally 'word differently'.

metaphysic ▶ **noun** a system of metaphysics.

metaphysical ▶ **adjective** **1** of or relating to metaphysics: *the essentially metaphysical question of the nature of mind.* ■ based on abstract (typically, excessively abstract) reasoning: *an empiricist rather than a metaphysical view of law.* ■ transcending physical matter or the laws of nature: *Good and Evil are inextricably linked in a metaphysical battle across space and time.*
2 of or characteristic of the metaphysical poets.
▶ **noun** (**the Metaphysicals**) the metaphysical poets.
– DERIVATIVES **metaphysically** adverb.

metaphysical poets a group of 17th-century poets whose work is characterized by the use of complex and elaborate images or conceits, typically using an intellectual form of argumentation to express emotional states. Members of the group include John Donne, George Herbert, Henry Vaughan, and Andrew Marvell.

metaphysics ▶ **plural noun** [usu. treated as sing.] the branch of philosophy that deals with the first principles of things, including abstract concepts such as being, knowing, substance, cause, identity, time, and space. ■ abstract theory or talk with no basis in reality: *his concept of society as an organic entity is, for market liberals, simply metaphysics.*

> Metaphysics has two main strands: that which holds that what exists lies beyond experience (as argued by Plato), and that which holds that objects of experience constitute the only reality (as argued by Kant, the logical positivists, and Hume). Metaphysics has also concerned itself with a discussion of whether what exists is made of one substance or many, and whether what exists is inevitable or driven by chance.

– DERIVATIVES **metaphysician** noun.
– ORIGIN mid 16th cent.: representing medieval Latin *metaphysica* (neuter plural), based on Greek *ta meta ta phusika* 'the things after the Physics', referring to the sequence of Aristotle's works: the title came to denote the branch of study treated in the books, later interpreted as meaning 'the science of things transcending what is physical or natural'.

metaplasia /ˌmɛtəˈpleɪzɪə/ ▶ **noun** [mass noun] Physiology abnormal change in the nature of a tissue.
– DERIVATIVES **metaplastic** adjective.
– ORIGIN late 19th cent.: modern Latin, from German *Metaplase*, based on Greek *metaplassein* 'mould into a new form'.

metapsychology ▶ **noun** [mass noun] speculation concerning mental processes and the mind–body relationship, beyond what can be studied experimentally.
– DERIVATIVES **metapsychological** adjective.

metasomatism /ˌmɛtəˈsəʊmətɪz(ə)m/ ▶ **noun** [mass noun] Geology change in the composition of a rock as a result of the introduction or removal of chemical constituents.
– DERIVATIVES **metasomatic** adjective, **metasomatize** (also **-ise**) verb.
– ORIGIN late 19th cent.: from **META-** (expressing change) + Greek *sōma*, *somat-* 'body' + **-ISM**.

metastable /ˌmɛtəˈsteɪb(ə)l/ ▶ **adjective** Physics (of a state of equilibrium) stable provided it is subjected to no more than small disturbances. ■ (of a substance or particle) theoretically unstable but so long-lived as to be stable for practical purposes.
– DERIVATIVES **metastability** noun.

metastasis /mɪˈtastəsɪs/ ▶ **noun** (pl. **metastases** /-siːz/) [mass noun] Medicine the development of secondary malignant growths at a distance from a primary site of cancer. ■ [count noun] a growth of this type.
– DERIVATIVES **metastatic** adjective.
– ORIGIN late 16th cent. (as a rhetorical term, meaning 'rapid transition from one point to another'): from Greek, literally 'removal or change', from *methistanai* 'to change'.

metastasize (also **-ise**) ▶ **verb** [no obj.] Medicine (of a cancer) spread to other sites in the body by metastasis: *cancers that metastasize to the brain.*

metatarsal ▶ **noun** any of the bones of the foot (metatarsus). ■ any of the equivalent bones in an animal's hindlimb.

metatarsus ▶ **noun** (pl. **metatarsi**) the group of bones in the foot, between the ankle and the toes. ■ this part of the foot.
– ORIGIN late Middle English: modern Latin (see **META-**, **TARSUS**).

metate /məˈtɑːteɪ/ (also **metate stone**) ▶ **noun** (in Central America) a flat or slightly hollowed oblong stone on which materials such as grain and cocoa are ground using a smaller stone.
– ORIGIN from American Spanish, from Nahuatl *métatl*.

Metatheria /ˌmɛtəˈθɪərɪə/ Zoology a group of mammals which comprises the marsupials. Compare with **EUTHERIA**.
• Infraclass Metatheria, subclass Theria.
– DERIVATIVES **metatherian** noun & adjective.
– ORIGIN modern Latin (plural), from **META-** (expressing change) + Greek *thēria*, plural of *thērion* 'wild animal'.

metathesis /mɪˈtaθɪsɪs/ ▶ **noun** (pl. **metatheses** /-siːz/) **1** [mass noun] Grammar the transposition of sounds or letters in a word.
2 (also **metathesis reaction**) Chemistry another term for **DOUBLE DECOMPOSITION**.
– DERIVATIVES **metathetic** /ˌmɛtəˈθɛtɪk/ adjective, **metathetical** adjective.
– ORIGIN late 16th cent.: from Greek, from *metatithenai* 'transpose, change the position of'.

metathorax ▶ **noun** Entomology the posterior segment of the thorax of an insect, bearing the hindwings.
– DERIVATIVES **metathoracic** adjective.

Metazoa /ˌmɛtə'zəʊə/ Zoology a major division of the animal kingdom that comprises all animals other than protozoans and sponges. They are multicellular animals with differentiated tissues.
- Subkingdom Metazoa, kingdom Animalia.
- ■ [as plural noun **metazoa**] animals of this division.
- DERIVATIVES **metazoan** noun & adjective.
- ORIGIN modern Latin (plural), from META- (expressing change) + zōia (plural of zōion 'animal').

mete[1] /miːt/ ▶ verb [with obj.] (**mete something out**) dispense or allot (justice, a punishment, or harsh treatment): he denounced the maltreatment meted out to minorities.
- ■ (in biblical use) measure out: with what measure ye mete, it shall be measured to you again.
- ORIGIN Old English metan 'measure, determine the quantity of', of Germanic origin; related to Dutch meten and German messen 'to measure', from an Indo-European root shared by Latin meditari 'meditate', Greek medesthai 'care for', also by MEET[2].

mete[2] /miːt/ ▶ noun (usu. **metes and bounds**) chiefly historical a boundary or boundary stone.
- ORIGIN late Middle English: from Old French, from Latin meta 'boundary, goal'.

metempsychosis /ˌmɛtɛmsaɪ'kəʊsɪs/ ▶ noun (pl. **metempsychoses** /-siːz/) [mass noun] the supposed transmigration at death of the soul of a human being or animal into a new body of the same or a different species.
- DERIVATIVES **metempsychosist** noun, **metempsychotic** adjective, **metempsychotically** adverb.
- ORIGIN late 16th cent.: via late Latin from Greek metempsukhōsis, from meta- (expressing change) + en 'in' + psukhē 'soul'.

meteor ▶ noun a small body of matter from outer space that enters the earth's atmosphere, becoming incandescent as a result of friction and appearing as a streak of light.
- ORIGIN mid 16th cent. (denoting any atmospheric phenomenon): from modern Latin meteorum, from Greek meteōron, neuter (used as a noun) of meteōros 'lofty'.

Meteora /ˌmɛtɪ'ɔːrə/ a group of monasteries in north central Greece, in the region of Thessaly. The monasteries, built between the 12th and the 16th centuries, are perched on the summits of curiously shaped rock formations.

meteoric ▶ adjective 1 of or relating to meteors or meteorites: meteoric iron.
- ■ figurative (of the development of something, especially a person's career) very rapid: her meteoric rise to the top of her profession.
- 2 chiefly Geology relating to or denoting water derived from the atmosphere by precipitation or condensation.
- DERIVATIVES **meteorically** adverb.

meteorite ▶ noun a piece of rock or metal that has fallen to the earth's surface from outer space as a meteor. Over 90 per cent of meteorites are of rock while the remainder consist wholly or partly of iron and nickel.
- DERIVATIVES **meteoritic** adjective.

meteorograph /'miːtɪərə(ʊ)grɑːf/ ▶ noun archaic an apparatus that records several meteorological phenomena at the same time.
- ORIGIN late 18th cent.: from French météorographe (see METEOR, -GRAPH).

meteoroid ▶ noun Astronomy a small body moving in the solar system that would become a meteor if it entered the earth's atmosphere.
- DERIVATIVES **meteoroidal** adjective.

Meteorological Office (in the UK) a government department providing weather forecasts.

meteorology /ˌmiːtɪə'rɒlədʒi/ ▶ noun [mass noun] the branch of science concerned with the processes and phenomena of the atmosphere, especially as a means of forecasting the weather.
- ■ the climate and weather of a region.
- DERIVATIVES **meteorological** adjective, **meteorologically** adverb, **meteorologist** noun.
- ORIGIN early 17th cent.: from Greek meteōrologia, from meteōron 'of the atmosphere' (see METEOR).

meteor shower ▶ noun Astronomy a number of meteors that appear to radiate from one point in the sky at a particular date each year, due to the earth regularly passing through them at that position in its orbit. Meteor showers are named after the constellation in which the radiant is situated, e.g. the Perseids.

meter[1] ▶ noun a device that measures and records the quantity, degree, or rate of something, especially the amount of electricity, gas, or water used: an electricity meter.
- ▶ verb [with obj.] [often as adj. **metered**] measure by means of a meter: a metered supply of water.
- ORIGIN Middle English (in the sense 'person who measures'): from METE[1] + -ER[1]. The current sense dates from the 19th cent.

meter[2] ▶ noun US spelling of METRE[1], METRE[2].

-meter ▶ combining form 1 in names of measuring instruments: thermometer.
- 2 Prosody in nouns denoting lines of poetry with a specified number of measures: hexameter.
- ORIGIN from Greek metron 'measure'.

meth ▶ noun [mass noun] informal 1 (also **crystal meth**) the drug methamphetamine.
- 2 short for METHADONE.
- 3 chiefly US another term for METHS.

methacrylic acid ▶ noun [mass noun] Chemistry a colourless, low-melting solid which polymerizes when distilled and is used in the manufacture of synthetic resins.
- ● Alternative name: **1-methylacrylic acid**; chem. formula: $CH_2=C(CH_3)COOH$.
- DERIVATIVES **methacrylate** noun.

methadone /'mɛθədəʊn/ ▶ noun [mass noun] a powerful synthetic analgesic drug which is similar to morphine in its effects but less sedative and is used as a substitute drug in the treatment of morphine and heroin addiction.
- ORIGIN 1940s: from its chemical name, (6-di)meth(yl)a(mino-4,4)-d(iphenyl-3-heptan)one.

methaemoglobin /ˌmɛθiːmə'gləʊbɪn, mɛt,hiː-/ ▶ noun [mass noun] Biochemistry a stable oxidized form of haemoglobin which is unable to release oxygen to the tissues, produced in some inherited abnormalities and by oxidizing drugs.

methaemoglobinaemia /ˌmɛθiːmə,gləʊbɪ'niːmɪə, mɛt,hiː-/ (US **methemoglobinemia**) ▶ noun [mass noun] Medicine the presence of methaemoglobin in the blood.

methamphetamine /ˌmɛθam'fɛtəmiːn, -ɪn/ ▶ noun [mass noun] a synthetic drug with more rapid and lasting effects than amphetamine, used illegally as a stimulant.
- ● A methyl derivative of amphetamine; chem. formula $C_6H_5CH_2CH(CH_3)NH(CH_3)$.

methanal /'mɛθənal/ ▶ noun systematic chemical name for FORMALDEHYDE.
- ORIGIN late 19th cent.: blend of METHANE and ALDEHYDE.

methane /'miːθeɪn, 'mɛθeɪn/ ▶ noun [mass noun] Chemistry a colourless, odourless flammable gas which is the main constituent of natural gas. It is the simplest member of the alkane series of hydrocarbons.
- ● Chem. formula: CH_4.
- ORIGIN mid 19th cent.: from METHYL + -ANE[2].

methanogen /'mɛθənə(ʊ)dʒ(ə)n, mɛ'θanə(ʊ)-/ ▶ noun Biology a methane-producing bacterium, especially an archaean which reduces carbon dioxide to methane.
- DERIVATIVES **methanogenic** adjective.

methanogenesis /ˌmɛθənə(ʊ)'dʒɛnɪsɪs, mɛ'θanə(ʊ)-/ ▶ noun [mass noun] Biology the production of methane by bacteria or other living organisms.

methanoic acid /ˌmɛθə'nəʊɪk/ ▶ noun systematic chemical name for FORMIC ACID.
- DERIVATIVES **methanoate** noun.
- ORIGIN late 19th cent.: methanoic, from METHANE + -oic (perhaps on the pattern of benzoic).

methanol /'mɛθənɒl/ ▶ noun [mass noun] Chemistry a toxic, colourless, volatile flammable liquid alcohol, originally made by distillation from wood and now chiefly by oxidizing methane. Also called METHYL ALCOHOL.
- ● Chem. formula: CH_3OH.
- ORIGIN late 19th cent.: from METHANE + -OL.

methedrine /'mɛθədrɪn, -driːn/ ▶ noun (trademark in the UK) another term for METHAMPHETAMINE.
- ORIGIN 1930s: blend of METHYL and BENZEDRINE.

metheglin /mɪ'θɛglɪn, 'mɛθəglɪn/ ▶ noun [mass noun] historical a spiced or medicated variety of mead, associated particularly with Wales.
- ORIGIN mid 16th cent.: from Welsh meddyglyn, from meddyg 'medicinal' (from Latin medicus) + llyn 'liquor'.

methemoglobinemia ▶ noun US spelling of METHAEMOGLOBINAEMIA.

methicillin /ˌmɛθɪ'sɪlɪn/ ▶ noun [mass noun] Medicine a semi-synthetic form of penicillin used against staphylococci which produce penicillinase.
- ORIGIN 1960s: from meth(yl) and (pen)icillin.

methinks ▶ verb (past **methought**) [no obj.] archaic or humorous it seems to me: life has been rather hard on her, methinks | [with clause] methought you knew all about it.
- ORIGIN Old English mē thyncth, from mē 'to me' + thyncth 'it seems' (from thyncan 'seem', related to, but distinct from, THINK).

methiocarb /mɪ'θʌɪəkɑːb/ ▶ noun [mass noun] a synthetic compound used in garden preparations to kill insects, snails, mites, and ticks.
- ORIGIN 1960s: from me(thyl) + THIO- + carb(amate).

methionine /mɪ'θʌɪəniːn/ ▶ noun [mass noun] Biochemistry a sulphur-containing amino acid which is a constituent of most proteins. It is an essential nutrient in the diet of vertebrates.
- ● Chem. formula: $CH_3S(CH_2)_2CH(NH_2)COOH$.
- ORIGIN 1920s: from METHYL + Greek theion 'sulphur'.

metho ▶ noun (pl. **-os**) [mass noun] Austral./NZ informal methylated spirit.
- ■ [count noun] a person addicted to drinking methylated spirit.
- ORIGIN 1930s: abbreviation.

method ▶ noun (often **method for/of**) a particular form of procedure for accomplishing or approaching something, especially a systematic or established one: a method for software maintenance | labour-intensive production methods.
- ■ [mass noun] orderliness of thought or behaviour; systematic planning or action: historical study is the rigorous combination of knowledge and method. ■ (often **Method**) short for METHOD ACTING.
- PHRASES **there is method in one's madness** there is a sensible foundation for what appears to be foolish or strange behaviour. [ORIGIN: from Shakespeare's Hamlet (II. ii. 211).]
- ORIGIN late Middle English (in the sense 'prescribed medical treatment for a disease'): via Latin from Greek methodos 'pursuit of knowledge', from meta- (expressing development) + hodos 'way'.

method acting ▶ noun [mass noun] a technique of acting in which an actor aspires to complete emotional identification with a part, based on the system evolved by Stanislavsky and brought into prominence in the US in the 1930s. Method acting was developed in institutions such as the Actors' Studio in New York City, notably by Elia Kazan and Lee Strasberg, and is particularly associated with actors such as Marlon Brando and Dustin Hoffman.
- DERIVATIVES **method actor** noun.

méthode champenoise /meɪˌtəʊd ʃɒpən'wɑːz/ ▶ noun [mass noun] [often as modifier] a method of making sparkling wine by allowing the last stage of fermentation to take place in the bottle.
- ■ sparkling wine made in this way, especially a kind not made in the Champagne region of France.
- ORIGIN French, literally 'champagne method'.

methodical ▶ adjective done according to a systematic or established form of procedure: a methodical approach to the evaluation of computer systems.
- ■ (of a person) orderly or systematic in thought or behaviour.
- DERIVATIVES **methodic** adjective, **methodically** adverb.
- ORIGIN late 16th cent.: via late Latin from Greek methodikos (from methodos: see METHOD) + -AL.

Methodist ▶ noun a member of a Christian Protestant denomination originating in the 18th-century evangelistic movement of Charles and John Wesley and George Whitefield.

The Methodist Church grew out of a religious society established within the Church of England, from which it formally separated in 1791. It is particularly strong in the US and now constitutes one of the largest Protestant denominations worldwide, with more than 30 million members. Methodism has a strong tradition of missionary work and concern with social welfare, and emphasizes the believer's personal relationship with God.

- ▶ adjective of or relating to Methodists or Methodism: a Methodist chapel.

- DERIVATIVES **Methodism** noun, **Methodistic** adjective, **Methodistical** adjective.
- ORIGIN probably from the notion of following a specified 'method' of Bible study.

Methodius, St /mɪˈθəʊdɪəs/ the brother of St Cyril (see **CYRIL, ST**).

methodize (also **-ise**) ▶ verb [with obj.] rare arrange in an orderly or systematic manner.
- DERIVATIVES **methodizer** noun.

methodology ▶ noun (pl. **-ies**) a system of methods used in a particular area of study or activity: *a methodology for investigating the concept of focal points* | [mass noun] *courses in research methodology and practice.*
- DERIVATIVES **methodological** adjective, **methodologically** adverb, **methodologist** noun.
- ORIGIN early 19th cent.: from modern Latin *methodologia* or French *méthodologie*.

methotrexate /ˌmɛθəˈtrɛkseɪt, ˌmiːθə-/ ▶ noun [mass noun] Medicine a synthetic compound that interferes with cell growth and is used to treat leukaemia and other forms of cancer.
- Alternative name: **4-amino-10-methylfolic acid**; chem. formula: $C_{20}H_{22}N_8O_5$.
- ORIGIN 1950s: from *meth-* (denoting a substance containing methyl groups) + elements of unknown origin.

methought past of **METHINKS**.

meths ▶ noun [mass noun] Brit. informal methylated spirit.

Methuselah /mɪˈθjuːz(ə)lə/ (in the Bible) a patriarch, the grandfather of Noah, who is said to have lived for 969 years (Gen. 5:27).
■ used to refer to a very old person: *I'm feeling older than Methuselah.*

methuselah ▶ noun a wine bottle of eight times the standard size.
- ORIGIN 1930s: from **METHUSELAH**.

methyl /ˈmiːθʌɪl, ˈmɛθ-, -θɪl/ ▶ noun [as modifier] Chemistry of or denoting the alkyl radical —CH₃, derived from methane and present in many organic compounds: *methyl bromide.*
- ORIGIN mid 19th cent.: from German *Methyl* or French *méthyle*, back-formations from German *Methylen* and French *méthylène* (see **METHYLENE**).

methyl alcohol ▶ noun another term for **METHANOL**.

methylate /ˈmɛθɪleɪt/ ▶ verb [with obj.] [often as adj. **methylated**] mix or impregnate with methanol or methylated spirit.
■ Chemistry introduce a methyl group into (a molecule or compound).
- DERIVATIVES **methylation** noun.

methylated spirit (also **methylated spirits**) ▶ noun [mass noun] alcohol for general use that has been made unfit for drinking by the addition of about 10 per cent methanol and typically also some pyridine and a violet dye.

methylbenzene ▶ noun systematic chemical name for **TOLUENE**.

methyl cyanide ▶ noun another term for **ACETONITRILE**.

methylene /ˈmɛθɪliːn/ ▶ noun [as modifier] Chemistry the divalent radical or group —CH₂—, derived from methane by loss of two hydrogen atoms: *methylene chloride.*
- ORIGIN mid 19th cent.: from French *méthylène* (formed irregularly from Greek *methu* 'wine' + *hulē* 'wood') + **-ENE**.

methylphenidate /ˌmiːθʌɪlˈfɛnɪdeɪt, ˌmɛθ-, -θɪl-/ ▶ noun [mass noun] Medicine a synthetic drug that stimulates the sympathetic and central nervous systems and is used to improve mental activity in attention deficit disorder and other conditions.

metic /ˈmɛtɪk/ ▶ noun a foreigner living in an ancient Greek city who had some of the privileges of citizenship.
- ORIGIN early 19th cent.: formed irregularly from Greek *metoikos*, from *meta-* (expressing change) + *oikos* 'dwelling'.

metical /ˌmɛtɪˈkal/ ▶ noun (pl. **meticais**) the basic monetary unit of Mòzambique, equal to 100 centavos.
- ORIGIN Portuguese, based on Arabic *miṭkāl*, from *ṯakala* 'to weigh'.

meticulous /mɪˈtɪkjʊləs/ ▶ adjective showing great attention to detail; very careful and precise: *he had always been so meticulous about his appearance.*
- DERIVATIVES **meticulously** adverb, **meticulousness** noun.

- ORIGIN mid 16th cent. (in the sense 'fearful or timid'): from Latin *meticulosus*, from *metus* 'fear'. The word came to mean 'overcareful about detail', hence the current sense (early 19th cent.).

métier /ˈmɛtjeɪ/ ▶ noun a trade, profession, or occupation: *the boy must begin to learn his métier as heir to the throne.*
■ an occupation or activity that one is good at: *television is rather more my métier.* ■ an outstanding or advantageous characteristic: *subtlety is not his métier.*
- ORIGIN late 18th cent.: French, based on Latin *ministerium* 'service'.

Metis /meɪˈtiːs/ ▶ noun (pl. same) (in Canada) a person of mixed race, especially the offspring of a white person and an American Indian.
▶ adjective denoting or relating to such people.
- ORIGIN from French *métis*, from Latin *mixtus* 'mixed' (see also **MESTIZO**).

Met Office ▶ noun see **MET**.

metol /ˈmɛtɒl/ ▶ noun [mass noun] a soluble white compound used as a photographic developer.
- A sulphate of 4-methylaminophenol (chem. formula: $CH_3NHC_6H_4OH$).
- ORIGIN late 19th cent.: from German, arbitrarily named by the inventor.

Metonic cycle /mɪˈtɒnɪk/ ▶ noun a period of 19 years (235 lunar months), after which the new and full moons return to the same day of the year. It was the basis of the ancient Greek calendar, and is still used for calculating movable feasts such as Easter.
- ORIGIN named after *Metōn*, an Athenian astronomer of the 5th cent. BC.

metonym /ˈmɛtənɪm/ ▶ noun a word, name, or expression used as a substitute for something else with which it is closely associated. For example, *Washington* is a metonym for the US government.
- ORIGIN mid 19th cent.: back-formation from **METONYMY**.

metonymy /mɪˈtɒnɪmi/ ▶ noun (pl. **-ies**) [mass noun] the substitution of the name of an attribute or adjunct for that of the thing meant, for example *suit* for *business executive*, or *the turf* for *horse racing.*
- DERIVATIVES **metonymic** adjective, **metonymical** adjective, **metonymically** adverb.
- ORIGIN mid 16th cent.: via Latin from Greek *metōnumia*, literally 'change of name'.

metope /ˈmɛtəʊp, ˈmɛtəpi/ ▶ noun Architecture a square space between triglyphs in a Doric frieze.
- ORIGIN mid 16th cent.: via Latin from Greek *metopē*, from *meta* 'between' + *opē* 'hole for a beam-end'.

metoprolol /mɪˈtɒprəlɒl/ ▶ noun [mass noun] Medicine a beta-blocking drug related to propranolol, used to treat hypertension and angina.
- ORIGIN 1970s: from *met-* (from **METHYL**) + *pro(prano)lol.*

metre¹ (US **meter**) ▶ noun the fundamental unit of length in the metric system, equal to 100 centimetres or approximately 39.37 inches.
■ (—— **metres**) a race over a specified number of metres: *the 200 metres.*
- DERIVATIVES **metreage** noun.
- ORIGIN late 18th cent.: from French *mètre*, from Greek *metron* 'measure'.

metre² (US **meter**) ▶ noun the rhythm of a piece of poetry, determined by the number and length of feet in a line: *the Horatian ode has an intricate governing metre* | [mass noun] *unexpected changes of stress and metre.*
■ the basic pulse and rhythm of a piece of music.
- ORIGIN Old English, reinforced in Middle English by Old French *metre*, from Latin *metrum*, from Greek *metron* 'measure'.

metre-kilogram-second (abbrev.: **mks**) ▶ adjective denoting a system of measure using the metre, kilogram, and second as the basic units of length, mass, and time.

metric¹ ▶ adjective 1 of or based on the metre as a unit of length; relating to the metric system: *all measurements are given in metric form.*
■ using the metric system: *we should have gone metric years ago.*
2 Mathematics & Physics relating to or denoting a metric.
▶ noun 1 technical a system or standard of measurement.
■ Mathematics & Physics a binary function of a topological space which gives, for any two points of the space, a

value equal to the distance between them, or to a value treated as analogous to distance for the purpose of analysis.
2 [mass noun] informal metric units, or the metric system: *it's easier to work in metric.*
- ORIGIN mid 19th cent. (as an adjective relating to length): from French *métrique*, from *mètre* (see **METRE¹**).

metric² ▶ adjective relating to or composed in a poetic metre.
▶ noun the metre of a poem.
- ORIGIN late 15th cent. (denoting the branch of study dealing with metre): via Latin from Greek *metrikos*, from *metron* (see **METRE²**).

-metric ▶ combining form in adjectives corresponding to nouns ending in *-meter* (such as *geometric* corresponding to *geometer* and *geometry*).
- DERIVATIVES **-metrically** combining form in corresponding adverbs.
- ORIGIN from French *-métrique*, from Latin (see **METRIC¹**).

metrical ▶ adjective 1 of, relating to, or composed in poetic metre: *metrical translations of the Psalms.*
2 of or involving measurement: *a metrical analysis of male and female scapulae.*
- DERIVATIVES **metrically** adverb.
- ORIGIN late Middle English: via Latin from Greek *metrikos* (from *metron*: see **METRE²**) + **-AL**.

-metrical ▶ combining form equivalent to **-METRIC**.

metricate ▶ verb [with obj.] change or adapt to a metric system of measurement.
- DERIVATIVES **metrication** noun.

metric hundredweight ▶ noun see **HUNDREDWEIGHT**.

metric mile ▶ noun a distance of 1,500 metres, or a race over this distance.

metric system ▶ noun the decimal measuring system based on the metre, litre, and gram as units of length, capacity, and weight or mass. The system was first proposed by the French astronomer and mathematician Gabriel Mouton (1618–94) in 1670 and was standardized in France under the Republican government in the 1790s.

metric ton (also **metric tonne**) ▶ noun a unit of weight equal to 1,000 kilograms (2,205 lb).

metritis /mɪˈtrʌɪtɪs/ ▶ noun [mass noun] Medicine inflammation of the womb.
- ORIGIN mid 19th cent.: from Greek *mētra* 'womb' + **-ITIS**.

metro ▶ noun (pl. **-os**) an underground railway system in a city, especially Paris.
■ an underground train, especially in Paris.
▶ adjective [attrib.] N. Amer. metropolitan: *the Detroit metro area.*
- ORIGIN early 20th cent.: from French *métro*, abbreviation of *métropolitain* (from *Chemin de Fer Métropolitain* 'Metropolitan Railway').

Metroland ▶ noun the area around London served by the underground railway, especially as viewed nostalgically as an ideal suburban environment of the 1920s and 1930s.
- ORIGIN 1920s: from **METROPOLITAN** + **LAND**.

metrology /mɪˈtrɒlədʒi/ ▶ noun [mass noun] the scientific study of measurement.
- DERIVATIVES **metrological** adjective.
- ORIGIN early 19th cent.: from Greek *metron* 'measure' + **-LOGY**.

metronidazole /ˌmɛtrəˈnʌɪdəzəʊl/ ▶ noun [mass noun] Medicine a synthetic drug used to treat trichomoniasis and some similar infections.
- A nitro-derivative of imidazole; chem. formula: $C_6H_9N_3O_3$.
- ORIGIN mid 20th cent.: from *me(thyl)* + *(ni)tro-* + *(im)idazole.*

metronome /ˈmɛtrənəʊm/ ▶ noun a device used by musicians that marks time at a selected rate by giving a regular tick.
- DERIVATIVES **metronomic** adjective, **metronomically** adverb.
- ORIGIN early 19th cent.: from Greek *metron* 'measure' + *nomos* 'law'.

metronymic /ˌmɛtrəˈnɪmɪk/ ▶ adjective & noun variant spelling of **MATRONYMIC**.

metroplex ▶ noun a very large metropolitan area, especially one which is an aggregation of two or more cities.
- ORIGIN 1960s: blend of **METROPOLITAN** and **COMPLEX**.

metropole /ˈmɛtrəpəʊl/ ▶ noun the parent state of a colony.
– ORIGIN late 15th cent.: from Old French *metropole*, based on Greek *mētēr, mētr-* 'mother' + *polis* 'city' (see METROPOLIS).

metropolis /mɪˈtrɒp(ə)lɪs/ ▶ noun the capital or chief city of a country or region.
■ a very large and densely populated industrial and commercial city.
– ORIGIN late Middle English (denoting the see of a Metropolitan): via late Latin from Greek *mētropolis* 'mother state', from *mētēr, mētr-* 'mother' + *polis* 'city'.

metropolitan ▶ adjective 1 of, relating to, or denoting a metropolis: *the Boston metropolitan area.*
2 of, relating to, or denoting the parent state of a colony or dependency: *metropolitan Spain.*
3 Christian Church of, relating to, or denoting a metropolitan or his see: *a metropolitan bishop.*
▶ noun 1 Christian Church a bishop having authority over the bishops of a province, in particular (in many Orthodox Churches) one ranking above archbishop and below patriarch.
2 an inhabitant of a metropolis: *the sophisticated metropolitan.*
– DERIVATIVES **metropolitanate** noun (only in sense 1 of the noun), **metropolitanism** noun, **metropolitical** adjective (only in sense 1 of the noun).
– ORIGIN late Middle English (in the ecclesiastical sense): from late Latin *metropolitanus*, from Greek *mētropolitēs* 'citizen of a mother state', from *mētropolis* (see METROPOLIS).

metropolitan county ▶ noun (in England) each of six units of local government centred on a large urban area (in existence since 1974, although their councils were abolished in 1986).

metropolitan magistrate ▶ noun (in the UK) a stipendiary magistrate who sits in petty sessional courts in London.

Metropolitan Museum of Art an important museum of art and archaeology in New York, founded in 1870.

metrorrhagia /ˌmiːtrəˈreɪdʒɪə/ ▶ noun [mass noun] abnormal bleeding from the womb.
– ORIGIN mid 19th cent.: modern Latin, from Greek *mētra* 'womb' + *-rrhag-*, stem of *rhēgnunai* 'to burst'.

-metry ▶ combining form in nouns denoting procedures and systems corresponding to names of instruments ending in *-meter* (such as *calorimetry* corresponding to *calorimeter*).
– ORIGIN from Greek *-metria*, from *-metrēs* 'measurer'.

Metternich /ˈmɛtənɪx, German ˈmɛtərnɪç/, Klemens Wenzel Nepomuk Lothar, Prince of Metternich-Winneburg-Beilstein (1773–1859), Austrian statesman. As Foreign Minister (1809–48), he was one of the organizers of the Congress of Vienna (1814–15), which devised the settlement of Europe after the Napoleonic Wars.

mettle ▶ noun [mass noun] a person's ability to cope well with difficulties or to face a demanding situation in a spirited and resilient way: *the team showed their true mettle in the second half.*
– PHRASES **be on one's mettle** be ready or forced to prove one's ability to cope well with a demanding situation. **put someone on their mettle** (of a demanding situation) test someone's ability to face difficulties.
– DERIVATIVES **mettlesome** adjective.
– ORIGIN mid 16th cent.: specialized spelling (used for figurative senses) of METAL.

Metz /mɛts/ a city in Lorraine, NE France, on the Moselle River; pop. 123,920 (1990).

meunière /məːˈnjɛː/ ▶ adjective [usu. postpositive] (especially of fish) cooked or served in lightly browned butter with lemon juice and parsley: *sole meunière.*
– ORIGIN from French (à la) *meunière* '(in the manner of) a miller's wife'.

Meursault /məːˈsəʊ, ˈməː-/ ▶ noun (pl. same) [mass noun] a burgundy wine, typically white, produced near Beaune.
– ORIGIN named after a commune in the Côte d'Or region of France.

Meuse /məːz/ a river of western Europe, which rises in NE France and flows 950 km (594 miles) through Belgium and the Netherlands to the North Sea south of Dordrecht. Flemish and Dutch name MAAS.

MeV ▶ abbreviation for mega-electronvolt(s).

mew[1] ▶ verb [no obj.] (of a cat or some kinds of bird) make a characteristic high-pitched crying noise: *a throng of cats and kittens mewing to be fed* | [as noun **mewing**] *the mewing of gulls.*
▶ noun the high-pitched crying noise made by a cat or bird: *a kitten's mew.*
– ORIGIN Middle English: imitative.

mew[2] Falconry ▶ noun (usu. **mews**) a cage or building for trained hawks, especially while they are moulting.
▶ verb 1 [no obj.] (especially of a trained hawk) moult.
2 [with obj.] confine (a trained hawk) to a cage or building at the time of moulting.
■ figurative confine in a restricting place or situation: *a lovely wife mewed up in an Oxfordshire farmhouse.*
– ORIGIN late Middle English: from Old French *mue*, from *muer* 'to moult', from Latin *mutare* 'to change'.

mew gull ▶ noun chiefly N. Amer. another term for COMMON GULL.
– ORIGIN mid 19th cent.: *mew* (in Old English *meau* 'mew gull'), of Germanic origin; related to Dutch *meeuw* and German *Möwe*.

mewl ▶ verb [no obj.] [often as adj. **mewling**] (especially of a baby) cry feebly or querulously; whimper: *dozens of mewling babies.*
■ (of a cat or bird) mew: *the mewling cry of a hawk.*
– ORIGIN late Middle English: imitative; compare with MIAUL.

mews ▶ noun (pl. same) Brit. a row or street of houses or flats that have been converted from stables or built to look like former stables.
■ a group of stables, typically with rooms above, built round a yard or along an alley.
– ORIGIN late Middle English: plural of MEW[2], originally referring to the royal stables on the site of the hawk mews at Charing Cross, London. The sense 'converted dwellings' dates from the early 19th cent.

MEX ▶ abbreviation for Mexico (international vehicle registration).

Mex ▶ adjective & noun informal Mexican.

Mexicali /ˌmɛksɪˈkɑːli/ the capital of the state of Baja California, in NW Mexico; pop. 602,400 (1990).

Mexican hairless ▶ noun a small dog of a breed lacking hair except for tufts on the head and tail.

Mexicano /ˌmɛksɪˈkɑːnəʊ/ ▶ noun & adjective informal, chiefly US Mexican.
– ORIGIN Spanish.

Mexican wave ▶ noun an effect resembling a moving wave produced by successive sections of the crowd in a stadium standing up, raising their arms, lowering them, and sitting down again.
– ORIGIN so named because of the repeated practice of this movement at the 1986 soccer World Cup finals in Mexico City.

Mexico a country in North America, with extensive coastlines on the Gulf of Mexico and the Pacific Ocean, bordered by the US to the north; pop. 81,140,920 (1990); official language, Spanish; capital, Mexico City.
■ a state of central Mexico, to the west of Mexico City; capital, Toluca de Lerdo.

> The centre of both Mayan and Aztec civilizations, Mexico was conquered and colonized by the Spanish in the early 16th century. It remained under Spanish rule until independence was achieved in 1821; a republic was established three years later. Texas rebelled and broke away in 1836, while all the remaining territory north of the Rio Grande was lost to the US in the Mexican War of 1846–8.

– DERIVATIVES **Mexican** adjective & noun.

Mexico, Gulf of a large extension of the western Atlantic Ocean. Bounded in a sweeping curve by the US to the west and south, and by Cuba to the south-east, it is linked to the Atlantic by the Straits of Florida and to the Caribbean Sea by the Yucatán Channel.

Mexico City the capital of Mexico; pop. 13,636,130 (1990). Founded in about 1300 as the Aztec capital Tenochtitlán, it was destroyed in 1521 by the Spanish conquistador Cortés, who rebuilt it as the capital of New Spain.

Meyerbeer /ˈmaɪəˌbɪə, German ˈmaɪərbeːɐ/, Giacomo (1791–1864), German composer; born *Jakob Liebmann Beer.* He settled in Paris, establishing himself as a leading exponent of French grand opera with a series of works including *Les Huguenots* (1836).

Meyerhof /ˈmaɪəhɒf, German ˈmaɪərhoːf/, Otto Fritz (1884–1951), German-born American biochemist. He worked on the biochemical processes involved in muscle action and provided the basis for understanding the process by which glucose is broken down to provide energy. Nobel Prize for Physiology or Medicine (1922).

meze /ˈmeɪzeɪ/ ▶ noun (pl. same or **mezes**) (in Turkish, Greek, and Middle Eastern cookery) a selection of hot and cold dishes, typically served as an hors-d'oeuvre.
– ORIGIN from Turkish, literally 'appetizer', from Persian *maza* 'to relish'.

mezereon /mɪˈzɪərɪən/ ▶ noun a Eurasian shrub with fragrant purplish-red flowers and poisonous red berries, found chiefly in calcareous woodland.
● *Daphne mezereum*, family Thymelaeaceae.
– ORIGIN late 15th cent.: from medieval Latin, from Arabic *māzaryūn*.

mezuzah /məˈzuːzə/ ▶ noun (pl. **mezuzahs** or **mezuzoth** /-zəʊt/) a parchment inscribed with religious texts and attached in a case to the doorpost of a Jewish house as a sign of faith.
– ORIGIN mid 17th cent.: from Hebrew *mĕzūzāh* 'doorpost'.

mezzanine /ˈmɛzəniːn, ˈmɛts-/ ▶ noun a low storey between two others in a building, typically between the ground and first floors.
■ N. Amer. the lowest balcony of a theatre, cinema, stadium, etc., or the front rows of the balcony.
▶ adjective [attrib.] Finance relating to or denoting unsecured, higher-yielding loans that are subordinate to bank loans and secured loans but rank above equity.
– ORIGIN early 18th cent.: from French, from Italian *mezzanino*, diminutive of *mezzano* 'middle', from Latin *medianus* 'median'.

mezza voce /ˌmɛtsə ˈvəʊtʃeɪ, ˈvɒtʃi/ Music ▶ adverb & adjective (especially as a direction) using about half the singer's vocal power.
▶ noun [mass noun] singing performed in this way.
– ORIGIN Italian, literally 'half voice'.

mezzo /ˈmɛtsəʊ/ ▶ noun (pl. **-os**) (also **mezzo-soprano**) a female singer with a voice pitched between soprano and contralto.
■ a singing voice of this type, or a part written for one.
– ORIGIN mid 18th cent.: Italian, from Latin *medius* 'middle'.

mezzo forte Music ▶ adverb & adjective (especially as a direction) moderately loud.
▶ noun [mass noun] a moderately high volume.

Mezzogiorno /ˌmɛtsəʊˈdʒɔːnəʊ, Italian meddzoˈdʒorno/ the southern part of Italy, including Sicily and Sardinia.
– ORIGIN Italian, literally 'midday'; compare with MIDI.

mezzo piano Music ▶ adverb & adjective (especially as a direction) moderately soft.
▶ noun [mass noun] a moderately low volume.

mezzo-relievo /ˌmɛtsəʊrɪˈljiːvəʊ/ ▶ noun (pl. **-os**) Sculpture another term for HALF RELIEF.
– ORIGIN late 16th cent.: Italian *mezzo-rilievo.*

mezzotint /ˈmɛtsəʊtɪnt, ˈmɛzəʊ-/ ▶ noun a print made from an engraved copper or steel plate on which the surface has been partially roughened, for shading, and partially scraped smooth, giving light areas. The technique was much used in the 17th, 18th, and early 19th centuries for the reproduction of paintings.
■ [mass noun] the technique or process of making pictures in this way.
▶ verb [with obj.] engrave (a picture) in mezzotint.
– DERIVATIVES **mezzotinter** noun.
– ORIGIN from Italian *mezzotinto*, from *mezzo* 'half' + *tinto* 'tint'.

MF ▶ abbreviation for medium frequency.

mf ▶ abbreviation for mezzo forte.

MFH ▶ abbreviation for Master of Foxhounds.

MFN ▶ abbreviation for most favoured nation.

MG ▶ abbreviation for ■ machine gun. ■ historical Morris Garages.

Mg ▶ symbol for the chemical element magnesium.

mg ▶ abbreviation for milligram(s): *100 mg paracetamol.*

MGM Metro-Goldwyn-Mayer, a film company formed in 1924 by Samuel Goldwyn and Louis B. Mayer.

MGR Brit. ▶ abbreviation for merry-go-round (train).

Mgr ▶ abbreviation for ■ (**mgr**) manager. ■ Monseigneur. ■ Monsignor: *Mgr O'Flaherty.*

MGy Sgt ▶ abbreviation for Master Gunnery Sergeant.

MHK ▶ abbreviation for (in the Isle of Man) Member of the House of Keys.

mho /məʊ/ ▶ noun (pl. -os) the reciprocal of an ohm, a former unit of electrical conductance.
– ORIGIN late 19th cent.: the word **OHM** reversed.

MHR ▶ abbreviation for (in the US and Australia) Member of the House of Representatives.

MHz ▶ abbreviation for megahertz.

MI ▶ abbreviation for ■ Michigan (in official postal use). ■ Brit. historical Military Intelligence: *MI5*.

mi ▶ noun variant spelling of **ME**².

mi. ▶ abbreviation for mile(s): *10 km/6 mi*.

MI5 (in the UK) the governmental agency responsible for dealing with internal security and counter-intelligence on British territory. Formed in 1909, the agency was officially named the Security Service in 1964, but the name MI5 remains in popular use.
– ORIGIN from *Military Intelligence section 5*.

MI6 (in the UK) the governmental agency responsible for dealing with matters of internal security and counter-intelligence overseas. Formed in 1912, the agency was officially named the Secret Intelligence Service in 1964, but the name MI6 remains in popular use.

MIA ▶ abbreviation for chiefly US missing in action.
■ [as noun] a member of the armed forces who is missing in action.

Miami /maɪˈami/ a city and port on the coast of SE Florida; pop. 358,550 (1990). Its subtropical climate and miles of beaches make this and the resort island of Miami Beach a year-round holiday resort.

mia-mia /ˈmaɪə͜miə/ ▶ noun Austral. an Aboriginal hut or shelter.
– ORIGIN an Aboriginal word.

Miao /mɪˈaʊ/ ▶ noun (pl. same) & adjective another term for **HMONG**.
– ORIGIN from Chinese *Miáo*, literally 'tribes'.

miaow (also **meow**) ▶ noun the characteristic crying sound of a cat.
▶ verb [no obj.] (of a cat) make such a sound.
– ORIGIN early 17th cent.: imitative.

miasm /ˈmaɪaz(ə)m/ ▶ noun (in homeopathy) a supposed predisposition to a particular disease, either inherited or acquired.
– ORIGIN mid 19th cent.: from German *Miasm*, from Greek *miasma* 'pollution'.

miasma /mɪˈazmə, maɪ-/ ▶ noun (pl. **miasmas**) poetic/literary a highly unpleasant or unhealthy smell or vapour: *a miasma of stale alcohol hung around him like marsh gas*.
■ figurative an oppressive or unpleasant atmosphere which surrounds or emanates from something: *a miasma of despair rose from the black workshops*.
– DERIVATIVES **miasmal** adjective, **miasmatic** adjective, **miasmic** adjective, **miasmically** adverb.
– ORIGIN mid 17th cent.: from Greek, literally 'defilement', from *miainein* 'pollute'.

miaul /mɪˈɔːl/ ▶ verb [no obj.] rare (of a cat) miaow.
– ORIGIN mid 17th cent.: from French *miauler*, of imitative origin.

Mic. ▶ abbreviation for Micah (in biblical references).

mic ▶ noun short for **MICROPHONE**.

mica /ˈmaɪkə/ ▶ noun [mass noun] a shiny silicate mineral with a layered structure, found as minute scales in granite and other rocks, or as crystals. It is used as a thermal or electrical insulator.
– DERIVATIVES **micaceous** /mɪˈkeɪʃəs/ adjective.
– ORIGIN early 18th cent.: from Latin, literally 'crumb'.

Micah /ˈmaɪkə/ (in the Bible) a Hebrew minor prophet.
■ a book of the Bible bearing his name, foretelling the destruction of Samaria and Jerusalem.

mica schist ▶ noun [mass noun] a metamorphic rock containing quartz and mica which resembles slate in being easily split.

Micawber /mɪˈkɔːbə/, Wilkins, a character in Dickens's novel *David Copperfield* (1850), an eternal optimist who, despite evidence to the contrary, continues to have faith that 'something will turn up'.
– DERIVATIVES **Micawberish** adjective, **Micawberism** noun.

mice plural form of **MOUSE**.

micelle /mɪˈsɛl, maɪˈsɛl/ ▶ noun Chemistry an aggregate of molecules in a colloidal solution, such as those formed by detergents.
– DERIVATIVES **micellar** adjective.
– ORIGIN late 19th cent.: coined as a diminutive of Latin *mica* 'crumb'.

Mich. ▶ abbreviation for Michigan.

Michael, St one of the archangels, typically represented slaying a dragon (see Rev. 12:7). Feast day, 29 September (Michaelmas Day).

Michaelis constant /mɪˈkeɪlɪs/ ▶ noun Biochemistry the concentration of a given enzyme which catalyses the associated reaction at half the maximum rate.
– ORIGIN 1930s: named after Leonor *Michaelis* (1875–1949), German-born American chemist.

Michaelmas /ˈmɪk(ə)lməs/ ▶ noun the feast of St Michael, 29 September.
– ORIGIN Old English *Sanct Michaeles mæsse* 'Saint Michael's Mass', referring to the Archangel.

Michaelmas daisy ▶ noun an autumn-flowering North American aster with numerous pinkish-lilac daisy-like flowers which bloom around Michaelmas.
● *Aster novi-belgii*, family Compositae: many cultivars.

Michaelmas term ▶ noun Brit. (in some universities) the autumn term.

Michelangelo /ˌmʌɪk(ə)lˈandʒələʊ/ (1475–1564), Italian sculptor, painter, architect, and poet; full name *Michelangelo Buonarroti*.

A leading figure of the High Renaissance, Michelangelo established his reputation with sculptures such as the *Pietà* (c.1497–1500) and *David* (1501–4). Under papal patronage he decorated the ceiling of the Sistine Chapel in Rome (1508–12) and painted the fresco *The Last Judgement* (1536–41), both important mannerist works. His architectural achievements include the completion of St Peter's in Rome (1546–64).

Michelin /ˈmɪtʃəlɪn, French miʃlɛ̃/, André (1853–1931) and Édouard (1859–1940), French industrialists. They founded the Michelin Tyre Company in 1888 and pioneered the use of pneumatic tyres on motor vehicles.

Michelozzo /ˌmiːkɛˈlɒtsəʊ/ (1396–1472), Italian architect and sculptor; full name *Michelozzo di Bartolommeo*. In partnership with Ghiberti and Donatello he led a revival of interest in Roman architecture.

Michelson /ˈmʌɪk(ə)ls(ə)n/, Albert Abraham (1852–1931), American physicist. He specialized in precision measurement in experimental physics, and in 1907 became the first American to be awarded a Nobel Prize.

Michelson–Morley experiment Physics an experiment performed in 1887 which attempted to measure the relative motion of the earth and the ether by measuring the speed of light in directions parallel and perpendicular to the earth's motion. The result disproved the existence of the ether, which contradicted Newtonian physics but was explained by Einstein's special theory of relativity.
– ORIGIN named after A. A. **MICHELSON** and E. W. **MORLEY**.

Michigan /ˈmɪʃɪg(ə)n/ a state in the northern US, bordered on the west, north, and east by Lakes Michigan, Superior, Huron, and Erie; pop. 9,295,300 (1990); capital, Lansing. It was acquired from Britain by the US in 1783, becoming the 26th state in 1837.
– DERIVATIVES **Michigander** /ˌmɪʃɪˈgandə/ noun.

Michigan, Lake one of the five Great Lakes of North America. Bordered by Michigan, Wisconsin, Illinois, and Indiana, it is the only one of the Great Lakes to lie wholly within the US.

Michoacán /ˌmiːtʃəʊəˈkɑːn/ a state of western Mexico, on the Pacific coast; capital, Morelia.

Mick ▶ noun informal, offensive **1** an Irishman (often as a form of address).
2 a Roman Catholic.
– ORIGIN mid 19th cent.: pet form of the given name *Michael*.

mick ▶ noun Austral. (in the game of two-up) the reverse side of a coin.
– ORIGIN early 20th cent.: of unknown origin.

mickery (also **mickerie**) ▶ noun (pl. -ies) Austral. a waterhole or excavated well, especially in a dry river bed.

– ORIGIN from Arabana Wahgaburu (an Aboriginal language) *migri*.

mickey ▶ noun (in phrase **take the mickey**) informal, chiefly Brit. tease or ridicule someone.
– DERIVATIVES **mickey-taking** noun.
– ORIGIN 1950s: of unknown origin.

Mickey Finn ▶ noun informal a surreptitiously drugged or doctored drink given to someone so as to make them drunk or insensible.
– ORIGIN 1920s: of unknown origin; sometimes said to be the name of a notorious Chicago saloon-keeper (c.1896–1906).

Mickey Mouse a Walt Disney cartoon character, who first appeared as Mortimer Mouse in 1927, becoming Mickey in 1928. During the 1930s he became established as the central Disney character.
■ [as modifier] informal of inferior quality: *people think you're a Mickey Mouse outfit if you work from home*.

mickle (also **muckle**) archaic or Scottish & N. English ▶ noun a large amount.
▶ adjective very large: *she had a great big elephant ... that's one of those mickle beasts from Africa*.
▶ determiner & pronoun much; a large amount.
– PHRASES **many a little makes a mickle** (also **many a mickle makes a muckle**) proverb many small amounts accumulate to make a large amount.
– ORIGIN Old English *micel* 'great, numerous, much', of Germanic origin; from an Indo-European root shared by Greek *megas, megal-*.

USAGE The original proverb **many a little makes a mickle** was misquoted (and first recorded in the writing of George Washington, 1793) as **many a mickle makes a muckle**. While **mickle** and **muckle** are, by origin, merely variants of the same (now dialect) word meaning 'a large amount', the misquotation spawned a misunderstanding that has now become widespread: that **mickle** means 'a small amount', and **muckle** means the opposite, 'a large amount'.

Micmac /ˈmɪkmak/ (also **Mi'kmaq**) ▶ noun (pl. same or **Micmacs**) **1** a member of an American Indian people inhabiting the Maritime Provinces of Canada.
2 [mass noun] the Algonquian language of this people, now with fewer than 8,000 speakers.
▶ adjective of or relating to this people or their language.
– ORIGIN via French from Micmac.

micrite /ˈmɪkrʌɪt/ ▶ noun [mass noun] Geology microcrystalline calcite present in some types of limestone.
■ limestone consisting chiefly of this.
– DERIVATIVES **micritic** adjective.
– ORIGIN 1950s: from *micr(ocrystalline)* + -ITE¹.

micro ▶ noun (pl. -os) **1** short for **MICROCOMPUTER**.
2 short for **MICROPROCESSOR**.
▶ adjective [attrib.] extremely small: *a micro buffet area*.
■ small-scale: CO_2 *emissions cannot be dealt with at the micro level*. Often contrasted with **MACRO**.

micro- ▶ combining form **1** small: *microcar*.
■ of reduced or restricted size: *microdot*.
2 (used commonly in units of measurement) denoting a factor of one millionth (10^{-6}): *microfarad*.
– ORIGIN from Greek *mikros* 'small'.

microaerophilic /ˌmʌɪkrəʊˌɛːrəˈfɪlɪk/ ▶ adjective Biology (of a micro-organism) requiring little free oxygen, or oxygen at a lower partial pressure than that of atmospheric oxygen.
– DERIVATIVES **microaerophile** noun.

microanalyser (US also **microanalyzer**) ▶ noun Chemistry an instrument in which a beam of electrons or other radiation is focused on to a minute area of a sample and the resulting secondary radiation (usually X-ray fluorescence) is analysed to yield chemical information.

microanalysis ▶ noun [mass noun] the quantitative analysis of chemical compounds using a sample of a few milligrams.
– DERIVATIVES **microanalytical** adjective.

microbalance ▶ noun a balance for weighing masses of a fraction of a gram.

microbe /ˈmʌɪkrəʊb/ ▶ noun a micro-organism, especially a bacterium causing disease or fermentation.
– DERIVATIVES **microbial** adjective, **microbic** adjective.
– ORIGIN late 19th cent.: from French, from Greek *mikros* 'small' + *bios* 'life'.

microbiology ▶ noun [mass noun] the branch of science that deals with micro-organisms.

– DERIVATIVES **microbiological** adjective, **microbiologically** adverb, **microbiologist** noun.

microbiota /ˌmʌɪkrəʊbʌɪˈəʊtə/ ▶ noun [mass noun] the micro-organisms of a particular site, habitat, or geological period.

microbrew ▶ noun chiefly N. Amer. a type of beer produced in a microbrewery.

microbrewery ▶ noun (pl. **-ies**) chiefly N. Amer. a brewery which produces limited quantities of beer, typically for consumption on its own premises.

microburst ▶ noun a sudden, powerful, localized air current, especially a downdraught.

microcapsule ▶ noun a minute capsule used to contain drugs, dyes, or other substances and render them temporarily inactive.

microcar ▶ noun a small and fuel-efficient car.

microcellular ▶ adjective containing or made up of minute cells.
■ (of a mobile telephone system) having small cells, typically with a radius of five hundred metres.

microcephaly /ˌmʌɪkrəʊˈsɛfəli, -ˈkɛfəli/ ▶ noun [mass noun] Medicine abnormal smallness of the head, a congenital condition associated with incomplete brain development.
– DERIVATIVES **microcephalic** adjective & noun, **microcephalous** adjective.

microcheck ▶ noun [usu. as modifier] a pattern of very small squares.

microchemistry ▶ noun [mass noun] the branch of chemistry concerned with the reactions and properties of substances in minute quantities, e.g. in living tissue.

microchip ▶ noun a tiny wafer of semiconducting material used to make an integrated circuit.

Microchiroptera /ˌmʌɪkrəʊkʌɪˈrɒpt(ə)rə/ Zoology a major division of bats which comprises all but the fruit bats.
● Suborder Microchiroptera, order Chiroptera: many families.
– DERIVATIVES **microchiropteran** noun & adjective.
– ORIGIN modern Latin (plural), from **MICRO-** 'small' + Greek *kheir* 'hand' + *pteron* 'wing'.

microcircuit ▶ noun a minute electric circuit, especially an integrated circuit.
– DERIVATIVES **microcircuitry** noun.

microcirculation ▶ noun [mass noun] circulation of the blood in the smallest blood vessels.
– DERIVATIVES **microcirculatory** adjective.

microclimate ▶ noun the climate of a very small or restricted area, especially when this differs from the climate of the surrounding area.
– DERIVATIVES **microclimatic** adjective, **microclimatically** adverb.

microcline /ˈmʌɪkrə(ʊ)klʌɪn/ ▶ noun [mass noun] a green, pink or brown crystalline mineral consisting of potassium-rich feldspar, characteristic of granite and pegmatites.
– ORIGIN mid 19th cent.: from German *Mikroklin*, from Greek *mikros* 'small' + *klinein* 'to lean' (because its angle of cleavage differs only slightly from 90 degrees).

micrococcus /ˌmʌɪkrəʊˈkɒkəs/ ▶ noun (pl. **micrococci** /-ˈkɒk(s)ʌɪ, -(s)iː/) a spherical bacterium that is typically found on dead or decaying organic matter.
● Family Micrococcaceae of Gram-positive non-motile bacteria, in particular the genera *Micrococcus* and *Staphylococcus*.
– DERIVATIVES **micrococcal** adjective.

microcode ▶ noun [mass noun] Computing a very low-level instruction set which is stored permanently in a computer or peripheral controller and controls the operation of the device.

microcomputer ▶ noun a small computer that contains a microprocessor as its central processor.

microcontinent ▶ noun Geology an isolated fragment of continental crust forming part of a small crust plate.

microcopy ▶ noun (pl. **-ies**) a copy of printed matter that has been reduced in size by microphotography.
▶ verb (**-ies, -ied**) [with obj.] make a microcopy of.

microcosm /ˈmʌɪkrə(ʊ)kɒz(ə)m/ ▶ noun a community, place, or situation regarded as encapsulating in miniature the characteristic qualities or features of something much larger: *Berlin is a microcosm of Germany, in unity as in division.*
■ humankind regarded as the epitome of the universe.
– PHRASES **in microcosm** in miniature.

– DERIVATIVES **microcosmic** /-ˈkɒzmɪk/ adjective, **microcosmically** /-ˈkɒzmɪk(ə)li/ adverb.
– ORIGIN Middle English: from Old French *microcosme* or medieval Latin *microcosmus*, from Greek *mikros kosmos* 'little world'.

microcosmic salt ▶ noun [mass noun] Chemistry a white crystalline salt obtained from human urine.
● Hydrated sodium ammonium hydrogen phosphate; chem. formula: HNaNH₄PO₄.4H₂O.
– ORIGIN late 18th cent.: translating Latin *sal microcosmicus*.

microcrystalline ▶ adjective (of a material) formed of microscopic crystals.

microcyte /ˈmʌɪkrə(ʊ)sʌɪt, ˈmɪ-/ ▶ noun Medicine an unusually small red blood cell, associated with certain anaemias.
– DERIVATIVES **microcytic** adjective.

microdensitometer ▶ noun a densitometer for measuring the density of very small areas of a photographic image.

microdot ▶ noun **1** a microphotograph, especially of a printed or written document, that is only about 1 mm across.
■ [usu. as modifier] denoting a pattern of very small dots. **2** a tablet of LSD: *more than 1000 microdots of LSD*.

microeconomics ▶ plural noun [treated as sing.] the part of economics concerned with single factors and the effects of individual decisions.
– DERIVATIVES **microeconomic** adjective.

microelectronics ▶ plural noun [usu. treated as sing.] the design, manufacture, and use of microchips and microcircuits.
– DERIVATIVES **microelectronic** adjective.

micro-environment ▶ noun Biology the immediate small-scale environment of an organism or a part of an organism, especially as a distinct part of a larger environment.

microevolution ▶ noun [mass noun] Biology evolutionary change within a species or small group of organisms, especially over a short period.
– DERIVATIVES **microevolutionary** adjective.

microfarad ▶ noun one millionth of a farad. (Symbol µF)

microfauna ▶ noun [mass noun] Ecology microscopic interstitial animals living in the soil.

microfibre (US also **microfiber**) ▶ noun a very fine synthetic yarn.

microfibril ▶ noun Biology a small fibril in the cytoplasm or wall of a cell, visible only under an electron microscope, and typically aggregated into coarser fibrils or structures.

microfiche /ˈmʌɪkrə(ʊ)fiːʃ/ ▶ noun a flat piece of film containing microphotographs of the pages of a newspaper, catalogue, or other document: *this new journal is available as a microfiche* | [mass noun] *the index will be made available on microfiche.*
▶ verb [with obj.] make a microfiche of (a newspaper, catalogue, or other document).

microfilament ▶ noun Biology a small rod-like structure, about 4–7 nanometres in diameter, present in numbers in the cytoplasm of many eukaryotic cells.

microfilaria /ˌmʌɪkrəʊfɪˈlɛːrɪə/ ▶ noun (pl. **microfilariae**) Zoology the minute larva of a filaria.

microfilm ▶ noun [mass noun] a length of film containing microphotographs of a newspaper, catalogue, or other document: *all those forms go on microfilm* | [count noun] *his vast hoard of microfilms.*
▶ verb [with obj.] make a microfilm of (a newspaper, catalogue, or other document).

microflora ▶ noun [mass noun] Biology the micro-organisms of a particular site or habitat, or living on or in a larger organism.

microform ▶ noun [mass noun] microphotographic reproduction on film or paper of a manuscript, map, or other document.

microfossil ▶ noun a fossil or fossil fragment that can only be seen with a microscope.

microfungus ▶ noun (pl. **microfungi**) Biology a fungus in which no sexual process has been observed or in which the reproductive organs are microscopic.

microgamete ▶ noun Biology (especially in protozoans) the smaller of a pair of conjugating gametes, usually regarded as male.

microglia /ˌmʌɪkrə(ʊ)ˈɡlʌɪə, ˌmɪ-/ ▶ plural noun Anatomy glial cells derived from mesoderm that

function as macrophages (scavengers) in the central nervous system and form part of the reticuloendothelial system.
– DERIVATIVES **microglial** adjective.

microgram ▶ noun one millionth of a gram. (Symbol: µg)

microgranite ▶ noun [mass noun] Geology granite that is recognizable as crystalline only under a microscope.

micrograph ▶ noun a photograph taken by means of a microscope.
– DERIVATIVES **micrographic** adjective, **micrographics** noun, **micrography** noun.

microgravity ▶ noun [mass noun] very weak gravity, as in an orbiting spacecraft.

microgroove ▶ noun a very narrow groove on a long-playing gramophone record.

microhabitat ▶ noun Ecology a habitat which is of small or limited extent and which differs in character from some surrounding more extensive habitat.

microinject ▶ verb [with obj.] Biology inject (something) into a microscopic object.
– DERIVATIVES **microinjection** noun.

microinstruction ▶ noun Computing a single instruction in microcode.

microkernel ▶ noun Computing a small modular part of an operating system kernel which implements its basic features.

microlepidoptera /ˌmʌɪkrə(ʊ)lɛpɪˈdɒpt(ə)rə/ ▶ plural noun Entomology the numerous small moths, which are of interest only to the specialist.
– ORIGIN modern Latin (plural), from **MICRO-** 'small' + **LEPIDOPTERA**.

microlight ▶ noun chiefly Brit. a very small, light, one- or two-seater aircraft.

microlith ▶ noun Archaeology a minute shaped flint, typically part of a composite tool such as a spear.
– DERIVATIVES **microlithic** adjective.

microlitre (US also **microliter**) ▶ noun one millionth of a litre. (Symbol µl)

micromanage ▶ verb [with obj.] N. Amer. control every part, however small, of (an enterprise or activity).
– DERIVATIVES **micromanagement** noun, **micromanager** noun.

micromesh ▶ noun [mass noun] a material, typically nylon, consisting of a very fine mesh.

micrometeorite ▶ noun a micrometeoroid that has entered the earth's atmosphere.

micrometeoroid ▶ noun a microscopic particle in space or of extraterrestrial origin which is small enough not to burn up in the earth's atmosphere but to drift to the surface instead.

micrometeorology ▶ noun [mass noun] the branch of meteorology concerned with small areas and with small-scale meteorological phenomena.
– DERIVATIVES **micrometeorological** adjective.

micrometer¹ /mʌɪˈkrɒmɪtə/ ▶ noun a gauge which measures small distances or thicknesses between its two faces, one of which can be moved away from or toward the other by turning a screw with a fine thread.
– DERIVATIVES **micrometry** noun.

micrometer² ▶ noun US spelling of **MICROMETRE**.

micrometre /ˈmʌɪkrə(ʊ)ˌmiːtə/ ▶ noun one millionth of a metre. (Symbol µm)

microminiaturization (also **-isation**) ▶ noun [mass noun] the manufacture of extremely small versions of electronic devices.

micron /ˈmʌɪkrɒn/ ▶ noun a unit of length equal to one millionth of a metre, used in many technological and scientific fields.
– ORIGIN late 19th cent.: from Greek *mikron*, neuter of *mikros* 'small'.

Micronesia /ˌmʌɪkrəʊˈniːzɪə, -ˈniːʒə/ **1** a region of the western Pacific to the north of Melanesia and north and west of Polynesia. It includes the Mariana, Caroline, and Marshall island groups and Kiribati.
2 a group of associated island states comprising the 600 islands of the Caroline Islands, in the western Pacific to the north of the equator; pop. 107,900 (est. 1990); languages, English (official), Austronesian languages; capital, Kolonia (on Pohnpei). The group was administered by the US as part of the Pacific Islands Trust Territory from 1947

and entered into free association with the US as an independent state in 1986. Full name **FEDERATED STATES OF MICRONESIA**.
– ORIGIN from Greek *mikros* 'small' + *nēsos* 'island'.

Micronesian ▶ adjective of or relating to Micronesia, its people, or their languages.
▶ noun **1** a native of Micronesia.
2 [mass noun] the group of Austronesian languages spoken in Micronesia.

micronize /ˈmaɪkrənʌɪz/ (also **-ise**) ▶ verb [with obj.] break (a substance) into very fine particles.
– DERIVATIVES **micronization** noun, **micronizer** noun.

micronutrient ▶ noun a chemical element or substance required in trace amounts for the normal growth and development of living organisms.

micro-organism ▶ noun a microscopic organism, especially a bacterium, virus, or fungus.

microphage ▶ noun Physiology a small phagocytic blood cell, in particular a polymorphonuclear leucocyte.

microphagous /maɪˈkrɒfəgəs/ ▶ adjective Zoology (of an invertebrate) feeding on minute particles or micro-organisms.
– DERIVATIVES **microphagic** adjective.

microphone ▶ noun an instrument for converting sound waves into electrical energy variations which may then be amplified, transmitted, or recorded.
– DERIVATIVES **microphonic** adjective.

microphotograph ▶ noun a photograph reduced to a very small size.
– DERIVATIVES **microphotographic** adjective, **microphotography** noun.

microphyll /ˈmaɪkrə(ʊ)fɪl/ ▶ noun Botany a very short leaf, such as in a moss or clubmoss, with a single unbranched vein and no leaf gaps in the stele.

microphysics ▶ plural noun [treated as sing.] the branch of physics that deals with bodies and phenomena on a microscopic or smaller scale, especially with molecules, atoms, and subatomic particles.
– DERIVATIVES **microphysical** adjective.

micropipette ▶ noun a very fine pipette for measuring, transferring, or injecting very small quantities of liquid.

micropore ▶ noun a very narrow pore, especially in a material.
– DERIVATIVES **microporosity** noun, **microporous** adjective.

microprint ▶ noun [mass noun] printed text reduced by microphotography.
– DERIVATIVES **microprinting** noun.

microprism ▶ adjective of or relating to an area of the focusing screen of some reflex cameras which is covered with a grid of tiny prisms and splits up the image when the subject is not in focus.
■(of focusing) using such a system.

microprobe ▶ noun another term for **MICROANALYSER**.

microprocessor ▶ noun an integrated circuit that contains all the functions of a central processing unit of a computer.

microprogram ▶ noun a microinstruction program that controls the functions of a central processing unit or peripheral controller of a computer.

micropropagation ▶ noun [mass noun] Botany the propagation of plants by growing plantlets in tissue culture and then planting them out.

micropsia /maɪˈkrɒpsɪə/ ▶ noun [mass noun] a condition of the eyes in which objects appear smaller than normal.
– ORIGIN mid 19th cent.: from **MICRO-** 'small' + Greek *-opsia* 'seeing'.

micropterous /maɪˈkrɒpt(ə)rəs/ ▶ adjective Entomology having small or reduced wings.

micropyle /ˈmaɪkrə(ʊ)pʌɪl/ ▶ noun Botany a small opening in the surface of an ovule, through which the pollen tube penetrates, often visible as a small pore in the ripe seed.
■a small opening in the egg of a fish, insect, etc., through which spermatozoa can enter.
– ORIGIN early 19th cent.: from **MICRO-** 'small' + Greek *pulē* 'gate'.

microreader ▶ noun an apparatus for producing

an enlarged readable image from a microfilm or microprint.

microscope ▶ noun an optical instrument used for viewing very small objects, such as mineral samples or animal or plant cells, typically magnified several hundred times.
– PHRASES **under the microscope** under critical examination.
– ORIGIN mid 17th cent.: from modern Latin *microscopium* (see **MICRO-**, **-SCOPE**).

microscope slide ▶ noun see **SLIDE** (sense 3).

microscopic ▶ adjective **1** so small as to be visible only with a microscope: *microscopic algae*.
■informal extremely small: *a microscopic skirt*. ■ concerned with minute detail: *such a vision is as microscopic as his is panoramic*.
2 of or relating to a microscope: *microscopic analysis of the soil*.
– DERIVATIVES **microscopical** adjective (only in sense 2), **microscopically** adverb.

Microscopium /ˌmaɪkrəˈskəʊpɪəm/ Astronomy a small and inconspicuous southern constellation (the Microscope), between Piscis Austrinus and Sagittarius.
■[as genitive **Microscopii** /-ˈskəʊpiː, -ˈskəʊpɪʌɪ/] used with preceding letter or numeral to designate a star in this constellation: *the star Gamma Microscopii*.
– ORIGIN modern Latin.

microscopy /maɪˈkrɒskəpi/ ▶ noun [mass noun] the use of the microscope.
– DERIVATIVES **microscopist** noun.

microsecond (Abbrev.: **µs**) ▶ noun one millionth of a second.

microseism /ˈmaɪkrəʊˌsʌɪz(ə)m/ ▶ noun Geology a very small earthquake, less than 2 on the Richter scale.
– DERIVATIVES **microseismic** adjective.

microsome /ˈmaɪkrəsəʊm/ ▶ noun Biology a fragment of endoplasmic reticulum and attached ribosomes obtained by the centrifugation of homogenized cells.
– DERIVATIVES **microsomal** adjective.

microspecies ▶ noun (pl. **same**) Biology a species differing only in minor characteristics from others of its group, typically one of limited geographical range forming part of an aggregate species.

microsphere ▶ noun a microscopic hollow sphere, especially of a protein or synthetic polymer.

microsporangium /ˌmaɪkrə(ʊ)spəˈrandʒɪəm/ ▶ noun (pl. **microsporangia** /-dʒɪə/) Botany a sporangium containing microspores.

microspore ▶ noun Botany the smaller of the two kinds of spore produced by some ferns. See also **MEGASPORE**.

microstructure ▶ noun the fine structure (in a metal or other material) which can be made visible and examined with a microscope.

microsurgery ▶ noun [mass noun] intricate surgery performed using miniaturized instruments and a microscope.
– DERIVATIVES **microsurgical** adjective.

microswitch ▶ noun an electric switch that can be operated rapidly by a small movement.

microtechnology ▶ noun [mass noun] technology that uses microelectronics.
– DERIVATIVES **microtechnological** adjective.

microtome /ˈmaɪkrə(ʊ)təʊm/ ▶ noun chiefly Biology an instrument for cutting extremely thin sections of material for examination under a microscope.

microtone ▶ noun Music an interval smaller than a semitone.
– DERIVATIVES **microtonal** adjective, **microtonality** noun, **microtonally** adverb.

microtubule ▶ noun Biology a microscopic tubular structure present in numbers in the cytoplasm of cells, sometimes aggregating to form more complex structures.

microvascular ▶ adjective of or relating to the smallest blood vessels.

microvillus ▶ noun (pl. **microvilli**) Biology each of a large number of minute projections from the surface of some cells.
– DERIVATIVES **microvillar** adjective.

microwave ▶ noun an electromagnetic wave with a wavelength in the range 0.001–0.3 m, shorter than that of a normal radio wave but longer than those of infrared radiation. Microwaves are used in

radar, in communications, and for heating in microwave ovens and in various industrial processes.
■short for **MICROWAVE OVEN**.
▶ verb [with obj.] cook (food) in a microwave oven.
– DERIVATIVES **microwaveable** (also **microwavable**) adjective.

microwave background ▶ noun Astronomy a weak uniform microwave radiation which is detectable in nearly every direction of the sky. It is believed to be evidence of the big bang.

microwave oven ▶ noun an oven that uses microwaves to cook or heat food.

micrurgy /ˈmaɪkrəːdʒi/ ▶ noun [mass noun] Biology the manipulation of individual cells under a microscope.
– DERIVATIVES **micrurgical** adjective.
– ORIGIN 1920s: from **MICRO-** 'small' + Greek *-ourgia* 'work'.

micturate /ˈmɪktjʊreɪt/ ▶ verb [no obj.] formal urinate.
– DERIVATIVES **micturition** noun.
– ORIGIN mid 19th cent.: back-formation from *micturition*, from Latin *micturit-* 'urinated', from the verb *micturire*.

mid¹ ▶ adjective [attrib.] of or in the middle part or position of a range: *the mid 17th century* | *a mid grey*.
■Phonetics (of a vowel) pronounced with the tongue neither high nor low: *a mid central vowel*.

mid² ▶ preposition poetic/literary in the middle of.
■in the course of.
– ORIGIN Shortening of **AMID**.

mid- ▶ combining form denoting the middle of: *midsection*.
■in the middle; medium; half: *midway*.
– ORIGIN Old English *midd*, of Germanic origin; from an Indo-European root shared by Latin *medius* and Greek *mesos*.

mid-air ▶ noun a part or section of the air above ground level or above another surface: *the plane exploded in mid-air* | [as modifier] *a mid-air collision*.

Midas /ˈmaɪdəs/ Greek Mythology a king of Phrygia, who, according to one story, was given by Dionysus the power of turning everything he touched into gold.
– PHRASES **the Midas touch** the ability to make money out of anything one undertakes.

mid-Atlantic ▶ adjective **1** situated or occurring in the middle of the Atlantic ocean: *the mid-Atlantic fault line*.
■having characteristics of both Britain and America, or designed to appeal to the people of both countries: *mid-Atlantic accents*.
2 of or relating to states on the middle Atlantic coast of the United States, including New York, Pennsylvannia, New Jersey, West Virginia, Delaware, and Maryland.

Mid-Atlantic Ridge a submarine ridge system extending the length of the Atlantic Ocean from the Arctic to the Antarctic. It is seismically and (in places) volcanically active; the islands of Iceland, the Azores, Ascension, St Helena, and Tristan da Cunha are situated on it.

midbrain ▶ noun Anatomy a small central part of the brainstem, developing from the middle of the primitive or embryonic brain. Also called **MESENCEPHALON**.

midday ▶ noun the middle of the day; noon: *he awoke at midday* | [as modifier] *the midday sun*.
– ORIGIN Old English *middæg* (see **MID-**, **DAY**).

middelmannetjie /ˈmɛd(ə)lˌmanəki/ ▶ noun (pl. **-ies**) S. African a ridge between the wheel-ruts of an unsurfaced road.
– ORIGIN Afrikaans, literally 'little man in the middle'.

midden /ˈmɪd(ə)n/ ▶ noun a dunghill or refuse heap.
■short for **KITCHEN MIDDEN**.
– ORIGIN late Middle English *myddyng*, of Scandinavian origin; compare with Danish *mødding* 'muck heap'.

middle ▶ adjective [attrib.] **1** at an equal distance from the extremities of something; central: *the early and middle part of life* | *middle and eastern Europe*.
■(of a member of a group, series, or sequence) so placed as to have the same number of members on each side: *the woman was in her middle forties*. ■ intermediate in rank, quality, or ability: *there is a dearth of talent at middle level*. ■ (of a language) of the period between the old and modern forms: *Middle High German*.

2 Grammar denoting a voice of verbs in some languages, such as Greek, which expresses reciprocal or reflexive action.

■ denoting a transitive verb in English which does not have an equivalent passive, e.g. *had* in *he had an idea.*

▶ **noun 1** [usu. in sing.] the point or position at an equal distance from the sides, edges, or ends of something: *she stood alone in the middle of the street.*

■ the point at or around the centre of a process or activity, period of time, etc.: *we were married in the middle of December.* ■ informal a person's waist or waist and stomach: *he had a towel round his middle.*

2 Grammar the form or voice of a verb expressing reflexive or reciprocal action.

3 short for **MIDDLE TERM**.

▶ **verb** [with obj.] (in cricket, tennis, etc.) strike (the ball) with the middle of the bat, racket, or club.

– PHRASES **down the middle** divided or dividing something equally into two parts. **in the middle of** engaged in or in the process of doing something. ■ involved in something, typically something unpleasant or dangerous: *he was caught in the middle of the emotional triangle.* **the middle of nowhere** informal a place that is very remote and isolated. **steer** (or **take**) **a middle course** adopt a policy which avoids extremes.

– ORIGIN Old English *middel*, of West Germanic origin; related to Dutch *middel* and German *Mittel*, also to **MID**.

middle age ▶ **noun** [mass noun] the period between youth and old age, about 45 to 60.

– DERIVATIVES **middle-aged** adjective.

middle-aged spread (also **middle-age spread**)
▶ **noun** [mass noun] the fat that may accumulate around the abdomen in middle age.

Middle Ages ▶ **plural noun** the period of European history from the fall of the Roman Empire in the West (5th century) to the fall of Constantinople (1453), or, more narrowly, from *c*.1000 to 1453.

> The earlier part of the period (*c*.500–*c*.1100) is sometimes distinguished as the Dark Ages, while the later part (*c*.1100–1453) is often thought of as the Middle Ages proper. The whole period is characterized by the emergence of separate kingdoms, the growth of trade and urban life, and the growth in power of monarchies and the Church. The growth of interest in classical models within art and scholarship in the 15th century is seen as marking the transition to the Renaissance period and the end of the Middle Ages.

Middle America ▶ **noun 1** the middle class in the United States, especially when regarded as a conservative political force.

■ the Midwest of the United States, regarded as the home of such people.

2 Mexico and Central America.

– DERIVATIVES **Middle American** adjective & noun.

middlebrow informal, chiefly derogatory ▶ **adjective** (of art or literature or a system of thought) demanding or involving only a moderate degree of intellectual application, typically as a result of not deviating from convention: *middlebrow fiction.*

▶ **noun** a person who is capable of or enjoys only a moderate degree of intellectual effort.

middle C ▶ **noun** Music the C near the middle of the piano keyboard, written on the first leger line below the treble stave or the first leger line above the bass stave.

middle class ▶ **noun** [treated as sing. or pl.] the social group between the upper and working classes, including professional and business workers and their families.

▶ **adjective** of, relating to, or characteristic of this section of society: *a middle-class suburb.*

■ attaching too much importance to convention, security, and material comfort: *the sterile goals of middle-class life.*

– DERIVATIVES **middle-classness** noun.

middle common room ▶ **noun** Brit. a common room for the use of postgraduate students in a university or college.

Middle Congo see **CONGO** (sense 2).

middle distance ▶ **noun 1** (**the middle distance**) the part of a real or painted landscape between the foreground and the background.

2 [usu. as modifier] Athletics a race distance of between 800 and 5,000 metres: *middle-distance runners.*

Middle Dutch ▶ **noun** [mass noun] the Dutch language from *c*.1100–1500.

middle ear ▶ **noun** the air-filled central cavity of the ear, behind the eardrum.

Middle East an extensive area of SW Asia and

northern Africa, stretching from the Mediterranean to Pakistan and including the Arabian peninsula.

– DERIVATIVES **Middle Eastern** adjective.

middle eight ▶ **noun** a short section (typically of eight bars) in the middle of a conventionally structured popular song, generally of a different character from the other parts of the song.

Middle England ▶ **noun** the middle classes in England outside London, especially as representative of conservative political views.

– DERIVATIVES **Middle Englander** noun.

Middle English ▶ **noun** [mass noun] the English language from *c*.1150 to *c*.1470.

Middle-European ▶ **adjective** of or relating to central Europe or its people.

middle finger ▶ **noun** the finger next to the forefinger.

middle game ▶ **noun** the phase of a chess game after the opening, when all or most of the pieces and pawns remain on the board.

middle ground ▶ **noun** (usu. **the middle ground**)
1 an area of compromise or possible agreement between two extreme positions, especially political ones: *each party wants to capture the votes of those perceived as occupying the middle ground.*

2 the middle distance of a painting or photograph.

Middle High German ▶ **noun** [mass noun] the language of southern Germany from *c*.1200–1500.

Middle Kingdom 1 a period of ancient Egyptian history (*c*.2040–1640 BC, 11th–14th dynasty).

2 historical China or its eighteen inner provinces.

middle life ▶ **noun** [mass noun] middle age.

Middle Low German ▶ **noun** [mass noun] the Low German language (spoken in northern Germany) from *c*.1200–1500.

middleman ▶ **noun** (pl. **-men**) a person who buys goods from producers and sells them to retailers or consumers: *we aim to maintain value for money by cutting out the middleman and selling direct.*

■ a person who arranges business or political deals between other people.

middle name ▶ **noun** a person's name (typically a personal name) placed after the first name and before the surname.

■ a quality for which a person is notable: *optimism is my middle name.*

middle-of-the-road ▶ **adjective** avoiding extremes; moderate: *the paper reflected the views of its middle-of-the-road readers.*

■ (of music) tuneful but somewhat bland and unadventurous.

middle passage ▶ **noun** historical the sea journey undertaken by slave ships from West Africa to the West Indies.

middle period ▶ **noun** the middle phase of a culture, an artist's or writer's work, etc.

Middle Persian ▶ **noun** [mass noun] the Persian language from *c*.300 BC to AD 800. See also **PAHLAVI**[2].

Middlesbrough /ˈmɪd(ə)lzbrə/ a port in NE England, on the estuary of the River Tees; pop. 141,100 (1991).

middle school ▶ **noun 1** (in the UK) a school for children from about 9 to 13 years old.

2 (in the US and Canada) a junior high school.

Middlesex a former county of SE England, situated to the north and west of London. In 1965 it was divided between Hertfordshire, Surrey, and Greater London.

middle-sized ▶ **adjective** of medium size: *a middle-sized farm.*

Middle Stone Age the Mesolithic period.

Middle Temple one of the two Inns of Court on the site of the Temple in London, England. Compare with **INNER TEMPLE**.

middle term ▶ **noun** Logic the term common to both premises of a syllogism.

Middleton, Thomas (*c*.1570–1627), English dramatist. He is best known for the tragedies *The Changeling* (1622), written with the dramatist William Rowley, and *Women Beware Women* (1620–7).

middleware ▶ **noun** [mass noun] Computing software that occupies a position in a hierarchy between the operating system and the applications, whose task

is to ensure that software from a variety of sources will work together correctly.

middle watch ▶ **noun** the period from midnight to 4 a.m. on board a ship.

middle way ▶ **noun 1** a policy or course of action which avoids extremes: *there is no middle way between central planning and capitalism.*

2 (**the Middle Way**) the eightfold path of Buddhism between indulgence and asceticism.

middleweight ▶ **noun** [mass noun] a weight in boxing and other sports intermediate between welterweight and light heavyweight. In the amateur boxing scale it ranges from 71–5 kg.

■ [count noun] a boxer or other competitor of this weight.

Middle West another term for **MIDWEST**.

middling ▶ **adjective** moderate or average in size, amount, or rank: *the village contained no poor households but a lot of middling ones.*

■ neither very good nor very bad: *he had had a good to middling season.* ■ [predic.] informal (of a person) in reasonably good but not perfect health.

▶ **noun** (**middlings**) bulk goods of medium grade, especially flour of medium fineness.

▶ **adverb** [as submodifier] informal, dated fairly or moderately: *middling rich.*

– DERIVATIVES **middlingly** adverb.

– ORIGIN late Middle English (originally Scots): probably from **MID-** + the adverbial suffix *-ling.*

Middx ▶ **abbreviation** for Middlesex.

middy[1] ▶ **noun** (pl. **-ies**) **1** informal a midshipman.

2 (also **middy blouse**) chiefly historical a woman's or child's loose blouse with a collar that is cut deep and square at the back and tapering to the front, resembling that worn by a sailor.

middy[2] ▶ **noun** (pl. **-ies**) Austral. informal a beer glass containing half a pint (285 ml).

– ORIGIN so named because it is considered to be a medium-sized measure.

Mideast US term for **MIDDLE EAST**.

mid-engined ▶ **adjective** (of a car) having the engine located centrally between the front and rear axles.

mid-European ▶ **adjective** another term for **MIDDLE-EUROPEAN**.

midfield ▶ **noun** (chiefly in soccer) the central part of the field.

■ the players on a team who play in a central position between attack and defence.

– DERIVATIVES **midfielder** noun.

Midgard /ˈmɪdɡɑːd/ Scandinavian Mythology the region, encircled by the sea, in which human beings live; the earth.

Midgard's serpent Scandinavian Mythology a monstrous serpent that was the offspring of Loki and was thrown by Odin into the sea, where, with its tail in its mouth, it encircled the earth.

midge ▶ **noun 1** a small or minute two-winged fly that is often seen in dancing swarms near water or marshy areas where it breeds.

● The families Chironomidae (the **non-biting midges**), and Ceratopogonidae (see **BITING MIDGE**): numerous species.

■ [with modifier] any of a number of small flies whose larvae can be pests of plants, typically producing galls or damaging leaves.

2 informal a small person.

– ORIGIN Old English *mycg(e)*, of Germanic origin; related to Dutch *mug* and German *Mücke*, from an Indo-European root shared by Latin *musca* and Greek *muia* 'fly'.

midget ▶ **noun** an extremely or unusually small person.

■ [usu. as modifier] Canadian a level of amateur sport typically involving children aged between sixteen and seventeen: *midget hockey.*

▶ **adjective** [attrib.] very small: *a midget submarine.*

– ORIGIN mid 19th cent.: from **MIDGE** + **-ET**[1].

Mid Glamorgan a former county of South Wales formed in 1974 from parts of Breconshire, Glamorgan, and Monmouthshire and dissolved in 1996.

midgut ▶ **noun** Zoology the middle part of the alimentary canal, including (in vertebrates) the small intestine.

midheaven ▶ **noun** Astrology (on an astrological chart) the point where the ecliptic intersects the meridian.

MIDI ▶ **noun** [mass noun] [usu. as modifier] a widely used

standard for interconnecting electronic musical instruments and computers: *a MIDI controller*.
– ORIGIN 1980s: acronym from *musical instrument digital interface*.

Midi /'mɪdi/ the south of France.
– ORIGIN French, literally 'midday'; compare with **MEZZOGIORNO**.

midi ▸ noun (pl. **midis**) a woman's calf-length skirt, dress, or coat.
– ORIGIN 1960s: from **MID**, on the pattern of *maxi* and *mini*.

midi- ▸ combining form medium-sized; of medium length: *midibus* | *midi-skirt*.
– ORIGIN from **MIDDLE**, on the pattern of *maxi-* and *mini-*.

midibus ▸ noun a bus seating up to about twenty-five passengers.

midinette /ˌmɪdɪˈnɛt, French midinɛt/ ▸ noun a seamstress or assistant in a Parisian fashion house.
– ORIGIN French, from *midi* 'midday' + *dînette* 'light dinner' (because only a short break was taken at lunchtime).

Midi-Pyrénées /ˌmɪdɪˌpɪrəˈneɪ, French midipiʀene/ a region of southern France, between the Pyrenees and the Massif Central, centred on Toulouse.

midiron ▸ noun Golf an iron with a medium degree of loft, such as a four-, five-, or six-iron.

midi system ▸ noun Brit. a set of compact stacking hi-fi equipment components.

midland ▸ noun the middle part of a country. ■ (**the Midlands**) the inland counties of central England. ■ (**Midland**) a part of the central United States, roughly bounded by Illinois, South Carolina, and Delaware. ▸ adjective of or in the middle part of a country. ■ (**Midland**) of or in the English Midlands. ■ (**Midland**) of or in the Midland of the United States.
– DERIVATIVES **midlander** noun.

midlife ▸ noun [mass noun] the central period of a person's life, between around 45 and 60 years old.

midlife crisis ▸ noun an emotional crisis of self-confidence that can occur in early middle age.

midline ▸ noun [often as modifier] a median line or plane of bilateral symmetry, especially that of the body: *the abdomen was opened by midline incision*.

Midlothian /mɪdˈləʊðɪən/ an administrative region and former county of central Scotland; administrative centre, Dalkeith.

midmost ▸ adjective & adverb poetic/literary in the very middle.

midnight ▸ noun twelve o'clock at night: *I left at midnight* | [as modifier] *a midnight deadline*. ■ [often as modifier] the middle period of the night: *the midnight hours*.
– ORIGIN Old English *midniht* (see **MID-**, **NIGHT**).

midnight blue ▸ noun [mass noun] a very dark blue.

midnight feast ▸ noun a meal eaten late at night, especially in secret by children.

midnight Mass ▸ noun a mass celebrated at or shortly before midnight, especially on Christmas Eve.

midnight sun ▸ noun the sun when seen at midnight during the summer in either the Arctic or Antarctic Circle.

mid-ocean ridge ▸ noun Geology a long, seismically active submarine ridge system situated in the middle of an ocean basin and marking the site of the upwelling of magma associated with sea-floor spreading. An example is the Mid-Atlantic Ridge.

mid-off ▸ noun Cricket a fielding position on the off side near the bowler. ■ a fielder at this position.

mid-on ▸ noun Cricket a fielding position on the on side near the bowler. ■ a fielder at this position.

mid range ▸ noun 1 Statistics the arithmetic mean of the largest and the smallest values in a sample or other group. 2 the middle part of the range of audible frequencies. ▸ adjective (of a product) in the middle of a range of products with regard to size, quality, or price.

Midrash /'mɪdraʃ, -rʌʃ/ ▸ noun (pl. **Midrashim** /-'ʃɪm/) an ancient commentary on part of the Hebrew scriptures, attached to the biblical text. The earliest Midrashim come from the 2nd century AD, although much of their content is older.
– ORIGIN from Hebrew *miḏraš* 'commentary', from *dāraš* 'expound'.

midrib ▸ noun a large strengthened vein along the midline of a leaf.

midriff ▸ noun the region of the front of the body between the chest and the waist. ■ Anatomy, dated the diaphragm.
– ORIGIN Old English *midhrif*, from **MID** + *hrif* 'belly'.

midsection ▸ noun the middle part of something. ■ the midriff.

midship ▸ noun [usu. as modifier] the middle part of a ship or boat: *her powerful midship section*.

midshipman ▸ noun (pl. **-men**) 1 a rank of officer in the Royal Navy, above naval cadet and below sub lieutenant. [ORIGIN: early 17th cent.: so named because the officer was stationed amidships; he was however allowed to walk the quarterdeck, to which he aspired in promotion.] ■ a naval cadet in the US navy. 2 an American toadfish with dorsal and anal fins that run most of the length of the body and rows of light organs on the underside. ● Genus *Porichthys*, family *Batrachoididae*: two or three species.

midships ▸ adverb & adjective another term for **AMIDSHIPS**.

mid shot ▸ noun Photography a shot taken at a medium distance.

midsole ▸ noun a layer of material between the inner and outer soles of a shoe, for absorbing shock.

midst ▸ preposition archaic or poetic/literary in the middle of. ▸ noun archaic the middle point or part.
– PHRASES **in the midst of** in the middle of: *he left his flat in the midst of a rainstorm*. **in our** (or **your, their,** etc.) **midst** among us (or you or them).
– ORIGIN late Middle English: from *in middes* 'in the middle'.

midstream ▸ noun the middle of a stream or river: *the ferry was moving out into midstream*. ▸ adjective Medicine (of urine) passed in the middle part of an act of urinating.
– PHRASES **in midstream** in the middle of a stream or river. ■ figurative (of an activity or process, especially one that is interrupted) part-way through its course: *our conversation was interrupted in midstream*.

midsummer ▸ noun [often as modifier] the middle part of summer: *the midsummer heat*. ■ another term for **SUMMER SOLSTICE**.
– ORIGIN Old English *midsumor* (see **MID-**, **SUMMER**[1]).

Midsummer Day (also **Midsummer's Day**) ▸ noun 24 June, a quarter day in England, Wales, and Ireland, originally coinciding with the summer solstice and in some countries marked by a summer festival.

midsummer madness ▸ noun [mass noun] foolish or reckless behaviour, considered to be at its height at midsummer.

midterm ▸ noun the middle of a period of office, an academic term, or a pregnancy: *Nixon resigned in midterm* | [as modifier] *midterm elections*. ■ N. Amer. an exam in the middle of an academic term.

midtown ▸ noun [usu. as modifier] N. Amer. the central part of a city between the downtown and uptown areas: *a huge midtown apartment*.

mid-Victorian ▸ adjective of or relating to the middle of the Victorian era.

midway ▸ adverb & adjective in or towards the middle of something: [as adv.] *Father Peter came to a halt midway down the street* | [as adj.] *midway profits roared from £130 m to £160 m*. ■ having some of the characteristics of one thing and some of another: [as adj.] *a midway path is chosen between the diverging aspirations of the two factions* | [as adv.] *the leaves have a unique smell midway between eucalyptus and mint*. ▸ noun N. Amer. an area of sideshows or other amusements at a fair or exhibition.

Midway Islands two small islands with a surrounding coral atoll, in the central Pacific in the western part of the Hawaiian chain. The islands were annexed by the US in 1867 and remain a US territory and naval base. They were the scene in 1942 of the decisive Battle of Midway, in which the US navy repelled a Japanese invasion fleet.

midweek ▸ noun the middle of the week, usually regarded as being from Tuesday to Thursday: *Clarkson suffered his injury playing in the reserves in midweek*. ▸ adjective & adverb in the middle of the week: [as adj.] *a special midweek reduction* | [as adv.] *we have opportunities to fish midweek*.

Midwest the region of northern states of the US from Ohio west to the Rocky Mountains. Formerly called **FAR WEST**.
– DERIVATIVES **Midwestern** adjective.

midwicket ▸ noun Cricket a fielding position on the leg side, level with the middle of the pitch. ■ a fielder at this position.

midwife ▸ noun (pl. **-wives**) a person (typically a woman) trained to assist women in childbirth. ■ figurative a person or thing that helps to bring something into being or assists its development: *he survived to be one of the midwives of the Reformation*. ▸ verb [with obj.] assist (a woman) during childbirth. ■ figurative bring into being: *revolutions midwifed by new technologies of communication*.
– DERIVATIVES **midwifery** /-ˈwɪf(ə)ri/ noun.
– ORIGIN Middle English: probably from the obsolete preposition *mid* 'with' + **WIFE** (in the archaic sense 'woman'), expressing the sense 'a woman who is with (the mother)'.

midwife toad ▸ noun a European toad, the male of which has a distinctive piping call in spring and carries the developing eggs wrapped around his hind legs. ● *Alytes obstetricans*, family Discoglossidae.

midwinter ▸ noun the middle part of winter: *in midwinter the track became a muddy morass*. ■ another term for **WINTER SOLSTICE**.
– ORIGIN Old English (see **MID-**, **WINTER**).

mielie ▸ noun variant spelling of **MEALIE**.

Mien /mjɛn/ ▸ noun another term for **YAO**[2].

mien /miːn/ ▸ noun a person's look or manner, especially one of a particular kind indicating their character or mood: *he has a cautious, academic mien*.
– ORIGIN early 16th cent.: probably from French *mine* 'expression', influenced by obsolete *demean* 'bearing, demeanour' (from **DEMEAN**[2]).

Mies van der Rohe /ˌmiːz van də ˈrəʊə, German ˌmiːs van deːɐ ˈroːə/, Ludwig (1886–1969), German-born architect and designer. He designed the German pavilion at the 1929 International Exhibition at Barcelona and the Seagram Building in New York (1954–8), and was noted for his tubular steel furniture. He was director of the Bauhaus 1930–3.
– DERIVATIVES **Miesian** adjective.

mifepristone /ˌmɪfɛˈprɪstəʊn/ ▸ noun [mass noun] Medicine a synthetic steroid that inhibits the action of progesterone, given orally in early pregnancy to induce abortion.
– ORIGIN 1980s: probably from Dutch *mifepriston*, from *mife-* (representing *aminophenol*) + *-pr-* (representing *propyl*) + *-ist-* (representing **OESTRADIOL**) + **-ONE**.

miff ▸ verb [with obj.] (usu. **be miffed**) informal annoy: *she was slightly miffed at not being invited*. ▸ noun archaic a petty quarrel or fit of pique.
– ORIGIN early 17th cent.: perhaps imitative; compare with early modern German *muff*, an exclamation of disgust.

miffy ▸ adjective informal, dated easily annoyed or irritated.

MiG ▸ noun a type of Russian fighter aircraft.
– ORIGIN 1940s: from the initial letters of the surnames of A. I. Mikoyan and M. I. Gurevich (Russian aircraft designers), linked by Russian *i* 'and'.

might[1] ▸ modal verb (3rd sing. present **might**) 1 past of **MAY**[1], used especially: ■ in reported speech, expressing possibility or permission: *he said he might be late*. ■ expressing a possibility based on a condition not fulfilled: *we might have won if we'd played better*. ■ expressing annoyance about something that someone has not done: *you might have told me!* ■ expressing purpose: *he avoided social engagements so that he might work*. 2 used in questions and requests: ■ tentatively asking permission: *might I just ask one question?* ■ expressing a polite request: *you might just call me Jane, if you don't mind*. ■ asking for

information, especially condescendingly: *and who might you be?*
3 expressing possibility: *this might be true.*
■ making a suggestion: *you might try non-prescription pain relievers.*
– PHRASES **might as well** **1** used to make an unenthusiastic suggestion: *I might as well begin.* **2** used to indicate that a situation is the same as if the hypothetical thing stated were true: *for readers seeking illumination, this book might as well have been written in Serbo-Croatian.* **might have known** (or **guessed**) used to express one's lack of surprise about something: *I might have known it was you.*

might[2] ▶ noun [mass noun] great and impressive power or strength, especially of a nation, large organization, or natural force: *a convincing display of military might.*
– PHRASES **might is right** those who are powerful can do what they wish unchallenged, even if their action is in fact unjustified. **with all one's might** using all one's power or strength. **with might and main** with all one's strength or power.
– ORIGIN Old English *miht, mieht*, of Germanic origin; related to **MAY**[1].

might-have-been ▶ noun informal a past possibility that no longer applies.

mightn't ▶ contraction of might not: *you mightn't believe it, but I saw him stop a fight.*

mighty ▶ adjective (**mightier**, **mightiest**) possessing great and impressive power or strength, especially on account of size: *three mighty industrial countries | mighty beasts.*
■ (of an action) performed with or requiring great strength: *a mighty heave* | figurative *a mighty blow against racism.* ■ informal very large: *she gave a mighty hiccup.*
▶ adverb [as submodifier] informal, chiefly N. Amer. extremely: *this is mighty early to be planning a presidential campaign.*
– DERIVATIVES **mightily** adverb, **mightiness** noun.
– ORIGIN Old English *mihtig* (see **MIGHT**[2], **-Y**[1]).

migmatite /ˈmɪɡmətʌɪt/ ▶ noun Geology a rock composed of two intermingled but distinguishable components, typically a granitic rock within a metamorphic host rock.
– ORIGIN early 20th cent.: from Greek *migma, migmat-* 'mixture' + **-ITE**[1].

mignonette /ˌmɪnjəˈnɛt/ ▶ noun a herbaceous plant with spikes of small fragrant greenish flowers.
• Genus *Reseda*, family Resedaceae: several species, in particular the North African *R. odorata*, which is cultivated as an ornamental and for its essential oil, and the European **wild mignonette** (*R. lutea*).
– ORIGIN early 18th cent.: from French *mignonnette*, diminutive of *mignon* 'small and sweet'.

migraine /ˈmiːɡreɪn, ˈmʌɪ-/ ▶ noun a recurrent throbbing headache that typically affects one side of the head and is often accompanied by nausea and disturbed vision.
– DERIVATIVES **migrainous** adjective.
– ORIGIN late Middle English: from French, via late Latin from Greek *hēmikrania*, from *hēmi-* 'half' + *kranion* 'skull'.

migrant ▶ noun an animal that migrates.
■ a worker who moves from place to place to do seasonal work.
▶ adjective [attrib.] tending to migrate or having migrated: *migrant birds.*

migrant labour system ▶ noun chiefly historical (in South Africa) the laws and structures under which black contract labourers from rural areas, the homelands, or neighbouring states were recruited to work in the cities and mines.

migrate /mʌɪˈɡreɪt, ˈmʌɪɡreɪt/ ▶ verb [no obj.] (of an animal, typically a bird or fish) move from one region or habitat to another, especially regularly according to the seasons: *as autumn arrives, the birds migrate south.*
■ (of a person) move from one area or country to settle in another, especially in search of work: *rural populations have* **migrated to** *urban areas.* ■ move from one specific part of something to another: *cells which can form pigment migrate beneath the skin.* ■ Computing change or cause to change from using one system to another. ■ [with obj.] Computing transfer (programs or hardware) from one system to another.
– DERIVATIVES **migration** /-ˈɡreɪʃ(ə)n/ noun, **migrational** adjective, **migrator** noun, **migratory** /ˈmʌɪɡrət(ə)ri, mʌɪˈɡreɪt(ə)ri/ adjective.
– ORIGIN early 17th cent. (in the general sense 'move from one place to another'): from Latin *migrat-* 'moved, shifted', from the verb *migrare*.

Mihailović /mɪˈhʌɪləvɪtʃ/, Draža (1893–1946), Yugoslav soldier; full name *Dragoljub Mihailović*. Leader of the Chetniks during the Second World War, in 1941 he became Minister of War for the Yugoslav government in exile. After the war he was executed on the charge of collaboration with the Germans.

mihrab /ˈmiːrɑːb/ ▶ noun a niche in the wall of a mosque, at the point nearest to Mecca, towards which the congregation faces to pray.
– ORIGIN from Arabic *miḥrāb* 'place for prayer'.

mikado /mɪˈkɑːdəʊ/ ▶ noun historical a title given to the emperor of Japan.
– ORIGIN Japanese, from *mi* 'august' + *kado* 'gate'; the title is a tranferred use of 'gate (to the Imperial palace)', an ancient place of audience. Compare with **PORTE**.

Mike ▶ noun a code word representing the letter M, used in radio communication.

mike[1] informal ▶ noun a microphone.
▶ verb [with obj.] place a microphone close to (someone or something) or in (a place).
– ORIGIN 1920s: abbreviation.

mike[2] Brit. informal, dated ▶ verb [no obj.] idle away one's time: *he thundered at anyone who was miking.*
▶ noun a period of idleness.
– ORIGIN early 19th cent.: of unknown origin.

Mi'kmaq ▶ noun & adjective variant spelling of **MICMAC**.

Míkonos /ˈmikɔnɔs/ Greek name for **MYKONOS**.

mikva /ˈmɪkvə/ ▶ noun a bath in which certain Jewish ritual purifications are performed.
■ [mass noun] the action of taking such a bath.
– ORIGIN mid 19th cent.: from Yiddish *mikve*, from Hebrew *miqweh*, literally 'collection (usually of water)'.

mil[1] informal ▶ abbreviation for ■ millimetres. ■ millilitres. ■ (used in sums of money) millions: *the insurance company coughed up five mil.*

mil[2] ▶ noun one thousandth of an inch.
– ORIGIN late 17th cent.: from Latin *millesimum* 'thousandth', from *mille* 'thousand'.

milady /mɪˈleɪdi/ ▶ noun (pl. **-ies**) historical or humorous used to address or refer to an English noblewoman or great lady: *I went off to milady's boudoir.*
– ORIGIN late 18th cent.: via French from English *my lady*; compare with **MILORD**.

milage ▶ noun variant spelling of **MILEAGE**.

Milan /mɪˈlan/ an industrial city in NW Italy, capital of Lombardy region; pop. 1,432,180 (1990). A powerful city in the past, particularly from the 13th to the 15th centuries, Milan is today a leading financial and commercial centre. Italian name **Milano** /miˈlano/.
– DERIVATIVES **Milanese** adjective & noun.

Milan, Edict of an edict made by the Roman emperor Constantine in 313 which recognized Christianity and gave freedom of worship in the Roman Empire.

Milanese silk ▶ noun [mass noun] finely knitted silk or viscose.

milch /mɪltʃ/ ▶ adjective denoting a cow or other domestic mammal giving or kept for milk.
– ORIGIN Middle English: from Old English *-milce*, only in *thrimilce* 'May' (when cows could be milked three times a day), from the Germanic base of **MILK**.

milch cow ▶ noun a person or organization that is a source of easy profit: *governments throughout the world are privatizing their milch cows.*

mild ▶ adjective gentle and not easily provoked: *she was implacable, despite her mild exterior.*
■ (of a rule or punishment) of only moderate severity: *he received a mild sentence.* ■ not keenly felt or seriously intended: *she looked at him in mild surprise.* ■ (of an illness or pain) not serious or dangerous. ■ (of weather) moderately warm, especially less cold than expected: *it is still mild enough to work outdoors.* ■ (of a medicine or cosmetic) acting gently and without causing harm. ■ (of food, drink, or tobacco) not sharp or strong in flavour: *a mild Italian cheese.*
▶ noun [mass noun] Brit. a kind of dark beer not strongly flavoured with hops.
– DERIVATIVES **mildish** adjective, **mildness** noun.
– ORIGIN Old English *milde* (originally in the sense 'gracious, not severe in command'), of Germanic origin; related to Dutch and German *mild*, from an Indo-European root shared by Latin *mollis* and Greek *malthakos* 'soft'.

mildew ▶ noun [mass noun] a thin whitish coating consisting of minute fungal hyphae, growing on plants or damp organic material such as paper or leather.
▶ verb affect or be affected with mildew.
– DERIVATIVES **mildewy** adjective.
– ORIGIN Old English *mildēaw* 'honeydew', of Germanic origin. The first element is related to Latin *mel* and Greek *meli* 'honey'.

mildly ▶ adverb in a mild manner, in particular without anger or severity.
■ not seriously or dangerously: *he had suffered mildly from the illness since he was 23.* ■ [as submodifier] to a slight extent: *he kept his voice mildly curious.*
– PHRASES **to put it mildly** (or **putting it mildly**) used to imply that the reality is more extreme, usually worse: *the proposals were, to put it mildly, unpopular.*

mild-mannered ▶ adjective (of a person) gentle and not given to extremes of emotion.

mild steel ▶ noun [mass noun] steel containing a small percentage of carbon, strong and tough but not readily tempered.

mile ▶ noun (also **statute mile**) a unit of linear measure equal to 1,760 yards (approximately 1.609 kilometres).
■ historical a Roman measure of 1,000 paces (approximately 1,620 yards). ■ (usu. **miles**) informal a very long way or a very great amount: *vistas which stretch for miles.* ■ a race extending over a mile.
▶ adverb [as submodifier] (**miles**) informal by a great amount or a long way: *the second tape is miles better.*
– PHRASES **be miles away** informal be lost in thought and so unaware of what is happening around one. **go the extra mile** be especially assiduous in one's attempt to achieve something. **a mile a minute** informal very quickly: *he talks a mile a minute.* **miles from anywhere** informal in a very isolated place. **run a mile** informal used to show that one is frightened by or very unwilling to do something: *if someone proposed to me I'd probably run a mile.* **see** (or **tell** or **spot**) **something a mile off** informal recognize something very easily: *the baddies can be spotted a mile off.* **stand** (or **stick**) **out a mile** informal be very obvious or incongruous.
– ORIGIN Old English *mīl*, based on Latin *mil(l)ia*, plural of *mille* 'thousand' (the original Roman unit of distance was *mille passus* 'a thousand paces').

mileage (also **milage**) ▶ noun **1** [usu. in sing.] a number of miles travelled or covered: *the car is in good condition, considering its mileage.*
■ [usu. as modifier] travelling expenses paid according to the number of miles travelled: *the mileage rate will be 30p per mile.*
2 [mass noun] informal the contribution made by something to one's aims or interests: *he was* **getting a lot of mileage out of** *the mix-up.*
■ the likely potential of someone or something: *there is bound to be a lot of mileage for the paperback.*

mileometer ▶ noun variant spelling of **MILOMETER**.

milepost ▶ noun chiefly N. Amer. & Austral. a marker set up to indicate how distant a particular place is.
■ a post one mile from the finishing post of a race. ■ figurative an action or event marking a significant change or stage in development: *three members of the team have all recently passed mileposts in their careers.*

miler ▶ noun informal a person or horse trained specially to run a mile.
– DERIVATIVES **miling** noun.

miles gloriosus /ˌmiːleɪz ɡlɔːrɪˈəʊsəs, ˌmʌɪliːz/ ▶ noun (pl. **milites gloriosi** /ˌmɪlɪteɪz ɡlɔːrɪˈəʊsiː/) (in literature) a boastful soldier as a stock figure.
– ORIGIN Latin, from the title of a comedy by Plautus.

Milesian /mʌɪˈliːʃɪən, -ʃ(ə)n/ ▶ noun a native or inhabitant of ancient Miletus.
▶ adjective of or relating to Miletus or its inhabitants.
– ORIGIN mid 16th cent.: via Latin from Greek *Milēsios* + **-AN**.

milestone ▶ noun a stone set up beside a road to mark the distance in miles to a particular place.
■ figurative an event marking a significant change or stage in the development of something: *the speech is being hailed as a* **milestone in** *race relations.*

Miletus /mʌɪˈliːtəs/ an ancient city of the Ionian Greeks in SW Asia Minor. In the 7th and 6th centuries BC it was a powerful port, from which more than sixty colonies were founded on the shores of the Black Sea and in Italy and Egypt.

milfoil /ˈmɪlfɔɪl/ ▶ noun **1** the common Eurasian yarrow.

2 (also **water milfoil**) a widely distributed aquatic plant with whorls of fine submerged leaves and wind-pollinated flowers.
• Genus *Myriophyllum*, family Haloragaceae.
– ORIGIN Middle English: via Old French from Latin *millefolium*, from *mille* 'thousand' + *folium* 'leaf'.

Milhaud /ˈmiːjəʊ/, Darius (1892–1974), French composer. A member of the group Les Six, he composed the music to Cocteau's ballet *Le Boeuf sur le toit* (1919). Much of his music was polytonal and influenced by jazz.

milia plural form of **MILIUM**.

miliaria /ˌmɪlɪˈɛːrɪə/ ▶ **noun** medical term for **PRICKLY HEAT**.
– ORIGIN early 19th cent.: modern Latin, from Latin *miliarius* (see **MILIARY**).

miliary /ˈmɪlɪəri/ ▶ **adjective** (of a disease) accompanied by a rash with lesions resembling millet seed: *miliary tuberculosis*.
– ORIGIN late 17th cent.: from Latin *miliarius*, from *milium* 'millet'.

milieu /ˈmiːljəː, mɪˈljəː/ ▶ **noun** (pl. **milieux** or **milieus** pronounced same or /-ljəːz/) a person's social environment: *Gregory came from the same aristocratic milieu as Sidonius*.
– ORIGIN mid 19th cent.: French, from *mi* 'mid' + *lieu* 'place'.

militant ▶ **adjective** combative and aggressive in support of a political or social cause, and typically favouring extreme, violent, or confrontational methods: *militant left-wing trade unionists*.
▶ **noun** a person who is active in this way.
– DERIVATIVES **militancy** noun, **militantly** adverb.
– ORIGIN late Middle English (in the sense 'engaged in warfare'): from Old French, or from Latin *militant-* 'serving as a soldier', from the verb *militare* (see **MILITATE**). The current sense dates from the early 20th cent.

militaria /ˌmɪlɪˈtɛːrɪə/ ▶ **plural noun** military articles of historical interest, such as weapons, uniforms, and equipment.
– ORIGIN 1960s: from **MILITARY** + **-IA**[2].

militarism ▶ **noun** [mass noun] chiefly derogatory the belief or desire of a government or people that a country should maintain a strong military capability and be prepared to use it aggressively to defend or promote national interests.
– DERIVATIVES **militarist** noun & adjective, **militaristic** adjective.
– ORIGIN mid 19th cent.: from French *militarisme*, from *militaire* (see **MILITARY**).

militarize (also **-ise**) ▶ **verb** [with obj.] [often as adj. **militarized**] give (something, especially an organization) a military character or style: *militarized police forces*.
■ equip or supply (a place) with soldiers and other military resources: *a militarized security zone*.
– DERIVATIVES **militarization** noun.

military ▶ **adjective** of, relating to, or characteristic of soldiers or armed forces: *both leaders condemned the build-up of military activity*.
▶ **noun** (**the military**) the armed forces of a country.
– DERIVATIVES **militarily** adverb.
– ORIGIN late Middle English: from French *militaire* or Latin *militaris*, from *miles*, *milit-* 'soldier'.

military academy ▶ **noun** an institution for training army cadets.

military age ▶ **noun** [mass noun] the age range within which a person is eligible for military service: *young men of military age*.

military attaché ▶ **noun** an army officer serving with an embassy or attached as an observer to a foreign army.

military band ▶ **noun** a group of musicians playing brass, woodwind, and percussion instruments, typically while marching. Also called **CONCERT BAND**.

Military Cross (abbrev.: **MC**) ▶ **noun** (in the UK and Commonwealth countries) a decoration awarded for distinguished active service on land, instituted in 1914 (originally for officers).

military honours ▶ **plural noun** ceremonies performed by troops as a mark of respect at the burial of a member of the armed forces: *he was buried with full military honours*.

military-industrial complex ▶ **noun** a country's military establishment and those industries producing arms or other military materials, regarded as a powerful vested interest.

military law ▶ **noun** [mass noun] the law governing an army, navy, or air force.

Military Medal (abbrev.: **MM**) ▶ **noun** (in the UK and Commonwealth countries) a decoration for distinguished active service on land, instituted in 1916 (originally for enlisted soldiers).

military police ▶ **noun** [treated as pl.] the corps responsible for police and disciplinary duties in an army.
– DERIVATIVES **military policeman** noun, **military policewoman** noun.

military tribune ▶ **noun** see **TRIBUNE**[1].

militate ▶ **verb** [no obj.] (**militate against**) (of a fact or circumstance) be a powerful or conclusive factor in preventing: *these fundamental differences will militate against the two communities coming together*.
– ORIGIN late 16th cent.: from Latin *militat-* 'served as a soldier', from the verb *militare*, from *miles*, *milit-* 'soldier'.

USAGE The verbs **militate** and **mitigate** are often confused. See **usage** at **MITIGATE**.

milites gloriosi plural form of **MILES GLORIOSUS**.

militia /mɪˈlɪʃə/ ▶ **noun** a military force that is raised from the civil population to supplement a regular army in an emergency.
■ a military force that engages in rebel or terror activities, typically in opposition to a regular army. ■ (in the US) all able-bodied civilians eligible by law for military service.
– ORIGIN late 16th cent.: from Latin, literally 'military service', from *miles*, *milit-* 'soldier'.

militiaman ▶ **noun** (pl. **-men**) a member of a militia.

milium /ˈmɪlɪəm/ ▶ **noun** (pl. **milia** /ˈmɪlɪə/) Medicine a small, hard, pale keratinous nodule formed on the skin, typically by a blocked sebaceous gland.
– ORIGIN mid 19th cent.: from Latin, literally 'millet' (because of a resemblance to a millet seed).

milk ▶ **noun** [mass noun] an opaque white fluid rich in fat and protein, secreted by female mammals for the nourishment of their young.
■ the milk of cows (or occasionally goats or ewes) as food for humans: *a glass of milk*. ■ the white juice of certain plants: *coconut milk*. ■ a creamy-textured liquid with a particular ingredient or use: *cleansing milk*.
▶ **verb** [with obj.] draw milk from (a cow or other animal), either by hand or mechanically.
■ [no obj.] (of an animal, especially a cow) produce or yield milk: *the breed does seem to milk better in harder conditions*. ■ extract sap, venom, or other substances from. ■ figurative exploit or defraud (someone), typically by taking regular small amounts of money over a period of time: [with complement] *he had milked his grandmother dry of all her money*. ■ figurative get all possible advantage from (a situation): *the newspapers were milking the story for every possible drop of drama*. ■ figurative elicit a favourable reaction from (an audience) and prolong it for as long as possible: *he milked the crowd for every last drop of applause*.
– PHRASES **in milk** (of an animal, especially a cow) producing milk. **it's no use crying over spilt** (or N. Amer. also **spilled**) **milk** proverb there is no point in regretting something which has already happened and cannot be changed or reversed. **milk and honey** prosperity and abundance. [ORIGIN: with biblical allusion to the prosperity of the Promised Land (Exod. 3:8).] **milk of human kindness** care and compassion for others. [ORIGIN: with allusion to Shakespeare's *Macbeth*.]
– ORIGIN Old English *milc*, *milcian*, of Germanic origin; related to Dutch *melk* and German *Milch*, from an Indo-European root shared by Latin *mulgere* and Greek *amelgein* 'to milk'.

milk-and-water ▶ **adjective** [attrib.] lacking the will or ability to act effectively: *a milk-and-water rebel*.

milk bar ▶ **noun** Brit. a snack bar that sells milk drinks and other refreshments.

milk cap ▶ **noun** a large woodland toadstool with a concave cap, the flesh exuding a white or coloured milky fluid when cut.
• Genus *Lactarius*, family Russulaceae, class Hymenomycetes: several species, including the edible **saffron milk cap** (*L. deliciosus*).

milk chocolate ▶ **noun** [mass noun] solid chocolate made in a similar way to plain chocolate but with the addition of milk.

milker ▶ **noun 1** a cow or other animal that is kept for milk, especially one of a specified productivity: *the cows were no more than fair milkers*.
2 a person that milks cows.

milk fever ▶ **noun** [mass noun] **1** an acute illness in female cows, goats, etc. that have just produced young, caused by calcium deficiency.
2 a fever in women caused by infection after childbirth, formerly supposed to be due to the swelling of the breasts with milk.

milkfish ▶ **noun** (pl. same or **-fishes**) a large active silvery fish of the Indo-Pacific region, farmed for food in SE Asia and the Philippines.
• *Chanos chanos*, the only member of the family Chanidae.

milk float ▶ **noun** Brit. an open-sided van, typically powered by electricity, that is used for delivering milk to houses.

milk-glass ▶ **noun** [mass noun] semi-translucent glass, whitened by the addition of various ingredients. Also called **OPALINE**.

milking parlour ▶ **noun** see **PARLOUR** (sense 3).

milking stool ▶ **noun** a short three-legged stool, of a kind traditionally used while milking cows.

milk-leg ▶ **noun** [mass noun] painful swelling of the leg after giving birth, caused by thrombophlebitis in the femoral vein.

milk loaf ▶ **noun** Brit. a loaf of bread made with milk instead of water.

milkmaid ▶ **noun** chiefly archaic a girl or woman who milks cows or does other work in a dairy.

milkman ▶ **noun** (pl. **-men**) a man who delivers and sells milk.

Milk of Magnesia ▶ **noun** [mass noun] Brit. trademark a white suspension of hydrated magnesium carbonate in water, used as an antacid or laxative.

milk powder ▶ **noun** [mass noun] milk dehydrated by evaporation.

milk pudding ▶ **noun** Brit. a baked pudding made of milk and rice or sometimes another grain, such as sago or tapioca.

milk punch ▶ **noun** a drink made of spirits mixed with milk and sometimes other ingredients.

milk round ▶ **noun** Brit. a regular milk delivery along a fixed route.
■ a regular journey that includes calls at several places. ■ a series of visits to universities and colleges by recruiting staff from large companies.

milk run ▶ **noun** a routine, uneventful journey, especially by plane.

milkshake ▶ **noun** a cold drink made of milk, a sweet flavouring such as fruit or chocolate, and typically ice cream, whisked until it is frothy.

milk-sickness ▶ **noun** [mass noun] a condition of cattle and sheep in the western US, caused by eating white snakeroot, which contains a toxic alcohol. It sometimes occurs in humans who have eaten meat or dairy produce from affected animals.

milk snake ▶ **noun** a harmless North American constrictor that is typically strongly marked with red and black on yellow or white. It was formerly supposed to suck milk from sleeping cows.
• Genus *Lampropeltis*, family Colubridae: several species, in particular *L. doliata*. Compare with **KINGSNAKE**.

milksop ▶ **noun** a man or boy who is indecisive and lacks courage.

milk stout ▶ **noun** [mass noun] a kind of sweet stout made with lactose.

milk sugar ▶ **noun** another term for **LACTOSE**.

milk thistle ▶ **noun** a European thistle with a solitary purple flower and glossy marbled leaves, naturalized in America and used in herbal medicine.
• *Silybum marianum*, family Compositae.
■ another term for **SOWTHISTLE**.

milk tooth ▶ **noun** any of a set of early, temporary (deciduous) teeth in children or young mammals which fall out as the permanent teeth erupt (in children between the ages of about 6 and 12).

milk train ▶ **noun** a train that runs very early in the morning to transport milk but also carries passengers.

milk vetch ▶ **noun** a yellow-flowered Eurasian plant of the pea family, grown in some regions as a fodder plant.
• *Astragalus glycyphyllos*, family Leguminosae.

milkweed ▶ **noun 1** [mass noun] a herbaceous American plant with milky sap. Some kinds attract

butterflies, some yield a variety of useful products, and some are grown as ornamentals.
● Genus *Asclepias*, family Asclepiadaceae.
2 (also **milkweed butterfly**) another term for **MONARCH** (in sense 2).

milk-white ▶ **adjective** of the opaque white colour of milk: *she had milk-white skin.*

milkwort ▶ **noun** a small plant with blue, pink, or white flowers, which was formerly believed to increase the milk yield of cows and nursing mothers.
● Genus *Polygala*, family Polygalaceae: several species, including the European **common milkwort** (*P. vulgaris*).

milky ▶ **adjective** (**milkier**, **milkiest**) **1** containing or mixed with a large amount of milk: *a cup of sweet milky coffee.*
■ (of a cow) producing a lot of milk. ■ resembling milk, especially in colour: *not a blemish marred her milky skin.* ■ (of something that is usually clear) cloudy: *the old man's milky, uncomprehending eyes.*
2 informal, dated weak and compliant: *they just talk that way to make you turn milky.*
– DERIVATIVES **milkiness** noun.

Milky Way a faint band of light crossing the sky, made up of vast numbers of faint stars. It corresponds to the plane of our Galaxy, in which most of its stars are located.

Mill, John Stuart (1806–73), English philosopher and economist. Mill is best known for his political and moral works, especially *On Liberty* (1859), which argued for the importance of individuality, and *Utilitarianism* (1861), which extensively developed Bentham's theory.
– DERIVATIVES **Millian** adjective.

mill[1] ▶ **noun 1** a building equipped with machinery for grinding grain into flour.
■ a piece of machinery of this type. ■ a domestic device for grinding a solid substance to powder or pulp: *a coffee mill.* ■ a building fitted with machinery for a manufacturing process: *a steel mill* | [as modifier] *a mill town.* ■ a piece of manufacturing machinery.
2 informal an engine.
3 informal, dated a boxing match or a fist fight.
▶ **verb 1** [with obj.] grind or crush (something) in a mill: *hard wheats are easily milled into white flour* | [as adj., with submodifier] (**milled**) *freshly milled black pepper.*
■ cut or shape (metal) with a rotating tool. [as adj. **milling**] *lathes and milling machines.* ■ [usu. as adj. **milled**] produce regular ribbed markings on the edge of (a coin) as a protection against illegal clipping.
2 [no obj.] (**mill about/around**) (of people or animals) move around in a confused mass: *people milled about the room, shaking hands* | [as adj. **milling**] *the milling crowds of guests.*
3 [with obj.] thicken (wool or another animal fibre) by fulling it.
– PHRASES **go** (or **put someone**) **through the mill** undergo (or cause someone to undergo) an unpleasant experience.
– DERIVATIVES **millable** adjective.
– ORIGIN Old English *mylen*, based on late Latin *molinum*, from Latin *mola* 'grindstone, mill', from *molere* 'to grind'.

mill[2] ▶ **noun** N. Amer. a monetary unit used only in calculations, worth one thousandth of a dollar.
– ORIGIN late 18th cent.: from Latin *millesimum* 'thousandth part'; compare with **CENT**.

Millais /ˈmɪleɪ/, Sir John Everett (1829–96), English painter. A founder member of the Pre-Raphaelite Brotherhood, he went on to produce lavishly painted portraits and landscapes. Notable works: *Christ in the House of his Parents* (1850) and *Bubbles* (1886).

millboard ▶ **noun** [mass noun] stiff grey pasteboard, used for the covers of books.

mill dam ▶ **noun** a dam built across a stream to raise the level of the water so that it will turn the wheel of a watermill.

Mille, Cecil B. de, see **DE MILLE**.

millefeuille /miːlˈfəːi/ ▶ **noun** a rich cake consisting of thin layers of puff pastry filled with jam and cream.
– ORIGIN French, literally 'thousand-leaf'.

millefiori /ˌmiːlɪfɪˈɔːri/ ▶ **noun** [mass noun] a kind of ornamental glass in which a number of glass rods of different sizes and colours are fused together and cut into sections which form various patterns, typically embedded in colourless transparent glass to make items such as paperweights.
– ORIGIN mid 19th cent.: from Italian *millefiore*, literally 'a thousand flowers'.

millefleurs /ˈmiːlflәː/ ▶ **noun** a pattern of flowers and leaves used in tapestry, on porcelain, or in other decorative items.
– ORIGIN mid 19th cent.: French, literally 'a thousand flowers'.

millenarian /ˌmɪlɪˈnɛːrɪən/ ▶ **adjective** relating to or believing in Christian millenarianism.
■ *figurative* believing in the imminence or inevitability of a golden age of peace, justice, and prosperity: *millenarian Marxists.* ■ denoting a religious or political group seeking solutions to present crises through rapid and radical change.
▶ **noun** a person who believes in the doctrine of the millennium.
– ORIGIN mid 17th cent.: from late Latin *millenarius* (see **MILLENARY**) + **-AN**.

millenarianism ▶ **noun** [mass noun] the doctrine of or belief in a future (and typically imminent) thousand-year age of blessedness, beginning with or culminating in the Second Coming of Christ. It is central to the teaching of groups such as Adventists, Mormons, and Jehovah's Witnesses.
■ belief in a future golden age of peace, justice, and prosperity.
– DERIVATIVES **millenarianist** noun & adjective.

millenary /mɪˈlɛnəri, ˈmɪlɪnəri/ ▶ **noun** (pl. **-ies**) a period of a thousand years. Compare with **MILLENNIUM**.
■ a thousandth anniversary.
▶ **adjective** consisting of a thousand people, years, etc.
– ORIGIN mid 16th cent.: from late Latin *millenarius* 'containing a thousand', based on Latin *mille* 'thousand'.

millennialism ▶ **noun** another term for **MILLENARIANISM**.
– DERIVATIVES **millennialist** noun & adjective.

millennium /mɪˈlɛnɪəm/ ▶ **noun** (pl. **millennia** /-nɪə/ or **millenniums**) a period of a thousand years, especially when calculated from the traditional date of the birth of Christ.
■ an anniversary of a thousand years: *the millennium of the Russian Orthodox Church.* ■ (**the millennium**) the point at which one period of a thousand years ends and another begins. ■ (**the millennium**) Christian Theology the prophesied thousand-year reign of Christ at the end of the age (Rev. 20:1–5). ■ (**the millennium**) figurative a utopian period of good government, great happiness, and prosperity.
– DERIVATIVES **millennial** adjective.
– ORIGIN mid 17th cent.: modern Latin, from Latin *mille* 'thousand', on the pattern of *biennium*.

USAGE The correct spelling is **millennium** not **millenium**. The latter is a common error (found in just over 10 per cent of citations in the British National Corpus), formed by analogy with other similar words correctly spelled with only one **n**, such as **millenarian** and **millenary**. The differences in spelling are explained by different origins. **Millennium** was formed by analogy with words like **biennium**, while **millenary** and **millenarian** were formed on the Latin **milleni**.

millennium bug ▶ **noun** a problem with some computers arising from an inability of the software to deal correctly with dates of 1 January 2000 or later.

millepede ▶ **noun** variant spelling of **MILLIPEDE**.

millepore /ˈmɪlɪpɔː/ ▶ **noun** Zoology a fire coral.
– ORIGIN mid 18th cent.: from French *millépore* or modern Latin *millepora*, from Latin *mille* 'thousand' + *porus* 'pore'.

Miller[1], Arthur (b.1915), American dramatist. He established his reputation with *Death of a Salesman* (1949). *The Crucible* (1953) used the Salem witch trials of 1692 as an allegory for McCarthyism in America in the 1950s.

Miller[2], (Alton) Glenn (1904–44), American jazz trombonist and bandleader. He led a celebrated swing big band, with whom he recorded his signature tune 'Moonlight Serenade'. He died when his aircraft disappeared over the English Channel.

Miller[3], Henry (Valentine) (1891–1980), American novelist. His autobiographical novels *Tropic of Cancer* (1934) and *Tropic of Capricorn* (1939) were banned in the US until the 1960s due to their frank depiction of sex and use of obscenities.

miller ▶ **noun** a person who owns or works in a corn mill.

millerite ▶ **noun** [mass noun] a mineral consisting of nickel sulphide and typically occurring as slender needle-shaped bronze crystals.
– ORIGIN mid 19th cent.: named after William H. *Miller* (1801–80), English scientist, + **-ITE**[1].

miller's thumb ▶ **noun** a small European freshwater fish of the sculpin family, having a broad flattened head and most active at night. Also called **BULLHEAD**.
● *Cottus gobio*, family Cottidae.

millesimal /mɪˈlɛsɪm(ə)l/ ▶ **adjective** consisting of thousandth parts; thousandth.
▶ **noun** a thousandth part.
– DERIVATIVES **millesimally** adverb.
– ORIGIN early 18th cent.: from Latin *millesimus* (from *mille* 'thousand') + **-AL**.

Millet /ˈmiːeɪ/, Jean (François) (1814–75), French painter. He was famous for the dignity he brought to the treatment of peasant subjects, which he concentrated on from 1850. Notable works: *The Gleaners* (1857).

millet ▶ **noun** [mass noun] a fast-growing cereal which is widely grown in warm countries and regions with poor soils. The numerous small seeds are widely used to make flour or alcoholic drinks.
● Several species in the family Gramineae, in particular **common millet** (*Panicum miliaceum*), of temperate regions, the tropical **finger millet** (*Eleusine caracana*), which is a staple in parts of Africa and India, and **pearl millet**.
– ORIGIN late Middle English: from French, diminutive of dialect *mil*, from Latin *milium*.

Millett /ˈmɪlɪt/, Kate (b.1934), American feminist; full name *Katherine Millett*. She became involved in the civil rights movement of the 1960s, and advocated a radical feminism in *Sexual Politics* (1970).

millhand ▶ **noun** a worker in a mill or factory.

milli- ▶ **combining form** (used commonly in units of measurement) a thousand, chiefly denoting a factor of one thousandth: *milligram* | *millipede.*
– ORIGIN from Latin *mille* 'thousand'.

milliammeter /ˌmɪlɪˈamɪtə/ ▶ **noun** an instrument for measuring electric current in milliamperes.

milliamp ▶ **noun** short for **MILLIAMPERE**.

milliampere ▶ **noun** one thousandth of an ampere, a measure for small electric currents.

milliard /ˈmɪlɪɑːd/ ▶ **noun** Brit. one thousand million (a term now largely superseded by billion).
– ORIGIN late 18th cent.: French, from *mille* 'thousand'.

millibar ▶ **noun** one thousandth of a bar, the cgs unit of atmospheric pressure equivalent to 100 pascals.

millieme /ˌmiː(l)ˈjɛm/ ▶ **noun** a monetary unit of Egypt, equal to one thousandth of a pound.
– ORIGIN from French *millième* 'thousandth'.

Milligan, Spike (b.1918), British comedian and writer, born in India; born *Terence Alan Milligan*. He came to prominence in the cult radio programme *The Goon Show* (1951–9).

milligram (also **milligramme**) (abbrev.: **mg**) ▶ **noun** one thousandth of a gram.

Millikan /ˈmɪlɪkən/, Robert Andrews (1868–1953), American physicist. He was the first to give an accurate figure for the electric charge on an electron. Nobel Prize for Physics (1923).

millilitre (US **milliliter**) (abbrev.: **ml**) ▶ **noun** one thousandth of a litre (0.002 pint).

millimetre (US **millimeter**) (abbrev.: **mm**) ▶ **noun** one thousandth of a metre (0.039 in.).

milliner ▶ **noun** a person who makes or sells women's hats.
– ORIGIN late Middle English (originally in the sense 'native of Milan', later 'a vendor of fancy goods from Milan'): from **MILAN** + **-ER**[1].

millinery ▶ **noun** (pl. **-ies**) [mass noun] women's hats.
■ the trade or business of a milliner.

million ▶ **cardinal number** (pl. **millions** or (with numeral or quantifying word) same) (**a/one million**) the number equivalent to the product of a thousand and a thousand; 1,000,000 or 10^6: *a million people will benefit* | *a population of half a million* | *a cost of more than £20 million.*
■ (**millions**) the numbers from a million to a billion. ■ (**millions**) several million things or people: *millions of TV viewers.* ■ informal an unspecified but very large number or amount of something: *I've got millions of beer bottles in my cellar* | *you're* **one in a million**. ■ (**the millions**) the bulk of the population: *movies for the*

millions. ■ a million pounds or dollars. *the author is set to make millions.*

– PHRASES **gone a million** Austral. informal (of a person) completely defeated or finished. **look** (or **feel**) (**like**) **a million dollars** informal (of a person) look or feel extremely good.

– DERIVATIVES **millionfold** adjective & adverb. **millionth** ordinal number.

– ORIGIN late Middle English: from Old French, probably from Italian *milione*, from *mille* 'thousand' + the augmentative suffix *-one*.

millionaire ▶ noun a person whose assets are worth one million pounds or dollars or more.

– ORIGIN early 19th cent.: from French *millionnaire*, from *million* (see **MILLION**).

millionairess ▶ noun a female millionaire.

millipede /ˈmɪlɪpiːd/ (also **millepede**) ▶ noun a myriapod invertebrate with an elongated body composed of many segments, most of which bear two pairs of legs. Most kinds are herbivorous and live in the soil or under stones and logs.

● Class Diplopoda: several orders.

– ORIGIN early 17th cent.: from Latin *millepeda* 'woodlouse', from *mille* 'thousand' + *pes, ped-* 'foot'.

millisecond ▶ noun one thousandth of a second.

millivolt ▶ noun one thousandth of a volt.

millpond ▶ noun the pool which is created by a mill dam and provides the head of water that powers a watermill.

■ figurative a very calm stretch of water.

mill race ▶ noun the channel carrying the swift current of water that drives a mill wheel.

Mills, Sir John (Lewis Ernest Watts) (b.1908), English actor. He is best known for his roles in war and adventure films, such as *Scott of the Antarctic* (1948). He won an Oscar for his portrayal of a village idiot in *Ryan's Daughter* (1971).

Mills and Boon ▶ noun [as modifier] trademark used to denote idealized and sentimental romantic situations of the kind associated with the type of fiction published by Mills & Boon Limited: *I'm not exactly the Mills and Boon tall dark stranger.*

Mills bomb ▶ noun historical an oval hand grenade.

– ORIGIN early 20th cent.: named after Sir William Mills (1856–1932), the English engineer who invented it.

millstone ▶ noun each of two circular stones used for grinding corn.

■ figurative a heavy and inescapable responsibility: *she threatened to become a millstone round his neck.*

millstone grit ▶ noun [mass noun] a coarse sandstone of the British Carboniferous, occurring immediately below the coal measures.

■ any hard siliceous rock suitable for making millstones.

millstream ▶ noun the flowing water that drives a mill wheel.

mill wheel ▶ noun a wheel used to drive a watermill.

millworker ▶ noun a worker in a mill or factory.

millwright ▶ noun a person who designs or builds corn mills or who maintains mill machinery.

Milne, A. A. (1882–1956), English writer of stories and poems for children; full name *Alan Alexander Milne*. He created the character Winnie the Pooh for his son Christopher Robin. Notable works: *Winnie-the-Pooh* (1926) and *When We Were Very Young* (verse collection, 1924).

milo /ˈmaɪləʊ/ ▶ noun [mass noun] sorghum of a drought-resistant variety which is an important cereal in the central US.

– ORIGIN late 19th cent.: from Sesotho *maili*.

milometer /maɪˈlɒmɪtə/ (also **mileometer**) ▶ noun Brit. an instrument on a vehicle for measuring the number of miles travelled.

milord ▶ noun historical or humorous used to address or refer to an English nobleman.

– ORIGIN early 17th cent.: via French from English *my lord*; compare with **MILADY**.

Mílos /ˈmiːlɒs/ Greek name for **MELOS**.

Milosevic /mɪˈlɒsəvɪtʃ/, Slobodan (b.1941), Serbian politician, President of Serbia 1989–97 and of Yugoslavia 1997–2000. His nationalist policies accelerated the breakup of Yugoslavia and led to war in Bosnia-Herzegovina, Croatia, and Kosovo.

Milquetoast /ˈmɪlktəʊst/ ▶ noun chiefly N. Amer. a

person who is timid or submissive: [as modifier] *a soppy, Milquetoast composer.*

– ORIGIN 1930s: from the name of a cartoon character, Caspar *Milquetoast*, created by H. T. Webster in 1924.

milreis /ˈmɪlreɪs/ ▶ noun (pl. same) a former monetary unit of Portugal and Brazil equal to one thousand reis.

– ORIGIN Portuguese, from *mil* 'thousand' + *reis*, plural of *real* (see **REAL**²).

milt ▶ noun [mass noun] the semen of a male fish.

■ [count noun] a sperm-filled reproductive gland of a male fish.

– ORIGIN Old English *milte* 'spleen', of Germanic origin; perhaps related to **MELT**. The current sense dates from the late 15th cent.

Milton, John (1608–74), English poet. His three major works, completed after he had gone blind (1652), show his mastery of blank verse: they are the epic poems *Paradise Lost* (1667, revised 1674) and *Paradise Regained* (1671), and the verse drama *Samson Agonistes* (1671).

– DERIVATIVES **Miltonian** adjective, **Miltonic** adjective.

Milton Keynes /ˈkiːnz/ a town in south central England; pop. 172,300 (1991). It was established as a new town in the late 1960s, and is the site of the headquarters of the Open University.

Milwaukee /mɪlˈwɔːki/ an industrial port and city in SE Wisconsin, on the west shore of Lake Michigan; pop. 628,090 (1990). It is noted for its brewing industry.

mim ▶ adjective Scottish affectedly modest or demure.

– ORIGIN late 16th cent.: imitative of pursing the lips.

Mimas /ˈmaɪmas, -məs/ Astronomy a satellite of Saturn, the seventh closest to the planet, which has a crater a third of its whole diameter and was discovered by W. Herschel in 1789 (diameter 390 km).

– ORIGIN named after a giant in Greek mythology, killed by Mars.

mimbar /ˈmɪmbɑː/ ▶ noun variant spelling of **MINBAR**.

mime ▶ noun 1 [mass noun] the theatrical technique of suggesting action, character, or emotion without words, using only gesture, expression, and movement.

■ [count noun] a theatrical performance or part of a performance using such a technique. ■ [count noun] an action or set of actions intended to convey the idea of another action or an idea or feeling: *he performed a brief mime of someone fencing.* ■ (also **mime artist**) [count noun] a practitioner of mime or a performer in a mime.

2 (in ancient Greece and Rome) a simple farcical drama including mimicry.

▶ verb [with obj.] use gesture and movement without words in the acting of (a play or role).

■ convey an impression of (an idea, emotion, or feeling) by gesture and movement, without using words; mimic (an action or set of actions) in this way: *he stands up and mimes throwing a spear.* ■ [no obj.] pretend to sing or play an instrument as a recording is being played: *singers and musicians on television often mime to pre-recorded tape tracks.*

– DERIVATIVES **mimer** noun.

– ORIGIN early 17th cent. (also in the sense 'mimic or jester'): from Latin *mimus*, from Greek *mimos*.

mimeo /ˈmɪmɪəʊ/ ▶ noun short for **MIMEOGRAPH**.

mimeograph ▶ noun a duplicating machine which produces copies from a stencil, now superseded by the photocopier.

■ a copy produced on such a machine.

▶ verb [with obj.] make a copy of (a document) with such a machine.

– ORIGIN late 19th cent.: formed irregularly from Greek *mimeomai* 'I imitate' + **-GRAPH**.

mimesis /mɪˈmiːsɪs, maɪ-/ ▶ noun formal or technical imitation, in particular:

■ representation or imitation of the real world in art and literature. ■ the deliberate imitation of the behaviour of one group of people by another as a factor in social change. ■ Zoology another term for **MIMICRY**.

– ORIGIN mid 16th cent.: from Greek *mimēsis*, from *mimeisthai* 'to imitate'.

mimetic /mɪˈmɛtɪk, maɪ-/ ▶ adjective formal or technical relating to, constituting, or habitually practising mimesis: *mimetic patterns in butterflies.*

– DERIVATIVES **mimetically** adverb.

– ORIGIN mid 17th cent.: from Greek *mimētikos* 'imitation', from *mimeisthai* 'to imitate'.

mimetite /ˈmɪmɪtaɪt, ˈmaɪ-/ ▶ noun [mass noun] a yellow or brown mineral consisting of a chloride and arsenate of lead, typically found as a crust or needle-like crystals in lead deposits.

– ORIGIN mid 19th cent.: from Greek *mimētēs* 'imitator' + **-ITE**¹.

mimic ▶ verb (**mimicked**, **mimicking**) [with obj.] imitate (someone or their actions or words), typically in order to entertain or ridicule: *she mimicked Eileen's voice.*

■ (of an animal or plant) resemble or imitate (another animal or plant), especially to deter predators or for camouflage. ■ (of a drug) replicate the physiological effects of (another substance). ■ (of a disease) exhibit symptoms that bear a deceptive resemblance to those of (another disease).

▶ noun a person skilled in imitating the voice, mannerisms, or movements of others in an entertaining way.

■ an animal or plant that exhibits mimicry.

▶ adjective [attrib.] imitative of something, especially for amusement: *they were waging mimic war.*

– DERIVATIVES **mimicker** noun.

– ORIGIN late 16th cent. (as noun and adjective): via Latin from Greek *mimikos*, from *mimos* 'mime'.

mimicry ▶ noun (pl. -ies) [mass noun] the action or art of imitating someone or something, typically in order to entertain or ridicule: *the word was spoken with gently teasing mimicry.*

■ Biology the close external resemblance of an animal or plant (or part of one) to another animal, plant, or inanimate object. See also **BATESIAN MIMICRY**, **MÜLLERIAN MIMICRY**.

mimosa /mɪˈməʊzə, -sə/ ▶ noun 1 an Australian acacia tree with delicate fern-like leaves and yellow flowers which are the mimosa of florists.

● *Acacia dealbata*, family Leguminosae.

2 a plant of a genus that includes the sensitive plant.

● Genus *Mimosa*, family Leguminosae.

3 N. Amer. a drink of champagne and orange juice.

– ORIGIN modern Latin, apparently from Latin *mimus* 'mime' (because the plant seemingly mimics the sensitivity of an animal) + the feminine suffix *-osa*.

mimsy ▶ adjective rather feeble and prim or over-restrained.

– ORIGIN 1871: nonsense word coined by Lewis Carroll; a blend of **MISERABLE** and **FLIMSY**.

mimulus /ˈmɪmjʊləs/ ▶ noun a plant of a genus which includes the musk plants and the monkey flower.

● Genus *Mimulus*, family Scrophulariaceae.

– ORIGIN modern Latin, apparently a diminutive of Latin *mimus* 'mime', perhaps with reference to its mask-like flowers.

Min ▶ noun [mass noun] a dialect of Chinese spoken by over 50 million people, mainly in Fujian province, Hainan, and Taiwan. It has two main forms, northern and southern.

– ORIGIN Chinese.

min. ▶ abbreviation for ■ minim (fluid measure). ■ minimum. ■ minute(s).

minacious /mɪˈneɪʃəs/ ▶ adjective rare menacing; threatening.

– ORIGIN mid 17th cent.: from Latin *minax, minac-* 'threatening' (from *minari* 'threaten') + **-OUS**.

Minamata disease /ˌmɪnəˈmɑːtə/ ▶ noun [mass noun] chronic poisoning by alkyl mercury compounds from industrial waste, characterized by (usually permanent) impairment of brain functions such as speech, sight, and muscular coordination.

– ORIGIN 1950s: named after *Minamata*, a town in Japan.

Minangkabau /ˌmiːnaŋkəˈbaʊ/ ▶ noun [mass noun] an Indonesian language spoken by over 6 million people in Sumatra and elsewhere.

– ORIGIN Malay and Indonesian.

minaret /ˈmɪnarɛt, ˌmɪnəˈrɛt/ ▶ noun a slender tower, typically part of a mosque, with a balcony from which a muezzin calls Muslims to prayer.

– DERIVATIVES **minareted** adjective.

– ORIGIN late 17th cent.: from French, or from Spanish *minarete*, Italian *minaretto*, via Turkish from Arabic *manār(a)* 'lighthouse, minaret', based on *nār* 'fire or light'.

Minas Gerais /ˌmiːnas ʒɛˈraɪs/ a state of SE Brazil; capital, Belo Horizonte. It has major deposits of iron ore, coal, gold, and diamonds.

minatory /ˈmɪnət(ə)ri/ ▶ **adjective** formal expressing or conveying a threat: *he is unlikely to be deterred by minatory finger-wagging.*
– ORIGIN mid 16th cent.: from late Latin *minatorius*, from *minat-* 'threatened', from the verb *minari*.

minaudière /ˌmɪnəʊˈdjɛː/ ▶ **noun** a small, decorative handbag without handles or a strap.
– ORIGIN French, literally 'coquettish woman', from *minauder* 'simper'.

minbar /ˈmɪnbɑː/ (also **mimbar**) ▶ **noun** a short flight of steps used as a platform by a preacher in a mosque.
– ORIGIN from Arabic *minbar*.

mince ▶ **verb** [with obj.] **1** [often as adj. **minced**] cut up or grind (food, especially meat) into very small pieces, typically in a machine with revolving blades: *minced beef.*
2 [no obj., with adverbial of direction] walk with an affected delicacy or fastidiousness, typically with short quick steps: *there were plenty of secretaries mincing about.*
▶ **noun** [mass noun] chiefly Brit. minced meat, especially beef.
– PHRASES **mince matters** [usu. with negative] dated use polite or moderate expressions to indicate disapproval. **not mince words** (or **one's words**) speak candidly and directly, especially when criticizing someone or something.
– DERIVATIVES **mincer** noun, **mincingly** adverb (only in sense 2).
– ORIGIN late Middle English: from Old French *mincier*, based on Latin *minutia* 'smallness'.

mincemeat ▶ **noun** [mass noun] **1** a mixture of currants, raisins, sugar, apples, candied peel, spices, and suet, typically baked in pastry.
2 minced meat.
– PHRASES **make mincemeat of someone** informal defeat someone decisively or easily in a fight, contest, or argument.

mince pie ▶ **noun** chiefly Brit. a small round pie or tart containing sweet mincemeat, typically eaten at Christmas.

Minch /mɪn(t)ʃ/ (**the Minch**) a channel of the Atlantic, between the mainland of Scotland and the Outer Hebrides. The northern stretch is called the **North Minch**, the southern stretch, north-west of Skye, is called the **Little Minch**. Also called **THE MINCHES**.

mind ▶ **noun 1** the element of a person that enables them to be aware of the world and their experiences, to think, and to feel; the faculty of consciousness and thought: *as the thoughts ran through his mind, he came to a conclusion | people have the price they are prepared to pay settled in their minds.*
■ a person's mental processes contrasted with physical action: *I wrote a letter in my mind.*
2 a person's intellect: *his keen mind.*
■ the state of normal mental functioning in a person: *the strain has affected his mind.* ■ a person's memory: *the company's name **slips** my **mind**.* ■ a person identified with their intellectual faculties: *he was one of the greatest minds of his time.*
3 a person's attention: *I expect my employees to keep their minds on the job.*
■ the will or determination to achieve something: *anyone can slim if they set their mind to it.*
▶ **verb** [with obj.] **1** [often with negative] be distressed, annoyed, or worried by: *I don't mind the rain.*
■ have an objection to: *what does that mean, if you don't mind my asking?* | [with clause] *do you mind if I have a cigarette?* ■ [with negative or in questions] (**mind doing something**) be reluctant to do something (often used in polite requests): *I don't mind admitting I was worried.* ■ (**would not mind something**) informal used to express one's strong enthusiasm for something: *I wouldn't mind some coaching from him!*
2 regard as important and worthy of attention: *never mind the opinion polls.*
■ [no obj.] feel concern: *why should she mind about a few snubs from people she didn't care for?* ■ [with clause, in imperative] used to urge someone to remember or take care to bring about something: *mind you look after the children.* ■ [no obj., in imperative] (also **mind you**) used to introduce a qualification to a previous statement: *we've got some decorations up—not a lot, mind you.* ■ [no obj., in imperative] informal used to make a command more insistent or to draw attention to a statement: *be early to bed tonight, mind.* ■ N. Amer. & Irish be obedient to: *you think about how much Cal does for you, and you mind her, you hear?* ■ Scottish remember: *I mind the time when he lost his false teeth.*
3 take care of temporarily: *we left our husbands to mind the children while we went out.*
■ [in imperative] used to warn someone to avoid injury or damage from a hazard: *mind your head on that cupboard!* ■ [no obj., in imperative] Brit. take care: *mind out—there's a step missing.* ■ [in imperative] be careful about the quality or nature of: *mind your manners!*
4 [with infinitive] (**be minded**) chiefly formal be inclined or disposed to do a particular thing: *he was minded to reject the application | the Board was given leave to object if it was so minded.*
– PHRASES **be in** (or chiefly N. Amer. **of**) **two minds** be unable to decide between alternatives. **be of one** (or **a different**) **mind** share the same (or hold a different) opinion. **close** (or **shut**) **one's mind to** (or **against**) refuse to consider or acknowledge. **come** (or **spring**) **to mind** (of a thought or idea) occur to someone. **don't mind if I do** informal used to accept an invitation: *'Have some breakfast.' 'Ta very much—don't mind if I do.'* **give someone a piece of one's mind** tell someone what one thinks of them, especially in anger. **have a** (or **a good** or **half a**) **mind to do something** be very much inclined to do something: *I've a good mind to write to the manager to complain.* **have someone or something in mind** be thinking of. ■ intend: *I **had it in mind** to ask you to work for me.* **have a mind of one's own** be capable of independent opinion or action. ■ (of an inanimate object) seem capable of thought and intention, especially by behaving contrary to the will of the person using it: *the trolley had a mind of its own.* **in one's mind's eye** in one's imagination or mental view. **mind over matter** the use of will power to overcome physical problems. **mind one's own business** refrain from prying or interfering. **mind one's Ps & Qs** be careful to behave well and avoid giving offence. [ORIGIN: of unknown origin; said by some to refer to the care a young pupil must pay in differentiating the tailed letters *p* and *q*.] **mind the shop** informal have charge of something temporarily. **never mind 1** used to urge someone not to feel anxiety or distress: *never mind—it's all right now.* ■ used to suggest that a problem or objection is not important: *that's getting off the subject but never mind.* **2** (also **never you mind**) used in refusing to answer a question: *never mind where I'm going.* **3** used to indicate that what has been said of one thing applies even more to another: *he was so tired that he found it hard to think, never mind talk.* **not pay someone any mind** N. Amer. not pay someone any attention. **on someone's mind** preoccupying someone, especially in a disquieting way: *new parents have many worries on their minds.* **an open mind** the readiness to consider something without prejudice. **open one's mind to** be receptive to: *he opened his mind to the ways of the rest of the world.* **out of one's mind** having lost control of one's mental faculties. ■ informal suffering from a particular condition to a very high degree: *she was bored out of her mind.* **put someone in mind of** resemble and so cause someone to think of or remember: *he was a small, well-dressed man who put her in mind of a jockey.* **put** (or **give** or **set**) **one's mind to** direct all one's attention to (achieving something): *she'd have made an excellent dancer, if she'd have put her mind to it.* **put someone/thing out of one's mind** deliberately forget someone or something. **to my mind** in my opinion: *this story is, to my mind, a masterpiece.*
– ORIGIN Old English *gemynd* 'memory, thought', of Germanic origin, from an Indo-European root meaning 'revolve in the mind, think', shared by Sanskrit *manas* and Latin *mens* 'mind'.

mind-altering ▶ **adjective** (of a hallucinogenic drug) producing mood changes or giving a sense of heightened awareness.

Mindanao /ˌmɪndəˈnaʊ/ the second largest island in the Philippines, in the south-east of the group. Its chief town is Davao.

mind-bending ▶ **adjective** informal (chiefly of a psychedelic drug) influencing or altering one's state of mind.
– DERIVATIVES **mind-bender** noun, **mind-bendingly** adverb.

mind-blowing ▶ **adjective** informal overwhelmingly impressive: *for a kid, Chicago was really mind-blowing.*
■ (of a drug) inducing hallucinations.
– DERIVATIVES **mind-blowingly** adverb.

mind-boggling ▶ **adjective** informal overwhelming; startling: *the implications are mind-boggling.*
– DERIVATIVES **mind-bogglingly** adverb.

minded ▶ **adjective** [in combination or with submodifier] inclined to think in a particular way: *liberal-minded scholars | I'm not scientifically minded.*
■ [in combination] interested in or enthusiastic about the thing specified: *conservation-minded citizens.*

Mindel /ˈmɪnd(ə)l/ ▶ **noun** [usu. as modifier] Geology a Pleistocene glaciation in the Alps preceding the Riss, possibly corresponding to the Elsterian of northern Europe.
■ the system of deposits laid down at this time.
– ORIGIN early 20th cent.: from the name of a river in southern Germany.

minder ▶ **noun** a person whose job it is to look after someone or something: [in combination] *a baby-minder.*
■ informal a bodyguard employed to protect a celebrity or criminal: *he was accompanied by his personal minder.*

mind-expanding ▶ **adjective** (especially of a hallucinogenic drug) giving a sense of heightened or broader awareness.

mindful ▶ **adjective** [predic.] conscious or aware of something: *we can be more **mindful of** the energy we use to heat our homes.*
■ [with infinitive] formal inclined or willing to do something: *the judge said that he was not mindful to postpone the eviction again.*
– DERIVATIVES **mindfully** adverb, **mindfulness** noun.

mind game ▶ **noun** a series of deliberate actions or responses planned for psychological effect on another, typically for amusement or competitive advantage.

mindless ▶ **adjective** (of a person) acting without concern for the consequences: *a generation of mindless vandals.*
■ (especially of harmful or evil behaviour) done for no particular reason: *mindless violence.* ■ [predic.] (**mindless of**) not thinking of or concerned about: *mindless of the fact she was in her nightie, she rushed to the door.* ■ (of an activity) so simple or repetitive as to be performed automatically without thought or skill: *the monotony of housework turns it into a mindless task.*
– DERIVATIVES **mindlessly** adverb, **mindlessness** noun.

mind-numbing ▶ **adjective** so extreme or intense as to prevent normal thought: *a landscape of mind-numbing boredom.*
– DERIVATIVES **mind-numbingly** adverb.

Mindoro /mɪnˈdɔːrəʊ/ an island in the Philippines, situated to the south-west of Luzon.

mind-reader ▶ **noun** a person who can supposedly discern what another person is thinking.
– DERIVATIVES **mind-reading** noun.

mindset ▶ **noun** [usu. in sing.] the established set of attitudes held by someone: *the region seems stuck in a medieval mindset.*

mind-your-own-business ▶ **noun** a creeping Mediterranean plant with masses of tiny pale green leaves, widely cultivated as a greenhouse or indoor plant. Also called **MOTHER OF THOUSANDS**.
• *Soleirolia soleirolia*, family Urticaceae.

mine[1] ▶ **possessive pronoun** used to refer to a thing or things belonging to or associated with the speaker: *you go your way and I'll go mine | some friends **of mine**.*
▶ **possessive determiner** archaic (used before a vowel) my: *tears did fill mine eyes.*
– ORIGIN Old English *mīn*, of Germanic origin; related to **ME**[1] and to Dutch *mijn* and German *mein*.

mine[2] ▶ **noun 1** an excavation in the earth for extracting coal or other minerals: *a copper mine.*
■ [in sing.] an abundant source of something: *the book contains **a mine of** information.*
2 a type of bomb placed on or just below the surface of the ground or in the water which detonates when activated by a person, vehicle, or ship.
■ historical a subterranean passage under the wall of a besieged fortress, especially one in which explosives are put to blow up fortifications.
▶ **verb** [with obj.] (often **be mined**) **1** obtain (coal or other minerals) from a mine.
■ dig in (the earth) for coal or other minerals: *the hills were **mined for** copper oxide* | [no obj.] *many English financiers managed to obtain concessions to **mine for** silver.* ■ dig or burrow in (the earth). ■ figurative delve into (an abundant source) to extract something of value, especially information or skill: *how do they manage to mine such **a rich vein of** talent?*
2 lay explosive mines on or just below the surface of (the ground or water): *the area was heavily mined.*
■ destroy by means of an explosive mine.
– DERIVATIVES **mineable** (also **minable**) adjective.
– ORIGIN late Middle English: from Old French *mine*

(noun), *miner* (verb), perhaps of Celtic origin; compare with Welsh *mwyn* 'ore', earlier 'mine'.

mine-detector ▶ noun an instrument used for detecting explosive mines.

mine dump ▶ noun S. African a large mound or hill of mining waste at the surface of a mine.

minefield ▶ noun an area planted with explosive mines.
■ figurative a subject or situation presenting unseen hazards: *tax is a minefield for the unwary.*

minehunter ▶ noun Brit. a warship used for detecting and destroying explosive mines.
– DERIVATIVES **minehunting** noun.

minelayer ▶ noun a warship, aircraft, or land vehicle from which explosive mines are laid.
– DERIVATIVES **minelaying** noun.

miner ▶ noun 1 a person who works in a mine.
■ historical a person who dug tunnels in order to destroy an enemy position with explosives. ■ short for LEAF MINER.
2 an Australian bird of the honeyeater family, having a loud call and typically nesting socially.
● Genus *Manorina*, family Meliphagidae: five species, including the **bell miner** or bellbird (*M. melanophrys*), with greenish plumage and a bell-like call.
3 a small South American bird of the ovenbird family, which excavates a long burrow for breeding.
● Genus *Geositta*, family Furnariidae: several species.
– ORIGIN Middle English: from Old French *minour*, from *miner* 'to mine' (see MINE²).

mineral ▶ noun 1 a solid inorganic substance of natural occurrence.
■ a substance obtained by mining. ■ an inorganic substance needed by the human body for good health.
2 (**minerals**) Brit. (in commercial use) effervescent soft drinks.
▶ adjective of or denoting a mineral: *mineral ingredients such as zinc oxide.*
– ORIGIN late Middle English: from medieval Latin *minerale*, neuter (used as a noun) of *mineralis*, from *minera* 'ore'.

mineralize (also **-ise**) ▶ verb [with obj.] convert (organic matter) wholly or partly into a mineral or inorganic material or structure.
■ impregnate (water or another liquid) with a mineral substance.
– DERIVATIVES **mineralization** noun.

mineralocorticoid /ˌmɪn(ə)rələ(ʊ)ˈkɔːtɪkɔɪd/ ▶ noun Biochemistry a corticosteroid which is involved with maintaining the salt balance in the body, such as aldosterone.

mineralogy ▶ noun [mass noun] the scientific study of minerals.
– DERIVATIVES **mineralogical** adjective, **mineralogically** adverb, **mineralogist** noun.

mineral oil ▶ noun [mass noun] petroleum.
■ a distillation product of petroleum, especially one used as a lubricant, moisturizer, or laxative.

mineral spirits ▶ noun North American term for WHITE SPIRIT.

mineral water ▶ noun [mass noun] water found in nature with some dissolved salts present.
■ an artificial imitation of this, especially soda water.

mineral wool ▶ noun [mass noun] a substance resembling matted wool and made from inorganic mineral material, used chiefly for packing or insulation.

miner's right ▶ noun Austral./NZ a licence to prospect and dig for gold or another mineral.

Minerva /mɪˈnɜːvə/ Roman Mythology the goddess of handicrafts, widely worshipped and regularly identified with Athene, which led to her being regarded also as the goddess of war.

Minervois /ˌmɪnɛːˈvwɑː, French minɛʁvwa/ ▶ noun [mass noun] a wine produced in the district of Minervois, in the department of Aude in southern France.

mineshaft ▶ noun a deep narrow vertical hole, or sometimes a horizontal tunnel, that gives access to a mine.

minestrone /ˌmɪnɪˈstrəʊni/ ▶ noun [mass noun] a fairly thick soup containing vegetables and pasta.
– ORIGIN Italian.

minesweeper ▶ noun a warship equipped for detecting and removing or destroying tethered explosive mines.
– DERIVATIVES **minesweeping** noun.

Ming ▶ noun the dynasty ruling China 1368–1644 founded by Zhu Yuanzhang (1328–98).
■ [mass noun] [usu. as modifier] Chinese porcelain made during the rule of the Ming dynasty, characterized by elaborate designs and vivid colours: *a priceless Ming vase.*
– ORIGIN Chinese, literally 'clear or bright'.

minge /mɪn(d)ʒ/ ▶ noun Brit. vulgar slang a woman's pubic hair or genitals.
– ORIGIN late 19th cent.: of unknown origin.

mingle ▶ verb mix or cause to mix together: [no obj.] *the sound of voices mingled with a scraping of chairs* | [with obj.] *a smell which mingled disinfectant and scouring soap.*
■ [no obj.] move freely around a place or at a social function, associating with others: *over aperitifs, there was a chance to mingle with friends old and new.*
– ORIGIN late Middle English: frequentative of obsolete *meng* 'mix or blend' (related to AMONG), perhaps influenced by Middle Dutch *mengelen*.

Mingus /ˈmɪŋɡəs/, Charles (1922–79), American jazz bassist and composer. A leading figure of the 1940s jazz scene, he experimented with atonality and was influenced by gospel and blues. His compositions include 'Goodbye Porkpie Hat'.

mingy /ˈmɪn(d)ʒi/ ▶ adjective (**mingier**, **mingiest**) informal mean: *you've been too mingy with the sunscreen.*
■ unexpectedly or undesirably small: *a mingy kitchenette tucked in the corner.*
– DERIVATIVES **mingily** adverb.
– ORIGIN early 20th cent.: perhaps a blend of MEAN² and STINGY.

Minho /ˈmiːnjʊ/ Portuguese name for MIÑO.

mini ▶ adjective [attrib.] denoting a miniature version of something: *a mini camera.*
▶ noun (pl. **minis**) 1 a very short skirt or dress.
2 short for MINICOMPUTER.
– ORIGIN 1960s: abbreviation.

mini- ▶ combining form very small or minor of its kind; miniature: *minicab* | *minicomputer.*
– ORIGIN from MINIATURE, reinforced by MINIMUM.

miniature ▶ adjective [attrib.] (especially of a replica of something) of a much smaller size than normal; very small: *children dressed as miniature adults.*
▶ noun a thing that is much smaller than normal, especially a small replica or model.
■ a very small bottle of spirits. ■ a plant or animal that is a small version of an existing variety or breed. ■ a very small and highly detailed portrait or other painting. ■ a picture or decorated letter in an illuminated manuscript.
▶ verb [with obj.] rare represent on a smaller scale; reduce to miniature dimensions.
– PHRASES **in miniature** on a small scale, but otherwise a replica: *a place that is Greece in miniature.*
– ORIGIN early 18th cent.: from Italian *miniatura*, via medieval Latin from Latin *miniare* 'rubricate, illuminate', from *minium* 'red lead, vermilion' (used to mark particular words in manuscripts).

miniaturist ▶ noun a painter of miniatures or an illuminator of manuscripts.

miniaturize (also **-ise**) ▶ verb [with obj.] [usu. as adj. **miniaturized**] make on a smaller or miniature scale.
– DERIVATIVES **miniaturization** noun.

minibar ▶ noun a refrigerator in a hotel room containing a selection of mainly alcoholic drinks that are charged for on the bill if used by the occupant.

minibeast ▶ noun Brit. informal a small invertebrate animal such as an insect or spider.

mini-break ▶ noun a very short holiday, especially a package holiday lasting only two or three days.

mini-budget ▶ noun a minor or interim budget, especially one prepared by a state or government.

minibus ▶ noun a small bus for about ten to fifteen passengers.

minicab ▶ noun Brit. a car that is used as a taxi but which must be ordered in advance because it is not licensed to pick up passengers who hail it in the street.

minicam ▶ noun a hand-held video camera.

minicomputer ▶ noun a computer of medium power, more than a microcomputer but less than a mainframe.

Minicoy Islands /ˈmɪnɪkɔɪ/ one of the groups of islands forming the Indian territory of Lakshadweep in the Indian Ocean.

minidisc ▶ noun a disc having a format similar to a small CD but able to record sound or data as well as play it back.

minidress ▶ noun a very short dress.

minifundium /ˌmɪnɪˈfʌndɪəm/ (/-dɪə/) ▶ noun (pl. **minifundia** /-dɪə/) a small farm or property in Latin America, especially one that is too small to support a single family.
– ORIGIN 1950s: modern Latin, or from Spanish *minifundio* 'smallholding'.

minigolf ▶ noun [mass noun] an informal version of golf played on a series of short constructed obstacle courses.

minikin ▶ adjective chiefly archaic small; insignificant: *capable men devoting their lives to such minikin pursuits.*

minim ▶ noun 1 Music, chiefly Brit. a note having the time value of two crotchets or half a semibreve, represented by a ring with a stem. Also called HALF NOTE.
2 a small Roman coin, typically of bronze.
3 one sixtieth of a fluid drachm, about one drop of liquid.
4 Calligraphy a short vertical stroke, as in the letters *i*, *m*, *n*, *u*.
– ORIGIN late Middle English: from Latin *minima*, from *minimus* 'smallest'.

minima plural form of MINIMUM.

minimal ▶ adjective 1 of a minimum amount, quantity, or degree; negligible: *a minimal amount of information* | *production costs are minimal.*
2 Art characterized by the use of simple or primary forms or structures, especially geometric or massive ones.
■ Music characterized by the repetition and gradual alteration of short phrases.
3 Linguistics (of a pair of forms) distinguished by only one feature: *'p' and 'b' are a minimal pair, distinguished by the feature of voicing.*
– DERIVATIVES **minimally** adverb.
– ORIGIN mid 17th cent.: from Latin *minimus* 'smallest' + -AL.

minimalism ▶ noun 1 a trend in sculpture and painting which arose in the 1950s and used simple, typically massive, forms.
2 an avant-garde movement in music characterized by the repetition of very short phrases which change gradually, producing a hypnotic effect.

minimalist ▶ noun 1 a person advocating minor or moderate reform in politics.
2 a person who advocates or practises minimalism in art or music.
▶ adjective 1 advocating moderate political policies.
2 of or relating to minimalism in art or music.
– ORIGIN early 20th cent.: first used with reference to the Russian Mensheviks. Usage in art and music dates from the 1960s.

mini-mall ▶ noun N. Amer. a shopping mall containing a relatively small number of retail outlets and with access to each shop from the outside rather than from an interior hallway.

minimart ▶ noun N. Amer. a convenience store.

minimax ▶ noun Mathematics the lowest of a set of maximum values. Compare with MAXIMIN.
■ [as modifier] denoting a method or strategy in game theory that minimizes the greatest risk to a participant in a game or other situation of conflict. ■ [as modifier] denoting the theory that in a game with two players, a player's smallest possible maximum loss is equal to the same player's greatest possible minimum gain.
– ORIGIN 1940s: blend of MINIMUM and MAXIMUM.

minimize (also **-ise**) ▶ verb [with obj.] reduce (something, especially something unwanted or unpleasant) to the smallest possible amount or degree: *the aim is to minimize costs.*
■ represent or estimate at less than the true value or importance: *they may minimize, or even overlook, the importance of such beliefs.*
– DERIVATIVES **minimization** noun, **minimizer** noun.

minimum ▶ noun (pl. **minima** or **minimums**) [usu. in sing.] the least or smallest amount or quantity possible, attainable, or required: *the need for economy kept packaging to a minimum* | *they checked passports with the minimum of fuss.*
■ the lowest or smallest amount of a varying quantity (e.g. temperature) allowed, attained, or recorded: *clients with a minimum of £500,000 to invest.*
▶ adjective [attrib.] smallest or lowest: *this can be done with the minimum amount of effort.*

minimum wage

– PHRASES **at a** (or **the**) **minimum** at the very least: *we zipped along at a minimum of 55 mph.*

– ORIGIN mid 17th cent.: from Latin, neuter of *minimus* 'least'.

minimum wage ▶ noun the lowest wage permitted by law or by a special agreement (such as one with a trade union).

mining ▶ noun [mass noun] the process or industry of obtaining coal or other minerals from a mine.

mining bee ▶ noun a solitary bee that builds long underground tunnels containing nest chambers. A number of individuals sometimes nest close together but there is no cooperation between them.
● *Andrena* and other genera, family Apidae.

minion /ˈmɪnjən/ ▶ noun a follower or underling of a powerful person, especially a servile or unimportant one.

– ORIGIN late 15th cent.: from French *mignon*, *mignonne*.

mini-pill ▶ noun a contraceptive pill containing a progestogen and not oestrogen.

mini roundabout ▶ noun Brit. a small traffic roundabout, indicated by road markings or a very low island.

mini rugby ▶ noun [mass noun] a simplified version of rugby with only nine players in a team.

miniseries ▶ noun (pl. same) a television drama shown in a number of episodes.
■ Brit. a television or radio series of about three or four programmes on a single or related themes.

miniskirt ▶ noun a very short skirt.

minister ▶ noun 1 a head of a government department: *the Defence Minister.*
■ a diplomatic agent, usually ranking below an ambassador, representing a state or sovereign in a foreign country.
2 (also **minister of religion**) a member of the clergy, especially in the Presbyterian and Nonconformist Churches.
■ (also **minister general**) the superior of some religious orders.
3 archaic a person or thing used to achieve or convey something: *the Angels are ministers of the Divine Will.*
▶ verb [no obj.] 1 (**minister to**) attend to the needs of (someone): *her doctor was busy ministering to the injured.*
■ [with obj.] archaic provide (something necessary or helpful): *the story was able to minister true consolation.*
2 act as a minister of religion.
■ [with obj.] administer (a sacrament).

– DERIVATIVES **ministership** noun.

– ORIGIN Middle English (in senses 2 and 3): from Old French *ministre* (noun), *ministrer* (verb), from Latin *minister* 'servant', from *minus* 'less'.

ministerial ▶ adjective 1 of or relating to a government minister or ministers: *a back-bencher who had never held ministerial office.*
2 of or relating to a minister of religion.
3 archaic acting as an agent, instrument, or means in achieving a purpose: *those uses of conversation which are ministerial to intellectual culture.*

– DERIVATIVES **ministerially** adverb.

– ORIGIN mid 16th cent.: from French *ministériel* or late Latin *ministerialis*, from Latin *ministerium* 'ministry'.

ministering angel ▶ noun often humorous a kind-hearted person, especially a woman, who nurses or comforts others.

– ORIGIN early 17th cent.: with biblical allusion to Mark 1:13.

Minister of State ▶ noun a government minister, in particular:
■ (in the UK) a minister ranking below a Secretary of State: *the Minister of State for Education.* ■ (in Canada) a federal government minister having responsibility for a certain policy area but without direct control over a department, a position superseded in 1993 by the creation of that of Secretary of State.

Minister of the Crown ▶ noun (in the UK and Canada) a member of the cabinet.

Minister without Portfolio ▶ noun (in the UK and some other countries) a government minister who has cabinet status, but is not in charge of a specific department of state.

ministration ▶ noun (usu. **ministrations**) chiefly formal or humorous the provision of assistance or care: *a kitchen made spotless by the ministrations of a cleaning lady.*
■ the services of a minister of religion or of a religious institution. ■ [mass noun] the action of administering the sacrament.

– DERIVATIVES **ministrant** noun.

– ORIGIN late Middle English: from Latin *ministratio(n-)*, from *ministrare* 'wait upon', from *minister* (see **MINISTER**).

ministry ▶ noun (pl. **-ies**) 1 a government department headed by a minister: *the Ministry of Defence.*
2 [usu. in sing.] the work or vocation of a minister of religion: *he is training for the ministry.*
■ the period of tenure of a minister of religion. ■ the spiritual work or service of any Christian or a group of Christians, especially evangelism: *a ministry of Christian healing.*
3 a period of government under one Prime Minister.
4 [mass noun] rare the action of ministering to someone: *the soldiers were no less in need of his ministry.*

– ORIGIN Middle English (in sense 2): from Latin *ministerium*, from *minister* (see **MINISTER**).

minitower ▶ noun a small vertical case for a computer, or a computer mounted in such a case.

minivan ▶ noun a small van, typically one fitted with seats in the back for transporting passengers.

miniver /ˈmɪnɪvə/ ▶ noun [mass noun] plain white fur used for lining or trimming clothes.

– ORIGIN Middle English: from Old French *menu vair* 'little vair', from *menu* 'little' + *vair* 'squirrel fur' (see **VAIR**).

minivet /ˈmɪnɪvɪt/ ▶ noun a boldly patterned Asian cuckoo-shrike, the male of which is typically red and black, and the female yellow and grey.
● Genus *Pericrocotus*, family Campephagidae: several species.

– ORIGIN mid 19th cent.: of unknown origin.

mink ▶ noun (pl. same or **minks**) a small semiaquatic stoat-like carnivore native to North America and Eurasia. The American mink is widely farmed for its fur, resulting in it becoming naturalized in many parts of Europe.
● Genus *Mustela*, family Mustelidae: the **American mink** (*M. vison*) and the smaller **European mink** (*M. lutreola*).
■ [mass noun] the thick brown fur of the mink. ■ a coat made of this.

– ORIGIN late Middle English (denoting the animal's fur): from Swedish.

minke /ˈmɪŋkə, -ki/ (also **minke whale**) ▶ noun a small rorqual whale with a dark grey back, white underparts, and pale markings on the fins and behind the head.
● *Balaenoptera acutorostrata*, family Balaenopteridae.

– ORIGIN 1930s: probably from *Meincke*, the name of a Norwegian whaler.

Minkowski /mɪŋˈkɒfski/, Hermann (1864–1909), Russian-born German mathematician. He worked on the properties of sets in multidimensional systems, and suggested the concept of four-dimensional space-time, which was the basis for Einstein's general theory of relativity.

min-min (also **min-min light**) ▶ noun Austral. a will-o'-the-wisp.

– ORIGIN probably from a Queensland Aboriginal language.

Minn. ▶ abbreviation for Minnesota.

Minneapolis /ˌmɪnɪˈapəlɪs/ an industrial city and port on the Mississippi in SE Minnesota; pop. 368,380 (1990). It is a major agricultural centre of the upper Midwest.

minneola /ˌmɪnɪˈəʊlə/ ▶ noun a deep reddish tangelo of a thin-skinned variety.

– ORIGIN mid 20th cent.: named after a town in Florida, US.

minnerichi /ˌmɪnəˈrɪtʃi/ (also **minnaritchi**) ▶ noun a small acacia of arid inland Australia, which typically has thin, peeling curls of reddish bark.
● *Acacia cyperophylla*, family Leguminosae.

– ORIGIN early 20th cent.: an Aboriginal word.

Minnesinger /ˈmɪnəsɪŋə/ ▶ noun a German lyric poet and singer of the 12th–14th centuries, who performed songs of courtly love.

– ORIGIN early 19th cent.: from German *Minnesinger* 'love-singer'.

Minnesota /ˌmɪnɪˈsəʊtə/ a state in the north central US, on the Canadian border; pop. 4,375,100 (1990); capital, St Paul. It became the 32nd state of the US in 1858.

– DERIVATIVES **Minnesotan** noun & adjective.

minnow ▶ noun a small freshwater Eurasian fish of

the carp family, which typically forms large shoals.
● *Phoxinus phoxinus*, family Cyprinidae.
■ used in names of similar small freshwater fishes, e.g. **mudminnow**, **topminnow**. ■ Fishing an artificial lure imitating a minnow. ■ a person or organization of relatively small size, power, or influence.

– ORIGIN late Middle English: probably related to Dutch *meun* and German *Münne*, influenced by Anglo-Norman French *menu* 'small, minnow'.

Miño /ˈmiːnjəʊ/ a river which rises in NW Spain and flows south to the Portuguese border, which it follows before entering the Atlantic north of Viana do Castelo. Portuguese name **MINHO**.

Minoan /mɪˈnəʊən/ ▶ adjective of, relating to, or denoting a Bronze Age civilization centred on Crete (c.3000–1050 BC), its people, or its language.
▶ noun 1 an inhabitant of Minoan Crete or member of the Minoan people.
2 [mass noun] the language or scripts associated with the Minoans.

> The Minoan civilization had reached its zenith by the beginning of the late Bronze Age; impressive remains reveal the existence of large urban centres dominated by palaces. The civilization is also noted for its script (see **LINEAR A**) and distinctive art and architecture.

– ORIGIN named after the legendary Cretan king **MINOS**, to whom a palace excavated at Knossos was attributed.

minor ▶ adjective 1 lesser in importance, seriousness, or significance: *she requested a number of minor alterations.*
■ (of a surgical operation) comparatively simple and not life-threatening.
2 Music (of a scale) having intervals of a semitone between the second and third degrees, and (usually) the fifth and sixth, and the seventh and eighth. Contrasted with **MAJOR**.
■ (of an interval) characteristic of a minor scale and less by a semitone than the equivalent major interval. Compare with **DIMINISHED**. ■ [usu. postpositive] (of a key or mode) based on a minor scale, tending to produce a sad or pensive effect: *Concerto in A minor.*
3 Brit. dated (following a surname in public schools) indicating the second or younger of two brothers or boys with the same family name: *Smith minor.*
4 Logic (of a term) occurring as the subject of the conclusion of a categorical syllogism.
■ (of a premise) containing the minor term in a categorical syllogism.
▶ noun 1 a person under the age of full legal responsibility.
2 Music a minor key, interval, or scale.
■ Bell-ringing a system of change-ringing using six bells.
3 (**minors**) N. Amer. the minor leagues in a particular professional sport, especially baseball or American football: *Salinas was one of six teams in the minors.*
4 N. Amer. a student's subsidiary subject or course: *a minor in American Indian studies.*
5 Logic a minor term or premise.
6 Bridge short for **MINOR SUIT**.
7 a small drab moth which has purplish caterpillars that feed on grass.
● Genus *Oligia*, family Noctuidae.

– PHRASES **in a minor key** (especially of a literary work) understated.

– ORIGIN Middle English: from Latin, 'smaller, less'; related to *minuere* 'lessen'. The term originally denoted a Franciscan friar, suggested by the Latin name *Fratres Minores* ('Lesser Brethren'), chosen by St Francis for the order.

▶ **minor in** N. Amer. study or qualify in as a subsidiary subject at college or university.

minor arcana ▶ noun see **ARCANA**.

minor axis ▶ noun Geometry the shorter axis of an ellipse that is perpendicular to its major axis.

Minorca /mɪˈnɔːkə/ the most easterly and second largest of the Balearic Islands; pop. 58,700 (1981); capital, Mahón. Spanish name **MENORCA**.

– DERIVATIVES **Minorcan** adjective & noun.

minor canon ▶ noun a member of the Christian clergy who assists in the daily services of a cathedral but is not a member of the chapter.

minor county ▶ noun Cricket, Brit. a county whose team does not take part in the County Championship.

Minorite /ˈmʌɪnərʌɪt/ a Franciscan friar or Friar Minor.

minority ▶ noun (pl. **-ies**) 1 the smaller number or part, especially a number which is less than half

the whole number: *harsher measures for* ***the minority of*** *really serious offenders* | [as modifier] *a minority party.*
■ the number of votes cast for or by the smaller party in a legislative assembly: *a blocking minority of 23 votes.* ■ a relatively small group of people, especially one commonly discriminated against in a community, society, or nation, differing from others in race, religion, language, or political persuasion: *representatives of ethnic minorities* | [as modifier] *minority rights.*
2 [mass noun] the state or period of being under the age of full legal responsibility.
– PHRASES **be** (or **find oneself**) **in a minority of one** often humorous be the sole person to be in favour of or against something. **in the minority** belonging to or constituting the smaller group or number.
– ORIGIN late 15th cent. (denoting the state of being a minor): from French *minorité* or medieval Latin *minoritas*, from Latin *minor* 'smaller' (see **MINOR**).

minority government ▶ noun a government in which the governing party has most seats but still less than half the total.

minority report ▶ noun a separate report presented by members of a committee or other group who disagree with the majority.

minor league ▶ noun [often as modifier] N. Amer. a league below the level of the major league in a particular professional sport, especially baseball or American football: *a minor-league team.*
– DERIVATIVES **minor-leaguer** noun.

minor orders ▶ plural noun chiefly historical the formal grades of Catholic or Orthodox clergy below the rank of deacon (most now discontinued).

minor piece ▶ noun Chess a bishop or knight.
– ORIGIN early 19th cent.: named in contrast to the rook or queen.

minor planet ▶ noun an asteroid. Often contrasted with **MAJOR PLANET**.

minor prophet ▶ noun any of the twelve prophets after whom the shorter prophetic books of the Bible, from Hosea to Malachi, are named.

minor suit ▶ noun Bridge diamonds or clubs.
– ORIGIN early 20th cent.: so named because of their lower scoring value.

minor tranquillizer ▶ noun a tranquillizer of the kind used to treat anxiety states, especially a benzodiazepine.

Minos /ˈmʌɪnɒs/ Greek Mythology a legendary king of Crete, son of Zeus and Europa. His wife Pasiphaë gave birth to the Minotaur; Minos later exacted tribute from Athens in the form of young people to be devoured by the monster.

Minos, Palace of a complex of buildings excavated and reconstructed by Sir Arthur Evans at Knossos, which yielded local coins portraying the labyrinth as the city's symbol and a Linear B religious tablet which refers to the 'lady of the labyrinth'.

Minotaur /ˈmɪnətɔː, ˈmʌɪ-/ Greek Mythology a creature who was half-man and half-bull, the offspring of Pasiphaë and a bull with which she fell in love. Confined in Crete in a labyrinth made by Daedalus and fed on human flesh, it was eventually slain by Theseus.
– ORIGIN from Old French, via Latin from Greek *Minōtauros*, from *Minōs* (see **MINOS**) + *tauros* 'bull'.

minotaur beetle ▶ noun a black Eurasian dung beetle with three horns on the thorax. It typically lives in sandy areas and favours rabbit and sheep droppings.
• *Typhaeus typhoeus*, family Geotrupidae.

minoxidil /mɪˈnɒksɪdɪl/ ▶ noun [mass noun] Medicine a synthetic drug which is used as a vasodilator in the treatment of hypertension, and is also used in lotions to promote hair growth.
– ORIGIN 1970s: from **AMINO** + **OXIDE** + *-dil* (perhaps representing **DILATE**).

Minsk /mɪnsk/ the capital of Belarus, an industrial city in the central region of the country; pop. 1,613,000 (1990).

minster ▶ noun a large or important church, typically one of cathedral status in the north of England that was built as part of a monastery: *York Minster.*
– ORIGIN Old English *mynster*, via ecclesiastical Latin from Greek *monastērion* (see **MONASTERY**).

minstrel ▶ noun a medieval singer or musician, especially one who sang or recited lyric or heroic poetry to a musical accompaniment for the nobility.
– ORIGIN Middle English: from Old French *menestral* 'entertainer, servant', via Provençal from late Latin *ministerialis* 'servant' (see **MINISTERIAL**).

minstrelsy ▶ noun [mass noun] the practice of performing as a minstrel: *a long tradition of minstrelsy.*
– ORIGIN Middle English: from Old French *menestralsie*, from *menestrel* (see **MINSTREL**).

mint[1] ▶ noun **1** an aromatic plant native to temperate regions of the Old World, several kinds of which are used as culinary herbs.
• Genus *Mentha*, family Labiatae (or Lamiaceae; the **mint family**): several species and hybrids, in particular the widely cultivated **common mint** or **spearmint** (*M. spicata*) and **peppermint** (*M.* × *piperita*). The mint family, the members of which have distinctive two-lobed flowers and square stems, also includes the dead-nettles and many aromatic herbs.
■ [mass noun] the flavour of mint, especially peppermint.
2 a peppermint sweet.
– DERIVATIVES **minty** adjective (**mintier**, **mintiest**).
– ORIGIN Old English *minte*, of West Germanic origin; related to German *Minze*, ultimately via Latin from Greek *minthē*.

mint[2] ▶ noun a place where money is coined, especially under state authority.
■ (**a mint**) informal a vast sum of money: *the curtains had* ***cost a mint****, but Aunt thought they were worth it.*
▶ adjective (of an object) in pristine condition; as new: *a pair of speakers including stands, mint, £160.* [ORIGIN: elliptically from *in mint condition*.]
▶ verb [with obj.] (often **be minted**) make (a coin) by stamping metal.
■ [usu. as adj., with submodifier] (**minted**) produce for the first time: *an example of newly minted technology.*
– PHRASES **in mint condition** (of an object) new or as if new.
– ORIGIN Old English *mynet* 'coin', of West Germanic origin; related to Dutch *munt* and German *Münze*, from Latin *moneta* 'money'.

mintage ▶ noun [mass noun] the minting of coins.
■ the number of copies issued of a particular coin: *an estimated mintage of about 800.*

minted ▶ adjective flavoured or seasoned with mint: *grilled lamb chops with minted potatoes.*

minter ▶ noun **1** a person who mints money.
2 Brit. informal something in mint condition, especially a second-hand car.

mint julep ▶ noun a long drink consisting of bourbon, crushed ice, sugar, and fresh mint and associated chiefly with the Southern states of the United States.

mint mark ▶ noun a mark on a coin indicating the mint at which it was struck.

mint master ▶ noun a superintendent at a mint.

Minton ▶ noun [mass noun] pottery made at Stoke-on-Trent by Thomas Minton (1766–1836) or his factory. Minton's company popularized the willow pattern.

mint sauce ▶ noun [mass noun] chopped spearmint in vinegar and sugar, traditionally eaten with lamb.

minuend /ˈmɪnjʊɛnd/ ▶ noun Mathematics a quantity or number from which another is to be subtracted.
– ORIGIN early 18th cent.: from Latin *minuendus*, gerundive of *minuere* 'diminish'.

minuet ▶ noun a slow, stately ballroom dance for two in triple time, popular especially in the 18th century.
■ a piece of music in triple time in the style of such a dance, typically as a movement in a suite, sonata, or symphony and frequently coupled with a trio.
▶ verb (**minueted**, **minueting**) [no obj.] dance a minuet.
– ORIGIN late 17th cent.: from French *menuet*, 'fine, delicate', diminutive (used as a noun) of *menu* 'small'.

minus ▶ preposition **1** with the subtraction of: *what's ninety three minus seven?*
■ informal lacking; deprived of: *he was minus a finger on each hand.*
2 (of temperature) below zero: *minus 40 degrees centigrade.*
▶ adjective **1** (before a number) below zero; negative: *minus five.*
2 (after a grade) rather worse than: *C minus, could do better.*
3 having a negative electric charge.
▶ noun **1** short for **MINUS SIGN**.
■ a mathematical operation of subtraction.
2 a disadvantage: *for every plus with this equipment there can be a minus.*
– ORIGIN late 15th cent.: from Latin, neuter of *minor* 'less'.

minuscule /ˈmɪnəskjuːl/ ▶ adjective **1** extremely small; tiny: *a minuscule fragment of DNA.*
■ informal so small as to be negligible or insufficient: *he believed the risk of infection was minuscule.*
2 of or in lower-case letters, as distinct from capitals or uncials.
■ of or in a small cursive script of the Roman alphabet, with ascenders and descenders, developed in the 7th century AD.
▶ noun [mass noun] minuscule script.
■ [count noun] a small or lower-case letter.
– DERIVATIVES **minuscular** /mɪˈnʌskjʊlə/ adjective.
– ORIGIN early 18th cent.: from French, from Latin *minuscula* (*littera*) 'somewhat smaller (letter)'.

USAGE The correct spelling is **minuscule** rather than **miniscule**. The latter is a common error, which has arisen by analogy with other words beginning with **mini-**, where the meaning is similarly 'very small'.

minus sign ▶ noun the symbol –, indicating subtraction or a negative value.

minute[1] /ˈmɪnɪt/ ▶ noun **1** a period of time equal to sixty seconds or a sixtieth of an hour: *he stood in the shower for twenty minutes* | ***in ten minutes' time*** *he could be on his way.*
■ the distance covered in this length of time by someone driving or walking: *the hotel is situated just ten* ***minutes from*** *the centre of the resort.* ■ informal a very short time: *come and sit down* ***for a minute****.* ■ an instant or a point of time: *she had been laughing* ***one minute*** *and crying* ***the next****.*
2 (also **arc minute** or **minute of arc**) a sixtieth of a degree of angular measurement (symbol: ʹ).
– PHRASES **any minute** (or **at any minute**) very soon. **at the minute** Brit. informal at the present time. **by the minute** (especially of the progress of a change) very rapidly: *matters grew worse by the minute.* **just** (or **wait**) **a minute 1** used as a request to delay an action, departure, or decision for a short time, usually to allow the speaker to do something: *wait a minute—I have to put my make-up on.* **2** as a prelude to a challenge, query, or objection: *wait a minute—that just isn't true.* **the minute** (or **the minute that**) as soon as. **not for a minute** not at all: *don't think for a minute that our pricing has affected our quality standards.* **this minute** (or **this very minute**) informal **1** at once; immediately. **2** Brit. only a short while ago: *I've* ***just this minute*** *got back to the flat.*
– ORIGIN late Middle English: via Old French from late Latin *minuta*, feminine (used as a noun) of *minutus* 'made small'. The senses 'period of sixty seconds' and 'sixtieth of a degree' derive from medieval Latin *pars minuta prima* 'first minute part'.

minute[2] /mʌɪˈnjuːt/ ▶ adjective (**minutest**) extremely small: *her flat was minute.*
■ so small as to verge on insignificance: *he will have no more than a minute chance of exercising significant influence.* ■ (of an inquiry or investigation, or an account of one) taking the smallest points into consideration; precise and meticulous: *a minute examination of the islands.*
– DERIVATIVES **minutely** adverb, **minuteness** noun.
– ORIGIN late Middle English (in the sense 'lesser', with reference to a tithe or tax): from Latin *minutus* 'lessened', past participle of *minuere*.

minute[3] /ˈmɪnɪt/ ▶ noun (**minutes**) a summarized record of the proceedings at a meeting.
■ an official memorandum authorizing or recommending a course of action.
▶ verb [with obj.] record or note (the proceedings of a meeting or a specified item among such proceedings).
■ send information to (someone) by means of a memorandum: *look up the case and minute me about it.*
– ORIGIN late Middle English (in the singular in the sense 'note or memorandum'): from French *minute*, from the notion of a rough copy in 'small writing' (Latin *scriptura minuta*) as distinct from the fair copy in book hand. The verb dates from the mid 16th cent.

minute gun ▶ noun a gun fired at intervals of a minute, especially at a funeral.

minuteman /ˈmɪnɪtman/ ▶ noun (pl. **-men**) historical a member of a class of militiamen of the American revolutionary period who volunteered to be ready for service at a minute's notice.

minute steak ▶ noun a thin slice of steak cooked very quickly.

minutiae /mɪˈnjuːʃiː, mʌɪ-, -ʃɪʌɪ/ (also **minutia** /-ʃɪə/) ▶ plural noun the small, precise, or trivial details of something: *the minutiae of everyday life.*
– ORIGIN mid 18th cent.: Latin, literally 'trifles', from *minutia* 'smallness', from *minutus* (see MINUTE²).

minx ▶ noun humorous or derogatory an impudent, cunning, or boldly flirtatious girl or young woman.
– DERIVATIVES **minxish** adjective.
– ORIGIN mid 16th cent. (denoting a pet dog): of unknown origin.

minyan /ˈmɪnjən/ ▶ noun (pl. **minyanim** /ˈmɪnjənɪm/) a quorum of ten men over the age of 13 required for traditional Jewish public worship.
■ a meeting of Jews for public worship.
– ORIGIN mid 18th cent.: from Hebrew *minyān*, literally 'reckoning'.

Miocene /ˈmʌɪə(ʊ)siːn/ ▶ adjective Geology of, relating to, or denoting the fourth epoch of the Tertiary period, between the Oligocene and Pliocene epochs.
■ [as noun **the Miocene**] the Miocene epoch or the system of rocks deposited during it.

The Miocene epoch lasted from 23.3 to 5.2 million years ago. During this time the Alps and Himalayas were being formed and there was diversification of the primates, including the first apes.

– ORIGIN mid 19th cent.: formed irregularly from Greek *meiōn* 'less' + *kainos* 'new'.

miosis /mʌɪˈəʊsɪs/ (also **myosis**) ▶ noun [mass noun] excessive constriction of the pupil of the eye.
– DERIVATIVES **miotic** adjective.
– ORIGIN early 19th cent.: from Greek *muein* 'shut the eyes' + -OSIS.

MIPS ▶ noun a unit of computing speed equivalent to a million instructions per second.
– ORIGIN 1970s: acronym.

Miquelet lock /ˈmɪkəlɪt/ ▶ noun historical a type of flintlock developed in Spain.
– ORIGIN late 17th cent.: via French from Spanish *miquelete*, from Catalan *Miquel*, equivalent of the given name Michael.

Miquelon see ST PIERRE AND MIQUELON.

Mir /mɪə/ a Soviet space station, launched in 1986 and designed to be permanently manned.

Mira /ˈmʌɪrə/ Astronomy a star in the constellation Cetus, regarded as the prototype of long-period variable stars.
– ORIGIN Latin, literally 'wonderful'.

Mirabeau /ˈmɪrəbəʊ, French miʁabo/, Honoré Gabriel Riqueti, Comte de (1749–91), French revolutionary politician. Pressing for a form of constitutional monarchy, Mirabeau was prominent in the early days of the French Revolution.

mirabelle /ˌmɪrəˈbɛl/ ▶ noun a sweet yellow plum-like fruit that is a variety of the greengage.
■ the tree that bears such fruit. ■ [mass noun] a liqueur distilled from such fruit.
– ORIGIN early 18th cent.: from French.

mirabile dictu /mɪˌrɑːbɪleɪ ˈdɪktuː/ ▶ adverb wonderful to relate.
– ORIGIN Latin.

miracidium /ˌmɪrəˈsɪdɪəm/ ▶ noun (pl. **miracidia**) Zoology a free-swimming ciliated larval stage in which a parasitic fluke passes from the egg to its first host, typically a snail.
– ORIGIN late 19th cent.: from Greek *meirakidion*, diminutive of *meirakion* 'boy, stripling'.

miracle ▶ noun a surprising and welcome event that is not explicable by natural or scientific laws and is therefore considered to be the work of a divine agency: *the miracle of rising from the grave.*
■ a highly improbable or extraordinary event, development, or accomplishment that brings very welcome consequences: *it was a miracle that more people hadn't been killed or injured* | [as modifier] *a miracle drug.* ■ an amazing product or achievement, or an outstanding example of something: *a machine which was a miracle of design.*
– ORIGIN Middle English: via Old French from Latin *miraculum* 'object of wonder', from *mirari* 'to wonder', from *mirus* 'wonderful'.

miracle play ▶ noun a mystery play.

miraculous ▶ adjective occurring through divine or supernatural intervention, or manifesting such power: *a miraculous cure.*
■ highly improbable and extraordinary and bringing

very welcome consequences: *I felt amazed and grateful for our miraculous escape.*
– DERIVATIVES **miraculously** adverb, **miraculousness** noun.
– ORIGIN late Middle English: from French *miraculeux* or medieval Latin *miraculosus*, from Latin *miraculum* (see MIRACLE).

mirador /ˌmɪrəˈdɔː, ˈmɪrədɔː/ ▶ noun a turret or tower attached to a building and providing an extensive view.
– ORIGIN late 17th cent.: from Spanish, from *mirar* 'to look'.

mirage /ˈmɪrɑːʒ, mɪˈrɑːʒ/ ▶ noun an optical illusion caused by atmospheric conditions, especially the appearance of a sheet of water in a desert or on a hot road caused by the refraction of light from the sky by heated air.
■ something that appears real or possible but is not in fact so: *to insist that science provides cast-iron knowledge is to believe in a mirage.*
– ORIGIN early 19th cent.: from French, from *se mirer* 'be reflected', from Latin *mirare* 'look at'.

Miranda¹ Astronomy a satellite of Uranus, the eleventh closest to the planet, having a complex terrain of cratered areas and tracts of grooves and ridges, discovered in 1948 (diameter 480 km).
– ORIGIN named after the daughter of Prospero in Shakespeare's *The Tempest.*

Miranda² ▶ adjective US Law denoting or relating to the duty of the police to inform a person taken into custody of their right to legal counsel and the right to remain silent under questioning: *the patrolman read Lee his Miranda rights.*
– ORIGIN mid 20th cent.: from *Miranda* versus *Arizona*, the case that led to this ruling by the Supreme Court.

MIRAS /ˈmʌɪrəs/ ▶ abbreviation for (in the UK) mortgage interest relief at source.

mirch /mɪətʃ/ ▶ noun Indian term for CHILLI or CHILLI POWDER.

mire ▶ noun a stretch of swampy or boggy ground.
■ [mass noun] soft and slushy mud or dirt. ■ figurative a situation or state of difficulty, distress, or embarrassment from which it is hard to extricate oneself: *he has been left to squirm in a mire of new allegations.* ■ Ecology a wetland area or ecosystem based on peat.
▶ verb [with obj.] (usu. **be mired**) cause to become stuck in mud: *sometimes a heavy truck gets mired down.*
■ cover or spatter with mud. ■ figurative (**mire someone/thing in**) involve someone or something in (difficulties): *the economy is mired in its longest recession since the second world war.*
– ORIGIN Middle English: from Old Norse *mýrr*, of Germanic origin; related to MOSS.

mirepoix /ˈmɪəˌpwɑː/ ▶ noun a mixture of sautéed chopped vegetables used in various sauces.
– ORIGIN French, named after the Duc de *Mirepoix* (1699–1757), French general.

mirex /ˈmʌɪrɛks/ ▶ noun [mass noun] a synthetic insecticide of the organochlorine type used chiefly against ants.
– ORIGIN 1960s: of unknown origin.

mirid /ˈmɪrɪd, ˈmʌɪrɪd/ ▶ noun an active plant bug of a large family that includes numerous plant pests. Formerly called CAPSID¹.
● Family Miridae (formerly Capsidae), suborder Heteroptera.
– ORIGIN 1940s: from modern Latin *Miridae*, from *mirus* 'wonderful'.

mirin /ˈmɪrɪn/ ▶ noun [mass noun] a rice wine used as a flavouring in Japanese cookery.
– ORIGIN Japanese.

mirk ▶ noun & adjective archaic spelling of MURK.

mirky ▶ adjective archaic spelling of MURKY.

mirliton /ˈmɪːlɪtɒn/ ▶ noun 1 a musical instrument with a nasal tone produced by a vibrating membrane, typically a toy instrument resembling a kazoo.
2 chiefly US another term for CHAYOTE (in sense 1).
– ORIGIN early 19th cent.: from French, 'reed pipe', of imitative origin.

Miró /mɪˈrəʊ/, Joan (1893–1983), Spanish painter. One of the most prominent figures of surrealism, he painted a brightly coloured fantasy world of variously spiky and amoebic calligraphic forms against plain backgrounds.

miro /ˈmɪərəʊ/ (also **miro tree**) ▶ noun (pl. **-os**) an evergreen coniferous New Zealand tree which yields useful timber.

● *Prumnopitys ferruginea*, family Podocarpaceae.
– ORIGIN mid 19th cent.: from Maori.

mirrnyong /ˈmɜːnjɒŋ/ (also **mirnyong**) ▶ noun Austral. a mound of shells, ashes, and other debris accumulated in a place used for cooking by Australian Aboriginals.
– ORIGIN probably from an Aboriginal language of Victoria.

mirror ▶ noun a reflective surface, now typically of glass coated with a metal amalgam, which reflects a clear image.
■ figurative something regarded as accurately representing something else: *the stage is supposed to be the mirror of life.* ■ (also **mirror site**) Computing a site on a network which stores some or all of the contents from another site.
▶ verb [with obj.] (of a reflective surface) show a reflection of: *the clear water mirrored the sky.*
■ figurative correspond to: *gradations of educational attainment that mirror differences in social background.* ■ Computing keep a copy of some or all of the contents of (a network site) at another site, typically in order to improve accessibility. ■ [usu. as noun **mirroring**] Computing store copies of data in (two or more hard disks) as a method of protecting it.
– DERIVATIVES **mirrored** adjective.
– ORIGIN Middle English: from Old French *mirour*, based on Latin *mirare* 'look at'. Early senses also included 'a crystal used in magic' and 'a person deserving imitation'.

mirrorball ▶ noun a revolving ball covered with small mirrored facets, used to provide lighting effects at discos or dances.

mirror carp ▶ noun a common carp of an ornamental variety that has a row of large shiny plate-like scales along each side. It has been naturalized in Britain and elsewhere.

mirror finish ▶ noun a very smooth reflective finish produced on the surface of a metal.

mirror glass ▶ noun [mass noun] glass with a reflective metallic coating, as used for mirrors.

mirror image ▶ noun an image or object which is identical in form to another, but with the structure reversed, as in a mirror.
■ a person or thing that closely resembles another: *each shop is a mirror image of all the others.*

mirror symmetry ▶ noun [mass noun] symmetry about a plane, like that between an object and its reflection.

mirror writing ▶ noun [mass noun] reversed writing resembling ordinary writing reflected in a mirror.

mirth ▶ noun [mass noun] amusement, especially as expressed in laughter: *his six-foot frame shook with mirth.*
– DERIVATIVES **mirthful** adjective, **mirthfully** adverb.
– ORIGIN Old English *myrgth*, of Germanic origin; related to MERRY.

mirthless ▶ adjective (of a smile or laugh) lacking real amusement and typically expressing irony.
– DERIVATIVES **mirthlessly** adverb, **mirthlessness** noun.

MIRV /mɜːv/ ▶ noun a type of intercontinental nuclear missile carrying several independent warheads.
– ORIGIN 1960s: acronym from *Multiple Independently targeted Re-entry Vehicle.*

miry /ˈmʌɪri/ ▶ adjective very muddy or boggy: *the roads were miry in winter.*

MIS Computing ▶ abbreviation for management information systems.

mis-¹ ▶ prefix (added to verbs and their derivatives) wrongly: *misapply.*
■ badly: *mismanage.* ■ unsuitably: *misname.*
– ORIGIN Old English, of Germanic origin.

mis-² ▶ prefix occurring in a few words adopted from French expressing a sense with negative force: *misadventure* | *mischief.*
– ORIGIN from Old French *mes-* (based on Latin *minus*), assimilated to MIS-¹.

misadventure ▶ noun 1 (also **death by misadventure**) [mass noun] Law death caused by a person accidentally while performing a legal act without negligence or intent to harm.
2 an unfortunate incident; a mishap: *the petty misdemeanours and misadventures of childhood.*
– ORIGIN Middle English (in sense 2): from Old French *mesaventure*, from *mesavenir* 'turn out badly'.

misaligned ▶ adjective having an incorrect position or alignment: *misaligned headlights.*

misalignment ▶ noun [mass noun] the incorrect arrangement or position of something in relation to something else.

misalliance ▶ noun an unsuitable, unhappy, or unworkable alliance or marriage.
– ORIGIN mid 18th cent.: from **MIS-**[1] 'awry' + **ALLIANCE**, on the pattern of French *mésalliance*.

misallocate ▶ verb [with obj.] fail to allocate (something) efficiently or fairly.
– DERIVATIVES **misallocation** noun.

misandry /mɪ'sandri/ ▶ noun [mass noun] the hatred of men (i.e. the male sex specifically).
– ORIGIN 1940s: from Greek *miso-* 'hating' + *aner, andr-* 'man', on the pattern of *misogyny*.

misanthrope /'mɪz(ə)nθrəʊp, mɪs-/ (also **misanthropist** /mɪ'zanθrəpɪst, mɪ'san-/) ▶ noun a person who dislikes humankind and avoids human society.
– DERIVATIVES **misanthropic** adjective, **misanthropical** adjective, **misanthropically** adverb.
– ORIGIN mid 16th cent.: from Greek *misanthrōpos*, from *misein* 'to hate' + *anthrōpos* 'man'.

misanthropy /mɪ'zanθrəpi, mɪ'san-/ ▶ noun [mass noun] a dislike of humankind.
– ORIGIN mid 17th cent.: from Greek *misanthrōpia*, from *miso-* 'hating' + *anthropos* 'man'.

misapply ▶ verb (-ies, -ied) [with obj.] (usu. **be misapplied**) use (something) for the wrong purpose or in the wrong way.
– DERIVATIVES **misapplication** noun.

misapprehension ▶ noun a mistaken belief about or interpretation of something: *people tried to exchange the vouchers* ***under the misapprehension that*** *they were book tokens.*
– DERIVATIVES **misapprehensive** adjective.

misappropriate ▶ verb [with obj.] (of a person) dishonestly or unfairly take (something, especially money, belonging to another) for one's own use: *the report revealed that department officials had misappropriated funds.*
– DERIVATIVES **misappropriation** noun.

misbegotten ▶ adjective badly conceived, designed, or planned: *someone's misbegotten idea of an English country house.*
■ contemptible (used as a term of abuse): *you misbegotten hound!* ■ archaic (of a child) illegitimate.

misbehave ▶ verb [no obj.] (of a person, especially a child) fail to conduct oneself in a way that is acceptable to others; behave badly.
■ (of a machine) fail to function correctly: *her regularly serviced car was misbehaving.*
– DERIVATIVES **misbehaviour** noun.

misbelief ▶ noun a wrong or false belief or opinion: *the misbelief that alcohol problems require a specialist response.*
■ less common term for **DISBELIEF**.
– DERIVATIVES **misbeliever** noun.

misc. ▶ abbreviation for miscellaneous.

miscalculate ▶ verb [with obj.] calculate (an amount, distance, or measurement) wrongly.
■ assess (a situation) wrongly.
– DERIVATIVES **miscalculation** noun.

miscall ▶ verb [with obj. and complement] call (something) by a wrong or inappropriate name.
■ [with obj.] archaic or dialect insult (someone) verbally.

miscarriage ▶ noun **1** the expulsion of a fetus from the womb before it is able to survive independently, especially spontaneously or as the result of accident: *his wife had a miscarriage* | [mass noun] *some pregnancies result in miscarriage.*
2 an unsuccessful outcome of something planned: *the miscarriage of the project.*

miscarriage of justice ▶ noun a failure of a court or judicial system to attain the ends of justice, especially one which results in the conviction of an innocent person.

miscarry ▶ verb (-ies, -ied) [no obj.] **1** (of a pregnant woman) have a miscarriage: *Wendy conceived, but she miscarried after five weeks* | [with obj.] *an ultrasound scan showed that she had miscarried her baby.*
2 (of something planned) fail to attain an intended or expected outcome: *such a rash crime, and one so very likely to miscarry!*
■ dated (of a letter) fail to reach its intended destination.

miscast ▶ verb (past and past participle **miscast**) [with obj.] (usu. **be miscast**) allot an unsuitable role to (a particular actor): *he is badly miscast in the romantic lead.*
■ allot the roles in (a play or film) to unsuitable actors.

miscegenation /ˌmɪsɪdʒɪ'neɪʃ(ə)n/ ▶ noun [mass noun] the interbreeding of people considered to be of different racial types.
– ORIGIN mid 19th cent.: formed irregularly from Latin *miscere* 'to mix' + *genus* 'race' + **-ATION**.

miscellanea /ˌmɪsə'leɪnɪə/ ▶ plural noun miscellaneous items, especially literary compositions, that have been collected together.
– ORIGIN late 16th cent.: from Latin, neuter plural of *miscellaneus* (see **MISCELLANEOUS**).

miscellaneous /ˌmɪsə'leɪnɪəs/ ▶ adjective (of items or people gathered or considered together) of various types or from different sources: *he picked up the miscellaneous papers in the in tray.*
■ (of a collection or group) composed of members or elements of different kinds: *a miscellaneous collection of well-known ne'er-do-wells.*
– DERIVATIVES **miscellaneously** adverb, **miscellaneousness** noun.
– ORIGIN early 17th cent.: from Latin *miscellaneus* (from *miscellus* 'mixed', from *miscere* 'to mix') + **-OUS**. In earlier use the word also described a person as 'having various qualities'.

miscellany /mɪ'sɛləni/ ▶ noun (pl. **-ies**) a group or collection of different items; a mixture: *to the east was a* ***miscellany of*** *houses.*
■ a book containing a collection of pieces of writing by different authors.
– ORIGIN late 16th cent.: from French *miscellanées* (feminine plural), from Latin *miscellanea* (see **MISCELLANEA**).

mischance ▶ noun [mass noun] bad luck: *by pure mischance the secret was revealed.*
■ [count noun] an unlucky occurrence: *innumerable mischances might ruin the enterprise.*
– ORIGIN Middle English: from Old French *mescheance*, from the verb *mescheoir*, from *mes-* 'adversely' + *cheoir* 'befall'.

mischief ▶ noun [mass noun] **1** playful misbehaviour or trouble-making, especially in children: *she'll make sure Danny doesn't* ***get into mischief.***
■ playfulness that is intended to tease, mock, or create trouble: *her eyes twinkled with irrepressible mischief.* ■ harm or trouble caused by someone or something: *she was bent on* ***making mischief.*** ■ [count noun] archaic a person responsible for harm or annoyance.
2 Law a wrong or hardship which it is the object of a statute to remove or for which the common law affords a remedy.
– PHRASES **do someone** (or **oneself**) **a mischief** informal injure someone or oneself.
– ORIGIN late Middle English (denoting misfortune or distress): from Old French *meschief*, from the verb *meschever*, from *mes-* 'adversely' + *chever* 'come to an end' (from *chef* 'head').

mischievous ▶ adjective (of a person or their behaviour) causing or showing a fondness for causing trouble in a playful way: *mixing up the signposts was a favourite pastime of the more mischievous pupils.*
■ (of an action or thing) causing or intended to cause harm or trouble: *a mischievous allegation for which there is not a shred of evidence.*
– DERIVATIVES **mischievously** adverb, **mischievousness** noun.
– ORIGIN Middle English: from Anglo-Norman French *meschevous*, from Old French *meschever* 'come to an unfortunate end' (see **MISCHIEF**). The early sense was 'unfortunate or calamitous', later 'having harmful effects'; the sense 'playfully troublesome' dates from the late 17th cent.

misch metal /mɪʃ/ ▶ noun [mass noun] an alloy of cerium, lanthanum, and other rare earth metals, used as an additive in various alloys, e.g. in flints for lighters.
– ORIGIN 1920s: from German *Mischmetall*, from *mischen* 'to mix' + *Metall* 'metal'.

miscible /'mɪsɪb(ə)l/ ▶ adjective (of liquids) forming a homogeneous mixture when added together: *sorbitol is* ***miscible with*** *glycerol.*
– DERIVATIVES **miscibility** noun.
– ORIGIN late 16th cent.: from medieval Latin *miscibilis*, from Latin *miscere* 'to mix'.

miscommunication ▶ noun [mass noun] failure to communicate adequately.

misconceive ▶ verb [with obj.] fail to understand correctly: *some academic latinists did misconceive Pound's poem in that way.*
■ (usu. **be misconceived**) judge or plan badly, typically on the basis of faulty understanding: *criticism of the trade surplus in Washington is misconceived* | [as adj. **misconceived**] *misconceived notions about gypsies.*
– DERIVATIVES **misconceiver** noun.

misconception ▶ noun a view or opinion that is incorrect because based on faulty thinking or understanding: *public* ***misconceptions about*** *Aids remain high.*

misconduct ▶ noun [mass noun] **1** unacceptable or improper behaviour, especially by an employee or professional person: *she was found guilty of professional misconduct by a disciplinary tribunal.*
■ [count noun] Ice Hockey a penalty assessed against a player for abusive conduct or other misbehaviour.
2 mismanagement, especially culpable neglect of duties.
▶ verb **1** (**misconduct oneself**) behave in an improper or unprofessional manner.
2 [with obj.] mismanage (duties or a project).

misconstruct ▶ verb [with obj.] rare misconstrue (something).
– DERIVATIVES **misconstruction** noun.

misconstrue ▶ verb (**misconstrues, misconstrued, misconstruing**) [with obj.] interpret (something, especially a person's words or actions) wrongly: *my advice was deliberately misconstrued.*
– DERIVATIVES **misconstruction** noun.

miscount ▶ verb [with obj.] count (something) incorrectly.
▶ noun an incorrect reckoning of the total number of something: *a miscount necessitates a recount.*

miscreant /'mɪskrɪənt/ ▶ noun a person who behaves badly or in a way that breaks the law.
■ archaic a heretic.
▶ adjective (of a person) behaving badly or in a way that breaks a law or rule: *her miscreant husband.*
■ archaic heretical.
– ORIGIN Middle English (as an adjective in the sense 'disbelieving'): from Old French *mescreant*, present participle of *mescreire* 'disbelieve', from *mes-* 'mis-' + *creire* 'believe' (from Latin *credere*).

miscue[1] ▶ noun (in billiards and snooker) a shot in which the player fails to strike the ball properly with the cue.
■ (in other sports) a faulty strike, kick, or catch. ■ figurative a miscalculated action; a mistake: *political miscues that led to resignations.*
▶ verb (**miscues, miscued, miscueing** or **miscuing**) [with obj.] (in snooker and other games) fail to strike (the ball or a shot) properly.

miscue[2] ▶ noun Linguistics an error in reading, especially one caused by failure to respond correctly to a phonetic or contextual cue in the text.

misdate ▶ verb [with obj.] assign an incorrect date to (a document, event, or work of art).

misdeal ▶ verb (past and past participle **misdealt**) [no obj.] make a mistake when dealing cards.
▶ noun a hand dealt wrongly.

misdeclaration ▶ noun an incorrect declaration, especially in an official context.

misdeed ▶ noun a wicked or illegal act.
– ORIGIN Old English *misdǣd* (see **MIS-**[1], **DEED**).

misdelivery ▶ noun [mass noun] delivery to the wrong person or at the wrong time.

misdemeanour (US **misdemeanor**) ▶ noun a minor wrongdoing: *the player can expect a lengthy suspension for his latest misdemeanour.*
■ Law a non-indictable offence, regarded in the US (and formerly in the UK) as less serious than a felony.

misdescribe ▶ verb [with obj.] describe inaccurately or misleadingly: *he misdescribed the play as a tragedy.*
– DERIVATIVES **misdescription** noun.

misdiagnose ▶ verb [with obj.] make an incorrect diagnosis of (a particular illness).
■ make an incorrect diagnosis of the illness from which (someone) is suffering: *the consultant misdiagnosed her as having cancer.*
– DERIVATIVES **misdiagnosis** noun.

misdial ▶ verb (**misdialled, misdialling**; US **misdialed, misdialing**) [no obj.] dial a telephone number incorrectly.
▶ noun an act of dialling a number incorrectly.

misdirect ▶ verb [with obj.] (often **be misdirected**) send (someone or something) to the wrong place or in the wrong direction: *voters were misdirected to the wrong polling station.*
■ aim (something) in the wrong direction: *he*

m

misdirected a clearance to allow a Spurs equalizer. ■ (of a judge) instruct wrongly: *the appeal court was satisfied that the trial judge had misdirected the jury.* ■ use or apply (something) wrongly or inappropriately: *their efforts have been largely misdirected.*
– DERIVATIVES **misdirection** noun.

misdoing ▶ **noun** a misdeed.

misdoubt ▶ **verb** [with obj.] chiefly archaic or dialect have doubts about the truth, reality, or existence of: *he was diffident and always misdoubted his own ability.*
■ fear or be suspicious about: *for I fear my father, and I misdoubt his hindrances.*

miseducate ▶ **verb** [with obj.] educate, teach, or inform wrongly.
– DERIVATIVES **miseducation** noun, **miseducative** adjective.

mise en place /ˌmiːz ɒ̃ ˈplas, French miz ɑ̃ plas/ ▶ **noun** [usu. in sing.] (in a professional kitchen) the preparation of dishes and ingredients before the beginning of service.
– ORIGIN French, literally 'putting in place'.

mise en scène /ˌmiːz ɒ̃ ˈsɛn, French miz ɑ̃ sɛn/ ▶ **noun** [usu. in sing.] the arrangement of scenery and stage properties in a play.
■ the setting or surroundings of an event or action.
– ORIGIN French, literally 'putting on stage'.

misemploy ▶ **verb** [with obj.] employ or use (something) wrongly or improperly.
– DERIVATIVES **misemployment** noun.

miser ▶ **noun** a person who hoards wealth and spends as little money as possible.
– ORIGIN late 15th cent. (as an adjective in the sense 'miserly'): from Latin, literally 'wretched'.

miserable ▶ **adjective** **1** (of a person) wretchedly unhappy or uncomfortable: *their happiness made Anne feel even more miserable.*
■ (of a situation or environment) causing someone to feel wretchedly unhappy or uncomfortable: *horribly wet and miserable conditions.* ■ (of a person) habitually morose: *a miserable man in his late sixties.*
2 pitiably small or inadequate: *all they pay me is a miserable £5000 a year.*
■ [attrib.] contemptible (used as a term of abuse or for emphasis): *don't call me a charlatan, you miserable old creep!* ■ Austral./NZ & Scottish (of a person) miserly: *a lousy dollar a day – could any government be more miserable?*
– DERIVATIVES **miserableness** noun, **miserably** adverb.
– ORIGIN late Middle English: from French *misérable*, from Latin *miserabilis* 'pitiable', from *miserari* 'to pity', from *miser* 'wretched'.

misère /mɪˈzɛː/ ▶ **noun** (in solo whist) a bid by which a player undertakes to win no tricks.
– ORIGIN early 19th cent.: French, literally 'poverty or misery'.

misère ouverte /mɪˌzɛː uːˈvɛːt/ ▶ **noun** (in solo whist) a bid by which a player undertakes to win no tricks, playing with all his or her cards exposed on the table.
– ORIGIN from **MISÈRE** + French *ouverte* (feminine) 'open (to view)'.

miserere /ˌmɪzəˈrɪəri, -ˈrɛː-/ ▶ **noun** **1** a psalm in which mercy is sought, especially Psalm 51 or the music written for it.
■ any prayer or cry for mercy.
2 another term for **MISERICORD** (in sense 1).
– ORIGIN Middle English: from Latin, 'have mercy!', imperative of *misereri*, from *miser* 'wretched'.

misericord /mɪˈzɛrɪkɔːd/ ▶ **noun** **1** a ledge projecting from the underside of a hinged seat in a choir stall which, when the seat is turned up, gives support to someone standing.
2 historical an apartment in a monastery in which some relaxations of the monastic rule were permitted.
3 historical a small dagger used to deliver a death stroke to a wounded enemy.
– ORIGIN Middle English (denoting pity): from Old French *misericorde*, from Latin *misericordia*, from *misericors* 'compassionate', from the stem of *misereri* 'to pity' + *cor, cord-* 'heart'.

miserly ▶ **adjective** of, relating to, or characteristic of a miser: *his miserly great-uncle proved to be worth nearly £1 million.*
■ (of a quantity) pitiably small or inadequate: *the prize for the winner will be a miserly £3,500.*
– DERIVATIVES **miserliness** noun.

misery ▶ **noun** (pl. **-ies**) [mass noun] a state or feeling of great distress or discomfort of mind or body: *she went upstairs and cried in misery* | [count noun] *he wrote endlessly about his frustrations and miseries.*
■ [count noun] (usu. **miseries**) a cause or source of great distress or discomfort: *the miseries of war.* ■ [count noun] Brit. informal a person who is constantly miserable or discontented: *have we really been such a bunch of miseries to work with?*
– PHRASES **make someone's life a misery** (or **make life a misery for someone**) cause someone severe distress by continued unpleasantness or harassment. **put someone/thing out of their misery** end the suffering of a person or animal in pain by killing them. ■ informal release someone from suspense or anxiety by telling them something they are anxious to know.
– ORIGIN late Middle English: from Old French *miserie*, from Latin *miseria*, from *miser* 'wretched'.

misfeasance /mɪsˈfiːz(ə)ns/ ▶ **noun** Law a transgression, especially the wrongful exercise of lawful authority.
– ORIGIN early 17th cent.: from Old French *mesfaisance*, from *mesfaire*, from *mes-* 'wrongly' + *faire* 'do' (from Latin *facere*). Compare with **MALFEASANCE**.

misfeed ▶ **noun** an instance of faulty feeding of something (typically paper) through a machine.

misfield ▶ **verb** [with obj.] (in cricket and rugby) field (a ball) badly or clumsily.
▶ **noun** (in cricket and rugby) a failure to field a ball correctly.

misfile ▶ **verb** [with obj.] file wrongly.

misfire ▶ **verb** [no obj.] (of a gun or missile) fail to discharge or fire properly.
■ (of an internal-combustion engine) undergo failure of the fuel to ignite correctly or at all: *the car would misfire occasionally from the cold.* ■ (especially of a plan) fail to produce the intended result: *the killer didn't know that his plan had misfired.* ■ (of a nerve cell) fail to transmit an electrical impulse at an appropriate moment.
▶ **noun** a failure of a gun or missile to fire correctly or of fuel in an internal-combustion engine to ignite.

misfit ▶ **noun** a person whose behaviour or attitude sets them apart from others in an uncomfortably conspicuous way: *a motley collection of social misfits.*
■ archaic something that does not fit or that fits badly.

misfit stream ▶ **noun** Geography a stream occupying a valley which is larger than would be predicted on the basis of the stream's present erosive power.

misfortune ▶ **noun** [mass noun] bad luck: *the project was dogged by misfortune.*
■ [count noun] an unfortunate condition or event: *never laugh at other people's misfortunes.*

misgive ▶ **verb** (past **misgave**; past participle **misgiven**) [with obj.] poetic/literary (of a person's mind or heart) fill (that person) with doubt, apprehension, or foreboding: *my heart misgave me when I saw him.*

misgiving ▶ **noun** (usu. **misgivings**) a feeling of doubt or apprehension about the outcome or consequences of something: *we have **misgivings about** the way the campaign is being run* | [mass noun] *I felt a sense of misgiving at the prospect of retirement.*

misgovern ▶ **verb** [with obj.] govern (a state or country) unfairly or inefficiently.
– DERIVATIVES **misgovernment** noun.

misguide ▶ **verb** [with obj.] rare mislead: *a long survey that can only baffle and misguide the general reader.*
– DERIVATIVES **misguidance** noun.

misguided ▶ **adjective** having or showing faulty judgement or reasoning: *the proposals ignore the reality of market forces in a misguided attempt to solve undesirable social objectives.*
– DERIVATIVES **misguidedly** adverb, **misguidedness** noun.

mishandle ▶ **verb** [with obj.] **1** manage or deal with (something) wrongly or ineffectively: *the officer had mishandled the situation.*
2 manipulate roughly or carelessly: *the equipment could be dangerous if mishandled.*

mishap ▶ **noun** an unlucky accident: *although there were a few minor mishaps, none of the pancakes stuck to the ceiling* | [mass noun] *the event passed without mishap.*

mishear ▶ **verb** (past and past participle **misheard**) [with obj.] fail to hear (a person or their words) correctly.

Mishima /ˈmɪʃɪmə/, Yukio (1925–70), Japanese writer; pseudonym of *Hiraoka Kimitake*. His books include the four-volume *The Sea of Fertility* (1965–70), which looks at reincarnation and the sterility of modern life. An avowed imperialist, he committed hara-kiri after failing to incite soldiers against the post-war regime.

mishit ▶ **verb** (**mishitting**; past and past participle **mishit**) [with obj.] (in various sports) hit or kick (a ball) badly or in the wrong direction.
▶ **noun** an instance of hitting or kicking a ball in such a way.

mishmash ▶ **noun** [in sing.] a confused mixture: *a mishmash of outmoded ideas.*
– ORIGIN late 15th cent.: reduplication of **MASH**.

Mishnah /ˈmɪʃnə/ ▶ **noun** (**the Mishnah**) an authoritative collection of exegetical material embodying the oral tradition of Jewish law and forming the first part of the Talmud.
– DERIVATIVES **Mishnaic** /-ˈneɪɪk/ adjective.
– ORIGIN from Hebrew *mišnāh* '(teaching by) repetition'.

mishugas ▶ **noun** variant spelling of **MESHUGAAS**.

misidentify /mɪsʌɪˈdɛntɪfʌɪ/ ▶ **verb** (**-ies**, **-ied**) [with obj.] identify (something or someone) incorrectly.
– DERIVATIVES **misidentification** /-fɪˈkeɪʃ(ə)n/ noun.

misinform ▶ **verb** [with obj.] (often **be misinformed**) give (someone) false or inaccurate information.

misinformation ▶ **noun** [mass noun] false or inaccurate information, especially that which is deliberately intended to deceive: *nuclear matters are often entangled in a web of secrecy and misinformation.*

misinterpret ▶ **verb** (**misinterpreted**, **misinterpreting**) [with obj.] interpret (something or someone) wrongly.
– DERIVATIVES **misinterpretation** noun, **misinterpreter** noun.

misjudge ▶ **verb** [with obj.] form a wrong opinion or conclusion about: *I've misjudged Doris—she hasn't told anyone.*
■ make an incorrect estimation or assessment of: *the horse misjudged the fence and Mrs Weaver was thrown off.*
– DERIVATIVES **misjudgement** (also **misjudgment**) noun.

miskey ▶ **verb** (**-eys**, **-eyed**) [with obj.] key (a word or piece of data) into a computer or other machine incorrectly.

miskick ▶ **verb** [with obj.] kick (a ball) badly or wrongly.
▶ **noun** an instance of kicking the ball in such a way.

Miskito /mɪˈskiːtəʊ/ (also **Mosquito**) ▶ **noun** (pl. same or **-os**) **1** a member of an American Indian people of the Atlantic coast of Nicaragua and Honduras.
2 [mass noun] the language of this people, possibly related to Chibchan.
▶ **adjective** of or relating to the Miskito or their language.
– ORIGIN the name in Miskito.

Miskolc /ˈmiːʃkɒlts/ a city in NE Hungary; pop. 191,000 (1993).

mislay ▶ **verb** (past and past participle **mislaid**) [with obj.] unintentionally put (an object) where it cannot readily be found and so lose it temporarily: *I seem to have mislaid my car keys.*

mislead ▶ **verb** (past and past participle **misled**) [with obj.] cause (someone) to have a wrong idea or impression about someone or something: *the government misled the public about the road's environmental impact.*
– DERIVATIVES **misleader** noun.

misleading ▶ **adjective** giving the wrong idea or impression: *your article contains a number of misleading statements.*
– DERIVATIVES **misleadingly** adverb, **misleadingness** noun.

mislike archaic ▶ **verb** [with obj.] consider to be unpleasant: *the pony snorted, misliking the smell of blood.*
▶ **noun** [mass noun] distaste; dislike.
– ORIGIN Old English *mislīcian* (see **MIS-**[1], **LIKE**[2]).

mismanage ▶ **verb** [with obj.] manage (something) badly or wrongly.
– DERIVATIVES **mismanagement** noun.

mismatch ▶ **noun** **1** a failure to correspond or match; a discrepancy: *a huge **mismatch between** supply and demand.*
2 an unequal or unfair sporting contest.
▶ **verb** [with obj.] [usu. as adj. **mismatched**] match (people or things) unsuitably or incorrectly: *a pair of mismatched cops.*

mismated ▶ **adjective** badly matched or not matching.

mismeasure ▶ **verb** [with obj.] measure or estimate incorrectly.
– DERIVATIVES **mismeasurement** noun.

misname ▶ **verb** [with obj.] give (something) a wrong or inappropriate name: *the place is misnamed—it's too well organized to be a wilderness.*

misnomer ▶ **noun** a wrong or inaccurate name or designation: *'King crab' is a misnomer—these creatures are not crustaceans at all.*
■ a wrong or inaccurate use of a name or term: *to call this neighbourhood policing would be a misnomer.*
– ORIGIN late Middle English: from Anglo-Norman French, from the Old French verb *mesnommer*, from *mes-* 'wrongly' + *nommer* 'to name' (based on Latin *nomen* 'name').

miso /ˈmiːsəʊ/ ▶ **noun** [mass noun] paste made from fermented soya beans and barley or rice malt, used in Japanese cookery.
– ORIGIN Japanese.

misogamy /mɪˈsɒɡəmi, mʌɪ-/ ▶ **noun** [mass noun] rare the hatred of marriage.
– DERIVATIVES **misogamist** noun.
– ORIGIN mid 17th cent.: from Greek *misos* 'hatred' + *gamos* 'marriage'.

misogynist /mɪˈsɒdʒ(ə)nɪst, mʌɪ-/ ▶ **noun** a man who hates women.
▶ **adjective** reflecting or inspired by a hatred of women: *a misogynist attitude.*
– DERIVATIVES **misogynistic** adjective.

misogyny /mɪˈsɒdʒ(ə)ni, mʌɪ-/ ▶ **noun** [mass noun] the hatred of women by men: *she felt she was struggling against thinly disguised misogyny.*
– DERIVATIVES **misogynous** adjective.
– ORIGIN mid 17th cent.: from Greek *misos* 'hatred' + *gunē* 'woman'.

misperceive ▶ **verb** [with obj.] perceive wrongly or incorrectly.
– DERIVATIVES **misperception** noun.

mispickel /ˈmɪspɪk(ə)l/ ▶ **noun** another term for **ARSENOPYRITE**.
– ORIGIN late 17th cent.: from German.

misplace ▶ **verb** [with obj.] (usu. **be misplaced**) put in the wrong place and lose temporarily because of this: *I'm sure the jewellery has just been misplaced, and not stolen.*
■ position incorrectly: *Crewe came back into the game when Strachan misplaced a pass in the midfield.*
– DERIVATIVES **misplacement** noun.

misplaced ▶ **adjective** **1** incorrectly positioned: *a million dollars had been lost because of a misplaced comma.*
■ not appropriate or correct in the circumstances: *a telling sign of misplaced priorities.* ■ (of an emotion) directed unwisely or to an inappropriate object: *he began to wonder if his sympathy was misplaced.*
2 [attrib.] temporarily lost: *her misplaced keys.*

misplay ▶ **verb** [with obj.] play (a ball or card) wrongly, badly, or in contravention of the rules.
▶ **noun** an instance of playing a ball or card in such a way.

misprint ▶ **noun** an error in printed text: *Galway might be a misprint for Galloway.*
▶ **verb** [with obj.] print (something) incorrectly.

misprision[1] /mɪsˈprɪʒ(ə)n/ (also **misprision of treason** or **felony**) ▶ **noun** Law, chiefly historical the deliberate concealment of one's knowledge of a treasonable act or a felony.
– ORIGIN late Middle English: from Old French *mesprision* 'error', from *mesprendre*, from *mes-* 'wrongly' + *prendre* 'to take'.

misprision[2] /mɪsˈprɪʒ(ə)n/ ▶ **noun** [mass noun] rare erroneous judgement, especially of the value or identity of something: *he despised himself for his misprision.*
– ORIGIN late 16th cent.: from **MISPRIZE**, influenced by **MISPRISION**[1].

misprize ▶ **verb** [with obj.] rare fail to appreciate the value of (something); undervalue.
– ORIGIN late 15th cent.: from Old French *mesprisier*, from *mes-* 'wrongly' + *prisier* 'estimate the value of'.

mispronounce ▶ **verb** [with obj.] pronounce (a word) incorrectly: *she mispronounced my name.*
– DERIVATIVES **mispronunciation** noun.

misquote ▶ **verb** [with obj.] quote (a person or a piece of written or spoken text) inaccurately: *the government insisted that the official had been misquoted.*
▶ **noun** a passage or remark quoted inaccurately: *a misquote from a poem by Robert Burns.*
– DERIVATIVES **misquotation** noun.

misread ▶ **verb** (past and past participle **misread**) [with obj.] read (a piece of text) wrongly.
■ judge or interpret (a situation or a person's manner or behaviour) incorrectly: *had she been completely misreading his intentions?*

misrecognize ▶ **verb** [with obj.] incorrectly identify while apparently recognizing.
– DERIVATIVES **misrecognition** noun.

misremember ▶ **verb** [with obj.] remember imperfectly or incorrectly.

misreport ▶ **verb** [with obj.] give a false or inaccurate account of (something): *the press exaggerated and misreported the response to the film.*
▶ **noun** a false or incorrect report.

misrepresent ▶ **verb** [with obj.] give a false or misleading account of the nature of: *you are misrepresenting the views of the government.*
– DERIVATIVES **misrepresentation** noun, **misrepresentative** adjective.

misroute ▶ **verb** [with obj.] divert or direct to the wrong place or by the wrong route.

misrule ▶ **noun** [mass noun] the unfair or inefficient conduct of the affairs of a country or state: *thirty years of misrule by the one-party socialist government.*
■ the disruption of peace; disorder: *there was a tradition of misrule before, during, and after games.*
▶ **verb** [with obj.] govern (a country or state) badly.

Miss. ▶ **abbreviation for** Mississippi.

miss[1] ▶ **verb** [with obj.] **1** fail to hit, reach, or come into contact with (something aimed at): *a laser-guided bomb had missed its target* | [no obj.] *he shot twice at the cashier, but missed both times.*
■ pass by without touching; chance not to hit: *a piece of shrapnel missed him by inches.* ■ fail to catch (something thrown or dropped). ■ be too late to catch (a passenger vehicle or the post): *we'll miss the train if he doesn't hurry.* ■ fail to notice, hear, or understand: *the villa is impossible to miss—it's right by the road.* ■ fail to attend, participate in, or watch (something one is expected to do or habitually does): *teachers were supposed to report those students who missed class that day.* ■ fail to see or have a meeting with (someone): *'Potter's been here this morning?' 'You've just missed him.'* ■ not be able to experience or fail to take advantage of (an opportunity or chance): *don't miss the chance to visit the breathtaking Dolomites* | [no obj.] *he failed to recover from a leg injury and* **missed out on** *a trip to Barcelona.* ■ avoid; escape: *Christmas shoppers go out early to miss the crowds.* ■ fail to include (someone or something); omit: *I'm sure Guy will fill in any bits I* **missed out**. ■ (of a woman) fail to have (a monthly period). ■ [no obj.] (of an engine or motor vehicle) undergo failure of ignition in one or more cylinders.
2 notice the loss or absence of: *he's rich—he won't miss the money* | *she slipped away when she thought she wouldn't be missed.*
■ feel regret or sadness at no longer being able to enjoy the presence of: *she misses all her old friends.* ■ feel regret or sadness at no longer being able to go to, do, or have: *I still miss France and I wish I could go back.*
▶ **noun** a failure to hit, catch, or reach something: *the penalty miss cost us the game.*
■ a failure, especially an unsuccessful record or film: *it is the public who decide whether a film is a hit or a miss.*
– PHRASES **give something a miss** Brit. informal decide not to do or have something: *we decided to give the popcorn a miss.* **miss a beat 1** (of the heart) temporarily fail or appear to fail to beat. **2** [usu. with negative] informal hesitate or falter, especially in demanding circumstances or when making a transition from one activity to another: *the Swiss handle metres of snow without missing a beat.* **miss the boat** (or **bus**) informal be too slow to take advantage of an opportunity: *people who've been holding off buying anything in case prices drop further could find they've missed the boat.* **a miss is as good as a mile** proverb the fact of failure or escape is not affected by the narrowness of the margin. **not miss a trick** informal never fail to take advantage of a situation.
– DERIVATIVES **missable** adjective.
– ORIGIN Old English *missan*, of Germanic origin; related to Dutch and German *missen*.

miss[2] ▶ **noun** **1** (**Miss**) a title prefixed to the name of an unmarried woman or girl, or to that of a married woman retaining her maiden name for professional purposes: *Miss Hazel Armstrong.*
■ used in the title of the winner in a beauty contest: *Miss World.* ■ used as a polite form of address to a young woman or to a waitress or female shop assistant: *'Where will you be staying in England, miss?' asked the Immigration man.* ■ chiefly Brit. used by children in addressing a female teacher: *please, Miss, can I be excused hockey?*
2 often derogatory or humorous a girl or young woman, especially one regarded as silly or headstrong: *there was none of the country bumpkin about this young miss.*
– DERIVATIVES **missish** adjective (in sense 2).
– ORIGIN mid 17th cent.: abbreviation of **MISTRESS**.

miss[3] ▶ **noun** informal a miscarriage.

missal /ˈmɪs(ə)l/ ▶ **noun** a book containing the texts used in the Catholic Mass throughout the year.
– ORIGIN Middle English: from medieval Latin *missale*, neuter of ecclesiastical Latin *missalis* 'relating to the Mass', from *missa* 'Mass'.

mis-sell ▶ **verb** [with obj.] [often as noun **mis-selling**] sell (something) to a customer for whom it is an inappropriate purchase.

missel thrush ▶ **noun** variant spelling of **MISTLE THRUSH**.

misshape ▶ **verb** [with obj.] archaic give a bad or ugly shape or form to; distort: *our meddling intellect misshapes the beauteous forms of things.*
▶ **noun** a misshapen chocolate or other item of food, sold cheaply.

misshapen ▶ **adjective** not having the normal or natural shape or form: *misshapen fruit.*
– DERIVATIVES **misshapenly** adverb, **misshapenness** noun.

missile ▶ **noun** an object which is forcibly propelled at a target, either by hand or from a mechanical weapon.
■ a weapon that is self-propelled or directed by remote control, carrying conventional or nuclear explosive.
– ORIGIN early 17th cent. (as an adjective in the sense 'suitable for throwing (at a target)'): from Latin *missile*, neuter (used as a noun) of *missilis*, from *miss-* 'sent', from the verb *mittere*.

missilery /ˈmɪsʌɪlri/ ▶ **noun** [mass noun] **1** the study of the use and characteristics of missiles.
2 missiles collectively.

missing ▶ **adjective** (of a thing) not able to be found because it is not in its expected place: *a quantity of cash has* **gone missing**.
■ not present or included when expected or supposed to be: *passion was an element that had been* **missing from** *her life for too long* | *you can fill in the missing details later.* ■ (of a person) absent from a place, especially home, and of unknown whereabouts: *she alerted police after her son* **went missing**. ■ (of a person) not yet traced or confirmed as alive, but not known to be dead, after an accident or during wartime: *servicemen listed as* **missing in action**.

missing link ▶ **noun** a thing that is needed in order to complete a series, provide continuity, or gain complete knowledge: *she is the missing link between the European ballad tradition and Anglo-American white soul.*
■ a hypothetical fossil form intermediate between two living forms, especially between humans and apes.

missiology ▶ **noun** [mass noun] the study of religious (typically Christian) missions and their methods and purposes.
– DERIVATIVES **missiological** adjective.
– ORIGIN 1930s: formed irregularly from **MISSION** + **-LOGY**.

mission ▶ **noun** an important assignment carried out for political, religious, or commercial purposes, typically involving travel abroad: *a fact-finding* **mission to** *China.*
■ [treated as sing. or pl.] a group of people taking part in such an assignment: *by then, the mission had journeyed over 3,500 miles.* ■ [in sing.] an organization or institution involved in a long-term assignment abroad: *the majestic garden of the West German mission* | [as modifier] *the mission school.* ■ the vocation or calling of a religious organization, especially a Christian one, to go out into the world and spread its faith: *the Christian mission* | [mass noun] *Gandhi's attitude to mission and conversion.* ■ a strongly felt aim, ambition, or calling: *his main mission in life has been to cut unemployment.* ■ an expedition into space. ■ an operation carried out by military aircraft at a time of conflict: *he was shot down on a supply mission.*
– ORIGIN mid 16th cent. (denoting the sending of the Holy Spirit into the world): from Latin *missio(n-)*, from *mittere* 'send'.

missionary ▶ **noun** (pl. **-ies**) a person sent on a religious mission, especially one sent to promote Christianity in a foreign country.

▶ **adjective** of, relating to, or characteristic of a missionary or a religious mission: *missionary work* | *our taxi driver shared a sense of missionary zeal with us.*
– ORIGIN mid 17th cent.: from modern Latin *missionarius*, from Latin *missio* (see **MISSION**).

missionary position ▶ **noun** informal a position for sexual intercourse in which a couple lie face to face with the woman underneath the man.
– ORIGIN said to be so named because early missionaries advocated the position as 'proper' to primitive peoples, to whom the practice was unknown.

mission-critical ▶ **adjective** Computing (of hardware or software) vital to the functioning of an organization.

missioner ▶ **noun 1** a person in charge of a religious or charitable mission.
2 a missionary.

mission statement ▶ **noun** a formal summary of the aims and values of a company, organization, or individual.

missis /ˈmɪsɪs, -ɪz/ ▶ **noun** variant spelling of **MISSUS**.

Mississauga /ˌmɪsɪˈsɔːgə/ a town in southern Ontario, on the western shores of Lake Ontario; pop. 463,400 (1991). It forms a southern suburb of Toronto.

Mississippi /ˌmɪsɪˈsɪpi/ **1** a major river of North America, which rises in Minnesota near the Canadian border and flows south to a delta on the Gulf of Mexico. With its chief tributary, the Missouri, it is 5,970 km (3,710 miles) long.
2 a state of the southern US, on the Gulf of Mexico, bounded to the west by the lower Mississippi River; pop. 2,573,200 (1990); capital, Jackson. A French colony in the first half of the 18th century, it was ceded to Britain in 1763 and to the US in 1783, becoming the 20th state in 1817.

Mississippian ▶ **adjective 1** of or relating to the state of Mississippi.
2 Geology of, relating to, or denoting the early part of the Carboniferous period in North America, following the Devonian and preceding the Pennsylvanian. This period corresponds to the Lower Carboniferous of Europe and lasted from about 363 to 323 million years ago.
■ Archaeology of, relating to, or denoting a settled culture of the south-eastern US, dated to about AD 800–1300.
▶ **noun 1** a native or inhabitant of Mississippi.
2 (**the Mississippian**) Geology the Mississippian period or the system of rocks deposited during it.
■ Archaeology the Mississippian culture or period.

Mississippi mud pie ▶ **noun** a type of rich mousse-like chocolate cake.

missive ▶ **noun** often humorous a letter, especially a long or official one: *yet another missive from the Foreign Office.*
■ Scots Law a document in the form of a letter interchanged by the parties to a contract.
– ORIGIN late Middle English (as an adjective, originally in the phrase **LETTER MISSIVE**): from medieval Latin *missivus*, from Latin *mittere* 'send'. The current sense dates from the early 16th cent.

Missolonghi /ˌmɪsəˈlɒŋgi/ a city in western Greece, on the north shore of the Gulf of Patras; pop. 10,900 (1991). It is noted as the place where the poet Byron, who had joined the fight for Greek independence from the Turks, died of malaria in 1824. Greek name **MESOLÓNGION**.

Missouri /mɪˈzʊəri/ **1** a major river of North America, one of the main tributaries of the Mississippi. It rises in the Rocky Mountains in Montana and flows 3,736 km (2,315 miles) to meet the Mississippi just north of St Louis.
2 a state of the US, bounded on the east by the Mississippi River; pop. 5,117,070 (1990); capital, Jefferson City. It was acquired as part of the Louisiana Purchase in 1803, becoming the 24th state of the US in 1821.
– DERIVATIVES **Missourian** noun & adjective.

misspeak ▶ **verb** (past **misspoke**; past participle **misspoken**) [no obj.] chiefly US express oneself insufficiently clearly or accurately.

misspell ▶ **verb** (past and past participle **misspelt** or **misspelled**) [with obj.] spell (a word) wrongly.

misspend ▶ **verb** (past and past participle **misspent**) [with obj.] [usu. as adj. **misspent**] spend (one's time or money) foolishly, wrongly, or wastefully: *perhaps I am atoning for my misspent youth.*

misstate ▶ **verb** [with obj.] make wrong or inaccurate statements about.
– DERIVATIVES **misstatement** noun.

misstep ▶ **noun** a clumsy or badly judged step: *for a mountain goat one misstep could be fatal.*
■ a mistake or blunder.

missus /ˈmɪsəz/ (also **missis**) ▶ **noun** [in sing.] informal or humorous a man's wife: *I promised* **the missus** *I'd be home by eleven.*
■ informal used as a form of address to a woman whose name is not known: *sit down, missus.*

missy ▶ **noun** (pl. **-ies**) used as an affectionate or disparaging form of address to a young girl: *'Don't tell lies, missy,' he said sternly.*

mist ▶ **noun** [mass noun] a cloud of tiny water droplets suspended in the atmosphere at or near the earth's surface limiting visibility (to a lesser extent than fog; strictly, with visibility remaining above 1 km): *the peaks were shrouded in mist* | [in sing.] *a mist rose out of the river.*
■ [in sing.] a condensed vapour settling in fine droplets on a surface: *a breeze cooled the mist of perspiration that had dampened her temples.* ■ [in sing.] a haze or film over the eyes, especially caused by tears, and resulting in blurred vision: *Ruth saw most of the scene through a mist of tears.* ■ [count noun] used in reference to something that blurs one's perceptions or memory: *Sardinia's origins are lost in* **the mists of time**.
▶ **verb** cover or become covered with mist: [with obj.] *the windows were* **misted up** *with condensation* | [no obj.] *the glass was beginning to* **mist up**.
■ [no obj.] (of a person's eyes) become covered with a film of tears causing blurred vision: *her eyes misted at this heroic image.* ■ [with obj.] spray (something, especially a plant) with a fine cloud of water droplets.
– ORIGIN Old English, of Germanic origin; from an Indo-European root shared by Greek *omikhlē* 'mist, fog'.

mistake ▶ **noun** an action or judgement that is misguided or wrong: *coming here was a mistake* | *she* **made the mistake of** *thinking they were important.*
■ something, especially a word, figure, or fact, which is not correct; an inaccuracy: *a couple of spelling mistakes.*
▶ **verb** (past **mistook**; past participle **mistaken**) [with obj.] be wrong about: *because I was inexperienced I mistook the nature of our relationship.*
■ (**mistake someone/thing for**) wrongly identify someone or something as: *she thought he'd mistaken her for someone else.*
– PHRASES **and no mistake** informal without any doubt: *it's a bad business and no mistake.* **by mistake** accidentally; in error: *she'd left her purse at home by mistake.* **make no mistake** (**about it**) informal do not be deceived into thinking otherwise. **there is no mistaking someone or something** it is impossible not to recognize someone or something.
– DERIVATIVES **mistakable** (also **mistakeable**) adjective, **mistakably** (also **mistakeably**) adverb.
– ORIGIN late Middle English (as a verb): from Old Norse *mistaka* 'take in error', probably influenced in sense by Old French *mesprendre*.

mistaken ▶ **adjective** [predic.] wrong in one's opinion or judgement: *she wondered whether she'd been mistaken about his intentions.*
■ [attrib.] (especially of a belief) based on or resulting from a misunderstanding or faulty judgement: *don't buy a hard bed in the mistaken belief that it is good for you* | *an unfortunate case of mistaken identity.*
– DERIVATIVES **mistakenly** adverb, **mistakenness** noun.

misteach ▶ **verb** (past and past participle **mistaught**) [with obj.] teach (someone) wrongly or incorrectly.

mister ▶ **noun** variant form of **MR**, often used humorously or with offensive emphasis: *look here, mister know-all.*
■ informal used as a form of address to a man whose name is not known: *thanks, mister.*
– ORIGIN mid 16th cent.: weakened form of **MASTER**[1] in unstressed use before a name.

mistime ▶ **verb** [with obj.] choose a bad or inappropriate moment to do or say (something).
– ORIGIN Old English *mistīmian* 'happen unfortunately' (see **MIS-**[1], **TIME**).

mistitle ▶ **verb** [with obj.] give the wrong title or name to: *Mr Hammond mistitles his source.*

mistle thrush /ˈmɪs(ə)l/ (also **missel thrush**) ▶ **noun** a large Eurasian thrush with a spotted breast and harsh rattling call, with a fondness for mistletoe berries.
● *Turdus viscivorus*, family Turdidae.
– ORIGIN early 17th cent.: *mistle* from Old English *mistel* (see **MISTLETOE**).

mistletoe ▶ **noun** a leathery-leaved parasitic plant which grows on apple, oak, and other broadleaf trees and bears white glutinous berries in winter.
● Several species in the family Viscaceae, in particular the Eurasian *Viscum album* and the North American *Phoradendron flavescens*.
– ORIGIN Old English *misteltān*, from *mistel* 'mistletoe' (of Germanic origin, related to Dutch *mistel* and German *Mistel*) + *tān* 'twig'.

mistletoebird ▶ **noun** an Australian flowerpecker that feeds mainly on mistletoe berries, the male of which has a bright red breast.
● *Dicaeum hirundinaceum*, family Dicaeidae. Alternative name: **mistletoe flowerpecker**.

mistook past of **MISTAKE**.

mistral /ˈmɪstr(ə)l, mɪˈstrɑːl/ ▶ **noun** a strong cold north-westerly wind that blows through the Rhône valley and southern France into the Mediterranean, mainly in winter.
– ORIGIN early 17th cent.: French, from Provençal, from Latin *magistralis* (*ventus*), literally 'master wind'.

mistranslate ▶ **verb** [with obj.] translate (something) incorrectly.
– DERIVATIVES **mistranslation** noun.

mistreat ▶ **verb** [with obj.] treat (a person or animal) badly, cruelly, or unfairly.
– DERIVATIVES **mistreatment** noun.

mistress ▶ **noun 1** a woman in a position of authority or control: *she is always* **mistress of** *the situation, coolly self-possessed.*
■ [with modifier] chiefly Brit. a female schoolteacher who teaches a particular subject: *a Geography mistress.* ■ a woman who is skilled in a particular subject or activity: *a* **mistress of** *the sound bite, she is famed for the acidity of her tongue.* ■ the female owner of a dog, cat, or other domesticated animal. ■ archaic a female head of a household: *he asked for the mistress of the house.* ■ (especially formerly) a female employer of domestic staff.
2 a woman (other than a wife) having a sexual relationship with a married man.
■ archaic or poetic/literary a woman loved and courted by a man.
3 (**Mistress**) archaic or dialect used as a title prefixed to the name of a married woman; Mrs.
– ORIGIN Middle English: from Old French *maistresse*, from *maistre* 'master'.

Mistress of the Robes ▶ **noun** (in the English royal household) a woman of high rank in charge of the Queen's wardrobe.

mistrial ▶ **noun** a trial rendered invalid through an error in the proceedings.
■ US an inconclusive trial, such as one in which the jury cannot agree on a verdict.

mistrust ▶ **verb** [with obj.] be suspicious of; have no confidence in: *she had no cause to mistrust him.*
▶ **noun** [mass noun] lack of trust: suspicion: *an atmosphere of continued mistrust of the business community.*

mistrustful ▶ **adjective** lacking in trust; suspicious: *he wondered if he had been unduly* **mistrustful of** *her.*
– DERIVATIVES **mistrustfully** adverb, **mistrustfulness** noun.

misty ▶ **adjective** (**mistier**, **mistiest**) full of, covered with, or accompanied by mist: *the evening was cold and misty* | *the misty air above the frozen river.*
■ (of a person's eyes) full of tears so as to blur the vision. ■ indistinct or dim in outline: *a misty out-of-focus silhouette* | figurative *a few misty memories.* ■ (of a colour) not bright; soft: *a misty pink.*
– DERIVATIVES **mistily** adverb, **mistiness** noun.
– ORIGIN Old English *mistig* (see **MIST**).

mistype ▶ **verb** [with obj.] make a mistake in typing (a word or letter).

misunderstand ▶ **verb** (past and past participle **misunderstood** /-ˈstʊd/) [with obj.] fail to interpret or understand (something) correctly: *he had misunderstood the policeman's hand signals* | [no obj.] *I must have misunderstood—I thought you were anxious to leave.*
■ fail to interpret or understand the words or actions of (someone) correctly: *don't misunderstand me—I'm not implying she should be working* | [as adj. **misunderstood**] *he is one of football's most misunderstood men.*

misunderstanding ▶**noun** a failure to understand something correctly: *a misunderstanding of the government's plans* | [mass noun] *there must have been some kind of misunderstanding.*
■ a disagreement or quarrel: *he left the army after a slight misunderstanding with his commanding officer.*

misusage ▶**noun** [mass noun] archaic unjust treatment: *they were determined to defend themselves from misusage.*

misuse ▶**verb** [with obj.] use (something) in the wrong way or for the wrong purpose: *he was found guilty of misusing public funds.*
■ treat (someone or something) badly or unfairly.
▶**noun** [mass noun] the wrong or improper use of something: *drugs of such potency that their misuse can have dire consequences* | [count noun] *a misuse of power.*
– DERIVATIVES **misuser** noun.

MIT ▶**abbreviation for** Massachusetts Institute of Technology.

Mitchell[1], Joni (b.1943), Canadian singer and songwriter; born *Roberta Joan Anderson*. Starting to record in 1968, she moved from folk to a fusion of folk, jazz, and rock. Notable albums: *Blue* (1971) and *Hejira* (1976).

Mitchell[2], Margaret (1900–49), American novelist, famous as the author of the best-selling and Pulitzer Prize-winning novel *Gone with the Wind* (1936), set during the American Civil War.

Mitchell[3], R. J. (1895–1937), English aeronautical engineer; full name *Reginald Joseph Mitchell*. He designed the Spitfire fighter aircraft.

Mitchum /ˈmɪtʃəm/, Robert (1917–97), American actor. He was a professional boxer before rising to stardom in films such as *Out of the Past* (1947), *Night of the Hunter* (1955), and *Farewell My Lovely* (1975).

mite[1] ▶**noun** a minute arachnid which has four pairs of legs when adult, related to the ticks. Many kinds live in the soil and a number are parasitic on plants or animals.
• Order (or subclass) Acari: numerous families.
– ORIGIN Old English *mīte*, of Germanic origin.

mite[2] ▶**noun 1** a small child or animal, especially when regarded as an object of sympathy: *the **poor little mite** looks half-starved.*
2 a very small amount: *his teacher thought he needed **a mite of** discipline.*
■ historical a small coin, in particular a small Flemish copper coin of very low face value. See also **WIDOW'S MITE**.
▶**adverb** (**a mite**) informal a little; slightly: *I haven't eaten yet and I'm feeling a mite peckish.*
– ORIGIN late Middle English (denoting a small Flemish copper coin): from Middle Dutch *mīte*; probably from the same Germanic word as **MITE**[1].

miter ▶**noun** & **verb** US spelling of **MITRE**.

Mitford /ˈmɪtfəd/, Nancy (Freeman) (1904–73) and her sister Jessica (Lucy) (1917–96), English writers. Nancy achieved fame with comic novels including *Love in a Cold Climate* (1949). Jessica became an American citizen in 1944, and is best known for her works on American culture, notably *The American Way of Death* (1963). Among their four sisters were Unity (1914–48), who was an admirer of Hitler, and Diana (b.1910), who married Sir Oswald Mosley in 1936.

mithai /mɪˈtʌɪ/ ▶**noun** [mass noun] Indian sweets, such as burfi or gulab jamun.
– ORIGIN from Hindi *miṭhāī*.

mithan /ˈmɪθ(ə)n/ ▶**noun** (pl. same) another term for **GAYAL**.
– ORIGIN mid 19th cent.: from Khasi (a Mon-Khmer language of NE India).

mither /ˈmʌɪðə/ ▶**verb** [no obj.] dialect, chiefly N. English make a fuss; moan: *oh men—don't they mither?*
■ [with obj.] pester or irritate (someone).
– ORIGIN late 17th cent.: of unknown origin; compare with Welsh *moedrodd* 'to worry, bother'.

Mithraeum /mɪˈθriːəm/ ▶**noun** (pl. **Mithraea** /-ˈθriːə/) a sanctuary or temple of the god Mithras.
– ORIGIN late Latin, from Latin *Mithras* (see **MITHRAS**).

Mithraism /ˈmɪθrəˌɪz(ə)m, ˈmɪθreɪ-/ ▶**noun** [mass noun] the cult of the god Mithras, which became popular among Roman soldiers of the later empire, and was the main rival to Christianity in the first three centuries AD.
– DERIVATIVES **Mithraic** /-ˈθreɪɪk/ adjective, **Mithraist** noun.

Mithras /ˈmɪθras/ Mythology a god of light, truth, and honour, the central figure of the cult of Mithraism but probably of Persian origin. He was also associated with merchants and the protection of warriors.

Mithridates VI /ˌmɪθrɪˈdeɪtiːz/ (also **Mithradates VI**) (c.132–63 BC), king of Pontus 120–63; known as **Mithridates the Great**. His expansionist policies led to three wars with Rome (88–85; 83–2; 74–66). He was finally defeated by Pompey.

mithridatize /mɪˈθrɪdətʌɪz/ (also **-ise**) ▶**verb** [with obj.] rare render immune against a poison by administering gradually increasing doses of the poison.
– ORIGIN mid 19th cent.: from the name of *Mithridates* (see **MITHRIDATES VI**), who reputedly made himself immune to poisons by constantly taking antidotes, + **-IZE**.

mitigate /ˈmɪtɪgeɪt/ ▶**verb** [with obj.] make less severe, serious, or painful: *drainage schemes have helped to mitigate this problem.*
■ lessen the gravity of (an offence or mistake): [as adj. **mitigating**] *he would have faced a prison sentence but for **mitigating circumstances**.*
– DERIVATIVES **mitigable** adjective, **mitigator** noun, **mitigatory** adjective.
– ORIGIN late Middle English: from Latin *mitigat-* 'softened, alleviated', from the verb *mitigare*, from *mitis* 'mild'.

USAGE The verbs **mitigate** and **militate** do not have the same meaning, although the similarity of the forms has led to them being often confused. **Mitigate** means 'make (something bad) less severe', as in *drainage schemes have helped to **mitigate** this problem*, while **militate** is nearly always used in constructions with **against** to mean 'be a powerful factor in preventing', as in *these disagreements will **militate against** the two communities coming together*. More than 10 per cent of citations for **mitigate** in the British National Corpus are for **mitigate against**, where the context implies that the sense of **militate against** is what is intended.

mitigation ▶**noun** [mass noun] the action of reducing the severity, seriousness, or painfulness of something: *the emphasis is on the identification and mitigation of pollution.*
– PHRASES **in mitigation** so as to make something, especially a crime, appear less serious and thus be punished more leniently: *in mitigation she said her client had been deeply depressed.*
– ORIGIN late Middle English: from Old French, or from Latin *mitigatio(n-)*, from the verb *mitigare* 'alleviate' (see **MITIGATE**).

Mitilíni /mitiˈlini/ Greek name for **MYTILENE**.

Mitla /ˈmiːtlə/ an ancient city in southern Mexico, to the east of the city of Oaxaca, now a noted archaeological site. Believed to have been established as a burial site by the Zapotecs, it was eventually overrun by the Mixtecs in about AD 1000.
– ORIGIN Nahuatl, literally 'place of the dead'.

mitochondrion /ˌmʌɪtə(ʊ)ˈkɒndrɪən/ ▶**noun** (pl. **mitochondria** /-rɪə/) Biology an organelle found in large numbers in most cells, in which the biochemical processes of respiration and energy production occur. It has a double membrane, the inner layer being folded inwards to form layers (cristae).
– DERIVATIVES **mitochondrial** adjective.
– ORIGIN early 20th cent.: modern Latin, from Greek *mitos* 'thread' + *khondrion* (diminutive of *khondros* 'granule').

mitogen /ˈmʌɪtədʒ(ə)n/ ▶**noun** Physiology a substance that induces or stimulates mitosis.
– DERIVATIVES **mitogenic** adjective.
– ORIGIN 1960s: from **MITOSIS** + **-GEN**.

mitosis /mʌɪˈtəʊsɪs/ ▶**noun** (pl. **mitoses**) [mass noun] Biology a type of cell division that results in two daughter cells each having the same number and kind of chromosomes as the parent nucleus, typical of ordinary tissue growth. Compare with **MEIOSIS**.
– DERIVATIVES **mitotic** adjective.
– ORIGIN late 19th cent.: modern Latin, from Greek *mitos* 'thread'.

mitral /ˈmʌɪtr(ə)l/ ▶**adjective** denoting or relating to the mitral valve.
– ORIGIN early 17th cent.: from modern Latin *mitralis*, from Latin *mitra* 'belt or turban'.

mitral valve ▶**noun** Anatomy the valve between the left atrium and the left ventricle of the heart, which has two tapered cusps.

mitre (US **miter**) ▶**noun 1** a tall headdress worn by bishops and senior abbots as a symbol of office, tapering to a point at front and back with a deep cleft between.
2 (also **mitre joint**) a joint made between two pieces of wood or other material at an angle of 90°, such that the line of junction bisects this angle.
■ a diagonal seam of two pieces of fabric that meet at a corner joining.
3 (also **mitre shell**) a mollusc of warm seas which has a sharply pointed shell with a narrow aperture, supposedly resembling a bishop's mitre.
• Family Mitridae, class Gastropoda: *Mitra* and other genera.
▶**verb** [with obj.] join by means of a mitre.
– ORIGIN late Middle English: from Old French, via Latin from Greek *mitra* 'belt or turban'.

mitre box (also **mitre block** or **mitre board**) ▶**noun** a guide to enable a saw to cut mitre joints at the desired angle.

mitred ▶**adjective 1** joined with a mitre joint or seam: *complete the sides with mitred corners.*
2 bearing, wearing, or entitled to wear a mitre: *the mitred abbot of Battle.*

mitre wheel ▶**noun** each of a pair of bevelled cogwheels with teeth set at 45° and axes at right angles.

Mitsiwa /mɪˈtsiːwə/ variant spelling of **MASSAWA**.

mitt ▶**noun** (usu. **mitts**) a mitten: *oven mitts.*
■ a glove leaving the fingers and thumb-tip exposed. ■ (also **baseball mitt**) Baseball a large fingerless glove worn by the catcher or first baseman. ■ informal a person's hand.
– PHRASES **get one's mitts on** informal get hold of; possess.
– ORIGIN mid 18th cent.: abbreviation of **MITTEN**.

Mittelland Canal /ˈmɪt(ə)lˌland, German ˈmɪtlˌlant/ a canal in NW Germany, which was constructed between 1905 and 1930. It is part of an inland waterway network linking the Rivers Rhine and Elbe.

Mittelstand /ˈmɪt(ə)lstand, German ˈmɪtlʃtant/ ▶**noun** the medium-sized companies in a country, viewed as an economic unit.
– ORIGIN German, literally 'middle group'.

mitten ▶**noun** (usu. **mittens**) a glove with two sections, one for the thumb and the other for all four fingers.
■ (**mittens**) informal boxing gloves.
– DERIVATIVES **mittened** adjective.
– ORIGIN Middle English: from Old French *mitaine*, perhaps from *mite* pet name for a cat (because mittens were often made of fur).

mitten crab ▶**noun** see **CHINESE MITTEN CRAB**.

Mitterrand /ˈmiːtərɒ̃, French mitɛʀɑ̃/, François (Maurice Marie) (1916–96), French statesman, President 1981–95. As President he initially moved to raise basic wages, increase social benefits, nationalize key industries, and decentralize government. The Socialist Party lost its majority vote in the 1986 general election and Mitterrand made the right-wing Jacques Chirac Prime Minister, resulting in a reversal of some policies.

Mitty see **WALTER MITTY**.

mitzvah /ˈmɪtsvə/ ▶**noun** (pl. **mitzvoth** /-vəʊt/) Judaism a precept or commandment.
■ a good deed done from religious duty.
– ORIGIN mid 17th cent.: from Hebrew *miṣwāh* 'commandment'.

mix ▶**verb** [with obj.] combine or put together to form one substance or mass: *peppercorns are sometimes **mixed with** other spices for a table condiment* | *these two chemicals, when **mixed together**, literally explode.*
■ [no obj.] [often with negative] (of different substances) be able to be combined in this way: *oil and water don't mix.* ■ make or prepare by combining various ingredients: *mixing concrete is hard physical work.* ■ (especially in sound recording) combine (two or more signals or soundtracks) into one: *up to eight tracks can be mixed simultaneously.* ■ produce (a sound signal or recording) by combining a number of separate signals or recorded soundtracks: *it was everyone's dream to mix their album in their front room.* ■ juxtapose or put together to form a whole whose constituent parts are still distinct: *he continues to **mix** an off-hand sense of humour with a sharp insight.* ■ [no obj.] (of a person) associate with others socially: *the people he **mixed with** were nothing to do with show*

business. ■ (**mix it**) informal be belligerent physically or verbally.
▶ **noun** [usu. in sing.] two or more different qualities, things, or people placed, combined, or considered together: *the decor is a fascinating mix of antique and modern.*
■ a group of people of different types within a particular society or community: *the school has a good social mix.* ■ [often with modifier] a commercially prepared mixture of ingredients for making a particular type of food or a product such as concrete: *cake mixes have made cooking easier.* ■ the proportion of different people or other constituents that make up a mixture: *arriving at the correct mix of full-time to part-time staff | trousers made from a cotton and polyester mix.* ■ [often with modifier] a version of a recording in which the component tracks are mixed in a different way from the original: *a dance mix version of 'This Charming Man'.* ■ an image or sound produced by the combination of two separate images or sounds.
– PHRASES **be** (or **get**) **mixed up in** be (or become) involved in (something regarded dubious or dishonest): *Steve was mixed up in an insurance swindle.* **be** (or **get**) **mixed up with** be (or become) associated with (someone unsuitable or unreliable). **mix and match** select and combine different but complementary items, such as clothing or pieces of equipment, to form a coordinated set: *mix and match this season's colours for a combination that says winter* | [as modifier] *a mix-and-match menu.* **mix one's drinks** drink different kinds of alcohol in close succession.
– DERIVATIVES **mixable** adjective.
– ORIGIN late Middle English: back-formation from **MIXED** (taken as a past participle).
▶ **mix something up** spoil the order or arrangement of a collection of things: *disconnect all the cables, mix them up then try to reconnect them.* ■ (**mix someone/thing up**) confuse someone or something with another person or thing: *I'd got her **mixed up** with her sister.*

mixed ▶ **adjective** consisting of different qualities or elements: *a varied, mixed diet | beaches with mixed sand and shingle.*
■ (of an assessment of, reaction to, or feeling about something) containing a mixture of both favourable and negative elements: *the film opened last Friday to mixed reviews | I had mixed feelings about seeing Laura again.* ■ composed of different varieties of the same thing: *crab on a bed of mixed salad.* ■ involving or showing a mixture of races or social classes: *people of mixed race.* ■ (especially of an educational establishment or a sports team or competition) of or for members of both sexes: *the college's mixed hockey team.*
– ORIGIN late Middle English *mixt*: from Old French *mixte*, from Latin *mixtus*, past participle of *miscere* 'to mix'.

mixed bag (also **mixed bunch**) ▶ **noun** [in sing.] a diverse assortment of things or people: *we have a mixed bag of destinations and holiday choices for you.*

mixed blessing ▶ **noun** a situation or thing that has disadvantages as well as advantages: *having children so early in their marriage was a mixed blessing.*

mixed company ▶ **noun** [mass noun] company consisting of members of both sexes.

mixed crystal ▶ **noun** a crystal formed from more than one substance.

mixed doubles ▶ **plural noun** [treated as sing.] (especially in tennis and badminton) a game or competition involving sides each consisting of a man and a woman.

mixed economy ▶ **noun** an economic system combining private and state enterprise.

mixed farming ▶ **noun** [mass noun] a system of farming which involves the growing of crops as well as the raising of livestock.

mixed fortunes ▶ **plural noun** a mixture of success and lack of success, or good and bad luck: *the company had mixed fortunes during the year.*

mixed grill ▶ **noun** Brit. a dish consisting of various items of grilled food, typically bacon, sausages, tomatoes, and mushrooms.

mixed marriage ▶ **noun** a marriage between people of different races or religions.

mixed media ▶ **noun** [mass noun] the use of a variety of media in an entertainment or work of art.
▶ **adjective** (**mixed-media**) another term for **MULTIMEDIA**.

mixed metaphor ▶ **noun** a combination of two or more incompatible metaphors, which produces a ridiculous effect (e.g. *this tower of strength will forge ahead*).

mixed number ▶ **noun** a number consisting of an integer and a proper fraction.

mixed spice ▶ **noun** [mass noun] a commercially prepared mixture of ground spices for cooking, typically including cinnamon, nutmeg, and cloves.

mixed-up ▶ **adjective** informal (of a person) suffering from psychological or emotional problems: *a lonely mixed-up teenager.*

mixer ▶ **noun 1** [often with modifier] a machine or device for mixing things, especially an electrical appliance for mixing foods: *a food mixer.*
2 [with adj.] a person considered in terms of their ability to mix socially with others: *media people need to be good mixers.*
3 a soft drink that can be mixed with alcohol.
■ [mass noun] a type of dry pet food which can be mixed with moist tinned food.
4 (in sound recording and cinematography) a device for merging input signals to produce a combined output in the form of sound or pictures.
■ [often with modifier] a person who operates such a device: *a sound mixer.*

mixer tap ▶ **noun** Brit. a tap through which both hot and cold water can be drawn at the same time by means of separate controls.

mixing desk ▶ **noun** a console where sound signals are mixed during recording or broadcasting.

Mixmaster ▶ **noun** trademark a type of electric food processor.
■ (**mixmaster**) informal a sound-recording engineer or disc jockey who is an accomplished mixer of music, during recording or as a disc jockey.

mixologist ▶ **noun** US informal a person who is skilled at mixing cocktails and other drinks.
– DERIVATIVES **mixology** noun.

Mixolydian mode /ˌmɪksəˈlɪdɪən/ ▶ **noun** Music the mode represented by the natural diatonic scale G–G (containing a minor 7th).
– ORIGIN late 16th cent.: *Mixolydian* from Greek *mixoludios* 'half-Lydian' + **-AN**.

Mixtec /ˈmɪstɛk/ ▶ **noun** (pl. same or **Mixtecs**) **1** a member of an American Indian people of southern Mexico, noted for their skill in pottery and metallurgy.
2 the Otomanguean language of this people, spoken by about 250,000 people in several dialects.
▶ **adjective** of or relating to the Mixtec or their language.
– ORIGIN Spanish, from Nahuatl *mixtecah* 'person from a cloudy place'.

mixture ▶ **noun** a substance made by mixing other substances together: *form the mixture into a manageable dough | shandy is **a mixture of** beer and lemonade.*
■ [mass noun] the process of mixing or being mixed. ■ (**a mixture of**) a combination of different qualities, things, or emotions in which the component elements are individually distinct: *she thumped the pillow with a mixture of anger and frustration | the old town is a mixture of narrow medieval streets and 18th-century architecture.* ■ a person regarded as a combination of qualities and attributes: *he was a curious mixture, an unpredictable man.* ■ Chemistry the product of the random distribution of one substance through another without any chemical reaction, as distinct from a compound. ■ the charge of gas or vapour mixed with air which is admitted to the cylinder of an internal-combustion engine, especially as regards the ratio of fuel to air: *newer pilots often leave their mixture rich during an entire flight.* ■ (also **mixture stop**) an organ stop in which each key sounds a group of small pipes, of different pitches, giving a very bright tone.
– PHRASES **the mixture as before** Brit. the same treatment repeated. [ORIGIN: used formerly as an instruction on a medicine bottle.]
– ORIGIN late Middle English: from French *mixture* or Latin *mixtura* (see **MIXED**).

mix-up ▶ **noun** informal a confusion of one thing with another, or a misunderstanding or mistake that results in confusion: *there's been a mix-up over the tickets.*
■ a combination of different things, especially one whose effect is inharmonious: *a ghastly mix-up of furniture styles.*

Mizo /ˈmiːzəʊ/ ▶ **noun** (pl. same or **-os**) **1** a member of a people inhabiting Mizoram.
2 [mass noun] the Tibeto-Burman language of this people, with about 340,000 speakers. Also called **LUSHAI**.
▶ **adjective** of or relating to this people or their language.
– ORIGIN the name in Mizo, literally 'highlander', from *mi-* 'person' + *zo* 'hill'.

Mizoram /ˈmɪzəʊram/ a state in the far north-east of India, lying between Bangladesh and Burma (Myanmar); capital, Aizawl. Separated from Assam in 1972, it was administered as a Union Territory in India until 1986, when it became a state.

mizuna /mɪˈzuːnə/ (also **mizuna greens**) ▶ **noun** [mass noun] an oriental rape of a variety with finely cut leaves that are eaten as a salad vegetable.
● *Brassica rapa* var. *nipposinica*, family Cruciferae.
– ORIGIN 1990s: from Japanese.

mizzen /ˈmɪz(ə)n/ (also **mizen**) ▶ **noun 1** (also **mizzenmast**) the mast aft of a ship's mainmast.
2 (also **mizzensail**) a sail on the mizzenmast of a ship, in particular the lowest sail on the mizzenmast of a square-rigged sailing ship.
– ORIGIN late Middle English: from Italian *mezzana* 'mizzensail', feminine (used as a noun) of *mezzano* 'middle', from Latin *medianus* (see **MEDIAN**).

mizzle¹ /ˈmɪz(ə)l/ chiefly dialect ▶ **noun** [mass noun] light rain; drizzle.
▶ **verb** [no obj.] (**it mizzles, it is mizzling**, etc.) rain lightly: *it was mizzling steadily.*
– DERIVATIVES **mizzly** adjective.
– ORIGIN late Middle English (as a verb): probably a frequentative from the base of **MIST**; compare with Low German *miseln* and Dutch dialect *miezelen.*

mizzle² /ˈmɪz(ə)l/ ▶ **verb** [no obj.] Brit. informal, dated go away suddenly; vanish: *he mizzled into the crowd.*
– ORIGIN late 18th cent.: of unknown origin.

Mk ▶ **abbreviation for** ■ the German mark. ■ the Gospel of Mark (in biblical references). ■ (followed by a numeral) Mark, used to denote a design or model of car, aircraft, or other machine: *a VW Golf Mk III.*

mks ▶ **abbreviation for** metre-kilogram-second.

Mkt ▶ **abbreviation for** Market (in place names).

ml ▶ **abbreviation for** ■ mile(s). ■ millilitre(s).

MLA ▶ **abbreviation for** ■ Member of the Legislative Assembly. ■ Modern Language Association (of America).

MLC ▶ **abbreviation for** Member of the Legislative Council.

MLD ▶ **abbreviation for** ■ minimum lethal dose. ■ moderate learning difficulties: [as modifier] *a school for MLD pupils.*

MLF ▶ **abbreviation for** multilateral nuclear force.

MLitt ▶ **abbreviation for** Master of Letters: *Susan Williams, M Litt.*
– ORIGIN from Latin *Magister Litterarum*.

Mlle (pl. **Mlles**) ▶ **abbreviation for** Mademoiselle.

MM ▶ **abbreviation for** ■ Maelzel's metronome (an indication of tempo in music, given as the number of beats per minute). [ORIGIN: with reference to the metronome invented by Johann N. Maelzel (died 1838).] ■ Messieurs. ■ (in the UK) Military Medal.

mm ▶ **abbreviation for** millimetre(s).

Mmabatho /məˈbɑːtəʊ, ˌəmmə-/ the capital of North-West Province in South Africa, near the border with Botswana; pop. 28,000 (1985).

Mme (pl. **Mmes**) ▶ **abbreviation for** Madame.

m.m.f. ▶ **abbreviation for** magnetomotive force.

MMR ▶ **abbreviation for** measles, mumps, and rubella, a vaccination given to small children.

MMus ▶ **abbreviation for** Master of Music.

MN ▶ **abbreviation for** ■ (in the UK) Merchant Navy. ■ Minnesota (in official postal use).

Mn ▶ **symbol for** the chemical element manganese.

MNA ▶ **abbreviation for** (in Canada) Member of the National Assembly (of Quebec).

M'Naghten rules variant spelling of **MCNAGHTEN RULES**.

mnemonic /nɪˈmɒnɪk/ ▶ **noun** a device such as a pattern of letters, ideas, or associations which assists in remembering something.
▶ **adjective** aiding or designed to aid the memory.
■ of or relating to the power of memory.

– DERIVATIVES **mnemonically** adverb, **mnemonist** /ˈniːmənɪst/ noun.
– ORIGIN mid 18th cent. (as an adjective): via medieval Latin from Greek *mnēmonikos*, from *mnēmōn* 'mindful'.

mnemonics ▶ **plural noun** [usu. treated as sing.] the study and development of systems for improving and assisting the memory.

Mnemosyne /niːˈmɒzɪni/ Greek Mythology the mother of the Muses.
– ORIGIN from Greek *mnēmosunē*, literally 'memory'.

mnemotechnics /ˌniːmə(ʊ)ˈtɛknɪks/ ▶ **plural noun** another term for **MNEMONICS**.
– DERIVATIVES **mnemotechnic** adjective & noun.
– ORIGIN mid 19th cent.: from Greek *mnēmē* 'memory' + *-technics* (see **TECHNIC**).

MO ▶ **abbreviation for** ■ Computing (of a disk or disk drive) magneto-optical. ■ Medical Officer. ■ Missouri (in official postal use). ■ modus operandi. ■ money order.

Mo ▶ **symbol for** the chemical element molybdenum.

mo ▶ **noun** [in sing.] informal, chiefly Brit. a short period of time: *hang on a mo!*
– ORIGIN late 19th cent.: abbreviation of **MOMENT**.

mo. N. Amer. ▶ **abbreviation for** month.

-mo /məʊ/ ▶ **suffix** forming nouns denoting a book size by the number of leaves into which a sheet of paper has been folded: *twelvemo*.
– ORIGIN from the final syllable of Latin ordinal numbers such as *duodecimo* (masculine ablative singular).

moa /ˈməʊə/ ▶ **noun** a large extinct flightless bird resembling the emu, formerly found in New Zealand.
● Family Dinornithidae: several genera and species; *Dinornis maximus* is the tallest known bird at over 3 m, but *Megalapteryx didinus*, which may have survived until the early 19th century, was much smaller.
– ORIGIN mid 19th cent.: from Maori.

Moab /ˈməʊab/ the ancient kingdom of the Moabites, situated to the east of the Dead Sea.

Moabite /ˈməʊəbʌɪt/ ▶ **noun** a member of a Semitic people living in Moab in biblical times, traditionally descended from Lot.
▶ **adjective** of or relating to Moab or its people.

Moabite Stone a monument erected by Mesha, king of Moab, in *c.*850 BC which describes (in an early form of the Hebrew language) the campaign between Moab and ancient Israel (2 Kings 3), and furnishes an early example of an inscription in the Phoenician alphabet. It is now in the Louvre in Paris.

moan ▶ **noun** a long, low sound made by a person expressing physical or mental suffering or sexual pleasure: *she gave a low moan of despair.*
■ a sound resembling this, especially one made by the wind: *the moan of the wind in the chimneys.* ■ informal a complaint which is perceived as trivial and not taken seriously by others: *there were moans about the car's feeble ventilation.*
▶ **verb** [no obj.] make a long, low sound expressing physical or mental suffering or sexual pleasure: *just then their patient moaned and opened his eyes* | [with direct speech] *'Oh God,' I moaned.*
■ (of a thing) make a sound resembling this: *the foghorn moaned at intervals.* ■ [reporting verb] informal complain or grumble, typically about something trivial: [no obj.] *passengers moaned about overcrowded coaches* | [with clause] *my husband moans that I'm not as slim as when we first met.* ■ poetic/literary lament.
– DERIVATIVES **moaner** noun, **moanful** adjective.
– ORIGIN Middle English (in the sense 'complaint or lamentation'): of unknown origin.

moat ▶ **noun** a deep, wide ditch surrounding a castle, fort, or town, typically filled with water and intended as a defence against attack.
▶ **verb** [with obj.] [often as adj. **moated**] surround (a place) with a moat: *a moated castle.*
– ORIGIN late Middle English: from Old French *mote* 'mound'.

mob ▶ **noun** a large crowd of people, especially one that is disorderly and intent on causing trouble or violence: *a mob of protesters.*
■ (usu. **the Mob**) N. Amer. the Mafia or a similar criminal organization. ■ Brit. informal a group of people in the same place or with something in common: *he stood out from the rest of the mob with his silver hair and stacked shoes.* ■ (**the mob**) the ordinary people: *the age-old fear that the mob may organize to destroy the last vestiges of civilized life.* ■ Austral. a flock or herd of animals: *a mob of cattle.*
▶ **verb** (**mobbed**, **mobbing**) [with obj.] (often **be mobbed**) crowd round (someone) in an unruly and excitable way in order to admire or attack them: *he was mobbed by autograph hunters.*
■ (of a group of birds or mammals) surround and attack (a predator or other source of threat) in order to drive it off. ■ N. Amer. crowd into (a building or place): *an unruly crowd mobbed the White House during an inaugural reception.*
– DERIVATIVES **mobber** noun.
– ORIGIN late 17th cent.: abbreviation of archaic *mobile*, short for Latin *mobile vulgus* 'excitable crowd'.

mob cap ▶ **noun** a large soft hat covering all of the hair and typically having a decorative frill, worn indoors by women in the 18th and early 19th centuries.
– ORIGIN mid 18th cent.: *mob*, variant of obsolete *mab* 'slut'. The word *mob* was first used in the sense 'prostitute' (mid to late 17th cent.), later denoting a négligé (mid 17th cent. to mid 18th cent.).

mob-handed ▶ **adverb** Brit. informal in considerable numbers: *they came mob-handed.*

Mobile /məʊˈbiːl/ an industrial city and port on the coast of southern Alabama; pop. 196,280 (1990). It is situated at the head of Mobile Bay, an inlet of the Gulf of Mexico.

mobile /ˈməʊbʌɪl/ ▶ **adjective** able to move or be moved freely or easily: *he has a major weight problem and is not very mobile* | *highly mobile international capital.*
■ (of the face or its features) indicating feelings with fluid and expressive movements: *her mobile features working overtime to register shock and disapproval.* ■ (of a shop, library, or other service) accommodated in a vehicle so as to travel around and serve various places. ■ (of a military or police unit) equipped and prepared to move quickly to any place it is needed: *creating a mobile reserve of police on a national basis.* ■ able or willing to move easily or freely between occupations, places of residence, or social classes: *an increasingly mobile and polarized society.*
▶ **noun 1** a decorative structure that is suspended so as to turn freely in the air.
2 short for **MOBILE PHONE**.
– PHRASES **upwardly** (or **downwardly**) **mobile** moving to a higher (or lower) social class; acquiring (or losing) wealth and status.
– ORIGIN late 15th cent.: via French from Latin *mobilis*, from *movere* 'to move'. The noun dates from the 1940s.

mobile home ▶ **noun** a large caravan that is parked in one particular place and used as permanent living accommodation.

mobile phone (also **mobile telephone**) ▶ **noun** a telephone with access to a cellular radio system so it can be used over a wide area, without a physical connection to a network.

mobile sculpture ▶ **noun** a sculpture with moving parts.

mobility ▶ **noun** [mass noun] the ability to move or be moved freely and easily: *this exercise helps retain mobility in the damaged joints.*
■ the ability to move between different levels in society or employment: *industrialization would open up increasing chances of social mobility.*

mobility allowance ▶ **noun** Brit. a state benefit paid to disabled people to assist them in travelling for regular medical attention or other purposes.

mobilize (also **-ise**) ▶ **verb** [with obj.] **1** (of a country or its government) prepare and organize (troops) for active service.
■ organize and encourage (people) to act or have effect in a concerted way in order to bring about a particular political objective: *he used the press to mobilize support for his party.* ■ bring (resources) into use in order to achieve a particular goal: *at sea we will mobilize any amount of resources to undertake a rescue.*
2 make (something) movable or capable of movement: *the physiotherapist might mobilize the patient's shoulder girdle.*
■ make (a substance) able to be transported by or as a liquid: *acid rain mobilizes the aluminium in forest soils.*
– DERIVATIVES **mobilizable** adjective, **mobilization** noun, **mobilizer** noun.
– ORIGIN mid 19th cent.: from French *mobiliser*, from *mobile* (see **MOBILE**).

Möbius strip /ˈməːbɪəs/ ▶ **noun** a surface with one continuous side formed by joining the ends of a rectangle after twisting one end through 180°.
– ORIGIN early 20th cent.: named after August F. *Möbius* (1790–1868), German mathematician .

mobocracy ▶ **noun** (pl. **-ies**) [mass noun] rule or domination by the masses.

mob rule ▶ **noun** [mass noun] control of a political situation by those outside the conventional or lawful realm, typically involving violence and intimidation.

mobster ▶ **noun** informal a member of a group of violent criminals; a gangster.

Mobutu /məˈbuːtuː/, Sese Seko (1930–97), Zairean statesman, President 1965–97; born *Joseph-Désiré Mobutu*. Seizing power in a military coup in 1965, he retained control despite opposition until 1997, when he was finally forced to stand down.

Mobutu Sese Seko, Lake /məˌbuːtuː ˌseɪseɪ ˈseɪkəʊ/ Zairean name for Lake Albert (see **ALBERT, LAKE**).

moc /mɒk/ ▶ **noun** N. Amer. informal short for **MOCCASIN**.

moccasin ▶ **noun 1** a soft leather slipper or shoe, strictly one without a separate heel, having the sole turned up on all sides and sewn to the upper in a simple gathered seam, in a style originating among North American Indians.
2 a venomous American pit viper.
● Genus *Agkistrodon*, family Viperidae: three species, in particular the **water** (or **cottonmouth**) **moccasin** (see **COTTONMOUTH**) and the **highland moccasin** (see **COPPERHEAD**.)
– ORIGIN early 17th cent.: from Virginia Algonquian *mockasin*. The word is also found in other American Indian languages.

moccasin telegraph ▶ **noun** Canadian term for **BUSH TELEGRAPH**.

mocha /ˈmɒkə/ ▶ **noun** [mass noun] **1** a fine-quality coffee.
■ a drink or flavouring made with or in imitation of this, typically with chocolate added. ■ a dark brown colour.
2 a soft kind of leather made from sheepskin.
– ORIGIN late 18th cent.: named after *Mocha*, a port on the Red Sea, from where the coffee and leather were first shipped.

mock ▶ **verb** [with obj.] tease or laugh at in a scornful or contemptuous manner: *opposition MPs mocked the government's decision* | [as adj. **mocking**] *the mocking hostility in his voice made her wince.*
■ make (something) seem laughably unreal or impossible: *at Christmas, arguments and friction mock our pretence at peace.* ■ mimic (someone or something) scornfully or contemptuously.
▶ **adjective** [attrib.] not authentic or real, but without the intention to deceive: *a mock-Georgian red brick house* | *Jim threw up his hands in mock horror.*
■ (of an examination, battle, etc.) arranged for training or practice: *a mock examination paper.*
▶ **noun 1** (**mocks**) Brit. informal mock examinations: *obtaining Grade A in mocks.*
2 dated an object of derision: *he has become the mock of all his contemporaries.*
– PHRASES **make (a) mock of** hold up to scorn or ridicule: *stop making a mock of other people's business.*
– DERIVATIVES **mockable** adjective, **mockingly** adverb.
– ORIGIN late Middle English: from Old French *mocquer* 'deride'.

mocker ▶ **noun** a person who mocks someone or something: *a mocker of authority.*
– PHRASES **put the mockers on** Brit. informal put an end to; thwart. ■ bring bad luck to: *someone has really put the mockers on the team.*

mockery ▶ **noun** (pl. **-ies**) [mass noun] derision; ridicule: *stung by her mockery, Frankie hung his head.*
■ [in sing.] an absurd misrepresentation or imitation of something: *after **a mockery of** a trial in London, he was executed.* ■ archaic ludicrously futile action: *in her bitterness she felt that all rejoicing was mockery.*
– PHRASES **make a mockery of** make (something) seem foolish or absurd: *the terrorists are making a mockery of security policy.*
– ORIGIN late Middle English: from Old French *moquerie*, from *mocquer* 'to deride'.

mock-heroic ▶ **adjective** (of a literary work or its style) imitating the style of heroic literature in order to satirize an unheroic subject.
▶ **noun** a burlesque imitation of the heroic character or literary style.

mockingbird ▶ **noun** a long-tailed thrush-like songbird with greyish plumage, found mainly in

tropical America and noted for its mimicry of the calls and songs of other birds.
• Family Mimidae (the **mockingbird family**): three genera and several species, especially the **northern mockingbird** (*Mimus polyglottos*), of North America. The mockingbird family also includes the catbirds, thrashers, and tremblers.

mock moon ▶ **noun** Astronomy a paraselene.

mockney ▶ **noun** [mass noun] Brit. informal a form of speech perceived as an affected imitation of cockney in accent and vocabulary.

mock orange ▶ **noun** a bushy shrub of north temperate regions, which is cultivated for its strongly scented white flowers, the perfume of which resembles orange blossom.
• Genus *Philadelphus*, family Hydrangeaceae (formerly Philadelphaceae): several species and hybrids, in particular *P. coronarius*.

mock sun ▶ **noun** Astronomy a parhelion.

mock turtle soup ▶ **noun** [mass noun] imitation turtle soup made from a calf's head.

mock-up ▶ **noun** a model or replica of a machine or structure, used for instructional or experimental purposes.
■ an arrangement of text and pictures to be printed: *a mock-up of the following day's front page.*

mocky US informal, dated, offensive, ▶ **noun** (pl. **-ies**) a Jew.
▶ **adjective** Jewish.
– ORIGIN 1930s: perhaps from Yiddish *makeh* 'a plague'.

mocock /məʊˈkɒk/ ▶ **noun** N. Amer. a container resembling a basket made from birchbark.
– ORIGIN late 18th cent.: from an American Indian language.

MOD ▶ **abbreviation for** (in the UK) Ministry of Defence.

Mod ▶ **noun** a Highland meeting for Gaelic literary and musical competitions.
– ORIGIN from Scottish Gaelic *mōd*.

mod[1] ▶ **adjective** informal modern.
▶ **noun** Brit. (especially in the early 1960s) a young person of a subculture characterized by a smart stylish appearance, the riding of motor scooters, and a liking for soul music.
– ORIGIN abbreviation of **MODERN** or **MODERNIST**.

mod[2] ▶ **preposition** Mathematics another term for **MODULO**.

mod[3] ▶ **noun** informal (usu. **mods**) short for **MODIFICATION**.

modacrylic /ˌmɒdəˈkrɪlɪk/ ▶ **adjective** of or denoting a synthetic textile fibre which is a polymer containing a high proportion of units derived from acrylonitrile.
▶ **noun** [mass noun] a textile fibre of this kind.
– ORIGIN 1950s: from *modified* (past participle of **MODIFY**) + **ACRYLIC**.

modal /ˈməʊd(ə)l/ ▶ **adjective 1** of or relating to mode or form as opposed to substance.
2 Grammar of or denoting the mood of a verb.
■ relating to a modal verb.
3 Statistics of or relating to a mode; occurring most frequently in a sample or population.
4 Music of or denoting music using melodies or harmonies based on modes other than the ordinary major and minor scales.
5 Logic (of a proposition) in which the predicate is affirmed of the subject with some qualification, or which involves the affirmation of possibility, impossibility, necessity, or contingency.
▶ **noun** Grammar a modal word or construction.
– DERIVATIVES **modally** adverb.
– ORIGIN mid 16th cent. (in sense 5): from medieval Latin *modalis*, from Latin *modus* (see **MODE**).

modalism ▶ **noun** [mass noun] **1** Theology the doctrine that the persons of the Trinity represent only three modes or aspects of the divine revelation, not distinct and coexisting parts of the divine nature.
2 Music the use of modal melodies and harmonies.
– DERIVATIVES **modalist** noun & adjective.

modality ▶ **noun** (pl. **-ies**) **1** [mass noun] modal quality: *the harmony had a touch of modality.*
2 a particular mode in which something exists or is experienced or expressed.
■ a particular method or procedure: *they addressed questions concerning the modalities of Soviet troop withdrawals.* ■ a particular form of sensory perception: *the visual and auditory modalities.*
– ORIGIN early 17th cent.: from medieval Latin *modalitas*, from *modalis* (see **MODAL**).

modal verb ▶ **noun** Grammar an auxiliary verb that expresses necessity or possibility. English modal verbs include *must, shall, will, should, would, can, could, may,* and *might*.

mod cons ▶ **plural noun** Brit. informal the amenities and appliances characteristic of a well-equipped modern house that contribute to an easier and more comfortable way of life: *the property has many interesting features and* ***all mod cons.***

mode ▶ **noun 1** a way or manner in which something occurs or is experienced, expressed, or done: *his preferred mode of travel was a kayak* | *differences between language modes, namely speech and writing.*
■ an option allowing a change in the method of operation of a device, especially a camera: *a camcorder* ***in automatic mode.*** ■ Computing a way of operating or using a system: *some computers provide several so-called processor modes.* ■ Physics any of the distinct kinds or patterns of vibration of an oscillating system. ■ Logic the character of a modal proposition (whether necessary, contingent, possible, or impossible). ■ Logic & Grammar another term for **MOOD**[2].
2 a fashion or style in clothes, art, literature, etc.: *in the Seventies the mode for active wear took hold.*
3 Statistics the value that occurs most frequently in a given set of data.
4 Music a set of musical notes forming a scale and from which melodies and harmonies are constructed.

> The modes of plainsong and later Western music (including the usual major and minor scales) correspond to the diatonic scales played on the white notes of a piano. They are named arbitrarily after ancient Greek modes: Ionian (or major), Dorian, Phrygian, Lydian, Mixolydian, Aeolian, and Locrian.

– ORIGIN late Middle English (in the musical and grammatical senses): from Latin *modus* 'measure', from an Indo-European root shared by **METE**[1]; compare with **MOOD**[2].

model ▶ **noun 1** a three-dimensional representation of a person or thing or of a proposed structure, typically on a smaller scale than the original: *a model of St Paul's Cathedral* | [as modifier] *a model aeroplane.*
■ (in sculpture) a figure or object made in clay or wax, to be reproduced in another more durable material.
2 a system or thing used as an example to follow or imitate: *the law became a model for dozens of laws banning nondegradable plastic products* | [as modifier] *a model farm.*
■ a simplified description, especially a mathematical one, of a system or process, to assist calculations and predictions: *a statistical model used for predicting the survival rates of endangered species.* ■ (**model of**) a person or thing regarded as an excellent example of a specified quality: *as she grew older, she became a model of self-control* | [as modifier] *he was a model husband and father.* ■ (**model for**) an actual person or place on which a specified fictional character or location is based: *Preston was the model for Coketown in 'Hard Times'.* ■ (**the Model**) the plan for the reorganization of the Parliamentary army, passed by the House of Commons in 1644–5. See also **NEW MODEL ARMY**.
3 a person, typically a woman, employed to display clothes by wearing them.
■ a person employed to pose for an artist, photographer, or sculptor: *an artist's model.*
4 a particular design or version of a product: *changing your car for a new model.*
■ a garment or a copy of a garment by a well-known designer.
▶ **verb** (**modelled**, **modelling**; US **modeled**, **modeling**) [with obj.] **1** fashion or shape (a three-dimensional figure or object) in a malleable material such as clay or wax: *use the icing to model a house.*
■ (in drawing or painting) represent so as to appear three-dimensional: *the body of the woman to the right is modelled in softer, riper forms.* ■ (**model something on/after**) use (especially a system or procedure) as an example to follow or imitate: *the research method will be modelled on previous work.* ■ (**model oneself on**) take (someone admired or respected) as an example to copy: *he models himself on rock legend Elvis Presley.* ■ devise a representation, especially a mathematical one, of (a phenomenon or system): *a computer program that can model how smoke behaves.*
2 display (clothes) by wearing them.
■ [no obj.] work as a model by displaying clothes or posing for an artist or sculptor.
– DERIVATIVES **modeller** noun.
– ORIGIN late 16th cent. (denoting a set of plans of a building): from French *modelle*, from Italian *modello*, from an alteration of Latin *modulus* (see **MODULUS**).

model home ▶ **noun** North American term for **SHOW HOUSE**.

modelling (US **modeling**) ▶ **noun** [mass noun] **1** the work of a fashion model.
2 the art or activity of making three-dimensional models.
■ [often with adj. or noun modifier] the devising or use of abstract or mathematical models: *macroeconomic modelling and policy analysis.*

model village ▶ **noun 1** historical a village providing a high standard of housing, typically built by an employer for the workforce.
2 a small copy of a village or a collection of models of famous buildings arranged as a village, typically built as a tourist attraction.

modem /ˈməʊdɛm/ ▶ **noun** a combined device for modulation and demodulation, for example, between the digital data of a computer and the analogue signal of a telephone line.
▶ **verb** [with obj. and adverbial of direction] send (data) by modem.
– ORIGIN mid 20th cent.: blend of *modulator* and *demodulator*.

Modena /ˈmɒdɪnə, Italian moˈdena/ a city in northern Italy, north-west of Bologna; pop. 177,500 (1990).

moderate ▶ **adjective** average in amount, intensity, quality, or degree: *we walked at a moderate pace.*
■ (of a person, party, or policy) not radical or excessively right- or left-wing: *a moderate reform programme.*
▶ **noun** /ˈmɒd(ə)rət/ a person who holds moderate views, especially in politics.
▶ **verb 1** make or become less extreme, intense, rigorous, or violent: [with obj.] *I shall not moderate my criticism* | [as adj. **moderating**] *his moderating influence in the army was now needed more than ever* | [no obj.] *the weather has moderated considerably.*
2 [with obj.] review (examination papers, results, or candidates) in relation to an agreed standard so as to ensure consistency of marking.
3 [with obj.] (in academic and ecclesiastical contexts) preside over (a deliberative body) or at (a debate): *a panel moderated by a Harvard University law professor.*
■ [no obj.] (especially in the Presbyterian Church in Scotland) preside; act as a moderator.
4 [with obj.] Physics retard (neutrons) with a moderator.
– DERIVATIVES **moderatism** noun.
– ORIGIN late Middle English: from Latin *moderat-* 'reduced, controlled', from the verb *moderare*; related to **MODEST**.

moderate breeze ▶ **noun** a wind of force 4 on the Beaufort scale (11–16 knots or 20–30 kph).

moderate gale ▶ **noun** another term for **NEAR GALE**.

moderately ▶ **adverb** [as submodifier] to a certain extent; quite; fairly: *these events were moderately successful* | *he answered all the questions moderately well.*
■ in a moderate manner: *growth continues moderately.*
■ within reasonable limits: *both hotels are moderately priced.*

moderation ▶ **noun** [mass noun] **1** the avoidance of excess or extremes, especially in one's behaviour or political opinions: *he urged the police to show moderation.*
■ the action of making something less extreme, intense, or violent: *the union's approach was based on increased dialogue and* ***the moderation of*** *demands.*
2 the action or process of moderating examination papers, results, or candidates.
■ (**Moderations**) the first public examination in some faculties for the BA degree at Oxford University.
3 Physics the retardation of neutrons by a moderator.
– PHRASES **in moderation** within reasonable limits; not to excess: *nuts can be eaten in moderation.*
– ORIGIN late Middle English: via Old French from Latin *moderatio(n-)*, from the verb *moderare* 'to control' (see **MODERATE**).

moderato /ˌmɒdəˈrɑːtəʊ/ Music ▶ **adverb & adjective** (especially as a direction) at a moderate pace: [postpositive as submodifier] *allegro moderato.*
▶ **noun** (pl. **-os**) a passage marked to be performed in such a way.
– ORIGIN Italian, literally 'moderate'.

moderator ▶ **noun 1** an arbitrator or mediator: *Egypt managed to assert its role as a regional moderator.*
■ a presiding officer, especially a chairman of a debate.

▪a Presbyterian minister presiding over an ecclesiastical body.
2 a person who reviews examination papers to ensure consistency, or otherwise oversees an examination.
3 Physics a substance used in a nuclear reactor to retard neutrons.
– DERIVATIVES **moderatorship** noun.

modern ▶ **adjective** of or relating to the present or recent times as opposed to the remote past: *the pace of modern life | modern Chinese history.*
▪characterized by or using the most up-to-date techniques, ideas, or equipment: *they do not have modern weapons.* ▪ [attrib.] denoting the form of a language that is currently used, as opposed to any earlier form: *modern German.* ▪ [attrib.] denoting a current or recent style or trend in art, architecture, or other cultural activity marked by a significant departure from traditional styles and values: *Matisse's contribution to modern art.*
▶ **noun** (usu. **moderns**) a person who advocates or practises a departure from traditional styles or values.
– DERIVATIVES **modernity** noun, **modernly** adverb, **modernness** noun.
– ORIGIN late Middle English: from late Latin *modernus*, from Latin *modo* 'just now'.

modern dance ▶ **noun** [mass noun] a free expressive style of dancing started in the early 20th century as a reaction to classical ballet. In recent years it has included elements not usually associated with dance, such as speech and film.

moderne /mə'dəːn/ ▶ **adjective** of or relating to a popularization of the art deco style marked by bright colours and geometric shapes.
▪often derogatory denoting an ultra-modern style.
– ORIGIN mid 20th cent.: French, 'modern'.

modern English ▶ **noun** [mass noun] the English language as it has been since about 1500.

Modern Greats ▶ **plural noun** (at Oxford University) the school of philosophy, politics, and economics.

modern history ▶ **noun** [mass noun] history up to the present day, from some arbitrary point taken to represent the end of the Middle Ages. In some contexts it may be contrasted with 'ancient' rather than 'medieval' history, and start (e.g.) from the fall of the Western Roman Empire.

modernism ▶ **noun** [mass noun] modern character or quality of thought, expression, or technique: *when he waxes philosophical, he comes over as a strange mix of nostalgia and modernism.*
▪a style or movement in the arts that aims to break with classical and traditional forms. ▪ a movement towards modifying traditional beliefs in accordance with modern ideas, especially in the Roman Catholic Church in the late 19th and early 20th centuries.

modernist ▶ **noun** a believer in or supporter of modernism, especially in the arts.
▶ **adjective** of or associated with modernism, especially in the arts.
– DERIVATIVES **modernistic** adjective.

modernize (also **-ise**) ▶ **verb** [with obj.] adapt (something) to modern needs or habits, typically by installing modern equipment or adopting modern ideas or methods: *he wanted to modernize the health service.*
– DERIVATIVES **modernization** noun, **modernizer** noun.

modern jazz ▶ **noun** [mass noun] jazz as developed in the 1940s and 1950s, especially bebop and the music that followed it.

modern languages ▶ **plural noun** European languages (especially French and German) as a subject of study, as contrasted with classical Latin and Greek.

modern Latin ▶ **noun** [mass noun] Latin as developed since 1500, used especially in scientific terminology.

modern pentathlon ▶ **noun** see **PENTATHLON**.

modest ▶ **adjective 1** unassuming or moderate in the estimation of one's abilities or achievements: *he was a very modest man, refusing to take any credit for the enterprise.*
2 (of an amount, rate, or level of something) relatively moderate, limited, or small: *drink modest amounts of alcohol | employment growth was relatively modest.*
▪(of a place in which one lives, eats, or stays) not excessively large, elaborate, or expensive: *a modest flat in Fulham.*
3 (of a woman) dressing or behaving so as to avoid impropriety or indecency, especially to avoid attracting sexual attention.
▪(of clothing) not revealing or emphasizing the figure: *modest dress means that hemlines must be below the knee.*
– DERIVATIVES **modestly** adverb.
– ORIGIN mid 16th cent.: from French *modeste*, from Latin *modestus* 'keeping due measure', related to *modus* 'measure'.

modesty ▶ **noun** [mass noun] the quality or state of being unassuming or moderate in the estimation of one's abilities: *with typical modesty he insisted on sharing the credit with others.*
▪the quality of being relatively moderate, limited, or small in amount, rate, or level: *the modesty of his political aspirations.* ▪ behaviour, manner, or appearance intended to avoid impropriety or indecency: *modesty forbade her to undress in front of so many people.*

modicum /'mɒdɪkəm/ ▶ **noun** [in sing.] a small quantity of a particular thing, especially something considered desirable or valuable: *his statement had more than **a modicum of** truth.*
– ORIGIN late 15th cent.: from Latin, neuter of *modicus* 'moderate', from *modus* 'measure'.

modification ▶ **noun** [mass noun] the action of modifying something: *the parts supplied should fit with little or no modification.*
▪[count noun] a change made: *a number of modifications are being carried out to the engines.*
– ORIGIN late 15th cent. (in Scots law, denoting the assessment of a payment): from French, or from Latin *modificatio(n-)*, from *modificare* (see **MODIFY**).

modifier ▶ **noun** a person or thing that makes partial or minor changes to something.
▪Grammar a word, especially an adjective or noun used attributively, that restricts or adds to the sense of a head noun (e.g. *good* and *family* in *a good family house*). ▪ Genetics a gene which modifies the phenotypic expression of a gene at another locus.

modify ▶ **verb** (**-ies**, **-ied**) [with obj.] make partial or minor changes to (something), typically so as to improve it or to make it less extreme: *she may be prepared to modify her views* | [as adj. **modified**] *a modified version of the aircraft.*
▪Biology transform (a structure) from its original anatomical form during development or evolution. ▪ Grammar (especially of an adjective) restrict or add to the sense of (a noun): *the target noun is modified by a 'direction' word.* ▪ Phonetics pronounce (a speech sound) in a way that is different from the norm for that sound.
– DERIVATIVES **modifiable** adjective, **modificatory** adjective.
– ORIGIN late Middle English: from Old French *modifier*, from Latin *modificare*, from *modus* (see **MODE**).

Modigliani /ˌmɒdɪ'ljɑːni/, Amedeo (1884–1920), Italian painter and sculptor, resident in France from 1906. His portraits and nudes are noted for their elongated forms, linear qualities, and earthy colours.

modillion /mə'dɪljən/ ▶ **noun** Architecture a projecting bracket under the corona of a cornice in the Corinthian and other orders.
– ORIGIN mid 16th cent.: from French *modillon*, from Italian *modiglione*, based on Latin *mutulus* 'mutule'.

modiolus /mə'dʌɪələs/ ▶ **noun** (pl. **modioli**) Anatomy the conical central axis of the cochlea of the ear.
– ORIGIN early 19th cent.: from Latin, literally 'nave of a wheel'.

modish /'məʊdɪʃ/ ▶ **adjective** often derogatory conforming to or following what is currently popular and fashionable: *it seems sad that such a scholar should feel compelled to use this modish jargon.*
– DERIVATIVES **modishly** adverb, **modishness** noun.

modiste /mɒ'diːst/ ▶ **noun** dated a fashionable milliner or dressmaker.
– ORIGIN mid 19th cent.: French, from *mode* 'fashion'.

Mods ▶ **plural noun** informal the Moderations examination at Oxford University.

modular ▶ **adjective** employing or involving a module or modules as the basis of design or construction: *modular housing units.*
▪of or relating to an educational course designed as a series of independent units of study that can be combined in a number of ways. ▪ Mathematics of or relating to a modulus.
– DERIVATIVES **modularity** noun.
– ORIGIN late 18th cent.: from modern Latin *modularis*, from Latin *modulus* (see **MODULUS**).

modulate /'mɒdjʊleɪt/ ▶ **verb** [with obj.] exert a modifying or controlling influence on: *the state attempts to modulate private business's cash flow.*
▪vary the strength, tone, or pitch of (one's voice): *we all modulate our voice by hearing it.* ▪ alter the amplitude or frequency of (an electromagnetic wave or other oscillation) in accordance with the variations of a second signal, typically one of a lower frequency: *radio waves are modulated to carry the analogue information of the voice.* ▪ [no obj.] Music change from one key to another: *the first half of the melody, **modulating from** E minor to G.* ▪ [no obj.] (**modulate into**) change from one form or condition into (another): *the fraught silence would modulate into conciliatory monosyllables.*
– DERIVATIVES **modulation** noun, **modulator** noun.
– ORIGIN mid 16th cent. (in the sense 'intone (a song)'): from Latin *modulat-* 'measured, made melody', from the verb *modulari*, from *modulus* 'measure' (see **MODULUS**).

module ▶ **noun** each of a set of standardized parts or independent units that can be used to construct a more complex structure, such as an item of furniture or a building.
▪each of a set of independent units of study or training that can be combined in a number of ways to form a course at a college or university. ▪ [usu. with modifier] an independent self-contained unit of a spacecraft. ▪ Computing any of a number of distinct but interrelated units from which a program may be built up or into which a complex activity may be analysed.
– ORIGIN late 16th cent. (in the senses 'allotted scale' and 'plan, model'): from French, or from Latin *modulus* (see **MODULUS**). Current senses date from the 1950s.

modulo /'mɒdjʊləʊ/ ▶ **preposition** Mathematics (in number theory) with respect to or using a modulus of a specified number. Two numbers are congruent modulo a given number if they give the same remainder when divided by that number.
▪[as modifier] using moduli: *modulo operations.*
– ORIGIN late 19th cent.: from Latin, ablative of *modulus* (see **MODULUS**).

modulus /'mɒdjʊləs/ Mathematics ▶ **noun** (pl. **moduli** /-lʌɪ, -liː/) **1** another term for **ABSOLUTE VALUE**.
▪the positive square root of the sum of the squares of the real and imaginary parts of a complex number.
2 a constant factor or ratio.
▪a constant indicating the relation between a physical effect and the force producing it.
3 a number used as a divisor for considering numbers in sets, numbers being considered congruent when giving the same remainder when divided by a particular modulus.
– ORIGIN mid 16th cent. (denoting an architectural unit of length): from Latin, literally 'measure', diminutive of *modus*.

modus operandi /ˌməʊdəs ɒpə'randiː, -dʌɪ/ ▶ **noun** (pl. **modi operandi** /ˌməʊdi/) [usu. in sing.] a particular way or method of doing something, especially one that is characteristic or well-established: *every killer has his own special modus operandi.*
▪the way something operates or works.
– ORIGIN Latin, literally 'way of operating'.

modus ponens /ˌməʊdəs 'pəʊnenz/ ▶ **noun** the rule of logic which states that if a conditional statement ('if *p* then *q*') is accepted, and the antecedent (*p*) holds, then the consequent (*q*) may be inferred.
▪an argument using this rule.
– ORIGIN Latin, literally 'mood that affirms'.

modus tollens /ˌməʊdəs 'tɒlenz/ ▶ **noun** the rule of logic which states that if a conditional statement ('if *p* then *q*') is accepted, and the consequent does not hold (*not-q*) then the negation of the antecedent (*not-p*) can be inferred.
▪an argument using this rule.
– ORIGIN Latin, literally 'mood that denies'.

modus vivendi /ˌməʊdəs vɪ'vendiː, -dʌɪ/ ▶ **noun** (pl. **modi vivendi** /ˌməʊdi/) [usu. in sing.] an arrangement or agreement allowing conflicting parties to coexist peacefully, either indefinitely or until a final settlement is reached.
▪a way of living.
– ORIGIN Latin, literally 'way of living'.

Moesia /'miːsɪə, 'miːʃə/ an ancient country of

southern Europe, corresponding to parts of modern Bulgaria and Serbia.

mofette /mɒˈfɛt/ ▶ noun archaic term for FUMAROLE.
– ORIGIN early 19th cent.: from French, from Neapolitan Italian *mofetta*.

moffie /ˈmɒfi/ ▶ noun (pl. **-ies**) S. African informal, derogatory a man perceived as effeminate or weak-spirited.
■ a male homosexual.
– ORIGIN Afrikaans, perhaps an abbreviation of *moffiedaal*, dialect variant of *hermafrodiet* 'hermaphrodite'.

mofo ▶ noun vulgar slang short for MOTHERFUCKER.

mog ▶ noun Brit. informal another term for MOGGIE.

Mogadishu /ˌmɒɡəˈdiʃuː/ the capital of Somalia, a port on the Indian Ocean; pop. 377,000 (1982). Also called MUQDISHO; Italian name MOGADISCIO /ˌmɒɡəˈdiʃʃo/.

Mogadon /ˈmɒɡədɒn/ ▶ noun trademark for NITRAZEPAM.

moggie (also **moggy**) ▶ noun (pl. **-ies**) Brit. informal a cat.
– ORIGIN late 17th cent.: variant of *Maggie*, pet form of the given name *Margaret*.

Mogilyov /mɑɡɪˈljɒf/ (also **Mogilev**) Russian name for MAHILYOW.

Mogul /ˈmoʊɡ(ə)l/ (also **Moghul** or **Mughal**) ▶ noun a member of the Muslim dynasty of Mongol origin founded by the successors of Tamerlane, which ruled much of India from the 16th to the 19th century: [as modifier] *Mogul architecture*.
■ (often **the Great Mogul**) historical the Mogul emperor of Delhi.
– ORIGIN from Persian *muġul* 'Mongol'.

mogul[1] /ˈmoʊɡ(ə)l/ ▶ noun **1** informal an important or powerful person, especially in the film or media industry.
2 (**Mogul**) a steam locomotive of 2-6-0 wheel arrangement.
– ORIGIN late 17th cent.: figurative use of MOGUL.

mogul[2] /ˈmoʊɡ(ə)l/ ▶ noun a bump on a ski slope formed by skiers turning: [as modifier] *a mogul field*.
– ORIGIN 1960s: probably from southern German dialect *Mugel*, *Mugl*.

MOH ▶ abbreviation for ■ Ministry of Health. ■ Medical Officer of Health (chief health executive of a local authority).

Mohács /ˈmoʊhɑːtʃ/ a river port and industrial town on the Danube in southern Hungary, close to the borders with Croatia and Serbia; pop. 20,120 (1993). It was the site of a battle in 1526 in which the Hungarians were defeated by a Turkish force, as a result of which Hungary became part of the Ottoman Empire.

mohair ▶ noun [mass noun] the hair of the angora goat.
■ a yarn or fabric made from this, typically mixed with wool: [as modifier] *a mohair sweater*.
– ORIGIN late 16th cent.: from Arabic *mukayyar* 'cloth made of goat's hair' (literally 'choice, select'). The change in ending was due to association with HAIR.

mohalla /moʊˈhʌlɑː/ ▶ noun Indian an area of a town or village; a community.
– ORIGIN from Arabic *mohālla*.

Mohammed ▶ noun see MUHAMMAD[1].

Mohammerah /məˈhamərɑ/ former name (until 1924) for KHORRAMSHAHR.

Mohave Desert variant spelling of MOJAVE DESERT.

Mohawk ▶ noun (pl. same or **Mohawks**) **1** a member of an American Indian people, originally inhabiting parts of what is now upper New York State.
2 [mass noun] the Iroquoian language of this people.
3 chiefly N. Amer. a Mohican haircut.
4 Skating a step from either edge of the skate to the same edge on the other foot in the opposite direction.
▶ adjective **1** of or relating to the Mohawks or their language.
2 chiefly N. Amer. denoting a Mohican haircut.
– ORIGIN from Narragansett *mohowawog*, literally 'maneaters'.

Mohegan /moʊˈhiːɡ(ə)n/ ▶ noun **1** a member of an American Indian people formerly inhabiting the western parts of Connecticut and Massachusetts. Compare with MAHICAN.

2 [mass noun] the extinct Algonquian language of this people.
▶ adjective of or relating to the Mohegans or their language.
– ORIGIN from Mohegan, literally 'people of the tidal waters'.

mohel /ˈmoʊ(h)(ə)l/ ▶ noun a Jew who performs the rite of circumcision.
– ORIGIN mid 17th cent.: from Hebrew *mōhēl*.

Mohenjo-Daro /məˌhɛndʒoʊˈdɑːroʊ/ an ancient city of the civilization of the Indus valley (*c.*2600–1700 BC), now a major archaeological site in Pakistan, south-west of Sukkur.

Mohican[1] /moʊˈhiːk(ə)n, məˈruːk(ə)n/ ▶ noun a hairstyle with the head shaved except for a strip of hair from the middle of the forehead to the back of the neck, typically stiffened to stand erect or in spikes: [as modifier] *a Mohican haircut*.
– ORIGIN 1960s: erroneously associated with the American Indian people (see HURON).

Mohican[2] /moʊˈhiːk(ə)n/ ▶ adjective & noun old-fashioned variant spelling of MAHICAN or MOHEGAN.

Moho /ˈmoʊhoʊ/ ▶ noun Geology short for MOHOROVIČIĆ DISCONTINUITY.

Moholy-Nagy /ˌmoʊhɔɪˈnɒdʒ/, László (1895–1946), Hungarian-born American painter, sculptor, and photographer. He pioneered the experimental use of plastic materials, light, photography, and film.

Mohorovičić discontinuity /ˌmoʊhəˈroʊvɪtʃɪtʃ/ ▶ noun Geology the boundary surface between the earth's crust and the mantle, lying at a depth of about 10–12 km under the ocean bed and 40–50 km under the continents.
– ORIGIN 1930s: named after Andrija *Mohorovičić* (1857–1936), Yugoslav seismologist.

Mohs' scale /moʊz/ ▶ noun a scale of hardness used in classifying minerals. It runs from 1 to 10 using a series of reference minerals, and position on the scale depends on ability to scratch minerals rated lower.
– ORIGIN late 19th cent.: named after Friedrich *Mohs*, (1773–1839), German mineralogist.

moi /mwʌ/ ▶ exclamation humorous me? (used when accused of something that one knows one is guilty of): *sarcastic, moi?*
– ORIGIN French, 'me'.

moidore /ˈmɔɪdɔː/ ▶ noun a Portuguese gold coin, current in England in the early 18th century and then worth about 27 shillings.
– ORIGIN from Portuguese *moeda d'ouro* 'money of gold'.

moiety /ˈmɔɪti/ ▶ noun (pl. **-ies**) formal or technical each of two parts into which a thing is or can be divided.
■ Anthropology each of two social or ritual groups into which a people is divided, especially among Australian Aboriginals and some American Indians.
■ a part or portion, especially a lesser share. ■ Chemistry a distinct part of a large molecule: *the enzyme removes the sulphate moiety*.
– ORIGIN late Middle English: from Old French *moite*, from Latin *medietas* 'middle', from *medius* 'mid, middle'.

moil /mɔɪl/ archaic, dialect, or N. Amer. ▶ verb [no obj.] work hard: *men who moiled for gold*.
■ [with adverbial] move around in confusion or agitation: *a crowd of men and women moiled in the smoky haze*.
▶ noun [mass noun] hard work; drudgery.
■ turmoil; confusion: *the moil of his intimate thoughts*.
– ORIGIN late Middle English (in the sense 'moisten or bedaub'): from Old French *moillier* 'paddle in mud, moisten', based on Latin *mollis* 'soft'. The sense 'work' dates from the mid 16th cent., often in the phrase *toil and moil*.

Moirai /ˈmɔɪrʌɪ/ Greek Mythology the Fates.

moire /mwɑː/ (also **moiré** /ˈmwɑːreɪ/) ▶ noun [mass noun] silk fabric that has been subjected to heat and pressure rollers after weaving to give it a rippled appearance.
▶ adjective (of silk) having a rippled, lustrous finish.
■ denoting or showing a pattern of irregular wavy lines like that of such silk, produced by the superposition at a slight angle of two sets of closely spaced lines.
– ORIGIN mid 17th cent.: French *moire* 'mohair' (the original fabric); the variant *moiré* 'given a watered appearance' (past participle of *moirer*, from *moire*).

Moissan /ˈmwʌsɒ̃, French mwasɑ̃/, Ferdinand Frédéric Henri (1852–1907), French chemist. In 1886

he succeeded in isolating the very reactive element fluorine. In 1892 he invented the electric-arc furnace that bears his name. Nobel Prize for Chemistry (1906).

moist ▶ adjective slightly wet; damp or humid: *the air was moist and heavy*.
■ (of the eyes) wet with tears: *her brother's eyes became moist*. ■ (of a climate) rainy. ■ Medicine marked by a fluid discharge.
– DERIVATIVES **moistly** adverb, **moistness** noun.
– ORIGIN late Middle English: from Old French *moiste*, based on Latin *mucidus* 'mouldy' (influenced by *musteus* 'fresh', from *mustum*: see MUST[2]).

moisten ▶ verb [with obj.] wet slightly: *she moistened her lips with the tip of her tongue*.
■ [no obj.] (of the eyes) fill with tears: *her eyes moistened*.

moisture ▶ noun [mass noun] water or other liquid diffused in a small quantity as vapour, within a solid, or condensed on a surface.
– DERIVATIVES **moistureless** adjective.
– ORIGIN late Middle English (denoting moistness): from Old French *moistour*, from *moiste* (see MOIST).

moisturize (also **-ise**) ▶ verb [with obj.] make (something, especially the skin) less dry.

moisturizer ▶ noun a cosmetic preparation used to prevent dryness in the skin.

moisty ▶ adjective archaic or informal (especially of weather) moist or damp.

mojarra /moʊˈhɑrə/ ▶ noun a small, typically silvery fish that lives in shallow coastal and brackish waters of tropical America.
● Family Gerreidae: several genera and numerous species.
– ORIGIN mid 19th cent.: from American Spanish.

Mojave Desert /moʊˈhɑːvi/ (also **Mohave**) a desert in southern California, to the south-east of the Sierra Nevada and north and east of Los Angeles.

mojo /ˈmoʊdʒoʊ/ ▶ noun (pl. **-os**) chiefly US a magic charm, talisman, or spell: *someone must have their mojo working over at the record company*.
■ [mass noun] magic power.
– ORIGIN early 20th cent.: probably of African origin; compare with Gullah *moco* 'witchcraft'.

moke ▶ noun Brit. informal a donkey.
■ Austral./NZ a horse, typically one of inferior quality.
– ORIGIN mid 19th cent.: of unknown origin.

moko /ˈmoʊkoʊ/ ▶ noun (pl. **-os**) NZ a traditional Maori tattoo, typically one on the face.
■ [mass noun] a pattern of such tattoos: *a tall woman with moko on her chin*.
– ORIGIN Maori.

moksha /ˈmoʊkʃə/ ▶ noun [mass noun] (in Hinduism and Jainism) release from the cycle of rebirth impelled by the law of karma.
■ the transcendent state attained by this liberation.
– ORIGIN from Sanskrit *mokṣa*.

mol /moʊl/ Chemistry ▶ abbreviation for MOLE[4].

mola /ˈmoʊlə/ ▶ noun (pl. same or **molas**) another term for SUNFISH (in sense 1).
– ORIGIN late 16th cent.: from Latin, literally 'millstone', with reference to the shape.

molal /ˈmoʊləl/ ▶ adjective Chemistry (of a solution) containing one mole of solute per kilogram of solvent.
– DERIVATIVES **molality** noun.

molar[1] (also **molar tooth**) ▶ noun a grinding tooth at the back of a mammal's mouth.
– ORIGIN late Middle English: from Latin *molaris*, from *mola* 'millstone'.

molar[2] ▶ adjective of or relating to mass; acting on or by means of large masses or units.
– ORIGIN mid 19th cent.: from Latin *moles* 'mass' + -AR[1].

molar[3] ▶ adjective Chemistry of or relating to one mole of a substance.
■ (of a solution) containing one mole of solute per litre of solvent.
– DERIVATIVES **molarity** noun.

molasses ▶ noun [mass noun] thick, dark brown uncrystallized juice obtained from raw sugar during the refining process.
■ N. Amer. a paler, sweeter version of this; golden syrup.
– ORIGIN mid 16th cent.: from Portuguese *melaço*, from late Latin *mellacium* 'must', based on *mel* 'honey'.

Mold /moʊld/ a town in NE Wales, administrative centre of Flintshire; pop. 8,589 (1981).

mold ▶ noun & verb US spelling of MOULD¹, MOULD², and MOULD³.

Moldau /ˈmɔldaʊ/ German name for VLTAVA.

Moldavia /mɒlˈdeɪvɪə/ **1** a former principality of SE Europe. Formerly a part of the Roman province of Dacia, the principality came under Turkish rule in the 16th century. In 1861 Moldavia united with Wallachia to form Romania. **2** another name for MOLDOVA.

Moldavian ▶ noun **1** a native or national of Moldavia. **2** [mass noun] the Romanian language as spoken and written (in the Cyrillic alphabet) in Moldavia. ▶ adjective of or relating to Moldavia, its inhabitants, or their language.

molder ▶ verb & noun US spelling of MOULDER.

molding ▶ noun US spelling of MOULDING.

Moldova /mɒlˈdəʊvə, mɒlˈdɒvə/ a landlocked country in SE Europe, between Romania and Ukraine; pop. 4,384,000 (1991); languages, Moldavian (official), Russian; capital, Chişinău. Also called MOLDAVIA.

A former constituent republic of the USSR, Moldova was formed from territory ceded by Romania in 1940. It became independent as a member of the Commonwealth of Independent States in 1991.

– DERIVATIVES **Moldovan** adjective & noun.

moldy ▶ adjective US spelling of MOULDY.

mole¹ /məʊl/ ▶ noun **1** a small burrowing insectivorous mammal with dark velvety fur, a long muzzle, and very small eyes.
● Family Talpidae: several genera and species, including the **European mole** (*Talpa europaea*).
2 a spy who achieves over a long period an important position within the security defences of a country.
■someone within an organization who anonymously betrays confidential information.
– ORIGIN late Middle English: from the Germanic base of Middle Dutch and Middle Low German *mol*.

mole² /məʊl/ ▶ noun a small, often slightly raised blemish on the skin made dark by a high concentration of melanin.
– ORIGIN Old English *māl* 'discoloured spot', of Germanic origin.

mole³ /məʊl/ ▶ noun a large solid structure on a shore serving as a pier, breakwater, or causeway.
■a harbour formed or protected by such a structure.
– ORIGIN mid 16th cent.: from French *môle*, from Latin *moles* 'mass'.

mole⁴ /məʊl/ ▶ noun Chemistry the SI unit of amount of substance, equal to the quantity containing as many elementary units as there are atoms in 0.012 kg of carbon-12.
– ORIGIN early 20th cent.: from German *Mol*, from *Molekul*, from Latin (see MOLECULE).

mole⁵ /məʊl/ ▶ noun Medicine an abnormal mass of tissue in the uterus. See also HYDATIDIFORM MOLE.
– ORIGIN late Middle English: from French *môle*, from Latin *mola* in the sense 'false conception'.

mole⁶ /ˈməʊleɪ/ ▶ noun [mass noun] a highly spiced Mexican sauce made chiefly from chilli peppers and chocolate, served with meat.
– ORIGIN Mexican Spanish, from Nahuatl *molli* 'sauce, stew'.

mole cricket ▶ noun a large burrowing nocturnal cricket-like insect with broad forelegs, the female of which lays her eggs in an underground nest and guards the young. Very rare in Britain, it can be a pest in some other areas.
● Family Gryllotalpidae: several genera.

molecular /məˈlɛkjʊlə/ ▶ adjective of, relating to, or consisting of molecules. *interactions between polymer and solvent at the molecular level | ozone is produced by dissociation of molecular oxygen.*
– DERIVATIVES **molecularity** noun, **molecularly** adverb.

molecular biology ▶ noun [mass noun] the branch of biology that deals with the structure and function of the macromolecules (e.g. proteins and nucleic acids) essential to life.

molecular sieve ▶ noun a crystalline substance (especially a zeolite) with pores of molecular dimensions which permit the passage of molecules below a certain size.

molecular weight ▶ noun another term for RELATIVE MOLECULAR MASS.

molecule /ˈmɒlɪkjuːl/ ▶ noun Chemistry a group of atoms bonded together, representing the smallest fundamental unit of a chemical compound that can take part in a chemical reaction.
– ORIGIN late 18th cent.: from French *molécule*, from modern Latin *molecula*, diminutive of Latin *moles* 'mass'.

molehill ▶ noun a small mound of earth thrown up by a mole burrowing near the surface.
– PHRASES **make a mountain out of a molehill** exaggerate the importance of something trivial.

mole plough ▶ noun a plough in which a pointed iron shoe attached to an upright support is drawn along beneath the surface, making a hollow drainage channel resembling a mole's burrow.

mole rat ▶ noun a herbivorous short-legged rat-like rodent that typically lives permanently underground, with long incisors that protrude from the mouth and are used in digging.
● Family Bathyergidae (African mole rats): several genera; also two subfamilies and three genera in the family Muridae (Eurasian blind mole rats and Asiatic mole rats).

mole salamander ▶ noun a stocky, broad-headed North American salamander which spends much of its life underground.
● Family Ambystomatidae: several genera, in particular *Ambystoma*, and numerous species, including *A. talpoideum*.

moleskin ▶ noun [mass noun] **1** the skin of a mole used as fur.
2 a thick, strong cotton fabric with a shaved pile surface: [as modifier] *moleskin trousers.*

molest ▶ verb [with obj.] pester or harass (someone), typically in an aggressive or persistent manner: *the crowd were shouting abuse and molesting the two police officers.*
■assault or abuse (a person, especially a woman or child) sexually.
– DERIVATIVES **molestation** noun, **molester** noun.
– ORIGIN late Middle English (in the sense 'cause trouble to, vex'): from Old French *molester* or Latin *molestare* 'annoy', from *molestus* 'troublesome'.

Molière /ˈmɒlɪeː, French mɔljɛːr/ (1622–73), French dramatist; pseudonym of *Jean-Baptiste Poquelin*. He wrote more than twenty comic plays about contemporary France, developing stock characters from Italian *commedia dell'arte*. Notable works: *Don Juan* (1665), *Le Misanthrope* (1666), and *Le Bourgeois gentilhomme* (1670).

moline /məˈlʌɪn/ ▶ adjective [postpositive] Heraldry (of a cross) having each extremity broadened, split, and curved back.
– ORIGIN mid 16th cent.: probably from Anglo-Norman French *moliné*, from *molin* 'mill', because of a resemblance to the iron support of a millstone.

Molise /mɒˈliːzeɪ/ a region of eastern Italy, on the Adriatic coast; capital, Campobasso.

moll ▶ noun informal **1** a gangster's female companion.
2 a prostitute.
– ORIGIN early 17th cent.: pet form of the given name *Mary*.

mollify /ˈmɒlɪfʌɪ/ ▶ verb (-ies, -ied) [with obj.] appease the anger or anxiety of (someone): *nature reserves were set up around the power stations to mollify local conservationists.*
■rare reduce the severity of (something); soften.
– DERIVATIVES **mollification** noun, **mollifier** noun.
– ORIGIN late Middle English (also in the sense 'make soft or supple'): from French *mollifier* or Latin *mollificare*, from *mollis* 'soft'.

mollisol /ˈmɒlɪsɒl/ ▶ noun Soil Science a soil of an order comprising temperate grassland soils with a dark, humus-rich surface layer containing high concentrations of calcium and magnesium.
– ORIGIN mid 20th cent.: from Latin *mollis* 'soft' + *solum* 'ground, soil'.

mollusc /ˈmɒləsk/ (US **mollusk**) ▶ noun an invertebrate of a large phylum which includes snails, slugs, mussels, and octopuses. They have a soft unsegmented body and live in aquatic or damp habitats, and most kinds have an external calcareous shell.
● Phylum Mollusca: several classes, in particular Gastropoda, Bivalvia, and Cephalopoda.
– DERIVATIVES **molluscan** /məˈlʌskən/ adjective.
– ORIGIN late 18th cent.: from modern Latin *mollusca*, neuter plural of Latin *molluscus*, from *mollis* 'soft'.

molluscum contagiosum /məˌlʌskəm kənˌteɪdʒɪˈəʊsəm/ ▶ noun [mass noun] Medicine a chronic viral disorder of the skin characterized by groups of small, smooth, painless pinkish nodules with a central depression, that yield a milky fluid when squeezed.
– ORIGIN early 19th cent.: from Latin *molluscum* (as a noun denoting a kind of fungus), neuter of *molluscus* + *contagiosum* (neuter of *contagiosus* 'contagious').

Mollweide projection /ˈmɒlvʌɪdə/ ▶ noun [mass noun] a projection of a map of the world on to an ellipse, with lines of latitude represented by straight lines (spaced more closely towards the poles) and meridians represented by equally spaced elliptical curves. This projection distorts shape but preserves relative area.
– ORIGIN early 20th cent.: named after Karl B. *Mollweide* (died 1825), German mathematician and astronomer.

molly (also **mollie**) ▶ noun a small live-bearing killifish which is popular in aquaria and has been bred in many colours, especially black.
● Genus *Poecilia*, family Poeciliidae: several species, in particular *P. sphenops*. See also SAILFIN MOLLY.
– ORIGIN 1930s: from modern Latin *Mollienisia* (former genus name), from the name of Count *Mollien* (1758–1850), French statesman.

mollycoddle ▶ verb [with obj.] treat (someone) very indulgently or protectively.
▶ noun an effeminate or ineffectual man or boy.
– ORIGIN mid 19th cent.: from *molly* 'girl or prostitute' (see MOLL) + CODDLE.

molly-dooker /ˈmɒlɪˌduːkə/ ▶ noun Austral. informal a left-handed person.
– ORIGIN 1940s: from *Molly* (pet form of the given name *Mary*) or from the slang term *mauley* 'hand' + *-dook* representing a pronunciation of DUKE (in sense 2) + -ER¹.

mollymawk ▶ noun chiefly Austral./NZ an albatross.
● Genus *Diomedea*, family Diomedeidae: several species, excluding the wandering and royal albatrosses.
– ORIGIN late 17th cent.: from Dutch *mallemok*, from *mal* 'foolish' + *mok* 'gull'.

Moloch /ˈməʊlɒk/ a Canaanite idol to whom children were sacrificed.
■[as noun **a Moloch**] a tyrannical object of sacrifices.
– ORIGIN via late Latin from Greek *Molokh*, from Hebrew *mōlek*.

moloch /ˈməʊlɒk/ ▶ noun a harmless spiny lizard of grotesque appearance which feeds chiefly on ants, found in arid inland Australia. Also called MOUNTAIN DEVIL, THORNY DEVIL.
● *Moloch horridus*, family Agamidae.

Molotov¹ /ˈmɒlətɒf/ former name (1940–57) for PERM.

Molotov² /ˈmɒlətɒf/, Vyacheslav (Mikhailovich) (1890–1986), Soviet statesman; born *Vyacheslav Mikhailovich Skryabin*. As Commissar (later Minister) for Foreign Affairs (1939–49; 1953–6), he negotiated the non-aggression pact with Nazi Germany (1939) and after 1945 represented the Soviet Union at meetings of the United Nations.

Molotov cocktail ▶ noun a crude incendiary device typically consisting of a bottle filled with flammable liquid and with a means of ignition. The production of similar grenades was organized by Vyacheslav Molotov during the Second World War.

molt ▶ verb & noun US spelling of MOULT.

molten /ˈməʊlt(ə)n/ ▶ adjective (especially of materials with a high melting point, such as metal and glass) liquefied by heat.
– ORIGIN Middle English: archaic past participle of MELT.

molto /ˈmɒltəʊ/ ▶ adverb Music (in directions) very: *molto maestoso* | [postpositive as submodifier] *allegro molto.*
– ORIGIN Italian, from Latin *multus* 'much'.

Molucca Islands /məˈlʌkə/ an island group in Indonesia, between Sulawesi and New Guinea; capital, Amboina. Settled by the Portuguese in the early 16th century, the islands were taken a century later by the Dutch. They were formerly known as the Spice Islands. Indonesian name MALUKU.
– DERIVATIVES **Moluccan** noun & adjective.

moly /ˈməʊli/ ▶ noun **1** a southern European plant related to the onions, with small yellow flowers.
● *Allium moly*, family Liliaceae (or Alliaceae).
2 a mythical herb with white flowers and black roots, endowed with magic properties.
– ORIGIN mid 16th cent. (in sense 2): via Latin from Greek *mōlu*.

molybdate /məˈlɪbdeɪt/ ▶ noun Chemistry a salt in which the anion contains both molybdenum and oxygen, especially one of the anion $MoO_4{}^{2-}$.
– ORIGIN late 18th cent.: from *molybdic* (*acid*), a parent acid of molybdates, + -ATE[1].

molybdenite /məˈlɪbdənʌɪt/ ▶ noun [mass noun] a blue-grey mineral, typically occurring as hexagonal crystals. It consists of molybdenum disulphide and is the most common ore of molybdenum.

molybdenum /məˈlɪbdənəm/ ▶ noun [mass noun] the chemical element of atomic number 42, a brittle silver-grey metal of the transition series, used in some alloy steels. (Symbol: **Mo**)
– ORIGIN early 19th cent.: modern Latin, earlier *molybdena* (originally denoting a salt of lead), from Greek *molubdaina* 'plummet', from *molubdos* 'lead'.

mom ▶ noun North American term for MUM[1].

Mombasa /mɒmˈbasə/ a seaport and industrial city in SE Kenya, on the Indian Ocean; pop. 465,000 (est. 1989). It is the leading port and second largest city of Kenya.

moment ▶ noun **1** a very brief period of time: *she was silent for a moment before replying* | *a few moments later he returned to the office.*
■ an exact point in time: *she would always remember the moment they met.* ■ an appropriate time for doing something; an opportunity: *I was waiting for the right moment.* ■ a particular stage in something's development or in a course of events: *one of the great moments in aviation history.*
2 [mass noun] formal importance: *the issues were of little moment to the electorate.*
3 Physics a turning effect produced by a force acting at a distance on an object.
■ the magnitude of such an effect, expressed as the product of the force and the distance from its line of action to a given point.
4 Statistics a quantity that expresses the average or expected value of the first, second, third, or fourth power of the deviation of each component of a frequency distribution from some given value, typically mean or zero. The **first moment** is the mean, the **second moment** the variance, the **third moment** the skew, and the **fourth moment** the kurtosis.
– PHRASES **any moment** (or **at any moment**) very soon. **at the** (or **this**) **moment** at the present time; now. **for the moment** for now. **have one's** (or **its**) **moments** have short periods that are better or more impressive than others: *I had my moments in the game.* **in a moment 1** very soon: *I'll be back in a moment.* **2** instantly: *the fugitive was captured in a moment.* **live for the moment** live or act without worrying about the future. **the moment** —— as soon as ——: *the heavens opened the moment we left the house.* **moment of truth** a time when a person or thing is tested, a decision has to be made, or a crisis has to be faced. [ORIGIN: with allusion to the final sword-thrust in a bullfight.] **not a moment too soon** almost too late. **not for a** (or **one**) **moment** not at all; never. **of the moment** currently popular, famous, or important: *the buzzword of the moment.* **one moment** (or **just a moment**) a request for someone to wait for a short period of time, especially to allow the speaker to do or say something.
– ORIGIN late Middle English: from Latin *momentum* (see MOMENTUM).

momenta plural form of MOMENTUM.

momentarily ▶ adverb **1** for a very short time: *as he passed Jenny's door, he paused momentarily.*
2 N. Amer. at any moment; very soon: *my husband will be here to pick me up momentarily.*

momentary ▶ adjective lasting for a very short time; brief: *a momentary lapse of concentration.*
– DERIVATIVES **momentariness** noun.
– ORIGIN late Middle English: from Latin *momentarius*, from *momentum* (see MOMENT).

momently ▶ adverb archaic or poetic/literary **1** from moment to moment; continually.
2 at any moment.
3 for a moment; briefly.

moment of inertia ▶ noun Physics a quantity expressing a body's tendency to resist angular acceleration, which is the sum of the products of the mass of each particle in the body with the square of its distance from the axis of rotation.

momentous ▶ adjective (of a decision, event, or change) of great importance or significance, especially in its bearing on the future: *a period of momentous changes in East–West relations.*
– DERIVATIVES **momentously** adverb, **momentousness** noun.

momentum /məˈmɛntəm/ ▶ noun (pl. **momenta** /-tə/) [mass noun] **1** Physics the quantity of motion of a moving body, measured as a product of its mass and velocity.
2 the impetus gained by a moving object: *the vehicle gained momentum as the road dipped.*
■ the impetus and driving force gained by the development of a process or course of events: *the investigation gathered momentum in the spring.*
– ORIGIN late 17th cent.: from Latin, from *movimentum*, from *movere* 'to move'.

momism /ˈmɒmɪz(ə)m/ ▶ noun [mass noun] US informal excessive attachment to or domination by one's mother.

momma ▶ noun North American term for MAMA.

Mommsen /ˈmɒmz(ə)n/, Theodor (1817–1903), German historian. He is noted for his three-volume *History of Rome* (1854–6; 1885) and his treatises on Roman constitutional law (1871–88). Nobel Prize for Literature (1902).

mommy ▶ noun (pl. **-ies**) North American term for MUMMY[1].

mompara /mɒmˈpɑːrə/ ▶ noun S. African derogatory an unsophisticated country person.
– ORIGIN Fanakalo, literally 'a fool', also 'waste material'.

Mon /məʊn/ ▶ noun (pl. same or **Mons**) **1** a member of a people now inhabiting parts of SE Burma (Myanmar) and western Thailand but having their ancient capital at Pegu in the south of Burma.
2 [mass noun] the language of this people, related to Khmer (Cambodian).
▶ adjective of or relating to this people or their language. See also MON-KHMER.
– ORIGIN the name in Mon.

Mon. ▶ abbreviation for Monday.

mon- ▶ combining form variant spelling of MONO-shortened before a vowel (as in *monamine*).

Monaco /ˈmɒnəkəʊ/ a principality forming an enclave within French territory, on the Mediterranean coast near the Italian frontier; pop. 29,880 (1990); official language, French.

The smallest sovereign state in the world apart from the Vatican, Monaco was ruled by the Genoese from medieval times and by the Grimaldi family from 1297, becoming a constitutional monarchy in 1911. It includes the resort of Monte Carlo.

monad /ˈmɒnad, ˈməʊ-/ ▶ noun technical a single unit; the number one.
■ Philosophy (in the philosophy of Leibniz) an indivisible and hence ultimately simple entity, such as an atom or a person. ■ Biology, dated a single-celled organism, especially a flagellate protozoan, or a single cell.
– DERIVATIVES **monadic** adjective, **monadism** noun (Philosophy).
– ORIGIN early 17th cent.: via late Latin from Greek *monas, monad-* 'unit', from *monos* 'alone'.

monadelphous /ˌmɒnəˈdɛlfəs/ ▶ adjective Botany (of stamens) united by their filaments so as to form one group.
– ORIGIN early 19th cent.: from Greek *monos* 'one' + *adelphos* 'brother' + -OUS.

monadnock /məˈnadnɒk/ ▶ noun an isolated hill or ridge or erosion-resistant rock rising above a peneplain.
– ORIGIN late 19th cent.: named after Mount *Monadnock* in New Hampshire, US.

Monaghan /ˈmɒnəhən/ a county of the Republic of Ireland, part of the old province of Ulster.
■ its county town; pop. 5,750 (1991).

monal /ˈmɒnɑːl/ ▶ noun (also **monal pheasant**) ▶ noun an Asian pheasant of mountainous wooded country, the male having dark plumage with colourful iridescence.
● Genus *Lophophorus*, family Phasianidae: three species, e.g. the crested **Himalayan monal** (*L. impeyanus*).
– ORIGIN mid 18th cent.: from Nepali *monāl*, from Hindi *munāl*.

Mona Lisa /ˌməʊnə ˈliːzə/ a painting (now in the Louvre in Paris) executed 1503–6 by Leonardo da Vinci. The sitter was the wife of Francesco del Giocondo; her enigmatic smile has become one of the most famous images in Western art. Also called LA GIOCONDA.

monamine ▶ noun variant spelling of MONOAMINE.

mona monkey /ˈməʊnə/ ▶ noun a West African guenon that has a bluish-grey face with a pink muzzle. The female has a distinctive moaning call.
● *Cercopithecus mona*, family Cercopithecidae.
– ORIGIN late 18th cent.: from *mona* from Spanish and Portuguese *mona, mono*, Italian *monna*.

monarch /ˈmɒnək/ ▶ noun **1** a sovereign head of state, especially a king, queen, or emperor.
2 (also **monarch butterfly**) a large migratory orange and black butterfly that occurs mainly in North America. The caterpillar feeds on milkweed, using the toxins in the plant to render both itself and the adult unpalatable to predators. Also called MILKWEED.
● *Danaus plexippus*, subfamily Danainae, family Nymphalidae.
3 (also **monarch flycatcher**) a flycatcher found in Africa, Asia, and Australasia, typically having boldly marked or colourful plumage.
● Family Monarchidae (the **monarch flycatcher family**): many genera and numerous species. This family also includes the fantail and paradise flycatchers, and the boatbills.
– DERIVATIVES **monarchal** adjective, **monarchial** adjective, **monarchic** adjective, **monarchical** adjective, **monarchically** adverb.
– ORIGIN late Middle English: from late Latin *monarcha*, from Greek *monarkhēs*, from *monos* 'alone' + *arkhein* 'to rule'.

Monarchian /məˈnɑːkɪən/ ▶ noun a Christian heretic of the 2nd or 3rd century who denied the doctrine of the Trinity.
▶ adjective of or relating to the Monarchians or their beliefs.
– ORIGIN from late Latin *monarchiani* (plural), from *monarchia* (see MONARCHY).

monarchism ▶ noun [mass noun] support for the principle of having monarchs.
– DERIVATIVES **monarchist** noun & adjective.
– ORIGIN mid 19th cent.: from French *monarchisme*.

monarchy ▶ noun (pl. **-ies**) [mass noun] a form of government with a monarch at the head. ■ [count noun] a state that has a monarch. ■ (**the monarchy**) the monarch and royal family of a country: *the monarchy is the focus of loyalty and service.*
– ORIGIN late Middle English: from Old French *monarchie*, via late Latin from Greek *monarkhia* 'the rule of one'.

monastery ▶ noun (pl. **-ies**) a community of monks living under religious vows.
– ORIGIN late Middle English: via ecclesiastical Latin from ecclesiastical Greek *monastērion*, from *monazein* 'live alone', from *monos* 'alone'.

monastic ▶ adjective of or relating to monks, nuns, or others living under religious vows, or the buildings in which they live: *a monastic order.*
■ resembling or suggestive of monks or their way of life, especially in being austere, solitary, or celibate: *she set her things round the monastic student bedroom.*
▶ noun a monk or other follower of a monastic rule.
– DERIVATIVES **monastically** adverb, **monasticism** noun.
– ORIGIN late Middle English (in the sense 'anchoritic'): from Latin *monasticus*, from Greek *monastikos*, from *monazein* 'live alone'.

Monastral /mɒˈnastr(ə)l/ ▶ noun trademark a synthetic pigment of high fastness.
– ORIGIN 1930s: of unknown origin.

monatomic /ˌmɒnəˈtɒmɪk/ ▶ adjective Chemistry consisting of one atom.

monaural /mɒnˈɔːr(ə)l/ ▶ adjective of or involving one ear.
■ another term for MONOPHONIC (in sense 1).
– DERIVATIVES **monaurally** adverb.

monazite /ˈmɒnəzʌɪt/ ▶ noun [mass noun] a brown crystalline mineral consisting of a phosphate of cerium, lanthanum, other rare earth elements, and thorium.
– ORIGIN mid 19th cent.: from German *Monazit*, from Greek *monazein* 'live alone' (because of its rare occurrence).

Monbazillac /mɒnˈbazɪlak, mɔˈbazijak/ ▶ noun [mass noun] a sweet white dessert wine, similar to Sauternes, produced at Monbazillac in the Dordogne.

Mönchengladbach /ˌmɒnʃ(ə)nˈgladbax, German ˌmынçənˈɡlatbax/ a city in NW Germany; pop. 262,580 (1991). It is the site of the NATO headquarters for northern Europe.

Monck /mʌŋk/, George, 1st Duke of Albemarle

(1608–70), English general. Initially a Royalist, he became a supporter of Oliver Cromwell and later suppressed the Royalists in Scotland (1651). Concerned at the growing unrest following Cromwell's death (1658), Monck negotiated the return of Charles II in 1660.

mondaine /mɒnˈdeɪn, French mɔ̃dɛn/ ▶ **adjective** belonging to fashionable society; worldly.
▶ **noun** dated a fashionable woman.
– ORIGIN French, feminine of *mondain* (see **MUNDANE**).

Monday ▶ **noun** the day of the week before Tuesday and following Sunday: *I saw him on Monday | the Monday before last | she's only in the office on Mondays.*
▶ **adverb** chiefly N. Amer. on Monday: *I'll ring you Monday.*
■ (**Mondays**) on Mondays; each Monday: *the restaurant is closed Mondays.*
– ORIGIN Old English *Mōnandæg* 'day of the moon', translation of late Latin *lunae dies*; compare with Dutch *maandag* and German *Montag*.

Monday morning quarterback ▶ **noun** N. Amer. informal a person who passes judgement on and criticizes something after the event.
– DERIVATIVES **Monday morning quarterbacking** noun.

mondial /ˈmɒndɪəl/ ▶ **adjective** of, affecting, or involving the whole world; worldwide.
– ORIGIN early 20th cent.: French.

mondo /ˈmɒndəʊ/ ▶ **adverb & adjective** informal, chiefly US used in reference to something very striking or remarkable of its kind (often in conjunction with a pseudo-Italian noun or adjective): [as adv.] *I think it's going to be mondo weirdo this year, Andy.*
– ORIGIN from Italian *Mondo Cane*, literally 'dog's world', the title of a film (1961) depicting bizarre behaviour.

Mondrian /ˈmɒndrɪɑːn/, Piet (1872–1944), Dutch painter; born *Pieter Cornelis Mondriaan*. He was a co-founder of the De Stijl movement and the originator of neo-plasticism, one of the earliest and strictest forms of geometrical abstract painting.

Monégasque /ˌmɒneɪˈgask, French mɔnegask/ ▶ **noun** a native or national of Monaco.
▶ **adjective** of or relating to Monaco or its inhabitants.
– ORIGIN French.

Monel /ˈməʊn(ə)l/ (also **Monel metal**) ▶ **noun** [mass noun] trademark a nickel-copper alloy with high tensile strength and resistance to corrosion.
– ORIGIN early 20th cent.: named after Ambrose *Monell* (died 1921), American businessman.

Monet /ˈmɒneɪ/, Claude (1840–1926), French painter. A founder member of the Impressionists, his fascination with the play of light on objects led him to produce series of paintings of single subjects painted at different times of day and under different weather conditions, such as the *Water-lilies* sequence (1899–1906; 1916 onwards).

monetarism ▶ **noun** [mass noun] the theory or practice of controlling the supply of money as the chief method of stabilizing the economy.
– DERIVATIVES **monetarist** noun & adjective.

monetarize /ˈmʌnɪtəraɪz/ ▶ **verb** another term for **MONETIZE**.

monetary ▶ **adjective** of or relating to money or currency: *documents with little or no monetary value.*
– DERIVATIVES **monetarily** adverb.
– ORIGIN early 19th cent.: from French *monétaire* or late Latin *monetarius*, from Latin *moneta* 'money'.

monetize /ˈmʌnɪtaɪz/ (also **-ise**) ▶ **verb** [with obj.] convert into or express in the form of currency.
■ [usu. as adj. **monetized**] adapt (a society) to the use of money: *a fully monetized society.*
– DERIVATIVES **monetization** noun.
– ORIGIN late 19th cent.: from French *monétiser*, from Latin *moneta* 'money'.

money ▶ **noun** [mass noun] a current medium of exchange in the form of coins and banknotes; coins and banknotes collectively: *I counted the money before putting it in my wallet | he borrowed money to modernize the shop.*
■ (**moneys** or **monies**) formal sums of money: *a statement of all moneys paid into and out of the account.* ■ the assets, property, and resources owned by someone or something; wealth: *the college is very short of money.* ■ financial gain: *the main aim of a commercial organization is to make money.* ■ payment for work; wages: *she accepted the job at the bank since the money was better.*
– PHRASES **be in the money** informal have or win a lot of money. **for my money** in my opinion or judgement: *for my money, they're one of the best bands around.* **money for old rope** (or **money for jam**) Brit. informal money or reward earned for little or no effort. (**the love of**) **money is the root of all evil** proverb avarice gives rise to selfish or wicked actions. **money talks** proverb wealth gives power and influence to those who possess it. **one's money's worth** good value for one's money. **on the money** chiefly N. Amer. accurate; correct: *every criticism she made was right on the money.* **put money** (or **put one's money**) **on 1** place a bet on. **2** used to express one's confidence in the truth or success of something: *she won't have him back—I'd put money on it.* **put one's money where one's mouth is** informal take action to support one's statements or opinions. **see the colour of someone's money** receive some proof that someone has enough money to pay for something. **throw one's money about/around** spend one's money extravagantly or carelessly. **throw money at something** try to solve a problem by recklessly spending money on it, without due consideration of what is required.
– DERIVATIVES **moneyless** adjective.
– ORIGIN Middle English: from Old French *moneie*, from Latin *moneta* 'mint, money', originally a title of the goddess Juno, in whose temple in Rome money was minted.

money-back ▶ **adjective** denoting an agreement or guarantee that provides for the customer's money to be refunded if they are not satisfied.

moneybags ▶ **plural noun** [usu. treated as sing.] informal a wealthy person.

money box ▶ **noun** Brit. a box used for saving money in, with a slit in the top through which the money is dropped.

money broker ▶ **noun** a person or company that negotiates loans between banks or other financial institutions.

money changer ▶ **noun** archaic a person whose business was the exchanging of one currency for another.

moneyed ▶ **adjective** having much money; affluent: *the industrial revolution created a new moneyed class.*
■ characterized by affluence: *a moneyed lifestyle.*

moneyer ▶ **noun** archaic a person who mints money.

money-grubbing ▶ **adjective** informal overeager to make money; grasping: *money-grubbing speculators.*
– DERIVATIVES **money-grubber** noun.

money illusion ▶ **noun** [mass noun] Economics belief that money has a fixed value in terms of its purchasing power, so that, for example, changes in prices represent real gains and losses.

moneylender ▶ **noun** a person whose business is lending money to others who pay interest.
– DERIVATIVES **moneylending** noun & adjective

moneymaker ▶ **noun** a person or thing that earns a lot of money: *the movie became one of the year's top moneymakers.*
– DERIVATIVES **moneymaking** noun & adjective.

money market ▶ **noun** the trade in short-term loans between banks and other financial institutions.

money of account ▶ **noun** see **ACCOUNT**.

money order ▶ **noun** a printed order for payment of a specified sum, issued by a bank or Post Office.

money spider ▶ **noun** a very small shiny black spider which is supposed to bring financial luck.
● Family Linyphiidae.

money-spinner ▶ **noun** chiefly Brit. a thing that brings in a profit.
– DERIVATIVES **money-spinning** adjective.

money supply ▶ **noun** the total amount of money in circulation or in existence in a country.

money tree ▶ **noun** US a source of easily obtained or unlimited money: *I knew how to shake the money tree.*
■ a real or artificial tree to which people attach paper money, especially as a gift or donation.

money wages ▶ **plural noun** income expressed in terms of its monetary value, with no account taken of its purchasing power.

moneywort ▶ **noun** another term for **CREEPING JENNY**.

mong /mʌŋ/ ▶ **noun** Austral. informal a mongrel.
– ORIGIN early 20th cent.: abbreviation.

-monger ▶ **combining form** denoting a dealer or trader in a specified commodity: *fishmonger | cheesemonger.*
■ a person who promotes a specified activity, situation, or feeling, especially one that is undesirable or discreditable: *rumour-monger | warmonger.*
– ORIGIN Old English *mangere*, from *mangian* 'to traffic', of Germanic origin, based on Latin *mango* 'dealer'.

mongo /ˈmɒŋgəʊ/ ▶ **noun** (pl. same or **-os**) a monetary unit of Mongolia, equal to one hundredth of a tugrik.
– ORIGIN from Mongolian *möngö* 'silver'.

Mongol /ˈmɒŋg(ə)l/ ▶ **adjective 1** of or relating to the people of Mongolia or their language.
2 (**mongol**) offensive suffering from Down's syndrome.
▶ **noun 1** a native or national of Mongolia; a Mongolian.
2 [mass noun] the language of this people; Mongolian.
3 (**mongol**) offensive a person suffering from Down's syndrome.

> In the 13th century AD the Mongol empire under Genghis Khan extended across central Asia from Manchuria in the east to European Russia in the west. Under Kublai Khan China was conquered and the Mongol capital moved to Khanbaliq (modern Beijing). The Mongol empire collapsed after a series of defeats culminating in the destruction of the Golden Horde by the Muscovites in 1380.

– ORIGIN Mongolian, perhaps from *mong* 'brave'.

> **USAGE** The term **mongol** was adopted in the late 19th century to refer to a person suffering from **Down's syndrome**, owing to the similarity of some of the physical symptoms of the disorder with the normal facial characteristics of East Asian people. In modern English, this use is now unacceptable and considered offensive. It has been replaced in scientific as well as in most general contexts by the term **Down's syndrome** (first recorded in the early 1960s).

Mongolia /mɒŋˈgəʊlɪə/ a large and sparsely populated country of east Asia, bordered by Siberian Russia and China; pop. 2,184,000 (est. 1991); official language, Mongolian; capital, Ulan Bator.

> The Gobi Desert occupies much of the southern half of the country. The centre of the medieval Mongol empire, Mongolia subsequently became a Chinese province, achieving de facto independence in 1911. In 1924 it became a communist state after the Soviet model; a new democratic constitution was introduced in 1992. It was formerly known as Outer Mongolia to distinguish it from Inner Mongolia, which remains a province of China.

Mongolian ▶ **adjective** of or relating to Mongolia, its people, or their language.
▶ **noun 1** a native or national of Mongolia.
2 [mass noun] the language of Mongolia, a member of the Altaic family with an unusual vertical cursive script. It has some 2 million speakers, and related forms are spoken by over 3 million people in northern China.

mongolism ▶ **noun** offensive another term for **DOWN'S SYNDROME**.

> **USAGE** See usage at **MONGOL**.

Mongoloid ▶ **adjective 1** of or relating to the broad division of humankind including the indigenous peoples of east Asia, SE Asia, and the Arctic region of North America.
2 (**mongoloid**) offensive affected with Down's syndrome.
▶ **noun 1** a person of a Mongoloid physical type.
2 offensive a person with Down's syndrome.

> **USAGE** The terms **Mongoloid**, **Negroid**, **Caucasoid**, and **Australoid** were introduced by 19th-century anthropologists such as Blumenbach attempting to classify human racial types, but today they are recognized as having very limited validity as scientific categories. Although occasionally used when making broad generalizations about the world's populations, in most modern contexts they are potentially offensive, especially when used of individuals. The names of specific peoples or nationalities should be used instead wherever possible.

mongoose ▶ **noun** (pl. **mongooses**) a small carnivorous mammal with a long body and tail and a grizzled or banded coat, native to Africa and Asia.
● Family Herpestidae (or Viverridae): several genera, in particular *Herpestes*, and many species.
– ORIGIN late 17th cent.: from Marathi *maṅgūs*.

mongrel ▶ noun a dog of no definable type or breed: [as modifier] *a mongrel bitch.*
■ any other animal resulting from the crossing of different breeds or types. ■ offensive a person of mixed descent.
– DERIVATIVES **mongrelism** noun.
– ORIGIN late Middle English: of Germanic origin, apparently from a base meaning 'mix', and related to **MINGLE** and **AMONG**.

mongrelize (also **-ise**) ▶ verb [with obj.] cause to become mixed in race, composition, or character: [as adj. **mongrelized**] *a patois of mongrelized French.*
– DERIVATIVES **mongrelization** noun.

'mongst ▶ preposition poetic/literary short for *amongst* (see **AMONG**).

monial /ˈməʊnɪəl/ ▶ noun a mullion.
– ORIGIN Middle English: from Old French *moinel* 'middle'.

monic /ˈmɒnɪk/ ▶ adjective Mathematics (of a polynomial) having the coefficient of the term of highest degree equal to one.

Monica, St (332–*c*.387), mother of St Augustine of Hippo. She is often regarded as the model of Christian mothers for her patience with her son's spiritual crises, which ended with his conversion in 386. Feast day, 27 August (formerly 4 May).

monies plural form of **MONEY**, as used in financial contexts.

moniker /ˈmɒnɪkə/ (also **monicker**) ▶ noun informal a name.
– DERIVATIVES **monikered** adjective.
– ORIGIN mid 19th cent.: of unknown origin.

monilia /məˈnɪlɪə/ ▶ noun (pl. usu. same or **moniliae** /-lɪaɪ/) former term for **CANDIDA**.
– ORIGIN modern Latin, from Latin *monile* 'necklace' (with reference to the chains of spores).

moniliform /məˈnɪlɪfɔːm/ ▶ adjective Zoology & Botany resembling a string of beads.
– ORIGIN early 19th cent.: from French *moniliforme* or modern Latin *moniliformis*, from Latin *monile* 'necklace' + **-IFORM**.

monism /ˈmɒnɪz(ə)m, ˈməʊ-/ ▶ noun Philosophy & Theology a theory or doctrine that denies the existence of a distinction or duality in some sphere, such as that between matter and mind, or God and the world.
■ the doctrine that only one supreme being exists. Compare with **PLURALISM**.
– DERIVATIVES **monist** noun & adjective, **monistic** adjective.
– ORIGIN mid 19th cent.: from modern Latin *monismus*, from Greek *monos* 'single'.

monition /məˈnɪʃ(ə)n/ ▶ noun rare a warning of impending danger.
■ a formal notice from a bishop or ecclesiastical court admonishing a person not to do something specified.
– ORIGIN late Middle English: via Old French from Latin *monitio(n-)*, from *monere* 'warn'.

monitor ▶ noun **1** an instrument or device used for observing, checking, or keeping a continuous record of a process or quantity: *a heart monitor.*
■ a person operating such an instrument or device. ■ a person who observes a process or activity to check that it is carried out fairly or correctly, especially in an official capacity: *the independent judicial monitor.* ■ a person who listens to and reports on foreign radio broadcasts and signals.
2 a school pupil with disciplinary or other special duties.
3 a television receiver used in a studio to select or verify the picture being broadcast from a particular camera.
■ a television which displays an image generated by a computer. ■ a loudspeaker, especially one used by performers on stage to hear themselves or in the studio to hear what has been recorded.
4 (also **monitor lizard**) a large tropical Old World lizard with a long neck, narrow head, forked tongue, strong claws, and a short body. Monitors were formerly believed to give warning of crocodiles. Called **GOANNA** in Australia.
● Family Varanidae and genus *Varanus*: many species. See also **KOMODO DRAGON**.
5 historical a shallow-draught warship mounting one or two heavy guns for bombardment.
▶ verb [with obj.] observe and check the progress or quality of (something) over a period of time; keep under systematic review: *equipment was installed to monitor air quality.*
■ maintain regular surveillance over: *he was a man of routine and it was easy for an enemy to monitor his movements.* ■ listen to and report on (a foreign radio broadcast or a telephone conversation). ■ check or regulate the technical quality of (a radio transmission or television signal).
– DERIVATIVES **monitorial** adjective, **monitorship** noun.
– ORIGIN early 16th cent. (in sense 2): from Latin, from *monit-* 'warned', from the verb *monere*. Sense 1 dates from the 1930s.

monitory ▶ adjective rare giving or serving as a warning: *the chill, monitory wail of an air-raid siren.*
▶ noun (pl. **-ies**) (in church use) a letter of admonition from the Pope or a bishop.

Monk, Thelonious (Sphere) (1917–82), American jazz pianist and composer, one of the founders of the bebop style in the early 1940s. Notable compositions: 'Round Midnight', 'Straight, No Chaser', and 'Well, You Needn't'.

monk ▶ noun a member of a religious community of men typically living under vows of poverty, chastity, and obedience.
– DERIVATIVES **monkish** adjective, **monkishly** adverb, **monkishness** noun.
– ORIGIN Old English *munuc*, based on Greek *monakhos* 'solitary', from *monos* 'alone'.

monkery ▶ noun [mass noun] derogatory monasticism.

monkey ▶ noun (pl. **-eys**) **1** a small to medium-sized primate that typically has a long tail, most kinds of which live in trees in tropical countries.
● Families Cebidae and Callitrichidae (or Callithricidae) (**New World monkeys**, with prehensile tails), and Cercopithecidae (**Old World monkeys**, without prehensile tails).
■ (in general use) any primate. ■ a mischievous person, especially a child: *where have you been, you little monkey!* ■ figurative a person who is dominated or controlled by another (with reference to the monkey traditionally kept by an organ-grinder).
2 Brit. informal a sum of £500.
3 (also **monkey engine**) a piledriving machine consisting of a heavy hammer or ram working vertically in a groove.
▶ verb (**-eys**, **-eyed**) [no obj.] (**monkey about/around**) behave in a silly or playful way.
■ (**monkey with**) tamper with: *don't monkey with that lock!* ■ [with obj.] archaic ape; mimic.
– PHRASES **as artful** (or **clever**) **as a wagonload** (or **cartload**) **of monkeys** Brit. informal extremely clever or mischievous. **make a monkey of** (or **out of**) **someone** humiliate someone by making them appear ridiculous. **a monkey on one's back** informal a burdensome problem. ■ a dependence on drugs. **not give a monkey's** informal be completely indifferent or unconcerned: *he doesn't give a monkey's what we think about him.*
– DERIVATIVES **monkeyish** adjective.
– ORIGIN mid 16th cent.: of unknown origin, perhaps from Low German.

monkey bars ▶ plural noun a piece of playground equipment consisting of a horizontally mounted overhead ladder, from which children may swing.

monkey business ▶ noun [mass noun] informal mischievous or deceitful behaviour.

monkey engine ▶ noun see **MONKEY** (sense 3).

monkey flower ▶ noun a plant of boggy ground, having yellow or red snapdragon-like flowers.
● Genus *Mimulus*, family Scrophulariaceae: several species, in particular *M. guttatus.*

monkey jacket ▶ noun a short, close-fitting jacket worn by sailors or waiters or by officers in their mess.

monkey nut ▶ noun Brit. a peanut.

monkey orange ▶ noun S. African a small evergreen tree of warm climates, which bears a hard-shelled edible fruit with poisonous seeds.
● Genus *Strychnos*, family Loganiaceae: two species.

monkey puzzle (also **monkey puzzle tree**) ▶ noun an evergreen coniferous tree with branches covered in spirals of tough spiny leaf-like scales, native to Chile.
● *Araucaria araucana*, family Araucariaceae.
– ORIGIN mid 19th cent.: said to be so named in response to a remark that an attempt to climb the tree would puzzle a monkey.

monkey rope ▶ noun S. African a liana.

monkeyshines ▶ plural noun informal North American term for **MONKEY TRICKS**.

monkey suit ▶ noun informal a man's evening dress or formal suit.

monkey's wedding ▶ noun S. African informal simultaneous rain and sunshine.
– ORIGIN perhaps based on Portuguese *casamento de raposa* 'vixen's wedding', in the same sense.

monkey tricks ▶ plural noun Brit. informal mischievous behaviour.

monkey wrench ▶ noun an adjustable spanner with large jaws which has its adjusting screw contained in the handle.
▶ verb (**monkey-wrench**) [with obj.] informal sabotage (something), especially as a form of protest: [as noun **monkey-wrenching**] *the five defendants received jail sentences for monkey-wrenching.*
– PHRASES **a monkey wrench in the works** see **WORK**.
– DERIVATIVES **monkey-wrencher** noun.

monkfish ▶ noun (pl. same or **-fishes**) **1** a bottom-dwelling anglerfish of European waters.
● *Lophius piscatorius*, family Lophiidae.
■ [mass noun] this fish as food.
2 see **ANGEL SHARK**.

Mon-Khmer /ˈmɔːnˌkmɛː/ ▶ noun [mass noun] a family of languages spoken throughout SE Asia, of which the most important are Mon and Khmer. They are distantly related to Munda, with which they form the Austro-Asiatic phylum or superfamily.
▶ adjective relating to or denoting this group of languages.

monk seal ▶ noun a seal with a dark back and pale underside, occurring in warm waters of the northern hemisphere.
● Genus *Monachus*, family Phocidae: two or three species, including the endangered *M. monachus* of the Mediterranean and adjacent seas.

monkshood ▶ noun an aconite with blue or purple flowers.
● Genus *Aconitum*, family Ranunculaceae: several species, including the European *A. napellus* and the North American *A. uncinatum.*

Monmouth /ˈmɒnməθ/, James Scott, Duke of (1649–85), English claimant to the throne of England. The illegitimate son of Charles II, he became the focus for Whig supporters of a Protestant succession. In 1685 he led a rebellion against the Catholic James II, but was defeated at the Battle of Sedgemoor and executed.

Monmouthshire a county of SE Wales, on the border with England; administrative centre, Cwmbran. Most of the county was part of Gwent 1974–96.

mono ▶ adjective **1** monophonic.
2 monochrome.
▶ noun (pl. **-os**) **1** a monophonic recording.
■ [mass noun] monophonic reproduction.
2 a monochrome picture.
■ [mass noun] monochrome reproduction.
3 N. Amer. short for **MONONUCLEOSIS**.
4 N. Amer. short for **MONOFILAMENT**.

mono- (also **mon-** before a vowel) ▶ combining form **1** one; alone; single: *monocoque.*
2 Chemistry (forming names of compounds) containing one atom or group of a specified kind: *monoamine.*
– ORIGIN from Greek *monos* 'alone'.

monoamine /ˌmɒnəʊˈeɪmiːn/ (also **monamine**) ▶ noun Chemistry a compound having a single amine group in its molecule, especially one which is a neurotransmitter (e.g. serotonin, noradrenaline).

monoamine oxidase ▶ noun [mass noun] Biochemistry an enzyme (present in most tissues) which catalyses the oxidation and inactivation of monoamine neurotransmitters.

monoamine oxidase inhibitor ▶ noun Medicine any of a group of antidepressant drugs which inhibit the activity of monoamine oxidase (so allowing accumulation of serotonin and noradrenaline in the brain).

monobasic ▶ adjective Chemistry (of an acid) having one replaceable hydrogen atom.

monobloc ▶ adjective made as, contained in, or involving a single casting.
– ORIGIN early 20th cent.: from French, from *mono-* (from Greek *monos* 'alone') + *bloc* 'block'.

monocarpic /ˌmɒnə(ʊ)ˈkɑːpɪk/ ▶ adjective Botany (of a plant) flowering only once and then dying.
– ORIGIN mid 19th cent.: from **MONO-** 'single' + Greek *karpos* 'fruit' + **-IC**.

monocausal ▶ adjective in terms of a sole cause: *the pitfalls of monocausal explanations.*

Monoceros /məˈnɒs(ə)rəs/ Astronomy an inconspicuous constellation (the Unicorn), lying on the celestial equator in the Milky Way between Canis Major and Canis Minor.
■ [as genitive **Monocerotis** /ˌmɒnɒs(ʊ)səˈrəʊtɪs/] used with preceding letter or numeral to designate a star in this constellation: *the star Alpha Monocerotis.*
– ORIGIN via Latin from Greek.

monochasium /ˌmɒnə(ʊ)ˈkeɪzɪəm/ ▶ noun (pl. **monochasia**) Botany a cyme in which each flowering branch gives rise to one lateral branch, so that the inflorescence is helicoid or asymmetrical.
– ORIGIN late 19th cent.: modern Latin, from **MONO-** 'one' + Greek *khasis* 'separation'.

monochord ▶ noun an instrument for comparing musical pitches, using a taut wire whose vibrating length can be adjusted with a movable bridge.
– ORIGIN late Middle English: from Old French *monacorde*, via late Latin from Greek *monokhordon*, neuter (used as a noun) of *monokhordos* 'having a single string'.

monochromatic ▶ adjective containing or using only one colour: *monochromatic light.*
■ Physics (of light or other radiation) of a single wavelength or frequency. ■ lacking in variety; monotonous: *her typically monochromatic acting style.*
– DERIVATIVES **monochromatically** adverb.

monochromatism ▶ noun [mass noun] complete colour blindness in which all colours appear as shades of one colour.

monochromator /ˈmɒnə(ʊ)krəˌmeɪtə, ˌmɒnə(ʊ)ˈkrɒmɪtə/ ▶ noun Physics a device used to select radiation of (or very close to) a single wavelength or energy.

monochrome ▶ noun a photograph or picture developed or executed in black and white or in varying tones of only one colour.
■ [mass noun] representation or reproduction in black and white or in varying tones of only one colour.
▶ adjective (of a photograph or picture, or a television screen) consisting of or displaying images in black and white or in varying tones of only one colour.
– DERIVATIVES **monochromic** adjective.
– ORIGIN mid 17th cent.: based on Greek *monokhrōmatos* 'of a single colour'.

monocle /ˈmɒnək(ə)l/ ▶ noun a single eyeglass, kept in position by the muscles around the eye.
– DERIVATIVES **monocled** adjective.
– ORIGIN mid 19th cent.: from French (earlier in the sense 'one-eyed'), from late Latin *monoculus* 'one-eyed'.

monocline /ˈmɒnə(ʊ)klʌɪn/ ▶ noun Geology a bend in rock strata that are otherwise uniformly dipping or horizontal.
– DERIVATIVES **monoclinal** adjective.
– ORIGIN late 19th cent.: from **MONO-** 'single' + Greek *klinein* 'to lean'.

monoclinic ▶ adjective of or denoting a crystal system or three-dimensional geometrical arrangement having three unequal axes of which one is at right angles to the other two.

monoclonal /ˌmɒnə(ʊ)ˈkləʊn(ə)l/ ▶ adjective Biology forming a clone which is derived asexually from a single individual or cell.

monoclonal antibody ▶ noun an antibody produced by a single clone of cells or cell line and consisting of identical antibody molecules.

monocoque /ˈmɒnə(ʊ)kɒk/ ▶ noun an aircraft or vehicle structure in which the chassis is integral with the body.
– ORIGIN early 20th cent.: from French, from *mono-* 'single' + *coque* 'shell'.

monocot ▶ noun Botany short for **MONOCOTYLEDON**.

monocotyledon /ˌmɒnə(ʊ)kɒtɪˈliːd(ə)n/ ▶ noun Botany a flowering plant with an embryo that bears a single cotyledon (seed leaf). Monocotyledons constitute the smaller of the two great divisions of flowering plants, and typically have elongated stalkless leaves with parallel veins (e.g. grasses, lilies, palms). Compare with **DICOTYLEDON**.
● Class Monocotyledoneae (or -donae, -dones; sometimes Liliopsida), subdivision Angiospermae.
– DERIVATIVES **monocotyledonous** adjective.

monocracy /məˈnɒkrəsi/ ▶ noun (pl. **-ies**) [mass noun] a system of government by one person only.
– DERIVATIVES **monocrat** noun, **monocratic** adjective.

monocrystalline ▶ adjective consisting of a single crystal.

monocular /məˈnɒkjʊlə/ ▶ adjective with, for, or in one eye: *he had only monocular vision.*
▶ noun an optical instrument for viewing distant objects with one eye, like one half of a pair of binoculars.
– ORIGIN mid 17th cent.: from late Latin *monoculus* 'having one eye' + **-AR**[1].

monoculture ▶ noun [mass noun] the cultivation of a single crop in a given area.

monocycle ▶ noun another term for **UNICYCLE**.

monocyclic /ˌmɒnə(ʊ)ˈsʌɪklɪk, -ˈsɪk-/ ▶ adjective
1 Chemistry having one ring of atoms in its molecule.
2 of or relating to a single cycle of activity.

monocyte /ˈmɒnə(ʊ)sʌɪt/ ▶ noun Physiology a large phagocytic white blood cell with a simple oval nucleus and clear, greyish cytoplasm.

Monod /ˈmɒnəʊ/, Jacques Lucien (1910–76), French biochemist. Together with fellow French biochemist François Jacob (b.1920), with whom he was awarded a Nobel Prize in 1965, he formulated a theory to explain how genes are activated and in 1961 proposed the existence of messenger RNA.

monodactyly /ˌmɒnə(ʊ)ˈdaktɪli/ ▶ noun [mass noun] Medicine & Zoology a condition in which there is only one finger or toe on each hand or foot.
– DERIVATIVES **monodactyl** adjective.
– ORIGIN late 19th cent.: from *monodactyl* (from Greek *monodaktulos* 'one-fingered') + **-Y**[3].

monodisperse /ˌmɒnə(ʊ)ˈdɪspəːs/ ▶ adjective Chemistry (of a colloid) containing particles of uniform size.

monodrama ▶ noun a dramatic piece for one performer.

monody /ˈmɒnədi/ ▶ noun (pl. **-ies**) **1** an ode sung by a single actor in a Greek tragedy.
2 a poem lamenting a person's death.
3 [mass noun] music with only one melodic line.
– DERIVATIVES **monodic** adjective, **monodist** noun.
– ORIGIN early 17th cent.: via late Latin from Greek *monōdia*, from *monōdos* 'singing alone'.

monoecious /məˈniːʃəs/ ▶ adjective Biology (of a plant or invertebrate animal) having both the male and female reproductive organs in the same individual; hermaphrodite. Compare with **DIOECIOUS**.
– DERIVATIVES **monoecy** noun.
– ORIGIN mid 18th cent.: from modern Latin *Monoecia* (denoting a class of such plants in Linnaeus's system), from Greek *monos* 'single' + *oikos* 'house'.

monofilament (also **monofil**) ▶ noun a single strand of man-made fibre.
■ [mass noun] a type of fishing line using such a strand.

monogamy /məˈnɒɡəmi/ ▶ noun [mass noun] the practice or state of being married to one person at a time.
■ the practice or state of having a sexual relationship with only one partner. ■ Zoology the habit of having only one mate at a time.
– DERIVATIVES **monogamist** noun, **monogamous** adjective, **monogamously** adverb.
– ORIGIN early 17th cent.: from French *monogamie*, via ecclesiastical Latin from Greek *monogamia*, from *monos* 'single' + *gamos* 'marriage'.

monogenean /ˌmɒnə(ʊ)dʒɪˈniːən, məˈnɒdʒɪnɪən/ Zoology ▶ adjective of or relating to a group of flukes that are chiefly external or gill parasites of fish and only require a single host. Compare with **DIGENEAN**.
▶ noun a monogenean fluke.
● Class Monogenea, phylum Platyhelminthes; sometimes treated as a subclass of the class Trematoda.
– ORIGIN 1960s: from modern Latin *Monogenea* (from Greek *monos* 'single' + *genea* 'generation') + **-AN**.

monogenesis /ˌmɒnə(ʊ)ˈdʒɛnɪsɪs/ ▶ noun [mass noun] the theory that humans are all descended from a single pair of ancestors. Also called **MONOGENY**.
■ Linguistics the hypothetical origination of language or of a surname from a single source at a particular place and time.

monogenic /ˌmɒnə(ʊ)ˈdʒɛnɪk/ ▶ adjective Genetics involving or controlled by a single gene.
– DERIVATIVES **monogenically** adverb.

monogeny /məˈnɒdʒəni/ ▶ noun another term for **MONOGENESIS**.
– DERIVATIVES **monogenism** noun, **monogenist** noun.

monoglot /ˈmɒnə(ʊ)ɡlɒt/ ▶ adjective using or speaking only one language: *monoglot Irish-speakers.*
▶ noun a person who speaks only one language.
– ORIGIN mid 19th cent.: from Greek *monoglōttos*, from *monos* 'single' + *glōtta* 'tongue'.

monogram ▶ noun a motif of two or more interwoven letters, typically a person's initials, used to identify a personal possession or as a logo.
▶ verb [with obj.] decorate with a monogram.
– DERIVATIVES **monogrammatic** adjective.
– ORIGIN late 17th cent.: from French *monogramme*, from late Latin *monogramma*, from Greek.

monograph ▶ noun a detailed written study of a single specialized subject or an aspect of it.
▶ verb [with obj.] write a monograph on; treat in a monograph.
– DERIVATIVES **monographer** noun, **monographist** noun.
– ORIGIN early 19th cent. (earlier *monography*): from modern Latin *monographia*, from *monographus* 'writer on a single genus or species'.

monographic ▶ adjective of or relating to a monograph.
■ (of an art gallery or exhibition) showing the works of a single artist.

monogyne /ˈmɒnədʒʌɪn/ ▶ adjective Entomology (of a social insect) having only one egg-laying queen in each colony.
– ORIGIN from **MONO-** 'one' + Greek *gunē* 'woman, wife'.

monohull ▶ noun a boat with only one hull, as opposed to a catamaran or multihull.

monohybrid ▶ noun Genetics a hybrid that is heterozygous with respect to a specified gene.

monohydrate ▶ noun Chemistry a hydrate containing one mole of water per mole of the compound.

monohydric ▶ adjective Chemistry (of an alcohol) containing one hydroxyl group.

monokini ▶ noun a woman's one-piece beach garment equivalent to the lower half of a bikini.
– ORIGIN 1960s: from **MONO-** 'one' + a shortened form of **BIKINI** (the first syllable misinterpreted as *bi-* 'two').

monolatry /məˈnɒlətri/ ▶ noun [mass noun] the worship of one god without denial of the existence of other gods.
– DERIVATIVES **monolater** noun, **monolatrist** noun, **monolatrous** adjective.

monolayer ▶ noun Chemistry a layer one molecule thick.
■ Biology & Medicine a cell culture in a layer one cell thick.

monolingual ▶ adjective (of a person or society) speaking only one language: *monolingual families.*
■ (of a text or conversation) written or conducted in only one language: *monolingual and bilingual editions.*
▶ noun a person who speaks only one language.
– DERIVATIVES **monolingualism** noun.

monolith ▶ noun **1** a large single upright block of stone, especially one shaped into or serving as a pillar or monument.
■ a very large and characterless building: *the 72-storey monolith overlooking the waterfront.* ■ a large block of concrete sunk in water, e.g. in the building of a dock.
2 a large impersonal political, corporate, or social structure regarded as intractably indivisible and uniform: *states struggling to break away from the Moscow-dominated communist monolith.*
– ORIGIN mid 19th cent.: from French *monolithe*, from Greek *monolithos*, from *monos* 'single' + *lithos* 'stone'.

monolithic ▶ adjective **1** formed of a single large block of stone.
■ (of a building) very large and characterless.
2 (of an organization or system) large, powerful, and intractably indivisible and uniform: *rejecting any move towards a monolithic European superstate.*
3 Electronics (of a solid-state circuit) composed of active and passive components formed in a single chip.

monologue ▶ noun a long speech by one actor in a play or film, or as part of a theatrical or broadcast programme.

■[mass noun] the form or style of such speeches: *the play oscillates between third-person narration and monologue.* ■ a long and typically tedious speech by one person during a conversation: *Fred carried on with his monologue as if I hadn't spoken.*
– DERIVATIVES **monologic** adjective, **monological** adjective, **monologist** (also **-loguist**) noun, **monologize** (also **-ise**) verb.
– ORIGIN mid 17th cent.: from French, from Greek *monologos* 'speaking alone'.

monomania ▶ noun [mass noun] exaggerated or obsessive enthusiasm for or preoccupation with one thing.
– DERIVATIVES **monomaniac** noun & adjective, **monomaniacal** adjective.

monomer /ˈmɒnəmə/ ▶ noun Chemistry a molecule that can be bonded to other identical molecules to form a polymer.
– DERIVATIVES **monomeric** adjective.

monometallic ▶ adjective consisting of one metal only.
■of, involving, or using a standard of currency based on one metal.
– DERIVATIVES **monometallism** noun, **monometallist** noun & adjective.

monometer /məˈnɒmɪtə/ ▶ noun Prosody a line consisting of one metrical foot.
– DERIVATIVES **monometric** adjective, **monometrical** adjective.

monomial /məˈnəʊmɪəl/ Mathematics ▶ adjective (of an algebraic expression) consisting of one term.
▶ noun an algebraic expression of this type.
– ORIGIN early 18th cent.: from **MONO-** 'one', on the pattern of *binomial*.

monomolecular ▶ adjective Chemistry (of a layer) one molecule thick.
■consisting of or involving one molecule.

monomorphemic /ˌmɒnə(ʊ)mɔːˈfiːmɪk/ ▶ adjective Linguistics consisting of a single morpheme.

monomorphic /ˌmɒnə(ʊ)ˈmɔːfɪk/ ▶ adjective chiefly Biology having or existing in only one form, in particular:
■(of a species or population) showing little or no variation in morphology or phenotype. ■(of an animal species) having sexes that are similar in size and appearance.
– DERIVATIVES **monomorphism** noun, **monomorphous** adjective.
– ORIGIN late 19th cent.: from **MONO-** 'single' + Greek *morphē* 'form'.

mononuclear ▶ adjective Biology (of a cell) having one nucleus.

mononucleosis /ˌmɒnə(ʊ)njuːklɪˈəʊsɪs/ ▶ noun [mass noun] Medicine an abnormally high proportion of monocytes in the blood, especially associated with glandular fever.

monophagous /məˈnɒfəɡəs/ ▶ adjective Zoology (of an animal) eating only one kind of food.

monophonic /ˌmɒnə(ʊ)ˈfɒnɪk/ ▶ adjective **1** (of sound reproduction) using only one channel of transmission. Compare with **STEREOPHONIC**.
2 Music homophonic.
– DERIVATIVES **monophonically** adverb, **monophony** noun.
– ORIGIN early 19th cent.: from **MONO-** 'one' + Greek *phonē* 'sound' + **-IC**.

monophthong /ˈmɒnəfθɒŋ/ ▶ noun Phonetics a vowel that has a single perceived auditory quality. Contrasted with **DIPHTHONG, TRIPHTHONG**.
– DERIVATIVES **monophthongal** adjective.
– ORIGIN early 17th cent.: from Greek *monophthongos*, from *monos* 'single' + *phthongos* 'sound'.

monophyletic /ˌmɒnə(ʊ)fʌɪˈlɛtɪk/ ▶ adjective Biology (of a group of organisms) descended from a common evolutionary ancestor or ancestral group, especially one not shared with any other group.

Monophysite /məˈnɒfɪsʌɪt/ ▶ noun Christian Theology a person who holds that there is only one inseparable nature (partly divine, partly and subordinately human) in the person of Christ.
– DERIVATIVES **Monophysitism** noun.
– ORIGIN late 17th cent.: via ecclesiastical Latin from ecclesiastical Greek *monophusitēs*, from *monos* 'single' + *phusis* 'nature'.

monoplane ▶ noun an aeroplane with one pair of wings. Often contrasted with **BIPLANE, TRIPLANE**.

monoplegia /ˌmɒnə(ʊ)ˈpliːdʒə/ ▶ noun [mass noun] paralysis restricted to one limb or region of the body. Compare with **PARAPLEGIA**.
– DERIVATIVES **monoplegic** adjective.

monoploid /ˈmɒnə(ʊ)plɔɪd/ ▶ adjective less common term for **HAPLOID**.

monopod ▶ noun a one-legged support for a camera or fishing rod.
– ORIGIN early 19th cent.: via Latin from Greek *monopodion*, from *monos* 'single' + *pous, pod-* 'foot'.

monopodium /ˌmɒnə(ʊ)ˈpəʊdɪəm/ ▶ noun (pl. **monopodia**) Botany a single continuous growth axis which extends at its apex and produces successive lateral shoots. Compare with **SYMPODIUM**.
– DERIVATIVES **monopodial** adjective.

monopole[1] ▶ noun **1** Physics a single electric charge or magnetic pole, especially a hypothetical isolated magnetic pole.
2 a radio aerial or pylon consisting of a single pole or rod.

monopole[2] ▶ noun a champagne that is exclusive to one shipper.
– ORIGIN late 19th cent.: from French 'monopoly'.

Monopolies and Mergers Commission a UK government body designed to investigate and report on activities relating to the setting up of trading monopolies, company mergers, and takeovers, in which the public has an interest.

monopolist ▶ noun a person or business that has a monopoly.
– DERIVATIVES **monopolistic** adjective, **monopolistically** adverb.

monopolistic competition ▶ noun another term for **IMPERFECT COMPETITION**.

monopolize (also **-ise**) ▶ verb [with obj.] (of an organization or group) obtain exclusive possession or control of (a trade, commodity, or service).
■have or take the greatest share of: *the bigger clubs monopolize the most profitable sponsorships and TV deals.* ■get or keep exclusively to oneself: *Sophie monopolized the guest of honour for most of the evening.*
– DERIVATIVES **monopolization** noun, **monopolizer** noun.

monopoly ▶ noun (pl. **-ies**) **1** the exclusive possession or control of the supply or trade in a commodity or service: *the state's monopoly of radio and television broadcasting.*
■[usu. with negative] the exclusive possession, control, or exercise of something: *men don't have a monopoly on unrequited love.* ■a company or group having exclusive control over a commodity or service. ■a commodity or service controlled in this way: *electricity, gas, and water were considered to be natural monopolies.*
2 (**Monopoly**) trademark a board game in which players engage in simulated property and financial dealings using imitation money. It was invented in the US and the name was coined by Charles Darrow c.1935.
– ORIGIN mid 16th cent.: via Latin from Greek *monopōlion*, from *monos* 'single' + *pōlein* 'sell'.

monopoly capitalism ▶ noun [mass noun] Economics a capitalist system typified by trade monopolies in the hands of a few people.

Monopoly money ▶ noun [mass noun] imitation money used in the game of Monopoly.
■figurative money having no real existence or value.

monopropellant ▶ noun a substance used as rocket fuel without an additional oxidizing agent.
▶ adjective using such a substance.

monopsony /məˈnɒpsəni/ ▶ noun (pl. **-ies**) Economics a market situation in which there is only one buyer.
– ORIGIN 1930s: from **MONO-** 'one' + Greek *opsōnein* 'buy provisions' + **-Y[3]**.

monopteros /məˈnɒptərɒs/ ▶ noun a classical temple consisting of a single circle of columns supporting a roof.
– DERIVATIVES **monopteral** adjective.
– ORIGIN late 17th cent.: from medieval Latin (adjective used as a noun), from Greek *monos* 'single' + *pteron* 'wing'.

monorail ▶ noun a railway in which the track consists of a single rail, typically elevated and with the trains suspended from it.

monorail camera ▶ noun a camera mounted on a rail which allows positional adjustment and may support additional components.

monorchid ▶ adjective (of a person or animal) having only one testicle.

▶ noun such a person or animal.
– DERIVATIVES **monorchidism** noun.
– ORIGIN early 19th cent.: from modern Latin *monorchis, monorchid-*, from Greek *monos* 'single' + *orkhis* 'testicle'.

monosaccharide ▶ noun Chemistry any of the class of sugars (e.g. glucose) that cannot be hydrolysed to give a simpler sugar.

monosemy /ˈmɒnə(ʊ)siːmi/ ▶ noun [mass noun] Linguistics the property of having only one meaning.
– DERIVATIVES **monosemous** adjective.
– ORIGIN 1950s: from **MONO-** 'one' + Greek *sēma* 'sign' + **-Y[3]**.

monoski ▶ noun a single broad ski attached to both feet.
– DERIVATIVES **monoskier** noun, **monoskiing** noun.

monosodium glutamate ▶ noun a compound which occurs naturally as a breakdown product of proteins and is used as a flavour enhancer in food (although itself tasteless). A traditional ingredient in oriental cooking, it was originally obtained from seaweed but is now mainly made from bean and cereal protein.
● Chem. formula: $HOOC(CH_2)_2(NH_2)COONa$.

monosome /ˈmɒnə(ʊ)səʊm/ ▶ noun Biology an unpaired (usually X) chromosome in a diploid chromosome complement.

monosomy /ˌmɒnə(ʊ)ˈsəʊmɪk/ ▶ noun [mass noun] Biology the condition of having a diploid chromosome complement in which one (usually the X) chromosome lacks its homologous partner.
– DERIVATIVES **monosomic** adjective.

monospecific ▶ adjective Biology relating to or consisting of only one species.
■(of an antibody) specific to one antigen.

monostable Electronics ▶ adjective (of a circuit or device) having only one stable position or state.
▶ noun a device or circuit of this type.

monostrophic /ˌmɒnə(ʊ)ˈstrɒfɪk, -ˈstrəʊf-/ ▶ adjective Prosody consisting of repetitions of the same strophic arrangement.

monosyllabic ▶ adjective (of a word or utterance) consisting of one syllable.
■(of a person) using brief words to signify reluctance to engage in conversation.
– DERIVATIVES **monosyllabically** adverb.

monosyllable ▶ noun a word consisting of only one syllable.
■(**monosyllables**) brief words, signifying reluctance to engage in conversation: *if she spoke at all it was in monosyllables.*

monosynaptic /ˌmɒnə(ʊ)sɪˈnaptɪk/ ▶ adjective Physiology (of a reflex pathway) involving a single synapse.

monotechnic ▶ adjective related to a single technical subject.
■(of a college) providing instruction in a single technical subject. Compare with **POLYTECHNIC**.

monotheism /ˈmɒnə(ʊ)θiːɪz(ə)m/ ▶ noun [mass noun] the doctrine or belief that there is only one God.
– DERIVATIVES **monotheist** noun & adjective, **monotheistic** adjective, **monotheistically** adverb.
– ORIGIN mid 17th cent.: from **MONO-** 'one' + Greek *theos* 'god' + **-ISM**.

Monothelite /məˈnɒθəlʌɪt/ (also **Monothelete** /-liːt/) ▶ noun Christian Theology an adherent of the doctrine that Jesus had only one will, proposed in the 7th century to reconcile Monophysite and orthodox parties in the Byzantine Empire but condemned as heresy.
– ORIGIN late Middle English: via ecclesiastical Latin from ecclesiastical Greek *monothelētēs*, from *monos* 'single' + *thelētēs* (from *thelein* 'to will').

monotint ▶ noun archaic term for **MONOCHROME**.

monotone /ˈmɒnətəʊn/ ▶ noun [usu. in sing.] a continuing sound, especially of someone's voice, that is unchanging in pitch and without intonation: *he sat and answered the questions in a monotone.*
▶ adjective (of a voice or other sound) unchanging in pitch; without intonation or expressiveness: *his monotone reading of the two-hour report.*
■figurative without colour, vividness, or variety; dull: *the monotone housing estates of the big cities.*
– ORIGIN mid 17th cent.: from modern Latin *monotonus*, from late Greek *monotonos*.

monotonic ▶ adjective **1** Mathematics (of a function or

quantity) varying in such a way that it either never decreases or never increases.
2 speaking or uttered with an unchanging pitch or tone: *her dour, monotonic husband.*
– DERIVATIVES **monotonically** adverb, **monotonicity** noun.

monotonous ▶ adjective dull, tedious, and repetitious; lacking in variety and interest: *the statistics that he quotes with monotonous regularity.*
■ (of a sound or utterance) lacking in variation in tone or pitch: *her slurred monotonous speech.*
– DERIVATIVES **monotonously** adverb.

monotony ▶ noun [mass noun] lack of variety and interest; tedious repetition and routine: *you can become resigned to the monotony of captivity.*
■ sameness of pitch or tone in a sound or utterance: *depression flattens the voice almost to monotony.*

monotreme /ˈmɒnə(ʊ)triːm/ ▶ noun Zoology a primitive mammal that lays large yolky eggs and has a common opening for the urogenital and digestive systems. Monotremes are now restricted to Australia and New Guinea, and comprise the platypus and the echidnas.
● Order Monotremata and subclass Prototheria: two families.
– ORIGIN mid 19th cent.: from **MONO-** 'single' + Greek *trēma* 'hole'.

monotropy /məˈnɒtrəpɪ/ ▶ noun [mass noun] Chemistry the existence of allotropes of an element, one of which is stable and the others metastable under all known conditions.
– DERIVATIVES **monotrope** noun.
– ORIGIN early 20th cent.: from **MONO-** 'one' + Greek *tropē* 'turning' + **-Y**³.

monotype ▶ noun **1** (**Monotype**) [usu. as modifier] Printing, trademark a typesetting machine, now little used, which casts type in metal, one character at a time: *Monotype machines.*
2 a single print taken from a design created in oil paint or printing ink on glass or metal.

monotypic /ˌmɒnə(ʊ)ˈtɪpɪk/ ▶ adjective chiefly Biology having only one type or representative, especially (of a genus) containing only one species.

monounsaturated ▶ adjective Chemistry (of an organic compound, especially a fat) saturated except for one multiple bond.

monovalent /ˌmɒnə(ʊ)ˈveɪl(ə)nt/ ▶ adjective Chemistry having a valency of one.

monoxide ▶ noun Chemistry an oxide containing one atom of oxygen in its molecule or empirical formula.

monozygotic /ˌmɒnə(ʊ)zʌɪˈɡɒtɪk/ ▶ adjective (of twins) derived from a single ovum, and so identical.
– ORIGIN early 20th cent.: from **MONO-** 'single' + **ZYGOTE** + **-IC**.

monozygous /ˌmɒnə(ʊ)ˈzʌɪɡəs/ ▶ adjective another term for **MONOZYGOTIC**.
– DERIVATIVES **monozygosity** noun.

Monroe¹ /mənˈrəʊ/, James (1758–1831), American Democratic Republican statesman, 5th President of the US 1817–25. In 1803, while minister to France under President Jefferson, he negotiated and ratified the Louisiana Purchase; he is chiefly remembered, however, as the originator of the Monroe doctrine.

Monroe² /mənˈrəʊ/, Marilyn (1926–62), American actress; born *Norma Jean Mortenson*; later *Norma Jean Baker*. Her film roles, largely in comedies, made her the definitive Hollywood sex symbol. She is thought to have died of an overdose of sleeping pills. Notable films: *Gentlemen Prefer Blondes* (1953), *Some Like it Hot* (1959), and *The Misfits* (1961).

Monroe doctrine a principle of US policy, originated by President James Monroe, that any intervention by external powers in the politics of the Americas is a potentially hostile act against the US.

Monrovia /mɒnˈrəʊvɪə/ the capital and chief port of Liberia; pop. 500,000 (est. 1985).

Mons /mɒnz/ a town in southern Belgium, capital of the province of Hainaut; pop. 91,730 (1991). It was the scene in August 1914 of the first major battle of the First World War between British and German forces. Flemish name **BERGEN**.

mons /mɒnz/ ▶ noun short for **MONS PUBIS**.

Monseigneur /ˌmɒnseɪˈnjəː, French mɔ̃sɛɲœr/ ▶ noun (pl. **Messeigneurs** /ˌmɛseɪnˈjəː, French mesɛɲœr/) a title or form of address used of or to a

French-speaking prince, cardinal, archbishop, or bishop.
– ORIGIN French, from *mon* 'my' + *seigneur* 'lord'.

Monsieur /məˈsjəː, French məsjø/ ▶ noun (pl. **Messieurs** /mɛˈsjəː, French mesjø/) a title or form of address used of or to a French-speaking man, corresponding to *Mr* or *sir*: *Monsieur Hulot.*
– ORIGIN French, from *mon* 'my' + *sieur* 'lord'.

Monsignor /mɒnˈsiːnjə, ˌmɒnsiːˈnjɔː/ ▶ noun (pl. **Monsignori** /-ˈnjɔːri/) the title of various senior Roman Catholic posts, such as a prelate or an officer of the papal court.
– ORIGIN Italian, on the pattern of French *Monseigneur.*

monsoon ▶ noun a seasonal prevailing wind in the region of the Indian subcontinent and SE Asia, blowing from the south-west between May and September and bringing rain (the **wet monsoon**), or from the north-east between October and April (the **dry monsoon**).
■ the rainy season accompanying the wet monsoon.
– DERIVATIVES **monsoonal** adjective.
– ORIGIN late 16th cent.: from Portuguese *monção*, from Arabic *mawsim* 'season', from *wasama* 'to mark, brand'.

mons pubis /ˌmɒnz ˈpjuːbɪs/ ▶ noun the rounded mass of fatty tissue lying over the joint of the pubic bones, in women typically more prominent and also called the **mons veneris**.
– ORIGIN late 19th cent.: Latin, 'mount of the pubes'.

monster ▶ noun an imaginary creature that is typically large, ugly, and frightening.
■ an inhumanly cruel or wicked person: *he was an unfeeling, treacherous monster.* ■ often humorous a person, typically a child, who is rude or badly behaved: *Christian is only a year old, but already he is a little monster.* ■ a thing or animal that is excessively or dauntingly large: *this is a monster of a book, almost 500 pages.* ■ a congenitally malformed or mutant animal or plant.
▶ adjective [attrib.] informal of an extraordinary and daunting size or extent: *a monster 36lb carp.*
▶ verb [with obj.] informal, chiefly Austral. criticize or reprimand severely: *my mum used to monster me for coming home so late.*
– ORIGIN late Middle English: from Old French *monstre*, from Latin *monstrum* 'portent or monster', from *monere* 'warn'.

monstera /mɒnˈstɪərə/ ▶ noun a large tropical American climbing plant of the arum family, which typically has divided or perforated leaves and corky aerial roots. Several kinds are cultivated as indoor plants when young.
● Genus *Monstera*, family Araceae: several species, including the Swiss cheese plant.
– ORIGIN modern Latin, perhaps from Latin *monstrum* 'monster' (because of the unusual appearance of the leaves in some species).

monster truck ▶ noun an extremely large pickup truck, typically with greatly oversized tyres. They are often used for racing across rough terrain.

monstrance /ˈmɒnstr(ə)ns/ ▶ noun (in the Roman Catholic Church) an open or transparent receptacle in which the consecrated Host is exposed for veneration.
– ORIGIN late Middle English (also in the sense 'demonstration or proof'): from medieval Latin *monstrantia*, from Latin *monstrare* 'to show'.

monstrosity ▶ noun (pl. **-ies**) **1** something, especially a building, which is very large and is considered unsightly: *the shopping centre, a multi-storey monstrosity of raw concrete.*
■ something which is outrageously or offensively wrong: *he rebelled against Nazi monstrosities.* ■ a grossly malformed animal, plant, or person.
2 [mass noun] the state or fact of being monstrous.
– ORIGIN mid 16th cent. (denoting an abnormality of growth): from late Latin *monstrositas*, from Latin *monstrosus* (see **MONSTROUS**).

monstrous ▶ adjective having the ugly or frightening appearance of a monster: *monstrous, bug-eyed fish.*
■ (of a person or an action) inhumanly or outrageously evil or wrong: *he wasn't lovable, he was monstrous and violent* | *it is a monstrous waste of money.* ■ extremely and dauntingly large: *the monstrous tidal wave swamped the surrounding countryside.*
– DERIVATIVES **monstrously** adverb, **monstrousness** noun.
– ORIGIN late Middle English (in the sense 'strange or unnatural'): from Old French *monstreux* or Latin

monstrosus, from *monstrum* (see **MONSTER**). Current senses date from the 16th cent.

mons Veneris /ˌmɒnz ˈvɛnərɪs/ ▶ noun (in women) the mons pubis.
– ORIGIN late 17th cent.: Latin, 'mount of Venus'.

Mont. ▶ abbreviation for Montana.

montage /mɒnˈtɑːʒ, ˈmɒntɑːʒ/ ▶ noun [mass noun] the process or technique of selecting, editing, and piecing together separate sections of film to form a continuous whole.
■ [count noun] a sequence of film resulting from this: *a montage of excerpts from the film.* ■ the technique of producing a new composite whole from fragments of pictures, text, or music.
– ORIGIN early 20th cent.: French, from *monter* 'to mount'.

Montagna /mɒnˈtɑːnjə/, Bartolommeo Cincani (c.1450–1523), Italian painter. He is noted for his altarpiece *Sacra Conversazione* (1499).

Montagnais /ˌmɒntanˈjeɪ/ ▶ noun (pl. same) **1** a member of an American Indian people living in a vast area of Canada from north of the Gulf of St Lawrence to the southern shores of Hudson Bay.
2 [mass noun] the Algonquian language of this people, closely related to Cree. It has about 7,000 speakers.
▶ adjective of or relating to this people or their language.
– ORIGIN from French, literally 'of the mountains'.

Montagnard /ˌmɒntəˈnjɑː(d)/ ▶ noun & adjective former term for **HMONG**.
– ORIGIN French, from *montagne* 'mountain'.

Montagu's harrier /ˈmɒntəɡjuːz/ ▶ noun a slender migratory Eurasian bird of prey, the male having pale grey plumage with black wing tips.
● *Circus pygargus*, family Accipitridae.
– ORIGIN mid 19th cent.: named after George Montagu (1751–1815), British naturalist.

Montaigne /mɒnˈteɪn, French mɔ̃tɛɲ/, Michel (Eyquem) de (1533–92), French essayist. Widely regarded as the originator of the modern essay, he wrote about prominent personalities and ideas of his age in his sceptical *Essays* (1580; 1588).

Montana¹ /mɒnˈtanə/ a state in the western US, on the Canadian border to the east of the Rocky Mountains; pop. 799,065 (1990); capital, Helena. Acquired from France as part of the Louisiana Purchase in 1803, it became the 41st state of the US in 1889.
– DERIVATIVES **Montanan** adjective & noun.

Montana² /mɒnˈteɪnə/, Joe (b.1956), American football player. He joined the San Francisco 49ers as quarterback in 1980 and played in four winning Super Bowls (1982; 1985; 1989; 1990).

montane /ˈmɒnteɪn/ ▶ adjective [attrib.] of or inhabiting mountainous country: *montane grasslands.*
– ORIGIN mid 19th cent.: from Latin *montanus*, from *mons, mont-* 'mountain'.

Montanism /ˈmɒntənɪz(ə)m/ ▶ noun the tenets of a heretical millenarian and ascetic Christian sect that set great store by prophecy, founded in Phrygia by the priest Montanus in the middle of the 2nd century.
– DERIVATIVES **Montanist** noun.

Mont Blanc /ˌmɒ̃ ˈblɑ̃(k), French mɔ̃ blɑ̃/ a peak in the Alps on the border between France and Italy, rising to 4,807 m (15,771 ft). It is the highest peak in the Alps and in western Europe.

montbretia /mɒn(t)ˈbriːʃə/ ▶ noun a plant of the iris family with bright orange-yellow trumpet-shaped flowers.
● *Crocosmia × crocosmiiflora*, family Iridaceae.
– ORIGIN late 19th cent.: modern Latin, named after A. F. E. Coquebert de *Montbret* (1780–1801), French botanist.

Montcalm /mɒnˈkɑːm, French mɔ̃kalm/, Louis Joseph de Montcalm-Gozon, Marquis de (1712–59), French general. He defended Quebec against British troops under General Wolfe, but was defeated and fatally wounded in the battle on the Plains of Abraham.

Mont Cervin /mɔ̃ sɛrvɛ̃/ French name for **MATTERHORN**.

monte /ˈmɒntɪ/ ▶ noun (usu. **three-card monte**) [mass noun] a game of Mexican origin played with three cards, similar to three-card trick.
– ORIGIN early 19th cent.: Spanish, literally

'mountain', also 'heap of cards left after dealing' (from an earlier game of chance played with forty-five cards).

Monte Albán /ˌmɒnteɪ alˈbɑːn/ an ancient city, now in ruins, in Oaxaca, southern Mexico. Occupied from the 8th century BC, it was a centre of the Zapotec culture from about the 1st century BC to the 8th century AD.

Monte Carlo /ˌmɒntɪ ˈkɑːləʊ/ a resort in Monaco, forming one of the four communes of the principality; pop. 12,000 (1985). It is famous as a gambling resort and as the terminus of the annual Monte Carlo rally.

Monte Carlo method ▶ noun *Statistics* a technique in which a large quantity of randomly generated numbers are studied using a probabilistic model to find an approximate solution to a numerical problem that would be difficult to solve by other methods.
– ORIGIN 1940s: named after *Monte Carlo* (see **MONTE CARLO**), once famous for its gambling casino.

Monte Cassino /ˌmɒnteɪ kaˈsiːnəʊ/ a hill in central Italy near the town of Cassino, the site of the principal monastery of the Benedictines, founded by St Benedict *c*.529. The monastery and the town were destroyed in 1944 during bitter fighting between Allied and German forces, but have since been restored.

Monte Cervino /ˌmonte tʃerˈviːno/ Italian name for **MATTERHORN**.

Montego Bay /mɒnˈtiːɡəʊ/ a free port and tourist resort on the north coast of Jamaica; pop. 82,000 (1991).

Montenegro /ˌmɒntɪˈniːɡrəʊ/ a mountainous, landlocked republic in the Balkans, part of Yugoslavia; pop. 632,000 (1988); official language, Serbo-Croat; capital, Podgorica.

> Joined with Serbia before the Turkish conquest of 1355, Montenegro became independent in 1851. In 1918 it became part of the federation of Yugoslavia, of which it remains, with Serbia, a constituent.

– DERIVATIVES **Montenegrin** adjective & noun.

Montepulciano /ˌmɒnteɪpʊlˈtʃɑːnəʊ, ˌmɒntɪ-/ ▶ noun [mass noun] a red wine made in the region of Montepulciano, a town in Tuscany.

Monterey /ˌmɒntəˈreɪ/ a city and fishing port on the coast of California, founded by the Spanish in the 18th century; pop. 31,950 (1990).

Monterey cypress ▶ noun another term for **MACROCARPA**.

Monterey Jack (also **Monterey cheese** or N. Amer. **Jack cheese**) ▶ noun [mass noun] a kind of cheese resembling Cheddar.
– ORIGIN from the name of *Monterey* County, California, where it was first made; the origin of *Jack* is unknown.

Monterrey /ˌmɒntəˈreɪ/ an industrial city in NE Mexico, capital of the state of Nuevo León; pop. 2,521,700 (1990).

Montespan /ˈmɒntɪspɒ̃, French mɔ̃tɛspɑ̃/, Françoise-Athénaïs de Rochechouart, Marquise de (1641–1707), French noblewoman. She was mistress of Louis XIV from 1667 to 1679, and had seven illegitimate children by him. She subsequently fell from favour when the king became attracted to the children's governess, Madame de Maintenon.

Montesquieu /ˈmɒntɪskjəː, -sjuː, French mɔ̃teskjø/, Charles Louis de Secondat, Baron de La Brède et de (1689–1755), French political philosopher. His reputation rests chiefly on *L'Esprit des lois* (1748), a comparative study of political systems in which he championed the separation of judicial, legislative, and executive powers as being most conducive to individual liberty.

Montessori[1] /ˌmɒntɪˈsɔːri/, Maria (1870–1952), Italian educationist. In her book *The Montessori Method* (1909) she advocated a child-centred approach to education, developed from her success with mentally handicapped children.

Montessori[2] /ˌmɒntɪˈsɔːri/ ▶ noun [usu. as modifier] a system of education for young children that seeks to develop natural interests and activities rather than use formal teaching methods: *a Montessori school*.

Monteverdi /ˌmɒntɪˈvɛːdi/, Claudio (1567–1643), Italian composer. His madrigals are noted for their use of harmonic dissonance; other important

works include his opera *Orfeo* (1607) and his sacred *Vespers* (1610).

Montevideo /ˌmɒntɪvɪˈdeɪəʊ, Spanish monteβiˈðeo/ the capital and chief port of Uruguay, on the River Plate; pop. 1,360,250 (est. 1991).

Montez /ˈmɒntez/, Lola (1818–61), Irish dancer; born *Marie Dolores Eliza Rosanna Gilbert*. She became the mistress of Ludwig I of Bavaria in 1846 and exercised great influence over him until banished the following year.

Montezuma II /ˌmɒntɪˈz(j)uːmə/ (1466–1520), Aztec emperor 1502–20. The last ruler of the Aztec empire in Mexico, he was defeated and imprisoned by the Spanish under Cortés in 1519. He was killed while trying to pacify some of his former subjects during an uprising against his captors.

Montezuma's revenge ▶ noun [mass noun] informal diarrhoea suffered by travellers, especially visitors to Mexico.

Montfort[1] /ˈmɒntfət/, Simon de (*c*.1165–1218), French soldier. From 1209 he led the Albigensian Crusade against the Cathars in southern France.

Montfort[2] /ˈmɒntfət/, Simon de, Earl of Leicester (*c*.1208–65), English soldier, born in Normandy. He was the son of Simon de Montfort. He led the baronial opposition to Henry III, defeating the king at Lewes in 1264 and summoning a Parliament (1265). He was defeated and killed by reorganized royal forces under Henry's son (later Edward I).

Montgolfier /mɒnˈɡɒlfɪeɪ, -fɪə, French mɔ̃ɡɔlfje/, Joseph Michel (1740–1810) and Jacques Étienne (1745–99), French inventors and pioneers in hot-air ballooning. In 1782 they built a large balloon from linen and paper and successfully lifted a number of animals; the first human ascents followed in 1783.

Montgomery[1] /mɒntˈɡʌməri, -ˈɡɒməri/ the state capital of Alabama; pop. 187,100 (1990).

Montgomery[2] /mɒntˈɡʌməri, -ˈɡɒməri/, Bernard Law, 1st Viscount Montgomery of Alamein (1887–1976), British Field Marshal; known as **Monty**. His victory at El Alamein in 1942 proved the first significant Allied success in the Second World War. He commanded the Allied ground forces in the invasion of Normandy in 1944 and accepted the German surrender on 7 May, 1945.

Montgomery[3] /mɒntˈɡʌməri, -ˈɡɒməri/, L. M. (1874–1942), Canadian novelist; full name *Lucy Maud Montgomery*. She is noted for her best-selling first novel *Anne of Green Gables* (1908).

Montgomeryshire /mɒntˈɡʌmərɪʃɪə, -ˈɡɒm-, -ʃə/ a former county of central Wales. It became a part of Powys in 1974.

month ▶ noun (also **calendar month**) each of the twelve named periods into which a year is divided: *the first six months of 1992* | *it was the end of the month.* ■ a period of time between the same dates in successive calendar months: *the president's rule was extended for six more months from March 3.* ■ a period of 28 days or four weeks. ■ a lunar month.
– PHRASES **a month of Sundays** informal a very long, seemingly endless period of time: *no one will find them in a month of Sundays.*
– ORIGIN Old English *mōnath*, of Germanic origin; related to Dutch *maand* and German *Monat*, also to **MOON**.

month-long ▶ adjective [attrib.] of a month's duration: *a month-long trial.*

monthly ▶ adjective [attrib.] done, produced, or occurring once a month: *the Council held monthly meetings.*
▶ adverb once a month; every month; from month to month: *most of us get paid monthly.*
▶ noun (pl. **-ies**) **1** a magazine that is published once a month.
2 (**monthlies**) informal a menstrual period.

Montmartre /mɒnˈmɑːtr(ə), French mɔ̃maʁtʁ/ a district in northern Paris, on a hill above the Seine, much frequented by artists in the late 19th and early 20th centuries when it was a separate village.

montmorillonite /ˌmɒntməˈrɪlənʌɪt/ ▶ noun [mass noun] an aluminium-rich clay mineral of the smectite group, containing some sodium and magnesium.
– ORIGIN mid 19th cent.: from *Montmorillon*, the name of a town in France, + **-ITE**[1].

Montonero /ˌmɒntəˈnɛːrəʊ/ ▶ noun (pl. **-os**) a member of a left-wing Peronist guerrilla organization in Argentina.

■ historical a peasant rebel against imperial Spain in South America.
– ORIGIN South American Spanish, literally 'guerrilla fighter', from Spanish *montón* 'crowd or mass'.

Montparnasse /ˌmɒnpɑːˈnas, French mɔ̃paʁnas/ a district of Paris, on the left bank of the River Seine. Frequented in the late 19th century by writers and artists, it is traditionally associated with Parisian cultural life.

Montpelier /mɒntˈpiːljə/ the state capital of Vermont; pop. 8,250 (1990).

Montpellier /mɒnˈpɛlɪeɪ, French mɔ̃pɛlje/ a city in southern France, near the Mediterranean coast, capital of Languedoc-Roussillon; pop. 210,870 (1990). A distinguished medical school and university, world-famous in medieval times, was founded there in 1221.

Montrachet /ˈmɒ̃trafeɪ/ ▶ noun [mass noun] a white wine produced in the Montrachet region of France.

Montreal /ˌmɒntrɪˈɔːl/ a port on the St Lawrence in Quebec, SE Canada; pop. 1,017,700 (1991); metropolitan area pop. 3,127,240 (1991). Founded in 1642, it was under French rule until 1763; almost two thirds of its present-day population are French-speaking. French name **MONTRÉAL** /mɔ̃real/.

Montreux /mɔ̃ˈtrəː, French mɔ̃tʁø/ a resort town in SW Switzerland, at the east end of Lake Geneva; pop. 19,850 (1990). Since the 1960s it has hosted annual festivals of both jazz and television.

Montrose /mɒnˈtrəʊz/, James Graham, 1st Marquis of (1612–50), Scottish general. Montrose supported Charles I in the English Civil War and inflicted a dramatic series of defeats on the stronger Covenanter forces in the north before being defeated. In 1650 he attempted to restore Charles II, but was betrayed to the Covenanters and hanged.

Mont St Michel /ˌmɔ̃ sã mɪˈʃɛl, French mɔ̃ sɛ̃ miʃel/ a rocky islet off the coast of Normandy, NW France. An island only at high tide, it is surrounded by sandbanks and linked to the mainland by a causeway. It is crowned by a medieval Benedictine abbey-fortress.

Montserrat /ˌmɒntsəˈrat, ˈmɒnsərat/ an island in the Caribbean, one of the Leeward Islands; pop. 12,000 (est. 1988); capital, Plymouth. It was colonized by Irish settlers in 1632 and is now a British dependency. Since 1995 it has been severely affected by the ongoing eruption of the Soufrière Hills volcano, causing the evacuation of the southern part of the island, including Plymouth.
– DERIVATIVES **Montserratian** adjective & noun /ˌmɒn(t)səˈraʃ(ə)n/.
– ORIGIN visited by Columbus in 1493, the island was named after a Benedictine monastery on the mountain of *Montserrat* in Catalonia, NE Spain.

montuno /mɒnˈtuːnəʊ/ ▶ noun (pl. **-os**) a traditional costume worn by men from Panama, consisting of white cotton short trousers and an embroidered shirt.
– ORIGIN American Spanish, literally 'native to mountains, untamed'.

monty ▶ noun (in phrase **the full monty**) Brit. informal the full amount expected, desired, or possible: *they'll do the full monty for a few thousand each.*
– ORIGIN of unknown origin; the phrase is only recorded recently. Among various (unsubstantiated) theories, one cites the phrase *the full Montague Burton*, apparently meaning 'Sunday-best three-piece suit' (from the name of a tailor of made-to-measure clothing in the early 20th cent.); another recounts the possibility of a military usage, *the full monty* being 'the full cooked English breakfast' insisted upon by Field Marshal Montgomery.

monument ▶ noun a statue, building, or other structure erected to commemorate a famous or notable person or event. ■ a statue or other structure placed by or over a grave in memory of the dead. ■ a building, structure, or site that is of historical importance or interest: *the amphitheatre is one of the many Greek monuments in Sicily.* ■ figurative an outstanding, enduring, and memorable example of something: *recordings that are a monument to the art of playing the piano.*
– ORIGIN Middle English (denoting a burial place): via French from Latin *monumentum*, from *monere* 'remind'.

monumental ▶ adjective great in importance, extent, or size: *it's been a monumental effort.*
■ (of a work of art) great in ambition and scope: *the ballet came across as one of MacMillan's most monumental works.* ■ of or serving as a monument: *additional details are found in monumental inscriptions.*
– DERIVATIVES **monumentality** noun, **monumentally** adverb.

monumentalism ▶ noun [mass noun] construction, especially of buildings, on a grand scale.

monumentalize (also **-ise**) ▶ verb [with obj.] make a permanent record of (something) by or as if by creating a monument: *the kind of ethic that monumentalizes the glory of a hero.*

monumental mason ▶ noun Brit. a person who makes tombstones and similar items.

-mony ▶ suffix forming nouns often denoting an action, state, or quality: *ceremony* | *harmony.*
– ORIGIN from Latin *-monia, -monium.*

monzonite /ˈmɒnzənʌɪt/ ▶ noun [mass noun] Geology a granular igneous rock with a composition intermediate between syenite and diorite, containing approximately equal amounts of orthoclase and plagioclase.
– DERIVATIVES **monzonitic** adjective.
– ORIGIN late 19th cent.: named after Mount *Monzoni* in the Tyrol, Italy, + **-ITE**[1].

moo ▶ verb (**moos**, **mooed**) [no obj.] make the characteristic deep resonant vocal sound of cattle.
▶ noun (pl. **moos**) 1 a sound of this kind.
2 Brit. informal an irritating or disliked woman: *you silly old moo.*
– ORIGIN mid 16th cent.: imitative.

mooch ▶ verb informal 1 [no obj.] (**mooch about/around**) Brit. loiter in a bored or listless manner: *he just mooched about my bedsit.*
2 [with obj.] N. Amer. ask for or obtain (something) without paying for it: *a bunch of your friends will show up, mooching food* | *I'm mooching off you all the time.*
▶ noun 1 [in sing.] Brit. an instance of loitering in a bored or listless manner.
2 N. Amer. a beggar or scrounger.
– DERIVATIVES **moocher** noun.
– ORIGIN late Middle English (in the sense 'to hoard'): probably from Anglo-Norman French *muscher* 'hide, skulk'. A dialect sense 'play truant' dates from the early 16th cent.; current senses date from the mid 19th cent.

moo-cow ▶ noun a child's name for a cow.

mood[1] ▶ noun a temporary state of mind or feeling: *he appeared to be in a very good mood about something.*
■ an angry, irritable, or sullen state of mind: *he was obviously in a mood.* ■ the atmosphere or pervading tone of something, especially a work of art: *Monet's Mornings on the Seine series, with their hushed and delicate mood.*
▶ adjective [attrib.] (especially of music) inducing or suggestive of a particular feeling or state of mind.
– PHRASES **in the** (or **in no**) **mood for/to do something** feeling (or not feeling) like doing or experiencing something.
– ORIGIN Old English *mōd* (also in the senses 'mind' and 'fierce courage'), of Germanic origin; related to Dutch *moed* and German *Mut.*

mood[2] ▶ noun 1 Grammar a category of verb use, typically expressing fact (indicative mood), command (imperative mood), question (interrogative mood), wish (optative mood), or conditionality (subjunctive mood).
■ a form or set of forms of a verb in an inflected language such as French, Latin, or Greek, serving to indicate whether it expresses fact, command, wish, or conditionality.
2 Logic any of the valid forms into which each of the figures of a categorical syllogism may occur.
– ORIGIN mid 16th cent.: variant of **MODE**, influenced by **MOOD**[1].

mood-altering ▶ adjective (of a drug) capable of inducing changes of mood.

mood swing ▶ noun an abrupt and unaccountable change of mood.

moody ▶ adjective (**moodier**, **moodiest**) (of a person) given to unpredictable changes of mood, especially sudden bouts of gloominess or sullenness: *she met his moody adolescent brother.*
■ giving an impression of melancholy or mystery: *grainy film which gives a soft, moody effect.*
– DERIVATIVES **moodily** adverb, **moodiness** noun.

– ORIGIN Old English *mōdig* 'brave or wilful' (see **MOOD**[1], **-Y**[1]).

mooi /mɔɪ/ ▶ adjective S. African pleasant; nice.
– ORIGIN Afrikaans, from Dutch, 'handsome, pretty'.

moolah /ˈmuːlə/ ▶ noun [mass noun] informal money.
– ORIGIN 1930s (originally US): of unknown origin.

mooli /ˈmuːli/ ▶ noun a radish of a variety with a large slender white root which is typically eaten cooked, especially in Eastern cuisine, and is also used for stockfeed.
– ORIGIN 1960s: from Hindi *mūlī,* from Sanskrit *mūla* 'root'.

moomba /ˈmuːmbə/ ▶ noun an annual pre-Lent festival held in Melbourne.
– ORIGIN an Aboriginal word.

Moon, Sun Myung (b.1920), Korean industrialist and religious leader. In 1954 he founded the Holy Spirit Association for the Unification of World Christianity, which became known as the Unification Church.

moon ▶ noun (also **Moon**) the natural satellite of the earth, visible (chiefly at night) by reflected light from the sun.
■ a natural satellite of any planet. ■ (**the moon**) figurative anything that one could desire: *you must know he'd give any of us the moon.* ■ poetic/literary or humorous a month: *that wonderful night four moons ago.*

> The moon orbits the earth in a period of 28 days, going through a series of phases from new moon to full moon and back again during that time. Its average distance from the earth is some 384,000 km and it is 3,476 km in diameter. The bright and dark features which outline the face of 'the Man in the Moon' are highland and lowland regions, the former heavily pockmarked by craters due to the impact of meteorites. The moon has no atmosphere, and the same side is always presented to the earth.

▶ verb 1 [no obj., with adverbial] behave or move in a listless and aimless manner: *I don't want her mooning about in the morning.*
■ act in a dreamily infatuated manner: *Timothy's mooning over her like a schoolboy.*
2 [no obj.] informal expose one's buttocks to someone in order to insult or amuse them.
– PHRASES **many moons ago** informal a long time ago. **over the moon** informal extremely happy; delighted. [ORIGIN: from *The Cow jumped over the Moon,* a line from a nursery rhyme.]
– DERIVATIVES **moonless** adjective, **moonlike** adjective.
– ORIGIN Old English *mōna,* of Germanic origin; related to Dutch *maan* and German *Mond,* also to **MONTH**, from an Indo-European root shared by Latin *mensis* and Greek *mēn* 'month', and also Latin *metiri* 'to measure' (the moon being used to measure time).

moonbeam ▶ noun a ray of moonlight.

moon blindness ▶ noun [mass noun] 1 (in horses) a recurrent inflammatory disease of the eyes, causing intermittent blindness.
2 night blindness.
– DERIVATIVES **moon-blind** adjective.

moon boot ▶ noun a warm, thickly padded boot with an outer surface of fabric or plastic.

moon buggy ▶ noun informal term for **LUNAR ROVING VEHICLE**.

moon cake ▶ noun a round cake eaten during the Chinese Moon Festival.

mooncalf ▶ noun (pl. **mooncalves**) a foolish person.

moon daisy ▶ noun another term for **OX-EYE DAISY**.

moon-eye ▶ noun a herring-like freshwater fish with large eyes, which lives in the south of the Great Lakes region of North America.
● *Hiodon tergisus,* family Hiodontidae.

moon-faced ▶ adjective having a round face: *he was a moon-faced, roly-poly little man.*

Moon Festival ▶ noun a Chinese festival held in the middle of the autumn.

moonfish ▶ noun (pl. same or **-fishes**) a deep-bodied laterally compressed marine fish, in particular:
■ a silvery fish of the jack family (Carangidae), including *Selene setapinnis* of the Atlantic. ■ an opah. ■ a fingerfish.

moonflower ▶ noun a tropical American climbing plant of the convolvulus family, with sweet-smelling trumpet-shaped white flowers which open at dusk and close at midday.
● *Ipomoea alba,* family Convolvulaceae.

moong ▶ noun variant spelling of **MUNG**.

moon gate ▶ noun (in China) a circular gateway in a wall.

Moonie ▶ noun [often as modifier] informal, often derogatory a member of the Unification Church.
– ORIGIN 1970s: from the name of its founder, Sun Myung *Moon.*

moonlet ▶ noun a small moon.
■ an artificial satellite.

moonlight ▶ noun [mass noun] the light of the moon: *I sat there in the moonlight.*
▶ adjective [attrib.] illuminated or happening by the light of the moon: *a moonlight stroll.*
▶ verb (past and past participle **-lighted**) [no obj.] informal have a second job, typically secretly and at night, in addition to one's regular employment.
– DERIVATIVES **moonlighter** noun.

moonlit ▶ adjective lit by the moon.

moon moth ▶ noun a large pale green silk moth with transparent eyespots on each wing and long tail-like projections on the hindwings.
● Several genera and species in the family Saturniidae, including the **Spanish moon moth** (*Graellsia isabellae*). See also **LUNA MOTH**.

moon pool ▶ noun a shaft through the bottom of a drilling ship, oil rig, etc. for lowering and raising equipment into or from the water.

moonquake ▶ noun a tremor of the moon's surface.

moonraker ▶ noun 1 dialect a native of the county of Wiltshire. [ORIGIN: with reference to the Wiltshire story of men caught raking a pond for kegs of smuggled brandy, who feigned madness to fool the revenue men, by saying they were raking out the moon.]
2 a small square sail set above a skysail on a sailing ship.

moonrat ▶ noun a shy insectivorous mammal of the hedgehog family, with a long snout and rat-like appearance, native to SE Asia and China. Also called **GYMNURE**.
● Subfamily Galericinae, family Erinaceidae: several genera and species, in particular *Echinosorex gymnurus.*

moonrise ▶ noun [in sing.] the rising or time of rising of the moon above the horizon: *it was actually about an hour after moonrise.*

moon roof ▶ noun another term for **SUNROOF**.

moonscape ▶ noun a landscape having features characteristic of the surface of the moon, especially in being rocky and barren: *the blistering, eroded moonscape of Rajasthan.*

moonseed ▶ noun a North American climbing plant with crescent-shaped seeds.
● *Menispermum canadense,* family Menispermaceae.

moonset ▶ noun [in sing.] the setting or time of setting of the moon below the horizon: *the best times to observe these meteors are after moonset.*

moon-shaped ▶ adjective 1 crescent-shaped: *blood cells which instead of being round are moon-shaped.*
2 round: *her moon-shaped face.*

moonshee /ˈmuːnʃi/ ▶ noun variant spelling of **MUNSHI**.

moon shell (also **moon snail**) ▶ noun a marine mollusc with a shiny, almost spherical, shell and a large foot.
● Family Naticidae, class Gastropoda: *Natica* and other genera.

moonshine ▶ noun [mass noun] 1 foolish talk or ideas: *whatever I said, it was moonshine.*
2 informal, chiefly N. Amer. illicitly distilled or smuggled liquor.

moonshiner ▶ noun informal, chiefly N. Amer. an illicit distiller or smuggler of liquor.

moon shot ▶ noun the launching of a spacecraft to the moon.

moonstomp ▶ noun an informal dance characterized by heavy rhythmic stamping.
▶ verb [no obj.] perform such a dance.

moonstone ▶ noun a pearly white semi-precious stone, especially one consisting of alkali feldspar.

moonstruck ▶ adjective unable to think or act normally, especially because of being in love.

moonwalk ▶ verb [no obj.] (usu. as noun **moonwalking**) walk on the moon.
■ move in a way which resembles the characteristic weightless movement of walking on the moon, typically as part of a dance or performance.
– DERIVATIVES **moonwalker** noun.

moonwort /ˈmuːnwəːt/ ▶ noun a widely distributed fern with a single small frond of fan-shaped lobes and a separate spike bearing the spore-producing

organs, growing typically in grassy uplands and old meadows.
● Genus *Botrychium*, family Ophioglossaceae: several species, in particular *B. lunaria*.

moony ▶ **adjective** (**moonier**, **mooniest**) dreamy and unaware of one's surroundings, for example because one is in love: *she's not drunk, but still smiling in the same moony way | little girls go moony over horses.*

Moor /mʊə, mɔː/ ▶ **noun** a member of a NW African Muslim people of mixed Berber and Arab descent. In the 8th century they conquered the Iberian peninsula, but were finally driven out of their last stronghold in Granada at the end of the 15th century.
– DERIVATIVES **Moorish** adjective.
– ORIGIN from Old French *More*, via Latin from Greek *Mauros* 'inhabitant of Mauretania'.

moor[1] /mʊə, mɔː/ ▶ **noun** a tract of open uncultivated upland, typically covered with heather.
■ a tract of such land preserved for shooting: [with modifier] *a grouse moor.* ■ US or dialect a fen.
– DERIVATIVES **moorish** adjective, **moory** adjective.
– ORIGIN Old English *mōr*, of Germanic origin.

moor[2] /mʊə, mɔː/ ▶ **verb** [with obj.] (often **be moored**) make fast (a boat) by attaching it by cable or rope to the shore or to an anchor: *twenty or so fishing boats were* **moored to** *the pierside.*
■ [no obj., with adverbial of place] (of a boat) be made fast somewhere in this way : *we moored alongside a jetty.*
– DERIVATIVES **moorage** noun.
– ORIGIN late 15th cent.: probably from the Germanic base of Dutch *meren*.

moorburn ▶ **noun** [mass noun] Scottish the seasonal burning of heather and other vegetation on a moor to make way for new growth.

moorcock ▶ **noun** Brit. a male red grouse.

Moore[1] /mʊə, mɔː/, Bobby (1941–93), English footballer; full name *Robert Frederick Moore*. A defender who spent most of his career with West Ham United, he captained the English team that won the World Cup in 1966.

Moore[2] /mʊə, mɔː/, Dudley (Stuart John) (b.1935), English actor, comedian, and musician. He appeared with Peter Cook in the television shows *Beyond the Fringe* (1959–64) and *Not Only … But Also* (1964–70). His films include *Arthur* (1981).

Moore[3] /mʊə, mɔː/, Francis (1657–c.1715), English physician, astrologer, and schoolmaster. His almanacs of meteorological and astrological predictions gave their name to the range of almanacs called 'Old Moore' available today.

Moore[4] /mʊə, mɔː/, George (Augustus) (1852–1933), Irish novelist. Notable works: *A Mummer's Wife* (1885) and *Esther Waters* (1894).

Moore[5] /mʊə, mɔː/, G. E. (1873–1958), English moral philosopher and member of the Bloomsbury Group; full name *George Edward Moore*. Notable works: *Principia Ethica* (1903).

Moore[6] /mʊə, mɔː/, Henry (Spencer) (1898–1986), English sculptor and draughtsman. His work is characterized by semi-abstract reclining forms, large upright figures, and family groups, which Moore intended to be viewed in the open air.

Moore[7] /mʊə, mɔː/, Sir John (1761–1809), British general. He commanded the British army during the Peninsular War and was killed at Corunna.

Moore[8] /mʊə, mɔː/, Thomas (1779–1852), Irish poet and musician. He wrote patriotic and nostalgic songs set to Irish tunes, notably 'The Harp that once through Tara's Halls' and 'The Minstrel Boy', and is also known for the oriental romance *Lalla Rookh* (1817).

Mooré /ˈmuːreɪ/ ▶ **noun** another term for **MORE**[2].

moorfowl ▶ **noun** (pl. same) Brit. another term for **RED GROUSE**.

moor grass ▶ **noun** [mass noun] either of two coarse upland grasses found in Eurasia:
● (**purple moor grass**) a purplish-green grass which grows in large tussocks, chiefly in wet and peaty areas (*Molinia caerulea*, family Gramineae). ● (**blue moor grass**) a wiry bluish-grey European grass which favours dry limestone soils (*Sesleria caerulea*, family Gramineae).

moorhen ▶ **noun** **1** a small aquatic rail with mainly blackish plumage.
● Family Rallidae: two genera and four species, in particular the widespread **common moorhen** or common gallinule (*Gallinula chloropus*), with a red and yellow bill.
2 Brit. a female red grouse.

mooring ▶ **noun** (often **moorings**) a place where a boat or ship is moored: *they tied up at Water Gypsy's permanent moorings.*
■ the ropes, chains, or anchors by or to which a boat, ship, or buoy is moored: *the great ship* **slipped her moorings** *and slid out into the Atlantic.*

Moorish idol ▶ **noun** a disc-shaped fish with bold vertical black-and-white bands and a very tall tapering dorsal fin, of coral reefs in the Indo-Pacific region. Also called **TOBY**.
● *Zanclus cornutus*, family Acanthuridae.

moorland ▶ **noun** [mass noun] (also **moorlands**) an extensive area of moor.

Moorpark ▶ **noun** an apricot of a large orange-fleshed variety.
– ORIGIN late 18th cent.: named after *Moor Park*, Hertfordshire, southern England, the house of Sir William Temple (1628–99), who cultivated this variety of fruit.

moose ▶ **noun** (pl. same) North American term for **ELK**.
– ORIGIN early 17th cent.: from Abnaki *mos*.

moose milk ▶ **noun** [mass noun] Canadian an alcoholic drink consisting typically of rum, milk, and other ingredients such as eggs.
■ home-made liquor.

moosewood ▶ **noun** a compact North American maple with large leaves and vertically striped bark. Moose often feed on the bark during severe winters.
● *Acer pennsylvanicum*, family Aceraceae.

moo shi /ˌmuː ˈʃiː/ (also **moo shoo** /ˌmuː ˈʃuː/ or **moo shu roo** /ˌmuː ˌʃuː ˈruː/) ▶ **noun** [mass noun] a Chinese dish consisting of shredded pork with vegetables and seasonings, rolled in thin pancakes.

moot ▶ **adjective** subject to debate, dispute, or uncertainty, and typically not admitting of a final decision: *whether the temperature rise was mainly due to the greenhouse effect was* **a moot point**.
■ having no practical significance, typically because the subject is too uncertain to allow a decision: *it is moot whether this phrase should be treated as metaphor or not.*
▶ **verb** [with obj.] (usu. **be mooted**) raise (a question or topic) for discussion; suggest (an idea or possibility).
▶ **noun** **1** Brit. an assembly held for debate, especially in Anglo-Saxon and medieval times.
■ a regular gathering of people having a common interest.
2 Law a mock trial set up to examine a hypothetical case as an academic exercise.
– ORIGIN Old English *mōt* 'assembly or meeting' and *mōtian* 'to converse', of Germanic origin; related to **MEET**[1]. The adjective (originally an attributive noun use: see **MOOT COURT**) dates from the mid 16th cent.; the current verb sense dates from the mid 17th cent.

moot court ▶ **noun** chiefly N. Amer. a mock court at which law students argue imaginary cases for practice.

mop[1] ▶ **noun** an implement consisting of a bundle of thick loose strings or a sponge attached to a handle, used for wiping floors or other surfaces.
■ a thick mass of disordered hair: *her tousled mop of blonde hair.* ■ [in sing.] an act of wiping something clean: *the kitchen needed a quick mop.*
▶ **verb** (**mopped**, **mopping**) [with obj.] clean or soak up liquid by wiping: *he was mopping his plate with a piece of bread.*
■ [with obj. and adverbial] wipe (something) away from a surface: *a barmaid rushed forward to* **mop up** *the spilt beer.* ■ wipe sweat or tears from (one's face or eyes).
– DERIVATIVES **moppy** adjective.
– ORIGIN late 15th cent.: perhaps ultimately related to Latin *mappa* 'napkin'.
▶ **mop something up** informal put an end to or dispose of something: *he aims to mop up corruption.*

mop[2] (also **mop fair**) ▶ **noun** Brit. historical an autumn fair or gathering at which farmhands and servants were hired.
– ORIGIN late 17th cent.: probably from the practice at the fair whereby a mop was carried by a maidservant seeking employment.

mopane /mɒˈpɑːni/ (also **mopani**) ▶ **noun** a tree found in arid regions of southern Africa, with bitter-tasting leaves that are shaped like butterfly wings and fold together in intense heat.
● *Colophospermum mopane*, family Leguminosae.
– ORIGIN mid 19th cent.: from Setswana.

mopane worm ▶ **noun** the spotted caterpillar of a southern African moth, which feeds on mopane leaves and is a source of food for local people.
● *Gonimbrasia belina*, family Saturniidae.

mopboard ▶ **noun** US term for **SKIRTING**.

mope ▶ **verb** [no obj.] be dejected and apathetic: *no use moping—things could be worse.*
■ (**mope around/about**) wander about listlessly and aimlessly because of unhappiness or boredom.
▶ **noun** a person given to prolonged spells of low spirits: *a bunch of totally depressed mopes.*
■ (**mopes**) dated low spirits; depression.
– DERIVATIVES **moper** noun, **mopey** (also **mopy**) adjective, **mopily** adverb, **mopiness** noun, **mopish** adjective.
– ORIGIN mid 16th cent. (the early noun sense being 'fool or simpleton'): perhaps of Scandinavian origin; compare with Swedish dialect *mopa* 'to sulk'.

moped /ˈməʊpɛd/ ▶ **noun** a light motor cycle, especially one with an engine capacity of not more than 50 cc.
– ORIGIN 1950s: from Swedish, from (*trampcykel med*) *mo*(*tor och*) *ped*(*aler*) 'pedal cycle with motor and pedals'.

mopery ▶ **noun** [mass noun] **1** feelings of apathy and dejection.
2 US informal the action of committing a minor or petty offence such as loitering: *we got guys doing stretches for passing bad checks and aggravated mopery.*

mop fair ▶ **noun** see **MOP**[2].

mopoke /ˈməʊpəʊk/ ▶ **noun** (also **morepork**) Austral./NZ another term for **BOOBOOK**.
■ a tawny frogmouth (see **FROGMOUTH**).
– ORIGIN early 19th cent.: imitative of the bird's cry.

moppet ▶ **noun** informal a small endearingly sweet child.
– ORIGIN early 17th cent.: from obsolete *moppe* 'baby or rag doll' + **-ET**[1].

Mopti /ˈmɒpti/ a city in central Mali, at the junction of the Niger and Bani Rivers; pop. 53,900 (1976).

moquette /mɒˈkɛt/ ▶ **noun** [mass noun] a thick pile fabric used for carpets and upholstery.
– ORIGIN 1930s: from French, perhaps from obsolete Italian *mocaiardo* 'mohair'.

MOR ▶ **abbreviation for** (of music) middle-of-the-road.

mor /mɔː/ ▶ **noun** [mass noun] Soil Science humus formed under acid conditions.
– ORIGIN 1930s: from Danish.

Moradabad /ˌmɔːrɑːdəˈbad/ a city and railway junction in northern India, in Uttar Pradesh; pop. 417,000 (1991).

moraine /məˈreɪn/ ▶ **noun** Geology a mass of rocks and sediment carried down and deposited by a glacier, typically as ridges at its edges or extremity.
– DERIVATIVES **morainal** adjective, **morainic** adjective.
– ORIGIN late 18th cent.: from French, from Italian dialect *morena*, from French dialect *morre* 'snout'; related to **MORION**[1].

moral ▶ **adjective** concerned with the principles of right and wrong behaviour and the goodness or badness of human character: *the moral dimensions of medical intervention | a moral judgement.*
■ concerned with or adhering to the code of interpersonal behaviour that is considered right or acceptable in a particular society: *an individual's ambitions may get out of step with the general moral code.* ■ [attrib.] examining the nature of ethics and the foundations of good and bad character and conduct: *moral philosophers.*
▶ **noun** **1** a lesson, especially one concerning what is right or prudent, that can be derived from a story, a piece of information, or an experience: ***the moral of this story*** *was that one must see the beauty in what one has.*
2 (**morals**) a person's standards of behaviour or beliefs concerning what is and is not acceptable for them to do: *the corruption of public morals.*
■ standards of behaviour which are considered good or acceptable: *they believe addicts have no morals and cannot be trusted.*
– ORIGIN late Middle English: from Latin *moralis*, from *mos*, *mor-* 'custom', (plural) *mores* 'morals'. As a noun the word was first used to translate Latin *Moralia*, the title of St Gregory the Great's moral exposition of the Book of Job, and was subsequently applied to the works of various classical writers.

morale /məˈrɑːl/ ▶ **noun** [mass noun] the confidence,

enthusiasm, and discipline of a person or group at a particular time: *their morale was high.*
– ORIGIN mid 18th cent.: from French *moral*, respelled to preserve the final stress in pronunciation.

moral hazard ▶ noun [mass noun] Economics lack of incentive to guard against risk where one is protected from its consequences, e.g. by insurance.

moralism ▶ noun [mass noun] the practice of moralizing, especially showing a tendency to make judgements about others' morality: *the patriotic moralism of many political leaders.*

moralist ▶ noun a person who teaches or promotes morality.
■ a person given to moralizing. ■ a person who behaves in a morally commendable way.
– DERIVATIVES **moralistic** adjective, **moralistically** adverb.

morality ▶ noun (pl. **-ies**) [mass noun] principles concerning the distinction between right and wrong or good and bad behaviour:
■ behaviour as it is affected by the observation of these principles: *the past few years have seen a sharp decline in morality.* ■ [count noun] a particular system of values and principles of conduct, especially one held by a specified person or society: *a bourgeois morality.* ■ the extent to which an action is right or wrong: *behind all the arguments lies the issue of **the morality of** the possession of nuclear weapons.* ■ behaviour or qualities judged to be good: *they saw the morality of equal pay.*
– ORIGIN late Middle English: from Old French *moralite* or late Latin *moralitas*, from Latin *moralis* (see **MORAL**).

morality play ▶ noun a kind of drama with personified abstract qualities as the main characters and presenting a lesson about good conduct and character, popular in the 15th and early 16th centuries.

moralize (also **-ise**) ▶ verb [no obj.] [often as noun **moralizing**] indulge in comment on issues of right and wrong, typically with an unfounded air of superiority: *the self-righteous moralizing of his aunt was ringing in his ears.*
■ [with obj.] interpret or explain as giving lessons on good and bad character and conduct: *mythographers normally moralize Narcissus as the man who wastes himself in pursuing worldly goods.* ■ [with obj.] reform the character and conduct of: *he endeavoured to moralize an immoral society.*
– DERIVATIVES **moralization** noun, **moralizer** noun, **moralizingly** adverb.
– ORIGIN late Middle English (in the sense 'explain the moral meaning of'): from French *moraliser* or medieval Latin *moralizare*, from late Latin *moralis* (see **MORAL**).

moral law ▶ noun (in some systems of ethics) an absolute principle defining the criteria of right action (whether conceived as a divine ordinance or a truth of reason).

morally ▶ adverb **1** in relation to standards of good and bad character or conduct: *theories which assert that all inequality is morally wrong.*
■ in a way which conforms to standards of good behaviour: *the task of education was to reinvigorate citizenship in order that pupils might act morally.*
2 [usu. as submodifier] on the basis of strong though not irresistible evidence or probability, especially regarding a person's character: *I am **morally certain** that he is incapable of deliberately harming anyone.*

moral majority ▶ noun [treated as pl.] the majority of people, regarded as favouring firm moral standards: *smokers are often made to feel like social outcasts by the moral majority.*
– ORIGIN 1970s: originally as *Moral Majority*, the name of a right-wing movement in the US.

moral philosophy ▶ noun [mass noun] the branch of philosophy concerned with ethics.

Moral Rearmament an organization founded by the American Lutheran evangelist Frank Buchman (1878–1961) and first popularized in Oxford in the 1920s (hence until about 1938 called the **Oxford Group Movement**). It emphasizes personal integrity and confession of faults, cooperation, and mutual respect, especially as a basis for social transformation.

moral science ▶ noun [mass noun] dated social sciences and/or philosophy.

moral sense ▶ noun [mass noun] the ability to distinguish between right and wrong.

moral support ▶ noun [mass noun] support or help the effect of which is psychological rather than physical.

moral victory ▶ noun a defeat that can be interpreted as a victory on moral terms, for example because the defeated party defended their principles.

moran /ˈmɒr(ə)n/ ▶ noun (pl. same) a member of the warrior group of the Masai people of East Africa, which comprises the younger unmarried males.
– ORIGIN Masai.

Morar, Loch /ˈmɔːrə/ a loch in western Scotland. At 310 m (1,017 ft), it is Scotland's deepest loch.

morass /məˈras/ ▶ noun an area of muddy or boggy ground.
■ figurative a complicated or confused situation: *she would become lost in **a morass of** lies and explanations.*
– ORIGIN late 15th cent.: from Dutch *moeras*, alteration (by assimilation to *moer* 'moor') of Middle Dutch *marasch*, from Old French *marais* 'marsh', from medieval Latin *mariscus*.

moratorium /ˌmɒrəˈtɔːrɪəm/ ▶ noun (pl. **moratoriums** or **moratoria** /-rɪə/) a temporary prohibition of an activity: *an indefinite **moratorium on** the use of drift nets.*
■ Law a legal authorization to debtors to postpone payment. ■ Law the period of this postponement.
– ORIGIN late 19th cent.: modern Latin, neuter (used as a noun) of late Latin *moratorius* 'delaying', from Latin *morat-* 'delayed', from the verb *morari*, from *mora* 'delay'.

Moravia /məˈreɪvɪə/ a region of the Czech Republic, situated between Bohemia in the west and the Carpathians in the east; chief town, Brno. A province of Bohemia from the 11th century, it was made an Austrian province in 1848, becoming a part of Czechoslovakia in 1918.

Moravian ▶ noun a native of Moravia.
■ a member of a Protestant Church founded in Saxony by emigrants from Moravia holding views derived from the Hussites and accepting the Bible as the only source of faith.
▶ adjective of or relating to Moravia or its people.
■ of or relating to the Moravian Church.

Moray /ˈmʌri/ (also **Morayshire** /ˈmʌrɪʃɪə, -ʃə/) an administrative region and former county of northern Scotland, bordered on the north by the Moray Firth; administrative centre, Elgin.

moray /mɒˈreɪ, ˈmɒreɪ/ (also **moray eel**) ▶ noun a mainly nocturnal eel-like predatory fish of warm seas, which typically hides in crevices with just the head protruding.
● Family Muraenidae: several genera and numerous species, including *Muraena helena* of the East Atlantic and Mediterranean.
– ORIGIN early 17th cent.: from Portuguese *moréia*, via Latin from Greek *muraina*.

Moray Firth a deep inlet of the North Sea on the NE coast of Scotland.

morbid ▶ adjective **1** characterized by or appealing to an abnormal and unhealthy interest in disturbing and unpleasant subjects, especially death and disease: *he had long held a morbid fascination with the horrors of contemporary warfare.*
2 Medicine of the nature of or indicative of disease: *the treatment of morbid obesity.*
– DERIVATIVES **morbidity** noun, **morbidly** adverb, **morbidness** noun.
– ORIGIN mid 17th cent. (in the medical sense): from Latin *morbidus*, from *morbus* 'disease'.

morbid anatomy ▶ noun [mass noun] the anatomy of diseased organs and tissues.

morbific /mɔːˈbɪfɪk/ ▶ adjective dated causing disease: *in cholera the morbific matter is taken into the alimentary canal.*
– ORIGIN mid 17th cent.: from French *morbifique* or modern Latin *morbificus*, from Latin *morbus* 'disease'.

morbilli /mɔːˈbɪlʌɪ, -liː/ ▶ plural noun technical term for **MEASLES**.
– ORIGIN mid 16th cent.: Latin, plural of *morbillus* 'pustule', from *morbus* 'disease'.

morbillivirus /mɔːˈbɪlɪˌvʌɪrəs/ ▶ noun Medicine any of a group of paramyxoviruses which causes measles, rinderpest, and canine distemper.
– ORIGIN 1970s: from Latin *morbilli* (plural of *morbillus* 'pustule', from *morbus* 'disease') + **VIRUS**.

morceau /mɔːˈsəʊ/ ▶ noun (pl. **morceaux**) a short literary or musical composition.
– ORIGIN mid 18th cent.: French, literally 'morsel, piece'.

morcha /ˈmɔːtʃɑː/ ▶ noun Indian an organized march or rally.
– ORIGIN from Hindi *morcā*.

mordacious /mɔːˈdeɪʃəs/ ▶ adjective formal **1** denoting or using biting sarcasm or invective.
2 (of a person or animal) given to biting.
– ORIGIN mid 17th cent.: from Latin *mordax, mordac-* 'biting' + **-IOUS**.

mordant /ˈmɔːd(ə)nt/ ▶ adjective (especially of humour) having or showing a sharp or critical quality; biting: *a mordant sense of humour.*
▶ noun a substance, typically an inorganic oxide, that combines with a dye or stain and thereby fixes it in a material.
■ an adhesive compound for fixing gold leaf. ■ a corrosive liquid used to etch the lines on a printing plate.
▶ verb [with obj.] impregnate or treat (a fabric) with a mordant.
– DERIVATIVES **mordancy** noun, **mordantly** adverb.
– ORIGIN late 15th cent.: from French, present participle of *mordre* 'to bite', from Latin *mordere*.

mordent /ˈmɔːd(ə)nt/ ▶ noun Music an ornament consisting of one rapid alternation of a written note with the note immediately below or above it in the scale (sometimes further distinguished as **lower mordent** and **upper mordent**). The term **inverted mordent** usually refers to the **upper mordent**.
– ORIGIN early 19th cent.: via German from Italian *mordente*, present participle of *mordere* 'to bite'.

Mordred /ˈmɔːdrɪd/ (in Arthurian legend) the nephew of King Arthur who abducted Guinevere and raised a rebellion against Arthur.

Mordvin /ˈmɔːdvɪn/ (also **Mordva** /ˈmɔːdvə/) ▶ noun **1** a member of a non-Russian people inhabiting Mordvinia.
2 [mass noun] the Finno-Ugric language of this people, which has two distinct dialects and over 1 million speakers altogether.
▶ adjective of or relating to this people or their language.

Mordvinia /mɔːˈdvɪnɪə/ an autonomous republic in European Russia, south-east of Nizhni Novgorod; pop. 964,000 (1990); capital, Saransk. Also called **MORDVINIAN AUTONOMOUS REPUBLIC**.

More[1] /mɔː/, Sir Thomas (1478–1535), English scholar and statesman, Lord Chancellor 1529–32; canonized as **St Thomas More**. His *Utopia* (1516), describing an ideal city state, established him as a leading humanist of the Renaissance. He was imprisoned in 1534 after opposing Henry's marriage to Anne Boleyn, and beheaded for opposing the Act of Supremacy. Feast day, 22 June.

More[2] /ˈmɔːri/ (also **Mooré**) ▶ noun [mass noun] the language of the Mossi people of Burkina, a member of the Gur family of languages with about 4 million speakers.
▶ adjective of or relating to this language.
– ORIGIN the name in More.

more ▶ determiner & pronoun a greater or additional amount or degree: [as determiner] *I helped myself to more tea* | [as pronoun] *tell me more* | *they proved **more of** a hindrance than a help.*
▶ adverb **1** forming the comparative of adjectives and adverbs, especially those of more than one syllable: *for them enthusiasm is more important than talent.*
2 to a greater extent: *in his experience females liked chocolate **more than** males.*
■ (**more than**) extremely (used before an adjective conveying a positive feeling or attitude): *she is more than happy to oblige.*
3 again: *repeat **once more**.*
4 moreover: *he was rich, and more, he was handsome.*
– PHRASES **more and more** at a continually increasing rate: *vacancies were becoming more and more rare.* **more like it** see **LIKE**[1]. **more or less** speaking imprecisely; to a certain extent: *they are more or less a waste of time.* ■ approximately: *more or less symmetrical.* **no more** **1** nothing further: *there was no more to be said about it.* **2** no further: *you must have some hot soup, but no more wine.* **3** (**be no more**) exist no longer. **4** never again: *mention his name no more to me.* **5** neither: *I had no complaints and no more did Tom.*
– ORIGIN Old English *māra*, of Germanic origin; related to Dutch *meer* and German *mehr*.

Moreau /mɒˈrəʊ, French mɔʀo/, Jeanne (b.1928), French actress. Notable films: *Les Liaisons dangereuses* (1959), *Jules et Jim* (1961), and *Nikita* (1990).

Morecambe /ˈmɔːkəm/, Eric (1926–84), English comedian; born *John Eric Bartholomew*. In 1941 he formed a double act with comedian Ernie Wise that led to the enduringly popular TV series *The Morecambe and Wise Show* (1961–76).

Morecambe Bay an inlet of the Irish Sea, on the NW coast of England between Cumbria and Lancashire.
– ORIGIN *Morecambe*, derived in the 18th cent. from a reference by Ptolemy, 2nd-cent. Greek geographer, to *mori kambē*, from *mori cambo* 'great bay', the old Celtic name for the Lune estuary.

moreen /məˈriːn/ (also **morine**) ▶ noun [mass noun] a strong, ribbed cotton fabric, used chiefly for curtains.
– ORIGIN mid 17th cent.: perhaps a fanciful formation from MOIRE.

moreish ▶ adjective Brit. informal so pleasant to eat that one wants more.

morel /məˈrɛl/ ▶ noun a widely distributed edible fungus which has a brown oval or pointed fruiting body with an irregular honeycombed surface bearing the spores.
● Genus *Morchella*, family Morchellaceae, subdivision Ascomycotina: several species, in particular the common *M. esculenta*.
– ORIGIN late 17th cent.: from French *morille*, from Dutch *morilje*; related to German *Morchel* 'fungus'.

Morelia /mɒˈreɪlɪə/ a city in central Mexico, capital of the state of Michoacán; pop. 489,760 (1990). Founded in 1541, it was known as Valladolid until 1828.
– ORIGIN renamed in honour of J. M. *Morelos y Pavón* (1765–1815), a key figure in Mexico's independence movement.

morello /mɒˈrɛləʊ/ ▶ noun (pl. **-os**) a dark cherry of a sour kind used in cooking: [as modifier] *morello cherries*.
– ORIGIN mid 17th cent.: from Italian *morello* 'blackish', from medieval Latin *morellus*, diminutive of Latin *Maurus* 'Moor'.

Morelos /mɒˈreɪlɒs/ a state of central Mexico, to the west of Mexico City; capital, Cuernavaca.

moreover ▶ adverb as a further matter; besides: *moreover, glass is electrically insulating*.

morepork /ˈmɔːpɔːk/ ▶ noun variant spelling of MOPOKE.

mores /ˈmɔːreɪz, -riːz/ ▶ plural noun the essential or characteristic customs and conventions of a community: *an offence against social mores*.
– ORIGIN late 19th cent.: from Latin, plural of *mos*, *mor-* 'custom'.

Moresco /məˈrɛskəʊ/ ▶ noun & adjective variant spelling of MORISCO.

Moresque /məˈrɛsk, mɔː-/ ▶ adjective (of art or architecture) Moorish in style or design.
– ORIGIN late Middle English (as a noun denoting arabesque ornament): from French, from Italian *moresco*, from *Moro* 'Moor'.

Moreton Bay chestnut ▶ noun a large tree with red and yellow flowers and decorative timber, native to Queensland, Australia. Its heavy pods contain large poisonous seeds yielding an alkaloid that appears to inhibit the Aids virus. Also called BLACK BEAN.
● *Castanospermum australe*, family Leguminosae.
– ORIGIN mid 19th cent.: so named because the tree was first found near *Moreton Bay*, Queensland.

Morgan[1], J. P. (1837–1913), American financier, philanthropist, and art collector; full name *John Pierpont Morgan*. He created General Electric (1891) and the United States Steel Corporation (1901). He bequeathed his large art collection to the Museum of Modern Art in New York.

Morgan[2], Thomas Hunt (1866–1945), American zoologist. His studies on inheritance using the fruit fly *Drosophila* showed that the genetic information was carried by genes arranged along the length of the chromosomes. Nobel Prize for Physiology or Medicine (1933).

Morgan[3] ▶ noun a horse of a light thickset breed developed in New England.
– ORIGIN mid 19th cent.: named after Justin *Morgan* (1747–98), American teacher and owner of the original sire of the breed.

morganatic /ˌmɔːɡəˈnatɪk/ ▶ adjective of or

denoting a marriage in which neither the spouse of lower rank, nor any children, have any claim to the possessions or title of the spouse of higher rank.
– DERIVATIVES **morganatically** adverb.
– ORIGIN early 18th cent.: from modern Latin *morganaticus*, from medieval Latin *matrimonium ad morganaticam* 'marriage with a morning gift' (because a morning gift, given by a husband to his wife on the morning after the marriage, was the wife's sole entitlement in a marriage of this kind).

morganite /ˈmɔːɡ(ə)nʌɪt/ ▶ noun [mass noun] a pink transparent variety of beryl, used as a gemstone.
– ORIGIN early 20th cent.: from the name of J. P. *Morgan* (see MORGAN[1]) + -ITE[1].

Morgan le Fay /ˌmɔːɡən lə ˈfeɪ/ (in Arthurian legend) an enchantress, sister of King Arthur.

morgen /ˈmɔːɡ(ə)n/ ▶ noun a measure of land, in particular:
■ (in the Netherlands, South Africa, and parts of the US) a measure of land equal to about 0.8 hectare or two acres. ■ (in Norway, Denmark, and Germany) a measure of land now equal to about 0.3 hectare or two thirds of an acre.
– ORIGIN early 17th cent.: from Dutch, or from German *Morgen* 'morning', apparently from the notion of 'an area of land that can be ploughed in a morning'.

morgue /mɔːɡ/ ▶ noun **1** a mortuary.
■ used in similes to refer to a place that is quiet, gloomy, or cold: *she put us in that draughty morgue of a sitting room.*
2 informal a newspaper's collection of miscellaneous information for use in future obituaries.
– ORIGIN early 19th cent.: from French, originally the name of a building in Paris where bodies were kept until identified.

moribund /ˈmɒrɪbʌnd/ ▶ adjective (of a person) at the point of death.
■ (of a thing) in terminal decline; lacking vitality or vigour: *the moribund commercial property market.*
– DERIVATIVES **moribundity** noun.
– ORIGIN early 18th cent.: from Latin *moribundus*, from *mori* 'to die'.

morine ▶ noun variant spelling of MOREEN.

morion[1] /ˈmɒrɪən/ ▶ noun a kind of helmet without beaver or visor, worn by soldiers in the 16th and 17th cents.
– ORIGIN French, from Spanish *morrión*, from *morro* 'round object'.

morion[2] /ˈmɒrɪən/ ▶ noun [mass noun] a brown or black variety of quartz.
– ORIGIN mid 18th cent.: from French, from Latin *morion*, a misreading (in Pliny) for *mormorion*.

Morisco /məˈrɪskəʊ/ (also **Moresco**) ▶ noun (pl. **-os** or **-oes**) historical a Moor in Spain, especially one who had accepted Christian baptism.
– ORIGIN Spanish, from *Moro* 'Moor'.

Morisot /ˈmɒrɪzəʊ, French mɔʀizo/, Berthe (Marie Pauline) (1841–95), French painter, the first woman to join the Impressionists. Her works typically depicted women and children and waterside scenes.

Morley /ˈmɔːli/, Edward Williams (1838–1923), American chemist. In 1887 he collaborated with Albert Michelson in an experiment to determine the speed of light, the result of which disproved the existence of the ether. See also MICHELSON–MORLEY EXPERIMENT.

Mormon /ˈmɔːmən/ ▶ noun a member of the Church of Jesus Christ of Latter-day Saints, a religion founded in the US in 1830 by Joseph Smith Jr.

Smith claimed to have found and translated *The Book of Mormon* by divine revelation. It tells the story of a group of Hebrews who migrated to America *c*.600 BC, and is taken as scriptural alongside the Bible. The Mormons came into conflict with the US government over their practice of polygamy (officially abandoned in 1890) and moved their headquarters from Illinois to Salt Lake City, Utah, in 1847 under Smith's successor, Brigham Young. Mormon doctrine emphasizes tithing, missionary work, and the Second Coming of Christ.

– DERIVATIVES **Mormonism** noun.
– ORIGIN the name of a prophet to whom Smith attributed *The Book of Mormon*.

morn ▶ noun poetic/literary term for MORNING.
– ORIGIN Old English *morgen*, of Germanic origin.

mornay /ˈmɔːneɪ/ ▶ adjective denoting or served in a cheese-flavoured white sauce: *mornay sauce* | [postpositive] *cauliflower mornay*.
– ORIGIN named after *Mornay*, the French cook and

eldest son of Joseph Voiron, chef of the restaurant Durand at the end of the 19th cent. and inventor of the sauce.

morning ▶ noun the period of time between midnight and noon, especially from sunrise to noon: *Market Square bustles with citizens from morning until night* | *it was a little after eight in the morning.*
■ this time on a particular day characterized by a specified type of activity or particular weather conditions: *it was a beautiful sunny morning.* ■ sunrise: *a hint of steely light showed that morning was on its way.*
▶ adverb (**mornings**) informal every morning: *mornings, she'd sleep late.*
▶ exclamation informal short for GOOD MORNING.
– PHRASES **morning, noon, and night** all of the time.
– ORIGIN Middle English: from MORN, on the pattern of *evening*.

morning-after pill ▶ noun a contraceptive pill that is effective within about thirty-six hours after intercourse.

morning coat ▶ noun a man's formal coat with a long back section cut into tails which curves up to join the waist at the front.

morning dress ▶ noun [mass noun] a man's morning coat and striped trousers, worn on formal occasions such as weddings, typically with a top hat.

morning glory ▶ noun a climbing plant of the convolvulus family, sometimes cultivated for its trumpet-shaped flowers.
● Genus *Ipomoea*, family Convolvulaceae: several species, in particular the purple-flowered *I. purpurea* of tropical America.

morning prayer ▶ noun (usu. **morning prayers**) a formal act of worship held in the morning, especially regularly or by a group assembled for this purpose.
■ [in sing.] (in the Anglican Church) the service of matins.

morning sickness ▶ noun [mass noun] nausea in pregnancy, typically occurring in the first few months. Despite its name, the nausea can affect pregnant women at any time of day.

Morningside ▶ adjective Scottish (of an accent or manners) affected and refined.
– ORIGIN 1950s: from the name of a residential district in Edinburgh, Scotland.

morning star ▶ noun **1** (**the morning star**) a planet, especially Venus, when visible in the east before sunrise.
2 historical a club with a heavy spiked head, sometimes attached to the handle by a chain. [ORIGIN: translating German *Morgenstern*, comparing the weapon's spikes to rays of the star.]

morning watch ▶ noun the period from 4 to 8 a.m. on board a ship.

Moro /ˈmɔːrəʊ/ ▶ noun (pl. **-os**) a Muslim inhabitant of the Philippines.
– ORIGIN Spanish, literally 'Moor'.

Morocco /məˈrɒkəʊ/ a country in NW Africa, with coastlines on the Mediterranean Sea and Atlantic Ocean; pop. 25,731,000 (est. 1991); languages, Arabic (official), Berber; capital, Rabat.

Conquered by the Arabs in the 7th century, Morocco later fell under French and Spanish influence, each country establishing protectorates in the early 20th century. It became an independent monarchy after the withdrawal of the colonial powers in 1956, the sultan becoming king.

– DERIVATIVES **Moroccan** adjective & noun.

morocco ▶ noun (pl. **-os**) [mass noun] fine flexible leather made (originally in Morocco) from goatskins tanned with sumac, used especially for book covers and shoes.

morocoy /ˈmɒrəkɔɪ/ ▶ noun W. Indian a large tortoise.
● Genus *Geochelone*, family Testudinidae: two species.
– ORIGIN from Spanish *morrocoyo* 'land tortoise'.

moron ▶ noun informal a stupid person.
– DERIVATIVES **moronic** adjective, **moronically** adverb.
– ORIGIN early 20th cent. (as a medical term denoting an adult with a mental age of about 8–12): from Greek *mōron*, neuter of *mōros* 'foolish'.

Moroni /məˈrəʊni/ the capital of Comoros, on the island of Grande Comore; pop. 22,000 (1988).

morose ▶ adjective sullen and ill-tempered.
– DERIVATIVES **morosely** adverb, **moroseness** noun.
– ORIGIN mid 16th cent.: from Latin *morosus* 'peevish', from *mos*, *mor-* 'manner'.

Morpeth /ˈmɔːpəθ/ a town in NE England, the

county town of Northumberland; pop. 15,000 (1981).

morph¹ /mɔːf/ ▶ noun an actual linguistic form: *the present participle in English is always the morph '-ing'.*
– ORIGIN 1940s: from Greek *morphē* 'form'.

morph² /mɔːf/ ▶ noun Biology each of several variant forms of an animal or plant.
– ORIGIN 1950s: from Greek *morphē* 'form'.

morph³ /mɔːf/ ▶ verb change or cause to change smoothly from one image to another by small gradual steps using computer animation techniques.
▶ noun an image that has been processed in this way. ■ an instance of changing an image in this way.
– ORIGIN 1990s: element from METAMORPHOSIS.

-morph ▶ combining form denoting something having a specified form or character: *endomorph | polymorph.*
– ORIGIN from Greek *morphē* 'form'.

morphallaxis /ˌmɔːfəˈlaksɪs/ ▶ noun [mass noun] Zoology regeneration by the transformation of existing body tissues.
– DERIVATIVES **morphallactic** adjective.
– ORIGIN late 19th cent.: from Greek *morphē* 'form' + *allaxis* 'exchange'.

morpheme /ˈmɔːfiːm/ ▶ noun Linguistics a meaningful morphological unit of a language that cannot be further divided (e.g. *in, come, -ing*, forming *incoming*).
■ a morphological element considered in respect of its functional relations in a linguistic system.
– DERIVATIVES **morphemic** adjective, **morphemically** adverb.
– ORIGIN late 19th cent.: from French *morphème*, from Greek *morphē* 'form', on the pattern of French *phonème* 'phoneme'.

morphemics /mɔːˈfiːmɪks/ ▶ plural noun [treated as sing.] Linguistics the study of word structure in terms of minimal meaningful units.

Morpheus /ˈmɔːfɪəs/ Roman Mythology the son of Somnus (god of sleep), the god of dreams and, in later writings, also god of sleep.

morphia /ˈmɔːfɪə/ ▶ noun old-fashioned term for MORPHINE.

morphic resonance ▶ noun [mass noun] (according to the theory developed by Rupert Sheldrake, British biologist b.1942) a paranormal influence by which a pattern of events or behaviour can facilitate subsequent occurrences of similar patterns.

morphine /ˈmɔːfiːn/ ▶ noun [mass noun] an analgesic and narcotic drug obtained from opium and used medicinally to relieve pain.
● An alkaloid; chem. formula: $C_{17}H_{19}NO_3$. Compare with HEROIN.
– ORIGIN early 19th cent.: from German *Morphin*, from the name of the Roman god *Morpheus* (see MORPHEUS).

morphinism /ˈmɔːfɪnɪz(ə)m/ ▶ noun [mass noun] Medicine dependence on or addiction to morphine.

morpho ▶ noun (pl. **-os**) a large tropical butterfly, the male of which has bright blue iridescent wings. Native to the Central and South American rainforests, large numbers are caught each year for use in the jewellery trade.
● Genus *Morpho*, subfamily Morphinae, family Nymphalidae.
– ORIGIN modern Latin, from Greek *Morphō*, an epithet of Aphrodite.

morphogen /ˈmɔːfədʒ(ə)n/ ▶ noun Biology a chemical agent able to cause or determine morphogenesis.

morphogenesis /ˌmɔːfəˈdʒɛnɪsɪs/ ▶ noun [mass noun] **1** Biology the origin and development of morphological characteristics. **2** Geology the formation of landforms or other structures.
– DERIVATIVES **morphogenetic** adjective, **morphogenic** adjective.
– ORIGIN late 19th cent.: modern Latin, from Greek *morphē* 'form' + GENESIS.

morpholine /ˈmɔːfəliːn/ ▶ noun [mass noun] Chemistry a synthetic compound used as a solvent for resins and dyes and (in the form of salts) as an ingredient of emulsifying soaps used in floor polishes.
● A cyclic amine; chem. formula: C_4H_9NO.
– ORIGIN late 19th cent.: from MORPHINE, with the insertion of the syllable *-ol-* (see -OL).

morphology /mɔːˈfɒlədʒi/ ▶ noun (pl. **-ies**) [mass noun] the study of the forms of things, in particular:

■ Biology the branch of biology that deals with the form of living organisms, and with relationships between their structures. ■ Linguistics the study of the forms of words, in particular inflected forms.
– DERIVATIVES **morphologic** adjective, **morphological** adjective, **morphologically** adverb, **morphologist** noun.
– ORIGIN mid 19th cent.: from Greek *morphē* 'form' + -LOGY.

morphometrics /ˌmɔːfə(ʊ)ˈmɛtrɪks/ ▶ plural noun [usu. treated as sing.] chiefly Biology morphometry, especially of living organisms.

morphometry /mɔːˈfɒmɪtri/ ▶ noun [mass noun] the process of measuring the external shape and dimensions of landforms, living organisms, or other objects.
– DERIVATIVES **morphometric** adjective, **morphometrically** adverb.

morphophoneme /ˌmɔːfə(ʊ)ˈfəʊniːm/ ▶ noun Phonetics any of the variant forms of a phoneme as determined by the context in which it is used.
– DERIVATIVES **morphophonemic** adjective.

morphophonemics ▶ noun another term for MORPHOPHONOLOGY.

morphophonology /ˌmɔːfə(ʊ)fəˈnɒlədʒi/ ▶ noun [mass noun] the branch of linguistics that deals with the phonological representation of morphemes.
– DERIVATIVES **morphophonological** adjective, **morphophonologically** adverb.

morphosyntactic /ˌmɔːfə(ʊ)sɪnˈtaktɪk/ ▶ adjective Linguistics involving both morphology and syntax.
– DERIVATIVES **morphosyntactically** adverb, **morphosyntax** noun.

Morris¹, William (1834–96), English designer, craftsman, poet, and writer. A leading figure in the Arts and Crafts Movement, in 1861 he established Morris & Company, an association of craftsmen whose members included Edward Burne-Jones and Dante Gabriel Rossetti, to produce hand-crafted goods for the home. His many writings include *News from Nowhere* (1891), which portrays a socialist Utopia.

Morris², William Richard, see NUFFIELD.

Morris chair ▶ noun a type of easy chair with open padded arms and an adjustable back.
– ORIGIN late 19th cent.: named after William *Morris* (see MORRIS¹).

morris dance ▶ noun a lively traditional English dance performed out of doors by groups known as 'sides'. Dancers wear a distinctive costume that is mainly black and white and has small bells attached, and often carry handkerchiefs or sticks.
– DERIVATIVES **morris dancer** noun, **morris dancing** noun.
– ORIGIN late Middle English: *morris* from *morys*, variant of *Moorish* (see MOOR); the association with the Moors remains unexplained.

Morrison¹, Jim (1943–71), American rock singer; full name *James Douglas Morrison*. Morrison was the lead singer of the Doors.

Morrison², Toni (b.1931), American novelist; full name *Chloe Anthony Morrison*. Her novels depict the black American experience and heritage. *Beloved* (1987) won the Pulitzer Prize, and Morrison became the first black woman writer to receive the Nobel Prize for Literature in 1993.

Morrison³, Van (b.1945), Northern Irish singer, instrumentalist, and songwriter; full name *George Ivan Morrison*. He has developed a distinctive personal style from a background of blues, soul, folk music, and rock. Notable albums: *Astral Weeks* (1968) and *Moondance* (1970).

Morrison shelter ▶ noun historical a movable air-raid shelter, shaped like a table and used indoors.
– ORIGIN named after Herbert S. *Morrison*, UK Secretary of State for Home Affairs and Home Security 1940–5, during which period the shelter was adopted.

morrow ▶ noun (**the morrow**) archaic or poetic/literary the following day: *on the morrow they attacked the city.*
■ the time following an event: *in the morrow of great victory, will they show some equanimity?* ■ the near future: *we have the religious enthusiast who takes no thought for the morrow.*
– ORIGIN Middle English *morwe*, from Old English *morgen* (see MORN).

Morse ▶ noun (also **Morse code**) [mass noun] an alphabet or code in which letters are represented

by combinations of long and short light or sound signals.
▶ verb [with obj.] signal (something) using Morse code.
– ORIGIN mid 19th cent.: named after Samuel F. B. *Morse* (1791–1872), American inventor.

morsel ▶ noun a small piece or amount of food; a mouthful: *Juliet pushed a last morsel of toast into her mouth* | figurative *estate agents think the mansion will be a very tasty morsel for an international company.*
■ a small piece or amount: *there was a morsel of consolation for the British team.* ■ a person who is regarded with pity or sympathy.
– ORIGIN Middle English: from Old French, diminutive of *mors* 'a bite', from Latin *mors-* 'bitten', from the verb *mordere.*

Morse taper ▶ noun a taper on a shank or socket that is one of a standard series having specified dimensions and angles.
– ORIGIN late 19th cent.: probably named after the *Morse* Twist Drill Co., Massachusetts, US.

mort ▶ noun Hunting, archaic the note sounded on a horn when the quarry is killed.
– ORIGIN Middle English: via Old French from Latin *mors, mort-* 'death'.

mortadella /ˌmɔːtəˈdɛlə/ ▶ noun [mass noun] a type of light pink, smooth-textured Italian sausage containing pieces of fat, typically served in slices.
– ORIGIN Italian diminutive, formed irregularly from Latin *murtatum* '(sausage) seasoned with myrtle berries'.

mortal ▶ adjective **1** (of a living human being, often in contrast to a divine being) subject to death: *all men are mortal.*
■ of or relating to humanity as subject to death: *the coffin held the mortal remains of her uncle.* ■ informal conceivable or imaginable: *punishment out of all mortal proportion to the offence.*
2 [attrib.] causing or liable to cause death; fatal: *a mortal disease* | figurative *the scandal appeared to have struck a mortal blow to the government.*
■ (of a battle) fought to the death: *from the outbuildings came the screams of men in mortal combat.* ■ (of an enemy or a state of hostility) admitting or allowing no reconciliation until death. ■ Christian Theology denoting a grave sin that is regarded as depriving the soul of divine grace. Often contrasted with VENIAL. ■ (of a feeling, especially fear) very intense: *parents live in mortal fear of children's diseases.* ■ informal very great: *he was in a mortal hurry.* ■ informal, dated long and tedious: *for three mortal days it rained.*
▶ noun **1** a human being subject to death, often contrasted with a divine being.
■ humorous a person contrasted with others regarded as being of higher status or ability: *an ambassador had to live in a style which was not expected of lesser mortals.*
– ORIGIN late Middle English: from Old French, or from Latin *mortalis*, from *mors, mort-* 'death'.

mortality ▶ noun (pl. **-ies**) [mass noun] **1** the state of being subject to death: *the work is increasingly haunted by thoughts of mortality.*
2 death, especially on a large scale: *the causes of mortality among infants and young children.*
■ (also **mortality rate**) the number of deaths in a given area or period, or from a particular cause: *post-operative mortality was 90 per cent for some operations.*
– ORIGIN late Middle English: via Old French from Latin *mortalitas*, from *mortalis* (see MORTAL).

mortally ▶ adverb in such a manner as to cause death: *the gunner was mortally wounded.*
■ very intensely or seriously: *I expected him to be mortally offended.*

mortar¹ ▶ noun **1** a short smooth-bore gun for firing shells (technically called bombs) at high angles.
■ a similar device used for firing a lifeline or firework. **2** a cup-shaped receptacle made of hard material, in which ingredients are crushed or ground, used especially in cooking or pharmacy: *a pestle and mortar.*
▶ verb [with obj.] attack or bombard with shells fired from a mortar.
– ORIGIN late Old English (in sense 2), from Old French *mortier*, from Latin *mortarium* (to which the English spelling was later assimilated).

mortar² ▶ noun [mass noun] a mixture of lime with cement, sand, and water, used in building to bond bricks or stones.
▶ verb [with obj.] fix or join using mortar: *the pipe can be mortared in place.*
– DERIVATIVES **mortarless** adjective, **mortary** adjective.

– ORIGIN Middle English: from Old French *mortier*, from Latin *mortarium*, probably a transferred sense of the word denoting a container (see **MORTAR**[1]).

mortar board ▶ **noun 1** an academic cap with a stiff, flat, square top and a tassel.
2 a small square board with a handle on the underside, used by bricklayers for holding mortar.

mortarium /mɔːˈtɛːrɪəm/ ▶ **noun** (pl. **mortaria**) Archaeology a Roman container for pounding or grinding.
– ORIGIN Latin.

mortgage /ˈmɔːgɪdʒ/ ▶ **noun** the charging of real (or personal) property by a debtor to a creditor as security for a debt (especially one incurred by the purchase of the property), on the condition that it shall be returned on payment of the debt within a certain period.
■ a deed effecting such a transaction. ■ a loan obtained through the conveyance of property as security: *I put down a hundred thousand in cash and took out a mortgage for the rest.*
▶ **verb** [with obj.] (often **be mortgaged**) convey (a property) to a creditor as security on a loan.
■ figurative expose to future risk or constraint for the sake of immediate advantage: *some people worry that selling off state assets mortgages the country's future.*
– DERIVATIVES **mortgageable** adjective.
– ORIGIN late Middle English: from Old French, literally 'dead pledge', from *mort* (from Latin *mortuus* 'dead') + *gage* 'pledge'.

mortgagee ▶ **noun** the lender in a mortgage, typically a bank, building society, or savings and loan association.

mortgage rate ▶ **noun** the rate of interest charged by a mortgage lender.

mortgagor /ˌmɔːgɪˈdʒɔː/ ▶ **noun** the borrower in a mortgage, typically a homeowner.

mortice ▶ **noun** & **verb** variant spelling of **MORTISE**.

mortician /mɔːˈtɪʃ(ə)n/ ▶ **noun** chiefly N. Amer. an undertaker.
– ORIGIN late 19th cent.: from Latin *mors*, *mort-* 'death' + **-ICIAN**.

mortify /ˈmɔːtɪfʌɪ/ ▶ **verb** (**-ies**, **-ied**) [with obj.] **1** (often **be mortified**) cause (someone) to feel embarrassed, ashamed, or humiliated: [with obj. and infinitive] *she was mortified to see her wrinkles in the mirror* | [as adj. **mortifying**] *she refused to accept this mortifying disgrace.*
2 subdue (the body or its needs and desires) by self-denial or discipline: *return to heaven by* ***mortifying the flesh.***
3 [no obj.] (of flesh) be affected by gangrene or necrosis: *a scratch or cut in Henry's arm had mortified.*
– DERIVATIVES **mortification** noun, **mortifyingly** adverb.
– ORIGIN late Middle English (in the senses 'put to death', 'deaden', and 'subdue by self-denial'): from Old French *mortifier*, from ecclesiastical Latin *mortificare* 'kill, subdue', from *mors*, *mort-* 'death'.

Mortimer, Roger de, 8th Baron of Wigmore and 1st Earl of March (*c*.1287–1330), English noble. In 1326 he invaded England with his lover Isabella of France, replacing her husband Edward II with her son, the future Edward III. When Edward III assumed royal power in 1330 he had Mortimer executed.

mortise /ˈmɔːtɪs/ (also **mortice**) ▶ **noun** a hole or recess cut into a part which is designed to receive a corresponding projection (a tenon) on another part so as to join or lock the parts together.
▶ **verb** [with obj. and adverbial] join securely by using a mortise and tenon.
■ [with obj.] [often as adj. **mortised**] cut a mortise in or through: *the mortised ports.*
– DERIVATIVES **mortiser** noun.
– ORIGIN late Middle English: from Old French *mortaise*.

mortise lock ▶ **noun** a lock which is set within the body of a door in a recess or mortise, as opposed to one attached to the door surface.

mortmain /ˈmɔːtmeɪn/ ▶ **noun** [mass noun] Law the status of lands or tenements held inalienably by an ecclesiastical or other corporation.
– ORIGIN late Middle English: from Anglo-Norman French, Old French *mortemain*, from medieval Latin *mortua manus* 'dead hand' (probably alluding to impersonal ownership).

Morton[1], Jelly Roll (1885–1941), American jazz pianist, composer, and bandleader; born *Ferdinand Joseph La Menthe Morton*. He was one of the principal links between ragtime and New Orleans jazz.

Morton[2], John (*c*.1420–1500), English prelate and statesman. He was appointed Archbishop of Canterbury in 1486 and Chancellor under Henry VII a year later. The Crown's stringent taxation policies made the regime in general and Morton in particular widely unpopular.

Morton's Fork an argument used by John Morton in demanding gifts for the royal treasury: if a man lived well he was obviously rich and if he lived frugally then he must have savings.

mortuary /ˈmɔːtjʊəri, -tʃʊ-/ ▶ **noun** (pl. **-ies**) a room or building in which dead bodies are kept, for hygienic storage or for examination, until burial or cremation.
▶ **adjective** [attrib.] of or relating to burial or tombs: *mortuary rituals* | *a mortuary temple.*
– ORIGIN late Middle English (denoting a gift claimed by a parish priest from a deceased person's estate): from Latin *mortuarius*, from *mortuus* 'dead'. The current noun sense dates from the mid 19th cent.

morula /ˈmɔːr(j)ʊlə/ ▶ **noun** (pl. **morulae** /-liː/) Embryology a solid ball of cells resulting from division of a fertilized ovum, and from which a blastula is formed.
– ORIGIN mid 19th cent.: modern Latin, diminutive of Latin *morum* 'mulberry'.

morwong /ˈmɔːwɒŋ/ ▶ **noun** a marine fish of Australian waters, typically brightly coloured and sometimes commercially fished.
● *Nemadactylus* and other genera, family Cheilodactylidae.
– ORIGIN late 19th cent.: probably from a New South Wales Aboriginal language.

Mosaic /məʊˈzeɪɪk/ ▶ **adjective** of or associated with Moses.
– ORIGIN mid 17th cent.: from French *mosaïque* or modern Latin *Mosaicus*.

mosaic /mə(ʊ)ˈzeɪɪk/ ▶ **noun 1** a picture or pattern produced by arranging together small variously coloured pieces of hard material, such as stone, tile, or glass: [as modifier] *a mosaic floor.*
■ [mass noun] decorative work of this kind: *the walls and vaults are decorated by marble and mosaic.* ■ a colourful and variegated pattern: *the bird's plumage was* ***a mosaic of*** *slate-grey, blue, and brown.* ■ a combination of diverse elements forming a more or less coherent whole: *an incompetently constructed* ***mosaic of*** *competing interests.* ■ an arrangement of photosensitive elements in a television camera.
2 Biology an individual (especially an animal) composed of cells of two genetically different types.
3 (also **mosaic disease**) a virus disease that results in leaf variegation in tobacco, maize, sugar cane, and other plants.
▶ **verb** (**mosaicked**, **mosaicking**) [with obj.] decorate with a mosaic: [as adj. **mosaicked**] *the mosaicked swimming pool.*
■ combine (distinct or disparate elements) to form a picture or pattern: *the digital data were combined, or mosaicked, to delineate counties.*
– DERIVATIVES **mosaicist** noun.
– ORIGIN late Middle English: from French *mosaïque*, based on Latin *musi(v)um* decoration with small square stones, perhaps ultimately from Greek *mousa* 'a muse'.

mosaic gold ▶ **noun** [mass noun] an imitation gold pigment consisting of tin disulphide.

mosaicism /məʊˈzeɪɪsɪz(ə)m/ ▶ **noun** [mass noun] Biology the property or state of being composed of cells of two genetically different types.

Mosaic Law ▶ **noun** another term for ***the Law of Moses*** (see **LAW** in sense 3).

Mosander /mɒˈsandə/, Carl Gustaf (1797–1858), Swedish chemist. Mosander continued Berzelius's work on the rare earth elements and discovered the new elements lanthanum, erbium, and terbium, and the supposed element didymium.

mosasaur /ˈməʊzəsɔː/ ▶ **noun** a large fossil marine reptile of the late Cretaceous period, with large toothed jaws, paddle-like limbs, and a long flattened tail, related to the monitor lizards.
● Family Mosasauridae, suborder Lacertilia: several genera, including *Mosasaurus*.
– ORIGIN mid 19th cent.: from modern Latin *Mosasaurus*, from Latin *Mosa*, 'Meuse' (the river near which it was first discovered) + Greek *sauros* 'lizard'.

mosbolletjie /mɒsˈbɒləki/ ▶ **noun** (pl. **-ies**) S. African a semi-sweet bun eaten fresh or dried.
– ORIGIN Afrikaans, from Dutch *most* 'new wine' (because the yeast is of partially fermented grape juice) + *bolletje* 'little ball'.

moscato /mɒˈskɑːtəʊ/ ▶ **noun** [mass noun] a sweet Italian dessert wine.
– ORIGIN Italian; related to **MUSCAT**.

moschatel /ˌmɒskəˈtɛl/ ▶ **noun** a small plant of north temperate regions, with pale green musk-scented flowers which grow at right angles to each other, forming five sides of a cube.
● *Adoxa moschatellina*, family Adoxaceae.
– ORIGIN mid 18th cent.: from French *moscatelle*, from Italian *moscatella*, from *moscato* 'musk'.

Moscow /ˈmɒskəʊ/ the capital of Russia, situated at the centre of the vast plain of European Russia, on the River Moskva; pop. 9,000,000 (1990). Russian name **MOSKVA**.

> Moscow became the capital when Ivan the Terrible proclaimed himself the first tsar of Russia in the 16th century. Peter the Great moved his capital to St Petersburg in 1712, but after the Bolshevik Revolution of 1917 Moscow was made the capital of the USSR and seat of the new Soviet government, with its centre in the Kremlin.

Mosel /ˈməʊz(ə)l/ (also **Moselle**) a river of western Europe, which rises in the Vosges mountains of NE France and flows 550 km (346 miles) north-east through Luxembourg and Germany to meet the Rhine at Koblenz.

Moseley /ˈməʊzli/, Henry Gwyn Jeffreys (1887–1915), English physicist. He determined the atomic numbers of elements from their X-ray spectra, demonstrated that an element's chemical properties are determined by this number, and showed that there are only ninety-two naturally occurring elements.

Moselle /mə(ʊ)ˈzɛl/ (also **Mosel**) ▶ **noun** [mass noun] a light medium-dry white wine produced in the valley of the River Moselle (see **MOSEL**).

Moses[1] (*fl.* *c*.14th–13th centuries BC), Hebrew prophet and lawgiver, brother of Aaron. According to the biblical account, he was born in Egypt and led the Israelites away from servitude there, across the desert towards the Promised Land. During the journey he was inspired by God on Mount Sinai to write down the Ten Commandments on tablets of stone (Exod. 20).

Moses[2], Grandma (1860–1961), American painter; byname of *Anna Mary Robertson Moses*. She took up painting as a hobby when widowed in 1927, producing more than a thousand paintings in naive style, mostly of American rural life.

Moses[3], Ed (b.1956), American athlete; full name *Edwin Corley Moses*. He won Olympic gold medals for the 400-metres hurdles in 1976 and 1984, and set four successive world records between 1976 and 1983.

Moses basket ▶ **noun** a carrycot or small portable cot made of wickerwork.
– ORIGIN *Moses*, with allusion to the biblical story of Moses, left in a basket among the bulrushes (Exod. 2:3).

mosey informal ▶ **verb** (**-eys**, **-eyed**) [no obj., with adverbial of direction] walk or move in a leisurely manner: *we decided to mosey on up to Montgomery.*
▶ **noun** chiefly Brit. a leisurely walk or drive: *I'll just have a mosey round.*
– ORIGIN early 19th cent.: of unknown origin. The original sense was 'go away quickly'.

MOSFET ▶ **noun** Electronics a field-effect transistor in which there is a thin layer of silicon oxide between the gate and the channel.
– ORIGIN 1960s: acronym from *metal oxide semiconductor field-effect transistor.*

mosh ▶ **verb** [no obj.] dance to rock music in a violent manner involving jumping up and down and deliberately colliding with other dancers.
– ORIGIN 1980s: perhaps from **MASH** or **MUSH**[1].

moshav /ˈməʊʃɑːv, məʊˈʃɑːv/ ▶ **noun** (pl. **moshavim**) a cooperative association of Israeli smallholders.
– ORIGIN from Hebrew *mōšāḇ*, literally 'dwelling'.

moskonfyt /ˈmɒskɒnˌfeɪt/ ▶ **noun** [mass noun] S. African a thick syrup prepared from grapes, used in wine production and as a sweetener in cookery.
– ORIGIN Afrikaans, from *mos* 'must' + *konfyt* 'jam'.

Moskva /məˈskva/ Russian name for **MOSCOW**.

Moslem /ˈmɒzləm/ ▶ **noun** & **adjective** variant spelling of **MUSLIM**.

Mosley /ˈməʊzli/, Sir Oswald (Ernald), 6th Baronet (1896–1980), English Fascist leader. Successively a Conservative, Independent, and Labour MP, he founded the British Union of Fascists, also known as the Blackshirts, in 1932. The party was effectively destroyed by the Public Order Act of 1936. In 1948 Mosley founded the right-wing Union Movement.
– DERIVATIVES **Mosleyite** noun & adjective.

Mosotho /məˈsuːtuː/ singular form of **BASOTHO**.

mosque ▶ **noun** a Muslim place of worship.

Mosques consist of an area reserved for communal prayers, frequently in a domed building with a minaret, and with a niche (mihrab) or other structure indicating the direction of Mecca. There may also be a platform for preaching (minbar), and an adjacent courtyard in which water is provided for the obligatory ablutions before prayer.

– ORIGIN late Middle English: from French *mosquée*, via Italian and Spanish from Egyptian Arabic *masgid*.

Mosquito ▶ **noun** (pl. **-os**) & **adjective** variant spelling of **MISKITO**.

mosquito ▶ **noun** (pl. **-oes**) a slender long-legged fly with aquatic larvae. The bite of the bloodsucking female can transmit a number of serious diseases including malaria and elephantiasis.
• *Culex, Anopheles*, and other genera, family Culicidae.
– ORIGIN late 16th cent.: from Spanish and Portuguese, diminutive of *mosca*, from Latin *musca* 'fly'.

Mosquito Coast a sparsely populated coastal strip of swamp, lagoon, and tropical forest comprising the Caribbean coast of Nicaragua and NE Honduras, occupied by the Miskito people after whom it is named.

mosquito coil ▶ **noun** a spiral made from a dried paste of pyrethrum powder, which when lit burns slowly to produce a mosquito-repellent smoke.

mosquito fish ▶ **noun** another term for **GAMBUSIA**.

mosquito hawk ▶ **noun** chiefly N. Amer. **1** a nighthawk.
2 a dragonfly.

mosquito net ▶ **noun** a fine net hung across a door or window or around a bed to keep mosquitoes away.

Moss, Sir Stirling (b.1929), English motor-racing driver. He won various Grands Prix and other competitions in the 1950s, though the world championship always eluded him.

moss ▶ **noun 1** [mass noun] a small flowerless green plant which lacks true roots, growing in low carpets or rounded cushions in damp habitats and reproducing by means of spores released from stalked capsules: *the trees are overgrown with vines and moss* | [count noun] *the bog is home to rare mosses.*
• Class Musci, division Bryophyta.
■used in names of algae, lichens, and higher plants resembling moss, e.g. **reindeer moss**, **Ceylon moss**, **Spanish moss**.
2 Scottish & N. English a bog, especially a peat bog.
▶ **verb** [usu. as adj. **mossed**] cover with moss.
– DERIVATIVES **moss-like** adjective.
– ORIGIN Old English *mos* 'bog or moss', of Germanic origin; related to Dutch *mos* and German *Moos*.

Mossad /mɒˈsad/ **1** the Supreme Institution for Intelligence and Special Assignments, the principal secret intelligence service of the state of Israel, founded in 1951.
2 the Institution for the Second Immigration, an earlier organization formed in 1938 for the purpose of bringing Jews from Europe to Palestine.
– ORIGIN from Hebrew *mōsāḏ* 'institution'.

moss agate ▶ **noun** [mass noun] agate with moss-like dendritic markings.

moss animal ▶ **noun** a sedentary colonial aquatic animal found chiefly in the sea, either encrusting rocks, seaweeds, or other surfaces, or forming stalked fronds. Each minute zooid filter-feeds by means of a crown of ciliated tentacles (lophophore). Also called ***bryozoan***, ***polyzoan***, ***ectoproct***.
• Phylum Bryozoa (or Polyzoa, Ectoprocta).

mossback ▶ **noun** N. Amer. informal an old-fashioned or extremely conservative person.
– DERIVATIVES **mossbacked** adjective.

Mössbauer effect /ˈmɜːsbaʊə/ ▶ **noun** [mass noun] Chemistry an effect in which certain atomic nuclei bound in a crystal emit gamma rays of sharply defined frequency which can be used as a probe of energy levels in other nuclei.
– ORIGIN 1960s: named after Rudolf L. *Mössbauer* (born 1929), German physicist.

moss campion ▶ **noun** an almost stemless campion with pink flowers, found on mountains and in arctic areas of both Eurasia and North America.
• *Silene acaulis*, family Caryophyllaceae.

moss green ▶ **noun** [mass noun] a bright green colour like that of moss.

moss-grown ▶ **adjective** overgrown with moss.

moss hag ▶ **noun** Scottish an area of broken ground or a hole from which peat has been taken.

Mossi /ˈmɒsi/ ▶ **noun** (pl. same or **Mossis**) a member of a people of Burkina in West Africa. Their language is More.
▶ **adjective** of or relating to this people.
– ORIGIN the name in More.

mossie ▶ **noun** (pl. **-ies**) **1** South African term for **CAPE SPARROW**. [ORIGIN: Afrikaans, from Dutch *mosje* 'little sparrow'.]
2 variant spelling of **MOZZIE**.

moss stitch ▶ **noun** [mass noun] alternate plain and purl stitches in knitting.

mosstrooper ▶ **noun** historical a person who lived by plundering property in the Scottish Borders during the 17th century.

mossy ▶ **adjective** (**mossier**, **mossiest**) covered in or resembling moss: *mossy tree trunks.*
■US informal old-fashioned or extremely conservative.
– DERIVATIVES **mossiness** noun.

mossy cyphel ▶ **noun** another term for **CYPHEL**.

most ▶ **determiner** & **pronoun** greatest in amount or degree: [as determiner] *they've had the most success* | [as pronoun] *they had the most to lose.*
■the majority of; nearly all of: [as determiner] *the two-pin sockets found in most European countries* | [as pronoun] *I spent* ***most of*** *the winter on the coast.*
▶ **adverb 1** to the greatest extent: *the things he most enjoyed* | *what she wanted* ***most of all***.
■forming the superlative of adjectives and adverbs, especially those of more than one syllable: *the most important event of my life* | *sandy plains where fire tends to spread most quickly.*
2 extremely; very: *it was most kind of you* | *that is most probably correct.*
3 N. Amer. informal almost: *most everyone understood.*
– PHRASES **at (the) most** not more than: *the walk took four minutes at the most.* **be the most** informal be the best of all. **for the most part** in most cases; usually: *the older members, for the most part, shun him.* **make the most of** use to the best advantage: *he was eager to make the most of his visit.* ■ represent at its best: *how to make the most of your features.*
– ORIGIN Old English *māst*, of Germanic origin; related to Dutch *meest* and German *meist*.

-most ▶ **suffix** forming superlative adjectives and adverbs from prepositions and other words indicating relative position: *innermost* | *uppermost.*
– ORIGIN Old English *-mest*, assimilated to **MOST**.

Mostar /mɒsˈtɑː/ a largely Muslim city in Bosnia-Herzegovina south-west of Sarajevo, the chief town of Herzegovina; pop. 126,000 (1991). Its chief landmark, an old Turkish bridge across the River Neretva, was destroyed during the siege of the city by Serb forces in 1993.

mostest ▶ **pronoun** humorous most: *the winner is the person who can get there quickest with the mostest.*

most favoured nation ▶ **noun** a country which has been granted the most favourable trading terms available by another country.

Most Honourable ▶ **noun** (in the UK) a title given to marquesses, members of the Privy Council, and holders of the Order of the Bath.

mostly ▶ **adverb** as regards the greater part or number: *this is mostly a grim and honest budget.*
■usually: *I practised mostly all day.*

Most Reverend ▶ **noun** the title of an Anglican archbishop or an Irish Roman Catholic bishop.

most significant bit (abbrev.: **MSB**) ▶ **noun** Computing the bit in a binary number which is of the greatest numerical value.

Mosul /ˈməʊsʊl/ a city in northern Iraq, on the River Tigris, opposite the ruins of Nineveh; pop. 570,900 (est. 1985).

MOT ▶ **noun** (also **MOT test**) (in the UK) a compulsory annual test for safety and exhaust emissions of motor vehicles of more than a specified age.
■(also **MOT certificate**) a document certifying that a vehicle has passed this test.
– ORIGIN abbreviation of *Ministry of Transport*, which introduced the original test.

mot¹ /məʊ, French mo/ ▶ **noun** (pl. pronounced same or /məʊz/) short for **BON MOT**.

mot² /mɒt/ ▶ **noun** Irish informal a girl or young woman, especially a man's girlfriend.
– ORIGIN mid 16th cent.: of unknown origin.

mote ▶ **noun** a tiny piece of a substance: *the tiniest mote of dust.*
– PHRASES **a mote in someone's eye** a fault in a person which is less serious than one in someone else who is being critical. [ORIGIN: with biblical allusion to Matt. 7:3.]
– ORIGIN Old English *mot*, related to Dutch *mot* 'dust, sawdust'.

motel ▶ **noun** a roadside hotel designed primarily for motorists, typically having the rooms arranged in low blocks with parking directly outside.
– ORIGIN 1920s: blend of **MOTOR** and **HOTEL**.

motet /məʊˈtɛt/ ▶ **noun** a short piece of sacred choral music.
– ORIGIN late Middle English: from Old French, diminutive of *mot* 'word'.

moth ▶ **noun** an insect with two pairs of broad wings covered in microscopic scales, typically drably coloured and held flat when at rest. Moths are chiefly nocturnal, and lack the clubbed antennae of butterflies.
• Most superfamilies of the order Lepidoptera. Formerly placed in a grouping known as the Heterocera.
■informal a clothes moth.
– PHRASES **like a moth to the flame** with an irresistible attraction for someone or something: *he drew women to him like moths to the flame.*
– ORIGIN Old English *moththe*, of Germanic origin; related to Dutch *mot* and German *Motte*.

mothball ▶ **noun** (usu. **mothballs**) a small pellet of a pungent substance, typically naphthalene, put in among stored clothes to keep away moths.
▶ **verb** [with obj.] store (clothes) among or in mothballs.
■stop using (a piece of equipment or a building) but keep it in good condition so that it can readily be used again. ■ cancel or postpone work on (a plan or project): *plans to invest in four superstores have been mothballed.*
– PHRASES **in mothballs** unused but kept in good condition for future use.

moth-eaten ▶ **adjective** damaged or destroyed by moths.
■old-fashioned and no longer appropriate or useful.

mother /ˈmʌðə/ ▶ **noun 1** a woman in relation to a child or children to whom she has given birth.
■a person who provides the care and affection normally associated with a female parent: *my adoptive mother.* ■ a female animal in relation to its offspring: [as modifier] *a mother penguin.* ■ archaic (especially as a form of address) an elderly woman. ■ (**Mother**, **Mother Superior**, or **Reverend Mother**) (especially as a title or form of address) the head of a female religious community. ■ [as modifier] denoting an institution or organization from which more recently founded institutions of the same type derive. ■ figurative something that is the origin of or stimulus for something else: *the wish was* ***the mother of*** *the deed.* ■ informal an extreme example or very large specimen of something: *I got stuck in* ***the mother of*** *all traffic jams.*
2 vulgar slang, chiefly N. Amer. short for **MOTHERFUCKER**.
▶ **verb** [with obj.] **1** [often as noun **mothering**] bring up (a child) with care and affection: *the art of mothering.*
■look after kindly and protectively, sometimes excessively so: *she mothered her husband, insisting he should take cod liver oil in the winter.*
2 dated give birth to.
– DERIVATIVES **motherhood** noun, **motherless** adjective, **motherlessness** noun, **mother-like** adjective & adverb.
– ORIGIN Old English *mōdor*, of Germanic origin; related to Dutch *moeder* and German *Mutter*, from an Indo-European root shared by Latin *mater* and Greek *mētēr*.

motherboard ▶ **noun** Computing a printed circuit board containing the principal components of a microcomputer or other device, with connectors for other circuit boards to be slotted into.

m

Mother Carey's chicken ▶ noun old-fashioned term for **STORM PETREL**.
– ORIGIN mid 18th cent.: of unknown origin.

mother country ▶ noun (often **the mother country**) a country in relation to its colonies.

mothercraft ▶ noun [mass noun] archaic skill in or knowledge of looking after children as a mother.

Mother Earth ▶ noun the earth considered as the source of all its living beings and inanimate things.

mother figure ▶ noun an older woman who is regarded as a source of nurture and support.

motherfucker ▶ noun vulgar slang, chiefly N. Amer. a despicable or very unpleasant person or thing.
– DERIVATIVES **motherfucking** adjective.

mother goddess ▶ noun a mother-figure deity, a central figure of many early nature cults where maintenance of fertility was of prime religious importance. Examples of such goddesses include Isis, Astarte, Cybele, and Demeter.

mother hen ▶ noun a hen with chicks.
■ a person who sees to the needs of others, especially in a fussy or interfering way.

mother house ▶ noun the founding house of a religious order.

Mother Hubbard ▶ noun a kind of cloak.
■ chiefly US a long, loose-fitting, shapeless woman's dress or undergarment.
– ORIGIN so named from early illustrations of the nursery rhyme.

Mothering Sunday ▶ noun Brit. the fourth Sunday in Lent, traditionally a day for visiting or giving a present to one's mother.

mother-in-law ▶ noun (pl. **mothers-in-law**) the mother of one's husband or wife.

mother-in-law's tongue ▶ noun a West African plant of the agave family, which has long slender leaves with yellow marginal stripes.
● *Sansevieria trifasciata*, family Agavaceae.

motherland ▶ noun (often **the motherland**) one's native country.

mother liquor ▶ noun [mass noun] Chemistry the liquid remaining after a substance has crystallized out.

mother lode ▶ noun Mining a principal vein of an ore or mineral.
■ figurative a rich source of something: *your portfolio holds a mother lode of opportunities.*

motherly ▶ adjective of, resembling, or characteristic of a mother, especially in being caring, protective, and kind: *she held both her arms wide in a gesture of motherly love.*
– DERIVATIVES **motherliness** noun.
– ORIGIN Old English *mōdorlic* (see **MOTHER**, **-LY**[1]).

mother-naked ▶ adjective [predic.] wearing no clothes at all: *Desmond was lying mother-naked.*

Mother Nature nature personified as a creative and controlling force affecting the world and humans.

Mother of God a name given to the Virgin Mary (as mother of the divine Christ).

mother-of-pearl ▶ noun [mass noun] a smooth shining iridescent substance forming the inner layer of the shell of some molluscs, especially oysters and abalones, used in ornamentation.

mother of thousands ▶ noun any of a number of small-leaved prolific creeping plants, in particular:
● another term for *ivy-leaved toadflax* (see **TOADFLAX**).
● another term for **MIND-YOUR-OWN-BUSINESS**.

mother's boy ▶ noun a boy or man who is excessively influenced by or attached to his mother.

Mother's Day ▶ noun a day of the year on which mothers are particularly honoured by their children. In North America it is the second Sunday in May; in Britain it has become another term for Mothering Sunday.

mother's help ▶ noun a person who helps a mother, mainly by looking after children.

mother ship ▶ noun a large spacecraft or ship from which smaller craft are launched or maintained.

Mother Shipton ▶ noun a day-flying European moth with a marking on the wing that is said to resemble the crone-like profile of a legendary English seer.
● *Callistega mi*, family Noctuidae.

mother's milk ▶ noun [mass noun] the milk of a particular child's own mother.
■ figurative something providing sustenance or regarded by a person as entirely appropriate to them: *the early work of Sturtevant and Morgan was mother's milk to geneticists.* ■ informal alcoholic drink.

mother's ruin ▶ noun Brit. informal term for **GIN**[1].

mother's son ▶ noun informal a man: *every mother's son personally knew his friendly local CIA agent.*

Mother Superior ▶ noun the head of a female religious community.

Mother Teresa see **TERESA, MOTHER**.

mother-to-be ▶ noun (pl. **mothers-to-be**) a woman who is expecting a baby.

mother tongue ▶ noun the language which a person has grown up speaking from early childhood.

mother wit ▶ noun [mass noun] natural ability to cope with everyday matters; common sense.

motherwort ▶ noun a tall strong-smelling European plant of the mint family. It is used in herbal medicine, especially in the treatment of gynaecological disorders.
● *Leonurus cardiaca*, family Labiatae.

mothproof ▶ adjective (of clothes or fabrics) treated with a substance which repels moths.
▶ verb [with obj.] treat with a substance which repels moths.

mothy ▶ adjective (**mothier**, **mothiest**) infested with or damaged by moths: *tattered mothy curtains.*

motif /məʊˈtiːf/ ▶ noun a decorative design or pattern: *the colourful hand-painted motifs which adorn narrowboats.*
■ a distinctive feature or dominant idea in an artistic or literary composition: *the prison motif in Little Dorrit.* ■ Music a leitmotif or figure (see **FIGURE** sense 4). ■ an ornament of lace, braid, etc. sewn separately on a garment. ■ Biochemistry a distinctive sequence on a protein or DNA, having a three-dimensional structure that allows binding interactions to occur.
– ORIGIN mid 19th cent.: from French.

motile /ˈməʊtʌɪl/ ▶ adjective 1 Zoology & Botany (of cells, gametes, and single-celled organisms) capable of motion.
2 Psychology of, relating to, or characterized by responses that involve muscular rather than audiovisual sensations.
– DERIVATIVES **motility** noun.
– ORIGIN mid 19th cent.: from Latin *motus* 'motion', on the pattern of *mobile*.

motion ▶ noun 1 [mass noun] the action or process of moving or being moved: *the laws of planetary motion* | *a cushioned shoe that doesn't restrict motion.*
■ [count noun] a gesture: *she made a motion with her free hand.* ■ [count noun] a piece of moving mechanism: *the earliest engines had the Gresley conjugated motion for the middle cylinder.*
2 a formal proposal put to a legislature or committee: *opposition parties tabled a no confidence motion.*
■ Law an application for a rule or order of court.
3 Brit. an evacuation of the bowels.
■ a portion of excrement: *her mother put on her nappy for her to pass a motion.*
▶ verb [with obj. and adverbial of direction] direct or command (someone) with a movement of the hand or head: *he motions her towards the lift* | [with obj. and infinitive] *he motioned the young officer to sit down.*
– PHRASES **go through the motions** do something perfunctorily, without any enthusiasm or commitment. ■ simulate an action: *a child goes through the motions of washing up.* **in motion** moving: *flowing blonde hair that was constantly in motion.* **set in motion** start something moving or working. ■ start or trigger a process or series of events: *plunging oil prices set in motion an economic collapse.*
– DERIVATIVES **motional** adjective, **motionless** adjective, **motionlessly** adverb.
– ORIGIN late Middle English: via Old French from Latin *motio(n-)*, from *movere* 'to move'.

motion picture ▶ noun chiefly N. Amer. another term for **FILM** (in sense 2): [as modifier] *the motion-picture industry.*

motion sickness ▶ noun [mass noun] nausea caused by motion, especially by travelling in a vehicle.

motivate ▶ verb [with obj.] provide (someone) with a motive for doing something: *he was primarily motivated by the desire for profit.*
■ stimulate (someone's) interest in or enthusiasm for

doing something: *it is the teacher's job to motivate the child at school.* ■ S. African request (something) and present facts and arguments in support of one's request: *he said he would motivate funds to upgrade the food stalls.*
– DERIVATIVES **motivator** noun.

motivation ▶ noun [mass noun] the reason or reasons one has for acting or behaving in a particular way: *the needs or wants that inspire individual motivation* | [count noun] *escape can be a strong motivation for travel.*
■ the general desire or willingness of someone to do something: *keep staff up to date and maintain interest and motivation.* ■ [count noun] S. African a set of facts and arguments used in support of a proposal.
– DERIVATIVES **motivational** adjective, **motivationally** adverb.
– ORIGIN late 19th cent.: from **MOTIVE**, reinforced by **MOTIVATE**.

motivation research ▶ noun [mass noun] the psychological or sociological investigation of motives, especially those influencing the decisions of consumers.

motive ▶ noun 1 a reason for doing something, especially one that is hidden or not obvious: *a motive for his murder.*
2 a motif in art, literature, or music.
▶ adjective [attrib.] 1 producing physical or mechanical motion: *the charge of gas is the motive force for every piston stroke.*
2 causing or being the reason for something: *the motive principle of a writer's work.*
– DERIVATIVES **motiveless** adjective, **motivelessly** adverb, **motivelessness** noun.
– ORIGIN late Middle English: from Old French *motif* (adjective used as a noun), from late Latin *motivus*, from *movere* 'to move'.

motive power ▶ noun [mass noun] the energy (in the form of steam, electricity, etc.) used to drive machinery.
■ the locomotive engines of a railway system collectively.

motivic /məʊˈtiːvɪk/ ▶ adjective Music of or relating to a motif or motifs.

mot juste /məʊ ˈʒuːst, French mo ʒyst/ ▶ noun (pl. **mots justes** pronunc. same) (**the mot juste**) the exact, appropriate word.

motley /ˈmɒtli/ ▶ adjective (**motlier**, **motliest**) incongruously varied in appearance or character; disparate: *a motley crew of discontents and zealots.*
▶ noun 1 [usu. in sing.] an incongruous mixture: *a motley of interacting interest groups.*
2 [mass noun] historical the particoloured costume of a jester: *life-size mannequins in full motley.*
– ORIGIN late Middle English: of unknown origin; perhaps ultimately related to **MOTE**.

motmot /ˈmɒtmɒt/ ▶ noun a tree-dwelling tropical American bird with colourful plumage, typically having two long racket-like tail feathers.
● Family Momotidae: several genera and species, in particular the widespread **blue-crowned motmot** (*Momotus momota*).
– ORIGIN mid 19th cent.: from Latin American Spanish, of imitative origin.

motocross ▶ noun [mass noun] cross-country racing on motorcycles.
– DERIVATIVES **motocrosser** noun.
– ORIGIN late 20th cent.: abbreviation of **MOTOR** + **CROSS**.

motoneuron /ˌməʊtə(ʊ)ˈnjʊərɒn/ ▶ noun another term for **MOTOR NEURON**.

moto perpetuo /ˌməʊtəʊ pəˈpɛtjʊəʊ/ ▶ noun (pl. **moto perpetui**) a piece of fast-moving instrumental music consisting mainly of notes of equal length.
– ORIGIN Italian, literally 'perpetual motion'.

motor ▶ noun a machine, especially one powered by electricity or internal combustion, that supplies motive power for a vehicle or for some other device with moving parts.
■ Brit. informal short for **MOTOR CAR**. ■ a source of power, energy, or motive force: *hormones are the motor of the sexual functions.*
▶ adjective 1 chiefly Brit. driven by a motor.
■ of or relating to motor vehicles: *motor insurance.*
2 giving, imparting, or producing motion or action: *demand is the principle motor force governing economic activity.*
■ Physiology relating to muscular movement or the nerves activating it: *the motor functions of each hand.*
▶ verb [no obj., with adverbial of direction] informal, chiefly Brit.

travel in a motor vehicle, typically a car: *they motored north up the M6.*
■ [with obj. and adverbial of direction] convey (someone) somewhere in a motor vehicle.
– ORIGIN late Middle English (denoting a person who imparts motion): from Latin, literally 'mover', based on *movere* 'to move'. The current sense of the noun dates from the mid 19th cent.

motorable ▶ adjective Brit. dated (of a road) able to be used by motor vehicles.

Motorail ▶ noun a rail service in which cars are transported together with their drivers and passengers.
– ORIGIN 1960s: blend of **MOTOR** and **RAIL**[1].

motor area ▶ noun Anatomy a part of the central nervous system concerned with muscular action, especially the motor cortex.

motorbike ▶ noun another term for **MOTORCYCLE**.

motor boat ▶ noun a boat powered by a motor.

motor bus ▶ noun old-fashioned term for **BUS** (in sense 1).

motorcade /ˈməʊtəkeɪd/ ▶ noun a procession of motor vehicles, typically carrying and escorting a prominent person.
– ORIGIN early 20th cent.: from **MOTOR**, on the pattern of *cavalcade.*

motor car ▶ noun **1** a car.
2 US a self-propelled railway vehicle used to carry railway workers.

motor coach ▶ noun **1** old-fashioned term for **COACH**[1] (in sense 1).
2 a self-propelled railway passenger carriage.

motor cortex ▶ noun Anatomy the part of the cerebral cortex in the brain in which originate the nerve impulses that initiate voluntary muscular activity.

motorcycle ▶ noun a two-wheeled vehicle that is powered by a motor and has no pedals.
– DERIVATIVES **motorcycling** noun, **motorcyclist** noun.

motor drive ▶ noun a battery-driven motor in a camera used to wind the film rapidly between exposures.

motor generator ▶ noun a device consisting of a mechanically coupled electric motor and generator which may be used to control the voltage, frequency, or phase of an electrical supply.

motorhome ▶ noun chiefly N. Amer. a motor caravan.

motorist ▶ noun the driver of a motor car.

motorize (also **-ise**) ▶ verb [with obj.] [usu. as adj. **motorized**] equip (a vehicle or device) with a motor to operate or propel it: *a motorized wheelchair.*
■ equip (troops) with motor transport: *three motorized divisions.*
– DERIVATIVES **motorization** noun.

motor lodge (also **motor hotel**) ▶ noun a motel.

motorman ▶ noun (pl. **-men**) the driver of a train or tram.

motormouth ▶ noun informal a person who talks very quickly and incessantly.
– DERIVATIVES **motormouthed** adjective.

motor nerve ▶ noun a nerve carrying impulses from the brain or spinal cord to a muscle or gland.

motor neuron ▶ noun a nerve cell forming part of a pathway along which impulses pass from the brain or spinal cord to a muscle or gland.

motor neuron disease ▶ noun [mass noun] a progressive disease involving degeneration of the motor neurons and wasting of the muscles.

motor racing ▶ noun [mass noun] the sport of racing motor vehicles, especially cars.

motorsailer ▶ noun a boat equipped with both sails and an engine.

motor scooter ▶ noun see **SCOOTER**.

motor sport ▶ noun another term for **MOTOR RACING**.

motor vehicle ▶ noun a road vehicle powered by an internal-combustion engine.

motorway ▶ noun Brit. a dual-carriageway road designed for fast traffic, with relatively few places for joining or leaving.
■ informal a wide, fast, easy ski run.

motor wind /wʌɪnd/ ▶ noun a camera winding mechanism driven by a motor.

motor yacht ▶ noun a motor-driven boat equipped for cruising.

Motown /ˈməʊtaʊn/ ▶ noun **1** (also trademark **Tamla Motown**) [mass noun] music released on or reminiscent of the US record label Tamla Motown. The first black-owned record company in the US, Tamla Motown was founded in Detroit in 1959 by Berry Gordy, and was important in popularizing soul music, producing artists such as the Supremes, Stevie Wonder, and Marvin Gaye.
2 informal name for **DETROIT**.
– ORIGIN mid 20th cent.: shortening of *Motor Town*, by association with the car manufacturing industry of Detroit.

motser /ˈmɒtsə/ (also **motza**) ▶ noun Austral. informal a large sum of money, especially as won in gambling.
– ORIGIN 1930s: probably from Yiddish *matse* 'bread'.

motte /mɒt/ ▶ noun historical a mound forming the site of a castle or camp.
– ORIGIN late 19th cent.: from French, 'mound', from Old French *mote* (see **MOAT**).

motte-and-bailey ▶ adjective denoting a castle consisting of a fort on a motte surrounded by a bailey.

mottle ▶ verb [with obj.] mark with spots or smears of colour: *the cow's coat was light red mottled with white* | [as adj. **mottled**] *a bird with mottled brown plumage.*
▶ noun an irregular arrangement of spots or patches of colour: *the ship was a mottle of khaki and black.*
■ a spot or patch forming part of such an arrangement: *a pale gray with lighter grey mottles.*
– ORIGIN late 18th cent.: probably a back-formation from **MOTLEY**.

motto ▶ noun (pl. **-oes** or **-os**) a short sentence or phrase chosen as encapsulating the beliefs or ideals guiding an individual, family, or institution: *the family motto is 'Faithful though Unfortunate'.*
■ Music a phrase which recurs throughout a musical work and has some symbolical significance.
– ORIGIN late 16th cent.: from Italian, 'word'.

Motu /ˈməʊtuː/ ▶ noun (pl. same) **1** a member of a Melanesian people of Papua New Guinea inhabiting the area around Port Moresby.
2 [mass noun] the language of this people, the base of a pidgin known as **Hiri Motu** or (formerly) **Police Motu**, widely used as a lingua franca for administrative purposes.
▶ adjective of or relating to this people or their language.
– ORIGIN the name in Melanesian.

motu proprio /ˌməʊtuː ˈprəʊprɪəʊ/ ▶ noun (pl. **-os**) an edict issued by the Pope personally to the Roman Catholic Church or to a part of it.
– ORIGIN Latin, literally 'of one's own volition'.

motza ▶ noun variant spelling of **MOTSER**.

moue /muː/ ▶ noun a pouting expression used to convey annoyance or distaste.
– ORIGIN mid 19th cent.: French, earlier having the sense 'lip'.

mouflon /ˈmuːflɒn/ (also **moufflon**) ▶ noun a small wild sheep with chestnut-brown wool, found in mountainous country from Iran to Asia Minor. It is the ancestor of the domestic sheep.
● *Ovis orientalis*, family Bovidae.
– ORIGIN late 18th cent.: from French, from Italian *muflone.*

mouillé /ˈmuːjeɪ/ ▶ adjective Phonetics (of a consonant) palatalized.
– ORIGIN French, 'wetted'.

mould[1] (US **mold**) ▶ noun a hollow container used to give shape to molten or hot liquid material (such as wax or metal) when it cools and hardens.
■ something made in this way, especially a pudding or savoury mousse: *lobster mould with a sauce of carrots and port.* ■ [in sing.] figurative a distinctive and typical style, form, or character: *he's a superb striker in the same mould as Gary Lineker.* ■ a frame or template for producing mouldings. ■ archaic the form or shape of something, especially the features or physique of a person or the build of an animal.
▶ verb [with obj.] form (an object with a particular shape) out of easily manipulated material: *mould the figure from white fondant.*
■ give a shape to (a malleable substance): *take the marzipan and mould it into a cone shape.* ■ influence the formation or development of: *the professionals who were helping to mould US policy.* ■ shape (clothing) to fit a particular part of the body: [as adj. **moulded**] *a shoe with moulded insole.* ■ [often as adj. **moulded**] shape (a column, ceiling, or other part of a building) to a

particular design, especially a decorative moulding: *a corridor with a moulded cornice.*
– PHRASES **break the mould** put an end to a restrictive pattern of events or behaviour by doing things in a markedly different way: *his work did much to break the mould of the old urban sociology.*
– DERIVATIVES **mouldable** adjective, **moulder** noun.
– ORIGIN Middle English: apparently from Old French *modle*, from Latin *modulus* (see **MODULUS**).

mould[2] (US **mold**) ▶ noun [mass noun] a furry growth of minute fungal hyphae occurring typically in moist warm conditions, especially on food or other organic matter.
● The fungi belong to the subdivision Deuteromycotina (or Ascomycotina).
– ORIGIN late Middle English: probably from obsolete *mould*, past participle of *moul* 'grow mouldy', of Scandinavian origin; compare with Old Norse *mygla* 'grow mouldy'.

mould[3] (US **mold**) ▶ noun [mass noun] chiefly Brit. soft loose earth. See also **LEAF MOULD**.
■ the upper soil of cultivated land, especially when rich in organic matter.
– ORIGIN Old English *molde*, from a Germanic base meaning 'pulverize or grind'; related to **MEAL**[2].

mould-board ▶ noun a board in a plough that turns the earth over.

moulder (US **molder**) ▶ verb [no obj.] [often as adj. **mouldering**] slowly decay or disintegrate, especially because of neglect: *there was a mushroomy smell of disuse and mouldering books* | figurative *I couldn't permit someone of your abilities to moulder away in a backwater.*
– ORIGIN mid 16th cent.: perhaps from **MOULD**[3], but compare with Norwegian dialect *muldra* 'crumble'.

moulding (US **molding**) ▶ noun an ornamentally shaped outline as an architectural feature, especially in a cornice.
■ [mass noun] material such as wood, plastic, or stone shaped for use as a decorative or architectural feature.

mouldwarp /ˈməʊldwɔːp/ (also **mouldiwarp**) ▶ noun archaic or dialect another term for **MOLE**[1] (in sense 1).
– ORIGIN Middle English: probably from Middle Low German *moldewerp*, from the Germanic bases of **MOULD**[3] and **WARP**; compare with Dutch *muldvarp.*

mouldy (US **moldy**) ▶ adjective (**mouldier**, **mouldiest**) covered with a fungal growth which causes decay, due to age or damp conditions: *mouldy bread.*
■ tediously old-fashioned: *mouldy conventions.* ■ informal, chiefly Brit. dull or depressing: *evenings filled with mouldy old shows.*
– DERIVATIVES **mouldiness** noun.

moules marinière /ˌmuːl marɪnˈjɛː/ (also **moules à la marinière**) ▶ plural noun mussels served in their shells and cooked in a wine and onion sauce.
– ORIGIN French, literally 'mussels in the marine style'.

Mouli /ˈmuːli/ ▶ noun trademark a type of kitchen utensil for grinding or puréeing food.
– ORIGIN 1930s: abbreviation of **MOULINETTE**.

moulin /ˈmuːlɪn/ ▶ noun a vertical or nearly vertical shaft in a glacier, formed by surface water percolating through a crack in the ice.
– ORIGIN mid 19th cent.: French, literally 'mill'.

Moulin Rouge /ˌmuːlã ˈruːʒ, French mulɛ̃ ʀuʒ/ a cabaret in Montmartre, Paris, a favourite resort of poets and artists around the end of the 19th century. Toulouse-Lautrec immortalized its dancers in his posters.
– ORIGIN French, literally 'red windmill'.

Moulmein /maʊlˈmeɪn/ a port in SE Burma (Myanmar); pop. 220,000 (1983).

moult (US **molt**) ▶ verb [no obj.] (of an animal) shed old feathers, hair, or skin, or an old shell, to make way for a new growth: *the adult birds were already moulting into their winter shades of grey* | [with obj.] *the snake moults its skin.*
■ (of hair or feathers) fall out to make way for new growth: *the last of his juvenile plumage had moulted.*
▶ noun a loss of plumage, skin, or hair, especially as a regular feature of an animal's life cycle.
– ORIGIN Middle English *moute*, from an Old English verb based on Latin *mutare* 'to change'. For the intrusive *-l-*, compare with words such as *fault.*

moulvi /ˈmuːlvi/ (also **maulvi**) ▶ noun (pl. **moulvis**)

(especially in the Indian subcontinent) a Muslim doctor of the law.
– ORIGIN from Urdu *maulvī*, from Arabic *mawlawī* 'judicial' (adjective used as a noun), from *mawlā* 'mullah'.

mound¹ ▶ **noun** a rounded mass projecting above a surface.
▪a raised mass of earth, stones, or other compacted material, sometimes created artificially for purposes of defence or burial. ▪a small hill. ▪(**a mound of/mounds of**) a large pile or quantity of something: *a mound of dirty crockery.* ▪Baseball a slight elevation from which the pitcher delivers the ball.
▶ **verb** [with obj.] heap up into a rounded pile: *try to mound up the cream quite high.*
▪archaic enclose, bound, or fortify with an embankment.
– PHRASES **take the mound** Baseball (of a pitcher) have a turn at pitching.
– ORIGIN early 16th cent. (as a verb in the sense 'enclose with a fence or hedge'): of obscure origin. An early sense of the noun was 'boundary hedge or fence'.

mound² ▶ **noun** archaic a ball representing the earth, used as part of royal regalia, e.g. on top of a crown, typically of gold and surmounted by a cross.
– ORIGIN Middle English (denoting the world): from Old French *monde*, from Latin *mundus* 'world'.

mound-builder ▶ **noun** another term for **MEGAPODE**.

mount¹ ▶ **verb** [with obj.] **1** climb up (stairs, a hill, or other rising surface): *he mounted the stairs.*
▪climb or move up on to (a raised surface): *the master of ceremonies mounted the platform.* ▪get up on (an animal or bicycle) in order to ride it. ▪(often **be mounted**) set (someone) on horseback; provide with a horse: *she was mounted on a white horse.* ▪(of a male mammal or bird) get on (a female) for the purpose of copulation. ▪[no obj.] (of the blood or its colour) rise into the cheeks: *feeling the blush mount in her cheeks, she looked down quickly.*
2 organize and initiate (a campaign or other significant course of action): *the company had successfully mounted takeover bids.*
▪establish; set up: *security forces mounted check points at every key road.* ▪produce (a play, exhibition, or other artistic event); present for public view or display.
3 [no obj.] grow larger or more numerous: *the costs **mount up** when you buy a home.*
▪(of a feeling) become stronger or more intense: *his anxiety mounted as messages were left unanswered.*
4 [with obj. and adverbial of place] place or fix (an object) on an elevated support: *fluorescent lights are **mounted on** the ceiling.*
▪fix (an object) in position: *the engine is mounted behind the rear seats.* ▪[with obj.] place (a gun) on a fixed mounting. ▪[with obj.] set in or attach to a backing or setting: *the photographs will be mounted and framed.* ▪[with obj.] fix (an object for viewing) on a microscope slide. ▪[with obj.] Computing make (a disk or disk drive) available for use.
▶ **noun 1** a backing or setting on which a photograph, gem, or work of art is set for display.
▪a glass microscope slide for securing a specimen to be viewed. ▪a stamp hinge.
2 a support for a gun, camera, or similar piece of equipment.
3 a horse being ridden or that is available for riding: *he hung on to his mount's bridle.*
▪an opportunity to ride a horse, especially as a jockey: *the jockey's injuries forced him to give up the coveted mount on Cool Ground.*
– PHRASES **mount guard** keep watch, especially for protection or to prevent escape.
– DERIVATIVES **mountable** adjective, **mounter** noun.
– ORIGIN Middle English: from Old French *munter*, based on Latin *mons, mont-* 'mountain'.

mount² ▶ **noun** a mountain or hill (archaic except in place names): *Mount Everest.*
▪any of several fleshy prominences on the palm of the hand regarded in palmistry as signifying the degree of influence of a particular planet: *mount of Mars.*
– ORIGIN Old English *munt*, from Latin *mons, mont-* 'mountain', reinforced in Middle English by Old French *mont*.

mountain ▶ **noun** a large natural elevation of the earth's surface rising abruptly from the surrounding level; a large steep hill.
▪(**mountains**) a region where there are many such features, characterized by remoteness and inaccessibility: *they sought refuge in the mountains.* ▪(**a mountain/mountains of**) a large pile or quantity of something: *a mountain of paperwork.* ▪[usu. with modifier] a large surplus stock of a commodity: *huge food mountains.*
– PHRASES **if the mountain won't come to Muhammad, Muhammad must go to the mountain** proverb if someone won't do as you wish or a situation can't be arranged to suit you, you must accept it and change your plans accordingly. [ORIGIN: with allusion to a well-known story about Muhammad told by Bacon (*Essays* xii).] **make a mountain out of a molehill** see **MOLEHILL**. **move mountains 1** achieve spectacular and apparently impossible results: *faith can move mountains.* **2** make every possible effort: *his fans move mountains to catch as many of his performances as possible.*
– DERIVATIVES **mountainy** adjective.
– ORIGIN Middle English: from Old French *montaigne*, based on Latin *mons, mont-* 'mountain'.

mountain ash ▶ **noun 1** a small deciduous tree of the rose family, with compound leaves, white flowers, and red berries. Compare with **ROWAN**.
• Genus *Sorbus*, family Rosaceae: several species, in particular the North American *S. americana*.
2 Austral. a eucalyptus tree that is widely used for timber.
• Genus *Eucalyptus*, family Myrtaceae: several species, in particular the very tall *E. regnans*.

mountain avens ▶ **noun** a creeping arctic-alpine plant with white flowers and glossy leaves. See also **DRYAS**.
• *Dryas octopetala*, family Rosaceae.

mountain beaver ▶ **noun** a burrowing forest-dwelling rodent occurring only on the west coast of North America. Also called **SEWELLEL**.
• *Aplodontia rufa*, the only member of the family Aplodontidae.

mountain bike ▶ **noun** a bicycle with a light sturdy frame, broad deep-treaded tyres, and multiple gears, originally designed for riding on mountainous terrain.
– DERIVATIVES **mountain biker** noun, **mountain biking** noun.

mountain chain ▶ **noun** a connected series of mountains.

mountain devil ▶ **noun** another term for **MOLOCH**.

mountain dew ▶ **noun** [mass noun] informal illicitly distilled liquor, especially whisky or rum.

mountaineer ▶ **noun** a person who takes part in mountaineering.
▪rare a person living in a mountainous area.

mountaineering ▶ **noun** [mass noun] the sport or activity of climbing mountains.

mountain everlasting ▶ **noun** another term for **CAT'S FOOT**.

mountain gem ▶ **noun** a green hummingbird found in the upland forests of Central America.
• Genus *Lampornis*, family Trochilidae: several species.

mountain goat ▶ **noun 1** (also **Rocky Mountain goat**) a goat-antelope with shaggy white hair and backward curving horns, living in the Rocky Mountains of North America.
• *Oreamnos americanus*, family Bovidae.
2 any goat that lives on mountains, proverbial for agility.

mountain hare ▶ **noun** a hare whose coat turns white in winter, found in upland and arctic areas of northern Eurasia. It is the only hare in Ireland. Also called **BLUE HARE**.
• *Lepus timidus*, family Leporidae.

mountain laurel ▶ **noun** a North American kalmia which bears clusters of bright pink flowers.
• *Kalmia latifolia*, family Ericaceae.

mountain lion ▶ **noun** North American term for **PUMA**.

mountainous ▶ **adjective** (of a region) having many mountains.
▪huge: *struggling under mountainous debts.*

mountain range ▶ **noun** a line of mountains connected by high ground.

mountain sheep ▶ **noun** see **BIGHORN**, **WELSH MOUNTAIN SHEEP**.

mountain sickness ▶ **noun** another term for **ALTITUDE SICKNESS**.

mountainside ▶ **noun** the sloping surface of a mountain.

Mountain State informal name for **WEST VIRGINIA**.

Mountain time the standard time in a zone including parts of Canada and the US in or near the Rocky Mountains, specifically:
• (**Mountain Standard Time** abbrev.: **MST**) standard time based on the mean solar time at the meridian 105° W., seven hours behind GMT. • (**Mountain Daylight Time** abbrev.: **MDT**) Mountain time during daylight saving, eight hours behind GMT.

mountant /ˈmaʊnt(ə)nt/ ▶ **noun** a substance used to mount photographs, microscope specimens, etc.
– ORIGIN late 19th cent.: from **MOUNT**¹, on the pattern of French *montant* 'mounting'.

Mount Ararat, Mount Carmel, etc. see **ARARAT, MOUNT**; **CARMEL, MOUNT**, etc.

Mountbatten /maʊntˈbat(ə)n/, Louis (Francis Albert Victor Nicholas), 1st Earl Mountbatten of Burma (1900–79), British admiral and administrator. He was supreme Allied commander in SE Asia (1943–5) and the last viceroy (1947) and first Governor General of India (1947–8). He was killed by an IRA bomb while on his yacht.

mountebank /ˈmaʊntɪbaŋk/ ▶ **noun** a person who deceives others, especially in order to trick them out of their money; a charlatan.
▪historical a person who sold patent medicines in public places.
– DERIVATIVES **mountebankery** noun.
– ORIGIN late 16th cent.: from Italian *montambanco*, from the imperative phrase *monta in banco!* 'climb on the bench!' (with allusion to the raised platform used to attract an audience).

mounted ▶ **adjective** [attrib.] riding an animal, typically a horse, especially for military or other duty: *mounted police controlled the crowd.*

Mountie ▶ **noun** informal a member of the Royal Canadian Mounted Police.

mounting ▶ **noun 1** a backing, setting, or support for something: *he pulled the curtain rail from its mounting.*
2 [mass noun] the action of mounting something: *the mounting of rapid-fire guns.*

mounting block ▶ **noun** a block of stone or low wooden steps from which a rider mounts a horse.

Mount Isa /ˈʌɪzə/ a lead and silver-mining town in NE Australia, in western Queensland; pop. 24,200 (est. 1987).

Mount of Olives the highest point in the range of hills to the east of Jerusalem. It is a holy place for both Judaism and Christianity and is frequently mentioned in the Bible. The Garden of Gethsemane is located nearby.

Mount Vernon /ˈvəːnən/ a property in NE Virginia, about 24 km (15 miles) from Washington DC, on a site overlooking the Potomac River. Built in 1743, it was the home of George Washington from 1747 until his death in 1799.

mourn ▶ **verb** [with obj.] feel or show deep sorrow or regret for (someone or their death), typically by following conventions such as the wearing of black clothes: *Isobel mourned her husband* | [no obj.] *she had to **mourn for** her friends who died in the accident.*
▪feel regret or sadness about (the loss or disappearance of something): *publishers mourned declining sales of hardback fiction.*
– ORIGIN Old English *murnan*, of Germanic origin.

Mourne Mountains /mɔːn/ a range of hills in SE Northern Ireland, in County Down.

mourner ▶ **noun 1** a person who attends a funeral as a relative or friend of the dead person.
▪chiefly historical a person hired to attend a funeral.
2 any of a number of drab coloured South American tyrant flycatchers and related birds.
• Families Tyrannidae, Pipridae, and Cotingidae: four genera and several species; the classification is uncertain.

mournful ▶ **adjective** feeling, expressing, or inducing sadness, regret, or grief: *her large, mournful eyes.*
– DERIVATIVES **mournfully** adverb, **mournfulness** noun.

mourning ▶ **noun** [mass noun] the expression of deep sorrow for someone who has died, typically involving following certain conventions such as wearing black clothes: *she's still **in mourning** after the death of her husband.*
▪black clothes worn as an expression of grief when someone dies.

mourning band ▶ **noun** a strip of black crape or other material that is worn round a person's sleeve or hat as a mark of respect for someone who has recently died.

b **b**ut | d **d**og | f **f**ew | g **g**et | h **h**e | j **y**es | k **c**at | l **l**eg | m **m**an | n **n**o | p **p**en | r **r**ed | s **s**it | t **t**op | v **v**oice | w **w**e | z **z**oo | ʃ **sh**e | ʒ deci**s**ion | θ **th**in | ð **th**is | ŋ ri**ng** | x lo**ch** | tʃ **ch**ip | dʒ **j**ar

mourning cloak ▶ noun North American term for **CAMBERWELL BEAUTY**.

mourning dove ▶ noun a North and Central American dove with a long tail, a grey-brown back, and a plaintive call.
• *Zenaida macroura*, family Columbidae.

mourning ring ▶ noun historical a ring worn to remind the wearer of someone who has died.

Mousalla variant spelling of **MUSALA, MOUNT**.

mouse ▶ noun (pl. **mice**) **1** a small rodent that typically has a pointed snout, relatively large ears and eyes, and a long tail.
• Family Muridae: many genera and numerous species. Also, some species in the families Heteromyidae, Zapodidae, and Muscardinidae.
■(in general use) any similar small mammal, such as a shrew or vole. ■ a shy, timid, and quiet person.
2 (pl. also **mouses**) Computing a small hand-held device which is dragged across a flat surface to move the cursor on a computer screen, typically having buttons which are pressed to control computer functions.
3 informal a lump or bruise, especially one on or near the eye.
▶verb /also maʊz/ [no obj.] **1** (of a cat or an owl) hunt for or catch mice.
■[with adverbial] prowl about as if searching: *he was mousing among the books of the old library.*
2 [with adverbial of direction] Computing, informal use a mouse to move a cursor on a computer screen: *mouse your way over to the window and click on it.*
– DERIVATIVES **mouse-like** adjective.
– ORIGIN Old English *mūs*, (plural) *mȳs*, of Germanic origin; related to Dutch *muis* and German *Maus*, from an Indo-European root shared by Latin and Greek *mus*.

mousebird ▶ noun a small gregarious African bird with mainly drab plumage, a crest, and a long tail.
• Genera *Colius* and *Urocolius*, family Coliidae: six species.

mouse-coloured ▶ adjective (of hair) dull light brown.

mouse deer ▶ noun another term for **CHEVROTAIN**.

mouse-ear (also **mouse-ear chickweed**) ▶ noun a small white-flowered creeping chickweed with softly hairy leaves which supposedly resemble the ears of mice.
• Genus *Cerastium*, family Caryophyllaceae.

mouse-eared bat ▶ noun a myotis bat that has mouse-like ears and mainly brownish fur.
• Genus *Myotis*, family Vespertilionidae: several species, in particular the large *M. myotis*, found from SW Europe to Asia Minor.

mouse hare ▶ noun another term for **PIKA**.

mouse lemur ▶ noun a small nocturnal Madagascan lemur with large ears, close-set eyes, and a long tail.
• Genus *Microcebus*, family Cheirogaleidae: three species. See also **DWARF LEMUR**.

mouse mat ▶ noun see **MAT**[1] (sense 2).

mouse opossum ▶ noun a mouse-like opossum with large ears and no marsupial pouch, native to Central and South America.
• Genus *Marmosa*, family Didelphidae: several species.

mouse potato ▶ noun informal a person who spends large amounts of leisure or working time operating a computer.
– ORIGIN 1990s: on the pattern of *couch potato*.

mouser ▶ noun an animal that catches mice, especially a cat.

mouse-tailed bat ▶ noun an insectivorous bat with a long mouse-like tail, native to Africa and Asia and often found in man-made structures.
• Family Rhinopomatidae and genus *Rhinopoma*: three species.

mousetrap ▶ noun a trap for catching and usually killing mice, especially one with a spring bar which snaps down on to the mouse when it touches a piece of cheese or other bait attached to the mechanism.
■(also **mousetrap cheese**) [mass noun] Brit. informal cheese of poor quality.
▶verb [with obj.] N. Amer. informal induce (someone) to do something by means of a trick: *the editor mousetrapped her into giving him an article.*

mousey ▶ adjective variant spelling of **MOUSY**.

moussaka /muːˈsɑːkə, ˌmuːsəˈkɑː/ ▶ noun [mass noun] a Greek dish made of minced lamb, aubergines, and tomatoes, with cheese sauce on top.
– ORIGIN from Turkish *musakka*, based on Arabic.

mousse ▶ noun a sweet or savoury dish made as a smooth light mass with whipped cream and beaten egg white, flavoured with chocolate, fish, etc., and typically served chilled: *avoid mousses and gateaux* | [mass noun] *sponge topped with chocolate mousse.*
■[mass noun] a soft, light, or aerated gel such as a soap preparation: *fragrant shower mousse.* ■ [mass noun] a frothy preparation that is applied to the hair, enabling it to be styled more easily. ■ (also **chocolate mousse**) [mass noun] a brown frothy emulsion of oil and seawater formed by weathering of an oil slick.
▶verb [with obj.] style (hair) using mousse.
– ORIGIN mid 19th cent.: from French, 'moss or froth'.

mousseline /ˈmuːsliːn/ ▶ noun **1** [mass noun] a very fine, semi-opaque fabric similar to muslin, typically made of silk, wool, or cotton.
2 a soft, light sweet or savoury mousse.
3 (also **sauce mousseline**) [mass noun] hollandaise sauce that has been made frothy with whipped cream or egg white, served mainly with fish or asparagus.
– ORIGIN late 17th cent.: from French (see **MUSLIN**).

mousseron /ˈmuːsərɒn/ ▶ noun an edible mushroom with a flattish white cap, pink gills, and a mealy smell.
• *Clitopilus prunulus*, family Agaricaceae, class Hymenomycetes.

mousseux /muːˈsəː, French musø/ ▶ adjective (of wine) sparkling: *vin mousseux.*
▶ noun (pl. same) [mass noun] sparkling wine.
– ORIGIN from French, from *mousse* 'froth'.

Moussorgsky variant spelling of **MUSSORGSKY**.

moustache (US also **mustache**) ▶ noun a strip of hair left to grow above the upper lip.
■(**moustaches**) a long moustache.
■a similar growth, or a marking that resembles it, round the mouth of some animals.
– DERIVATIVES **moustached** adjective.
– ORIGIN late 16th cent.: from French, from Italian *mostaccio*, from Greek *mustax, mustak-*.

moustache cup ▶ noun a cup with a partial cover that protects the moustache of the person drinking from it.

Mousterian /muːˈstɪərɪən/ ▶ adjective Archaeology of, relating to, or denoting the main culture of the Middle Palaeolithic period in Europe, between the Acheulian and Aurignacian periods (chiefly 80,000–35,000 years ago). It is associated with Neanderthal peoples and is typified by flints worked on one side only. See also **LEVALLOIS**.
■[as noun **the Mousterian**] the Mousterian culture or period.
– ORIGIN late 19th cent.: from French *moustiérien*, from *Le Moustier*, a cave in SW France where objects from this culture were found.

mousy (also **mousey**) ▶ adjective (**mousier**, **mousiest**) of or like a mouse.
■(of hair) of a dull light brown colour. ■ (of a person) nervous, shy, or timid; lacking in presence or charisma: *he had a small mousy wife.*
– DERIVATIVES **mousiness** noun.

Moutan /ˈmuːt(ə)n/ (also **Moutan peony**) ▶ noun a tall shrubby peony with pink or white blotched flowers, native to China and Tibet and the parent of many garden varieties.
• *Paeonia suffruticosa*, family Paeoniaceae.
– ORIGIN early 19th cent.: from Chinese *mudan*.

mouth ▶ noun (pl. **mouths**) **1** the opening in the lower part of the human face, surrounded by the lips, through which food is taken in and from which speech and other sounds are emitted.
■the cavity behind this, containing the teeth and tongue. ■ the corresponding opening through which an animal takes in food (at the front of the head in vertebrates and many other creatures), or the cavity behind this. ■ [usu. with adj.] a horse's readiness to feel and obey the pressure of the bit in its mouth: *the horse had a **hard mouth**.* ■ the character or quality of a wine as judged by its feel or flavour in the mouth (rather than its aroma). ■ [mass noun] informal talkativeness; impudence: *you've got more mouth on you than any woman I've ever known.*
2 an opening or entrance to a structure that is hollow, concave, or almost completely enclosed: *standing before the mouth of a cave.*
■the opening for filling or emptying something used as a container: *the mouth of the bottle.* ■ the muzzle of a gun. ■ the opening or entrance to a harbour or bay: *walking to the mouth of the bay to absorb the view.* ■ the place where a river enters the sea.
▶verb [with obj.] **1** say (something dull or unoriginal), especially in a pompous or affected way: *this clergyman mouths platitudes in breathy, soothing tones.*
■utter very clearly and distinctly: *she would carefully mouth the right pronunciation.* ■ move the lips as if saying (something) or in a grimace: *she mouthed a silent farewell* | [with direct speech] *'Come on,' he mouthed.*
2 take in or touch with the mouth: *puppies may mouth each other's collars during play.*
■train the mouth of (a horse) so that it responds to a bit.
– PHRASES **a mouth to feed** a person, typically a child, who has to be looked after and fed. **be all mouth (and no trousers)** informal tend to talk boastfully without any intention of acting on one's words. **give mouth** (of a dog) bark; bay. **keep one's mouth shut** informal not say anything, especially not reveal a secret: *would he keep his mouth shut under interrogation?* **open one's mouth** informal say something: *sorry, I'll never open my mouth about you again.* **watch one's mouth** informal be careful about what one says.
– DERIVATIVES **mouthed** adjective [in combination] *wide-mouthed*, **mouther** /ˈmaʊðə/ noun, **mouthless** adjective.
– ORIGIN Old English *mūth*, of Germanic origin; related to Dutch *mond* and German *Mund*, from an Indo-European root shared by Latin *mentum* 'chin'.
▶**mouth off** informal talk in an unpleasantly loud and boastful or opinionated way: *he was mouthing off about society in general.* ■ (**mouth off at**) loudly criticize or abuse.

mouthbrooder ▶ noun a freshwater cichlid fish which protects its eggs (and in some cases its young) by carrying them in its mouth.
• *Sarotherodon* and other genera, family Cichlidae.

mouthful ▶ noun (pl. **-fuls**) **1** a quantity of food or drink that fills or can be put in the mouth: *he took **a mouthful of** beer.*
2 a long or complicated word or phrase that is difficult to say: *poliomyelitis is **a bit of a mouthful**.*
– PHRASES **give someone a mouthful** Brit. informal talk to or shout at someone in an angry, abusive, or severely critical way. **say a mouthful** N. Amer. informal say something noteworthy.

mouth organ ▶ noun another term for **HARMONICA**.

mouthpart ▶ noun (usu. **mouthparts**) Zoology any of the appendages, typically found in pairs, surrounding the mouth of an insect or other arthropod and adapted for feeding.

mouthpiece ▶ noun **1** a thing designed to be put in or against the mouth: *the snorkel's mouthpiece.*
■a part of a musical instrument placed between or against the lips. ■ the part of a telephone for speaking into. ■ the part of a tobacco pipe placed between the lips. ■ a gumshield.
2 chiefly derogatory a person or organization who speaks on behalf of another person or organization: *the media acts as a mouthpiece for the Party.*
■informal, chiefly N. Amer. a lawyer.

mouth-to-mouth ▶ adjective denoting a method of artificial respiration in which a person breathes into an unconscious patient's lungs through their mouth: *mouth-to-mouth resuscitation.*
▶ noun [mass noun] respiration of this kind.

mouthwash ▶ noun [mass noun] a liquid used for rinsing the mouth or gargling with. It may contain antiseptic.

mouth-watering ▶ adjective smelling, looking, or sounding delicious: *a mouth-watering mixture of French and English cuisine.*
■highly attractive or tempting: *mouth-watering views of the mountains.*

mouthy ▶ adjective (**mouthier**, **mouthiest**) informal inclined to talk a lot, especially in a cheeky way.

mouton /ˈmuːtɒn/ ▶ noun [mass noun] sheepskin cut and dyed to resemble beaver fur or sealskin.
– ORIGIN mid 20th cent.: from French, literally 'sheep'.

movable (also **moveable**) ▶ adjective **1** capable of being moved: *they stripped the town of all movable objects and fled.*
■(of a feast or festival) variable in date from year to year. See also **MOVABLE FEAST**.
2 Law (of property) of the nature of a chattel, as

distinct from land or buildings. Compare with **HERITABLE**.

▶**noun** (usu. **movables**) property or possessions not including land or buildings.
■ an article of furniture that may be removed from a house, as distinct from a fixture.

– DERIVATIVES **movability** noun, **movably** adverb.

– ORIGIN late Middle English: from Old French, from *moveir* 'to move'.

movable-doh ▶ **adjective** [attrib.] denoting a system of solmization (such as tonic sol-fa) in which doh is the keynote of any major scale. Compare with **FIXED-DOH**.

movable feast ▶ **noun** a religious feast day that does not occur on the same calendar date each year. The term refers most often to Easter Day and other Christian holy days whose dates are related to it.

movant /ˈmuːv(ə)nt/ ▶ **noun** US Law a person who applies to or petitions a court or judge for a ruling in his or her favour.

– ORIGIN late 19th cent.: from **MOVE** + **-ANT**.

move ▶ **verb 1** [no obj., usu. with adverbial of direction] go in a specified direction or manner; change position: *she stood up and moved to the door | he let his eyes move across the rows of faces.*
■ [with obj. and often with adverbial of direction] change the place or position of: *she moved the tray to a side table.* ■ change one's place of residence or work: *his family moved to London when he was a child.* ■ [with obj.] exchange (one's job or place of residence) for another: *they moved house four days after the baby was born.* ■ [with obj.] cause (someone) to change their job or place of residence: *the Employment Minister was moved to the Department of the Environment.* ■ [with obj.] change the date or time of (an event). ■ (of a player) change the position of a piece in a board game: *White has forced his opponent to move | [with obj.] if Black moves his bishop he loses a pawn.*
2 change or cause to change from one state, opinion, sphere, or activity to another: [no obj., with adverbial] *the school moved over to the new course in 1987 |* [with obj. and adverbial] *she deftly moved the conversation to safer territory.*
■ [with obj. and infinitive] influence or prompt (someone) to do something: *his deep love of music moved him to take lessons with Dr Hill.* ■ [no obj.] take action: *hardliners may yet* **move against** *him, but their success might be limited.* ■ [with obj.] (usu. **be moved**) provoke a strong feeling, especially of sorrow or sympathy, in: *he was* **moved to tears** *by a get-well message from the Queen.* ■ [with obj.] archaic stir up (an emotion) in someone: *he justly moves one's derision.*
3 [no obj., with adverbial] make progress; develop in a particular manner or direction: *aircraft design had moved forward a long way | councillors are anxious to* **get things moving** *as soon as possible.*
■ [no obj.] informal depart; start off: *let's move—it's time we started shopping.* ■ [in imperative] (**move it**) informal used to urge or command someone to hurry up: *come on—move it!* ■ [no obj.] informal go quickly: *Kennings was really moving when he made contact with a tyre at the hairpin and flipped over.* ■ [no obj.] (of merchandise) be sold: *despite the high prices, goods are moving.* ■ [with obj.] sell (merchandise).
4 [no obj.] (**move in/within**) spend one's time or be socially active in (a particular sphere) or among (a particular group of people): *she moved in the pop and art worlds.*
5 [with obj.] propose for discussion and resolution at a meeting or legislative assembly: *she intends to move an amendment to the Bill |* [with clause] *I beg to move that this House deplores the government's economic policies.*
■ make a formal request or application to (a court or assembly) for something: *his family* **moved** *the Special Court* **for** *adequate 'maintenance expenses' to run the household.*
6 [with obj.] empty (one's bowels).
■ [no obj.] (of the bowels) be emptied.

▶**noun** a change of place or position: *she made a sudden move towards me | his eyes followed her every move.*
■ a change of house or business premises. ■ a change of job, career, or business direction: *a career move.* ■ a change of state or opinion: *the country's move to independence.* ■ an action that initiates or advances a process or plan: *my next move is to talk to Matthew.* ■ a manoeuvre in a sport or game: *Robson began a move which saw Webb run from the halfway line down the right.* ■ a change of position of a piece in a board game. ■ a player's turn to make such a change.

– PHRASES **get a move on** [often in imperative] informal hurry up. **get moving** [often in imperative] informal make a prompt start (on a journey or task): *you're here to work, so get moving.* **make a move** take action: *each army was waiting for the other side to make a move.* ■ Brit. set off; leave somewhere: *I think I'd better be making a move.* **make a move on** (or **put the moves on**) informal make a proposition to (someone), especially of a sexual nature. **move the goalposts** see **GOALPOST**. **move heaven and earth** see **HEAVEN**. **move mountains** see **MOUNTAIN**. **move up a gear** see **GEAR**. **move with the times** keep abreast of current thinking or developments. **not move a muscle** see **MUSCLE**. **on the move** in the process of moving from one place or job to another: *it's difficult to contact her because she's always on the move.* ■ making progress: *the economy appeared to be on the move.*

– ORIGIN Middle English: from Old French *moveir*, from Latin *movere*.

▶**move along** [often in imperative] change to a new position, especially to avoid causing an obstruction: *'Move along, move along,' said the constable.*

move aside see *move over* below.

move in 1 take possession of a new house or business premises. ■ (**move in with**) start to share accommodation with (an existing resident). **2** intervene, especially so as to take control of a situation: *this riot could have been avoided had the police moved in earlier.*

move in on approach, especially so as to take action: *the police moved in on him.* ■ become involved with so as to take control of or put pressure on: *the Bank did not usually move in on doubtful institutions until they were almost bankrupt.*

move on (or **move someone on**) go or cause to leave somewhere, especially because one is causing an obstruction: *the Mounties briskly ordered them to move on.* ■ (**move on**) progress: *ballet has moved on, leaving Russia behind.*

move out (or **move someone out**) leave or cause to leave one's place of residence or work.

move over (or **aside**) adjust one's position to make room for someone else: *Jo motioned to the girls on the couch to move over.* ■ relinquish a job or leading position, typically because of being superseded by someone or something more competent or important: *it's time for the film establishment to move aside and make way for a new generation.*

move up adjust one's position, either to be nearer or make room for someone else: *do move up, there's just room for me if you do.*

moveable ▶ **adjective** & **noun** variant spelling of **MOVABLE**.

moveless ▶ **adjective** chiefly poetic/literary not moving or capable of moving or being moved.

movement ▶ **noun 1** an act of changing physical location or position or of having this changed: *a slight movement of the upper body |* [mass noun] *the EC is on the verge of allowing free movement of labour.*
■ an arrival or departure of an aircraft. ■ (also **bowel movement**) an act of defecation. ■ (**movements**) the activities and whereabouts of someone, especially during a particular period of time: *your movements and telephone conversations are recorded.* ■ [mass noun] the general activity or bustle of people or things in a particular place: *the scene was almost devoid of movement.* ■ [mass noun] the quality of suggesting motion in a work of art: *the painting was a busy landscape, full of detail and movement.* ■ [mass noun] the progressive development of a poem or story: *the novel shows minimal concern for narrative movement.*
2 [often with modifier] a group of people working together to advance their shared political, social, or artistic ideas: *the labour movement.*
■ [usu. in sing.] a campaign undertaken by such a group: *a* **movement** *to declare war on poverty.* ■ a change or development in something: *movements in the underlying financial markets.* ■ a change in policy or general attitudes seen as positive: *the* **movement towards** *greater sexual equality.*
3 Music a principal division of a longer musical work, self-sufficient in terms of key, tempo, and structure: *the slow movement of his violin concerto.*
4 the moving parts of a mechanism, especially a clock or watch.

– ORIGIN late Middle English: via Old French from medieval Latin *movimentum*, from Latin *movere* 'to move'.

mover ▶ **noun 1** a person or thing in motion, especially an animal: *she's a lovely mover and jumper.*
■ [usu. with modifier] a person undertaking or undergoing a move or change in a particular aspect of their life: *transferability of pension rights for job movers.* ■ chiefly N. Amer. a person whose job is to remove and transport furniture from one house to another.
2 a person who makes a formal proposal at a meeting or in an assembly: *the mover and seconder of the Loyal Address.*
■ a person who instigates or organizes something: *she was key mover in making this successful conference happen.*

– PHRASES **a mover and shaker** a powerful person who initiates events and influences people. [ORIGIN: from *movers and shakers*, a phrase from O'Shaughnessy's *Music & Moonlight* (1874).]

movie ▶ **noun** chiefly N. Amer. a cinema film.
■ (**the movies**) films generally or the film industry: *a lifelong love of the movies.*

movie theatre (also **movie house**) ▶ **noun** N. Amer. a cinema.

moving ▶ **adjective 1** [often with submodifier] in motion: *a fast-moving river.*
2 producing strong emotion, especially sadness or sympathy: *an unforgettable and moving book.*

– DERIVATIVES **movingly** adverb (in sense 2).

moving average ▶ **noun** Statistics a succession of averages derived from successive segments (typically of constant size and overlapping) of a series of values.

moving-coil ▶ **adjective** [attrib.] (of an electrical device such as a voltmeter or microphone) containing a wire coil suspended in a magnetic field, so that the coil either moves in response to a current or produces a current when it is made to move.

moving pavement ▶ **noun** a mechanism resembling a conveyor belt for pedestrians in a place such as an airport.

moving picture ▶ **noun** dated a cinematographic film.

moving staircase ▶ **noun** Brit. another term for **ESCALATOR**.

moviola /ˌmuːvɪˈəʊlə/ ▶ **noun** trademark a device which reproduces the picture and sound of a film on a small scale, to allow checking and editing.

– ORIGIN 1920s: from **MOVIE** + *-ola* (probably from **PIANOLA**).

mow[1] ▶ **verb** (past participle **mowed** or **mown**) [with obj.] cut down (an area of grass) with a machine: *Roger mowed the lawn |* [as adj. **mown**] *the delicious smell of newly mown grass.*
■ chiefly historical cut down (grass or a cereal crop) with a scythe.

– DERIVATIVES **mower** noun.

– ORIGIN Old English *māwan*, of Germanic origin; related to Dutch *maaien*, German *mähen* 'mow', also to **MEAD**[2].

▶**mow someone down** kill someone with a fusillade of bullets or other missiles. ■ recklessly knock down someone with a car or other vehicle.

mow[2] ▶ **noun** [often with modifier] N. Amer. or dialect a stack of hay, corn, or other crop.
■ a place in a barn where such a stack is put.

– ORIGIN Old English *mūga*; of unknown ultimate origin; compare with Swedish and Norwegian *muga* 'heap'.

mowing ▶ **noun** [mass noun] the action of mowing.
■ (**mowings**) loose pieces of grass resulting from mowing. ■ [count noun] US a field of grass grown for hay.

MOX ▶ **noun** [mass noun] a type of nuclear fuel designed for use in breeder reactors, consisting of a blend of uranium and plutonium oxides.

– ORIGIN from *m(ixed) ox(ides)*.

moxa /ˈmɒksə/ ▶ **noun** [mass noun] a downy substance obtained from the dried leaves of an Asian plant related to mugwort. It is burnt on or near the skin in Eastern medicine as a counterirritant.
• The plant is *Crossostephium artemisioides*, family Compositae.

– ORIGIN late 17th cent.: from Japanese *mogusa*, from *moe kusa* 'burning herb'.

moxibustion /ˌmɒksɪˈbʌstʃ(ə)n/ ▶ **noun** [mass noun] (in Eastern medicine) the burning of moxa on or near a person's skin as a counterirritant.

moxie /ˈmɒksi/ ▶ **noun** [mass noun] N. Amer. informal force of character, determination, or nerve: *when you've got the moxie, you need the clothes to match.*

– ORIGIN mid 20th cent.: from *Moxie*, the proprietary name of a soft drink.

Moygashel /ˈmɔɪgəʃ(ə)l/ ▶ **noun** trademark a type of Irish linen.

– ORIGIN 1930s: named after a village in Co. Tyrone, Northern Ireland.

Mozambique /ˌməʊzamˈbiːk/ a country on the east coast of southern Africa; pop. 16,142,000 (est. 1991); languages, Portuguese (official), Bantu languages; capital, Maputo.

First visited by Vasco da Gama, Mozambique was colonized by the Portuguese in the early 16th century. It was a centre of the slave trade in the 17th and 18th centuries. Mozambique became an independent republic in 1975, after a ten-year armed struggle by the Frelimo liberation movement; civil war between the Frelimo government and the Renamo opposition followed until a peace agreement was signed in 1992.

– DERIVATIVES **Mozambican** adjective & noun.

Mozambique Channel an arm of the Indian Ocean separating the eastern coast of mainland Africa from the island of Madagascar.

Mozarabic /məʊˈzarabɪk/ ▶ adjective historical of or relating to the Christian inhabitants of Spain under the Muslim Moorish kings.
– DERIVATIVES **Mozarab** noun.
– ORIGIN late 17th cent.: from Spanish *mozárabe* (from Arabic *mustaʿrib*, literally 'making oneself an Arab') + -IC.

Mozart /ˈməʊtsɑːt, German ˈmoːtsart/, (Johann Chrysostom) Wolfgang Amadeus (1756–91), Austrian composer.

A child prodigy as a harpsichordist, pianist, and composer, he came to epitomize classical music in its purity of form and melody. A prolific composer, he wrote more than forty symphonies, nearly thirty piano concertos, over twenty string quartets, and sixteen operas, including *The Marriage of Figaro* (1786), *Don Giovanni* (1787), *Così fan tutte* (1790), and *The Magic Flute* (1791).

– DERIVATIVES **Mozartian** adjective & noun.

mozo /ˈməʊzəʊ, Spanish ˈmoθo, ˈmoso/ ▶ noun (pl. **-os**) (in Spanish-speaking countries) a male servant or attendant.
– ORIGIN Spanish, literally 'boy'.

mozz ▶ verb [with obj.] (also **put the mozz on**) Austral. informal exert a malign influence on (someone); jinx.
– ORIGIN 1920s: abbreviation of MOZZLE.

mozzarella /ˌmɒtsəˈrɛlə/ ▶ noun [mass noun] a firm white Italian cheese made from buffalo or cow's milk, used in pizzas and salads.
– ORIGIN Italian, diminutive of *mozza*, denoting a kind of cheese, from *mozzare* 'cut off'.

mozzetta /məʊˈzɛtə, məʊˈtsɛtə/ (also **mozetta**) ▶ noun (pl. **mozzette**) a short cape with a hood, worn by the Pope, cardinals, and some other ecclesiastics.
– ORIGIN late 18th cent.: Italian, shortened form of *almozzetta*, from medieval Latin *almucia* 'amice' + the diminutive suffix *-etta*.

mozzie (also **mossie**) ▶ noun (pl. **-ies**) informal, chiefly Austral. a mosquito.

mozzle ▶ noun [mass noun] Austral. informal luck; fortune.
– ORIGIN late 19th cent.: from Hebrew *mazzāl* 'star or luck'.

MP ▶ abbreviation for ■ Member of Parliament: *Robert Brown, MP.* ■ military police. ■ military policeman.

mp ▶ abbreviation for mezzo piano.

m.p. ▶ abbreviation for melting point.

MPC ▶ abbreviation for multimedia personal computer.

MPD ▶ abbreviation for multiple personality disorder.

MPEG /ˈɛmpɛg/ ▶ noun [mass noun] Computing an international standard for encoding and compressing video images.
– ORIGIN late 20th cent.: from *Motion Pictures Experts Group*.

mpg ▶ abbreviation for miles per gallon (a measurement of a vehicle's rate of fuel consumption).

mph ▶ abbreviation for miles per hour.

MPhil ▶ abbreviation for Master of Philosophy.

MPLA the Popular Movement for the Liberation of Angola, a Marxist organization founded in the 1950s that emerged as the ruling party in Angola after independence from Portugal in 1975. Once in power the MPLA fought UNITA and other rival groups for many years.
– ORIGIN abbreviation of Portuguese *Movimento Popular de Libertação de Angola*.

Mpumalanga /(ə)mˌpuːməˈlaŋgə/ a province of NE South Africa, formerly part of Transvaal; capital, Nelspruit.

MPV ▶ abbreviation for multi-purpose vehicle, a large van-like car.

MR ▶ abbreviation for Master of the Rolls.

Mr ▶ noun a title used before a surname or full name to address or refer to a man without a higher or honorific or professional title: *Mr Robert Smith.* ■ used before the name of an office to address a man who holds it: *yes, Mr President.* ■ (in the UK) used before a surname to address or refer to a male surgeon. ■ used in the armed forces to address a senior warrant officer, officer cadet, or junior naval officer.
– ORIGIN late Middle English: originally an abbreviation of MASTER[1]; compare with MISTER.

MRA ▶ abbreviation for Moral Rearmament.

MRBM ▶ abbreviation for medium-range ballistic missile.

MRC ▶ abbreviation for (in the UK) Medical Research Council.

MRCP ▶ abbreviation for Member of the Royal College of Physicians.

MRCVS ▶ abbreviation for Member of the Royal College of Veterinary Surgeons.

MRE ▶ abbreviation for meal ready to eat (a pre-cooked and pre-packaged meal used by US military personnel).

MRI ▶ abbreviation for magnetic resonance imaging.

MRIA ▶ abbreviation for Member of the Royal Irish Academy.

mridangam /mrɪˈdaŋəm/ ▶ noun a barrel-shaped double-headed drum with one head larger than the other, used in southern Indian music.
– ORIGIN late 19th cent.: Tamil alteration of Sanskrit *mrdanga*.

mRNA Biology ▶ abbreviation for messenger RNA.

MRPhS ▶ abbreviation for Member of the Royal Pharmaceutical Society.

Mr Right ▶ noun informal the ideal future husband: *I expect you're waiting for Mr Right.*

Mrs ▶ noun the title used before a surname or full name to address or refer to a married woman without a higher or honorific or professional title: *Mrs Sally Jones.*
– ORIGIN early 17th cent.: abbreviation of MISTRESS; compare with MISSUS.

MRSA ▶ abbreviation for methicillin-resistant *Staphylococcus aureus*, a strain of antibiotic resistant bacteria.

Mrs Grundy ▶ noun (pl. **Mrs Grundys**) a person with very conventional standards of propriety.
– ORIGIN early 19th cent.: a person repeatedly mentioned in T. Morton's comedy *Speed the Plough* (1798), often in the phrase 'What will Mrs Grundy say?', which became a popular catchphrase.

MS ▶ abbreviation for ■ manuscript. ■ Master of Surgery. ■ Master of Science. ■ Mississippi (in official postal use). ■ multiple sclerosis. ■ motor ship. ■ Master Seaman.

Ms ▶ noun a title used before the surname or full name of any woman regardless of her marital status (a neutral alternative to **Mrs** or **Miss**): *Ms Sarah Brown.*
– ORIGIN 1950s: combination of MRS and MISS[2].

msasa /(ə)mˈsɑːsə/ ▶ noun a tree of central Africa (especially Zimbabwe), with fragrant white flowers and compound leaves which are crimson and bronze in spring.
● *Brachystegia spiciformis*, family Leguminosae.
– ORIGIN early 20th cent.: from Shona.

MSB ▶ abbreviation for most significant bit.

MSC ▶ abbreviation for (in the UK) Manpower Services Commission.

MSc ▶ abbreviation for Master of Science.

MS-DOS Computing, trademark ▶ abbreviation for Microsoft disk operating system.

MSF ▶ abbreviation for (in the UK) Manufacturing, Science, and Finance (a trade union representing skilled and professional workers).

MSG ▶ abbreviation for monosodium glutamate.

Msgr N. Amer. ▶ abbreviation for ■ Monseigneur. ■ Monsignor.

MSgt ▶ abbreviation for Master Sergeant.

MSS /ˈɛmˈɛsɪz/ ▶ abbreviation for manuscripts.

MST ▶ abbreviation for (in North America) Mountain Standard Time (see MOUNTAIN TIME).

MSY ▶ abbreviation for maximum sustainable yield.

MT ▶ abbreviation for ■ machine translation. ■ Montana (in official postal use).

Mt ▶ abbreviation for ■ the Gospel of Matthew (in biblical references). ■ [in place names] Mount: *Mt Everest.*
▶ symbol for the chemical element meitnerium.

MTB ▶ abbreviation for ■ Brit. motor torpedo boat. ■ mountain bike.

MTBF ▶ abbreviation for mean time between failures, a measure of the reliability of a device or system.

MTech ▶ abbreviation for Master of Technology.

MTV trademark a cable and satellite television channel which broadcasts popular music and promotional music videos.
– ORIGIN late 20th cent.: abbreviation of *music television*.

mu /mjuː/ ▶ noun the twelfth letter of the Greek alphabet (M, μ), transliterated as 'm'. ■ (**Mu**) [followed by Latin genitive] Astronomy the twelfth star in a constellation: *Mu Cassiopeiae.* ■ [as modifier] Physics relating to muons: *mu particle.*
▶ symbol for ■ (μ) micron. ■ (μ) [in combination] 'micro-' in symbols for units: *the recommended daily amount is 750µg.* ■ (μ) permeability.
– ORIGIN Greek.

Mubarak /muːˈbɑːrak/, (Muhammad) Hosni (Said) (b.1928), Egyptian statesman, President since 1981. He did much to establish closer links between Egypt and other Arab nations, though he aligned Egypt against Iraq in the Gulf War of 1991.

much ▶ determiner & pronoun (**more**, **most**) [often with negative or in questions] a large amount: [as determiner] *I did not get much sleep* | *I did so much shopping* | [as pronoun] *he does not eat much* | *they must bear much of the blame.*
■ [as pronoun] [with negative] used to refer disparagingly to someone or something as being a poor specimen: *I'm not much of a gardener.*
▶ adverb to a great extent; a great deal: *did it hurt much?* | *thanks very much* | *they did not mind, much to my surprise* | [with comparative] *they look much better* | [with superlative] *Nicolai's English was much the worst.*
■ [usu. with negative or in questions] for a large part of one's time; often: *I'm not there much.*
– PHRASES **as much** the same: *I am sure she would do as much for me.* **a bit much** informal somewhat excessive or unreasonable: *his earnestness can be a bit much.* **how much** used to ask what a particular amount or cost is. (**as**) **much as** even though: *much as I had enjoyed my adventure it was good to be back.* **much less** see LESS. **not much in it** little difference between things being compared. **so much the better** (or **worse**) that is even better (or worse): *we want to hear your say, but if you make it short, so much the better.* **this much** the fact about to be stated: *I know this much, you would defy the world to get what you wanted.* **too much** an intolerable, impossible, or exhausting situation or experience: *the effort proved too much for her.*
– DERIVATIVES **muchly** adverb (humorous).
– ORIGIN Middle English: shortened from *muchel*, from Old English *micel* (see MICKLE).

Mucha /ˈmuːkə/, Alphonse (1860–1939), Czech painter and designer; born *Alfons Maria*. He was a leading figure in the art nouveau movement, noted for his flowing poster designs, typically featuring the actress Sarah Bernhardt.

muchacha /muːˈtʃatʃə/ ▶ noun (in Spanish-speaking countries) a young woman; a female servant.
– ORIGIN Spanish, feminine of *muchacho* (see MUCHACHO).

muchacho /muːˈtʃatʃəʊ/ ▶ noun (pl. **-os**) (in Spanish-speaking countries) a young man; a male servant.
– ORIGIN Spanish.

Muchinga Mountains /muːˈtʃɪŋgə/ a range of mountains in eastern Zambia.

muchness ▶ noun [in sing.] greatness in quantity or degree: *a human muchness encountering no bounds.*
– PHRASES (**much**) **of a muchness** informal very similar: *the polls looked much of a muchness but concealed politically crucial variations.*

mucho /ˈmɒtʃəʊ, ˈmʌtʃəʊ/ informal, humorous ▶ determiner much or many: *that caused me mucho problems.*
▶ adverb [usu. as submodifier] very: *he was being mucho macho.*
– ORIGIN Spanish.

mucilage /ˈmjuːsɪlɪdʒ/ ▶ noun [mass noun] a viscous secretion or bodily fluid.

▪a polysaccharide substance extracted as a viscous or gelatinous solution from plant roots, seeds, etc., and used in medicines and adhesives. ▪N. Amer. an adhesive solution; gum, glue.
– DERIVATIVES **mucilaginous** /-ˈladʒɪnəs/ adjective.
– ORIGIN late Middle English: via French from late Latin *mucilago* 'musty juice', from Latin *mucus* (see **MUCUS**).

mucin /ˈmjuːsɪn/ ▶**noun** [mass noun] Biochemistry a glycoprotein constituent of mucus.
– ORIGIN mid 19th cent.: from **MUCUS** + **-IN**[1].

mucinous ▶**adjective** of, relating to, or covered with mucus.

muck ▶**noun** [mass noun] dirt, rubbish, or waste matter: *I'll just clean the muck off the windscreen.*
▪farmyard manure, widely used as fertilizer. ▪informal something regarded as worthless, sordid, or corrupt: *the muck that passes for music in the pop charts.*
▶**verb** [with obj.] **1** (**muck something up**) informal mishandle a job or situation; spoil something: *she had mucked up her first few weeks at college.*
2 (**muck something out**) chiefly Brit. remove manure and other dirt from a horse's stable or other animal's dwelling.
3 rare spread manure on (land).
– PHRASES **as common as muck** Brit. informal of low social status. **make a muck of** Brit. informal handle incompetently. **where there's muck there's brass** proverb dirty or unpleasant activities are also lucrative.
– ORIGIN Middle English *muk*, probably of Scandinavian origin: compare with Old Norse *myki* 'dung', from a Germanic base meaning 'soft', shared by **MEEK**.
▶**muck about/around** Brit. informal behave in a silly or aimless way, especially by wasting time when serious activity is expected: *we just muck around in training and have a laugh.* ▪(**muck about/around with**) spoil (something) by interfering with it.
muck someone about/around Brit. informal treat someone inconsiderately, typically by disrupting their activities or plans.
muck in Brit. informal share tasks or accommodation without expecting a privileged position: *she really enjoys **mucking in with** the lads.*

muckamuck /ˈmʌkəmʌk/ (also **mucky-muck**) ▶**noun** N. Amer. informal a person of great importance or self-importance.
– ORIGIN mid 19th cent.: from Chinook Jargon, shortening of **HIGH MUCK-A-MUCK**.

mucker ▶**noun 1** Brit. informal a friend or companion: *we felt like old muckers.* [ORIGIN: 1940s: probably from *muck in* (see **MUCK**).]
2 US informal, dated a rough or coarse person. [ORIGIN: late 19th cent.: probably from German *Mucker* 'sulky person'.]
3 a person who removes dirt and waste, especially from mines or stables. [ORIGIN: late 19th cent.: from **MUCK** + **-ER**[1].]
– PHRASES **come a mucker** Brit. informal, dated another way of saying ***come a cropper*** (see **CROPPER**).

muckle ▶**noun, adjective, determiner, & pronoun** variant form of **MICKLE**.

USAGE On the confused use of **muckle** and **mickle**, see **usage** at **MICKLE**.

muckraking ▶**noun** [mass noun] the action of searching out and publicizing scandal about famous people in an underhand way.
▶**adjective** [attrib.] searching out and publicizing scandal in such a way: *a muckraking journalist.*
– DERIVATIVES **muckrake** verb, **muckraker** noun.
– ORIGIN coined by President Roosevelt in a speech (1906) alluding to Bunyan's *Pilgrim's Progress* and the man with the *muck rake*.

muck spreader ▶**noun** Brit. a machine used to spread manure on fields.
– DERIVATIVES **muck-spreading** noun.

muck sweat ▶**noun** informal a state of perspiring profusely: *I got there in a muck sweat.*

mucky ▶**adjective** (**muckier**, **muckiest**) covered with or consisting of dirt or filth: *guests carried their food on trays to mucky tables.*
▪informal corrupt, typically in sexual or financial matters; sordid or indecent: *a mucky mix of political wheeler-dealing and multinational corruption.*
– DERIVATIVES **muckiness** noun.

muco- ▶**combining form** Biochemistry representing **MUCUS**.

mucoid /ˈmjuːkɔɪd/ ▶**adjective** of, involving, resembling, or of the nature of mucus.

mucopolysaccharide /ˌmjuːkəʊpɒlɪˈsakərʌɪd/ ▶**noun** Biochemistry any of a group of compounds occurring chiefly as components of connective tissue. They are complex polysaccharides containing amino groups.

mucosa /mjuːˈkəʊsə/ ▶**noun** (pl. **mucosae** /-siː/) a mucous membrane: *the intestinal mucosa.*
– DERIVATIVES **mucosal** adjective.
– ORIGIN late 19th cent.: modern Latin, feminine of *mucosus* (see **MUCOUS**).

mucous /ˈmjuːkəs/ ▶**adjective** relating to, producing, covered with, or of the nature of mucus.
– DERIVATIVES **mucosity** noun.
– ORIGIN mid 17th cent.: from Latin *mucosus* (see **MUCUS**).

mucous membrane ▶**noun** an epithelial tissue which secretes mucus, and lines many body cavities and tubular organs including the gut and respiratory passages.

mucro /ˈmjuːkrəʊ/ ▶**noun** Botany & Zoology a short sharp point at the end of a part or organ.
– ORIGIN mid 17th cent.: from Latin, 'sharp point'.

mucronate /ˈmjuːkrənеɪt/ ▶**adjective** Botany & Zoology ending abruptly in a short sharp point or mucro.
– ORIGIN late 18th cent.: from Latin *mucronatus*, from *mucro, mucron-* 'point'.

mucus /ˈmjuːkəs/ ▶**noun** [mass noun] a slimy substance, typically not miscible with water, secreted by the mucous membranes and glands of animals for lubrication, protection, etc.
▪a gummy substance found in plants; mucilage.
– ORIGIN mid 17th cent.: from Latin.

MUD ▶**noun** a computer-based text or virtual reality game which several players play at the same time, interacting with each other as well as with characters controlled by the computer.
– ORIGIN late 20th cent.: from *multi-user dungeon* or *multi-user dimension*.

mud ▶**noun** [mass noun] soft, sticky matter resulting from the mixing of earth and water.
▪figurative information or allegations regarded as damaging, typically concerned with corruption: *they are trying to **sling mud** at me to cover up their defeat.*
– PHRASES **as clear as mud** informal not at all easy to understand. **drag someone through the mud** slander or denigrate someone publicly. **here's mud in your eye!** Brit. informal used to express friendly feelings towards one's companions before drinking. **one's name is mud** informal one is in disgrace or unpopular: *if you forget their birthdays your name is mud.*
– ORIGIN late Middle English: probably from Middle Low German *mudde*.

mudbank ▶**noun** a bank of mud on the bed of a river or the bottom of the sea.

mudbath ▶**noun** a bath in the mud of mineral springs, taken especially to relieve rheumatic complaints.
▪a muddy place: *the pitch was a mudbath.*

mudbug ▶**noun** N. Amer. a freshwater crayfish.

mud dauber ▶**noun** a solitary wasp which builds a mud nest that typically consists of a series of tube-like cells on an exposed surface.
• Several genera in the family Sphecidae.

muddle ▶**verb** [with obj.] bring into a disordered or confusing state: *they were **muddling up** the cards.*
▪confuse (a person or their thoughts). ▪[no obj., with adverbial] busy oneself in a confused and ineffective way: *he was muddling about in the kitchen.* ▪US mix (a drink) or stir (an ingredient) into a drink.
▶**noun** [usu. in sing.] an untidy and disorganized state or collection: *a muddle of plasticine, string, and electric flex | the finances were **in a muddle** |* [mass noun] *an admirable chairman, she cut through confusion and muddle.*
▪a mistake arising from or resulting in confusion: *a bureaucratic muddle.*
– DERIVATIVES **muddlingly** adverb, **muddly** adjective.
– ORIGIN late Middle English (in the sense 'wallow in mud'): perhaps from Middle Dutch *moddelen*, frequentative of *modden* 'dabble in mud'; compare with **MUD**. The sense 'confuse' was initially associated with alcoholic drink (late 17th cent.), giving rise to 'busy oneself in a confused way' and 'jumble up' (mid 19th cent.).
▶**muddle along/through** cope more or less satisfactorily despite lack of expertise, planning, or equipment: *students are often left to muddle along.*
muddle something up confuse two or more things with each other: *the words seemed to have **got muddled up**.*

muddled ▶**adjective** in a state of bewildered or bewildering confusion or disorder: *the statement betrayed muddled thinking on refugee issues.*

muddle-headed ▶**adjective** mentally disorganized or confused: *a muddle-headed idealist with utopian views.*
– DERIVATIVES **muddle-headedness** noun.

muddler ▶**noun 1** a person who creates muddles, especially because of a disorganized method of thinking or working.
2 (also **muddler minnow**) a type of fly used in trout-fishing.

muddy ▶**adjective** (**muddier**, **muddiest**) covered in or full of mud: *they changed their muddy boots | it was very muddy underfoot.*
▪(of a liquid) discoloured and made cloudy by mud. ▪(of a colour) dull and dirty-looking: *the original colours were blurred into muddy pink and yellow.* ▪(of a sound, especially in music) not clearly defined: *an awful muddy sound that renders his vocal incoherent.* ▪confused, vague, or illogical: *some sentences are so muddy that their meaning can only be guessed.*
▶**verb** (**-ies**, **-ied**) [with obj.] cause to become covered in or full of mud: *the linoleum flooring was muddied |* [as adj. **muddied**] *cold, muddied feet.*
▪make (something) hard to perceive or understand: *the first year's results muddy rather than clarify the situation.*
– PHRASES **muddy the waters** make an issue or a situation more confusing and harder to understand by introducing complications.
– DERIVATIVES **muddily** adverb, **muddiness** noun.

Mudejar /muːˈdeɪhɑː/ ▶**adjective** of or denoting a partly Gothic, partly Islamic style of architecture and art prevalent in Spain in the 12th to 15th centuries.
▪of or relating to Muslim subjects of Christian monarchs during the reconquest of the Iberian peninsula from the Moors.
▶**noun** (pl. **Mudejares** /-reɪz/) a subject Muslim during the Christian reconquest of the Iberian peninsula from the Moors (11th–15th centuries) who, until 1492, was allowed to retain Islamic laws and religion in return for loyalty to a Christian monarch.
– ORIGIN via Spanish from Arabic *mudajjan* 'allowed to stay'.

mud fever ▶**noun** [mass noun] a bacterial skin infection which chiefly affects the lower legs of horses exposed to wet and muddy conditions, causing cracking and soreness of the skin and hair loss in the affected area.
• This condition is caused by the bacterium *Dermatophilus congolensis*.

mudfish ▶**noun** (pl. same or **-fishes**) **1** any of a number of elongated fish that are able to survive long periods of drought by burrowing in the mud:
• a New Zealand fish (genus *Neochanna*, family Galaxiidae).
• an African lungfish (*Protopterus annectens*, family Protopteridae).
2 another term for **BOWFIN**.

mudflap ▶**noun** a flap that hangs behind the wheel of a vehicle and is designed to prevent water and stones thrown up from the road from hitting the bodywork or any following vehicles.

mudflat ▶**noun** (usu. **mudflats**) a stretch of muddy land left uncovered at low tide.

mudflow ▶**noun** a fluid or hardened stream or avalanche of mud.

mudguard ▶**noun** a curved strip or cover over a wheel of a vehicle, especially a bicycle or motorcycle, designed to protect the vehicle and rider from water and dirt thrown up from the road.

mudlark (also **mudlarker**) ▶**noun** a person who scavenges in river mud for objects of value.
▪historical a street urchin.

mudminnow ▶**noun** a small stout-bodied freshwater fish of both Eurasia and North America, able to survive low concentrations of oxygen and very low temperatures.
• Genus *Umbra*, family Umbridae: several species.

mud-nester ▶**noun** a gregarious Australian bird of a family that comprises the apostlebird and the white-winged chough, which make nests of mud.
• Family Corcoracidae; sometimes placed with the magpie lark in the family Grallinidae.

mud pack ▸ noun a paste of fuller's earth or a similar substance, applied thickly to the face to improve the condition of the skin.

mud pie ▸ noun mud made into a pie shape by a child.

mud puppy ▸ noun a large aquatic salamander of the eastern US, reaching sexual maturity while retaining an immature body form with feathery external gills.
● *Necturus maculosus*, family Proteidae. Compare with **WATERDOG**.

mudra /ˈmʊdrə/ ▸ noun a symbolic hand gesture used in Hindu ceremonies and statuary, and in Indian dance.
■ a movement or pose in yoga.
– ORIGIN from Sanskrit *mudrā* 'sign or token'.

mudskipper ▸ noun a goby (fish) with its eyes on raised bumps on top of the head, found in mangrove swamps from East Africa to Australia. It moves about on land with great agility, often basking on mud or mangrove roots.
● *Periophthalmodon* and related genera, family Gobiidae: several species, including the common and widespread *P. schlosseri* (or *barbarus*).

mudslide ▸ noun a mass of mud and other earthy material that is falling or has fallen down a hillside or other slope.

mud-slinging ▸ noun [mass noun] informal the use of insults and accusations, especially unjust ones, with the aim of damaging the reputation of an opponent.
– DERIVATIVES **mud-sling** verb, **mud-slinger** noun.

mudstone ▸ noun [mass noun] a dark sedimentary rock formed from consolidated mud and lacking the laminations of shale.

mud turtle ▸ noun any of a number of drab-coloured freshwater turtles that often haul out on to mud banks, in particular:
● an American turtle with scent glands that produce an unpleasant odour (genus *Kinosternon*, family Kinosternidae). ● an African side-necked turtle (genus *Pelusios*, family Pelomedusidae). ● an Asian softshell (genera *Lissemys* and *Pelochelys*, family Trionychidae).

mud volcano ▸ noun a small vent or fissure in the ground discharging hot mud.

mudwort ▸ noun a very small creeping plant that grows in mud and damp soils in north temperate regions.
● *Limosella aquatica*, family Scrophulariaceae.

muesli /ˈm(j)uːzli/ ▸ noun (pl. **mueslis**) [mass noun] a mixture of cereals (especially rolled oats), dried fruit, and nuts, typically eaten with milk at breakfast.
– ORIGIN Swiss German.

muezzin /muːˈɛzɪn/ ▸ noun a man who calls Muslims to prayer from the minaret of a mosque.
– ORIGIN late 16th cent.: dialect variant of Arabic *muʾaddin*, active participle of *addana* 'proclaim'.

muff[1] ▸ noun 1 a tube made of fur or other warm material into which the hands are placed for warmth.
■ a warm or protective covering for other parts of the body.
2 vulgar slang a woman's genitals.
– ORIGIN mid 16th cent.: from Dutch *mof*, Middle Dutch *muffel*, from medieval Latin *muff(u)la*, of unknown ultimate origin.

muff[2] informal ▸ verb [with obj.] handle (a situation, task, or opportunity) clumsily or badly: *the administration muffed several of its biggest projects.*
▸ noun a mistake or failure, especially a failure to catch or receive a ball cleanly.
■ dated, chiefly Brit. a person who is awkward or stupid, especially in relation to a sport or manual skill.
– ORIGIN early 19th cent.: of unknown origin.

muff diver ▸ noun vulgar slang a person who performs cunnilingus.
– DERIVATIVES **muff diving** noun.

muffin ▸ noun 1 chiefly Brit. a flat circular spongy bread roll made from yeast dough and eaten split, toasted, and buttered.
2 chiefly N. Amer. a small domed spongy cake made with eggs and baking powder.
– ORIGIN early 18th cent.: of unknown origin.

muffle ▸ verb [with obj.] (often **be muffled**) wrap or cover for warmth: *it was very cold and everyone was muffled up in coats and scarves.*
■ cover or wrap up (a source of sound) to reduce its loudness: [as adj.] **muffled**] *the soft beat of a muffled*

drum. ■ make (a sound) quieter or less distinct: *his voice was muffled.* ■ restrain or conceal (someone) with wrappings: *the boy was bound and muffled.*
▸ noun [usu. as modifier] a receptacle in a furnace or kiln in which things can be heated without contact with combustion products: *a muffle furnace.*
– ORIGIN late Middle English (as a verb): perhaps a shortening of Old French *enmoufler*; the noun (mid 17th cent.) from Old French *moufle* 'thick glove'.

muffler ▸ noun 1 a wrap or scarf worn around the neck and face for warmth.
2 a device used to deaden the sound of a drum, bell, piano, or other instrument.
■ N. Amer. a silencer for a motor vehicle exhaust.

mufti[1] /ˈmʌfti/ ▸ noun (pl. **muftis**) a Muslim legal expert who is empowered to give rulings on religious matters.
– ORIGIN late 16th cent.: from Arabic *muftī*, active participle of *'aftā* 'decide a point of law'.

mufti[2] /ˈmʌfti/ ▸ noun [mass noun] plain clothes worn by a person who wears a uniform for their job, such as a soldier or police officer: *a High Court judge in mufti.*
– ORIGIN early 19th cent.: perhaps humorously from **MUFTI**[1].

mug[1] ▸ noun 1 a large cup, typically cylindrical and with a handle and used without a saucer.
■ the contents of such a cup: *a large mug of tea vanished in a single gulp.*
2 informal a person's face.
3 Brit. informal a stupid or gullible person.
4 US informal a hoodlum or thug.
▸ verb (**mugged**, **mugging**) informal 1 [with obj.] (often **be mugged**) attack and rob (someone) in a public place: *he was mugged by three men who stole his bike* | [as noun **mugging**] *a brutal mugging.*
■ dated fight or hit (someone).
2 [no obj.] make faces, especially silly or exaggerated ones, before an audience or a camera: *he mugged for the camera.*
– PHRASES **a mug's game** informal an activity in which it is foolish to engage because it is likely to be unsuccessful or dangerous: *playing with drugs is a mug's game.*
– DERIVATIVES **mugful** noun (pl. **-fuls**).
– ORIGIN early 16th cent. (originally Scots and northern English, denoting an earthenware bowl): probably of Scandinavian origin; compare with Norwegian *mugge*, Swedish *mugg* 'pitcher with a handle'.

mug[2] ▸ verb (**mugged**, **mugging**) [with obj.] (**mug something up**) Brit. informal learn or revise a subject as far as possible in a short time: *I'm constantly having to mug up things ahead of teaching them* | [no obj.] *we had mugged up on all things Venetian before the start of the course.*
– ORIGIN mid 19th cent.: of unknown origin.

Mugabe /mʊˈɡɑːbi/, Robert (Gabriel) (b.1924), Zimbabwean statesman, Prime Minister 1980–7 and President since 1987. He became Prime Minister in Zimbabwe's first post-independence elections. In 1987 his party ZANU merged with ZAPU and Mugabe became executive President of a one-party state.

Muganda /mʊˈɡandə/ ▸ noun singular form of **BAGANDA**.

mugger[1] ▸ noun a person who attacks and robs another in a public place.

mugger[2] ▸ noun a large short-snouted Indian crocodile, venerated by many Hindus.
● *Crocodylus palustris*, family Crocodylidae.
– ORIGIN mid 19th cent.: from Hindi *magar*.

muggins ▸ noun (pl. same or **mugginses**) Brit. informal a foolish and gullible person.
■ humorous used to refer to oneself in order to suggest that one has been stupid, especially in allowing oneself to be exploited: *muggins has volunteered to do the catering.*
– ORIGIN mid 19th cent.: perhaps a use of the surname *Muggins*, with allusion to **MUG**[1].

Muggletonian /ˌmʌɡ(ə)lˈtəʊnɪən/ ▸ noun a member of a small Christian sect founded in England c.1651 by Lodowicke Muggleton (1609–98) and John Reeve (1608–58), who claimed to be the two witnesses mentioned in the book of Revelation (Rev. 11:3–6). Despite many eccentric doctrines, the sect survived into the late 19th century.
▸ adjective of or relating to this sect.

muggy ▸ adjective (**muggier**, **muggiest**) (of the weather) unpleasantly warm and humid.
– DERIVATIVES **mugginess** noun.
– ORIGIN mid 18th cent.: from dialect *mug* 'mist, drizzle', from Old Norse *mugga*.

Mughal /ˈmuːɡɑːl/ variant spelling of **MOGUL**.

mugshot ▸ noun informal a photograph of a person's face made for an official purpose, especially police records.
■ humorous any photograph of a person's face.

mugwort ▸ noun a plant of the daisy family, with aromatic divided leaves that are dark green above and whitish below, native to north temperate regions.
● Genus *Artemisia*, family Compositae: several species, in particular the common English hedgerow plant *A. vulgaris*, which has long been connected with magic and superstition.
– ORIGIN Old English *mucgwyrt* (see **MIDGE, WORT**).

mugwump /ˈmʌɡwʌmp/ ▸ noun N. Amer. a person who remains aloof or independent, especially from party politics.
– ORIGIN mid 19th cent.: from Algonquian *mugquomp* 'great chief'.

Muhammad[1] /məˈhamɪd/ (also **Mohammed**) (c.570–632), Arab prophet and founder of Islam.

In c.610 in Mecca he received the first of a series of revelations which, as the Koran, became the doctrinal and legislative basis of Islam. In the face of opposition to his preaching he and his small group of supporters were forced to flee to Medina in 622 (the Hegira). Muhammad led his followers into a series of battles against the Meccans. In 630 Mecca capitulated, and by his death Muhammad had united most of Arabia.

Muhammad[2] /məˈhamɪd/, Mahathir (b.1925), Malaysian statesman, Prime Minister since 1981.

Muhammad Ahmad[1] /ˈɑːmad/ see **MAHDI**.

Muhammad Ali[1] /ˈɑːli, ɑːˈliː/ (1769–1849), Ottoman viceroy and pasha of Egypt 1805–49, possibly of Albanian descent. He modernized Egypt's infrastructure, making it the leading power in the eastern Mediterranean, and established a dynasty that survived until 1952.

Muhammad Ali[2] /ˈɑːli, ɑːˈliː/ (b.1942), American boxer; born *Cassius Marcellus Clay*. He won the world heavyweight title in 1964, 1974, and 1978, becoming the only boxer to be world champion three times. He retired in 1981.

Muhammadan /məˈhaməd(ə)n/ (also **Mohammedan**) ▸ noun & adjective archaic term for **MUSLIM** (not favoured by Muslims).
– DERIVATIVES **Muhammadanism** noun.
– ORIGIN late 17th cent.: from the name of the prophet *Muhammad* (see **MUHAMMAD**[1], + **-AN**).

Muharram /məˈharəm/ ▸ noun the first month of the year in the Islamic calendar.
■ an annual celebration in this month commemorating the death of Husayn, grandson of Muhammad, and his retinue.
– ORIGIN from Arabic *muharram* 'inviolable'.

Mühlhausen /ˈmyːlˌhaʊzn/ German name for **MULHOUSE**.

Muir[1] /mjʊə/, Jean (Elizabeth) (1933–95), English fashion designer. Her designs are noted for their subtle, restrained, and fluid styles.

Muir[2] /mjʊə/, John (1838–1914), Scottish-born American naturalist, a pioneer of environmental conservation. Muir was largely responsible for the establishment of Yosemite and Sequoia National Parks in California (1890).

muishond /ˈmeɪs(h)ɒnt/ ▸ noun (pl. same or **muishonds** or **muishonde**) S. African any of a number of small carnivorous mammals, especially of the weasel or mongoose families.
– ORIGIN late 18th cent.: from South African Dutch, transferred use of Dutch *muishond* 'weasel'.

mujahedin /ˌmʊdʒaːhɪˈdiːn/ (also **mujahidin, mujaheddin**, or **mujahideen**) ▸ plural noun guerrilla fighters in Islamic countries, especially those who are Islamic fundamentalists.
– ORIGIN from Persian and Arabic *mujāhidīn*, colloquial plural of *mujāhid*, denoting a person who fights a jihad.

Mujibur Rahman /mʊˌdʒɪbʊə rəˈmɑːn/ (1920–75), Bangladeshi statesman, first Prime Minister of independent Bangladesh 1972–5 and President 1975; known as **Sheikh Mujib**. After failing to establish parliamentary democracy as Prime Minister, he assumed dictatorial powers in 1975. He and his family were assassinated in a military coup.

mujtahid /mʊdʒ'tɑːhɪd/ ▶noun (pl. **mujtahids** or **mujtahidūn**) Islam a person accepted as an original authority in Islamic law. Such authorities continue to be recognized in the Shia tradition, but Sunni Muslims accord this status only to the great lawmakers of early Islam.
– ORIGIN Persian, from Arabic, active participle of *ijtahada* 'strive'.

Mukalla /mʊ'kalə/ a port on the south coast of Yemen, in the Gulf of Aden; pop. 154,360 (1987).

Mukden /'mʊkdən/ former name for **SHENYANG**.

mukhtar /'mʊktɑː/ ▶noun (in Turkey and some Arab countries) the head of local government of a town or village.
– ORIGIN from Arabic *muḵtār*, passive participle of *iḵtāra* 'choose'.

mukluk /'mʌklʌk/ ▶noun N. Amer. a high, soft boot that is worn in the American Arctic and is traditionally made from sealskin.
– ORIGIN mid 19th cent.: from Yupik *maklak* 'bearded seal'.

mukti /'mʌkti, 'mʊkti/ ▶noun another term for **MOKSHA**.
– ORIGIN Sanskrit, literally 'release'.

muktuk /'mʌktʌk/ ▶noun [mass noun] the skin and blubber of a whale, typically the narwhal or the beluga, used as food by the Inuit.
– ORIGIN from Inuit *maktak*.

mulatto /m(j)uː'latəʊ/ dated ▶noun (pl. **-oes** or **-os**) a person with one white and one black parent.
▶adjective relating to or denoting a mulatto or mulattoes.
– ORIGIN late 16th cent.: from Spanish *mulato* 'young mule or mulatto', formed irregularly from *mulo* 'mule'.

mulberry ▶noun 1 (also **mulberry tree** or **bush**) a small deciduous tree with broad leaves, native to the Far East and long cultivated elsewhere.
● Genus *Morus*, family Moraceae, in particular the **white mulberry** (*M. alba*), originally grown for feeding silkworms, and the **black** (or **common**) **mulberry** (*M. nigra*), grown for its fruit. See also **PAPER MULBERRY**.
■the dark red or white loganberry-like fruit of this tree.
2 [mass noun] a dark red or purple colour: [as modifier] *a mulberry carpet*.
– ORIGIN Old English *mōrberie*, from Latin *morum* + **BERRY**; related to Dutch *moerbezie* and German *Maulbeere*.

mulch /mʌl(t)ʃ/ ▶noun [mass noun] a material (such as decaying leaves, bark, or compost) spread around or over a plant to enrich or insulate the soil.
■[count noun] an application of such a material: *regular mulches keep down annual weeds.* ■ a formless mass or pulp: *a mulch of sodden brown stems.*
▶verb [no obj.] apply a mulch.
■[with obj.] treat or cover with mulch.
– ORIGIN mid 17th cent.: probably from dialect *mulch* 'soft' used as a noun, from Old English *melsc, mylsc*.

mulct /mʌlkt/ formal ▶verb [with obj.] extract money from by fine or taxation.
■(**mulct something of**) take money or possessions from (someone) by fraudulent means: *a rapacious old moneybag who would never miss the few dollars mulcted of her.*
▶noun a fine or compulsory payment.
– ORIGIN late 15th cent.: from Latin *mulctare, multare*, from *mulcta* 'a fine'.

Muldoon /mʌl'duːn/, Sir Robert (David) (1921–92), New Zealand statesman, Prime Minister 1975–84. His Premiership was marked by domestic measures to tackle low economic growth and high inflation.

mule¹ ▶noun 1 the offspring of a donkey and a horse (strictly, a male donkey and a female horse), typically sterile and used as a beast of burden. Compare with **HINNY¹**.
■a person compared to a mule, especially in being stupid or obstinate. ■ informal a courier for illegal drugs. ■ a small tractor or locomotive, typically one that is electrically powered.
2 a hybrid plant or animal, especially a sterile one.
■any of several standard cross-bred varieties of sheep.
3 (also **spinning mule**) a kind of spinning machine producing yarn on spindles, invented by Samuel Crompton in 1779.
4 a coin with the obverse and reverse of designs not originally intended to be used together.
– ORIGIN Old English *mūl*, probably of Germanic origin, from Latin *mulus, mula*; reinforced in Middle English by Old French *mule*.

mule² ▶noun a slipper or light shoe without a back.
– ORIGIN mid 16th cent.: from French, 'slipper'.

mule deer ▶noun a North American deer with long ears and black markings on the tail.
● *Odocoileus hemionus*, family Cervidae.

mulesing /'mjuːlzɪŋ/ ▶noun [mass noun] the process of removing folds of skin from the tail area of a sheep, intended to reduce fly strike.
– ORIGIN 1940s: from the name of John H. W. *Mules* (1876–1946), the Australian sheep farmer who developed the process, + **-ING**.

muleta /mə'leɪtə/ ▶noun a red cloth fixed to a stick, brandished by a matador during a bullfight.
– ORIGIN Spanish.

muleteer /ˌmjuːlɪ'tɪə/ ▶noun a person who drives mules.
– ORIGIN mid 16th cent.: from French *muletier*, from *mulet*, diminutive of Old French *mul* 'mule'.

muley¹ /'mjuːli/ ▶adjective chiefly US (of cattle) hornless.
– ORIGIN late 16th cent. (as noun): perhaps from Irish *maol* or Welsh *moel*, literally 'bald', used in the sense 'hornless cow'. The adjective dates from the mid 19th cent.

muley² /'mjuːli/ (also **mulie**) ▶noun (pl. **-eys** or **-ies**) US informal a mule deer.

mulga /'mʌlɡə/ ▶noun (also **mulga tree** or **bush**) a small Australian acacia tree or shrub with greyish foliage, which forms dense scrubby growth and yields brown and yellow timber.
● *Acacia aneura*, family Leguminosae.
■[mass noun] an area of scrub or bush dominated by this plant. ■ (**the mulga**) Austral. informal the outback.
– ORIGIN mid 19th cent.: from Yuwaalaraay (an Aboriginal language of New South Wales).

mulgara /məl'ɡɑːrə/ ▶noun a rat-sized carnivorous marsupial with a pointed snout, large eyes, and a short crested tail, native to central Australia.
● *Dasycercus cristicauda*, family Dasyuridae.
– ORIGIN 1940s: probably from Wangganguru (an Aboriginal language) *mardagura*.

Mulhacén /ˌmuːlə'sɛn, Spanish mula'θen, -sen/ a mountain in southern Spain, south-east of Granada, in the Sierra Nevada range. Rising to 3,482 m (11,424 ft), it is the highest mountain in the country.

Mülheim /'muːlhaɪm, German 'myːlhaɪm/ an industrial city in western Germany, in North Rhine-Westphalia south-west of Essen; pop. 177,040 (1991). Full name **MÜLHEIM AN DER RUHR** /ˌan dɛː 'rʊə, German ˌan dɛːɐ 'ruːɐ/.

Mulhouse /muː'luːz/ an industrial city in NE France, in Alsace; pop. 109,900 (1990). It was a free imperial city until it joined the French Republic in 1798. In 1871, after the Franco-Prussian War, the city became part of the German Empire until it was reunited with France in 1918. German name **MÜHLHAUSEN**.

muliebrity /ˌmjuːlɪ'ɛbrɪti/ ▶noun [mass noun] poetic/literary womanly qualities; womanhood.
– ORIGIN late 16th cent.: from late Latin *muliebritas*, from Latin *mulier* 'woman'.

mulish /'mjuːlɪʃ/ ▶adjective resembling or likened to a mule in being stubborn: *Belinda's face took on a mulish expression.*
– DERIVATIVES **mulishly** adverb, **mulishness** noun.

Mull a large island of the Inner Hebrides; chief town, Tobermory. It is separated from the coast of Scotland near Oban by the Sound of Mull.

mull¹ ▶verb [with obj.] think about (a fact, proposal, or request) deeply and at length: *she began to mull over the various possibilities.*
– ORIGIN mid 19th cent.: of uncertain origin.

mull² ▶verb [with obj.] [usu. as adj. **mulled**] warm (an alcoholic drink, especially wine or beer) and add sugar and spices to it: *delicious mulled wine.*
– ORIGIN early 17th cent.: of unknown origin.

mull³ ▶noun [in place names] Scottish term for **PROMONTORY**: *the Mull of Kintyre.*
– ORIGIN Middle English: compare with Scottish Gaelic *maol* and Icelandic *múli.*

mull⁴ ▶noun [mass noun] humus formed under non-acid conditions.
– ORIGIN 1920s: from Danish *muld* 'soil'.

mull⁵ ▶noun [mass noun] thin, soft plain muslin, used in bookbinding for joining the spine of a book to its cover.

– ORIGIN late 17th cent.: abbreviation, from Hindi *malmal.*

mullah /'mʌlə, 'mʊlə/ ▶noun a Muslim learned in Islamic theology and sacred law.
– ORIGIN early 17th cent.: from Persian, Turkish, and Urdu *mullā*, from Arabic *mawlā.*

mullein /'mʌlɪn/ ▶noun a herbaceous Eurasian plant with woolly leaves and tall spikes of yellow flowers.
● Genus *Verbascum*, family Scrophulariaceae: several species, in particular the **common** (or **great**) **mullein** (*V. thapsus*).
– ORIGIN late Middle English: from Old French *moleine*, of Celtic origin; compare with Breton *melen*, Cornish and Welsh *melyn* 'yellow'.

Muller /'mʌlə/, Hermann Joseph (1890–1967), American geneticist. He discovered that X-rays induce mutations in the genetic material of the fruit fly *Drosophila* and thus recognized the danger of X-radiation to living things. Nobel Prize for Physiology or Medicine (1946).

Müller¹ /'mʊlə, German 'mylɐ/, (Friedrich) Max (1823–1900), German-born British philologist. He is remembered for his edition of the Sanskrit *Rig-veda* (1849–75).

Müller² /'mʊlə, German 'mylɐ/, Johannes Peter (1801–58), German anatomist and zoologist. He was a pioneer of comparative and microscopical methods in biology.

Müller³ /'mʊlə, German 'mylɐ/, Paul Hermann (1899–1965), Swiss chemist. He synthesized DDT in 1939 and soon patented it as an insecticide. Nobel Prize for Physiology or Medicine (1948).

muller /'mʌlə/ ▶noun a stone or other heavy weight used for grinding artists' pigments or other material on a slab.
– ORIGIN late Middle English: perhaps from Anglo-Norman French *moldre* 'to grind'.

Müllerian mimicry /mʊ'lɪərɪən/ ▶noun [mass noun] Zoology a form of mimicry in which two or more noxious animals develop similar appearances as a shared protective device.
– ORIGIN late 19th cent.: named after Johann F. T. *Müller* (1821–97), German zoologist.

Müller–Thurgau /ˌmʊlə'tʊəɡaʊ, German ˌmylɐ'tuːɐɡaʊ/ ▶noun [mass noun] a variety of white grape used for making wine, developed as a cross between the Sylvaner and the Riesling vines.
■a wine made from this.
– ORIGIN named after Hermann *Müller-Thurgau*, Swiss viniculturist.

mullet¹ ▶noun any of various chiefly marine fish that are widely caught for food.
● Families Mullidae (see **RED MULLET**) and Mugilidae (see **GREY MULLET**).
– ORIGIN late Middle English: from Old French *mulet*, diminutive of Latin *mullus* 'red mullet', from Greek *mullos.*

mullet² ▶noun Heraldry a star with five (or more) straight-edged points or rays, as a charge or a mark of cadency for a third son.
– ORIGIN late Middle English: from Old French *molette* 'rowel', diminutive of *meule* 'millstone', from Latin *mola* 'grindstone'.

mulligan /'mʌlɪɡ(ə)n/ ▶noun informal, chiefly N. Amer. 1 a stew made from odds and ends of food.
2 (in informal golf) an extra stroke allowed after a poor shot, not counted on the scorecard.
– ORIGIN early 20th cent.: apparently from the surname *Mulligan.*

mulligatawny /ˌmʌlɪɡə'tɔːni/ (also **mulligatawny soup**) ▶noun [mass noun] a spicy meat soup originally made in India.
– ORIGIN from Tamil *miḻaku-taṇṇi* 'pepper-water'.

Mullingar /ˌmʌlɪn'ɡɑː/ the county town of Westmeath, in the Republic of Ireland; pop. 7,470 (1981).

mullion /'mʌljən/ ▶noun a vertical bar between the panes of glass in a window. Compare with **TRANSOM**.
– DERIVATIVES **mullioned** adjective.
– ORIGIN mid 16th cent.: probably an altered form of **MONIAL**.

mullock /'mʌlək/ ▶noun [mass noun] Austral./NZ or dialect worthless material; rubbish.
■Austral./NZ rock which contains no gold or from which gold has been extracted. ■ Austral./NZ worthless information; nonsense.
– PHRASES **poke mullock at** Austral./NZ informal ridicule (someone).

– ORIGIN late Middle English: diminutive of earlier *mul* 'dust, rubbish', from Middle Dutch.

mulloway /ˈmʌləweɪ/ ▶ noun a large edible fast-swimming predatory fish of Australian coastal waters, which is popular with anglers. Also called **JEWFISH**.
● *Johnius antarctica*, family Sciaenidae.
– ORIGIN mid 19th cent.: from Yaralde (an Aboriginal language of South Australia).

Mulready /mʌlˈriːdi/ ▶ noun a postage envelope with a design by the Irish painter William Mulready (1786–1863), the designer of the first penny postage envelope (1840).

Mulroney /mʌlˈruːni/, (Martin) Brian (b.1939), Canadian Progressive Conservative statesman, Prime Minister 1984–93.

Multan /mʊlˈtɑːn/ a commercial city in Punjab province, east central Pakistan; pop. 980,000 (1991).

multangular /mʌlˈtaŋɡjʊlə/ ▶ adjective rare (of a polygon) having many angles.
– ORIGIN late 17th cent.: from medieval Latin *multangularis*.

multi- ▶ combining form more than one; many: *multicolour | multicultural*.
– ORIGIN from Latin *multus* 'much, many'.

multi-access ▶ adjective (of a computer system) allowing the simultaneous connection of a number of terminals.

multi-agency ▶ adjective involving cooperation between several organizations, especially in crime prevention, social welfare programmes, or research: *a multi-agency conference*.

multiaxial ▶ adjective involving or possessing several or many axes.

multibuy ▶ noun [usu. as modifier] a purchase of two or more articles at a special discount compared to the price when bought separately: *multibuy discounts*.

multicast ▶ verb (past and past participle **multicast**) [with obj.] send (data) across a computer network to several users at the same time.
▶ noun a set of data sent across a computer network to many users at the same time.

multicellular ▶ adjective Biology (of an organism or part) having or consisting of many cells.
– DERIVATIVES **multicellularity** noun.

multichannel ▶ adjective employing or possessing many communication or television channels.

multicoloured (also **multicolour**) ▶ adjective having many colours.

multicultural ▶ adjective of, relating to, or constituting several cultural or ethnic groups within a society: *multicultural education*.
– DERIVATIVES **multiculturalism** noun, **multiculturalist** noun & adjective, **multiculturally** adverb.

multidimensional ▶ adjective of or involving several dimensions: *multidimensional space*.
– DERIVATIVES **multidimensionality** noun, **multidimensionally** adverb.

multidirectional ▶ adjective of, involving, or operating in several directions: *a multidirectional antenna*.

multidisciplinary ▶ adjective combining or involving several academic disciplines or professional specializations in an approach to a topic or problem.

multi-ethnic ▶ adjective of, relating to, or constituting several ethnic groups: *a multi-ethnic society*.

multifaceted ▶ adjective having many facets: *the play of light on the diamond's multifaceted surface* | figurative *this is a rapidly moving and multifaceted subject*.

multifactorial ▶ adjective involving or dependent on a number of factors or causes.

multi-faith ▶ adjective involving or characterized by a variety of religions: *the multi-faith approach aims to develop an attitude of tolerance*.

multifarious /ˌmʌltɪˈfɛːrɪəs/ ▶ adjective many and of various types: *multifarious activities*.
■having many varied parts or aspects: *a vast multifarious organization*.
– DERIVATIVES **multifariously** adverb, **multifariousness** noun.
– ORIGIN late 16th cent.: from Latin *multifarius* + -OUS.

multifid /ˈmʌltɪfɪd/ ▶ adjective Botany & Zoology divided into several or many parts by deep clefts or notches.
– ORIGIN mid 18th cent.: from Latin *multifidus*, from *multus* 'much, many' + -*fid* from *fidus* 'cleft, split'.

multifilament ▶ adjective denoting a cord or yarn composed of a number of strands or filaments wound together.

multiflora (also **multiflora rose**) ▶ noun an East Asian shrubby or climbing rose which bears clusters of small single pink or white flowers.
● *Rosa multiflora*, family Rosaceae.
– ORIGIN early 19th cent.: from late Latin, feminine of *multiflorus* 'multiflorous'.

multifocal ▶ adjective chiefly Medicine & Optics having more than one focus.

multifoil ▶ noun Architecture an ornament consisting of more than five foils.

multifold ▶ adjective manifold.

multiform ▶ adjective existing in many forms or kinds: *a very complex, multiform illness like cancer*.
– DERIVATIVES **multiformity** noun.

multifunctional (also **multifunction**) ▶ adjective having or fulfilling several functions: *a multifunctional optical-disk drive*.

multigenerational ▶ adjective of or relating to several generations: *multigenerational families*.

multigrade ▶ noun 1 an engine oil meeting the requirements of several standard grades.
2 (trademark in the US) a kind of photographic paper made with two emulsions of different sensitivities, from which prints with different levels of contrast can be made using colour filters.

multigrain ▶ adjective (of bread) made from more than one kind of grain.

multigravida /ˌmʌltɪˈɡravɪdə/ ▶ noun (pl. **multigravidae** /-diː/) Medicine & Zoology a woman (or female animal) that is or has been pregnant for at least a second time.
– ORIGIN late 19th cent.: from MULTI- 'many', on the pattern of *primigravida*.

multigym ▶ noun an apparatus on which a number of weightlifting and other exercises can be performed to improve muscle tone.

multihull ▶ noun a boat with two or more hulls, especially three.

multilateral ▶ adjective agreed upon or participated in by three or more parties, especially the governments of different countries: *multilateral negotiations | multilateral nuclear disarmament*.
■having members or contributors from several groups, especially several different countries: *multilateral aid agencies*.
– DERIVATIVES **multilateralism** noun, **multilateralist** adjective & noun, **multilaterally** adverb.

multilayer chiefly technical ▶ adjective relating to or consisting of several or many layers: *a multilayer circuit board*.
▶ noun a coating or deposit consisting of several or many layers.

multilayered ▶ adjective having or involving several or many layers.

multilevel (also **multilevelled**) ▶ adjective of, relating to, or involving many levels.

multilingual ▶ adjective in or using several languages: *a multilingual dictionary*.
– DERIVATIVES **multilingualism** noun, **multilingually** adverb.

multimedia ▶ adjective (of art, education, etc.) using more than one medium of expression or communication.
▶ noun [mass noun] an extension of hypertext allowing the provision of audio and video material cross-referenced to a computer text.

multimeter ▶ noun an instrument designed to measure electric current, voltage, and usually resistance, typically over several ranges of value.

multimillion ▶ adjective [attrib.] costing or involving several million of a currency: [in combination] *a multimillion-dollar advertising campaign*.

multimillionaire ▶ noun a person with assets worth several million pounds or dollars.

multimode (also **multimodal**) ▶ adjective characterized by several different modes of activity or occurrence.
■Statistics (of a frequency curve or distribution) having several modes or maxima. ■ Statistics (of a property) occurring with such a distribution.

multinational ▶ adjective including or involving several countries or individuals of several nationalities: *1,500 troops were sent to join the multinational force*.
■(of a business organization) operating in several countries: *multinational corporations*.
▶ noun a company operating in several countries.
– DERIVATIVES **multinationally** adverb.

multinomial /ˌmʌltɪˈnəʊmɪəl/ ▶ adjective & noun Mathematics another term for POLYNOMIAL.
– ORIGIN early 17th cent.: from MULTI- 'many', on the pattern of *binomial*.

multi-occupy ▶ verb [with obj.] [usu. as adj. **multi-occupied**] occupy (a building) as one of a number of independent occupants or families of occupants, typically as tenants: *a multi-occupied building*.
– DERIVATIVES **multi-occupancy** noun, **multi-occupation** noun.

multipack ▶ noun a package containing a number of similar or identical products sold at a discount compared to the price when bought separately.

multipara /mʌlˈtɪp(ə)rə/ ▶ noun (pl. **multiparae** /-riː/) Medicine & Zoology a woman (or female animal) that has had more than one pregnancy resulting in viable offspring.
– ORIGIN mid 19th cent.: modern Latin, feminine of *multiparus* 'multiparous'.

multiparous /mʌlˈtɪp(ə)rəs/ ▶ adjective Medicine (of a woman) having borne more than one child.
■chiefly Zoology producing more than one young at a birth.

multipartite /ˌmʌltɪˈpɑːtʌɪt/ ▶ adjective having several or many parts or divisions.
■Biology (of a virus) existing as two or more separate but incomplete particles. ■another term for MULTIPARTY.

multiparty ▶ adjective of or involving several political parties: *multiparty elections*.

multiphase ▶ adjective in, of, or relating to more than one phase.
■(of an electrical device or circuit) polyphase.

multiplay ▶ adjective denoting a compact disc player which can be stacked with a number of discs before needing to be reloaded.

multiplayer ▶ noun 1 a compact disc player which can play a number of discs in succession.
2 a multimedia computer and home entertainment system that integrates a number of conventional and interactive audio and video functions with those of a personal computer.
▶ adjective denoting a computer game designed for or involving several players.

multiple ▶ adjective having or involving several parts, elements, or members: *multiple occupancy | a multiple pile-up | a multiple birth*.
■numerous and often varied: *words with multiple meanings*. ■(of a disease, injury, or disability) complex in its nature or effects; affecting several parts of the body: *a multiple fracture of the femur*.
▶ noun 1 a number that may be divided by another a certain number of times without a remainder: *15, 20, or any multiple of five*.
2 (also **multiple shop** or **store**) chiefly Brit. a shop with branches in many places, especially one selling a specific type of product.
– ORIGIN mid 17th cent.: from French, from late Latin *multiplus*, alteration of Latin *multiplex* (see MULTIPLEX).

multiple-choice ▶ adjective (of a question in an examination) accompanied by several possible answers from which the candidate must try to choose the correct one.

multiple fruit ▶ noun Botany a fruit formed from carpels derived from several flowers, such as a pineapple.

multiple personality ▶ noun [often as modifier] Psychology a rare dissociative disorder in which two or more personalities with distinct memories and behaviour patterns apparently exist in one individual: *multiple-personality disorder*.

multiple sclerosis ▶ noun see SCLEROSIS.

multiple star ▶ noun a group of stars very close together as seen from the earth, especially one whose members are in fact close together and rotate around a common centre.

multiplet ▶ noun Physics a group of closely associated things, especially closely spaced spectral lines or atomic energy levels, or subatomic

particles differing only in a single property (e.g. charge or strangeness).
– ORIGIN 1920s: from **MULTIPLE**, on the pattern of words such as *doublet* and *triplet*.

multiple unit ▶ noun a diesel or electric passenger train of two or more carriages powered by integral motors which drive a number of axles throughout the train.

multiplex ▶ adjective consisting of many elements in a complex relationship: *multiplex ties of work and friendship.*
  ■ involving simultaneous transmission of several messages along a single channel of communication. ■ (of a cinema) having several separate screens within one building.
▶ noun 1 a system or signal involving simultaneous transmission of several messages along a single channel of communication.
  2 a cinema with several separate screens.
▶ verb [with obj.] incorporate into a multiplex signal or system.
– DERIVATIVES **multiplexer** (also **multiplexor**) noun.
– ORIGIN late Middle English in the mathematical sense 'multiple': from Latin.

multipliable ▶ adjective able to be multiplied.

multiplicable /ˈmʌltɪˌplɪkəb(ə)l/ ▶ adjective able to be multiplied.
– ORIGIN late 15th cent.: from Old French, from medieval Latin *multiplicabilis*, from Latin, from *multiplex, multiplic-* (see **MULTIPLEX**).

multiplicand /ˌmʌltɪplɪˈkand, ˈmʌltɪplɪˌkand/ ▶ noun a quantity which is to be multiplied by another (the multiplier).
– ORIGIN late 16th cent.: from medieval Latin *multiplicandus* 'to be multiplied', gerundive of Latin *multiplicare* (see **MULTIPLY**[1]).

multiplication ▶ noun [mass noun] the process or skill of multiplying: *we need to use both multiplication and division to find the answers* | [count noun] *these formulae involve a number of multiplications.*
  ■ Mathematics the process of combining matrices, vectors, or other quantities under specific rules to obtain their product.
– ORIGIN late Middle English: from Old French, or from Latin *multiplicatio(n-)*, from *multiplicare* (see **MULTIPLY**[1]).

multiplication sign ▶ noun the sign ×, used to indicate that one quantity is to be multiplied by another, as in $2 \times 3 = 6$.

multiplication table ▶ noun a list of multiples of a particular number, typically from 1 to 12.

multiplicative /ˈmʌltɪˌplɪkətɪv/ ▶ noun subject to or of the nature of multiplication: *coronary risk factors are multiplicative.*

multiplicity ▶ noun (pl. **-ies**) a large number: *his climbing record lists a multiplicity of ascents.*
  ■ a large variety: *the rainforests and the multiplicity of species which they harbour.*
– ORIGIN late Middle English: from late Latin *multiplicitas*, from Latin *multiplex* (see **MULTIPLEX**).

multiplier ▶ noun a quantity by which a given number (the multiplicand) is to be multiplied.
  ■ Economics a factor by which an increment of income exceeds the resulting increment of saving or investment. ■ a device for increasing by repetition the intensity of an electric current, force, etc. to a measurable level. ■ a type of fishing reel with a geared spool.

multiply[1] /ˈmʌltɪplʌɪ/ ▶ verb (**-ies, -ied**) [with obj.] obtain from (a number) another which contains the first number a specified number of times: *I asked you to multiply fourteen by nineteen* | [no obj.] *we all know how to multiply by ten.*
  ■ increase or cause to increase greatly in number or quantity: [no obj.] *ever since I became a landlord my troubles have multiplied tenfold* | [with obj.] *cigarette smoking combines with other factors to multiply the risks of atherosclerosis.* ■ [no obj.] (of an animal or other organism) increase in number by reproducing. ■ propagate (plants).
– ORIGIN Middle English: from Old French *multiplier*, from Latin *multiplicare.*

multiply[2] /ˈmʌltɪplɪ/ ▶ adverb [often as submodifier] in several different ways or respects: *multiply injured patients.*

multipolar ▶ adjective 1 having many poles or extremities.
  2 polarized in several ways or directions.
– DERIVATIVES **multipolarity** noun, **multipole** noun.

multiprocessing (also **multiprogramming**)
▶ noun Computing another term for **MULTITASKING**.

multiprocessor ▶ noun a computer with more than one central processor.

multi-purpose ▶ adjective having several purposes or functions: *two tools may do a better job than one multi-purpose tool.*

multiracial ▶ adjective made up of or relating to people of many races: *multiracial education.*
– DERIVATIVES **multiracialism** noun, **multiracialist** adjective & noun, **multiracially** adverb.

multi-role ▶ adjective [attrib.] (chiefly of an aircraft) capable of performing several roles.

multisession ▶ adjective Computing denoting a format for recording digital information on to a CD-ROM disc over two or more separate sessions.

multispectral ▶ adjective operating in or involving several regions of the electromagnetic spectrum: *multispectral images from satellites.*

multistage ▶ adjective [attrib.] consisting of or relating to several stages or processes: *a multistage decision-making process.*
  ■ (of a rocket) having at least two sections which contain their own motor and are jettisoned as their fuel runs out. ■ (of a pump, turbine, or similar device) having more than one rotor.

multi-storey ▶ adjective [attrib.] (of a building) having several storeys.
▶ noun Brit. informal a car park with several storeys.

multitasking ▶ noun [mass noun] Computing the execution of more than one program or task simultaneously by sharing the resources of the computer processor between them.
– DERIVATIVES **multitask** verb.

multithreading ▶ noun [mass noun] Computing a technique by which a single set of code can be used by several processors at different stages of execution.
– DERIVATIVES **multithreaded** adjective.

multi-track ▶ adjective relating to or made by the mixing of several separately recorded tracks of sound: *the advent of multi-track recording facilities.*
▶ noun a recording made from the mixing of several separately recorded tracks.
▶ verb [with obj.] record using multi-track recording: [as adj. **multi-tracked**] *multi-tracked vocals.*

multituberculate /ˌmʌltɪtjuːˈbəːkjʊlət/ ▶ noun a small primitive fossil mammal of a mainly Cretaceous and Palaeocene order, distinguished by having molar teeth with several cusps arranged in two or three rows.
  ● Order Multituberculata, subclass Allotheria.
– ORIGIN late 19th cent.: from modern Latin *Multituberculata*, from **MULTI-** 'many' + Latin *tuberculum* 'tubercle'.

multitude ▶ noun a large number: *a multitude of medical conditions are due to being overweight.*
  ■ (the multitudes) large numbers of people: *the multitudes using the roads.* ■ (the multitude) a large gathering of people: *Father Peter addressed the multitude.* ■ (the multitude) the mass of ordinary people without power or influence: *placing ultimate political power in the hands of the multitude.* ■ [mass noun] archaic the state of being numerous: *they would swarm over the river in their multitude.*
– ORIGIN Middle English: via Old French from Latin *multitudo*, from *multus* 'many'.

multitudinous /ˌmʌltɪˈtjuːdɪnəs/ ▶ adjective very numerous: *multitudinous rugs kept us warm.*
  ■ consisting of or containing many individuals or elements: *the multitudinous array of chemical substances that exist in the natural world.* ■ poetic/literary (of a body of water) vast.
– DERIVATIVES **multitudinously** adverb, **multitudinousness** noun.
– ORIGIN early 17th cent.: from Latin *multitudo* (see **MULTITUDE**) + **-OUS**.

multi-user ▶ adjective [attrib.] (of a computer system) able to be used by a number of people simultaneously.
  ■ denoting a computer game in which several players interact simultaneously using the Internet or other communications.

multivalent /ˌmʌltɪˈveɪl(ə)nt/ ▶ adjective 1 having or susceptible of many applications, interpretations, meanings, or values: *visually complex and multivalent work.*
  2 Medicine (of an antigen or antibody) having several

sites at which attachment to an antibody or antigen can occur: *a multivalent antiserum.* Compare with **POLYVALENT**.
  3 Chemistry another term for **POLYVALENT**.
– DERIVATIVES **multivalence** noun, **multivalency** noun.

multivalve ▶ adjective [attrib.] (of an internal-combustion engine) having more than two valves per cylinder, typically four (two inlet and two exhaust).

multivariate /ˌmʌltɪˈvɛːrɪət/ ▶ adjective Statistics involving two or more variable quantities.

multivendor ▶ adjective [attrib.] denoting or relating to computer hardware or software products or network services from more than one supplier.

multiverse ▶ noun an infinite realm of being or potential being of which the universe is regarded as a part or instance.

multivibrator ▶ noun Electronics a device consisting of two amplifying transistors or valves, each with its output connected to the input of the other, which produces an oscillatory signal.

multivitamin ▶ adjective [attrib.] containing a combination of vitamins: *multivitamin tablets.*

multiway ▶ adjective having several paths, routes, or channels: *a multiway switch.*

multum in parvo /ˌmʌltəm ɪn ˈpɑːvəʊ/ ▶ noun a great deal in a small space.
– ORIGIN Latin, literally 'much in little'.

multure /ˈmʌltʃə/ ▶ noun [mass noun] historical a toll of grain or flour due to a miller in return for grinding corn.
  ■ the right to collect this.
– ORIGIN Middle English: from Old French *moulture*, from medieval Latin *molitura*, from *molit-* 'ground', from the verb *molere*.

mum[1] ▶ noun Brit. informal one's mother.
– ORIGIN mid 17th cent.: abbreviation of **MUMMY**[1].

mum[2] ▶ adjective
– PHRASES **keep mum** informal remain silent, especially so as not to reveal a secret: *he was keeping mum about a possible move to West Ham.* **mum's the word** informal (as a request or warning) say nothing; don't reveal a secret.
– ORIGIN late Middle English: imitative of a sound made with closed lips.

mum[3] ▶ verb (**mummed, mumming**) [no obj.] act in a traditional masked mime or a mummers' play.
– ORIGIN late Middle English: compare with **MUM**[2] and Middle Low German *mummen*.

Mumbai /mʊmˈbʌɪ/ official name (from 1995) for **BOMBAY**.

mumble ▶ verb 1 [reporting verb] say something indistinctly and quietly, making it difficult for others to hear: [with obj.] *he mumbled something she didn't catch* | [with direct speech] *'Sorry,' she mumbled.*
  2 [with obj.] bite or chew with toothless gums or eat without making much use of the teeth.
▶ noun [usu. in sing.] a quiet and indistinct utterance: *Rosie had replied in a mumble.*
– DERIVATIVES **mumbler** noun, **mumblingly** adverb.
– ORIGIN Middle English: frequentative of **MUM**[2].

mumblety-peg /ˈmʌmb(ə)ltɪ/ ▶ noun [mass noun] chiefly US a game in which each player in turn throws a knife or pointed stick from a series of positions, continuing until it fails to stick in the ground.
– ORIGIN early 17th cent.: also in the form *mumble the peg*, from *mumble* in the late 16th-cent. sense 'bite as if with toothless gums', from the requirement of the game that an unsuccessful player withdraw a peg from the ground using the mouth.

mumbo-jumbo ▶ noun [mass noun] informal language or ritual causing or intended to cause confusion or bewilderment: *a maze of legal mumbo jumbo.*
– ORIGIN mid 18th cent. (as *Mumbo Jumbo*, denoting a supposed African idol): of unknown origin; the current sense dates from the late 19th cent.

mumchance /ˈmʌmtʃɑːns/ ▶ adjective archaic silent; tongue-tied.
– ORIGIN late 17th cent.: from Middle Low German *mummenschanze*, denoting a game of dice (also an early sense in English from the early 16th cent. to the mid 17th cent.).

mu-meson ▶ noun another term for **MUON**.

mummer ▶ noun an actor in a traditional masked mime or a mummers' play.

■archaic or derogatory an actor in the theatre.
— ORIGIN late Middle English: from Old French *momeur*, from *momer* 'act in a mime'; perhaps of Germanic origin.

Mummerset ▶ noun [mass noun] an imitation rustic West Country accent used by actors.
— ORIGIN 1950s: probably from **MUMMER**, on the pattern of *Somerset*.

mummers' play (also **mumming play**) ▶ noun a traditional English folk play, of a type often associated with Christmas and popular in the 18th and early 19th centuries. The plot typically features Saint George and involves the miraculous resurrection of a character.

mummery ▶ noun (pl. **-ies**) a performance by mummers.
■[mass noun] ridiculous ceremonial, especially of a religious nature: *that's all it is, mere mummery.*
— ORIGIN mid 16th cent.: from Old French *momerie*, from *momer* (see **MUMMER**).

mummichog /ˈmʌmɪtʃɒg/ ▶ noun a small marine killifish which lives along the sheltered shores and estuaries of eastern North America. It is widely kept in aquaria and is also used as bait and for biological research.
● *Fundulus heteroclitus*, family Cyprinodontidae (or Fundulidae).
— ORIGIN late 18th cent.: from Narragansett *moamitteaug.*

mummify ▶ verb (**-ies**, **-ied**) [with obj.] [usu. as adj. **mummified**] (especially in ancient Egypt) preserve (a body) by embalming and wrapping it in cloth.
■shrivel or dry up (a body or a thing), thus preserving it: *the wind must have dehydrated and mummified the body.*
— DERIVATIVES **mummification** noun.

mummy[1] ▶ noun (pl. **-ies**) Brit. informal one's mother (chiefly as a child's term).
— ORIGIN late 18th cent.: perhaps an alteration of earlier **MAMMY**.

mummy[2] ▶ noun (pl. **-ies**) (especially in ancient Egypt) a body of a human being or animal that has been ceremonially preserved by removal of the internal organs, treatment with natron and resin, and wrapping in bandages. In Egypt the preservation of the body was regarded as important for the afterlife.
— ORIGIN late Middle English (denoting a substance taken from embalmed bodies and used in medicines): from French *momie*, from medieval Latin *mumia* and Arabic *mūmiyā* 'embalmed body', perhaps from Persian *mūm* 'wax'.

mumpish ▶ adjective informal, dated sullen or sulky.
— ORIGIN early 18th cent.: from obsolete *mump* 'grimace, have a miserable expression' + **-ISH**[1].

mumps ▶ plural noun [treated as sing.] a contagious and infectious viral disease causing swelling of the parotid salivary glands in the face, and a risk of sterility in adult males.
— ORIGIN late 16th cent.: from obsolete *mump* 'grimace, have a miserable expression'.

mumpsimus /ˈmʌmpsɪməs/ ▶ noun (pl. **mumpsimuses**) a traditional custom or notion adhered to although shown to be unreasonable.
■a person who obstinately adheres to such a custom or notion.
— ORIGIN mid 16th cent.: erroneously for Latin *sumpsimus* in *quod in ore sumpsimus* 'which we have taken into the mouth' (Eucharist), in a story of an illiterate priest who, when corrected, replied 'I will not change my old mumpsimus for your new sumpsimus'.

mumsy Brit. informal ▶ adjective (of a woman) giving an impression of dull domesticity; homely and unfashionable: *she wore a big mumsy dress.*
▶ noun [usu. as name] chiefly humorous one's mother.
— ORIGIN late 19th cent.: humorous variant of **MUMMY**[1].

mun /mʌn/ ▶ auxiliary verb dialect form of **MUST**[1].
— ORIGIN Middle English: from Old Norse *muna*, from the Germanic base of **MIND**.

Munch /mʊŋk/, Edvard (1863–1944), Norwegian painter and engraver. He infused his subjects with an intense emotionalism, exploring the use of vivid colour and linear distortion to express feelings about life and death. Notable works: his *Frieze of Life* sequence, incorporating *The Scream* (1893).

munch ▶ verb [with obj.] eat (something) with a continuous and often audible action of the jaws.

— DERIVATIVES **muncher** noun.
— ORIGIN late Middle English: imitative; compare with **CRUNCH**.

Munchausen, Baron /ˈmɒn(t)ʃˌhaʊz(ə)n, German ˈmʏnç.haʊz/ the hero of a book of fantastic travellers' tales (1785) written in English by a German, Rudolph Erich Raspe. The original Baron Munchausen is said to have lived 1720–97, to have served in the Russian army against the Turks, and to have related extravagant tales of his prowess.

Munchausen's syndrome /ˈmɒn(t)ʃˌhaʊz(ə)nz/ ▶ noun [mass noun] Psychiatry a mental disorder in which a person repeatedly feigns severe illness so as to obtain hospital treatment.
■(**Munchausen's syndrome by proxy**) a mental disorder in which a person seeks attention by inducing or feigning illness in another person, typically a child.

München /ˈmʏnçn/ German name for **MUNICH**.

munchie ▶ noun (pl. **-ies**) (usu. **munchies**) informal a snack or small item of food.
■(**the munchies**) a sudden strong desire for food: *I bought a pork pie to stave off the munchies.*

munchkin ▶ noun N. Amer. informal a child.
— ORIGIN from the *Munchkins*, depicted as a race of small childlike creatures, in L. Frank Baum's *The Wonderful Wizard of Oz* (1900).

Munda /ˈmʊndə/ ▶ noun (pl. same or **Mundas**) 1 a member of a group of indigenous peoples living scattered in a region from east central India to Nepal and Bangladesh.
2 [mass noun] a family of languages spoken by these peoples, distantly related to the Mon-Khmer family, with which they are sometimes classified as Austro-Asiatic. They have over 5 million speakers altogether; the most widely spoken is Santali.
■any language of this family.
▶ adjective relating to or denoting the Munda or their languages.
— ORIGIN the name in Munda.

mundane /ˈmʌndeɪn, mʌnˈdeɪn/ ▶ adjective 1 lacking interest or excitement; dull: *seeking a way out of his mundane, humdrum existence.*
2 of this earthly world rather than a heavenly or spiritual one.
■of, relating to, or denoting the branch of astrology that deals with political, social, economic, and geophysical events and processes.
— DERIVATIVES **mundanely** adverb, **mundaneness** noun, **mundanity** /-ˈdaniti/ noun (pl. **-ies**).
— ORIGIN late Middle English (in sense 2): from Old French *mondain*, from late Latin *mundanus*, from Latin *mundus* 'world'. Sense 1 dates from the late 19th cent.

mung /mʌŋ, muːŋ/ (also **moong** or **mung bean**) ▶ noun 1 a small round green bean.
2 the tropical Old World plant that yields these beans, commonly grown as a source of bean sprouts.
● *Vigna radiata* (or *Phaseolus aureus*), family Leguminosae.
— ORIGIN early 19th cent.: from Hindi *mūng*.

mungo /ˈmʌŋgəʊ/ ▶ noun [mass noun] cloth made from recycled woven or felted material.
— ORIGIN mid 19th cent.: of unknown origin.

muni[1] /ˈmjuːni/ ▶ noun (pl. **munis**) US short for **MUNICIPAL BOND**.

muni[2] /ˈmʊni/ ▶ noun (pl. **munis**) (especially in India) an inspired holy person; an ascetic, hermit, or sage.
— ORIGIN from Sanskrit, literally 'silent', from *man* 'think'.

munia /ˈmuːnɪə/ ▶ noun a South Asian waxbill, especially a mannikin or an avadavat.

Munich /ˈmjuːnɪk/ a city in SE Germany, capital of Bavaria; pop. 1,229,050 (1991). German name **MÜNCHEN**.

Munich Agreement an agreement between Britain, France, Germany, and Italy, signed at Munich on 29 September 1938, under which the Sudetenland was ceded to Germany.

municipal /mjʊˈnɪsɪp(ə)l/ ▶ adjective of or relating to a town or district or its governing body: *national and municipal elections | municipal offices.*
— DERIVATIVES **municipally** adverb.
— ORIGIN mid 16th cent. (originally relating to the internal affairs of a state as distinct from its foreign relations): from Latin *municipalis* (from *municipium* 'free city', from *municeps, municip-* 'citizen with privileges', from *munia* 'civic offices') + *capere* 'take'.

municipal bond ▶ noun (chiefly in the US) a

security issued by or on behalf of a local authority.

municipality ▶ noun (pl. **-ies**) a town or district that has local government.
■the governing body of such an area.
— ORIGIN late 18th cent.: from French *municipalité*, from *municipal* (see **MUNICIPAL**).

municipalize (also **-ise**) ▶ verb [with obj.] bring under the control or ownership of the authorities of a town or district: *an expensive commitment to municipalize rented housing.*
— DERIVATIVES **municipalization** noun.

munificent /mjʊˈnɪfɪs(ə)nt/ ▶ adjective (of a gift or sum of money) larger or more generous than is usual or necessary: *a munificent gesture.*
■(of a person) very generous.
— DERIVATIVES **munificence** noun, **munificently** adverb.
— ORIGIN late 16th cent.: from Latin *munificent-* (stem of *munificentior*, comparative of *munificus* 'bountiful', from *munus* 'gift'.

muniment /ˈmjuːnɪm(ə)nt/ ▶ noun (usu. **muniments**) a document or record, especially one kept in an archive.
— ORIGIN late Middle English: via Old French from Latin *munimentum* 'defence' (in medieval Latin 'title deed'), from *munire* 'fortify'.

munition /mjʊˈnɪʃ(ə)n/ ▶ plural noun (**munitions**) military weapons, ammunition, equipment, and stores: *reserves of nuclear, chemical, and conventional munitions* | [as modifier] (**munition**) *munition factories.*
▶ verb [with obj.] supply with munitions.
— DERIVATIVES **munitioner** noun (rare).
— ORIGIN late Middle English (denoting a granted right or privilege): from French, from Latin *munitio(n-)* 'fortification', from *munire* 'fortify or secure'.

Munro[1] /mənˈrəʊ/, H. H., see **SAKI**.

Munro[2] /mʌnˈrəʊ/ ▶ noun (pl. **-os**) any of the 277 mountains in Scotland that are at least 3,000 feet high (approximately 914 metres).
— ORIGIN early 20th cent.: named after Sir Hugh Thomas Munro (1856–1919), who published a list of all such mountains in the Journal of the Scottish Mountaineering Club for 1891.

Munsell /ˈmʌns(ə)l/ ▶ noun [as modifier] denoting a system of classifying colours according to their hue, value (or lightness), and chroma (or intensity of colour).
— ORIGIN early 20th cent.: named after Albert H. Munsell (1858–1918), American painter.

munshi /ˈmuːnʃiː/ (also **moonshee**) ▶ noun (pl. **munshis**) a secretary or language teacher in the Indian subcontinent.

Munsi /ˈmʊnsi/ ▶ noun see **DELAWARE**[2] (sense 2).
— ORIGIN the name in Munsi.

munsif /ˈmuːnsɪf/ ▶ noun Indian a judge.
— ORIGIN Persian and Urdu, from Arabic *munsif* 'just or honest'.

Munster /ˈmʌnstə/ a province of the Republic of Ireland, in the south-west of the country.

Münster /ˈmʌnstə, German ˈmʏnstɐ/ a city in NW Germany; pop. 249,900 (1991). It was formerly the capital of Westphalia; the Treaty of Westphalia, ending the Thirty Years War, was signed simultaneously there and at Osnabrück in 1648.

munt /mʊnt/ ▶ noun S. African informal, offensive a black African.
— ORIGIN shortening of Zulu *umuntu* 'person'.

muntin /ˈmʌntɪn/ ▶ noun US term for **GLAZING BAR**.
— DERIVATIVES **muntined** adjective.
— ORIGIN early 17th cent.: variant of obsolete *montant* (from French, literally 'rising').

muntjac /ˈmʌntdʒak/ ▶ noun a small SE Asian deer, the male of which has tusks, small antlers, and a doglike bark. Also called **BARKING DEER**.
● Genus *Muntiacus*, family Cervidae: several species, including the **Chinese muntjac** (*M. reevesi*), which is naturalized in England and France.
— ORIGIN late 18th cent.: from Sundanese *minchek*.

Muntz metal /mʌnts/ ▶ noun [mass noun] a form of brass consisting of 60 per cent copper and 40 per cent zinc, used for casting and working at high temperatures.
— ORIGIN mid 19th cent.: named after George F. Muntz (1794–1857), English manufacturer.

munyeroo /ˌmʌnjəˈruː/ (also **munyeru**) ▶ noun Austral. a succulent plant whose seeds and leaves are used for food.

● *Portulaca oleracea* (or sometimes *Calandrinia balonensis*), family Portulacaceae.
– ORIGIN late 19th cent.: from Diyari (an Aboriginal language of South Australia).

muon /ˈmjuːɒn/ ▶ **noun** Physics an unstable subatomic particle of the same class as an electron (a lepton), but with a mass around 200 times greater. Muons make up much of the cosmic radiation reaching the earth's surface.
– DERIVATIVES **muonic** adjective.
– ORIGIN 1950s: contraction of **MU-MESON**; the particle, however, is no longer regarded as a meson.

Muqdisho /mʊkˈdɪʃəʊ/ another name for **MOGADISHU**.

murage /ˈmjʊərɪdʒ/ ▶ **noun** [mass noun] Brit. historical tax levied for building or repairing the walls of a town.
– ORIGIN late Middle English: from Old French from *mur* 'wall', from Latin *murus*.

mural /ˈmjʊər(ə)l/ ▶ **noun** a painting or other work of art executed directly on a wall.
▶ **adjective** [attrib.] of, like, or relating to a wall: *a mural escarpment*.
■ Medicine of, relating to, or occurring in the wall of a body cavity or blood vessel: *mural thrombosis*.
– DERIVATIVES **muralist** noun.
– ORIGIN late Middle English: from French, from Latin *muralis*, from *murus* 'wall'. The adjective was first used in **MURAL CROWN**; later (mid 16th cent.) the sense 'placed or executed on a wall' arose, reflected in the current noun use (dating from the early 20th cent.).

mural crown ▶ **noun 1** Heraldry a representation of a city wall in the form of a crown, borne above the shield in the arms of distinguished soldiers and of some civic authorities.
2 (in ancient Roman times) a crown or garland given to the soldier who was first to scale the wall of a besieged town.

Murano glass /mjʊˈrɑːnəʊ/ ▶ **noun** [mass noun] decorative glassware of a type associated with the island of Murano near Venice.

Murat /mjʊəˈrɑː, French myʀa/, Joachim (*c*.1767–1815), French general, king of Naples 1808–15. Murat made his name as a cavalry commander in Napoleon's Italian campaign (1800) and was made king of Naples. He attempted to become king of all Italy in 1815, but was captured in Calabria and executed.

Murchison Falls /ˈməːtʃɪs(ə)n/ former name for **KABALEGA FALLS**.

Murchison Rapids former name for **KAPACHIRA FALLS**.

Murcia /ˈmʊəsɪə, Spanish ˈmurθja, ˈmursja/ an autonomous region in SE Spain. In the Middle Ages, along with Albacete, it formed an ancient Moorish kingdom.
■ its capital city; pop. 328,840 (1991).

murder ▶ **noun** the unlawful premeditated killing of one human being by another: *the brutal murder of a German holidaymaker* | [mass noun] *he was put on trial for attempted murder*.
■ [mass noun] informal a very difficult or unpleasant task or experience: *the 40-mile-per-hour winds here are murder*. ■ [mass noun] informal something causing great discomfort to a part of the body: *that exercise is* **murder on** *the lumbar regions*.
▶ **verb** [with obj.] kill (someone) unlawfully and with premeditation: *somebody tried to murder Joe*.
■ informal punish severely or be very angry with: *my father will murder me if I'm home late*. ■ informal conclusively defeat (an opponent) in a game or sport. ■ spoil by lack of skill or knowledge: *the only thing he had murdered was the English language*. ■ informal, chiefly Brit. consume (food or drink) greedily or with relish: *I could murder some chips*.
– PHRASES **get away with (blue) murder** informal succeed in doing whatever one chooses without being punished or suffering any disadvantage. **murder one** (or **two**) N. Amer. informal first-degree (or second-degree) murder. **murder will out** murder cannot remain undetected. **scream** (or **yell**) **blue** (or N. Amer. **bloody**) **murder** informal make an extravagant and noisy protest: *if it gets into the papers, she'll be down here screaming blue murder*.
– DERIVATIVES **murderer** noun, **murderess** noun.
– ORIGIN Old English *morthor*, of Germanic origin; related to Dutch *moord* and German *Mord*, from an Indo-European root shared by Sanskrit *mará* 'death' and Latin *mors*; reinforced in Middle English by Old French *murdre*.

murderous ▶ **adjective** capable of or intending to murder; dangerously violent: *a brutal and murderous despot* | *her estranged husband was seized with murderous jealousy*.
■ (of an action, event, or plan) involving murder or extreme violence: *murderous acts of terrorism*. ■ informal extremely arduous or unpleasant: *the team had a murderous schedule of four games in ten days*. ■ informal (of a person or their expression) extremely angry: *Mary emerged from the changing room, looking murderous*.
– DERIVATIVES **murderously** adverb, **murderousness** noun.

Murdoch[1] /ˈməːdɒk/, Dame (Jean) Iris (1919–99), British novelist and philosopher, born in Ireland. She is primarily known for her novels, many of which explore complex sexual relationships and spiritual life. Notable novels: *The Sandcastle* (1957) and *The Sea, The Sea* (Booker Prize, 1978).

Murdoch[2] /ˈməːdɒk/, (Keith) Rupert (b.1931), Australian-born American publisher and media entrepreneur. As the founder and head of the News International Communications empire he owns major newspapers in Australia, Britain, and the US, together with film and television companies and the publishing firm HarperCollins.

mure /mjʊə/ ▶ **verb** [with obj.] archaic shut up in an enclosed space; imprison: *they are not a little tired of being* **mured up** *in the cottage*.
– ORIGIN late Middle English: from Old French *murer*, from Latin *murare*, from *murus* 'wall'.

murex /ˈmjʊərɛks/ ▶ **noun** (pl. **murices** /-rɪsiːz/ or **murexes**) a predatory tropical marine mollusc, the shell of which bears spines and forms a long narrow canal extending downwards from the aperture.
● Genus *Murex*, family Muricidae, class Gastropoda.
– ORIGIN late 16th cent.: from Latin; perhaps related to Greek *muax* 'sea mussel'.

muriatic acid /ˌmjʊərɪˈatɪk/ ▶ **noun** archaic term for **HYDROCHLORIC ACID**.
– DERIVATIVES **muriate** noun.
– ORIGIN late 17th cent.: *muriatic* from Latin *muriaticus*, from *muria* 'brine'.

muricate /ˈmjʊərɪkət/ ▶ **adjective** Botany & Zoology studded with short rough points.
– ORIGIN mid 17th cent.: from Latin *muricatus* 'shaped like a murex'.

murid[1] /mjʊˈriːd, mʊ-/ ▶ **noun** a follower of a Muslim holy man, especially a Sufi disciple.
■ (**Murid**) a member of any of several Muslim movements, especially one which advocated rebellion against the Russians in the Caucasus in the late 19th century.
– ORIGIN from Arabic *murīd*, literally 'he who desires'.

murid[2] /ˈmjʊərɪd/ ▶ **noun** Zoology a rodent of a very large family (Muridae) which includes most kinds of rats, mice, and voles.
– ORIGIN early 20th cent.: from modern Latin *Muridae* (plural), based on Latin *mus*, *mur-* 'mouse'.

Murillo /mʊˈriːjəʊ, -ˈriːljəʊ/, Bartolomé Esteban (*c*.1618–82), Spanish painter. He is noted for his genre scenes of urchins and peasants and for his devotional pictures.

murine /ˈmjʊərʌɪn, -rɪn/ ▶ **adjective** Zoology of, relating to, or affecting mice or related rodents.
● Murine rodents belong to the family Muridae, in particular the subfamily Murinae of the Old World.
– ORIGIN early 17th cent.: from Latin *murinus*, from *mus*, *mur-* 'mouse'.

muriqui /mjʊˈriːkwi/ ▶ **noun** (pl. **muriquis**) another term for **WOOLLY SPIDER MONKEY**.

murk ▶ **noun** [mass noun] darkness or thick mist that makes it difficult to see: *my eyes were straining to see through the murk of the rainy evening*.
▶ **adjective** archaic murky; gloomy.
– ORIGIN Old English *mirce*, of Germanic origin; reinforced in Middle English by Old Norse *myrkr*.

murky ▶ **adjective** (**murkier**, **murkiest**) dark and gloomy, especially due to thick mist: *the sky was murky and a thin drizzle was falling*.
■ (of liquid) dark and dirty; not clear: *the murky silt of a muddy pond*. ■ not fully explained or understood, especially with concealed dishonesty or immorality: *the murky world of espionage*.
– DERIVATIVES **murkily** adverb, **murkiness** noun.

Murmansk /mʊəˈmansk/ a port in NW Russia, on the northern coast of the Kola Peninsula, in the Barents Sea; pop. 472,000 (1990). It is the largest city north of the Arctic Circle and its port is ice-free throughout the year.

murmur ▶ **noun** a soft, indistinct sound made by a person or group of people speaking quietly or at a distance: *his voice was little more than a murmur*.
■ a softly spoken or almost inaudible utterance: *she accepted his offer with a quiet murmur of thanks*. ■ the quiet or subdued expression of a particular feeling by a group of people: *there was a murmur of approval from the crowd*. ■ a rumour: *he had heard hints only, murmurs*. ■ a low continuous sound: *the murmur of bees in the rhododendrons*. ■ Medicine a recurring sound heard in the heart through a stethoscope that is usually a sign of disease or damage. ■ informal a condition in which the heart produces or is apt to produce such a sound: *she had been born with a heart murmur*.
▶ **verb** [reporting verb] say something in a low, soft, or indistinct voice: [with obj.] *Nina murmured an excuse and hurried away* | [with direct speech] *'How interesting,' he murmured quietly*.
■ say something cautiously and discreetly: [no obj.] *they began to murmur of an uprising*. ■ [no obj.] (**murmur against**) archaic express one's discontent about (someone or something) in a subdued manner. ■ [no obj.] make a low continuous sound: *the wind was murmuring through the trees*.
– PHRASES **without a murmur** without complaining.
– DERIVATIVES **murmurer** noun, **murmurous** adjective.
– ORIGIN late Middle English: from Old French *murmure*, from *murmurer* 'to murmur', from Latin *murmurare*, from *murmur* 'a murmur'.

murmuration ▶ **noun** poetic/literary **1** [mass noun] the action of murmuring: *the murmuration of a flock of warblers*.
2 rare a flock of starlings.
– ORIGIN late Middle English: from French, from Latin *murmuratio(n-)*, from *murmurare* 'to murmur'. The usage as a collective noun dates from the late 15th cent.

murmuring ▶ **noun** a soft, low, or indistinct sound produced by a person or group of people speaking quietly or at a distance.
■ (usu. **murmurings**) a subdued or private expression of discontent or dissatisfaction: *murmurings of discontent from the fans*. ■ (usu. **murmurings**) an insinuation: *his father's life had been ruined by the murmurings and innuendoes of lesser men*. ■ [mass noun] a low continuous sound: *the murmuring of the River Derwent*.
– DERIVATIVES **murmuringly** adverb.

Murnau /ˈmʊənaʊ, German ˈmʊrnaʊ/, F. W. (1888–1931), German film director; born *Frederick Wilhelm Plumpe*. His revolutionary use of cinematic techniques to record and interpret human emotion paralleled the expressionist movement in art and drama. Notable films: *Nosferatu* (1922), *Der letzte Mann* (1924), and *Sunrise* (1927), which won three Oscars.

murphy ▶ **noun** (pl. **-ies**) informal a potato.
– ORIGIN early 19th cent.: from *Murphy*, an Irish surname.

Murphy's Law a supposed law of nature, expressed in various humorous popular sayings, to the effect that anything that can go wrong will go wrong.

murrain /ˈmʌrɪn/ ▶ **noun 1** [mass noun] redwater fever or a similar infectious disease affecting cattle or other animals.
2 archaic or humorous a plague, epidemic, or crop blight.
■ the potato blight during the Irish famine in the mid 19th century.
– ORIGIN late Middle English: from Old French *morine*, based on Latin *mori* 'to die'.

murram /ˈmʌrəm/ ▶ **noun** [mass noun] a form of laterite used for road surfaces in tropical Africa.
– ORIGIN 1920s: a local word.

Murray[1] /ˈmʌri/, (George) Gilbert (Aimé) (1866–1957), Australian-born British classical scholar. His translations of Greek dramatists helped to revive interest in Greek drama. He was also a founder of the League of Nations and later a joint president of the United Nations.

Murray[2] /ˈmʌri/, Sir James (Augustus Henry) (1837–1915), Scottish lexicographer. He was chief editor of the *Oxford English Dictionary*, but did not live to see the work completed.

Murray River the principal river of Australia, which rises in the Great Dividing Range in New South Wales and flows 2,590 km (1,610 miles) generally north-westwards, forming part of the border between the states of Victoria and New South Wales, before turning southwards in South Australia to empty into the Indian Ocean south-east of Adelaide.

murre /məː/ ▶ noun N. Amer. a guillemot with a white breast.
● Genus *Uria*, family Alcidae: two species.
– ORIGIN late 16th cent.: of unknown origin.

murrelet /ˈməːlɪt/ ▶ noun a small North Pacific auk, typically having a grey back and white underparts.
● Genera *Brachyramphus* and *Synthliboramphus*, family Alcidae: six species.

murrey /ˈmʌri/ ▶ noun [mass noun] archaic a deep purple-red cloth.
■ the deep purple-red colour of a mulberry. ■ Heraldry another term for SANGUINE.
– ORIGIN late Middle English: via Old French from medieval Latin *moratus*, from *morum* 'mulberry'.

Murrumbidgee /ˌmʌrəmˈbɪdʒiː/ a river of SE Australia, in New South Wales. Rising in the Great Dividing Range, it flows 1,759 km (1,099 miles) westwards to join the Murray, of which it is a major tributary.

murther /ˈməːðə/ ▶ noun & verb archaic spelling of MURDER.

Mururoa /ˌmuərʊˈrəʊə/ a remote South Pacific atoll in the Tuamotu archipelago, in French Polynesia, used as a nuclear testing site since 1966.

Musala, Mount /muːˈsɑːlə/ (also **Mousalla**) the highest peak in Bulgaria, in the Rila Mountains, rising to 2,925 m (9,596 ft).

musambi /mʊˈsambi/ ▶ noun an orange of a variety with green skin and yellow flesh.
– ORIGIN alteration of MOZAMBIQUE.

MusB (also **Mus Bac**) ▶ abbreviation for Bachelor of Music.
– ORIGIN from Latin *Musicae Baccalaureus*.

Musca /ˈmʌskə/ Astronomy a small southern constellation (the Fly), lying in the Milky Way between the Southern Cross and the south celestial pole.
■ [as genitive **Muscae** /-kiː/] used with preceding letter or numeral to designate a star in this constellation: *the star Beta Muscae*.
– ORIGIN Latin.

muscadel /ˌmʌskəˈdɛl/ ▶ noun variant spelling of MUSCATEL.

Muscadelle /ˌmʌskəˈdɛl/ ▶ noun [mass noun] a variety of white grape mainly grown for sweet white wines in Bordeaux and Australia.

Muscadet /ˈmʌskədeɪ, ˈmʊsk-, French myskadɛ/ ▶ noun [mass noun] a dry white wine from the part of the Loire region in France nearest the west coast.
– ORIGIN French, from *muscade* 'nutmeg', from *musc* 'musk'.

muscadine /ˈmʌskədɪn, -ʌɪn/ ▶ noun any of a group of species and varieties of wine grape native to Mexico and the south-eastern US, typically having thick skins and a musky flavour.
● Genus *Vitis* (section *Muscadinia*): several species, in particular *V. rotundifolia*.
– ORIGIN probably an alteration of MUSCATEL.

muscae volitantes /ˌmʌsiː ˌvɒlɪˈtantiːz/ ▶ plural noun Medicine dark specks appearing to float before the eyes, generally caused by particles in the vitreous humour of the eye.
– ORIGIN mid 18th cent.: Latin, literally 'flying flies'.

muscarine /ˈmʌskəriːn, -ɪn/ ▶ noun [mass noun] Chemistry a poisonous compound present in certain fungi, including the fly agaric.
● An alkaloid; chem. formula: $C_9H_{21}NO_3$.
– ORIGIN late 19th cent.: based on Latin *musca* 'fly'.

muscarinic /ˌmʌskəˈrɪnɪk/ ▶ adjective Physiology of or relating to a type of acetylcholine receptor in the nervous system which is capable of responding to muscarine.

Muscat /ˈmʌskat/ the capital of Oman, a port on the SE coast of the Arabian peninsula; pop. 40,850 (1993).

muscat /ˈmʌskat/ ▶ noun [mass noun] [often as modifier] a variety of white, red, or black grape with a musky scent, grown in warm climates for wine or raisins or as table grapes.
■ a wine made from a muscat grape, especially a sweet or fortified white wine.
– ORIGIN French, from Provençal, from *musc* 'musk'.

Muscat and Oman former name (until 1970) for OMAN.

muscatel /ˌmʌskəˈtɛl/ (also **muscadel**) ▶ noun a muscat grape, especially as grown for drying to make raisins.
■ a raisin made from such a grape. ■ [mass noun] a wine made from such a grape.
– ORIGIN via Old French from Provençal, diminutive of *muscat* (see MUSCAT).

Muscat Hamburg ▶ noun see HAMBURG[2] (sense 2).

Muschelkalk /ˈmʊʃ(ə)lkalk/ ▶ noun [mass noun] Geology a limestone or chalk deposit from the Middle Triassic in Europe, especially in Germany.
– ORIGIN mid 19th cent.: from German, literally 'mussel chalk'.

Musci /ˈmʌskiː/ Botany a class of lower plants that comprises the mosses.
– ORIGIN modern Latin, literally 'mosses'.

muscid /ˈmʌsɪd/ ▶ noun Entomology an insect of the housefly family (Muscidae).
– ORIGIN late 19th cent.: from modern Latin *Muscidae* (plural), from Latin *musca* 'fly'.

muscimol /ˈmʌskɪmɒl/ ▶ noun [mass noun] Chemistry a narcotic and hallucinogenic compound found in the fly agaric and other fungi.
● An alkaloid related to oxazole; chem. formula: $C_4H_6N_2O_2$.
– ORIGIN 1960s: from modern Latin *muscaria* (see MUSCARINE) + *im(ine)* + -OL.

muscle ▶ noun **1** a band or bundle of fibrous tissue in a human or animal body that has the ability to contract, producing movement in or maintaining the position of parts of the body: *the calf muscle* | [mass noun] *the sheet of muscle between the abdomen and chest.*
■ such a band or bundle of tissue when well developed or prominently visible under the skin: *showing off our muscles to prove how strong we were.*

Muscles are formed of bands, sheets, or columns of elongated cells (or fibres) containing interlocking parallel arrays of the proteins actin and myosin. Projections on the myosin molecules respond to chemical signals by forming and reforming chemical bonds to the actin, so that the filaments move past each other and interlock more deeply. This converts chemical energy into the mechanical force of contraction, and also generates heat.

2 [mass noun] physical power; strength: *he had muscle but no brains.*
■ informal a man or men exhibiting such power or strength: *an ex-marine of enormous proportions who'd been brought along as muscle.* ■ power or influence, especially in a commercial or political context: *he had enough muscle and resources to hold his position on the council.*
▶ verb [with obj. and adverbial] N. Amer. informal move (an object) in a particular direction by using one's physical strength: *they were muscling baggage into the hold of the plane.*
■ informal, chiefly N. Amer. coerce by violence or by economic or political pressure: *he was eventually muscled out of his market.*
– PHRASES **flex one's muscles** give a show of strength or power. **not move a muscle** be completely motionless.
– DERIVATIVES **muscled** adjective [in combination] hard-muscled, **muscleless** adjective.
– ORIGIN late Middle English: from French, from Latin *musculus*, diminutive of *mus* 'mouse' (some muscles being thought to be mouse-like in form).
▶ **muscle in/into** informal force one's way into (something), typically in order to gain an advantage: *he was determined to muscle in on the union's affairs.*
muscle up US informal build up one's muscles.

muscle-bound ▶ adjective having well-developed or over-developed muscles: *a muscle-bound hunk.*

muscleman ▶ noun (pl. **-men**) a large, strong man, especially one employed to protect someone or intimidate people.

muscle tone ▶ noun see TONE (sense 6).

muscly ▶ adjective muscular: *his muscly forearms.*

muscovado /ˌmʌskəˈvɑːdəʊ/ (also **muscovado sugar**) ▶ noun [mass noun] unrefined sugar made from the juice of sugar cane by evaporating it and draining off the molasses.
– ORIGIN early 17th cent.: from Portuguese *mascabado (açúcar)* '(sugar) of the lowest quality'.

Muscovite /ˈmʌskəvʌɪt/ ▶ noun a native or citizen of Moscow.
■ archaic a Russian.

▶ adjective of or relating to Moscow.
■ archaic of or relating to Russia.
– ORIGIN from modern Latin *Muscovita*, from *Muscovia* (see MUSCOVY).

muscovite /ˈmʌskəvʌɪt/ ▶ noun [mass noun] a silver-grey form of mica occurring in many igneous and metamorphic rocks.
– ORIGIN mid 19th cent.: from obsolete *Muscovy glass* (in the same sense) + -ITE[1].

Muscovy /ˈmʌskəvi/ a medieval principality in west central Russia, centred on Moscow, which formed the nucleus of modern Russia. As Muscovy expanded, princes of Muscovy became the rulers of Russia; in 1472 Ivan III, grand duke of Muscovy, completed the unification of the country, and 1547 Ivan the Terrible became the first tsar of Russia.
■ archaic name for Russia.
– ORIGIN from obsolete French *Muscovie*, from modern Latin *Moscovia*, from Russian *Moskva* 'Moscow'.

Muscovy duck ▶ noun a large tropical American tree-nesting duck, having glossy greenish-black plumage in the wild but bred in a variety of colours as a domestic bird.
● Cairina moschata, family Anatidae.

muscular ▶ adjective of or affecting the muscles: *energy is needed for muscular activity* | *muscular tension.*
■ having well-developed muscles: *his legs were strong and muscular.* ■ figurative vigorously robust: *a muscular economy.*
– DERIVATIVES **muscularity** noun, **muscularly** adverb.
– ORIGIN late 17th cent.: alteration of earlier *musculous*, in the same sense.

muscular Christianity ▶ noun [mass noun] a Christian life of brave and cheerful physical activity, especially as popularly associated with the writings of Charles Kingsley and with boys' public schools of the Victorian British Empire.

muscular dystrophy ▶ noun [mass noun] a hereditary condition marked by progressive weakening and wasting of the muscles.

muscular rheumatism ▶ noun [mass noun] aching pain in the muscles and joints.

musculature /ˈmʌskjʊlətʃə/ ▶ noun [mass noun] the system or arrangement of muscles in a body, part of the body, or an organ.
– ORIGIN late 19th cent.: from French, from Latin *musculus* (see MUSCLE).

musculoskeletal /ˌmʌskjʊləʊˈskɛlɪt(ə)l/ ▶ adjective relating to or denoting the musculature and skeleton together.

MusD (also **Mus Doc**) ▶ abbreviation for Doctor of Music.
– ORIGIN from Latin *Musicae Doctor*.

muse[1] ▶ noun (**Muse**) (in Greek and Roman mythology) each of nine goddesses, the daughters of Zeus and Mnemosyne, who preside over the arts and sciences.
■ a woman, or a force personified as a woman, who is the source of inspiration for a creative artist.

The Muses are generally listed as Calliope (epic poetry), Clio (history), Euterpe (flute playing and lyric poetry), Terpsichore (choral dancing and song), Erato (lyre playing and lyric poetry), Melpomene (tragedy), Thalia (comedy and light verse), Polyhymnia (hymns, and later mime), and Urania (astronomy).

– ORIGIN late Middle English: from Old French, or from Latin *musa*, from Greek *mousa*.

muse[2] ▶ verb [no obj.] be absorbed in thought: *he was musing on the problems he faced.*
■ [with direct speech] say to oneself in a thoughtful manner: *'I think I've seen him somewhere before,' mused Rachel.* ■ (**muse on**) gaze thoughtfully at: *the sergeant stood, his eyes musing on the pretty police constable.*
▶ noun dated an instance or period of reflection.
– DERIVATIVES **musingly** adverb.
– ORIGIN Middle English: from Old French *muser* 'meditate, waste time', perhaps from medieval Latin *musum* 'muzzle'.

museography /ˌmjuːzɪˈɒɡrəfi/ ▶ noun another term for MUSEOLOGY.
■ rare the systematic description of objects in museums.
– DERIVATIVES **museographic** adjective, **museographical** adjective.

museology /ˌmjuːzɪˈɒlədʒi/ ▶ noun [mass noun] the science or practice of organizing, arranging, and managing museums.

– DERIVATIVES **museological** adjective, **museologist** noun.

musette /mjuːˈzɛt/ ▶ noun **1** a kind of small bagpipe played with bellows, common in the French court in the 17th–18th centuries and in later folk music. ■a tune or piece of music imitating the sound of this, typically with a drone. ■a dance to such a tune, especially in the 18th-century French court. ■a small simple variety of oboe, used chiefly in 19th-century France.
2 (also **musette bag**) US a small knapsack.
– ORIGIN late Middle English: from Old French, diminutive of *muse* 'bagpipe'.

museum ▶ noun a building in which objects of historical, scientific, artistic, or cultural interest are stored and exhibited.
– ORIGIN early 17th cent. (denoting a university building, specifically one erected at Alexandria by Ptolemy Soter): via Latin from Greek *mouseion* 'seat of the Muses', based on *mousa* 'muse'.

museum beetle ▶ noun a small dark beetle whose larvae can cause severe damage to carpets, stored goods, and zoological and entomological collections.
● *Anthrenus museorum* and related species, family Dermestidae.

museum piece ▶ noun an object that is worthy of display in a museum.
■Brit. a person or object regarded as old-fashioned, irrelevant, or useless: *we're nothing but museum pieces—machines can do everything that we can do.*

Museveni /ˌmʊsəˈveɪni/, Yoweri (Kaguta) (b.1944), Ugandan statesman, President since 1986. He came to power after ousting Milton Obote, and brought some stability to a country that had suffered under the dictatorial Obote and Idi Amin.

mush¹ /mʌʃ/ ▶ noun [mass noun] **1** a soft, wet, pulpy mass: *she trudged through the mush of fallen leaves* | [count noun] *the flowers had been flattened into a sodden pink mush.*
■figurative feeble or cloying sentimentality: *the film's not just romantic mush.*
2 [count noun] Brit. informal a person's mouth or face.
3 N. Amer. thick maize porridge.
▶ verb [with obj., usu. as adj. **mushed**] reduce (a substance) to a soft, wet, pulpy mass: *a cake combining layers of mushed prune and pastry.*
– ORIGIN late 17th cent. (in sense 3): apparently a variant of **MASH**.

mush² /mʌʃ/ N. Amer. ▶ verb [no obj., with adverbial of direction] go on a journey across snow with a dog sled: *Sepala mushed through the land of the midnight sun.*
■[with obj.] urge on (the dogs) during such a journey.
▶ exclamation a command urging on dogs during such a journey.
▶ noun a journey across snow with a dog sled.
– ORIGIN mid 19th cent.: probably an alteration of French *marchez!* or *marchons!*, imperatives of *marcher* 'to advance'.

mush³ /mʊʃ/ ▶ noun Brit. used as an informal term of address: *what you doing round here, mush?*
– ORIGIN 1930s: of unknown origin.

mushaira /mʊˈʃʌɪərə/ ▶ noun Indian an evening social gathering at which Urdu poetry is read, typically taking the form of a contest.
– ORIGIN from Hindi *muṣaira*.

musher¹ ▶ noun N. Amer. the driver of a dog sled.

musher² ▶ noun Brit. informal a person who owns and drives a taxi cab.
– ORIGIN late 19th cent.: from slang *mush* 'owner-driver of a cab', from **MUSHROOM**, apparently referring to the increase in the number of vehicles owned with growth in business.

mushrat /ˈmʌʃrat/ ▶ noun North American term for **MUSKRAT**.

mushroom ▶ noun a fungal growth that typically takes the form of a domed cap on a stalk, with gills on the underside of the cap.
■a thing resembling a mushroom in shape: *a mushroom of smoke and flames.* ■[mass noun] a pale pinkish-brown colour: [as modifier] *a mushroom leather bag.* ■figurative a person or thing that appears or develops suddenly and is ephemeral: *he was one of those showbiz mushrooms who spring up overnight.*

Mushrooms are fruiting bodies that produce spores, growing from the hyphae of fungi concealed in soil or wood. They are proverbial for rapid growth. Toadstools are often called mushrooms when they are considered to be edible.

▶ verb [no obj.] **1** increase, spread, or develop rapidly: *environmental concern mushroomed in the 1960s.*
2 (of the smoke, fire, or flames produced by an explosion) spread into the air in a shape resembling that of a mushroom: *the grenade mushroomed into red fire as it hit the hillside.*
■(of a bullet) expand and flatten on reaching its target.
3 [usu. as noun **mushrooming**] (of a person) gather mushrooms.
– DERIVATIVES **mushroomy** adjective.
– ORIGIN late Middle English (originally denoting any fungus having a fleshy fruiting body): from Old French *mousseron*, from late Latin *mussirio(n-)*.

mushroom cloud ▶ noun a mushroom-shaped cloud of dust and debris formed after a nuclear explosion.

mushroom growth ▶ noun a sudden development or expansion: *a mushroom growth of grant-aided housing associations.*

mushy ▶ adjective (**mushier**, **mushiest**) soft and pulpy: *cook until the fruit is mushy* | *mushy vegetables.*
■(of a motor-vehicle's brakes) lacking firmness; spongy. ■figurative excessively sentimental: *a mushy film.*
– DERIVATIVES **mushily** adverb, **mushiness** noun.

music ▶ noun [mass noun] **1** the art or science of combining vocal or instrumental sounds (or both) to produce beauty of form, harmony, and expression of emotion: *he devoted his life to music.*
■the vocal or instrumental sound produced in this way: *couples were dancing to the music* | *baroque music.* ■a sound perceived as pleasingly harmonious: *the background music of softly lapping water.*
2 the written or printed signs representing such sound: *Tony learned to read music.*
■the score or scores of a musical composition or compositions: *the music was open on a stand.*
– PHRASES **music of the spheres** see **SPHERE**. **music to one's ears** something that is very pleasant or gratifying to hear or discover: *the commission's report was music to the ears of the government.*
– ORIGIN Middle English: from Old French *musique*, via Latin from Greek *mousikē* (*tekhnē*) '(art) of the Muses', from *mousa* 'muse'.

musica ficta /ˌmjuːzɪkə ˈfɪktə/ ▶ noun [mass noun] Music (in early contrapuntal music) the introduction by a performer of sharps, flats, or other accidentals to avoid unacceptable intervals.
– ORIGIN early 19th cent.: Latin, literally 'feigned music'.

musical ▶ adjective **1** of or relating to music: *they shared similar musical tastes.*
■set to or accompanied by music: *an evening of musical entertainment.* ■fond of or skilled in music: *Henry was very musical, but his wife was tone-deaf.*
2 having a pleasant sound; melodious; tuneful: *they burst out into rich, musical laughter.*
▶ noun a play or film in which singing and dancing play an essential part. Musicals developed from light opera in the early 20th century.
– DERIVATIVES **musically** adverb.
– ORIGIN late Middle English: from Old French, from medieval Latin *musicalis*, from Latin *musica* (see **MUSIC**).

musical box ▶ noun Brit. a small box which plays a tune when the lid is opened.

musical bumps ▶ noun [mass noun] Brit. a party game similar to musical chairs, in which the player who is last to sit on the floor when the music stops is eliminated in each round.

musical chairs ▶ noun [mass noun] a party game in which players compete for a decreasing number of chairs, the losers in successive rounds being those unable to find a chair to sit on when the accompanying music is abruptly stopped.
■a series of changes or exchanges of position, especially in a political or commercial organization.

musical comedy ▶ noun a light play or film with songs, dialogue, and dancing, connected by a slender plot.

musical director ▶ noun the person responsible for the musical aspects of a performance or production, typically the conductor or leader of a music group.

musicale /ˌmjuːzɪˈkɑːl/ ▶ noun N. Amer. a musical gathering or concert.
– ORIGIN late 19th cent.: French, from *soirée musicale* 'evening of music'.

musical film ▶ noun a film in which music is an important feature.

musical glasses ▶ plural noun a graduated series of glass bowls or tubes played as a musical instrument by rubbing with the fingers.

musical instrument ▶ noun see **INSTRUMENT** (sense 3).

musicality ▶ noun [mass noun] the quality of being musical: *she sings with unfailing musicality.*
■awareness of music and rhythm, especially in dance.

musicalize (also **-ise**) ▶ verb [with obj.] set (a novel, play, or poem) to music.

musical saw ▶ noun a saw, typically held between the knees and played with a bow like a cello, the note varying with the degree of bending of the blade.

musical sound ▶ noun see **SOUND¹**.

music box ▶ noun another term for **MUSICAL BOX**.

music cassette ▶ noun a tape cassette of pre-recorded music.

music centre ▶ noun Brit. a combined radio, cassette player, and record or compact disc player.

music drama ▶ noun an opera whose structure is governed by considerations of dramatic effectiveness, rather than by the convention of having a series of formal arias.

music hall ▶ noun [mass noun] a form of variety entertainment popular in Britain from c.1850, consisting of singing, dancing, comedy, acrobatics, and novelty acts. Its popularity declined after the First World War with the rise of the cinema.
■[count noun] a theatre where such entertainment took place.

musician ▶ noun a person who is talented or skilled in music.
■a person who plays a musical instrument, especially professionally.
– DERIVATIVES **musicianly** adjective, **musicianship** noun.
– ORIGIN late Middle English: from Old French *musicien*, from Latin *musica* (see **MUSIC**).

musicology ▶ noun [mass noun] the study of music as an academic subject, as distinct from training in performance or composition; scholarly research into music.
– DERIVATIVES **musicological** adjective, **musicologist** noun.
– ORIGIN early 20th cent.: from French *musicologie*.

music stand ▶ noun a rest or light frame on which sheet music or a score is supported.

music stool ▶ noun a stool for a pianist, typically adjustable in height and sometimes having a hinged top covering a storage space for musical scores.

music theatre ▶ noun [mass noun] a combination of music and drama in modern form distinct from traditional opera, typically for a small group of performers.

Musil /ˈmuːzɪl/, Robert (1880–1942), Austrian novelist. He is best known for his unfinished novel *The Man Without Qualities* (1930–43), about the disintegration of traditional Austrian society just before the outbreak of the First World War.

musique concrète /mjuːˌziːk kɒˈkrɛt/ ▶ noun [mass noun] music constructed by mixing recorded sounds, first developed by experimental composers in the 1940s.
– ORIGIN French, literally 'concrete music'.

musk ▶ noun **1** [mass noun] a strong-smelling reddish-brown substance which is secreted by the male musk deer for scent-marking and is an important ingredient in perfumery.
2 (also **musk plant**) a relative of the monkey flower that was formerly cultivated for its musky perfume, which has been lost in the development of modern varieties.
● Genus *Mimulus*, family Scrophulariaceae: several species, in particular *M. moschatus*.
■Austral. see **MUSK TREE**.
– ORIGIN late Middle English: from late Latin *muscus*, from Persian *mušk*, perhaps from Sanskrit *muska* 'scrotum' (because of the similarity in shape of a musk deer's musk bag).

musk beetle ▶ noun a slender longhorn beetle that is dark metallic green and emits a musk-like scent.
● *Aromia moschata*, family Cerambycidae.

musk deer ▶ noun a small solitary deer-like East Asian mammal without antlers, the male having long protruding upper canine teeth. Musk is produced in a sac on the abdomen of the male.
● Family Moschidae and genus *Moschus*: several species.

musk duck ▶ noun an Australian stiff-tailed duck with dark grey plumage and a musky smell, the male having a large black lobe of skin hanging below the bill.
● *Biziura lobata*, family Anatidae.

muskeg /ˈmʌskɛɡ/ ▶ noun a swamp or bog in northern North America.
– ORIGIN early 19th cent.: from Cree.

muskellunge /ˈmʌskəˌlʌn(d)ʒ/ ▶ noun a large pike that occurs only in the Great Lakes region of North America. Also called **MASKINONGE**.
● *Esox masquinongy*, family Esocidae.
– ORIGIN late 18th cent.: based on Ojibwa, 'great fish'.

musket ▶ noun historical an infantryman's light gun with a long barrel, typically smooth-bored and fired from the shoulder.
– ORIGIN late 16th cent.: from French *mousquet*, from Italian *moschetto* 'crossbow bolt', from *mosca* 'a fly'.

musketeer ▶ noun historical **1** a soldier armed with a musket.
2 a member of the household troops of the French king in the 17th and 18th centuries.

musketry ▶ noun [mass noun] musket fire.
■ soldiers armed with muskets: *the Prussian musketry*. ■ the art or technique of handling a musket.

musk melon ▶ noun a yellow or green melon of a variety which has a raised network of markings on the skin.

Muskogean /ˌmʌskəˈɡiːən, mʌˈskəʊɡɪən/ ▶ noun a family of American Indian languages spoken in SE North America, including Creek and Choctaw.
▶ adjective of or relating to this language family.
– ORIGIN from **MUSKOGEE** + **-AN**.

Muskogee /mʌˈskəʊɡi/ ▶ noun (pl. same or **Muskogees**) **1** a member of an American Indian people of SE North America, who formed part of the Creek Indian confederacy.
2 [mass noun] the Muskogean language of this people, now all but extinct.
▶ adjective of or relating to the Muskogees or their language.
– ORIGIN from Creek *maˈskóːki*.

musk ox ▶ noun a large heavily built goat-antelope with a thick shaggy coat and a horny boss on the head, native to the tundra of North America and Greenland.
● *Ovibos moschatus*, family Bovidae.

muskrat ▶ noun a large semiaquatic North American rodent with a musky smell, valued for its fur.
● *Ondatra zibethicus*, family Muridae.
■ [mass noun] the fur of the muskrat.

musk rose ▶ noun a rambling rose with large white musk-scented flowers.
● *Rosa moschata*, family Rosaceae.

musk shrew ▶ noun an African shrew, the male of which has large scent glands on the flanks that produce a strong musky odour.
● Genus *Crocidura*, family Soricidae: several species.

musk thistle ▶ noun a thistle which has a solitary drooping flower with a musky fragrance.
● *Carduus nutans*, family Compositae.

musk tree ▶ noun either of two Australian trees with a musky smell. Also called **MUSKWOOD**.
● (also **musk**) a small tree or shrub that has musky leaves with silvery undersides (*Olearia argyrophylla*, family Compositae). ● a rainforest tree with musky timber (*Alangium villosum*, family Alangiaceae).

musk turtle ▶ noun a small drab-coloured American freshwater turtle which has scent glands that produce an unpleasant musky odour when the turtle is disturbed.
● Genus *Kinosternon* (or *Sternotherus*), family Kinosternidae: several species, including the stinkpot.

muskwood ▶ noun [mass noun] timber with a musky smell, especially that of a musk tree.
■ another term for **MUSK TREE**.

musky ▶ adjective (**muskier**, **muskiest**) of or having a smell or taste of musk, or suggestive of musk.
– DERIVATIVES **muskiness** noun.

Muslim /ˈmʊzlɪm, ˈmʌz-, -s-/ (also **Moslem**) ▶ noun a follower of the religion of Islam.

▶ adjective of or relating to the Muslims or their religion.
– ORIGIN early 17th cent.: from Arabic, active participle of *'aslama* (see **ISLAM**).

Muslim Brotherhood an Islamic religious and political organization dedicated to the establishment of a nation based on Islamic principles. Founded in Egypt in 1928, it has become a radical underground force in Egypt and other Sunni countries, promoting strict moral discipline and opposing Western influence, often by violence.

Muslim League one of the main political parties in Pakistan. It was formed in 1906 in India to represent the rights of Indian Muslims; its demands from 1940 for an independent Muslim state led ultimately to the establishment of Pakistan.

muslin ▶ noun [mass noun] lightweight cotton cloth in a plain weave: *a white muslin dress*.
– DERIVATIVES **muslined** adjective.
– ORIGIN early 17th cent.: from French *mousseline*, from Italian *mussolina*, from *Mussolo* 'Mosul' (the name of the place of manufacture in Iraq).

muso /ˈmjuːzəʊ/ ▶ noun (pl. **-os**) Brit. informal a musician, especially one over-concerned with technique.
■ a keen music fan, especially one who has expensive hi-fi equipment.
– ORIGIN 1960s: abbreviation.

musquash /ˈmʌskwɒʃ/ ▶ noun archaic term for **MUSKRAT**.
■ [mass noun] Brit. the fur of the muskrat.
– ORIGIN early 17th cent.: from Abnaki *mòskwas*.

muss informal, chiefly N. Amer. ▶ verb [with obj.] make (someone's hair or clothes) untidy or messy: *the wind was mussing up his hair*.
▶ noun [usu. in sing.] a state of disorder.
– DERIVATIVES **mussy** adjective (dated).
– ORIGIN mid 19th cent. (also as a noun in the sense 'disturbance or row'): apparently a variant of **MESS**.

mussel ▶ noun any of a number of bivalve molluscs with a brown or purplish-black shell.
● a marine bivalve which uses byssus threads to anchor to a firm surface (family Mytilidae, order Mytiloidea), including the **edible mussel** (*Mytilus edulis*). ● a freshwater bivalve which typically lies on the bed of a river, some species forming small pearls (family Unionidae, order Unionoida).
– ORIGIN Old English *mus(c)le*, superseded by forms from Middle Low German *mussel*, Middle Dutch *mosscele*; ultimately from late Latin *muscula*, from Latin *musculus* (see **MUSCLE**).

musselcracker ▶ noun S. African a large sea bream with powerful jaws, feeding on shellfish and crustaceans and popular with anglers.
● *Lithognathus* and other genera, family Sparidae: several species.

Mussolini /ˌmʊsəˈliːni/, Benito (Amilcaro Andrea) (1883–1945), Italian Fascist statesman, Prime Minister 1922–43; known as Il Duce ('the leader'). He founded the Italian Fascist Party in 1919. He annexed Abyssinia in 1936 and entered the Second World War on Germany's side in 1940. Forced to resign after the Allied invasion of Sicily, he was rescued from imprisonment by German paratroopers, but was captured and executed by Italian communist partisans.

Mussorgsky /mʊˈsɔːɡski/ (also **Moussorgsky**), Modest (Petrovich) (1839–81), Russian composer. His best-known works include the opera *Boris Godunov* (1874), *Songs and Dances of Death* (1875–7) and the piano suite *Pictures at an Exhibition* (1874).

Mussulman /ˈmʌs(ə)lmən/ ▶ noun (pl. **Mussulmans** or **Mussulmen**) & adjective archaic term for **MUSLIM**.
– ORIGIN late 16th cent.: from Persian *musulmān* (originally an adjective), from *muslim* (see **MUSLIM**).

must[1] ▶ modal verb (past **had to** or in reported speech **must**) **1** be obliged to; should (expressing necessity): *I must go* | *it mustn't be over 2,000 words* | *she said she must be going*.
■ expressing insistence: *you must try some of this fish* | *if you must smoke you could at least go in the living room*. ■ used in ironic questions expressing irritation: *Charlotte, must you put spanners in the works?*
2 expressing an opinion about something that is logically very likely: *there must be something wrong* | *you must be tired*.
▶ noun informal something that should not be overlooked or missed: *this video is a must for everyone*.

– PHRASES **I must say** see **SAY**. **must needs do something** see **NEEDS**.
– ORIGIN Old English *mōste*, past tense of *mōt* 'may', of Germanic origin; related to Dutch *moeten* and German *müssen*.

must[2] ▶ noun [mass noun] grape juice before or during fermentation.
– ORIGIN Old English, from Latin *mustum*, neuter (used as a noun) of *mustus* 'new'.

must[3] ▶ noun [mass noun] mustiness, dampness, or mould: *a pervasive smell of must*.
– ORIGIN early 17th cent.: back-formation from **MUSTY**.

must[4] (also **musth**) ▶ noun [mass noun] the frenzied state of certain male animals, especially elephants or camels, that is associated with the rutting season: *a big old bull elephant in must* | [as modifier] *the must gland*.
– ORIGIN late 19th cent.: via Urdu from Persian *mast* 'intoxicated'.

mustache ▶ noun US spelling of **MOUSTACHE**.

mustachios /məˈstɑːʃɪəʊz/ ▶ plural noun a long or elaborate moustache.
– DERIVATIVES **mustachioed** adjective.
– ORIGIN mid 16th cent.: from Spanish *mostacho* (singular), from Italian *mostaccio* (see **MOUSTACHE**).

mustang /ˈmʌstaŋ/ ▶ noun an American feral horse which is typically small and lightly built.
– ORIGIN early 19th cent.: from a blend of Spanish *mestengo* (from *mesta* 'company of graziers') and *mostrenco*, both meaning 'wild or masterless cattle'.

mustard ▶ noun [mass noun] **1** a hot-tasting yellow or brown paste made from the crushed seeds of certain plants, typically eaten with meat or used as a cooking ingredient.
2 the yellow-flowered Eurasian plant of the cabbage family whose seeds are used to make this paste.
● Genera *Brassica* and *Sinapis*, family Cruciferae: several species, in particular **black mustard** (*B. nigra*) and **white mustard** (*S. alba*), which is commonly eaten as a seedling in 'mustard and cress'.
■ used in names of related plants, only some of which are used to produce mustard for the table, e.g. **hedge mustard**.
3 a dark yellow colour.
– DERIVATIVES **mustardy** adjective.
– ORIGIN Middle English: from Old French *moustarde*, from Latin *mustum* 'must' (the condiment being originally prepared with 'must').

mustard gas ▶ noun a colourless oily liquid whose vapour is a powerful irritant and vesicant, used in chemical weapons.
● Chem. formula: $(ClCH_2CH_2)_2S$.

mustard greens ▶ plural noun chiefly US the leaves of the mustard plant used in salads.

mustard plaster ▶ noun a poultice made with mustard.

mustelid /ˈmʌstɪlɪd, mʌˈstɛlɪd/ ▶ noun Zoology a mammal of the weasel family (Mustelidae), distinguished by having a long body, short legs, and musky scent glands under the tail.
– ORIGIN early 20th cent.: from modern Latin *Mustelidae* (plural), from Latin *mustela* 'weasel'.

muster ▶ verb [with obj.] **1** assemble (troops), especially for inspection or in preparation for battle.
■ [no obj., with adverbial] (of troops) come together in this way: *the cavalrymen mustered beside the other regiments*. ■ [no obj., with adverbial of place] (of a group of people) gather together: *reporters mustered outside her house*. ■ Austral./NZ round up (livestock).
2 collect or assemble (a number or amount): *we couldn't muster up enough members for a quorum*.
■ summon up (a particular feeling, attitude, or response): *he replied with as much dignity as he could muster*.
▶ noun a formal gathering of troops, especially for inspection, display, or exercise.
■ short for **MUSTER ROLL**. ■ Austral./NZ a rounding up of livestock. ■ Austral. informal the number of people attending a meeting.
– PHRASES **pass muster** be accepted as adequate or satisfactory: *this manifesto would not pass muster with the voters*.
– ORIGIN late Middle English: from Old French *moustrer* (verb), *moustre* (noun), from Latin *monstrare* 'to show'.
▶ **muster someone in** (or **out**) US enrol someone into (or discharge someone from) military service.

muster book ▶ **noun** historical a book in which military personnel were registered.

musterer ▶ **noun** Austral./NZ a person who rounds up livestock.

muster roll ▶ **noun** an official list of officers and men in a military unit or ship's company.

musth ▶ **noun** variant spelling of MUST[4].

Mustique /mʌˈstiːk, mʊ-/ a small resort island in the northern Grenadines, in the Caribbean to the south of St Vincent.

mustn't ▶ **contraction of** must not.

musty ▶ **adjective** (**mustier**, **mustiest**) having a stale, mouldy, or damp smell: *a dark musty library filled with old books.*
▪having a stale taste: *the beer tasted sour, thin, and musty.* ▪ figurative lacking originality or interest: *when I read it again, the play seemed musty.*
– DERIVATIVES **mustily** adverb, **mustiness** noun.
– ORIGIN early 16th cent.: perhaps an alteration of *moisty* 'moist', influenced by MUST[2].

Mut /mʊt/ Egyptian Mythology a goddess who was the wife of Amun and mother of Khonsu.

mutable /ˈmjuːtəb(ə)l/ ▶ **adjective** liable to change: *the mutable nature of fashion.*
▪poetic/literary inconstant in one's affections: *youth is said to be fickle and mutable.*
– DERIVATIVES **mutability** noun.
– ORIGIN late Middle English: from Latin *mutabilis*, from *mutare* 'to change'.

mutagen /ˈmjuːtədʒ(ə)n/ ▶ **noun** an agent, such as radiation or a chemical substance, which causes genetic mutation.
– DERIVATIVES **mutagenesis** noun, **mutagenic** adjective.
– ORIGIN 1940s: from MUTATION + -GEN.

mutagenize /ˈmjuːtədʒənʌɪz/ (also **-ise**) ▶ **verb** [with obj.] [usu. as adj. **mutagenized**] Biology treat (a cell, organism, etc.) with mutagenic agents: *mutagenized DNA.*

mutant ▶ **adjective** resulting from or showing the effect of mutation: *a mutant gene.*
▶ **noun** a mutant form.
– ORIGIN early 20th cent.: from Latin *mutant-* 'changing', from the verb *mutare*.

Mutare /muːˈtɑːri/ an industrial town in the eastern highlands of Zimbabwe; pop. 69,620 (1982). Former name (until 1982) **UMTALI**.

mutate ▶ **verb** change or cause to change in form or nature: [no obj.] *technology continues to mutate at an alarming rate* | [with obj.] *each side is mutating their image of the opposing culture into something evil and sinister.*
▪Biology (with reference to a cell, DNA molecule, etc.) undergo or cause to undergo change in a gene or genes: [no obj.] *the virus is able to* **mutate into** *new forms that are immune to the vaccine* | [with obj.] *certain nucleotides were mutated.*
– DERIVATIVES **mutator** noun.
– ORIGIN early 19th cent.: back-formation from MUTATION.

mutation ▶ **noun** [mass noun] **1** the action or process of mutating: *the mutation of ethnic politics into nationalist politics* | [count noun] *his first novel went through several mutations.*
2 the changing of the structure of a gene, resulting in a variant form which may be transmitted to subsequent generations, caused by the alteration of single base units in DNA, or the deletion, insertion, or rearrangement of larger sections of genes or chromosomes.
▪[count noun] a distinct form resulting from such a change.
3 Linguistics regular change of a sound when it occurs adjacent to another, in particular:
▪(in Celtic languages) change of an initial consonant in a word caused (historically) by the preceding word. See also LENITION. ▪(in Germanic languages) the process by which the quality of a vowel was altered in certain phonetic contexts; umlaut.
– DERIVATIVES **mutational** adjective, **mutationally** adverb, **mutative** adjective.
– ORIGIN late Middle English: from Latin *mutatio(n-)*, from *mutare* 'to change'.

mutatis mutandis /muːˌtɑːtɪs muːˈtandɪs, mjuː-, -iːs/ ▶ **adverb** (used when comparing two or more cases or situations) making necessary alterations while not affecting the main point at issue: *what is true of undergraduate teaching in England is equally true, mutatis mutandis, of American graduate schools.*
– ORIGIN Latin, literally 'things being changed that have to be changed'.

mutch ▶ **noun** chiefly historical a linen cap, especially one worn by older women or children.
– ORIGIN late Middle English (denoting a nightcap): from Middle Dutch *mutse*, from medieval Latin *almucia* 'amice'.

mutchkin ▶ **noun** a Scottish unit of capacity equal to a quarter of the old Scottish pint, or roughly three quarters of an imperial pint (0.43 litres).
– ORIGIN late Middle English: from early modern Dutch *mudsekin*, diminutive of *mud* 'hectolitre'.

mute /mjuːt/ ▶ **adjective 1** refraining from speech or temporarily speechless: *Irene, the talkative one, was now mute.*
▪not expressed in speech: *she gazed at him in mute appeal.* ▪characterized by an absence of sound; quiet: *the great church was mute and dark.* ▪ dated (of a person) without the power of speech. ▪(of hounds) not giving tongue while hunting.
2 (of a letter) not pronounced: *mute e is generally dropped before suffixes beginning with a vowel.*
▶ **noun 1** dated a person without the power of speech.
▪historical (in some Asian countries) a servant who was deprived of the power of speech. ▪ historical an actor in a dumbshow. ▪ historical a professional attendant or mourner at a funeral.
2 a device which softens the sound (and typically alters the tone) of a musical instrument, in particular:
▪a clamp placed over the bridge of a stringed instrument to deaden the resonance without affecting the vibration of the strings. ▪ a pad or cone placed in the opening of a brass or other wind instrument.
▶ **verb** [with obj.] (often **be muted**) deaden, muffle, or soften the sound of: *her footsteps were muted by the thick carpet.*
▪muffle the sound of (a musical instrument), especially by the use of a mute. ▪ figurative reduce the strength or intensity of: *his professional contentment was muted by personal sadness at the death of his mother.*
– DERIVATIVES **mutely** adverb, **muteness** noun.
– ORIGIN Middle English: from Old French *muet*, diminutive of *mu*, from Latin *mutus*.

USAGE To describe a person without the power of speech as **mute** (especially as in **deaf mute**) is today likely to cause offence. Nevertheless, there are no accepted alternative terms in general use.

mute button ▶ **noun** a device on a telephone that one can press to temporarily prevent oneself from being heard.

muted ▶ **adjective** (of a sound or voice) quiet and soft: *they discussed the accident in muted voices.*
▪(of a musical instrument) having a muffled sound as a result of being fitted with a mute. ▪ figurative not expressed strongly or openly: *muted anger.* ▪(of colour or lighting) not bright; subdued: *a dress in muted tones of powder blue and dusty pink.*

mute swan ▶ **noun** the commonest Eurasian swan, having white plumage and an orange-red bill with a black knob at the base.
• *Cygnus olor*, family Anatidae.

mutha /ˈmʌðə/ ▶ **noun** chiefly US variant spelling of MOTHER (especially in sense 2).

muti /ˈmuːti/ ▶ **noun** [mass noun] S. African informal African medicinal or magical charms.
– ORIGIN from Zulu *umuthi* 'plant or medicine'.

mutilate ▶ **verb** [with obj.] (usu. **be mutilated**) inflict a violent and disfiguring injury on: *Brian's body was badly mutilated* | [as adj. **mutilated**] *mutilated bodies.*
▪inflict serious damage on: *the 14th-century church had been partly mutilated in the 18th century.*
– DERIVATIVES **mutilation** noun, **mutilator** noun.
– ORIGIN early 16th cent.: from Latin *mutilat-* 'maimed, mutilated, lopped off', from the verb *mutilare*, from *mutilus* 'maimed'.

mutineer ▶ **noun** a person, especially a soldier or sailor, who rebels or refuses to obey the orders of a person in authority.
– ORIGIN early 17th cent.: from French *mutinier*, from *mutin* 'rebellious', from *muete* 'movement', based on Latin *movere* 'to move'.

mutinous ▶ **adjective** (of a soldier or sailor) refusing to obey the orders of a person in authority.
▪wilful or disobedient: *Antoinette looked mutinous, but she obeyed.*
– DERIVATIVES **mutinously** adverb.
– ORIGIN late 16th cent.: from obsolete *mutine* 'rebellion' (see MUTINY) + -OUS.

mutiny ▶ **noun** (pl. **-ies**) an open rebellion against the proper authorities, especially by soldiers or sailors against their officers: *a mutiny by those manning the weapons could trigger a global war* | [mass noun] *the crew were on the verge of mutiny.*
▶ **verb** (**-ies**, **-ied**) [no obj.] refuse to obey the orders of a person in authority.
– ORIGIN mid 16th cent.: from obsolete *mutine* 'rebellion', from French *mutin* 'mutineer', based on Latin *movere* 'to move'.

mutism /ˈmjuːtɪz(ə)m/ ▶ **noun** [mass noun] inability to speak, typically as a result of congenital deafness or brain damage.
▪(in full **elective mutism**) unwillingness or refusal to speak, arising from psychological causes such as depression or trauma.
– ORIGIN early 19th cent.: from French *mutisme*, from Latin *mutus* 'mute'.

muton /ˈmjuːtɒn/ ▶ **noun** Biology the smallest element of genetic material capable of undergoing a distinct mutation, usually identified as a single pair of nucleotides.

Mutsuhito /ˌmʊtsuːˈhiːtəʊ/ see MEIJI TENNO.

mutt ▶ **noun** informal **1** humorous or derogatory a dog, especially a mongrel.
2 a person regarded as stupid or incompetent: *he pitied the poor mutt who ever fell for her charms.*
– ORIGIN late 19th cent.: abbreviation of MUTTONHEAD.

mutter ▶ **verb** [reporting verb] say something in a low or barely audible voice, especially in dissatisfaction or irritation: [with obj.] *he muttered something under his breath* | [with direct speech] *'I knew she was a troublemaker,' Rebecca muttered* | [no obj.] *she muttered in annoyance as the keys slid from her fingers.*
▪[no obj.] speak privately or unofficially about someone or something; spread rumours: *back-benchers were muttering about the next reshuffle.*
▶ **noun** a barely audible utterance, especially a dissatisfied or irritated one: *a little mutter of disgust.*
– DERIVATIVES **mutterer** noun, **mutteringly** adverb.
– ORIGIN late Middle English: imitative; compare with German dialect *muttern*.

mutton ▶ **noun** [mass noun] the flesh of (mature adult) sheep used as food: *a leg of mutton.*
– PHRASES **dead as mutton** quite dead. **mutton dressed as lamb** Brit. informal, derogatory a middle-aged or old woman dressed in a style suitable for a much younger woman.
– DERIVATIVES **muttony** adjective.
– ORIGIN Middle English: from Old French *moton*, from medieval Latin *multo(n-)*, probably of Celtic origin; compare with Scottish Gaelic *mult*, Welsh *mollt*, and Breton *maout*.

mutton bird ▶ **noun** a shearwater or petrel of the southern oceans.
• Family Procellariidae: several species, in particular (in Australia) the **short-tailed shearwater** (*Puffinus tenuirostris*), and (in New Zealand) the **sooty shearwater** (*P. griseus*)
– ORIGIN early 19th cent.: because when cooked, the flesh of some species resembles mutton in flavour.

mutton chop ▶ **noun** (usu. **mutton chop whiskers**) the whiskers on a man's cheek when shaped like a meat chop, narrow at the top and broad and rounded at the bottom.

muttonhead ▶ **noun** informal, dated a dull or stupid person (often used as a general term of abuse).
– DERIVATIVES **muttonheaded** adjective.

mutual /ˈmjuːtʃʊəl, -tjʊəl/ ▶ **adjective 1** (of a feeling or action) experienced or done by each of two or more parties towards the other or others: *a partnership based on mutual respect and understanding* | *my father hated him from the start and the feeling was mutual.*
▪(of two or more people) having the same specified relationship to each other: *they cooperated as potentially mutual beneficiaries of the settlement.*
2 held in common by two or more parties: *we were introduced by a mutual friend.*
▪denoting a building society or insurance company owned by its members and dividing some or all of its profits between them.
▶ **noun** a mutual building society or insurance company.
– ORIGIN late 15th cent.: from Old French *mutuel*, from Latin *mutuus* 'mutual, borrowed'; related to *mutare* 'to change'.

USAGE Traditionally it has long been held that the only correct use of **mutual** is in describing a reciprocal relationship: **mutual respect**, for example, means that the parties involved feel respect for each other. The other use of **mutual** meaning 'held in common', as in **mutual friend**, is held to be incorrect. This latter use has a long and respectable history, however. It was first recorded in Shakespeare, and has since appeared in the writing of Sir Walter Scott, George Eliot, and, most famously, as the title of Dickens's novel *Our Mutual Friend*. It is now generally accepted as part of standard English.

mutual conductance ▸ noun Electronics another term for **TRANSCONDUCTANCE**.

mutual fund ▸ noun North American term for **UNIT TRUST**.

mutual inductance ▸ noun Physics a measure or coefficient of mutual induction, usually expressed in henries.
■the property of a circuit which permits mutual induction.

mutual induction ▸ noun [mass noun] Physics the production of an electromotive force in a circuit by a change in the current in an adjacent circuit which is linked to the first by the flux lines of a magnetic field.

mutualism ▸ noun [mass noun] the doctrine that mutual dependence is necessary to social well-being.
■Biology symbiosis which is beneficial to both organisms involved.
– DERIVATIVES **mutualist** noun & adjective, **mutualistic** adjective, **mutualistically** adverb.

mutuality ▸ noun [mass noun] mutual character, quality, or activity: *a high degree of mutuality of respect for each other's expertise.*

mutualize (also **-ise**) ▸ verb [with obj.] organize (a company or business) on mutual principles.
■share out (something, especially insurance losses) between involved parties.

mutually ▸ adverb with mutual action; in a mutual relationship: [as submodifier] *adoption and fostering are not necessarily mutually exclusive alternatives.*

mutuel /ˈmjuːtʃʊəl, -tjʊəl/ ▸ noun chiefly US (in betting) a totalizator or a pari-mutuel.
– ORIGIN early 20th cent.: shortening of **PARI-MUTUEL**.

mutule /ˈmjuːtjuːl/ ▸ noun Architecture a stone block projecting under a cornice in the Doric order.
– ORIGIN mid 17th cent.: from French, from Latin *mutulus*.

muumuu /ˈmuːmuː/ ▸ noun a woman's loose, brightly coloured dress, especially one traditionally worn in Hawaii.
– ORIGIN early 20th cent.: from Hawaiian *mu'u mu'u*, literally 'cut off'.

mux ▸ noun a multiplexer.
▸ verb short for **MULTIPLEX**.

Muzaffarabad /ˌmʊzəˌfarəˈbad/ a town in NE Pakistan, the administrative centre of Azad Kashmir.

muzak /ˈmjuːzak/ ▸ noun [mass noun] trademark recorded light background music played through speakers in public places.
– ORIGIN 1930s: alteration of **MUSIC**.

muzhik /muːˈʒɪk, ˈmuːʒɪk/ ▸ noun historical a Russian peasant.
– ORIGIN Russian.

Muztag /muːsˈtɑːg/ a mountain in western China, on the north Tibetan border close to the Karamiran Shankou pass. Rising to 7,723 m (25,338 ft), it is the highest peak in the Kunlun Shan range.

muzz ▸ noun [mass noun] informal a muddle or blur: *in the echoey hall, every other word is lost in the muzz.*
– ORIGIN mid 18th cent. (as a verb in the sense 'study intently'): of unknown origin; based partly perhaps on an alteration of **MUSE**².

muzzle ▸ noun 1 the projecting part of the face, including the nose and mouth, of an animal such as a dog or horse.
■a guard, typically made of straps or wire, fitted over this part of an animal's face to stop it biting or feeding. ■ informal the part of a person's face including the nose, mouth, and chin.
2 the open end of the barrel of a firearm: *Devlin jammed the muzzle of the gun into the man's neck.*
▸ verb [with obj.] put a muzzle on (an animal).

■figurative prevent (a person or an institution, especially the press) from expressing their opinions freely: *the politicians want to muzzle us and control what we write.*
– ORIGIN late Middle English: from Old French *musel*, diminutive of medieval Latin *musum*, of unknown ultimate origin.

muzzle-loader ▸ noun historical a gun that is loaded through its muzzle.

muzzle velocity ▸ noun the velocity with which a bullet or shell leaves the muzzle of a gun.

muzzy ▸ adjective (**muzzier, muzziest**) 1 unable to think clearly; confused: *she was shivering and her head felt muzzy from sleep.*
■not thought out clearly; vague: *society's muzzy notion of tolerance.*
2 (of a person's eyes or a visual image) blurred: *a slightly muzzy picture.*
■(of a sound) indistinct: *the bass and drums are, even on CD, appallingly muzzy.*
– DERIVATIVES **muzzily** adverb, **muzziness** noun.
– ORIGIN early 18th cent.: of unknown origin.

MV ▸ abbreviation for ■ megavolt(s). ■ motor vessel: *on board the MV Alcinous.* ■ muzzle velocity.

MVD the Ministry of Internal Affairs, the secret police of the former USSR from 1946 to 1953.
– ORIGIN abbreviation of Russian *Ministerstvo vnutrennikh del.*

MVO ▸ abbreviation for Member of the Royal Victorian Order.

MVP N. Amer. ▸ abbreviation for most valuable player (an award given in various sports to the best player in a team).

MW ▸ abbreviation for ■ Malawi (international vehicle registration). ■ medium wave. ■ megawatt(s).

mW ▸ abbreviation for milliwatt(s).

MWO ▸ abbreviation for Master Warrant Officer.

Mx ▸ abbreviation for ■ maxwell(s). ■ Middlesex (a former county in England).

MY ▸ abbreviation for motor yacht: *MY Fleury.*

my ▸ possessive determiner 1 belonging to or associated with the speaker: *my name is John | my friend.*
■informal used with a name to refer to a member of the speaker's family: *my Johnny, see, he was smart.* ■ used with forms of address in affectionate, sympathetic, humorous, or patronizing contexts: *my dear boy | my poor baby.*
2 used in various expressions of surprise: *my goodness! | oh my!*
– PHRASES **My Lady** (or **Lord**) a polite form of address to certain titled people.
– ORIGIN Middle English *mi* (originally before words beginning with any consonant except *h-*), reduced from *min*, from Old English *mīn* (see **MINE**¹).

my- ▸ combining form variant spelling of **MYO-** shortened before a vowel (as in *myalgia*).

myalgia /maɪˈaldʒə/ ▸ noun [mass noun] pain in a muscle or group of muscles.
– DERIVATIVES **myalgic** adjective.
– ORIGIN mid 19th cent.: modern Latin, from Greek *mus* 'muscle' + **-ALGIA**.

myalgic encephalomyelitis (abbrev.: **ME**) ▸ noun another term for **CHRONIC FATIGUE SYNDROME**.

myalism /ˈmaɪəlɪz(ə)m/ ▸ noun [mass noun] a Jamaican folk religion focused on the power of ancestors, typically involving drumming, dancing, spirit possession, ritual sacrifice, and herbalism.
– ORIGIN mid 19th cent.: from *myal*, in the same sense (perhaps from Hausa *mayl* 'sorcerer'), + **-ISM**.

myall /ˈmaɪɔːl/ ▸ noun 1 an Australian acacia tree with hard decorative timber that is used for tobacco pipes and other fancy work. [ORIGIN: mid 19th cent.: perhaps a transferred use of sense 2, with reference to trade in wood between Dharuk-speakers and Kamilaroi-speakers.]
●Genus *Acacia*, family Leguminosae: several species, in particular *A. pendula*, which has violet-scented timber.
2 Austral. an Australian Aboriginal living in a traditional way. [ORIGIN: from Dharuk *mayal, miyal* 'person of another tribe'.]

Myanmar /ˌmaɪanˈmaː, ˈmjama:/ see **BURMA**.

myasthenia /ˌmaɪəsˈθiːnɪə/ ▸ noun [mass noun] a condition causing abnormal weakness of certain muscles.
■(in full **myasthenia gravis** /ˈgraːvɪs, ˈgravɪs/) a rare chronic autoimmune disease marked by muscular weakness without atrophy, and caused by a defect in

the action of acetylcholine at neuromuscular junctions.
– ORIGIN mid 19th cent.: modern Latin, from Greek *mus* 'muscle' + **ASTHENIA**.

mycelium /maɪˈsiːlɪəm/ ▸ noun (pl. **mycelia** /-lɪə/) Botany the vegetative part of a fungus, consisting of a network of fine white filaments (hyphae).
– DERIVATIVES **mycelial** adjective.
– ORIGIN mid 19th cent.: modern Latin, from Greek *mukēs* 'fungus', on the pattern of *epithelium*.

Mycenae /maɪˈsiːniː/ an ancient city in Greece, situated near the coast in the NE Peloponnese, the centre of the late Bronze Age Mycenaean civilization. The capital of King Agamemnon, it was at its most prosperous *c*.1400–1200 BC; systematic excavation of the site began in 1840.

Mycenaean /ˌmaɪsɪˈniːən/ (also **Mycenean**) Archaeology ▸ adjective of, relating to, or denoting a late Bronze Age civilization in Greece represented by finds at Mycenae and other ancient cities of the Peloponnese.
▸ noun an inhabitant of Mycenae or member of the Mycenaean people.

The Mycenaeans controlled the Aegean after the fall of the Minoan civilization *c*.1400 BC, and built fortified citadels and impressive palaces. They spoke a form of Greek, written in a distinctive script (see **LINEAR B**), and their culture is identified with that portrayed in the Homeric poems. Their power declined during widespread upheavals at the end of the Mediterranean Bronze Age, around 1100 BC.

mycetoma /ˌmaɪsɪˈtəʊmə/ ▸ noun [mass noun] Medicine chronic inflammation of the tissues caused by infection with a fungus or with certain bacteria.
– ORIGIN late 19th cent.: modern Latin, from Greek *mukēs, mukēt-* 'fungus' + **-OMA**.

-mycin ▸ combining form in names of antibiotic compounds derived from fungi: *streptomycin.*
– ORIGIN based on **MYCO-**.

myco- ▸ combining form relating to fungi: *mycoprotein.*
– ORIGIN formed irregularly from Greek *mukēs* 'fungus, mushroom'.

mycobacterium /ˌmaɪkə(ʊ)bakˈtɪərɪəm/ ▸ noun (pl. **mycobacteria** /-rɪə/) a bacterium of a group which includes the causative agents of leprosy and tuberculosis.
●Genus *Mycobacterium* and family Mycobacteriaceae; Gram-positive aerobic acid-fast bacteria.
– DERIVATIVES **mycobacterial** adjective.

mycology /maɪˈkɒlədʒi/ ▸ noun [mass noun] the scientific study of fungi.
– DERIVATIVES **mycological** adjective, **mycologically** adverb, **mycologist** noun.

mycoplasma /ˌmaɪkə(ʊ)ˈplazmə/ ▸ noun (pl. **mycoplasmas** or **mycoplasmata** /-mətə/) any of a group of small typically parasitic bacteria that lack cell walls and sometimes cause diseases.
●Class Mollicutes and order Mycoplasmatales.

mycoprotein ▸ noun [mass noun] protein derived from fungi, especially as produced for human consumption.

mycorrhiza /ˌmaɪkə(ʊ)ˈraɪzə/ ▸ noun (pl. **mycorrhizae** /-ziː/) Botany a fungus which grows in association with the roots of a plant in a symbiotic or mildly pathogenic relationship.
– DERIVATIVES **mycorrhizal** adjective.
– ORIGIN late 19th cent.: modern Latin, from **MYCO-** 'of fungi' + Greek *rhiza* 'root'.

mycosis /maɪˈkəʊsɪs/ ▸ noun (pl. **mycoses** /-siːz/) a disease caused by infection with a fungus, such as ringworm or thrush.
– DERIVATIVES **mycotic** /-ˈkɒtɪk/ adjective.

mycotoxin ▸ noun any toxic substance produced by a fungus.

mycotrophic /ˌmaɪkə(ʊ)ˈtrəʊfɪk, -ˈtrɒfɪk/ ▸ adjective Botany (of a plant) living in association with a mycorrhiza or another fungus which appears to improve the uptake of nutrients.
– DERIVATIVES **mycotrophy** noun.
– ORIGIN 1920s: from **MYCO-** 'of fungi' + Greek *trophē* 'nourishment'.

mydriasis /ˌmɪdrɪˈeɪsɪs, mɪˈdraɪəsɪs/ ▸ noun [mass noun] Medicine dilation of the pupil of the eye.
– ORIGIN early 19th cent.: via Latin from Greek *mudriasis.*

myelin /ˈmaɪəlɪn/ ▸ noun [mass noun] Anatomy & Physiology a mixture of proteins and phospholipids forming a whitish insulating sheath around many nerve

fibres, which increases the speed at which impulses are conducted.
– DERIVATIVES **myelinated** adjective, **myelination** noun.
– ORIGIN late 19th cent.: from Greek *muelos* 'marrow' + -IN[1].

myelitis /ˌmʌɪəˈlʌɪtɪs/ ▶ noun [mass noun] Medicine inflammation of the spinal cord.
– ORIGIN mid 19th cent.: modern Latin, from Greek *muelos* 'marrow' + -ITIS.

myeloid /ˈmʌɪəlɔɪd/ ▶ adjective **1** of or relating to bone marrow.
■(of leukaemia) characterized by the proliferation of cells originating in the bone marrow.
2 of or relating to the spinal cord.
– ORIGIN mid 19th cent.: from Greek *muelos* 'marrow' + -OID.

myeloma /ˌmʌɪəˈləʊmə/ ▶ noun (pl. **myelomas** or **myelomata** /-mətə/) Medicine a malignant tumour of the bone marrow.
– ORIGIN mid 19th cent.: modern Latin, from Greek *muelos* 'marrow' + -OMA.

myelopathy /ˌmʌɪəˈlɒpəθi/ ▶ noun [mass noun] Medicine disease of the spinal cord.

myenteric /ˌmʌɪɛnˈtɛrɪk/ ▶ adjective Anatomy relating to or denoting a plexus of nerves of the sympathetic and parasympathetic systems situated between and supplying the two layers of muscle in the small intestine.

mygalomorph /ˈmɪɡ(ə)ləmɔːf/ ▶ noun Zoology a large spider of a group that includes the tarantulas, trapdoor spiders, and funnel-web spiders. Mygalomorphs have several primitive features, including fangs that stab downwards rather than towards one another.
●Suborder Mygalomorphae, order Araneae.
– ORIGIN 1920s: from modern Latin *Mygalomorphae*, from Greek *mugalē* 'shrew' + *morphē* 'form'.

Mykolayiv /ˌmɪkəˈlʌɪf/ an industrial city in southern Ukraine, on the Southern Bug river near the northern tip of the Black Sea; pop. 507,900 (1990). Russian name **NIKOLAEV**.

Mykonos /ˈmɪkɒnɒs/ a Greek island in the Aegean, one of the Cyclades. Greek name **MÍKONOS**.

Mylar /ˈmʌɪlɑː/ ▶ noun [mass noun] trademark a form of polyester resin used to make heat-resistant plastic films and sheets. It is made by copolymerizing ethylene glycol and terephthalic acid.
– ORIGIN 1950s: an arbitrary formation.

mylodon /ˈmʌɪləd(ə)n/ ▶ noun an extinct giant ground sloth found in Pleistocene ice age deposits in South America. It died out only 11,000 years ago.
●Genus *Glossotherium* (formerly *Mylodon*), family Mylodontidae.
– ORIGIN mid 19th cent.: modern Latin, from Greek *mulē* 'mill, molar' + *odous*, *odont-* 'tooth'.

mylonite /ˈmʌɪlənʌɪt/ ▶ noun [mass noun] Geology a fine-grained metamorphic rock, typically banded, resulting from the grinding or crushing of other rocks.
– ORIGIN late 19th cent.: from Greek *mulōn* 'mill' + -ITE[1].

Mymensingh /ˌmʌɪmənˈsɪŋ/ a port on the Brahmaputra River in central Bangladesh; pop. 186,000 (1991).

mynah /ˈmʌɪnə/ (also **mynah bird**) (also **myna**) ▶ noun an Asian and Australasian starling that typically has dark plumage, gregarious behaviour, and a loud call.
●Family Sturnidae: several genera and species, in particular the **hill mynah** or **southern grackle** (*Gracula religiosa*), which is popular as a cage bird because of its ability to mimic the human voice.
– ORIGIN mid 18th cent.: from Hindi *mainā*.

myo- (also **my-** before a vowel) ▶ combining form of muscle; relating to muscles: *myocardium* | *myometrium*.
– ORIGIN from Greek *mus*, *mu-* 'mouse or muscle'.

myocarditis /ˌmʌɪəʊkɑːˈdʌɪtɪs/ ▶ noun [mass noun] Medicine inflammation of the heart muscle.

myocardium /ˌmʌɪəʊˈkɑːdɪəm/ ▶ noun [mass noun] Anatomy the muscular tissue of the heart.
– DERIVATIVES **myocardial** adjective.
– ORIGIN late 19th cent.: modern Latin, from MYO- 'muscle' + Greek *kardia* 'heart'.

myoclonus /ˌmʌɪə(ʊ)ˈkləʊnəs/ ▶ noun [mass noun] Medicine spasmodic jerky contraction of groups of muscles.
– DERIVATIVES **myoclonic** adjective.

myofibril /ˌmʌɪə(ʊ)ˈfʌɪbrɪl/ ▶ noun any of the elongated contractile threads found in striated muscle cells.

myogenic /ˌmʌɪə(ʊ)ˈdʒɛnɪk/ ▶ adjective Physiology originating in muscle tissue (rather than from nerve impulses).

myoglobin /ˌmʌɪə(ʊ)ˈɡləʊbɪn/ ▶ noun [mass noun] Biochemistry a red protein containing haem, which carries and stores oxygen in muscle cells. It is structurally similar to a subunit of haemoglobin.

myology /mʌɪˈɒlədʒi/ ▶ noun [mass noun] the study of the structure, arrangement, and action of muscles.
– DERIVATIVES **myological** adjective, **myologist** noun.

myomere /ˈmʌɪə(ʊ)mɪə/ ▶ noun see MYOTOME.

myometrium /ˌmʌɪə(ʊ)ˈmiːtrɪəm/ ▶ noun [mass noun] Anatomy the smooth muscle tissue of the womb.
– ORIGIN early 20th cent.: modern Latin, from MYO- 'muscle' + Greek *mētra* 'womb'.

Myomorpha /ˌmʌɪə(ʊ)ˈmɔːfə/ Zoology a major division of the rodents that includes the rats, mice, voles, hamsters, and their relatives.
●Suborder Myomorpha, order Rodentia.
– ORIGIN modern Latin (plural), from Greek *mus*, *mu-* 'mouse' + *morphē* 'form'.

myopathy /mʌɪˈɒpəθi/ ▶ noun (pl. **-ies**) Medicine a disease of muscle tissue.
– DERIVATIVES **myopathic** adjective.

myope /ˈmʌɪəʊp/ ▶ noun a short-sighted person.
– ORIGIN early 18th cent.: from French, via late Latin from Greek *muōps*, from *muein* 'to shut' + *ōps* 'eye'.

myopia /mʌɪˈəʊpɪə/ ▶ noun [mass noun] short-sightedness.
■lack of imagination, foresight, or intellectual insight: *historians have been censured for their myopia in treating modern science as a western phenomenon.*
– ORIGIN early 18th cent.: modern Latin, from late Greek *muōpia*, from Greek *muōps* (see MYOPE).

myopic /mʌɪˈɒpɪk/ ▶ adjective (of a person or their eyes) short-sighted.
■lacking imagination, foresight, or intellectual insight: *the government still has a myopic attitude to public spending.*
– DERIVATIVES **myopically** /-ˈɒpɪk(ə)li/ adverb.

myosin /ˈmʌɪə(ʊ)sɪn/ ▶ noun [mass noun] Biochemistry a fibrous protein which forms (together with actin) the contractile filaments of muscle cells and is also involved in motion in other types of cell.

myosis ▶ noun variant spelling of MIOSIS.

myositis /ˌmʌɪə(ʊ)ˈsʌɪtɪs/ ▶ noun [mass noun] Medicine inflammation and degeneration of muscle tissue.
– ORIGIN early 19th cent.: formed irregularly from Greek *mus*, *mu-* 'muscle' + -ITIS.

myosotis /ˌmʌɪə(ʊ)ˈsəʊtɪs/ ▶ noun a plant of a genus which includes the forget-me-nots.
●Genus *Myosotis*, family Boraginaceae.
– ORIGIN modern Latin, from Greek *muosōtis*, from *mus*, *mu-* 'mouse' + *ous*, *ōt-* 'ear'.

myotis /mʌɪˈəʊtɪs/ ▶ noun an insectivorous bat with a slender muzzle and with the flight membrane extending between the hind legs and the tip of the tail.
●Genus *Myotis*, family Vespertilionidae: numerous species.
– ORIGIN modern Latin, based on Greek *mus*, *mu-* 'mouse'.

myotome /ˈmʌɪətəʊm/ ▶ noun Embryology the dorsal part of each somite in a vertebrate embryo, giving rise to the skeletal musculature. Compare with DERMATOME, SCLEROTOME.
■each of the muscle blocks along either side of the spine in vertebrates (especially fish and amphibians). Also called MYOMERE.

myotonia /ˌmʌɪə(ʊ)ˈtəʊnɪə/ ▶ noun [mass noun] inability to relax voluntary muscle after vigorous effort.
– DERIVATIVES **myotonic** adjective.
– ORIGIN late 19th cent.: from MYO- 'muscle' + Greek *tonos* 'tone'.

myotonic dystrophy ▶ noun [mass noun] Medicine a form of muscular dystrophy accompanied by myotonia.

myriad /ˈmɪrɪəd/ poetic/literary ▶ noun **1** a countless or extremely great number: *myriads of insects danced around the light above my head.*
2 (chiefly in classical history) a unit of ten thousand.
▶ adjective countless or extremely great in number: *he gazed at the myriad lights of the city.*

■having countless or very many elements or aspects: *the myriad political scene.*
– ORIGIN mid 16th cent. (in sense 2 of the noun): via late Latin from Greek *murias*, *muriad-*, from *murioi* '10,000'.

myriapod /ˈmɪrɪəpɒd/ ▶ noun Zoology an arthropod of a group that includes the centipedes, millipedes, and related animals. Myriapods have elongated bodies with numerous leg-bearing segments.
●Classes Chilopoda, Diplopoda, Pauropoda, and Symphyla; formerly placed together in the class Myriapoda.
– ORIGIN early 19th cent.: from modern Latin *Myriapoda*, from Greek *murias* (see MYRIAD) + *pous*, *pod-* 'foot'.

myringotomy /ˌmɪrɪnˈɡɒtəmi, -ˈɡɒtəmi/ ▶ noun [mass noun] surgical incision into the eardrum, to relieve pressure or drain fluid.
– ORIGIN late 19th cent.: from modern Latin *myringa* 'eardrum' + -TOMY.

myristic acid /mʌɪˈrɪstɪk, mɪ-/ ▶ noun [mass noun] Chemistry a compound present in oil of nutmeg and other natural fats.
●A straight-chain fatty acid; chem. formula: $CH_3(CH_2)_{12}COOH$.
– DERIVATIVES **myristate** noun.
– ORIGIN mid 19th cent.: *myristic* from modern Latin *Myristica* (genus name), from medieval Latin (*nux*) *myristica* 'nutmeg', from Greek *murizein* 'anoint'.

myrmecology /ˌmɜːmɪˈkɒlədʒi/ ▶ noun [mass noun] the branch of entomology that deals with ants.
– DERIVATIVES **myrmecological** adjective, **myrmecologist** noun.
– ORIGIN late 19th cent.: from Greek *murmēx*, *murmēk-* 'ant' + -LOGY.

myrmecophile /ˈmɜːmɪkə(ʊ)fʌɪl, mə-ˈmiːkə(ʊ)-/ ▶ noun Biology an invertebrate or plant which has a symbiotic relationship with ants, such as being tended and protected by ants or living inside an ants' nest.
– DERIVATIVES **myrmecophilous** adjective, **myrmecophily** noun.
– ORIGIN late 19th cent.: from Greek *murmēx*, *murmēk-* 'ant' + -PHILE.

myrmidon /ˈmɜːmɪd(ə)n/ ▶ noun a member of a warlike Thessalian people led by Achilles at the siege of Troy.
■a hired ruffian or unscrupulous subordinate: *he wrote to one of Hitler's myrmidons.*
– ORIGIN late Middle English: from Latin *Myrmidones* (plural), from Greek *Murmidones*.

myrobalan /mʌɪˈrɒbələn/ ▶ noun **1** (also **myrobalan plum**) another term for CHERRY PLUM.
2 a tropical tree of a characteristic pagoda shape, which yields a number of useful items including dye, timber, and medicinal products.
●Genus *Terminalia*, family Combretaceae: several species, in particular *T. chebula*.
■(also **myrobalan nut**) the fruit of this tree, used especially for tanning leather.
– ORIGIN late Middle English: from French *myrobolan* or Latin *myrobalanum*, from Greek *murobalanos*, from *muron* 'unguent' + *balanos* 'acorn'.

Myron /ˈmʌɪ(ə)rən/ (*fl. c.*480–440 BC), Greek sculptor. None of his work is known to survive, but there are two certain copies, one being the *Discobolus* (*c.*450 BC), a figure of a man throwing the discus, which demonstrates a remarkable interest in symmetry and movement.

myrrh[1] /mɜː/ ▶ noun [mass noun] a fragrant gum resin obtained from certain trees and used, especially in the Near East, in perfumery, medicines, and incense.
●The trees belong to the genus *Commiphora*, family Burseraceae, in particular *C. myrrha*.
– DERIVATIVES **myrrhy** adjective.
– ORIGIN Old English *myrra*, *myrre*, via Latin from Greek *murra*, of Semitic origin; compare with Arabic *murr* 'bitter'.

myrrh[2] /mɜː/ ▶ noun another term for SWEET CICELY.
– ORIGIN late 16th cent.: from Latin *myrris*, from Greek *murris*.

myrtaceous /mɜːˈteɪʃəs/ ▶ adjective Botany of, relating to, or denoting plants of the myrtle family (Myrtaceae).
– ORIGIN mid 19th cent.: from modern Latin *Myrtaceae* (plural), from the genus name *Myrtus* (see MYRTLE), + -OUS.

myrtle ▶ noun **1** an evergreen shrub which has glossy aromatic foliage and white flowers followed by purple-black oval berries.
●*Myrtus communis*, family Myrtaceae (the **myrtle family**).

This family also includes several aromatic plants (clove, allspice) and many characteristic Australian plants (eucalyptus trees, bottlebrushes).

2 N. Amer. the lesser periwinkle.

• *Vinca minor*, family Apocynaceae. See **PERIWINKLE**[1].

– ORIGIN late Middle English: from medieval Latin *myrtilla*, *myrtillus*, diminutive of Latin *myrta*, *myrtus*, from Greek *murtos*.

myself ▶ **pronoun** [first person singular] **1** [reflexive] used by a speaker to refer to himself or herself as the object of a verb or preposition when he or she is the subject of the clause: *I hurt myself by accident* | *I strolled around, muttering to myself.*

2 [emphatic] I or me personally (used to emphasize the speaker): *I myself am unsure how this problem should be handled* | *I wrote it myself.*

3 poetic/literary term for **I**[2]: *myself presented to him a bronze sword.*

– PHRASES **(not) be myself** see ***be oneself, not be oneself*** at **BE**. **by myself** see ***by oneself*** at **BY**.

– ORIGIN Old English *me self*, from **ME**[1] + **SELF** (used adjectivally); the change of *me* to *my* occurred in Middle English.

Mysia /ˈmɪsɪə/ an ancient region of NW Asia Minor, on the Mediterranean coast south of the Sea of Marmara.

– DERIVATIVES **Mysian** adjective & noun.

mysid /ˈmʌɪsɪd/ ▶ **noun** Zoology a crustacean of an order that comprises the opossum shrimps.

• Order Mysidacea, class Malacostraca.

– ORIGIN mid 20th cent.: from modern Latin *Mysis* (genus name) + **-ID**[3].

Mysore /mʌɪˈsɔː/ **1** a city in the Indian state of Karnataka; pop. 480,000 (1991). It was the capital of the princely state of Mysore and is noted for the production of silk, incense, and sandalwood oil.

2 former name (until 1973) for **KARNATAKA**.

mystagogue /ˈmɪstəɡɒɡ/ ▶ **noun** a teacher or propounder of mystical doctrines.

– DERIVATIVES **mystagogy** noun.

– ORIGIN mid 16th cent.: from French, or via Latin from Greek *mustagōgos*, from *mustēs* 'initiated person' + *agōgos* 'leading'.

mysterious ▶ **adjective 1** difficult or impossible to understand, explain, or identify: *his colleague had vanished in mysterious circumstances* | *a mysterious benefactor provided the money.*

▪(of a location) having an atmosphere of strangeness or secrecy: *a dark, mysterious, windowless building.*

2 (of a person) deliberately enigmatic: *she was mysterious about herself but said plenty about her husband.*

– DERIVATIVES **mysteriously** adverb, **mysteriousness** noun.

– ORIGIN late 16th cent.: from French *mystérieux*, from *mystère* 'mystery'.

mystery[1] ▶ **noun** (pl. **-ies**) **1** something that is difficult or impossible to understand or explain: *the mysteries of outer space* | *hoping that the inquest would solve the mystery.*

▪[mass noun] the condition or quality of being secret, strange, or difficult to explain: *much of her past is shrouded in mystery.* ▪a person or thing whose identity or nature is puzzling or unknown: *'He's a bit of a mystery,' said Nina* | [as modifier] *a mystery guest.*

2 a novel, play, or film dealing with a puzzling crime, especially a murder.

3 (**mysteries**) the secret rites of Greek and Roman pagan religion, or of any ancient or tribal religion, to which only initiates are admitted.

▪the practices, skills, or lore peculiar to a particular trade or activity and regarded as baffling to those without specialized knowledge: *the mysteries of analytical psychology.* ▪ archaic the Christian Eucharist.

4 chiefly Christian Theology a religious belief based on divine revelation, especially one regarded as beyond human understanding: *the mystery of Christ.*

▪an incident in the life of Jesus or of a saint as a focus of devotion in the Roman Catholic Church, especially each of those commemorated during recitation of successive decades of the rosary.

– ORIGIN Middle English (in the sense 'mystic presence, hidden religious symbolism'): from Old French *mistere* or Latin *mysterium*, from Greek *mustērion*; related to **MYSTIC**.

mystery[2] ▶ **noun** (pl. **-ies**) archaic a handicraft or trade, especially when referred to in indentures.

– ORIGIN late Middle English: from medieval Latin *misterium*, contraction of *ministerium* 'ministry', by association with *mysterium* (see **MYSTERY**[1]).

mystery play ▶ **noun** a popular medieval play based on biblical stories or the lives of the saints. Also called **MIRACLE PLAY**.

Mystery plays were performed by members of trade guilds in Europe from the 13th century, in churches or later on wagons or temporary stages along a route, frequently introducing apocryphal and satirical elements. Several cycles of plays survive in association with particular English cities and towns.

mystery religion ▶ **noun** a religion centred on secret or mystical rites for initiates, especially any of a number of cults popular during the late Roman Empire.

mystery tour ▶ **noun** Brit. a pleasure excursion to an unspecified destination.

mystic ▶ **noun** a person who seeks by contemplation and self-surrender to obtain unity with or absorption into the Deity or the absolute, or who believes in the spiritual apprehension of truths that are beyond the intellect.

▶ **adjective** another term for **MYSTICAL**.

– ORIGIN Middle English (in the sense 'mystical meaning'): from Old French *mystique*, or via Latin from Greek *mustikos*, from *mustēs* 'initiated person' from *muein* 'close the eyes or lips', also 'initiate'. The current sense of the noun dates from the late 17th cent.

mystical ▶ **adjective 1** of or relating to mystics or religious mysticism: *the mystical experience.*

▪spiritually allegorical or symbolic; transcending human understanding: *the mystical body of Christ.* ▪ of or relating to ancient religious mysteries or other occult or esoteric rites: *the mystical practices of the Pythagoreans.* ▪ of hidden or esoteric meaning: *a geometric figure of mystical significance.*

2 inspiring a sense of spiritual mystery, awe, and fascination: *the mystical forces of nature.*

▪concerned with the soul or the spirit, rather than with material things: *the beliefs of a more mystical age.*

– DERIVATIVES **mystically** adverb.

Mysticeti /ˌmɪstɪˈsiːtiː/ Zoology a division of the whales that comprises the baleen whales.

• Suborder Mysticeti, order Cetacea.

– DERIVATIVES **mysticete** noun & adjective.

– ORIGIN modern Latin (plural), from Greek *mustikētos* representing (in old editions of Aristotle) the phrase *ho mus to kētos* 'the mouse, the whale so called'.

mysticism ▶ **noun** [mass noun] **1** belief that union with or absorption into the Deity or the absolute, or the spiritual apprehension of knowledge inaccessible to the intellect, may be attained through contemplation and self-surrender.

2 belief characterized by self-delusion or dreamy confusion of thought, especially when based on the assumption of occult qualities or mysterious agencies.

mystify ▶ **verb** (**-ies**, **-ied**) [with obj.] utterly bewilder or perplex (someone): *I was completely mystified by his disappearance* | [as adj. **mystifying**] *a mystifying phenomenon.*

▪dated take advantage of the credulity of; hoax: *he took a childlike delight in mystifying his officials.* ▪ make obscure or mysterious: *lawyers who mystify the legal system so that laymen find it unintelligible.*

– DERIVATIVES **mystification** noun, **mystifier** noun, **mystifyingly** adverb.

– ORIGIN early 19th cent.: from French *mystifier*, formed irregularly from *mystique* 'mystic' or from *mystère* 'mystery'.

mystique ▶ **noun** [mass noun] a fascinating aura of mystery, awe, and power surrounding someone or something: *the mystique surrounding the monarchy* | *the tiger has a mystique that man has always respected and revered.*

▪an air of secrecy surrounding a particular activity or subject that makes it impressive or baffling to those without specialized knowledge: *eliminating the mystique normally associated with computers.*

– ORIGIN late 19th cent.: from French, from Old French (see **MYSTIC**).

myth ▶ **noun 1** a traditional story, especially one concerning the early history of a people or explaining some natural or social phenomenon, and typically involving supernatural beings or events.

▪[mass noun] such stories collectively: *the heroes of Greek myth.*

2 a widely held but false belief or idea: *dispelling the myth that croquet is a genteel Sunday afternoon pastime* | [mass noun] *contrary to popular myth, the south-east does not consist entirely of rich people.*

▪a misrepresentation of the truth: *attacking the party's irresponsible myths about privatization.* ▪ a fictitious or imaginary person or thing. ▪ an exaggerated or idealized conception of a person or thing: *the book is a scholarly study of the Churchill myth.*

– ORIGIN mid 19th cent.: from modern Latin *mythus*, via late Latin from Greek *muthos*.

mythi plural form of **MYTHUS**.

mythic ▶ **adjective** of, relating to, or resembling myth: *we explain spiritual forces in mythic language.*

▪exaggerated or idealized: *Scott of the Antarctic was a national hero of mythic proportions.* ▪ fictitious: *a mythic land of plenty.*

– ORIGIN mid 17th cent.: via late Latin from Greek *muthikos*, from *muthos* 'myth'.

mythical ▶ **adjective** occurring in or characteristic of myths or folk tales: *one of Denmark's greatest mythical heroes.*

▪idealized, especially with reference to the past: *a mythical age of contentment and social order.* ▪ fictitious: *a mythical customer whose name appears in brochures.*

– DERIVATIVES **mythically** adverb.

mythicize (also **-ise**) ▶ **verb** [with obj.] turn into myth; interpret mythically.

– DERIVATIVES **mythicism** noun, **mythicist** noun.

mytho- ▶ **combining form** of or relating to myth: *mythography.*

– ORIGIN from Greek *muthos*, or from **MYTH**.

mythographer ▶ **noun** a writer or collector of myths.

mythography ▶ **noun** [mass noun] **1** the representation of myths, especially in the plastic arts.

2 the creation or collection of myths.

mythologize (also **-ise**) ▶ **verb** [with obj.] convert into myth or mythology; make the subject of a myth: *there is a grave danger of mythologizing the past.*

– DERIVATIVES **mythologizer** noun.

mythology ▶ **noun** (pl. **-ies**) [mass noun] **1** a collection of myths, especially one belonging to a particular religious or cultural tradition: *Ganesa was the god of wisdom and success in Hindu mythology* | [count noun] *a book discussing Jewish and Christian mythologies.*

▪a set of stories or beliefs about a particular person, institution, or situation, especially when exaggerated or fictitious: *we look for change in our thirties, not in our forties, as popular mythology has it.*

2 the study of myths.

– DERIVATIVES **mythologer** noun, **mythologic** adjective, **mythological** adjective, **mythologically** adverb, **mythologist** noun.

– ORIGIN late Middle English: from French *mythologie*, or via late Latin from Greek *muthologia*, from *muthos* 'myth' + *-logia* (see **-LOGY**).

mythomania ▶ **noun** [mass noun] an abnormal or pathological tendency to exaggerate or tell lies.

– DERIVATIVES **mythomaniac** noun & adjective.

mythopoeia /ˌmɪθə(ʊ)ˈpiːə/ ▶ **noun** [mass noun] the making of a myth or myths.

– DERIVATIVES **mythopoeic** adjective.

– ORIGIN 1950s: from Greek *muthopoiia*, from *muthos* 'myth' + *poiein* 'make'.

mythopoetic /ˌmɪθə(ʊ)pəʊˈɛtɪk/ ▶ **adjective** of or relating to the making of a myth or myths.

▪relating to or denoting a movement for men that uses activities such as storytelling and poetry reading as a means of self-understanding.

mythos /ˈmʌɪθɒs, ˈmɪθɒs/ ▶ **noun** (pl. **mythoi** /-θɔɪ/) chiefly technical a myth or mythology.

▪a traditional or recurrent narrative theme or plot structure. ▪ a set of beliefs or assumptions about something: *the rhetoric and mythos of science create the comforting image of linear progression toward truth.*

– ORIGIN mid 18th cent.: from Greek.

mythus /ˈmʌɪθəs, ˈmɪθəs/ ▶ **noun** (pl. **mythi** /-θʌɪ/) a myth or mythos.

– ORIGIN early 19th cent.: modern Latin.

Mytilene /ˌmɪtɪˈliːni/ the chief town of the Greek island of Lesbos; pop. 23,970 (1991). Greek name **MITILÍNI**.

myxo- (also **myx-**) ▶ **combining form** relating to mucus: *myxodoema* | *myxovirus.*

– ORIGIN from Greek *muxa* 'slime, mucus'.

myxoedema /ˌmɪksɪˈdiːmə/ (US **myxedema**) ▶ **noun** [mass noun] Medicine swelling of the skin and underlying tissues giving a waxy consistency, typical of patients with underactive thyroid glands.

m

■the more general condition associated with hypothyroidism, including weight gain, mental dullness, and sensitivity to cold.

myxoma /mɪkˈsəʊmə/ ▶ noun (pl. **myxomas** or **myxomata** /-mətə/) Medicine a benign tumour of connective tissue containing mucous or gelatinous material.

– DERIVATIVES **myxomatous** adjective.

myxomatosis /ˌmɪksəməˈtəʊsɪs/ ▶ noun [mass noun] a highly infectious and usually fatal viral disease of rabbits, causing swelling of the mucous membranes and inflammation and discharge around the eyes.

myxomycete /ˌmɪksə(ʊ)ˈmʌɪsiːt/ ▶ noun Biology a slime mould, especially an acellular one whose vegetative stage is a multinucleate plasmodium.

● Division Myxomycota, kingdom Fungi, in particular the class Myxomycetes; also treated as protozoan (phylum Gymnomyxa, kingdom Protista).

– ORIGIN late 19th cent.: from modern Latin *Myxomycetes*, from MYXO- 'slime' + Greek *mukētes* 'fungi'.

myxovirus /ˈmɪksə(ʊ)ˌvʌɪrəs/ ▶ noun any of a group of RNA viruses including the influenza virus.

Nn

N¹ (also **n**) ▶ **noun** (pl. **Ns** or **N's**) the fourteenth letter of the alphabet. See also **EN**.
■ denoting the next after M in a set of items, categories, etc.

N² ▶ **abbreviation for** ■ (used in recording moves in chess) knight: *17.Na4?* [ORIGIN: representing the pronunciation of *kn*-, since the initial letter *k*-represents 'king'.] ■ (on a gear lever) neutral. ■ (chiefly in place names) New: *N Zealand.* ■ Physics newton(s). ■ Chemistry (with reference to solutions) normal: *the pH was adjusted to 7.0 with 1 N HCl.* ■ North or Northern: *78° N | N Ireland.* ■ Norway (international vehicle registration). ■ nuclear: *the N bomb.*
▶ **symbol for** the chemical element nitrogen.

n ▶ **abbreviation for** ■ [in combination] (in units of measurement) nano- (10^{-9}): *the plates were coated with 500 ng of protein in sodium carbonate buffer.* ■ Grammar neuter. ■ (n-) [in combination] Chemistry normal (denoting straight-chain hydrocarbons): *n-hexane.* ■ note (used in a book's index to refer to a footnote): *450n.* ■ Grammar noun.
▶ **symbol for** an unspecified or variable number: *at the limit where n equals infinity.* See also **NTH**.

'n (also **'n'**) ▶ **contraction** of and (conventionally used in informal contexts to coordinate two closely connected elements): *rock 'n roll | fish 'n chips.*

-n¹ ▶ **suffix** variant spelling of **-EN²**.

-n² ▶ **suffix** variant spelling of **-EN³**.

Na ▶ **symbol for** the chemical element sodium.
– ORIGIN from modern Latin *natrium*.

na ▶ **adverb** Scottish form of **NOT**, used after an auxiliary verb: *we couldna spaek tae dem.*

n/a ▶ **abbreviation for** ■ not applicable. ■ not available.

NAACP ▶ **abbreviation for** National Association for the Advancement of Colored People.

NAAFI /'nafi/ ▶ **abbreviation for** Navy, Army, and Air Force Institutes, an organization running canteens and shops for British service personnel.
■ [as noun] a canteen or shop run by this organization.

naan ▶ **noun** variant spelling of **NAN²**.

naartjie /'nɑːtʃi, 'nɑːki/ ▶ **noun** (pl. **-ies**) S. African a mandarin orange of a soft-skinned variety.
– ORIGIN late 18th cent.: from Afrikaans, from Tamil *nārattai* 'citrus'.

Naas /neɪs/ the county town of Kildare in the Republic of Ireland; pop. 11,140 (1991).

nab ▶ **verb** (**nabbed**, **nabbing**) [with obj.] informal catch (someone) doing something wrong: *Olympic drug tests nabbed another athlete yesterday.*
■ take or grab (something): *Dan nabbed the seat next to mine.* ■ steal.
– ORIGIN late 17th cent. (also as *napp*; compare with **KIDNAP**): of unknown origin.

Nabataean /ˌnabəˈtiːən/ (also **Nabatean**) ▶ **noun 1** a member of an ancient Arabian people who from 312 BC formed an independent kingdom with its capital at Petra (now in Jordan). The kingdom was allied to the Roman Empire from AD 63 and incorporated as the province of Arabia in AD 106.
2 [mass noun] the extinct language of this people, a form of Aramaic strongly influenced by Arabic.
▶ **adjective** of or relating to the Nabataeans or their language.

– ORIGIN from Latin *Nabat(h)aeus*, Greek *Nabat(h)aios* (compare with the Arabic adjective *Nabaṭī* 'relating to the Nabataeans)' + **-AN**.

nabe ▶ **noun** US informal a neighbourhood.
■ a local cinema. ■ a neighbour.

Nabeul /naˈbəːl/ a resort town in NE Tunisia, on the Cape Bon peninsula; pop. 39,500 (1984).

Nabi Group /'nɑːbi/ a group of late 19th-century French painters, largely symbolist in their approach and heavily indebted to Gauguin. Members of the group included Maurice Denis, Pierre Bonnard, and Edouard Vuillard.
– ORIGIN *Nabi* from Hebrew *nāḇī* 'prophet'.

Nablus /'nɑːbləs/ a town in the West Bank; pop. 80,000 (est. 1984).

nabob /'neɪbɒb/ ▶ **noun** historical a Muslim official or governor under the Mogul empire.
■ a person of conspicuous wealth or high status. ■ chiefly historical a person who returned from India to Europe with a fortune.
– ORIGIN from Portuguese *nababo* or Spanish *nabab*, from Urdu; see also **NAWAB**.

Nabokov /'nabəkɒf, nəˈbəʊkɒf/, Vladimir (Vladimorovich) (1899–1977), Russian-born American novelist and poet. He is best known for *Lolita* (1958), his novel about a middle-aged man's obsession with a twelve-year-old girl.

Nacala /nəˈkɑːlə/ a deep-water port on the east coast of Mozambique; pop. 104,300 (1990). It is linked by rail with landlocked Malawi.

nacarat /'nakərat/ ▶ **noun** [mass noun] rare a bright orange-red colour.
– ORIGIN mid 18th cent.: from French, perhaps from Spanish and Portuguese *nacarado* 'orange-red in colour' (referring to the colour of the pinna shell that yields mother-of-pearl), from *nacar* 'nacre'.

nacelle /nəˈsɛl/ ▶ **noun** a streamlined housing or tank for something on the outside of an aircraft or motor vehicle.
■ the outer casing of an aircraft engine. ■ chiefly historical the car of an airship.
– ORIGIN early 20th cent. (originally denoting the car of an airship): from French, from late Latin *navicella*, diminutive of Latin *navis* 'ship'.

naches /'nʌxəs/ (also **nachas** pronunc. same) ▶ **noun** [mass noun] US pride or gratification, especially at the achievements of one's children.
■ congratulations: *naches to Miriam Goldstein on her acceptance into rabbinic school.*
– ORIGIN early 20th cent.: from Yiddish *nakhes*, from Hebrew *naḥaṭ* 'contentment'.

nacho /'natʃəʊ/ ▶ **noun** (pl. **-os**) a small piece of tortilla, typically topped with melted cheese and spices.
– ORIGIN perhaps from Mexican Spanish *Nacho*, pet form of *Ignacio*, given name of the chef credited with creation of the dish. An alternative derivation is from Spanish *nacho* 'flat-nosed'.

NACODS /'neɪkɒds/ ▶ **abbreviation for** (in the UK) National Association of Colliery Overmen, Deputies, and Shotfirers.

nacre /'neɪkə/ ▶ **noun** [mass noun] mother-of-pearl.
– DERIVATIVES **nacreous** adjective.
– ORIGIN late 16th cent.: from French, of unknown origin.

NAD Biochemistry ▶ **abbreviation for** nicotinamide adenine dinucleotide, a coenzyme important in many biological oxidation reactions.

nada /'nɑːdə, 'nadə/ ▶ **pronoun** N. Amer. informal nothing.
– ORIGIN Spanish.

Na-Dene /nɑːˈdɛneɪ, -ni/ ▶ **adjective** denoting or belonging to a postulated phylum of North American Indian languages including the Athabaskan family, Tlingit, and (in some classifications) Haida.
▶ **noun** [mass noun] this language group.
– ORIGIN early 20th cent.: from Tlingit *naa* 'tribe' (related to Haida *náa* 'dwell') + North Athabaskan *dene* 'tribe'.

Nader /'neɪdə/, Ralph (b.1934), American lawyer and reformer. He campaigned on behalf of public safety and prompted legislation concerning car design, radiation hazards, food packaging, and insecticides.

nadir /'neɪdɪə, 'nadɪə/ ▶ **noun** [in sing.] the lowest point in the fortunes of a person or organization: *the 1420s marked the nadir of French fortunes.*
■ Astronomy the point on the celestial sphere directly below an observer. The opposite of **ZENITH**.
– ORIGIN late Middle English (in the astronomical sense): via French from Arabic *naẓīr (as-samt)* 'opposite (to the zenith)'.

nae ▶ **determiner, exclamation, adverb,** & **noun** Scottish form of **NO**.
▶ **adverb** & **noun** Scottish form of **NOT**.

naevus /'niːvəs/ (US **nevus**) ▶ **noun** (pl. **naevi** /-vʌɪ, -viː/) a birthmark or a mole on the skin, especially a birthmark in the form of a raised red patch.
– ORIGIN mid 19th cent.: from Latin.

naff¹ ▶ **verb** Brit., usu. in imperative] (**naff off**) Brit. informal go away: *she told press photographers to naff off.*
■ [as adj. **naffing**] used for emphasis, especially to express annoyance: *more naffing guidelines!*
– ORIGIN 1950s: euphemism for **FUCK**; compare with **EFF**.

naff² ▶ **adjective** Brit. informal lacking taste or style: *he always went for the most obvious melody he could get, no matter how naff it sounded.*
– DERIVATIVES **naffness** noun.
– ORIGIN 1960s: of unknown origin.

NAFTA (also **Nafta**) ▶ **abbreviation for** North American Free Trade Agreement.

nag¹ ▶ **verb** (**nagged**, **nagging**) [with obj.] harass (someone) constantly to do something that they are averse to: *she constantly nags her daughter about getting married* | [with infinitive] *she nagged him to do the housework* | [no obj.] *he's always nagging at her for staying out late.*
■ [often as adj. **nagging**] be persistently painful, troublesome, or worrying to: *there was a nagging pain in his chest* | [no obj.] *something nagged at the back of his mind.*
▶ **noun** a person who nags someone to do something.
■ a persistent feeling of anxiety: *he felt once again that little nag of doubt.*
– DERIVATIVES **nagger** noun, **naggingly** adverb, **naggy** adjective.
– ORIGIN early 19th cent. (originally dialect in the sense 'gnaw'): perhaps of Scandinavian or Low German origin; compare with Norwegian and

Swedish *nagga* 'gnaw, irritate' and Low German (g)*naggen* 'provoke'.

nag² ▶ **noun** informal, often derogatory a horse, especially one that is old or in poor health.
■archaic a horse suitable for riding rather than as a draught animal.
– ORIGIN Middle English: of unknown origin.

Naga /ˈnɑːɡə/ ▶ **noun** **1** a member of a group of peoples living in or near the Naga Hills of Burma (Myanmar) and NE India.
2 [mass noun] any of the Tibeto-Burman languages of these peoples, with about 340,000 speakers altogether.
▶ **adjective** of or relating to the Nagas or their language.
– ORIGIN perhaps from Sanskrit *nagna* 'naked' or *naga* 'mountain'.

naga¹ /ˈnɑːɡə/ ▶ **noun** (in Indian mythology) a member of a semi-divine race, part human, part cobra in form, associated with water and sometimes with mystical initiation.
– ORIGIN from Sanskrit *nāga* 'serpent'.

naga² /ˈnɑːɡɑː/ ▶ **noun** (in some Hindu sects) a naked wandering ascetic, in particular one belonging to a sect whose members carry arms and serve as mercenaries.
– ORIGIN from Hindi *nāgā* 'naked'.

Nagaland /ˈnɑːɡəland/ a state in the far north-east of India, on the border with Burma (Myanmar); capital, Kohima. It was created in 1962 from parts of Assam.

nagana /nəˈɡɑːnə/ ▶ **noun** [mass noun] a disease of cattle, antelope, and other livestock in southern Africa, characterized by fever, lethargy, and oedema, and caused by trypanosome parasites transmitted by the tsetse fly.
– ORIGIN late 19th cent.: from Zulu *nakane*.

Nagasaki /ˌnaɡəˈsɑːki/ a city and port in SW Japan, on the west coast of Kyushu island; pop. 444,620 (1990). It was the target of the second atom bomb, dropped by the United States on 9 August 1945.

Nagorno-Karabakh /nəˌɡɔːnəʊˌkarəˈbax/ a region of Azerbaijan in the southern foothills of the Caucasus; pop. 192,000 (1990); capital, Xankändi.

Formerly a khanate, it was absorbed into the Russian empire in the 19th century, later becoming an autonomous region of the Soviet Union within Azerbaijan. Fighting between Azerbaijan and Armenia began in 1985, with the majority Armenian population desiring to be separated from Muslim Azerbaijan and united with Armenia; the region declared unilateral independence in 1991. A ceasefire was signed in 1994.

Nagoya /nəˈɡɔɪə/ a city in central Japan, on the south coast of the island of Honshu, capital of Chubu region; pop. 2,154,660 (1990).

Nagpur /naɡˈpʊə/ a city in central India, in the state of Maharashtra; pop. 1,622,000 (1991).

nagware ▶ **noun** [mass noun] informal computer software which is free for a trial period and thereafter frequently reminds the user to pay for it.

Nagy /nɒdʒ/, Imre (1896–1958), Hungarian communist statesman, Prime Minister 1953–5 and 1956. In 1956 he withdrew Hungary from the Warsaw Pact, seeking neutral status for it. He was executed after the Red Army crushed the uprising of 1956 later that year.

Nah. ▶ **abbreviation for** Nahum (in biblical references).

nah ▶ **determiner, exclamation, adverb, & noun** non-standard spelling of **NO**, used in representing southern English (especially cockney) speech: [as exclamation] *'Want a lift?' 'Nah, that's okay.'*
▶ **adverb, conjunction, & adjective** non-standard spelling of **NOW**, used in representing such speech.

Naha /ˈnɑːhə/ a port in southern Japan, capital of Okinawa island; pop. 304,900 (1990).

Nahuatl /ˈnɑːwɑːt(ə)l, nɑːˈwɑːt(ə)l/ ▶ **noun** **1** a member of a group of peoples native to southern Mexico and Central America, including the Aztecs.
2 [mass noun] the Uto-Aztecan language of these peoples, which still has over 1 million speakers.
▶ **adjective** of or relating to these peoples or their language.
– ORIGIN via Spanish from Nahuatl.

Nahum /ˈneɪhəm/ (in the Bible) a Hebrew minor prophet.
■a book of the Bible containing his prophecy of the fall of Nineveh (early 7th century BC).

naiad /ˈnʌɪad/ ▶ **noun** (pl. **naiads** or **naiades** /ˈnʌɪəˌdiːz/) **1** (in classical mythology) a water nymph said to inhabit a river, spring, or waterfall.
2 the aquatic larva or nymph of a dragonfly, mayfly, or stonefly.
3 a submerged aquatic plant with narrow leaves and minute flowers.
● Genus *Najas*, family Najadaceae.
– ORIGIN via Latin from Greek *Naias*, *Naiad-*, from *naein* 'to flow'. Use as a term in entomology and botany dates from the early 20th cent.

naiant /ˈneɪənt/ ▶ **adjective** [postpositive] Heraldry (of a fish or marine creature) swimming horizontally.
– ORIGIN mid 16th cent.: from Anglo-Norman French, variant of Old French *noiant* 'swimming', present participle of *noier*, from Latin *natare* 'to swim'.

naif /nʌɪˈiːf, nɑːˈiːf/ ▶ **adjective** naive or ingenuous.
▶ **noun** a naive or ingenuous person.
– ORIGIN from French *naïf*.

nail ▶ **noun** **1** a small metal spike with a broadened flat head, driven typically into wood with a hammer to join things together or to serve as a peg or hook.
2 a horny covering on the upper surface of the tip of the finger and toe in humans and other primates.
■an animal's claw. ■a hard growth on the upper mandible of some soft-billed birds.
3 historical a medieval unit of measurement:
■a measure of length for cloth, equal to 2¼ inches. ■a measure of wool, beef, or other commodity, roughly equal to 7 or 8 pounds.
▶ **verb** [with obj.] **1** [with obj. and adverbial of place] fasten to a surface or to something else with a nail or nails: *the strips are simply nailed to the roof.*
2 informal expose (someone) as deceitful or criminal; catch or arrest: *have you nailed the killer?*
■expose (a lie or other instance of deception).
3 informal (of a player in a game) strike (a ball) forcefully and successfully: *she was stretched to the limit and failed to nail the smash.*
■Baseball (of a fielder) put (a runner) out by throwing to a base. ■chiefly N. Amer. (of a player) defeat or outwit (an opponent): *Navratilova tried to nail her on the backhand side.* ■(of a player) secure (especially a victory) conclusively.
4 vulgar slang, chiefly US (of a man) have sexual intercourse with.
– PHRASES **fight tooth and nail** see **TOOTH**. **hard as nails** (of a person) very tough; completely callous or unfeeling. **nail one's colours to the mast** see **MAST¹**. **a nail in the coffin** an action or event regarded as likely to have a detrimental or destructive effect on a situation, enterprise, or person: *this was going to put the final nail in the coffin of his career.* **on the nail** (N. Amer. also **on the barrelhead**) (of payment) without delay.
– DERIVATIVES **nailed** adjective [in combination] *dirty-nailed fingers*, **nailless** adjective.
– ORIGIN Old English *nægel* (noun), *næglan* (verb), of Germanic origin; related to Dutch *nagel* and German *Nagel*, from an Indo-European root shared by Latin *unguis* and Greek *onux*.
▶**nail someone down** elicit a firm promise or commitment from someone: *I can't nail her down to a specific date.*
nail something down **1** fasten something securely with nails. **2** identify something precisely: *something seems unexpected—I can't nail it down, but it makes me uneasy.* **3** secure something, especially an agreement.
nail something up fasten a door or window with nails so that it cannot be opened.

nail-biting ▶ **adjective** causing great anxiety or tension: *a nail-biting final game.*

nail brush ▶ **noun** a small brush designed for cleaning the finger- and toenails.

nail enamel ▶ **noun** N. Amer. nail polish.

nailer ▶ **noun** **1** chiefly historical a maker of nails.
2 a power tool for inserting nails.
– DERIVATIVES **nailery** noun.

nail file ▶ **noun** a strip of roughened metal or an emery board used for smoothing and shaping the fingernails and toenails.

nail gall ▶ **noun** a small conical nail-shaped gall which forms on the leaves of lime trees in response to the presence of mites.
● The mite is *Eriophyes tiliae*, family Eriophyidae.

nail head ▶ **noun** an ornament like the head of a nail, used chiefly in architecture and on clothing.

nail polish ▶ **noun** [mass noun] varnish applied to the fingernails or toenails to colour them or make them shiny.

nail punch (also **nail set**) ▶ **noun** a tool hit with a hammer to sink the head of a nail below a surface.

nail scissors ▶ **plural noun** small scissors for cutting the fingernails or toenails.

nail sickness ▶ **noun** [mass noun] the condition of a structure which is held together with corroded nails.

nailtail wallaby ▶ **noun** a brightly marked Australian wallaby with white stripes on the cheeks, hips, and behind the arms, and a small horny nail at the end of its long slender tail.
● Genus *Onychogalea*, family Macropodidae: three species.

nail varnish ▶ **noun** Brit. nail polish.

nainsook /ˈneɪnsʊk/ ▶ **noun** [mass noun] a fine, soft cotton fabric, originally from the Indian subcontinent.
– ORIGIN late 18th cent.: from Hindi *nainsukh*, from *nain* 'eye' + *sukh* 'pleasure'.

Naipaul /ˈnʌɪpɔːl/, V. S. (b.1932), Trinidadian writer of Indian descent, resident in Britain since 1950; full name *Sir Vidiadhar Surajprasad Naipaul*. He is best known for his satirical novels, such as *A House for Mr Biswas* (1961); *In a Free State* (1971) won the Booker Prize.

naira /ˈnʌɪrə/ ▶ **noun** the basic monetary unit of Nigeria, equal to 100 kobo.
– ORIGIN contraction of **NIGERIA**.

Nairnshire /ˈnɛːnʃɪə, -ʃə/ a former county of NE Scotland, on the Moray Firth. It became a part of Highland region in 1975.

Nairobi /nʌɪˈrəʊbi/ the capital of Kenya; pop. 1,346,000 (est. 1989). It is situated on the central Kenyan plateau at an altitude of 1,680 m (5,500 ft).

naissant /ˈneɪs(ə)nt/ ▶ **adjective** Heraldry (of a charge, especially an animal) issuing from the middle of an ordinary, especially a fess.
– ORIGIN late 16th cent.: from French, literally 'being born', present participle of *naître*, from Latin *nasci* 'be born'.

naive /nʌɪˈiːv, nɑːˈiːv/ (also **naïve**) ▶ **adjective** (of a person or action) showing a lack of experience, wisdom, or judgement: *the rather naive young man had been totally misled.*
■(of a person) natural and unaffected; innocent: *Andy had a sweet, naive look when he smiled.* ■of or denoting art produced in a straightforward style which deliberately rejects sophisticated artistic techniques and has a bold directness resembling a child's work, typically in bright colours with little or no perspective.
– DERIVATIVES **naively** adverb, **naiveness** noun.
– ORIGIN mid 17th cent.: from French *naïve*, feminine of *naïf*, from Latin *nativus* 'native, natural'.

naivety /nʌɪˈiːvti, nɑːˈiːvti/ (also **naïvety**) ▶ **noun** [mass noun] lack of experience, wisdom, or judgement: *his appalling naivety in going to the press.*
■innocence or unsophistication: *the charm and naivety of the early to mid fifties.*
– ORIGIN late 17th cent.: from French *naïveté*, from *naïf*, *-ive* (see **NAIVE**).

Najaf /ˈnadʒaf/ (also **An Najaf**) a city in southern Iraq, on the Euphrates; pop. 242,600 (est. 1985). It contains the shrine of Ali, the prophet Muhammad's son-in-law, and is a holy city for the Shiite Muslims.

naked ▶ **adjective** (of a person or part of the body) without clothes: *he'd never seen a naked woman before | he was stripped naked.*
■(of an object) without the usual covering or protection: *her room was lit by a single naked bulb.* ■(of a tree, plant, or animal) without leaves, hairs, scales, shell, etc.: *the twisted trunks and naked branches of the trees.* ■figurative exposed to harm; unprotected or vulnerable: *John looked naked and defenceless without his spectacles.* ■[attrib.] (of something such as feelings or behaviour) undisguised; blatant: *naked fear made him tremble | naked, unprovoked aggression | the naked truth.*
– PHRASES **naked of** devoid of.
– DERIVATIVES **nakedly** adverb, **nakedness** noun.
– ORIGIN Old English *nacod*, of Germanic origin; related to Dutch *naakt* and German *nackt*, from an Indo-European root shared by Latin *nudus* and Sanskrit *nagna*.

naked bat ▶ noun another term for **HAIRLESS BAT**.

naked eye ▶ noun (usu. **the naked eye**) unassisted vision, without a telescope, microscope, or other device: *threadworm eggs are so small that they cannot be seen with the naked eye.*

naked ladies (also **naked boys**) ▶ plural noun the meadow saffron.

naked mole rat ▶ noun a blind and hairless mole rat living in large underground colonies in East Africa. The colony structure is similar to that of social insects, with only one pair breeding and most other individuals acting as workers.
• *Heterocephalus glaber*, family Bathyergidae.

naker /ˈneɪkə/ ▶ noun historical a kettledrum.
– ORIGIN late Middle English: from Old French *nacaire*, from Arabic *naḳḳāra* 'drum'.

Nakhichevan /naxʲitʃiˈvan/ Russian name for **NAXÇIVAN**.

Nakuru /naˈkuːruː/ an industrial city in western Kenya; pop. 162,800 (1989). Nearby is Lake Nakuru, famous for its spectacular flocks of flamingos.

Nalchik /ˈnaltʃɪk/ a city in the Caucasus, SW Russia, capital of the republic of Kabardino-Balkaria; pop. 237,000 (1990).

nalidixic acid /ˌnalɪˈdɪksɪk/ ▶ noun [mass noun] Medicine a synthetic compound which inhibits the multiplication of bacteria, used chiefly to treat urinary infections.
• A heterocyclic compound; chem. formula: $C_{12}H_{12}N_2O_3$.
– ORIGIN 1960s: *nalidixic* by rearrangement of elements from **NAPHTHALENE**, *carboxylic*, and **DI-**[1] (forming the systematic name).

naloxone /nəˈlɒksəʊn/ ▶ noun [mass noun] Medicine a synthetic drug, similar to morphine, which blocks opiate receptors in the nervous system.
– ORIGIN 1960s: contraction of *N-allylnoroxymorphone*.

naltrexone /nalˈtrɛksəʊn/ ▶ noun [mass noun] Medicine a synthetic drug, similar to morphine, which blocks opiate receptors in the nervous system and is used chiefly in the treatment of heroin addiction.
– ORIGIN 1970s: from a contraction of *N-al(lylnoroxymorph)one* (see **NALOXONE**), with the insertion of the arbitrary element *-trex-*.

Nam (also **'Nam**) informal name for **VIETNAM** (in the context of the Vietnam War).

Nama /ˈnɑːmə/ ▶ noun (pl. same or **Namas**) **1** a member of one of the Khoikhoi peoples of South Africa and SW Namibia. Traditionally nomadic hunter-gatherers, they were displaced from the region near the Cape by Dutch settlers.
2 [mass noun] the language of this people, which belongs to the Khoisan family and is the only language of the Khoikhoi peoples still spoken by a substantial number (over 100,000).
▶ adjective of or relating to this people or their language.
– ORIGIN the name in Nama.

> USAGE **Nama** is the standard accepted term. The term **Hottentot**, an older term with a somewhat broader meaning, is obsolete and may now cause offence. See usage at **HOTTENTOT**.

Namangan /ˌnamənˈɡɑːn/ a city in eastern Uzbekistan, near the border with Kyrgyzstan; pop. 312,000 (1990).

Namaqualand /nəˈmɑːkwəland/ a region of SW Africa, the homeland of the Nama people. **Little Namaqualand** lies immediately to the south of the Orange River and is in the South African province of Northern Cape, while **Great Namaqualand** lies to the north of the river, in Namibia.

Namaqualand daisy ▶ noun a widely cultivated annual African daisy.
• *Dimorphotheca sinuata*, family Compositae.

namaskar /ˌnʌmʌsˈkɑː/ ▶ noun a traditional Indian greeting or gesture of respect, made by bringing the palms together before the face or chest and bowing.
– ORIGIN via Hindi from Sanskrit *namaskāra*, from *namas* 'bowing' + *kāra* 'action'.

namaste /ˈnʌməsteɪ/ ▶ exclamation a respectful greeting said when giving a namaskar.
▶ noun another term for **NAMASKAR**.
– ORIGIN via Hindi from Sanskrit *namas* 'bowing' + *te* 'to you'.

namby-pamby derogatory ▶ adjective lacking energy, strength, or courage; feeble or effeminate in behaviour or expression: *these weren't namby-pamby fights, but brutal affairs where heads hit the sidewalk.*
▶ noun (pl. **-ies**) a feeble or effeminate person.
– ORIGIN mid 18th cent.: fanciful formation based on the given name of *Ambrose* Philips (died 1749), an English writer whose pastorals were ridiculed by Carey and Pope.

name ▶ noun **1** a word or set of words by which a person, animal, place, or thing is known, addressed, or referred to: *my name is Parsons, John Parsons* | *Kalkwasser is the German **name for** limewater.*
■ someone or something regarded as existing merely as a word and lacking substance or reality: *Nathan Bryce was still simply a name in a gossip column.*
2 a famous person: *as usual, the big race will lure the top names.*
■ [in sing.] a reputation, especially a good one: *he set up a school which gained a name for excellence.*
3 (in the UK) an insurance underwriter belonging to a Lloyd's syndicate.
▶ verb [with obj.] **1** give a name to: *hundreds of diseases had not yet been isolated or named* | [with obj. and complement] *she decided to name the child Edward.*
■ identify by name; give the correct name for: *the dead man has been **named as** John Mackintosh.* ■ give a particular title or epithet to: *she was **named as** Student of the Year.* ■ mention or cite by name: *the sea is as crystal clear as any spot in the Caribbean you might care to name.* ■ specify (a sum, time, or place) as something desired, suggested, or decided on: *the club have asked Ballymena to name their price for the Scottish striker.* ■ chiefly Brit. (of the Speaker) mention (a member of the legislative assembly) by name as disobedient to the chair and thereby subject to a ban from the House.
▶ adjective [attrib.] (of a person or commercial product) having a name that is widely known: *countless specialized name brands geared to niche markets.*
– PHRASES **by name** using the name of someone or something: *ask for the street by name.* **by** (or **of**) **the name of** called: *a woman by the name of Smeeton.* **call someone names** insult someone verbally. **give one's name to** invent, discover, or found something which then becomes known by one's name: *the company's founder, Henry Ford, gave his name to Fordism.* **something has someone's name on it** a person is destined or particularly suited to receive or experience a specified thing: *he dared not go out for fear of encountering a bullet with his name on it.* **have to one's name** [often with negative] in one's possession: *Jimmy hadn't a bean to his name.* **in all but name** existing in a particular state but not formally recognized as such: *these polytechnics had been universities in all but name for many years.* **in someone's name 1** formally registered as belonging to or reserved for someone: *the house was in her name.* **2** on behalf of someone: *he began to question what had been done in his name.* **in the name of** bearing or using the name of a specified person or organization: *a driving licence in the name of William Sanders.* ■ for the sake of: *he withdrew his candidacy for the nation's top post in the name of party unity.* ■ by the authority of: *crimes committed in the name of religion.* ■ **(in the name of Christ/God/Allah/heaven** etc.) used for emphasis: *what in the name of God do you think you're doing?* **in name only** by description but not in reality: *a college in name only.* **make a name for oneself** become famous. **name the day** arrange a date for a specific occasion, especially a wedding. **one's name is mud** see **MUD**. **name names** mention specific names, especially of people involved in something wrong or illegal: *if you're convinced my staff are part of this operation, then name names.* **the name of the game** informal the main purpose or most important aspect of a situation. **no names, no pack drill** see **PACK DRILL**. **put down** (or **enter**) **one's** (or **someone's**) **name** apply to enter an educational institution, course, competition, etc.: *I **put** my name **down for** the course.* **put a name to** remember or tell someone what someone or something is called. **take someone's name in vain** see **VAIN**. **to name** (**but**) **a few** giving only these as examples, even though more could be cited: *the ingredients used are drawn from nature—avocado, lemon grass, and chamomile to name a few.* **what's in a name?** names are arbitrary labels: *'But was it still an opera?' 'What's in a name?' he replied.* **you name it** informal whatever you can think of (used to express the extent or variety of something): *easy-to-assemble kits of locos, cars, lorries, ships … you name it.*
– DERIVATIVES **nameable** adjective.
– ORIGIN Old English *nama*, *noma* (noun), *(ge)namian* (verb), of Germanic origin; related to Dutch *naam* and German *Name*, from a root shared by Latin *nomen* and Greek *onoma*.
▶ **name someone/thing after** (N. Amer. also **for**) call someone or something by the same name as: *Nathaniel **was named after** his maternal grandfather.*

name-calling ▶ noun [mass noun] abusive language or insults.

namecheck ▶ noun a public mention or listing of the name of a person or thing such as a product, especially in acknowledgement or for publicity purposes.
▶ verb [with obj.] publicly mention or list the name of.

name-child ▶ noun Brit. archaic a person named after another.

name day ▶ noun the feast day of a saint after whom a person is named.

name-dropping ▶ noun [mass noun] the practice of casually mentioning the names of famous people one knows or claims to know in order to impress others.
– DERIVATIVES **name-drop** verb, **name-dropper** noun.

nameless ▶ adjective **1** having no name or no known name.
■ deliberately not identified; anonymous: *the director of a voluntary organization which shall remain nameless.* ■ archaic (of a child) illegitimate.
2 (especially of an emotion) not easy to describe; indefinable: *a nameless yearning for transcendence.*
■ too loathsome or horrific to be described: *the myths talk about nameless horrors infesting our universe.*
– DERIVATIVES **namelessly** adverb, **namelessness** noun.

namely ▶ adverb that is to say; to be specific (used to introduce detailed information or a specific example): *the menu makes good use of Scottish produce, namely game and seafood.*

Namen /ˈnɑːmə(n)/ Flemish name for **NAMUR**.

name part ▶ noun Brit. another term for **TITLE ROLE**.

nameplate ▶ noun a metal plate or sign displaying the name of someone such as the person working in a building or the builder of a ship.

namesake ▶ noun a person or thing that has the same name as another.
– ORIGIN mid 17th cent.: from the phrase *for the name's sake*.

name tape ▶ noun a piece of cloth tape bearing the name of a person, fixed to a garment of theirs to identify it.

Namib Desert /ˈnɑːmɪb/ a desert of SW Africa. It extends for 1,900 km (1,200 miles) along the Atlantic coast, from the Curoca River in SW Angola through Namibia to the border between Namibia and South Africa.

Namibia /nəˈmɪbɪə/ a country in southern Africa, on the Atlantic Ocean; pop. 1,834,000 (est. 1991); languages, English (official), various Bantu languages, Khoisan languages, Afrikaans; capital, Windhoek.

> An arid country with large tracts of desert, Namibia was made the protectorate of German South West Africa in 1884. In 1920 it was mandated to South Africa by the League of Nations, becoming known as South West Africa. Despite international pressure South Africa continued to administer the country after the ending of the UN mandate in 1964, agreeing to withdraw only after several years of fighting by SWAPO guerrillas. Namibia became fully independent in 1990.

– DERIVATIVES **Namibian** adjective & noun.

namkin /nʌmˈkiːn/ ▶ noun [mass noun] Indian any savoury snack.
– ORIGIN from Hindi *namkīn*.

namma ▶ noun variant spelling of **GNAMMA**.

Namur /naˈmʊə/ a province in central Belgium. It was the scene of the last German offensive in the Ardennes in 1945. Flemish name **NAMEN**.
■ the capital of this province, at the junction of the Meuse and Sambre Rivers; pop. 103,440 (1991).

nan[1] /nan/ ▶ noun Brit. informal one's grandmother.
– ORIGIN 1940s: abbreviation of **NANNY**, or a child's pronunciation of **GRAN**.

nan[2] /nɑːn/ (also **naan**) ▶ noun (in Indian cookery) a type of leavened bread, typically of teardrop shape and traditionally cooked in a clay oven.
– ORIGIN from Urdu and Persian *nān*.

nana[1] /ˈnɑːnə/ ▶ noun Brit. informal a silly person; a fool

n

(often as a general term of abuse): *I was made to look a right nana.*
– ORIGIN 1960s: perhaps a shortening of **BANANA**.

nana[2] /ˈnanə/ (Brit. also **nanna**) ▶ noun informal one's grandmother.
– ORIGIN mid 19th cent.: child's pronunciation of **NANNY** or **GRAN**.

Nanaimo /nəˈnaɪməʊ/ a port on the east coast of Vancouver Island in British Columbia, Canada; pop. 63,730 (1991).

Nanak /ˈnɑːnʌk/ (1469–1539), Indian religious leader and founder of Sikhism; known as **Guru Nanak.** Not seeking to create a new religion, he preached that spiritual liberation could be achieved through meditating on the name of God. His teachings are contained in a number of hymns which form part of the Adi Granth.

nance ▶ noun another term for **NANCY.**

Nanchang /nanˈtʃaŋ/ a city in SE China, capital of Jiangxi province; pop. 1,330,000 (1990).

Nancy /ˈnɒsi/ a city in NE France, chief town of Lorraine; pop. 102,410 (1990).

nancy informal, derogatory ▶ noun (pl. **-ies**) (also **nancy boy**) an effeminate or homosexual man.
▶ adjective effeminate.
– ORIGIN early 20th cent.: pet form of the given name *Ann.*

nancy story ▶ noun W. Indian a traditional African folk tale about Anancy the spider, who overcomes others by cunning rather than physical strength.
■ an evasive story or lie, typically an elaborate one: *the minister had left the country and so could not give his side of the nancy story.* ■ a superstitious belief: *God is a nancy story, you hear.*
– ORIGIN *nancy,* shortening of *Anancy,* from Twi *ananse* 'spider'.

NAND ▶ noun Electronics a Boolean operator which gives the value zero if and only if all the operands have a value of one, and otherwise has a value of one (equivalent to NOT AND).
■ (also **NAND gate**) a circuit which produces an output signal until there are signals on all of its inputs.

Nandi /ˈnʌndi/ Hinduism a bull which serves as the mount of Shiva and symbolizes fertility.
– ORIGIN Sanskrit.

nandina /nanˈdʌɪnə, -ˈdiːnə/ ▶ noun an evergreen East Asian shrub that resembles bamboo, cultivated for its foliage which turns red or bronze in autumn. Also called **CELESTIAL BAMBOO, SACRED BAMBOO.**
● *Nandina domestica,* family Berberidaceae.
– ORIGIN mid 19th cent.: modern Latin (genus name), adapted from Japanese *nanten.*

Nanga Parbat /ˌnʌŋɡə ˈpɑːbʌt/ a mountain in northern Pakistan, in the western Himalayas. It rises to 8,126 m (26,660 ft).

Nanjing /nanˈdʒɪŋ/ (also **Nanking** /-ˈkɪŋ/) a city in eastern China, on the Yangtze River, capital of Jiangsu province; pop. 2,470,000 (1990). It was the capital of various ruling dynasties and China from 1368 until replaced by Beijing in 1421.

nankeen /nanˈkiːn, nan-/ ▶ noun [mass noun] a yellowish cotton cloth.
■ (**nankeens**) historical trousers made of this cloth. ■ the characteristic yellowish-buff colour of this cloth.
▶ adjective of this colour.
– ORIGIN mid 18th cent.: from the name of the city of *Nanking* (see **NANJING**), where it was first made.

nanna ▶ noun variant spelling of **NANA**[2].

Nanning /nanˈnɪŋ/ the capital of Guangxi Zhuang autonomous region in southern China; pop. 1,070,000 (1990).

nannofossil (also **nanofossil**) ▶ noun the fossil of a minute planktonic organism, especially a calcareous unicellular alga.
– ORIGIN 1960s: *nanno-* from *nannoplankton* (variant of **NANOPLANKTON**) + **FOSSIL.**

nanny ▶ noun (pl. **-ies**) **1** a person, typically a woman, employed to look after a child in its own home.
■ figurative a person or institution regarded as interfering and overprotective: [as modifier] *a precarious path between freedom and the nanny state.*
2 (in full **nanny goat**) a female goat.
▶ verb (**-ies, -ied**) [with obj.] [usu. as noun **nannying**] be overprotective towards: *his well-intentioned nannying.*
– ORIGIN early 18th cent. (as a noun): pet form of the given name *Ann.* The verb dates from the 1950s.

nannygai /ˈnanɪɡʌɪ/ ▶ noun (pl. **nannygais**) the redfish of Australia (*Centroberyx affinis*).
– ORIGIN late 19th cent.: from a New South Wales Aboriginal language.

nano ▶ noun informal short for **NANOTECHNOLOGY.**

nano- /ˈnanəʊ/ ▶ combining form denoting a factor of 10^{-9} (used commonly in units of measurement): *nanosecond.*
– ORIGIN via Latin from Greek *nanos* 'dwarf'.

nanometre /ˈnanə(ʊ)ˌmiːtə/ (US **nanometer**) (abbrev.: **nm**) ▶ noun one thousand millionth of a metre.

nanoplankton ▶ noun [mass noun] Biology very small unicellular plankton, at the limits of resolution of light microscopy.
– ORIGIN early 20th cent.: from German, from Greek *nanos* 'dwarf' + **PLANKTON.**

nanosecond (abbrev.: **ns**) ▶ noun one thousand millionth of a second.

nanotechnology ▶ noun [mass noun] the branch of technology that deals with dimensions and tolerances of less than 100 nanometres, especially the manipulation of individual atoms and molecules.
– DERIVATIVES **nanotechnological** adjective, **nanotechnologist** noun.

nanotube ▶ noun Chemistry a cylindrical molecule of a fullerene.

Nansen /ˈnans(ə)n/, Fridtjof (1861–1930), Norwegian Arctic explorer. In 1888 he led the first expedition to cross the Greenland ice fields, and five years later he sailed from Siberia for the North Pole, which he failed to reach, on board the *Fram.*

Nansen passport ▶ noun historical a document of identification issued to stateless people after the First World War.

Nantes /nɒt/ a city in western France, on the Loire, chief town of Pays de la Loire region; pop. 252,030 (1990).

Nantes, Edict of an edict of 1598 signed by Henry IV of France granting toleration to Protestants and ending the French Wars of Religion. It was revoked by Louis XIV in 1685.

Nantucket /nanˈtʌkɪt/ an island off the coast of Massachusetts, south of Cape Cod and east of Martha's Vineyard. It was an important whaling centre in the 18th and 19th centuries.

naos /ˈneɪɒs/ ▶ noun (pl. **naoi** /ˈneɪɔɪ/) the inner chamber or sanctuary of a Greek or other ancient temple.
■ the main body or nave of a Byzantine church.
– ORIGIN Greek, literally 'temple'.

nap[1] ▶ verb (**napped, napping**) [no obj.] sleep lightly or briefly, especially during the day.
▶ noun a short sleep, especially during the day: *excuse me, I'll just take a little nap.*
– PHRASES **catch someone napping** informal (of an action or event) find someone off guard and unprepared to respond: *the goalkeeper was caught napping by a shot from Carpenter.*
– ORIGIN Old English *hnappian,* probably of Germanic origin.

nap[2] ▶ noun [in sing.] **1** the raised hairs, threads, or similar small projections on the surface of fabric or suede leather (used especially with reference to the direction in which they naturally lie): *carefully machine the seam, following the direction of the nap.*
2 Austral. informal a bedroll used for sleeping on in the open. [ORIGIN: late 19th cent.: probably from **KNAPSACK.**]
– DERIVATIVES **napless** adjective.
– ORIGIN late Middle English *noppe,* from Middle Dutch, Middle Low German *noppe* 'nap', *noppen* 'trim the nap from'.

nap[3] ▶ noun **1** [mass noun] a card game resembling whist in which players declare the number of tricks they expect to take, up to five.
2 Brit. the betting of all one's money on one prospective winner.
■ a tipster's choice for this.
▶ verb (**napped, napping**) [with obj.] Brit. name (a horse or greyhound) as a probable winner of a race.
– PHRASES **go nap** attempt to take all five tricks in nap. ■ score or win five times: *Tranmere Rovers went nap to inflict a heavy 5–1 defeat on West Ham.* ■ risk everything in one attempt. **not go nap on** Austral. informal not be too keen on.

– ORIGIN early 19th cent.: abbreviation of **NAPOLEON**, the original name of the card game.

nap[4] ▶ verb (**napped, napping**) [no obj.] (of a horse) refuse, especially habitually, to go on at the rider's instruction; jib.
– ORIGIN 1950s: back-formation from *nappy,* an adjective first used to describe heady beer (late Middle English), later used in the sense 'intoxicated by drink' (early 18th cent.), and since the 1920s used to describe a disobedient horse.

napa ▶ noun variant spelling of **NAPPA.**

napa cabbage /ˈnapə/ ▶ noun chiefly N. Amer. a variety of Chinese leaf.
– ORIGIN *napa,* of unknown origin.

napalm /ˈneɪpɑːm/ ▶ noun [mass noun] a highly flammable sticky jelly used in incendiary bombs and flame-throwers, consisting of petrol thickened with special soaps.
▶ verb [with obj.] attack with bombs containing napalm.
– ORIGIN 1940s: from *na(phthenic)* and *palm(itic acid).*

nape ▶ noun (also **nape of the/one's neck**) the back of a person's neck.
– ORIGIN Middle English: of unknown origin.

napery /ˈneɪp(ə)ri/ ▶ noun [mass noun] archaic household linen, especially tablecloths and napkins.
– ORIGIN Middle English: from Old French *naperie,* from *nape* 'tablecloth'.

nap hand ▶ noun informal a series of five winning points, victories, etc. in a game or sport.

Naphtali /ˈnaftəlʌɪ/ (in the Bible) a Hebrew patriarch, son of Jacob and Bilhah (Gen. 30:7–8).
■ the tribe of Israel traditionally descended from him.

naphtha /ˈnafθə/ ▶ noun [mass noun] Chemistry a flammable oil containing various hydrocarbons, obtained by the dry distillation of organic substances such as coal, shale, or petroleum.
– ORIGIN late Middle English *napte,* from Latin *naphtha* from Greek, of oriental origin; the Latin spelling was introduced in the late 16th cent.

naphthalene /ˈnafθəliːn/ ▶ noun [mass noun] Chemistry a volatile white crystalline compound produced by the distillation of coal tar, used in mothballs and as a raw material for chemical manufacture.
● A bicyclic aromatic hydrocarbon; chem. formula: $C_{10}H_8$.
– DERIVATIVES **naphthalic** adjective.
– ORIGIN early 19th cent.: from **NAPHTHA** + **-ENE**, with the insertion of -*l-* for ease of pronunciation.

naphthene /ˈnafθiːn/ ▶ noun Chemistry any of a group of cyclic aliphatic hydrocarbons (e.g. cyclohexane) obtained from petroleum.
– DERIVATIVES **naphthenic** adjective.

naphthol /ˈnafθɒl/ ▶ noun [mass noun] Chemistry a crystalline solid derived from naphthalene, used to make antiseptics and dyes.
● Chem. formula: $C_{10}H_7OH$; two isomers, especially naphthalen-2-ol (**β-naphthol**).

Napier[1] /ˈneɪpɪə/ a seaport on Hawke Bay, North Island, New Zealand; pop. 52,470 (1991). Originally a whaling port, the town was named after the British general and colonial administrator Sir Charles Napier (1809–54).

Napier[2] /ˈneɪpɪə/, John (1550–1617), Scottish mathematician. He was the inventor of logarithms.

Napierian logarithm /neɪˈpɪərɪən/ ▶ noun another term for **NATURAL LOGARITHM.**
– ORIGIN early 19th cent.: named after J. *Napier* (see **NAPIER**[2]).

Napier's bones ▶ plural noun Mathematics slips of ivory or other material divided into sections marked with digits, devised by John Napier and formerly used to facilitate multiplication and division.

napkin ▶ noun **1** (also **table napkin**) a square piece of cloth or paper used at a meal to wipe the fingers or lips and to protect garments, or to serve food on.
2 Brit. dated a baby's nappy.
3 (also **sanitary napkin**) chiefly N. Amer. another term for **SANITARY TOWEL.**
– ORIGIN late Middle English: from Old French *nappe* 'tablecloth' (from Latin *mappa:* see **MAP**) + **-KIN.**

napkin ring ▶ noun a ring used to hold (and distinguish) a person's table napkin when not in use.

Naples /ˈneɪp(ə)lz/ a city and port on the west coast of Italy, capital of Campania region; pop. 1,206,000 (1990). It was formerly the capital of the kingdom of Naples and Sicily (1816–60). Italian name **NAPOLI.**

– ORIGIN from Latin *Neapolis*, from Greek *neos* 'new' + *polis* 'city'.

Naples yellow ▶ **noun** [mass noun] a pale yellow pigment containing lead and antimony oxides.
▪ the pale yellow colour of this pigment, now commonly produced using cadmium, zinc, or iron-based substitutes.
– ORIGIN mid 18th cent.: named after **NAPLES**, the city where such a pigment was originally made.

Napoleon /nəˈpəʊlɪən/ the name of three rulers of France:
▪ Napoleon I (1769–1821), emperor 1804–14 and 1815; full name *Napoleon Bonaparte*; known as **Napoleon**. In 1799 Napoleon joined a conspiracy which overthrew the Directory, becoming the supreme ruler of France. He declared himself emperor in 1804, establishing an empire stretching from Spain to Poland. After defeats at Trafalgar (1805) and in Russia (1812), he abdicated and was exiled to the island of Elba (1814). He returned to power in 1815, but was defeated at Waterloo and exiled to the island of St Helena.
▪ Napoleon II (1811–1832), son of Napoleon I and Empress Marie-Louise; full name *Napoleon François Charles Joseph Bonaparte*. In 1814 Napoleon I abdicated on behalf of himself and Napoleon II, who had no active political role.
▪ Napoleon III (1808–73), emperor 1852–70; full name *Charles Louis Napoleon Bonaparte*; known as **Louis-Napoleon**. A nephew of Napoleon I, Napoleon III was elected President of the Second Republic in 1848 and staged a coup in 1851. He abdicated in 1870 after defeat in the Franco-Prussian War.

napoleon ▶ **noun 1** historical a gold twenty-franc French coin minted in the reign of Napoleon I.
2 (also **napoleon boot**) historical a 19th-century man's boot reaching above the knee in front and with a piece cut out behind, originally worn by cavalrymen.
3 N. Amer. a flaky rectangular pastry with a sweet filling.

Napoleonic Wars a series of campaigns (1800–15) of French armies under Napoleon against Austria, Russia, Great Britain, Portugal, Prussia, and other European powers. They ended with Napoleon's defeat at the Battle of Waterloo.

Napoli /ˈnapoli/ Italian name for **NAPLES**.

nappa /ˈnapə/ (also **napa**) ▶ **noun** [mass noun] a soft leather made by a special tawing process from the skin of sheep or goats.
– ORIGIN late 19th cent.: from *Napa*, the name of a valley in California.

nappe /nap/ ▶ **noun** Geology a sheet of rock that has moved sideways over neighbouring strata as a result of an overthrust or folding.
– ORIGIN late 19th cent.: from French *nappe* 'tablecloth'.

napped[1] ▶ **adjective** [usu. in combination] (of a textile) having a nap, usually of a specified kind: *a long-napped paint roller.*

napped[2] ▶ **adjective** (of food) served in a sauce or other liquid: *mushrooms **napped with** melted butter.*
– ORIGIN 1970s: from French *napper* 'coat with (a sauce)', from *nappe* 'cloth', figuratively 'pool of liquid', + **-ED**[2].

napper ▶ **noun** Brit. informal a person's head: *a couple of shaven nappers.*
– ORIGIN late 18th cent.: from thieves' slang, of unknown origin.

nappy[1] ▶ **noun** (pl. **-ies**) Brit. a piece of towelling or other absorbent material wrapped round a baby's bottom and between its legs to absorb and retain urine and faeces.
– ORIGIN early 20th cent.: abbreviation of **NAPKIN**.

nappy[2] ▶ **adjective** US informal (of a black person's hair) frizzy.
– ORIGIN late 15th cent. (in the sense 'shaggy'): from Middle Dutch *noppigh*, Middle Low German *noppich*, from *noppe* (see **NAP**[2]). The current sense dates from the early 20th cent.

nappy liner ▶ **noun** see **LINER**[2].

nappy rash ▶ **noun** [mass noun] Brit. inflammation of a baby's skin caused by prolonged contact with a damp nappy.

naproxen /naˈprɒksɛn/ ▶ **noun** [mass noun] Medicine a synthetic compound used as an anti-inflammatory drug, especially in the treatment of headache and arthritis.
• Chem. formula: $C_{14}H_{14}O_3$.
– ORIGIN 1970s: from *na(phthyl)* + *pr(opionic)* + *ox(y-)*, + *-en* on the pattern of words such as *tamoxifen*.

Nara /ˈnɑːrə/ a city in central Japan, on the island of Honshu; pop. 349,360 (1990). It was the first capital of Japan (710–84) and an important centre of Japanese Buddhism.

Narayan /nəˈrɑːjən, nʌˈrʌɪʌn/, R. K. (b.1906), Indian novelist and short-story writer; full name *Rasipuram Krishnaswamy Narayan*. His best-known novels are set in an imaginary small Indian town, and portray its inhabitants in an affectionate yet ironic manner; they include *Swami and Friends* (1935) and *The Man-Eater of Malgudi* (1961)

Narayanan /nəˈrɑːjən(ə)n/, K. R. (b.1920), Indian statesman, President since 1997; full name *Kocheril Raman Narayanan*. A member of the Congress party, Narayanan served as Vice-President 1992–7.

Narayanganj /nəˈrɑːjən,gʌndʒ/ a river port in Bangladesh, on the Ganges delta south-east of Dhaka; pop. 406,000 (1991).

Narbonne /nɑːˈbɒn, French naʀbɔn/ a city in southern France, in Languedoc-Roussillon, just inland from the Mediterranean; pop. 47,090 (1990). It was founded by the Romans in 118 BC and was a prosperous port of medieval France until its harbour silted up in the 14th century.

narc (also **nark**) ▶ **noun** informal, chiefly N. Amer. an official narcotics agent.
– ORIGIN 1960s: abbreviation of **NARCOTIC**.

narcissism /ˈnɑːsɪsɪz(ə)m, nɑːˈsɪs-/ ▶ **noun** [mass noun] excessive or erotic interest in oneself and one's physical appearance.
▪ Psychology extreme selfishness, with a grandiose view of one's own talents and a craving for admiration, as characterizing a personality type. ▪ Psychoanalysis self-centredness arising from failure to distinguish the self from external objects, either in very young babies or as a feature of mental disorder.
– DERIVATIVES **narcissist** noun, **narcissistic** adjective, **narcissistically** adverb.
– ORIGIN early 19th cent.: via Latin from the Greek name *Narkissos* (see **NARCISSUS**) + **-ISM**.

Narcissus /nɑːˈsɪsəs/ Greek Mythology a beautiful youth who rejected the nymph Echo and fell in love with his own reflection in a pool. He pined away and was changed into the flower that bears his name.

narcissus /nɑːˈsɪsəs/ ▶ **noun** (pl. **narcissi** /-sʌɪ/ or **narcissuses**) a bulbous Eurasian plant of a genus that includes the daffodil, especially (in gardening) one with flowers that have white or pale outer petals and a shallow orange or yellow cup in the centre.
• Genus *Narcissus*, family Liliaceae (or Amaryllidaceae): many species and varieties, in particular *N. poeticus*.
– ORIGIN via Latin from Greek *narkissos*, perhaps from *narkē* 'numbness', with reference to its narcotic effects.

narcissus fly ▶ **noun** another term for **BULB FLY**.

narco ▶ **noun** (pl. **-os**) US informal short for **NARCOTIC**.
▪ a dealer in drugs. ▪ an official narcotics agent.

narco- ▶ **combining form** relating to a state of insensibility: *narcolepsy.*
▪ relating to narcotic drugs or their use: *narcoterrorism.*
– ORIGIN from Greek *narkē* 'numbness'.

narcolepsy /ˈnɑːkə(ʊ)lɛpsi/ ▶ **noun** [mass noun] Medicine a condition characterized by an extreme tendency to fall asleep whenever in relaxing surroundings.
– DERIVATIVES **narcoleptic** adjective & noun.
– ORIGIN late 19th cent.: from Greek *narkē* 'numbness', on the pattern of *epilepsy.*

narcosis /nɑːˈkəʊsɪs/ ▶ **noun** [mass noun] Medicine a state of stupor, drowsiness, or unconsciousness produced by drugs. See also **NITROGEN NARCOSIS**.
– ORIGIN late 17th cent.: from Greek *narkōsis*, from *narkoun* 'make numb'.

narcoterrorism ▶ **noun** [mass noun] terrorism associated with the trade in illicit drugs.
– DERIVATIVES **narcoterrorist** noun.
– ORIGIN 1980s: from **NARCO-** 'relating to illegal narcotics' + *terrorism* (see **TERRORIST**).

narcotic ▶ **noun** a drug or other substance affecting mood or behaviour and sold for non-medical purposes, especially an illegal one.
▪ Medicine a drug which induces drowsiness, stupor, or insensibility, and relieves pain.
▶ **adjective** relating to or denoting narcotics or their effects or use: *the substance has a mild narcotic effect.*
– DERIVATIVES **narcotically** adverb, **narcotism** noun.
– ORIGIN late Middle English: from Old French *narcotique*, via medieval Latin from Greek *narkōtikos*, from *narkoun* 'make numb'.

narcotize (also **-ise**) ▶ **verb** [with obj.] stupefy with or as if with a drug.
▪ make (something) have a soporific or narcotic effect: *the essence of apple blossom narcotizes the air.*
– DERIVATIVES **narcotization** noun.

nard ▶ **noun** the Himalayan spikenard.
– ORIGIN late Old English, via Latin from Greek *nardos*; related to Sanskrit *nalada, narada.*

nardoo /nɑːˈduː, ˈnɑːduː/ ▶ **noun** an Australian fern with long stalks bearing either silvery-green clover-like lobes or woody globular cases containing spores, growing typically in water in areas of intermittent flooding.
• *Marsilea drummondii*, family Marsiliaceae.
▪ [mass noun] a food made from the spores of this fern, eaten by Aboriginals: [as modifier] *nardoo flour.*
– ORIGIN mid 19th cent.: from an Aboriginal language.

nares /ˈnɛːriːz/ ▶ **plural noun** (sing. **naris**) Anatomy & Zoology the nostrils.
– DERIVATIVES **narial** adjective.
– ORIGIN late 17th cent.: plural of Latin *naris* 'nostril, nose'.

narghile /ˈnɑːgɪleɪ, -li/ ▶ **noun** an oriental tobacco pipe with a long tube that draws the smoke through water; a hookah.
– ORIGIN mid 18th cent.: from Persian *nārgīl* 'coconut, hookah', from Sanskrit *nārikela* 'coconut'.

naris singular form of **NARES**.

nariyal /ˈnɑːrɪəl/ ▶ **noun** Indian term for **COCONUT**.
– ORIGIN from Hindi *nāriyal.*

nark informal ▶ **noun 1** chiefly Brit. a police informer: *I'm not a copper's nark.*
2 Austral./NZ an annoying person or thing.
3 chiefly N. Amer. variant spelling of **NARC**.
▶ **verb** [with obj.] (usu. **be narked**) chiefly Brit. annoy or exasperate: *I was narked at being pushed around.*
– PHRASES **nark it!** stop that!
– ORIGIN mid 19th cent.: from Romany *nāk* 'nose'.

narky ▶ **adjective** (**narkier**, **narkiest**) Brit. informal bad-tempered or irritable.

Narmada /ˈnəːmədə/ a river which rises in Madhya Pradesh, central India, and flows generally westwards for 1,245 km (778 miles) to the Gulf of Cambay. It is regarded by Hindus as sacred.

Narragansett /,narəˈgansət/ (also **Narraganset**) ▶ **noun** (pl. same or **Narragansetts**) **1** a member of an American Indian people originally of Rhode Island. They came into conflict with the British in the 17th century, and few now remain.
2 [mass noun] the extinct Algonquian language of this people.
– ORIGIN the name in Narragansett, literally 'people of the promontory'.

narrate ▶ **verb** [with obj.] (often **be narrated**) give a spoken or written account of: *the title story is narrated entirely by the heroine* | [with clause] *Actaeon is not free to narrate what he has seen.*
▪ provide a spoken commentary to accompany (a film, broadcast, piece of music, etc.).
– DERIVATIVES **narratable** adjective, **narration** noun.
– ORIGIN mid 17th cent.: from Latin *narrat-* 'related, told', from the verb *narrare* (from *gnarus* 'knowing').

narrative ▶ **noun** a spoken or written account of connected events; a story: *the hero of his modest narrative.*
▪ [mass noun] the narrated part or parts of a literary work, as distinct from dialogue. ▪ [mass noun] the practice or art of narration: *traditions of oral narrative.*
▶ **adjective** in the form of or concerned with narration: *a narrative poem* | *narrative technique.*
– DERIVATIVES **narratively** adverb.
– ORIGIN late Middle English (as an adjective): from French *narratif, -ive*, from late Latin *narrativus* 'telling a story', from the verb *narrare* (see **NARRATE**).

narrativity ▶ **noun** [mass noun] the quality or condition of presenting a narrative: *music has developed a narrativity which lends it the character of language.*
– ORIGIN 1970s: from French *narrativité.*

narrativize (also **-ise**) ▶ **verb** [with obj.] present or interpret (something such as experience or theory) in the form of a story or narrative.

narratology ▶ **noun** [mass noun] the branch of

n

knowledge or criticism that deals with the structure and function of narrative and its themes, conventions, and symbols.
– DERIVATIVES **narratological** adjective, **narratologist** noun.

narrator ▶ noun a person who narrates something, especially a character who recounts the events of a novel or narrative poem.
▪ a person who delivers a commentary accompanying a film, broadcast, piece of music, etc.
– DERIVATIVES **narratorial** adjective.

narrow ▶ adjective (**narrower**, **narrowest**) **1** (especially of something that is considerably longer or higher than it is wide) of small width: *he made his way down the narrow road.*
2 limited in extent, amount, or scope; restricted: *his ability to get good results within narrow constraints of money and manpower.*
▪ (of a person's attitude or beliefs) limited in range and lacking willingness or ability to appreciate alternative views: *companies fail through their narrow view of what contributes to profit.* ▪ precise or strict in meaning: *some of the narrower definitions of democracy.* ▪ (of a phonetic transcription) showing fine details of accent. ▪ Phonetics denoting a vowel pronounced with the root of the tongue drawn back so as to narrow the pharynx.
3 (especially of a victory, defeat, or escape) with only a small margin; barely achieved.
▶ verb **1** become or make less wide: [no obj.] *the road narrowed and crossed an old bridge* | [with obj.] *the Victoria Embankment was built to narrow the river.*
▪ [no obj.] (of a person's eyes) almost close so as to focus on something or someone, or to indicate anger, suspicion, or other emotion. ▪ [with obj.] (of a person) cause (one's eyes) to do this.
2 become or make more limited or restricted in extent or scope: [no obj.] *the trade surplus* ***narrowed to*** *£70 m in January* | [with obj.] *England had narrowed Wales's lead from 13 points to 4.*
▶ noun (**narrows**) a narrow channel connecting two larger areas of water: *there was a car ferry across the narrows of Loch Long.*
– DERIVATIVES **narrowish** adjective, **narrowness** noun.
– ORIGIN Old English *nearu*, of Germanic origin; related to Dutch *naar* 'dismal, unpleasant' and German *Narbe* 'scar'. Early senses in English included 'constricted' and 'mean'.
▶ **narrow something down** reduce the number of possibilities or options of something.

narrowband ▶ adjective of or involving signals over a narrow range of frequencies.

narrowboat ▶ noun Brit. a canal boat less than 7 ft (2.1 metres) wide with a maximum length of 70 ft (21.3 metres) and steered with a tiller rather than a wheel.

narrowcast ▶ verb (past and past participle **narrowcast** or **narrowcasted**) [no obj.] transmit a television programme, especially by cable, or otherwise disseminate information, to a comparatively small audience defined by special interest or geographical location: *the channel narrowcasts to over 5,800 pubs and clubs* | [as noun **narrowcasting**] *one journal has avoided the narrowcasting that seems to enslave so many mainstream magazines.*
▶ noun [mass noun] transmission or dissemination in this way: [as modifier] *dozens of narrowcast niche channels* | [count noun] *most narrowcasts were a service of the BBC.*
– DERIVATIVES **narrowcaster** noun.
– ORIGIN 1930s: back-formation from *narrowcasting*, on the pattern of *broadcasting*.

narrow circumstances ▶ plural noun poverty.

narrow gauge ▶ noun a railway gauge which is narrower than the standard gauge of 4 ft 8½ inches (1.435 m).

narrowly ▶ adverb **1** only just; by only a small margin: *the party was narrowly defeated in the elections.*
2 closely or carefully: *he was looking at her narrowly.*
3 in a limited or restricted way: *narrowly defined tasks.*

narrow-minded ▶ adjective not willing to listen to or tolerate other people's views; prejudiced.
– DERIVATIVES **narrow-mindedly** adverb, **narrow-mindedness** noun.

narrow money ▶ noun [mass noun] Economics money in forms that can be used as a medium of exchange, generally notes, coins, and certain balances held by banks.

narrow seas ▶ plural noun Brit. archaic the English Channel and the Irish Sea.

narrow squeak ▶ noun [in sing.] Brit. informal an escape or victory that is narrowly achieved: *Hunt's championship was a narrow squeak, achieved in a car that was far from perfect.*

narthex /ˈnɑːθɛks/ ▶ noun an antechamber, porch, or distinct area at the western entrance of some early Christian churches, separated off by a railing and used by catechumens, penitents, etc.
▪ an antechamber or large porch in a modern church.
– ORIGIN late 17th cent.: via Latin from Greek *narthēx*.

Narvik /ˈnɑːvɪk/ an ice-free port on the NW coast of Norway, north of the Arctic Circle; pop. 18,640 (1990).

narwhal /ˈnɑːw(ə)l/ ▶ noun a small Arctic whale, the male of which has a long forward-pointing spirally twisted tusk developed from one of its teeth.
• *Monodon monoceros*, family Monodontidae.
– ORIGIN mid 17th cent.: from Dutch *narwal*, Danish *narhval*, based on Old Norse *nár* 'corpse', with reference to skin colour.

nary /ˈnɛːri/ ▶ adjective informal or dialect form of NOT: *nary a murmur or complaint.*
– ORIGIN mid 18th cent.: from the phrase *ne'er a.*

NAS ▶ abbreviation for (in the UK) Noise Abatement Society.

NASA /ˈnasə/ ▶ abbreviation for (in the US) National Aeronautics and Space Administration.

nasal /ˈneɪz(ə)l/ ▶ adjective **1** of, for, or relating to the nose: *the nasal passages* | *a nasal spray.*
2 (of a speech sound) pronounced by the breath resonating in the nose, e.g. *m*, *n*, *ng*, or French *en*, *un*.
▪ (of the voice or speech) produced or characterized by resonating in the nose as well as the mouth.
▶ noun **1** a nasal speech sound.
2 historical a nosepiece on a helmet.
– DERIVATIVES **nasality** noun, **nasally** adverb.
– ORIGIN Middle English (in sense 2 of the noun): from medieval Latin *nasalis*, from Latin *nasus* 'nose'.

nasal concha ▶ noun see CONCHA.

nasalize (also **-ise**) ▶ verb [with obj.] pronounce or utter (a speech sound) with the breath resonating in the nose: [as adj. **nasalized**] *a nasalized vowel.*
– DERIVATIVES **nasalization** noun.

nascent /ˈnas(ə)nt, ˈneɪ-/ ▶ adjective (especially of a process or organization) just coming into existence and beginning to display signs of future potential: *the nascent space industry.*
▪ Chemistry (chiefly of hydrogen) freshly generated in a reactive form.
– DERIVATIVES **nascency** /ˈnas(ə)nsi, ˈneɪ-/ noun.
– ORIGIN early 17th cent.: from Latin *nascent-* 'being born', from the verb *nasci*.

NASDAQ /ˈnazdak/ ▶ abbreviation for (in the US) National Association of Securities Dealers Automated Quotations, a computerized system for trading in securities.

naseberry /ˈneɪzb(ə)ri, -bɛri/ ▶ noun another term for SAPODILLA or *sapodilla plum*.
– ORIGIN late 17th cent.: from Spanish and Portuguese *néspera* 'medlar' + BERRY.

Naseby, Battle of /ˈneɪzbi/ a major battle of the English Civil War, which took place in 1645 near the village of Naseby in Northamptonshire. The Royalist army of Prince Rupert and King Charles I was decisively defeated by the New Model Army under General Fairfax and Oliver Cromwell.

Nash[1], (Frederic) Ogden (1902–71), American poet. His sophisticated light verse comprises puns, epigrams, and other verbal eccentricities.

Nash[2], John (1752–1835), English town planner and architect. He planned the layout of Regent's Park (1811–25), Trafalgar Square (1826–c.1835), and many other parts of London, and designed the Marble Arch.

Nash[3], Paul (1889–1946), English painter and designer. He was a war artist in both World Wars. Notable works: *Totes Meer* (1940–1).

Nash[4], Richard (1674–1762), Welsh dandy; known as Beau Nash. He was an arbiter of fashion and etiquette in the early Georgian age.

Nashe /naʃ/, Thomas (1567–1601), English pamphleteer, prose writer, and dramatist. Notable works: *The Unfortunate Traveller* (1594).

Nash equilibrium ▶ noun (in economics and game theory) a stable state of a system involving the interaction of different participants, in which no participant can gain by a unilateral change of strategy if the strategies of the others remain unchanged.

nashi /ˈnaʃiː/ (also **nashi pear**) ▶ noun the crisp apple-shaped fruit of a tree that is native to Japan and China and cultivated in Australia and New Zealand. Also called ASIAN PEAR.
• This fruit is obtained from varieties of *Pyrus pyrifolia*, family Rosaceae.
– ORIGIN 1960s: from Japanese, literally 'pear'.

Nashville the state capital of Tennessee; pop. 510,780 (1990). The city is noted for its music industry and the Country Music Hall of Fame.

Nasik /ˈnɑːsɪk/ a city in western India, in Maharashtra, on the Godavari River north-east of Bombay; pop. 647,000 (1991).

Nasmyth /ˈneɪsmɪθ/, James (1808–90), British engineer. He invented the steam hammer (1839).

naso- /ˈneɪzəʊ/ ▶ combining form relating to the nose: *nasogastric.*
– ORIGIN from Latin *nasus* 'nose'.

nasogastric ▶ adjective reaching or supplying the stomach via the nose: *she had to be fed by a nasogastric tube.*

nasopharynx ▶ noun Anatomy the upper part of the pharynx, connecting with the nasal cavity above the soft palate.
– DERIVATIVES **nasopharyngeal** adjective.

Nassau 1 /ˈnasaʊ/ a former duchy of western Germany, centred on the small town of Nassau, from which a branch of the House of Orange arose. It corresponds to parts of the present-day states of Hesse and Rhineland-Palatinate.
2 /ˈnasɔː/ a port on the island of New Providence, capital of the Bahamas; pop. 172,000 (1990).

Nasser /ˈnɑːsə, ˈnas-/, Gamal Abdel (1918–70), Egyptian colonel and statesman, Prime Minister 1954–6 and President 1956–70. He deposed King Farouk in 1952 and President Muhammad Neguib in 1954. His nationalization of the Suez Canal brought war with Britain, France, and Israel in 1956; he also waged two unsuccessful wars against Israel (1956 and 1967).

Nasser, Lake a lake in SE Egypt created in the 1960s by the building of the two dams on the Nile at Aswan.

nastic /ˈnastɪk/ ▶ adjective Botany (of the movement of plant parts) caused by an external stimulus but unaffected in direction by it.
– ORIGIN early 20th cent.: from Greek *nastos* 'squeezed together' (from *nassein* 'to press') + -IC.

nasturtium /nəˈstəːʃ(ə)m/ ▶ noun a South American trailing plant with round leaves and bright orange, yellow, or red flowers, which is widely grown as an ornamental.
• *Tropaeolum majus*, family Tropaeolaceae.
– ORIGIN Old English, from Latin, apparently from *naris* 'nose' + *torquere* 'to twist'.

nasty ▶ adjective (**nastier**, **nastiest**) **1** highly unpleasant, especially to the senses; physically nauseating: *plastic bags burn with a nasty, acrid smell.*
▪ (of the weather) unpleasantly cold or wet: *it's a nasty old night.* ▪ repugnant to the mind; morally bad: *her stories are very nasty, full of murder and violence.*
2 (of a person or animal) behaving in an unpleasant or spiteful way: *Harry was a nasty, foul-mouthed old devil* | *when she confronted him he turned nasty.*
▪ annoying or unwelcome: *life has a nasty habit of repeating itself.*
3 physically or mentally damaging or harmful: *a nasty, vicious-looking hatchet.*
▪ (of an injury, illness, or accident) having caused harm; severe: *a nasty bang on the head.*
▶ noun (pl. **-ies**) (often **nasties**) informal an unpleasant or harmful person or thing: *a water conditioner to neutralize chlorine and other nasties.*
▪ a horror video or film. See also VIDEO NASTY.
– PHRASES **a nasty one** informal an awkward question or task. **a nasty piece** (or **bit**) **of work** informal an unpleasant or untrustworthy person. **a nasty taste in the mouth** see TASTE. **something nasty in the woodshed** see WOODSHED.
– DERIVATIVES **nastily** adverb, **nastiness** noun.

– ORIGIN late Middle English: of unknown origin.

NASUWT ▶ abbreviation for (in the UK) National Association of Schoolmasters and Union of Women Teachers.

Nat. ▶ abbreviation for ■ national. ■ nationalist. ■ natural.

Natal /nə'tal, -'tɑːl/ **1** a former province of South Africa, situated on the east coast. Having been a Boer republic and then a British colony, it acquired internal self-government in 1893 and became a province of the Union of South Africa in 1910. The province was renamed KwaZulu/Natal in 1994. [ORIGIN: from Latin *Terra Natalis* 'land of the day of birth', a name given by Vasco da Gama in 1497, because he sighted the entrance to what is now Durban harbour on Christmas Day.] **2** a port on the Atlantic coast of NE Brazil, capital of the state of Rio Grande do Norte; pop. 606,280 (1990).

natal[1] /'neɪt(ə)l/ ▶ adjective of or relating to the place or time of one's birth: *after puberty a Hindu girl does not stay long in her natal home.*
– ORIGIN late Middle English: from Latin *natalis*, from *nat-* 'born', from the verb *nasci.*

natal[2] /'neɪt(ə)l/ ▶ adjective Anatomy of or relating to the buttocks: *the natal cleft.*
– ORIGIN late 19th cent.: from **NATES** + **-AL**.

natality /nə'talɪti/ ▶ noun [mass noun] the ratio of the number of births to the size of the population; birth rate: *in spite of falling natality, the population as a whole went up.*
– ORIGIN late 19th cent.: from French *natalité*, from *nat-* 'born', from the verb *nasci.*

natant /'neɪt(ə)nt/ ▶ adjective formal, rare swimming or floating.
– ORIGIN mid 18th cent.: from Latin *natant-* 'swimming', from the verb *natare.*

natation /nə'teɪʃ(ə)n/ ▶ noun [mass noun] technical or poetic/literary swimming.
– DERIVATIVES **natatorial** /ˌneɪtə'tɔːrɪəl/ adjective, **natatory** /'neɪtət(ə)ri, nə'teɪt(ə)ri/ adjective.
– ORIGIN mid 16th cent.: from Latin *natatio(n-)*, from *natare* 'to swim'.

natatorium /ˌneɪtə'tɔːrɪəm/ ▶ noun N. Amer. a swimming pool, especially one that is indoors.
– ORIGIN late 19th cent.: from late Latin, neuter (used as a noun) of *natatorius* 'relating to a swimmer', from *natare* 'to swim'.

natch ▶ adverb informal term for **NATURALLY**.

nates /'neɪtiːz/ ▶ plural noun Anatomy the buttocks.
– ORIGIN late 17th cent.: Latin, plural of *natis* 'buttock, rump'.

NATFHE ▶ abbreviation for (in the UK) National Association of Teachers in Further and Higher Education.

natheless /'neɪθlɪs/ (also **nathless**) ▶ adverb archaic nevertheless.
– ORIGIN Old English.

nation ▶ noun a large aggregate of people united by common descent, history, culture, or language, inhabiting a particular state or territory: *leading industrialized nations.*
■ a North American Indian people or confederation of peoples.
– PHRASES **one nation** [often as modifier] a nation not divided by social inequality: *one-nation Tories.*
– DERIVATIVES **nationhood** noun.
– ORIGIN Middle English: via Old French from Latin *natio(n-)*, from *nat-* 'born', from the verb *nasci.*

national ▶ adjective of or relating to a nation; common to or characteristic of a whole nation: *this policy may have been in the national interest | a national newspaper.*
■ owned, controlled, or financially supported by the state: *plans for a national art library.*
▶ noun **1** a citizen of a particular country, typically entitled to hold that country's passport: *a German national | the new law on foreign nationals.*
2 (usu. **nationals**) a national newspaper as opposed to a local one.
3 (**the National**) another name for **GRAND NATIONAL**.
– DERIVATIVES **nationally** adverb [sentence adverb] *nationally, there has been a 2.5% drop in car crime.*
– ORIGIN late 16th cent.: from French, from Latin *natio(n-)* 'birth, race of people' (see **NATION**).

national anthem ▶ noun see **ANTHEM** (sense 1).

National Assembly ▶ noun an elected legislature in various countries.
■ historical the elected legislature in France during the first part of the Revolution, 1789–91.

National Assistance ▶ noun [mass noun] welfare payment made to people on low incomes in Britain between 1948 and 1965.

National Association for the Advancement of Colored People (abbrev.: **NAACP**) a US civil rights organization set up in 1909 to oppose racial segregation and discrimination by non-violent means.

national bank ▶ noun another term for **CENTRAL BANK**.
■ a commercial bank which is chartered under the federal government and is a member of the Federal Reserve System.

national convention ▶ noun US a convention of a major political party, especially one that nominates a candidate for the presidency.

national curriculum ▶ noun a common programme of study in schools that is designed to ensure nationwide uniformity of content and standards in education.

national debt ▶ noun the total amount of money which a country's government has borrowed, by various means.

national football ▶ noun [mass noun] Austral. Australian Rules football.

National Front (abbrev.: **NF**) a right-wing UK political party, formed in 1967, with extreme reactionary views on immigration.

National Gallery an art gallery in Trafalgar Square, London, holding one of the chief national collections of pictures. The collection began in 1824, and the present main building was opened in 1838.

national government ▶ noun a coalition government, especially one subordinating party differences to the national interest in a time of crisis, as in Britain under Ramsay MacDonald in 1931–5.

national grid ▶ noun Brit. **1** the network of high-voltage power lines between major power stations.
■ a similar network of pipes or cables.
2 the metric system of geographical coordinates used in maps of the British Isles.

National Guard ▶ noun **1** (in the US) the primary reserve military force partly maintained by the states but also available for federal use.
■ the primary military force of some other countries.
■ a member of such a force.
2 an armed force existing in France at various times between 1789 and 1871, first commanded by the Marquis de Lafayette.
■ a member of this force.

National Health Service (also **National Health**) (abbrev.: **NHS**) (in the UK) a system of national medical care paid for mainly by taxation and started by the Labour government in 1948.

National Hunt (also **National Hunt Committee**) ▶ noun the body controlling steeplechasing and hurdle racing in Great Britain.

national income ▶ noun the total amount of money earned within a country.

National Insurance (in the UK) the system of compulsory payments by employees and employers to provide state assistance for people who are sick, unemployed, or retired.

nationalism ▶ noun [mass noun] patriotic feeling, principles, or efforts.
■ an extreme form of this, especially marked by a feeling of superiority over other countries: *playing with right-wing nationalism.* ■ advocacy of political independence for a particular country: *Scottish nationalism.*

nationalist ▶ noun a person who advocates political independence for a country: *a Scottish nationalist.*
■ a person with strong patriotic feelings, especially one who believes in the superiority of their country over others.
▶ adjective of or relating to nationalists or nationalism: *a nationalist movement.*
– DERIVATIVES **nationalistic** adjective, **nationalistically** adverb.

nationality ▶ noun (pl. **-ies**) **1** [mass noun] the status

of belonging to a particular nation: *they changed their nationality and became Lebanese.*
■ distinctive national or ethnic character: *the change of a name does not discard nationality.* ■ patriotic sentiment; nationalism.
2 an ethnic group forming a part of one or more political nations: *all the main nationalities of Ethiopia.*

nationalize (also **-ise**) ▶ verb [with obj.] **1** transfer (a major branch of industry or commerce) from private to state ownership or control.
2 make distinctively national; give a national character to: *in the 13th and 14th centuries church designs were further nationalized.*
3 [usu. as adj. **nationalized**] naturalize (a foreigner): *he is now a nationalized Frenchman.*
– DERIVATIVES **nationalization** noun, **nationalizer** noun.

national minority ▶ noun a minority group within a country felt to be distinct from the majority because of historical differences of language, religion, culture, etc.

national park ▶ noun an area of countryside, or occasionally sea or fresh water, protected by the state for the enjoyment of the general public or the preservation of wildlife.

National Party an Australian political party established in 1914 (as the Country Party) to represent agricultural and rural interests. It has been in power, in coalition with the Liberal Party of Australia since 1997 and for most of the period since the second world war.

National Party of South Africa a political party that held power in South Africa from 1948 until the country's first democratic elections in 1994. Formed in 1914 as an Afrikaner party, it favoured racial segregation and instituted apartheid.

National Portrait Gallery an art gallery in London holding the national collection of portraits of eminent or well-known British men and women. Founded in 1856, it moved to its present site next to the National Gallery in 1896.

national road ▶ noun (in South Africa) any of a network of major intercity roads.

National Security Agency (abbrev.: **NSA**) (in the US) a secret body established after the Second World War to gather intelligence, deal with coded communications from around the world, and safeguard US transmissions.

National Security Council (abbrev.: **NSC**) (in the US) a body created by Congress after the Second World War to advise the President (who chairs it) on issues relating to national security in domestic, foreign, and military policy.

national service ▶ noun [mass noun] a period of compulsory service in the armed forces during peacetime (phased out in the UK by 1963).

National Socialism ▶ noun [mass noun] historical the political doctrine of the Nazi Party of Germany. See **NAZI**.
– DERIVATIVES **National Socialist** noun.

National Trust (abbrev.: **NT**) a trust for the preservation of places of historic interest or natural beauty in England, Wales, and Northern Ireland, founded in 1895 and supported by endowment and private subscription. The National Trust for Scotland was founded in 1931.

National Vocational Qualification (abbrev.: **NVQ**) (in the UK) a qualification in a vocational subject set at various levels and (at levels two and three) corresponding in standard to GCSE and GCE A levels.

Nation of Islam an exclusively black Islamic sect proposing a separate black nation, founded in Detroit c.1930. It came to prominence under the influence of Malcolm X.

nation state ▶ noun a sovereign state of which most of the citizens or subjects are united also by factors which define a nation, such as language or common descent.

nationwide ▶ adjective extending or reaching throughout the whole nation: *a nationwide hunt.*
▶ adverb throughout a whole nation: *it employs 6,000 people nationwide.*

native ▶ noun a person born in a specified place or who is associated with a place by birth, whether subsequently resident there or not: *a native of Montreal | an eighteen-year-old Brooklyn native.*

■ a local inhabitant: *New York in the summer was too hot even for the natives.* ■ dated, chiefly offensive one of the original inhabitants of a country, especially a non-white as regarded by European colonists or travellers. ■ (in Australia) a white person born in the country, as distinguished from an immigrant and from an Aboriginal. ■ an animal or plant indigenous to a place: *the marigold is **a native of** southern Europe.* ■ Brit. an oyster reared in British waters.

▶ **adjective 1** associated with the country, region, or circumstances of a person's birth: *he's a native New Yorker | her native country.* ■ of the indigenous inhabitants of a place: *a ceremonial native dance from Fiji.* **2** (of a plant or animal) of indigenous origin or growth: *eagle owls aren't **native to** Britain | Scotland's few remaining native pinewoods.* ■ Austral./NZ used in names of animals or plants resembling others familiar elsewhere, e.g. **native bear**. **3** (of a quality) belonging to a person's character from birth rather than acquired; innate: *some last vestige of native wit prompted Guy to say nothing | a jealousy and rage **native to** him.* ■ Computing designed for or built into a given system, especially denoting the language associated with a given processor, computer, or compiler, and programs written in it. **4** (of a metal or other mineral) found in a pure or uncombined state.

– PHRASES **go native** humorous or derogatory (of a person living away from their own country or region) abandon one's own culture, customs, or way of life and adopt those of the country or region one is living in.

– DERIVATIVES **natively** adverb, **nativeness** noun.

– ORIGIN late Middle English: from Latin *nativus*, from *nat-* 'born', from the verb *nasci*.

USAGE In contexts such as *a **native** of Boston* the use of the noun **native** is quite acceptable. But when used as a noun without qualification, as in *this dance is a favourite with the **natives***, it is more problematic. In modern use it is used humorously to refer to the local inhabitants of a particular place (*New York in the summer was too hot even for the **natives***). In other contexts it has an old-fashioned feel and, because of being closely associated with a colonial European outlook on non-white peoples living in remote places, it may cause offence.

Native American ▶ **noun** a member of any of the indigenous peoples of North and South America and the Caribbean Islands.

▶ **adjective** of or relating to these peoples.

USAGE In the US, **Native American** is now the current accepted term in many contexts. The term **American Indian** is still used elsewhere, by American Indians themselves, among others, and is the form used in this dictionary. See **usage** at **AMERICAN INDIAN**.

native bear ▶ **noun** Australian term for **KOALA**.

native bush ▶ **noun** [mass noun] woodland or forest in New Zealand consisting of indigenous trees and shrubs.

native cat ▶ **noun** Australian term for **QUOLL**.

native hen ▶ **noun** a moorhen found in Australia, with mainly dark plumage and a greenish bill. Also called **WATERHEN** or **GALLINULE**.
• Genus *Gallinula*, family Rallidae: *G. ventralis* of Australia and *G. mortierii* of Tasmania.

native rock ▶ **noun** [mass noun] rock in its original place, i.e. that has not been moved or quarried.

native speaker ▶ **noun** a person who has spoken the language in question from earliest childhood.

nativism /ˈneɪtɪvɪz(ə)m/ ▶ **noun** [mass noun] **1** the theory or doctrine that concepts, mental capacities, and mental structures are innate rather than acquired or learned. **2** historical, chiefly US the policy of protecting the interests of native-born or established inhabitants against those of immigrants. **3** a return to or emphasis on traditional or local customs, in opposition to outside influences.

– DERIVATIVES **nativist** noun & adjective, **nativistic** adjective.

nativity ▶ **noun** (pl. **-ies**) the occasion of a person's birth: *the place of my nativity.* ■ (usu. **the Nativity**) the birth of Jesus Christ. ■ a picture, carving, or model representing Jesus Christ's birth. ■ a nativity play. ■ the Christian festival of Christ's birth; Christmas. ■ Astrology, dated a horoscope relating to the time of birth; a birth chart.

– ORIGIN Middle English: from Old French *nativite*, from late Latin *nativitas*, from Latin *nativus* 'arisen by birth' (see **NATIVE**).

nativity play ▶ **noun** a play, typically performed by children at Christmas, based on the events surrounding the birth of Jesus Christ.

nativity scene ▶ **noun** a model or tableau representing the scene of Jesus Christ's birth, displayed in homes or public places at Christmas.

NATO (also **Nato**) ▶ **abbreviation for** North Atlantic Treaty Organization.

natriuresis /ˌneɪtrɪjʊ(ə)ˈriːsɪs, ˌnat-/ ▶ **noun** [mass noun] Physiology excretion of sodium in the urine.

– DERIVATIVES **natriuretic** adjective.

– ORIGIN 1950s: from **NATRON** + Greek *ourēsis* 'urination'.

natron /ˈneɪtr(ə)n, ˈnat-/ ▶ **noun** [mass noun] a mineral salt found in dried lake beds, consisting of hydrated sodium carbonate.

– ORIGIN late 17th cent.: from French, from Spanish *natrón*, via Arabic from Greek *nitron* (see **NITRE**).

Natron, Lake /ˈneɪtrən/ a lake in northern Tanzania, on the border with Kenya, containing large deposits of salt and soda.

natter informal, chiefly Brit. ▶ **verb** [no obj.] talk casually, especially on unimportant matters; chatter: *they **nattered away** for hours while out riding.*

▶ **noun** [in sing.] a casual and leisurely conversation: *I could do with a drink and a natter.*

– DERIVATIVES **natterer** noun.

– ORIGIN early 19th cent. (in the dialect sense 'grumble, fret'): imitative.

Natterer's bat /ˈnatərəz/ ▶ **noun** a small greyish-brown myotis bat native to Europe and North Africa.
• *Myotis nattereri*, family Vespertilionidae.

– ORIGIN late 19th cent.: named after Johann Natterer (1787–1843), Austrian naturalist.

natterjack (also **natterjack toad**) ▶ **noun** a small European toad which has a bright yellow stripe down its back and runs in short bursts.
• *Bufo calamita*, family Bufonidae.

– ORIGIN mid 18th cent.: perhaps from **NATTER** (because of its loud croak) + **JACK**[1].

Nattier blue /ˈnatjeɪ/ ▶ **noun** [mass noun] dated a soft shade of blue, especially in fine textiles.

– ORIGIN early 20th cent.: a colour much used by Jean-Marc Nattier (1685–1766), French painter.

natty[1] ▶ **adjective** (**nattier**, **nattiest**) informal (especially of a person or an article of clothing) smart and fashionable: *a natty blue blazer and designer jeans.* ■ well designed: *it's a natty little invention to ensure that the bottle is absolutely watertight.*

– DERIVATIVES **nattily** adverb, **nattiness** noun.

– ORIGIN late 18th cent. (originally slang): perhaps related to **NEAT**1.

natty[2] ▶ **adjective** [attrib.] black English (among Rastafarians) denoting hair that is uncombed or matted, as in dreadlocks.

– ORIGIN variant of **KNOTTY**.

natty dread ▶ **noun** black English a Rastafarian, typically a male with dreadlocks.

Natufian /nɑːˈtuːfɪən/ ▶ **adjective** Archaeology of, relating to, or denoting a late Mesolithic culture of the Middle East, dated to about 12,500–10,000 years ago. It provides evidence for the first settled villages, and is characterized by the use of microliths and of bone for implements. ■ [as noun **the Natufian**] the Natufian culture or period.

– ORIGIN 1930s: from Wadi *an-Natuf*, the type site (a cave north-west of Jerusalem), + **-IAN**.

natural ▶ **adjective 1** existing in or caused by nature; not made or caused by humankind: *carrots contain a natural antiseptic which fights bacteria | natural disasters such as earthquakes.* ■ (of fabric) having a colour characteristic of the unbleached and undyed state; off-white, creamy-beige. **2** of or in agreement with the character or make-up of, or circumstances surrounding, someone or something: *sharks have no natural enemies.* ■ [attrib.] (of a person) born with a particular skill, quality, or ability: *he was a natural entertainer.* ■ (of a skill, quality, or ability) coming instinctively to a person; innate: *writing appears to demand muscular movements which are not **natural to** children.* ■ (of a person or their behaviour) relaxed and unaffected; spontaneous: *he replied with just a little too much nonchalance to sound natural.* ■ occurring as a matter of course and without debate; inevitable: *on giving up as a player, Ken was a natural choice for chairman.* ■ [attrib.] (of law or justice) based on innate moral sense; instinctively felt to be right and fair. See also **NATURAL LAW**. ■ Bridge (of a bid) straightforwardly reflecting one's holding of cards. Often contrasted with **CONVENTIONAL** or **ARTIFICIAL**. **3** [attrib.] (of a parent or child) related by blood: *such adopted children always knew who their natural parents were.* ■ chiefly archaic illegitimate: *the Baron left a natural son by his mistress.* **4** Music (of a note) not sharpened or flattened: *the bassoon plays G natural instead of A flat.* ■ (of a brass instrument) having no valves and able to play only the notes of the harmonic series above a fundamental note. ■ of or relating to the notes and intervals of the harmonic series. **5** Christian Theology relating to earthly or unredeemed human or physical nature as distinct from the spiritual or supernatural realm.

▶ **noun 1** a person regarded as having an innate gift or talent for a particular task or activity: *she was a **natural for** the sort of television work required of her.* ■ a thing that is particularly suited for something: *a nice wide hall is a **natural for** dining.* **2** Music a sign (♮) denoting a natural note when a previous sign or the key signature would otherwise demand a sharp or a flat. ■ a natural note. ■ any of the longer, lower keys on a keyboard instrument that are normally white. **3** a creamy beige colour. **4** a hand of cards, throw of dice, or other result which wins immediately, in particular: ■ a hand of two cards making 21 in the first deal in blackjack and similar games. ■ a first throw of 7 or 11 at craps. **5** Fishing an insect or other small creature used as bait, rather than an artificial imitation. **6** archaic, offensive a person mentally handicapped from birth.

▶ **adverb** informal or dialect naturally: *keep walking—just act natural.*

– DERIVATIVES **naturalness** noun.

– ORIGIN Middle English (in the sense 'having a certain status by birth'): from Old French, from Latin *naturalis*, from *natura* 'birth, nature, quality' (see **NATURE**).

natural-born ▶ **adjective** having a specified innate characteristic or ability: *Glen was a natural-born sailor.* ■ archaic having a position by birth.

natural childbirth ▶ **noun** [mass noun] childbirth with minimal medical or technological intervention, usually involving special breathing and relaxation techniques.

natural classification ▶ **noun** a scientific classification according to features which are held to be objectively significant, rather than being selected for convenience.

natural food ▶ **noun** [mass noun] a food which has undergone a minimum of processing or preservative treatment.

natural frequency ▶ **noun** Physics the frequency at which a system oscillates when not subjected to a continuous or repeated external force.

natural gas ▶ **noun** [mass noun] flammable gas, consisting largely of methane and other hydrocarbons, occurring naturally underground (often in association with petroleum) and used as fuel.

natural history ▶ **noun** [mass noun] **1** the scientific study of animals or plants, especially as concerned with observation rather than experiment, and presented in popular rather than academic form. ■ the study of the whole natural world, including mineralogy and palaeontology. ■ natural phenomena which are the subject of scientific observation: *Pembrokeshire has an abundance of wildlife and natural history.* **2** Medicine the usual course of development of a disease or condition, especially in the absence of treatment.

– DERIVATIVES **natural historian** noun.

Natural History Museum a museum of zoological, botanical, palaeontological, and mineralogical items in South Kensington, London.

naturalism ▶ **noun** [mass noun] **1** (in art and literature) a style and theory of representation based on the accurate depiction of detail.

The name 'Naturalism' was given to a 19th-century artistic and literary movement, influenced by contemporary ideas of science and society, which rejected the idealization of experience and adopted an objective and often uncompromisingly realistic approach to art. Notable figures include the novelist Zola and the painter Rousseau.

2 a philosophical viewpoint according to which everything arises from natural properties and causes, and supernatural or spiritual explanations are excluded or discounted. [ORIGIN: translating French *naturalisme*.]
■(in moral philosophy) the theory that ethical statements can be derived from non-ethical ones. ■ another term for **NATURAL RELIGION**.

naturalist ▶ **noun 1** an expert in or student of natural history.
2 a person who practises naturalism in art or literature.
■a person who adopts philosophical naturalism.
▶ **adjective** another term for **NATURALISTIC**.

naturalistic ▶ **adjective 1** derived from real life or nature, or imitating it very closely: *verbatim records of children's speech in naturalistic settings.*
2 based on the theory of naturalism in art or literature: *naturalistic paintings of the city.*
■of or according to the philosophy of naturalism: *phenomena once considered supernatural have yielded to naturalistic explanation.*
– DERIVATIVES **naturalistically** adverb.

naturalize (also **-ise**) ▶ **verb** [with obj.] **1** (often **be/become naturalized**) admit (a foreigner) to the citizenship of a country: *he was born in a foreign country and had never been naturalized* | [as adj. **naturalized**] *a naturalized US citizen born in Germany.*
■[no obj.] (of a foreigner) be admitted to the citizenship of a country. ■ alter (an adopted foreign word) so that it conforms more closely to the phonology or orthography of the adopting language: *the* stoccafisso *of Liguria was naturalized in Nice as* stocoficada.
2 [usu. as adj. **naturalized**] Biology establish (a plant or animal) so that it lives wild in a region where it is not indigenous: *native and naturalized species* | *black mustard has become naturalized in Britain and America.*
■establish (a cultivated plant) in a natural situation: *this species of crocus* ***naturalizes itself*** *very easily.* ■ [no obj.] (of a cultivated plant) become established in a natural situation: *these perennials should be planted where they can naturalize.*
3 regard as or cause to appear natural: *although women do more childcare than men, feminists should beware of naturalizing that fact.*
■explain (a phenomenon) in a naturalistic way.
– DERIVATIVES **naturalization** noun.
– ORIGIN mid 16th cent.: from French *naturaliser*, from Old French *natural* (see **NATURAL**).

natural killer cell ▶ **noun** Medicine a lymphocyte able to bind to certain tumour cells and virus-infected cells without the stimulation of antigens, and kill them by the insertion of granules containing perforin.

natural language ▶ **noun** a language that has developed naturally in use (as contrasted with an artificial language or computer code).

natural law ▶ **noun 1** [mass noun] a body of unchanging moral principles regarded as a basis for all human conduct.
2 an observable law relating to natural phenomena: *the natural laws of perspective.*
■[mass noun] such laws collectively.

natural life ▶ **noun** the expected span of a person's life on Earth or a thing's existence under normal circumstances: *the natural life of a hen is seven years.*

natural logarithm (abbrev.: **ln** or $\log_e$) ▶ **noun** Mathematics a logarithm to the base *e* (2.71828...).

naturally ▶ **adverb 1** in a natural manner, in particular:
■in a normal manner; without distortion or exaggeration: *act naturally.* ■ as a natural result: *one leads naturally into the other.* ■ without special help or intervention: *naturally curly hair.*
2 [sentence adverb] as may be expected; of course: *naturally, I hoped for the best.*

natural magic ▶ **noun** [mass noun] (in the Middle Ages) magic practised for beneficial purposes, involving the making of images, healing, and the use of herbs.

natural numbers ▶ **plural noun** the positive integers (whole numbers) 1, 2, 3, etc., and sometimes zero as well.

natural philosophy ▶ **noun** [mass noun] archaic natural science, especially physical science.
– DERIVATIVES **natural philosopher** noun.

natural religion ▶ **noun** [mass noun] religion based on reason rather than divine revelation, especially deism.

natural resources ▶ **plural noun** materials or substances occurring in nature which can be exploited for economic gain.

natural science ▶ **noun** (usu. **natural sciences**) a branch of science which deals with the physical world, e.g. physics, chemistry, geology, biology.
■[mass noun] the branch of knowledge which deals with the study of the physical world.

natural selection ▶ **noun** [mass noun] Biology the process whereby organisms better adapted to their environment tend to survive and produce more offspring. The theory of its action was first fully expounded by Charles Darwin and is now believed to be the main process that brings about evolution. Compare with ***survival of the fittest*** (see **SURVIVAL**).

natural theology ▶ **noun** [mass noun] theology or knowledge of God based on observed facts and experience apart from divine revelation.

natural virtues ▶ **plural noun** the traditional chief moral virtues of justice, prudence, temperance, and fortitude. Often contrasted with **THEOLOGICAL VIRTUE**.

natural wastage ▶ **noun** see **WASTAGE** (sense 2).

natural year ▶ **noun** the tropical or solar year. See **YEAR** (sense 1).

nature ▶ **noun 1** [mass noun] the phenomena of the physical world collectively, including plants, animals, the landscape, and other features and products of the earth, as opposed to humans or human creations: *the breathtaking beauty of nature.*
■the physical force regarded as causing and regulating these phenomena: *it is impossible to change the laws of nature.* See also **MOTHER NATURE**. ■ the countryside, especially when picturesque. ■ archaic a living thing's vital functions or needs.
2 [in sing.] the basic or inherent features of something, especially when seen as characteristic of it: *helping them to realize the nature of their problems* | *there are a lot of other documents of that nature.*
■the innate or essential qualities or character of a person or animal: *it's not in her nature to listen to advice* | *I'm not violent* ***by nature***. See also **HUMAN NATURE**. ■ [mass noun] inborn or hereditary characteristics as an influence on or determinant of personality. Often contrasted with **NURTURE**. ■ [with adj.] archaic a person of a specified character: *Emerson was so much more luminous a nature.*
– PHRASES **against nature** unnatural; immoral. **someone's better nature** the good side of a person's character; their capacity for tolerance, generosity, or sympathy: *Charlotte planned to appeal to his better nature.* **call of nature** used euphemistically to refer to a need to urinate or defecate. **from nature** (in art) using natural scenes or objects as models. **get** (or **go**) **back to nature** return to the type of life (regarded as being more in tune with nature) that existed before the development of complex industrial societies. **in the nature of** similar in type to or having the characteristics of: *a week at home would be in the nature of a holiday.* **in the nature of things 1** inevitable: *it is in the nature of things that the majority of music prizes get set up for performers rather than composers.* **2** inevitably: *in the nature of things, old people spend much more time indoors.* **in a state of nature 1** in an uncivilized or uncultivated state. **2** totally naked. **3** Christian Theology in a morally unregenerate condition, unredeemed by divine grace. **the nature of the beast** informal the inherent or essential quality or character of something, which cannot be changed.
– ORIGIN Middle English (denoting the physical power of a person): from Old French, from Latin *natura* 'birth, nature, quality', from *nat-* 'born', from the verb *nasci*.

nature cure ▶ **noun** another term for **NATUROPATHY**.

natured ▶ **adjective** [in combination] having a nature or disposition of a specified kind: *a good-natured man.*

nature printing ▶ **noun** [mass noun] a method of producing a print of a natural object (such as a leaf) or a textile (such as lace) by making an impression of it directly on to a soft metal printing plate under great pressure and then taking an inked impression on paper.

nature reserve ▶ **noun** a tract of land managed so as to preserve its flora, fauna, and physical features.

nature strip ▶ **noun** Austral. a piece of publicly owned land between the front boundary of a dwelling or other building and the street, typically planted with grass.

nature study ▶ **noun** [mass noun] the practical study of plants, animals, and natural phenomena as a school subject.

nature trail ▶ **noun** a signposted path through the countryside designed to draw attention to natural features.

naturism ▶ **noun** [mass noun] **1** the practice of wearing no clothes in a holiday camp or for other leisure activities; nudism.
2 the worship of nature or natural objects.
– DERIVATIVES **naturist** noun & adjective.

naturopathy /ˌneɪtʃəˈrɒpəθi/ ▶ **noun** [mass noun] a system of alternative medicine based on the theory that diseases can be successfully treated or prevented without the use of drugs, by techniques such as control of diet, exercise, and massage.
– DERIVATIVES **naturopath** noun, **naturopathic** adjective.

Naugahyde /ˈnɔːgəhʌɪd/ ▶ **noun** [mass noun] N. Amer. (trademark in the US) an artificial material designed to resemble leather, made from fabric coated with rubber or vinyl resin.
– ORIGIN mid 20th cent.: from *Nauga(tuk)*, the name of a town in Connecticut, US, where rubber is manufactured, + *-hyde* (alteration of **HIDE**[2]).

naught ▶ **pronoun** archaic nothing: *he's naught but a worthless fool.*
▶ **noun** N. Amer. variant spelling of **NOUGHT**.
– PHRASES **bring to naught** archaic ruin; foil. **come to naught** be ruined or foiled. **set at naught** archaic disregard; despise.
– ORIGIN Old English *nāwiht, -wuht*, from *nā* 'no' + *wiht* 'thing' (see **WIGHT**).

naughty ▶ **adjective** (**naughtier**, **naughtiest**) **1** (especially of children) disobedient; badly behaved: *you've been a really naughty boy.*
2 informal mildly rude or indecent, typically because related to sex: *naughty drawings* | *naughty goings-on.*
3 archaic wicked.
– DERIVATIVES **naughtily** adverb, **naughtiness** noun.
– ORIGIN late Middle English: from **NAUGHT** + **-Y**[1]. The earliest recorded sense was 'possessing nothing'; the sense 'wicked' also dates from late Middle English, and gave rise to the current senses.

naughty bits ▶ **plural noun** informal, humorous the parts of a person's body connected with sexual activity or attraction, especially their genitals.

naughty nineties ▶ **plural noun** the 1890s, regarded as a time of liberalism and permissiveness, especially in Britain and France.

nauplius /ˈnɔːplɪəs/ ▶ **noun** (pl. **nauplii** /-plɪʌɪ, -plɪiː/) Zoology the first larval stage of many crustaceans, having an unsegmented body and a single eye.
– ORIGIN mid 19th cent.: from Latin, denoting a kind of shellfish, or from the Greek name *Nauplios*, the son of Poseidon.

Nauru /nɑːˈuːruː/ an island country in the SW Pacific, near the equator; pop. 10,000 (1993); official languages, Nauruan (an Austronesian language) and English; no official capital. Since 1968 it has been an independent republic with a limited form of membership of the Commonwealth. It has the world's richest deposits of phosphates.
– DERIVATIVES **Nauruan** adjective & noun.

nausea /ˈnɔːsɪə, -z-/ ▶ **noun** [mass noun] a feeling of sickness with an inclination to vomit.
■loathing; revulsion: *intended to induce a feeling of nostalgia, it only induces in me a feeling of nausea.*
– ORIGIN late Middle English: via Latin from Greek *nausia*, from *naus* 'ship'.

nauseate ▶ **verb** [with obj.] make (someone) feel sick; affect with nausea: *the thought of food nauseated her* | [as adj. **nauseating**] *the stench became nauseating.*
■fill (someone) with revulsion; disgust: *they were nauseated by the jingoism.*
– DERIVATIVES **nauseatingly** adverb.
– ORIGIN mid 17th cent.: from Latin *nauseat-* 'made to feel sick', from the verb *nauseare*, from *nausea* (see **NAUSEA**).

nauseous ▶ **adjective 1** affected with nausea;

inclined to vomit: *a rancid, cloying odour that made him nauseous.*
2 causing nausea; offensive to the taste or smell: *the smell was nauseous.*
■ disgusting, repellent, or offensive: *this nauseous account of a court case.*
– DERIVATIVES **nauseously** adverb, **nauseousness** noun.
– ORIGIN early 17th cent.: from Latin *nauseosus* (from *nausea* 'seasickness').

nautch /nɔːtʃ/ ▶ noun (in the Indian subcontinent) a traditional dance performed by professional dancing girls.
– ORIGIN from Hindi *nāc*, from Prakrit *nachcha*, from Sanskrit *nṛtya* 'dancing'.

nautical ▶ adjective of or concerning sailors or navigation; maritime: *nautical charts.*
– DERIVATIVES **nautically** adverb.
– ORIGIN mid 16th cent.: from French *nautique*, or via Latin from Greek *nautikos*, from *nautēs* 'sailor', from *naus* 'ship'.

nautical almanac ▶ noun a yearbook containing astronomical and tidal information for navigators.

nautical mile ▶ noun a unit used in measuring distances at sea, equal to 1,852 metres (2,025 yards) approximately. Compare with **SEA MILE**.

nautiloid /ˈnɔːtɪlɔɪd/ ▶ noun Zoology a mollusc of a group of mainly extinct marine molluscs which includes the pearly nautilus.
● Subclass Nautiloidea, class Cephalopoda: *Nautilus* is the only surviving genus.
– ORIGIN mid 19th cent.: from the modern Latin genus name *Nautilus* (from Greek *nautilos* 'sailor') + -OID.

Nautilus /ˈnɔːtɪləs/ the first nuclear-powered submarine, launched in 1954. This US navy vessel made a historic journey (1–5 August 1958) under the ice of the North Pole.
– ORIGIN a name previously given to Robert Fulton's 'diving boat' (1800), also to the fictitious submarine in Jules Verne's *Twenty Thousand Leagues under the Sea.*

nautilus /ˈnɔːtɪləs/ ▶ noun (pl. **nautiluses** or **nautili** /-lʌɪ, -liː/) **1** a cephalopod mollusc with a light external spiral shell and numerous short tentacles around the mouth. Nautiluses swim with the buoyant gas-filled shell upright and descend to greater depths during the day.
● Genus *Nautilus*, the only surviving genus of the subclass Nautiloidea: several species, in particular the **pearly nautilus.**
2 (also **paper nautilus**) another term for **ARGONAUT.**
– ORIGIN modern Latin, from Latin, from Greek *nautilos*, literally 'sailor'.

NAV ▶ abbreviation for net asset value.

nav ▶ noun informal short for **NAVIGATION.**
■ short for **NAVIGATOR.**

navaid /ˈnaveɪd/ ▶ noun a navigational device in an aircraft, ship, or other vehicle.
– ORIGIN 1950s: from *navigational aid.*

Navajo /ˈnavəhəʊ/ (also **Navaho**) ▶ noun (pl. same or **-os**) **1** a member of an American Indian people of New Mexico and Arizona.
2 [mass noun] the Athabaskan language of this people, with about 130,000 speakers.
▶ adjective of or relating to this people or their language.
– ORIGIN from Spanish *Apaches de Navajó* 'apaches from Navajo', from Tewa *navahu:* 'fields adjoining an arroyo'.

naval ▶ adjective of, in, or relating to a navy or navies: *a naval base | a naval officer | naval operations.*
– ORIGIN late Middle English: from Latin *navalis*, from *navis* 'ship'.

naval architecture ▶ noun [mass noun] the designing of ships.
– DERIVATIVES **naval architect** noun.

naval stores ▶ plural noun articles or materials used in shipping.

Navan /ˈnavən/ the county town of Meath, in the Republic of Ireland; pop. 3,410 (1991).

Navanagar /ˌnʌvəˈnʌgə/ a former princely state of NW India, centred on the city of Jamnagar. It is now part of the state of Gujarat.

Navaratri /ˌnʌvəˈrʌtri/ (also **Navaratra**) ▶ noun a Hindu autumn festival extending over the nine nights before Dussehra. It is associated with many local observances, especially the Bengali festival of Durga.
– ORIGIN Sanskrit, literally 'nine nights'.

navarin /ˈnavərɪn, -rã/ ▶ noun a casserole of lamb or mutton with vegetables.
– ORIGIN French.

Navarino, Battle of /ˌnavəˈriːnəʊ/ a decisive naval battle in the Greek struggle for independence from the Ottoman Empire, fought in 1827 in the Bay of Navarino off Pylos in the Peloponnese. Britain, Russia, and France sent a combined fleet which destroyed the Egyptian and Turkish fleet.

Navarre /nəˈvɑː/ an autonomous region of northern Spain, on the border with France; capital, Pamplona. It represents the southern part of the former kingdom of Navarre, which was conquered by Ferdinand in 1512 and attached to Spain, while the northern part passed to France in 1589 through inheritance by Henry IV. Spanish name **NAVARRA** /naˈβarra/.

nave¹ ▶ noun the central part of a church building, intended to accommodate most of the congregation. In traditional Western churches it is rectangular, separated from the chancel by a step or rail, and from adjacent aisles by pillars.
– ORIGIN late 17th cent.: from Latin *navis* 'ship'.

nave² ▶ noun the hub of a wheel.
– ORIGIN Old English *nafu, nafa*, of Germanic origin; related to Dutch *naaf* and German *Nabe*, from an Indo-European root shared by Sanskrit *nābhis* 'nave, navel'. Compare with **NAVEL.**

navel ▶ noun a rounded knotty depression in the centre of a person's belly caused by the detachment of the umbilical cord after birth; the umbilicus.
■ figurative the central point of a place: *the Incas saw Cuzco as the navel of the world.*
– PHRASES **contemplate one's navel** spend time complacently considering oneself or one's own interests; concentrate on one issue at the expense of a wider view.
– ORIGIN Old English *nafela*, of Germanic origin; related to Dutch *navel* and German *Nabel*, from an Indo-European root shared by Latin *umbo* 'boss of a shield', *umbilicus* 'navel', and Greek *omphalos* 'boss, navel'. Compare with **NAVE²**.

navel-gazing ▶ noun [mass noun] complacent self-absorption; concentration on a single issue at the expense of a wider view.

navel orange ▶ noun a large seedless orange of a variety which has a navel-like depression at the top and contains a small secondary fruit underneath it.

navelwort ▶ noun another term for **PENNYWORT.**

navicular /nəˈvɪkjʊlə/ ▶ adjective chiefly archaic boat-shaped.
▶ noun **1** (also **navicular bone**) a boat-shaped bone in the ankle or wrist, especially that in the ankle, between the talus and the cuneiform bones.
2 (also **navicular disease** or **navicular syndrome**) [mass noun] a chronic disorder of the navicular bone in horses, causing lameness in the front feet.
– ORIGIN late Middle English: from French *naviculaire* or late Latin *navicularis*, from Latin *navicula* 'little ship', diminutive of *navis.*

navigable ▶ adjective (of a waterway or sea) able to be sailed on by ships or boats.
■ (of a track or road) suitable for other forms of transport: *a good cart track, navigable by cars.*
– DERIVATIVES **navigability** noun.
– ORIGIN early 16th cent.: from French *navigable* or Latin *navigabilis*, from the verb *navigare* 'to sail' (see **NAVIGATE**).

navigate ▶ verb **1** [no obj.] plan and direct the route or course of a ship, aircraft, or other form of transport, especially by using instruments or maps: *they navigated by the stars.*
■ [no obj., with adverbial of direction] travel on a desired course after planning a route: *he taught them how to navigate across the oceans.* ■ (of an animal or bird) find its way, especially over a long distance: *whales use their own inbuilt sonar system to navigate.* ■ (of a passenger in a vehicle) assist the driver by map-reading and planning a route.
2 [with obj.] sail or travel over (a stretch of water or terrain), especially carefully or with difficulty: *ships had been lost while navigating the narrows.*
■ [no obj.] (of a ship or boat) sail; proceed: [with adverbial of direction] *we sailed out surrounded by loose ice while navigating around larger grounded icebergs.* ■ guide (a vessel or vehicle) over a specified route or terrain: *she navigated the car safely through the traffic.* ■ make one's way with difficulty over (a route or terrain): *the drivers skilfully navigated a twisting and muddy course.* ■ informal guide or steer (someone), especially through a crowd.
– ORIGIN late 16th cent. (in the sense 'travel in a ship'): from Latin *navigat-* 'sailed', from the verb *navigare*, from *navis* 'ship' + *agere* 'drive'.

navigation ▶ noun [mass noun] **1** the process or activity of accurately ascertaining one's position and planning and following a route.
2 the passage of ships: *transporter bridges to span rivers without hindering navigation.*
■ [count noun] chiefly dialect a navigable inland waterway, especially a canal.
– DERIVATIVES **navigational** adjective.
– ORIGIN early 16th cent. (denoting the action of travelling on water): from French, or from Latin *navigatio(n-)*, from the verb *navigare* (see **NAVIGATE**).

navigation lights ▶ plural noun a set of lights shown by a ship or aircraft at night to indicate its position and orientation.

navigator ▶ noun a person who directs the route or course of a ship, aircraft, or other form of transport, especially by using instruments and maps.
■ historical a person who explores by sea. ■ an instrument or device which assists in directing the course of a vessel or aircraft. ■ Computing a browser program for accessing data on the World Wide Web or another information system.

Navratilova /nəˌvratɪˈləʊvə/, Martina (b.1956), Czech-born American tennis player. Her major successes include nine Wimbledon singles titles (1978–9; 1982–7; 1990), two world championships (1980; 1984), and eight successive grand slam doubles titles.

navvy ▶ noun (pl. **-ies**) Brit. dated a labourer employed in the excavation and construction of a road, railway, or canal.
– ORIGIN early 19th cent.: abbreviation of **NAVIGATOR.**

navy ▶ noun (pl. **-ies**) **1** (often **the navy**) the branch of the armed services of a state which conducts military operations at sea.
■ the ships of a navy: *a 600-ship navy | we built their navy.* ■ poetic/literary a fleet of ships.
2 (also **navy blue**) [mass noun] a dark blue colour: [as modifier] *a navy-blue suit.*
– ORIGIN late Middle English (in the sense 'ships collectively, fleet'): from Old French *navie* 'ship, fleet', from popular Latin *navia* 'ship', from Latin *navis* 'ship'.

navy bean ▶ noun chiefly N. Amer. another term for **HARICOT.**

Navy Department (in the US) the government department in charge of the navy.

Navy List (in the UK) an official list of the commissioned officers in the Royal Navy and the Royal Marines.

navy yard ▶ noun (in the US) a shipyard for the construction, repair, and equipping of naval vessels.

naw ▶ determiner, exclamation, adverb, & noun Scottish, N. English & N. Amer. informal variant spelling of **NO**, representing a dialect or non-standard pronunciation.

nawab /nʌˈwɑːb/ ▶ noun Indian historical a native governor during the time of the Mogul empire: [as title] *Nawab Haider Beg.*
■ a Muslim nobleman or person of high status.
– ORIGIN from Urdu *nawwāb*, variant of Arabic *nuwwāb*, plural (used as singular) of *nā'ib* 'deputy'; compare with **NABOB.**

Naxalite /ˈnaksəlʌɪt/ ▶ noun (in the Indian subcontinent) a member of an armed revolutionary group advocating Maoist communism.
– ORIGIN 1960s: from *Naxal(bari)*, a place name in West Bengal, India, + -ITE¹.

Naxçivan /ˌnaxtʃɪˈvɑːn/ a predominantly Muslim Azerbaijani autonomous republic, situated on the borders of Turkey and northern Iran and separated from the rest of Azerbaijan by a narrow strip of Armenia; pop. 300,000 (est. 1987). Russian name **NAKHICHEVAN.**
■ the capital city of this republic; pop. 51,000 (est. 1987).

Persian from the 13th to the 19th century, it became part of the Russian empire in 1828 and an autonomous republic of the Soviet Union in 1924. In 1990 it was the first Soviet territory to declare unilateral independence. It has a predominantly Azerbaijani population and, along with Nagorno-Karabakh, is a point of conflict between Armenia and Azerbaijan.

Naxos /ˈnaksɒs/ a Greek island in the southern Aegean, the largest of the Cyclades.

nay ▶ **adverb 1** or rather; and more than that (used to emphasize a more appropriate word than one just used): *it will take months, nay years.*
2 archaic or dialect no: *nay, I must not think thus.*
▶ **noun** a negative answer: *the cabinet sits to give the final yea or nay to policies.*
– ORIGIN Middle English (in sense 2): from Old Norse *nei*, from *ne* 'not' + *ei* 'ever' (compare with **AYE**[2]).

Nayarit /ˌnɑːjɑːˈriːt/ a state of western Mexico, on the Pacific coast; capital, Tepic.

naysay ▶ **verb** (past and past participle **-said**) [with obj.] chiefly US say no to; deny or oppose: *I'm not going to naysay anything he does.*
– DERIVATIVES **naysayer** noun.

Nazarene /ˈnazəriːn, ˌnazəˈriːn/ ▶ **noun 1** a native or inhabitant of Nazareth.
■ (**the Nazarene**) Jesus Christ. ■ (chiefly in Jewish or Muslim use) a Christian. ■ a member of an early sect or faction of Jewish Christians, especially one in 4th-century Syria using an Aramaic version of the Gospels and observing much of the Jewish law. ■ a member of the Church of the Nazarene, a Christian denomination originating in the American holiness movement.
2 a member of a group of German painters (working mainly in Rome) who from 1809 sought to revive the art and techniques of medieval Germany and early Renaissance Italy.
▶ **adjective** of or relating to Nazareth or Nazarenes.
– ORIGIN via late Latin from Greek *Nazarēnos*, from *Nazaret* 'Nazareth'.

Nazareth /ˈnazərəθ/ a historic town in lower Galilee, in present-day northern Israel; pop. 39,000 (1982). Mentioned in the Gospels as the home of Mary and Joseph, it is closely associated with the childhood of Jesus and is a centre of Christian pilgrimage.

Nazca Lines /ˈnazkə/ a group of huge abstract designs, including representations of birds and animals, and straight lines on the coastal plain north of Nazca in southern Peru, clearly visible from the air but almost indecipherable from ground level. Made by exposing the underlying sand, they belong to a pre-Inca culture, and their purpose is uncertain; some hold the designs to represent a vast calendar or astronomical information.

Nazi /ˈnɑːtsi, ˈnɑːzi/ ▶ **noun** (pl. **Nazis**) historical a member of the National Socialist German Workers' Party.
■ a member of an organization with similar ideology. ■ derogatory a person who holds and acts brutally in accordance with extreme racist or authoritarian views.

The Nazi Party was formed in Munich after the First World War. It advocated right-wing authoritarian nationalist government, and developed a racist ideology based on anti-Semitism and a belief in the superiority of 'Aryan' Germans. Its leader, Adolf Hitler, who was elected Chancellor in 1933, established a totalitarian dictatorship, rearmed Germany in support of expansionist foreign policies in central Europe, and so precipitated the Second World War. The Nazi Party collapsed at the end of the War and was outlawed.

▶ **adjective** of or concerning the Nazis or Nazism.
– DERIVATIVES **Nazidom** noun, **Nazify** verb (**-ies**, **-ied**), **Naziism** noun, **Nazism** noun.
– ORIGIN German, abbreviation representing the pronunciation of *Nati-* in *Nationalsozialist* 'national socialist'.

Nazirite /ˈnazərʌɪt/ (also **Nazarite**) ▶ **noun** historical an Israelite consecrated to the service of God, under vows to abstain from alcohol, let the hair grow, and avoid defilement by contact with corpses (Num. 6).
– ORIGIN from Hebrew *nāzīr* 'consecrated one', from *nāzar* 'to separate or consecrate oneself', + **-ITE**[1].

Nazi salute ▶ **noun** a gesture or salute in which the right arm is inclined upwards, with the hand open and palm down.

NB ▶ **abbreviation for** ■ New Brunswick (in official postal use). ■ nota bene; take special note (used to precede a written note). [ORIGIN: Latin.]

Nb ▶ **symbol for** the chemical element niobium.

nb Cricket ▶ **abbreviation for** no-ball.

NBA ▶ **abbreviation for** ■ (in North America) National Basketball Association. ■ (in the US) National Boxing Association. ■ net book agreement.

NBC ▶ **abbreviation for** ■ (in the US) National Broadcasting Company. ■ (of weapons or warfare) nuclear, biological, and chemical.

NBG informal ▶ **abbreviation for** no bloody good.

NC ▶ **abbreviation for** ■ network computer, a personal computer with reduced functionality intended to be used to access services on a network. ■ North Carolina (in official postal use). ■ numerical control.

NC-17 ▶ **symbol for** (in the US) films classified as suitable for adults only.
– ORIGIN representing *no children (under) 17.*

NCC ▶ **abbreviation for** (in the UK) ■ National Curriculum Council. ■ Nature Conservancy Council (dissolved 1991).

NCO ▶ **abbreviation for** non-commissioned officer.

NCT ▶ **abbreviation for** (in the UK) National Childbirth Trust, an organization which runs prenatal classes and promotes breastfeeding.

NCU ▶ **abbreviation for** (in the UK) National Communications Union.

ND ▶ **abbreviation for** North Dakota (in official postal use).

Nd ▶ **symbol for** the chemical element neodymium.

n.d. ▶ **abbreviation for** no date (used especially in bibliographies).

-nd ▶ **suffix** variant spelling of **-AND**, **-END**.

N. Dak. ▶ **abbreviation for** North Dakota.

Ndebele /ˌ(ə)ndəˈbiːli, -ˈbeɪli/ ▶ **noun** (pl. same or **Ndebeles**) **1** a member of a people of Zimbabwe and NE South Africa. See also **MATABELE**.
2 [mass noun] the Bantu language of this people, with over 1 million speakers. Also called **SINDEBELE**.
▶ **adjective** of or relating to this people or their language.
– ORIGIN the name in the Nguni languages.

N'Djamena /ˌ(ə)ndʒaˈmeɪnə/ the capital of Chad; pop. 530,965 (1993). Former name (1900–1973) Fort Lamy.

Ndola /(ə)nˈdəʊlə/ a city in the Copperbelt region of central Zambia; pop. 376,000 (1990).

NE ▶ **abbreviation for** ■ Nebraska (in official postal use). ■ New England. ■ north-east or north-eastern.

Ne ▶ **symbol for** the chemical element neon.

né /neɪ/ ▶ **adjective** originally called; born (used before the name by which a man was originally known): *Al Kelly, né Kabish.*
– ORIGIN 1930s: French, literally 'born', masculine past participle of *naître*; compare with **NÉE**.

Neagh, Lough /neɪ/ a shallow lake in Northern Ireland, the largest freshwater lake in the British Isles.

Neanderthal /nɪˈandətɑːl/ ▶ **noun** (also **Neanderthal man**) an extinct human that was widely distributed in ice age Europe between *c.*120,000–35,000 years ago, with a receding forehead and prominent brow ridges. The Neanderthals were associated with the Mousterian flint industry of the Middle Palaeolithic.
● *Homo neanderthalensis*; now usually regarded as a separate species from *H. sapiens* and probably at the end of a different evolutionary line.
■ figurative an uncivilized, unintelligent, or uncouth person, especially a man: *the stereotype of the mechanic as a macho Neanderthal.*
▶ **adjective** of or relating to this extinct human.
■ figurative (especially of a man) uncivilized, unintelligent, or uncouth: *your attitude to women is Neanderthal.*
– ORIGIN mid 19th cent.: from *Neanderthal*, the name of a region in Germany, where remains of Neanderthal man were found.

neap /niːp/ ▶ **noun** (usu. **neap tide**) a tide just after the first or third quarters of the moon when there is least difference between high and low water.
▶ **verb** (**be neaped**) (of a boat) be kept aground or in harbour by a neap tide.
■ [no obj.] archaic (of a tide) tend towards or reach the highest point of a neap tide.
– ORIGIN late Middle English, originally an adjective from Old English *nēp*, first element of *nēpflōd* 'neap flood', of unknown origin.

Neapolitan /nɪəˈpɒlɪt(ə)n/ ▶ **noun** a native or citizen of Naples.
▶ **adjective** of or relating to Naples.
– ORIGIN from Latin *Neapolitanus*, from Latin *Neapolis* 'Naples', from Greek *neos* 'new' + *polis* 'city'.

Neapolitan ice cream ▶ **noun** [mass noun] ice cream made in layers of different colours.

near ▶ **adverb 1** at or to a short distance away; nearby: *a bomb exploding somewhere near* | [comparative] *she took a step nearer.*
2 a short time away in the future: *the time for his retirement was drawing near.*
3 [as submodifier] almost: *a near perfect fit.*
4 archaic or dialect almost: *I near fell out of the chair.*
▶ **preposition** (also **near to**) **1** at or to a short distance away from (a place): *the car park near the sawmill* | *do you live near here?* | [superlative] *the table nearest the door.*
2 a short period of time from: *near the end of the war* | [comparative] *details will be given nearer the date.*
3 close to (a state); verging on: *she gave a tiny smile, brave but near tears* | *she was near to death.*
■ (used before an amount) a small amount below (something); approaching: *temperatures near 2 million degrees K.*
4 similar to: *a shape near to the original.*
▶ **adjective 1** located a short distance away: *a big house in the near distance* | [superlative] *I was fifteen miles from the nearest village.*
2 only a short time ahead: *the conflict is unlikely to be resolved in the near future.*
3 similar: [superlative] *walking in these shoes is the nearest thing to floating on air.*
■ [attrib.] close to being (the thing mentioned): *his state of near despair* | *a near disaster.* ■ [attrib.] having a close family connection: *the loss of a child or other near relative.*
4 [attrib.] located on the side of a vehicle that is normally closest to the kerb; nearside: *the near right-hand end window of the caravan.* Compare with **OFF** (in sense 3).
5 archaic (of a person) mean; miserly.
▶ **verb** [with obj.] come near to (someone or something); approach: *soon the cab would be nearing Oxford Street* | [no obj.] *lunchtime neared.*
– PHRASES **near at hand** within easy reach. ■ about to happen or come about: *an all-electric future was near at hand.* **near enough** sufficiently close to being the case for all practical purposes. **one's nearest and dearest** one's close friends and relatives. **so near and yet so far** a rueful comment on someone's narrow failure to achieve an aim.
– DERIVATIVES **nearish** adjective, **nearness** noun.
– ORIGIN Middle English: from Old Norse *nær* 'nearer', comparative of *ná*, corresponding to Old English *nēah* 'nigh'.

nearby ▶ **adjective** close at hand; not far away: *he slung his jacket over a nearby chair.*
▶ **adverb** (also **near by**) close by: *his four sisters live nearby.*

Nearctic /nɪˈɑːktɪk/ ▶ **adjective** Zoology of, relating to, or denoting a zoogeographical region comprising North America as far south as northern Mexico, together with Greenland. The fauna is closely related to that of the Palaearctic region. Compare with **HOLARCTIC**.
■ [as noun **the Nearctic**] the Nearctic region.
– ORIGIN mid 19th cent.: from **NEO-** 'new' + **ARCTIC**.

near-death experience ▶ **noun** an unusual experience taking place on the brink of death and recounted by a person on recovery, typically an out-of-body experience or a vision of a tunnel of light.

Near East (**the Near East**) a term originally applied to the Balkan states of SE Europe, but now generally applied to the countries of SW Asia between the Mediterranean and India (including the Middle East), especially in historical contexts.
– DERIVATIVES **Near Eastern** adjective.

near gale ▶ **noun** a wind of force 7 on the Beaufort scale (28–33 knots or 51–62 kph).

near go ▶ **noun** Brit. dated informal term for **NEAR MISS**.

nearly ▶ **adverb 1** very close to; almost: *David was nearly asleep* | *a rise of nearly 25 per cent.*
2 closely: *in the absence of anyone more nearly related, I had been designated next of kin.*
– PHRASES **not nearly** nothing like; far from: *you're not nearly as clever as you think you are.*

nearly man ▶ **noun** Brit. informal someone who

narrowly fails to achieve the success or position expected of them in their particular field.

near miss ▶ noun **1** a narrowly avoided collision, especially between two aircraft.
▪something narrowly avoided; a lucky escape: *she had a near miss when her horse was nearly sucked into a dyke.*
2 a bomb or shot that just misses its target.
▪something almost achieved: *a victory in Houston and a near miss in the semi-finals of the French Open.*

near money ▶ noun [mass noun] Finance assets which can readily be converted into cash, such as bills of exchange.

nearshore ▶ adjective [attrib.] relating to or denoting the region of the sea or seabed relatively close to a shore.

nearside ▶ noun (usu. **the nearside**) chiefly Brit. the side of a vehicle nearest the kerb (in Britain, the left). Compare with **OFFSIDE**.
▪the left side of a horse.

near-sighted ▶ adjective another term for **SHORT-SIGHTED**.
– DERIVATIVES **near-sightedly** adverb, **near-sightedness** noun.

near-term ▶ adjective short-term.
▪(of a pregnant female or a fetus) close to the time of birth: *near-term sheep fetuses.*

neat[1] ▶ adjective **1** (of a place or thing) arranged in a tidy way; in good order: *the books had been stacked up in neat piles.*
▪(of a person) habitually tidy, smart, or well organized: *her daughter was always neat and clean.* ▪ having a pleasing shape or appearance; well formed or regular: *Alan noted down the orders in his neat, precise script.* ▪ informal, chiefly N. Amer. very good or pleasant; excellent: *I've been taking lessons in tracking from this really neat Indian guide.*
2 done with or demonstrating skill or efficiency: *Hapgood's neat, precise tackling.*
▪tending to disregard specifics for the sake of convenience; slick or facile: *this neat division does not take into account a host of associated factors.*
3 (of liquid, especially spirits) not diluted or mixed with anything else: *he drank neat Scotch.*
– DERIVATIVES **neatly** adverb, **neatness** noun.
– ORIGIN late 15th cent. (in the sense 'clean, free from impurities'): from French *net*, from Latin *nitidus* 'shining', from *nitere* 'to shine'; related to **NET**[2]. The sense 'bright' (now obsolete) was recorded in English in the late 16th cent.

neat[2] ▶ noun archaic a bovine animal.
▪[mass noun] cattle.
– ORIGIN Old English, of Germanic origin; related to Dutch *noot*, also to the base of dialect *nait* meaning 'companion'.

neaten ▶ verb [with obj.] make tidy.

Neath /niːθ/ an industrial town in South Wales on the River Neath; pop. 49,130 (1981). Welsh name **CASTELL-NEDD**.

neath ▶ preposition chiefly poetic/literary beneath: *neath the trees.*

neat's-foot oil ▶ noun [mass noun] oil obtained by boiling the feet of cattle, used to dress leather.

NEB ▶ abbreviation for ▪ (in the UK) National Enterprise Board. ▪ New English Bible.

Neb. ▶ abbreviation for Nebraska.

neb ▶ noun Scottish & N. English a projecting part of something, in particular:
▪a nose or snout. ▪ a bird's beak or bill. ▪ the peak of a cap.
– ORIGIN Old English *nebb*, of Germanic origin; related to Dutch *neb(be)*; compare with **NIB**.

Nebbiolo /ˌnɛbɪˈəʊləʊ, Italian nebˈbjɔlo/ ▶ noun [mass noun] a variety of black wine grape grown in Piedmont in northern Italy.
▪a red wine made from this.
– ORIGIN Italian, from *nebbia* 'mist' (because the grape ripens in the autumn).

nebbish ▶ noun informal a person, especially a man, who is regarded as pitifully ineffectual, timid, or submissive.
– DERIVATIVES **nebbishy** adjective.
– ORIGIN late 19th cent.: from Yiddish *nebekh* 'poor thing'.

Neblina, Pico da see **PICO DA NEBLINA**.

Nebr. ▶ abbreviation for Nebraska.

Nebraska /nɪˈbraskə/ a state in the central US to the west of the Missouri; pop. 1,578,385 (1990); capital, Lincoln. It was acquired as part of the Louisiana Purchase in 1803 and became the 37th state of the US in 1867.
– DERIVATIVES **Nebraskan** adjective & noun.

Nebuchadnezzar /ˌnɛbjʊkədˈnɛzə/ ▶ noun a very large wine bottle, equivalent in capacity to about twenty regular bottles.
– ORIGIN early 20th cent.: from *Nebuchadnezzar* (see **NEBUCHADNEZZAR II**).

Nebuchadnezzar II (*c.*630–562 BC), king of Babylon 605–562 BC. He rebuilt the city with massive walls, a huge temple, and a ziggurat, and extended his rule over neighbouring countries. In 586 BC he captured and destroyed Jerusalem and deported many Israelites in what is known as the Babylonian Captivity.

nebula /ˈnɛbjʊlə/ ▶ noun (pl. **nebulae** /-liː/ or **nebulas**) **1** Astronomy a cloud of gas and dust in outer space, visible in the night sky either as an indistinct bright patch or as a dark silhouette against other luminous matter.
▪(in general use) any indistinct bright area in the night sky, e.g. a distant galaxy.
2 Medicine a clouded spot on the cornea causing defective vision.
– ORIGIN mid 17th cent. (as a medical term): from Latin, literally 'mist'.

nebular ▶ adjective of, relating to, or denoting a nebula or nebulae: *a vast nebular cloud.*

nebular theory (also **nebular hypothesis**) ▶ noun the theory that the solar and stellar systems were developed from a primeval nebula.

nebulizer /ˈnɛbjʊlʌɪzə/ (also **-iser**) ▶ noun a device for producing a fine spray of liquid, used for example for inhaling a medicinal drug.
– DERIVATIVES **nebulize** (also **-ise**) verb.
– ORIGIN late 19th cent.: from Latin *nebula* 'mist' + *-izer* (see **-IZE**).

nebulous /ˈnɛbjʊləs/ ▶ adjective in the form of a cloud or haze; hazy: *a giant nebulous glow.*
▪(of a concept or idea) unclear, vague, or ill-defined: *nebulous concepts like quality of life.* ▪ another term for **NEBULAR**.
– DERIVATIVES **nebulosity** noun, **nebulously** adverb, **nebulousness** noun.
– ORIGIN late Middle English (in the sense 'cloudy'): from French *nébuleux* or Latin *nebulosus*, from *nebula* 'mist'. The sense 'cloud-like, vague' dates from the early 19th cent.

nebulous star ▶ noun Astronomy a small cluster of indistinct stars, or a star in a luminous haze.

nebuly /ˈnɛbjʊli/ ▶ adjective Heraldry divided or edged with a line formed of deeply interlocking curves.
– ORIGIN mid 16th cent.: from French *nébulé*, from medieval Latin *nebulatus* 'clouded' (the curves being thought of as representing clouds), from Latin *nebula* 'mist'.

NEC ▶ abbreviation for ▪ National Executive Committee. ▪ (in the UK) National Exhibition Centre.

nécessaire /ˌnɛsɛˈsɛː/ ▶ noun a small ornamental case for pencils, scissors, tweezers, and other small items.
– ORIGIN early 19th cent.: French, literally 'necessary (thing)'.

necessarian /ˌnɛsɪˈsɛːrɪən/ ▶ noun & adjective another term for **NECESSITARIAN**.
– DERIVATIVES **necessarianism** noun.

necessarily /ˈnɛsəs(ə)rɪli, ˌnɛsəˈsɛrɪli/ ▶ adverb as a necessary result; inevitably: *the prognosis can necessarily be only an educated guess.*
– PHRASES **not necessarily** (as a reponse) what has been said or suggested may not be true or unavoidable.

necessary ▶ adjective **1** required to be done, achieved, or present; needed; essential: *they granted the necessary planning permission | it's not necessary for you to be here.*
2 determined, existing, or happening by natural laws or predestination; inevitable: *a necessary consequence.*
▪Philosophy (of a concept, statement, judgement, etc.) inevitably resulting from or produced by the nature of things, so that the contrary is impossible. ▪ Philosophy (of an agent) having no independent volition.
▶ noun (usu. **necessaries**) (also **necessaries of life**) the basic requirements of life, such as food and warmth.
▪(**the necessary**) informal an action or item needed for a purpose: *see when they need a tactful word of advice or encouragement and do the necessary.* ▪ (**the necessary**) Brit. informal enough money for a particular purpose.
– PHRASES **a necessary evil** something that is undesirable but must be accepted.
– ORIGIN late Middle English: from Latin *necessarius*, from *necesse* 'needful'.

necessitarian /nəˌsɛsɪˈtɛːrɪən/ ▶ noun Philosophy another term for ***determinist*** (see **DETERMINISM**).
– DERIVATIVES **necessitarianism** noun.

necessitate ▶ verb [with obj.] make (something) necessary as a result or consequence: *a cut which necessitated eighteen stitches.*
▪[with obj. and present participle] force or compel (someone) to do something: *the late arrival had necessitated her getting out of bed.*
– ORIGIN early 17th cent.: from medieval Latin *necessitat-* 'compelled', from the verb *necessitare*, based on Latin *necesse* 'needful'.

necessitous ▶ adjective (of a person) lacking the necessities of life; needy.
– ORIGIN early 17th cent.: from French *nécessiteux*, or from **NECESSITY** + **-OUS**.

necessity ▶ noun (pl. **-ies**) **1** [mass noun] the fact of being necessary.
▪(**necessity of/for/to do something**) the fact of being required or indispensable: *the necessity for law and order.* ▪ unavoidability: *the **necessity of** growing old.* ▪ a state of things or circumstances enforcing a certain course: *created more by necessity than design.*
2 an indispensable thing: *a good book is a necessity when travelling.*
3 [mass noun] Philosophy the principle according to which something must be so, by virtue either of logic or of natural law.
▪[count noun] a condition that cannot be otherwise, or a statement asserting this.
– PHRASES **necessity is the mother of invention** proverb when the need for something becomes imperative, you are forced to find ways of getting or achieving it. **of necessity** unavoidably.
– ORIGIN late Middle English: from Old French *necessite*, from Latin *necessitas*, from *necesse* 'needful'.

Nechtansmere, Battle of /ˈnɛktənzˌmɪə/ a battle which took place in 685 at Nechtansmere, near Forfar, Scotland, in which the Picts defeated the Northumbrians, stopping their expansion northward and forcing their withdrawal.

neck ▶ noun **1** the part of a person's or animal's body connecting the head to the rest of the body: *a silver crucifix around her neck | [as modifier] the neck muscles.*
▪the part of a shirt, dress, or other garment that is around or close to the neck: *her dress had three buttons at the neck undone | a round neck.* ▪ [mass noun] meat from an animal's neck: *neck of lamb made an excellent stew.* ▪ figurative a person's neck regarded as bearing a burden of responsibility or guilt for something: *he'll be stuck with a loan **around his neck**.*
2 a narrow part of something, resembling a neck in shape or position:
▪the part of a bottle or other container near the mouth. ▪ a narrow piece of terrain or sea, such as an isthmus, channel, or pass. ▪ Anatomy a narrow part near one end of an organ, such as the uterus. ▪ the part of a violin, guitar, or other similar instrument that bears the fingerboard. ▪ Architecture another term for **NECKING**. ▪ (often **volcanic neck**) Geology a column of solidified lava or igneous rock formed in a volcanic vent, especially when exposed by erosion. ▪ Botany a narrow supporting part in a plant, especially the terminal part of the fruiting body in a fern, bryophyte, or fungus.
3 the length of a horse's head and neck as a measure of its lead in a race: *Dolpour won by a neck from Wood Dancer.*
▶ verb **1** [no obj.] informal (of two people) kiss and caress amorously: *we started necking on the sofa.*
2 [with obj.] Brit. informal swallow (something, especially a drink): *after necking some beers, we left the bar.*
3 [no obj.] form a narrowed part at a particular point when subjected to tension: *the nylon filament **necks down** to a fraction of its original diameter.*
– PHRASES **break one's neck 1** dislocate or seriously damage a vertebra or the spinal cord in one's neck. **2** (**break one's neck to do something**) informal exert oneself to the utmost to achieve something. **get** (or **catch**) **it in the neck** informal be severely criticized or punished. **have the neck to do something** informal have the impudence or nerve to do something. **neck and neck** level in a race, competition, or comparison. **neck of the woods** informal a particular

area or locality: *fancy seeing her in this neck of the woods.* **up to one's neck in** informal heavily, deeply, or busily involved in: *they were up to their necks in debt | I'm up to my neck in rearranging the match.*
– DERIVATIVES **necked** adjective [in combination] *an open-necked shirt | a red-necked grebe,* **necker** noun, **neckless** adjective.
– ORIGIN Old English *hnecca* 'back of the neck', of Germanic origin; related to Dutch *nek* 'neck' and German *Nacken* 'nape'.

Neckar /ˈnɛkɑː, German ˈnɛkar/ a river of western Germany, which rises in the Black Forest and flows 367 km (228 miles) north and west through Stuttgart to meet the Rhine at Mannheim.

neckband ▶ noun a strip of material round the neck of a garment.

neckcloth ▶ noun a cravat.

Necker /ˈnɛkə, French nɛkɛʀ/, Jacques (1732–1804), Swiss-born banker and director general of French finances (1777–81; 1788–9). In 1789 he recommended summoning the States General and was dismissed, this being one of the factors which resulted in the storming of the Bastille.

neckerchief ▶ noun a square of cloth worn round the neck.

Necker cube ▶ noun a line drawing of a transparent cube, with opposite sides drawn parallel, so that the perspective is ambiguous.
– ORIGIN early 20th cent.: named after L. A. Necker (1786–1861), Swiss naturalist.

necking ▶ noun Architecture a short plain concave section between the capital and the shaft of a classical Doric or Tuscan column.

necklace ▶ noun **1** an ornamental chain or string of beads, jewels, or links worn round the neck.
2 (chiefly in South Africa) a tyre doused or filled with petrol, placed round a victim's neck and set alight.
▶ verb [with obj.] (chiefly in South Africa) kill (someone) with a tyre necklace.

necklace shell ▶ noun a burrowing predatory mollusc which drills into the shells of, and feeds upon, burrowing bivalves. It lays a mass of eggs that resemble a string of beads.
• Genus *Natica*, family Naticidae, class Gastropoda.

necklet ▶ noun a fairly close-fitting and typically rigid ornament worn around the neck.

neckline ▶ noun the edge of a woman's garment at or below the neck, used with reference to its height or shape: *a sundress with a square neckline.*

necktie ▶ noun N. Amer. or dated another term for **TIE** (in sense 2).

necktie party ▶ noun N. Amer. informal a lynching or hanging.

neckwear ▶ noun [mass noun] items worn around the neck, such as collars or ties, collectively.

necro- ▶ combining form relating to a corpse or death: *necromancy.*
– ORIGIN from Greek *nekros* 'corpse'.

necrobiosis /ˌnɛkrə(ʊ)bʌɪˈəʊsɪs/ ▶ noun [mass noun] Medicine gradual degeneration and death of cells in the body tissues.
– DERIVATIVES **necrobiotic** /-ˈɒtɪk/ adjective.

necrologist /nɛˈkrɒlədʒɪst/ ▶ noun the author of an obituary notice.

necrology /nɛˈkrɒlədʒi/ ▶ noun (pl. **-ies**) formal **1** an obituary notice.
2 a list of deaths.
– DERIVATIVES **necrological** adjective.

necromancy /ˈnɛkrə(ʊ)ˌmansi/ ▶ noun [mass noun] the supposed practice of communicating with the dead, especially in order to predict the future.
▪ witchcraft, sorcery, or black magic in general.
– DERIVATIVES **necromancer** noun, **necromantic** adjective.
– ORIGIN Middle English *nigromancie*, via Old French from medieval Latin *nigromantia*, changed (by association with Latin *niger, nigr-* 'black') from late Latin *necromantia*, from Greek (see **NECRO-**, **-MANCY**). The spelling was changed in the 16th cent. to conform with the late Latin form.

necrophilia /ˌnɛkrə(ʊ)ˈfɪlɪə/ ▶ noun [mass noun] sexual intercourse with or attraction towards corpses.
– DERIVATIVES **necrophile** noun, **necrophiliac** noun, **necrophilic** adjective, **necrophilism** noun, **necrophilist** noun.

necrophobia ▶ noun [mass noun] extreme or irrational fear of death or dead bodies.

necropolis /nɛˈkrɒpəlɪs/ ▶ noun a cemetery, especially a large one belonging to an ancient city.
– ORIGIN early 19th cent.: from Greek, from *nekros* 'dead person' + *polis* 'city'.

necropsy /ˈnɛkrɒpsi, nɛˈkrɒpsi/ ▶ noun (pl. **-ies**) another term for **AUTOPSY**.

necrosis /nɛˈkrəʊsɪs/ ▶ noun [mass noun] Medicine the death of most or all of the cells in an organ or tissue due to disease, injury, or failure of the blood supply.
– DERIVATIVES **necrotic** adjective.
– ORIGIN mid 17th cent.: modern Latin, from Greek *nekrōsis* (see **NECRO-**, **-OSIS**).

necrotizing /ˈnɛkrəˌtʌɪzɪŋ/ (also **-ising**) ▶ adjective [attrib.] causing or accompanied by necrosis.
– DERIVATIVES **necrotized** adjective.

necrotizing fasciitis ▶ noun [mass noun] Medicine an acute disease in which inflammation of the fasciae of muscles or other organs results in rapid destruction of overlying tissues.
• This disease is caused by the bacterium *Streptococcus pyogenes.*

nectar ▶ noun [mass noun] **1** a sugary fluid secreted by plants, especially within flowers to encourage pollination by insects and other animals. It is collected by bees to make into honey.
2 (in Greek and Roman mythology) the drink of the gods.
▪ a delicious drink: *the cold pint at the pub was nectar.*
– DERIVATIVES **nectarean** adjective, **nectareous** adjective, **nectarous** adjective.
– ORIGIN mid 16th cent. (in sense 2): via Latin from Greek *nektar.*

nectariferous /ˌnɛktəˈrɪf(ə)rəs/ ▶ adjective Botany (of a flower) producing nectar.

nectarine /ˈnɛktərɪn, -iːn/ ▶ noun a peach of a variety with smooth, thin, brightly coloured skin and rich firm flesh.
▪ the tree bearing this fruit.
– ORIGIN early 17th cent. (also used as an adjective meaning 'nectar-like'): from **NECTAR** + **-INE**[4].

nectarivorous /ˌnɛktəˈrɪv(ə)rəs/ ▶ adjective Zoology (of an animal) feeding on nectar.

nectary ▶ noun (pl. **-ies**) Botany a nectar-secreting glandular organ in a flower (floral) or on a leaf or stem (extrafloral).
– ORIGIN mid 18th cent.: from modern Latin *nectarium*, from *nectar* (see **NECTAR**).

neddy informal ▶ noun (pl. **-ies**) Brit. informal, dated a child's word for a donkey.
▪ Austral. a horse, especially a racehorse.
– ORIGIN mid 16th cent.: diminutive of *Ned*, pet form of the given name *Edward.*

Nederland /ˈneːdərlɑnt/ Dutch name for **NETHERLANDS**.

née /neɪ/ ▶ adjective originally called; born (used in adding a married woman's maiden name after her surname): *Mary Toogood, née Johnson.*
– ORIGIN mid 18th cent.: French, literally 'born', feminine past participle of *naître*; compare with **NÉ**.

need ▶ verb [with obj.] **1** require (something) because it is essential or very important rather than just desirable: *I need help now* | [with present participle] *this shirt needs washing* | [with infinitive] *they need to win tomorrow.*
▪ (**not need something**) not want to be subjected to something: *I don't need your sarcasm.*
2 [as modal verb] [with negative or in questions] expressing necessity or obligation: *need I say more?* | *all you need bring are sheets.*
3 [no obj.] archaic be necessary: *lest you, even more than needs, embitter our parting.*
▶ noun **1** [mass noun] circumstances in which something is necessary, or which require some course of action; necessity: *the basic human* **need** *for food* | [with infinitive] *there's no need to cry.*
2 (often **needs**) a thing that is wanted or required: *his day-to-day needs.*
3 [mass noun] the state of lacking basic necessities such as food or money: *a family whose need was particularly pressing.*
▪ the state of requiring help or support: *help us in our hour of need.*
– PHRASES **at need** archaic when needed; in an emergency: *men whose experience could be called upon at need.* **had need** archaic ought to: *you had need hire men to chip it all over artistically.* **have need of/to do something** formal need: *Alida had need of company.* **if need be** if necessary. **in need** requiring help: *children in need.* **in need of** requiring or needing (something): *he was in desperate need of medical care.*
– ORIGIN Old English *nēodian* (verb), *nēod, nēd* (noun), of Germanic origin; related to Dutch *nood* and German *Not* 'danger'.

USAGE **1** In modern English, there are two quite distinct uses for the verb **need**. In the first place it is used as a normal verb meaning 'require': *I* ***need*** *some money; I* ***need*** *to see her today.* Second, it is one of a small class of verbs called *modals* (like **can**, **could**, and **might**, for example), which cannot stand alone without another verb and do not take normal verb endings or normal negative constructions, e.g. *he* ***need not*** *worry,* not *he* ***needs not*** *worry; he* ***can't*** *swim,* not *he* ***doesn't can*** *swim.* Because of this dual grammatical status, it is sometimes called a *semi-modal.*
2 The two constructions in *that shirt* ***needs washing*** (verb + present participle) and *that shirt* ***needs to be washed*** (verb + infinitive and past participle) have more or less the same meaning. Both these constructions are acceptable in standard English, but a third construction, *that shirt* ***needs washed*** (verb + bare past participle), is restricted to certain dialects of Scotland and North America and is not considered acceptable in standard English.

needful ▶ adjective **1** formal necessary; requisite: *a further word was needful.*
2 needy: *she gave her money away to needful people.*
▶ noun (**the needful**) what is necessary: *I call upon the authorities to do the needful.*
– DERIVATIVES **needfully** adverb, **needfulness** noun.

Needham /ˈniːdəm/, Joseph (1900–95), English scientist and historian. Notable works: *History of Embryology* (1934) and *Science and Civilization in China* (1954).

needle ▶ noun **1** a very fine slender piece of polished metal with a point at one end and a hole or eye for thread at the other, used in sewing.
2 something resembling a sewing needle in use, shape, or appearance:
▪ such an instrument used in crafts such as crochet, knitting, and lacemaking. ▪ the pointed hollow end of a hypodermic syringe. ▪ a very fine metal spike used in acupuncture. ▪ a thin, typically metal pointer on a dial, compass, or other instrument. ▪ an etching tool. ▪ the sharp stiff slender leaf of a fir or pine tree. ▪ a pointed rock or peak. ▪ (**the Needles**) a group of rocks in the sea off the western tip of the Isle of Wight in southern England. ▪ a stylus used to play records. ▪ an obelisk: *Cleopatra's Needle.* ▪ a steel pin exploding the cartridge of a breech-loading gun. ▪ a beam used as a temporary support during underpinning.
3 [mass noun] Brit. informal hostility or antagonism, especially provoked by rivalry: *there is already a little bit of needle between the sides* | [as modifier] *a needle match.*
▶ verb [with obj.] **1** prick or pierce (something) with or as if with a needle: *dust needled his eyes.*
2 informal provoke or annoy (someone), especially by continual criticism or questioning: *I just said that to Charlie to needle him.*
– PHRASES **the eye of a needle** a tiny aperture or opening through which it would seem impossible to pass (especially with reference to Matt. 19:24). **a needle in a haystack** something that is almost impossible to find because it is hidden among so many other things.
– ORIGIN Old English *nǣdl*, of Germanic origin; related to Dutch *naald* and German *Nadel*, from an Indo-European root shared by Latin *nere* 'to spin' and Greek *nēma* 'thread'.

needlecord ▶ noun [mass noun] Brit. fine-ribbed corduroy fabric.

needlecraft ▶ noun [mass noun] needlework.

needlefish ▶ noun (pl. same or **-fishes**) North American term for **GARFISH**.

needlelace ▶ noun another term for **NEEDLEPOINT** (in sense 2).

needlepoint ▶ noun **1** [mass noun] embroidery worked over canvas.
2 (also **needlepoint lace**) [mass noun] lace made by hand using a needle rather than bobbins.

needler ▶ noun (in science fiction) a weapon which fires needle-like projectiles.

needless ▶ adjective (of something bad) unnecessary; avoidable: *I deplore needless waste.*

– PHRASES **needless to say** of course.
– DERIVATIVES **needlessly** adverb, **needlessness** noun.

needletail (also **needle-tailed swift**) ▶ **noun** an Asian spine-tailed swift, believed to be the world's fastest flying bird.
• Genus *Hirundapus*, family Apodidae: four species.

needle time ▶ **noun** [mass noun] Brit. an agreed maximum allowance of time for broadcasting recorded music.
– ORIGIN 1960s: with reference to the 'needle' in the groove of a gramophone record.

needle valve ▶ **noun** a valve closed by a thin tapering part.

needlewoman ▶ **noun** (pl. **-women**) a woman or girl who has particular sewing skills or who sews for a living.

needlework ▶ **noun** [mass noun] the art or practice of sewing or embroidery: *a dab hand at needlework.*
■ sewn or embroidered items collectively: *exhibits include European and Eastern needlework.*
– DERIVATIVES **needleworker** noun.

needn't ▶ **contraction of** need not.

needs ▶ **adverb** archaic of necessity.
– PHRASES **must needs** (or **needs must**) **do something** cannot avoid or help doing something: *they must needs depart.* **needs must** it is or was necessary or unavoidable: *if needs must, they will eat any food.* **needs must when the Devil drives** proverb sometimes you have to do something you would rather not.
– ORIGIN Old English *nēdes* (see **NEED**, **-S**[3]).

needy ▶ **adjective** (**needier**, **neediest**) (of a person) lacking the necessities of life; very poor: *needy and elderly people.*
■ (of circumstances) characterized by poverty: *those from needy backgrounds.*
– DERIVATIVES **neediness** noun.

neem /niːm/ ▶ **noun** a tropical Old World tree, which yields mahogany-like timber, oil, medicinal products, and insecticide.
• *Azadirachta indica*, family Meliaceae.
– ORIGIN early 19th cent.: via Hindi from Sanskrit *nimba*.

neep ▶ **noun** Scottish & N. English a turnip.
– ORIGIN Old English *nǣp*, from Latin *napus*.

ne'er /nɛː/ poetic/literary or dialect ▶ **contraction of** never.

ne'er-do-well ▶ **noun** a person who is lazy and irresponsible.
▶ **adjective** [attrib.] lazy and irresponsible.

nef ▶ **noun** an elaborate table decoration in the shape of a ship for holding such things as table napkins and condiments.
– ORIGIN mid 19th cent.: from French, literally 'ship' (see **NAVE**[1]).

nefarious /nɪˈfɛːrɪəs/ ▶ **adjective** (typically of an action or activity) wicked or criminal: *the nefarious activities of the organized-crime syndicates.*
– DERIVATIVES **nefariously** adverb, **nefariousness** noun.
– ORIGIN early 17th cent.: from Latin *nefarius*, from *nefas*, *nefar-* 'wrong' (from *ne-* 'not' + *fas* 'divine law') + **-OUS**.

Nefertiti /ˌnɛfəˈtiːtiː/ (also **Nofretete**) (*fl.* 14th century BC), Egyptian queen, wife of Akhenaten. She is best known from the painted limestone bust of her, now in Berlin.

neg ▶ **noun** informal a photographic negative.
– ORIGIN late 19th cent.: abbreviation.

neg. ▶ **abbreviation for** negative: *HIV neg.*

nega- ▶ **combining form** informal denoting the negative counterpart of a unit of measurement, in particular a unit of energy saved as a result of conservation measures.
– ORIGIN abbreviation of **NEGATIVE**.

negate /nɪˈɡeɪt/ ▶ **verb** [with obj.] **1** nullify; make ineffective: *alcohol negates the effects of the drug.*
2 Logic & Grammar make (a clause, sentence, or proposition) negative in meaning.
3 deny the existence of (something): *negating the political nature of education.*
– ORIGIN early 17th cent. (in senses 1 and 3): from Latin *negat-* 'denied', from the verb *negare*.

negation ▶ **noun** [mass noun] **1** the contradiction or denial of something: *there should be confirmation—or negation—of the findings.*
■ Grammar denial of the truth of a clause or sentence, typically involving the use of a negative word (e.g. *not, no, never*) or a word or affix with negative force (e.g. *nothing, non-*). ■ [count noun] Logic a proposition whose assertion specifically denies the truth of another proposition: *the negation of A is, briefly, 'not A'.* ■ Mathematics inversion: [count noun] *these formulae and their negations.*
2 the absence or opposite of something actual or positive: *evil is not merely the negation of goodness.*
– DERIVATIVES **negatory** /nɪˈɡeɪt(ə)ri, ˈnɛɡət(ə)ri/ adjective.
– ORIGIN late Middle English: from Latin *negatio(n-)*, from the verb *negare* 'deny' (see **NEGATE**).

negative ▶ **adjective 1** consisting in or characterized by the absence rather than the presence of distinguishing features.
■ (of a statement or decision) expressing or implying denial, disagreement, or refusal: *that, I take it, was a negative answer.* ■ (of the results of a test or experiment) indicating that a certain substance or condition is not present or does not exist: *so far all the patients have tested negative for TB.* ■ [in combination] (of a person or their blood) not having a specified substance or condition: *HIV-negative.* ■ (of a person or an attitude or response) not optimistic; harmful or unwelcome: *the new tax was having a very negative effect on car sales | not all the news is negative.* ■ US informal denoting a complete lack of something: *they were described as having negative vulnerability to water entry.* ■ [as exclamation] no (usually used in a military context): *'Any snags, Captain?' 'Negative, she's running like clockwork.'* ■ Grammar & Logic (of a word, clause, or proposition) expressing denial, negation, or refutation; stating or asserting that something is not the case. Contrasted with **AFFIRMATIVE** and **INTERROGATIVE**.
2 (of a quantity) less than zero, to be subtracted from others or from zero.
■ denoting a direction of decrease or reversal: *negative interest rates | the industry suffered negative growth in 1992.*
3 of, containing, producing, or denoting the kind of electric charge carried by electrons.
4 (of a photographic image) showing light and shade or colours reversed from those of the original.
5 Astrology relating to or denoting any of the earth or water signs, considered passive in nature.
6 Brit. (in Parliament) relating to or denoting proposed legislation which will come into force after a specified period unless explicitly rejected in a parliamentary vote.
▶ **noun 1** a word or statement that expresses denial, disagreement, or refusal: *she replied **in the negative**.*
■ (usu. **the negative**) a bad, unwelcome, or unpleasant quality, characteristic, or aspect of a situation: *confidence will not be instilled by harping solely on the negative.* ■ Grammar a word, affix, or phrase expressing negation. ■ Logic another term for **NEGATION**.
2 a photographic image made on film or specially prepared glass which shows the light and shade or colour values reversed from the original, and from which positive prints may be made.
3 a result of a test or experiment indicating that a certain substance or condition is not present or does not exist: *the percentage of false negatives generated by a cancer test was of great concern.*
4 [mass noun] the part of an electric circuit that is at a lower electrical potential than another part designated as having zero electrical potential.
5 a number less than zero.
▶ **verb** [with obj.] **1** reject; refuse to accept; veto: *the bill was negatived on second reading by 130 votes to 129.*
■ disprove; contradict: *the insurer's main arguments were negatived by Lawrence.*
2 render ineffective; neutralize: *should criminal law allow consent to negative what would otherwise be a crime?*
– DERIVATIVES **negatively** adverb, **negativeness** noun, **negativity** noun.
– ORIGIN late Middle English: from late Latin *negativus*, from *negare* 'deny' (see **NEGATE**).

negative equity ▶ **noun** [mass noun] potential indebtedness arising when the market value of a property falls below the outstanding amount of a mortgage secured on it.

negative evidence ▶ **noun** [mass noun] evidence for a theory provided by the non-occurrence or absence of something.

negative feedback ▶ **noun** [mass noun] chiefly Biology the diminution or counteraction of an effect by its own influence on the process giving rise to it, as when a high level of a particular hormone in the blood may inhibit further secretion of that hormone, or where the result of a certain action may inhibit further performance of that action.
■ Electronics the return of part of an output signal to the input, which is out of phase with it, so that amplifier gain is reduced and the output is improved.

negative geotropism ▶ **noun** [mass noun] the tendency of plant stems and other parts to grow upwards.

negative income tax ▶ **noun** [mass noun] money credited as allowances to a taxed income, and paid as benefit when it exceeds debited tax.

negative instance ▶ **noun** a piece of negative evidence.

negative pole ▶ **noun** the south-seeking pole of a magnet.

negative sign ▶ **noun** another term for **MINUS SIGN**.

negativism ▶ **noun** [mass noun] the practice of being or tendency to be negative or sceptical in attitude while failing to offer positive suggestions or views.
– DERIVATIVES **negativist** noun & adjective, **negativistic** adjective.

negator /nɪˈɡeɪtə/ ▶ **noun** Grammar a word expressing negation, especially (in English) the word *not*.

negentropic /ˌnɛɡɛnˈtrɒpɪk/ ▶ **adjective** Physics of or characterized by a reduction in entropy (and corresponding increase in order).
– DERIVATIVES **negentropy** noun.
– ORIGIN mid 20th cent.: from **NEGATIVE** + *entropic* (see **ENTROPY**).

Negev /ˈnɛɡɛv/ (**the Negev**) an arid region forming most of southern Israel, between Beersheba and the Gulf of Aqaba, on the Egyptian border. Large areas are irrigated for agriculture.

neglect ▶ **verb** [with obj.] fail to care for properly: *the old churchyard has been sadly neglected |* [as adj. **neglected**] *some severely neglected children.*
■ not pay proper attention to; disregard: *you neglect our advice at your peril.* ■ [with infinitive] fail to do something: *he neglected to write to her.*
▶ **noun** [mass noun] the state or fact of being uncared for: *animals dying through disease or neglect.*
■ the action of not taking proper care of someone or something: *she was accused of child neglect.* ■ failure to do something: *he was reported for **neglect of** duty.*
– DERIVATIVES **neglectful** adjective, **neglectfully** adverb, **neglectfulness** noun.
– ORIGIN early 16th cent.: from Latin *neglect-* 'disregarded', from the verb *neglegere*, from *neg-* 'not' + *legere* 'choose, pick up'.

negligee /ˈnɛɡlɪʒeɪ/ (also **négligée**) ▶ **noun** a woman's light dressing gown, typically made of a filmy, soft fabric.
– ORIGIN mid 18th cent. (denoting a kind of loose gown worn by women in the 18th cent.): from French, literally 'given little thought or attention', feminine past participle of *négliger* 'to neglect'.

negligence ▶ **noun** [mass noun] failure to take proper care over something: *a scheme to protect investors in the event of negligence by their financial advisers.*
■ Law breach of a duty of care which results in damage.

negligent ▶ **adjective** failing to take proper care over something: *the council had been negligent in its supervision of the children in care.*
– DERIVATIVES **negligently** adverb.
– ORIGIN late Middle English: from Old French, or from Latin *negligent-* 'disregarding', from the verb *negligere* (variant of *neglegere* 'disregard, slight': see **NEGLECT**).

negligible ▶ **adjective** so small or unimportant as to be not worth considering; insignificant: *he said that the risks were negligible.*
– DERIVATIVES **negligibility** /-ˈbɪlɪti/ noun, **negligibly** adverb.
– ORIGIN early 19th cent.: from obsolete French, from *négliger* 'to neglect'.

Negombo /nɪˈɡɒmbəʊ/ a port and resort on the west coast of Sri Lanka; pop. 60,700 (1981).

negotiable ▶ **adjective** open to discussion or modification: *the price was not negotiable.*
■ (of a document) able to be transferred or assigned to the legal ownership of another person, who thus becomes entitled to any benefit to which the previous owner was entitled. ■ (of an obstacle or pathway) able to be traversed; passable: *such walkways must be accessible and negotiable for all users.*
– DERIVATIVES **negotiability** noun.

negotiate ▶ **verb 1** [no obj.] try to reach an

agreement or compromise by discussion with others: *his government's willingness to negotiate.*
■[with obj.] obtain or bring about by negotiating: *he negotiated a new contract with the sellers.*
2 [with obj.] find a way over or through (an obstacle or difficult path): *there was a puddle to be negotiated.*
3 [with obj.] transfer (a cheque, bill, or other document) to the legal ownership of another person, who thus becomes entitled to any benefit. ■convert (a cheque) into cash or notes.
– DERIVATIVES **negotiant** noun (archaic), **negotiator** noun.
– ORIGIN early 17th cent.: from Latin *negotiat-* 'done in the course of business', from the verb *negotiari*, from *negotium* 'business', from *neg-* 'not' + *otium* 'leisure'.

negotiation ▶ **noun** [mass noun] (also **negotiations**) discussion aimed at reaching an agreement: *a worldwide ban is currently* ***under negotiation*** | [count noun] ***negotiations between*** *unions and employers.*
■the action or process of negotiating: *negotiation of the deals.* ■the action or process of transferring ownership of a document.
– ORIGIN late 15th cent. (denoting an act of dealing with another person): from Latin *negotiatio(n-)*, from the verb *negotiari* (see **NEGOTIATE**).

Negress /ˈniːgrɪs, -grɛs/ ▶ **noun** a woman or girl of black African origin. See **usage** at **NEGRO**.
– ORIGIN late 18th cent.: from French *négresse*, feminine of *nègre* 'negro'.

Negrillo /nɪˈgrɪləʊ/ ▶ **noun** (pl. **-os**) a member of a black people of short stature native to central and southern Africa.
– ORIGIN Spanish, diminutive of *negro* 'black' (see **NEGRO**); compare with **NEGRITO**.

Negri Sembilan /ˌnɛgriː sɛmˈbiːlən/ a state of Malaysia, on the SW coast of the Malay Peninsula; capital, Seremban.

Negrito /nɪˈgriːtəʊ/ ▶ **noun** (pl. **-os**) a member of a black people of short stature native to the Austronesian region.
– ORIGIN Spanish, diminutive of *negro* 'black' (see **NEGRO**); compare with **NEGRILLO**.

Negritude /ˈnɛgrɪtjuːd/ ▶ **noun** [mass noun] the quality or fact of being of black African origin.
■the affirmation or consciousness of the value of black or African culture, heritage, and identity: *Negritude helped to guide Senegal into independence with pride.*
– ORIGIN 1950s: from French *négritude* 'blackness'.

Negro /ˈniːgrəʊ/ ▶ **noun** (pl. **-oes**) a member of a dark-skinned group of peoples originally native to Africa south of the Sahara.
▶ **adjective** of or relating to such people.
– ORIGIN via Spanish and Portuguese from Latin *niger, nigr-* 'black'.

USAGE The word **Negro** was adopted from Spanish and Portuguese and first recorded from the mid 16th century. It remained the standard term throughout the 17th–19th centuries and was used by prominent black American campaigners such as W. E. B. DuBois and Booker T. Washington in the early 20th century. Since the Black Power movement of the 1960s, however, when the term **black** was favoured as the term to express racial pride, **Negro** (together with related words such as **Negress**) has dropped out of favour and now seems out of date or even offensive in both British and US English.

Negroid ▶ **adjective** of or relating to the division of humankind represented by the indigenous peoples of central and southern Africa.

USAGE The term **Negroid** belongs to a set of terms introduced by 19th-century anthropologists attempting to categorize human races. Such terms are associated with outdated notions of racial types, and so are now potentially offensive and best avoided. See **usage** at **MONGOLOID**.

negroni /nɪˈgrəʊni/ ▶ **noun** a cocktail made from gin, vermouth, and Campari.
– ORIGIN Italian.

Negrophobia ▶ **noun** [mass noun] intense or irrational dislike or fear of black people.
– DERIVATIVES **Negrophobe** noun.

Negros /ˈneɪgrɒs/ an island, the fourth largest of the Philippines; pop. 3,182,180 (1991); chief city, Bacolod.

Negro spiritual ▶ **noun** see **SPIRITUAL**.

Negus /ˈniːgəs/ ▶ **noun** historical a ruler, or the supreme ruler, of Ethiopia.
– ORIGIN from Amharic *n'gus* 'king'.

negus /ˈniːgəs/ ▶ **noun** historical a hot drink of port, sugar, lemon, and spice.
– ORIGIN named after Colonel Francis *Negus* (died 1732), who created it.

Neh. ▶ **abbreviation for** Nehemiah (in biblical references).

Nehemiah /nɪəˈmʌɪə/ (5th century BC) a Hebrew leader who supervised the rebuilding of the walls of Jerusalem (*c.*444) and introduced moral and religious reforms (*c.*432).
■a book of the Bible telling of this rebuilding and of the reforms.

Nehru /ˈnɛːruː/, Jawaharlal (1889–1964), Indian statesman, Prime Minister 1947–64; known as **Pandit Nehru**. Nehru was elected leader of the Indian National Congress in 1929. He was imprisoned nine times by the British for his nationalist campaigns, but went on to become the first Prime Minister of independent India.

neigh /neɪ/ ▶ **noun** a characteristic high whinnying sound made by a horse.
▶ **verb** [no obj.] (of a horse) make such a sound; utter a neigh.
■(of a person) make a similar sound: *they neighed dutifully at jokes they did not understand.*
– ORIGIN Old English *hnǣgan* (verb), of imitative origin; compare with Dutch dialect *neijen*.

neighbour (US **neighbor**) ▶ **noun** a person living next door to or very near to the speaker or person referred to: *our garden was the envy of the neighbours.*
■a person or place in relation to others next or near to it: *I chatted with my neighbour on the flight to New York | matching our investment levels with those of our European neighbours.* ■any person in need of one's help or kindness (after biblical use): *love thy neighbour as thyself.*
▶ **verb** [with obj.] (of a place or thing) be situated next to or very near (another): *the square neighbours the old quarter of the town* | [as adj. **neighbouring**] *neighbouring countries | a couple at a neighbouring table.*
– DERIVATIVES **neighbourless** adjective.
– ORIGIN Old English *nēahgebūr*, from *nēah* 'nigh, near' + *gebūr* 'inhabitant, peasant, farmer' (compare with **BOOR**).

neighbourhood (US **neighborhood**) ▶ **noun** a district, especially one forming a community within a town or city: *she lived in a wealthy neighbourhood of Boston.*
■[mass noun] neighbourly feeling or conduct: *the importance of neighbourhood to old people.* ■the area surrounding a particular place, person, or object: *he was reluctant to leave the neighbourhood of London.* ■Mathematics the set of points whose distance from a given point is less than (or less than or equal to) some value.
– PHRASES **in the neighbourhood of** approximately; about: *the cost would be in the neighbourhood of three billion.*

neighbourhood watch ▶ **noun** a scheme of systematic local vigilance by householders to discourage crime, especially burglary.

neighbourly (US **neighborly**) ▶ **adjective** characteristic of a good neighbour, especially helpful, friendly, or kind.
– DERIVATIVES **neighbourliness** noun.

Neisse /ˈnʌɪsə/ **1** a river in central Europe, which rises in the north of the Czech Republic and flows over 225 km (140 miles) generally northwards, forming the southern part of the border between Germany and Poland (the Oder–Neisse Line) and joining the River Oder north-east of Cottbus. German name **LAUSITZER NEISSE**; Polish name **NYSA**.
2 a river of southern Poland, which rises near the border with the Czech Republic and flows 195 km (120 miles) generally north-eastwards, through the town of Nysa, joining the River Oder south-east of Wrocław. German name **GLATZER NEISSE**.

neither /ˈnʌɪðə, ˈniː-/ ▶ **determiner & pronoun** not the one nor the other of two people or things; not either: [as determiner] *neither side of the brain is dominant over the other* | [as pronoun] ***neither of*** *us believes it.*
▶ **adverb 1** used before the first of two (or occasionally more) alternatives that are being specified (the others being introduced by 'nor') to indicate that they are each untrue or each do not happen: *I am neither a liberal nor a conservative.*
2 used to introduce a further negative statement: *he didn't remember, and neither did I.*
– PHRASES **neither here nor there** see **HERE**.
– ORIGIN Middle English: alteration (by association with **EITHER**) of Old English *nawther*, contraction of *nāhwæther* (from *nā* 'no' + *hwæther* 'whether').

USAGE 1 The use of **neither** with another negative, as in *I* ***don't*** *like him* ***neither*** or ***not*** *much good at reading* ***neither*** is recorded from the 16th century onwards, but is not thought to be good English. This is because it is an example of a **double negative**, which, though standard in some other languages such as Spanish and found in many dialects of English, is not acceptable in standard English. In the sentences above, **either** should be used instead. For more information, see **usage** at **DOUBLE NEGATIVE**.
2 When **neither** is followed by **nor**, it is important in good English style that the two halves of the structure mirror each other: *she saw herself as* ***neither*** *wife* ***nor*** *mother* rather than *she* ***neither*** *saw herself as wife* ***nor*** *mother.* For more details, see **usage** at **EITHER**.

Nejd /nɛdʒd/ an arid plateau region in central Saudi Arabia, north of the Rub' al Khali desert, at an altitude of about 1,500 m (5,000 ft).

nek /nɛk/ ▶ **noun** S. African a mountain col.
– ORIGIN South African Dutch, literally 'neck'.

nekton /ˈnɛkt(ə)n, -tɒn/ ▶ **noun** [mass noun] Zoology aquatic animals that are able to swim and move independently of water currents. Often contrasted with **PLANKTON**.
– DERIVATIVES **nektonic** adjective.
– ORIGIN late 19th cent.: via German from Greek *nēkton*, neuter of *nēktos* 'swimming', from *nēkhein* 'to swim'.

Nellore /nɛˈlɔː/ a city and river port in SE India, in Andhra Pradesh, on the River Penner; pop. 316,000 (1991). Situated close to the mouth of the river, it is one of the chief ports of the Coromandel Coast.

nelly ▶ **noun** (pl. **-ies**) informal **1** a silly person.
2 offensive an effeminate homosexual man.
– PHRASES **not on your nelly** Brit. certainly not. [ORIGIN: originally as *not on your Nelly Duff*, rhyming slang for 'puff' (i.e. breath of life); modelled on the phrase *not on your life.*]
– ORIGIN mid 20th cent.: from the given name *Nelly*.

Nelson[1] a port in New Zealand, on the north coast of South Island; pop. 47,390 (1991). It was founded in 1841 by the New Zealand Company and named after the British admiral Lord Nelson.

Nelson[2], Horatio, Viscount Nelson, Duke of Bronte (1758–1805), British admiral. Nelson became a national hero as a result of his victories at sea in the Napoleonic Wars, especially the Battle of Trafalgar, in which he was mortally wounded.

Nelson[3], Willie (b.1933), American country singer and songwriter. He is noted for hits such as 'A Good Hearted Woman' (1976) and the album *Red Haired Stranger* (1975).

nelson ▶ **noun** a wrestling hold in which one arm is passed under the opponent's arm from behind and the hand is applied to the neck (**half nelson**), or both arms and hands are applied (**full nelson**).
– ORIGIN late 19th cent.: apparently from the surname *Nelson*, but the reference is unknown.

Nelson's Column a memorial to Lord Nelson in Trafalgar Square, London, consisting of a column 58 metres (170 feet) high surmounted by his statue.

Nelson touch ▶ **noun** (**the Nelson touch**) Brit. a masterly or sympathetic approach to a problem.
– ORIGIN early 19th cent.: with allusion to the skills of Admiral Horatio **NELSON**[2].

Nelspruit /ˈnɛlsprɔɪt/ a town in eastern South Africa, the capital of the province of Mpumalanga, situated on the Crocodile River to the west of Kruger National Park.

Neman /ˈnɛmən/ a river of eastern Europe, which rises south of Minsk in Belarus and flows 955 km (597 miles) west and north to the Baltic Sea. Its lower course, which forms the boundary between Lithuania and the Russian enclave of Kaliningrad, is called the Memel. Lithuanian name **NEMUNAS**, Belorussian name **NYOMAN**.

nematic /nɪˈmatɪk/ ▶ **adjective** relating to or denoting a state of a liquid crystal in which the molecules are oriented in parallel but not arranged in well-defined planes. Compare with **SMECTIC**.
▶ **noun** a nematic substance.

– ORIGIN early 20th cent.: from Greek *nēma*, *nēmat-* 'thread' + -IC.

nemato- /nɪˈmatəʊ, ˈnɛmətəʊ/ (also **nemat-** before a vowel) ▶ combining form denoting something thread-like in shape: *nematocyst*.
■ relating to Nematoda: *nematocide*.
– ORIGIN from Greek *nēma*, *nēmat-* 'thread'.

nematocide /nɪˈmatə(ʊ)sʌɪd, ˈnɛmətə(ʊ)-/ (also **nematicide** /nɪˈmatɪ-, ˈnɛmətɪ-/) ▶ noun a substance used to kill nematode worms.
– DERIVATIVES **nematocidal** adjective.
– ORIGIN late 19th cent.: from **NEMATO-** 'of nematode worms' + -CIDE.

nematocyst /nɪˈmatə(ʊ)sɪst, ˈnɛmət-/ ▶ noun Zoology a specialized cell in the tentacles of a jellyfish or other coelenterate, containing a barbed or venomous coiled thread that can be projected in self-defence or to capture prey.
– ORIGIN late 19th cent.: from **NEMATO-** 'of thread-like shape' + CYST.

Nematoda /ˌnɛməˈtəʊdə/ Zoology a large phylum of worms with slender, unsegmented, cylindrical bodies, including the roundworms, threadworms, and eelworms. They are found abundantly in soil and water, and many are parasites.
– DERIVATIVES **nematode** /ˈnɛmətəʊd/ noun.
– ORIGIN modern Latin (plural), from Greek *nēma*, *nēmat-* 'thread'.

nematology /ˌnɛməˈtɒlədʒi/ ▶ noun [mass noun] the scientific study of nematode worms.
– DERIVATIVES **nematologist** noun.

Nematomorpha /nɛˌmatəˈmɔːfə/ Zoology a small phylum that comprises the horsehair worms.
– DERIVATIVES **nematomorph** noun.
– ORIGIN modern Latin (plural), from Greek *nēma*, *nēmat-* 'thread' + *morphē* 'form'.

Nembutal /ˈnɛmbjʊt(ə)l, -tɑːl/ ▶ noun (trademark in the US) the drug sodium pentobarbitone (see **PENTOBARBITONE**).
– ORIGIN mid 20th cent.: from *N(a)* (symbol for sodium) + *e(thyl)*, *m(ethyl)*, *but(yl)*, elements of the systematic name, + -AL.

nem. con. ▶ abbreviation for nemine contradicente, with no one dissenting; unanimously: *the motions were carried nem. con.*
– ORIGIN Latin.

Nemertea /ˌnɛməˈtiːə, nɪˈməːtɪə/ Zoology a small phylum that comprises the ribbon worms.
– DERIVATIVES **nemertean** adjective & noun, **nemertine** /ˈnɛmətiːn, ˈnɛmətʌɪn/ adjective & noun.
– ORIGIN modern Latin (plural), from Greek *Nēmertēs*, the name of a sea nymph.

nemesia /nɪˈmiːʒə/ ▶ noun a plant related to the snapdragon, which is cultivated for its colourful, obliquely funnel-shaped flowers.
● Genus *Nemesia*, family Scrophulariaceae: several species, in particular *N. strumosa* and its hybrids.
– ORIGIN modern Latin, from Greek *nemesion*, denoting various similar plants.

Nemesis /ˈnɛmɪsɪs/ Greek Mythology a goddess usually portrayed as the agent of divine punishment for wrongdoing or presumption (hubris).

nemesis /ˈnɛmɪsɪs/ ▶ noun (pl. **nemeses** /-siːz/) (usu. **one's nemesis**) the inescapable or implacable agent of someone's or something's downfall, especially when deserved: *I am either your saviour or your nemesis.*
■ a downfall caused by such an agent: *one risks nemesis by uttering such words.* ■ (often **Nemesis**) retributive justice: *Nemesis is notoriously slow.*
– ORIGIN late 16th cent.: Greek, literally 'retribution', from *nemein* 'give what is due'.

nemo dat quod non habet /ˌniːməʊ ˈdat, ˈnɛməʊ/ (in full **nemo dat quod non habet**) ▶ noun Law the basic principle that a person who does not own property, especially a thief, cannot confer it on another except with the true owner's authority.
– ORIGIN Latin, literally 'no one gives (what he or she does not have)'.

Nemunas /ˈnjamʊnəs/ Lithuanian name for **NEMAN**.

nene /ˈneɪneɪ/ (also **ne-ne**) ▶ noun (pl. same or **nenes**) another term for **HAWAIIAN GOOSE**.
– ORIGIN early 20th cent.: from Hawaiian.

Nenets /ˈnɛnɛts/ ▶ noun (pl. same or **Nentsy** or **Nentsi**) **1** a member of a nomadic people of Siberia, whose main traditional occupation is reindeer herding.

2 [mass noun] the language of this people, the most widely used of the Samoyedic languages, with about 27,000 speakers.
– ORIGIN the name in Russian.

Nennius /ˈnɛnɪəs/ (*fl. c*.800), Welsh chronicler. He is traditionally credited with the compilation or revision of the *Historia Britonum*, which includes one of the earliest known accounts of King Arthur.

neo- /ˈniːəʊ/ ▶ combining form **1** new: *neonate*.
2 a new or revived form of: *neo-Georgian.*
– ORIGIN from Greek *neos* 'new'.

neoclassical (also **neoclassic**) ▶ adjective of or relating to neoclassicism.

neoclassicism ▶ noun [mass noun] the revival of a classical style or treatment in art, literature, architecture, or music.

As an aesthetic and artistic style this originated in Rome in the mid 18th century, combining a reaction against the late baroque and rococo with a new interest in antiquity. In music, the term refers to a return by composers of the early 20th century to the forms and styles of the 17th and 18th centuries, as a reaction against 19th-century Romanticism.

– DERIVATIVES **neoclassicist** noun & adjective.

neocolonialism ▶ noun [mass noun] the use of economic, political, cultural, or other pressures to control or influence other countries, especially former dependencies.
– DERIVATIVES **neocolonial** adjective, **neocolonialist** noun & adjective.

neocon chiefly US ▶ adjective neoconservative, especially in advocating democratic capitalism.
▶ noun a neoconservative.

neo-Confucianism ▶ noun a movement in religious philosophy derived from Confucianism in China around AD 1000 in response to the ideas of Taoism and Buddhism.
– DERIVATIVES **neo-Confucian** adjective.

neoconservative ▶ adjective of or relating to an approach to politics, literary criticism, theology, history, or any other branch of thought, which represents a return to a modified form of a traditional viewpoint, in contrast to more radical or liberal schools of thought.
▶ noun a person with neoconservative views.
– DERIVATIVES **neoconservatism** noun.

neocortex ▶ noun (pl. **neocortices**) Anatomy a part of the cerebral cortex concerned with sight and hearing in mammals, regarded as the most recently evolved part of the cortex.
– DERIVATIVES **neocortical** adjective.

neo-Darwinian ▶ adjective Biology of or relating to the modern version of Darwin's theory of evolution by natural selection, incorporating the findings of genetics.
– DERIVATIVES **neo-Darwinism** noun, **neo-Darwinist** noun.

neodymium /ˌniːə(ʊ)ˈdɪmɪəm/ ▶ noun [mass noun] the chemical element of atomic number 60, a silvery-white metal of the lanthanide series. Neodymium is a component of misch metal and some other alloys, and its compounds are used in colouring glass and ceramics. (Symbol: **Nd**)
– ORIGIN late 19th cent.: from **NEO-** 'new' + a shortened form of **DIDYMIUM**.

neo-fascist ▶ noun a member of an organization similar to the Italian Fascist movement of the early 20th century.
▶ adjective of or relating to neo-fascists or neo-fascism.
– DERIVATIVES **neo-fascism** noun.

Neogaea /ˌniːə(ʊ)ˈdʒiːə/ (US **Neogea**) Zoology a zoogeographical area comprising the Neotropical region.
– DERIVATIVES **Neogaean** adjective.
– ORIGIN modern Latin, from Greek *neos* 'new' + *gaia* 'earth'.

Neogene /ˈniːə(ʊ)dʒiːn/ ▶ adjective Geology of, relating to, or denoting the later division of the Tertiary period, comprising the Miocene and Pliocene epochs.
■ [as noun **the Neogene**] the Neogene sub-period or the system of rocks deposited during it.

The Neogene lasted from about 23 to 1.6 million years ago. The mammals continued to evolve during this time, developing into the forms that are familiar today.

– ORIGIN late 19th cent.: from **NEO-** 'new' + Greek *-genēs* 'born, of a specified kind' (see -GEN).

neo-Georgian ▶ adjective of, relating to, or imitative of a revival of a Georgian style in architecture.

neo-Gothic ▶ adjective of or in an artistic style that originated in the 19th century, characterized by the revival of Gothic and other medieval forms. In architecture it is manifested in pointed arches, vaulted ceilings, and mock fortifications.
▶ noun the neo-Gothic style.

Neogrammarian /ˌniːə(ʊ)grəˈmɛːrɪən/ ▶ noun any of a group of 19th-century German scholars who, having noticed that sound changes in language are regular and that therefore lost word forms can be reconstructed, postulated the forms of entire lost languages such as Proto-Indo-European by the comparison of related forms in existing languages.
– ORIGIN translation of German *Junggrammatiker*.

neo-Impressionism ▶ noun [mass noun] a late 19th-century movement in French painting which sought to improve on Impressionism through a systematic approach to form and colour, particularly using pointillist technique. The movement's leading figures included Georges Seurat, Paul Signac, and Camille Pissarro.
– DERIVATIVES **neo-Impressionist** adjective & noun.

neo-liberal ▶ adjective relating to or denoting a modified form of liberalism tending to favour free-market capitalism.
▶ noun a person holding such views.
– DERIVATIVES **neo-liberalism** noun.

Neolithic /ˌniːə(ʊ)ˈlɪθɪk/ ▶ adjective Archaeology of, relating to, or denoting the later part of the Stone Age, when ground or polished stone weapons and implements prevailed.
■ [as noun **the Neolithic**] the Neolithic period. Also called **NEW STONE AGE**.

In the Neolithic period farm animals were first domesticated and agriculture was introduced, beginning in the Near East by the 8th millennium BC and spreading to northern Europe by the 4th millennium BC. Neolithic societies in NW Europe left such monuments as causewayed camps, henges, long barrows, and chambered tombs.

– ORIGIN mid 19th cent.: from **NEO-** 'new' + Greek *lithos* 'stone' + -IC.

neologism /nɪˈɒlədʒɪz(ə)m/ ▶ noun a newly coined word or expression.
■ [mass noun] the coining or use of new words.
– DERIVATIVES **neologist** noun, **neologize** (also -ise) verb.
– ORIGIN early 19th cent.: from French *néologisme*.

neo-Malthusianism /ˌniːəʊmal'θjuːzɪənɪz(ə)m/ ▶ noun [mass noun] the view that the rate of increase of a population should be controlled.
– DERIVATIVES **neo-Malthusian** adjective & noun.

neo-Marxist ▶ adjective of or relating to forms of political philosophy which arise from the adaptation of Marxist thought to accommodate or confront modern issues such as the global economy, the capitalist welfare state, and the stability of liberal democracies.
▶ noun a person with neo-Marxist views.
– DERIVATIVES **neo-Marxism** noun.

Neo-Melanesian ▶ noun another term for **TOK PISIN**.

neomycin /ˌniːə(ʊ)ˈmʌɪsɪn/ ▶ noun [mass noun] Medicine an antibiotic related to streptomycin, active against a wide variety of bacterial infections.
● This antibiotic is obtained from the bacterium *Streptomyces fradiae*.

neon ▶ noun [mass noun] the chemical element of atomic number 10, an inert gaseous element of the noble gas group. It is obtained by the distillation of liquid air and is used in fluorescent lamps and advertising signs. (Symbol: **Ne**)
■ fluorescent lighting or signs (whether containing neon or some other gas): *the lobby of the hotel was bright with neon.* ■ [count noun] a small lamp containing neon. ■ [count noun] short for **NEON TETRA**. ■ a very bright or fluorescent colour: *a denim cap outlined in neon* | [as modifier] *we bought ourselves neon bandannas.*
– ORIGIN late 19th cent.: from Greek, literally 'something new', neuter of the adjective *neos*.

neonatal /ˌniːə(ʊ)ˈneɪt(ə)l/ ▶ adjective of or relating to newborn children (or mammals).
– DERIVATIVES **neonatologist** noun, **neonatology** noun.

neonate /ˈniːə(ʊ)neɪt/ ▶ noun a newborn child or mammal.
■ Medicine an infant less than four weeks old.
– ORIGIN 1930s: from modern Latin *neonatus*, from

Greek *neos* 'new' + Latin *nat-* 'born' (from the verb *nasci*).

neo-Nazi ▶ noun (pl. **neo-Nazis**) a member of an organization similar to the German Nazi Party.
■ a person of extreme racist or nationalist views.
▶ adjective of or relating to neo-Nazis or neo-Nazism.
– DERIVATIVES **neo-Nazism** noun.

neon tetra ▶ noun a small Amazonian characin (fish) with a shining blue-green stripe along each side and a red band near the tail, popular in aquaria.
● *Paracheirodon innesi*, family Characidae.

neontology /ˌniːɒnˈtɒlədʒi/ ▶ noun [mass noun] the branch of zoology dealing with living forms as distinct from fossils. Often contrasted with PALAEONTOLOGY.
– DERIVATIVES **neontological** adjective.
– ORIGIN late 19th cent.: from NEO- 'new', on the pattern of *palaeontology*.

neopaganism ▶ noun [mass noun] a modern religious movement which seeks to incorporate beliefs or ritual practices from traditions outside the main world religions, especially those of pre-Christian Europe and North America.
– DERIVATIVES **neopagan** noun & adjective.

neophobia ▶ noun [mass noun] extreme or irrational fear or dislike of anything new, novel, or unfamiliar.
– DERIVATIVES **neophobic** adjective.

neophyte /ˈniːəfʌɪt/ ▶ noun a person who is new to a subject, skill, or belief.
■ a new convert to a religion. ■ a novice in a religious order, or a newly ordained priest.
– ORIGIN late Middle English: via ecclesiastical Latin from Greek *neophutos*, literally 'newly planted' but first used in the sense 'new convert' by St Paul (1 Tim. 3:6), from *neos* 'new' + *phuton* 'plant'.

neoplasia /ˌniːə(ʊ)ˈpleɪzɪə/ ▶ noun [mass noun] Medicine the presence or formation of new, abnormal growth of tissue.

neoplasm ▶ noun a new and abnormal growth of tissue in some part of the body, especially as a characteristic of cancer.
– ORIGIN mid 19th cent.: from NEO- 'new' + Greek *plasma* 'formation' (see PLASMA).

neoplastic¹ ▶ adjective Medicine of or relating to a neoplasm or neoplasia.

neoplastic² ▶ adjective Art of or relating to neoplasticism.
– ORIGIN 1930s: back-formation from NEOPLASTICISM.

neoplasticism ▶ noun [mass noun] a style of abstract painting developed by Piet Mondrian, using only vertical and horizontal lines and rectangular shapes in black, white, grey, and primary colours.
– ORIGIN 1920s: coined by Piet Mondrian.

Neoplatonism /ˌniːəʊˈpleɪt(ə)nɪz(ə)m/ ▶ noun a philosophical and religious system developed by the followers of Plotinus in the 3rd century AD.

Neoplatonism combined ideas from Plato, Aristotle, Pythagoras, and the Stoics with oriental mysticism. Predominant in pagan Europe until the early 6th century, it was a major influence on early Christian writers, on later medieval and Renaissance thought, and on Islamic philosophy. It envisages the human soul rising above the imperfect material world through virtue and contemplation towards knowledge of the transcendent One.

– DERIVATIVES **Neoplatonic** adjective, **Neoplatonist** noun.

neoprene /ˈniːə(ʊ)priːn/ ▶ noun [mass noun] a synthetic polymer resembling rubber, resistant to oil, heat, and weathering.
– ORIGIN 1930s: from NEO- 'new' + *prene* (perhaps from PROPYL + -ENE), on the pattern of words such as *chloroprene*.

Neoptolemus /ˌniːɒpˈtɒləməs/ Greek Mythology the son of Achilles and killer of Priam after the fall of Troy.

neo-realism ▶ noun [mass noun] a movement or school in art or philosophy representing a modified form of realism.
■ a naturalistic movement in Italian literature and cinema that emerged in the 1940s. Important exponents include the writer Italo Calvino and the film director Federico Fellini.
– DERIVATIVES **neo-realist** noun & adjective.

neostigmine /ˌniːə(ʊ)ˈstɪɡmiːn/ ▶ noun [mass noun] Medicine a synthetic compound with the property of inhibiting cholinesterase and used to treat ileus, glaucoma, and myasthenia gravis.

– ORIGIN 1940s: from NEO- 'new', on the pattern of *physostigmine*.

neoteny /niːˈɒt(ə)ni/ ▶ noun [mass noun] Zoology the retention of juvenile features in the adult animal. Also called PAEDOMORPHOSIS.
■ the sexual maturity of an animal while it is still in a mainly larval state, as in the axolotl. Also called PAEDOGENESIS.
– DERIVATIVES **neotenic** adjective, **neotenous** adjective.
– ORIGIN late 19th cent.: coined in German as *Neotenie*, from Greek *neos* 'new' (in the sense 'juvenile') + *teinein* 'extend'.

neoteric /ˌniːə(ʊ)ˈtɛrɪk/ ▶ adjective recent; new; modern: *another effort by the White House to display its neoteric wizardry went awry.*
– ORIGIN late 16th cent.: via late Latin from Greek *neōterikos*, from *neōteros* 'newer', comparative of *neos*.

Neotropical ▶ adjective Zoology of, relating to, or denoting a zoogeographical region comprising Central and South America, including the tropical southern part of Mexico and the Caribbean. Distinctive animals include edentates, opossums, marmosets, and tamarins. Compare with NEOGAEA.
■ Botany of, relating to, or denoting a phytogeographical kingdom comprising Central and South America but excluding the southern parts of Chile and Argentina.
– DERIVATIVES **neotropics** plural noun.

Nepal /nɪˈpɔːl/ a mountainous landlocked country in southern Asia, in the Himalayas (and including Mount Everest); pop. 19,406,000 (est. 1991); official language, Nepali; capital, Kathmandu.

The country was conquered by the Gurkhas in the 18th century and has maintained its independence despite border defeats by the British in the 19th century. Nepal was for long an absolute monarchy, but in 1990 democratic elections were held under a new constitution.

– DERIVATIVES **Nepalese** adjective & noun.

Nepali /nɪˈpɔːli/ ▶ noun (pl. same or **Nepalis**) a native or national of Nepal.
■ [mass noun] the official language of Nepal, a member of the Indic branch of the Indo-European language family. It is also used in Sikkim and has about 8 million speakers altogether. Also called GURKHALI.
▶ adjective of or relating to Nepal or its language or people.

nepenthes /nɪˈpɛnθiːz/ ▶ noun 1 (also **nepenthe**) [mass noun] poetic/literary a drug described in Homer's *Odyssey* as banishing grief or trouble from a person's mind.
■ any drug or potion bringing welcome forgetfulness. [ORIGIN: via Latin from Greek *nēpenthēs* 'dispelling pain', from *nē-* 'not' + *penthos* 'grief'.]
2 a plant of a genus that comprises the Old World pitcher plants. [ORIGIN: modern Latin.]
● Genus *Nepenthes* and family Nepenthaceae.

neper /ˈniːpə, ˈneɪ-/ ▶ noun Physics a unit used in comparing voltages, currents, and power levels, especially in communication circuits. The difference between two values in nepers is equal to the natural logarithm of their ratio for voltages and currents or to half of this for power differences.
– ORIGIN early 20th cent.: from *Neperus*, Latinized form of NAPIER².

nepeta /nɪˈpiːtə/ ▶ noun a plant of a genus that includes catmint and several kinds cultivated for their spikes of blue or violet flowers.
● Genus *Nepeta*, family Labiatae.
– ORIGIN modern Latin, from Latin *nepeta* 'calamint' (formerly in this genus).

nepheline /ˈnɛf(ə)lɪn/ ▶ noun [mass noun] a colourless, greenish, or brownish mineral consisting of an aluminosilicate of sodium (often with potassium) and occurring as crystals and grains in igneous rocks.
– ORIGIN early 19th cent.: from French *néphéline*, from Greek *nephelē* 'cloud' (because its fragments are made cloudy on immersion in nitric acid) + -INE².

nepheline-syenite ▶ noun [mass noun] Geology a plutonic rock resembling syenite but containing nepheline and lacking quartz.

nephelinite /ˈnɛf(ə)lɪnʌɪt/ ▶ noun [mass noun] Geology a fine-grained basaltic rock containing nepheline in place of plagioclase feldspar.

nephelometer /ˌnɛfəˈlɒmɪtə/ ▶ noun an instrument

for measuring the size and concentration of particles suspended in a liquid or gas, especially by means of the light they scatter.
– ORIGIN late 19th cent.: from Greek *nephelē* 'cloud' + -METER.

nephew ▶ noun a son of one's brother or sister, or of one's brother-in-law or sister-in-law.
– ORIGIN Middle English: from Old French *neveu*, from Latin *nepos* 'grandson, nephew', from an Indo-European root shared by Dutch *neef* and German *Neffe*.

nephology /nɪˈfɒlədʒi/ ▶ noun [mass noun] the study or contemplation of clouds.
– ORIGIN late 19th cent.: from Greek *nephos* 'cloud' + -LOGY.

nephr- /nɪfr/ ▶ combining form variant spelling of NEPHRO- shortened before a vowel (as in *nephrectomy*).

nephrectomy /nɪˈfrɛktəmi/ ▶ noun (pl. -ies) surgical removal of one or both of the kidneys.

nephridiopore /nɪˈfrɪdɪəpɔː/ ▶ noun Zoology the external opening of a nephridium.

nephridium /nɪˈfrɪdɪəm/ ▶ noun (pl. **nephridia**) Zoology (in many invertebrate animals) a tubule open to the exterior which acts as an organ of excretion or osmoregulation. It typically has ciliated or flagellated cells and absorptive walls.
– DERIVATIVES **nephridial** adjective.
– ORIGIN late 19th cent.: modern Latin, from Greek *nephrion* (diminutive of *nephros* 'kidney') + the diminutive ending -*idium*.

nephrite /ˈnɛfrʌɪt/ ▶ noun [mass noun] a hard pale green or white mineral which is one of the forms of jade. It is a silicate of calcium and magnesium.
– ORIGIN late 18th cent.: from German *Nephrit*, from Greek *nephros* 'kidney' (with reference to its supposed efficacy in treating kidney disease).

nephritic /nɪˈfrɪtɪk/ ▶ adjective of or in the kidneys; renal.
■ of or relating to nephritis.
– ORIGIN early 19th cent.: via late Latin from Greek *nephritikos* 'of the kidneys' (see NEPHRITIS).

nephritis /nɪˈfrʌɪtɪs/ ▶ noun [mass noun] Medicine inflammation of the kidneys. Also called BRIGHT'S DISEASE.
– ORIGIN late 16th cent.: via late Latin from Greek, from *nephros* 'kidney'.

nephro- (also **nephr-** before a vowel) ▶ combining form of a kidney; relating to the kidneys: *nephrotoxic*.
– ORIGIN from Greek *nephros* 'kidney'.

nephrology /nɛˈfrɒlədʒi/ ▶ noun [mass noun] the branch of medicine that deals with the physiology and diseases of the kidneys.
– DERIVATIVES **nephrological** adjective, **nephrologist** noun.

nephron /ˈnɛfrɒn/ ▶ noun Anatomy each of the functional units in the kidney, consisting of a glomerulus and its associated tubule, through which the glomerular filtrate passes before emerging as urine.
– ORIGIN 1930s: via German from Greek *nephros* 'kidney'.

nephrosis /nɪˈfrəʊsɪs/ ▶ noun [mass noun] kidney disease, especially when characterized by oedema and the loss of protein from the plasma into the urine due to increased glomerular permeability (also called **nephrotic syndrome**).
– DERIVATIVES **nephrotic** adjective.

nephrotoxic /ˌnɛfrə(ʊ)ˈtɒksɪk/ ▶ adjective damaging or destructive to the kidneys.
– DERIVATIVES **nephrotoxicity** noun, **nephrotoxin** noun.

Nepia /ˈniːpɪə/, George (1905–86), New Zealand rugby union player. He played a record thirty-eight consecutive matches for his country (1929–30).

ne plus ultra /ˌneɪ plʌs ˈʊltrɑː/ ▶ noun (the ne plus ultra) the perfect or most extreme example of its kind; the ultimate: *he became the ne plus ultra of bebop trombonists.*
– ORIGIN Latin, literally 'not further beyond', the supposed inscription on the Pillars of Hercules prohibiting passage by ships.

nepotism /ˈnɛpətɪz(ə)m/ ▶ noun [mass noun] the practice among those with power or influence of favouring relatives or friends, especially by giving them jobs.
– DERIVATIVES **nepotist** noun, **nepotistic** adjective.
– ORIGIN mid 17th cent.: from French *népotisme*,

from Italian *nepotismo*, from *nipote* 'nephew' (with reference to privileges bestowed on the 'nephews' of popes, who were in many cases their illegitimate sons).

Neptune 1 Roman Mythology the god of water and of the sea. Greek equivalent **POSEIDON**. [ORIGIN: from Latin *Neptunus*.]
2 Astronomy a distant planet of the solar system, eighth in order from the sun, discovered in 1846.

Neptune orbits between Uranus and Pluto at an average distance of 4,497 million km from the sun (but temporarily outside the orbit of Pluto 1979–99). It is the fourth largest planet, with an equatorial diameter of 48,600 km, and the most remote of the gas giants. The planet is predominantly blue, with an upper atmosphere mainly of hydrogen and helium with some methane. There are at least eight satellites, the largest of which is Triton, and a faint ring system.

Neptunian ▶ **adjective 1** of or relating to the Roman sea god Neptune or to the sea.
2 of or relating to the planet Neptune.
3 Geology, historical advocating Neptunism.

neptunian dyke ▶ **noun** Geology a deposit of sand cutting through sedimentary strata in the manner of an igneous dyke, formed by the filling of an underwater fissure.

Neptunism ▶ **noun** [mass noun] Geology, historical the erroneous theory that rocks such as granite were formed by crystallization from the waters of a primeval ocean. The chief advocate of this theory was Abraham Gottlob Werner. Compare with **PLUTONISM**.
– DERIVATIVES **Neptunist** noun & adjective.

neptunium /nɛp'tju:nɪəm/ ▶ **noun** [mass noun] the chemical element of atomic number 93, a radioactive metal of the actinide series. Neptunium was discovered as a product of the bombardment of uranium with neutrons, and occurs only in trace amounts in nature. (Symbol: **Np**)
– ORIGIN late 19th cent.: from **NEPTUNE**, on the pattern of *uranium* (Neptune being the next planet beyond Uranus).

NERC ▶ **abbreviation for** (in the UK) Natural Environment Research Council.

nerd (also **nurd**) ▶ **noun** informal, chiefly US a foolish or contemptible person who lacks social skills or is boringly studious: *I was a serious computer nerd until I discovered girls and cars.*
– DERIVATIVES **nerdish** adjective, **nerdishness** noun, **nerdy** adjective.
– ORIGIN 1950s: of unknown origin.

Nereid /'nɪərɪɪd/ **1** Greek Mythology any of the sea nymphs, daughters of Nereus. They include Thetis, mother of Achilles.
2 Astronomy a satellite of Neptune, the furthest from the planet, discovered in 1949. It has an irregular shape (with a diameter of about 340 km) and an eccentric orbit.

nereid ▶ **noun** Zoology a bristle worm of the ragworm family (Nereidae).
– ORIGIN mid 19th cent.: from modern Latin *Nereidae*, from the Greek name *Nēreus* (see **NEREID**).

Nereus /'nɪərɪəs/ Greek Mythology an old sea god, the father of the nereids. Like Proteus he had the power of assuming various forms.

nerine /nɪ'rʌɪni, nə'ri:nə/ ▶ **noun** a bulbous South African plant with narrow strap-shaped petals that are typically crimped and twisted and appear when there are no leaves.
• Genus *Nerine*, family Liliaceae (or Amaryllidaceae).
– ORIGIN modern Latin, derivative of Greek *Nērēis*, the name of a water nymph.

nerite /'nɪərʌɪt/ ▶ **noun** a chiefly tropical mollusc with a somewhat globe-shaped and brightly marked shell, typically found in water.
• Superfamily Neritacea, class Gastropoda: several genera and species, including the European freshwater snail *Theodoxus fluviatilis*.
– ORIGIN early 18th cent.: from Latin *nerita*, from Greek *nēritēs* 'sea mussel', from the name of the sea god **NEREUS**.

neritic /nɪ'rɪtɪk/ ▶ **adjective** Biology & Geology of, relating to, or denoting the shallow part of the sea near a coast and overlying the continental shelf.
– ORIGIN late 19th cent.: from **NERITE** + **-IC**.

nerk ▶ **noun** Brit. informal a foolish, objectionable, or insignificant person: *you little nerk.*
– ORIGIN 1960s: of uncertain origin; compare with **NERD** and **JERK**[1].

Nernst /nɛ:nst, German 'nɛrnst/, Hermann Walther (1864–1941), German physical chemist. He is best known for his discovery of the third law of thermodynamics (also known as **Nernst's heat theorem**). Nobel Prize for Chemistry (1920).

Nero /'nɪərəʊ/ (AD 37–68), Roman emperor 54–68; full name *Nero Claudius Caesar Augustus Germanicus*. Infamous for his cruelty, he wantonly executed leading Romans. His reign witnessed a fire which destroyed half of Rome in 64.

neroli /'nɪərəli/ (also **neroli oil**) ▶ **noun** [mass noun] an essential oil distilled from the flowers of the Seville orange, used in perfumery.
– ORIGIN late 17th cent.: via French from Italian *neroli*, said to be from the name of an Italian princess.

Neruda /nə'ru:də/, Pablo (1904–73), Chilean poet and diplomat; born *Ricardo Eliezer Neftalí Reyes*. He took his pseudonym from the Czech poet Jan Neruda. His *Canto General* (completed 1950), is an epic covering the history of the Americas.

Nerva /'nə:və/, Marcus Cocceius (*c.*30–98 AD), Roman emperor 96–8. He returned to a liberal and constitutional form of rule after the autocracy of his predecessor, Domitian.

nervation ▶ **noun** [mass noun] Botany the arrangement of nerves in a leaf.
– ORIGIN early 18th cent.: from French, based on *nerf* 'nerve'.

nerve ▶ **noun 1** (in the body) a whitish fibre or bundle of fibres that transmits impulses of sensation to the brain or spinal cord, and impulses from these to the muscles and organs: *the optic nerve.*
2 (**nerves**) a person's mental state, in particular the extent to which they are agitated or worried: *an amazing journey which tested her nerves to the full.*
■ nervousness or anxiety: *his first-night nerves soon disappeared.*
3 [mass noun] (usu. **one's nerve**) a person's steadiness, courage, and sense of purpose when facing a demanding situation: *she* **kept her nerve** *and won five games in a row | the army's commanders were beginning to* **lose their nerve**.
■ informal impudence or audacity: *he* **had the nerve to** *insult my cooking |* **she's got a nerve** *wearing that short skirt with those legs.*
4 Botany a prominent unbranched rib in a leaf, especially in the midrib of the leaf of a moss.
▶ **verb** (**nerve oneself**) brace oneself mentally to face a demanding situation: *she nerved herself to enter the room | he nerved himself for a final effort.*
– PHRASES **a bag** (or **bundle**) **of nerves** informal someone who is extremely timid or tense. **get on someone's nerves** informal irritate or annoy someone. **have nerves of steel** not be easily upset or frightened. **live on one's nerves** (or **one's nerve ends**) be extremely anxious or tense. **strain every nerve** make every possible effort. [ORIGIN: from the earlier sense of *nerve* as 'tendon, sinew'.] **touch** (or **hit**) **a nerve** (or **a raw nerve**) provoke a reaction by referring to a sensitive topic. **war of nerves** a struggle in which opponents try to wear each other down by psychological means.
– DERIVATIVES **nerved** adjective [usu. in combination] *she was still raw-nerved from reliving the past.*
– ORIGIN late Middle English (also in the sense 'tendon, sinew'): from Latin *nervus*; related to Greek *neuron* 'nerve' (see **NEURON**).

nerve block ▶ **noun** Medicine the production of insensibility in a part of the body by injecting an anaesthetic close to the nerves that supply it.

nerve cell ▶ **noun** a neuron.

nerve centre ▶ **noun** a group of closely connected nerve cells that perform a particular function in the body; a ganglion.
■ the control centre of an organization or operation: *Frankfurt is the economic nerve centre of Germany.*

nerve cord ▶ **noun** Zoology the major cord of nerve fibres running the length of an animal's body, especially a ventral cord in invertebrates that connects segmental nerve ganglia.

nerve fibre ▶ **noun** the axon of a neuron. A nerve is formed of a bundle of many such fibres, with their sheaths.

nerve gas ▶ **noun** [mass noun] a poisonous vapour which has a rapid disabling or lethal effect by disrupting the transmission of nerve impulses.

nerve impulse ▶ **noun** a signal transmitted along a nerve fibre. It consists of a wave of electrical depolarization that reverses the potential difference across the nerve cell membranes.

nerveless ▶ **adjective 1** inert; lacking vigour or feeling: *the knife dropped from Grant's nerveless fingers.*
■ (of literary or artistic style) diffuse or insipid: *Wilde and his art are described as 'nerveless and effeminate'.*
2 confident; not nervous: *with nerveless panache.*
3 Anatomy & Biology lacking nerves or nervures.
– DERIVATIVES **nervelessly** adverb, **nervelessness** noun.

nerve net ▶ **noun** Zoology (in invertebrates such as coelenterates and flatworms) a diffuse network of neurons which conducts impulses in all directions from a point of stimulus.

nerve-racking (also **nerve-wracking**) ▶ **adjective** causing stress or anxiety: *his driving test was a nerve-racking ordeal.*

Nervi /'nɛ:vi, Italian 'nɛrvi/, Pier Luigi (1891–1979), Italian engineer and architect. A pioneer of reinforced concrete, he co-designed the UNESCO building in Paris (1953) and designed the Pirelli skyscraper in Milan (1958) and San Francisco cathedral (1970).

nervine /'nə:vʌɪn, -i:n/ ▶ **adjective** (of a medicine) used to calm the nerves.
▶ **noun** a medicine of this kind.
– ORIGIN mid 17th cent.: from medieval Latin *nervinus* 'of the nerves or sinews', or suggested by French *nervin*.

nervous ▶ **adjective 1** easily agitated or alarmed; tending to be anxious; highly strung: *a sensitive, nervous person | these quick, nervous birds.*
■ anxious or apprehensive: *staying in the house on her own made her nervous | the gunners were* **nervous of** *hitting their own planes.* ■ (of a feeling or reaction) resulting from anxiety or anticipation: *nervous energy.*
2 relating to or affecting the nerves: *a nervous disorder.*
– DERIVATIVES **nervously** adverb, **nervousness** noun.
– ORIGIN late Middle English (in the senses 'containing nerves' and 'relating to the nerves'): from Latin *nervosus* 'sinewy, vigorous', from Latin *nervus* 'sinew' (see **NERVE**). Sense 1 dates from the mid 18th cent.

nervous breakdown ▶ **noun** a period of mental illness resulting from severe depression, stress, or anxiety.

nervous system ▶ **noun** the network of nerve cells and fibres which transmits nerve impulses between parts of the body. See also **AUTONOMIC NERVOUS SYSTEM**, **CENTRAL NERVOUS SYSTEM**, **PERIPHERAL NERVOUS SYSTEM**.

nervous wreck ▶ **noun** informal a person suffering from stress or emotional exhaustion: *by the end of the day I was a nervous wreck.*

nervure /'nə:vjʊə/ ▶ **noun** Entomology each of the hollow veins that form the framework of an insect's wing.
■ Botany the principal vein of a leaf.
– ORIGIN early 19th cent.: from French, from *nerf* 'nerve'.

nervy ▶ **adjective** (**nervier**, **nerviest**) **1** chiefly Brit. easily agitated or alarmed; nervous: *he was nervy and on edge.*
■ characterized or produced by apprehension or uncertainty: *they made a nervy start.*
2 N. Amer. informal bold or impudent: *it was kind of nervy for Billy to be telling him how to play.*
3 archaic or poetic/literary sinewy or strong.
– DERIVATIVES **nervily** adverb, **nerviness** noun.

Nesbit /'nɛzbɪt/, E. (1858–1924), English novelist; full name *Edith Nesbit*. She is best known for her children's books, including *Five Children and It* (1902) and *The Railway Children* (1906).

nescient /'nɛsɪənt/ ▶ **adjective** poetic/literary lacking knowledge; ignorant: *I ventured into the new Korean restaurant with some equally nescient companions.*
– DERIVATIVES **nescience** noun.
– ORIGIN late Middle English: from Latin *nescient-* 'not knowing', from the verb *nescire*, from *ne-* 'not' + *scire* 'know'.

nesh ▶ **adjective** dialect (especially of a person) weak and delicate; feeble: *it was nesh to go to school in a topcoat.*
– DERIVATIVES **neshness** noun.
– ORIGIN Old English *hnesce*, of Germanic origin; related to Dutch dialect *nes* 'soft or foolish'.

ness ▶ **noun** [usu. in place names] a headland or promontory: *Orford Ness.*
– ORIGIN Old English *næs*, perhaps reinforced in Middle English by Old Norse *nes*; related to Old English *nasu* 'nose'.

-ness forming nouns chiefly from adjectives: ▶ **suffix 1** denoting a state or condition: *liveliness* | *sadness.*
■ an instance of this: *a kindness.*
2 something in a certain state: *wilderness.*
– ORIGIN Old English *-nes, -ness*, of Germanic origin.

Nessie informal name for **LOCH NESS MONSTER**.

Ness, Loch see **LOCH NESS**.

Nessus /ˈnɛsəs/ Greek Mythology a centaur who was killed by Hercules, but whose blood soaked Hercules's tunic and consumed him in fire.
– PHRASES **Nessus shirt** (or **shirt of Nessus**) used to refer to a destructive or expurgatory force or influence: *after the lost election of 1979 he found himself wearing this shirt of Nessus.*

nest ▶ **noun 1** a structure or place made or chosen by a bird for laying eggs and sheltering its young.
■ a place where an animal or insect breeds or shelters: *an ants' nest.* ■ a person's snug or secluded retreat or shelter. ■ a bowl-shaped object likened to a bird's nest: *potato nests filled with okra.* ■ a place filled with or frequented by undesirable people or things: ***a nest of** spies.*
2 a set of similar objects of graduated sizes, made so that each smaller one fits into the next in size for storage: ***a nest of** tables.*
▶ **verb 1** [no obj.] (of a bird or other animal) use or build a nest: *the owls often nest in barns* | [as adj. **nesting**] *do not disturb nesting birds.*
2 [with obj.] (often **be nested**) fit (an object or objects) inside a larger one: *the town is nested inside a large crater on the flanks of a volcano.*
■ (especially in computing and linguistics) place (an object or element) in a hierarchical arrangement, typically in a lower position: [as adj. **nested**] *organisms classified in a series of nested sets* | *a nested relative clause.*
– DERIVATIVES **nestful** noun (pl. **-fuls**), **nest-like** adjective.
– ORIGIN Old English *nest*, of Germanic origin; related to Latin *nidus*, from the Indo-European bases of **NETHER** (meaning 'down') and **SIT**.

nest box (also **nesting box**) ▶ **noun** a box provided for a bird to make its nest in.

nest egg ▶ **noun 1** a sum of money saved for the future: *I worked hard to build up a nice little nest egg.*
2 a real or artificial egg left in a nest to induce hens to lay eggs there.

nester ▶ **noun** [usu. with adj. or noun modifier] a bird that nests in a specified manner or place: *a scarce nester in Britain* | *hole-nesters.* See also **EMPTY NESTER**.

nestle ▶ **verb** [no obj., with adverbial of place] settle or lie comfortably within or against something: *the baby deer nestled in her arms* | [with obj.] *she nestled her head against his shoulder.*
■ (of a place) lie or be situated in a half-hidden or obscured position: *picturesque villages nestle in the wooded hills* | (**be nestled**) *the hotel is nestled between two headlands.*
– ORIGIN Old English *nestlian*, from **NEST**; compare with Dutch *nestelen*.

nestling ▶ **noun** a bird that is too young to leave its nest.

Nestor /ˈnɛstə/ Greek Mythology a king of Pylos in the Peloponnese, who in old age led his subjects to the Trojan War. His wisdom was proverbial.

Nestorianism /nɛˈstɔːrɪənɪz(ə)m/ ▶ **noun** [mass noun] the Christian doctrine that there were two separate persons, one human and one divine, in the incarnate Christ. It is named after Nestorius, patriarch of Constantinople (428–31), and was maintained by some ancient Churches of the Middle East. A small Nestorian Church still exists in Iraq.
– DERIVATIVES **Nestorian** adjective & noun.

net[1] ▶ **noun 1** a length of open-meshed material made of twine, cord, rope, or something similar, used typically for catching fish or other animals.
■ a piece of such material supported by a frame at the end of a handle, used for catching fish or other aquatic animals, or insects. ■ a length of such material supported on a frame and forming part of the goal in various games such as football: *Wales did find the net in the 32nd minute.* ■ a length of such material supported on a cord between two posts to divide the playing area in tennis, badminton, volleyball, etc. ■ Cricket a strip of ground enclosed by a net, for batting and bowling practice. ■ Cricket a session of practice on such a strip: *he had time for a second net against the quick bowlers.* ■ the total amount of fish caught in one session or expedition: *good nets of roach, chub, and perch.* ■ a safety net. ■ a hairnet.
2 [mass noun] a fine fabric with a very open weave: [as modifier] *net curtains.*
■ (**nets**) Brit. informal net curtains.
3 figurative a system or procedure for catching or entrapping someone; a trap: *the search was delayed, allowing the murderers to escape the net.*
■ a system or procedure for selecting or recruiting someone: *he spread his net far and wide in his search for success.*
4 a network, in particular:
■ a communications or broadcasting network, especially of maritime radio: *the radio net was brought to life with a mayday.* ■ a network of interconnected computers: *a computer news net.* ■ (**the Net**) the Internet.
▶ **verb** (**netted**, **netting**) [with obj.] **1** catch or land (a fish or other animal) with a net.
■ fish with nets in (a river): *netting the River Naver.*
■ figurative acquire or obtain as if with a net: *customs officials have netted large caches of drugs.*
2 (in sport) hit (a ball) into the net: score (a goal): *Butler netted 14 goals* | [no obj.] *Aldridge netted twice.*
3 cover with a net: *we fenced off a rabbit-proof area for vegetables and netted the top.*
– PHRASES **slip** (or **fall**) **through the net** escape from or be missed by something organized to catch or deal with one: *she slipped through the net of all the care agencies.*
– DERIVATIVES **netful** noun (pl. **-fuls**), **netter** noun [in combination] *drift-netters.*
– ORIGIN Old English *net, nett*, of Germanic origin; related to Dutch *net* and German *Netz*.

net[2] (Brit. also **nett**) ▶ **adjective 1** (of an amount, value, or price) remaining after a deduction, such as tax or a discount, has been made: *net earnings per share rose* | *the net worth of the business* | *the camera will cost you, net of VAT, about £300.* Often contrasted with **GROSS** (in sense 2).
■ (of a price) to be paid in full; not reducible. ■ (of a weight) excluding that of the packaging or container. ■ (of a score in golf) adjusted to take account of a player's handicap.
2 (of an effect or result) final or overall: *the net result is the same.*
▶ **verb** (**netted**, **netting**) [with obj.] acquire or obtain (a sum of money) as clear profit: *they sold their 20% stake, netting a huge profit in the process.*
■ [with two objs] return (profit or income) for (someone): *the land netted its owner a turnover of $800,000.* ■ (**net something down/off/out**) exclude a non-net amount, such as tax, when making a calculation, in order to reduce the amount left to a net sum: *the scrap or salvage value should be netted off against the original purchase price.*
– ORIGIN Middle English (in the senses 'clean' and 'smart'): from French *net* 'neat'; see **NEAT**[1]. The sense 'free from deductions' is first recorded in late Middle English commercial documents.

neta /ˈneɪtɑː/ ▶ **noun** Indian a leader of an organization or a politician.
– ORIGIN via Bengali from Sanskrit *netā* 'leader'.

Netanyahu /ˌnɛt(ə)nˈjɑːhuː/, Benjamin (b.1949), Israeli Likud statesman, Prime Minister 1996–9. Leader of the right-wing Likud coalition 1993–9, he narrowly defeated Shimon Peres in the elections of 1996, but lost to Ehud Barak in 1999.

netball ▶ **noun** [mass noun] a seven-a-side game in which goals are scored by throwing an inflated ball so that it falls through an elevated horizontal ring from which a net hangs. By contrast with basketball, a player receiving the ball must stand still until they have passed it to another player.
■ [count noun] the ball used in this game.

Net Book Agreement (in the UK) an agreement set up in 1900 between booksellers and publishers, by which booksellers will not, with certain exceptions, offer books for less than the price marked on the cover. The agreement effectively collapsed in September 1995 when several major publishers withdrew their support.

net current assets ▶ **plural noun** another term for **WORKING CAPITAL**.

nether /ˈnɛðə/ ▶ **adjective** lower in position: *the ballast is suspended from its nether end.*
– DERIVATIVES **nethermost** adjective.
– ORIGIN Old English *nithera, neothera*, of Germanic origin; related to Dutch *neder-* (found in compounds), *neer*, and German *nieder*, from an Indo-European root meaning 'down'.

Netherlands a country in western Europe, on the North Sea; pop. 15,010,445 (1991); official language, Dutch; capital, Amsterdam; seat of government, The Hague. Dutch name **NEDERLAND**. Also called **HOLLAND**.
■ historical the Low Countries.

> Following a struggle against the Spanish Habsburg empire, the northern (Dutch) part of the Low Countries won full independence in 1648 and became a leading imperial power. In 1814 north and south were united under a monarchy, but the south revolted in 1830 and became an independent kingdom, Belgium, in 1839. In 1948 the Netherlands formed the Benelux Customs Union with Belgium and Luxembourg, becoming a founder member of the EEC in 1957. The name **Holland** strictly refers only to the western coastal provinces of the country.

– DERIVATIVES **Netherlander** noun, **Netherlandish** adjective.

Netherlands Antilles two widely separated groups of Dutch islands in the Caribbean, in the Lesser Antilles; capital, Willemstad, on Curaçao; pop. 189,470 (1992).

> The southernmost group, situated just off the north coast of Venezuela, comprises the islands of Bonaire and Curaçao. The northern group comprises the islands of St Eustatius, St Martin, and Saba. The islands were originally visited in the 16th century by the Spanish and were settled by the Dutch in the mid 17th century. In 1954 the islands were granted self-government and became an autonomous region of the Netherlands.

Netherlands Reformed Church the largest Protestant Church in the Netherlands, established in 1816 as the successor to the Dutch Reformed Church.

nether regions ▶ **plural noun** (**the nether regions**) the lowest or furthest parts of a place, especially with allusion to hell or the underworld.
■ (**one's nether regions**) used euphemistically to refer to a person's genitals and bottom.

netherworld ▶ **noun** (**the netherworld**) the underworld of the dead; hell.
■ a hidden underworld or ill-defined area: *the narcotic netherworld thriving in post-war America.*

netiquette ▶ **noun** [mass noun] the correct or acceptable way of using the Internet.
– ORIGIN 1990s: blend of **NET**[1] and **ETIQUETTE**.

netizen ▶ **noun** a user of the Internet, especially a habitual or keen one.
– ORIGIN 1990s: blend of **NET**[1] and **CITIZEN**.

net national product (abbrev.: **NNP**) ▶ **noun** the total value of goods produced and services provided in a country during one year, after depreciation of capital goods has been allowed for.

net present value ▶ **noun** see **PRESENT VALUE**.

net profit ▶ **noun** the actual profit after working expenses not included in the calculation of gross profit have been paid.

netsuke /ˈnɛtski, ˈnɛtsʊki/ ▶ **noun** (pl. same or **netsukes**) a carved button-like ornament, especially of ivory or wood, formerly worn in Japan to suspend articles from the sash of a kimono.
– ORIGIN late 19th cent.: from Japanese.

nett ▶ **adjective** & **verb** Brit. variant spelling of **NET**[2].

netting ▶ **noun** [mass noun] open-meshed material made by knotting together twine, wire, rope, or thread.

nettle ▶ **noun** a herbaceous plant which has jagged leaves covered with stinging hairs.
● Genus *Urtica*, family Urticaceae: several species, in particular the Eurasian **stinging nettle** (*U. dioica*).
■ used in names of other plants of a similar appearance, e.g. **dead-nettle**.
▶ **verb** [with obj.] **1** irritate or annoy (someone).
2 archaic beat or sting (someone) with nettles.
– PHRASES **grasp the nettle** see **GRASP**.
– ORIGIN Old English *netle, netele*, of Germanic origin; related to Dutch *netel* and German *Nessel*. The verb dates from late Middle English.

nettlerash ▶ **noun** another term for **URTICARIA** (from its resemblance to the sting of a nettle).

nettlesome ▶ **adjective** chiefly US causing annoyance or difficulty: *nettlesome regional disputes.*

nettle tree ▶ **noun** an Old World tree related to the hackberries, with a straight silvery-grey trunk and rough, toothed nettle-like leaves.
● Genus *Celtis*, family Ulmaceae: several species, in particular

C. australis, which is a popular street and shade tree in Mediterranean countries.

nettle-tree butterfly ▶ noun a brown and orange snout butterfly of central Europe, the caterpillar of which feeds on nettle trees.
● _Libythea celtis_, subfamily Libytheinae, family Nymphalidae.

net ton ▶ noun another term for TON¹ (in sense 1).

netty ▶ noun (pl. **-ies**) N. English a toilet, especially an earth closet.
– ORIGIN from Northumberland dialect.

network ▶ noun **1** an arrangement of intersecting horizontal and vertical lines.
■ a complex system of railways, roads, or other transport routes: _the railway network_.
2 a group or system of interconnected people or things: _a trade network_.
■ a group of people who exchange information, contacts, and experience for professional or social purposes: _a support network_. ■ a group of broadcasting stations that connect for the simultaneous broadcast of a programme: [as modifier] _network television_. ■ a number of interconnected computers, machines, or operations. ■ a system of connected electrical conductors.
▶ verb [with obj.] connect as or operate with a network: _compared with the railways the canals were inflexible and less effectively networked_.
■ Brit. broadcast (a programme) on a network: _the Spurs match which ITV had networked_. ■ link (machines, especially computers) to operate interactively: [as adj. **networked**] _networked workstations_. ■ [no obj.] [often as noun **networking**] interact with other people to exchange information and develop contacts, especially to further one's career.
– DERIVATIVES **networkable** adjective.

network analysis ▶ noun [mass noun] the mathematical analysis of complex working procedures in terms of a network of related activities.
■ calculation of the electric currents flowing in the various meshes of a network, often carried out by a device used to model the network.

networker ▶ noun **1** Computing a person who operates from home or from an external office via a computer network.
2 a person who interacts or exchanges information with others working in a similar field, especially to further their career.

Neuchâtel, Lake /nɜːʃaˈtɛl, French nøʃatɛl/ the largest lake lying wholly within Switzerland, situated at the foot of the Jura Mountains in western Switzerland.

Neue Sachlichkeit /ˌnɔɪə ˈzaxlɪxkaɪt, German ˌnɔʏə ˈzaxlɪçkaɪt/ a movement in the fine arts, music, and literature, which developed in Germany during the 1920s and was characterized by realism and a deliberate rejection of romantic attitudes.
– ORIGIN German, literally 'new objectivity'.

Neumann /ˈnɔɪmən/, John von (1903–57), Hungarian-born American mathematician and computer pioneer. He pioneered game theory and the design and operation of electronic computers.

neume /njuːm/ (also **neum**) ▶ noun Music (in plainsong) a note or group of notes to be sung to a single syllable.
■ a sign indicating this.
– ORIGIN late Middle English: from Old French _neume_, from medieval Latin _neu(p)ma_, from Greek _pneuma_ 'breath'.

neural ▶ adjective of or relating to a nerve or the nervous system: _patterns of neural activity_.
– DERIVATIVES **neurally** adverb.
– ORIGIN mid 19th cent.: from Greek _neuron_ in the sense 'nerve' + -AL.

neural arch ▶ noun Anatomy the curved rear (dorsal) section of a vertebra, enclosing the canal through which the spinal cord passes.

neuralgia /njʊəˈraldʒə/ ▶ noun [mass noun] intense, typically intermittent pain along the course of a nerve, especially in the head or face.
– DERIVATIVES **neuralgic** adjective.

neural network (also **neural net**) ▶ noun a computer system modelled on the human brain and nervous system.

neural tube ▶ noun Zoology & Medicine (in an embryo) a hollow structure from which the brain and spinal cord form. Defects in its development can result in congenital abnormalities such as spina bifida.

neuraminic acid /ˌnjʊərəˈmɪnɪk/ ▶ noun [mass noun] Biochemistry a crystalline compound of which derivatives occur in many animal substances, chiefly as sialic acids.
● A sugar with amino and acid groups; chem. formula: C₉H₁₇NO₈.
– ORIGIN mid 20th cent.: _neuraminic_ from NEURO- (because it was originally isolated from brain tissue) + AMINE + -IC.

neuraminidase /ˌnjʊərəˈmɪnɪdeɪz/ ▶ noun [mass noun] Biochemistry an enzyme, present in many pathogenic or symbiotic micro-organisms, which catalyses the breakdown of glycosides containing neuraminic acid.

neurasthenia /ˌnjʊərəsˈθiːnɪə/ ▶ noun [mass noun] an ill-defined medical condition characterized by lassitude, fatigue, headache, and irritability, associated chiefly with emotional disturbance.
– DERIVATIVES **neurasthenic** adjective & noun.

neurectomy /ˌnjʊəˈrɛktəmi/ ▶ noun [mass noun] Medicine surgical removal of all or part of a nerve.

neurilemma /ˌnjʊərɪˈlɛmə/ ▶ noun (pl. **neurilemmas** or **neurilemmata**) Anatomy the thin sheath around a nerve axon (including myelin where this is present)
– DERIVATIVES **neurilemmal** adjective.

neuritis /njʊəˈraɪtɪs/ ▶ noun [mass noun] Medicine inflammation of a peripheral nerve or nerves, usually causing pain and loss of function.
■ (in general use) neuropathy.
– DERIVATIVES **neuritic** adjective.

neuro- ▶ combining form relating to nerves or the nervous system: _neuroanatomy_ | _neurohormone_.
– ORIGIN from Greek _neuron_ 'nerve, sinew, tendon'.

neuroanatomy ▶ noun [mass noun] the anatomy of the nervous system.
– DERIVATIVES **neuroanatomical** adjective, **neuroanatomist** noun.

neurobiology ▶ noun [mass noun] the biology of the nervous system.
– DERIVATIVES **neurobiological** adjective, **neurobiologist** noun.

neuroblast /ˈnjʊərə(ʊ)blast/ ▶ noun Embryology an embryonic cell from which nerve fibres originate.

neuroblastoma /ˌnjʊərə(ʊ)blaˈstəʊmə/ ▶ noun [mass noun] Medicine a malignant tumour composed of neuroblasts, most commonly in the adrenal gland.

neuroepithelium /ˌnjʊərəʊˌɛpɪˈθiːlɪəm/ ▶ noun [mass noun] Anatomy **1** a type of epithelium containing sensory nerve endings and found in certain sense organs (e.g. the retina, the inner ear, the nasal membranes, and the taste buds).
2 (in embryology) ectoderm that develops into nerve tissue.
– DERIVATIVES **neuroepithelial** adjective.

neurofibril /ˌnjʊərə(ʊ)ˈfaɪbrɪl/ ▶ noun Anatomy a fibril in the cytoplasm of a nerve cell, visible by light microscopy.
– DERIVATIVES **neurofibrillary** adjective.

neurofibroma /ˌnjʊərə(ʊ)faɪˈbrəʊmə/ ▶ noun (pl. **neurofibromas** or **neurofibromata** /-mətə/) Medicine a tumour formed on a nerve cell sheath, frequently symptomless but occasionally malignant.

neurofibromatosis /ˌnjʊərə(ʊ)faɪˌbrəʊmətˈəʊsɪs/ ▶ noun [mass noun] Medicine a disease in which neurofibromas form throughout the body. Also called VON RECKLINGHAUSEN'S DISEASE.

neurogenesis /ˌnjʊərə(ʊ)ˈdʒɛnɪsɪs/ ▶ noun [mass noun] Physiology the growth and development of nervous tissue.

neurogenic /ˌnjʊərə(ʊ)ˈdʒɛnɪk/ ▶ adjective Physiology caused or controlled by or arising in the nervous system.

neuroglia /njʊəˈrɒglɪə/ ▶ noun another term for GLIA.
– ORIGIN mid 19th cent.: from NEURO- 'of nerves' + Greek _glia_ 'glue'.

neurohormone ▶ noun Physiology a hormone (such as vasopressin or noradrenaline) produced by nerve cells and secreted into the circulation.

neurohypophysis /ˌnjʊərəʊhaɪˈpɒfɪsɪs/ ▶ noun (pl. **neurohypophyses** /-siːz/) Anatomy the posterior lobe of the hypophysis (pituitary gland), which stores and releases oxytocin and vasopressin produced in the hypothalamus.

neuroleptic /ˌnjʊərə(ʊ)ˈlɛptɪk/ Medicine ▶ adjective (chiefly of a drug) tending to reduce nervous tension by depressing nerve functions.
▶ noun a drug of this kind; a major tranquillizer.

– ORIGIN mid 20th cent.: from NEURO- 'relating to nerves', on the pattern of _psycholeptic_.

neurolinguistic programming (abbrev.: NLP) ▶ noun [mass noun] a system of alternative therapy intended to educate people in self-awareness and effective communication, and to model and change their patterns of mental and emotional behaviour.

neurolinguistics ▶ plural noun [treated as sing.] the branch of linguistics dealing with the relationship between language and the structure and functioning of the brain.
– DERIVATIVES **neurolinguistic** adjective.

neurology /ˌnjʊəˈrɒlədʒi/ ▶ noun [mass noun] the branch of medicine or biology that deals with the anatomy, functions, and organic disorders of nerves and the nervous system.
– DERIVATIVES **neurological** adjective, **neurologically** adverb, **neurologist** noun.
– ORIGIN late 17th cent.: from modern Latin _neurologia_, from NEURO- + -LOGY.

neuroma /ˌnjʊəˈrəʊmə/ ▶ noun (pl. **neuromas** or **neuromata** /-mətə/) another term for NEUROFIBROMA.

neuromast /ˈnjʊərə(ʊ)mast/ ▶ noun Zoology a sensory organ of fishes and larval or aquatic amphibians, typically forming part of the lateral line system.
– ORIGIN early 20th cent.: from NEURO- 'of nerves' + Greek _mastos_ 'breast'.

neuromuscular ▶ adjective of or relating to nerves and muscles.

neuron /ˈnjʊərɒn/ (also **neurone** /-rəʊn/) ▶ noun a specialized cell transmitting nerve impulses; a nerve cell.
– DERIVATIVES **neuronal** /-ˈrəʊn(ə)l/ adjective, **neuronic** /-ˈrɒnɪk/ adjective.
– ORIGIN late 19th cent.: from Greek _neuron_, special use of the literal sense 'sinew, tendon'. See NERVE.

USAGE In scientific sources the standard spelling is **neuron**. The spelling **neurone** is found only in non-technical sources.

neuropath /ˈnjʊərə(ʊ)paθ/ ▶ noun dated a person affected by nervous disease, or with an abnormally sensitive nervous system.

neuropathology ▶ noun [mass noun] the branch of medicine concerned with diseases of the nervous system.
– DERIVATIVES **neuropathological** adjective, **neuropathologist** noun.

neuropathy /njʊəˈrɒpəθi/ ▶ noun [mass noun] Medicine disease or dysfunction of one or more peripheral nerves, typically causing numbness or weakness.
– DERIVATIVES **neuropathic** adjective.

neuropeptide ▶ noun Biochemistry any of a group of compounds which act as neurotransmitters and are short-chain polypeptides.

neuropharmacology ▶ noun [mass noun] the branch of pharmacology that deals with the action of drugs on the nervous system.
– DERIVATIVES **neuropharmacologic** adjective, **neuropharmacological** adjective, **neuropharmacologist** noun.

neurophysiology ▶ noun [mass noun] the physiology of the nervous system.
– DERIVATIVES **neurophysiological** adjective, **neurophysiologist** noun.

neuropil /ˈnjʊərə(ʊ)pɪl/ (also **neuropile** /-paɪl/) ▶ noun Anatomy & Zoology a dense network of interwoven unmyelinated nerve fibres and their branches and synapses, together with glial filaments.
– ORIGIN late 19th cent.: probably an abbreviation of obsolete _neuropilema_, from Greek _neuron_ 'nerve' + _pilema_ 'felt'.

neuropsychiatry ▶ noun [mass noun] psychiatry relating mental or emotional disturbance to disordered brain function.
– DERIVATIVES **neuropsychiatric** adjective, **neuropsychiatrist** noun.

neuropsychology ▶ noun [mass noun] the study of the relationship between behaviour, emotion, and cognition on the one hand, and brain function on the other.
– DERIVATIVES **neuropsychological** adjective, **neuropsychologist** noun.

Neuroptera /ˌnjʊəˈrɒpt(ə)rə/ Entomology an order of predatory flying insects that includes the lacewings, alderflies, snake flies, and ant lions. They have four finely veined membranous wings.

■(**neuroptera**) [as plural noun] insects of this order.
– DERIVATIVES **neuropteran** noun & adjective, **neuropterous** adjective.
– ORIGIN modern Latin (plural), from **NEURO-** in the sense 'veined' + Greek *pteron* 'wing'.

neuroscience ▶ noun any of the sciences, such as neurochemistry and experimental psychology, which deal with the structure or function of the nervous system and brain.
■[mass noun] such sciences collectively.
– DERIVATIVES **neuroscientist** noun.

neurosis /ˌnjʊəˈrəʊsɪs/ ▶ noun (pl. **neuroses** /-siːz/) Medicine a relatively mild mental illness that is not caused by organic disease, involving symptoms of stress (depression, anxiety, obsessive behaviour, hypochondria) but not a radical loss of touch with reality. Compare with **PSYCHOSIS**.
■(in non-technical use) excessive and irrational anxiety or obsession: *apprehension over mounting debt has created a collective neurosis in the business world.*
– ORIGIN mid 18th cent.: modern Latin, from **NEURO-** 'of nerves' + **-OSIS**.

neurosurgery ▶ noun [mass noun] surgery performed on the nervous system, especially the brain and spinal cord.
– DERIVATIVES **neurosurgeon** noun, **neurosurgical** adjective.

neurosyphilis ▶ noun [mass noun] syphilis that involves the central nervous system.
– DERIVATIVES **neurosyphilitic** adjective & noun.

neurotic ▶ adjective Medicine suffering from, caused by, or relating to neurosis.
■abnormally sensitive, obsessive, or tense and anxious: *Alex was too jumpy, too neurotic.*
▶ noun a neurotic person.
– DERIVATIVES **neurotically** adverb, **neuroticism** noun.

neurotomy /ˌnjʊəˈrɒtəmi/ ▶ noun [mass noun] the surgical cutting of a nerve to produce sensory loss and relief of pain or to suppress involuntary movements.

neurotoxin /ˌnjʊərəʊˈtɒksɪn/ ▶ noun a poison which acts on the nervous system.
– DERIVATIVES **neurotoxic** adjective, **neurotoxicity** noun, **neurotoxicology** noun.

neurotransmitter ▶ noun Physiology a chemical substance which is released at the end of a nerve fibre by the arrival of a nerve impulse and, by diffusing across the synapse or junction, effects the transfer of the impulse to another nerve fibre, a muscle fibre, or some other structure.
– DERIVATIVES **neurotransmission** noun.

neurotrophic /ˌnjʊərə(ʊ)ˈtrəʊfɪk, -ˈtrɒfɪk/ ▶ adjective Physiology of or relating to the growth of nervous tissue.

neurotropic /ˌnjʊərə(ʊ)ˈtrəʊpɪk, -ˈtrɒpɪk/ ▶ adjective Medicine (of a virus, toxin, or chemical) tending to attack or affect the nervous system preferentially.
– DERIVATIVES **neurotropism** noun.

Neusiedler See /ˈnɔɪziːdlə ˌzeɪ/ a shallow lake in the steppe region between eastern Austria and NW Hungary. Hungarian name **FERTŐ TÓ**.

neuston /ˈnjuːstɒn/ ▶ noun [mass noun] Biology small aquatic organisms inhabiting the surface layer or moving on the surface film.
– DERIVATIVES **neustonic** adjective.
– ORIGIN early 20th cent.: via German from Greek, neuter of *neustos* 'swimming', on the pattern of *plankton*.

neuter ▶ adjective **1** of or denoting a gender of nouns in some languages, typically contrasting with masculine and feminine or common: *it is a neuter word in Greek.*
2 (of an animal) lacking developed sexual organs, or having had them removed.
■(of a plant or flower) having neither functional pistils nor functional stamens. ■(of a person) apparently having no sexual characteristics; asexual.
▶ noun **1** Grammar a neuter word.
■(**the neuter**) the neuter gender.
2 a non-fertile caste of social insect, especially a worker bee or ant.
■a castrated or spayed domestic animal. ■a person who appears to lack sexual characteristics.
▶ verb [with obj.] castrate or spay (a domestic animal): [as adj. **neutered**] *a neutered tomcat.*
■render ineffective; deprive of vigour or force: *disarmament negotiations that will neuter their military power.*
– ORIGIN late Middle English: via Old French from Latin *neuter* 'neither', from *ne-* 'not' + *uter* 'either'.

neutral ▶ adjective **1** not helping or supporting either of two opposing sides, especially states at war; impartial: *during the Second World War Portugal was neutral.*
■belonging to an impartial party, state, or group: *on neutral ground.* ■unbiased; disinterested: *neutral, expert scientific advice.*
2 having no strongly marked or positive characteristics or features: *the tone was neutral, devoid of sentiment | a fairly neutral background.*
■Chemistry neither acid nor alkaline; having a pH of about 7. ■electrically neither positive nor negative.
▶ noun **1** an impartial and uninvolved state or person: *he acted as a neutral between the parties | Sweden and its fellow neutrals.*
■an unbiased person.
2 [mass noun] a neutral colour or shade, especially light grey or beige.
3 [mass noun] a disengaged position of gears in which the engine is disconnected from the driven parts: *she slipped the gear into neutral.*
4 an electrically neutral point, terminal, conductor, or wire.
– DERIVATIVES **neutrality** noun, **neutrally** adverb.
– ORIGIN late Middle English (as a noun): from Latin *neutralis* 'of neuter gender', from Latin *neuter* (see **NEUTER**).

neutral axis ▶ noun Engineering a line or plane through a beam or plate connecting points at which no extension or compression occurs when it is bent.

neutral density filter ▶ noun a photographic or optical filter that absorbs light of all wavelengths to the same extent, causing overall dimming but no change in colour.

neutralism ▶ noun [mass noun] a policy of political neutrality.
– DERIVATIVES **neutralist** noun.

neutralize (also **-ise**) ▶ verb [with obj.] render (something) ineffective or harmless by applying an opposite force or effect: *impatience at his frailty began to neutralize her fear.*
■make (an acidic or alkaline substance) chemically neutral. ■disarm (a bomb or similar weapon). ■a euphemistic way of saying kill or destroy, especially in a covert or military operation.
– DERIVATIVES **neutralization** noun, **neutralizer** noun.
– ORIGIN mid 17th cent.: from French *neutraliser*, from medieval Latin *neutralizare*, from Latin *neutralis* (see **NEUTRAL**).

neutral zone ▶ noun the central area of an ice-hockey rink, lying between the two blue lines.

neutrino /njuːˈtriːnəʊ/ ▶ noun (pl. **-os**) a neutral subatomic particle with a mass close to zero and half-integral spin, which rarely reacts with normal matter. Three kinds of neutrinos are known, associated with the electron, muon, and tau particle.
– ORIGIN mid 20th cent.: from Italian, diminutive of *neutro* 'neutral'.

neutron ▶ noun a subatomic particle of about the same mass as a proton but without an electric charge, present in all atomic nuclei except those of ordinary hydrogen.
– ORIGIN early 20th cent.: from **NEUTRAL** + **-ON**.

neutron bomb ▶ noun a nuclear weapon that produces large numbers of neutrons rather than heat or blast like conventional nuclear weapons.

neutron star ▶ noun Astronomy a celestial object of very small radius (typically 30 km) and very high density, composed predominantly of closely packed neutrons. Neutron stars are thought to form by the gravitational collapse of the remnant of a massive star after a supernova explosion, provided that the star is insufficiently massive to produce a black hole.

neutrophil /ˈnjuːtrə(ʊ)fɪl/ ▶ noun Physiology a neutrophilic white blood cell.

neutrophilic ▶ adjective Physiology (of a cell or its contents) readily stained only by neutral dyes.
– ORIGIN late 19th cent.: from **NEUTRAL** + *-philic* (see **-PHILIA**).

Nev. ▶ abbreviation for Nevada.

Neva /ˈniːvə, njɪˈvɑː/ a river in NW Russia which flows 74 km (46 miles) westwards from Lake Ladoga to the Gulf of Finland, passing through St Petersburg.

Nevada /nɪˈvɑːdə/ a state of the western US; pop. 1,201,830 (1990); capital, Carson City. Acquired from Mexico in 1848, it became the 36th state of the US in 1864.
– DERIVATIVES **Nevadan** adjective & noun.

névé /ˈnɛveɪ/ ▶ noun another term for **FIRN**.
– ORIGIN mid 19th cent.: from Swiss French, literally 'glacier', based on Latin *nix*, *niv-* 'snow'.

never ▶ adverb **1** at no time in the past or future; on no occasion; not ever: *they had never been camping in their lives | I will **never ever** forget it.*
2 not at all: *he never turned up.*
■[as exclamation] Brit. informal (expressing surprise) surely not: *What, you, Annabel? Never!*
– PHRASES **never fear** see **FEAR**. **never mind** see **MIND**. **never a one** none; not one: *the gaunt figures strode ever onwards; never a one turned his head from his goal.* **never say die** see **DIE**[1]. **well I never!** (or **I never did!**) informal expressing great surprise or indignation: *Well I never—that's not like you!*
– ORIGIN Old English *nǣfre*, from *ne* 'not' + *ǣfre* 'ever'.

never-ending ▶ adjective (especially of something unpleasant) having or seeming to have no end.

nevermore ▶ adverb poetic/literary at no future time; never again: *I order you gone, nevermore to return.*

Never-Never 1 the unpopulated desert country of the interior of Australia; the remote outback.
2 (**Never-Never Land** (or **Country**)) a region of Northern Territory, Australia, south-east of Darwin; chief town, Katherine.
– ORIGIN so named from the notion that one might never return from such remote country.

never-never ▶ noun (**the never-never**) Brit. informal hire purchase: *buying a telly **on the never-never**.*

never-never land ▶ noun an imaginary utopian place or situation: *a never-never land of unreal prices and easy bank loans.*
– ORIGIN often with allusion to the ideal country in J. M. Barrie's *Peter Pan*.

Nevers /nəˈvɛː, French nɛvɛʀ/ a city in central France, on the Loire; pop. 43,890 (1990). It was capital of the former province of Nivernais.

nevertheless ▶ adverb in spite of that; notwithstanding; all the same: *statements which, although literally true, are nevertheless misleading.*

Neville /ˈnɛvɪl/, Richard, see **WARWICK**[2].

Nevis /ˈniːvɪs/ one of the Leeward Islands in the Caribbean, part of St Kitts and Nevis; capital, Charlestown.
– DERIVATIVES **Nevisian** /niːˈvɪsɪən/ noun & adjective.

Nevsky, Alexander, see **ALEXANDER NEVSKY**.

nevus ▶ noun (pl. **nevi**) US spelling of **NAEVUS**.

new ▶ adjective **1** not existing before; made, introduced, or discovered recently or now for the first time: *new crop varieties | this tendency is not new |* [as noun **the new**] *a fascinating mix of the old and the new.*
■in original condition; not worn or used: *check that the wiring is new and in good condition.* ■not previously used or owned: *a second-hand bus cost a fraction of a new one.* ■of recent origin or arrival: *a new baby.* ■(of food or drink) freshly or recently produced. ■(of vegetables) dug or harvested early in the season: *new potatoes.*
2 already existing but seen, experienced, or acquired recently or now for the first time: *her new bike | a new sensation.*
■[predic.] (**new to**) unfamiliar or strange to (someone): *a way of living that was new to me.* ■[predic.] (**new to/at**) (of a person) inexperienced at or unaccustomed to doing (something): *I'm quite new to gardening.* ■different from a recent previous one: *I have a new assistant | this would be her new home.* ■in addition to another or others already existing: *recruiting new pilots overseas.* ■[in place names] discovered or founded later than and named after: *New York.*
3 just beginning and regarded as better than what went before: *starting a new life.*
■(of a person) reinvigorated or restored: *a bottle of pills would make him a new man.* ■(**the new**) renewed or reformed: *the new South Africa.* ■superseding another or others of the same kind, and advanced in method or theory: *the new architecture.* ■reviving another or others of the same kind: *the New Bohemians.* ■recently affected or produced by social change: *the new rich.*
▶ adverb [usu. in combination] newly; recently: *new-mown hay | he was enjoying his **new-found** freedom.*

– PHRASES **a new one** informal an account, idea, or joke not previously encountered by someone: *its separate vapour tank was a new one on me.* **what's new 1** (said on greeting someone) what's going on? how are you? **2** as is the usual situation: *United were unlucky ... so what's new?*
– DERIVATIVES **newish** adjective, **newness** noun.
– ORIGIN Old English *nīwe*, *nēowe*, of Germanic origin; related to Dutch *nieuw* and German *neu*, from an Indo-European root shared by Sanskrit *nava*, Latin *novus*, and Greek *neos* 'new'.

New Age ▶ noun [mass noun] a broad movement characterized by alternative approaches to traditional Western culture, with an interest in spirituality, mysticism, holism, and environmentalism: [as modifier] *the New Age movement.*
– DERIVATIVES **New Ager** noun, **New Agey** adjective.

New Age music ▶ noun [mass noun] a style of chiefly instrumental music characterized by light melodic harmonies, improvisation, and sounds reproduced from the natural world, intended to promote serenity.

New Age traveller ▶ noun see TRAVELLER.

New Amsterdam former name for NEW YORK.

Newark /ˈnjuːək/ an industrial city in New Jersey; pop. 275,220 (1990).

newbie ▶ noun (pl. **-ies**) an inexperienced newcomer, especially in computing.

newborn ▶ adjective (of a child or animal) recently or just born: *newborn babies* | figurative *a newborn star.*
■ figurative regenerated: *Birmingham is establishing its image as a thriving newborn European city.*
▶ noun a recently born child or animal.

New Britain a mountainous island in the South Pacific, administratively part of Papua New Guinea, lying off the NE coast of New Guinea; pop. 311,955 (1990); capital, Rabaul.

New Brunswick a maritime province on the SE coast of Canada; pop. 726,000 (1991); capital, Fredericton. It was first settled by the French and ceded to Britain in 1713. It became one of the original four provinces in the Dominion of Canada in 1867.

newbuilding ▶ noun (also **newbuild**) a newly constructed ship.
■ [mass noun] the construction of ships.

Newby, (George) Eric (b.1919), English travel writer. Notable works: *A Short Walk in the Hindu Kush* (1958), *A Traveller's Life* (1982), and *A Small Place in Italy* (1994).

New Caledonia an island in the South Pacific, east of Australia; pop. 178,000 (1994); capital, Nouméa. Since 1946 it has formed, with its dependencies, a French overseas territory; the French annexed the island in 1853. French name NOUVELLE-CALÉDONIE.
– DERIVATIVES **New Caledonian** noun & adjective.
– ORIGIN named, by Captain Cook in 1774, after the Roman name *Caledonia* 'Scotland'.

New Carthage see CARTAGENA (sense 1).

Newcastle[1] **1** an industrial city in NE England, a port on the River Tyne; pop. 263,000 (1991). Full name NEWCASTLE-UPON-TYNE.
2 an industrial town in Staffordshire, just south-west of Stoke-on-Trent; pop. 117,400 (1991). Full name NEWCASTLE-UNDER-LYME.
3 an industrial port on the SE coast of Australia, in New South Wales; pop. 262,160 (1991).

Newcastle[2], Thomas Pelham-Holles, 1st Duke of (1693–1768), British Whig statesman, Prime Minister 1754–6 and 1757–62. During his second term in office he headed a coalition with William Pitt the Elder.

Newcastle disease ▶ noun [mass noun] an acute infectious viral fever affecting birds, especially poultry. Also called FOWL PEST.
– ORIGIN 1920s: so named because it was first recorded near Newcastle in 1927.

New Comedy a style of ancient Greek comedy associated with Menander, in which young lovers typically undergo endless vicissitudes in the company of stock fictional characters.

Newcomen /ˈnjuːˌkʌmən/, Thomas (1663–1729), English engineer, developer of the first practical steam engine. His beam engine to operate a pump for the removal of water from mines was first erected in Worcestershire in 1712.

newcomer ▶ noun a person who has recently arrived in a place or joined a group.
■ a novice in a particular activity or situation.

New Commonwealth those countries which have achieved self-government within the Commonwealth since 1945.

New Criticism an influential movement in literary criticism in the mid 20th century, which stressed the importance of focusing on the text itself rather than being concerned with external biographical or social considerations. Associated with the movement were John Crowe Ransom, who first used the term in 1941, I. A. Richards, and Cleanth Brooks.

New Deal the economic measures introduced by Franklin D. Roosevelt in 1933 to counteract the effects of the Great Depression. It involved a massive public works programme, complemented by the large-scale granting of loans, and succeeded in reducing unemployment by between 7 and 10 million.

New Delhi see DELHI.

newel /ˈnjuːəl/ ▶ noun the central supporting pillar of a spiral or winding staircase.
■ (also **newel post**) a post at the head or foot of a flight of stairs, supporting a handrail.
– ORIGIN late Middle English: from Old French *nouel* 'knob', from medieval Latin *nodellus*, diminutive of Latin *nodus* 'knot'.

New England an area on the NE coast of the US, comprising the states of Maine, New Hampshire, Vermont, Massachusetts, Rhode Island, and Connecticut.
– DERIVATIVES **New Englander** noun.

New English Bible (abbrev.: **NEB**) ▶ noun a modern English translation of the Bible, published in the UK in 1961–70 and revised (as the **Revised English Bible**) in 1989.

newfangled ▶ adjective derogatory different from what one is used to; objectionably new: *I've no time for such newfangled nonsense.*
– ORIGIN Middle English: from *newfangle* (now dialect) 'liking what is new', from the adverb NEW + a second element related to an Old English word meaning 'to take'.

new-fashioned ▶ adjective of a new type or style; up to date: *the development of a new-fashioned kind of language awareness.*

New Forest an area of heath and woodland in southern Hampshire. It has been reserved as Crown property since 1079, originally by William I as a royal hunting area, and is noted for its ponies.

Newfoundland[1] /ˈnjuːfəndlənd, -land, -ˈfaʊndlənd/ a large island off the east coast of Canada, at the mouth of the St Lawrence River. In 1949 it was united with Labrador (as Newfoundland and Labrador) to form a province of Canada.
– DERIVATIVES **Newfoundlander** noun.

Newfoundland[2] /ˈnjuːf(ə)n(d)lənd, -land, njuːˈfaʊndlənd/ (in full **Newfoundland dog**) ▶ noun a dog of a very large breed with a thick coarse coat.

Newfoundland and Labrador a province of Canada, comprising the island of Newfoundland and the Labrador coast of eastern Canada; pop. 573,500 (1991); capital, St John's. It joined the confederation of Canada in 1949.

Newgate a former London prison whose unsanitary conditions became notorious in the 18th century before the building was burnt down in the Gordon Riots of 1780. A new edifice was erected on the same spot but was demolished in 1902 to make way for the Central Criminal Court.

New Georgia a group of islands in the Solomon Islands, north-west of Guadalcanal.
■ the largest of these islands.

New Guinea an island in the western South Pacific, off the north coast of Australia, the second largest island in the world (following Greenland). It is divided into two parts; the western half comprises part of Irian Jaya, a province of Indonesia, the eastern half forms part of Papua New Guinea.
– DERIVATIVES **New Guinean** noun & adjective.

New Hampshire a state in the north-eastern US, on the Atlantic coast; pop. 1,109,250 (1990); capital, Concord. It was settled from England in the 17th century and was one of the original thirteen states of the Union (1788).

New Hebrides former name (until 1980) for VANUATU.

newie ▶ noun (pl. **-ies**) informal, chiefly Brit. something or someone new, especially a newly released music record.

Ne Win /ˌneɪ ˈwɪn/ (b.1911), Burmese general and socialist statesman, Prime Minister 1958–60, head of state 1962–74, and President 1974–81. After the military coup in 1962 he established a military dictatorship and formed a one-party state.

New International Version (abbrev.: **NIV**) ▶ noun a modern English translation of the Bible published in 1973–8.

New Ireland an island in the South Pacific, administratively part of Papua New Guinea, lying to the north of New Britain; pop. 87,190 (1990); capital, Kavieng.

New Jersey a state in the north-eastern US, on the Atlantic coast; pop. 7,730,190 (1990); capital, Trenton. Colonized by Dutch settlers and ceded to Britain in 1664, it became one of the original thirteen states of the Union (1787).
– DERIVATIVES **New Jerseyan** noun & adjective.

New Jerusalem Christian Theology the abode of the blessed in heaven (with reference to Rev. 21:2).
■ [as noun **a New Jerusalem**] an ideal place or situation.

New Jerusalem Church a Christian sect instituted by followers of Emanuel Swedenborg.

New Kingdom a period of ancient Egyptian history (c.1550–1070 BC, 18th–20th dynasty).

new-laid ▶ adjective (of an egg) freshly laid.

Newlands, John Alexander Reina (1837–98), English industrial chemist. He proposed a form of periodic table shortly before Dmitri Mendeleev, based on a supposed **law of octaves** according to which similar chemical properties recurred in every eighth element.

New Look a style of women's clothing introduced in 1947 by Christian Dior, featuring calf-length full skirts and a generous use of material in contrast to wartime austerity.

newly ▶ adverb **1** recently: *a newly acquired hi-fi system.*
2 afresh; again: *social confidence for the newly single.*
■ in a new or different manner.

newly-wed ▶ noun (usu. **newly-weds**) a recently married person.

Newman[1], Barnett (1905–70), American painter. A seminal figure in colour-field painting, he juxtaposed large blocks of uniform colour with narrow marginal strips of contrasting colours.

Newman[2], John Henry (1801–90), English prelate and theologian. A founder of the Oxford Movement, in 1845 he turned to Roman Catholicism, becoming a cardinal in 1879.

Newman[3], Paul (b.1925), American actor and film director. Among his many films are *Butch Cassidy and the Sundance Kid* (1969), *The Sting* (1973), *The Color of Money* (1987), for which he won an Oscar, and *The Glass Menagerie* (1987), which he also directed.

new man ▶ noun a man who rejects sexist attitudes and the traditional male role, especially in the context of domestic responsibilities and childcare.

Newman–Keuls test /kɜːls/ ▶ noun Statistics a test for assessing the significance of differences between all possible pairs of different sets of observations, with a fixed error rate for the whole set of comparisons.
– ORIGIN mid 20th cent.: named after D. *Newman* (fl. 1939), English statistician, and M. *Keuls* (fl. 1952), Dutch horticulturalist.

Newmarket[1] a town in eastern England, in Suffolk; pop. 16,130 (1981). It is a noted horse-racing centre and headquarters of the Jockey Club.

Newmarket[2] ▶ noun **1** [mass noun] a card game in which the players put down cards in sequence, hoping to be the first to play all their cards and also to play certain special cards on which bets have been placed.
2 (also **Newmarket coat**) a close-fitting overcoat of a style originally worn for riding.

new maths (N. Amer. **new math**) ▶ noun [mass noun] a system of teaching mathematics to younger children, with emphasis on investigation and discovery by them and on set theory.

New Mexico a state in the south-western US, on the border with Mexico; pop. 1,515,070 (1990);

capital, Santa Fe. It was obtained from Mexico in 1848 and 1854, and in 1912 it became the 47th state of the US.
– DERIVATIVES **New Mexican** adjective & noun.

New Model Army an army created in 1645 by Oliver Cromwell to fight for the Parliamentary cause in the English Civil War. Led by Thomas Fairfax, it was a disciplined and well-trained army which later came to possess considerable political influence.

new moon ▶ noun the phase of the moon when it first appears as a slender crescent, shortly after its conjunction with the sun. ■ (mass noun) the time when this occurs. ■ (mass noun) Astronomy the time at which the moon is in conjunction with the sun, when it is not visible from the earth.

new order ▶ noun a new system, regime, or government: *a new economic order.* ■ (**New Order**) Hitler's planned reorganization of Europe under Nazi rule.

New Orleans /ˈɔːliːnz, ɔːˈliːnz/ a city and port in SE Louisiana, on the Mississippi; pop. 496,940 (1990). It was founded by the French in 1718 and named after the Duc d'Orléans, regent of France. It is noted for its annual Mardi Gras celebrations and for its association with the development of blues and jazz.

New Plymouth a port in New Zealand, on the west coast of North Island; pop. 48,520 (1991).

Newport an industrial town and port in South Wales, on the Bristol Channel; pop. 129,900 (1991). Welsh name **CASNEWYDD**.

Newport News a city in SE Virginia, at the mouth of the James River on the Hampton Roads estuary; pop. 170,045 (1990).

New Red Sandstone ▶ noun Geology a series of sedimentary rocks, chiefly soft red sandstones, belonging to the Permo–Triassic system of NW Europe.

New Revised Standard Version (abbrev.: **NRSV**) ▶ noun a modern English translation of the Bible, based on the Revised Standard Version and published in 1990.

New Romantic ▶ adjective denoting a style of popular music and fashion popular in Britain in the early 1980s in which both men and women wore make-up and dressed in flamboyant clothes. ▶ noun a performer or enthusiast of New Romantic music.

Newry /ˈnjʊəri/ a port in the south-east of Northern Ireland, in County Down; pop. 19,400 (1981).

news ▶ noun (mass noun) newly received or noteworthy information, especially about recent or important events: *I've got some good news for you.* ■ (**the news**) a broadcast or published report of news: *he was back in the news again.* ■ (**news to**) informal information not previously known to someone: *this was hardly news to her.* ■ a person or thing considered interesting enough to be reported in the news: *Chanel became the hottest news in fashion.*
– PHRASES **be good news** be an asset; be commendable or admirable. **no news is good news** proverb without information to the contrary you can assume that all is well.
– ORIGIN late Middle English: plural of **NEW**, translating Old French *noveles* or medieval Latin *nova* 'new things'.

news agency ▶ noun an organization that collects news items and distributes them to newspapers or broadcasters.

newsagent ▶ noun Brit. a person or a shop selling newspapers, magazines, and other items such as stationery and confectionery.

newsboy ▶ noun a boy who sells or delivers newspapers.

news bulletin ▶ noun Brit. a short radio or television broadcast of news reports.

newscast ▶ noun a radio or television broadcast of news reports.

newscaster ▶ noun a newsreader.

news conference ▶ noun a press conference.

news desk ▶ noun the department of a broadcasting organization or newspaper responsible for collecting and reporting the news.

newsflash ▶ noun a single item of important news broadcast separately and often interrupting other programmes.

newsgroup ▶ noun a group of Internet users who exchange e-mail messages on a topic of mutual interest.

news hound ▶ noun informal a newspaper reporter.

newsie ▶ noun (pl. **-ies**) variant spelling of **NEWSY**.

newsletter ▶ noun a bulletin issued periodically to the members of a society, business, or organization.

newsman ▶ noun (pl. **-men**) a male reporter or journalist.

New South Wales a state of SE Australia; pop. 5,827,400 (1990); capital, Sydney. First colonized from Britain in 1788, it was federated with the other states of Australia in 1901.

New Spain a former Spanish viceroyalty established in Central and North America in 1535, centred on present-day Mexico City. It comprised all the land under Spanish control north of the Isthmus of Panama, including parts of the southern US. It also came to include the Spanish possessions in the Caribbean and the Philippines. The viceroyalty was abolished in 1821, when Mexico achieved independence.

newspaper ▶ noun a printed publication (usually issued daily or weekly) consisting of folded unstapled sheets and containing news, articles, advertisements, and correspondence.

newspaperman ▶ noun (pl. **-men**) a male newspaper journalist.

newspaperwoman ▶ noun (pl. **-women**) a female newspaper journalist.

newspeak ▶ noun (mass noun) ambiguous euphemistic language used chiefly in political propaganda.
– ORIGIN 1949: the name of an artificial official language in George Orwell's *Nineteen Eighty-Four.*

newsprint ▶ noun (mass noun) cheap, low-quality absorbent printing paper made from coarse wood pulp and used chiefly for newspapers.

newsreader ▶ noun Brit. a person who reads out broadcast news bulletins. ■ Computing a computer program for reading e-mail messages posted to newsgroups.

newsreel ▶ noun a short film of news and current affairs, formerly made for showing as part of the programme in a cinema.

newsroom ▶ noun the area in a newspaper or broadcasting office where news is processed.

news-sheet ▶ noun a simple form of newspaper; a newsletter.

news-stand ▶ noun a stand or stall for the sale of newspapers.

New Stone Age the Neolithic period.

New Style (abbrev.: **NS**) ▶ noun (mass noun) the method of calculating dates using the Gregorian calendar. It superseded the use of the Julian calendar in Scotland in 1600 and in England and Wales in 1752.

newsvendor ▶ noun Brit. a newspaper seller.

news wire ▶ noun an up-to-date news service on the Internet.

newsworthy ▶ adjective topical; noteworthy as news: *a newsworthy event.*
– DERIVATIVES **newsworthiness** noun.

newsy ▶ adjective (**newsier, newsiest**) informal full of news, especially of a personal kind: *short, newsy letters.* ▶ noun (also **newsie**) (pl. **-ies**) informal, chiefly US a reporter. ■ informal, chiefly US & Austral. a newsboy.

newt ▶ noun a small slender-bodied amphibian with lungs and a well-developed tail, typically spending its adult life on land and returning to water to breed.
● *Triturus* and other genera, family Salamandridae: numerous species.
– ORIGIN late Middle English: from *an ewt* (ewt from Old English *efeta*: see **EFT**), interpreted (by wrong division) as *a newt.*

New Territories part of Hong Kong on the south coast of mainland China, lying to the north of the Kowloon peninsula and including the islands of Lantau, Tsing Yi, and Lamma.

New Testament ▶ noun the second part of the Christian Bible, written originally in Greek and recording the life and teachings of Christ and his

earliest followers. It includes the four Gospels, the Acts of the Apostles, twenty-one Epistles by St Paul and others, and the book of Revelation.

Newton, Sir Isaac (1642–1727), English mathematician and physicist, considered the greatest single influence on theoretical physics until Einstein.

In his *Principia Mathematica* (1687), Newton gave a mathematical description of the laws of mechanics and gravitation, and applied these to planetary motion. *Opticks* (1704) records his optical experiments and theories, including the discovery that white light is made up of a mixture of colours. His work in mathematics included the binomial theorem and differential calculus.

newton (abbrev.: **N**) ▶ noun Physics the SI unit of force. It is equal to the force that would give a mass of one kilogram an acceleration of one metre per second per second, and is equivalent to 100,000 dynes.
– ORIGIN early 20th cent.: named after Sir Isaac **NEWTON**.

Newtonian ▶ adjective relating to or arising from the work of Sir Isaac Newton. ■ formulated or behaving according to the principles of classical physics.

Newtonian mechanics ▶ plural noun [usu. treated as sing.] the system of mechanics which relies on Newton's laws of motion concerning the relations between forces acting and motions occurring.

Newtonian telescope ▶ noun Astronomy a reflecting telescope in which the light from the main mirror is deflected by a small, flat secondary mirror set at 45°, sending it to a magnifying eyepiece in the side of the telescope.

Newton's laws of motion Physics three fundamental laws of classical physics. The first states that a body continues in a state of rest or uniform motion in a straight line unless it is acted on by an external force. The second states that the rate of change of momentum of a moving body is proportional to the force acting to produce the change. The third states that if one body exerts a force on another, there is an equal and opposite force (or reaction) exerted by the second body on the first.

Newton's rings ▶ plural noun Optics a set of concentric circular fringes seen around the point of contact when a convex lens is placed on a plane surface (or on another lens), caused by interference between light reflected from the upper and lower surfaces.

new town ▶ noun a planned urban centre created in an undeveloped or rural area, especially with government sponsorship.

new wave ▶ noun (mass noun) **1** another term for **NOUVELLE VAGUE**. **2** a style of rock music popular in the 1970s, deriving from punk but generally more poppy in sound and less aggressive in performance.

New World North and South America regarded collectively in relation to Europe, especially after the early voyages of European explorers.

new year ▶ noun the calendar year just begun or about to begin: *Happy New Year!* ■ the first few days or weeks of a year: *the band is playing at Wembley in the new year.* ■ the period immediately before and after 31 December: *the facilities are closed over Christmas and New Year.*
– PHRASES **New Year's** informal, chiefly N. Amer. New Year's Eve or New Year's Day. **see the new year in** stay up until after midnight on 31 December to celebrate the start of a new year.

New Year's Day ▶ noun the first day of the year; in the modern Western calendar, 1 January.

New Year's Eve ▶ noun the last day of the year; in the modern Western calendar, 31 December. ■ the evening of this day, typically marked with a celebration.

New York 1 a state in the north-eastern US; pop. 17,990,445 (1990); capital, Albany. It stretches from the Canadian border and Lake Ontario in the northwest to the Atlantic in the east. Originally settled by the Dutch, it was surrendered to the British in 1664 and was one of the original thirteen states of the Union (1788). **2** a major city and port in the south-east of New York State, situated on the Atlantic coast at the mouth of the Hudson River; pop. 7,322,560 (1990). The city is situated mainly on islands, linked by

n

bridges, and comprises five boroughs: Manhattan, Brooklyn, the Bronx, Queens, and Staten Island. Manhattan is the economic and cultural heart of the city, containing the Stock Exchange in Wall Street and the headquarters of the United Nations. Former name (until 1664) **New Amsterdam**.
– DERIVATIVES **New Yorker** noun.

New Zealand an island country in the South Pacific about 1,900 km (1,200 miles) east of Australia; pop. 3,434,950 (1991); languages, English (official), Maori; capital, Wellington. Maori name **Aotearoa**.

New Zealand consists of two major islands (North and South Islands) separated by Cook Strait, and several smaller islands. The original discoverers of the country were the Maoris. The first European to sight New Zealand was the Dutch navigator Abel Tasman in 1642; the islands were circumnavigated by Captain James Cook, and came under British sovereignty in 1840. Full dominion status was granted in 1907, and independence in 1931 within the Commonwealth.

– DERIVATIVES **New Zealander** noun.

New Zealand flatworm ▶ noun a speckled brown terrestrial flatworm up to 15 cm in length, accidentally introduced from New Zealand to Britain where it is destroying earthworm populations.
• *Artioposthia triangulata*, order Tricladida, class Turbellaria.

New Zealand flax ▶ noun another term for **flax-lily**.

New Zealand rug ▶ noun a strong waterproof rug for a horse, used during the winter.

next ▶ adjective **1** (of a time or season) coming immediately after the time of writing or speaking: *we'll go next year | next week's Cup Final.*
■ (of a day of the week) nearest (or the nearest but one) after the present: *not this Wednesday, next Wednesday |* [postpositive] *on Monday next.* ■ (of an event or occasion) occurring directly after the present one in time, without anything of the same kind intervening: *the next election | next time I'll bring a hat.*
2 coming immediately after the present one in order or space: *the woman in the next room | the next chapter | who's next?*
■ coming immediately after the present one in rank: *building materials were next in importance.*
▶ adverb on the first or soonest occasion after the present; immediately afterwards: *wondering what would happen next | next, I heard the sound of voices.*
■ [with superlative] following in the specified order: *Jo was the next oldest after Martin.*
▶ noun the next person or thing: *one moment he wasn't there, the next he was | the week* ***after next.***
▶ preposition archaic next to: *he plodded along next him.*
▶ determiner **(a next)** W. Indian another: *every year sales down by a next ten per cent again.*
– PHRASES **next in line** immediately below the present holder of a position in order of succession: *he is* ***next in line*** *to the throne.* **next to 1** in or into a position immediately to one side of; beside: *we sat next to each other.* **2** following in order or importance: *next to buying a whole new wardrobe, nothing lifts the spirits quite like a new hairdo!* **3** almost: *Charles knew* ***next to nothing*** *about farming.* **4** in comparison with: *next to her I felt like a fraud.* **the next world** (according to some religious beliefs) the place where one goes after death. **what next** (or **whatever next**) an expression of surprise or amazement.
– ORIGIN Old English *nēhsta* 'nearest', superlative of *nēah* 'nigh'; compare with Dutch *naast* and German *nächste*.

next best ▶ adjective [attrib.] second in order of preference; to be preferred if one's first choice is not available: ***the next best thing*** *to flying is gliding.*

next door ▶ adverb in or to the next house or room: *the caretaker lives next door.*
▶ adjective **(next-door)** living or situated next door: *next-door neighbours.*
▶ noun [mass noun] the building, room, or people next door: *next door's dog | a bleary-eyed man emerged from next door.*
– PHRASES **the boy** (or **girl**) **next door** a person or type of person perceived as familiar, approachable, and dependable, typically in the context of a romantic partnership. **next door to** in the next house or room to: *the newsagent next door to Mr Afzal's store.* ■ nearly; almost; near to: *she thought George was next door to a saint.*

next of kin ▶ noun [treated as sing. or pl.] a person's closest living relative or relatives.

nexus /ˈnɛksəs/ ▶ noun (pl. same or **nexuses**) a connection or series of connections linking two or more things: *the nexus between industry and political power.*
■ a connected group or series: *a nexus of ideas.* ■ the central and most important point or place: *the nexus of any government in this country is No. 10.*
– ORIGIN mid 17th cent.: from Latin, 'a binding together', from *nex-* 'bound', from the verb *nectere*.

Ney /neɪ/, Michel (1768–1815), French marshal. He was one of Napoleon's leading generals, and commanded the French cavalry at Waterloo (1815).

Nez Percé /nɛz ˈpəːs, ˈpɛːseɪ/ ▶ noun (pl. same or **Nez Percés**) **1** a member of an American Indian people of central Idaho.
2 [mass noun] the Penutian language of this people, now with few speakers.
▶ adjective of or relating to this people or their language.
– ORIGIN French, literally 'pierced nose'.

NF ▶ abbreviation for ■ National Front. ■ Newfoundland (in official postal use).

NFL ▶ abbreviation for National Football League (the top professional league for American football in the US).

Nfld ▶ abbreviation for Newfoundland.

NFU ▶ abbreviation for (in the UK) National Farmers' Union.

ngaio /ˈnʌɪəʊ/ ▶ noun (pl. **-os**) a small New Zealand tree with edible fruit and light white timber.
• *Myoporum laetum*, family Myoporaceae.
– ORIGIN mid 19th cent.: from Maori.

Ngaliema, Mount /(ə)ŋ,gɑːlɪˈeɪmə/ Zairean name for Mount Stanley (see **Stanley, Mount**).

Ngamiland /(ə)ŋˈgɑːmɪland/ a region in NW Botswana, north of the Kalahari Desert. It includes the Okavango marshes and Lake Ngami.

Ngata /ˈnɑːtə/, Sir Apirana Turupa (1874–1950), New Zealand Maori leader and politician. As Minister for Native Affairs he devoted much time to Maori resettlement, seeking to preserve the characteristic elements of their life and culture.

Ngbandi /(ə)ŋˈbandi/ ▶ noun [mass noun] a Bantu language of northern Zaire (Democratic Republic of Congo).
▶ adjective of or relating to this language.
– ORIGIN the name in Ngbandi.

NGO ▶ abbreviation for non-governmental organization.

ngoma /(ə)ŋˈgəʊmə/ ▶ noun (in East Africa) a dance; a night of dancing and music.
– ORIGIN Kiswahili, literally 'drum, dance, music'.

Ngoni /(ə)ŋˈgəʊni/ ▶ noun (pl. same or **Ngonis**) **1** a member of a people now living chiefly in Malawi.
2 **(ngoni)** a kind of traditional African drum.
▶ adjective of or relating to the Ngoni.
– ORIGIN a local name.

Ngorongoro /(ə)ŋ,gɔːr(ə)ŋˈgɔːrəʊ/ a huge extinct volcanic crater in the Great Rift Valley in NE Tanzania, 326 sq. km (126 sq. miles) in area.

ngultrum /(ə)ŋˈgʊltrəm/ ▶ noun (pl. same) the basic monetary unit of Bhutan, equal to 100 chetrum.
– ORIGIN Dzongkha.

Nguni /(ə)ŋˈguːni/ ▶ noun (pl. same) **1** a member of a group of Bantu-speaking peoples living mainly in southern Africa.
2 [mass noun] the group of closely related Bantu languages, including Xhosa, Zulu, Swazi, and Ndebele, spoken by this group of peoples.
▶ adjective of or relating to this group of peoples or their languages.
– ORIGIN from Zulu.

ngwee /(ə)ŋˈgweɪ/ ▶ noun (pl. same) a monetary unit of Zambia, equal to one hundredth of a kwacha.
– ORIGIN a local word.

NH ▶ abbreviation for New Hampshire (in official postal use).

NHS ▶ abbreviation for (in the UK) National Health Service.

Nhulunbuy /,njuːlənˈbʌɪ/ a bauxite-mining centre on the NE coast of Arnhem Land in Northern Territory, Australia; pop. 3,800 (1986).

NI ▶ abbreviation for ■ (in the UK) National Insurance. ■ Northern Ireland. ■ (in New Zealand) North Island.

Ni ▶ symbol for the chemical element nickel.

niacin /ˈnʌɪəsɪn/ ▶ noun another term for **nicotinic acid**.

Niagara Falls /nʌɪˈag(ə)rə/ the waterfalls on the Niagara River, consisting of two principal parts separated by Goat Island: the Horseshoe Falls adjoining the west (Canadian) bank, which fall 47 m (158 ft), and the American Falls adjoining the east (American) bank, which fall 50 m (167 ft).
■ a city in upper New York State situated on the right bank of the Niagara River beside the Falls; pop. 61,840 (1990). ■ a city in Canada, in southern Ontario, situated on the left bank of the Niagara River beside the Falls, opposite the city of Niagara Falls, US, to which it is linked by bridges; pop. 75,400 (1991).

Niagara River a river of North America, flowing northwards for 56 km (35 miles) from Lake Erie to Lake Ontario, and forming part of the border between Canada and the US.

Niamey /njɑːˈmeɪ/ the capital of Niger, a port on the River Niger; pop. 410,000 (1994).

nib ▶ noun **1** the pointed end part of a pen, which distributes the ink on the writing surface.
■ a pointed or projecting part of an object.
2 **(nibs)** shelled and crushed coffee or cocoa beans.
3 a speck of solid matter in a coat of paint or varnish.
– DERIVATIVES **nibbed** adjective.
– ORIGIN late 16th cent. (in the sense 'beak, nose'): probably from Middle Dutch *nib* or Middle Low German *nibbe*, variant of *nebbe* 'beak' (see **neb**).

nibble ▶ verb take small bites out of: [with obj.] *he sat nibbling a biscuit |* [no obj.] *she* ***nibbled at*** *her food.*
■ [no obj.] eat in small amounts, especially between meals. ■ gently bite at (a part of the body), especially amorously or nervously: [with obj.] *Tamar nibbled her bottom lip |* [no obj.] *he* ***nibbled at*** *her earlobe.* ■ figurative gradually erode or eat away: [no obj.] *inflation was* ***nibbling away at*** *spending power.* ■ [no obj.] figurative show cautious interest in a project or proposal: *there's an American agent nibbling.*
▶ noun [in sing.] an instance of nibbling something.
■ a small piece of food bitten off. ■ **(nibbles)** informal small savoury snacks, typically eaten before a meal or with drinks.
– ORIGIN late 15th cent.: probably of Low German or Dutch origin; compare with Low German *nibbeln* 'gnaw'.

nibbler ▶ noun **1** a person who habitually nibbles at food.
2 a cutting tool in which a rapidly reciprocating punch knocks out a line of overlapping small holes from a metal sheet.

Nibelung /ˈniːbəlʊŋ/ ▶ noun (pl. **Nibelungs** or **Nibelungen** /-,lʊŋ(ə)n/) Germanic Mythology **1** a member of a Scandinavian race of dwarfs, owners of a hoard of gold and magic treasures, who were ruled by Nibelung, king of Nibelheim (land of mist).
2 (in the Nibelungenlied) a supporter of Siegfried or one of the Burgundians who stole the hoard from him.
– ORIGIN from Old High German, from *nibel* 'mist' + the patronymic ending *-ung*.

Nibelungenlied /ˈniːbəlʊŋən,liːd, German ˈniːbəlʊŋən,liːt/ a 13th-century German poem, embodying a story found in the (Poetic) Edda, telling of the life and death of Siegfried, a prince of the Netherlands. There have been many adaptations of the story, including Wagner's epic music drama *Der Ring des Nibelungen* (1848–74).
– ORIGIN German, from the name **Nibelung** + *Lied* 'song'.

niblet ▶ noun a small piece of food.
– ORIGIN late 19th cent.: from **nibble** + **-let**.

niblick /ˈnɪblɪk/ ▶ noun Golf, dated an iron with a heavy, lofted head, such as a nine-iron, used especially for playing out of bunkers.
– ORIGIN mid 19th cent.: of unknown origin.

nibs ▶ noun **(his nibs)** informal a mock title used to refer to a self-important man, especially one in authority.
– ORIGIN early 19th cent.: of unknown origin; compare with earlier *nabs*, used similarly with a possessive adjective as in *his nabs*, on the pattern of references to the aristocracy such as *his lordship*.

NIC ▶ abbreviation for ■ (in the UK) National Insurance contribution. ■ newly industrialized country. ■ Nicaragua (international vehicle registration).

NiCad /ˈnʌɪkad/ (also US trademark **Nicad**) ▶ noun [usu. as

modifier] a battery or cell with a nickel anode, a cadmium cathode, and a potassium hydroxide electrolyte. NiCads are used chiefly as a rechargeable power source for portable equipment.
– ORIGIN 1950s: blend of **NICKEL** and **CADMIUM**.

Nicaea /nʌɪˈsiːə/ an ancient city in Asia Minor, on the site of modern Iznik, which was important in Roman and Byzantine times. It was the site of two ecumenical councils of the early Christian Church (in 325 and 787). See also **NICENE CREED**.

Nicam /ˈnʌɪkam/ (also **NICAM**) ▶ **noun** [mass noun] a digital system used in British television to provide video signals with high-quality stereo sound.
– ORIGIN 1980s: acronym from *near instantaneously companded* (i.e. compressed and expanded) *audio multiplex*.

Nicaragua /ˌnɪkəˈragjʊə, -ˈragwə/ the largest country in Central America, with a coastline on both the Atlantic and the Pacific Ocean; pop. 3,975,000 (est. 1991); official language, Spanish; capital, Managua.

Colonized by the Spaniards, Nicaragua broke away from Spain in 1821 and, after brief membership of the United Provinces of Central America, became an independent republic in 1838. In 1979 the dictator Anastasio Somoza was overthrown by a popular revolution; the new left-wing Sandinista regime then faced a counter-revolutionary guerrilla campaign by the US-backed Contras. In the 1990 election the Sandinistas lost power to an opposition coalition.

– DERIVATIVES **Nicaraguan** adjective & noun.

Nicaragua, Lake a lake near the west coast of Nicaragua, the largest lake in Central America.

Nice /niːs/ a resort city on the French Riviera, near the border with Italy; pop. 345,670 (1990).

nice ▶ **adjective 1** pleasant; agreeable; satisfactory: *we had a very nice time | that wasn't very* ***nice of*** *him | Jeremy had been very* ***nice to*** *her | a nice hot cup of tea.*
■(of a person) pleasant in manner; good-natured; kind: *he's a really nice guy.*
2 fine or subtle: *a nice distinction.*
■requiring careful thought or attention: *a nice point.*
3 archaic fastidious; scrupulous.
– PHRASES **make nice** (or **nice-nice**) N. Amer. informal be pleasant or polite to someone, typically in a hypocritical way. **nice and ——** satisfactorily or adequately in terms of the quality described: *it's nice and warm in here.* **nice one** informal expressing approval or commendation. **nice to meet you** a polite formula used on being introduced to someone. **nice work** informal expressing approval of a task well done. **nice work if you can get it** informal used to express envy of what is perceived to be another person's more favourable situation, especially if they seem to have reached it with little effort.
– DERIVATIVES **niceness** noun.
– ORIGIN Middle English (in the sense 'stupid'): from Old French, from Latin *nescius* 'ignorant', from *nescire* 'not know'. Other early senses included 'coy, reserved', giving rise to 'fastidious, scrupulous': this led both to the sense 'fine, subtle' (regarded by some as the 'correct' sense), and to the main current senses.

nicely ▶ **adverb** in a pleasant, agreeable, or attractive manner: *nicely dressed in flowered cotton.*
■satisfactorily; perfectly well: *we're doing very nicely now.*

Nicene Creed /nʌɪˈsiːn, ˈnʌɪ-/ a formal statement of Christian belief which is very widely used in Christian liturgies, based on that adopted at the first Council of Nicaea in 325.

nicety /ˈnʌɪsɪti/ ▶ **noun** (pl. **-ies**) (usu. **niceties**) a fine detail or distinction, especially one regarded as intricate and fussy: *she was never interested in the niceties of Greek and Latin.*
■[mass noun] accuracy or precision: *she prided herself on her nicety of pronunciation.* ■ a minor aspect of polite social behaviour; a detail of etiquette: *we were brought up to observe the niceties.*
– PHRASES **to a nicety** precisely.
– ORIGIN Middle English (in the sense 'folly, foolish conduct'): from Old French *nicete*, based on Latin *nescius* 'ignorant' (see **NICE**).

niche /niːʃ, nɪtʃ/ ▶ **noun** a shallow recess, especially one in a wall to display a statue or other ornament.
■(**one's niche**) a comfortable or suitable position in life or employment. ■ a specialized but profitable corner of the market: [as modifier] *important new niche markets.* ■ Ecology a position or role taken by a kind of organism within its community. Such a position may be occupied by different organisms in different localities, e.g. antelopes in Africa and kangaroos in Australia.
▶ **verb** [with obj.] place or position (something) in a niche.
– ORIGIN early 17th cent.: from French, literally 'recess', from *nicher* 'make a nest', based on Latin *nidus* 'nest'.

Nichiren /ˈnɪʃərən/ (also **Nichiren Buddhism**) ▶ **noun** [mass noun] a Japanese Buddhist sect founded by the religious teacher Nichiren (1222–82) with the Lotus Sutra as its central scripture. See also **SOKA GAKKAI**.

Nicholas the name of two tsars of Russia:
■Nicholas I (1796–1855), brother of Alexander I, reigned 1825–55. At home he pursued rigidly conservative policies while his expansionism in the Near East led to the Crimean War.
■Nicholas II (1868–1918), son of Alexander III, reigned 1894–1917. Forced to abdicate after the Russian Revolution in 1917, he was shot along with his family a year later.

Nicholas, St (4th century), Christian prelate. Said to have been bishop of Myra in Lycia, he is patron saint of children, sailors, Greece, and Russia. The cult of Santa Claus (a corruption of his name) comes from the Dutch custom of giving gifts to children on his feast day (6 December).

Nicholson[1], Ben (1894–1982), English painter; full name *Benjamin Lauder Nicholson*. He was a pioneer of British abstract art, noted for his painted reliefs with circular and rectangular motifs.

Nicholson[2], Jack (b.1937), American actor. He won Oscars for *One Flew Over the Cuckoo's Nest* (1975) and *Terms of Endearment* (1983). Other films include *The Shining* (1980) and *Batman* (1989).

nichrome /ˈnʌɪkrəʊm/ ▶ **noun** [mass noun] trademark an alloy of nickel with chromium (10 to 20 per cent) and sometimes iron (up to 25 per cent), used chiefly in high-temperature applications such as electrical heating elements.
– ORIGIN early 20th cent.: blend of **NICKEL** and **CHROME**.

nick[1] ▶ **noun 1** a small cut or notch.
2 (**the nick**) Brit. informal prison.
■a police station: *he was being fingerprinted in the nick.*
3 the junction between the floor and side walls in a squash court or real tennis court.
▶ **verb** [with obj.] **1** make a nick or nicks in: *he had nicked himself while shaving.*
2 Brit. informal steal: *he'd had his car nicked by joyriders.*
■arrest or apprehend (someone): *I'd got* ***nicked*** *for burglary.* ■ (**nick someone for**) N. Amer. informal cheat someone of (something, typically a sum of money): *banks and life insurance companies will be nicked for an extra $40 million.* ■ (especially in sports journalism) score (a goal) undeservedly or unexpectedly.
– PHRASES **in —— nick** Brit. informal in a specified condition: *you've kept the car* ***in good nick***. **in the nick of time** only just in time.
– ORIGIN late Middle English: of unknown origin.

nick[2] ▶ **verb** [no obj., with adverbial of direction] Austral. informal go quickly or surreptitiously: *they nicked across the road.*
■(**nick off**) depart; go away.
– ORIGIN late 19th cent.: probably a figurative use of the verb **NICK**[1] in the sense 'to steal'.

nickel ▶ **noun 1** [mass noun] a silvery-white metal, the chemical element of atomic number 28. (Symbol: **Ni**)

Nickel occurs naturally in various minerals and the earth's core is believed to consist largely of metallic iron and nickel. Its chief use is in alloys, especially with iron, to which it imparts strength and resistance to corrosion, and with copper for coinage.

2 N. Amer. informal a five-cent coin; five cents.
▶ **verb** (**nickelled**, **nickelling**; US **nickeled**, **nickeling**) [with obj.] coat with nickel.
– ORIGIN mid 18th cent.: shortening of German *Kupfernickel*, the copper-coloured ore from which nickel was first obtained, from *Kupfer* 'copper' + *Nickel* 'demon' (with reference to the ore's failure to yield copper).

nickel-and-dime N. Amer. ▶ **verb** [with obj.] put a financial strain on (someone) by charging small amounts for many minor services.
▶ **adjective** [attrib.] of little importance; petty: *the only games this weekend are nickel-and-dime stuff.*
– ORIGIN 1970s: originally designating a store selling articles costing five or ten cents.

nickel brass ▶ **noun** [mass noun] an alloy of copper, zinc, and a small amount of nickel.

nickelodeon /ˌnɪkəˈləʊdɪən/ N. Amer. ▶ **noun 1** informal, dated a jukebox, originally one operated by the insertion of a nickel coin.
2 historical a cinema with an admission fee of one nickel.
– ORIGIN early 20th cent.: from **NICKEL** in the sense 'five-cent coin' + a shortened form of **MELODEON**.

nickel silver ▶ **noun** another term for **GERMAN SILVER**.

nickel steel ▶ **noun** [mass noun] a type of stainless steel containing chromium and nickel.

nicker[1] ▶ **noun** (pl. same) Brit. informal a pound sterling.
– ORIGIN early 20th cent.: of unknown origin.

nicker[2] ▶ **verb** [no obj.] (of a horse) give a soft breathy whinny.
▶ **noun** a sound of this kind.
– ORIGIN late 16th cent.: imitative.

Nicklaus /ˈnɪklaʊs, -ləs/, Jack William (b.1940), American golfer. He has won more than eighty tournaments during his professional career.

nick-nack ▶ **noun** variant spelling of **KNICK-KNACK**.

nickname ▶ **noun** a familiar or humorous name given to a person or thing instead of or as well as the real name.
▶ **verb** [with obj. and complement] give a nickname to; call by a nickname: *an area nicknamed Sniper's Alley.*
– ORIGIN late Middle English: from *an eke-name* (*eke* meaning 'addition': see **EKE**[2]), misinterpreted, by wrong division, as *a neke name*.

nick point ▶ **noun** variant spelling of **KNICK POINT**.

Nicobarese /ˌnɪkəbəˈriːz/ ▶ **noun** (pl. same) **1** a native or inhabitant of the Nicobar Islands.
2 [mass noun] an ancient language spoken in the Nicobar Islands, distantly related to the Mon-Khmer and Munda families. It now has fewer than 20,000 speakers.
▶ **adjective** of or relating to the Nicobar Islands, their inhabitants, or their language.

Nicobar Islands see **ANDAMAN AND NICOBAR ISLANDS**.

Niçois /niːˈswɑː/ ▶ **noun** (fem. **Niçoise** /niːˈswɑːz/) a native or inhabitant of the city of Nice.
▶ **adjective** of, relating to, or characteristic of Nice or its inhabitants: *the Niçois dialect.*
■[postpositive] denoting food that is characteristic of Nice or the surrounding region, typically garnished with tomatoes, capers, and anchovies: *salade Niçoise.*
– ORIGIN French.

Nicol prism /ˈnɪk(ə)l/ ▶ **noun** a device for producing plane-polarized light, consisting of two pieces of optically clear calcite or Iceland spar cemented together with Canada balsam in the shape of a prism.
– ORIGIN mid 19th cent.: named after William Nicol (died 1851), the Scottish physicist who invented it.

Nicosia /ˌnɪkəˈsɪə/ the capital of Cyprus; pop. 186,400 (est. 1993). Since 1974 it has been divided into Greek and Turkish sectors.

nicotiana /ˌnɪkɒtɪˈɑːnə, -kəʊʃ-/ ▶ **noun** an ornamental plant related to tobacco, with tubular flowers that are particularly fragrant at night. Also called **TOBACCO PLANT**.
• Genus *Nicotiana*, family Solanaceae: several species, in particular *N. alata*.
– ORIGIN from modern Latin *nicotiana* (*herba*) 'tobacco (plant)', named after Jaques *Nicot*, a 16th-cent. French diplomat who introduced tobacco to France in 1560.

nicotinamide /ˌnɪkəˈtɪnəmʌɪd/ ▶ **noun** [mass noun] Biochemistry a compound which is the form in which nicotinic acid often occurs in nature.
• The amide of nicotinic acid; chem. formula: $(C_5H_4N)CONH_2$.

nicotinamide adenine dinucleotide ▶ **noun** see **NAD**.

nicotine ▶ **noun** [mass noun] a toxic colourless or yellowish oily liquid which is the chief active constituent of tobacco. It acts as a stimulant in small doses, but in larger amounts blocks the action of autonomic nerve and skeletal muscle cells.
• An alkaloid; chem. formula: $C_{10}H_{14}N_2$.
– ORIGIN early 19th cent.: from French, from **NICOTIANA** + **-INE**[4].

nicotine patch ▶ **noun** a patch impregnated with nicotine, which is worn on the skin by a person

n

trying to give up smoking. Nicotine is gradually absorbed into the bloodstream, helping reduce the craving for cigarettes.

nicotinic acid ▶ noun [mass noun] Biochemistry a vitamin of the B complex which is widely distributed in foods such as milk, wheat germ, and meat, and can be synthesized in the body from tryptophan. Its deficiency causes pellagra.
● Alternative name: **3-pyridinecarboxylic acid**; chem. formula: $(C_5H_4N)COOH$.
– DERIVATIVES **nicotinate** noun.

nictation ▶ noun [mass noun] technical the action or process of blinking.
– ORIGIN late 18th cent.: from Latin *nictatio(n-)*, from the verb *nictare* 'to blink'.

nictitating membrane ▶ noun Zoology a whitish or translucent membrane that forms an inner eyelid in birds, reptiles, and some mammals. It can be drawn across the eye to protect it from dust and keep it moist. Also called **THIRD EYELID**.
– ORIGIN early 18th cent.: *nictitating* based on medieval Latin *nictitat-* 'blinked', frequentative of *nictare*.

nidation /naɪˈdeɪʃ(ə)n/ ▶ noun another term for **IMPLANTATION**.
– ORIGIN late 19th cent.: from Latin *nidus* 'nest' + **-ATION**.

nide /naɪd/ ▶ noun archaic a brood or nest of pheasants.
– ORIGIN late 17th cent.: from French *nid* or Latin *nidus* 'nest'.

nidicolous /nɪˈdɪk(ə)ləs/ ▶ adjective another term for **ALTRICIAL**.
– ORIGIN early 20th cent.: from Latin *nidus* 'nest' + *-colus* 'inhabiting' (from the verb *colere* 'live in, cultivate').

nidification /ˌnɪdɪfɪˈkeɪʃ(ə)n/ ▶ noun Zoology nest-building.
– ORIGIN mid 17th cent.: from Latin *nidificat-* 'made into a nest' (from the verb *nidificare*, from *nidus* 'nest') + **-ATION**.

nidifugous /nɪˈdɪfjʊɡəs/ ▶ adjective another term for **PRECOCIAL**.
– ORIGIN early 20th cent.: from Latin *nidus* 'nest' + *fugere* 'flee' + **-OUS**.

nidus /ˈnaɪdəs/ ▶ noun (pl. **nidi** /-dʌɪ/ or **niduses**) a place in which something is formed or deposited; a site of origin.
■ Medicine a place in which bacteria have multiplied or may multiply; a focus of infection.
– ORIGIN early 18th cent. (in the medical sense 'focus of infection'): from Latin, literally 'nest'.

niece ▶ noun a daughter of one's brother or sister, or of one's brother-in-law or sister-in-law.
– ORIGIN Middle English: from Old French, based on Latin *neptis* 'granddaughter', feminine of *nepos* 'nephew, grandson' (see **NEPHEW**), from an Indo-European root shared by Dutch *nicht*, German *Nichte*.

Niederösterreich /ˈniːdɐˌøːstəraɪç/ German name for **LOWER AUSTRIA**.

Niedersachsen /ˈniːdɐˌzaksn/ German name for **LOWER SAXONY**.

niello /nɪˈɛləʊ/ ▶ noun [mass noun] a black compound of sulphur with silver, lead, or copper, used for filling in engraved designs in silver or other metals.
■ objects decorated with this.
– DERIVATIVES **nielloed** adjective.
– ORIGIN early 19th cent.: from Italian, from Latin *nigellus*, diminutive of *niger* 'black'.

nielsbohrium /niːlzˈbɔːrɪəm/ ▶ noun [mass noun] a name proposed by the American Chemical Society for the chemical element of atomic number 107, now called **bohrium**.
– ORIGIN modern Latin, from the name of the scientist *Niels Bohr* (see **BOHR**). The term was originally proposed (*c*.1971) by Soviet scientists for element 105 (hahnium).

Nielsen /ˈniːls(ə)n/, Carl August (1865–1931), Danish composer. He is best known for his six symphonies (1890–1925).

Niemeyer /ˈniːmʌɪə/, Oscar (b.1907), Brazilian architect. An early exponent of modernist architecture in Latin America, he designed the main public buildings of Brasilia (1950–60).

Niemöller /ˈniːmɜːlə, German ˈniːmœlɐ/, Martin (1892–1984), German Lutheran pastor. An outspoken opponent of Nazism, he was imprisoned

in Sachsenhausen and Dachau concentration camps (1937–45).

niente /nɪˈɛnteɪ/ ▶ adverb & adjective Music (especially as a direction) with the sound or tone gradually fading to nothing.
– ORIGIN Italian, literally 'nothing'.

Niersteiner /ˈnɪəˌʃtʌɪnə, German ˈniːɐˌʃtaɪnɐ/ ▶ noun [mass noun] a white Rhine wine produced in the region around Nierstein, a town in Germany.

Nietzsche /ˈniːtʃə/, Friedrich Wilhelm (1844–1900), German philosopher. He is known for repudiating Christianity's compassion for the weak, exalting the 'will to power', and formulating the idea of the *Übermensch* (superman), who can rise above the restrictions of ordinary morality.
– DERIVATIVES **Nietzschean** adjective & noun, **Nietzscheanism** noun.

nifedipine /nʌɪˈfɛdɪpiːn/ ▶ noun [mass noun] Medicine a synthetic compound which acts as a calcium antagonist and is used as a coronary vasodilator in the treatment of cardiac and circulatory disorders.
– ORIGIN 1970s: from *ni(tro-)* + *fe* (alteration of **PHENYL**) + **DI-**[1] + *p(yrid)ine*, elements of the systematic name.

niff Brit. informal ▶ noun an unpleasant smell.
▶ verb [no obj.] have an unpleasant smell.
– DERIVATIVES **niffy** adjective (**niffier**, **niffiest**).
– ORIGIN early 20th cent. (originally dialect): perhaps from **SNIFF**.

Niflheim /ˈnɪv(ə)l̩ˌheɪm, -ˌhʌɪm/ Scandinavian Mythology an underworld of eternal cold, darkness, and mist inhabited by those who died of old age or illness.
– ORIGIN from Old Norse *Niflheimr*, literally 'world of mist'.

nifty ▶ adjective (**niftier**, **niftiest**) informal particularly good, skilful, or effective: *nifty footwork*.
■ fashionable; stylish: *a nifty blue shirt*.
– DERIVATIVES **niftily** adverb, **niftiness** noun.
– ORIGIN mid 19th cent.: of unknown origin.

nigella /nʌɪˈdʒɛlə/ ▶ noun a plant of a genus which includes love-in-a-mist.
● Genus *Nigella*, family Ranunculaceae.
– ORIGIN modern Latin, feminine of Latin *nigellus*, diminutive of *niger* 'black'.

Niger /ˈnaɪdʒə/ **1** a river in NW Africa, which rises on the NE border of Sierra Leone and flows in a great arc for 4,100 km (2,550 miles) north-east to Mali, then south-east through western Niger and Nigeria, before turning southwards into the Gulf of Guinea.
2 a landlocked country in West Africa, on the southern edge of the Sahara. pop. 7,909,000 (est. 1991): languages, French (official), Hausa, and other West African languages: capital, Niamey. Part of French West Africa from 1922, it became an autonomous republic within the French Community in 1958 and fully independent in 1960.

Niger–Congo ▶ adjective denoting or belonging to a large phylum of languages in Africa, named after the rivers Niger and Congo. It comprises most of the languages spoken by the indigenous peoples of Africa south of the Sahara and includes the Bantu, Mande, Gur, and Kwa families.

Nigeria /nʌɪˈdʒɪərɪə/ a country on the coast of West Africa, bordered by the River Niger to the north; pop. 88,514,500 (1991); languages, English (official), Hausa, Ibo, Yoruba, and others; capital, Abuja.

The site of highly developed kingdoms in the Middle Ages, the area came under British influence during the 19th century and was made into a single colony in 1914. Independence came in 1960 and the state became a federal republic in 1963, remaining a member of the Commonwealth. Oil was discovered in the 1960s and 1970s, since when Nigeria has emerged as one of the world's major exporters. The country was suspended from the Commonwealth 1995–9 following the execution of the writer and activist Ken Saro-Wiwa.

– DERIVATIVES **Nigerian** adjective & noun.

niggard /ˈnɪɡəd/ ▶ noun a mean or stingy person.
▶ adjective archaic term for **NIGGARDLY**.
– ORIGIN late Middle English: alteration of earlier *nigon*.

niggardly ▶ adjective ungenerous; stingy: *mean, niggardly, and unnecessary regulations.*
■ meagre; scanty: *their share is a niggardly 2.7 per cent.*
▶ adverb archaic in a stingy or meagre manner.
– DERIVATIVES **niggardliness** noun.

nigger ▶ noun offensive a contemptuous term for a black person.
– ORIGIN late 17th cent. (as an adjective): from

earlier *neger*, from French *nègre*, from Spanish *negro* 'black' (see **NEGRO**).

USAGE The word **nigger** was first used as an adjective denoting a black person in the 17th century and has had strong offensive connotations ever since. Today it remains one of the most racially offensive words in the language. Ironically, it has acquired a new strand of use in recent years, being used by black people as a mildly disparaging way of referring to other black people.

niggerhead ▶ noun chiefly N. Amer. & NZ **1** a tangled mass of the roots and decayed remains of sedges projecting from a swamp.
2 a rounded rock, stone, or coral, especially a black one.
3 [mass noun] strong black tobacco.

niggle ▶ verb **1** [no obj.] cause slight but persistent annoyance, discomfort, or anxiety: *a suspicion niggled at the back of her mind* | [as adj. **niggling**] *niggling aches and pains.*
■ [with obj.] find fault with (someone) in a petty way: *people niggling me for doing too much work.*
▶ noun a trifling complaint, dispute, or criticism.
– DERIVATIVES **nigglingly** adverb.
– ORIGIN early 17th cent. (in the sense 'do something in a fiddling or ineffectual way'): apparently of Scandinavian origin; compare with Norwegian *nigla*. Current senses date from the late 18th cent.

nigh ▶ adverb, preposition, & adjective archaic near: [as adj.] *the Day of Judgement is nigh* | [as adv.] *they drew nigh unto the city.*
■ almost: [as adv.] *a car weighing nigh on two tons* | *recovery will be well nigh impossible.*
– ORIGIN Old English *nēh*, *nēah*, of Germanic origin; related to Dutch *na*, German *nah*. Compare with **NEAR**.

night ▶ noun **1** the period of darkness in each twenty-four hours; the time from sunset to sunrise: *a moonless night* | *the office door is always locked at night.*
■ this as the interval between two days: *supplements per person per night* | *somebody put him up for the night.*
■ the darkness of night: *a line of watchfires stretched away into the night.* ■ poetic/literary nightfall.
2 the period of time between afternoon and bedtime; an evening: *he was not allowed to go out on weekday nights.*
■ [with modifier] an evening appointed for some activity, or spent or regarded in a certain way: *a Quiz Night has been organized for July 19th* | *wasn't it a great night out?*
▶ exclamation informal short for **GOODNIGHT**.
– PHRASES **night and day** all the time; constantly: *she studied night and day.*
– DERIVATIVES **nightless** adjective.
– ORIGIN Old English *neaht*, *niht*, of Germanic origin; related to Dutch *nacht* and German *Nacht*, from an Indo-European root shared by Latin *nox* and Greek *nux*.

night adder ▶ noun a venomous nocturnal African viper.
● Genus *Causus*, family Viperidae: several species, in particular the grey and black *C. rhombeatus*, common in southern Africa.
■ S. African any of a number of non-venomous nocturnal colubrid snakes.

nightbird ▶ noun another term for **NIGHT OWL**.

night blindness ▶ noun less technical term for **NYCTALOPIA**.

night-blooming cereus ▶ noun a tropical climbing cactus with aerial roots and heavily scented flowers that open only at night and are typically pollinated by bats.
● Genera *Hylocereus* and *Selenicereus*, family Cactaceae: several species, in particular *H. undatus*.

nightcap ▶ noun **1** historical a cap worn in bed.
2 a hot or alcoholic drink taken before going to bed.

nightclothes ▶ plural noun clothes worn in bed.

nightclub ▶ noun a club that is open from the evening until early morning, having facilities such as a bar and disco or other entertainment.
– DERIVATIVES **nightclubber** noun, **nightclubbing** noun.

night crawler ▶ noun chiefly N. Amer. an earthworm, in particular one which comes to the surface at night and is collected for use as fishing bait.

nightdress ▶ noun a light, loose garment worn by a woman or child in bed.

nightfall ▶ noun the onset of night; dusk.

night fighter ▶ noun a fighter aircraft used or designed for use at night.

nightgown ▶ noun **1** another term for **NIGHTDRESS**.
2 historical a dressing gown.

nighthawk ▶ noun **1** an American nightjar with sharply pointed wings.
● Family Caprimulgidae: four genera and several species, in particular the **common nighthawk** (*Chordeiles minor*) of North America.
2 North American term for **NIGHT OWL**.

night heron ▶ noun a small short-necked heron that is active mainly at night.
● Genus *Nycticorax*, family Ardeidae: several species.

nightie ▶ noun informal a nightdress.

Nightingale, Florence (1820–1910), English nurse and medical reformer. In 1854, during the Crimean War, she improved sanitation and medical procedures at the army hospital at Scutari, achieving a dramatic reduction in the mortality rate.

nightingale ▶ noun a small migratory thrush with drab brownish plumage, noted for its rich melodious song which can often be heard at night.
● *Luscinia megarhynchos*, family Turdidae.
– ORIGIN Old English *nihtegala*, of Germanic origin; related to Dutch *nachtegaal* and German *Nachtigall*, from the base of **NIGHT** and a base meaning 'sing'.

nightjar ▶ noun a nocturnal insectivorous bird with grey-brown camouflaged plumage, large eyes and gape, and a distinctive call.
● Family Caprimulgidae (the **nightjar family**): several genera, especially *Caprimulgus*, and many species, including the **European nightjar** (*C. europaeus*), which has a chirring call. The nightjar family also includes the nighthawks, pauraques, poorwills, whippoorwills, and chuck-will's-widow.

Night Journey (in Muslim tradition) the journey through the air made by Muhammad, guided by the archangel Gabriel. They flew first to Jerusalem, where Muhammad prayed with earlier prophets including Abraham, Moses, and Jesus, before entering the presence of Allah in heaven.

nightlife ▶ noun [mass noun] social activities or entertainment available at night in a town or city.

night light ▶ noun a lamp or candle providing a dim light during the night.

night lizard ▶ noun a small dull-coloured nocturnal lizard with large scales or bony plates on the head, occurring from the south-western US to Central America.
● Family Xantusiidae: several genera and species, including the **desert night lizard** (*Xantusia vigilis*).

night-long ▶ adjective lasting throughout the night: *its tragic, night-long struggle to survive.*

nightly ▶ adjective **1** happening or done every night: *his prime-time, nightly TV talk show.*
2 happening, done, or existing in the night.
▶ adverb every night: *the hotel features live music nightly.*

nightmare ▶ noun a frightening or unpleasant dream: *I had nightmares after watching the horror movie.*
■ a terrifying or very unpleasant experience or prospect: *the nightmare of racial hatred* | *an astronaut's worst nightmare is getting detached during an extra-vehicle activity.* ■ a person, thing, or situation that is very difficult to deal with: *buying wine can be a nightmare if you don't know enough about it.*
– DERIVATIVES **nightmarish** adjective, **nightmarishly** adverb.
– ORIGIN Middle English (denoting a female evil spirit thought to lie upon and suffocate sleepers): from **NIGHT** + Old English *mære* 'incubus'.

night monkey ▶ noun another term for **DOUROUCOULI**.

night of the long knives ▶ noun a treacherous massacre or betrayal, especially the massacre of the Brownshirts on Hitler's orders in June 1934.

night owl ▶ noun informal a person who is habitually active or wakeful at night.

nights ▶ adverb informal during the night; at night: *investments that won't keep us awake nights with worry.*

night safe ▶ noun Brit. a safe with access from the outer wall of a bank for the deposit of money or other valuables when the bank is closed.

night school ▶ noun an institution providing evening classes for those working during the day.

nightshade ▶ noun a plant related to the potato, typically having poisonous black or red berries. Several kinds of nightshade have been used in the production of herbal medicines.
● *Solanum* and other genera, family Solanaceae (the

nightshade family): several species, including the European **woody nightshade** (*S. dulcamara*), a climber with purple flowers and red berries. The nightshade family includes many commercially important plants (potato, tomato, capsicum peppers, tobacco) as well as a number of highly poisonous ones (henbane, thorn apple). See also **DEADLY NIGHTSHADE**.
– ORIGIN Old English *nihtscada*, apparently from **NIGHT** + **SHADE**, probably with reference to the dark colour and poisonous properties of the berries. Compare with German *Nachtschatten*.

night shift ▶ noun the period of time worked at night in a hospital, factory, or other institution.
■ the group of people working during this period.

nightshirt ▶ noun a long shirt worn in bed especially by boys or men.

nightside ▶ noun **1** Astronomy the side of a planet or moon that is facing away from the sun and is therefore in darkness.
2 [mass noun] chiefly US the world at night; activities that take place during the night.

night soil ▶ noun [mass noun] human excrement collected at night from buckets, cesspools, and privies and sometimes used as manure.

nightspot ▶ noun informal a nightclub.

nightstick ▶ noun N. Amer. a police officer's truncheon.

night table (also **nightstand**) ▶ noun N. Amer. a small low bedside table, typically having drawers.

night terrors ▶ plural noun feelings of great fear experienced on suddenly waking in the night.

night-time ▶ noun the time between evening and morning; the time of darkness: [as modifier] *they asked police for extra night-time patrols.*

night vision ▶ noun [mass noun] the faculty of seeing in the dark, especially when the eye has become adapted to the low level of light.
▶ adjective (**night-vision**) denoting devices that enable the user to see in the dark.

nightwatchman ▶ noun (pl. **-men**) **1** a person whose job is to guard a building at night.
2 Cricket an inferior batsman sent in to bat when a wicket falls just before the end of a day's play, to avoid the dismissal of a better one in adverse conditions.

nightwear ▶ noun [mass noun] clothing suitable for wearing in bed.

nigrescent /nɪˈɡrɛs(ə)nt, nʌɪ-/ ▶ adjective rare blackish.
– DERIVATIVES **nigrescence** noun.
– ORIGIN mid 18th cent.: from Latin *nigrescent-* 'growing black', from the verb *nigrescere*, from *niger, nigr-* 'black'.

nigritude /ˈnɪɡrɪtjuːd/ ▶ noun [mass noun] rare blackness.
– ORIGIN mid 17th cent.: from Latin *nigritudo* 'blackness', from *niger, nigr-* 'black'.

nihilism /ˈnʌɪ(h)ɪlɪz(ə)m/ ▶ noun [mass noun] the rejection of all religious and moral principles, often in the belief that life is meaningless.
■ Philosophy extreme scepticism maintaining that nothing in the world has a real existence. ■ historical the doctrine of an extreme Russian revolutionary party *c*.1900 which found nothing to approve of in the established social order.
– DERIVATIVES **nihilist** noun, **nihilistic** adjective.
– ORIGIN early 19th cent.: from Latin *nihil* 'nothing' + -ISM.

nihility /nʌɪˈhɪlɪti, nɪ-/ ▶ noun [mass noun] rare non-existence; nothingness.
– ORIGIN late 17th cent.: from medieval Latin *nihilitas*, from Latin *nihil* 'nothing'.

nihil obstat /ˌnʌɪhɪl ˈɒbstat, ˌnɪhɪl/ ▶ noun (in the Roman Catholic Church) a certificate that a book is not open to objection on doctrinal or moral grounds.
– ORIGIN Latin, literally 'nothing hinders'.

Niigata /ˌniːɪˈɡɑːtə/ an industrial port in central Japan, on the NW coast of the island of Honshu; pop. 486,090 (1990).

Nijinsky /nɪˈdʒɪnski/, Vaslav (Fomich) (1890–1950), Russian ballet dancer and choreographer. The leading dancer with Diaghilev's Ballets Russes from 1909, he went on to choreograph Debussy's *L'Après-midi d'un faune* (1912) and Stravinsky's *The Rite of Spring* (1913).

Nijmegen /ˈnʌɪmeɪɡ(ə)n/ an industrial town in the eastern Netherlands, south of Arnhem; pop. 145,780 (1991).

-nik ▶ suffix (forming nouns) denoting a person associated with a specified thing or quality: *beatnik* | *refusenik.*
– ORIGIN from Russian (on the pattern of (*sput*)*nik*) and Yiddish.

nikah /nɪˈkɑːhə/ ▶ noun a Muslim marriage.
– ORIGIN Urdu and Arabic.

Nike /ˈnʌɪki/ Greek Mythology the goddess of victory.
– ORIGIN Greek, literally 'victory'.

Nikkei index /ˈnɪkeɪ/ a figure indicating the relative price of representative shares on the Tokyo Stock Exchange. Also called **NIKKEI AVERAGE**.
– ORIGIN 1970s: *Nikkei*, abbreviation of *Ni(hon) Kei(zai) Shimbun* 'Japanese Economic Journal'.

Nikolaev /nɪkaˈlajɪf/ Russian name for **MYKOLAYIV**.

nil ▶ noun nothing, especially as the score in certain games; zero: *they beat us three-nil.*
▶ adjective non-existent: *the chances of seeing wild barn owls in Britain are virtually nil.*
– ORIGIN mid 19th cent.: from Latin, contraction of *nihil* 'nothing'.

nil desperandum /ˌdɛspəˈrandəm/ ▶ exclamation do not despair; never despair.
– ORIGIN from Latin *nil desperandum Teucro duce* 'no need to despair with Teucer as your leader', from Horace's *Odes* 1.vii.27.

Nile a river in eastern Africa, the longest river in the world, which rises in east central Africa near Lake Victoria and flows 6,695 km (4,160 miles) generally northwards through Uganda, Sudan, and Egypt to empty through a large delta into the Mediterranean. See also **BLUE NILE, ALBERT NILE, VICTORIA NILE, WHITE NILE**.

Nile, Battle of the another name for **ABOUKIR BAY, BATTLE OF**.

Nile blue ▶ noun [mass noun] a pale greenish blue.
– ORIGIN late 19th cent.: suggested by French *eau de Nil*.

Nile crocodile ▶ noun a large crocodile with a long narrow head, native to Africa and Madagascar.
● *Crocodilus niloticus*, family Crocodylidae.

Nile green ▶ noun [mass noun] a pale bluish green.

Nile monitor ▶ noun a large heavily built African lizard that has greyish-olive skin with yellow markings and is semiaquatic.
● *Varanus niloticus*, family Varanidae.

Nile perch ▶ noun a large predatory fish found in lakes and rivers in NE and central Africa, widely caught for food and sport.
● *Lates niloticus*, family Centropomidae.

nilgai /ˈnɪlɡʌɪ/ ▶ noun a large Indian antelope, the male of which has a blue-grey coat and short horns, and the female a tawny coat and no horns.
● *Boselaphus tragocamelus*, family Bovidae.
– ORIGIN late 18th cent.: from Hindi *nīlgāī*, from *nīl* 'blue' + *gāī* 'cow'.

Nilgiri Hills /ˈnɪlɡɪri/ a range of hills in southern India, in western Tamil Nadu. They form a branch of the Western Ghats.

Nilo-Saharan /ˌnʌɪləʊsəˈhɑːr(ə)n/ ▶ adjective denoting or belonging to a phylum of languages that includes the Nilotic family together with certain other languages of northern and eastern Africa.
▶ noun [mass noun] this phylum of languages.

Nilotic /nʌɪˈlɒtɪk/ ▶ adjective **1** of or relating to the River Nile or to the Nile region of Africa.
2 denoting or belonging to a family of languages spoken in Egypt, Sudan, Kenya, and Tanzania. The western group includes Luo and Dinka; the eastern group includes Masai and Turkana.
– ORIGIN via Latin from Greek *Neilōtikos*, from *Neilos* 'Nile'.

nilpotent /nɪlˈpəʊt(ə)nt/ ▶ adjective Mathematics becoming zero when raised to some positive integral power.
– ORIGIN late 19th cent.: from **NIL** + Latin *potens, potent-* 'power'.

Nilsson /ˈnɪls(ə)n/, (Märta) Birgit (b.1918), Swedish operatic soprano. She gained international success in the 1950s, being particularly noted for her interpretation of Wagnerian roles.

nim ▶ noun [mass noun] a game in which two players alternately take one or more objects from one of a number of heaps, each trying to take, or to compel the other to take, the last remaining object.
– ORIGIN early 20th cent.: apparently from archaic

nim 'to take' or from German *nimm!* 'take!', imperative of *nehmen*.

nimble ▶ **adjective** (**nimbler**, **nimblest**) quick and light in movement or action; agile: *with a deft motion of her nimble fingers.*
■(of the mind) quick to comprehend; clever.
– DERIVATIVES **nimbleness** noun, **nimbly** adverb.
– ORIGIN Old English *næmel* 'quick to seize or comprehend', related to *niman* 'take', of Germanic origin. The *-b-* was added for ease of pronunciation.

nimbostratus /ˌnɪmbə(ʊ)'strɑːtəs, -'streɪtəs/ ▶ **noun** [mass noun] cloud forming a thick uniform grey layer at low altitude, from which rain or snow often falls (without any lightning or thunder).
– ORIGIN late 19th cent.: modern Latin, from **NIMBUS** + **STRATUS**.

nimbus /'nɪmbəs/ ▶ **noun** (pl. **nimbi** /-bʌɪ/ or **nimbuses**) **1** a luminous cloud or a halo surrounding a supernatural being or a saint.
2 a large grey rain cloud: [as modifier] *nimbus clouds.*
– ORIGIN early 17th cent.: from Latin, literally 'cloud, aureole'.

Nimby /'nɪmbi/ ▶ **noun** (pl. **Nimbys**) a person who objects to the siting of something perceived as unpleasant or hazardous in their own neighbourhood, especially while raising no such objections to similar developments elsewhere.
– DERIVATIVES **Nimbyism** noun.
– ORIGIN 1980s: acronym from *not in my back yard*.

Nîmes /niːm/ a city in southern France; pop. 133,600 (1990). It is noted for its many well-preserved Roman remains.

niminy-piminy ▶ **adjective** affectedly prim or refined: *she had a niminy-piminy ladylike air.*
– ORIGIN late 18th cent.: fanciful coinage; compare with **NAMBY-PAMBY**.

nimrod /'nɪmrɒd/ ▶ **noun** chiefly humorous a skilful hunter.
– ORIGIN late 16th cent.: from Hebrew *Nimrōḏ*, the name of the great-grandson of Noah, reputed for his skill as a hunter (see Gen. 10:8–9).

Nimrud /'nɪmrʊd/ modern name of an ancient Mesopotamian city on the east bank of the Tigris south of Nineveh, near the modern city of Mosul. It was the capital of Assyria 879–722 BC. The city was known in biblical times as Calah (Gen. 10:11); the modern name arose through association in Islamic mythology with the biblical figure of Nimrod.

Nin, Anaïs (1903–77), American writer. She published her first novel, *House of Incest*, in 1936 and went on to produce collections of short stories, essays, diaries, and erotica.

nincompoop /'nɪŋkəmpuːp/ ▶ **noun** a foolish or stupid person.
– ORIGIN late 17th cent.: perhaps from the given name *Nicholas* or from *Nicodemus* (by association with the Pharisee of this name, and his naive questioning of Christ; compare with French *nicodème* 'simpleton').

nine ▶ **cardinal number** equivalent to the product of three and three; one more than eight, or one less than ten; 9: *nine European countries | nine of the twelve members.* (Roman numeral: **ix** or **IX**.)
■a group or unit of nine individuals. ■ nine years old: *I was only nine.* ■ nine o'clock: *it's ten to nine.* ■ a size of garment or other merchandise denoted by nine. ■ a playing card with nine pips. ■ (**the Nine**) Greek Mythology the nine Muses.
– PHRASES **dressed to** (or Brit. **up to**) **the nines** dressed very smartly or elaborately. **nine tenths** nearly all. **nine times out of ten** on nearly every occasion; almost always.
– ORIGIN Old English *nigon*, of Germanic origin; related to Dutch *negen* and German *neun*, from an Indo-European root shared by Sanskrit *nava*, Latin *novem*, and Greek *ennea*.

ninefold ▶ **adjective** nine times as great or as numerous: *a ninefold increase in the amount of traffic.*
■having nine parts or elements.
▶ **adverb** by nine times; to nine times the number or amount: *consumption increased ninefold.*

ninepins ▶ **plural noun** [usu. treated as sing.] the traditional form of the game of skittles, using nine pins and played in an alley.
■[treated as pl.] skittles used in this game.
– PHRASES **go down** (or **drop** or **fall**) **like ninepins** succumb in large numbers or without much opposition.

nineteen ▶ **cardinal number** one more than eighteen; nine more than ten; 19: *nineteen of the interviewees had never worked.* (Roman numeral: **xix** or **XIX**.)
■nineteen years old: *she married at nineteen.* ■ a size of garment or other merchandise denoted by nineteen.
– PHRASES **talk nineteen to the dozen** see **DOZEN**.
– DERIVATIVES **nineteenth** ordinal number.
– ORIGIN Old English *nigontȳne*.

nineteenth hole ▶ **noun** informal, humorous the bar in a golf clubhouse, as reached after a standard round of eighteen holes.

nineteenth man ▶ **noun** Austral./NZ the first reserve in an Australian Rules football team.

nine-to-five ▶ **adjective** used in reference to typical office hours, often to express an idea of routine or predictability: *a nine-to-five job.*
▶ **noun** an occupation involving such hours.
– DERIVATIVES **nine-to-fiver** noun.

ninety ▶ **cardinal number** (pl. **-ies**) equivalent to the product of nine and ten; ten less than one hundred; 90. (Roman numeral: **xc** or **XC**.)
■(**nineties**) the numbers from 90 to 99, especially the years of a century or of a person's life: *art in the nineties.* ■ ninety years old: *she is nearly ninety.* ■ ninety miles an hour: *we passed the junction doing about ninety.*
– DERIVATIVES **ninetieth** ordinal number, **ninetyfold** adjective & adverb.
– ORIGIN Old English *nigontig*.

ninety-nine ▶ **noun** (usu. **99**) Brit. a cone of ice cream with a stick of flaky chocolate in it.

Nineveh /'nɪnɪvə/ an ancient city located on the east bank of the Tigris, opposite the modern city of Mosul. It was the oldest city of the ancient Assyrian empire and its capital until it was destroyed by a coalition of Babylonians and Medes in 612 BC.

ning-nong ▶ **noun** Austral. informal a fool.
– ORIGIN mid 19th cent.: of unknown origin.

Ningxia /nɪŋ'ʃjɑː/ (also **Ningsia**) an autonomous region of north central China; capital, Yinchuan.

ninhydrin /nɪn'hʌɪdrɪn/ ▶ **noun** [mass noun] Chemistry a synthetic crystalline compound which forms deeply coloured products with primary amines and is used in analytical tests for amino acids.
• A ketone derivative of indene; chem. formula: $C_9H_6O_4$.
– ORIGIN early 20th cent.: from *nin-* (of unknown origin) + **HYDRO-** + **-IN**[1].

Ninian, St /'nɪnɪən/ (*c*.360–*c*.432), Scottish bishop and missionary. According to Bede he founded a church at Whithorn in SW Scotland (*c*.400) and from there evangelized the southern Picts.

ninja /'nɪndʒə/ ▶ **noun** a person skilled in ninjutsu.
– ORIGIN Japanese, literally 'spy'.

ninjutsu /nɪn'dʒʌtsuː/ ▶ **noun** [mass noun] the traditional Japanese technique of espionage, characterized by stealthy movement and camouflage. It was developed in feudal times for military purposes and subsequently used in the training of samurai.
– ORIGIN Japanese, from *nin* 'stealth' + *jutsu* 'art, science'.

ninny ▶ **noun** (pl. **-ies**) informal a foolish and weak person.
– ORIGIN late 16th cent.: perhaps from **INNOCENT**.

ninon /'niːnɒn/ ▶ **noun** [mass noun] a lightweight silk dress fabric.
– ORIGIN early 20th cent.: from French.

ninth ▶ **ordinal number** constituting number nine in a sequence; 9th: *the ninth century | the ninth of March.*
■(**a ninth/one ninth**) each of nine equal parts into which something is or may be divided. ■ the ninth finisher or position in a race or competition: *he came in ninth.* ■ Music an interval spanning nine consecutive notes in a diatonic scale. ■ Music the note which is higher by this interval than the tonic of a diatonic scale or root of a chord. ■ Music a chord in which the ninth note of the scale forms an important component.
– DERIVATIVES **ninthly** adverb.

Niobe /'nʌɪəbi/ Greek Mythology the daughter of Tantalus. Apollo and Artemis, enraged because Niobe boasted herself superior to their mother Leto, slew her children and turned her into a stone.

niobium /nʌɪ'əʊbɪəm/ ▶ **noun** [mass noun] the chemical element of atomic number 41, a silver-grey metal of the transition series, used in superconducting alloys. (Symbol: **Nb**)
– ORIGIN mid 19th cent.: modern Latin, from **NIOBE**, by association with her father Tantalus (so named because the element was first found in **TANTALITE**).

Nip ▶ **noun** informal, offensive a Japanese person.
– ORIGIN mid 20th cent.: abbreviation of the synonym *Nipponese*, from *Nippon* (see **NIPPON**).

nip[1] ▶ **verb** (**nipped**, **nipping**) **1** [with obj.] pinch, squeeze, or bite sharply: *one of the dogs nipped him on the leg* | [no obj.] *his teeth* **nipped at** *her ear.*
■(of the cold or frost) cause sharp pain or harm to: *the vegetable garden, nipped now by frost.* ■ (**nip something off**) remove something by pinching or squeezing sharply.
2 [no obj., with adverbial of direction] Brit. informal go quickly: *I'm just nipping down to the Post Office.*
3 [with obj.] US informal steal or snatch (something).
▶ **noun** a sharp pinch, squeeze, or bite.
■a feeling of biting cold: *there was a real winter nip in the air.*
– PHRASES **nip something in the bud** suppress or destroy something, especially at an early stage.
– ORIGIN late Middle English: probably of Low German or Dutch origin.

nip[2] ▶ **noun** a small quantity or sip of spirits.
▶ **verb** (**nipped**, **nipping**) [no obj.] take a sip or sips of spirits: *the men nipped from the bottle.*
– ORIGIN late 18th cent. (originally denoting a half-pint of ale): probably an abbreviation of the rare term *nipperkin* 'small measure'; compare with Low German and Dutch *nippen* 'to sip'.

nipa /'niːpə, 'nʌɪpə/ (also **nipa palm**) ▶ **noun** a palm tree with creeping roots, characteristic of mangrove swamps in India and the Pacific islands.
• *Nypa fruticans*, family Palmae.
– ORIGIN late 16th cent. (denoting an alcoholic drink made from the sap of the tree): via Spanish or Portuguese from Malay *nīpah*.

nip and tuck ▶ **adverb** & **adjective** neck and neck; closely contested: [as adv.] *it was nip and tuck to 7–7 until Best took the lead.*
▶ **noun** informal a cosmetic surgical operation.

nipper ▶ **noun** **1** informal a child, especially a small boy.
2 (**nippers**) pliers, pincers, forceps, or a similar tool for gripping or cutting.
3 an insect or other creature that nips or bites.
■(usu. **nippers**) the grasping claw of a crab or lobster.
4 Austral. a burrowing marine prawn, widely used as bait in fishing. Also called **YABBY**.
• Infraorder Thalassinidea, order Decapoda.

nipple ▶ **noun** **1** the small projection of a woman's or girl's breast in which the mammary ducts terminate and from which milk can be secreted.
■the corresponding vestigial structure in a male. ■ the teat of a female animal. ■ N. Amer. the teat of a feeding bottle.
2 a small projection on a device or machine, especially one from which oil, grease, or other fluid is dispensed in small amounts.
■a short section of pipe with a screw thread at each end for coupling.
▶ **verb** [with obj.] (usu. **be nippled**) provide (something) with a projection like a nipple: *rocks nippled with limpets.*
– ORIGIN mid 16th cent. (also as *neble*, *nible*): perhaps a diminutive of **NEB**.

nipplewort /'nɪp(ə)lwəːt/ ▶ **noun** a yellow-flowered European plant of the daisy family, growing in woods and waste places.
• *Lapsana communis*, family Compositae.

Nippon /'nɪpɒn/ Japanese name for **JAPAN**.
– ORIGIN literally 'land where the sun rises or originates'.

nippy ▶ **adjective** (**nippier**, **nippiest**) informal **1** (of a person or their actions) quick; nimble: *he used to be a very nippy scrum half | nippy footwork.*
■(of a motor vehicle) able to accelerate quickly.
2 (of the weather) rather cold; chilly.
▶ **noun** (**Nippy**) (pl. **-ies**) informal, historical a waitress in any of the restaurants of J. Lyons & Co. Ltd in London from about 1920 to 1950.
– DERIVATIVES **nippily** adverb.

NIREX /'nʌɪrɛks/ ▶ **abbreviation for** (in the UK) Nuclear Industry Radioactive Waste Executive.

Niro, Robert De, see **DE NIRO**.

nirvana /nɪə'vɑːnə/ ▶ **noun** [mass noun] Buddhism a transcendent state in which there is neither suffering, desire, nor sense of self, and the subject is released from the effects of karma. It represents the final goal of Buddhism.
■a state of perfect happiness; an ideal or idyllic place.

– ORIGIN from Sanskrit *nirvāṇa*, from *nirvā* 'be extinguished', from *nis* 'out' + *vā-* 'to blow'.

Nirvana principle Psychoanalysis yearning for a state of oblivion, as a manifestation of the death instinct.

Niš /niːʃ/ (also **Nish**) a historically dominant industrial city in SE Serbia, on the Nišava river near its confluence with the Morava; pop. 175,400 (1991).

Nisan /'nɪs(ə)n, 'niːsɑːn/ ▶ noun (in the Jewish calendar) the seventh month of the civil and first of the religious year, usually coinciding with parts of March and April.
– ORIGIN from Hebrew *nīsān*.

nisei /'niːseɪ, niːˈseɪ/ ▶ noun (pl. same or **niseis**) N. Amer. an American or Canadian whose parents were immigrants from Japan. Compare with **ISSEI** and **SANSEI**.
– ORIGIN 1940s: from Japanese, literally 'second generation'.

Nish variant spelling of **NIŠ**.

nisi /'naɪsaɪ/ ▶ adjective [postpositive] Law (of a decree, order, or rule) that takes effect or is valid only after certain conditions are met. See also **DECREE NISI**.
– ORIGIN mid 19th cent.: from Latin, literally 'unless'.

nisin /'naɪsɪn/ ▶ noun [mass noun] an antibiotic substance which is a mixture of related polypeptides and is used in some countries as a food preservative.
● This substance is produced by the bacterium *Streptococcus lactis*.
– ORIGIN 1940s: from (Group) N i(nhibitory) s(ubstance) + -**IN**[1].

Nissen hut /'nɪs(ə)n/ ▶ noun chiefly Brit. a tunnel-shaped hut made of corrugated iron with a cement floor.
– ORIGIN early 20th cent.: named after Peter N. *Nissen* (1871–1930), the British engineer who invented it.

nit[1] ▶ noun informal **1** the egg or young form of a louse or other parasitic insect, especially the egg of a human head louse attached to a hair. **2** Brit. a stupid person (often as a general term of abuse): *you stupid nit!*
– PHRASES **pick nits** chiefly N. Amer. look for and criticize small or insignificant faults or errors; nit-pick.
– DERIVATIVES **nitty** adjective.
– ORIGIN Old English *hnitu*, of West Germanic origin; related to Dutch *neet* and German *Nisse*.

nit[2] ▶ exclamation Austral. informal used as a warning that someone is approaching.
– PHRASES **keep nit** keep watch or act as a guard.
– ORIGIN late 19th cent.: probably from **NIX**[3].

nite ▶ noun informal, chiefly N. Amer. non-standard spelling of **NIGHT**: *the Golden Tiara Nite Club*.

niter ▶ noun US spelling of **NITRE**.

niterie /'naɪtəri/ ▶ noun informal (pl. -**ies**) a nightclub.

Niterói /ˌniːtəˈrɔɪ/ an industrial port on the coast of SE Brazil, on Guanabara Bay opposite the city of Rio de Janeiro; pop. 436,155 (1991).

nitinol /'nɪtɪnɒl/ ▶ noun [mass noun] an alloy of nickel and titanium.
– ORIGIN 1960s: from the chemical symbols **Ni** and **Ti** + the initial letters of *Naval Ordnance Laboratory* (in Maryland, US).

nit-picking informal ▶ adjective looking for small or unimportant errors or faults, especially in order to criticize unnecessarily: *a nit-picking legalistic exercise.*
▶ noun [mass noun] such fault-finding.
– DERIVATIVES **nit-pick** verb, **nit-picker** noun.

nitrate Chemistry ▶ noun /'naɪtreɪt/ a salt or ester of nitric acid, containing the anion NO_3^- or the group $-NO_3$.
▶ verb /naɪ'treɪt/ [with obj.] treat (a substance) with nitric acid (typically a concentrated mixture of nitric and sulphuric acids), especially so as to introduce nitro groups.
– DERIVATIVES **nitration** noun.
– ORIGIN late 18th cent.: from French (see **NITRE**, -**ATE**[1]).

nitrazepam /naɪ'treɪzɪpam, -'traːzə-/ ▶ noun [mass noun] Medicine a short-acting hypnotic drug of the benzodiazepine group, used to treat insomnia.
– ORIGIN 1960s: from nitr(o) + az(o-) + ep(ine) + am(ide).

nitre /'naɪtə/ (US **niter**) ▶ noun another term for **SALTPETRE**.

– ORIGIN late Middle English: from Old French, from Latin *nitrum*, from Greek *nitron*.

nitric acid ▶ noun [mass noun] Chemistry a colourless or pale yellow corrosive poisonous liquid acid with strong oxidizing properties, made in the laboratory by distilling nitrates with sulphuric acid.
● Chem. formula: HNO_3.
– ORIGIN late 18th cent.: from French *acide nitrique*.

nitric oxide ▶ noun another term for **NITROGEN MONOXIDE**.

nitride /'naɪtraɪd/ ▶ noun Chemistry a binary compound of nitrogen with a more electropositive element.
▶ verb [with obj.] [usu. as noun **nitriding**] Metallurgy heat steel in the presence of ammonia or other nitrogenous material so as to increase hardness and corrosion resistance.
– ORIGIN mid 19th cent.: from **NITRE** + -**IDE**.

nitrify /'naɪtrɪfaɪ/ ▶ verb (-**ies**, -**ied**) [with obj.] Chemistry convert (ammonia or other nitrogen compound) into nitrites or nitrates.
– DERIVATIVES **nitrification** noun.
– ORIGIN early 19th cent.: from French *nitrifier*.

nitrile /'naɪtraɪl/ ▶ noun Chemistry an organic compound containing a cyanide group $-CN$ bound to an alkyl group.
– ORIGIN mid 19th cent.: from **NITRE** + -*ile* (alteration of -**YL**).

nitrite /'naɪtraɪt/ ▶ noun Chemistry a salt or ester of nitrous acid, containing the anion NO_2^- or the group $-NO_2$.
– ORIGIN early 19th cent.: from **NITRE** + -**ITE**[1].

nitro ▶ noun short for **NITROGLYCERINE**.

nitro- /'naɪtrəʊ/ ▶ combining form of or containing nitric acid, nitrates, or nitrogen: *nitrogenous*.
■ Chemistry containing a nitro group: *nitromethane*.
– ORIGIN from **NITRE** or **NITROGEN**.

nitrobenzene ▶ noun [mass noun] Chemistry a yellow oily liquid made by nitrating benzene, used in chemical synthesis.
● Chem. formula: $C_6H_5NO_2$.

nitroblue tetrazolium ▶ noun see **TETRAZOLIUM**.

nitrocellulose ▶ noun [mass noun] Chemistry a highly flammable material made by treating cellulose with concentrated nitric acid, used to make explosives (e.g. guncotton) and celluloid.

nitrochalk ▶ noun [mass noun] a mixture of chalk and ammonium nitrate, used as fertilizer.

nitrofurantoin /ˌnaɪtrə(ʊ)fjʊˈrantəʊɪn/ ▶ noun [mass noun] Medicine a synthetic compound with antibacterial properties, used to treat infections of the urinary tract.
● A bicyclic furan derivative; chem. formula: $C_8H_6N_4O_5$.

nitrogen /'naɪtrədʒ(ə)n/ ▶ noun [mass noun] the chemical element of atomic number 7, a colourless, odourless unreactive gas that forms about 78 per cent of the earth's atmosphere. Liquid nitrogen (made by distilling liquid air) boils at 77.4 kelvins (−195.8°C) and is used as a coolant. (Symbol: **N**)
– ORIGIN late 18th cent.: from French *nitrogène* (see **NITRO-**, -**GEN**).

nitrogen cycle ▶ noun Ecology the series of processes by which nitrogen and its compounds are interconverted in the environment and in living organisms, including nitrogen fixation and decomposition.

nitrogen dioxide ▶ noun [mass noun] Chemistry a reddish-brown poisonous gas formed when many metals dissolve in nitric acid.
● Chem. formula: NO_2. It usually exists in equilibrium with **dinitrogen tetroxide**, N_2O_4.

nitrogen fixation ▶ noun [mass noun] Biology the chemical processes by which atmospheric nitrogen is assimilated into organic compounds, especially by certain micro-organisms as part of the nitrogen cycle.

nitrogen monoxide ▶ noun [mass noun] Chemistry a colourless toxic gas formed in many reactions in which nitric acid is reduced. It reacts immediately with oxygen to form nitrogen dioxide.
● Chem. formula: NO. Also called **NITRIC OXIDE**.

nitrogen mustard ▶ noun Chemistry any of a group of organic compounds containing the group $-N(CH_2CH_2Cl)_2$. They are powerful cytotoxic alkylating agents and some are used in chemotherapy to treat cancer.
– ORIGIN 1940s: *mustard* denoting a substance chemically similar to **MUSTARD GAS**.

nitrogen narcosis ▶ noun [mass noun] Medicine a drowsy state induced by breathing air under pressure, e.g. in deep-sea diving.

nitrogenous /naɪ'trɒdʒɪnəs/ ▶ adjective containing nitrogen in chemical combination.

nitroglycerine (also **nitroglycerin**) ▶ noun [mass noun] Chemistry an explosive yellow liquid made by nitrating glycerol, used in explosives such as dynamite.
● Alternative name: **glyceryl trinitrate**; chem. formula: $CH_2(NO_3)CH(NO_3)CH_2(NO_3)$.

nitro group ▶ noun Chemistry a group $-NO_2$, attached to an organic group in a molecule.

nitromethane ▶ noun [mass noun] Chemistry an oily liquid which is used as a solvent and as rocket fuel.
● Chem. formula: CH_3NO_2.

nitrophilous /naɪ'trɒfɪləs/ ▶ adjective Botany (of a plant) preferring soils rich in nitrogen.

nitrosamine /naɪ'trəʊsəmiːn/ ▶ noun Chemistry a compound containing the group $=NNO$ attached to two organic groups. Compounds of this kind are generally carcinogenic.
– ORIGIN late 19th cent.: from *nitroso-* (relating to nitric oxide in combination) + **AMINE**.

nitrous /'naɪtrəs/ ▶ adjective of nitrogen; nitrogenous: *the effect of nitrous emissions on acid rain.*
– ORIGIN early 17th cent.: from Latin *nitrosus* 'nitrous'.

nitrous acid ▶ noun [mass noun] Chemistry an unstable, weak acid, existing only in solution and in the gas phase, made by the action of acids on nitrites.
● Chem. formula: HNO_2.

nitrous oxide ▶ noun [mass noun] Chemistry a colourless gas with a sweetish odour, prepared by heating ammonium nitrate. It produces exhilaration or anaesthesia when inhaled and is used (mixed with oxygen) as an anaesthetic and as an aerosol propellant.
● Chem. formula: N_2O.

nitty-gritty ▶ noun (**the nitty-gritty**) informal the most important aspects or practical details of a subject or situation.
– ORIGIN 1960s: of unknown origin.

nitwit ▶ noun informal a silly or foolish person (often as a general term of abuse).
– DERIVATIVES **nitwitted** adjective, **nitwittedness** noun, **nitwittery** noun.
– ORIGIN early 20th cent.: apparently from **NIT**[1] + **WIT**[1].

Niue /nɪˈuːeɪ/ an island territory in the South Pacific to the east of Tonga; pop. 2,239 (1991); languages, English (official), local Austronesian; capital, Alofi. Annexed by New Zealand in 1901, the island achieved self-government in free association with New Zealand in 1974. Niue is the world's largest coral island.

NIV ▶ abbreviation for New International Version (of the Bible)

nival /'naɪv(ə)l/ ▶ adjective of, relating to, or characteristic of a region of perpetual snow.
– ORIGIN mid 17th cent.: from Latin *nivalis*, from *nix*, *niv-* 'snow'.

nivation /naɪ'veɪʃ(ə)n/ ▶ noun [mass noun] Geography erosion of the ground beneath and at the sides of a snow bank, mainly as a result of alternate freezing and thawing.
– ORIGIN early 20th cent.: from Latin *nix*, *niv-* 'snow' + -**ATION**.

niveous /'nɪvɪəs/ ▶ adjective poetic/literary snowy or resembling snow.
– ORIGIN early 17th cent.: from Latin *niveus* (from *nix*, *niv-* 'snow') + -**OUS**.

Nivernais /ˌniːvəˈneɪ, French nivɛʀnɛ/ a former duchy and province of central France. Its capital was the city of Nevers.

Nivose /nɪ'vəʊz/ (also **Nivôse** /French nivoz/) ▶ noun the fourth month of the French Republican calendar (1793–1805), originally running from 21 December to 19 January.
– ORIGIN French *Nivôse*, from Latin *nivosus* 'snowy', from *nix*, *niv-* 'snow'.

nix[1] informal ▶ pronoun nothing: *apart from that, nix.*
▶ exclamation expressing denial or refusal.
▶ verb [with obj.] put an end to; cancel: *he nixed the deal just before it was to be signed.*
– ORIGIN late 18th cent. (as a noun): from German, colloquial variant of *nichts* 'nothing'.

nix[2] ▶ **noun** (fem. **nixie**) rare a water sprite.
– ORIGIN mid 19th cent.: from German; related to the archaic English word *nicker*, denoting a water demon believed to live in the sea.

nix[3] ▶ **exclamation** Brit. informal, dated used as a signal or warning that a person in authority is approaching.
– ORIGIN mid 19th cent.: perhaps from the phrase *keep nix* 'to watch, guard' (see **NIX**[1]).

Nixon, Richard (Milhous) (1913–94), American Republican statesman, 37th President of the US 1969–74. His period of office was overshadowed by the Vietnam War. Re-elected in 1972, he became the first President to resign from office, owing to his involvement in the Watergate scandal.

Nizam /nɪˈzɑːm/ ▶ **noun** historical **1** the title of the hereditary ruler of Hyderabad. [ORIGIN: abbreviation of Urdu *nizām-al-mulk* 'administrator of the realm'.]
2 (**the nizam**) the Turkish regular army. [ORIGIN: abbreviation of Turkish *nizām askeri* 'regular soldier'.]

Nizari /nɪˈzɑːri/ ▶ **noun** a member of a Muslim sect that split from the Ismaili branch in 1094 over disagreement about the succession to the caliphate. The majority of Nizaris now live in the Indian subcontinent; their leader is the Aga Khan.

Nizhni Novgorod /ˌniːʒnɪ ˈnɒvgərɒd/ a river port in European Russia on the Volga; pop. 1,443,000 (1990). Between 1932 and 1991 it was named Gorky after the writer Maxim Gorky, who was born there.

Nizhni Tagil /ˌniːʒnɪ təˈgiːl/ an industrial and metal-mining city in central Russia, in the Urals north of Ekaterinburg; pop. 440,000 (1990).

NJ ▶ **abbreviation for** New Jersey (in official postal use).

NK cell ▶ **abbreviation for** natural killer cell.

Nkomo /(ə)ŋˈkəʊməʊ/, Joshua (Mqabuko Nyongolo) (1917–99), Zimbabwean statesman. He became leader of the ZAPU party in 1961; in 1976 he formed the Patriotic Front with Robert Mugabe, leader of ZANU, and he held a cabinet post in the first post-independence government. He was Vice-President 1990–9.

Nkrumah /(ə)ŋˈkruːmə/, Kwame (1909–72), Ghanaian statesman, Prime Minister 1957–60, President 1960–66. The first Prime Minister after independence, he became increasingly dictatorial and was finally overthrown in a military coup.

NKVD the secret police agency in the former USSR which absorbed the functions of the former OGPU in 1934. It merged with the MVD in 1946.
– ORIGIN abbreviation of Russian *Narodnyĭ komissariat vnutrennikh del* 'People's Commissariat of Internal Affairs'.

NL ▶ **abbreviation for** the Netherlands (international car registration).

NLP ▶ **abbreviation for** ■ natural language processing. ■ neurolinguistic programming.

NM ▶ **abbreviation for** New Mexico (in official postal use).

nm ▶ **abbreviation for** ■ nanometre. ■ nautical mile.

n.m. ▶ **abbreviation for** nautical mile.

N.Mex. ▶ **abbreviation for** New Mexico.

NMR Physics ▶ **abbreviation for** nuclear magnetic resonance.

NNE ▶ **abbreviation for** north-north-east.

NNP ▶ **abbreviation for** net national product.

NNW ▶ **abbreviation for** north-north-west.

No[1] ▶ **symbol for** the chemical element nobelium.

No[2] ▶ **noun** variant spelling of **NOH**.

No. ▶ **abbreviation for** ■ US North. ■ (also **no.**) number: *No. 27.* [ORIGIN: from Latin *numero*, ablative of *numerus* 'number'.]

no ▶ **determiner 1** not any: *there is no excuse | no two plants are alike.*
2 used to indicate that something is quite the opposite of what is being specified: *it was no easy task persuading her | Toby is no fool.*
3 hardly any: *you'll be back in no time.*
4 used in notices or slogans forbidding or rejecting something specified: *No Smoking signs | no nukes.*
▶ **exclamation** used to give a negative response: *'Is anything wrong?' 'No.'*
■ expressing disagreement or contradiction: *'This is boring.' 'No, it's not!'* ■ expressing agreement with or affirmation of a negative statement: *they would never cause a fuss, oh no.* ■ expressing shock or disappointment at something one has heard or discovered: *oh no, look at this!*
▶ **adverb 1** [with comparative] not at all; to no extent: *they were no more able to perform the task than I was.*
2 Scottish not: *I'll no be a minute.*
▶ **noun** (pl. **noes**) a negative answer or decision, especially in voting.
– PHRASES **no can do** informal I am unable to do it. **the noes have it** the negative votes are in the majority. **no less** see **LESS**. **no longer** not now as formerly: *they no longer live here.* **no man** no person; no one. **no more** see **MORE**. **no place** N. Amer. nowhere. **no sooner —— than** see **SOON**. **no through road** an indication that passage along a street is blocked or prohibited. **not take no for an answer** persist in spite of refusals. **no two ways about it** used to convey that there can be no doubt about something. **no way** informal under no circumstances; not at all: *You think she's alone? No way.* **or no** or not: *she'd have ridden there, winter or no.* **—— or no ——** regardless of the specified thing: *recession or no recession there is always going to be a shortage of good people.*
– ORIGIN Old English *nō*, *nā* (adverb), from *ne* 'not' + *ō*, *ā* 'ever'. The determiner arose in Middle English (originally before words beginning with any consonant except *h*-), reduced from *non*, from Old English *nān* (see **NONE**[1]).

n.o. Cricket ▶ **abbreviation for** not out.

no-account informal, chiefly N. Amer. ▶ **adjective** of little or no importance, value, or use; worthless.
▶ **noun** such a person.

Noachian /nəʊˈeɪkɪən/ ▶ **adjective 1** of or relating to the biblical patriarch Noah or his time.
2 Astronomy of, relating to, or denoting an early geological period on the planet Mars.

Noah /ˈnəʊə/ (in the Bible) a Hebrew patriarch represented as tenth in descent from Adam. According to a story in Genesis he made the ark which saved his family and specimens of every animal from the Flood.

noah ▶ **noun** Austral. informal a shark.
– ORIGIN 1940s: from rhyming slang *Noah's ark*.

Noah's ark ▶ **noun 1** the ship in which Noah, his family, and the animals were saved from the Flood, according to the biblical account (Genesis 6–8).
■ a model of this as a child's toy.
2 a small bivalve mollusc with a boat-shaped shell, found in the Mediterranean and off the Atlantic coasts of Africa and southern Europe.
● *Arca noae*, family Arcidae. See also ***ark shell***.

nob[1] ▶ **noun** Brit. informal a person of wealth or high social position.
– DERIVATIVES **nobby** adjective.
– ORIGIN late 17th cent. (originally Scots as *knab*): of unknown origin.

nob[2] ▶ **noun** informal a person's head.
– PHRASES **one for his nob** Cribbage a bonus point scored for holding the jack of the same suit as the card turned up by the dealer.
– ORIGIN late 17th cent.: apparently a variant of **KNOB**.

no-ball Cricket ▶ **noun** an unlawfully delivered ball, counting one as an extra to the batting side if not otherwise scored from.
▶ **verb** [with obj.] (often **be no-balled**) (of an umpire) declare (a bowler) to have bowled a no-ball.
■ declare (a delivery) to be a no-ball.

nobble ▶ **verb** [with obj.] Brit. informal **1** try to influence or thwart (someone or something) by underhand or unfair methods: *an attempt to nobble the jury | the industry will try to nobble plans for further competition.*
■ accost (someone), especially in order to persuade them to do something: *people always tried to nobble her at parties.* ■ tamper with (a racehorse or greyhound) to prevent it from winning a race, especially by giving it a drug.
2 obtain dishonestly; steal: *he intended to nobble Rose's money.*
■ seize: *they nobbled him and threw him on to the train.*
– ORIGIN mid 19th cent.: probably a variant of dialect *knobble*, *knubble* 'knock, strike with the knuckles'.

nobbler informal ▶ **noun 1** Brit. a person who nobbles someone or something.
2 Austral./NZ a glass or drink of liquor.

nobbut /ˈnɒbət/ ▶ **adverb** N. English nothing but; just: *he looked a lot like his uncle when he was nobbut a lad.*
– ORIGIN Middle English: from the adverb **NO** + the preposition **BUT**[1].

Nobel /nəʊˈbɛl/, Alfred Bernhard (1833–96), Swedish chemist and engineer. He invented dynamite (1866), gelignite, and other high explosives, making a large fortune which enabled him to endow the prizes that bear his name.

Nobelist /nəʊˈbɛlɪst/ ▶ **noun** chiefly N. Amer. a winner of a Nobel Prize.

nobelium /nə(ʊ)ˈbiːlɪəm, -ˈbɛl-/ ▶ **noun** [mass noun] the chemical element of atomic number 102, a radioactive metal of the actinide series. Nobelium does not occur naturally and was first produced by bombarding curium with carbon nuclei. (Symbol: **No**)
– ORIGIN 1950s: modern Latin, from the name **NOBEL** + **-IUM**.

Nobel Prize ▶ **noun** any of six international prizes awarded annually for outstanding work in physics, chemistry, physiology or medicine, literature, economics, and the promotion of peace. The Nobel Prizes, first awarded in 1901, are decided by members of Swedish learned societies or the Norwegian Parliament.
– DERIVATIVES **Nobel prizewinner** noun.

nobiliary /nə(ʊ)ˈbɪljəri/ ▶ **adjective** rare of or relating to the nobility.
– ORIGIN mid 18th cent.: from French *nobiliaire*, based on Latin *nobilis* (see **NOBLE**).

nobiliary particle ▶ **noun** a preposition forming part of a title of the nobility (e.g. French *de*, German *von*).

nobility ▶ **noun** (pl. **-ies**) **1** [mass noun] the quality of being noble in character, mind, birth, or rank.
2 (usu. **the nobility**) the group of people belonging to the highest social class in a country; the aristocracy: *a member of the English nobility.*
– ORIGIN late Middle English: from Old French *nobilite* or Latin *nobilitas*, from *nobilis* 'noted, high-born' (see **NOBLE**).

noble ▶ **adjective** (**nobler**, **noblest**) **1** belonging by rank, title, or birth to the aristocracy.
2 having or showing fine personal qualities or high moral principles and ideals: *the promotion of human rights was a noble aspiration.*
■ of imposing or magnificent size or appearance. ■ of excellent or superior quality.
▶ **noun 1** (especially in former times) a person of noble rank or birth.
2 a former English gold coin first issued in 1351.
– PHRASES **the noble art** (or **science**) (**of self-defence**) chiefly archaic boxing.
– DERIVATIVES **nobleness** noun, **nobly** adverb.
– ORIGIN Middle English: from Old French, from Latin (*g*)*nobilis* 'noted, high-born', from an Indo-European root shared by **KNOW**.

noble gas ▶ **noun** Chemistry any of the gaseous elements helium, neon, argon, krypton, xenon, and radon, occupying Group 0 (18) of the periodic table. They were long believed to be totally unreactive but compounds of xenon, krypton, and radon are now known.

nobleman ▶ **noun** (pl. **-men**) a man who belongs by rank, title, or birth to the aristocracy; a peer.

noble metal ▶ **noun** Chemistry a metal (e.g. gold, silver, or platinum) that resists chemical action, does not corrode, and is not easily attacked by acids.

noble rot ▶ **noun** [mass noun] a grey mould that is deliberately cultivated on grapes in order to perfect certain wines.
● The fungus is *Botrytis cinerea*, subdivision Deuteromycotina.
– ORIGIN 1930s: translation of French *pourriture noble*.

noble savage ▶ **noun** (usu. **the noble savage**) a representative of primitive mankind as idealized in Romantic literature, symbolizing the innate goodness of humanity when free from the corrupting influence of civilization.

noblesse /nəʊˈblɛs/ ▶ **noun** [mass noun] the nobility of a foreign country.
– PHRASES **noblesse oblige** /ɒˈbliːʒ/ privilege entails responsibility: *the notion of noblesse oblige was part of the ethic of the country gentleman.*
– ORIGIN French, literally 'nobility'.

noblewoman ▶ **noun** (pl. **-women**) a woman who belongs by rank, title, or birth to the aristocracy; a peeress.

nobody ▶ **pronoun** no person; no one: *nobody was at home | nobody could predict how it might end.*

▶ **noun** (pl. **-ies**) a person of no importance or authority: *they went from nobodies to superstars.*
– PHRASES **be nobody's fool** see **FOOL**[1]. **like nobody's business** see **BUSINESS**.
– ORIGIN Middle English: originally as *no body*.

no-brainer ▶ **noun** N. Amer. informal something that requires or involves little or no mental effort.

nociceptive /ˌnəʊsɪˈsɛptɪv/ ▶ **adjective** Physiology of, relating to, or denoting pain arising from the stimulation of nerve cells (often as distinct from that arising from damage or disease in the nerves themselves).
– ORIGIN early 20th cent.: from Latin *nocere* 'to harm' + **RECEPTIVE**.

nociceptor /ˈnəʊsɪˌsɛptə/ ▶ **noun** Physiology a sensory receptor for painful stimuli.
– ORIGIN early 20th cent.: from Latin *nocere* 'to harm' + **RECEPTOR**.

nock ▶ **noun** Archery a notch at either end of a bow for holding the string.
■ a notch at the butt-end of an arrow for receiving the bowstring.
▶ **verb** [with obj.] fit (an arrow) to the bowstring ready for shooting.
– ORIGIN late Middle English: perhaps from Middle Dutch *nocke* 'point, tip'.

no-claims bonus (also **no-claims discount**) ▶ **noun** Brit. a reduction in the premium charged for insurance when no claim has been made during an agreed preceding period.

noctambulist /nɒkˈtambjʊlɪst/ ▶ **noun** rare a sleepwalker.
– DERIVATIVES **noctambulism** noun.
– ORIGIN mid 18th cent.: from Latin *nox, noct-* 'night' + *ambulare* 'walk' + **-IST**.

noctiluca /ˌnɒktɪˈluːkə/ ▶ **noun** (pl. **noctilucae** /-kiː/) a roughly spherical marine dinoflagellate which is strongly phosphorescent, especially when disturbed.
● Genus *Noctiluca*, division (or phylum) Dinophyta.
– ORIGIN modern Latin, from Latin, literally 'night light, lantern'.

noctilucent cloud /ˌnɒktɪˈluːs(ə)nt/ ▶ **noun** a luminous cloud of a kind occasionally seen at night in summer in high latitudes, at the altitude of the mesopause.
– ORIGIN late 19th cent.: from Latin *nox, noct-* 'night' + *lucere* 'to shine' + **-ENT**.

noctuid /ˈnɒktjʊɪd/ ▶ **noun** Entomology a moth of a large family (Noctuidae), whose members typically have dull forewings and pale or colourful hindwings. Also called **OWLET**.
– ORIGIN late 19th cent.: from modern Latin *Noctuidae* (plural), based on Latin *noctua* 'night owl'.

noctule /ˈnɒktjuːl/ ▶ **noun** a large golden-brown bat native to Eurasia and North Africa with long slender wings, rounded ears, and a short muzzle.
● *Nyctalus noctula*, family Vespertilionidae.
– ORIGIN late 18th cent.: from French, from Italian *nottola* 'bat', literally 'small night creature'.

nocturn ▶ **noun** (in the Roman Catholic Church) a part of matins originally said at night.
– ORIGIN Middle English: from Old French *nocturne* or ecclesiastical Latin *nocturnum*, neuter of Latin *nocturnus* 'of the night'.

nocturnal ▶ **adjective** done, occurring, or active at night: *most owls are nocturnal.*
– DERIVATIVES **nocturnally** adverb.
– ORIGIN late 15th cent.: from late Latin *nocturnalis*, from Latin *nocturnus* 'of the night', from *nox, noct-* 'night'.

nocturnal emission ▶ **noun** an involuntary ejaculation of semen during sleep.

nocturne /ˈnɒktəːn/ ▶ **noun 1** Music a short composition of a romantic nature, typically for piano.
2 Art a picture of a night scene.
– ORIGIN mid 19th cent.: French, from Latin *nocturnus* 'of the night'.

nocuous /ˈnɒkjʊəs/ ▶ **adjective** poetic/literary noxious, harmful, or poisonous.
– ORIGIN mid 17th cent.: from Latin *nocuus* (from *nocere* 'to hurt') + **-OUS**.

nod ▶ **verb** (**nodded, nodding**) **1** [no obj.] lower and raise one's head slightly and briefly, especially in greeting, assent, or understanding, or to give someone a signal: *he nodded to Mona to unlock the door* | [with obj.] *she nodded her head in agreement.*
■ [with obj.] signify or express (greeting, assent, or understanding) in this way: *he nodded his consent.* ■ [no obj., with adverbial of direction] draw or direct attention to someone or something by moving one's head: *he nodded towards the corner of the room.* ■ move one's head up and down repeatedly: *he shut his eyes, nodding to the beat* | figurative *foxgloves nodding by the path.*
2 [no obj.] let one's head fall forward when drowsy or asleep: *Anna nodded over her book.*
■ make a mistake due to a momentary lack of alertness or attention: *scientific reason, like Homer, sometimes nods.* [ORIGIN: with allusion to Latin *dormitat Homerus* (Horace *Ars Poet.* 359).]
3 [with obj. and adverbial of direction] Soccer head (the ball) in a specified direction without great force.
▶ **noun** an act of nodding the head: *at a nod from his father he left the room.*
■ figurative a gesture of acknowledgement or concession: *the device is* **a nod to** *the conventions of slapstick.*
– PHRASES **a nodding acquaintance** a slight acquaintance with a person or knowledge of a subject: *students will need* **a nodding acquaintance** *with three other languages.* **be on nodding terms** know someone slightly. **get the nod 1** be selected or approved. **2** receive a signal or information. **give someone/thing the nod 1** select or approve someone or something: *they banned one book but gave the other the nod.* **2** give someone a signal. **a nod's as good as a wink to a blind horse** proverb used to convey that a hint or suggestion can be or has been understood without the need of further elaboration or explanation. **on the nod** Brit. informal **1** by general agreement and without discussion: *parliamentary approval of the treaty went through on the nod.* **2** dated on credit.
– ORIGIN late Middle English (as a verb): perhaps of Low German origin; compare with Middle High German *notten* 'move about, shake'. The noun dates from the mid 16th cent.
▶ **nod off** informal fall asleep, especially briefly or unintentionally: *some of the congregation nodded off during the sermon.*
nod something through informal approve by general agreement and without discussion: *the DTI nodded through the bid from Airtours.*

noddle[1] ▶ **noun** informal, dated a person's head.
– ORIGIN late Middle English (denoting the back of the head): of unknown origin.

noddle[2] ▶ **verb** [with obj.] archaic, informal nod or wag (one's head).
– ORIGIN mid 18th cent.: frequentative of the verb **NOD**.

Noddy a character in the writings of Enid Blyton, a toy figure of a boy whose head is fixed in such a way that he has to nod when he speaks.

noddy ▶ **noun** (pl. **-ies**) **1** dated a silly or foolish person (often as a general term of abuse). [ORIGIN: perhaps from the verb **NOD** + **-Y**[1].]
2 a tropical tern with mainly dark-coloured plumage. [ORIGIN: perhaps from the nodding behaviour of the birds during courtship.]
● Genera *Anous* and *Procelsterna*, family Sternidae (or Laridae): four species.
3 informal a brief shot in a filmed interview in which the interviewer or interviewee nods in agreement or acknowledgement.

node ▶ **noun** technical **1** a point in a network or diagram at which lines or pathways intersect or branch.
■ a piece of equipment, such as a computer or peripheral, attached to a network. ■ (in generative grammar) a vertex or end point in a tree diagram. ■ Mathematics a point at which a curve intersects itself. ■ Astronomy either of the two points at which a planet's orbit intersects the plane of the ecliptic or the celestial equator.
2 Botany the part of a plant stem from which one or more leaves emerge, often forming a slight swelling or knob.
3 Anatomy a lymph node or other structure consisting of a small mass of differentiated tissue.
4 Physics & Mathematics a point at which the amplitude of vibration in a standing wave system is zero.
■ a point at which a harmonic function has the value zero, especially a point of zero electron density in an orbital. ■ a point of zero current or voltage.
– DERIVATIVES **nodal** adjective.
– ORIGIN late Middle English (denoting a knotty swelling or a protuberance): from Latin *nodus* 'knot'.

node of Ranvier /ˈrɑːnvɪeɪ, French rɑ̃vje/ (also **Ranvier's node**) ▶ **noun** Anatomy a gap in the myelin sheath of a nerve, between adjacent Schwann cells.
– ORIGIN late 19th cent.: named after Louis Antoine *Ranvier* (1835–1922), French histologist.

nodical ▶ **adjective** Astronomy of or relating to a node or the nodes of an orbit.

nodose /nəʊˈdəʊs/ ▶ **adjective** technical having or characterized by hard or tight lumps; knotty.
– DERIVATIVES **nodosity** noun.
– ORIGIN early 18th cent.: from Latin *nodosus*, from *nodus* 'knot'.

nodule ▶ **noun 1** a small swelling or aggregation of cells in the body, especially an abnormal one.
■ (usu. **root nodule**) a swelling on a root of a leguminous plant, containing nitrogen-fixing bacteria.
2 a small rounded lump of matter distinct from its surroundings, e.g. of flint in chalk, carbon in cast iron, or a mineral on the seabed.
– DERIVATIVES **nodular** adjective, **nodulated** adjective, **nodulation** noun, **nodulose** adjective, **nodulous** adjective.
– ORIGIN late Middle English: from Latin *nodulus*, diminutive of *nodus* 'knot'.

nodus /ˈnəʊdəs/ ▶ **noun** (pl. **nodi** /-dʌɪ/) rare a problem, difficulty, or complication.
– ORIGIN late Middle English (denoting a knotty swelling): from Latin, literally 'knot'.

Noel ▶ **noun** Christmas, especially as a refrain in carols and on Christmas cards.
– ORIGIN early 19th cent.: French *Noël* 'Christmas'.

Noether /ˈnəːtə, German ˈnøːtɐ/, Emmy (1882–1935), German mathematician. Despite prejudices against women mathematicians she inaugurated the modern period in algebraic geometry and abstract algebra.

noetic /nəʊˈɛtɪk/ ▶ **adjective** of or relating to mental activity or the intellect.
– ORIGIN mid 17th cent.: from Greek *noētikos*, from *noētos* 'intellectual', from *noein* 'perceive'.

no-fault ▶ **adjective** [attrib.] involving no fault or blame, in particular:
■ chiefly N. Amer. denoting an insurance policy that is valid regardless of whether the policyholder was at fault. ■ denoting an insurance or compensation scheme (especially one covering medical or industrial accidents) whereby a claimant need not legally prove negligence against any party. ■ of or denoting a form of divorce granted without requiring one party to prove the other is to blame for the breakdown of the marriage.

no-fly zone ▶ **noun** an area over which aircraft are forbidden to fly, especially during a conflict.

Nofretete /ˌnɒfrəˈtiːtiː/ variant of **NEFERTITI**.

no-frills ▶ **adjective** [attrib.] without unnecessary extras, especially ones for decoration or additional comfort: *cheap fast food in no-frills surroundings.*

nog[1] ▶ **noun** archaic a small block or peg of wood.
– ORIGIN early 17th cent.: of unknown origin.

nog[2] ▶ **noun** [mass noun] Brit. archaic a kind of strong beer, brewed in East Anglia.
– ORIGIN late 17th cent.: of unknown origin.

nogal /ˈnɒxal/ ▶ **adverb** [sentence adverb] S. African informal what is more; moreover: *the picture would be ready in three minutes and for free nogal.*
– ORIGIN Afrikaans, literally 'fairly, rather'.

noggin ▶ **noun** informal **1** a person's head.
2 a small quantity of alcoholic drink, typically a quarter of a pint.
– ORIGIN mid 17th cent. (in the sense 'small drinking cup'): of unknown origin.

nogging ▶ **noun** [mass noun] Building brickwork in a timber frame.
■ [count noun] a horizontal piece of wood fixed to a framework to strengthen it.
– ORIGIN early 19th cent.: from **NOG**[1] + **-ING**[1].

no go ▶ **adjective** informal impossible, hopeless, or forbidden: *I tried to start the engine again, but it was no go.*

no-go area ▶ **noun** Brit. an area which is dangerous or impossible to enter or to which entry is restricted or forbidden.

no-good ▶ **adjective** [attrib.] informal (of a person) contemptible; worthless: *a no-good layabout.*
▶ **noun** a worthless or contemptible person.

Noh /nəʊ/ (also **No**) ▶ **noun** [mass noun] traditional Japanese masked drama with dance and song, evolved from Shinto rites.

Noh dates from the 14th and 15th centuries, and its subject matter is taken mainly from Japan's classical literature. Traditionally the players were all male, with the chorus playing a passive narrative role.

– ORIGIN Japanese.

no-hitter ▶ **noun** Baseball a game in which a pitcher yields no hits to the opposing team.

no-hoper ▶ **noun** informal a person who is not expected to be successful.

nohow ▶ **adverb 1** chiefly US used, especially in uneducated speech, to emphasize a negative: *they never executes nobody nohow.*
2 archaic not attractive, well, or in good order.

noil /nɔɪl/ ▶ **noun** [mass noun] (usu. **noils**) short strands and knots combed out of wool fibre before spinning.
– ORIGIN early 17th cent.: probably from Old French *noel*, from medieval Latin *nodellus*, diminutive of Latin *nodus* 'knot'.

noise ▶ **noun 1** a sound, especially one that is loud or unpleasant or that causes disturbance: *making a noise like a pig in a trough | what's that rustling noise outside the door?*
■ [mass noun] a series or combination of loud, confused sounds, especially when causing disturbance: *dazed with the heat and noise | vibration and noise from traffic.* ■ (**noises**) conventional remarks or speech-like sounds made to express some emotion or quality: *the government made tough noises about defending sterling.*
2 [mass noun] technical irregular fluctuations that accompany a transmitted electrical signal but are not part of it and tend to obscure it.
■ random fluctuations that obscure or do not contain meaningful data or other information: *over half the magnitude of the differences came from noise in the data.*
▶ **verb** [with obj.] (usu. **be noised about**) dated talk about or make known publicly.
■ [no obj.] poetic/literary make much noise.
– PHRASES **make a noise** speak or act in a way designed to attract a lot of attention or publicity: *he knows how to make a noise and claim police harassment.*
– ORIGIN Middle English (also in the sense 'quarrelling'): from Old French, from Latin *nausea* 'seasickness' (see **NAUSEA**).

noiseless ▶ **adjective** silent; quiet: *the cycle is a benign form of transport, being noiseless and non-polluting | given to almost noiseless fits of giggling.*
■ technical accompanied by or introducing no random fluctuations that would obscure the real signal or data.
– DERIVATIVES **noiselessly** adverb, **noiselessness** noun.

noisemaker ▶ **noun** N. Amer. a device for making a loud noise at a festivity or sports match.

noise pollution ▶ **noun** [mass noun] harmful or annoying levels of noise.

noises off ▶ **plural noun** sounds made offstage to be heard by the audience of a play.
■ distracting or intrusive background noise.

noisette /nwʌˈzɛt/ ▶ **noun 1** a small round piece of meat, especially lamb. [ORIGIN: French, diminutive of *noix* 'nut'.]
2 a chocolate made with hazelnuts. [ORIGIN: French, in the sense 'hazelnut'.]

noisome /ˈnɔɪs(ə)m/ ▶ **adjective** poetic/literary having an extremely offensive smell.
■ disagreeable; unpleasant.
– DERIVATIVES **noisomeness** noun.
– ORIGIN late Middle English: from obsolete *noy* (shortened form of **ANNOY**) + **-SOME**[1].

noisy ▶ **adjective** (**noisier**, **noisiest**) **1** making or given to making a lot of noise: *a noisy, giggling group of children | diesel cars can be very noisy.*
■ (of a person or group of people) stridently seeking to attract attention to their views.
2 full of or characterized by noise: *noisy scenes outside the court building | the pub was crowded and noisy.*
■ technical accompanied by or introducing random fluctuations that obscure the real signal or data.
– DERIVATIVES **noisily** adverb, **noisiness** noun.

Nok /nɒk/ ▶ **noun** [usu. as modifier] Archaeology an ancient civilization of northern Nigeria, dated to the 5th–3rd centuries BC. It is characterized by the production of distinctive terracotta figurines and is significant for its development of iron-working.
– ORIGIN from the name of the site where remains of this culture were found.

no-knock ▶ **adjective** US denoting or relating to a search or raid by the police made without permission or warning: *during a no-knock raid.*

Nolan /ˈnəʊlən/, Sir Sidney Robert (1917–93), Australian painter, known for his paintings of famous characters and events from Australian history.

nolens volens /ˌnəʊlɛnz ˈvəʊlɛnz/ ▶ **adverb** formal whether a person wants or likes something or not.
– ORIGIN Latin, from *nolens* 'not willing' and *volens* 'willing'.

noli me tangere /ˌnəʊlʌɪ miː ˈtan(d)ʒəri, ˌnəʊli meɪ ˈtaŋg(ə)ri/ ▶ **noun 1** a warning or prohibition against meddling or interference.
■ a painting representing the appearance of Jesus to Mary Magdalen at the sepulchre (*John* 20:17).
2 another term for **TOUCH-ME-NOT**.
– ORIGIN Latin, literally 'do not touch me'.

nolle pros /ˌnɒli ˈprɒs, ˈprəʊs/ ▶ **verb** (**prossed**, **prossing**) [with obj.] US Law abandon or dismiss (a suit) by issuing a nolle prosequi.

nolle prosequi /ˌnɒli ˈprɒsɪkwʌɪ/ ▶ **noun** Law a formal notice of abandonment by a plaintiff or prosecutor of all or part of a suit.
■ (in the UK) the dismissal or termination of legal proceedings by the Attorney General. ■ the entry of this in a court record.
– ORIGIN Latin, literally 'refuse to pursue'.

no-load ▶ **adjective** N. Amer. (of shares in a mutual fund) sold directly to a buyer by the mutual fund itself without a commission being charged.

nolo contendere /ˌnəʊləʊ kɒnˈtɛndəri/ ▶ **noun** [mass noun] US Law a plea by which a defendant in a criminal prosecution accepts conviction as in the case of a plea of guilty but does not admit guilt.
– ORIGIN Latin, literally 'I do not wish to contend'.

nom. ▶ **abbreviation for** nominal.

nomad ▶ **noun** a member of a people travelling from place to place to find fresh pasture for its animals and having no permanent home.
■ a person who does not stay long in the same place; a wanderer.
▶ **adjective** relating to or characteristic of nomads.
– DERIVATIVES **nomadic** adjective, **nomadically** adverb, **nomadism** noun.
– ORIGIN late 16th cent.: from French *nomade*, via Latin from Greek *nomas, nomad-* 'roaming in search of pasture', from the base of *nemein* 'to pasture'.

no-man's-land ▶ **noun** [mass noun] disputed ground between the front lines or trenches of two opposing armies: *enemy soldiers facing you across no-man's-land | figurative the farmers are caught in no-man's-land, between the free market and old style Marxism.*
■ [count noun] a piece of unowned land or wasteland.
– ORIGIN Middle English: originally the name of a plot of ground lying outside the north wall of the city of London, the site of a place of execution.

nomarch /ˈnɒmɑːk/ ▶ **noun 1** the governor of an ancient Egyptian nome.
2 the senior administrator of a modern Greek nomarchy.
– ORIGIN mid 17th cent.: from Greek *nomarkhēs* or *nomarkhos*, from *nomos* 'nome' + *arkhēs* 'governor'.

nomarchy /ˈnɒmɑːki/ ▶ **noun** (pl. **-ies**) formerly a province, now a smaller administrative division, of modern Greece.
– ORIGIN mid 17th cent.: from Greek *nomarkhia*, from *nomos* 'nome' + *arkhē* 'government'.

nombril /ˈnɒmbrɪl/ ▶ **noun** Heraldry the point halfway between fess point and the base of the shield.
– ORIGIN mid 16th cent.: from French, literally 'navel'.

nom de guerre /ˌnɒm də ˈɡɛː/ ▶ **noun** (pl. **noms de guerre** pronunc. same) an assumed name under which a person engages in combat or some other activity or enterprise.
– ORIGIN French, literally 'war name'.

nom de plume /ˌnɒm də ˈpluːm/ ▶ **noun** (pl. **noms de plume** pronunc. same) an assumed name used by a writer instead of their real name; a pen-name.
– ORIGIN early 19th cent.: formed in English from French words, to render the sense 'pen name', on the pattern of *nom de guerre*.

Nome /nəʊm/ a city in western Alaska, on the south coast of the Seward Peninsula. Founded in 1896 as a gold-mining camp, it became a centre of the Alaskan gold rush at the turn of the century.

nome /nəʊm/ ▶ **noun 1** one of the thirty-six territorial divisions of ancient Egypt.
2 an administrative division of modern Greece.
– ORIGIN early 18th cent.: from Greek *nomos* 'division', from *nemein* 'to divide'.

nomen /ˈnəʊmən/ ▶ **noun** Roman History the second personal name of a citizen of ancient Rome that indicates the gens to which he or she belonged, e.g. Marcus *Tullius* Cicero.
– ORIGIN Latin, literally 'name'.

nomenclature /nə(ʊ)ˈmɛŋklətʃə, ˈnəʊmənˌkleɪtʃə/ ▶ **noun** [mass noun] the devising or choosing of names for things, especially in a science or other discipline.
■ the body or system of such names in a particular field. ■ formal the term or terms applied to someone or something: *'Customers' was preferred to the original nomenclature 'passengers'.*
– DERIVATIVES **nomenclatural** /-ˈklatʃ(ə)r(ə)l, -kləˈtʃʊər(ə)l/ adjective.
– ORIGIN early 17th cent.: from French, from Latin *nomenclatura*, from *nomen* 'name' + *clatura* 'calling, summoning' (from *calare* 'to call').

nomenklatura /nɒˌmɛnkləˈtjʊərə/ ▶ **noun** (in the former Soviet Union) a list of influential posts in government and industry to be filled by Party appointees.
■ [mass noun] the holders of such posts collectively.
– ORIGIN Russian, from Latin *nomenclatura* (see **NOMENCLATURE**).

nominal ▶ **adjective 1** (of a role or status) existing in name only: *Thailand retained nominal independence under Japanese military occupation.*
■ of, relating to, or consisting of names. ■ Grammar relating to, headed by, or having the function of a noun: *a nominal group.*
2 (of a price or sum of money) very small; far below the real value or cost: *some firms charge only a nominal fee for the service.*
3 (of a quantity or dimension, especially of manufactured articles) that is stated or expressed but does not necessarily correspond exactly to the real value: *EEC legislation allowed variation around the nominal weight (that printed on each packet).*
■ Economics (of a rate or other figure) expressed in terms of current prices or figures, without making allowance for changes over time: *the nominal exchange rate.*
4 informal (chiefly in the context of space travel) functioning normally or acceptably.
– DERIVATIVES **nominally** adverb.
– ORIGIN late 15th cent. (as a term in grammar): from Latin *nominalis*, from *nomen, nomin-* 'name'.

nominal account ▶ **noun** Finance an account recording the financial transactions of a business in a particular category, rather than with a person or other organization.

nominal definition ▶ **noun** Logic a definition that describes something in terms of its properties, in order to distinguish it from other things, but without describing its underlying structure or 'essence'.

nominalism ▶ **noun** [mass noun] Philosophy the doctrine that universals or general ideas are mere names without any corresponding reality. Only particular objects exist, and properties, numbers, and sets are merely features of the way of considering the things that exist. Important in medieval scholastic thought, nominalism is associated particularly with William of Occam. Often contrasted with **REALISM** (sense 3).
– DERIVATIVES **nominalist** noun, **nominalistic** adjective.
– ORIGIN mid 19th cent.: from French *nominalisme*, from *nominal* 'relating to names' (see **NOMINAL**).

nominalize (also **-ise**) ▶ **verb** [with obj.] Grammar form (a noun) from a verb or adjective, e.g. *output, truth*, from *put out, true.*
– DERIVATIVES **nominalization** noun.

nominal ledger ▶ **noun** Finance a ledger containing nominal accounts, or one containing both nominal and real accounts.

nominal value ▶ **noun** Economics the value that is stated on a coin or note; face value.
■ the price of a share, bond, or stock when it was issued, rather than its current market value.

nominate ▶ **verb** [with obj.] **1** propose or formally enter as a candidate for election or for an honour or award: *the film was nominated for several Oscars.*
■ appoint to a job or position: *the company nominated her as a delegate to the convention.*
2 specify (something) formally, typically the date or

place for an event: *a day was nominated for the exchange of contracts.*

▶ **adjective** Zoology & Botany denoting a race or subspecies which is given the same epithet as the species to which it belongs, e.g. *Homo sapiens sapiens.*

– DERIVATIVES **nominator** noun.

– ORIGIN late Middle English (as an adjective in the sense 'named'): from Latin *nominat-* 'named', from the verb *nominare*, from *nomen, nomin-* 'a name'. The verb senses are first found in English in the 16th cent.

nomination ▶ **noun** [mass noun] the action of nominating or state of being nominated: *women's groups opposed the nomination of the judge* | [count noun] *the film received five nominations.*
■ [count noun] a person or thing nominated: *send your nominations in by 30th November.* ■ the right of nominating someone to a job or position: *senior Tories argued that the nomination should lie with the majority party.*

nominative /ˈnɒmɪnətɪv/ ▶ **adjective 1** Grammar relating to or denoting a case of nouns, pronouns, and adjectives in Latin, Greek, and other inflected languages, used for the subject of a verb.
2 /ˈnɒmɪˌneɪtɪv/ of or appointed by nomination as distinct from election.
▶ **noun** Grammar a word in the nominative case.
■ **(the nominative)** the nominative case.

– ORIGIN late Middle English: from Latin *nominativus* 'relating to naming', translation of Greek *onomastikē (ptōsis)* 'naming (case)'.

nominee ▶ **noun 1** a person who is proposed or formally entered as a candidate for an office or as the recipient of a grant or award.
2 a person or company, not the owner, in whose name a stock, bond, or company is registered.

– ORIGIN mid 17th cent.: from **NOMINATE** + **-EE**.

nomogram /ˈnɒməɡram, ˈnəʊm-/ (also **nomograph**) ▶ **noun** a diagram representing the relations between three or more variable quantities by means of a number of scales, so arranged that the value of one variable can be found by a simple geometrical construction, e.g. by drawing a straight line intersecting the other scales at the appropriate values.

– DERIVATIVES **nomographic** adjective, **nomographically** adverb, **nomography** /nəˈmɒɡrəfi/ noun.

– ORIGIN early 20th cent.: from Greek *nomos* 'law' + **-GRAM**[1].

nomological /ˌnɒməˈlɒdʒɪk(ə)l/ ▶ **adjective** relating to or denoting law-like principles, especially those laws of nature which are neither logically necessary nor theoretically explicable, but just are so.
■ another term for **NOMOTHETIC**.

– DERIVATIVES **nomologically** adverb.

– ORIGIN mid 19th cent.: from Greek *nomos* 'law' + *-logical* (see **-LOGY**).

nomothetic /ˌnɒməˈθɛtɪk, ˌnəʊm-/ ▶ **adjective** of or relating to the study or discovery of general scientific laws. Often contrasted with **IDIOGRAPHIC**.

– ORIGIN mid 17th cent.: from obsolete *nomothete* 'legislator' (from Greek *nomothetēs*) + **-IC**.

-nomy ▶ **combining form** denoting a specified area of knowledge or the laws governing it: *astronomy* | *gastronomy.*

– ORIGIN from Greek *-nomia*; related to *nomos* 'law' and *nemein* 'distribute'.

non- ▶ **prefix 1** not doing; not involved with: *non-aggression* | *non-recognition.*
2 not of the kind or class described: *non-believer* | *nonconformist.*
■ also forming nouns used attributively (such as *non-union* in *non-union miners*).
3 not of the importance implied: *non-issue.*
4 a lack of: *non-aggression.*
5 (added to adverbs) not in the way described: *non-uniformly.*
6 (added to verbs to form adjectives) not causing or requiring: *non-skid* | *non-iron.*
7 expressing a neutral negative sense when a corresponding form beginning with *in-* or *un-* has a special connotation (such as *non-human* compared with *inhuman*).

– ORIGIN from Latin *non* 'not'.

USAGE The prefixes **non-** and **un-** both have the meaning 'not', but tend to be used with a difference of emphasis. See usage at **UN-**[1].

nona- /ˈnɒnə, ˈnəʊnə/ ▶ **combining form** nine; having nine: *nonagon.*

– ORIGIN from Latin *nonus* 'ninth'.

non-addictive ▶ **adjective** (of a drug or other substance) not causing addiction.

nonage /ˈnəʊnɪdʒ, ˈnɒn-/ ▶ **noun** [in sing.] formal the period of immaturity or youth.

– ORIGIN late Middle English: from Old French *nonage*, from *non-* 'non-' + *age* 'age'.

nonagenarian /ˌnɒnədʒɪˈnɛːrɪən, ˌnəʊn-/ ▶ **noun** a person who is between 90 and 99 years old.

– ORIGIN early 19th cent.: from Latin *nonagenarius* (based on *nonaginta* 'ninety') + **-AN**.

non-aggression ▶ **noun** [mass noun] absence of the desire or intention to be aggressive, especially on the part of nations or governments: [as modifier] *a non-aggression pact.*

nonagon /ˈnɒnəɡ(ə)n/ ▶ **noun** a plane figure with nine straight sides and nine angles.

– DERIVATIVES **nonagonal** adjective.

– ORIGIN mid 17th cent.: formed irregularly from Latin *nonus* 'ninth', on the pattern of words such as *hexagon.*

non-alcoholic ▶ **adjective** (of a drink) not containing alcohol.

non-aligned ▶ **adjective** not aligned with something else.
■ of or relating to a state in the Non-Aligned Movement.

– DERIVATIVES **non-alignment** noun.

Non-Aligned Movement a grouping of chiefly developing countries pursuing a policy of neutrality towards the superpowers (i.e. the US and formerly the USSR) in world politics.

non-allergenic ▶ **adjective** not causing an allergic reaction.

non-allergic ▶ **adjective** another term for **NON-ALLERGENIC**.
■ not having an allergy to something.

no-name chiefly N. Amer. ▶ **adjective** (of a product) having no brand name: *cheap, no-name cigarettes.*
■ (of a person) unknown, especially in a particular profession: *no-name, no-frills chefs.*
▶ **noun** such a person.

nonane /ˈnəʊneɪn, ˈnɒn-/ ▶ **noun** [mass noun] Chemistry a colourless liquid hydrocarbon of the alkane series, present in petroleum spirit.
● Chem. formula: C_9H_{20}; many isomers, especially the straight-chain isomer (*n*-**nonane**).

– ORIGIN mid 19th cent.: from **NONA-** (denoting nine carbon atoms) + **-ANE**[2].

non-appearance ▶ **noun** [mass noun] failure to appear or be present, especially at a gathering or engagement.
■ Law failure to appear or be present in a court of law, especially as a witness, defendant, or plaintiff.

nonary /ˈnəʊnəri/ ▶ **adjective** rare relating to or based on the number nine.

– ORIGIN mid 17th cent. (as a noun): from Latin *nonus* 'ninth', on the pattern of words such as *denary.*

non-associative ▶ **adjective 1** not characterized by association, especially of ideas: *the development of chaffinch song is most obviously classified as non-associative learning.*
2 Mathematics involving the condition that a group of quantities connected by operations gives a result dependent upon the order in which the operations are performed.

non-attendance ▶ **noun** [mass noun] failure to attend or be present at a place where you are expected to be: *pupils' non-attendance at school.*

non-attributable ▶ **adjective** not able to be attributed to a particular source or cause.

– DERIVATIVES **non-attributably** adverb.

non-availability ▶ **noun** [mass noun] the state of not being available, free, or able to be used.

non-bank ▶ **adjective** [attrib.] not relating to, connected with, or transacted by a bank.
▶ **noun** a financial institution that is not a bank.

non-being ▶ **noun** [mass noun] the state of not being; non-existence.

non-believer ▶ **noun** a person who does not believe in something, especially one who has no religious faith.

non-belligerent ▶ **adjective** not aggressive or engaged in a war or conflict.

▶ **noun** a nation or person that is not engaged in a war or conflict.

– DERIVATIVES **non-belligerence** noun.

non-biodegradable ▶ **adjective** not biodegradable: *non-biodegradable plastics.*

non-biological ▶ **adjective** not involving, relating to, or derived from biology or living organisms.
■ (of a detergent) not containing enzymes.

non-capital ▶ **adjective** Law (of an offence) not punishable by death.

nonce[1] /nɒns/ ▶ **adjective** (of a word or expression) coined for one occasion: *a nonce word.*

– PHRASES **for the nonce** for the present; temporarily: *the room had been converted for the nonce into a nursery.*

– ORIGIN Middle English: from *then anes* 'the one (purpose)' (from *then*, obsolete oblique form of **THE** + *ane* 'one' + **-s**[3]), altered by misdivision; compare with **NEWT** and **NICKNAME**.

nonce[2] /nɒns/ ▶ **noun** Brit. informal a person convicted of a sexual offence, especially child molesting.

– ORIGIN 1970s: of unknown origin.

nonchalant /ˈnɒnʃ(ə)l(ə)nt/ ▶ **adjective** (of a person or manner) feeling or appearing casually calm and relaxed; not displaying anxiety, interest, or enthusiasm: *she gave a nonchalant shrug.*

– DERIVATIVES **nonchalance** noun, **nonchalantly** adverb.

– ORIGIN mid 18th cent.: from French, literally 'not being concerned', from the verb *nonchaloir.*

non-citizen ▶ **noun** a person who is not an inhabitant or national of a particular state or town.

non-classified ▶ **adjective** (of information or documents) not designated as officially secret; freely available (tending to be less forceful in meaning than **unclassified**).

non-clerical ▶ **adjective 1** (of a job or a person) not doing or involving routine clerical work in an office.
2 not relating to or belonging to the clergy.

non-clinical ▶ **adjective** not clinical.
■ not accompanied by directly observable symptoms.

non-coding ▶ **adjective** Biology (of a section of a nucleic acid molecule) not directing the production of a peptide sequence.

non-collegiate ▶ **adjective** (of a university) not composed of different colleges.
■ not attached or belonging to a particular college within a university.

non-com ▶ **noun** Military, informal a non-commissioned officer.

non-combatant ▶ **noun** a person who is not engaged in fighting during a war, especially a civilian, army chaplain, or army doctor.

non-comedogenic ▶ **adjective** denoting a skincare product or cosmetic that is specially formulated so as not to cause blocked pores.

non-commissioned ▶ **adjective** Military (of an officer in the army, navy, or air force) not holding a rank conferred by a commission.

non-committal ▶ **adjective** (of a person or a person's behaviour or manner) not expressing or revealing commitment to a definite opinion or course of action: *her tone was non-committal, and her face gave nothing away.*

– DERIVATIVES **non-committally** adverb.

non-communicant ▶ **noun** (in church use) a person who does not receive Holy Communion, especially regularly or at a particular service.

non-competitive ▶ **adjective** (of a person or activity) not involving competition; not competitive: *they joined in non-competitive activities like friendship week.*

non-compliance ▶ **noun** [mass noun] failure to act in accordance with a wish or command.

non compos mentis /ˌnɒn ˌkɒmpɒs ˈmɛntɪs/ (also **non compos**) ▶ **adjective** not sane or in one's right mind.

– ORIGIN Latin, literally 'not having control of one's mind'.

non-conductor ▶ **noun** a substance that does not conduct heat or electricity.

– DERIVATIVES **non-conducting** adjective.

nonconformist ▶ **noun 1** (**Nonconformist**) a member of a Protestant Church which dissents from the established Church of England.

2 a person who does not conform to prevailing ideas or practices in their behaviour or views.
▶ adjective **1** (**Nonconformist**) of or relating to Nonconformists or their principles and practices.
2 of or characterized by behaviour or views that do not conform to prevailing ideas or practices.
– DERIVATIVES **nonconformism** noun.

nonconformity ▶ noun [mass noun]
1 (**Nonconformity**) Nonconformists as a body, especially Protestants dissenting from the Anglican Church.
■ the principles or practice of Nonconformists, especially Protestant dissent.
2 failure or refusal to conform to a prevailing rule or practice.
■ lack of similarity in form or type.

non-content ▶ noun a member of the British House of Lords who votes against a particular motion.

non-contentious ▶ adjective **1** not causing or likely to cause an argument.
2 Law not involving differences between contending parties.

non-contradiction ▶ noun a lack or absence of contradiction, especially as a principle of logic that a proposition and its opposite cannot both be true.
– DERIVATIVES **non-contradictory** adjective.

non-contributory ▶ adjective (of a pension or pension scheme) funded by regular payments by the employer, not the employee.
■ (of a state benefit) paid to eligible people regardless of how much tax or other contributions they have made: *non-contributory invalidity benefits.*

non-controversial ▶ adjective not giving or likely to give rise to disagreement (tending to be less forceful in meaning than **uncontroversial**).

non-cooperation ▶ noun [mass noun] failure or refusal to cooperate, especially as a form of protest.

non-count ▶ adjective Grammar (of a noun) not countable.

nonda /ˈnɒndə/ ▶ noun a tropical Australian tree which bears an edible, yellow plum-like fruit and grows in groves on sand ridges.
● *Parinari nonda,* family Chrysobalanaceae.
– ORIGIN mid 19th cent.: probably from a Queensland Aboriginal language.

non-dairy ▶ adjective containing no milk or milk products: *a non-dairy creamer.*

non-delivery ▶ noun [mass noun] chiefly Law failure to provide or deliver goods.

non-denominational ▶ adjective open or acceptable to people of any Christian denomination.

nondescript /ˈnɒndɪskrɪpt/ ▶ adjective lacking distinctive or interesting features or characteristics: *she lived in a nondescript suburban apartment block.*
▶ noun a nondescript person or thing.
– DERIVATIVES **nondescriptly** adverb, **nondescriptness** noun.
– ORIGIN late 17th cent. (in the sense 'not previously described or identified scientifically'): from **NON-** + obsolete *descript* 'described, engraved' (from Latin *descriptus*).

non-destructive ▶ adjective technical not involving damage or destruction, especially of an object or material that is being tested.

non-directional ▶ adjective lacking directional properties.
■ (of sound, light, radio waves, etc.) equally sensitive, intense, etc., in every direction.

non-disjunction ▶ noun [mass noun] Genetics the failure of one or more pairs of homologous chromosomes or sister chromatids to separate normally during nuclear division, usually resulting in an abnormal distribution of chromosomes in the daughter nuclei.

non-drinker ▶ noun a person who does not drink alcohol.

non-drip ▶ adjective (of paint) specially formulated so that it does not drip or run when wet.

non-driver ▶ noun a person who does not or cannot drive a motor vehicle.

none¹ /nʌn/ ▶ pronoun not any: *none of you want to work | don't use any more water, or there'll be none left for me.*
■ no person; no one: *none could match her looks.*
▶ adverb (**none the**) [with comparative] by no amount; not

at all: *it is made none the easier by the differences in approach.*
– PHRASES **none the less** see **NONETHELESS**. **none other than** used to emphasize the surprising identity of a person or thing: *her first customer was none other than Henry du Pont.* **be none the wiser** see **WISE¹**. **none the worse for** see **WORSE**. **none too** see **TOO**. **will have** (or **want**) **none of something** refuse to accept something (especially with reference to behaviour): *I will have none of it.*
– ORIGIN Old English *nān,* from *ne* 'not' + *ān* 'one', of Germanic origin; compare with German *nein* 'no!'.

USAGE It is sometimes held that **none** can only take a singular verb, never a plural verb: *none of them is coming tonight* rather than *none of them are coming tonight.* There is little justification, historical or grammatical, for this view. **None** is descended from Old English **nān** meaning 'not one' and has been used for around a thousand years with both a singular and a plural verb, depending on the context and the emphasis needed.

none² /nəʊn/ (also **nones**) ▶ noun a service forming part of the Divine Office of the Western Christian Church, traditionally said (or chanted) at the ninth hour of the day (3 p.m.).
– ORIGIN mid 19th cent.: from French, from Latin *nona,* feminine singular of *nonus* 'ninth'. Compare with **NOON**.

non-empty ▶ adjective Mathematics & Logic (of a set or class) not empty; having at least one element or member.

nonentity /nɒˈnɛntɪti/ ▶ noun (pl. **-ies**) **1** a person or thing with no special or interesting qualities; an unimportant person or thing: *a political nonentity.*
■ [mass noun] the quality or condition of being uninteresting or unimportant.
2 [mass noun] non-existence: *asserting the nonentity of evil.*
– ORIGIN late 16th cent.: from medieval Latin *nonentitas* 'non-existence'.

nones /nəʊnz/ ▶ plural noun **1** in the ancient Roman calendar, the ninth day before the ides by inclusive reckoning, i.e. the 7th day of March, May, July, October, the 5th of other months.
2 another term for **NONE²**.
– ORIGIN via Old French from Latin *nonas,* feminine accusative plural of *nonus* 'ninth'.

non-essential ▶ adjective not absolutely necessary (tending to be less forceful in meaning than **inessential**): *during the strike non-essential hospital services were halted.*
▶ noun (usu. **non-essentials**) a non-essential thing.

non est factum /ˌnɒn ɛst ˈfaktəm/ ▶ noun Law a plea that a written agreement is invalid because the defendant was mistaken about its character when signing it.
– ORIGIN Latin, literally 'it was not done'.

nonesuch ▶ noun variant spelling of **NONSUCH**.

nonet /nəʊˈnɛt, nɒˈnɛt/ ▶ noun a group of nine people or things, especially musicians.
■ a musical composition for nine voices or instruments.
– ORIGIN mid 19th cent.: from Italian *nonetto,* from *nono* 'ninth', from Latin *nonus.*

nonetheless (also **none the less**) ▶ adverb in spite of that; nevertheless: *the rally, which the government had declared illegal, was nonetheless attended by some 6,000.*

non-Euclidean ▶ adjective Geometry denying or going beyond Euclidean principles in geometry, especially contravening the postulate that only one line through a given point can be parallel to a given line.

non-event ▶ noun a disappointing or insignificant event or occasion, especially one that was expected or intended to be exciting or interesting.
■ an event that did not happen.

non-executive ▶ adjective not having an executive function: *a non-executive chairman.*
▶ noun a person without executive responsibilities.

non-existent ▶ adjective not existing or not real or present: *she pretended to tie a non-existent shoelace.*
– DERIVATIVES **non-existence** noun.

non-factive ▶ adjective Linguistics denoting a verb that takes a clausal object which may or may not designate a true fact, e.g. *believe* as opposed to *know.* Contrasted with **CONTRAFACTIVE, FACTIVE**.

non-fat ▶ adjective (of a food) containing little or no fat: *non-fat buttermilk.*

non-fattening ▶ adjective (of food) not causing an increase in weight when eaten in normal amounts.

nonfeasance /nɒnˈfiːz(ə)ns/ ▶ noun [mass noun] Law failure to perform an act that is required by law.

non-ferrous ▶ adjective relating to or denoting a metal other than iron or steel.

non-fiction ▶ noun [mass noun] prose writing that is informative or factual rather than fictional.
– DERIVATIVES **non-fictional** adjective.

non-figurative ▶ adjective not figurative.
■ (of an artist or work of art) abstract.

non-finite ▶ adjective not finite.
■ Grammar (of a verb form) not limited by tense, person, or number. Contrasted with **FINITE**.

non-flam ▶ adjective short for **NON-FLAMMABLE**.

non-flammable ▶ adjective not catching fire easily; not flammable.

USAGE The adjectives **non-flammable** and **non-inflammable** have the same meaning: see **usage** at **FLAMMABLE**.

non-fulfilment ▶ noun [mass noun] failure to fulfil or carry out something desired, planned, or promised.

non-functional ▶ adjective not having any particular purpose or function.
■ not operating or in working order.

nong /nɒŋ/ ▶ noun Austral. informal a foolish or stupid person (often as a general term of abuse).
– ORIGIN 1940s: of unknown origin.

non-governmental ▶ adjective (especially of an organization) not belonging to or associated with any government.

non-Hodgkin's lymphoma ▶ noun [mass noun] Medicine a form of malignant lymphoma distinguished from Hodgkin's disease only by the absence of binucleate giant cells.

non-human ▶ adjective of, relating to, or characteristic of a creature or thing that is not a human being: *non-human material objects.*
▶ noun a creature that is not a human being.

non-infectious ▶ adjective (of a disease or disease-causing organism) not liable to be transmitted through the environment.
■ not liable to spread infection.

non-inflammable ▶ adjective not catching fire easily; not inflammable.

USAGE The adjectives **non-inflammable** and **non-flammable** have the same meaning: see **usage** at **INFLAMMABLE**.

non-inherent ▶ adjective (of an adjective) having the relevant meaning only when used attributively with reference to a particular individual; for example *poor* and *old* in *the poor old chap,* which is not equivalent to *the chap was poor and old.* Contrasted with **INHERENT**.

non-insulin-dependent ▶ adjective Medicine relating to or denoting a type of diabetes in which there is some insulin secretion. Such diabetes typically develops in adulthood and can frequently be managed by diet and hypoglycaemic agents.

non-interference ▶ noun [mass noun] failure or refusal to intervene without invitation or necessity, especially in political matters.

non-interlaced ▶ adjective denoting, relating to, or capable of a mode of video or computer graphic display in which adjacent lines or picture elements are displayed in succession, so as to form a single scanning sequence.

non-intervention ▶ noun [mass noun] the principle or practice of not becoming involved in the affairs of others.
■ such a policy adopted by a country in its international relations.
– DERIVATIVES **non-interventionism** noun, **non-interventionist** adjective & noun.

non-invasive ▶ adjective **1** (of medical procedures) not involving the introduction of instruments into the body: *non-invasive techniques such as ultrasound.*
2 (of a cancerous disease) not tending to spread.
■ (of plants) not tending to spread undesirably.

non-iron ▶ adjective (of clothes or fabric) not needing to be ironed.

non-ism ▶ noun [mass noun] US general abstention

from activities and substances regarded as damaging to one's health or well-being.

non-issue ▶ noun a topic of little or no importance.

non-judgemental ▶ adjective not judgemental; avoiding moral judgements.

Nonjuror ▶ noun a member of the clergy who refused to take the oath of allegiance to William and Mary in 1689.

non-jury ▶ adjective Law denoting a trial or legal action not having or requiring a jury.

non licet /nɒn ˈlʌɪsɛt/ ▶ adjective not allowed; unlawful.
– ORIGIN Latin.

non-linear ▶ adjective 1 not denoting, involving, or arranged in a straight line.
■Mathematics designating or involving an equation whose terms are not of the first degree. ■ Physics involving a lack of linearity between two related qualities such as input and output. ■ Mathematics involving measurement in more than one dimension. ■ not linear, sequential, or straightforward; random: *Joyce's stream-of-consciousness, non-linear narrative*.
2 of or denoting digital editing whereby a sequence of edits is stored on computer as opposed to videotape, thus facilitating further editing.
– PHRASES **go non-linear** informal become very excited or angry, especially about a particular obsession.
– DERIVATIVES **non-linearity** noun, **non-linearly** adverb.

non-logical ▶ adjective not derived from or according to the rules of logic or formal argument (less forceful in meaning than **illogical**).
– DERIVATIVES **non-logically** adverb.

non-magnetic ▶ adjective (of a substance) not magnetic.

non-malignant ▶ adjective (of a tumour) benign; not cancerous.

non-member ▶ noun a person, body, or country that is not a member of a particular organization.
– DERIVATIVES **non-membership** noun.

non-metal ▶ noun an element or substance that is not a metal.
– DERIVATIVES **non-metallic** adjective.

non-military ▶ adjective not belonging to, characteristic of, or involving the armed forces; civilian: *the widespread destruction of non-military targets*.

non-moral ▶ adjective not holding or manifesting moral principles: *non-moral value judgements*.

non-native ▶ adjective (of a person, plant, or animal) not indigenous or native to a particular place.
■(of a speaker) not having spoken the language in question from earliest childhood.

non-natural ▶ adjective not involving or manifesting natural means or processes.
■Philosophy existing but not part of the natural world (a term used by G.E. Moore of ethical properties).

non-negative ▶ adjective not negative.
■Mathematics either positive or equal to zero.

non-negotiable ▶ adjective not open to discussion or modification.
■(of a document) not able to be transferred or assigned to the legal ownership of another person.

non-net ▶ adjective Brit. (of a book) not subject to a minimum selling price under the terms of the Net Book Agreement.

non-nuclear ▶ adjective 1 not involving or relating to nuclear energy or nuclear weapons.
■(of a state) not possessing nuclear weapons.
2 Physics not involving, relating to, or forming part of a nucleus or nuclei.

no-no ▶ noun (pl. **-os**) informal a thing that is not possible or acceptable: *perming highlighted hair used to be a definite no-no, but it's now possible*.

non-objective ▶ adjective 1 (of a person or their judgement) influenced by personal feeling or opinions in considering and representing facts.
2 of or relating to abstract art.

non-observance ▶ noun [mass noun] failure to fulfil or comply with an obligation, rule, or custom.

no-nonsense ▶ adjective simple and straightforward; sensible.

non-operational ▶ adjective not engaged in or involving active duties: *his current non-operational job as a fire prevention office*.
■not working or in use: *non-operational equipment*.

non-organic ▶ adjective not organic, in particular:
■not relating to or derived from living matter: *non-organic archaeological finds*. ■ (especially of food or farming methods) not produced, relating to, or involving production by organic methods: *non-organic hens' eggs | non-organic pesticides*.

non-parametric ▶ adjective Statistics not involving any assumptions as to the form or parameters of a frequency distribution.

nonpareil /ˌnɒnpəˈreɪl/ ▶ adjective having no match or equal; unrivalled: *he is a nonpareil storyteller* | [postpositive] *a film critic nonpareil*.
▶ noun 1 an unrivalled or matchless person or thing.
2 US a flat round confection made of chocolate covered with white sugar sprinkles.
3 [mass noun] Printing an old type size equal to six points (larger than ruby).
– ORIGIN late Middle English: from French, from *non-* 'not' + *pareil* 'equal' (from popular Latin *pariculus*, diminutive of Latin *par* 'equal').

non-participating ▶ adjective 1 not involved or taking part in an activity.
2 (of an insurance policy) not allowing the holder a share of the profits, typically in the form of a bonus, made by the company.

non-partisan ▶ adjective not biased or partisan, especially towards any particular political group.

non-party ▶ adjective independent of any political party.

non-penetrative ▶ adjective (of sexual activity) in which penetration by the penis does not take place.

non-person ▶ noun a person regarded as non-existent or unimportant, or as having no rights; an ignored or forgotten person: *these players were famous within their own communities, but non-persons outside them*. Compare with **UNPERSON**.

non-personal ▶ adjective not personal: *non-personal tax allowances*.

non-physical ▶ adjective not physical, in particular:
■not relating to or concerning the body: *both physical and non-physical ill-treatment*. ■ not tangible or concrete: *a tactile alternative to non-physical digital money*.
– DERIVATIVES **non-physically** adverb.

non placet /nɒn ˈpleɪsɛt/ ▶ noun a negative vote in a Church or university assembly.
– ORIGIN Latin, literally 'it does not please'.

non-playing ▶ adjective (of a team captain or other member of a team or club) not playing in a game or sport.

nonplus /nɒnˈplʌs/ ▶ verb (**nonplussed**, **nonplussing**) [with obj.] (usu. **be nonplussed**) surprise and confuse (someone) so much that they are unsure how to react: *Diane was nonplussed by such an odd question*.
▶ noun a state of being surprised and confused in this way.
– ORIGIN late 16th cent.: from Latin *non plus* 'not more'. The noun originally meant 'a state in which no more can be said or done'.

nonplussed ▶ adjective 1 (of a person) surprised and confused so much that they are unsure how to react: *Henry looked completely nonplussed*.
2 N. Amer. informal (of a person) not disconcerted; unperturbed.

> **USAGE** In standard use **nonplussed** means 'surprised and confused', as in *she was nonplussed at his eagerness to help out*. In North American English a new use has developed in recent years, meaning 'unperturbed'—more or less the opposite of its traditional meaning—as in *he was clearly trying to appear nonplussed*. This new use probably arose on the assumption that **non-** was the normal negative prefix and must therefore have a negative meaning. Although the use is common it is not yet considered standard.

non-political ▶ adjective not relating to or motivated by politics: *non-political speeches*.

non possumus /nɒn ˈpɒsjʊməs/ ▶ noun used as a statement expressing inability to act in a matter.
– ORIGIN Latin, literally 'we cannot'.

non-prescription ▶ adjective (of a medicine) available for sale without a prescription.
■denoting such sale or purchase.

non-price competition ▶ noun [mass noun] Economics a form of competition in which two or more producers use such factors as packaging, delivery, or customer service rather than price to increase demand for their products.

non-productive ▶ adjective not producing or able to produce goods, crops, or economic benefit (tending to be less forceful in meaning than **unproductive**).
■achieving little.
– DERIVATIVES **non-productively** adverb.

non-professional ▶ adjective relating to or engaged in a paid occupation that does not require advanced education or training: *non-professional grades of staff*.
■relating to or engaged in an activity (especially an interest or hobby) which is not a person's main paid occupation: *non-professional actors*.
▶ noun a non-professional person.

non-profit ▶ adjective [attrib.] not making or conducted primarily to make a profit: *charities and other non-profit organizations*.

non-proliferation ▶ noun [mass noun] the prevention of an increase or spread of something, especially the number of countries possessing nuclear weapons: [as modifier] *a nuclear non-proliferation treaty*.

non-proprietary ▶ adjective (especially of computer hardware or software) conforming to standards that are in the public domain or are widely licensed, and so not restricted to one manufacturer.
■not registered or protected as a trademark or brand name; generic.

non-racial ▶ adjective not involving racial factors or racial discrimination.

non-random ▶ adjective not random; not ordered randomly: *our sample was non-random*.

non-reader ▶ noun a person who cannot or does not read.

non-resident ▶ adjective not living in a particular place, especially a country or a place of work: *the building had a non-resident, part-time caretaker*.
■(of a company or trust) not based in or administered from a particular country: *the Revenue only seek to charge the 35 per cent rate if the income of the non-resident trust has a UK source*. ■ (of a job or course) not requiring the holder or participant to reside at the place of work or instruction. ■ Computing (of software) not kept permanently in memory but available to be loaded from a backing store or external device.
▶ noun a person not living in a particular place.
– DERIVATIVES **non-residence** noun.

non-residential ▶ adjective not requiring or providing facilities for people to live on the premises: *two-day non-residential workshops*.
■(of property or land) containing or suitable for commercial premises rather than private houses.

non-resistance ▶ noun [mass noun] the practice or principle of not resisting authority, even when it is unjustly exercised.

non-restrictive ▶ adjective 1 not involving restrictions or limitations.
2 Grammar (of a relative clause or descriptive phrase) giving additional information about a noun phrase whose particular reference has already been specified.

> **USAGE** On the use of restrictive and non-restrictive relative clauses, see usage at **RESTRICTIVE**.

non-return ▶ adjective permitting the flow of air or liquid in one direction only: *a non-return valve*.

non-returnable ▶ adjective (especially of a deposit) not repayable in any circumstances.
■(of bottles or other containers) not intended to be returned empty to the suppliers.

non-rhotic ▶ noun Phonetics relating to or denoting a dialect of English in which *r* is pronounced in prevocalic position only. Standard British English is non-rhotic.

non-rigid ▶ adjective (especially of materials) not rigid.
■denoting an airship whose shape is maintained solely by the pressure of the gas inside.

non-scene ▶ adjective informal (of a homosexual) not inclined to participate in the social environment frequented predominantly by other homosexuals.

non-scheduled ▶ adjective denoting or relating to an airline that operates without fixed or published flying schedules: *measures for non-scheduled sites are being considered.*

non-scientific ▶ adjective not involving or relating to science or scientific methods.
– DERIVATIVES **non-scientist** noun.

non-secretor /ˌnɒnsɪˈkriːtə/ ▶ noun a person whose saliva and other secretions do not contain blood-group antigens.

non-sectarian ▶ adjective not involving or relating to different religious sects or political groups.

nonsense ▶ noun [mass noun] **1** spoken or written words that have no meaning or make no sense: *he was talking absolute nonsense.*
■ [as exclamation] used to show strong disagreement: *'Nonsense! No one can do that.'* ■ [as modifier] denoting verse or other writing intended to be amusing by virtue of its absurd or whimsical language: *nonsense poetry.*
2 foolish or unacceptable behaviour: *she's a strong woman who stands no nonsense.*
■ [count noun] something that one disagrees with or disapproves of: *they dismissed the concept of large mergers as a nonsense.*
– PHRASES **make (a) nonsense** reduce the value of something to a ridiculous degree: *the proposal would make a nonsense of their plans.*
– DERIVATIVES **nonsensical** adjective, **nonsensicality** noun, **nonsensically** adverb.

nonsense syllable ▶ noun an arbitrarily formed syllable with no meaning, used in memory experiments and tests.

nonsense word ▶ noun a word having no conventionally accepted meaning.

non sequitur /nɒn ˈsɛkwɪtə/ ▶ noun a conclusion or statement that does not logically follow from the previous argument or statement.
– ORIGIN Latin, literally 'it does not follow'.

non-sexual ▶ adjective not involving or relating to sex or sexual reproduction.
– DERIVATIVES **non-sexually** adverb.

non-skid ▶ adjective designed to prevent sliding or skidding: *non-skid tyres.*

non-slip ▶ adjective designed to prevent slipping: *a non-slip bath mat.*

non-smoker ▶ noun **1** a person who does not smoke tobacco.
2 Brit. informal a train compartment in which smoking is forbidden.

non-smoking ▶ adjective denoting a place where smoking tobacco is forbidden.
■ denoting a person who does not smoke.
▶ noun [mass noun] the practice or habit of not smoking.

non-solid colour ▶ noun Computing a colour simulated by a pattern of dots of other colours, extending the range of colours available.

non-specific ▶ adjective not detailed or exact; general.
■ Medicine not assignable to a particular cause, condition, or category.

non-specific urethritis (abbrev.: **NSU**) ▶ noun [mass noun] Medicine inflammation of the urethra due to infection by chlamydiae or other organisms (other than gonococci).

non-standard ▶ adjective not average, normal, or usual: *people working non-standard hours.*
■ (of language) not of the form that is accepted as standard.

non-starter ▶ noun a person or animal that fails to take part in a race.
■ informal a person, plan, or idea that has no chance of succeeding or being effective.

non-stick ▶ adjective (of a pan or surface) covered with a substance that prevents food sticking to it during cooking: *a non-stick frying pan.*

non-stoichiometric ▶ adjective Chemistry relating to or denoting quantities of reactants which are not in a simple integral ratio or are not in the ratio expected from an ideal formula or equation.

non-stop ▶ adjective continuing without stopping or pausing: *we had two days of almost non-stop rain.*
■ (of a passenger vehicle or journey) not having or making stops on the way to its destination: *the non-stop London shuttle runs until 10pm | a non-stop flight to Los Angeles.* ■ oppressively constant; relentless; unremitting: *the show was axed after non-stop criticism.*

▶ adverb without stopping or pausing: *Stephen had been working non-stop.*
▶ noun a non-stop flight or train.

nonsuch /ˈnɒnsʌtʃ/ ▶ noun **1** (also **nonesuch**) archaic a person or thing that is regarded as perfect or excellent.
2 a small Eurasian medick which is widely grown as a constituent of grazing pasture.
● *Medicago lupulina*, family Leguminosae.
– ORIGIN early 17th cent.: coined on the pattern of *nonpareil.*

nonsuit Law ▶ verb [with obj.] (of a judge or court) subject (a plaintiff) to the stoppage of their suit on the grounds of failure to make a legal case or bring sufficient evidence.
▶ noun the stoppage of a suit on such grounds.
– ORIGIN late Middle English (as a noun): from Anglo-Norman French, literally 'not pursuing' (see **NON-, SUIT**).

non-swimmer ▶ noun a person who cannot or does not swim.

non-technical ▶ adjective not relating to or involving science or technology: *a simple, non-technical procedure.*
■ without specialized or technical knowledge: *a non-technical background.* ■ not using technical terms or requiring specialized knowledge.

non-toxic ▶ adjective not poisonous or toxic: *non-toxic waste.*

non-transferable ▶ adjective not able to be transferred or made over to the possession of another person: *a special ticket which was non-transferable.*

non-treaty ▶ adjective N. Amer., chiefly historical of or relating to an American Indian person or people not subject to a treaty made with the government.

non-trivial ▶ adjective not trivial; significant.
■ Mathematics having some variables or terms that are not equal to zero or an identity.

non-tropical sprue ▶ noun see **SPRUE**[2].

non-U ▶ adjective informal, chiefly Brit. (of language or social behaviour) not characteristic of the upper social classes; not socially acceptable to certain people.
– ORIGIN 1950s: from **NON-** + **U**[3].

non-uniform ▶ adjective not uniform, regular, or constant; varying.
– DERIVATIVES **non-uniformity** noun, **non-uniformly** adverb.

non-union ▶ adjective not belonging or relating to a trade union: *non-union agreements.*
■ (of a company) not having trade union members. ■ not done or produced by members of a trade union.

non-usage ▶ noun another term for **NON-USE**.

non-use ▶ noun [mass noun] the refusal or failure to use something.
– DERIVATIVES **non-user** noun.

non-verbal ▶ adjective not involving or using words or speech: *forms of non-verbal communication.*
– DERIVATIVES **non-verbally** adverb.

non-vintage ▶ adjective denoting a wine that is not made from the crop of a single identified district in a good year.

non-violence ▶ noun [mass noun] the use of peaceful means, not force, to bring about political or social change.

non-violent ▶ adjective (especially of political action or resistance) characterized by non-violence.
■ (especially of a person) not using violence.
– DERIVATIVES **non-violently** adverb.

non-volatile ▶ adjective not volatile.
■ Computing (of a computer's memory) retaining data even if there is a break in the power supply.

non-white ▶ adjective denoting or relating to a person whose origin is not predominantly European.
▶ noun a person whose origin is not predominantly European.

> **USAGE** The term **non-white** has been objected to as politically incorrect, on the grounds that it assumes that the norm is white. However, although alternatives such as **person of colour** have been put forward in recent years, these have not yet become widespread in British or US English. **Non-white** continues to be broadly accepted where a collective term is required.

non-word ▶ noun a group of letters or speech

sounds that looks or sounds like a word but that is not accepted as such by native speakers.

nonyl /ˈnɒnʌɪl, -nɪl, ˈnəʊn-/ ▶ noun [as modifier] Chemistry of or denoting an alkyl radical —C_9H_{19}, derived from nonane.

non-zero ▶ adjective having a positive or negative value; not equal to zero.

noodle[1] ▶ noun (usu. **noodles**) a very thin, long strip of pasta or a similar flour paste, usually eaten with a sauce or in a soup.
– ORIGIN late 18th cent.: from German *Nudel*, of unknown origin.

noodle[2] ▶ noun informal a stupid or silly person.
■ a person's head.
– ORIGIN mid 18th cent.: of unknown origin. The sense 'head' dates from the early 20th cent.

noodle[3] ▶ verb [with obj.] Austral. informal search (an opal dump) for opals.
– ORIGIN early 20th cent.: of unknown origin.

Noogoora burr /nʊˈɡuːrə/ ▶ noun Austral. a plant of the daisy family which has become naturalized in Australia, where it is considered a noxious weed because its hooked burrs become entangled in sheep's fleeces.
● *Xanthium occidentale*, family Compositae.
– ORIGIN late 19th cent.: *Noogoora* from the name of a sheep station in Queensland.

nook ▶ noun a corner or recess, especially one offering seclusion or security: *the nook beside the fire.*
– PHRASES **every nook and cranny** every part or aspect of something: *the party reached into every nook and cranny of people's lives.*
– ORIGIN Middle English (denoting a corner or fragment): of unknown origin.

nooky (also **nookie**) ▶ noun [mass noun] informal sexual activity or intercourse.
– ORIGIN early 20th cent.: perhaps from **NOOK**.

noon ▶ noun twelve o'clock in the day; midday: *the service starts at twelve noon.*
– ORIGIN Old English *nōn* 'the ninth hour from sunrise, i.e. approximately 3 p.m.', from Latin *nona* (*hora*) 'ninth hour'; compare with **NONE**[2].

noonday ▶ noun the middle of the day: [as modifier] *the blinds were lowered to keep out the noonday sun.*

no one ▶ pronoun no person; not a single person: *no one came | she told no one she was going.*

nooner ▶ noun N. Amer. informal an event that occurs in the middle of the day, especially an act of sexual intercourse.

nooning ▶ noun N. Amer. dialect a rest or meal at midday.

noonoo ▶ noun (pl. **noonoos**) variant spelling of **NUNU**.

noontide (also **noontime**) ▶ noun poetic/literary noon.

noose ▶ noun a loop with a running knot, tightening as the rope or wire is pulled and typically used to hang people or trap animals.
■ (**the noose**) death by hanging.
▶ verb [with obj.] put a noose on (someone): *she was noosed and hooded, then strangled by the executioner.*
■ catch (an animal) with a noose. ■ form (a rope) into a noose.
– PHRASES **put one's head in a noose** bring about one's own downfall.
– ORIGIN late Middle English: probably via Old French *no(u)s* from Latin *nodus* 'knot'.

noosphere /ˈnəʊəsfɪə/ ▶ noun a postulated sphere or stage of evolutionary development dominated by consciousness, the mind, and interpersonal relationships.
– ORIGIN 1940s: from French *noösphère*, based on Greek *noos* 'mind'.

Nootka /ˈnuːtkə, ˈnɒt-/ ▶ noun (pl. same or **Nootkas**) **1** a member of an American Indian people of Vancouver Island, Canada.
2 [mass noun] the Wakashan language of this people, now with few speakers.
▶ adjective of or relating to this people or their language.
– ORIGIN named after *Nootka* Sound, an inlet on the coast of Vancouver Island.

Nootka cypress ▶ noun a conical cypress whose foliage has an unpleasant turpentine smell when crushed, native to western North America and typically growing at high altitudes.
● *Chamaecyparis nootkatensis*, family Cupressaceae.

nootropic /ˌnəʊəˈtrɒpɪk, -ˈtrəʊp-/ ▶ adjective (of a

drug) used to enhance memory or other cognitive functions.
▶**noun** a drug of this kind.
– ORIGIN 1970s: from French *nootrope* (from Greek *noos* 'mind' + *tropē* 'turning') + **-IC**.

nopal /ˈnəʊp(ə)l, ˈnəʊpal/ ▶**noun** a cactus which is a major food plant of the bugs from which cochineal is obtained.
• Genus *Nopalea*, family Cactaceae: several species, in particular *N. cochinellifera*.
▪(**nopales** /nəʊˈpɑːlɛz/) the edible fleshy pads of this cactus used as a staple in Mexican cuisine.
– ORIGIN mid 18th cent.: via French and Spanish from Nahuatl *nopalli* 'cactus'.

nope ▶**exclamation** informal variant of **NO**.

nor ▶**conjunction** & **adverb 1** used before the second or further of two or more alternatives (the first being introduced by a negative such as 'neither' or 'not') to indicate that they are each untrue or each do not happen: *they were neither cheap nor convenient* | *the sheets were never washed, nor the towels, nor his shirts.*
▪[as adv.] poetic/literary term for **NEITHER**: *nor God nor demon can undo the done.*
2 used to introduce a further negative statement: *the struggle did not end, nor was it any less diminished.*
3 [conjunction or prep.] archaic or dialect than: *she thinks she knows better nor me.*
▶**noun** (usu. **NOR**) Electronics a Boolean operator which gives the value one if and only if all operands have a value of zero and otherwise has a value of zero.
▪(also **NOR gate**) a circuit which produces an output signal only when there are no signals on any of the input connections.
– ORIGIN Middle English: contraction of Old English *nother* 'neither'.

nor' ▶**abbreviation for** (especially in compounds) north.

nor- ▶**prefix** Chemistry denoting an organic compound derived from another, in particular by the shortening of a chain or ring by the removal of one methylene group or by the replacement of one or more methyl side chains by hydrogen atoms: *noradrenaline.*
– ORIGIN from *nor(mal)*.

noradrenaline /ˌnɔːrəˈdrɛn(ə)lɪn/ ▶**noun** [mass noun] Biochemistry a hormone which is released by the adrenal medulla and by the sympathetic nerves and functions as a neurotransmitter. It is also used as a drug to raise blood pressure.
• Chem. formula: $(HO)_2C_6H_3CHOHCH_2NH_2$.
– ORIGIN 1930s: from **NOR-** + **ADRENALIN**.

Norbertine /ˈnɔːbətɪn, -ʌɪn/ ▶**noun** another term for **PREMONSTRATENSIAN**.
– ORIGIN late 17th cent.: named after St *Norbert* (*c.*1080–1134), founder of the order.

Nordic ▶**adjective** of or relating to Scandinavia, Finland, and Iceland.
▪relating to or denoting a physical type of northern European peoples characterized by tall stature, a bony frame, light colouring, and a dolichocephalic head. ▪(in skiing) relating to or denoting the disciplines of cross-country skiing or ski jumping. Often contrasted with **ALPINE**.
▶**noun** a native of Scandinavia, Finland, or Iceland.
– ORIGIN from French *nordique*, from *nord* 'north'.

Nordkapp /ˈnuːrkap/ Norwegian name for **NORTH CAPE**.

Nordkyn /ˈnʊətʃʊn/ a promontory on the north coast of Norway, to the east of North Cape. At 71° 8′ N, it is the northernmost point of the European mainland, North Cape being on an island.

Nord-Pas-de-Calais /ˌnɔːpɑːdəˈkaleɪ, French nɔʀpadəkalɛ/ a region of northern France, on the border with Belgium.

Nordrhein-Westfalen /ˌnɔrtraɪnvɛstˈfaːlən/ German name for **NORTH RHINE-WESTPHALIA**.

norepinephrine /ˌnɔːrɛpɪˈnɛfrɪn, -riːn/ ▶**noun** another term for **NORADRENALINE**.
– ORIGIN 1940s: from **NOR-** + **EPINEPHRINE**.

Norfolk /ˈnɔːfək/ a county on the east coast of England, east of the Wash; county town, Norwich.

Norfolk Island an island in the Pacific Ocean, off the east coast of Australia, administered since 1913 as an external territory of Australia; pop. 1,912 (1991). Discovered by Captain James Cook in 1774, it was occupied from 1788 to 1814 as a penal colony.

Norfolk Island pine (also **Norfolk pine**) ▶**noun** an evergreen tree related to the monkey puzzle, having horizontal branches with upswept shoots bearing small scale-like leaves. Native to Norfolk Island, it is often grown in Mediterranean countries.
• *Araucaria heterophylla*, family Araucariaceae.

Norfolk jacket ▶**noun** a loose belted jacket with box pleats, typically made of tweed.

Norfolk reed ▶**noun** the common reed, which is cultivated in eastern England for use in thatching.
• *Phragmites australis*, family Gramineae.

Norfolk terrier ▶**noun** a small thickset terrier of a breed with a rough red or black-and-tan coat and drop ears.

Norge /ˈnɒrgə/ Norwegian name for **NORWAY**.

nori /ˈnɔːri/ ▶**noun** [mass noun] an edible seaweed, eaten either fresh or dried in sheets, especially by the Japanese.
– ORIGIN Japanese.

noria /ˈnɔːrɪə/ ▶**noun** a device for raising water from a stream or river, consisting of a chain of pots or buckets revolving round a wheel driven by the water current.
– ORIGIN via Spanish from Arabic *nāʿūra*.

Noriega /ˌnɒrɪˈeɪgə/, Manuel (Antonio Morena) (b.1940), Panamanian statesman and general, head of state 1983–9. Charged with drug trafficking by a US grand jury in 1988, he eventually surrendered to US troops sent into Panama and was brought to trial and convicted in 1992.

norite /ˈnɔːrʌɪt/ ▶**noun** [mass noun] Geology a coarse-grained plutonic rock similar to gabbro but containing hypersthene.
– ORIGIN late 19th cent.: from **NORWAY** + **-ITE**[1].

nork ▶**noun** (usu. **norks**) Austral. informal a woman's breast.
– ORIGIN 1960s: of unknown origin.

norm ▶**noun 1** (**the norm**) something that is usual, typical, or standard: *strikes were the norm.*
▪(usu. **norms**) a standard or pattern, especially of social behaviour, that is typical or expected of a group: *the norms of good behaviour in the Civil Service.* ▪a required standard; a level to be complied with or reached: [as modifier] *the 7% pay norm had been breached again.*
2 Mathematics the product of a complex number and its conjugate, equal to the sum of the squares of its real and imaginary components, or the positive square root of this sum.
▪an analogous quantity used to represent the magnitude of a vector.
– ORIGIN early 19th cent.: from Latin *norma* 'precept, rule, carpenter's square'.

Norma /ˈnɔːmə/ Astronomy a small and inconspicuous southern constellation (the Rule), lying partly in the Milky Way between Lupus and Ara.
▪[as genitive **Normae** /-miː/] used with preceding letter or numeral to designate a star in this constellation: *the star Gamma Normae.*
– ORIGIN Latin, 'carpenter's square'.

normal ▶**adjective 1** conforming to a standard; usual, typical, or expected: *it's quite* ***normal*** *for puppies to bolt their food* | *normal working hours.*
▪(of a person) free from physical or mental disorders.
2 technical (of a line, ray, or other linear feature) intersecting a given line or surface at right angles.
3 Medicine (of a salt solution) containing the same salt concentration as the blood.
▪Chemistry dated (of a solution) containing one gram-equivalent of solute per litre.
4 Geology denoting a fault or faulting in which a relative downward movement occurred in the strata situated on the upper side of the fault plane.
▶**noun** [mass noun] **1** the usual, average, or typical state or condition: *her temperature was* ***above normal*** | *the service will be* ***back to normal*** *next week.*
▪[count noun] a person who is physically or mentally healthy.
2 [count noun] technical a line at right angles to a given line or surface.
– DERIVATIVES **normalcy** noun chiefly N. Amer., **normality** noun.
– ORIGIN mid 17th cent. (in the sense 'right-angled'): from Latin *normalis*, from *norma* 'carpenter's square' (see **NORM**). Current senses date from the early 19th cent.

normal distribution ▶**noun** Statistics a function that represents the distribution of many random variables as a symmetrical bell-shaped graph.

normal form ▶**noun 1** Computing a defined standard structure for relational databases in which a relation may not be nested within another relation.
2 Philosophy a standard structure or format in which all propositions in a (usually symbolic) language can be expressed.

normalize (also **-ise**) ▶**verb 1** [with obj.] bring or return to a normal or standard condition or state: *Vietnam and China agreed to normalize diplomatic relations in 1991* | [no obj.] *the situation had normalized.*
▪(in South Africa) desegregate and remove racial bias from (an activity).
2 [with obj.] (often **be normalized**) Mathematics multiply (a series, function or item of data) by a factor that makes the norm or some associated quantity such as an integral equal to a desired value (usually 1).
▪Computing (in floating-point representation) express (a number) in the standard form as regards the position of the radix point, usually immediately preceding the first non-zero digit.
– DERIVATIVES **normalization** noun, **normalizer** noun.

normally ▶**adverb 1** [sentence adverb] under normal or usual conditions; as a rule: *normally, it takes three or four years to complete the training.*
2 in a normal manner; in the usual way: *try to breathe normally.*
3 technical at right angles to a given line or surface.

normally aspirated ▶**adjective** (of an engine) not turbocharged or supercharged.

normal school ▶**noun** (especially in North America and France) a school or college for the training of teachers.

Norman[1] ▶**noun 1** a member of a people of mixed Frankish and Scandinavian origin who settled in Normandy from about AD 912 and became a dominant military power in western Europe and the Mediterranean in the 11th century.
▪in particular, any of the Normans who conquered England in 1066 or their descendants. ▪a native or inhabitant of modern Normandy. ▪any of the English kings from William I to Stephen.
2 [mass noun] the form of French spoken by the Normans.
▶**adjective** of, relating to, or denoting the Normans.
▪denoting, relating to, or built in the style of Romanesque architecture used in Britain under the Normans. ▪of or relating to modern Normandy.
– DERIVATIVES **Normanesque** adjective, **Normanism** noun, **Normanize** (also **-ise**) verb.
– ORIGIN Middle English: from Old French *Normans*, plural of *Normant*, from Old Norse *Northmathr* 'Northman'.

Norman[2], Greg (b.1955), Australian golfer; full name *Gregory John Norman*. He has won the world match-play championship three times (1980; 1983; 1986) and the British Open twice (1986; 1993).

Norman[3], Jessye (b.1945), American operatic soprano. She is noted for her interpretations of the works of Wagner, Schubert, and Mahler.

Norman Conquest the conquest of England by William of Normandy (William the Conqueror) after the Battle of Hastings in 1066.

Normandy a former province of NW France with its coastline on the English Channel, now divided into the two regions of Lower Normandy (Basse-Normandie) and Upper Normandy (Haute-Normandie); chief town, Rouen.

Norman French ▶**noun** [mass noun] the northern form of Old French spoken by the Normans.
▪the variety of this used in English law courts from the 11th to 13th centuries; Anglo-Norman French. ▪the French dialect of modern Normandy.

normative ▶**adjective** formal establishing, relating to or deriving from a standard or norm, especially of behaviour: *negative sanctions to enforce normative behaviour.*
– DERIVATIVES **normatively** adverb, **normativeness** noun.
– ORIGIN late 19th cent.: from French *normatif, -ive*, from Latin *norma* 'carpenter's square' (see **NORM**).

normoglycaemia /ˌnɔːmə(ʊ)glʌɪˈsiːmɪə/ (US **normoglycemia**) ▶**noun** [mass noun] Medicine a normal concentration of sugar in the blood (as contrasted with hyper- or hypoglycaemia).
– DERIVATIVES **normoglycaemic** adjective.

normotensive /ˌnɔːmə(ʊ)ˈtɛnsɪv/ ▶**adjective** Medicine having or denoting a normal blood pressure.

Norn /nɔːn/ ▶**noun** [mass noun] a form of Norse

n

formerly spoken in Orkney and Shetland but largely extinct by the 19th century.
▶ **adjective** of or relating to this language.
– ORIGIN from Old Norse *norræn* 'Norn, northern', from *northr* 'north'.

Norns /'nɔːnz/ Scandinavian Mythology the three virgin goddesses of destiny (Urd or Urdar, Verdandi, and Skuld), who sit by the well of fate at the base of the ash tree Yggdrasil and spin the web of fate.
– ORIGIN from Old Norse, of unknown origin.

Norplant ▶ **noun** [mass noun] trademark a contraceptive for women consisting of small rods implanted under the skin which gradually release the hormone levonorgestrel over a number of years.
– ORIGIN 1980s: from (*levo*)*nor*(*gestrel*) (*im*)*plant*.

Norrköping /'nɔː,tʃøː,pɪŋ/ an industrial city and seaport on an inlet of the Baltic Sea in SE Sweden; pop. 120,520 (1990).

Norroy /'nɒrɔɪ/ (in full **Norroy and Ulster**) ▶ **noun** Heraldry (in the UK) the title given to the third King of Arms, with jurisdiction north of the Trent and (since 1943) in Northern Ireland.
– ORIGIN late Middle English: from Old French *nord* 'north' + *roi* 'king'.

Norse /nɔːs/ ▶ **noun** 1 [mass noun] the Norwegian language, especially in an ancient or medieval form, or the Scandinavian language group.
2 [treated as pl.] Norwegians or Scandinavians, especially in ancient or medieval times.
▶ **adjective** of or relating to ancient or medieval Norway or Scandinavia, or their inhabitants or language.
– DERIVATIVES **Norseman** noun (pl. **-men**).
– ORIGIN from Dutch *noor*(*d*)*sch*, from *noord* 'north'; compare with Swedish, Danish, and Norwegian *Norsk*.

norteño /nɔː'tɛnjəʊ/ ▶ **noun** 1 (pl. **-os** /-ɒs/) an inhabitant or native of northern Mexico.
2 (also **norteña** /nɔː'tɛnja/ [mass noun] a style of folk music, associated particularly with northern Mexico and Texas, typically featuring an accordion and using polkas and other rhythms found in the music of central European immigrants.
– ORIGIN Spanish, literally 'northerner'.

North, Frederick, Lord (1732–92), British Tory statesman, Prime Minister 1770–82. He sought to avoid the War of American Independence, but was regarded as responsible for the loss of the American colonies.

north ▶ **noun** (usu. **the north**) 1 the direction in which a compass needle normally points, towards the horizon on the left-hand side of a person facing east, or the part of the horizon lying in this direction: *a bitter wind blew from the north* | *Mount Kenya is* **to the north of** *Nairobi*.
■ the compass point corresponding to this. ■ a direction in space parallel to the earth's axis of rotation and towards the point on the celestial sphere around which the stars appear to turn anticlockwise.
2 the northern part of the world or of a specified country, region, or town: *there will be heavy wintry showers, particularly in the north*.
■ (usu. **the North**) the northern part of England. ■ (usu. **the North**) the NE states of the United States, especially those opposed to slavery during the Civil War. ■ (usu. **the North**) the industrialized and economically advanced nations of the world.
3 (**North**) [as name] Bridge the player occupying a designated position at the table, sitting opposite and partnering South.
▶ **adjective** [attrib.] 1 lying towards, near, or facing the north: *the north bank of the river* | *the north door*.
■ (of a wind) blowing from the north.
2 of or denoting the northern part of a specified area, city, or country or its inhabitants: *North Wales* | *North African*.
▶ **adverb** to or towards the north: *the town is twenty-five miles north of Newport* | *a north-facing wall*.
– PHRASES **north by east** (or **west**) between north and north-north-east (or north-north-west). **up north** informal to or in the north of a country, especially England: *he's taken a teaching job up north*.
– ORIGIN Old English, of Germanic origin; related to Dutch *noord* and German *nord*.

North Africa the northern part of the African continent, especially the countries bordering the Mediterranean and the Red Sea.

Northallerton /nɔː'θalət(ə)n/ a town in the north

of England, the administrative centre of North Yorkshire; pop. 13,860 (1981).

North America a continent comprising the northern half of the American land mass, connected to South America by the Isthmus of Panama. It contains Canada, the United States, Mexico, and the countries of Central America.

North American ▶ **adjective** of or relating to North America.
▶ **noun** a native or inhabitant of North America, especially a citizen of the US or Canada.

North American English ▶ **noun** [mass noun] the English language as spoken and written in Canada and the US. See also **AMERICAN ENGLISH**.

North American Free Trade Agreement (abbrev.: **NAFTA**) an agreement which came into effect in January 1994 between the US, Canada, and Mexico to remove barriers to trade between the three countries over a ten-year period.

Northampton /nɔː'θampt(ə)n/ a town in SE central England, on the River Nene, the county town of Northamptonshire; pop. 178,200 (1991).

Northamptonshire a county of central England; county town, Northampton.

Northants /nɔː'θants/ ▶ **abbreviation** for Northamptonshire.

North Atlantic Drift a continuation of the Gulf Stream across the Atlantic Ocean and along the coast of NW Europe, where it has a significant warming effect on the climate.

North Atlantic Ocean see **ATLANTIC OCEAN**.

North Atlantic Treaty Organization (abbrev.: **NATO**) an association of European and North American states, formed in 1949 for the defence of Europe and the North Atlantic against the perceived threat of Soviet aggression. It includes most major Western powers, although France withdrew from the military side of the alliance in 1966.

northbound ▶ **adjective** travelling or leading towards the north: *the northbound carriageway of the M5* | *northbound traffic*.

North Cape a promontory on Magerøya, an island off the north coast of Norway. North Cape is the northernmost point of the world accessible by road. Norwegian name **NORDKAPP**.

North Carolina a state of the east central US, on the Atlantic coast; pop. 6,628,640 (1990); capital, Raleigh. Originally settled by the English, it was one of the original thirteen states of the Union (1788).
– DERIVATIVES **North Carolinian** noun & adjective.
– ORIGIN *Carolina* from *Carolus*, the Latin name of Charles I.

North Channel the stretch of sea separating SW Scotland from Northern Ireland and connecting the Irish Sea to the Atlantic Ocean.

Northcliffe, Alfred Charles William Harmsworth, 1st Viscount (1865–1922), British newspaper proprietor. He built up a large newspaper empire, including *The Times*, the *Daily Mail*, and the *Daily Mirror*.

north country the northern part of a country, for example the part of England north of the River Humber.

North Dakota an agricultural state in the north central US, on the border with Canada; pop. 638,800 (1990); capital, Bismarck. Acquired partly by the Louisiana Purchase in 1803 and partly from Britain by treaty in 1818, it became the 39th state of the US in 1889.
– DERIVATIVES **North Dakotan** noun & adjective.

north-east ▶ **noun** 1 (usu. **the north-east**) the point of the horizon midway between north and east: *I pointed to the north-east*.
■ the compass point corresponding to this. ■ the direction in which this lies.
2 the north-eastern part of a country, region, or town: *the north-east of Scotland*.
▶ **adjective** 1 lying towards, near, or facing the north-east.
■ (of a wind) coming from the north-east: *there was a strong north-east wind*.
2 of or denoting the north-eastern part of a specified country, region, or town.
▶ **adverb** to or towards the north-east: *the ship sailed north-east* | *the north-east-facing slopes*.
– DERIVATIVES **north-eastern** adjective.

northeaster ▶ **noun** a wind blowing from the north-east.

north-easterly ▶ **adjective** & **adverb** another term for **NORTH-EAST**.
▶ **noun** another term for **NORTHEASTER**.

North-East Passage a passage for ships along the northern coast of Europe and Asia, from the Atlantic to the Pacific via the Arctic Ocean, sought for many years as a possible trade route to the East. It was first navigated in 1878–9 by the Swedish Arctic explorer Baron Nordenskjöld (1832–1901).

north-eastward ▶ **adverb** (also **north-eastwards**) towards the north-east; in a north-east direction.
▶ **adjective** situated in, directed towards, or facing the north-east.

North Equatorial Current an ocean current that flows westwards across the Pacific Ocean just north of the equator.

norther ▶ **noun** US a strong cold north wind blowing in autumn and winter over Texas, Florida, and the Gulf of Mexico.

northerly ▶ **adjective** & **adverb** in a northward position or direction: [as adj.] *he set off in a northerly direction*.
■ (of wind) blowing from the north: [as adv.] *the wind was gusting northerly*.
▶ **noun** (often **northerlies**) a wind blowing from the north.

northern ▶ **adjective** 1 [attrib.] situated in the north, or directed towards or facing the north: *the northern slopes* | *northern Europe*.
■ (of a wind) blowing from the north.
2 living in or originating from the north: *northern breeds of cattle*.
■ of, relating to, or characteristic of the north or its inhabitants: *she had a broad northern accent*.
– DERIVATIVES **northernmost** adjective.
– ORIGIN Old English *northerne* (see **NORTH**, **-ERN**).

Northern blot ▶ **noun** Biology an adaptation of the Southern blot procedure used to detect specific sequences of RNA by hybridization with complementary DNA.

Northern Cape a province of western South Africa, formerly part of Cape Province; capital, Kimberley.

Northern Circars /'sɜːkɑːz/ a former name for the coastal region of eastern India between the Krishna River and Orissa, now in Andhra Pradesh.

northerner ▶ **noun** a native or inhabitant of the north, especially of northern England or the northern United States.

northern hemisphere the half of the earth that is north of the equator.

Northern Ireland a province of the United Kingdom occupying the NE part of Ireland; pop. 1,569,790 (1991); capital, Belfast.

Northern Ireland, which comprises six of the counties of Ulster, was established as a self-governing province in 1920. Northern Ireland has always been dominated by Unionist parties, which represent the Protestant majority. Many members of the Roman Catholic minority favour union with the Republic of Ireland. Discrimination against the latter group led to violent conflicts and (from 1969) the presence of British army units in an attempt to keep the peace. Terrorism and sectarian violence by the Provisional IRA and other paramilitary groups, both Republican and Loyalist, resulted in the imposition of direct rule from Westminster in 1972. Multi-party talks begun in 1996 led to an agreement between most political parties in 1998. In 1999 a devolved parliament was inaugurated, with representation from both Nationalist and Unionist groups.

Northern Lights another name for the aurora borealis. See **AURORA**.

Northern Marianas a self-governing territory in the western Pacific, comprising the Mariana Islands with the exception of the southernmost, Guam; pop. 43,345 (1990); languages, English (official), Austronesian languages; capital, Chalan Kanoa (on Saipan). The Northern Marianas are constituted as a self-governing commonwealth in union with the United States.

Northern Paiute ▶ **noun** & **adjective** see **PAIUTE**.

Northern Province a province of northern South Africa, formerly part of Transvaal; capital, Pietersburg.

Northern Rhodesia former name (until 1964) for **ZAMBIA**.

Northern Territory a state of north central Australia; pop. 158,400 (1990); capital, Darwin. The territory was annexed by the state of South Australia in 1863, and administered by the Commonwealth of Australia from 1911. It became a self-governing territory in 1978 and a full state in 1995.

North Frisian Islands see FRISIAN ISLANDS.

North Germanic ▶ noun [mass noun] a subdivision of the Germanic group of languages, comprising the Scandinavian languages.
▶ adjective of or relating to North Germanic.

northing ▶ noun [mass noun] distance travelled or measured northward, especially at sea.
■ [count noun] a figure or line representing northward distance on a map (expressed by convention as the second part of a grid reference, after easting).

North Island the northernmost of the two main islands of New Zealand, separated from South Island by Cook Strait.

North Korea a country in the Far East, occupying the northern part of the peninsula of Korea; pop. 22,227,000 (est. 1992); official language, Korean; capital, Pyongyang. Official name DEMOCRATIC PEOPLE'S REPUBLIC OF KOREA.

North Korea was formed in 1948 when Korea was partitioned along the 38th parallel. In 1950 North Korean forces invaded the south, but in the war that followed were forced back to more or less the previous border (see KOREAN WAR). A communist state which was long dominated by the personality of Kim Il Sung, its leader from 1948 to 1994, North Korea has always sought Korean reunification.

– DERIVATIVES **North Korean** adjective & noun.

northland ▶ noun [mass noun] (also **northlands**) poetic/literary the northern part of a country or region.
– ORIGIN Old English (see NORTH, LAND).

north light ▶ noun [mass noun] good natural light without direct sun, especially as desired by artists.

Northman ▶ noun (pl. **-men**) archaic a native or inhabitant of Scandinavia, especially of Norway.
– ORIGIN Old English (see NORTH, MAN).

North Minch see MINCH.

north-north-east ▶ noun the compass point or direction midway between north and north-east.

north-north-west ▶ noun the compass point or direction midway between north and north-west.

North Ossetia an autonomous republic of Russia, in the Caucasus on the border with Georgia; pop. 638,000 (1990); capital, Vladikavkaz. See also OSSETIA.

North Pole ▶ noun see POLE².

North Rhine-Westphalia a state of western Germany; capital, Düsseldorf. German name NORDRHEIN-WESTFALEN.

North Sea an arm of the Atlantic Ocean lying between the mainland of Europe and the coast of Britain, important for its oil and gas deposits.

North Star Astronomy the Pole Star.

North Star State informal name for MINNESOTA.

North Uist see UIST.

Northumb. ▶ abbreviation for Northumberland.

Northumberland /nɔːˈθʌmbələnd/ a county in NE England, on the Scottish border; county town, Morpeth.

Northumbria /nɔːˈθʌmbrɪə/ an area of NE England comprising Northumberland, Durham, and Tyne and Wear.
■ an ancient Anglo-Saxon kingdom in NE England extending from the Humber to the Forth.
– DERIVATIVES **Northumbrian** adjective & noun.
– ORIGIN from obsolete *Northumber*, denoting a person living beyond the Humber.

North Utsire see UTSIRE.

northward ▶ adjective in a northerly direction.
▶ adverb (also **northwards**) towards the north.
▶ noun (**the northward**) the direction or region to the north.
– DERIVATIVES **northwardly** adjective & adverb.

north-west ▶ noun (usu. **the north-west**) 1 the point of the horizon midway between north and west: *he pointed to the north-west.*
■ the compass point corresponding to this. ■ the direction in which this lies.
2 the north-western part of a country, region, or town: *the north-west of London.*

▶ adjective 1 lying towards, near, or facing the north-west: *the north-west corner of the square.*
■ (of a wind) blowing from the north-west.
2 of or denoting the north-western part of a country, region, or town, or its inhabitants: *north-west Europe.*
▶ adverb to or towards the north-west: *he turned on to the motorway and headed north-west.*
– DERIVATIVES **north-western** adjective.

northwester ▶ noun a wind blowing from the north-west.

north-westerly ▶ adjective & adverb another term for NORTH-WEST.
▶ noun another term for NORTHWESTER.

North-West Frontier Province a province of NW Pakistan, on the border with Afghanistan; capital, Peshawar.

North-West Passage a sea passage along the northern coast of the American continent, through the Canadian Arctic from the Atlantic to the Pacific. It was sought for many years as a possible trade route by explorers including Sebastian Cabot, Sir Francis Drake, and Martin Frobisher; it was first navigated in 1903–6 by Roald Amundsen.

North-West Province a province of northern South Africa, formed in 1994 from the NE part of Cape Province and SW Transvaal; capital, Mmabatho.

Northwest Territories a territory of northern Canada extending northwards from the 60th parallel and westwards from Hudson Bay to the Rocky Mountains; pop. 57,650 (1991); capital, Yellowknife. From 1670 the southern part of this territory was part of Rupert's Land; the remainder was under nominal British rule until 1870, when both parts were ceded to Canada.

Northwest Territory a region and former territory of the US lying between the Mississippi and Ohio rivers and the Great Lakes. It was acquired in 1783 after the War of American Independence and now forms the states of Indiana, Ohio, Michigan, Illinois, and Wisconsin.

north-westward ▶ adverb (also **north-westwards**) towards the north-west; in a north-west direction.
▶ adjective situated in, directed towards, or facing the north-west.

North Yorkshire a county in NE England; administrative centre, Northallerton. It was formed in 1974 from parts of the former North, East, and West Ridings of Yorkshire.

Norway a mountainous European country on the northern and western coastline of Scandinavia; pop. 4,249,830 (1991); official language, Norwegian; capital, Oslo. Norwegian name NORGE.

Norway was united with Denmark and Sweden by the Union of Kalmar in 1397, but after Sweden's withdrawal in 1523 became subject to Denmark. Ceded to Sweden in 1814, Norway emerged as an independent kingdom in 1905. An invitation to join the EC was rejected after a referendum in 1972; an application to join the European Union twenty years later was accepted by the European Parliament but failed to win approval in a referendum (1994).

Norway lobster ▶ noun a small slender, commercially important European lobster. Also called DUBLIN BAY PRAWN.
● *Nephrops norvegicus*, class Malacostraca.

Norway maple ▶ noun a Eurasian maple with yellow flowers that appear before the lobed leaves, widely planted as an ornamental.
● *Acer platanoides*, family Aceraceae.

Norway rat ▶ noun another term for BROWN RAT.

Norway spruce ▶ noun a long-coned European spruce which is widely grown for timber and pulp. In Britain it is often used as a Christmas tree.
● *Picea abies*, family Pinaceae.

Norwegian /nɔːˈwiːdʒ(ə)n/ ▶ adjective of or relating to Norway or its people or language.
▶ noun 1 a native or national of Norway, or a person of Norwegian descent.
2 [mass noun] the language of Norway, a member of the Scandinavian language group.

Norwegian today exists in two forms, *Bokmål*, the more widely used, a modified form of Danish, and *Nynorsk* ('new Norwegian'), a 19th-century literary form devised from the country dialects most closely descended from Old Norse, and considered to be a purer form of the language than *Bokmål*.

– ORIGIN from medieval Latin *Norvegia* 'Norway' (from Old Norse *Norvegr*, literally 'north way') + -AN.

Norwegian Sea a sea which lies between Iceland and Norway and links the Arctic Ocean with the NE Atlantic.

nor'wester ▶ noun 1 short for NORTHWESTER.
2 an oilskin jacket or sou'wester.

Norwich /ˈnɒrɪdʒ, -rɪtʃ/ a city in eastern England, the county town of Norfolk; pop. 121,000 (1991).

Norwich School an English regional school of landscape painting associated with John Sell Cotman and John Crome.

Norwich terrier ▶ noun a small thickset terrier of a breed with a rough red or black-and-tan coat and pricked ears.

nos ▶ abbreviation for numbers.
– ORIGIN plural of No..

no-score draw ▶ noun a goalless draw in soccer, especially as distinguished from a score draw in football pools.

nose ▶ noun 1 the part projecting above the mouth on the face of a person or animal, containing the nostrils and used for breathing and smelling.
■ [in sing.] the sense of smell, especially a dog's ability to track something by its scent: *a dog with a keen nose.*
■ [in sing.] figurative an instinctive talent for detecting something: *he has a nose for a good script.* ■ the aroma of a particular substance, especially wine.
2 the front end of an aircraft, car, or other vehicle.
■ a projecting part of something: *the nose of the saddle.*
3 [in sing.] a look, especially out of curiosity: *she wanted a good nose round the house.*
■ informal a police informer.
▶ verb 1 [no obj., with adverbial of place] (of an animal) thrust its nose against or into something, especially in order to smell it: *the pony nosed at the straw.*
■ [with obj.] smell or sniff (something).
2 [no obj.] investigate or pry into something: *I was anxious to get inside and nose around her house | she's always nosing into my business*
■ [with obj.] detect in such a way.
3 [no obj., with adverbial of direction] (of a vehicle or its driver) make one's way cautiously forward: *he turned left and nosed into an empty parking space.*
■ (of a competitor) manage to achieve a winning or leading position, especially by a small margin: *they nosed ahead by one point.*
– PHRASES **by a nose** (of a victory) by a very narrow margin. **count noses** count people, typically in order to determine the numbers in a vote. **cut off one's nose to spite one's face** disadvantage oneself in the course of trying to disadvantage another. **get one's nose in front** (of a competitor) manage to achieve a winning or leading position. **get up someone's nose** informal irritate or annoy someone. **give someone a bloody nose** inflict a resounding defeat on someone. **have one's nose in a book** be reading studiously or intently. **keep one's nose clean** informal stay out of trouble. **keep one's nose out of** refrain from interfering in (someone else's affairs). **keep one's nose to the grindstone** see GRINDSTONE. **nose to tail** (of vehicles) moving or standing close behind one another, especially in heavy traffic. **not see further than one's (or the end of one's) nose** be unwilling or fail to consider different possibilities or to foresee the consequences of one's actions. **on the nose 1** to a person's sense of smell: *the wine is pungently smoky and peppery on the nose.* **2** informal, chiefly N. Amer. precisely: *at ten on the nose the van pulled up.* **3** Austral. informal distasteful; offensive. **4** informal (of betting) on a horse to win (as opposed to being placed). **put someone's nose out of joint** informal upset or annoy someone. **speak through one's nose** pronounce words with a nasal twang. **turn one's nose up at something** informal show distaste or contempt for something: *he turned his nose up at the job.* **under someone's nose** informal directly in front of someone: *he thrust the paper under the Inspector's nose.* ■ (of an action) committed openly and boldly, but without someone noticing or noticing in time to prevent it. **with one's nose in the air** haughtily: *she walked past the cars with her nose in the air.*
– DERIVATIVES **nosed** adjective [in combination] snub-nosed, **noseless** adjective.
– ORIGIN Old English *nosu*, of West Germanic origin; related to Dutch *neus*, and more remotely to German *Nase*, Latin *nasus*, and Sanskrit *nāsā*; also to NESS.

nosebag ▶ noun a strong canvas or leather bag containing fodder, hung from a horse's head.

noseband ▶ noun the strap of a bridle or head collar, which passes over the horse's nose and under its chin.

nosebleed ▶ noun an instance of bleeding from the nose.
■ [as modifier] N. Amer. informal denoting cheap seating located in an extremely high position in a sports stadium, large theatre, or concert hall.

nose candy ▶ noun [mass noun] N. Amer. informal an illegal drug that is inhaled, in particular, cocaine.

nose-cone ▶ noun the cone-shaped nose of a rocket or aircraft.

nosedive ▶ noun a steep downward plunge by an aircraft.
■ figurative a sudden dramatic deterioration: the player's fortunes took a nosedive.
▶ verb [no obj.] (of an aircraft) make a nosedive.
■ figurative deteriorate suddenly and dramatically: massive strikes caused the economy to nosedive.

no-see-um /ˈnəʊsiːəm/ ▶ noun N. Amer. a minute bloodsucking insect, especially a biting midge.

nose flute ▶ noun a musical instrument of the flute type played by blowing through the nose rather than the mouth, associated especially with SE Asia and the Pacific islands.

nosegay ▶ noun a small bunch of flowers, typically one that is sweet-scented.
– ORIGIN late Middle English: from NOSE + GAY in the obsolete sense 'ornament'.

nose guard ▶ noun American Football the defensive lineman whose position is opposite the offensive centre.

nose job ▶ noun informal an operation involving rhinoplasty or cosmetic surgery on a person's nose.

nose leaf ▶ noun a fleshy leaf-shaped structure on the nose of many bats, used for echolocation.

nosema /nəʊˈsiːmə/ ▶ noun a spore-forming parasitic protozoan that chiefly affects insects.
● Genus Nosema, phylum Microspora, kingdom Protista: several species, in particular N. apis, which causes infectious dysentery (**nosema disease**) in honeybees.
– ORIGIN modern Latin, from Greek nosēma 'disease'.

nosepiece ▶ noun 1 the part of a helmet or headdress that protects a person's nose.
■ chiefly N. Amer. another term for NOSEBAND. ■ the central part of a pair of glasses that fits over the bridge of the nose.
2 the part of a microscope to which the objective lenses are attached.

nose rag ▶ noun informal a handkerchief.

nose ring ▶ noun a ring fixed in the nose of an animal, typically a bull, for leading it.
■ a ring worn in a person's nose as a piece of jewellery.

nose tackle ▶ noun American Football a defensive lineman positioned opposite the offensive centre.

nose wheel ▶ noun a landing wheel under the nose of an aircraft.

nosey ▶ adjective & verb variant spelling of NOSY.

nosh informal ▶ noun [mass noun] food: filling the freezer with all kinds of nosh.
■ [count noun] N. Amer. a small item of food: have plenty of noshes and nibbles conveniently placed. ■ [count noun] a light meal; a snack: in between noshes we explored the city.
▶ verb [no obj.] eat food enthusiastically or greedily: there are several restaurants, so you can nosh to your heart's content | [with obj.] there I sat, noshing my favourite food.
– ORIGIN early 20th cent. (denoting a snack bar): Yiddish.

noshery ▶ noun (pl. -ies) informal a restaurant or snack bar.

no-show ▶ noun a person who has made a reservation, booking, or appointment but neither keeps nor cancels it.

nosh-up ▶ noun Brit. informal a large meal: the grand nosh-up after the ceremony.

no side ▶ noun [in sing.] Rugby the end of a game: the whistle went for no side.

nosing ▶ noun a rounded edge of a step or moulding.
■ a metal shield for such an edge.

nosocomial /ˌnɒsə(ʊ)ˈkəʊmɪəl/ ▶ adjective Medicine (of a disease) originating in a hospital.
– ORIGIN mid 19th cent.: from Greek nosokomos 'person who tends the sick' + -IAL.

nosode /ˈnɒsəʊd/ ▶ noun (in homeopathy) a preparation of substances secreted in the course of a disease, used in the treatment of that disease.
– ORIGIN late 19th cent.: from Greek nosos 'disease' + -ODE[1].

nosography /nɒˈsɒɡrəfi/ ▶ noun [mass noun] the systematic description of diseases.
– DERIVATIVES **nosographic** adjective.
– ORIGIN mid 17th cent.: from Greek nosos 'disease' + -GRAPHY.

nosology /nɒˈsɒlədʒi/ ▶ noun [mass noun] the branch of medical science dealing with the classification of diseases.
– DERIVATIVES **nosological** adjective, **nosologist** noun.
– ORIGIN early 18th cent.: from Greek nosos 'disease' + -LOGY.

nostalgia ▶ noun [mass noun] a sentimental longing or wistful affection for the past, typically for a period or place with happy personal associations: I was overcome with acute nostalgia for my days at university.
■ the evocation of these feelings or tendencies, especially in commercialized form: an evening of TV nostalgia.
– DERIVATIVES **nostalgic** adjective, **nostalgically** adverb, **nostalgist** noun.
– ORIGIN late 18th cent. (in the sense 'acute homesickness'): modern Latin (translating German Heimweh 'homesickness'), from Greek nostos 'return home' + algos 'pain'.

nostalgie de la boue /ˌnɒstalˈ(d)ʒiː də la ˌbuː/ ▶ noun [mass noun] a desire for degradation and depravity.
– ORIGIN French, literally 'mud nostalgia'.

nostoc /ˈnɒstɒk/ ▶ noun Biology a micro-organism composed of beaded filaments which aggregate to form a gelatinous mass, growing in water and damp places and able to fix nitrogen from the atmosphere.
● Genus Nostoc, division Cyanobacteria.
– ORIGIN name invented by Paracelsus.

Nostradamus /ˌnɒstrəˈdɑːməs, -ˈdeɪ-/ (1503–66), French astrologer and physician; Latinized name of Michel de Nostredame. His cryptic and apocalyptic predictions in rhyming quatrains appeared in two collections (1555; 1558); their interpretation continues to be the subject of controversy.

Nostratic /nɒˈstratɪk/ ▶ noun a hypothetical phylum of languages of which the principal members are the Indo-European, Semitic, Altaic, and Dravidian families.
▶ adjective of or relating to this language phylum.
– ORIGIN 1960s: from German nostratisch, based on Latin nostras, nostrat- 'of our country'.

nostril ▶ noun either of two external openings of the nasal cavity in vertebrates that admit air to the lungs and smells to the olfactory nerves.
– DERIVATIVES **nostrilled** adjective [in combination].
– ORIGIN Old English nosterl, nosthyrl, from nosu 'nose' + thȳr(e)l 'hole'.

nostril fly ▶ noun a parasitic fly that lays its eggs in the nostrils of sheep, goats, and deer. The larvae develop in the nasal cavities before being sneezed out.
● The **sheep nostril fly** or sheep bot (Oestrus ovis) and the **deer nostril flies** (genus Cephenemyia), both in the family Oestridae.

nostro account /ˈnɒstrəʊ/ ▶ noun a bank account held by a UK bank with a foreign bank, usually in the currency of that country.

nostrum /ˈnɒstrəm/ ▶ noun a medicine prepared by an unqualified person, especially one that is not considered effective.
■ a pet scheme or favourite remedy, especially one for bringing about some social or political reform or improvement: right-wing nostrums such as a wage freeze and cutting public spending.
– ORIGIN early 17th cent.: from Latin, used in the sense 'something of our own making', neuter of noster 'our'.

nosy (also **nosey**) informal ▶ adjective (**nosier**, **nosiest**) (of a person or their behaviour) showing too much curiosity about other people's affairs: get on with your work and stop being so nosy!
▶ verb [no obj., with adverbial] pry into something: they don't nosy into your business like some people.
– DERIVATIVES **nosily** adverb, **nosiness** noun.

nosy parker ▶ noun informal, chiefly Brit. an overly inquisitive person.
– ORIGIN early 20th cent.: from the picture postcard caption, 'The adventures of Nosey Parker', referring to a peeping Tom in Hyde Park.

not ▶ adverb 1 (also **n't** joined to a preceding verb) used with an auxiliary verb or 'be' to form the negative: he would not say | she isn't there | didn't you tell me?
■ used in some constructions with other verbs: [with infinitive] he has been warned not to touch | the pain of not knowing | she **not** only wrote the text **but also** researched the photographs.
2 used as a short substitute for a negative clause: maybe I'll regret it, but I hope not | 'Don't you keep in touch?' 'I'm afraid not.' | they wouldn't know if I was telling the truth or **not**.
3 used to express the negative of other words: not a single attempt was made | treating the symptoms and not the cause | 'How was it?' 'Not so bad.'
■ used with a quantifier to exclude a person or part of a group: not all the poems are serious. ■ less than (used to indicate a surprisingly small quantity): the brakes went on not ten feet from him.
4 used in understatements to suggest that the opposite of a following word or phrase is true: the not too distant future | not a million miles away.
■ informal, humorous following and emphatically negating a statement: that sounds like quality entertainment—not. [ORIGIN: a usage popularized by the film Wayne's World.]
▶ noun (often **NOT**) Electronics a Boolean operator with only one variable that has the value one when the variable is zero and vice versa.
■ (also **not gate**) a circuit which produces an output signal only when there is not a signal on its input.
▶ adjective (often **Not**) Art (of paper) not hot-pressed, and having a slightly textured surface.
– PHRASES **not at all 1** used as a polite response to thanks. **2** definitely not: 'You don't mind?' 'Not at all.' **not but what** archaic nevertheless: not but what the picture has its darker side. **not half** see HALF. **not least** see LEAST. **not quite** see QUITE. **not that** it is not to be inferred that: I'll never be allowed back—not that I'd want to go back. **not a thing** nothing at all. **not very** see VERY.
– ORIGIN Middle English: contraction of the adverb NOUGHT.

nota bene /ˌnəʊtə ˈbɛneɪ/ ▶ verb [in imperative] formal (used in written text to draw attention to what follows) observe carefully or take special notice.
– ORIGIN Latin, literally 'note well!'

notability ▶ noun (pl. -ies) a famous or important person: a Fleet Street notability.

notable ▶ adjective worthy of attention or notice; remarkable: the gardens are notable for their collection of magnolias and camellias | the results, with one notable exception, have been superb.
▶ noun (usu. **notables**) a famous or important person: businessmen and local notables.
– ORIGIN Middle English: from Old French, from Latin notabilis 'worthy of note', from the verb notare 'to note, mark'.

notably ▶ adverb especially, in particular: a diet low in animal fat protects against potentially fatal diseases, notably diabetes.
■ in a way that is striking or remarkable: [as submodifier] such a statement is notably absent from the government's proposals.

notam /ˈnəʊtəm/ ▶ noun a written notification issued to pilots before a flight, advising them of circumstances relating to the state of flying.
– ORIGIN 1940s: from no(tice) t(o) a(ir)m(en).

notaphily /nəʊˈtafɪli/ ▶ noun [mass noun] the collecting of banknotes as a hobby.
– DERIVATIVES **notaphilic** adjective, **notaphilist** noun.

notarize (also **-ise**) ▶ verb [with obj.] have (a document) legalized by a notary.

notary /ˈnəʊt(ə)ri/ (in full **notary public**) ▶ noun (pl. -ies) a person authorized to perform certain legal formalities, especially to draw up or certify contracts, deeds, and other documents for use in other jurisdictions.
– DERIVATIVES **notarial** adjective.
– ORIGIN Middle English (in the sense 'clerk or secretary'): from Latin notarius 'secretary', from nota 'mark'.

notate ▶ verb [with obj.] write (something, typically music) in notation.
– DERIVATIVES **notator** noun.
– ORIGIN early 20th cent.: back-formation from NOTATION.

notation ▶ **noun 1** [mass noun] a series or system of written symbols used to represent numbers, amounts, or elements in something such as music or mathematics: *algebraic notation* | [count noun] *new terminologies and notations.*
2 a note or annotation: *he noticed the notations in the margin.*
3 short for ***scale of notation*** (see **SCALE**[3] in sense 2).
– DERIVATIVES **notational** adjective.
– ORIGIN late 16th cent.: from Latin *notatio(n-)*, from the verb *notare*, from *nota* 'mark'.

not-being ▶ **noun** [mass noun] non-existence.

notch ▶ **noun 1** an indentation or incision on an edge or surface: *there was a notch in the end of the arrow for the bowstring.*
■ each of a series of holes for the tongue of a buckle: *he tightened his belt an extra notch.* ■ a nick made on something in order to keep a score or record. ■ a point or degree in a scale: *her opinion of Nicole dropped a few notches.*
2 N. Amer. a deep narrow mountain pass.
▶ **verb** [with obj.] **1** make notches in: [as adj. **notched**] *notched bamboo sticks.*
■ secure or insert by means of notches: *she notched her belt tighter.*
2 score or achieve (something): *he **notched up** fifteen years' service with the company.*
– DERIVATIVES **notcher** noun.
– ORIGIN mid 16th cent.: probably from Anglo-Norman French *noche*, variant of Old French *osche*, of unknown origin.

notchback ▶ **noun** a car with a back that extends approximately horizontally from the bottom of the rear window so as to make a distinct angle with it.

notch effect ▶ **noun** Engineering the increase in the susceptibility of a specimen to fracture caused by a notch.

notch filter ▶ **noun** Electronics a filter that attenuates signals within a very narrow band of frequencies.

notchy ▶ **adjective** (**notchier**, **notchiest**) (of a manual gear-changing mechanism) difficult to use because the lever has to be moved accurately (as if into a narrow notch).

note ▶ **noun 1** a brief record of facts, topics, or thoughts, written down as an aid to memory: *I'll **make a note** in my diary* | *Robyn arranged her notes on the lectern.*
■ a short comment on or explanation of a word or passage in a book or article; an annotation: *see note iv above.*
2 a short informal letter or written message: *I left her a note explaining where I was going.*
■ an official letter sent from the representative of one government to another. ■ [usu. with adj. or noun modifier] a short official document that certifies a particular thing: *you need a sick note from your doctor.*
3 Brit. a banknote: *a ten-pound note.*
■ a written promise or notice of payment of various kinds: *a credit note.*
4 a single tone of definite pitch made by a musical instrument or the human voice: *the last notes of the symphony died away.*
■ a written sign representing the pitch and duration of such a sound. ■ a key of a piano or similar instrument: *black notes* | *white notes.* ■ a bird's song or call, or a single tone in this: *the tawny owl has a harsh flight note.*
5 [in sing.] a particular quality or tone that reflects or expresses a mood or attitude: *there was a note of scorn in her voice* | *the decade could have ended on an optimistic note.*
■ any of the basic components of a fragrance or flavour: *the fresh note of bergamot.*
▶ **verb** [with obj.] **1** notice or pay particular attention to (something): *noting his mother's unusual gaiety* | [with clause] *please note that you will not receive a reminder that final payment is due.*
■ remark upon (something), typically in order to draw someone's attention to it: *we noted earlier the difficulties inherent in this strategy.*
2 record (something) in writing: *he **noted down** her address on a piece of paper.*
– PHRASES **hit** (or **strike**) **the right** (or **wrong**) **note** say or do something in exactly the right (or wrong) way. **of note 1** worth paying attention to: *many of his comments are worthy of note.* **2** important; distinguished: *Roman historians of note include Livy, Tacitus, and Sallust.* **strike a false note** appear insincere or inappropriate: *she greeted him gushingly, and that struck a false note.* **strike** (or **sound**) **a note of** express (a particular feeling or view) about something: *he sounded a note of caution about the trend towards health foods.* **take note** pay attention: *employers should **take note of** the needs of disabled people.*
– ORIGIN Middle English (in sense 4 of the noun and sense 1 of the verb): from Old French *note* (noun), *noter* (verb), from Latin *nota* 'a mark', *notare* 'to mark'.

notebook ▶ **noun** a small book with blank or ruled pages for writing notes in.
■ a portable computer that is smaller than a laptop.

notecard ▶ **noun** a decorative card with a blank space for a short message.

notecase ▶ **noun** Brit. dated a small flat folding case or wallet for holding banknotes.

note cluster ▶ **noun** Music a chord containing a number of closely adjacent notes. Also called **TONE CLUSTER**.

noted ▶ **adjective** well known; famous: *the restaurant is **noted for** its high standards of cuisine* | *a noted patron of the arts.*

notelet ▶ **noun** a small folded sheet of paper, typically with a decorative design on the front, on which a note or informal letter may be written.

notepad ▶ **noun** a pad of blank or ruled pages for writing notes on.
■ (also **notepad computer**) a pocket-sized personal computer in which the user writes with a stylus on the screen to input text.

notepaper ▶ **noun** [mass noun] paper for writing letters on.

notes inégales /ˌnəʊts ɪneɪˈɡɑːl/ ▶ **plural noun** (in baroque music) notes performed by convention in an uneven rhythm though notated as equal in the score.

noteworthy ▶ **adjective** interesting, significant, or unusual: [with clause] *it is noteworthy that no one at the Bank has accepted responsibility for the failure.*
– DERIVATIVES **noteworthiness** noun.

'nother ▶ **determiner** & **pronoun** informal non-standard spelling of **ANOTHER**, used to represent informal speech: *'nother thing just occurred to me.*

nothing ▶ **pronoun** not anything; no single thing: *I said nothing* | *there's nothing you can do* | *they found nothing wrong.*
■ something of no importance or concern: *'What are you laughing at?' 'Oh, nothing, sir.'* | *they are nothing to him* | [as noun] *no longer could we be treated as nothings.* ■ (in calculations) no amount; nought.
▶ **adjective** [attrib.] informal having no prospect of progress; of no value: *he had a series of nothing jobs.*
▶ **adverb** not at all: *she cares nothing for others* | *he looks **nothing like** the others.*
■ [postpositive] N. Amer. informal used to contradict something emphatically: *'This is a surprise.' 'Surprise nothing.'*
– PHRASES **be nothing to do with** see **DO**[1]. **for nothing 1** at no cost; without payment: *working for nothing.* **2** to no purpose: *he died anyway, so it had all been for nothing.* **have nothing on someone** see **HAVE**. **have nothing to do with** see **DO**[1]. **no nothing** informal (concluding a list of negatives) nothing at all: *how could you solve it with no clues, no witnesses, no nothing?* **not for nothing** for a very good reason: *not for nothing have I a brother-in-law who cooks professionally.* **nothing but** only: *nothing but the best will do.* **nothing daunted** see **DAUNT**. **nothing doing** informal **1** there is no prospect of success or agreement: *He wants to marry her. Nothing doing!* **2** nothing is happening: *there's nothing doing, and I've been waiting for weeks.* **nothing** (or **nothing else**) **for it** Brit. no alternative: *there was **nothing for it but to** follow.* **nothing less than** used to emphasize how extreme something is: *it was nothing less than sexual harassment.* **nothing much** not a great amount; nothing of importance. **there is nothing to it** there is no difficulty involved. **stop at nothing** see **STOP**. **sweet nothings** words of affection exchanged by lovers: *whispering sweet nothings in her ear.* **think nothing of it** do not apologize or feel bound to show gratitude (used as a polite response). **you ain't seen nothing yet** informal used to indicate that although something may be considered extreme or impressive, there is something even more extreme or impressive in store: *if you think that was muddy, you ain't seen nothing yet.*
– ORIGIN Old English *nān thing* (see **NO**, **THING**).

nothingness ▶ **noun** [mass noun] the absence or cessation of life or existence: *the fear of the total nothingness of death.*
■ worthlessness; insignificance; unimportance: *the nothingness of it all overwhelmed him.*

nothosaur /ˈnəʊtəsɔː, ˈnəʊθ-/ ▶ **noun** a semiaquatic fossil carnivorous reptile of the Triassic period, having a slender body and long neck, related to the plesiosaurs.
• Infraorder Nothosauria, superorder Sauropterygia.
– ORIGIN 1930s: from modern Latin *Nothosauria*, from Greek *nothos* 'false' + *sauros* 'lizard'.

notice ▶ **noun 1** [mass noun] attention; observation: *their silence did not escape my notice* | *it has **come to our notice** that you have been missing school.*
2 [mass noun] notification or warning of something, especially to allow preparations to be made: *interest rates are subject to fluctuation without notice.*
■ a formal declaration of one's intention to end an agreement, typically one concerning employment or tenancy, at a specified time: *she handed in her notice.*
3 a displayed sheet or placard giving news or information: *the jobs were advertised in a notice posted in the common room.*
■ a small advertisement or announcement in a newspaper or magazine: *an obituary notice.* ■ (usu. **notices**) a short published review or comment about a new film, play, or book: *she had good notices in her first film.*
▶ **verb** [with obj.] become aware of: *he noticed the youths behaving suspiciously* | [with clause] *I noticed that she was looking tired* | [no obj.] *they were too drunk to notice.*
■ (usu. **be noticed**) treat (someone) with some degree of attention or recognition: *it was only last year that the singer really began to be noticed.* ■ archaic remark upon: *she looked so much better that Sir Charles noticed it to Lady Harriet.*
– PHRASES **at short** (or **a moment's**) **notice** with little warning or time for preparation: *tours may be cancelled at short notice.* **put someone on notice** (or **serve notice**) warn someone of something about or likely to occur, especially in a formal or threatening manner: *we're going to put foreign governments on notice that we want a change of trade policy.* **take no notice** pay no attention to someone or something. **take notice** pay attention; show signs of interest.
– ORIGIN late Middle English (in sense 2): from Old French, from Latin *notitia* 'being known', from *notus* 'known' (see **NOTION**).

noticeable ▶ **adjective** easily seen or noticed; clear or apparent: *a noticeable increase in staff motivation.*
■ noteworthy: *a noticeable new phenomenon.*
– DERIVATIVES **noticeably** adverb.

noticeboard ▶ **noun** chiefly Brit. a board for displaying notices.

notifiable ▶ **adjective** denoting something, typically a serious, infectious disease, that must be reported to the appropriate authorities.

notify ▶ **verb** (**-ies**, **-ied**) [with obj.] inform (someone) of something, typically in a formal or official manner: *you will be **notified of** our decision as soon as possible* | [with obj. and clause] *they were notified that John had been taken prisoner.*
■ give notice of or report (something) formally or officially: *births and deaths are required by law to be **notified to** the Registrar.*
– DERIVATIVES **notification** noun.
– ORIGIN late Middle English: from Old French *notifier*, from Latin *notificare* 'make known', from *notus* 'known' (see **NOTION**) + *facere* 'make'.

notion ▶ **noun 1** a conception of or belief about something: *children have different notions about the roles of their parents.*
■ a vague awareness or understanding of the nature of something: *I had no notion of what her words meant.*
2 an impulse or desire, especially one of a whimsical kind: *she had a notion to ring her friend at work.*
3 (**notions**) chiefly N. Amer. items used in sewing, such as buttons, pins, and hooks.
– ORIGIN late Middle English: from Latin *notio(n-)* 'idea', from *notus* 'known', past participle of *noscere*.

notional ▶ **adjective 1** existing only in theory or as a suggestion or idea: *notional budgets for hospital and community health services.*
■ existing only in the imagination: *Lizzie seemed to vanish into thin air, as if her presence were merely notional.*
2 Linguistics denoting or relating to an approach to grammar which is dependent on the definition of terminology (e.g. 'a verb is a doing word') as

n

opposed to identification of structures and processes.

3 (in language teaching) denoting or relating to a syllabus that aims to develop communicative competence.

− DERIVATIVES **notionally** adverb.

− ORIGIN late Middle English (in the Latin sense): from obsolete French, or from medieval Latin *notionalis* 'relating to an idea', from *notio(n-)* 'idea' (see **NOTION**).

notitia /nəʊˈtɪʃɪə/ ▶ noun a register or list of ecclesiastical sees or districts.

− ORIGIN early 18th cent.: from Latin, literally 'knowledge', later 'list or account', from *notus* 'known'.

notochord /ˈnəʊtə(ʊ)kɔːd/ ▶ noun Zoology a cartilaginous skeletal rod supporting the body in all embryonic and some adult chordate animals.

− ORIGIN mid 19th cent.: from Greek *nōton* 'back' + **CHORD**[2].

Notogaea /ˌnəʊtə(ʊ)ˈdʒiːə/ (US also **Notogea**) Zoology a zoogeographical area comprising the Australian region.

− DERIVATIVES **Notogaean** adjective.

− ORIGIN mid 19th cent.: modern Latin, from Greek *notos* 'south wind' + *gaia* 'earth'.

notorious ▶ adjective famous or well known, typically for some bad quality or deed: *Los Angeles is notorious for its smog | he was a notorious drinker and womanizer.*

− DERIVATIVES **notoriety** noun, **notoriously** adverb.

− ORIGIN late 15th cent. (in the sense 'generally known'): from medieval Latin *notorius* (from Latin *notus* 'known') + **-OUS**.

notornis /nə(ʊ)ˈtɔːnɪs/ ▶ noun another term for **TAKAHE**.

− ORIGIN mid 19th cent.: from Greek *notos* 'south' + *ornis* 'bird'.

notoungulate /ˌnəʊtəʊˈʌŋɡjʊlət/ ▶ noun an extinct hoofed mammal of a large and varied group that lived in South America throughout the Tertiary period, finally dying out in the Pleistocene.

● Order Notoungulata: many families.

− ORIGIN late 20th cent.: from modern Latin *Notoungulata*, from Greek *notos* 'south' + Latin *ungula* 'nail'.

not-out Cricket ▶ adjective [attrib.] denoting a batsman who is not out when the team's innings ends or a score or innings made by such a batsman.

▶ noun a not-out score or innings.

Notre-Dame /ˌnɒtrəˈdɑːm, French nɔtR(ə)dam/ a Gothic cathedral church in Paris, dedicated to the Virgin Mary, on the Île de la Cité (an island in the Seine). It was built between 1163 and 1250 and is especially noted for its innovatory flying buttresses and sculptured facade.

− ORIGIN French, literally 'our lady'.

no-trumper ▶ noun Bridge a hand on which a no-trump bid can suitably be made or has been made.

no trumps ▶ noun Bridge a situation in which no suit is designated as trumps.

Nottingham /ˈnɒtɪŋəm/ a city in east central England, the county town of Nottinghamshire; pop. 261,500 (1991).

Nottingham lace ▶ noun [mass noun] a type of machine-made flat lace.

Nottinghamshire a county in central England; county town, Nottingham.

Notting Hill a district of NW central London, the scene of an annual street carnival.

Notts. ▶ abbreviation for Nottinghamshire.

notum /ˈnəʊtəm/ ▶ noun (pl. **nota**) Entomology (in an insect) the tergum or dorsal exoskeleton of the thorax.

− DERIVATIVES **notal** adjective.

− ORIGIN late 19th cent.: from Greek *nōton* 'back'.

notwithstanding ▶ preposition in spite of: *notwithstanding the evidence, the consensus is that the jury will not reach a verdict | [postpositive] this small contretemps notwithstanding, they both had a good time.*

▶ adverb nevertheless; in spite of this: *she tells us she is an intellectual; notwithstanding, she faces the future as unprovided for as a beauty queen.*

▶ conjunction although; in spite of the fact that: *notwithstanding that the hall was packed with bullies, our champion played on steadily and patiently.*

− ORIGIN late Middle English: from **NOT** + *withstanding*, present participle of **WITHSTAND**, on

the pattern of Old French *non obstant* 'not providing an obstacle to'.

Nouadhibou /ˌnwadɪˈbuː/ the principal port of Mauritania, on the Atlantic coast at the border with Western Sahara; pop. 22,000 (1976). Former name **PORT ÉTIENNE**.

Nouakchott /nwakˈʃɒt/ the capital of Mauritania, situated on the Atlantic coast; pop. 850,000 (est. 1994).

nougat /ˈnuːɡɑː, ˈnʌɡət/ ▶ noun [mass noun] a sweet made from sugar or honey, nuts, and egg white.

− ORIGIN early 19th cent.: from French, from Provençal *nogat*, from *noga* 'nut'.

nougatine /ˌnuːɡəˈtiːn/ ▶ noun [mass noun] nougat covered with chocolate.

− ORIGIN late 19th cent.: from **NOUGAT** + *-ine* 'resembling' (see **-INE**[1]).

nought ▶ noun the digit 0.

▶ pronoun variant spelling of **NAUGHT**.

noughts and crosses ▶ plural noun chiefly Brit. a game in which two players seek to complete a row of either three noughts or three crosses drawn alternately in the spaces of a grid of nine squares.

Nouméa /nuːˈmeɪə/ the capital of the island of New Caledonia; pop. 65,000 (1994). Former name **PORT DE FRANCE**.

noumenon /ˈnaʊmənɒn/ ▶ noun (pl. **noumena**) (in Kantian philosophy) a thing as it is in itself, as distinct from a thing as it is knowable by the senses through phenomenal attributes.

− DERIVATIVES **noumenal** adjective.

− ORIGIN late 18th cent.: via German from Greek, literally '(something) conceived', from *noien* 'conceive, apprehend'.

noun ▶ noun Grammar a word (other than a pronoun) used to identify any of a class of people, places, or things (**common noun**), or to name a particular one of these (**proper noun**).

− DERIVATIVES **nounal** adjective.

− ORIGIN late Middle English: from Anglo-Norman French, from Latin *nomen* 'name'.

noun phrase ▶ noun Grammar a word or group of words that function in a sentence as subject, object, or prepositional object.

nourish ▶ verb [with obj.] **1** provide with the food or other substances necessary for growth, health, and good condition: *I was doing everything I could to nourish and protect the baby | figurative spiritual resources which nourished her in her darkest hours.*

■ enhance the fertility of (soil): *a clay base nourished with plant detritus.*

2 keep (a feeling or belief) in one's mind, typically for a long time: *he has long nourished an ambition to bring the show to Broadway.*

− DERIVATIVES **nourisher** noun.

− ORIGIN Middle English: from Old French *noriss-*, lengthened stem of *norir*, from Latin *nutrire* 'feed, cherish'.

nourishing ▶ adjective (of food) containing substances necessary for growth, health, and good condition: *a simple but nourishing meal.*

− DERIVATIVES **nourishingly** adverb.

nourishment ▶ noun [mass noun] the substances necessary for growth, health, and good condition: *tubers from which plants obtain nourishment.*

■ food: *they often go days with little or no nourishment.* ■ the action of nourishing someone or something: *God's gifts to us for the nourishment of our bodies.*

nous /naʊs/ ▶ noun [mass noun] **1** Brit. informal common sense; practical intelligence: *if he had any nous at all, he'd sell the film rights.*

2 Philosophy the mind or intellect.

− ORIGIN late 17th cent. (in sense 2): from Greek, 'mind, intelligence, intuitive apprehension'.

nouveau /ˈnuːvəʊ, French nuvo/ ▶ adjective informal

1 short for **NOUVEAU RICHE**.

2 modern; up to date.

nouveau riche /ˌnuːvəʊ ˈriːʃ, French nuvo Riʃ/ ▶ noun [treated as pl.] (usu. **the nouveau riche**) people who have recently acquired wealth, typically those perceived as ostentatious or lacking in good taste.

▶ adjective of, relating to, or characteristic of such people: *nouveau-riche social climbers.*

− ORIGIN French, literally 'new rich'.

nouveau roman /ˌnuːvəʊ rəʊˈmɑːn, French nuvo Rɔmã/ ▶ noun [mass noun] a style of avant-garde French novel that came to prominence in the 1950s. It rejected the plot, characters, and omniscient

narrator central to the traditional novel in an attempt to reflect more faithfully the sometimes random nature of experience.

− ORIGIN French, literally 'new novel'.

nouvelle /nuːˈvɛl/ ▶ adjective of, relating to, or specializing in nouvelle cuisine: *nouvelle bistros.*

Nouvelle-Calédonie /nuvɛlkaledɔni/ French name for **NEW CALEDONIA**.

nouvelle cuisine /kwiːˈziːn/ ▶ noun [mass noun] a modern style of cookery that avoids rich, heavy foods and emphasizes the freshness of the ingredients and the presentation of the dishes.

− ORIGIN French, literally 'new cookery'.

nouvelle vague /nuːˌvɛl ˈvɑːɡ, French nuvɛl vag/ ▶ noun [mass noun] a grouping of French film directors in the late 1950s and 1960s who reacted against established French cinema and sought to make more individualistic and stylistically innovative films. Exponents included Claude Chabrol, Jean-Luc Godard, Alain Resnais, and François Truffaut.

− ORIGIN French, literally 'new wave'.

Nov. ▶ abbreviation for November.

nova /ˈnəʊvə/ ▶ noun (pl. **novae** /-viː/ or **novas**) Astronomy a star showing a sudden large increase in brightness and then slowly returning to its original state over a few months. See also **SUPERNOVA**.

− ORIGIN late 19th cent.: from Latin, feminine of *novus* 'new' (because such stars were thought to be newly formed).

novaculite /nə(ʊ)ˈvakjʊlʌɪt/ ▶ noun [mass noun] Geology a hard, dense, fine-grained siliceous rock resembling chert, with a high content of microcrystalline quartz.

− ORIGIN late 18th cent.: from Latin *novacula* 'razor' + **-ITE**[1].

Nova Lisboa /ˌnəʊvə lɪzˈbəʊə/ former name (until 1978) for **HUAMBO**.

Nova Scotia /ˌnəʊvə ˈskəʊʃə/ **1** a peninsula on the SE coast of Canada, projecting into the Atlantic Ocean and separating the Bay of Fundy from the Gulf of St Lawrence.

2 a province of eastern Canada, comprising the peninsula of Nova Scotia and the adjoining Cape Breton Island; pop. 900,600 (1991); capital, Halifax. Settled by the French in the early 18th century as Acadia, it changed hands several times between French and English before being awarded to Britain in 1713. It became one of the original four provinces in the Dominion of Canada in 1867.

− DERIVATIVES **Nova Scotian** adjective & noun.

novation /nə(ʊ)ˈveɪʃ(ə)n/ ▶ noun [mass noun] Law the substitution of a new contract in place of an old one.

− DERIVATIVES **novate** verb.

− ORIGIN early 16th cent.: from late Latin *novatio(n-)*, from the verb *novare* 'make new'.

Novaya Zemlya /ˌnəʊvəjə zɪmˈljɑː/ two large uninhabited islands in the Arctic Ocean off the north coast of Siberian Russia. The name means 'new land'.

novel[1] ▶ noun a fictitious prose narrative of book length, typically representing character and action with some degree of realism: *the novels of Jane Austen.*

■ a book containing such a narrative: *she was reading a paperback novel.* ■ (**the novel**) the literary genre represented or exemplified by such works: *the novel is the most adaptable of all literary forms.*

− ORIGIN mid 16th cent.: from Italian *novella* (*storia*) 'new (story)', feminine of *novello* 'new', from Latin *novellus*, from *novus* 'new'. The word is also found from late Middle English until the 18th cent. in the sense 'a novelty, a piece of news', from Old French *novelle* (see **NOVEL**[2]).

novel[2] ▶ adjective interestingly new or unusual: *he hit on a novel idea to solve his financial problems.*

− DERIVATIVES **novelly** adverb.

− ORIGIN late Middle English (in the sense 'recent'): from Old French, from Latin *novellus*, from *novus* 'new'.

novelese ▶ noun [mass noun] derogatory a style of writing supposedly characteristic of inferior novels.

novelette ▶ noun chiefly derogatory a short novel, typically one that is light and romantic or sentimental in character.

− DERIVATIVES **novelettish** adjective.

novelist ▶ noun a writer of novels.

novelistic ▶ **adjective** characteristic of or used in novels: *the novelistic detail of his film.*

novelize (also **-ise**) ▶ **verb** [with obj.] [usu. as adj. **novelized**] convert (a story, typically one in the form of a film or screenplay) into a novel.
– DERIVATIVES **novelization** noun.

novella /nəˈvɛlə/ ▶ **noun** a short novel or long short story.
– ORIGIN early 20th cent.: from Italian, 'novel'.

Novello /nəˈvɛləʊ/, Ivor (1893–1951), Welsh composer, songwriter, actor, and dramatist; born *David Ivor Davies.*

novelty ▶ **noun** (pl. **-ies**) **1** [mass noun] the quality of being new, original, or unusual: *the novelty of being a married woman wore off.*
■ [count noun] a new or unfamiliar thing or experience: *in 1914 air travel was still a novelty.* ■ [as modifier] denoting something intended to be amusing as a result of its new or unusual quality: *a novelty teapot.*
2 a small and inexpensive toy or ornament: *he bought chocolate novelties to decorate the Christmas tree.*
– ORIGIN late Middle English: from Old French *novelte*, from *novel* 'new, fresh' (see **NOVEL**[2]).

November ▶ **noun** **1** the eleventh month of the year, in the northern hemisphere usually considered the last month of autumn: *the shop opened in November | he hasn't played for England since last November.*
2 a code word representing the letter N, used in radio communication.
– ORIGIN Old English, from Latin, from *novem* 'nine' (being originally the ninth month of the Roman year).

novena /nə(ʊ)ˈviːnə/ ▶ **noun** (in the Roman Catholic church) a form of worship consisting of special prayers or services on nine successive days.
– ORIGIN mid 19th cent.: from medieval Latin, from Latin *novem* 'nine'.

Noverre /nɒˈvɛː, French nɔvɛʀ/, Jean-Georges (1727–1810), French choreographer and dance theorist, who stressed the importance of dramatic motivation in ballet as opposed to technical virtuosity.

Novgorod /ˈnɒvgərɒd/ a city in NW Russia, on the Volkhov River at the northern tip of Lake Ilmen; pop. 232,000 (1990). Russia's oldest city, it was settled by the Varangian chief Rurik in 862 and ruled by Alexander Nevsky between 1238 and 1263, when it was an important centre of medieval eastern Europe.

novice /ˈnɒvɪs/ ▶ **noun** a person new to or inexperienced in the field or situation in which they are placed: *he was a complete novice in foreign affairs.*
■ a person who has entered a religious order and is under probation, before taking vows. ■ an animal, especially a racehorse, that has not yet won a major prize or reached a level of performance to qualify for important events.
– ORIGIN Middle English: from Old French, from late Latin *novicius*, from *novus* 'new'.

Novi Sad /ˌnəʊvɪ ˈsad/ an industrial city in Serbia, on the River Danube, capital of the autonomous province of Vojvodina; pop. 178,800 (1991).

novitiate /nə(ʊ)ˈvɪʃɪət, -ɪeɪt/ (also **noviciate**) ▶ **noun** [mass noun] chiefly US the period or state of being a novice, especially in a religious order.
■ a novice, especially in a religious order. ■ a place housing religious novices.
– ORIGIN early 17th cent.: from ecclesiastical Latin *noviciatus*, from Latin *novicius* 'new' (see **NOVICE**).

novocaine /ˈnəʊvəkeɪn/ ▶ **noun** another term for **PROCAINE**.
– ORIGIN early 20th cent.: from Latin *novus* 'new' + *-caine* (from **COCAINE**).

Novokuznetsk /ˌnəʊvəkʊzˈnjɛtsk/ an industrial city in the Kuznets Basin in south central Siberian Russia; pop. 601,000 (1990).

Novosibirsk /ˌnəʊvəsɪˈbɪəsk/ a city in central Siberian Russia, to the west of the Kuznets Basin, on the River Ob; pop. 1,443,000 (1990).

no vote ▶ **noun** a vote in opposition to a proposal.

Novotný /ˈnɒvɒtˌniː/, Antonín (1904–75), Czechoslovak communist statesman, President 1957–68. A founder member of the Czechoslovak Communist Party (1921), he played a major part in the communist seizure of power in 1948. He was ousted by the reform movement in 1968.

now ▶ **adverb** **1** at the present time or moment: *where are you living now? | it's the most popular style of jazz* **right now** *| not now, I'm late |* [after prep.] *they should be back* **by now**.
■ at the time directly following the present moment; immediately: *if we leave now we can be home by ten | I'd rather do it now than leave it till later.* ■ under the present circumstances; as a result of something that has recently happened: *it is now clear that we should not pursue this policy | I didn't receive the letter, but it hardly matters now.* ■ on this further occasion, typically as the latest in a series of annoying situations or events: *what do you want now?* ■ used to emphasize a particular length of time: *they've been married four years now.* ■ (in a narrative or account of past events) at the time spoken of or referred to: *it had happened three times now | she was nineteen now, and she was alone.*
2 used, especially in conversation, to draw attention to a particular statement or point in a narrative: *now, my first impulse was to run away | I don't like Scotch. Now, if it had been Irish Whiskey you'd offered me.*
3 used in or as a request, instruction, or question, typically to give a slight emphasis to one's words: *now, if you'll excuse me? | we can hardly send her back, now can we? | run along now.*
■ used when pausing or considering one's next words: *let me see now, oh yes, I remember.*
4 used at the end of an ironic question echoing a previous statement: *'Mum says you might let me have some of your stamps.' 'Does she now?'*
▶ **conjunction** as a consequence of the fact: *they spent a lot of time together* **now that** *he had retired | now you mention it, I haven't seen her around for ages.*
▶ **adjective** informal fashionable; up to date: *seventies disco dancing—very now.*
– PHRASES **for now** until a later time: *that's all the news there is for now.* **now and again** (or **then**) from time to time. **now now** used as an expression of mild remonstrance: *now now, that's not the way to behave.* **now ——, now ——** at one moment ——, at the next ——: *a wind whipped about the house, now this way, now that.* **now or never** used to convey urgency: ***it was now or never****—I had to move fast.* **now then** **1** used to get someone's attention or to invite a response: *now then, who's for a coffee?* **2** used as an expression of mild remonstrance or warning: *now then, Emily, I think Sarah has suffered enough.* **now you're talking** used to express one's enthusiastic agreement with or approval of a statement or suggestion: *The Beatles! Now you're talking.*
– DERIVATIVES **nowness** noun.
– ORIGIN Old English *nū*, of Germanic origin; related to Dutch *nu*, German *nun*, from an Indo-European root shared by Latin *nunc* and Greek *nun*.

nowadays ▶ **adverb** at the present time, in contrast with the past: *the sort of clothes worn by almost all young people nowadays |* [sentence adverb] *nowadays, many people condemn hunting.*

noway (also **noways**) ▶ **adverb** chiefly archaic or US not at all; by no means.

nowed /naʊd/ ▶ **adjective** [often postpositive] Heraldry knotted; (of a snake) depicted interlaced in a knot.
– ORIGIN late 16th cent.: from French *noué* 'knotted'.

Nowel (also **Nowell**) ▶ **noun** archaic spelling of **NOEL**.

nowhere ▶ **adverb** not in or to any place; not anywhere: *plants and animals found nowhere else in the world | the constable was nowhere to be seen.*
▶ **pronoun** **1** no place: *there was nowhere for her to sit | there's nowhere better to experience the wonders of the Pyrenees.*
2 a place that is remote, uninteresting, or nondescript: *a stretch of road between nowhere and nowhere |* [as noun] *the town is a particularly American nowhere.*
▶ **adjective** [attrib.] informal having no prospect of progress or success: *she's involved in a nowhere affair with a married executive.*
– PHRASES **be** (or **come**) **nowhere** be badly beaten or completely unsuccessful in a race or competition. **from** (or **out of**) **nowhere** appearing or happening suddenly and unexpectedly: *they came from nowhere to win in the last three strokes of the race.* **get** (or **go**) **nowhere** make no progress: *he'll* **get nowhere** *with her, he's too young.* **get someone nowhere** be of no use or benefit to someone: *being angry would get her nowhere.* **nowhere near** not nearly: *he's* **nowhere near as** *popular as he used to be.* **a road to nowhere** a situation or course of action offering no prospects of progress or advancement.
– ORIGIN Old English *nāhwǣr* (see **NO**, **WHERE**).

no-win ▶ **adjective** of or denoting a situation in which success or a favourable outcome is impossible.

nowise ▶ **adverb** archaic in no way or manner; not at all: *I can nowise accept the accusation.*

now-now ▶ **adverb** S. African informal used to refer to a time very shortly before or very soon after the moment of speaking: *I'll be back now-now.*

nowt /naʊt/ ▶ **pronoun** & **adverb** N. English nothing: *it's nowt to do with me.*

NOx ▶ **noun** [mass noun] oxides of nitrogen, especially as atmospheric pollutants.

noxious /ˈnɒkʃəs/ ▶ **adjective** harmful, poisonous, or very unpleasant: *they were overcome by the noxious fumes.*
– DERIVATIVES **noxiously** adverb, **noxiousness** noun.
– ORIGIN late 15th cent.: from Latin *noxius* (from *noxa* 'harm') + **-OUS**.

noyade /nwɑːˈjɑːd/ ▶ **noun** historical an execution carried out by drowning.
– ORIGIN early 19th cent. (referring especially to a mass execution by drowning, carried out in France in 1794): from French, literally 'drowning', from the verb *noyer*, from Latin *necare* 'kill without use of a weapon', later 'drown'.

noyau /nwʌˈjəʊ/ ▶ **noun** (pl. **noyaux** /-jəʊz/) [mass noun] a liqueur made of brandy flavoured with fruit kernels.
– ORIGIN French, literally 'kernel', based on Latin *nux, nuc-* 'nut'.

nozzle ▶ **noun** a cylindrical or round spout at the end of a pipe, hose, or tube used to control a jet of gas or liquid.
– ORIGIN early 17th cent.: from **NOSE** + **-LE**[2].

NP ▶ **abbreviation for** notary public.

Np ▶ **symbol for** the chemical element neptunium.

n.p. ▶ **abbreviation for** ■ new paragraph. ■ no place of publication (used especially in book classification).

NPA ▶ **abbreviation for** (in the UK) Newspaper Publishers' Association.

NPL ▶ **abbreviation for** (in the UK) National Physical Laboratory.

NPN ▶ **adjective** Electronics denoting a semiconductor device in which a *p*-type region is sandwiched between two *n*-type regions.

NPV ▶ **abbreviation for** net present value. See **PRESENT VALUE**.

nr ▶ **abbreviation for** near.

NRA ▶ **abbreviation for** ■ (in the US) National Rifle Association. ■ (in the UK) National Rivers Authority.

NRSV ▶ **abbreviation for** New Revised Standard Version (of the Bible).

NS ▶ **abbreviation for** ■ New Style. ■ Nova Scotia (in official postal use).

ns ▶ **abbreviation for** nanosecond.

n/s ▶ **abbreviation for** non-smoker; non-smoking (used in personal advertisements).

NSA ▶ **abbreviation for** (in the US) National Security Agency.

NSB ▶ **abbreviation for** (in the UK) National Savings Bank.

NSC ▶ **abbreviation for** (in the US) National Security Council.

NSF ▶ **abbreviation for** (in the US) National Science Foundation.

NSPCC ▶ **abbreviation for** (in the UK) National Society for the Prevention of Cruelty to Children.

NSU Medicine ▶ **abbreviation for** non-specific urethritis.

NSW ▶ **abbreviation for** New South Wales.

NT ▶ **abbreviation for** ■ National Trust. ■ New Testament. ■ Northern Territory. ■ Northwest Territories (in official postal use). ■ Bridge no trump(s).

-n't ▶ **contraction of** not, used with auxiliary verbs (e.g. *can't, won't, didn't,* and *isn't*).

Nth ▶ **abbreviation for** North.

nth ▶ **adjective** Mathematics denoting an unspecified member of a series of numbers or enumerated items: *systematic sampling by taking every nth name from the list.*
■ (in general use) denoting an unspecified item or instance in a series, typically the last or latest in a

n

long series: *he had just been booted out of his digs for the nth time.*
– PHRASES **to the nth degree** to the utmost: *the gullibility of the electorate was tested to the nth degree by such promises.*

NTP Chemistry ▶ **abbreviation for** normal temperature and pressure.

NTSC ▶ noun [mass noun] the television broadcasting system used in North America and Japan.
– ORIGIN 1950s: acronym from *National Television Standard Committee.*

n-tuple ▶ noun Mathematics an ordered set with *n* elements.

n-type ▶ adjective Electronics denoting a region in a semiconductor in which electrical conduction is due chiefly to the movement of electrons. Often contrasted with **P-TYPE**.

nu /njuː/ ▶ noun the thirteenth letter of the Greek alphabet (N, v), transliterated as 'n'.
■ (**Nu**) [followed by Latin genitive] Astronomy the thirteenth star in a constellation: *Nu Draconis.*
▶ **symbol for** (v) frequency.
– ORIGIN Greek.

nuance /ˈnjuːɑːns/ ▶ noun a subtle difference in or shade of meaning, expression, or sound: *the nuances of facial expression and body language.*
▶ verb [with obj.] (usu. **be nuanced**) give nuances to: *the effect of the music is nuanced by the social situation of listeners.*
– ORIGIN late 18th cent.: from French, 'shade, subtlety', from *nuer* 'to shade', based on Latin *nubes* 'cloud'.

nub ▶ noun **1** (**the nub**) the crux or central point of a matter: *the nub of the problem lies elsewhere.*
2 a small lump or protuberance: *he pressed down on the two nubs on top of the phone.*
■ a small chunk or nugget of metal or rock: *a nub of gold.*
– ORIGIN late 17th cent.: apparently a variant of dialect *knub* 'protuberance', from Middle Low German *knubbe, knobbe* 'knob'.

Nuba /ˈnuːbə/ ▶ noun (pl. same or **Nubas**) a member of a Nilotic people inhabiting southern Kordofan in Sudan.
▶ adjective of or relating to this people.
– ORIGIN from Latin *Nubae* 'Nubians'.

nubbin /ˈnʌbɪn/ ▶ noun a small lump or residual part: *nubbins of bone or cartilage.*
– ORIGIN late 17th cent.: diminutive of **NUB**.

nubby (also **nubbly**) ▶ adjective chiefly US (of fabric) coarse or knobbly in texture: *upholstered in nubby blue cotton.*
■ stubby; lumpy: *the nubby points of the new leaves.*
– ORIGIN early 19th cent. (as *nubbly*): derivative of *nubble* 'small lump'.

Nubia /ˈnjuːbɪə/ an ancient region of southern Egypt and northern Sudan, including the Nile valley between Aswan and Khartoum and the surrounding area. Much of Nubia is now drowned by the waters of Lake Nasser, formed by the building of the two dams at Aswan. Nubians constitute an ethnic minority group in Egypt.

Nubian ▶ adjective of or relating to Nubia, its people, or their language.
▶ noun **1** a native or inhabitant of Nubia.
2 [mass noun] the Nilo-Saharan language spoken by the Nubians.
3 a goat of a short-haired breed with long pendant ears and long legs, originally from Africa.
– ORIGIN from medieval Latin *Nubianus,* from *Nubia* 'Nubia', from Latin *Nubae* 'Nubians'.

nubile /ˈnjuːbʌɪl/ ▶ adjective (of a girl or young woman) sexually mature; suitable for marriage.
■ (of a girl or young woman) sexually attractive: *he employed a procession of nubile young secretaries.*
– DERIVATIVES **nubility** noun.
– ORIGIN mid 17th cent.: from Latin *nubilis* 'marriageable', from *nubere* 'cover or veil oneself for a bridegroom' (from *nubes* 'cloud').

Nubuck /ˈnjuːbʌk/ ▶ noun [mass noun] cowhide leather which has been rubbed on the flesh side to give it a feel like that of suede.

nucellus /njuːˈsɛləs/ ▶ noun (pl. **nucelli**) Botany the central part of an ovule, containing the embryo sac.
– DERIVATIVES **nucellar** adjective.
– ORIGIN late 19th cent.: modern Latin, apparently an irregular diminutive of **NUCLEUS**.

nuchal /ˈnjuːk(ə)l/ ▶ adjective Anatomy of or relating to the nape of the neck.
– ORIGIN mid 19th cent.: from obsolete *nucha* 'nape' (from medieval Latin *nucha* 'medulla oblongata', from Arabic *nuḵaʿ* 'spinal marrow') + **-AL**.

nuci- /ˈnjuːsɪ/ ▶ **combining form** of a nut or nuts: *nuciferous.*
– ORIGIN from Latin *nux, nuc-* 'nut'.

nuciferous /njuːˈsɪf(ə)rəs/ ▶ adjective Botany (of a tree or bush) bearing nuts.

nuclear ▶ adjective **1** of or relating to the nucleus of an atom.
■ denoting, relating to, or powered by the energy released in nuclear fission or fusion: *nuclear submarines.* ■ denoting, possessing, or involving weapons using this energy: *a nuclear bomb.*
2 Biology of or relating to the nucleus of a cell: *nuclear DNA.*
– ORIGIN mid 19th cent.: from **NUCLEUS** + **-AR**[1].

USAGE The standard pronunciation of the word **nuclear** in British and US English rhymes with **clear**. A variant pronunciation exists in US English, famously used by Presidents Eisenhower and Carter, which pronounces the second part of the word like **-ular** in **circular** or **particular**. This pronunciation is not acceptable in standard British or US English, although it is still widely heard.

nuclear club ▶ noun the nations possessing nuclear weapons.

nuclear family ▶ noun a couple and their dependent children, regarded as a basic social unit.

nuclear fission ▶ noun [mass noun] a nuclear reaction in which a heavy nucleus splits spontaneously or on impact with another particle, with the release of energy.

nuclear flask ▶ noun see **FLASK**.

nuclear force ▶ noun Physics a strong attractive force between nucleons in the atomic nucleus that holds the nucleus together.

nuclear-free ▶ adjective (of a country or region) not having or allowing any nuclear weapons, materials, or power: *a nuclear-free zone.*

nuclear fuel ▶ noun a substance that will sustain a fission chain reaction so that it can be used as a source of nuclear energy.

nuclear fusion ▶ noun [mass noun] a nuclear reaction in which atomic nuclei of low atomic number fuse to form a heavier nucleus with the release of energy.

nuclear isomer ▶ noun another term for **ISOMER** (in sense 2).

nuclear magnetic resonance (abbrev.: **NMR.**) ▶ noun [mass noun] the absorption of electromagnetic radiation by a nucleus having a magnetic moment when in an external magnetic field, used mainly as an analytical technique and in diagnostic body imaging.

nuclear medicine ▶ noun [mass noun] the branch of medicine that deals with the use of radioactive substances in research, diagnosis, and treatment.

nuclear physics ▶ plural noun [treated as sing.] the physics of atomic nuclei and their interactions, especially in the generation of nuclear energy.

nuclear power ▶ noun **1** [mass noun] electric or motive power generated by a nuclear reactor.
2 a country that has nuclear weapons.
– DERIVATIVES **nuclear-powered** adjective.

nuclear reactor ▶ noun see **REACTOR**.

nuclear threshold ▶ noun a point in a conflict at which nuclear weapons are or would be brought into use.

nuclear umbrella ▶ noun the supposed protection gained from an alliance with a country possessing nuclear weapons.

nuclear waste ▶ noun [mass noun] radioactive waste material, for example from the use or reprocessing of nuclear fuel.

nuclear winter ▶ noun a period of abnormal cold and darkness predicted to follow a nuclear war, caused by a layer of smoke and dust in the atmosphere blocking the sun's rays.

nuclease /ˈnjuːklɪeɪz/ ▶ noun Biochemistry an enzyme that cleaves the chains of nucleotides in nucleic acids into smaller units.

nucleate ▶ adjective /ˈnjuːklɪət/ chiefly Biology having a nucleus.

▶ verb /ˈnjuːklɪeɪt/ [no obj.] [usu. as adj. **nucleated**] form a nucleus.
■ form around a central area: *a nucleated village.*
– DERIVATIVES **nucleation** noun.

nuclei plural form of **NUCLEUS**.

nucleic acid /njuːˈkliːɪk, -ˈkleɪɪk/ ▶ noun Biochemistry a complex organic substance present in living cells, especially DNA or RNA, whose molecules consist of many nucleotides linked in a long chain.

nucleo- combining form representing **NUCLEUS**, **NUCLEAR**, or **NUCLEIC ACID**.

nucleocapsid /ˌnjuːklɪə(ʊ)ˈkapsɪd/ ▶ noun Biology the capsid of a virus with the enclosed nucleic acid.

nucleolus /ˌnjuːklɪˈəʊləs/ ▶ noun (pl. **nucleoli** /-lʌɪ/) Biology a small dense spherical structure in the nucleus of a cell during interphase.
– DERIVATIVES **nucleolar** adjective.
– ORIGIN mid 19th cent.: from late Latin, diminutive of Latin *nucleus* 'inner part, kernel' (see **NUCLEUS**).

nucleon /ˈnjuːklɒn/ ▶ noun Physics a proton or neutron.

nucleonics /ˌnjuːklɪˈɒnɪks/ ▶ plural noun [treated as sing.] the branch of science and technology concerned with atomic nuclei and nucleons, especially the exploitation of nuclear power.
– DERIVATIVES **nucleonic** adjective.
– ORIGIN 1940s: from **NUCLEAR**, on the pattern of *electronics.*

nucleophilic /ˌnjuːklɪə(ʊ)ˈfɪlɪk/ ▶ adjective Chemistry (of a molecule or group) having a tendency to donate electrons or react at electron-poor sites such as protons. Often contrasted with **ELECTROPHILIC**.
– DERIVATIVES **nucleophile** noun.

nucleoplasm ▶ noun [mass noun] Biology the substance of a cell nucleus, especially that not forming part of a nucleolus.

nucleoprotein ▶ noun Biochemistry a complex consisting of a nucleic acid bonded to a protein.

nucleoside ▶ noun Biochemistry a compound (e.g. adenosine or cytidine) consisting of a purine or pyrimidine base linked to a sugar.

nucleosome /ˈnjuːklɪə(ʊ)səʊm/ ▶ noun Biology a structural unit of a eukaryotic chromosome, consisting of a length of DNA coiled around a core of histones.
– DERIVATIVES **nucleosomal** adjective.

nucleosynthesis ▶ noun [mass noun] Astronomy the cosmic formation of atoms more complex than the hydrogen atom.
– DERIVATIVES **nucleosynthetic** adjective.

nucleotide ▶ noun Biochemistry a compound consisting of a nucleoside linked to a phosphate group. Nucleotides form the basic structural unit of nucleic acids such as DNA.

nucleus /ˈnjuːklɪəs/ ▶ noun (pl. **nuclei** /-lʌɪ/) the central and most important part of an object, movement, or group, forming the basis for its activity and growth: *the nucleus of a British film-producing industry.*
■ Astronomy the solid part of a comet's head. ■ Physics the positively charged central core of an atom that contains most of its mass. ■ Biology a dense organelle present in most eukaryotic cells, typically a single rounded structure bounded by a double membrane, containing the genetic material. ■ a discrete mass of grey matter in the central nervous system.
– ORIGIN early 18th cent.: from Latin, literally 'kernel, inner part', diminutive of *nux, nuc-* 'nut'.

nuclide /ˈnjuːklʌɪd/ ▶ noun Physics a distinct kind of atom or nucleus characterized by a specific number of protons and neutrons.
– DERIVATIVES **nuclidic** adjective.
– ORIGIN 1940s: from **NUCLEUS** + *-ide* (from Greek *eidos* 'form').

nuddy ▶ noun (in phrase **in the nuddy**) informal in the nude.
– ORIGIN 1950s: humorous alteration of **NUDE**.

nude ▶ adjective wearing no clothes; naked: *a painting of a nude model.*
■ [attrib.] depicting or performed by naked people: *he was asked to act in a frank nude scene.*
▶ noun a naked human figure, typically as the subject of a painting, sculpture, or photograph: *a study of a kneeling nude.*
■ (**the nude**) the representation of the naked human figure as a genre in art.

- PHRASES **in the nude** in an unclothed state: *I like to swim in the nude.*
- ORIGIN late Middle English (in the sense 'plain, explicit'): from Latin *nudus*. The current sense is first found in noun use in the early 18th cent.

nudge ▶ verb [with obj.] prod (someone) gently with one's elbow in order to draw their attention to something: *people were nudging each other and pointing at me.* ■ touch or push (something) gently or gradually: *the canoe nudged a bank of reeds.* ■ figurative coax or gently encourage (someone) to do something: *we have to nudge the politicians in the right direction.* ■ approach (an age, figure, or level) very closely: *both men were nudging fifty.* ▶ noun a light touch or push: figurative *she appreciated the nudge to her memory.*
- PHRASES **nudge nudge (wink wink)** used to draw attention to a sexual innuendo in the previous statement: *haven't seen much of the beach—we've been catching up on our sleep (nudge nudge).* [ORIGIN: a catchphrase from *Monty Python's Flying Circus*, a British television comedy programme.]
- DERIVATIVES **nudger** noun.
- ORIGIN late 17th cent. (as a verb): of unknown origin; compare with Norwegian dialect *nugga*, *nyggja* 'to push, rub'.

nudge bar ▶ noun another term for BULL BAR.

Nudibranchia /ˌnjuːdɪˈbraŋkɪə/ Zoology an order of shell-less marine molluscs which comprises the sea slugs.
● Order Nudibranchia, class Gastropoda.
- DERIVATIVES **nudibranch** /ˈnjuːdɪbraŋk/ noun.
- ORIGIN modern Latin (plural), from Latin *nudus* 'nude' + BRANCHIA.

nudie ▶ noun (pl. **-ies**) informal a publication, entertainment, or venue featuring nude performers or models: [as modifier] *a nudie calendar.*

nudist ▶ noun a person who engages in the practice of going naked wherever possible: [as modifier] *a nudist beach.*
- DERIVATIVES **nudism** noun.

nudity ▶ noun [mass noun] the state or fact of being naked: *scenes of full frontal nudity.*

nudnik /ˈnʊdnɪk/ (also **nudnick**) ▶ noun N. Amer. informal a pestering, nagging, or irritating person; a bore.
- ORIGIN mid 20th cent.: Yiddish, from Russian *nudnyi* 'tedious'.

nuée ardente /ˌnjuːeɪ ɑːˈdɒt/ ▶ noun Geology an incandescent cloud of gas, ash, and lava fragments ejected from a volcano, typically as part of a pyroclastic flow.
- ORIGIN French, literally 'burning cloud'.

Nuer /ˈnuːə/ ▶ noun (pl. same or **Nuers**) 1 a member of an African people of SE Sudan and Ethiopia, traditionally pastoralists and cattle-rearers. 2 [mass noun] the Nilotic language of this people, with about 840,000 speakers. ▶ adjective of or relating to this people or their language.
- ORIGIN the name in Dinka.

Nuevo León /ˌnweɪvəʊ leɪˈɒn, Spanish ˌnweβo leˈon/ a state of NE Mexico, on the border with the US; capital, Monterrey.

nuevo sol /ˌnweɪvəʊ ˈsɒl, Spanish ˌnweβo ˈsol/ ▶ noun another term for SOL³.
- ORIGIN Spanish, 'new sol'.

nuff ▶ determiner, pronoun, & adverb non-standard spelling of ENOUGH, representing informal speech: *The pen is mightier than the sword. Nuff said.* ■ [as determiner] black English much: *nuff respect goes out to Galliano.*

Nuffield /ˈnʌfiːld/, William Richard Morris, 1st Viscount (1877–1963), British motor manufacturer and philanthropist, who opened the first Morris automobile factory in Oxford in 1912. He endowed Nuffield College, Oxford (1937) and created the Nuffield Foundation (1943) for medical, social, and scientific research.

nuffin (also **nuffink**) ▶ pronoun, adjective, & adverb non-standard spelling of NOTHING, representing informal speech: *'There was nuffin in it,' Carrie retorted.*

nugacity /njuːˈɡasɪti/ ▶ noun (pl. **-ies**) [mass noun] rare triviality; frivolity. ■ [count noun] a trivial or frivolous thing or idea.
- ORIGIN late 16th cent.: from late Latin *nugacitas*, from Latin *nugax*, *nugac-* 'trifling, frivolous'.

nugatory /ˈnjuːɡət(ə)ri, ˈnuː-/ ▶ adjective of no value or importance: *a nugatory and pointless observation.* ■ useless; futile: *the teacher shortages will render nugatory the hopes of implementing the new curriculum.*
- ORIGIN early 17th cent.: from Latin *nugatorius*, from *nugari* 'to trifle', from *nugae* 'jests'.

nugget ▶ noun a small lump of gold or other precious metal found ready-formed in the earth. ■ a small chunk or lump of another substance: *a nugget of food.* ■ a valuable idea or fact: *nuggets of information.*
- ORIGIN mid 19th cent.: apparently from dialect *nug* 'lump', of unknown origin.

nuggety (also **nuggetty**) ▶ adjective chiefly Austral./NZ 1 occurring as nuggets: *nuggety gold.* ■ rich in nuggets: *nuggety gullies.* 2 (of a person) stocky; thickset.

nuisance ▶ noun a person, thing, or circumstance causing inconvenience or annoyance: *an unreasonable landlord could become a nuisance* | *I hope you're not going to make a nuisance of yourself.* ■ (also **private nuisance**) Law an unlawful interference with the use and enjoyment of land. ■ Law see PUBLIC NUISANCE.
- ORIGIN late Middle English (in the sense 'injury, hurt'): from Old French, 'hurt', from the verb *nuire*, from Latin *nocere* 'to harm'.

nuisance grounds ▶ plural noun Canadian a rubbish dump.

nuisance value ▶ noun [mass noun] the significance or a person or thing arising from their capacity to cause inconvenience or annoyance.

nuit blanche /ˌnwiː ˈblɒʃ/ ▶ noun (pl. **nuits blanches**) a sleepless night.
- ORIGIN French, literally 'white night'.

Nuits St George /ˌnwiː sæ̃ ˈʒɔːʒ, French nɥi sɛ̃ ʒɔʁʒ/ ▶ noun [mass noun] a red burgundy wine, produced in the district of Nuits St Georges, France.

NUJ ▶ abbreviation for (in the UK) National Union of Journalists.

Nujol /ˈnjuːdʒɒl/ ▶ noun [mass noun] (trademark in the US) a paraffin oil used as an emulsifying agent in pharmacy and for making mulls in infrared spectroscopy.
- ORIGIN early 20th cent.: perhaps from *New J(ersey)*, site of the original manufacturing company, + Latin *oleum* 'oil'.

nuke informal ▶ noun a nuclear weapon. ■ a nuclear power station. ■ a nuclear-powered vessel. ▶ verb [with obj.] attack or destroy with nuclear weapons. ■ chiefly N. Amer. destroy; get rid of: *I fertilized the lawn and nuked the weeds.* ■ chiefly N. Amer. cook or heat up (food) in a microwave oven: *I nuked a quick burger.*
- ORIGIN 1950s: abbreviation of NUCLEAR.

Nuku'alofa /ˌnuːkuːˈɑːləʊfə/ the capital of Tonga, situated on the island of Tongatapu; pop. 30,000 (1994).

null ▶ adjective 1 [predic.] having no legal or binding force; invalid: *the establishment of a new interim government was declared null and void.* 2 having or associated with the value zero. ■ Mathematics (of a set or matrix) having no elements, or only zeros as elements. ■ lacking distinctive qualities; having no positive substance or content: *his curiously null life.* ▶ noun poetic/literary a zero. ■ a dummy letter in a cipher. ■ Electronics a condition of no signal. ■ a direction in which no electromagnetic radiation is detected or emitted. ▶ verb [with obj.] Electronics combine (a signal) with another in order to create a null; cancel out.
- ORIGIN late Middle English: from French *nul*, *nulle*, from Latin *nullus* 'none', from *ne* 'not' + *ullus* 'any'.

nullah /ˈnʌlə/ ▶ noun Indian a dry river bed or ravine.
- ORIGIN late 18th cent.: from Hindi *nāla*.

nulla-nulla /ˌnʌlənˈʌlə/ (also **nulla**) ▶ noun a hardwood club used as a weapon by Australian Aboriginals.
- ORIGIN from Dharuk *ngalla-ngalla*.

Nullarbor Plain /ˈnʌləbɔː/ a vast arid plain in SW Australia, stretching inland from the Great Australian Bight. It contains no surface water, has sparse vegetation, and is almost uninhabited.
- ORIGIN *Nullarbor* from Latin *nullus arbor* 'no tree'.

null character ▶ noun Computing a character denoting nothing, usually represented by a binary zero.

null hypothesis ▶ noun (in a statistical test) the hypothesis that there is no significant difference between specified populations, any observed difference being due to sampling or experimental error.

nullifidian /ˌnʌlɪˈfɪdɪən/ rare ▶ noun a person having no faith or religious belief. ▶ adjective having no faith or religious belief.
- ORIGIN mid 16th cent.: from medieval Latin *nullifidius* (from *nullus* 'no, none' + *fides* 'faith') + -AN.

nullify /ˈnʌlɪfʌɪ/ ▶ verb (**-ies**, **-ied**) [with obj.] make legally null and void; invalidate: *judges were unwilling to nullify government decisions.* ■ make of no use or value; cancel out: *insulin can block the release of the hormone and thereby nullify the effects of training.*
- DERIVATIVES **nullification** noun, **nullifier** noun.

null instrument (also **null indicator**) ▶ noun an instrument used to measure an electrical quantity by adjusting known quantities in the circuit until a reading of zero is obtained.

nullipara /nʌˈlɪp(ə)rə/ ▶ noun (pl. **nulliparae** /nʌˈlɪp(ə)riː/) Medicine & Zoology a woman (or female animal) that has never given birth. Compare with PRIMIPARA.
- DERIVATIVES **nulliparous** adjective.
- ORIGIN late 19th cent.: modern Latin, from Latin *nullus* 'none' + *-para* (feminine of *-parus*), from *parere* 'bear children'.

nullity ▶ noun (pl. **-ies**) 1 Law an act or thing that is legally void. ■ [mass noun] the state of being legally void; invalidity, especially of a marriage. 2 a thing of no importance or worth. ■ [mass noun] nothingness.
- ORIGIN mid 16th cent.: from French *nullité*, from medieval Latin *nullitas*, from Latin *nullus* 'none'.

null link ▶ noun Computing a reference incorporated into the last item in a list to indicate there are no further items in the list.

NUM ▶ abbreviation for (in the UK) National Union of Mineworkers.

Num. ▶ abbreviation for Numbers (in biblical references).

Numa Pompilius /ˌnjuːmə pɒmˈpɪlɪəs/ the legendary second king of Rome, successor to Romulus, revered by the ancient Romans as the founder of nearly all their religious institutions.

numb ▶ adjective deprived of the power of sensation: *my feet were numb with cold* | figurative *the tragic events left us shocked and numb.* ▶ verb [with obj.] deprive of feeling or responsiveness: *the cold had numbed her senses.* ■ cause (a sensation) to be felt less intensely; deaden: *vodka might numb the pain in my hand.*
- DERIVATIVES **numbly** adverb, **numbness** noun.
- ORIGIN late Middle English *nome(n)*, past participle of obsolete *nim* 'take'.

numbat /ˈnʌmbat/ ▶ noun a small termite-eating Australian marsupial with a black-and-white striped back and a bushy tail. Also called BANDED ANTEATER.
● *Myrmecobius fasciatus*, family Myrmecobiidae.
- ORIGIN early 20th cent.: from Nyungar.

number ▶ noun 1 an arithmetical value, expressed by a word, symbol, or figure, representing a particular quantity and used in counting and making calculations and for showing order in a series or for identification: *she dialled the number carefully* | *an even number.* ■ (**numbers**) dated arithmetic: *the boy was adept at numbers.* 2 a quantity or amount: *the company is seeking to increase the number of women on its staff* | *the exhibition attracted vast numbers of visitors.* ■ (**a number of**) several: *we have discussed the matter on a number of occasions.* ■ a group or company of people: *there were some distinguished names among our number.* ■ (**numbers**) a large quantity or amount, often in contrast to a smaller one; numerical preponderance: *the weight of numbers turned the battle against them.* 3 a single issue of a magazine: *the October number of 'Travel'.* ■ a song, dance, piece of music, etc., especially one of several in a performance: *they go from one melodious number to another.* ■ [usu. with adj. or noun modifier] informal a thing, typically an item of clothing, of a particular type, regarded with approval or admiration: *Yvonne was wearing a little black number.* 4 [mass noun] a grammatical classification of words

that consists typically of singular and plural, and, in Greek and certain other languages, dual.
■ a particular form so classified.
▶ **verb** [with obj.] **1** amount to (a specified figure or quantity); comprise: *the demonstrators numbered more than 5,000.*
■ include or classify as a member of a group: *the orchestra numbers Brahms among its past conductors.*
2 (often **be numbered**) mark with a number or assign a number to, typically to indicate position in a series: *each document was numbered consecutively.*
■ count: *strategies like ours can be numbered on the fingers of one hand.* ■ assess or estimate the size or quantity of (something) to be a specified figure: *he numbers the fleet at a thousand.*
– PHRASES **any number of** any particular whole quantity of: *the game can involve any number of players.* ■ a large and unlimited quantity or amount of: *the results can be read any number of ways.* **by numbers** following simple instructions identified by numbers or as if identified: *painting by numbers.* **someone's/thing's days are numbered** someone or something will not survive or remain in a position of power or advantage for much longer: *my days as director were numbered.* **do a number on** N. Amer. informal treat someone badly, typically by deceiving, humiliating, or criticizing them in a calculated and thorough way. **have someone's number** informal understand a person's real motives or character and thereby gain some advantage. **have someone's number on it** informal (of a bomb, bullet, or other missile) destined to find a specified person as its target. **someone's number is up** informal the time has come when someone is doomed to die or suffer some other disaster or setback. [ORIGIN: with reference to a lottery number or a number by which one may be identified.] **without number** too many to count: *they forgot the message times without number.*
– ORIGIN Middle English: from Old French *nombre* (noun), *nombrer* (verb), from Latin *numerus.*

USAGE The construction **the number of** + plural noun is used with a singular verb (as in *the number of people affected remains small*). Thus it is the noun **number** rather than the noun **people** which is taken to agree with the verb (and which is therefore functioning as the head noun). By contrast, the apparently similar construction *a number of* + plural noun is used with a plural verb (as in *a number of people remain to be contacted*). In this case it is the noun **people** which acts as the head noun and with which the verb agrees. In the latter case, **a number of** works as if it were a single word, such as **some** or **several**. See also **usage** at **LOT.**

number cruncher ▶ **noun** informal **1** a computer or software capable of performing rapid calculations with large amounts of data.
2 often derogatory a statistician, accountant, or other person whose job involves dealing with large amounts of numerical data.
– DERIVATIVES **number crunching** noun.

numbered account ▶ **noun** a bank account, especially in a Swiss bank, identified only by a number and not bearing the owner's name.

number eight ▶ **noun 1** Rugby Union the forward at the back of the scrum.
2 [mass noun] NZ a wire of 4 mm gauge, used especially for fences: [as modifier] *number eight wire.*

numberless ▶ **adjective** too many to be counted; innumerable.

number line ▶ **noun** Mathematics a line on which numbers are marked at intervals, used to illustrate simple numerical operations.

number one informal ▶ **noun 1** oneself: *you must look after number one.*
2 a person or thing that is the most important in an activity or area: *businesses that were number one in their markets.*
■ a best-selling record or book: *an album featuring seventeen top movie themes and six number ones.*
3 used euphemistically to refer to urine.
4 a first lieutenant in the navy.
▶ **adjective** most important or prevalent: *a number-one priority.*
■ best-selling: *a number-one album.*

number opera ▶ **noun** an opera in which arias and other sections are clearly separable.

number plate ▶ **noun** Brit. a sign affixed to the front and rear of a vehicle displaying its registration number.

Numbers the fourth book of the Bible, relating the experiences of the Israelites in the wilderness after Moses led them out of Egypt.
– ORIGIN named in English from the book's accounts of a census; the title in Hebrew means 'in the wilderness'.

numbers game ▶ **noun** often derogatory the use or manipulation of statistics or figures, especially in support of an argument: *MPs were today playing the numbers game as the vote drew closer*
■ (also **numbers pool** or **numbers racket**) N. Amer. a lottery based on the occurrence of unpredictable numbers in the results of races etc.

Number Ten 10 Downing Street, the official London home of the British Prime Minister.

number theory ▶ **noun** [mass noun] the branch of mathematics that deals with the properties and relationships of numbers, especially the positive integers.

number two ▶ **noun** informal **1** a second in command: *he is currently number two at the Department of Employment.*
2 used euphemistically to refer to faeces.

number work ▶ **noun** [mass noun] simple arithmetic.

numbfish ▶ **noun** (pl. same or **-fishes**) an electric ray, especially a heavy-bodied Australian ray that lies partly buried on sand flats and estuaries and can give a severe electric shock.
● Family Torpedinidae: many species, in particular *Hypnos monopterygium.*

numbles ▶ **plural noun** Brit. archaic the entrails of an animal, especially a deer, as used for food.
– ORIGIN Middle English (denoting the back and loins of a deer): from Old French, from Latin *lumbulus,* diminutive of *lumbus* 'loin'. Compare with UMBLES.

numbskull (also **numskull**) ▶ **noun** informal a stupid or foolish person.

numdah /ˈnʌmdə/ ▶ **noun** (in the Indian subcontinent and the Middle East) an embroidered rug or carpet made of felt or coarse woollen cloth.
■ [mass noun] cloth of this type.
– ORIGIN from Urdu *namdā,* from Persian *namad* 'carpet'.

numen /ˈnjuːmən/ ▶ **noun** (pl. **numina** /-mɪnə/) the spirit or divine power presiding over a thing or place.
– ORIGIN early 17th cent.: from Latin.

numerable ▶ **adjective** able to be counted.
– ORIGIN mid 16th cent.: from Latin *numerabilis,* from *numerare* 'to number'.

numeracy ▶ **noun** [mass noun] the ability to understand and work with numbers.

numeraire /ˈnjuːmərɛː/ ▶ **noun** Economics an item or commodity acting as a measure of value or as a standard for currency exchange.
– ORIGIN 1960s: from French *numéraire,* from late Latin *numerarius,* from Latin *numerus* 'a number'.

numeral ▶ **noun** a figure, symbol, or group of these denoting a number.
■ a word expressing a number.
▶ **adjective** of or denoting a number.
– ORIGIN late Middle English (as an adjective): from late Latin *numeralis,* adjective from Latin *numerus* 'a number' (see NUMBER).

numerate /ˈnjuːm(ə)rət/ ▶ **adjective** having a good basic knowledge of arithmetic; able to understand and work with numbers.
– ORIGIN 1950s: from Latin *numerus* 'a number', on the pattern of *literate.*

numeration ▶ **noun** [mass noun] the action or process of calculating or assigning a number to something.
■ [count noun] a method or process of numbering, counting, or computing.
– ORIGIN late Middle English: from Latin *numeratio(n-)* 'payment' (in late Latin 'numbering'), from the verb *numerare* 'to number'.

numerator ▶ **noun** the number above the line in a vulgar fraction showing how many of the parts indicated by the denominator are taken, for example, 2 in ⅔.

numerical ▶ **adjective** of, relating to, or expressed as a number or numbers: *the lists are in numerical order.*
– DERIVATIVES **numerically** adverb.
– ORIGIN early 17th cent.: from medieval Latin *numericus* (from Latin *numerus* 'a number') + -AL.

numerical analysis ▶ **noun** [mass noun] the branch

of mathematics that deals with the development and use of numerical methods for solving problems.

numerical control ▶ **noun** [mass noun] Engineering computer control of machine tools, where operations are directed by numerical data.

numerology /ˌnjuːməˈrɒlədʒi/ ▶ **noun** [mass noun] the branch of knowledge that deals with the occult significance of numbers.
– DERIVATIVES **numerological** adjective, **numerologist** noun.
– ORIGIN early 20th cent.: from Latin *numerus* 'a number' + -LOGY.

numero uno /ˌnjuːmərəʊ ˈuːnəʊ/ ▶ **noun** (pl. **-os**) informal the best or most important person or thing.
– ORIGIN Italian, literally 'number one'.

numerous ▶ **adjective** great in number; many: *he has attended numerous meetings and social events.*
■ consisting of many members: *the orchestra and chorus were numerous.*
– DERIVATIVES **numerously** adverb, **numerousness** noun.
– ORIGIN late Middle English: from Latin *numerosus,* from *numerus* 'a number'.

numerus clausus /ˌnjuːmərəs ˈklaʊsəs/ ▶ **noun** a fixed maximum number of entrants admissible to an academic institution.
– ORIGIN Latin, literally 'closed number'.

Numidia /njuːˈmɪdɪə/ an ancient kingdom, later a Roman province, situated in North Africa in an area north of the Sahara corresponding roughly to present-day Algeria.
– DERIVATIVES **Numidian** adjective & noun.

numina plural form of NUMEN.

numinous /ˈnjuːmɪnəs/ ▶ **adjective** having a strong religious or spiritual quality; indicating or suggesting the presence of a divinity: *the strange, numinous beauty of this ancient landmark.*
– ORIGIN mid 17th cent.: from Latin *numen, numin-* 'divine will' + -OUS.

numismatic /ˌnjuːmɪzˈmatɪk/ ▶ **adjective** of, relating to, or consisting of coins or medals.
– DERIVATIVES **numismatically** adverb.
– ORIGIN late 18th cent.: from French *numismatique,* via Latin from Greek *nomisma, nomismat-* 'current coin', from *nomizein* 'use currently'.

numismatics ▶ **plural noun** [usu. treated as sing.] the study or collection of coins, banknotes, and medals.
– DERIVATIVES **numismatist** /njuːˈmɪzmətɪst/ noun.

numismatology /ˌnjuːmɪzməˈtɒlədʒi, njuːˌmɪz-/ ▶ **noun** [mass noun] numismatics.

nummular /ˈnʌmjʊlə/ ▶ **adjective** resembling a coin or coins.
– ORIGIN mid 18th cent.: from Latin *nummulus* (diminutive of *nummus* 'coin') + -AR[1].

nummulite /ˈnʌmjʊlʌɪt/ ▶ **noun** Palaeontology the flat disc-shaped calcareous shell of a foraminiferan, found commonly as a fossil up to 8 cm across in marine Tertiary deposits.
● Family Nummulitidae, order Foraminiferida: several genera, including *Nummulites.*
– ORIGIN early 19th cent.: from Latin *nummulus* (diminutive of *nummus* 'coin') + -ITE[1].

nummy ▶ **adjective** N. Amer. informal (of food) delicious.
– ORIGIN early 20th cent.: variant of YUMMY.

numnah /ˈnʌmnə/ ▶ **noun** a pad, typically made of sheepskin or foam, which is placed under a saddle.
– ORIGIN mid 19th cent.: from Urdu *namdā.*

num-num /ˈnʌmnʌm/ ▶ **noun** S. African a white-flowered spiny southern African shrub or small tree which yields edible fruit.
● Genus *Carissa,* family Apocynaceae.
– ORIGIN early 19th cent.: from Afrikaans *noem-noem,* perhaps from Nama.

numskull ▶ **noun** variant spelling of NUMBSKULL.

nun ▶ **noun** a member of a religious community of women, typically one living under vows of poverty, chastity, and obedience.
■ any of a number of birds whose plumage resembles a nun's habit, especially an Asian mannikin. ■ a pigeon of a breed with a crest on its neck.
– DERIVATIVES **nunlike** adjective, **nunnish** adjective.
– ORIGIN Old English *nonne,* from ecclesiastical Latin *nonna,* feminine of *nonnus* 'monk', reinforced by Old French *nonne.*

nunatak /ˈnʌnətak/ ▶ **noun** an isolated peak of rock projecting above a surface of inland ice or snow.

– ORIGIN late 19th cent.: from Eskimo *nunataq*.

Nunavut /ˈnʊnəvʊt/ a province of northern Canada, created in 1999 as an Inuit territory; capital, Iqaluit.

nunbird ▶ noun a tropical American puffbird with mainly dark grey or blackish plumage.
• Genus *Monasa* (and *Hapaloptila*), family Bucconidae: five species.

nun buoy ▶ noun US a buoy which is circular in the middle and tapering to each end.
– ORIGIN early 18th cent.: from obsolete *nun* 'child's top' and **BUOY**.

Nunc Dimittis /ˌnʌŋk dɪˈmɪtɪs/ ▶ noun the Song of Simeon (Luke 2:29–32) used as a canticle in Christian liturgy, especially at compline and evensong.
– ORIGIN Latin, the opening words of the canticle, '(Lord), now you let (your servant) depart'.

nunchaku /nʌnˈtʃakuː/ ▶ noun (pl. same or **nunchakus**) a Japanese martial arts weapon consisting of two hardwood sticks joined together by a chain, rope, or thong.
– ORIGIN Japanese, from Okinawa dialect.

nunciature /ˈnʌnsɪəˌtjʊə, -ʃə-/ ▶ noun the office or tenure of a nuncio in the Roman Catholic Church.
– ORIGIN early 17th cent.: from Italian *nunziatura*, from *nunzio* 'message-bearer' (see **NUNCIO**).

nuncio /ˈnʌnsɪəʊ, ˈnʌnʃɪəʊ/ ▶ noun (pl. **-os**) (in the Roman Catholic Church) a papal ambassador to a foreign court or government.
– ORIGIN early 16th cent.: from Italian, from Latin *nuntius* 'messenger'.

nuncle ▶ noun archaic or dialect a person's uncle.
– ORIGIN late 16th cent.: by misdivision of *mine uncle*.

nuncupative /ˈnʌŋkjʊˌpətɪv/ ▶ adjective Law (of a will or testament) declared orally as opposed to in writing, especially by a mortally wounded soldier.
– ORIGIN mid 16th cent.: from late Latin *nuncupativus*, from Latin *nuncupat-* 'named, declared', from the verb *nuncupare*.

Nuneaton /nʌˈniːt(ə)n/ a town in north Warwickshire in central England, near Coventry; pop. 81,880 (1981).

nunnery ▶ noun (pl. **-ies**) a building or group of buildings in which nuns live as a religious community; a convent.

nunu /ˈnuːnuː/ (also **noonoo**) ▶ noun (pl. **nunus**) S. African informal an insect, spider, worm, or similar small creature.
– ORIGIN from Zulu *inunu* 'horrible object or animal'.

nuoc mam /nwɒk ˈmɑːm/ ▶ noun [mass noun] a spicy Vietnamese fish sauce.
– ORIGIN Vietnamese.

Nupe /ˈnuːpeɪ/ ▶ noun (pl. same or **Nupes**) **1** a member of a people of central Nigeria.
2 [mass noun] the Benue-Congo language of this people, with over 1 million speakers.
▶ adjective of or relating to this people or their language.
– ORIGIN the name of a former kingdom at the confluence of the Niger and Benue rivers in West Africa.

nuptial /ˈnʌpʃ(ə)l/ ▶ adjective of or relating to marriage or weddings: *moments of nuptial bliss.*
■ Zoology denoting the characteristic breeding behaviour, coloration, or structures of some animals: *nuptial plumage.*
▶ noun (usu. **nuptials**) a wedding: *the forthcoming nuptials between Richard and Jocelyn.*
– ORIGIN late 15th cent.: from Old French, or from Latin *nuptialis*, from *nuptiae* 'wedding', from *nubere* 'to wed'; related to **NUBILE**.

nuptiality ▶ noun [mass noun] the frequency or incidence of marriage within a population.

nuptial mass ▶ noun (in the Roman Catholic Church) a mass celebrated as part of a wedding ceremony.

nuptial pad ▶ noun Zoology a pigmented swelling on the inner side of the hand in some male frogs and toads, assisting grip during copulation.

nuragh /ˈnʊəraɡ/ (also **nuraghe** /-ɡi/) ▶ noun (pl. **nuraghi** /-ɡi/) a type of massive stone tower found in Sardinia, dating from the Bronze and Iron Ages.
– DERIVATIVES **nuraghic** adjective.
– ORIGIN Sardinian.

nurd ▶ noun variant spelling of **NERD**.

Nuremberg /ˈnjʊərəmbəːɡ/ a city in southern Germany, in Bavaria; pop. 497,500 (1991). In the 1930s the Nazi Party congresses and annual rallies were held in the city and in 1945–6 it was the scene of the Nuremberg war trials, in which Nazi war criminals were tried by international military tribunal. German name **NÜRNBERG**.

Nureyev /nəˈreɪef, ˈnjʊərɪef/, Rudolf (1939–93), Russian-born ballet dancer and choreographer. He defected to the West in 1961, joining the Royal Ballet in London, where he began his noted partnership with Margot Fonteyn. He became a naturalized Austrian citizen in 1982.

Nürnberg /ˈnyrnbɛrk/ German name for **NUREMBERG**.

Nurofen /ˈnjʊərəfɛn/ ▶ noun trademark for **IBUPROFEN**.

nurse[1] ▶ noun a person trained to care for the sick or infirm, especially in a hospital.
■ dated a person employed or trained to take charge of young children: *her mother's old nurse.* ■ archaic a wet nurse. ■ [often as modifier] Forestry a tree or crop planted as a shelter to others. ■ Entomology a worker bee, ant, or other social insect, caring for a young brood.
▶ verb [with obj.] **1** give medical and other attention to (a sick person): *he was gradually nursed back to health.*
■ [no obj.] care for the sick and infirm, especially as a profession: *she nursed at the hospital for 30 years.* ■ try to cure or alleviate (an injury, injured part, or illness) by treating it carefully and protectively: figurative *he nursed his hurt pride.* ■ hold closely and carefully or caressingly: *he nursed his small case on his lap.* ■ hold (a cup or glass) in one's hands, drinking from it occasionally: *I nursed a double brandy.* ■ harbour (a belief or feeling), especially for a long time: *I still nurse anger and resentment.* ■ take special care of, especially to promote development or well-being: *our political unity needs to be protected and nursed.* ■ Billiards & Snooker try to play strokes which keep (the balls) close together.
2 feed (a baby) at the breast: [as adj. **nursing**] *nursing mothers.*
■ [no obj.] be fed at the breast: *the baby snuffled as he nursed.* ■ (**be nursed in**) dated be brought up in (a specified condition): *he was nursed in the lap of plenty.*
– ORIGIN late Middle English: contraction of earlier *nourice*, from Old French, from late Latin *nutricia*, feminine of Latin *nutricius* '(person) that nourishes', from *nutrix*, *nutric-* 'nurse', from *nutrire* 'nourish'. The verb was originally a contraction of **NOURISH**, altered under the influence of the noun.

nurse[2] (also **grey nurse**) ▶ noun a greyish Australian shark of shallow inshore waters. Compare with **NURSE SHARK, NURSE HOUND**.
• *Odontaspis arenarius*, family Odontaspididae.
– ORIGIN late 15th cent.: originally as *nusse*, perhaps derived (by wrong division) from *an huss* (see **HUSS**).

nurse hound ▶ noun a large spotted dogfish of the NE Atlantic, which is caught for food. Also called **BULL HUSS** in Britain.
• *Scyliorhinus stellaris*, family Scyliorhinidae.

nurseling ▶ noun archaic spelling of **NURSLING**.

nursemaid ▶ noun a woman or girl employed to look after a young child or children.
▶ verb [with obj.] look after or be overprotective towards.

nursery ▶ noun (pl. **-ies**) a room in a house for the special use of young children.
■ (also **day nursery**) a place where young children are cared for during the working day; a nursery school. ■ a place where young plants and trees are grown for sale or for planting elsewhere. ■ a place or habitat which breeds or supports animals. ■ an institution or environment in which certain types of people or qualities are fostered or bred: *that nursery of traitors.* ■ [as modifier] denoting a race for two-year-old horses.
– ORIGIN late Middle English: from Old French *nourice* 'nurse' (see **NURSE**[1]) + **-ERY**.

nursery cannon ▶ noun Billiards a cannon which keeps the balls close together.

nursery class ▶ noun a class for the education of children mainly between the ages of three and five.

nurseryman ▶ noun (pl. **-men**) a worker in or owner of a plant or tree nursery.

nursery nurse ▶ noun Brit. a person trained to look after young children and babies in nurseries, crèches, etc.

nursery rhyme ▶ noun a simple traditional song or poem for children.

nursery school ▶ noun a school for young children, mainly between the ages of three and five.

nursery slope ▶ noun Skiing, Brit. a gentle slope suitable for beginners.

nursery stakes ▶ plural noun Brit. a race for two-year-old horses.

nurse shark ▶ noun a shark with barbels on the snout.
• Three species in the family Orectolobidae (or Ginglymostomatidae), in particular *Ginglymostoma cirratum*, a slow-swimming brownish shark of warm Atlantic waters.

nursey (also **nursie**) ▶ noun informal a nurse.

nursing ▶ noun [mass noun] the profession or practice of providing care for the sick and infirm.

nursing home ▶ noun a small private institution providing residential accommodation with health care, especially for the elderly.

nursing officer ▶ noun Brit. a senior nurse with administrative responsibility.

nursling ▶ noun a baby that is being breastfed.

nurturance ▶ noun [mass noun] emotional and physical nourishment and care given to someone.
– DERIVATIVES **nurturant** adjective.

nurture /ˈnəːtʃə/ ▶ verb [with obj.] care for and encourage the growth or development of: figurative *my father nurtured my love of art.*
■ cherish (a hope, belief, or ambition): *for a long time she had nurtured the dream of buying a shop.*
▶ noun [mass noun] the process of caring for and encouraging the growth or development of someone or something: *the nurture of ethics and integrity.*
■ upbringing, education, and environment, contrasted with inborn characteristics as an influence on or determinant of personality. Often contrasted with **NATURE**.
– DERIVATIVES **nurturer** noun.
– ORIGIN Middle English: from Old French *noureture* 'nourishment', based on Latin *nutrire* 'feed, cherish'.

NUS ▶ abbreviation for ■ (in the UK) National Union of Students.

Nusselt number /ˈnʊs(ə)lt/ ▶ noun Physics a dimensionless parameter used in calculations of heat transfer between a moving fluid and a solid body.
• It is equal to hD/k, where h is the rate of heat loss per unit area per degree difference in temperature between the body and its surroundings, D is a characteristic length of the body, and k is the thermal conductivity of the fluid.
– ORIGIN mid 20th cent.: named after Ernst K. W. *Nusselt* (1882–1957), German engineer.

NUT ▶ abbreviation for (in the UK) National Union of Teachers.

Nut /nʊt/ Egyptian Mythology the sky goddess, thought to swallow the sun at night and give birth to it in the morning.

nut ▶ noun **1** a fruit consisting of a hard or tough shell around an edible kernel.
■ the hard kernel of such a fruit. ■ informal a person's head. ■ (usu. **nuts**) a small lump or knob of something, especially coal. ■ (usu. **nuts**) compressed animal feed in the form of small cylindrical pellets. ■ (**nuts**) vulgar slang a man's testicles.
2 a small flat piece of metal or other material, typically square or hexagonal, with a threaded hole through it for screwing on to a bolt as a fastener.
■ the part at the lower end of the bow of a violin or similar instrument, with a screw for adjusting the tension of the hair.
3 informal a crazy or eccentric person.
■ [with adj. or noun modifier] a person who is excessively interested in or enthusiastic about a specified thing: *a football nut.*
4 the fixed ridge on the neck of a stringed instrument over which the strings pass.
▶ verb (**nutted**, **nutting**) **1** [with obj.] informal butt (someone) with one's head.
2 [no obj.] [usu. as noun **nutting**] archaic gather nuts.
– PHRASES **do one's nut** Brit. informal be extremely angry or agitated. **nuts and bolts** informal the basic practical details: *the nuts and bolts of public policy.* **off one's nut** informal out of one's mind; crazy. **a tough** (or **hard**) **nut** informal someone who is difficult to deal with; a formidable person. **a tough** (or **hard**) **nut to crack** informal a difficult problem or an opponent hard to beat. **use** (or **take**) **a sledgehammer to crack a nut** informal use disproportionately drastic measures to deal with a simple problem.
– DERIVATIVES **nut-like** adjective.

n

– ORIGIN Old English *hnutu*, of Germanic origin; related to Dutch *noot* and German *Nuss*.

nutation /njuːˈteɪʃ(ə)n/ ▶ noun [mass noun] a periodic variation in the inclination of the axis of a rotating object.
■ Astronomy a periodic oscillation of the earth's axis which causes the precession of the poles to follow a wavy rather than a circular path. ■ Botany the circular swaying movement of the tip of a growing shoot.
– ORIGIN early 17th cent. (denoting nodding of the head): from Latin *nutatio(n-)*, from *nutare* 'to nod'.

nut-brown ▶ adjective of a rich dark brown colour: *a nut-brown face.*

nutcase ▶ noun informal a mad or foolish person.

nutcracker ▶ noun 1 (usu. **nutcrackers**) a device for cracking nuts.
■ [as modifier] denoting a person's nose and chin with the points near each other, either naturally or as a result of the loss of teeth.
2 a crow that feeds on the seeds of conifers, found widely in Eurasia and in western North America.
● Genus *Nucifraga*, family Corvidae: the Eurasian **spotted nutcracker** (*N. caryocatactes*), with white-spotted brown plumage, and the North American **Clark's nutcracker** (*N. columbiana*), with pale grey and black plumage.

Nutcracker man ▶ noun the nickname of a fossil hominid with massive jaws and molar teeth, especially the original specimen found near Olduvai Gorge in 1959.
● *Australopithecus* (or *Zinjanthropus*) *boisei*, family Hominidae. See **AUSTRALOPITHECUS**, **PARANTHROPUS**.

nut cutlet ▶ noun Brit. a cutlet-shaped savoury cake made of chopped nuts, breadcrumbs, etc.

nutgall ▶ noun 1 another term for **ALEPPO GALL**.
2 a gall which forms inside the buds of hazel bushes in response to the presence of mites, causing the buds to enlarge greatly.
● The mite is *Phytoptus avellanae*, family Eriophyidae.

nuthatch ▶ noun a small songbird with a stiffened tail, which climbs up and down tree trunks and feeds on nuts, seeds, and insects.
● Family Sittidae and genus *Sitta*: several species, including the widespread (**Eurasian**) **nuthatch** (*S. europaea*), with a grey back, black eyestripe, and white or buff underparts.
– ORIGIN Middle English: from **NUT** + obsolete *hatch* (related to **HACK**[1]), from the bird's habit of hacking with the beak at nuts wedged in a crevice.

nuthin ▶ pronoun, adjective, & adverb informal non-standard spelling of **NOTHING**, used to represent informal speech.

nuthouse ▶ noun informal a home or hospital for people with mental illnesses.

nutlet ▶ noun Botany a small nut, especially an achene.

nut loaf ▶ noun a baked vegetarian dish made from ground or chopped nuts, vegetables, and herbs.

nutmeg ▶ noun 1 the hard, aromatic, almost spherical seed of a tropical tree.
■ [mass noun] this seed grated and used as a spice.
2 the evergreen tree that bears these seeds, native to the Moluccas.
● *Myristica fragrans*, family Myristicaceae.
3 Soccer an instance of playing the ball through an opponent's legs. [ORIGIN: extended use of obsolete *nutmegs* 'testicles'.]
▶ verb (**nutmegged**, **nutmegging**) [with obj.] Soccer play the ball through the legs of (an opponent). [ORIGIN: see nut sense 3.]
– ORIGIN late Middle English *notemuge*, partial translation of Old French *nois muguede*, based on Latin *nux* 'nut' + late Latin *muscus* 'musk'.

Nutmeg State informal name for **CONNECTICUT**.

nut oil ▶ noun [mass noun] oil obtained from the kernels of nuts and used in cooking and to make paints and varnishes.

nutraceutical /ˌnjuːtrəˈsjuːtɪk(ə)l/ ▶ noun another term for **FUNCTIONAL FOOD**.
– ORIGIN 1990s: from Latin *nutrire* 'nourish' + **PHARMACEUTICAL**.

nutria /ˈnjuːtrɪə/ ▶ noun [mass noun] the skin or fur of the coypu.
– ORIGIN early 19th cent.: from Spanish, literally 'otter'.

nutrient ▶ noun a substance that provides nourishment essential for the maintenance of life and for growth: *fish is a source of many important nutrients, including protein, vitamins, and minerals.*
– ORIGIN mid 17th cent.: from Latin *nutrient-* 'nourishing', from the verb *nutrire*.

nutriment ▶ noun [mass noun] rare nourishment; sustenance.
– DERIVATIVES **nutrimental** /-ˈmɛnt(ə)l/ adjective.
– ORIGIN late Middle English: from Latin *nutrimentum*, from *nutrire* 'feed, nourish'.

nutrition ▶ noun [mass noun] the process of providing or obtaining the food necessary for health and growth: *a guide to good nutrition.*
■ food; nourishment: *a feeding tube gives her nutrition and water.* ■ the branch of science that deals with nutrients and nutrition, particularly in humans.
– DERIVATIVES **nutritional** adjective, **nutritionally** adverb.
– ORIGIN late Middle English: from late Latin *nutritio(n-)*, from *nutrire* 'feed, nourish'.

nutritionist (also **nutritionalist**) ▶ noun a person who studies or is an expert in nutrition.

nutritious ▶ adjective efficient as food; nourishing: *home-cooked burgers make a nutritious meal.*
– DERIVATIVES **nutritiously** adverb, **nutritiousness** noun.
– ORIGIN mid 17th cent.: from Latin *nutritius* 'that nourishes' (from *nutrex* 'a nurse') + **-OUS**.

nutritive ▶ adjective of or relating to nutrition: *the food was low in nutritive value.*
■ providing nourishment; nutritious: *nutritive food.*
– ORIGIN late Middle English: from medieval Latin *nutritivus*, from *nutrire* 'feed, nourish'.

nut roast ▶ noun [mass noun] a baked vegetarian dish made from a mixture of ground or chopped nuts, vegetables, and herbs.

nuts ▶ adjective [predic.] informal mad: *the way he turns on the television as soon as he walks in drives me nuts.*
▶ exclamation informal (often **nuts to you/him**) an expression of contempt or derision.
– PHRASES **be nuts about** (or Brit. **on**) informal like very much: *I was nuts about him.*

nutshell ▶ noun 1 the hard woody covering around the kernel of a nut.
2 (**nut shell**) any of a number of bivalve molluscs occurring chiefly in cool seas, in particular:
● a small oval-shelled bivalve (genus *Nuculana*, family Nuculanidae). ● a bivalve with a rectangular shell which is rounded at the front and angled behind (genus *Nucula*, family Nuculidae).
– PHRASES **in a nutshell** in the fewest possible words: *she put the matter in a nutshell.*

nutso N. Amer. informal ▶ adjective mad.
▶ noun (pl. **-os**) a mad or eccentric person.

nutsy ▶ adjective (**-ier**, **-iest**) N. Amer. informal mad.

nutter ▶ noun Brit. informal a mad or eccentric person.

nut tree ▶ noun a tree that bears nuts, especially the hazel.

nutty ▶ adjective (**nuttier**, **nuttiest**) 1 tasting like nuts: *wild rice has a very nutty flavour.*
■ containing a lot of nuts: *a nutty vegetable bake.*
2 informal mad: *he came up with a few nutty proposals.*
– PHRASES **be nutty about** informal like very much: *he is nutty about boats.* (as) **nutty as a fruitcake** informal completely mad.
– DERIVATIVES **nuttiness** noun.

Nuuk /nuːk/ the capital of Greenland, a port on the Davis Strait; pop. 12,480 (est. 1994). It was known by the Danish name Godthåb until 1979.

nux vomica /ˌnʌks ˈvɒmɪkə/ ▶ noun [mass noun] a spiny southern Asian tree with berry-like fruit and toxic seeds that are a commercial source of strychnine.
● *Strychnos nux-vomica*, family Loganiaceae.
■ a homeopathic preparation of this plant used especially for the treatment of symptoms of overeating and overdrinking.
– ORIGIN late Middle English: from medieval Latin, from Latin *nux* 'nut' + *vomica* 'causing vomiting' (from *vomere* 'to vomit').

nuzzle ▶ verb [with obj.] rub or push against gently with the nose and mouth: *he nuzzled her hair* | [no obj.] *the foal nuzzled at its mother.*
■ [no obj.] (**nuzzle up to/against**) lean or snuggle against: *the dog nuzzled up against me.*
– ORIGIN late Middle English (in the sense 'grovel'): frequentative from **NOSE**, reinforced by Dutch *neuzelen* 'poke with the nose'.

NV ▶ abbreviation for Nevada (in official postal use).

NVI ▶ abbreviation for no value indicated, a postage stamp that does not bear a monetary value on it but instead shows which postal service it is valid for.

NVQ ▶ abbreviation for (in the UK) National Vocational Qualification.

NW ▶ abbreviation for ■ north-west. ■ north-western.

NY ▶ abbreviation for New York (in official postal use).

nyaff /njaf/ ▶ noun Scottish informal a stupid, irritating, or insignificant person.
– ORIGIN Scots variant of **NAFF**[2].

nyala /ˈnjɑːlə/ ▶ noun (pl. same) a southern African antelope, which has a conspicuous crest on the neck and back and lyre-shaped horns.
● *Tragelaphus angasi*, family Bovidae.
– ORIGIN late 19th cent.: from Zulu.

Nyamwezi /ˌnjamˈweɪzi/ ▶ noun (pl. same or **Nyamwezis**) 1 a member of a people inhabiting western Tanzania.
2 [mass noun] the Bantu language of this people, related to Sukuma and having about 900,000 speakers.
▶ adjective of or relating to this people or their language.
– ORIGIN a local name.

Nyanja /ˈnjandʒə/ ▶ noun (pl. same or **Nyanjas**) 1 a member of a people of Malawi and eastern and central Zambia.
2 [mass noun] the Bantu language of this people, with over 3 million speakers.
▶ adjective of or relating to this people or their language.
– ORIGIN a local name. literally 'lake'.

Nyasa, Lake /ˈnjɑːsə/ a lake in east central Africa, the third largest lake in Africa. About 580 km (360 miles) long, it forms most of the eastern border of Malawi with Mozambique and Tanzania. Also called **LAKE MALAWI**.
– ORIGIN *Nyasa*, literally 'lake'.

Nyasaland /ˈnjɑːsəland/ former name (until 1966) for **MALAWI**.

NYC ▶ abbreviation for New York City.

nyctalopia /ˌnɪktəˈləʊpɪə/ ▶ noun [mass noun] Medicine a condition characterized by the inability to see in dim light or at night.
– ORIGIN late 17th cent.: via late Latin from Greek *nuktalōps*, from *nux, nukt-* 'night' + *alaos* 'blind' + *ōps* 'eye'.

nyctinastic /ˌnɪktɪˈnastɪk/ ▶ adjective Botany (of the periodic movement of flowers or leaves) caused by nightly changes in light intensity or temperature.
– DERIVATIVES **nyctinasty** /ˈnɪktɪˌnasti/ noun.
– ORIGIN early 20th cent.: from Greek *nux, nukt-* 'night' + *nastos* 'pressed' + **-IC**.

nyctophobia /ˌnɪktə(ʊ)ˈfəʊbɪə/ ▶ noun [mass noun] extreme or irrational fear of the night or of darkness.
– ORIGIN early 20th cent.: from Greek *nux, nukt-* 'night' + **PHOBIA**.

Nyerere /njɛˈrɛːri/, Julius Kambarage (1922–99), Tanzanian statesman, President of Tanganyika 1962–4 and of Tanzania 1964–85. He led Tanganyika to independence in 1961 and in 1964 successfully negotiated a union with Zanzibar, creating the new state of Tanzania.

nylon ▶ noun [mass noun] a tough, lightweight, elastic synthetic polymer with a protein-like chemical structure, able to be produced as filaments, sheets, or moulded objects.
■ fabric or yarn made from nylon fibres. ■ (**nylons**) stockings or tights made of nylon.
– ORIGIN 1930s: an invented word, on the pattern of *cotton* and *rayon*.

Nyman /ˈnaɪmən/, Michael (b.1944), English composer, best known for his film scores for director Peter Greenaway.

nymph ▶ noun 1 a mythological spirit of nature imagined as a beautiful maiden inhabiting rivers, woods, or other locations.
■ chiefly poetic/literary a beautiful young woman.
2 an immature form of an insect that does not change greatly as it grows, e.g. a dragonfly, mayfly, or locust. Compare with **LARVA**.
■ an artificial fishing fly made to resemble the aquatic nymph of an insect.
3 a mainly brown butterfly that frequents woods and forest glades.
● Several genera in the subfamily Satyrinae, family Nymphalidae. See also **WOOD NYMPH**.
– DERIVATIVES **nymphal** adjective, **nymphean** adjective, **nymph-like** adjective.

– ORIGIN late Middle English: from Old French *nimphe*, from Latin *nympha*, from Greek *numphē* 'nymph, bride'; related to Latin *nubere* 'be the wife of'.

nymphaeum /nɪmˈfiːəm/ ▶ noun (pl. **nymphaea**) a grotto or shrine dedicated to a nymph or nymphs.
– ORIGIN via Latin from Greek.

nymphalid /nɪmˈfalɪd/ ▶ noun Entomology an insect of a large family of strikingly marked butterflies which have small forelegs that are not used for walking, including many familiar butterflies of temperate regions. Compare with **VANESSID**.
● Family Nymphalidae (sometimes restricted to those that are now usually placed in the subfamily Nymphalinae).
– ORIGIN late 19th cent.: from modern Latin *Nymphalidae*, from Latin *nympha* 'nymph'.

nymphet /ˈnɪmfɛt, nɪmˈfɛt/ (also **nymphette**) ▶ noun an attractive and sexually mature young girl.
– ORIGIN 1950s: from **NYMPH** + **-ET**[1].

nympho ▶ noun informal a nymphomaniac.

nympholepsy /ˈnɪmfə(ʊ)ˌlɛpsi/ ▶ noun [mass noun] poetic/literary passion aroused in men by beautiful young girls.
■ wild frenzy caused by desire for an unattainable ideal.
– ORIGIN late 18th cent.: from **NYMPHOLEPT**, on the pattern of *epilepsy*.

nympholept /ˈnɪmfə(ʊ)lɛpt/ ▶ noun a person affected by nympholepsy.

– DERIVATIVES **nympholeptic** adjective.
– ORIGIN early 19th cent.: from Greek *numpholēptos* 'caught by nymphs', from *numphē* 'nymph' + *lambanein* 'take'.

nymphomania ▶ noun [mass noun] uncontrollable or excessive sexual desire in a woman.
– DERIVATIVES **nymphomaniac** noun & adjective, **nymphomaniacal** adjective.
– ORIGIN late 18th cent.: modern Latin, from Latin *nympha* (see **NYMPH**) + **-MANIA**.

Nynorsk /ˈnjuːnɔːsk/ ▶ noun [mass noun] a literary form of the Norwegian language, based on certain country dialects and constructed in the 19th century to serve as a national language more clearly distinct from Danish than Bokmål. See **NORWEGIAN** (sense 2).
– ORIGIN Norwegian, from *ny* 'new' + *Norsk* 'Norwegian'.

Nyoman /ˈnjɒmən/ Belorussian name for **NEMAN**.

Nyquist criterion /ˈnaɪkwɪst/ ▶ noun Electronics a criterion for determining the stability or instability of a feedback system.
– ORIGIN 1930s named after Harry *Nyquist* (1889–1976), Swedish-born American engineer.

Nyquist diagram (also **Nyquist plot**) ▶ noun Electronics a representation of the vector response of a feedback system (especially an amplifier) as a complex graphical plot showing the relationship between feedback and gain.

– ORIGIN 1930s: see **NYQUIST CRITERION**.

Nyquist frequency (also **Nyquist rate**) ▶ noun Electronics the minimum rate at which a signal can be sampled without introducing errors, which is twice the highest frequency present in the signal.
– ORIGIN 1930s: see **NYQUIST CRITERION**.

Nysa /ˈniːsa/ Polish name for **NEISSE**.

NYSE ▶ abbreviation for New York Stock Exchange.

nystagmus /nɪˈstagməs/ ▶ noun [mass noun] rapid involuntary movements of the eyes.
– DERIVATIVES **nystagmic** adjective.
– ORIGIN early 19th cent.: from Greek *nustagmos* 'nodding, drowsiness', from *nustazein* 'nod, be sleepy'.

nystatin /ˈnʌɪstətɪn, ˈnɪs-/ ▶ noun [mass noun] an antibiotic used chiefly to treat fungal infections.
● This antibiotic is obtained from the bacterium *Streptomyces noursei*.
– ORIGIN 1950s: from *N(ew) Y(ork) Stat(e)* (where it was developed) + **-IN**[1].

Nyungar /ˈnjʊŋə/ ▶ noun [mass noun] an Aboriginal language of SW Australia, now extinct.
– ORIGIN the name in Nyungar, literally 'man'.

Nyx /nɪks/ Greek Mythology the female personification of the night, daughter of Chaos.

NZ ▶ abbreviation for New Zealand.

Oo

O¹ (also **o**) ▶ noun (pl. **Os** or **O's**) **1** the fifteenth letter of the alphabet.
■denoting the next after N in a set of items, categories, etc. ■ a human blood type (in the ABO system) lacking both the A and B antigens. In blood transfusion, a person with blood of this group is a potential universal donor.
2 (also **oh**) nought or zero (in a sequence of numerals, especially when spoken).
3 a shape like that of a capital O; a circle.

O² ▶ abbreviation for ■ US Ohio. ■ Cricket (on scorecards) over(s).
▶ symbol for the chemical element oxygen.

O³ ▶ exclamation **1** archaic spelling of **OH¹**.
2 archaic used before a name in the vocative: *give peace in our time, O Lord.*
– ORIGIN natural exclamation: first recorded in Middle English.

O' ▶ prefix in Irish patronymic names such as *O'Neill.*
– ORIGIN mid 18th cent.: from Irish *ó*, *ua* 'descendant'.

o ▶ abbreviation for (**o-**) [in combination] Chemistry ortho-: *o-xylene.*

o' ▶ preposition short for **OF**, used to represent an informal pronunciation: *a cup o' coffee.*

-o ▶ suffix forming chiefly informal or slang variants or derivatives such as *beano, wino.*
– ORIGIN perhaps from **OH¹**, reinforced by abbreviated forms such as *hippo, photo.*

-o- ▶ suffix used as the terminal vowel of combining forms: *chemico-* | *Gallo-.*
– ORIGIN from Greek.

USAGE The suffix **-o-** is often elided before a vowel, as in neuralgia.

oaf ▶ noun a stupid, uncultured, or clumsy man.
– DERIVATIVES **oafish** adjective, **oafishly** adverb, **oafishness** noun.
– ORIGIN early 17th cent.: variant of obsolete *auf*, from Old Norse *álfr* 'elf'. The original meaning was 'elf's child, changeling', later 'idiot child' and 'halfwit', generalized in the current sense.

Oahu /əʊˈɑːhuː/ the third largest of the Hawaiian islands; pop. 838,500 (1988). Its principal town, Honolulu, is the state capital of Hawaii. It is the site of the US naval base Pearl Harbor.

oak ▶ noun **1** (also **oak tree**) a large tree which bears acorns and typically has lobed deciduous leaves. Oaks are dominant in many north temperate forests and are an important source of hard and durable timber used chiefly in building, furniture, and (formerly) ships.
● Genus *Quercus*, family Fagaceae: many species, including the deciduous **common** (or **English**) **oak** (*Q. robur*), and the evergreen **holm oak**.
■[mass noun] a smoky flavour or nose characteristic of wine aged in barrels made from this wood. ■ chiefly Austral. used in names of other trees or plants that resemble the oaks in some way, e.g. **she-oak**, **silky oak**.
2 (**the Oaks**) an annual flat horse race for three-year-old fillies run on Epsom Downs, over the same course as the Derby. It was first run in 1779. [ORIGIN: named after a nearby estate.]
■[usu. with modifier] a similar race run at another course: *the Irish Oaks.*

– PHRASES **great oaks from little acorns grow** proverb something of small or modest proportions may grow into something very large or impressive. **sport the** (or **one's**) **oak** Brit. (in certain universities) shut the outer door of one's room as a sign that one does not wish to be disturbed. [ORIGIN: such outer doors were often formerly of oak.]
– DERIVATIVES **oaken** adjective, **oaky** adjective.
– ORIGIN Old English *āc*, of Germanic origin; related to Dutch *eik* and German *Eiche*.

oak apple ▶ noun a spongy spherical gall which forms on oak trees in response to the developing larvae of a gall wasp.
● The wasp is *Biorhiza pallida* (in Europe) or *Amphibolips confluenta* (in America), family Cynipidae.

oak eggar ▶ noun a large brown and yellow European eggar moth which frequents open country and light woodland.
● *Lasiocampa quercus*, family Lasiocampidae.

oak fern ▶ noun a delicate fern of woods and damp places in the uplands of northern Eurasia and North America.
● Genus *Gymnocarpium* (formerly *Thelypteris*), family Woodsiaceae: two species, in particular *G. dryopteris*.

oak kermes ▶ noun see **KERMES** (sense 2).

Oakland an industrial port on the east side of San Francisco Bay in California; pop. 372,240 (1990).

oak leaf (also **oak leaf lettuce**) ▶ noun [mass noun] a red or green variety of lettuce which has leaves with serrated edges and a slightly bitter taste.

oak leaf cluster ▶ noun (in the US) an insignia of bronze or silver oak leaves and acorns awarded to the holders of certain military decorations to mark actions worthy of a subsequent award of the same decoration.

Oakley, Annie (1860–1926), American markswoman; full name *Phoebe Anne Oakley Mozee*. In 1885 she joined Buffalo Bill's Wild West Show, of which she became a star attraction for the next seventeen years.

oaktag ▶ noun [mass noun] a type of craft paper.

oakum ▶ noun [mass noun] chiefly historical loose fibre obtained by untwisting old rope, used especially in caulking wooden ships.
– ORIGIN Old English *ācumbe*, literally 'off-combings'. The current sense dates from Middle English.

oak wilt ▶ noun [mass noun] a fungal disease of oaks and other trees which makes the foliage wilt and eventually kills the tree.
● The fungus is *Ceratocystis fagacearum*, subdivision Ascomycotina.

OAM ▶ abbreviation for Medal of the Order of Australia.

O. & M. ▶ abbreviation for ■ operations and maintenance. ■ organization and methods.

OAP Brit. ▶ abbreviation for old-age pensioner.

OAPEC /ˈɔʊpɛk/ ▶ abbreviation for Organization of Arab Petroleum Exporting Countries.

oar ▶ noun a pole with a flat blade, used to row or steer a boat through the water.
■an oarsman; a rower.
– PHRASES **put** (or **stick**) **one's oar in** informal give an opinion without being asked.
– DERIVATIVES **oarless** adjective.

– ORIGIN Old English *ār*, of Germanic origin; related to Danish and Norwegian *åre*.

oared ▶ adjective [attrib.] (of a boat) having an oar or oars: [in combination] *four-oared sculls.*

oarfish ▶ noun (pl. same or **-fishes**) a very long, narrow, silvery marine fish of deep water, with a deep red dorsal fin running the length of the body. Also called **RIBBONFISH, KING OF THE HERRINGS**.
● *Regalecus glesne*, family Regalecidae.

oarlock ▶ noun N. Amer. a rowlock.

oarsman ▶ noun (pl. **-men**) a rower, especially as a member of a racing team.
– DERIVATIVES **oarsmanship** noun.

oarswoman ▶ noun (pl. **-women**) a female rower, especially as a member of a racing team.

oarweed ▶ noun [mass noun] a large brown kelp with a long hard stalk and a large oar-shaped frond divided into ribbon-like strips, growing on rocky shores. Also called **TANGLE²**.
● Genus *Laminaria*, class Phaeophyceae, in particular *L. digitata*.

OAS ▶ abbreviation for Organization of American States.

oasis /əʊˈeɪsɪs/ ▶ noun (pl. **oases** /-siːz/) **1** a fertile spot in a desert, where water is found.
■figurative a pleasant or peaceful area or period in the midst of a difficult, troubled, or hectic place or situation: *an oasis of calm in the centre of the city.*
2 (**Oasis**) [mass noun] trademark a type of rigid foam into which the stems of flowers can be secured in flower arranging.
– ORIGIN early 17th cent.: via late Latin from Greek, apparently of Egyptian origin.

oast /əʊst/ ▶ noun a kiln used for drying hops.
– ORIGIN Old English *āst* (originally denoting any kiln), of Germanic origin; related to Dutch *eest*, from an Indo-European root meaning 'burn'.

oast house ▶ noun a building containing an oast, typically built of brick in a conical shape with a cowl on top.

oat ▶ noun an Old World cereal which is cultivated chiefly in cool climates and is widely used for animal food.
● *Avena sativa*, family Gramineae.
■(**oats**) the grain yielded by this, used as food. ■ used in names of wild grasses related to the cultivated oat, e.g. **wild oat**.
– PHRASES **feel one's oats** US informal feel lively and energetic. **get one's oats** Brit. informal have sexual intercourse. **sow one's wild oats** go through a period of wild or promiscuous behaviour while young.
– DERIVATIVES **oaten** adjective (archaic), **oaty** adjective.
– ORIGIN Old English *āte*, plural *ātan*, of unknown origin. Unlike other names of cereals (such as *wheat, barley*, etc.), *oat* is not a mass noun and may originally have denoted the individual grain, which may imply that oats were eaten in grains and not as meal.

oatcake ▶ noun a thin, unleavened, savoury oatmeal biscuit, traditionally made in Scotland.

oater ▶ noun informal, chiefly US a western film.
– ORIGIN 1950s: derivative of **OAT**, with allusion to horse feed; compare with the synonym **HORSE OPERA**.

---

b **b**ut | d **d**og | f **f**ew | g **g**et | h **h**e | j **y**es | k **c**at | l **l**eg | m **m**an | n **n**o | p **p**en | r **r**ed | s **s**it | t **t**op | v **v**oice | w **w**e | z **z**oo | ʃ **sh**e | ʒ deci**s**ion | θ **th**in | ð **th**is | ŋ ri**ng** | x lo**ch** | tʃ **ch**ip | dʒ **j**ar

Oates, Titus (1649–1705), English clergyman and conspirator, remembered as the fabricator of the Popish Plot. Convicted of perjury in 1685, Oates was imprisoned in the same year, but subsequently released and granted a pension.

oat grass ▶ noun [mass noun] a wild grass which resembles the oat.
● *Avenula* and other genera, family Gramineae.

oath ▶ noun (pl. **oaths**) **1** a solemn promise, often invoking a divine witness, regarding one's future action or behaviour: *they took an oath of allegiance to the king.*
■ a sworn declaration that one will tell the truth, especially in a court of law.
2 a profane or offensive expression used to express anger or other strong emotions.
– PHRASES **my oath** Austral./NZ an exclamation of agreement or endorsement. **under** (or Brit. **on**) **oath** having sworn to tell the truth, especially in a court of law.
– ORIGIN Old English *āth*, of Germanic origin; related to Dutch *eed* and German *Eid*.

oatmeal ▶ noun [mass noun] **1** meal made from ground oats used in porridge, oatcakes, or other food.
2 a greyish-fawn colour flecked with brown: [as modifier] *an oatmeal jacket.*

OAU ▶ abbreviation for Organization of African Unity.

Oaxaca /wəˈhɑːkə/ a state of southern Mexico.
■ its capital city; pop. 212,940 (1990). Full name **OAXACA DE JUÁREZ** /deɪ ˈhwɑːrɛz/.

OB Brit. ▶ abbreviation for outside broadcast.

Ob /ɒb/ the principal river of the western Siberian lowlands and one of the largest rivers in Russia. Rising in the Altai Mountains, it flows generally north and west for 5,410 km (3,481 miles) before entering the Gulf of Ob (or Ob Bay), an inlet of the Kara Sea, a part of the Arctic Ocean.

ob. ▶ abbreviation he or she died: *ob. 1867.*
– ORIGIN from Latin *obiit*.

ob- ▶ prefix **1** denoting exposure or openness: *obverse.*
■ expressing meeting or facing: *occasion.*
2 denoting opposition, hostility, or resistance: *opponent.*
■ denoting hindrance, blocking, or concealment: *obviate.*
3 denoting finality or completeness: *obsolete.*
4 (in modern technical words) inversely; in a direction or manner contrary to the usual: *obconical.*
– ORIGIN from Latin *ob* 'towards, against, in the way of'.

USAGE **Ob-** occurs mainly in words of Latin origin; it is also found assimilated in the following forms: **oc-** before **c**; **of-** before **f**; **op-** before **p**.

oba /ˈɒbə/ ▶ noun a local chief in Nigeria.
– ORIGIN Yoruba, originally the name of the absolute ruler of the ancient West African kingdom of Benin, now part of Nigeria.

Obad. ▶ abbreviation for Obadiah (in biblical references).

Obadiah /ˌəʊbəˈdʌɪə/ (in the Bible) a Hebrew minor prophet.
■ the shortest book of the Bible, bearing his name.

Oban /ˈəʊb(ə)n/ a port and tourist resort on the west coast of Scotland, in Argyll and Bute, opposite the island of Mull; pop. 8,110 (1981).

obbligato /ˌɒblɪˈɡɑːtəʊ/ (US also **obligato**) ▶ noun (pl. **obbligatos** or **obbligati**) [usu. with or as modifier] an instrumental part, typically distinctive in effect, which is integral to a piece of music and should not be omitted in performance.
– ORIGIN Italian, literally 'obligatory', from Latin *obligatus*, past participle of *obligare* (see **OBLIGE**).

obconical /ɒbˈkɒnɪk(ə)l/ ▶ adjective Botany in the form of an inverted cone.

obcordate /ɒbˈkɔːdeɪt/ ▶ adjective Botany (of a leaf) in the shape of a heart with the pointed end at the base.

obduction ▶ noun [mass noun] Geology the sideways and upwards movement of the edge of a crustal plate over the margin of an adjacent plate.
– DERIVATIVES **obduct** verb.
– ORIGIN 1970s: from Latin *obduct-* 'covered over', from the verb *obducere*, from *ob-* 'against, towards' + *ducere* 'to lead'.

obdurate /ˈɒbdjʊrət/ ▶ adjective stubbornly refusing to change one's opinion or course of action.
– DERIVATIVES **obduracy** noun, **obdurately** adverb, **obdurateness** noun.
– ORIGIN late Middle English (originally in the sense 'hardened in sin, impenitent'): from Latin *obduratus*, past participle of *obdurare*, from *ob-* 'in opposition' + *durare* 'harden' (from *durus* 'hard').

OBE ▶ abbreviation for Officer of the Order of the British Empire.

obeah /ˈəʊbɪə/ (also **obi**) ▶ noun [mass noun] a kind of sorcery practised especially in the Caribbean.
– ORIGIN Twi, from *bayi* 'sorcery'.

obeche /əʊˈbiːtʃi/ ▶ noun a tropical tree native to West and central Africa, grown for its pale timber which is used for plywood and veneers.
● *Triplochiton scleroxylon*, family Sterculiaceae.
– ORIGIN early 20th cent.: a term used in Nigeria.

obedience ▶ noun [mass noun] compliance with someone's wishes or orders or acknowledgement of their authority: *unquestioning obedience to the Prime Minister.*
■ submission to a law or rule: *obedience to moral standards.* ■ observance of a monastic rule: *vows of poverty, chastity, and obedience.*
– PHRASES **in obedience to** in accordance with: *the Communist Party supported sanctions, in obedience to Soviet policy.*
– ORIGIN Middle English: via Old French from Latin *oboedientia*, from the verb *oboedire* (see **OBEY**).

obedient ▶ adjective complying or willing to comply with orders or requests; submissive to another's will: *she was totally obedient to him.*
– PHRASES **your obedient servant** dated a formula used to end a letter.
– DERIVATIVES **obediently** adverb.
– ORIGIN Middle English: via Old French from Latin *oboedient-* 'obeying', from the verb *oboedire* (see **OBEY**).

obedientiary /ə(ʊ)ˌbiːdɪˈɛnʃ(ə)ri/ ▶ noun (pl. **-ies**) the holder of a position of responsibility in a monastery or convent under a superior.
– ORIGIN mid 16th cent. (denoting a vassal): from medieval Latin *oboedientiarius*, from *oboedientia* (see **OBEDIENCE**).

obeisance /ə(ʊ)ˈbeɪs(ə)ns/ ▶ noun [mass noun] deferential respect: *they paid obeisance to the Prince.*
■ [count noun] a gesture expressing deferential respect, such as a bow or curtsy: *she made a deep obeisance.*
– DERIVATIVES **obeisant** adjective.
– ORIGIN late Middle English (in the sense 'obedience'): from Old French *obeissance*, from *obeissant* 'obeying', present participle of *obeir.*

obeli plural form of **OBELUS**.

obelia /ə(ʊ)ˈbiːlɪə/ ▶ noun Zoology a sedentary colonial coelenterate with upright branching stems bearing minute cups in which the polyps sit.
● Genus *Obelia*, class Hydrozoa.
– ORIGIN modern Latin, from Greek *obelos* 'tapering column'.

obelisk /ˈɒb(ə)lɪsk/ ▶ noun **1** stone pillar, typically having a square or rectangular cross section, set up as a monument or landmark.
■ a mountain, tree, or other natural object of similar shape.
2 another term for **OBELUS**.
– ORIGIN mid 16th cent.: via Latin from Greek *obeliskos*, diminutive of *obelos* 'pointed pillar'.

obelize /ˈɒb(ə)lʌɪz/ (also **-ise**) ▶ verb [with obj.] mark (a word or passage) with an obelus to show that it is spurious, corrupt, or doubtful.
– ORIGIN mid 17th cent.: from Greek *obelizein*, in the same sense.

obelus /ˈɒb(ə)ləs/ ▶ noun (pl. **obeli** /-lʌɪ, -liː/) **1** a symbol (†) used as a reference mark in printed matter, or to indicate that a person is deceased.
2 a mark (– or ÷) used in ancient manuscripts to mark a word or passage as spurious, corrupt or doubtful.
– ORIGIN late Middle English: via Latin from Greek *obelos* 'pointed pillar', also 'critical mark'.

Oberammergau /ˌəʊbərˈaməɡaʊ, German ˌoːbəˈraməɡaʊ/ a village in the Bavarian Alps of SW Germany; pop. 4,800 (1983). It is the site of the most famous of the few surviving passion plays, which has been performed by the villagers every tenth year (with few exceptions) from 1634 as a result of a vow made during an epidemic of plague.

Oberhausen /ˈəʊbəˌhaʊz(ə)n, German ˈoːbɐˌhaʊzn̩/ an industrial city in western Germany, in the Ruhr valley of North Rhine-Westphalia; pop. 224,560 (1991).

Oberon /ˈəʊbərɒn/ Astronomy a satellite of Uranus, the furthest from the planet, which has a heavily cratered surface and was discovered by W. Herschel in 1787 (diameter 1,550 km).
– ORIGIN from the name of the king of the fairies in Shakespeare's *A Midsummer Night's Dream*.

Oberösterreich /ˈoːbɐˌøːstəraɪç/ German name for **UPPER AUSTRIA**.

obese ▶ adjective grossly fat or overweight.
– DERIVATIVES **obesity** noun.
– ORIGIN mid 17th cent.: from Latin *obesus* 'having eaten until fat', from *ob-* 'away, completely' + *esus* (past participle of *edere* 'eat').

obey ▶ verb [with obj.] comply with the command, direction, or request of (a person or a law); submit to the authority of: *I always obey my father.*
■ carry out (a command or instruction): *the officer was convicted for refusing to obey orders* | [no obj.] *when the order was repeated, he refused to obey.* ■ behave in accordance with (a general principle, natural law, etc.): *the universe was complex but it obeyed certain rules.*
– DERIVATIVES **obeyer** noun.
– ORIGIN Middle English: from Old French *obeir*, from Latin *oboedire*, from *ob-* 'in the direction of' + *audire* 'hear'.

obfuscate /ˈɒbfʌskeɪt/ ▶ verb [with obj.] render obscure, unclear, or unintelligible: *the spelling changes will deform some familiar words and obfuscate their etymological origins.*
■ bewilder (someone): *it is more likely to obfuscate people than enlighten them.*
– DERIVATIVES **obfuscation** noun, **obfuscatory** adjective.
– ORIGIN late Middle English: from late Latin *obfuscat-* 'darkened', from the verb *obfuscare*, based on Latin *fuscus* 'dark'.

obi[1] /ˈəʊbi/ ▶ noun variant form of **OBEAH**.

obi[2] /ˈəʊbi/ ▶ noun (pl. **obis**) a broad sash worn round the waist of a Japanese kimono.
– ORIGIN Japanese, literally 'belt'.

obit /ˈɒbɪt, ˈəʊ-/ ▶ noun informal an obituary.
– ORIGIN late Middle English: now regarded as an abbreviation of **OBITUARY**, but originally also used in the senses 'death' and 'funeral service', from Latin *obitus* 'going down, death'.

obiter /ˈɒbɪtə/ ▶ adverb & adjective (chiefly in legal contexts) made or said in passing.
▶ noun short for **OBITER DICTUM**.
– ORIGIN Latin, originally as the phrase *ob itur* 'by the way'.

obiter dictum /ˈdɪktəm/ ▶ noun (pl. **obiter dicta** /ˈdɪktə/) Law a judge's expression of opinion uttered in court or giving judgement, but not essential to the decision and not part of the ratio decidendi.
■ an incidental remark.
– ORIGIN Latin *obiter* 'in passing' + *dictum* 'something that is said'.

obituary /ə(ʊ)ˈbɪtʃʊəri, -tʃəri, -tjʊəri/ ▶ noun (pl. **-ies**) a notice of a death, especially in a newspaper, typically including a brief biography of the deceased person.
– DERIVATIVES **obituarist** noun.
– ORIGIN early 18th cent.: from medieval Latin *obituarius*, from Latin *obitus* 'death', from *obit-* 'perished', from the verb *obire*.

object ▶ noun /ˈɒbdʒɪkt, -dʒɛkt/ **1** a material thing that can be seen and touched: *he was dragging a large object* | *small objects such as shells.*
■ Philosophy a thing external to the thinking mind or subject.
2 a person or thing to which a specified action or feeling is directed: *disease became the object of investigation.*
■ a goal or purpose: *the Institute was opened with the object of promoting scientific study.* ■ Grammar a noun phrase governed by an active transitive verb or by a preposition. ■ Computing a data construct that provides a description of virtually anything known to a computer (such as a processor, a peripheral, a document, or a piece of code) and defines its status, its method of operation, and how it interacts with other objects.
▶ verb /əbˈdʒɛkt/ [reporting verb] say something to express one's disapproval of or disagreement with something: [no obj.] *residents object to the volume of traffic* | [with clause] *the boy's father objected that the police had arrested him unlawfully.*

▪ [with obj.] archaic adduce as a reason against something: *Bryant objects this very circumstance to the authenticity of the Iliad.*
– PHRASES **no object** not influencing or restricting choices or decisions: *a tycoon for whom* **money is no object**. **the object of the exercise** the main point or purpose of an activity. **object of virtu** see **VIRTU**.
– DERIVATIVES **objectless** adjective, **objector** noun.
– ORIGIN late Middle English: from medieval Latin *objectum* 'thing presented to the mind', neuter past participle (used as a noun) of Latin *obicere*, from *ob-* 'in the way of' + *jacere* 'to throw'; the verb may also partly represent the Latin frequentative *objectare*.

object ball ▶ noun Billiards & Snooker the ball at which a player aims the cue ball.

object choice ▶ noun Psychoanalysis a person or thing external to the ego chosen as a focus of desire or sexual activity.

object code ▶ noun [mass noun] Computing code produced by a compiler or assembler.

object-glass ▶ noun another term for **OBJECTIVE** (in sense 3).

objectify ▶ verb (**-ies**, **-ied**) [with obj.] express (something abstract) in a concrete form: *good poetry objectifies feeling.*
▪ degrade to the status of a mere object: *a deeply sexist attitude that objectifies women.*
– DERIVATIVES **objectification** noun.

objection ▶ noun an expression or feeling of disapproval or opposition; a reason for disagreeing: *they have raised no objections to the latest plans.*
▪ [mass noun] the action of challenging or disagreeing with something: *his view is open to objection.*
– ORIGIN late Middle English: from Old French, or from late Latin *objectio(n-)*, from the verb *obicere* (see **OBJECT**).

objectionable ▶ adjective arousing distaste or opposition; unpleasant or offensive. *I find his theory objectionable in its racist undertones.*
– DERIVATIVES **objectionableness** noun, **objectionably** adverb.

objective ▶ adjective **1** (of a person or their judgement) not influenced by personal feelings or opinions in considering and representing facts: *historians try to be objective and impartial.* Contrasted with **SUBJECTIVE**.
▪ not dependent on the mind for existence; actual: *a matter of objective fact.*
2 [attrib.] Grammar of, relating to, or denoting a case of nouns and pronouns used for the object of a transitive verb or a preposition.
▶ noun **1** a thing aimed at or sought; a goal: *the system has achieved its objective.*
2 (**the objective**) Grammar the objective case.
3 (also **objective lens**) the lens in a telescope or microscope nearest to the object observed.
– DERIVATIVES **objectively** adverb, **objectiveness** noun, **objectivity** noun, **objectivization** noun, **objectivize** (also **-ise**) verb.
– ORIGIN early 17th cent.: from medieval Latin *objectivus*, from *objectum* (see **OBJECT**).

objective correlative ▶ noun the artistic and literary technique of representing or evoking a particular emotion by means of symbols which become indicative of that emotion and are associated with it.

objective danger ▶ noun Climbing a danger such as a rock fall that does not arise from a lack of skill on the part of the climber.

objective function ▶ noun Mathematics (in linear programming) the function that it is desired to maximize or minimize.

objectivism ▶ noun [mass noun] **1** the tendency to lay stress on what is external to or independent of the mind.
2 Philosophy the belief that certain things, especially moral truths, exist independently of human knowledge or perception of them.
– DERIVATIVES **objectivist** noun & adjective, **objectivistic** adjective.

object language ▶ noun **1** a language described by means of another language. Compare with **METALANGUAGE**, **TARGET LANGUAGE**.
2 Computing a language into which a program is translated by means of a compiler or assembler.

object lesson ▶ noun a striking practical example of some principle or ideal: *they responded to daily emergencies in a way that was an object lesson to us all.*

object-oriented ▶ adjective Computing (of a programming language) using a methodology which enables a system to be modelled as a set of objects which can be controlled and manipulated in a modular manner.

object program ▶ noun Computing a program into which some other program is translated by an assembler or compiler.

object-relationship ▶ noun Psychoanalysis a relationship felt, or the emotional energy directed, by the self or ego towards a chosen object.

objects clause ▶ noun Law a clause in a memorandum of association specifying the objects for which the company was established.

object world ▶ noun the world external to the self, apprehended through the objects in it.

objet /ˈɒbʒeɪ/ ▶ noun an object displayed or intended for display as an ornament.
– ORIGIN French, literally 'object'.

objet d'art /ˈdɑː/ ▶ noun (pl. **objets d'art** pronunc. same) a small decorative or artistic object, typically when regarded as a collectable item.
– ORIGIN French, literally 'object of art'.

objet trouvé /ˈtruːveɪ/ ▶ noun (pl. **objets trouvés** pronunc. same) an object found or picked up at random and considered as a work of art.
– ORIGIN French, literally 'found object'.

objurgate /ˈɒbdʒəgeɪt/ ▶ verb [with obj.] rare rebuke severely; scold.
– DERIVATIVES **objurgation** noun, **objurgatory** adjective.
– ORIGIN early 17th cent.: from Latin *objurgat-* 'chided, rebuked', from the verb *objurgare*, based on *jurgium* 'strife'.

oblast /ˈɒblast/ ▶ noun an administrative division or region in Russia and the former Soviet Union, and in some constituent republics of the former Soviet Union.
– ORIGIN Russian.

oblate[1] /ˈɒbleɪt/ ▶ noun a person dedicated to a religious life, but typically having not taken full monastic vows.
– ORIGIN late 17th cent.: from French, from medieval Latin *oblatus*, past participle (used as a noun) of Latin *offerre* 'to offer'.

oblate[2] /ˈɒbleɪt/ ▶ adjective Geometry (of a spheroid) flattened at the poles. Often contrasted with **PROLATE**.
– ORIGIN early 18th cent.: from modern Latin *oblatus* (from *ob-* 'inversely' + *-latus* 'carried'), on the pattern of Latin *prolatus* 'prolonged'.

oblation ▶ noun a thing presented or offered to God or a god.
▪ [mass noun] Christian Church the presentation of bread and wine to God in the Eucharist.
– DERIVATIVES **oblational** adjective, **oblatory** adjective.
– ORIGIN late Middle English: from Old French, or from late Latin *oblatio(n-)*, from Latin *offerre* 'to offer'.

oblietjie /ɒˈbliːki/ ▶ noun (pl. **-ies**) S. African a rolled wafer-thin teacake.
– ORIGIN Afrikaans, from French *oublie* 'offering, wafer' + the Afrikaans diminutive suffix *-tjie*.

obligate ▶ verb **1** [with obj. and infinitive] bind or compel (someone), especially legally or morally: *the medical establishment is obligated to take action in the best interest of the public.*
2 [with obj.] US commit (assets) as security: *the money must be obligated within 30 days.*
▶ adjective [attrib.] Biology restricted to a particular function or mode of life: *an obligate intracellular parasite.* Often contrasted with **FACULTATIVE**.
– DERIVATIVES **obligator** noun.
– ORIGIN late Middle English (as an adjective in the sense 'bound by law'): from Latin *obligatus*, past participle of *obligare* (see **OBLIGE**). The current adjectival use dates from the late 19th cent.

obligation ▶ noun an act or course of action to which a person is morally or legally bound; a duty or commitment: [with infinitive] *I have an obligation to look after her.*
▪ [mass noun] the condition of being morally or legally bound to do something: *they are* **under no obligation** *to stick to the scheme.* ▪ a debt of gratitude for a service or favour: *she didn't want to be under an obligation to him.*
– PHRASES **day of obligation** (in the Roman Catholic Church) a day on which all are required to attend Mass.
– DERIVATIVES **obligational** adjective.
– ORIGIN Middle English (in the sense 'formal promise'): via Old French from Latin *obligatio(n-)*, from the verb *obligare* (see **OBLIGE**).

obligato ▶ noun US variant spelling of **OBBLIGATO**.

obligatory /əˈblɪgət(ə)ri/ ▶ adjective required by a legal, moral, or other rule; compulsory: *use of seat belts in cars is now obligatory.*
▪ often humorous so customary or fashionable as to be expected of everyone or on every occasion: *after the obligatory preamble on the weather he got down to business.* ▪ (of a ruling) having binding force: *a sovereign whose laws are obligatory.*
– DERIVATIVES **obligatorily** adverb.
– ORIGIN late Middle English: from late Latin *obligatorius*, from Latin *obligat-* 'obliged', from the verb *obligare* (see **OBLIGE**).

oblige ▶ verb [with obj. and infinitive] make (someone) legally or morally bound to an action or course of action: *doctors are obliged by law to keep patients alive while there is a chance of recovery.*
▪ [with obj.] do as (someone) asks or desires in order to help or please them: **oblige** *me* **by** *not being sorry for yourself* | [no obj.] *tell me what you want to know and I'll see if I can oblige.* ▪ (**be obliged**) be indebted or grateful: *if you can give me a few minutes of your time I'll be much obliged.* ▪ [with obj.] archaic bind (someone) by an oath, promise, or contract.
– DERIVATIVES **obliger** noun.
– ORIGIN Middle English (in the sense 'bind by oath'): from Old French *obliger*, from Latin *obligare*, from *ob-* 'towards' + *ligare* 'to bind'.

obligee /ˌɒblɪˈdʒiː/ ▶ noun Law a person to whom another is bound by contract or other legal procedure. Compare with **OBLIGOR**.

obligement ▶ noun chiefly Scottish a kindness; a favour.

obliging ▶ adjective willing to do a service or kindness; helpful.
– DERIVATIVES **obligingly** adverb, **obligingness** noun.

obligor /ˈɒblɪgɔː, ˌɒblɪˈgɔː/ ▶ noun Law a person who is bound to another by contract or other legal procedure. Compare with **OBLIGEE**.

oblique /əˈbliːk/ ▶ adjective **1** neither parallel nor at right angles to a specified or implied line; slanting: *we sat on the settee oblique to the fireplace.*
▪ not explicit or direct in addressing a point: *he issued an oblique attack on the President.* ▪ Geometry (of a line, plane figure, or surface) inclined at other than a right angle. ▪ Geometry (of an angle) acute or obtuse. ▪ Geometry (of a cone, cylinder, etc.) with an axis not perpendicular to the plane of its base. ▪ Anatomy (especially of a muscle) neither parallel nor perpendicular to the long axis of a body or limb.
2 Grammar denoting any case other than the nominative or vocative.
▶ noun **1** Brit. another term for **SLASH** (in sense 2).
2 a muscle neither parallel nor perpendicular to the long axis of a body or limb.
– DERIVATIVES **obliquely** adverb, **obliqueness** noun, **obliquity** /əˈblɪkwɪti/ noun.
– ORIGIN late Middle English: from Latin *obliquus*.

obliterate /əˈblɪtəreɪt/ ▶ verb [with obj.] destroy utterly; wipe out: *the memory was so painful that he obliterated it from his mind.*
▪ cause to become invisible or indistinct; blot out: *clouds were darkening, obliterating the sun.* ▪ cancel (something, especially a postage stamp) to prevent further use.
– DERIVATIVES **obliteration** noun, **obliterative** /-rətɪv/ adjective, **obliterator** noun.
– ORIGIN mid 16th cent.: from Latin *obliterat-* 'struck out, erased', from the verb *obliterare*, based on *littera* 'letter, something written'.

oblivion ▶ noun [mass noun] **1** the state of being unaware or unconscious of what is happening: *they drank themselves into oblivion.*
▪ the state of being forgotten, especially by the public: *his name will fade into oblivion.* ▪ figurative extinction: *only our armed forces stood between us and oblivion.*
2 Law historical amnesty or pardon.
– ORIGIN late Middle English: via Old French from Latin *oblivio(n-)*, from *oblivisci* 'forget'.

oblivious ▶ adjective not aware of or not concerned about what is happening around one: *she became absorbed,* **oblivious to** *the passage of time.*
– DERIVATIVES **obliviously** adverb, **obliviousness** noun.
– ORIGIN late Middle English: from Latin *obliviosus*, from *oblivio(n-)* (see **OBLIVION**).

oblong ▶ adjective having an elongated and typically rectangular shape.
▶ noun an object or flat figure in this shape.
– ORIGIN late Middle English: from Latin *oblongus* 'longish'.

obloquy /ˈɒbləkwi/ ▶ noun [mass noun] strong public criticism or verbal abuse: *he endured years of contempt and obloquy.*
■ disgrace, especially that brought about by public abuse: *conduct to which no more obloquy could reasonably attach.*
– ORIGIN late Middle English: from late Latin *obloquium* 'contradiction', from Latin *obloqui*, from *ob-* 'against' + *loqui* 'speak'.

obnoxious /əbˈnɒkʃəs/ ▶ adjective extremely unpleasant.
– DERIVATIVES **obnoxiously** adverb, **obnoxiousness** noun.
– ORIGIN late 16th cent. (in the sense 'vulnerable (to harm)'): from Latin *obnoxiosus*, from *obnoxius* 'exposed to harm', from *ob-* 'towards' + *noxa* 'harm'. The current sense, influenced by **NOXIOUS**, dates from the late 17th cent.

obnubilate /ɒbˈnjuːbɪleɪt/ ▶ verb [with obj.] poetic/literary darken, dim, or cover with or as if with a cloud; obscure.
– DERIVATIVES **obnubilation** noun.
– ORIGIN late 16th cent.: from Latin *obnubilat-* 'covered with clouds or fog', from the verb *obnubilare*.

obo N. Amer. ▶ abbreviation for or best offer: $2,700 *obo.*

oboe /ˈəʊbəʊ/ ▶ noun a woodwind instrument of treble pitch, played with a double reed and having an incisive tone.
■ an organ stop resembling an oboe in tone.
– DERIVATIVES **oboist** noun.
– ORIGIN early 18th cent.: from Italian, or from French *hautbois*, from *haut* 'high' + *bois* 'wood'.

oboe d'amore /daˈmɔːreɪ/ ▶ noun a type of oboe with a bulbous bell, sounding a minor third lower than the ordinary oboe. It has a soft tone and is used in baroque music.
– ORIGIN late 19th cent.: from Italian, literally 'oboe of love'.

obol /ˈɒb(ə)l/ ▶ noun an ancient Greek coin worth one sixth of a drachma.
– ORIGIN via Latin from Greek *obolos*, variant of *obelos* (see **OBELUS**).

O-Bon /əʊˈbɒn/ ▶ noun another name for **BON**.

Obote /əˈbəʊteɪ, -ti/, (Apollo) Milton (b.1924), Ugandan statesman, Prime Minister 1962–6, President 1966–71 and 1980–5. Overthrown by Idi Amin in 1971, he was re-elected President in 1980. He was removed in a second military coup in 1985.

obovate /ɒbˈəʊveɪt/ ▶ adjective Botany (of a leaf) ovate with the narrower end at the base.

O'Brien[1], Edna (b.1932), Irish novelist and short-story writer, noted especially for her novel *The Country Girls* (1960).

O'Brien[2], Flann (1911–66), Irish novelist and journalist; pseudonym of *Brian O'Nolan*. Writing under the name of Myles na Gopaleen, he contributed a satirical column to the *Irish Times* for nearly twenty years. Notable novels: *At Swim-Two-Birds* (1939); *The Third Policeman* (1967).

obscene ▶ adjective (of the portrayal or description of sexual matters) offensive or disgusting by accepted standards of morality and decency: *obscene jokes | obscene literature.*
■ offending against moral principles; repugnant: *using animals' skins for fur coats is obscene.*
– DERIVATIVES **obscenely** adverb.
– ORIGIN late 16th cent.: from French *obscène* or Latin *obscaenus* 'ill-omened or abominable'.

obscenity ▶ noun (pl. **-ies**) [mass noun] the state or quality of being obscene; obscene behaviour, language, or images: *the book was banned for obscenity.*
■ [count noun] an extremely offensive word or expression: *the men scowled and muttered obscenities.*
– ORIGIN late 16th cent.: from French *obscénité* or Latin *obscaenitas*, from *obscaenus* (see **OBSCENE**).

obscurantism /ˌɒbskjʊˈrantɪz(ə)m/ ▶ noun [mass noun] the practice of deliberately preventing the facts or full details of something from becoming known.
– DERIVATIVES **obscurant** noun & adjective, **obscurantist** noun & adjective.
– ORIGIN mid 19th cent.: from earlier *obscurant*, denoting a person who obscures something, via German from Latin *obscurant-* 'making dark', from the verb *obscurare*.

obscure ▶ adjective (**obscurer**, **obscurest**) not discovered or known about; uncertain: *his origins and parentage are obscure.*
■ not clearly expressed or easily understood: *obscure references to Proust.* ■ not important or well known: *an obscure religious sect.* ■ hard to make out or define; vague: *I feel an obscure resentment.* ■ (of a colour) not sharply defined; dim or dingy.
▶ verb [with obj.] keep from being seen; conceal: *grey clouds obscure the sun.*
■ make unclear and difficult to understand: *the debate has become obscured by conflicting ideological perspectives.* ■ overshadow: *none of this should obscure the skill, experience, and perseverance of CP workers.*
– DERIVATIVES **obscuration** noun, **obscurely** adverb.
– ORIGIN late Middle English: from Old French *obscur*, from Latin *obscurus* 'dark', from an Indo-European root meaning 'cover'.

obscurity ▶ noun (pl. **-ies**) [mass noun] the state of being unknown, inconspicuous, or unimportant: *he is too good a player to slide into obscurity.*
■ the quality of being difficult to understand: *poems of impenetrable obscurity.* ■ [count noun] a thing that is unclear or difficult to understand: *the obscurities in his poems and plays.*
– ORIGIN late Middle English: from Old French *obscurite*, from Latin *obscuritas*, from *obscurus* 'dark'.

obsecration /ˌɒbsɪˈkreɪʃ(ə)n/ ▶ noun [mass noun] rare earnest pleading or supplication.
– ORIGIN late Middle English: from Latin *obsecratio(n-)*, from *obsecrare* 'entreat', based on *sacer*, *sacr-* 'sacred'.

obsequies /ˈɒbsɪkwɪz/ ▶ plural noun funeral rites.
– ORIGIN late Middle English: plural of obsolete *obsequy*, from Anglo-Norman French *obsequie*, from the medieval Latin plural *obsequiae* (from Latin *exsequiae* 'funeral rites', influenced by *obsequium* 'dutiful service').

obsequious /əbˈsiːkwɪəs/ ▶ adjective obedient or attentive to an excessive or servile degree: *they were served by obsequious waiters.*
– DERIVATIVES **obsequiously** adverb, **obsequiousness** noun.
– ORIGIN late 15th cent. (not depreciatory in sense in early use): from Latin *obsequiosus*, from *obsequium* 'compliance', from *obsequi* 'follow, comply with'.

observance ▶ noun [mass noun] **1** the action or practice of fulfilling or respecting the requirements of law, morality, or ritual: *strict observance of the rules | the decline in religious observance.*
■ [count noun] (usu. **observances**) an act performed for religious or ceremonial reasons: *official anniversary observances.* ■ [count noun] a rule to be followed by a religious order: *he drew up a body of monastic observances.* ■ archaic respect; deference: *the tramp gave them no observance.*
2 the action of watching or noticing something: *the baby's motionless observance of me.*
– ORIGIN Middle English: via Old French from Latin *observantia*, from *observant-* 'watching, paying attention to', from the verb *observare* (see **OBSERVE**).

observant ▶ adjective **1** quick to notice things: *her observant eye took in every detail.*
2 adhering strictly to the rules of a particular religion, especially Judaism.
▶ noun (**Observant**) historical a member of a branch of the Franciscan order that followed a strict rule.
– ORIGIN late Middle English (as a noun): from French, literally 'watching', present participle of *observer* (see **OBSERVE**).

observation ▶ noun **1** [mass noun] the action or process of observing something or someone carefully or in order to gain information: *she was brought into hospital for observation | [count noun] detailed observations were carried out on the students' behaviour.*
■ the ability to notice things, especially significant details: *his powers of observation.* ■ the taking of the sun's or another celestial body's altitude to find a latitude or longitude.
2 a remark, statement, or comment based on something one has seen, heard, or noticed: *he made a telling observation about Hughie.*
– PHRASES **under observation** (especially of a patient or a suspected criminal) being closely and constantly watched or monitored: *he spent two nights in hospital under observation.*
– DERIVATIVES **observational** adjective, **observationally** adverb.
– ORIGIN late Middle English (in the sense 'respectful adherence to the requirements of (rules, a ritual, etc.)'): from Latin *observatio(n-)*, from the verb *observare* (see **OBSERVE**).

observation car ▶ noun a railway carriage with large windows designed to provide a good view of passing scenery.

observation post ▶ noun Military a post for watching the movement of enemy forces or the effect of artillery fire.

observatory ▶ noun (pl. **-ies**) a room or building housing an astronomical telescope or other scientific equipment for the study of natural phenomena.
– ORIGIN late 17th cent.: from modern Latin *observatorium*, from Latin *observat-* 'watched', from the verb *observare* (see **OBSERVE**).

observe ▶ verb [with obj.] **1** notice or perceive (something) and register it as being significant: [with clause] *young people observe that decisions are made by others.*
■ watch (someone or something) carefully and attentively: *Rob stood in the hallway, from where he could observe the happenings on the street.* ■ take note of or detect (something) in the course of a scientific study: *the behaviour observed in groups of chimpanzees.* ■ [reporting verb] make a remark or comment: [with direct speech] *'It's chilly,' she observed* | [with clause] *a stockbroker once observed that dealers live and work in hell.*
2 fulfil or comply with (a social, legal, ethical, or religious obligation): *a tribunal must observe the principles of natural justice.*
■ (usu. **be observed**) maintain (silence) in compliance with a rule or custom, or temporarily as a mark of respect: *a minute's silence will be observed.* ■ perform or take part in (a rite or ceremony): *relations gather to observe the funeral rites.* ■ celebrate or acknowledge (an anniversary): *many Delawareans last week observed the one-year anniversary of the flood.*
– DERIVATIVES **observable** adjective, **observably** adverb.
– ORIGIN late Middle English (in sense 2): from Old French *observer*, from Latin *observare* 'to watch', from *ob-* 'towards' + *servare* 'attend to, look at'.

observer ▶ noun a person who watches or notices something: *to a casual observer, he was at peace.*
■ a person who follows events, especially political ones, closely and comments publicly on them: *some observers expect interest rates to rise.* ■ a person posted in an official capacity to an area to monitor political or military events: *elections scrutinized by international observers.* ■ a person who attends a conference, inquiry, etc., to note the proceedings without participating in them. ■ (in science or art) a real or hypothetical observer regarded as having a particular viewpoint or effect. ■ a person trained to spot and identify enemy aircraft or to reconnoitre enemy positions from the air.

obsess ▶ verb [with obj.] (usu. **be obsessed**) preoccupy or fill the mind of (someone) continually, intrusively, and to a troubling extent: *he was obsessed with thoughts of suicide* | [as adj. **obsessed**] *he became completely obsessed about germs.*
■ [no obj.] chiefly N. Amer. (of a person) be preoccupied in this way: *her husband, who is* **obsessing about** *the wrong she has done him.*
– DERIVATIVES **obsessive** adjective & noun, **obsessively** adverb, **obsessiveness** noun.
– ORIGIN late Middle English (in the sense 'haunt, possess', referring to an evil spirit): from Latin *obsess-* 'besieged', from the verb *obsidere*, from *ob-* 'opposite' + *sedere* 'sit'. The current sense dates from the late 19th cent.

obsession ▶ noun [mass noun] the state of being obsessed with someone or something: *she cared for him with a devotion bordering on obsession.*
■ [count noun] an idea or thought that continually preoccupies or intrudes on a person's mind: *he was in the grip of an obsession he was powerless to resist.*
– DERIVATIVES **obsessional** adjective, **obsessionally** adverb.
– ORIGIN early 16th cent. (in the sense 'siege'): from Latin *obsessio(n-)*, from the verb *obsidere* (see **OBSESS**).

obsessive–compulsive ▶ adjective Psychiatry denoting or relating to an anxiety disorder in which a person feels compelled to perform certain

O

stereotyped actions repeatedly to alleviate persistent fears or intrusive thoughts, typically resulting in severe disruption of daily life.

obsidian /əbˈsɪdɪən/ ▶ **noun** [mass noun] a hard, dark, glass-like volcanic rock formed by the rapid solidification of lava without crystallization.
– ORIGIN mid 17th cent.: from Latin *obsidianus*, error for *obsianus*, from *Obsius*, the name (in Pliny) of the discoverer of a similar stone.

obsolescent /ˌɒbsəˈlɛs(ə)nt/ ▶ **adjective** becoming obsolete: *obsolescent equipment | obsolescent slang.*
– DERIVATIVES **obsolesce** verb *existing systems begin to obsolesce*, **obsolescence** noun.
– ORIGIN mid 18th cent.: from Latin *obsolescent-* 'falling into disuse', from the verb *obsolescere*.

obsolete ▶ **adjective** **1** no longer produced or used; out of date: *the disposal of old and obsolete machinery | the phrase was obsolete after 1625.*
2 Biology (of a part or characteristic of an organism) less developed than formerly or in a related species; rudimentary; vestigial.
▶ **verb** [with obj.] chiefly US cause (a product or idea) to be or become obsolete by replacing it with something new: *we're trying to stimulate the business by obsoleting last year's designs.*
– DERIVATIVES **obsoletely** adverb, **obsoleteness** noun, **obsoletism** noun.
– ORIGIN late 16th cent.: from Latin *obsoletus* 'grown old, worn out', past participle of *obsolescere* 'fall into disuse'.

obstacle ▶ **noun** a thing that blocks one's way or prevents or hinders progress: *the major* **obstacle to** *achieving that goal is money.*
– ORIGIN Middle English: via Old French from Latin *obstaculum*, from *obstare* 'impede', from *ob-* 'against' + *stare* 'stand'.

obstacle race ▶ **noun** a race in which various obstacles, such as fences, pits, and climbing nets, have to be negotiated.

obstetric ▶ **adjective** of or relating to childbirth and the processes associated with it.
– DERIVATIVES **obstetrical** adjective (chiefly N. Amer.), **obstetrically** adverb.
– ORIGIN mid 18th cent.: from modern Latin *obstetricus* from Latin *obstetricius* (based on *obstetrix* 'midwife'), from *obstare* 'be present'.

obstetrician /ˌɒbstəˈtrɪʃ(ə)n/ ▶ **noun** a physician or surgeon qualified to practise in obstetrics.

obstetrics ▶ **plural noun** [usu. treated as sing.] the branch of medicine and surgery concerned with childbirth and midwifery.

obstinate ▶ **adjective** stubbornly refusing to change one's opinion or chosen course of action, despite attempts to persuade one to do so.
■(of an unwelcome phenomenon or situation) very difficult to change or overcome: *the obstinate problem of unemployment.*
– DERIVATIVES **obstinacy** noun, **obstinately** adverb.
– ORIGIN Middle English: from Latin *obstinatus*, past participle of *obstinare* 'persist'.

obstipation /ˌɒbstɪˈpeɪʃ(ə)n/ ▶ **noun** [mass noun] Medicine severe or complete constipation.
– ORIGIN late 16th cent.: alteration of **CONSTIPATION**, by substitution of the prefix **OB-** for *con-*.

obstreperous /əbˈstrɛp(ə)rəs/ ▶ **adjective** noisy and difficult to control: *the boy is cocky and obstreperous.*
– DERIVATIVES **obstreperously** adverb, **obstreperousness** noun.
– ORIGIN late 16th cent. (in the sense 'clamorous, vociferous'): from Latin *obstreperus* (from *obstrepere*, from *ob-* 'against' + *strepere* 'make a noise') + **-OUS**.

obstruct ▶ **verb** [with obj.] block (an opening, path, road, etc.); be or get in the way of: *she was obstructing the entrance.*
■prevent or hinder (movement or someone or something in motion): *they had to alter the course of the stream and obstruct the natural flow of the water.* ■ figurative put difficulties in the way of: *fears that the regime would obstruct the distribution of food.* ■ Law commit the offence of intentionally hindering (a police officer). ■(in various sports) impede (a player in the opposing team) in a manner which constitutes an offence.
– DERIVATIVES **obstructor** noun.
– ORIGIN late 16th cent.: from Latin *obstruct-* 'blocked up', from the verb *obstruere*, from *ob-* 'against' + *struere* 'build, pile up'.

obstruction ▶ **noun** [mass noun] the action of obstructing or the state of being obstructed: *they faced obstruction in carrying out their research | walkers could proceed with the minimum of obstruction.*
■[count noun] a thing that impedes or prevents passage or progress; an obstacle or blockage: *the tractor hit an obstruction.* ■(in various sports) the action of unlawfully obstructing a player in the opposing team. ■ Medicine blockage of a bodily passage, especially the gut: *they presented with severe intestinal obstruction.* ■ Law the action of impeding the movement of traffic on a highway. ■ Law the action of deliberately hindering the police in their duties.
– ORIGIN mid 16th cent.: from Latin *obstructio(n-)*, from the verb *obstruere* (see **OBSTRUCT**).

obstructionism ▶ **noun** [mass noun] the practice of deliberately impeding or delaying the course of legal, legislative, or other procedures.
– DERIVATIVES **obstructionist** noun & adjective.

obstructive ▶ **adjective** **1** causing a blockage or obstruction: *all tubing should be cleared of obstructive algae and detritus.*
■of or relating to obstruction of a passage in the body, especially the gut or the bronchi: *the child developed severe obstructive symptoms.*
2 causing or tending to cause deliberate difficulties and delays: *instead of being helpful, she had been a shade obstructive.*
– DERIVATIVES **obstructively** adverb, **obstructiveness** noun.

obstructive jaundice ▶ **noun** [mass noun] Medicine jaundice resulting from blockage of the bile ducts or abnormal retention of bile in the liver.

obstruent /ˈɒbstrʊənt/ ▶ **noun** Phonetics a fricative or plosive speech sound.
– ORIGIN mid 17th cent.: from Latin *obstruent-* 'blocking up', from the verb *obstruere*.

obtain ▶ **verb** **1** [with obj.] get, acquire, or secure (something): *adequate insurance cover is difficult to obtain.*
2 [no obj.] formal be prevalent, customary, or established: *the price of silver fell to that obtaining elsewhere in the ancient world.*
– DERIVATIVES **obtainability** noun, **obtainable** adjective, **obtainer** noun, **obtainment** noun, **obtention** noun.
– ORIGIN late Middle English: from Old French *obtenir*, from Latin *obtinere* 'obtain, gain'.

obtect (also **obtected**) ▶ **adjective** Entomology (of an insect pupa or chrysalis) covered in a hard case with the legs and wings attached immovably against the body.
– ORIGIN late 19th cent.: from Latin *obtectus*, past participle of *obtegere* 'cover over'.

obtrude ▶ **verb** [no obj.] become noticeable in an unwelcome or intrusive way: *a sound from the reception hall obtruded into his thoughts.*
■[with obj.] impose or force (something) on someone in such a way: *I felt unable to obtrude my private sorrow upon anyone.*
– DERIVATIVES **obtruder** noun, **obtrusion** noun.
– ORIGIN mid 16th cent.: from Latin *obtrudere*, from *ob-* 'towards' + *trudere* 'to push'.

obtrusive ▶ **adjective** noticeable or prominent in an unwelcome or intrusive way: *period artifice is not so obtrusive in his plays.*
– DERIVATIVES **obtrusively** adverb, **obtrusiveness** noun.
– ORIGIN mid 17th cent.: from Latin *obtrus-* 'thrust forward', from the verb *obtrudere* (see **OBTRUDE**).

obtund /əbˈtʌnd/ ▶ **verb** [with obj.] dated, chiefly Medicine dull the sensitivity of; blunt; deaden.
– ORIGIN late Middle English: from Latin *obtundere*, from *ob-* 'against' + *tundere* 'to beat'.

obturate /əbˈtjʊəreɪt/ ▶ **verb** [with obj.] formal or technical block up; obstruct.
– DERIVATIVES **obturation** noun.
– ORIGIN mid 17th cent.: from Latin *obturat-* 'stopped up', from the verb *obturare*.

obturator /ˈɒbtjʊəreɪtə/ ▶ **noun** Anatomy either of two muscles covering the outer front part of the pelvis on each side and involved in movements of the thigh and hip.
■[as modifier] relating to this muscle or to the obturator foramen.
– ORIGIN early 18th cent.: from medieval Latin, literally 'obstructor', from *obturare* 'stop up'.

obturator foramen ▶ **noun** Anatomy a large opening in the hip bone between the pubis and the ischium.

obtuse ▶ **adjective** **1** annoyingly insensitive or slow to understand: *he wondered if the doctor was being deliberately obtuse.*
■difficult to understand: *some of the lyrics are a bit obtuse.*
2 (of an angle) more than 90° and less than 180°.
■not sharp-pointed or sharp-edged; blunt.
– DERIVATIVES **obtusely** adverb, **obtuseness** noun, **obtusity** noun.
– ORIGIN late Middle English (in the sense 'blunt'): from Latin *obtusus*, past participle of *obtundere* 'beat against' (see **OBTUND**).

Ob-Ugrian /ɒbˈuːgrɪən, -ˈjuː-/ (also **Ob-Ugric**) ▶ **adjective** of or denoting a branch of the Finno-Ugric language family containing two languages of western Siberia, related to Hungarian.
▶ **noun** [mass noun] this group of languages.
– ORIGIN 1930s: from *Ob*, the name of a Siberian river, + **UGRIAN**.

obverse ▶ **noun** [usu. in sing.] **1** the side of a coin or medal bearing the head or principal design.
■the design or inscription on this side.
2 the opposite or counterpart of a fact or truth: *true solitude is the obverse of true society.*
▶ **adjective** [attrib.] **1** of or denoting the obverse of a coin or medal.
2 corresponding to something else as its opposite or counterpart.
– DERIVATIVES **obversely** adverb.
– ORIGIN mid 17th cent. (in the sense 'turned towards the observer'): from Latin *obversus*, past participle of *obvertere* 'turn towards' (see **OBVERT**).

obvert ▶ **verb** [with obj.] Logic alter (a proposition) so as to infer another proposition with a contradictory predicate, e.g. *'no men are immortal'* to *'all men are mortal'.*
– DERIVATIVES **obversion** noun.
– ORIGIN early 17th cent. (in the sense 'turn something until it is facing'): from Latin *obvertere*, from *ob-* 'towards' + *vertere* 'to turn'.

obviate /ˈɒbvɪeɪt/ ▶ **verb** [with obj.] remove (a need or difficulty): *the presence of roller blinds obviated the need for curtains.*
■avoid; prevent: *a parachute can be used to obviate disaster.*
– DERIVATIVES **obviation** noun.
– ORIGIN late 16th cent.: from late Latin *obviat-* 'prevented', from the verb *obviare*, based on Latin *via* 'way'.

obvious ▶ **adjective** easily perceived or understood; clear, self-evident, or apparent: *unemployment has been the most obvious cost of the recession |* [with clause] *it was obvious a storm was coming in.*
■derogatory predictable and lacking in subtlety: *it was an obvious remark to make.*
– DERIVATIVES **obviously** adverb, **obviousness** noun.
– ORIGIN late 16th cent. (in the sense 'frequently encountered'): from Latin *obvius* (from the phrase *ob viam* 'in the way') + **-OUS**.

OC ▶ **abbreviation for** ■ Officer Commanding. ■ Officer of the Order of Canada.

oc- ▶ **prefix** variant spelling of **OB-** assimilated before *c* (as in *occasion, occlude*).

oca /ˈəʊkə/ ▶ **noun** a South American plant related to wood sorrel, long cultivated in Peru for its edible tubers.
• *Oxalis tuberosa*, family Oxalidaceae.
– ORIGIN early 17th cent.: from American Spanish, from Quechua *ócca*.

ocarina /ˌɒkəˈriːnə/ ▶ **noun** a small egg-shaped ceramic (especially terracotta) or metal wind instrument with holes for the fingers.
– ORIGIN late 19th cent.: from Italian, from *oca* 'goose' (from its shape).

OCAS ▶ **abbreviation for** Organization of Central American States.

O'Casey, Sean (1880–1964), Irish dramatist. Notable plays: *The Shadow of a Gunman* (1923); *Juno and the Paycock* (1924).

Occam /ˈɒkəm/ ▶ **noun** [mass noun] a computer programming language devised for use in parallel processing.
– ORIGIN 1980s: from the name of **WILLIAM OF OCCAM**.

Occam, William of see **WILLIAM OF OCCAM**.

Occam's razor (also **Ockham's razor**) the principle (attributed to William of Occam) that in explaining a thing no more assumptions should be made than are necessary. The principle is often invoked to defend reductionism or nominalism.

occasion ▶ **noun 1** a particular time or instance of an event: *on one occasion I stayed up until two in the morning.*
■ a special or noteworthy event, ceremony, or celebration: *she was presented with a gold watch to mark the occasion* | [mass noun] *Sunday lunch has a suitable sense of occasion about it.* ■ a suitable or opportune time for doing something: *by-elections are traditionally an occasion for registering protest votes.*
2 [mass noun] formal reason; cause: [with infinitive] *it's the first time that I've had occasion to complain.*
▶ **verb** [with obj.] formal cause (something): *something vital must have occasioned this visit* | [with two objs] *his death occasioned her much grief.*
– PHRASES **on occasion** (or **occasions**) occasionally; from time to time: *on occasion, the state was asked to intervene.* **rise to the occasion** perform better than usual in response to a special situation or event. **take occasion** archaic make use of an opportunity to do something.
– ORIGIN late Middle English: from Latin *occasio(n-)* 'juncture, reason', from *occidere* 'go down, set', from *ob-* 'towards' + *cadere* 'to fall'.

occasional ▶ **adjective** occurring, appearing, or done infrequently and irregularly: *the occasional car went by but no taxis.*
■ (of furniture) made or adapted for use on a particular occasion or for irregular use: *an occasional table.* ■ (of a literary composition, speech, religious service, etc.) produced on or intended for a special occasion: *he wrote occasional verse for patrons.* ■ dated employed for a particular occasion or on an irregular basis: *occasional freelancer seeks full-time position.*
– DERIVATIVES **occasionality** noun, **occasionally** adverb.

occasionalism ▶ **noun** [mass noun] Philosophy the doctrine ascribing the connection between mental and bodily events to the continuing intervention of God.

Occident /ˈɒksɪd(ə)nt/ ▶ **noun** (**the Occident**) formal or poetic/literary the countries of the West, especially Europe and America.
– ORIGIN late Middle English: via Old French from Latin *occident-* 'going down, setting', from the verb *occidere.*

occidental ▶ **adjective** of or relating to the countries of the West: *an Asian challenge to occidental dominance.*
▶ **noun** (**Occidental**) a native or inhabitant of the Occident.
– DERIVATIVES **occidentalism** noun, **occidentalize** (also **-ise**) verb.
– ORIGIN late Middle English: from Old French, or from Latin *occidentalis*, from *occident-* 'going down' (see **OCCIDENT**).

occipital bone /ɒkˈsɪpɪt(ə)l/ ▶ **noun** Anatomy the bone which forms the back and base of the skull and encircles the spinal cord.

occipital condyle ▶ **noun** Anatomy each of two rounded knobs at the base of the skull which articulate with the first vertebra.

occipital lobe ▶ **noun** Anatomy the rearmost lobe in each cerebral hemisphere of the brain.

occipito- /ɒkˈsɪpɪtəʊ/ ▶ **combining form** relating to the occipital lobe or the occipital bone: *occipitotemporal.*
– ORIGIN from medieval Latin *occipitalis*, from Latin *caput, capit-* 'head'.

occipitotemporal /ɒkˌsɪpɪtə(ʊ)ˈtɛmp(ə)r(ə)l/ ▶ **adjective** Anatomy of or relating to the occipital and temporal bones.

occiput /ˈɒksɪpʌt/ ▶ **noun** Anatomy the back of the head.
– DERIVATIVES **occipital** adjective.
– ORIGIN late Middle English: from Latin *occiput*, from *ob-* 'against' + *caput* 'head'.

Occitan /ˈɒksɪt(ə)n/ ▶ **noun** [mass noun] the medieval or modern language of Languedoc, including literary Provençal of the 12th–14th centuries.
▶ **adjective** of or relating to this language.
– DERIVATIVES **Occitanian** noun & adjective.
– ORIGIN French (see also **LANGUE D'OC**).

occlude /əˈkluːd/ ▶ **verb** formal or technical **1** [with obj.] stop, close up, or obstruct (an opening, orifice, or passage): *thick make-up can occlude the pores.*
■ shut (something) in: *they were occluding the waterfront with a wall of buildings.* ■ technical cover (an eye) to prevent its use: *it is placed at eye level with one eye occluded.* ■ Chemistry (of a solid) absorb and retain (a gas or impurity).
2 [no obj.] (of a tooth) come into contact with another tooth in the opposite jaw.
– ORIGIN late 16th cent.: from Latin *occludere* 'shut up'.

occluded front ▶ **noun** Meteorology a composite front produced by occlusion.

occlusal ▶ **adjective** Dentistry of, relating to, or involved in the occlusion of teeth.
■ denoting a surface of a tooth that comes into contact with a tooth in the other jaw.

occlusion ▶ **noun** [mass noun] **1** Medicine the blockage or closing of a blood vessel or hollow organ.
2 [count noun] Meteorology a process by which the cold front of a rotating low-pressure system catches up the warm front, so that the warm air between them is forced upwards off the earth's surface between wedges of cold air.
■ [count noun] an occluded front.
3 Dentistry the position of the teeth when the jaws are closed.
– DERIVATIVES **occlusive** adjective.
– ORIGIN mid 17th cent.: from Latin *occlus-* 'shut up' (from the verb *occludere*) + **-ION**.

occult /ɒˈkʌlt, ˈɒkʌlt/ ▶ **noun** (**the occult**) supernatural, mystical, or magical beliefs, practices, or phenomena: *a secret society to study alchemy and the occult.*
▶ **adjective 1** of, involving, or relating to supernatural, mystical, or magical powers or phenomena: *an occult ceremony.*
■ beyond the range of ordinary knowledge or experience; mysterious: *a weird occult sensation of having experienced the identical situation before.* ■ communicated only to the initiated; esoteric: *the typically occult language of the time.*
2 Medicine (of a disease or process) not accompanied by readily discernible signs or symptoms.
■ (of blood) abnormally present, e.g. in faeces, but detectable only chemically or microscopically.
▶ **verb** /ɒˈkʌlt/ [with obj.] cut off from view by interposing something: *a wooden screen designed to occult the competitors.*
■ Astronomy (of a celestial body) conceal (an apparently smaller body) from view by passing or being in front of it.
– DERIVATIVES **occultation** noun, **occultism** noun, **occultist** noun, **occultly** adverb, **occultness** noun.
– ORIGIN late 15th cent. (as a verb): from Latin *occultare* 'secrete', frequentative of *occulere* 'conceal', based on *celare* 'to hide'; the adjective and noun from *occult-* 'covered over', from the verb *occulere.*

occulting light ▶ **noun** a light in a lighthouse or buoy which shines for a longer period than that for which it is cut off.

occupance ▶ **noun** another term for **OCCUPANCY**.
■ Geography the inhabiting and modification of an area by humans.
– ORIGIN early 19th cent.: from **OCCUPANT** + **-ANCE**.

occupancy ▶ **noun** [mass noun] the action or fact of occupying a place: *the palace proved unready for occupancy.*
■ the proportion of accommodation occupied or used, typically in a hotel: *the 70 per cent occupancy needed to give a profit.*

occupant ▶ **noun** a person who resides or is present in a house, vehicle, seat, place, etc. at a given time.
■ the holder of a position or office: *the first occupant of the Chair of Botany.* ■ Law a person holding property, especially land, in actual possession.
– ORIGIN late 16th cent. (in the legal sense 'person who establishes a title'): from French, or from Latin *occupant-* 'seizing', from the verb *occupare.*

occupation ▶ **noun 1** a job or profession: *people in professional occupations.*
■ a way of spending time: *a game of cards is a pretty harmless occupation.*
2 [mass noun] the action, state, or period of occupying or being occupied by military force: *the Roman* ***occupation of*** *Britain* | *crimes committed during the Nazi occupation.*
■ the action of entering and taking control of a building: *the workers remained* ***in occupation*** *until 16 October.*
3 [mass noun] the action or fact of living in or using a building or other place: *a property suitable for occupation by older people.*
▶ **adjective** Brit. for the sole use of the occupiers of the land concerned.
– ORIGIN Middle English: via Old French from Latin *occupatio(n-)*, from the verb *occupare* (see **OCCUPY**). Sense 2 dates from the mid 16th cent.

occupational ▶ **adjective** of or relating to a job or profession: *an occupational pension scheme.*
– DERIVATIVES **occupationally** adverb.

occupational hazard (also **occupational risk**) ▶ **noun** a risk accepted as a consequence of a particular occupation.

occupational psychology ▶ **noun** [mass noun] the study of human behaviour at work, including methods of selecting personnel, improving productivity, and coping with stress.
– DERIVATIVES **occupational psychologist** noun.

occupational therapy ▶ **noun** [mass noun] activity encouraged in the ill or infirm to maximize their capabilities, independence, or recuperation from physical or mental illness.
– DERIVATIVES **occupational therapist** noun.

occupier ▶ **noun 1** Brit. a person or company residing in or using a property as its owner or tenant, or (illegally) as a squatter.
2 a member of a group that takes possession of a country by force.

occupy ▶ **verb** (**-ies**, **-ied**) [with obj.] **1** reside or have one's place of business in (a building): *the rented flat she occupies in Hampstead.*
■ fill or take up (a space or time): *two long windows occupied almost the whole of the end wall.* ■ be situated in or at (a place or position in a system or hierarchy): *the Bank of England occupies a central position in the UK financial system.* ■ hold (a position or job).
2 (often **be occupied with/in**) fill or preoccupy (the mind or thoughts): *her mind was occupied with alarming questions.*
■ keep (someone) busy and active: *Sarah* ***occupied herself*** *taking the coffee cups over to the sink* | [as adj. **occupied**] *tasks which kept her occupied for the remainder of the afternoon.*
3 take control of (a place, especially a country) by military conquest or settlement: *Syria was occupied by France under a League of Nations mandate.*
■ enter, take control of, and stay in (a building) illegally and often forcibly, especially as a form of protest: *the workers occupied the factory.*
– ORIGIN Middle English: formed irregularly from Old French *occuper*, from Latin *occupare* 'seize'. A now obsolete vulgar sense 'have sexual relations with' seems to have led to the general avoidance of the word in the 17th and most of the 18th cent.

occur ▶ **verb** (**occurred**, **occurring**) [no obj., with adverbial] happen; take place: *the accident occurred at about 3.30p.m.*
■ exist or be found to be present in a place or under a particular set of conditions: *radon occurs naturally in rocks such as granite.* ■ (**occur to**) (of a thought or idea) come into the mind of (someone): [with clause] *it occurred to him that he hadn't eaten.*
– ORIGIN late 15th cent.: from Latin *occurrere* 'go to meet, present itself', from *ob-* 'against' + *currere* 'to run'.

occurrence /əˈkʌr(ə)ns/ ▶ **noun** an incident or event: *vandalism used to be a rare occurrence.*
■ [mass noun] the fact or frequency of something happening: *the occurrence of cancer increases with age.* ■ [mass noun] the fact of something existing or being found in a place or under a particular set of conditions: *the occurrence of natural gas fields.*
– ORIGIN mid 16th cent.: probably from the plural of archaic *occurrent*, in the same sense, via French from Latin *occurrent-* 'befalling', from the verb *occurrere* (see **OCCUR**).

occurrent ▶ **adjective** actually occurring or observable, not potential or hypothetical.
– ORIGIN late 15th cent.: from French, or from Latin *occurrent-* 'befalling', from the verb *occurrere.*

OCD ▶ **abbreviation for** obsessive–compulsive disorder.

ocean ▶ **noun** a very large expanse of sea, in particular, each of the main areas into which the sea is divided geographically: *the Atlantic Ocean.*
■ (usu. **the ocean**) the sea: [as modifier] *the ocean floor.* ■ (**an ocean of/oceans of**) informal a very large expanse or quantity: *she had oceans of energy.*
– DERIVATIVES **oceanward** (also **-wards**) adverb & adjective.
– ORIGIN Middle English: from Old French *occean*, via Latin from Greek *ōkeanos* 'great stream encircling the earth's disc'. 'The ocean' originally denoted the whole body of water regarded as encompassing the earth's single land mass.

oceanarium /ˌəʊʃəˈnɛːrɪəm/ ▶ **noun** (pl.

O

oceanariums or **oceanaria** /-rɪə/) a large seawater aquarium in which marine animals are kept for study and public entertainment.
– ORIGIN 1940s: from **OCEAN**, on the pattern of *aquarium.*·

ocean basin ▶ noun a depression of the earth's surface in which an ocean lies.

ocean-going ▶ adjective (of a ship) designed to cross oceans.

Oceania /ˌəʊsɪˈɑːnɪə, -ʃɪ-/ the islands of the Pacific Ocean and adjacent seas.
– DERIVATIVES **Oceanian** adjective & noun.
– ORIGIN modern Latin, from French *Océanie*.

oceanic /ˌəʊsɪˈanɪk, -ʃɪ-/ ▶ adjective **1** of or relating to the ocean: *oceanic atolls.*
■ of or inhabiting the part of the ocean beyond the edge of a continental shelf: *stocks of oceanic fish.* ■ (of a climate) governed by the proximity of the sea. ■ figurative of enormous size or extent; huge; vast: *an oceanic failure.*
2 (**Oceanic**) of or relating to Oceania: *a gallery specializing in Oceanic art.*

oceanic bonito ▶ noun another term for **SKIPJACK** (in sense 1).

oceanic crust ▶ noun Geology the relatively thin part of the earth's crust which underlies the ocean basins. It is geologically young compared with the continental crust and consists of basaltic rock overlain by sediments.

Oceanid /əʊˈsiːənɪd, -ʃʊˈ(ə)nɪd/ ▶ noun (pl. **Oceanids** or **Oceanides** /ˌəʊsɪˈanɪdiːz, ˌəʊʃɪ-/) Greek Mythology a sea nymph.
– ORIGIN from French *Océanide*, from Greek *ōkeanis, ōkeanid-*.

Ocean Island another name for **BANABA**.

oceanography ▶ noun [mass noun] the branch of science that deals with the physical and biological properties and phenomena of the sea.
– DERIVATIVES **oceanographer** noun, **oceanographic** adjective, **oceanographical** adjective.

oceanology ▶ noun another term for **OCEANOGRAPHY**.
■ the branch of technology and economics dealing with human use of the sea.
– DERIVATIVES **oceanological** adjective, **oceanologist** noun.

Ocean State informal name for **RHODE ISLAND**.

ocean trench ▶ noun see **TRENCH**.

Oceanus /əʊˈsiːənəs, ˌəʊsɪˈeɪn-, ˌəʊsɪˈɑːn-/ Greek Mythology the son of Uranus (Heaven) and Gaia (Earth), the personification of the great river believed to encircle the whole world.

ocellated /ˈɒsɪleɪtɪd/ ▶ adjective (of an animal, or its plumage or body surface) having eye-like markings.

ocellus /əˈsɛləs/ ▶ noun (pl. **ocelli** /-lʌɪ, -liː/) Zoology
1 another term for **SIMPLE EYE**.
2 another term for **EYESPOT** (in senses 1 and 2).
– DERIVATIVES **ocellar** adjective.
– ORIGIN early 19th cent.: from Latin, diminutive of *oculus* 'eye'.

ocelot /ˈɒsɪlɒt, ˈəʊs-/ ▶ noun a medium-sized wild cat that has an orange-yellow coat marked with black stripes and spots, native to South and Central America.
● *Felis pardalis*, family Felidae.
■ [mass noun] the fur of the ocelot.
– ORIGIN late 18th cent.: from French, from Nahuatl *tlatlocelotl*, literally 'field tiger'.

och /ɒx, ɒx/ ▶ exclamation Scottish & Irish used to express a range of emotions, typically surprise, regret, or disbelief: *Och, you're kidding.*

oche /ˈɒki/ (also **hockey**) ▶ noun Brit. the line behind which darts players stand when throwing.
– ORIGIN mid 20th cent.: perhaps related to Old French *ocher* 'cut a deep notch in'.

ocher ▶ noun US spelling of **OCHRE**.

ochlocracy /ɒkˈlɒkrəsi/ ▶ noun [mass noun] government by the populace; mob rule.
– DERIVATIVES **ochlocrat** noun, **ochlocratic** adjective.
– ORIGIN late 16th cent.: via French from Greek *okhlokratia*, from *okhlos* 'mob' + *-kratia* 'power'.

ochone /əʊˈhəʊn, ɒˈxəʊn/ (also **ohone**) ▶ exclamation Irish & Scottish poetic/literary used to express regret or sorrow.
– ORIGIN from Scottish Gaelic *ochòin*, Irish *ochón*.

ochre /ˈəʊkə/ (US also **ocher**) ▶ noun [mass noun] an earthy pigment containing ferric oxide, typically

with clay, varying from light yellow to brown or red.
■ a pale brownish yellow colour.
– DERIVATIVES **ochreish** adjective, **ochreous** /ˈəʊkrɪəs/ adjective, **ochroid** adjective, **ochrous** adjective, **ochry** adjective.
– ORIGIN Middle English: from Old French *ocre*, via Latin from Greek *ōkhra* 'yellow ochre'.

ochrea /ˈɒkrɪə/ ▶ noun (pl. **ochreas** or **ochreae** /ˈɒkriiː/) Botany a dry sheath round a stem formed by the cohesion of two or more stipules, characteristic of the dock family.
– ORIGIN mid 19th cent.: from Latin, literally 'protective legging'.

-ock ▶ suffix forming nouns originally with diminutive sense: *haddock* | *pollock.*
■ also occasionally forming words from other sources: *bannock* | *hassock.*
– ORIGIN Old English *-uc, -oc*.

ocker informal ▶ noun Austral. a boorish or aggressive Australian.
▶ adjective denoting or characteristic of such a man: *an ocker sports writer.*
– ORIGIN alteration of *Oscar*, popularized by the name of a character in an Australian television series (1965–68).

Ockham's razor variant spelling of **OCCAM'S RAZOR**.

Ockham, William of see **WILLIAM OF OCCAM**.

o'clock ▶ adverb used to specify the hour when telling the time: *the gates will open at eight o'clock.*

ocnophil /ˈɒknə(ʊ)fɪl/ ▶ noun Psychology a personality type characterized by the avoidance of dangerous or unfamiliar situations and reliance on external objects or other people for security. Often contrasted with **PHILOBAT**.
– ORIGIN mid 20th cent.: from Greek *oknein* 'hesitate' + **-PHIL**.

O'Connell, Daniel (1775–1847), Irish nationalist leader and social reformer; known as **the Liberator**. His election to Parliament in 1828 forced the British government to grant Catholic Emancipation in order to enable him to take his seat in the House of Commons. In 1839 he established the Repeal Association to abolish the union with Britain.

O'Connor, (Mary) Flannery (1925–64), American novelist and short-story writer. Notable novels: *Wise Blood* (1952) and *The Violent Bear It Away* (1960).

ocotillo /ˌɒkəˈtiːjəʊ, -ˈteɪjəʊ/ ▶ noun (pl. **-os**) chiefly US a spiny scarlet-flowered desert shrub of the south-western US and Mexico, which is sometimes planted as a spiny hedge.
● *Fouquieria splendens*, family Fouquieriaceae.
– ORIGIN mid 19th cent.: via American Spanish (diminutive form) from Nahuatl *ocotl* 'torch'.

OCR ▶ abbreviation for optical character recognition.

Oct. ▶ abbreviation for October.

oct. ▶ abbreviation for octavo.

oct- ▶ combining form variant spelling of **OCTA-** and **OCTO-** assimilated before a vowel (as in *octennial*).

octa- (also **oct-** before a vowel) ▶ combining form eight; having eight: *octahedron.*
– ORIGIN from Greek *oktō* 'eight'.

octad /ˈɒktad/ ▶ noun technical a group or set of eight.
– ORIGIN mid 19th cent.: via late Latin from Greek *oktas, oktad-*, from *oktō* 'eight'.

octagon ▶ noun a plane figure with eight straight sides and eight angles.
■ an object or building with a plan or cross section of this shape.
– DERIVATIVES **octagonal** adjective, **octagonally** adverb.
– ORIGIN late 16th cent.: via Latin from Greek *oktagōnos* 'eight-angled'.

octahedron /ˌɒktəˈhiːdrən, -ˈhɛd-/ ▶ noun (pl. **octahedra** /-drə/ or **octahedrons**) a three-dimensional shape having eight plane faces, especially a regular solid figure with eight equal triangular faces.
■ a body, especially a crystal, in the form of a regular octahedron.
– DERIVATIVES **octahedral** adjective.
– ORIGIN late 16th cent.: from Greek *oktaedron*, neuter (used as a noun) of *oktaedros* 'eight-faced'.

octal /ˈɒkt(ə)l/ ▶ adjective relating to or using a system of numerical notation that has 8 rather than 10 as a base.
▶ noun [mass noun] the octal system; octal notation.

octamerous /ɒkˈtam(ə)rəs/ ▶ adjective Botany & Zoology having parts arranged in groups of eight.
■ consisting of eight joints or parts.

octameter /ɒkˈtamɪtə/ ▶ noun Prosody a line of verse consisting of eight metrical feet.

octane ▶ noun [mass noun] Chemistry a colourless flammable hydrocarbon of the alkane series, present in petroleum spirit.
● Chem. formula: C_8H_{18}; many isomers, especially the straight-chain isomer (*n*-**octane**). See also **ISOOCTANE**.
– ORIGIN late 19th cent.: from **OCTO-** 'eight' (denoting eight carbon atoms) + **-ANE**[2].

octane number (also **octane rating**) ▶ noun a figure indicating the anti-knock properties of a fuel, based on a comparison with a mixture of isooctane and heptane.

octangular ▶ adjective having eight angles.

Octans /ˈɒktanz/ Astronomy a faint southern constellation (the Octant), containing the south celestial pole.
■ [as genitive **Octantis** /ɒkˈtantɪs/] used with preceding letter or numeral to designate a star in this constellation: *the star Delta Octantis.*
– ORIGIN Latin.

octant /ˈɒkt(ə)nt/ ▶ noun an arc of a circle equal to one eighth of its circumference, or the area enclosed by such an arc with two radii at the circle.
■ each of eight parts into which a space or solid body is divided by three planes which intersect (especially at right angles) at a single point. ■ an obsolete instrument in the form of a graduated eighth of a circle, used in astronomy and navigation.
– ORIGIN late 17th cent.: from Latin *octans, octant-* 'half-quadrant', from *octo* 'eight'.

octastyle ▶ adjective (of a building or portico) having eight columns at the end or in front.
▶ noun a portico or building in this style.
– ORIGIN early 18th cent.: via Latin from Greek *oktastulos*, from *okta-* 'eight' + *stulos* 'pillar'.

octavalent /ˌɒktəˈveɪl(ə)nt/ ▶ adjective Chemistry having a valency of eight.

octave /ˈɒktɪv/ ▶ noun **1** Music a series of eight notes occupying the interval between (and including) two notes, one having twice or half the frequency of vibration of the other.
■ the interval between these two notes. ■ each of the two notes at the extremes of this interval. ■ these two notes sounding together.
2 a group or stanza of eight lines; an octet.
3 the seventh day after a Church festival.
■ a period of eight days beginning with the day of such a festival.
4 Fencing the last of eight parrying positions.
5 Brit. a wine cask holding an eighth of a pipe.
– PHRASES **law of octaves** Chemistry, historical see **NEWLANDS**.
– ORIGIN Middle English (in sense 3): via Old French from Latin *octava dies* 'eighth day'.

octave coupler ▶ noun another term for **COUPLER**.

Octavian /ɒkˈteɪvɪən/ see **AUGUSTUS**.

octavo /ɒkˈtɑːvəʊ, -ˈteɪ-/ (abbrev.: **8vo**) ▶ noun (pl. **-os**) a size of book page that results from folding each printed sheet into eight leaves (sixteen pages).
■ a book of this size.
– ORIGIN late 16th cent.: from Latin *in octavo* 'in an eighth', from *octavus* 'eighth'.

octennial ▶ adjective rare recurring every eight years.
■ lasting for or relating to a period of eight years.
– ORIGIN mid 17th cent.: from late Latin *octennium* 'period of eight years' + **-AL**.

octet /ɒkˈtɛt/ ▶ noun a group of eight people or things, in particular:
■ a group of eight musicians. ■ a musical composition for eight voices or instruments. ■ the first eight lines of a sonnet. ■ Chemistry a stable group of eight electrons occupying a single shell in an atom.
– ORIGIN mid 19th cent.: from Italian *ottetto* or German *Oktett*, on the pattern of *duet* and *quartet*.

octo- (also **oct-** before a vowel) ▶ combining form eight; having eight: *octosyllabic.*
– ORIGIN from Latin *octo* or Greek *oktō* 'eight'.

October ▶ noun the tenth month of the year, in the northern hemisphere usually considered the second month of autumn: *the project started in October* | *one of the wettest Octobers on record.*
– ORIGIN late Old English, from Latin, from *octo*

'eight' (being originally the eighth month of the Roman year).

October Revolution ▶ noun see **RUSSIAN REVOLUTION**.

October War Arab name for **YOM KIPPUR WAR**.

Octobrist /ɒkˈtəʊbrɪst/ ▶ noun historical a member of the moderate party in the Russian Duma, which supported Tsar Nicholas II's reforming manifesto of 30 October 1905.
– ORIGIN suggested by Russian *oktyabrist*.

octocentenary ▶ noun (pl. **-ies**) the eight-hundredth anniversary of a significant event.

octodecimo /ˌɒktəʊˈdɛsɪməʊ/ ▶ noun (pl. **-os**) a size of book page resulting from folding each printed sheet into eighteen leaves (36 pages).
■ a book of this size.
– ORIGIN mid 19th cent.: from Latin *in octodecimo* 'in an eighteenth', from *octodecimus* 'eighteenth'.

octofoil ▶ adjective having or consisting of eight leaves or lobes.
▶ noun an octofoil ornamental or heraldic figure.

octogenarian /ˌɒktə(ʊ)dʒɪˈnɛːrɪən/ ▶ noun a person who is between 80 and 89 years old.
– ORIGIN early 19th cent.: from Latin *octogenarius* (based on *octoginta* 'eighty') + **-AN**.

octonary /ˈɒktə(ʊ)n(ə)ri/ ▶ adjective rare relating to or based on the number eight.

octopamine /ɒkˈtəʊpəmiːn/ ▶ noun [mass noun] Biochemistry a compound which can accumulate in nerves as a result of the use of monoamine oxidase inhibitors and cause a rise in blood pressure.
• An amine related to noradrenaline; chem. formula: $HOC_6H_4CHOHCH_2NH_2$.
– ORIGIN 1940s: from **OCTOPUS** (from which it was first extracted) + **AMINE**.

Octopoda /ˌɒktəˈpəʊdə/ Zoology an order of cephalopod molluscs that comprises the octopuses.
– DERIVATIVES **octopod** noun.
– ORIGIN modern Latin (plural), from Greek *oktōpous*, *oktōpod-*, from *oktō* 'eight' + *pous, pod-* 'foot'.

octopus ▶ noun (pl. **octopuses**) **1** a cephalopod mollusc with eight sucker-bearing arms, a soft sac-like body, strong beak-like jaws, and no internal shell.
• Order Octopoda, class Cephalopoda: *Octopus* and other genera.
2 figurative an organization or system perceived to have far-reaching and typically harmful effects: *the octopus of destructive politics*.
– DERIVATIVES **octopoid** adjective.
– ORIGIN mid 18th cent.: from Greek *oktōpous* (see also **OCTOPODA**).

USAGE The standard plural in English of **octopus** is **octopuses**. However, the word **octopus** comes from Greek and the Greek plural form **octopodes** is still occasionally used. The plural form **octopi**, formed according to rules for Latin plurals, is incorrect.

octoroon /ˌɒktəˈruːn/ ▶ noun archaic a person whose parents are a quadroon and a white person and who is therefore one-eighth black by descent.
– ORIGIN mid 19th cent.: from **OCTO-** 'eight', on the pattern of *quadroon*.

octosyllabic ▶ adjective having or written in lines that have eight syllables.
▶ noun a line of verse that has eight syllables.

octosyllable ▶ noun a word or line of verse with eight syllables.

octothorp /ˈɒktə(ʊ)θɔːp/ (also **octothorpe**) ▶ noun chiefly N. Amer. another term for the symbol #.
– ORIGIN 1970s: of uncertain origin; probably from **OCTO-** (referring to the eight points on the symbol) + the surname *Thorpe*.

octroi /ˈɒktrwɑː/ ▶ noun a duty levied in some countries on various goods entering a town or city.
– ORIGIN late 16th cent. (in the sense 'concession', especially one giving an exclusive right of trade): from French *octroyer* 'to grant', based on medieval Latin *auctorizare* (see **AUTHORIZE**). Current senses date from the early 18th cent.

octuple /ˈɒktjʊp(ə)l, ɒkˈtjuːp(ə)l/ ▶ adjective [attrib.] consisting of eight parts or things.
■ eight times as many or as much.
▶ verb make or become eight times as numerous or as large.
– ORIGIN early 17th cent.: from French *octuple* or Latin *octuplus* (both adjectives), from *octo* 'eight' + *-plus* (as in *duplus* 'double').

octuplet ▶ noun (usu. **octuplets**) each of eight children born at one birth.

octyl /ˈɒktʌɪl, -tɪl/ ▶ noun [as modifier] Chemistry of or denoting an alkyl radical $—C_8H_{17}$, derived from octane.

ocular /ˈɒkjʊlə/ ▶ adjective [attrib.] Medicine of or connected with the eyes or vision: *ocular trauma*.
▶ noun another term for **EYEPIECE**.
– DERIVATIVES **ocularly** adverb.
– ORIGIN late 16th cent.: from late Latin *ocularis*, from Latin *oculus* 'eye'.

ocular dominance ▶ noun the priority of one eye over the other as regards preference of use or acuity of vision.

ocularist ▶ noun a person who makes artificial eyes.
– ORIGIN mid 19th cent.: from French *oculariste*, from late Latin *ocularis* (see **OCULAR**).

oculist /ˈɒkjʊlɪst/ ▶ noun a person who specializes in the medical treatment of diseases or defects of the eye; an ophthalmologist.
– ORIGIN late 16th cent.: from French *oculiste*, from Latin *oculus* 'eye'.

oculo- /ˈɒkjʊləʊ/ ▶ combining form relating to the eye or the sense of vision: *oculomotor*.
– ORIGIN from Latin *oculus* 'eye'.

oculomotor /ˈɒkjʊlə(ʊ)ˌməʊtə/ ▶ adjective of or relating to the motion of the eye.

oculomotor nerve ▶ noun Anatomy each of the third pair of cranial nerves, supplying most of the muscles around and within the eyeballs.

oculus /ˈɒkjʊləs/ ▶ noun (pl. **oculi** /-lʌɪ, -liː/) Architecture a round or eye-like opening or design, in particular:
■ a circular window. ■ the central boss of a volute. ■ an opening at the apex of a dome.
– ORIGIN mid 19th cent.: from Latin, literally 'eye'.

OD[1] ▶ abbreviation for ordnance datum.

OD[2] informal ▶ verb (**OD's, OD'd, OD'ing**) [no obj.] take an overdose of a drug: *Spike had OD'd on barbiturates*.
■ humorous have too much of something: *I almost OD'd on mushroom salad*.
▶ noun an overdose of a narcotic drug.

od[1] ▶ noun historical a hypothetical power once thought to pervade nature and account for various scientific phenomena.
– ORIGIN mid 19th cent.: arbitrary term coined in German by Baron von Reichenbach (1788–1869), German scientist.

od[2] ▶ noun an archaic euphemism for God, used in exclamations: *ods blood!*

odalisque /ˈəʊd(ə)lɪsk/ ▶ noun historical a female slave or concubine in a harem, especially one in the seraglio of the Sultan of Turkey.
■ an exotic, sexually attractive woman.
– ORIGIN late 17th cent.: from French, from Turkish *odalık*, from *oda* 'chamber' + *lık* 'function'.

odd ▶ adjective **1** different to what is usual or expected; strange: *the neighbours thought him very odd* | [with clause] *it's odd that she didn't recognize me*.
2 (of whole numbers such as 3 and 5) having one left over as a remainder when divided by two.
■ (of things numbered consecutively) represented or indicated by such a number: *he has come to us every odd year since 1981*. ■ [postpositive] [in combination] in the region of or somewhat more than a particular number or quantity: *she looked younger than her fifty-odd years*. ■ denoting a single goal by which one side defeats another, especially where each side scores at least once: *they lost a close-fought game by the odd goal in five*.
3 [attrib.] happening or occurring infrequently and irregularly; occasional: *we have the odd drink together* | *neither did she want a secret affair, snatching odd moments together*.
■ spare; unoccupied: *when you've got an odd five minutes, could I have a word?*
4 separated from a usual pair or set and therefore out of place or mismatched: *he's wearing odd socks*.
– PHRASES **odd one** (or **man**) **out** a person or thing differing from all other members of a particular group or set in some way.
– DERIVATIVES **oddish** adjective (only in sense 1), **oddly** adverb (only in sense 1) [sentence adverb] *oddly enough, I didn't feel nervous* | [as submodifier] *she felt oddly guilty*, **oddness** noun.
– ORIGIN Middle English (in sense 2): from Old Norse *odda-*, found in combinations such as *odda-mathr* 'third or odd man', from *oddi* 'angle'.

oddball informal ▶ noun a strange or eccentric person.
▶ adjective strange; bizarre: *oddball training methods*.

Oddfellow ▶ noun (usu. **Oddfellows**) a member of a fraternity similar to the Freemasons.

oddity ▶ noun (pl. **-ies**) a strange or peculiar person, thing, or trait: *she was regarded as a bit of an oddity*.
■ [mass noun] the quality of being strange or peculiar: *realizing the* **oddity** *of the remark, he retracted it*.

odd job ▶ noun (usu. **odd jobs**) a casual or isolated piece of work, especially one of a routine domestic or manual nature.
– DERIVATIVES **odd-jobbing** noun.

odd-job man (also **odd-jobber**) ▶ noun a man who does odd jobs.

odd lot ▶ noun an incomplete set or random mixture of things.
■ Finance, US a transaction involving an unusually small number of shares.

oddment ▶ noun (usu. **oddments**) an item or piece of something, typically one left over from a larger piece or set: *a quilt made from oddments of silk*.

odd pricing ▶ noun [mass noun] the action of setting the price of something to end in an odd number such as £9.99 in order to make it appear cheaper.

odds ▶ plural noun the ratio between the amounts staked by the parties to a bet, based on the expected probability either way: *with Nicer starting* **at odds of** *8–1* | *it is possible for the race to be won* **at very long odds**.
■ (usu. **the odds**) the chances or likelihood of something happening or being the case: **the odds are that** *he is no longer alive* | **the odds against** *this ever happening are high*. ■ (usu. **the odds**) the balance of advantage; superiority in strength, power, or resources: *she clung to the lead* **against all the odds** | **the odds were** *overwhelmingly* **in favour of** *the banks rather than the customer*.
– PHRASES **at odds** in conflict or at variance: *his behaviour is* **at odds with** *the interests of the company*. **by all odds** N. Amer. certainly. **it makes no odds** informal, chiefly Brit. it does not matter. [ORIGIN: from an earlier use of *odds* in the sense 'difference in advantage or effect'.] **lay** (or **give**) **odds** offer a bet with odds favourable to the other better. ■ figurative be very sure about something: *I'd lay odds that the person responsible is an insider*. **over the odds** Brit. above what is generally considered acceptable, especially for a price: *you could be paying over the odds for perfume*. **take odds** offer a bet with odds unfavourable to the other better. **what's the odds?** informal what does it matter? [ORIGIN: from an earlier sense of *odds*; compare with *it makes no odds*.]
– ORIGIN early 16th cent.: apparently the plural of the obsolete noun *odd* 'odd number or odd person'.

odds and ends ▶ plural noun miscellaneous articles or remnants.

odds and sods ▶ plural noun informal, chiefly Brit. miscellaneous people or articles.

odds-on ▶ adjective (especially of a horse) rated at evens or less to win: *the odds-on favourite*.
■ figurative very likely to happen or succeed: *it seemed odds-on that Jones would add another century to his 157*.

odd-toed ungulate ▶ noun a hoofed mammal of an order which includes horses, rhinoceroses, and tapirs. Mammals of this group have either one or three toes on each foot. Compare with **EVEN-TOED UNGULATE**.
• Order Perissodactyla: three families.

ode ▶ noun a lyric poem, typically one in the form of an address to a particular subject, written in varied or irregular metre.
■ a classical poem of a kind originally meant to be sung.
– ORIGIN late 16th cent.: from French, from late Latin *oda*, from Greek *ōidē*, Attic form of *aoidē* 'song', from *aeidein* 'sing'.

-ode[1] ▶ combining form of the nature of a specified thing: *geode*.
– ORIGIN from Greek adjectival ending *-ōdēs*.

-ode[2] ▶ combining form in names of electrodes, or devices having them: *diode*.
– ORIGIN from Greek *hodos* 'way'.

Odense /ˈəʊd(ə)nsə/ a port in eastern Denmark, on the island of Fyn; pop. 177,640 (1991).

odeon /ˈəʊdɪən/ ▶ noun **1** variant spelling of **ODEUM**.
2 (**Odeon**) a cinema. [ORIGIN: from the name of a chain built in the 1930s.]

– ORIGIN from Greek *ōideion*, from *ōidē* 'song' (see **ODE**).

Oder /ˈəʊdə/ a river of central Europe which rises in the mountains in the west of the Czech Republic and flows northwards through western Poland to meet the River Neisse, then continues northwards forming the northern part of the border between Poland and Germany before flowing into the Baltic Sea. Czech and Polish name **ODRA**.

Odessa /əʊˈdɛsə/ a city and port on the south coast of Ukraine, on the Black Sea; pop. 1,106,000 (1990). Ukrainian name **ODESA** /ɔˈdɛsa/.

Odets /əʊˈdɛts/, Clifford (1906–63), American dramatist. He was a founder member in 1931 of the avant-garde Group Theatre, which staged his best-known play, *Waiting for Lefty* (1935).

odeum /ˈəʊdɪəm/ (also **odeon** /ˈəʊdɪən/) ▶ noun (pl. **odeums** or **odea** /-dɪə/) (especially in ancient Greece or Rome) a building used for musical performances.
– ORIGIN from French *odéum* or Latin *odeum*, from Greek *ōideion* (see **ODE**).

odiferous /əʊˈdɪf(ə)rəs/ ▶ adjective variant spelling of **ODORIFEROUS**.

Odin /ˈəʊdɪn/ (also **Woden** or **Wotan**) Scandinavian Mythology the supreme god and creator, god of victory and the dead. Wednesday is named after him.

odious ▶ adjective extremely unpleasant; repulsive.
– DERIVATIVES **odiously** adverb, **odiousness** noun.
– ORIGIN late Middle English: from Old French *odieus*, from Latin *odiosus*, from *odium* 'hatred'.

odium /ˈəʊdɪəm/ ▶ noun [mass noun] general or widespread hatred or disgust incurred by someone as a result of their actions.
– ORIGIN early 17th cent.: from Latin, 'hatred', from the verb stem *od-* 'hate'.

odometer /əʊˈdɒmɪtə/ ▶ noun chiefly US an instrument for measuring the distance travelled by a wheeled vehicle.
– ORIGIN late 18th cent.: from French *odomètre*, from Greek *hodos* 'way' + **-METER**.

Odonata /ˌəʊdəˈnɑːtə/ Entomology an order of predatory insects that comprises the dragonflies and damselflies. They have long slender bodies, two pairs of membranous wings, large compound eyes, and aquatic larvae.
■ [as plural noun **odonata**] insects of this order; dragonflies and damselflies.
– DERIVATIVES **odonate** noun & adjective.
– ORIGIN modern Latin (plural), formed irregularly from Greek *odōn* (variant of *odous*) 'tooth', with reference to the insect's mandibles.

odontalgia /ˌɒdɒnˈtaldʒə/ ▶ noun [mass noun] technical toothache.
– DERIVATIVES **odontalgic** adjective.

odonto- ▶ combining form relating to a tooth or teeth: *odontology* | *odontophore*.
– ORIGIN from Greek *odous, odont-* 'tooth'.

odontoblast /ɒˈdɒntə(ʊ)blɑːst/ ▶ noun Anatomy a cell in the pulp of a tooth that produces dentine.

Odontoceti /əʊˌdɒntə(ʊ)ˈsiːtiː/ Zoology a division of the whales that comprises the toothed whales.
● Suborder Odontoceti, order Cetacea.
– DERIVATIVES **odontocete** noun & adjective.
– ORIGIN modern Latin (plural), from Greek *odous, odont-* 'tooth' + *cēti* 'of a whale' (genitive of *cetus*, from Greek *kētos* 'whale').

odontoid /əˈ(ʊ)ɒntɔɪd/ (also **odontoid process**) ▶ noun Anatomy a projection from the second cervical vertebra (axis) on which the first (atlas) can pivot: [as modifier] *the anterior odontoid joint*.
– ORIGIN early 19th cent.: from Greek *odontoeidēs*, from *odous, odont-* 'tooth' + *eidos* 'form'.

odontology /ˌɒdɒnˈtɒlədʒi, ˌəʊdɒn-/ ▶ noun [mass noun] the scientific study of the structure and diseases of teeth.
– DERIVATIVES **odontological** adjective, **odontologist** noun.

odontophore /əˈdɒntə(ʊ)fɔː/ ▶ noun Zoology a cartilaginous projection in the mouth of a mollusc, on which the radula is supported.
– DERIVATIVES **odontophoral** adjective.

odor ▶ noun US spelling of **ODOUR**.

odorant ▶ noun a substance giving off a smell, especially one used to give a particular scent or odour to a product.

– ORIGIN late Middle English (as an adjective in the sense 'odorous'): from Old French, present participle of *odorer*, from Latin *odorare* 'give an odour to'. The current sense dates from the 1940s.

odoriferous /ˌəʊdəˈrɪf(ə)rəs/ ▶ adjective having or giving off a smell, especially an unpleasant one: *an odoriferous pile of fish remains*.
– DERIVATIVES **odoriferously** adverb.
– ORIGIN late Middle English: from Latin *odorifer* 'odour-bearing' + **-OUS**.

odorize (also **-ise**) ▶ verb [with obj.] give an odour or scent to.
– DERIVATIVES **odorizer** noun.
– ORIGIN late 19th cent.: from Latin *odor* 'odour' + **-IZE**.

odorous ▶ adjective having or giving off a smell.
– ORIGIN late Middle English: from Latin *odorus* 'fragrant' (from *odor* 'odour') + **-OUS**.

odour (US **odor**) ▶ noun a distinctive smell, especially an unpleasant one: *the odour of cigarette smoke*.
■ figurative a lingering quality, impression, or feeling attaching to something: *an odour of suspicion*. ■ [mass noun] [with adj.] figurative the state of being held in a specified regard: *a decade of bad odour between Britain and the European Community*.
– PHRASES **be in good** (or **bad**) **odour with** be in (or out of) favour with (someone). **odour of sanctity** a sweet odour reputedly emitted by the bodies of saints at or near death. ■ figurative a state of holiness.
– DERIVATIVES **odourless** adjective.
– ORIGIN Middle English: from Anglo-Norman French, from Latin *odor* 'smell, scent'.

Odra /ˈɒdrɑ/ Polish name for **ODER**.

Odysseus /əˈdɪsɪəs/ Greek Mythology the king of Ithaca and central figure of the *Odyssey*, renowned for his cunning and resourcefulness. Roman name **ULYSSES**.

Odyssey /ˈɒdɪsi/ a Greek hexameter epic poem traditionally ascribed to Homer, describing the travels of Odysseus during his ten years of wandering after the sack of Troy. He eventually returned home to Ithaca and killed the suitors who had plagued his wife Penelope during his absence.
– DERIVATIVES **Odyssean** /ˌɒdɪˈsiːən/ adjective.

odyssey /ˈɒdɪsi/ ▶ noun (pl. **-eys**) a long and eventful or adventurous journey: figurative *his odyssey from military man to politician*.
– DERIVATIVES **odyssean** adjective.
– ORIGIN late 19th cent.: via Latin from Greek *Odusseia* (see **ODYSSEY**).

OE ▶ abbreviation for Old English.

Oe ▶ abbreviation for oersted(s).

Oea /ˈiːə/ ancient name for **TRIPOLI** (in sense 1).

OECD ▶ abbreviation for Organization for Economic Cooperation and Development.

oecology ▶ noun archaic spelling of **ECOLOGY**.

oeconomics ▶ plural noun archaic spelling of **ECONOMICS**.

oecumenical ▶ adjective archaic spelling of **ECUMENICAL**.

OED ▶ abbreviation for Oxford English Dictionary.

oedema /ɪˈdiːmə/ (US **edema**) ▶ noun [mass noun] a condition characterized by an excess of watery fluid collecting in the cavities or tissues of the body. Also called **DROPSY**.
– DERIVATIVES **oedematous** adjective.
– ORIGIN late Middle English: modern Latin, from Greek *oidēma*, from *oidein* 'to swell'.

Oedipus /ˈiːdɪpəs/ Greek Mythology the son of Jocasta and of Laius, king of Thebes.

> Left to die on a mountain by Laius, who had been told by an oracle that he would be killed by his own son, the infant Oedipus was saved by a shepherd. Returning eventually to Thebes, Oedipus solved the riddle of the sphinx, but unwittingly killed his father and married Jocasta. On discovering what he had done he put out his own eyes in a fit of madness, while Jocasta hanged herself.

Oedipus complex ▶ noun Psychoanalysis (in Freudian theory) the complex of emotions aroused in a young child, typically around the age of four, by an unconscious sexual desire for the parent of the opposite sex and wish to exclude the parent of the same sex. (The term was originally applied to boys, the equivalent in girls being called the **Electra complex**.)
– DERIVATIVES **Oedipal** adjective.

– ORIGIN early 20th cent.: by association with **OEDIPUS**.

oeil-de-boeuf /ˌɔːdəˈbəːf/ ▶ noun (pl. **oeils-de-boeuf** pronunc. same) a small round window.
– ORIGIN mid 18th cent.: French, literally 'ox-eye'.

OEM ▶ abbreviation for original equipment manufacturer (an organization that makes devices from component parts bought from other organizations).

oenology /iːˈnɒlədʒi/ (US also **enology**) ▶ noun [mass noun] the study of wines.
– DERIVATIVES **oenological** adjective, **oenologist** noun.
– ORIGIN early 19th cent.: from Greek *oinos* 'wine' + **-LOGY**.

Oenone /iːˈnəʊni/ Greek Mythology a nymph of Mount Ida and lover of Paris, who deserted her for Helen.

oenophile /ˈiːnə(ʊ)fʌɪl/ ▶ noun a connoisseur of wines.
– DERIVATIVES **oenophilist** /iːˈnɒfɪlɪst/ noun.

o'er ▶ adverb & preposition archaic or poetic/literary term for **OVER**.

Oersted /ˈəːstɛd/, Hans Christian (1777–1851), Danish physicist, discoverer of the magnetic effect of an electric current. He also worked on the compressibility of gases and liquids, and on diamagnetism.

oersted (abbrev.: **Oe**) ▶ noun Physics a unit of magnetic field strength equivalent to 79.58 amperes per metre.
– ORIGIN late 19th cent.: named after H. C. **OERSTED**.

oesophagitis /ɪˌsɒfəgəˈdʒʌɪtɪs/ (US **esophagitis**) ▶ noun [mass noun] Medicine inflammation of the oesophagus.

oesophagoscope /ɪˈsɒfədʒəˌskəʊp/ (US **esophagoscope**) ▶ noun an instrument for the inspection or treatment of the oesophagus.

oesophagus /ɪˈsɒfəgəs/ (US **esophagus**) ▶ noun (pl. **oesophagi** /-dʒʌɪ/ or **oesophaguses**) the part of the alimentary canal which connects the throat to the stomach; the gullet. In humans and other vertebrates it is a muscular tube lined with mucous membrane.
– DERIVATIVES **oesophageal** /ɪˌsɒfəˈdʒiːəl, ˌiːsəˈfadʒɪəl/ adjective.
– ORIGIN late Middle English: modern Latin, from Greek *oisophagos*.

oestradiol /ˌiːstrəˈdʌɪɒl, ˌɛstrə-/ (US **estradiol**) ▶ noun [mass noun] Biochemistry a major oestrogen produced in the ovaries.
– ORIGIN 1930s: from **OESTRUS** + **DI-**[1] + **-OL**.

oestriol /ˈiːstrɪɒl, ˈɛstrɪɒl/ (US also **estriol**) ▶ noun [mass noun] Biochemistry an oestrogen which is one of the metabolic products of oestradiol.
– ORIGIN 1930s: from *oestrane* (the parent molecule of most oestrogens) + **TRI-** + **-OL**.

oestrogen /ˈiːstrədʒ(ə)n, ˈɛstrə-/ (US **estrogen**) ▶ noun any of a group of steroid hormones which promote the development and maintenance of female characteristics of the body. Such hormones are also produced artificially for use in oral contraceptives or to treat menopausal and menstrual disorders.
– DERIVATIVES **oestrogenic** adjective.
– ORIGIN 1920s: from **OESTRUS** + **-GEN**.

oestrone /ˈiːstrəʊn, ˈɛstrəʊn/ (US **estrone**) ▶ noun [mass noun] Biochemistry an oestrogen similar to but less potent than oestradiol.
– ORIGIN 1930s: from *oestrane* (parent molecule of most oestrogens) + **-ONE**.

oestrus /ˈiːstrəs, ˈɛstrəs/ (US **estrus**) ▶ noun [mass noun] a recurring period of sexual receptivity and fertility in many female mammals; heat: *a mare in oestrus*.
– DERIVATIVES **oestrous** adjective.
– ORIGIN late 17th cent.: from Greek *oistros* 'gadfly or frenzy'.

oeuvre /ˈəːvr(ə)/ ▶ noun the works of a painter, composer, or author regarded collectively: *the complete oeuvre of Mozart*.
■ a work of art, music, or literature: *an early oeuvre*.
– ORIGIN late 19th cent.: French, literally 'work'.

OF ▶ abbreviation for Old French.

of ▶ preposition **1** expressing the relationship between a part and a whole:
■ with the word denoting the part functioning as the head of the phrase: *the sleeve of his coat* | *in the back of the car* | *the days of the week*. ■ after a number, quantifier, or partitive noun, with the word denoting

the whole functioning as the head of the phrase: *nine of the children came to the show* | *a series of programmes* | [with mass noun] *a piece of cake* | *a lot of money* | *a cup of tea.*
2 expressing the relationship between a scale or measure and a value: *an increase of 5%* | *a height of 10 metres.*
■expressing an age: *a boy of 15.*
3 indicating an association between two entities, typically one of belonging, in which the first is the head of the phrase and the second is something associated with it: *the son of a friend* | *the government of India* | *a photograph of the bride* | [with a possessive] *a former colleague of John's.*
■expressing the relationship between an author, artist, or composer and their works collectively: *the plays of Shakespeare* | *the paintings of Rembrandt.*
4 expressing the relationship between a direction and a point of reference: *north of Watford* | *on the left of the picture.*
5 expressing the relationship between a general category and the thing being specified which belongs to such a category: *the city of Prague* | *the idea of a just society* | *the set of all genes.*
■governed by a noun expressing the fact that a category is vague: *this type of book* | *the general kind of answer that would satisfy me.*
6 expressing the relationship between an abstract concept having a verb-like meaning and a noun denoting the subject of the underlying verb: *the opinion of the directors* | *the decision of the County Council.*
■where the second noun denotes the object of the underlying verb: *the murder of two boys* | *payment of his debts* | *an admirer of Dickens.* ■ where the head of the phrase is a predicative adjective: *it was kind of you to ask* | *I am certain of that.*
7 indicating the relationship between a verb and an indirect object:
■with a verb expressing a mental state: *they must be persuaded of the severity of the problem* | *I don't know of anything that would be suitable.* ■ expressing a cause: *he died of cancer.*
8 indicating the material or substance constituting something: *the house was built of bricks* | *walls of stone.*
9 N. Amer. expressing time in relation to the following hour: *it would be just a quarter of three in New York.*
– PHRASES **be of** possess intrinsically; give rise to: *this work is of great interest and value.* **of all** denoting the least likely or expected example: *Jordan, of all people, committed a flagrant foul.* **of all the nerve** (or Brit. **cheek**) an expression of indignation. **of an evening** (or **morning** etc.) informal **1** on most evenings (or mornings etc.). **2** at some time in the evenings (or mornings etc.).
– ORIGIN Old English, of Germanic origin; related to Dutch *af* and German *ab*, from an Indo-European root shared by Latin *ab* and Greek *apo*.

USAGE It is a mistake to use **of** instead of **have** in constructions such as *you should **have** asked* (not *you should **of** asked*). For more information, see **usage** at **HAVE**.

of- ▶ **prefix** variant spelling of **OB-** assimilated before *f* (as in *offend*).

ofay /ˈəʊfeɪ/ ▶ **noun** US a derogatory term for a white person used by black people.
– ORIGIN 1920s: of unknown origin.

Off. ▶ **abbreviation for** ■ Office. ■ Officer.

off ▶ **adverb 1** away from the place in question; to or at a distance: *the man ran off* | *she dashed off to her room* | *we must be off now.*
■away from the main route: *turning off for Ripon.*
2 so as to be removed or separated: *he whipped off his coat* | *a section of the runway had been cordoned off.*
■absent; away from work: *take a day off* | *he is off on sick leave.*
3 starting a journey or race; leaving: *we're off on holiday tomorrow* | *the gunmen made off on foot* | *they're off!*
4 so as to bring to an end or be discontinued: *the Christmas party rounded off a hugely successful year* | *she broke off her reading to look at her husband.*
■cancelled: *tell them the wedding's off.* ■ Brit. informal (of a menu item) temporarily unavailable: *strawberries are off.*
5 (of an electrical appliance or power supply) not functioning or so as to cease to function: *switch the TV off* | *the electricity was off for four days.*
6 having access to or possession of material goods or wealth to the extent specified: *we'd been rather **badly off** for books* | *how are you off for money?*
7 chiefly Brit. (with preceding numeral) denoting a quantity produced at one time.
▶ **preposition 1** moving away and often down from: *he rolled off the bed* | *the coat slipped off his arms* | *trying to get us off the stage.*
2 situated or leading in a direction away from (a main route or intersection): *single wires leading off the main lines* | *in a little street off Whitehall.*
■out at sea from (a place on the coast): *anchoring off Blue Bay* | *six miles off Dunkirk.*
3 so as to be removed or separated from: *threatening to tear it off its hinges* | *they are knocking $2,000 off the price* | figurative *it's a huge burden off my shoulders.*
■absent from: *I took a couple of days off work.* ■ informal abstaining from: *he managed to stay off alcohol.*
4 informal having a dislike (usually temporary) of: *he's running a temperature and he's off his food.*
▶ **adjective 1** [attrib.] characterized by someone performing or feeling worse than usual; unsatisfactory or inadequate: *even the greatest athletes have **off days**.*
2 [predic.] (of food) no longer fresh: *the fish was a bit off.*
3 [attrib.] located on the side of a vehicle that is normally furthest from the kerb; offside. Compare with **NEAR** (in sense 4).
4 [predic.] Brit. informal annoying or unfair: *His boss deducted the money from his pay. That was a bit off.*
5 [predic.] Brit. informal unwell: *I felt decidedly off.*
6 [predic.] Brit. informal unfriendly or hostile: *there's no one there except the barmaid, and she's a bit off.*
▶ **noun 1** (also **off side**) Cricket the half of the field (as divided lengthways through the pitch) towards which the batsman's feet are pointed when standing to receive the ball. The opposite of **LEG**.
2 Brit. informal the start of a race; the beginning; the departure: *now Ian is **ready for the off**.*
3 S. African informal a day or part of a day when one does not have to work: *she only sees her children during her off on Sunday afternoons.*
▶ **verb** informal **1** [no obj.] leave: *supposedly loyal workers suddenly **upped and offed** to the new megafirms.*
2 [with obj.] N. Amer. kill; murder: *she might off a cop, but she wouldn't shoot her boyfriend.*
– PHRASES **off and on** intermittently; now and then.
– ORIGIN Old English, originally a variant of **OF** (which combined the senses of 'of' and 'off').

USAGE The compound preposition **off of** is used interchangeably with the preposition **off** in a context such as *she picked it up **off of** the floor* (compared with *she picked it up **off** the floor*). The use of **off of** is recorded from the 16th century (and was used commonly by Shakespeare, for example) and is logically parallel to the standard **out of**, but is not accepted in standard modern English. Today **off of** is restricted to dialect and informal contexts, particularly in the US.

Offa /ˈɒfə/ (d.796), king of Mercia 757–96. He organized the construction of Offa's Dyke.

offa ▶ **preposition** US informal off from.

off-air ▶ **adjective** & **adverb 1** not being broadcast: [as adv.] *he is exactly the same off-air as he is on.*
2 of or relating to the reception of broadcast programmes.

offal ▶ **noun** [mass noun] the entrails and internal organs of an animal used as food.
■refuse or waste material. ■ decomposing animal flesh.
– ORIGIN late Middle English (in the sense 'refuse from a process'): probably suggested by Middle Dutch *afval*, from *af* 'off' + *vallen* 'to fall'.

Offaly /ˈɒfəli/ a county in the central part of the Republic of Ireland, in the province of Leinster; county town, Tullamore.

Offa's Dyke a series of earthworks marking the traditional boundary between England and Wales, running from near the mouth of the Wye to near the mouth of the Dee, originally constructed by Offa in the second half of the 8th century to mark the boundary established by his wars with the Welsh.

offbeat ▶ **adjective 1** Music not coinciding with the beat.
2 informal unconventional; unusual: *she's a little offbeat but she's a wonderful actress.*
▶ **noun** Music any of the normally unaccented beats in a bar.

off-brand ▶ **adjective** denoting or relating to an item of goods of an unknown, unpopular, or inferior brand.
▶ **noun** an unknown, unpopular, or inferior brand.

off break ▶ **noun** Cricket a ball which deviates from the off side towards the leg side after pitching.

off-Broadway ▶ **adjective** (of a theatre, play, or performer) located in, appearing in, or associated with an area of New York other than Broadway, typically with reference to experimental and less commercial productions.
▶ **noun** [mass noun] such theatres and productions collectively.

off-campus ▶ **adjective** & **adverb** away from a university or college campus.

off-centre ▶ **adjective** & **adverb** not quite in the centre of something.

off colour ▶ **adjective 1** Brit. slightly unwell: *I'm feeling a bit off colour.*
2 slightly indecent or obscene: *off-colour jokes.*

offcomer ▶ **noun** dialect an outsider or newcomer to a district.

off-course ▶ **adjective** situated or taking place away from a racecourse: *off-course betting.*

offcut ▶ **noun** a piece of waste material that is left behind after cutting a larger piece.

off-cutter ▶ **noun** Cricket a fast off break.

off-diagonal ▶ **adjective** Mathematics denoting an element of a square matrix that is not on the diagonal running from the upper left to the lower right.

off drive Cricket ▶ **noun** a drive to the off side.
▶ **verb** [with obj.] (**off-drive**) drive (the ball) to the off side; drive a ball from (a bowler) to the off side.

off-dry ▶ **adjective** (of wine) having an almost dry flavour, with just a trace of sweetness.

Offenbach /ˈɒf(ə)nbɑːx/, Jacques (1819–80), German composer, resident in France from 1833; born *Jacob Offenbach*. He is associated with the rise of the operetta, whose style is typified by his *Orpheus in the Underworld* (1858). Other notable works: *The Tales of Hoffmann* (1881).

offence (US **offense**) ▶ **noun 1** a breach of a law or rule; an illegal act: *the new offence of obtaining property by deception.*
■a thing that constitutes a violation of what is judged to be right or natural: *the outcome is an **offence to** basic justice.*
2 [mass noun] annoyance or resentment brought about by a perceived insult to or disregard for oneself or one's standards or principles: *he went out, making it clear he'd **taken offence*** | *I didn't intend to **give offence**.*
3 [mass noun] the action of attacking: [as modifier] *reductions in strategic offence arsenals.*
■N. Amer. the attacking team or players in a sport, especially in American football.
– PHRASES **no offence** informal do not be offended.
– ORIGIN late Middle English: from Old French *offens* 'misdeed', from Latin *offensus* 'annoyance', reinforced by French *offense*, from Latin *offensa* 'a striking against, a hurt, or displeasure'; based on Latin *offendere* 'strike against'.

offend ▶ **verb 1** [with obj.] (often **be offended**) cause to feel upset, annoyed, or resentful: *17 per cent of viewers said they had been offended by bad language.*
■be displeasing to: *he didn't smoke and the smell of ash offended him* | [as adj. **offending**] *the Department of Transport must redesign the offending section of road.*
2 [no obj.] commit an illegal act: *a small hard core of young criminals who offend again and again.*
■break a commonly accepted rule or principle: *those activities which **offend against** public order and decency.*
– DERIVATIVES **offendedly** adverb, **offender** noun.
– ORIGIN late Middle English: from Old French *offendre*, from Latin *offendere* 'strike against'.

offense ▶ **noun** US spelling of **OFFENCE**.

offensive ▶ **adjective 1** causing someone to feel deeply hurt, upset, or angry: *the allegations made are deeply offensive to us* | *offensive language.*
■(of a sight or smell) disgusting; repulsive: *an offensive odour.*
2 [attrib.] actively aggressive; attacking: *offensive operations against the insurgents.*
■(of a weapon) meant for use in attack. ■ chiefly N. Amer. of or relating to the team in possession of the ball or puck in a game.
▶ **noun** an attacking military campaign: *an impending military offensive against the guerrillas.*

O

■ an organized and forceful campaign to achieve something, typically a political or social end: *the need to launch an offensive against crime.*

– PHRASES **be on the offensive** act or be ready to act aggressively. **go on** (**to** or **take**) **the offensive** take the initiative by beginning to attack or act aggressively: *security forces took the offensive ten days ago.*

– DERIVATIVES **offensively** adverb, **offensiveness** noun.

– ORIGIN mid 16th cent.: from French *offensif, -ive* or medieval Latin *offensivus*, from Latin *offens-* 'struck against', from the verb *offendere* (see **OFFEND**).

OFFER ▶ **abbreviation for** (in the UK) Office of Electricity Regulation, a regulatory body supervising the operation of the electricity industry.

offer ▶ **verb** [with two objs] present or proffer (something) for (someone) to accept or reject as so desired: *may I offer you a drink? | you may be offered a job on the spot.*

■ [reporting verb] express readiness or the intention to do something for or on behalf of someone: [with infinitive] *he offered to fix the gate* | [with direct speech] *'Can I help you, dear?' a kindly voice offered.* ■ [with obj.] (usu. **be offered**) make available for sale: *the product is offered at a very competitive price.* ■ [with obj.] provide (something): *the Coast Road offers easy access to the Nine Glens of Antrim.* ■ [with obj.] present (something, especially an opportunity) for consideration and possible exploitation: *a good understanding of what a particular career can offer.* ■ [no obj.] dated (of an opportunity or chance) present itself; occur: *whenever a favourable opportunity offered, he obligingly allowed me the use of a boat.* ■ [with obj.] present (a prayer or sacrifice) to a deity: *the three imams* **offer up** *prayers on behalf of the dead.* ■ [with obj.] make an attempt at or show one's readiness for (violence or resistance): *he had to offer some resistance to her tirade.* ■ [with obj.] archaic give an opportunity for (battle) to an enemy: *Darius was about to meet him and to offer battle.*

▶ **noun** an expression of readiness to do or give something if desired: [with infinitive] *he had accepted Mallory's offer to buy him a drink | a job offer.*

■ an amount of money that someone is willing to pay for something: *the prospective purchaser who made the highest offer.* ■ a specially reduced price for something: *the offer runs right up until Christmas Eve.* ■ a proposal of marriage.

– PHRASES **have something to offer** have something available to be used or appreciated. **offer one's hand** extend one's hand to be shaken as a sign of friendship. **on offer** available: *the number of permanent jobs on offer is relatively small.* ■ (also **on special offer**) Brit. available for sale at a reduced price: *the fruit cocktail trifle is on offer at 99p.* **open to offers** willing to sell something or do a job for a reasonable price.

– DERIVATIVES **offerer** (or **offeror**) noun.

– ORIGIN Old English *offrian* 'sacrifice (something) to a deity', of Germanic origin, from Latin *offerre* 'bestow, present' (in ecclesiastical Latin 'offer to God'), reinforced by French *offrir* (which continued to express the primary sense). The noun (late Middle English) is from French *offre*.

▶ **offer something up** technical put something in place to test or assess its appearance or fit: *the infill panels are offered up and bolted in position.*

offer document ▶ **noun** a document containing details of a takeover bid which is sent to the shareholders of the target company.

offering ▶ **noun** a thing offered, especially as a gift or contribution: *everyone transported their offerings to the bring-and-buy stall.*

■ a thing produced or manufactured for entertainment or sale: *the latest offerings from the garage showrooms.* ■ a contribution, especially of money, to a church. ■ a thing offered as a religious sacrifice or token of devotion.

offer price ▶ **noun** the price at which a market-maker or institution is prepared to sell securities or other assets. Compare with **BID PRICE**.

offertory /ˈɒfət(ə)ri/ ▶ **noun** (pl. **-ies**) Christian Church **1** the offering of the bread and wine at the Eucharist.

■ an anthem accompanying this.

2 an offering or collection of money made at a religious service.

– ORIGIN late Middle English: from ecclesiastical Latin *offertorium* 'offering', from late Latin *offert-* (which replaced Latin *oblat-*) 'offered', from the verb *offerre* (see **OFFER**).

off-gas ▶ **noun** a gas which is given off, especially one emitted as the by-product of a chemical process.

▶ **verb** [no obj.] give off a chemical, especially a harmful one, in the form of a gas.

off-glide ▶ **noun** Phonetics a glide terminating the articulation of a speech sound, when the vocal organs either return to a neutral position or adopt a position anticipating the formation of the next sound. Compare with **ON-GLIDE**.

offhand ▶ **adjective** ungraciously or offensively nonchalant or cool in manner: *you were a bit offhand with her this afternoon.*

▶ **adverb** without previous thought or consideration: *I can't think of a better answer offhand.*

– DERIVATIVES **offhanded** adjective, **offhandedly** adverb, **offhandedness** noun.

off-hours ▶ **plural noun** N. Amer. the time when one is not at work; one's leisure time.

office ▶ **noun 1** a room, set of rooms, or building used as a place of business for non-manual work: *computers first appeared in offices in the late 1970s* | [as modifier] *an office job.*

■ the local centre of a large business: *a company which has four US and four European offices.* ■ a room, department, or building used to provide a particular service: *a ticket office | a Post Office.* ■ N. Amer. the consulting room of a professional person. ■ (**offices**) Brit. dated the parts of a house given over to household work or to storage. ■ (usu. **usual offices**) Brit. dated used euphemistically to refer to a toilet.

2 a position of authority, trust, or service, typically one of a public nature: *the office of Director General of Fair Trading.*

■ [mass noun] tenure of an official position, especially that of a Minister of State or of the party forming the government: *a year ago, when the President* **took office** | *he was ejected from office in 1988.* ■ (**Office**) the quarters, staff, or collective authority of a particular government department or agency: *the Foreign Office.*

3 (usu. **offices**) a service or kindness done for another person or group of people.

■ dated a duty attaching to one's position; a task or function: *the offices of a nurse | his family had escaped to Canada* **through the good offices of** *a Jewish agency in 1923.*

4 (also **Divine Office**) Christian Church the series of services of prayers and psalms said (or chanted) daily by Catholic priests, members of religious orders, and other clergy.

■ one of these services: *the noon office.*

– ORIGIN Middle English: via Old French from Latin *officium* 'performance of a task' (in medieval Latin also 'office, divine service'), based on *opus* 'work' + *facere* 'do'.

office-bearer ▶ **noun** a person holding a position of authority in an organization.

office block ▶ **noun** a large multi-storey building containing the offices of one or more companies.

office boy (also **office girl**) ▶ **noun** a young man (or woman) employed to do less important jobs in a business office.

office hours ▶ **plural noun** the hours during which business is normally conducted.

office lady ▶ **noun** (in Japan) a woman working in an office, typically in a secretarial or relatively menial position.

office of arms ▶ **noun** Heraldry the College of Arms, or a similar body in another country.

officer ▶ **noun 1** a person holding a position of authority, especially one with a commission, in the armed services, the mercantile marine, or on a passenger ship.

■ a policeman or policewoman. ■ a bailiff.

2 a holder of a public, civil, or ecclesiastical office: *a probation officer | the Chief Medical Officer.*

■ a holder of a post in a society, company, or other organization, especially one who is involved at a senior level in its management: *a chief executive officer.*

3 a member of a certain grade in some honorary orders, such as the grade next below commander in the Order of the British Empire.

▶ **verb** [with obj.] provide with military officers: *the aristocracy continued to wield considerable political power, officering the army.*

■ act as the commander of (a unit): *foreign mercenaries were hired to officer new regiments.*

– ORIGIN Middle English: via Anglo-Norman French from medieval Latin *officiarius*, from Latin *officium* (see **OFFICE**).

officer of arms ▶ **noun** Heraldry a heraldic official; a herald or pursuivant.

official ▶ **adjective** of or relating to an authority or public body and its duties, actions, and responsibilities: *the prime minister's official engagements.*

■ having the approval or authorization of such a body: *members would know when industrial action is official.* ■ employed by such a body in a position of authority or trust: *an official spokesman.* ■ emanating from or attributable to a person in office; properly authorized: *official statistics.* ■ often derogatory perceived as characteristic of officials and bureaucracy; officious: *he sat up straight and became official.*

▶ **noun** a person holding public office or having official duties, especially as a representative of an organization or government department: *a union official.*

■ (also **official principal**) Brit. the presiding officer or judge of an archbishop's, bishop's, or archdeacon's court.

– DERIVATIVES **officialdom** noun, **officialism** noun, **officialize** (also **officialise**) verb.

– ORIGIN Middle English (originally as a noun): via Old French from Latin *officialis*, from *officium* (see **OFFICE**).

official assignee ▶ **noun** New Zealand term for **OFFICIAL RECEIVER**.

official birthday ▶ **noun** (in the UK) a day in June chosen for the observance of the sovereign's birthday.

officialese ▶ **noun** [mass noun] derogatory the formal and typically verbose style of writing considered to be characteristic of official documents, especially when it is difficult to understand.

officially ▶ **adverb** in a formal and public way: *on June 24 the election campaign will officially begin.*

■ with the authority of the government or some other organization: *it was officially acknowledged that the economy was in recession.* ■ in public and for official purposes but not necessarily so in reality: [sentence adverb] *there is a possibility he was murdered—officially, he died in a car smash.*

official receiver ▶ **noun** Brit. another term for **RECEIVER** (in sense 3).

official secret ▶ **noun** Brit. a piece of confidential information that is important for national security.

Official Secrets Act (in the UK) the legislation that controls access to confidential information important for national security.

officiant /əˈfɪʃɪənt, -ʃ(ə)nt/ ▶ **noun** a person, typically a priest or minister, who performs a religious service or ceremony.

– ORIGIN mid 19th cent.: from medieval Latin *officiant-* 'performing divine service', from the verb *officiare*.

officiate /əˈfɪʃɪeɪt/ ▶ **verb** [no obj.] act as an official in charge of something, especially a sporting event: *three judges will officiate at the two Grands Prix.*

■ perform a religious service or ceremony: *he baptized children and officiated at weddings.*

– DERIVATIVES **officiation** noun, **officiator** noun.

– ORIGIN mid 17th cent.: from medieval Latin *officiare* 'perform divine service', from *officium* (see **OFFICE**).

officinal /əˈfɪsɪn(ə)l, ɒfɪˈsiːn(ə)l/ ▶ **adjective** chiefly historical (of a herb or drug) standardly used in medicine.

– DERIVATIVES **officinally** adverb.

– ORIGIN late 17th cent. (as a noun denoting an officinal medicine): from medieval Latin *officinalis* 'storeroom for medicines', from Latin *officina* 'workshop'.

officious ▶ **adjective** assertive of authority in an annoyingly domineering way, especially with regard to petty or trivial matters. *the security people in the foyer were even more officious.*

■ intrusively enthusiastic in offering help or advice; interfering: *an officious bystander.*

– DERIVATIVES **officiously** adverb, **officiousness** noun.

– ORIGIN late 15th cent.: from Latin *officiosus* 'obliging', from *officium* (see **OFFICE**). The original sense was 'performing its function, efficacious', whence 'ready to help or please' (mid 16th cent.), later becoming depreciatory (late 16th cent.).

offie (also **offy**) ▶ **noun** (pl. **-ies**) Brit. informal an off-licence.

– ORIGIN 1970s: abbreviation.

offing ▶ noun the more distant part of the sea in view.
– PHRASES **in the offing** likely to happen or appear soon: *there are several initiatives in the offing.*
– ORIGIN early 17th cent.: perhaps from **OFF** + **-ING**[1].

offish ▶ adjective informal aloof or distant in manner; not friendly: *he was being offish with her.*
– DERIVATIVES **offishly** adverb, **offishness** noun.

off-island ▶ adverb away from an island.
▶ noun an island off the shore of a larger or central island.
▶ adjective located on or coming from such an island.

off-key ▶ adjective & adverb (of music) not having the correct pitch; out of tune.
■ not in accordance with what is appropriate or correct in the circumstances: [as adv.] *some of the cinematic effects are distractingly off-key.*

off-licence ▶ noun Brit. a shop selling alcoholic drink for consumption elsewhere.
■ a licence for this.

off-limits ▶ adjective (of a place) not to be entered; out of bounds: *the site was off-limits to the public.*

off-line Computing ▶ adjective not controlled by or directly connected to a computer.
▶ adverb while not directly controlled by or connected to a computer.
■ with a delay between the production of data and its processing.

offload ▶ verb [with obj.] unload (a cargo): *a delivery could be offloaded immediately on arrival.*
■ rid oneself of (something) by selling or passing it on to someone else: *a dealer offloaded 5,000 of these shares on a client.* ■ relieve oneself of (a problem or worry) by talking to someone else: *it would be nice to have been able to offload your worries on to someone.* ■ Computing move (data or a task) from one processor to another in order to free the first processor for other tasks: *a system designed to offload the text on to a host computer.*

off-message ▶ adjective (of a politician) departing from the official party line.

off-off-Broadway ▶ adjective denoting or relating to avant-garde, experimental theatrical productions in New York taking place in small or informal venues away from off-Broadway.
▶ noun theatrical productions of this kind.

off-patent ▶ adjective & adverb out of patent restrictions.

off-peak ▶ adjective & adverb at a time when demand is less: [as adj.] *off-peak travel.*

off-piste ▶ adjective & adverb Skiing away from prepared ski runs: [as adj.] *off-piste slopes* | [as adv.] *heli-skiing is an expensive way of skiing off-piste.*

off-pitch ▶ adjective Music not of the correct pitch.

off-plan ▶ adverb & adjective (of the selling or purchasing of property) before the property is built and with only the plans available for inspection.

off-price N. Amer. ▶ noun [mass noun] a method of retailing in which branded goods (especially clothing) are sold for less than the usual retail price: [as modifier] *an off-price store.*
▶ adverb using this method: *selling goods off-price.*

offprint ▶ noun a printed copy of an article that originally appeared as part of a larger publication.

off-putting ▶ adjective unpleasant, disconcerting, or repellent: *his scar is somewhat off-putting.*
– DERIVATIVES **off-puttingly** adverb.

off-ramp ▶ noun N. Amer. a sloping one-way road leading off a main highway.

off-road ▶ adverb away from the road; on rough terrain.
▶ adjective denoting a vehicle or bicycle for use over rough terrain.

off-roading ▶ noun [mass noun] the activity or sport of driving a motor vehicle over rough terrain.
– DERIVATIVES **off-roader** noun.

offsaddle ▶ verb [with obj.] S. African take the saddle off (a horse).

off-sale ▶ noun [mass noun] the sale of alcoholic drink for consumption elsewhere than at the place of sale.

off-sales ▶ noun (in South Africa) a retail outlet attached to a hotel, where alcohol is sold for consumption off the premises.

offscourings ▶ plural noun refuse, rubbish, or dregs.

off-screen ▶ adjective not appearing on a cinema,

television, or VDU screen: *he drawls to an off-screen interrogator.*
■ [attrib.] happening in reality rather than fictionally on-screen: *they were off-screen lovers.*
▶ adverb outside what can be seen on a television or cinema screen: *the girl is looking off-screen to the right.*
■ in real life rather than fictionally in a film or on television: *happy endings rarely happen off-screen.*

off season ▶ noun a time of year when a particular activity, typically a sport, is not engaged in.
■ a time of year when business in a particular sphere is slack.

offset ▶ noun **1** a consideration or amount that diminishes or balances the effect of a contrary one: *widow's bereavement allowance is an offset against income.*
2 the amount or distance by which something is out of line: *these wheels have an offset of four inches.*
■ Surveying a short distance measured perpendicularly from the main line of measurement. ■ Electronics a small deviation or bias in a voltage or current.
3 a side shoot from a plant serving for propagation.
■ a spur in a mountain range.
4 Architecture a sloping ledge in a wall or other feature where the thickness of the part above is diminished.
5 a bend in a pipe to carry it past an obstacle.
6 [mass noun] [often as modifier] a method of printing in which ink is transferred from a plate or stone to a uniform rubber surface and from that to the paper.
▶ verb (**-setting**; past and past participle **-set**) **1** [with obj.] (often **be offset**) counteract (something) by having an equal and opposite force or effect: *donations to charities can be offset against tax* | *his unfortunate appearance was offset by a compelling personality.*
2 [with obj.] place out of line: *several places where the ridge was offset at right angles to its length.*
3 [no obj.] (of ink or a freshly printed page) transfer an impression to the next leaf or sheet.

off-shears ▶ adjective Austral./NZ (of a sheep) recently shorn.

offshoot ▶ noun a side shoot or branch on a plant.
■ a thing that originated or developed from something else: *commercial offshoots of universities.*

offshore ▶ adjective & adverb **1** situated at sea some distance from the shore: [as adj.] *this huge stretch of coastline is dominated by offshore barrier islands* | [as adv.] *we dropped anchor offshore.*
■ (of the wind) blowing towards the sea from the land. ■ of or relating to the business of extracting oil or gas from the seabed.
2 made, situated, or registered abroad, especially in order to take advantage of lower taxes or costs or less stringent regulation: [as adj.] *deposits in offshore accounts.*
■ of, relating to, or derived from a foreign country: [as adj.] *American offshore politics.*

offside ▶ adjective & adverb (of a player, especially in soccer, rugby, or hockey) occupying a position on the field where playing the ball or puck is not allowed, generally through being between the ball and the opponents' goal: [as adv.] *the attacker looked offside by several yards* | figurative *his radicalism caught him offside with the law.*
▶ noun **1** the fact or an instance of being offside: *the goal was disallowed for offside.*
2 (usu. **the off side**) chiefly Brit. the side of a vehicle furthest from the kerb (in Britain, the right). Compare with **NEARSIDE**. See also **off side** at **OFF** (sense 1).
■ the right side of a horse.

offsider ▶ noun Austral./NZ informal a partner, assistant, or deputy.

off spin ▶ noun [mass noun] Cricket a type of spin bowling that causes the ball to deviate from the off side towards the leg side after pitching; off breaks.
– DERIVATIVES **off-spinner** noun.

offspring ▶ noun (pl. same) a person's child or children: *the offspring of middle-class parents.*
■ an animal's young. ■ figurative the product or result of something: *German nationalism was the offspring of military ambition.*
– ORIGIN Old English *ofspring* (see **OFF**, **SPRING**).

offstage ▶ adjective & adverb (in a theatre) not on the stage and so not visible to the audience.

off-street ▶ adjective [attrib.] (of parking facilities) not on a public road.

off stump ▶ noun Cricket the stump on the off side of a wicket.

off-tackle ▶ adjective American Football of, directed towards, or occurring in a part of the offensive line immediately to the outside of either of the tackles.

offtake ▶ noun [mass noun] the removal of oil from a reservoir or supply.

off-the-ball ▶ adjective & adverb Soccer not in contact with or playing the ball.

off-the-shoulder ▶ adjective (especially of a dress or blouse) not covering the shoulders.

off-track ▶ adjective N. Amer. situated or taking place away from a racetrack.

off-trade ▶ noun [mass noun] the part of the market in alcoholic drinks which is made up of off-sales.

off-white ▶ noun [mass noun] a white colour with a grey or yellowish tinge.

off-width ▶ adjective Climbing (of a crack in the rock) considered too wide to be a jam and too narrow to be a chimney.

offy ▶ noun (pl. **-ies**) variant spelling of **OFFIE**.

off year ▶ noun US a year in which there is no major election, especially one in which there is a Congressional election but no Presidential election.

Ofgas /ˈɒfgas/ ▶ abbreviation for (in the UK) Office of Gas Supply, a regulatory body supervising the operation of the gas industry.

Oflag /ˈɒflag/ ▶ noun historical a German prison camp for captured enemy officers. Compare with **STALAG**.
– ORIGIN German, contraction of *Offizier(s)lager* 'officers' camp'.

Ofsted /ˈɒfstɛd/ ▶ abbreviation for (in the UK) Office for Standards in Education, an organization monitoring standards in schools by means of regular inspections.

OFT ▶ abbreviation for (in the UK) Office of Fair Trading.

oft ▶ adverb archaic or poetic/literary form of **OFTEN**: [in combination] *an oft-quoted tenet.*
– ORIGIN Old English, of Germanic origin; related to German *oft.*

Oftel /ˈɒftɛl/ ▶ abbreviation for (in the UK) Office of Telecommunications, a regulatory body supervising the operation of the telecommunications industry.

often /ˈɒf(ə)n, ˈɒft(ə)n/ ▶ adverb (**oftener**, **oftenest**) frequently; many times: *he often goes for long walks by himself* | *how often do you have your hair cut?*
■ in many instances: *vocabulary often reflects social standing.*
– PHRASES **as often as not** quite frequently or commonly: *I had two homes really, because as often as not I was down at her house.* **more often than not** usually: *food is scarce and more often than not they go hungry.*
– ORIGIN Middle English: extended form of **OFT**, probably influenced by *selden* 'seldom'. Early examples appear to be northern English; the word became general in the 16th cent.

oftentimes ▶ adverb archaic or North American form of **OFTEN**.
– ORIGIN late Middle English: extended form of **OFT-TIMES**, influenced by **OFTEN**.

oft-times ▶ adverb archaic or poetic/literary form of **OFTEN**.

Ofwat /ˈɒfwɒt/ ▶ abbreviation for (in the UK) Office of Water Services, a regulatory body supervising the operation of the water industry.

Ogaden /ˌɒgəˈdɛn/ (**the Ogaden**) a desert region in SE Ethiopia, largely inhabited by Somali nomads. It has been claimed by successive governments of neighbouring Somalia.

ogam ▶ noun variant spelling of **OGHAM**.

Ogbomosho /ˌɒgbəˈməʊʃəʊ/ a city and agricultural market in SW Nigeria, north of Ibadan; pop. 660,600 (1992).

ogdoad /ˈɒgdəʊad/ ▶ noun rare a group or set of eight.
– ORIGIN early 17th cent.: via late Latin from Greek *ogdoas, ogdoad-*, from *ogdoos* 'eighth', from *oktō* 'eight'.

ogee /ˈəʊdʒiː, əʊˈdʒiː/ Architecture ▶ adjective showing in section a double continuous S-shaped curve.
▶ noun an S-shaped line or moulding.
– DERIVATIVES **ogeed** adjective.
– ORIGIN late Middle English: apparently from **OGIVE** (with which it was originally synonymous). The current sense arose in the late 17th cent.

ogee arch ▶ noun Architecture an arch with two ogee curves meeting at the apex.

Ogen /ˈəʊgən/ (also **Ogen melon**) ▶ noun a small melon with pale orange flesh and an orange skin ribbed with green.
– ORIGIN 1960s: from the name of a kibbutz in Israel.

ogham /ˈɒgəm/ (also **ogam**) ▶ noun [mass noun] an ancient British and Irish alphabet, consisting of twenty characters formed by parallel strokes on either side of or across a continuous line.
■ [count noun] an inscription in this alphabet. ■ [count noun] each of its characters.
– ORIGIN early 18th cent.: from Irish *ogam*, connected with *Ogma*, the name of its mythical inventor.

ogive /ˈəʊdʒaɪv, əʊˈdʒaɪv/ ▶ noun **1** Architecture a pointed or Gothic arch.
■ one of the diagonal groins or ribs of a vault. ■ a thing having the profile of an ogive, especially the head of a projectile or the nose cone of a rocket.
2 Statistics a cumulative frequency graph.
– DERIVATIVES **ogival** adjective.
– ORIGIN late Middle English: from French, of unknown origin.

ogle ▶ verb [with obj.] stare at in a lecherous manner: *he was ogling her breasts* | [no obj.] *men who had turned up to ogle.*
▶ noun a lecherous look.
– DERIVATIVES **ogler** noun.
– ORIGIN late 17th cent.: probably from Low German or Dutch; compare with Low German *oegeln*, frequentative of *oegen* 'look at'.

OGPU (also **Ogpu**) an organization for investigating and combating counter-revolutionary activities in the former Soviet Union, existing from 1922 (1922–3 as the GPU) to 1934 and replacing the Cheka. It was absorbed into the NKVD in 1934.
– ORIGIN acronym from Russian *Ob"edinënnoe gosudarstvennoe politicheskoe upravlenie* 'United State Political Directorate'.

O grade ▶ noun short for **ORDINARY GRADE**.

ogre ▶ noun (in folklore) a man-eating giant.
■ a cruel or terrifying person.
– DERIVATIVES **ogreish** (also **ogrish**) adjective.
– ORIGIN early 18th cent.: from French, first used by the French writer Perrault in 1697.

ogress ▶ noun a female ogre.

OH ▶ abbreviation for Ohio (in official postal use).

oh¹ ▶ exclamation used to express a range of emotions including surprise, anger, disappointment, or joy, or when reacting to something that has just been said: *'Oh no,' said Daisy, appalled* | *Me? Oh, I'm fine* | *oh, shut up.*
– PHRASES **oh boy** used to express surprise or excitement. **oh well** used to express resignation: *oh well, please yourself.* **oh yeah?** used to express disbelief.
– ORIGIN mid 16th cent.: variant of **O³**.

oh² ▶ noun variant spelling of **O¹** (in sense 2).

OHC ▶ abbreviation for overhead camshaft.

O'Higgins, Bernardo (*c.*1778–1842), Chilean revolutionary leader and statesman, head of state 1817–23. With the help of José de San Martín he led the army which defeated Spanish forces in 1817 and paved the way for Chilean independence the following year.

Ohio /əʊˈhʌɪəʊ/ a state in the north-eastern US, bordering on Lake Erie; pop. 10,847,115 (1990); capital, Columbus. Acquired by Britain from France in 1763 and by the US in 1783, it became the 17th state of the US in 1803.
– DERIVATIVES **Ohioan** adjective & noun.

Ohm /əʊm/, Georg Simon (1789–1854), German physicist. The units ohm and mho are named after him, as is Ohm's Law on electricity.

ohm ▶ noun the SI unit of electrical resistance, transmitting a current of one ampere when subjected to a potential difference of one volt. (Symbol: Ω)
– DERIVATIVES **ohmic** adjective, **ohmically** adverb.
– ORIGIN mid 19th cent.: named after G. S. **Ohm**.

ohmmeter /ˈəʊmˌmiːtə/ ▶ noun an instrument for measuring electrical resistance.

OHMS ▶ abbreviation for on Her (or His) Majesty's Service.

Ohm's law Physics a law stating that electric current is proportional to voltage and inversely proportional to resistance.

oho ▶ exclamation used to express pleased surprise or recognition.
– ORIGIN Middle English: from **O³** + **HO²**.

oh-oh ▶ exclamation an expression of alarm or realization of a difficulty.

-oholic ▶ suffix variant spelling of **-AHOLIC**.

ohone ▶ exclamation variant spelling of **OCHONE**.

OHP Brit. ▶ abbreviation for overhead projector.

Ohrid, Lake /ˈɒxrɪd/ a lake in SE Europe, on the border between Macedonia and Albania.

oh-so ▶ adverb [as submodifier] informal extremely: *their oh-so-ordinary lives.*

ohu /ˈəʊhuː/ ▶ noun (pl. same or **ohus**) NZ a working party or camp.
– ORIGIN Maori.

OHV ▶ abbreviation for overhead valve.

oi ▶ exclamation (also **oy**) informal used to attract someone's attention, especially in a rough or angry way.
▶ noun [mass noun] a type of harsh, aggressive punk music originally popular in the late 1970s and early 1980s.
– ORIGIN variant of **HOY¹**: first recorded in the 1930s.

-oid ▶ suffix forming adjectives and nouns: **1** Zoology denoting an animal belonging to a higher taxon with a name ending in *-oidea*: *hominoid* | *percoid.*
2 denoting form or resemblance: *asteroid* | *rhomboid.*
– DERIVATIVES **-oidal** suffix forming corresponding adjectives, **-oidally** suffix forming corresponding adverbs.
– ORIGIN from modern Latin *-oides*, from Greek *-oeidēs*; related to *eidos* 'form'.

oidium /əʊˈɪdɪəm/ ▶ noun (pl. **oidia** /-dɪə/) **1** Botany a type of fungal spore (conidium) formed by the breaking up of fungal hyphae into cells, especially as produced by powdery mildews.
2 [mass noun] a fungal disease affecting vines, caused by a powdery mildew.
● The fungus is *Uncinula necator* (formerly *Oidium tuckeri*), family Erysiphaceae, subdivision Ascomycotina.
– ORIGIN mid 19th cent.: modern Latin, from Greek *ōion* 'egg' + the diminutive suffix *-idion.*

OIEO Brit. ▶ abbreviation for offers in excess of (used in advertisements).

oik (also **oick**) ▶ noun informal an uncouth or obnoxious person.
– ORIGIN 1930s: of unknown origin.

oil ▶ noun **1** [mass noun] a viscous liquid derived from petroleum, especially for use as a fuel or lubricant.
■ petroleum. ■ [with modifier] any of various thick, viscous, typically flammable liquids which are insoluble in water but soluble in organic solvents and are obtained from animals or plants: *potatoes fried in vegetable oil.* ■ a liquid preparation used on the hair or skin as a cosmetic: *suntan oil.* ■ [count noun] Chemistry any of a group of natural esters of glycerol and various fatty acids, which are liquid at room temperature. Compare with **FAT**.
2 (often **oils**) oil paint: *a portrait in oils.*
▶ verb [with obj.] [often as adj. **oiled**] **1** lubricate or coat (something) with oil: *a lightly oiled baking tray.*
■ impregnate or treat (something) with oil: *her hair was heavily oiled.* ■ (**be oiled**) (of a place) be polluted with oil: *parts of the shoreline are oiled to a heavy degree.*
2 supply with oil as fuel: *attempts should not be made to oil individual tanks too quickly.*
– PHRASES **oil and water** used to refer to two elements, factors, or people that do not agree or blend together. **oil the wheels** help something go smoothly: *compliments oil the wheels of life.*
– DERIVATIVES **oil-less** adjective.
– ORIGIN Middle English: from Old Northern French *olie*, Old French *oile*, from Latin *oleum* '(olive) oil'; compare with *olea* 'olive'.

oil bath ▶ noun a receptacle containing oil, especially one used for cooling, heating, lubricating, or insulating apparatus immersed in it.

oil beetle ▶ noun a slow-moving flightless beetle that releases a foul-smelling oily secretion when disturbed. The larvae develop as parasites in the nests of solitary bees.
● *Meloe* and other genera, family Meloidae.

oilbird ▶ noun a large nocturnal fruit-eating bird that resembles a nightjar, living in caves in Central and South America. Called **GUACHARO** in America.
● *Steatornis caripensis*, the only member of the family Steatornithidae.

oil-burner ▶ noun a diesel vehicle.
– DERIVATIVES **oil-burning** adjective.

oilcake ▶ noun a mass of compressed linseed or other plant material left after oil has been extracted, used as fodder or fertilizer.

oilcan ▶ noun a can containing oil, especially one with a long nozzle for oiling machinery.

oilcloth ▶ noun [mass noun] cotton fabric treated on one side with oil to make it waterproof.
■ [count noun] a canvas coated with linseed or other oil and used to cover a table or floor.

oil colour ▶ noun another term for **OIL PAINT**.

oil drum ▶ noun a metal drum used for transporting oil.

oiled silk ▶ noun [mass noun] silk treated on one side with oil to make it waterproof.

oil engine ▶ noun an internal-combustion engine in which the fuel enters the cylinder as a liquid.

oiler ▶ noun **1** a thing that holds or supplies oil, in particular:
■ an oil tanker. ■ an oilcan. ■ N. Amer. informal an oil well.
2 (**oilers**) N. Amer. informal oilskin garments.

oilfield ▶ noun an area of land or seabed underlain by strata yielding mineral oil, especially in amounts that justify commercial exploitation.

oil-fired ▶ adjective (especially of a heating system or power station) using oil as fuel.

oilfish ▶ noun (pl. same or **-fishes**) a large violet or purple-brown escolar, the flesh of which is oily and unpalatable.
● *Ruvettus pretiosus*, family Gempylidae.

oil gas ▶ noun [mass noun] a gaseous mixture derived from mineral oils by destructive distillation.

oil-gilding ▶ noun [mass noun] gilding in which gold leaf is laid on a surface formed of linseed oil mixed with a yellow pigment.

oil gland ▶ noun Botany & Zoology a gland which secretes oil.
■ Ornithology another term for **PREEN GLAND**.

oil lamp ▶ noun a lamp using oil as fuel.

oilman ▶ noun (pl. **-men**) an owner or employee of an oil company.

oil-meal ▶ noun [mass noun] ground oilcake.

oil-mill ▶ noun a machine or a factory in which seeds, fruits, or other plant parts are crushed or pressed to extract oil.

oil of cloves ▶ noun see **CLOVE¹** (sense 1).

oil of turpentine ▶ noun see **TURPENTINE** (sense 1).

oil of vitriol ▶ noun archaic term for **SULPHURIC ACID**.

oil paint ▶ noun a paste made with ground pigment and a drying oil such as linseed oil, used chiefly by artists.

oil painting ▶ noun [mass noun] the art of painting in oils.
■ [count noun] a picture painted in oils.
– PHRASES **be no oil painting** Brit. informal be not very attractive.

oil palm ▶ noun a tropical West African palm which is the chief source of palm oil, widely cultivated in the tropics.
● *Elaeis guineensis*, family Palmae: several cultivars.

oil pan ▶ noun an engine sump.

oil paper ▶ noun [mass noun] paper made transparent or waterproof by soaking in oil.

oil platform ▶ noun a structure designed to stand on the seabed to provide a stable base above water for the drilling and regulation of oil wells.

oil-press ▶ noun an apparatus for pressing oil from seeds, fruits, etc.

oil rig ▶ noun a structure with equipment for drilling an oil well; an oil platform.

oil sand ▶ noun (often **oil sands**) a deposit of loose sand or partially consolidated sandstone containing bitumen.

oilseed ▶ noun [mass noun] any of a number of seeds from cultivated crops yielding oil, e.g. rape, peanut, or cotton.

oilseed rape ▶ noun see **RAPE²**.

oil shale ▶ noun [mass noun] fine-grained sedimentary rock from which oil can be extracted.

oilskin ▶ noun [mass noun] heavy cotton cloth waterproofed with oil.

■(**oilskins**) a set of garments made of such cloth.

oil slick ▶ **noun** a film or layer of oil floating on an expanse of water.

oil-spot ▶ **noun** an oily patch or mark.
■a silvery marking on brown Chinese porcelain (especially of the Song period) caused by precipitation of iron in firing.

oilstone ▶ **noun** a fine-grained flat stone used with oil for sharpening chisels, planes, or other tools.

oil tanker ▶ **noun** a ship designed to carry oil in bulk.

oil well ▶ **noun** an artificially made well or shaft in rock from which mineral oil is drawn.

oily ▶ **adjective** (**oilier**, **oiliest**) **1** containing oil: *taramasalata and hummus are both oily and rich.*
■covered or soaked with oil: *an oily rag.* ■ resembling oil in appearance or behaviour: *the oily swell of the river.*
2 figurative (of a person or their behaviour) unpleasantly smooth and ingratiating: *his oily smile.*
– DERIVATIVES **oilily** adverb, **oiliness** noun.

oink ▶ **noun** the characteristic grunting sound of a pig.
▶ **verb** [no obj.] make such a sound.
– ORIGIN 1940s: imitative.

ointment ▶ **noun** [mass noun] a smooth oily substance that is rubbed on the skin for medicinal purposes or as a cosmetic.
– ORIGIN Middle English: alteration of Old French *oignement*, from a popular Latin form of Latin *unguentum* (see **UNGUENT**); influenced by obsolete *oint* 'anoint' (from Old French, past participle of *oindre* 'anoint').

Oireachtas /ˈɛrəktəs, Irish ˈorʲəxtəs/ the legislature of the Irish Republic: the President, Dáil, and Seanad.
– ORIGIN Irish, literally 'assembly, convocation'.

OIRO Brit. ▶ **abbreviation for** offers in the region of (used in advertisements).

Oirot-Tura /ˌɔɪrɒtˈtuːrə/ former name (1932–48) for **GORNO-ALTAISK**.

Oisin /ˈəʊʃiːn/ another name for **OSSIAN**.

Ojibwa /ə(ʊ)ˈdʒɪbweɪ/ ▶ **noun** (pl. same or **Ojibwas**) **1** a member of an American Indian people inhabiting a wide area around Lake Superior. Also called **CHIPPEWA**.
2 [mass noun] the Algonquian language of this people.
▶ **adjective** of or relating to this people or their language.
– ORIGIN from Ojibwa *ojibwe*, said to mean 'puckered', with reference to their moccasins.

OK[1] (also **okay**) informal ▶ **exclamation** used to express assent, agreement, or acceptance: *OK, I'll pass on your message | OK, OK, I give in.*
■used to introduce an utterance: *'OK, let's go'.*
▶ **adjective** [predic.] satisfactory but not exceptionally or especially good: *the flight was OK.*
■(of a person) in a satisfactory physical or mental state: *are you okay, Ben?* ■ permissible; allowable: *I'm not sure if it's OK to say that to a teacher.*
▶ **adverb** in a satisfactory manner or to a satisfactory extent: *the computer continues to work OK.*
▶ **noun** [in sing.] an authorization or approval: *do you know how long it takes for those pen-pushers to* **give** *us* **the OK**?
▶ **verb** (**OK's**, **OK'd**, **OK'ing**) [with obj.] sanction or give approval to: *the Governor recently OK'd the execution of a man who had committed murder.*
– ORIGIN mid 19th cent. (originally US): probably an abbreviation of *orl korrect*, humorous form of *all correct*, popularized as a slogan during President Van Buren's re-election campaign of 1840 in the US; his nickname *Old Kinderhook* (derived from his birthplace) provided the initials.

OK[2] ▶ **abbreviation for** Oklahoma (in official postal use).

Oka /ˈəʊkə/ ▶ **noun** [mass noun] a variety of cured Canadian cheese, made by Trappist monks.
– ORIGIN named after a town in southern Quebec, where the cheese is made.

oka /ˈɒkə/ (also **oke**) ▶ **noun** **1** an Egyptian and former Turkish unit of weight, variable but now usually equal to approximately 1.3 kg (2¾ lb).
2 an Egyptian and former Turkish unit of capacity equal to approximately 0.2 litre (⅓ pint).
– ORIGIN early 17th cent.: via Italian and French *oque* from Turkish *okka*, from Arabic *ūḳiya*, based on Latin *uncia* 'ounce'.

okapi /ə(ʊ)ˈkɑːpi/ ▶ **noun** (pl. same or **okapis**) a large browsing mammal of the giraffe family that lives in the rainforests of northern Zaire (Democratic Republic of Congo). It has a dark chestnut coat with stripes on the hindquarters and upper legs.
● *Okapia johnstoni*, family Giraffidae.
– ORIGIN early 20th cent.: a local word.

Okara /əʊˈkɑːrə/ a commercial city in NE Pakistan, in Punjab province; pop. 154,000 (1981).

Okavango /ˌəʊkəˈvaŋgəʊ/ a river of SW Africa which rises in central Angola and flows 1,600 km (1,000 miles) south-eastwards to Namibia, where it turns eastwards to form part of the border between Angola and Namibia before entering Botswana, where it drains into the extensive Okavango marshes of Ngamiland. Also called **CUBANGO**.

okay ▶ **exclamation**, **adjective**, **adverb**, **noun**, & **verb** variant spelling of **OK**[1].

Okayama /ˌəʊkəˈjɑːmə/ an industrial city and major railway junction in SW Japan, on the SW coast of the island of Honshu; pop. 593,740 (1990).

oke[1] ▶ **noun** variant spelling of **OKA**.

oke[2] ▶ **exclamation**, **adjective**, etc. another term for **OKAY**.

oke[3] (also **okie**) ▶ **noun** (pl. **okes** or **okies**) S. African informal a man: *who's that oke talking to your sister?*
■(**okie**) used to refer to or address a boy or, patronizingly, a man.
– ORIGIN shortened form of *okie*, Anglicized form of Afrikaans *outjie* 'little chap'.

Okeechobee, Lake /ˌəʊkəˈtʃəʊbiː/ a lake in southern Florida. It forms part of the Okeechobee Waterway, which crosses the Florida peninsula from west to east, linking the Gulf of Mexico with the Atlantic.

O'Keeffe /əʊˈkiːf/, Georgia (1887–1986), American painter. Her best-known paintings depict enlarged studies, particularly of flowers, and are often regarded as being sexually symbolic (for example *Black Iris*, 1926).

Okefenokee Swamp /ˌəʊkəfəˈnəʊkiː/ an area of swampland in SE Georgia and NE Florida.

okey-dokey (also **okey-doke**) ▶ **exclamation**, **adjective**, & **adverb** variant form of **OK**[1].

Okhotsk, Sea of /əʊˈxɒtsk/ an inlet of the northern Pacific Ocean on the east coast of Russia, between the Kamchatka peninsula and the Kurile Islands.

Okie ▶ **noun** (pl. **-ies**) US informal a native or inhabitant of Oklahoma.
■historical, derogatory a migrant agricultural worker from Oklahoma who had been forced to leave a farm during the depression of the 1930s.

Okinawa /ˌəʊkɪˈnɑːwə/ a region in southern Japan, in the southern Ryukyu Islands; capital, Naha.

Okla ▶ **abbreviation for** Oklahoma.

Oklahoma /ˌəʊkləˈhəʊmə/ a state in the south central US, north of Texas; pop. 3,145,585 (1990); capital, Oklahoma City. In 1803 it was acquired from the French as part of the Louisiana Purchase. It became the 46th state of the US in 1907.
– DERIVATIVES **Oklahoman** noun & adjective.

Oklahoma City the state capital of Oklahoma; pop. 444,720 (1990).

okra /ˈɒkrə, ˈəʊkrə/ ▶ **noun** [mass noun] a plant of the mallow family with long ridged seed pods, native to the Old World tropics.
● *Abelmoschus esculentus*, family Malvaceae.
■the immature seed pods of this plant eaten as a vegetable and also used to thicken soups and stews. Also called **BHINDI**, **GUMBO**, or **LADIES' FINGERS**.
– ORIGIN early 18th cent.: a West African word, perhaps from the root *nkru*; compare with *nkran*, the name of the town Europeanized as *Accra*.

okrug /ˈɒkrʊg/ ▶ **noun** (in Russia and Bulgaria) a territorial division for administrative and other purposes.
– ORIGIN Russian *okrug*, Bulgarian *okrăg*.

okta /ˈɒktə/ ▶ **noun** (pl. same or **oktas**) Meteorology a unit used in expressing the extent of cloud cover, equal to one eighth of the sky.
– ORIGIN 1950s: alteration of **OCTA-**.

-ol ▶ **suffix** Chemistry forming names of organic compounds: **1** denoting alcohols and phenols: *glycerol | retinol.*
2 denoting oils and oil-derived compounds: *benzol.*
– ORIGIN sense 1 from *(alcoh)ol*; sense 2 from Latin *oleum* 'oil'. See also **-OLE**.

Olaf /ˈəʊlaf/ the name of five kings of Norway:
■**Olaf I Tryggvason** (969–1000), reigned 995–1000.
■**Olaf II Haraldsson** (c.995–1030), reigned 1016–30; canonized as **St Olaf** for his attempts to spread Christianity in his kingdom. He is the patron saint of Norway. Feast day, 29 July.
■**Olaf III Haraldsson** (d.1093), reigned 1066–93.
■**Olaf IV Haakonson** (1370–87), reigned 1380–7.
■**Olaf V** (b.1903), reigned 1957–91; full name *Olaf Alexander Edmund Christian Frederik*.

Öland /ˈəːland/ a narrow island in the Baltic Sea off the SE coast of Sweden, separated from the mainland by Kalmar Sound.

Olbers' Paradox /ˈɒlbəz/ Astronomy the apparent paradox that if stars are distributed evenly throughout an infinite universe, the sky should be as bright by night as by day, since more distant stars would be fainter but more numerous. This is not the case because the universe is of finite age, and the light from the more distant stars is dimmed because they are receding from the observer as the universe expands.
– ORIGIN 1950s: named after Heinrich W. M. *Olbers* (1758–1840), the German astronomer who propounded it in 1826.

old ▶ **adjective** (**older**, **oldest**) See also **ELDER**[1], **ELDEST**. **1** having lived for a long time; no longer young: *the old man lay propped up on cushions.*
■made or built long ago: *the old quarter of the town.* ■ possessed or used for a long time: *he gave his old clothes away.* ■ having the characteristics or showing the signs of age: *he complained of being old beyond his years.*
2 [attrib.] belonging only or chiefly to the past; former or previous: *valuation under the old rating system was inexact.*
■used to refer to the first of two or more similar things: *I was going to try to get my old job back.* ■ dating from far back; long-established or known: *we greet each other like old friends | I get sick of the* **same old** *routine.* ■ denoting someone who formerly attended a specified school: *an old Etonian.* ■ (of a form of a language) as used in former or earliest times.
3 [in combination] of a specified age: *he was fourteen years old | a seven-month-old baby.*
■[as noun] [in combination] a person or animal of the age specified: *a nineteen-year-old.*
4 [attrib.] informal used to express affection, familiarity, or contempt: *it wasn't a bad old life | 'Good old Mum,' she said.*
– PHRASES **any old** any item of a specified type (used to show that no particular or special individual is in question): *any old room would have done.* **any old how** in no particular order: *they've dropped things just any old how.* **as old as the hills** of very long standing or very great age (often used in exaggerated statements). **for old times' sake** see **SAKE**[1]. **of old** **1** in or belonging to the past: *he was more reticent than of old.* **2** starting long ago; for a long time: *they knew him of old.* **the old days** a period in the past, often seen as significantly different from the present, especially noticeably better or worse: *it was easier in the old days | we are less confident than in* **the good old days** *|* **the bad old days** *of incoherence and irresponsibility.* **old enough to be someone's father** (or **mother**) informal of a much greater age than someone (especially used to suggest that a romantic or sexual relationship between the people concerned is inappropriate). **you can't put an old head on young shoulders** proverb you can't expect a young person to have the wisdom or maturity associated with older people.
– DERIVATIVES **oldish** adjective, **oldness** noun.
– ORIGIN Old English *ald*, of West Germanic origin; related to Dutch *oud* and German *alt*, from an Indo-European root meaning 'grown-up, adult', shared by Latin *alere* 'nourish'.

old age ▶ **noun** [mass noun] the later part of normal life: *loneliness affects many people* **in old age**.
■the state of being old: *old age itself is not a disease.*

old-age pension ▶ **noun** another term for **RETIREMENT PENSION**.

old-age pensioner ▶ **noun** an old person, especially one receiving an old-age pension.

Old Bailey the Central Criminal Court in London, formerly standing in an ancient bailey of the London city wall. The present court was built in 1903–6 on the site of Newgate Prison.

O

old bean ▶ noun see **BEAN**.

Old Believer ▶ noun a member of a Russian Orthodox group which refused to accept the liturgical reforms of the patriarch Nikon (1605–81).

Old Bill ▶ noun see **BILL**.

old boy ▶ noun **1** a former male pupil of a school, college, or university.
■ a former male member of a sports team, company, or other organization.
2 informal an elderly man.
■ an affectionate form of address to a boy or man.

old boy network (also **old boys' network**) ▶ noun an informal system of support and friendship through which men are thought to use their positions of influence to help others who went to the same school or university as they did, or who share a similar social background.

Old Catholic ▶ noun a member of any of various religious groups which have separated from the Roman Catholic Church since the Reformation, especially the Church of Utrecht (which broke with Rome over the condemnation of Jansenism in 1724), and a number of German-speaking Churches which refused to accept papal infallibility after the First Vatican Council.
■ a member of an English family that have remained Roman Catholic since the Reformation.

Old Church Slavonic ▶ noun [mass noun] the oldest recorded Slavic language, as used by the apostles Cyril and Methodius and surviving in texts from the 9th–12th centuries. It is related particularly to the Southern Slavic languages. See also **CHURCH SLAVONIC**.

Old Colony informal name for **MASSACHUSETTS**.

Old Contemptibles the veterans of the British Expeditionary Force sent to France in the First World War (1914), so named because of a supposed German reference to the 'contemptible little army' facing them.

old country ▶ noun **(the old country)** the native country of a person who has gone to live abroad.

Old Dart ▶ noun Austral./NZ informal England.
– ORIGIN *Dart* as a figurative use representing a pronunciation of *dirt*, from **PAY DIRT**.

old dear ▶ noun informal a patronizing term for an elderly woman.

Old Delhi see **DELHI**.

Old Dominion informal name for **VIRGINIA**[1].

olde /əʊld, ˈəʊldi/ ▶ adjective [attrib.] pseudo-archaic in or relating to on old-fashioned style that is intended to be quaint and attractive: *Ye Olde Tea Shoppe*.

olden ▶ adjective [attrib.] archaic of or relating to former times: *the olden days*.

Old English ▶ noun [mass noun] the language of the Anglo-Saxons (up to about 1150), an inflected language with a Germanic vocabulary, very different from modern English. Also called **ANGLO-SAXON**.

Old English sheepdog ▶ noun a large sheepdog of a breed with a shaggy blue-grey and white coat.

olde worlde /ˈwɜːldi/ ▶ adjective pseudo-archaic in or relating to an old-fashioned style that is intended to be quaint and attractive (often used to suggest a lack of authenticity): *picturesque villages with olde worlde inns*.

old-fangled ▶ adjective characterized by adherence to what is old; old-fashioned.

old-fashioned ▶ adjective in or according to styles or types no longer current or common; not modern: *an old-fashioned kitchen range*.
■ (of a person or their views) favouring traditional and usually restrictive styles, ideas, or customs: *she's stuffy and old-fashioned*. ■ (of a facial expression) disapproving: *Jonas gave her an old-fashioned look*.
▶ noun [mass noun] N. Amer. a cocktail consisting chiefly of whisky, bitters, water, and sugar.
– DERIVATIVES **old-fashionedness** noun.

old-fashioned rose ▶ noun another term for **OLD ROSE** (in sense 1).

old-fashioned waltz ▶ noun a waltz played in quick time.

Oldfield, Bruce (b.1950), English fashion designer.

old field ▶ noun US a piece of formerly cultivated land left fallow because it has been exhausted.

Old French ▶ noun [mass noun] the French language up to c.1400.

Old Frisian ▶ noun [mass noun] the Frisian language up to c.1400, closely related to both Old English and Old Saxon.

old fruit ▶ noun Brit. informal, dated a friendly form of address to a man.

old fustic ▶ noun see **FUSTIC** (sense 2).

old girl ▶ noun **1** a former female pupil of a school, college, or university.
■ a former female member of a sports team, company, or other organization.
2 informal an elderly woman.
■ an affectionate term of address to a girl or woman.

Old Glory US an informal name for the US national flag.

old gold ▶ noun [mass noun] a dull brownish-gold colour.

old guard ▶ noun (usu. **the old guard**) the original or long-standing members of a group or party, especially ones who are unwilling to accept change or new ideas: *the ageing right-wing old guard*.

Oldham /ˈəʊldəm/ an industrial town in NW England, near Manchester; pop. 100,000 (1991).

old hand ▶ noun a person with a lot of experience in something: *the examiner is an old hand at the game*.

old hat ▶ adjective informal tediously predictable or old-fashioned: *last year's electronics are already old hat*.

Old High German ▶ noun [mass noun] the language of southern Germany up to c.1200, from which modern standard German is derived. See **GERMAN**.

Old Icelandic ▶ noun [mass noun] Icelandic up to the 16th century, a form of Old Norse in which the medieval sagas were composed.

old identity ▶ noun Austral./NZ a person long resident or well known in a place.

oldie ▶ noun informal an old song, film, or television programme that is still well known or popular.
■ an older person.

Old Irish ▶ noun [mass noun] the Irish Gaelic language up to c.1000, from which modern Irish and Scottish Gaelic are derived.

Old Kingdom a period of ancient Egyptian history (c.2575–2134 BC, 4th–8th dynasty).

old lady ▶ noun **1** an elderly woman.
■ informal one's mother or wife.
2 a brownish European moth with a creamy pattern on the wings.
● *Mormo maura*, family Noctuidae.

Old Lady of Threadneedle Street the nickname of the Bank of England, which stands in this street.

old lag ▶ noun see **LAG**[3].

Old Latin ▶ noun [mass noun] Latin before about 100 BC.

Old Left ▶ noun (**the Old Left**) a name given to the older liberal elements in the socialist movement.
■ a name given to the more left wing elements of the British Labour Party, as distinct from the more centrist elements who became dominant in the 1980s and 1990s.

old-line ▶ adjective N. Amer. **1** holding conservative views.
2 well established.
– DERIVATIVES **old-liner** noun.

Old Line State informal name for **MARYLAND**.

Old Low German ▶ noun [mass noun] the language of northern Germany and the Netherlands up to c.1200, from which modern Dutch and modern Low German are derived.

old maid ▶ noun **1** derogatory a single woman regarded as too old for marriage.
■ a prim and fussy person: *he said James was an old maid*.
2 [mass noun] a card game in which players collect pairs and try not to be left with an odd penalty card, typically a queen.
3 chiefly W. Indian another term for **PERIWINKLE**[1].
– DERIVATIVES **old-maidish** adjective.

old man ▶ noun **1** an elderly male person.
■ (**one's old man**) informal a person's father or a woman's husband or partner. ■ (**the old man**) informal a person in authority over others, especially an employer or commanding officer. ■ Brit. informal an affectionate term of address between men or boys: *are you all right, old man?* ■ informal used with a surname instead of Mr: *old man Roberts*.
2 another term for **SOUTHERNWOOD**.

old man's beard ▶ noun [mass noun] **1** a wild

clematis which has grey fluffy hairs around the seeds.
● Genus *Clematis*, family Ranunculaceae: several species, in particular (in Britain) traveller's joy.
2 a large lichen that forms shaggy greyish beard-like growths on the branches of trees.
● *Usnea barbata* and related species, order Parmeliales.

old master ▶ noun a great artist of former times, especially of the 13th–17th century in Europe.
■ a painting by such a painter: *he formed a large collection of old masters*.

old moon ▶ noun the moon in its last quarter, before the new moon.

Old Nick an informal name for the Devil.
– ORIGIN mid 17th cent.: probably from a pet form of the given name *Nicholas*.

Old Norse ▶ noun [mass noun] the North Germanic language of medieval Norway, Iceland, Denmark, and Sweden up to the 14th century, from which the modern Scandinavian languages are derived. See also **OLD ICELANDIC**.

Old North State informal name for **NORTH CAROLINA**.

Oldowan /ˈɒldə(ʊ)wən/ ▶ adjective Archaeology of, relating to, or denoting an early Lower Palaeolithic culture of Africa, dated to about 2.0–1.5 million years ago. It is characterized by primitive stone tools that are associated chiefly with *Homo habilis*.
■ [as noun **the Oldowan**] the Oldowan culture or period.
– ORIGIN 1930s: from *Oldoway*, alteration of **OLDUVAI GORGE**, Tanzania, + -**AN**.

Old Pals Act ▶ noun Brit. informal used humorously to imply that someone is using a position of influence to help their friends.

Old Persian ▶ noun [mass noun] the Persian language up to the 3rd century BC, used in the ancient Persian empire and written in cuneiform.

Old Pretender see **STUART**[2].

Old Prussian ▶ noun [mass noun] a Baltic language, related to Lithuanian, spoken in Prussia until the 17th century.

Old Red Sandstone ▶ noun [mass noun] Geology a series of sedimentary rocks, chiefly red sandstones, belonging to the Devonian system of NW Europe.

old religion ▶ noun a religion replaced or ousted by another, in particular:
■ paganism. ■ witchcraft. ■ Roman Catholicism.

old rose ▶ noun **1** a double-flowered rose of a variety or hybrid evolved before the development of the hybrid tea rose.
2 [mass noun] a shade of deep pink.

Old Sarum a hill in southern England 3 km (2 miles) north of Salisbury, the site of an ancient Iron Age settlement and hill fort, and later of a Norman castle and town. It fell into decline after the new cathedral and town of Salisbury were established in 1220, and the site was deserted.

Old Saxon ▶ noun **1** a member of the Saxon peoples who remained in Germany, as opposed to an Anglo-Saxon.
2 [mass noun] the dialect of Old Low German spoken in Saxony up to c.1200.
▶ adjective of or relating to the Old Saxons or their language.

old school ▶ noun used, usually approvingly, to refer to someone or something that is old-fashioned or conservative: *he was one of the old school of English gentlemen*.

old school tie ▶ noun chiefly Brit. a necktie with a characteristic pattern worn by the former pupils of a particular school, especially a public school.
■ used to refer to the group loyalty, mutual assistance, social class, and traditional attitudes associated with people who attended public schools: *appointments based on social class and the old school tie*.

Old Slavonic ▶ noun another name for **CHURCH SLAVONIC**.

old soldier ▶ noun a man who used to serve in the army.
– PHRASES **come** (or **play**) **the old soldier** informal use one's greater age or experience of life to deceive someone or to shirk a duty.

Old South ▶ noun (**the Old South**) the Southern states of the US before the civil war of 1861–5.

old Spanish custom (also **Spanish practice**) ▶ noun informal an irregular practice in a company aimed at decreasing working hours or increasing financial rewards or perquisites.

oldspeak ▶ noun [mass noun] chiefly humorous normal English usage as opposed to technical or propagandist language.
– ORIGIN 1949: from George Orwell's *Nineteen Eighty-Four* (see **NEWSPEAK**).

oldsquaw ▶ noun North American term for **LONG-TAILED DUCK**.

old stager ▶ noun a person who is experienced at something or who has been in a place or position for a long time: *the changes aroused the suspicion and hostility of the old stagers*.

oldster ▶ noun informal, chiefly N. Amer. an older person.
– ORIGIN early 19th cent.: from **OLD**, on the pattern of *youngster*.

Old Stone Age the Palaeolithic period.

Old Style (abbrev.: **OS**) ▶ noun [mass noun] [often as modifier] the method of calculating dates using the Julian calendar.

old sweat ▶ noun informal a veteran soldier.

old talk W. Indian ▶ noun [mass noun] small talk; chatter: *they would start big old talk with the travellers, finding out what was happening in Trinidad.*
  ▪ empty or insincere talk: *the old talk and empty promises by the politicians.*
  ▶ verb (**old-talk**) [no obj.] engage in such talk.

Old Testament ▶ noun the first part of the Christian Bible, comprising thirty-nine books and corresponding approximately to the Hebrew Bible. Most of the books were written in Hebrew, some in Aramaic, between about 1200 and 100 BC. They comprise the chief texts of the law, history, prophecy, and wisdom literature of the ancient people of Israel.

old thing ▶ noun **1** informal a familiar form of address.
  2 Austral. a meal of beef and damper.

old-time ▶ adjective [attrib.] used to refer to something old-fashioned in an approving or nostalgic way: *old-time dancing.*
  ▪ US denoting traditional or folk styles of American popular music, such as gospel or bluegrass.
– PHRASES **for old times' sake** see **SAKE**[1].

old-timer ▶ noun informal a person who has been in a place or position or doing something for a long time.
  ▪ derogatory an old person.

Olduvai Gorge /ˈɒlduvaɪ/ a gorge in northern Tanzania, 48 km (30 miles) long and up to 90 metres (300 ft) deep. The exposed strata contain numerous fossils (especially hominids) spanning the full range of the Pleistocene period.

Old Vic the popular name of the Royal Victoria Theatre in London. Under the management of Lilian Baylis from 1912 it gained an enduring reputation for its Shakespearean productions.

Old Welsh ▶ noun [mass noun] the Welsh language up to c.1150.

old wife ▶ noun any of a number of deep-bodied edible marine fishes, in particular:
  ● a brightly patterned tropical Atlantic triggerfish (*Balistes vetula*, family Balistidae). ● a small brightly patterned Australian fish (*Enoplosus armatus*, the only member of the family Enoplosidae). ● the black sea bream of European Atlantic waters (*Spondyliosoma cantharus*, family Sparidae).

old witch grass ▶ noun see **WITCH GRASS**.

old wives' tale ▶ noun a widely held traditional belief that is now thought to be unscientific or incorrect.

old woman ▶ noun an elderly female person.
  ▪ informal (**one's old woman**) a person's mother or a man's wife or partner. ▪ derogatory a fussy or timid person, especially a man: *he's always telling me I'm an old woman about security.*
– DERIVATIVES **old-womanish** adjective.

Old World Europe, Asia, and Africa, regarded collectively as the part of the world known before the discovery of the Americas. Compare with **NEW WORLD**.

old-world ▶ adjective belonging to or associated with former times, especially when considered quaint and attractive: *medieval towns which still retain old-world charm.*

old year ▶ noun the year just ended or just about to end.

OLE Computing ▶ abbreviation for object linking and embedding, denoting a set of techniques for

transferring an object from one application to another.

ole ▶ adjective US informal old.
– ORIGIN mid 19th cent.: representing a pronunciation.

-ole ▶ combining form in names of organic compounds, especially heterocyclic compounds: *thiazole.*
– ORIGIN from Latin *oleum* 'oil' (compare with **-OL**).

olé /əʊˈleɪ/ ▶ exclamation bravo.
– ORIGIN Spanish.

oleaceous /ˌəʊlɪˈeɪʃəs/ ▶ adjective Botany of, relating to, or denoting plants of the olive family (Oleaceae).
– ORIGIN mid 19th cent.: from modern Latin *Oleaceae* (plural), based on Latin *olea* 'olive tree', + **-OUS**.

oleaginous /ˌəʊlɪˈadʒɪnəs/ ▶ adjective rich in, covered with, or producing oil; oily or greasy.
  ▪ figurative exaggeratedly and distastefully complimentary; obsequious: *candidates made oleaginous speeches praising government policies.*
– ORIGIN late Middle English: from French *oléagineux*, from Latin *oleaginus* 'of the olive tree', from *oleum* 'oil'.

oleander /ˌəʊlɪˈandə/ ▶ noun a poisonous evergreen Old World shrub which is widely grown in warm countries for its clusters of white, pink, or red flowers.
  ● *Nerium oleander*, family Apocynaceae.
– ORIGIN early 16th cent.: from medieval Latin, of unknown ultimate origin.

oleaster /ˌəʊlɪˈastə/ ▶ noun a Eurasian shrub or small tree which is sometimes cultivated as an ornamental.
  ● Genus *Elaeagnus*, family Elaeagnaceae: several species, in particular *E. angustifolia*, which bears edible yellow olive-shaped fruit (also called **RUSSIAN OLIVE** in North America).
– ORIGIN late Middle English: from Latin, from *olea* 'olive tree'.

olecranon /əʊˈlɛkrənɒn, ˌəʊlɪˈkreɪnən/ ▶ noun Anatomy a bony prominence at the elbow, on the upper end of the ulna.
– ORIGIN early 18th cent.: from Greek *ōle(no)kranon*, from *ōlenē* 'elbow' + *kranion* 'head'.

olefin /ˈəʊlɪfɪn/ (also **olefine**) ▶ noun Chemistry another term for **ALKENE**.
– DERIVATIVES **olefinic** adjective.
– ORIGIN mid 19th cent.: from French *oléfiant* 'oil-forming' (with reference to oily ethylene dichloride).

oleic acid /əʊˈliːɪk/ ▶ noun [mass noun] Chemistry an unsaturated fatty acid present in many fats and soaps.
  ● Chem. formula: $CH_3(CH_2)_7CH=CH(CH_2)_7COOH$.
– DERIVATIVES **oleate** /ˈəʊlɪət/ noun.
– ORIGIN early 19th cent.: *oleic* from Latin *oleum* 'oil'.

oleiferous /ˌəʊlɪˈɪf(ə)rəs/ ▶ adjective Botany (of seeds, glands, etc.) producing oil.
– ORIGIN early 19th cent.: from Latin *oleum* 'oil' + **-FEROUS**.

oleo- /ˈəʊlɪəʊ, ˈɒlɪəʊ/ ▶ combining form relating to or containing oil: *oleomargarine | oleoresin.*
– ORIGIN from Latin *oleum* 'oil'.

oleograph ▶ noun a print textured to resemble an oil painting.
– DERIVATIVES **oleographic** adjective, **oleography** noun.

oleomargarine ▶ noun [mass noun] a fatty substance extracted from beef fat and widely used in the manufacture of margarine.
  ▪ N. Amer. old-fashioned term for **MARGARINE**.

oleoresin ▶ noun a natural or artificial mixture of essential oils and a resin, e.g. balsam.
– DERIVATIVES **oleoresinous** adjective.

Olestra /ɒˈlɛstrə/ ▶ noun [mass noun] trademark a synthetic compound used as a calorie-free substitute for fat in various foods because of its ability to pass through the body without being absorbed. It is a polyester derived from sucrose.
– ORIGIN 1980s: from (*p*)*ol*(*y*)*est*(*e*)*r* + the suffix *-a*.

oleum /ˈəʊlɪəm/ ▶ noun [mass noun] a dense, corrosive liquid consisting of concentrated sulphuric acid containing excess sulphur trioxide in solution.
– ORIGIN early 20th cent.: from Latin, literally 'oil'.

O level ▶ noun short for **ORDINARY LEVEL**.
  ▪ an exam or pass at this level.

olfaction /ɒlˈfakʃ(ə)n/ ▶ noun [mass noun] technical the action or capacity of smelling; the sense of smell.
– DERIVATIVES **olfactive** adjective.

– ORIGIN mid 19th cent.: from Latin *olfactus* 'a smell' (from *olere* 'to smell' + *fact-* 'made', from the verb *facere*) + **-ION**.

olfactometer /ˌɒlfakˈtɒmɪtə/ ▶ noun an instrument for measuring the intensity of an odour or the sensitivity of someone or something to an odour.
– DERIVATIVES **olfactometry** noun.

olfactory /ɒlˈfakt(ə)ri/ ▶ adjective of or relating to the sense of smell: *the olfactory organs.*
– ORIGIN mid 17th cent.: from Latin *olfactare* (frequentative of *olfacere* 'to smell') + **-ORY**[2].

olfactory nerve ▶ noun Anatomy each of the first pair of cranial nerves, supplying the smell receptors in the mucous membrane of the nose.

olibanum /ɒˈlɪbənəm/ ▶ noun another term for **FRANKINCENSE**.
– ORIGIN late Middle English: from medieval Latin, from Late Latin *libanus*, from Greek *libanos* 'frankincense'.

oligaemia /ˌɒlɪˈgiːmɪə/ (US **oligemia**) ▶ noun another term for **HYPOVOLAEMIA**.
– DERIVATIVES **oligaemic** adjective.
– ORIGIN mid 19th cent.: from French *oligaimie*, from Greek *oligaimia*.

oligarch /ˈɒlɪgɑːk/ ▶ noun a ruler in an oligarchy.
– ORIGIN late 19th cent.: from Greek *oligarkhēs*, from *oligoi* 'few' + *arkhein* 'to rule'.

oligarchy ▶ noun (pl. **-ies**) a small group of people having control of a country, organization, or institution: *the ruling oligarchy of military men around the president.*
  ▪ a state governed by such a group: *he believed that Britain was an oligarchy.* ▪ [mass noun] government by such a group.
– DERIVATIVES **oligarchic** adjective, **oligarchical** adjective, **oligarchically** adverb.
– ORIGIN late 15th cent.: from Greek *oligarkhia* (probably via medieval Latin).

oligo ▶ noun (pl. **-os**) Biochemistry short for **OLIGONUCLEOTIDE**.

oligo- ▶ combining form having few; containing a relatively small number of units: *oligopoly | oligosaccharide.*
– ORIGIN from Greek *oligos* 'small', *oligoi* 'few'.

Oligocene /ˈɒlɪgə(ʊ)siːn/ ▶ adjective Geology of, relating to, or denoting the third epoch of the Tertiary period, between the Eocene and Miocene epochs.
  ▪ [as noun **the Oligocene**] the Oligocene epoch or the system of rocks deposited during it.

The Oligocene epoch lasted from 35.4 to 23.3 million years ago. It was a time of falling temperatures, with evidence of the first primates.

– ORIGIN mid 19th cent.: from **OLIGO-** 'few' + Greek *kainos* 'new'.

Oligochaeta /ˌɒlɪgə(ʊ)ˈkiːtə/ Zoology a class of annelid worms which includes the earthworms. They have simple setae projecting from each segment and a small head lacking sensory appendages.
– DERIVATIVES **oligochaete** noun.
– ORIGIN modern Latin (plural), from **OLIGO-** 'few' + Greek *khaitē* 'long hair' (taken to mean 'bristle'), because they have fewer setae than polychaetes.

oligoclase /ˈɒlɪgə(ʊ)kleɪz/ ▶ noun [mass noun] a feldspar mineral common in siliceous igneous rocks, consisting of a sodium-rich plagioclase (with more calcium than albite).
– ORIGIN mid 19th cent.: from **OLIGO-** 'relatively little' + Greek *klasis* 'breaking' (because thought to have a less perfect cleavage than albite).

oligodendrocyte /ˌɒlɪgə(ʊ)ˈdɛndrəsʌɪt/ ▶ noun Anatomy a glial cell similar to an astrocyte but with fewer protuberances, concerned with the production of myelin in the central nervous system.
– ORIGIN 1930s: from **OLIGODENDROGLIA** + **-CYTE**.

oligodendroglia /ˌɒlɪgə(ʊ)dɛndrə'glʌɪə/ ▶ plural noun Anatomy oligodendrocytes collectively.
– DERIVATIVES **oligodendroglial** adjective.
– ORIGIN 1920s: from **OLIGO-** 'few' + **DENDRO-** 'branching' + a shortened form of **NEUROGLIA**.

oligodendroglioma /ˌɒlɪgə(ʊ)ˌdɛndrə(ʊ)glɪˈəʊmə/ ▶ noun (pl. **oligodendrogliomas** or **oligodendrogliomata** /-mətə/) Medicine a tumour derived from oligodendroglia.

oligomer /ɒˈlɪgəmə, ˈɒlɪg-/ ▶ noun Chemistry a polymer

whose molecules consist of relatively few repeating units.

oligomerize /ə'lɪɡəmərʌɪz/ (also **-ise**) ▶ verb [with obj.] Chemistry join a number of molecules of (a monomer) together to form an oligomer.
– DERIVATIVES **oligomerization** noun.

oligomerous /ˌɒlɪ'ɡɒmərəs/ ▶ adjective Biology having a small number of segments or parts.

oligonucleotide /ˌɒlɪɡə(ʊ)'nju:klɪətʌɪd/ ▶ noun Biochemistry a polynucleotide whose molecules contain a relatively small number of nucleotides.

oligopeptide /ˌɒlɪɡə(ʊ)'pɛptʌɪd/ ▶ noun Biochemistry a peptide whose molecules contain a relatively small number of amino-acid residues.

oligopoly /ˌɒlɪ'ɡɒp(ə)li/ ▶ noun (pl. **-ies**) a state of limited competition, in which a market is shared by a small number of producers or sellers.
– DERIVATIVES **oligopolist** noun, **oligopolistic** adjective.
– ORIGIN late 19th cent.: from OLIGO- 'small number', on the pattern of *monopoly*.

oligopsony /ˌɒlɪ'ɡɒps(ə)ni/ ▶ noun (pl. **-ies**) a state of the market in which only a small number of buyers exists for a product.
– DERIVATIVES **oligopsonistic** adjective.
– ORIGIN 1940s: from OLIGO- 'small number' + Greek *opsōnein* 'buy provisions', on the pattern of *monopsony*.

oligosaccharide /ˌɒlɪɡə(ʊ)'sakərʌɪd/ ▶ noun Biochemistry a carbohydrate whose molecules are composed of a relatively small number of monosaccharide units.

oligospermia /ˌɒlɪɡə(ʊ)'spɜ:mɪə/ ▶ noun [mass noun] Medicine deficiency of sperm cells in the semen.

oligotrophic /ˌɒlɪɡə(ʊ)'trəʊfɪk, -'trɒfɪk/ ▶ adjective Ecology (especially of a lake) relatively poor in plant nutrients and containing abundant oxygen in the deeper parts. Compare with DYSTROPHIC, EUTROPHIC.
– DERIVATIVES **oligotrophy** noun.

oliguria /ɒlɪ'ɡjʊərɪə/ ▶ noun [mass noun] Medicine the production of abnormally small amounts of urine.
– DERIVATIVES **oliguric** adjective.

olingo /ɒ'lɪŋɡəʊ/ ▶ noun (pl. **-os**) a small nocturnal mammal resembling the kinkajou but with a long muzzle and a bushy non-prehensile tail, living in tropical American rainforests.
● Genus *Bassaricyon*, family Procyonidae: between one and five species.
– ORIGIN 1920s: via American Spanish from Mayan.

olio /'əʊlɪəʊ/ ▶ noun (pl. **-os**) a highly spiced stew of various meats and vegetables originating from Spain and Portugal.
■ a miscellaneous collection of things. ■ a variety act or show.
– ORIGIN mid 17th cent.: from Spanish *olla* 'stew', from Latin *olla* 'cooking pot'.

olivaceous /ˌɒlɪ'veɪʃəs/ ▶ adjective technical of a dusky yellowish green colour; olive green.

olivary /'ɒlɪv(ə)ri/ ▶ adjective Anatomy relating to or denoting the nucleus situated in the olive of the medulla oblongata in the brain.
– ORIGIN late Middle English: from Latin *olivarius* 'relating to olives', from *oliva* (see OLIVE).

olive ▶ noun 1 a small oval fruit with a hard stone and bitter flesh, green when unripe and bluish black when ripe, used as food and as a source of oil.
■ Anatomy each of a pair of smooth, oval swellings in the medulla oblongata. ■ a slice of beef or veal made into a roll with stuffing inside and stewed.
2 (also **olive tree**) the small evergreen tree which yields this fruit, native to warm regions of the Old World. It has slender leathery leaves with silvery undersides and is widely cultivated.
● *Olea europaea*, family Oleaceae (the **olive family**). This family also includes the ash, lilac, jasmine, and privet.
■ used in names of other trees which are related to the olive, resemble it, or bear similar fruit, e.g. **Russian olive**.
3 (also **olive green**) [mass noun] a greyish-green colour like that of an unripe olive.
4 a metal ring or fitting which is tightened under a threaded nut to form a seal, as in a compression joint.
5 (also **olive shell**) a marine mollusc with a smooth, roughly cylindrical shell which is typically brightly coloured.
● Genus *Oliva*, family Olividae, class Gastropoda.

▶ adjective greyish-green, like an unripe olive: *a small figure in olive fatigues*.
■ (of the complexion) yellowish brown; sallow.
– ORIGIN Middle English: via Old French from Latin *oliva*, from Greek *elaia*, from *elaion* 'oil'.

olive branch ▶ noun the branch of an olive tree, traditionally regarded as a symbol of peace (in allusion to the story of Noah in Gen. 8:1, in which a dove returns with an olive branch after the Flood).
■ an offer of reconciliation: *the government is holding out an olive branch to the demonstrators*.

olive brown ▶ noun [mass noun] a dull shade of yellowish brown.

olive drab ▶ noun [mass noun] a dull olive-green colour, used in some military uniforms.

olive oil ▶ noun [mass noun] an oil obtained from olives, used in cookery and salad dressings.

Oliver the companion of Roland in the *Chanson de Roland* (see ROLAND).

Olives, Mount of see MOUNT OF OLIVES.

olivette /ɒlɪ'vɛt/ ▶ noun a small oval weight threaded on a fishing line.
– ORIGIN early 19th cent. (in the sense 'an oval button or bead').

Olivier /ə'lɪvɪeɪ/, Laurence (Kerr), Baron Olivier of Brighton (1907–89), English actor and director. Following his professional debut in 1924, he performed all the major Shakespearean roles; he was also director of the National Theatre (1963–73). His films include *Rebecca* (1940), *Henry V* (1944), and *Hamlet* (1948).

olivine /'ɒlɪvi:n, -ʌɪn/ ▶ noun [mass noun] an olive-green, grey-green, or brown mineral occurring widely in basalt, peridotite, and other basic igneous rocks. It is a silicate containing varying proportions of magnesium, iron, and other elements.
– ORIGIN late 18th cent.: from Latin *oliva* (see OLIVE) + -INE[1].

olla podrida /ˌɒlə pə(ʊ)'dri:də, Spanish ˌoja po'ðriða/ ▶ noun another term for OLIO.
– ORIGIN Spanish, literally 'rotten pot', from Latin *olla* 'jar' + *putridus* 'rotten'.

ollie ▶ noun (pl. **-ies**) (in skateboarding and snowboarding) a jump performed without the aid of a take-off ramp, executed by pressing the foot down on the tail of the board to rebound the deck off the ground.
▶ verb (**ollieing**) [no obj.] perform such a jump.
– ORIGIN 1980s: of unknown origin.

ollycrock /'ɒlɪkrɒk/ ▶ noun S. African a turban shell which is eaten as seafood and used as bait.
● *Turbo sarmaticus*, family Turbinidae, class Gastropoda.
– ORIGIN Anglicized form of Afrikaans *alikreukel*.

olm /əʊlm, ɒlm/ ▶ noun a pale-skinned blind salamander with external gills which lives in limestone caves in SE Europe.
● *Proteus anguinus*, family Proteidae.
– ORIGIN late 19th cent.: from German.

Olmec /'ɒlmɛk/ ▶ noun (pl. same or **Olmecs**) 1 a member of a prehistoric people inhabiting the coast of Veracruz and western Tabasco on the Gulf of Mexico (c.1200–400 BC), who established what was probably the first developed civilization of Meso-America.
2 a native people living in the same general area during the 15th and 16th centuries.
– ORIGIN from Nahuatl *Olmecatl*, (plural) *Olmeca*, literally 'inhabitants of the rubber country'.

Olmos /'ɒlmɒs/ a small town on the eastern edge of the Sechura Desert in NW Peru, which gave its name to a major irrigation project initiated in 1926.

ology ▶ noun (pl. **-ies**) informal, humorous a subject of study; a branch of knowledge.
– DERIVATIVES **ologist** noun.

-ology ▶ combining form common form of -LOGY.

Olomouc /'ɒləməʊts/ an industrial city on the Morava river in northern Moravia in the Czech Republic; pop. 105,690 (1991).

oloroso /ˌɒlə'rəʊsəʊ/ ▶ noun [mass noun] a heavy, dark, medium-sweet sherry.
■ sherry which does not have a covering of flor (yeast) during production, used to make oloroso and cream sherries. Compare with FINO.
– ORIGIN Spanish, literally 'fragrant'.

Olsztyn /'ɒlʃtɪn/ a city in northern Poland, in the lakeland area of Masuria; pop. 163,935 (1990). Founded in 1348 by the Teutonic Knights, it was a part of Prussia between 1772 and 1945. German name ALLENSTEIN.

Olympia 1 a plain in Greece, in the western Peloponnese. In ancient Greece it was the site of the chief sanctuary of the god Zeus, the place where the original Olympic Games were held, after which the site is named.
2 the capital of the state of Washington, a port on Puget Sound; pop. 33,840 (1990).

Olympiad /ə'lɪmpɪad/ ▶ noun a celebration of the ancient or modern Olympic Games.
■ a period of four years between Olympic Games, used by the ancient Greeks in dating events. ■ a major national or international contest in some activity, notably chess or bridge.
– ORIGIN via French or Latin from Greek *Olumpias*, *Olumpiad-*, from *Olumpios* (see also OLYMPIAN and OLYMPIC).

Olympian ▶ adjective 1 associated with Mount Olympus in NE Greece, or with the Greek gods whose home was traditionally held to be there: *a temple of Olympian Zeus*.
■ resembling or appropriate to a god, especially in superiority and aloofness: *the court is capable of an Olympian detachment and impartiality*.
2 [attrib.] relating to the ancient or modern Olympic Games: *an Olympian champion*.
▶ noun 1 any of the pantheon of twelve gods regarded as living on Olympus.
■ a person of great attainments or exalted position.
2 a competitor in the Olympic Games.
– ORIGIN late 15th cent.: sense 1 from Latin *Olympus* (see OLYMPUS) + -IAN; sense 2 from *Olympia* (see OLYMPIA) + -AN.

Olympic ▶ adjective [attrib.] of or relating to ancient Olympia or the Olympic Games: *an Olympic champion*.
▶ noun (**the Olympics**) the Olympic Games.
– ORIGIN late 16th cent.: via Latin from Greek *Olumpikos* 'of Olympus or Olympia', the latter (see OLYMPIA) being the site of games in honour of Zeus of Olympus.

Olympic Games (also **the Olympics**) a sports festival held every four years in different venues, instigated by the Frenchman Baron de Coubertin (1863–1937) in 1896. Athletes representing nearly 150 countries now compete for gold, silver, and bronze medals in more than twenty sports.
■ an ancient Greek festival with athletic, literary, and musical competitions held at Olympia every four years, traditionally from 776 BC until abolished by the Roman emperor Theodosius I in AD 393.

Olympic-sized (also **Olympic-size**) ▶ adjective (of a swimming pool or other sports venue) of the dimensions prescribed for modern Olympic competitions.

Olympus Greek Mythology the home of the twelve greater gods, identified in later antiquity with Mount Olympus in Greece.

Olympus, Mount 1 a mountain in northern Greece, at the eastern end of the range dividing Thessaly from Macedonia; height 2,917 m (9,570 ft).
2 a mountain in Cyprus, in the Troodos range. Rising to 1,951 m (6,400 ft), it is the highest peak on the island.

OM ▶ abbreviation for (in the UK) Order of Merit.

om /əʊm/ ▶ noun Hinduism & Tibetan Buddhism a mystic syllable, considered the most sacred mantra. It appears at the beginning and end of most Sanskrit recitations, prayers, and texts.
– ORIGIN Sanskrit, sometimes regarded as three sounds, *a-u-m*, symbolic of the three major Hindu deities.

-oma ▶ suffix (forming nouns) denoting tumours and other abnormal growths: *carcinoma*.
– ORIGIN modern Latin, from a Greek suffix denoting the result of verbal action.

omadhaun /'ɒmədɔːn/ (also **omadawn** or **omadhawn**) ▶ noun N. Amer. & Irish a foolish person.
– ORIGIN early 19th cent.: from Irish *amadán*.

Omagh /əʊ'mɑː, 'əʊmə/ a town in Northern Ireland, principal town of County Tyrone; pop. 14,600 (1981).

Omaha[1] /'əʊməhɑː/ a city in eastern Nebraska, on the Missouri River; pop. 335,795 (1990).

Omaha[2] /'əʊməhɑː/ ▶ noun (pl. same or **Omahas**) 1 a

member of an American Indian people of NE Nebraska.

2 [mass noun] the Siouan language of this people, now all but extinct.

▶ **adjective** of or relating to this people or their language.

– ORIGIN from Omaha *umonhon* 'upstream people'.

Oman /əʊˈmɑːn/ a country at the eastern corner of the Arabian peninsula; pop. 1,600,000 (est. 1991); official language, Arabic; capital, Muscat.

An independent sultanate, known as Muscat and Oman until 1970, Oman was the most influential power in the region in the 19th century, controlling Zanzibar and other territory. Since the late 19th century Oman has had strong links with Britain. The economy is dependent on oil, discovered in 1964.

– DERIVATIVES **Omani** adjective & noun.

Oman, Gulf of an inlet of the Arabian Sea, connected by the Strait of Hormuz to the Persian Gulf.

Omar I /ˈəʊmɑː/ (*c*.581–644), Muslim caliph 634–44. He conquered Syria, Palestine, and Egypt.

Omar Khayyám /kʌɪˈɑːm/ (d.1123), Persian poet, mathematician, and astronomer. His *rubáiyát* (quatrains), found in *The Rubáiyát of Omar Khayyám* (translation published 1859), are meditations on the mysteries of existence and celebrations of worldly pleasures.

omasum /əʊˈmeɪsəm/ ▶ **noun** (pl. **omasa** /-sə/) Zoology the muscular third stomach of a ruminant animal, between the reticulum and the abomasum. Also called **PSALTERIUM**.

– ORIGIN early 18th cent.: from Latin, literally 'bullock's tripe'.

Omayyad /əʊˈmʌɪjad/ variant spelling of **UMAYYAD**.

ombre /ˈɒmbə, ˈɒmbreɪ/ ▶ **noun** [mass noun] a trick-taking card game for three people using a pack of forty cards, popular in Europe in the 17th–18th centuries.

– ORIGIN from Spanish *hombre* 'man', with reference to one player seeking to win the pool.

ombré /ˈɒmbreɪ/ ▶ **adjective** (of a fabric) having a dyed, printed, or woven design in which the colour is graduated from light to dark.

– ORIGIN French, past participle of *ombrer* 'to shade'.

ombro- ▶ **combining form** relating to rain: *ombrotrophic*.

– ORIGIN from Greek *ombros* 'rain shower'.

ombrogenous /ɒmˈbrɒdʒɪnəs/ ▶ **adjective** Ecology (of a bog or peat) dependent on rain for its formation.

ombrotrophic /ˌɒmbrə(ʊ)ˈtrəʊfɪk, -ˈtrɒfɪk/ ▶ **adjective** Ecology (of a bog or its vegetation) dependent on atmospheric moisture for its nutrients.

ombudsman /ˈɒmbʊdzmən/ ▶ **noun** (pl. **-men**) an official appointed to investigate individuals' complaints against maladministration, especially that of public authorities.

■ (**the Ombudsman**) Brit. informal term for **PARLIAMENTARY COMMISSIONER FOR ADMINISTRATION**.

– ORIGIN 1950s: from Swedish, 'legal representative'.

ombudsperson ▶ **noun** chiefly N. Amer. a person acting as an ombudsman (used as a neutral alternative).

Omdurman /ˌɒmdəˈmɑːn/ a city in central Sudan, on the Nile opposite Khartoum; pop. 228,700 (1993). In 1898 it was the site of a battle which marked the final British defeat of the Mahdist forces.

-ome ▶ **suffix** chiefly Biology forming nouns denoting objects or parts having a specified nature: *rhizome* | *trichome*.

– ORIGIN variant form of **-OMA**.

omega /ˈəʊmɪgə/ ▶ **noun** the last letter of the Greek alphabet (Ω, ω), transliterated as 'o' or 'ō'.

■ the last of a series; the final development: [as modifier] *the omega point*. ■ (**Omega**) [followed by Latin genitive] Astronomy the twenty-fourth star in a constellation: *Omega Scorpii*.

▶ **symbol for** ■ (Ω) ohm(s): *a 100Ω resistor*. ■ (ω) angular frequency.

– ORIGIN from Greek *ō mega* 'the great O'.

omega-3 fatty acid ▶ **noun** an unsaturated fatty acid of a kind occurring chiefly in fish oils, with three double bonds at particular positions in the hydrocarbon chain.

omelette (US also **omelet**) ▶ **noun** a dish of beaten eggs cooked in a frying pan and served plain or with a savoury or sweet topping or filling.

– PHRASES **one can't make an omelette without**

breaking eggs proverb one cannot accomplish something without adverse effects elsewhere.

[ORIGIN: translating French *On ne saurait faire une omelette sans casser des œufs.*]

– ORIGIN French, earlier *amelette* (alteration of *alumette*), variant of *alumelle*, from *lemele* 'knife blade', from Latin *lamella* (see **LAMELLA**). The association with 'knife blade' is probably because of the thin flat shape of an omelette.

omen ▶ **noun** an event regarded as a portent of good or evil: *the ghost's appearance was an ill omen* | *a rise in imports might be an omen of recovery*.

■ [mass noun] prophetic significance: *the raven seemed a bird of evil omen*.

– ORIGIN late 16th cent.: from Latin.

omentum /əʊˈmɛntəm/ ▶ **noun** (pl. **omenta** /-tə/) Anatomy a fold of peritoneum connecting the stomach with other abdominal organs.

– DERIVATIVES **omental** adjective.

– ORIGIN late Middle English: from Latin.

omer /ˈəʊmə/ ▶ **noun 1** an ancient Hebrew dry measure, the tenth part of an ephah.

2 (**Omer**) Judaism a sheaf of corn or omer of grain presented as an offering on the second day of Passover.

■ the period of 49 days between this day and Pentecost.

– ORIGIN from Hebrew 'ōmer.

omertà /əʊmɛːˈtɑː, Italian omerˈta/ ▶ **noun** [mass noun] (as practised by the Mafia) a code of silence about criminal activity and a refusal to give evidence to the police.

– ORIGIN Italian dialect, variant of *umiltà* 'humility'.

omicron /əʊ(ʊ)ˈmʌɪkrɒn/ ▶ **noun** the fifteenth letter of the Greek alphabet (Ο, ο), transliterated as 'o'.

■ (**Omicron**) [followed by Latin genitive] Astronomy the fifteenth star in a constellation: *Omicron Piscium*.

– ORIGIN from Greek *o mikron* 'small o'.

ominous ▶ **adjective** giving the worrying impression that something bad or unpleasant is going to happen; threateningly inauspicious: *there were ominous dark clouds gathering overhead*.

– DERIVATIVES **ominously** adverb, **ominousness** noun.

– ORIGIN late 16th cent.: from Latin *ominosus*, from *omen, omin-* 'omen'.

omission ▶ **noun** someone or something that has been left out or excluded: *there are glaring omissions in the report*.

■ [mass noun] the action of excluding or leaving out someone or something: *the omission of recent publications from his bibliography*. ■ a failure to do something, especially something that one has a moral or legal obligation to do: *to pay compensation for a wrongful act or omission*.

– DERIVATIVES **omissive** adjective.

– ORIGIN late Middle English: from late Latin *omissio(n-)*, from the verb *omittere* (see **OMIT**).

omit ▶ **verb** (**omitted**, **omitting**) [with obj.] (often be **omitted**) leave out or exclude (someone or something), either intentionally or forgetfully: *he was controversially omitted from the second Test*.

■ fail or neglect to do (something); leave undone: *the final rinse is omitted* | [with infinitive] *he modestly omits to mention that he was British pole-vault champion*.

– DERIVATIVES **omissible** adjective.

– ORIGIN late Middle English: from Latin *omittere*, from *ob-* 'down' + *mittere* 'let go'.

ommatidium /ˌɒməˈtɪdɪəm/ ▶ **noun** (pl. **ommatidia** /-dɪə/) Entomology each of the optical units that make up the compound eye of an insect.

– ORIGIN late 19th cent.: modern Latin, from Greek *ommatidion*, diminutive of *omma, ommat-* 'eye'.

ommatophore /ˈɒmətəfɔː/ ▶ **noun** Zoology a part of an invertebrate animal, especially a tentacle, which bears an eye.

– ORIGIN late 19th cent.: from Greek *omma, ommat-* 'eye' + **-PHORE**.

omni- ▶ **combining form** all; of all things: *omniscient* | *omnifarious*.

■ in all ways or places: *omnicompetent* | *omnipresent*.

– ORIGIN from Latin *omnis* 'all'.

omnibus ▶ **noun 1** a volume containing several novels or other items previously published separately: *an omnibus of her first trilogy*.

■ chiefly Brit. a single edition of two or more consecutive programmes, especially soap operas, previously broadcast separately.

2 dated a bus.

▶ **adjective** comprising several items: *omnibus editions of novels*.

– ORIGIN early 19th cent.: via French from Latin, literally 'for all', dative plural of *omnis*.

omnicompetent ▶ **adjective** able to deal with all matters or solve all problems.

■ (of a legislative body) having powers to legislate on all matters.

– DERIVATIVES **omnicompetence** noun.

omnidirectional ▶ **adjective** Telecommunications receiving signals from or transmitting in all directions.

omnifarious /ˌɒmnɪˈfɛːrɪəs/ ▶ **adjective** formal comprising or relating to all sorts or varieties.

– ORIGIN mid 17th cent.: from late Latin *omnifarius* + **-OUS**; compare with **MULTIFARIOUS**.

Omnimax /ˈɒmnɪmaks/ ▶ **noun** [mass noun] trademark a technique of widescreen cinematography in which 70 mm film is projected through a fisheye lens on to a hemispherical screen.

– ORIGIN 1970s: from **OMNI-** 'everywhere' + **MAXIMUM**.

omnipotent /ɒmˈnɪpət(ə)nt/ ▶ **adjective** (of a deity) having unlimited power; able to do anything.

■ having great power and influence: *an omnipotent sovereign*.

– DERIVATIVES **omnipotence** noun, **omnipotently** adverb.

– ORIGIN Middle English (as a divine attribute): via Old French from Latin *omnipotent-* 'all-powerful'.

omnipresent ▶ **adjective** (of God) present everywhere at the same time.

■ widely or constantly encountered; common or widespread: *the omnipresent threat of natural disasters*.

– DERIVATIVES **omnipresence** noun.

– ORIGIN early 17th cent.: from medieval Latin *omnipraesent-*.

omnirange ▶ **noun** a navigation system in which short-range omnidirectional VHF transmitters serve as radio beacons.

omniscient /ɒmˈnɪsɪənt/ ▶ **adjective** knowing everything: *a third person omniscient narrator*.

– DERIVATIVES **omniscience** noun, **omnisciently** adverb.

– ORIGIN early 17th cent.: from medieval Latin *omniscient-* 'all-knowing', based on *scire* 'to know'.

omnisexual ▶ **adjective** involving, related to, or characterized by a diverse sexual propensity.

– DERIVATIVES **omnisexuality** noun.

omnium gatherum /ˌɒmnɪəm ˈgaðərəm/ ▶ **noun** a collection of miscellaneous people or things.

– ORIGIN early 16th cent.: mock Latin, from Latin *omnium* 'of all' and **GATHER** + the Latin suffix *-um*.

omnivore /ˈɒmnɪvɔː/ ▶ **noun** an animal or person that eats a variety of food of both plant and animal origin.

– ORIGIN late 19th cent.: from French, from Latin *omnivorus* 'omnivorous'.

omnivorous /ɒmˈnɪv(ə)rəs/ ▶ **adjective** (of an animal or person) feeding on a variety of food of both plant and animal origin.

■ indiscriminate in taking in or using whatever is available: *an omnivorous reader*.

– DERIVATIVES **omnivorously** adverb, **omnivorousness** noun.

– ORIGIN mid 17th cent.: from Latin *omnivorus* + **-OUS**.

omophagy /ɒ(ʊ)ˈmɒfədʒɪ/ (also **omophagia**) ▶ **noun** [mass noun] the eating of raw food, especially raw meat.

– DERIVATIVES **omophagic** adjective, **omophagous** adjective.

– ORIGIN early 18th cent.: from Greek *ōmophagia*, from *ōmos* 'raw' + *-phagia* (from *phagein* 'eat').

Omotic /əʊˈmɒtɪk/ ▶ **noun** [mass noun] a subfamily of Afro-Asiatic languages spoken in Ethiopia, with over thirty members, all having comparatively few speakers.

▶ **adjective** denoting or belonging to this subfamily.

– ORIGIN 1970s: from *Omo*, the name of a river in SW Ethiopia, + **-OTIC**.

omphalo- /ˈɒmfələʊ/ ▶ **combining form** relating to the navel: *omphalocele*.

– ORIGIN from Greek *omphalos* 'navel'.

omphalocele /ˈɒmfələʊˌsiːl/ ▶ **noun** Medicine a hernia in which abdominal organs protrude into a baby's umbilical cord.

omphalos /ˈɒmfələs/ ▶ **noun** (pl. **omphaloi** /-lɔɪ/)

poetic/literary the centre or hub of something: *this was the omphalos of confusion and strife.*
■a conical stone (especially that at Delphi) representing the navel of the earth in ancient Greek mythology. ■ a boss on an ancient Greek shield.
– ORIGIN Greek, literally 'navel, boss'.

Omsk /ɒmsk/ a city in south central Russia, on the Irtysh River; pop. 1,159,000 (1990).

ON[1] ▶ **abbreviation for** Ontario (in official postal use).

ON[2] ▶ **abbreviation for** Old Norse.

on ▶ **preposition 1** physically in contact with and supported by (a surface): *on the table was a water jug | she was lying on the floor | a sign on the front gate.*
■located somewhere in the general surface area of (a place): *an internment camp on the island | the house on the corner.* ■ as a result of accidental physical contact with: *one of the children had cut a foot on some glass | he banged his head on a beam.* ■ supported by (a part of the body): *he was lying on his back.* ■ on to: *put it on the table.* ■ in the possession of (the person referred to): *she only had a few pounds on her.*
2 forming a distinctive or marked part of (the surface of something): *a scratch on her arm | a smile on her face.*
3 having (the thing mentioned) as a topic: *a book on careers | essays on a wide range of issues.*
■having (the thing mentioned) as a basis: *modelled on the Act of 1954 | dependent on availability.*
4 as a member of (a committee, jury, or other body): *they would be allowed to serve on committees.*
5 having (the place or thing mentioned) as a target: *five air raids on Schweinfurt | thousands marching on Washington.*
■having (the thing mentioned) as a target for visual focus: *her eyes were fixed on his dark profile.*
6 (often followed by a noun without a determiner) having (the thing mentioned) as a medium for transmitting or storing information: *put your ideas down on paper | stored on the client's own computer.*
■being broadcast by (a radio or television channel): *a new 12-part TV series on Channel 4.*
7 in the course of (a journey): *he was on his way to see his mother.*
■while travelling in (a public service vehicle): *John got some sleep on the plane.* ■ on to (a public vehicle) with the intention of travelling in it: *we got on the train.*
8 indicating the day or part of a day during which an event takes place: *reported on September 26 | on a very hot evening in July.*
■at the time of: *she was booed on arriving home.*
9 engaged in: *his attendant was out on errands.*
10 regularly taking (a drug or medicine): *he is on morphine to relieve the pain.*
11 paid for by: *the drinks are on me.*
12 added to: *a few pence on the electricity bill is nothing compared with your security.*
▶ **adverb 1** physically in contact with and supported by a surface: *make sure the lid is on.*
■(of clothing) being worn by a person: *sitting with her coat on | get your shoes on.*
2 indicating continuation of a movement or action: *she burbled on | he drove on | and so on.*
■further forward; in an advanced state: *later on | time's getting on.*
3 (of an entertainment or other event) taking place or being presented: *what's on at the May Festival | there's a good film on this afternoon.*
■due to take place as planned: *the reorganization is still on.*
4 (of an electrical appliance or power supply) functioning: *they always left the lights on.*
■(of an actor) on stage. ■ (of an employee) on duty.
▶ **noun** (also **on side**) Cricket the leg side.
– PHRASES **be on about** Brit. informal talk tediously and at length: *she's always on about doing one's duty.* **be on at someone** Brit. informal nag or grumble at someone. **be on to someone** informal be close to discovering the truth about an illegal or undesirable activity that someone is engaging in. **be on to something** informal have an idea or information that is likely to lead to an important discovery. **it's not on** informal it's impractical or unacceptable. **on and off** intermittently: *it rained on and off most of the afternoon.* **on and on** continually; at tedious length: *he went on and on about his grandad's trombone.* **on it** Austral. informal drinking heavily. **on side** supporting or part of the same team as someone else. **on to 1** moving to a location on (the surface of something): *they went up on to the ridge.* **2** moving aboard (a public service vehicle) with the intention of travelling in it: *we got on to the train.* **what are you on?** informal said to express incredulity at someone's behaviour, with the implication that they must be under the influence of drugs. **you're on** informal said by way of accepting a challenge or bet.
– ORIGIN Old English *on, an*, of Germanic origin; related to Dutch *aan* and German *an*, from an Indo-European root shared by Greek *ana*.

-on ▶ **suffix** Physics, Biochemistry, & Chemistry forming nouns: **1** denoting subatomic particles or quanta: *neutron | photon.*
2 denoting molecular units: *codon.*
3 denoting substances: *interferon.*
– ORIGIN sense 1 originally in *electron*, from **ION**, influenced (as in sense 2) by Greek *on* 'being'; sense 3 is on the pattern of words such as *cotton* or from German *-on*.

onager /ˈɒnəgə/ ▶ **noun** an animal of a race of the Asian wild ass native to northern Iran.
● *Equus hemionus onager*, family Equidae. Compare with **KIANG, KULAN**.
– ORIGIN Middle English: via Latin from Greek *onagros*, from *onos* 'ass' + *agrios* 'wild'.

onanism /ˈəʊnənɪz(ə)m/ ▶ **noun** [mass noun] formal
1 masturbation.
2 coitus interruptus.
– DERIVATIVES **onanist** noun, **onanistic** adjective.
– ORIGIN early 18th cent.: from French *onanisme* or modern Latin *onanismus*, from the name *Onan* (Gen. 38:9).

Onassis[1] /əʊˈnasɪs/, Aristotle (Socrates) (1906–75), Greek shipping magnate and international businessman. He owned a substantial shipping empire and founded the Greek national airline, Olympic Airways (1957).

Onassis[2] /əʊˈnasɪs/, Jacqueline Lee Bouvier Kennedy (1929–94), American First Lady; known as **Jackie O.** She married John F. Kennedy in 1953. After he was assassinated she married Aristotle Onassis in 1968.

on-board ▶ **adjective** [attrib.] **1** available or situated on board a ship, aircraft, or other vehicle.
2 Computing denoting or controlled from a facility or feature incorporated into the main circuit board of a computer or computerized device.

ONC historical ▶ **abbreviation for** (in the UK) Ordinary National Certificate (a technical qualification).

once ▶ **adverb 1** on one occasion or for one time only: *they deliver once a week* | [as noun **the once**] informal *he'd only met her the once.*
■[usu. with negative or **if**] at all; on even one occasion (used for emphasis): *he never once complained | if she once got an idea in her head you'd never move it.*
2 at some time in the past; formerly: *Gran had once been a famous singer.*
3 multiplied by one: *once two is two.*
▶ **conjunction** as soon as; when: *once the grapes were pressed, the juice was put into barrels.*
– PHRASES **all at once 1** without warning; suddenly: *all at once the noise stopped.* **2** all at the same time: *a lot of beans are ready all at once.* **at once 1** immediately: *I fell asleep at once.* **2** simultaneously: *computers that can do many things at once.* **for once** (or **this once**) on this occasion only, as an exception: *I hope you'll forgive me this once.* **once a ——, always a ——** proverb a person cannot change their fundamental nature: *once a whinger, always a whinger.* **once again** (or **more**) one more time. **once and for all** (or **once for all**) now and for the last time; finally. **once and future** denoting someone or something that is eternal, enduring, or constant: *side two contains four once and future hit singles.* [ORIGIN: 1950s: from T. H. White's *Once and Future King* (1958).] **once bitten, twice shy** see **BITE**. **once** (or **every once**) **in a while** from time to time; occasionally. **once or twice** a few times. **once upon a time** at some time in the past (used as a conventional opening of a story). ■ formerly: *once upon a time she would have been jealous, but no longer.*
– ORIGIN Middle English *ones*, genitive of **ONE**. The spelling change in the 16th cent. was in order to retain the unvoiced sound of the final consonant.

once-over ▶ **noun** informal a rapid inspection or search: *some doctor came and gave us all a once-over.*
■a piece of work that is done quickly: *a quick once-over with a broom.*

oncer ▶ **noun** informal **1** Brit. historical a one-pound note.
2 Brit. a person who does a particular thing only once.
3 Austral. an MP regarded as likely to serve only one term.

on-chip ▶ **adjective** Electronics denoting or relating to circuitry included in a single integrated circuit or in the same integrated circuit as a given device.

onchocerciasis /ˌɒŋkəʊsəːˈsʌɪəsɪs, -ˈkʌɪəsɪs/ ▶ **noun** technical term for **RIVER BLINDNESS**.
– ORIGIN early 20th cent.: from modern Latin *Onchocerca* (from Greek *onkos* 'barb' + *kerkos* 'tail') + **-IASIS**.

onco- ▶ **combining form** of or relating to tumours: *oncology.*
– ORIGIN from Greek *onkos* 'mass'.

oncogene /ˈɒŋkə(ʊ)dʒiːn/ ▶ **noun** Medicine a gene which in certain circumstances can transform a cell into a tumour cell.

oncogenic /ˌɒŋkə(ʊ)ˈdʒɛnɪk/ ▶ **adjective** Medicine causing development of a tumour or tumours.
– DERIVATIVES **oncogenesis** noun, **oncogenicity** noun.

oncology /ɒŋˈkɒlədʒi/ ▶ **noun** [mass noun] Medicine the study and treatment of tumours.
– DERIVATIVES **oncological** adjective, **oncologist** noun.

oncoming ▶ **adjective** [attrib.] approaching from the front; moving towards one: *she walked into the path of an oncoming car.*
■figurative due to happen or occur in the near future: *the oncoming Antarctic winter.*
▶ **noun** [mass noun] the fact of being about to happen in the near future: *the oncoming of age.*

oncost ▶ **noun** Brit. an overhead expense.

OND historical ▶ **abbreviation for** (in the UK) Ordinary National Diploma (a qualification in technical subjects).

Ondaatje /ɒnˈdɑːtjə/, (Philip) Michael (b.1943), Sri Lankan-born Canadian writer. Notable works: *Running in the Family* (autobiography, 1982); *The English Patient* (novel; Booker Prize, 1992).

ondes martenot /ɒ̃d ˈmɑːt(ə)nəʊ, French ɔ̃d martəno/ ▶ **noun** (pl. same) Music an electronic keyboard producing one note of variable pitch.
– ORIGIN 1950s: from French *ondes musicales*, literally 'musical waves' (the original name of the instrument) and the name of Maurice *Martenot* (1898–1980), its French inventor.

on dit /ɒ̃ ˈdiː/ ▶ **noun** (pl. **on dits** pronunc. same) a piece of gossip; a rumour.

on drive Cricket ▶ **noun** a drive to the on side.
▶ **verb** [with obj.] (**on-drive**) drive (the ball) to the on side; drive a ball delivered by (a bowler) to the on side.

one ▶ **cardinal number** the lowest cardinal number; half of two; 1: *there's only room for one person | two could live as cheaply as one | one hundred miles | World War One | a one-bedroom flat.* (Roman numeral: **i, I**)
■a single person or thing, viewed as taking the place of a group: *they would straggle home in ones and twos.* ■ single; just one as opposed to any more or to none at all (used for emphasis): *her one concern is to save her daughter.* ■ denoting a particular item of a pair or number of items: *electronics is one of his hobbies | he put one hand over her shoulder and one around her waist | a glass tube closed at one end.* ■ denoting a particular but unspecified occasion or period: *one afternoon in late October.* ■ used before a name to denote a person who is not familiar or has not been previously mentioned; a certain: *he worked as a clerk for one Mr Ming.* ■ informal, chiefly N. Amer. a noteworthy example of (used for emphasis): *the actor was one smart-mouthed troublemaker | he was **one hell of a** snappy dresser.* ■ identical; the same: *all types of training meet one common standard.* ■ identical and united; forming a unity: *the two things are **one and the same**.* ■ W. Indian alone: *the time when you one tackled a field of cane and finished before the others had even started.* [ORIGIN: a use recorded in Old English, becoming obsolete in standard use in the mid 16th cent.] ■ one year old. ■ one o'clock: *it's half past one | I'll be there at one.* ■ informal an alcoholic drink: *a cool one after a day on the water.* ■ informal a joke or story: *the one about the Englishman, the Irishman, and the Yank.* ■ a size of garment or other merchandise denoted by one. ■ a domino or dice with one spot.
▶ **pronoun 1** referring to a person or thing previously mentioned: *her mood changed from one of moroseness to one of joy | her best apron, the white one.*
■used as the object of a verb or preposition to refer to any example of a noun previously mentioned or easily identified: *they had to buy their own copies rather than waiting to borrow one | do you want one?*
2 a person of a specified kind: *you're the one who*

ruined her life | Eleanor was never one to be trifled with | my friends and **loved ones**.

■ a person who is remarkable or extraordinary in some way: *you never saw **such a one** for figures.*

3 [third person singular] used to refer to any person as representing people in general: *one must admire him for his willingness.*

■ referring to the speaker as representing people in general: *one gets the impression that he is ahead.*

– PHRASES **at one** in agreement or harmony: *they were completely **at one with** their environment.* **for one** used to stress that the person named holds the specified view, even if no one else does: *I for one am getting a little sick of writing about it.* **get something in one** informal understand or succeed in guessing something immediately. **have one over the eight** see **EIGHT**. **one after another** (or **the other**) following one another in quick succession: *one after another the buses drew up.* **one and all** everyone: *well done one and all!* **one and only** unique; single (used for emphasis or as a designation of a celebrity): *the title of his one and only book | the one and only Muhammad Ali.* **one by one** separately and in succession; singly. **one day** at a particular but unspecified time in the past or future: *one day a boy started teasing Grady | he would one day be a great President.* **one for one** denoting or referring to a situation or arrangement in which one thing corresponds to or is exchanged for another: *these donations would be matched on a one-for-one basis with public revenues.* **one of a kind** see **KIND**[1]. **one on one** (or **one to one**) denoting or referring to a situation in which two parties come into direct contact, opposition, or correspondence: *maybe we should talk to them one on one.* ■ (**one-to-one**) Mathematics in which each member of one set is associated with one member of another. **one or another** (or **the other**) denoting or referring to a particular but unspecified one out of a set of items: *not all instances fall neatly into one or another of these categories.* **one or two** informal a few: *there are one or two signs worth watching for.* **one thing and another** informal used to cover various unspecified matters, events, or tasks: ***what with one thing and another** she hadn't had much sleep recently.*

– ORIGIN Old English *ān*, of Germanic origin; related to Dutch *een* and German *ein*, from an Indo-European root shared by Latin *unus*. The initial *w* sound developed before the 15th cent. and was occasionally represented in the spelling; it was not accepted into standard English until the late 17th cent.

USAGE **1** **One** is used as a pronoun to mean 'anyone' or 'me and people in general', as in ***one** must try **one's** best.* In modern English it is generally only used in formal and written contexts, outside which it is likely to be regarded as pompous or over-formal. In informal and spoken contexts the normal alternative is **you**, as in ***you** have to do what **you** can, don't **you**?*
2 Until quite recently, sentences in which **one** is followed by **his** or **him** were considered perfectly correct: ***one** must try **his** best.* These uses are now held to be ungrammatical: **one's** should be used instead.

-one ▶ **suffix** Chemistry forming nouns denoting various compounds, especially ketones: *acetone | quinone.*

– ORIGIN from Greek patronymic *-ōnē*.

one-acter ▶ **noun** a one-act play.

one another ▶ **pronoun** each other: *the children used to tease one another.*

one-armed bandit ▶ **noun** informal a fruit machine operated by pulling a long handle at the side.

one-design ▶ **noun** a yacht built from a standard design: [as modifier] *one-design racing.*

one-dimensional ▶ **adjective** having or relating to a single dimension: *one-dimensional curves.*

■ lacking depth; superficial: *the supporting roles are alarmingly one-dimensional creations.*

– DERIVATIVES **one-dimensionality** noun.

one-down ▶ **adjective** informal at a psychological disadvantage in a game or a competitive situation.

onefold ▶ **adjective** consisting of only one part or element.

Onega, Lake /əʊˈnjeɪɡə/ a lake in NW Russia, near the border with Finland, the second largest European lake.

one-horse ▶ **adjective** drawn by or using a single horse.

– PHRASES **one-horse race** a contest in which one candidate or competitor is clearly superior to all the others and seems certain to win. **one-horse town** informal a small town with few and poor facilities.

Oneida /əʊˈnʌɪdə/ ▶ **noun** (pl. same or **Oneidas**) **1** a member of an American Indian people formerly inhabiting upper New York State, one of the five peoples comprising the original Iroquois confederacy.

2 [mass noun] the extinct Iroquoian language of this people.

▶ **adjective** of or relating to this people or their language.

– ORIGIN from a local word meaning 'erected stone', the name of successive principal Oneida settlements, near which, by tradition, a large syenite boulder was erected.

Oneida Community a religious community, founded in New York State in 1848 and originally embracing primitive Christian beliefs and radical social and economic ideas, later relaxed. It became a joint-stock company in 1881.

O'Neill, Eugene (Gladstone) (1888–1953), American dramatist. He was awarded the Pulitzer Prize for his first full-length play, *Beyond the Horizon* (1920). Other notable works: *Mourning Becomes Electra* (1931) and *The Iceman Cometh* (1946). Nobel Prize for Literature (1936).

oneiric /ə(ʊ)ˈnʌɪrɪk/ ▶ **adjective** formal of or relating to dreams or dreaming.

– ORIGIN mid 19th cent.: from Greek *oneiros* 'dream' + **-IC**.

oneiro- /ə(ʊ)ˈnʌɪrəʊ/ ▶ **combining form** relating to dreams or dreaming: *oneiromancy.*

– ORIGIN from Greek *oneiros* 'dream'.

oneiromancy /əˈnʌɪrə(ʊ)ˌmansi/ ▶ **noun** [mass noun] the interpretation of dreams in order to foretell the future.

one-liner ▶ **noun** informal a short joke or witty remark.

one-lunger ▶ **noun** informal a single-cylinder engine.

■ a vehicle or boat driven by such an engine.

one-man ▶ **adjective** [attrib.] involving, done, or operated by only one person: *a one-man show.*

one-man band ▶ **noun** a street entertainer who plays many instruments at the same time.

■ a person who runs a business alone.

oneness ▶ **noun** [mass noun] **1** the fact or state of being unified or whole, though comprised of two or more parts: *the oneness of man and nature.*

■ identity or harmony with someone or something: *a strong sense of oneness is felt with all things.*

2 the fact or state of being one in number: *holding to the oneness of God the Father as the only God.*

one-nighter ▶ **noun** another term for **ONE-NIGHT STAND**.

one-night stand ▶ **noun** **1** informal a sexual relationship lasting only one night.

■ a person with whom one has such a relationship.

2 a single performance of a play or show in a particular place.

one-off informal, chiefly Brit. ▶ **adjective** done, made, or happening only once and not repeated: *one-off tax deductible donations to charity.*

▶ **noun** something done, made, or happening only once, not as part of a regular sequence: *the meeting is a one-off.*

■ a person who is unusual or unique, especially in an admirable way: *he's a one-off, no one else has his skills.*

one-parent ▶ **adjective** of or relating to a person bringing up a child or children without a partner.

one-piece ▶ **adjective** [attrib.] (especially of an article of clothing) made or consisting of a single piece.

▶ **noun** an article of clothing made or consisting of a single piece: *I was wearing a tight black one-piece.*

oner ▶ **noun** Brit. informal **1** something denoted or characterized in some way by the number one: *when one conker has broken another it becomes a oner.*

■ one pound (of money).

2 archaic a remarkable person or thing.

onerous /ˈəʊn(ə)rəs, ˈɒn-/ ▶ **adjective** (of a task, duty, or responsibility) involving an amount of effort and difficulty which is oppressively burdensome: *he found his duties increasingly onerous.*

■ Law involving heavy obligations: *an onerous lease.*

– DERIVATIVES **onerously** adverb, **onerousness** noun.

– ORIGIN late Middle English: from Old French *onereus*, from Latin *onerosus*, from *onus*, *oner-* 'burden'.

oneself ▶ **pronoun** [third person singular] **1** [reflexive] used as the object of a verb or preposition when this is the same as the subject of the clause and the subject is stated or understood as 'one': *it is difficult to wrest oneself away | resolves that one makes to oneself.*

2 [emphatic] used to emphasize that one does something individually or unaided: *the idea of publishing a book oneself.*

3 in one's normal and individual state of body or mind; not influenced by others: *freedom to be oneself.*

– PHRASES **by oneself** see **BY**.

one-sided ▶ **adjective** unfairly giving or dealing with only one side of a contentious issue or question; biased or partial: *the press was accused of being one-sided, of not giving a balanced picture.*

■ (of a contest or conflict) having a gross inequality of strength or ability between the opponents. ■ (of a relationship or conversation) having all the effort or activity coming from one participant. ■ having or occurring on one side of something only: *one-sided documents.* ■ physically larger or more developed on one side: *a one-sided swelling.*

– DERIVATIVES **one-sidedly** adverb, **one-sidedness** noun.

one-star ▶ **adjective** having one star in a grading system (especially of accommodation) in which this denotes the lowest standard: *a good one-star hotel.*

■ having or denoting the fifth-highest military rank, distinguished in the US armed forces by one star on the uniform: *a one-star general.*

one-step ▶ **noun** a vigorous kind of foxtrot in duple time.

one-stop ▶ **adjective** (of a shop or other business) capable of supplying all a customer's needs within a particular range of goods or services.

one-tailed ▶ **adjective** Statistics denoting a test for deviation from the null hypothesis in one direction only.

one-time ▶ **adjective** **1** former: *a one-time football player.*

2 of or relating to a single occasion: *a one-time charge.*

▶ **adverb** (**one time**) W. Indian all at once; immediately: *he does eat six roti one time.*

one-time pad ▶ **noun** a pad of keys for a cipher, each page being destroyed after one use, so that each message is sent using a different key.

one-touch ▶ **adjective** [attrib.] **1** (of an electrical device or facility) able to be operated simply at or as though at the touch of a button.

2 Soccer denoting fast-moving play in which players manage to control and pass the ball with the first touch of the foot.

one-track mind ▶ **noun** used in reference to a person whose thoughts are preoccupied with one subject or interest.

one-two ▶ **noun** a pair of punches in quick succession, especially with alternate hands.

■ chiefly Soccer a move in which a player plays a short pass to a teammate and moves forward to receive an immediate return pass.

one-up informal ▶ **adjective** having a psychological advantage over someone: *you're always trying to be **one-up on** whoever you're with.*

▶ **verb** [with obj.] do better than (someone): *he deftly one-upped the interrogator.*

one-upmanship ▶ **noun** [mass noun] informal the technique or practice of gaining a feeling of superiority over another person.

one-way ▶ **adjective** moving or allowing movement in one direction only: *a one-way valve.*

■ (of a road or system of roads) along which traffic may pass in one direction only. ■ (of a ticket) allowing a person to travel to a place but not back again; single. ■ (of glass or a mirror) seen as a mirror from one side but transparent from the other. ■ denoting a relationship in which all the action or contribution of a particular kind comes from only one member: *interaction between the organism and the environment is not a one-way process.*

one-woman ▶ **adjective** involving, done, or operated by only one woman.

one-world ▶ **adjective** of, relating to, or holding the view that the world's inhabitants are interdependent and should behave accordingly.

– DERIVATIVES **one-worlder** noun, **one-worldism** noun.

on-field ▶ **adjective** situated or taking place at or on a sports field.

onflow ▶ **noun** [mass noun] the action or process of flowing or moving steadily onward.

onglaze ▶ **adjective** (of painting or decoration) done on a glazed surface.

on-glide ▶ **noun** Phonetics a glide produced at the beginning of articulating a speech sound. Compare with **OFF-GLIDE**.

ongoing ▶ **adjective** continuing; still in progress: *ongoing negotiations.*

– DERIVATIVES **ongoingness** noun.

onion ▶ **noun** **1** a swollen edible bulb with a pungent taste and smell, composed of several concentric layers, used in cooking as a vegetable and flavouring.

2 the plant that produces this bulb, with long rolled or strap-like leaves and spherical heads of greenish-white flowers.

• *Allium cepa*, family Liliaceae (or Alliaceae).

– PHRASES **know one's onions** informal be very knowledgeable about something.

– DERIVATIVES **oniony** adjective.

– ORIGIN Middle English: from Old French *oignon*, based on Latin *unio(n-)*, denoting a kind of onion.

onion bag ▶ **noun** Soccer, informal a goal net (used especially in the context of scoring a goal).

onion dome ▶ **noun** a dome which bulges in the middle and rises to a point, used especially in Russian church architecture.

– DERIVATIVES **onion-domed** adjective.

onion fly ▶ **noun** a small fly whose larvae are a pest of onions.

• The European *Delia antiqua* (family Anthomyiidae), and the American *Tritoxa flexa* (family Otitidae), which also attacks garlic.

onion hoe ▶ **noun** a small hoe with a curved neck, used for weeding between onions and other closely grown plants.

onion set ▶ **noun** a small onion bulb planted instead of seed to yield a mature bulb.

onion skin (also **onion-skin paper**) ▶ **noun** [mass noun] very fine smooth translucent paper.

onkus /ˈɒŋkəs/ ▶ **adjective** Austral. informal

1 unpleasant.

2 disorganized.

– ORIGIN early 20th cent.: of unknown origin.

on-lend ▶ **verb** [with obj.] lend (borrowed money) to a third party.

onliest ▶ **adjective** black English superlative of **ONLY**: *you're the onliest man I've seen who has everything.*

online Computing ▶ **adjective** controlled by or connected to a computer.

▶ **adverb** **1** while connected to a computer or under computer control.

■ with processing of data carried out simultaneously with its production.

2 in or into operation or existence: *the town's new high-tech power plant is expected to go online this month.*

onlooker ▶ **noun** a non-participating observer; a spectator: *a crowd of fascinated onlookers.*

– DERIVATIVES **onlooking** adjective.

only ▶ **adverb** **1** and no one or nothing more besides; solely or exclusively: *there are only a limited number of tickets available | only their faith sustained them.*

■ no more than (implying that more was hoped for or expected); merely: *deaths from heart disease have only declined by 10 per cent | she was still only in her mid thirties.* ■ no longer ago than: *genes that were discovered only last year.* ■ not until: *a final report reached him only on January 15.*

2 [with infinitive] with the negative or unfortunate result that: *she turned into the car park, only to find her way blocked.*

■ [with modal] inevitably, although unfortunate or undesirable: *if banks cancelled the debts, these countries **would only** borrow more | rebellion **will only** bring more unhappiness.*

▶ **adjective** [attrib.] alone of its or their kind; single or solitary: *the only medal we had ever won | he was an only child.*

■ alone deserving consideration: *it's simply the only place to be seen these days.*

▶ **conjunction** informal except that; but for the fact that: *he is still a young man, only he seems older because of his careworn expression.*

■ but then: *the man was going to be hanged, only he took poison first.*

– PHRASES **only just** by a very small margin; almost not: *the building survived the earthquake, but only just.* ■ very recently: *I'd only just arrived back from Paris.* **only too** —— used to emphasize that something is the case to an extreme or regrettable extent: *you should be only too glad to be rid of him | they found that the rumour was only too true.*

– ORIGIN Old English *ānlic* (adjective) (see **ONE**, **-LY**[1]).

> **USAGE** The traditional view is that the adverb **only** should be placed next to the word or words whose meaning it restricts: *I have seen him **only once*** rather than *I have **only** seen him **once***. The argument for this, a topic which has occupied grammarians for more than 200 years, is that if **only** is not placed correctly the scope or emphasis is wrong, and could even result in ambiguity. But in normal, everyday English, the impulse is to state **only** as early as possible in the sentence, generally just before the verb. The result is, in fact, hardly ever ambiguous: few native speakers would be confused by the sentence *I have **only** seen him **once***, and the supposed 'logical' sense often emerges only with further clarification, as in *I've **only seen** him once, but I've heard him many times.*

only-begotten ▶ **adjective** poetic/literary used to denote an only child.

on-message ▶ **adjective** (of a politician) stating the official party line.

Ono /ˈəʊnəʊ/, Yoko (b.1933), American musician and artist, born in Japan. She married John Lennon in 1969 and collaborated with him on various experimental recordings.

o.n.o. Brit. ▶ **abbreviation for** or nearest offer (used in advertisements): *beginner's guitar £150 o.n.o.*

on-off ▶ **adjective** **1** (of a switch) having two positions, 'on' and 'off'.

2 (of a relationship) not continuous or steady.

onomasiology /ˌɒnə(ʊ)meɪsɪˈɒlədʒi/ ▶ **noun** [mass noun] the branch of knowledge that deals with terminology, in particular contrasting terms for similar concepts, as in a thesaurus. Compare with **SEMASIOLOGY**.

– DERIVATIVES **onomasiological** adjective.

– ORIGIN early 20th cent.: from Greek *onomasia* 'term' + **-LOGY**.

onomast /ˈɒnəmast/ ▶ **noun** a person who studies proper names, especially personal names.

– ORIGIN 1980s: back-formation from **ONOMASTIC**.

onomastic /ɒnəˈmastɪk/ ▶ **adjective** of or relating to the study of the history and origin of proper names.

– ORIGIN late 16th cent. (as a noun in the sense 'alphabetical list of proper nouns', later also 'lexicographer'): from Greek *onomastikos*, from *onoma* 'name'. The adjective dates from the early 18th cent.

onomastics ▶ **plural noun** [usu. treated as sing.] the study of the history and origin of proper names, especially personal names.

onomatopoeia /ˌɒnə(ʊ)matəˈpiːə/ ▶ **noun** [mass noun] the formation of a word from a sound associated with what is named (e.g. *cuckoo, sizzle*).

■ the use of such words for rhetorical effect.

– DERIVATIVES **onomatopoeic** adjective, **onomatopoeically** adverb.

– ORIGIN late 16th cent.: via late Latin from Greek *onomatopoiia* 'word-making', from *onoma, onomat-* 'name' + *-poios* 'making' (from *poiein* 'to make').

Onondaga /ˌɒnənˈdɑːgə/ ▶ **noun** (pl. same or **Onondagas**) **1** a member of an Iroquois people, one of the five comprising the original Iroquois confederacy, formerly inhabiting an area near Syracuse, New York.

2 [mass noun] the extinct Iroquoian language of this people.

▶ **adjective** of or relating to this people or their language.

– ORIGIN from the Iroquoian name of their main settlement, literally 'on the hill'.

on-pack ▶ **adjective** displayed on or attached to the packaging of a product.

on-road ▶ **adjective** denoting or relating to events or conditions on a road, especially a vehicle's performance.

onrush ▶ **noun** a surging rush forward: *the mesmerizing onrush of the sea.*

▶ **verb** [no obj.] [usu. as adj. **onrushing**] move forward in a surging rush: *the walls of onrushing white water.*

on-screen ▶ **adjective** & **adverb** shown or appearing in a film or television programme: [as adj.] *on-screen violence.*

■ making use of or performed with the aid of a VDU screen: [as adj.] *on-screen editing facilities.*

onset ▶ **noun** the beginning of something, especially something unpleasant: *the **onset of** winter.*

■ archaic a military attack.

on-set ▶ **adjective** taking place during or relating to the rehearsing of a play or the making of a film.

onshore ▶ **adjective** & **adverb** situated or occurring on land (often used in relation to the oil and gas industry): [as adj.] *an onshore oilfield.*

■ (especially of the direction of the wind) from the sea towards the land.

onside ▶ **adjective** & **adverb** (of a player, especially in soccer, rugby, or hockey) occupying a position on the field where playing the ball or puck is allowed; not offside.

■ [as adv.] informal in or into a position of agreement: *the assurances helped bring officials onside.*

onside kick (also **onsides kick**) ▶ **noun** American Football an intentionally short kick-off that travels forward only slightly further than the legally required distance of 10 yards, and which the kicking team attempts to recover.

on-site ▶ **adjective** & **adverb** taking place or available on a particular site or premises.

onslaught ▶ **noun** a fierce or destructive attack: *a series of **onslaughts on** the citadel.*

■ a large quantity of people or things that is difficult to cope with: *the lending library market began to subside under the onslaught of cheap paperbacks.*

– ORIGIN early 17th cent. (also in the form *anslaight*): from Middle Dutch *aenslag*, from *aen* 'on' + *slag* 'blow'. The change in the ending was due to association with (now obsolete) *slaught* 'slaughter'.

onstage ▶ **adjective** & **adverb** (in a theatre) on the stage and so visible to the audience.

on-stream ▶ **adverb** in or into industrial production or useful operation.

▶ **adjective** of or relating to normal industrial production.

on-street ▶ **adjective** [attrib.] (of parking facilities) at the side of a public road.

Ont. ▶ **abbreviation for** Ontario.

-ont ▶ **combining form** Biology denoting an individual or cell of a specified type: *schizont.*

– ORIGIN from Greek *ont-* 'being', present participle of *eimi* 'be'.

on-target ▶ **adjective** & **adverb** hitting a target or achieving an aim.

Ontario /ɒnˈtɛːrɪəʊ/ a province of eastern Canada, between Hudson Bay and the Great Lakes; pop. 9,914,200 (1991); capital, Toronto. It was settled by the French and English in the 17th century, ceded to Britain in 1763, and became one of the original four provinces in the Dominion of Canada in 1867.

– DERIVATIVES **Ontarian** adjective & noun.

Ontario, Lake the smallest and most easterly of the Great Lakes, lying on the US–Canadian border between Ontario and New York State.

ontic /ˈɒntɪk/ ▶ **adjective** Philosophy of or relating to entities and the facts about them; relating to real as opposed to phenomenal existence.

– ORIGIN 1940s: from Greek *ōn, ont-* 'being' + **-IC**.

onto ▶ **preposition** variant form of *on to* (see **ON**).

■ Mathematics expressing the relationship of a set to its image under a mapping when every element of the image set has an inverse image in the first set: [as modifier] *an onto mapping.*

> **USAGE** The preposition **onto** written as one word (instead of **on to**) is recorded from the early 18th century and has been widely used ever since, but is still not wholly accepted as part of standard English (unlike **into**, for example). Many style guides still advise writing it as two words, and that is the practice followed in this dictionary. However, in US English **onto** is more or less the standard form and this is likely to become the case in British English before long. When used in the specialized mathematics sense, the form is invariably **onto**.
> Nevertheless, it is important to maintain a distinction between the preposition **onto** or **on to** and the use of the adverb **on** followed by the preposition **to**: *she climbed **on to*** (or ***onto***) *the roof* but *let's go **on to*** (not ***onto***) *the next point.*

ontogenesis /ˌɒntə(ʊ)ˈdʒɛnɪsɪs/ ▶ **noun** [mass noun]

Biology the development of an individual organism or anatomical or behavioural feature from the earliest stage to maturity. Compare with **PHYLOGENESIS**.

– DERIVATIVES **ontogenetic** adjective, **ontogenetically** adverb.
– ORIGIN late 19th cent.: from Greek *ōn, ont-* 'being' + *genesis* 'birth'.

ontogeny /ɒnˈtɒdʒəni/ ▶ noun [mass noun] the branch of biology that deals with ontogenesis. Compare with **PHYLOGENY**.
■ another term for **ONTOGENESIS**.
– DERIVATIVES **ontogenic** adjective, **ontogenically** adverb.
– ORIGIN late 19th cent.: from Greek *ōn, ont-* 'being' + **-GENY**.

ontological argument ▶ noun Philosophy the argument that God, being defined as most great or perfect, must exist, since a God who exists is greater than a God who does not. Compare with **COSMOLOGICAL ARGUMENT** and **TELEOLOGICAL ARGUMENT**.

ontology /ɒnˈtɒlədʒi/ ▶ noun [mass noun] the branch of metaphysics dealing with the nature of being.
– DERIVATIVES **ontological** adjective, **ontologically** adverb, **ontologist** noun.
– ORIGIN early 18th cent.: from modern Latin *ontologia*, from Greek *ōn, ont-* 'being' + **-LOGY**.

onus /ˈəʊnəs/ ▶ noun (**the onus**) something that is one's duty or responsibility: *the onus is on you to show that you have suffered loss.*
– ORIGIN mid 17th cent.: from Latin, literally 'load or burden'.

onward ▶ adverb (also **onwards**) in a continuing forward direction; ahead: *she stumbled onward.*
■ forward in time: *the period from 1969 onward.* ■ figurative so as to make progress or become more successful: *the business moved onward and upward.*
▶ adjective (of a journey) going further rather than coming to an end or halt; moving forward: *informing passengers where to change for their onward journey* | figurative *the onward march of history.*

Onychophora /ˌɒnɪˈkɒf(ə)rə/ Zoology a small phylum of terrestrial invertebrates which comprises the velvet worms such as peripatus. They share characteristics with the arthropods and annelids, having a long soft segmented body with stubby legs (lobopods).
– DERIVATIVES **onychophoran** adjective & noun.
– ORIGIN modern Latin (plural), from Greek *onux, onukh-* 'nail, claw' + *-phoros* 'bearing'.

onymous /ˈɒnɪməs/ ▶ adjective having a name. The opposite of **ANONYMOUS**.
■ (of a writing) bearing the name of the author. ■ (of an author) giving his or her name.
– ORIGIN late 18th cent.: shortening of **ANONYMOUS**.

onyx /ˈɒnɪks, ˈəʊnɪks/ ▶ noun [mass noun] a semi-precious variety of agate with different colours in layers.
– ORIGIN Middle English: from Old French *oniche, onix*, via Latin from Greek *onux* 'fingernail or onyx'.

onyx marble ▶ noun [mass noun] banded calcite or other stone used as a decorative material.

oo- /ˈəʊə/ ▶ combining form Biology relating to or denoting an egg or ovum.
– ORIGIN from Greek *ōion* 'egg'.

o-o /ˈəʊəʊ/ (also **oo**) ▶ noun an endangered honeyeater found in Hawaii, which has a thin curved bill and climbs about on tree trunks. Compare with **ou**[2].
● Genus *Moho*, family Meliphagidae: only two of four species survive.
– ORIGIN late 19th cent.: from Hawaiian.

oocyst /ˈəʊəsɪst/ ▶ noun Zoology a cyst containing a zygote formed by a parasitic protozoan such as the malaria parasite.

oocyte /ˈəʊəsʌɪt/ ▶ noun Biology a cell in an ovary which may undergo meiotic division to form an ovum.

oodles ▶ plural noun informal a very great number or amount of something: *if only I had oodles of cash.*
– ORIGIN mid 19th cent. (originally US): of unknown origin.

oo-er ▶ exclamation expressing surprise or alarm.
– ORIGIN early 20th cent.: from the interjections **OOH** and **ER**.

oof[1] ▶ exclamation expressing alarm, annoyance, or relief.

– ORIGIN natural exclamation: first recorded in English in the mid 19th cent.

oof[2] ▶ noun [mass noun] informal money; cash.
– ORIGIN late 19th cent.: from Yiddish *oyf* 'on', *tish* 'table', i.e. 'on the table' (referring to money in gambling).

oofy ▶ adjective (**-ier, -iest**) informal, dated rich; wealthy.
– DERIVATIVES **oofiness** noun.
– ORIGIN late 19th cent.: from **OOF**[2] + **-Y**[1].

oogamous /əʊˈɒɡəməs/ ▶ adjective Biology relating to or denoting reproduction by the union of mobile male and immobile female gametes.
– DERIVATIVES **oogamously** adverb, **oogamy** noun.

oogenesis /ˌəʊəˈdʒɛnɪsɪs/ ▶ noun [mass noun] Biology the production or development of an ovum.

oogonium /ˌəʊəˈɡəʊnɪəm/ ▶ noun (pl. **oogonia**) **1** Botany the female sex organ of certain algae and fungi, typically a rounded cell or sac containing one or more oospheres. **2** Biology an immature female reproductive cell that gives rise to primary oocytes by mitosis.
– ORIGIN mid 19th cent.: from **OO-** 'of an egg' + Greek *gonos* 'generation' + **-IUM**.

ooh ▶ exclamation used to express a range of emotions including surprise, delight, or pain: *ooh, this is fun* | *ooh, my feet!*
▶ noun an utterance of such an exclamation: *the oohs and aahs of the enthusiastic audience.*
▶ verb (**oohed, oohing**) [no obj.] utter such an exclamation: *visitors oohed and aahed at the Christmas tree.*
– ORIGIN natural exclamation: first recorded in English in the early 20th cent.

oojah /ˈuːdʒɑː/ (also **oojamaflip** /ˈuːdʒəməflɪp/) ▶ noun informal used when one cannot think of or does not wish to use the name of something.
– ORIGIN early 20th cent.: of unknown origin.

oolite /ˈəʊəlʌɪt/ ▶ noun [mass noun] Geology limestone consisting of a mass of rounded grains (ooliths) made up of concentric layers.
– DERIVATIVES **oolitic** adjective.
– ORIGIN early 19th cent.: from French *oölithe*, modern Latin *oolites* (see **OO-, -LITE**).

oolith /ˈəʊəlɪθ/ ▶ noun Geology any of the rounded grains making up oolite.

oology /əʊˈɒlədʒi/ ▶ noun [mass noun] the study or collecting of birds' eggs.
– DERIVATIVES **oological** adjective, **oologist** noun.

oolong /ˈuːlɒŋ/ ▶ noun [mass noun] a kind of dark-coloured China tea made by fermenting the withered leaves to about half the degree usual for black teas.
– ORIGIN mid 19th cent.: from Chinese *wūlóng*, literally 'black dragon'.

oom /ʊəm/ ▶ noun S. African a man, especially an older one.
■ used as a respectful and affectionate form of address to a man older than the speaker.
– ORIGIN Afrikaans, from Dutch.

oompah (also **oompah-pah**) informal ▶ noun [mass noun] used to refer to the rhythmical sound of deep-toned brass instruments in a band.
▶ verb (**oompahed, oompahing**) [no obj.] make such a sound.
– ORIGIN late 19th cent.: imitative.

oomph (also **umph**) ▶ noun [mass noun] informal the quality of being exciting, energetic, or sexually attractive: *he showed entrepreneurial oomph.*
– ORIGIN 1930s: perhaps imitative.

-oon ▶ suffix forming nouns, originally from French words having the final stressed syllable *-on*: *balloon* | *buffoon.*
– ORIGIN from Latin *-onis* sometimes via Italian *-one.*

USAGE In words ending in *-on* adopted from French in Middle English, the spelling *-on* was retained in English (pronounced /(ə)n/, as the last syllable in **button**), reflecting a shift of stress away from this final syllable. Words borrowed during the 16th–18th centuries retained the stress on the final syllable with the spelling *-oon* (pronounced /ˈuːn/, as in **balloon**). Later borrowings have tended to retain the French spelling *-on* (e.g. **carton**).

oophorectomy /ˌəʊəfəˈrɛktəmi/ ▶ noun (pl. **-ies**) [mass noun] surgical removal of one or both ovaries; ovariectomy.
– ORIGIN late 19th cent.: from modern Latin *oophoron*

'ovary' (from Greek *ōophoros* 'egg-bearing') + **-ECTOMY**.

oophoritis /ˌəʊəfəˈrʌɪtɪs/ ▶ noun [mass noun] Medicine inflammation of an ovary.

oops ▶ exclamation informal used to show recognition of a mistake or minor accident, often as part of an apology: *'Oops! I'm sorry. I just made you miss your bus'.*
– ORIGIN natural exclamation: first recorded in English in the 1930s.

oops-a-daisy ▶ exclamation variant spelling of **UPSY-DAISY**.

Oort /ɔːt/, Jan Hendrik (1900–92), Dutch astronomer. He proved that the Galaxy is rotating, and determined the position and orbital period of the sun within it.

Oort cloud /ɔːt, ʊət/ Astronomy a spherical cloud of small rocky and icy bodies postulated to orbit the sun beyond the orbit of Pluto and up to 1.5 light years from the sun, and to act as a reservoir of comets. Its existence was proposed by J. H. Oort.

oosphere /ˈəʊəsfɪə/ ▶ noun Botany the female reproductive cell of certain algae or fungi, which is formed in the oogonium and when fertilized becomes the oospore.

oospore /ˈəʊəspɔː/ ▶ noun Botany the thick-walled zygote of certain algae and fungi, formed by fertilization of an oosphere. Compare with **ZYGOSPORE**.

Oostende /ɔːstˈɛndə/ Flemish name for **OSTEND**.

ootheca /ˌəʊəˈθiːkə/ ▶ noun (pl. **oothecae** /-kiː/) Entomology the egg case of cockroaches, mantises, and related insects.
– ORIGIN mid 19th cent.: from **OO-** 'of an egg' + Greek *thēkē* 'receptacle'.

ootid /ˈəʊətɪd/ ▶ noun Biology a haploid cell formed by the meiotic division of a secondary oocyte, especially the ovum, as distinct from the polar bodies.
– ORIGIN early 20th cent.: from **OO-** 'egg', on the pattern of *spermatid.*

ooze[1] ▶ verb [no obj., with adverbial of direction] (of a fluid) slowly trickle or seep out of something; move in a slow, creeping way: *blood was oozing from a wound in his scalp* | *honey oozed out of the comb.*
■ [no obj.] slowly exude or discharge a viscous fluid: *her mosquito bites were oozing and itching like mad.* ■ [with obj.] figurative (of a person) give a powerful impression of (a quality): *she oozes a raunchy sex appeal.*
▶ noun **1** [mass noun] the sluggish flow of a fluid. **2** an infusion of oak bark or other vegetable matter, used in tanning.
– DERIVATIVES **oozy** adjective.
– ORIGIN Old English *wōs* 'juice or sap'; the verb dates from late Middle English.

ooze[2] ▶ noun [mass noun] wet mud or slime, especially that found at the bottom of a river, lake, or sea.
■ Geology a deposit of white or grey calcareous matter largely composed of foraminiferan remains, covering extensive areas of the ocean floor.
– DERIVATIVES **oozy** adjective.
– ORIGIN Old English *wāse*; related to Old Norse *veisa* 'stagnant pool'. In Middle English and the 16th cent. the spelling was *wose* (rhyming with *repose*), but from 1550 spellings imply a change in pronunciation and influence by **OOZE**[1].

OP ▶ abbreviation for ■ observation post. ■ (in the theatre) opposite prompt. ■ organophosphate(s). ■ (in the Roman Catholic Church) *Ordo Praedicatorum* Order of Preachers (Dominican).

Op. (also **op.**) ▶ abbreviation for Music opus (before a number given to each work of a particular composer, usually indicating the order of publication).

op ▶ noun informal a surgical operation: *a minor op.*
■ (**ops**) military operations: [as modifier] *the ops room.* ■ a radio or telephone operator.

op- ▶ prefix variant spelling of **OB-** assimilated before *p* (as in *oppress, oppugn*).

o.p. ▶ abbreviation for ■ (of a book) out of print. ■ (of alcohol) overproof.

opacify /əˈ(ʊ)pasɪfʌɪ/ ▶ verb (**-ies, -ied**) technical make or become opaque.
– DERIVATIVES **opacifier** noun.

opacity /əˈ(ʊ)pasɪti/ ▶ noun [mass noun] the condition of lacking transparency or translucence: *thinner paints need black added to increase opacity.*
■ figurative obscurity of meaning: *the difficulty and opacity in Barthes' texts.*

– ORIGIN mid 16th cent.: from French *opacité*, from Latin *opacitas*, from *opacus* 'darkened'.

opah /ˈəʊpə/ ▶ **noun** a large deep-bodied fish with a deep blue back, silvery belly, and crimson fins, which lives in deep oceanic waters. Also called **MOONFISH**.
• *Lampris guttatus*, family Lampridae.
– ORIGIN mid 18th cent.: a West African word.

opal ▶ **noun** a gemstone consisting of a quartz-like form of hydrated silica, typically semi-transparent and showing many small points of shifting colour against a pale or dark ground.
– ORIGIN late 16th cent.: from French *opale* or Latin *opalus*, probably based on Sanskrit *upala* 'precious stone' (having been first brought from India).

opalescent ▶ **adjective** showing many small points of shifting colour against a pale or dark ground.
– DERIVATIVES **opalescence** noun.

opal glass ▶ **noun** [mass noun] a type of semi-translucent white glass.

opaline /ˈəʊp(ə)lʌɪn, -lɪn/ ▶ **adjective** another term for **OPALESCENT**.
▶ **noun** another term for **MILK-GLASS**.
■ translucent glass of a colour other than white.

op-amp ▶ **abbreviation for** operational amplifier.

opanka /ɒpˈaŋkə/ ▶ **noun** (pl. **opankas** or **opanci**) a kind of Serbian shoe made of soft leather and fastened with straps, similar in style to a moccasin.
– ORIGIN early 19th cent.: from Serbo-Croat *opanak*.

opaque /ə(ʊ)ˈpeɪk/ ▶ **adjective** (**opaquer**, **opaquest**) not able to be seen through; not transparent: *the windows were opaque with ancient grime.*
■ figurative (especially of language) hard or impossible to understand; unfathomable: *technical jargon that was opaque to her.*
▶ **noun** an opaque thing or substance.
■ [mass noun] Photography a substance for producing opaque areas on negatives.
– DERIVATIVES **opaquely** adverb, **opaqueness** noun.
– ORIGIN late Middle English *opake*, from Latin *opacus* 'darkened'. The current spelling (rare before the 19th cent.) has been influenced by the French form.

op art (also **optical art**) ▶ **noun** [mass noun] a form of abstract art that gives the illusion of movement by the precise use of pattern and colour, or in which conflicting patterns emerge and overlap. Bridget Riley and Victor Vasarely are its most famous exponents.
– ORIGIN 1960s: on the pattern of *pop art*.

op. cit. ▶ **adverb** in the work already cited.
– ORIGIN from Latin *opere citato*.

opcode ▶ **noun** Computing short for **OPERATION CODE**.

ope ▶ **adjective** & **verb** poetic/literary or archaic form of **OPEN**.

OPEC ▶ **abbreviation for** Organization of the Petroleum Exporting Countries.

Op-Ed (also **Op-Ed page**) ▶ **noun** N. Amer. a newspaper page opposite the editorial page, devoted to personal comment, feature articles, etc.

Opel /ˈəʊp(ə)l/, Wilhelm von (1871–1948), German motor manufacturer. His company was the first in Germany to introduce assembly-line production, selling over one million cars.

open ▶ **adjective 1** allowing access, passage, or a view through an empty space; not closed or blocked up: *it was a warm evening and the window was open* | *the door was* **wide open** | *the cupboard's been ripped open.*
■ (of a container) not fastened or sealed; in a position or with the lid or other covering in a position allowing access to the inside part or the contents: *the case burst open and its contents flew all over the place.* ■ (of a garment or its fastenings) not done up: *his tie was knotted below the open collar of his shirt.* ■ (of the mouth or eyes) with lips or lids parted: *his eyes were open but he could see nothing.* ■ Phonetics (of a vowel) produced with a relatively wide opening of the mouth and the tongue kept low. ■ Phonetics (of a syllable) ending in a vowel. ■ free from obstructions: *the pass is kept open all year by snowploughs.* ■ (of the bowels) not constipated. ■ (of a game or style of play) characterized by action which is spread out over the field.
2 [attrib.] exposed to the air or to view; not covered: *an open fire burned in the grate.*
■ (of an area of land) not covered with buildings or trees: *the plans allow increasing numbers of new houses in open countryside.* ■ (of a fabric) loosely knitted or woven. ■ (of a goalmouth or other object of attack in a game) unprotected; vulnerable. ■ (of a boat) without a deck. ■ [predic.] (**open to**) likely to suffer from or be affected by; vulnerable or subject to: *the system is open to abuse.* ■ (of a town or city) officially declared to be undefended, and so immune under international law from bombardment. ■ with the outer edges or sides drawn away from each other; unfolded: *the trees had buds and a few open flowers.* ■ (of a book or file) with the covers parted allowing it to be read: *she was copying verses from an open Bible* | figurative *her mind was an open book to him.* ■ (of a hand) not clenched into a fist. ■ [as complement] damaged or injured by a deep cut in the surface: *he had his arm slashed open.*
3 [predic.] (of a shop, place of entertainment, etc.) officially admitting customers or visitors; available for business: *the bar was open, but did not seem ready for business* | *the shop stays open until 9pm.*
■ (of a bank account) available for transactions. ■ (of a telephone line) ready to take calls: *our free advice line is open from 8.30 to 17.30.* ■ (of a choice, offer, or opportunity) still available; such that people can take advantage of it: *the offer is open while stocks last* | *we need to consider what options are left open.*
4 (of a person) frank and communicative; not given to deception or concealment: *she was open and naive* | *I was quite open about my views.*
■ not concealed; manifest: *his eyes showed open admiration as they swept over her.* ■ [attrib.] (of conflict) fully developed and unconcealed: *the dispute erupted into open war.* ■ involving no concealment, restraint, or deception; welcoming discussion, criticism, and enquiry: *he outlined the party's commitment to democracy and open government.*
5 (of a question, case, or decision) not finally settled; still admitting of debate: *students' choice of degree can be kept open until the second year.*
■ (of the mind) accessible to new ideas; unprejudiced: *I'm keeping an open mind about my future.* ■ [predic.] (**open to**) receptive to: *the union was open to suggestions for improvements.* ■ [predic.] (**open to**) admitting of; making possible: *the message is open to different interpretations.* ■ freely available or accessible; offered without restriction: *the service is* **open to** *all students at the University.* ■ with no restrictions on those allowed to attend or participate: *an open audition was announced.* ■ (also **Open**) (of an award or the competition for it) unrestricted as to who may compete: *each horse had won two open races.* ■ (also **Open**) (of a victor) having won a contest with no restrictions upon entrants. ■ (of a ticket) not restricted as to day of travel. ■ Brit. (of a cheque) not crossed.
6 Music (of a string) allowed to vibrate along its whole length.
■ (of a pipe) unstopped at each end. ■ (of a note) sounded from an open string or pipe.
7 (of an electric circuit) having a break in the conducting path.
8 Mathematics (of a set) not containing any of its limit points.
▶ **verb** [with obj.] **1** move or adjust (a door or window) so as to leave a space allowing access and vision: *she opened the door and went in* | [no obj., in imperative] *'Open up!' he said.*
■ [no obj.] (of a door or window) be moved or adjusted to leave a space allowing access: *the door opened and a man came out.* ■ undo or remove the lid, cover, or fastening of (a container) to get access to the contents: *he opened a bottle inexpertly, spilling some of the wine.* ■ remove the covers or wrapping from: *can we open the presents now?* ■ part the lips or lids of (a mouth or eye): *she opened her mouth to argue.* ■ [no obj.] (of the mouth of eyes) have the lips of lids parted in this way: *her eyes slowly opened.* ■ improve or make possible access to or passage through: *the President announced that his government would open the border.* ■ cause evacuation of (the bowels). ■ [no obj.] (**open on to/into**) (of a room, door, or window) give access to: *the kitchen opened into a pleasant sitting room.* ■ [no obj., with adverbial] (of a prospect) come into view; spread out before someone: *stop to marvel at the views that* **open out** *below.* ■ Nautical achieve a clear view of (a place) by sailing past a headland or other obstruction: *we shall open Torbay shortly.*
2 spread out; unfold: *the eagle opened its wings and circled up into the air* | *the tail looks like a fan when it is* **opened out** *fully.*
■ [no obj.] be unfolded; spread out to the full extent: *the flowers only open during bright weather.* ■ part the covers of (a book or file) to read it: *she opened her book at the prologue.* ■ [no obj.] (**open out**) become wider or more spacious: *the path opened out into a glade.*
3 allow public access to: *one woman raised $731 by opening her home and selling coffee and tea.*
■ make available: *the new plan proposed to* **open up** *opportunities to immigrants.* ■ make more widely known; reveal: *the move may force the company to* **open up** *its plans for the future.* ■ [no obj.] (**open out/up**) become more communicative or confiding: *he was very reserved and only opened out to her slowly.* ■ make (one's mind or heart) more receptive or sympathetic: **open** *your mind* **to** *what is going on around you.* ■ (**open someone to/up to**) make someone vulnerable to: *the process is going to open them to a legal threat.*
4 establish (a new business, movement, or enterprise): *he* **opened up** *a new business.*
■ [no obj.] (of an enterprise, especially a commercial one) be established: *two new restaurants open this week.* ■ take the action required to make ready for use: *they have the £10 necessary to open a savings account* | *click twice to open a file for the piece of software selected.* ■ [no obj.] (of a meeting or a sporting or artistic event) formally begin: *the incident occurred just before the Olympic Games were due to open.* ■ [no obj.] (of a piece of writing or music) begin: *the chapter opens with a discussion of Anglo-Irish relations.* ■ (**open up**) [no obj.] (of a process) start to develop: *a new and dramatic phase was opening up.* ■ ceremonially declare (a building, road, etc.) to be completed and ready for use: *we will have to wait until a new bypass is opened before we can tackle the problem of congestion.* ■ [no obj.] (of a shop, place of entertainment, etc.) be officially ready to receive customers or visitors; become ready for business: *the shops didn't open until 10.* ■ (of a counsel in a law court) make a preliminary statement in (a case) before calling witnesses. ■ Cricket another term for **open the batting** below. ■ [with obj.] Bridge make (the first bid) in the auction.
5 break the conducting path of (an electric circuit): *the switch opens the motor circuit.*
■ [no obj.] (of an electric circuit or device) suffer a break in its conducting path.
▶ **noun 1** (**Open**) a championship or competition with no restrictions on who may compete.
2 an accidental break in the conducting path for an electric current.
– PHRASES **be open with** speak frankly to; conceal nothing from: *I had always been completely open with my mother.* **in** (or **into**) **the open** out of doors; not under cover. ■ not subject to concealment or obfuscation; made public: *we have never let our dislike for him come into the open.* **in open court** in a court of law, before the judge and the public. **open-and-shut** (of a case or argument) admitting no doubt or dispute; straightforward. **open the batting** Cricket play as one of the pair of batsmen who begin a side's innings. **open the door to** see **DOOR**. **open someone's eyes** see **EYE**. **open fire** begin to shoot. **an open mind** see **MIND**. **with one's eyes open** (or **with open eyes**) fully aware of the risks and other implications of an action or situation: *I went into the job with my eyes open—everyone knows what happens to an unsuccessful manager.* **with open arms** see **ARM**[1].
– DERIVATIVES **openable** adjective, **openness** noun.
– ORIGIN Old English *open* (adjective), *openian* (verb), of Germanic origin; related to Dutch *open* and German *offen*, from the root of the adverb **UP**.
▶ **open up** begin shooting: *the enemy artillery had opened up.*
open something up 1 accelerate a motor vehicle.
2 (of a sports player or team) create an advantage for one's side: *he opened up a lead of 14–8.*

open access ▶ **noun** [mass noun] availability to all.
■ a system where users of a library have direct access to bookshelves.

open air ▶ **noun** a free or unenclosed space outdoors: *getting out* **in the open air**.
▶ **adjective** positioned or taking place out of doors: *an open-air swimming pool.*

open bar ▶ **noun** a bar at a special function at which the drinks have been paid for by the host or are prepaid through the admission fee.

openbill (also **openbill** (or **open-billed**) **stork**) ▶ **noun** an African and South Asian stork with a bill that meets only at the tip, feeding on water snails.
• Genus *Anastomus*, family Ciconiidae: the all-dark **African openbill** (*A. lamelligerus*) and the mainly pale grey **Asian openbill** (*A. oscitans*).

open bite ▶ **noun** [mass noun] Dentistry lack of occlusion of the front teeth when the jaw is closed normally.

Open Brethren one of the two principal divisions of the Plymouth Brethren (the other is the Exclusive Brethren), formed in 1849 as a result of doctrinal and other differences. The Open Brethren are less rigorous and less exclusive in matters such as conditions for membership and contact with outsiders than the Exclusive Brethren.

opencast ▶ **adjective** Brit. denoting a method of mining in which coal or ore is extracted at or from a level near the earth's surface, rather than from shafts.
▶ **noun** [mass noun] the process of mining in such a way.

open chain ▶ **noun** Chemistry a molecular structure consisting of a chain of atoms with no closed rings.

open circuit ▶ **noun** an electric circuit that is incomplete.
▶ **adjective** consisting of or containing an open circuit.
– DERIVATIVES **open-circuited** adjective.

open cluster ▶ **noun** Astronomy a loose grouping of stars.

Open College (in the UK) an organization established to provide retraining opportunities, chiefly by arranging managerial and technical courses for the staff of companies.

open communion ▶ **noun** [mass noun] Christian Church communion administered to any Christian believer.

open date ▶ **noun** US a future available date for which no sports fixture has yet been arranged.

open day ▶ **noun** Brit. a day when members of the public may visit a place or institution to which they do not usually have access.

open door ▶ **noun** [in sing.] a free or unrestricted means of admission or access: *being homeless is not an open door to decent housing.*
■ the policy or practice by which a country allows the free admission of immigrants or foreign imports: [as modifier] *an open-door immigration policy.*

open-ended (also **open-end**) ▶ **adjective** having no predetermined limit or boundary.
– DERIVATIVES **open-endedness** noun.

open enrolment ▶ **noun** [mass noun] the unrestricted enrolment of students at schools, colleges, or universities of their choice.

opener ▶ **noun 1** [usu. with modifier] a device for opening something, especially a container: *a bottle opener | a tin opener | a letter opener.*
2 informal the first of a series of sporting or cultural events or other items: *last night's opener was sharply edited and tautly scripted.*
■ the first goal in a sporting event. ■ a remark used as an excuse to initiate a conversation: *we blurted out the obvious opener.* ■ Cricket a batsman who opens the batting. ■ Bridge the player who makes the first bid in the auction.
– PHRASES **for openers** informal to start with; first of all: *for openers we chose potted lobster.*

open-faced ▶ **adjective 1** having a frank or ingenuous expression.
2 (of a watch) having no cover other than the glass.
■ (also **open-face**) chiefly N. Amer. (of a sandwich or pie) without an upper layer of bread or pastry.

open-field system ▶ **noun** the traditional medieval system of farming in England, in which land was divided into strips and managed by an individual only in the growing season, being available to the community for grazing animals during the rest of the year.

open go ▶ **noun** Austral. informal a fair chance.

open-handed ▶ **adjective 1** (of a blow) delivered with the palm of the hand.
2 giving freely; generous: *open-handed philanthropy.*
– DERIVATIVES **open-handedly** adverb, **open-handedness** noun.

open-hearted ▶ **adjective** expressing or displaying one's warm and kindly feelings without concealment: *Betty's open-hearted goodwill.*
– DERIVATIVES **open-heartedness** noun.

open-hearth process ▶ **noun** a steel-making process in which scrap iron or steel, limestone, and pig iron are melted together in a shallow reverberatory furnace, the mixture being heated from above using gaseous fuel and air which oxidizes impurities in the iron.

open-heart surgery ▶ **noun** [mass noun] surgery in which the heart is exposed and the blood made to bypass it.

open house ▶ **noun** a place or situation in which all visitors are welcome: [mass noun] *they kept open house, entertaining a wide variety of guests and writers.*
■ North American term for **OPEN DAY**.

open ice ▶ **noun** [mass noun] ice-covered water through which navigation is possible.

opening ▶ **noun 1** an aperture or gap, especially one allowing access: *she peered through one of the smaller openings.*
■ figurative an opportunity to achieve something: *they seem to have exploited fully the openings offered.* ■ an available job or position: *there are few openings for the ex-footballer.*
2 a beginning; an initial part: *Maya started tapping out the opening of her story.*
■ the occasion of the first performance of a play, film, etc., of the start of an exhibition, or of a public building being officially ready for use, marked by a ceremony or celebratory gathering. ■ Chess a recognized sequence of moves at the beginning of a game. ■ a counsel's preliminary statement of a case in a law court.
▶ **adjective** [attrib.] coming at the beginning of something; initial: *she stole the show with her opening remark.*

opening gambit ▶ **noun** an introductory remark or stratagem, especially one designed to make social contact or secure one's own position.

opening hours ▶ **plural noun** the times during which a shop, bank, etc., is open for business.

opening night ▶ **noun** the first night of a theatrical play or other entertainment.

opening time ▶ **noun** Brit. the time at which public houses may legally open for custom.

open interest ▶ **noun** [mass noun] Finance the number of contracts or commitments outstanding in futures and options trading on an official exchange at any one time.

open learning ▶ **noun** [mass noun] learning based on independent study or initiative rather than formal classroom instruction.

open letter ▶ **noun** a letter addressed to a particular person or group of people but intended for publication in a newspaper or journal.

open line ▶ **noun** a telephone line on which conversations can be overheard or intercepted by others.
▶ **adjective** denoting a radio or television programme in which the public can participate by telephone.

openly ▶ **adverb** without concealment, deception, or prevarication, especially where these might be expected; frankly or honestly: *a lecturer who had openly criticized the government.*
– ORIGIN Old English *openlíce* (see **OPEN**, **-LY²**).

open market ▶ **noun** (often **the open market**) an unrestricted market with free access by and competition of buyers and sellers.

open mike ▶ **noun** [often as modifier] chiefly N. Amer. a session in a club where anyone is welcome to sing or perform stand-up comedy.

open-minded ▶ **adjective** willing to consider new ideas; unprejudiced.
– DERIVATIVES **open-mindedly** adverb, **open-mindedness** noun.

open-mouthed ▶ **adjective** with the mouth open, especially in surprise or excitement.

open-necked ▶ **adjective** (of a shirt) worn with the collar unbuttoned and without a tie.

open outcry ▶ **noun** [mass noun] a system of financial trading in which dealers shout their bids and contracts aloud.

open-pit ▶ **adjective** North American term for **OPENCAST**.

open-plan ▶ **adjective** (of a room or building) having large rooms with few or no internal dividing walls.

open primary ▶ **noun** US a primary election open to all registered voters.

open prison ▶ **noun** Brit. a prison with the minimum of restrictions on prisoners' movements and activities.

open question ▶ **noun** a matter on which differences of opinion are possible; a matter not yet decided.

open range ▶ **noun** N. Amer. a tract of land without fences or other barriers.

open-reel ▶ **adjective** (of a tape recorder) having reels of tape requiring individual threading, as distinct from a cassette.

open road ▶ **noun** a main road, especially one outside an urban area.

open sandal ▶ **noun** a sandal that does not cover the toes.

open sandwich ▶ **noun** a sandwich without a top slice of bread.

open sea ▶ **noun** (usu. **the open sea**) an expanse of sea away from land.

open season ▶ **noun** [in sing.] the annual period when restrictions on the killing of certain types of wildlife, especially for sport, are lifted.
■ a period when all restrictions on a particular activity, especially on attacking or criticizing a particular group, are abandoned or ignored: *it's open season on public figures.*

open secret ▶ **noun** a supposed secret that is in fact known to many people.

open sesame ▶ **noun** see **SESAME**.

open shop ▶ **noun** a system whereby employees in a place of work do not have to join a trade union.
■ a place of work following such a system.

open side ▶ **noun** [in sing.] Rugby the side of the scrum on which the main line of the opponents' backs is ranged.

open slather ▶ **noun** Austral./NZ informal an opportunity or state of freedom to operate without interference; a free-for-all.

open society ▶ **noun** a society characterized by a flexible structure, freedom of belief, and wide dissemination of information.

open system ▶ **noun 1** Computing a system in which the components and protocols conform to standards independent of a particular supplier.
2 Physics a material system in which mass or energy can be lost to or gained from the environment.

open texture ▶ **noun** chiefly Philosophy the inability of certain concepts to be fully or precisely defined or of regulations to be exhaustive and leave no room for interpretation.

open-toed ▶ **adjective** (of a shoe) having an upper that does not cover the toes.

open-top (also **open-topped**) ▶ **adjective** [attrib.] (of a vehicle) not having a roof or having a folding or detachable roof.

Open University (in the UK) a university that teaches mainly by broadcasting, correspondence, and summer schools, and is open to those without formal academic qualifications.

open verdict ▶ **noun** Law a verdict of a coroner's jury affirming the occurrence of a suspicious death but not specifying the cause.

open water ▶ **noun** [mass noun] a stretch of water which is not enclosed by land, ice, or other barriers.
■ Canadian the melting of ice on rivers and lakes in spring. ■ Canadian the time when this happens.

openwork ▶ **noun** [mass noun] [usu. as modifier] ornamental work in cloth, metal, leather, or other material with regular patterns of openings and holes.

opepe /əʊˈpiːpi/ ▶ **noun** a tropical West African tree which yields timber that is used in harbour work because of its resistance to marine borers.
● *Nauclea diderichii*, family Rubiaceae.
– ORIGIN late 19th cent.: from Yoruba.

opera¹ ▶ **noun** a dramatic work in one or more acts, set to music for singers and instrumentalists.
■ [mass noun] such works as a genre of classical music. ■ a building for the performance of opera.
– ORIGIN mid 17th cent.: from Italian, from Latin, literally 'labour, work'.

opera² plural form of **OPUS**.

operable ▶ **adjective 1** able to be used: *less than half the rail network was operable.*
2 able to be treated by means of a surgical operation: *operable breast cancer.*
– DERIVATIVES **operability** noun.
– ORIGIN mid 17th cent.: from late Latin *operabilis*, from Latin *operari* 'expend labour on' (see **OPERATE**).

opéra bouffe /ˌɒp(ə)rɑ ˈbuːf, French ɔpera buf/ ▶ **noun** (pl. **opéras bouffes**) a French comic opera, with dialogue in recitative and characters drawn from everyday life.
– ORIGIN French, from Italian (see **OPERA BUFFA**).

opera buffa /ˌɒp(ə)rə ˈbuːfə/ ▶ **noun** a comic opera (usually in Italian), especially one with characters drawn from everyday life.
– ORIGIN Italian.

opera cloak ▶ **noun** a cloak of rich material worn over evening clothes, especially by women.

opéra comique /ˌɒp(ə)rə kɒˈmiːk, French ɔpeʀa kɔmik/ ▶ **noun** an opera (usually in French) on a light-hearted theme, with spoken dialogue.

opera glasses ▶ **plural noun** small binoculars for use at the opera or theatre.

opera hat ▶ **noun** a collapsible top hat.

opera house ▶ **noun** a theatre designed for the performance of opera.

operand /ˈɒpərand/ ▶ **noun** Mathematics the quantity on which an operation is to be done.
– ORIGIN late 19th cent.: from Latin *operandum*, neuter gerundive of *operari* 'expend labour on' (see **OPERATE**).

operant /ˈɒp(ə)r(ə)nt/ Psychology ▶ **adjective** involving the modification of behaviour by the reinforcing or inhibiting effect of its own consequences (instrumental conditioning).
▶ **noun** an item of behaviour that is not a response to a prior stimulus but something which is initially spontaneous, which may reinforce or inhibit recurrence of that behaviour.
– ORIGIN late Middle English: from Latin *operant-* 'being at work', from the verb *operari*.

opera seria /ˈsɪərɪə/ ▶ **noun** an opera (especially one of the 18th century in Italian) on a serious, usually classical or mythological theme.
– ORIGIN Italian, literally 'serious opera'.

operate ▶ **verb 1** [with obj.] (of a person) control the functioning of (a machine, process, or system): *a shortage of workers to operate new machines | the Prime Minister operates a system of divide and rule.*
■ [no obj., with adverbial] (of a machine, process, or system) function in a specified manner: *market forces were allowed to operate freely.* ■ [no obj.] be in effect: *there is a powerful law which operates in politics.* ■ (of a person or organization) manage and run (a business): *many foreign companies operate factories in the United States.* ■ [no obj., with adverbial] (of an organization) be managed and run in a specified way: *neither company had operated within the terms of its constitution.* ■ [no obj., with adverbial] (of an armed force) conduct military activities in a specified area or from a specified base.
2 [no obj.] perform a surgical operation: *my brother had to be* **operated on** *last week | the surgeons refused to operate.*
– ORIGIN early 17th cent.: from Latin *operat-* 'done by labour', from the verb *operari*, from *opus, oper-* 'work'.

operatic ▶ **adjective** of, relating to, or characteristic of opera: *operatic arias.*
■ extravagantly theatrical; histrionic: *she wrung her hands in operatic despair.*
– DERIVATIVES **operatically** adverb.
– ORIGIN mid 18th cent.: formed irregularly from **OPERA**[1], on the pattern of words such as *dramatic*.

operatics ▶ **plural noun** [often treated as sing.] the production or performance of operas.
■ theatrically exaggerated or overemotional behaviour.

operating profit ▶ **noun** a gross profit before deduction of expenses.

operating system ▶ **noun** the low-level software that supports a computer's basic functions, such as scheduling tasks and controlling peripherals.

operating table ▶ **noun** a table on which a patient is placed during a surgical operation.

operating theatre (N. Amer. **operating room**) ▶ **noun** a room in a hospital in which surgical operations are performed.

operation ▶ **noun 1** [mass noun] the fact or condition of functioning or being active: *the construction and operation of power stations | some of these ideas could be* **put into operation**.
2 an act of surgery performed on a patient.
3 [often with adj. or noun modifier] a piece of organized and concerted activity involving a number of people, especially members of the armed forces or the police: *a rescue operation.*
■ (**Operation**) preceding a code name for such an activity: *Operation Desert Storm.* ■ a business organization; a company: *he reopened his operation under a different name.* ■ an activity in which such an organization is involved: *the company is selling most of its continental commercial banking operations.* ■ an active process; a discharge of a function: *the operations of the mind.*
4 Mathematics a process in which a number, quantity, expression, etc., is altered or manipulated according to set formal rules, such as those of addition, multiplication, and differentiation.
– ORIGIN late Middle English: via Old French from Latin *operatio(n-)*, from the verb *operari* 'expend labour on' (see **OPERATE**).

operational ▶ **adjective** in or ready for use: *the new laboratory is fully operational.*
■ of or relating to the routine functioning and activities of a business or organization: *the coffee bar's initial operational costs.* ■ engaged in or relating to active operations of the armed forces, police, or emergency services: *an operational fighter squadron.* ■ Philosophy of, relating to, or in accordance with operationalism.
– DERIVATIVES **operationally** adverb.

operational amplifier (abbrev.: **op-amp**) ▶ **noun** Electronics an amplifier with high gain and high input impedance (usually with external feedback), used especially in circuits for performing mathematical operations on an input voltage.

operational area ▶ **noun** (in South Africa) an area in which control is vested in the defence forces rather than the police.

operationalism ▶ **noun** [mass noun] Philosophy a form of positivism which defines scientific concepts in terms of the operations used to determine or prove them.
– DERIVATIVES **operationalist** noun & adjective.

operationalize (also **-ise**) ▶ **verb** [with obj.] **1** put into operation or use.
2 Philosophy express or define (something) in terms of the operations used to determine or prove it.

operational research (also **operations research**) ▶ **noun** [mass noun] a method of mathematically based analysis for providing a quantitive basis for management decisions.

operation code ▶ **noun** Computing the part of a machine code instruction that defines the operation to be performed.

operations room ▶ **noun** a room from which military or police operations are directed.

operative ▶ **adjective 1** functioning; having effect: *the transmitter is operative | the mining ban would remain operative.*
■ [attrib.] (of a word) having the most relevance or significance in a phrase or sentence: *I was madly—the operative word—in love.*
2 [attrib.] of or relating to surgery: *they had wounds needing operative treatment.*
▶ **noun** a worker, especially a skilled one in a manufacturing industry.
■ a private detective or secret agent.
– DERIVATIVES **operatively** adverb, **operativeness** noun.
– ORIGIN late Middle English: from late Latin *operativus*, from Latin *operat-* 'done by labour', from the verb *operari* (see **OPERATE**).

operator ▶ **noun 1** [often with modifier] a person who operates equipment or a machine: *a radio operator.*
■ (usu. **the operator**) a person who works at the switchboard of a telephone exchange.
2 [usu. with modifier] a person or company that engages in or runs a business or enterprise: *a tour operator.*
3 [with adj.] informal a person who acts in a specified, especially manipulative, way: *her reputation as a cool, clever operator.*
4 Mathematics a symbol or function denoting an operation (e.g. ×, +).

operatorship ▶ **noun** (in the oil and gas industries) the right to operate a well, field, or other oil source.

opera window ▶ **noun** chiefly US a small, typically triangular window at the back of either side of a motor car, usually behind a rear side window.

operculum /ə(ʊ)ˈpəːkjʊləm/ ▶ **noun** (pl. **opercula** /-lə/) Zoology & Botany a structure that closes or covers an aperture, in particular:
■ technical term for **GILL COVER**. ■ a secreted plate that serves to close the aperture of a gastropod mollusc's shell when the animal is retracted. ■ a lid-like structure of the spore-containing capsule of a moss.
– DERIVATIVES **opercular** adjective, **operculate** adjective, **operculi-** combining form.
– ORIGIN early 18th cent.: from Latin, literally 'lid, covering', from *operire* 'to cover'.

operetta ▶ **noun** a short opera, usually on a light or humorous theme and typically having spoken dialogue. Notable composers of operettas include Offenbach, Johan Strauss, Franz Lehár, and Gilbert and Sullivan.
– ORIGIN late 18th cent.: from Italian, diminutive of *opera* (see **OPERA**[1]).

operon /ˈɒpərɒn/ ▶ **noun** Biology a unit made up of linked genes which is thought to regulate other genes responsible for protein synthesis.
– ORIGIN 1960s: from French *opérer* 'to effect, work' + **-ON**.

operose /ˈɒpərəʊs/ ▶ **adjective** rare involving or displaying much industry or effort.
– ORIGIN late 17th cent.: from Latin *operosus*, from *opus* 'work'.

ophicleide /ˈɒfɪklʌɪd/ ▶ **noun** an obsolete bass brass instrument with keys, used in bands in the 19th century but superseded by the tuba.
– ORIGIN mid 19th cent.: from French *ophicléide*, from Greek *ophis* 'serpent' + *kleis, kleid-* 'key'.

Ophidia /ɒˈfɪdɪə/ Zoology a group of reptiles which comprises the snakes. Also called **SERPENTES**.
• Suborder Ophidia, order Squamata.
– DERIVATIVES **ophidian** noun & adjective.
– ORIGIN modern Latin (plural), from Greek *ophis, ophid-* 'snake'.

ophiolite /ˈɒfɪəlʌɪt/ ▶ **noun** [mass noun] Geology an igneous rock consisting largely of serpentine, believed to have been formed from the submarine eruption of oceanic crustal and upper mantle material.
– DERIVATIVES **ophiolitic** adjective.
– ORIGIN mid 19th cent.: from Greek *ophis* 'snake' + **-LITE**.

Ophir /ˈəʊfə/ (in the Bible) an unidentified region, perhaps in SE Arabia, famous for its fine gold and precious stones.

ophitic /əˈfɪtɪk/ ▶ **adjective** Geology relating to or denoting a poikilitic rock texture in which crystals of feldspar are interposed between plates of augite.
– ORIGIN late 19th cent.: via Latin from Greek *ophitēs* 'serpentine stone' (from *ophis* 'snake') + **-IC**.

Ophiuchus /ɒˈfjuːkəs/ Astronomy a large constellation (the Serpent Bearer or Holder), said to represent a man in the coils of a snake. Both the celestial equator and the ecliptic pass through it, but it is not counted among the signs of the zodiac.
■ [as genitive **Ophiuchi** /ɒˈfjuːkʌɪ/] used with preceding letter or numeral to designate a star in this constellation: *the star Eta Ophiuchi.*
– ORIGIN via Latin from Greek *Ophioukos*.

Ophiuroidea /ˌɒfɪ(j)ʊəˈrɔɪdɪə/ Zoology a class of echinoderms that comprises the brittlestars.
– DERIVATIVES **ophiuroid** noun & adjective.
– ORIGIN modern Latin (plural), based on the genus name *Ophiura*, from Greek *ophis* 'snake' + *oura* 'tail'.

ophthalmia /ɒfˈθalmɪə/ ▶ **noun** [mass noun] Medicine inflammation of the eye, especially conjunctivitis.
– ORIGIN late Middle English: via late Latin from Greek, from *ophthalmos* 'eye'.

ophthalmic ▶ **adjective** [attrib.] of or relating to the eye and its diseases.
– ORIGIN early 17th cent.: via Latin from Greek *ophthalmikos*, from *ophthalmos* 'eye'.

ophthalmic optician ▶ **noun** Brit. an optician qualified to prescribe and dispense glasses and contact lenses and to detect eye diseases.

ophthalmitis /ˌɒfθalˈmʌɪtɪs/ ▶ **noun** [mass noun] Medicine inflammation of the eye.

ophthalmo- ▶ **combining form** Medicine relating to the eyes: *ophthalmoscope.*
– ORIGIN from Greek *ophthalmos* 'eye'.

ophthalmology /ˌɒfθalˈmɒlədʒi/ ▶ **noun** [mass noun] the branch of medicine concerned with the study and treatment of disorders and diseases of the eye.
– DERIVATIVES **ophthalmological** adjective, **ophthalmologist** noun.

ophthalmoplegia /ɒfˌθalmə(ʊ)ˈpliːdʒə/ ▶ **noun** [mass noun] Medicine paralysis of the muscles within or surrounding the eye.
– DERIVATIVES **ophthalmoplegic** adjective.

ophthalmoscope /ɒfˈθalməskəʊp/ ▶ **noun** an instrument for inspecting the retina and other parts of the eye.
– DERIVATIVES **ophthalmoscopic** adjective, **ophthalmoscopy** noun.

-opia ▶ **combining form** denoting a visual disorder: *myopia.*
– ORIGIN from Greek *ōps, ōp-* 'eye, face'.

opiate ▶ **adjective** /ˈəʊpɪət/ relating to, resembling, or containing opium.
▶ **noun** /ˈəʊpɪət/ a drug derived from or related to opium.
■ figurative a thing which soothes or stupefies.

▶**verb** /ˈəʊpɪeɪt/ [with obj.] [often as adj. **opiated**] impregnate with opium.
– ORIGIN late Middle English (as a noun): from medieval Latin *opiatus* (adjective), *opiatus* (noun), based on Latin *opium* (see **OPIUM**).

Opie /ˈəʊpi/, John (1761–1807), English painter. His work includes portraits and history paintings such as *The Murder of Rizzio* (1787).

opine ▶**verb** [reporting verb] formal hold and state as one's opinion: [with direct speech] *'The man is a genius,' he opined* | [with clause] *the headmistress opined that the outing would make a nice change for Flora.*
– ORIGIN late Middle English: from Latin *opinari* 'think, believe'.

opinion ▶**noun** a view or judgement formed about something, not necessarily based on fact or knowledge: *I'm writing to voice my opinion on an issue of great importance* | *that, **in my opinion**, is dead right.*
■[mass noun] the beliefs or views of a large number or majority of people about a particular thing: *the changing climate of opinion.* ■(**opinion of**) an estimation of the quality or worth of someone or something: *I had a higher opinion of myself than I deserved.* ■ a formal statement of advice by an expert on a professional matter: *if in doubt, get a second opinion.* ■ Law a formal statement of reasons for a judgement given. ■ Law a barrister's advice on the merits of a case.
– PHRASES **be of the opinion that** believe or maintain that. **a matter of opinion** something not capable of being proven either way.
– ORIGIN Middle English: via Old French from Latin *opinio(n-)*, from the stem of *opinari* 'think, believe'.

opinionated ▶**adjective** characterized by conceited assertiveness and dogmatism: *an arrogant and opinionated man.*
– ORIGIN early 17th cent.: from the (rare) verb *opinionate* 'hold the opinion (that)', from **OPINION**.

opinion poll ▶**noun** an assessment of public opinion by questioning a representative sample, especially as the basis for forecasting the results of voting.

opioid /ˈəʊpɪɔɪd/ Biochemistry ▶**noun** a compound resembling opium in addictive properties or physiological effects.
▶**adjective** relating to or denoting such compounds.
– ORIGIN 1950s: from **OPIUM** + **-OID**.

opistho- /əˈpɪsθəʊ/ ▶**prefix** behind; to the rear: *opisthosoma.*
– ORIGIN from Greek *opisthen* 'behind'.

Opisthobranchia /əˌpɪsθə(ʊ)ˈbraŋkɪə/ Zoology a group of molluscs which includes the sea slugs and sea hares. They have a small or absent shell and are typically brightly coloured with conspicuous external gills.
• Subclass Opisthobranchia, class Gastropoda.
– DERIVATIVES **opisthobranch** /əˈpɪsθə(ʊ)braŋk/ noun.
– ORIGIN modern Latin (plural), from **OPISTHO-** 'to the rear' + *brankhia* 'gills'.

opisthosoma /əˌpɪsθəˈsəʊmə/ ▶**noun** Zoology the abdomen of a spider or other arachnid.

opisthotonos /ˌɒpɪsˈθɒt(ə)nəs/ (also **opisthotonus**) ▶**noun** [mass noun] Medicine spasm of the muscles causing backward arching of the head, neck, and spine, as in severe tetanus, some kinds of meningitis, and strychnine poisoning.
– ORIGIN mid 17th cent.: via late Latin from Greek *opisthotonos* 'drawn backwards'.

opium ▶**noun** [mass noun] a reddish-brown heavy-scented addictive drug prepared from the juice of the opium poppy, used illicitly as a narcotic and occasionally in medicine as an analgesic.
– PHRASES **the opium of the people** (or **masses**) something regarded as inducing a false and unrealistic sense of contentment among people. [ORIGIN: translating the German phrase *Opium des Volks*, used by Marx in reference to religion (1844).]
– ORIGIN late Middle English: via Latin from Greek *opion* 'poppy juice', from *opos* 'juice', from an Indo-European root meaning 'water'.

opium den ▶**noun** a public room where opium is sold and smoked.

opium dream ▶**noun** a dream during an opium-induced sleep.

opium poppy ▶**noun** a Eurasian poppy with ornamental white, red, pink, or purple flowers. Its immature capsules yield a latex from which opium is obtained.
• *Papaver somniferum*, family Papaveraceae.

Opium Wars two wars involving China regarding the question of commercial rights.

> That between Britain and China (1839–42) followed China's attempt to prohibit the illegal importation of opium from British India into China. The second, involving Britain and France against China (1856–60), followed Chinese restrictions on foreign trade. Defeat of the Chinese resulted in the ceding of Hong Kong to Britain and the opening of five 'treaty ports' to traders.

opopanax /ə(ʊ)ˈpɒpənaks/ (also **opoponax**) ▶**noun** **1** an acacia tree with violet-scented flowers that yield an essential oil used in perfumery, native to warm regions of America and cultivated elsewhere.
• *Acacia farnesiana*, family Leguminosae.
2 a yellow-flowered Mediterranean plant of the parsley family.
• *Opopanax chironium*, family Umbelliferae.
■(also **gum opopanax**) [mass noun] a fetid gum resin obtained from the roots of this plant, used in perfumery.
3 [mass noun] a fragrant gum resin which is used in perfumery.
• This resin is obtained from the tree *Commiphora kataf*, family Burseraceae.
– ORIGIN late Middle English: via Latin from Greek, from *opos* 'juice' + *panax* 'all-healing'; compare with **PANACEA**.

Oporto /əʊˈpɔːtuː/ the principal city and port of northern Portugal, near the mouth of the River Douro, famous for port wine; pop. 310,640 (1991). Portuguese name **PORTO**.

opossum /əˈpɒs(ə)m/ ▶**noun** an American marsupial which has a naked prehensile tail and hind feet with an opposable thumb.
• Family Didelphidae: several genera and numerous species. See also **VIRGINIA OPOSSUM**.
■Austral. a possum.
– ORIGIN early 17th cent.: from Virginia Algonquian *opassom*, from *op* 'white' + *assom* 'dog'.

opossum shrimp ▶**noun** a small shrimp-like crustacean which has a long abdomen and conspicuous eyes and is typically transparent. The eggs and young are carried in a ventral brood pouch.
• Order Mysidacea: *Praunus* and other genera. See also **MYSID**.

opp. ▶**abbreviation for** opposite.

Oppenheimer /ˈɒp(ə)nˌhʌɪmə/, Julius Robert (1904–67), American theoretical physicist. He was director of the laboratory at Los Alamos during the development of the first atom bomb, but opposed the development of the hydrogen bomb after the Second World War.

oppidum /ˈɒpɪdəm/ ▶**noun** (pl. **oppida**) an ancient Celtic fortified town, especially one under Roman rule.
– ORIGIN Latin, 'town'.

oppo ▶**noun** (pl. **-os**) Brit. informal a colleague or friend.
– ORIGIN 1930s: abbreviation of *opposite number.*

opponens /əˈpəʊnənz/ ▶**noun** Anatomy another term for **OPPONENT MUSCLE**.
– ORIGIN late 18th cent.: from Latin, literally 'setting against'.

opponent ▶**noun** someone who competes with or fights another in a contest, game, or argument; a rival or adversary: *he beat his Republican opponent by a landslide margin.*
■a person who disagrees with or resists a proposal or practice: *an **opponent of** the economic reforms.*
– ORIGIN late 16th cent. (denoting a person opening an academic debate by proposing objections to a philosophical or religious thesis): from Latin *opponent-* 'setting against', from the verb *opponere*, from *ob-* 'against' + *ponere* 'place'.

opponent muscle ▶**noun** Anatomy any of several muscles enabling the thumb to be placed front to front against a finger of the same hand.

opportune /ˈɒpətjuːn, ˌɒpəˈtjuːn/ ▶**adjective** (of a time) at which a particular action or event occurs, especially conveniently or appropriately: *he couldn't have arrived at a less opportune moment.*
■done or occurring at a favourable or useful time; well-timed: *the opportune use of humour to lower tension.*
– DERIVATIVES **opportunely** adverb, **opportuneness** noun.
– ORIGIN late Middle English: from Old French *opportun(e)*, from Latin *opportunus*, from *ob-* 'in the direction of' + *portus* 'harbour', originally describing the wind driving towards the harbour, hence 'seasonable'.

opportunist ▶**noun** a person who exploits circumstances to gain immediate advantage rather than being guided by consistent principles or plans: *most burglaries are committed by casual opportunists.*
▶**adjective** opportunistic: *the calculating and opportunist politician.*
– DERIVATIVES **opportunism** noun.
– ORIGIN late 19th cent.: from **OPPORTUNE** + **-IST**.

opportunistic ▶**adjective** exploiting chances offered by immediate circumstances without reference to a general plan or moral principle: *the change was cynical and opportunistic.*
■Ecology (of a plant or animal) able to spread quickly in a previously unexploited habitat. ■ Medicine (of a micro-organism or an infection caused by it) rarely affecting patients except in unusual circumstances, typically when the immune system is depressed.
– DERIVATIVES **opportunistically** adverb.

opportunity ▶**noun** (pl. **-ies**) a set of circumstances that makes it possible to do something: *we may see increased **opportunities for** export* | *the collection gives students the **opportunity of** reading works by well-known authors.*
■a chance for employment or promotion: *career opportunities in our New York Headquarters.*
– PHRASES **opportunity knocks** a chance of success occurs.
– ORIGIN late Middle English: from Old French *opportunite*, from Latin *opportunitas*, from *opportunus* (see **OPPORTUNE**).

opportunity cost ▶**noun** Economics the loss of other alternatives when one alternative is chosen.

opportunity shop ▶**noun** Austral./NZ a charity shop.

opposable ▶**adjective** Zoology (of the thumb of a primate) capable of facing and touching the other digits on the same hand.

oppose ▶**verb** [with obj.] disapprove of and attempt to prevent, especially by argument: *a majority of the electorate opposed EC membership.*
■actively resist or refuse to comply with (a person or a system): *a workers' movement opposed the regime.* ■ compete with (someone) in a contest: *a candidate to oppose the leader in the presidential contest.*
– DERIVATIVES **opposer** noun.
– ORIGIN late Middle English: from Old French *opposer*, from Latin *opponere* (see **OPPONENT**), but influenced by Latin *oppositus* 'set or placed against' and Old French *poser* 'to place'.

O

opposed ▶**adjective** **1** [predic.] (**opposed to**) anxious to prevent or put an end to; disapproving of or disagreeing with: *he was opposed to discrimination.*
■in conflict or disagreement with; hostile to: *parties opposed to the ruling party.*
2 (of two or more things) contrasting or conflicting with each other: *the agency is being asked to do two **diametrically opposed** things.*
– PHRASES **as opposed to** distinguished from or in contrast with: *an approach that is theoretical as opposed to practical.*

opposing ▶**adjective** [attrib.] in conflict or competition with a specified or implied subject: *the opposing team.*
■(of two or more subjects) differing from or in conflict with each other: *the brothers fought on opposing sides in the war.* ■ facing; opposite: *on the opposing page there were two addresses.*

opposite ▶**adjective** **1** [attrib.] having a position on the other or further side when seen from a specified or implicit viewpoint; facing something, especially something of the same type: *a crowd gathered on the opposite side of the street.*
■[postpositive] facing the speaker or a specified person or thing: *he went into the shop opposite.* ■(of angles) between opposite sides of the intersection of two lines. ■ Botany (of leaves or shoots) arising in pairs at the same level on opposite sides of the stem.
2 diametrically different; of a contrary kind: *a word that is **opposite** in meaning **to** another* | *currents flowing **in opposite directions**.*
■[attrib.] being the other of a contrasted pair: *the opposite ends of the price range.*
▶**noun** a person or thing that is totally different from or the reverse of someone or something else: *we **were opposites** in temperament* | *the literal is **the opposite of** the figurative.*
▶**adverb** in a position facing a specified or implied subject: *she was sitting almost opposite.*
▶**preposition** in a position on the other side of a

specific area from; facing: *they sat opposite one another.*

■figurative (of someone taking a leading part in a play or film) in a complementary role to (another performer).

– PHRASES **the opposite sex** women in relation to men or vice versa.

– DERIVATIVES **oppositely** adverb, **oppositeness** noun.

– ORIGIN late Middle English: via Old French from Latin *oppositus*, past participle of *opponere* 'set against'.

opposite number ▶ noun (**someone's opposite number**) a person whose position in another group, organization, or country is equivalent to that held by someone already mentioned.

opposite prompt ▶ noun Brit. the offstage area of a theatre stage to the right of an actor facing the audience.

opposition ▶ noun [mass noun] resistance or dissent, expressed in action or argument: *there was considerable* ***opposition to*** *the proposal | the regime cracked down against the threat of opposition.*

■(often **the opposition**) a group of adversaries or competitors, especially a rival political party or sporting team. ■(also **the Opposition**) Brit. the principal parliamentary party opposed to that in office. ■[count noun] a contrast or antithesis: *a nature-culture opposition.* ■Astronomy & Astrology the apparent position of two celestial objects that are directly opposite each other in the sky, especially when a superior planet is opposite the sun.

– PHRASES **in opposition** in contrast or conflict: *they found themselves* ***in opposition to*** *state policy.* ■(with reference to a major political party) not forming the government.

– DERIVATIVES **oppositional** adjective.

– ORIGIN late Middle English: from Latin *oppositio(n-)*, from *opponere* 'set against'.

oppress ▶ verb [with obj.] (often **be oppressed**) **1** keep (someone) in subjection and hardship, especially by the unjust exercise of authority: *a system which oppressed working people* | [as adj. **oppressed**] *oppressed racial minorities.*

■cause (someone) to feel distressed, anxious, or uncomfortable: *he was oppressed by some secret worry.*

2 Heraldry another term for **DEBRUISE**.

– DERIVATIVES **oppressor** noun.

– ORIGIN late Middle English: from Old French *oppresser*, from medieval Latin *oppressare*, from Latin *oppress-* 'pressed against', from the verb *opprimere*.

oppression ▶ noun [mass noun] prolonged cruel or unjust treatment or exercise of control or authority: *a region shattered by oppression and killing.*

■the state of being subject to such treatment or exercise of authority: *a response to collective poverty and oppression.* ■mental pressure or distress: *Beatrice's mood had initially been alarm and a sense of oppression.*

– ORIGIN Middle English: from Old French, from Latin *oppressio(n-)*, from the verb *opprimere* (see **OPPRESS**).

oppressive ▶ adjective unjustly inflicting hardship and constraint, especially on a minority or other subordinate group: *an oppressive dictatorship.*

■weighing heavily on the mind or spirits; causing depression or discomfort: *the offices present an oppressive atmosphere.* ■(of weather) close and sultry.

– DERIVATIVES **oppressively** adverb, **oppressiveness** noun.

– ORIGIN late 16th cent.: from medieval Latin *oppressivus*, from *oppress-* 'pressed against', from the verb *opprimere* (see **OPPRESS**).

opprobrious /ə'prəʊbrɪəs/ ▶ adjective (of language) expressing scorn.

– DERIVATIVES **opprobriously** adverb.

– ORIGIN late Middle English: from late Latin *opprobriosus*, from *opprobrium* (see **OPPROBRIUM**).

opprobrium /ə'prəʊbrɪəm/ ▶ noun [mass noun] harsh criticism or censure: *the critical opprobrium generated by his films.*

■the public disgrace arising from someone's shameful conduct: *the opprobrium of being closely associated with thugs and gangsters.* ■[count noun] archaic an occasion or cause of reproach or disgrace.

– ORIGIN mid 17th cent.: from Latin, literally 'infamy', from *opprobrum*, from *ob-* 'against' + *probrum* 'disgraceful act'.

oppugn /ə'pjuːn/ ▶ verb [with obj.] archaic call into question the truth or validity of.

– DERIVATIVES **oppugner** noun.

– ORIGIN late Middle English (in the sense 'fight against'): from Latin *oppugnare* 'attack, besiege', from *ob-* 'against' + *pugnare* 'to fight'.

oppugnant /ə'pʌgnənt/ ▶ adjective rare opposing; antagonistic.

– DERIVATIVES **oppugnancy** noun.

– ORIGIN early 16th cent.: from Latin *oppugnant-* 'fighting against', from the verb *oppugnare* (see **OPPUGN**).

op shop (also **opp shop**) ▶ noun Austral./NZ short for **OPPORTUNITY SHOP**.

opsimath /'ɒpsɪmaθ/ ▶ noun rare a person who begins to learn or study only late in life.

– ORIGIN late 19th cent.: from Greek *opsimathēs*, from *opse* 'late' + the stem *math-* 'learn'.

opsin /'ɒpsɪn/ ▶ noun [mass noun] Biochemistry a protein which forms part of the visual pigment rhodopsin and is released by the action of light.

– ORIGIN 1950s: shortening of **RHODOPSIN**.

opsonin /'ɒpsənɪn/ ▶ noun Biochemistry an antibody or other substance which binds to foreign microorganisms or cells making them more susceptible to phagocytosis.

– DERIVATIVES **opsonic** adjective.

– ORIGIN early 20th cent.: from Latin *opsonare* 'buy provisions' (from Greek *opsōnein*) + **-IN**[1].

opsonize (also **-ise**) ▶ verb [with obj.] Medicine make (a foreign cell) more susceptible to phagocytosis.

– DERIVATIVES **opsonization** noun.

opt ▶ verb [no obj.] make a choice from a range of possibilities: *consumers will* ***opt for*** *low-priced goods* | [with infinitive] *pupils opting to continue with physics.*

– ORIGIN late 19th cent.: from French *opter*, from Latin *optare* 'choose, wish'.

▶**opt in** choose to participate: *the database would not include a person's name unless he opted in.*

opt out choose not to participate in or carry on with something: *the treaty gives any country the right to* ***opt out of*** *a single currency.* ■Brit. (of a school or hospital) decide to withdraw from local authority control.

optant ▶ noun a person who chooses or has chosen.

■a person who may choose one of two nationalities.

– ORIGIN early 20th cent.: via German and Danish from Latin *optant-* 'choosing', from the verb *optare*.

optative /'ɒptətɪv, ɒp'teɪtɪv/ Grammar ▶ adjective relating to or denoting a mood of verbs in Greek and certain other languages, expressing a wish, equivalent in meaning to English *let's* or *if only.*

▶noun a verb in the optative mood.

■(**the optative**) the optative mood.

– DERIVATIVES **optatively** adverb.

– ORIGIN mid 16th cent.: from French *optatif, -ive*, from late Latin *optativus*, from *optat-* 'chosen', from the verb *optare* (see **OPT**).

optic ▶ adjective of or relating to the eye or vision.

▶noun **1** a lens or other optical component in an optical instrument.

2 archaic or humorous the eye.

3 Brit. trademark a device fastened to the neck of an inverted bottle for measuring out spirits.

– ORIGIN late Middle English: from French *optique* or medieval Latin *opticus*, from Greek *optikos*, from *optos* 'seen'.

optical ▶ adjective **1** of or relating to sight, especially in relation to the physical action of light: *optical illusions.*

■constructed to assist sight: *an optical aid.* ■devised on the principles of optics.

2 Physics operating in or employing the visible part of the electromagnetic spectrum: *optical telescopes.*

■Electronics (of a device) requiring electromagnetic radiation for its operation: *integrated optical circuits.*

– DERIVATIVES **optically** adverb.

optical activity ▶ noun [mass noun] Chemistry the property (displayed by solutions of some compounds, notably many sugars) of rotating the plane of polarization of plane-polarized light.

optical art ▶ noun another term for **OP ART**.

optical axis ▶ noun Physics a line passing through the centre of curvature of a lens or spherical mirror and parallel to the axis of symmetry.

■Crystallography a direction in a doubly refracting crystal along which a light ray does not undergo double refraction.

optical bench ▶ noun a straight rigid bar, typically marked with a scale, to which supports for lenses, light sources, and other optical components can be attached.

optical brightener ▶ noun a fluorescent substance added to detergents in order to produce a whitening effect on laundry.

optical character recognition ▶ noun [mass noun] the identification of printed characters using photoelectric devices and computer software.

optical density ▶ noun Physics the degree to which a refractive medium retards transmitted rays of light.

optical disk ▶ noun see **DISC** (sense 1).

optical double ▶ noun Astronomy a group of two stars which appear to constitute a double star due to their being in the same line of sight as seen from the earth, but are actually at different distances.

optical fibre ▶ noun a thin glass fibre through which light can be transmitted.

optical glass ▶ noun [mass noun] a very pure kind of glass used for lenses.

optical illusion ▶ noun an experience of seeming to see something which does not exist or is other than it appears to one.

■something that deceives one's eyes and causes such an experience.

optical indicatrix ▶ noun see **INDICATRIX**.

optical isomer ▶ noun Chemistry each of two or more forms of a compound which have the same structure but are mirror images of each other and typically differ in optical activity.

– DERIVATIVES **optical isomerism** noun.

optically active ▶ adjective Chemistry (of a substance) displaying optical activity.

optical microscope ▶ noun a microscope using visible light, typically viewed directly by the eye.

optical path ▶ noun Physics the distance which in a vacuum would contain the same number of wavelengths as the actual path taken by a ray of light.

optical rotation ▶ noun [mass noun] Chemistry the rotation of the plane of polarization of plane-polarized light by an optically active substance.

optical scanner ▶ noun Electronics a device which performs optical character recognition and produces coded signals corresponding to the characters identified.

optic angle ▶ noun the angle formed by notional lines from the extremities of an object to the eye, or by lines from the eyes to a given point.

optic axis ▶ noun another term for **OPTICAL AXIS**.

optic chiasma ▶ noun Anatomy the X-shaped structure formed at the point below the brain where the two optic nerves cross over each other.

optic cup ▶ noun Anatomy a cup-like outgrowth of the brain of an embryo which develops into the retina.

optic disc ▶ noun Anatomy the raised disc on the retina at the point of entry of the optic nerve, lacking visual receptors and so creating a blind spot.

optician ▶ noun a person qualified to prescribe and dispense glasses and contact lenses, and to detect eye diseases (**ophthalmic optician**), or to make and supply glasses and contact lenses (**dispensing optician**).

■rare a person who makes or sells optical instruments.

– ORIGIN late 17th cent.: from French *opticien*, from medieval Latin *optica* 'optics'.

optic lobe ▶ noun Anatomy a lobe in the midbrain from which the optic nerve partly arises.

optic nerve ▶ noun Anatomy each of the second pair of cranial nerves, transmitting impulses to the brain from the retina at the back of the eye.

optic neuritis ▶ noun [mass noun] Medicine inflammation of an optic nerve, causing blurred vision.

optics ▶ plural noun [usu. treated as sing.] the scientific study of sight and the behaviour of light, or the properties of transmission and deflection of other forms of radiation.

optic tectum ▶ noun see **TECTUM**.

optic tract ▶ noun Anatomy the pathway between the optic chiasma and the brain.

optima plural form of **OPTIMUM**.

optimal ▶ adjective best or most favourable; optimum: *seeking the optimal solution.*

– DERIVATIVES **optimality** noun, **optimally** adverb.

– ORIGIN late 19th cent.: from Latin *optimus* 'best' + **-AL**.

optimific /ˌɒptɪˈmɪfɪk/ ▶ adjective Philosophy producing the maximum good consequences.
– ORIGIN mid 20th cent.: from Latin *optimus* 'best' + **-IFIC**.

optimism ▶ noun [mass noun] **1** hopefulness and confidence about the future or the successful outcome of something: *the talks had been amicable and there were grounds for optimism.*
2 Philosophy the doctrine, especially as set forth by Leibniz, that this world is the best of all possible worlds.
■ the belief that good must ultimately prevail over evil in the universe.
– DERIVATIVES **optimist** noun.
– ORIGIN mid 18th cent.: from French *optimisme*, from Latin *optimum* 'best thing' (see **OPTIMUM**).

optimistic ▶ adjective hopeful and confident about the future: *the optimistic mood of the Sixties* | *he was optimistic about the deal.*
■ involving an overestimate: *previous estimates of whale numbers may be wildly optimistic.*
– DERIVATIVES **optimistically** adverb.

optimize (also **-ise**) ▶ verb [with obj.] make the best or most effective use of (a situation, opportunity, or resource).
– DERIVATIVES **optimization** noun, **optimizer** noun.
– ORIGIN early 19th cent.: from Latin *optimus* 'best' + **-IZE**.

optimum ▶ adjective most conducive to a favourable outcome; best: *the optimum childbearing age.*
▶ noun (pl. **optima** or **optimums**) the most favourable conditions or level for growth, reproduction, or success.
– ORIGIN late 19th cent.: from Latin, neuter (used as a noun) of *optimus* 'best'.

option ▶ noun a thing that is or may be chosen: *choose the cheapest options for supplying energy.*
■ [in sing.] the freedom, power, or right to choose something: *she was given the option of resigning or being dismissed* | *he has no option but to pay up.* ■ a right to buy or sell a particular thing at a specified price within a set time: *Columbia Pictures has an option on the script.*
▶ verb [with obj.] buy or sell an option on (something).
– PHRASES **keep** (or **leave**) **one's options open** not commit oneself. **not be an option** not be feasible.
– ORIGIN mid 16th cent.: from French, or from Latin *optio(n-)*, from the stem of *optare* 'choose'. The verb dates from the 1930s.

optional ▶ adjective available to be chosen but not obligatory: *a wide range of optional excursions is offered.*
– DERIVATIVES **optionality** noun, **optionally** adverb.

optional extra ▶ noun a non-essential additional item which is available for purchase.

option card ▶ noun **1** Computing an expansion card.
2 a credit card issued for use in a particular store or chain of stores.

optocoupler ▶ noun Electronics a device containing light-emitting and light-sensitive components, used to couple isolated circuits.

optoelectronics ▶ plural noun [treated as sing.] the branch of technology concerned with the combined use of electronics and light.
■ [treated as pl.] circuitry constructed using this technology.
– DERIVATIVES **optoelectronic** adjective.

optometer /ɒpˈtɒmɪtə/ ▶ noun an instrument for testing the refractive power of the eye.
– ORIGIN mid 18th cent.: from Greek *optos* 'seen' + **-METER**.

optometrist ▶ noun chiefly N. Amer. a person who practises optometry.

optometry ▶ noun [mass noun] the occupation of measuring eyesight, prescribing corrective lenses, and detecting eye disease.
– DERIVATIVES **optometric** adjective.

opt-out ▶ noun an instance of choosing not to participate in something: *opt-outs from key parts of the treaty.*
■ Brit. an instance of a school or hospital withdrawing from local authority control.

optronics ▶ plural noun [treated as sing.] short for **OPTOELECTRONICS**.
– DERIVATIVES **optronic** adjective.

opulent ▶ adjective ostentatiously rich and luxurious or lavish: *the opulent comfort of a limousine.*
■ wealthy: *his more opulent tenants.*
– DERIVATIVES **opulence** noun, **opulently** adverb.
– ORIGIN mid 16th cent. (in the sense 'wealthy, affluent'): from Latin *opulent-* 'wealthy, splendid', from *opes* 'wealth'.

opuntia /ɒˈpʌnʃɪə, ə(ʊ)-/ ▶ noun a cactus of a genus that comprises the prickly pears.
● Genus *Opuntia*, family Cactaceae.
– ORIGIN early 17th cent.: from Latin, a name given to a plant growing around *Opus* (stem *Opunt-*), a city in Locris in ancient Greece. The term was later used as a genus name.

opus /ˈəʊpəs, ˈɒp-/ ▶ noun (pl. **opuses** or **opera** /ˈɒp(ə)rə/) **1** Music a separate composition or set of compositions. See also **OP.**
2 any artistic work, especially one on a large scale.
– ORIGIN early 18th cent.: from Latin, literally 'work'.

opuscule /əˈpʌskjuːl/ (also **opusculum** /əˈpʌskjʊləm/) ▶ noun (pl. **opuscules** or **opuscula** /-lə/) rare a small or minor literary or musical work.
– ORIGIN mid 17th cent.: from French, from Latin *opusculum*, diminutive of *opus* 'work'.

opus Dei /ˌəʊpəs ˈdeɪiː, ˈɒpəs/ ▶ noun **1** [mass noun] liturgical worship regarded as man's primary duty to God.
2 (**Opus Dei**) a Roman Catholic organization of laymen and priests founded in Spain in 1928 with the aim of re-establishing Christian ideals in society.
– ORIGIN late 19th cent.: from medieval Latin, literally 'work of God'.

OR ▶ abbreviation for ■ operational research. ■ Oregon (in official postal use). ■ Military, Brit. other ranks (as opposed to commissioned officers).

or[1] ▶ conjunction **1** used to link alternatives: *a cup of tea or coffee* | *are you coming or not?* | *she couldn't read or write* | *I either take taxis or walk everywhere* | *it doesn't matter whether the theory is right or wrong.*
2 introducing a synonym or explanation of a preceding word or phrase: *the espionage novel, or, as it is known in the trade, the thriller.*
3 otherwise (used to introduce the consequences of something not being done or not being the case): *hurry up, or you'll miss it.*
4 introducing an afterthought, usually in the form of a question: *John's indifference—or was it?—left her unsettled.*
5 poetic/literary either: *to love is the one way to know or God or man.*
▶ noun (often **OR**) Electronics a Boolean operator which gives the value one if at least one operand (or input) has a value of one, and otherwise has a value of zero.
■ (also **OR gate**) a circuit which gives an output signal if there is a signal on any of its inputs.
– PHRASES **or else** see **ELSE**. **or so** (after a quantity) approximately: *a dozen or so people.*
– ORIGIN Middle English: a reduced form of the obsolete conjunction *other* (which superseded Old English *oththe* 'or'), of uncertain ultimate origin.

USAGE **1** Where a verb follows a list separated by **or**, the traditional rule is that the verb should be singular, as long as the things in the list are individually singular, as in *a sandwich or other snack is included in the price* (rather than *a sandwich or other snack are included in the price*). The argument is that each of the elements agrees separately with the verb. The opposite rule applies when the elements are joined by **and**: here, the verb should be plural: *a sandwich and a cup of coffee are included in the price.* These traditional rules are observed in good English writing style but are often disregarded in speech. **2** On the use of **either … or**, see usage at **EITHER**.

or[2] ▶ noun [mass noun] gold or yellow, as a heraldic tincture: [postpositive] *azure a bend or.*
– ORIGIN early 16th cent.: from French, from Latin *aurum* 'gold'.

-or[1] ▶ suffix (forming nouns) denoting a person or thing performing the action of a verb, or denoting another agent: *escalator* | *governor* | *resistor.*
– ORIGIN from Latin, sometimes via Anglo-Norman French *-eour* or Old French *-eor* (see also **-ATOR**, **-ITOR**).

-or[2] ▶ suffix forming nouns denoting a state or condition: *error* | *pallor* | *terror.*
– ORIGIN from Latin, sometimes via Old French *-or*, *-ur*.

-or[3] ▶ suffix forming adjectives expressing a comparative sense: *junior* | *major.*
– ORIGIN via Anglo-Norman French from Latin.

-or[4] ▶ suffix US form of **-OUR**[1].

ora plural form of **os**[2].

orache /ˈɒrətʃ/ (also **orach**) ▶ noun a plant of the goosefoot family with leaves that are sometimes covered in a white mealy substance. Several kinds are edible and can be used as a substitute for spinach or sorrel.
● Genus *Atriplex*, family Chenopodiaceae: several species, in particular the **common orache** (*A. hortensis*), which is cultivated in some areas.
– ORIGIN Middle English *orage*, from Anglo-Norman French *arasche*, from Latin *atriplex*, from Greek *atraphaxus*.

oracle ▶ noun **1** a priest or priestess acting as a medium through whom advice or prophecy was sought from the gods in classical antiquity.
■ a place at which such advice or prophecy was sought. ■ a person or thing regarded as an infallible authority or guide on something: *he reigned supreme as the Colonial Office's oracle on Africa.*
2 a response or message given by an oracle, especially one that is ambiguous or obscure.
– ORIGIN late Middle English: via Old French from Latin *oraculum*, from *orare* 'speak'.

oracle bones ▶ plural noun bones used in ancient China for divination.

oracular /ɒˈrakjʊlə/ ▶ adjective of or relating to an oracle: *the oracular shrine.*
■ (of an utterance, advice, etc.) hard to interpret; enigmatic: *an ambiguous, oracular remark.* ■ holding or claiming the authority of an oracle: *he holds forth in oracular fashion.*
– DERIVATIVES **oracularity** noun, **oracularly** adverb.
– ORIGIN mid 17th cent.: from Latin *oraculum* (see **ORACLE**) + **-AR**[1].

oracy /ˈɔːrəsi/ ▶ noun [mass noun] Brit. the ability to express oneself fluently and grammatically in speech.
– ORIGIN 1960s: from Latin *os, or-* 'mouth', on the pattern of *literacy.*

Oradea /ɒˈrɑːdɪə/ an industrial city in western Romania, near the border with Hungary; pop. 221,550 (1993).

oral ▶ adjective **1** by word of mouth; spoken rather than written: *they had reached an oral agreement.*
■ relating to the transmission of information or literature by word of mouth rather than in writing: *oral literature.* ■ (of a society) not having reached the stage of literacy.
2 of or relating to the mouth: *oral hygiene.*
■ done or taken by the mouth: *oral contraceptives.* ■ Psychoanalysis (in Freudian theory) relating to or denoting a stage of infantile psychosexual development in which the mouth is the main source of pleasure and the centre of experience.
▶ noun a spoken examination or test: *a French oral.*
– DERIVATIVES **orally** adverb.
– ORIGIN early 17th cent.: from late Latin *oralis*, from Latin *os, or-* 'mouth'.

oral-formulaic ▶ adjective relating to or denoting poetry belonging to an early spoken tradition characterized by the use of poetic formulae.

oral history ▶ noun [mass noun] the collection and study of historical information using sound recordings of interviews with people having personal knowledge of past events.

oralism ▶ noun [mass noun] the system of teaching profoundly deaf people to communicate by the use of speech and lip-reading rather than sign language.

oralist ▶ adjective relating to or advocating oralism.
▶ noun a profoundly deaf person who uses speech and lip-reading to communicate, rather than sign language.

orality ▶ noun [mass noun] **1** the quality of being spoken or verbally communicated.
■ preference for or tendency to use spoken forms of language.
2 Psychoanalysis the focusing of sexual energy and feeling on the mouth.

Oral Law ▶ noun [mass noun] Judaism the part of Jewish religious law believed to have been passed down by oral tradition before being collected in the Mishnah.

oral sex ▶ noun [mass noun] sexual activity in which

the genitals of one partner are stimulated by the mouth of the other; fellatio or cunnilingus.

Oran /ɔːˈrɑːn/ a port on the Mediterranean coast of Algeria; pop. 664,000 (1989).

orang /ɔːˈraŋ, əˈraŋ/ ▶ **noun** short for **ORANG-UTAN**.

Orang Asli /ˌɒrəŋ ˈazli/ ▶ **noun** [treated as pl.] a collective term for the indigenous peoples of Malaysia.
– ORIGIN Malay, from *orang* 'person' and *as(a)li* 'of ancient origin' (from *asal* 'source or origin').

Orange[1] a town in southern France, on the Rhône, home of the ancestors of the Dutch royal house. See **ORANGE, HOUSE OF**.

Orange[2] ▶ **adjective** [attrib.] of or relating to the Orange Order.
– DERIVATIVES **Orangeism** noun.

orange ▶ **noun 1** a large round juicy citrus fruit with a tough bright reddish-yellow rind.
■[mass noun] a drink made from or flavoured with orange: *a vodka and orange.*
2 (also **orange tree**) the leathery-leaved evergreen tree which bears this fruit, native to warm regions of south and SE Asia. Oranges are a major commercial crop in many warm regions of the world.
• Genus *Citrus*, family Rutaceae: several species, in particular the **sweet orange** (*C. sinensis*) and the **Seville orange**.
■used in names of other plants with similar fruit or flowers, e.g. **mock orange**.
3 [mass noun] a bright reddish-yellow colour like that of the skin of a ripe orange.
4 [with modifier] a butterfly with mainly or partly orange wings.
• Several species in the family Pieridae, in particular American species in the genera *Colias* and *Eurema*.
▶ **adjective** reddish yellow, like a ripe orange in colour: *an orange glow in the sky.*
– DERIVATIVES **orangey** (also **orangy**) adjective, **orangish** adjective.
– ORIGIN late Middle English: from Old French *orenge* (in the phrase *pomme d'orenge*), based on Arabic *nāranj*, from Persian *nārang*.

Orange, House of the Dutch royal house, originally a princely dynasty of the principality centred on the town of Orange in the 16th century.

Members of the family held the position of stadtholder or magistrate from the mid 16th until the late 18th century. In 1689 William of Orange became King William III of Great Britain and Ireland and the son of the last stadtholder became King William I of the United Netherlands in 1815.

O

Orange, William of William III of Great Britain and Ireland (see **WILLIAM**).

orangeade ▶ **noun** [mass noun] Brit. a fizzy non-alcoholic drink flavoured with orange.

orange badge ▶ **noun** Brit. an orange windscreen badge displayed by a disabled driver indicating that he or she is entitled to parking concessions.

orange flower water ▶ **noun** [mass noun] a solution of neroli in water, used in perfumery and as a food flavouring.

Orange Free State an area and former province in central South Africa, situated to the north of the Orange River. First settled by Boers after the Great Trek, the area became a province of the Union of South Africa in 1910 and in 1994 became one of the new provinces of South Africa. Province named **FREE STATE** in 1995.

Orange Lodge another name for **ORANGE ORDER**.

Orangeman ▶ **noun** (pl. **-men**) a member of the Orange Order.

Orange Order a Protestant political society in Ireland, especially in Northern Ireland.

The Orange Order was formed in 1795 (as the Association of Orangemen) for the defence of Protestantism and maintenance of Protestant ascendancy in Ireland. It was probably named from the wearing of orange badges as a symbol of adherence to William III (William of Orange). In the early 20th century it was strengthened in the north of Ireland in its campaign to resist the Home Rule bill and has continued to form a core of Protestant Unionist opinion since.

orange peel ▶ **noun** [mass noun] the skin of an orange.
■[usu. as modifier] a finely dimpled surface resembling this: *pockets of orange-peel skin.*

orange pekoe ▶ **noun** [mass noun] a type of black tea made from young leaves.

orangequit /ˈɒrɪn(d)ʒkwɪt/ ▶ **noun** a Jamaican tanager, the male of which has grey-blue plumage with a reddish throat.
• *Euneornios campestris*, family Emberizidae (subfamily Thraupinae).
– ORIGIN mid 19th cent.: from **ORANGE** (because it feeds on oranges) + **QUIT**[2].

Orange River the longest river in South Africa, which rises in the Drakensberg Mountains in NE Lesotho and flows generally westward for 1,859 km (1,155 miles) to the Atlantic, forming the border between Namibia and South Africa in its lower course.

orangery ▶ **noun** (pl. **-ies**) a building like a large conservatory where orange trees are grown.

orange stick ▶ **noun** a thin stick, pointed at one end and typically made of orange wood, used for manicuring the fingernails.

orange tip ▶ **noun** a cream-coloured butterfly of both Eurasia and North America, the male (and sometimes the female) of which has orange tips to the forewings.
• *Anthocharis* and other genera, family Pieridae: several species.

orang-utan /ɔːˌraŋuːˈtan, əˈraŋuːtan/ (also **-utang** or **-outang** /-uːˈtaŋ/) ▶ **noun** a large mainly solitary arboreal ape with long red hair, long arms, and hooked hands and feet, native to Borneo and Sumatra. The mature male develops fleshy cheek pads and a throat pouch.
• *Pongo pygmaeus*, family Pongidae.
– ORIGIN late 17th cent.: from Malay *orang huan* 'forest person'.

Oranjestad /ɒˈranjəˌstɑːt/ the capital of the Dutch island of Aruba in the Caribbean; pop. 25,000 (1994).

Oraşul Stalin /ɒˌraʃʊl ˈstɑːlɪn/ former name for **BRAŞOV**.

orate /ˈɔːreɪt, ɒˈreɪt/ ▶ **verb** [no obj.] make a speech, especially pompously or at length.
– ORIGIN early 17th cent.: back-formation from **ORATION**.

oration ▶ **noun** a formal speech, especially one given on a ceremonial occasion.
■[mass noun] the style or manner in which such a speech is given: *there is nothing quite like his messianic oration.*
– ORIGIN late Middle English (denoting a prayer): from Latin *oratio(n-)* 'discourse, prayer', from *orare* 'speak, pray'.

orator ▶ **noun** a public speaker, especially one who is eloquent or skilled.
■(also **public orator**) an official speaking for a university on ceremonial occasions.
– DERIVATIVES **oratorial** adjective.
– ORIGIN late Middle English: from Anglo-Norman French *oratour*, from Latin *orator* 'speaker, pleader'.

oratorio /ˌɒrəˈtɔːrɪəʊ/ ▶ **noun** (pl. **-os**) a large-scale, usually narrative musical work for orchestra and voices, typically on a sacred theme, performed without costume, scenery, or action. Well-known examples include Bach's *Christmas Oratorio*, Handel's *Messiah*, and Haydn's *The Creation*.
– ORIGIN Italian, from ecclesiastical Latin *oratorium* 'oratory', from the musical services held in the Church of the Oratory of St Philip Neri in Rome.

oratory[1] /ˈɒrət(ə)ri/ ▶ **noun** (pl. **-ies**) **1** a small chapel, especially for private worship. [ORIGIN: Middle English: from Anglo-Norman French *oratorie*, from ecclesiastical Latin *oratorium*, based on Latin *orare* 'pray, speak'.]
2 (**Oratory**) (in the Roman Catholic Church) a religious society of secular priests founded in Rome in 1564 to provide plain preaching and popular services and established in various countries. [ORIGIN: from *Congregation of the Fathers of the Oratory*.]
– DERIVATIVES **Oratorian** noun & adjective (in sense 2).

oratory[2] ▶ **noun** [mass noun] the art or practice of formal speaking in public.
■exaggerated, eloquent, or highly coloured language: *learned discussions degenerated into pompous oratory.*
– DERIVATIVES **oratorical** /-ˈtɒrɪk(ə)l/ adjective.
– ORIGIN early 16th cent.: from Latin *oratoria*, feminine (used as a noun) of *oratorius* 'relating to an orator'.

orb ▶ **noun** a spherical body; a globe.
■a golden globe surmounted by a cross, forming part of the regalia of a monarch. ■ poetic/literary a celestial body. ■ (usu. **orbs**) poetic/literary an eyeball; an eye. ■ Astrology a circle of up to 10° radius around the position of a celestial object: *within an orb of 1° of Mars.*
▶ **verb** [with obj.] poetic/literary encircle; enclose.
■form (something) into an orb; make circular or globular.
– ORIGIN late Middle English (denoting a circle): from Latin *orbis* 'ring'.

orbat ▶ **noun** Military short for ***order of battle*** (see **ORDER**).

orbicular /ɔːˈbɪkjʊlə/ ▶ **adjective** technical **1** having the shape of a flat ring or disc.
2 having a rounded convex or globular shape.
■Geology (of a rock) containing spheroidal igneous inclusions.
– DERIVATIVES **orbicularity** noun, **orbicularly** adverb.
– ORIGIN late Middle English: from late Latin *orbicularis*, from Latin *orbiculus*, diminutive of *orbis* 'ring'.

Orbison /ˈɔːbɪs(ə)n/, Roy (1936–88), American singer and composer. Notable songs: 'Only the Lonely' (1960) and 'Oh, Pretty Woman' (1964).

orbit ▶ **noun 1** the regularly repeated elliptical course of a celestial object or spacecraft about a star or planet.
■one complete circuit round an orbited body. ■ [mass noun] the state of being on or moving in such a course: *the earth is **in orbit** around the sun.* ■ the path of an electron round an atomic nucleus.
2 a sphere of activity, interest, or application: *audiences drawn largely from outside the Party orbit.*
3 Anatomy the cavity in the skull of a vertebrate that contains the eye; the eye socket.
■the area around the eye of a bird or other animal.
▶ **verb** (**orbited**, **orbiting**) [with obj.] (of a celestial object or spacecraft) move in orbit round (a star or planet): *Mercury orbits the Sun.*
■[no obj.] fly or move round in a circle: *the mobile's disks spun and orbited slowly.* ■ put (a satellite) into orbit.
– PHRASES **into orbit** informal into a state of heightened performance, activity, anger, or excitement: *his goal sent the fans into orbit.*
– ORIGIN mid 16th cent. (in sense 3): from Latin *orbita* 'course, track' (in medieval Latin 'eye socket'), feminine of *orbitus* 'circular', from *orbis* 'ring'.

orbital ▶ **adjective** of or relating to an orbit or orbits.
■Brit. (of a road) passing round the outside of a town.
▶ **noun** Physics each of the actual or potential patterns of electron density which may be formed in an atom or molecule by one or more electrons, and can be represented as a wave function.
– ORIGIN mid 16th cent. (referring to the eye socket): probably from medieval Latin *orbitalis*, from Latin *orbita* (see **ORBIT**).

orbital sander ▶ **noun** a sander in which the sanding surface has a minute circular motion without rotating relative to the workpiece.

orbiter ▶ **noun** a spacecraft designed to go into orbit, especially one that does not subsequently land. Compare with **LANDER**.

orbitosphenoid (also **orbitosphenoid bone**) ▶ **noun** Anatomy & Zoology a bone in the floor of the mammalian cranium, in the region of the optic nerve. In the human skull it is represented by the lesser wings of the sphenoid bone.

orb web ▶ **noun** a circular vertical spider's web formed of threads radiating from a central point, crossed by radial links that spiral in from the edge.

orb-web spider ▶ **noun** a spider of a kind that builds orb webs. Many species are large and brightly coloured, and wait either in the centre of the web or in a retreat at the edge.
• Family Araneidae.

orc ▶ **noun** (in fantasy literature and games) a member of an imaginary race of human-like creatures, characterized as ugly, warlike, and malevolent.
– ORIGIN late 16th cent. (denoting an ogre): perhaps from Latin *orcus* 'hell' or Italian *orco* 'demon, monster', influenced by obsolete *orc* 'ferocious sea creature' and by Old English *orcneas* 'monsters'. The current sense is due to the use of the word in Tolkien's fantasy adventures.

orca /ˈɔːkə/ ▶ **noun** another term for **KILLER WHALE**.
– ORIGIN mid 19th cent.: from French *orque* or Latin *orca*, denoting a kind of whale.

Orcadian /ɔːˈkeɪdɪən/ ▶ **adjective** of or relating to the Orkney Islands or their inhabitants.
▶ **noun** a native or inhabitant of the Orkney Islands.

b but | d dog | f few | g get | h he | j yes | k cat | l leg | m man | n no | p pen | r red | s sit | t top | v voice | w we | z zoo | ʃ she | ʒ decision | θ thin | ð this | ŋ ring | x loch | tʃ chip | dʒ jar

– ORIGIN from *Orcades*, the Latin name for the Orkney Islands, + **-IAN**.

Orcagna /ɔːˈkɑːnjə/ (*c.*1308–68), Italian painter, sculptor, and architect; born *Andrea di Cione*. His paintings include frescoes and an altarpiece in the church of Santa Maria Novella, Florence (1357).

orcein /ˈɔːsiːɪn/ ▶ **noun** [mass noun] Chemistry a red dye obtained from orchil, used as a microscopic stain.
– ORIGIN mid 19th cent.: alteration of *orcin*, another name for **ORCINOL**.

orch. ▶ **abbreviation for** ■ orchestra. ■ orchestrated by.

orchard ▶ **noun** a piece of enclosed land planted with fruit trees.
– DERIVATIVES **orchardist** noun.
– ORIGIN Old English *ortgeard*; the first element from Latin *hortus* 'garden', the second representing **YARD**[2].

orchard grass ▶ **noun** North American term for **COCKSFOOT**.

orchestra ▶ **noun 1** [treated as sing. or pl.] a group of instrumentalists, especially one combining string, woodwind, brass, and percussion sections and playing classical music.
2 (also **orchestra pit**) the part of a theatre where the orchestra plays, typically in front of the stage and on a lower level.
■ N. Amer. the stalls in a theatre.
3 the semicircular space in front of an ancient Greek theatre stage where the chorus danced and sang.
– ORIGIN early 17th cent.: via Latin from Greek *orkhēstra*, from *orkheisthai* 'to dance'.

orchestral ▶ **adjective** written for an orchestra to play: *orchestral music*.
■ of or relating to an orchestra: *an orchestral conductor*.
– DERIVATIVES **orchestrally** adverb.

orchestra stalls ▶ **plural noun** Brit. the front part of the stalls in a theatre.

orchestrate ▶ **verb** [with obj.] **1** arrange or score (music) for orchestral performance.
2 arrange or direct the elements of (a situation) to produce a desired effect, especially surreptitiously: *the situation has been orchestrated by a tiny minority*.
– DERIVATIVES **orchestration** noun, **orchestrator** noun.
– ORIGIN late 19th cent.: from **ORCHESTRA**, perhaps suggested by French *orchestrer*.

orchestrion /ɔːˈkɛstrɪən/ (also **orchestrina** /ˌɔːkɪˈstriːnə/) ▶ **noun** a large mechanical musical instrument designed to imitate the sound of an orchestra.
– ORIGIN mid 19th cent.: from **ORCHESTRA**, on the pattern of *accordion*.

orchid ▶ **noun** a plant with complex flowers that are often showy or bizarrely shaped, having a large specialized lip (labellum) and frequently a spur. Orchids occur worldwide, especially as epiphytes in tropical forests, and are valuable hothouse plants.
• Family Orchidaceae: numerous genera and species.
■ the flowering stem of a cultivated orchid.
– DERIVATIVES **orchidist** noun.
– ORIGIN mid 19th cent.: from modern Latin *Orchid(ac)eae*, formed irregularly from Latin *orchis* (see **ORCHIS**).

orchidaceous ▶ **adjective** Botany of, relating to, or denoting plants of the orchid family (Orchidaceae).
– ORIGIN mid 19th cent.: from modern Latin *Orchidaceae* (plural) + **-OUS**.

orchidectomy ▶ **noun** [mass noun] surgical removal of one or both testicles.
– ORIGIN late 19th cent.: from modern Latin *orchido-* (from a Latinized stem of Greek *orkhis* 'testicle') + **-ECTOMY**.

orchil /ˈɔːtʃɪl/ ▶ **noun 1** [mass noun] a red or violet dye obtained from certain lichens, used as a source of litmus, orcinol, and other pigments.
2 a lichen with flattened fronds from which such a dye may be obtained.
• *Roccella* (order Graphidiales) and other genera: several species, including the Mediterranean *R. tinctoria*, used for dyeing, and the Madagascan *R. montagnei*, used for litmus.
– ORIGIN late 15th cent.: from Old French *orcheil*, related to Spanish *urchilla*; of uncertain origin.

orchis /ˈɔːkɪs/ ▶ **noun** an orchid of (or formerly of) a genus native to north temperate regions, characterized by a tuberous root and an erect fleshy stem bearing a spike of typically purple or pinkish flowers.
• Genus *Orchis* (or *Dactylorhiza*), family Orchidaceae.
■ [with modifier] dated any wild orchid occurring in temperate regions.
– ORIGIN modern Latin, based on Greek *orkhis*, literally 'testicle' (with reference to the shape of its tuber).

orchitis /ɔːˈkʌɪtɪs/ ▶ **noun** [mass noun] Medicine inflammation of one or both of the testicles.
– ORIGIN late 18th cent.: modern Latin, from Greek *orkhis* 'testicle' + **-ITIS**.

orcinol /ˈɔːsɪnɒl/ ▶ **noun** [mass noun] Chemistry a crystalline compound extracted from certain lichens and used to make dyes.
• Alternative name: **2-hydroxyphenylmethanol**; chem. formula: $C_7H_8O_2$.
– ORIGIN mid 19th cent.: from modern Latin *orcina*, from Italian *orcello* 'orchil'.

Orczy /ˈɔːtsi/, Baroness Emmusca (1865–1947), Hungarian-born British novelist. Her best-known novel is *The Scarlet Pimpernel* (1905).

ord. ▶ **abbreviation for** ■ order. ■ ordinary.

ordain ▶ **verb** [with obj.] **1** make (someone) a priest or minister; confer holy orders on.
2 order or decree (something) officially: *equal punishment was ordained for the two crimes* | [with clause] *the king ordained that these courts should be revived*.
■ (especially of God or fate) prescribe; determine (something): *the path ordained by God*.
– DERIVATIVES **ordainer** noun, **ordainment** noun.
– ORIGIN Middle English (also in the sense 'put in order'): from Anglo-Norman French *ordeiner*, from Latin *ordinare*, from *ordo*, *ordin-* (see **ORDER**).

ordeal ▶ **noun 1** a painful or horrific experience, especially a protracted one: *the* **ordeal** *of having to give evidence*.
2 historical an ancient test of guilt or innocence by subjection of the accused to severe pain, survival of which was taken as divine proof of innocence.
– ORIGIN Old English *ordāl*, *ordēl*, of Germanic origin; related to German *urteilen* 'give judgement', from a base meaning 'share out'. The word is not found in Middle English (except once in Chaucer's *Troylus*); modern use of sense 2 began in the late 16th cent., whence sense 1 (mid 17th cent.).

order ▶ **noun 1** [mass noun] the arrangement or disposition of people or things in relation to each other according to a particular sequence, pattern, or method: *I filed the cards in alphabetical order*.
■ a state in which everything is in its correct or appropriate place: *she tried to put her shattered thoughts into some semblance of order*. ■ a state in which the laws and rules regulating the public behaviour of members of a community are observed and authority is obeyed: *the army was deployed to keep order*. ■ [with adj.] the overall state or condition of something: *the house had only just been vacated and was in good order*. ■ a particular social, political, or economic system: *if only the peasantry would rise up against the established order* | *the social order of Britain*. ■ the prescribed or established procedure followed by a meeting, legislative assembly, debate, or court of law: *the meeting was* **called to order**. ■ a stated form of liturgical service, or of administration of a rite or ceremony, prescribed by ecclesiastical authority.
2 an authoritative command, direction, or instruction: *he was not going to take orders from a mere administrator* | [with infinitive] *the skipper gave the order to abandon ship*.
■ a verbal or written request for something to be made, supplied, or served: *the firm has won an order for six tankers*. ■ a thing made, supplied, or served as a result of such a request: *he would deliver special orders for the Sunday dinner*. ■ a written direction of a court or judge: *she was admitted to hospital under a guardianship order*. ■ a written direction to pay money or deliver property. ■ Brit. archaic a pass admitting the bearer to a theatre, museum, or private house free or cheaply.
3 (often **orders**) a social class: *the upper social orders*.
■ a grade or rank in the Christian ministry, especially that of bishop, priest, or deacon. ■ (**orders**) the rank or position of a member of the clergy or an ordained minister of the Church: *he took priest's orders*. See also **HOLY ORDERS**. ■ Biology a principal taxonomic category that ranks below class and above family. ■ Theology any of the nine grades of angelic beings in the celestial hierarchy as formulated by Pseudo-Dionysius.
4 (also **Order**) a society of monks, nuns, or friars living under the same religious, moral, and social regulations and discipline: *the Franciscan Order*.
■ historical a society of knights bound by a common rule of life and having a combined military and monastic character. ■ an institution founded by a monarch along the lines of certain medieval crusading monastic orders for the purpose of conferring an honour or honours for merit on those appointed to it. ■ the insignia worn by members of such an institution. ■ a Masonic or similar fraternity.
5 [in sing.] used to describe the quality, nature, or importance of something: *Mendonca's finishing was of the highest* **order**.
6 any of the five classical styles of architecture (Doric, Ionic, Corinthian, Tuscan, and Composite) based on the proportions of columns, amount of decoration, etc.
■ any style or mode of architecture subject to uniform established proportions.
7 [mass noun] [with modifier] Military equipment or uniform for a specified purpose or of a specified type: *the platoon changed from drill order into PT kit*.
■ (**the order**) the position in which a rifle is held after ordering arms. See ***order arms*** below.
8 Mathematics the degree of complexity of an equation, expression, etc., as denoted by an ordinal number.
■ the number of differentiations required to reach the highest derivative in a differential equation. ■ the number of elements in a finite group. ■ the number of rows or columns in a square matrix.
▶ **verb 1** [reporting verb] give an authoritative direction or instruction to do something: [with obj. and infinitive] *she ordered me to leave* | [with direct speech] *'Stop frowning,' he ordered* | [with clause] *the court ordered that the case should be heard at the end of August* | [with obj.] *her father ordered her back home* | *the judge ordered a retrial*.
■ [with obj.] (**order someone about/around**) continually tell someone to do things in an overbearing way. ■ [with obj. and complement] N. Amer. command (something) to be done or (someone) to be treated in a particular way: *Gorbachev ordered the resolution suspended*.
2 [with obj.] request (something) to be made, supplied, or served: *my mate ordered the tickets last week* | [with two objs] *I asked the security guard to order me a taxi* | [no obj.] *Are you ready to order, sir?*
3 [with obj.] arrange (something) in a methodical or appropriate way: *all entries are ordered by date* | [as adj., in combination **-ordered**] *her normally well-ordered life*.
– PHRASES **by order** according to directions given by the proper authority. **in order 1** according to a particular sequence. **2** in the correct condition for operation or use. **3** in accordance with the rules of procedure at a meeting, legislative assembly, etc. ■ appropriate in the circumstances: *a little bit of flattery was now in order*. **in order for** so that: *staff must be committed to the change in order for it to succeed*. **in order that** with the intention; so that: *she used her mother's kitchen in order that the turkey might be properly cooked*. **in order to do something** with the purpose of doing something: *he slouched into his seat in order to avoid drawing attention to himself*. **of the order of 1** approximately: *sales increases are of the order of 20%*. **2** Mathematics having the order of magnitude specified by. **on order** (of goods) requested but not yet received from the supplier or manufacturer. **on the order of 1** another term for ***of the order of*** (in sense 1) above. **2** N. Amer. along the lines of; similar to: *singers on the order of Janis Joplin*. **Order!** (or **Order! Order!**) a call for silence or the observance of the prescribed procedures by someone in charge of a meeting, legislative assembly, etc. **order arms** Military hold a rifle with its butt on the ground close to one's right side. **order of battle** the units, formations, and equipment of a military force. **orders are orders** commands must be obeyed, however much one may disagree with them. **order to view** Brit. an estate agent's request to an occupier to allow inspection of their premises by a client. **out of order 1** (of an electrical or mechanical device) not working properly or at all. **2** not in the correct sequence. **3** not according to the rules of a meeting, legislative assembly, etc. ■ Brit. informal (of a person or their behaviour) unacceptable or wrong: *he's getting away with things that are out of order*. **to order** according to a customer's particular requirements: *the jumpers are knitted to order*.
– ORIGIN Middle English: from Old French *ordre*, from Latin *ordo*, *ordin-* 'row, series, rank'.

order book ▶ **noun 1** chiefly Brit. a book in which orders are entered as they are received by a business.
2 Brit. a booklet of vouchers which are exchanged for weekly payments of a pension or other benefit at a post office.

O

ordered pair ▶ noun Mathematics a pair of elements *a, b* having the property that (*a, b*) = (*u, v*) if and only if *a* = *u*, *b* = *v*.

order form ▶ noun a printed form on which a customer writes the details of a product or service they wish to order.

Order in Council ▶ noun Brit. a sovereign's order on an administrative matter, given on the advice of the Privy Council.

orderly ▶ adjective **1** neatly and methodically arranged: *an orderly arrangement of objects.*
■ (of a person or group) well behaved; disciplined.
2 [attrib.] Military charged with the conveyance or execution of orders: *the orderly sergeant.*
▶ noun (pl. **-ies**) **1** an attendant in a hospital responsible for the non-medical care of patients and the maintenance of order and cleanliness.
2 a soldier who carries orders or performs minor tasks for an officer.
– DERIVATIVES **orderliness** noun.

orderly book ▶ noun Military, Brit. a regimental or company book in which orders are entered.

orderly officer ▶ noun Military, Brit. the officer who is in charge of the security and administration of a unit or establishment for a day at a time.

orderly room ▶ noun Military the room in a barracks used for regimental or company business.

order mark ▶ noun Brit. a punishment in a school for bad behaviour.

Order of Australia an order instituted in 1975 to honour Australians for outstanding achievement and divided into four classes: Companion (AC), Officer (AO), Member (AM), and Medal of the Order of Australia (OAM). A fifth class of Knight or Dame, above Companion, was abolished in 1986.

Order of Canada an order instituted in 1967 to honour Canadians for outstanding achievement and divided into three classes: Companion (CC), Officer (OC), and Member (CM).

order of magnitude ▶ noun a class in a system of classification determined by size, each class being a number of times (usually ten) greater or smaller than the one before.
■ [mass noun] size or quantity: *the new problems were of a different order of magnitude.* ■ [mass noun] the arrangement of a number of items determined by their relative size: *the items are arranged in ascending order of magnitude.*

Order of Merit (in the UK) an order founded in 1902, for distinguished achievement, with membership limited to twenty-four people.

Order of St Michael and St George (in the UK) an order of knighthood instituted in 1818, divided into three classes: Knight or Dame Grand Cross of the Order of St Michael and St George (GCMG), Knight or Dame Commander (KCMG/DCMG), and Companion (CMG).

Order of the Bath (in the UK) an order of knighthood, so called from the ceremonial bath which originally preceded installation. It has four classes of membership, which are: Knight or Dame Grand Cross of the Order of the Bath (GCB), Knight or Dame Commander (KCB/DCB), and Companion (CB).

Order of the British Empire (in the UK) an order of knighthood instituted in 1917 and divided into five classes, each with military and civilian divisions. The classes are: Knight or Dame Grand Cross of the Order of the British Empire (GBE), Knight or Dame Commander (KBE/DBE), Commander (CBE), Officer (OBE), and Member (MBE). The two highest classes entail the awarding of a knighthood.

order of the day ▶ noun (**the order of the day**)
1 the prevailing state of things: *confusion would seem to be the order of the day.*
2 something that is required or recommended: *on Sundays, a black suit was the order of the day.*
3 a programme or agenda.

Order of the Garter the highest order of English knighthood, founded by Edward III *c.*1344. According to tradition, the garter was that of the Countess of Salisbury, which the king placed on his own leg after it fell off while she was dancing with him. The king's comment to those present, 'Honi soit qui mal y pense' (shame be to him who thinks evil of it), was adopted as the motto of the order.

Order of the Thistle a Scottish order of knighthood instituted in 1687 by James II.

Order Paper ▶ noun Brit. & Canadian a paper on which the day's business for a legislative assembly is entered.
– PHRASES **die on the Order Paper** Canadian (of a bill) fail to be voted on before the end of a legislative session.

ordinal ▶ noun **1** short for **ORDINAL NUMBER**.
2 Christian Church, chiefly historical a service book, especially one with the forms of service used at ordinations.
▶ adjective of or relating to a thing's position in a series: *ordinal scales.*
■ of or relating to an ordinal number. ■ Biology of or relating to a taxonomic order.
– ORIGIN Middle English (in sense 2): the noun from medieval Latin *ordinale* (neuter); the adjective from late Latin *ordinalis* 'relating to order in a series', from Latin *ordo, ordin-* (see **ORDER**).

ordinal number ▶ noun a number defining a thing's position in a series, such as 'first', 'second', or 'third'. Ordinal numbers are used as adjectives, nouns, and pronouns. Compare with **CARDINAL NUMBER**.

ordinance ▶ noun formal **1** N. Amer. a by-law.
2 a religious rite.
3 archaic term for **ORDONNANCE**.
– ORIGIN Middle English (also in the sense 'arrangement in ranks'): from Old French *ordenance*, from medieval Latin *ordinantia*, from Latin *ordinare* 'put in order' (see **ORDAIN**).

ordinand /ˈɔːdɪnand/ ▶ noun a person who is training to be ordained as a priest or minister.
– ORIGIN mid 19th cent.: from Latin *ordinandus*, gerundive of *ordinare* 'put in order' (see **ORDAIN**).

ordinarily /ˈɔːd(ə)n(ə)rɪli, ˌɔːdɪˈnɛrɪli/ ▶ adverb
1 [sentence adverb] usually: *a person who is ordinarily resident in the United Kingdom.*
2 in a normal way: *an effort to behave ordinarily.*

ordinary ▶ adjective **1** with no special or distinctive features; normal: *he sets out to depict ordinary people* | *it was just an ordinary evening.*
■ uninteresting; commonplace: *she seemed very ordinary.*
2 (especially of a judge or bishop) exercising authority by virtue of office and not by deputation.
▶ noun (pl. **-ies**) **1** Law, Brit. a person, especially a judge, exercising authority by virtue of office and not by deputation.
2 (**the Ordinary**) an archbishop in a province.
■ a bishop in a diocese.
3 (usu. **Ordinary**) those parts of a Roman Catholic service, especially the Mass, which do not vary from day to day.
■ a rule or book laying down the order of divine service.
4 Heraldry any of the simplest principal charges used in coats of arms (especially chief, pale, bend, fess, bar, chevron, cross, saltire).
5 short for **ORDINARY SHARE**.
6 Brit. archaic a meal provided at a fixed time and price at an inn.
■ an inn providing this.
7 historical, chiefly US an early type of bicycle with one large and one very small wheel; a penny-farthing.
– PHRASES **in ordinary** Brit. (in titles) by permanent appointment, especially to the royal household: *painter in ordinary to Her Majesty.* **in the ordinary way** chiefly Brit. if the circumstances are or were not exceptional; normally. **out of the ordinary** unusual: *nothing out of the ordinary happened.*
– DERIVATIVES **ordinariness** noun.
– ORIGIN late Middle English: the noun partly via Old French; the adjective from Latin *ordinarius* 'orderly' (reinforced by French *ordinaire*), from *ordo, ordin-* 'order'.

ordinary grade ▶ noun (in Scotland) the lower of the two main levels of the Scottish Certificate of Education examination. Compare with **HIGHER**.

ordinary level ▶ noun [mass noun] historical (in the UK except Scotland) the lower of the two main levels of the GCE examination. Compare with **ADVANCED LEVEL**.

ordinary ray ▶ noun Optics (in double refraction) the ray that obeys the ordinary laws of refraction.

ordinary seaman ▶ noun the lowest rank of sailor in the Royal Navy, below able seaman.

ordinary share ▶ noun Brit. a share entitling its holder to dividends which vary in amount and may even be missed, depending on the fortunes of the company. Compare with **PREFERENCE SHARE**.

ordinate /ˈɔːdɪnət/ ▶ noun Mathematics a straight line from any point drawn parallel to one coordinate axis and meeting the other, especially a coordinate measured parallel to the vertical. Compare with **ABSCISSA**.
– ORIGIN late 17th cent.: from Latin *linea ordinata applicata* 'line applied parallel', from *ordinare* 'put in order'.

ordination ▶ noun **1** [mass noun] the action of ordaining or conferring holy orders on someone.
■ [count noun] a ceremony in which someone is ordained.
2 chiefly Ecology a statistical technique in which data from a large number of sites or populations are represented as points in a multidimensional space.
– ORIGIN late Middle English (in the general sense 'arrangement in order'): from Latin *ordinatio(n-)*, from Latin *ordinare* 'put in order' (see **ORDAIN**).

ordnance /ˈɔːdnəns/ ▶ noun [mass noun] **1** mounted guns; cannon.
■ missiles or bombs.
2 a branch of government service dealing especially with military stores and materials.
– ORIGIN late Middle English: variant of **ORDINANCE**.

ordnance datum ▶ noun Brit. the mean sea level as defined for Ordnance Survey.

Ordnance Survey (in the UK) an official survey organization, originally under the Master of the Ordnance, preparing large-scale detailed maps of the whole country.

ordonnance /ˈɔːdənəns/ ▶ noun [mass noun] the systematic or orderly arrangement of parts, especially in art and architecture.
– ORIGIN mid 17th cent.: from French, alteration of Old French *ordenance* (see **ORDINANCE**).

Ordovician /ˌɔːdəˈvɪʃən/ ▶ adjective Geology of, relating to, or denoting the second period of the Palaeozoic era, between the Cambrian and Silurian periods.
■ [as noun **the Ordovician**] the Ordovician period or the system of rocks deposited during it.

The Ordovician lasted from about 510 to 439 million years ago. It saw the diversification of many invertebrate groups and the appearance of the first vertebrates (jawless fish).

– ORIGIN late 19th cent.: from *Ordovices*, the Latin name of an ancient British tribe in North Wales, + **-IAN**.

ordure /ˈɔːdjʊə/ ▶ noun [mass noun] excrement; dung.
■ something regarded as vile or abhorrent: *can you give credence to this ordure?*
– ORIGIN late Middle English: from Old French, from *ord* 'foul', from Latin *horridus* (see **HORRID**).

Ordzhonikidze /ˌɔːdʒɒnəˈkɪdzi/ former name (1954–93) for **VLADIKAVKAZ**.

Ore. ▶ abbreviation for Oregon.

ore ▶ noun a naturally occurring solid material from which a metal or valuable mineral can be extracted profitably.
– ORIGIN Old English *ōra* 'unwrought metal', of West Germanic origin; influenced in form by Old English *ār* 'bronze' (related to Latin *aes* 'crude metal, bronze').

øre /ˈøːrə/ ▶ noun (pl. same) a monetary unit of Denmark and Norway, equal to one hundredth of a krone.
– ORIGIN Danish and Norwegian.

öre /ˈøːrə/ ▶ noun (pl. same) a monetary unit of Sweden, equal to one hundredth of a krona.
– ORIGIN Swedish.

oread /ˈɔːrɪad/ ▶ noun Greek & Roman Mythology a nymph believed to inhabit mountains.
– ORIGIN from Latin *Oreas, Oread-*, from Greek *Oreias*, from *oros* 'mountain'.

orebody ▶ noun a connected mass of ore in a mine or suitable for mining.

Örebro /ˌøːrəˈbruː/ an industrial city in south central Sweden; pop. 120,940 (1990).

orecchiette /ˌɒrɛkiˈɛti/ ▶ plural noun small pieces of ear-shaped pasta.
– ORIGIN Italian, literally 'little ears'.

orectic /ɒˈrɛktɪk/ ▶ adjective technical, rare of or concerning desire or appetite.
– ORIGIN late 17th cent. (as a noun in the sense 'stimulant for the appetite'): from Greek *orektikos*, from *oregein* 'stretch out, reach for'. The current sense dates from the late 18th cent.

Oreg. ▶ abbreviation for Oregon.

oregano /ˌɒrɪˈɡɑːnəʊ, ɔːˈrɛɡənəʊ/ ▶ noun [mass noun] an aromatic Eurasian plant related to marjoram, with small purple flowers and leaves used as a culinary herb.
● *Origanum vulgare*, family Labiatae.
– ORIGIN late 18th cent.: from Spanish, variant of **ORIGANUM**.

Oregon /ˈɒrɪɡ(ə)n/ a state in the north-western US, on the Pacific coast; pop. 2,842,320 (1990); capital, Salem. British claims to Oregon were formally ceded to the US in 1846 and it became the 33rd state in 1859.
– DERIVATIVES **Oregonian** adjective & noun.

Oregon grape ▶ noun a North American mahonia which forms a spreading bush with spiny leaves.
● *Mahonia aquifolium*, family Berberidaceae.

Oregon pine ▶ noun another term for **DOUGLAS FIR**.

Oregon Trail a route across the central US, from the Missouri to Oregon, some 3,000 km (2,000 miles) in length. It was used chiefly in the 1840s by settlers moving west.

Orel /ɒˈrɛl/ an industrial city in SW Russia; pop. 342,000 (1990).

Ore Mountains another name for the **ERZGEBIRGE**.

Orenburg /ˈɒrənbɜːɡ/ a city in southern Russia, on the Ural River; pop. 552,000 (1990). It was known as Chkalov from 1938 to 1957.

orenda /ɒˈrɛndə/ ▶ noun [mass noun] invisible magic power believed by the Iroquois to pervade all natural objects as a spiritual energy.
– ORIGIN early 20th cent.: coined in English as the supposed Huron form of a Mohawk word.

Oreo /ˈɔːrɪəʊ/ ▶ noun (pl. **-os**) US trademark a chocolate biscuit with a white cream filling.
■ derogatory an American black who is seen, especially by other blacks, as wishing to be part of the white establishment.

Orestes /ɒˈrɛstiːz/ Greek Mythology the son of Agamemnon and Clytemnestra. He killed his mother and her lover Aegisthus to avenge the murder of Agamemnon.

Øresund /ˌɜːrəˈsʊnd/ a narrow channel between Sweden and the Danish island of Zealand. Also called **THE SOUND**.

orf ▶ noun [mass noun] an infectious disease of sheep and goats caused by a poxvirus, characterized by skin lesions and secondary bacterial infection.
– ORIGIN mid 19th cent.: probably from Old Norse *hrufa*.

orfe /ɔːf/ ▶ noun a silvery freshwater fish of the carp family, which is fished commercially in eastern Europe. Also called **IDE**.
● *Leuciscus idus*, family Cyprinidae. See also **GOLDEN ORFE**.
– ORIGIN late 19th cent.: from German; perhaps related to French *orphe*, Latin *orphus*, and Greek *orphos* 'sea perch'.

Orff /ɔːf/, Carl (1895–1982), German composer. He is best known for his secular cantata *Carmina Burana* (1937), based on a collection of characteristically bawdy medieval Latin poems.

organ ▶ noun **1** a large musical instrument having rows of pipes supplied with air from bellows (now usually electrically powered), and played using a keyboard or by an automatic mechanism. The pipes are generally arranged in ranks of a particular type, each controlled by a stop, and often into larger sets linked to separate keyboards.
■ a smaller instrument without pipes, producing similar sounds electronically. See also **REED ORGAN**.
2 a part of an organism which is typically self-contained and has a specific vital function.
■ used euphemistically to refer to the penis. ■ archaic a region of the brain formerly held to be the seat of a particular faculty. ■ a department or organization that performs a specified function: *the central organs of administration and business.* ■ a medium of communication, especially a newspaper or periodical which serves as the mouthpiece of a political party or movement: *the People's Daily, the official organ of the Chinese Communist Party.*
– ORIGIN late Old English, via Latin from Greek *organon* 'tool, instrument, sense organ', reinforced in Middle English by Old French *organe*.

organ-blower ▶ noun a person or mechanism working the bellows of an organ.

organdie /ˈɔːɡ(ə)ndi, ɔːˈɡandi/ (US also **organdy**) ▶ noun (pl. **-ies**) [mass noun] a fine translucent cotton muslin that is usually stiffened and is used for women's clothing.
– ORIGIN early 19th cent.: from French *organdi*, of unknown origin.

organelle /ˌɔːɡəˈnɛl/ ▶ noun Biology any of a number of organized or specialized structures within a living cell.
– ORIGIN early 20th cent.: from modern Latin *organella*, diminutive of *organum* 'instrument, tool' (see **ORGAN**).

organ-grinder ▶ noun a street musician who plays a barrel organ.
■ figurative a person in control of another. [ORIGIN: with reference to the tradition of an organ-grinder's keeping a monkey trained to collect money.]

organic ▶ adjective **1** of, relating to, or derived from living matter: *organic soils.*
■ Chemistry of, relating to, or denoting compounds containing carbon (other than simple binary compounds and salts) and chiefly or ultimately of biological origin. Compare with **INORGANIC**. ■ (of food or farming methods) produced or involving production without the use of chemical fertilizers, pesticides, or other artificial chemicals.
2 Physiology of or relating to a bodily organ or organs.
■ Medicine (of a disease) affecting the structure of an organ.
3 denoting a relation between elements of something such that they fit together harmoniously as necessary parts of a whole: *the organic unity of the integral work of art.*
■ characterized by continuous or natural development: *companies expand as much by acquisition as by organic growth.*
– DERIVATIVES **organically** adverb.
– ORIGIN late Middle English: via Latin from Greek *organikos* 'relating to an organ or instrument'.

organicism ▶ noun [mass noun] **1** the doctrine that everything in nature has an organic basis or is part of an organic whole.
2 the use or advocacy of literary or artistic forms in which the parts are connected or coordinated in the whole.
– DERIVATIVES **organicist** adjective & noun, **organicistic** adjective.
– ORIGIN mid 19th cent.: from French *organicisme*.

organic law ▶ noun a law stating the formal constitution of a nation.

organigram /ɔːˈɡanɪɡram/ (also **organogram**) ▶ noun another term for **ORGANIZATION CHART**.
– ORIGIN 1960s: from **ORGANIZATION** + **-GRAM**[1].

organism ▶ noun an individual animal, plant, or single-celled life form.
■ the material structure of such an individual: *the heart's contribution to the maintenance of the human organism.* ■ a whole with interdependent parts compared to a living being: *the Church is a divinely constituted organism.*
– DERIVATIVES **organismal** adjective, **organismic** adjective.
– ORIGIN early 18th cent. (in the sense 'organization', from **ORGANIZE**): current senses derive from French *organisme*.

organist ▶ noun a person who plays the organ.

organization (also **-isation**) ▶ noun **1** [mass noun] the action of organizing something: *the organization of conferences and seminars.*
■ the structure or arrangement of related or connected items: *the spatial organization of the cells.* ■ an efficient and orderly approach to tasks: *his lack of organization.*
2 an organized body of people with a particular purpose, especially a business, government department, or charity: *a research organization.*
– DERIVATIVES **organizational** adjective, **organizationally** adverb.

organization chart ▶ noun a graphic representation of the structure of an organization showing the relationships of the positions or jobs within it.

Organization for Economic Cooperation and Development (abbrev.: **OECD**) an organization formed in 1961 to assist the economy of its member nations and to promote world trade. Its members include the industrialized countries of western Europe together with Australia, Japan, New Zealand, and the US. Its headquarters are in Paris.

Organization for European Economic Cooperation an organization established in 1948 by sixteen West European countries to promote trade and stability. It was replaced by the Organization for Economic Cooperation and Development in 1961.

organization man ▶ noun derogatory a man who lets his individuality and personal life be dominated by the organization he serves.

Organization of African Unity (abbrev.: **OAU**) an association of African states founded in 1963 for mutual cooperation and the elimination of colonialism in Africa. It is based in Addis Ababa.

Organization of American States (abbrev.: **OAS**) an association including most of the countries of North and South America, originally founded in 1890 for largely commercial purposes. From 1948 it has aimed to work for peace and prosperity in the region and to uphold the sovereignty of member nations. Its headquarters are in Washington DC.

Organization of Arab Petroleum Exporting Countries (abbrev.: **OAPEC**) an association of Arab countries, founded in 1968 to promote economic cooperation and safeguard its members' interests and to ensure the supply of oil to consumer markets. Its headquarters are in Safat, Kuwait.

Organization of Central American States (abbrev.: **OCAS**) an association of Guatemala, Honduras, El Salvador, and Costa Rica founded in 1951 for economic and political cooperation.

Organization of the Petroleum Exporting Countries (abbrev.: **OPEC**) an association of the thirteen major oil-producing countries, founded in 1960 to coordinate policies. Its headquarters are in Vienna.

organize (also **-ise**) ▶ verb [with obj.] **1** arrange into a structured whole; order: *organize lessons in a planned way | it will enable individuals to organize their lives.*
■ coordinate the activities of (a person or group of people) efficiently: *she was unsuited to anything where she had to organize herself.* ■ form (a number of people) into a trade union or other political group: *we all believed in the need to organize women.* ■ form (a trade union or other political group). ■ archaic arrange or form into a living being or tissue: *the soul doth organize the body.*
2 Brit. make arrangements or preparations for (an event or activity); coordinate: *social and cultural programmes are organized by the school.*
■ take responsibility for providing or arranging: *he is sometimes asked to stay behind, organizing transport.*
– DERIVATIVES **organizable** adjective.
– ORIGIN late Middle English: from medieval Latin *organizare*, from Latin *organum* 'instrument, tool' (see **ORGAN**).

organized ▶ adjective arranged in a systematic way, especially on a large scale: *organized crime.*
■ having one's affairs in order so as to deal with them efficiently. ■ having formed a trade union or other political group: *a repressive regime which crushed organized labour.*

organizer ▶ noun **1** a person who arranges an event or activity.
2 a thing used for organizing. See also **PERSONAL ORGANIZER**.

organ loft ▶ noun a gallery in a church or concert hall for an organ.

organo- /ˈɔːɡ(ə)nəʊ, ɔːˈɡanəʊ/ ▶ combining form **1** chiefly Biology relating to bodily organs: *organogenesis.*
2 Chemistry (forming names of classes of organic compounds containing a particular element or group) organic: *organochlorine | organophosphate.*
– ORIGIN from Greek *organon* 'organ'; sense 2 from **ORGANIC**.

organochlorine ▶ noun [often as modifier] any of a large group of pesticides and other synthetic organic compounds with chlorinated aromatic molecules.

organ of Corti ▶ noun Anatomy a structure in the cochlea of the inner ear which produces nerve impulses in response to sound vibrations.
– ORIGIN late 19th cent.: named after Alfonso *Corti* (1822–76), Italian anatomist.

organogenesis /ˌɔːɡ(ə)nə(ʊ)ˈdʒɛnɪsɪs, ɔːˌɡan(ə)-/ ▶ noun [mass noun] Biology the production and development of the organs of an animal or plant.

organogeny /ˌɔːɡəˈnɒdʒəni/ ▶ **noun** dated another term for **ORGANOGENESIS**.

organogram ▶ **noun** variant spelling of **ORGANIGRAM**.

organoleptic /ˌɔːɡ(ə)nə(ʊ)ˈlɛptɪk/ ▶ **adjective** acting on, or involving the use of, the sense organs.
– ORIGIN mid 19th cent.: from French *organoleptique*, from Greek *organon* 'organ' + *lēptikos* 'disposed to take' (from *lambanein* 'take').

organometallic ▶ **adjective** Chemistry (of a compound) containing a metal atom bonded to an organic group or groups.

organon /ˈɔːɡ(ə)nɒn/ ▶ **noun** an instrument of thought, especially a means of reasoning or a system of logic.
– ORIGIN late 16th cent. (denoting a bodily organ): from Greek, literally 'instrument, organ'. *Organon* was the title of Aristotle's logical treatises.

organophosphorus /ˌɔːɡ(ə)nəʊˈfɒsf(ə)rəs/ ▶ **adjective** denoting synthetic organic compounds containing phosphorus, especially pesticides and nerve gases of this kind.
– DERIVATIVES **organophosphate** noun.

organotherapy ▶ **noun** [mass noun] the treatment of disease with extracts from animal organs, especially glands.
– DERIVATIVES **organotherapeutic** adjective.

organ pipe cactus ▶ **noun** a large cactus native to the south-western US, having columnar stems or branches and typically flowering at night.
• Several species in the family Cactaceae, including *Lemaireocereus marginatus* and *Cereus thurberi*.

organ-pipe coral ▶ **noun** a tropical coral which forms narrow parallel calcareous tubes linked by transverse plates.
• Genus *Tubipora*, order Stolonifera.

organ-screen ▶ **noun** an ornamental screen above which the organ is placed in some cathedrals and large churches, typically between the choir and the nave.

organ stop ▶ **noun** a set of pipes of a similar tone in an organ.
■ the handle of the mechanism that brings such a set into action.

organum /ˈɔːɡ(ə)nəm/ ▶ **noun** (pl. **organa** /-nə/) (in medieval music) a part sung as an accompaniment below or above a melody.
– ORIGIN Latin, from Greek *organon*, literally 'instrument, organ'.

organza /ɔːˈɡanzə/ ▶ **noun** [mass noun] a thin, stiff, transparent dress fabric made of silk or a synthetic yarn.
– ORIGIN early 19th cent.: probably from *Lorganza*, a US trademark.

organzine /ˈɔːɡ(ə)nziːn, -ˈɡanziːn/ ▶ **noun** [mass noun] a silk thread made of strands twisted together in the contrary direction to that of each individual strand.
– ORIGIN late 17th cent.: from French *organsin*, from Italian *organzino*, of unknown ultimate origin.

orgasm ▶ **noun** a sexual climax characterized by feelings of pleasure centred in the genitals and (in men) experienced as an accompaniment to ejaculation.
▶ **verb** [no obj.] experience an orgasm.
– ORIGIN late 17th cent.: from French *orgasme*, or from modern Latin *orgasmus*, from Greek *orgasmos*, from *organ* 'swell or be excited'.

orgasmic ▶ **adjective** of or relating to orgasm.
■ (of a person) able to achieve orgasm. ■ informal, figurative very enjoyable or exciting: *the album is an orgasmic whirl of techno soundscapes.*
– DERIVATIVES **orgasmically** adverb, **orgastic** adjective, **orgastically** adverb.

OR gate ▶ **noun** see **OR**[1].

orgeat /ˈɔːdʒɪət/ ▶ **noun** [mass noun] a cooling drink made from orange flower water and either barley or almonds.
– ORIGIN French, from Provençal *orjat*, from *ordi* 'barley', from Latin *hordeum* 'barley'.

orgiastic ▶ **adjective** of or resembling an orgy.
– DERIVATIVES **orgiastically** adverb.
– ORIGIN late 17th cent.: from Greek *orgiastikos*, from *orgiastēs*, agent noun from *orgiazein* 'hold an orgy'.

orgone /ˈɔːɡəʊn/ ▶ **noun** [mass noun] a supposed excess sexual energy or life force distributed throughout the universe which can be collected and stored for subsequent therapeutic use.
– ORIGIN 1940s: from the psychoanalytical theory of Wilhelm Reich (1897–1957).

orgulous /ˈɔːɡjʊləs/ ▶ **adjective** poetic/literary haughty.
– ORIGIN Middle English: from Old French *orguillus*, from *orguill* 'pride'. The word was rare from the 16th cent. until used by Robert Southey and Sir Walter Scott as a historical archaism and affected by 19th-cent. journalists.

orgy ▶ **noun** (pl. **-ies**) **1** a wild party, especially one involving excessive drinking and indiscriminate sexual activity: *he had a reputation for drunken orgies.*
■ excessive indulgence in a specified activity: *an orgy of buying.*
2 (usu. **orgies**) secret rites used in the worship of Bacchus, Dionysus, and other Greek and Roman deities, celebrated with dancing, drunkenness, and singing.
– ORIGIN early 16th cent.: originally plural, from French *orgies*, via Latin from Greek *orgia* 'secret rites or revels'.

oribi /ˈɒrɪbi/ ▶ **noun** (pl. same or **oribis**) a small antelope of the African savannah, having a reddish-fawn back, white underparts, and short vertical horns.
• *Ourebia ourebi*, family Bovidae.
– ORIGIN late 18th cent.: from Afrikaans, from Khoikhoi.

orichalc /ˈɒrɪkalk/ (also **orichalcum**) ▶ **noun** [mass noun] a yellow metal prized in ancient times, probably a form of brass or a similar alloy.
– ORIGIN late Middle English: via Latin from Greek *oreikhalkon*, literally 'mountain copper'.

oriel /ˈɔːrɪəl/ ▶ **noun** a large polygonal recess in a building, typically built out from an upper storey and supported from the ground or on corbels.
■ (also **oriel window**) a window in such a structure. ■ a projecting window of an upper storey.
– ORIGIN late Middle English: from Old French *oriol* 'gallery', of unknown origin; compare with medieval Latin *oriolum* 'upper chamber'.

orient ▶ **noun** /ˈɔːrɪənt, ˈɒr-/ **1** (**the Orient**) poetic/literary the countries of the East, especially east Asia.
2 [mass noun] the special lustre of a pearl of the finest quality.
■ [count noun] a pearl with such a lustre.
▶ **adjective** /ˈɔːrɪənt, ˈɒr-/ poetic/literary situated in or belonging to the east; oriental.
■ (of the sun, daylight, etc.) rising: *the orient moon of Islam.* ■ (especially of precious stones) lustrous (with reference to fine pearls from the East).
▶ **verb** /ˈɔːrɪɛnt, ˈɒr-/ **1** [with obj. and adverbial] align or position (something) relative to the points of a compass or other specified positions: *the fires are oriented in direct line with the midsummer sunset.*
■ adjust or tailor (something) to specified circumstances or needs: *magazines oriented to the business community* | [as adj., in combination **-oriented**] *market-oriented economic reforms.* ■ (often **be oriented**) guide (someone) physically in a specified direction.
2 (**orient oneself**) find one's position in relation to new and strange surroundings: *there are no street names which would enable her to orient herself.*
– ORIGIN late Middle English: via Old French from Latin *orient-* 'rising or east', from *oriri* 'to rise'.

oriental (also **Oriental**) ▶ **adjective** **1** of, from, or characteristic of the Far East: *oriental countries.*
■ (**Oriental**) Zoology of, relating to, or denoting a zoogeographical region comprising Asia south of the Himalayas and Indonesia west of Wallace's line. Distinctive animals include pandas, gibbons, tree shrews, tarsiers, and moonrats.
2 (of a pearl or other jewel) orient.
▶ **noun** often offensive a person of Far Eastern descent.
– DERIVATIVES **orientalism** noun, **orientalist** noun, **orientalize** (also **-ise**) verb, **orientally** adverb.
– ORIGIN late Middle English: from Old French, or from Latin *orientalis*, from *orient-* (see **ORIENT**).

> **USAGE** The term **oriental** has an out-of-date feel as a term denoting people from the Far East; it tends to be associated with a rather offensive stereotype of the people and their customs as inscrutable and exotic. In US English, **Asian** is the standard accepted term in modern use; in British English, where **Asian** tends to denote people from the Indian subcontinent, specific terms such as **Chinese** or **Japanese** are more likely to be used.

orientalia /ˌɔːrɪɛnˈteɪlɪə, ɒr-/ ▶ **plural noun** books and other items relating to or characteristic of the Orient.
– ORIGIN early 20th cent.: from Latin, neuter plural of *orientalis* 'oriental'.

oriental poppy ▶ **noun** a SW Asian poppy with coarse deeply cut hairy leaves and large scarlet flowers with a black mark at the base of each petal, widely grown as a garden perennial.
• *Papaver orientale*, family Papaveraceae.

oriental sore ▶ **noun** [mass noun] Medicine a form of leishmaniasis occurring in Asia and Africa, causing open ulcers.

oriental topaz ▶ **noun** a yellow sapphire.

orientate ▶ **verb** another term for **ORIENT**.
– ORIGIN mid 19th cent.: probably a back-formation from **ORIENTATION**.

orientation ▶ **noun** [mass noun] the determination of the relative position of something or someone (especially oneself): *the pupil's surroundings provide clues to help in orientation.*
■ [count noun] the relative physical position or direction of something: *two complex shapes, presented in different orientations.* ■ Zoology an animal's change of position in response to an external stimulus, especially with respect to compass directions. ■ familiarization with something: *many judges give instructions to assist jury orientation.* ■ the direction of someone's interest or attitude, especially political or sexual: *a common age of consent regardless of gender or sexual orientation.*
– DERIVATIVES **orientational** adjective.
– ORIGIN mid 19th cent.: apparently from **ORIENT**.

orientation course ▶ **noun** chiefly N. Amer. a course giving information to newcomers to a university or other institution.

orienteer ▶ **noun** a person who takes part in orienteering.
▶ **verb** [no obj.] take part in orienteering.

orienteering ▶ **noun** [mass noun] a competitive sport in which runners have to find their way across rough country with the aid of a map and compass.
– ORIGIN 1940s: from Swedish *orientering*.

Orient Express a train which ran between Paris and Istanbul and other Balkan cities, via Vienna, from 1883 to 1961.

orifice /ˈɒrɪfɪs/ ▶ **noun** an opening, particularly one in the body such as a nostril or the anus.
– ORIGIN late Middle English: from French, from late Latin *orificium*, from *os*, *or-* 'mouth' + *facere* 'make'.

oriflamme /ˈɒrɪflam/ ▶ **noun** poetic/literary (in historical use) a scarlet banner or knight's standard.
■ a principle or ideal that serves as a rallying point in a struggle. ■ a bright, conspicuous object: *her hair is swept up to a glossy oriflamme.*
– ORIGIN late Middle English: from Old French, from Latin *aurum* 'gold' + *flamma* 'flame'.

origami /ˌɒrɪˈɡɑːmi/ ▶ **noun** [mass noun] the Japanese art of folding paper into decorative shapes and figures.
– ORIGIN Japanese, from *oru*, *-ori* 'fold' + *kami* 'paper'.

origanum /ɒˈrɪɡ(ə)nəm/ ▶ **noun** an aromatic plant of a genus that includes marjoram and oregano.
• Genus *Origanum*, family Labiatae.
– ORIGIN Latin, from Greek *origanon*, perhaps from *oros* 'mountain' + *ganos* 'brightness'.

Origen /ˈɒrɪdʒ(ə)n/ (*c.*185–*c.*254), Christian scholar and theologian, probably born in Alexandria. His most famous work was the *Hexapla*, an edition of the Old Testament with six or more parallel versions. His Neoplatonist theology was ultimately rejected by Church orthodoxy.

origin ▶ **noun** **1** the beginning of something's existence: *a novel theory about the origin of oil* | *the name is Norse* ***in origin.***
■ a person's social background or ancestry: *a family of peasant origin* | *a voice that betrays his Welsh origins.* ■ the place or situation from which something comes: *a label of origin on imported eggs.*
2 Anatomy the place or point where a muscle, nerve, or other body part arises, in particular:
■ the more fixed end or attachment of a muscle. ■ a place where a nerve or blood vessel begins or branches from a main nerve or blood vessel.
3 Mathematics a fixed point from which coordinates are measured.
– ORIGIN early 16th cent.: from French *origine*, from Latin *origo*, *origin-*, from *oriri* 'to rise'.

original ▶ **adjective** **1** used or produced at the creation or earliest stage of something: *costumes made afresh from the original designs* | *the plasterwork is probably original.*

■[attrib.] present or existing at the beginning of a series or process; first: *the original owner of the house.* **2** created directly and personally by a particular artist; not an imitation: *original Rembrandts.* **3** not dependent on other people's ideas; inventive and unusual: *a subtle and original thinker.*
▶**noun 1** something serving as a model or basis for imitations or copies: *the portrait may be a copy of the original | one set of originals and four photocopies.* ■(**the original**) the form or language in which something was first produced or created: *the study of Russian texts in the original.* ■(**the original of**) a person or place on which a character or location in a literary work is based: *the house is reputed to be the original of Mansfield Park.* ■a song, picture, etc. produced by a performer or artist personally: *a mix of traditional tunes and originals.* ■a book or recording that has not been previously made available in a different form: *paperback originals.* ■a garment made to order from a design specially prepared for a fashion collection. **2** an eccentric or unusual person: *he was one of the true originals.*
– ORIGIN Middle English (the earliest use being in the phrase *original sin*): from Old French, or from Latin *originalis*, from *origin-* (see **ORIGIN**).

original gravity ▶**noun** [mass noun] the relative density of the wort before it is fermented to produce beer, being chiefly dependent on the quantity of fermentable sugars in solution. It is regarded as a guide to the alcoholic strength of the finished beer.

original instrument ▶**noun** a musical instrument, or a copy of one, dating from the time the music played on it was composed.

originality ▶**noun** [mass noun] the ability to think independently and creatively: *a writer of great originality.* ■the quality of being novel or unusual: *he congratulated her on the originality of her costume.*

originally ▶**adverb 1** from or in the beginning; at first: *potatoes originally came from South America.* **2** in a novel and inventive way: *the suggestions so originally and persuasively outlined.*

original print ▶**noun** Art a print made directly from an artist's own woodcut, etching, or other original production, and printed under the artist's supervision.

original sin ▶**noun** [mass noun] Christian Theology the tendency to evil supposedly innate in all human beings, held to be inherited from Adam in consequence of the Fall. The concept of original sin was established by the writings of St Augustine.

originate ▶**verb** [no obj., with adverbial] have a specified beginning: *the word originated as a marketing term.* ■[with obj.] create or initiate (something): *he is responsible for originating this particular cliché.*
– DERIVATIVES **origination** noun, **originative** adjective, **originator** noun.
– ORIGIN mid 17th cent.: from medieval Latin *originat-* 'caused to begin', from Latin *origo, origin-* 'source, origin'.

origination fee ▶**noun** Finance a fee charged by a lender on entering into a loan agreement to cover the cost of processing the loan.

Orimulsion /ˌɒrɪˈmʌlʃ(ə)n/ ▶**noun** [mass noun] trademark a fuel consisting of an emulsion of bitumen in water.
– ORIGIN 1980s: blend of *Orinoco* (the name of an oil belt in Venezuela, where the bitumen was originally extracted) and **EMULSION**.

O-ring ▶**noun** a gasket or seal in the form of a ring with a circular cross section, typically made of rubber and used especially in swivelling joints.

Orinoco /ˌɒrɪˈnəʊkəʊ/ a river in northern South America, which rises in SE Venezuela and flows 2,060 km (1,280 miles), entering the Atlantic Ocean through a vast delta. For part of its length it forms the border between Colombia and Venezuela.

oriole /ˈɔːrɪəʊl, ˈɔːrɪəl/ ▶**noun 1** an Old World bird which is related to the starlings and feeds on fruit and insects, the male typically having bright yellow and black plumage.
● Family Oriolidae and genus *Oriolus*: many species, including the **golden oriole**.
2 a New World bird of the American blackbird family, with black and orange or yellow plumage.
● Genus *Icterus*, family Icteridae (sometimes called the **American oriole family**): many species.
– ORIGIN late 18th cent.: from medieval Latin *oriolus* (in Old French *oriol*), from Latin *aureolus*, diminutive of *aureus* 'golden', from *aurum* 'gold'.

Orion /əˈrʌɪən/ **1** Greek Mythology a giant and hunter who was changed into a constellation at his death. **2** Astronomy a conspicuous constellation (the Hunter), said to represent a hunter holding a club and shield. It lies on the celestial equator and contains many bright stars, including Rigel, Betelgeuse, and a line of three that form **Orion's Belt**. ■[as genitive **Orionis** /ɒrɪˈəʊnɪs/] used with preceding letter or numeral to designate a star in this constellation: *the multiple star Theta Orionis.*
– ORIGIN via Latin from Greek.

Orisha /əˈrɪʃə/ ▶**noun** (pl. same) (in southern Nigeria) any of several minor gods. The term is also used in various black religious cults of South America and the Caribbean.
– ORIGIN Yoruba.

orison /ˈɒrɪz(ə)n, -s(ə)n/ ▶**noun** (usu. **orisons**) archaic a prayer.
– ORIGIN Middle English: from Old French *oreison*, from Latin *oratio(n-)* 'speech' (see **ORATION**).

Orissa /əˈrɪsə/ a state in eastern India, on the Bay of Bengal; capital, Bhubaneswar.

-orium ▶**suffix** forming nouns denoting a place for a particular function: *auditorium | sanatorium.*
– ORIGIN from Latin; compare with **-ORY**[1].

Oriya /ɒˈriːjə/ ▶**adjective 1** of or relating to Odra, an ancient region corresponding to the modern state of Orissa in India. **2** of or relating to Orissa, its people, or their language.
▶**noun** (pl. same or **Oriyas**) **1** a native or inhabitant of Orissa or Odra. **2** [mass noun] the language of these people, an Indic language closely related to Bengali and spoken today by over 20 million people.
– ORIGIN from Hindi *Uṛiyā*.

Orkney Islands /ˈɔːkni/ (also **Orkney** or **the Orkneys**) a group of more than seventy islands off the NE tip of Scotland, constituting an administrative region of Scotland; pop. 19,450 (1991); chief town, Kirkwall. They came into Scottish possession in 1472, having previously been ruled by Norway and Denmark.

Orlando /ɔːˈlandəʊ/ a city in central Florida; pop. 164,690 (1990). It is a popular tourist resort.

orle /ɔːl/ ▶**noun** Heraldry a narrow border inset from the edge of a shield. ■a series of charges placed in orle.
– PHRASES **in orle** (of a series of charges) arranged around the edge of a shield.
– ORIGIN late 16th cent.: from French *ourle*, from *ourler* 'to hem', based on Latin *ora* 'edge'.

Orleanist /ˈɔːlɪənɪst, ɔːˈliːənɪst/ ▶**noun** historical a person supporting the claim to the French throne of the descendants of the Duke of Orleans (1640–1701), younger brother of Louis XIV, especially Louis Philippe (King of France, 1830–48).
– ORIGIN from French *Orléaniste*, from *Orléans*.

Orleans /ɔːˈliːənz/ a city in central France, on the Loire; pop. 107,965 (1990). In 1429 it was the scene of Joan of Arc's first victory over the English during the Hundred Years War. French name **ORLÉANS** /ɔrleɑ̃/.

Orlon /ˈɔːlɒn/ ▶**noun** [mass noun] trademark a synthetic acrylic fibre used for textiles and knitwear, or a fabric made from it.
– ORIGIN 1950s: invented word, on the pattern of *nylon*.

orlop /ˈɔːlɒp/ (also **orlop deck**) ▶**noun** the lowest deck of a wooden sailing-ship with three or more decks.
– ORIGIN late Middle English: from Dutch *overloop* 'covering', from *overlopen* 'run over'.

Ormazd /ˈɔːməzd/ another name for **AHURA MAZDA**.

ormer /ˈɔːmə/ ▶**noun** an abalone (mollusc), especially one used as food in the Channel Islands.
● Genus *Haliotis*, in particular *H. tuberculata*.
– ORIGIN mid 17th cent.: Channel Islands French, from French *ormier*, from Latin *auris maris* 'ear of the sea' (because of its ear-like shape).

ormolu /ˈɔːməluː/ ▶**noun** [mass noun] a gold-coloured alloy of copper, zinc, and tin used in decoration and making ornaments.
– ORIGIN mid 18th cent.: from French *or moulu* 'powdered gold' (used in gilding).

Ormuz /ˈɔːmʊz, ɔːˈmuːz/ variant spelling of **HORMUZ**.

ornament ▶**noun** /ˈɔːnəm(ə)nt/ a thing used or serving to adorn something but usually having no practical purpose, especially a small object such as a figurine. ■a quality or person adding grace, beauty, or honour to something: *the design would be a great **ornament** to the metropolis.* ■[mass noun] decoration added to embellish something, especially a building: *it served more for ornament than for protection.* ■(**ornaments**) Music embellishments and decorations made to a melody. ■(usu. **ornaments**) Christian Church the accessories of worship, such as the altar, chalice, and sacred vessels.
▶**verb** /ˈɔːnəmɛnt/ [with obj.] adorn; beautify: *a jewel to ornament your wife's lovely throat.*
– ORIGIN Middle English (also in the sense 'accessory'): from Old French *ournement*, from Latin *ornamentum* 'equipment, ornament', from *ornare* 'adorn'. The verb dates from the early 18th cent.

ornamental ▶**adjective** serving or intended as an ornament; decorative: *an ornamental fountain.*
▶**noun** a plant grown for its attractive appearance.
– DERIVATIVES **ornamentalism** noun, **ornamentalist** noun, **ornamentally** adverb.

ornamentation ▶**noun** [mass noun] things added to something to provide decoration: *a baroque chandelier with plasterwork ornamentation.* ■the action of decorating something or making it more elaborate: *the rhetorical ornamentation of text.*

ornate ▶**adjective** made in an intricate shape or decorated with complex patterns: *an ornate wrought-iron railing.* ■(of literary style) using unusual words and complex constructions: *peculiarly ornate and metaphorical language.* ■(of musical composition or performance) using many ornaments such as grace notes and trills.
– DERIVATIVES **ornately** adverb, **ornateness** noun.
– ORIGIN late Middle English: from Latin *ornatus* 'adorned', past participle of *ornare*.

ornery /ˈɔːnəri/ ▶**adjective** N. Amer. informal **1** bad-tempered and intolerant. **2** ordinary.
– DERIVATIVES **orneriness** noun.
– ORIGIN early 19th cent.: variant of **ORDINARY**, representing a dialect pronunciation.

ornithine /ˈɔːnɪθiːn/ ▶**noun** [mass noun] Biochemistry an amino acid which is produced by the body and is important in protein metabolism.
● Chem. formula: $NH_2(CH_2)_3CH(NH_2)COOH$.
– ORIGIN late 19th cent.: from **ORNITHO-** (with reference to a constituent found in bird excrement) + **-INE**[4].

ornithischian /ˌɔːnɪˈθɪskɪən, -ˈθɪʃɪən/ Palaeontology ▶**adjective** of, relating to, or denoting herbivorous dinosaurs of an order distinguished by having a pelvic structure resembling that of birds. Compare with **SAURISCHIAN**.
▶**noun** an ornithischian dinosaur.
● Order Ornithischia, superorder Dinosauria; comprises the stegosaurs, ankylosaurs, ornithopods, pachycephalosaurs, and ceratopsians.
– ORIGIN early 20th cent.: from modern Latin *Ornithiscia*, from Greek *ornis, ornith-* 'bird' + *iskhion* 'hip joint'.

ornitho- ▶**combining form** relating to or resembling a bird or birds: *ornithology | ornithopod.*
– ORIGIN from Greek *ornis, ornith-* 'bird'.

ornithology /ˌɔːnɪˈθɒlədʒi/ ▶**noun** [mass noun] the scientific study of birds.
– DERIVATIVES **ornithological** adjective, **ornithologically** adverb, **ornithologist** noun.
– ORIGIN late 17th cent.: from modern Latin *ornithologia*, from Greek *ornithologos* 'treating of birds'.

ornithomimosaur /ˌɔːnɪθə(ʊ)ˈmʌɪməsɔː/ ▶**noun** technical term for **OSTRICH DINOSAUR**.
– ORIGIN 1980s: from modern Latin *Ornithomimosauria*, from Greek *ornis, ornith-* 'bird' + *mimos* 'mime' + *sauros* 'lizard'.

ornithopod /ˈɔːnɪθəˌpɒd/ ▶**noun** a mainly bipedal herbivorous dinosaur.
● Infraorder Ornithopoda, order Ornithischia; includes the hadrosaurs, iguanodon, hypsilophodon, etc.
– ORIGIN late 19th cent.: from modern Latin *Ornithopoda*, from Greek *ornis, ornith-* 'bird' + *pous, pod-* 'foot'.

ornithopter /ˈɔːnɪˌθɒptə/ ▶**noun** chiefly historical a machine designed to achieve flight by means of flapping wings.

– ORIGIN early 20th cent.: coined in French as *ornithoptère*.

ornithosis /ˌɔːnɪˈθəʊsɪs/ ▶ noun another term for **PSITTACOSIS**.

oro- ▶ combining form of or relating to mountains: *orogeny*.
– ORIGIN from Greek *oros* 'mountain'.

orogen /ˈɒrədʒ(ə)n/ ▶ noun Geology a belt of the earth's crust involved in the formation of mountains.
– ORIGIN 1920s: from Greek *oros* 'mountain' + -GEN.

orogeny /ɒˈrɒdʒəni/ ▶ noun [mass noun] Geology a process in which a section of the earth's crust is folded and deformed by lateral compression to form a mountain range.
– DERIVATIVES **orogenesis** noun, **orogenic** adjective.

orographic /ˌɒrəˈɡrafɪk/ ▶ adjective of or relating to mountains, especially as regards their position and form.
■(of clouds or rainfall) resulting from the effects of mountains in forcing moist air to rise.
– DERIVATIVES **orographical** adjective.

Oromo /ˈɒrəməʊ/ ▶ noun (pl. same or -os) **1** a member of an East African people, the largest ethnic group in Ethiopia.
2 [mass noun] the Cushitic language of this people, spoken by some 17 million people in several different dialects.
▶ adjective of or relating to this people or their language.
– ORIGIN the name in Oromo. An earlier term was *Galla*, which remains in use but is not favoured by the Oromo themselves.

Orontes /ɒˈrɒntiːz/ a river in SW Asia which rises near Baalbek in northern Lebanon and flows 571 km (355 miles) through western and northern Syria before turning west through southern Turkey to enter the Mediterranean. It is an important source of water for irrigation, especially in Syria.

oropendola /ˌɒrəˈpɛndələ/ ▶ noun a large gregarious tropical American bird of the American blackbird family, which has brown or black plumage with yellow outer tail feathers, and constructs a pendulous nest.
● Genus *Psarocolius*, family Icteridae: several species.
– ORIGIN late 19th cent.: from Spanish, literally 'golden oriole'.

oropharynx /ˌɔːrə(ʊ)ˈfarɪŋks/ ▶ noun (pl. **oropharynges** or **oropharynxes**) Anatomy the part of the pharynx that lies between the soft palate and the hyoid bone.
– DERIVATIVES **oropharyngeal** adjective.
– ORIGIN late 19th cent.: formed irregularly from Latin *os, -or* 'mouth' + **PHARYNX**.

orotund /ˈɒrə(ʊ)tʌnd, ˈɔː-/ ▶ adjective (of the voice or phrasing) full, round, and imposing.
■(of writing, style, or expression) pompous; pretentious.
– DERIVATIVES **orotundity** noun.
– ORIGIN late 18th cent.: from Latin *ore rotundo* 'with rounded mouth'.

orphan ▶ noun **1** a child whose parents are dead.
2 Printing the first line of a paragraph set as the last line of a page or column, considered undesirable.
▶ verb [with obj.] (usu. **be orphaned**) make (a person or animal) an orphan: *John was orphaned at 12*.
– DERIVATIVES **orphanhood** noun.
– ORIGIN late Middle English: via late Latin from Greek *orphanos* 'bereaved'.

orphanage ▶ noun a residential institution for the care and education of orphans.
■[mass noun] archaic the state or condition of being an orphan.

orphan drug ▶ noun a synthetic pharmaceutical which remains commercially undeveloped.

orpharion /ɔːˈfarɪən/ ▶ noun Music a stringed instrument of the 16th and 17th centuries, resembling a bandora but tuned like an ordinary lute.
– ORIGIN late 16th cent.: blend of the names *Orpheus* (see **ORPHEUS**) and *Arion*, musicians in Greek mythology.

Orpheus /ˈɔːfiəs/ Greek Mythology a poet who could entrance wild beasts with the beauty of his singing and lyre playing. He went to the underworld after the death of his wife Eurydice and secured her release from the dead, but lost her because he failed to obey the condition that he must not look

back at her until they had reached the world of the living.
– DERIVATIVES **Orphean** adjective.

Orphic ▶ adjective of or concerning Orpheus or Orphism.
– ORIGIN late 17th cent.: via Latin from Greek *Orphikos*, from *Orpheus* (see **ORPHEUS**).

Orphism /ˈɔːfɪz(ə)m/ ▶ noun [mass noun] **1** a mystic religion of ancient Greece, originating in the 7th or 6th century BC and based on poems (now lost) attributed to Orpheus, emphasizing the necessity for individuals to rid themselves of the evil part of their nature by ritual and moral purification throughout a series of reincarnations.
2 a short-lived art movement (*c.*1912) within cubism, pioneered by a group of French painters (including Robert Delaunay, Sonia Delaunay-Terk, and Fernand Léger) and emphasizing the lyrical use of colour rather than the austere intellectual cubism of Picasso, Braque, and Gris.

orphrey /ˈɔːfri/ ▶ noun (pl. **-eys**) an ornamental stripe or border, especially one on an ecclesiastical vestment such as a chasuble.
– ORIGIN Middle English: from Old French *orfreis*, from a medieval Latin alteration of *auriphrygium*, from Latin *aurum* 'gold' + *Phrygius* 'Phrygian' (also used in the sense 'embroidered').

orpiment /ˈɔːpɪm(ə)nt/ ▶ noun [mass noun] a bright yellow mineral consisting of arsenic trisulphide, formerly used as a dye and artist's pigment.
– ORIGIN late Middle English: via Old French from Latin *auripigmentum*, from *aurum* 'gold' + *pigmentum* 'pigment'.

orpine /ˈɔːpɪn/ (also **orpin**) ▶ noun a purple-flowered Eurasian stonecrop.
● *Sedum telephium*, family Crassulaceae.
– ORIGIN Middle English: from Old French *orpine*, probably an alteration of **ORPIMENT**, originally applied to a yellow-flowered sedum.

Orpington /ˈɔːpɪŋt(ə)n/ ▶ noun **1** a chicken of a buff, white, or black breed.
2 a duck of a buff or white breed, kept for its meat.
– ORIGIN late 19th cent.: from *Orpington*, the name of a town in Kent.

orra /ˈɒrə/ ▶ adjective Scottish **1** separated from a usual pair or set; odd.
2 used irregularly or only occasionally; extra.
– ORIGIN late 16th cent.: of unknown origin.

orrery /ˈɒrəri/ ▶ noun (pl. **-ies**) a clockwork model of the solar system, or of just the sun, earth, and moon.
– ORIGIN early 18th cent.: named after the fourth Earl of *Orrery*, for whom one was made.

orris /ˈɒrɪs/ (also **orris root**) ▶ noun [mass noun] a preparation of the fragrant rootstock of an iris, used in perfumery and formerly in medicine.
● The root is usually taken from *Iris × germanica* var. 'Florentina'.
– ORIGIN mid 16th cent.: apparently an unexplained alteration of **IRIS**.

Orsk /ɔːsk/ a city in southern Russia, in the Urals on the Ural River near the border with Kazakhstan; pop. 271,000 (1990).

ortanique /ˌɔːtəˈniːk/ ▶ noun a citrus fruit which is a cross between an orange and a tangerine, developed in Jamaica in the 1920s.
● *Citrus sinensis × reticulata*, family Rutaceae.
– ORIGIN blend of **ORANGE**, **TANGERINE**, and **UNIQUE**.

Ortega /ɔːˈteɪɡə/, Daniel (b.1945), Nicaraguan statesman, President 1985–90; full name *Daniel Ortega Saavedra*. He became the leader of the Sandinista National Liberation Front (FSLN) in 1966 and became President after the Sandinista election victory in 1984.

Ortega y Gasset /ɔːˌteɪɡə iː ɡaˈsɛt/, José (1883–1955), Spanish philosopher. His works include *The Revolt of the Masses* (1930), in which he proposed leadership by an intellectual elite.

ortho- ▶ combining form **1** straight; rectangular; upright: *orthodontics*.
■right; correct: *orthoepy*.
2 Chemistry denoting substitution at two adjacent carbon atoms in a benzene ring, e.g. in 1,2 positions: *orthodichlorobenzene*. Compare with **META-** and **PARA-**[1].
3 Chemistry denoting a compound from which a *meta*-compound is formed by dehydration: *orthophosphoric acid*.
– ORIGIN from Greek *orthos* 'straight, right'.

orthochromatic ▶ adjective (of black-and-white photographic film) sensitive to all visible light except red. Orthochromatic film can therefore be handled in red light in the darkroom but does not produce black-and-white tones that correspond very closely to the colours seen by the eye. Often contrasted with **PANCHROMATIC**.

orthoclase /ˈɔːθəkleɪz/ ▶ noun [mass noun] a common rock-forming mineral occurring typically as white or pink crystals. It is a potassium-rich alkali feldspar and is used in ceramics and glass-making.
– ORIGIN mid 19th cent.: from **ORTHO-** 'straight' + Greek *klasis* 'breaking' (because of the characteristic two cleavages at right angles).

orthocone /ˈɔːθəkəʊn/ ▶ noun Palaeontology the straight shell typical of early nautiloid cephalopods.
■a fossil cephalopod with such a shell.
– DERIVATIVES **orthoconic** adjective.

orthodontics /ˌɔːθəˈdɒntɪks/ (also **orthodontia** /-ˈdɒntɪə/) ▶ plural noun [treated as sing.] the treatment of irregularities in the teeth and jaws.
– DERIVATIVES **orthodontic** adjective, **orthodontically** adverb, **orthodontist** noun.
– ORIGIN early 20th cent.: from **ORTHO-** 'straight' + Greek *odous, odont-* 'tooth'.

orthodox ▶ adjective **1** (of a person or their views, especially religious or political ones, or other beliefs or practices) conforming to what is generally or traditionally accepted as right or true; established and approved: *Burke's views were orthodox in his time* | *orthodox medical treatment* | *orthodox Hindus*.
■(of a person) not independent-minded; conventional and unoriginal: *a relatively orthodox artist*.
2 (of a thing) of the ordinary or usual type; normal: *they avoided orthodox jazz venues*.
3 (usu. **Orthodox**) of or relating to Orthodox Judaism.
4 (usu. **Orthodox**) of or relating to the Orthodox Church.
– DERIVATIVES **orthodoxly** adverb.
– ORIGIN late Middle English: from Greek *orthodoxos* (probably via ecclesiastical Latin), from *orthos* 'straight or right' + *doxa* 'opinion'.

Orthodox Church a Christian Church or federation of Churches originating in the Greek-speaking Church of the Byzantine Empire, not accepting the authority of the Pope of Rome, and using elaborate and archaic forms of service.

The chief Orthodox Churches (often known collectively as the **Eastern Orthodox Church**) include the national Churches of Greece, Russia, Bulgaria, Romania, and Serbia. The term is also used by other ancient Churches, mainly of African or Asian origin, e.g. the Coptic, Syrian, and Ethiopian Churches.

Orthodox Judaism a major branch within Judaism which teaches strict adherence to rabbinical interpretation of Jewish law and its traditional observances. There are more than 600 rules governing religious and everyday life. Orthodox Jews maintain the separation of the sexes in synagogue worship.

orthodoxy ▶ noun (pl. **-ies**) [mass noun] **1** authorized or generally accepted theory, doctrine, or practice: *monetarist orthodoxy* | [count noun] *he challenged many of the established orthodoxies*.
■the quality of conforming to such theories, doctrines, or practices: *writings of unimpeachable orthodoxy*.
2 the whole community of Orthodox Jews or Orthodox Christians.
– ORIGIN mid 17th cent.: via late Latin from late Greek *orthodoxia* 'sound doctrine', from *orthodoxos* (see **ORTHODOX**).

orthodromic /ˌɔːθəˈdrɒmɪk/ ▶ adjective Physiology (of an impulse) travelling in the normal direction in a nerve fibre. The opposite of **ANTIDROMIC**.
– ORIGIN 1940s: from **ORTHO-** 'right, correct' + Greek *dromos* 'running' + -IC.

orthoepy /ˈɔːθəʊɛpi, -ɪpi, ɔːˈθəʊɪpi/ ▶ noun [mass noun] the correct or accepted pronunciation of words.
■the study of correct or accepted pronunciation.
– DERIVATIVES **orthoepic** /-ˈɛpɪk/ adjective, **orthoepist** noun.
– ORIGIN mid 17th cent.: from Greek *orthoepeia* 'correct speech', from *orthos* 'right or straight' + *epos, epe-* 'word'.

orthogenesis /ˌɔːθə(ʊ)ˈdʒɛnɪsɪs/ ▶ noun [mass noun] Biology, chiefly historical evolution in which variations

follow a particular direction and are not merely sporadic and fortuitous.
– DERIVATIVES **orthogenesist** noun, **orthogenetic** adjective, **orthogenetically** adverb.

orthognathous /ˌɔːθəɡˈneɪθəs, ɔːˈθɒɡnəθəs/ ▶ adjective Anatomy (especially of a person) having a jaw which does not project forwards and a facial angle approaching a right angle.
– ORIGIN mid 19th cent.: from **ORTHO-** 'straight' + Greek *gnathos* 'jaw' + **-OUS**.

orthogonal /ɔːˈθɒɡ(ə)n(ə)l/ ▶ adjective 1 of or involving right angles; at right angles.
2 Statistics (of variates) statistically independent.
■ (of an experiment) having variates which can be treated as statistically independent.
– DERIVATIVES **orthogonality** noun, **orthogonally** adverb.
– ORIGIN late 16th cent.: from French, based on Greek *orthogōnios* 'right-angled'.

orthogonal projection ▶ noun [mass noun] Engineering a system of making engineering drawings showing several different views of an object at right angles to each other on a single drawing.
■ [count noun] a drawing made using this method.

orthographic projection ▶ noun [mass noun] Engineering a method of projection in which an object is depicted using parallel lines to project its outline on to a plane.
■ [count noun] a drawing made using this method.

orthography /ɔːˈθɒɡrəfi/ ▶ noun (pl. **-ies**) 1 the conventional spelling system of a language.
■ [mass noun] the study of spelling and how letters combine to represent sounds and form words.
2 another term for **ORTHOGRAPHIC PROJECTION**.
– DERIVATIVES **orthographer** noun (only in sense 1), **orthographic** adjective, **orthographical** adjective, **orthographically** adverb.
– ORIGIN late Middle English: via Old French and Latin from Greek *orthographia*, from *orthos* 'correct' + *-graphia* writing.

orthomorphic /ˌɔːθəˈmɔːfɪk/ ▶ adjective Geography (of a map projection) preserving the correct shape of small areas.

Orthonectida /ˌɔːθə(ʊ)ˈnɛktɪdə/ Zoology a minor phylum of mesozoan worms which are internal parasites of a range of marine invertebrates.
– DERIVATIVES **orthonectid** noun & adjective.
– ORIGIN modern Latin (plural), from Greek *orthos* 'straight' + *nektos* 'swimming' (see **NEKTON**).

orthonormal ▶ adjective Mathematics both orthogonal and normalized.
– DERIVATIVES **orthonormality** noun, **orthonormalization** noun.

orthopaedics /ˌɔːθəˈpiːdɪks/ (US **-pedics**) ▶ plural noun [treated as sing.] the branch of medicine dealing with the correction of deformities of bones or muscles. [ORIGIN: originally relating specifically to children.]
– DERIVATIVES **orthopaedic** adjective, **orthopaedically** adverb, **orthopaedist** noun.
– ORIGIN mid 19th cent.: from French *orthopédie*, from Greek *orthos* 'right or straight' + *paideia* 'rearing of children'.

orthophosphoric acid /ˌɔːθə(ʊ)fɒsˈfɒrɪk/ ▶ noun another term for **PHOSPHORIC ACID**.
– DERIVATIVES **orthophosphate** noun.

orthopsychiatry ▶ noun [mass noun] the branch of psychiatry concerned with the prevention of mental or behavioural disorders, especially by studying borderline cases.
– DERIVATIVES **orthopsychiatric** adjective, **orthopsychiatrist** noun.

orthopter /ɔːˈθɒptə/ ▶ noun another term for **ORNITHOPTER**.

Orthoptera /ɔːˈθɒpt(ə)rə/ Entomology an order of insects that comprises the grasshoppers, crickets, and their relatives. They have a saddle-shaped thorax, hind legs that are typically long and modified for jumping, and a characteristic song which the male produces by stridulation.
■ [as plural noun **orthoptera**] insects of this order.
– DERIVATIVES **orthopteran** noun & adjective, **orthopterous** adjective.
– ORIGIN modern Latin (plural), from **ORTHO-** 'straight' + Greek *pteros* 'wing'.

orthopteroid /ɔːˈθɒptərɔɪd/ ▶ adjective Entomology of or relating to a group of insect orders that are related to the grasshoppers and crickets, including

also the stoneflies, stick insects, earwigs, cockroaches, mantises, and termites.

orthoptics /ɔːˈθɒptɪks/ ▶ plural noun [treated as sing.] the study or treatment of irregularities of the eyes, especially those of the eye muscles that prevent normal binocular vision.
– DERIVATIVES **orthoptic** adjective, **orthoptist** noun.
– ORIGIN late 19th cent.: from **ORTHO-** 'correct' + Greek *optikos* (see **OPTIC**).

orthopyroxene /ˌɔːθə(ʊ)pʌɪˈrɒksiːn/ ▶ noun [mass noun] a mineral of the pyroxene group crystallizing in the orthorhombic system.

orthorhombic /ˌɔːθə(ʊ)ˈrɒmbɪk/ ▶ adjective of or denoting a crystal system or three-dimensional geometrical arrangement having three unequal axes at right angles.

orthosis /ɔːˈθəʊsɪs/ ▶ noun (pl. **orthoses** /-siːz/) Medicine a brace, splint, or other artificial external device serving to support the limbs or spine or to prevent or assist relative movement.
– ORIGIN 1950s: from Greek *orthōsis* 'making straight', from *orthoun* 'set straight'.

orthostat /ˈɔːθə(ʊ)stat/ ▶ noun Archaeology an upright stone or slab forming part of a structure or set in the ground.
– ORIGIN early 20th cent.: from Greek *orthostatēs*, from *orthos* 'right or straight' + *statos* 'standing'.

orthostatic ▶ adjective 1 Medicine relating to or caused by an upright posture.
2 Archaeology (of a stone) set on end.
■ (of a structure) built of such stones.

orthostichy /ɔːˈθɒstɪki/ ▶ noun (pl. **-ies**) Botany (in phyllotaxis) a vertical row of leaves arranged one directly above another. Contrasted with **PARASTICHY**.
– ORIGIN late 19th cent.: from **ORTHO-** 'upright, straight' + Greek *stikhos* 'row, rank'.

orthotic ▶ adjective relating to orthotics.
▶ noun an artificial support or brace for the limbs or spine.

orthotics /ɔːˈθɒtɪks/ ▶ plural noun [treated as sing.] the branch of medicine that deals with the provision and use of artificial devices such as splints and braces.
– DERIVATIVES **orthotist** noun.

orthotropic /ˌɔːθə(ʊ)ˈtrəʊpɪk, -ˈtrɒpɪk/ ▶ adjective 1 Botany (of a shoot, stem, or axis) growing vertically.
2 Engineering having three mutually perpendicular planes of elastic symmetry at each point.

ortolan /ˈɔːt(ə)lən/ (also **ortolan bunting**) ▶ noun a small Eurasian songbird that was formerly eaten as a delicacy, the male having an olive-green head and yellow throat.
● *Emberiza hortulana*, family Emberizidae (subfamily Emberizinae).
– ORIGIN early 16th cent.: from French, from Provençal, literally 'gardener', based on a diminutive of Latin *hortus* 'garden'.

Orton[1], Arthur (1834–98), English butcher; known as the **Tichborne claimant**. In 1866 he returned to England from Australia claiming to be the heir to the valuable Tichborne estate. He lost his claim and was tried and imprisoned for perjury.

Orton[2], Joe (1933–67), English dramatist; born *John Kingsley Orton*. He wrote a number of unconventional black comedies, examining corruption, sexuality, and violence; they include *Entertaining Mr Sloane* (1964) and *Loot* (1965). Orton was murdered by his homosexual lover, who committed suicide.
– DERIVATIVES **Ortonesque** adjective.

orts /ɔːts/ ▶ plural noun archaic or dialect scraps; remains.
– ORIGIN late Middle English: from Middle Low German *orte* 'food remains', originally a compound the second element of which is related to **EAT**.

Oruro /əˈrʊərəʊ/ a city in western Bolivia; pop. 183,190 (1992). It is the centre of an important mining region, with rich deposits of tin, zinc, silver, copper, and gold.

Orvieto[1] /ɔːˈvjɛtəʊ, Italian orˈvjeto/ a town in Umbria, central Italy; pop. 21,575 (1990). It lies at the centre of a wine-producing area.

Orvieto[2] /ˌɔːvɪˈɛtəʊ/ ▶ noun [mass noun] a white wine made near Orvieto.

Orwell, George (1903–50), British novelist and essayist, born in India; pseudonym of *Eric Arthur Blair*. His work is characterized by his concern

about social injustice. His most famous works are *Animal Farm* (1945), a satire on Communism as it developed under Stalin, and *Nineteen Eighty-four* (1949), a dystopian account of a future state in which every aspect of life is controlled by Big Brother.
– DERIVATIVES **Orwellian** adjective.

-ory[1] ▶ suffix (forming nouns) denoting a place for a particular function: *dormitory* | *repository*.
– DERIVATIVES **-orial** suffix forming corresponding adjectives.
– ORIGIN from Latin *-oria*, *-orium*, sometimes via Anglo-Norman French *-orie*, Old French *-oire*.

-ory[2] ▶ suffix forming adjectives (and occasionally nouns) relating to or involving a verbal action: *compulsory* | *directory* | *mandatory*.
– ORIGIN from Latin *-orius*, sometimes via Anglo-Norman French *-ori(e)*.

oryx /ˈɒrɪks/ ▶ noun a large antelope living in arid regions of Africa and Arabia, having dark markings on the face and long horns.
● Genus *Oryx*, family Bovidae: three species, including the **Arabian oryx** (*O. leucoryx*). See also **BEISA**, **SCIMITAR ORYX**.
– ORIGIN late Middle English: via Latin from Greek *orux* 'stonemason's pickaxe' (because of its pointed horns).

orzo /ˈɔːtsəʊ/ ▶ noun [mass noun] small pieces of pasta, shaped like grains of barley or rice.
– ORIGIN Italian, literally 'barley'.

OS ▶ abbreviation for ■ (in calculating dates) Old Style. ■ Computing operating system. ■ Ordinary Seaman. ■ (in the UK) Ordnance Survey. ■ (as a size of clothing) outsize. ■ out of stock.

Os ▶ symbol for the chemical element osmium.

os[1] /ɒs/ ▶ noun (pl. **ossa** /ˈɒsə/) Anatomy a bone (used chiefly in Latin names of individual bones, e.g. *os trapezium*).
– ORIGIN Latin.

os[2] /ɒs/ ▶ noun (pl. **ora** /ˈɔːrə/) Anatomy an opening or entrance to a passage, especially one at either end of the cervix of the womb.
– ORIGIN mid 18th cent.: from Latin *os* 'mouth'.

Osage /əʊˈseɪdʒ, ˈəʊseɪdʒ/ ▶ noun (pl. same or **Osages**) 1 a member of an American Indian people formerly inhabiting the Osage river valley in Missouri.
2 [mass noun] the Siouan language of this people, now virtually extinct.
▶ adjective of or relating to this people or their language.
– ORIGIN alteration of Osage *Wazhazhe*, the name of one of the three groups that compose this people.

Osage orange ▶ noun a small spiny North American deciduous tree which bears inedible green orange-like fruit. Its durable orange-coloured timber was formerly used by American Indians for bows and other weapons.
● *Maclura pomifera*, family Moraceae.

Osaka /əʊˈsɑːkə/ a port and commercial city in central Japan, on the island of Honshu, capital of Kinki region; pop. 2,642,000 (1990).

Osborne, John (James) (1929–94), English dramatist. His first play, *Look Back in Anger* (1956), ushered in a new era of kitchen-sink drama; its hero Jimmy Porter personified contemporary disillusioned youth, the so-called 'angry young man'.

Oscan /ˈɒsk(ə)n/ ▶ noun [mass noun] an extinct Italic language of southern Italy, related to Umbrian and surviving in inscriptions mainly of the 4th to 1st centuries BC.
▶ adjective of or relating to this language.
– ORIGIN late 16th cent.: from Latin *Oscus* 'Oscan' + **-AN**.

Oscar[1] ▶ noun 1 (trademark in the US) the nickname for a gold statuette given as an Academy award. [ORIGIN: one of the several speculative stories of its origin claims that the statuette reminded Margaret Herrick, an executive director of the Academy of Motion Picture Arts and Sciences, of her uncle Oscar.]
2 a code word representing the letter O, used in radio communication.

Oscar[2] ▶ noun [mass noun] Austral./NZ informal money.
– ORIGIN early 20th cent.: from the name *Oscar Asche* (1871–1936), Australian actor, used as rhyming slang for 'cash'.

oscar (also **oscar cichlid**) ▶ noun a South American cichlid fish with velvety brown young and multicoloured adults, popular in aquaria.
● *Astronotus ocellatus*, family Cichlidae. Alternative name: **velvet cichlid**.

oscillate /ˈɒsɪleɪt/ ▶ verb [no obj.] **1** move or swing back and forth at a regular speed: *it oscillates in a plane at right angles to the cam axis*.
■ [with adverbial] figurative waver between extremes of opinion, action, or quality: *he was oscillating between fear and bravery*.
2 Physics vary in magnitude or position in a regular manner around a central point.
■ (of a circuit or device) cause the electric current or voltage running through it to behave in this way.
– DERIVATIVES **oscillation** noun, **oscillatory** /ɒˈsɪlət(ə)ri, ˈɒsɪlə,t(ə)ri/ adjective.
– ORIGIN early 18th cent.: from Latin *oscillat-* 'swung', from the verb *oscillare*.

oscillator ▶ noun a device for generating oscillatory electric currents or voltages by non-mechanical means.

oscillo- /əˈsɪləʊ/ ▶ combining form relating to oscillation, especially of electric current: *oscilloscope*.

oscillogram ▶ noun a record produced by an oscillograph.

oscillograph ▶ noun a device for recording oscillations, especially those of an electric current.
– DERIVATIVES **oscillographic** adjective, **oscillography** noun.

oscilloscope ▶ noun a device for viewing oscillations by a display on the screen of a cathode ray tube.
– DERIVATIVES **oscilloscopic** adjective.

oscine /ˈɒsʌɪn, -sɪn/ ▶ adjective Ornithology of, relating to or denoting passerine birds of a large division that includes the songbirds. Compare with **SUBOSCINE**.
● Suborder Oscines, order Passeriformes.
– ORIGIN late 19th cent.: from Latin *oscen, oscin-* 'songbird' + **-INE**[1].

Osco-Umbrian ▶ noun **1** [mass noun] a group of ancient Italic languages including Oscan and Umbrian, spoken in Italy in the 1st millennium BC, before the emergence of Latin as a standard language.
2 a member of any of the peoples who spoke a language in this group.
▶ adjective of or relating to these peoples or their languages.

oscula plural form of **OSCULUM**.

oscular /ˈɒskjʊlə/ ▶ adjective **1** humorous of or relating to kissing.
2 Zoology of or relating to an osculum.
– ORIGIN early 19th cent.: from Latin *osculum* 'mouth, kiss' (diminutive of *os* 'mouth') + **-AR**[1].

osculate /ˈɒskjʊleɪt/ ▶ verb [with obj.] **1** Mathematics (of a curve or surface) touch (another curve or surface) so as to have a common tangent at the point of contact: [as adj. **osculating**] *the plots have been drawn using osculating orbital elements*.
2 formal or humorous kiss.
– DERIVATIVES **osculant** adjective, **osculation** noun, **osculatory** adjective.
– ORIGIN mid 17th cent.: from Latin *osculat-* 'kissed', from the verb *osculari*, from *osculum* 'little mouth or kiss'.

osculum /ˈɒskjʊləm/ ▶ noun (pl. **oscula** /-lə/) Zoology a large aperture in a sponge through which water is expelled.
– ORIGIN early 17th cent.: from Latin 'little mouth'.

-ose[1] ▶ suffix (forming adjectives) having a specified quality: *bellicose | comatose | verbose*.
– DERIVATIVES **-osely** suffix forming corresponding adverbs, **-oseness** suffix forming corresponding nouns. Compare with **-OSITY**.
– ORIGIN from Latin *-osus*.

-ose[2] ▶ suffix Chemistry forming names of sugars and other carbohydrates: *cellulose | glucose*.
– ORIGIN on the pattern of (*gluc*)*ose*.

Osh /ɒʃ/ a city in western Kyrgyzstan, near the border with Uzbekistan; pop. 236,200 (1990). It was, until the 15th century, an important post on an ancient trade route to China and India.

OSHA ▶ abbreviation for (in the US) Occupational Safety and Health Administration.

Oshawa /ˈɒʃəwə/ a city in Ontario, on the northern shores of Lake Ontario east of Toronto; pop. 174,010 (1991).

oshi /ˈɒʃi/ ▶ noun [pl. same] (in sumo wrestling) a move in which an opponent is pushed backwards or down.
– ORIGIN Japanese.

osier /ˈəʊzɪə/ ▶ noun a small Eurasian willow which grows mostly in wet habitats. It is usually coppiced, being a major source of the long flexible shoots (withies) used in basketwork.
● *Salix viminalis*, family Salicaceae.
■ a shoot of a willow. ■ dated any willow tree.
– ORIGIN late Middle English: from Old French; compare with medieval Latin *auseria* 'osier bed'.

osier bed ▶ noun a place where osiers are grown.

Osijek /ˈɒsɪjɛk/ a city in eastern Croatia, on the River Drava; pop. 104,700 (1991).

Osiris /ə(ʊ)ˈsʌɪrɪs/ Egyptian Mythology a god originally connected with fertility, husband of Isis and father of Horus. He is known chiefly through the story of his death at the hands of his brother Seth and his subsequent restoration to a new life as ruler of the afterlife.
– DERIVATIVES **Osirian** adjective.

-osis ▶ suffix (pl. **-oses**) denoting a process or condition: *metamorphosis*.
■ denoting a pathological state: *neurosis | thrombosis*.
– ORIGIN via Latin from Greek *-ōsis*, verbal noun ending.

-osity ▶ suffix forming nouns from adjectives ending in *-ose* (such as *verbosity* from *verbose*) and from adjectives ending in *-ous* (such as *pomposity* from *pompous*).
– ORIGIN from French *-osité* or Latin *-ositas*.

Oslo /ˈɒzləʊ/ the capital and chief port of Norway, on the south coast at the head of Oslofjord; pop. 458,360 (1990). Founded in the 11th century, it was known as Christiania (or Kristiania) from 1624 until 1924 in honour of Christian IV of Norway and Denmark (1577–1648).

Osman I /ˈɒzmən/ (also **Othman**) (1259–1326), Turkish conqueror, founder of the Ottoman (Osmanli) dynasty and empire. Osman reigned as sultan of the Seljuk Turks from 1288, conquering NW Asia Minor. He assumed the title of emir in 1299.

Osmanli /ɒzˈmanli/ ▶ adjective & noun (pl. same or **Osmanlis**) old-fashioned term for **OTTOMAN**.
– ORIGIN Turkish, from the name *Osman*, from Arabic *'uṯmān* (see **OTTOMAN**), + the adjectival suffix *-li*.

osmic /ˈɒzmɪk/ ▶ adjective relating to odours or the sense of smell.
– DERIVATIVES **osmically** adverb.
– ORIGIN mid 20th cent.: from Greek *osmē* 'smell, odour' + **-IC**.

osmic acid ▶ noun [mass noun] Chemistry a solution of osmium tetroxide.
– ORIGIN mid 19th cent.: *osmic* from **OSMIUM** + **-IC**.

osmium /ˈɒzmɪəm/ ▶ noun [mass noun] the chemical element of atomic number 76, a hard, dense, silvery-white metal of the transition series. (Symbol: **Os**)
– ORIGIN early 19th cent.: modern Latin, from Greek *osmē* 'smell' (from the pungent smell of its tetroxide).

osmium tetroxide ▶ noun [mass noun] a poisonous pale yellow solid with a distinctive pungent smell, used in solution as a biological stain (especially for lipids) and fixative.
● Chem. formula: OsO_4.

osmo- ▶ combining form representing **OSMOSIS**.

osmolality /ˌɒzmə(ʊ)ˈlalɪti/ ▶ noun Chemistry the concentration of a solution expressed as the total number of solute particles per kilogram.
– ORIGIN 1950s: blend of *osmotic* (see **OSMOSIS**) and **MOLAL**, + **-ITY**.

osmolarity /ˌɒzmə(ʊ)ˈlarɪti/ ▶ noun Chemistry the concentration of a solution expressed as the total number of solute particles per litre.
– ORIGIN 1950s: blend of *osmotic* (see **OSMOSIS**) and **MOLAR**[3], + **-ITY**.

osmometer /ɒzˈmɒmɪtə/ ▶ noun an instrument for demonstrating or measuring osmotic pressure.
– DERIVATIVES **osmometric** adjective, **osmometry** noun.

osmoregulation ▶ noun [mass noun] Biology the maintenance of constant osmotic pressure in the fluids of an organism by the control of water and salt concentrations.
– DERIVATIVES **osmoregulatory** adjective.

osmose /ˈɒzməʊs/ ▶ verb [no obj.] rare pass by or as if by osmosis.
– ORIGIN mid 19th cent. (as a noun in the sense 'osmosis'): from the element common to *endosmose* and *exosmose*.

osmosis /ɒzˈməʊsɪs/ ▶ noun [mass noun] Biology & Chemistry a process by which molecules of a solvent tend to pass through a semipermeable membrane from a less concentrated solution into a more concentrated one.
■ figurative the process of gradual or unconscious assimilation of ideas, knowledge, etc.: *by some strange political osmosis, private reputations became public*.
– DERIVATIVES **osmotic** adjective, **osmotically** adverb.
– ORIGIN mid 19th cent.: Latinized form of earlier *osmose*, from Greek *ōsmos* 'a push'.

osmotic pressure /ɒzˈmɒtɪk/ ▶ noun Chemistry the pressure that would have to be applied to a pure solvent to prevent it from passing into a given solution by osmosis, often used to express the concentration of the solution.

osmunda /ɒzˈmʌndə/ ▶ noun a plant of a genus that includes the royal and cinnamon ferns.
● Genus *Osmunda*, family Osmundaceae.
– ORIGIN Anglo-Latin, from Anglo-Norman French *osmunde*, of unknown origin.

Osnabrück /ˈɒznəbrʊk, German ˌɒsnaˈbrʏk/ a city in NW Germany, in Lower Saxony; pop. 165,140 (1991). In 1648 the Treaty of Westphalia, ending the Thirty Years War, was signed there and in Münster.

osnaburg /ˈɒznəbəːɡ/ ▶ noun [mass noun] a kind of coarse linen or cotton used for such items as furnishings and sacks.
– ORIGIN late Middle English: alteration of **OSNABRÜCK**, where the cloth was originally produced.

os penis ▶ noun Zoology a bone in the penis of carnivores and some other mammals. Also called **BACULUM**.

osprey /ˈɒspri, -preɪ/ ▶ noun (pl. **-eys**) a large fish-eating bird of prey with long narrow wings and a white underside and crown, found throughout the world. Also called **FISH HAWK**.
● *Pandion haliaetus*, the only member of the family Pandionidae.
– ORIGIN late Middle English: from Old French *ospres*, apparently based on Latin *ossifraga* (mentioned by Pliny and identified with the lammergeier), from *os* 'bone' + *frangere* 'to break', probably because of the lammergeier's habit of dropping bones from a height to break them and reach the marrow.

OSS ▶ abbreviation for (in the US) Office of Strategic Services, an intelligence organization.

ossa plural form of **OS**[1].

Ossa, Mount /ˈɒsə/ **1** a mountain in Thessaly, NE Greece, south of Mount Olympus, rising to a height of 1,978 m (6,489 ft). In Greek mythology the giants were said to have piled Mount Olympus and Mount Ossa on to Mount Pelion in an attempt to reach heaven and destroy the gods.
2 the highest mountain on the island of Tasmania, rising to a height of 1,617 m (5,305 ft).

osseous /ˈɒsɪəs/ ▶ adjective chiefly Zoology & Medicine consisting of or turned into bone; ossified.
– ORIGIN late Middle English: from Latin *osseus* 'bony' + **-OUS**.

Ossete /ˈɒsiːt/ ▶ noun **1** a native or inhabitant of Ossetia.
2 another term for **OSSETIAN** (the language).
▶ adjective of or relating to Ossetia or the Ossetes.
– ORIGIN from Russian *osetin*, from Georgian.

Ossetia /ɒˈsiːʃə/ a region of the central Caucasus. It is divided by the boundary between Russia and Georgia into two parts, North Ossetia and South Ossetia, and between 1989 and 1992 was the scene of ethnic conflict.

Ossetian ▶ noun **1** [mass noun] the language of the Ossetes, belonging to the Iranian group.
2 a native or inhabitant of Ossetia.
▶ adjective of or relating to the Ossetes or their language.
– DERIVATIVES **Ossetic** adjective & noun.

Ossi /ˈɒsi/ ▶ noun (pl. **Ossies** or **Ossis**) informal, often

derogatory (in Germany) a citizen of the former German Democratic Republic.
− ORIGIN German, probably an abbreviation of *Ostdeutsche* 'East German'.

Ossian /'ɒʃən, 'ɒsɪ-/ a legendary Irish warrior and bard, whose name became well known in 1760–3 when the Scottish poet James Macpherson (1736– 96) published his own verse as an alleged translation of 3rd-century Gaelic tales. Irish name **OISIN**.

ossicle /'ɒsɪk(ə)l/ ▶ noun Anatomy & Zoology a very small bone, especially one of those in the middle ear.
 ■ Zoology a small piece of calcified material forming part of the skeleton of an invertebrate animal such as an echinoderm.
− ORIGIN late 16th cent.: from Latin *ossiculum*, diminutive of *os* 'bone'.

Ossie ▶ noun variant spelling of **AUSSIE**.

ossify /'ɒsɪfʌɪ/ ▶ verb (**-ies**, **-ied**) [no obj.] turn into bone or bony tissue: *these tracheal cartilages may ossify.*
 ■ [often as adj. **ossified**] figurative cease developing; stagnate: *ossified political institutions.*
− DERIVATIVES **ossification** noun.
− ORIGIN early 18th cent.: from French *ossifier*, from Latin *os, oss-* 'bone'.

Ossining Correctional Facility official name for **SING SING**.

osso bucco /ˌɒsəʊ 'buːkəʊ/ ▶ noun [mass noun] an Italian dish made of shin of veal containing marrowbone, stewed in wine with vegetables.
− ORIGIN Italian, literally 'marrowbone'.

ossuary /'ɒsjʊəri/ ▶ noun (pl. **-ies**) a container or room into which the bones of dead people are placed.
− ORIGIN mid 17th cent.: from late Latin *ossuarium*, formed irregularly from Latin *os, oss-* 'bone'.

Ostade /ɒ'staːdə/, Adriaen van (1610–85), Dutch painter and engraver. His work chiefly depicts lively genre scenes of peasants carousing or brawling in crowded taverns or barns.

Osteichthyes /ˌɒstɪ'ɪkθiːz/ Zoology a class of fishes that includes those with a bony skeleton. Compare with **CHONDRICHTHYES**.
− ORIGIN modern Latin (plural), from Greek *osteon* 'bone' + *ikhthus* 'fish'.

osteitis /ˌɒstɪ'ʌɪtɪs/ ▶ noun [mass noun] Medicine inflammation of the substance of a bone.
 ■ (**osteitis fibrosa cystica** /fʌɪˌbrəʊsə 'sɪstɪkə/) another term for **VON RECKLINGHAUSEN'S DISEASE** (in sense 2). ■ (**osteitis deformans** /dɪ'fɔːmanz/) another term for **PAGET'S DISEASE** (in sense 1).
− ORIGIN mid 19th cent.: from Greek *osteon* 'bone' + **-ITIS**.

Ostend /ɒ'stɛnd/ a port on the North Sea coast of NW Belgium, in West Flanders; pop. 68,500 (1991). It is a major ferry port with links to Dover. Flemish name **OOSTENDE**; French name **OSTENDE** /ɒstɑ̃d/.

ostensible /ɒ'stɛnsɪb(ə)l/ ▶ adjective [attrib.] stated or appearing to be true, but not necessarily so: *the real dispute which lay behind the ostensible complaint.*
− DERIVATIVES **ostensibility** noun.
− ORIGIN mid 18th cent.: from French, from medieval Latin *ostensibilis* from Latin *ostens-* 'stretched out to view', from the verb *ostendere*, from *ob-* 'in view of' + *tendere* 'to stretch'.

ostensibly ▶ adverb [sentence adverb] apparently: *the party secretary resigned, ostensibly from ill health.*

ostensive ▶ adjective Linguistics denoting a way of defining by direct demonstration, e.g. pointing.
− DERIVATIVES **ostensively** adverb, **ostensiveness** noun.
− ORIGIN mid 16th cent.: from late Latin *ostensivus*, from *ostens-* 'stretched out to view' (see **OSTENSIBLE**).

ostensory /ɒ'stɛns(ə)ri/ ▶ noun (pl. **-ies**) another term for **MONSTRANCE**.
− ORIGIN early 18th cent.: from medieval Latin *ostensorium*, from *ostens-* 'stretched out to view' (see **OSTENSIBLE**).

ostentation ▶ noun [mass noun] pretentious and vulgar display, especially of wealth and luxury, designed to impress or attract notice.
− ORIGIN late Middle English: via Old French from Latin *ostentatio(n-)*, from the verb *ostentare*, frequentative of *ostendere* 'stretch out to view'.

ostentatious /ˌɒstɛn'teɪʃəs/ ▶ adjective character- ized by vulgar or pretentious display; designed to

impress or attract notice: *a simple design that is glamorous without being ostentatious.*
− DERIVATIVES **ostentatiously** adverb, **ostenta- tiousness** noun.

osteo- ▶ combining form of or relating to the bones: *osteoporosis.*
− ORIGIN from Greek *osteon* 'bone'.

osteoarthritis ▶ noun [mass noun] Medicine degeneration of joint cartilage and the underlying bone, most common from middle age onward. It causes pain and stiffness, especially in the hip, knee, and thumb joints. Compare with **RHEUMATOID ARTHRITIS**.
− DERIVATIVES **osteoarthritic** adjective.

osteoblast /'ɒstɪə(ʊ)blast/ ▶ noun Physiology a cell which secretes the substance of bone.
− DERIVATIVES **osteoblastic** adjective.

osteoclast /'ɒstɪə(ʊ)klast/ ▶ noun Physiology a large multinucleate bone cell which absorbs bone tissue during growth and healing.
− DERIVATIVES **osteoclastic** adjective.
− ORIGIN late 19th cent.: from **OSTEO-** 'bone' + Greek *klastēs* 'breaker'.

osteocyte /'ɒstɪə(ʊ)sʌɪt/ ▶ noun Physiology a bone cell, formed when an osteoblast becomes embedded in the material it has secreted.
− DERIVATIVES **osteocytic** adjective.

osteogenesis /ˌɒstɪə(ʊ)'dʒɛnɪsɪs/ ▶ noun [mass noun] the formation of bone.
− DERIVATIVES **osteogenetic** adjective, **osteogenic** adjective.

osteogenesis imperfecta /ˌɪmpəː'fɛktə/ ▶ noun [mass noun] Medicine an inherited disorder characterized by extreme fragility of the bones.
− ORIGIN modern Latin, from **OSTEOGENESIS** + Latin *imperfecta* 'imperfect' (feminine of *imperfectus*).

osteoid /'ɒstɪɔɪd/ Physiology & Medicine ▶ adjective resembling bone in appearance or structure.
▶ noun [mass noun] the unmineralized organic component of bone.

osteology /ˌɒstɪ'ɒlədʒi/ ▶ noun [mass noun] the study of the structure and function of the skeleton and bony structures.
− DERIVATIVES **osteological** adjective, **osteologically** adverb, **osteologist** noun.

osteolysis /ˌɒstɪ'ɒlɪsɪs/ ▶ noun [mass noun] Medicine the pathological destruction or disappearance of bone tissue.
− DERIVATIVES **osteolytic** adjective.

osteomalacia /ˌɒstɪəmə'leɪʃɪə/ ▶ noun [mass noun] softening of the bones, typically through a deficiency of vitamin D or calcium.
− DERIVATIVES **osteomalacic** /-'lasɪk/ adjective.
− ORIGIN early 19th cent.: modern Latin, from **OSTEO-** 'bone' + Greek *malakos* 'soft'.

osteomyelitis /ˌɒstɪəʊmʌɪ'lʌɪtɪs/ ▶ noun [mass noun] Medicine inflammation of bone or bone marrow, usually due to infection.

osteonecrosis /ˌɒstɪəʊnɛ'krəʊsɪs/ ▶ noun [mass noun] Medicine the death of bone tissue.
− DERIVATIVES **osteonecrotic** adjective.

osteopathy /ˌɒstɪ'ɒpəθi/ ▶ noun [mass noun] a system of complementary medicine involving the treatment of medical disorders through the manipulation and massage of the skeleton and musculature.
− DERIVATIVES **osteopath** noun, **osteopathic** adjective, **osteopathically** adverb.

osteophyte /'ɒstɪə(ʊ)fʌɪt/ ▶ noun Medicine a bony projection associated with the degeneration of cartilage at joints.
− DERIVATIVES **osteophytic** adjective.

osteoporosis /ˌɒstɪəʊpə'rəʊsɪs/ ▶ noun [mass noun] a medical condition in which the bones become brittle and fragile from loss of tissue, typically as a result of hormonal changes, or deficiency of calcium or vitamin D.
− DERIVATIVES **osteoporotic** adjective.
− ORIGIN mid 19th cent.: from **OSTEO-** 'bone' + Greek *poros* 'passage, pore' + **-OSIS**.

osteosarcoma /ˌɒstɪəʊsɑː'kəʊmə/ ▶ noun (pl. **osteosarcomas** or **osteosarcomata** /-mətə/) Medicine a malignant tumour of bone in which there is a proliferation of osteoblasts.

osteotome /'ɒstɪətəʊm/ ▶ noun a surgical instrument for cutting bone, typically resembling a chisel.

osteotomy /ˌɒstɪ'ɒtəmi/ ▶ noun (pl. **-ies**) [mass noun] the surgical cutting of a bone, especially to allow realignment.

Österreich /'øːstəˌrʌɪç/ German name for **AUSTRIA**.

Ostia /'ɒstɪə/ an ancient city and harbour which was situated on the western coast of Italy at the mouth of the River Tiber. It was the first colony founded by ancient Rome and was a major port and commercial centre.

ostinato /ˌɒstɪ'nɑːtəʊ/ ▶ noun (pl. **ostinatos** or **ostinati** /-ti/) a continually repeated musical phrase or rhythm.
− ORIGIN Italian, literally 'obstinate'.

ostiole /'ɒstɪəʊl/ ▶ noun Botany (in some small algae and fungi) a small pore through which spores are discharged.
− ORIGIN mid 19th cent.: from Latin *ostiolum*, diminutive of *ostium* 'opening'.

ostium /'ɒstɪəm/ ▶ noun (pl. **ostia** /'ɒstɪə/) Anatomy & Zoology an opening into a vessel or cavity of the body.
 ■ Zoology each of a number of pores in the wall of a sponge, through which water is drawn in.
− ORIGIN early 17th cent.: from Latin, 'door, opening'.

ostler /'ɒslə/ (also **hostler**) ▶ noun historical a man employed to look after the horses of people staying at an inn.
− ORIGIN late Middle English: from Old French *hostelier* 'innkeeper', from *hostel* (see **HOSTEL**).

Ostmark /'ɒstmɑːk/ ▶ noun historical the basic monetary unit of the former German Democratic Republic, equal to 100 pfennigs.
− ORIGIN German, literally 'east mark' (see **MARK²**).

Ostpolitik /'ɒstpɒlɪˌtiːk/ ▶ noun [mass noun] historical the foreign policy of détente of western European countries with reference to the former communist bloc, especially the opening of relations with the Eastern bloc by the Federal Republic of Germany (West Germany) in the 1960s.
− ORIGIN German, from *Ost* 'east' + *Politik* 'politics'.

ostracize /'ɒstrəsʌɪz/ (also **-ise**) ▶ verb [with obj.] exclude (someone) from a society or group: *she called for those who helped the bombers to be ostracized.*
 ■ (in ancient Greece) banish (an unpopular or too powerful citizen) from a city for five or ten years by popular vote.
− DERIVATIVES **ostracism** noun.
− ORIGIN mid 17th cent.: from Greek *ostrakizein*, from *ostrakon* 'shell or potsherd' (on which names were written, in voting to banish unpopular citizens).

Ostracoda /ˌɒstrə'kəʊdə/ Zoology a class of minute aquatic crustaceans that have a hinged shell from which the antennae protrude, and a reduced number of appendages.
− DERIVATIVES **ostracod** /'ɒstrəkɒd/ noun.
− ORIGIN modern Latin (plural), from Greek *ostrakōdēs* 'testaceous', from *ostrakon* 'shell'.

ostracoderm /ɒ'strakədəːm/ ▶ noun an early fossil jawless fish of the Cambrian to Devonian periods, having a heavily armoured body.
 ● Class Agnatha: several orders.
− ORIGIN late 19th cent.: from modern Latin *Ostracodermi* (former taxonomic name), from Greek *ostrakon* 'shell' + *derma* 'skin'.

ostracon /'ɒstrəkɒn/ (also **ostrakon**) ▶ noun (pl. **ostraca** or **ostraka**) a potsherd used as a writing surface.
− ORIGIN Greek, 'hard shell or potsherd'.

Ostrava /'ɒstrəvə/ an industrial city in the Moravian lowlands of the NE Czech Republic; pop. 327,550 (1991). It is situated in the coal-mining region of Silesia.

ostrich ▶ noun **1** a flightless swift-running African bird with a long neck, long legs, and two toes on each foot. It is the largest living bird, with males reaching a height of up to 2.75 m.
 ● *Struthio camelus*, the only member of the family Struthionidae.
 2 a person who refuses to face reality or accept facts. [ORIGIN: from the popular belief that ostriches bury their heads in the sand if pursued.]
− ORIGIN Middle English: from Old French *ostriche*, from Latin *avis* 'bird' + late Latin *struthio* (from Greek *strouthiōn* 'ostrich', from *strouthos* 'sparrow or ostrich').

ostrich dinosaur ▶ noun a lightly built toothless bipedal dinosaur of the late Cretaceous period,

adapted for running and somewhat resembling an ostrich. Also called **ORNITHOMIMOSAUR**.
• Infraorder Ornithomimisauria, suborder Theropoda, order Saurischia: several genera, including *Gallimimus*, *Ornithomimus*, and *Struthiomimus*.

Ostrogoth /ˈɒstrəgɒθ/ ▶ **noun** a member of the eastern branch of the Goths, who conquered Italy in the 5th–6th centuries AD.
– DERIVATIVES **Ostrogothic** adjective.
– ORIGIN from late Latin *Ostrogothi* (plural), from the Germanic base of **EAST** + late Latin *Gothi* 'Goths'.

Ostwald /ˈɒstvalt/, Friedrich Wilhelm (1853–1932), German physical chemist. He established physical chemistry as a separate discipline and contributed to pioneering work on catalysis, chemical affinities, and the development of a new quantitative colour theory. Nobel Prize for Chemistry (1909).

Oswald, Lee Harvey (1939–63), American alleged assassin of John F. Kennedy. He denied the charge of assassinating the president, but was murdered before he could be brought to trial.

Oswald of York, St (d.992), English prelate and Benedictine monk. As Archbishop of York, he founded several monasteries and, with St Dunstan, revived the Church and learning in 10th-century England. Feast day, 28 February.

oswego tea /ɒˈzwiːgəʊ/ ▶ **noun** see **BERGAMOT**[1] (sense 3).
– ORIGIN mid 18th cent.: named after a river and town in the northern part of the state of New York.

OT ▶ **abbreviation for** ■ occupational therapist. ■ occupational therapy. ■ Old Testament.

-ot[1] ▶ **suffix** forming nouns which were originally diminutives: *ballot* | *parrot*.
– ORIGIN from French.

-ot[2] ▶ **suffix** (forming nouns) denoting a person of a particular type: *harlot* | *idiot*.
■ denoting a native of a place: *Cypriot*.
– ORIGIN via French and Latin from Greek *ōtēs*.

Otago /ɒˈtɑːgəʊ/ a region of New Zealand, on the SE coast of South Island.

otaku /əʊˈtɑːkuː/ ▶ **plural noun** (in Japan) young people who are highly skilled in or obsessed with computer technology to the detriment of their social skills.
– ORIGIN Japanese, literally 'your house', alluding to the reluctance of such young people to leave the house.

O

otalgia /əʊˈtaldʒə/ ▶ **noun** [mass noun] Medicine earache.
– ORIGIN mid 17th cent.: from Greek *ōtalgia*, from *ous, ōt-* 'ear' + *algos* 'pain'.

OTC ▶ **abbreviation for** ■ (in the UK) Officers' Training Corps. ■ over the counter.

OTE ▶ **abbreviation for** on-target earnings, as used to indicate the expected salary of a salesperson, with bonuses and commission.

other ▶ **adjective** & **pronoun 1** used to refer to a person or thing that is different or distinct from one already mentioned or known about: [as adj.] *stick the camera on a tripod or* ***some other*** *means of support* | *other people found her difficult* | [as pronoun] *a language unrelated to any other*.
■ alternative of two: [as adj.] *the other side of the page* | [as pronoun] *flinging up first one arm and then the other* | ***one or other*** *of his parents*. ■ those remaining in a group; those not already mentioned: [as adj.] *they took the other three away in an ambulance* | [as pronoun] *Freddie set off and* ***the others*** *followed*.
2 further; additional: [as adj.] *one other word of advice* | [as pronoun] *Labour would have 49 MPs plus ten others*.
3 [pronoun] (**the other**) informal used euphemistically to refer to sexual intercourse: *a bit of the other*.
4 [pronoun] (**the other**) Philosophy & Sociology that which is distinct from, different from, or opposite to something or oneself.
– PHRASES **no other** archaic nothing else: *we can do no other*. **other than** [with negative or in questions] apart from; except: *he claims not to own anything other than his home*. ■ differently or different from; otherwise than: *there is no suggestion that we are to take this other than literally*. **on the other hand** see **HAND**. **the other day** (or **night**, **week**, etc.) a few days (or nights, weeks, etc.) ago. **the other thing** Brit. dated, chiefly humorous an unexpressed alternative: *if you keep a lot of rules I'll reward you, and if you don't I'll do the other thing*. **someone** (or **something** or **somehow** etc.) **or other** some unspecified or unknown person, thing, manner, etc. (used to express vagueness or uncertainty): *they were protesting about something or other*.
– ORIGIN Old English *ōther*, of Germanic origin; related to Dutch and German *ander*, from an Indo-European root meaning 'different'.

other half ▶ **noun** (**one's other half**) Brit. informal a person's wife, husband, or partner.
– PHRASES **how the other half lives** used to express or allude to the way of life of a different group in society, especially a wealthier one.

otherness ▶ **noun** [mass noun] the quality or fact of being different: *the developed world has been celebrating African music while altogether denying its otherness*.

other place ▶ **noun** (**the other place**) Brit. humorous hell, as opposed to heaven.
■ Oxford University as regarded by Cambridge, and vice versa. ■ the House of Lords as regarded by the House of Commons, and vice versa.

other ranks ▶ **plural noun** Brit. (in the armed forces) all those who are not commissioned officers.

otherwhere ▶ **adverb** & **pronoun** archaic or poetic/literary elsewhere.

otherwise ▶ **adverb 1** in circumstances different from those present or considered; or else: *the collection is a good draw that brings visitors who might not come otherwise* | *I'm not motivated by money, otherwise I would have quit*.
2 in other respects; apart from that: *an otherwise totally black cat with a single white whisker*.
3 in a different way: *he means mischief—it's no good pretending otherwise* | *all the staff were* ***otherwise engaged***.
■ as an alternative: *the Cosa Nostra,* ***otherwise known as*** *the Brotherhood*.
▶ **adjective** [predic.] in a different state or situation: *I would that it were otherwise*.
– PHRASES **or** (or **and**) **otherwise** indicating the opposite of or a contrast to something stated: *we don't want a president, elected or otherwise*.
– ORIGIN Old English *on ōthre wisan* (see **OTHER**, **WISE**[2]).

other woman ▶ **noun** (**the other woman**) the lover of a married or similarly attached man.

other world ▶ **noun** (**the other world**) the spiritual world or afterlife.

other-worldly ▶ **adjective** of or relating to an imaginary or spiritual world: *music of an almost other-worldly beauty*.
■ unworldly: *celibate clerics with a very other-worldly outlook*.
– DERIVATIVES **other-worldliness** noun.

Othman /ˈɒθmən/ variant form of **OSMAN I**.

Otho /ˈəʊθəʊ/, Marcus Salvius (AD 32–69), Roman emperor January–April 69. He was proclaimed emperor after he had procured the death of Galba in a conspiracy of the praetorian guard, but the German legions, led by their imperial candidate, Vitellius, defeated his troops and Otho committed suicide.

otic /ˈəʊtɪk, ˈɒtɪk/ ▶ **adjective** Anatomy of or relating to the ear.
– ORIGIN mid 17th cent.: from Greek *ōtikos*, from *ous, ōt-* 'ear'.

-otic ▶ **suffix** forming adjectives and nouns corresponding to nouns ending in *-osis* (such as *neurotic* corresponding to *neurosis*).
– DERIVATIVES **-otically** suffix forming corresponding adverbs.
– ORIGIN from French *-otique*, via Latin from the Greek adjectival ending *-ōtikos*.

otiose /ˈəʊtɪəʊs, ˈəʊʃɪ-, -z/ ▶ **adjective** serving no practical purpose or result: *the linking commentary is often otiose*.
■ archaic indolent; idle.
– DERIVATIVES **otiosely** adverb.
– ORIGIN late 18th cent.: from Latin *otiosus*, from *otium* 'leisure'.

Otis /ˈəʊtɪs/, Elisha Graves (1811–61), American inventor and manufacturer. He produced the first efficient elevator with a safety device in 1852.

otitis /ə(ʊ)ˈtʌɪtɪs/ ▶ **noun** [mass noun] Medicine inflammation of the ear, usually distinguished as **otitis externa** (of the passage of the outer ear), **otitis media** (of the middle ear), and **otitis interna** (of the inner ear; labyrinthitis).
– ORIGIN late 18th cent.: modern Latin, from Greek *ous, ōt-* 'ear' + **-ITIS**.

oto- /ˈəʊtəʊ/ ▶ **combining form** (used chiefly in medical terms) of or relating to the ears: *otoscope*.
– ORIGIN from Greek *ous, ōt-* 'ear'.

otocyst ▶ **noun** another term for **STATOCYST**.

otolaryngology /ˌəʊtə(ʊ)larɪŋˈgɒlədʒi/ ▶ **noun** [mass noun] the study of diseases of the ear and throat.
– DERIVATIVES **otolaryngological** adjective, **otolaryngologist** noun.

otolith ▶ **noun** Zoology each of three small oval calcareous bodies in the inner ear of vertebrates, involved in sensing gravity and movement.
– DERIVATIVES **otolithic** adjective.

otology /əʊˈtɒlədʒi/ ▶ **noun** [mass noun] the study of the anatomy and diseases of the ear.
– DERIVATIVES **otological** adjective, **otologist** noun.

Otomanguean /ˌəʊtə(ʊ)ˈmaŋgɪən, -ˈmaŋgwɪən/ ▶ **adjective** of, relating to, or denoting a family of American Indian languages of central and southern Mexico, including Mixtec, Otomi, and Zapotec.
– ORIGIN 1940s: from **OTOMI** + *Mangue* (an extinct language of Costa Rica) + **-AN**.

Otomi /ˌəʊtəˈmiː/ ▶ **noun** (pl. same) **1** a member of an American Indian people inhabiting parts of central Mexico.
2 [mass noun] the Otomanguean language of this people.
▶ **adjective** of or relating to this people or their language.
– ORIGIN via American Spanish from Nahuatl *otomih*, literally 'unknown'.

O'Toole, Peter (Seamus) (b.1932), Irish-born British actor. Notable films include *Lawrence of Arabia* (1962) and *Goodbye Mr Chips* (1969); he is especially noted for his portrayals of eccentric characters.

otoplasty /ˈəʊtə(ʊ)ˌplasti/ ▶ **noun** (pl. **-ies**) a surgical operation to restore or enhance the appearance of an ear or the ears.

otorhinolaryngology /ˌəʊtə(ʊ)ˌrʌɪnəʊˌlarɪŋˈgɒlədʒi/ ▶ **noun** [mass noun] the study of diseases of the ear, nose, and throat.
– DERIVATIVES **otorhinolaryngologist** noun.

otosclerosis ▶ **noun** [mass noun] Medicine a hereditary disorder causing progressive deafness due to overgrowth of bone in the inner ear.
– DERIVATIVES **otosclerotic** adjective.

otoscope ▶ **noun** an instrument designed for visual examination of the eardrum and the passage of the outer ear, typically having a light and a set of lenses. Also called **AURISCOPE**.
– DERIVATIVES **otoscopic** adjective, **otoscopically** adverb.

ototoxic ▶ **adjective** Medicine having a toxic effect on the ear or its nerve supply.
– DERIVATIVES **ototoxicity** noun.

Otranto, Strait of /ɒˈtrantəʊ/ a channel linking the Adriatic Sea with the Ionian Sea and separating the 'heel' of Italy from Albania.

OTT Brit. informal ▶ **abbreviation for** over the top: *it's manic and unashamedly OTT*.

ottava rima /ɒˌtɑːvə ˈriːmə/ ▶ **noun** [mass noun] a form of poetry consisting of stanzas of eight lines of ten or eleven syllables, rhyming *abababcc*.
– ORIGIN late 18th cent.: from Italian, literally 'eighth rhyme'.

Ottawa /ˈɒtəwə, -wɑː/ the federal capital of Canada, on the Ottawa River (a tributary of the St Lawrence); pop. 313,990 (1991); metropolitan area pop. 920,860. Founded in 1827, it was named Bytown until 1854 after Colonel John By (1779–1836).

otter ▶ **noun 1** a semiaquatic fish-eating mammal of the weasel family, with an elongated body, dense fur, and webbed feet.
• *Lutra* and other genera, family Mustelidae: several species, including the **European otter** (*L. lutra*). See also **SEA OTTER**.
2 a piece of board used to carry fishing bait in water.
– ORIGIN Old English *otr, ot(t)or*, of Germanic origin; related to Greek *hudros* 'water snake'.

otter board ▶ **noun** either of a pair of boards or metal plates, attached to each side of the mouth of a trawl net at an angle which keeps the net open as it is pulled through the water.

otter dog (also **otter hound**) ▶ **noun** a large hound of a breed with a long rough coat, used in otter hunting.

otter shell ▶ noun a burrowing marine bivalve mollusc with a relatively thin elliptical shell.
● Genus *Lutraria*, family Mactridae: numerous species, including the **common otter shell** (*L. lutraria*).

otter shrew ▶ noun a semiaquatic mammal of the tenrec family, with a sleek body and long tail, native to central and West Africa.
● Genera *Potamogale* and *Micropotamogale*, family Tenrecidae: three species, including the **giant otter shrew** (*P. velox*), which resembles an otter.

otter trawl ▶ noun a trawl net fitted with an otter board.

Otto, Nikolaus August (1832–91), German engineer, whose name is given to the four-stroke cycle on which most internal-combustion engines work.

otto ▶ noun another term for **ATTAR**.

ottocento /ˌɒtə(ʊ)ˈtʃɛntəʊ/ ▶ adjective of or relating to the 19th century in Italy.
– ORIGIN Italian, literally '800' (shortened from *milottocento* '1800'), used with reference to the years 1800–99.

Otto I (912–73), king of the Germans 936–73, Holy Roman emperor 962–73; known as **Otto the Great**. As king of the Germans he carried out a policy of eastward expansion and as Holy Roman emperor he established a presence in Italy to rival that of the papacy.

Ottoman /ˈɒtəmən/ ▶ adjective historical **1** of or relating to the Turkish dynasty of Osman I (Othman I).
■ of or relating to the branch of the Turks to which he belonged. ■ of or relating to the Ottoman Empire ruled by his successors. **2** Turkish.
▶ noun (pl. **Ottomans**) a Turk, especially of the period of the Ottoman Empire.
– ORIGIN based on Arabic *'uṯmānī* (adjective), from *'Uṯmān* 'Othman'.

ottoman ▶ noun (pl. **ottomans**) **1** a low upholstered seat without a back or arms that typically serves also as a box, with the seat hinged to form a lid. **2** [mass noun] a heavy ribbed fabric made from silk and either cotton or wool.
– ORIGIN early 19th cent.: from French *ottomane*, feminine of *ottoman* 'Ottoman'.

Ottoman Empire the Turkish empire, established in northern Anatolia by Osman I at the end of the 13th century and expanded by his successors to include all of Asia Minor and much of SE Europe. After setbacks caused by the invasion of the Mongol ruler Tamerlane in 1402, Constantinople was captured in 1453 and the empire reached its zenith under Suleiman in the mid 16th century. It had greatly declined by the 19th century and collapsed after the First World War.

Ottoman Porte see **PORTE**.

Otto the Great see **OTTO I**.

Otway, Thomas (1652–85), English dramatist. He is chiefly remembered for his two blank verse tragedies, *The Orphan* (1680) and *Venice Preserved* (1682).

OU ▶ abbreviation for (in the UK) Open University.

ou¹ /əʊ/ ▶ noun (pl. **ouens** /ˈəʊənz/ or **ous**) S. African informal a man.
■ a person of unspecified sex.
– ORIGIN Afrikaans, probably from Dutch *ouwe* 'old man'.

ou² /ˈəʊuː/ ▶ noun a fruit-eating Hawaiian honeycreeper with a stout bill and green and yellow plumage. Compare with **O-O**.
● *Psittirostra psittacea*, family Drepanididae.
– ORIGIN late 19th cent.: the name in Hawaiian.

ouabain /ˈuːəbeɪn/ ▶ noun [mass noun] Chemistry a toxic compound obtained from certain trees, used as a very rapid cardiac stimulant. It is a polycyclic glycoside.
– ORIGIN late 19th cent.: via French from Somali *wabayo*, denoting a tree that yields poison (used on arrow points) containing ouabain.

Ouagadougou /ˌwaɡəˈduːɡuː/ the capital of Burkina; pop. 634,480 (est. 1991).

ouananiche /ˌwanəˈniːʃ/ ▶ noun (pl. same) Canadian an Atlantic salmon of landlocked populations living in lakes in Labrador and Newfoundland.
– ORIGIN late 19th cent.: via Canadian French from Algonquian.

oubaas /ˈəʊbɑːs/ ▶ noun S. African a head of a family.

■ an elderly man.
– ORIGIN Afrikaans, from Dutch *oud* 'old' + **BAAS**.

oubliette /ˌuːblɪˈɛt/ ▶ noun a secret dungeon with access only through a trapdoor in its ceiling.
– ORIGIN late 18th cent.: from French, from *oublier* 'forget'.

ouboet /ˈəʊbʊt/ ▶ noun S. African informal used as an affectionate way of addressing or referring to an older brother or male friend.
– ORIGIN Afrikaans, from *ou* 'old' + *boet* 'mate' (from Dutch dialect *boet* 'youngster').

ouch ▶ exclamation used to express pain.
– ORIGIN natural exclamation: first recorded in English in the mid 17th cent.

oud /uːd/ ▶ noun a form of lute or mandolin played principally in Arab countries.
– ORIGIN mid 18th cent.: from Arabic *al-'ūd*.

Oudenarde, Battle of /ˈuːdənɑːd/ a battle which took place in 1708 during the War of the Spanish Succession, near the town of Oudenarde in eastern Flanders, Belgium. A force of allied British and Austrian troops defeated the French.

Oudh /aʊd/ (also **Audh** or **Awadh**) a region of northern India. In 1877 it joined with Agra and in 1902 it formed the United Provinces of Agra and Oudh. This was renamed Uttar Pradesh in 1950.

oudstryder /ˈəʊtˌstreɪdə/ ▶ noun S. African a war veteran.
– ORIGIN Afrikaans, 'old soldier'.

ouens plural form of **OU¹**.

ought¹ ▶ modal verb (3rd sing. present and past **ought**) [with infinitive] **1** used to indicate duty or correctness, typically when criticizing someone's actions: *they ought to respect the law* | *it ought not to be allowed*.
■ used to indicate a desirable or expected state: *he ought to be able to take the initiative*. ■ used to give or ask advice: *what ought I to do?*
2 used to indicate something that is probable: *five minutes ought to be enough time*.
– ORIGIN Old English *āhte*, past tense of *āgan* 'owe' (see **OWE**).

> **USAGE** The verb **ought** is a modal verb and this means that, grammatically, it does not behave like ordinary verbs. In particular, the negative is formed with the word **not** alone and not also with auxiliary verbs such as **do** or **have**. Thus the standard construction for the negative is *he ought not to have gone*. The alternative forms *he **didn't** ought to have gone* and *he **hadn't** ought to have gone*, formed as if **ought** were an ordinary verb rather than a modal verb, are found in dialect from the 19th century but are not acceptable in standard modern English.

ought² (also **aught**) ▶ noun archaic term for **NOUGHT**.
– ORIGIN mid 19th cent.: perhaps from *an ought*, by wrong division of *a nought*; compare with **ADDER¹**.

ought³ ▶ pronoun variant spelling of **AUGHT¹**.

oughtn't ▶ contraction of ought not.

ouguiya /uːˈɡiːjə/ (also **ougiya**) ▶ noun the basic monetary unit of Mauritania, equal to five khoums.
– ORIGIN via French from Mauritanian Arabic, from Arabic *'ūkiyya*, from Greek *ounkia*, from Latin *uncia* 'ounce'.

Ouida /ˈwiːdə/ (1839–1908), English novelist; pseudonym of *Marie Louise de la Ramée*. Her novels, such as *Under Two Flags* (1867), are romances that are typically set in a fashionable world far removed from reality.

Ouija board /ˈwiːdʒə/ ▶ noun trademark a board with letters, numbers, and other signs around its edge, to which a planchette, movable pointer, or upturned glass points supposedly in answer to questions from people at a seance.
– ORIGIN late 19th cent.: *Ouija* from French *oui* 'yes' + German *ja* 'yes'.

ouklip /ˈəʊklɪp/ ▶ noun [mass noun] S. African an iron-rich lateritic conglomerate formed from the decomposition of underlying rocks by subsurface chemical weathering.
– ORIGIN late 19th cent.: from Afrikaans, from *ou* 'old' + *klip* 'rock, stone'.

Oulu /ˈəʊluː/ a city in central Finland, on the west coast, capital of a province of the same name; pop. 101,380 (1990). Swedish name **ULEÅBORG**.

ouma /ˈəʊmə/ ▶ noun S. African used as a respectful or affectionate form of address for a grandmother or elderly woman.

– ORIGIN Afrikaans, 'grandmother'.

ounce¹ ▶ noun **1** (abbrev.: **oz**) a unit of weight of one sixteenth of a pound avoirdupois (approximately 28 grams).
■ a unit of one twelfth of a pound troy or apothecaries' measure, equal to 480 grains (approximately 31 grams).
2 a very small amount of something: *Robyn summoned up every ounce of strength*.
– ORIGIN Middle English: from Old French *unce*, from Latin *uncia* 'twelfth part (of a pound or foot)'; compare with **INCH¹**.

ounce² ▶ noun another term for **SNOW LEOPARD**.
– ORIGIN Middle English: from Old French *once*, earlier *lonce* (the l- being misinterpreted as the definite article), based on Latin *lynx*, *lync-* (see **LYNX**).

oupa /ˈəʊpə/ ▶ noun S. African used as a respectful or affectionate form of address for a grandfather or elderly man.
– ORIGIN Afrikaans, 'grandfather'.

our ▶ possessive determiner **1** belonging to or associated with the speaker and one or more other people previously mentioned or easily identified: *Jo and I had our hair cut*.
■ belonging to or associated with people in general: *when we hear a sound, our brains identify the source quickly*.
2 used in formal contexts by a royal person or a writer or editor to refer to something belonging to or associated with himself or herself: *we want to know what you, our readers, think*.
3 informal, chiefly N. English used with a name to refer to a relative, friend, or colleague of the speaker: *really, she is a one, our Gillian*.
– ORIGIN Old English *ūre*, of Germanic origin; related to **US** and German *unser*.

-our¹ ▶ suffix variant spelling of **-OR²** surviving in some nouns such as *ardour*, *colour*.

-our² ▶ suffix variant spelling of **-OR¹** (as in *saviour*).

Our Father used as a title for God.
■ a name for the Lord's Prayer.

Our Lady used as a title for the Virgin Mary.

Our Lord used as a title for God or Jesus Christ.

ouroboros /jʊərəʊˈbɒrəs/ ▶ noun variant spelling of **UROBOROS**.

ours ▶ possessive pronoun used to refer to a thing or things belonging to or associated with the speaker and one or more other people previously mentioned or easily identified: *ours was the ugliest house on the block* | *this chat of ours is strictly between us*.

ourself ▶ pronoun [first person plural] **1** used instead of 'ourselves' typically when 'we' refers to people in general rather than a definite group of people: [reflexive] *we must choose which aspects of ourself to express to the world* | [emphatic] *this is our affair—we deal with it ourself*.
2 archaic used instead of 'myself' by a sovereign or other person in authority.

> **USAGE** The standard reflexive form corresponding to we and us is ourselves, as in *we can only blame ourselves*. The singular form **ourself**, first recorded in the 15th century, is sometimes used in modern English, typically where 'we' refers to people in general. This use, though logical, is uncommon and not widely accepted in standard English.

ourselves ▶ pronoun [first person plural] **1** [reflexive] used as the object of a verb or preposition when this is the same as the subject of the clause and the subject is the speaker and one or more other people considered together: *for this we can only blame ourselves*.
2 [emphatic] we or us personally (used to emphasize the speaker and one or more other people considered together): *we invented it ourselves*.
– PHRASES **(not) be ourselves** see *be oneself*, *not be oneself* at **BE**. **by ourselves** see *by oneself* at **BY**.

-ous ▶ suffix forming adjectives: **1** characterized by; of the nature of: *dangerous* | *mountainous*.
2 Chemistry denoting an element in a lower valency: *ferrous* | *sulphurous*. Compare with **-IC**.
– DERIVATIVES **-ously** suffix forming corresponding adverbs, **-ousness** suffix forming corresponding nouns.
– ORIGIN from Anglo-Norman French, or Old French *-eus*, from Latin *-osus*.

Ouse /uːz/ **1** (also **Great Ouse**) a river of eastern England, which rises in Northamptonshire and

flows 257 km (160 miles) eastwards then northwards through East Anglia to the Wash near King's Lynn.
2 a river of NE England, formed at the confluence of the Ure and Swale in North Yorkshire and flowing 92 km (57 miles) south-eastwards through York to the Humber estuary.
3 a river of SE England, which rises in the Weald of West Sussex and flows 48 km (30 miles) south-eastwards to the English Channel.
4 (also **Little Ouse**) a river of East Anglia, which forms a tributary of the Great Ouse.

ousel ▶ **noun** variant spelling of OUZEL.

oust /aʊst/ ▶ **verb** [with obj.] drive out or expel (someone) from a position or place: *the reformists were ousted from power.*
■ Law deprive (someone) of or exclude (someone) from possession of something. ■ take away (a court's jurisdiction) in a matter.
– ORIGIN late Middle English (as a legal term): from Anglo-Norman French *ouster* 'take away', from Latin *obstare* 'oppose, hinder'.

ouster ▶ **noun** [mass noun] **1** Law ejection from a freehold or other possession; deprivation of an inheritance.
■ removal from the jurisdiction of the courts. ■ [count noun] a clause that is or is claimed to be outside the jurisdiction of the courts.
2 chiefly N. Amer. dismissal or expulsion from a position: *a showdown which may lead to his ouster as leader of the Party.*

out ▶ **adverb** **1** moving or appearing to move away from a particular place, especially one that is enclosed or hidden: *he walked out into the street | watch the stars come out.*
■ situated or operating in the open air, away from buildings: *the search-and-rescue team have been out looking for you.* ■ no longer detained in prison: *they would be out on bail in no time.*
2 away from one's usual base or residence: *the team had put on a marvellous display out in Georgia.*
■ in a public place for purposes of pleasure or entertainment: *an evening out at a restaurant.*
3 to sea, away from the land: *the Persian fleet put out from Cyprus.*
■ (of the tide) falling or at its lowest level: *the tide was going out.*
4 indicating a specified distance away from the goal line or finishing line: *he scored from 70 metres out.*
5 so as to be revealed or known: *find out what you can.*
■ aloud; so as to be heard: *Miss Beard cried out in horror.*
6 at or to an end: *the romance fizzled out.*
■ so as to be finished or complete: *I'll leave them to fight it out | I typed out the poem.* ■ in various other completive uses: *the crowd had thinned out | he crossed out a word.*
7 (of a light or fire) so as to be extinguished or no longer burning: *at ten o'clock the lights went out.*
■ (of a stain or mark) no longer visible; removed: *try and get the stain out.*
▶ **preposition** non-standard contraction of OUT OF: *he ran out the door.*
▶ **adjective** [predic.] **1** not at home or at one's place of work: *if he called, she'd pretend to be out.*
2 revealed or made public: *the secret was soon out.*
■ (of a flower) in bloom; open. ■ published: *the book should be out before the end of the month.* ■ informal in existence or use: *it works as well as any system that's out.* ■ open about one's homosexuality: *I had been out since I was 17.*
3 no longer alight; extinguished: *the fire was nearly out.*
4 at an end: *school was out for the summer.*
■ informal no longer in fashion: *grunge is out.*
5 not possible or worth considering: *a trip to the seaside is out for a start.*
6 in a state of unconsciousness.
■ Boxing unable to rise from the floor.
7 mistaken; in error: *he was slightly out in his calculations.*
8 (of the ball in tennis and similar games) outside the designated playing area.
9 Cricket & Baseball no longer batting or at bat, having had one's innings or at bat ended by the fielding side: *England were all out for 159.*
▶ **noun** **1** informal a way of escaping from a problem or dilemma: *he was desperately looking for an out.*
2 Baseball an act of putting a player out.
3 (**the outs**) the political party out of office.
▶ **verb** [with obj.] **1** knock out (someone).
2 informal reveal the homosexuality of (a prominent person).
3 W. Indian extinguish: *out the lamp when you're ready.*
4 dated expel, reject, or dismiss (someone or something): *they had outed Asquith quite easily.*
– PHRASES **at outs** (N. Amer. **on the outs**) in dispute: *you were* **at outs with** *my uncle Ned.* **not out** Cricket (of a side or batsman) having begun an innings and not been dismissed. **out and about** (of a person, especially after an illness) engaging in normal activity. **out for** intent on having: *he was out for a good time.* **out of 1** moving or situated away from (a place, typically one that is enclosed or hidden): *he came out of prison.* ■ situated a specified distance from (a place): *they lived eight miles out of town.* ■ taken or appearing to be taken from (a particular type of writing, genre, or artistic performance): *a romance straight out of a fairy tale.* ■ eliminated from (a competition): *Oxford United are out of the FA Cup.* **2** spoken by: *still not a word out of Pearsall.* **3** using (a particular thing) as raw material: *a bench fashioned out of a fallen tree trunk.* ■ using (a particular thing) as a source of some benefit: *you should not expect too much out of life.* ■ having (the thing mentioned) as a motivation: *she did it out of spite.* ■ indicating the dam of a pedigree animal, especially a horse. **4** from among (a number): *nine times out of ten.* **5** not having (a particular thing): *they had run out of cash.* **out of it** informal **1** not included; rejected: *I hate feeling out of it.* **2** unaware of what is happening as a result of being uninformed. ■ N. Amer. unable to think or react properly as a result of being drowsy. ■ Brit. drunk. **out to do something** keenly striving to do something: *they were out to impress.* **out with it** [in imperative] say what you are thinking.
– ORIGIN Old English *ūt* (adverb), *ūtian* (verb), of Germanic origin; related to Dutch *uit* and German *aus.*

USAGE The use of **out** as a preposition (rather than the standard prepositional phrase **out of**), as in *he threw it* **out** *the window,* is common in informal contexts but is not widely accepted in standard English.

out- ▶ **prefix** **1** to the point of surpassing or exceeding: *outfight | outperform.*
2 external; separate; from outside: *outbuildings | outpatient.*
3 away from; outward: *outbound | outpost.*

outa ▶ **preposition** variant spelling of OUTTA.

outact ▶ **verb** [with obj.] surpass (someone) in acting or performing something.

outage /ˈaʊtɪdʒ/ ▶ **noun** a period when a power supply or other service is not available or when equipment is closed down.

out and out ▶ **adjective** [attrib.] in every respect; absolute: *an out-and-out rogue.*
▶ **adverb** completely: *he was induced to part out and out with all the money.*

out-and-outer ▶ **noun** archaic, informal an out-and-out possessor of a particular quality.

outasight ▶ **exclamation** informal an expression of surprise and delight.

outback ▶ **noun** (**the outback**) the remote and usually uninhabited inland districts of Australia.
■ any remote or sparsely populated inland region.
– DERIVATIVES **outbacker** noun.

outbalance ▶ **verb** [with obj.] be more valuable, important, or influential than: *their high capacity outbalances this defect.*

outbid ▶ **verb** (**-bidding**; past and past participle **-bid**) [with obj.] offer to pay a higher price for something than (another person): *residential builders could always outbid any farmer for the land round London.*

outboard ▶ **adjective** & **adverb** on, towards, or near the outside of a ship or aircraft: [as adj.] *the outboard wing panels* | [as adv.] *the chart table faces outboard.*
■ [as adj.] (of a motor) portable and attachable to the outside of the stern of a boat. ■ [as adj.] (of an electronic accessory) in a separate container from the device with which it is used.
▶ **noun** an outboard motor.
■ a boat with such a motor.
– PHRASES **outboard of** to the outside or on the far side of: *the controls are placed just outboard of the wheel.*

outbound ▶ **adjective** & **adverb** travelling away from a particular place, especially on the first leg of a return journey: [as adj.] *an outbound flight* | [as adv.] *flying outbound.*

outbox ▶ **verb** [with obj.] Boxing defeat (an opponent) by superior boxing ability.

outbrave ▶ **verb** [with obj.] archaic outdo in bravery: *I would outbrave the hart most daring on the earth.*
■ face (something) with a show of brave defiance: *the Duke sat outfacing his accusers, and outbraving their accusations.*

outbreak ▶ **noun** the sudden or violent start of something unwelcome, such as war, disease, etc.: *the outbreak of World War II.*

outbreed ▶ **verb** (past and past participle **-bred**) [with obj.] [usu. as noun **outbreeding**] breed from parents not closely related: *many specific genetic factors are known which regulate the degree of outbreeding.*

outbuilding ▶ **noun** a detached building such as a shed, barn, or garage that belongs to a more important one, such as a house or farm.

outburst ▶ **noun** a sudden release of strong emotion: *an angry outburst from the prime minister.*
■ a sudden outbreak of a particular activity: *a wild outburst of applause.* ■ a volcanic eruption. ■ Physics a sudden emission of energy or particles: *a very dramatic outburst of neutrons.*

outcall ▶ **noun** a house call made by a prostitute.

outcast ▶ **noun** a person who has been rejected by their society or social group.
▶ **adjective** (of a person) rejected or cast out: *they can be made to feel outcast and inadequate.*

outcaste ▶ **noun** (in Hindu society) a person who has no caste; a person expelled from their caste.
▶ **verb** [with obj.] cause (someone) to lose their caste: *he has deliberately elected to outcaste himself.*

outclass ▶ **verb** [with obj.] be far superior to: *Villa totally outclassed us in the first half.*

outcome ▶ **noun** the way a thing turns out; a consequence: *it is the outcome of the vote that counts.*

outcompete ▶ **verb** [with obj.] surpass (someone) in competition: *they were outcompeted by their foreign rivals.*
■ Biology displace (another species) in the competition for space, food, or other resources.

outcrop ▶ **noun** a rock formation that is visible on the surface: *dramatic limestone outcrops.*
▶ **verb** (**-cropped**, **-cropping**) [no obj.] [often as noun **outcropping**] appear as an outcrop: *jumbled outcroppings of bedrock.*

outcross ▶ **verb** [with obj.] breed (an animal or plant) with one not closely related.
▶ **noun** an animal or plant produced as the result of such cross-breeding.

outcry ▶ **noun** (pl. **-ies**) an exclamation or shout: *an outcry of spontaneous passion.*
■ a strong expression of public disapproval or anger: *the public outcry over the bombing.*

outcurve ▶ **noun** Baseball a ball pitched so as to curve away from the batter.

outdated ▶ **adjective** out of date; obsolete.
– DERIVATIVES **outdatedness** noun.

outdistance ▶ **verb** [with obj.] leave (a competitor or pursuer) far behind: *she could maintain a fast enough pace to outdistance any pursuers.*

outdo ▶ **verb** (**-does**, **-doing**; past **-did**; past participle **-done**) [with obj.] be more successful than: *the men tried to outdo each other in their generosity |* **not to be outdone**, *Vicky and Laura reached the same standard.*

outdoor ▶ **adjective** [attrib.] done, situated, or used out of doors: *a huge outdoor concert.*
■ (of a person) fond of the open air or open-air activities.

outdoor pursuits ▶ **plural noun** Brit. open-air sporting or leisure activities, such as orienteering, mountaineering, and canoeing.

outdoors ▶ **adverb** in or into the open air; outside a building or shelter: *it was warm enough to eat outdoors.*
▶ **noun** (usu. **the outdoors**) any area outside buildings or shelter, typically that far away from human habitation: *a lover of* **the great outdoors**.

outdoorsman ▶ **noun** (pl. **-men**) a man who spends a lot of time outdoors or doing outdoor activities.

outdoorsy ▶ **adjective** informal, chiefly N. Amer. of, associated with, or fond of the outdoors: *the outdoorsy fragrance of pines.*

outdrive ▶ **verb** (past **-drove**; past participle **-driven**) [with obj.] **1** drive a golf ball further than (another player): *Buck outdrove him by forty yards.*

2 drive a vehicle better or faster than (someone else): *he knew he couldn't outdrive the police.*
▶ noun an outboard motor.

outer ▶ adjective [attrib.] outside; external: *the outer door.*
■ further from the centre or inside: *the outer city bypass.* ■ (especially in place names) more remote: *Outer Mongolia.* ■ objective or physical; not subjective.
▶ noun an external or further out thing or part, in particular:
■ Brit. the division of a target furthest from the bullseye; a shot that strikes this. ■ Brit. an outer garment or part of one: *boots with stiff leather outers.* ■ Brit. a container in which packaged objects are placed for transport or display. ■ Austral. informal the part of a racecourse outside the enclosure.
– ORIGIN late Middle English: from **OUT** + **-ER**², replacing earlier **UTTER**¹.

outer bar ▶ noun (**the outer bar**) (in the UK) a collective term for barristers who are not Queen's or King's Counsels.

Outer Hebrides see **HEBRIDES**.

Outer House (in full **the Outer House of the Court of Session**) (in Scotland) a law court that hears cases in the first instance, presided over by a single judge (a Lord Ordinary).

Outer Mongolia see **MONGOLIA**.

outermost ▶ adjective [attrib.] furthest from the centre: *the outermost layer of the earth.*
▶ pronoun the one that is furthest from the centre: *the orbit of the outermost of these eight planets.*

outer planet ▶ noun a planet whose orbit lies outside the asteroid belt, i.e. Jupiter, Saturn, Uranus, Neptune, or Pluto.

outer space ▶ noun [mass noun] the physical universe beyond the earth's atmosphere.

outerwear ▶ noun [mass noun] clothing worn over other clothes, especially outdoors.

outface ▶ verb [with obj.] disconcert or defeat (an opponent) by confronting them boldly: *these achievements were based on outfacing militant unions.*

outfall ▶ noun the place where a river, drain, or sewer empties into the sea, a river, or a lake.

outfield ▶ noun **1** the outer part of the field of play in various sports, in particular:
■ Cricket the part of the field furthest from the wicket. ■ Baseball the grassy area beyond the infield. ■ [treated as sing. or pl.] the players stationed in the outfield, collectively.
2 the outlying land of a farm.
– DERIVATIVES **outfielder** noun.

outfight ▶ verb (past and past participle **-fought**) [with obj.] fight better than and beat (an opponent).

outfit ▶ noun a set of clothes worn together, especially for a particular occasion or purpose: *a riding outfit.*
■ [usu. with adj. or noun modifier] informal a group of people undertaking a particular activity together, especially a group of musicians, a sports team, or a business concern: *Scotland's best jazz outfit.* ■ [with adj. or noun modifier] a complete set of equipment or articles needed for a particular purpose: *a first-aid outfit.*
▶ verb (**-fitted**, **-fitting**) [with obj.] (usu. **be outfitted**) provide (someone) with a set of clothes: *warders outfitted in special suits.*
■ provide with equipment: *planes outfitted with sophisticated electronic gear.*

outfitter (also **outfitters**) ▶ noun Brit. dated an establishment that sells men's clothing.
■ N. Amer. an establishment that sells equipment, typically for outdoor pursuits: *a canoe outfitter.*

outflank ▶ verb [with obj.] move round the side of (an enemy) so as to outmanoeuvre them: *the Germans had sought to outflank them from the north-east.*
■ figurative outwit: *an attempt to outflank the opposition.*

outflow ▶ noun a large amount of money, liquid, or people that moves or is transferred out of a place: *an outflow of foreign currency* | [mass noun] *capital outflow took place on a very large scale.*

outfox ▶ verb [with obj.] informal defeat (someone) by being more clever or cunning than them.

outgas ▶ verb (**-gases**, **-gassing**, **-gassed**) [with obj.] release or give off (a substance) as a gas or vapour: *glue may outgas smelly volatile organic compounds* | [no obj.] *samples are heated and begin to outgas.*

outgeneral ▶ verb (**-generalled**, **-generalling**; US **-generaled**, **-generaling**) [with obj.] get the better of by superior strategy or tactics: *he had outgeneraled a few Indians at the battle.*

outgo archaic ▶ verb (**-goes**; past **-went**; past participle **-gone**) [with obj.] go faster than: *he on horseback outgoes him on foot.*
▶ noun [mass noun] the outlay of money: *the secret of success lies in the relation of income to outgo.*

outgoing ▶ adjective **1** friendly and socially confident.
2 [attrib.] leaving an office or position, especially after an election or term of office: *the outgoing Prime Minister.*
■ going out or away from a particular place: *incoming and outgoing calls.*
▶ noun Brit. **1** (**outgoings**) a person's regular expenditure.
2 an instance of going out: *the inward deliveries and outgoings of raw materials.*

outgross ▶ verb [with obj.] surpass in gross takings or profit: *the film has outgrossed all other movie comedies.*

out-group ▶ noun **1** Sociology those people who do not belong to a specific in-group.
2 Biology a group of organisms not belonging to the group whose evolutionary relationships are being investigated. Such a group is used for comparison, to assess which characteristics of the group being studied are more widely distributed and may therefore be older in origin.

outgrow ▶ verb (past **-grew**; past participle **-grown**) [with obj.] grow too big for (something): *the cradle which Patrick had outgrown.*
■ leave behind as one matures: *her chest infections were long outgrown.* ■ grow faster or taller than: *the more vigorous plants outgrow their weaker neighbours.*
– PHRASES **outgrow one's strength** Brit. become lanky and weak through excessively rapid growth.

outgrowth ▶ noun something that grows out of something else: *the eye first appears as an outgrowth from the brain.*
■ a natural development or result of something: *the book is an imaginative outgrowth of practical criticism.* ■ [mass noun] the process of growing out: *with further outgrowth the radius and ulna develop.*

outguess ▶ verb [with obj.] outwit (someone) by guessing correctly what they intend to do: *a brilliant military commander outguesses the enemy.*

outgun ▶ verb (**-gunned**, **-gunning**) [with obj.] [often as adj. **outgunned**] have better or more weaponry than: *the outgunned Muslims* | figurative *the prime minister was outgunned at the summit.*
■ shoot better than: *the correspondents proudly outgunned the army sharpshooters.*

out-half ▶ noun Rugby another term for **STAND-OFF HALF**.

outhaul ▶ noun Sailing a rope used to haul out the clew of a sail.

outhouse ▶ noun a building such as a shed or barn that is built on to or in the grounds of a house.
■ an outside toilet.
▶ verb [with obj.] store or accommodate away from the main storage or accommodation area: *books outhoused in the annex take longer to deliver.*

outie /'aʊti/ ▶ noun (pl. **-ies**) S. African informal a homeless person.

outing ▶ noun **1** a trip taken for pleasure, especially one lasting a day or less: *they would go on family outings to the movies.*
■ a brief journey from home: *her daily outing to the shops.* ■ informal an appearance in something, especially a sporting event or film: *Madonna's first screen outing in three years.*
2 [mass noun] the practice or policy of revealing the homosexuality of a prominent person.
– ORIGIN late Middle English (in the sense 'the action of going out or of expelling'): from the verb **OUT** + **-ING**¹.

outing flannel ▶ noun [mass noun] US a type of flannelette.

out island ▶ noun an island situated away from the mainland.

outjie /'əʊki, -tʃi/ ▶ noun (pl. **-ies**) S. African informal a child.
– ORIGIN Afrikaans, from *ou* 'old' + the diminutive suffix *-jie*.

outjockey ▶ verb (**-eys**, **-eyed**) [with obj.] dated outwit by deception.

outjutting ▶ adjective protruding.

outlander ▶ noun chiefly N. Amer. a foreigner; a stranger.

outlandish ▶ adjective **1** looking or sounding bizarre or unfamiliar: *the most outlandish ideas.*
2 archaic foreign; alien: *three wise, outlandish kings.*
– DERIVATIVES **outlandishly** adverb, **outlandishness** noun.
– ORIGIN Old English *ūtlendisc* 'not native', from *ūtland* 'foreign country'.

outlast ▶ verb [with obj.] outlive; last longer than: *the kind of beauty that will outlast youth.*

outlaw ▶ noun a person who has broken the law, especially one who remains at large or is a fugitive.
■ historical a person deprived of the benefit and protection of the law.
▶ verb [with obj.] ban; make illegal: *secondary picketing has been outlawed* | [as adj. **outlawed**] *the outlawed terrorist group.*
■ historical deprive (someone) of the benefit and protection of the law.
– DERIVATIVES **outlawry** noun.
– ORIGIN late Old English *ūtlaga* (noun), *ūtlagian* (verb), from Old Norse *útlagi*, noun from *útlagr* 'outlawed or banished'.

outlay ▶ noun an amount of money spent on something.

outlet ▶ noun a means by which something escapes or is released, in particular:
■ a pipe or hole through which water or gas may escape. ■ the mouth of a river. ■ an output socket in an electrical device. ■ a point from which goods are sold or distributed: *a fast-food outlet.* ■ a market for goods: *the state system provided an outlet for farm produce.* ■ figurative a means of expressing one's talents, energy, or emotions: *writing became the main outlet for his energies.*
– ORIGIN Middle English: from **OUT-** + the verb **LET**¹.

outlet box ▶ noun a box giving access to connections to electric wiring where it is led out of conduits.

outlet pass ▶ noun Basketball a pass from a player who has just taken a rebound to a teammate who can initiate an offensive break.

outlier /'aʊtlʌɪə/ ▶ noun a person or thing situated away or detached from the main body or system: *less accessible islands and outliers.*
■ Geology a younger rock formation isolated among older rocks. ■ Statistics a data point on a graph or in a set of results that is very much bigger or smaller than the next nearest data point.

outline ▶ noun **1** a line or set of lines enclosing or indicating the shape of an object in a sketch or diagram.
■ a line or set of lines of this type, perceived as defining the contours or bounds of an object: *the outlines of her face.* ■ a representation of a word in shorthand.
2 a general plan showing the essential features but not the detail: *a course outline.*
■ the main features or general principles of something: *the main outlines of Eustace's career.*
▶ verb [with obj.] **1** draw, trace, or define the outer edge or shape of (something): *her large eyes were darkly outlined with kohl.*
2 give a summary of (something): *she outlined the case briefly.*
– PHRASES **in outline** in broad terms: *the plan has been agreed in outline.*

outliner ▶ noun a computer program, or part of a program, which allows its user to create and edit a hierarchically arranged outline of the logical structure of a document.

outlive ▶ verb [with obj.] (of a person) live longer than (another person): *women generally outlive men.*
■ survive or last beyond (a specified period or expected lifespan): *the organization had largely outlived its usefulness.* ■ archaic live through (an experience): *the world has outlived much.*

outlook ▶ noun a person's point of view or general attitude to life: *broaden your outlook on life.*
■ a view: *the pleasant outlook from the club window.* ■ the prospect for the future: *the deteriorating economic outlook.* ■ the weather as forecast for the near future.

outlying ▶ adjective [attrib.] situated far from a centre; remote: *an outlying village.*

outman ▶ verb (**-manned**, **-manning**) [with obj.] outnumber: [as adj. **outmanned**] *outgunned and outmanned armies.*

outmanoeuvre ▶ verb [with obj.] evade (an opponent) by moving faster or with greater agility: *the YF-22 can outmanoeuvre any fighter flying today.*

■use skill and cunning to secure an advantage over (someone): *he would be able to outmanoeuvre his critics.*

outmatch ▶verb [with obj.] be superior to (an opponent or rival).

outmeasure ▶verb [with obj.] archaic exceed in quantity or extent: *there are some days that might outmeasure years.*

outmigrant ▶noun a person who has migrated from one place to another, especially within a country.
– DERIVATIVES **outmigration** noun.

outmoded ▶adjective old-fashioned.
– DERIVATIVES **outmodedness** noun.

outmost ▶adjective chiefly archaic furthest away: *the outmost reaches of the empire.*
– ORIGIN Middle English: variant of *utmest* 'utmost'.

outnumber ▶verb [with obj.] be more numerous than: *women outnumbered men by three to one.*

out-of-area ▶adjective (of a military operation) conducted away from the place of origin or expected place of action of the force concerned.

out-of-body experience ▶noun a sensation of being outside one's body, typically of floating and being able to observe oneself from a distance.

out-of-court ▶adjective [attrib.] (of a settlement) made or done without the intervention of a court.

out of date ▶adjective old-fashioned: *everything in her wardrobe must be hopelessly out of date.*
■no longer valid or relevant: *your passport is out of date.*

out-of-town ▶adjective situated, originating from, or taking place outside a town: *an out-of-town hypermarket.*

outpace ▶verb [with obj.] go faster than: *any modern GTi hatchback will comfortably outpace it.*

outpatient ▶noun a patient who attends a hospital for treatment without staying there overnight: [as modifier] *an outpatient clinic.*

outperform ▶verb [with obj.] perform better than: *an experienced employee will outperform the novice.*
■(of an investment) be more profitable than: *Georgian silver has outperformed the stock market.*
– DERIVATIVES **outperformance** noun.

outplacement ▶noun [mass noun] the provision of assistance to redundant employees in finding new employment, either as a benefit provided by the employer directly, or through a specialist service.

outplay ▶verb [with obj.] (often **be outplayed**) play better than: *we were absolutely and totally outplayed.*

outpoint ▶verb [with obj.] Boxing defeat (an opponent) on points: *Berbick outpointed him easily.*

outport ▶noun **1** a subsidiary port built near an existing one.
■Brit. any British port other than London.
2 Canadian (especially in Newfoundland) a small remote fishing village.

outpost ▶noun a small military camp or position at some distance from the main army, used especially as a guard against surprise attack.
■a remote part of a country or empire. ■figurative something regarded as an isolated or remote branch of something: *the community is the last outpost of civilization in the far north.*

outpouring ▶noun something that streams out rapidly: *a massive outpouring of high-energy gamma rays.*
■(often **outpourings**) an outburst of strong emotion: *outpourings of nationalist discontent.*

output ▶noun **1** [mass noun] the amount of something produced by a person, machine, or industry: *output from the mine ceased in May* | [count noun] *efficiency can lead to higher outputs.*
■the action or process of producing something: *the output of epinephrine.* ■the power, energy, or other results supplied by a device or system.
2 Electronics a place where power or information leaves a system.
▶verb (**-putting**; past and past participle **-put** or **-putted**) [with obj.] (of a computer or other device) produce, deliver, or supply (data): *you can output the image directly to a video recording system.*

output gap ▶noun Economics the amount by which the actual output of an economy falls short of its potential output.

outrace ▶verb [with obj.] exceed in speed, amount, or extent: *demand for trained clergy is outracing the supply.*

outrage ▶noun [mass noun] an extremely strong reaction of anger, shock, or indignation: *her voice trembled with outrage.*
■[count noun] an action or event causing such a reaction: *the decision was an outrage.*
▶verb [with obj.] (usu. **be outraged**) arouse fierce anger, shock, or indignation in (someone): *the public were outraged at the brutality involved.*
■violate or infringe flagrantly (a principle, law, etc.): *their behaviour outraged all civilized standards.*
– ORIGIN Middle English (in the senses 'lack of moderation' and 'violent behaviour'): from Old French *ou(l)trage*, based on Latin *ultra* 'beyond'. Sense development has been affected by the belief that the word is a compound of **OUT** and **RAGE**.

outrageous ▶adjective **1** shockingly bad or excessive: *an outrageous act of bribery.*
■wildly exaggerated or improbable: *the outrageous claims made by the previous government.*
2 very bold and unusual and rather shocking: *her outrageous leotards and sexy routines.*
– DERIVATIVES **outrageously** adverb, **outrageousness** noun.
– ORIGIN late Middle English: from Old French *outrageus*, from *outrage* 'excess' (see **OUTRAGE**).

outran past of **OUTRUN**.

outrank ▶verb [with obj.] have a higher rank than (someone else).
■be better, more important, or more significant than.

outré /'u:treɪ/ ▶adjective unusual and typically rather improper or shocking: *the composer's more outré harmonies.*
– ORIGIN French, literally 'exceeded', past participle of *outrer* (see **OUTRAGE**).

outreach ▶verb /aʊt'ri:tʃ/ [with obj.] reach further than: *their pack outweighed, outreached, and outwitted the Welsh team.*
■[no obj.] poetic/literary stretch out one's arms.
▶noun /'aʊtri:tʃ/ [mass noun] the extent or length of reaching out: *the loving outreach of God to the world.*
■an organization's involvement with or influence in the community, especially in the context of religion or social welfare: [as modifier] *outreach work.*

out relief ▶noun [mass noun] Brit. historical assistance given to very poor people not living in a workhouse.

Outremer /'u:trəmɛ:/ a name applied to the medieval French crusader states, including Armenia, Antioch, Tripoli, and Jerusalem.
– ORIGIN from French *outremer* (adverb) 'overseas', from *outre* 'beyond' + *mer* 'sea'.

outride ▶verb (past **-rode**; past participle **-ridden**) [with obj.] **1** ride better, faster, or further than.
2 archaic (of a ship) come safely through (a storm).

outrider ▶noun a person in a motor vehicle or on horseback who goes in front of or beside a vehicle as an escort or guard.
■US a mounted official who escorts racehorses to the starting post. ■US a mounted herdsman who prevents cattle from straying beyond a certain limit.
– DERIVATIVES **outriding** noun.

outrigger ▶noun a beam, spar, or framework projecting from or over a boat's side.
■a float or secondary hull fixed parallel to a canoe or small ship to stabilize it. ■a boat fitted with such a structure. ■a similar projecting support in another structure or vehicle.
– DERIVATIVES **outrigged** adjective.
– ORIGIN mid 18th cent.: perhaps influenced by the obsolete nautical term *outligger*, in the same sense.

outright ▶adverb **1** altogether: *logging has been banned outright.*
■without reservation; openly: *she couldn't ask him outright.*
2 immediately: *the impact killed four horses outright.*
■not by degrees or instalments: *they decided to buy the company outright.*
▶adjective [attrib.] open and direct: *an outright refusal.*
■total: *the outright abolition of the death penalty.*
■undisputed; clear: *an outright victory.*

outrival ▶verb (**-rivalled**, **-rivalling**; US **-rivaled**, **-rivaling**) [with obj.] archaic surpass in competition or comparison.

outro ▶noun (pl. **-os**) informal the concluding section of a piece of music or a radio or television programme.
– ORIGIN 1970s: from **OUT**, on the pattern of *intro*.

outrode past of **OUTRIDE**.

outrun ▶verb (**-running**; past **-ran**; past participle **-run**) [with obj.] run or travel faster or further than.
■escape from: *it's harder than anyone imagines to outrun destiny.* ■go beyond; exceed: *his courage outran his prudence.*

outrush ▶verb [with obj.] American Football surpass in rushing.

outsail ▶verb [with obj.] sail better or faster than (a competitor).

outsat past and past participle of **OUTSIT**.

outscore ▶verb [with obj.] score more than (an opponent) in a game.

outsell ▶verb (past and past participle **-sold**) [with obj.] be sold in greater quantities than: *CD outsells vinyl for the first time.*
■(of a person) sell more of something than (someone else): *Garth Brooks is outselling Michael Jackson.*

outsert ▶noun a piece of promotional material which is placed on the outside of a package, publication, or other product.
– ORIGIN 1960s: from **OUT** + **INSERT**.

outset ▶noun [in sing.] the start or beginning of something: *the imposition of surcharges was something the federation had opposed since its outset.*
– PHRASES **at** (or **from**) **the outset** at or from the beginning.

outshine ▶verb (past and past participle **-shone**) [with obj.] shine more brightly than.
■be much better than (someone) in a particular area: *it is a shame when a mother outshines a daughter.*

outshoot ▶verb (past and past participle **-shot**) [with obj.] shoot better than (someone else).
■score more goals or points or make more shots than (another player or team).

outshop ▶verb (**-shopped**, **-shopping**) [with obj.] (usu. **be outshopped**) Brit. send (a railway vehicle) out from a workshop or factory after construction or overhaul.

outshout ▶verb [with obj.] shout louder than.

outside ▶noun the external side or surface of something: *record the date on the outside of the file.*
■the part of a path nearer to a road or further from a wall. ■the side of a bend or curve where the edge or surface is longer in extent. ■the side of a racetrack further from the centre, where the lanes are longer. ■(**outsides**) the outer sheets of a ream of paper. ■the external appearance of someone or something: *was he as straight as he appeared **on the outside**?*
▶adjective [attrib.] **1** situated on or near the exterior or external surface of something: *the outside rim.*
■(in hockey, soccer, and other sports) denoting positions nearer to the sides of the field.
2 not belonging to or coming from within a particular group: *I have some outside help.*
■beyond one's own immediate personal concerns: *I was able to face the outside world again.*
▶preposition & adverb **1** situated or moving beyond the boundaries of (a room, building, or other enclosed space): [as prep.] *there was a boy outside the door* | [as adv.] *the dog was still barking outside* | *outside, the wind was as wild as ever.*
■situated beyond the boundaries of (a particular location): [as prep.] *major conurbations outside London* | [as adv.] *those in the occupied territories and those outside.* ■not being a member of (a particular group): [as prep.] *critics outside the government.* ■(in soccer, rugby, and other sports) closer to the side of the field than (another player): [as prep.] *Swift appeared outside him with the powerful Fallon overlapping on his left.*
2 [prep.] beyond the limits or scope of: *the high cost of shipping has put it outside their price range.*
– PHRASES **at the outside** (of an estimate) at the most: *every minute, or at the outside, every ninety seconds.* **get outside of** informal eat or drink (something): *we'll get outside of a feed of bacon and egg.* **on the outside** away from or not belonging to a particular circle or institution. **on the outside looking in** (of a person) excluded from a group or activity. **an outside chance** a remote possibility. **outside of** informal, chiefly N. Amer. beyond the boundaries of: *a village 20 miles outside of New York.* ■apart from: *outside of an unfortunate sermon, he never put a foot wrong.*

USAGE **Outside** and **outside of**: is there any difference between *the books have been distributed **outside** Europe* and *the books have been distributed **outside of** Europe*? Broadly speaking, both have the same meaning and either is acceptable in standard English. However, the use of **outside of** is much commoner and better established in North American than in British English.

outside broadcast ▶noun Brit. a radio or

television programme that is recorded, filmed, or broadcast live on location and not in a studio.

outside cabin ▶ noun a ship's cabin with an outside window or porthole.

outside director ▶ noun a director of a company who is not employed by that company, typically an employee of an associated company.

outside interest ▶ noun an interest not connected with one's work or studies.

outside line ▶ noun a telephone connection with an external exchange.

outside loop ▶ noun a looping movement made by an aircraft in which the back of the aircraft is on the outside of the curve.

outside money ▶ noun [mass noun] Economics money held in a form such as gold which is an asset for the holder and does not represent a corresponding liability for someone else.

outsider ▶ noun **1** a person who does not belong to a particular group.
■ a person who is not accepted by or who isolates themselves from society.
2 a competitor, applicant, etc. thought to have little chance of success: *he started as a rank outsider for the title.*

outsider art ▶ noun [mass noun] art produced by untrained artists, for example children or the mentally ill.
– DERIVATIVES **outsider artist** noun.

outside track ▶ noun the outer, longer side of a racecourse or running track.

outsing ▶ verb (past **-sang**; past participle **-sung**) [with obj.] sing better or louder than (someone else).

outsize ▶ adjective (also **outsized**) exceptionally large.
▶ noun an exceptionally large person or thing, especially a garment made to measurements larger than the standard.

outskirts ▶ plural noun the outer parts of a town or city.

outsmart ▶ verb [with obj.] informal defeat or get the better of (someone) by being clever or cunning: *the hero is invariably outsmarted by the heroine.*

outsold past and past participle of OUTSELL.

outsole ▶ noun the outer sole of a boot or shoe, especially a sports shoe.

outsource ▶ verb [with obj.] obtain (goods or a service) by contract from an outside supplier: [as noun **outsourcing**] *outsourcing can dramatically lower total costs.*
■ contract (work) out: *you may choose to outsource this function to another company or do it yourself.*

outspan S. African ▶ verb (**-spanned**, **-spanning**) [with obj.] unharness (an animal) from a wagon: *the wagons were drawn up beside the road and the oxen outspanned* | [no obj.] *they outspanned at the hotel.*
■ [no obj.] rest or camp at the side of the road while travelling by wagon: *we used to outspan for five or six hours in the heat of the day.*
▶ noun a place for grazing or camping on a wagon journey.
– ORIGIN early 19th cent.: from Dutch *uitspannen* 'unyoke'.

outspeed ▶ verb (past and past participle **-sped**) [with obj.] move faster than.

outspend ▶ verb (past and past participle **-spent**) [with obj.] spend more than (someone else).

outspoken ▶ adjective frank in stating one's opinions, especially if they are shocking or controversial: *he has been outspoken in his criticism.*
– DERIVATIVES **outspokenly** adverb, **outspokenness** noun.

outspread ▶ adjective fully extended or expanded: *outspread hands.*
▶ verb (past and past participle **-spread**) [with obj.] poetic/literary spread out: *that eagle outspreading his wings for flight.*

outstanding ▶ adjective **1** exceptionally good: *the team's outstanding performance.*
■ clearly noticeable: *works of outstanding banality.*
2 remaining to be done or dealt with.
■ (of a debt) remaining to be paid or dealt with: *there was a small charge outstanding.*

outstandingly ▶ adverb [usu. as submodifier] exceptionally: *outstandingly beautiful gardens.*

outstare ▶ verb [with obj.] stare at (someone) for longer than they can stare back, typically in order to intimidate or disconcert them.

outstation ▶ noun a branch of an organization situated at some distance from its headquarters.
■ [as modifier] Indian (of a person) working in a place where one does not live: *an outstation journalist.* ■ Austral./NZ a part of a farming estate that is separate from the main estate. ■ Austral. an autonomous Aboriginal community situated at some distance from a centre on which it depends.

outstation cheque ▶ noun Indian a cheque issued at one place but cashed elsewhere.

outstay ▶ verb [with obj.] stay beyond the limit of (one's expected or permitted time): *employees who had outstayed their coffee break.*
■ endure or last longer than (another competitor): *his mount tenaciously outstayed Melody for second place.*
– PHRASES **outstay one's welcome** see WELCOME.

outstep ▶ verb (**-stepped**, **-stepping**) [with obj.] rare exceed.

outstretch ▶ verb [with obj.] [usu. as adj. **outstretched**] extend or stretch out (something, especially a hand or arm): *I walked with my arms outstretched.*
■ go beyond the limit of: *their good intentions far outstretched their capacity to offer help.*

outstrip ▶ verb (**-stripped**, **-stripping**) [with obj.] move faster than and overtake (someone else).
■ exceed: *supply far outstripped demand.*

outswinger ▶ noun Cricket a ball bowled with a swerve or swing from the leg to the off side.
– DERIVATIVES **outswing** noun, **outswinging** adjective.

outta (also **outa**) ▶ preposition a non-standard contraction of 'out of', used in representing informal speech: *we'd better get outta here.*

out-take ▶ noun a scene or sequence filmed or recorded for a film or programme but not included in the final version.

out-talk ▶ verb [with obj.] outdo or overcome in talking: *he was out-talked by his mother.*

out-think ▶ verb [with obj.] outdo in thinking; outwit: *machines that can out-think humans.*

out-thrust ▶ adjective extended outward: *with his out-thrust foot he sent the man keeling over.*
▶ noun a thing which projects or is extended outward: *root hairs are out-thrusts from the root surface.*

out-top ▶ verb [with obj.] rare surpass in number, amount, height, or extent: *Nellie out-topped him by three inches.*

out tray ▶ noun a tray on someone's desk for outgoing letters and other documents that have been dealt with.

out-turn ▶ noun the amount of something produced, especially money: *the financial out-turn.*
■ the result of a process or sequence of events: *an entirely implausible out-turn.*

outvalue ▶ verb (**-values**, **-valued**, **-valuing**) [with obj.] chiefly archaic be of greater value than: *a ray of beauty outvalues all the utilities of the world.*

outvote ▶ verb [with obj.] defeat by gaining more votes.

outwait ▶ verb [with obj.] wait longer than.

outwalk ▶ verb [with obj.] chiefly archaic walk faster or farther than (someone else).

outward ▶ adjective [attrib.] **1** of, on, or from the outside: *the vehicle's outward and interior appearance.*
■ relating to the external appearance of something rather than its true nature or substance: *an outward display of friendliness.* ■ archaic outer: *the outward physical body.*
2 going out or away from a place: *the outward voyage.*
▶ adverb outwards.
– DERIVATIVES **outwardness** noun.
– ORIGIN Old English *ūtweard* (see OUT-, -WARD).

outward bound ▶ adjective (of a ship or passenger) going away from home: *they were outward bound for the Great Barrier Reef.*
▶ noun (**Outward Bound**) [usu. as modifier] trademark an organization that provides naval and adventure training and other outdoor activities for young people: *Outward Bound training.*

outwardly ▶ adverb [often as submodifier] on the surface: *an outwardly normal life* | [sentence adverb] *outwardly she seemed no different.*
■ on or from the outside: *outwardly featureless modern offices* | [sentence adverb] *outwardly it's not a bad-looking car.*

outwards ▶ adverb away from the centre or a particular point; towards the outside: *a window that opens outwards.*

outwash ▶ noun [mass noun] material carried away from a glacier by meltwater and deposited beyond the moraine.

outwatch ▶ verb [with obj.] archaic watch (something) until it disappears.
■ keep awake beyond the end of.

outwear ▶ verb (past **-wore**; past participle **-worn**) [with obj.] last longer than: *a material that will outwear any other waterproof sheeting.*

outweigh ▶ verb [with obj.] be heavier, greater, or more significant than: *the advantages greatly outweigh the disadvantages.*

outwent past of OUTGO.

outwit ▶ verb (**-witted**, **-witting**) [with obj.] deceive by greater ingenuity: *Ray had outwitted many an opponent.*

outwith ▶ preposition Scottish outside; beyond: *he has lived outwith Scotland for only five years.*

outwore past of OUTWEAR.

outwork ▶ noun **1** a section of a fortification or system of defence which is in front of the main part.
2 [mass noun] Brit. work done outside the factory or office which provides it.
– DERIVATIVES **outworker** noun (only in sense 2).

outworking ▶ noun [mass noun] **1** the action or process of working something out: *the brain is involved in the outworking of mental processes.*
2 the action or process of doing work outside the factory or office which provides it.

outworld ▶ noun (in science fiction) an outlying or alien planet.
– DERIVATIVES **outworlder** noun.

outworn past participle of OUTWEAR. ▶ adjective out of date: *outworn prejudices.*
■ no longer usable or serviceable: *outworn lead flashings.*

outyield ▶ verb [with obj.] produce or yield more than: *plantations outyield managed natural forest.*

ouzel /ˈuːz(ə)l/ (also **ousel**) ▶ noun a bird that resembles the blackbird, especially the ring ouzel. See also WATER OUZEL.
– ORIGIN Old English *ōsle* 'blackbird', of Germanic origin; related to German *Amsel* 'blackbird'.

ouzo /ˈuːzəʊ/ ▶ noun [mass noun] a Greek aniseed-flavoured spirit.
– ORIGIN modern Greek.

ova plural form of OVUM.

oval ▶ adjective having a rounded and slightly elongated outline or shape like that of an egg: *her smooth oval face* | *the game with the oval ball.*
▶ noun a body, object, or design with such a shape or outline: *cut out two small ovals from the felt.*
■ an oval sports field or racing track. ■ Austral. a ground for Australian Rules football.
– DERIVATIVES **ovality** noun, **ovalness** noun.
– ORIGIN mid 16th cent.: from French, or modern Latin *ovalis*, from Latin *ovum* 'egg'.

ovalbumin /əʊˈvalbjʊmɪn/ ▶ noun [mass noun] Biochemistry albumin derived from the white of eggs.
– ORIGIN mid 19th cent.: from Latin *ovi albumen* 'albumen of egg', altered on the pattern of *albumin.*

Oval Office the office of the US President in the White House.

oval window ▶ noun informal term for *fenestra ovalis* (see FENESTRA).

Ovambo /əʊˈvambəʊ/ ▶ noun (pl. same or **-os**) **1** a member of a people of northern Namibia.
2 [mass noun] the Bantu language of this people.
▶ adjective of or relating to the Ovambo or their language.
– ORIGIN a local name, from *ova-* (prefix denoting a plural) + *ambo* 'man of leisure'.

Ovamboland a semi-arid region of northern Namibia, the homeland of the Ovambo people.

ovarian /əʊˈvɛːrɪən/ ▶ adjective of or relating to an ovary or the ovaries: *an ovarian cyst.*

ovarian follicle ▶ noun another term for GRAAFIAN FOLLICLE.

ovariectomy /ˌəʊvərɪˈɛktəmi/ ▶ noun (pl. **-ies**) [mass noun] surgical removal of one or both ovaries; oophorectomy.

ovariotomy /ˌəʊvərɪˈɒtəmi/ ▶ noun another term for OVARIECTOMY.

ovaritis /ˌəʊvəˈrʌɪtɪs/ ▶ noun another term for OOPHORITIS.

ovary /ˈəʊv(ə)ri/ ▶ noun (pl. **-ies**) a female

reproductive organ in which ova or eggs are produced, present in humans and other vertebrates as a pair.
■Botany the hollow base of the carpel of a flower, containing one or more ovules.
– ORIGIN mid 17th cent.: from modern Latin *ovarium*, from Latin *ovum* 'egg'.

ovate[1] /ˈəʊveɪt/ ▶ **adjective** chiefly Biology having an oval outline or ovoid shape, like an egg.
– ORIGIN mid 18th cent.: from Latin *ovatus* 'egg-shaped'.

ovate[2] /ˈɒvət/ ▶ **noun** a member of an order of Welsh bards recognized at an Eisteddfod.
■historical an ancient Celtic priest or natural philosopher.
– ORIGIN early 18th cent.: from the Greek plural *ouateis* 'soothsayers'.

ovation ▶ **noun 1** a sustained and enthusiastic show of appreciation from an audience, especially by means of applause.
2 Roman History a processional entrance into Rome by a victorious commander, of lesser honour than a triumph.
– ORIGIN early 16th cent. (in sense 2): from Latin *ovatio(n-)*, from *ovare* 'exult'. The word had the sense 'exultation' from the mid 17th to early 19th cent.

oven ▶ **noun** an enclosed compartment, usually part of a cooker, for cooking and heating food.
■a small furnace or kiln. ■a cremation chamber in a Nazi concentration camp.
– ORIGIN Old English *ofen*, of Germanic origin; related to Dutch *oven*, German *Ofen*, from an Indo-European root shared by Greek *ipnos*.

ovenbird ▶ **noun 1** a small, drab tropical American bird belonging to a diverse family, many members of which make domed oven-like nests of mud.
• Family Furnariidae (the **ovenbird family**): many genera and numerous species. The ovenbird family comprises the horneros, miners, spinetails, and many others.
2 a migratory brown North American warbler that builds a domed oven-like nest of vegetation on the ground.
• *Seiurus aurocapillus*, family Parulidae.

oven glove ▶ **noun** a padded glove for handling dishes in or from a hot oven.

ovenproof ▶ **adjective** (of cookware) suitable for use in an oven; heat-resistant.

oven-ready ▶ **adjective** (of food) prepared before sale so as to be ready for cooking in an oven.

O

ovenware ▶ **noun** [mass noun] dishes that can be used for cooking food in the oven.

over ▶ **preposition 1** extending directly upwards from: *I saw flames over Berlin.*
■above so as to cover or protect: *an oxygen tent over the bed | ladle this sauce over fresh pasta.* ■extending above (a general area) from a vantage point: *views over Hyde Park.* ■at the other side of; beyond: *over the hill is a small village.*
2 expressing passage or trajectory across: *she trudged over the lawn.*
■beyond and falling or hanging from: *it toppled over the cliff.* ■expressing duration: *inventories have been refined over many years | she told me over coffee.* ■by means of; by the medium of: *over the loudspeaker.*
3 at a higher level or layer than: *his flat was over the shop.*
■higher in grade or rank than: *over him is the financial director.* ■expressing authority or control: *editorial control over what is included.* ■expressing preference: *I'd choose the well-known brand over that one.* ■expressing majority: *the predominance of Asian over African managers in the sample.* ■higher in volume or pitch than: *he shouted over the noise of the taxis.*
4 higher than (a specified number or quantity): *over 40 degrees C | they have lived together for over a year.*
5 on the subject of: *a heated debate over unemployment.*
▶ **adverb 1** expressing passage or trajectory across an area: *he leant over and tapped me on the hand.*
■beyond and falling or hanging from a point: *listing over at an acute angle.*
2 in or to the place mentioned or indicated: *over here | come over and cheer us up.*
3 used to express action and result: *the car flipped over | hand the money over.*
■finished: *the match is over | message understood, over and out.*
4 used to express repetition of a process: *twice over | the sums will have to be done over again.*
▶ **noun** Cricket a sequence of six balls bowled by a bowler from one end of the pitch, after which another bowler takes over from the other end.
– PHRASES **be over** no longer be affected by: *we were over the worst.* **get something over with** do or undergo something unpleasant or difficult, so as to be rid of it. **over against** adjacent to: *over against the wall.* ■in contrast with: *over against heaven is hell.* **over and above** in addition to: *exceptional service over and above what normally might be expected.* **over and done with** completely finished. **over and over** again and again.
– ORIGIN Old English *ofer*, of Germanic origin; related to Dutch *over* and German *über*, from an Indo-European word (originally a comparative of the element represented by *-ove* in *above*) which is also the base of Latin *super* and Greek *huper*.

over- ▶ **prefix 1** excessively; to an unwanted degree: *overambitious | overcareful.*
■completely; utterly: *overawe | overjoyed.*
2 upper; outer; extra: *overcoat | overtime.*
■over; above: *overcast | overhang.*

over-abundant ▶ **adjective** excessive in quantity: *over-abundant microbial growth.*
– DERIVATIVES **over-abundance** noun, **over-abundantly** adverb.

overachieve ▶ **verb** [no obj.] do better than is expected, especially in school work: *David continued to overachieve all through high school.*
■be excessively dedicated to the achievement of success in one's work.
– DERIVATIVES **overachievement** noun, **over-achiever** noun.

overact ▶ **verb** [no obj.] (of an actor or actress) act a role in an exaggerated manner: *a weepy actress with a strong tendency to overact | [as noun **overacting**] there was a certain amount of overacting.*

overactive ▶ **adjective** excessively active: *the product of an overactive imagination.*
– DERIVATIVES **overactivity** noun.

overage ▶ **noun** an excess or surplus, especially the amount by which a sum of money is greater than a previous estimate.

over age ▶ **adjective** over a certain age limit: *they were banned after fielding over-age players.*

overall ▶ **adjective** [attrib.] total: *an overall cut of 30 per cent.*
■taking everything into account: *the overall effect is impressive.*
▶ **adverb** [sentence adverb] in all parts; taken as a whole: *overall, 10,000 jobs will go.*
▶ **noun** (usu. **overalls**) Brit. a loose-fitting garment such as a coat or dungarees worn, typically over ordinary clothes, for protection against dirt or heavy wear.
■(**overalls**) Brit. close-fitting trousers formerly worn as part of an army uniform, now only on ceremonial or formal occasions.
– DERIVATIVES **overalled** adjective.

overambitious ▶ **adjective** excessively ambitious.
– DERIVATIVES **overambition** noun, **overambitiously** adverb.

overanxious ▶ **adjective** excessively anxious.
– DERIVATIVES **overanxiety** noun, **overanxiously** adverb.

overarch ▶ **verb** [with obj.] form an arch over: *an old dirt road, overarched by forest.*

overarching ▶ **adjective** [attrib.] forming an arch over something: *the overarching mangroves.*
■comprehensive; all-embracing: *a single overarching principle.*

overarm ▶ **adjective** & **adverb** (chiefly of a throw or a stroke with a racket) made with the hand or arm passing above the level of the shoulder: [as adj.] *the bowler was happy to demonstrate his overarm technique* | [as adv.] *competitors can throw overarm or underarm.*

overate past of **OVEREAT**.

overawe ▶ **verb** [with obj.] (usu. **be overawed**) impress (someone) so much that they are silent or inhibited: *the eleven-year-old was overawed by the atmosphere.*

overbalance ▶ **verb** chiefly Brit. fall or cause to fall over from loss of balance: [no obj.] *the ladder overbalanced on top of her.*
■[with obj.] outweigh: *I fault the university for many things, but all are overbalanced by its unparalleled resources.*
▶ **noun** [mass noun] archaic excess of weight, value, or amount: *overbalance of propriety.*

overbear ▶ **verb** (past **-bore**; past participle **-borne**) [with obj.] overcome by emotional pressure or physical force: *his will had not been overborne by another's influence.*

overbearing ▶ **adjective** unpleasantly overpowering: *an overbearing, ill-tempered brute.*
– DERIVATIVES **overbearingly** adverb, **overbearingness** noun.

overbid ▶ **verb** (**-bidding**; past and past participle **-bid**) [no obj.] **1** (in an auction) make a higher bid than a previous bid: *I'd once seen him blithely overbid for a tiny James I miniature portrait.*
2 (in competitive tendering, the auction at bridge, etc.) bid more than is warranted or manageable.
▶ **noun** a bid that is higher than another or higher than is justified.
– DERIVATIVES **overbidder** noun.

overbite ▶ **noun** [mass noun] Dentistry the overlapping of the lower teeth by the upper.

overblouse ▶ **noun** a blouse designed to be worn without being tucked into a skirt or trousers.

overblowing ▶ **noun** [mass noun] a technique for playing high notes on a wind instrument by producing harmonics.

overblown ▶ **adjective 1** excessively inflated or pretentious: *a world of overblown egos.*
2 (of a flower) past its prime: *an overblown rose.*

overboard ▶ **adverb** from a ship into the water: *the severe storm washed a man overboard.*
– PHRASES **go overboard 1** be very enthusiastic: *Garry went overboard for you.* **2** react in an immoderate way: *Chris has a bit of a temper and can sometimes go overboard.* **throw something overboard** abandon or discard something.

overbold ▶ **adjective** excessively bold.
– DERIVATIVES **overboldly** adverb, **overboldness** noun.

overbook ▶ **verb** [with obj.] accept more reservations for (a flight or hotel) than there is room for: *airlines deliberately overbook some scheduled flights.*

overboot ▶ **noun** a boot worn over another boot or shoe to protect it or to provide extra warmth.

overbore past of **OVERBEAR**.

overborne past participle of **OVERBEAR**.

overbought past and past participle of **OVERBUY**.

overbreathe ▶ **verb** another term for **HYPERVENTILATE**.

overbridge ▶ **noun** a bridge over a railway or road.

overbrim ▶ **verb** [with obj.] archaic flow over the brim of: *the liquor that o'erbrims the cup.*
■[no obj.] (of a container or liquid) overflow at the brim.

overbrimming ▶ **adjective** abundant, especially excessively so: *overbrimming confidence.*

overbuild ▶ **verb** (past and past participle **-built**) [with obj.] **1** put up too many buildings in (an area): *investors overbuilt the Atlantic and Mediterranean coasts.*
■build too many: *to overbuild hotels would destroy the setting.* ■build (something) elaborately or to a very high standard, especially unnecessarily: *overbuilding something will always be safer than taking short cuts.*
2 [often as noun **overbuilding**] build on top of: *the preservation of the medieval field pattern by direct overbuilding.*

overburden ▶ **verb** [with obj.] (often **be overburdened**) load (someone) with too many things to carry: *they were overburdened with luggage.*
■give (someone) more work or pressure than they can deal with: *ministers are overburdened with engagements.*
▶ **noun** [mass noun] rock or soil overlying a mineral deposit, archaeological site, or other underground feature.
■[count noun] an excessive burden: *an overburden of costs.*
– DERIVATIVES **overburdensome** /əʊvəˈbəːd(ə)ns(ə)m/ adjective.

overbusy ▶ **adjective** excessively busy: *their overbusy lives.*

overbuy ▶ **verb** (past and past participle **-bought**) [with obj.] buy more of (something) than one needs.

overcall Bridge ▶ **verb** [no obj.] make a higher bid than an opponent's bid.
▶ **noun** an act or instance of making such a bid.

overcame past of **OVERCOME**.

overcapacity ▶ **noun** [mass noun] the situation in which an industry or factory cannot sell as much as its plant is designed to produce.

overcapitalize (also **-ise**) ▶ **verb** [with obj.] [usu. as adj. **overcapitalized**] provide (a company) with more capital than is advisable or necessary: *a bleak time for the overcapitalized firm.*

▪estimate the capital value of (a company) at too high an amount.
– DERIVATIVES **overcapitalization** noun.

overcareful ▶ adjective excessively careful.
– DERIVATIVES **overcarefully** adverb.

overcast ▶ adjective **1** (of the sky or weather) marked by a covering of grey cloud; dull.
2 (in sewing) edged with stitching to prevent fraying.
▶ noun [mass noun] cloud covering a large part of the sky.
▶ verb (past and past participle **-cast**) [with obj.] **1** cover with clouds or shade: *the pebbled beach, overcast with the shadows of the high cliffs.*
2 stitch over (a raw edge) to prevent fraying: *finish off the raw edge of the hem by overcasting it.*

overcautious ▶ adjective excessively cautious.
– DERIVATIVES **overcaution** noun, **overcautiously** adverb, **overcautiousness** noun.

overcharge ▶ verb [with obj.] **1** charge (someone) too high a price for goods or a service: *they are being overcharged for an inadequate service.*
▪charge someone (a sum) beyond the correct amount: [with two objs] *customers have been overcharged £12 million in the last year.*
2 put too much electric charge into (a battery): *large generators can overcharge batteries.*
▪put exaggerated or excessive detail into (a text or work of art): *the scenes are overcharged.*
▶ noun an excessive charge for goods or a service.

overcheck[1] ▶ noun a check pattern superimposed on a colour or design.

overcheck[2] ▶ noun a strap passing over a horse's head between the ears, to pull up on the bit and make breathing easier.

overclass ▶ noun a privileged, wealthy, or powerful section of society.

overcloud ▶ verb [with obj.] mar, dim, or obscure: *the darkness of the beginning overclouds the set.*

overcoat ▶ noun **1** a long warm coat.
2 a top, final layer of paint or a similar covering.

overcome ▶ verb (past **-came**; past participle **-come**) [with obj.] succeed in dealing with (a problem or difficulty): *she worked hard to overcome her paralysing shyness.*
▪defeat (an opponent): *an experienced England side overcame the determined home team* | [no obj.] *we shall overcome.* ▪(usu. **be overcome**) (of an emotion) overpower or overwhelm: *she was obviously overcome with excitement.*
– ORIGIN Old English *ofercuman* (see **OVER-**, **COME**).

overcommit ▶ verb (**-committed**, **-committing**) [with obj.] oblige (someone) to do more than they are capable of, especially to repay a loan they cannot afford: *multiple borrowers who may be overcommitting themselves.*
▪allocate more (resources) to a purpose than can be provided: *they could easily overcommit their budgets.*
– DERIVATIVES **overcommitment** noun.

overcompensate ▶ verb [no obj.] take excessive measures in attempting to correct or make amends for an error, weakness, or problem: *he was overcompensating for fears about the future.*
– DERIVATIVES **overcompensatingly** adverb, **overcompensation** noun, **overcompensatory** adjective.

overconfident ▶ adjective excessively confident.
– DERIVATIVES **overconfidence** noun, **overconfidently** adverb.

overcook ▶ verb [with obj.] cook too much or for too long.
▪[no obj.] (of food) be cooked too much or for too long: *ensure that the food doesn't overcook during reheating.*

overcritical ▶ adjective inclined to find fault too readily.

overcrop ▶ verb (**-cropped**, **-cropping**) [with obj.] [usu. as noun **overcropping**] exhaust (land) by growing crops continuously on it.

overcrowd ▶ verb [with obj.] fill (accommodation or a space) beyond what is usual or comfortable: [as adj. **overcrowded**] *overcrowded and insanitary conditions* | [as noun **overcrowding**] *severe overcrowding at a football match.*
▪house (people or animals) in accommodation that is too small: *my family weren't bad, we were just overcrowded.*

overcurious ▶ adjective excessively eager to know or learn something.
– DERIVATIVES **overcuriosity** /ˌəʊvəkjʊərɪˈɒsɪti/ noun.

overdamp ▶ verb [with obj.] Physics damp (a system) to a greater extent than the minimum needed to prevent oscillations.

overdate ▶ noun a variety of a coin in which one date has been superimposed over another.
– DERIVATIVES **overdating** noun.

overdelicate ▶ adjective excessively delicate.
– DERIVATIVES **overdelicacy** noun.

overdetermine ▶ verb [with obj.] technical determine, account for, or cause (something) in more than one way or with more conditions than are necessary: *there is evidence that housing tenure overdetermines party support.*
– DERIVATIVES **overdetermination** noun.

overdevelop ▶ verb (**-developed**, **-developing**) [with obj.] develop too much or to excess: *cycling may overdevelop the calf muscles* | [as adj. **overdeveloped**] *Majorca's overdeveloped coastline.*
▪Photography treat with developer for too long: *you can overdevelop the film to make up for underexposure.*
– DERIVATIVES **overdevelopment** noun.

overdo ▶ verb (**-does**; past **-did**; past participle **-done**) [with obj.] carry to excess; exaggerate: *she rather overdoes the early cockney scenes.*
▪use too much of (something): *I'd overdone the garlic in the curry.* ▪(**overdo it/things**) exhaust oneself by overwork or overexertion: *I'd simply overdone it in the gym.* ▪[often as adj. **overdone**] overcook (food): *chewing his overdone steak.*
– ORIGIN Old English *oferdōn* (see **OVER-**, **DO**[1]).

overdose ▶ noun an excessive and dangerous dose of a drug: *she took an overdose the day her husband left.*
▶ verb [no obj.] take an overdose of a drug: *he was admitted to hospital after **overdosing on** cocaine.*
▪[with obj.] give an overdose to.
– DERIVATIVES **overdosage** /ˈəʊvəˈdəʊsɪdʒ/ noun.

overdraft ▶ noun a deficit in a bank account caused by drawing more money than the account holds.

overdramatize (also **-ise**) ▶ verb [with obj.] react to or portray (something) in an excessively dramatic manner.
– DERIVATIVES **overdramatic** adjective.

overdraw ▶ verb (past **-drew**; past participle **-drawn**) [with obj.] **1** (usu. **be overdrawn**) draw money from (one's bank account) in excess of what the account holds: *you only pay interest if your account is overdrawn.*
▪(**be overdrawn**) (of a person) have taken money out of an account in excess of what it holds: *I'm already overdrawn this month.*
2 exaggerate in describing or depicting (someone or something): *some of the characters were overdrawn.*

overdress ▶ verb [no obj.] (also **be overdressed**) dress with too much display or formality: *Eugenie did not wish to overdress* | *she felt wildly overdressed in her velvet suit.*
▶ noun chiefly Brit. a dress worn over another dress or other clothing.

overdrink ▶ verb (past **-drank**; past participle **-drunk**) [no obj.] [usu. as noun **overdrinking**] drink too much alcohol.

overdrive ▶ noun a gear in a motor vehicle providing a gear ratio higher than that of direct drive (the usual top gear), so that the engine speed can be reduced at high road speeds to lessen fuel consumption or to allow further acceleration.
▪[mass noun] a state of high or excessive activity: *the city's worried public relations arm **went into overdrive**.* ▪a mechanism which permits the exceeding of some normal operating level in a piece of equipment, especially the amplifier of an electric guitar.
▶ verb [with obj.] [usu. as adj. **overdriven**] drive or work to exhaustion: *the overdriven mothers of ten or eleven hungry children.*

overdub ▶ verb (**-dubbed**, **-dubbing**) [with obj.] record (additional sounds) on an existing recording: *he overdubbed vocals in the US.*
▶ noun an instance of overdubbing: *a guitar overdub.*

overdue ▶ adjective not yet having arrived, happened, or been done, though after the expected time: *reform is now overdue.*
▪(of a payment) not having been made, although required: *the rent was nearly three months overdue.* ▪(of a woman) not having had a menstrual period at the expected time: *I was already a week-and-a-half overdue.* ▪(of a baby) not having been born at the expected time: *our daughter was six days overdue.* ▪having deserved or needed something for some time: *she was **overdue for** some leave.* ▪(of a library book) retained longer than the period allowed.

overeager ▶ adjective excessively eager.
– DERIVATIVES **overeagerly** adverb, **overeagerness** noun.

over easy ▶ adjective N. Amer. (of a fried egg) turned over when almost cooked and fried lightly on the other side, so that the yolk remains slightly liquid.

overeat ▶ verb (past **-ate**; past participle **-eaten**) [no obj.] [usu. as noun **overeating**] eat too much: *the effect of overeating is weight gain.*
– DERIVATIVES **overeater** noun.

over-egg ▶ verb (in phrase **over-egg the pudding**) used to suggest that one has gone too far in embellishing, exaggerating, or doing something.

over-elaborate ▶ adjective excessively elaborate.
▶ verb [with obj.] explain or treat (something) in excessive detail: *if they don't over-elaborate the story I don't question it.*
– DERIVATIVES **over-elaborately** adverb, **over-elaborateness** noun, **over-elaboration** noun.

overemotional ▶ adjective (of a person) having feelings that are too easily excited and displayed: *we're not an overemotional family.*
– DERIVATIVES **overemotionally** adverb.

overemphasis ▶ noun [mass noun] excessive emphasis.

overemphasize (also **-ise**) ▶ verb [with obj.] (usu. **be overemphasized**) place excessive emphasis on: *the importance of adequate preparation cannot be overemphasized.*

overenthusiasm ▶ noun [mass noun] excessive enthusiasm.
– DERIVATIVES **overenthusiastic** adjective, **overenthusiastically** adverb.

overestimate ▶ verb [with obj.] estimate (something) to be better, larger, or more important than it really is: *his influence cannot be overestimated.*
▶ noun an excessively high estimate.
– DERIVATIVES **overestimation** noun.

overexcite ▶ verb [with obj.] [often as adj. **overexcited**] excite excessively: *an overexcited schoolgirl at a birthday party.*
– DERIVATIVES **overexcitable** adjective, **overexcitement** noun.

over-exercise ▶ verb [no obj.] take too much exercise.
▶ noun [mass noun] excessive exercise.

overexert ▶ verb (**overexert oneself**) engage in too much or too strenuous exertion.
– DERIVATIVES **overexertion** noun.

overexpose ▶ verb [with obj.] expose too much, especially to the public eye or to risk: *many UK banks were overexposed to overseas lending risks.*
▪Photography expose (film or a part of an image) for too long a time: *the sunlit background is overexposed.*
– DERIVATIVES **overexposure** noun.

overextend ▶ verb [with obj.] (usu. **be overextended**) **1** make too long: *at nine minutes plus the song is somewhat overextended.*
2 impose on (someone) an excessive burden of work or commitments: *he should not overextend himself on the mortgage.*
– DERIVATIVES **overextension** noun.

overfall ▶ noun a turbulent stretch of open water caused by a strong current or tide over a submarine ridge, or by a meeting of currents.
▪a place where surplus water overflows from a dam, weir, or pool.

overfamiliar ▶ adjective too well known: *the overfamiliar teacher's voice.*
▪[predic.] (**overfamiliar with**) too well acquainted with: *the researcher is overfamiliar with the community.* ▪behaving or speaking in an inappropriately informal way: *her private detective was dismissed for being **overfamiliar with** her.*
– DERIVATIVES **overfamiliarity** noun.

overfatigue ▶ noun [mass noun] excessive fatigue.

overfeed ▶ verb (past and past participle **-fed**) [with obj.] give too much food to: *the general view was that you cannot overfeed a baby.*

overfill ▶ verb [with obj.] put more into (a container) than it either should or can contain.

overfine ▶ adjective excessively or extremely fine: *the distinction may seem overfine to westerners.*

overfish ▶ verb [with obj.] deplete the stock of fish in (a body of water) by too much fishing: *this part of the Mediterranean is terribly overfished.*

■ deplete the stock of (a fish): *yellowfin tuna has been overfished.*

overflow ▶ **verb** [no obj.] (especially of a liquid) flow over the brim of a receptacle: *chemicals overflowed from a storage tank* | [with obj.] *the river overflowed its banks.*
■ (of a container) be so full that the contents go over the sides: *boxes* ***overflowing with*** *bright flowers* | [as adj. **overflowing**] *an overflowing ashtray.* ■ (of a space) be so crowded that people spill out: *the waiting area was overflowing.* ■ [with obj.] flood or flow over (a surface or area): *her hair overflowed her shoulders.* ■ (**overflow with**) figurative be very full of (an emotion or quality): *her heart overflowed with joy.*
▶ **noun 1** [mass noun] the flowing over of a liquid: *there was some overflow after heavy rainfall* | [count noun] *an overflow of sewage.*
■ [in sing.] the excess or surplus not able to be accommodated by an available space: *to accommodate the overflow five more offices have been built.*
2 (also **overflow pipe**) (in a bath or sink) an outlet for excess water.
3 [mass noun] Computing the generation of a number or other data item which is too large for the assigned location or memory space.
– PHRASES **full to overflowing** completely full.
– ORIGIN Old English *oferflōwan* (see **OVER-**, **FLOW**).

overfly ▶ **verb** (**-flies**; past **-flew**; past participle **-flown**) [with obj.] fly over (a place or territory): *there was a delay in obtaining clearance to overfly Israel.*
■ fly beyond (a place or thing): *overfly the radio beacon by approximately 15 seconds.*
– DERIVATIVES **overflight** noun.

overfold ▶ **noun** a part of something which is folded over another part: *the tunic is belted over a long overfold.*
■ Geology a fold in which both the limbs dip in the same direction so that strata in the middle part are upside down.

overfond ▶ **adjective** having too great an affection or liking for someone or something: *he's been getting* ***overfond of*** *this Pinot Grigio.*
– DERIVATIVES **overfondly** adverb, **overfondness** noun.

overfulfil (US **-fulfill**) ▶ **verb** (**-fulfilled**, **-fulfilling**) [with obj.] fulfil (a contract or quota) earlier or in greater quantity than required: *he overfulfilled the quota by forty per cent.*
– DERIVATIVES **overfulfilment** noun.

overfull ▶ **adjective** containing an excessive amount of something: *an overfull cup of tea.*

overgarment ▶ **noun** a garment that is worn over others.

overgeneralize (also **-ise**) ▶ **verb** [with obj.] draw a conclusion or make a statement about (something) that is more general than is justified by the available evidence.
– DERIVATIVES **overgeneralization** noun.

overgenerous ▶ **adjective** excessively generous: *she was not* ***overgenerous with*** *praise.*
– DERIVATIVES **overgenerosity** noun, **overgenerously** adverb.

overglaze ▶ **noun** [mass noun] decoration or a second glaze applied to glazed ceramic ware.
▶ **adjective** (of painting, printing, or other decoration) done on a glazed surface: *overglaze enamel.*

overgrainer ▶ **noun** a brush used in interior decorating to give a marbled or woodgrain effect.

overgraze ▶ **verb** [with obj.] graze (grassland) so heavily that the vegetation is damaged and the ground becomes liable to erosion: *their own pastures were overgrazed and arid* | [as noun **overgrazing**] *the failure of the rains led to overgrazing and deforestation.*

overground ▶ **adverb** & **adjective** on or above the ground: [as adv.] *it has suggested that a new line be built overground* | [as attrib. adj.] *a huge heating system pipes heat along overground tubes.*
■ [as attrib. adj.] legitimate; not subversive: *they devised plans for using overground political processes.*

overgrow ▶ **verb** (past **-grew**; past participle **-grown**) [with obj.] grow or spread over (something), especially so as to choke or stifle it: *the mussels overgrow and smother whatever is underneath.*

overgrown ▶ **adjective 1** covered with plants that have been allowed to grow wild: *the garden was overgrown and deserted.*
2 grown too large or beyond its normal size: *the town is only an overgrown village.*
■ chiefly derogatory used to describe an adult behaving in a childish manner: *a pair of overgrown schoolboys.*

overgrowth ▶ **noun** [mass noun] excessive growth: *intestinal bacterial overgrowth.*

overhand ▶ **adjective** & **adverb** another term for **OVERARM**.
■ with the palm of the hand downward or inward: [as adj.] *an overhand grip.*

overhand knot ▶ **noun** a simple knot made by forming a loop and passing a free end round the standing part and through the loop.

overhang ▶ **verb** (past and past participle **-hung**) [with obj.] hang or extend outwards over: *a concrete path overhung by jacaranda trees* | [as adj. **overhanging**] *overhanging branches.*
■ figurative loom over: *the film's mood is overhung with impending death.*
▶ **noun** a part of something that sticks out or hangs over another thing: *he crouched beneath an overhang of bushes.*

overhasty ▶ **adjective** excessively hasty.
– DERIVATIVES **overhastily** adverb.

overhaul ▶ **verb** [with obj.] **1** take apart (a piece of machinery or equipment) in order to examine it and repair it if necessary: *the steering box was recently overhauled* | figurative *moves to overhaul the income tax system.*
2 Brit. overtake (someone), especially in a sporting event: *Jodami overhauled his chief rival.*
▶ **noun** a thorough examination of machinery or a system, with repairs or changes made if necessary: *a major overhaul of environmental policies.*
– ORIGIN early 17th cent. (originally in nautical use in the sense 'release (rope tackle) by slackening'): from **OVER-** + **HAUL**.

overhead ▶ **adverb** above the level of the head; in the sky: *a helicopter buzzed overhead.*
▶ **adjective 1** situated above the level of the head, especially in the sky: *the sun was directly overhead.*
2 (of a driving mechanism) above the object driven: *an overhead cam four-cylinder engine.*
3 [attrib.] (of a cost or expense) incurred in the upkeep or running of a plant, premises, or business and not attributable to individual products or items.
▶ **noun 1** (usu. **overheads**) an overhead cost or expense.
2 a transparency designed for use with an overhead projector.

overhead projector ▶ **noun** a device that projects an enlarged image of an acetate or other transparency placed on it on to a wall or screen by means of an overhead mirror.

overhear ▶ **verb** (past and past participle **-heard**) [with obj.] hear (someone or something) without meaning to or without the knowledge of the speaker: *I couldn't help overhearing your conversation.*

overheat ▶ **verb** make or become too hot: [no obj.] *her car started to overheat* | [with obj.] *it's vital not to overheat the liquid.*
■ Economics (of a country's economy) show marked inflation when increased demand results in rising prices rather then increased output: [no obj.] *in 1987 the Treasury had allowed the economy to overheat.*

Overijssel /ˌəʊvərˈʌɪs(ə)l/ a province of the east central Netherlands, north of the IJssel River, on the border with Germany; capital, Zwolle.

overindulge ▶ **verb** [no obj.] have too much of something enjoyable, especially food or drink: *it is easy to* ***overindulge in*** *these kinds of food.*
■ [with obj.] gratify the wishes of (someone) to an excessive extent: *his mother had overindulged him.*
– DERIVATIVES **overindulgence** noun, **overindulgent** adjective.

overinflated ▶ **adjective 1** (of a price or value) excessive: *overinflated land values.*
■ exaggerated: *there have been so many overinflated claims and unfulfilled promises.*
2 filled with too much air: *an overinflated balloon.*
– DERIVATIVES **overinflation** noun.

overinsured ▶ **adjective** having excessive insurance cover.
– DERIVATIVES **overinsurance** noun.

overissue ▶ **verb** (**-issues**, **-issued**, **-issuing**) [with obj.] issue (banknotes, shares, etc.) beyond the authorized amount or the issuer's ability to pay them on demand: *the Bank could deliberately overissue Treasury bills.*
▶ **noun** [mass noun] the action of overissuing banknotes, shares, etc.

overjoyed ▶ **adjective** extremely happy.

overkill ▶ **noun** [mass noun] the amount by which destruction or the capacity for destruction exceeds what is necessary: *the existing nuclear overkill.*
■ excessive use, treatment, or action; too much of something: *animators now face a dilemma of technology overkill.*

overladen ▶ **adjective** having too large or too heavy a load: *an overladen trolley* | figurative *the film is overladen with tear-jerking moments.*

overlaid past and past participle of **OVERLAY**[1].

overlain past participle of **OVERLIE**.

overland ▶ **adjective** & **adverb** by land: [as adj.] *an overland trade route* | [as adv.] *she journeyed overland.*
▶ **verb** [with obj. and adverbial of direction] Austral./NZ drive (livestock) over a long distance: *100,000 cattle were overlanded out of the Territory annually.*
■ [no obj., with adverbial of direction] travel by land, especially over a long distance: *they left the ship and overlanded to Coolgardie.*

overlander ▶ **noun** Austral./NZ a person who drives livestock over a long distance.
■ a person who travels a long distance overland, especially under arduous conditions. ■ informal a tramp.

overlap ▶ **verb** (**-lapped**, **-lapping**) [with obj.] extend over so as to cover partly: *the canopy overlaps the house roof at one end* | [no obj.] *the curtains overlap at the centre when closed.*
■ [no obj.] cover part of the same area of interest, responsibility, etc.: *the union's commitments* ***overlapped with*** *those of NATO.* ■ [no obj.] partly coincide in time: *two new series overlapped.*
▶ **noun** a part or amount which overlaps: *an overlap of about half an inch.*
■ a common area of interest, responsibility, etc.: *there are many overlaps between the approaches* | [mass noun] *there is some overlap in requirements.* ■ a period of time in which two events or activities happen together.

overlarge ▶ **adjective** too large: *an overlarge meal.*

overlay[1] ▶ **verb** (past and past participle **-laid**) [with obj.] (often **be overlaid with**) cover the surface of (a thing) with a coating: *their fingernails were overlaid with silver or gold.*
■ lie on top of: *a third screen which will overlay the others.* ■ figurative (of a quality or feeling) become more prominent than (a previous quality or feeling): *his openness had been overlaid by his new self-confidence.*
▶ **noun 1** something laid as a covering over something else: *a durable, cost-effective floor overlay.*
■ a transparent sheet placed over artwork or something such as a map, giving additional information or detail. ■ a graphical computer display which can be superimposed on another.
2 [mass noun] Computing the process of transferring a block of program code or other data into internal memory, replacing what is already stored.
■ [count noun] a block of code or other data transferred in such a way.

overlay[2] past of **OVERLIE**.

overleaf ▶ **adverb** on the other side of the page: *an information sheet is printed overleaf.*

overleap ▶ **verb** (past and past participle **-leaped** or **-leapt**) [with obj.] archaic jump over or across: *a stream that any five-years' child might overleap.*
■ omit; ignore: *whatever objection made by us, he finds too heavy to remove, he overleaps it.*
– ORIGIN Old English *oferhlēapan* (see **OVER**, **LEAP**).

overlie ▶ **verb** (**-lying**; past **-lay**; past participle **-lain**) [with obj.] lie on top of: *soft clays overlie the basalt* | figurative *the national situation was overlain by sharp regional differences.*

overload ▶ **verb** [with obj.] load with too great a burden or cargo: [as adj. **overloaded**] *overloaded vehicles are dangerous.*
■ give too much of something, typically something undesirable, to (someone): *the staff are heavily overloaded with casework.* ■ put too great a demand on (an electrical system): *the wiring had been overloaded.*
▶ **noun** [in sing.] an excessive amount: *an overload of stress.*

overlock ▶ **verb** [with obj.] strengthen and prevent fraying of (an edge of cloth) by oversewing it.
– DERIVATIVES **overlocker** noun.

overlong ▶ **adjective** & **adverb** too long: [as adj.] *an overlong sermon* | [as adv.] *the pass was delayed overlong.*

overlook ▶ **verb** [with obj.] **1** fail to notice

(something): *he seems to have overlooked one important fact.* ■ignore or disregard (something, especially a fault or offence): *she was more than ready to overlook his faults.* ■ pass over (someone) in favour of another: *he was overlooked by the Nobel committee.* **2** have a view of from above: *the chateau overlooks fields of corn and olive trees.* ■(**be overlooked**) (of a place) be open to view and so lack privacy: *it's better if the property isn't overlooked.* **3** archaic supervise: *he was overlooking his harvest men.* **4** archaic bewitch with the evil eye: *they told them they were overlooked by some unlucky Person.* ▶ noun N. Amer. a commanding position or view: *the overlook to the townsite.*

overlooker ▶ noun a person whose job it is to supervise the work of others.

overlord ▶ noun a ruler, especially a feudal lord.
– DERIVATIVES **overlordship** noun.

overly ▶ adverb [as submodifier] excessively: *she was a jealous and overly possessive woman.*

overlying present participle of **OVERLIE**.

overman ▶ verb (**-manned**, **-manning**) [with obj.] provide with more people than necessary: *the company was vastly overmanned.*
▶ noun (pl. **-men**) **1** an overseer in a colliery. **2** Philosophy another term for **SUPERMAN**. [ORIGIN: translation of Nietzsche's *Übermensch*.]

overmantel ▶ noun an ornamental structure over a mantelpiece, typically of plaster or carved wood and sometimes including a mirror.

overmaster ▶ verb poetic/literary [with obj.] overcome; conquer: *he was overmastered by events* | [as adj. **overmastering**] *an overmastering force of bombers.*

overmatch ▶ verb [with obj.] [usu. as adj. **overmatched**] chiefly N. Amer. be stronger, better armed, or more skilful than: *Bosnia's overmatched forces.*

overmighty ▶ adjective Brit. excessively powerful.

overmuch ▶ adverb, determiner, & pronoun too much: [as adv.] *I would not worry myself overmuch* | [as determiner] *the police may have overmuch regard for public order considerations* | [as pronoun] *she was requiring overmuch from him.*

overnice ▶ adjective dated excessively fussy or fastidious: *Mildred was overnice in regard to their father.*

overnight ▶ adverb for the duration of a night: *they refused to stay overnight.* ■during the course of a night: *you can recharge the battery overnight.* ■ very quickly; suddenly: *the picture made Wallis famous overnight.*
▶ adjective [attrib.] for use overnight: *an overnight bag.* ■done or happening overnight: *an overnight stay.* ■ sudden, rapid, or instant: *Tom became an overnight celebrity.*
▶ verb [no obj., with adverbial of place] stay for the night in a particular place: *I overnighted at the Beverly Wilshire.* ■[with obj.] N. Amer. convey (goods) at night, so that they arrive the next day: *Forster overnighted the sample to headquarters by courier.*
▶ noun a stop or stay lasting one night.

overnighter ▶ noun a person who stops at a place overnight. ■an overnight bag. ■ N. Amer. an overnight trip or stay.

over-optimistic ▶ adjective unjustifiably optimistic.
– DERIVATIVES **over-optimism** noun, **over-optimistically** adverb.

overpaid past and past participle of **OVERPAY**.

overpaint ▶ verb [with obj.] cover with a layer of paint.
▶ noun [mass noun] paint added as a covering layer.

overparted ▶ adjective chiefly Brit. having too difficult a part or role or too many parts or roles to play: *a sadly overparted soprano.*

over-particular ▶ adjective fussy: *passengers who were not over-particular about their time of arrival.*

overpass ▶ noun a bridge by which a road or railway line passes over another.
▶ verb [with obj.] rare surpass: *did not its sublimity overpass a little the bounds of the ridiculous?* ■archaic come to the end of (something): *the time of respite now being overpast, the king demanded surrender.*

overpay ▶ verb (past and past participle **-paid**) [with obj.] pay (someone) too highly: *many fans think our top players are overpaid.* ■pay (money) in excess of what is due: [as adj. **overpaid**] *the recovery of overpaid tax.*

– DERIVATIVES **overpayment** noun.

overpitch ▶ verb [with obj.] [often as adj. **overpitched**] **1** Cricket bowl (a ball) so that it pitches or would pitch too far up the pitch. **2** Brit. exaggerate: *the tone of his writing now seems overpitched.*

overplay ▶ verb [with obj.] give undue importance to; overemphasize: *he thinks the idea of a special relationship between sitter and artist is much overplayed.*
– PHRASES **overplay one's hand** spoil one's chance of success through excessive confidence in one's position.

overplus ▶ noun dated a surplus or excess: *an overplus of one ingredient.*
– ORIGIN late Middle English: partial translation of French *surplus* or medieval Latin *superplus*.

overpopulate ▶ verb [with obj.] populate (an area) in too large numbers: *the country was overpopulated.* ■[no obj.] (of an animal) breed too rapidly: *without natural predators, deer would overpopulate.*
– DERIVATIVES **overpopulation** noun.

overpower ▶ verb [with obj.] defeat or overcome with superior strength. ■be too intense for; overwhelm: *they were overpowered by the fumes* | [as adj. **overpowering**] *a feeling of overpowering sadness.*
– DERIVATIVES **overpoweringly** adverb.

overprescribe ▶ verb [with obj.] prescribe (a drug or treatment) in greater amounts or on more occasions than necessary: *doctors have been overprescribing antibiotics for decades.*
– DERIVATIVES **overprescription** noun.

overprice ▶ verb [with obj.] [often as adj. **overpriced**] charge too high a price for: *overpriced hotels.*

overprint ▶ verb [with obj.] **1** print additional matter on (a stamp or other surface already bearing print): *menus will be overprinted with company logos.* ■print (additional matter) on something already printed: *details specific to the issue in question were overprinted.* **2** print too many copies or too much of: [as noun **overprinting**] *the overprinting of paper money.* **3** Photography make (a print or other positive) darker than intended.
▶ noun [mass noun] words or other matter printed on to something already bearing print. ■[count noun] an overprinted postage stamp.

overproduce ▶ verb [with obj.] **1** produce more of (a product or commodity) than is wanted or needed: *our unplanned manufacturing system continually overproduces consumer products.* **2** [often as adj. **overproduced**] record or produce (a song or film) in such an elaborate way that the spontaneity or artistry of the original material is lost: *a series of overproduced albums.*
– DERIVATIVES **overproduction** noun.

overproof ▶ adjective containing more alcohol than proof spirit does: *overproof rum.*

overprotective ▶ adjective having a tendency to protect someone, especially a child, excessively.
– DERIVATIVES **overprotect** verb, **overprotection** noun, **overprotectiveness** noun.

overqualified ▶ adjective too highly qualified for a particular job.

overran past of **OVERRUN**.

overrate ▶ verb [with obj.] [often as adj. **overrated**] have a higher opinion of (someone or something) than is deserved: *an overrated player.*

overreach ▶ verb **1** [no obj.] strain oneself by reaching too far: *never lean sideways from a ladder or overreach.* ■(**overreach oneself**) defeat one's object by trying to do more than is possible: *the Church overreached itself in securing a territory that would prove impossible to hold.* ■ (of a horse, dog, or other quadruped) bring the hind feet so far forward that they fall alongside or strike the forefeet: *the horse overreached jumping the first hurdle.* **2** [with obj.] get the better of (someone) by cunning: *Faustus's lunacy in thinking he can overreach the devil.*
▶ noun an injury to a forefoot of a horse resulting from it having overreached.

overreacher ▶ noun N. Amer. a fraudster.

overreact ▶ verb [no obj.] respond more emotionally or forcibly than is justified: *the Authority are urging people not to overreact to the problem.*
– DERIVATIVES **overreaction** noun.

over-refine ▶ verb [with obj.] refine (something, especially food) too much.
– DERIVATIVES **over-refinement** noun.

over-report ▶ verb [with obj.] report (an event or instance of something) with disproportionately great frequency or emphasis: *newspapers over-reported sexual offences.*

over-represent ▶ verb [with obj.] include a disproportionately large number of (a particular category or type of person), especially as part of a statistical exercise: *using telephone owners as the sampling list would seriously over-represent the better off.* ■(**be over-represented**) form a disproportionately large percentage: *ethnic minorities are relatively over-represented in semi-skilled occupations.*
– DERIVATIVES **over-representation** noun.

override ▶ verb (past **-rode**; past participle **-ridden**) [with obj.] **1** use one's authority to reject or cancel (a decision, view, etc.): *the government can override all opposition.* ■interrupt the action of (an automatic device), typically in order to take manual control: *you can override the cut-out by releasing the switch.* ■ be more important than: *this commitment should override all other considerations.* **2** technical extend over; overlap: *the external rendering should not override the damp-proof membrane.* **3** travel or move over (a place or thing): [as noun **overriding**] *overriding by vehicles is implicated in over half the cases of footway damage.*
▶ noun **1** a device for suspending an automatic function on a machine. ■[mass noun] the action or process of suspending an automatic function. **2** an excess or increase on a budget, salary, or cost: *commission overrides give established carriers an unfair advantage.* **3** chiefly US a cancellation of a decision by exertion of authority or winning of votes.

overrider ▶ noun Brit. either of a pair of projecting pieces on the bumper of a car.

overriding ▶ adjective **1** more important than any other considerations: *their overriding need will be for advice.* **2** technical extending or moving over something, especially while remaining in close contact: *oceanic lithosphere beneath an overriding continental plate.*

overripe ▶ adjective too ripe; past its best: *overripe tomatoes.*

overrode past of **OVERRIDE**.

overruff ▶ verb [no obj.] (in bridge, whist, and similar card games) play a trump that is higher than one already played in the same trick: *there was a danger that West would be able to overruff.*
▶ noun an act of overruffing.

overrule ▶ verb [with obj.] reject or disallow by exercising one's superior authority: *Chief Judge Moran overruled the government's objections.* ■reject the decision or argument of (someone): *welfare staff overruled an experienced detective.*

overrun ▶ verb (**-running**; past **-ran**; past participle **-run**) [with obj.] **1** spread over or occupy (a place) in large numbers: *the Mediterranean has been overrun by tourists.* ■conquer or occupy (territory) by force: *the northern frontier was overrun by invaders.* ■ move or extend over or beyond: *let the text overrun the right-hand margin.* ■ run over or beyond (a thing or place): *Rufus overran third base.* ■ rotate faster than (another part of a machine): [as adj. **overrunning**] *an overrunning clutch.* **2** continue beyond or above (an expected or allowed time or cost): *he mustn't overrun his budget* | [no obj.] *he inadvertently allowed the match to overrun by 2 minutes.*
▶ noun **1** an instance of something exceeding an expected or allowed time or cost: *the cost overrun caused the company's share price to fall* | [mass noun] *an increase in the budgeted fee due to overrun of the project.* **2** [mass noun] the movement or extension of something beyond an allotted or particular position or space: *the system acts as a brake to prevent cable overrun.* ■[count noun] a clear area beyond the end of a runway. **3** [mass noun] the movement of a vehicle at a speed greater than is imparted by the engine.
– ORIGIN Old English *oferyrnan* (see **OVER-**, **RUN**).

oversail ▶ verb [with obj.] (of a part of a building) project beyond (a lower part): *a sloping stone coping oversailing a gutter.*

– ORIGIN late 17th cent. (originally Scots): from **OVER** + French *saillir* 'jut out'.

oversampling ▶ **noun** [mass noun] Electronics the technique of increasing the apparent sampling frequency of a digital signal by repeating each digit a number of times, in order to facilitate the subsequent filtering of unwanted noise.

oversaw past of **OVERSEE**.

overscan ▶ **noun** [mass noun] the facility on some computer screens or televisions to adjust the picture size so that the picture is bigger but the edges of the picture are lost.

overscrupulous ▶ **adjective** excessively scrupulous.
– DERIVATIVES **overscrupulousness** noun.

overseas ▶ **adverb** (Brit. also **oversea**) in or to a foreign country, especially one across the sea: *he spent quite a lot of time working overseas.*
▶ **adjective** [attrib.] (Brit. also **oversea**) from, to, or relating to a foreign country, especially one across the sea: *overseas trips.*
– PHRASES **from overseas** from abroad.

oversee ▶ **verb** (**-sees**; past **-saw**; past participle **-seen**) [with obj.] supervise (a person or their work), especially in an official capacity: *the Home Secretary oversees the police service.*
– ORIGIN Old English *ofersēon* 'look at from above' (see **OVER-**, **SEE**[1]).

overseer ▶ **noun** a person who supervises others, especially workers.
– ORIGIN late Middle English (also denoting a person appointed by a testator to assist the executor of a will): from **OVERSEE**.

overseer of the poor ▶ **noun** Brit. historical a parish official who administered funds to the poor. The office was established by the Poor Laws of Elizabeth I and abolished in 1925.

oversell ▶ **verb** (past and past participle **-sold**) [with obj.] sell more of (something) than exists or can be delivered: *he defrauded investors by deliberately overselling time shares.*
■ exaggerate the merits of: *computer-aided software engineering has been oversold.*

oversensitive ▶ **adjective** (especially of a person or an instrument) excessively sensitive: *Bentley was oversensitive to criticism.*
– DERIVATIVES **oversensitiveness** noun, **oversensitivity** noun.

overset ▶ **verb** (**-setting**; past and past participle **-set**) [with obj.] **1** upset emotionally: *the small kindness nearly overset her again.*
2 archaic overturn: *he jumped up and overset the canoe.*

oversew ▶ **verb** (past participle **-sewn** or **-sewed**) [with obj.] sew (the edges of two pieces of fabric) with every stitch passing over the join: *oversew the two long edges together.*
■ join the sections of (a book) in such a way.

oversexed ▶ **adjective** having unusually strong sexual desires.

overshadow ▶ **verb** [with obj.] tower above and cast a shadow over: *an enormous oak tree stood overshadowing the cottage.*
■ figurative cast a gloom over: *it is easy to let this feeling of tragedy overshadow his story.* ■ appear much more prominent or important than: *his competitive nature often overshadows the other qualities.* ■ (often **be overshadowed**) be more impressive or successful than (another person): *he was always overshadowed by his brilliant elder brother.*
– ORIGIN Old English *ofersceadwian* (see **OVER-**, **SHADOW**).

overshoe ▶ **noun** a shoe worn over a normal shoe, typically made either of rubber to protect the normal shoe or of felt to protect a floor surface.

overshoot ▶ **verb** (past and past participle **-shot**) [with obj.] go past (a point) unintentionally, especially through travelling too fast or being unable to stop: *they overshot their intended destination* | [no obj.] *he had overshot by fifty yards but backed up to the junction.*
■ (of an aircraft) fly beyond or taxi too far along (the runway) when landing or taking off: *he has overshot the landing strip again.* ■ exceed (a financial target or limit): *the department may overshoot its cash limit.*
▶ **noun** an act of going past or beyond a point, target, or limit.
■ an amount by which a financial target is exceeded.
– PHRASES **overshoot the mark** go beyond what is intended or acceptable.

overshot past and past participle of **OVERSHOOT**.
▶ **adjective** **1** (of a waterwheel) turned by water falling on to it from a channel.
2 denoting an upper jaw which projects beyond the lower jaw.

overside ▶ **adverb** over the side of a ship: *we saw him dumped unceremoniously overside by the guards.*

oversight ▶ **noun** **1** an unintentional failure to notice or do something: *he had simply missed Parsons out by an oversight* | [mass noun] *was the mistake due to oversight?*
2 [mass noun] the action of overseeing something: *effective oversight of the financial reporting process.*

oversimplify ▶ **verb** (**-ies**, **-ied**) [with obj.] [often as adj. **oversimplified**] simplify (something) so much that a distorted impression of it is given: *a false and oversimplified view of human personality.*
– DERIVATIVES **oversimplification** noun.

oversite ▶ **noun** a layer of concrete used to seal the earth under the ground floor of a house.

oversized (also **oversize**) ▶ **adjective** bigger than the usual size: *an oversized T-shirt.*

overskirt ▶ **noun** an outer skirt, worn over the skirt of a dress.

overslaugh /ˈəʊvəslɔː/ ▶ **verb** [with obj.] US pass over (someone) in favour of another: *during the war officers were often overslaughed.*
– ORIGIN mid 18th cent.: from Dutch *overslag* (noun), from *overslaan* 'pass over'.

oversleep ▶ **verb** (past and past participle **-slept**) [no obj.] sleep longer or later than one intended: *we talked until the early hours and consequently I overslept.*

oversleeve ▶ **noun** a protective sleeve covering an ordinary sleeve.

oversold past and past participle of **OVERSELL**.

oversolicitous ▶ **adjective** showing excessive concern for another person's welfare or interests.
– DERIVATIVES **oversolicitude** noun.

oversoul ▶ **noun** [in sing.] a divine spirit supposed to pervade the universe and to encompass all human souls. The term is associated particularly with Transcendentalism.

overspecialize (also **-ise**) ▶ **verb** [no obj.] concentrate too much on one aspect or area of something: [as adj. **overspecialized**] *overspecialized medicine.*
– DERIVATIVES **overspecialization** noun.

overspend ▶ **verb** (past and past participle **-spent**) [no obj.] spend too much: *she overspent on her husband's funeral.*
■ [with obj.] spend more than (a specified amount): *the department can see that it is going to overspend its budget.*
▶ **noun** [in sing.] an act of overspending a limit.
■ an amount by which a limit is overspent.

overspill ▶ **noun** [mass noun] Brit. people or things that spill over or are in excess, especially the surplus population moving or forced to move from an overcrowded to a less heavily populated area.

overspray ▶ **noun** [mass noun] excess paint or other liquid which spreads or blows beyond an area being sprayed.

overspread ▶ **verb** (past and past participle **-spread**) [with obj.] cover the surface of; spread over: *a giant bramble had overspread the path.*
– ORIGIN Old English *ofersprǣdan* (see **OVER-**, **SPREAD**).

overstaff ▶ **verb** [with obj.] provide with more members of staff than are necessary: *government departments are always overstaffed.*

overstate ▶ **verb** [with obj.] express or state too strongly; exaggerate: *I may have overstated my case to make my point.*
– DERIVATIVES **overstatement** noun.

overstay ▶ **verb** [with obj.] stay longer than the time, limits, or duration of: *he was arrested for overstaying his visa.*
– PHRASES **overstay one's welcome** see **WELCOME**.
– DERIVATIVES **overstayer** noun.

oversteer ▶ **verb** [no obj.] (of a motor vehicle) have a tendency to turn more sharply than was intended.
▶ **noun** [mass noun] the tendency of a vehicle to turn in such a way.

overstep ▶ **verb** (**-stepped**, **-stepping**) pass beyond (a limit): *you must not overstep your borrowing limit.*
■ violate (a rule or standard of behaviour): *he has overstepped the bounds of acceptable discipline.*
– PHRASES **overstep the mark** behave in an unacceptable way.

overstimulate ▶ **verb** [with obj.] stimulate physiologically or mentally to an excessive degree: *hot water overstimulates the sebaceous glands.*
– DERIVATIVES **overstimulation** noun.

overstitch ▶ **noun** a stitch made over an edge or over another stitch.
▶ **verb** [with obj.] sew with such a stitch: [as adj. **overstitched**] *the baggy, overstitched look.*

overstock ▶ **verb** [with obj.] supply with more of something than is necessary or required: *do not overstock the kitchen with food.*
■ put more animals in (an area) than it is capable of supporting in terms of food or space.
▶ **noun** [mass noun] chiefly US (especially in a manufacturing or retailing context) a supply or quantity in excess of demand or requirement: *factory overstock* | [count noun] *publishers' overstocks and remainders.*

overstrain ▶ **verb** [with obj.] subject to an excessive demand on strength, resources, or abilities: *there was a risk he might overstrain his heart.*
▶ **noun** [mass noun] the action or result of subjecting someone or something to such a demand: *overstrain had brought on tuberculosis.*

overstress ▶ **verb** [with obj.] (often **be overstressed**) subject to or cause too much physical or mental stress in: *they are prone to nervous breakdowns if overstressed.*
■ lay too much emphasis on: *the value of good legal assistance cannot be overstressed.*
▶ **noun** [mass noun] excessive stress.

overstretch ▶ **verb** [with obj.] [often as adj. **overstretched**] stretch too much: *the aches and pains of overstretched muscles.*
■ figurative make excessive demands on: *classes are very large and facilities are overstretched.*

overstrike ▶ **noun** [mass noun] the superimposing of one printed character or one coin design on another.
■ [count noun] a coin showing one design superimposed on another.
– DERIVATIVES **overstriking** noun.

overstrung ▶ **adjective** **1** /ˈəʊvəstrʌŋ/ (of a piano) with strings in sets crossing each other obliquely.
2 /əʊvəˈstrʌŋ/ dated (of a person) extremely nervous or tense.

overstuff ▶ **verb** [with obj.] [usu. as adj. **overstuffed**] **1** force too much into (a container): *an overstuffed briefcase.*
2 cover (furniture) completely with upholstery: *an overstuffed armchair.*

oversubscribed ▶ **adjective** (of something for sale) applied for in greater quantities than are available: *shares on sale in Europe were oversubscribed.*
■ (of a course or an institution) having more applications than available places.

oversubtle ▶ **adjective** making excessively fine distinctions: *an oversubtle argument.*

oversupply ▶ **noun** an excessive supply: *an oversupply of teachers* | [mass noun] *oversupply causes prices to fall.*
▶ **verb** (**-ies**, **-ied**) [with obj.] (usu. **be oversupplied**) supply with too much or too many: *the country was oversupplied with lawyers.*

oversusceptible ▶ **adjective** too susceptible or vulnerable.

overt /əʊˈvəːt, ˈəʊvəːt/ ▶ **adjective** done or shown openly; plainly or readily apparent, not secret or hidden: *an overt act of aggression* | *people with HIV progressing to overt Aids.*
– DERIVATIVES **overtly** adverb, **overtness** noun.
– ORIGIN Middle English: from Old French, past participle of *ovrir* 'to open', from Latin *aperire.*

overtake ▶ **verb** (past **-took**; past participle **-taken**) [with obj.] **1** catch up with and pass while travelling in the same direction: *the driver overtook a line of vehicles* | [no obj.] *he overtook in the face of oncoming traffic.*
■ become greater or more successful than: *Germany rapidly overtook Britain in industrial output.*
2 (especially of misfortune) come suddenly or unexpectedly upon: *the report was* **overtaken by events**.
■ (of a feeling) affect (someone) suddenly and powerfully: *weariness overtook him and he retired to bed.*

overtask ▶ **verb** [with obj.] impose too much work on: [as adj. **overtasked**] *an overtasked school system.*

overtax ▶ **verb** [with obj.] **1** require to pay too much

tax: *the UK is not overtaxed compared to other countries.* **2** make excessive demands on (a person's strength, abilities, etc.): *do athletes overtax their hearts?*
– DERIVATIVES **overtaxation** noun (only in sense 1).

overthrow ▶ verb (past **-threw**; past participle **-thrown**) [with obj.] **1** remove forcibly from power: *military coups which had attempted to overthrow the King.*
■ put an end to (something), typically by the use of force or violence: *their subversive activities are calculated to overthrow parliamentary democracy.* ■ archaic knock or throw to the ground: *one who is already prostrate cannot be overthrown.*
2 throw (a ball) further than the intended distance: *he grips the ball too tight and overthrows it.*
■ chiefly N. Amer. throw a ball beyond (a receiving player): *Perkins jumped on him for overthrowing wideout Mark Carrier early in the game.*
▶ noun **1** [in sing.] a removal from power; a defeat or downfall: *plotting the overthrow of the government.*
2 (in cricket, baseball, and other games) a throw which sends a ball past its intended recipient or target.
■ a score made because the ball has been overthrown: *his throw missed the stumps and went for four overthrows.*
3 a panel of decorated wrought-iron work above an arch or gateway.

overthrust Geology ▶ noun the thrust of one series of rock strata over another, especially along a fault line at a shallow angle to the horizontal.
▶ verb (past and past participle **-thrust**) [with obj.] force (a body of rock) over another: [as noun **overthrusting**] *the increased overburden resulting from overthrusting.*
■ (of a body of rock) be forced over (another formation): *the shales are overthrust by Carboniferous rocks.*

overtime ▶ noun [mass noun] time worked in addition to one's normal working hours: *fewer opportunities for overtime* | [as modifier] *an overtime ban.*
■ payment for such extra work. ■ N. Amer. extra time played at the end of a game that is tied at the end of the regulation time: *they lost in overtime.*
▶ adverb in addition to normal working hours: *they were working overtime to fulfil a big order* | figurative *his brain was working overtime.*

overtire ▶ verb [with obj.] exhaust (someone): *walk at a pace that does not overtire you.*

overtone ▶ noun **1** a musical tone which is a part of the harmonic series above a fundamental note, and may be heard with it.
■ Physics a component of any oscillation whose frequency is an integral multiple of the fundamental frequency.
2 (often **overtones**) a subtle or subsidiary quality, implication, or connotation: *the decision may have political overtones.*
– ORIGIN mid 19th cent.: from **OVER-** + **TONE**, suggested by German *Oberton.*

overtop ▶ verb (**-topped**, **-topping**) [with obj.] exceed in height: *no building is allowed to overtop the cathedral.*
■ (especially of water) rise over the top of (a barrier constructed to hold it back): *the old sea wall is regularly overtopped by high tides.* ■ archaic be superior to in quality: *none can overtop him in goodness.*
▶ adverb & preposition chiefly Canadian over: [as adv.] *the fence broke as he climbed overtop* | [as prep.] *sprinkle the mixture overtop the batter.*

overtrade ▶ verb [no obj.] engage in more business than can be supported by the market or by the funds or resources available.

overtrain ▶ verb [no obj.] (especially of an athlete) train too hard or for too long.
■ [with obj.] subject to excessive training: *the team overtrained their young players.*

overtrick ▶ noun Bridge a trick taken by the declarer in excess of the contract.

overtrousers ▶ plural noun waterproof trousers, typically worn over other trousers.

overtrump ▶ verb another term for **OVERRUFF**.

overture ▶ noun an orchestral piece at the beginning of an opera, suite, play, oratorio, or other extended composition.
■ an independent orchestral composition in one movement. ■ an introduction to something more substantial: *the talks were no more than an overture to a long debate.* ■ (usu. **overtures**) an approach or proposal made to someone with the aim of opening negotiations or establishing a relationship: *Coleen listened to his overtures of love.*
– ORIGIN late Middle English (in the sense 'aperture'): from Old French, from Latin *apertura* 'aperture'.

overturn ▶ verb [with obj.] **1** tip (something) over so that it is on its side or upside down: *the crowd proceeded to overturn cars and set them on fire.*
■ [no obj.] turn over and come to rest upside down, typically as the result of an accident: *a coach hit a car and overturned.*
2 abolish, invalidate, or turn around (an established fact, system, etc.): *the results overturned previous findings.*
■ reverse (a legal decision): *he fought for eight years to overturn a conviction for armed robbery.*
▶ noun rare an act of turning over or upsetting something; a revolution, subversion, or reversal.
■ [mass noun] Ecology the occasional (typically twice yearly) mixing of the water of a thermally stratified lake.

overtype ▶ verb [with obj.] type over (another character) on a computer screen: *overtype it with the correct number and press Return.*
▶ noun [mass noun] a facility or operating mode allowing overtyping.

overuse ▶ verb [with obj.] use too much: *young children sometimes overuse 'and' in their writing.*
▶ noun [mass noun] excessive use: *overuse of natural resources.*

overvalue ▶ verb (**-values**, **-valued**, **-valuing**) [with obj.] overestimate the importance of: *intelligence can be overvalued.*
■ fix the value of (something, especially a currency) at too high a level: *sterling was overvalued against the dollar.*
– DERIVATIVES **overvaluation** noun.

overview ▶ noun a general review or summary of a subject: *a brief overview of the survey.*
▶ verb [with obj.] give a general review or summary of: *the report overviews the needs of the community.*

overwater ▶ verb [with obj.] water (a plant, a sports field, etc.) too much: *your cutting needs some water, but make sure you don't overwater it.*
▶ adjective situated or taking place above water: *the airline is to initiate long-haul overwater operations.*

overweening ▶ adjective showing excessive confidence or pride: *overweening ambition.*
– DERIVATIVES **overweeningly** adverb.

overweight ▶ adjective above a weight considered normal or desirable: *she was a stone overweight.*
■ above an allowed weight: *an overweight lorry.*
▶ noun [mass noun] excessive or extra weight.
▶ verb [with obj.] [usu. as adj. **overweighted**] put too much weight on; overload.

overwhelm ▶ verb [with obj.] bury or drown beneath a huge mass: *the embankment was overwhelmed and water surrounded the mosque.*
■ defeat completely: [with obj. and complement] *the Irish side was overwhelmed 15–3 by Scotland.* ■ (often **be overwhelmed**) give too much of a thing to (someone); inundate: *they were overwhelmed by farewell messages.* ■ (usu. **be overwhelmed**) have a strong emotional effect on: *I was overwhelmed with guilt.* ■ be too strong for; overpower: *the Stilton doesn't overwhelm the flavour of the trout.*

overwhelming ▶ adjective very great in amount: *his party won overwhelming support.*
■ (especially of an emotion) very strong: *she felt an overwhelming desire to giggle.*
– DERIVATIVES **overwhelmingly** adverb, **overwhelmingness** noun.

overwind ▶ verb (past and past participle **-wound**) [with obj.] wind (a mechanism, especially a watch) beyond the proper stopping point.

overwinter ▶ verb [no obj.] **1** [with adverbial of place] spend the winter: *many birds overwinter in equatorial regions.*
2 (of an insect, plant, etc.) live through the winter: *the germinated seeds will overwinter.*
■ [with obj.] keep (an animal or plant) alive through the winter: *check any begonias that you intend to overwinter.*

overwork ▶ verb [with obj.] exhaust with too much work: *executives who are overworked and worried* | [as adj. **overworked**] *tired, overworked, demoralized staff.*
■ [no obj.] (of a person) work too hard: *the doctor advised a complete rest because he had been overworking.* ■ (usu. **be overworked**) make excessive use of: *our lifts are overworked.* ■ [usu. as adj. **overworked**] use (a word or idea) too much and so make it weaker in meaning or effect: *'Breathtaking' is an overworked brochure cliché.*
▶ noun [mass noun] excessive work: *his health broke down under the strain of overwork.*

overwound past and past participle of **OVERWIND**.

overwrap ▶ verb (**-wrapped**, **-wrapping**) [with obj.] cover with a wrapping: *when the food is cold, overwrap it tightly with foil.*
■ wrap or envelop too much: *the risk of cot death is reduced if infants are not overwrapped or overheated.*
▶ noun an outer wrapping: *a cellophane overwrap.*

overwrite ▶ verb (past **-wrote**; past participle **-written**) [with obj.] **1** write on top of (other writing): *many names had been scratched out or overwritten.*
■ Computing destroy (data) or the data in (a file) by entering new data in its place: *an entry stating who is allowed to overwrite the file.* ■ another term for **OVERTYPE**.
2 write too elaborately or ornately: *there is a tendency to overwrite their parts and fall into cliché.*
3 [no obj.] [usu. as noun **overwriting**] (in insurance) accept more risk than the premium income limits allow.

overwrought ▶ adjective **1** in a state of nervous excitement or anxiety: *she was too overwrought to listen to reason.*
2 (of a piece of writing or a work of art) too elaborate or complicated in design or construction.
– ORIGIN late Middle English: archaic past participle of **OVERWORK**.

overzealous ▶ adjective too zealous in one's attitude or behaviour: *he's been overzealous in handing out parking tickets.*

ovi- ▶ combining form chiefly Zoology of or relating to eggs or ova: *oviparous.*
– ORIGIN from Latin *ovum* 'egg'.

Ovid /ˈɒvɪd/ (43 BC–*c.*17 AD), Roman poet; full name *Publius Ovidius Naso.* He is particularly known for his elegiac love poems (such as the *Amores* and the *Ars Amatoria*) and for the *Metamorphoses*, a hexametric epic which retells Greek and Roman myths.

oviduct /ˈəʊvɪdʌkt/ ▶ noun Anatomy & Zoology the tube through which an ovum or egg passes from an ovary.
– DERIVATIVES **oviducal** /-ˈdjuːk(ə)l/ adjective, **oviductal** adjective.

Oviedo /ˌɒvɪˈeɪdəʊ, Spanish oˈβjeðo/ a city in NW Spain, capital of the Asturias; pop. 203,190 (1991).

oviform /ˈəʊvɪfɔːm/ ▶ adjective egg-shaped.

Ovimbundu see **MBUNDU**.

ovine /ˈəʊvʌɪn/ ▶ adjective of, relating to, affecting, or resembling sheep: *the ovine immune system.*
– ORIGIN early 19th cent.: from late Latin *ovinus*, from Latin *ovis* 'sheep'.

oviparous /əʊˈvɪp(ə)rəs/ ▶ adjective Zoology (of an animal) producing young by means of eggs which are hatched after they have been laid by the parent, as in birds. Compare with **VIVIPAROUS** and **OVOVIVIPAROUS**.
– DERIVATIVES **oviparity** noun.

oviposit /ˌəʊvɪˈpɒzɪt/ ▶ verb (**oviposited**, **ovipositing**) [no obj.] Zoology (especially of an insect) lay an egg or eggs: *larger females have the potential to oviposit on a greater number of hosts.*
– DERIVATIVES **oviposition** noun.
– ORIGIN early 19th cent.: from **OVI-** 'egg' + Latin *posit-* 'placed' (from the verb *ponere*).

ovipositor /ˌəʊvɪˈpɒzɪtə/ ▶ noun Zoology a tubular organ through which a female insect or fish deposits eggs.

ovoid /ˈəʊvɔɪd/ ▶ adjective (of a solid or a three-dimensional surface) more or less egg-shaped.
■ (of a plane figure) oval, especially with one end more pointed than the other.
▶ noun an ovoid body or surface.
– ORIGIN early 19th cent.: from French *ovoïde*, from modern Latin *ovoides*, from Latin *ovum* 'egg'.

ovolo /ˈəʊvələʊ/ ▶ noun (pl. **ovoli** /-liː/) Architecture a rounded convex moulding.
– ORIGIN mid 17th cent.: from Italian, diminutive of *ovo* 'egg', from Latin *ovum.*

ovotestis /ˌəʊvəʊˈtɛstɪs/ ▶ noun (pl. **ovotestes** /-tiːz/) Zoology an organ producing both ova and spermatozoa, especially in some gastropod molluscs.
– ORIGIN late 19th cent.: from **OVUM** + **TESTIS**.

ovoviviparous /ˌəʊvəʊvɪˈvɪp(ə)rəs/ ▶ adjective Zoology (of an animal) producing young by means of eggs which are hatched within the body of the parent, as in some snakes. Compare with **OVIPAROUS** and **VIVIPAROUS**.
– DERIVATIVES **ovoviviparity** noun.

ovulate /ˈɒvjʊleɪt/ ▶ verb [no obj.] discharge ova or

ovules from the ovary: *women who ovulate but cannot conceive* | [with obj.] *all the eggs that will be ovulated are present at birth.*
– DERIVATIVES **ovulation** noun, **ovulatory** adjective.
– ORIGIN late 19th cent.: back-formation from *ovulation*, or from medieval Latin *ovulum* 'little egg' (see **OVULE**) + **-ATE**[3].

ovule /ˈɒvjuːl, ˈəʊ-/ ▶ **noun** Botany the part of the ovary of seed plants that contains the female germ cell and after fertilization becomes the seed.
– DERIVATIVES **ovular** adjective.
– ORIGIN early 19th cent.: from French, from medieval Latin *ovulum*, diminutive of **OVUM**.

ovum /ˈəʊvəm/ ▶ **noun** (pl. **ova** /ˈəʊvə/) Biology a mature female reproductive cell, especially of a human or other animal, which can divide to give rise to an embryo usually only after fertilization by a male cell.
– ORIGIN early 18th cent.: from Latin, literally 'egg'.

ow ▶ **exclamation** used to express sudden pain: *Ow! You're hurting me!*
– ORIGIN natural exclamation: first recorded in English in the mid 19th cent.

owe ▶ **verb** [with obj.] have an obligation to pay or repay (something, especially money) in return for something received: *they have denied they owe money to the company* | [with two objs] *you owe me £19.50 for the electricity bill.*
■ owe something, especially money, to (someone): *I owe you for the taxi.* ■ be under a moral obligation to give someone (gratitude, respect, etc.): *I* **owe it to** *him to explain what's happened* | [with two objs] *I owe you an apology.* ■ **(owe something to)** have something because of (someone or something): *champagne houses owe their success to brand image.* ■ be indebted to someone or something for (something): *I owe my life to you.*
– PHRASES **owe someone a grudge** see **GRUDGE**. **owe it to oneself (to do something)** need to do something to protect one's own interests: *you owe it to yourself to take care of your body.* **owe someone one** informal feel indebted to someone: *thanks, I owe you one for this.* **someone/thing owes one a living** used to express disapproval of someone who expects to receive financial support or other benefits without doing any work: *they think the world owes them a living.*
– ORIGIN Old English *āgan* 'own, have it as an obligation', of Germanic origin; from an Indo-European root shared by Sanskrit *īś* 'possess, own'. Compare with **OUGHT**[1].

O

Owen[1], Sir Richard (1804–92), English anatomist and palaeontologist. Owen made important contributions to evolution, taxonomy, and palaeontology and coined the word *dinosaur* in 1841. He was a strong opponent of Darwinism.

Owen[2], Robert (1771–1858), Welsh social reformer and industrialist. A pioneer socialist thinker, he founded a model industrial community in Scotland, organized on principles of mutual cooperation, the first of a series of cooperative communities.

Owen[3], Wilfred (1893–1918), English poet. His experiences of fighting in the First World War inspired his best-known works, such as 'Anthem for Doomed Youth'.

Owens, Jesse (1913–80), American athlete; born *James Cleveland Owens*. In 1935 he equalled or broke six world records in 45 minutes, and in 1936 won four gold medals at the Olympic Games in Berlin. The success in Berlin of Owens, as a black man, outraged Hitler.

owing ▶ **adjective** [predic.] (of money) yet to be paid: *no rent was owing.*
– PHRASES **owing to** because of or on account of: *his reading was hesitant owing to a stammer.*

owl ▶ **noun** a nocturnal bird of prey with large eyes, a facial disc, a hooked beak, and typically a loud hooting call.
● Order Strigiformes: families Strigidae (**typical owls** such as tawny owls and eagle owls) and Tytonidae (**barn owls** and their relatives).
■ informal a person compared to an owl, especially in being active or wakeful at night. Often contrasted with **LARK**[1].
– DERIVATIVES **owl-like** adjective.
– ORIGIN Old English *ūle*, of Germanic origin; related to Dutch *uil* and German *Eule*, from a base imitative of the bird's call.

owl butterfly ▶ **noun** a very large South American butterfly which flies at dusk, with a large eye-like marking on the underside of each hindwing.
● Genus *Caligo*, subfamily Brassolinae, family Nymphalidae.

owlet ▶ **noun 1** a small owl found chiefly in Asia and Africa.
● Genus *Glaucidium* and *Athene*, family Strigidae: several species.
■ a young owl of any kind.
2 another term for **NOCTUID**.

owlet-nightjar ▶ **noun** a nocturnal Australasian bird resembling a small nightjar, with an owl-like face and a large gape.
● Family Aegothelidae and genus *Aegotheles*: several species.

owl-faced monkey ▶ **noun** a guenon that has a black face with white and yellow markings and bright blue skin on the rump, living in the forests of central Africa.
● *Cercopithecus hamlyni*, family Cercopithecidae.

owlish ▶ **adjective** like an owl, especially in acting or appearing wise or solemn: *he had an owlish and solemn air.*
■ (of glasses) resembling the large round eyes of an owl.
– DERIVATIVES **owlishly** adverb, **owlishness** noun.

owl light ▶ **noun** dusk; twilight.

owl monkey ▶ **noun** another term for **DOUROUCOULI**.

owl parrot ▶ **noun** another term for **KAKAPO**.

own ▶ **adjective** & **pronoun** used with a possessive to emphasize that someone or something belongs or relates to the person mentioned: [as adj.] *they can't handle their own children* | *I was an outcast among my own kind* | [as pronoun] *the Church would look after its own.*
■ done or produced by and for the person specified: [as adj.] *I used to design all my own clothes* | [as pronoun] *they claimed the work as their own.* ■ particular to the person or thing mentioned; individual: [as adj.] *the style had its own charm* | [as pronoun] *the film had a quality all its own.* ■ [as attrib. adj.] S. African historical (without a possessive) relating exclusively to a particular ethnic group: *an own nation.*
▶ **verb 1** [with obj.] have (something) as one's own; possess: *his father owns a restaurant* | [as adj., in combination **-owned**] *a state-owned company.*
2 [no obj.] formal admit or acknowledge that something is the case or that one feels a certain way: *she* **owned to** *a feeling of profound jealousy* | [with clause] *he was reluctant to own that he was indebted.*
■ [with obj.] archaic acknowledge paternity, authorship, or possession of: *he has published little, trivial things which he will not own.*
– PHRASES **as if** (or **like**) **one owns the place** informal in an overbearing or self-important manner. **be one's own man** (or **woman**) act independently and with confidence. ■ archaic be in full possession of one's faculties. **come into its** (or **one's**) **own** become fully effective, used, or recognized: *the two folk languages will at last come into their own.* **get one's own back** informal take action in retaliation for a wrongdoing or insult. **hold one's own** retain a position of strength in a challenging situation. **of one's own** belonging to oneself alone: *at last I've got a place of my own.* **on one's own** unaccompanied by others; alone or unaided.
– ORIGIN Old English *āgen* (adjective and pronoun) 'owned, possessed', past participle of *āgan* 'owe'; the verb (Old English *āgnian* 'possess', also 'make own's own') was originally from the adjective, later probably reintroduced from **OWNER**.
▶ **own up** admit or confess to having done something wrong or embarrassing: *he* **owns up to** *few mistakes.*

own affair ▶ **noun** historical (in South Africa) a matter defined as being specific to a particular ethnic group, and controlled by that group through a chamber of the tricameral parliament.

own brand ▶ **noun** Brit. **1** a product manufactured specially for a retailer and bearing the retailer's name.
2 a kind or variety of something particular to a person or group: *his own brand of humour.*

owner ▶ **noun** a person who owns something: *the proud owner of a huge Dalmatian.*
■ informal the captain of a ship.
– DERIVATIVES **ownerless** adjective, **ownership** noun.

owner-occupier ▶ **noun** Brit. a person who owns the house, flat, etc. in which he or she lives.
– DERIVATIVES **owner-occupied** adjective.

own goal ▶ **noun** (in soccer) a goal scored when a player inadvertently strikes or deflects the ball into their own team's goal.
■ informal an act that unintentionally harms one's own interests.

own-label ▶ **adjective** [attrib.] (of a product) manufactured for a retailer and sold under the retailer's name rather than the manufacturer's brand name.
▶ **noun** a product sold by a retail business under its own name.

owt /aʊt/ ▶ **pronoun** N. English anything: *I've never seen owt like it.*
– ORIGIN mid 19th cent.: variant of **AUGHT**[1].

ox ▶ **noun** (pl. **oxen** /ˈɒks(ə)n/) a domesticated bovine animal kept for milk or meat; a cow or bull. See **CATTLE** (sense 1).
■ a castrated male of this, formerly much used as a draught animal: [as modifier] *an ox cart.* ■ an animal of a group related to the domestic ox. See **CATTLE** (sense 2).
– ORIGIN Old English *oxa*, of Germanic origin; related to Dutch *os* and German *Ochse*, from an Indo-European root shared by Sanskrit *ukṣán* 'bull'.

ox- ▶ **combining form** variant spelling of **OXY-**[2] reduced before a vowel (as in *oxazole*).

oxacillin /ˌɒksəˈsɪlɪn/ ▶ **noun** [mass noun] Medicine an antibiotic drug made by chemical modification of penicillin and used to treat bacterial infections.
– ORIGIN 1960s: blend of **OXAZOLE** and **PENICILLIN**.

oxalic acid /ɒkˈsalɪk/ ▶ **noun** [mass noun] Chemistry a poisonous crystalline acid with a sour taste, present in rhubarb leaves, wood sorrel, and other plants.
● Alternative name: **ethanedioic acid**; chem. formula: $(COOH)_2$.
– DERIVATIVES **oxalate** /ˈɒksəleɪt/ noun.
– ORIGIN late 18th cent.: *oxalic* from French *oxalique*, via Latin from Greek *oxalis* 'wood sorrel'.

oxalis /ˈɒksəlɪs, ɒkˈsɑːlɪs/ ▶ **noun** a plant of a genus which includes the wood sorrel, typically having three-lobed leaves and white, yellow, or pink flowers.
● Genus *Oxalis*, family Oxalidaceae.
– ORIGIN early 17th cent.: via Latin from Greek, from *oxus* 'sour' (because of its sharp-tasting leaves).

oxazole /ˈɒksəzəʊl/ ▶ **noun** [mass noun] Chemistry a volatile liquid with weakly basic properties, whose molecule contains a five-membered ring important as the basis of a number of medicinal drugs.
● A heterocyclic compound; chem. formula: C_3H_3NO.
– ORIGIN late 19th cent.: from **OX-** 'oxygen' + **AZO-** + **-OLE**.

oxbow /ˈɒksbəʊ/ ▶ **noun 1** a loop formed by a horseshoe bend in a river.
■ short for **OXBOW LAKE**.
2 a U-shaped collar of an ox-yoke.

oxbow lake ▶ **noun** a curved lake formed from a horseshoe bend in a river where the main stream has cut across the narrow end and no longer flows around the loop of the bend.

Oxbridge ▶ **noun** Oxford and Cambridge universities regarded together: [as modifier] *Oxbridge colleges.*
– ORIGIN mid 19th cent.: blend of **OXFORD** and **CAMBRIDGE**.

oxen plural form of **OX**.

oxer ▶ **noun** an ox-fence or a fence resembling this.
■ (in showjumping) a jump consisting of a brush fence with a guard rail on one or both sides.

ox-eye ▶ **noun** a yellow-flowered North American plant of the daisy family.
● *Heliopsis helianthoides*, family Compositae.

ox-eye daisy ▶ **noun** a Eurasian daisy which has large white flowers with yellow centres. Also called **MOON DAISY** or **MARGUERITE**.
● *Leucanthemum vulgare*, family Compositae.

Oxf. ▶ **abbreviation for** Oxford.

Oxfam a British charity founded in Oxford in 1942, dedicated to helping victims of famine and natural disasters as well as raising living standards in developing countries.
– ORIGIN from Ox*(ford Committee for)* Fam*(ine Relief)*.

ox-fence ▶ **noun** a strong fence for confining cattle, consisting of a hedge with a strong guard rail on one side, and usually a ditch on the other.

Oxford a city in central England, on the River Thames, the county town of Oxfordshire; pop. 109,000 (1991).

oxford (also **oxford shoe**) ▶ noun a type of lace-up shoe with a low heel.

Oxford bags ▶ plural noun Brit. wide baggy trousers.
– ORIGIN 1920s: named after the city of **OXFORD**.

Oxford blue ▶ noun Brit. **1** [mass noun] a dark blue, typically with a purple tinge.
2 a person who has represented Oxford University in a particular sport.

Oxford cloth ▶ noun [mass noun] a heavy cotton cloth chiefly used to make shirts.

Oxford English Dictionary (abbrev.: **OED**) the largest dictionary of the English language, prepared in Oxford and originally issued in instalments between 1884 and 1928.

Oxford Group a Christian movement popularized in Oxford in the late 1920s, advocating discussion of personal problems by groups. Later known as **MORAL REARMAMENT**.

Oxfordian ▶ adjective **1** Geology of, relating to, or denoting an age in the Upper Jurassic period, lasting from about 157 to 155 million years ago. Also called **CORALLIAN**.
2 relating to or denoting the theory that Edward de Vere (1550–1604), Earl of Oxford, wrote the plays attributed to Shakespeare.
▶ noun **1** (**the Oxfordian**) Geology the Oxfordian age or the system of rocks (chiefly coral-derived limestones) deposited during it.
2 a supporter of the Oxfordian theory.

Oxford Movement a Christian movement started in Oxford in 1833, seeking to restore traditional Catholic teachings and ceremonial within the Church of England. Its leaders were John Keble, Edward Pusey, and (until he became a Roman Catholic) John Henry Newman. It formed the basis of the present Anglo-Catholic (or High Church) tradition. Also called **TRACTARIANISM**.

Oxfordshire a county of south central England; county town, Oxford.

Oxford University the oldest English university, comprising a federation of thirty-nine colleges, the first of which, University College, was formally founded in 1249. The university was established at Oxford soon after 1167.

oxherd ▶ noun archaic a cowherd.
– ORIGIN Old English, from **OX** + obsolete *herd* 'herdsman'.

oxhide ▶ noun [mass noun] leather made from the hide of an ox.

oxic /ˈɒksɪk/ ▶ adjective (of a process or environment) in which oxygen is involved or present.
– ORIGIN 1960s: from *ox*(*ide*) or *ox*(*ygen*) + **-IC**.

oxidant /ˈɒksɪd(ə)nt/ ▶ noun an oxidizing agent.
– ORIGIN late 19th cent.: from French (modern French *oxydant*), present participle of *oxider* 'oxidize'.

oxidase /ˈɒksɪdeɪz/ ▶ noun Biochemistry an enzyme which promotes the transfer of a hydrogen atom from a particular substrate to an oxygen molecule, forming water or hydrogen peroxide.
– ORIGIN late 19th cent.: from French *oxydase*, from *oxyde* 'oxide'.

oxidation /ˌ/ ▶ noun [mass noun] Chemistry the process or result of oxidizing or being oxidized.
– DERIVATIVES **oxidational** adjective, **oxidative** adjective.
– ORIGIN late 18th cent.: from French (modern French *oxydation*), from *oxider* 'oxidize'.

oxidation number (also **oxidation state**) ▶ noun Chemistry a number assigned to an element in chemical combination which represents the number of electrons lost (or gained, if the number is negative), by an atom of that element in the compound.

oxide /ˈɒksʌɪd/ ▶ noun Chemistry a binary compound of oxygen with another element or group.
– ORIGIN late 18th cent.: from French, from *oxygène* 'oxygen' + *-ide* (as in *acide* 'acid').

oxidize /ˈɒksɪdʌɪz/ (also **-ise**) ▶ verb combine or become combined chemically with oxygen: [with obj.] *when coal is burnt any sulphur is oxidized to sulphur dioxide* | [no obj.] *the fats in the food will oxidize, turning it rancid*.
■ Chemistry undergo or cause to undergo a reaction in which electrons are lost to another species. The opposite of **REDUCE**.
– DERIVATIVES **oxidizable** adjective, **oxidation** noun, **oxidizer** noun.

oxidizing agent ▶ noun Chemistry a substance that tends to bring about oxidation by being reduced and gaining electrons.

oximeter /ɒkˈsɪmɪtə/ ▶ noun an instrument for measuring the proportion of oxygenated haemoglobin in the blood.
– DERIVATIVES **oximetry** noun.

oxisol /ˈɒksɪsɒl/ ▶ noun Soil Science a soil of an order comprising stable, highly weathered, tropical mineral soils with highly oxidized subsurface horizons.
– ORIGIN 1960s: from **OXIC** + **-SOL**.

oxlip ▶ noun a woodland Eurasian primula with yellow flowers that hang down one side of the stem.
● *Primula elatior*, family Primulaceae.
■ (also **false oxlip**) a natural hybrid between a primrose and a cowslip.
– ORIGIN Old English *oxanslyppe*, from *oxa* 'ox' + *slyppe* 'slime'; compare with **COWSLIP**.

Oxon /ˈɒks(ə)n, -sɒn/ ▶ abbreviation for ■ Oxfordshire.
■ (especially in degree titles) of Oxford University: *BA, Oxon.*
– ORIGIN from medieval Latin *Oxoniensis*, from *Oxonia* (see **OXONIAN**).

Oxonian /ɒkˈsəʊnɪən/ ▶ adjective of or relating to Oxford or Oxford University.
▶ noun a native or inhabitant of Oxford.
■ a member of Oxford University.
– ORIGIN mid 16th cent.: from *Oxonia* (Latinized name of Oxford, from its old form *Oxenford*) + **-AN**.

oxpecker ▶ noun a brown African bird related to the starlings, feeding on parasites that infest the skins of large grazing mammals.
● Genus *Buphagus*, family Sturnidae (or Buphagidae): two species.

oxtail ▶ noun the tail of a cow.
■ [mass noun] meat from this, used especially for making soup.

oxter /ˈɒkstə/ ▶ noun Scottish & N. English a person's armpit.
– ORIGIN Old English *ōhsta*, *ōxta*.

ox-tongue ▶ noun **1** the tongue of an ox.
■ [mass noun] the meat from this when cooked as food.
2 an Old World plant of the daisy family with yellow dandelion-like flowers and prickly hairs on the stem and leaves.
● Genus *Picris*, family Compositae.

Oxus /ˈɒksəs/ ancient name for **AMU DARYA**.

ox-wagon ▶ noun a heavy wagon drawn by oxen, used by settlers and pioneers in South Africa.
■ S. African used as a symbol of reactionary and unprogressive views: [as modifier] *the former ox-wagon tempo of change.*

oxy-¹ ▶ combining form denoting sharpness: *oxytone*.
– ORIGIN from Greek *oxus* 'sharp'.

oxy-² (also **ox-**) ▶ combining form Chemistry representing **OXYGEN**.

oxyacetylene ▶ adjective [attrib.] of or denoting welding or cutting techniques using a very hot flame produced by mixing acetylene and oxygen.

oxyacid ▶ noun Chemistry an inorganic acid whose molecules contain oxygen, such as sulphuric or nitric acid.

oxyanion /ˌɒksɪˈanʌɪən/ ▶ noun Chemistry an anion containing one or more oxygen atoms bonded to another element (as in the sulphate and carbonate ions).

oxygen ▶ noun [mass noun] a colourless, odourless reactive gas, the chemical element of atomic number 8 and the life-supporting component of the air. Oxygen forms about 20 per cent of the earth's atmosphere, and is the most abundant element in the earth's crust, mainly in the form of oxides, silicates, and carbonates. (Symbol: **O**)
– DERIVATIVES **oxygenous** adjective.
– ORIGIN late 18th cent.: from French (*principe*) *oxygène* 'acidifying constituent' (because at first it was held to be the essential component in the formation of acids).

oxygenate /ˈɒksɪdʒəneɪt, ɒkˈsɪdʒ-/ ▶ verb [with obj.] supply, treat, charge, or enrich with oxygen: [as adj.] **oxygenated**] *a good supply of oxygenated blood.*
– DERIVATIVES **oxygenation** noun.
– ORIGIN late 18th cent.: from French *oxygéner* 'supply with oxygen' + **-ATE³**.

oxygenator ▶ noun Medicine an apparatus for oxygenating the blood.
■ an aquatic plant which enriches the surrounding water with oxygen, especially in a pond or aquarium.

oxygenize (also **-ise**) ▶ verb rare term for **OXYGENATE**.

oxygen mask ▶ noun a mask placed over the nose and mouth and connected to a supply of oxygen, used when the body is not able to gain enough oxygen by breathing air, for example at high altitudes, or because of a medical condition.

oxygen tent ▶ noun a tent-like enclosure within which the air supply can be enriched with oxygen to aid a patient's breathing.

oxyhaemoglobin ▶ noun [mass noun] Biochemistry a bright red substance formed by the combination of haemoglobin with oxygen, present in oxygenated blood.

oxymoron /ˌɒksɪˈmɔːrɒn/ ▶ noun a figure of speech in which apparently contradictory terms appear in conjunction (e.g. *faith unfaithful kept him falsely true*).
– DERIVATIVES **oxymoronic** adjective.
– ORIGIN mid 17th cent.: from Greek *oxumōron*, neuter (used as a noun) of *oxumōros* 'pointedly foolish', from *oxus* 'sharp' + *mōros* 'foolish'.

oxyntic /ɒkˈsɪntɪk/ ▶ adjective of or denoting the secretory cells which produce hydrochloric acid in the main part of the stomach, or the glands which they compose.
– ORIGIN late 19th cent.: from Greek *oxunteos* (verbal noun from *oxunein* 'sharpen') + **-IC**.

oxytetracycline /ˌɒksɪtɛtrəˈsʌɪkliːn/ ▶ noun [mass noun] Medicine an antibiotic related to tetracycline, used to treat a variety of bacterial infections.

oxytocin /ˌɒksɪˈtəʊsɪn/ ▶ noun [mass noun] Biochemistry a hormone released by the pituitary gland that causes increased contraction of the womb during labour and stimulates the ejection of milk into the ducts of the breasts.
– ORIGIN 1920s: from Greek *oxutokia* 'sudden delivery' (from *oxus* 'sharp' + *tokos* 'childbirth') + **-IN¹**.

oxytone /ˈɒksɪtəʊn/ ▶ adjective (especially in ancient Greek) having an acute accent on the last syllable.
▶ noun a word of this kind.
– ORIGIN mid 18th cent.: from Greek *oxutonos*, from *oxus* 'sharp' + *tonos* 'tone'.

oy ▶ exclamation **1** variant spelling of **OI**.
2 see **OY VEH**.

oyer and terminer /ˌɔɪə(r) ən(d) ˈtəːmɪnə/ ▶ noun historical a commission issued to judges on a circuit to hold courts: *a court of oyer and terminer.*
– ORIGIN late Middle English: from Anglo-Norman French *oyer et terminer* 'hear and determine'.

oyez /əʊˈjɛs, -ˈjɛz, -ˈjeɪ/ (also **oyes**) ▶ exclamation a call given, typically three times, by a public crier or a court officer to command silence and attention before an announcement.
– ORIGIN late Middle English: from Old French *oiez!*, *oyez!* 'hear!', imperative plural of *oir*, from Latin *audire* 'hear'.

oyster ▶ noun **1** any of a number of bivalve molluscs with rough irregular shells. Several kinds are eaten (especially raw) as a delicacy and may be farmed for food or pearls:
● a true oyster (family Ostreidae), in particular the edible **common European oyster** (*Ostrea edulis*) and **American oyster** (*Crassostrea virginica*). ● [with modifier] a similar bivalve of another family, in particular the **thorny oysters** (Spondylidae), **wing oysters** (Pteriidae), and **saddle oysters** (Anomiidae).
■ [mass noun] the colour oyster white.
2 an oyster-shaped morsel of meat on each side of the backbone in poultry.
– PHRASES **the world is your oyster** you are in a position to take the opportunities that life has to offer. [ORIGIN: from Shakespeare's *Merry Wives of Windsor* (II. ii. 5).]
– ORIGIN Middle English: from Old French *oistre*, via Latin from Greek *ostreon*; related to *osteon* 'bone' and *ostrakon* 'shell or tile'.

oyster bar ▶ noun **1** a hotel bar, small restaurant, or other place where oysters are served.
2 (especially in the south-eastern US) an oyster bed.

oyster bed ▶ noun a part of the sea bottom where oysters breed or are bred.

oystercatcher ▶ noun a wading bird with black-and-white or all-black plumage and a strong orange-red bill, typically found on the coast and feeding chiefly on shellfish.
● Family Haematopodidae and genus *Haematopus*: several species, e.g. the black and white *H. ostralegus* of Eurasia.

oyster farm ▸ noun an area of the seabed used for breeding oysters.

oyster mushroom ▸ noun a widely distributed edible fungus which has a greyish-brown oyster-shaped cap and a very short or absent stem, growing on the wood of broadleaved trees and causing rot.
● *Pleurotus ostreatus*, family Pleurotaceae, class Hymenomycetes.

oyster plant ▸ noun **1** another term for **SALSIFY**.
2 a blue-flowered thick-leaved creeping plant of the borage family, native to northern Europe and growing chiefly on stony beaches.
● *Mertensia maritima*, family Boraginaceae.

oyster sauce ▸ noun [mass noun] a sauce made with oysters and soy sauce, used especially in oriental cookery.

oyster white ▸ noun [mass noun] a shade of greyish-white.

oy vey /ɔɪ ˈveɪ/ (also **oy**) ▸ exclamation indicating dismay or grief (used mainly by Yiddish-speakers).
– ORIGIN late 19th cent.: Yiddish, literally 'oh woe'.

Oz Austral. informal ▸ adjective Australian: *Oz hospitality.*
▸ noun **1** Australia.
■ a person from Australia.
– ORIGIN 1940s: representing a pronunciation of an abbreviation of **AUSTRALIA**.

oz ▸ abbreviation for ounce(s).

– ORIGIN from Italian *onza* 'ounce'.

Ozalid /ˈəʊzəlɪd, ˈɒz-/ ▸ noun trademark a photocopy made by a process in which a diazonium salt and coupler are present in the paper coating, so that the image develops in the presence of ammonia.
– ORIGIN 1920s: by reversal of **DIAZO** and insertion of -*l*.

Ozark Mountains /ˈəʊzɑːk/ (also **the Ozarks**) a heavily forested highland plateau dissected by rivers, valleys, and streams, lying between the Missouri and Arkansas rivers and within the states of Missouri, Arkansas, Oklahoma, Kansas, and Illinois.

ozokerite /əʊˈzəʊkərʌɪt, -sərʌɪt, ˌəʊzə(ʊ)ˈsɪərʌɪt/ ▸ noun [mass noun] a brown or black paraffin wax occurring naturally in some shales and sandstones and formerly used in candles, polishes, and electrical insulation.
– ORIGIN mid 19th cent.: from German *Ozokerit*, from Greek *ozein* 'to smell' + *kēros* 'wax'.

ozone ▸ noun [mass noun] a colourless unstable toxic gas with a pungent odour and powerful oxidizing properties, formed from oxygen by electrical discharges or ultraviolet light. It differs from normal oxygen (O_2) in having three atoms in its molecule (O_3).
■ informal fresh invigorating air, especially that blowing on to the shore from the sea.
– DERIVATIVES **ozonic** adjective.

– ORIGIN mid 19th cent.: from German *Ozon*, from Greek *ozein* 'to smell'.

ozone-friendly ▸ adjective (of manufactured products) not containing chemicals that are destructive to the ozone layer.

ozone hole ▸ noun a region of marked thinning of the ozone layer in high latitudes, chiefly in winter, attributed to the chemical action of CFCs and other atmospheric pollutants. The resulting increase in ultraviolet light at ground level gives rise to an increased risk of skin cancer.

ozone layer ▸ noun a layer in the earth's stratosphere at an altitude of about 10 km (6.2 miles) containing a high concentration of ozone, which absorbs most of the ultraviolet radiation reaching the earth from the sun.

ozonide /ˈəʊzənʌɪd/ ▸ noun Chemistry any of a class of unstable cyclic compounds formed by the addition of ozone to a carbon–carbon double bond.
■ a salt of the anion O_3^-, derived from ozone.

ozonize /ˈəʊzənʌɪz/ (also **-ise**) ▸ verb [with obj.] [often as adj. **ozonized**] convert (oxygen) into ozone.
■ enrich or treat with ozone: *ozonized air.*
– DERIVATIVES **ozonization** noun, **ozonizer** noun.

ozonosphere /əʊˈzəʊnəsfɪə/ ▸ noun technical term for **OZONE LAYER**.

Ozzie ▸ noun variant spelling of **AUSSIE**.

Pp

P¹ (also **p**) ▶ noun (pl. **Ps** or **P's**) the sixteenth letter of the alphabet.
■ denoting the next after O (or N if O is omitted) in a set of items, categories, etc.
– PHRASES **mind ones Ps and Qs** see MIND.

P² ▶ abbreviation for ■ (in tables of sports results) games played. ■ (on an automatic gear shift) park. ■ (on road signs and street plans) parking. ■ [in combination] (in units of measurement) peta- (10¹⁵): *27 PBq of radioactive material.* ■ Physics poise (unit of viscosity). ■ Portugal (international vehicle registration). ■ proprietary.
▶ symbol for ■ the chemical element phosphorus.

p ▶ abbreviation for ■ page. ■ (*p-*) [in combination] Chemistry para-: *p-xylene.* ■ Brit. penny or pence. ■ Music piano (softly). ■ [in combination] (in units of measurement) pico- (10⁻¹²): *a 220 pf capacitor.* ■ Chemistry denoting electrons and orbitals possessing one unit of angular momentum. [ORIGIN: from *principal*, originally applied to lines in atomic spectra.]
▶ symbol for ■ Physics pressure. ■ Statistics probability.

PA ▶ abbreviation for ■ Panama (international vehicle registration). ■ Pennsylvania (in official postal use). ■ Brit. personal assistant. ■ Press Association. ■ public address.

Pa ▶ symbol for the chemical element protactinium.

pa ▶ noun informal father: [as name] *Pa is busy on the telephone.*
– ORIGIN early 19th cent.: abbreviation of PAPA.

p.a. ▶ abbreviation for per annum.

paan /pɑːn/ (also **pan**) ▶ noun [mass noun] Indian betel leaves prepared and used as a stimulant.
– ORIGIN via Hindi from Sanskrit *parṇa* 'feather, leaf'.

pa'anga /pɑːˈɑːŋgə/ ▶ noun (pl. same) the basic monetary unit of Tonga, equal to 100 seniti.
– ORIGIN Tongan.

Paarl /pɑːl/ a town in SW South Africa, in the province of Western Cape, north-east of Cape Town; pop. 71,300 (1980). It is at the centre of a noted wine-producing region.

pablum /ˈpabləm/ ▶ noun variant spelling of PABULUM.

pabulum /ˈpabjʊləm/ (also **pablum**) ▶ noun [mass noun] bland or insipid intellectual fare, entertainment, etc.; pap.
– ORIGIN mid 17th cent. (in the sense 'food'): from Latin, from the stem of *pascere* 'to feed'.

PABX ▶ abbreviation for private automatic branch exchange, a private telephone switchboard.

PAC ▶ abbreviation for Pan-Africanist Congress.

paca /ˈpakə/ ▶ noun a robust nocturnal South American rodent that has a reddish-brown coat patterned with rows of white spots. It is hunted for its flesh, which commands high prices.
● Genus *Agouti*, family Dasyproctidae: two species, in particular *A. paca.*
– ORIGIN mid 17th cent.: via Spanish and Portuguese from Tupi.

pacamac ▶ noun variant spelling of PAKAMAC.

pacarana /ˌpakəˈrɑːnə/ ▶ noun a slow-moving South American cavy-like rodent that has coarse dark hair with white stripes along the back, and a short furry tail.

● *Dinomys branickii,* the only member of the family Dinomyidae.
– ORIGIN from Tupi, literally 'false paca'.

PACE Brit. ▶ abbreviation for Police and Criminal Evidence Act. This act, which was passed in 1984, dealt principally with the conditions under which suspects can be detained without charge and with the rights of those detained.

pace¹ /peɪs/ ▶ noun **1** a single step taken when walking or running.
■ a unit of length representing the distance between two successive steps in walking. ■ a gait of a horse or other animal, especially one of the recognized trained gaits of a horse. ■ [mass noun] poetic/literary a person's manner of walking or running: *I steal with quiet pace.*
2 [mass noun] consistent and continuous speed in walking, running, or moving: *he's an aggressive player with plenty of pace* | [in sing.] *the ring road allows traffic to flow at a remarkably fast pace.*
■ the speed or rate at which something happens, changes, or develops: *the industrial boom gathered pace* | [in sing.] *the story rips along at a cracking pace.* ■ Cricket the state of a wicket as affecting the speed of the ball.
▶ verb [no obj., with adverbial of direction] walk at a steady and consistent speed, especially without a particular destination and as an expression of one's anxiety or annoyance: *we paced up and down in exasperation* | [with obj.] *she had been pacing the room.*
■ [with obj.] measure (a distance) by walking it and counting the number of steps taken: *I paced out the dimensions of my new home.* ■ [no obj.] (of a horse) move in a distinctive lateral gait in which both legs on the same side are lifted together, seen mostly in specially bred or trained horses. ■ [with obj.] lead (another runner in a race) in order to establish a competitive speed: *McKenna paced us for four miles.* ■ (**pace oneself**) do something at a slow and steady rate or speed in order to avoid overexerting oneself: *Frank was pacing himself for the long night and day ahead.* ■ [with obj. and adverbial] move or develop (something) at a particular rate or speed: *the action is paced to the beat of a perky march* | [as adj., in combination **-paced**] *our fast-paced daily lives.*
– PHRASES **change of pace** chiefly N. Amer. a change from what one is used to: *the magenta is a change of pace from traditional red.* **keep pace with** move, develop, or progress at the same speed as: *fees have had to be raised a little to keep pace with inflation.* **off the pace** behind the leader or leading group in a race or contest. **put someone** (or **something**) **through their** (or **its**) **paces** make someone (or something) demonstrate their (or its) qualities or abilities. **set the pace** be the fastest runner in the early part of a race. ■ lead the way in doing or achieving something: *space movies have set the pace for the development of special effects.* **stand** (or **stay**) **the pace** be able to keep up with another or others.
– ORIGIN Middle English: from Old French *pas*, from Latin *passus* 'stretch (of the leg)', from *pandere* 'to stretch'.

pace² /ˈpɑːteɪ, ˈpeɪsi/ ▶ preposition with due respect to (someone or their opinion), used to express polite disagreement or contradiction: *narrative history, pace some theorists, is by no means dead.*
– ORIGIN Latin, literally 'in peace', ablative of *pax*, as in *pace tua* 'by your leave'.

pace bowler ▶ noun Cricket a fast bowler.

pace car ▶ noun Motor Racing a car that sets the pace for the warm-up lap before a race but does not take part in it, or that controls the pace in temporarily hazardous conditions.

pacemaker ▶ noun **1** a runner or competitor who sets the pace at the beginning of a race or competition, sometimes in order to help another runner break a record.
■ a person viewed as taking the lead or setting standards of achievement for others.
2 an artificial device for stimulating the heart muscle and regulating its contractions.
■ the part of the heart muscle (the sino-atrial node) which normally performs this role. ■ the part of an organ or of the body which controls any other rhythmic physiological activity.
– DERIVATIVES **pacemaking** adjective & noun.

paceman ▶ noun (pl. **-men**) Cricket a fast bowler.

pace notes ▶ plural noun (in rally driving) notes made before a race by a competitor about the characteristics of a particular course, especially with regard to advisable speeds for each section.

pacer ▶ noun **1** a pacemaker.
2 chiefly US a horse bred or trained to have a distinctive lateral gait in which both legs on the same side are lifted together, which is used in some types of racing.

pacesetter ▶ noun another term for PACEMAKER (in sense 1).
– DERIVATIVES **pacesetting** adjective & noun.

pacey ▶ adjective variant spelling of PACY.

pacha ▶ noun variant spelling of PASHA (in sense 1).

Pachelbel /ˈpax(ə)lbɛl/, Johann (1653–1706), German composer and organist. His compositions include seventy-eight chorale preludes, thirteen settings of the Magnificat, and the Canon and Gigue in D for three violins and continuo.

pachinko /pəˈtʃɪŋkəʊ/ ▶ noun [mass noun] a Japanese form of pinball.
– ORIGIN Japanese.

pachisi /pəˈtʃiːzi/ (also US trademark **Parcheesi**) ▶ noun a four-handed Indian board game in which six cowries are used like dice.
– ORIGIN from Hindi *paccīsī*, literally '(throw) of 25' (the highest of the game).

Pachuca de Soto /pəˌtʃuːkə deɪ ˈsəʊtəʊ/ (also **Pachuca**) a city in Mexico, capital of the state of Hidalgo; pop. 179,440 (1990).

pachuco /pəˈtʃuːkəʊ/ ▶ noun (pl. **-os** /-əʊz/) chiefly US, dated a juvenile gang member of Mexican-American ethnic origin.
– ORIGIN Mexican Spanish, literally 'flashily dressed'.

pachycephalosaur /ˌpakɪˈsɛfələsɔː, -ˈkɛf-/ ▶ noun a bipedal herbivorous dinosaur of the late Cretaceous period, with a thick domed skull.
● Infraorder Pachycephalosauria, order Ornithischia: several genera, including *Pachycephalosaurus.*
– ORIGIN from Greek *pakhus* 'thick' + *kephalē* 'head' + *sauros* 'lizard'.

pachyderm /ˈpakɪdəːm/ ▶ noun a very large mammal with thick skin, especially an elephant, rhinoceros, or hippopotamus.
– DERIVATIVES **pachydermal** adjective, **pachydermatous** adjective, **pachydermic** adjective.

– ORIGIN mid 19th cent.: from French *pachyderme*, from Greek *pakhudermos*, from *pakhus* 'thick' + *derma* 'skin'.

pachysandra /ˌpakɪˈsandrə/ ▶ **noun** an evergreen creeping shrubby plant of the box family.
• Genus *Pachysandra*, family Buxaceae: several species, in particular the Japanese *P. terminalis*.
– ORIGIN formed irregularly from Greek *pakhus* 'thick' + *anēr, andr-* 'male' (with reference to the thick stamens).

pachytene /ˈpakɪtiːn/ ▶ **noun** [mass noun] Biology the third stage of the prophase of meiosis, following zygotene, during which the paired chromosomes shorten and thicken, the two chromatids of each separate, and exchange of segments between chromatids may occur.
– ORIGIN early 20th cent.: from Greek *pakhus* 'thick' + *tainia* 'band'.

pacific ▶ **adjective 1** peaceful in character or intent: *a pacific gesture.*
2 (**Pacific**) of or relating to the Pacific Ocean: *the Pacific War.*
▶ **noun** (**Pacific**) **1** (**the Pacific**) short for **PACIFIC OCEAN**.
2 a steam locomotive of 4–6–2 wheel arrangement.
– DERIVATIVES **pacifically** adverb.
– ORIGIN mid 16th cent.: from French *pacifique* or Latin *pacificus* 'peacemaking', from *pax, pac-* 'peace'.

Pacific Islander ▶ **noun** a native or inhabitant of any of the islands in the South Pacific, especially an aboriginal native of Polynesia.

Pacific Ocean the largest of the world's oceans, lying between America to the east and Asia and Australasia to the west.

Pacific Rim the countries and regions bordering the Pacific Ocean, especially the small nations of east Asia.

Pacific Security Treaty another name for **ANZUS**.

Pacific time the standard time in a zone including the Pacific coastal region of Canada and the US, specifically:
• (**Pacific Standard Time**, abbrev.: **PST**) standard time based on the mean solar time at longitude 120° W, eight hours behind GMT. • (**Pacific Daylight Time**, abbrev.: **PDT**) Pacific time during daylight saving, nine hours behind GMT.

pacifier ▶ **noun** a person or thing that pacifies.
■ N. Amer. a baby's dummy.

pacifism ▶ **noun** [mass noun] the belief that war and violence are unjustifiable and that all disputes should be settled by peaceful means.
– DERIVATIVES **pacifist** noun & adjective.
– ORIGIN early 20th cent.: from French *pacifisme*, from *pacifier* 'pacify'.

p

pacify ▶ **verb** (**-ies, -ied**) [with obj.] quell the anger, agitation, or excitement of: *he had to pacify angry spectators.*
■ bring peace to (a country or warring factions), especially by the use or threatened use of military force: *the general pacified northern Italy.*
– DERIVATIVES **pacification** noun, **pacificatory** adjective.
– ORIGIN late 15th cent.: from Old French *pacefier*, from Latin *pacificare*, based on *pax, pac-* 'peace'.

Pacinian corpuscle /pəˈsɪnɪən/ ▶ **noun** Anatomy an encapsulated ending of a sensory nerve that acts as a receptor for pressure and vibration.
– ORIGIN late 19th cent.: named after Filippo *Pacini* (1812–83), Italian anatomist.

Pacino /pəˈtʃiːnəʊ/, Al (b.1940), American film actor; full name *Alfred Pacino*. Nominated for an Oscar eight times and winning one for *Scent of a Woman* (1992), he first achieved recognition with *The Godfather* (1972).

pack[1] ▶ **noun 1** a small cardboard or paper container and the items contained within it: ***a pack** of cigarettes.*
■ a collection of related documents, especially one kept in a folder: *an information pack.* ■ Brit. a set of playing cards. ■ a rucksack. ■ (often **the pack**) a quantity of fish, fruit, or other foods packed or canned in a particular season or year.
2 a group of wild animals, especially wolves, living and hunting together.
■ a group of hounds kept and used for hunting, especially fox-hunting. ■ (usu. **Pack**) an organized group of Cub Scouts or Brownies. ■ Rugby a team's forwards considered as a group. ■ (**the pack**) the main body of competitors following the leader or leaders in a race or competition: figurative *the company was demonstrating the kind of innovations needed to keep it ahead of the pack.* ■ chiefly derogatory a group or set of similar things or people: *the reports were **a pack of** lies.* ■ (also **ice pack**) an expanse of large pieces of floating ice driven together into a nearly continuous mass, as occurs in polar seas.
3 a hot or cold pad of absorbent material, especially as used for treating an injury.
■ short for **FACE PACK**.
▶ **verb** [with obj.] fill (a suitcase or bag), especially with clothes and other items needed when away from home: *I packed a bag with a few of my favourite clothes* | [no obj.] *she had packed and checked out of the hotel.*
■ place (something) in a container, especially for transport or storage: *I **packed up** my stuff and drove to Detroit.* ■ [no obj.] be capable of being folded up for transport or storage: *a pneumatic igloo tent that packs away compactly.* ■ (**pack something in**) store something perishable in (a specified substance) in order to preserve it: *the organs were packed in ice.* ■ informal carry (a gun): *a sixteen-year-old can make a fortune selling drugs and pack a gun in the process.* ■ (often **be packed**) cram a large number of things into: *it was a large room, packed with beds jammed side by side.* ■ [often as adj. **packed**] (of a large number of people) crowd into and fill (a room, building, or place): *the waiting room was packed* | [as adj. **packed**] *a packed Merseyside pub.* ■ cover, surround, or fill (something): *if you have a nosebleed, try packing the nostrils with cotton wool.* ■ [no obj.] Rugby (of players) form or take their places in a scrum: *we often **packed down** with only seven men.*
– PHRASES **go to the pack** Austral./NZ informal deteriorate; go to pieces. **pack heat** N. Amer. informal carry a gun. **pack it in** informal stop what one is doing. **pack a punch** be capable of hitting with skill or force: *Rosie, although small, could pack a hefty punch.* ■ have a powerful effect: *the Spanish wine packed quite a punch.* **packed out** Brit. informal (of a place) very crowded. **send someone packing** informal make someone leave in an abrupt or peremptory way.
– DERIVATIVES **packable** adjective.
– ORIGIN Middle English: from Middle Dutch, Middle Low German *pak* (noun), *pakken* (verb). The verb appears appears early in Anglo-Latin and Anglo-Norman French in connection with the wool trade; trade in English wool was chiefly with the Low Countries.
▶ **pack something in** informal give up an activity or job.
pack someone off informal send someone somewhere without much warning or notice: *I was packed off to hospital for surgery.*
pack something out N. Amer. pack something up and take it away: *pack out any garbage you have left.*
pack up Brit. informal (of a machine) break down: *the immersion heater has packed up.*

pack[2] ▶ **verb** [with obj.] fill (a jury, committee, etc.) with people likely to support a particular verdict or decision: *his efforts to **pack** the Supreme Court **with** men who shared his ideology.*
– ORIGIN early 16th cent. (in the sense 'enter into a private agreement)'): probably from the obsolete verb *pact* 'enter into an agreement with', the final *-t* being interpreted as an inflection of the past tense.

package ▶ **noun** an object or group of objects wrapped in paper or packed in a box.
■ the box or bag in which things are packed. ■ N. Amer. a packet: *a package of peanuts.* ■ (also **package deal**) a set of proposals or terms offered or agreed as a whole: *a package of measures announced by the government.* ■ informal a package holiday. ■ Computing a collection of programs or subroutines with related functionality.
▶ **verb** [with obj.] (usu. **be packaged**) put into a box or wrapping, especially for sale: *choose products which are packaged in recyclable materials* | [as adj. **packaged**] *packaged foods.*
■ present (someone or something) in a particular way, especially to make them more attractive: [as adj., with submodifier] (**packaged**) *everything became a carefully packaged photo opportunity.* ■ combine (various products) for sale as one unit: *films would be packaged with the pictures of a production company.* ■ commission and produce (a book, typically a highly illustrated one) to sell as a complete product to publishers: *it's a question of trying to package the book properly.*
– DERIVATIVES **packager** noun.
– ORIGIN mid 16th cent. (as a noun denoting the action or mode of packing goods): from the verb **PACK**[1] + **-AGE**; compare with Anglo-Latin *paccagium*. The verb dates from the 1920s.

package holiday (also **package tour**) ▶ **noun** a holiday organized by a travel agent, with arrangements for transport, accommodation, etc. made at an inclusive price.

packaging ▶ **noun** [mass noun] materials used to wrap or protect goods.
■ the business or process of packing goods. ■ the presentation of a person, product, or action in a particular way: *diplomatic packaging of the key provisions will make a confrontation unlikely.*

pack animal ▶ **noun 1** an animal used to carry packs.
2 an animal that lives and hunts in a pack.

packcloth ▶ **noun** [mass noun] a stout coarse cloth used for packing.

pack drill ▶ **noun** a military punishment of marching up and down carrying full equipment.
– PHRASES **no names, no pack drill** punishment will be prevented if names and details are not mentioned.

packed lunch ▶ **noun** a cold lunch prepared at home and carried in a bag or box to work or school or on an excursion.

Packer, Kerry (Francis Bullmore) (b.1937), Australian media entrepreneur. He launched the 'World Series Cricket' tournaments (1977–9), engaging many leading cricketers in defiance of the wishes of cricket's ruling bodies.

packer ▶ **noun** a person or machine that packs something, especially someone who prepares and packs food for transportation and sale.

packet ▶ **noun 1** a paper or cardboard container, typically one in which goods are packed to be sold: ***a packet** of cigarettes.*
■ the contents of such a container. ■ a block of data transmitted across a network.
2 informal, chiefly Brit. a large sum of money: *a hectic social life could **cost a packet**.*
3 (also **packet boat**) dated a ship travelling at regular intervals between two ports, originally for the conveyance of mail.
▶ **verb** (**packeted**, **packeting**) [with obj.] [often as adj. **packeted**] make up into or wrap up in a packet: *packeted pastry fruit pies.*
– ORIGIN mid 16th cent.: diminutive of **PACK**[1], perhaps from Anglo-Norman French; compare with Anglo-Latin *paccettum*.

packetize ▶ **verb** [with obj.] Computing partition or separate (data) into units for transmission in a packet-switching network: *this layer packetizes and reassembles messages.*

packet radio ▶ **noun** [mass noun] a method of broadcasting that makes use of radio signals carrying packets of data.

packet switching ▶ **noun** [mass noun] Computing & Telecommunications a mode of data transmission in which a message is broken into a number of parts which are sent independently, over whatever route is optimum for each packet, and reassembled at the destination. Compare with **MESSAGE SWITCHING**.

packframe ▶ **noun** a frame into which a knapsack or other pack is fitted to make it easier to carry.

packhorse ▶ **noun** a horse used to carry loads.

pack ice ▶ **noun** [mass noun] a mass of ice floating in the sea, formed by smaller pieces freezing together.

packing ▶ **noun** [mass noun] the action or process of packing something: *she finished her packing.*
■ a charge made when delivering goods to cover the cost of packing them. ■ material used to protect fragile goods, especially in transit: *polystyrene packing.* ■ material used to seal a join or assist in lubricating an axle.

packing case ▶ **noun** a large strong box, typically a wooden one, in which goods are packed for transportation or storage.

packing density ▶ **noun** Computing the density of stored information in terms of bits per unit occupied of its storage medium.

packing station ▶ **noun** an official depot where eggs are graded and packed.

packman ▶ **noun** (pl. **-men**) archaic a pedlar.

pack rat ▶ **noun** another term for **WOODRAT**.
■ N. Amer. derogatory a person who hoards things.

packsack ▶ **noun** N. Amer. a rucksack.

packsaddle ▶ **noun** chiefly N. Amer. a horse's saddle adapted for supporting packs.

pack shot ▶ **noun** (in advertising) a close-up picture of the advertised product in its packaging.

packthread ▶ **noun** [mass noun] stout thread for sewing or tying up packs.

Pac-Man trademark an electronic computer game in which a player attempts to guide a voracious, blob-shaped character through a maze while eluding attacks from opposing images which it may in turn devour. It is also the name of the blob-shaped character itself.
– ORIGIN 1980s: *Pac*, probably a respelling of **PACK**[1] (from the character's action of 'packing away' (i.e. eating) obstacles in its path) + **MAN**.

pact ▶ **noun** a formal agreement between individuals or parties.
– ORIGIN late Middle English: from Old French, from Latin *pactum* 'something agreed', neuter past participle (used as a noun) of *paciscere* 'agree'.

pacu /paˈkuː, ˈpakuː/ ▶ **noun** (pl. same) a deep-bodied herbivorous freshwater fish native to northern South America, which has been introduced into the Old World.
• *Colossoma nigripinnis*, family Characidae.
– ORIGIN early 19th cent.: from Tupi *pacú*.

pacy (also **pacey**) ▶ **adjective** (**pacier**, **paciest**) moving or progressing quickly: *a pacy thriller.*

pad[1] ▶ **noun** **1** a thick piece of soft material used to reduce friction or jarring, enlarge or change the shape of something, or hold or absorb liquid: *a pad of cotton wool.*
■ short for **INK-PAD**. ■ the fleshy underpart of an animal's foot or of a human finger. ■ a protective guard worn by a sports player to protect a part of the body (especially the leg or ankle) from blows.
2 a number of sheets of blank paper fastened together at one edge, used for writing or drawing on.
3 a flat-topped structure or area used for helicopter take-off and landing or for rocket-launching.
■ Electronics a flat area on a track of a printed circuit or on the edge of an integrated circuit to which wires or component leads can be attached to make an electrical connection.
4 informal, dated a person's home: *the police raided my pad.*
5 short for **LILY PAD**.
▶ **verb** (**padded**, **padding**) [with obj.] [often as adj. **padded**] fill or cover (something) with a soft material in order to give it a particular shape, protect it, or make it more comfortable: *a padded envelope.*
■ chiefly N. Amer. defraud by adding false items to (an expenses claim or bill): *faked repairs and padded expenses for government work reaped billions of dollars for the Mafia.*
– ORIGIN mid 16th cent. (in the sense 'bundle of straw to lie on'): the senses may not be of common origin; the meaning 'underpart of an animal's foot' is perhaps related to Low German *pad* 'sole of the foot'; the history remains obscure.
▶ **pad something out** lengthen something, especially written or spoken matter, with unnecessary material.
pad up put on protective pads in order to play a sport, especially cricket. ■ Cricket (of a batsman) deliberately use one's pads to block a ball.

pad[2] ▶ **verb** (**padded**, **padding**) [no obj., with adverbial of direction] walk with steady steps making a soft dull sound: *she padded along the corridor.*
■ [with obj.] tramp along (a road or route) on foot: *he was padding the streets.*
▶ **noun** [in sing.] the soft dull sound of steady steps: *he heard the pad of feet.*
– ORIGIN mid 16th cent.: from Low German *padden* 'to tread, go along a path', partly imitative.

Padang /pəˈdaŋ/ a seaport of Indonesia, the largest city on the west coast of Sumatra; pop. 480,920 (1980).

padauk /paˈdaʊk/ (also **padouk**) ▶ **noun** **1** [mass noun] timber from a tropical tree of the pea family, resembling rosewood.
2 the large hardwood tree of the Old World tropics which is widely grown for this timber. Some kinds yield a red dye which is used for religious and ritual purposes.
• Genus *Pterocarpus*, family Leguminosae: three species, in particular **African padauk** (*P. soyauxii*).
– ORIGIN mid 19th cent.: from Burmese.

padded cell ▶ **noun** a room in a psychiatric hospital with padding on the walls to prevent violent patients from injuring themselves.

padding ▶ **noun** [mass noun] soft material such as foam or cloth used to pad or stuff something.
■ superfluous material in a book, speech, etc. introduced in order to make it reach a desired length.

paddle[1] ▶ **noun** a short pole with a broad blade at one or both ends, used without a rowlock to move a small boat or canoe through the water.
■ an act of using a paddle in a boat: *a gentle paddle on sluggish water.* ■ a short-handled bat used in various ball games, especially table tennis. ■ a paddle-shaped instrument used for mixing food, or stirring or mixing in industrial processes. ■ N. Amer. informal a paddle-shaped instrument used for administering corporal punishment. ■ each of the boards fitted round the circumference of a paddle wheel or mill wheel. ■ a flat array of solar cells projecting from a spacecraft. ■ the fin or flipper of an aquatic mammal or bird. ■ Medicine a plastic-covered electrode used in cardiac stimulation. ■ short for **BIDDING PADDLE**.
▶ **verb** **1** [no obj., with adverbial of direction] move through the water in a boat using a paddle or paddles: *he paddled along the coast.*
■ [with obj.] propel (a small boat or canoe) with a paddle or paddles: *he was teaching trainees to paddle canoes.* ■ [with obj.] travel along (a stretch of water) using such a method: *a legal right to paddle Scottish rivers.* ■ (of bird or other animal) swim with short fast strokes: *the swan paddled away.*
2 [with obj.] informal, chiefly N. Amer. beat (someone) with a paddle as a punishment: *ask the mother if she minds the offspring getting paddled from time to time.*
– PHRASES **paddle one's own canoe** informal be independent and self-sufficient.
– DERIVATIVES **paddler** noun.
– ORIGIN late Middle English (denoting a small spade-like implement): of unknown origin. Current senses date from the 17th cent.

paddle[2] ▶ **verb** [no obj.] walk with bare feet in shallow water: *the children paddled at the water's edge.*
■ dabble the feet or hands in water: *Peter paddled idly in the water with his fingers.*
▶ **noun** [in sing.] an act of walking with bare feet in shallow water.
– DERIVATIVES **paddler** noun.
– ORIGIN mid 16th cent.: of obscure origin; compare with Low German *paddeln* 'tramp about'; the association with water remains unexplained.

paddleball ▶ **noun** [mass noun] a game played with a light ball and wooden bat in a four-walled handball court.

paddlefish ▶ **noun** (pl. same or **-fishes**) a large mainly freshwater fish related to the sturgeon, with an elongated snout.
• The plankton-feeding *Polyodon spathula* of the Mississippi basin, and the fish-eating *Psephurus gladius* of the Yangtze River, the only surviving members of the family Polyodontidae.

paddle steamer (also **paddle boat**) ▶ **noun** a boat powered by steam and propelled by paddle wheels.

paddle tennis ▶ **noun** [mass noun] a type of tennis played in a small court with a sponge-rubber ball and wooden or plastic bat.

paddle wheel ▶ **noun** a large steam-driven wheel with boards round its circumference, situated at the stern or side of a ship so as to propel the ship through the water by its rotation.

paddling pool ▶ **noun** a shallow artificial pool for children to paddle in.

paddock ▶ **noun** a small field or enclosure where horses are kept or exercised.
■ an enclosure adjoining a racecourse or track where horses or cars are gathered and displayed before a race. ■ Austral./NZ a field or plot of land enclosed by fencing or defined by natural boundaries.
▶ **verb** [with obj.] (usu. **be paddocked**) keep or enclose (a horse) in a paddock: *horses paddocked on a hillside.*
– ORIGIN early 17th cent.: apparently a variant of dialect *parrock*, of unknown ultimate origin.

Paddy ▶ **noun** (pl. **-ies**) informal, chiefly offensive an Irishman (often as a form of address).
– ORIGIN late 18th cent.: pet form of the Irish given name *Padraig*.

paddy[1] ▶ **noun** (pl. **-ies**) (also **paddy field**) a field where rice is grown.
■ [mass noun] rice before threshing or in the husk.
– ORIGIN early 17th cent.: from Malay *pādī*.

paddy[2] ▶ **noun** (pl. **-ies**) [in sing.] Brit. informal a fit of temper: *John drove off in a paddy.*
– ORIGIN late 19th cent.: from **PADDY**, associated with obsolete *paddywhack* 'Irishman (given to brawling)'.

paddymelon[1] ▶ **noun** Austral. a plant of the gourd family, especially a trailing or climbing annual that has become naturalized in inland Australia.
• Several species in the family Cucurbitaceae, in particular *Cucumis myriocarpus*, which has bristly melon-like fruits and is native to Africa.
– ORIGIN late 19th cent.: probably by erroneous association with **PADDYMELON**[2].

paddymelon[2] ▶ **noun** variant spelling of **PADEMELON**.

paddy wagon ▶ **noun** N. Amer. informal a police van.
– ORIGIN 1930s: *paddy* from **PADDY**, perhaps because formerly many American police officers were of Irish descent.

pademelon /ˈpadɪˌmɛlən/ (also **paddymelon**) ▶ **noun** a small wallaby inhabiting the coastal scrub of Australia and New Guinea. Also called **SCRUB WALLABY**.
• Genus *Thylogale*, family Macropodidae: three species.
– ORIGIN early 19th cent. (earlier as *paddymelon*): probably an alteration of Dharuk *badimalion*.

Paderewski /ˌpadəˈrɛfski/, Ignacy Jan (1860–1941), Polish pianist, composer, and statesman, Prime Minister 1919. He was the first Prime Minister of independent Poland, but resigned after only ten months in office and resumed his musical career.

pad eye ▶ **noun** a flat metal plate with a projecting loop or ring, made all in one piece.

padkos /ˈpatkɒs/ ▶ **noun** [mass noun] S. African food taken to eat on a journey.
– ORIGIN Afrikaans, from *pad* 'road' + *kos* 'food'.

padlock ▶ **noun** a detachable lock hanging by a pivoted hook on the object fastened.
▶ **verb** [with obj.] [usu. as adj. **padlocked**] secure with such a lock: *a padlocked door.*
– ORIGIN late 15th cent.: from *pad-* (of unknown origin) + the noun **LOCK**[1].

padloper /ˈpatˌlʊəpə/ ▶ **noun** S. African a small tortoise native to southern Africa, often seen on roads and paths.
• Genus *Homopus*, family Testudinidae: several species.
– ORIGIN Afrikaans, literally 'vagabond', from *pad* 'path' + *loper* 'runner'.

Padma /ˈpadmə/ a river of southern Bangladesh, formed by the confluence of the Ganges and the Brahmaputra near Rajbari.

padouk /pəˈduːk/ ▶ **noun** variant spelling of **PADAUK**.

Padova /ˈpadova/ Italian name for **PADUA**.

padre /ˈpɑːdreɪ, -dri/ ▶ **noun** informal a chaplain in any of the armed services.
■ (also **padri**) Indian a Christian priest: [as title] *Padre Saheb's gardener told me he was dead.*
– ORIGIN late 16th cent.: from Italian, Spanish, and Portuguese, literally 'father, priest', from Latin *pater, patr-* 'father'.

padrino /paˈdriːnəʊ/ ▶ **noun** (pl. **-os**) a godfather; a patron.
■ a best man at a wedding.
– ORIGIN Spanish.

padrona /paˈdrəʊnə/ ▶ **noun** (pl. **padronas**) a female boss or proprietress.
– ORIGIN Italian.

padrone /paˈdrəʊneɪ, -ni/ ▶ **noun** (pl. **padrones**) a patron or master, in particular:
■ a Mafia boss. ■ informal, chiefly US an employer, especially one who exploits immigrant workers. ■ (in Italy) the proprietor of a hotel.
– ORIGIN Italian.

padsaw ▶ **noun** a small saw with a narrow blade, for cutting curves.

pad thai /pad ˈtʌɪ/ ▶ **noun** [mass noun] a Thai dish based on rice noodles.
– ORIGIN Thai.

Padua /ˈpadjʊə/ a city in NE Italy; pop. 218,190 (1990). It was the birthplace of Livy, and Galileo taught at its university from 1592 to 1610. Italian name **PADOVA**.
– DERIVATIVES **Paduan** adjective.

paduasoy /ˈpadjʊəˌsɔɪ/ ▶ **noun** [mass noun] a heavy, rich corded or embossed silk fabric, popular in the 18th century.
– ORIGIN late 16th cent. (as *poudesoy*), from French *pou-de-soie*, of unknown origin; altered by association with *Padua say*, denoting a cloth resembling serge.

paean /ˈpiːən/ ▶ **noun** a song of praise or triumph.
■ a thing that expresses enthusiastic praise: *she uses photography to create a poignant paean to life itself.*

p

– ORIGIN late 16th cent.: via Latin from Greek *paian* 'hymn of thanksgiving to Apollo' (invoked by the name *Paian*, originally the Homeric name for the physician of the gods).

paederast ▶ **noun** variant spelling of **PEDERAST**.

paederasty ▶ **noun** variant spelling of **PEDERASTY**.

paediatrics /ˌpiːdɪˈatrɪks/ (US **pediatrics**) ▶ **plural noun** [treated as sing.] the branch of medicine dealing with children and their diseases.
– DERIVATIVES **paediatric** adjective, **paediatrician** noun.
– ORIGIN late 19th cent.: from **PAEDO-** 'of children' + Greek *iatros* 'physician' + **-ICS**.

paedo- (US **pedo-**) ▶ **combining form** of a child; relating to children: *paedophile*.
– ORIGIN from Greek *pais, paid-* 'child, boy'.

paedodontics /ˌpiːdəʊˈdɒntɪks/ (US **pedodontics**) ▶ **plural noun** [treated as sing.] the branch of dentistry that deals with children's teeth.
– DERIVATIVES **paedodontic** adjective, **paedodontist** noun.

paedogenesis /ˌpiːdə(ʊ)ˈdʒɛnɪsɪs/ ▶ **noun** Zoology see **NEOTENY**.
– DERIVATIVES **paedogenetic** adjective.

paedomorphosis /ˌpiːdə(ʊ)ˈmɔːfəsɪs, -mɔːˈfəʊsɪs/ ▶ **noun** Zoology see **NEOTENY**.
– DERIVATIVES **paedomorphic** adjective.

paedophile (US **pedophile**) ▶ **noun** a person who is sexually attracted to children.

paedophilia (US **pedophilia**) ▶ **noun** [mass noun] sexual feelings directed towards children.
– DERIVATIVES **paedophiliac** noun & adjective.

paella /pʌɪˈɛlə/ ▶ **noun** [mass noun] a Spanish dish of rice, saffron, chicken, seafood, etc., cooked and served in a large shallow pan.
– ORIGIN Catalan, from Old French *paele*, from Latin *patella* 'pan'.

paeon /ˈpiːən/ ▶ **noun** a metrical foot of one long syllable and three short syllables in any order.
– DERIVATIVES **paeonic** /piːˈɒnɪk/ adjective.
– ORIGIN early 17th cent.: via Latin from Greek *paiōn*, the Attic form of *paian* 'hymn of thanksgiving to Apollo' (see **PAEAN**).

paeony ▶ **noun** variant spelling of **PEONY**.

Pagan /pəˈgɑːn/ a town in Burma, situated on the Irrawaddy south-east of Mandalay. It is the site of an ancient city, founded in about AD 849, which was the capital of a powerful Buddhist dynasty from the 11th to the end of the 13th centuries.

pagan /ˈpeɪg(ə)n/ ▶ **noun** a person holding religious beliefs other than those of the main world religions.
■ dated, derogatory a non-Christian. ■ an adherent of neopaganism.
▶ **adjective** of or relating to such people or beliefs: *a pagan god*.
– DERIVATIVES **paganish** adjective, **paganism** noun, **paganize** (also **-ise**) verb.
– ORIGIN late Middle English: from Latin *paganus* 'villager, rustic', from *pagus* 'country district'. Latin *paganus* also meant 'civilian', becoming, in Christian Latin, 'heathen' (i.e. one not enrolled in the army of Christ).

Paganini /ˌpagəˈniːni/, Niccolò (1782–1840), Italian violinist and composer. His virtuoso violin recitals, including widespread use of pizzicato and harmonics, established him as a major figure of the romantic movement.

Page, Sir Frederick Handley (1885–1962), English aircraft designer. He is noted for designing the first twin-engined bomber (1915), as well as the Halifax heavy bombers of the Second World War.

page¹ ▶ **noun** one side of a sheet of paper in a collection of sheets bound together, especially as a book, magazine, or newspaper.
■ the material written or printed on such a sheet of paper: *she silently read several pages*. ■ a sheet of paper of such a kind considered as a whole, comprising both sides. ■ [with modifier] a page of a newspaper or magazine set aside for a particular topic. ■ Computing a section of stored data, especially that which can be displayed on a screen at one time. ■ a significant episode or period considered as a part of a longer history: *a shameful page in British imperial history*.
▶ **verb** [no obj.] (**page through**) leaf through (a book, magazine, or newspaper): *she was paging through an immense pile of Sunday newspapers*.
■ Computing move through and display (text) one page at a time. ■ [usu. as noun **paging**] Computing divide (a piece of software or data) into sections, keeping the most frequently accessed in main memory and storing the rest in virtual memory. ■ [with obj.] assign numbers to the pages in (a book or periodical); paginate. ■ [as adj., in combination **-paged**] having pages of a particular kind or number: *a many-paged volume*.
– PHRASES **on the same page** US (of two or more people) in agreement.
– ORIGIN late 16th cent.: from French, from Latin *pagina*, from *pangere* 'fasten'.

page² ▶ **noun** a boy or young man, usually in uniform, employed in a hotel or club to run errands, open doors, etc.
■ a young boy attending a bride at a wedding. ■ historical a boy in training for knighthood, ranking next below a squire in the personal service of a knight. ■ historical a man or boy employed as the personal attendant of a person of rank.
▶ **verb** [with obj.] summon (an individual) by name, typically over a public address system, so as to pass on a message: *no need to interrupt the background music just to page the concierge*.
■ [often as noun **paging**] contact (someone) by means of a pager: *many systems have paging as a standard feature*.
– ORIGIN Middle English (in the sense 'youth, male of uncouth manners'): from Old French, perhaps from Italian *paggio*, from Greek *paidion*, diminutive of *pais, paid-* 'boy'. Early use of the verb (mid 16th cent.) was in the sense 'follow as or like a page'; its current sense dates from the early 20th cent.

pageant /ˈpadʒ(ə)nt/ ▶ **noun** a public entertainment consisting of a procession of people in elaborate, colourful costumes, or an outdoor performance of a historical scene.
■ a thing that looks impressive or grand, but is actually shallow and empty. ■ historical a scene erected on a fixed stage or moving vehicle as a public show. ■ (also **beauty pageant**) N. Amer. a beauty contest.
– ORIGIN late Middle English *pagyn*, of unknown origin.

pageantry ▶ **noun** [mass noun] elaborate display or ceremony.

pageboy ▶ **noun 1** a woman's hairstyle consisting of a shoulder-length bob with the ends rolled under.
2 a page, especially in a hotel or attending a bride at a wedding.

page-one ▶ **adjective** N. Amer. worthy of being featured on the front page of a newspaper or magazine: *page-one news*.

page proof ▶ **noun** a printer's proof of a page to be published.

pager ▶ **noun** a small radio device, activated from a central point which emits a series of bleeps or vibrates to inform the wearer that someone wishes to contact them or that it has received a short text message.

Page Three ▶ **noun** Brit. trademark a feature which formerly appeared daily on page three of the *Sun* newspaper and included a picture of a topless young woman: [as modifier] *Page Three girls*.

Paget's disease /ˈpadʒɪts/ ▶ **noun** [mass noun] **1** a chronic disease of the elderly characterized by alteration of bone tissue, especially in the spine, skull, or pelvis, sometimes causing severe pain; osteitis deformans.
2 an inflammation of the nipple associated with breast cancer.
– ORIGIN late 19th cent.: named after Sir James Paget (1814–99), English surgeon.

page-turner ▶ **noun** informal an exciting book.

page-turning ▶ **adjective** informal (of a book) very exciting: *the punchy, page-turning storyline of a detective novel*.
– DERIVATIVES **page-turningly** adverb.

paginal /ˈpadʒɪn(ə)l/ ▶ **adjective** of or relating to the pages of a book or periodical.
– ORIGIN mid 17th cent.: from late Latin *paginalis*, from *pagina* (see **PAGE**¹).

pagination /ˌpadʒɪˈneɪʃ(ə)n/ ▶ **noun** [mass noun] the sequence of numbers assigned to pages in a book or periodical.
– DERIVATIVES **paginate** verb.
– ORIGIN mid 19th cent.: noun of action from *paginate*, from French *paginer*, based on Latin *pagina* 'a page' (see **PAGE**¹).

Pagnol /paˈnjɒl/, Marcel (1895–1974), French dramatist, film director, and writer. His novels include *La Gloire de mon père* (1957) and *Le Chateau de ma mère* (1958); the films *Jean de Florette* and *Manon des Sources* (both 1986) were based on Pagnol's *L'Eau des collines* (1963).

pagoda /pəˈgəʊdə/ ▶ **noun** a Hindu or Buddhist temple or sacred building, typically a many-tiered tower, in India and the Far East.
■ an ornamental imitation of this.
– ORIGIN late 16th cent.: from Portuguese *pagode*, perhaps based on Persian *butkada* 'temple of idols', influenced by Prakrit *bhagodī* 'divine'.

pagoda sleeve ▶ **noun** a funnel-shaped outer sleeve turned back to expose an inner sleeve and lining.

pagoda tree ▶ **noun** a SE Asian tree of the pea family, which has hanging clusters of cream flowers and is cultivated as an ornamental.
• *Sophora japonica*, family Leguminosae.

pagri /ˈpʌgriː/ ▶ **noun** (pl. **pagris**) a turban worn by employees of exclusive establishments in the Indian subcontinent.
– ORIGIN from Hindi *pagrī* 'turban'.

pah ▶ **exclamation** used to express disgust or contempt: *'Pah! They know nothing.'*
– ORIGIN natural utterance: first recorded in English in the late 16th cent.

Pahang /pəˈhaŋ/ a mountainous forested state of Malaysia, on the east coast of the Malay Peninsula; capital, Kuantan.

Pahlavi¹ /ˈpɑːləvi/ the name of two shahs of Iran:
■ **Reza** (1878–1944), ruled 1925–41; born *Reza Khan*. An army officer, he took control of the Persian government after a coup in 1921. He was elected Shah in 1925 but abdicated following the occupation of Iran by British and Soviet forces.
■ **Muhammad Reza** (1919–80), ruled 1941–79, son of Reza Pahlavi; also known as **Reza Shah**. Opposition to his regime culminated in the Islamic revolution of 1979 under Ayatollah Khomeini; Reza Shah was forced into exile and died in Egypt.

Pahlavi² /ˈpɑːləvi/ (also **Pehlevi**) ▶ **noun** [mass noun] an Aramaic-based writing system used in Persia from the 2nd century BC to the advent of Islam in the 7th century AD. It was also used for the recording of ancient Avestan sacred texts.
■ the form of the Middle Persian language written in this script, used in the Sassanian empire.
– ORIGIN from Persian *pahlawī*, from *pahlav*, from *parthava* 'Parthia'.

pahoehoe /pəˈhəʊɪhəʊi/ ▶ **noun** [mass noun] Geology basaltic lava forming smooth undulating or ropy masses. Often contrasted with **AA**.
– ORIGIN mid 19th cent.: from Hawaiian.

paid past and past participle of **PAY**¹. ▶ **adjective** (of work or leave) for or during which one receives pay: *they get a certain number of weeks paid holiday a year*.
■ [attrib.] (of a person in a specified occupation) in receipt of pay: *a paid, anonymous informer*.
– PHRASES **put paid to** informal stop abruptly; destroy: *Denmark's victory put paid to our hopes of qualifying*.

paideia /pʌɪˈdʌɪə/ ▶ **noun** [mass noun] (in ancient Greece) education or upbringing.
■ the culture of a society.
– ORIGIN Greek.

paid-up ▶ **adjective** [attrib.] (of a member of an organization, especially a trade union) having paid all the necessary subscriptions in full.
■ firmly committed to an organization or movement: *a fully paid-up Thatcher supporter*. ■ denoting the part of the subscribed capital of an undertaking which has actually been paid: *paid-up capital*. ■ denoting an endowment policy in which the policyholder has stopped paying premiums, resulting in the surrender value being used to purchase a single-premium whole-of-life assurance.

Paignton /ˈpeɪnt(ə)n/ a resort town in SW England, on the south coast of Devon; pop. 40,820 (1981).

pail ▶ **noun** a bucket.
– DERIVATIVES **pailful** noun (pl. **-fuls**).
– ORIGIN Middle English: origin uncertain; compare with Old English *pægel* 'gill, small measure' and Old French *paelle* 'pan, liquid measure, brazier'.

Pailin /ˈpeɪlɪn/ a ruby-mining town in western Cambodia, close to the border with Thailand.

paillasse ▶ **noun** variant spelling of **PALLIASSE**.

paillette /palˈjɛt, pʌɪˈjɛt/ ▶ **noun** a piece of glittering material used to ornament clothing; a spangle.
■ a piece of bright metal used in enamel painting.
– ORIGIN mid 19th cent.: from French, diminutive of *paille*, from Latin *palea* 'straw, chaff'.

pain ▶ **noun 1** [mass noun] physical suffering or

discomfort caused by illness or injury: *she's* **in** *great* **pain** | *those who suffer from back pain.* ■[count noun] a feeling of marked discomfort in a particular part of the body: *he had severe pains in his stomach* | *chest pains.* ■ mental suffering or distress: *the pain of loss.* ■ (also **pain in the neck** or vulgar slang **arse**) [in sing.] informal an annoying or tedious person or thing: *she's a pain.*
2 (**pains**) careful effort; great care or trouble: *she* **took pains** *to see that everyone ate well* | *he* **is at pains** *to point out that he isn't like that.*
▶**verb** [with obj.] cause mental or physical pain to: *it pains me to say this* | *her legs had been paining her.* ■[no obj.] chiefly N. Amer. (of a part of the body) hurt: *sometimes my right hand would pain.*
– PHRASES **for one's pains** informal as an unfairly bad return for efforts or trouble: *he was sued for his pains.* **no pain, no gain** chiefly N. Amer. suffering is necessary in order to achieve something. [ORIGIN: originally used as a slogan in fitness classes.] **on** (or **under**) **pain of** the penalty for disobedience or shortcoming being: *they proscribed all such practices and observances on pain of death.*
– ORIGIN Middle English (in the sense 'suffering inflicted as punishment for an offence'): from Old French *peine*, from Latin *poena* 'penalty', later 'pain'.

pain barrier ▶**noun** the state of greatest pain, especially during physical exertion, beyond which the pain diminishes: *marathon runners go through the pain barrier.*

Paine, Thomas (1737–1809), English political writer. His pamphlet *Common Sense* (1776) called for American independence and *The Rights of Man* (1791) defended the French Revolution. His radical views prompted the British government to indict him for treason and he fled to France. Other notable works: *The Age of Reason* (1794).

pained ▶**adjective** affected with pain, especially mental pain; hurt or troubled: *a pained expression came over his face* | *Susan looked pained.*

Paine Towers /ˈpʌmi, -neɪ/ a group of spectacular granite peaks in southern Chile, rising to a height of 2,668 m (8,755 ft).

painful ▶**adjective** (of part of the body) affected with pain: *her ankle was very painful* | *painful feet.* ■causing physical pain: *a painful knock.* ■ causing distress or trouble: *a painful experience* | *change is inevitably slow and painful.*
– DERIVATIVES **painfulness** noun.

painfully ▶**adverb** in a painful manner or to a painful degree: *she coughed painfully.* ■[as submodifier] (with reference to something bad) exceedingly; acutely: *progress was painfully slow.*

painkiller ▶**noun** a drug or a medicine for relieving pain.
– DERIVATIVES **painkilling** adjective.

painless ▶**adjective** not causing or suffering physical pain: *a painless death.* ■involving little effort or stress: *a painless way to travel.*
– DERIVATIVES **painlessly** adverb, **painlessness** noun.

painstaking ▶**adjective** done with or employing great care and thoroughness: *painstaking attention to detail* | *he is a gentle, painstaking man.*
– DERIVATIVES **painstakingly** adverb, **painstakingness** noun.

paint ▶**noun 1** [mass noun] a coloured substance which is spread over a surface and dries to leave a thin decorative or protective coating: *a tin of paint* | [count noun] *bituminous paints.* ■[count noun] an act of covering something with paint: *it looked in need of a good paint.* ■ informal cosmetic make-up: *one has false curls, another too much paint.* ■ Basketball the rectangular area marked near the basket at each end of the court: *the two players jostled* **in the paint.** ■ Computing the function or capability of producing graphics, especially those that mimic the effect of real paint: [as modifier] *a paint program.*
2 N. Amer. a piebald horse: [as modifier] *a paint mare.*
▶**verb** [with obj.] **1** (often **be painted**) cover the surface of (something) with paint, as decoration or protection: *the window surrounds have been painted* | [with obj. and complement] *the ceiling was painted dark grey* | [as adj., with submodifier] (**painted**) *a brightly painted caravan.* ■apply cosmetics to (the face or skin): *she couldn't have been more than fourteen but her face was thickly painted.* ■ apply (a liquid) to a surface with a brush. ■ (**paint something out**) efface something with paint: *the markings on the plane were hurriedly painted out.* ■ Computing create (a graphic or screen display) using a paint program. ■ display a mark representing (an aircraft or vehicle) on a radar screen.
2 depict (an object, person, or scene) with paint: *I painted a woman sitting next to a table lamp.* ■produce (a picture) in such a way: *Marr is a self-taught artist who paints portraits* | [no obj.] *she paints and she makes sculptures and things.* ■ give a description of (someone or something): *the city is not as bad as it is painted.*
– PHRASES **like watching paint dry** (of an activity or experience) extremely boring. **paint oneself into a corner** leave oneself no means of escape or room to manoeuvre. **paint the town red** informal go out and enjoy oneself flamboyantly.
– DERIVATIVES **paintable** adjective, **painty** adjective (**paintier, paintiest**).
– ORIGIN Middle English: from *peint* 'painted', past participle of Old French *peindre*, from Latin *pingere* 'to paint'.

paintball ▶**noun** [mass noun] a game in which participants simulate military combat using air guns to shoot capsules of paint at each other. ■[count noun] a capsule of paint used in this game.
– DERIVATIVES **paintballer** noun.

paintbox ▶**noun** a box holding dry paints for painting pictures. ■(**Paintbox**) trademark an electronic system used to create video graphics by storing filmed material on disk and manipulating it using a graphics tablet.

paintbrush ▶**noun 1** a brush for applying paint.
2 [with modifier] a North American plant which bears brightly coloured flowering spikes with a brush-like appearance. See also **DEVIL'S PAINTBRUSH**.
● Genus *Castilleja*, family Scrophulariaceae: several species, including the **Indian paintbrush** (*C. coccinea*).

paint-by-number ▶**adjective** denoting a child's picture marked out in advance into sections which are numbered according to the colour to be used. ■figurative denoting something mechanical or formulaic rather than imaginative, original, or natural: *a paint-by-number way to feel or act.*

paint chip ▶**noun 1** a small area on a painted surface where the paint has been chipped away.
2 N. Amer. a card showing a colour or a range of related colours available in a type of paint.

painted bat ▶**noun** a SE Asian bat with scarlet or orange fur and fingers and black wing membranes.
● *Kerivoula picta*, family Vespertilionidae.

painted lady ▶**noun 1** a migratory butterfly with predominantly orange-brown wings and darker markings.
● Genus *Cynthia*, subfamily Nymphalinae, family Nymphalidae: the widely distributed *C. cardui*, with black-and-white markings, and the **American painted lady** (*C. virginiensis*), with eyemarks on the undersides of the wings.
2 South African term for **GLADIOLUS**.

painted snipe ▶**noun** a small long-billed wading bird which has brown plumage with bold and colourful markings.
● Family Rostratulidae: two species, in particular *Rostratula benghalensis* of the Old World.

painted turtle ▶**noun** a small American freshwater turtle with a smooth patterned shell.
● *Chrysemys picta*, family Emydidae.

painter[1] ▶**noun 1** an artist who paints pictures: *a German landscape painter.*
2 a person who paints windows, doors, and other parts of a house, especially as a job.
– ORIGIN Middle English: from Anglo-Norman French *peintour*, based on Latin *pictor*, from the verb *pingere* 'to paint'.

painter[2] ▶**noun** a rope attached to the bow of a boat for tying it to a quay.
– ORIGIN Middle English: of uncertain origin; compare with Old French *pentoir* 'something from which to hang things'.

painterly ▶**adjective** of or appropriate to a painter; artistic: *she has a painterly eye.* ■(of a painting or its style) characterized by qualities of colour, stroke, and texture rather than of line.
– DERIVATIVES **painterliness** noun.

paint frame ▶**noun** a movable iron framework for moving scenes from the stage to the platform on which a scene-painter stands.

paint gun ▶**noun** a gun-shaped tool for applying paint. ■an air gun firing capsules of paint, used in the game of paintball.

pain threshold ▶**noun** the point beyond which a stimulus causes pain. ■the upper limit of tolerance to pain.

painting ▶**noun** [mass noun] the process or art of using paint, either in a picture or as decoration. ■[count noun] a painted picture: *an oil painting.*

paint kettle ▶**noun** a container with a handle used to hold paint during use.

paint shop ▶**noun** the part of a factory where goods are painted, typically by spraying.

paintstick ▶**noun** a stick of water-soluble paint used like a crayon.

paintwork ▶**noun** [mass noun] chiefly Brit. painted surfaces in a building or vehicle.

pair ▶**noun** a set of two things used together or regarded as a unit: *a pair of gloves* | *a pair of shoes.* ■an article or object consisting of two joined or corresponding parts not used separately: *a pair of jeans* | *a pair of scissors* | *she resolved to buy him a new pair.* ■ two playing cards of the same denomination: *Jacobs had two pairs.* ■ two people related in some way or considered together: *a company run by a pair of brothers* | *get out,* **the pair of you,** *before I change my mind* | *students work alone or* **in pairs.** ■ the second member of a pair in relation to the first: *each course member tries to persuade his pair of the merits of his model.* ■ a mated couple of animals: *76 pairs of red kites.* ■ two horses harnessed side by side. ■ either or both of two members of a legislative assembly on opposite sides who absent themselves from voting by mutual arrangement, leaving the relative position of the parties unaffected.
▶**verb** [with obj.] (often **be paired**) join or connect to form a pair: *a cardigan* **paired with** *a matching skirt.* ■[no obj.] (of animals) mate: *individuals pair later in the season for breeding in the following year.* ■ [no obj.] (**pair off/up**) form a couple: *Rachel has* **paired up with** *Tommy.* ■ give (a member of a legislative assembly) another member as a pair, to allow both to absent themselves from a vote without affecting the result.
– PHRASES **pair of hands** used in reference to a person seen in terms of their participation in a task: *we can always do with an extra pair of hands.*
– DERIVATIVES **pairwise** adjective & adverb.
– ORIGIN Middle English: from Old French *paire*, from Latin *paria* 'equal things', neuter plural of *par* 'equal'. Formerly phrases such as *a pair of gloves* were expressed without *of*, as in *a pair gloves* (compare with German *ein Paar Handschuhe*).

pair-bond ▶**verb** [no obj.] (of an animal or person) form a close relationship through courtship and sexual activity with one other animal or person.
▶**noun** (**pair bond**) a relationship so formed.

paired ▶**adjective** occurring in pairs or as a pair: *a characteristic arrangement of paired fins.*

pairing ▶**noun** an arrangement or match resulting from organizing or forming people or things into pairs: *the dancers made a fine pairing.* ■[mass noun] the action of pairing things or people: *the pairing of food and wine.*

pair production ▶**noun** [mass noun] Physics the conversion of a radiation quantum into an electron and a positron.

paisa /ˈpʌɪsɑː, -sə/ ▶**noun** (pl. **paise** /-seɪ or -sə/) a monetary unit of India, Pakistan, and Nepal, equal to one hundredth of a rupee.
– ORIGIN from Hindi *paisā*.

paisan /pʌɪˈzɑːn/ ▶**noun** US informal (among people of Italian or Spanish descent) a fellow countryman or friend (often as a term of address).
– ORIGIN from Italian *paisano* 'peasant, rustic'.

paisano /pʌɪˈsɑːnəʊ, -ˈzɑː-/ ▶**noun** (pl. **-os** /-əʊz/) US a peasant of Spanish or Italian ethnic origin.
– ORIGIN Spanish.

Paisley[1] /ˈpeɪzli/ a town in central Scotland, to the west of Glasgow, administrative centre of Renfrewshire; pop. 75,500 (1991).

Paisley[2] /ˈpeɪzli/, Ian (Richard Kyle) (b.1926), Northern Irish clergyman and politician. MP for North Antrim since 1970 and co-founder of the Ulster Democratic Unionist Party (1972), he has been a vociferous and outspoken defender of the Protestant Unionist position in Northern Ireland.

paisley /ˈpeɪzli/ ▶**noun** [mass noun] [usu. as modifier] a distinctive intricate pattern of curved feather-shaped figures based on an Indian pine cone design: *a paisley silk tie.*
– ORIGIN early 19th cent.: named after the town of

Paisley (see **PAISLEY**[1]), the original place of manufacture.

Paiute /ˈpʌɪuːt/ ▶ **noun** (pl. same or **Paiutes**) **1** a member of either of two culturally similar but geographically separate and linguistically distinct American Indian peoples (the **Southern Paiute** and the **Northern Paiute**) of the western US.
2 [mass noun] either of the Uto-Aztecan languages of these peoples, now with few speakers.
▶ **adjective** of or relating to the Paiute or their languages.
– ORIGIN from Spanish *Payuchi*, *Payuta*, influenced by **UTE**.

pajamas ▶ **plural noun** US spelling of **PYJAMAS**.

PAK ▶ **abbreviation for** Pakistan or Pakistani.

pakamac /ˈpakəmak/ (also **pacamac**) ▶ **noun** Brit. a kind of lightweight plastic mackintosh that can be folded up into a small pack when not required.
– ORIGIN 1950s: phonetic respelling of *pack a mac*.

pakapoo /ˈpakəpuː, ˌpakəˈpuː/ (also **pakapu**) ▶ **noun** [mass noun] Austral. a Chinese form of lottery played with slips of paper marked with columns of characters.
– ORIGIN early 20th cent.: from Chinese, literally 'white pigeon ticket', perhaps with reference to a Cantonese competition which involved releasing pigeons and assessing distance flown and the number likely to return.

pak choi /pak ˈtʃɔɪ/ (also N. Amer. **bok choy**) ▶ **noun** [mass noun] a Chinese cabbage of a variety with smooth-edged tapering leaves.
– ORIGIN from Chinese (Cantonese dialect) *paâk ts'oì* 'white vegetable'.

pakeha /ˈpɑːkɪhɑː/ ▶ **noun** Austral./NZ a white New Zealander, as opposed to a Maori.
▶ **adjective** of or relating to white New Zealanders and their languages and culture.
– ORIGIN Maori.

Paki ▶ **noun** (pl. **Pakis**) Brit. informal, offensive a person from Pakistan or the Indian subcontinent by birth or descent, especially one living in Britain.
– ORIGIN 1960s: abbreviation.

Pakistan /ˌpɑːkɪˈstɑːn, ˌpakɪ-, -ˈstan/ a country in the Indian subcontinent; pop. 115,588,000 (est. 1991); languages, Urdu (official), Punjabi, Sindhi, Pashto; capital, Islamabad.

> Pakistan was created as a separate country in 1947, following the British withdrawal from India. It originally comprised two territories, respectively to the east and west of India, in which the population was predominantly Muslim. Civil war in East Pakistan led to the establishment of the independent state of Bangladesh in 1972. Pakistan withdrew from the Commonwealth in 1972 as a protest against international recognition of Bangladesh, but rejoined in 1989; it was suspended in 1999 following a military coup.

– DERIVATIVES **Pakistani** adjective & noun.
– ORIGIN from Punjab, Afghan Frontier, Kashmir, Baluchistan, lands where Muslims predominated.

Pakistan People's Party (abbrev.: **PPP**) one of the main political parties in Pakistan. It was founded in 1967 by Zulfikar Ali Bhutto, and has been led since 1984 by his daughter Benazir Bhutto.

pakora /pəˈkɔːrə/ ▶ **noun** (in Indian cookery) a piece of vegetable or meat, coated in seasoned batter and deep-fried.
– ORIGIN from Hindi *pakoṛā*, denoting a dish of vegetables in gram flour.

pa kua /pɑːˈkwɑː/ ▶ **noun** variant spelling of **BA GUA**.

PAL ▶ **noun** [mass noun] the television broadcasting system used in most of Europe.
– ORIGIN acronym from *Phase Alternate Line* (so named because the colour information in alternate lines is inverted in phase).

pal informal ▶ **noun** a friend.
■ used as a form of address, especially to indicate anger or aggression: *back off, pal.*
▶ **verb** (**palled**, **palling**) [no obj.] (**pal up**) form a friendship: *she* ***palled up with*** *a lot of English chaps.*
■ (**pal around**) spend time with a friend: *we got acquainted but we never really palled around.*
– ORIGIN late 17th cent.: from Romany, 'brother, mate', based on Sanskrit *bhrātṛ* 'brother'.

palace ▶ **noun** the official residence of a sovereign, president, archbishop, or bishop: *the royal palace.*
■ informal a large, splendid house.
– ORIGIN Middle English: from Old French *paleis*, from Latin *Palatium*, the name of the Palatine hill in Rome, where the house of the emperor was situated.

Palace of Westminster see **WESTMINSTER, PALACE OF**.

palace revolution (also **palace coup**) ▶ **noun** the non-violent overthrow of a sovereign or government by senior officials within the ruling group.

palacsinta /ˌpalətsˈsɪntə/ ▶ **noun** (pl. same or **palacsintas**) (in Hungarian cuisine) a thin pancake eaten as a dessert, typically with a filling.
– ORIGIN Hungarian.

paladin /ˈpalədɪn/ ▶ **noun** historical any of the twelve peers of Charlemagne's court, of whom the Count Palatine was the chief.
■ a knight renowned for heroism and chivalry.
– ORIGIN late 16th cent.: from French *paladin*, from Italian *paladino*, from Latin *palatinus* '(officer) of the palace' (see **PALATINE**[1]).

Palaearctic /ˌpalɪˈɑːktɪk, ˌpeɪ-/ (also chiefly US **Palearctic**) ▶ **adjective** Zoology of, relating to, or denoting a zoogeographical region comprising Eurasia north of the Himalayas, together with North Africa and the temperate part of the Arabian peninsula. The fauna is closely related to that of the Nearctic region. Compare with **HOLARCTIC**.
■ [as noun **the Palaearctic**] the Palaearctic region.

palaeo- /ˈpalɪəʊ, ˈpeɪlɪəʊ/ (US **paleo-**) ▶ **combining form** older or ancient, especially relating to the geological past: *Palaeolithic* | *palaeomagnetism.*
– ORIGIN from Greek *palaios* 'ancient'.

palaeoanthropology (US **paleoanthropology**) ▶ **noun** the branch of anthropology concerned with fossil hominids.
– DERIVATIVES **palaeoanthropological** adjective, **palaeoanthropologist** noun.

palaeobiology (US **paleobiology**) ▶ **noun** [mass noun] the biology of fossil animals and plants.
– DERIVATIVES **palaeobiological** adjective, **palaeobiologist** noun.

palaeobotany (US **paleobotany**) ▶ **noun** [mass noun] the study of fossil plants.
– DERIVATIVES **palaeobotanical** adjective, **palaeobotanist** noun.

Palaeocene /ˈpalɪə(ʊ)siːn, ˈpeɪ-/ (US **Paleocene**) ▶ **adjective** Geology of, relating to, or denoting the earliest epoch of the Tertiary period, between the Cretaceous period and the Eocene epoch.
■ [as noun **the Palaeocene**] the Palaeocene epoch or the system of rocks deposited during it.

> The Paleocene epoch lasted from 65.0 to 56.5 million years ago. It was a time of sudden diversification among the mammals, probably as a result of the mass extinctions (notably of the dinosaurs) which occurred at the end of the Cretaceous period (see **CRETACEOUS–TERTIARY BOUNDARY**).

– ORIGIN late 19th cent.: from **PALAEO-** (relating to prehistoric times) + Greek *kainos* 'new'.

palaeoclimate (US **paleoclimate**) ▶ **noun** a climate prevalent at a particular time in the geological past.
– DERIVATIVES **palaeoclimatic** adjective, **palaeoclimatologist** noun, **palaeoclimatology** noun.

palaeocurrent (US **paleocurrent**) ▶ **noun** a current which existed at some time in the geological past, as inferred from the features of sedimentary rocks.

palaeodemography ▶ **noun** [mass noun] the branch of knowledge that deals with the demographic features of past cultures.

palaeoecology (US **paleoecology**) ▶ **noun** [mass noun] the ecology of fossil animals and plants.
– DERIVATIVES **palaeoecological** adjective, **palaeoecologist** noun.

palaeoenvironment ▶ **noun** an environment at a period in the geological past.
– DERIVATIVES **palaeoenvironmental** adjective.

Palaeo-Eskimo (US **Paleo-Eskimo**) ▶ **noun** a member of the earliest prehistoric Inuit people, inhabiting the Arctic from Greenland to Siberia.
▶ **adjective** of or relating to this people.

palaeoethnobotany (US **paleoethnobotany**) ▶ **noun** [mass noun] the branch of ethnobotany that deals archaeologically with the remains of plants cultivated or used by human beings.
– DERIVATIVES **palaeoethnobotanical** adjective, **palaeoethnobotanist** noun.

Palaeogene /ˈpalɪə(ʊ)dʒiːn, ˈpeɪ-/ (US **Paleogene**) ▶ **adjective** Geology of, relating to, or denoting the earlier division of the Tertiary period, comprising the Palaeocene, Eocene, and Oligocene epochs. Compare with **NEOGENE**.
■ [as noun **the Palaeogene**] the Palaeogene sub-period or the system of rocks deposited during it.

> The Palaeogene lasted from about 65 to 23 million years ago. The mammals diversified following the demise of the dinosaurs, and many bizarre and gigantic forms appeared.

– ORIGIN late 19th cent.: from **PALAEO-** (relating to prehistoric times) + Greek *genēs* 'of a specified kind' (see **-GEN**).

palaeogeography (US **paleogeography**) ▶ **noun** [mass noun] the study of geographical features at periods in the geological past.
– DERIVATIVES **palaeogeographer** noun, **palaeogeographical** adjective.

palaeography /ˌpalɪˈɒgrəfi, peɪ-/ (US **paleography**) ▶ **noun** [mass noun] the study of ancient writing systems and the deciphering and dating of historical manuscripts.
– DERIVATIVES **palaeographer** noun, **palaeographic** adjective, **palaeographical** /-əˈgrafɪk(ə)l/ adjective, **palaeographically** adverb.

Palaeo-Indian (US **Paleo-Indian**) ▶ **adjective** of, relating to, or denoting the earliest human inhabitants of the Americas, to *c.*5000 BC. The date of their first arrival in America is debated (possibly up to 30,000 or 40,000 years ago, but artefacts do not become numerous until the Clovis period).
▶ **noun 1** (**the Palaeo-Indian**) the Palaeo-Indian culture or period.
2 a member of the Palaeo-Indian peoples.

palaeolatitude (US **paleolatitude**) ▶ **noun** the latitude of a place at some time in the past, measured relative to the earth's magnetic poles in the same period. Differences between this and the present latitude are caused by continental drift and movement of the earth's magnetic poles.

Palaeolithic /ˌpalɪə(ʊ)ˈlɪθɪk, ˌpeɪ-/ (US **Paleolithic**) ▶ **adjective** Archaeology of, relating to, or denoting the early phase of the Stone Age, lasting about 2.5 million years, when primitive stone implements were used.
■ [as noun **the Palaeolithic**] the Palaeolithic period. Also called **OLD STONE AGE**.

> The Palaeolithic period extends from the first appearance of artefacts to the end of the last ice age (about 8,500 years BC). The period has been divided into the **Lower Palaeolithic**, with the earliest forms of humankind and the emergence of hand-axe industries (ending about 120,000 years ago), the **Middle Palaeolithic**, the era of Neanderthal man (ending about 35,000 years ago), and the **Upper Palaeolithic**, during which only modern *Homo sapiens* is known to have existed.

– ORIGIN mid 19th cent.: from **PALAEO-** 'of prehistoric times' + Greek *lithos* 'stone' + **-IC**.

palaeomagnetism (US **paleomagnetism**) ▶ **noun** [mass noun] the branch of geophysics concerned with the magnetism in rocks that was induced by the earth's magnetic field at the time of their formation.
– DERIVATIVES **palaeomagnetic** adjective.

palaeontology /ˌpalɪɒnˈtɒlədʒi, ˌpeɪ-/ (US **paleontology**) ▶ **noun** [mass noun] the branch of science concerned with fossil animals and plants.
– DERIVATIVES **palaeontological** adjective, **palaeontologist** noun.
– ORIGIN mid 19th cent.: from **PALAEO-** 'of prehistoric times' + Greek *onta* 'beings' (neuter plural of *ōn*, present participle of *einai* 'be') + **-LOGY**.

palaeopathology (US **paleopathology**) ▶ **noun** [mass noun] the branch of science concerned with the pathological conditions found in ancient human and animal remains.
– DERIVATIVES **palaeopathological** adjective, **palaeopathologist** noun.

palaeopole (US **paleopole**) ▶ **noun** a magnetic pole of the earth as it was situated at a time in the distant past.

Palaeo-Siberian ▶ **adjective** denoting or belonging to a group of languages spoken in eastern Siberia, formerly thought to constitute a phylum or superfamily. The most important of them is Chukchi.

palaeosol /ˈpalɪə(ʊ)sɒl, ˈpeɪ-/ (US **paleosol**) ▶ **noun** Geology a stratum or soil horizon which was formed as a soil in a past geological age.

palaeotemperature (US **paleotemperature**)

▶ **noun** Geology the temperature or mean temperature of a locality at a time in the geological past.

Palaeotropical (US **Paleotropical**) ▶ **adjective** Botany of, relating to, or denoting a phytogeographical kingdom comprising Africa, tropical Asia, New Guinea, and many Pacific islands (excluding Australia and New Zealand).
■ Zoology of, relating to, or denoting a zoogeographical region comprising the tropical parts of the Old World.

Palaeozoic /ˌpalɪə(ʊ)ˈzəʊɪk, ˌpeɪ-/ (US **Paleozoic**) ▶ **adjective** Geology of, relating to, or denoting the era between the Precambrian aeon and the Mesozoic era. Formerly called **PRIMARY**.
■ [as noun **the Palaeozoic**] the Palaeozoic era or the system of rocks deposited during it.

The Palaeozoic lasted from about 570 to 245 million years ago, its end being marked by mass extinctions. The **Lower Palaeozoic** sub-era comprises the Cambrian, Ordovician, and Silurian periods, and the **Upper Palaeozoic** sub-era comprises the Devonian, Carboniferous, and Permian periods. The era began with the first invertebrates with hard external skeletons, notably trilobites, and ended with the rise to dominance of the reptiles.

– ORIGIN mid 19th cent.: from **PALAEO-** 'of prehistoric times' + Greek *zōē* 'life' + **-IC**.

palaestra /pəˈliːstrə, -ˈlʌɪstrə/ (also **palestra**) ▶ **noun** (in ancient Greece and Rome) a wrestling school or gymnasium.
– ORIGIN via Latin from Greek *palaistra*, from *palaiein* 'wrestle'.

palagi /ˈpɑːlɑŋi/ (also **papalagi**) ▶ **noun** (pl. same) (in Samoa) a white or non-Samoan person.
– ORIGIN from Samoan *papālagi*.

palais /ˈpaleɪ/ ▶ **noun** [often as name] Brit. a public hall for dancing: *Hammersmith Palais*.
– ORIGIN early 20th cent.: from French *palais (de danse)* '(dancing) hall'.

palais de danse /ˌpaleɪ də ˈdɒ̃s, French palɛ də dɑ̃s/ ▶ **noun** (pl. same) a dance hall.
– ORIGIN early 20th cent.: from French.

Palais de Justice /ˌpaleɪ də juːˈstiːs, French palɛ də ʒystis/ ▶ **noun** (pl. same) (in France and French-speaking countries) a court of law.
– ORIGIN French, literally 'palace of justice'.

Palais de l'Elysée /palɛ də lelize/ French name for **ELYSÉE PALACE**.

palanquin /ˌpalənˈkiːn/ (also **palankeen**) ▶ **noun** (in India and the East) a covered litter for one passenger, consisting of a large box carried on two horizontal poles by four or six bearers.
– ORIGIN late 16th cent.: from Portuguese *palanquim*, from Oriya *pālańki*, based on Sanskrit *palyanka* 'bed, couch'.

Palantype /ˈpalәntʌɪp/ ▶ **noun** [mass noun] trademark a system of shorthand which can be typed using a machine designed for the purpose, often used in transcribing speech for deaf people.
■ [count noun] a machine for typing this form of shorthand.
– ORIGIN 1940s: from the name of Clementine Camille Marie *Palanque*, English manufacturer, + the noun **TYPE**.

palapa /pəˈlapə/ ▶ **noun** a traditional Mexican shelter roofed with palm leaves or branches.
■ US a structure, especially on a beach, of a similar kind.
– ORIGIN Mexican Spanish, denoting the palm *Orbignya cohune*.

palatable /ˈpalətəb(ə)l/ ▶ **adjective** (of food or drink) pleasant to taste: *a very palatable local red wine*.
■ (of an action or proposal) acceptable or satisfactory: *a device that made increased taxation more palatable*.
– DERIVATIVES **palatability** noun, **palatably** adverb.

palatal /ˈpalət(ə)l/ ▶ **adjective** technical of or relating to the palate: *a palatal lesion*.
■ Phonetics (of a speech sound) made by placing the blade of the tongue against or near the hard palate (e.g. *y* in *yes*).
▶ **noun** Phonetics a palatal sound.
– DERIVATIVES **palatally** adverb.
– ORIGIN early 18th cent.: from French, from Latin *palatum* (see **PALATE**).

palatalize (also **-ise**) ▶ **verb** [with obj.] Phonetics make (a speech sound) palatal, especially by changing a velar to a palatal by moving the point of contact between tongue and palate further forward in the mouth.
■ [no obj.] (of a speech sound) become palatal.
– DERIVATIVES **palatalization** noun.

palate ▶ **noun 1** the roof of the mouth, separating the cavities of the mouth and nose in vertebrates.
2 a person's sense of appreciation of taste and flavour, especially when sophisticated and discriminating: *a fine range of drink for sophisticated palates*.
■ a person's taste or liking: *the suggestions may not suit everyone's palate*. ■ taste or flavour of wine or beer: *a wine with a zingy, peachy palate*.
– ORIGIN late Middle English: from Latin *palatum*.

palatial ▶ **adjective** resembling a palace in being spacious and splendid: *her palatial apartment in Mayfair*.
– DERIVATIVES **palatially** adverb.
– ORIGIN mid 18th cent.: from Latin *palatium* 'palace' (see **PALACE**) + **-AL**.

palatinate /pəˈlatɪnət/ ▶ **noun** historical a territory under the jurisdiction of a Count Palatine.
■ (**the Palatinate**) the territory of the German Empire ruled by the Count Palatine of the Rhine.

palatine[1] /ˈpalətʌɪn, -tɪn/ ▶ **adjective** [usu. postpositive] chiefly historical (of an official or feudal lord) having local authority that elsewhere belongs only to a sovereign.
■ (of a territory) subject to this authority.
– ORIGIN late Middle English: from French *palatin(e)*, from Latin *palatinus* 'of the palace'.

palatine[2] /ˈpalətʌɪn, -tɪn/ chiefly Anatomy ▶ **adjective** of or relating to the palate or especially the palatine bone.
▶ **noun** (also **palatine bone**) each of two bones within the skull forming parts of the eye socket, the nasal cavity, and the hard palate.
– ORIGIN mid 17th cent.: from French *palatin(e)*, from Latin *palatum* 'palate'.

palatine uvula ▶ **noun** see **UVULA**.

Palau /pəˈlaʊ/ (also **Belau**) a group of islands in the western Pacific Ocean, an independent republic since 1990; pop. 18,000 (est. 1994); capital, Koror. It was part of the US Trust Territory of the Pacific Islands 1947–80.

Palaung /pəˈlaʊŋ/ ▶ **noun** (pl. same or **Palaungs**) **1** a member of an indigenous people of the northern Shan states of Burma (Myanmar).
2 [mass noun] the Mon-Khmer language of this people.
▶ **adjective** of or relating to this people or their language.
– ORIGIN the name in Palaung.

palaver /pəˈlɑːvə/ informal ▶ **noun** [mass noun] prolonged and tedious fuss or discussion: *mucking around with finances and all that palaver*.
■ [count noun] dated a parley or improvised conference between two sides.
▶ **verb** [no obj.] talk unnecessarily at length: *it's too hot for palavering*.
– ORIGIN mid 18th cent. (in the sense 'a talk between tribespeople and traders'): from Portuguese *palavra* 'word', from Latin *parabola* 'comparison' (see **PARABLE**).

Palawan /pəˈlɑːwən/ a long, narrow island in the western Philippines, separating the Sulu Sea from the South China Sea; chief town, Puerto Princesa.

palazzo /pəˈlatsəʊ/ ▶ **noun** (pl. **palazzos** or **palazzi** /-tsi/) a palatial building, especially in Italy.
– ORIGIN Italian, 'palace'.

palazzo pants ▶ **plural noun** women's loose wide-legged trousers.

pale[1] ▶ **adjective** light in colour or having little colour: *choose pale floral patterns for walls*.
■ (of a person's face or complexion) having less colour than usual, typically as a result of shock, fear, or ill health: *she looked pale and drawn*. ■ figurative feeble and unimpressive: *it is a pale imitation of continental cheeses*.
▶ **verb** [no obj.] **1** become pale in one's face from shock or fear: *I paled at the thought of what she might say*.
2 seem less impressive or important: *all else pales by comparison | his own problems* ***paled into insignificance*** *compared to the plight of this child*.
– DERIVATIVES **palely** adverb, **paleness** noun, **palish** adjective.
– ORIGIN Middle English: from Old French *pale*, from Latin *pallidus*; the verb is from Old French *palir*.

pale[2] ▶ **noun 1** a wooden stake or post used as an upright along with others to form a fence.
■ figurative a boundary: *bring these things back within the pale of decency*. ■ archaic or historical an area within determined bounds, or subject to a particular jurisdiction.
2 (**the Pale**) historical another term for **ENGLISH PALE**.
■ the areas of Russia to which Jewish residence was restricted.
3 Heraldry a broad vertical stripe down the middle of a shield.
– PHRASES **beyond the pale** outside the bounds of acceptable behaviour: *the language my father used was beyond the pale*. **in pale** Heraldry arranged vertically. **per pale** Heraldry divided by a vertical line.
– ORIGIN Middle English: from Old French *pal*, from Latin *palus* 'stake'.

palea /ˈpeɪlɪə/ ▶ **noun** (pl. **paleae** /-lɪiː/) Botany the upper bract of the floret of a grass. Compare with **LEMMA**[2].
– ORIGIN mid 18th cent.: from Latin, literally 'chaff'.

Palearctic ▶ **adjective** chiefly US variant spelling of **PALAEARCTIC**.

paleface ▶ **noun** a name supposedly used by the North American Indians for a white person.

Palekh /ˈpɑːlɛk/ ▶ **noun** [as modifier] denoting a type of Russian iconography or a style of miniature painting on boxes, trays, and other small items.
– ORIGIN from the name of a town north-east of Moscow renowned for this type of work.

Palembang /ˌpɑːləmˈbɑːŋ, pɑːˈlɛmbɑːŋ/ a city in Indonesia, in the SE part of the island of Sumatra, a river port on the Musi River; pop. 1,140,900 (1990).

Palenque /pəˈlɛŋkeɪ/ the site of a former Mayan city in SE Mexico, south-east of present-day Villahermosa. The well-preserved ruins of the city, which existed from about AD 300 to 900, include notable examples of Mayan architecture and extensive hieroglyphic texts.

paleo- ▶ **combining form** US spelling of **PALAEO-**.

paleo-conservative ▶ **noun** N. Amer. a person who advocates old or traditional forms of conservatism; an extremely right-wing conservative.

Palermo /pəˈlɛːməʊ, Italian paˈlɛrmo/ the capital of the Italian island of Sicily, a port on the north coast; pop. 734,240 (1990).

Palestine /ˈpalɪstʌɪn/ a territory in the Middle East on the eastern coast of the Mediterranean Sea.

In biblical times Palestine comprised the kingdoms of Israel and Judah. The land was controlled at various times by the Egyptian, Assyrian, Persian, and Roman empires before being conquered by the Arabs in AD 634. It was part of the Ottoman Empire from 1516 to 1918. The name Palestine was used as the official political title for the land west of the Jordan mandated to Britain in 1920; in 1948 the state of Israel was established in what was traditionally Palestine, but the name continued to be used in the context of the struggle for territory and political rights of displaced Palestinian Arabs. In 1993 an agreement was signed between Israel and the Palestine Liberation Organization giving some autonomy to the Gaza Strip and the West Bank and setting up the Palestine National Authority and a police force.

– ORIGIN from Greek *Palaistinē* (used in early Christian writing), from Latin *(Syria) Palaestina* (the name of a Roman province), from *Philistia* 'land of the Philistines'.

Palestine Liberation Organization (abbrev.: **PLO**) a political and military organization formed in 1964 to unite various Palestinian Arab groups and ultimately to bring about an independent state of Palestine. Since 1968 it has been led by Yasser Arafat.

Palestinian /ˌpalɪˈstɪnɪən/ ▶ **adjective** of or relating to Palestine or its peoples.
▶ **noun** a member of the native Arab population of the region of Palestine (including the modern state of Israel).

palestra /pəˈlɛstrə/ ▶ **noun** variant spelling of **PALAESTRA**.

Palestrina /ˌpaləˈstriːnə/, Giovanni Pierluigi da (*c*.1525–94), Italian composer. Palestrina is chiefly known for his sacred music, including 105 masses, over 250 motets, and the *Missa Papae Marcelli* (1567).

palette /ˈpalɪt/ ▶ **noun** a thin board or slab on which an artist lays and mixes colours.
■ the range of colours used by a particular artist or in a particular picture: *I choose a palette of natural, earthy colours*. ■ figurative the range or variety of tonal or instrumental colour in a musical piece: *he commands the sort of tonal palette which this music needs*. ■ (in computer graphics) the range of colours or shapes available to the user.
– ORIGIN late 18th cent.: from French, diminutive of *pale* 'shovel', from Latin *pala* 'spade'.

p

palette knife ▶**noun 1** a thin steel blade with a handle for mixing colours or applying or removing paint.
2 Brit. a kitchen knife or spatula with a long, blunt, flexible, round-ended blade.

palfrey /ˈpɔːlfri, ˈpal-/ ▶**noun** (pl. **-eys**) archaic a docile horse used for ordinary riding, especially by women.
– ORIGIN Middle English: from Old French *palefrei*, from medieval Latin *palefredus*, alteration of late Latin *paraveredus*, from Greek *para* 'beside, extra' + Latin *veredus* 'light horse'.

Palgrave /ˈpalɡreɪv, ˈpɔːl-/, Francis Turner (1824–97), English critic and poet, known for his anthology *The Golden Treasury of Songs and Lyrical Poems in the English Language* (1861).

Pali /ˈpɑːliː/ ▶**noun** [mass noun] an Indic language, closely related to Sanskrit, in which the sacred texts of southern Buddhism are written. Pali developed in northern India in the 5th–2nd centuries BC.
▶**adjective** of or relating to this language.
– ORIGIN from Pali *pāli(-bhāsā)* 'canonical texts'.

pali /ˈpɑːliː/ ▶**noun** (pl. same or **palis**) (in Hawaii) a cliff.
– ORIGIN Hawaiian.

palilalia /ˌpalɪˈleɪlɪə/ ▶**noun** [mass noun] Medicine a speech disorder characterized by involuntary repetition of words, phrases, or sentences.
– ORIGIN early 20th cent.: from French *palilalie*, from Greek *palin* 'again' + *lalia* 'speech, chatter'.

palimony /ˈpalɪməni/ ▶**noun** [mass noun] informal, chiefly US compensation made by one member of an unmarried couple to the other after separation.
– ORIGIN 1970s: from **PAL** + a shortened form of **ALIMONY**.

palimpsest /ˈpalɪm(p)sɛst/ ▶**noun** a manuscript or piece of writing material on which later writing has been superimposed on effaced earlier writing.
■figurative something reused or altered but still bearing visible traces of its earlier form: *Sutton Place is a palimpsest of the taste of successive owners.*
– DERIVATIVES **palimpsestic** adjective.
– ORIGIN mid 17th cent.: via Latin from Greek *palimpsēstos*, from *palin* 'again' + *psēstos* 'rubbed smooth'.

palindrome /ˈpalɪndrəʊm/ ▶**noun** a word, phrase, or sequence that reads the same backwards as forwards, e.g. *madam* or *nurses run*.
– DERIVATIVES **palindromic** /-ˈdrɒmɪk/ adjective, **palindromist** noun.
– ORIGIN early 17th cent.: from Greek *palindromos* 'running back again', from *palin* 'again' + *drom-* (from *dramein* 'to run').

paling /ˈpeɪlɪŋ/ ▶**noun** a fence made from pointed wooden or metal stakes.
■a stake used in such a fence.

palingenesis /ˌpalɪnˈdʒɛnɪsɪs/ ▶**noun** [mass noun] Biology the exact reproduction of ancestral characteristics in ontogenesis.
– DERIVATIVES **palingenetic** adjective.
– ORIGIN early 19th cent.: from Greek *palin* 'again' + *genesis* 'birth'.

palinode /ˈpalɪnəʊd/ ▶**noun** a poem in which the poet retracts a view or sentiment expressed in a former poem.
– ORIGIN late 16th cent.: via Latin from Greek *palinōidia*, from *palin* 'again' + *ōidē* 'song'.

Palio /ˈpalɪəʊ, Italian ˈpalio/ (pl. **Palii** /-ɪiː, Italian -ii/) a traditional horse race held in Siena twice a year, in July and August.
– ORIGIN Italian, from Latin *pallium* 'covering' (with reference to the cloth given as a prize).

palisade /ˌpalɪˈseɪd/ ▶**noun** a fence of wooden stakes or iron railings fixed in the ground, forming an enclosure or defence.
■historical a strong pointed wooden stake fixed deeply in the ground with others in a close row, used as a defence. ■ (**palisades**) US a line of high cliffs. ■ (**the Palisades**) a ridge of high basalt cliffs on the west bank of the Hudson River, in NE New Jersey.
▶**verb** [with obj.] [usu. as adj. **palisaded**] enclose or provide (a building or place) with a palisade.
– ORIGIN early 17th cent.: from French *palissade*, from Provençal *palissada*, from *palissa* 'paling', based on Latin *palus* 'stake'.

palisade layer ▶**noun** Botany a layer of parallel elongated cells below the epidermis of a leaf.

Palissy /ˈpalɪsi/, Bernard (*c.*1510–90), French potter, known for his richly coloured earthenware decorated with reliefs of plants and animals.

Palk Strait /pɔːlk/ an inlet of the Bay of Bengal separating northern Sri Lanka from the coast of Tamil Nadu in India. It lies to the north of Adam's Bridge, which separates it from the Gulf of Mannar.

pall[1] /pɔːl/ ▶**noun 1** a cloth spread over a coffin, hearse, or tomb.
■figurative a dark cloud or covering of smoke, dust, or similar: *a pall of black smoke hung over the quarry.* ■ figurative something regarded as enveloping a situation with an air of gloom, heaviness, or fear: *torture and murder have cast a pall of terror over the villages.*
2 an ecclesiastical pallium.
■Heraldry a Y-shaped charge representing the front of an ecclesiastical pallium.
– ORIGIN Old English *pæll* 'rich (purple) cloth', 'cloth cover for a chalice', from Latin *pallium* 'covering, cloak'.

pall[2] /pɔːl/ ▶**verb** [no obj.] become less appealing or interesting through familiarity: *the novelty of the quiet life palled | their talk must* **pall on** *people.*
– ORIGIN late Middle English: shortening of **APPAL**.

palladia plural form of **PALLADIUM**[2].

Palladian /pəˈleɪdɪən/ ▶**adjective** Architecture of, relating to, or denoting the neoclassical style of Andrea Palladio, in particular with reference to the phase of English architecture from *c.*1715, when there was a revival of interest in Palladio and his English follower, Inigo Jones, and a reaction against the baroque.
– DERIVATIVES **Palladianism** noun.

Palladian window ▶**noun** chiefly US a large window consisting of a central arched section flanked by two narrow rectangular sections.

Palladio /pəˈlɑːdɪəʊ/, Andrea (1508–80), Italian architect. He led a revival of classical architecture, in particular promoting the Roman ideals of harmonic proportions and symmetrical planning. A notable example of his many villas, palaces, and churches is the church of San Giorgio Maggiore in Venice.

palladium[1] /pəˈleɪdɪəm/ ▶**noun** [mass noun] the chemical element of atomic number 46, a rare silvery-white metal resembling platinum. (Symbol: **Pd**)
– ORIGIN early 19th cent.: modern Latin, from *Pallas*, the name given to an asteroid discovered (1803) just before the element.

palladium[2] /pəˈleɪdɪəm/ ▶**noun** (pl. **palladia** /-dɪə/) archaic a safeguard or source of protection.
– ORIGIN late Middle English (in the Greek sense): via Latin from Greek *palladion*, denoting an image of the goddess Pallas (Athene), on which the safety of Troy was believed to depend.

Pallas /ˈpaləs/ **1** Greek Mythology (also **Pallas Athene**) one of the names (of unknown meaning) of **ATHENE**.
2 Astronomy asteroid 2, discovered in 1802. It is the second largest (diameter 523 km).

pallasite /ˈpaləsʌɪt/ ▶**noun** a meteorite consisting of roughly equal proportions of iron and olivine.
– ORIGIN mid 19th cent.: from the name of Peter S. *Pallas* (1741–1811), German naturalist, + **-ITE**[1].

Pallas's cat /ˈpaləsɪz/ ▶**noun** a small wild cat that has a long orange-grey coat with black-and-white head markings, occurring in the mountains of central Asia. Also called **MANUL**.
• *Felis manul*, family Felidae.
– ORIGIN mid 19th cent.: named after Peter S. *Pallas* (1741–1811), German naturalist.

pall-bearer ▶**noun** a person helping to carry or officially escorting a coffin at a funeral.

pallet[1] ▶**noun** a straw mattress.
■a crude or makeshift bed.
– ORIGIN Middle English: from Anglo-Norman French *paillete*, from *paille* 'straw', from Latin *palea*.

pallet[2] ▶**noun 1** a portable platform on which goods can be moved, stacked, and stored, especially with the aid of a forklift truck.
2 a flat wooden blade with a handle, used to shape clay or plaster.
3 an artist's palette.
4 a projection on a machine part, serving to change the mode of motion of a wheel.
■(in a clock or watch) a projection transmitting motion from an escapement to a pendulum or balance wheel.
– ORIGIN late Middle English (in sense 2): from French *palette* 'little blade', from Latin *pala* 'spade' (related to *palus* 'stake').

pallet[3] ▶**noun** Heraldry the diminutive of the pale, a narrow vertical strip, usually borne in groups of two or three.
– ORIGIN late 15th cent.: diminutive of the noun **PALE**[2].

palletize (also **-ise**) ▶**verb** [with obj.] [usu. as adj. **palletized**] place, stack, or transport (goods) on a pallet or pallets.

pallia plural form of **PALLIUM**.

palliasse /ˈpalɪas/ (also **paillasse**) ▶**noun** a straw mattress.
– ORIGIN early 16th cent. (originally Scots): from French *paillasse*, based on Latin *palea* 'straw'.

palliate /ˈpalɪeɪt/ ▶**verb** [with obj.] make (a disease or its symptoms) less severe or unpleasant without removing the cause: *treatment works by palliating symptoms.*
■allay or moderate (fears or suspicions): *this eliminated, or at least palliated, suspicions aroused by German unity.* ■ disguise the seriousness or gravity of (an offence): *there is no way to excuse or palliate his dirty deed.*
– DERIVATIVES **palliation** noun, **palliator** noun.
– ORIGIN late Middle English: from late Latin *palliat-* 'cloaked', from the verb *palliare*, from *pallium* 'cloak'.

palliative /ˈpalɪətɪv/ ▶**adjective** (of a treatment or medicine) relieving pain or alleviating a problem without dealing with the underlying cause: *short-term, palliative measures had been taken.*
▶**noun** a remedy, medicine, etc. of such a kind.
– DERIVATIVES **palliatively** adverb.
– ORIGIN late Middle English (as an adjective): from French *palliatif, -ive* or medieval Latin *palliativus*, from the verb *palliare* 'to cloak' (see **PALLIATE**).

palliative care ▶**noun** [mass noun] care for the terminally ill and their families, especially that provided by an organized health service.

pallid ▶**adjective** (of a person's face) pale, typically because of poor health.
■derogatory feeble or insipid: *a pallid ray of winter sun.*
– DERIVATIVES **pallidly** adverb, **pallidness** noun.
– ORIGIN late 16th cent.: from Latin *pallidus* 'pale' (related to *pallere* 'be pale').

pallium /ˈpalɪəm/ ▶**noun** (pl. **pallia** /-lɪə/ or **palliums**) **1** a woollen vestment conferred by the Pope on an archbishop, consisting of a narrow circular band placed round the shoulders with a short lappet hanging from front and back.
2 historical a man's large rectangular cloak, especially as worn by Greek philosophical and religious teachers.
3 Zoology the mantle of a mollusc or brachiopod.
4 Anatomy the outer wall of the mammalian cerebrum, corresponding to the cerebral cortex.
– DERIVATIVES **pallial** adjective (only in senses 3 and 4).
– ORIGIN Middle English: from Latin, literally 'covering'.

pall-mall /palˈmal/ ▶**noun** [mass noun] historical a 16th- and 17th-century game in which a boxwood ball was driven through an iron ring suspended at the end of a long alley. The street Pall Mall in London was on the site of a pall-mall alley.
– ORIGIN from obsolete French *pallemaille*, from Italian *pallamaglio*, from *palla* 'ball' + *maglio* 'mallet'.

pallor ▶**noun** [in sing.] an unhealthy pale appearance.
– ORIGIN late Middle English: from Latin, from *pallere* 'be pale'.

pally ▶**adjective** (**pallier**, **palliest**) [predic.] informal having a close, friendly relationship: *I see you're getting quite* **pally with** *Carlos.*

palm[1] ▶**noun** (also **palm tree**) an unbranched evergreen tree with a crown of very long feathered or fan-shaped leaves, and typically having old leaf scars forming a regular pattern on the trunk. Palms grow in tropical and warm regions.
• Family Palmae (or Arecaceae): numerous genera and species, some of which are of great commercial importance, e.g. the **oil palm**, **date palm**, and coconut.
■a leaf of such a tree awarded as a prize or viewed as a symbol of victory or triumph: *the consensus was that the palm should go to Doerner.*
– ORIGIN Old English *palm(a)*, of Germanic origin; related to Dutch *palm* and German *Palme*, from

Latin *palma* 'palm (of a hand)', its leaf being likened to a spread hand.

palm[2] ▶ **noun** the inner surface of the hand between the wrist and fingers.
■ a part of a glove that covers this part of the hand. ■ a hard shield worn on the hand by sailmakers to protect the palm. ■ the palmate part of a deer's antler.
▶ **verb 1** [with obj.] conceal (a card or other small object) in the hand, especially as part of a trick or theft.
2 [with obj. and adverbial of direction] (of a goalkeeper) deflect (the ball) with the palm of the hand: *Jason palmed the ball out of danger.*
– PHRASES **have** (or **hold**) **someone in the palm of one's hand** have someone under one's control or influence: *she had the audience in the palm of her hand.* **read someone's palm** tell someone's fortune by looking at the lines on their palm.
– DERIVATIVES **palmar** /'palmə/ adjective, **palmed** adjective [in combination] *sweaty-palmed*, **palmful** noun.
– ORIGIN Middle English: from Old French *paume*, from Latin *palma*. Current senses of the verb date from the late 17th cent.
▶ **palm someone off** informal persuade someone to accept something by deception: *most sellers are* ***palmed off with*** *a fraction of what something is worth.* **palm something off** sell or dispose of something by misrepresentation or fraud: *they* ***palmed off*** *their shoddiest products* ***on*** *the Russians.*

Palma /'pɑːmə, 'palmə/ the capital of the Balearic Islands, an industrial port and resort on the island of Majorca; pop. 308,620 (1991). Full name **Palma de Mallorca**.

Palmas /'palmas/ a town in central Brazil, on the Tocantins River, capital of the state of Tocantins; pop. 5,750 (1990).

palmate /'palmeɪt/ ▶ **adjective 1** Botany (of a leaf) having five or more lobes whose midribs all radiate from one point.
2 Zoology (of an antler) in which the angles between the tines are partly filled in to form a broad flat surface, as in fallow deer and moose.
– DERIVATIVES **palmated** adjective.
– ORIGIN mid 18th cent.: from Latin *palmatus*, from *palma* 'palm' (see **palm**[2]).

palmate newt ▶ **noun** a small olive-brown smooth-skinned newt native to western Europe, with partially webbed feet.
● *Triturus helveticus*, family Salamandridae.

palm ball ▶ **noun** a baseball pitch in which the ball is released from the palm and thumb rather than the fingers.

Palm Beach a resort town in SE Florida, situated on an island just off the coast; pop. 9,810 (1990).

palm civet ▶ **noun** a mainly arboreal civet that typically has pale spots or stripes on a dark coat, and powerful curved claws, native to Africa and Asia. It is often a pest of banana plantations.
● *Paradoxurus* and other genera, family Viverridae: several species, including the **common palm civet** or toddy cat (*P. hermaphroditus*) of Asia.

palmcorder ▶ **noun** a small, hand-held camcorder.
– ORIGIN 1980s: blend of **palm**[2] and **recorder**.

Palme /'pɑːlmə/, (Sven) Olof (Joachim) (1927–86), Swedish statesman, Prime Minister 1969–76 and 1982–6. He was killed by an unknown assassin.

Palmer[1], Arnold (Daniel) (b.1929), American golfer. His many championship victories include the Masters (1958; 1960; 1962; 1964), the US Open (1960), and the British Open (1961–2).

Palmer[2], Samuel (1805–91), English painter and etcher. His friendship with William Blake resulted in the mystical, visionary landscape paintings, such as *Repose of the Holy Family* (1824), for which he is best known. He was leader of a group of artists called The Ancients.

palmer ▶ **noun 1** historical a pilgrim, especially one who had returned from the Holy Land with a palm branch or leaf as a sign of having undertaken the pilgrimage.
■ historical an itinerant monk travelling from shrine to shrine under a vow of poverty.
2 a hairy artificial fly used in angling.
– ORIGIN Middle English: from Anglo-Norman French, from medieval Latin *palmarius* 'pilgrim', from Latin *palma* 'palm'.

Palmerston /'pɑːməst(ə)n/, Henry John Temple, 3rd Viscount (1784–1865), British Whig statesman, Prime Minister 1855–8 and 1859–65. Palmerston declared the second Opium War against China in 1856, and oversaw the successful conclusion of the Crimean War in 1856 and the suppression of the Indian Mutiny in 1858.

Palmerston North a city in the SW part of North Island, New Zealand; pop. 69,300 (1990).

palmette /pal'mɛt/ ▶ **noun** Archaeology an ornament of radiating petals like a palm leaf.
– ORIGIN mid 19th cent.: from French, literally 'small palm', diminutive of *palme*.

palmetto /pal'mɛtəʊ/ ▶ **noun** (pl. **-os**) a fan palm, especially one of a number occurring from the southern US to northern South America.
● *Sabal* and other genera, family Palmae: several species, in particular the **cabbage palmetto** (*S. palmetto*), which is the state tree of Florida.
– ORIGIN mid 16th cent.: from Spanish *palmito*, literally 'small palm', diminutive of *palma*, assimilated to Italian words ending in *-etto*.

Palmetto State informal name for **South Carolina**.

palmier /'palmɪeɪ/ ▶ **noun** (pl. pronounced same) a sweet crisp pastry shaped like a palm leaf.
– ORIGIN French, literally 'palm tree'.

palmistry ▶ **noun** [mass noun] the art or practice of supposedly interpreting a person's character or predicting their future by examining the lines and other features of the hand, especially the palm and fingers.
– DERIVATIVES **palmist** noun.
– ORIGIN late Middle English: from **palm**[2] + *-estry* (of unknown origin), later altered to *-istry*, perhaps on the pattern of *sophistry*.

palmitic acid /pal'mɪtɪk/ ▶ **noun** Chemistry a solid saturated fatty acid obtained from palm oil and other vegetable and animal fats.
● Chem. formula: $CH_3(CH_2)_{14}COOH$.
– DERIVATIVES **palmitate** /'palmɪteɪt/ noun.
– ORIGIN mid 19th cent.: *palmitic* from French *palmitique*, from *palme* (see **palm**[1]).

palm oil ▶ **noun** [mass noun] oil from the fruit of certain palms, especially the West African oil palm.

Palm Springs a resort city in the desert area of southern California, east of Los Angeles, noted for its hot mineral springs; pop. 40,180 (1990).

palm squirrel ▶ **noun** an Old World squirrel that frequents palm trees, especially a tree squirrel with a striped back and a shrill birdlike call that is native to the Indian subcontinent.
● Genus *Funambulus* and other genera, family Sciuridae: several species, in particular the **five-striped northern palm squirrel** (*F. pennanti*) which is common in and around human habitation in northern India.

Palm Sunday ▶ **noun** the Sunday before Easter, on which Christ's entry into Jerusalem is celebrated in many Christian churches by processions in which branches of palms are carried.

palmtop ▶ **noun** a computer small and light enough to be held in one hand.

palm wine ▶ **noun** [mass noun] an alcoholic drink made from fermented palm sap.

palmy ▶ **adjective** (**palmier**, **palmiest**) **1** (especially of a previous period of time) flourishing or successful: *the palmy days of the 1970s.*
2 covered with palms.

Palmyra /pal'mʌɪrə/ an ancient city of Syria, an oasis in the Syrian desert north-east of Damascus on the site of present-day Tadmur.
– ORIGIN Greek form of the city's modern and ancient pre-Semitic name Tadmur or Tadmor, meaning 'city of palms'.

palmyra ▶ **noun** an Asian fan palm which yields a wide range of useful products, including timber, fibre, and fruit.
● *Borassus flabellifer*, family Palmae.
– ORIGIN late 17th cent.: from Portuguese *palmeira* 'palm tree'. The change in the ending was due to association with the name of the ancient city of **Palmyra**.

Palo Alto /ˌpaləʊ 'altəʊ/ a city in western California, south of San Francisco; pop. 55,900 (1990). It is a noted centre for electronics and computer technology, and the site of Stanford University.

palolo worm /pə'ləʊləʊ/ ▶ **noun** a marine bristle worm which swarms in response to changes in light intensity, particularly that of the moon. The worm's posterior segments detach themselves and swim to the surface where the reproductive cells are released into the sea.
● Several species in Eunicidae and other families, in particular the **Samoan palolo worm** (*Palola* (or *Eunice*) *viridis*), which occurs on South Pacific reefs.
– ORIGIN late 19th cent.: *palolo* from Samoan or Tongan.

Palomar, Mount /'paləmɑː/ a mountain in southern California, north-east of San Diego, rising to a height of 1,867 m (6,126 ft). It is the site of an astronomical observatory.
– ORIGIN Spanish *Palomar*, literally 'place of the pigeon'.

palomino /ˌpalə'miːnəʊ/ ▶ **noun 1** (pl. **-os**) a pale golden or tan-coloured horse with a white mane and tail, originally bred in the south-western US.
2 [mass noun] a variety of white grape, originally grown around Jerez in southern Spain, used especially to make sherry and fortified wines.
– ORIGIN early 20th cent.: from Latin American Spanish, from Spanish *palomino* 'young pigeon', from Latin *palumbinus* 'resembling a dove'.

palooka /pə'luːkə/ ▶ **noun** US informal, dated an inferior or average prizefighter.
■ N. Amer. a stupid, uncouth person; a lout.
– ORIGIN 1920s: of unknown origin.

Palouse /pə'luːz/ ▶ **noun** (pl. same or **Palouses**) a member of an American Indian people inhabiting the Palouse river valley in SW Washington and NW Idaho.
▶ **adjective** of or relating to this people.
– ORIGIN the name in their own language.

paloverde /ˌpaləʊ'vəːdi/ ▶ **noun** a thorny yellow-flowered tree that grows along water courses in the warm desert areas of America.
● Genus *Cercidium*, family Leguminosae.
– ORIGIN early 19th cent.: from Latin American Spanish, literally 'green tree'.

palp /palp/ (also **palpus**) ▶ **noun** (pl. **palps** or **palpi** /-pʌɪ, -piː/) Zoology each of a pair of elongated segmented appendages near the mouth of an arthropod, usually concerned with the senses of touch and taste.
– DERIVATIVES **palpal** adjective.
– ORIGIN mid 19th cent.: from Latin *palpus*, from *palpare* 'to feel'.

palpable /'palpəb(ə)l/ ▶ **adjective** able to be touched or felt: *the palpable bump at the bridge of the nose.*
■ (especially of a feeling or atmosphere) so intense as to be almost touched or felt: *a palpable sense of loss.* ■ clear to the mind or plain to see: *to talk of dawn raids in the circumstances is palpable nonsense.*
– DERIVATIVES **palpability** noun, **palpably** adverb.
– ORIGIN late Middle English: from late Latin *palpabilis*, from Latin *palpare* 'feel, touch gently'.

palpate /pal'peɪt/ ▶ **verb** [with obj.] examine (a part of the body) by touch, especially for medical purposes.
– DERIVATIVES **palpation** noun.
– ORIGIN mid 19th cent.: from Latin *palpat-* 'touched gently', from the verb *palpare*.

palpebral /'palpɪbr(ə)l/ ▶ **adjective** [attrib.] Anatomy of or relating to the eyelids.
– ORIGIN mid 19th cent.: from late Latin *palpebralis*, from Latin *palpebra* 'eyelid'.

palpitant ▶ **adjective** rare palpitating.
– ORIGIN mid 19th cent.: from French, present participle of *palpiter*, from Latin *palpitare* 'continue to pat'.

palpitate /'palpɪteɪt/ ▶ **verb** [no obj.] [often as adj. **palpitating**] (of the heart) beat rapidly, strongly, or irregularly.
■ shake; tremble: *she was palpitating with terror.*
– ORIGIN early 17th cent.: from Latin *palpitat-* 'patted', from the verb *palpitare*, frequentative of *palpare* 'touch gently'.

palpitation ▶ **noun** (usu. **palpitations**) a noticeably rapid, strong, or irregular heartbeat due to agitation, exertion, or illness.
– ORIGIN late Middle English: from Latin *palpitatio(n-)*, from the verb *palpitare* (see **palpitate**).

palpus /'palpəs/ ▶ **noun** another term for **palp**.
– ORIGIN early 19th cent.: from Latin, literally 'feeler'.

palsgrave /'pɔːlzgreɪv/ ▶ **noun** historical a Count Palatine.
– ORIGIN mid 16th cent.: from early modern Dutch *paltsgrave*, from *palts* 'palatinate' + *grave* 'count'.

p

palstave /ˈpɔːlsteɪv/ ▶ noun Archaeology a type of chisel, typically made of bronze, which is shaped to fit into a split handle rather than having a socket for the handle.
– ORIGIN mid 19th cent.: from Danish *paalstav*, from Old Norse *pálstafr*, from *páll* 'hoe' (compare with Latin *palus* 'stake') + *stafr* 'staff'.

palsy /ˈpɔːlzi, ˈpɒl-/ ▶ noun (pl. **-ies**) [mass noun] dated paralysis, especially that which is accompanied by involuntary tremors: *a kind of palsy had seized him.*
■ archaic a condition of incapacity or helplessness.
▶ verb (**-ies, -ied**) [with obj.] (often **be palsied**) affect with paralysis and involuntary tremors.
– ORIGIN Middle English: from Old French *paralisie*, from an alteration of Latin *paralysis* (see **PARALYSIS**).

palsy-walsy ▶ adjective informal very friendly or intimate.
– ORIGIN 1930s (as a noun in the sense 'friend'): from the noun **PAL** + **-SY**, by reduplication.

palter /ˈpɔːltə, ˈpɒl-/ ▶ verb [no obj.] archaic **1** equivocate or prevaricate in action or speech.
2 (**palter with**) trifle with: *this great work should not be paltered with.*
– DERIVATIVES **palterer** noun.
– ORIGIN mid 16th cent. (in the sense 'mumble or babble'): of unknown origin; no corresponding verb is known in any other language.

paltry ▶ adjective (**paltrier, paltriest**) (of an amount) very small or meagre: *she would earn a paltry £33 more each month | funding of the arts is paltry.*
■ petty; trivial: *naval glory struck him as paltry.*
– DERIVATIVES **paltriness** noun.
– ORIGIN mid 16th cent.: apparently based on dialect *pelt* 'rubbish, especially rags'; compare with Low German *paltrig* 'ragged'.

paludal /pəˈl(j)uːd(ə)l, ˈpal(j)ʊd(ə)l/ ▶ adjective Ecology (of a plant, animal, or soil) living or occurring in a marshy habitat.
– ORIGIN early 19th cent.: from Latin *palus, palud-* 'marsh' + **-AL**.

Paludrine /ˈpal(j)ʊdrɪn, -iːn/ ▶ noun trademark for PROGUANIL.
– ORIGIN 1940s: from Latin *palus, palud-* 'marsh' + *-rine*, on the pattern of *Atabrine* and *mepacrine*.

paly /ˈpeɪli/ ▶ adjective Heraldry divided into equal vertical stripes: *paly of six, argent and gules.*
– ORIGIN late Middle English: from Old French *pale* 'divided by stakes', from *pal* 'pale, stake'.

palynology /ˌpalɪˈnɒlədʒi/ ▶ noun [mass noun] the study of pollen grains and other spores, especially as found in archaeological or geological deposits. Pollen extracted from such deposits may be used for radiocarbon dating and for studying past climates and environments by identifying plants then growing.
– DERIVATIVES **palynological** adjective, **palynologist** noun.
– ORIGIN 1940s: from Greek *palunein* 'sprinkle' + **-LOGY**.

pama /ˈpɑːmə/ ▶ noun variant spelling of BAMA.

Pama-Nyungan /ˌpɑːməˈnjʌŋɡən/ ▶ adjective of, relating to, or denoting the main family of Australian Aboriginal languages, covering much of the continent except for a northern fringe. Most have become extinct during the 20th century.
▶ noun this family of languages.

Pamir Mountains /pəˈmɪə/ (also **the Pamirs**) a mountain system of central Asia, centred in Tajikistan and extending into Kyrgyzstan, Afghanistan, Pakistan, and western China. The highest peak in the Pamirs, Communism Peak in Tajikistan, rises to 7,495 m (24,590 ft).

pampas /ˈpampəs, -z/ ▶ noun [treated as sing. or pl.] large treeless plains in South America.
– ORIGIN early 18th cent.: via Spanish from Quechua *pampa* 'plain'.

pampas grass ▶ noun [mass noun] a tall South American grass with silky flowering plumes, widely grown as a specimen lawn plant.
● *Cortaderia selloana*, family Gramineae.

pampelmoes /ˌpamp(ə)lˈmuːs/ ▶ noun South African term for POMELO.

pamper ▶ verb [with obj.] indulge with every attention, comfort, and kindness; spoil: *famous people just love being pampered.*
– ORIGIN late Middle English (in the sense 'cram with food'): probably of Low German or Dutch

origin; compare with German dialect *pampfen* 'cram, gorge'; perhaps related to PAP¹.

pampero /pamˈpɛːrəʊ/ ▶ noun (pl. **-os**) a strong, cold south-westerly wind in South America, blowing from the Andes across the pampas towards the Atlantic.
– ORIGIN late 18th cent.: from Spanish *pampas* 'plain'.

pamphlet /ˈpamflɪt/ ▶ noun a small booklet or leaflet containing information or arguments about a single subject.
▶ verb (**pamphleted, pamphleting**) [with obj.] distribute pamphlets to.
– ORIGIN late Middle English: from *Pamphilet*, the familiar name of the 12th-cent. Latin love poem *Pamphilus, seu de Amore.*

pamphleteer ▶ noun a writer of pamphlets, especially ones of a political and controversial nature.
▶ verb [no obj.] [usu. as noun **pamphleteering**] write and issue such pamphlets.

Pamphylia /pamˈfɪlɪə/ an ancient coastal region of southern Asia Minor, between Lycia and Cilicia, to the east of the modern port of Antalya.
– DERIVATIVES **Pamphylian** adjective & noun.

Pamplona /pamˈpləʊnə/ a city in northern Spain, capital of the former kingdom and modern region of Navarre; pop. 191,110 (1991). It is noted for the fiesta of San Fermín, held there in July, which is celebrated with the running of bulls through the streets of the city.

Pan Greek Mythology a god of flocks and herds, typically represented with the horns, ears, and legs of a goat on a man's body. His sudden appearance was supposed to cause terror similar to that of a frightened and stampeding herd, and the word *panic* is derived from his name.
– ORIGIN probably originally in the sense 'the feeder' (i.e. herdsman), although the name was regularly associated with Greek *pas* or *pan* (= 'all'), giving rise to his identification as a god of nature or the universe.

pan¹ /pan/ ▶ noun **1** a container made of metal and used for cooking food in.
■ an amount of something contained in such a container: *a pan of hot water.* ■ a large container used in a technical or manufacturing process for subjecting a material to heat or a mechanical or chemical process. ■ a bowl fitted at either end of a pair of scales. ■ another term for STEEL DRUM. ■ a shallow bowl in which gold is separated from gravel and mud by agitation and washing. ■ Brit. the bowl of a toilet. ■ a hollow in the ground in which water may collect or in which a deposit of salt remains after water has evaporated. ■ Scottish & Irish short for PAN-LOAF. ■ a part of the lock that held the priming in old types of gun.
2 US informal a face.
3 a hard stratum of compacted soil.
▶ verb (**panned, panning**) [with obj.] **1** (often **be panned**) informal criticize (someone or something) severely: *the movie was panned by the critics.*
2 wash gravel in a pan to separate out (gold): *the old-timers panned gold* | [no obj.] *prospectors panned for gold in the Yukon.*
– PHRASES **go down the pan** informal reach a stage of abject failure or uselessness: *communities crumble, hospitals are shut, and the economy goes down the pan.*
– DERIVATIVES **panful** noun (pl. **-fuls**), **pan-like** adjective.
– ORIGIN Old English *panne*, of West Germanic origin; related to Dutch *pan*, German *Pfanne*, perhaps based on Latin *patina* 'dish'.
▶ **pan out** (of gravel) yield gold. ■ turn out well: *Harold's idea had been a good one even if it hadn't panned out.* ■ end up; conclude: *he's happy with the way the deal panned out.*

pan² /pan/ ▶ verb (**panned, panning**) [with obj. and adverbial of direction] swing (a video or film camera) in a horizontal or vertical plane, typically to give a panoramic effect or follow a subject.
■ [no obj., with adverbial of direction] (of a camera) be swung in such a way: *the camera panned to the dead dictator.*
▶ noun a panning movement: *that slow pan over London.*
– PHRASES **pan and scan** a technique for narrowing the aspect ratio of a widescreen film to fit the squarer shape of a television screen by continuously selecting the portion of the original picture with the most significance, rather than just the middle portion.

– ORIGIN early 20th cent.: abbreviation of PANORAMA.

pan³ /paːn/ ▶ noun variant spelling of PAAN.

pan- ▶ combining form all-inclusive, especially in relation to the whole of a continent, racial group, religion, etc.: *pan-African | pansexual.*
– ORIGIN from Greek *pan*, neuter of *pas* 'all'.

panacea /ˌpanəˈsiːə/ ▶ noun a solution or remedy for all difficulties or diseases: *the panacea for all corporate ills | the time-honoured panacea, cod liver oil.*
– DERIVATIVES **panacean** adjective.
– ORIGIN mid 16th cent.: via Latin from Greek *panakeia*, from *panakēs* 'all-healing', from *pan* 'all' + *akos* 'remedy'.

panache /pəˈnaʃ/ ▶ noun **1** [mass noun] flamboyant confidence of style or manner.
2 historical a tuft or plume of feathers, especially as a headdress or on a helmet.
– ORIGIN mid 16th cent.: from French, from Italian *pennacchio*, from late Latin *pinnaculum*, diminutive of *pinna* 'feather'.

panada /pəˈnɑːdə/ ▶ noun [mass noun] a simple dish consisting of bread boiled to a pulp and flavoured.
– ORIGIN late 16th cent.: from Spanish and Portuguese, based on Latin *panis* 'bread'.

Panadol ▶ noun trademark for PARACETAMOL.
– ORIGIN 1950s: of unknown origin.

pan-African ▶ adjective of or relating to all people of African birth or descent.

pan-Africanism ▶ noun [mass noun] the principle or advocacy of the political union of all the indigenous inhabitants of Africa.
– DERIVATIVES **pan-Africanist** noun.

Pan-Africanist Congress (in full **Pan-Africanist Congress of Azania**) (abbrev.: **PAC**) a South African political movement formed in 1959 as a militant offshoot of the African National Congress. It was outlawed in 1960 after the Sharpeville massacre, but continued its armed opposition to the South African government until it was legalized in 1990.

Panaji /ˈpʌnədʒi/ (also **Panjim**) a city in western India, a port on the Arabian Sea; pop. 85,200 (1991). It is the capital of the state of Goa.

Panama /ˈpanəmɑː, ˌpanəˈmɑː/ a country in Central America; pop. 2,329,330 (1990); official language, Spanish; capital, Panama City.

Panama occupies the isthmus connecting North and South America. Colonized by Spain in the early 16th century, Panama was freed from imperial control in 1821, becoming a Colombian province. It gained full independence in 1903, although the construction of the Panama Canal and the leasing of the zone around it to the US (until 1979) split the country in two; the canal itself was ceded to Panama in 1999.

– DERIVATIVES **Panamanian** adjective & noun.

panama (also **panama hat**) ▶ noun a man's wide-brimmed hat of straw-like material, originally made from the leaves of a particular tropical palm tree.
– ORIGIN mid 19th cent.: named after the country of PANAMA.

Panama Canal a canal about 80 km (50 miles) long, across the Isthmus of Panama, connecting the Atlantic and Pacific Oceans. Its construction, begun by Ferdinand de Lesseps in 1881 but abandoned in 1889, was completed by the US between 1904 and 1914. Control of the canal remained with the US until 1999, at which date it was ceded to Panama.

Panama City the capital of Panama, situated on the Pacific coast close to the Panama Canal; pop. 584,800 (1990).

Panama disease ▶ noun [mass noun] a fungal disease of bananas producing yellowing and wilting of the leaves.
● The fungus is *Fusarium oxysporum* f. sp. *cubense*, subdivision Deuteromycotina.

Panamax ▶ adjective denoting a ship with a deadweight tonnage of not more than 69,000, the maximum size for a ship navigating the Panama canal.
– ORIGIN 1980s: blend of PANAMA and the adjective MAXIMUM.

pan-American ▶ adjective of, relating to, representing, or involving all the countries of North and South America.

pan-Americanism ▶ noun [mass noun] the principle or advocacy of political or commercial and cultural cooperation among all the countries of North and South America.

pan-and-tilt ▸ adjective denoting a stand, tripod, or other item of mounting equipment that allows a camera to move in both horizontal and vertical planes.

pan-Arabism ▸ noun [mass noun] the principle or advocacy of political alliance or union of all the Arab states.
– DERIVATIVES **pan-Arab** adjective.

panatella /ˌpanəˈtɛlə/ ▸ noun a long thin cigar.
– ORIGIN mid 19th cent.: from Latin American Spanish *panatela*, denoting a long thin biscuit, from Italian *panatello* 'small loaf', diminutive of *panata*.

Panay /paˈnʌɪ/ an island in the central Philippines; chief town, Iloilo.

pancake ▸ noun a thin, flat cake of batter, fried and turned in a pan and typically rolled up with a sweet or savoury filling.
■(also **pancake make-up**) [mass noun] make-up consisting of a flat solid layer of compressed powder, widely used in the theatre.
▸ verb **1** [no obj.] (of an aircraft) make a pancake landing.
■[with obj.] (of a pilot) cause (an aircraft) to make such a landing: *he pancaked it in about twenty metres.*
2 informal flatten or become flattened: [with obj.] *Hurley's car was pancaked.*
– PHRASES (**as**) **flat as a pancake** completely flat.
– ORIGIN late Middle English: from **PAN**[1] + **CAKE**.

Pancake Day ▸ noun Shrove Tuesday, when pancakes are traditionally eaten.

pancake landing ▸ noun an emergency landing in which an aircraft levels out close to the ground and drops vertically with its undercarriage still retracted.

pancake race ▸ noun a race in which each competitor must toss a pancake from a pan as they run, traditionally held in some places on Shrove Tuesday.

pancetta /panˈtʃɛtə/ ▸ noun [mass noun] Italian cured belly of pork.
– ORIGIN Italian, diminutive of *pancio* 'belly'.

panchayat /pʌnˈtʃʌɪjət/ ▸ noun Indian a village council.
– ORIGIN from Hindi (originally denoting a council consisting of five members), from Sanskrit *panca* 'five' + *āyatta* 'depending upon'.

Panchen Lama /ˈpantʃ(ə)n ˈlɑːmə/ ▸ noun a Tibetan lama ranking next after the Dalai Lama.
– ORIGIN Tibetan *panchen*, abbreviation of *panditachen-po* 'great learned one'; compare with **PUNDIT**.

panchromatic ▸ adjective Photography (of photographic film) sensitive to all visible colours of the spectrum. Often contrasted with **ORTHOCHROMATIC**.

pancreas /ˈpaŋkrɪəs/ ▸ noun (pl. **pancreases**) a large gland behind the stomach which secretes digestive enzymes into the duodenum. Embedded in the pancreas are the islets of Langerhans, which secrete into the blood the hormones insulin and glucagon.
– DERIVATIVES **pancreatic** adjective.
– ORIGIN late 16th cent.: from modern Latin, from Greek *pankreas*, from *pan* 'all' + *kreas* 'flesh'.

pancreatectomy /ˌpaŋkrɪəˈtɛktəmi/ ▸ noun (pl. **-ies**) [mass noun] surgical removal of the pancreas.

pancreatic juice ▸ noun [mass noun] the clear alkaline digestive fluid secreted by the pancreas.

pancreatin /ˈpaŋkrɪətɪn/ ▸ noun [mass noun] a mixture of enzymes obtained from animal pancreases, given as a medicine to aid digestion.

pancreatitis /ˌpaŋkrɪəˈtʌɪtɪs/ ▸ noun [mass noun] Medicine inflammation of the pancreas.

pancreozymin /ˌpaŋkrɪə(ʊ)ˈzʌɪmɪn/ ▸ noun [mass noun] Biochemistry a hormone which stimulates the production of enzymes by the pancreas.

pancytopenia /ˌpansʌɪtə(ʊ)ˈpiːnɪə/ ▸ noun [mass noun] Medicine deficiency of all three cellular components of the blood (red cells, white cells, and platelets).
– ORIGIN mid 20th cent.: from **PAN-** 'all' + **CYTO-** 'cell' + Greek *penia* 'poverty, lack'.

panda[1] /ˈpandə/ (also **giant panda**) ▸ noun a large bear-like mammal with characteristic black-and-white markings, native to certain mountain forests in China. It feeds almost entirely on bamboo and has become increasingly rare. See also **RED PANDA**.
● *Ailuropoda melanoleuca*; it is now usually placed with the bears (family Ursidae), but was formerly thought to belong with the raccoons (family Procyonidae).
– ORIGIN mid 19th cent.: from Nepali.

panda[2] /ˈpandə/ ▸ noun a Brahmin expert in genealogy, who provides religious guidance and acts as a family priest.
– ORIGIN via Hindi from Sanskrit *paṇḍita* 'learned, wise'.

panda car ▸ noun Brit. informal a small police patrol car (originally black and white or blue and white).

pandal /ˈpand(ə)l, panˈdɑːl/ ▸ noun Indian a marquee.
– ORIGIN from Tamil *pantal*.

pandanus /panˈdeɪnəs, -ˈdan-/ (also **pandan**) ▸ noun a tropical tree or shrub which has a twisted and branched stem, stilt roots, spiral tufts of long, narrow typically spiny leaves, and fibrous edible fruit. Also called **SCREW PINE**.
● Genus *Pandanus*, family Pandanaceae.
■[mass noun] fibre from the leaves of this plant, or material woven from this fibre.
– ORIGIN modern Latin, from Malay *pandan*.

Pandarus /ˈpandərəs/ Greek Mythology a Lycian fighting on the side of the Trojans, described in the *Iliad* as breaking the truce with the Greeks by wounding Menelaus with an arrow. The role as the lovers' go-between that he plays in Chaucer's (and later Shakespeare's) story of Troilus and Cressida originated with Boccaccio and is also the origin of the word *pander*.

pandect /ˈpandɛkt/ ▸ noun chiefly historical a complete body of the laws of a country.
■(usu. **the Pandects**) a compendium in 50 books of the Roman civil law made by order of Justinian in the 6th century.
– DERIVATIVES **pandectist** noun.
– ORIGIN mid 16th cent.: from French *pandecte*, from Latin *pandecta*, from Greek *pandektēs* 'all-receiver', from *pan* 'all' + *dektēs* (from *dekhesthai* 'receive').

pandemic /panˈdɛmɪk/ ▸ adjective (of a disease) prevalent over a whole country or the world.
▸ noun an outbreak of such a disease.
– ORIGIN mid 17th cent.: from Greek *pandēmos* (from *pan* 'all' + *dēmos* 'people') + **-IC**.

pandemonium /ˌpandɪˈməʊnɪəm/ ▸ noun [mass noun] wild and noisy disorder or confusion; uproar.
– ORIGIN mid 17th cent.: modern Latin (denoting the place of all demons, in Milton's *Paradise Lost*), from **PAN-** 'all' + Greek *daimōn* 'demon'.

pander ▸ verb [no obj.] (**pander to**) gratify or indulge (an immoral or distasteful desire, need, or habit or a person with such a desire, need, etc.): *newspapers are pandering to people's baser instincts.*
▸ noun dated a pimp.
■archaic a person who assists the baser urges or evil designs of others: *the lowest panders of a venal press.*
– ORIGIN late Middle English (as a noun): from *Pandare*, the name of a character in Chaucer's *Troilus and Criseyde* (see **PANDARUS**). The verb dates from the early 17th cent.

Pandit /ˈpʌndɪt/, Vijaya (Lakshmi) (1900–90), Indian politician and diplomat, sister of Jawaharlal Nehru. Having been imprisoned three times by the British for nationalist activities, after independence she became the first woman to serve as president of the United Nations General Assembly (1953–4).

pandit (also **pundit**) ▸ noun a Hindu scholar learned in Sanskrit and Hindu philosophy and religion, typically also a practising priest: [as title] *Pandit Misir.*
■Indian a wise man or teacher. ■Indian a talented musician (used as a respectful title or form of address).

P & L ▸ abbreviation for profit and loss account.

P. & O. ▸ abbreviation for Peninsular and Oriental Shipping Company (or Line).

Pandora Greek Mythology the first mortal woman. In one story she was created by Zeus and sent to earth with a jar or box of evils in revenge for Prometheus' having brought the gift of fire back to the world. Pandora let out all the evils from the jar to infect the earth; hope alone remained to assuage the lot of humankind.
– ORIGIN from the Greek name *Pandōra* 'all-gifted' (from *pan* 'all' + *dōron* 'gift').

pandora (also **pandora shell** or **Pandora's box shell**) ▸ noun a burrowing bivalve mollusc with a fragile shell, the unequal valves of which form a 'box' with a lid.
● Genus *Pandora*, family Pandoridae.
– ORIGIN modern Latin, from Greek *pandoura* 'three-stringed lute' (because of the shell's resemblance to the soundbox of a stringed instrument).

Pandora's box ▸ noun a process that generates many complicated problems as the result of unwise interference in something.

pandowdy /panˈdaʊdi/ ▸ noun (pl. **-ies**) N. Amer. a kind of spiced apple pudding baked in a deep dish.
– ORIGIN of unknown origin.

p. & p. Brit. ▸ abbreviation for postage and packing.

pane ▸ noun a single sheet of glass in a window or door.
■Computing a separate defined area within a window for the display of, or interaction with, a specified part of that window's application or output. ■a sheet or page of stamps.
– ORIGIN late Middle English (originally denoting a section or piece of something, such as a fence or strip of cloth): from Old French *pan*, from Latin *pannus* 'piece of cloth'.

paneer /paˈnɪə/ (also **panir**) ▸ noun [mass noun] a type of milk curd cheese used in Indian, Iranian, and Afghan cooking.
– ORIGIN from Hindi or Persian *panīr* 'cheese'.

panegyric /ˌpanɪˈdʒɪrɪk/ ▸ noun a public speech or published text in praise of someone or something: *panegyrics on the pleasures of malt whisky.*
– DERIVATIVES **panegyrical** adjective.
– ORIGIN early 17th cent.: from French *panégyrique*, via Latin from Greek *panēgurikos* 'of public assembly', from *pan* 'all' + *aguris* 'agora, assembly'.

panegyrize /ˈpanɪdʒɪrʌɪz/ (also **-ise**) ▸ verb [with obj.] archaic speak or write in praise of; eulogize.
– DERIVATIVES **panegyrist** noun.

panel ▸ noun **1** a thin, typically rectangular piece of wood or glass forming or set into the surface of a door, wall, or ceiling.
■a thin piece of metal forming part of the outer shell of a vehicle: *body panels for the car trade.* ■a flat board on which instruments or controls are fixed: *a control panel.* ■a decorated area within a larger design containing a separate subject: *the central panel depicts the Crucifixion.* ■one of several drawings making up a cartoon strip. ■a piece of material forming part of a garment.
2 a small group of people brought together to discuss, investigate, or decide upon a particular matter, especially in the context of business or government: *an interview panel.*
■Brit. a list of medical practitioners registered in a district as accepting patients under the National Health Service or, formerly, the National Insurance Act. ■chiefly N. Amer. a list of available jurors or a jury. ■Scots Law a person or people charged with a crime or offence.
▸ verb (**panelled**, **panelling**; US **paneled**, **paneling**) [with obj.] [usu. as adj. **panelled**] cover (a wall or other surface) with panels: *his panelled rooms at All Souls.*
– ORIGIN Middle English: from Old French, literally 'piece of cloth', based on Latin *pannus* '(piece of) cloth'. The early sense 'piece of parchment' was extended to mean 'list', whence the notion 'advisory group'. Sense 1 derives from the late Middle English sense 'distinct (usually framed) section of a surface'.

panel beater ▸ noun Brit. a person whose job is to beat out the bodywork of motor vehicles.

panel game ▸ noun Brit. a broadcast quiz played by a panel or team of people.

panel heating ▸ noun [mass noun] a system of heating rooms by panels in the walls and ceiling that contain hot-water pipes or another source of heat.

panelling (US **paneling**) ▸ noun [mass noun] panels collectively, when used to decorate a wall.

panellist (US **panelist**) ▸ noun a member of a panel, especially in a broadcast game or discussion.

panel pin ▸ noun Brit. a light, thin nail with a very small head.

panel saw ▸ noun Brit. a light saw with small teeth, for cutting thin wood.

panel study ▸ noun an investigation of attitude changes using a constant set of people and comparing each individual's opinions at different times.

panel truck ▶ noun N. Amer. a small enclosed delivery truck.

panel van ▶ noun Austral./NZ & S. African a small van, especially one with windows and passenger seats.

panentheism /pan'ɛnθiːɪʒ(ə)m/ ▶ noun [mass noun] the belief or doctrine that God is greater than the universe and includes and interpenetrates it.
– DERIVATIVES **panentheistic** adjective.

panettone /ˌpanɪ'təʊneɪ, -ni/ ▶ noun (pl. **panettoni** /ˌpanɪ'təʊni/) a rich Italian bread made with eggs, fruit, and butter and typically eaten at Christmas.
– ORIGIN Italian, from *panetto* 'cake', diminutive of *pane* 'bread' (from Latin *panis* 'bread').

panfish N. Amer. ▶ noun (pl. same or **-fishes**) a fish suitable for frying whole in a pan, especially one caught by an angler rather than bought.
▶ verb [no obj.] [often as noun **panfishing**] catch, or try to catch, such fish.

panforte /pan'fɔːteɪ, -ti, Italian panˈfɔrte/ ▶ noun [mass noun] a hard, spicy Sienese cake containing nuts, candied peel, and honey.
– ORIGIN Italian, from *pane* 'bread' + *forte* 'strong'.

pan-fry ▶ verb [with obj.] [often as adj. **pan-fried**] fry in a pan in shallow fat: *pan-fried trout.*

pang ▶ noun a sudden sharp pain or painful emotion: *Lindsey experienced a sharp pang of guilt | the snack bar will keep those hunger pangs at bay.*
– ORIGIN late 15th cent.: perhaps an alteration of **PRONG**.

panga /ˈpaŋɡə/ ▶ noun a bladed African tool like a machete.
– ORIGIN Kiswahili.

Pangaea /panˈdʒiːə/ a vast continental area or supercontinent comprising all the continental crust of the earth, which is postulated to have existed in late Palaeozoic and Mesozoic times before breaking up into Gondwana and Laurasia.
– ORIGIN early 20th cent.: from **PAN-** 'all' + Greek *gaia* 'earth'.

pan-German ▶ adjective of, relating to, or advocating pan-Germanism.
■ of, relating to, or including both East and West Germany.
– DERIVATIVES **pan-Germanic** adjective.

pan-Germanism ▶ noun [mass noun] the idea or principle of a political unification of all Europeans speaking German or a Germanic language.

Pangloss /ˈpaŋɡlɒs/ ▶ noun a person who is optimistic regardless of the circumstances.
– DERIVATIVES **Panglossian** adjective.
– ORIGIN mid 19th cent.: from the name of the tutor and philosopher in Voltaire's *Candide* (1759).

pangolin /paŋˈɡəʊlɪn/ ▶ noun an African and Asian mammal that has a body covered with horny overlapping scales, a small head with elongated snout, a long sticky tongue for catching ants and termites, and a stout tapering tail. Also called **SCALY ANTEATER**.
● Family Manidae and order Pholidota: genera *Manis* (three species in Asia) and *Phataginus* (four species in Africa).
– ORIGIN late 18th cent.: from Malay *peng-guling*, literally 'roller' (from its habit of rolling into a ball).

panhandle N. Amer. ▶ noun [often in place names] a narrow strip of territory projecting from the main territory of one state into another: *the Oklahoma Panhandle.*
▶ verb [no obj.] informal beg in the street.
– DERIVATIVES **panhandler** noun.

Panhellenic /ˌpanhɛˈlɛnɪk, -hiːˈliː-/ ▶ adjective of, concerning, or representing all people of Greek origin or ancestry.
■ relating to, advocating, or denoting the idea of a political union of all Greeks.

pani /ˈpɑːni/ ▶ noun Indian term for **WATER**.
– ORIGIN from Hindi *pānī.*

panic[1] ▶ noun [mass noun] sudden uncontrollable fear or anxiety, often causing wildly unthinking behaviour: *she hit him in panic | [in sing.] he ran to the library in a blind panic.*
■ widespread financial or commercial apprehension provoking hasty action: *he caused an economic panic by his sudden resignation | [as modifier] panic selling.* ■ informal frenzied hurry to do something.
▶ verb (**panicked, panicking**) [no obj.] be affected by panic: *the crowd panicked and stampeded for the exit.*
■ [with obj.] cause to feel panic: *talk of love panicked her.* ■ [with obj.] (**panic someone into**) drive or force

someone through panic into (hasty or rash action): *we are not going to be panicked into a decision.*
– PHRASES **panic stations** Brit. informal a state of alarm or emergency: *many quite reasonable people were at panic stations because of popular unrest.*
– DERIVATIVES **panicky** adjective.
– ORIGIN early 17th cent.: from French *panique*, from modern Latin *panicus*, from Greek *panikos*, from the name of the god **PAN**, noted for causing terror, to whom woodland noises were attributed.

panic[2] (also **panic grass**) ▶ noun [mass noun] any of a number of cereal and fodder grasses related to millet.
● *Panicum* and related genera, family Gramineae.
– ORIGIN late Middle English: from Latin *panicum*, from *panus* 'ear of millet' (literally 'thread wound on a bobbin'), based on Greek *pēnos* 'web', *pēnion* 'bobbin'.

panic attack ▶ noun a sudden overwhelming feeling of acute and disabling anxiety.

panic button ▶ noun a button for summoning help in an emergency.
– PHRASES **press** (or **push** or **hit**) **the panic button** informal respond to a situation by panicking or taking emergency measures.

panicle /ˈpanɪk(ə)l/ ▶ noun Botany a loose branching cluster of flowers, as in oats.
– DERIVATIVES **panicled** adjective.
– ORIGIN late 16th cent.: from Latin *panicula*, diminutive of *panus* 'ear of millet' (see **PANIC**[2]).

panic-stricken (also **panic-struck**) ▶ adjective affected with panic; very frightened: *the panic-stricken victims rushed out of their blazing homes.*

pan-Indian ▶ adjective 1 of or relating to the whole of India, or to all its ethnic, religious, or linguistic groups.
2 denoting or relating to a cultural movement or religious practice participated in by many or all American Indian peoples.

Panini /ˈpɑːnɪni/, Indian grammarian. Sources vary as to when he lived, with dates ranging from the 4th to the 7th century BC. He is noted as the author of the *Eight Lectures*, a grammar of Sanskrit.

pani puri /ˈpɑːni ˈpuːri/ ▶ noun (in Indian cookery) a puff-pastry ball filled with spiced mashed potato and tamarind juice and fried.
– ORIGIN from Hindi *pānī* 'water' and *pūrī* from Sanskrit *pūrikā* 'small, fried wheaten cake'.

panir ▶ noun variant spelling of **PANEER**.

Panjabi ▶ noun (pl. **Panjabis**) & adjective variant spelling of **PUNJABI**.

panjandrum /panˈdʒandrəm/ ▶ noun a person who has or claims to have a great deal of authority or influence.
– ORIGIN late 19th cent.: from *Grand Panjandrum*, an invented phrase in a nonsense verse (1755) by S. Foote.

Panjim /ˈpʌndʒɪm/ another name for **PANAJI**.

Pankhurst /ˈpaŋkhəːst/, Mrs Emmeline (1858–1928), Christabel (1880–1958), and (Estelle) Sylvia (1882–1960), English suffragettes. In 1903 Emmeline and her daughters founded the Women's Social and Political Union, with the motto 'Votes for Women'. Following the imprisonment of Christabel in 1905, Emmeline initiated the militant suffragette campaign which continued until the outbreak of the First World War.

pan-loaf ▶ noun Scottish & Irish a loaf baked in a pan or tin.

panmixia /panˈmɪksɪə/ ▶ noun [mass noun] Zoology random mating within a breeding population.
– DERIVATIVES **panmictic** adjective.
– ORIGIN late 19th cent.: modern Latin, from German *Panmixie*, from Greek *pan* 'all' + *mixis* 'mixing'.

pannage /ˈpanɪdʒ/ ▶ noun [mass noun] chiefly historical the right or privilege of feeding pigs or other animals in a wood.
■ pasturage for pigs in woodland.
– ORIGIN late Middle English: from Old French *pasnage*, from medieval Latin *pastionaticum*, from *pastio(n-)* 'pasturing', from the verb *pascere* 'to feed'.

panne /pan/ (also **panne velvet**) ▶ noun [mass noun] a lustrous fabric resembling velvet, made of silk or rayon and having a flattened pile.
– ORIGIN late 18th cent.: from French, of unknown origin.

pannier ▶ noun 1 a basket, especially one of a pair carried by a beast of burden.
■ each of a pair of bags or boxes fitted on either side of the rear wheel of a bicycle or motorcycle.
2 historical part of a skirt looped up round the hips.
■ a frame supporting this.
– ORIGIN Middle English: from Old French *panier*, from Latin *panarium* 'bread basket', from *panis* 'bread'.

pannier tank ▶ noun a small steam locomotive with an overhanging rectilinear water tank along each side of the boiler.

pannikin /ˈpanɪkɪn/ ▶ noun a small metal drinking cup.
– ORIGIN early 19th cent.: from **PAN**[1], on the pattern of *cannikin*.

pannikin boss ▶ noun Austral. informal a minor overseer or foreman.

pannist ▶ noun W. Indian a person who plays a pan in a steel band. See **PAN**[1] (sense 1).

Pannonia /pəˈnəʊnɪə/ an ancient country of southern Europe lying south and west of the Danube, in present-day Austria, Hungary, Slovenia, and Croatia.

pannus /ˈpanəs/ ▶ noun [mass noun] Medicine a condition in which a layer of vascular fibrous tissue extends over the surface of an organ or other specialized anatomical structure, especially the cornea.
– ORIGIN late Middle English: perhaps from Latin, literally 'cloth'.

panoply /ˈpanəpli/ ▶ noun a complete or impressive collection of things: *a deliciously inventive panoply of insults.*
■ a splendid display: *all the panoply of Western religious liturgy.* ■ historical or poetic/literary a complete set of arms or suit of armour.
– DERIVATIVES **panoplied** adjective.
– ORIGIN late 16th cent. (in the sense 'complete protection for spiritual warfare', often with biblical allusion to Eph. 6:11, 13): from French *panoplie* or modern Latin *panoplia* 'full armour', from Greek, from *pan* 'all' + *hopla* 'arms'.

panoptic /panˈɒptɪk/ ▶ adjective showing or seeing the whole at one view: *a panoptic aerial view.*
– ORIGIN early 19th cent.: from Greek *panoptos* 'seen by all', from *panoptēs* 'all-seeing' + **-IC**.

panopticon /panˈɒptɪk(ə)n/ ▶ noun historical a circular prison with cells arranged around a central well, from which prisoners could at all times be observed.
– ORIGIN mid 18th cent.: from **PAN-** 'all' + Greek *optikon*, neuter of *optikos* 'optic'.

panorama ▶ noun an unbroken view of the whole region surrounding an observer: *the tower offers a wonderful panorama of Prague.*
■ a picture or photograph containing a wide view. ■ a complete survey or presentation of a subject or sequence of events.
– DERIVATIVES **panoramic** adjective, **panoramically** adverb.
– ORIGIN late 18th cent.: from **PAN-** 'all' + Greek *horama* 'view' (from *horan* 'see').

pan-pan ▶ noun an international radio distress signal, of less urgency than a mayday signal.
– ORIGIN 1920s: *pan* from French *panne* 'breakdown'.

pan pipes ▶ plural noun a musical instrument made from a row of short pipes of varying length fixed together and played by blowing across the top.
– ORIGIN originally associated with the Greek rural god **PAN**.

panpsychism /panˈsʌɪkɪz(ə)m/ ▶ noun [mass noun] the doctrine or belief that everything material, however small, has an element of individual consciousness.
– DERIVATIVES **panpsychist** adjective & noun.

pansexual ▶ adjective not limited or inhibited in sexual choice with regard to gender or activity.
▶ noun a person who is sexually inclusive in this way.
– DERIVATIVES **pansexuality** noun.

pansified /ˈpanzɪfʌɪd/ ▶ adjective informal markedly effeminate or affected.

panslavism /panˈslɑːvɪz(ə)m/ ▶ noun [mass noun] the principle or advocacy of the union of all Slavs or all Slavic peoples in one political organization.
– DERIVATIVES **panslavist** adjective & noun.

panspermia /panˈspəːmɪə/ ▶ noun [mass noun] the theory that life on the earth originated from micro-organisms or chemical precursors of life present in outer space and able to initiate life on reaching a suitable environment.

– ORIGIN mid 19th cent.: from Greek, from *panspermos* 'containing all kinds of seed'.

panstick ▶ noun [mass noun] a kind of matt cosmetic foundation in stick form, widely used in theatrical make-up.

– ORIGIN 1940s: from **PANCAKE** + **STICK**[1].

pansy ▶ noun **1** a popular cultivated viola with flowers in rich colours, with both summer- and winter-flowering varieties.
● Genus *Viola*, family Violaceae: several species and hybrids, in particular *V.* × *wittrockiana*.
2 informal an effeminate or homosexual man.
3 S. African a sand dollar with a flower-like purple marking on the shell.
● *Echinodiscus bisperforatus*, class Echinoidea.

– ORIGIN late Middle English: from French *pensée* 'thought, pansy', from *penser* 'think', from Latin *pensare*, frequentative of *pendere* 'weigh, consider'.

pant ▶ verb [no obj.] breathe with short, quick breaths, typically from exertion or excitement: *he was panting when he reached the top*.
■ [with adverbial of direction] run or go in a specified direction while panting: *they panted up the stairs*. ■ [with direct speech] say something breathlessly: *'We'll never have time,' she panted*. ■ long for or to do something: *it makes you pant for more*. ■ poetic/literary (of the heart or chest) throb violently from strong emotions.
▶ noun a short, quick breath.
■ poetic/literary a throb or heave of a person's heart or chest.

– DERIVATIVES **pantingly** adverb.

– ORIGIN Middle English: related to Old French *pantaisier* 'be agitated, gasp', based on Greek *phantasioun* 'cause to imagine', from *phantasia* (see **FANTASY**).

Pantagruelian /ˌpantəgruːˈɛlɪən/ ▶ adjective rare enormous: *a Pantagruelian banquet*.

– ORIGIN late 17th cent.: from *Pantagruel* (the name of an enormous giant in Rabelais's *Gargantua and Pantagruel*) + **-IAN**.

pantalettes (chiefly N. Amer. also **pantalets**) ▶ plural noun long underpants with a frill at the bottom of each leg, worn by women and girls in the 19th century.

pantaloon ▶ noun **1** (**pantaloons**) women's baggy trousers gathered at the ankles.
■ historical men's close-fitting breeches fastened below the calf or at the foot. ■ informal trousers.
2 (**Pantaloon**) a Venetian character in Italian commedia dell'arte represented as a foolish old man wearing pantaloons.

– ORIGIN late 16th cent. (in sense 2): from French *pantalon*, from the Italian name *Pantalone* 'Pantaloon' (see sense 2).

Pantanal /ˌpantəˈnɑːl/ a vast region of tropical swampland in the upper reaches of the Paraguay River in SW Brazil.

pantec (also **pantech**) ▶ noun Austral. informal a container trailer forming the rear part of an articulated lorry.

– ORIGIN 1970s: abbreviation of **PANTECHNICON**.

pantechnicon /panˈtɛknɪk(ə)n/ ▶ noun Brit. dated a large van for transporting furniture.

– ORIGIN mid 19th cent.: from **PAN-** 'all' + *tekhnikon* 'piece of art', originally the name of a bazaar in London for all kinds of artistic work, later converted into a furniture warehouse.

Pantelleria /ˌpantɛlɛˈrɪə/ a volcanic Italian island in the Mediterranean, situated between Sicily and the coast of Tunisia. It was used as a place of exile by the ancient Romans, who called it Cossyra.

Panthalassa /ˌpanθəˈlasə/ a universal sea or single ocean, such as would have surrounded Pangaea.

– ORIGIN late 19th cent.: from **PAN-** 'all' + Greek *thalassa* 'sea'.

pantheism /ˈpanθiːɪz(ə)m/ ▶ noun [mass noun] **1** a doctrine which identifies God with the universe, or regards the universe as a manifestation of God.
2 rare worship that admits or tolerates all gods.

– DERIVATIVES **pantheist** noun, **pantheistic** adjective, **pantheistical** adjective, **pantheistically** adverb.

– ORIGIN mid 18th cent.: from **PAN-** 'all' + Greek *theos* 'god' + **-ISM**.

pantheon /ˈpanθɪən/ ▶ noun all the gods of a people or religion collectively: *the deities of the Hindu and Shinto pantheons*.

■ (especially in ancient Greece and Rome) a temple dedicated to all the gods. ■ a building in which the illustrious dead of a nation are buried or honoured. ■ a group of particularly respected, famous, or important people: *the pantheon of the all-time greats*.

– ORIGIN late Middle English (referring especially to the circular temple built by Hadrian, Severus, and Caracalla in Rome): via Latin from Greek *pantheion*, from *pan* 'all' + *theion* 'holy' (from *theos* 'god').

panther ▶ noun a leopard, especially a black one.
■ N. Amer. a puma or a jaguar.

– ORIGIN Middle English: from Old French *pantere*, from Latin *panthera*, from Greek *panthēr*. In Latin, *pardus* 'leopard' also existed; the two terms led to confusion: until the mid 19th cent. many taxonomists regarded the panther and the leopard as separate species.

panther cap ▶ noun a poisonous toadstool which has a brownish-grey cap with fluffy white spots and white gills, found in woodland in both Eurasia and North America.
● *Amanita pantherina*, family Amanitaceae, class Hymenomycetes.

panties ▶ plural noun informal legless underpants worn by women and girls; knickers.

pantihose ▶ plural noun variant spelling of **PANTYHOSE**.

pantile /ˈpantʌɪl/ ▶ noun a roof tile curved to form an S-shaped section, fitted to overlap its neighbour.

– DERIVATIVES **pantiled** adjective.

– ORIGIN mid 17th cent.: from **PAN**[1] + **TILE**, probably suggested by Dutch *dakpan*, literally 'roof pan'.

Pantisocracy /ˌpantɪˈsɒkrəsi/ ▶ noun [mass noun] a form of utopian social organization in which all are equal in social position and responsibility.

– DERIVATIVES **Pantisocratic** adjective.

– ORIGIN late 18th cent.: from **PANTO-** 'all' + Greek *isokratia* 'equality of power'.

panto ▶ noun (pl. **-os**) Brit. informal short for **PANTOMIME** (in sense 1).

panto- ▶ combining form all; universal: *pantograph* | *pantomime*.

– ORIGIN from Greek *pas, pant-* 'all'.

Pantocrator /panˈtɒkrətə/ ▶ noun a title of Christ represented as the ruler of the universe, especially in Byzantine church decoration.

– ORIGIN late 19th cent.: via Latin from Greek, 'ruler over all'.

pantograph ▶ noun **1** an instrument for copying a plan or drawing on a different scale by a system of hinged and jointed rods.
2 a jointed framework conveying a current to a train, tram, or other electric vehicle from overhead wires.

– DERIVATIVES **pantographic** adjective.

– ORIGIN early 18th cent.: from **PANTO-** 'all, universal' + Greek *-graphos* 'writing'.

pantomime ▶ noun **1** Brit. a theatrical entertainment, mainly for children, which involves music, topical jokes, and slapstick comedy and is based on a fairy tale or nursery story, usually produced around Christmas. Modern British pantomime developed from the harlequinade and the cast typically includes a man in the chief comic female role ('principal dame'), a woman in the main male role ('principal boy'), and an animal played by actors in comic costume.
2 a dramatic entertainment, originating in Roman mime, in which performers express meaning through gestures accompanied by music.
■ an absurdly exaggerated piece of behaviour: *he made a pantomime of checking his watch*. ■ informal a ridiculous or confused situation or event: *the drive to town was a pantomime*.
▶ verb [with obj.] express or represent (something) by extravagant and exaggerated mime.

– DERIVATIVES **pantomimic** adjective.

– ORIGIN late 16th cent. (first used in the Latin form and denoting an actor using mime): from French *pantomime* or Latin *pantomimus*, from Greek *pantomimos* 'imitator of all' (see **PANTO-, MIME**).

pantomime dame ▶ noun Brit. an actor, traditionally a male actor, playing a comic female character in a pantomime.

pantomime horse ▶ noun Brit. a comic character in the form of a horse, played by two actors in one costume, one providing the front legs and operating the head, the other providing the back legs.

Pantone ▶ noun [usu. as modifier] trademark a system for matching colours, used in specifying printing inks: *Pantone colours*.

pantothenic acid /ˌpantəˈθɛnɪk/ ▶ noun [mass noun] Biochemistry a vitamin of the B complex, found in rice, bran, and many other foods, and essential for the oxidation of fats and carbohydrates.

– DERIVATIVES **pantothenate** noun.

– ORIGIN 1930s: *pantothenic* from Greek *pantothen* 'from every side' (with allusion to its widespread occurrence).

pantoum /panˈtuːm/ (also **pantun**) ▶ noun a Malay verse form, also imitated in French and English, with a rhyme scheme *abab*.

– ORIGIN late 18th cent.: Malay *pantun*.

pantry ▶ noun (pl. **-ies**) a small room or cupboard in which food, crockery, and cutlery are kept.

– ORIGIN Middle English: from Anglo-Norman French *paneter* 'baker', based on late Latin *panarius* 'bread seller', from Latin *panis* 'bread'.

pantryman ▶ noun (pl. **-men**) a butler or a butler's assistant.

pants ▶ plural noun **1** Brit. underpants or knickers.
2 chiefly N. Amer. trousers: *baggy corduroy pants* | [as modifier] (**pant**) *his pant leg*.

– PHRASES **catch someone with their pants** (or **trousers**) **down** informal catch someone in an embarrassingly unprepared state. **fly** (or **drive**) **by the seat of one's pants** informal rely on instinct rather than logic or knowledge. **scare** (or **bore** etc.) **the pants off someone** informal make someone extremely scared, bored, etc.

– ORIGIN mid 19th cent.: abbreviation of *pantaloons* (see **PANTALOON**).

pantsuit (also **pants suit**) ▶ noun chiefly N. Amer. a trouser suit.

pantsula /panˈtsuːlə/ ▶ noun (pl. **pantsulas** or **mapantsula**) S. African informal **1** a fashionable young urban black person, especially a man.
2 [mass noun] a dance style in which each person performs a solo turn within a circle of dancers doing a repetitive, shuffling step.

– ORIGIN perhaps related to Zulu *p(h)ansula* 'strike sharply (with a whip)', with reference to elements of the dance style.

pantun /panˈtuːn/ ▶ noun variant spelling of **PANTOUM**.

panty girdle (also **pantie girdle**) ▶ noun a woman's control undergarment with a crotch shaped like pants.

pantyhose (also **pantihose**) ▶ plural noun N. Amer. women's thin nylon tights.

pantywaist N. Amer. informal ▶ noun a feeble or effeminate person.
▶ adjective [attrib.] effeminate or feeble.

– ORIGIN 1930s: extended use of the term's literal sense 'child's garment consisting of panties attached to a bodice'.

panzanella /ˌpanzəˈnɛlə, ˌpantsə-/ ▶ noun [mass noun] a type of Tuscan salad made with anchovies, chopped salad vegetables, and bread soaked in dressing.

– ORIGIN Italian, from *pane* 'bread' + *zanella* 'small basket'.

panzer /ˈpanzə/ ▶ noun [usu. as modifier] a German armoured unit: *panzer divisions*.

– ORIGIN from German *Panzer*, literally 'coat of mail'.

Paolozzi /paʊˈlɒtsi/, Eduardo (Luigi) (b.1924), Scottish artist and sculptor, of Italian descent. He was a key figure in the development of pop art in Britain in the 1950s. His work is typified by mechanistic sculptures in a figurative style, often surfaced with cog wheels and machine parts.

pap[1] ▶ noun [mass noun] often derogatory bland soft or semi-liquid food such as that suitable for babies or invalids: *trying to eat a trayful of tasteless pap*.
■ derogatory reading matter or entertainment that is worthless or lacking in substance: *limitless channels serving up an undemanding diet of pap*. ■ (in Africa and the Caribbean) porridge, usually made with maize meal.
▶ adjective S. African (of food) lacking flavour.
■ (of a person) lacking physical or emotional strength; feeble. ■ (of an inflatable object) under-inflated; flat.

– ORIGIN late Middle English: probably from Middle Low German, Middle Dutch *pappe*, probably based on Latin *pappare* 'eat'.

pap² ▶ noun archaic or dialect a woman's breast or nipple.
– ORIGIN Middle English: probably of Scandinavian origin, from a base imitative of the sound of sucking.

papa /pə'pɑː, 'pɑːpə/ ▶ noun 1 N. Amer. or dated one's father: [as name] *Papa had taught her to ride a bicycle.* 2 a code word representing the letter P, used in radio communication.
– ORIGIN late 17th cent.: from French, via late Latin from Greek *papas.*

papabile /pə'pɑːbɪleɪ, -li/ ▶ adjective rare worthy of being or eligible to be pope.
– ORIGIN Italian, from Latin *papa* 'pope'.

papacy /'peɪpəsi/ ▶ noun (pl. **-ies**) (usu. **the papacy**) the office or authority of the Pope.
■ the tenure of office of a pope: *during the papacy of Pope John.*
– ORIGIN late Middle English: from medieval Latin *papatia,* from *papa* 'pope'.

Papago /'pɑːpəɡəʊ, 'pɑː-/ ▶ noun (pl. same or **-os**) 1 a member of an American Indian people of the south-western US and northern Mexico. 2 [mass noun] the Uto-Aztecan language of this people, a form of Pima with around 10,000 speakers.
▶ adjective of or relating to this people or their language.
– ORIGIN via Spanish from an American Indian word.

papain /pə'peɪɪn, pə'pʌɪɪn/ ▶ noun [mass noun] a protein-digesting enzyme obtained from unripe papaya fruit, used to tenderize meat and as a food supplement to aid digestion.
– ORIGIN late 19th cent.: from PAPAYA + -IN¹.

papal /'peɪp(ə)l/ ▶ adjective of or relating to a pope or to the papacy.
– DERIVATIVES **papally** adverb.
– ORIGIN late Middle English: from Old French, from medieval Latin *papalis,* from ecclesiastical Latin *papa* 'bishop (of Rome)'.

papalagi /pɑ'pɑːləŋi/ ▶ noun (pl. same) another term for PALAGI.
– ORIGIN from Samoan *papālagi.*

papal infallibility ▶ noun see INFALLIBILITY.

papalist chiefly historical ▶ noun a supporter of the papacy, especially an advocate of papal supremacy.
▶ adjective supporting the papacy.

Papal States historical the temporal dominions belonging to the Pope, especially in central Italy.

paparazzo /ˌpapə'ratsəʊ/ ▶ noun (pl. **paparazzi** /-tsi/) (usu. **paparazzi**) a freelance photographer who pursues celebrities to get photographs of them.
– ORIGIN mid 20th cent.: from Italian, from the name of a character in Fellini's film *La Dolce Vita* (1960).

papaveraceous /pəˌpeɪvə'reɪʃəs, -ˌpav-/ ▶ adjective Botany of, relating to, or denoting plants of the poppy family (Papaveraceae).
– ORIGIN mid 19th cent.: from modern Latin *Papaveraceae* (plural), based on Latin *papaver* 'poppy', + -OUS.

papaverine /pə'peɪvərʌɪn, -'pav-, -i:n/ ▶ noun [mass noun] Chemistry a compound present in opium used medicinally to alleviate muscle spasm and asthma.
● An alkaloid; chem. formula: $C_{20}H_{21}NO_4$.
– ORIGIN mid 19th cent.: from Latin *papaver* 'poppy' + -INE⁴.

papaw /pə'pɔː/ ▶ noun variant spelling of PAWPAW.

papaya /pə'pʌɪə/ ▶ noun 1 a tropical fruit shaped like an elongated melon, with edible orange flesh and small black seeds. Also called PAWPAW or PAWPAW. 2 (also **papaya tree**) the fast-growing tree which bears this fruit, native to warm regions of America. It is widely cultivated for its fruit, both for eating and for papain production.
● *Carica papaya,* family Caricaceae.
– ORIGIN late 16th cent.: from Spanish and Portuguese (see PAWPAW).

pap boat ▶ noun historical a boat-shaped container for holding soft food for feeding babies.

Papeete /ˌpɑːpɪ'eɪti, -'i:ti/ the capital of French Polynesia, situated on the NW coast of Tahiti; pop. 24,200 (1994).

paper ▶ noun 1 [mass noun] material manufactured in thin sheets from the pulp of wood or other fibrous substances, used for writing, drawing, or printing

on, or as wrapping material: *a sheet of paper* | [as modifier] *a paper napkin.*
■ [count noun] a newspaper. ■ wallpaper. ■ [count noun] (usu. **papers**) a piece or sheet of paper with something written or drawn on it: *he riffled through the papers on his desk.* ■ (**papers**) significant or important documents belonging to a person. ■ [as modifier] denoting something that is officially documented but has no real existence or little merit or use: *a paper profit.* ■ [count noun] a government report or policy document: *a recently leaked cabinet paper.* ■ (**papers**) documents attesting identity; credentials: *two men stopped us and asked us for our papers.* ■ [count noun] a piece of paper used for wrapping or enclosing something or made into a packet: *toffee papers.* ■ short for COMMERCIAL PAPER. ■ short for CIGARETTE PAPER.
2 a set of examination questions to be answered at one session: *we had to sit a three-hour paper.*
■ the written answers to such questions. ■ an essay or dissertation, especially one read at an academic lecture or seminar or published in an academic journal.
3 [mass noun] theatrical slang free passes of admission to a theatre or other entertainment.
▶ verb [with obj.] 1 (often **be papered**) apply wallpaper to (a wall or room): *the walls were papered in a Regency stripe.*
■ [no obj.] (**paper over**) cover (a hole or blemish) with wallpaper. ■ (**paper over**) disguise (an awkward problem) instead of resolving it: *the ill feeling between her and Jenny must have been papered over.*
2 theatrical slang fill (a theatre) by giving out free tickets.
– PHRASES **be not worth the paper it is written on** be of no value or validity whatsoever despite having been written down. **make the papers** be written about in newspapers and thus become famous or notorious. **on paper** in writing. ■ in theory rather than in reality: *the combatants were, on paper at least, evenly matched.* **paper over the cracks** disguise problems or divisions rather than trying to solve them.
– DERIVATIVES **paperer** noun, **paperless** adjective.
– ORIGIN Middle English: from Anglo-Norman French *papir,* from Latin *papyrus* 'paper-reed' (see PAPYRUS). The verb dates from the late 16th cent.

paperback ▶ adjective (of a book) bound in stiff paper or flexible card.
▶ noun a book bound in stiff paper or flexible card.
– PHRASES **in paperback** in an edition bound in stiff paper or flexible card: *now available in paperback.*

paper bag ▶ noun a small bag made of paper.
– PHRASES **be unable to punch one's way out of a paper bag** informal be completely ineffectual or inept.

paperbark ▶ noun a cajuput tree.
■ used in names of other trees which have a peeling papery bark, e.g. **paperbark maple, paperbark birch.**

paper birch (also **paperbark birch**) ▶ noun a North American birch with large leaves and peeling white bark.
● *Betula papyrifera,* family Betulaceae.

paperboard ▶ noun [mass noun] cardboard or pasteboard.

paper boy ▶ noun a boy who delivers newspapers to people's homes.

paper chain ▶ noun a chain made of paper links and used for decorating a room, especially at Christmas.

paperchase ▶ noun 1 Brit. a cross-country race in which the runners follow a trail marked by torn-up paper.
2 informal an administration characterized by excessive bureaucracy.

paper clip ▶ noun a piece of bent wire or plastic used for holding several sheets of paper together.

paper cup ▶ noun a disposable cup made of thin cardboard.

paper doll ▶ noun a piece of paper cut or folded into the shape of a human figure.

paper feed ▶ noun a device for inserting sheets of paper into a typewriter, printer, or similar machine.

paper girl ▶ noun a girl who delivers newspapers to people's homes.

paperhanger ▶ noun a person who decorates with wallpaper, especially professionally.

paperknife ▶ noun (pl. **paperknives**) a blunt knife

used for cutting paper, such as when opening envelopes or slitting the uncut pages of books.

paper money ▶ noun [mass noun] money in the form of banknotes.

paper mulberry ▶ noun a small tree of the mulberry family, the inner bark of which is used for making paper and tapa cloth, occurring from east Asia to Polynesia.
● *Broussonetia papyrifera,* family Moraceae.

paper nautilus ▶ noun another term for ARGONAUT.

paper plate ▶ noun a disposable plate made of cardboard.

paper-pusher ▶ noun informal, chiefly US a bureaucrat or menial clerical worker.
– DERIVATIVES **paper-pushing** noun & adjective.

paper round (N. Amer. **paper route**) ▶ noun a job of regularly delivering newspapers.

paper taffeta ▶ noun [mass noun] a lightweight taffeta with a crisp papery finish.

paper tape ▶ noun [mass noun] paper in the form of a long narrow strip.
■ such tape having holes punched in it, used in older computer systems for conveying data or instructions.

paper-thin ▶ adjective very thin or insubstantial: *paper-thin pancakes* | *her sophistication was paper-thin.*

paper tiger ▶ noun a person or thing that appears threatening but is ineffectual.

paper trail ▶ noun chiefly N. Amer. the total amount of written evidence of someone's activities.

paper wasp ▶ noun a social wasp that forms a small umbrella-shaped nest made from wood pulp.
● Genus *Polistes,* family Vespidae.

paperweight ▶ noun a small, heavy object for keeping loose papers in place.

paperwork ▶ noun [mass noun] routine work involving written documents such as forms, records, or letters: *I need to catch up on some paperwork.*
■ such written documents.

papery ▶ adjective thin and dry like paper.

Paphlagonia /ˌpaflə'ɡəʊnɪə/ an ancient region of northern Asia Minor, on the Black Sea coast between Bithynia and Pontus, to the north of Galatia.
– DERIVATIVES **Paphlagonian** adjective & noun.

Papiementu /ˌpapɪə'mɛntuː/ (also **Papiemento** /-'mɛntəʊ/) ▶ noun [mass noun] the Creole language of the Caribbean islands of Aruba, Bonaire, and Curaçao, based on African, Spanish, Portuguese, and Dutch.
– ORIGIN from Spanish *Papiamento.*

papier collé /ˌpapɪeɪ 'kɒleɪ/ ▶ noun (pl. **papiers collés** pronunc. same) [mass noun] the technique of using paper for collage.
■ [count noun] a collage made from paper.
– ORIGIN French, literally 'glued paper'.

papier mâché /'maʃeɪ/ ▶ noun [mass noun] a malleable mixture of paper and glue, or paper, flour, and water, that becomes hard when dry, used to make boxes, trays, or ornaments.
– ORIGIN French, literally 'chewed paper'.

papilionaceous /pəˌpɪlɪə'neɪʃəs/ ▶ adjective Botany of, relating to, or denoting leguminous plants of a group (subfamily Papilionoideae or family Papilionaceae) with flowers that resemble a butterfly.
– ORIGIN mid 17th cent.: from modern Latin *Papilionaceae* (plural), based on Latin *papilio* 'butterfly', + -OUS.

papilionid /pəˌpɪlɪ'əʊnɪd/ ▶ noun Entomology a butterfly of a family (Papilionidae) which includes the swallowtails, birdwings, and apollos. They are typically large and boldly marked, and most kinds have tail-like projections on the hindwings.
– ORIGIN late 19th cent.: from modern Latin *Papilionidae* (plural), from Latin *papilio(n-)* 'butterfly'.

papilla /pə'pɪlə/ ▶ noun (pl. **papillae** /-liː/) a small rounded protuberance on a part or organ of the body.
■ a small fleshy projection on a plant.
– DERIVATIVES **papillary** adjective, **papillate** /'papɪleɪt, pə'pɪlət/ adjective, **papillose** /'papɪləʊs/ adjective.
– ORIGIN late 17th cent.: from Latin, literally 'nipple', diminutive of *papula* 'small protuberance'.

papilloma /ˌpapɪ'ləʊmə/ ▶ noun (pl. **papillomas** or

papillomata /-mətə/ Medicine a small wart-like growth on the skin or on a mucous membrane, derived from the epidermis and usually benign.
– ORIGIN mid 19th cent.: from PAPILLA + -OMA.

papillon /ˈpapɪlon, ˈpapɪjõ/ ▸ noun a dog of a toy breed with ears suggesting the form of a butterfly.
– ORIGIN early 20th cent.: from French, literally 'butterfly', from Latin papilio(n-).

papist /ˈpeɪpɪst/ chiefly derogatory ▸ noun a Roman Catholic.
■ another term for PAPALIST.
▸ adjective of, relating to, or associated with the Roman Catholic Church.
– DERIVATIVES **papism** noun, **papistical** adjective (archaic), **papistry** noun.
– ORIGIN mid 16th cent.: from French papiste or modern Latin papista, from ecclesiastical Latin papa 'bishop of Rome'.

papoose /pəˈpuːs/ ▸ noun **1** chiefly offensive a young North American Indian child.
2 a type of bag used to carry a child on one's back.
– ORIGIN mid 17th cent.: from Algonquian papoos.

papovavirus /pəˈpəʊvə͵vʌɪrəs/ ▸ noun Medicine any of a group of small DNA viruses, most of which infect mammals and can cause sarcoma and warts.
– ORIGIN 1960s: from pa(pilloma) + po(lyoma) + va(cuolating) + VIRUS.

pappardelle /͵papaːˈdɛleɪ, Italian ͵papaʳˈdelle/ ▸ plural noun pasta in the form of broad flat ribbons, usually served with a meat sauce.
– ORIGIN Italian, from pappare 'eat hungrily'.

Pappus /ˈpapəs/ (fl. c.300–350 AD), Greek mathematician; known as **Pappus of Alexandria**. Little is known of his life, but his Collection of six books (another two are missing) is the principal source of knowledge of the mathematics of his predecessors.

pappus /ˈpapəs/ ▸ noun (pl. **pappi** /-pʌɪ, -piː/) Botany the tuft of hairs on each seed of thistles, dandelions, and similar plants, which assists dispersal by the wind.
– DERIVATIVES **pappose** adjective.
– ORIGIN early 18th cent.: via Latin from Greek pappos.

pappy[1] ▸ noun (pl. **-ies**) [usu. as name] a child's word for father: Pappy was always busy.
– ORIGIN mid 18th cent.: from PAPA + -Y[2].

pappy[2] ▸ adjective of the nature of pap.

pappyshow ▸ noun [in sing.] W. Indian a person or thing that is a parody or mockery of something else: with the best of intentions, he is merely making a pappyshow of the volunteer litter wardens.
– ORIGIN variant of puppet show.

paprika /ˈpaprɪkə, pəˈpriːkə/ ▸ noun [mass noun] a powdered spice with a deep orange-red colour and a mildly pungent flavour, made from the dried and ground fruits of certain varieties of sweet pepper.
■ a deep orange-red colour like that of paprika.
– ORIGIN late 19th cent.: from Hungarian.

Pap test /pap/ ▸ noun a test carried out on a cervical smear to detect cancer of the cervix or womb.
– ORIGIN 1960s: named after George N. Papanicolaou (1883–1962), Greek-born American scientist.

Papua /ˈpapwə, pəˈpuːə, ˈpapjʊə/ the SE part of the island of New Guinea, now part of the independent state of Papua New Guinea.
– ORIGIN named by a Portuguese navigator who visited it in 1526–7, from a Malay word meaning 'woolly-haired'.

Papuan ▸ noun **1** a native or inhabitant of Papua, or of Papua New Guinea.
2 [mass noun] a heterogeneous group of around 750 languages spoken by some 3 million people in Papua New Guinea and neighbouring islands.
▸ adjective of or relating to Papua or its people or their languages.

Papua New Guinea a country in the western Pacific comprising the eastern half of the island of New Guinea together with some neighbouring islands; pop. 3,529,540 (1990); languages, English (official), Tok Pisin, and several hundred native Austronesian and Papuan languages; capital, Port Moresby.

Papua New Guinea was formed from the administrative union, in 1949, of Papua, an Australian Territory since 1906, and the Trust Territory of New Guinea (NE New Guinea), formerly under German control and an Australian trusteeship since 1921. In 1975 Papua New Guinea became an independent state within the Commonwealth.

– DERIVATIVES **Papua New Guinean** adjective & noun.

papule /ˈpapjuːl/ (also **papula** /-jʊlə/) ▸ noun (pl. **papules** or **papulae** /-jʊliː/) Medicine a small, raised, solid pimple or swelling, often forming part of a rash on the skin and typically inflamed but not producing pus.
– DERIVATIVES **papular** adjective, **papulose** adjective, **papulous** adjective.
– ORIGIN early 18th cent.: from Latin papula.

papyrology /͵papɪˈrolədʒi/ ▸ noun [mass noun] the branch of study that deals with ancient papyri.
– DERIVATIVES **papyrological** adjective, **papyrologist** noun.

papyrus /pəˈpʌɪrəs/ ▸ noun (pl. **papyri** /-rʌɪ, -riː/ or **papyruses**) [mass noun] **1** a material prepared in ancient Egypt from the pithy stem of a water plant, used in sheets throughout the ancient Mediterranean world for writing or painting on and also for making articles such as rope, sandals, and boats.
■ [count noun] a document written on papyrus.
2 the tall aquatic sedge from which this material is obtained, native to central Africa and the Nile valley.
● Cyperus papyrus, family Cyperaceae.
– ORIGIN late Middle English (in sense 2): via Latin from Greek papuros. Sense 1 dates from the early 18th cent.

par[1] ▸ noun **1** Golf the number of strokes a first-class player should normally require for a particular hole or course: Woosnam had advanced from his overnight position of three under par | the sixteenth is a par five.
■ a score of this number of strokes at a hole: a card that showed 16 pars, one eagle, and one birdie.
2 Stock Exchange the face value of a share or other security, as distinct from its market value.
■ (also **par of exchange**) the recognized value of one country's currency in terms of another's.
▸ verb (**parred**, **parring**) [with obj.] Golf play (a hole) in par.
– PHRASES **above** (or **below** or **under**) **par** better (or worse) than is usual or expected: poor nutrition can leave you feeling below par. **on a par with** equal in importance or quality to; on an equal level with: this home cooking is on a par with the best in the world. **par for the course** what is normal or expected in any given circumstances: given the high standards of the food, the prices seem par for the course. **up to par** at an expected or usual level or quality.
– ORIGIN late 16th cent. (in the sense 'equality of value or standing'): from Latin, 'equal', also 'equality'. The golf term dates from the late 19th cent.

par[2] ▸ noun informal a paragraph.
– ORIGIN mid 19th cent.: abbreviation.

par. (also **para.**) ▸ abbreviation for paragraph.

par- ▸ combining form variant spelling of PARA-[1] shortened before a vowel or h (as in paraldehyde, parody, parhelion).

Pará /pəˈraː/ a state in northern Brazil, on the Atlantic coast at the delta of the Amazon; capital, Belém. It is a region of dense rainforest.

para[1] /ˈparə/ informal ▸ noun **1** a paratrooper.
2 a paragraph.
▸ adjective [predic.] Brit. unreasonably anxious or worried, especially as the result of taking drugs; paranoid: I'm always para when I haven't been sleeping. [ORIGIN: abbreviation of PARANOID.]

para[2] /ˈparə/ ▸ noun (pl. same or **paras**) a monetary unit of Bosnia–Herzegovina, Montenegro, and Serbia, equal to one hundredth of a dinar.
– ORIGIN Turkish, from Persian pāra 'piece, portion'.

para-[1] (also **par-**) ▸ prefix **1** beside; adjacent to: parataxis | parathyroid.
■ beyond or distinct from, but analogous to: paramilitary | paratyphoid.
2 Chemistry denoting substitution at diametrically opposite carbon atoms in a benzene ring, e.g. in 1, 4 positions: paradichlorobenzene. Compare with META- and ORTHO-.
– ORIGIN from Greek para 'beside'; in combinations often meaning 'amiss, irregular' and denoting alteration or modification.

para-[2] ▸ combining form denoting something that protects or wards off: parachute | parasol.
– ORIGIN from French, from the Italian imperative singular of parare 'defend, shield' (originally meaning 'prepare', from Latin parare).

para-aminobenzoic acid /͵parə͵amiːnəʊbɛnˈzəʊɪk, -ə'mʌɪnəʊ-, -͵amɪnəʊ-/ ▸ noun [mass noun] Biochemistry a crystalline acid which is widely distributed in plant and animal tissue, and has been used to treat rickettsial infections.
● Chem. formula: $NH_2C_6H_4COOH$.

parabasis /pəˈrabəsɪs/ ▸ noun (pl. **parabases** /-siːz/) (in ancient Greek comedy) a direct address to the audience, sung or chanted by the chorus on behalf of the author.
– ORIGIN early 19th cent.: from Greek, from parabainein 'go aside'.

parabiosis /͵parəbʌɪˈəʊsɪs/ ▸ noun [mass noun] Biology the anatomical joining of two individuals, especially artificially in physiological research.
– DERIVATIVES **parabiotic** adjective.
– ORIGIN early 20th cent.: modern Latin, from PARA-[1] 'beside, distinct from' + Greek biōsis 'mode of life' (from bios 'life').

parable ▸ noun a simple story used to illustrate a moral or spiritual lesson, as told by Jesus in the Gospels.
– ORIGIN Middle English: from Old French parabole, from an ecclesiastical Latin sense 'discourse, allegory' of Latin parabola 'comparison', from Greek parabolē (see PARABOLA).

parabola /pəˈrab(ə)lə/ ▸ noun (pl. **parabolas** or **parabolae** /-liː/) a symmetrical open plane curve formed by the intersection of a cone with a plane parallel to its side. The path of a projectile under the influence of gravity follows a curve of this shape.
– ORIGIN late 16th cent.: modern Latin, from Greek parabolē 'placing side by side, application', from para- 'beside' + bolē 'a throw' (from the verb ballein).

parabolic /parəˈbɒlɪk/ ▸ adjective **1** of or like a parabola or part of one.
2 of or expressed in parables: parabolic teaching.
– DERIVATIVES **parabolical** adjective, **parabolically** adverb.
– ORIGIN late Middle English: via late Latin from Greek parabolikos, from parabolē 'application' (see PARABOLA).

paraboloid /pəˈrab(ə)lɔɪd/ ▸ noun **1** (also **paraboloid of revolution**) a solid generated by the rotation of a parabola about its axis of symmetry.
2 a solid having two or more non-parallel parabolic cross sections.
– DERIVATIVES **paraboloidal** adjective.

Paracel Islands /͵parəˈsɛl/ (also **the Paracels**) a group of about 130 small barren coral islands and reefs in the South China Sea to the south-east of the Chinese island of Hainan. The islands are claimed by both China and Vietnam.

paracellular ▸ adjective Biology passing or situated beside or between cells.

Paracelsus /͵parəˈsɛlsəs/ (c.1493–1541), Swiss physician: born Theophrastus Phillipus Aureolus Bombastus von Hohenheim. He developed a new approach to medicine and philosophy based on observation and experience. He saw illness as having a specific external cause (rather than an imbalance of the bodily humours), and introduced chemical remedies to replace traditional ones.

paracentesis /͵parəsɛnˈtiːsɪs/ ▸ noun (pl. **paracenteses** /-siːz/) [mass noun] Medicine the perforation of a cavity of the body or of a cyst or similar outgrowth, especially with a hollow needle to remove fluid or gas.
– ORIGIN late 16th cent.: via Latin from Greek parakentēsis, from parakentein 'pierce at the side'.

paracentric inversion ▸ noun Genetics a reversal of the normal order of genes in a chromosome segment involving only the part of a chromosome at one side of the centromere.

paracetamol /parəˈsiːtəmɒl, -ˈsɛt-/ ▸ noun (pl. same or **paracetamols**) [mass noun] Brit. a synthetic compound used very widely as a drug to relieve headaches and other pain and also to reduce fever.
● Alternative name: **para-acetylaminophenol**; chem. formula: $C_8H_9NO_2$. Compare with ACETAMINOPHEN.
■ [count noun] a tablet of this drug.

parachronism /pəˈrakrənɪz(ə)m/ ▸ noun an error in chronology, especially by assigning too late a date.

– ORIGIN mid 17th cent.: from **PARA-**[1] 'beyond' + Greek *khronos* 'time' + **-ISM**, perhaps suggested by **ANACHRONISM**.

parachute ▶ **noun** a cloth canopy which fills with air and allows a person or heavy object attached to it to descend slowly when dropped from an aircraft, or which is released from the rear of an aircraft on landing to act as a brake.
▶ **verb** drop or cause to drop from an aircraft by parachute: [no obj.] *airborne units **parachuted in** to secure the airport* | [with obj.] *an air operation to **parachute** relief supplies **into** Bosnia.*
– ORIGIN late 18th cent.: from French *para-* 'protection against' + *chute* 'fall'.

parachute flare ▶ **noun** a pyrotechnic signal flare which is carried up into the air by a rocket and floats suspended from a small parachute.

parachutist ▶ **noun** a person who uses a parachute.

Paraclete /ˈparəkliːt/ ▶ **noun** (in Christian theology) the Holy Spirit as advocate or counsellor (John 14:16, 26).
– ORIGIN via late Latin from Greek *paraklētos* 'called in aid', from *para-* 'alongside' + *klētos* (from *kalein* 'to call').

paraclinical ▶ **adjective** of or relating to the branches of medicine, especially the laboratory sciences, that provide a service for patients without direct involvement in care.

paracrine /ˈparəkrʌɪn/ ▶ **adjective** Physiology of, relating to, or denoting a hormone which has effect only in the vicinity of the gland secreting it.
– ORIGIN 1970s: from **PARA-**[1] 'beside' + *krinein* 'to separate'.

paracrystal ▶ **noun** Chemistry a piece of a substance that is not a true crystal but has some degree of order in its structure.
– DERIVATIVES **paracrystalline** adjective.

parade ▶ **noun 1** a public procession, especially one celebrating a special day or event.
■ a formal march or gathering of troops for inspection or display: *a military parade* | [mass noun] *the men massed for parade.* ■ a series of people or things appearing or being displayed one after the other: *the parade of Hollywood celebrities who troop on to his show.* ■ a distasteful manifestation of a particular quality or kind of behaviour: *the parade of lunacy and corruption will continue.*
2 Brit. a public square or promenade.
■ a row of shops: *a shopping parade.* ■ a parade ground.
▶ **verb** [no obj.] walk or march in public in a formal procession or in an ostentatious or attention-seeking way: *officers will parade through the town centre.*
■ [with obj.] walk or march in such a way along (the streets of a town): *carefree young men were parading the streets.* ■ [with obj.] display (someone or something) while marching or moving around a place: *they paraded national flags.* ■ [with obj.] display (something) publicly in order to impress or attract attention: *he paraded his knowledge.* ■ (**parade as**) appear falsely as; masquerade as: *these untruths parading as history.* ■ [no obj.] (of troops) assemble for a formal inspection or ceremonial occasion: *the recruits were due to parade that day.*
– PHRASES **on parade** taking part in a parade. ■ on public display: *politicians are always on parade.*
– DERIVATIVES **parader** noun.
– ORIGIN mid 17th cent.: from French, literally 'a showing', from Spanish *parada* and Italian *parata*, based on Latin *parare* 'prepare, furnish'.

parade ground ▶ **noun** a place where troops gather for parade.

parade ring ▶ **noun** a circuit at a racecourse round which horses can be walked to warm up before a race.

paradiddle /ˈparəˌdɪd(ə)l/ ▶ **noun** Music one of the basic patterns (rudiments) of drumming, consisting of four even strokes played in the order 'left right left left' or 'right left right right'.
– ORIGIN 1920s: imitative.

paradigm /ˈparədʌɪm/ ▶ **noun 1** technical a typical example or pattern of something; a pattern or model: *there is a new paradigm for public art in this country.*
■ a world view underlying the theories and methodology of a particular scientific subject.
2 a set of linguistics items that form mutually exclusive choices in particular syntactic roles: *English determiners form a paradigm: we can say 'a book' or 'his book' but not 'a his book'.* Often contrasted with **SYNTAGM**.
■ (in the traditional grammar of Latin, Greek, and other inflected languages) a table of all the inflected forms of a particular verb, noun, or adjective, serving as a model for other words of the same conjugation or declension.
– ORIGIN late 15th cent.: via late Latin from Greek *paradeigma*, from *paradeiknunai* 'show side by side', from *para-* 'beside' + *deiknunai* 'to show'.

paradigmatic /parədɪɡˈmatɪk/ ▶ **adjective** of or denoting the relationship between a set of linguistic items that form mutually exclusive choices in particular syntactic roles. Contrasted with **SYNTAGMATIC**.
– DERIVATIVES **paradigmatically** adverb.

paradigm shift ▶ **noun** a fundamental change in approach or underlying assumptions.
– ORIGIN 1970s: term used in the writings of Thomas S. Kuhn (1922–96), philosopher of science.

paradise /ˈparədʌɪs/ ▶ **noun** (in some religions) heaven as the ultimate abode of the just.
■ (**Paradise**) the abode of Adam and Eve before the Fall in the biblical account of the Creation; the garden of Eden. ■ an ideal or idyllic place or state: *the surrounding countryside is a walker's paradise* | *my idea of paradise is to relax on the seafront.*
– DERIVATIVES **paradisal** adjective, **paradisiacal** /-dɪˈsʌɪək(ə)l/ (also **paradisaical** /-dɪˈseɪɪk(ə)l/ or **paradisical** /-ˈdɪsɪk(ə)l/) adjective.
– ORIGIN Middle English: from Old French *paradis*, via ecclesiastical Latin from Greek *paradeisos* 'royal (enclosed) park', from Avestan *pairidaēza* 'enclosure, park'.

paradise fish ▶ **noun** a small colourful labyrinth fish that is native to SE Asia and popular in aquaria.
• Genus *Macropodus*, family Belontiidae: several species, including *M. opercularis*.

paradise flycatcher ▶ **noun** a tropical monarch flycatcher with brown, black, and white plumage, the male having very long central tail feathers.
• Genus *Terpsiphone*, family Monarchidae: several species.

paradise kingfisher ▶ **noun** a tropical Australasian forest kingfisher with brightly coloured plumage and a long tail.
• Genus *Tanysiptera*, family Alcedinidae: several species.

parador /ˈparədɔː, ˌparəˈdɔː/ ▶ **noun** (pl. **paradors** or **paradores** /-ˈdɔːreɪz/) a hotel in Spain owned and administered by the Spanish government.
– ORIGIN Spanish.

parados /ˈparədɒs/ ▶ **noun** an elevation of earth behind a fortified place as a protection against attack from the rear, especially a mound along the back of a trench.
– ORIGIN mid 19th cent.: from French, from *para-* 'protection against' + *dos* 'back' (from Latin *dorsum*).

paradox ▶ **noun** a statement or proposition which, despite sound (or apparently sound) reasoning from acceptable premises, leads to a conclusion that seems senseless, logically unacceptable, or self-contradictory.
■ a seemingly absurd or self-contradictory statement or proposition which when investigated or explained may prove to be well founded or true. ■ a situation, person, or thing that combines contradictory features or qualities: *cathedrals facing the paradox of having enormous wealth in treasures but huge annual expenses.*
– ORIGIN mid 16th cent. (originally denoting a statement contrary to accepted opinion): via late Latin from Greek *paradoxon* 'contrary (opinion)', neuter adjective used as a noun, from *para-* 'distinct from' + *doxa* 'opinion'.

paradoxical ▶ **adjective** seemingly absurd or self-contradictory: *by glorifying the acts of violence they achieve the paradoxical effect of making them trivial.*
– DERIVATIVES **paradoxically** adverb [sentence adverb] *paradoxically, the more fuel a star starts off with, the sooner it runs out.*

paradrop ▶ **noun** a descent or delivery by parachute.
▶ **verb** (**paradropped**, **paradropping**) [with obj.] drop (someone or something) by parachute.
– DERIVATIVES **paradropper** noun.

paraesthesia /ˌparɪsˈθiːzɪə/ (US **paresthesia**) ▶ **noun** (pl. **paraesthesiae** /-zɪiː/ or **paraesthesias**) [mass noun] Medicine an abnormal sensation, typically tingling or pricking ('pins and needles'), caused chiefly by pressure on or damage to peripheral nerves.
– ORIGIN late 19th cent.: from **PARA-**[1] 'alongside, irregular' + Greek *aisthēsis* 'sensation' + **-IA**[1].

paraffin ▶ **noun** (Brit. **paraffin wax**) [mass noun] a flammable, whitish, translucent, waxy solid consisting of a mixture of saturated hydrocarbons, obtained by distillation from petroleum or shale and used in candles, cosmetics, polishes, and sealing and waterproofing compounds.
■ (also **paraffin oil** or **liquid paraffin**) Brit. a colourless, flammable, oily liquid similarly obtained and used as fuel, especially kerosene. ■ [count noun] Chemistry old-fashioned term for **ALKANE**.
– ORIGIN mid 19th cent.: from German, from Latin *parum* 'little' + *affinis* 'related' (from its low reactivity).

paragenesis /ˌparəˈdʒɛnɪsɪs/ ▶ **noun** (pl. **parageneses**) /-siːz/ Geology a set of minerals which were formed together, especially in a rock, or with a specified mineral.
– DERIVATIVES **paragenetic** /-dʒɪˈnɛtɪk/ adjective.

paragliding ▶ **noun** [mass noun] a sport in which a wide canopy resembling a parachute is attached to a person's body by a harness in order to allow them to glide through the air after jumping from or being hauled to a height.
– DERIVATIVES **paraglide** verb, **paraglider** noun.

paragon ▶ **noun** a person or thing regarded as a perfect example of a particular quality: *it would have taken a paragon of virtue not to feel viciously jealous.*
■ a person or thing viewed as a model of excellence: *your cook is a paragon.* ■ a perfect diamond of 100 carats or more.
– ORIGIN mid 16th cent.: from obsolete French, from Italian *paragone* 'touchstone to try good (gold) from bad', from medieval Greek *parakonē* 'whetstone'.

paragrammatism /ˌparəˈɡramətɪz(ə)m/ ▶ **noun** [mass noun] Psychiatry confused or incomplete use of grammatical structures, found in certain forms of speech disturbance.
– DERIVATIVES **paragrammatical** adjective.

paragraph ▶ **noun** a distinct section of a piece of writing, usually dealing with a single theme and indicated by a new line, indentation, or numbering.
▶ **verb** [with obj.] arrange (a piece of writing) in paragraphs.
– DERIVATIVES **paragraphic** adjective.
– ORIGIN late 15th cent.: from French *paragraphe*, via medieval Latin from Greek *paragraphos* 'short stroke marking a break in sense', from *para-* 'beside' + *graphein* 'write'.

paragraph mark (also **paragraph symbol**) ▶ **noun** a symbol (usually ¶) used in printed text to mark a new paragraph or as a reference mark.

Paraguay /ˈparəɡwʌɪ, Spanish paraˈɣwaj/ a landlocked country in central South America; pop. 4,120,000 (1992); languages, Spanish (official), Guarani; capital, Asunción.

The territory was occupied by semi-nomadic Guarani peoples before Spanish rule was established in the 16th century. Paraguay achieved independence in 1811. It was devastated, losing more than half of its population, in war against Brazil, Argentina, and Uruguay in 1865–70, but gained land in the Chaco War with Bolivia in 1932–5. The country was ruled by the military dictator Alfredo Stroessner (b.1912) from 1954 to 1989.

– DERIVATIVES **Paraguayan** adjective & noun.

Paraíba /ˌparaˈiːbə/ a state of eastern Brazil, on the Atlantic coast; capital, João Pessoa.

parainfluenza ▶ **noun** [mass noun] Medicine a disease caused by any of a group of viruses which resemble the influenza viruses.

parakeet /ˈparəkiːt/ (also **parrakeet**) ▶ **noun** a small parrot with predominantly green plumage and a long tail.
• Family Psittacidae: five genera, e.g. *Psittacula* of Asia and Africa and *Cyanoramphus* of Australasia, and many species.
– ORIGIN mid 16th cent.: from Old French *paroquet*, Italian *parrocchetto*, and Spanish *periquito*; origin uncertain, perhaps (via Italian) based on a diminutive meaning 'little wig', referring to head plumage, or (via Spanish) based on a diminutive of the given name *Pedro*.

paralanguage ▶ **noun** [mass noun] the non-lexical component of communication by speech, for example intonation, pitch and speed of speaking, hesitation noises, gesture, and facial expression.

paraldehyde /pəˈraldɪhʌɪd/ ▶ **noun** [mass noun]

p

Chemistry a liquid made by treating acetaldehyde with acid, used medicinally as a sedative, hypnotic, and anticonvulsant.
• A cyclic trimer of acetaldehyde; chem. formula: $(CH_3CHO)_3$.

paralegal chiefly N. Amer. ▶ **noun** a person trained in subsidiary legal matters but not fully qualified as a lawyer.
▶ **adjective** of or relating to auxiliary aspects of the law.

paralinguistic ▶ **adjective** of, relating to, or denoting paralanguage or the non-lexical elements of communication by speech.

paralipomena /ˌparəlɪˈpɒmɪnə/ (also **paraleipomena** /-lʌɪ-/) ▶ **plural noun** (sing. **paralipomenon**) formal things omitted from a work and added as a supplement.
■ (usu. **Paralipomenon**) archaic (in the Vulgate Bible and some other versions) the name of the books of Chronicles, regarded as supplementary to the books of Kings.
– ORIGIN late Middle English: via ecclesiastical Latin from Greek *paraleipomena*, from *paraleipein* 'omit', from *para-* 'to one side' + *leipein* 'to leave'.

paralipsis /ˌparəˈlɪpsɪs/ ▶ **noun** [mass noun] Rhetoric the device of giving emphasis by professing to say little or nothing of a subject, as in *not to mention their unpaid debts of several millions.*
– ORIGIN late 16th cent.: via late Latin from Greek *paraleipsis* 'passing over', from *paraleipein* 'omit', from *para-* 'aside' + *leipein* 'to leave'.

parallax /ˈparəlaks/ ▶ **noun** [mass noun] the effect whereby the position or direction of an object appears to differ when viewed from different positions, e.g. through the viewfinder and the lens of a camera.
■ [count noun] the angular amount of this in a particular case, especially that of a star viewed from different points in the earth's orbit.
– DERIVATIVES **parallactic** adjective.
– ORIGIN late 16th cent. (also in the general sense 'fact of seeing wrongly'): from French *parallaxe*, from Greek *parallaxis* 'a change', from *parallassein* 'to alternate', based on *allassein* 'to exchange' (from *allos* 'other').

parallel ▶ **adjective** (of lines, planes, surfaces, or objects) side by side and having the same distance continuously between them: *parallel lines never meet | the road **runs parallel to** the Ottawa river.*
■ occurring or existing at the same time or in a similar way; corresponding: *a parallel universe | they shared a flat in London while establishing parallel careers.* ■ Computing involving the simultaneous performance of operations. ■ of or denoting electrical components or circuits connected to common points at each end, rather than one to another in sequence. The opposite of **SERIES**. ■ S. African of or relating to schools in which two languages are used in separate classes.
▶ **noun 1** a person or thing that is similar or analogous to another: *a challenge which has no **parallel** in peacetime this century.*
■ a similarity: *he points to a **parallel between** biological evolution and cognitive development.* ■ a comparison: *he draws a **parallel between** personal destiny and social forces.*
2 (also **parallel of latitude**) each of the imaginary parallel circles of constant latitude on the earth's surface.
■ a corresponding line on a map. ■ Printing two parallel lines (‖) as a reference mark.
▶ **verb** (**paralleled**, **paralleling**) [with obj.] (of something extending in a line) be side by side with (something extending in a line), always keeping the same distance: *a big concrete gutter that paralleled the road.*
■ be similar or corresponding to (something): *US naval and air superiority was paralleled by Soviet superiority in land-based missile systems.*
– PHRASES **in parallel** occurring at the same time and having some connection. ■ (of electrical components or circuits) connected to common points at each end; not in series.
– ORIGIN mid 16th cent.: from French *parallèle*, via Latin from Greek *parallēlos*, from *para-* 'alongside' + *allēlos* 'one another'.

parallel bars ▶ **plural noun** a pair of parallel rails on posts used in gymnastics.

parallel cousin ▶ **noun** the offspring of a parent's sibling; a first cousin.

parallel distributed processing (abbrev.: **PDP**) ▶ **noun** another term for **CONNECTIONISM**.

parallelepiped /ˌparəlɛləˈpʌɪpɛd, ˌparəlɛˈlɛpɪpɛd/ ▶ **noun** Geometry a solid body of which each face is a parallelogram.
– ORIGIN late 16th cent.: from Greek *parallēlepipedon*, from *parallēlos* 'beside another' + *epipedon* 'plane surface'.

parallel imports ▶ **plural noun** goods imported by unlicensed distributors for sale at less than the manufacturer's official retail price.
– DERIVATIVES **parallel importing** noun.

parallelism ▶ **noun** [mass noun] the state of being parallel or of corresponding in some way.
■ the use of successive verbal constructions in poetry or prose which correspond in grammatical structure, sound, metre, meaning, etc. ■ the use of parallel processing in computer systems.
– DERIVATIVES **parallelistic** adjective.

parallelize /ˈparəlɛlʌɪz/ (also **-ise**) ▶ **verb** [with obj.] Computing adapt (a program) to be suitable for running on a parallel processing system.
– DERIVATIVES **parallelization** noun.

parallel market ▶ **noun** an unofficial market in goods or currencies, especially in a country with a controlled economy.

parallelogram /ˌparəˈlɛləgram/ ▶ **noun** a four-sided plane rectilinear figure with opposite sides parallel.
– PHRASES **parallelogram of forces** a parallelogram illustrating the theorem that if two forces acting at a point are represented in magnitude and direction by two sides of a parallelogram meeting at that point, their resultant is represented by the diagonal drawn from that point.
– ORIGIN late 16th cent.: from French *parallélogramme*, via late Latin from Greek *parallēlogrammon*, from *parallēlos* 'alongside another' + *grammē* 'line'.

parallel port ▶ **noun** Computing a connector for a device that sends or receives several bits of data simultaneously by using more than one wire.

parallel processing ▶ **noun** [mass noun] a mode of computer operation in which a process is split into parts, which execute simultaneously on different processors attached to the same computer.

parallel ruler ▶ **noun** an instrument for drawing parallel lines, consisting of two or more rulers connected by jointed crosspieces so as to be always parallel, at whatever distance they are set.

parallel turn ▶ **noun** Skiing a turn with the skis kept parallel to each other.

paralogical ▶ **adjective** of or relating to a form of reasoning which does not conform to the rules of logic.
– DERIVATIVES **paralogically** adverb.

paralogism /pəˈralədʒɪz(ə)m/ ▶ **noun** Logic a piece of illogical or fallacious reasoning, especially one which appears superficially logical or which the reasoner believes to be logical.
– DERIVATIVES **paralogist** noun.
– ORIGIN mid 16th cent.: from French *paralogisme*, via late Latin from Greek *paralogismos*, from *paralogizesthai* 'reason falsely'.

paralogous /pəˈraləgəs/ ▶ **adjective** Genetics of or relating to genes that are descended from the same ancestral gene by gene duplication in the course of evolution, especially when present in different species which have diverged after the duplication.

paralogy /pəˈralədʒi/ ▶ **noun** [mass noun] **1** Genetics the state of being paralogous.
2 paralogical reasoning.

Paralympics ▶ **plural noun** an international athletic competition for disabled athletes.
– DERIVATIVES **Paralympic** adjective.
– ORIGIN 1950s: blend of *paraplegic* (see **PARAPLEGIA**) and *Olympics* (plural of **OLYMPIC**).

paralyse (chiefly US also **paralyze**) ▶ **verb** [with obj.] (often **be paralysed**) cause (a person or part of the body) to become partly or wholly incapable of movement: *Mrs Burrows had been paralysed by a stroke* | [as adj. **paralysed**] *he became partially paralysed.*
■ render (someone) unable to think or act normally, especially through panic or fear: *some people are paralysed by the thought of failure* | [as adj. **paralysing**] *her paralysing shyness.* ■ bring (a system, place, or organization) to a standstill by causing disruption or chaos: *the regional capital was paralysed by a general strike.*
– DERIVATIVES **paralysingly** adverb.
– ORIGIN early 19th cent.: from French *paralyser*, from *paralysie* 'paralysis'.

paralysis /pəˈralɪsɪs/ ▶ **noun** (pl. **paralyses** /-siːz/) [mass noun] the loss of the ability to move (and sometimes to feel anything) in part or most of the body, typically as a result of illness, poison, or injury.
■ inability to act or function in a person, organization, or place: *the paralysis gripping the country.*
– ORIGIN late Old English, via Latin from Greek *paralusis*, from *paraluesthai* 'be disabled at the side', from *para* 'beside' + *luein* 'loosen'.

paralysis agitans /ˈadʒɪtanz/ ▶ **noun** less common term for **PARKINSON'S DISEASE**.
– ORIGIN Latin, literally 'shaking paralysis'.

paralytic ▶ **adjective** of or relating to paralysis: *the incidence of paralytic disease.*
■ [predic.] informal, chiefly Brit. extremely drunk: *a leaving party which left everyone paralytic.*
▶ **noun** a person affected by paralysis.
– DERIVATIVES **paralytically** adverb.
– ORIGIN late Middle English: from Old French *paralytique*, via Latin from Greek *paralutikos* 'relating to paralysis' (see **PARALYSIS**).

paramagnetic ▶ **adjective** (of a substance or body) very weakly attracted by the poles of a magnet, but not retaining any permanent magnetism.
– DERIVATIVES **paramagnetism** noun.

Paramaribo /ˌparəˈmarɪbəʊ/ the capital of Suriname, a port on the Atlantic coast; pop. 200,920 (est. 1993).

paramatta ▶ **noun** variant spelling of **PARRAMATTA**.

paramecium /ˌparəˈmiːsɪəm/ ▶ **noun** Zoology a single-celled freshwater animal which has a characteristic slipper-like shape and is covered with cilia.
• Genus *Paramecium*, phylum Ciliophora, kingdom Protista.
– ORIGIN mid 18th cent.: modern Latin, from Greek *paramēkēs* 'oval' from *para-* 'against' + *mēkos* 'length'.

paramedic ▶ **noun** a person who is trained to do medical work, especially emergency first aid, but is not a fully qualified doctor.

paramedical ▶ **adjective** of or relating to services and professions which supplement and support medical work but do not require a fully qualified doctor (such as nursing, radiography, emergency first aid, physiotherapy, and dietetics).

parameter /pəˈramɪtə/ ▶ **noun** technical a numerical or other measurable factor forming one of a set that defines a system or sets the conditions of its operation.
■ Mathematics a quantity whose value is selected for the particular circumstances and in relation to which other variable quantities may be expressed. ■ Statistics a numerical characteristic of a population, as distinct from a statistic of a sample. ■ (in general use) a limit or boundary which defines the scope of a particular process or activity: *the parameters within which the media work.*
– ORIGIN mid 17th cent.: modern Latin, from Greek *para-* 'beside' + *metron* 'measure'.

USAGE Until recently, use of the word **parameter** was confined to mathematics and related technical fields. Since around the mid 20th century, however, it has been used in non-technical fields as a technical-sounding word for 'a limit or boundary', as in *they set the **parameters** of the debate.* This use, probably influenced by the word **perimeter**, has been criticized for being a weakening of the technical sense. However, it is now generally accepted as part of standard English.

parameterize /pəˈramɪt(ə)rʌɪz/ (also **parametrize** /pəˈramɪtrʌɪz/) ▶ **verb** [with obj.] technical describe or represent in terms of a parameter or parameters.
– DERIVATIVES **parameterization** noun.

parametric ▶ **adjective** of, relating to, or expressed in terms of a parameter or parameters.
■ Statistics assuming the value of a parameter for the purpose of analysis. ■ Electronics relating to or denoting a process in which amplification or frequency conversion is obtained using a device modulated by a pumping frequency, which enables power to be transferred from the pumping frequency to the signal.

parametric equalizer ▶ **noun** an electronic device or computer program which allows any specific part of the frequency range of a signal to be selected and altered in strength.

paramilitary ▶ **adjective** (of an unofficial force) organized similarly to a military force: *illegal paramilitary groups.*

▶ **noun** (pl. **-ies**) a member of an unofficial paramilitary organization, especially in Northern Ireland.

paramnesia /ˌparəmˈniːzɪə/ ▶ **noun** [mass noun] Psychiatry a condition or phenomenon involving distorted memory or confusions of fact and fantasy, such as confabulation or déjà vu.

paramo /ˈparəməʊ/ ▶ **noun** (pl. **-os**) a high treeless plateau in tropical South America.
– ORIGIN Spanish and Portuguese, from Latin *paramus*.

paramoecium ▶ **noun** old-fashioned spelling of **PARAMECIUM**.

Paramount a US film production and distribution company established in 1914. A major studio of the silent era, Paramount acted as an outlet for many of the films of Cecil B. De Mille and helped to create stars such as Mary Pickford and Rudolf Valentino.

paramount ▶ **adjective** more important than anything else; supreme: *the interests of the child are of paramount importance.*
■[attrib.] having supreme power: *a paramount chief.*
– DERIVATIVES **paramountcy** noun, **paramountly** adverb.
– ORIGIN mid 16th cent. (in the sense 'highest in jurisdiction' in the phrases *lord paramount* and *paramount chief*): from Anglo-Norman French *paramont*, from Old French *par* 'by' + *amont* 'above'.

paramour ▶ **noun** archaic or derogatory a lover, especially the illicit partner of a married person.
– ORIGIN Middle English: from Old French *par amour* 'by love'; in English the phrase was written from an early date as one word and came to be treated as a noun.

paramyxovirus /ˌparəˈmɪksə(ʊ),vʌɪrəs/ ▶ **noun** Medicine any of a group of RNA viruses similar to the myxoviruses but larger and haemolytic, including those causing mumps, measles, distemper, rinderpest, and various respiratory infections (parainfluenza).

Paraná /ˌparəˈnɑː/ **1** a river of South America, which rises in SE Brazil and flows some 3,300 km (2,060 miles) southwards to the River Plate estuary in Argentina. For part of its length it forms the SE border of Paraguay.
2 a river port in eastern Argentina, on the Paraná River; pop. 276,000 (1991).
3 a state of southern Brazil, on the Atlantic coast; capital, Curitiba.

parang[1] /ˈpɑːraŋ, ˈpa-/ ▶ **noun** a Malayan machete.
– ORIGIN Malay.

parang[2] /paˈraŋ/ ▶ **noun** [mass noun] a variety of Trinidadian folk music, traditionally played at Christmas by groups which travel from house to house.
– ORIGIN Spanish creole, based on Spanish *parranda* 'spree, binge'.

paranoia /ˌparəˈnɔɪə/ ▶ **noun** [mass noun] a mental condition characterized by delusions of persecution, unwarranted jealousy, or exaggerated self-importance, typically worked into an organized system. It may be an aspect of chronic personality disorder, of drug abuse, or of a serious condition such as schizophrenia in which the person loses touch with reality.
■suspicion and mistrust of people or their actions without evidence or justification.
– DERIVATIVES **paranoiac** adjective & noun, **paranoiacally** adverb, **paranoic** /-ˈnəʊɪk, -ˈnɔɪɪk/ adjective, **paranoically** /-ˈnəʊɪk(ə)li, -ˈnɔɪk(ə)li/ adverb.
– ORIGIN early 19th cent.: modern Latin, from Greek, from *paranoos* 'distracted', from *para* 'irregular' + *noos* 'mind'.

paranoid ▶ **adjective** of, characterized by, or suffering from the mental condition of paranoia: *paranoid schizophrenia.*
■unreasonably or obsessively anxious, suspicious, or mistrustful: *you think I'm paranoid but I tell you there is something going on.*
▶ **noun** a person who is paranoid.

paranormal ▶ **adjective** denoting events or phenomena such as telekinesis or clairvoyance that are beyond the scope of normal scientific understanding: *a mystic who can prove he has paranormal powers* | [as noun **the paranormal**] *an investigator of the paranormal.*
– DERIVATIVES **paranormally** adverb.

Paranthropus /pəˈranθrəpəs/ ▶ **noun** a genus name often applied to robust fossil hominids first found in South Africa in 1938.
● *Australopithecus robustus* and *A.* (or *Zinjanthropus*) *boisei*, family Hominidae. See **AUSTRALOPITHECUS**.
– ORIGIN modern Latin, from Greek *para-* (expressing relationship) + *anthrōpos* 'man'.

paranumismatica /ˌparənjuːmɪzˈmatɪkə/ ▶ **plural noun** Brit. collectable items that are similar to coins and medals, such as tokens and medallions.

paraparesis /ˌparəpəˈriːsɪs/ ▶ **noun** [mass noun] partial paralysis of the lower limbs.
– DERIVATIVES **paraparetic** adjective.

parapente /ˈparəpɒnt/ ▶ **noun** [mass noun] the activity of gliding by means of an aerofoil parachute launched from high ground.
■[count noun] the parachute used for this purpose.
▶ **verb** [no obj.] glide using an aerofoil parachute.
– DERIVATIVES **parapenter** noun.
– ORIGIN 1980s: from French, from *para(chute)* + *pente* 'slope'.

parapet /ˈparəpɪt/ ▶ **noun** a low protective wall along the edge of a roof, bridge, or balcony.
■a protective wall or earth defence along the top of a trench or other place of concealment for troops.
– DERIVATIVES **parapeted** adjective.
– ORIGIN late 16th cent.: from French, or from Italian *parapetto* 'breast-high wall', from *para-* 'protecting' + *petto* 'breast' (from Latin *pectus*).

paraph /ˈparaf/ ▶ **noun** a flourish after a signature, originally as a precaution against forgery.
– ORIGIN late Middle English (denoting a paragraph): from French *paraphe*, from medieval Latin *paraphus* (contraction of *paragraphus* 'short horizontal stroke').

paraphasia /ˌparəˈfeɪzɪə/ ▶ **noun** [mass noun] Psychology speech disturbance resulting from brain damage in which words are jumbled and sentences meaningless: [count noun] *her conversation was largely free of paraphasias.*
– DERIVATIVES **paraphasic** adjective.

paraphernalia /ˌparəfəˈneɪlɪə/ ▶ **noun** [treated as sing. or pl.] miscellaneous articles, especially the equipment needed for a particular activity.
■trappings associated with a particular institution or activity that are regarded as superfluous: *the rituals and paraphernalia of government.*
– ORIGIN mid 17th cent. (denoting property owned by a married woman): from medieval Latin, based on Greek *parapherna* 'property apart from a dowry', from *para* 'distinct from' + *pherna* (from *phernē* 'dower').

paraphilia /ˌparəˈfɪlɪə/ ▶ **noun** [mass noun] Psychiatry a condition characterized by abnormal sexual desires, typically involving extreme or dangerous activities.
– DERIVATIVES **paraphiliac** adjective & noun.

paraphrase ▶ **verb** [with obj.] express the meaning of (something written or spoken or the writer or speaker) using different words, especially to achieve greater clarity: *you can either quote or paraphrase literary texts.*
▶ **noun** a rewording of something written or spoken by someone else.
– DERIVATIVES **paraphrasable** adjective, **paraphrastic** adjective.
– ORIGIN mid 16th cent. (as a noun): via Latin from Greek *paraphrasis*, from *paraphrazein*, from *para-* (expressing modification) + *phrazein* 'tell'.

paraphyletic /ˌparəfʌɪˈlɛtɪk/ ▶ **adjective** Biology (of a group of organisms) descended from a common evolutionary ancestor or ancestral group, but not including all the descendant groups.

paraphysis /pəˈrafɪsɪs/ ▶ **noun** (pl. **paraphyses** /-siːz/) Botany a sterile hair-like filament present among the reproductive organs in many lower plants, especially bryophytes, algae, and fungi.
– ORIGIN mid 19th cent.: modern Latin, from Greek *para-* 'beside, subsidiary' + *phusis* 'growth'.

paraplegia /ˌparəˈpliːdʒə/ ▶ **noun** [mass noun] paralysis of the legs and lower body, typically caused by spinal injury or disease.
– DERIVATIVES **paraplegic** adjective & noun.
– ORIGIN mid 17th cent.: modern Latin, from Greek *paraplēgia*, from *paraplēssein* 'strike at the side', from *para* 'beside' + *plēssein* 'to strike'.

parapodium /ˌparəˈpəʊdɪəm/ ▶ **noun** (pl. **parapodia** /-ɪə/) Zoology (in a polychaete worm) each of a number of paired muscular bristle-bearing appendages used in locomotion, sensation, or respiration.
■(in a sea slug or other mollusc) a lateral extension of the foot used as an undulating fin for swimming.
– DERIVATIVES **parapodial** adjective.
– ORIGIN late 19th cent.: modern Latin, from Greek *para-* 'subsidiary' + *pous, pod-* 'foot'.

paraprofessional chiefly N. Amer. ▶ **noun** a person to whom a particular aspect of a professional task is delegated but who is not licensed to practise as a fully qualified professional.
▶ **adjective** of, relating to, or denoting such a person.

paraprotein ▶ **noun** Medicine a protein found in the blood only as a result of cancer or other disease.

parapsychic ▶ **adjective** of, relating to, or denoting mental phenomena for which no adequate scientific explanation exists.

parapsychology ▶ **noun** [mass noun] the study of mental phenomena which are excluded from or inexplicable by orthodox scientific psychology (such as hypnosis, telepathy, etc.).
– DERIVATIVES **parapsychological** adjective, **parapsychologist** noun.

paraquat /ˈparəkwɒt, -kwat/ ▶ **noun** [mass noun] a toxic fast-acting herbicide, which becomes deactivated in the soil.
– ORIGIN 1960s: from **PARA-**[1] (in sense 2) + **QUATERNARY** (it is a quaternary ammonium salt containing pyridine rings linked at the para-position).

pararhyme ▶ **noun** [mass noun] partial rhyme between words with the same pattern of consonants but different vowels.

parasagittal /ˌparəˈsadʒɪt(ə)l/ ▶ **adjective** Anatomy relating to or situated in a plane adjacent or parallel to the plane which divides the body into right and left halves.
– DERIVATIVES **parasagittally** adverb.

parasail ▶ **verb** [no obj.] [often as noun **parasailing**] glide through the air wearing an open parachute while being towed by a motor boat.
▶ **noun** a parachute designed for parasailing.

parascending ▶ **noun** Brit. the sport or activity of paragliding or parasailing.
– DERIVATIVES **parascend** verb, **parascender** noun.

paraselene /ˌparəsɪˈliːni/ ▶ **noun** (pl. **paraselenae** /-niː/) a bright spot in the sky similar to a parhelion but formed by moonlight.
– ORIGIN mid 17th cent.: modern Latin, from Greek *para-* 'beside' + *selēnē* 'moon'.

parasitaemia /ˌparəsɪˈtiːmɪə/ (US **parasitemia**) ▶ **noun** [mass noun] Medicine the demonstrable presence of parasites in the blood.

parasite ▶ **noun** an organism which lives in or on another organism (its host) and benefits by deriving nutrients at the other's expense.
■derogatory a person who habitually relies on or exploits others and gives nothing in return.

> Parasites exist in huge variety, including animals, plants, and micro-organisms. They may live as exoparasites on the surface of the host (e.g. arthropods such as ticks, mites, lice, fleas, and many insects infesting plants) or as endoparasites in the gut or tissues (e.g. many kinds of worm), and cause varying degrees of damage or disease to the host.

– ORIGIN mid 16th cent.: via Latin from Greek *parasitos* '(person) eating at another's table', from *para-* 'alongside' + *sitos* 'food'.

parasitic ▶ **adjective** (of an organism) living as a parasite: *mistletoe is **parasitic on** trees.*
■resulting from infestation by a parasite: *mortality from parasitic diseases.* ■ derogatory habitually relying on or exploiting others: *attacks on the parasitic existence of Party functionaries.* ■ Phonetics (of a speech sound) inserted without etymological justification (e.g. the *b* in *thimble*); epenthetic.
– DERIVATIVES **parasitical** adjective, **parasitically** adverb, **parasitism** noun.
– ORIGIN early 17th cent.: via Latin from Greek *parasitikos*, from *parasitos* '(person) eating at another's table'.

parasitic bronchitis ▶ **noun** technical term for **HUSK**[2] (in sense 1).

parasiticide /ˌparəˈsɪtɪsʌɪd/ ▶ **noun** a substance used in medicine and veterinary medicine to kill parasites (especially those other than bacteria or fungi).

parasitize /ˈparəsʌɪtʌɪz, -sɪ-/ (also **-ise**) ▶ **verb** [with obj.] infest or exploit (an organism or part) as a parasite.

– DERIVATIVES **parasitization** noun.

parasitoid /ˈparəsɪtɔɪd/ Entomology ▶ **noun** an insect whose larvae live as parasites which eventually kill their hosts, e.g. an ichneumon wasp.
▶ **adjective** of, relating to, or denoting such an insect.

parasitology /ˌparəsɪˈtɒlədʒi/ ▶ **noun** [mass noun] the branch of biology or medicine concerned with the study of parasitic organisms.
– DERIVATIVES **parasitological** adjective, **parasitologist** noun.

parasol ▶ **noun 1** a light umbrella used to give shade from the sun.
2 (also **parasol mushroom**) a widely distributed large mushroom with a broad scaly greyish-brown cap and a tall slender stalk, growing typically in grassy places.
● Genus *Lepiota*, family Lepiotaceae, class Hymenomycetes: numerous species, especially the edible *L. procera*.
– ORIGIN early 17th cent.: from French, from Italian *parasole*, from *para-* 'protecting against' + *sole* 'sun' (from Latin *sol*).

parastatal /ˌparəˈsteɪt(ə)l/ ▶ **adjective** (of an organization or industry) having some political authority and serving the state indirectly, especially in some African countries.
▶ **noun** a parastatal organization.

parasternal /ˌparəˈstəːnəl/ ▶ **adjective** Anatomy situated beside the sternum.

parastichy /pəˈrastɪki/ ▶ **noun** (pl. **-ies**) Botany (in phyllotaxis) an oblique row of leaves arranged in a secondary spiral. Contrasted with **ORTHOSTICHY**.
– ORIGIN late 19th cent.: from **PARA-**[1] 'adjacent' + Greek *stikhos* 'row, rank'.

parasuicide ▶ **noun** [mass noun] Psychiatry apparent attempted suicide without the actual intention of killing oneself.

parasympathetic ▶ **adjective** Physiology of or relating to the part of the autonomic nervous system which balances the action of the sympathetic nerves. It consists of nerves arising from the brain and the lower end of the spinal cord and supplying the internal organs, blood vessels, and glands.
– ORIGIN early 20th cent.: from **PARA-**[1] 'alongside' + **SYMPATHETIC**, because some of these nerves run alongside sympathetic nerves.

parasynthesis ▶ **noun** Linguistics a process by which a term is formed by adding a bound morpheme (e.g. *-ed*) to a combination of existing words (e.g. *black-eyed* from *black eye(s)* + *-ed*).
– DERIVATIVES **parasynthetic** adjective, **parasynthetically** adverb.
– ORIGIN mid 19th cent.: from Greek *parasunthesis*, from *para-* 'subsidiary' + **SYNTHESIS**.

parataxis /ˌparəˈtaksɪs/ ▶ **noun** Grammar the placing of clauses or phrases one after another, without words to indicate coordination or subordination, as in *Tell me, how are you?* Contrasted with **HYPOTAXIS**.
– DERIVATIVES **paratactic** adjective, **paratactically** adverb.
– ORIGIN mid 19th cent.: from Greek *parataxis*, from *para-* 'beside' + *taxis* 'arrangement' (from *tassein* 'arrange').

paratha /pəˈrɑːtə/ ▶ **noun** (in Indian cookery) a flat, thick piece of unleavened bread fried on a griddle.
– ORIGIN from Hindi *parāṭhā*.

parathion /ˌparəˈθʌɪən/ ▶ **noun** [mass noun] a highly toxic synthetic organophosphorus compound containing phosphorus and sulphur, used as an agricultural insecticide.
– ORIGIN 1940s: from **PARA-**[1] (in sense 2) + **THIO-** + **-ON**.

parathormone /ˌparəˈθɔːməʊn/ ▶ **noun** [mass noun] Physiology parathyroid hormone.

parathyroid ▶ **noun** Anatomy a gland next to the thyroid which secretes a hormone (**parathyroid hormone**) that regulates calcium levels in a person's body: [as modifier] *parathyroid tissue.*

paratrooper ▶ **noun** a member of a paratroop regiment or airborne unit.

paratroops ▶ **plural noun** troops equipped to be dropped by parachute from aircraft: [as modifier] (usu. **paratroop**) *a paratroop regiment.*
– ORIGIN 1940s: from an abbreviation of **PARACHUTE** + *troops* (plural of **TROOP**).

paratyphoid ▶ **noun** [mass noun] a fever resembling typhoid but caused by different (though related) bacteria.
● The bacteria are species of the genus *Salmonella*, in particular (in humans) *S. paratyphi*.
▶ **adjective** [attrib.] of or relating to such a fever or the bacteria causing it: *paratyphoid fever.*

paravane ▶ **noun** a device towed behind a boat at a depth regulated by its vanes or planes, so that the cable to which it is attached can cut the moorings of submerged mines.
– ORIGIN early 20th cent.: from **PARA-**[2] 'protecting' + **VANE**.

paraventricular /ˌparəvɛnˈtrɪkjələ/ ▶ **adjective** Anatomy situated next to a ventricle of the brain.

par avion /pɑː(r) aˈvjɔ̃, French paʀ avjɔ̃/ ▶ **adverb** by airmail (written on a letter or parcel to indicate how it is to reach its destination).
– ORIGIN French, literally 'by aeroplane'.

parawing ▶ **noun** a type of parachute or kite having a flattened shape like a wing, to give greater manoeuvrability.

paraxial /pəˈraksɪəl/ ▶ **adjective** Anatomy & Zoology situated alongside, or on each side of, an axis, especially the central axis of the body.

parboil ▶ **verb** [with obj.] partly cook (food) by boiling.
– ORIGIN late Middle English: from Old French *parbouillir*, from late Latin *perbullire* 'boil thoroughly', from Latin *per-* 'through, thoroughly' (later confused with **PART**) + *bullire* 'to boil'.

parbuckle /ˈpɑːbʌk(ə)l/ ▶ **noun** a loop of rope arranged like a sling, used for raising or lowering casks and other cylindrical objects.
▶ **verb** [with obj.] raise or lower with such a device.
– ORIGIN early 17th cent.: from earlier *parbunkle*, of unknown origin. The change in the ending was due to association with **BUCKLE**.

Parcae /ˈpɑːkʌɪ, ˈpɑːsiː/ Roman Mythology Roman name for ***the Fates*** (see **FATE**).

parcel ▶ **noun 1** a thing or collection of things wrapped in paper in order to be carried or sent by post.
2 a quantity or amount of something, in particular:
■ a piece of land, especially one considered as part of an estate. ■ a quantity dealt with in one commercial transaction: *a parcel of shares.* ■ technical a portion of a larger body of air or other fluid considered as a discrete element.
▶ **verb** (**parcelled**, **parcelling**; US **parceled**, **parceling**) [with obj.] make (something) into a parcel by wrapping it: *he parcelled up his only winter suit to take to the pawnbroker.*
■ (**parcel something out**) divide into portions and then distribute: *the farmers argue that parcelling out commercial farmland in small plots will reduce productivity.* ■ Nautical wrap (rope) with strips of tarred canvas, before binding it with yarn as part of a traditional technique to reduce chafing.
– PHRASES **pass the parcel** a children's game in which a parcel is passed around to the accompaniment of music, the child holding the parcel when the music stops being allowed to unwrap a layer.
– ORIGIN late Middle English (chiefly in the sense 'small portion'): from Old French *parcelle*, from Latin *particula* 'small part'.

parcel bomb ▶ **noun** an explosive device hidden in a package and sent with the intention of causing harm or injury to the recipient.

parcel-gilt ▶ **adjective** (of an item of furniture, silverware, or similar) partly gilded, especially on the inner surface only.

parcel post ▶ **noun** the branch of the postal service dealing with parcels.

parcel shelf ▶ **noun** a shelf in a motor vehicle behind the rear seat.

parch ▶ **verb** make or become dry through intense heat: [with obj.] *a piece of grassland parched by the sun* | [no obj.] *his crops parched during the last two summers.*
■ [with obj.] roast (corn, peas, etc.) lightly.
– ORIGIN late Middle English: of unknown origin.

parched ▶ **adjective** dried out with heat.
■ [predic.] informal extremely thirsty: *I'm parched—I'll die without a drink.* ■ lightly roasted: *parched corn.*

parcheesi ▶ **noun** variant spelling of **PACHISI**.

parchment ▶ **noun** [mass noun] a stiff, flat, thin material made from the prepared skin of an animal, usually a sheep or goat, and used as a durable writing surface in ancient and medieval times.
■ [count noun] a manuscript written on this material: *a large collection of ancient parchments.* ■ (also **parchment paper**) [mass noun] a type of stiff translucent paper treated to resemble parchment and used for lampshades, as a writing surface, and in baking. ■ [count noun] informal a diploma or other formal document.
– ORIGIN Middle English: from Old French *parchemin*, from a blend of late Latin *pergamina* 'writing material from Pergamum' and *Parthica pellis* 'Parthian skin' (a kind of scarlet leather).

parclose /ˈpɑːkləʊz/ ▶ **noun** a screen or railing in a church enclosing a tomb or altar or separating off a side chapel.
– ORIGIN Middle English: from Old French *parclos(e)* 'enclosed', past participle of *parclore* (from Latin *per-* 'thoroughly' + *claudere* 'to close').

pard ▶ **noun** archaic or poetic/literary a leopard.
– ORIGIN late Middle English: from Old French, via Latin from Greek *pardos*.

pardalote /ˈpɑːdələʊt/ ▶ **noun** a small short-billed Australian songbird related to the flowerpeckers, typically having white spots or streaks on the dark wings and crown. Also called **DIAMOND-BIRD** in Australia.
● Genus *Pardalotus*, family Dicaeidae (or Pardalotidae): several species.
– ORIGIN mid 19th cent.: from modern Latin *Pardalotus*, from Greek *pardalōtos* 'spotted like a leopard', based on *pardos* (see **PARD**).

pardner ▶ **noun** US dated or humorous variant spelling of **PARTNER**, used to represent US dialect speech: *you and me, pardner, against the world.*

pardon ▶ **noun** [mass noun] the action of forgiving or being forgiven for an error or offence: *he obtained pardon for his sins.*
■ [count noun] a remission of the legal consequences of an offence or conviction: *he offered a full pardon to five convicted men.* ■ [count noun] Christian Church, historical an indulgence, as widely sold in medieval Europe.
▶ **verb** [with obj.] forgive or excuse (a person, error, or offence).
■ release (an offender) from the legal consequences of an offence or conviction, and often implicitly from blame: *he was pardoned for his treason.* ■ (usu. **be pardoned**) used to indicate that the actions or thoughts of someone are justified or understandable given the circumstances: *one can be pardoned the suspicion that some of his errors were deliberate.*
▶ **exclamation** a request to a speaker to repeat something because one did not hear or understand it: *'Pardon?' I said, cupping a hand to my ear.*
– PHRASES **beg someone's pardon** express polite apology: *I beg your pardon for intruding.* **I beg your pardon** (or N. Amer. **pardon me**) used to indicate that one has not heard or understood something. ■ used to express one's anger or indignation at what someone has just said.
– DERIVATIVES **pardonable** adjective, **pardonably** adverb.
– ORIGIN Middle English: from Old French *pardun* (noun), *pardoner* (verb), from medieval Latin *perdonare* 'concede, remit', from *per-* 'completely' + *donare* 'give'.

pardoner ▶ **noun** historical a person licensed to sell papal pardons or indulgences.
– ORIGIN Middle English: from Anglo-Norman French.

pare ▶ **verb** [with obj.] trim (something) by cutting away its outer edges.
■ cut off the outer skin of (something): *pare off the rind using a peeler.* ■ reduce (something) in size, extent, quantity, or number, usually in a number of small successive stages: *union leaders publicly pared down their demands | we pared costs by doing our own cleaning.*
– DERIVATIVES **parer** noun.
– ORIGIN Middle English: from Old French *parer* 'adorn, prepare', also 'peel, trim', from Latin *parare* 'prepare'.

paregoric /ˌparɪˈɡɒrɪk/ ▶ **noun** [mass noun] historical a medicine consisting of opium flavoured with camphor, aniseed, and benzoic acid, formerly used to treat diarrhoea and coughing in children.
– ORIGIN late 17th cent.: via late Latin from Greek *parēgorikos* 'soothing', from the verb *parēgorein* literally 'speak in the assembly', hence 'soothe, console'.

paren /pəˈrɛn/ ▶ **noun** (usu. **parens**) Printing a round bracket.
– ORIGIN early 20th cent.: abbreviation of **PARENTHESIS**.

parenchyma /pəˈrɛŋkɪmə/ ▶ **noun** [mass noun] Anatomy

p

the functional tissue of an organ as distinguished from the connective and supporting tissue.
■ Botany the cellular tissue, typically soft and succulent, found chiefly in the softer parts of leaves, pulp of fruits, bark and pith of stems, etc. ■ Zoology cellular tissue lying between the body wall and the organs of invertebrate animals lacking a coelom, such as flatworms.
– DERIVATIVES **parenchymal** adjective (chiefly Anatomy), **parenchymatous** adjective (chiefly Botany).
– ORIGIN mid 17th cent.: from Greek *parenkhuma* 'something poured in besides', from *para-* 'beside' + *enkhuma* 'infusion'.

parens patriae /ˌparɛnz ˈpatrɪiː/ ▶ **noun** Law the monarch, or any other authority, regarded as the legal protector of citizens unable to protect themselves.
■ [mass noun] the principle that political authority carries with it the responsibility for such protection.
– ORIGIN modern Latin, literally 'parent of the country'.

parent ▶ **noun** a father or mother: *the parents of the bride | his adoptive parents.*
■ archaic a forefather or ancestor. ■ an animal or plant from which younger ones are derived. ■ a source or origin of a smaller or less important part. ■ [often as modifier] an organization or company which owns or controls a number of subsidiary organizations or companies: *policy considerations were determined largely by the parent institution.*
▶ **verb** [with obj.] [often as noun **parenting**] be or act as a mother or father to (someone).
– DERIVATIVES **parental** adjective, **parentally** adverb, **parenthood** noun.
– ORIGIN late Middle English: from Old French, from Latin *parent-* 'bringing forth', from the verb *parere*. The verb dates from the mid 17th cent.

parentage ▶ **noun** [mass noun] the identity and origins of one's parents: *a boy of Jamaican parentage.*
■ figurative the origin of something: *this ice cream boasts American parentage.*
– ORIGIN late 15th cent.: from Old French.

parentcraft ▶ **noun** [mass noun] the aggregate of skills and knowledge that facilitate the rearing of children.

parenteral /pəˈrɛnt(ə)r(ə)l/ ▶ **adjective** Medicine administered or occurring elsewhere in the body than the mouth and alimentary canal: *parenteral nutrition.* Often contrasted with **ENTERAL**.
– DERIVATIVES **parenterally** adverb.
– ORIGIN early 20th cent.: from **PARA-**[1] 'beside' + Greek *enteron* 'intestine' + **-AL**.

parenthesis /pəˈrɛnθɪsɪs/ ▶ **noun** (pl. **parentheses** /-siːz/) a word, clause, or sentence inserted as an explanation or afterthought into a passage which is grammatically complete without it, in writing usually marked off by brackets, dashes, or commas.
■ (usu. **parentheses**) a pair of round brackets () used to include such a word, clause, or sentence. ■ an interlude or interval: *the three months of coalition government were a lamentable political parenthesis.*
– PHRASES **in parenthesis** as a digression or afterthought.
– ORIGIN mid 16th cent.: via late Latin from Greek, from *parentithenai* 'put in beside'.

parenthesize (also **-ise**) ▶ **verb** [with obj.] [usu. as adj. **parenthesized**] put (a word, phrase, or clause) into brackets: *parenthesized clauses.*
■ insert as a parenthesis; express or state in parenthesis.

parenthetic /ˌpar(ə)nˈθɛtɪk/ ▶ **adjective** of, relating to, or inserted as a parenthesis: *parenthetic remarks.*
– DERIVATIVES **parenthetical** adjective, **parenthetically** adverb.
– ORIGIN late 18th cent.: from **PARENTHESIS**, on the pattern of pairs such as *synthesis, synthetic.*

parent-teacher association ▶ **noun** Brit. a local organization of parents and teachers for promoting closer relations and improving educational facilities at a school.

parergon /pəˈrəːgɒn/ ▶ **noun** (pl. **parerga** /-gə/) a piece of work that is supplementary to or a by-product of a larger work.
■ archaic work that is subsidiary to one's ordinary employment: *he pursued astronomy as a parergon.*
– ORIGIN early 17th cent.: via Latin from Greek *parergon*, from *para-* 'beside, additional' + *ergon* 'work'.

paresis /pəˈriːsɪs, ˈparɪsɪs/ ▶ **noun** (pl. **pareses** /-siːz/) Medicine a condition of muscular weakness caused by nerve damage or disease; partial paralysis.
■ (also **general paresis**) [mass noun] inflammation of the brain in the later stages of syphilis, causing progressive dementia and paralysis.
– DERIVATIVES **paretic** adjective.
– ORIGIN late 17th cent.: modern Latin, from Greek *parienai* 'let go', from *para-* 'alongside' + *hienai* 'let go'.

paresthesia ▶ **noun** US spelling of **PARAESTHESIA**.

Pareto /paˈreɪtəʊ, -ˈriːtəʊ/ ▶ **adjective** [attrib.] denoting or involving the theories and methods of the Italian economist and sociologist Vilfredo Pareto (1848–1923), especially a formula used to express the income distribution of a society.

Pareto-optimal ▶ **adjective** relating to or denoting a distribution of wealth such that any redistribution or other change beneficial to one individual is detrimental to one or more others.
– DERIVATIVES **Pareto-optimality** noun.

pareu /ˈpɑːreɪuː/ ▶ **noun** a kind of sarong made of a single straight piece of printed cotton cloth, worn by people from Polynesia.
– ORIGIN Tahitian.

par excellence /pɑːr ˈɛks(ə)l(ə)ns, French paʀ ɛksɛlɑ̃s/ ▶ **adjective** [postpositive] better or more than all others of the same kind: *Nash is, to many, the Regency architect par excellence.*
– ORIGIN French, literally 'by excellence'.

parfait /ˈpɑːfeɪ/ ▶ **noun** [mass noun] **1** a rich cold dessert made with whipped cream, eggs, and often fruit.
2 a dessert consisting of layers of ice cream, meringue, and fruit, served in a tall glass.
– ORIGIN from the French adjective *parfait*, literally 'perfect'.

parfleche /ˈpɑːflɛʃ/ ▶ **noun** (in American Indian culture) a hide, especially a buffalo's hide, with the hair removed, dried by being stretched on a frame.
■ an article, especially a bag, made from this.
– ORIGIN from Canadian French *parflèche*, from French *parer* 'ward off' + *flèche* 'arrow'.

parfumerie /pɑːˈfjuːm(ə)ri/ ▶ **noun** (pl. **-ies**) a place where perfume is sold or made.
– ORIGIN French.

pargana /pəˈgʌnə/ (also **pergunnah** or **pergana**) ▶ **noun** a group of villages or a subdivision of a district in India.
– ORIGIN Urdu, literally 'district'.

parget /ˈpɑːdʒɪt/ (also **parge** /pɑːdʒ/) ▶ **verb** (**pargeted**, **pargeting**) [with obj.] cover (a part of a building, especially a flue or an external brick wall) with plaster or mortar that typically bears an ornamental pattern.
▶ **noun** another term for **PARGETING**.
– ORIGIN late Middle English: from Old French *parjeter*, from *par-* 'all over' + *jeter* 'to throw'.

pargeting (also **parging**) ▶ **noun** [mass noun] plaster or mortar applied in a layer over a part of a building, especially ornamental plasterwork.

parhelion /pɑːˈhiːlɪən/ ▶ **noun** (pl. **parhelia** /-lɪə/) a bright spot in the sky appearing on either side of the sun, formed by refraction of sunlight through ice crystals high in the atmosphere.
– ORIGIN mid 17th cent.: from Latin *parelion*, from Greek *para-* 'beside' + *hēlios* 'sun'.

pariah /pəˈrʌɪə/ ▶ **noun** **1** an outcast: *they were treated as social pariahs.*
2 historical a member of a low caste or of no caste in southern India.
– ORIGIN early 17th cent.: from Tamil *paraiyar*, plural of *paraiyan* '(hereditary) drummer', from *parai* 'a drum' (pariahs not being allowed to join in with a religious procession).

pariah dog ▶ **noun** another term for **PYE-DOG**.

Parian /ˈpɛːrɪən/ ▶ **adjective** of or relating to Paros or the fine white marble for which it is renowned.
■ denoting a form of fine white unglazed hard-paste porcelain likened to Parian marble.
▶ **noun** **1** a native or inhabitant of Paros.
2 [mass noun] Parian ware (porcelain).

parietal /pəˈrʌɪt(ə)l/ ▶ **adjective** **1** Anatomy & Biology of, relating to, attached to, or denoting the wall of the body or of a body cavity or hollow structure.
■ of the parietal lobe: *the parietal cortex.*
2 N. Amer. relating to residence within a college and especially to visits from members of the opposite sex: *parietal rules.*
3 Archaeology denoting prehistoric art found on rock walls.
▶ **noun** **1** Anatomy & Zoology a parietal structure.
■ short for **PARIETAL BONE**.
2 (**parietals**) US informal college dormitory rules governing visits from members of the opposite sex.
– ORIGIN late Middle English: from late Latin *parietalis*, from Latin *paries, pariet-* 'wall'.

parietal bone ▶ **noun** a bone forming the central side and upper back part of each side of the skull.

parietal cell ▶ **noun** an oxyntic (acid-secreting) cell of the stomach wall.

parietal lobe ▶ **noun** either of the paired lobes of the brain at the top of the head, including areas concerned with the reception and correlation of sensory information.

pari-mutuel /ˌpɑːrɪˈmjuːtʃʊəl, -ˈtjʊəl/ ▶ **noun** [often as modifier] a form of betting in which those backing the first three places divide the losers' stakes (less the operator's commission): *pari-mutuel betting.*
■ a booth for placing bets under such a system.
– ORIGIN French, literally 'mutual stake'.

parings ▶ **plural noun** thin strips that have been pared off from something: *fingernail parings.*

pari passu /ˌpɑːrɪ ˈpasuː, ˌparɪ/ ▶ **adverb** side by side; at the same rate or on an equal footing: *early opera developed* **pari passu with** *solo song.*
– ORIGIN Latin, literally 'with equal step'.

Paris[1] /ˈparɪs, French paʀi/ the capital of France, on the River Seine; pop. 2,175,200 (1990).

> Paris was held by the Romans, who called it Lutetia, and the Franks, and was established as the capital in 987 under Hugh Capet. It was organized into three parts, the Île de la Cité (an island in the Seine), the Right Bank, and the Left Bank, during the reign of Philippe-Auguste (1180–1223). The city's neoclassical architecture dates from the modernization of the Napoleonic era; this continued under Napoleon III, when the bridges and boulevards of the modern city were built.

– ORIGIN named after the *Parisii*, a Gallic people who settled on the Île de la Cité.

Paris[2] /ˈparɪs/ Greek Mythology a Trojan prince, the son of Priam and Hecuba. Appointed by the gods to decide who among the three goddesses Hera, Athene, and Aphrodite should win a prize for beauty, he awarded it to Aphrodite, who promised him the most beautiful woman in the world—Helen, wife of Menelaus king of Sparta. He abducted Helen, bringing about the Trojan War, in which he killed Achilles but was later himself killed.

Paris[3], Matthew, see **MATTHEW PARIS**.

Paris club a group of the major creditor nations of the International Monetary Fund, meeting informally in Paris to discuss the financial relations of the IMF member nations.

Paris Commune ▶ **noun** see **COMMUNE**[1] (sense 3).

Paris green ▶ **noun** [mass noun] a vivid green toxic crystalline salt of copper and arsenic, used as a preservative, pigment, and insecticide.

parish ▶ **noun** (in the Christian Church) a small administrative district typically having its own church and a priest or pastor: [as modifier] *a parish church.*
■ (also **civil parish**) Brit. a small country district; the smallest unit of local government, constituted only in rural areas. ■ US (in Louisiana) a territorial division corresponding to a county in other states.
– ORIGIN Middle English: from Anglo-Norman French and Old French *paroche*, from late Latin *parochia*, from Greek *paroikia* 'sojourning', based on *para-* 'beside, subsidiary' + *oikos* 'dwelling'.

parishad /ˈpʌrɪʃʌd/ ▶ **noun** Indian a council or assembly.
– ORIGIN from Sanskrit, from *pari* 'around' + *sad-* 'sit'.

parish clerk ▶ **noun** an official performing various mainly administrative duties concerned with the Church or with a civil parish.

parish council ▶ **noun** Brit. the administrative body in a civil parish.

parishioner ▶ **noun** an inhabitant of a parish, especially one who belongs to or attends a particular church.

parish-pump ▶ **adjective** [attrib.] Brit. of local importance or interest only; parochial: *I looked down on parish-pump politics.*

parish register ▶ **noun** a book recording

christenings, marriages, and burials at a parish church.

Parisian /pəˈrɪzɪən/ ▶**adjective** of or relating to Paris.
▶**noun** a native or inhabitant of Paris.
– ORIGIN late Middle English: from French *parisien*.

Parisienne /paˌrɪzɪˈɛn, French parizjɛn/ ▶**noun** a Parisian girl or woman.
▶**adjective** (especially of a girl or woman) Parisian.
– ORIGIN mid 17th cent.: French, feminine of *parisien* 'Parisian'.

parison /ˈparɪs(ə)n/ ▶**noun** a rounded mass of glass formed by rolling the substance immediately after removal from the furnace.
– ORIGIN early 19th cent.: from French *paraison*, from *parer* 'prepare', from Latin *parare*.

parity[1] /ˈparɪti/ ▶**noun** [mass noun] **1** the state or condition of being equal, especially as regards status or pay: *parity of incomes between rural workers and those in industrial occupations.*
■the value of one currency in terms of another at an established exchange rate.
2 Mathematics (of a number) the fact of being even or odd.
■Physics the property of a spatial wave equation that either remains the same (**even parity**) or changes sign (**odd parity**) under a given transformation. ■Physics the value of a quantum number corresponding to this property. ■Computing a function whose being even (or odd) provides a check on a set of binary values.
– ORIGIN late 16th cent.: from late Latin *paritas*, from *par* 'equal'.

parity[2] /ˈparɪti/ ▶**noun** [mass noun] Medicine the fact or condition of having borne children.
■the number of children previously borne: *very high parity (six children or more).*
– ORIGIN late 19th cent.: from *parous* 'having borne offspring' (back-formation from adjectives ending in **-PAROUS**) + **-ITY**.

parity bit ▶**noun** Computing a bit which acts as a check on a set of binary values, calculated in such a way that the number of 1s in the set plus the parity bit should always be even (or occasionally, should always be odd).

Park, Mungo (1771–1806), Scottish explorer. He undertook a series of explorations in West Africa (1795–7), among them the navigation of the Niger. He drowned on a second expedition to the Niger (1805–6).

park ▶**noun 1** a large public garden in a town, used for recreation: *a walk round the park.*
■a large enclosed piece of ground, typically with woodland and pasture, attached to a large country house: *the house is set in its own park.* ■a large area of land kept in its natural state for public recreational use. ■(also **wildlife park**) a large enclosed area of land used to accommodate wild animals in captivity. ■(usu. **the park**) Brit. informal a football field: *he was the liveliest player on the park.* ■N. Amer. an enclosed sports ground.
2 [with adj. or noun modifier] an area devoted to a specified purpose: *an industrial park.*
■[with modifier] chiefly Brit. an area for motor vehicles to be left in: *a coach park.*
3 (in a car with automatic transmission) the position of the gear selector in which the gears are locked, preventing the vehicle's movement.
▶**verb** [with obj.] bring (a vehicle that one is driving) to a halt and leave it temporarily, typically in a car park or by the side of the road: *he parked his car outside her house* | [no obj.] *he couldn't find anywhere to park.*
■[with obj. and adverbial of place] informal deposit and leave in a convenient place until required: *come on in, and park your bag by the door.* ■(**park oneself in/on**) informal sit down on or in: *after dinner, we parked ourselves on a pair of couches.*
– ORIGIN Middle English: from Old French *parc*, from medieval Latin *parricus*, of Germanic origin; related to German *Pferch* 'pen, fold', also to **PADDOCK**. The word was originally a legal term designating land held by royal grant for keeping game animals: this was enclosed and therefore distinct from a *forest* or *chase*, and (also unlike a *forest*) had no special laws or officers. A military sense 'space occupied by artillery, wagons, stores, etc. in an encampment' (late 17th cent.) is the origin of the verb sense (mid 19th cent.) and of sense 2 (early 20th cent.).

parka ▶**noun** a large windproof jacket with a hood, designed to be worn in cold weather.
■a hooded jacket made of animal skin, worn by Eskimos.
– ORIGIN late 18th cent.: via Aleut from Russian.

parkade ▶**noun** Canadian a multi-storey car park.
– ORIGIN 1950s: from **PARK**, on the pattern of *arcade*.

park-and-ride ▶**noun** [often as modifier] a system for reducing urban traffic congestion, in which drivers leave their cars in car parks on the outskirts of a city and travel to the city centre on public transport.

park cattle (also **white park cattle**) ▶**plural noun** animals of a breed of primitive cattle that are maintained in a semi-wild state in several parks in Britain. They are typically white in colour with dark ears and muzzles.

Park Chung Hee /ˌpɑːk tʃʊŋ ˈhiː/ (1917–79), South Korean statesman, President 1963–79. After staging a coup in 1961 he was elected President, assuming dictatorial powers in 1971. Under Park's presidency South Korea emerged as a leading industrial nation.

Parker[1], Charlie (1920–55), American saxophonist; full name *Charles Christopher Parker*; known as **Bird** or **Yardbird**. From 1944 he played with Thelonious Monk and Dizzy Gillespie, and became one of the key figures of the bebop movement.

Parker[2], Dorothy (Rothschild) (1893–1967), American humorist, literary critic, and writer. From 1927 Parker wrote book reviews and short stories for the *New Yorker* magazine, becoming one of its legendary wits.

parkerizing ▶**noun** [mass noun] a process for rustproofing iron or steel by brief immersion in a hot acidic solution of a metal phosphate.
– DERIVATIVES **parkerized** adjective.
– ORIGIN 1920s: from *Parker* Rust-Proof Company of America (which introduced the process) + **-IZE** + **-ING**[1].

parkie (also **parky**) ▶**noun** (pl. **-ies**) informal a park-keeper.

parkin ▶**noun** [mass noun] Brit. a kind of dark gingerbread, typically with a soft, dry texture, made with oatmeal and treacle or molasses, especially in Yorkshire around Bonfire Night.
– ORIGIN early 19th cent.: perhaps from the family name *Parkin*, diminutive of *Per* 'Peter'.

parking light ▶**noun** a small light on the side of a vehicle, for use when parking the vehicle at night.

parking lot ▶**noun** see **LOT** (sense 5).

parking meter ▶**noun** a machine next to a parking space in a street, into which the driver puts money so as to be authorized to park the vehicle for a particular length of time.

parking ticket ▶**noun** a notice telling a driver of a fine imposed on them for parking illegally, typically written by a traffic warden and attached to a car windscreen.

Parkinsonism ▶**noun** another term for **PARKINSON'S DISEASE**.

Parkinson's disease ▶**noun** [mass noun] a progressive disease of the nervous system marked by tremor, muscular rigidity, and slow, imprecise movement, chiefly affecting middle-aged and elderly people. It is associated with degeneration of the basal ganglia of the brain and a deficiency of the neurotransmitter dopamine.
– ORIGIN late 19th cent.: named after James *Parkinson* (1755–1824), English surgeon.

Parkinson's law the notion that work expands so as to fill the time available for its completion.
– ORIGIN 1950s: named after Cyril Northcote *Parkinson* (1909–93), English writer.

parkland ▶**noun** [mass noun] (also **parklands**) open land consisting of fields and scattered groups of trees.

parkway ▶**noun 1** N. Amer. an open landscaped highway.
2 [in names] Brit. a railway station with extensive parking facilities: *Didcot Parkway.*

parky[1] ▶**adjective** (**parkier**, **parkiest**) Brit. informal chilly: *it was parky on Bradfield Moors last week.*
– ORIGIN late 19th cent.: of unknown origin.

parky[2] ▶**noun** variant spelling of **PARKIE**.

Parl. Brit. ▶**abbreviation** for ■Parliament. ■Parliamentary.

parlance /ˈpɑːl(ə)ns/ ▶**noun** [mass noun] a particular way of speaking or using words, especially a way common to those with a particular job or interest: *dated terms that were once in common parlance* | *medical parlance.*
– ORIGIN late 16th cent. (denoting speech or debate): from Old French, from *parler* 'speak', from Latin *parabola* 'comparison' (in late Latin 'speech').

parlando /pɑːˈlandəʊ/ Music ▶**adverb** & **adjective** (with reference to singing) expressive or declamatory in the manner of speech.
▶**noun** [mass noun] composition or performance in this manner.
– ORIGIN Italian, literally 'speaking'.

parlay /ˈpɑːleɪ/ N. Amer. ▶**verb** [with obj.] (**parlay something into**) turn an initial stake or winnings from a previous bet into (a greater amount) by gambling: *it involved parlaying a small bankroll into big winnings.*
▶**noun** a cumulative series of bets in which winnings accruing from each transaction are used as a stake for a further bet.
– ORIGIN late 19th cent.: from French *paroli*, from Italian, from *paro* 'like', from Latin *par* 'equal'.

parley /ˈpɑːli/ ▶**noun** (pl. **-eys**) a conference between opposing sides in a dispute, especially a discussion of terms for an armistice.
▶**verb** (**-eys**, **-eyed**) [no obj.] hold a conference with the opposing side to discuss terms: *they disagreed over whether to* ***parley with*** *the enemy.*
– ORIGIN late Middle English (denoting speech or debate): perhaps from Old French *parlee* 'spoken', feminine past participle of the verb *parler*.

parliament /ˈpɑːləm(ə)nt/ ▶**noun** (**Parliament**) (in the UK) the highest legislature, consisting of the Sovereign, the House of Lords, and the House of Commons: *the Secretary of State will lay proposals before Parliament* | *an Act of Parliament.*
■the members of this legislature for a particular period, especially between one dissolution and the next: *the act was passed by the last parliament of the reign.* ■a similar legislature in other nations and states: *the Russian parliament.*
– ORIGIN Middle English: from Old French *parlement* 'speaking', from the verb *parler*.

parliamentarian ▶**noun 1** a member of a parliament, especially one well versed in parliamentary procedure and experienced in debate.
2 historical a supporter of parliament in the English Civil War; a Roundhead.
▶**adjective 1** of or relating to parliament or its members: *parliamentarian committees.*
2 historical of or relating to the Roundheads.
– DERIVATIVES **parliamentarianism** noun.

parliamentary ▶**adjective** relating to, enacted by, or suitable for a parliament: *a parliamentary candidate* | *parliamentary legislation.*

Parliamentary Commissioner for Administration ▶**noun** (in the UK) an official appointed to investigate complaints by individuals against public authorities. Also called the **OMBUDSMAN**.

Parliamentary Counsel ▶**noun** (in the UK) a group of barristers employed as civil servants to draft government bills and amendments.

parliamentary party ▶**noun** the members of a political party who are in parliament, as distinguished from the party in the country as a whole.

parliamentary private secretary ▶**noun** (in the UK) a Member of Parliament assisting a government minister.

parliamentary undersecretary ▶**noun** (in the UK) a Member of Parliament in a department of state, ranking below a minister.

parlour (US **parlor**) ▶**noun 1** dated a sitting room in a private house.
■a room in a public building for receiving guests: *the mayor's parlour.* ■a room in a monastery or convent that is set aside for conversation.
2 [usu. with modifier] chiefly N. Amer. a shop or business providing specified goods or services: *an ice-cream parlour* | *a funeral parlour.*
3 (also **milking parlour**) a room or building equipped for milking cows.
▶**adjective** [attrib.] dated, derogatory denoting a person who professes but does not actively give support for a specified (especially radical) political view: *the so-called radicalism of the new 'parlour communists'.*
– ORIGIN Middle English: from Anglo-Norman

French *parlur* 'place for speaking', from Latin *parlare* 'speak'.

parlour car ▶ noun N. Amer. a luxuriously fitted railway carriage, typically with individually reserved seats.

parlour game ▶ noun an indoor game, especially a word game.

parlourmaid ▶ noun historical a maid employed to wait at table.

parlour palm ▶ noun a small Central American palm which is a popular pot plant.
● *Chamaedorea elegans*, family Palmae.

parlous /ˈpɑːləs/ ▶ adjective archaic or humorous full of danger or uncertainty; precarious: *the parlous state of the economy | the General's position was parlous.*
▶ adverb archaic greatly or excessively: *she is parlous handsome.*
– DERIVATIVES **parlously** adverb, **parlousness** noun.
– ORIGIN late Middle English: contraction of **PERILOUS**.

Parma /ˈpɑːmə, Italian ˈparma/ a province of northern Italy, south of the River Po in Emilia-Romagna.
■ its capital; pop. 193,990 (1990). Founded by the Romans in 183 BC, it became a bishopric in the 9th century AD and capital of the duchy of Parma and Piacenza in about 1547.

Parma ham ▶ noun [mass noun] a type of ham which is eaten uncooked.

Parma violet ▶ noun a sweet violet of a variety with a heavy scent and lavender-coloured flowers which are often crystallized and used for food decoration.

parma wallaby ▶ noun a small dark brown Australian wallaby, restricted to the rainforests of New South Wales.
● *Macropus parma*, family Macropodidae.
– ORIGIN mid 19th cent.: *parma* (probably from a New South Wales Aboriginal language) was applied by George Robert Waterhouse (1810–88), English naturalist.

Parmenides /pɑːˈmɛnɪdiːz/ (fl. 5th century BC), Greek philosopher. Born in Elea in SW Italy, he founded the Eleatic school of philosophers. In his work *On Nature*, written in hexameter verse, he maintained that the apparent motion and changing forms of the universe are in fact manifestations of an unchanging and indivisible reality.

Parmentier /ˈpɑːmɒtɪeɪ/ ▶ adjective [postpositive] cooked or served with potatoes.
– ORIGIN from the name of Antoine A. *Parmentier* (1737–1813), the French agriculturalist who popularized the potato in France.

Parmesan /pɑːmɪˈzan/ ▶ noun [mass noun] a hard, dry cheese used in grated form, especially on Italian dishes.
– ORIGIN early 16th cent.: from French, from Italian *parmigiano* 'of Parma', where it was originally made.

Parmigiana /ˌpɑːmɪˈdʒɑːnə, Italian ˌparmiˈdʒana/ ▶ adjective [postpositive] cooked or served with Parmesan cheese.
▶ noun a dish cooked in this way.
– ORIGIN Italian, feminine of *Parmigiano* 'of Parma'.

Parmigianino /ˌpɑːmɪdʒaˈniːnəʊ, Italian ˌparmidʒaˈnino/ (also **Parmigiano** /-ˈdʒɑːnəʊ, Italian -ˈdʒano/) (1503–40), Italian painter; born *Girolano Francesco Maria Mazzola*. He made an important contribution to early mannerism with the graceful figure style of his frescoes and portraits. Notable works: *Madonna with the Long Neck* (1534).

Parnassian /pɑːˈnasɪən/ ▶ adjective **1** relating to poetry; poetic.
2 of or relating to a group of French poets of the late 19th century who emphasized strictness of form, named from the anthology *Le Parnasse contemporain* (1866).
▶ noun a member of this group of French poets.

Parnassus, grass of ▶ noun see **GRASS OF PARNASSUS**.

Parnassus, Mount /pɑːˈnasəs/ a mountain in central Greece, just north of Delphi, rising to a height of 2,457 m (8,064 ft). Held to be sacred by the ancient Greeks, as was the spring of Castalia on its southern slopes, it was associated with Apollo and the Muses and regarded as a symbol of poetry. Greek name **PARNASSÓS** /ˌparnaˈsɔs/.

Parnell /pɑːˈnɛl/, Charles Stewart (1846–91), Irish

nationalist leader. Parnell became leader of the Irish Home Rule faction in 1880 and raised the profile of Irish affairs through obstructive parliamentary tactics. He was forced to retire from public life in 1890 after the exposure of his adultery with Mrs Kitty O'Shea.
– DERIVATIVES **Parnellite** adjective & noun.

parochial /pəˈrəʊkɪəl/ ▶ adjective of or relating to a Church parish: *the parochial church council.*
■ having a limited or narrow outlook or scope: *parochial attitudes | their interests are too parochial.*
– DERIVATIVES **parochialism** noun, **parochiality** noun, **parochially** adverb.
– ORIGIN late Middle English: from Old French, from ecclesiastical Latin *parochialis* 'relating to an ecclesiastical district', from *parochia* (see **PARISH**).

parochial school ▶ noun North American term for **CHURCH SCHOOL**.

parody ▶ noun (pl. **-ies**) an imitation of the style of a particular writer, artist, or genre with deliberate exaggeration for comic effect: *the film is a parody of the horror genre | [mass noun] his provocative use of parody.*
■ an imitation or a version of something that falls far short of the real thing; a travesty: *he gave her a parody of a smile.*
▶ verb (**-ies, -ied**) [with obj.] produce a humorously exaggerated imitation of (a writer, artist, or genre).
■ mimic humorously: *he parodied his friend's voice.*
– DERIVATIVES **parodic** adjective, **parodist** noun.
– ORIGIN late 16th cent.: via late Latin from Greek *parōidia* 'burlesque poem', from *para-* 'beside' (expressing alteration) + *ōidē* 'ode'.

par of exchange ▶ noun see **PAR**¹ (sense 2).

parol /pəˈrəʊl, ˈpar(ə)l/ ▶ adjective Law given or expressed orally: *the parol evidence.*
■ (of a document) agreed orally, or in writing but not under seal: *there was a parol agreement.*
– PHRASES **by parol** by oral declaration.
– ORIGIN late 15th cent. (as a noun): from Old French *parole* 'word' (see **PAROLE**).

parole ▶ noun [mass noun] **1** the release of a prisoner temporarily (for a special purpose) or permanently before the expiry of a sentence, on the promise of good behaviour: *he committed a burglary while on parole.*
■ [count noun] historical a promise or undertaking given by a prisoner of war not to escape or, if released, to return to custody under stated conditions.
2 Linguistics the actual linguistic behaviour or performance of individuals, in contrast to the linguistic system of a community. Contrasted with **LANGUE**.
▶ verb [with obj.] (usu. **be paroled**) release (a prisoner) on parole: *he was paroled after serving nine months of a two-year sentence.*
– DERIVATIVES **parolee** noun.
– ORIGIN late 15th cent.: from Old French, literally 'word', also 'formal promise', from ecclesiastical Latin *parabola* 'speech'; compare with **PAROL**.

paronomasia /ˌparənəˈmeɪzɪə/ ▶ noun a play on words; a pun.
– ORIGIN late 16th cent.: via Latin from Greek *paronomasia*, from *para-* 'beside' (expressing alteration) + *onomasia* 'naming' (from *onomazein* 'to name', from *onoma* 'a name').

paronym /ˈparənɪm/ ▶ noun Linguistics a word which is a derivative of another and has a related meaning: *'wisdom' is a paronym of 'wise'.*
■ a word formed by adaptation of a foreign word: *'preface' is a paronym of Latin 'prefatio'.* Contrasted with **HETERONYM**.
– DERIVATIVES **paronymic** adjective, **paronymous** adjective, **paronymy** noun.
– ORIGIN mid 19th cent.: from Greek *parōnumon*, neuter (used as a noun) of *parōnumos* 'naming by modification', from *para-* 'beside' + *onuma* 'a name'.

Paros /ˈparɒs, ˈpɛːrɒs/ a Greek island in the southern Aegean, in the Cyclades. It is noted for the translucent white Parian marble which has been quarried there since the 6th century BC.

parotid /pəˈrɒtɪd/ Anatomy ▶ adjective relating to, situated near, or affecting a parotid gland.
▶ noun short for **PAROTID GLAND**.
– ORIGIN late 17th cent.: via Latin from Greek *parōtis*, *parōtid-*, from *para-* 'beside' + *ous*, *ōt-* 'ear'.

parotid gland ▶ noun Anatomy either of a pair of large salivary glands situated just in front of each ear.

parotitis /ˌparəˈtʌɪtɪs/ ▶ noun [mass noun] Medicine inflammation of a parotid gland, especially (**infectious parotitis**) mumps.

-parous ▶ combining form Biology bearing offspring of a specified number or reproducing in a specified manner: *multiparous | viviparous.*
– ORIGIN from Latin *-parus* '-bearing' (from *parere* 'bring forth, produce') + **-OUS**.

Parousia /pəˈruːzɪə/ ▶ noun Christian Theology another term for **SECOND COMING**.
– ORIGIN Greek, literally 'being present'.

paroxysm /ˈparəksɪz(ə)m/ ▶ noun a sudden attack or violent expression of a particular emotion or activity: *a paroxysm of weeping.*
■ Medicine a sudden recurrence or attack of a disease; a sudden worsening of symptoms.
– DERIVATIVES **paroxysmal** adjective.
– ORIGIN late Middle English: from French *paroxysme*, via medieval Latin from Greek *paroxusmos*, from *paroxunein* 'exasperate', from *para-* 'beyond' + *oxunein* 'sharpen' (from *oxus* 'sharp').

paroxytone /pəˈrɒksɪtəʊn/ ▶ adjective (especially in ancient Greek) having an acute accent on the last syllable but one.
▶ noun a word with such an accent.
– ORIGIN mid 18th cent.: from modern Latin *paroxytonus*, from Greek *paroxutonos*, from *para-* 'alongside' + *oxutonos* 'sharp pitch'.

parp informal ▶ noun a honking sound produced by, or like that produced by, a car horn.
▶ verb [no obj.] make such a sound.
– ORIGIN 1950s: imitative.

parpen /ˈpɑːp(ə)n/ ▶ noun a stone passing through a wall from side to side, with two smooth vertical faces.
– ORIGIN Middle English: from Old French *parpain* 'length of a stone', probably based on Latin *perpes* 'continuous'.

parquet /ˈpɑːkɪ, ˈpɑːkeɪ/ ▶ noun **1** (also **parquet flooring**) [mass noun] flooring composed of wooden blocks arranged in a geometric pattern.
2 N. Amer. the ground floor of a theatre or auditorium, especially the orchestra pit.
3 (**the Parquet**) (in France and French-speaking countries) the branch of the administration of the law that deals with the prosecution of crime.
– ORIGIN late 17th cent. (as a verb, especially as *parqueted*): from French, literally 'small park (i.e. delineated area)'. The noun dates from the early 19th cent.

parquetry /ˈpɑːkɪtri/ ▶ noun [mass noun] inlaid work of blocks of various woods arranged in a geometric pattern, especially for flooring or furniture.

Parr, Katherine (1512–48), sixth and last wife of Henry VIII. Having married the king in 1543, she influenced his decision to restore the succession to his daughters Mary and Elizabeth (later Mary I and Elizabeth I respectively).

parr ▶ noun (pl. same) a young salmon (or trout) between the stages of fry and smolt, distinguished by dark rounded patches evenly spaced along its sides.
– ORIGIN early 18th cent.: of unknown origin.

parrakeet ▶ noun variant spelling of **PARAKEET**.

parramatta /ˌparəˈmatə/ (also **paramatta**) ▶ noun [mass noun] a fine-quality twill fabric with a weft of worsted and a warp of cotton or silk, used originally as a dress material and now particularly in the making of rubber-proofed garments.
– ORIGIN early 19th cent.: named after *Parramatta*, a city in New South Wales, Australia, which was the site of a prison whose inmates manufactured the cloth for clothing supplied to the convict servants of settlers.

parricide /ˈparɪsʌɪd/ ▶ noun [mass noun] the killing of a parent or other near relative.
■ [count noun] a person who commits parricide.
– DERIVATIVES **parricidal** adjective.
– ORIGIN late 16th cent.: from French, from Latin *parricidium* 'murder of a parent', with first element of unknown origin, but for long associated with Latin *pater* 'father' and *parens* 'parent'.

parrot ▶ noun a bird, often vividly coloured, with a short downcurved hooked bill, grasping feet, and a raucous voice, found especially in the tropics and feeding on fruits and seeds. Many are popular as cage birds, and some are able to mimic the human voice.

• Order Psittaciformes: numerous species, sometimes all placed in the family Psittacidae. The order also contains the cockatoos, lories, lovebirds, macaws, conures, and budgerigar.

▶ **verb** (**parroted**, **parroting**) [with obj.] repeat mechanically: *encouraging students to parrot back information.*

– ORIGIN early 16th cent.: probably from dialect French *perrot*, diminutive of the male given name *Pierre* 'Peter'. Compare with **PARAKEET**.

parrotbill ▶ **noun** a tit-like Asian songbird with brown and grey plumage and a short arched bill.
• Family Panuridae (or Paradoxornithidae): two genera and several species, including the bearded tit or reedling.

parrot-fashion ▶ **adverb** without thought or understanding; mechanically: *she repeated the phrase parrot-fashion.*

parrot fever ▶ **noun** less formal term for **PSITTACOSIS**.

parrotfish ▶ **noun** (pl. same or **-fishes**) **1** any of a number of brightly coloured marine fish with a parrot-like beak, which they use to scrape food from coral and other hard surfaces:
• a widespread fish of warm seas which may secrete a mucous cocoon to deter predators (family Scaridae: *Scarus* and other genera). • an edible fish of the southern Indian ocean (*Oplegnathus conwayi*, family Oplegnathidae).
2 Austral. a brightly coloured marine fish, especially one of the wrasse family.
• Several species in the family Labridae.

parrotlet ▶ **noun** a tiny tropical American parrot with mainly green plumage and a short tail.
• Family Psittacidae: three genera, in particular *Forpus* and *Touit*, and several species.

parrot tulip ▶ **noun** a cultivated tulip of a variety which has irregularly fringed or wavy petals, typically of two colours.

Parry, Sir (Charles) Hubert (Hastings) (1848–1918), English composer. Parry's best-known work is his setting of William Blake's poem 'Jerusalem' (1916), which has acquired the status of a national song.

parry ▶ **verb** (**-ies**, **-ied**) [with obj.] ward off (a weapon or attack), especially with a countermove: *he parried the blow by holding his sword vertically.*
■ answer (a question or accusation) evasively: *he parried questions from reporters outside the building.*

▶ **noun** (pl. **-ies**) an act of warding off a blow.
■ an evasive reply: *her question met with a polite parry.*

– ORIGIN late 17th cent.: probably representing French *parez!* 'ward off!', imperative of *parer*, from Italian *parare* 'ward off'.

parse /pɑːz/ ▶ **verb** [with obj.] resolve (a sentence) into its component parts and describe their syntactic roles.
■ Computing analyse (a string or text) into logical syntactic components, typically in order to test conformability to a logical grammar.

▶ **noun** Computing an act of or the result obtained by parsing a string or a text.

– ORIGIN mid 16th cent.: perhaps from Middle English *pars* 'parts of speech', from Old French *pars* 'parts' (influenced by Latin *pars* 'part').

parsec /ˈpɑːsɛk/ ▶ **noun** a unit of distance used in astronomy, equal to about 3.25 light years (3.08×10^{16} metres). One parsec corresponds to the distance at which the mean radius of the earth's orbit subtends an angle of one second of arc.

– ORIGIN early 20th cent.: blend of **PARALLAX** and **SECOND**[2].

Parsee /pɑːˈsiː, ˈpɑːsiː/ ▶ **noun** an adherent of Zoroastrianism, especially a descendant of those Zoroastrians who fled to India from Muslim persecution in Persia during the 7th–8th centuries.

– ORIGIN from Persian *pārsī* 'Persian', from *pārs* 'Persia'.

parser ▶ **noun** Computing a program for parsing.

parse tree ▶ **noun** Linguistics a diagrammatic representation of the parsed structure of a sentence or string.

Parsifal /ˈpɑːsɪf(ə)l/ another name for **PERCEVAL**[1].

parsimonious /ˌpɑːsɪˈməʊnɪəs/ ▶ **adjective** very unwilling to spend money or use resources: *even the parsimonious Littler paid for drinks all round.*

– DERIVATIVES **parsimoniously** adverb, **parsimoniousness** noun.

parsimony /ˈpɑːsɪməni/ ▶ **noun** [mass noun] extreme unwillingness to spend money or use resources: *a great tradition of public design has been shattered by government parsimony.*

– PHRASES **principle** (or **law**) **of parsimony** the scientific principle that things are usually connected or behave in the simplest or most economical way, especially with reference to alternative evolutionary pathways. Compare with **OCCAM'S RAZOR**.

– ORIGIN late Middle English: from Latin *parsimonia*, *parcimonia*, from *parcere* 'be sparing'.

parsley ▶ **noun** [mass noun] a biennial plant with white flowers and aromatic leaves which are either crinkly or flat and are used as a culinary herb and for garnishing food.
• *Petroselinum crispum*, family Umbelliferae (or Apiaceae; the **parsley family**). Members of this family have their flowers arranged in umbels and are known as umbellifers; typical members include hogweed and hemlock as well as many food plants and herbs (carrot, parsnip, celery, fennel, anise).

– ORIGIN Old English *petersilie*, via late Latin based on Greek *petroselinon*, from *petra* 'rock' + *selinon* 'parsley', influenced in Middle English by Old French *peresil*, of the same origin.

parsley fern ▶ **noun** a fern with finely divided fronds resembling parsley leaves, found typically on rocky ground in mountainous and boreal areas.
• Genus *Cryptogramma*, family Adiantaceae: several species.

parsley piert /ˌpɑːslɪ ˈpɪət/ ▶ **noun** a small hairy European plant with divided leaves, growing as a weed of fields and waste places.
• *Aphanes arvensis*, family Rosaceae.

– ORIGIN late 16th cent.: probably an altered form of French *perce-pierre*, literally 'pierce stone', used to denote various plants living in rock or wall crevices.

parsnip ▶ **noun 1** a long tapering cream-coloured root with a sweet flavour.
2 the Eurasian plant of the parsley family which yields this root.
• *Pastinaca sativa*, family Umbelliferae.

– ORIGIN late Middle English: from Old French *pasnaie*, from Latin *pastinaca* (related to *pastinare* 'dig and trench the ground'). The change in the ending was due to association with **NEEP**.

parson ▶ **noun** a beneficed member of the clergy; a rector or a vicar.
■ informal any member of the clergy, especially a Protestant one.

– DERIVATIVES **parsonic** adjective, **parsonical** adjective.

– ORIGIN Middle English: from Old French *persone*, from Latin *persona* 'person' (in medieval Latin 'rector').

parsonage ▶ **noun** a church house provided for a member of the clergy.

parson-bird ▶ **noun** NZ another term for **TUI**.

Parsons, Sir Charles (Algernon) (1854–1931), British engineer, scientist, and manufacturer. He patented and built the first practical steam turbine in 1884, designed to drive electricity generators. He also developed steam turbines for marine propulsion, and his experimental vessel *Turbinia* caused a sensation in 1897.

parson's nose ▶ **noun** informal the fatty extremity of the rump of a cooked fowl.

pars pro toto /ˌpɑːz prəʊ ˈtəʊtəʊ/ ▶ **noun** formal a part or aspect of something taken as representative of the whole.

– ORIGIN Latin, literally 'part on behalf of the whole'.

part ▶ **noun 1** a piece or segment of something such as an object, activity, or period of time, which combined with other pieces makes up the whole: *divide the circle into three equal parts | the early part of 1989.*
■ an element or constituent that belongs to something and is essential to its nature: *I was part of the family.* ■ a component of a machine: *the production of aircraft parts.* ■ a measure allowing comparison between the amounts of different ingredients used in a mixture: *use a mix of one part cement to five parts ballast.* ■ a specified fraction of a whole: *they paid a twentieth part of the cost.* ■ a division of a book treated as a unit in which a particular topic is discussed. ■ the amount of a serial that is published or broadcast at one time. ■ (**parts**) informal short for **PRIVATE PARTS**.
2 some but not all of something: *the painting tells only part of the story.*
■ a point on or area of something: *hold the furthest part of your leg that you can reach.* ■ (**parts**) informal a region, especially one not clearly specified or delimited: *they wanted to know why he was loitering in these parts.*
3 a character as represented in a play or film; a role played by an actor or actress: *she played a lot of leading parts | he took the part of Prospero.*
■ the words and directions to be learned and performed by an actor in such a role: *she was memorizing a part.* ■ Music a melody or other constituent of harmony assigned to a particular voice or instrument in a musical work: *he coped well with the percussion part.* ■ the contribution made by someone or something to an action or situation: *he played a key part in ending the revolt | he may be jailed for his part in the robbery.* ■ the behaviour appropriate to or expected of a person in a particular role or situation; a person's duty: *in such a place his part is to make good.* ■ the chance to be involved in something: *they were legislating for a future they had no part in.*
4 (**parts**) archaic abilities.
5 N. Amer. a parting in the hair.

▶ **verb** [no obj.] (of two things) move away from each other: *his lips parted in a smile.*
■ divide to leave a central space: *at that moment the mist parted.* ■ [with obj.] cause to divide or move apart, leaving a central space: *she parted the ferns and looked between them.* ■ leave someone's company: *there was a good deal of kissing and more congratulations before we parted.* ■ (**be parted**) leave the company of someone: *she can't bear to be parted from her daughter again.* ■ (**part with**) give up possession of; hand over: *even quite small companies parted with large sums.* ■ [with obj.] separate (the hair of the head on either side of the parting) with a comb.

▶ **adverb** to some extent; partly (often used to contrast different parts of something): *the city is now part slum, part consumer paradise.*

– PHRASES **be part and parcel of** be an essential feature or element of: *it's best to accept that some inconveniences are part and parcel of travel.* **for my** (or **his**, **her**, etc.) **part** used to focus attention on one person or group and distinguish them from others involved in a situation: *I for my part find the story less than convincing.* **in part** to some extent though not entirely: *the cause of the illness is at least in part psychological.* **look the part** have an appearance or style of dress appropriate to a particular role or situation. **a man of** (**many**) **parts** a man showing great ability in many different areas. **on the part of** (or **on my**, **their**, etc. **part**) used to ascribe responsibility for something to someone: *there was a series of errors on my part.* **part company** (of two or more people) cease to be together; go in different directions: *they parted company outside the Red Lion.* ■ (of two or more parties) cease to associate with each other, especially as the result of a disagreement: *the chairman has **parted company with** the club.* **take part** join in an activity; be involved: *we have come here to **take part in** a major game | they ran away and took no part in the battle.* **take the part of** give support and encouragement to (someone) in a dispute.

– ORIGIN Old English (denoting a part of speech), from Latin *pars*, *part-*. The verb (originally in Middle English in the sense 'divide into parts') is from Old French *partir*, from Latin *partire*, *partiri* 'divide, share'.

partake ▶ **verb** (past **partook**; past participle **partaken**) [no obj.] (**partake in**) formal join in (an activity): *visitors can partake in golfing or clay pigeon shooting.*
■ (**partake of**) be characterized by (a quality): *the birth of twins became an event which partook of the mythic.* ■ (**partake of**) eat or drink (something): *she had partaken of a cheese sandwich and a cup of coffee.*

– DERIVATIVES **partaker** noun.

– ORIGIN mid 16th cent.: back-formation from earlier *partaker* 'person who takes a part'.

parter ▶ **noun** [in combination] a broadcast or published work with a specified number of parts: *the first in a six-parter.*

parterre /pɑːˈtɛː/ ▶ **noun 1** a level space in a garden occupied by an ornamental arrangement of flower beds.
2 chiefly US the part of the ground floor of a theatre auditorium behind the orchestra pit, especially the part beneath the balconies.

– ORIGIN early 17th cent.: from French, from *par terre* 'on the ground'.

part exchange Brit. ▶ **noun** [mass noun] a method of buying something in which an article that one already owns is given as part of the payment for another, more expensive, article: *he sold the car **in part exchange** for another vehicle.*

▶ **verb** (**part-exchange**) [with obj.] give or take (an article) as part of such a transaction.

parthenocarpy /ˈpɑːθɪnə(ʊ)ˌkɑːpi/ ▶ **noun** [mass noun] Botany the development of a fruit without prior fertilization.

p

– DERIVATIVES **parthenocarpic** adjective.
– ORIGIN early 20th cent.: from German *Parthenocarpie*, from Greek *parthenos* 'virgin' + *karpos* 'fruit'.

parthenogenesis /ˌpɑːθɪnə(ʊ)ˈdʒɛnɪsɪs/ ▶ **noun** [mass noun] Biology reproduction from an ovum without fertilization, especially as a normal process in some invertebrates and lower plants.
– DERIVATIVES **parthenogenetic** adjective, **parthenogenetically** adverb.
– ORIGIN mid 19th cent.: modern Latin, from Greek *parthenos* 'virgin' + *genesis* 'creation'.

Parthenon /ˈpɑːθɪnən/ the temple of Athene Parthenos, built on the Acropolis in 447–432 BC by Pericles to honour Athens' patron goddess and to commemorate the recent Greek victory over the Persians. It was designed by Ictinus and Callicrates with sculptures by Phidias.
– ORIGIN from Greek *parthenos* 'virgin'.

Parthia /ˈpɑːθɪə/ an ancient kingdom which lay SE of the Caspian Sea in present-day Iran. From *c.*250 BC to *c.*230 AD the Parthians ruled an empire stretching from the Euphrates to the Indus.
– DERIVATIVES **Parthian** noun & adjective.

Parthian shot ▶ **noun** another term for **PARTING SHOT**.
– ORIGIN late 19th cent.: so named because of the trick used by Parthians of shooting arrows backwards while in real or pretended flight.

partial ▶ **adjective 1** existing only in part; incomplete: *a question to which we have only partial answers.*
2 favouring one side in a dispute above the other; biased: *the paper gave a distorted and very partial view of the situation.*
■ [predic.] (**partial to**) having a liking for: *you know I'm very partial to bacon and eggs.*
▶ **noun** Music a component of a musical sound; an overtone or harmonic.
– DERIVATIVES **partially** adverb [as submodifier] *a partially open door*, **partialness** noun.
– ORIGIN late Middle English (in the sense 'inclined to favour one party in a cause'): from Old French *parcial* (sense 2), French *partiel* (sense 1), from late Latin *partialis*, from *pars, part-* 'part'.

partial derivative ▶ **noun** Mathematics a derivative of a function of two or more variables with respect to one variable, the other(s) being treated as constant.

partial differential equation ▶ **noun** Mathematics an equation containing one or more partial derivatives.

partial eclipse ▶ **noun** an eclipse of a celestial body in which only part of the luminary is obscured or darkened.

partial fraction ▶ **noun** Mathematics each of two or more fractions into which a more complex fraction can be decomposed as a sum.

partiality ▶ **noun** [mass noun] unfair bias in favour of one thing or person compared with another; favouritism: *an attack on the partiality of judges.*
■ [count noun] a particular liking or fondness for something: *he had a distinct **partiality for** Bath Olivers.*
– ORIGIN late Middle English: from Old French *parcialite*, from medieval Latin *partialitas*, based on Latin *pars, part-* 'part'.

partially sighted ▶ **adjective** having a visual impairment: *a partially sighted child.*

partial order (also **partial ordering**) ▶ **noun** Mathematics a transitive antisymmetric relation among the elements of a set, which does not necessarily apply to each pair of elements.

partial pressure ▶ **noun** Chemistry the pressure that would be exerted by one of the gases in a mixture if it occupied the same volume on its own.

partial product ▶ **noun** Mathematics the product of one term of a multiplicand and one term of its multiplier.
■ the product of the first *n* terms of a large or infinite series, where *n* is a finite integer (including 1).

partible ▶ **adjective** involving or denoting a system of inheritance in which a deceased person's estate is divided equally among the heirs.
– DERIVATIVES **partibility** noun.
– ORIGIN late Middle English (in the sense 'able to be parted'): from late Latin *partibilis*, from Latin *partiri* 'divide into parts'.

participant ▶ **noun** a person who takes part in something: *staff are to be active **participants in** the decision-making process.*
– ORIGIN late Middle English: from Latin *participant-*, literally 'sharing in', from the verb *participare* (see **PARTICIPATE**).

participate ▶ **verb** [no obj.] **1** take part: *thousands **participated in** a nationwide strike.*
2 (**participate of**) archaic have or possess (a particular quality): *both members participate of harmony.*
– DERIVATIVES **participation** noun, **participative** adjective, **participator** noun, **participatory** adjective.
– ORIGIN early 16th cent.: from Latin *participat-* 'shared in', from the verb *participare*, based on *pars, part-* 'part' + *capere* 'take'.

participial adjective ▶ **noun** Grammar an adjective that is a participle in origin and form, such as *burnt, cutting, engaged.*

participle /ˈpɑːtɪsɪp(ə)l/ ▶ **noun** Grammar a word formed from a verb (e.g. *going, gone, being, been*) and used as an adjective (e.g. *working woman, burnt toast*) or a noun (e.g. *good breeding*). In English participles are also used to make compound verb forms (e.g. *is going, has been*). Compare with **GERUND**.
– DERIVATIVES **participial** /-ˈsɪpɪəl/ adjective, **participially** /-ˈsɪpɪəli/ adverb.
– ORIGIN late Middle English: from Old French, by-form of *participe*, from Latin *participium* '(verbal form) sharing (the functions of a noun)', from *participare* 'share in'.

particle ▶ **noun 1** a minute portion of matter: *tiny **particles of** dust.*
■ (also **subatomic** or **elementary particle**) Physics any of numerous subatomic constituents of the physical world that interact with each other, including electrons, neutrinos, photons, and alpha particles. ■ [with negative] the least possible amount: *he agrees without hearing the least particle of evidence.* ■ Mathematics a hypothetical object having mass but no physical size.
2 Grammar a minor function word that has comparatively little meaning and does not inflect, in particular:
■ (in English) any of the class of words such as *in, up, off, over*, used with verbs to make phrasal verbs. ■ (in ancient Greek) any of the class of words such as *de* and *ge*, used for contrast and emphasis.
– ORIGIN late Middle English: from Latin *particula* 'little part', diminutive of *pars, part-*.

particle accelerator ▶ **noun** an apparatus for accelerating subatomic particles to high velocities by means of electric or electromagnetic fields. The accelerated particles are generally made to collide with other particles, either as a research technique or for the generation of high-energy X-rays and gamma rays.

particle board ▶ **noun** another term for **CHIPBOARD**.

particle physics ▶ **plural noun** [treated as sing.] the branch of physics that deals with the properties, relationships, and interactions of subatomic particles.

particoloured (US **particolored**) ▶ **adjective** having or consisting of two or more different colours: *particoloured Devon cattle.*
– ORIGIN early 16th cent.: from the adjective **PARTY**[2] + **COLOURED**.

particoloured bat ▶ **noun** a Eurasian bat with narrow pointed wings and dark brown fur with a frosted appearance on the back and a paler underside.
• *Vespertilio murinus*, family Vespertilionidae.

particular ▶ **adjective 1** [attrib.] used to single out an individual member of a specified group or class: *the action seems to discriminate against a particular group of companies.*
■ Logic denoting a proposition in which something is asserted of some but not all of a class. Contrasted with **UNIVERSAL**.
2 [attrib.] especially great or intense: *when handling or checking cash the cashier should exercise particular care.*
3 insisting that something should be correct or suitable in every detail; fastidious: *she is very **particular about** cleanliness.*
▶ **noun 1** Philosophy an individual item, as contrasted with a universal quality.
2 a detail: *he is wrong **in every particular**.*
■ (**particulars**) detailed information about someone or something: *a clerk took the woman's particulars.*
– PHRASES **in particular** especially (used to show that a statement applies to one person or thing more than any other): *he socialized with the other young people, one boy in particular.*
– ORIGIN late Middle English: from Old French *particuler*, from Latin *particularis* 'concerning a small part', from *particula* 'small part'.

Particular Baptist ▶ **noun** a member of a Baptist denomination holding the doctrine of the election and redemption of some but not all people.

particular integral ▶ **noun** Mathematics another term for **PARTICULAR SOLUTION**.

particular intention ▶ **noun** another term for **SPECIAL INTENTION**.

particularism ▶ **noun** [mass noun] exclusive attachment to one's own group, party, or nation.
■ the principle of leaving each state in an empire or federation free to govern itself and promote its own interests, without reference to those of the whole. ■ Theology the doctrine that some but not all people are elected and redeemed.
– DERIVATIVES **particularist** noun & adjective, **particularistic** adjective.
– ORIGIN early 19th cent.: from French *particularisme*, modern Latin *particularismus*, and German *Partikularismus*, based on Latin *particularis* 'concerning a small part'.

particularity ▶ **noun** (pl. **-ies**) [mass noun] the quality of being individual.
■ fullness or minuteness of detail in the treatment of something: *parties must present their case with some degree of accuracy and particularity.* ■ (**particularities**) small details: *the tedious particularities of daily life | he wanted to disregard the particularities and establish general laws.* ■ Christian Theology the doctrine of God's incarnation as Jesus as a particular person at a particular time and place.
– ORIGIN early 16th cent. (as *particularities* 'details'): from Old French *particularite* or late Latin *particularitas*, from Latin *particularis* 'concerning a small part'.

particularize (also **-ise**) ▶ **verb** [with obj.] formal mention or describe particularly; treat individually or in detail: *he was the first to particularize themes in the poetry.*
– DERIVATIVES **particularization** noun.

particularly ▶ **adverb 1** to a higher degree than is usual or average: *I don't particularly want to be reminded of that time |* [as submodifier] *particularly able students.*
■ used to single out a subject to which a statement is especially applicable: *the team's defence is excellent, particularly their two centre backs.*
2 so as to give special emphasis to a point; specifically: *he particularly asked that I should help you.*

particular solution ▶ **noun** Mathematics the most general form of the solution of a differential equation, containing arbitrary constants.

particulate /pɑːˈtɪkjʊlət, -eɪt, pə-/ ▶ **adjective** of, relating to, or in the form of minute separate particles: *particulate pollution.*
▶ **noun** (**particulates**) matter in such a form.
– ORIGIN late 19th cent.: from Latin *particula* 'particle' + **-ATE**[2].

parting ▶ **noun** [mass noun] **1** the action of leaving or being separated from someone: *they exchanged a few words on parting.*
■ [count noun] a leave-taking or departure: *the wrench of her parting from Stephen | anguished partings at railway stations.*
2 the action of dividing something into parts: *the parting of the Red Sea.*
■ [count noun] Brit. a line of scalp revealed in a person's hair by combing the hair away in opposite directions on either side: *his hair was dark, with a side parting.*
– PHRASES **a** (or **the**) **parting of the ways** a point at which two people must separate or at which a decision must be taken: *the best course is to seek an amicable parting of the ways.*

parting shot ▶ **noun** a final remark, typically a cutting one, made by someone at the moment of departure: *as her parting shot she told me never to phone her again.*

parti pris /ˌpɑːtɪ ˈpriː/ ▶ **noun** (pl. **partis pris** pronunc. same) a preconceived view; a bias.
▶ **adjective** prejudiced; biased.
– ORIGIN French, literally 'side taken'.

partisan /ˈpɑːtɪzan, ˌpɑːtɪˈzan/ ▶ **noun 1** a strong supporter of a party, cause, or person.
2 a member of an armed group formed to fight secretly against an occupying force, in particular

one operating in enemy-occupied Yugoslavia, Italy, and parts of eastern Europe in the Second World War.
▶**adjective** prejudiced in favour of a particular cause: *newspapers have become increasingly partisan.*
– DERIVATIVES **partisanship** noun.
– ORIGIN mid 16th cent.: from French, via Italian dialect from Italian *partigiano*, from *parte* 'part' (from Latin *pars, part-*).

partita /pɑːˈtiːtə/ ▶**noun** (pl. **partitas** or **partite** /-teɪ, -tiː/) Music a suite, typically for a solo instrument or chamber ensemble.
– ORIGIN late 19th cent.: from Italian, literally 'divided off', feminine past participle of *partire*.

partite /ˈpɑːtʌɪt/ ▶**adjective** [usu. in combination] divided into parts.
■Botany & Zoology (especially of a leaf or an insect's wing) divided to or nearly to the base.
– ORIGIN late 16th cent.: from Latin *partitus* 'divided up', past participle of *partiri*.

partition ▶**noun** [mass noun] (especially with reference to a country with separate areas of government) the action or state of dividing or being divided into parts: *the country's partition into separate states.*
■[count noun] a structure dividing a space into two parts, especially a light interior wall. ■Chemistry the distribution of a solute between two immiscible or slightly miscible solvents in contact with one another, in accordance with its differing solubility in each. ■[count noun] Computing each of a number of portions into which some operating systems divide memory or storage.
▶**verb** [with obj.] divide into parts: *an agreement was reached to partition the country.*
■divide (a room) into smaller rooms or areas by erecting partitions: *the hall was partitioned to contain the noise of the computers.* ■(**partition something off**) separate a part of a room from the rest by erecting a partition: *partition off part of a large bedroom to create a small bathroom.*
– DERIVATIVES **partitioner** noun, **partitionist** noun.
– ORIGIN late Middle English: from Latin *partitio(n-)*, from *partiri* 'divide into parts'.

partition coefficient ▶**noun** Chemistry the ratio of the concentrations of a solute in two immiscible or slightly miscible liquids, or in two solids, when it is in equilibrium across the interface between them.

partitive /ˈpɑːtɪtɪv/ Grammar ▶**adjective** denoting a grammatical construction used to indicate that only a part of a whole is referred to, for example *a slice of bacon, a series of accidents, some of the children.*
▶**noun** such a construction.
■a noun or pronoun used as the first term in such a construction.
– DERIVATIVES **partitively** adverb.

partitive genitive ▶**noun** Grammar a genitive used to indicate a whole divided into or regarded in parts, expressed in English by *of* as in *most of us.*

partizan ▶**noun** & **adjective** old-fashioned spelling of **PARTISAN**.

partly ▶**adverb** to some extent; not completely: *the result is partly a matter of skill and partly of chance | you're only partly right.*

partner ▶**noun** a person who takes part in an undertaking with another or others, especially in a business or firm with shared risks and profits.
■either of two people dancing together or playing a game or sport on the same side. ■either member of a married couple or of an established unmarried couple (often used neutrally to avoid specifying whether a couple is married or not): *she lived with her partner.* ■a person with whom one has sex; a lover. ■US dated or dialect a friendly form of address by one man to another: *how you doing, partner?*
▶**verb** [with obj.] be the partner of: *young farmers who partnered Isabel to the village dance.*
■[no obj.] N. Amer. associate as partners: *I never expected to partner with a man like you.*
– DERIVATIVES **partnerless** adjective.
– ORIGIN Middle English: alteration of *parcener* 'partner, joint heir', from Anglo-Norman French *parcener*, based on Latin *partitio(n-)* 'partition'. The change in the first syllable was due to association with **PART**.

partners' desk (also **partnership desk**) ▶**noun** a large flat-topped pedestal desk with space for two people to sit opposite each other.

partnership ▶**noun** [mass noun] the state of being a partner or partners: *we should go on working together in partnership.*
■[count noun] an association of two or more people as partners: *an increase in partnerships with housing associations.* ■[count noun] a business or firm owned and run by two or more partners. ■[count noun] a position as one of the partners in a business or firm. ■[count noun] Cricket the number of runs added by a pair of batsmen before one of them is dismissed or the innings ends.

part of speech ▶**noun** a category to which a word is assigned in accordance with its syntactic functions. In English the main parts of speech are noun, pronoun, adjective, determiner, verb, adverb, preposition, conjunction, and interjection. Also called **WORD CLASS**.

Parton, Dolly (Rebecca) (b.1946), American singer and songwriter. She is best known as a country music singer; her hits include 'Jolene' (1974).

partook past of **PARTAKE**.

partridge ▶**noun** (pl. same or **partridges**) a short-tailed game bird with mainly brown plumage, found chiefly in Europe and Asia.
● Family Phasianidae: several genera and many species, in particular the European **grey partridge** (*Perdix perdix*) and **red-legged partridge** (*Alectoris rufa*).
– ORIGIN Middle English *partrich*, from Old French *pertriz, perdriz*, from Latin *perdix*.

partridgeberry ▶**noun** (pl. **-ies**) either of two North American plants with edible red berries that are eaten by game birds.
● *Mitchella repens*, family Rubiaceae. ● the cowberry.
■the fruit of either of these plants.

partridge pea ▶**noun** a field pea of a variety with speckled seeds.

part-song ▶**noun** a secular song with three or more voice parts, typically unaccompanied, and homophonic rather than contrapuntal in style.

part-time ▶**adjective** & **adverb** for only part of the usual working day or week: [as adj.] *part-time jobs | a part-time teacher* | [as adv.] *he only worked part-time.*
– DERIVATIVES **part-timer** noun.

parturient /pɑːˈtjʊərɪənt/ ▶**adjective** technical (of a woman or female mammal) about to give birth; in labour.
▶**noun** a parturient woman.
– ORIGIN late 16th cent.: from Latin *parturient-* 'being in labour', from the verb *parturire*, inceptive of *parere* 'bring forth'.

parturition /ˌpɑːtjʊˈrɪʃ(ə)n/ ▶**noun** [mass noun] formal or technical the action of giving birth to young; childbirth: *the weeks following parturition.*
– ORIGIN mid 17th cent.: from late Latin *parturitio(n-)*, from *parturire* 'be in labour' (see **PARTURIENT**).

part-way ▶**adverb** part of the way: *part-way along the corridor he stopped.*

part-work ▶**noun** Brit. a publication appearing in several parts over a period of time.

party¹ ▶**noun** (pl. **-ies**) **1** a social gathering of invited guests, typically involving eating, drinking, and entertainment: *an engagement party.*
2 a formally constituted political group, typically operating on a national basis, that contests elections and attempts to form or take part in a government: *draft the party's election manifesto.*
■a group of people taking part in a particular activity or trip, especially one for which they have been chosen.
3 a person or people forming one side in an agreement or dispute: *a contract between two parties.*
■informal a person, especially one with specified characteristics: *an old party has been coming in to clean.*
▶**verb** (**-ies, -ied**) [no obj.] informal enjoy oneself at a party or other lively gathering, typically with drinking and music: *put on your glad rags and party!*
– PHRASES **be party** (or **a party**) **to** be involved in: *the manipulations I'd been party to.*
– ORIGIN Middle English (denoting a body of people united in opposition to others, also in sense 2): from Old French *partie*, based on Latin *partiri* 'divide into parts'. Sense 1 dates from the early 18th cent.

party² ▶**adjective** Heraldry divided into parts of different tinctures: *party per fess, or, and azure.*
– ORIGIN Middle English (in the sense 'particoloured'): from Old French *parti* 'parted', based on Latin *partitus* 'divided into parts' (from the verb *partiri*).

party boat ▶**noun** N. Amer. a boat available for hiring by a group of people who want to go fishing.

party line ▶**noun** **1** a policy, or the policies collectively, officially adopted by a political party: *they rarely fail to toe the party line.*
2 a telephone line or circuit shared by two or more subscribers.

party list ▶**noun** [mass noun] a voting system used with proportional representation, in which people vote for a party rather than a candidate. Each party is assigned a number of seats which reflects its share of the vote.
■[count noun] a list of candidates representing a party in this system.

party piece ▶**noun** Brit. a poem, song, or trick regularly performed by someone in order to entertain others.

party plan ▶**noun** [mass noun] a sales strategy involving the demonstration of goods at parties in people's homes.

party political ▶**adjective** of, relating to, or involved in party politics: *thinly disguised party political propaganda.*

party political broadcast ▶**noun** a television or radio programme on which a representative of a political party presents material intended to foster support for it.

party politics ▶**plural noun** [also treated as sing.] politics that relate to political parties rather than to the good of the general public.

party-pooper ▶**noun** informal a person who throws gloom over social enjoyment: *I hate to be a party-pooper, but I've got to catch the last train.*
– DERIVATIVES **party-pooping** noun.

party popper ▶**noun** a device used as an amusement at parties, which explodes when a string is pulled, ejecting thin paper streamers.

party wall ▶**noun** a wall common to two adjoining buildings or rooms.

parure /pəˈrʊə/ ▶**noun** a set of jewels intended to be worn together.
– ORIGIN early 19th cent.: from French, from *parer* 'adorn'.

Parvati /ˈpɑːvəti/ Hinduism a benevolent goddess, wife of Shiva, mother of Ganesha and Skanda, often identified in her malevolent aspect with Durga and Kali.
– ORIGIN from Sanskrit *Pārvatī*, literally 'daughter of the mountain'.

parvenu /ˈpɑːvənuː, -njuː/ often derogatory ▶**noun** a person of obscure origin who has gained wealth, influence, or celebrity: *the political inexperience of a parvenu.*
▶**adjective** having recently achieved, or associated with someone who has recently achieved wealth, influence, or celebrity despite obscure origins: *he concealed the details of his parvenu lifestyle.*
– ORIGIN early 19th cent.: from French, literally 'arrived', past participle of *parvenir*, from Latin *pervenire* 'come to, reach'.

parvis /ˈpɑːvɪs/ (also **parvise**) ▶**noun** an enclosed area in front of a cathedral or church, typically one that is surrounded with colonnades or porticoes.
– ORIGIN late Middle English: from Old French, based on late Latin *paradisus* 'paradise', in the Middle Ages denoting a court in front of St Peter's, Rome.

parvovirus /ˈpɑːvəʊˌvʌɪrəs/ ▶**noun** Medicine any of a class of very small viruses chiefly affecting animals, especially one (**canine parvovirus**) which causes contagious disease in dogs.
– ORIGIN 1960s: from Latin *parvus* 'small' + **VIRUS**.

PAS ▶**abbreviation for** power-assisted steering.

pas /pɑː/ ▶**noun** (pl. same) a step in dancing, especially in classical ballet.
– ORIGIN French.

Pasadena /ˌpasəˈdiːnə/ a city in California, in the San Gabriel Mountains on the NE side of the Los Angeles conurbation; pop. 131,590 (1990). It is the site of the Rose Bowl stadium, venue for the American Football Super Bowl.

Pascal¹ /pasˈkɑːl, French paskal/, Blaise (1623–62), French mathematician, physicist, and religious philosopher. He founded the theory of probabilities and developed a forerunner of integral calculus, but is best known for deriving the principle that the pressure of a fluid at rest is transmitted equally in all directions. His *Lettres Provinciales* (1656–7) and *Pensées* (1670) argue for his Jansenist Christianity.

p

Pascal² /ˈpask(ə)l/ (also **PASCAL**) ▶ **noun** [mass noun] a high-level structured computer programming language used for teaching and general programming.

pascal /ˈpask(ə)l/ ▶ **noun** the SI unit of pressure, equal to one newton per square metre (approximately 0.000145 pounds per square inch, or 9.9 × 10⁻⁶ atmospheres).
– ORIGIN 1950s: named after B. *Pascal* (see **PASCAL**¹).

Pascal's triangle ▶ **noun** Mathematics a triangular array of numbers in which those at the ends of the rows are 1 and each of the others is the sum of the nearest two numbers in the row above (the apex, 1, being at the top).

Pascal's wager ▶ **noun** [in sing.] Philosophy the argument that it is in one's own best interest to behave as if God exists, since the possibility of eternal punishment in hell outweighs any advantage in believing otherwise.

paschal /ˈpask(ə)l, ˈpɑːs-/ ▶ **adjective** formal **1** of or relating to Easter.
2 of or relating to the Jewish Passover.
– ORIGIN late Middle English: from Old French, from ecclesiastical Latin *paschalis*, from *pascha* 'feast of Passover', via Greek and Aramaic from Hebrew *Pesaḥ* 'Passover'.

paschal candle ▶ **noun** Christian Church a large candle blessed and lit on Holy Saturday and placed by the altar until Pentecost.

paschal lamb ▶ **noun 1** a lamb sacrificed at Passover.
2 Christ.

Paschen series /ˈpaʃ(ə)n/ Physics a series of lines in the infrared spectrum of atomic hydrogen, between 1.88 and 0.82 micrometres.
– ORIGIN 1920s: named after L. C. H. Friedrich *Paschen* (1865–1947), German physicist.

pas de basque /ˌpɑː də ˈbask, ˈbɑːsk/ ▶ **noun** (pl. same) a ballet step in three beats, with a circular movement of the right leg on the second beat.
■ (especially in jigs and reels) a step in three beats with one long and two short movements, transferring weight from one foot to the other on the spot.
– ORIGIN French, literally 'step of a Basque'.

pas de bourrée /ˌpɑː də ˈbʊəreɪ/ ▶ **noun** Ballet a sideways step in which one foot crosses behind or in front of the other.
– ORIGIN French, literally 'bourrée step'.

pas de chat /ˌpɑː də ˈʃa/ ▶ **noun** (pl. same) Ballet a jump in which each foot in turn is raised to the opposite knee.
– ORIGIN French, literally 'step of a cat'.

pas de deux /ˌpɑː də ˈdəː/ ▶ **noun** (pl. same) a dance for two people, typically a man and a woman.
– ORIGIN French, literally 'step of two'.

pas de quatre /ˌpɑː də ˈkatr(ə)/ ▶ **noun** (pl. same) a dance for four people.
– ORIGIN French, literally 'step of four'.

pas de trois /ˌpɑː də ˈtrwʌ/ ▶ **noun** (pl. same) a dance for three people.
– ORIGIN French, literally 'step of three'.

paseo /paˈseɪəʊ/ ▶ **noun** (pl. **-os** /-əʊz/) chiefly US a leisurely walk or stroll, especially one taken in the evening; a promenade (used with reference to the tradition of taking such a walk in Spain or Spanish-speaking communities).
– ORIGIN Spanish, literally 'step'.

pash ▶ **noun** informal, dated a brief infatuation: *Kath's got a* **pash on** *him.*
– ORIGIN early 20th cent.: abbreviation of **PASSION**.

pasha /ˈpaʃə/ ▶ **noun 1** (also **pacha**) historical the title of a Turkish officer of high rank.
2 (**two-tailed pasha**) a large orange-brown butterfly with two tails on each hindwing and complex patterns on the underwings, occurring around the Mediterranean and in Africa.
• *Charaxes jasius*, subfamily Nymphalinae, family Nymphalidae.
– ORIGIN mid 17th cent.: from Turkish *paşa*, from Pahlavi *pati* 'lord' + *šāh* 'shah'.

pashka /ˈpaʃkə/ (also **paskha**) ▶ **noun** [mass noun] a rich Russian dessert made with curd cheese, dried fruit, nuts, and spices, and traditionally eaten at Easter.
– ORIGIN Russian, literally 'Easter'.

pashm /ˈpaʃ(ə)m/ ▶ **noun** [mass noun] the soft underfur of some Tibetan animals, of which cashmere represents a particularly fine and soft type.
– ORIGIN late 19th cent.: from Persian *pašm* 'wool'.

pashmina /pʌʃˈmiːnə/ ▶ **noun** [mass noun] fine-quality material made from goat's wool.
– ORIGIN Persian, from *pašm* 'wool, down'.

Pashto /ˈpʌʃtəʊ/ ▶ **noun** [mass noun] the language of the Pathans, which belongs to the Iranian group. It is the official language of Afghanistan and is also spoken in northern areas of Pakistan.
▶ **adjective** of or relating to this language.
– ORIGIN the name in Pashto.

Pašić /ˈpaʃɪtʃ/, Nikola (1845–1926), Serbian statesman, Prime Minister of Serbia five times between 1891 and 1918, and of the Kingdom of Serbs, Croats, and Slovenes 1921–4 and 1924–6. He was a party to the formation of the Kingdom of Serbs, Croats, and Slovenes (called Yugoslavia from 1929) in 1918.

Pasiphaë /pəˈsɪfiː/ Greek Mythology the wife of Minos and mother of the Minotaur.

paskha /ˈpaskə/ ▶ **noun** variant spelling of **PASHKA**.

paso doble /ˌpasə(ʊ) ˈdəʊbleɪ/ ▶ **noun** (pl. **paso dobles**) a fast-paced ballroom dance based on a Latin American style of marching.
■ a piece of music for this dance, typically in duple time.
– ORIGIN 1920s: from Spanish, literally 'double step'.

Pasolini /ˌpasəˈliːni/, Pier Paolo (1922–75), Italian film director and novelist. A Marxist, he drew on his experiences in the slums of Rome for his work, but became recognized for his controversial, bawdy literary adaptations, such as *The Gospel According to St Matthew* (1964) and *The Canterbury Tales* (1973).

pas op /pas ˈɒp/ ▶ **exclamation** S. African informal look out!
– ORIGIN Afrikaans, imperative of Dutch *oppassen* 'be on guard'.

paspalum /ˈpasp(ə)ləm/ ▶ **noun** [mass noun] a grass of warm and tropical regions, which is grown for fodder, erosion control, and as a pasture grass.
• Genus *Paspalum*, family Gramineae.
– ORIGIN modern Latin, from Greek *paspalos*, denoting a kind of millet.

pasque flower /pask, pɑːsk/ ▶ **noun** a spring-flowering European plant related to the anemones, with purple flowers and fern-like foliage.
• *Pulsatilla vulgaris*, family Ranunculaceae.
– ORIGIN late 16th cent. (as *passeflower*): from French *passe-fleur*. The change in spelling of the first word was due to association with archaic *pasque* 'Easter' (because of the plant's early flowering).

pasquinade /ˌpaskwɪˈneɪd/ ▶ **noun** a satire or lampoon, originally one displayed or delivered publicly in a public place.
– ORIGIN late 16th cent.: from Italian *pasquinata*, from *Pasquino*, the name of a statue in Rome on which abusive Latin verses were posted annually.

pass¹ ▶ **verb 1** [no obj., with adverbial of direction] move in a specified direction: *he passed through towns and villages | the shells from the Allied guns were passing very low overhead.*
■ [with obj. and adverbial of direction] cause (something) to move or lie in a specified direction or position: *he passed a weary hand across his forehead | pass an electric current through it.* ■ change from one state or condition to another: *homes which have passed from public to private ownership.* ■ [no obj.] die (used euphemistically): *she* **passed away** *peacefully in her sleep.*
2 [with obj.] go past or across; leave behind or on one side in proceeding: *on the way to the tube station she passed a cinema | the two vehicles had no room to pass each other |* [no obj.] *we will not let you pass.*
■ go beyond the limits of; surpass; exceed: *the Portuguese trade passed its peak in the 1760s | this item has passed its sell-by date.* ■ Tennis hit a winning shot past (an opponent).
3 [no obj.] (of time or a point in time) elapse; go by: *the day and night passed slowly | the moment had passed.*
■ happen; be done or said: *not another word* **passed between** *them |* [with complement] *this fact has passed almost unnoticed.* ■ [with obj.] spend or use up (a period of time): *this was how they* **passed the time**. ■ come to an end: *the danger had passed.*
4 [with obj. and usu. with adverbial of direction] transfer (something) to someone, especially by handing or bequeathing it to the next person in a series: *your letter has been passed to Mr Rich for action | pass the milk |* [with two objs] *he passed her a cup.*
■ [no obj., with adverbial] be transferred from one person or place to another, especially by inheritance: *the poem was passed from generation to generation.* ■ (in soccer, rugby, and other games) kick, hit, or throw (the ball) to another player of one's own side. ■ put (something, especially money) into circulation: *persons who have passed bad cheques.* ■ [no obj.] (especially of money) circulate; be current: *racegoers had formed card schools, and cash was passing briskly.*
5 [with obj.] (of a candidate) be successful in (an examination, test, or course): *she passed her driving test.*
■ judge the performance or standard of (someone or something) to be satisfactory: [with obj. and complement] *he was passed fit by army doctors.* ■ [no obj.] (**pass as/for**) be accepted as or taken for: *he could pass for a native of Sweden.*
6 [with obj.] (of a legislative or other official body) approve or put into effect (a proposal or law) by voting on it: *the bill was passed despite fierce opposition.*
■ (of a proposal or law) be examined and approved by (a parliamentary body or process): *bills that passed committees last year.* ■ [no obj.] (of a proposal) be approved: *the Bill passed by 164 votes to 107.*
7 [with obj.] pronounce (a judgement or judicial sentence): ***passing*** *judgement* ***on*** *these crucial issues | it is now my duty to* **pass** *sentence* **upon** *you.*
■ utter (something, especially criticism): *she would pass remarks about the Peebles in their own house.* ■ [no obj.] (**pass on/upon**) archaic adjudicate or give a judgement on: *a jury could not be trusted to pass upon the question of Endacott's good faith.*
8 [with obj.] discharge (something, especially urine or faeces) from the body: *frequency of passing urine.*
9 [no obj.] forgo one's turn in a game or an offered opportunity to do or have something: *we* **pass on** *pudding and have coffee.*
■ [as exclamation] said when one does not know the answer to a question, for example in a quiz: *to the enigmatic question we answered 'Pass'.* ■ [with obj.] (of a company) not declare or pay (a dividend). ■ Bridge make no bid when it is one's turn during an auction. ■ [with obj.] Bridge make no bid in response to (one's partner's bid): *East had passed his partner's opening bid of one club.*
▶ **noun 1** an act or instance of moving past or through something: *repeated passes with the swipe card | an unmarked plane had been making passes over his house.*
■ informal an amorous or sexual advance made to someone: *she* **made a pass at** *Stephen.* ■ an act of passing the hands over anything, as in conjuring or hypnotism. ■ a thrust in fencing. ■ a juggling trick. ■ Bridge an act of refraining from bidding during the auction. ■ Computing a single scan through a set of data or a program.
2 a success in an examination: *an A-level pass in Music |* [as modifier] *a 100 per cent pass rate.*
■ Brit. an achievement of a university degree without honours: [as modifier] *a pass degree.*
3 a card, ticket, or permit giving authorization for the holder to enter or have access to a place, form of transport, or event.
■ historical (in South Africa) a temporary permit allowing movement from one district to another. ■ historical (in South Africa) an identity book which black people had to carry between 1952 and 1986, used to limit the movement of black people to urban areas: [as modifier] *the pass laws.*
4 (in soccer, rugby, and other games) an act of kicking, hitting, or throwing the ball to another player on the same side.
5 a state or situation of a specified, usually bad or difficult, nature: *this is a sad pass for a fixture which used to crackle with excitement.*
– PHRASES **come to a pretty pass** reach a bad or regrettable state of affairs. **pass the baton** see **BATON**. **pass the buck** see **BUCK**³. **pass one's eye over** read (a document) cursorily. **pass the hat (round)** see **HAT**. **pass one's lips** see **LIP**. **pass muster** see **MUSTER**. **pass the parcel** see **PARCEL**. **pass the time of day** see **TIME**. **pass water** urinate.
– DERIVATIVES **passer** noun *he's a good passer of the ball.*
– ORIGIN Middle English: from Old French *passer*, based on Latin *passus* 'pace'.
▶ **pass someone by** happen without being noticed or fully experienced by someone: *sometimes I feel that life is passing me by.*
pass off (of proceedings) happen or be carried through in a specified, usually satisfactory way: *the weekend had passed off entirely without incident.*
pass something off 1 evade or lightly dismiss an awkward remark: *he made a light joke and passed it off.* **2** Basketball throw the ball to a teammate who is unmarked: *he scored eight times and passed off forty-*

one assists.

pass someone/thing off as falsely represent a person or thing as (something else): *the drink was packaged in champagne bottles and was being passed off as the real stuff.*

pass out 1 become unconscious: *he consumed enough alcohol to make him pass out.* **2** Brit. complete one's initial training in the armed forces.

pass someone over ignore the claims of someone to promotion or advancement: *he was passed over for a cabinet job.*

pass something over avoid mentioning or considering something: *I shall pass over the matter of the transitional period.*

pass something up refrain from taking up an opportunity: *he passed up a career in pro baseball.*

pass² ▶ **noun** a route over or through mountains: *the pass over the mountain was open again after the snows* | [in place names] *the Khyber Pass.*

■a passage for fish over or past a weir or dam.

– PHRASES **head** (or **cut**) **someone/thing off at the pass** forestall someone or something: *he came up with this story at the last minute, just to cut me off at the pass.* **sell the pass** Brit. betray a cause: *he is merciless to other poets whom he considers to have sold the pass.*

– ORIGIN Middle English (in the sense 'division of a text, passage through'): variant of **PACE**¹, influenced by **PASS**¹ and French *pas*.

passable ▶ **adjective 1** just good enough to be acceptable; satisfactory: *he spoke passable English.*

2 (of a route or road) clear of obstacles and able to be travelled along or on: *the road was passable with care.*

– DERIVATIVES **passably** adverb.

– ORIGIN late Middle English: from Old French, from *passer* 'to pass'.

passacaglia /ˌpasəˈkɑːlɪə/ ▶ **noun** Music a composition similar to a chaconne, typically in slow triple time with variations over a ground bass.

– ORIGIN Italian, from Spanish *pasacalle*, from *pasar* 'to pass' + *calle* 'street' (because originally it was a dance often played in the streets).

passade /pəˈseɪd/ ▶ **noun** a movement performed in advanced dressage and classical riding, in which the horse performs a 180° turn, with its forelegs describing a large circle and its hind legs a smaller one.

– ORIGIN mid 17th cent.: French, from Italian *passata* or Provençal *passada*, from medieval Latin *passare* 'to pass'.

passage¹ /ˈpasɪdʒ/ ▶ **noun 1** [mass noun] the act or process of moving through, under, over, or past something on the way from one place to another: *there were moorings for boats wanting passage through the lock.*

■the act or process of moving forward: *despite the passage of time she still loved him.* ■the right to pass through somewhere: *we obtained a permit for safe passage from the embassy.* ■[count noun] a journey or ticket for a journey by sea or air: *I booked a passage on the next ship.* ■Ornithology (of a migrating bird) the action of passing through a place en route to its final destination: *the species occurs regularly* **on passage** | [as modifier] *a passage migrant.* ■Medicine & Biology /paˈsɑːʒ/ the process of propagating micro-organisms or cells in a series of host organisms or culture media, so as to maintain them or modify their virulence.

2 a narrow way, typically having walls either side, allowing access between buildings or to different rooms within a building; a passageway.

■a duct, vessel, or other channel in the body.

3 [mass noun] the process of transition from one state to another: *an allegory on the theme of the passage from ignorance to knowledge.*

■the passing of a bill into law: *a catalyst for the unrest was the passage of a privatization law.*

4 a short extract from a book or other printed material: *he picked up the newspaper and read the passage again.*

■a section of a piece of music: *nothing obscures the outlines of an orchestral passage more than a drum roll on an unrelated note.* ■an episode in a longer activity such as a sporting event: *a neat passage of midfield play.*

▶ **verb** /paˈsɑːʒ/ [with obj.] Medicine & Biology subject (a strain of micro-organisms or cells) to a passage: *each recombinant virus was passaged nine times successively.*

– PHRASES **passage of** (or **at**) **arms** a fight or dispute. **work one's passage** work in return for a free place on a voyage: *he worked his passage home as a steward.*

– ORIGIN Middle English: from Old French, based on Latin *passus* 'pace'.

passage² /paˈsɑːʒ/ ▶ **noun** a movement performed in advanced dressage and classical riding, in which the horse executes a slow elevated trot, giving the impression of dancing.

– ORIGIN early 18th cent.: from French *passage* from an alteration of Italian *passeggiare* 'to walk, pace', based on Latin *passus* 'pace'.

passage grave ▶ **noun** Archaeology a prehistoric megalithic burial chamber of a type found chiefly in western Europe, with a passage leading to the exterior. Passage graves were originally covered by a mound, which in many cases has disappeared, and most date from the Neolithic period.

passage hawk ▶ **noun** a hawk caught for training while on migration, especially as an immature bird of less than twelve months. Compare with **HAGGARD**.

passageway ▶ **noun** a long, narrow way, typically having walls either side, that allows access between buildings or to different rooms within a building.

passagework ▶ **noun** [mass noun] music notable chiefly for the scope it affords for virtuoso playing: *some of the passagework in early Beethoven is very awkward.*

Passamaquoddy /ˌpasəməˈkwɒdi/ ▶ **noun** (pl. same or **-ies**) **1** a member of an American Indian people inhabiting parts of SE Maine and, formerly, SW New Brunswick.

2 [mass noun] the Algonquian language of this people, now with few speakers.

▶ **adjective** of or relating to this people or their language.

– ORIGIN from a Micmac name for *Passamaquoddy* Bay, literally 'place where pollack are plentiful'.

passant /ˈpas(ə)nt/ ▶ **adjective** [usu. postpositive] Heraldry (of an animal) represented as walking, with the right front foot raised. The animal is depicted in profile facing the dexter side with the tail raised, unless otherwise specified (e.g. as 'passant guardant').

– ORIGIN late Middle English: from Old French, literally 'proceeding', present participle of *passer.*

passata /pəˈsɑːtə/ ▶ **noun** [mass noun] a thick paste made from sieved tomatoes and used especially in Italian cooking.

– ORIGIN Italian.

passband ▶ **noun** a frequency band within which signals are transmitted by a filter without attenuation.

passbook ▶ **noun 1** a book issued by a bank or building society to an account-holder, recording sums deposited and withdrawn.

2 historical (in South Africa under apartheid) a black person's pass.

Passchendaele, Battle of /ˈpaʃ(ə)ndeɪl/ (also **Passendale**) a prolonged episode of trench warfare involving appalling loss of life during the First World War in 1917, near the village of Passchendaele in western Belgium. It is also known as the third Battle of Ypres.

pass door ▶ **noun** a door in a theatre connecting the backstage area and the auditorium.

passé /ˈpaseɪ/ ▶ **adjective** [predic.] no longer fashionable; out of date: *minis are passé—the best skirts are knee-length.*

■archaic (especially of a woman) past one's prime.

– ORIGIN French, literally 'gone by', past participle of *passer.*

passed pawn ▶ **noun** Chess a pawn that no enemy pawn can stop from queening.

passeggiata /ˌpaseˈdʒɑːtə/ ▶ **noun** (pl. **passeggiate** /-teɪ/) a leisurely walk or stroll, especially one taken in the evening; a promenade (used with reference to the tradition of taking such a walk in Italy or Italian-speaking communities).

– ORIGIN Italian.

passel /ˈpas(ə)l/ ▶ **noun** informal, chiefly US a large group of people or things of indeterminate number; a pack: *a passel of journalists.*

– ORIGIN mid 19th cent.: representing a pronunciation of **PARCEL**.

passementerie /ˈpasm(ə)ntri/ ▶ **noun** [mass noun] decorative textile trimming consisting of gold or silver lace, gimp, or braid.

– ORIGIN early 17th cent.: from French, from *passement* 'gold lace'.

Passendale, Battle of /ˈpas(ə)ndeɪl/ variant spelling of **PASSCHENDAELE, BATTLE OF**.

passenger ▶ **noun** a traveller on a public or private conveyance other than the driver, pilot, or crew.

■a member of a team or group who does far less effective work than the other members.

– ORIGIN Middle English: from the Old French adjective *passager* 'passing, transitory', used as a noun, from *passage* (see **PASSAGE**¹).

passenger mile ▶ **noun** one mile travelled by one passenger, as a unit of traffic.

passenger pigeon ▶ **noun** an extinct long-tailed North American pigeon, noted for its long migrations in huge flocks. It was relentlessly hunted, the last individual dying in captivity in 1914.

• *Ectopistes migratorius*, family Columbidae.

passepartout /ˌpaspɑːˈtuː, ˌpɑːs-/ ▶ **noun 1** (also **passepartout frame**) a picture or photograph simply mounted between a piece of glass and a sheet of card (or two pieces of glass) stuck together at the edges with adhesive tape.

■[mass noun] adhesive tape or paper used in making such a frame.

2 archaic a master key.

– ORIGIN late 17th cent.: from French, literally 'passes everywhere'.

passepied /ˌpasˈpjeɪ/ ▶ **noun** a Breton dance like a quick minuet, popular in the 17th and 18th centuries.

– ORIGIN French, from *passer* 'to pass' + *pied* 'foot'.

passer-by ▶ **noun** (pl. **passers-by**) a person who happens to be going past something, especially on foot.

passerine /ˈpasərʌɪn, -riːn/ Ornithology ▶ **adjective** of, relating to, or denoting birds of a large order distinguished by having feet that are adapted for perching, including all songbirds.

▶ **noun** a passerine bird; a perching bird.

> The order Passeriformes comprises more than half of all bird species, the remainder being known informally as the **non-passerines**. All passerines in Europe belong to the suborder Oscines (the **oscine passerines**), so that the term is effectively synonymous with 'songbird' there (see **SONGBIRD**). Those of the suborder Deutero-Oscines (the **suboscine passerines**) are found mainly in America.

– ORIGIN late 18th cent.: from Latin *passer* 'sparrow' + **-INE**¹.

pas seul /pɑː ˈsəːl/ ▶ **noun** a dance for one person.

– ORIGIN French, literally 'single step'.

passible /ˈpasɪb(ə)l/ ▶ **adjective** Christian Theology capable of feeling or suffering; susceptible to sensation or emotion: *only the humanity of Jesus is regarded as passible.*

– DERIVATIVES **passibility** noun.

– ORIGIN late Middle English: from Old French, from late Latin *passibilis*, from Latin *pass-* 'suffered', from the verb *pati.*

passim /ˈpasɪm/ ▶ **adverb** (of allusions or references in a published work) to be found at various places throughout the text.

– ORIGIN Latin, from *passus* 'scattered', from the verb *pandere.*

passing ▶ **adjective** [attrib.] **1** going past: *passing cars.*

2 (of a period of time) going by: *she detested him more with every passing second.*

■carried out quickly and lightly: *a passing glance.*

▶ **noun** [in sing.] **1** the passage of something, especially time: *with* **the passing of** *the years she had become a little eccentric.*

■[mass noun] the action of kicking, hitting, or throwing a ball to another team member during a sports match: *his play showed good passing and good control* | [as modifier] *a good passing movement.*

2 used euphemistically to refer to a person's death: *her passing will be felt deeply by many people.*

■the end of something: **the passing of** *the cold war and the rise of a new Europe.*

– PHRASES **in passing** briefly and casually: *the research was mentioned only in passing.*

– DERIVATIVES **passingly** adverb.

passing bell ▶ **noun** chiefly historical a bell rung immediately after a death as a signal for prayers.

passing note ▶ **noun** Music a note not belonging to the harmony but interposed to secure a smooth transition.

passing shot ▶ **noun** Tennis a shot aiming the ball beyond and out of reach of one's opponent.

p

passion ▶ **noun 1** [mass noun] strong and barely controllable emotion: *a man of impetuous passion.*
■ [count noun] a state or outburst of such emotion: *oratory in which he gradually works himself up into a passion.* ■ intense sexual love: *their all-consuming passion for each other* | [count noun] *she nurses a passion for Thomas.* ■ [count noun] an intense desire or enthusiasm for something: *the English have* ***a passion for*** *gardens.* ■ [count noun] a thing arousing enthusiasm: *modern furniture is a particular passion of Bill's.*
2 (**the Passion**) the suffering and death of Jesus: *meditations on the Passion of Christ.*
■ a narrative of this from any of the Gospels. ■ a musical setting of any of these narratives: *an aria from Bach's St. Matthew Passion.*
– DERIVATIVES **passionless** adjective.
– ORIGIN Middle English: from Old French, from late Latin *passio(n-)* (chiefly a term in Christian theology), from Latin *pati* 'suffer'.

passional ▶ **adjective** rare of, relating to, or marked by passion: *a current of passional electric energy.*
▶ **noun** Christian Church a book about the sufferings of saints and martyrs, for reading on their feast days.

passionate ▶ **adjective** showing or caused by strong feelings or a strong belief: *passionate pleas for help* | *he's* ***passionate about*** *football.*
■ showing or caused by intense feelings of sexual love: *a passionate kiss.* ■ dominated by or easily affected by intense emotion: *a strong-minded and passionate man.*
– DERIVATIVES **passionately** adverb, **passionateness** noun.
– ORIGIN late Middle English (also in the senses 'easily moved to passion' and 'enraged'): from medieval Latin *passionatus* 'full of passion', from *passio* (see **PASSION**).

passion flower ▶ **noun** an evergreen climbing plant of warm regions, which bears distinctive flowers with parts that supposedly resemble instruments of the Crucifixion.
● Genus *Passiflora*, family Passifloraceae.

passion fruit ▶ **noun** the edible purple fruit of a kind of passion flower that is grown commercially, especially in tropical America and the Caribbean. Also called **GRANADILLA**.
● This fruit is obtained from *Passiflora edulis*, family Passifloraceae.

passion play ▶ **noun** a dramatic performance representing Christ's Passion from the Last Supper to the Crucifixion.

Passion Sunday ▶ **noun** the fifth Sunday in Lent.

Passiontide ▶ **noun** the last two weeks of Lent.

Passion Week ▶ **noun 1** the week between Passion Sunday and Palm Sunday.
2 older name for **HOLY WEEK**.

passivate /ˈpasɪveɪt/ ▶ **verb** [with obj.] [usu. as adj. **passivated**] make (a metal or other substance) unreactive by altering the surface layer or coating the surface with a thin inert layer.
■ Electronics coat (a semiconductor) with inert material to protect it from contamination.
– DERIVATIVES **passivation** noun.

passive ▶ **adjective 1** accepting or allowing what happens or what others do, without active response or resistance: *the women were portrayed as passive victims.*
■ Chemistry (of a metal) made unreactive by a thin inert surface layer of oxide. ■ (of a circuit or device) containing no source of electromotive force. ■ (of radar or a satellite) receiving or reflecting radiation from a transmitter or target rather than generating its own signal. ■ relating to or denoting heating systems that make use of incident sunlight as an energy source.
2 Grammar denoting or relating to a voice of verbs in which the subject undergoes the action of the verb (e.g. *they were killed* as opposed to *he killed them*). The opposite of **ACTIVE**.
▶ **noun** Grammar a passive form of a verb.
■ (**the passive**) the passive voice.
– DERIVATIVES **passively** adverb, **passiveness** noun, **passivity** noun.
– ORIGIN late Middle English (in sense 2, also in the sense '(exposed to) suffering, acted on by an external agency'): from Latin *passivus*, from *pass-* 'suffered', from the verb *pati*.

passive-aggressive ▶ **adjective** of or denoting a type of behaviour or personality characterized by indirect resistance to the demands of others and an avoidance of direct confrontation.

passive immunity ▶ **noun** [mass noun] Physiology the short-term immunity which results from the introduction of antibodies from another person or animal. Compare with **ACTIVE IMMUNITY**.

passive matrix ▶ **noun** Electronics a display system in which individual pixels are selected using two control voltages for the row and column.

passive resistance ▶ **noun** [mass noun] non-violent opposition to authority, especially a refusal to cooperate with legal requirements: *they called for protest in the form of passive resistance.*

passive smoking ▶ **noun** [mass noun] the involuntary inhaling of smoke from other people's cigarettes, cigars, or pipes: *children are more susceptible to the effects of passive smoking.*

passivize (also **-ise**) ▶ **verb** [with obj.] Grammar convert (a verb or clause) into the passive form: *a sentence that has been passivized.*
■ [no obj.] (of a verb or clause) be convertible in this way: *transitive verbs in idiomatic expressions frequently will not passivize.*
– DERIVATIVES **passivizable** adjective, **passivization** noun.

pass key ▶ **noun 1** a key to the door of a restricted area, given only to those who are officially allowed access.
2 a master key.

pass laws ▶ **plural noun** a body of laws formerly in operation in South Africa, controlling the rights of black people to residence and travel and implemented by means of identity documents compulsorily carried.

pass mark ▶ **noun** the minimum mark needed to pass an examination.

Passos, John Dos, see **DOS PASSOS**.

Passover ▶ **noun** the major Jewish spring festival which commemorates the liberation of the Israelites from Egyptian bondage, lasting seven or eight days from the 15th day of Nisan.
■ another term for **PASCHAL LAMB**.
– ORIGIN from *pass over* 'pass without touching', with reference to the exemption of the Israelites from the death of their firstborn (Exod. 12).

passport ▶ **noun** an official document issued by a government, certifying the holder's identity and citizenship and entitling them to travel under its protection to and from foreign countries.
■ [in sing.] a thing that ensures admission to or the achievement of something: *good qualifications are a* ***passport to*** *success.*
– ORIGIN late 15th cent. (denoting authorization to depart from a port): from French *passeport*, from *passer* 'to pass' + *port* 'seaport'.

passus /ˈpasəs/ ▶ **noun** (pl. same) a section, division, or canto of a story or poem, especially a medieval one.
– ORIGIN late 16th cent.: from Latin, literally 'step, pace', in medieval Latin 'passage of a book'.

password ▶ **noun** a secret word or phrase that must be used to gain admission to something.
■ a string of characters that allows someone access to a computer system.

past ▶ **adjective** gone by in time and no longer existing: *the danger is now past.*
■ [attrib.] belonging to a former time: *they made a study of the reasons why past attempts had failed* | *he is a past chairman of the society.* ■ [attrib.] (of a specified period of time) occurring before and leading up to the time of speaking or writing: *the band has changed over the past twelve months.* ■ Grammar (of a tense) expressing an action that has happened or a state that previously existed.
▶ **noun 1** (usu. **the past**) the time or a period of time before the moment of speaking or writing: *she found it hard to make ends meet in the past.*
■ the events of an earlier time: *the war-damaged church is preserved as a reminder of the past.* ■ the history of a person, country, or institution: *the monuments act as guidelines through the country's colourful past.*
2 Grammar a past tense or form of a verb: *a simple past of the first conjugation.*
▶ **preposition** to or on the further side of: *he rode on past the crossroads.*
■ in front of or from one side to the other of: *he began to drive slowly past the houses.* ■ beyond in time; later than: *by this time it was past 3.30.* ■ no longer capable of: *he is past giving the best advice.* ■ beyond the scope of: *my hair was past praying for.*
▶ **adverb 1** so as to pass from one side of something to the other: *a flotilla of glossy limousines swept past.*
■ used to indicate the lapse of time: *a week went past and nothing changed.*
2 at a time later by a specified amount than a particular known hour: *we're having speeches in the dining room at half past.*
– PHRASES **not put it past someone** believe someone to be capable of doing something wrong or rash: *I wouldn't put it past him to slip something into the drinks.* **past it** informal too old to be of any use or any good at anything.
– DERIVATIVES **pastness** noun.
– ORIGIN Middle English: variant of *passed*, past participle of **PASS**[1].

pasta ▶ **noun** [mass noun] a dish originally from Italy consisting of dough made from durum wheat and water, extruded or stamped into various shapes and typically cooked in boiling water.
– ORIGIN late 19th cent.: from Italian, literally 'paste'.

paste ▶ **noun** [mass noun] a thick, soft, moist substance, usually produced by mixing dry ingredients with a liquid: *blend onions, sugar, and oil to a paste.*
■ a substance such as this that is used as an adhesive, especially for sticking paper and other light materials: *wallpaper paste.* ■ a mixture consisting mainly of clay and water that is used in making ceramic ware, especially a mixture of low plasticity based on kaolin for making porcelain. ■ a hard vitreous composition used in making imitation gems: [as modifier] *paste brooches.*
▶ **verb** [with obj.] **1** coat with paste: *when coating walls with fabric, paste the wall, not the fabric.*
■ [with obj. and adverbial of place] fasten or stick (something) on to something with paste: *the posters were pasted up on to street noticeboards.* ■ Computing insert (text) into a document.
2 informal beat or defeat severely: *he pasted the guy and tied his ankles together.*
– ORIGIN late Middle English: from Old French, from late Latin *pasta* 'medicinal preparation in the shape of a small square', probably from Greek *pastē*, (plural) *pasta* 'barley porridge', from *pastos* 'sprinkled'.

pasteboard ▶ **noun** [mass noun] a type of thin board made by pasting together sheets of paper.

paste-down ▶ **noun** (in bookbinding) the part of an endpaper which is pasted to the inside of the cover.

pastel ▶ **noun 1** a crayon made of powdered pigments bound with gum or resin.
■ a work of art created using such crayons: *a pastel entitled 'Girl braiding her hair'.*
2 a soft and delicate shade of a colour: *the subtlest of pastels and creams.*
▶ **adjective** of a soft and delicate shade or colour: *pastel blue curtains.*
– DERIVATIVES **pastellist** (also **pastelist**) noun.
– ORIGIN mid 17th cent.: via French from Italian *pastello*, diminutive of *pasta* 'paste'.

pastern /ˈpast(ə)n/ ▶ **noun** the sloping part of a horse's foot between the fetlock and the hoof.
■ a corresponding part in some other domestic animals.
– ORIGIN Middle English: from Old French *pasturon*, from *pasture* 'strap for hobbling a horse', transferred in sense to the joint of the foot.

Pasternak /ˈpastənak/, Boris (Leonidovich) (1890–1960), Russian poet, novelist, and translator. His best-known novel, *Doctor Zhivago* (1957), describes the experience of the Russian intelligentsia during the Revolution; it was banned in the Soviet Union.

paste-up ▶ **noun** a document prepared for copying or printing by combining and pasting various sections on a backing.

Pasteur /paˈstəː, French pastœʀ/, Louis (1822–95), French chemist and bacteriologist. He introduced pasteurization and made pioneering studies in vaccination techniques.

pasteurellosis /ˌpɑːstərɛˈləʊsɪs, ˌpastərɛˈləʊsɪs/ ▶ **noun** [mass noun] a bacterial infection commonly affecting animals and sometimes transferred to humans through bites and scratches.
● The causative bacteria are Gram-negative rods of the genus *Pasteurella*, in particular *P. multocida*.
– ORIGIN early 20th cent.: from French *pasteurellose* (from the name **PASTEUR**) + **-OSIS**.

pasteurize /ˈpɑːstʃərʌɪz, -stjə-, ˈpas-/ (also **-ise**) ▶ **verb** [with obj.] [often as adj. **pasteurized**] subject (milk, wine, or other products) to a process of partial sterilization, especially one involving heat treatment or irradiation, thus making the product safe for consumption and improving its keeping quality: *pasteurized milk*.

- DERIVATIVES **pasteurization** noun, **pasteurizer** noun.
- ORIGIN late 19th cent.: from the name of L. **PASTEUR** + **-IZE**.

Pasteur pipette ▶ noun a simple glass pipette drawn into a capillary tube at one end, used with a rubber teat fitted to the other.

pasticcio /paˈstɪtʃəʊ/ ▶ noun (pl. **-os**) another term for **PASTICHE**.
- ORIGIN Italian.

pastiche /paˈstiːʃ/ ▶ noun an artistic work in a style that imitates that of another work, artist, or period: *the operetta is a pastiche of 18th century style* | [mass noun] *the songs amount to much more than blatant pastiche*.
- ■an artistic work consisting of a medley of pieces imitating various sources.
▶ verb [with obj.] imitate the style of (an artist or work): *Gauguin took himself to a Pacific island and pastiched the primitive art he found there.*
- ORIGIN late 19th cent.: from French, from Italian *pasticcio*, based on late Latin *pasta* 'paste'.

pasticheur /ˌpastiːˈʃəː/ ▶ noun an artist who imitates the style of another: *the early paintings reveal him as merely a pasticheur with panache.*

pastie ▶ noun (pl. **-ies**) **1** /ˈpeɪsti/ (usu. **pasties**) informal a decorative covering for the nipple worn by a stripper.
2 /ˈpasti/ variant spelling of **PASTY**[1].

pastille /ˈpast(ə)l, -tɪl/ ▶ noun a small sweet or lozenge.
- ■a small pellet of aromatic paste burnt as a perfume or deodorizer.
- ORIGIN mid 17th cent.: from French, from Latin *pastillus* 'little loaf, lozenge', from *panis* 'loaf'.

pastime ▶ noun an activity that someone does regularly for enjoyment rather than work; a hobby: *his favourite pastimes were shooting and golf.*
- ORIGIN late 15th cent.: from the verb **PASS**[1] + **TIME**, translating French *passe-temps.*

pasting /ˈpeɪstɪŋ/ ▶ noun informal a severe beating or defeat: *another pasting for England's bowlers.*

pastis /ˈpastɪs, paˈstiːs/ ▶ noun (pl. same) [mass noun] an aniseed-flavoured aperitif.
- ORIGIN French.

past master ▶ noun **1** a person who is particularly skilled at a specified activity or art: *he's a past master at keeping his whereabouts secret.*
2 a person who has held the position of master in an organization: *he was a past master of the City Company of Grocers.*

pastor /ˈpɑːstə/ ▶ noun **1** a minister in charge of a Christian church or congregation, especially in some non-episcopal churches.
2 see **ROSY PASTOR**.
▶ verb [with obj.] be pastor of (a church or a congregation): *he pastored Peninsula Bible Church in Palo Alto* | [no obj.] *he continued to study law while pastoring in Chelsea.*
- DERIVATIVES **pastorship** noun.
- ORIGIN late Middle English: from Anglo-Norman French *pastour*, from Latin *pastor* 'shepherd', from *past-* 'fed, grazed', from the verb *pascere.*

pastoral /ˈpɑːst(ə)r(ə)l/ ▶ adjective **1** (especially of land or a farm) used for or related to the keeping or grazing of sheep or cattle: *scattered pastoral farms.*
- ■associated with country life: *the view was pastoral, with rolling fields and grazing sheep.* ■ (of a work of art) portraying or evoking country life, typically in a romanticized or idealized form.
2 (in the Christian Church) concerning or appropriate to the giving of spiritual guidance: *pastoral and doctrinal issues* | *clergy doing pastoral work.*
- ■relating to or denoting a teacher's responsibility for the general well-being of pupils or students: *does the school operate a pastoral or guidance and counselling system?*
▶ noun a work of literature portraying an idealized version of country life: *the story, though a pastoral, has an actual connection with the life of agricultural labour.*
- DERIVATIVES **pastoralism** noun, **pastorally** adverb.
- ORIGIN late Middle English: from Latin *pastoralis* 'relating to a shepherd', from *pastor* 'shepherd' (see **PASTOR**).

pastorale /ˌpastəˈrɑːl/ ▶ noun (pl. **pastorales** or **pastorali** /-liː/) **1** a slow instrumental composition in compound time, usually with drone notes in the bass.
2 a simple musical play with a rural subject.
- ORIGIN early 18th cent.: from Italian, literally 'pastoral' (adjective used as a noun).

Pastoral Epistles the books of the New Testament comprising the two letters of Paul to Timothy and the one to Titus.

pastoralist ▶ noun **1** (especially in Australia) a sheep or cattle farmer.
2 archaic a writer of pastorals.

pastoral letter ▶ noun an official letter from a bishop to all the clergy or members of his or her diocese.

pastoral staff ▶ noun a bishop's crozier.

pastoral theology ▶ noun [mass noun] Christian theology that considers religious truth in relation to spiritual needs.

pastorate ▶ noun the office or period of office of a pastor: *a four-year pastorate in Scotland.*
- ■pastors collectively.

pastorie /ˌpastʊˈri/ ▶ noun (in South Africa) the residence of a minister of one of the Dutch Reformed Churches.
- ORIGIN Afrikaans, from medieval Latin *pastoria* 'place belonging to a shepherd'.

pastourelle /ˌpastʊˈrɛl/ (also **pastorela** /ˌpastəˈrɛlə/) ▶ noun (pl. same or **pastourelles** or **pastorelas**) a medieval lyric whose theme is love for a shepherdess.
- ORIGIN French, feminine of *pastoureau* 'shepherd'.

past participle ▶ noun Grammar the form of a verb, typically ending in *-ed* in English, which is used in forming perfect and passive tenses and sometimes as an adjective, e.g. *looked* in *have you looked?*, *lost* in *lost property.*

past perfect ▶ adjective & noun another term for **PLUPERFECT**.

pastrami /paˈstrɑːmi/ ▶ noun [mass noun] highly seasoned smoked beef, typically served in thin slices.
- ORIGIN Yiddish.

pastry ▶ noun (pl. **-ies**) [mass noun] a dough of flour, fat, and water, used as a base and covering in baked dishes such as pies.
- ■[count noun] an item of food consisting of sweet pastry with a cream, jam, or fruit filling.
- ORIGIN late Middle English (as a collective term): from **PASTE**, influenced by Old French *pastaierie.*

pastry cook ▶ noun a professional cook who specializes in making pastry.

pastry cream ▶ noun [mass noun] a thick, creamy custard used as a filling for cakes or flans.

pasturage ▶ noun [mass noun] land used for pasture.
- ■the occupation or process of pasturing cattle, sheep, or other grazing animals: *the human species has only engaged in pasturage for 12,000 to 15,000 years.*
- ORIGIN early 16th cent.: from Old French, from *pasture* (see **PASTURE**).

pasture ▶ noun [mass noun] land covered with grass and other low plants suitable for grazing animals, especially cattle or sheep.
- ■the grass and herbage growing on such land: [as modifier] *a range of pasture grasses.* ■ [count noun] figurative a place or activity regarded as offering new opportunities: *she left the office for pastures new.* [ORIGIN: sense suggested by 'Tomorrow to fresh woods and pastures new' (Milton's *Lycidas*).]
▶ verb [with obj.] put (animals) to graze in a pasture: *they pastured their cows in the water meadow.*
- ■[no obj.] (of animals) graze: *the livestock pastured and the crops grew.*
- PHRASES **put someone out to pasture** force someone to retire.
- ORIGIN Middle English: from Old French, from late Latin *pastura* 'grazing', from *past-* 'grazed', from the verb *pascere.*

pastureland ▶ noun land used as pasture.

pasty[1] /ˈpasti/ (also **pastie**) ▶ noun (pl. **-ies**) chiefly Brit. a folded pastry case filled with seasoned meat and vegetables.
- ORIGIN Middle English: from Old French *paste(e)*, based on late Latin *pasta* 'paste'.

pasty[2] /ˈpeɪsti/ ▶ adjective (**pastier, pastiest**) **1** (of a person's face) unhealthily pale: *a pasty complexion.*
2 of or like paste: *a pasty mixture.*

- DERIVATIVES **pastiness** noun.

Pat ▶ noun Brit. informal, often offensive a nickname for an Irishman.
- ORIGIN early 19th cent.: abbreviation of the male given name *Patrick.*

Pat. ▶ abbreviation for Patent.

pat[1] ▶ verb (**patted, patting**) [with obj.] touch quickly and gently with the flat of the hand: *he patted him consolingly on the shoulder* | [with obj. and complement] *a nurse washed her all over and patted her dry.*
- ■draw attention to (something) by tapping it gently: *he patted the bench beside him and I sat down.* ■ [with obj. and adverbial] mould into shape or put in position with gentle taps: *she patted down the earth in each pot.*
▶ noun **1** a light stroke with the hand: *giving him a friendly pat on the arm, she went off to join the others.*
2 a compact mass of soft material: *a pat of butter.*
- PHRASES **a pat on the back** an expression of approval or congratulation: *they deserve a pat on the back for a job well done.* **pat someone on the back** express approval of or admiration for someone.
- ORIGIN late Middle English (as a noun denoting a blow with something flat): probably imitative. The verb dates from the mid 16th cent.

pat[2] ▶ adjective simple and somewhat glib or unconvincing: *there are no pat answers to these questions.*
▶ adverb at exactly the right moment or in the right way; conveniently or opportunely: *the happy ending came rather pat.*
- PHRASES **have something off** (or **down**) **pat** have something memorized perfectly: *she has her answer off pat.* **stand pat** chiefly N. Amer. stick stubbornly to one's opinion or decision: *many ranchers stood pat with the old strains of cattle.* ■ (in poker and blackjack) retain one's hand as dealt, without drawing other cards.
- DERIVATIVES **patly** adverb, **patness** noun.
- ORIGIN late 16th cent.: related to **PAT**[1]; apparently originally symbolic: a frequently found early use was *hit pat* (i.e. hit as if with flat blow).

pataca /pəˈtɑːkə/ ▶ noun the basic monetary unit of Macao, equivalent to 100 avos.
- ORIGIN Spanish and Portuguese.

pat-a-cake ▶ noun [mass noun] a children's game in which participants gently clap their hands in time to the words of a rhyme.

patagium /ˌpatəˈdʒʌɪəm/ ▶ noun (pl. **patagia** /-ˈdʒʌɪə/) Zoology a membrane or fold of skin between the forelimbs and hindlimbs on each side of a bat or gliding mammal.
- ■Entomology a lobe that covers the wing joint in many moths.
- ORIGIN early 19th cent.: from Latin, denoting gold edging on the edge of a Roman lady's tunic, from Greek *patageion.*

Patagonia /ˌpatəˈɡəʊnɪə/ a region of South America, in southern Argentina and Chile. Consisting largely of a dry barren plateau, it extends from the Colorado River in central Argentina to the Strait of Magellan and from the Andes to the Atlantic coast.
- DERIVATIVES **Patagonian** adjective & noun.
- ORIGIN from obsolete *Patagon*, denoting a member of a native people alleged by travellers of the 17th and 18th cents to be the tallest known.

Patagonian cavy (also **Patagonian hare**) ▶ noun another term for **MARA**.

Pataliputra /ˌpɑːtlɪˈpʊtrə/ ancient name for **PATNA**.

pata-pata /ˌpɑːtaˈpɑːta/ ▶ noun [mass noun] S. African a sexually suggestive dance style in which pairs of dancers touch each other's bodies with their hands.
- ■kwela music arranged to suit this style of dance. ■ informal sexual intercourse.
- ORIGIN from Xhosa and Zulu *phatha* 'to touch, feel'.

pataphysics /ˌpatəˈfɪzɪks/ ▶ plural noun [usu. treated as sing.] the branch of philosophy that deals with an imaginary realm additional to metaphysics.
- ORIGIN 1940s: from Greek *ta epi ta metaphusika*, literally 'the (works) imposed on the Metaphysics'. The concept was introduced by Alfred Jarry (1873–1907), French writer of the Absurd.

patas monkey /ˈpatɑː/ ▶ noun a central African guenon with reddish-brown fur, a black face, and a white moustache.
- ● *Erythrocebus patas*, family Cercopithecidae.

– ORIGIN mid 18th cent.: *patas* from Senegalese French, from Wolof *pata*.

Patau's syndrome /ˈpataʊz/ ▶ noun [mass noun] Medicine a congenital disorder in which there are three copies of chromosome 13, 14, or 15 instead of the usual two. This results in brain, heart, and kidney defects which are usually fatal soon after birth.
– ORIGIN 1960s: named after Klaus *Patau*, 20th-cent. German physician.

Patavium /pəˈteɪvɪəm/ Latin name for **PADUA**.

patball ▶ noun [mass noun] Brit. a simple game in which a ball is hit back and forth between two players.

patch ▶ noun **1** a piece of cloth or other material used to mend or strengthen a torn or weak point. ■ a pad or shield worn over a sightless or injured eye or an eye socket. ■ a piece of cloth sewn on to clothing as a badge or distinguishing mark. ■ Computing a small piece of code inserted into a program to improve its functioning or to correct a fault. ■ an adhesive piece of drug-impregnated material worn on the skin so that the drug may be absorbed gradually over a period of time. ■ (on an animal or bird) an area of hair or plumage different in colour from that on most of the rest of the body. ■ a part of something marked out from the rest by a particular characteristic: *his hair was combed forward to hide a growing bald patch.* ■ a small area or amount of something: *patches of bluebells in the grass.* ■ historical a small disc of black silk attached to the face, especially as worn by women in the 17th and 18th centuries for adornment. **2** a small piece of ground, especially one used for gardening: *they spent Sundays digging their vegetable patch.*
■ Brit. informal an area for which someone is responsible or in which they operate: *we didn't want any secret organizations on our patch.* **3** Brit. informal a period of time seen as a distinct unit with a characteristic quality: *he may have been going through a bad patch.* **4** a temporary electrical or telephone connection.
■ a preset configuration or sound data file in an electronic musical instrument, especially a synthesizer.
▶ verb [with obj.] **1** mend or strengthen (fabric or an item of clothing) by putting a piece of material over a hole or weak point in it: *her jeans were neatly patched.*
■ Medicine place a patch over (a good eye) in order to encourage a lazy eye to work. ■ Computing correct, enhance, or modify (a routine or program) by inserting a patch. ■ (usu. **be patched**) cover small areas of (a surface) with something different, causing it to appear variegated: *the grass was patched with sandy stretches.* ■ (**patch someone/thing up**) informal treat someone's injuries or repair the damage to something, especially hastily: *they did their best to patch up the gaping wounds.* ■ (**patch something together**) construct something hastily from unsuitable components: *lean-tos patched together from aluminium siding and planks* | figurative *they were trying to patch together an arrangement for cooperation.* ■ (**patch something up**) informal restore peaceful or friendly relations after a quarrel or dispute: *any ill feeling could be patched up with a phone call* | *they sent him home to patch things up with his wife.*
2 [with obj. and adverbial] connect by a temporary electrical, radio, or telephonic connection: *patch me through to number nine.*
■ [no obj., with adverbial] become connected in this way: *stay on the open line and we'll patch in on you.*
– PHRASES **not a patch on** Brit. informal greatly inferior to: *he no longer looked so handsome—he wasn't a patch on Peter.*
– DERIVATIVES **patcher** noun.
– ORIGIN late Middle English: perhaps from a variant of Old French *pieche*, dialect variant of *piece* 'piece'.

patchboard (also **patch panel**) ▶ noun a board in a switchboard, computer, or other device with a number of electric sockets that may be connected in various combinations.

patch box ▶ noun historical a decorated box for holding black silk patches for the face, used especially by women in the 17th and 18th centuries.

patch cord (also **patch lead**) ▶ noun an insulated lead with a plug at each end, for use with a patchboard.

patchouli /ˈpatʃʊli, pəˈtʃuːli/ ▶ noun [mass noun] **1** an

aromatic oil obtained from a SE Asian shrub, which is used in perfumery, insecticides, and medicine. **2** the strongly scented shrub of the mint family from which this oil is obtained.
● *Pogostemon cablin*, family Labiatae.
– ORIGIN mid 19th cent.: from Tamil *paccuḷi*.

patch panel ▶ noun another term for **PATCHBOARD**.

patch pocket ▶ noun a pocket made of a separate piece of cloth sewn on to the outside of a garment.

patch reef ▶ noun a small isolated platform of coral.

patch test ▶ noun a test to discover whether a person is allergic to any of a range of substances which are applied to the skin in light scratches or under a plaster.

patchwork ▶ noun [mass noun] needlework in which small pieces of cloth in different designs, colours, or textures are sewn together: *a piece of patchwork* | [as modifier] *a patchwork bedspread.*
■ the craft of sewing in this way: *specialists in quilting and patchwork.* ■ [count noun] a thing composed of many different elements so as to appear variegated: *a patchwork of stone walls and green fields.*

patchy ▶ adjective (**patchier, patchiest**) existing or happening in small, isolated areas: *patchy fog.*
■ not of the same quality throughout; inconsistent: *your coursework was patchy.* ■ incomplete: *my knowledge of Egyptology is patchy.*
– DERIVATIVES **patchily** adverb, **patchiness** noun.

pate /peɪt/ ▶ noun archaic or humorous a person's head: *he scratched his balding pate.*
– ORIGIN Middle English: of unknown origin.

pâte /paːt/ ▶ noun [mass noun] the paste of which porcelain is made.
– ORIGIN mid 19th cent.: French, literally 'paste'.

pâté /ˈpateɪ/ ▶ noun [mass noun] a rich, savoury paste made from finely minced or mashed ingredients, typically seasoned meat or fish.
– ORIGIN French, from Old French *paste* 'pie of seasoned meat'.

pâté de campagne /də kɒmˈpaːnjə/ ▶ noun [mass noun] coarse pork and liver pâté.
– ORIGIN French, literally 'country pâté'.

pâté de foie gras /ˌpateɪ də fwaː ˈɡraː/ ▶ noun [mass noun] a smooth rich paste made from fatted goose liver.
– ORIGIN French.

patée ▶ adjective variant spelling of **PATTÉE**.

patella /pəˈtɛlə/ ▶ noun (pl. **patellae** /-liː/) Anatomy the kneecap.
– DERIVATIVES **patellar** adjective, **patellate** /-lət/ adjective.
– ORIGIN late 16th cent.: from Latin, diminutive of *patina* 'shallow dish'.

paten /ˈpat(ə)n/ ▶ noun a plate, typically made of gold or silver, used for holding the bread during the Eucharist and sometimes as a cover for the chalice.
■ a shallow metal plate or dish.
– ORIGIN Middle English: from Old French *patene*, from Latin *patina* 'shallow dish', from Greek *patanē* 'a plate'.

patency /ˈpeɪt(ə)nsi/ ▶ noun [mass noun] Medicine the condition of being open, expanded, or unobstructed.
■ the condition of showing detectable parasite infection.

patent ▶ noun /ˈpat(ə)nt, ˈpeɪt-/ a government authority or licence to an individual or organization conferring a right or title for a set period, especially the sole right to make, use, or sell some invention: *he took out a patent for an improved steam hammer.* [ORIGIN: Compare with **LETTERS PATENT**.]
▶ adjective **1** /ˈpeɪt(ə)nt/ easily recognizable; obvious: *she was smiling with patent insincerity.*
2 Medicine /ˈpat(ə)nt, ˈpeɪt-/ (of a vessel, duct, or aperture) open and unobstructed; failing to close.
■ (of a parasitic infection) showing detectable parasites in the tissues or faeces.
3 [attrib.] made and marketed under a patent; proprietary: *patent milk powder.*
▶ verb /ˈpat(ə)nt, ˈpeɪt-/ [with obj.] obtain a patent for (an invention): *an invention is not your own until it is patented.*
– DERIVATIVES **patentable** adjective, **patently** /ˈpeɪt(ə)ntli/ adverb (only in sense 1 of the adjective).

– ORIGIN late Middle English: from Old French, from Latin *patent-* 'lying open', from the verb *patere*.

patentee /ˌpeɪt(ə)nˈtiː, ˌpat-/ ▶ noun a person or organization that obtains or holds a patent for something.

patent leather ▶ noun [mass noun] leather with a glossy varnished surface, used chiefly for shoes, belts, and handbags.

patent log ▶ noun a mechanical device towed in the water behind a boat to measure its speed and distance travelled.

patent medicine ▶ noun a proprietary medicine made and marketed under a patent and available without prescription.

patent office ▶ noun an office from which patents are issued.

patent right ▶ noun the exclusive right conferred by a patent: *one of the collaborators has agreed to waive its patent rights to the cowpea gene.*

Patent Roll ▶ noun historical (in the UK) a parchment roll listing the patents issued in a particular year.

patent still ▶ noun a type of still using steam-heating to produce spirits of greater strength and purity than a pot still.
– ORIGIN so named having been *patented* by Aeneas Coffey in 1830.

Pater /ˈpeɪtə/, Walter (Horatio) (1839–94), English essayist and critic. His *Studies in the History of the Renaissance* (1873) had a major impact on the development of the Aesthetic Movement.

pater /ˈpeɪtə/ ▶ noun **1** Brit. informal, dated father: *the pater gives her fifty pounds a year as a dress allowance.*
2 Anthropology a person's legal father. Often contrasted with **GENITOR**.
– ORIGIN Latin.

patera /ˈpat(ə)rə/ ▶ noun (pl. **paterae** /-riː/) a broad shallow dish used in ancient Rome for pouring libations.
■ Architecture a flat, round ornament resembling a shallow dish.
– ORIGIN Latin, from *patere* 'be or lie open'.

paterfamilias /ˌpeɪtəfəˈmɪlɪas, ˌpatə-/ ▶ noun (pl. **patresfamilias** /ˌpeɪtriːz-, ˌpatriːz-/) the male head of a family or household.
– ORIGIN Latin, literally 'father of the family'.

paternal ▶ adjective of or appropriate to a father: *he reasserted his paternal authority.*
■ showing a kindness and care associated with a father; fatherly: *my elders in the newsroom kept a paternal eye on me.* ■ [attrib.] related through the father: *his father and paternal grandfather were porcelain painters.*
– DERIVATIVES **paternally** adverb.
– ORIGIN late Middle English: from late Latin *paternalis*, from Latin *paternus* 'fatherly, belonging to a father', from *pater* 'father'.

paternalism ▶ noun [mass noun] the policy or practice on the part of people in positions of authority of restricting the freedom and responsibilities of those subordinate to or otherwise dependent on them in their supposed interest: *attitudes in society reinforce a degree of paternalism among doctors.*
– DERIVATIVES **paternalist** noun & adjective, **paternalistic** adjective, **paternalistically** adverb.

paternity ▶ noun [mass noun] **1** (especially in legal contexts) the state of being someone's father: *he refused to admit paternity of the child.*
2 paternal origin: *his enemies made great play of the supposed dubiety of his paternity.*
– ORIGIN late Middle English: from Old French *paternité*, from late Latin *paternitas*, from *paternus* 'relating to a father'.

paternity suit ▶ noun chiefly US a court case held to establish formally the identity of a child's father, typically in order to require the man to support the child financially.

paternity test ▶ noun a medical test, typically a blood test, to determine whether a man may be the father of a particular child.

paternoster /ˌpatəˈnɒstə/ ▶ noun **1** (in the Roman Catholic Church) the Lord's Prayer, especially in Latin.
■ any of a number of special beads occurring at regular intervals in a rosary, indicating that the Lord's Prayer is to be recited.
2 (also **paternoster lift**) a lift consisting of a series

of linked doorless compartments moving continuously on an endless belt.
3 (also **paternoster line**) a fishing line to which hooks or weights are attached at intervals.
– ORIGIN Old English, from Latin *pater noster* 'our father', the first words of the Lord's Prayer.

path ▶ **noun** (pl. **paths**) a way or track laid down for walking or made by continual treading.
■[with modifier] such a way or track designed for a particular purpose: *cycle path.* ■ the course or direction in which a person or thing is moving: *the missile traced a fiery path in the sky* | figurative *a chosen career path.* ■ a course of action or conduct: *adoption of the recommendation is now seen as the best path towards a settlement of the dispute.* ■ Computing a definition of the order in which an operating system or program searches for a file or executable program. ■ a schedule available for allocation to an individual railway train over a given route.
– PHRASES **the path of least resistance** see **RESISTANCE**.
– DERIVATIVES **pathless** adjective.
– ORIGIN Old English *pæth*, of West Germanic origin; related to Dutch *pad*, German *Pfad*, of unknown ultimate origin.

-path ▶ **combining form 1** denoting a practitioner of curative treatment: *homeopath.*
2 denoting a person who suffers from a disease: *psychopath.*
– ORIGIN back-formation from **-PATHY**, or from Greek *-pathēs* '-sufferer'.

Pathan /pəˈtɑːn/ ▶ **noun** a member of a Pashto-speaking people inhabiting NW Pakistan and SE Afghanistan.
– ORIGIN from Hindi *Paṭhān.*

path-breaking ▶ **adjective** pioneering; innovative: *their path-breaking work opened up a new era in cancer research.*
– DERIVATIVES **path-breaker** noun.

Pathé /ˈpaθeɪ/, Charles (1863–1957), French film pioneer. In 1896 he and his brothers founded a company which came to dominate the production and distribution of films. It became internationally known for its newsreels, first introduced in France in 1909.

pathetic ▶ **adjective 1** arousing pity, especially through vulnerability or sadness: *she looked so pathetic that I bent down to comfort her.*
■informal miserably inadequate: *his ball control was pathetic.*
2 archaic relating to the emotions.
– DERIVATIVES **pathetically** adverb.
– ORIGIN late 16th cent. (in the sense 'affecting the emotions'): via late Latin from Greek *pathētikos* 'sensitive', based on *pathos* 'suffering'.

pathetic fallacy ▶ **noun** [mass noun] the attribution of human feelings and responses to inanimate things or animals, especially in art and literature.

Pathfinder (in full **Mars Pathfinder**) an unmanned American spacecraft which landed on Mars in 1997, deploying a small robotic rover (Sojourner) to explore the surface and examine the rocks.

pathfinder ▶ **noun** a person who goes ahead and discovers or shows others a path or way.
■an aircraft or its pilot sent ahead to locate and mark the target area for bombing. ■[usu. as modifier] an experimental plan or forecast: *a pathfinder prospectus.*

path length ▶ **noun** Physics the overall length of the path followed by a light ray or sound wave.

pathname ▶ **noun** Computing a description of where a file or other item is to be found in a hierarchy of directories.

patho- ▶ **combining form** relating to disease: *pathogenesis* | *pathology.*
– ORIGIN from Greek *pathos* 'suffering, disease'.

pathogen /ˈpaθədʒ(ə)n/ ▶ **noun** Medicine a bacterium, virus, or other micro-organism that can cause disease.
– DERIVATIVES **pathogenic** adjective, **pathogenicity** noun, **pathogenous** /-ˈθɒdʒɪnəs/ adjective.

pathogenesis /ˌpaθə(ʊ)ˈdʒɛnɪsɪs/ ▶ **noun** Medicine the manner of development of a disease.
– DERIVATIVES **pathogenetic** adjective.

pathognomonic /ˌpaθəgnə(ʊ)ˈmɒnɪk/ ▶ **adjective** Medicine (of a sign or symptom) specifically characteristic or indicative of a particular disease or condition.
– ORIGIN early 17th cent.: from Greek *pathognōmonikos* 'skilled in diagnosis', from *pathos* 'suffering' + *gnōmōn* 'judge'.

pathography /pəˈθɒgrəfi/ ▶ **noun** (pl. **-ies**) a study of the life of an individual or the history of a community with regard to the influence of a particular disease or psychological disorder.
■[mass noun] writing of such a type as a branch of literature.

pathological (US **pathologic**) ▶ **adjective** of or relating to pathology: *the interpretation of pathological studies.*
■involving, caused by, or of the nature of a physical or mental disease: *pathological changes associated with senile dementia.* ■ informal compulsive; obsessive: *a pathological gambler.*
– DERIVATIVES **pathologically** adverb.

pathology ▶ **noun** [mass noun] the science of the causes and effects of diseases, especially the branch of medicine that deals with the laboratory examination of samples of body tissue for diagnostic or forensic purposes: *research people skilled in experimental pathology.*
■Medicine pathological features considered collectively; the typical behaviour of a disease: *the pathology of Huntington's disease.* ■ Medicine a pathological condition: *the dominant pathology is multiple sclerosis.* ■ [usu. with modifier] mental, social, or linguistic abnormality or malfunction: *the city's inability to cope with the pathology of a burgeoning underclass.*
– DERIVATIVES **pathologist** noun.
– ORIGIN early 17th cent.: from modern or medieval Latin *pathologia* (see **PATHO-**, **-LOGY**).

pathophysiology ▶ **noun** [mass noun] Medicine the disordered physiological processes associated with disease or injury: *intracranial hypertension contributes to the pathophysiology of this condition.*
– DERIVATIVES **pathophysiologic** adjective, **pathophysiological** adjective, **pathophysiologically** adverb, **pathophysiologist** noun.

pathos /ˈpeɪθɒs/ ▶ **noun** [mass noun] a quality that evokes pity or sadness: *the actor injects his customary humour and pathos into the role.*
– ORIGIN mid 17th cent.: from Greek *pathos* 'suffering'; related to *paskhein* 'suffer' and *penthos* 'grief'.

pathway ▶ **noun** a way that constitutes or serves as a path.
■Physiology a route, formed by a chain of nerve cells, along which impulses of a particular kind usually travel. ■ (also **metabolic pathway**) Biochemistry a sequence of chemical reactions undergone by a compound or class of compounds in a living organism.

-pathy ▶ **combining form 1** denoting feelings: *telepathy.*
2 denoting disorder in a particular part of the body: *neuropathy.*
3 relating to curative treatment of a specified kind: *hydropathy.*
– ORIGIN from Greek *patheia* 'suffering, feeling'.

patience ▶ **noun** [mass noun] **1** the capacity to accept or tolerate delay, trouble, or suffering without getting angry or upset: *you can find bargains if you have the patience to sift through the dross.*
2 chiefly Brit. any of various forms of card game for one player, the object of which is to use up all one's cards by forming particular arrangements and sequences.
– PHRASES **lose patience** (or **lose one's patience**) become unable to keep one's temper: *even Laurence finally **lost patience with** him.*
– ORIGIN Middle English: from Old French, from Latin *patientia*, from *patient-* 'suffering', from the verb *pati.*

patient ▶ **adjective** able to wait without becoming annoyed or anxious: *be patient, your time will come.*
■slow to lose one's temper with irritating people or situations: *he was always kindly, patient, and considerate.*
▶ **noun 1** a person receiving or registered to receive medical treatment.
2 Linguistics the semantic role of a noun phrase denoting something that is affected or acted upon by the action of a verb.
– DERIVATIVES **patiently** adverb.
– ORIGIN Middle English: from Old French, from Latin *patient-* 'suffering', from the verb *pati.*

patient Lucy ▶ **noun** North American term for **BUSY LIZZIE**.

patina /ˈpatɪnə/ ▶ **noun** a green or brown film on the surface of bronze or similar metals, produced by oxidation over a long period.
■a gloss or sheen on wooden furniture produced by age and polishing. ■ an acquired change in the appearance of a surface: *plankton added a golden patina to the shallow, slowly moving water.* ■ figurative an impression or appearance of something: *he carries the patina of old money and good breeding.*
– DERIVATIVES **patinated** adjective, **patination** noun.
– ORIGIN mid 18th cent.: from Italian, from Latin *patina* 'shallow dish'.

patio ▶ **noun** (pl. **-os**) a paved outdoor area adjoining a house.
■a roofless inner courtyard in a Spanish or Spanish-American house.
– ORIGIN early 19th cent.: from Spanish, denoting an inner courtyard.

patio door ▶ **noun** a large glass sliding door leading to a patio, garden, or balcony.

patio rose ▶ **noun** a miniature floribunda rose.

patisserie /pəˈtiːs(ə)ri, -ˈtɪs-/ ▶ **noun** a shop where pastries and cakes are sold.
■[mass noun] pastries and cakes collectively: *cream cakes and French patisserie.*
– ORIGIN late 16th cent.: from French *pâtisserie*, from medieval Latin *pasticium* 'pastry', from *pasta* 'paste'.

Pat Malone ▶ **noun** (in phrase **on one's Pat Malone** or **pat**) Austral. informal on one's own.
– ORIGIN early 20th cent.: rhyming slang.

Patmore, Coventry (Kersey Dighton) (1823–96), English poet. His most important work is *The Angel in the House* (1854–63), a sequence of poems in praise of married love.

Patmos /ˈpatmɒs/ a Greek island in the Aegean Sea, one of the Dodecanese group. It is believed that St John was living there in exile (from AD 95) when he had the visions described in Revelation.

Patna /ˈpatnə/ a city in NE India, on the Ganges, capital of the state of Bihar; pop. 917,000 (1991). An important city in ancient times, it had become deserted by the 7th century but was refounded in 1541 by the Moguls and became a viceregal capital. Former name **PATALIPUTRA**.

Patna rice ▶ **noun** [mass noun] rice of a variety with long firm grains, which was originally produced at Patna.

patois /ˈpatwɑː/ ▶ **noun** (pl. same /-wɑːz/) the dialect of the common people of a region, differing in various respects from the standard language of the rest of the country: *the nurse talked to me in a patois that even Italians would have had difficulty in understanding.*
■the jargon or informal speech used by a particular social group: *the raunchy patois of inner-city kids.*
– ORIGIN mid 17th cent.: French, literally 'rough speech', perhaps from Old French *patoier* 'treat roughly', from *patte* 'paw'.

Paton /ˈpeɪt(ə)n/, Alan (Stewart) (1903–88), South African writer and politician. He is best known for his novel *Cry, the Beloved Country* (1948), a passionate indictment of the apartheid system.

patonce /pəˈtɒns/ ▶ **adjective** [postpositive] Heraldry (of a cross) with limbs which broaden from the centre and end in three pointed lobes: *a cross patonce.*
– ORIGIN mid 16th cent.: probably related to French *potencé*, a heraldic term denoting T-shaped endings to each limb of a cross, based on medieval Latin *potentia* 'crutch'.

patootie /pəˈtuːti/ ▶ **noun** (pl. **-ies**) N. Amer. informal
1 dated a girlfriend or a pretty girl.
2 derogatory a person's or animal's buttocks.
– ORIGIN 1920s: perhaps an alteration of **POTATO**.

Patras /pəˈtras, ˈpatrəs/ an industrial port in the NW Peloponnese, on the Gulf of Patras; pop. 155,000 (1991). Taken by the Turks in the 18th century, it was the site in 1821 of the outbreak of the Greek war of independence. It was finally freed in 1828. Greek name **PÁTRAI** /ˈpatrɛ/.

patresfamilias plural form of **PATERFAMILIAS**.

patria /ˈpatrɪə, ˈpeɪtrɪə/ ▶ **noun** one's native country or homeland.
■archaic heaven, regarded as the true home from which the soul is exiled while on earth.
– ORIGIN Latin.

patrial /ˈpeɪtrɪəl/ ▶ **noun** Brit. historical a person with the right to live in the UK through the British birth of a parent or grandparent.
– DERIVATIVES **patriality** /-ˈalɪti/ noun.

– ORIGIN early 17th cent.: from French, or from medieval Latin *patrialis*, from Latin *patria* 'fatherland', from *pater* 'father'.

patriarch /ˈpeɪtrɪɑːk/ ▶ **noun 1** the male head of a family or tribe.
■ a man who is the oldest or most venerable of a group: *Hollywood's reigning patriarch rose to speak.* ■ a man who behaves in a commanding manner: *Cunningham's authoritative energy marks him out as patriarch within his own company.* ■ a person or thing that is regarded as the founder of something: *the patriarch of all spin doctors.*
2 any of those biblical figures regarded as fathers of the human race, especially Abraham, Isaac, and Jacob, and their forefathers, or the sons of Jacob.
3 the title of a most senior Orthodox or Catholic bishop, in particular:
■ a bishop of one of the most ancient Christian sees (Alexandria, Antioch, Constantinople, Jerusalem, and formerly Rome). ■ the head of an autocephalous or independent Orthodox Church. ■ a Roman Catholic bishop ranking above primates and metropolitans and immediately below the Pope, often the head of a Uniate community.
– ORIGIN Middle English: from Old French *patriarche*, via ecclesiastical Latin from Greek *patriarkhēs*, from *patria* 'family' + *arkhēs* 'ruling'.

patriarchal ▶ **adjective 1** of, relating to, or characteristic of a patriarch.
2 of, relating to, or characteristic of a system of society or government controlled by men: *patriarchal values.*
– DERIVATIVES **patriarchally** adverb.

patriarchate ▶ **noun** the office, see, or residence of an ecclesiastical patriarch.

patriarchy ▶ **noun** (pl. **-ies**) [mass noun] a system of society or government in which the father or eldest male is head of the family and descent is reckoned through the male line.
■ a system of society or government in which men hold the power and women are largely excluded from it. ■ [count noun] a society or community organized in this way.
– ORIGIN mid 17th cent.: via medieval Latin from Greek *patriarkhia*, from *patriarkhēs* 'ruling father' (see **PATRIARCH**).

patriate /ˈpatrɪeɪt, ˈpeɪtrɪeɪt/ ▶ **verb** [with obj.] transfer control over (a constitution) from a mother country to its former dependency: *the Canadian government moved to patriate the constitution from Great Britain.*

patrician /pəˈtrɪʃ(ə)n/ ▶ **noun** an aristocrat or nobleman.
■ N. Amer. a member of a long-established wealthy family. ■ a member of a noble family or class in ancient Rome.
▶ **adjective** belonging to or characteristic of the aristocracy: *a proud, patrician face.*
■ N. Amer. belonging to or characteristic of a long-established and wealthy family. ■ belonging to the nobility of ancient Rome.
– ORIGIN late Middle English: from Old French *patricien*, from Latin *patricius* 'having a noble father', from *pater, patr-* 'father'.

patriciate ▶ **noun** a noble order or class: *the Venetian merchants became a great hereditary patriciate.*
■ the position or rank of patrician in ancient Rome.

patricide /ˈpatrɪsʌɪd/ ▶ **noun** [mass noun] the killing of one's father.
■ [count noun] a person who kills their father.
– DERIVATIVES **patricidal** adjective.
– ORIGIN early 17th cent.: from late Latin *patricidium*, alteration of Latin *parricidium* (see **PARRICIDE**).

Patrick, St (5th century), Apostle and patron saint of Ireland. Of Romano-British parentage, he was taken as a slave to Ireland, where he experienced a religious conversion. He founded the archiepiscopal see of Armagh in about 454. Feast day, 17 March.

patrilineal ▶ **adjective** of, relating to, or based on relationship to the father or descent through the male line: *in Polynesia inheritance of land was predominantly patrilineal.*
– ORIGIN early 20th cent.: from Latin *pater, patr-* 'father' + **LINEAL**.

patrilocal ▶ **adjective** of or relating to a pattern of marriage in which the couple settles in the husband's home or community: *the residence pattern is patrilocal.* Also called **VIRILOCAL**.
– DERIVATIVES **patrilocality** noun.
– ORIGIN early 20th cent.: from Latin *pater, patr-* 'father' + **LOCAL**.

patrimony /ˈpatrɪməni/ ▶ **noun** (pl. **-ies**) [mass noun] property inherited from one's father or male ancestor: *owners refuse to part with their patrimony in the interests of agricultural development.*
■ heritage: *an organization that saves the world's cultural patrimony by restoring historic buildings.* ■ chiefly historical the estate or property belonging by ancient endowment or right to a church or other institution.
– DERIVATIVES **patrimonial** /-ˈməʊnɪəl/ adjective.
– ORIGIN Middle English: from Old French *patrimoine*, from Latin *patrimonium*, from *pater, patr-* 'father'.

patriot /ˈpatrɪət, ˈpeɪt-/ ▶ **noun** a person who vigorously supports their country and is prepared to defend it against enemies or detractors.
– DERIVATIVES **patriotism** noun.
– ORIGIN late 16th cent. (in the late Latin sense): from French *patriote*, from late Latin *patriota* 'fellow countryman', from Greek *patriōtēs*, from *patrios* 'of one's fathers', from *patris* 'fatherland'.

patriotic ▶ **adjective** having or expressing devotion to and vigorous support for one's country: *he felt a surge of patriotic emotion.*
– DERIVATIVES **patriotically** adverb.
– ORIGIN mid 17th cent.: via late Latin from Greek *patriōtikos* 'relating to a fellow countryman' (see **PATRIOT**).

patriotic front ▶ **noun** a militant nationalist political organization.

patristic /pəˈtrɪstɪk/ ▶ **adjective** of or relating to the early Christian theologians or to patristics.
– ORIGIN mid 19th cent.: from German *patristisch*, from Latin *pater, patr-* 'father'.

patristics ▶ **plural noun** [treated as sing.] the branch of Christian theology that deals with the lives, writings, and doctrines of the early Christian theologians.

Patroclus /pəˈtrɒkləs/ Greek Mythology a Greek hero of the Trojan War, the close friend of Achilles.

patrol ▶ **noun** a person or group of people sent to keep watch over an area, especially a detachment of guards or police: *a police patrol stopped the man and searched him.*
■ [mass noun] the action of keeping watch over an area by walking or driving around it at regular intervals: *the policemen were* **on patrol** *when they were ordered to investigate the incident.* ■ an expedition to carry out reconnaissance: *we were ordered to investigate on a night patrol.* ■ a detachment of troops sent out to reconnoitre: *you couldn't go through the country without meeting an enemy patrol.* ■ a routine operational voyage of a ship or aircraft: *a submarine patrol.* ■ a unit of six to eight Scouts or Guides forming part of a troop. ■ Brit. an official who controls traffic where children cross the road: *there were two schools but no* **crossing patrol**.
▶ **verb** (**patrolled**, **patrolling**) [with obj.] keep watch over (an area) by regularly walking or travelling around it: *the garrison had to patrol the streets to maintain order* | [no obj.] *pairs of men were patrolling on each side of the thoroughfare.*
– DERIVATIVES **patroller** noun.
– ORIGIN mid 17th cent. (as a noun): from German *Patrolle*, from French *patrouille*, from *patrouiller* 'paddle in mud', from *patte* 'paw' + dialect (*gad*)*rouille* 'dirty water'.

patrolman ▶ **noun** (pl. **-men**) N. Amer. a patrolling police officer.

patrology /pəˈtrɒlədʒi/ ▶ **noun** another term for **PATRISTICS**.
– DERIVATIVES **patrologist** noun.
– ORIGIN early 17th cent.: from Greek *patēr, patr-* 'father' + **-LOGY**.

patron ▶ **noun 1** a person who gives financial or other support to a person, organization, cause, or activity: *a celebrated patron of the arts.*
■ a distinguished person who takes an honorary position in a charity: *the Mental Health Foundation, of which Her Royal Highness is Patron.*
2 a customer of a shop, restaurant, hotel, or theatre, especially a regular one: *we surveyed the plushness of the hotel and its sleek, well-dressed patrons.*
3 (in ancient Rome) a patrician in relation to a client. See also **CLIENT** (sense 3).
■ (in ancient Rome) the former owner and (frequently) protector of a freed slave.
4 Brit., chiefly historical a person or institution with the right to grant a benefice to a member of the clergy.
– ORIGIN Middle English: from Old French, from Latin *patronus* 'protector of clients, defender', from *pater, patr-* 'father'.

patronage /ˈpatr(ə)nɪdʒ, ˈpeɪt-/ ▶ **noun** [mass noun] **1** the support given by a patron: *the arts could no longer depend on private patronage.*
2 the power to control appointments to office or the right to privileges: *recruits are selected on merit, not through political patronage.*
3 a patronizing or condescending manner: *a twang of self-satisfaction—even patronage—about him.*
4 the regular custom given to a shop, restaurant, or public service by a person or group: *the direct train link was ending because of poor patronage.*
5 (in ancient Rome) the rights and duties or position of a patron.
– ORIGIN late Middle English: from Old French, from *patron* 'protector, advocate' (see **PATRON**).

Patronage Secretary ▶ **noun** (in the UK) the member of the government through whom patronage is administered.

patronal /pəˈtrəʊn(ə)l/ ▶ **adjective** of or relating to a patron saint: *the patronal festival of the parish church of St Peter.*

patroness ▶ **noun** a female patron.

patronize (also **-ise**) ▶ **verb 1** [often as adj. **patronizing**] treat with an apparent kindness which betrays a feeling of superiority: *'She's a good-hearted girl,' he said in a patronizing voice* | *she was determined not to be put down or patronized.*
2 frequent (a shop, theatre, restaurant, or other establishment) as a customer: *restaurants remaining open in the evening were well patronized.*
■ give encouragement and financial support to (a person, especially an artist, or a cause): *local churches and voluntary organizations were patronized by the family.*
– DERIVATIVES **patronization** noun, **patronizer** noun, **patronizingly** adverb.

patronne /paˈtrɒn/ ▶ **noun** a woman who is the owner, or the wife of the owner, of a business, especially a cafe, hotel, or restaurant.
– ORIGIN French, feminine of *patron*.

patron saint ▶ **noun** the protecting or guiding saint of a person or place.

patronymic /ˌpatrəˈnɪmɪk/ ▶ **noun** a name derived from the name of a father or ancestor, e.g. *Johnson, O'Brien, Ivanovich.*
– ORIGIN early 17th cent.: via late Latin from Greek *patrōnumikos*, from *patrōnumos*, from *patēr, patr-* 'father' + *onuma* 'name'.

patroon /pəˈtruːn/ ▶ **noun** US historical a person given land and granted certain manorial privileges under the former Dutch governments of New York and New Jersey.
– ORIGIN mid 17th cent.: from Dutch.

patsy ▶ **noun** (pl. **-ies**) informal, chiefly N. Amer. a person who is easily taken advantage of, especially by being cheated or blamed for something.
– ORIGIN early 20th cent.: of unknown origin.

patta /ˈpʌtə/ ▶ **noun** Indian a title deed to a property.
– ORIGIN Hindi, perhaps from Sanskrit *pattra* 'document'.

Pattaya /paˈtʌɪə/ a resort on the coast of southern Thailand, south-east of Bangkok.

pattée /ˈpateɪ, -ti/ (also **patée**) ▶ **adjective** [postpositive] (of a cross) having almost triangular arms, very narrow at the centre and broadening to squared ends: *a cross pattée.*
– ORIGIN late 15th cent.: from French, from *patte* 'paw'.

patten /ˈpat(ə)n/ ▶ **noun** historical a shoe or clog with a raised sole or set on an iron ring, worn to raise one's feet above wet or muddy ground when walking outdoors.
– ORIGIN late Middle English: from Old French *patin*, perhaps from *patte* 'paw'.

patter[1] ▶ **verb** [no obj.] make a repeated light tapping sound: *a flurry of rain pattered against the window.*
■ run with quick light steps: *plovers pattered at the edge of the marsh.*
▶ **noun** [in sing.] a repeated light tapping: *the rain had stopped its vibrating patter above him.*
– ORIGIN early 17th cent.: frequentative of **PAT**[1].

patter[2] ▶ **noun** [mass noun] rapid or smooth-flowing continuous talk, such as that used by a comedian or salesman: *slick black hair, flashy clothes and a New York line of patter.*

■ rapid speech included in a song, especially for comic effect: [as modifier] *a patter song of invective.* ■ the special language or jargon of a profession or other group: *he picked up the patter from watching his dad.*
▶ **verb** [no obj.] talk at length without saying anything significant: *she pattered on incessantly.*
– ORIGIN late Middle English (as a verb in the sense 'recite (a prayer, charm, etc.) rapidly'): from **PATERNOSTER**. The noun dates from the mid 18th cent.

pattern ▶ **noun 1** a repeated decorative design: *a neat blue herringbone pattern.*
■ an arrangement or sequence regularly found in comparable objects or events: *the house had been built on the usual pattern.* ■ a regular and intelligible form or sequence discernible in certain actions or situations: *a complicating factor is the change in working patterns.*
2 a model or design used as a guide in needlework and other crafts.
■ a set of instructions to be followed in making a sewn or knitted item. ■ a wooden or metal model from which a mould is made for a casting. ■ an example for others to follow: *he set the pattern for subsequent study.* ■ a sample of cloth or wallpaper.
▶ **verb** [with obj.] **1** [usu. as adj. **patterned**] decorate with a recurring design: *rosebud patterned wallpapers | violet-tinged flowers patterned the grassy banks.*
2 give a regular or intelligible form to: *the brain not only receives information, but interprets and patterns it.*
■ (**pattern something on/after**) give something a form based on that of (something else): *the clothing is patterned on athletes' wear.*
– ORIGIN Middle English *patron* 'something serving as a model', from Old French (see **PATRON**). The change in sense is from the idea of a patron giving an example to be copied. Metathesis in the second syllable occurred in the 16th cent. By 1700 *patron* ceased to be used of things, and the two forms became differentiated in sense.

pattern baldness ▶ **noun** [mass noun] genetically determined baldness in which hair is gradually lost according to a characteristic pattern.

pattern bombing ▶ **noun** [mass noun] the bombing of (a target) from a number of aircraft according to a prescribed pattern intended to produce the maximum effect.

pattern book ▶ **noun** a book containing samples of patterns and designs of cloth or wallpaper.

pattern drill ▶ **noun** another term for **PATTERN PRACTICE**.

patterned ground ▶ **noun** [mass noun] Geology ground showing a pattern of stones, fissures, and vegetation, typically forming polygons, rings, or stripes caused by repeated freezing and thawing.

patternless ▶ **adjective** having no pattern; plain and undecorated: *smooth, patternless paper for covering poor or uneven walls.*
■ forming no discernible pattern: *phenomena that are completely patternless and disorganized.*

pattern practice ▶ **noun** [mass noun] the intensive repetition of the distinctive constructions and patterns of a foreign language as a means of learning.

pattern welding ▶ **noun** [mass noun] Archaeology a technique in which metal bars and strips of different type and colour were welded together and hammered out to give a patterned artefact.

patty ▶ **noun** (pl. **-ies**) a small flat cake of minced or finely chopped food, especially meat.
■ a small pie or pasty. ■ N. Amer. a small, round, flat chocolate-covered peppermint sweet.
– ORIGIN mid 17th cent.: alteration of French *pâté*, by association with **PASTY**[1].

pattypan (also **pattypan squash**) ▶ **noun** chiefly US a squash of a saucer-shaped variety with a scalloped rim and creamy white flesh.
– ORIGIN so named from the resemblance in shape to a pan for baking a patty.

patulous /ˈpatjʊləs/ ▶ **adjective** rare (especially of the branches of a tree) spreading.
– ORIGIN early 17th cent.: from Latin *patulus* (from *patere* 'be or lie open') + **-OUS**.

patwari /pʌtˈwɑːri/ ▶ **noun** (pl. **patwaris**) Indian a government official who keeps records regarding the ownership of land.
– ORIGIN from Hindi *paṭwārī*, from Sanskrit *paṭṭa* 'document' + *pāla* 'keeper'.

patzer /ˈpɑːtsə, ˈpat-/ ▶ **noun** informal a poor player at chess.
– ORIGIN 1940s: perhaps related to German *patzen* 'to bungle'.

paua /ˈpɑːwə, ˈpaʊə/ ▶ **noun** NZ a large edible abalone (mollusc).
■ the ornamental shell of this. ■ a Maori fish-hook made from this shell.
– ORIGIN mid 19th cent.: from Maori.

paucity /ˈpɔːsɪti/ ▶ **noun** [in sing.] the presence of something in only small or insufficient quantities or amounts: *a* ***paucity of*** *information.*
– ORIGIN late Middle English: from Old French *paucite* or Latin *paucitas*, from *paucus* 'few'.

Paul, Les (b.1915), American jazz guitarist and guitar designer; born *Lester Polfus*. In 1946 he invented the solid-body electric guitar.

Paul III (1468–1549), Italian pope 1534–49; born *Alessandro Farnese*. He excommunicated Henry VIII of England in 1538, instituted the order of the Jesuits in 1540, and initiated the Council of Trent in 1545.

Paul, St (died *c.*64), missionary of Jewish descent; known as **Paul the Apostle**, or **Saul of Tarsus**, or **the Apostle of the Gentiles**. He first opposed the followers of Jesus, assisting at the martyrdom of St Stephen. On a mission to Damascus he was converted to Christianity after a vision and became one of the first major Christian missionaries and theologians. His epistles form part of the New Testament. Feast day, 29 June.

Paul–Bunnell test ▶ **noun** Medicine a test in which an antibody reaction to sheep red blood cells confirms a diagnosis of infectious mononucleosis (glandular fever).
– ORIGIN 1930s: named after John R. *Paul* (1893–1936) and Walls W. *Bunnell* (1902–1965), American physicians.

Pauli /ˈpaʊli/, Wolfgang (1900–58), Austrian-born American physicist. He made a major contribution to quantum theory with his **exclusion principle**, according to which only two electrons in an atom could occupy the same quantum level, provided they had opposite spins. In 1931 he postulated the existence of the neutrino, later discovered by Enrico Fermi. Nobel Prize for Physics (1945).

Paulician /pɔːˈlɪʃ(ə)n/ ▶ **noun** Church History a member of a sect which arose in Armenia in the 7th century AD, professing a modified form of Manichaeism.
– DERIVATIVES **Paulicianism** noun.
– ORIGIN from medieval Latin *Pauliciani*, Greek *Paulikianoi*, of unknown origin.

Pauli exclusion principle (also **Pauli's exclusion principle**) Physics the assertion that no two fermions can have the same quantum number.
– ORIGIN 1920s: named after W. **PAULI**.

Pauline /ˈpɔːlʌɪn/ ▶ **adjective** Christian Theology of, relating to, or characteristic of St Paul, his writings, or his doctrines.
■ (in the Roman Catholic Church) of or relating to Pope Paul VI, or the liturgical and doctrinal reforms pursued during his pontificate (1963–78) as a result of the Second Vatican Council.

Pauling /ˈpɔːlɪŋ/, Linus Carl (1901–94), American chemist. He is renowned for his study of molecular structure and chemical bonding, for which he received the 1954 Nobel Prize for Chemistry. His suggestion of a helical structure for proteins formed the foundation for the elucidation of the structure of DNA.

Paul Jones ▶ **noun** a ballroom dance in which the dancers change partners after circling in concentric rings of men and women.
– ORIGIN 1920s: named after John *Paul Jones* (1747–92), Scottish-born American admiral.

paulownia /pɔːˈləʊnɪə, -ˈlɒvnɪə/ ▶ **noun** a small SE Asian tree with heart-shaped leaves and fragrant lilac flowers.
• Genus *Paulownia*, family Scrophulariaceae.
– ORIGIN modern Latin, named after Anna *Pavlovna* (1795–1865), a Russian princess.

Paul Pry ▶ **noun** informal, dated an inquisitive person.
– ORIGIN from the name of a character in a US song of 1820.

paunch ▶ **noun 1** a large or protruding abdomen or stomach.
2 Nautical, archaic a thick strong mat used to give protection from chafing on a mast or spar.
▶ **verb** [with obj.] disembowel (an animal): *one of the things I had to do was to paunch and skin a hare.*
– DERIVATIVES **paunchiness** noun, **paunchy** adjective.
– ORIGIN late Middle English: from Anglo-Norman French *pa(u)nche*, based on Latin *pantex*, *pantic-*, usually in the plural in the sense 'intestines'.

pauper ▶ **noun** a very poor person.
■ historical a recipient of relief under the provisions of the Poor Law or of public charity.
– DERIVATIVES **pauperdom** noun, **pauperism** noun, **pauperization** noun, **pauperize** (also **-ise**) verb.
– ORIGIN late 15th cent.: from Latin, literally 'poor'. The word's use in English originated in the Latin legal phrase *in forma pauperis*, literally 'in the form of a poor person' (allowing non-payment of costs).

paupiette /pɔːˈpjɛt/ ▶ **noun** a long, thin slice of fish or meat, rolled and stuffed with a filling.
– ORIGIN French, probably from Italian *polpetta*, from Latin *pulpa* 'pulp'.

pauraque /paʊˈrɑːkeɪ/ ▶ **noun** a long-tailed nightjar found mainly in Central and South America.
• Family Caprimulgidae: two genera and species, in particular the **common pauraque** (*Nyctidromus albicollis*).
– ORIGIN probably a Hispanicized form of a local word.

Pauropoda /ˈpɔːrəpɒdə/ Zoology a small class of myriapod invertebrates which resemble the centipedes. They are small soft-bodied animals with one pair of legs per segment, living chiefly in forest litter.
– DERIVATIVES **pauropod** noun, **pauropodan** noun & adjective.
– ORIGIN modern Latin (plural), from Greek *pauros* 'small' + *pous*, *pod-* 'foot'.

Pausanias /pɔːˈseɪnɪəs/ (2nd century), Greek geographer and historian. His *Description of Greece* (also called the *Itinerary of Greece*) is a guide to the topography and remains of ancient Greece and is still considered an invaluable source of information.

pause ▶ **noun** a temporary stop in action or speech: *she dropped me outside during a brief pause in the rain |* [mass noun] *the admiral chattered away* ***without pause.***
■ Music a mark (𝄐) over a note or rest that is to be lengthened by an unspecified amount. ■ (also **pause button**) a control allowing the temporary interruption of an electronic (or mechanical) process, especially video or audio-tape recording or reproduction.
▶ **verb** [no obj.] interrupt action or speech briefly: *she paused, at a loss for words.*
■ [with obj.] temporarily interrupt the operation of (a video or audio tape or computer program): *she had paused a tape on the VCR.*
– PHRASES **give pause to someone** (or **give pause for thought**) cause someone to think carefully or hesitate before doing something: *the sight of these gives any would-be attacker pause for thought.*
– ORIGIN late Middle English: from Old French, from Latin *pausa*, from Greek *pausis*, from *pausein* 'to stop'.

pavage /ˈpeɪvɪdʒ/ ▶ **noun** [mass noun] historical a tax or toll to cover the cost of the paving of streets.
– ORIGIN late Middle English: from Old French, from *paver* 'to pave'.

pavane /pəˈvan, -ˈvɑːn/ (also **pavan** /ˈpav(ə)n/) ▶ **noun** a stately dance in slow duple time, popular in the 16th and 17th centuries and performed in elaborate clothing.
■ a piece of music for this dance.
– ORIGIN mid 16th cent.: from French *pavane*, from Italian *pavana*, feminine adjective from *Pavo*, dialect name of Padua.

Pavarotti /ˌpavəˈrɒti/, Luciano (b.1935), Italian operatic tenor. He made his debut as Rodolfo in Puccini's *La Bohème* in 1961 and has since gained international acclaim and popularity for his bel canto singing.

pave ▶ **verb** [with obj.] (often **be paved with**) cover (a piece of ground) with flat stones or bricks; lay paving over: *the yard at the front was paved with flagstones |* [as adj. **paved**] *chrysanthemums provide a cheerful border for the paved area |* figurative *the streets of the big city are not* ***paved with gold.***
– PHRASES **pave the way for** create the circumstances to enable (something) to happen or be done: *the proposals will pave the way for a speedy resolution to the problem.*
– DERIVATIVES **paver** noun.
– ORIGIN Middle English: from Old French *paver* 'pave'.

pavé /ˈpaveɪ/ ▶ **noun 1** a setting of precious stones

placed so closely together that no metal shows: *a solid diamond pavé.*
2 archaic a paved street, road, or path.
– ORIGIN French, literally 'paved', past participle of *paver.*

pavement ▶ **noun** Brit. a raised paved or asphalted path for pedestrians at the side of a road.
■ any paved area or surface used as a walkway. ■ [mass noun] N. Amer. the hard surface of a road or street. ■ Geology a horizontal expanse of bare rock or cemented fragments.
– ORIGIN Middle English: from Old French, from Latin *pavimentum* 'trodden down floor', from *pavire* 'beat, tread down'.

pavement artist ▶ **noun** Brit. an artist who draws with coloured chalks on paving stones or paper laid on a pavement, hoping to be given money by passers-by.

Pavese /paˈveɪzeɪ, -zi/, Cesare (1908–50), Italian novelist, poet, and translator. He is best known for his last novel *La Luna e i falò* (1950), in which he portrays isolation and the failure of communication as a general human predicament.

pavilion ▶ **noun** a building or similar structure used for a specific purpose, in particular:
■ Brit. a building at a cricket ground or other sports ground in which players change their clothes and in which refreshments are served. ■ a summer house or other decorative building used as a shelter in a park or large garden. ■ in the names of buildings used for theatrical or other entertainments: *the resort's Spa Pavilion.* ■ a detached or semi-detached block at a hospital or other building complex. ■ a large tent with a peak and crenellated decorations, used at a show or fair or in re-enactments of medieval events. ■ a temporary building, stand, or other structure in which items are displayed by a trader or exhibitor at a trade exhibition.
– ORIGIN Middle English (denoting a large decorated tent): from Old French *pavillon*, from Latin *papilio(n-)* 'butterfly or tent'.

paving ▶ **noun** [mass noun] a surface made up of flat stones laid in a pattern.
■ the stones used for such a surface.

paving stone ▶ **noun** a large, flat piece of stone or similar material, used in paving.

paviour /ˈpeɪvɪə/ (also **pavior**) ▶ **noun** a paving stone.
■ a person who lays paving stones.
– ORIGIN Middle English: from Old French *paveur*, from *paver* 'pave'.

Pavlov /ˈpavlɒf/, Ivan (Petrovich) (1849–1936), Russian physiologist. He was awarded a Nobel Prize in 1904 for his work on digestion, but is best known for his studies on the conditioned reflex. He showed by experiment with dogs how the secretion of saliva can be stimulated not only by food but also by the sound of a bell associated with the presentation of food.

p

Pavlova /pavˈləʊvə/ Anna (Pavlovna) (1881–1931), Russian dancer, resident in Britain from 1912. Her highly acclaimed solo dance *The Dying Swan* was created for her by Michel Fokine in 1905. On settling in Britain she formed her own company.

pavlova ▶ **noun** a dessert consisting of a meringue base or shell filled with whipped cream and fruit.
– ORIGIN named after A. **PAVLOVA**.

Pavlovian /pavˈləʊvɪən/ ▶ **adjective** of or relating to classical conditioning as described by I. P. Pavlov: *the sound of the tea trolley created a Pavlovian reaction among the men.*

Pavo /ˈpɑːvəʊ/ Astronomy a southern constellation (the Peacock), between Grus and Triangulum Australe. Its brightest star is itself sometimes called 'the Peacock'.
■ [as genitive **Pavonis** /pɑːˈvəʊnɪs/] used with preceding letter or numeral to designate a star in this constellation: *the star Beta Pavonis.*
– ORIGIN Latin.

pavonine /ˈpavənʌɪn/ ▶ **adjective** poetic/literary, rare of or like a peacock.
– ORIGIN mid 17th cent.: from Latin *pavoninus*, from *pavo, pavon-* 'peacock'.

paw ▶ **noun** an animal's foot having claws and pads.
■ chiefly derogatory a person's hand: *touch her with your filthy paws and I'll ram my fist into your face.*
▶ **verb** [with obj.] (of an animal) feel or scrape with a paw or hoof: *the horse rose on its strong haunches, its forelegs pawing the air* | [no obj.] *young dogs may* ***paw at*** *the floor and whine.*
■ informal (of a person) touch or handle awkwardly or roughly; touch (someone) in a lascivious and offensive way: *some overweight, ugly Casanova had tried to paw her.*
– ORIGIN Middle English: from Old French *poue*, probably of Germanic origin and related to Dutch *poot*.

pawky ▶ **adjective** (**pawkier**, **pawkiest**) chiefly Scottish & N. English having or showing a sly sense of humour: *a gentle man with a pawky wit.*
■ shrewd: *she shakes her head with a look of pawky, knowing scepticism.*
– DERIVATIVES **pawkily** adverb, **pawkiness** noun.
– ORIGIN mid 17th cent.: from Scots and northern English *pawk* 'trick', of unknown origin.

pawl /pɔːl/ ▶ **noun** a pivoted curved bar or lever whose free end engages with the teeth of a cogwheel or ratchet so that the wheel or ratchet can only turn or move one way.
■ each of a set of short stout bars that engage with the whelps and prevent a capstan, windlass, or winch from recoiling.
– ORIGIN early 17th cent.: perhaps from Low German and Dutch *pal* (related to *pal* 'fixed').

pawn[1] ▶ **noun** a chess piece of the smallest size and value, that moves one square forwards along its file if unobstructed (or two on the first move), or one square diagonally forwards when making a capture. Each player begins with eight pawns on the second rank, and can promote a pawn to become any other piece (typically a queen) if it reaches the opponent's end of the board.
■ a person used by others for their own purposes.
– ORIGIN late Middle English: from Anglo-Norman French *poun*, from medieval Latin *pedo, pedon-* 'foot soldier', from Latin *pes, ped-* 'foot'. Compare with **PEON**.

pawn[2] ▶ **verb** [with obj.] deposit (an object) with a pawnbroker as security for money lent: *I pawned the necklace to cover the loan.*
▶ **noun** archaic an object left as security for money lent.
– PHRASES **in pawn** (of an object) held as security by a pawnbroker: *all our money was gone and everything was in pawn.*
– ORIGIN late 15th cent. (as a noun): from Old French *pan* 'pledge, security', of West Germanic origin; related to Dutch *pand* and German *Pfand*.
▶ **pawn someone/thing off** pass off someone or something unwanted: *newly industrialized economies are racing to* ***pawn off*** *old processes* ***on*** *poorer countries.*

pawnbroker ▶ **noun** a person who lends money at interest on the security of an article pawned.
– DERIVATIVES **pawnbroking** noun.

Pawnee /pɔːˈniː/ ▶ **noun** (pl. same or **Pawnees**) **1** a member of an American Indian confederacy formerly living in Nebraska, and now mainly in Oklahoma.
2 [mass noun] the language of these people, belonging to the Caddoan family and now almost extinct.
▶ **adjective** of or relating to these people or their language.
– ORIGIN from Canadian French *Pani*, from a North American Indian language.

pawnshop ▶ **noun** a pawnbroker's shop.

pawn ticket ▶ **noun** a ticket issued by a pawnbroker in exchange for an article pawned, bearing particulars of the loan.

pawpaw /ˈpɔːpɔː/ (also **papaw**) ▶ **noun** **1** another term for **PAPAYA**.
2 (also **pawpaw tree**) US a North American tree of the custard apple family, with purple flowers and edible oblong yellow fruit with sweet pulp.
● *Asimina triloba*, family Annonaceae.
■ the fruit of this tree.
– ORIGIN early 17th cent.: from Spanish and Portuguese *papaya*, of Carib origin. The change in spelling is unexplained.

Pax Roman Mythology the goddess of peace. Greek equivalent **EIRENE**.

pax ▶ **noun** **1** [as exclamation] Brit. informal, dated a call for a truce, used especially by schoolchildren when playing: *Pax! No offence meant, honest old chum.*
2 chiefly historical (in the Christian Church) the kissing by all the participants at a mass of a tablet depicting the Crucifixion or other sacred object; the kiss of peace.
– ORIGIN Latin, literally 'peace'.

Pax Romana /ˌpaks rəʊˈmɑːnə/ ▶ **noun** [mass noun] historical the peace which existed between nationalities within the Roman Empire.
– ORIGIN Latin, literally 'Roman peace'.

Paxton, Sir Joseph (1801–65), English gardener and architect. He became head gardener at Chatsworth House in Derbyshire in 1826 and designed a series of glass-and-iron greenhouses. He later reworked these in his design for the Crystal Palace (1851).

pay[1] ▶ **verb** (past and past participle **paid**) **1** [with obj.] give (someone) money that is due for work done, goods received, or a debt incurred: [with obj. and infinitive] *the traveller was able to pay a guide to show him across* | [no obj.] *TV licences can be* ***paid for*** *by direct debit.*
■ give (a sum of money) in exchange for goods or work done or in discharge of a debt: *the company was rumoured to have paid 450p a share* | [with two objs] *a museum paid him a four-figure sum for it.* ■ hand over or transfer the amount due of (a debt, wages, etc.) to someone: *bonuses were paid to savers whose policies completed their full term.* ■ (of work, an investment, etc.) yield or provide someone with (a specified sum of money): *jobs that pay $5 or $6 an hour.* ■ [no obj.] (of a business, undertaking, or an attitude) be profitable or advantageous to someone: *crime doesn't pay* | [with infinitive] *it pays to choose varieties carefully.*
2 [no obj.] suffer a loss or other misfortune as a consequence of an action: *the destroyer would have to* ***pay with*** *his life.*
■ [with obj.] give what is due or deserved to (someone); reward or punish: *it was his way of* ***paying out*** *Maguire for giving him the push.*
3 [with two objs] give or bestow (attention, respect, or a compliment) on (someone): *no one paid them any attention.*
■ make (a visit or a call) to (someone): *she has been prevailed upon to pay us a visit.*
▶ **noun** [mass noun] the money paid to someone for regular work: *those working on contract may receive higher rates of pay.*
– PHRASES **he who pays the piper calls the tune** proverb the person who provides the money for something has the right to determine how it's spent. **in the pay of** employed by. **pay one's compliments** see **COMPLIMENT**. **pay court to** see **COURT**. **pay dearly** obtain something at a high cost or great effort: *his master must have paid dearly for such a magnificent beast.* ■ suffer for a misdemeanour or failure: *they paid dearly for wasting goalscoring opportunities.* **pay one's dues** see **DUE**. **pay for itself** (of an object or system) earn or save enough money to cover the cost of its purchase. **pay its** (or **one's**) **way** (of an enterprise or person) earn enough to cover its or one's costs. **pay one's last respects** show respect towards a dead person by attending their funeral. **pay one's respects** make a polite visit to someone: *we went to pay our respects to the head lama.* **pay through the nose** informal pay much more than a fair price. **you pays your money and you takes your choice** informal used to convey that there is little to choose between one alternative and another.
– DERIVATIVES **payer** noun.
– ORIGIN Middle English (in the sense 'pacify'): from Old French *paie* (noun), *payer* (verb), from Latin *pacare* 'appease', from *pax, pac-* 'peace'. The notion of 'payment' arose from the sense of 'pacifying' a creditor.
▶ **pay someone back** repay a loan to someone: *a regular amount was deducted from my wages to pay her back.* ■ figurative take revenge on someone: *he had left him out to* ***pay*** *him* ***back for*** *stealing his wife.*
pay something back repay a loan to someone: *the money should be paid back with interest* | [with two objs] *they did pay me back the money.*
pay something in pay money into a bank account.
pay off informal (of a course of action) yield good results; succeed: *all the hard work I had done over the summer paid off.*
pay someone off dismiss someone with a final payment: *when directors are fired, they should not be lavishly paid off.*
pay something off pay a debt in full: *you may have saved up enough to pay off your second mortgage.*
pay something out (or **pay out**) **1** pay a large sum of money from funds under one's control: *insurers can refuse to pay out.* **2** let out (a rope) by slackening it: *I began paying out the nylon line.*
pay up (or **pay something up**) pay a debt in full: *you got ninety days to pay up the principal.*

pay[2] ▶ **verb** (past and past participle **payed**) [with obj.] Nautical seal (the deck or seams of a wooden ship) with pitch or tar to prevent leakage.

– ORIGIN early 17th cent.: from Old Northern French *peier*, from Latin *picare*, from *pix, pic-* 'pitch'.

payable ▶ adjective [predic.] **1** (of money) required to be paid; due: *interest is payable on the money owing* | *send a cheque, payable to the RSPCA*.
2 able to be paid: *it costs just $195, payable in five monthly instalments*.
▶ noun (**payables**) debts owed by a business; liabilities.

pay and display ▶ noun [mass noun] [usu. as modifier] a parking system in which a motorist buys a temporary permit from a coin-operated machine and displays it in the window of the vehicle.

pay as you earn (abbrev.: **PAYE**) ▶ noun (in the UK) a system by which an employer deducts income tax from an employee's wages before paying them to the employee and sends the deduction to the Inland Revenue.

pay as you go ▶ noun a system of paying debts or meeting costs as they arise.

payback ▶ noun **1** [mass noun] financial return or reward, especially profit from an investment equal to the initial outlay.
2 an act of revenge or retaliation.

payback period ▶ noun the length of time required for an investment to recover its initial outlay in terms of profits or savings.

pay bed ▶ noun (in the UK) a hospital bed for private patients in a National Health Service hospital.

pay cable ▶ noun [mass noun] US a cable television service available on a subscription basis.

pay channel ▶ noun a television channel for which viewers pay a subscription fee, in contrast to those channels provided at no extra cost on the payment of a basic subscription fee to a cable or satellite television service.

pay day ▶ noun a day on which someone is paid or expects to be paid their wages.
■ informal an amount of money won or available to be won, especially in a sporting contest: *the win landed him the second-biggest pay day of his career—nearly £5,400*.

pay dirt ▶ noun [mass noun] Mining, chiefly N. Amer. ground containing ore in sufficient quantity to be profitably extracted.
■ informal profit; reward: *the gig pays three hundred bucks a week—looks like I just hit pay dirt*.

PAYE Brit. ▶ abbreviation for pay as you earn.

payee ▶ noun a person to whom money is paid or is to be paid, especially the person to whom a cheque is made payable.

pay envelope ▶ noun North American term for **PAY PACKET**.

payess /ˈpeɪɛs/ ▶ plural noun chiefly N. Amer. uncut sidelocks worn by male Orthodox Jews.
– ORIGIN mid 20th cent.: Yiddish, from Hebrew *pēˈōt* 'corners' (see Lev. 19:27).

paying guest ▶ noun a person who lives in someone else's house and pays for food and accommodation; a lodger.

payload ▶ noun the part of a vehicle's load, especially an aircraft's, from which revenue is derived; passengers and cargo.
■ an explosive warhead carried by an aircraft or missile. ■ equipment, personnel, or satellites carried by a spacecraft.

paymaster ▶ noun **1** a person or organization having control over someone because of payment given: *inventing what they think their new-found paymasters want to hear*.
2 an official who pays troops or workers.
■ (in full **Paymaster General**) Brit. the minister at the head of the Treasury department responsible for payments.

payment ▶ noun **1** [mass noun] the action or process of paying someone or something or of being paid: *ask for a discount for payment by cash* | [count noun] *three interest-free monthly payments*.
2 an amount paid or payable: *an interim compensation payment of £2500*.
■ [mass noun] figurative something given as a reward or in recompense for something done: *a suit with a velvet collar that I got as payment for being in the show*.
– ORIGIN late Middle English: from Old French *paiement*, from *payer* 'to pay'.

Payne's grey ▶ noun [mass noun] Printing a composite pigment composed of blue, red, black, and white

permanent pigments, used especially for watercolours.
– ORIGIN mid 19th cent.: named after William *Payne* (*fl.* 1800), English artist.

paynim /ˈpeɪnɪm/ ▶ noun archaic a pagan.
■ a non-Christian, especially a Muslim.
– ORIGIN Middle English: from Old French *paienime*, from ecclesiastical Latin *paganismus* 'heathenism', from *paganus* 'heathen' (see **PAGAN**).

pay-off ▶ noun informal a payment made to someone, especially as a bribe or reward, or on leaving a job: *he left the company with an £800,000 pay-off last autumn*.
■ the return on investment or on a bet. ■ a final outcome; a conclusion.

payola /peɪˈəʊlə/ ▶ noun [mass noun] chiefly US the practice of bribing someone to use their influence or position to promote a particular product or interest: *if a record company spends enough money on payola, it can make any record a hit*.
– ORIGIN 1930s: from **PAY**[1] + *-ola* as in *Victrola*, the name of a make of gramophone.

payout ▶ noun a large payment of money, especially as compensation or a dividend: *an insurance payout*.

pay packet ▶ noun Brit. an envelope containing an employee's wages.
■ figurative a salary or income: *she was looking for other jobs to supplement her pay packet*.

payphone ▶ noun a public telephone that is operated by coins or by a credit or prepaid card.

payroll ▶ noun a list of a company's employees and the amount of money they are to be paid: *there are just three employees on the payroll*.
■ the total amount of wages and salaries paid by a company to its employees: *small employers with a payroll of less than £45,000*.

paysage /peɪˈzɑːʒ/ ▶ noun a rural scene depicted in art.
■ [mass noun] landscape painting.
– DERIVATIVES **paysagist** /ˈpeɪzədʒɪst/ noun.
– ORIGIN French, literally 'countryside', from *pays* 'country'.

paysan /peɪˈzɑ̃, French peizɑ̃/ ▶ noun a peasant or countryman, especially in France.
– ORIGIN French.

Pays Basque /pei bask/ French name for **BASQUE COUNTRY**.

Pays de la Loire /ˌpeɪ də la ˈlwɑː, French pei də la lwɑʀ/ a region of western France centred on the Loire valley.

payslip ▶ noun a note given to an employee when they have been paid, detailing the amount of pay given, and the tax and insurance deducted.

pay spine ▶ noun see **SPINE** (sense 1).

pay station ▶ noun US term for **PAYPHONE**.

pay TV (also **pay television**) ▶ noun [mass noun] television broadcasting in which viewers pay by subscription to watch a particular channel.

Paz /paz/, Octavio (1914–98), Mexican poet and essayist. His poems reflect a preoccupation with Aztec mythology. He is also noted for his essays written in response to the brutal suppression of student demonstrations in 1968. Nobel Prize for Literature (1990).

Pb ▶ symbol for the chemical element lead.
– ORIGIN from Latin *plumbum*.

pb ▶ abbreviation for paperback: *hb £7.99, pb £2.99*.

PBX ▶ abbreviation for private branch exchange, a private telephone switchboard.

PC ▶ abbreviation for ■ personal computer. ■ police constable: *PC Bartholomew made his report*. ■ (also **pc**) politically correct; political correctness: *PC language* | *the cult of PC*. ■ Privy Counsellor.

p.c. ▶ abbreviation for ■ per cent. ■ postcard.

PCAS historical ▶ abbreviation for (in the UK) Polytechnics Central Admissions System (incorporated into UCAS in the 1993–4 academic year).

PCB ▶ abbreviation for ■ Electronics printed circuit board. ■ Chemistry polychlorinated biphenyl.

PC card ▶ noun Computing a printed circuit board for a personal computer, especially one built to the PCMCIA standard.

P-Celtic ▶ noun & adjective another term for **BRYTHONIC**.
– ORIGIN *P*, from the development of the Indo-

European *kw* sound into *p* in this group of languages.

PCI ▶ noun [mass noun] Computing a standard for connecting computers and their peripherals.
– ORIGIN late 20th cent.: abbreviation of *Peripheral Component Interconnect*.

PCM ▶ abbreviation for pulse code modulation.

PCMCIA ▶ abbreviation for Computing Personal Computer Memory Card International Association, denoting a standard specification for memory cards and interfaces in personal computers.

PCN ▶ abbreviation for personal communications network, a digital mobile telephony system.

p-code ▶ noun another term for **PSEUDOCODE**.

PCP ▶ abbreviation for ■ pentachlorophenol. ■ phencyclidine. ■ pneumocystis carinii pneumonia.

PC Plod ▶ noun see **PLOD** (sense 2).

PCS ▶ abbreviation for personal communications services, a digital mobile telephony system.

pct. N. Amer. ▶ abbreviation for per cent.

PCV Brit. ▶ abbreviation for passenger-carrying vehicle.

PD ▶ abbreviation for ■ US Police Department: *the Chicago PD*. ■ public domain: *PD software*.

Pd ▶ symbol for the chemical element palladium.

pd ▶ abbreviation for paid.

PDA ▶ noun a palmtop computer used to store information such as addresses and telephone numbers, and for simple word processing and spreadsheeting.
– ORIGIN late 20th cent.: abbreviation of *personal digital assistant*.

PDC ▶ abbreviation for programme delivery control, a system for broadcasting a coded signal at the beginning and end of a television programme which can be recognized by a video recorder and used to begin and end recording.

PDP ▶ abbreviation for parallel distributed processing.

p.d.q. informal ▶ abbreviation for pretty damn quick.

PDSA ▶ abbreviation for (in the UK) People's Dispensary for Sick Animals.

PDT ▶ abbreviation for Pacific Daylight Time (see **PACIFIC TIME**).

PE ▶ abbreviation for ■ Peru (international vehicle registration). ■ physical education. ■ Prince Edward Island (in official postal use).

pea ▶ noun **1** a spherical green seed which is widely eaten as a vegetable.
■ [with modifier] any of a number of edible spherical seeds of the pea family, e.g. **chick pea** and **pigeon pea**. ■ W. Indian any legume, including peas, beans, or lentils, eaten as a vegetable.
2 the hardy Eurasian climbing plant which yields pods containing these seeds.
● *Pisum sativum*, family Leguminosae (or Fabaceae; the **pea family**). The members of this family (known as legumes) are sometimes divided among three smaller families: Papilionaceae (peas, beans, clovers, vetches, brooms, laburnums, etc.), Mimosaceae (mimosas, acacias), and Caesalpiniaceae (cassia, carob, and many tropical timber trees).
■ used in names of other plants of this family which yield round seeds or have flowers resembling those of the pea, e.g. **sweet pea**.
– PHRASES **like peas** (or **two peas**) **in a pod** so similar as to be indistinguishable or nearly so.
– ORIGIN mid 17th cent.: back-formation from **PEASE** (interpreted as plural).

pea bean ▶ noun a variety of kidney bean with small rounded seeds.

peaberry ▶ noun (pl. **-ies**) a coffee berry containing one rounded seed instead of the usual two, through non-fertilization of one ovule or subsequent abortion. Such beans are esteemed for their fine strong flavour.

pea-brain ▶ noun informal a stupid person.

pea-brained ▶ adjective informal stupid; foolish.

peace ▶ noun [mass noun] **1** freedom from disturbance; quiet and tranquillity: *you can while away an hour or two in peace and seclusion*.
■ mental calm; serenity: *the peace of mind this insurance gives you*.
2 freedom from or the cessation of war or violence: *the Straits were to be open to warships in time of peace*.
■ [in sing.] a period of this: *the peace didn't last*. ■ [in sing.] a treaty agreeing the cessation of war between states at war: *support for a negotiated peace*. ■ freedom from civil disorder: *police action to restore peace*. ■ freedom from dispute or dissension between individuals or

groups: *the 8.8 per cent offer which promises peace with Nalgo.*

3 (**the peace**) a ceremonial handshake or kiss exchanged during a service in some Churches (now usually only in the Eucharist), symbolizing Christian love and unity. See also *kiss of peace* at **KISS**.

– PHRASES **at peace 1** free from anxiety or distress. ■ dead (used to suggest that someone has escaped from the difficulties of life). **2** in a state of friendliness: *a man at peace with the world.* **hold one's peace** remain silent about something. **keep the peace** refrain or prevent others from disturbing civil order. **make (one's) peace** re-establish friendly relations; become reconciled: *Labour should make its peace with the Lib-Dems.* **no peace for the wicked** see *no rest for the wicked* at **WICKED**.

– ORIGIN Middle English: from Old French *pais*, from Latin *pax, pac-* 'peace'.

peaceable ▶ adjective inclined to avoid argument or violent conflict: *they were famed as an industrious, peaceable, practical people.*
■ free from argument or conflict; peaceful: *the mainly peaceable daily demonstrations for democratic reform.*

– DERIVATIVES **peaceableness** noun, **peaceably** adverb.
– ORIGIN Middle English: from Old French *peisible*, alteration of *plaisible*, from late Latin *placibilis* 'pleasing', from Latin *placere* 'to please'.

peace camp ▶ noun an informal encampment set up as a public protest against a military establishment or some aspect of military policy.

Peace Corps an organization sending young people to work as volunteers in developing countries.

peace dividend ▶ noun a sum of public money which becomes available for other purposes when spending on defence is reduced.

peaceful ▶ adjective **1** free from disturbance; tranquil: *everything was so quiet and peaceful in the early morning.*
2 not involving war or violence: *a soldier was shot and seriously wounded at an otherwise peaceful demonstration.*
■ (of a person) inclined to avoid conflict; not aggressive: *Dad was a peaceful, law-abiding citizen.*
– DERIVATIVES **peacefulness** noun.

peacefully ▶ adverb **1** without disturbance; tranquilly: *the baby slept peacefully in its cradle.*
■ (of death) without pain: *she suffered a stroke and died peacefully in her sleep.*
2 without war or violence: *the siege ended peacefully.*

Peace Garden State informal name for **NORTH DAKOTA**.

peacekeeping ▶ noun [usu. as modifier] the active maintenance of a truce between nations or communities, especially by an international military force: *the 2,300-strong UN peacekeeping force.*
– DERIVATIVES **peacekeeper** noun.

peacemaker ▶ noun a person who brings about peace, especially by reconciling adversaries.
– DERIVATIVES **peacemaking** noun & adjective.

peace movement ▶ noun a broad movement opposed to preparations for war, especially a movement in Britain and western Europe attempting since the 1950s to bring about a reduction in or elimination of nuclear weapons.

peacenik ▶ noun informal, often derogatory a member of a pacifist movement.
– ORIGIN coined during peace protests in the 1960s.

peace offering ▶ noun **1** a propitiatory or conciliatory gift: *he took the flowers to Jean as a peace offering.*
2 (in biblical use) an offering presented as a thanksgiving to God.

peace officer ▶ noun chiefly N. Amer. a civil officer appointed to preserve law and order, such as a sheriff or policeman.

peace pipe ▶ noun a tobacco pipe offered and smoked as a token of peace among North American Indians.

Peace Pledge Union (abbrev.: **PPU**) a pacifist organization formed in 1936 and supported by a number of socialist writers and intellectuals including Bertrand Russell, Siegfried Sassoon, and Aldous Huxley.

peace sign ▶ noun a sign of peace made by

holding up the hand with palm out-turned and the first two fingers extended in a V-shape.

peace talk ▶ noun (usu. **peace talks**) a discussion about peace or the ending of hostilities, especially a conference or series of discussions aimed at achieving peace.

peacetime ▶ noun [mass noun] a period when a country is not at war.

peach¹ ▶ noun **1** a round stone fruit with juicy yellow flesh and downy pinkish-yellow skin.
■ [mass noun] a pinkish-yellow colour like that of a peach. ■ informal an exceptionally good or attractive person or thing: *what a peach of a shot!*
2 (also **peach tree**) the Chinese tree which bears this fruit.
● *Prunus persica*, family Rosaceae: many cultivars, including the nectarine.
– PHRASES **peaches and cream** (of a person's complexion) of a cream colour with downy pink cheeks.
– DERIVATIVES **peachiness** noun.
– ORIGIN late Middle English: from Old French *pesche*, from medieval Latin *persica*, from Latin *persicum (malum)*, literally 'Persian apple'.

peach² ▶ verb [no obj.] (**peach on**) informal inform on: *the other members of the gang would not hesitate to peach on him if it would serve their purpose.*
– ORIGIN late Middle English: shortening of archaic *appeach*, from Old French *empechier* 'impede' (see **IMPEACH**).

peach-bloom ▶ noun [mass noun] a matte glaze of reddish pink, mottled with green and brown, used on fine Chinese porcelain since around 1700.
■ a delicate purplish-pink colour.
– ORIGIN early 19th cent.: applied to the porcelain glaze from the 1880s.

peach blossom ▶ noun a European woodland moth that has brownish wings with pink markings.
● *Thyatira batis*, family Geometridae.

peach-blow ▶ noun [mass noun] another term for **PEACH-BLOOM**.
■ a type of late 19th-century American coloured glass.
– ORIGIN early 19th cent.: from **PEACH¹** + the noun **BLOW³**.

peach fuzz ▶ noun [mass noun] N. Amer. informal the down on the chin of an adolescent boy whose beard has not yet developed.

peachick ▶ noun a young peafowl.

peach Melba ▶ noun a dish of ice cream and peaches with liqueur or sauce.
– ORIGIN named after Dame Nellie *Melba* (see **MELBA¹**).

Peach State informal name for the US state of **GEORGIA**.

peachy ▶ adjective (**peachier, peachiest**) of the nature or appearance of a peach.
■ informal, chiefly N. Amer. attractive; excellent: *everything is just peachy.*

peachy-keen ▶ adjective informal, chiefly N. Amer. attractive; outstanding: *I enjoy my life, but it's not that peachy-keen.*
– ORIGIN mid 20th cent.: from **PEACHY** in the sense 'excellent' and **KEEN¹** in the sense 'wonderful'.

pea coat ▶ noun another term for **PEA JACKET**.

Peacock, Thomas Love (1785–1866), English novelist and poet. He is chiefly remembered for his prose satires, including *Nightmare Abbey* (1818) and *Crotchet Castle* (1831), lampooning the romantic poets.

peacock ▶ noun a male peafowl, which has very long tail feathers that have eye-like markings and can be erected and expanded in display like a fan.
– ORIGIN Middle English: from Old English *pēa* (from Latin *pavo*) 'peacock' + **COCK¹**.

peacock blue ▶ noun [mass noun] a greenish-blue colour like that of a peacock's neck.

peacock butterfly ▶ noun a brightly coloured Eurasian butterfly with conspicuous eyespots on its wings.
● *Inachis io*, subfamily Nymphalinae, family Nymphalidae.

peacock ore ▶ noun another term for **BORNITE**.

peacock worm ▶ noun a colourful European fan worm of shallow waters.
● *Sabella pavonina*, class Polychaeta.

pea crab ▶ noun a minute soft-bodied crab that lives inside the shell of a bivalve mollusc, where it

filters food particles from the water drawn into the shell by its host.
● Family Pinnotheridae: *Pinnotheres* and other genera.

pea flour ▶ noun [mass noun] flour made from dried split peas.

pea flower ▶ noun a flower that is characteristic of many leguminous plants and typified by that of the pea. See **PAPILIONACEOUS**.

peafowl ▶ noun a large crested pheasant found mainly in Asia. See **PEACOCK, PEAHEN**.
● Two genera and three species in the family Phasianidae, in particular the widely introduced **common peafowl** (*Pavo cristatus*).

pea green ▶ noun [mass noun] a bright green colour like that of a pea.

peahen ▶ noun a female peafowl, which has drabber colours and a shorter tail than the male.

pea jacket (also **pea coat**) ▶ noun a short double-breasted overcoat of coarse woollen cloth, formerly worn by sailors.
– ORIGIN early 18th cent.: probably from Dutch *pijjakker*, from *pij* 'coat of coarse cloth' + *jekker* 'jacket'. The change in the ending was due to association with **JACKET**.

peak¹ ▶ noun the pointed top of a mountain.
■ a mountain, especially one with a pointed top. ■ a projecting pointed part or shape: *whisk 2 egg whites to stiff peaks.* ■ a stiff brim at the front of a cap. ■ the narrow part of a ship's hold at the bow or stern. ■ the upper, outer corner of a sail extended by a gaff. ■ a point in a curve or on a graph, or a value of a physical quantity, higher than those around it. ■ the point of highest activity, quality, or achievement: *anyone who saw Best at his peak looked upon genius.*
▶ verb [no obj., with adverbial] reach a highest point, either of a specified value or at a specified time: *its popularity peaked in the 1940s.*
▶ adjective [attrib.] greatest; maximum: *he did not expect to be anywhere near peak fitness until Christmas.*
■ characterized by maximum activity or demand: *at peak hours, traffic speeds are reduced considerably.*
– ORIGIN mid 16th cent.: probably a back-formation from *peaked*, variant of dialect *picked* 'pointed'.

peak² ▶ verb [no obj.] archaic decline in health and spirits; waste away.
– ORIGIN early 17th cent.: of unknown origin. The phrase *peak and pine* derives its currency from Shakespeare.

peak cap ▶ noun a flat cap with a peak at the front.

Peak District a limestone plateau in Derbyshire, at the southern end of the Pennines, rising to 636 m (2,088 ft) at Kinder Scout.

Peake, Mervyn (Laurence) (1911–68), British novelist, poet, and artist, born in China. He is principally remembered for the trilogy comprising *Titus Groan* (1946), *Gormenghast* (1950), and *Titus Alone* (1959), set in the surreal world of Gormenghast Castle.

peaked¹ ▶ adjective (of a cap) having a peak.

peaked² ▶ adjective [predic.] (of a person) gaunt and pale from illness or fatigue: *you do look a little peaked.*

peak flow meter ▶ noun Medicine a calibrated instrument used to measure lung capacity in monitoring breathing disorders such as asthma.

peak load ▶ noun the maximum of electrical power demand.

peak-to-peak ▶ adjective & adverb measured between the greatest peaks of a periodically varying quantity.

peaky ▶ adjective (**peakier, peakiest**) (of a person) pale from illness or fatigue; sickly: *you're looking a bit peaky—a change of scene would do you good.*

peal ▶ noun **1** a loud ringing of a bell or bells.
■ Bell-ringing a series of changes (strictly, at least five thousand) rung on a set of bells. ■ a set of bells.
2 a loud repeated or reverberating sound of thunder or laughter.
▶ verb [no obj.] (of a bell or bells) ring loudly or in a peal: *all the bells of the city began to peal.*
■ (of laughter or thunder) sound in a peal. ■ [with obj.] convey or give out by the ringing of bells: *the carillon pealed out the news to the waiting city.*
– ORIGIN late Middle English: shortening of **APPEAL**.

pean /piːn/ ▶ noun [mass noun] Heraldry fur resembling ermine but with gold spots on a black ground.
– ORIGIN mid 16th cent.: of unknown origin.

Peano axioms /peɪˈɑːnəʊ/ ▶ plural noun Mathematics a

set of axioms from which the properties of the natural numbers may be deduced.

– ORIGIN early 20th cent.: named after Giuseppe *Peano* (1858–1932), Italian mathematician.

peanut ▸ noun **1** the oval seed of a South American plant, often roasted and salted and eaten as a snack.

■ **(peanuts)** informal a paltry thing or amount, especially a very small amount of money: *he pays peanuts.* **2** the plant of the pea family that bears these seeds, which develop in pods that ripen underground. It is widely cultivated, especially in the southern US, and large quantities go to make oil or animal feed.

● *Arachis hypogaea*, family Leguminosae.

peanut butter ▸ noun [mass noun] a paste of ground roasted peanuts, usually eaten spread on bread.

peanut gallery ▸ noun N. Amer. informal the top gallery in a theatre where the cheaper seats are located.

peanut oil ▸ noun [mass noun] oil produced from peanuts and used mainly for culinary purposes, but also in some soaps and pharmaceuticals. Also called **ARACHIS OIL**.

peanut worm ▸ noun an unsegmented burrowing marine worm with a stout body and a slender anterior part. The latter bears a terminal mouth surrounded by tentacles, and can be retracted into the trunk.

● Phylum Sipuncula.

pear ▸ noun **1** a yellowish- or brownish-green edible fruit which is typically narrow at the stalk and wider towards the tip, with sweet, slightly gritty flesh. **2** (also **pear tree**) the Eurasian tree which bears this fruit.

● Genus *Pyrus*, family Rosaceae: several species and hybrids, in particular *P. communis*.

– ORIGIN Old English *pere*, *peru*, of West Germanic origin; related to Dutch *peer*, from Latin *pirum*.

pear drop ▸ noun a small boiled sweet in the shape of a pear, with the distinctive aroma of amyl acetate.

pearl[1] ▸ noun a hard, lustrous spherical mass, typically white or bluish-grey, formed within the shell of a pearl oyster or other bivalve mollusc and highly prized as a gem.

■ an artificial imitation of this. ■ **(pearls)** a necklace of pearls. ■ something resembling a pearl in appearance: *the sweat stood in pearls along his forehead.* ■ short for **MOTHER-OF-PEARL**. ■ figurative a precious thing; the finest example of something: *the nation's media were assembled to hear his pearls of wisdom.* ■ [mass noun] a very pale bluish grey or white like the colour of a pearl.

▸ verb [no obj.] **1** poetic/literary form pearl-like drops: *the juice on the blade pearled into droplets.* ■ [with obj.] make bluish-grey like a pearl: *the peaked hills, blue and pearled with clouds.* **2** [usu. as noun **pearling**] dive or fish for pearl oysters.

– PHRASES **pearls before swine** valuable things offered or given to people who do not appreciate them.

– DERIVATIVES **pearler** noun.

– ORIGIN late Middle English: from Old French *perle*, perhaps based on Latin *perna* 'leg', extended to denote a leg-of-mutton-shaped bivalve.

pearl[2] ▸ noun Brit. another term for **PICOT**.

pearl ash ▸ noun [mass noun] archaic commercial potassium carbonate.

pearl barley ▸ noun [mass noun] barley reduced to small round grains by grinding.

pearl bulb ▸ noun Brit. an electric light bulb with translucent glass.

pearl button ▸ noun a button made of real or imitation mother-of-pearl.

pearl diver ▸ noun a person who dives for pearl oysters.

pearled ▸ adjective **1** adorned with pearls: *we saw her pearled like the Queen.* **2** poetic/literary bluish-grey, like a pearl.

pearlescent ▸ adjective having a lustre resembling that of mother-of-pearl: *pearlescent colours.*

pearl everlasting ▸ noun variant of **PEARLY EVERLASTING**.

pearleye ▸ noun a long-bodied active fish of open oceans, with tubular eyes which are directed upward and bear a glistening white spot that may be a light organ.

● Family Scopelarchidae: several genera and species.

pearlfish ▸ noun (pl. same or **-fishes**) **1** a long slender fish found chiefly in warmer seas, which lives inside the shells of bivalve molluscs or the body cavities of sea cucumbers and other invertebrates.

● Family Carapidae: several genera and species.

2 a small Argentinian killifish, popular in aquaria.

● *Cynolebius belotti*, family Cyprinodontidae.

Pearl Harbor a harbour on the island of Oahu, in Hawaii, the site of a major American naval base, where a surprise attack on 7 December 1941 by Japanese carrier-borne aircraft inflicted heavy damage and brought the US into the Second World War.

pearlite ▸ noun [mass noun] Metallurgy a finely laminated mixture of ferrite and cementite present in cast iron and steel, formed by the cooling of austenite.

– ORIGIN late 19th cent.: from **PEARL**[1] + **-ITE**[1].

pearlized (also **-ised**) ▸ adjective made to have or give a lustre like that of mother-of-pearl.

pearl millet ▸ noun a tall tropical cereal with long cylindrical ears, which is an important food crop in the driest areas of Africa and the Indian subcontinent.

● *Pennisetum glaucum* (or *typhoides*), family Gramineae.

pearl mussel ▸ noun an elongated freshwater bivalve mollusc which occasionally produces small pearls, found in large rivers of the northern hemisphere.

● *Margaritifera margaritifera*, family Margaritiferidae.

pearl onion ▸ noun a very small onion used for pickling.

pearl oyster ▸ noun a tropical marine bivalve mollusc with a ridged scaly shell, which produces pearls.

● Genus *Pinctada*, family Pteriidae: several species, in particular *P. margaritifera*, a major source of commercial pearls.

Pearl River a river of southern China, flowing from Guangzhou (Canton) southwards to the South China Sea and forming part of the delta of the Xi River. Its lower reaches widen to form the Pearl River estuary, the inlet between Hong Kong and Macao.

pearlware ▸ noun [mass noun] fine glazed earthenware pottery, typically white, of a type introduced by Josiah Wedgwood in 1779.

pearlwort ▸ noun a small plant of the pink family, with inconspicuous white flowers, native to north temperate regions.

● Genus *Sagina*, family Caryophyllaceae.

pearly ▸ adjective (**pearlier**, **pearliest**) resembling a pearl in lustre or colour: *the pearly light of a clear, still dawn.*

■ containing or adorned with pearls or mother-of-pearl.

▸ noun (pl. **-ies**) (**pearlies**) Brit. **1** pearly kings and queens.

■ a pearly king's or queen's clothes or pearl buttons. **2** informal a person's teeth.

– PHRASES **pearly whites** Brit. informal a person's teeth.

– DERIVATIVES **pearliness** noun.

pearly everlasting (also **pearl everlasting**) ▸ noun an ornamental North American plant with grey-green foliage and pearly white flower heads, used in dry flower arrangements.

● *Anaphalis margaritacea*, family Compositae.

pearly eye ▸ noun a brown American butterfly with pearly markings and distinctive eyespots on the undersides of the wings.

● Genus *Lethe*, subfamily Satyrinae, family Nymphalidae.

Pearly Gates ▸ plural noun informal the gates of heaven: *I am getting less fond of poems about old age as I near the Pearly Gates.*

pearly king (also **pearly queen**) ▸ noun a London costermonger wearing traditional ceremonial clothes covered with pearl buttons.

pearly nautilus ▸ noun a common nautilus of the Indo-Pacific, with a light spiral shell that is white with brownish bands on the outside and lined with mother-of-pearl on the inside.

● *Nautilus pompilius*, subclass Nautiloidea.

Pearmain /'pɛːmeɪn, 'pəː-, pəˈmeɪn/ ▸ noun a pear-shaped dessert apple of a variety with firm white flesh.

– ORIGIN Middle English (denoting an old variety of baking pear): from Old French *parmain*, probably based on Latin *parmensis* 'of Parma'.

Pears /pɪəz/, Sir Peter (1910–86), English operatic tenor. In his lifelong partnership with Benjamin Britten he performed the title roles in all Britten's operas and with Britten co-founded the Aldeburgh Festival in 1948.

pear-shaped ▸ adjective shaped like a pear; tapering towards the top.

■ (of a person) having hips that are disproportionately wide in relation to the upper part of the body.

– PHRASES **go pear-shaped** Brit. informal go wrong: *one of those days when everything went pear-shaped.* [ORIGIN: originally RAF slang.]

Pearson[1], Karl (1857–1936), English mathematician, the principal founder of 20th-century statistics. He defined the concept of standard deviation and devised the chi-square test.

Pearson[2], Lester Bowles (1897–1972), Canadian diplomat and Liberal statesman, Prime Minister 1963–8. As Secretary of State for External Affairs (1948–57) he acted as a mediator in the resolution of the Suez crisis (1956). Nobel Peace Prize (1957).

Pearson's correlation coefficient (also **Pearson's product-moment correlation coefficient**) ▸ noun Statistics a statistic measuring the linear interdependence between two variables or two sets of data.

– ORIGIN early 20th cent.: named after K. *Pearson* (see **PEARSON**[1]).

peart /pɪət, pjəːt/ ▸ adjective US dialect lively; cheerful.

– ORIGIN late 15th cent.: variant of **PERT**.

Peary /'pɪəri/, Robert Edwin (1856–1920), American explorer. He made eight Arctic voyages before becoming the first person to reach the North Pole, on 6 April 1909.

Peary Land a mountainous region on the Arctic coast of northern Greenland.

peasant ▸ noun a poor farmer of low social status who owns or rents a small piece of land for cultivation (chiefly in historical use or with reference to subsistence farming in poorer countries).

■ informal an ignorant, rude, or unsophisticated person; a person of low social status.

– DERIVATIVES **peasantry** noun, **peasanty** adjective.

– ORIGIN late Middle English: from Old French *paisent* 'country dweller', from *pais* 'country', based on Latin *pagus* 'country district'.

peasant economy ▸ noun an agricultural economy in which the family is the basic unit of production.

Peasants' Revolt an uprising in 1381 among the peasant and artisan classes in England, particularly in Kent and Essex. The rebels marched on London, occupying the city and executing unpopular ministers, but after the death of their leader, Wat Tyler, they were persuaded to disperse by Richard II.

pease /piːz/ ▸ plural noun archaic peas.

– ORIGIN Old English *pise* 'pea', (plural) *pisan*, via Latin from Greek *pison*. Compare with **PEA**.

pease pudding ▸ noun [mass noun] chiefly Brit. a dish of split peas boiled with onion and carrot and mashed to a pulp.

pea-shooter ▸ noun a toy weapon consisting of a small tube which is blown down in order to shoot out dried peas.

pea soup ▸ noun [mass noun] soup made from peas, especially a thick, yellow soup made from dried split peas.

pea-souper ▸ noun **1** Brit. informal a very thick yellowish fog. **2** Canadian derogatory a French Canadian.

peat ▸ noun [mass noun] a brown soil-like material characteristic of boggy, acid ground, consisting of partly decomposed vegetable matter and widely cut and dried for use in gardening and as fuel.

■ [count noun] (usu. **peats**) a cut piece of this.

– DERIVATIVES **peaty** adjective.

– ORIGIN Middle English: from Anglo-Latin *peta*, perhaps of Celtic origin.

peat hag ▸ noun another term for **HAG**[2] (in sense 1).

■Zoology a stalk-like part by which an organ is attached to an animal's body, or by which a barnacle or other sedentary animal is attached to a substrate.
– DERIVATIVES **peduncular** /pɪˈdʌŋkjʊlə/ adjective.
– ORIGIN mid 18th cent.: from modern Latin *pedunculus*, from Latin *pes*, *ped-* 'foot'.

pedunculate /pɪˈdʌŋkjʊlət/ ▶**adjective** Botany & Zoology having a peduncle.

pedunculate oak ▶**noun** the common or English oak.

pedway ▶**noun** chiefly N. Amer. a footway built for pedestrians in an urban area.
– ORIGIN 1960s: from **PEDESTRIAN** + **WAY**.

pee informal ▶**verb** (**pees**, **peed**, **peeing**) [no obj.] urinate: *the puppy was peeing on the carpet.*
■[with obj.] (**pee oneself/one's pants**) wet one's underpants by urinating involuntarily (often used to suggest the notion of losing control of oneself through fear or hilarity): *Mom just about* **pees herself** *laughing.*
▶**noun** [in sing.] an act of urinating: *she was bursting for a pee.*
■[mass noun] urine.
– PHRASES **peed off** annoyed; irritated.
– ORIGIN late 18th cent. (as a verb): euphemistic use of the initial letter of **PISS**.

Peeblesshire /ˈpiːb(ə)lzˌʃɪə, -ʃə/ a former county of southern Scotland. It became a part of Borders region (now Scottish Borders) in 1975.

peek ▶**verb** [no obj., with adverbial] look quickly, typically in a furtive manner: *faces peeked from behind twitched curtains.*
■figurative protrude slightly so as to be just visible: *his socks were so full of holes his toes peeked through.*
▶**noun 1** a quick and typically furtive look: *a peek through the window showed that the taxi had arrived.*
2 (usu. **PEEK**) Computing a statement or function in BASIC for reading the contents of a specified memory location. Compare with **POKE**[1] (sense 3).
– ORIGIN late Middle English *pike*, *pyke*, of unknown origin.

peekaboo (also **peek-a-boo**) ▶**noun** [mass noun] a game played with a young child, which involves hiding behind something and suddenly reappearing, saying 'peekaboo'.
▶**adjective** [attrib.] (of a garment) revealing glimpses of the skin or body: *a black lace peekaboo dress.*
■(of a hairstyle) concealing one eye with a fringe or wave.
– ORIGIN late 16th cent. (as a noun): from the verb **PEEK** + **BOO**.

Peel, Sir Robert (1788–1850), British Conservative statesman, Prime Minister 1834–5 and 1841–6. As Home Secretary (1828–30) he established the Metropolitan Police (hence the nicknames *bobby* and *peeler*). His repeal of the Corn Laws in 1846 split the Conservatives and forced his resignation.

peel[1] ▶**verb 1** [with obj.] remove the outer covering or skin from (a fruit, vegetable, or prawn): *she watched him peel an apple with deliberate care.*
■remove (the outer covering or skin) from a fruit or vegetable: **peel off** *the skins and thickly slice the potatoes.* ■ [no obj.] (of a fruit or vegetable) have a skin that can be removed: *oranges that peel easily.* ■ (**peel something away/off**) remove or separate a thin covering or part from the outside or surface of something: *carefully peel away the lining paper from the bottom of the roulade.* ■ remove (an article of clothing): *Suzy peeled off her white pullover.*
2 [no obj.] (of a surface or object) lose parts of its outer layer or covering in small strips or pieces: *the walls are peeling.*
■[with adverbial] (of an outer layer or covering) come off, especially in strips or small pieces.
▶**noun** [mass noun] the outer covering or rind of a fruit or vegetable.
– ORIGIN Middle English (in the sense 'to plunder'): variant of dialect *pill*, from Latin *pilare* 'to strip hair from', from *pilus* 'hair'. The differentiation of *peel* and *pill* may have been by association with the French verbs *peler* 'to peel' and *piller* 'to pillage'.
▶**peel off 1** (of a member of a formation) leave the formation by veering away to one side: *the pace was much too hot for Beris, and he peeled off after five laps.* **2** Brit. informal remove some or all of one's clothes: *you look hot, why don't you peel off?*
peel out N. Amer. informal leave quickly: *he peeled out down the street.*

peel[2] ▶**noun** archaic a shovel, especially a baker's shovel for carrying loaves into or out of an oven.
– ORIGIN late Middle English: from Old French *pele*, from Latin *pala*, from the base of *pangere* 'to fix, plant'.

peel[3] (also **pele** or **peel tower**) ▶**noun** a small square defensive tower of a kind built in the 16th century in the border counties of England and Scotland.
– ORIGIN probably short for synonymous *peel-house*: *peel* from Anglo-Norman French *pel* 'stake, palisade', from Latin *palus* 'stake'.

peel[4] ▶**verb** [with obj.] Croquet send (another player's ball) through a hoop: *the better players are capable of peeling a ball through two or three hoops.*
– ORIGIN late 19th cent.: from the name of Walter H. Peel, founder of the All England Croquet Association, a leading exponent of the practice.

peeler[1] ▶**noun** [usu. with modifier] a device for removing the skin from fruit and vegetables: *a potato peeler.*

peeler[2] ▶**noun** Brit. informal, dated a police officer.
– ORIGIN early 19th cent. (originally denoting a member of the Irish constabulary): from the name of Sir Robert **PEEL**.

peelings ▶**plural noun** [usu. with modifier] strips of the outer skin of a vegetable or fruit: *potato peelings.*

Peelite ▶**noun** historical a Conservative supporting Sir Robert Peel, especially with reference to his repeal of the Corn Laws (1846).

peely-wally /ˈpiːlɪwɒli, ˌpiːlɪˈwali/ (also **peely-wallie**) ▶**adjective** Scottish pale and sickly in appearance: *his face assumes a peely-wally hue.*
– ORIGIN mid 19th cent.: probably imitative of a whining sound.

peen /piːn/ (also **pein**) ▶**noun** the end of a hammer head opposite the face, typically wedge-shaped, curved, or spherical.
▶**verb** [with obj.] strike with a hammer or the peen of a hammer.
■another term for **SHOT-PEEN**.
– ORIGIN early 16th cent. (as a verb): probably of Scandinavian origin; compare with Swedish dialect *pena (ut)*, Danish dialect *pene (ud)* 'beat (out)'.

Peenemunde /ˌpeɪnəˈmʊndə/ a village in NE Germany, on a small island just off the Baltic coast. During the Second World War it was the chief site of German rocket research and testing.

peep[1] ▶**verb** [no obj.] look quickly and furtively at something, especially through a narrow opening: *his door was ajar and she couldn't resist peeping in.*
■(**peep out**) be just visible; appear slowly or partly or through a small opening: *the sun began to peep out.*
▶**noun** [usu. in sing.] a quick or furtive look: *Jonathan took a little peep at his watch.*
■a momentary or partial view of something: *black curls and a peep of gold earring.*
– ORIGIN late 15th cent.: symbolic; compare with **PEEK**.

peep[2] ▶**noun** a feeble, high-pitched sound made by a young bird or mammal.
■[with negative] a slight sound, utterance, or complaint: *not a peep out of them since shortly after eight.* ■ a brief, high-pitched sound produced mechanically or electronically: *the phone gives three sharp peeps.* ■ (usu. **peeps**) N. Amer. informal a small sandpiper or similar wading bird.
▶**verb** [no obj.] make a high-pitched sound of this kind.
– ORIGIN late Middle English: imitative; compare with **CHEEP**.

peep-bo ▶**noun** another term for **PEEKABOO**.

pee-pee ▶**noun** N. Amer. informal a child's word for an act of urinating.
■[mass noun] urine. ■ a penis.

peeper[1] ▶**noun** a person who peeps at someone or something, especially in a voyeuristic way.
■(**peepers**) informal a person's eyes: *keep your peepers peeled for a familiar face.*

peeper[2] (also **spring peeper**) ▶**noun** a small North American tree frog that has brownish-grey skin with a dark cross on the back, the males of which sing in early spring.
• *Hyla crucifer*, family Hylidae.

peephole ▶**noun** a small hole that may be looked through, especially one in a door through which callers may be identified before the door is opened.

peeping Tom ▶**noun** a person who gets sexual pleasure from secretly watching people undressing or engaging in sexual activity.
– ORIGIN from the name of the person said to have watched Lady **GODIVA** ride naked through Coventry.

peep show ▶**noun** a sequence of pictures viewed through a lens or hole set into a box, traditionally offered as a public entertainment.
■an erotic or pornographic film or show viewed from a coin-operated booth.

peep sight ▶**noun** a backsight for rifles with a circular hole through which the foresight is brought into line with the object aimed at.

peep-toe ▶**adjective** Brit. (of a shoe) having the tip cut away to leave the large toe partially exposed.
▶**noun** a shoe of such a type.

peepul /ˈpiːpʌl/ (also **pipal**) ▶**noun** another term for **BO TREE**.
– ORIGIN late 18th cent.: via Hindi from Sanskrit *pippala*.

peer[1] ▶**verb** [no obj., with adverbial] look keenly or with difficulty at someone or something: *Blake screwed up his eyes, trying to peer through the fog.*
■be just visible: *the two towers peer over the roofs.* ■ [no obj.] archaic come into view; appear.
– ORIGIN late 16th cent.: perhaps a variant of dialect *pire*; perhaps partly from a shortening of **APPEAR**.

peer[2] ▶**noun 1** a member of the nobility in Britain or Ireland, comprising the ranks of duke, marquess, earl, viscount, and baron.

> In the British peerage, earldoms and baronetcies were the earliest to be conferred; dukes were created from 1337, marquesses from the end of the 14th century, and viscounts from 1440. Such peerages are hereditary, although since 1958 there have also been non-hereditary life peerages. Peers are entitled to a seat in the House of Lords and exemption from jury service; they are debarred from election to the House of Commons.

2 a person of the same age, status, or ability as another specified person: *he has incurred much criticism from his academic peers.*
▶**verb** archaic make or become equal with or of the same rank.
– PHRASES **without peer** unequalled; unrivalled: *he is a goalkeeper without peer.*
– ORIGIN Middle English: from Old French *peer*, from Latin *par* 'equal'.

peerage ▶**noun** the title and rank of peer or peeress: *on his retirement as cabinet secretary, he was given a peerage.*
■(**the peerage**) peers as a class; the nobility: *he was elevated to the peerage two years ago.* ■ a book containing a list of peers and peeresses, with their genealogy and history.

peeress /ˈpɪərɪs, -rɛs/ ▶**noun** a woman holding the rank of a peer in her own right.
■the wife or widow of a peer.

peer group ▶**noun** a group of people of approximately the same age, status, and interests.

peerie /ˈpiːri/ ▶**adjective** Scottish tiny; insubstantial.
– ORIGIN early 19th cent.: of unknown origin.

peerless ▶**adjective** unequalled; unrivalled.
– DERIVATIVES **peerlessly** adverb.

peer of the realm ▶**noun** a member of the class of peers who has the right to sit in the House of Lords.

peer pressure ▶**noun** [mass noun] influence from members of one's peer group: *his behaviour was affected by drink and peer pressure.*

peer review ▶**noun** [mass noun] evaluation of scientific, academic, or professional work by others working in the same field.
▶**verb** [with obj.] (**peer-review**) subject (someone or something) to such evaluation.

peer-to-peer ▶**adjective** [attrib.] denoting computer networks in which each computer can act as a server for the others, allowing shared access to files and peripherals without the need for a central server.

peery /ˈpɪəri/ ▶**noun** (pl. **-ies**) Scottish & N. English a child's spinning top.
– ORIGIN mid 17th cent.: from *peer* (Scots spelling of **PEAR**) + **-Y**[1].

peeve informal ▶**verb** [with obj.] (usu. **be peeved**) annoy; irritate: *he was peeved at being left out of the cabinet* | [as adj. **peeved**] *a somewhat peeved tone.*
▶**noun** a cause of annoyance: *his pet peeve is not having answers for questions from players.*
– ORIGIN early 20th cent.: back-formation from **PEEVISH**.

peever ▶**noun** (often **peevers**) Scottish term for **HOPSCOTCH**.
– ORIGIN mid 19th cent. (denoting the stone or piece of pottery used in the game): of unknown origin.

peevish ▶ adjective easily irritated, especially by unimportant things: *all this makes Stephen fretful and peevish.*
■ querulous: *a peevish, whining voice.*
– DERIVATIVES **peevishly** adverb, **peevishness** noun.
– ORIGIN late Middle English (in the sense 'foolish, mad, spiteful'): of unknown origin.

peewee ▶ noun **1** any of a number of birds with a call that resembles the word 'peewee':
■ Austral. another term for **MAGPIE LARK**. ■ Scottish the northern lapwing. ■ N. Amer. variant spelling of **PEWEE**.
2 [usu. as modifier] N. Amer. a level of amateur sport, involving children aged eight or nine (in the US) or twelve or thirteen (in Canada): *a peewee baseball team.*
■ a player at such a level of amateur sport.
3 a small marble.

peewit (also **pewit**) ▶ noun Brit. the northern lapwing.
– ORIGIN early 16th cent.: imitative of the bird's call.

PEG ▶ abbreviation for polyethylene glycol.

peg ▶ noun **1** a short cylindrical piece of wood, metal, or plastic, typically tapered at one end, that is used for holding things together, hanging things on, or marking a position.
■ such an object attached to a wall on which to hang garments. ■ (also **tent peg**) such an object driven into the ground to hold one of the ropes or corners of a tent in position. ■ short for **TUNING PEG**. ■ Brit. short for **CLOTHES PEG**. ■ a bung for stoppering a cask. ■ a place allotted to a competitor to fish or shoot from. ■ informal a person's leg. ■ a point or limit on a scale, especially of exchange rates. ■ informal a footrest on a motorbike.
2 chiefly Indian a measure of spirits: *have a peg of whisky.*
3 US informal a strong throw, especially in baseball.
▶ verb (**pegged**, **pegging**) **1** [with obj. and adverbial] fix or make fast with a peg or pegs: *drape individual plants with nets, pegging down the edges.*
■ hang (washing) on a line with clothes pegs: *clothes were pegged out on a line.* ■ [with obj.] mark (the score) with pegs on a cribbage board. ■ (usu. **be pegged**) allot a specified place to (a competitor) in a fishing or shooting competition by means of a marker: *we've been pegged next to the winning team.*
2 [with obj.] fix (a price, rate, or amount) at a particular level.
■ N. Amer. informal form a fixed opinion of; categorize: *the officer probably has us pegged as anarchists.*
3 N. Amer. informal throw (a ball) hard and low, especially in baseball: *the catcher pegs the ball to the first baseman.*
– PHRASES **off the peg** chiefly Brit. (of clothes) ready-made rather than made to order. **a peg to hang a matter on** something used as a pretext or occasion for the discussion or treatment of a wider subject. **a square peg in a round hole** a person in a situation unsuited to their abilities or character. **take someone down a peg or two** make someone realize that they are less talented or important than they think are.
– ORIGIN late Middle English: probably of Low German origin; compare with Dutch dialect *peg* 'plug, peg'. The verb dates from the mid 16th cent.
▶ **peg away** informal continue working hard at or trying to achieve something, especially over a long period.
peg someone back reduce or eradicate the lead of an opponent in a race or game.
peg out 1 informal, chiefly Brit. die. **2** score the winning point at cribbage. **3** Croquet hit the peg with the ball as the final stroke in a game.
peg something out mark the boundaries of an area of land: *I went out to peg out our assembly area.*

Pegasus /ˈpɛgəsəs/ **1** Greek Mythology a winged horse which sprang from the blood of Medusa when Perseus cut off her head.
2 Astronomy a large northern constellation, said to represent a winged horse. The three brightest stars, together with one star of Andromeda, form the prominent **Square of Pegasus**.
■ [as genitive **Pegasi** /-saɪ/] used with preceding letter or numeral to designate a star in this constellation: *the star Zeta Pegasi.*
– ORIGIN via Latin from Greek.

pegboard ▶ noun a board having a regular pattern of small holes for pegs, used chiefly for games or the display of information.

pegbox ▶ noun a structure at the head of a stringed instrument where the strings are attached to the tuning pegs.

pegged ▶ adjective North American term for **PEGTOP**.

peggy ▶ noun (pl. **-ies**) Nautical slang a steward in a ship's mess (often used as a form of address).
– ORIGIN early 20th cent. (earlier denoting a man of feminine habits): alteration of *Meggy*, pet form of the given name *Margaret*.

peg leg ▶ noun informal an artificial leg, especially a wooden one.
■ a person with such an artificial leg.

pegmatite /ˈpɛgmətaɪt/ ▶ noun Geology a coarsely crystalline granite or other igneous rock with crystals several centimetres in length.
– ORIGIN mid 19th cent.: from Greek *pēgma, pēgmat-* 'thing joined together' + **-ITE**[1].

pego /ˈpiːgəʊ/ ▶ noun (pl. **-os**) vulgar slang a penis.
– ORIGIN late 17th cent.: of unknown origin.

pegtop ▶ noun a pear-shaped spinning top with a metal pin or peg forming the point, spun by the rapid uncoiling of a string wound round it.
▶ adjective dated (of a garment) wide at the top and narrow at the bottom: *pegtop trousers were very wide in the hips.*

Pegu /pɛˈguː/ a city and river port of southern Burma (Myanmar), on the Pegu River north-east of Rangoon; pop. 150,400 (1983). Founded in 825 as the capital of the Mon kingdom, it is a centre of Buddhist culture.

Pehlevi /ˈpeɪləvi/ ▶ noun variant spelling of **PAHLAVI**[2].

PEI ▶ abbreviation for Prince Edward Island.

Pei /peɪ/, I. M. (b.1917), American architect, born in China; full name *Ieoh Ming Pei*. Notable works include the John F. Kennedy Memorial Library at Harvard University (1964) and the glass and steel pyramid in the forecourt of the Louvre (1989).

Peigan /ˈpiːgən/ (also **Piegan**) ▶ noun (pl. same or **Peigans**) a member of a North American Indian people of the Blackfoot confederacy.
▶ adjective of or relating to this people.
– ORIGIN from Blackfoot *Piikániwa*.

peignoir /ˈpeɪnwɑː/ ▶ noun a woman's light dressing gown or negligee.
– ORIGIN French, from *peigner* 'to comb' (because the garment was originally worn while combing the hair).

pein ▶ noun & verb variant spelling of **PEEN**.

peine forte et dure /pɛn ˌfɔːt eɪ ˈd(j)ʊə/ ▶ noun [mass noun] historical a medieval form of torture in which the body was pressed with heavy weights.
– ORIGIN French, literally 'strong and hard suffering'.

Peirce /pɪəs/, Charles Sanders (1839–1914), American philosopher and logician. A founder of American pragmatism, he argued that the meaning of a belief is to be understood by the actions and uses to which it gives rise.

Peisistratus variant spelling of **PISISTRATUS**.

pejorative /pɪˈdʒɒrətɪv/ ▶ adjective expressing contempt or disapproval: *permissiveness is used almost universally as a pejorative term.*
▶ noun a word expressing contempt or disapproval.
– DERIVATIVES **pejoratively** adverb.
– ORIGIN late 19th cent.: from French *péjoratif, -ive*, from late Latin *pejorare* 'make worse', from Latin *pejor* 'worse'.

pekan /ˈpɛk(ə)n/ ▶ noun North American term for **FISHER**.
– ORIGIN mid 18th cent.: from Canadian French, from Algonquian.

peke ▶ noun informal a Pekinese dog.
– ORIGIN early 20th cent.: abbreviation.

Pekinese /ˌpiːkɪˈniːz/ (also **Pekingese**) ▶ noun (pl. same) a lapdog of a short-legged breed with long hair and a snub nose, originally brought to Europe from the Summer Palace at Beijing (Peking) in 1860.
▶ adjective of or relating to Beijing, its citizens, or their culture or cuisine.

Peking /piːˈkɪŋ/ variant of **BEIJING**.

Peking duck ▶ noun [mass noun] a Chinese dish consisting of strips of roast duck served with shredded vegetables and a sweet sauce.

Peking man ▶ noun a fossil hominid of the middle Pleistocene period, identified from remains found near Beijing in 1926.
● A late form of *Homo erectus* (formerly *Sinanthropus pekinensis*), family Hominidae.

Peking opera ▶ noun [mass noun] a stylized Chinese form of opera dating from the late 18th century, in which speech, singing, mime, and acrobatics are performed to an instrumental accompaniment.

Pekin robin ▶ noun another term for **LEIOTHRIX**.

pekoe /ˈpiːkəʊ, ˈpɛ-/ ▶ noun [mass noun] a high-quality black tea made from young leaves.
– ORIGIN early 18th cent.: from Chinese dialect *pekho*, from *pek* 'white' + *ho* 'down' (the leaves being picked young when covered with down).

pelage /ˈpɛlɪdʒ/ ▶ noun [mass noun] Zoology the fur, hair, or wool of a mammal.
– ORIGIN early 19th cent.: from French, from Old French *pel* 'hair'.

pelagic /pɪˈladʒɪk/ ▶ adjective technical of or relating to the open sea: *the kittiwakes return from their pelagic winter wanderings.*
■ (chiefly of fish) inhabiting the upper layers of the open sea. Often contrasted with **DEMERSAL**.
– ORIGIN mid 17th cent.: via Latin from Greek *pelagikos*, from *pelagios* 'of the sea' (from *pelagos* 'level surface of the sea').

Pelagius /pɪˈleɪdʒɪəs/ (c.360–c.420), British or Irish monk. He denied the doctrines of original sin and predestination, defending innate human goodness and free will. His beliefs were opposed by St Augustine of Hippo and condemned as heretical by the Synod of Carthage in about 418.
– DERIVATIVES **Pelagian** adjective & noun, **Pelagianism** noun.

pelargonium /ˌpɛləˈgəʊnɪəm/ ▶ noun a tender shrubby plant which is widely cultivated for its red, pink, or white flowers. Some kinds have fragrant leaves which yield an essential oil. See also **GERANIUM**.
● Genus *Pelargonium*, family Geraniaceae: many species and several hybrid groups, including the **zonal pelargoniums** (*P. × hortorum*), with rounded leaves bearing coloured zones, and the trailing **ivy-leaved pelargoniums** (*P. peltatum*).
– ORIGIN modern Latin, from Greek *pelargos* 'stork', apparently on the pattern of *geranium* (based on Greek *geranos* 'crane').

Pelasgian /pɪˈlazgɪən/ ▶ adjective relating to or denoting an ancient people inhabiting the coasts and islands of the Aegean Sea and eastern Mediterranean before the arrival of Greek-speaking peoples in the Bronze Age (12th century BC).
▶ noun a member of this people.
– ORIGIN late 15th cent.: via Latin from Greek *Pelasgos* + **-IAN**.

pelau /pəˈlaʊ/ ▶ noun [mass noun] a spicy dish consisting of meat (typically chicken), rice, and pigeon peas.
– ORIGIN from French Creole *pêlao*.

Pelé /ˈpɛleɪ/ (b.1940), Brazilian footballer; born *Edson Arantes do Nascimento*. Regarded as one of the greatest footballers of all time, he appeared 111 times for Brazil and is credited with over 1,200 goals in first-class soccer.

pele ▶ noun variant spelling of **PEEL**[3].

pelecypod /pɪˈlɛsɪpɒd/ ▶ noun another term for **BIVALVE**.
– ORIGIN late 19th cent.: from modern Latin *Pelecypoda* (alternative class name), from Greek *pelekus* 'hatchet' + *-podos* 'footed'.

Pelée, Mount /pəˈleɪ/ a volcano on the island of Martinique, in the Caribbean. Its eruption in 1902 destroyed the island's then capital St Pierre, killing its population of some 30,000.

pelerine /ˈpɛlərɪn, ˈpɛləriːn/ ▶ noun historical a woman's cape of lace or silk with pointed ends at the centre front, popular in the 19th century.
– ORIGIN mid 18th cent.: from French *pèlerine*, the sense being a transferred use of the feminine of *pèlerin* 'pilgrim'.

Pele's hair /ˈpɛleɪz/ ▶ noun [mass noun] fine threads of volcanic glass, formed when a spray of lava droplets cools rapidly in the air.
– ORIGIN mid 19th cent.: translating Hawaiian *lauoho o Pele*, Pele being the goddess of volcanoes in Hawaiian mythology.

Peleus /ˈpiːljuːs/ Greek Mythology a king of Phthia in Thessaly, who was given as his wife the sea nymph Thetis; their child was Achilles.

pelf ▶ **noun** [mass noun] archaic money, especially when gained in a dishonest or dishonourable way.
– ORIGIN late Middle English (in the sense 'booty, pilfered property'): from a variant of Old French *pelfre* 'spoils', of unknown origin. Compare with **PILFER**.

Pelham /ˈpɛləm/, Henry (1696–1754), British Whig statesman, Prime Minister 1743–54.

pelham ▶ **noun** a horse's bit which combines the action of a curb bit and a snaffle.
– ORIGIN mid 19th cent.: from the surname *Pelham*.

pelican ▶ **noun** a large gregarious waterbird with a long bill, an extensible throat pouch for scooping up fish, and mainly white or grey plumage.
• Family Pelecanidae and genus *Pelecanus*: several species.
■ a heraldic or artistic representation of a pelican, typically depicted pecking its own breast as a symbol of Christ. [ORIGIN: from an ancient legend that the pelican fed its young on its own blood.]
– ORIGIN late Old English *pellicane*, via late Latin from Greek *pelekan*, probably based on *pelekus* 'axe' (with reference to its bill).

pelican crossing ▶ **noun** (in the UK) a pedestrian crossing with traffic lights operated by pedestrians.
– ORIGIN 1960s: *pelican* from *pe(destrian) li(ght) (con)trolled*, altered to conform with the bird's name.

pelican's foot shell ▶ **noun** a burrowing European mollusc which has a heavily sculptured spiral shell with a flared lip that extends into several points.
• *Aporrhais pespelecani*, family Aporrhaidae, class Gastropoda.

Pelican State informal name for **LOUISIANA**.

pelike /ˈpɛlɪki, pɛˈliːki/ ▶ **noun** (pl. **pelikai** /ˈpɛlɪkʌɪ/) a wide-mouthed amphora with a broad base, used in ancient Greece for holding wine or water.
– ORIGIN from Greek *pelika*.

Pelion /ˈpiːlɪən/ a wooded mountain in Greece, near the coast of SE Thessaly, rising to 1,548 m (5,079 ft). It was held in Greek mythology to be the home of the centaurs, and the giants were said to have piled Mounts Olympus and Ossa on its summit in their attempt to reach heaven and destroy the gods.
– PHRASES **pile** (or **heap**) **Pelion on Ossa** add an extra difficulty or task to something which is already difficult or onerous.

pelisse /pɪˈliːs/ ▶ **noun** historical a woman's cloak with armholes or sleeves, reaching to the ankles.
■ a fur-lined cloak, especially as part of a hussar's uniform.
– ORIGIN early 18th cent.: from French, from medieval Latin *pellicia* (*vestis*) '(garment) of fur', from *pellis* 'skin'.

P

pelite /ˈpiːlʌɪt/ ▶ **noun** Geology a sediment or sedimentary rock composed of very fine clay or mud particles.
– ORIGIN late 19th cent.: from Greek *pēlos* 'clay, mud' + **-ITE**[1].

pellagra /pɛˈlagrə, -ˈleɪgrə/ ▶ **noun** [mass noun] a deficiency disease caused by a lack of nicotinic acid or its precursor tryptophan in the diet. It is characterized by dermatitis, diarrhoea, and mental disturbance, and is often linked to over-dependence on maize as a staple food.
– DERIVATIVES **pellagrous** adjective.
– ORIGIN early 19th cent.: from Italian, from *pelle* 'skin', on the pattern of *podagra*.

pellet ▶ **noun** a small, rounded, compressed mass of a substance: *fish food pellets*.
■ a piece of small shot or other lightweight bullet. ■ Ornithology a small mass of bones and feathers regurgitated by a bird of prey or other bird. ■ a small round piece of animal faeces, especially from a rabbit or rodent.
▶ **verb** (**pelleted**, **pelleting**) [with obj.] **1** form or shape (a substance, especially animal food) into pellets.
2 hit with or as though with pellets: *the last drops of rain were pelleting the windshield.*
– ORIGIN late Middle English: from Old French *pelote* 'metal ball', from a diminutive of Latin *pila* 'ball'.

Pelletier /ˌpɛlɛˈtɪeɪ/, Pierre-Joseph (1788–1842), French chemist. With his friend **Joseph-Bienaimé Caventou** (1795–1877) he isolated a number of alkaloids for the first time. Pelletier and Caventou also isolated the green pigment of leaves and gave it the name *chlorophyll*.

pelletize (also **-ise**) ▶ **verb** [with obj.] form or shape (a substance) into pellets.

pellicle /ˈpɛlɪk(ə)l/ ▶ **noun** technical a thin skin, cuticle, membrane, or film.
– DERIVATIVES **pellicular** /-ˈlɪkjʊlə/ adjective.
– ORIGIN late Middle English: from French *pellicule*, from Latin *pellicula* 'small piece of skin', diminutive of *pellis*.

pellitory /ˈpɛlɪtəri/ (also **pellitory of the wall**) ▶ **noun** a European plant of the nettle family with greenish flowers, which grows on or at the foot of walls or in stony places.
• *Parietaria judaica*, family Urticaceae.
– ORIGIN late Middle English: alteration of obsolete *parietary*, from Old French *paritaire*, based on Latin *paries*, *pariet-* 'wall'.

pell-mell ▶ **adverb** in a confused, rushed, or disorderly manner: *the contents of the sacks were thrown pell-mell to the ground.*
▶ **adjective** recklessly hasty or disorganized; headlong: *steering the pell-mell development of Europe on to a new and more gradual course.*
▶ **noun** [in sing.] a state of affairs or collection of things characterized by haste or confusion: *the pell-mell of ascending gables and roof tiles.*
– ORIGIN late 16th cent.: from French *pêle-mêle*, from earlier *pesle mesle*, *mesle pesle*, reduplication from *mesler* 'to mix'.

pellucid /pɪˈluːsɪd, pɛ-, -ˈljuːsɪd/ ▶ **adjective** translucently clear: *mountains reflected in the pellucid waters.*
■ lucid in style or meaning; easily understood: *he writes, as always, in pellucid prose.* ■ (of music or other sound) clear and pure in tone: *a smooth legato and pellucid singing tone are his calling cards.*
– DERIVATIVES **pellucidly** adverb.
– ORIGIN early 17th cent.: from Latin *pellucidus*, from *perlucere* 'shine through'.

Pelmanism /ˈpɛlmənɪz(ə)m/ ▶ **noun** [mass noun] a system of memory training originally devised by the Pelman Institute for the Scientific Development of Mind, Memory, and Personality in London.
■ a game based on memorizing cards or other objects placed before the players.

pelmet ▶ **noun** a narrow border of cloth or wood, fitted across the top of a door or window to conceal the curtain fittings.
– ORIGIN early 20th cent.: probably an alteration of French *palmette*, literally 'small palm' (see **PALMETTE**).

Peloponnese /ˌpɛləpəˈniːz/ (**the Peloponnese**) the mountainous southern peninsula of Greece, connected to central Greece by the Isthmus of Corinth. Greek name **PELOPÓNNISOS** /ˌpɛləˈpɒnɪsɒs/, also called **PELOPONNESUS** /-ˈniːsəs/.
– ORIGIN from Greek, literally 'island of Pelops'.

Peloponnesian War /ˌpɛləpəˈniːʃ(ə)n, -ˈniːʒ(ə)n/ the war of 431–404 BC fought between Athens and Sparta with their respective allies, occasioned largely by Spartan opposition to the Delian League. It ended in the total defeat of Athens and the transfer, for a brief period, of the leadership of Greece to Sparta.

Pelops /ˈpiːlɒps/ Greek Mythology son of Tantalus, brother of Niobe, and father of Atreus. He was killed by his father and served up as food to the gods, but only one shoulder was eaten, and he was restored to life with an ivory shoulder replacing the one that was missing.

pelorus /pɪˈlɔːrəs/ ▶ **noun** a sighting device on a ship for taking the relative bearings of a distant object.
– ORIGIN mid 19th cent.: perhaps from *Pelorus*, said to be the name of Hannibal's pilot.

pelota /pɪˈlɒtə, -ˈləʊtə/ ▶ **noun** [mass noun] a Basque or Spanish game played in a walled court with a ball and basket-like rackets attached to the hand.
■ [count noun] the ball used in such a game.
– ORIGIN Spanish, literally 'ball', augmentative of *pella*, from Latin *pila* 'ball'.

peloton /ˈpɛlətɒn/ ▶ **noun** the main field or group of cyclists in a race.
– ORIGIN 1950s: from French, literally 'small ball' (because of the concentrated grouping of the pack).

pelt[1] ▶ **verb** [with obj.] attack (someone) by repeatedly hurling things at them: *two little boys* **pelted** *him* **with** *rotten apples.*
■ hurl (something) at someone or something in this way: *he spotted four boys aged about ten pelting stones at ducks.* ■ [no obj.] (**pelt down**) (of rain, hail, or snow) fall quickly and very heavily: *the rain was pelting down.* ■ [no obj., with adverbial of direction] informal run somewhere very quickly: *I pelted across the road.*
▶ **noun** archaic an act of hurling something at someone.
– PHRASES (**at**) **full pelt** with great speed; as fast as possible: *I ran full pelt away from the harbour.*
– ORIGIN late 15th cent.: of unknown origin.

pelt[2] ▶ **noun** the skin of an animal with the fur, wool, or hair still on it.
■ an animal's coat of fur or hair. ■ the raw skin of a sheep or goat, stripped and ready for tanning. ■ informal a person's hair.
– ORIGIN Middle English: either from obsolete *pellet* 'skin', from an Old French diminutive of *pel* 'skin', from Latin *pellis* 'skin', or a back-formation from **PELTRY**.

pelta /ˈpɛltə/ ▶ **noun** (pl. **peltae** /-tiː/) a small light shield, as used by the ancient Greeks and Romans.
■ an ornamental motif resembling a shield.
– ORIGIN from Latin, from Greek *peltē*.

peltate /ˈpɛlteɪt/ ▶ **adjective** chiefly Botany shield-shaped.
■ (of a leaf) more or less circular, with the stalk attached at a point on the underside.

Peltier effect /ˈpɛltɪeɪ/ ▶ **noun** Physics an effect whereby heat is given out or absorbed when an electric current passes across a junction between two materials.
– ORIGIN mid 19th cent.: named after Jean C. A. *Peltier* (1785–1845), French amateur scientist.

peltry ▶ **noun** [mass noun] (also **peltries**) animal pelts collectively.
– ORIGIN late Middle English: from Anglo-Norman French *pelterie*, based on Old French *pel* 'skin', from Latin *pellis*.

pelvic ▶ **adjective** of, relating to, or situated within the bony pelvis.
■ of or relating to the renal pelvis.

pelvic fin ▶ **noun** Zoology each of a pair of fins on the underside of a fish's body, attached to the pelvic girdle and helping to control direction. Also called **VENTRAL FIN**.

pelvic floor ▶ **noun** the muscular base of the abdomen, attached to the pelvis.

pelvic girdle ▶ **noun** (in vertebrates) the enclosing structure formed by the pelvis, providing attachment for the hindlimbs or pelvic fins.

pelvic inflammatory disease (abbrev.: **PID**) ▶ **noun** [mass noun] inflammation of the female genital tract, accompanied by fever and lower abdominal pain.

pelvimetry /pɛlˈvɪmɪtri/ ▶ **noun** [mass noun] Medicine measurement of the dimensions of the pelvis, undertaken chiefly to help determine whether a woman can give birth normally or will require a Caesarean section.

pelvis ▶ **noun** (pl. **pelvises** or **pelves** /-viːz/) **1** the large bony structure near the base of the spine to which the hindlimbs or legs are attached in humans and many other vertebrates.
■ the part of the abdomen including or enclosed by the pelvis.

> In humans the pelvis, fused to the base of the spine, forms a basin-shaped hollow frame at the hips, partly supporting the internal organs and providing attachment for the bones and muscles of the legs.

2 (also **renal pelvis**) the broadened top part of the ureter into which the kidney tubules drain.
– ORIGIN early 17th cent.: from Latin, literally 'basin'.

pelycosaur /ˈpɛlɪkəsɔː/ ▶ **noun** a large fossil reptile of the late Carboniferous and Permian periods, typically having a line of long bony spines along the back supporting a sail-like crest.
• Order Pelycosauria, subclass Synapsida: several families and genera, including *Dimetrodon* and *Edaphosaurus*.
– ORIGIN mid 20th cent.: from Greek *pelux*, *peluk-* 'bowl' + *sauros* 'lizard'.

Pemba /ˈpɛmbə/ **1** a seaport in northern Mozambique, on the Indian Ocean; pop. 41,200 (1980).
2 an island off the coast of Tanzania, in the western Indian Ocean north of Zanzibar.

Pembroke /ˈpɛmbrʊk/ a port in SW Wales, in Pembrokeshire; pop. 15,600 (1981). It was a Norman stronghold from the 11th century. Welsh name **PENFRO**.

Pembrokeshire a county of SW Wales; administrative centre, Haverfordwest. It was part of Dyfed from 1974 to 1996.

Pembroke table ▶ **noun** a small table with fixed legs and a drop-leaf on each side.

Pembs. ▶ **abbreviation for** Pembrokeshire.

pemmican /ˈpɛmɪk(ə)n/ ▶ **noun** [mass noun] a paste of dried and pounded meat mixed with melted fat and other ingredients, originally made by North American Indians and later adapted by Arctic explorers.
– ORIGIN from Cree *pimecan*, from *pime* 'fat'.

pemphigoid /ˈpɛmfɪɡɔɪd/ ▶ **noun** [mass noun] Medicine a skin disease resembling pemphigus, chiefly affecting the elderly.

pemphigus /ˈpɛmfɪɡəs/ ▶ **noun** [mass noun] Medicine a skin disease in which watery blisters form on the skin.
– ORIGIN late 18th cent.: modern Latin, from Greek *pemphix*, *pemphig-* 'bubble'.

PEN ▶ **abbreviation for** International Association of Poets, Playwrights, Editors, Essayists, and Novelists.

Pen. ▶ **abbreviation for** Peninsula.

pen[1] ▶ **noun 1** an instrument for writing or drawing with ink, typically consisting of a metal nib or ball, or a nylon tip, fitted into a metal or plastic holder. ■ (**the pen**) the occupation or practice of writing: *she was forced to support herself not only by the pen, but as a secret agent.* ■ an electronic pen-like device used in conjunction with a writing surface to enter commands or data into a computer.
2 Zoology the tapering cartilaginous internal shell of a squid.
▶ **verb** (**penned**, **penning**) [with obj.] write or compose: *he had not penned a line to Lizzie in three years.*
– PHRASES **pen and ink** Brit. rhyming slang a stink. **the pen is mightier than the sword** proverb writing is more effective than military power or violence. **put** (or **set**) **pen to paper** write or begin to write something.
– ORIGIN Middle English (originally denoting a feather with a sharpened quill): from Old French *penne*, from Latin *penna* 'feather' (in late Latin 'pen').

pen[2] ▶ **noun** a small enclosure in which sheep, pigs, cattle, or other domestic animals are kept. ■ a number of animals in or sufficient to fill such an enclosure: *a pen of twenty-five Cheviots.* ■ any small enclosure in which someone or something can be confined. ■ a covered dock for a submarine or other warship. ■ (in the West Indies) a farm or plantation.
▶ **verb** (**penned**, **penning**) [with obj.] put or keep (an animal) in a pen: *it was the practice to pen the sheep for clipping.* ■ (**pen someone up/in**) confine someone in a restricted space: *they had been penned up day and night in the house.*
– ORIGIN Old English *penn*, of unknown origin.

pen[3] ▶ **noun** a female swan.
– ORIGIN mid 16th cent.: of unknown origin.

pen[4] ▶ **noun** N. Amer. informal short for **PENITENTIARY** (in sense 1).

penal ▶ **adjective** of, relating to, or prescribing the punishment of offenders under the legal system: *the campaign for penal reform.* ■ used or designated as a place of punishment: *a former penal colony.* ■ (of an act or offence) punishable by law. ■ (especially of taxation or interest rates) extremely severe.
– DERIVATIVES **penally** adverb.
– ORIGIN late Middle English: from Old French *penal*, from Latin *poenalis*, from *poena* 'pain, penalty'.

penalize (also **-ise**) ▶ **verb** [with obj.] (often **be penalized**) subject to some form of punishment: *high spending councils will be penalized.* ■ (in various sports) punish (a player or team) for a breach of the rules by awarding an advantage to the opposition. ■ put in an unfavourable position or at an unfair disadvantage: *if the bill is not amended genuine claimants will be penalized.* ■ Law make or declare (an act or offence) legally punishable: *section twenty penalizes possession of a firearm when trespassing.*
– DERIVATIVES **penalization** noun.

Penal Laws ▶ **plural noun** various statutes passed in Britain and Ireland during the 16th and 17th centuries that imposed harsh restrictions on Roman Catholics. The laws were repealed by various Acts between 1791 and 1926. See also **CATHOLIC EMANCIPATION**, **TEST ACT**.

penal servitude ▶ **noun** [mass noun] imprisonment with hard labour.

penalty ▶ **noun** (pl. **-ies**) **1** a punishment imposed for breaking a law, rule, or contract: *the charge carries a maximum penalty of ten years' imprisonment.* ■ a disadvantage or unpleasant experience suffered as the result of an action or circumstance: *the cold never leaves my bones these days—one of the penalties of age.*
2 (in sports and games) a disadvantage or handicap imposed on a player or team, typically for infringement of rules. ■ a kick or shot awarded to a team because of an infringement of the rules by an opponent. ■ Bridge points won by the defenders when a declarer fails to make the contract.
– PHRASES **under** (or **on**) **penalty of** under the threat of: *he ordered enterprises to fulfil contracts under penalty of strict fines.*
– ORIGIN early 16th cent.: probably via Anglo-Norman French, from medieval Latin *poenalitas*, based on *poena* 'pain'.

penalty area ▶ **noun** Soccer the rectangular area marked out in front of each goal, within which a foul by a defender involves the award of a penalty kick and outside which the goalkeeper is not allowed to handle the ball.

penalty box ▶ **noun 1** Soccer another term for **PENALTY AREA**.
2 Ice Hockey an area beside the rink reserved for penalized players and an official who records penalties.

penalty double ▶ **noun** Bridge another term for **BUSINESS DOUBLE**.

penalty kick ▶ **noun 1** Soccer a free kick at the goal from the penalty spot (which only the goalkeeper is allowed to defend), awarded to the attacking team after a foul within the penalty area by an opponent.
2 Rugby a place kick awarded to a team after an offence by an opponent.

penalty killer ▶ **noun** Ice Hockey a player specializing in preventing the opposing side from scoring while their own team's strength is reduced through penalties.
– DERIVATIVES **penalty killing** noun.

penalty point ▶ **noun** (in the UK) a punishment awarded by the courts for a driving offence and recorded cumulatively on a person's driving licence.

penalty rate ▶ **noun** Austral. an increased rate of pay for overtime or for work performed under abnormal conditions.

penalty shoot-out ▶ **noun** see **SHOOT-OUT**.

penalty spot ▶ **noun** Soccer the point within the penalty area from which penalty kicks are taken.

penalty try ▶ **noun** Rugby a try awarded to a side by the referee when a touchdown is prevented by an offence by the opposition.

penance ▶ **noun** [mass noun] **1** voluntary self-punishment inflicted as an outward expression of repentance for having done wrong: *he had* **done** *public* **penance for** *those hasty words.*
2 a sacrament in which a member of the Church confesses sins to a priest and is given absolution. In the Roman Catholic Church often called **SACRAMENT OF RECONCILIATION**. ■ a religious observance or other duty required of a person by a priest as part of this sacrament to indicate repentance.
▶ **verb** [with obj.] archaic impose a penance on: *a hair shirt to penance him for his folly in offending.*
– ORIGIN Middle English: from Old French, from Latin *paenitentia* 'repentance', from the verb *paenitere* 'be sorry'.

Penang /pɪˈnaŋ/ (also **Pinang**) an island of Malaysia, situated off the west coast of the Malay Peninsula. In 1786 it was ceded to the East India Company as a British colony by the sultan of Kedah. Known as Prince of Wales Island until 1867, it united with Malacca and Singapore in a union of 1826, which in 1867 became the British colony called the Straits Settlements. It joined the federation of Malaya in 1948. ■ a state of Malaysia, consisting of this island and a coastal strip on the mainland; capital, George Town (on Penang island). The mainland strip was united with the island in 1798 as part of the British colony. ■ another name for **GEORGE TOWN** (in sense 2).

penannular /pɛˈnanjʊlə/ ▶ **adjective** Archaeology in the form of a ring but with a small part of the circumference missing: *penannular neck ornaments.*
– ORIGIN mid 19th cent.: from Latin *paene* 'almost' + **ANNULAR**.

penates /pɪˈnɑːtiːz, -ˈneɪt-/ ▶ **plural noun** Roman History household gods worshipped in conjunction with Vesta and the lares by the ancient Romans.
– ORIGIN Latin, from *penus* 'provision of food'; related to *penes* 'within'.

pence plural form of **PENNY**.

> **USAGE** Both **pence** and **pennies** have existed as plural forms of **penny** since at least the 16th century. The two forms now tend to be used for different purposes: **pence** refers to sums of money (*five pounds and sixty-nine* **pence**) while **pennies** refers to the coins themselves (*I left two* **pennies** *on the table*).
> In recent years, **pence** rather than **penny** has sometimes been used in the singular to refer to sums of money amounting to one penny: *the chancellor will put* **one pence** *on income tax*. This singular use is not widely accepted in standard English, though.

penchant /ˈpɒ̃ʃɒ̃/ ▶ **noun** [usu. in sing.] a strong or habitual liking for something or tendency to do something: *he has a* **penchant for** *adopting stray dogs.*
– ORIGIN late 17th cent.: from French, 'leaning, inclining', present participle of the verb *pencher*.

pencil ▶ **noun** an instrument for writing or drawing, consisting of a thin stick of graphite or a similar substance enclosed in a long thin piece of wood or fixed in a metal or plastic case. ■ [mass noun] graphite or a similar substance used in such a way as a medium for writing or drawing: *the words were scribbled in pencil.* ■ [usu. with modifier] a cosmetic in a long thin stick, designed to be applied to a particular part of the face: *an eyebrow pencil.* ■ something with the shape of a pencil: *a pencil of light* | [as modifier] *a pencil torch.* ■ Physics & Geometry a set of light rays, lines, etc. converging to or diverging narrowly from a single point.
▶ **verb** (**pencilled**, **pencilling**; US **penciled**, **penciling**) [with obj.] write, draw, or colour (something) with a pencil: *a previous owner has pencilled their name inside the cover* | [as adj. **pencilled**] *a pencilled note.*
– DERIVATIVES **penciller** noun.
– ORIGIN Middle English (denoting a fine paintbrush): from Old French *pincel*, from a diminutive of Latin *peniculus* 'brush', diminutive of *penis* 'tail'. The verb was originally (early 16th cent.) in the sense 'paint with a fine brush'.
▶ **pencil something in 1** fill in an area or shape with pencil strokes: *a lot of the outlines had been pencilled in.* **2** arrange, forecast, or note down something provisionally or tentatively: *May 15 was pencilled in as the date for the meeting.* ■ (**pencil someone in**) make a provisional or tentative arrangement with or for someone: *he was pencilled in for surgery at the end of the month.*

pencil moustache ▶ **noun** a very thin moustache.

pencil-pusher ▶ **noun** N. Amer. another term for **PEN-PUSHER**.

pencil sharpener ▶ **noun** a device for sharpening a pencil by rotating it against a cutting edge.

pencil skirt ▶ **noun** a very narrow straight skirt.

pendant ▶ **noun 1** a piece of jewellery that hangs from a chain worn round the neck. ■ a necklace with such a piece of jewellery. ■ a light designed to hang from the ceiling. ■ the part of a pocket watch by which it is suspended. ■ a short rope hanging from the head of a ship's mast, yardarm, or clew of a sail, used for attaching tackles.
2 Brit. a pennant or tapering flag.
3 /ˈpɛnd(ə)nt, ˈpɒ̃dɒ̃/ an artistic, literary, or musical composition intended to match or complement another: *the triptych's pendant will occupy the corresponding wall in the south transept.*
▶ **adjective** hanging downwards; pendent: *pendant flowers on frail stems.*
– ORIGIN Middle English (denoting an architectural decoration projecting downwards): from Old French, literally 'hanging', present participle of the verb *pendre*, from Latin *pendere*.

pendent ▶ **adjective 1** hanging down or overhanging: *pendent catkins.*
2 undecided; pending: *the use of jurisdiction to decide pendent claims.*
3 Grammar (especially of a sentence) incomplete; not having a finite verb.
– DERIVATIVES **pendency** noun.

pensile /ˈpɛnsʌɪl/ ▶ adjective hanging down; pendulous: *pensile nests*.
– ORIGIN early 17th cent.: from Latin *pensilis*, from the verb *pendere* 'hang'.

pension¹ /ˈpɛnʃ(ə)n/ ▶ noun (Brit. also **state pension**) a regular payment made by the state to people of or above the official retirement age and to some widows and disabled people.
■ a regular payment made during a person's retirement from an investment fund to which that person or their employer has contributed during their working life. ■ chiefly historical a regular payment made to a royal favourite or to an artist or scholar to enable them to carry on work which is of public interest or value.
▶ verb [with obj.] (**pension someone off**) dismiss someone from employment, typically because of age or ill health, and pay them a pension: *he was pensioned off from the army at the end of the war.*
– DERIVATIVES **pensionless** adjective.
– ORIGIN late Middle English (in the sense 'payment, tax, regular sum paid to retain allegiance'): from Old French, from Latin *pensio(n-)* 'payment', from *pendere* 'to pay'. The current verb sense dates from the mid 19th cent.

pension² /pɒ̃ˈsjɔ̃, French pɑ̃sjɔ̃/ ▶ noun a boarding house in France and other European countries, providing full or half board at a fixed rate.
– ORIGIN French.

pensionable ▶ adjective entitling to or qualifying for a pension: *single and widowed women over pensionable age.*
– DERIVATIVES **pensionability** noun.

pension book ▶ noun Brit. a book of vouchers supplied by the government for the weekly payment of a person's pension.

pensione /ˌpɛnsiˈəʊneɪ/ ▶ noun (pl. **pensioni** /-ni/) a small hotel or boarding house in Italy.
– ORIGIN Italian.

pensioner ▶ noun a person who receives a pension, especially the retirement pension.

pension fund ▶ noun a fund from which pensions are paid, accumulated from contributions from employers, employees, or both.

pension mortgage ▶ noun a mortgage in which the borrower repays interest only and also contributes to a pension plan designed to provide an eventual tax-free lump sum, part of which is used to repay the capital at the end of the mortgage period and the rest to provide a pension for the borrower's retirement.

pensionnat /ˌpɒ̃sjɒˈna, French pɑ̃sjɔna/ ▶ noun (pl. pronounced same) in France and other European countries, a boarding school.
– ORIGIN French.

pensive ▶ adjective engaged in, involving, or reflecting deep or serious thought: *a pensive mood.*
– DERIVATIVES **pensively** adverb, **pensiveness** noun.
– ORIGIN late Middle English: from Old French *pensif*, *-ive*, from *penser* 'think', from Latin *pensare* 'ponder', frequentative of *pendere* 'weigh'.

penstemon /pɛnˈstiːmən, -ˈstɛmən, ˈpɛnstɪmən/ (also **pentstemon**) ▶ noun a North American plant with stems of showy snapdragon-like flowers.
● Genus *Penstemon*, family Scrophulariaceae.
– ORIGIN modern Latin, formed irregularly from PENTA- 'five' + Greek *stēmōn* 'warp', used to mean 'stamen'.

penstock ▶ noun a sluice or floodgate for regulating the flow of a body of water.
■ N. Amer. a channel for conveying water to a waterwheel or turbine.
– ORIGIN early 17th cent.: from PEN² (in the sense 'mill dam') + STOCK.

pent ▶ adjective chiefly poetic/literary another term for PENT-UP: *with pent breath she waited out the meeting.*

penta- ▶ combining form five; having five: *pentagram | pentadactyl.*
– ORIGIN from Greek *pente* 'five'.

pentachlorophenol /ˌpɛntəˌklɔːrəʊˈfiːnɒl/ ▶ noun [mass noun] Chemistry a colourless crystalline synthetic compound used in insecticides, fungicides, weedkillers, and wood preservatives.
● Chem. formula: C_6Cl_5OH.

pentachord ▶ noun a musical instrument with five strings.
■ a series of five musical notes.

pentacle /ˈpɛntək(ə)l/ ▶ noun a talisman or magical object, typically disc-shaped and inscribed with a pentagram or other figure, and used as a symbol of the element of earth.
■ another term for PENTAGRAM. ■ (**pentacles**) one of the suits in some tarot packs, corresponding to coins in others.
– ORIGIN late 16th cent.: from medieval Latin *pentaculum*, apparently based on Greek *penta-* 'five'.

pentad /ˈpɛntad/ ▶ noun technical a group or set of five.
– ORIGIN mid 17th cent.: from Greek *pentas*, *pentad-*, from *pente* 'five'.

pentadactyl /ˌpɛntəˈdaktɪl/ ▶ adjective Zoology (of a vertebrate limb) having five toes or fingers, or derived from such a form, as characteristic of all tetrapods.
– DERIVATIVES **pentadactyly** /-ˈdaktɪli/ noun.
– ORIGIN early 19th cent.: from PENTA- 'five' + Greek *daktulos* 'finger'.

pentagastrin /ˌpɛntəˈɡastrɪn/ ▶ noun [mass noun] Biochemistry a synthetic peptide which has the same action as the hormone gastrin. It is used to promote gastric secretions prior to sampling them for tests.

pentagon ▶ noun 1 a plane figure with five straight sides and five angles.
2 (**the Pentagon**) the pentagonal building serving as the headquarters of the US Department of Defense, near Washington DC.
■ the US Department of Defense: *the Pentagon said 19 of its soldiers had been killed.*
– DERIVATIVES **pentagonal** adjective.
– ORIGIN late 16th cent.: via Latin from Greek *pentagōnon*, neuter (used as a noun) of *pentagōnos* 'five-angled'.

Pentagonese /ˌpɛntəɡəˈniːz/ ▶ noun [mass noun] US informal the euphemistic or cryptic language supposedly used among high-ranking US military personnel.
– ORIGIN 1950s: from (*the*) *Pentagon* (see sense 2 of PENTAGON) + -ESE.

pentagram ▶ noun a five-pointed star that is formed by drawing a continuous line in five straight segments, often used as a mystic and magical symbol. Compare with PENTACLE.
– ORIGIN mid 19th cent.: from Greek *pentagrammon* (see PENTA-, -GRAM¹).

pentahedron /ˌpɛntəˈhiːdr(ə)n, -ˈhɛd-/ ▶ noun (pl. **pentahedra** /-drə/ or **pentahedrons**) a solid figure with five plane faces.
– DERIVATIVES **pentahedral** adjective.
– ORIGIN late 18th cent.: from PENTA- 'five' + -HEDRON, on the pattern of words such as *polyhedron*.

pentamer /ˈpɛntəmə/ ▶ noun Chemistry a polymer comprising five monomer units.
– DERIVATIVES **pentameric** /ˌpɛntəˈmɛrɪk/ adjective.

pentameral /pɛnˈtamərəl/ ▶ adjective Zoology (of symmetry) fivefold, as typical of many echinoderms. Compare with PENTAMEROUS.
– DERIVATIVES **pentamerally** adverb, **pentamery** noun.

pentamerous /pɛnˈtam(ə)rəs/ ▶ adjective Botany & Zoology having parts arranged in groups of five.
■ consisting of five joints or parts. Compare with PENTAMERAL.

pentameter /pɛnˈtamɪtə/ ▶ noun Prosody a line of verse consisting of five metrical feet, or (in Greek and Latin verse) of two halves each of two feet and a long syllable.
– ORIGIN early 16th cent.: via Latin from Greek *pentametros* (see PENTA-, -METER).

pentamidine /pɛnˈtamɪdiːn/ ▶ noun [mass noun] Medicine a synthetic antibiotic drug used chiefly in the treatment of PCP infection.
– ORIGIN 1940s: from PENTANE + AMIDE + -INE4.

pentane /ˈpɛnteɪn/ ▶ noun [mass noun] Chemistry a volatile liquid hydrocarbon of the alkane series, present in petroleum spirit.
● Chem. formula: C_5H_{12}; three isomers, especially the straight-chain isomer (*n-pentane*).
– ORIGIN late 19th cent.: from Greek *pente* 'five' (denoting five carbon atoms) + a shortened form of ALKANE.

pentangle ▶ noun another term for PENTAGRAM.
– ORIGIN late Middle English: perhaps from medieval Latin *pentaculum* 'pentacle' (*-aculum* assimilated to Latin *angulus* 'an angle').

pentanoic acid /ˌpɛntəˈnəʊɪk/ ▶ noun [mass noun] Chemistry a colourless liquid fatty acid present in various plant oils, used in making perfumes.
● Chem. formula: $CH_3(CH_2)_3COOH$.
– DERIVATIVES **pentanoate** noun.
– ORIGIN 1920s: *pentanoic* from PENTANE.

pentaploid /ˈpɛntəplɔɪd/ Genetics ▶ adjective (of a cell or nucleus) containing five homologous sets of chromosomes.
■ (of an organism or species) composed of pentaploid cells.
▶ noun a pentaploid organism, variety, or species.

pentaprism ▶ noun a five-sided prism with two silvered surfaces giving a constant deviation of all rays of light through 90°, used chiefly in the viewfinders of single-lens reflex cameras.

Pentateuch /ˈpɛntətjuːk/ the first five books of the Old Testament (Genesis, Exodus, Leviticus, Numbers, and Deuteronomy). Traditionally ascribed to Moses, it is now held by scholars to be a compilation from texts of the 9th to 5th centuries BC. Jewish name TORAH.
– DERIVATIVES **Pentateuchal** adjective.
– ORIGIN via ecclesiastical Latin from ecclesiastical Greek *pentateukhos*, from *penta-* 'five' + *teukhos* 'implement, book'.

pentathlon ▶ noun an athletic event comprising five different events for each competitor, in particular (also **modern pentathlon**) a men's event involving fencing, shooting, swimming, riding, and cross-country running.
– DERIVATIVES **pentathlete** noun.
– ORIGIN early 17th cent. (denoting the original five events of leaping, running, discus-throwing, spear-throwing, and wrestling): from Greek, from *pente* 'five' + *athlon* 'contest'.

pentathol ▶ noun variant spelling of PENTOTHAL, regarded as a misspelling in technical use.

pentatonic /ˌpɛntəˈtɒnɪk/ ▶ adjective Music relating to, based on, or denoting a scale of five notes, especially one without semitones equivalent to an ordinary major scale with the fourth and seventh omitted.
– DERIVATIVES **pentatonicism** noun.

pentavalent /ˌpɛntəˈveɪl(ə)nt/ ▶ adjective Chemistry having a valency of five.

pentazocine /pɛnˈtazə(ʊ)siːn/ ▶ noun [mass noun] Medicine a synthetic compound that is a potent non-addictive analgesic, often given during childbirth.
● A tricyclic compound; chem. formula: $C_{19}H_{27}NO$.
– ORIGIN 1960s: from PENTANE + AZO- + OCTA- + -INE⁴.

Pentecost /ˈpɛntɪkɒst/ ▶ noun 1 the Christian festival celebrating the descent of the Holy Spirit on the disciples of Jesus after his Ascension, held on the seventh Sunday after Easter.
■ the day on which this festival is held. Also called WHIT SUNDAY.
2 the Jewish festival of Shavuoth.
– ORIGIN Old English *pentecosten*, via ecclesiastical Latin from Greek *pentēkostē* (*hēmera*) 'fiftieth (day)' (because the Jewish festival is held on the fiftieth day after the second day of Passover).

Pentecostal ▶ adjective 1 of or relating to Pentecost.
2 of, relating to, or denoting any of a number of Christian sects and individuals emphasizing baptism in the Holy Spirit, evidenced by 'speaking in tongues', prophecy, healing, and exorcism. [ORIGIN: with reference to the baptism in the Holy Spirit at the first Pentecost (Acts 2: 9–11).]
▶ noun a member of a Pentecostal sect.
– DERIVATIVES **Pentecostalism** noun, **Pentecostalist** noun.

Pentelic marble /pɛnˈtɛlɪk/ ▶ noun [mass noun] a white marble quarried on Mount Pentelicus near Athens.

Penthesilea /ˌpɛnθɛsɪˈliːə/ Greek Mythology the queen of the Amazons, who came to the help of Troy after the death of Hector and was killed by Achilles.

penthouse ▶ noun 1 a flat on the top floor of a tall building, typically luxuriously fitted and offering fine views.
2 archaic an outhouse or shelter built on to the side of a building, having a sloping roof.
– ORIGIN Middle English *pentis* (in sense 2), shortening of Old French *apentis*, based on late Latin *appendicium* 'appendage', from Latin *appendere* 'hang on'. The change of form in the 16th cent. was by association with French *pente* 'slope' and HOUSE.

pentimento /ˌpɛntɪˈmɛntəʊ/ ▶ noun (pl. **pentimenti**

/-tiː/) a visible trace of earlier painting beneath a layer or layers of paint on a canvas.
– ORIGIN early 20th cent.: from Italian, literally 'repentance'.

Pentland Firth a channel separating the Orkney Islands from the northern tip of mainland Scotland. It links the North Sea with the Atlantic.

pentlandite /ˈpɛntləndʌɪt/ ▶ noun [mass noun] a bronze-yellow mineral which consists of a sulphide of iron and nickel and is the principal ore of nickel.
– ORIGIN mid 19th cent.: from the name of Joseph B. Pentland (1797–1873), Irish traveller, + -ITE[1].

pentobarbital ▶ noun US term for PENTOBARBITONE.

pentobarbitone /ˌpɛntə(ʊ)ˈbɑːbɪtəʊn/ ▶ noun [mass noun] Medicine a narcotic and sedative barbiturate drug formerly used to relieve insomnia.
● Alternative name: **5-ethyl-5-(1-methylbutyl)-barbituric acid**; often used as the sodium salt (**sodium pentobarbitone**, Nembutal).
– ORIGIN 1930s: from PENTANE + BARBITONE (or BARBITAL).

pentode /ˈpɛntəʊd/ ▶ noun Electronics a thermionic valve having five electrodes.
– ORIGIN early 20th cent.: from Greek pente 'five' + hodos 'way'.

pentose /ˈpɛntəʊz, -s/ ▶ noun Chemistry any of the class of simple sugars whose molecules contain five carbon atoms, such as ribose and xylose. They generally have the chemical formula $C_5H_{10}O_5$.
– ORIGIN late 19th cent.: from PENTA- 'five' + -OSE[2].

Pentothal /ˈpɛntəθal/ ▶ noun trademark for THIOPENTONE.

pentoxide /pɛnˈtɒksʌɪd/ ▶ noun Chemistry an oxide containing five atoms of oxygen in its molecule or empirical formula.

pent roof ▶ noun a roof consisting of a single sloping surface.
– ORIGIN mid 19th cent.: from PENTHOUSE + ROOF.

pentstemon /pɛntˈstiːmən, -ˈstɛmən, ˈpɛntstɪmən/ ▶ noun variant spelling of PENSTEMON.

pent-up ▶ adjective closely confined or held back: pent-up frustrations.

pentyl /ˈpɛntʌɪl, -tɪl/ ▶ noun [as modifier] Chemistry of or denoting an alkyl radical —C_5H_{11}, derived from pentane. Compare with AMYL.

penult /pɪˈnʌlt, ˈpɛnʌlt/ ▶ noun Linguistics the penultimate syllable of a word.
▶ adjective archaic term for PENULTIMATE.

penultimate ▶ adjective [attrib.] last but one in a series of things; second last: the penultimate chapter of the book.
– ORIGIN late 17th cent.: from Latin paenultimus, from paene 'almost' + ultimus 'last', on the pattern of ultimate.

penumbra /pɪˈnʌmbrə/ ▶ noun (pl. **penumbrae** /-briː/ or **penumbras**) the partially shaded outer region of the shadow cast by an opaque object.
■ Astronomy the shadow cast by the earth or moon over an area experiencing a partial eclipse. ■ Astronomy the less dark outer part of a sunspot, surrounding the dark core. ■ any area of partial shade.
– DERIVATIVES **penumbral** adjective.
– ORIGIN mid 17th cent.: modern Latin, from Latin paene 'almost' + umbra 'shadow'.

penurious /pɪˈnjʊərɪəs/ ▶ adjective formal 1 extremely poor; poverty-stricken: a penurious old tramp.
■ characterized by poverty or need: penurious years.
2 parsimonious; mean: he was generous and hospitable in contrast to his stingy and penurious wife.
– DERIVATIVES **penuriously** adverb, **penuriousness** noun.
– ORIGIN late 16th cent.: from medieval Latin penuriosus, from Latin penuria 'need, scarcity' (see PENURY).

penury /ˈpɛnjʊri/ ▶ noun [mass noun] extreme poverty; destitution: he died in a state of virtual penury.
– ORIGIN late Middle English: from Latin penuria 'need, scarcity'; perhaps related to paene 'almost'.

Penutian /pəˈnuːʃən, -ˈnuːtɪən/ ▶ noun [mass noun] a proposed superfamily or phylum of American Indian languages, most of which are now extinct or nearly so. Some scholars include certain living languages of Central and South America, principally Mayan and Mapuche, in this group.
▶ adjective of, relating to, or denoting these languages or any of the peoples speaking them.

– ORIGIN from pen and uti, words for 'two' in two groups of Penutian languages + -AN.

Penza /ˈpjɛnzə/ a city in south central Russia; pop. 548,000 (1990). Situated on the River Sura, a tributary of the Volga, it is an industrial and transportation centre.

Penzance /pɛnˈzans/ a resort town in SW England, on the south coast of Cornwall near Land's End; pop. 19,600 (1981).

peon /ˈpiːən/ ▶ noun 1 /also peɪˈɒn/ a Spanish-American day labourer or unskilled farm worker.
■ historical a debtor held in servitude by a creditor, especially in the southern US and Mexico. ■ chiefly N. Amer. a person who does menial work; a drudge: racing drivers aren't exactly normal nine-to-five peons.
2 /also pjuːn/ (in the Indian subcontinent and SE Asia) someone of low rank.
3 (pl. **peones** /peɪˈəʊneɪz/) another term for BANDERILLERO.
– DERIVATIVES **peonage** noun.
– ORIGIN from Portuguese peão and Spanish peón, from medieval Latin pedo, pedon- 'walker, foot soldier', from Latin pes, ped- 'foot'. Compare with PAWN[1].

peony /ˈpiːəni/ (also **paeony**) ▶ noun a herbaceous or shrubby plant of north temperate regions, which has long been cultivated for its showy flowers.
● Genus Paeonia, family Paeoniaceae.
– ORIGIN Old English peonie, via Latin from Greek paiōnia, from Paiōn, the name of the physician of the gods.

people ▶ plural noun 1 human beings in general or considered collectively: the earthquake killed 30,000 people.
■ (the people) the citizens of a country, especially when considered in relation to those who govern them: his economic reforms no longer have the support of the people. ■ (the people) those without special rank or position in society; the populace: he is very much a man of the people. ■ (one's people) dated a person's parents or relatives: my people live in Warwickshire. ■ (one's people) the supporters or employees of a person in a position of power or authority: I've had my people watching the house for some time now. ■ (the People) US the state prosecution in a trial: pre-trial statements made by the People's witnesses.
2 (pl. **peoples**) [treated as sing. or pl.] the men, women, and children of a particular nation, community, or ethnic group: the native peoples of Canada.
▶ verb [with obj.] (usu. **be peopled**) (of a particular group of people) inhabit (an area or place): an arid mountain region peopled by warring clans.
■ fill or be present in (a place, environment, or domain): in her imagination the flat was suddenly peopled with the ghosts of glamorous women. ■ fill (an area or place) with a particular group of inhabitants: it was his intention to people the town with English colonists.
– DERIVATIVES **peoplehood** noun (in sense 2 of the noun).
– ORIGIN Middle English: from Anglo-Norman French poeple, from Latin populus 'populace'.

people carrier ▶ noun a motor vehicle with three rows of seats, enabling the transport of more passengers than the average car.

people meter ▶ noun (in North America) an electronic device used to record the television viewing habits of a household so that the information obtained can be used to compile ratings.

people mover ▶ noun informal a means of transport, in particular any of a number of automated systems for carrying large numbers of people over short distances.

people person ▶ noun informal a person who enjoys or is particularly good at interacting with others.

people's court ▶ noun S. African 1 a small claims court.
2 an unofficial court set up by a vigilante group in a black urban area.

people's democracy ▶ noun a political system in which power is regarded as being invested in the people.

People's Liberation Army (abbrev.: **PLA**) the armed forces of the People's Republic of China, including all its land, sea, and air forces. The PLA traces its origins to an unsuccessful uprising by communist-led troops against pro-Nationalist forces in Kiangsi province on 1 August 1927, a date celebrated annually as its anniversary.

Peoples of the Sea another term for SEA PEOPLES.

People's Republic ▶ noun used in the official title of several present or former communist or left-wing states.
■ (the People's Republic) short for PEOPLE'S REPUBLIC OF CHINA.

People's Republic of China official name (since 1949) of CHINA.

Peoria /piːˈɔːrɪə/ a river port and industrial city in central Illinois, on the Illinois River; pop. 113,500 (1990). The city developed around a fort built by the French in 1680.
– ORIGIN named after the American Indians who occupied the area when the French arrived.

PEP Brit. ▶ abbreviation for ■ personal equity plan. ■ Political and Economic Planning.

pep informal ▶ noun [mass noun] energy and high spirits; liveliness: he was an enthusiastic player, full of pep and fight.
▶ verb (**pepped**, **pepping**) [with obj.] (**pep someone/thing up**) add liveliness or vigour to someone or something: measures to pep up the economy.
– ORIGIN early 20th cent.: abbreviation of PEPPER.

peperomia /ˌpɛpəˈrəʊmɪə/ ▶ noun a small fleshy-leaved tropical plant of the pepper family. Many are grown as house plants, chiefly for their decorative foliage.
● Genus Peperomia, family Piperaceae.
– ORIGIN modern Latin, from Greek peperi.

peperoni ▶ noun variant spelling of PEPPERONI.

pepino /pɛˈpiːnəʊ/ ▶ noun (pl. **-os**) a spiny plant of the nightshade family, with edible purple-streaked yellow fruit, native to the Andes.
● Solanum muricatum, family Solanaceae.
– ORIGIN mid 19th cent.: from Spanish, literally 'cucumber' (because of the elongated shape of the fruit).

peplos /ˈpɛplɒs/ ▶ noun (pl. **peploses** or **peplos**) a rich outer robe or shawl worn by women in ancient Greece, hanging in loose folds and sometimes drawn over the head.
– ORIGIN Greek.

peplum /ˈpɛpləm/ ▶ noun a short flared, gathered, or pleated strip of fabric attached at the waist of a woman's jacket, dress, or blouse to create a hanging frill or flounce.
■ (in ancient Greece) a woman's loose outer tunic or shawl. [ORIGIN: via Latin from Greek peplos.]

pepo /ˈpiːpəʊ/ ▶ noun (pl. **-os**) any fleshy watery fruit of the melon or cucumber type, with numerous seeds and a firm rind.
– ORIGIN mid 19th cent.: from Latin, literally 'pumpkin', from Greek pepōn (from pepōn sikuos 'ripe gourd').

pepper ▶ noun [mass noun] 1 a pungent hot-tasting powder prepared from dried and ground peppercorns, commonly used as a spice or condiment to flavour food.
■ a reddish and typically hot-tasting spice prepared from various forms of capsicum. See also CAYENNE. ■ [count noun] a capsicum, especially a sweet pepper.
2 a climbing vine with berries that are dried as black or white peppercorns.
● Piper nigrum, family Piperaceae.
■ used in names of other plants which are related to this, have hot-tasting leaves, or have fruits used as a pungent spice, e.g. **Jamaica pepper**, **water pepper**.
3 Baseball a practice game in which a fielder throws at close range to a batter who hits back to the fielder.
▶ verb [with obj.] sprinkle or season (food) with pepper: [as adj.] **peppered**] peppered beef.
■ (usu. **be peppered with**) cover or fill with a liberal amount of scattered items: the script is peppered with four-letter words. ■ hit repeatedly with small missiles or gunshot: another burst of enemy bullets peppered his defenceless body | figurative he peppered me with questions. ■ archaic inflict severe punishment or suffering upon.
– ORIGIN Old English piper, pipor, of West Germanic origin; related to Dutch peper and German Pfeffer; via Latin from Greek peperi, from Sanskrit pippali 'berry, peppercorn'.

pepper-and-salt ▶ adjective flecked or speckled with intermingled dark and light shades.

pepperbox ▶ noun 1 a gun or piece of artillery with a revolving set of barrels.
2 archaic a pepper pot.

peppercorn ▶ **noun** the dried berry of a climbing vine, used whole as a spice or crushed or ground to make pepper. See **PEPPER** (sense 2).
■(**peppercorns**) S. African a person's hair growing in sparse, tight, curly tufts, characteristic of the Khoikhoi and San peoples.

peppercorn rent ▶ **noun** Brit. a very low or nominal rent.
– ORIGIN from the (formerly common) practice of stipulating the payment of a peppercorn as a nominal rent.

pepper dulse ▶ **noun** a dark red seaweed with branching fronds, growing on rocks.
● *Laurencia pinnatifida*, division Rhodophyta.

peppered moth ▶ **noun** a European moth of woods and gardens, which is typically white with black speckling. In industrial areas sooty brown forms predominate as a result of industrial melanism.
● *Biston betularia*, family Geometridae.

peppergrass ▶ **noun** US term for **PEPPERWORT**.

pepperidge ▶ **noun** a deciduous North American tree with colourful autumn foliage. Also called **TUPELO**.
● *Nyssa sylvatica*, family Nyssaceae.
– ORIGIN late 17th cent.: alteration of dialect *pipperidge*, denoting the barberry and its fruit, of unknown origin.

pepper mill ▶ **noun** a device for grinding peppercorns by hand to make pepper.

peppermint ▶ **noun 1** [mass noun] the aromatic leaves of a plant of the mint family, or an essential oil obtained from them, used as a flavouring in food.
■[count noun] a sweet flavoured with such oil.
2 [mass noun] the cultivated Old World plant which yields these leaves or oil.
● *Mentha* × *piperita*, family Labiatae.
3 Austral. any of a number of trees or shrubs with peppermint-scented foliage, in particular:
● a gum tree with leaves that yield an aromatic essential oil (genus *Eucalyptus*, family Myrtaceae). ● a myrtle grown as an ornamental tree or shrub (genus *Agonis*, family Myrtaceae).
– DERIVATIVES **pepperminty** adjective.

pepperoni /ˌpɛpəˈrəʊni/ (also **peperoni**) ▶ **noun** [mass noun] beef and pork sausage seasoned with pepper.
– ORIGIN from Italian *peperone* 'chilli'.

pepper pot ▶ **noun 1** (US **pepper shaker**) Brit. a container with a perforated top for sprinkling pepper.
2 a West Indian dish consisting of stewed meat or fish with vegetables, typically flavoured with cassareep.

pepper-shrike ▶ **noun** a tropical American songbird with mainly green and yellow plumage and a heavy bill like that of a shrike.
● Genus *Cyclarhis*, now in the family Vireonidae: two species.

pepper tree ▶ **noun** any of a number of shrubs or trees which have aromatic leaves or fruit with a pepper-like smell, in particular:
● an evergreen Peruvian tree, grown as a shade tree in hot countries (*Schinus molle*, family Anacardiaceae). ● another term for **KAWA-KAWA**.

pepperwort ▶ **noun** a wild cress, particularly one with pungent leaves.
● Genus *Lepidium*, family Cruciferae.

peppery ▶ **adjective** strongly flavoured with pepper or other hot spices: *a hot, peppery dish.*
■having a flavour or scent like that of pepper. ■(of a person) irritable and sharp-tongued: *retired generals are expected to be peppery.*
– DERIVATIVES **pepperiness** noun.

pep pill ▶ **noun** informal a pill containing a stimulant drug.

peppy ▶ **adjective** (**peppier**, **peppiest**) informal, chiefly N. Amer. lively and high-spirited: *stickers bearing peppy slogans.*
– DERIVATIVES **peppily** adverb, **peppiness** noun.

pep rally ▶ **noun** N. Amer. informal a meeting aimed at inspiring enthusiasm, especially one held before a sporting event.

pepsin ▶ **noun** [mass noun] Biochemistry the chief digestive enzyme in the stomach, which breaks down proteins into polypeptides.
– ORIGIN mid 19th cent.: from Greek *pepsis* 'digestion' + **-IN**[1].

pepsinogen /pɛpˈsɪnədʒ(ə)n/ ▶ **noun** [mass noun] Biochemistry a substance which is secreted by the stomach wall and converted into the enzyme pepsin by gastric acid.

pep talk ▶ **noun** informal a talk intended to make someone feel more courageous or enthusiastic.

peptic ▶ **adjective** of or relating to digestion, especially that in which pepsin is concerned.
– ORIGIN mid 17th cent.: from Greek *peptikos* 'able to digest'.

peptic gland ▶ **noun** Anatomy a gland that secretes the gastric juice containing pepsin.

peptic ulcer ▶ **noun** a lesion in the lining (mucosa) of the digestive tract, typically in the stomach or duodenum, caused by the digestive action of pepsin and stomach acid.

peptidase /ˈpɛptɪdeɪz/ ▶ **noun** Biochemistry an enzyme which breaks down peptides into amino acids.

peptide /ˈpɛptʌɪd/ ▶ **noun** Biochemistry a compound consisting of two or more amino acids linked in a chain, the carboxyl group of each acid being joined to the amino group of the next by a bond of the type —OC—NH—.
– ORIGIN early 20th cent.: from German *Peptid*, back-formation from *Polypeptid* 'polypeptide'.

peptidoglycan /pɛpˌtʌɪdə(ʊ)ˈglʌɪkan/ ▶ **noun** [mass noun] Biochemistry a substance forming the cell walls of many bacteria, consisting of glycosaminoglycan chains interlinked with short peptides.

peptone /ˈpɛptəʊn/ ▶ **noun** [mass noun] Biochemistry a soluble protein formed in the early stage of protein breakdown during digestion.
■(also **peptone water**) a solution of this in saline, used as a liquid medium for growing bacteria.
– ORIGIN mid 19th cent.: from German *Pepton*, from Greek *pepton*, neuter of *peptos* 'cooked, digested'.

Pepys /piːps/, Samuel (1633–1703), English diarist and naval administrator. He is particularly remembered for his *Diary* (1660–9), which describes events such as the Great Plague and the Fire of London.

Péquiste /peɪˈkiːst/ ▶ **noun** Canadian a member or supporter of the Parti Québecois, a political party originally advocating independent rule for Quebec.
– ORIGIN from the French pronunciation of the abbreviation *PQ* + the noun suffix *-iste*.

Pequot /ˈpiːkwɒt/ ▶ **noun** (pl. same or **Pequots**) **1** a member of an American Indian people of southern New England.
2 [mass noun] the extinct Algonquian language of this people.
▶ **adjective** of or relating to this people or their language.
– ORIGIN from Narragansett *paquatanog* 'destroyers'.

per ▶ **preposition 1** for each (used with units to express a rate): *he charges £2 per square yard.*
2 archaic by means of: *send it per express.*
3 (**as per**) in accordance with: *made as per instructions.*
4 Heraldry divided by a line in the direction of: *per bend* | *per pale* | *per saltire.*
– PHRASES **as per usual** as usual.
– ORIGIN Latin, 'through, by means of'; partly via Old French.

per- ▶ **prefix 1** through; all over: *percuss* | *perforation* | *pervade.*
■completely; very: *perfect* | *perturb.* ■to destruction; to ill effect: *perdition* | *pervert.*
2 Chemistry having the maximum proportion of some element in combination: *peroxide* | *perchloric* | *permanganate.*
– ORIGIN from Latin (see **PER**).

peracute ▶ **adjective** chiefly Veterinary Medicine (of a disease) very severe and of very short duration, generally proving quickly fatal.
– ORIGIN late Middle English: from Latin *peracutus* 'very sharp'.

peradventure archaic or humorous ▶ **adverb** perhaps: *peradventure I'm not as wealthy as he is.*
▶ **noun** [mass noun] uncertainty or doubt as to whether something is the case: *that shows **beyond peradventure** the strength of the economy.*
– ORIGIN Middle English: from Old French *per* (or *par*) *auenture* 'by chance'.

Perak /ˈpɛːrə, pɛˈrak/ a state of Malaysia, on the west side of the Malay Peninsula; capital, Ipoh. It is a major tin-mining centre.

peralkaline ▶ **adjective** Geology (of an igneous rock) containing a higher proportion (taken together) of sodium and potassium than of aluminium.

peraluminous ▶ **adjective** Geology (of an igneous rock) containing a higher proportion of aluminium than of sodium and potassium (taken together).

perambulate /pəˈrambjʊleɪt/ ▶ **verb** [with obj.] formal walk or travel through or round (a place or area), especially for pleasure and in a leisurely way: *she perambulated the square.*
■[no obj.] walk from place to place; walk about: *he grew weary of perambulating over rough countryside in bad weather.* ■Brit. historical walk round (a parish, forest, etc.) in order to officially assert and record its boundaries; beat the bounds of.
– DERIVATIVES **perambulation** noun, **perambulatory** adjective.
– ORIGIN late Middle English: from Latin *perambulat-* 'walked about', from the verb *perambulare*, from *per-* 'all over' + *ambulare* 'to walk'.

perambulator ▶ **noun** formal term for **PRAM**[1].

per annum ▶ **adverb** for each year (used in financial contexts): *an average growth rate of around 2 per cent per annum.*
– ORIGIN early 17th cent.: Latin.

p/e ratio ▶ **abbreviation for** price-earnings ratio.

p/e ration ▶ **abbreviation for** price-earnings ratio.

perborate /pəˈbɔːreɪt/ ▶ **noun** Chemistry a salt which is an oxidized borate containing a peroxide linkage, especially a sodium salt of this kind used as a bleach.

percale /pəˈkeɪl/ ▶ **noun** [mass noun] a closely woven fine cotton fabric resembling calico.
– ORIGIN early 17th cent.: from French, of unknown origin.

per capita /pəː ˈkapɪtə/ (also **per caput** /ˈkapʊt/) ▶ **adverb** & **adjective** for each person; in relation to people taken individually: [as adv.] *the state had fewer banks per capita than elsewhere* | [as adj.] *per capita spending.*
– ORIGIN late 17th cent.: Latin, literally 'by heads'.

perceive ▶ **verb** [with obj.] **1** become aware or conscious of (something); come to realize or understand: *his mouth fell open as he perceived the truth* | [with clause] *he was quick to perceive that there was little future in such arguments.*
■become aware of (something) by the use of one of the senses, especially that of sight: *he perceived the faintest of flushes creeping up her neck.*
2 interpret or look on (someone or something) in a particular way; regard as: *if Guy does not **perceive** himself **as** disabled, nobody else should* | [with obj. and infinitive] *some geographers perceive hydrology to be a separate field of scientific enquiry.*
– DERIVATIVES **perceivable** adjective, **perceiver** noun.
– ORIGIN Middle English: from a variant of Old French *perçoivre*, from Latin *percipere* 'seize, understand', from *per-* 'entirely' + *capere* 'take'.

per cent ▶ **adverb** by a specified amount in or for every hundred: *new car sales may be down nineteen per cent* | *staff rejected a 1.8 per cent increase.*
▶ **noun** one part in every hundred: *a reduction of half a per cent or so in price.*
■the rate, number, or amount in each hundred.
– ORIGIN mid 16th cent.: from **PER** + **CENT**, perhaps an abbreviation of pseudo-Latin *per centum.*

percentage ▶ **noun** a rate, number, or amount in each hundred: *the percentage of Caesareans at the hospital was three per cent higher than the national average* | [as modifier] *a large percentage increase in the population aged over 85.*
■an amount, such as an allowance or commission, that is a proportion of a larger sum of money: *I hope to be on a percentage.* ■any proportion or share in relation to a whole: *only a tiny percentage of the day trippers are aware of the village's gastronomic distinction.* ■[in sing.] informal personal benefit or advantage: *you explain to me **the percentage in** looking like a hoodlum.*
– PHRASES **play the percentages** (or **the percentage game**) informal choose a safe and methodical course of action when calculating the odds in favour of success. [ORIGIN: referring to the calculated percentage of success from statistics.]

-percenter ▶ **combining form 1** denoting a member of a group forming a specified and usually small percentage of the population: *he was a one-percenter, riding outside of the law.*
2 denoting a person who takes commission at a specified rate: [as modifier] *ten-percenter agents.*
■denoting something whose value is estimated as a specified percentage: [as modifier] *five-percenter Treasury bonds.*

p

percentile /pəˈsɛntʌɪl/ ▶ noun Statistics each of the 100 equal groups into which a population can be divided according to the distribution of values of a particular variable.
■each of the 99 intermediate values of a random variable which divide a frequency distribution into 100 such groups.

percept /ˈpəːsɛpt/ ▶ noun Philosophy an object of perception; something that is perceived.
■a mental concept that is developed as a consequence of the process of perception.
– ORIGIN mid 19th cent.: from Latin *perceptum* 'something perceived', neuter past participle of *percipere* 'seize, understand', on the pattern of *concept*.

perceptible ▶ adjective (especially of a slight movement or change of state) able to be seen or noticed: *a perceptible decline in public confidence.*
– DERIVATIVES **perceptibility** noun, **perceptibly** adverb.
– ORIGIN late Middle English: from late Latin *perceptibilis*, from Latin *percipere* 'seize, understand' (see **PERCEIVE**).

perception ▶ noun [mass noun] the ability to see, hear, or become aware of something through the senses: *the normal limits to human perception.*
■the state of being or process of becoming aware of something in such a way: *the perception of pain.* ■a way of regarding, understanding, or interpreting something; a mental impression: *Hollywood's perception of the tastes of the American public* | [count noun] *we need to challenge many popular perceptions of old age.* ■intuitive understanding and insight: *'He wouldn't have accepted,' said my mother with unusual perception.* ■ Psychology & Zoology the neurophysiological processes, including memory, by which an organism becomes aware of and interprets external stimuli.
– DERIVATIVES **perceptional** adjective.
– ORIGIN late Middle English: from Latin *perceptio(n-)*, from the verb *percipere* 'seize, understand' (see **PERCEIVE**).

perceptive ▶ adjective having or showing sensitive insight: *an extraordinarily perceptive account of their relationship.*
– DERIVATIVES **perceptively** adverb, **perceptiveness** noun, **perceptivity** /-ˈtɪvɪti/ noun.

perceptron /pəˈsɛptrɒn/ ▶ noun a computer model or computerized machine devised to represent or simulate the ability of the brain to recognize and discriminate.

perceptual ▶ adjective of or relating to the ability to interpret or become aware of something through the senses: *a patient with perceptual problems who cannot judge distances.*
– DERIVATIVES **perceptually** adverb.

Perceval[1] /ˈpəːsɪv(ə)l/ a legendary figure dating back to ancient times, found in French, German, and English poetry from the late 12th century onwards. He is the father of Lohengrin and the hero of a number of legends, some of which are associated with the Holy Grail. Also called **PARSIFAL**.

Perceval[2] /ˈpəːsɪv(ə)l/, Spencer (1762–1812), British Tory statesman, Prime Minister 1809–12. He was shot dead in the lobby of the House of Commons by a bankrupt merchant who blamed the government for his insolvency.

perch[1] ▶ noun a thing on which a bird alights or roosts, typically a branch or a horizontal rod or bar in a birdcage.
■a place where someone or something rests or sits, especially one that is high or precarious: *Marian looked down from her perch in a beech tree above the road.* ▶ verb [no obj., with adverbial of place] (of a bird) alight or rest on something: *a herring gull perched on the rails for most of the crossing.* ■(of a person) sit somewhere, especially on something high or narrow: *Eve perched on the side of the armchair.* ■ (be perched) (of a building) be situated above or on the edge of something: *the fortress is perched on a crag in the mountains.* [with obj.] (perch someone/thing on) set or balance someone or something on (something): *Peter perched a pair of gold-rimmed spectacles on his nose.*
– PHRASES **knock someone off their perch** informal cause someone to lose a position of superiority or pre-eminence: *will this knock London off its perch as Europe's leading financial centre?*
– ORIGIN late Middle English: the noun from **PERCH**[3]; the verb from Old French *percher*.

perch[2] ▶ noun (pl. same or **perches**) an edible freshwater fish with a high spiny dorsal fin, dark vertical bars on the body, and orange lower fins.
● Genus *Perca*, family Percidae (the **perch family**): three species, in particular *P. fluviatilis* of Europe (also called **BASS**[2]), and the almost identical **yellow perch** (*P. flavescens*) of North America. The perch family also includes the pikeperches, ruffe, and darters.
■used in names of other freshwater and marine fishes resembling or related to this, e.g. **climbing perch**, **pikeperch**, **sea perch**, **surfperch**.
– ORIGIN late Middle English: from Old French *perche*, via Latin from Greek *perkē*.

perch[3] ▶ noun historical, chiefly Brit. **1** a measure of length, especially for land, equal to a quarter of a chain or 5½ yards (approximately 5.029 m). Also called **POLE**[1], **ROD**.
2 (also **square perch**) a measure of area, especially for land, equal to 160th of an acre or 30¼ square yards (approximately 25.29 sq. metres). Also called **POLE**[1], **ROD**, **SQUARE POLE**, **SQUARE ROD**.
– ORIGIN Middle English (in the general sense 'pole, stick'): from Old French *perche*, from Latin *pertica* 'measuring rod, pole'.

perchance ▶ adverb archaic or poetic/literary by some chance; perhaps: *we dare not go ashore lest perchance we should fall into some snare.*
– ORIGIN Middle English: from Old French *par cheance* 'by chance'.

percheron /ˈpəːʃ(ə)rɒn/ ▶ noun a powerful draught horse of a grey or black breed, originally from France.
– ORIGIN late 19th cent.: from French, originally bred in le *Perche*, the name of a district of northern France.

perchloric acid /pəˈklɔːrɪk/ ▶ noun [mass noun] Chemistry a fuming toxic liquid with powerful oxidizing properties.
● Chem. formula: $HClO_4$.
– DERIVATIVES **perchlorate** noun.

perchloroethylene /pəˌklɔːrəʊˈɛθɪliːn/ ▶ noun [mass noun] a toxic colourless volatile solvent used commonly as a dry-cleaning fluid. Also called **TETRACHLOROETHYLENE**.
● Chem. formula: $Cl_2C{=}CCl_2$.

percid /ˈpəːkɪd/ ▶ noun Zoology a fish of the perch family (Percidae).
– ORIGIN late 19th cent.: from modern Latin *Percidae* (plural), from Latin *perca* 'perch'.

perciform /ˈpəːsɪfɔːm/ ▶ adjective Zoology of or relating to fishes of an order (Perciformes) that comprises those resembling the perches. This is the largest vertebrate order and includes nearly half of all bony fishes.
– ORIGIN late 19th cent.: from modern Latin *Perciformes* (plural), from Latin *perca* 'perch' + *forma* 'shape'.

percipient /pəˈsɪpɪənt/ ▶ adjective (of a person) having a good understanding of things; perceptive: *he is a percipient interpreter of the public mood.*
▶ noun (especially in philosophy or with reference to psychic phenomena) a person who is able to perceive things.
– DERIVATIVES **percipience** noun, **percipiently** adverb.
– ORIGIN mid 17th cent.: from Latin *percipient-* 'seizing, understanding', from the verb *percipere*.

percoid /ˈpəːkɔɪd/ Zoology ▶ noun a fish of a large group that includes the perches, basses, jacks, snappers, grunts, sea breams, and drums.
● Superfamily Percoidea: many families.
▶ adjective of or relating to fish of this group.
– ORIGIN mid 19th cent.: from modern Latin *Percoïdes* (plural), from Latin *perca* 'perch'.

percolate ▶ verb **1** [no obj., with adverbial of direction] (of a liquid or gas) filter gradually through a porous surface or substance: *the water percolating through the soil may leach out minerals.*
■figurative (of information or an idea or feeling) spread gradually through an area or group of people: *this idea soon percolated into the Christian Church.*
2 [no obj.] (of coffee) be prepared in a percolator: *he put some coffee on to percolate.*
■[with obj.] prepare (coffee) in a percolator: [as adj. **percolated**] *freshly percolated coffee.* ■ figurative US be or become full of lively activity or excitement: *the night was percolating with an expectant energy.*
– DERIVATIVES **percolation** noun.
– ORIGIN early 17th cent.: from Latin *percolat-* 'strained through', from the verb *percolare*, from *per-* 'through' + *colare* 'to strain' (from *colum* 'strainer').

percolator ▶ noun a machine for making coffee, consisting of a pot in which boiling water is circulated through a small chamber that holds the ground beans.

per contra /pəː ˈkɒntrə/ ▶ adverb formal on the other hand: *he had worked very hard on the place; she, per contra, had little to do.*
▶ noun the opposite side of an account or an assessment.
– ORIGIN mid 16th cent.: from Italian.

per curiam /ˈkjʊərɪam/ Law ▶ adverb by decision of a judge, or of a court in unanimous agreement.
▶ noun such a decision: *in only a few cases did the panel publish a per curiam.*
– ORIGIN Latin, literally 'by a court'.

percuss /pəˈkʌs/ ▶ verb [with obj.] Medicine gently tap (a part of the body) with a finger or an instrument as part of a diagnosis: *the bladder was percussed.*
– ORIGIN mid 16th cent. (in the general sense 'give a blow to'): from Latin *percuss-* 'struck forcibly', from the verb *percutere*, from *per-* 'through' + *quatere* 'to shake, strike'.

percussion ▶ noun [mass noun] **1** musical instruments played by striking with the hand or with a hand-held or pedal-operated stick or beater, or by shaking, including drums, cymbals, xylophones, gongs, bells, and rattles: [as modifier] *percussion instruments* | *the percussion section.*
2 the striking of one solid object with or against another with some degree of force: *the clattering percussion of objects striking the walls and the shutters.*
■Medicine the action of tapping a part of the body as part of a diagnosis: *the chest sounded dull on percussion.*
– DERIVATIVES **percussionist** noun (in sense 1), **percussive** adjective, **percussively** adverb, **percussiveness** noun.
– ORIGIN late Middle English: from Latin *percussio(n-)*, from the verb *percutere* 'to strike forcibly' (see **PERCUSS**).

percussion cap ▶ noun a small amount of explosive powder contained in metal or paper and exploded by striking. Percussion caps are used chiefly in toy guns and formerly in some firearms.

percussion drill ▶ noun another term for **HAMMER DRILL**.

percutaneous /ˌpəːkjʊˈteɪnɪəs/ ▶ adjective Medicine made, done, or effected through the skin.
– DERIVATIVES **percutaneously** adverb.
– ORIGIN late 19th cent.: from Latin *per cutem* 'through the skin' + **-ANEOUS**.

Percy, Sir Henry (1364–1403), English soldier; known as **Hotspur** or **Harry Hotspur**. Son of the 1st Earl of Northumberland, he was killed at the battle of Shrewsbury during his father's revolt against Henry IV.

per diem /pəː ˈdiːɛm, ˈdʌɪɛm/ ▶ adverb & adjective for each day (used in financial contexts): [as adv.] *he agreed to pay at certain specified rates per diem* | [as adj.] *they are now demanding a per diem rate.*
▶ noun an allowance or payment made for each day.
– ORIGIN early 16th cent.: Latin.

perdition /pəˈdɪʃ(ə)n/ ▶ noun [mass noun] (in Christian theology) a state of eternal punishment and damnation into which a sinful and unpenitent person passes after death.
– ORIGIN late Middle English: from Old French *perdiciun*, from ecclesiastical Latin *perditio(n-)*, from Latin *perdere* 'destroy', from *per-* 'completely, to destruction' + the base of *dare* 'put'.

perdurable /pəˈdjʊərəb(ə)l/ ▶ adjective formal enduring continuously; imperishable.
– DERIVATIVES **perdurability** noun, **perdurably** adverb.
– ORIGIN late Middle English: via Old French from late Latin *perdurabilis*, from Latin *perdurare* 'endure'.

perdure /pəˈdjʊə/ ▶ verb [no obj.] formal, chiefly US remain in existence throughout a substantial period of time; endure: *bell music has perdured in Venice throughout five centuries.*
– DERIVATIVES **perdurance** noun.
– ORIGIN late 15th cent.: from Old French *perdurer*, from Latin *perdurare* 'endure', from *per-* 'through' + *durare* 'to last'.

père /pɛː/ ▶ noun used after a surname to distinguish a father from a son of the same name: *Alexandre Dumas père.* Compare with **FILS**[2].

– ORIGIN French, literally 'father'.

Père David's deer ▶ **noun** a large deer with a red summer coat that turns dark grey in winter, and long antlers with backward pointing tines. Formerly a native of China, it is now found only in captivity.
● *Elaphurus davidianus*, family Cervidae.
– ORIGIN late 19th cent.: named after Father Armand *David* (1826–1900), French missionary and naturalist.

peregrinate /ˈpɛrɪgrɪˌneɪt/ ▶ **verb** [no obj., with adverbial] archaic or humorous travel or wander around from place to place.
– DERIVATIVES **peregrination** noun, **peregrinator** noun.
– ORIGIN late 16th cent.: from Latin *peregrinat-* 'travelled abroad', from the verb *peregrinari*, from *peregrinus* 'foreign, travelling'.

peregrine /ˈpɛrɪgrɪn/ ▶ **noun** (also **peregrine falcon**) a powerful falcon found on most continents, breeding chiefly on mountains and coastal cliffs and much used for falconry. [ORIGIN: translating the modern Latin taxonomic name, literally 'pilgrim falcon', because the bird was caught full-grown as a passage hawk, not taken from the nest.]
● *Falco peregrinus*, family Falconidae.
▶ **adjective** archaic coming from another country; foreign or outlandish: *peregrine species of grass.*
– ORIGIN late Middle English: from Latin *peregrinus* 'foreign', from *peregre* 'abroad', from *per-* 'through' + *ager* 'field'.

pereiopod /pəˈrʌɪəpɒd, -ˈriː-/ ▶ **noun** Zoology each of the eight walking limbs of a crustacean such as a crab or lobster, growing from the thorax.
– ORIGIN late 19th cent.: from Greek *peraioōn* 'transporting' (present participle of *peraioun*) + *pous, pod-* 'foot'.

Perelman /ˈpɛrəlmən/, S. J. (1904–79), American humorist and writer; full name *Sidney Joseph Perelman*. In the early 1930s he worked in Hollywood as a scriptwriter, and from 1934 his name is linked with the *New Yorker* magazine, for whom he wrote most of his short stories and sketches.

peremptory /pəˈrɛm(p)t(ə)ri, ˈpɛrɪm-/ ▶ **adjective** (especially of a person's manner or actions) insisting on immediate attention or obedience, especially in a brusquely imperious way: *'Just do it!' came the peremptory reply.*
■ Law not open to appeal or challenge; final: *there has been no disobedience of a peremptory order of the court.*
– DERIVATIVES **peremptorily** adverb, **peremptoriness** noun.
– ORIGIN late Middle English (as a legal term): via Anglo-Norman French from Latin *peremptorius* 'deadly, decisive', from *perempt-* 'destroyed, cut off', from the verb *perimere*, from *per-* 'completely' + *emere* 'take, buy'.

peremptory challenge ▶ **noun** Law a defendant's or lawyer's objection to a proposed juror, made without needing to give a reason.

perennate /pəˈrɛneɪt/ ▶ **verb** [no obj.] [usu. as adj. **perennating**] Botany (of a plant or part of a plant) live through a number of years, usually with an annual quiescent period.
– DERIVATIVES **perennation** noun.
– ORIGIN early 17th cent.: from Latin *perennat-* 'continued for many years' (from the verb *perennare*) + **-ATE**³.

perennial ▶ **adjective** lasting or existing for a long or apparently infinite time; enduring: *his perennial distrust of the media.*
■ (of a plant) living for several years: *cow parsley is perennial.* Compare with **ANNUAL**, **BIENNIAL**. ■ (especially of a problem or difficult situation) continually occurring: *perennial manifestations of urban crisis.* ■ [attrib.] (of a person) apparently permanently engaged in a specified role or way of life: *he's a perennial student.* ■ (of a stream or spring) flowing throughout the year.
▶ **noun** a perennial plant.
– DERIVATIVES **perennially** adverb.
– ORIGIN mid 17th cent. (in the sense 'remaining leafy throughout the year, evergreen'): from Latin *perennis* 'lasting the year through' + **-IAL**.

perentie /pəˈrɛnti, ˈprɛnti/ (also **perenty**) ▶ **noun** (pl. **-ies**) a large brown and yellow monitor lizard which lives in arid regions of Australia.
● *Varanus giganteus*, family Varanidae.

– ORIGIN early 20th cent.: probably from Diyara *pirindi*.

Peres /ˈpɛrɛz/, Shimon (b.1923), Polish-born Israeli statesman, Prime Minister 1984–6 and 1995–6; Polish name *Szymon Perski*. As Foreign Minister under Yitzhak Rabin he played a major role in negotiating the PLO–Israeli peace accord (1993). Nobel Peace Prize (1994), shared with Rabin and Yasser Arafat.

perestroika /ˌpɛrɪˈstrɔɪkə/ ▶ **noun** [mass noun] (in the former Soviet Union) the policy or practice of restructuring or reforming the economic and political system. First proposed by Leonid Brezhnev in 1979 and actively promoted by Mikhail Gorbachev, perestroika originally referred to increased automation and labour efficiency, but came to entail greater awareness of economic markets and the ending of central planning. See also **GLASNOST**.
– ORIGIN Russian, literally 'restructuring'.

Pérez de Cuéllar /ˌpɛrɛz də ˈkwɛjɑː, Spanish ˌperes de ˈkwejar, ˌpereθ/, Javier (b.1920), Peruvian diplomat, Secretary General of the United Nations 1982–91.

perfect ▶ **adjective** /ˈpəːfɪkt/ **1** having all the required or desirable elements, qualities, or characteristics; as good as it is possible to be: *she strove to be the perfect wife | life certainly isn't perfect at the moment.*
■ free from any flaw or defect in condition or quality; faultless: *the equipment was in perfect condition.* ■ precisely accurate; exact: *a perfect circle.* ■ highly suitable for someone or something; exactly right: *Giles was perfect for her—ten years older and with his own career.* ■ dated thoroughly trained in or conversant with: *she was perfect in French.*
2 [attrib.] absolute; complete (used for emphasis): *a perfect stranger | all that Joseph said made perfect sense to me.*
3 Mathematics (of a number) equal to the sum of its positive divisors, e.g. the number 6, whose divisors (1, 2, 3) also add up to 6.
4 Grammar (of a tense) denoting a completed action or a state or habitual action which began in the past. The perfect tense is formed in English with *have* or *has* and the past participle, as in *they have eaten* and *they have been eating (since dawn)* (**present perfect**), *they had eaten* (**past perfect**), and *they will have eaten* (**future perfect**).
5 Botany (of a flower) having both stamens and carpels present and functional.
■ Botany denoting the stage or state of a fungus in which the sexually produced spores are formed. ■ Entomology (of an insect) fully adult and (typically) winged.
▶ **verb** /pəˈfɛkt/ [with obj.] make (something) completely free from faults or defects, or as close to such a condition as possible: *he's busy perfecting his bowling technique.*
■ archaic bring to completion; finish. ■ complete (a printed sheet of paper) by printing the second side. ■ Law satisfy the necessary conditions or requirements for the transfer of (a gift, title, etc.): *equity will not perfect an imperfect gift.*
▶ **noun** /ˈpəːfɪkt/ (**the perfect**) Grammar the perfect tense.
– DERIVATIVES **perfecter** noun, **perfectibility** noun, **perfectible** adjective, **perfectness** noun.
– ORIGIN Middle English: from Old French *perfet*, from Latin *perfectus* 'completed', from the verb *perficere*, from *per-* 'through, completely' + *facere* 'do'.

perfecta /pəˈfɛktə/ ▶ **noun** N. Amer. a bet in which the first two places in a race must be predicted in the correct order. Compare with **QUINELLA**.
– ORIGIN 1970s: from Latin American Spanish *quiniela perfecta* 'perfect quinella'.

perfect binding ▶ **noun** [mass noun] a form of bookbinding in which the leaves are bound by gluing, after the back folds have been cut off, rather than sewing.

perfect cadence ▶ **noun** Music a cadence in which the chord of the dominant immediately precedes that of the tonic.

perfect competition ▶ **noun** [mass noun] the situation prevailing in a market in which buyers and sellers are so numerous and well informed that all elements of monopoly are absent and the market price of a commodity is beyond the control of individual buyers and sellers.

perfect fifth ▶ **noun** Music see **FIFTH**.

perfect fourth ▶ **noun** Music see **FOURTH**.

perfect gas ▶ **noun** another term for **IDEAL GAS**.

perfection ▶ **noun** [mass noun] the condition, state, or quality of being free or as free as possible from all flaws or defects: *the satiny perfection of her skin | his pursuit of golfing perfection.*
■ a person or thing perceived as the embodiment of such a condition, state, or quality: *I am told that she is perfection itself.* ■ the action or process of improving something until it is faultless or as faultless as possible: *among the key tasks was the perfection of new mechanisms of economic management.*
– PHRASES **to perfection** in a manner or way that could not be better; perfectly: *a blue suit that showed off her blonde hair to perfection.*
– ORIGIN Middle English (in the sense 'completeness'): via Old French from Latin *perfectio(n-)*, from *perficere* 'to complete' (see **PERFECT**).

perfectionism ▶ **noun** [mass noun] refusal to accept any standard short of perfection.
■ Philosophy a doctrine holding that religious, moral, social, or political perfection is attainable, especially the theory that human moral or spiritual perfection should be or has been attained.
– DERIVATIVES **perfectionist** noun & adjective, **perfectionistic** adjective.

perfective Grammar ▶ **adjective** denoting or relating to an aspect of verbs in Slavic languages that expresses completed action. The opposite of **IMPERFECTIVE**.
▶ **noun** a perfective form of a verb.
■ (**the perfective**) the perfective aspect.
– ORIGIN early 17th cent. (in the general sense 'tending to make complete'): from medieval Latin *perfectivus*, from Latin *perfectus* 'accomplished' (see **PERFECT**).

perfectly ▶ **adverb** in a manner or way that could not be better: *the ring fitted perfectly | [as submodifier] perfectly clean glass bottles.*
■ [as submodifier] used for emphasis, especially in order to assert something that has been challenged or doubted: *you know perfectly well I can't stay.*

perfecto ▶ **noun** (pl. **-os**) a type of cigar that is thick in the centre and tapered at each end.
– ORIGIN late 19th cent.: from Spanish, literally 'perfect'.

perfect pitch ▶ **noun** [mass noun] the ability to recognize the pitch of a note or produce any given note; a sense of absolute pitch.

perfect square ▶ **noun** another term for **SQUARE NUMBER**.

perfervid /pəˈfəːvɪd/ ▶ **adjective** poetic/literary intense and impassioned: *perfervid nationalism.*
– DERIVATIVES **perfervidly** adverb.
– ORIGIN mid 19th cent.: from modern Latin *perfervidus*, from Latin *per-* 'utterly' + *fervidus* 'glowing hot, fiery'.

perfidious /pəˈfɪdɪəs/ ▶ **adjective** poetic/literary deceitful and untrustworthy: *a perfidious lover.*
– DERIVATIVES **perfidiously** adverb, **perfidiousness** noun.
– ORIGIN late 16th cent.: from Latin *perfidiosus*, from *perfidia* 'treachery'.

perfidy /ˈpəːfɪdi/ ▶ **noun** [mass noun] poetic/literary deceitfulness; untrustworthiness.
– ORIGIN late 16th cent.: via French from Latin *perfidia*, from *perfidus* 'treacherous', based on *per-* 'to ill effect' + *fides* 'faith'.

perfin /ˈpəːfɪn/ ▶ **noun** Philately a postage stamp perforated with the initials or insignia of an organization, especially to prevent misuse.
– ORIGIN 1950s: from *perf(orated) in(itials)*.

perfoliate /pəˈfəʊlɪət/ ▶ **adjective** Botany (of a stalkless leaf or bract) extended at the base to encircle the node, so that the stem apparently passes through it.
■ (of a plant) having such leaves.
– ORIGIN late 17th cent.: from modern Latin *perfoliatus*, from Latin *per-* 'through' + *foliatus* 'leaved'.

perforate ▶ **verb** /ˈpəːfəreɪt/ [with obj.] pierce and make a hole or holes in: *fragments of an explosive bullet perforated his intestines in a dozen places | [as adj.* **perforated**] *a perforated appendix.*
■ make a row of small holes in (paper) so that a part may be torn off easily.
▶ **adjective** /ˈpəːf(ə)rət/ Biology & Medicine perforated: *a perforate shell.*

– DERIVATIVES **perforator** /ˈpəːfəreɪtə/ noun.
– ORIGIN late Middle English (as an adjective): from Latin *perforat-* 'pierced through', from the verb *perforare*, from *per-* 'through' + *forare* 'pierce'.

perforation ▶ noun a hole made by boring or piercing; an aperture passing through or into something: *the perforations allow water to enter the well.*
■ a small hole or row of small holes punched in a sheet of paper, e.g. of postage stamps, so that a part can be torn off easily. ■ [mass noun] the action or state of perforating or being perforated: *there was evidence of intestinal perforation.*
– ORIGIN late Middle English: from medieval Latin *perforatio(n-)*, from the verb *perforare* (see **PERFORATE**).

perforce ▶ adverb formal used to express necessity or inevitability: *amateurs, perforce, have to settle for less expensive solutions.*
– ORIGIN Middle English: from Old French *par force* 'by force'.

perforin /ˈpəːfərɪn/ ▶ noun [mass noun] Biochemistry a protein, released by killer cells of the immune system, which destroys targeted cells by creating lesions like pores in their membranes.
– ORIGIN 1980s: from the verb **PERFORATE** + **-IN**[1].

perform ▶ verb [with obj.] **1** carry out, accomplish, or fulfil (an action, task, or function): *I have my duties to perform.*
■ [no obj., with adverbial] work, function, or do something to a specified standard: *the car performs well at low speeds.* ■ [no obj.] (of an investment) yield a profitable return: *our £120 million investment in the company is not performing at present.* ■ [no obj.] informal have successful or satisfactory sexual intercourse with someone.
2 present (a form of entertainment) to an audience: *the play has already been performed in Britain.*
■ [no obj.] entertain an audience, typically by acting, singing, or dancing on stage: *the band will be performing live in Hyde Park.*
– DERIVATIVES **performability** noun, **performable** adjective, **performer** noun.
– ORIGIN Middle English: from Anglo-Norman French *parfourmer*, alteration (by association with *forme* 'form') of Old French *parfournir*, from *par* 'through, to completion' + *fournir* 'furnish, provide'.

performance ▶ noun **1** an act of staging or presenting a play, concert, or other form of entertainment: *Don Giovanni had its first performance in 1787.*
■ a person's rendering of a dramatic role, song, or piece of music: *Bailey gives a sound performance as the doctor.* ■ [in sing.] informal a display of exaggerated behaviour or a process involving a great deal of unnecessary time and effort; a fuss: *he stopped to fasten his shoelace and seemed to be* ***making*** *quite a* ***performance*** *of it.*
2 [mass noun] the action or process of carrying out or accomplishing an action, task, or function: *the continual performance of a single task reduces a man to the level of a machine.*
■ an action, task, or operation, seen in terms of how successfully it was performed: *pay increases are now being linked more closely to performance* | [count noun] *it was a tremendous all-round performance by Wigan.* ■ the capabilities of a machine or product, especially when observed under particular conditions: *the hardware is put through tests which assess the performance of the processor.* ■ a vehicle's capacity to gain speed rapidly and move efficiently and safely at high speed. ■ the extent to which an investment is profitable, especially in relation to other investments. ■ (also **linguistic performance**) Linguistics an individual's use of a language, i.e. what a speaker actually says, including hesitations, false starts, and errors. Often contrasted with **COMPETENCE**.

performance art ▶ noun [mass noun] an artform that combines visual art with dramatic performance.
– DERIVATIVES **performance artist** noun.

performance bond ▶ noun a bond issued by a bank or other financial institution, guaranteeing the fulfilment of a particular contract.

performance poetry ▶ noun [mass noun] a form of poetry intended to be performed as a dramatic monologue or exchange and frequently involving extemporization.
– DERIVATIVES **performance poet** noun.

performance testing ▶ noun [mass noun] the evaluation of a person's mental or manual ability.
■ the evaluation of the heritable characteristics of a bull or other breeding animal, as determined from the known characteristics of the offspring.

performative Linguistics & Philosophy ▶ adjective relating to or denoting an utterance by means of which the speaker performs a particular act (e.g. *I bet, I apologize, I promise*). Often contrasted with **CONSTATIVE**.
▶ noun a performative verb, sentence, or utterance.

performing arts ▶ plural noun forms of creative activity that are performed in front of an audience, such as drama, music, and dance.

perfume /ˈpəːfjuːm/ ▶ noun [mass noun] a fragrant liquid typically made from essential oils extracted from flowers and spices, used to impart a pleasant smell to one's body or clothes: *I caught a whiff of her fresh lemony perfume* | [count noun] *musk-based perfumes.*
■ a pleasant smell: *the heady perfume of lilacs.*
▶ verb /also pəˈfjuːm/ [with obj.] impart a pleasant smell to: *just one bloom of jasmine has the power to perfume a whole room.*
■ (usu. **be perfumed**) impregnate (something) with perfume or a sweet-smelling ingredient: *the cream is perfumed with rosemary and iris extracts.* ■ apply perfume to (someone or something): *her hair was oiled and perfumed.*
– DERIVATIVES **perfumy** adjective.
– ORIGIN mid 16th cent. (originally denoting pleasant-smelling smoke from a burning substance, especially one used in fumigation): from French *parfum* (noun), *parfumer* (verb), from obsolete Italian *parfumare*, literally 'to smoke through'.

perfumed ▶ adjective naturally having or producing a sweet, pleasant smell: *the perfumed richness of the wine.*
■ impregnated with a sweet-smelling substance: *perfumed soap.* ■ denoting something to which perfume has been applied: *her plump perfumed arms.*

perfumer ▶ noun a producer or seller of perfumes.

perfumery ▶ noun (pl. **-ies**) [mass noun] the action or business of producing or selling perfumes: *an oil used in perfumery.*
■ [count noun] a shop that sells perfumes.

perfunctory /pəˈfʌŋ(k)t(ə)ri/ ▶ adjective (of an action or gesture) carried out with a minimum of effort or reflection: *he gave a perfunctory nod.*
– DERIVATIVES **perfunctorily** adverb, **perfunctoriness** noun.
– ORIGIN late 16th cent.: from late Latin *perfunctorius* 'careless', from Latin *perfunct-* 'done with, discharged', from the verb *perfungi*.

perfusate /pəˈfjuːzeɪt/ ▶ noun Medicine a fluid used in perfusion.

perfuse ▶ verb [with obj.] permeate or suffuse (something) with a liquid, colour, quality, etc.: *Glaser perfused the yellow light with white* | figurative *such expression is perfused by rhetoric.*
■ Medicine supply (an organ, tissue, or body) with a fluid, typically treated blood or a blood substitute, by circulating it through blood vessels or other natural channels.
– DERIVATIVES **perfusion** noun, **perfusionist** noun.
– ORIGIN late Middle English (in the sense 'cause to flow through or away'): from Latin *perfus-* 'poured through', from the verb *perfundere*, from *per-* 'through' + *fundere* 'pour'.

Pergamum /ˈpəːɡəməm/ a city in ancient Mysia, in western Asia Minor, situated to the north of Izmir on a rocky hill close to the Aegean coast. The capital in the 3rd and 2nd centuries BC of the Attalid dynasty, it was one of the greatest and most beautiful of the Hellenistic cities and was famed for its cultural institutions, especially its library, which was second only to that at Alexandria.
– DERIVATIVES **Pergamene** /-ˌmiːn/ adjective & noun.

pergana ▶ noun variant spelling of **PARGANA**.

pergola /ˈpəːɡələ/ ▶ noun an archway in a garden or park consisting of a framework covered with trained climbing or trailing plants.
– ORIGIN mid 17th cent.: from Italian, from Latin *pergula* 'projecting roof', from *pergere* 'come or go forward'.

pergunnah ▶ noun variant spelling of **PARGANA**.

perhaps ▶ adverb used to express uncertainty or possibility: *perhaps I should have been frank with him.*
■ used when one does not wish to be too definite or assertive in the expression of an opinion: *perhaps not surprisingly, he was cautious about committing himself.* ■ used when making a polite request, offer, or suggestion: *would you perhaps consent to act as our guide?* ■ used to express reluctant or qualified agreement or acceptance: *'She understood him better than his wife ever did.' 'Perhaps so. But …'*
– ORIGIN late 15th cent.: from **PER** + **HAP**.

peri /ˈpɪəri/ ▶ noun (pl. **peris**) (in Persian mythology) a mythical superhuman being, originally represented as evil but subsequently as a good or graceful genie or fairy.
– ORIGIN from Persian *perī*.

peri- ▶ prefix **1** round; about: *pericardium* | *peristyle.*
2 Astronomy denoting the point nearest to a specified celestial body: *perihelion* | *perilune.* Compare with **APO-**.
– ORIGIN from Greek *peri* 'about, around'.

perianal /ˌpɛrɪˈeɪnəl/ ▶ adjective Medicine situated in or affecting the area around the anus.

perianth /ˈpɛrɪanθ/ ▶ noun Botany the outer part of a flower, consisting of the calyx (sepals) and corolla (petals).
– ORIGIN early 18th cent.: from French *périanthe*, from modern Latin *perianthium*, from Greek *peri* 'around' + *anthos* 'flower'.

periapsis /ˌpɛrɪˈapsɪs/ ▶ noun (pl. **periapses** /-siːz/) Astronomy the point in the path of an orbiting body at which it is nearest to the body that it orbits.

periapt /ˈpɛrɪapt/ ▶ noun archaic an item worn as a charm or amulet.
– ORIGIN late 16th cent.: from French *périapte*, from Greek *periapton*, from *peri* 'around' + *haptein* 'fasten'.

periarticular /ˌpɛrɪɑːˈtɪkjʊlə/ ▶ adjective Medicine situated or occurring around a joint of the body.

periastron /ˌpɛrɪˈastrən/ ▶ noun Astronomy the point nearest to a star in the path of a body orbiting that star.
– ORIGIN mid 19th cent.: from **PERI-** 'around' + Greek *astron* 'star', on the pattern of *perigee* and *perihelion*.

pericarditis /ˌpɛrɪkɑːˈdʌɪtɪs/ ▶ noun [mass noun] Medicine inflammation of the pericardium.

pericardium /ˌpɛrɪˈkɑːdɪəm/ ▶ noun (pl. **pericardia** /-dɪə/) Anatomy the membrane enclosing the heart, consisting of an outer fibrous layer and an inner double layer of serous membrane.
– DERIVATIVES **pericardial** adjective.
– ORIGIN late Middle English: modern Latin, from Greek *perikardion*, from *peri* 'around' + *kardia* 'heart'.

pericarp ▶ noun Botany the part of a fruit formed from the wall of the ripened ovary.
– ORIGIN late 17th cent.: from French *péricarpe*, from Greek *perikarpion* 'pod, shell', from *peri-* 'around' + *karpos* 'fruit'.

pericentric inversion /ˌpɛrɪˈsɛntrɪk/ ▶ noun Genetics a reversal of the normal order of genes in a chromosome segment involving parts of a chromosome at both sides of the centromere.

perichondrium /ˌpɛrɪˈkɒndrɪəm/ ▶ noun Anatomy the connective tissue that envelops cartilage where it is not at a joint.
– ORIGIN mid 18th cent.: modern Latin, from **PERI-** 'around' + Greek *khondros* 'cartilage'.

periclase /ˈpɛrɪkleɪz, -s/ ▶ noun [mass noun] a colourless mineral consisting of magnesium oxide, occurring chiefly in marble and limestone.
– ORIGIN mid 19th cent.: from modern Latin *periclasia*, erroneously from Greek *peri* 'utterly' + *klasis* 'breaking' (because it cleaves perfectly).

Pericles /ˈpɛrɪkliːz/ (*c.*495–429 BC), Athenian statesman and general. A champion of Athenian democracy, he pursued an imperialist policy and masterminded Athenian strategy in the Peloponnesian War. He commissioned the building of the Parthenon in 447 and promoted the culture of Athens in a golden age that produced such figures as Aeschylus, Socrates, and Phidias.

periclinal /ˌpɛrɪˈklʌɪn(ə)l/ ▶ adjective Botany (of a cell wall) parallel to the surface of the meristem.
■ (of cell division) taking place by the formation of periclinal walls.
– DERIVATIVES **periclinally** adverb.
– ORIGIN late 19th cent.: from Greek *periklinēs* 'sloping on all sides', from *peri-* 'around' + *klinēs* 'sloping' (from the verb *klinein*).

pericope /pəˈrɪkəpi/ ▶ noun an extract from a text, especially a passage from the Bible.
– ORIGIN mid 17th cent.: via late Latin from Greek

p

perikopē 'section', from *peri-* 'around' + *kopē* 'cutting' (from *koptein* 'to cut').

pericranium ▶ **noun** Anatomy the periosteum enveloping the skull.
– ORIGIN late Middle English: modern Latin, from Greek *peri-* 'around' + *kranion* 'skull'.

pericycle ▶ **noun** Botany a thin layer of plant tissue between the endodermis and the phloem.
– ORIGIN late 19th cent.: from Greek *perikuklos* 'spherical', from *perikukloun* 'encircle'.

pericyclic /ˌpɛrɪˈsʌɪklɪk, -ˈsɪk-/ ▶ **adjective** **1** Chemistry relating to or denoting a reaction that involves a concerted rearrangement of bonding in which all the bonds broken or formed in the reaction lie on a closed ring, whether or not a cyclic molecule is involved.
2 Botany of or relating to a pericycle.

periderm ▶ **noun** [mass noun] Botany the corky outer layer of a plant stem formed in secondary thickening or as a response to injury or infection.
– DERIVATIVES **peridermal** adjective.
– ORIGIN mid 19th cent.: from **PERI-** 'around' + Greek *derma* 'skin'.

peridium /pɪˈrɪdɪəm/ ▶ **noun** (pl. **peridia** /-dɪə/) Botany the outer skin of a sporangium or other fruiting body of a fungus.
– ORIGIN early 19th cent.: from Greek *pēridion*, literally 'small wallet', diminutive of *pēra*.

peridot /ˈpɛrɪdɒt/ ▶ **noun** [mass noun] a green semi-precious variety of forsterite (olivine).
– ORIGIN early 18th cent.: from French, from Old French *peritot*, of unknown origin.

peridotite /ˈpɛrɪdɒtʌɪt/ ▶ **noun** [mass noun] Geology a dense, coarse-grained plutonic rock containing a large amount of olivine, believed to be the main constituent of the earth's mantle.
– DERIVATIVES **peridotitic** adjective.

perigee /ˈpɛrɪdʒiː/ ▶ **noun** Astronomy the point in the orbit of the moon or a satellite at which it is nearest to the earth. The opposite of **APOGEE**.
– ORIGIN late 16th cent.: from French *périgée*, via modern Latin from Greek *perigeion* 'close round the earth', from *peri-* 'around' + *gē* 'earth'.

periglacial ▶ **adjective** Geology relating to or denoting an area adjacent to a glacier or ice sheet or otherwise subject to repeated freezing and thawing.

Périgord /ˈpɛrɪgɔː, French pɛrigɔr/ an area of SW France, in the SW Massif Central. A former countship, it became a part of Navarre in 1470, becoming united with France in 1670.

perigynous /pəˈrɪdʒɪnəs/ ▶ **adjective** Botany (of a plant or flower) having the stamens and other floral parts at the same level as the carpels. Compare with **EPIGYNOUS**, **HYPOGYNOUS**.
– DERIVATIVES **perigyny** noun.
– ORIGIN early 19th cent.: from modern Latin *perigynus* (from Greek *peri-* 'around' + *gunē* 'woman') + **-OUS**.

perihelion /ˌpɛrɪˈhiːlɪən/ ▶ **noun** (pl. **perihelia** /-lɪə/) Astronomy the point in the orbit of a planet, asteroid, or comet at which it is closest to the sun. The opposite of **APHELION**.
– ORIGIN mid 17th cent.: alteration of modern Latin *perihelium* (by substitution of the Greek inflection *-on*), from Greek *peri-* 'around' + *hēlios* 'sun'.

perikaryon /ˌpɛrɪˈkarɪɒn/ ▶ **noun** (pl. **perikarya** /-ˈkarɪə/) Physiology the cell body of a neuron, containing the nucleus.
– DERIVATIVES **perikaryal** adjective.

peril ▶ **noun** [mass noun] serious and immediate danger: *you could well place us both in peril* | [count noun] *a setback to the state could present a peril to the regime.*
■(**perils**) the dangers or difficulties that arise from a particular situation or activity: *she first witnessed the perils of pop stardom a decade ago.*
▶ **verb** (**perilled**, **perilling**; US **periled**, **periling**) [with obj.] archaic expose to danger; threaten: *Jonathon perilled his life for love of David.*
– PHRASES **at one's peril** at one's own risk (used especially in warnings): *neglect our advice at your peril.* **in** (or **at**) **peril of** very likely to incur or to suffer from: *the movement is in peril of dying.* ■ at risk of losing or injuring: *anyone linked with the Republican cause would be in peril of their life.*
– ORIGIN Middle English: from Old French, from Latin *peric(u)lum* 'danger', from the base of *experiri* 'to try'. The verb dates from the mid 16th cent.

perilous ▶ **adjective** full of danger or risk: *a perilous journey south.*
■exposed to imminent risk of disaster or ruin: *the economy is in a perilous state.*
– DERIVATIVES **perilously** adverb, **perilousness** noun.
– ORIGIN Middle English: from Old French *perillous*, from Latin *periculosus*, from *periculum* 'danger' (see **PERIL**).

perilune /ˈpɛrɪluːn/ ▶ **noun** [mass noun] the point at which a spacecraft in lunar orbit is closest to the moon. The opposite of **APOLUNE**.
– ORIGIN 1960s: from **PERI-** 'around' + Latin *luna* 'moon', on the pattern of *perigee*.

perilymph ▶ **noun** [mass noun] Anatomy the fluid between the membraneous labyrinth of the ear and the bone which encloses it.
– DERIVATIVES **perilymphatic** adjective.

perimeter ▶ **noun** **1** the continuous line forming the boundary of a closed geometrical figure: *the perimeter of a rectangle.*
■the length of such a line: *the rectangle has a perimeter of 30 cm.* ■ the outermost parts or boundary of an area or object: *the perimeter of the garden* | figurative *my presence on the perimeter of his life.* ■ a defended boundary of a military position or base. ■ Basketball an area away from the basket, beyond the reach of the defensive team.
2 an instrument for measuring the extent and characteristics of a person's field of vision.
– DERIVATIVES **perimetric** adjective.
– ORIGIN late Middle English: via Latin from Greek *perimetros*, based on *peri-* 'around' + *metron* 'measure'.

perimetry ▶ **noun** [mass noun] measurement of a person's field of vision.

perimysium /ˌpɛrɪˈmɪsɪəm/ ▶ **noun** [mass noun] Anatomy the sheath of connective tissue surrounding a bundle of muscle fibres.
– DERIVATIVES **perimysial** adjective.
– ORIGIN mid 19th cent.: modern Latin, from Greek *peri-* 'around' + *mus* 'muscle'.

perinatal ▶ **adjective** Medicine of or relating to the time, usually a number of weeks, immediately before and after birth.
– DERIVATIVES **perinatally** adverb.

perinatology /ˌpɛrɪneɪˈtɒlədʒi/ ▶ **noun** [mass noun] Medicine the branch of obstetrics dealing with the period around childbirth.
– DERIVATIVES **perinatologist** noun.

per incuriam /ˌpə(r) ɪnˈkjʊərɪam/ ▶ **adverb** Law through lack of due regard to the law or the facts: *the decision was made per incuriam.*
– ORIGIN Latin, literally 'through lack of care'.

perineum /ˌpɛrɪˈniːəm/ ▶ **noun** Anatomy the area between the anus and the scrotum or vulva.
– DERIVATIVES **perineal** adjective.
– ORIGIN late Middle English: from late Latin, from Greek *perinaion*.

perineurium /ˌpɛrɪˈnjʊərɪəm/ ▶ **noun** [mass noun] Anatomy the sheath of connective tissue surrounding a bundle (fascicle) of nerve fibres within a nerve.
– DERIVATIVES **perineurial** adjective.
– ORIGIN mid 19th cent.: modern Latin, from Greek *peri-* 'around' + *neuron* 'sinew'.

perinuclear /ˌpɛrɪˈnjuːklɪə/ ▶ **adjective** Biology situated or occurring around the nucleus of a cell.

period ▶ **noun** **1** a length or portion of time: *he had long periods of depression* | *the ale will be available for a limited period* | *the period 1977–85.*
■a portion of time in the life of a person, nation, or civilization characterized by the same prevalent features or conditions: *the early medieval period.* ■ one of the set divisions of the day in a school allocated to a lesson or other activity. ■ [with modifier] a set period of time during which a particular activity takes place: *the training period is between 16 and 18 months.* ■ each of the intervals into which the playing time of a sporting event is divided. ■ a major division of geological time that is a subdivision of an era and is itself subdivided into epochs, corresponding to a system in chronostratigraphy.
2 Physics the interval of time between successive occurrences of the same state in an oscillatory or cyclic phenomenon, such as a mechanical vibration, an alternating current, a variable star, or an electromagnetic wave.
■Astronomy the time taken by a celestial object to rotate about its axis, or to make one circuit of its orbit. ■ Mathematics the interval between successive equal values of a periodic function.
3 (also **menstrual period**) a flow of blood and other material from the lining of the uterus, lasting for a few days and occurring in sexually mature women who are not pregnant at intervals of about one lunar month until the menopause.
4 chiefly N. Amer. a full stop.
■informal added to the end of a statement to indicate that no further discussion is possible or desirable: *he is the sole owner of the trademark, period.*
5 Chemistry a set of elements occupying a horizontal row in the periodic table.
6 Rhetoric a complex sentence, especially one consisting of several clauses, constructed as part of a formal speech or oration.
■Music a complete idea, typically consisting of two or four phrases.
▶ **adjective** [attrib.] belonging to or characteristic of a past historical time, especially in style or design: *a splendid selection of period furniture.*
– PHRASES **put a period to** dated put an end to; bring to a conclusion: *in dry climates, the onset of summer drought may put a period to plant activity.*
– ORIGIN late Middle English (denoting the time during which something, especially a disease, runs its course): from Old French *periode*, via Latin from Greek *periodos* 'orbit, recurrence, course', from *peri-* 'around' + *hodos* 'way, course'. The sense 'portion of time' dates from the early 17th cent.

periodic /ˌpɪərɪˈɒdɪk/ ▶ **adjective** **1** appearing or occurring at intervals: *the periodic visits she made to her father.*
2 Chemistry relating to the periodic table of the elements or the pattern of chemical properties which underlies it: *the periodic law.*
3 of or relating to a rhetorical period. See **PERIOD** (sense 6).
– ORIGIN mid 17th cent.: from French *périodique*, or via Latin from Greek *periodikos* 'coming round at intervals', from *periodos* (see **PERIOD**).

periodic acid /ˌpəːrʌɪˈɒdɪk/ ▶ **noun** [mass noun] Chemistry a hygroscopic solid acid with strong oxidizing properties.
• Chem. formula: H_5IO_6.
– DERIVATIVES **periodate** /pəˈrʌɪədeɪt/ noun.
– ORIGIN mid 19th cent.: from sense 2 of **PER-** + **IODIC ACID**.

periodical ▶ **noun** a magazine or newspaper published at regular intervals.
▶ **adjective** [attrib.] occurring or appearing at intervals; occasional: *she took periodical gulps of her tea.*
■(of a magazine or newspaper) published at regular intervals: *Britain's best periodical art magazine.*
– DERIVATIVES **periodically** adverb.

periodical cicada ▶ **noun** an American cicada whose nymphs emerge in large numbers periodically in a seventeen-year (or, in the south, a thirteen-year) cycle.
• *Magicicada septendecim*, family Cicadidae, suborder Homoptera. Alternative name: **seventeen-year cicada**.

periodic function ▶ **noun** Mathematics a function returning to the same value at regular intervals.

periodicity /ˌpɪərɪəˈdɪsɪti/ ▶ **noun** [mass noun] chiefly technical the quality or character of being periodic; the tendency to recur at intervals: *the periodicity of the sunspot cycle.*

periodic table ▶ **noun** Chemistry a table of the chemical elements arranged in order of atomic number, usually in rows, so that elements with similar atomic structure (and hence similar chemical properties) appear in vertical columns.

periodize (also **-ise**) ▶ **verb** [with obj.] formal divide (a portion of time) into periods.
– DERIVATIVES **periodization** noun.

periodontics /ˌpɛrɪəˈdɒntɪks/ ▶ **plural noun** [treated as sing.] the branch of dentistry concerned with the structures surrounding and supporting the teeth.
– DERIVATIVES **periodontal** adjective, **periodontist** noun.
– ORIGIN 1940s: from **PERI-** 'around' + Greek *odous*, *odont-* 'tooth' + **-ICS**.

periodontitis /ˌpɛrɪədɒnˈtʌɪtɪs/ ▶ **noun** [mass noun] Medicine inflammation of the tissue around the teeth, often causing shrinkage of the gums and loosening of the teeth.

periodontology /ˌpɛrɪədɒnˈtɒlədʒi/ ▶ **noun** another term for **PERIODONTICS**.

period piece ▶ **noun** an object or work that is set in or strongly reminiscent of an earlier historical period.

perioperative ▶ **adjective** Medicine (of a process or treatment) occurring or performed at or around the time of an operation.

periosteum /ˌpɛrɪˈɒstɪəm/ ▶ **noun** (pl. **periostea** /-tɪə/) Anatomy a dense layer of vascular connective tissue enveloping the bones except at the surfaces of the joints.
– DERIVATIVES **periosteal** adjective.
– ORIGIN late 16th cent.: modern Latin, from Greek *periosteon*, from *peri-* 'around' + *osteon* 'bone'.

periostitis /ˌpɛrɪɒˈstʌɪtɪs/ ▶ **noun** [mass noun] Medicine inflammation of the membrane enveloping a bone.

peripatetic /ˌpɛrɪpəˈtɛtɪk/ ▶ **adjective 1** travelling from place to place, especially working or based in various places for relatively short periods: *the peripatetic nature of military life.*
■ [attrib.] (of a teacher) working in more than one school or college: *a peripatetic music teacher.*
2 (**Peripatetic**) Aristotelian. [ORIGIN: with reference to Aristotle's practice of walking to and fro while teaching.]
▶ **noun 1** a person who travels from place to place, especially a teacher who works in more than one school or college.
2 (**Peripatetic**) an Aristotelian philosopher.
– DERIVATIVES **peripatetically** adverb, **peripateticism** noun.
– ORIGIN late Middle English (denoting an Aristotelian philosopher): from Old French *peripatetique*, via Latin from Greek *peripatētikos* 'walking up and down', from the verb *peripatein*.

peripatus /pəˈrɪpətəs/ ▶ **noun** Zoology a tropical terrestrial invertebrate with a soft worm-like body and stumpy legs. See **ONYCHOPHORA**.
● Genus *Peripatus*, phylum Onychophora.
– ORIGIN modern Latin, from Greek *peripatos* 'that walks about'.

peri-peri /ˌpɛrɪˈpɛri/ ▶ **noun** South African term for **PIRI-PIRI**.

peripeteia /ˌpɛrɪpɪˈtʌɪə, -ˈtiːə/ ▶ **noun** formal a sudden reversal of fortune or change in circumstances, especially in reference to fictional narrative.
– ORIGIN late 16th cent.: from Greek *peripeteia* 'sudden change', from *peri-* 'around' + the stem of *piptein* 'to fall'.

peripheral ▶ **adjective** of, relating to, or situated on the edge or periphery of something: *the peripheral areas of Europe.*
■ of secondary or minor importance; marginal: *she will see their problems as* ***peripheral to*** *her own.* ■ [attrib.] (of a device) able to be attached to and used with a computer, though not an integral part of it. ■ Anatomy near the surface of the body, with special reference to the circulation and nervous system: *lymphocytes from peripheral blood.*
▶ **noun** Computing a peripheral device.
– DERIVATIVES **peripherality** noun, **peripheralization** (also **-isation**) noun, **peripheralize** (also **-ise**) verb, **peripherally** adverb.

peripheral nervous system ▶ **noun** Anatomy the nervous system outside the brain and spinal cord.

periphery /pəˈrɪf(ə)ri/ ▶ **noun** (pl. **-ies**) the outer limits or edge of an area or object: *new buildings* ***on the periphery of*** *the hospital site.*
■ a marginal or secondary position in, or part or aspect of, a group, subject, or sphere of activity: *a shift in power from the centre to the periphery.*
– ORIGIN late 16th cent. (denoting a line that forms the boundary of something): via late Latin from Greek *periphereia* 'circumference', from *peripherēs* 'revolving around', from *peri-* 'around' + *pherein* 'to bear'.

periphrasis /pəˈrɪfrəsɪs/ ▶ **noun** (pl. **periphrases** /-siːz/) [mass noun] the use of indirect and circumlocutory speech or writing.
■ [count noun] an indirect and circumlocutory phrase. ■ Grammar the use of separate words to express a grammatical relationship that is otherwise expressed by inflection, e.g. *did go* as opposed to *went* and *more intelligent* as opposed to *cleverer*.
– ORIGIN mid 16th cent.: via Latin from Greek, from *periphrazein*, from *peri-* 'around' + *phrazein* 'declare'.

periphrastic /ˌpɛrɪˈfrastɪk/ ▶ **adjective** (of speech or writing) indirect and circumlocutory: *the periphrastic nature of legal syntax.*
■ Grammar (of a case or tense) formed by a combination of words rather than by inflection (such as *did go* and *of the people* rather than *went* and *the people's*).
– DERIVATIVES **periphrastically** adverb.
– ORIGIN early 19th cent.: from Greek *periphrastikos*, from *periphrazein* 'declare in a roundabout way'.

periphyton /pəˈrɪfɪtɒn/ ▶ **noun** [mass noun] Ecology freshwater organisms attached to or clinging to plants and other objects projecting above the bottom sediments.
– DERIVATIVES **periphytic** adjective.
– ORIGIN 1960s: from Greek *peri-* 'around' + *phuton* 'plant'.

peripteral /pəˈrɪpt(ə)r(ə)l/ ▶ **adjective** Architecture (of a building) having a single row of pillars on all sides in the style of the temples of ancient Greece.
– ORIGIN early 19th cent.: from Greek *peripteron* (from *peri-* 'around' + *pteron* 'wing') + **-AL**.

perique /pɛˈriːk/ ▶ **noun** [mass noun] a strong dark tobacco from Louisiana.
– ORIGIN late 19th cent.: Louisiana French, apparently from the nickname of Pierre Chenet, who first grew it.

periscope ▶ **noun** an apparatus consisting of a tube attached to a set of mirrors or prisms, by which an observer (typically in a submerged submarine or behind a high obstacle) can see things that are otherwise out of sight.

periscopic ▶ **adjective** of or relating to a periscope.
■ (of a lens or an optical instrument) giving a wide field of view: *a periscopic sextant.*
– DERIVATIVES **periscopically** adverb.

perish ▶ **verb 1** [no obj.] suffer death, typically in a violent, sudden, or untimely way: *a great part of his army perished of hunger and disease.*
■ suffer complete ruin or destruction: *if inflation is let rip, the government would almost certainly perish at the polls.* ■ (of rubber, a foodstuff, or other organic substance) lose its normal qualities; rot or decay: *most domestic building was in wood and has perished.*
2 (**be perished**) Brit. be suffering from extreme cold: *I was often perished with cold before the end of the day.*
– PHRASES **perish the thought** informal used, often ironically, to show that one finds a suggestion or idea completely ridiculous or unwelcome: *he wasn't out to get drunk—perish the thought!*
– ORIGIN Middle English: from Old French *periss-*, lengthened stem of *perir*, from Latin *perire* 'pass away', from *per-* 'through, completely' + *ire* 'go'.

perishable ▶ **adjective** (especially of food) likely to decay or go bad quickly.
■ (of something abstract) having a brief life or significance; transitory: *ballet is the most perishable of arts.*
▶ **noun** (**perishables**) things, especially foodstuffs, likely to decay or go bad quickly.
– DERIVATIVES **perishability** noun.

perisher ▶ **noun** Brit. informal a term used, often affectionately, for a mischievous or awkward person or thing, especially a child: *some pushy little perisher.*

perishing ▶ **adjective** Brit. informal **1** dated used for emphasis or to express annoyance: *I could murder that perishing kid!* | [as submodifier] *you've been a perishing long time with that coffee!*
2 [predic.] extremely cold: *it's perishing in the tent.*
– DERIVATIVES **perishingly** adverb.

perisperm ▶ **noun** Botany (in some seeds) a mass of nutritive material outside the embryo sac.
– ORIGIN early 19th cent.: from **PERI-** 'around' + Greek *sperma* 'seed'.

Perissodactyla /ˌpərɪsə(ʊ)ˈdaktɪlə/ Zoology an order of mammals that comprises the odd-toed ungulates. Compare with **ARTIODACTYLA**.
– DERIVATIVES **perissodactyl** noun & adjective.
– ORIGIN modern Latin (plural), from Greek *perissos* 'uneven' + *daktulos* 'finger, toe'.

peristalsis /ˌpɛrɪˈstalsɪs/ ▶ **noun** [mass noun] Physiology the involuntary constriction and relaxation of the muscles of the intestine or another canal, creating wave-like movements which push the contents of the canal forward.
– DERIVATIVES **peristaltic** adjective, **peristaltically** adverb.
– ORIGIN mid 19th cent.: modern Latin, from Greek *peristallein* 'wrap around', from *peri-* 'around' + *stallein* 'to place'.

peristaltic pump ▶ **noun** a mechanical pump in which pressure is provided by the movement of a constriction along a tube, similar to biological peristalsis.

peristome /ˈpɛrɪstəʊm/ ▶ **noun** Zoology the parts surrounding the mouth of various invertebrates.
■ Botany a fringe of small projections around the mouth of a capsule in mosses and certain fungi.
– ORIGIN late 18th cent.: from modern Latin *peristoma*, from Greek *peri-* 'around' + *stoma* 'mouth'.

peristyle ▶ **noun** Architecture a row of columns surrounding a space within a building such as a court or internal garden or edging a veranda or porch.
■ an architectural space such as a court or porch that is surrounded or edged by such columns.
– ORIGIN early 17th cent.: from French *péristyle*, from Latin *peristylum*, from Greek *peristulon*, from *peri-* 'around' + *stulos* 'pillar'.

perithecium /ˌpɛrɪˈθiːsɪəm/ ▶ **noun** (pl. **perithecia** /-sɪə/) Botany (in some fungi) a round or flask-shaped fruiting body with a pore through which the spores are discharged.
– ORIGIN mid 19th cent.: modern Latin, from **PERI-** 'around' + Greek *thēkē* 'case'.

peritoneum /ˌpɛrɪtəˈniːəm/ ▶ **noun** (pl. **peritoneums** or **peritonea** /-ˈniːə/) Anatomy the serous membrane lining the cavity of the abdomen and covering the abdominal organs.
– DERIVATIVES **peritoneal** adjective.
– ORIGIN late Middle English: via late Latin from Greek *peritonaion*, from *peritonos* 'stretched round', from *peri-* 'around' + *-tonos* 'stretched'.

peritonitis /ˌpɛrɪtəˈnʌɪtɪs/ ▶ **noun** [mass noun] Medicine inflammation of the peritoneum, typically caused by bacterial infection either via the blood or after rupture of an abdominal organ.

peri-track ▶ **noun** another term for **TAXIWAY**.
– ORIGIN contraction of *perimeter track*.

peritus /pəˈrʌɪtəs/ ▶ **noun** (pl. **periti** /-tʌɪ, -tiː/) a theological adviser or consultant to a council of the Roman Catholic Church.
– ORIGIN 1960s: from Latin; related to *expertus* 'expert'.

perivascular ▶ **adjective** Medicine situated or occurring around a blood vessel.

periventricular /ˌpɛrɪvɛnˈtrɪkjʊlə/ ▶ **noun** Anatomy & Medicine situated or occurring around a ventricle, especially a ventricle of the brain.

periwig ▶ **noun** a highly styled wig worn formerly as a fashionable headdress by both women and men and retained by judges and barristers as part of their professional dress.
■ archaic term for **WIG**[1].
– DERIVATIVES **periwigged** adjective.
– ORIGIN early 16th cent.: alteration of **PERUKE**, with *-wi-* representing the French *-u-* sound.

periwinkle[1] ▶ **noun** an Old World plant with flat five-petalled flowers and glossy leaves. Some kinds are grown as ornamentals and some contain alkaloids used in medicine.
● Genera *Vinca* and *Catharanthus*, family Apocynaceae.
– ORIGIN late Old English *peruince*, from late Latin *pervinca*, reinforced in Middle English by Anglo-Norman French *pervenke*. The change of *-v-* to *-w-* and the addition of *-le* seem to have occurred before the appearance of **PERIWINKLE**[2].

periwinkle[2] ▶ **noun** another term for **WINKLE**.
– ORIGIN mid 16th cent.: of unknown origin.

perjure ▶ **verb** (**perjure oneself**) Law wilfully tell an untruth when giving evidence to a court; commit perjury: *she admitted that she had perjured herself.*
– DERIVATIVES **perjurer** noun.
– ORIGIN late Middle English (as *perjured* in the sense 'guilty of perjury'): from Old French *parjurer*, from Latin *perjurare* 'swear falsely', from *per-* 'to ill effect' + *jurare* 'swear'.

perjured ▶ **adjective** Law (of evidence) involving wilfully told untruths.
■ (of a person) guilty of perjury: *a perjured witness.*

perjury /ˈpəːdʒ(ə)ri/ ▶ **noun** (pl. **-ies**) [mass noun] Law the offence of wilfully telling an untruth in a court after having taken an oath or affirmation.
– DERIVATIVES **perjurious** /-ˈdʒʊərɪəs/ adjective.
– ORIGIN late Middle English: from Anglo-Norman French *perjurie*, from Latin *perjurium* 'false oath', from the verb *perjurare* (see **PERJURE**).

perk[1] ▶ **verb** [no obj.] (**perk up**) become more cheerful, lively, or interesting: *in the second half the dance perked up* | *she'd been depressed, but she seemed to perk up last week.*

▪[with obj.] (**perk someone/thing up**) make someone or something more cheerful, lively, or interesting: *the coffee had perked him up long enough to tackle the reviews.*
▶**adjective** dialect perky; pert.
– ORIGIN late Middle English (in the senses 'perch' and 'be lively'): perhaps from an Old French dialect variant of *percher* 'to perch'.

perk² ▶**noun** (usu. **perks**) informal money, goods, or another benefit to which one is entitled as an employee or as a shareholder of a company: *many agencies are helping to keep personnel at their jobs by providing perks.*
▪an advantage or benefit following from a job or situation: *they were busy discovering the perks of town life.*
– ORIGIN early 19th cent.: abbreviation of PERQUISITE.

perk³ informal ▶**verb** [no obj.] (of coffee) percolate: *while the coffee perks, head out for the morning paper.*
▪[with obj.] percolate (coffee).
▶**noun** a coffee percolator.
– ORIGIN 1930s: abbreviation of PERCOLATE.

Perkin, Sir William Henry (1838–1907), English chemist and pioneer of the synthetic organic chemical industry. He prepared and manufactured the first synthetic dyestuff, mauve, from aniline.

perky ▶**adjective** (**perkier**, **perkiest**) cheerful and lively: *she certainly looked less than her usual perky self.*
▪cheeky: *don't be perky, miss!*
– DERIVATIVES **perkily** adverb, **perkiness** noun.

perlé /pəːˈleɪ/ ▶**noun** [mass noun] a semi-sweet, slightly sparkling wine produced in South Africa.
– ORIGIN French, literally 'beaded', perhaps from an abbreviation of German *Perlwein*, denoting a slightly sparkling wine, from *Perle* 'pearl, bubble' + *Wein* 'wine'.

perlemoen /ˌpəːləˈmʊn/ ▶**noun** (pl. same) S. African an abalone.
– ORIGIN Afrikaans, from obsolete *perlemoer* 'mother of pearl' (referring to the pearlized layer inside the shell).

Perlis /ˈpəːlɪs/ the smallest state of Malaysia and the most northerly of those on the Malay Peninsula; capital, Kangar.

perlite /ˈpəːlʌɪt/ ▶**noun** [mass noun] a form of obsidian consisting of glassy globules, used as insulation or in plant growth media.
– ORIGIN mid 19th cent.: from French, from *perle* 'pearl'.

perlocution ▶**noun** Philosophy & Linguistics an act of speaking or writing which has an action as its aim but which in itself does not effect or constitute the action, for example persuading or convincing. Compare with ILLOCUTION.
– DERIVATIVES **perlocutionary** adjective.
– ORIGIN 1950s: from modern Latin *perlocutio(n-)*, from *per-* 'throughout' + *locutio(n-)* 'speaking'.

Perm /pəːm/ an industrial city in Russia, in the western foothills of the Ural Mountains; pop. 1,094,000 (1990). Former name (1940–57) MOLOTOV.

perm¹ ▶**noun** (also **permanent wave**) a method of setting the hair in waves or curls and then treating it with chemicals so that the style lasts for several months.
▶**verb** [with obj.] (often **be permed**) treat (the hair) in such a way: *her hair was permed and then set.*
– ORIGIN 1920s: abbreviation of PERMANENT.

perm² Brit. informal ▶**noun** a permutation, especially a selection of a specified number of matches in a football pool: *a full perm of 8 from 11.*
▶**verb** [with obj.] make a selection of (so many) from a larger number: *one of the teams was to perm any 11 from 20.*
– ORIGIN 1950s: abbreviation of PERMUTATION.

permaculture ▶**noun** [mass noun] the development of agricultural ecosystems intended to be sustainable and self-sufficient.
– ORIGIN 1970s: blend of PERMANENT and AGRICULTURE.

permafrost ▶**noun** [mass noun] a thick subsurface layer of soil that remains below freezing point throughout the year, occurring chiefly in polar regions.
– ORIGIN 1940s: from PERMANENT + FROST.

permalloy /ˈpəːmælɔɪ/ ▶**noun** [mass noun] an alloy of nickel and iron that is easily magnetized and demagnetized, used in electrical equipment.
– ORIGIN 1920s: from PERMEABLE + ALLOY.

permanence ▶**noun** [mass noun] the state or quality of lasting or remaining unchanged indefinitely: *the clarity and permanence of the dyes.*
– DERIVATIVES **permanency** noun.
– ORIGIN late Middle English: from medieval Latin *permanentia* (perhaps via French), from *permanent-* 'remaining to the end', from the verb *permanere*.

permanent ▶**adjective** lasting or intended to last or remain unchanged indefinitely: *a permanent ban on the dumping of radioactive waste at sea | damage was not thought to be permanent | some temporary workers did not want a permanent job.*
▪lasting or continuing without interruption: *he's in a permanent state of rage.*
▶**noun** N. Amer. a perm for the hair.
– DERIVATIVES **permanentize** (also **-ise**) verb (rare), **permanently** adverb.
– ORIGIN late Middle English: from Latin *permanent-* 'remaining to the end' (perhaps via Old French), from *per-* 'through' + *manere* 'remain'.

Permanent Force ▶**noun** the standing army of South Africa.

permanent hardness ▶**noun** [mass noun] the presence in water of mineral salts (chiefly calcium sulphate) that are not removed by boiling.

permanent magnet ▶**noun** a magnet that retains its magnetic properties in the absence of an inducing field or current.

permanent revolution ▶**noun** [mass noun] the state or condition, envisaged by Leon Trotsky, of a country's continuing revolutionary progress being dependent on a continuing process of revolution in other countries.

permanent set ▶**noun** an irreversible deformation that remains in a structure or material after it has been subjected to stress.

permanent tooth ▶**noun** a tooth in a mammal that replaces a temporary milk tooth and lasts for most of the mammal's life.

Permanent Undersecretary (also **Permanent Secretary**) ▶**noun** (in the UK) a senior civil servant who is a permanent adviser to a Secretary of State.

permanent wave ▶**noun** see PERM¹.

permanent way ▶**noun** [mass noun] Brit. the finished roadbed of a railway together with the track and other permanent equipment.

permanganate /pəˈmaŋgənət, -eɪt/ ▶**noun** Chemistry a salt containing the anion MnO_4^-, typically deep purplish-red and with strong oxidizing properties.

permeability ▶**noun** [mass noun] **1** the state or quality of a material or membrane that causes it to allow liquids or gases to pass through it.
2 Physics a quantity measuring the influence of a substance on the magnetic flux in the region it occupies.

permeabilize /ˈpəːmɪəbɪˌlʌɪz/ (also **-ise**) ▶**verb** [with obj.] [often as adj. **permeabilized**] technical make permeable.
– DERIVATIVES **permeabilization** noun.

permeable ▶**adjective** (of a material or membrane) allowing liquids or gases to pass through it: *a frog's skin is permeable to water.*
– ORIGIN late Middle English: from Latin *permeabilis*, from *permeare* 'pass through' (see PERMEATE).

permeance /ˈpəːmɪəns/ ▶**noun** Physics the property of allowing the passage of lines of magnetic flux.

permeate ▶**verb** [with obj.] spread throughout (something); pervade: *the aroma of soup permeated the air | [no obj.] his personality has begun to permeate through the whole organization.*
– DERIVATIVES **permeation** noun.
– ORIGIN mid 17th cent.: from Latin *permeat-* 'passed through', from the verb *permeare*, from *per-* 'through' + *meare* 'pass, go'.

permeator ▶**noun** a container divided into two by a semipermeable membrane, used in the large-scale removal of solutes from a liquid by reverse osmosis.

permethrin /pəˈmiːθrɪn/ ▶**noun** [mass noun] a synthetic insecticide of the pyrethroid class, used chiefly against disease-carrying insects.
– ORIGIN 1970s: from sense 2 of PER- + *(res)methrin*, denoting a synthetic pyrethroid.

Permian /ˈpəːmɪən/ ▶**adjective** Geology of, relating to, or denoting the last period of the Palaeozoic era, between the Carboniferous and Triassic periods. See also PERMO-TRIASSIC.
▪[as noun **the Permian**] the Permian period or the system of rocks deposited during it.

The Permian lasted from about 290 to 245 million years ago. The climate was hot and dry in many parts of the world during this period, which saw the extinction of many marine animals, including trilobites, and the proliferation of reptiles.

– ORIGIN late 16th cent.: from the name of the Russian province PERM, from the extensive development of such strata there.

per mille /pəː ˈmɪleɪ, ˈmɪli/ (also **per mil** /mɪl/) ▶**noun** one part in every thousand: *foreign holidays account for 30 per mille of the cost of living.*
– ORIGIN late 17th cent.: Latin.

permineralized ▶**adjective** Geology (of organic material) fossilized through the precipitation of dissolved minerals which have collected in the interstices of hard tissue.
– DERIVATIVES **permineralization** noun.

permissible ▶**adjective** permitted; allowed: *it is permissible to edit and rephrase the statement.*
– DERIVATIVES **permissibility** noun, **permissibly** adverb.
– ORIGIN late Middle English: from medieval Latin *permissibilis*, from *permiss-* 'allowed', from the verb *permittere* (see PERMIT¹).

permission ▶**noun** [mass noun] consent; authorization: *they had entered the country without permission | [with infinitive] he had received permission to go to Brussels.*
▪[count noun] an official document giving authorization: *permissions to reproduce copyright material.*
– ORIGIN late Middle English: from Latin *permissio(n-)*, from the verb *permittere* 'allow' (see PERMIT¹).

permissive ▶**adjective 1** allowing or characterized by great or excessive freedom of behaviour: *I was not a permissive parent | the permissive society of the 60s and 70s.*
2 Law allowed but not obligatory; optional: *the Hague Convention was permissive, not mandatory.*
▪denoting a path available for public use by the landowner's consent, not as a legal right of way.
3 Biology allowing a biological or biochemical process to occur: *the mutants grow well at the permissive temperature.*
▪allowing the infection and replication of viruses.
– DERIVATIVES **permissively** adverb, **permissiveness** noun.
– ORIGIN late 15th cent. (in the sense 'tolerated, allowed'): from Old French, or from medieval Latin *permissivus*, from *permiss-* 'allowed', from the verb *permittere* (see PERMIT¹).

permit¹ ▶**verb** /pəˈmɪt/ (**permitted**, **permitting**) [with obj. and infinitive] give authorization or consent to (someone) to do something: *the law permits councils to monitor any factory emitting smoke | [with two objs] he would not permit anybody access to the library.*
▪[with obj.] authorize or give permission for (something): *the country is not ready to permit any rice imports.* ▪[with obj.] (of a thing, circumstance, or condition) provide an opportunity or scope for (something) to take place; make possible: *the car park was too rutted and stony to permit ball games | [no obj.] when weather permits, lunches are served outside.* ▪[no obj.] (**permit of**) formal allow for; admit of: *the camp permits of no really successful defence.*
▶**noun** /ˈpəːmɪt/ [often with modifier] an official document giving someone authorization to do something: *he is only in Britain on a work permit.*
▪[mass noun] official or formal permission to do something: *parking on University grounds is by permit only.*
– PHRASES **permit me** dated used for politeness before making a suggestion or expressing an intention: *permit me to correct you.* —— **permitting** if the specified thing does not prevent one from doing something: *weather permitting, guests can dine outside on the veranda.*
– DERIVATIVES **permittee** noun, **permitter** noun.
– ORIGIN late Middle English (originally in the sense 'commit, hand over'): from Latin *permittere*, from *per-* 'through' + *mittere* 'send, let go'.

permit² /ˈpəːmɪt/ ▶**noun** a deep-bodied fish of the jack family, found in warm waters of the western Atlantic and Caribbean and caught for food and sport.
• *Trachinotus falcatus*, family Carangidae.
– ORIGIN alteration of Spanish *palometa* 'little dove'.

permittivity /ˌpəːmɪˈtɪvɪti/ ▶**noun** Physics the ability

of a substance to store electrical energy in an electric field.

Permo–Carboniferous /ˈpəːməʊ/ ▶ **adjective** Geology of, relating to, or linking the Permian and Carboniferous periods or rock systems together.

Permo–Triassic ▶ **adjective** Geology of, relating to, or occurring at the boundary of the Permian and Triassic periods, about 245 million years ago. Mass extinctions occurred at this time, marking the end of the Palaeozoic era.
■of or relating to the Permian and Triassic periods or rock systems considered as a unit. ■ [as noun **the Permo–Triassic** or **Permo–Trias**] the Permian and Triassic periods together or the system of rocks deposited during them.

permutate /ˈpəːmjʊteɪt/ ▶ **verb** [with obj.] change the order or arrangement of: *statistics may be sorted and permutated according to requirements.*
– ORIGIN late 19th cent.: regarded as a back-formation from **PERMUTATION**.

permutation ▶ **noun** a way, especially one of several possible variations, in which a set or number of things can be ordered or arranged: *his thoughts raced ahead to fifty different permutations of what he must do.*
■[mass noun] Mathematics the action of changing the arrangement, especially the linear order, of a set of items. ■ Brit. a selection of a specified number of matches in a football pool.
– DERIVATIVES **permutational** adjective.
– ORIGIN late Middle English (in the sense 'exchange, barter'): via Old French from Latin *permutatio(n-)*, from the verb *permutare* 'change completely' (see **PERMUTE**).

permute ▶ **verb** [with obj.] technical submit to a process of alteration, rearrangement, or permutation: *we wish to permute the order of the bytes.*
– ORIGIN late Middle English (also in the sense 'interchange'): from Latin *permutare* 'change completely', from *per-* 'through, completely' + *mutare* 'to change'.

Pernambuco /ˌpəːnamˈbuːkuː/ a state of eastern Brazil, on the Atlantic coast; capital, Recife.
■former name for **RECIFE**.

pernambuco (also **pernambuco wood**) ▶ **noun** [mass noun] the hard reddish timber of a Brazilian tree, used for making violin bows and as a source of red dye.
• The tree is *Caesalpinia echinata*, family Leguminosae.
– ORIGIN late 16th cent.: from the name of the Brazilian state **PERNAMBUCO**.

pernicious /pəˈnɪʃəs/ ▶ **adjective** having a harmful effect, especially in a gradual or subtle way: *the pernicious influences of the mass media.*
– DERIVATIVES **perniciously** adverb, **perniciousness** noun.
– ORIGIN late Middle English: from Latin *perniciosus* 'destructive', from *pernicies* 'ruin', based on *nex, nec-* 'death'.

pernicious anaemia ▶ **noun** [mass noun] a deficiency in the production of red blood cells through a lack of vitamin B_{12}.

pernickety ▶ **adjective** informal placing too much emphasis on trivial or minor details; fussy: *she's very pernickety about her food.*
■requiring a particularly precise or careful approach: *the system does not encourage additional enquiries on detailed and pernickety points.*
– ORIGIN early 19th cent. (originally Scots): of unknown origin.

pernoctate /ˈpəːnɒkteɪt, pəˈnɒkteɪt/ ▶ **verb** [no obj.] formal pass the night somewhere.
– DERIVATIVES **pernoctation** noun.
– ORIGIN early 17th cent.: from Latin *pernoctat-* 'spent the night', from the verb *pernoctare*, from *per-* 'through' + *nox, noct-* 'night'.

Pernod /ˈpəːnəʊ/ ▶ **noun** [mass noun] trademark an aniseed-flavoured aperitif.
– ORIGIN named after the manufacturing firm *Pernod Fils*.

peroba /pəˈrəʊbə/ ▶ **noun** [mass noun] the timber of certain Brazilian hardwood trees:
• (**white peroba**) timber used for furniture and storage vats, from the tree *Paratecoma peroba* (family Bignoniaceae).
• (**red peroba**) similar but less versatile timber from trees of the genus *Aspidosperma* (family Apocynaceae).
– ORIGIN early 19th cent.: via Portuguese from Tupi *iperoba*, literally 'bitter bark'.

perogi ▶ **noun** variant spelling of **PIROGI**.

Perón[1] /pɛˈrɒn/, Eva (1919–52), Argentinian politician, second wife of Juan Perón; full name *María Eva Duarte de Perón*; known as **Evita**. A former actress, after her marriage in 1945 she became de facto Minister of Health and of Labour until her death from cancer; her social reforms earned her great popularity with the poor.

Perón[2] /pɛˈrɒn/, Juan Domingo (1895–1974), Argentinian soldier and statesman, President 1946–55 and 1973–4. He participated in the 1943 military coup, and was later elected President, winning popular support with his social reforms. The faltering economy and conflict with the Church led to his removal and exile.
– DERIVATIVES **Peronism** /ˈpɛrəˌnɪz(ə)m/ noun, **Peronist** adjective & noun.

peroneal /ˌpɛrəˈniːəl/ ▶ **adjective** Anatomy relating to or situated in the outer side of the calf of the leg.
– ORIGIN mid 19th cent.: from modern Latin *peronaeus* 'peroneal muscle' (based on Greek *peronē* 'pin, fibula') + **-AL**.

perorate /ˈpɛrəreɪt/ ▶ **verb** [no obj.] formal speak at length: *he reportedly would perorate against his colleague.*
■archaic sum up and conclude a speech: *the following innocent conclusion with which she perorates.*
– ORIGIN early 17th cent.: from Latin *perorat-* 'spoken at length', from the verb *perorare*, from *per-* 'through' + *orare* 'speak'.

peroration ▶ **noun** the concluding part of a speech, typically intended to inspire enthusiasm in the audience.
– ORIGIN late Middle English: from Latin *peroratio(n-)*, from *perorare* 'speak at length' (see **PERORATE**).

perovskite /pəˈrɒfskʌɪt/ ▶ **noun** [mass noun] a yellow, brown, or black mineral consisting largely of calcium titanate.
■[count noun] any of a group of related minerals and ceramics having the same crystal structure as this.
– ORIGIN mid 19th cent.: from the name of L. A. *Perovsky* (1792–1856), Russian mineralogist, + **-ITE**[1].

peroxidase /pəˈrɒksɪdeɪz/ ▶ **noun** Biochemistry an enzyme that catalyses the oxidation of a particular substrate by hydrogen peroxide.

peroxide ▶ **noun** Chemistry a compound containing two oxygen atoms bonded together in its molecule or as the anion O_2^{2-}.
■[mass noun] hydrogen peroxide, especially as used as a bleach for the hair: [as modifier] *a peroxide blonde.*
▶ **verb** [with obj.] bleach (hair) with peroxide.
– ORIGIN early 19th cent.: from sense 2 of **PER-** + **OXIDE**.

peroxisome /pəˈrɒksɪsəʊm/ ▶ **noun** Biology a small organelle present in the cytoplasm of many cells, which contains the reducing enzyme catalase and usually some oxidases.
– DERIVATIVES **peroxisomal** adjective.
– ORIGIN 1960s: from **PEROXIDE** + **-SOME**[3].

perp ▶ **noun** N. Amer. informal the perpetrator of a crime.
– ORIGIN 1980s: abbreviation.

perpend /ˈpəːpɛnd/ ▶ **noun** a vertical layer of mortar between two bricks.

perpendicular /ˌpəːp(ə)nˈdɪkjʊlə/ ▶ **adjective** **1** at an angle of 90° to a given line, plane, or surface: *dormers and gables that extend perpendicular to the main roofline.*
■at an angle of 90° to the ground; vertical: *the perpendicular cliff.* ■ (of something with a slope) so steep as to be almost vertical: *guest houses seem to cling by blind faith to the perpendicular hillside.*
2 (**Perpendicular**) denoting the latest stage of English Gothic church architecture, prevalent from the late 14th to mid 16th centuries and characterized by broad arches, elaborate fan vaulting, and large windows with vertical tracery: *the handsome Perpendicular church of St Andrew.*
▶ **noun** a straight line at an angle of 90° to a given line, plane, or surface: *at each division draw a perpendicular representing the surface line.*
■[mass noun] (usu. **the perpendicular**) perpendicular position or direction: *the wall declines from the perpendicular a little inward.*
– DERIVATIVES **perpendicularity** noun, **perpendicularly** adverb.
– ORIGIN late Middle English (as an adverb meaning 'at right angles'): via Old French from Latin *perpendicularis*, from *perpendiculum* 'plumb line', from *per-* 'through' + *pendere* 'to hang'.

perpetrate /ˈpəːpɪtreɪt/ ▶ **verb** [with obj.] carry out or commit (a harmful, illegal, or immoral action): *a crime has been perpetrated against a sovereign state.*
– DERIVATIVES **perpetration** noun, **perpetrator** noun.
– ORIGIN mid 16th cent.: from Latin *perpetrat-* 'performed', from the verb *perpetrare*, from *per-* 'to completion' + *patrare* 'bring about'. In Latin the act perpetrated might be good or bad; in English the verb was first used in the statutes referring to crime, hence the negative association.

perpetual /pəˈpɛtʃʊəl, -tjʊəl/ ▶ **adjective** **1** never ending or changing: *deep caves in perpetual darkness.*
■[attrib.] denoting or having a position, job, or trophy held for life rather than a limited period: *a perpetual secretary of the society.* ■ (of an investment) having no fixed maturity date; irredeemable: *a perpetual bond.*
2 occurring repeatedly; so frequent as to seem endless and uninterrupted: *their perpetual money worries.*
■(of a plant) blooming or fruiting several times in one season: *he grows perpetual flowering carnations.*
– DERIVATIVES **perpetually** adverb.
– ORIGIN Middle English: from Old French *perpetuel*, from Latin *perpetualis*, from *perpetuus* 'continuing throughout', from *perpes, perpet-* 'continuous'.

perpetual calendar ▶ **noun** a calendar in which the day, the month, and the date are adjusted independently to show any combination of the three.

perpetual check ▶ **noun** [mass noun] Chess the situation of play when a draw is obtained by repeated checking of the king.

perpetual motion ▶ **noun** [mass noun] a state in which movement or action is or appears to be continuous and unceasing.
■the motion of a hypothetical machine which, once activated, would run forever unless subject to an external force or to wear.

perpetual spinach ▶ **noun** another term for **SPINACH BEET**.

perpetuate /pəˈpɛtʃʊeɪt, -tjʊ-/ ▶ **verb** [with obj.] make (something, typically an undesirable situation or an unfounded belief) continue indefinitely: *the confusion was perpetuated through inadvertence.*
– DERIVATIVES **perpetuance** noun, **perpetuation** noun, **perpetuator** noun.
– ORIGIN early 16th cent.: from Latin *perpetuat-* 'made permanent', from the verb *perpetuare*, from *perpetuus* 'continuing throughout' (see **PERPETUAL**).

perpetuity ▶ **noun** (pl. **-ies**) **1** a thing that lasts forever or for an indefinite period, in particular:
■a bond or other security with no fixed maturity date.
■ Law a restriction making an estate inalienable perpetually or for a period beyond certain limits fixed by law. ■ Law an estate so restricted.
2 [mass noun] the state or quality of lasting forever: *he did not believe in the perpetuity of military rule.*
– PHRASES **in** (or **for**) **perpetuity** forever: *all the Bonapartes were banished from France in perpetuity.*
– ORIGIN late Middle English: from Old French *perpetuite*, from Latin *perpetuitas*, from *perpetuus* 'continuing throughout' (see **PERPETUAL**).

perpetuum mobile /pəːˌpɛtjʊəm ˈməʊbɪleɪ, ˈməʊbɪli/ ▶ **noun** **1** another term for **PERPETUAL MOTION**.
2 Music another term for **MOTO PERPETUO**.
– ORIGIN Latin, literally 'continuously moving (thing)', on the pattern of *primum mobile*.

Perpignan /ˈpəːpɪnjɒn, French pɛʀpiɲɑ̃/ a city in southern France, in the NE foothills of the Pyrenees, close to the border with Spain; pop. 108,050 (1990). A former fortress town, it was the capital of the old province of Roussillon.

perplex ▶ **verb** [with obj.] (often **be perplexed**) (of something complicated or unaccountable) cause (someone) to feel completely baffled: *she was perplexed by her husband's moodiness* | [as adj. **perplexing**] *a perplexing problem.*
■dated complicate or confuse (a matter): *they were perplexing a subject plain in itself.*
– DERIVATIVES **perplexedly** adverb, **perplexingly** adverb.
– ORIGIN late 15th cent. (as the adjective *perplexed*): from the obsolete adjective *perplex* 'bewildered', from Latin *perplexus* 'entangled', based on *plexus* 'interwoven', from the verb *plectere*.

perplexity ▶ **noun** (pl. **-ies**) [mass noun] **1** inability to deal with or understand something complicated or unaccountable: *she paused in perplexity.*
■[count noun] (usu. **perplexities**) a complicated or

baffling situation or thing: *the perplexities of international relations.*
2 archaic an entangled state: *the dense perplexity of dwarf palm, garlanded creepers, glossy undergrowth.*
– ORIGIN Middle English: from Old French *perplexite* or late Latin *perplexitas*, from Latin *perplexus* 'entangled, confused' (see **PERPLEX**).

per pro. /pəː ˈprəʊ/ ▶ **abbreviation for** per procurationem (used when signing a letter on behalf of someone else; now usually abbreviated to **pp**). See usage at **PP**.
– ORIGIN Latin.

perquisite /ˈpəːkwɪzɪt/ ▶ **noun** formal another term for **PERK**².
■ a thing regarded as a special right or privilege enjoyed as a result of one's position: *the wife of a president has all the perquisites of stardom.* ■ historical a thing which has served its primary use and to which a subordinate or employee has a customary right.
– ORIGIN late Middle English: from medieval Latin *perquisitum* 'acquisition', from Latin *perquirere* 'search diligently for', from *per-* 'thoroughly' + *quaerere* 'seek'.

Perrault /pɛˈrəʊ, French pɛʀo/, Charles (1628–1703), French writer. He is remembered for his *Mother Goose Tales* (1697), containing such fairy tales as 'Sleeping Beauty', 'Little Red Riding Hood', 'Puss in Boots', and 'Cinderella'.

Perrin /pɛˈrã, French pɛʀɛ̃/, Jean Baptiste (1870–1942), French physical chemist. He provided the definitive proof of the existence of atoms, proved that cathode rays are negatively charged, and investigated Brownian motion. Nobel Prize for Physics (1926).

perron /ˈpɛrən/ ▶ **noun** Architecture an exterior set of steps and a platform at the main entrance to a large building such as a church or mansion.
– ORIGIN late Middle English: from Old French, literally 'large stone', from Latin *petra* 'stone'.

Perry, Fred (1909–95), British-born American tennis player; full name *Frederick John Perry*. His record of winning three consecutive singles titles at Wimbledon (1934–6) was unequalled until 1978.

perry ▶ **noun** (pl. **-ies**) [mass noun] an alcoholic drink made from the fermented juice of pears.
– ORIGIN Middle English: from Old French *pere*, from an alteration of Latin *pirum* 'pear'.

per se /pəː ˈseɪ/ ▶ **adverb** by or in itself or themselves; intrinsically: *it is not these facts per se that are important.*
– ORIGIN Latin.

persecute ▶ **verb** [with obj.] (often **be persecuted**) subject (someone) to hostility and ill-treatment, especially because of their race or political or religious beliefs: *Jews who had been persecuted by the Nazi regime.*
■ harass or annoy (someone) persistently: *Hilda was persecuted by some of the other girls.*
– DERIVATIVES **persecution** noun, **persecutor** noun, **persecutory** adjective.
– ORIGIN late Middle English: from Old French *persecuter*, from Latin *persecut-* 'followed with hostility', from the verb *persequi*, from *per-* 'through, utterly' *sequi* 'follow, pursue'.

persecution complex ▶ **noun** an irrational and obsessive feeling or fear that one is the object of collective hostility or ill-treatment on the part of others.

Perseids /ˈpəːsɪˌɪdz/ Astronomy an annual meteor shower with a radiant in the constellation Perseus, reaching a peak about 12 August.

Persephone /pəˈsɛfəni/ Greek Mythology a goddess, the daughter of Zeus and Demeter. Roman name **PROSERPINA**.

> She was carried off by Hades and made queen of the underworld. Demeter, vainly seeking her, refused to let the earth produce its fruits until her daughter was restored to her, but because Persephone had eaten some pomegranate seeds in the other world, she was obliged to spend part of every year there. Her story symbolizes the return of spring and the life and growth of corn.

Persepolis /pəˈsɛpəlɪs/ a city in ancient Persia, situated to the north-east of Shiraz. It was founded in the late 6th century BC by Darius I as the ceremonial capital of Persia under the Achaemenid dynasty. The city's impressive ruins include functional and ceremonial buildings and cuneiform inscriptions in Old Persian, Elamite, and Akkadian.

Perseus /ˈpəːsɪəs, -sjuːs/ **1** Greek Mythology the son of Zeus and Danae, a hero celebrated for many achievements. He cut off the head of the gorgon Medusa and gave it to Athene; he also rescued and married Andromeda, and became king of Tiryns in Greece.
2 Astronomy a large northern constellation which includes a dense part of the Milky Way. It contains several star clusters and the variable star Algol.
■ [as genitive **Persei** /-sɪaɪ/] used with preceding letter or numeral to designate a star in this constellation: *the star Delta Persei.*

perseverance ▶ **noun** [mass noun] steadfastness in doing something despite difficulty or delay in achieving success: *medicine is a field which requires dedication and perseverance.*
– ORIGIN Middle English: from Old French, from Latin *perseverantia*, from *perseverant-* 'abiding by strictly', from the verb *perseverare* (see **PERSEVERE**).

perseverate /pəˈsɛvəreɪt/ ▶ **verb** [no obj.] Psychology repeat or prolong an action, thought, or utterance after the stimulus that prompted it has ceased.
– DERIVATIVES **perseveration** noun.
– ORIGIN early 20th cent.: from Latin *perseverat-* 'strictly abided by', from the verb *perseverare* (see **PERSEVERE**).

persevere ▶ **verb** [no obj.] continue in a course of action even in the face of difficulty or with little or no indication of success: *his family **persevered with** his treatment.*
– DERIVATIVES **perseverance** noun, **perseveringly** adverb.
– ORIGIN late Middle English: from Old French *perseverer*, from Latin *perseverare* 'abide by strictly', from *perseverus* 'very strict', from *per-* 'thoroughly' + *severus* 'severe'.

Persia /ˈpəːʃə, ˈpəːʒə/ a former country of SW Asia, now called Iran.

> Under Cyrus the Great in the 6th century BC Persia became the centre of a powerful empire which included all of western Asia, Egypt, and parts of eastern Europe; it was eventually overthrown by Alexander the Great in 330 BC. The country was conquered by the Muslim Arabs between AD 633 and 651. It was renamed Iran in 1935.

Persian ▶ **noun 1** a native or national of ancient or modern Persia (or Iran), or a person of Persian descent.
■ (also **Persian cat**) a long-haired domestic cat of a breed originating in Persia, having a broad round head, stocky body, and short thick legs. ■ a sheep of a breed common in South Africa.
2 [mass noun] the language of modern Iran, an Indo-European language written in Arabic script. Also called **FARSI**.
■ an earlier form of this language spoken in ancient or medieval Persia.
▶ **adjective** of or relating to ancient Persia or modern Iran or its people or language.

> Persian (or Farsi) is spoken by over 30 million people in Iran, by about 5 million in Afghanistan (as Dari), and by another 2.2 million in Tajikistan (as Tajik). Old Persian, written in cuneiform and attested from the 6th century BC, was the language of the Persian empire, which once spread from the Mediterranean to India. In the 2nd century BC the Persians created their own alphabet (Pahlavi), which was used until the Islamic conquest in the 7th century.

– ORIGIN Middle English: from Old French *persien*, from Latin *Persia*, via Greek from Old Persian *pārsa* 'Persia' (modern Persian *pārs*, Arabic *fārs*).

Persian blue ▶ **noun** [mass noun] a shade of bright pale blue.

Persian carpet (also **Persian rug**) ▶ **noun** a carpet or rug woven in Iran in a traditional design incorporating stylized symbolic imagery, or made elsewhere in such a style.

Persian cat ▶ **noun** see **PERSIAN** (sense 1).

Persian Gulf an arm of the Arabian Sea, to which it is connected by the Strait of Hormuz and the Gulf of Oman. It extends north-westwards between the Arabian peninsula and the coast of SW Iran. Also called **ARABIAN GULF**; informally **THE GULF**.

Persian lamb ▶ **noun** [mass noun] a silky, tightly curled fur made from or resembling the fleece of a young karakul, used to make clothing.

Persian silk ▶ **noun** [mass noun] a thin soft silk, chiefly used as a lining material.

Persian Wars the wars fought between Greece and Persia in the 5th century BC, in which the Persians sought to extend their territory over the Greek world.

> The wars began in 490 BC when Darius I sent an expedition to punish the Greeks for having supported the Ionian cities in their unsuccessful revolt against Persian rule; the Persians were defeated by a small force of Athenians at Marathon. Ten years later Darius' son Xerxes I attempted an invasion. He devastated Attica, but Persian forces were defeated on land at Plataea and in a sea battle at Salamis (480 BC), and retreated. Intermittent war continued in various areas until peace was signed in 449 BC.

persiflage /ˈpəːsɪflɑːʒ/ ▶ **noun** [mass noun] formal light and slightly contemptuous mockery or banter.
– ORIGIN mid 18th cent.: from French *persifler* 'to banter', based on *siffler* 'to whistle'.

persimmon /pəˈsɪmən/ ▶ **noun 1** an edible fruit that resembles a large tomato and has very sweet flesh.
2 the tree which yields this fruit, related to ebony.
● Genus *Diospyros*, family Ebenaceae: the evergreen American *D. virginiana*, with dark red fruit, and the **Japanese persimmon** (*D. kaki*), cultivated for its orange fruit.
– ORIGIN early 17th cent.: alteration of Algonquian *pessemmins*.

persist ▶ **verb** [no obj.] continue firmly or obstinately in an opinion or a course of action in spite of difficulty, opposition, or failure: *the minority of drivers who **persist in** drinking | we are **persisting with** policies that will create jobs for the future.*
■ continue to exist; be prolonged: *if the symptoms persist for more than a few days, then contact your doctor.*
– ORIGIN mid 16th cent.: from Latin *persistere*, from *per-* 'through, steadfastly' + *sistere* 'to stand'.

persistence ▶ **noun** [mass noun] firm or obstinate continuance in a course of action in spite of difficulty or opposition: *Cardiff's persistence was rewarded with a try.*
■ the continued or prolonged existence of something: *the persistence of huge environmental problems.*
– DERIVATIVES **persistency** noun.
– ORIGIN mid 16th cent.: from French *persistance*, from the verb *persister*; influenced in spelling by Latin *persistent-* 'continuing steadfastly'.

persistent ▶ **adjective 1** continuing firmly or obstinately in a course of action in spite of difficulty or opposition: *one of the government's most persistent critics.*
■ [attrib.] characterized by a specified habitual behaviour pattern, especially a dishonest or undesirable one: *an attempt to stop persistent drink-drivers.*
2 continuing to exist or endure over a prolonged period: *persistent rain will affect many areas.*
■ occurring repeatedly over a prolonged period: *persistent reports of human rights abuses by the military.* ■ (of a chemical or radioactivity) remaining within the environment for a long time after its introduction: *PCBs are persistent environmental contaminants.*
3 Botany & Zoology (of a part of an animal or plant, such as a horn, leaf, etc.) remaining attached instead of falling off in the normal manner.
– DERIVATIVES **persistently** adverb.

persistent vegetative state ▶ **noun** a condition in which a medical patient is completely unresponsive to psychological and physical stimuli and displays no sign of higher brain function, being kept alive only by medical intervention.

persnickety ▶ **adjective** North American term for **PERNICKETY**.

person ▶ **noun** (pl. **people** or **persons**) **1** a human being regarded as an individual: *the porter was the last person to see her prior to her disappearance | she is a person of astonishing energy.*
■ used in legal or formal contexts to refer to an unspecified individual: *the entrance fee is £2.00 per person.* ■ S. African informal used by speakers to refer to themselves or to people in general: *how many times must a person tell you—I don't smoke.* ■ [in sing.] [with modifier] an individual characterized by a preference or liking for a specified thing: *she's not a cat person.* ■ an individual's body: *I would have publicity photographs **on my person** at all times.* ■ dated (especially in legal contexts) used euphemistically to refer to a person's genitals, especially those of a man. ■ a character in a play or story: *his previous roles in the person of a fallible cop.*
2 Grammar a category used in the classification of pronouns, possessive determiners, and verb forms, according to whether they indicate the speaker (**first person**), the addressee (**second person**), or a third party (**third person**).
3 Christian Theology each of the three modes of being of God, namely the Father, the Son, or the Holy Ghost, who together constitute the Trinity.

– PHRASES **be one's own person** do or be what one wishes or in accordance with one's own character rather than as influenced by others. **in one's own person** archaic oneself; in person (used for emphasis). **in person** with the personal presence or action of the individual specified: *he had to pick up his welfare cheque in person.* **in the person of** in the physical form of: *trouble arrived in the person of a short, moustached Berliner.*

– ORIGIN Middle English: from Old French *persone*, from Latin *persona* 'actor's mask, character in a play', later 'human being'.

USAGE The words **people** and **persons** can both be used as the plural of **person** but they are not used in exactly the same way. **People** is by far the commoner of the two words and is used in most ordinary contexts: *a group of* ***people****; there were only about ten* ***people****; several thousand* ***people*** *have been rehoused.* **Persons**, on the other hand, tends now to be restricted to official or formal contexts, as in *this vehicle is authorized to carry twenty* ***persons****; no* ***persons*** *admitted without a pass.*

-person ▶ **combining form** used as a neutral alternative to *-man* in nouns denoting professional status, a position of authority, etc.: *chairperson* | *salesperson* | *sportsperson.*

persona /pə'səʊnə, pəː-/ ▶ **noun** (pl. **personas** or **personae** /-niː/) the aspect of someone's character that is presented to or perceived by others: *her public persona.* In psychology, often contrasted with **ANIMA**.

■ a role or character adopted by an author or an actor.

– ORIGIN early 20th cent.: Latin, literally 'mask, character played by an actor'.

personable ▶ **adjective** (of a person) having a pleasant appearance and manner.

– DERIVATIVES **personableness** noun, **personably** adverb.

personage ▶ **noun** a person (often used to express their significance, importance, or elevated status): *it was no less a personage than the bishop.*

■ a character in a play or other work.

– ORIGIN late Middle English: from Old French, reinforced by medieval Latin *personagium* 'effigy'. In early use the word was qualified by words such as *honourable, eminent*, but since the 19th cent. the notion 'significant, notable' has been implied in the word itself.

persona grata /pəˌsəʊnə 'grɑːtə, pəː-/ ▶ **noun** (pl. **personae gratae** /-niː, -tiː/) a person, especially a diplomat, acceptable to certain others: *in my last term I became* persona grata *to a group of Newnham College girls.*

– ORIGIN Latin, from *persona* (see **PERSONA**) + *grata*, feminine of *gratus* 'pleasing'.

personal ▶ **adjective** **1** [attrib.] of, affecting, or belonging to a particular person rather than anyone else: *her personal fortune was recently estimated at £37 million.*

■ done or made by a particular person; involving the actual presence or action of a particular individual: *the President and his wife made personal appearances for the re-election of the state governor.* ■ done, intended, or made for a particular person: *a personal loan.*

2 of or concerning one's private life, relationships, and emotions rather than matters connected with one's public or professional career: *the book describes his sporting career and gives little information about his personal life.*

■ referring to an individual's character, appearance, or private life, especially in a hostile or critical way: *he had the cheek to make personal remarks* | *you look like a drowned rat—nothing personal.*

3 [attrib.] of or relating to a person's body: *personal hygiene.*

4 [attrib.] Grammar of or denoting one of the three persons. See **PERSON** (sense 2).

5 existing as a self-aware entity, not as an abstraction or an impersonal force: *Jews, Christians, and Muslims believe in a personal God.*

▶ **noun** (usu. **personals**) chiefly N. Amer. an advertisement or message in the personal column of a newspaper.

– ORIGIN late Middle English: from Old French, from Latin *personalis* 'of a person', from *persona* (see **PERSON**).

personal action ▶ **noun** Law an action brought for compensation or damages for loss of a thing from the person responsible, rather than for recovery of the thing itself.

personal ad ▶ **noun** informal a private advertisement or message placed in the personal column of a newspaper.

personal assistant ▶ **noun** a secretary or administrative assistant working exclusively for one particular person.

personal column ▶ **noun** a section of a newspaper devoted to private advertisements or messages.

personal computer ▶ **noun** a microcomputer designed for use by one person at a time.

personal equity plan ▶ **noun** (in the UK) an investment scheme whereby personal investors may invest a limited sum each year in shares or unit trusts in British companies without liability for tax on dividends or capital gains (replaced in 1999 by the ISA).

personal estate ▶ **noun** Law another term for **PERSONAL PROPERTY**.

personal identification number (abbrev.: **PIN**) ▶ **noun** a number allocated to an individual and used to validate electronic transactions.

personal information manager ▶ **noun** a computer program functioning as an address book, organizer, diary, etc.

personal injury ▶ **noun** [mass noun] Law physical injury inflicted to a person's body, as opposed to damage to property or reputation.

personalism ▶ **noun** [mass noun] the quality of being personal, especially a theory or system based on subjective ideas or applications: *his sculpture investigating pure form from which all expressive personalism was eliminated.*

■ Philosophy the theory that probabilities do not have objective meaning but are expressions of a personal perspective on the occurrence of events. ■ Philosophy a system of thought which maintains the primacy of the human or divine person on the basis that reality has meaning only through the conscious mind. ■ allegiance to a person, especially a political leader, rather than to a party or ideology.

– DERIVATIVES **personalist** noun, **personalistic** adjective.

personality ▶ **noun** (pl. **-ies**) **1** the combination of characteristics or qualities that form an individual's distinctive character: *she had a sunny personality that was very engaging* | figurative *each brand of gin has its own personality* | [mass noun] *she has triumphed by sheer force of personality.*

■ [mass noun] qualities that make someone interesting or popular: *she's always had loads of personality.*

2 a famous person, especially in entertainment or sport: *an official opening by a famous personality.*

3 [mass noun] archaic the quality or fact of being a person as distinct from a thing or animal.

4 (**personalities**) archaic disparaging remarks about an individual.

– ORIGIN late Middle English (in sense 3): from Old French *personalite*, from medieval Latin *personalitas*, from Latin *personalis* 'of a person' (see **PERSONAL**). Sense 1 dates from the late 18th cent.

personality cult ▶ **noun** excessive public admiration for or devotion to a famous person, especially a political leader.

personality disorder ▶ **noun** Psychiatry a deeply ingrained and maladaptive pattern of behaviour of a specified kind, typically manifest by adolescence and causing long-term difficulties in personal relationships or in functioning in society.

personality inventory ▶ **noun** a type of questionnaire designed to reveal the respondent's personality traits.

personality type ▶ **noun** Psychology a collection of personality traits which are thought to occur together consistently, especially as determined by a certain pattern of responses to a personality inventory.

personalize (also **-ise**) ▶ **verb** [with obj.] **1** (usu. **be personalized**) design or produce (something) to meet someone's individual requirements: *the wedding invitations will be personalized to your exact requirements.*

■ make (something) identifiable as belonging to a particular person, especially by marking it with their name or initials: [as adj. **personalized**] *a personalized number plate.*

2 cause (something, especially an issue, argument, or debate) to become concerned with personalities or feelings rather than with general or abstract matters: *the mass media's tendency to personalize politics.*

3 (often **be personalized**) personify (something, especially a deity or spirit): *evil spirits personalized in Satan.*

– DERIVATIVES **personalization** noun.

personally ▶ **adverb** **1** with the personal presence or action of the individual specified; in person: *she stayed to thank O'Brien personally.*

■ used to indicate that a specified person and no other is involved in something: [as submodifier] *he never forgave his father, holding him* ***personally responsible*** *for this betrayal.* ■ used to indicate that one knows or has contact with someone in person rather than indirectly through their work, reputation, or a third party: *every pupil is known personally.*

2 from someone's personal standpoint or according to their particular nature; in a subjective rather than an objective way: *he had spoken personally and emotionally.*

■ [sentence adverb] used to emphasize that one is expressing one's personal opinion: *personally, I think he made a very sensible move.* ■ with regard to one's personal and private rather than public or professional capacity: *nothing had gone well personally or politically.*

– PHRASES **take something personally** interpret a remark or action as directed against oneself and be upset or offended by it, even if that was not the speaker's intention: *at first I took it personally when he yelled at me.*

personal organizer ▶ **noun** a loose-leaf notebook consisting of separate sections including a diary and pages for recording addresses and telephone numbers.

■ a hand-held microcomputer serving the same purpose.

personal pension ▶ **noun** a pension scheme that is independent of the contributor's employer.

personal pronoun ▶ **noun** each of the pronouns in English (*I, you, he, she, it, we, they, me, him, her, us,* and *them*) comprising a set that shows contrasts of person, gender, number, and case.

USAGE The correct use of personal pronouns is one of the most debated areas of English usage. **I**, **we**, **they**, **he**, and **she** are **subjective** personal pronouns, which means they are used as the subject of the sentence, often coming before the verb (***she*** *lives in Paris*; ***we*** *are leaving*). **Me**, **us**, **them**, **him**, and **her**, on the other hand, are **objective** personal pronouns, which means that they are used as the object of a verb or preposition (*John hates* ***me****; his father left* ***him****; I did it for* ***her***). This explains why it is not correct to say *John and* ***me*** *went to the shops*: the personal pronoun is in subject position, so it must be **I** not **me**. Using the pronoun alone makes the incorrect use obvious: ***me*** *went to the shops* is clearly not acceptable. This analysis also explains why it is not correct to say *he came with you and* ***I***: the personal pronoun is governed by a preposition (**with**) and is therefore objective, so it must be **me** not **I**. Again, a simple test for correctness is to use the pronoun alone: *he came with* ***I*** is clearly not acceptable. (See also **usage** at **BETWEEN**.)
Where a personal pronoun is used alone without the context of a verb or a preposition, however, the traditional analysis starts to break down. Traditionalists sometimes argue, for example, that *she's younger than* ***me*** and *I've not been here as long as* ***her*** are incorrect and that the correct forms are *she's younger than* ***I*** and *I've not been here as long as* ***she***. This is based on the assumption that **than** and **as** are conjunctions and so the personal pronoun is still subjective even though there is no verb (in full form it would be *she's younger than* ***I am***). Yet for most native speakers the supposed 'correct' form does not sound natural at all and is almost never used in speech. It would perhaps be more accurate to say that, in modern English, those personal pronouns listed above as being **objective** are used neutrally—i.e. they are used in all cases where the pronoun is not explicitly **subjective**. From this it follows that, despite the objections of prescriptive grammarians (whose arguments are based on Latin rather than English), it is standard accepted English to use any of the following: *Who is it? It's* ***me****!; she's taller than* ***him****; I didn't do as well as* ***her***.

personal property ▶ **noun** [mass noun] Law all of someone's property except land and those interests in land that pass to their heirs. Compare with **REAL PROPERTY**.

personal representative ▶ **noun** Law an

executor or administrator of the estate of a deceased person.
■a person who is responsible for representing someone else or an establishment, especially in a political or legal capacity.

personal service ▶ noun a commercial service that involves direct and personal communication between the company and the customer.
■(**personal services**) used to refer collectively to the commercial services such as catering and cleaning that supply the personal needs of customers.

personal shopper ▶ noun an individual who is paid to assist another to purchase goods, either by accompanying them while shopping or by shopping on their behalf.

personal space ▶ noun [mass noun] the physical space immediately surrounding someone, into which any encroachment feels threatening to or uncomfortable for them: *he was invading her personal space.*
■space designated for the use of an individual within a larger communal area such as an office. ■ time in which someone is undisturbed and free to concentrate on their own thoughts and needs.

personal stereo ▶ noun a small portable audio cassette player or compact disc player, used with lightweight headphones.

personal touch ▶ noun an element or feature contributed by someone to make something less impersonal: *customers prefer to write the messages themselves for more of a personal touch.*

personalty /ˈpəːs(ə)n(ə)lti/ ▶ noun [mass noun] Law a person's personal property. The opposite of **REALTY**.
– ORIGIN mid 16th cent. (in the legal phrase *in the personalty* 'for damages'): from Anglo-Norman French *personaltie*, from medieval Latin *personalitas* (see **PERSONALITY**).

personal watercraft ▶ noun another term for **JET SKI**.

persona non grata ▶ noun (pl. **personae non gratae**) an unacceptable or unwelcome person: *Nabokov was* persona non grata *with the regime.*
– ORIGIN Latin, from *persona* (see **PERSONA**) + *non* 'not' + *grata*, feminine of *gratus* 'pleasing'.

personate ▶ verb [with obj.] formal play the part of (a character in a drama).
■pretend to be (someone else), especially for fraudulent purposes such as casting a vote in another person's name.
– DERIVATIVES **personation** noun, **personator** noun.
– ORIGIN late 16th cent.: from late Latin *personat-* 'represented by acting', from Latin *persona* 'mask' (see **PERSON**).

p

personhood ▶ noun [mass noun] the quality or condition of being an individual person.

personification ▶ noun [mass noun] the attribution of a personal nature or human characteristics to something non-human, or the representation of an abstract quality in human form.
■[count noun] a figure intended to represent an abstract quality: *the knight is accompanied by two feminine personifications of vice.* ■ [in sing.] a person, animal, or object regarded as representing or embodying a quality, concept, or thing: *he was* **the** *very* **personification of** *British pluck and diplomacy.*

personify ▶ verb (-ies, -ied) [with obj.] represent (a quality or concept) by a figure in human form: *public pageants and dramas in which virtues and vices were personified.*
■(usu. **be personified**) attribute a personal nature or human characteristics to (something non-human): *in the poem the oak trees are personified.* ■ represent or embody (a quality, concept, or thing) in a physical form: *the car personified motoring fun for two decades.*
– DERIVATIVES **personifier** noun.
– ORIGIN early 18th cent.: from French *personnifier*, from *personne* 'person'.

personnel ▶ plural noun people employed in an organization or engaged in an organized undertaking such as military service: *many of the personnel involved require training | sales personnel.*
■short for **PERSONNEL DEPARTMENT**.
– ORIGIN early 19th cent.: from French (adjective used as a noun), contrasted with *matériel* 'equipment or materials used in an organization or undertaking'.

personnel carrier ▶ noun an armoured vehicle for transporting troops.

personnel department ▶ noun the part of an organization concerned with the appointment, training, and welfare of employees.

person of colour ▶ noun a person who is not white or of European parentage.

USAGE The term **person of colour** is first recorded at the end of the 18th century. It has been revived in the 1990s as the recommended term to use in some official contexts, especially in US English, to refer to a person who is not white. The term is not common in general use, however, where terms such as **non-white** are still used.

person-to-person ▶ adjective & adverb taking place directly between individuals: [as adj.] *person-to-person transmission of the disease* | [as adv.] *making contact with him person to person.*
■(in the US) denoting a phone call booked through the operator to a specified person and paid for from the time that person answers the phone.

perspective ▶ noun **1** [mass noun] the art of drawing solid objects on a two-dimensional surface so as to give the right impression of their height, width, depth, and position in relation to each other when viewed from a particular point: [as modifier] *a perspective drawing.* See also **LINEAR PERSPECTIVE** and **AERIAL PERSPECTIVE**.
■[count noun] a picture drawn in such a way, especially one appearing to enlarge or extend the actual space, or to give the effect of distance. ■ a view or prospect. ■ Geometry the relation of two figures in the same plane, such that pairs of corresponding points lie on concurrent lines, and corresponding lines meet in collinear points.
2 a particular attitude towards or way of regarding something; a point of view: *most guidebook history is written from the editor's perspective.*
■[mass noun] true understanding of the relative importance of things; a sense of proportion: *we must keep a sense of perspective about what he's done.*
3 an apparent spatial distribution in perceived sound.
– PHRASES **in** (or **out of**) **perspective** showing the right (or wrong) relationship between visible objects. ■ correctly (or incorrectly) regarded in terms of relative importance: *though these figures shock, they need to be* **put into perspective**.
– DERIVATIVES **perspectival** adjective.
– ORIGIN late Middle English (in the sense 'optics'): from medieval Latin *perspectiva (ars)* 'science of optics', from *perspect-* 'looked at closely', from the verb *perspicere*, from *per-* 'through' + *specere* 'to look'.

perspectivism ▶ noun [mass noun] **1** Philosophy the theory that knowledge of a subject is inevitably partial and limited by the individual perspective from which it is viewed. See also **RELATIVISM**.
2 the practice of regarding and analysing a situation or work of art from different points of view.
– DERIVATIVES **perspectivist** noun.

perspex ▶ noun [mass noun] trademark solid transparent plastic made of polymethyl methacrylate (the same material as plexiglas or lucite).
– ORIGIN 1930s: formed irregularly from Latin *perspicere* 'look through', from *per-* 'through' + *specere* 'to look'.

perspicacious /ˌpəːspɪˈkeɪʃəs/ ▶ adjective having a ready insight into and understanding of things: *it offers quite a few facts to the perspicacious reporter.*
– DERIVATIVES **perspicaciously** adverb, **perspicacity** noun.
– ORIGIN early 17th cent.: from Latin *perspicax, perspicac-* 'seeing clearly' + **-ACIOUS**.

perspicuous /pəˈspɪkjʊəs/ ▶ adjective formal (of an account or representation) clearly expressed and easily understood; lucid: *it provides simpler and more perspicuous explanations than its rivals.*
■(of a person) able to give an account or express an idea clearly.
– DERIVATIVES **perspicuity** noun, **perspicuously** adverb.
– ORIGIN late 15th cent. (in the sense 'transparent'): from Latin *perspicuus* 'transparent, clear' (from the verb *perspicere* 'look at closely') + **-OUS**.

perspiration ▶ noun [mass noun] the process of sweating: *it causes perspiration and a speeded-up heartbeat.*
■sweat: *perspiration ran down his forehead.*
– DERIVATIVES **perspiratory** adjective.
– ORIGIN early 17th cent.: from French, from *perspirer* (see **PERSPIRE**).

perspire ▶ verb [no obj.] give out sweat through the pores of the skin as the result of heat, physical exertion, or stress: *Will was perspiring heavily.*
– ORIGIN mid 17th cent.: from French *perspirer*, from Latin *perspirare*, from *per-* 'through' + *spirare* 'breathe'.

persuade ▶ verb [with obj. and infinitive] cause (someone) to do something through reasoning or argument: *it wasn't easy, but I persuaded him to do the right thing.*
■[with obj.] cause (someone) to believe something, especially after a sustained effort; convince: *health boards were finally* **persuaded of** *the desirability of psychiatric units in district general hospitals* | [with obj. and clause] *he did everything he could to persuade the police that he was the robber.* ■ (of a situation or event) provide a sound reason for (someone) to do something: *the cost of the manor's restoration persuaded them to take in guests.*
– DERIVATIVES **persuadability** noun, **persuadable** adjective, **persuasible** adjective.
– ORIGIN late 15th cent.: from Latin *persuadere*, from *per-* 'through, to completion' + *suadere* 'advise'.

USAGE For a discussion of the difference between **persuade** and **convince**, see **usage** at **CONVINCE**.

persuader ▶ noun a person who persuades someone to do something.
■informal a thing used to compel submission or obedience, typically a gun or other weapon.

persuasion ▶ noun **1** [mass noun] the action or process of persuading someone or of being persuaded to do or believe something: *Monica needed plenty of persuasion before she actually left.*
■[count noun] a means of persuading someone to do or believe something; an argument or inducement: *he gave way to the persuasions of his half-brother.*
2 a belief or set of beliefs, especially religious or political ones: *writers of all political persuasions.*
■a group or sect holding a particular religious belief: *the village had two chapels for those of the Primitive Methodist persuasion.* ■ humorous any group or type of person or thing linked by a specified characteristic, quality, or attribute: *an ancient gas oven* **of the** *enamel* **persuasion**.
– ORIGIN late Middle English: from Latin *persuasio(n-)*, from the verb *persuadere* (see **PERSUADE**).

persuasive ▶ adjective good at persuading someone to do or believe something through reasoning or the use of temptation: *an informative and persuasive speech.*
– DERIVATIVES **persuasively** adverb, **persuasiveness** noun.
– ORIGIN late 15th cent.: from French *persuasif, -ive* or medieval Latin *persuasivus*, from *persuas-* 'convinced by reasoning', from the verb *persuadere* (see **PERSUADE**).

PERT ▶ abbreviation for programme evaluation and review technique.

pert ▶ adjective (of a girl or young woman) sexually attractive because lively or cheeky: *a pert, slightly plump girl called Rose.*
■(of a bodily feature or garment) attractive because neat and jaunty: *she had a pert nose and deep blue eyes.* ■ (of a young person or their speech or behaviour) impudent: *no need to be pert, miss.* ■ another term for **PEART**.
– DERIVATIVES **pertly** adverb, **pertness** noun.
– ORIGIN Middle English (in the sense 'manifest'): from Old French *apert*, from Latin *apertus* 'opened', past participle of *aperire*, reinforced by Old French *aspert*, from Latin *expertus* (see **EXPERT**).

pertain ▶ verb [no obj.] be appropriate, related, or applicable: *matters* **pertaining to** *the organization of government.*
■chiefly Law belong to something as a part, appendage, or accessory: *the shop premises and stock and all assets* **pertaining to** *the business.* ■ [with adverbial] be in effect or existence in a specified place or at a specified time: *their economic circumstances are vastly different from those which pertained in their land of origin.*
– ORIGIN late Middle English: from Old French *partenir*, from Latin *pertinere* 'extend to, have reference to', from *per-* 'through' + *tenere* 'to hold'.

Pertex /ˈpəːtɛks/ ▶ noun [mass noun] trademark a lightweight breathable fabric used to make clothing and equipment for camping, climbing, and other outdoor pursuits.

Perth 1 a town in eastern Scotland, at the head of the Tay estuary; pop. 41,450 (1991). The administrative centre of Perth and Kinross region, it was the capital of Scotland from 1210 until 1452. **2** the capital of the state of Western Australia, on the Indian Ocean; pop. 1,018,700 (1991) (including the port of Fremantle). Founded by the British in 1829, it developed rapidly after the discovery in 1890 of gold in the region and the opening in 1897 of the harbour at Fremantle.

Perthes, Jacques Boucher de, see **BOUCHER DE PERTHES**.

Perthshire a former county of central Scotland. It became a part of Tayside region in 1975 and of Perth and Kinross in 1996.

pertinacious /ˌpəːtɪˈneɪʃəs/ ▶ adjective formal holding firmly to an opinion or a course of action: *he worked with a pertinacious resistance to interruptions.*
– DERIVATIVES **pertinaciously** adverb, **pertinaciousness** noun, **pertinacity** noun.
– ORIGIN early 17th cent.: from Latin *pertinax*, *pertinac-* 'holding fast' + -OUS.

pertinent ▶ adjective relevant or applicable to a particular matter; apposite: *she asked me a lot of very pertinent questions | practitioners must consider all factors pertinent to a situation.*
– DERIVATIVES **pertinence** noun, **pertinency** noun, **pertinently** adverb.
– ORIGIN late Middle English: from Old French, or from Latin *pertinent-* 'having reference to', from the verb *pertinere* (see **PERTAIN**).

perturb ▶ verb [with obj.] **1** (often **be perturbed**) make (someone) anxious or unsettled: *they were perturbed by her capricious behaviour |* [with obj. and clause] *he was perturbed that his bleeper wouldn't work.*
2 subject (a system, moving object, or process) to an influence tending to alter its normal or regular state or path: *nuclear weapons could be used to perturb the orbit of an asteroid.*
– DERIVATIVES **perturbable** adjective, **perturbative** /pəˈtəːbətɪv, ˈpəːtəbeɪtɪv/ adjective (in sense 2), **perturbingly** adverb.
– ORIGIN late Middle English: from Old French *pertourber*, from Latin *perturbare*, from *per-* 'completely' + *turbare* 'disturb'.

perturbation ▶ noun **1** [mass noun] anxiety; mental uneasiness: *she sensed her friend's perturbation.*
■ [count noun] a cause of such anxiety or uneasiness: *Frank's atheism was more than a perturbation to Michael.*
2 a deviation of a system, moving object, or process from its regular or normal state of path, caused by an outside influence: *some minor perturbation in his house's cash flow.*
■ Physics a slight alteration of a physical system, for example of the electrons in an atom, caused by a secondary influence. ■ Astronomy a minor deviation in the course of a celestial body, caused by the attraction of a neighbouring body.
– ORIGIN late Middle English: from Latin *perturbatio(n-)*, from the verb *perturbare* 'disturb greatly' (see **PERTURB**).

pertussis /pəˈtʌsɪs/ ▶ noun medical term for **WHOOPING COUGH**.
– ORIGIN late 18th cent.: modern Latin, from PER- 'away, extremely' + Latin *tussis* 'a cough'.

Peru /pəˈruː/ a country in South America on the Pacific coast, traversed throughout its length by the Andes; pop. 22,048,350 (1993); official languages, Spanish and Quechua; capital, Lima.

The centre of the Inca empire, Peru was conquered by the Spanish conquistador Pizarro in 1532. Peru was liberated by Simón Bolívar and José de San Martín in 1820–4, and a republic established. It lost territory in the south in a war with Chile (1879–83) and also had border disputes with Colombia and Ecuador in the 1930s and 1940s. Peru has been troubled by revolutionary guerrilla and terrorist activity in recent years.

– DERIVATIVES **Peruvian** adjective & noun.

Perugia /pəˈruːdʒə/ a city in central Italy, the capital of Umbria; pop. 150,580 (1990). It flourished in the 15th century as a centre of the Umbrian school of painting. A papal possession from 1540, it became a part of united Italy in 1860.

peruke /pəˈruːk/ ▶ noun archaic term for **PERIWIG**.
■ archaic term for **WIG**[1].
– ORIGIN mid 16th cent. (denoting a natural head of hair): from French *perruque*, from Italian *perrucca*, of unknown origin.

perusal ▶ noun [mass noun] formal the action of reading or examining something: *I continued my perusal of the instructions.*

peruse /pəˈruːz/ ▶ verb [with obj.] formal read thoroughly or carefully: *the pursed lips of an auditor perusing an unsatisfactory set of accounts.*
■ examine carefully or at length: *Laura perused a Caravaggio.*
– DERIVATIVES **peruser** noun.
– ORIGIN late 15th cent. (in the sense 'use up, wear out'): perhaps from PER- 'thoroughly' + USE, but compare with Anglo-Norman French *peruser* 'examine'.

USAGE The verb **peruse** means 'read thoroughly and carefully'. It is sometimes mistakenly taken to mean 'read through quickly; glance over', as in *later documents will be perused* rather than *analysed thoroughly.*

Peruvian bark ▶ noun [mass noun] cinchona bark.

Peruvian Current a cold ocean current that moves northwards from the Southern Ocean along the Pacific coast of Chile and Peru before turning westwards into the South Equatorial Current.

perv (also **perve**) informal ▶ noun **1** a sexual pervert. **2** [in sing.] Austral./NZ a lustful or lecherous look at someone or something: *come out here for a perv.*
▶ verb [no obj.] Austral./NZ gaze lustfully or lecherously: *we perved on them from a distance.*
– DERIVATIVES **pervy** (**pervier**, **perviest**) adjective.
– ORIGIN 1940s: abbreviation of the noun **PERVERT**.

pervade ▶ verb [with obj.] (especially of a smell) spread through and be perceived in every part of: *a smell of stale cabbage pervaded the air.*
■ (of an influence, feeling, or quality) be present and apparent throughout: *the sense of crisis which pervaded Europe in the 1930s.*
– DERIVATIVES **pervader** noun, **pervasion** noun.
– ORIGIN mid 17th cent. (also in the sense 'traverse'): from Latin *pervadere*, from *per-* 'throughout' + *vadere* 'go'.

pervasive ▶ adjective (especially of an unwelcome influence or physical effect) spreading widely throughout an area or a group of people: *ageism is pervasive and entrenched in our society.*
– DERIVATIVES **pervasively** adverb, **pervasiveness** noun.
– ORIGIN mid 18th cent.: from Latin *pervas-* 'passed through' (from the verb *pervadere*) + -IVE.

perverse ▶ adjective (of a person or their actions) showing a deliberate and obstinate desire to behave in a way that is unreasonable or unacceptable, often in spite of the consequences: *Kate's perverse decision not to cooperate held good.*
■ contrary to the accepted or expected standard or practice: *in two general elections the outcome was quite perverse.* ■ Law (of a verdict) against the weight of evidence or the direction of the judge on a point of law. ■ sexually perverted.
– DERIVATIVES **perversely** adverb [sentence adverb] *perversely, she felt nearer to tears now than at any other moment in the conversation,* **perverseness** noun, **perversity** noun (pl. **-ies**).
– ORIGIN late Middle English (in the sense 'turned away from what is right or good'): from Old French *pervers(e)*, from Latin *perversus* 'turned about', from the verb *pervertere* (see **PERVERT**).

perversion ▶ noun [mass noun] the alteration of something from its original course, meaning, or state to a distortion or corruption of what was first intended: *the perversion of Marxist theory to justify Soviet policy-making |* [count noun] *a scandalous perversion of the law.*
■ sexual behaviour or desire that is considered abnormal or unacceptable.
– ORIGIN late Middle English: from Latin *perversio(n-)*, from the verb *pervertere* 'turn about' (see **PERVERT**).

pervert ▶ verb [with obj.] alter (something) from its original course, meaning, or state to a distortion or corruption of what was first intended: *he was charged with conspiring to pervert the course of justice.*
■ lead (someone) away from what is considered right, natural, or acceptable: *Hector is a man who is simply perverted by his time.*
▶ noun a person whose sexual behaviour is regarded as abnormal and unacceptable.
– DERIVATIVES **perverter** noun.
– ORIGIN late Middle English (as a verb): from Old French *pervertir*, from Latin *pervertere*, from *per-* 'thoroughly, to ill effect' + *vertere* 'to turn'. The current noun sense dates from the late 19th cent.

perverted ▶ adjective (of a person or their actions) characterized by sexually abnormal and unacceptable practices or tendencies.
■ (of a thing) having been corrupted or distorted from its original course, meaning, or state: *this sudden surge of perverted patriotism.*
– DERIVATIVES **pervertedly** adverb.

pervious /ˈpəːvɪəs/ ▶ adjective (of a substance) allowing water to pass through; permeable: *pervious rocks.*
– DERIVATIVES **perviousness** noun.
– ORIGIN early 17th cent.: from Latin *pervius* 'having a passage through' (based on *via* 'way') + -OUS.

pes /peɪz, piːz/ ▶ noun (pl. **pedes** /ˈpɛdeɪz, ˈpɛdiːz/) technical the human foot, or the corresponding terminal segment of the hindlimb of a vertebrate animal.
– ORIGIN mid 19th cent.: from Latin, 'foot'.

Pesach /ˈpeɪsɑːx/ ▶ noun Jewish term for Passover festival.
– ORIGIN from Hebrew *Pesaḥ*.

pes cavus /ˈkeɪvəs, ˈkɑːvəs/ ▶ noun technical term for **CLAW FOOT** (in sense 2).
– ORIGIN Latin.

peseta /pəˈseɪtə/ ▶ noun (until the introduction of the euro in 2002) the basic monetary unit of Spain, equal to 100 centimos.
■ historical a silver coin.
– ORIGIN Spanish, diminutive of *pesa* 'weight', from Latin *pensa* 'things weighed', from the verb *pendere* 'weigh'.

pesewa /pɛˈsiːwə/ ▶ noun a monetary unit of Ghana, equal to one hundredth of a cedi.
– ORIGIN Akan, literally 'penny'.

Peshawar /pəˈʃɑːwə/ the capital of North-West Frontier Province, in Pakistan; pop. 555,000 (1981). Mentioned in early Sanskrit literature, it is one of Pakistan's oldest cities. Under Sikh rule from 1834, it was occupied by the British between 1849 and 1947. Situated near the Khyber Pass on the border with Afghanistan, it is of strategic and military importance.

Peshitta /pəˈʃiːtə/ ▶ noun the ancient Syriac version of the Bible, used in Syriac-speaking Christian countries from the early 5th century and still the official Bible of the Syrian Christian Churches.
– ORIGIN Syriac, literally 'simple, plain'.

peshmerga /pɛʃˈməːɡə/ ▶ noun (pl. same or **peshmergas**) a member of a Kurdish nationalist guerrilla organization.
– ORIGIN from Kurdish *pêshmerge*, from *pêsh* 'before' + *merg* 'death'.

pesky ▶ adjective (**peskier**, **peskiest**) informal causing trouble; annoying: *a pesky younger brother.*
– DERIVATIVES **peskily** adverb, **peskiness** noun.
– ORIGIN late 18th cent.: perhaps related to **PEST**.

peso /ˈpeɪsəʊ/ ▶ noun (pl. **-os**) the basic monetary unit of several Latin American countries and of the Philippines, equal to 100 centésimos in Uruguay and 100 centavos elsewhere.
– ORIGIN Spanish, literally 'weight', from Latin *pensum* 'something weighed', from the verb *pendere* 'weigh'.

pes planus /ˈpleɪnəs, ˈplɑːnəs/ ▶ noun technical term for **FLAT FOOT**.
– ORIGIN Latin.

pessary /ˈpɛs(ə)ri/ ▶ noun (pl. **-ies**) a small soluble block that is inserted into the vagina to treat infection or as a contraceptive.
■ an elastic or rigid device that is inserted into the vagina to support the uterus.
– ORIGIN late Middle English: from late Latin *pessarium*, based on Greek *pessos* 'oval stone' (used in board games).

pessimism ▶ noun [mass noun] a tendency to see the worst aspect of things or believe that the worst will happen; a lack of hope or confidence in the future: *the dispute cast an air of deep pessimism over the future of the peace talks.*
■ Philosophy a belief that this world is as bad as it could be or that evil will ultimately prevail over good.
– DERIVATIVES **pessimist** noun.
– ORIGIN late 18th cent.: from Latin *pessimus* 'worst', on the pattern of *optimism*.

pessimistic ▶ adjective seeing or having a tendency to see the worst aspect of things or believe that the worst will happen; lacking in hope and confidence in the future: *he was pessimistic about the prospects.*
– DERIVATIVES **pessimistically** adverb.

pest ▶ noun a destructive insect or other animal that attacks crops, food, livestock, etc.

■informal an annoying person or thing; a nuisance: *he was a real pest.* ■ (**the pest**) archaic bubonic plague.
– ORIGIN late 15th cent. (denoting the bubonic plague): from French *peste* or Latin *pestis* 'plague'.

Pestalozzi /ˌpɛstəˈlɒtsi/, Johann Heinrich (1746–1827), Swiss educational reformer. He pioneered education for poor children and had a major impact on the development of primary education.

pester ▶**verb** [with obj.] trouble or annoy (someone) with frequent or persistent requests or interruptions: *she constantly pestered him with telephone calls.*
– DERIVATIVES **pesterer** noun.
– ORIGIN mid 16th cent. (in the senses 'overcrowd (a place)' and 'impede (a person)'): from French *empestrer* 'encumber', influenced by **PEST**. The current sense is an extension of an earlier use, 'infest', referring to vermin.

pest-house ▶**noun** historical a hospital for people suffering from infectious diseases, especially the plague.

pesticide ▶**noun** a substance used for destroying insects or other organisms harmful to cultivated plants or to animals.
– DERIVATIVES **pesticidal** adjective.

pestiferous ▶**adjective** poetic/literary harbouring infection and disease: *the pestiferous area around the prison.*
■humorous constituting a pest or nuisance; annoying: *that pestiferous nephew of yours.*
– ORIGIN late Middle English (in the sense 'morally corrupting'): from Latin *pestifer* 'bringing pestilence' + **-OUS**.

pestilence ▶**noun** archaic a fatal epidemic disease, especially bubonic plague.
– ORIGIN Middle English (also denoting something morally corrupting): from Old French, from Latin *pestilentia*, based on *pestis* 'a plague'.

pestilent ▶**adjective** destructive to life; deadly: *pestilent diseases.*
■informal, dated causing annoyance; troublesome: *he regarded journalists as a whole as a pestilent race.* ■ archaic, figurative harmful or dangerous to morals or public order; pernicious: *the pestilent sect of Luther.*
– DERIVATIVES **pestilently** adverb.
– ORIGIN late Middle English: from Latin *pestilens, pestilent-* 'unhealthy, destructive', from *pestis* 'plague'.

pestilential ▶**adjective** of, relating to, or tending to cause infectious diseases: *pestilential fever.*
■ of the nature of a pest; very widespread and troublesome: *a pestilential weed.* ■ informal annoying: *what a pestilential man!*
– DERIVATIVES **pestilentially** adverb.

pestle /ˈpɛs(ə)l/ ▶**noun** a heavy tool with a rounded end, used for crushing and grinding substances such as spices or drugs, usually in a mortar.
■a mechanical device for grinding, pounding, or stamping something.
▶**verb** [with obj.] crush or grind (a substance such as a spice or drug) with a pestle: *she measured seeds into the mortar and pestled them to powder.*
– ORIGIN Middle English: from Old French *pestel*, from Latin *pistillum*, from *pist-* 'pounded', from the verb *pinsere*.

pesto /ˈpɛstəʊ/ ▶**noun** [mass noun] a sauce of crushed basil leaves, pine nuts, garlic, Parmesan cheese, and olive oil, typically served with pasta.
– ORIGIN Italian, from *pestare* 'pound, crush'.

PET ▶**abbreviation for** ■ polyethylene terephthalate. ■ positron emission tomography, a form of tomography used especially for brain scans.

Pet. ▶**abbreviation for** Peter (in biblical references).

pet[1] ▶**noun** a domestic or tamed animal or bird kept for companionship or pleasure and treated with care and affection: *the pony was a family pet.*
■a person treated with special favour, especially in a way that others regard as unfair: *Liz was teacher's pet.* ■ used as an affectionate form of address: *don't cry, pet, it's all right.*
▶**adjective** [attrib.] (of an animal or bird) kept as a pet: *a pet cat.*
■of or relating to pet animals: *a pet shop | pet food.* ■ denoting a thing that one devotes special attention to or feels particularly strongly about: *another of her pet projects was the arts centre | my pet hate is woodwork.* ■ denoting a person or establishment that one regards with particular favour or affection: *I found the chairs at my pet antiques dealer in Cannes.*
▶**verb** (**petted, petting**) [with obj.] stroke or pat (an animal) affectionately: *the cats came to be petted.*
■treat (someone) with affection or favouritism; pamper: *I was cosseted and petted and never shouted at.* ■ [no obj.] engage in sexually stimulating caressing and touching: *she watched the couples necking and petting in the cars.*
– DERIVATIVES **petter** noun.
– ORIGIN early 16th cent. (as a noun; originally Scots and northern English): of unknown origin.

pet[2] ▶**noun** [in sing.] a fit of sulking or ill humour: *Mother's* ***in a pet.***
– ORIGIN late 16th cent.: of unknown origin.

PETA ▶**abbreviation for** People for the Ethical Treatment of Animals.

peta- /ˈpɛtə/ ▶**combining form** (used in units of measurement) denoting a factor of 10^{15}: *petabytes.*
– ORIGIN from *pe(n)ta-* (see **PENTA-**), based on the supposed analogy of *tera-* and *tetra-*.

Pétain /peɪˈtã, French petɛ̃/, (Henri) Philippe (Omer) (1856–1951), French general and statesman, head of state 1940–2. He concluded an armistice with Nazi Germany in 1940 and established the French government at Vichy (effectively a puppet regime for the Third Reich) until the German occupation in 1942. After the war Pétain received a death sentence for collaboration, but this was commuted to life imprisonment.

petal ▶**noun** each of the segments of the corolla of a flower, which are modified leaves and are typically coloured.
– DERIVATIVES **petaline** adjective, **petalled** adjective [in combination] *pink-petalled trailing phlox*, **petal-like** adjective, **petaloid** adjective.
– ORIGIN early 18th cent.: from modern Latin *petalum* (in late Latin 'metal plate'), from Greek *petalon* 'leaf', neuter (used as a noun) of *petalos* 'outspread'.

pétanque /pəˈtaŋk, French petɑ̃k/ ▶**noun** [mass noun] a game similar to boule played chiefly in Provence.
– ORIGIN French, from Provençal *pèd tanco*, literally 'foot fixed (to the ground)', describing the start position.

petard /pɪˈtɑːd/ ▶**noun** historical a small bomb made of a metal or wooden box filled with powder, used to blast down a door or to make a hole in a wall.
■a kind of firework that explodes with a sharp report.
– PHRASES **hoist with** (or **by**) **one's own petard** have one's plans to cause trouble for others backfire on one. [ORIGIN: from Shakespeare's *Hamlet* (III. iv. 207); *hoist* is in the sense 'lifted and removed', past participle of dialect *hoise* (see **HOIST**).]
– ORIGIN mid 16th cent.: from French *pétard*, from *péter* 'break wind'.

petasus /ˈpɛtəsəs/ ▶**noun** a hat with a low crown and broad brim, worn in ancient Greece.
■Greek Mythology a winged hat of such a type worn by the god Hermes.
– ORIGIN via Latin from Greek *petasos*.

petcock ▶**noun** a small valve positioned in the pipe of a steam boiler or cylinder of a steam engine for drainage or testing.

petechia /pɪˈtiːkɪə/ ▶**noun** (pl. **petechiae** /-kɪiː/) Medicine a small red or purple spot caused by bleeding into the skin.
– DERIVATIVES **petechial** adjective.
– ORIGIN late 18th cent.: modern Latin, from Italian *petecchia*, denoting a freckle or spot on the face, from Latin *petigo* 'scab, eruption'.

peter[1] ▶**verb** [no obj.] decrease or fade gradually before coming to an end: *the storm had* ***petered out.***
– ORIGIN early 19th cent.: of unknown origin.

peter[2] ▶**noun** informal **1** a man's penis.
2 Austral./NZ a prison cell.
3 a safe.
– ORIGIN late Middle English: from the given name *Peter*, applied in many transferred uses. Current senses date from the 19th cent.

peter[3] ▶**noun** & **verb** Bridge another term for **ECHO**.
– ORIGIN late 19th cent.: from **BLUE PETER** (the invitation to one's partner to play a further lead in the suit being likened to the raising of this flag).

Peter I (1672–1725), tsar of Russia 1682–1725; known as **Peter the Great**. Peter modernized his armed forces before waging the Great Northern War (1700–21) and expanding his territory in the Baltic. His extensive administrative reforms were instrumental in transforming Russia into a significant European power. In 1703 he made the new city of St Petersburg his capital.

Peter, St an Apostle; born *Simon*. Peter ('stone') is the name given him by Jesus, signifying the rock on which he would establish his church. He is regarded by Roman Catholics as the first bishop of the Church at Rome, where he is said to have been martyred in about AD 67. He is often represented as the keeper of the door of heaven. Feast day, 29 June.
■either of the two epistles in the New Testament ascribed to St Peter.

Peterborough /ˈpiːtəˌbərə, -ˌbʌrə/ an industrial city in east central England, a unitary council formerly in Cambridgeshire; pop. 148,800 (1991). An old city with a 12th-century cathedral, it has been developed as a planned urban centre since the late sixties.

Peterborough ware ▶**noun** [mass noun] Archaeology prehistoric pottery of the mid to late Neolithic in Britain (*c.*3400–2500 BC), characterized by a round base and decorated with the impressions of twisted cord and bird bones. Unlike the contemporary grooved ware, it is not associated with henge monuments.
– ORIGIN named after **PETERBOROUGH**, where certain neolithic sites were located.

Peterloo massacre an attack by Manchester yeomanry on 16 August 1819 against a large but peaceable crowd. Sent to arrest the speaker at a rally of supporters of political reform in St Peter's Field, Manchester, the local yeomanry charged the crowd, killing 11 civilians and injuring more than 500.
– ORIGIN so named in ironical reference to the Battle of Waterloo.

peterman ▶**noun** (pl. **-men**) archaic a safe-breaker.
– ORIGIN early 20th cent.: from slang *peter* 'a safe' + **MAN**.

Peter Pan the hero of J. M. Barrie's play of the same name (1904), a boy with magical powers who never grew up.
■[as noun **a Peter Pan**] a person who retains youthful features, or who is immature.

Peter Pan collar ▶**noun** a flat collar with rounded points.

Peter Principle the principle that members of a hierarchy are promoted until they reach the level at which they are no longer competent.
– ORIGIN 1960s: named after Laurence J. *Peter* (1919–90), the American educationalist who put forward the theory.

petersham ▶**noun** [mass noun] a corded tape used in dressmaking and millinery for stiffening.
– ORIGIN early 19th cent.: named after Lord *Petersham* (1790–1851), English army officer.

Peterson[1], Oscar (Emmanuel) (b.1925), Canadian jazz pianist and composer. He became internationally famous in the 1960s, when he often appeared with Ella Fitzgerald.

Peterson[2], Roger Tory (1908–96), American ornithologist and artist. Peterson produced his first book for identifying birds in the field in 1934, introducing the concept of illustrating similar birds in similar postures with their differences highlighted. The format of his field guides has become standard in field guides for all groups of animals and plants.

Peter's pence ▶**plural noun** **1** historical an annual tax of one penny from every householder having land of a certain value, paid to the papal see at Rome from Anglo-Saxon times until discontinued in 1534 after Henry VIII's break with Rome.
2 a voluntary payment by Roman Catholics to the papal treasury, made since 1860.
– ORIGIN named after St *Peter*, the first Pope (see **PETER, ST**).

Peters projection a world map projection in which areas are shown in correct proportion at the expense of distorted shape, using a rectangular decimal grid to replace latitude and longitude. It was devised in 1973 to be a fairer representation of equatorial (i.e. mainly developing) countries, whose area is under-represented by the usual projections such as Mercator's.
– ORIGIN named after Arno *Peters* (born 1916), German historian.

Peter the Hermit (*c.*1050–1115), French monk. His preaching on the First Crusade was a rallying

p

cry for thousands of peasants throughout Europe to journey to the Holy Land; most were massacred by the Turks in Asia Minor. Peter later became prior of an Augustinian monastery in Flanders.

pethidine /ˈpɛθɪdiːn/ ▶ **noun** [mass noun] Medicine a synthetic compound used as a painkilling drug, especially for women in labour.
– ORIGIN 1940s: from *p(iper)idine* (from which the drug is derived), with the insertion of *eth(yl)*.

pétillant /ˈpɛtɪjɒ̃/ ▶ **adjective** (of wine) slightly sparkling.
– ORIGIN French.

petiole /ˈpɛtɪəʊl/ ▶ **noun** Botany the stalk that joins a leaf to a stem.
■ Zoology a slender stalk between two structures, especially that between the abdomen and thorax of a wasp or ant.
– DERIVATIVES **petiolar** adjective, **petiolate** /-lət/ adjective.
– ORIGIN mid 18th cent.: from French *pétiole*, from Latin *petiolus* 'little foot, stalk'.

Petipa /ˈpɛtɪpɑː/, Marius (Ivanovich) (1818–1910), French ballet dancer and choreographer, resident in Russia from 1847. Petipa choreographed more than fifty ballets, working with Tchaikovsky on *Sleeping Beauty* (1890) and *The Nutcracker* (1892).

petit /ˈpɛti/ ▶ **adjective** Law (of a crime) petty: *petit larceny*.
– ORIGIN late Middle English (in the sense 'small or insignificant'): from Old French, 'small'; the same word as **PETTY**, with retention of the French spelling.

petit battement ▶ **noun** Ballet a movement in which one leg is extended and lightly moved forwards and backwards from the ankle of the supporting leg.

petit beurre /ˌpəti ˈbəː/ (also **petit beurre biscuit**) ▶ **noun** (pl. **petits beurres** pronunc. same) a sweet butter biscuit.
– ORIGIN French, literally 'little butter'.

petit bourgeois ▶ **adjective** of or characteristic of the lower middle class, especially with reference to a perceived conventionalism and conservatism: *the frail facade of petit bourgeois respectability*.
▶ **noun** (pl. **petits bourgeois** pronunc. same) a member of the lower middle class, especially when perceived as conventional and conservative.
– ORIGIN French, literally 'little citizen'.

petite ▶ **adjective** (of a woman) having a small and attractively dainty build: *she was petite and vivacious*.
■ (of a size of women's clothing) smaller than standard: *it is available in petite sizes*. ■ used as an affectionate form of address to a woman: *what is wrong, petite?*
– ORIGIN late 18th cent.: French, feminine of *petit* 'small'.

petite bourgeoisie (also **petit bourgeoisie**) ▶ **noun** (**the petite bourgeoisie**) [treated as sing. or pl.] the lower middle class.
– ORIGIN French, literally 'little townsfolk'.

petite marmite /pəˌtiːt mɑːˈmiːt/ ▶ **noun** [mass noun] soup served in an earthenware pot.
– ORIGIN French, literally 'little earthenware pot'.

petit four /ˌpəti ˈfɔː, ˌpɛti/ ▶ **noun** (pl. **petits fours** /ˈfɔːz/) a very small fancy cake, biscuit, or sweet, typically made with marzipan and traditionally served after a meal.
– ORIGIN French, literally 'little oven'.

petitgrain /ˈpɛtɪgreɪn/ ▶ **noun** [mass noun] an essential oil with a floral scent distilled from parts of the orange tree, particularly the leaves and bark, and other citrus plants, used in perfumery.
– ORIGIN from French *petit grain* 'little grain' (from the small green fruits originally used).

petition ▶ **noun** a formal written request, typically one signed by many people, appealing to authority in respect of a particular cause: *she was asked to sign a petition against plans to build on the local playing fields*.
■ an appeal or request, especially a solemn or humble one to a deity or a superior. ■ Law an application to a court for a writ, judicial action in a suit, etc.: *a divorce petition*.
▶ **verb** [with obj.] make or present a formal request to (an authority) in respect of a particular cause: *the organization is* **petitioning** *the EC* **for** *a moratorium on the patenting of life* | [with obj. and infinitive] *the islanders petitioned the government to help them leave St Kilda*.
■ make a solemn or humble appeal to (a figure of authority): *a Highland chief* **petitioned** *her father* **for** *her hand in marriage*. ■ Law make a formal application to (a court) for a writ, judicial action in a suit, etc.: *the custodial parent* **petitioned** *the court* **for** *payment of the arrears* | [no obj.] *the Act allowed couples to* **petition for** *divorce after one year of marriage*.
– DERIVATIVES **petitionary** adjective, **petitioner** noun.
– ORIGIN Middle English: from Latin *petitio(n-)*, from *petit-* 'aimed at, sought, laid claim to', from the verb *petere*.

Petition of Right ▶ **noun 1** Brit. historical a parliamentary declaration of rights and liberties of the people assented to by Charles I in 1628.
2 English Law, chiefly historical a common-law remedy against the Crown for the recovery of property.

petitio principii /pɪˌtɪʃɪəʊ prɪnˈsɪpɪʌɪ, prɪŋˈkɪp-/ ▶ **noun** Logic a fallacy in which a conclusion is taken for granted in the premises; begging the question.
– ORIGIN Latin, literally 'laying claim to a principle'.

petit jeté ▶ **noun** Ballet a jump in which a dancer brushes one leg out to the side in the air then brings it back in again and lands on it with the other leg lifted and bent behind the body.

petit-maître /ˌpətɪˈmeɪtr(ə), French p(ə)timɛtʀ/ ▶ **noun 1** a dandy or fop.
2 a musician, writer, or other artist, of minor importance.
– ORIGIN French, literally 'little master'.

petit mal /mal/ ▶ **noun** [mass noun] a mild form of epilepsy characterized by brief spells of unconsciousness without loss of posture. Compare with **GRAND MAL**.
■ [count noun] an epileptic fit of this kind.
– ORIGIN late 19th cent.: from French, literally 'little sickness'.

petit pain /ˌpəti ˈpã/ ▶ **noun** (pl. **petits pains**) a small bread roll.
– ORIGIN French, literally 'little loaf'.

petit point /pɔɪnt, pwã/ ▶ **noun** [mass noun] a type of embroidery on a canvas ground, consisting of small, diagonal, adjacent stitches.
– ORIGIN late 19th cent.: from French, literally 'little stitch'.

petits pois /ˌpəti ˈpwɑː/ ▶ **plural noun** young peas that are picked before they are grown to full size; small, fine peas.
– ORIGIN French, literally 'small peas'.

pet name ▶ **noun** a name that is used instead of someone's usual first name to express fondness or familiarity.

Petra /ˈpɛtrə/ an ancient city of SW Asia, in present-day Jordan. The city, which lies in a hollow surrounded by cliffs, is accessible only through narrow gorges. Its extensive ruins include temples and tombs hewn from the rose-red sandstone cliffs.

Petrarch /ˈpɛtrɑːk/ (1304–74), Italian poet; Italian name *Francesco Petrarca*. His reputation is chiefly based on the *Canzoniere* (*c.*1351–3), a sonnet sequence in praise of a woman he calls Laura.

Petrarchan /pɪˈtrɑːk(ə)n/ ▶ **adjective** denoting a sonnet of the kind used by the Italian poet Petrarch, with an octave rhyming *abbaabba*, and a sestet typically rhyming *cdcdcd* or *cdecde*.

petrel /ˈpɛtr(ə)l/ ▶ **noun** a seabird related to the shearwaters, typically flying far from land.
• Order Procellariiformes, in particular the families Procellariidae (e.g. the **giant petrel** and **pintado petrel**) or Hydrobatidae (the **storm petrels**). See also **DIVING PETREL**.
– ORIGIN early 17th cent.: associated with St Peter, from the bird's habit of flying low with legs dangling, giving the appearance of walking on the water (see Matt. 14:30).

Petri dish /ˈpɛtri, ˈpiːtri/ ▶ **noun** a shallow, circular, transparent dish with a flat lid, used for the culture of micro-organisms.
– ORIGIN late 19th cent.: named after Julius R. Petri (1852–1922), German bacteriologist.

Petrie /ˈpiːtri/, Sir (William Matthew) Flinders (1853–1942), English archaeologist and Egyptologist. He began excavating the Great Pyramid in 1880. Petrie pioneered the use of mathematical calculation and became the first to establish the system of sequence dating, now standard archaeological practice, by which sites are excavated layer by layer and historical chronology determined by the dating of artefacts found *in situ*.

petrifaction ▶ **noun** another term for **PETRIFICATION**.

petrification ▶ **noun** [mass noun] the process by which organic matter exposed to minerals over a long period is turned into a stony substance.
■ a state of extreme fear making someone unable to move: *his heavy footfalls served to spur Paul out of his petrification*. ■ [count noun] an organic object which has been been turned to stone.

petrify ▶ **verb (-ies, -ied)** [with obj.] **1** make (someone) so frightened that they are unable to move or think: *his icy controlled quietness petrified her* | [as adj. **petrified**] *the petrified child clung to the side of her mother*.
2 change (organic matter) into a stony concretion by encrusting or replacing its original substance with a calcareous, siliceous, or other mineral deposit.
■ [no obj.] (of organic matter) become converted into stone or a stony substance in such a way. ■ figurative deprive or become deprived of vitality or the capacity for change: [with obj.] *death merely petrifies things for those who go on living* | [no obj.] *the inner life of the communist parties petrified*.
– ORIGIN late Middle English: from French *pétrifier*, from medieval Latin *petrificare*, from Latin *petra* 'rock', from Greek.

Petrine /ˈpiːtrʌɪn/ ▶ **adjective 1** Christian Theology of or relating to St Peter or his writings or teachings.
■ of or relating to the authority of the Pope over the Church, in his role as the successor of St Peter.
2 of or relating to Peter I of Russia: *the Petrine reforms of the early 18th century*.

petro- /ˈpɛtrəʊ/ ▶ **combining form 1** of rock; relating to rocks: *petrography*.
2 relating to petroleum: *petrodollar*.
– ORIGIN sense 1 from Greek *petros* 'stone', *petra* 'rock'; sense 2 from **PETROLEUM**.

petrochemical ▶ **adjective** relating to or denoting substances obtained by the refining and processing of petroleum or natural gas: *a huge petrochemical works producing plastics*.
■ of or relating to petrochemistry.
▶ **noun** (usu. **petrochemicals**) a chemical obtained from petroleum and natural gas.

petrochemistry ▶ **noun** [mass noun] **1** the branch of chemistry concerned with the composition and formation of rocks (as distinct from minerals and ore deposits).
2 the branch of chemistry concerned with petroleum and natural gas, and with their refining and processing.

petrodollar ▶ **noun** a notional unit of currency earned by a country from the export of petroleum: *petrodollars were pouring into the kingdom*.

petrogenesis ▶ **noun** [mass noun] Geology the formation of rocks, especially igneous and metamorphic rocks.
– DERIVATIVES **petrogenetic** adjective.

petroglyph /ˈpɛtrə(ʊ)glɪf/ ▶ **noun** a rock carving, especially a prehistoric one.
– ORIGIN late 19th cent.: from **PETRO-** 'rock' + Greek *glyphē* 'carving'.

Petrograd /ˈpɛtrə(ʊ)grad/ former name (1914–24) for **ST PETERSBURG**.

petrography /pɛˈtrɒgrəfi/ ▶ **noun** [mass noun] the branch of science concerned with the composition and properties of rocks.
– DERIVATIVES **petrographer** noun, **petrographic** adjective, **petrographical** adjective.

petrol ▶ **noun** [mass noun] Brit. refined petroleum used as a fuel in motor vehicles.
– ORIGIN late 19th cent.: from French *pétrole*, from medieval Latin *petroleum* (see **PETROLEUM**).

petrolatum /ˌpɛtrəˈleɪtəm/ ▶ **noun** North American term for **PETROLEUM JELLY**.
– ORIGIN late 19th cent.: modern Latin, from **PETROL** + the Latin suffix *-atum*.

petrol blue ▶ **noun** [mass noun] a shade of intense greenish or greyish blue.

petrol bomb ▶ **noun** Brit. a crude bomb consisting of a bottle containing petrol and an improvised cloth wick that is ignited just before the bottle is thrown at the target.

petroleum ▶ **noun** [mass noun] a liquid mixture of hydrocarbons which is present in suitable rock strata and can be extracted and refined to produce fuels including petrol, paraffin, and diesel oil; oil.
– ORIGIN late Middle English: from medieval Latin, from Latin *petra* 'rock' (from Greek) + Latin *oleum* 'oil'.

p

petroleum coke ▸ noun [mass noun] the solid non-volatile carbon residue left after the distillation and cracking of petroleum.

petroleum ether ▸ noun [mass noun] a volatile liquid distilled from petroleum, consisting of a mixture of hydrocarbons.

petroleum jelly ▸ noun [mass noun] a translucent jelly consisting of a mixture of hydrocarbons, used as a lubricant or ointment.

petroliferous /ˌpɛtrəˈlɪf(ə)rəs/ ▸ adjective (of rock) yielding or containing petroleum.

petrology /pɪˈtrɒlədʒi/ ▸ noun [mass noun] the branch of science concerned with the origin, structure, and composition of rocks. Compare with **LITHOLOGY**.
– DERIVATIVES **petrologic** adjective, **petrological** adjective, **petrologist** noun.

petrol station ▸ noun Brit. an establishment selling petrol and oil (and sometimes also other supplies and services) for motor vehicles.

Petronius /pɪˈtrəʊnɪəs/, Gaius (d. AD 66), Roman writer; known as **Petronius Arbiter**. Petronius is generally accepted as the author of the *Satyricon*, a work in prose and verse satirizing the excesses of Roman society.

Petropavlovsk /ˌpɛtrəˈpavlɒfsk/ **1** a Russian fishing port and naval base on the east coast of the Kamchatka peninsula in eastern Siberia; pop. 245,000 (1990). Full name **PETROPAVLOVSK-KAMCHATSKY** /ˌpɛtrəˌpavlɒfskkamˈtʃatski/. **2** a city in northern Kazakstan; pop. 239,000 (1995 est.).

petrophysics ▸ plural noun [treated as sing.] the branch of geology concerned with the physical properties and behaviour of rocks.
– DERIVATIVES **petrophysical** adjective, **petrophysicist** noun.

petrosal /pɪˈtrəʊs(ə)l/ Anatomy ▸ noun the dense part of the temporal bone at the base of the skull, surrounding the inner ear.
▸ adjective relating to or denoting this part of the temporal bone, or the nerves which pass through it.
– ORIGIN mid 18th cent.: from Latin *petrosus* 'stony, rocky' (from *petra* 'rock') + **-AL**.

petrotectonics /ˌpɛtrəʊtɛkˈtɒnɪks/ ▸ plural noun [treated as sing.] the branch of geology concerned with the structure of rocks, especially as a guide to their past movements.
– DERIVATIVES **petrotectonic** adjective.

petrous /ˈpɛtrəs/ ▸ adjective Anatomy another term for **PETROSAL**.
– ORIGIN late Middle English: from Latin *petrosus* 'stony, rocky', from *petra* 'rock', from Greek.

Petrozavodsk /ˌpɛtrəzaˈvɒdsk/ a city in NW Russia, on Lake Onega, capital of the republic of Karelia; pop. 252,000 (1990).

pe tsai /peɪ ˈtsʌɪ/ ▸ noun [mass noun] Chinese leaf of a variety which resembles lettuce.
– ORIGIN late 18th cent.: from Chinese (Cantonese dialect) *báicài*, literally 'white vegetable'.

Petsamo /ˈpɛtsəməʊ/ former name (1920–44) for **PECHENGA**.

petticoat ▸ noun a woman's light, loose undergarment hanging from the shoulders or the waist, worn under a skirt or dress.
■ [as modifier] informal, often derogatory used to denote female control of something regarded as more commonly dominated by men: *he was in danger of succumbing to the petticoat government of Mary and Sarah.*
– DERIVATIVES **petticoated** adjective.
– ORIGIN late Middle English: from *petty coat*, literally 'small coat'.

pettifog ▸ verb (**pettifogged**, **pettifogging**) [no obj.] archaic quibble about petty points.
■ practise legal deception or trickery.
– DERIVATIVES **pettifoggery** noun.
– ORIGIN early 17th cent.: back-formation from **PETTIFOGGER**.

pettifogger ▸ noun archaic an inferior legal practitioner, especially one who deals with petty cases or employs dubious practices.
– ORIGIN mid 16th cent.: from **PETTY** + obsolete *fogger* 'underhand dealer', probably from *Fugger*, the name of a family of merchants in Augsburg in the 15th and 16th cents.

pettifogging ▸ adjective petty; trivial: *I'm working*
on the broad business vision here, not pettifogging little details.*
■ (of a person) placing undue emphasis on petty details.

petting zoo ▸ noun N. Amer. a zoo at which visitors, especially children, may handle and feed the animals.

pettish ▸ adjective (of a person or their behaviour) childishly bad-tempered and petulant: *he comes across in his journal entries as spoiled and pettish.*
– DERIVATIVES **pettishly** adverb, **pettishness** noun.

petty ▸ adjective (**pettier**, **pettiest**) **1** of little importance; trivial: *the petty divisions of party politics.*
■ (of behaviour) characterized by an undue concern for trivial matters, especially in a small-minded or spiteful way: *he was prone to petty revenge on friends and family.*
2 [attrib.] of secondary or lesser importance, rank, or scale; minor: *a petty official.*
■ Law (of a crime) of lesser importance: *petty theft.* Compare with **GRAND**.
– DERIVATIVES **pettily** adverb, **pettiness** noun.
– ORIGIN late Middle English (in the sense 'small in size'): from a phonetic spelling of the pronunciation of French *petit* 'small'. Compare with **PETIT**.

petty apartheid ▸ noun [mass noun] segregation as applied in trivial applications or everyday situations: *he deliberately set about ending Ulster's petty apartheid by visiting Catholic schools.*

petty bourgeois ▸ noun another term for **PETIT BOURGEOIS**.

petty bourgeoisie ▸ noun another term for **PETITE BOURGEOISIE**.

petty cash ▸ noun [mass noun] an accessible store of money kept by an organization for expenditure on small items.

petty larceny ▸ noun [mass noun] Law (in many US states and formerly in Britain) theft of personal property having a value less than a legally specified amount.

petty officer ▸ noun a rank of non-commissioned officer in the navy, above leading seaman or seaman and below chief petty officer.

petty serjeanty ▸ noun see **SERJEANTY**.

petty sessions ▸ noun (in the UK) a magistrates' court for the summary trial of certain offences.

petty treason ▸ noun see **TREASON**.

petty whin ▸ noun a small spiny European broom of heath and moorland.
● *Genista anglica*, family Leguminosae.
– ORIGIN mid 16th cent.: from **PETTY** + **WHIN**[1].

petulant /ˈpɛtjʊl(ə)nt/ ▸ adjective (of a person or their manner) childishly sulky or bad-tempered: *he was moody and petulant* | *a petulant shake of the head.*
– DERIVATIVES **petulance** noun, **petulantly** adverb.
– ORIGIN late 16th cent. (in the sense 'immodest'): from French *pétulant*, from Latin *petulant-* 'impudent' (related to *petere* 'aim at, seek'). The current sense (mid 18th cent.) is influenced by **PETTISH**.

petunia ▸ noun a South American plant of the nightshade family which has white, purple, or red funnel-shaped flowers, with many ornamental varieties.
● *Petunia* × *hybrida*, family Solanaceae.
– ORIGIN modern Latin, from French *petun*, from Guarani *petỹ* 'tobacco' (to which these plants are related).

petuntse /peɪˈtʊntsə, pɪˈtʌntsə/ ▸ noun [mass noun] a type of fine china stone used to make Chinese porcelain.
– ORIGIN early 18th cent.: from Chinese (Mandarin dialect) *báidūnzi*, from *bái* 'white' + *dūn* 'stone' + the suffix *-zi*.

Pevsner /ˈpɛvznə/, Antoine (1886–1962), Russian-born French sculptor and painter, brother of Naum Gabo. With his brother he was a founder of Russian constructivism; the theoretical basis of the movement was put forward in their *Realistic Manifesto* (1920).

pew ▸ noun a long bench with a back, placed in rows in the main part of some churches to seat the congregation.
■ an enclosure or compartment containing a number of seats, used in some churches to seat a particular worshipper or group of worshippers. ■ Brit. informal a seat: *'Take a pew. What'll you have?'*
– ORIGIN late Middle English (originally denoting a raised, enclosed place in a church, provided for particular worshippers): from Old French *puye* 'balcony', from Latin *podia*, plural of *podium* 'elevated place'.

pewee /ˈpiːwiː/ (also **peewee**) ▸ noun a North American tyrant flycatcher with dark olive-grey plumage.
● Genus *Contopus*, family Tyrannidae: several species.
– ORIGIN late 18th cent.: imitative.

pewit ▸ noun variant spelling of **PEEWIT**.

pewter ▸ noun [mass noun] a grey alloy of tin with copper and antimony (formerly, tin and lead).
■ utensils made of this: *the kitchen pewter.* ■ a shade of bluish or silver grey: *looking back at that pewter sky.*
– DERIVATIVES **pewterer** noun.
– ORIGIN Middle English: from Old French *peutre*, of unknown origin.

Peyer's patches /ˈpʌɪəz/ ▸ plural noun Anatomy the numerous areas of lymphoid tissue in the wall of the small intestine which are involved in the development of immunity to antigens present there.
– ORIGIN mid 19th cent.: named after Johann K. *Peyer* (1653–1712), Swiss anatomist.

peyote /peɪˈəʊti/ ▸ noun a small soft blue-green spineless cactus, native to Mexico and the southern US. Also called **MESCAL**.
● *Lophophora williamsii*, family Cactaceae.
■ [mass noun] a hallucinogenic drug prepared from this cactus, containing mescaline.
– ORIGIN mid 19th cent.: from Latin American Spanish, from Nahuatl *peyotl*.

peyote buttons ▸ plural noun the disc-shaped dried tops of the peyote cactus, eaten or chewed for their hallucinogenic effects.

Peyronie's disease /ˈpɛrəniːz/ ▸ noun [mass noun] a condition in which a fibrous region forms in the erectile tissue of the penis, causing pain and curvature during erection.
– ORIGIN early 20th cent.: named after F. de la *Peyronie* (1678–1747), French physician.

Pf. ▸ abbreviation for pfennig.

Pfc. ▸ abbreviation for Private First Class.

PFD ▸ abbreviation for personal flotation device, a life jacket or similar buoyancy aid.

pfennig /ˈ(p)fɛnɪg/ ▸ noun a former monetary unit of Germany, equal to one hundredth of a mark.
– ORIGIN from German *Pfennig*; related to **PENNY**.

pfft /(p)ft/ ▸ exclamation US term for **PHUT**.

pfui /ˈ(p)fuːi/ ▸ exclamation US variant spelling of **PHOOEY**.
– ORIGIN mid 19th cent.: from German.

PG ▸ abbreviation for ■ parental guidance, a film classification indicating that some parents may find the film unsuitable for their children. ■ paying guest.

PGA ▸ abbreviation for trademark Professional Golfers' Association.

pH ▸ noun Chemistry a figure expressing the acidity or alkalinity of a solution on a logarithmic scale on which 7 is neutral, lower values are more acid and higher values more alkaline. The pH is equal to $-\log_{10} c$ where c is the hydrogen ion concentration in moles per litre.
– ORIGIN early 20th cent.: from *p* representing German *Potenz* 'power' + **H**[2], the symbol for hydrogen.

phacelia /fəˈsiːlɪə/ ▸ noun a herbaceous American plant with clustered blue, violet, or white flowers.
● Genus *Phacelia*, family Hydrophyllaceae.
– ORIGIN modern Latin, from Greek *phakelos* 'cluster'.

Phaeacian /fiːˈeɪʃ(ə)n/ ▸ noun (in the *Odyssey*) an inhabitant of Scheria (Corfu), whose people were noted for their hedonism.
– ORIGIN from Latin *Phaeacia*, Greek *Phaiakia*, the name of the island of Scheria, + **-AN**.

Phaedra /ˈfiːdrə/ Greek Mythology the wife of Theseus. She fell in love with her stepson Hippolytus, who rejected her, whereupon she hanged herself, leaving behind a letter which accused him of raping her. Theseus would not believe his son's protestations of innocence and banished him.

Phaeophyceae /ˌfiːə(ʊ)ˈfʌɪsiː/ ▶ Botany a class of lower plants that comprises the brown algae.
● Class Phaeophyceae, division Heterokontophyta (or phylum Heterokonta, kingdom Protista); formerly division Phaeophyta.
– ORIGIN modern Latin (plural), from Greek *phaios* 'dusky' + *phukos* 'seaweed'.

Phaethon /ˈfeɪəθən/ Greek Mythology the son of Helios the sun god. He asked to drive his father's solar chariot for a day, but could not control the immortal horses and the chariot plunged too near to the earth until Zeus killed Phaethon with a thunderbolt in order to save the earth from destruction.

phaeton /ˈfeɪt(ə)n/ ▶ noun historical a light, open, four-wheeled horse-drawn carriage.
■ US a vintage touring car.
– ORIGIN mid 18th cent.: from French *phaéton*, via Latin from the Greek name *Phaethon* (see **PHAETHON**).

phage /feɪdʒ, fɑːʒ/ ▶ noun short for **BACTERIOPHAGE**.

phage display ▶ noun [mass noun] Biochemistry a technique for the production and screening of novel proteins and polypeptides by inserting a gene fragment into a gene responsible for the surface protein of a bacteriophage. The new protein appears in the surface coating of the phage, in which it can be manipulated and tested for biological activity.

phagocyte /ˈfagə(ʊ)sʌɪt/ ▶ noun Physiology a type of cell within the body capable of engulfing and absorbing bacteria and other small cells and particles.
– DERIVATIVES **phagocytic** adjective.
– ORIGIN late 19th cent.: from Greek *phago-* 'eating' (from the verb *phagein*) + **-CYTE**.

phagocytosis /ˌfagə(ʊ)sʌɪˈtəʊsɪs/ ▶ noun [mass noun] Biology the ingestion of bacteria or other material by phagocytes and amoeboid protozoans.
– DERIVATIVES **phagocytize** (also **-ise**) verb, **phagocytose** verb.

phagosome /ˈfagə(ʊ)səʊm/ ▶ noun Biology a vacuole in the cytoplasm of a cell, containing a phagocytosed particle enclosed within a part of the cell membrane.
– DERIVATIVES **phagosomal** adjective.

-phagous ▶ combining form feeding or subsisting on a specified food: *coprophagous*.
– ORIGIN from Latin *-phagus*, Greek *-phagos* (from *phagein* 'eat') + **-OUS**.

-phagy ▶ combining form denoting the practice of eating a specified food: *anthropophagy*.
– ORIGIN from Greek *-phagia*, from *phagein* 'eat'.

phalange /ˈfalan(d)ʒ/ ▶ noun 1 Anatomy another term for **PHALANX** (in sense 2). [ORIGIN: mid 19th cent.: back-formation from *phalanges*, plural of **PHALANX**.]
2 (**Phalange**) a right-wing Maronite party in Lebanon founded in 1936 by Pierre Gemayel. [ORIGIN: mid 20th cent.: shortened from French *Phalanges Libanaises* 'Lebanese phalanxes'.]
– DERIVATIVES **Phalangist** noun & adjective (only in sense 2).

phalangeal ▶ adjective Anatomy of or relating to a phalanx or the phalanges.

phalanger ▶ noun a lemur-like tree-dwelling marsupial native to Australia and New Guinea.
● Family Phalangeridae: several genera, in particular *Phalanger* and *Spilocuscus*, and including the cuscuses; the **common phalanger** is either the spotted cuscus or the grey cuscus. See also **FLYING PHALANGER**.
– ORIGIN late 18th cent.: from French, from Greek *phalangion* 'spider's web' (because of the webbed toes of their hind feet).

phalanges plural form of **PHALANX** (in sense 2).

phalanstery /ˈfalanˌst(ə)ri/ ▶ noun (pl. **-ies**) a group of people living together in community, free of external regulation and holding property in common.
– ORIGIN mid 19th cent.: from French *phalanstère* (used by Fourier in his socialist scheme for the reorganization of society), blend of Latin *phalanx* 'band (of soldiers), group' and French *monastère* 'monastery'.

phalanx /ˈfalaŋks/ ▶ noun 1 (pl. **phalanxes**) a group of people or things of a similar type forming a compact body or brought together for a common purpose: *a phalanx of elegant apartment blocks*.
■ a body of troops or police officers, standing or moving in close formation: *six hundred marchers set*

off, led by a phalanx of police. ■ (in ancient Greece) a body of Macedonian infantry drawn up in close order with shields touching and long spears overlapping.
2 (pl. **phalanges** /fəˈlan(d)ʒiːz/) Anatomy a bone of the finger or toe.
– ORIGIN mid 16th cent. (denoting a body of Macedonian infantry): via Latin from Greek.

phalarope /ˈfalərəʊp/ ▶ noun a small wading or swimming bird with a straight bill and lobed feet, unusual in that the female is more brightly coloured than the male.
● Genus *Phalaropus*, family Scolopacidae (subfamily Phalaropodinae): three species.
– ORIGIN late 18th cent.: from French, from modern Latin *Phalaropus*, formed irregularly from Greek *phalaris* 'coot' + *pous, pod-* 'foot'.

phalera /ˈfalərə/ ▶ noun (pl. **phalerae** /-riː/) (in ancient Greece and Rome) a bright metal disc worn on the chest as an ornament by men, or used to adorn the harness of horses.
– ORIGIN Latin, from the Greek plural *phalara*.

phalli plural form of **PHALLUS**.

phallic ▶ adjective of, relating to, or resembling a phallus or erect penis: *a phallic symbol*.
■ Psychoanalysis of or denoting the genital phase of psychosexual development, especially in males.
– DERIVATIVES **phallically** adverb.
– ORIGIN late 18th cent.: from French *phallique*, from Greek *phallikos*, from *phallos* (see **PHALLUS**).

phallocentric /ˌfalə(ʊ)ˈsɛntrɪk/ ▶ adjective focused on or concerned with the phallus or penis as a symbol of male dominance: *the apartment block was an architectural monument to a phallocentric world*.
– DERIVATIVES **phallocentricity** noun, **phallocentrism** noun.

phallocracy /faˈlɒkrəsi/ ▶ noun (pl. **-ies**) a society or system which is dominated by men and in which the male sex is thought superior.
– DERIVATIVES **phallocratic** adjective.
– ORIGIN 1970s: from Greek *phallos* 'phallus' + **-CRACY**.

phalloidin /faˈlɔɪdɪn/ ▶ noun [mass noun] Chemistry the toxin present in the death cap toadstool. It is a peptide with seven amino acids in a ring structure bridged by a sulphur atom.
– ORIGIN 1930s: from modern Latin *phalloides*, specific epithet of the death cap toadstool *Amanita phalloides* (based on Greek *phallos* 'phallus') + **-IN**[1].

phalloplasty /ˈfalə(ʊ)ˌplasti/ ▶ noun [mass noun] plastic surgery performed to construct, repair, or enlarge the penis.
– ORIGIN late 19th cent.: from Greek *phallos* 'phallus' + **-PLASTY**.

phallus /ˈfaləs/ ▶ noun (pl. **phalli** /-lʌɪ, -liː/ or **phalluses**) a penis, especially when erect (typically used with reference to male potency or dominance).
■ an image or representation of an erect penis, typically symbolizing fertility or potency.
– DERIVATIVES **phallicism** noun, **phallism** noun.
– ORIGIN early 17th cent.: via late Latin from Greek *phallos*.

Phanariot /fəˈnarɪət/ ▶ noun a Greek official in Constantinople under the Ottoman Empire.
– ORIGIN from modern Greek *phanariōtēs*, from *Phanar*, chief Greek quarter of Istanbul, from Greek *phanarion* 'lighthouse' (one being situated in this area).

phanerogam /ˈfan(ə)rə(ʊ)gam/ ▶ noun Botany old-fashioned term for **SPERMATOPHYTE**.
– DERIVATIVES **phanerogamic** adjective, **phanerogamous** adjective.
– ORIGIN mid 19th cent.: from French *phanérogame*, from Greek *phaneros* 'visible' + *gamos* 'marriage'.

Phanerozoic /ˌfan(ə)rə(ʊ)ˈzəʊɪk/ ▶ adjective Geology of, relating to, or denoting the aeon covering the whole of time since the beginning of the Cambrian period, and comprising the Palaeozoic, Mesozoic, and Cenozoic eras. Compare with **CRYPTOZOIC**.
■ [as noun **the Phanerozoic**] the Phanerozoic aeon or the system of rocks deposited during it.

The Phanerozoic began about 570 million years ago, and covers the period in which rocks contain evidence of abundant life in the form of obvious mineralized fossils.

– ORIGIN late 19th cent.: from Greek *phaneros* 'visible, evident' + *zōion* 'animal' + **-IC**.

phantasize ▶ verb variant spelling of **FANTASIZE**

(restricted to archaic uses or, in modern use, to the fields of psychology and psychiatry).

phantasm /ˈfantaz(ə)m/ ▶ noun poetic/literary a figment of the imagination; an illusion or apparition: *the cart seemed to glide like a terrible phantasm*.
■ archaic an illusory likeness of something: *every phantasm of a hope was quickly nullified*.
– DERIVATIVES **phantasmal** adjective, **phantasmic** adjective.
– ORIGIN Middle English (in the sense 'deceptive appearance'): from Old French *fantasme*, via Latin from Greek *phantasma*, from *phantazein* 'make visible', from *phainein* 'to show'. The change from *f-* to *ph-* in the 16th cent. was influenced by the Latin spelling.

phantasmagoria /ˌfantazməˈɡɒrɪə, -ˈɡɔːrɪə/ ▶ noun a sequence of real or imaginary images like that seen in a dream: *what happened next was a phantasmagoria of horror and mystery*.
– DERIVATIVES **phantasmagoric** adjective, **phantasmagorical** adjective.
– ORIGIN early 19th cent. (originally the name of a London exhibition (1802) of optical illusions produced chiefly by magic lantern): probably from French *fantasmagorie*, from *fantasme* 'phantasm' + a fanciful suffix.

phantast ▶ noun variant spelling of **FANTAST**.

phantasy ▶ noun variant spelling of **FANTASY** (restricted to archaic uses or, in modern use, to the fields of psychology and psychiatry).

phantom ▶ noun a ghost: *a phantom who haunts lonely roads* | figurative *the centrist and conservative parties were mere phantoms in 1943* | [as modifier] *a phantom ship*.
■ a figment of the imagination: *he tried to clear the phantoms from his head and grasp reality* | [as modifier] *the women suffered from phantom pain that no physician could ever find*. ■ [as modifier] denoting a financial arrangement or transaction which has been invented for fraudulent purposes but which does not really exist: *he diverted an estimated £1,500,000 into 'phantom' bank accounts*. ■ [as modifier] denoting something, especially something illegal, that is done by an unknown person: *a series of phantom withdrawals from cash machines*.
– ORIGIN Middle English (also in the sense 'illusion, delusion'): from Old French *fantosme*, based on Greek *phantasma* (see **PHANTASM**).

phantom circuit ▶ noun an arrangement of telegraph or other electric wires equivalent to an extra circuit.

phantom limb ▶ noun a sensation experienced by someone who has had a limb amputated that the limb is still there.

phantom pregnancy ▶ noun Medicine an abnormal condition in which signs of pregnancy such as amenorrhoea, nausea, and abdominal swelling are present in a woman who is not pregnant.

pharaoh /ˈfɛːrəʊ/ ▶ noun a ruler in ancient Egypt.
– DERIVATIVES **pharaonic** /ˌfɛːreɪˈɒnɪk/ adjective.
– ORIGIN Middle English: via ecclesiastical Latin from Greek *Pharaō*, from Hebrew *par'ōh*, from Egyptian *pr-'o* 'great house'.

pharaoh ant (also **pharaoh's ant**) ▶ noun a small yellowish African ant that has established itself worldwide, living as a pest in heated buildings.
● *Monomorium pharaonis*, family Formicidae.
– ORIGIN so named because such ants were believed (erroneously) to be one of the plagues of ancient Egypt.

Pharaoh hound ▶ noun a hunting dog of a short-coated tan-coloured breed with large, pointed ears.
– ORIGIN 1960s: so named because the breed is said to have been first introduced to Gozo and Malta by Phoenician sailors.

Pharaoh's serpent ▶ noun an indoor firework that produces ash in a coiled, serpentine form as it burns.
– ORIGIN named by association with Aaron's staff which turned into a serpent before the Pharaoh (Exod. 7:9).

Pharisee /ˈfarɪsiː/ ▶ noun a member of an ancient Jewish sect, distinguished by strict observance of the traditional and written law, and commonly held to have pretensions to superior sanctity.
■ a self-righteous person; a hypocrite.

p

The Pharisees are mentioned only by Josephus and in the New Testament. Unlike the Sadducees, who tried to apply Mosaic law strictly, the Pharisees allowed some freedom of interpretation. Although in the Gospels they are represented as the chief opponents of Christ they seem to have been less hostile than the Sadducees to the nascent Church, with which they shared belief in the Resurrection.

– DERIVATIVES **Pharisaic** /ˌfarɪˈseɪɪk/ adjective, **Pharisaical** adjective, **Pharisaism** /ˈfarɪseɪˌɪz(ə)m/ noun.
– ORIGIN Old English *fariseus*, via ecclesiastical Latin from Greek *Pharisaios*, from Aramaic *prīšayyā* 'separated ones' (related to Hebrew *pārūš* 'separated').

pharmaceutical /ˌfɑːməˈsjuːtɪk(ə)l/ ▶ **adjective** of or relating to medicinal drugs, or their preparation, use, or sale.
▶ **noun** (usu. **pharmaceuticals**) a compound manufactured for use as a medicinal drug.
■ (**pharmaceuticals**) shares in companies manufacturing medicinal drugs.
– DERIVATIVES **pharmaceutically** adverb, **pharmaceutics** plural noun.
– ORIGIN mid 17th cent.: via late Latin from Greek *pharmakeutikos* (from *pharmakeutēs* 'druggist', from *pharmakon* 'drug') + **-AL**.

pharmacist ▶ **noun** a person who is professionally qualified to prepare and dispense medicinal drugs.

pharmaco- /ˈfɑːməkəʊ/ ▶ **combining form** relating to drugs: *pharmacogenetics.*
– ORIGIN from Greek *pharmakon* 'drug, medicine'.

pharmacodynamics ▶ **plural noun** [treated as sing.] the branch of pharmacology concerned with the effects of drugs and the mechanism of their action.
– DERIVATIVES **pharmacodynamic** adjective.

pharmacogenetics ▶ **plural noun** [treated as sing.] the branch of pharmacology concerned with the effect of genetic factors on reactions to drugs.

pharmacognosy /ˌfɑːməˈkɒɡnəsi/ ▶ **noun** [mass noun] the branch of knowledge concerned with medicinal drugs obtained from plants or other natural sources.
– DERIVATIVES **pharmacognosist** noun.
– ORIGIN mid 19th cent.: from **PHARMACO-** 'of drugs' + *gnōsis* 'knowledge'.

pharmacokinetics ▶ **plural noun** [treated as sing.] the branch of pharmacology concerned with the movement of drugs within the body.
– DERIVATIVES **pharmacokinetic** adjective.

pharmacology ▶ **noun** [mass noun] the branch of medicine concerned with the uses, effects, and modes of action of drugs.
– DERIVATIVES **pharmacologic** adjective, **pharmacological** adjective, **pharmacologically** adverb, **pharmacologist** noun.
– ORIGIN early 18th cent.: from modern Latin *pharmacologia*, from Greek *pharmakon* 'drug'.

pharmacopoeia /ˌfɑːməkəˈpiːə/ (US also **pharmacopeia**) ▶ **noun** a book, especially an official publication, containing a list of medicinal drugs with their effects and directions for their use.
■ a stock of medicinal drugs.
– ORIGIN early 17th cent.: modern Latin, from Greek *pharmakopoiia* 'art of preparing drugs', based on *pharmakon* 'drug' + *-poios* 'making'.

pharmacotherapy ▶ **noun** [mass noun] medical treatment by means of drugs.

pharmacy ▶ **noun** (pl. **-ies**) a shop or hospital dispensary where medicinal drugs are provided or sold.
■ [mass noun] the science or practice of the preparation and dispensing of medicinal drugs.
– ORIGIN late Middle English (denoting the administration of drugs): from Old French *farmacie*, via medieval Latin from Greek *pharmakeia* 'practice of the druggist', based on *pharmakon* 'drug'.

Pharos /ˈfɛːrɒs/ a lighthouse, often considered one of the Seven Wonders of the World, erected by Ptolemy II (308–246 BC) in *c.*280 BC on the island of Pharos, off the coast of Alexandria.
■ [as noun **a pharos**] a lighthouse or a beacon to guide sailors.

pharyngeal /fəˈrɪn(d)ʒɪəl, ˌfarɪnˈdʒiːəl/ ▶ **adjective** of or relating to the pharynx.
■ Phonetics (of a speech sound) produced by articulating the root of the tongue with the pharynx, a feature of certain consonants in Arabic, for example.
▶ **noun** Phonetics a pharyngeal consonant.
– ORIGIN early 19th cent.: from modern Latin *pharyngeus* (from Greek *pharunx, pharung-* 'throat') + **-AL**.

pharyngealize /fəˈrɪn(d)ʒɪəlʌɪz/ (also **-ise**) ▶ **verb** [with obj.] Phonetics articulate (a speech sound) with constriction of the pharynx.
– DERIVATIVES **pharyngealization** noun.

pharyngitis /ˌfarɪnˈdʒʌɪtɪs/ ▶ **noun** [mass noun] Medicine inflammation of the pharynx, causing a sore throat.

pharyngo- /fəˈrɪŋɡəʊ/ ▶ **combining form** of or relating to the pharynx: *pharyngotomy.*
– ORIGIN from modern Latin *pharynx, pharyng-.*

pharyngotomy /ˌfarɪŋˈɡɒtəmi/ ▶ **noun** (pl. **-ies**) a surgical incision into the pharynx.

pharynx /ˈfarɪŋks/ ▶ **noun** (pl. **pharynges** /-ˈrɪn(d)ʒiːz/) Anatomy & Zoology the membrane-lined cavity behind the nose and mouth, connecting them to the oesophagus.
■ Zoology the part of the alimentary canal immediately behind the mouth in invertebrates.
– ORIGIN late 17th cent.: modern Latin, from Greek *pharunx, pharung-.*

phascogale /faˈskɒɡəliː/ ▶ **noun** a small arboreal flesh- and nectar-eating Australian marsupial with a pointed snout, large eyes and ears, and a bushy tail.
• Genus *Phascogale*, family Dasyuridae: two species.
– ORIGIN modern Latin, from Greek *phaskōlos* 'purse' + *galē* 'weasel'.

phase /feɪz/ ▶ **noun 1** a distinct period or stage in a process of change or forming part of something's development: *the final phases of the war* | [as modifier] *phase two of the development is in progress.*
■ a stage in a person's psychological development, especially a period of temporary unhappiness or difficulty during adolescence or a particular stage during childhood: *most of your fans are* ***going through a phase.*** ■ each of the aspects of the moon or a planet, according to the amount of its illumination, especially the new moon, the first quarter, the full moon, and the last quarter. ■ each of the separate events in an eventing competition.
2 Zoology a genetic or seasonal variety of an animal's coloration.
■ a stage in the life cycle or annual cycle of an animal.
3 Chemistry a distinct and homogeneous form of matter (i.e. a particular solid, liquid, or gas) separated by its surface from other forms.
4 Physics the relationship in time between the successive states or cycles of an oscillating or repeating system (such as an alternating electric current or a light or sound wave) and either a fixed reference point or the states or cycles of another system with which it may or may not be in synchrony.
■ each of the electrical windings or connections of a polyphase machine or circuit.
5 Linguistics (in systemic grammar) the relationship between a catenative verb and the verb that follows it, as in *she hoped to succeed* and *I like swimming.*
■ a structure containing two verbs in such a relationship.
▶ **verb** [with obj.] (usu. **be phased**) **1** carry out (something) in gradual stages: *the work is being phased over a number of years* | [as adj. **phased**] *a phased withdrawal of troops.*
■ (**phase something in/out**) introduce into (or withdraw from) use in gradual stages: *our armed forces policy was to be phased in over 10 years.*
2 Physics adjust the phase of (something), especially so as to synchronize it with something else.
– PHRASES **in** (or **out of**) **phase** being or happening in (or out of) synchrony or harmony: *the cabling work should be carried out* ***in phase with*** *the building work.*
– ORIGIN early 19th cent. (denoting each aspect of the moon): from French *phase*, based on Greek *phasis* 'appearance', from the base of *phainein* 'to show'.

phase angle ▶ **noun** Physics an angle representing a difference in phase, 360 degrees (2π radians) corresponding to one complete cycle.
■ Astronomy the angle between the lines joining a given planet to the sun and to the earth.

phase contrast ▶ **noun** [mass noun] the technique in microscopy of introducing a phase difference between parts of the light supplied by the condenser so as to enhance the outlines of the sample, or the boundaries between parts differing in optical density.

phase diagram ▶ **noun** Chemistry a diagram representing the limits of stability of the various phases in a chemical system at equilibrium, with respect to variables such as composition and temperature.

phase-lock ▶ **verb** [with obj.] Electronics fix the frequency of (an oscillator or a laser) relative to a stable oscillator of lower frequency by a method that utilizes a correction signal derived from the phase difference generated by any shift in the frequency.

phase modulation ▶ **noun** [mass noun] Electronics variation of the phase of a radio or other wave as a means of carrying information such as an audio signal.

phaser ▶ **noun 1** an instrument that alters a sound signal by phasing it.
2 (in science fiction) a weapon that delivers a beam that can stun or annihilate.

phase rule ▶ **noun** Chemistry a rule relating the possible numbers of phases, constituents, and degrees of freedom in a chemical system.

phase shift ▶ **noun** Physics a change in the phase of a waveform.

phase space ▶ **noun** Physics a multidimensional space in which each axis corresponds to one of the coordinates required to specify the state of a physical system, all the coordinates being thus represented so that a point in the space corresponds to a state of the system.

phase velocity ▶ **noun** Physics the speed of propagation of a sine wave or a sinusoidal component of a complex wave, equal to the product of its wavelength and frequency.

phasic /ˈfeɪzɪk/ ▶ **adjective** of or relating to a phase or phases.
■ chiefly Physiology characterized by occurrence in phases rather than continuously: *phasic and tonic stretch reflexes.*

phasing ▶ **noun** [mass noun] the relationship between the timing of two or more events, or the adjustment of this relationship: *graphical techniques were used to investigate the phasing of traffic lights.*
■ the modification of the sound signal from an electric guitar or other electronic instrument by introducing a phase shift into either of two copies of it and then recombining them. ■ the action of dividing a large task or process into several stages: *the phasing of the overall project.*

Phasmida /ˈfazmɪdə/ **1** Entomology an order of insects that comprises the stick insects and leaf insects. They have very long bodies that resemble twigs or leaves.
2 Zoology a class of nematodes that includes the parasitic hookworms and roundworms. Also called **SECERNENTEA**.
– DERIVATIVES **phasmid** noun & adjective.
– ORIGIN modern Latin (plural), from Latin *phasma* 'apparition', from Greek.

phasor /ˈfeɪzə/ ▶ **noun** Physics a line used to represent a complex electrical quantity as a vector.
– ORIGIN 1940s: from **PHASE**, on the pattern of *vector.*

phat /fat/ ▶ **adjective** black slang excellent: *a London crew with a really phat funk sound.*
– ORIGIN 1970s (originally used to describe a woman, in the sense 'sexy, attractive'): of uncertain origin.

phatic /ˈfatɪk/ ▶ **adjective** denoting or relating to language used for general purposes of social interaction, rather than to convey information or ask questions. Utterances such as *hello, how are you?* and *nice morning, isn't it?* are phatic.
– ORIGIN 1920s: from Greek *phatos* 'spoken' or *phatikos* 'affirming'.

PhD ▶ **abbreviation for** Doctor of Philosophy.
– ORIGIN from Latin *philosophiae doctor.*

pheasant ▶ **noun** a large long-tailed game bird native to Asia, the male of which typically has very showy plumage.
• Family Phasianidae: several genera and many species, in particular the **common pheasant** (*Phasianus colchicus*), which has been widely introduced for shooting.
– ORIGIN Middle English: from Old French *fesan*, via Latin from Greek *phasianos* '(bird) of Phasis', the name of a river in the Caucasus, from which the bird is said to have spread westwards.

pheasantry ▶ **noun** (pl. **-ies**) a place where pheasants are reared or kept.

pheasant's eye ▶ **noun** a plant of the buttercup

family which has scarlet flowers with dark centres, native to southern Europe and SW Asia.
● *Adonis annua*, family Ranunculaceae.

pheasant shell ▶ **noun** a small marine mollusc which has a glossy white shell with red-brown markings. The foot bears a conspicuous white operculum.
● Family Phasianellidae, class Gastropoda: *Phasianella, Tricolia*, and other genera, including the European *T. pullus*.

Pheidippides /fʌɪˈdɪpɪdiːz/ (5th century BC), Athenian messenger. He was sent to Sparta to ask for help after the Persian landing at Marathon in 490 and is said to have covered the 250 km (150 miles) in two days on foot.

phen- ▶ **combining form** variant spelling of **PHENO-** shortened before a vowel (as in *phenelzine*).

phenanthrene /fɪˈnanθriːn/ ▶ **noun** [mass noun] Chemistry a crystalline hydrocarbon present in coal tar.
● A tricyclic compound: chem. formula: $C_{14}H_{10}$.

phencyclidine /fɛnˈsʌɪklɪdiːn/ (abbrev.: **PCP**) ▶ **noun** [mass noun] a synthetic compound derived from piperidine, used as a veterinary anaesthetic and in hallucinogenic drugs such as angel dust.
– ORIGIN 1950s: from **PHENO-** + **CYCLO-** + a shortened form of **PIPERIDINE**.

phenelzine /fəˈnɛlziːn/ ▶ **noun** [mass noun] Medicine a synthetic compound used as a monoamine oxidase inhibitor.
– ORIGIN 1950s: from **PHENO-** + *e(thy)l* + (*hydra*)*zine*.

pheno- (also **phen-** before a vowel) ▶ **combining form**
1 Chemistry derived from benzene: *phenobarbitone*.
2 showing: *phenotype*.
– ORIGIN sense 1 from French *phényle* 'phenyl', from Greek *phaino-* 'shining'; both senses from Greek *phainein* 'to show'.

phenobarbital /ˌfiːnə(ʊ)ˈbɑːbɪt(ə)l, ˌfɛn-/ ▶ **noun** US term for **PHENOBARBITONE**.

phenobarbitone /ˌfiːnə(ʊ)ˈbɑːbɪtəʊn, ˌfɛn-/ ▶ **noun** [mass noun] Medicine a narcotic and sedative barbiturate drug used chiefly to treat epilepsy.

phenocopy /ˈfiːnə(ʊ)kɒpi/ ▶ **noun** (pl. **-ies**) Genetics an individual showing features characteristic of a genotype other than its own, but produced environmentally rather than genetically.

phenocryst /ˈfiːnə(ʊ)krɪst, ˈfɛn-/ ▶ **noun** Geology a large or conspicuous crystal in a porphyritic rock, distinct from the groundmass.
– ORIGIN late 19th cent.: from French *phénocryste*, from Greek *phainein* 'to show' + *krustallos* 'crystal'.

phenol /ˈfiːnɒl/ ▶ **noun** [mass noun] Chemistry a mildly acidic toxic white crystalline solid obtained from coal tar and used in chemical manufacture, and in dilute form (under the name **carbolic**) as a disinfectant.
● Chem. formula: C_6H_5OH.
■ [count noun] any compound with a hydroxyl group linked directly to a benzene ring.
– DERIVATIVES **phenolic** adjective.
– ORIGIN mid 19th cent.: from French *phénole*, based on *phène* 'benzene'.

phenology /fɪˈnɒlədʒi/ ▶ **noun** [mass noun] the study of cyclic and seasonal natural phenomena, especially in relation to climate and plant and animal life.
– DERIVATIVES **phenological** adjective.
– ORIGIN late 19th cent.: from **PHENOMENON** + **-LOGY**.

phenolphthalein /ˌfiːnɒl(ˈf)θaliːn, -ˈ(f)θeɪl-/ ▶ **noun** [mass noun] Chemistry a colourless crystalline solid (pink in alkaline solution) used as an acid–base indicator and medicinally as a laxative.
● Chem. formula: $C_{20}H_{14}O_4$.
– ORIGIN late 19th cent.: from **PHENOL** + *-phthal-* (from **NAPHTHALENE**) + **-IN**[1].

phenol red ▶ **noun** [mass noun] Chemistry a red dye which is used as a pH indicator and (in medicine) injected in testing kidney function.

phenom ▶ **noun** N. Amer. informal a person who is outstandingly talented or admired; a star.
– ORIGIN late 19th cent.: abbreviation of **PHENOMENON**.

phenomena plural form of **PHENOMENON**.

phenomenal ▶ **adjective 1** very remarkable; extraordinary: *the town expanded at a phenomenal rate.*
2 perceptible by the senses or through immediate experience: *the phenomenal world.*

– DERIVATIVES **phenomenalize** (also **-ise**) verb (only in sense 2), **phenomenally** adverb.

phenomenalism ▶ **noun** [mass noun] Philosophy the doctrine that human knowledge is confined to or founded on the realities or appearances presented to the senses.
– DERIVATIVES **phenomenalist** noun & adjective, **phenomenalistic** adjective.

phenomenology /fɪˌnɒmɪˈnɒlədʒi/ ▶ **noun** [mass noun] Philosophy the science of phenomena as distinct from that of the nature of being.
■ an approach that concentrates on the study of consciousness and the objects of direct experience.
– DERIVATIVES **phenomenological** adjective, **phenomenologically** adverb, **phenomenologist** noun.

phenomenon ▶ **noun** (pl. **phenomena**) **1** a fact or situation that is observed to exist or happen, especially one whose cause or explanation is in question: *glaciers are unique and interesting natural phenomena.*
■ a remarkable person, thing, or event.
2 Philosophy the object of a person's perception; what the senses or the mind notice.
– ORIGIN late 16th cent.: via late Latin from Greek *phainomenon* 'thing appearing to view', based on *phainein* 'to show'.

USAGE The word **phenomenon** comes from Greek, and its plural form is **phenomena**, as in *these phenomena are not fully understood.* It is a mistake to treat **phenomena** as if it were a singular form, as in *this is a strange phenomena.*

phenothiazine /ˌfiːnəʊˈθʌɪəziːn, ˌfɛnəʊ-/ ▶ **noun** [mass noun] Chemistry a synthetic compound which is used in veterinary medicine to treat parasitic infestations of animals.
● A heterocyclic compound; chem. formula: $C_{12}H_9NS$.
■ [count noun] Psychiatry any of a group of derivatives of this compound with tranquillizing properties, used as tranquillizers in the treatment of mental illness.

phenotype /ˈfiːnə(ʊ)tʌɪp/ ▶ **noun** Biology the set of observable characteristics of an individual resulting from the interaction of its genotype with the environment.
– DERIVATIVES **phenotypic** adjective, **phenotypical** adjective, **phenotypically** adverb.
– ORIGIN early 20th cent.: from German *Phaenotypus* (see **PHENO-**, **TYPE**).

phentolamine /fɛnˈtɒləmiːn/ ▶ **noun** [mass noun] Medicine a synthetic compound used as a vasodilator, especially in certain cases of hypertension.
– ORIGIN 1950s: from **PHEN-** + *tol(yl)* (an isomeric cyclic radical derived from toluene) + **AMINE**.

phenyl /ˈfiːnʌɪl, ˈfɛnɪl/ ▶ **noun** [as modifier] Chemistry of or denoting the radical —C_6H_5, derived from benzene by removal of a hydrogen atom: *a phenyl group.*
– ORIGIN mid 19th cent.: from French *phényle*, from Greek *phaino-* 'shining' (because first used in names of compounds denoting by-products of the manufacture of gas used for illumination).

phenylalanine /ˌfiːnʌɪlˈaləniːn, ˌfɛnɪl-/ ▶ **noun** [mass noun] Biochemistry an amino acid widely distributed in plant proteins. It is an essential nutrient in the diet of vertebrates.
● Chem. formula: $C_6H_5CH_2CH(NH_2)COOH$.

phenylbutazone /ˌfiːnʌɪlˈbjuːtəzəʊn, ˌfɛnɪl-/ ▶ **noun** [mass noun] a synthetic compound used as an analgesic drug in veterinary medicine.
– ORIGIN 1950s: from **PHENYL** + *but(yl)* + **AZO-** + **-ONE**.

phenylenediamine /ˌfɛnɪliːnˌdʌɪˈiːmiːn, -dʌɪˈam-, ˈdʌɪəmiːn/ ▶ **noun** [mass noun] Chemistry a synthetic crystalline compound used widely in the manufacture of dyes and other chemicals and as a photographic developer.
● Chem. formula: $C_6H_4(NH_2)_2$: three isomers.

phenylephrine /ˌfiːnʌɪlˈɛfrɪn, ˌfɛnɪl-, -ˈɛfriːn/ ▶ **noun** [mass noun] Medicine a synthetic compound related to adrenalin, used as a vasoconstrictor and nasal decongestant.
– ORIGIN 1940s: from **PHENYL** + a contraction of **EPINEPHRINE**.

phenylketonuria /ˌfiːnʌɪlˌkiːtə(ʊ)ˈnjʊərɪə, ˌfɛnɪl-/ (abbrev.: **PKU**) ▶ **noun** [mass noun] Medicine an inherited inability to metabolize phenylalanine which, if untreated, causes brain and nerve damage.

phenylthiocarbamide /ˌfiːnʌɪlˌθʌɪə(ʊ)ˈkɑːbəmʌɪd, ˌfɛnɪl-/ ▶ **noun** [mass noun] Chemistry a crystalline solid

which has a bitter taste to people possessing a certain dominant gene and is tasteless to others.
● Chem. formula: $NH_2CSNHC_6H_5$.

phenytoin /fɛˈnɪtəʊɪn/ ▶ **noun** [mass noun] Medicine a synthetic compound related to hydantoin, used as an anticonvulsant in the treatment of epilepsy.
– ORIGIN 1940s: blend of **PHENYL** and **HYDANTOIN**.

pheromone /ˈfɛrəməʊn/ ▶ **noun** Zoology a chemical substance produced and released into the environment by an animal, especially a mammal or an insect, affecting the behaviour or physiology of others of its species.
– DERIVATIVES **pheromonal** adjective.
– ORIGIN 1950s: from Greek *pherein* 'convey' + **HORMONE**.

phew ▶ **exclamation** informal expressing a strong reaction of relief: *phew, what a year!*
– ORIGIN early 17th cent.: imitative of puffing.

phi /fʌɪ/ ▶ **noun** the twenty-first letter of the Greek alphabet (Φ, φ), transliterated as 'ph' or (in modern Greek) 'f'.
■ (Phi) [followed by Latin genitive] Astronomy the twenty-first star in a constellation: *Phi Eridani.*
▶ **symbol for** ■ (φ) a plane angle. ■ (φ) a polar coordinate. Often coupled with θ.
– ORIGIN Greek.

phial /ˈfʌɪəl/ ▶ **noun** a small cylindrical glass bottle, typically used for medical samples or for potions or medicines: *a phial of blood.*
– ORIGIN Middle English: from Old French *fiole*, via Latin from Greek *phialē*, denoting a broad flat container. Compare with **VIAL**.

Phi Beta Kappa /ˌfʌɪ ˌbiːtə ˈkapə/ ▶ **noun** (in the US) an honorary society of undergraduates and some graduates to which members are elected on the basis of high academic achievement.
■ a member of this society.
– ORIGIN from the initial letters of a Greek motto *philosophia biou kubernētēs* 'philosophy is the guide to life'.

Phidias /ˈfɪdɪas, ˈfʌɪd-/ (5th century BC), Athenian sculptor. He is noted for the Elgin marbles and his vast statue of Zeus at Olympia (c.430), which was one of the Seven Wonders of the World.

Phil. ▶ **abbreviation for** ■ Epistle to the Philippians (in biblical references). ■ Philadelphia. ■ Philharmonic.

phil- ▶ **combining form** variant spelling of **PHILO-** shortened before a vowel or *h* (as in *philanthrope*, *philharmonic*).

-phil ▶ **combining form** having a chemical affinity for a substance: *acidophil | neutrophil.*
– ORIGIN see **-PHILE**.

Philadelphia /ˌfɪləˈdɛlfɪə/ the chief city of Pennsylvania, on the Delaware River; pop. 1,585,580 (1990). Established as a Quaker colony by William Penn and others in 1681, it was the site in 1776 of the signing of the Declaration of Independence and in 1787 of the adoption of the Constitution of the United States.
– DERIVATIVES **Philadelphian** noun & adjective.
– ORIGIN from Greek *philadelphia* 'brotherly love'.

Philadelphia chromosome ▶ **noun** Genetics an abnormal small chromosome sometimes found in the leucocytes of leukaemia patients.

Philadelphia lawyer ▶ **noun** informal a very shrewd lawyer expert in the exploitation of legal technicalities.
– ORIGIN with reference to Andrew Hamilton of Philadelphia, who successfully defended John Zenger (1735), an American journalist and publisher, from libel charges.

philadelphus /ˌfɪləˈdɛlfəs/ ▶ **noun** a mock orange.
– ORIGIN late 18th cent.: modern Latin (adopted by Linnaeus as a genus name), from Greek *philadelphos* 'loving one's brother'.

philander /fɪˈlandə/ ▶ **verb** [no obj.] (of a man) readily or frequently enter into casual sexual relationships with women: *they accepted that their husbands would philander with other women.*
– DERIVATIVES **philanderer** noun.
– ORIGIN mid 18th cent.: from the earlier noun *philander* 'man, husband', often used in literature as the given name of a lover, from Greek *philandros* 'fond of men', from *philein* 'to love' + *anēr* 'man'.

philanthrope /ˈfɪlənˌθrəʊp/ ▶ **noun** archaic term for **PHILANTHROPIST**.

– ORIGIN mid 18th cent.: from Greek *philanthrōpos*, from *philein* 'to love' + *anthrōpos* 'human being'.

philanthropic /ˌfɪlən'θrɒpɪk/ ▶ **adjective** (of a person or organization) seeking to promote the welfare of others; generous and benevolent: *they receive financial support from philanthropic bodies.*
– DERIVATIVES **philanthropically** adverb.
– ORIGIN late 18th cent.: from French *philanthropique*, from Greek *philanthrōpos* 'man-loving' (see **PHILANTHROPE**).

philanthropist ▶ **noun** a person who seeks to promote the welfare of others, especially by the generous donation of money to good causes.

philanthropy /fɪ'lanθrəpi/ ▶ **noun** [mass noun] the desire to promote the welfare of others, expressed especially by the generous donation of money to good causes.
■ [count noun] N. Amer. a philanthropic institution; a charity.
– DERIVATIVES **philanthropism** noun, **philanthropize** (also **-ise**) verb.
– ORIGIN early 17th cent.: via late Latin from Greek *philanthrōpia*, from *philanthrōpos* 'man-loving' (see **PHILANTHROPE**).

philately /fɪ'lat(ə)li/ ▶ **noun** [mass noun] the collection and study of postage stamps.
– DERIVATIVES **philatelic** adjective, **philatelically** adverb, **philatelist** noun.
– ORIGIN mid 19th cent.: from French *philatélie*, from *philo-* 'loving' + Greek *ateleia* 'exemption from payment' (from *a-* 'not' + *telos* 'toll, tax'), used to mean a franking mark or postage stamp exempting the recipient from payment.

Philby /'fɪlbi/, Kim (1912–88), British Foreign Office official and spy; born *Harold Adrian Russell Philby*. While working at the British Embassy in Washington DC (1949–51), Philby was asked to resign on suspicion of being a Soviet agent, although there was no firm evidence to this effect. He defected to the USSR in 1963 and was officially revealed to have spied for the Soviets from 1933.

-phile ▶ **combining form** denoting fondness for a specified thing: *bibliophile | Francophile.*
– ORIGIN from Greek *philos* 'loving'.

Philem. ▶ **abbreviation** for Philemon (in biblical references).

Philemon /fɪ'li:mən/ Greek Mythology a good old countryman living with his wife Baucis in Phrygia who offered hospitality to Zeus and Hermes when the two gods came to earth, without revealing their identities, to test people's piety. Philemon and Baucis were subsequently saved from a flood which covered the district.

Philemon, Epistle to a book of the New Testament, an epistle of St Paul to a well-to-do Christian living probably at Colossae in Phrygia.

philharmonic ▶ **adjective** devoted to music (chiefly used in the names of orchestras): *the Boston Philharmonic Orchestra.*
– ORIGIN mid 18th cent.: from French *philharmonique*, from Italian *filarmonico* 'loving harmony' (see **PHIL-**, **HARMONIC**).

philhellene /'fɪlhɛˌli:n, fɪl'hɛli:n/ ▶ **noun** a lover of Greece and Greek culture: *a romantic philhellene.*
■ historical a supporter of Greek independence.
– DERIVATIVES **philhellenic** adjective, **philhellenism** noun.
– ORIGIN early 19th cent.: from Greek *philellēn* 'loving the Greeks' (see **PHIL-**, **HELLENE**).

-philia ▶ **combining form** denoting fondness, especially an abnormal love for a specified thing: *paedophilia.*
■ denoting undue inclination: *spasmophilia.*
– DERIVATIVES **-philiac** combining form in corresponding nouns and adjectives, **-philic** combining form in corresponding adjectives, **-philous** combining form in corresponding adjectives.
– ORIGIN from Greek *philia* 'fondness'.

philibeg /'fɪləbɛg/ ▶ **noun** variant spelling of **FILIBEG**.

Philip[1] the name of five kings of ancient Macedonia, notably:
■ Philip II (382–336 BC), father of Alexander the Great, reigned 359–336; known as **Philip II of Macedon**. He unified and expanded ancient Macedonia as well as carrying out a number of army reforms. His victory over Athens and Thebes at the battle of Chaeronea in 338 established his hegemony over Greece.
■ Philip V (238–179 BC), reigned 221–179. His

expansionist policies led to a series of confrontations with Rome, culminating in his defeat and his resultant loss of control over Greece.

Philip[2] the name of six kings of France:
■ Philip I (1052–1108), reigned 1059–1108.
■ Philip II (1165–1223), son of Louis VII, reigned 1180–1223; known as **Philip Augustus**. After mounting a series of campaigns against the English kings Henry II, Richard I, and John, Philip succeeded in regaining Normandy (1204), Anjou (1204), and most of Poitou (1204–5).
■ Philip III (1245–1285), reigned 1270–85; known as **Philip the Bold**.
■ Philip IV (1268–1314), son of Philip III, reigned 1285–1314; known as **Philip the Fair**. He continued to extend French dominions, waging wars with England (1294–1303) and Flanders (1302–5).
■ Philip V (1293–1322), reigned 1316–1322; known as **Philip the Tall**.
■ Philip VI (1293–1350), reigned 1328–50; known as **Philip of Valois**. The founder of the Valois dynasty, Philip came to the throne on the death of Charles IV, whose only child was a girl and barred from ruling. His claim was challenged by Edward III of England; the dispute developed into the Hundred Years War.

Philip[3] the name of five kings of Spain:
■ Philip I (1478–1506), reigned 1504–6; known as **Philip the Handsome**. Son of the Holy Roman emperor Maximilian I, in 1496 Philip married the infanta Joanna, daughter of Ferdinand of Aragon and Isabella of Castile. After Isabella's death he ruled Castile jointly with Joanna, establishing the Habsburgs as the ruling dynasty in Spain.
■ Philip II (1527–98), son of Charles I, reigned 1556–98. Philip came to the throne following his father's abdication. His reign was dominated by an anti-Protestant crusade which exhausted the Spanish economy. His Armada against England (1588) ended in defeat.
■ Philip III (1578–1621), reigned 1598–1621.
■ Philip IV (1605–1665), reigned 1621–1665.
■ Philip V (1683–1746), grandson of Louis XIV, reigned 1700–24 and 1724–46. The selection of Philip as successor to Charles II, and Louis XIV's insistence that Philip remain an heir to the French throne, gave rise to War of the Spanish Succession (1701–14). In 1724 Philip abdicated in favour of his son Louis I, but returned to the throne following Louis's death.

Philip, Prince, Duke of Edinburgh (b.1921), husband of Elizabeth II. The son of Prince Andrew of Greece and Denmark, he married Princess Elizabeth in 1947; on the eve of his marriage he was created Duke of Edinburgh.

Philip, St[1], an Apostle. He is commemorated with St James the Less on 1 May.

Philip, St[2], deacon of the early Christian Church; known as **St Philip the Evangelist**. He was one of seven deacons appointed to superintend the secular business of the Church at Jerusalem (Acts 6:5–6). Feast day, 6 June.

Philip II of Macedon /'masɪdɒn, -d(ə)n/, Philip II of Macedonia (see **PHILIP**[1]).

Philip Augustus, Philip II of France (see **PHILIP**[2]).

Philip of Valois, Philip VI of France (see **PHILIP**[2]).

Philippi /'fɪlɪpʌɪ, fɪ'lɪpʌɪ/ a city in ancient Macedonia, the scene in 42 BC of two battles in which Mark Antony and Octavian defeated Brutus and Cassius. The ruins lie close to the Aegean coast in NE Greece, near the port of Kaválla (ancient Neapolis). Greek name **FILIPPOI**.

Philippians, Epistle to the /fɪ'lɪpɪənz/ a book of the New Testament, an epistle of St Paul to the Church at Philippi in Macedonia.

philippic /fɪ'lɪpɪk/ ▶ **noun** poetic/literary a bitter attack or denunciation, especially a verbal one.
– ORIGIN late 16th cent.: via Latin from Greek *philippikos*, the name given to Demosthenes' speeches against Philip II of Macedon, also to those of Cicero against Mark Antony.

Philippine /'fɪlɪpi:n/ ▶ **adjective** of or relating to the Philippines. See also **FILIPINO**.

Philippines /'fɪlɪpi:nz/ a country in SE Asia consisting of an archipelago of over 7,000 islands separated from the Asian mainland by the South China Sea; pop. 60,684,890 (1990); official languages, Pilipino and English; capital, Manila.

The main islands are Luzon, Mindanao, Mindoro, Leyte, Samar, Negros, and Panay. Conquered by Spain in 1565, the islands were ceded to the US following the Spanish-American War in 1898. The Philippines achieved full independence as a republic in 1946. From 1965 the country was under the increasingly dictatorial rule of President Ferdinand Marcos (1917–89); he was driven from power in 1986 and replaced by Corazón Aquino (b.1933), President 1986–92.

Philippopolis /ˌfɪlɪ'pɒpəlɪs/ ancient Greek name for **PLOVDIV**.

Philip the Bold, Philip III of France (see **PHILIP**[2]).

Philip the Fair, Philip IV of France (see **PHILIP**[2]).

Philip the Handsome, Philip I of Spain (see **PHILIP**[3]).

Philip the Tall, Philip V of France (see **PHILIP**[2]).

Philistine /'fɪlɪstʌɪn/ ▶ **noun 1** a member of a non-Semitic people of southern Palestine in ancient times, who came into conflict with the Israelites during the 12th and 11th centuries BC.

The Philistines, from whom the country of Palestine took its name, were one of the Sea Peoples who, according to the Bible, came from Crete and settled the southern coastal plain of Canaan in the 12th century BC.

2 (usu. **philistine**) a person who is hostile or indifferent to culture and the arts, or who has no understanding of them: [as modifier] *a philistine government.*
– DERIVATIVES **philistinism** /-stɪnɪz(ə)m/ noun.
– ORIGIN from French *Philistin*, via late Latin from Greek *Philistinos*, from Hebrew *pĕlištī*. Sense 2 arose as a result of a confrontation between town and gown in Jena, Germany, in the late 17th cent.; a sermon on the conflict quoted: 'the Philistines are upon you' (Judges 16), which led to an association between the townspeople and those hostile to culture.

Phillips ▶ **adjective** trademark denoting a screw with a cross-shaped slot for turning, or a corresponding screwdriver.
– ORIGIN 1930s: from the name of Henry F. *Phillips* (died 1958), the original American manufacturer.

Phillips curve ▶ **noun** Economics a supposed inverse relationship between the level of unemployment and the rate of inflation.
– ORIGIN 1960s: named after Alban W. H. *Phillips* (1914–75), New Zealand economist.

phillumenist /fɪ'lu:mənɪst/ ▶ **noun** a collector of matchbox or matchbook labels.
– DERIVATIVES **phillumeny** noun.
– ORIGIN 1940s: from **PHIL-** 'loving' + Latin *lumen* 'light' + **-IST**.

Philly ▶ **noun** US informal Philadelphia.

philo- (also **phil-** before a vowel or *h*) ▶ **combining form** denoting a liking for a specified thing: *philogynist | philopatric.*
– ORIGIN from Greek *philein* 'to love' or *philos* 'loving'.

philobat /'fɪlə(ʊ)bat/ ▶ **noun** Psychology a personality type characterized by enjoyment of the challenge of coping alone with dangerous and uncertain situations. Often contrasted with **OCNOPHIL**.
– ORIGIN 1950s: from **PHILO-**, on the pattern of *acrobat*.

philodendron /ˌfɪlə'dɛndrən/ ▶ **noun** (pl. **philodendrons** or **philodendra** /-drə/) a tropical American climbing plant which is widely grown as a greenhouse or indoor plant.
● Genus *Philodendron*, family Araceae.
– ORIGIN late 19th cent.: from **PHILO-** 'loving' + Greek *dendron* 'tree'.

philogynist /fɪ'lɒdʒɪnɪst/ ▶ **noun** formal a person who likes or admires women.
– DERIVATIVES **philogyny** noun.
– ORIGIN mid 19th cent.: from **PHILO-** 'loving' + Greek *gunē* 'woman' + **-IST**.

Philo Judaeus /ˌfʌɪləʊ dʒuː'di:əs/ (c.15 BC–c.50 AD), Jewish philosopher of Alexandria. He is particularly known for his commentaries on the Pentateuch (written in Greek), which he interpreted allegorically in the light of Platonic and Aristotelian philosophy.

philology ▶ **noun** [mass noun] the branch of knowledge that deals with the structure, historical development, and relationships of a language or languages.
■ chiefly US literary or classical scholarship.
– DERIVATIVES **philologian** noun, **philological** adjective, **philologically** adverb, **philologist** noun.
– ORIGIN late Middle English (in the Greek sense):

current usage (late 17th cent.) from French *philologie*, via Latin from Greek *philologia* 'love of learning' (see **PHILO-**, **-LOGY**).

Philomel /ˈfɪləmɛl/ (also **Philomela** /ˌfɪləˈmiːlə/) Greek Mythology the daughter of Pandion, king of Athens. She was turned into a swallow and her sister Procne into a nightingale (or, in Latin versions, into a nightingale with Procne the swallow) when they were being pursued by the cruel Tereus, who had married Procne and raped Philomel.
– ORIGIN earlier as *philomene*, from medieval Latin *philomena*, from Latin *philomela* 'nightingale', from Greek *philomēla*.

philopatric /ˌfɪlə(ʊ)ˈpatrɪk/ ▶ **adjective** Zoology (of an animal or species) tending to return to or remain near a particular site or area.
– DERIVATIVES **philopatry** noun.
– ORIGIN 1940s: from **PHILO-** 'liking' + Greek *patra* 'fatherland' + **-IC**.

philoprogenitive /ˌfɪlə(ʊ)prə(ʊ)ˈdʒɛnɪtɪv/ ▶ **adjective** formal having many offspring: *a philoprogenitive ill-paid artisan.*
■ showing love towards one's offspring.
– DERIVATIVES **philoprogenitiveness** noun.

philosopher ▶ **noun** a person engaged or learned in philosophy, especially as an academic discipline.
– ORIGIN Middle English: from a variant of Old French *philosophe*, via Latin from Greek *philosophos* 'lover of wisdom', from *philein* 'to love' + *sophos* 'wise'.

philosopher kings ▶ **plural noun** (in the political theory of Plato) the elite whose knowledge enables them to rule justly.

philosopher's stone ▶ **noun** (**the philosopher's stone**) a mythical substance supposed to change any metal into gold or silver and, according to some, to cure all diseases and prolong life indefinitely. Its discovery was the supreme object of alchemy.

philosophia perennis /fɪləˌsɒfɪə pəˈrɛnɪs/ ▶ **noun** Philosophy a core of philosophical truths which is hypothesized to exist independently of and unaffected by time or place.
– ORIGIN mid 19th cent.: Latin, literally 'perennial philosophy'.

philosophical ▶ **adjective** **1** of or relating to the study of the fundamental nature of knowledge, reality, and existence: *philosophical discussions about free will.*
■ devoted to the study of such issues: *the Cambridge Philosophical Society.*
2 having or showing a calm attitude towards disappointments or difficulties: *he was* ***philosophical about*** *losing the contract.*
– DERIVATIVES **philosophic** adjective, **philosophically** adverb.

philosophical analysis ▶ **noun** [mass noun] the branch of philosophy that deals with the clarification of existing concepts and knowledge.

philosophize (also **-ise**) ▶ **verb** [no obj.] speculate or theorize about fundamental or serious issues, especially in a tedious or pompous way: *he paused for a while to philosophize on racial equality.*
■ [with obj.] explain or argue (a point or idea) in terms of one's philosophical theories.
– DERIVATIVES **philosophizer** noun.

philosophy ▶ **noun** (pl. **-ies**) [mass noun] the study of the fundamental nature of knowledge, reality, and existence, especially when considered as an academic discipline. See also **NATURAL PHILOSOPHY**.
■ [count noun] a set of views and theories of a particular philosopher concerning such study or an aspect of it: *a clash of rival socialist philosophies.* ■ the study of the theoretical basis of a particular branch of knowledge or experience: *the* ***philosophy of*** *science.* ■ [count noun] a theory or attitude held by a person or organization that acts as a guiding principle for behaviour: *don't expect anything and you won't be disappointed, that's my philosophy.*
– ORIGIN Middle English: from Old French *philosophie*, via Latin from Greek *philosophia* 'love of wisdom'.

philtre /ˈfɪltə/ (US **philter**) ▶ **noun** a drink supposed to excite sexual love in the drinker; a love potion.
– ORIGIN late 16th cent.: from French *philtre*, via Latin from Greek *philtron*, from *philein* 'to love'.

-phily ▶ **combining form** equivalent to **-PHILIA**.

phimosis /fʌɪˈməʊsɪs/ ▶ **noun** [mass noun] Medicine a congenital narrowing of the opening of the foreskin so that it cannot be retracted.
– DERIVATIVES **phimotic** adjective.
– ORIGIN late 17th cent.: modern Latin, from Greek, literally 'muzzling'.

Phintias /ˈfɪntɪas/ see **DAMON**.

Phiz /fɪz/ (1815–82), English illustrator; pseudonym of *Hablot Knight Browne*. He illustrated many of Dickens's works, including *Martin Chuzzlewit*, *Pickwick Papers*, and *Bleak House*. He took his pseudonym to complement Dickens's 'Boz'.

phiz /fɪz/ (also **phizog**, **fizzog** /ˈfɪzɒg/) ▶ **noun** Brit. informal a person's face or expression.
– ORIGIN late 17th cent.: abbreviation of **PHYSIOGNOMY**.

phlebitis /flɪˈbʌɪtɪs/ ▶ **noun** [mass noun] Medicine inflammation of the walls of a vein.
– DERIVATIVES **phlebitic** adjective.
– ORIGIN early 19th cent.: modern Latin, from Greek, from *phleps*, *phleb-* 'vein'.

phlebography /flɪˈbɒgrəfi/ ▶ **noun** [mass noun] Medicine radiography of the veins carried out after injection of a radiopaque substance.
– DERIVATIVES **phlebographic** adjective.

phlebotomy /flɪˈbɒtəmi/ ▶ **noun** (pl. **-ies**) [mass noun] the surgical opening or puncture of a vein in order to withdraw blood, to introduce a fluid, or (historically) as part of the procedure of letting blood.
– DERIVATIVES **phlebotomist** noun, **phlebotomize** (also **-ise**) verb (archaic).
– ORIGIN late Middle English: via Old French from late Latin *phlebotomia* from Greek, from *phleps*, *phleb-* 'vein' + *-tomia* 'cutting'.

phlegm /flɛm/ ▶ **noun** [mass noun] the thick viscous substance secreted by the mucous membranes of the respiratory passages, especially when produced in excessive or abnormal quantities e.g. when someone is suffering from a cold.
■ (in medieval science and medicine) one of the four bodily humours, believed to be associated with a calm, stolid, or apathetic temperament. ■ calmness of temperament: *phlegm and determination carried them through many difficult situations.*
– DERIVATIVES **phlegmy** adjective.
– ORIGIN Middle English *fleem*, *fleume*, from Old French *fleume*, from late Latin *phlegma* 'clammy moisture (of the body)', from Greek *phlegma* 'inflammation', from *phlegein* 'to burn'. The spelling change in the 16th cent. was due to association with the Latin and Greek.

phlegmatic /flɛgˈmatɪk/ ▶ **adjective** (of a person) having an unemotional and stolidly calm disposition: *the phlegmatic British character.*
– DERIVATIVES **phlegmatically** adverb.
– ORIGIN Middle English (in the sense 'relating to the humour phlegm'): from Old French *fleumatique*, via Latin from Greek *phlegmatikos*, from *phlegma* 'inflammation' (see **PHLEGM**).

phloem /ˈfləʊɛm/ ▶ **noun** [mass noun] Botany the vascular tissue in plants which conducts sugars and other metabolic products downwards from the leaves.
– ORIGIN late 19th cent.: from Greek *phloos* 'bark' + the passive suffix *-ēma*.

phlogiston /fləˈdʒɪst(ə)n, -ˈgɪst-/ ▶ **noun** [mass noun] a substance supposed by 18th-century chemists to exist in all combustible bodies, and to be released in combustion.
– ORIGIN mid 18th cent.: modern Latin, from Greek *phlogizein* 'set on fire', from *phlox*, *phlog-* 'flame', from the base of *phlegein* 'to burn'.

phlogopite /ˈflɒgəpʌɪt/ ▶ **noun** [mass noun] a brown micaceous mineral which occurs chiefly in metamorphosed limestone and magnesium-rich igneous rocks.
– ORIGIN mid 19th cent.: from Greek *phlogōpos* 'fiery' (from the base of *phlegein* 'to burn') + *ōps*, *ōp-* 'face' + **-ITE**[1].

phlox /flɒks/ ▶ **noun** a North American plant that typically has dense clusters of colourful scented flowers, widely grown as an alpine or border plant.
● Genus *Phlox*, family Polemoniaceae.
– ORIGIN modern Latin, from Latin, denoting a flame-coloured flower, from Greek, literally 'flame'.

Phnom Penh /nɒm ˈpɛn/ the capital of Cambodia, a port at the junction of the Mekong and Tonlé Sap Rivers; pop. 920,000 (est. 1994). It became the capital of a Khmer kingdom in the mid 15th century. Between 1975 and 1979 the Khmer Rouge forced a great many of its population (then 2.5 million) to leave the city and resettle in the country.

-phobe ▶ **combining form** denoting a person having a fear or dislike of what is specified: *homophobe* | *xenophobe.*
– ORIGIN from French, via Latin *-phobus* from Greek *-phobos* 'fearing', from *phobos* 'fear'.

phobia /ˈfəʊbɪə/ ▶ **noun** an extreme or irrational fear of or aversion to something: *she suffered from a phobia about birds.*
– DERIVATIVES **phobic** adjective & noun.
– ORIGIN late 18th cent.: independent usage of **-PHOBIA**.

-phobia ▶ **combining form** extreme or irrational fear or dislike of a specified thing or group: *arachnophobia* | *Russophobia.*
– DERIVATIVES **-phobic** combining form in corresponding adjectives.
– ORIGIN via Latin from Greek.

Phobos /ˈfəʊbɒs/ Astronomy the inner of the two small satellites of Mars, discovered in 1877 (27 km long and 22 km across).
– ORIGIN named after one of the sons of the Greek war god **ARES**.

phocine /ˈfəʊsʌɪn/ ▶ **adjective** Zoology of, relating to, or affecting the true (earless) seals.
– ORIGIN mid 19th cent.: from modern Latin *Phocinae* (subfamily name), from Greek *phōkē* 'seal'.

phocomelia /ˌfəʊkə(ʊ)ˈmiːlɪə/ ▶ **noun** [mass noun] Medicine a rare congenital deformity in which the hands or feet are attached close to the trunk, the limbs being grossly underdeveloped or absent. This condition was a side effect of the drug thalidomide taken during early pregnancy.
– ORIGIN late 19th cent.: modern Latin, from Greek *phōkē* 'seal' + *melos* 'limb'.

Phoebe /ˈfiːbi/ **1** Greek Mythology a Titaness, daughter of Uranus (Heaven) and Gaia (Earth). She became the mother of Leto and thus the grandmother of Apollo and Artemis. In the later Greek writers her name was often used for Selene (Moon).
2 Astronomy a satellite of Saturn, the furthest from the planet and with an eccentric retrograde orbit, discovered in 1898 (average diameter 220 km).
– ORIGIN from Greek *Phoibē*, literally 'bright one'.

phoebe ▶ **noun** an American tyrant flycatcher with mainly grey-brown or blackish plumage.
● Genus *Sayornis*, family Tyrannidae: three species, in particular the common **eastern phoebe** (*S. phoebe*).
– ORIGIN early 18th cent.: imitative; influenced by the name **PHOEBE**.

Phoebus /ˈfiːbəs/ Greek Mythology an epithet of Apollo, used in contexts where the god was identified with the sun.
– ORIGIN from Greek *Phoibos*, literally 'bright one'.

Phoenicia /fəˈniːʃə/ an ancient country on the shores of the eastern Mediterranean, corresponding to modern Lebanon and the coastal plains of Syria. It consisted of a number of city states, including Tyre and Sidon, and was a flourishing centre of Mediterranean trade and colonization during the early part of the 1st millennium BC.
– ORIGIN from Latin, from Greek *Phoinikē*.

Phoenician /fəˈnɪʃ(ə)n, -ˈniː-/ ▶ **noun** **1** a member of a Semitic people inhabiting ancient Phoenicia and its colonies. The Phoenicians prospered from trade and manufacturing until the capital, Tyre, was sacked by Alexander the Great in 332 BC.
2 [mass noun] the Semitic language of this people, written in an alphabet that was the ancestor of the Greek and Roman alphabets.
▶ **adjective** of or relating to Phoenicia or its colonies, or its people, language, or alphabet.

Phoenix[1] /ˈfiːnɪks/ Astronomy a southern constellation (the Phoenix), west of Grus.
■ [as genitive **Phoenicis** /fɪˈniːsɪs/] used with preceding letter or numeral to designate a star in this constellation: *the star Delta Phoenicis.*
– ORIGIN Latin.

Phoenix[2] /ˈfiːnɪks/ the state capital of Arizona; pop. 983,400 (1990). Its dry climate makes it a popular winter resort.

phoenix ▶ **noun** (in classical mythology) a unique bird that lived for five or six centuries in the Arabian desert, after this time burning itself on a funeral pyre and rising from the ashes with renewed youth to live through another cycle.

■a person or thing regarded as uniquely remarkable in some respect.
– PHRASES **rise like a phoenix from the ashes** emerge renewed after apparent disaster or destruction.
– ORIGIN from Old French *fenix*, via Latin from Greek *phoinix* 'Phoenician, reddish purple, or phoenix'. The relationship between the Greek senses is obscure: it could not be 'the Phoenician bird' because the legend centres on the temple at Heliopolis in Egypt, where the phoenix is said to have burnt itself on the altar. Perhaps the basic sense is 'purple', symbolic of fire and possibly the primary sense of *Phoenicia* as the purple land (or land of the sunrise).

Phoenix Islands a group of eight islands lying just south of the equator in the western Pacific. They form a part of Kiribati.

Pholidota /ˌfɒlɪˈdəʊtə/ Zoology a small order of mammals that comprises the pangolins.
– ORIGIN modern Latin (plural), from Greek *pholidōtos* 'scaly', from *pholis*, *pholid-* 'scale'.

phon /fɒn/ ▶ noun a unit of the perceived loudness of sounds.
– ORIGIN 1930s: from Greek *phōnē* 'sound'.

phonaesthesia /ˌfəʊnəsˈθiːzɪə/ (US also **phonesthesia**) ▶ noun [mass noun] attribution of common elements of meaning or connotation to certain sound sequences, especially consonant clusters, for example initial *sl-*, as in *slow*, *sleep*, *slush*, *slide*, *slip*.
– ORIGIN mid 20th cent.: modern Latin, from Greek *phōnē* 'sound' + *aesthesthai* 'perceive'.

phonaesthetics /ˌfəʊnəsˈθɛtɪks/ (US also **phonesthetics**) ▶ plural noun [treated as sing.] the study of the aesthetic properties of speech sound, in particular the study of sound sequences, as in phonaesthesia.
– DERIVATIVES **phonaesthetic** adjective.

phonation /fə(ʊ)ˈneɪʃ(ə)n/ ▶ noun [mass noun] Phonetics the production or utterance of speech sounds.
– DERIVATIVES **phonate** /fə(ʊ)ˈneɪt/ verb, **phonatory** /ˈfəʊnət(ə)ri/ adjective.
– ORIGIN mid 19th cent.: from Greek *phōnē* 'sound, voice' + -ATION.

phone¹ ▶ noun short for TELEPHONE.
■(phones) informal headphones or earphones.
▶ verb short for TELEPHONE.

phone² ▶ noun Phonetics a speech sound; the smallest discrete segment of sound in a stream of speech.
– ORIGIN mid 19th cent.: from Greek *phōnē* 'sound, voice'.

-phone ▶ combining form 1 denoting an instrument using or connected with sound: *megaphone*.
2 denoting a person who uses a specified language: *francophone*.
– ORIGIN from Greek *phōnē* 'sound, voice'.

phone bank ▶ noun US a battery of telephones.

phone book ▶ noun a telephone directory.

phonecard ▶ noun a prepaid card which allows the user to make telephone calls up to a specified number of units using a cardphone.

phone-in ▶ noun a radio or television programme during which the listeners or viewers telephone the studio and participate.
■[as modifier] denoting something conducted by people leaving answers or messages by telephone: *a phone-in contest* | *a phone-in poll*.

phonematic /ˌfəʊnɪˈmatɪk, ˌfɒn-/ ▶ adjective (in prosodic analysis) denoting a segmental element of vowel or consonant features which combines with other elements such as intonation or stress.
– ORIGIN 1930s: from Greek *phōnēma*, *phōnēmatik-* 'relating to a sound'.

phoneme /ˈfəʊniːm/ ▶ noun Phonetics any of the perceptually distinct units of sound in a specified language that distinguish one word from another, for example *p*, *b*, *d*, and *t* in the English words *pad*, *pat*, *bad*, and *bat*. Compare with ALLOPHONE.
– DERIVATIVES **phonemic** /-ˈniːmɪk/ adjective, **phonemics** noun.
– ORIGIN late 19th cent.: from French *phonème*, from Greek *phōnēma* 'sound, speech', from *phōnein* 'speak'.

phone sex ▶ noun [mass noun] a commercial service providing its customers with sexually explicit telephone conversation for the purposes of sexual gratification.

phonetic /fəˈnɛtɪk/ ▶ adjective Phonetics of or relating to speech sounds: *detailed phonetic information*.
■(of a system of writing) having a direct correspondence between symbols and sounds: *a phonetic alphabet*. ■of or relating to phonetics: *phonetic training*.
– DERIVATIVES **phonetically** adverb, **phoneticism** noun, **phoneticist** (also **-ise**) verb.
– ORIGIN early 19th cent.: from modern Latin *phoneticus*, from Greek *phōnētikos*, from *phōnein* 'speak'.

phonetics ▶ plural noun [treated as sing.] the study and classification of speech sounds.
– DERIVATIVES **phonetician** noun.

phoney (also **phony**) informal ▶ adjective (**phonier**, **phoniest**) not genuine; fraudulent: *I thought your accent was a bit phoney*.
▶ noun (pl. **-eys** or **-ies**) a fraudulent person or thing.
– DERIVATIVES **phonily** adverb, **phoniness** noun.
– ORIGIN late 19th cent.: of unknown origin.

phoney war the period of comparative inaction at the beginning of the Second World War between the German invasion of Poland (September 1939) and that of Norway (April 1940).

phonic /ˈfəʊnɪk, ˈfɒnɪk/ ▶ adjective of or relating to speech sounds.
■of or relating to phonics: *the English language presents difficulties if a purely phonic approach is attempted*.
– DERIVATIVES **phonically** adverb.
– ORIGIN early 19th cent.: from Greek *phōnē* 'voice' + -IC.

phonics ▶ plural noun [treated as sing.] a method of teaching people to read by correlating sounds with symbols in an alphabetic writing system.

phono ▶ adjective [usu. attrib.] denoting a type of plug, and the corresponding socket, used with audio and video equipment, in which one conductor is cylindrical and the other is a central prong that extends beyond it.
– ORIGIN 1940s: abbreviation of PHONOGRAPH.

phono- /ˈfəʊnəʊ, ˈfɒn-/ ▶ combining form relating to sound: *phonograph*.
– ORIGIN from Greek *phōnē* 'sound, voice'.

phonocardiogram ▶ noun Medicine a chart or record of the sounds made by the heart.

phonograph ▶ noun Brit. an early form of gramophone using cylinders and able to record as well as reproduce sound.
■N. Amer. a record player.
– DERIVATIVES **phonographic** adjective.

phonograph record ▶ noun N. Amer. fuller form of RECORD (in sense 4).

phonolite /ˈfəʊnəlʌɪt/ ▶ noun [mass noun] Geology a fine-grained volcanic igneous rock composed of alkali feldspars and nepheline.
– ORIGIN early 19th cent.: from PHONO- 'relating to sound' (because of its resonance when struck) + -ITE¹.

phonology /fəˈnɒlədʒi/ ▶ noun [mass noun] the system of contrastive relationships among the speech sounds that constitute the fundamental components of a language.
■the study of these relationships within a language or between different languages.
– DERIVATIVES **phonological** adjective, **phonologically** adverb, **phonologist** noun.

phonon /ˈfəʊnɒn/ ▶ noun Physics a quantum of energy or a quasiparticle associated with a compressional wave such as sound or a vibration of a crystal lattice.
– ORIGIN 1930s: from Greek *phōnē* 'sound', on the pattern of *photon*.

phonotactics /ˌfəʊnə(ʊ)ˈtaktɪks/ ▶ plural noun [treated as sing.] the study of the rules governing the possible phoneme sequences in a language.
– DERIVATIVES **phonotactic** adjective.

phony ▶ adjective & noun variant spelling of PHONEY.

phooey informal ▶ exclamation (US also **pfui**) used to express disdain or disbelief: *so phooey to sophistication*.
▶ noun [mass noun] nonsense: *they dismiss it all as movie phooey*.
– ORIGIN 1920s: imitative.

phorbol /ˈfɔːbɒl/ ▶ noun Chemistry a compound present (in the form of highly carcinogenic esters) in croton oil.
●A tetracyclic alcohol; chem. formula: $C_{20}H_{28}O_6$.

– ORIGIN 1930s: from Greek *phorbē* 'fodder' (from *pherbein* 'to feed') + -OL.

-phore ▶ combining form denoting an agent or bearer of a specified thing: *ionophore* | *semaphore*.
– DERIVATIVES **-phorous** combining form in corresponding adjectives.
– ORIGIN from modern Latin *-phorus*, from Greek *-phoros*, *-phoron* 'bearing, bearer', from *pherein* 'to bear'.

phoresy /fəˈriːsi, ˈfɒrəsi/ ▶ noun [mass noun] Zoology an association between two organisms in which one (e.g. a mite) travels on the body of another, without being a parasite.
– DERIVATIVES **phoretic** /fəˈrɛtɪk/ adjective.
– ORIGIN 1920s: from French *phorésie*, from Greek *phorēsis* 'being carried'.

phormium /ˈfɔːmɪəm/ ▶ noun the flax-lily of New Zealand.
– ORIGIN early 19th cent.: modern Latin, from Greek *phormion* 'small basket' (with reference to the use made of the fibres).

Phoronida /fəˈrɒnɪdə/ Zoology a small phylum of worm-like invertebrates that comprises the horseshoe worms.
– DERIVATIVES **phoronid** noun.
– ORIGIN modern Latin (plural), from Latin *Phoronis*, *Phoronid-*, the name of a character in Greek mythology.

phosgene /ˈfɒzdʒiːn/ ▶ noun [mass noun] Chemistry a colourless poisonous gas made by the reaction of chlorine and carbon dioxide. It was used as a poison gas, notably in the First World War.
●Alternative name: **carbonyl chloride**; chem. formula: $COCl_2$.
– ORIGIN early 19th cent.: from Greek *phōs* 'light' + -GEN, with reference to its original production by the action of sunlight on chlorine and carbon monoxide.

phosphatase /ˈfɒsfəteɪz/ ▶ noun [mass noun] Biochemistry an enzyme that catalyses the hydrolysis of organic phosphates in a specified (acid or alkaline) environment.

phosphate /ˈfɒsfeɪt/ ▶ noun Chemistry a salt or ester of phosphoric acid, containing PO_4^{3-} or a related anion or a group such as —$OPO(OH)_2$.
– ORIGIN late 18th cent.: from French, from *phosphore* 'phosphorus'.

phosphatic /fɒsˈfatɪk/ ▶ adjective (chiefly of rocks and fertilizer) containing or consisting of phosphates.

phosphatide /ˈfɒsfətʌɪd/ ▶ noun Biochemistry any of a class of compounds which are fatty acid esters of glycerol phosphate with a nitrogen base linked to the phosphate group.

phosphatidylcholine /ˌfɒsˌfatɪdʌɪlˈkəʊliːn, -dɪl-/ ▶ noun [mass noun] Biochemistry a substance widely distributed in animal tissues, egg yolk, and some higher plants, consisting of phospholipids linked to choline.

phosphene /ˈfɒsfiːn/ ▶ noun a ring or spot of light produced by pressure on the eyeball or direct stimulation of the visual system other than by light.
– ORIGIN late 19th cent.: formed irregularly from Greek *phōs* 'light' + *phainein* 'to show'.

phosphide /ˈfɒsfʌɪd/ ▶ noun Chemistry a binary compound of phosphorus with another element or group.

phosphine /ˈfɒsfiːn/ ▶ noun [mass noun] Chemistry a colourless foul-smelling gaseous compound of phosphorus and hydrogen, analogous to ammonia.
●Chem. formula: PH_3. It forms salts containing the **phosphonium** ion, PH_4^+.
– ORIGIN late 19th cent.: from PHOSPHO- 'relating to phosphorus' + -INE⁴, on the pattern of *amine*.

phosphite /ˈfɒsfʌɪt/ ▶ noun Chemistry old-fashioned term for *phosphonate* (see PHOSPHONIC ACID).

phospho- ▶ combining form representing PHOSPHORUS.

phosphocreatine /ˌfɒsfə(ʊ)ˈkriːəti:n/ ▶ noun [mass noun] Biochemistry a phosphate ester of creatine found in vertebrate muscle, where it serves to store phosphates to provide energy for muscular contraction.

phosphodiesterase /ˌfɒsfə(ʊ)dʌɪˈɛstəreɪz/ ▶ noun [mass noun] Biochemistry an enzyme which breaks a phosphodiester bond in an oligonucleotide.

phosphodiester bond /ˌfɒsfə(ʊ)dʌɪˈɛstə/ ▶ noun

Biochemistry a chemical bond of the kind joining successive sugar molecules in a polynucleotide.

phospholipase /ˈfɒsfə(ʊ)ˈlɪpeɪz, -ˈlʌɪpeɪz/ ▶ noun Biochemistry an enzyme which hydrolyses phosphatidylcholine or a similar phospholipid.

phospholipid /ˌfɒsfə(ʊ)ˈlɪpɪd/ ▶ noun Biochemistry a lipid containing a phosphate group in its molecule, e.g. phosphatidylcholine.

phosphonic acid /fɒsˈfɒnɪk/ ▶ noun [mass noun] Chemistry a crystalline acid obtained by the reaction of phosphorus trioxide with water.
● A dibasic acid; chem. formula: HPO(OH)$_2$.
– DERIVATIVES **phosphonate** noun.
– ORIGIN late 19th cent.: *phosphonic* from **PHOSPHO-** 'relating to phosphorus', on the pattern of *sulphonic*.

phosphonium /fɒsˈfəʊnɪəm/ ▶ noun see **PHOSPHINE**.
– ORIGIN late 19th cent.: blend of **PHOSPHORUS** and **AMMONIUM**.

phosphoprotein ▶ noun Biochemistry a protein that contains phosphorus (other than in a nucleic acid or a phospholipid).

phosphor /ˈfɒsfə/ ▶ noun a synthetic fluorescent or phosphorescent substance, especially any of those used to coat the screens of cathode ray tubes.
■ old-fashioned term for **PHOSPHORUS**.
– ORIGIN early 17th cent.: from Latin *phosphorus* (see **PHOSPHORUS**).

phosphorated ▶ adjective combined or impregnated with phosphorus.

phosphor bronze ▶ noun [mass noun] a tough, hard form of bronze containing a small amount of phosphorus, used especially for bearings.

phosphoresce /ˌfɒsfəˈrɛs/ ▶ verb [no obj.] emit light or radiation by phosphorescence.

phosphorescence ▶ noun [mass noun] light emitted by a substance without combustion or perceptible heat: *the stones overhead gleamed with phosphorescence.*
■ Physics the emission of radiation in a similar manner to fluorescence but on a longer timescale, so that emission continues after excitation ceases.
– DERIVATIVES **phosphorescent** adjective.

phosphoric /fɒsˈfɒrɪk/ ▶ adjective relating to or containing phosphorus.
■ Chemistry of phosphorus with a valency of five. Compare with **PHOSPHOROUS**.
– ORIGIN late 18th cent.: from French *phosphorique*, from *phosphore* 'phosphorus'.

phosphoric acid ▶ noun [mass noun] Chemistry a crystalline acid obtained e.g. by treating phosphates with sulphuric acid, and used in fertilizer and soap manufacture and food processing.
● A tribasic acid; chem. formula: H$_3$PO$_4$.

phosphorite /ˈfɒsfərʌɪt/ ▶ noun [mass noun] a sedimentary rock containing a high proportion of calcium phosphate.
– ORIGIN late 18th cent.: from **PHOSPHORUS** + **-ITE**^{1}.

phosphorous /ˈfɒsf(ə)rəs/ ▶ adjective relating to or containing phosphorus. Compare with **PHOSPHORIC**.
■ Chemistry of phosphorus with a valency of three.
■ phosphorescent.

USAGE The correct spelling for the noun denoting the chemical element is **phosphorus**, while the correct spelling for the adjective meaning 'relating to or containing phosphorus' is **phosphorous**. A common mistake is to use the spelling **phosphorous** for the noun as well as the adjective. Approximately 6 per cent of citations for this word in the British National Corpus use this incorrect spelling.

phosphorous acid ▶ noun another term for **PHOSPHONIC ACID**.

phosphorus /ˈfɒsf(ə)rəs/ ▶ noun [mass noun] the chemical element of atomic number 15, a poisonous, combustible non-metal which exists in two common allotropic forms, **white phosphorus**, a yellowish waxy solid which ignites spontaneously in air and glows in the dark, and **red phosphorus**, a less reactive form used in making matches. (Symbol: **P**)
– ORIGIN late 17th cent.: from Latin, from Greek *phōsphoros*, from *phōs* 'light' + *-phoros* '-bringing'.

phosphoryl /ˈfɒsfərʌɪl, -rɪl/ ▶ noun [as modifier] Chemistry the trivalent group ≡PO.

■ Biochemistry the monovalent phosphate group —PO(OH)$_2$.
– ORIGIN late 19th cent.: from **PHOSPHORUS** + **-YL**.

phosphorylase /fɒsˈfɒrɪleɪz/ ▶ noun [mass noun] Biochemistry an enzyme which introduces a phosphate group into an organic molecule, notably glucose.

phosphorylate /fɒsˈfɒrɪleɪt/ ▶ verb [with obj.] (often **be phosphorylated**) chiefly Biochemistry introduce a phosphate group into (a molecule or compound).
– DERIVATIVES **phosphorylation** noun.

phossy jaw /ˈfɒsi/ ▶ noun [mass noun] historical, informal gangrene of the jawbone caused by phosphorus poisoning.
– ORIGIN late 19th cent.: *phossy* by abbreviation of *phosphorus necrosis*, denoting gangrene of the jaw.

phot /fəʊt/ ▶ noun a unit of illumination equal to one lumen per square centimetre.
– ORIGIN early 20th cent.: from Greek *phōs, phōt-* 'light'.

photic ▶ adjective technical of or relating to light, especially as an agent of chemical change or physiological response.
■ Ecology denoting the layers of the ocean reached by sufficient sunlight to allow plant growth: *an average depth for the photic zone is about 100 m.*

photino /fəˈ(ʊ)ˈtiːnəʊ/ ▶ noun (pl. **-os**) Physics the hypothetical supersymmetric counterpart of the photon, with spin $-\frac{1}{2}$.
– ORIGIN 1970s: from **PHOTON** + *-ino* from **NEUTRINO**.

Photius /ˈfəʊtɪəs/ (*c.*820–*c.*891), Byzantine scholar and patriarch of Constantinople. His most important work is the *Bibliotheca*, a critical account of 280 earlier prose works and an invaluable source of information about many works now lost.

photo ▶ noun (pl. **-os**) a photograph.
■ informal a photo finish.
▶ verb (**-oes, -oed**) [with obj.] informal take a photograph of.
– ORIGIN mid 19th cent.: abbreviation.

photo- /ˈfəʊtəʊ/ ▶ combining form **1** relating to light: *photochemical.*
2 relating to photography: *photofit.*
– ORIGIN sense 1 from Greek *phōs, phōt-* 'light'; sense 2, abbreviation of **PHOTOGRAPHY**.

photoactive ▶ adjective (of a substance) capable of a chemical or physical change in response to illumination.

photobiology ▶ noun [mass noun] the study of the effects of light on living organisms.

photobleaching ▶ noun [mass noun] Biochemistry loss of colour by a pigment (such as chlorophyll or rhodopsin) when illuminated.

photocall ▶ noun Brit. an occasion on which famous people pose for photographers by arrangement.

photocatalysis /ˌfəʊtə(ʊ)kəˈtalɪsɪs/ ▶ noun [mass noun] Chemistry the acceleration of a chemical reaction by light.
– DERIVATIVES **photocatalytic** adjective.

photocathode ▶ noun a cathode which emits electrons when illuminated, causing an electric current.

photo CD ▶ noun a compact disc from which still photographs can be displayed on a television screen.
■ [mass noun] the storing and reproducing of photographs in this way: *photo CD is used in medicine and data storage*

photocell ▶ noun short for **PHOTOELECTRIC CELL**.

photochemical ▶ adjective of, relating to, or caused by the chemical action of light: *photochemical smog.*
■ of or relating to photochemistry.
– DERIVATIVES **photochemically** adverb.

photochemistry ▶ noun [mass noun] the branch of chemistry concerned with the chemical effects of light.

photochromic ▶ adjective (of a substance) undergoing a reversible change in colour or shade when exposed to light of a particular frequency or intensity: *photochromic sunglasses.*
– DERIVATIVES **photochromism** noun.
– ORIGIN 1950s: from **PHOTO-** 'relating to light' + Greek *khrōma* 'colour' + **-IC**.

photocoagulation /ˌfəʊtə(ʊ)kəʊˌagjʊˈleɪʃ(ə)n/ ▶ noun [mass noun] Medicine the use of a laser beam or other intense light source to coagulate and destroy

or fuse small areas of tissue, especially in the retina.

photocomposition ▶ noun another term for **FILMSETTING**.

photoconductivity /ˌfəʊtə(ʊ)kɒndʌkˈtɪvɪti/ ▶ noun [mass noun] increased electrical conductivity caused by the presence of light.
– DERIVATIVES **photoconductive** adjective, **photoconductor** noun.

photocopier ▶ noun a machine for making photocopies.

photocopy ▶ noun (pl. **-ies**) a photographic copy of printed or written material produced by a process involving the action of light on a specially prepared surface.
▶ verb (**-ies, -ied**) [with obj.] make a photocopy of.
– DERIVATIVES **photocopiable** adjective.

photocurrent ▶ noun an electric current induced by the action of light.

photodegradable ▶ adjective capable of being decomposed by the action of light, especially sunlight: *photodegradable plastic.*

photodetector ▶ noun a device that detects or responds to incident light by using the electrical effect of individual photons.

photodiode ▶ noun a semiconductor diode which, when exposed to light, generates a potential difference or changes its electrical resistance.

photodissociation ▶ noun [mass noun] Chemistry dissociation of a chemical compound by the action of light.

photodynamic ▶ adjective Medicine denoting treatment for cancer involving the injection of a cytotoxic compound which is relatively inactive until activated by a laser beam after collecting in the tumour.

photoelectric ▶ adjective characterized by or involving the emission of electrons from a surface by the action of light.
– DERIVATIVES **photoelectricity** noun.

photoelectric cell ▶ noun a device using a photoelectric effect to generate current.

photoelectron ▶ noun an electron emitted from an atom by interaction with a photon, especially an electron emitted from a solid surface by the action of light.
– DERIVATIVES **photoelectronic** adjective.

photoemission ▶ noun [mass noun] the emission of electrons from a surface caused by the action of light striking it.
– DERIVATIVES **photoemitter** noun.

photoessay ▶ noun an essay or short article consisting of text matter and numerous photographs.

photo finish ▶ noun a close finish of a race in which the winner is identifiable only from a photograph taken as the competitors cross the line.

photofit ▶ noun Brit. a reconstructed picture of a person, especially one sought by the police, made from composite photographs of facial features.

photog /fəˈtɒg/ ▶ noun N. Amer. informal a photographer.

photogenic /ˌfəʊtə(ʊ)ˈdʒɛnɪk, -ˈdʒiːn-/ ▶ adjective
1 (especially of a person) looking attractive in photographs or on film: *a photogenic child.*
2 Biology (of an organism or tissue) producing or emitting light.
– DERIVATIVES **photogenically** adverb.

photogeology ▶ noun [mass noun] the field of study concerned with the geological interpretation of aerial photographs.
– DERIVATIVES **photogeological** adjective, **photogeologist** noun.

photogram ▶ noun a picture produced with photographic materials, such as light-sensitive paper, but without a camera.
■ archaic a photograph.

photogrammetry /ˌfəʊtə(ʊ)ˈgramɪtri/ ▶ noun [mass noun] the use of photography in surveying and mapping to ascertain measurements between objects.
– DERIVATIVES **photogrammetric** adjective, **photogrammetrist** noun.

photograph ▶ noun a picture made using a camera, in which an image is focused on to film or other light-sensitive material and then made visible and permanent by chemical treatment.

p

Modern photography is based on the property of silver compounds of decomposing to metallic silver when exposed to light. The light-sensitive salts are held in an emulsion (in colour film, layers of emulsion) usually mounted on transparent roll film.

▶ **verb** [with obj.] take a photograph of.
■ [no obj., with adverbial] appear in a particular way when in a photograph: *that cityscape photographs well.*
– DERIVATIVES **photographable** adjective, **photographer** noun, **photographic** adjective, **photographically** adverb.

photographic memory ▶ **noun** the ability to remember information or visual images in great detail.

photography ▶ **noun** [mass noun] the art or practice of taking and processing photographs.

photogravure /ˌfəʊtə(ʊ)grəˈvjʊə/ ▶ **noun** an image produced from a photographic negative transferred to a metal plate and etched in.
■ [mass noun] the production of images in this way.
– ORIGIN late 19th cent.: from French, from *photo-* 'relating to light' + *gravure* 'engraving'.

photoionization /ˌfəʊtəʊˌʌɪənʌɪˈzeɪʃ(ə)n/ (also **-isation**) ▶ **noun** [mass noun] Physics ionization produced in a medium by the action of electromagnetic radiation.

photojournalism ▶ **noun** [mass noun] the art or practice of communicating news by photographs, especially in magazines.
– DERIVATIVES **photojournalist** noun.

photolithography (also **photolitho**) ▶ **noun** [mass noun] lithography using plates made photographically.
– DERIVATIVES **photolithographic** adjective, **photolithographically** adverb.

photolysis /fə(ʊ)ˈtɒlɪsɪs/ ▶ **noun** [mass noun] Chemistry the decomposition or separation of molecules by the action of light.
– DERIVATIVES **photolyse** verb, **photolytic** adjective.

photomap ▶ **noun** a map made from or drawn on photographs of the area concerned.

photomask ▶ **noun** Electronics a photographic pattern used in making microcircuits, ultraviolet light being shone through the mask on to a photoresist in order to transfer the pattern.

photomechanical ▶ **adjective** relating to or denoting processes in which photography is involved in the making of a printing plate.
– DERIVATIVES **photomechanically** adverb.

photometer /fə(ʊ)ˈtɒmɪtə/ ▶ **noun** an instrument for measuring the intensity of light.
– DERIVATIVES **photometric** adjective, **photometrically** adverb, **photometry** noun.

photomicrograph ▶ **noun** a photograph of a microscopic object, taken with the aid of a microscope.
– DERIVATIVES **photomicrographer** noun, **photomicrography** noun.

photomontage /ˌfəʊtəʊmɒnˈtɑːʒ/ ▶ **noun** a montage constructed from photographic images.
■ [mass noun] the technique of constructing such a montage.

photomorphogenesis /ˌfəʊtə(ʊ)mɔːfəˈdʒɛnɪsɪs/ ▶ **noun** [mass noun] Botany development of form and structure in plants which is affected by light, other than that occurring for photosynthesis.

photomosaic ▶ **noun** a large-scale detailed picture or map built up by combining photographs of small areas.

photomultiplier ▶ **noun** an instrument containing a photoelectric cell and a series of electrodes, used to detect and amplify the light from very faint sources.

photon /ˈfəʊtɒn/ ▶ **noun** Physics a particle representing a quantum of light or other electromagnetic radiation. A photon carries energy proportional to the radiation frequency but has zero rest mass.
– ORIGIN early 20th cent.: from Greek *phōs, phōt-* 'light', on the pattern of *electron*.

photonegative ▶ **adjective** 1 Biology (of an organism) tending to move away from light.
2 Physics (of a substance) exhibiting a decrease in electrical conductivity under illumination.

photonics /fəʊˈtɒnɪks/ ▶ **plural noun** [treated as sing.] the branch of technology concerned with the properties and transmission of photons, for example in fibre optics.

photo-offset ▶ **noun** [mass noun] offset printing using plates made photographically.

photo op ▶ **noun** chiefly N. Amer. informal term for PHOTO OPPORTUNITY.

photo opportunity ▶ **noun** another term for PHOTOCALL.

photo-oxidation ▶ **noun** [mass noun] Chemistry oxidation caused by the action of light.

photoperiod ▶ **noun** Botany & Zoology the period of time each day during which an organism receives illumination; day length.
– DERIVATIVES **photoperiodic** adjective.

photoperiodism ▶ **noun** [mass noun] Botany & Zoology the response of an organism to seasonal changes in day length.

photophobia ▶ **noun** [mass noun] extreme sensitivity to light.
– DERIVATIVES **photophobic** adjective.

photophore /ˈfəʊtə(ʊ)fɔː/ ▶ **noun** Zoology a light-producing organ in certain fishes and other animals.
– ORIGIN late 19th cent.: from Greek *phōtophoros* 'light-bearing'.

photopic /fəʊˈtɒpɪk, fəʊˈtəʊpɪk/ ▶ **adjective** Physiology relating to or denoting vision in daylight or other bright light, believed to involve chiefly the cones of the retina. Often contrasted with SCOTOPIC.
– ORIGIN early 20th cent.: from PHOTO- 'light' + -OPIA + -IC.

photopigment ▶ **noun** a pigment whose chemical state depends on its degree of illumination, such as those in the retina of the eye.

photopolarimeter /ˌfəʊtəʊpəʊləˈrɪmɪtə/ ▶ **noun** a telescopic apparatus for photographing stars, galaxies, etc. and measuring the polarization of light from them.

photopolymer ▶ **noun** a light-sensitive polymeric material, especially one used in printing plates or microfilms.

photopositive ▶ **adjective** 1 Biology (of an organism) tending to move towards light.
2 Physics (of a substance) exhibiting an increase in electrical conductivity under illumination.

photoproduct ▶ **noun** a product of a photochemical reaction.

photoprotein ▶ **noun** Biochemistry a protein active in the emission of light by a living creature.

photorealism ▶ **noun** [mass noun] 1 detailed and unidealized representation in art, especially of banal, mundane, or sordid aspects of life.
2 detailed visual representation, like that obtained in a photograph, in a non-photographic medium such as animation or computer graphics.
– DERIVATIVES **photorealist** noun & adjective, **photorealistic** adjective.

photoreceptor ▶ **noun** a structure in a living organism, especially a sensory cell or sense organ, that responds to light falling on it.
– DERIVATIVES **photoreceptive** adjective.

photoreconnaissance ▶ **noun** [mass noun] military reconnaissance carried out by means of aerial photography.

photoresist ▶ **noun** a photosensitive resist which, when exposed to light, loses its resistance or its susceptibility to attack by an etchant or solvent. Such materials are used in making microcircuits.

photorespiration ▶ **noun** [mass noun] Botany a respiratory process in many higher plants by which they take up oxygen in the light and give out some carbon dioxide, contrary to the general pattern of photosynthesis.

photoresponse ▶ **noun** Biology a response of a plant or other organism to light, mediated otherwise than through photosynthesis.

photosensitive ▶ **adjective** having a chemical, electrical, or other response to light: *photosensitive cells | photosensitive drugs.*
– DERIVATIVES **photosensitivity** noun.

photo session ▶ **noun** a pre-arranged session in which a photographer takes photographs of someone for publication.

photosetter ▶ **noun** a machine for filmsetting.

photosetting ▶ **noun** another term for FILMSETTING.
– DERIVATIVES **photoset** verb (past and past participle **-set**)

photo shoot ▶ **noun** another term for PHOTO SESSION.

photosphere ▶ **noun** Astronomy the luminous envelope of a star from which its light and heat radiate.
– DERIVATIVES **photospheric** adjective.

photostat /ˈfəʊtə(ʊ)stat/ ▶ **noun** trademark a type of machine for making photocopies on special paper.
■ a copy made by this means.
▶ **verb** (**photostatted, photostatting**) [with obj.] make a copy of (a document) using a photostat machine.
– DERIVATIVES **photostatic** adjective.

photostory ▶ **noun** a strip cartoon with photographs in place of drawings.

photosynthate /ˌfəʊtəˈsɪnθeɪt/ ▶ **noun** Biochemistry a sugar or other substance made by photosynthesis.

photosynthesis ▶ **noun** [mass noun] the process by which green plants and some other organisms use sunlight to synthesize foods from carbon dioxide and water. Photosynthesis in plants generally involves the green pigment chlorophyll and generates oxygen as a by-product.
– DERIVATIVES **photosynthetic** adjective, **photosynthetically** adverb.

photosynthesize (also **-ise**) ▶ **verb** [no obj.] (of a plant) synthesize sugars or other substances by means of photosynthesis.

photosystem ▶ **noun** a biochemical mechanism in plants by which chlorophyll absorbs light energy for photosynthesis. There are two such mechanisms (**photosystems I** and **II**) involving different chlorophyll–protein complexes.

phototaxis /ˌfəʊtəʊˈtaksɪs/ ▶ **noun** (pl. **phototaxes**) [mass noun] Biology the bodily movement of a motile organism in response to light, either towards the source of light (**positive phototaxis**) or away from it (**negative phototaxis**). Compare with PHOTOTROPISM.
■ [count noun] a movement of this kind.
– DERIVATIVES **phototactic** adjective.

phototherapy ▶ **noun** [mass noun] the use of light in the treatment of physical or mental illness.

phototransistor ▶ **noun** a transistor that responds to light striking it by generating and amplifying an electric current.

phototroph /ˈfəʊtə(ʊ)trəʊf/ ▶ **noun** Biology a phototrophic organism.

phototrophic ▶ **adjective** Biology (of an organism) obtaining energy from sunlight to synthesize organic compounds for nutrition.

phototropism /ˌfəʊtə(ʊ)ˈtrəʊpɪz(ə)m, fəʊˈtɒtrəˌpɪz(ə)m/ ▶ **noun** [mass noun] Biology the orientation of a plant or other organism in response to light, either towards the source of light (**positive phototropism**) or away from it (**negative phototropism**). Compare with HELIOTROPISM, PHOTOTAXIS.
– DERIVATIVES **phototropic** adjective.

phototube ▶ **noun** Electronics a photocell in the form of an electron tube with a photoemissive cathode.

phototypesetter ▶ **noun** a machine for filmsetting.
– DERIVATIVES **phototypeset** adjective, **phototypesetting** noun.

photovoltaic /ˌfəʊtəʊvɒlˈteɪk/ ▶ **adjective** relating to the production of electric current at the junction of two substances exposed to light.

photovoltaics ▶ **plural noun** [treated as sing.] the branch of technology concerned with the production of electric current at the junction of two substances.
■ [treated as pl.] devices having such a junction.

phragmites /fragˈmʌɪtiːz/ ▶ **noun** [mass noun] a common and invasive tall reed.
● Genus *Phragmites*, family Gramineae: several species, in particular the common or Norfolk reed.
– ORIGIN modern Latin, from Greek *phragmitēs* 'growing in hedges', from *phragma* 'hedge'.

phrasal ▶ **adjective** [attrib.] Grammar consisting of a phrase or phrases: *the text fragments itself into phrasal units.*
– DERIVATIVES **phrasally** adverb.

phrasal verb ▶ **noun** Grammar an idiomatic phrase consisting of a verb and another element, typically either an adverb, as in *break down*, or a preposition, for example *see to*, or a combination of both, such as *look down on.*

phrase ▶ noun a small group of words standing together as a conceptual unit, typically forming a component of a clause.
■ an idiomatic or short pithy expression: *his favourite phrase is 'it's a pleasure'.* ■ Music a group of notes forming a distinct unit within a longer passage. ■ Ballet a group of steps within a longer sequence or dance.
▶ verb [with obj. and adverbial] put into a particular form of words: *it's important to phrase the question correctly.*
■ divide (music) into phrases in a particular way, especially in performance: [as noun **phrasing**] *original phrasing brought out unexpected aspects of the music.*
– PHRASES **a —— turn of phrase** a person's particular or characteristic manner of expression: *a vituperative turn of phrase.*
– ORIGIN mid 16th cent. (in the sense 'style or manner of expression'): via late Latin from Greek *phrasis,* from *phrazein* 'declare, tell'.

phrase book ▶ noun a book for people visiting a foreign country, listing useful expressions in the language of the country together with their equivalent in the visitor's own language.

phraseology /ˌfreɪzɪˈɒlədʒi/ ▶ noun (pl. **-ies**) a particular mode of expression, especially one characteristic of a particular speaker or writer: *legal phraseology.*
– DERIVATIVES **phraseological** adjective.
– ORIGIN mid 17th cent.: from modern Latin *phraseologia,* from Greek *phraseōn,* genitive plural of *phrasis* 'a phrase' + *-logia* (see **-LOGY**).

phratry /ˈfreɪtri/ ▶ noun (pl. **-ies**) Anthropology a descent group or kinship group in some tribal societies.
– ORIGIN mid 19th cent.: from Greek *phratria,* from *phratēr* 'clansman'.

phreaking ▶ noun [mass noun] informal, chiefly US the action of hacking into telecommunications systems, especially to obtain free calls.
– DERIVATIVES **phreak** noun, **phreaker** noun.
– ORIGIN 1970s: alteration of *freaking* (see **FREAK**). The change from *f-* to *ph-* was due to association with **PHONE**[1].

phreatic /frɪˈatɪk/ ▶ adjective Geology relating to or denoting underground water in the zone of saturation (beneath the water table). Compare with **VADOSE**.
■ (of a volcanic eruption) caused by the heating and expansion of groundwater.
– ORIGIN late 19th cent.: from Greek *phrear, phreat-* 'a well' + **-IC**.

phreatomagmatic /frɪˌatə(ʊ)magˈmatɪk/ ▶ adjective Geology (of a volcanic eruption) in which both magmatic gases and steam from groundwater are expelled.
– ORIGIN mid 20th cent.: from Greek *phrear, phreat-* 'a well' + *magmatic* (see **MAGMA**).

phreatophyte /frɪˈatəfʌɪt/ ▶ noun Botany a plant with a deep root system that draws its water supply from near the water table.
– DERIVATIVES **phreatophytic** adjective.
– ORIGIN 1920s: from Greek *phrear, phreat-* 'a well' + **-PHYTE**.

phrenic /ˈfrɛnɪk/ ▶ adjective [attrib.] Anatomy of or relating to the diaphragm: *the phrenic nerves.*
– ORIGIN early 18th cent.: from French *phrénique,* from Greek *phrēn, phren-* 'diaphragm, mind' (because the mind was once thought to lie in the diaphragm).

phrenology /frɪˈnɒlədʒi/ ▶ noun [mass noun] chiefly historical the detailed study of the shape and size of the cranium as a supposed indication of character and mental abilities.
– DERIVATIVES **phrenological** adjective, **phrenologist** noun.
– ORIGIN early 19th cent.: from Greek *phrēn, phren-* 'mind' + **-LOGY**.

Phrygia /ˈfrɪdʒɪə/ an ancient region of west central Asia Minor, to the south of Bithynia. Centred on the city of Gordium, it dominated Asia Minor after the decline of the Hittites in the 12th century BC, reaching the peak of its power in the 8th century under King Midas. It was eventually absorbed into the kingdom of Lydia in the 6th century BC.

Phrygian ▶ adjective of or relating to Phrygia, its people, or their language.
▶ noun **1** a native or inhabitant of ancient Phrygia.
2 [mass noun] the language of the ancient Phrygians, of which only a few inscriptions survive. It is generally classified as an Indo-European language, with affinities to Greek and Armenian.

Phrygian bonnet (also **Phrygian cap**) ▶ noun a conical cap with the top bent forwards, worn in ancient times and now identified with the **CAP OF LIBERTY**.

Phrygian mode ▶ noun Music the mode represented by the natural diatonic scale E–E (containing a minor 2nd, 3rd, 6th, and 7th).

phthalic acid /ˈ(f)θalɪk/ ▶ noun Chemistry a crystalline acid derived from benzene, with two carboxylic acid groups attached to the benzene ring.
● Chem. formula: $C_6H_4(COOH)_2$; three isomers.
– DERIVATIVES **phthalate** noun.
– ORIGIN mid 19th cent.: *phthalic,* shortening of *naphthalic* (see **NAPHTHALENE**).

phthalic anhydride ▶ noun [mass noun] Chemistry a crystalline compound made by oxidizing naphthalene, used as an intermediate in the manufacture of plastics, resins, and dyes.
● A bicyclic anhydride; chem. formula: $C_6H_4(CO)_2O$.
– ORIGIN mid 19th cent.: *phthalic,* shortening of *naphthalic* (see **NAPHTHALENE**).

phthalocyanine /ˈ(f)θaləʊˈsʌɪəniːn/ ▶ noun [mass noun] Chemistry a greenish-blue crystalline dye of the porphyrin group.
● Chem. formula: $C_{32}H_{18}N_8$.
■ [count noun] any of a large class of green or blue pigments and dyes which are chelate complexes of this compound or one of its derivatives with a metal (in particular, copper).
– ORIGIN 1930s: from *phthalic* (see **PHTHALIC ACID**) + Greek *kuan(e)os* 'dark blue' + **-INE**[1].

Phthiraptera /(f)θɪˈraptərə/ Entomology an order of insects that is sometimes used, comprising both the sucking lice and the biting lice.
– ORIGIN modern Latin (plural), from Greek *phtheir* 'louse' + *pteron* 'wing'.

phthisis /ˈ(f)θʌɪsɪs, ˈtʌɪ-/ ▶ noun [mass noun] Medicine, archaic pulmonary tuberculosis or a similar progressive wasting disease.
– DERIVATIVES **phthisic** adjective, **phthisical** adjective.
– ORIGIN mid 16th cent.: via Latin from Greek, from *phthinein* 'to decay'.

Phuket /puːˈkɛt/ **1** an island of Thailand, situated at the head of the Strait of Malacca off the west coast of the Malay Peninsula.
2 a port at the south end of Phuket island, a major resort centre and outlet to the Indian Ocean.

phulkari /pʊlˈkaːri/ ▶ noun (pl. **phulkaris**) (in the Indian subcontinent) an ornamental cloth or shawl embroidered with silk flowers made for ceremonial occasions.
■ [mass noun] embroidery in such a pattern.
– ORIGIN from Hindi *phūlkārī,* based on *phūl* 'flower'.

phut ▶ exclamation used to represent a dull abrupt sound as of a slight impact or explosion.
– PHRASES **go phut** informal fail to work properly or at all.
– ORIGIN late 19th cent.: perhaps from Hindi *phaṭnā* 'to burst'.

phwoah /ˈfwɔːə/ (also **phwoor**) ▶ exclamation Brit. informal used to express desire, especially of a sexual nature.
– ORIGIN 1990s: imitative.

phyco- ▶ combining form relating to seaweed: *phycology.*
– ORIGIN from Greek *phukos* 'seaweed'.

phycobilin /ˌfʌɪkəʊˈbʌɪlɪn/ ▶ noun Biochemistry any of a group of red or blue photosynthetic pigments present in some algae.

phycocyanin /ˌfʌɪkəʊˈsʌɪnɪn/ ▶ noun Biochemistry any of a group of blue photosynthetic pigments present in cyanobacteria.

phycoerythrin /ˌfʌɪkəʊˈɛrɪθrɪn/ ▶ noun Biochemistry any of a group of red photosynthetic pigments present in red algae and some cyanobacteria.

phycology /fʌɪˈkɒlədʒi/ ▶ noun [mass noun] the branch of botany concerned with seaweeds and other algae.
– DERIVATIVES **phycological** adjective, **phycologist** noun.

phycomycete /ˌfʌɪkəʊˈmʌɪsiːt/ ▶ noun Botany any of the lower fungi, which typically form a non-septate mycelium.
● Subdivisions Mastigomycotina and Zygomycotina; formerly placed in a class Phycomycetes.

phycomycosis /ˌfʌɪkəʊmʌɪˈkəʊsɪs/ ▶ noun [mass noun] Medicine & Veterinary Medicine infection with a parasitic fungus which affects the sinuses and the tissues of the lungs, skin, and nerves.
● The fungus is typically a phycomycete, especially of the genus *Rhizopus, Absidia,* or *Mucor.*

phyla plural form of **PHYLUM**.

phylactery /fɪˈlakt(ə)ri/ ▶ noun (pl. **-ies**) a small leather box containing Hebrew texts on vellum, worn by Jewish men at morning prayer as a reminder to keep the law.
– ORIGIN late Middle English: via late Latin from Greek *phulaktērion* 'amulet', from *phulassein* 'to guard'.

phyletic /fʌɪˈlɛtɪk/ ▶ adjective Biology relating to or denoting the evolutionary development of a species or other group.
– DERIVATIVES **phyletically** adverb.
– ORIGIN late 19th cent.: from Greek *phuletikos,* from *phuletēs* 'tribesman', from *phulē* 'tribe'.

phyllite /ˈfɪlʌɪt/ ▶ noun [mass noun] Geology a fine-grained metamorphic rock with a well-developed laminar structure, intermediate between slate and schist.
– ORIGIN late 19th cent.: from Greek *phullon* 'leaf' + **-ITE**[1].

phyllo ▶ noun variant spelling of **FILO**.

phyllo- ▶ combining form of a leaf; relating to leaves: *phyllotaxis.*
– ORIGIN from Greek *phullon* 'leaf'.

phylloclade /ˈfɪlə(ʊ)kleɪd/ ▶ noun Botany a flattened branch or stem-joint resembling and functioning as a leaf.
– ORIGIN mid 19th cent.: from modern Latin *phyllocladium,* from Greek *phullōdēs* 'leaf-like', from *phullon* 'leaf'.

phyllode /ˈfɪləʊd/ ▶ noun Botany a winged leaf stalk which functions as a leaf.
– ORIGIN mid 19th cent.: from modern Latin *phyllodium,* from Greek *phullōdēs* 'leaf-like', from *phullon* 'leaf'.

phyllopod /ˈfɪlə(ʊ)pɒd/ ▶ noun Zoology, dated a branchiopod crustacean.
– ORIGIN from modern Latin *Phyllopoda* (former class name), from Greek *phullon* 'leaf' + *pous, pod-* 'foot'.

phylloquinone /ˌfɪlə(ʊ)ˈkwɪnəʊn/ ▶ noun [mass noun] Biochemistry one of the K vitamins, found in cabbage, spinach, and other leafy green vegetables, and essential for the blood-clotting process. Also called *vitamin K₁.*

phyllotaxis /ˌfɪlə(ʊ)ˈtaksɪs/ (also **phyllotaxy** /-ˈtaksi/) ▶ noun [mass noun] Botany the arrangement of leaves on an axis or stem.
– DERIVATIVES **phyllotactic** adjective.

phylloxera /ˌfɪlɒkˈsɪərə, fɪˈlɒksərə/ ▶ noun a plant louse that is a pest of vines.
● *Phylloxera vitifoliae,* family Phylloxeridae, suborder Homoptera.
– ORIGIN mid 19th cent.: modern Latin, from Greek *phullon* 'leaf' + *xēros* 'dry'.

phylogenesis /ˌfʌɪlə(ʊ)ˈdʒɛnɪsɪs/ ▶ noun [mass noun] Biology the evolutionary development and diversification of a species or group of organisms, or of a particular feature of an organism. Compare with **ONTOGENESIS**.
– DERIVATIVES **phylogenetic** adjective, **phylogenetically** adverb.
– ORIGIN late 19th cent.: from Greek *phulon, phulē* 'race, tribe' + **GENESIS**.

phylogeny /fʌɪˈlɒdʒ(ə)ni/ ▶ noun [mass noun] the branch of biology that deals with phylogenesis. Compare with **ONTOGENY**.
■ another term for **PHYLOGENESIS**.
– DERIVATIVES **phylogenic** adjective, **phylogenically** adverb.
– ORIGIN late 19th cent.: from Greek *phulon, phulē* 'race, tribe' + **-GENY**.

phylum /ˈfʌɪləm/ ▶ noun (pl. **phyla** /-lə/) Zoology a principal taxonomic category that ranks above class and below kingdom, equivalent to the division in botany.
■ Linguistics a group of languages related to each other less closely than those forming a family, especially one in which the relationships are disputed or unclear.
– ORIGIN late 19th cent.: modern Latin from Greek, *phulon* 'race'.

physalis /ˈfʌɪsəlɪs, ˈfɪs-, fʌɪˈseɪlɪs/ ▶ noun a plant of a genus that includes the Cape gooseberry and

p

Chinese lantern, which have an inflated lantern-like calyx.
- ● Genus *Physalis*, family Solanaceae: many species.
- ORIGIN modern Latin, from Greek *phusallis* 'bladder' (because of the inflated calyx).

Physeptone /ˈfʌɪsɛptəʊn/ ▶ noun trademark for **METHADONE**.
- ORIGIN 1940s: of unknown origin.

physiatrics /ˌfɪzɪˈatrɪks/ ▶ plural noun [treated as sing.] North American term for **PHYSIOTHERAPY**.
- DERIVATIVES **physiatrist** noun.

physic archaic ▶ noun [mass noun] medicinal drugs.
- ■ the art of healing.
- ▶ verb (**physicked**, **physicking**) [with obj.] treat with a medicine.
- ORIGIN Middle English: from Old French *fisique* 'medicine', from Latin *physica*, from Greek *phusikē* (*epistēmē*) '(knowledge) of nature'.

physical ▶ adjective 1 of or relating to the body as opposed to the mind: *a whole range of physical and mental challenges.*
- ■ involving bodily contact or activity: *less physical sports such as bowls | a physical relationship.*
- 2 of or relating to things perceived through the senses as opposed to the mind; tangible or concrete: *physical assets such as houses or cars.*
- ■ of or relating to physics or the operation of natural forces generally: *physical laws.*
- ▶ noun 1 (also **physical examination**) a medical examination to determine a person's bodily fitness.
- 2 (**physicals**) Stock Exchange stocks held in actual commodities for immediate exchange, for example as opposed to futures.
- PHRASES **get physical** informal become aggressive or violent. ■ become sexually intimate with someone.
- DERIVATIVES **physicality** /-ˈkalɪti/ noun, **physically** adverb, **physicalness** noun.
- ORIGIN late Middle English (in the sense 'medicinal, relating to medicine'): from medieval Latin *physicalis*, from Latin *physica* 'things relating to nature' (see **PHYSIC**). Sense 2 dates from the late 16th cent. and sense 1 from the late 18th cent.

physical anthropology ▶ noun see **ANTHROPOLOGY**.

physical chemistry ▶ noun [mass noun] the branch of chemistry concerned with the application of the techniques and theories of physics to the study of chemical systems.

physical culture ▶ noun [mass noun] dated the development of the body by exercise.

physical education ▶ noun [mass noun] instruction in physical exercise and games, especially in schools.

physical geography ▶ noun [mass noun] the branch of geography dealing with natural features.

physicalism ▶ noun [mass noun] Philosophy the doctrine that the real world consists simply of the physical world.
- DERIVATIVES **physicalist** noun & adjective, **physicalistic** adjective.

physicalize ▶ verb [with obj.] express or represent by physical means or in physical terms: *physicalizing your anger can help release tension.*
- DERIVATIVES **physicalization** noun.

physical jerks ▶ plural noun Brit. informal energetic exercises done as part of a fitness routine.

physical sciences ▶ plural noun the sciences concerned with the study of inanimate natural objects, including physics, chemistry, astronomy, and related subjects. Often contrasted with **LIFE SCIENCES**.

physical theatre ▶ noun [mass noun] a form of theatre which emphasizes the use of physical movement, as in dance and mime, for expression.

physical therapy ▶ noun US term for **PHYSIOTHERAPY**.
- DERIVATIVES **physical therapist** noun.

physical training ▶ noun [mass noun] the systematic use of exercises to promote bodily fitness and strength.

physic garden ▶ noun a garden for cultivating medicinal herbs.

physician ▶ noun a person qualified to practise medicine, especially one who specializes in diagnosis and medical treatment as distinct from surgery.
- ■ a healer: *physicians of the soul.*

- PHRASES **physician, heal thyself** proverb before attempting to correct others, make sure that you aren't guilty of the same faults yourself. [ORIGIN with biblical allusion to Luke 4:23.]
- ORIGIN Middle English: from Old French *fisicien*, based on Latin *physica* 'things relating to nature' (see **PHYSIC**).

physicist ▶ noun an expert in or student of physics.

physico- ▶ combining form physical; physical and ...: *physico-mental.*
- ORIGIN from **PHYSICS**.

physico-chemical ▶ adjective of or relating to physics and chemistry or to physical chemistry.

physics ▶ plural noun [treated as sing.] the branch of science concerned with the nature and properties of matter and energy. The subject matter of physics, distinguished from that of chemistry and biology, includes mechanics, heat, light and other radiation, sound, electricity, magnetism, and the structure of atoms.
- ■ the physical properties and phenomena of something: *the physics of plasmas.*
- ORIGIN late 15th cent. (denoting natural science in general, especially the Aristotelian system): plural of obsolete *physic* 'physical (thing)', suggested by Latin *physica*, Greek *phusika* 'natural things' from *phusis* 'nature'.

physio ▶ noun (pl. **-os**) informal a physiotherapist.
- ■ [mass noun] physiotherapy.
- ORIGIN 1960s: abbreviation.

physio- ▶ combining form 1 relating to nature and natural phenomena: *physiography.*
- 2 representing **PHYSIOLOGY**.
- ORIGIN from Greek *phusis* 'nature'.

physiochemical ▶ adjective of or relating to physiological chemistry.

physiocrat ▶ noun a member of an 18th-century group of French economists who believed that agriculture was the source of all wealth and that agricultural products should be highly priced. Advocating adherence to a supposed natural order of social institutions, they also stressed the necessity of free trade.
- DERIVATIVES **physiocracy** noun, **physiocratic** adjective.
- ORIGIN late 18th cent.: from French *physiocrate*, from *physiocratie* 'physiocracy' (see **PHYSIO-**, **-CRACY**).

physiognomist ▶ noun a person supposedly able to judge character (or, formerly, to predict the future) from facial characteristics.
- ORIGIN late 16th cent.: from Old French *physionomiste*.

physiognomy /ˌfɪzɪˈɒ(g)nəmi/ ▶ noun (pl. **-ies**) a person's facial features or expression, especially when regarded as indicative of character or ethnic origin.
- ■ [mass noun] the supposed art of judging character from facial characteristics. ■ the general form or appearance of something: *the physiognomy of the landscape.*
- DERIVATIVES **physiognomic** adjective, **physiognomical** adjective, **physiognomically** adverb.
- ORIGIN late Middle English: from Old French *phisonomie*, via medieval Latin from Greek *phusiognōmonia* 'judging of a man's nature (by his features)', based on *gnōmōn* 'a judge, interpreter'.

physiography ▶ noun another term for **PHYSICAL GEOGRAPHY**.
- DERIVATIVES **physiographer** noun, **physiographic** adjective, **physiographical** adjective, **physiographically** adverb.
- ORIGIN early 19th cent.: from French *physiographie* (see **PHYSIO-**, **-GRAPHY**).

physiological saline ▶ noun a solution of salts that is isotonic with the body fluids.

physiology ▶ noun [mass noun] the branch of biology that deals with the normal functions of living organisms and their parts.
- ■ the way in which a living organism or bodily part functions: *the physiology of the brain.*
- DERIVATIVES **physiologic** adjective, **physiological** adjective, **physiologically** adverb, **physiologist** noun.
- ORIGIN early 17th cent.: from Latin *physiologia* (perhaps via French), from Greek *phusiologia* 'natural philosophy' (see **PHYSIO-**, **-LOGY**).

physiotherapy (US **physical therapy**) ▶ noun [mass noun] the treatment of disease, injury, or deformity by physical methods such as massage, heat

treatment, and exercise rather than by drugs or surgery.
- DERIVATIVES **physiotherapist** noun.

physique /fɪˈziːk/ ▶ noun the form, size, and development of a person's body: *a sturdy, muscular physique | [mass noun] they were much alike in physique.*
- ORIGIN early 19th cent.: from French, literally 'physical' (used as a noun).

physostigmine /ˌfʌɪsəʊˈstɪgmiːn/ ▶ noun [mass noun] Chemistry a compound which is the active ingredient of the Calabar bean and is used medicinally in eye drops on account of its anticholinesterase activity.
- ● A tricyclic alkaloid; chem. formula: $C_{15}H_{21}N_3O_2$.
- ORIGIN mid 19th cent.: from the modern Latin genus name *Physostigma* (to which the Calabar bean belongs) + **-INE**[4].

-phyte ▶ combining form denoting a plant or plant-like organism: *epiphyte.*
- DERIVATIVES **-phytic** combining form in corresponding adjectives.
- ORIGIN from Greek *phuton* 'a plant', from *phuein* 'come into being'.

phyto- ▶ combining form of a plant; relating to plants: *phytogeography.*
- ORIGIN from Greek *phuton* 'a plant', from *phuein* 'come into being'.

phytoalexin /ˌfʌɪtəʊəˈlɛksɪn/ ▶ noun Botany a substance that is produced by plant tissues in response to contact with a parasite and specifically inhibits the growth of that parasite.
- ORIGIN 1940s: from **PHYTO-** 'of plants' + *alexin*, a name for a class of substances found in blood serum, able to destroy bacteria.

phytochemistry ▶ noun [mass noun] the branch of chemistry concerned with plants and plant products.
- DERIVATIVES **phytochemical** adjective, **phytochemist** noun.

phytochrome ▶ noun [mass noun] Biochemistry a blue-green pigment found in many plants, in which it regulates various developmental processes.
- ORIGIN late 19th cent.: from **PHYTO-** 'relating to plants' + Greek *khrōma* 'colour'.

phytogenetic ▶ adjective Botany of or relating to the origin and evolution of plants.

phytogeographical kingdom ▶ noun Botany each of a number of major areas of the earth distinguished on the basis of the characteristic plants present. They usually include the Boreal, Palaeotropical, Neotropical, Australian, and Antarctic kingdoms. Also called **FLORAL KINGDOM**.

phytogeography ▶ noun [mass noun] the branch of botany that deals with the geographical distribution of plants. Also called **PLANT GEOGRAPHY**.
- DERIVATIVES **phytogeographer** noun, **phytogeographic** adjective, **phytogeographical** adjective, **phytogeographically** adverb.

phytohaemagglutinin /ˌfʌɪtə(ʊ)hiːməˈgluːtɪnɪn/ (US **phytohemagglutinin**) ▶ noun [mass noun] Biochemistry a plant protein, especially that extracted from the French bean, that causes red blood cells to clump together.

phytolith /ˈfʌɪtə(ʊ)lɪθ/ ▶ noun Botany a minute mineral particle formed inside a plant.
- ■ Palaeontology a fossilized particle of plant tissue.

phytopathology ▶ noun [mass noun] the study of plant diseases.
- DERIVATIVES **phytopathological** adjective, **phytopathologist** noun.

phytophagous /fʌɪˈtɒfəgəs/ ▶ adjective Zoology (especially of an insect or other invertebrate) feeding on plants.
- DERIVATIVES **phytophagy** noun.

phytoplankton /ˈfʌɪtə(ʊ)ˌplaŋktən/ ▶ noun [mass noun] Biology plankton consisting of microscopic plants.

phytosanitary ▶ adjective relating to the health of plants, especially with respect to the requirements of international trade.
- ■ denoting a certificate stating that plants are free from infectious diseases.

phytotoxic ▶ adjective Botany poisonous to plants.
- DERIVATIVES **phytotoxicity** noun.

phytotoxin ▶ noun Botany a poisonous substance derived from a plant.
- ■ a substance that is phytotoxic, especially one produced by a parasite.

pi[1] /pʌɪ/ ▶**noun** the sixteenth letter of the Greek alphabet (Π, π), transliterated as 'p'.
■the numerical value of the ratio of the circumference of a circle to its diameter (approximately 3.14159). [ORIGIN: from the initial letter of Greek *periphereia* 'circumference'.] ■(**Pi**) [followed by Latin genitive] Astronomy the sixteenth star in a constellation: *Pi Herculis*. ■ Chemistry & Physics relating to or denoting an electron or orbital with one unit of angular momentum about an internuclear axis.
▶**symbol for** ■(π) the numerical value of pi. ■(Π) osmotic pressure. ■(Π) mathematical product.
– ORIGIN Greek.

pi[2] /pʌɪ/ ▶**adjective** Brit. informal short for **PIOUS**.

pia /ˈpʌɪə, ˈpiːə/ (in full **pia mater**) ▶**noun** [mass noun] Anatomy the delicate innermost membrane enveloping the brain and spinal cord. See also **MENINGES**.
– DERIVATIVES **pial** adjective.
– ORIGIN late 19th cent.: from medieval Latin, in full literally 'tender mother', translating Arabic *al-'umm ar-raḳīḳa*.

piacular /pʌɪˈakjʊlə/ ▶**adjective** rare making or requiring atonement.
– ORIGIN early 17th cent.: from Latin *piacularis*, from *piaculum* 'expiation', from *piare* 'appease'.

Piaf /ˈpiːaf/, Edith (1915–63), French singer; born *Edith Giovanna Gassion*. She became known as a cabaret and music-hall singer in the late 1930s. Her songs included 'La Vie en rose' and 'Je ne regrette rien'.

piaffe /pɪˈaf/ ▶**noun** (also **piaffer** /pɪˈafə/) a movement performed in advanced dressage and classical riding, in which the horse executes a slow elevated trot without moving forward.
▶**verb** [no obj.] (of a horse) perform such a movement.
– ORIGIN mid 18th cent.: from French *piaffer* 'to strut'.

Piaget /pɪˈaʒeɪ/, Jean (1896–1980), Swiss psychologist. Piaget's work on the intellectual and logical abilities of children provided the single biggest impact on the study of the development of human thought processes. He described the mind as proceeding through a series of fixed stages of cognitive development, each being a prerequisite for the next.

pia mater /ˈmeɪtə, ˈmɑːtə/ ▶**noun** see **PIA**.

piani plural form of **PIANO**[2].

pianism /ˈpɪənɪz(ə)m/ ▶**noun** [mass noun] technical skill or artistry in playing the piano, or in composing piano music.
– DERIVATIVES **pianistic** adjective, **pianistically** adverb.

pianissimo /ˌpɪəˈnɪsɪməʊ/ Music ▶**adverb** & **adjective** (especially as a direction) very soft or softly.
▶**noun** (pl. **pianissimos** or **pianissimi** /-miː/) a passage performed or marked to be performed very softly.
– ORIGIN Italian, superlative of *piano* (see **PIANO**[2]).

pianist ▶**noun** a person who plays the piano, especially professionally.
– ORIGIN mid 19th cent.: from French *pianiste*, from *piano* (see **PIANO**[1]).

piano[1] /pɪˈanəʊ/ ▶**noun** (pl. **-os**) a large keyboard musical instrument with a wooden case enclosing a soundboard and metal strings, which are struck by hammers when the keys are depressed. The strings' vibration is stopped by dampers when the keys are released and can be regulated for length and volume by two or three pedals.
– ORIGIN early 19th cent.: from Italian, abbreviation of **PIANOFORTE**.

piano[2] /ˈpjɑːnəʊ/ Music ▶**adverb** & **adjective** (especially as a direction) soft or softly.
▶**noun** (pl. **pianos** or **piani** /-ni/) a passage performed or marked to be performed softly.
– ORIGIN Italian, literally 'soft'.

piano accordion ▶**noun** an accordion with the melody played on a small vertical keyboard like that of a piano.

pianoforte /pɪˌanəʊˈfɔːteɪ, -ˈfɔːti/ ▶**noun** formal term for **PIANO**[1].
– ORIGIN mid 18th cent.: from Italian, earlier *piano e forte* 'soft and loud', expressing the gradation in tone.

pianola /ˌpɪəˈnəʊlə/ ▶**noun** trademark a piano equipped to be played automatically using a piano roll.
– ORIGIN late 19th cent.: apparently a diminutive of **PIANO**[1].

piano nobile /ˌpjɑːnəʊ ˈnəʊbɪleɪ/ ▶**noun** Architecture the main storey of a large house (usually the first floor), containing the principal rooms.
– ORIGIN Italian, literally 'noble floor'.

piano organ ▶**noun** a mechanical piano constructed like a barrel organ.

piano roll ▶**noun** a roll of perforated paper which controls the movement of the keys in a pianola or similar instrument, so producing a particular melody.

piano trio ▶**noun** a trio for piano and two stringed instruments, usually violin and cello.

piano wire ▶**noun** [mass noun] strong steel wire used for piano strings.

piapiac /ˈpɪəpɪak/ ▶**noun** a black long-tailed African crow that often feeds gregariously among grazing mammals.
● *Philostomus afer*, family Corvidae.
– ORIGIN probably imitative.

piassava /ˌpiːəˈsɑːvə/ ▶**noun** [mass noun] a stout fibre obtained from the leaf stalks of a number of South American and African palm trees.
– ORIGIN mid 19th cent.: via Portuguese from Tupi *piaçába*.

piastre /pɪˈastə/ (US also **piaster**) ▶**noun** a monetary unit of several Middle Eastern countries, equal to one hundredth of a pound.
– ORIGIN from French, from Italian *piastra* (*d'argento*) 'plate (of silver)'.

Piauí /pjaʊˈiː/ a state of NE Brazil, on the Atlantic coast; capital, Teresina.

piazza /pɪˈatsə/ ▶**noun** 1 a public square or marketplace, especially in an Italian town.
2 US archaic the veranda of a house.
– ORIGIN late 16th cent.: Italian.

pibroch /ˈpiːbrɒk, -brɒx/ ▶**noun** [mass noun] a form of music for the Scottish bagpipes involving elaborate variations on a theme, typically of a martial or funerary character.
■[count noun] a piece of such music.
– ORIGIN early 18th cent.: from Scottish Gaelic *piobaireachd* 'art of piping', from *piobair* 'piper', from *piob*, from English **PIPE**.

pic ▶**noun** informal a photograph or cinema film; a picture.
– ORIGIN late 19th cent.: abbreviation.

pica[1] /ˈpʌɪkə/ ▶**noun** Printing a unit of type size and line length equal to 12 points (about ⅙ inch or 4.2 mm).
■[mass noun] a size of letter in typewriting, with 10 characters to the inch (about 3.9 to the centimetre).
– ORIGIN late 16th cent.: from Anglo-Latin *pica* (literally 'magpie'), commonly identified with a 15th-cent. book of rules about Church feasts, but no edition of such a *pica* printed in 'pica' type is known.

pica[2] /ˈpʌɪkə/ ▶**noun** [mass noun] Medicine a tendency or craving to eat substances other than normal food (such as clay, plaster, or ashes), occurring during childhood or pregnancy, or as a symptom of disease.
– ORIGIN mid 16th cent.: modern Latin, from Latin, literally 'magpie', probably translating Greek *kissa* 'magpie', also 'false appetite'.

picador /ˈpɪkədɔː/ ▶**noun** (in bullfighting) a person on horseback who goads the bull with a lance.
– ORIGIN Spanish, from *picar* 'to prick'.

picante /pɪˈkanteɪ/ ▶**adjective** (of food) spicy.
– ORIGIN Spanish, literally 'pricking, biting'.

Picardy /ˈpɪkədi/ a region and former province of northern France, centred on the city of Amiens. It was the scene of heavy fighting in the First World War. French name **PICARDIE** /pikardi/

picaresque /ˌpɪkəˈrɛsk/ ▶**adjective** of or relating to an episodic style of fiction dealing with the adventures of a rough and dishonest but appealing hero.
– ORIGIN early 19th cent.: from French, from Spanish *picaresco*, from *pícaro* 'rogue'.

picaro /ˈpɪkərəʊ/ ▶**noun** (pl. **-os**) a rogue.
– ORIGIN early 17th cent.: from Spanish.

picaroon /ˌpɪkəˈruːn/ ▶**noun** archaic a rogue or scoundrel.
– ORIGIN early 17th cent.: from Spanish *picarón*, augmentative of *pícaro* 'rogue'.

Picasso /pɪˈkasəʊ/, Pablo (1881–1973), Spanish painter, sculptor, and graphic artist, resident in France from 1904.

His prolific inventiveness and technical versatility made him the dominant figure in avant-garde art in the first half of the 20th century. Following his Blue Period (1901–4) and Rose Period (1905–6), *Les Demoiselles d'Avignon* (1907) signalled his development of cubism (1908–14). In the 1920s and 1930s he adopted a neoclassical figurative style and produced semi-surrealist paintings using increasingly violent imagery, notably *The Three Dancers* (1935) and *Guernica* (1937).

– DERIVATIVES **Picassoesque** adjective.

picayune /ˌpɪkəˈjuːn/ N. Amer. ▶**adjective** informal petty; worthless: *the picayune squabbling of party politicians*.
▶**noun** a small coin of little value, especially a 5-cent piece.
■informal an insignificant person or thing.
– ORIGIN early 19th cent.: from French *picaillon*, denoting a Piedmontese copper coin, also used to mean 'cash', from Provençal *picaioun*, of unknown ultimate origin.

Piccadilly /ˌpɪkəˈdɪli/ a street in central London, extending from Hyde Park eastwards to Piccadilly Circus, noted for its fashionable shops, hotels, and restaurants.

piccalilli /ˌpɪkəˈlɪli/ ▶**noun** (pl. **piccalillies** or **piccalillis**) [mass noun] a pickle of chopped vegetables, mustard, and hot spices.
– ORIGIN mid 18th cent.: probably from a blend of **PICKLE** and **CHILLI**.

piccaninny /ˈpɪkənɪni/ (US **pickaninny**) ▶**noun** (pl. **-ies**) often offensive a small black or Australian Aboriginal child.
▶**adjective** archaic very small.
– ORIGIN mid 17th cent.: from West Indian creole, from Spanish *pequeño* or Portuguese *pequeno* 'little', *pequenino* 'tiny'.

piccolo ▶**noun** (pl. **-os**) a small flute sounding an octave higher than the ordinary one.
■a player of this instrument in an orchestra.
– ORIGIN mid 19th cent.: from Italian, 'small (flute)'.

piccy ▶**noun** (pl. **-ies**) informal a picture.
– ORIGIN mid 19th cent.: abbreviation.

pice /pʌɪs/ ▶**noun** (pl. same) a former monetary unit in the Indian subcontinent, equal to one quarter of an anna.
– ORIGIN from Hindi *paisā*.

pichi /ˈpɪtʃi/ ▶**noun** a small armadillo living in open pampas country in southern South America.
● *Zaedyus pichiy*, family Dasypodidae.
– ORIGIN early 19th cent.: via American Spanish from Araucanian, literally 'small'.

pichiciego /ˌpɪtʃɪˈsjeɪgəʊ/ ▶**noun** (pl. **-os**) another term for **FAIRY ARMADILLO**.
– ORIGIN early 19th cent.: from Spanish, perhaps from Guarani *pichey* 'armadillo' + Spanish *ciego* 'blind' (from Latin *caecus*).

pick[1] ▶**verb** 1 [with obj.] take hold of and remove (a flower, fruit, or vegetable) from where it is growing: *I went to pick some flowers for Jenny's room*.
■[with obj. and adverbial] take hold of and lift or move: *he picked a match out of the ashtray | **picking** her **up**, he carried her into the next room*. ■[no obj.] (**pick up**) Golf take hold of and lift up one's ball, especially when conceding a hole.
2 [with obj.] choose (someone or something) from a number of alternatives, typically after careful thought: *maybe I picked the wrong career after all* | [no obj.] *Maggie **picked on** a nice reliable chap*.
■(**pick one's way**) [with adverbial of direction] walk slowly and carefully, selecting the best or safest places to put one's feet: *he picked his way along the edge of the track, avoiding the potholes*.
3 [no obj.] repeatedly pull at something with one's fingers: *the old woman was **picking at** the sheet*.
■[with obj.] make (a hole) in fabric by doing this. ■eat food or a meal in small amounts or without much appetite: *she **picked at** her breakfast*. ■criticize someone in a niggling way: *now, please don't start **picking at** Ruth*. ■[with obj.] remove unwanted matter from (one's nose or teeth) by using one's finger or a pointed instrument. ■[with obj.] pluck the strings of (a guitar or banjo). ■[with obj.] (**pick something out**) play a tune on such an instrument slowly or with difficulty: *she began to pick out a rough melody on the guitar*.
▶**noun** 1 [in sing.] an act or the right of selecting something from among a group of alternatives: ***take your pick** from our extensive menu | Laura should have first pick*.
■(**the pick of**) informal the person or thing perceived as

p

the best in a particular group: *he was the pick of the bunch.* ■ chiefly US someone or something that has been selected: *the club made him their first pick.*
2 Basketball an act of blocking or screening a defensive player from the ball handler.
– PHRASES **pick and choose** select only the best or most desirable from among a number of alternatives. **pick someone's brains** (or **brain**) informal obtain information by questioning someone who is better informed about a subject than oneself. **pick something clean** completely remove the flesh from a bone or carcass. **pick one's feet up** raise one's feet clear of the ground when walking. **pick a fight** (or **quarrel**) talk or behave in such a way as to provoke an argument or fight. **pick holes in** find fault with. **pick a lock** open a lock with an instrument other than the proper key. **pick someone's pockets** steal something surreptitiously from another person's pocket. **pick someone/thing to pieces** (or **apart**) criticize someone or something severely and in detail. **pick up the pieces** restore one's life or a situation to a more normal state, typically after a shock or disaster. **pick up** (or **get up**) **speed** (or **steam**) (of a vehicle) go faster; accelerate. **pick up the threads** resume something that has been interrupted.
– DERIVATIVES **pickable** adjective.
– ORIGIN Middle English (earlier as *pike*, which continues in dialect use): of unknown origin. Compare with Dutch *pikken* 'pick, peck', and German *picken* 'peck, puncture', also with French *piquer* 'to prick'.
▶**pick someone/thing off** shoot a member of a group of people or things, aiming carefully from a distance. ■ Baseball put out a runner by throwing the ball to a base.
pick on repeatedly single (someone) out for blame, criticism, or unkind treatment in a way perceived to be unfair.
pick someone/thing out distinguish someone or something among a group of people or things: *Lester picked out two familiar voices.* ■ (of a light) illuminate an object by shining directly on it. ■ (usu. **be picked out**) distinguish shapes or letters from their surroundings by painting or fashioning them in a contrasting colour or medium: *the initials are picked out in diamonds.*
pick something over (or **pick through**) examine or sort through a number of items carefully: *they picked through the charred remains of their home.*
pick up become better; improve: *my luck's picked up.* ■ become stronger; increase: *the wind has picked up.*
pick oneself up stand up again after a fall.
pick someone up 1 go somewhere to collect someone, typically in one's car and according to a prior arrangement. ■ stop for someone and take them into one's vehicle or vessel. ■ informal arrest someone. ■ informal casually strike up a relationship with someone one has never met before as a sexual overture. **2** return to a point or remark made by someone in order to criticize it: *she picked him up on one niggling point.*
pick something up 1 collect something that has been left elsewhere: *Wanda came over to pick up her things.* ■ informal pay the bill for something, typically something expensive. ■ N. Amer. tidy a room or building. **2** obtain, acquire, or learn something, especially without formal arrangements or instruction: *he had picked up a little Russian from his father.* ■ catch an illness or infection. **3** detect or receive a signal or sound, especially by means of electronic apparatus. ■ (also **pick up on**) become aware of or sensitive to something: *women are very quick to pick up emotional atmospheres.* ■ find and take a particular road or route. **4** (also **pick up**) resume something: *they picked up their friendship without the slightest difficulty.* ■ (also **pick up on**) refer to or develop a point or topic mentioned earlier: *Dawson picked up her earlier remark.* ■ (of an object or colour) attractively accentuate the colour of something else by being of a similar shade.
pick up after chiefly US tidy up things left strewn around by (someone).

pick[2] ▶ **noun 1** a tool consisting of a long handle set at right angles in the middle of a curved iron or steel bar with a point at one end and a chisel edge or point at the other, used for breaking up hard ground or rock.
■ short for **ICE PICK**.
2 an instrument for picking: [with modifier] *an ebony hair pick.*
■ short for **TOOTHPICK**. ■ informal a plectrum.
– ORIGIN Middle English: variant of **PIKE**[2].

pickaback ▶ **noun**, **adverb**, & **verb** old-fashioned term for **PIGGYBACK**.

pick-and-mix (also **pick 'n' mix**) ▶ **adjective** denoting a method of assembling something by choosing elements or items from among a large variety of different possibilities: *enjoy the freedom and choice of our pick-and-mix holidays.*

pickaninny ▶ **noun** US spelling of **PICCANINNY**.

pickaxe (US also **pickax**) ▶ **noun** another term for **PICK**[2] (in sense 1).
▶**verb** [with obj.] break or strike with a pickaxe.
– ORIGIN Middle English *pikoys*, from Old French *picois*; related to **PIKE**[2]. The change in the ending was due to association with **AXE**.

pickelhaube /ˈpɪk(ə)lˌ(h)aʊbə/ ▶ **noun** historical a spiked helmet worn by German soldiers.
– ORIGIN German.

picker ▶ **noun** [usu. with modifier] a person or machine that gathers or collects something: *a potato picker.*

pickerel /ˈpɪk(ə)r(ə)l/ ▶ **noun** (pl. same or **pickerels**) a small pike occurring in North America.
• Genus *Esox*, family Esocidae: several species, including the **redfin** (or **grass**) **pickerel** (*E. americanus*).
■ a young pike.
– ORIGIN Middle English: diminutive of **PIKE**[1].

pickerelweed ▶ **noun** [mass noun] either of two broadleaved freshwater plants which were formerly believed to give rise to, or provide food for, young pike:
• a North American plant with spikes of blue flowers (*Pontederia cordata*, family Pontederiaceae). • Brit. dialect term for **PONDWEED**.

Pickering, William Hayward (b.1910), New Zealand-born American engineer, director of the Jet Propulsion Laboratory at the California Institute of Technology 1954–76. During his directorate the JPL launched America's first satellite, Explorer I (1958), and several unmanned probes to the moon and planets.

picket ▶ **noun 1** a person or group of people standing outside a place of work or other venue, protesting about something or trying to persuade others not to enter during a strike.
■ a blockade of a workplace or other venue staged by such a person or group.
2 (also **picquet**) a small body of troops or a single soldier sent out to watch for the enemy.
■ a soldier or party of soldiers performing a particular duty: *a* ***picket of*** *soldiers fired a volley over the coffin.*
3 [usu. as modifier] a pointed wooden stake driven into the ground, typically to form a fence or palisade or to tether a horse.
▶**verb** (**picketed**, **picketing**) [with obj.] act as a picket outside (a place of work or other venue): *strikers picketed the newspaper's main building.*
– DERIVATIVES **picketer** noun.
– ORIGIN late 17th cent. (denoting a pointed stake, on which a soldier was required to stand on one foot as a military punishment): from French *piquet* 'pointed stake', from *piquer* 'to prick', from *pic* 'pike'.

picket fence ▶ **noun** a wooden fence made of spaced uprights connected by two or more horizontal rails.

picket line ▶ **noun** a boundary established by workers on strike, especially at the entrance to the place of work, which others are asked not to cross.

Pickford, Mary (1893–1979), Canadian-born American actress; born *Gladys Mary Smith*. She was a star of silent films such as *Pollyanna* (1920). She also co-founded United Artists (1919).

pickings ▶ **plural noun 1** profits or gains that are made effortlessly or dishonestly: *Thornton exploited the* ***rich pickings*** *of the Dutch East Indies.*
2 remaining scraps or leftovers.

pickle ▶ **noun 1** [mass noun] food, typically vegetables or fruit, preserved in vinegar, brine, or mustard and used as a relish.
■ [count noun] N. Amer. a cucumber preserved in this way. ■ the liquid used to preserve food or other perishable items. ■ an acid solution for cleaning metal objects.
2 [in sing.] informal a difficult or messy situation: *I am* ***in a pickle.***
3 [in sing.] Brit. informal, dated used as an affectionate form of address to a mischievous child.
▶**verb** [with obj.] preserve (food or other perishable items) in pickle: *chunks of fish* ***pickled in*** *brine.*
■ immerse (a metal object) in an acid or other chemical solution for cleaning.
– ORIGIN late Middle English (denoting a spicy sauce served with meat): from Middle Dutch, Middle Low German *pekel*, of unknown ultimate origin.

pickled ▶ **adjective** (of food) preserved in vinegar or brine: *pickled onions.*
■ [predic.] informal drunk.

pickled fish ▶ **noun** [mass noun] a traditional South African dish of fish prepared with onions in a vinegar sauce and flavoured with curry powder, turmeric, and other spices.

pickler ▶ **noun** a vegetable or fruit suitable for pickling.

pickling ▶ **adjective** [attrib.] (of food) suitable for being pickled or used in making pickles.

picklock ▶ **noun** a person who picks locks.
■ an instrument for picking locks.

pick-me-up ▶ **noun** informal a thing that makes one feel more energetic or cheerful: *ginseng has long been used as a pick-me-up.*

pickney /ˈpɪkni/ ▶ **noun** black English a child: *me and the pickney have to survive some way.* Compare with **PICCANINNY**.
– ORIGIN contraction of **PICCANINNY**.

pick 'n' mix ▶ **adjective** variant of **PICK-AND-MIX**.

pickoff ▶ **noun 1** Baseball the catching of a runner off base, involving a sudden throw of the ball to that base by the pitcher or the catcher.
2 a device in the control or guidance system of an aircraft or boat which emits or alters an electrical, optical, or pneumatic output in response to a change in motion.

pickpocket ▶ **noun** a person who steals from people's pockets.
– DERIVATIVES **pickpocketing** noun.

Pick's disease ▶ **noun** [mass noun] a rare form of progressive dementia, typically in late middle age and often familial, involving localized atrophy of the brain.
– ORIGIN early 20th cent.: named after Arnold *Pick* (1851–1924), Bohemian neurologist.

pickup ▶ **noun 1** (also **pickup truck**) a small van or truck with low sides.
2 [often as modifier] an act of collecting a person or goods, especially in a vehicle: *travel by coach from your local pickup point to your hotel.*
■ [mass noun] the reception of signals, especially interference or noise, by electrical apparatus.
3 informal a casual encounter with someone with a view to having sexual intercourse.
■ a person met in such an encounter.
4 an improvement in an economic indicator: *signs of a* ***pickup*** *in demand.*
5 a device that produces an electrical signal in response to some other kind of signal or change, in particular:
■ the cartridge of a record player, carrying the stylus. ■ a device on a musical instrument, particularly an electric guitar, which converts sound vibrations into electrical signals for amplification.
6 Music a series of introductory notes leading into the opening part of a tune.
7 Fishing a semicircular loop of metal for guiding the line back on to the spool as it is reeled in.

Pickwickian /pɪkˈwɪkɪən/ ▶ **adjective** of or like Mr Pickwick in Dickens's *Pickwick Papers*, especially in being jovial, plump, or generous.
■ (of words or their sense) misunderstood or misused, especially to avoid offence.

picky ▶ **adjective** (**pickier**, **pickiest**) informal fastidious, especially excessively so: *she had been a picky eater as a child.*
– DERIVATIVES **pickiness** noun.

pick-your-own ▶ **adjective** [attrib.] of or relating to a system in which commercially grown fruit or vegetables are dug or picked by the customer for purchase at the place of production.

picnic ▶ **noun** an outing or occasion that involves taking a packed meal to be eaten outdoors.
■ a meal eaten outdoors on such an occasion.
▶**verb** (**picnicked**, **picnicking**) [no obj.] have or take part in a picnic.
– PHRASES **no picnic** informal used of something difficult or unpleasant: *being a freelance was no picnic.*
– DERIVATIVES **picnicker** noun.

– ORIGIN mid 18th cent.: from French *pique-nique*, of unknown origin.

picnic races ▶ **plural noun** Austral./NZ a race meeting for amateurs held in a rural area.

pico- /ˈpiːkəʊ, ˈpʌɪkəʊ/ ▶ **combining form** (used in units of measurement) denoting a factor of 10^{-12}: *picosecond*.
– ORIGIN from Spanish *pico*, literally 'beak, peak, little bit'.

Pico da Neblina /ˌpiːkuː dɑː nɛˈbliːnə/ a mountain in NW Brazil, close to the border with Venezuela. Rising to 3,014 m (9,888 ft), it is the highest peak in Brazil.

Pico de Orizaba /ˌpiko ðe oriˈθaβa, -ˈsaβa/ Spanish name for **CITLALTÉPETL**.

picong /ˈpiːkɒŋ/ ▶ **noun** [mass noun] W. Indian taunting or ridicule: *the boys might start to give Frederick picong*.
– ORIGIN from Spanish *picón*.

picornavirus /pɪˈkɔːnəˌvʌɪrəs/ ▶ **noun** any of a group of very small RNA viruses which includes enteroviruses, rhinoviruses, and the virus of foot-and-mouth disease.
– ORIGIN 1960s: from **PICO-** + **RNA** + **VIRUS**.

picot /ˈpiːkəʊ/ ▶ **noun** [often as modifier] a small loop or series of small loops of twisted thread in lace or embroidery, typically decorating the border of a fabric.
– ORIGIN early 17th cent.: from French, literally 'small peak or point', diminutive of *pic*.

picotee /ˌpɪkəˈtiː/ ▶ **noun** a type of carnation of which the flowers have a light ground and dark-edged petals.
– ORIGIN early 18th cent.: from French *picoté(e)* 'marked with points', past participle of *picoter* 'to prick'.

picquet ▶ **noun** variant spelling of **PICKET** (in sense 2).

picric acid /ˈpɪkrɪk/ ▶ **noun** [mass noun] Chemistry a bitter yellow compound obtained by nitrating phenol, used as a dye and in the manufacture of explosives.
• Alternative name: **2,4,6-trinitrophenol**; chem. formula: $C_6H_2(NO_2)_3OH$.
– DERIVATIVES **picrate** /-reɪt/ noun.
– ORIGIN mid 19th cent.: *picric* from Greek *pikros* 'bitter' + **-IC**.

picrite /ˈpɪkrʌɪt/ ▶ **noun** [mass noun] Geology a dark basaltic igneous rock rich in olivine.
– DERIVATIVES **picritic** /pɪˈkrɪtɪk/ adjective.
– ORIGIN early 19th cent.: from Greek *pikros* 'bitter' + **-ITE**[1].

picrotoxin /ˌpɪkrə(ʊ)ˈtɒksɪn/ ▶ **noun** [mass noun] Medicine a bitter compound used to stimulate the respiratory and nervous system, especially in treating barbiturate poisoning.
• This toxin is obtained from the seeds of the shrub *Anamirta cocculus* (family Menispermaceae).
– ORIGIN mid 19th cent.: from Greek *pikros* 'bitter' + **TOXIN**.

Pict ▶ **noun** a member of an ancient people inhabiting northern Scotland in Roman times.

Roman writings of around 300 AD apply the term *Picti* to the hostile tribes of the area north of the Antonine Wall. Their origins are uncertain, but they may have been a loose confederation of Celtic tribes.

– DERIVATIVES **Pictish** adjective & noun.
– ORIGIN from late Latin *Picti*, perhaps from *pict-* 'painted, tattooed' (from *pingere* 'to paint'), or perhaps influenced by a local name.

pictograph (also **pictogram**) ▶ **noun** a pictorial symbol for a word or phrase. Pictographs were used as the earliest known form of writing, examples having been discovered in Egypt and Mesopotamia from before 3000 BC.
▪ a pictorial representation of statistics on a chart, graph, or computer screen.
– DERIVATIVES **pictographic** adjective, **pictography** noun.
– ORIGIN mid 19th cent.: from Latin *pict-* 'painted' (from the verb *pingere*) + **-GRAPH**.

Pictor /ˈpɪktə/ Astronomy an inconspicuous southern constellation (the Easel or Painter), close to the star Canopus in Puppis.
▪ [as genitive **Pictoris** /pɪkˈtɔːrɪs/] used with preceding letter or numeral to designate a star in this constellation: *the star Beta Pictoris*.
– ORIGIN Latin.

pictorial ▶ **adjective** of or expressed in pictures; illustrated: *feelings presented in a pictorial form*.
▶ **noun** [usu. in names] a newspaper or periodical with pictures as a main feature: *he reported on cricket for the* Sunday Pictorial.
– DERIVATIVES **pictorially** adverb.
– ORIGIN mid 17th cent.: from late Latin *pictorius* (from Latin *pictor* 'painter', from the verb *pingere* 'to paint') + **-AL**.

picture ▶ **noun** a painting or drawing: *draw a picture of a tree*.
▪ a photograph: *we were warned not to* **take pictures**. ▪ a portrait: *have her picture painted*. ▪ archaic a person or thing resembling another closely. ▪ figurative an impression of something formed from an account or description: *a full picture of the disaster had not yet emerged*. ▪ an image on a television screen. ▪ a cinema film: *the movie took five honours including best picture*. ▪ (**the pictures**) the cinema: *I'm* **going to the pictures** *with my mates*.
▶ **verb** [with obj.] (often **be pictured**) represent (someone or something) in a photograph or picture.
▪ describe (someone or something) in a certain way: *the markets in London and New York are usually pictured in contrasting terms*. ▪ form a mental image of: *she pictured Benjamin waiting*.
– PHRASES **be in pictures** chiefly N. Amer. act in films or work for the film industry. **be** (or **look**) **a picture** be beautiful. ▪ look amusingly startled: *her face was a picture*. **get the picture** informal understand a situation. **in the picture** fully informed about something. **out of the picture** so as to be no longer involved; irrelevant: *hostages were better left out of the picture*. **a** (or **the**) **picture of ——** the embodiment of a specified state or emotion: *she looked a picture of health*. **(as) pretty as a picture** very pretty.
– ORIGIN late Middle English: from Latin *pictura*, from *pict-* 'painted' (from the verb *pingere*).

picture book ▶ **noun** a book containing many illustrations, especially one for children.

picture card ▶ **noun** an illustrated card used in games or as a teaching aid.
▪ another term for **COURT CARD**.

picture element ▶ **noun** see **PIXEL**.

picture hat ▶ **noun** a woman's highly decorated hat with a wide brim, as shown in pictures by 18th-century English painters such as Reynolds and Gainsborough.

picture palace ▶ **noun** Brit. dated a cinema.

picture-plane ▶ **noun** (in perspective), the imaginary plane corresponding to the surface of a picture, perpendicular to the viewer's line of sight.

picture postcard ▶ **noun** a postcard with a picture on one side.
▪ [as modifier] prettily picturesque, like the scenes typically shown on such postcards.

picture rail ▶ **noun** a horizontal strip of wood on a wall from which pictures can be hung.

picture space ▶ **noun** [mass noun] the apparent space behind the picture-plane of a painting, created by perspective and other techniques.

picturesque ▶ **adjective** visually attractive, especially in a quaint or pretty style: *ruined abbeys and picturesque villages*.
▪ (of language) unusual and vivid: *the salad has no regional or picturesque name*.
– DERIVATIVES **picturesquely** adverb, **picturesqueness** noun.
– ORIGIN early 18th cent.: from French *pittoresque*, from Italian *pittoresco*, from *pittore* 'painter' (from Latin *pictor*). The change from *-tt-* to *-ct-* was due to association with **PICTURE**.

picture theatre ▶ **noun** dated, chiefly N. Amer. a cinema.

picture tube ▶ **noun** Electronics the cathode ray tube of a television set designed for the reproduction of television pictures.

picture window ▶ **noun** a large window consisting of one pane of glass, typically facing an attractive view.

picture-writing ▶ **noun** [mass noun] a mode of recording events by pictorial symbols; pictography.

piculet /ˈpɪkjʊlɪt/ ▶ **noun** a tiny tropical woodpecker with a short unstiffened tail, found chiefly in Central and South America.
• *Picumnus* and other genera, family Picidae: numerous species.
– ORIGIN mid 19th cent.: apparently a double diminutive of Latin *picus* 'woodpecker'.

PID ▶ **abbreviation for** pelvic inflammatory disease.

piddle informal ▶ **verb** [no obj.] urinate.
▶ **noun** [in sing.] an act of urinating.
▪ [mass noun] urine.
– DERIVATIVES **piddler** noun.
– ORIGIN late 18th cent.: probably from a blend of **PISS** and **PUDDLE**.
▶ **piddle about** (or **around**) spend time in trifling activities; potter: *I piddled around the house all day*. [ORIGIN: mid 16th cent. (as *piddle*): of unknown origin; compare with the rare synonym *peddle*.]

piddling ▶ **adjective** informal pathetically trivial; trifling: *piddling little questions*.

piddock /ˈpɪdək/ ▶ **noun** a bivalve mollusc which bores into soft rock or other firm surfaces. The valves of the shell have a conspicuous gap between them and rough frontal ridges to aid in boring.
• *Pholas* and other genera, family Pholadidae.
– ORIGIN mid 19th cent.: of unknown origin.

pidgin /ˈpɪdʒɪn/ ▶ **noun** [often as modifier] a grammatically simplified form of a language, typically English, Dutch, or Portuguese, with a limited vocabulary, some elements of which are taken from local languages, used for communication between people not sharing a common language. Pidgins are not normally found as native languages, but arise out of language contact between speakers of other languages.
▪ (**Pidgin**) another term for **TOK PISIN**.
– ORIGIN late 19th cent.: Chinese alteration of English *business*.

pi-dog ▶ **noun** variant spelling of **PYE-DOG**.

pie[1] ▶ **noun** a baked dish of fruit, or meat and vegetables, typically with a top and base of pastry.
– PHRASES **(as) —— as pie** informal very ——: *using the camera was as easy as pie*. **(as) nice** (or **sweet**) **as pie** extremely pleasant or polite. **a piece** (or **slice**) **of the pie** a share of an amount of money or business available to be claimed or distributed: *orchestras have seen cultural rivals get a bigger piece of the pie*. **pie in the sky** informal used to describe or refer to something that is pleasant to contemplate but is very unlikely to be realized.
– ORIGIN Middle English: probably the same word as **PIE**[2], the various combinations of ingredients being compared to objects randomly collected by a magpie.

pie[2] ▶ **noun** used in names of birds that resemble the magpie, especially in having black-and-white plumage, e.g. **sea-pie**, **tree pie**.
– ORIGIN Middle English: from Old French, from Latin *pica* 'magpie' (related to *picus* 'green woodpecker').

pie[3] ▶ **noun** a former monetary unit in the Indian subcontinent, equal to one twelfth of an anna.
– ORIGIN from Hindi *pā'ī*, from Sanskrit *pada*, *padī* 'quarter'.

piebald ▶ **adjective** (of a horse) having irregular patches of two colours, typically black and white.
▶ **noun** a piebald horse or other animal.
– ORIGIN late 16th cent.: from **PIE**[2] (because of the magpie's black-and-white plumage) + **BALD** (in the obsolete sense 'streaked with white').

piece ▶ **noun 1** a portion of an object or of material, produced by cutting, tearing, or breaking the whole: ***a piece of** cheese* | *the dish lay* ***in pieces*** *upon the floor* | *toddlers who tore books* ***to pieces*** *at her feet*.
▪ one of the items which were put together to make something and into which it naturally divides: ***take** a car* ***to pieces***. ▪ an item of a particular type, especially one forming part of a set: ***a piece of** luggage*. ▪ an instance or example: *a crucial piece of evidence*. ▪ a financial share: *each employee owns a piece of the company*. ▪ a written, musical, or artistic creation or composition: *a hauntingly beautiful piece of music*. ▪ [with modifier] a coin of specified value: *a 10p piece*. ▪ a figure or token used to make moves in a board game. ▪ Chess a king, queen, bishop, knight, or rook, as opposed to a pawn. ▪ informal, chiefly N. Amer. a firearm. ▪ Scottish a sandwich or other item of food taken as a snack. ▪ informal, offensive a woman.
▶ **verb** [with obj.] **1** (**piece something together**) assemble something from individual parts: *the children took it in turns to piece together each other's jigsaw*.
▪ slowly make sense of something from separate facts and pieces of evidence: *Daniel had pieced the story together from the radio*.
2 (**piece something out**) archaic extend.
3 archaic patch: *if it be broken it must be pieced*.

P

– PHRASES **a piece of ass** (or **tail**) vulgar slang a woman regarded as sexually attractive. **a piece of cake** see **CAKE**. **a piece** (or **slice**) **of the action** informal a share in the excitement of something. ■ a share in the profits accruing from something. **go to pieces** become so nervous or upset that one is unable to behave or perform normally. **in one piece** unharmed or undamaged, especially after a dangerous experience. (**all**) **of a piece** (**with something**) (entirely) consistent (with something). **piece by piece** in slow and small stages. **piece of water** a small lake or pond. **say one's piece** give one's opinion or make a prepared statement. **tear** (or **pull**) **someone/thing to pieces** criticize someone or something harshly.

– ORIGIN Middle English: from Old French *piece* (compare with medieval Latin *pecia*, *petium*), of obscure ultimate origin.

pièce de résistance /ˌpjɛs də reɪˈzɪstɒ̃s, French pjɛs də ʀezistɑ̃s/ ▶ **noun** [in sing.] (especially with reference to creative work) the most important or remarkable feature: *the pièce de résistance of the meal was flaming ice cream.*

– ORIGIN French, literally 'piece (i.e. means) of resistance'.

piece goods ▶ **plural noun** fabrics woven in standard lengths for sale.

piecemeal ▶ **adjective** & **adverb** characterized by unsystematic partial measures taken over a period of time: [as adj.] *the village is slowly being killed off by piecemeal development* | [as adv.] *many organizations have been built up piecemeal.*

– ORIGIN Middle English: from the noun **PIECE** + *-meal* from Old English *mǣlum*, in the sense 'measure, quantity taken at one time'.

piece of eight ▶ **noun** historical a Spanish dollar, equivalent to 8 reals.

piecer ▶ **noun** a person who patches or creates a garment or item from pieces of fabric.
■ historical a child employed in a spinning mill to join the ends of broken threads.

piece rate ▶ **noun** a rate of payment for piecework.

piecework ▶ **noun** [mass noun] work paid for according to the amount produced.

– DERIVATIVES **pieceworker** noun.

pie chart ▶ **noun** a type of graph in which a circle is divided into sectors that each represent a proportion of the whole.

– ORIGIN 1920s: because of the resemblance of the graph to a pie divided into portions.

piecrust ▶ **noun** the baked pastry crust of a pie.
■ [mass noun] N. Amer. shortcrust pastry.

piecrust table ▶ **noun** a table with an indented edge like a piecrust.

pied /pʌɪd/ ▶ **adjective** having two or more different colours: *the pied flycatcher.*

– ORIGIN Middle English (originally in the sense 'black and white like a magpie'): from **PIE**[2] + **-ED**[1].

pied-à-terre /ˌpjeɪdɑːˈtɛː, French pjetatɛʀ/ ▶ **noun** (pl. **pieds-à-terre** pronunc. same) a small flat, house, or room kept for occasional use.

– ORIGIN early 19th cent.: French, literally 'foot to earth'.

Piedfort /ˈpjeɪfɔːt/ ▶ **noun** a coin that is thicker than a normal issue, made as a collector's item.

– ORIGIN from French *pied* 'foot' + *fort* 'strong'.

Piedmont /ˈpiːdmɒnt/ a region of NW Italy, in the foothills of the Alps; capital, Turin. Dominated by Savoy from 1400, it became a part of the kingdom of Sardinia in 1720. It was the centre of the movement for a united Italy in the 19th century. Italian name **PIEMONTE**.

– DERIVATIVES **Piedmontese** noun & adjective.

– ORIGIN from Italian *piemonte* 'mountain foot'.

piedmont ▶ **noun** a gentle slope leading from the foot of mountains to a region of flat land.
■ (**the Piedmont**) a hilly region of the eastern US, between the Appalachians and the coastal plain.

– ORIGIN mid 19th cent.: from Italian *piemonte* 'mountain foot' (see **PIEDMONT**).

pied noir /pjeɪ ˈnwɑː, French pje nwaʀ/ ▶ **noun** (pl. **pieds noirs** pronunc. same) a person of European origin who lived in Algeria during French rule, especially one who returned to Europe after Algeria was granted independence.

– ORIGIN French, literally 'black foot', so named because of the western-style black leather shoes worn by the first colonists.

pie-dog ▶ **noun** variant spelling of **PYE-DOG**.

Pied Piper the hero of *The Pied Piper of Hamelin*, a poem by Robert Browning (1842), based on an old German legend. The piper, dressed in particoloured costume, rid the town of Hamelin (Hameln) in Brunswick of rats by enticing them away with his music, and when refused the promised payment he lured away the children of the citizens.
■ [as noun **a Pied Piper**] a person who entices people to follow them, especially to their doom.

pied wagtail ▶ **noun** a bird of a black-and-white race of the white wagtail, found in the British Isles, Spain, and Morocco.
● *Motacilla alba yarrelli*, family Motacillidae.

pie-eyed ▶ **adjective** informal very drunk.

pie-faced ▶ **adjective** informal having a roundish face and typically a blank or stupid expression.

Piegan ▶ **noun** (pl. same or **Piegans**) & **adjective** variant spelling of **PEIGAN**.

pieman ▶ **noun** (pl. **-men**) archaic a pie seller.

Piemonte /pjeˈmonte/ Italian name for **PIEDMONT**.

piemontite /ˈpiːmɒntʌɪt/ ▶ **noun** [mass noun] a brown or black mineral consisting of a silicate of calcium, aluminium, iron, and manganese.

– ORIGIN late 19th cent.: from Italian *Piemonte* (see **PIEDMONT**) + **-ITE**[1].

pie plate (also **pie pan**) ▶ **noun** a shallow metal or glass dish with sloping sides in which pies are baked.

pier ▶ **noun 1** a structure leading out from the shore into the water, in particular:
■ Brit. a platform supported on pillars or girders leading out to sea and used as a promenade, typically incorporating entertainment arcades and places to eat. ■ a similar structure or a solid one, used as a landing stage for boats. ■ a breakwater or mole.
2 Brit. a long narrow structure projecting from an airport terminal, along which passengers walk to and from an aircraft.
3 a solid support designed to sustain vertical pressure, in particular:
■ the pillar of an arch or supporting a bridge. ■ a wall between windows or other adjacent openings.

– ORIGIN Middle English: from medieval Latin *pera*, of unknown origin.

Pierce, Franklin (1804–69), American Democratic statesman, 14th President of the US 1853–7.

pierce ▶ **verb** [with obj.] (of a sharp pointed object) go into or through (something): *a splinter had pierced the skin.*
■ make (a hole) with a sharp instrument. ■ make a hole in (the ears, nose, or other parts of the body) so as to wear jewellery in them: [as adj. **pierced**] *a punk with a pierced nose.* ■ (usu. **be pierced**) bore a hole or tunnel through: *the dividing wall is pierced by arches and piers.* ■ force or cut a way through: *they were seeking to pierce the anti-ballistic-missile defences* | *a shrill voice pierced the air.*

– PHRASES **pierce someone's heart** affect someone keenly or deeply.

– ORIGIN Middle English: from Old French *percer*, based on Latin *pertus-* 'bored through', from the verb *pertundere*, from *per* 'through' + *tundere* 'thrust'.

piercer ▶ **noun** a person or thing that pierces something.
■ [often with modifier] a person who pierces the ears, nose, or other parts of the body so jewellery can be worn in them.

piercing ▶ **adjective** (of eyes or a look) appearing to see through someone; searching: *he stared at me with those piercing eyes.*
■ (of a voice or sound) extremely high, loud, or shrill: *she let out a piercing scream.* ■ (of wind or extreme temperature) seeming to cut through one: *the piercing cold.* ■ (of a feeling) affecting one keenly or deeply. ■ (of mental attributes) sharp; profound: *her piercing analysis.*

– DERIVATIVES **piercingly** adverb.

pier glass ▶ **noun** a large mirror, used originally to fill wall space between windows.

pierid /ˈpʌɪərɪd/ ▶ **noun** Entomology a butterfly of a family (Pieridae) which includes the whites, brimstones, and sulphurs.

– ORIGIN late 19th cent.: from modern Latin *Pieridae* (plural), from Latin *pieris* 'Muse'.

pieris /ˈpɪərɪs, ˈpʌɪ-/ ▶ **noun** an evergreen shrub of the heather family, typically having pink or red young leaves and loose clusters of waxy white bell-shaped flowers. It is native to North America and Asia.
● Genus *Pieris*, family Ericaceae.

– ORIGIN modern Latin, from Latin, literally 'Muse', from *Pieria*, the name of a district in northern Thessaly, said to be the home of the Muses.

Piero della Francesca /ˌpjɛːrəʊ ˌdɛlə franˈtʃɛskə/ (1416–92), Italian painter. He used perspective, proportion, and geometrical relationships to create ordered and harmonious pictures in which the figures appear to inhabit real space. He is best known for his frescoes, notably a cycle in Arezzo depicting the story of the True Cross (begun 1452).

pierogi /pɪəˈrəʊgi/ ▶ **noun** variant spelling of **PIROGI**.

Pierre /pɪə/ the state capital of South Dakota, situated on the Missouri River; pop. 12,900 (1990).

Pierrot /ˈpɪərəʊ, ˈpjɛrəʊ/ ▶ **noun** a stock male character in French pantomime, with a sad white-painted face, a loose white costume, and a pointed hat.

– ORIGIN French, diminutive of the male given name *Pierre* 'Peter'.

pier table ▶ **noun** a low table or bracket in the space between two windows, typically placed under a pier glass.

Piesporter /ˈpiːzˌpɔːtə/ ▶ **noun** [mass noun] a white Moselle wine produced in the Piesport region of Germany.

pietà /pjeɪˈtɑː/ ▶ **noun** a picture or sculpture of the Virgin Mary holding the dead body of Christ on her lap or in her arms.

– ORIGIN Italian, from Latin *pietas* 'dutifulness'.

pietas /ˈpʌɪətɑːs, piːˈeɪtɑːs/ ▶ **noun** [mass noun] respect due to an ancestor, a country, an institution, etc.

– ORIGIN Latin, literally 'dutifulness'.

Pietermaritzburg /ˌpiːtəˈmarɪtsbəːg/ a city in eastern South Africa, the capital of KwaZulu/Natal; pop. 228,550 (1991).

Pietersburg /ˈpiːtəzbəːg/ a town in northern South Africa, the capital of Northern Province; pop. 29,000 (1985).

pietism /ˈpʌɪətɪz(ə)m/ ▶ **noun** [mass noun] pious sentiment, especially of an exaggerated or affected nature.
■ (usu. **Pietism**) a 17th-century movement for the revival of piety in the Lutheran Church. [ORIGIN: from German *Pietismus*, from modern Latin, based on Latin *pietas* (see **PIETY**).]

– DERIVATIVES **pietist** noun, **pietistic** adjective, **pietistical** adjective, **pietistically** adverb.

piet-my-vrou /ˈpɪtmeɪˌfrəʊ/ ▶ **noun** S. African an African cuckoo, which has a russet band on the upper part of the breast.
● *Cuculus solitarius*, family Cuculidae. Alternative name: **red-chested cuckoo**.

– ORIGIN mid 18th cent.: from South African Dutch, imitative of the bird's three-note call.

pietra dura /ˌpjɛtrə ˈdʊːrə/ ▶ **noun** [mass noun] pictorial mosaic work using semi-precious stones, typically for table-tops and other furniture.

– ORIGIN early 19th cent.: from Italian (plural *pietre dure*), literally 'hard stone'.

piety /ˈpʌɪəti/ ▶ **noun** [mass noun] the quality of being religious or reverent: *acts of piety and charity.*
■ [count noun] (pl. **-ies**) a belief or point of view which is accepted with unthinking conventional reverence: *the accepted pieties of our time.*

– ORIGIN early 16th cent. (in the sense 'devotion to religious observances'): from Old French *piete*, from Latin *pietas* 'dutifulness', from *pius* (see **PIOUS**).

piezo /pʌɪˈiːzəʊ, ˈpiːzəʊ/ ▶ **adjective** piezoelectric.

piezoelectricity ▶ **noun** [mass noun] electric polarization in a substance (especially certain crystals) resulting from the application of mechanical stress.

Piezoelectric substances are able to convert mechanical signals (such as sound waves) into electrical signals, and vice versa. They are therefore widely used in microphones, gramophone pickups, and earphones, and also to generate a spark for lighting gas.

– DERIVATIVES **piezoelectric** adjective, **piezoelectrically** adverb.

– ORIGIN late 19th cent.: from Greek *piezein* 'press, squeeze' + **ELECTRICITY**.

piezometer /ˌpʌɪɪˈzɒmɪtə/ ▶ **noun** an instrument for measuring the pressure of a liquid or gas, or

something related to pressure (such as the compressibility of liquid). Piezometers are often placed in boreholes to monitor the pressure or depth of groundwater.
– ORIGIN early 19th cent.: from Greek *piezein* 'press, squeeze' + -METER.

piffle ▶ noun [mass noun] informal nonsense.
– ORIGIN mid 19th cent.: diminutive of imitative *piff-*.

piffling ▶ adjective informal trivial; unimportant.

pig ▶ noun **1** an omnivorous domesticated hoofed mammal with sparse bristly hair and a flat snout for rooting in the soil, kept for its meat.
● *Sus domesticus*, family Suidae (the **pig family**), descended from the wild boar and domesticated over 8,000 years ago. The pig family also includes the warthog and babirusa, but the similar peccaries are placed in their own family.
■ a wild animal of this family. Also called HOG. ■ N. Amer. a young pig; a piglet. ■ [mass noun] the flesh of a pig, especially a young one, as food. ■ informal a greedy, dirty, or unpleasant person: *I bet he has scoffed them all, greedy pig.* ■ informal, chiefly N. Amer. a police officer. ■ Brit. informal an unpleasant or difficult thing or task: *it's a pig of a job.*
2 an oblong mass of iron or lead from a smelting furnace. See also PIG IRON.
■ a device which fits snugly inside an oil or gas pipeline and is sent through it to clean or test the inside, or to act as a barrier.
▶ verb (**pigged**, **pigging**) [no obj.] **1** informal gorge oneself with food: *lovesick people pig out on chocolate.*
2 informal crowd together with other people in disorderly or dirty conditions: *he didn't approve of the proposal to pig it in the studio.*
3 (of a sow) give birth to piglets; farrow.
4 operate a pig within an oil or gas pipeline.
– PHRASES **bleed like a (stuck) pig** bleed copiously. **in pig** (of a sow) pregnant. **in a pig's eye** informal, chiefly N. Amer. expressing scornful disbelief at a statement. **make a pig of oneself** informal overeat. **make a pig's ear of** Brit. informal handle ineptly. **pig in the middle** see *piggy in the middle* at PIGGY. **a pig in a poke** something that is bought or accepted without knowing its value or seeing it first. **pigs might (or can) fly** chiefly Brit. used ironically to express disbelief. **squeal (or yell) like a stuck pig** squeal or yell loudly and shrilly. **sweat like a pig** informal sweat profusely.
– DERIVATIVES **piglike** adjective, **pigling** noun.
– ORIGIN Middle English: probably from the first element of Old English *picbrēd* 'acorn', literally 'pig bread' (i.e. food for pigs).

pigeon[1] ▶ noun **1** a stout seed- or fruit-eating bird with a small head, short legs, and a cooing voice, typically having grey and white plumage. See also DOVE[1] (sense 1).
● Family Columbidae: numerous genera and species.
■ (also **domestic** or **feral pigeon**) a pigeon descended from the wild rock dove, kept for racing, showing, and carrying messages, and common as a feral bird in towns.
2 informal, chiefly US a gullible person, especially someone swindled in gambling or the victim of a confidence trick.
3 military slang an aircraft from one's own side.
– ORIGIN late Middle English: from Old French *pijon*, denoting a young bird, especially a young dove, from an alteration of late Latin *pipio(n-)*, 'young cheeping bird' of imitative origin.

pigeon[2] ▶ noun **1** archaic spelling of PIDGIN.
2 (**one's pigeon**) informal, chiefly Brit. a person's particular responsibility or business: *Hermia will have to tell them first, it's her pigeon.*

pigeon breast (also **pigeon chest**) ▶ noun a deformed human chest with a projecting breastbone.
– DERIVATIVES **pigeon-breasted** (also **pigeon-chested**) adjective.

pigeon hawk ▶ noun N. Amer. old-fashioned term for MERLIN.

pigeon-hearted ▶ adjective timid; cowardly.

pigeon-hole ▶ noun a small recess for a domestic pigeon to nest in.
■ a small compartment, open at the front and forming part of a set, where letters or messages may be left for someone. ■ a similar compartment built into a desk for keeping documents in. ■ figurative a category to which someone or something is assigned: *'laddism' is a journalistic pigeon-hole for boisterously antisocial young men.*
▶ verb [with obj.] deposit (a document) in a pigeon-hole.

■ assign to a particular category or class, especially in a manner that is too rigid or exclusive: *we won't pigeon-hole you as a scientist.* ■ put aside for future consideration: *she pigeon-holed her worry about him.*

pigeonite ▶ noun [mass noun] a calcium-poor pyroxene mineral occurring chiefly in basalt.
– ORIGIN early 20th cent.: named after *Pigeon* Point, Minnesota, + -ITE[1].

pigeon pair ▶ noun dialect a boy and girl as twins, or as the only children in a family.

pigeon pea ▶ noun **1** a dark red tropical pealike seed.
2 the woody Old World plant which yields these seeds, with pods and foliage that are used as fodder.
● *Cajanus cajan*, family Leguminosae.

pigeon's milk ▶ noun [mass noun] a curd-like secretion from a pigeon's crop, which it regurgitates and feeds to its young.

pigeon-toed ▶ adjective (of a person or horse) having the toes or feet turned inwards.

pigface ▶ noun Austral. a succulent creeping plant with bright flowers, related to Hottentot fig.
● Genera *Carpobrotus* and *Disphyma* (both formerly *Mesembryanthemum*), family Aizoaceae.
– ORIGIN early 19th cent.: named with reference to the large pink flowers.

pigfish ▶ noun (pl. same or **-fishes**) **1** a deep-bodied scaleless fish with a protuberant snout, which lives in the cooler seas of the southern hemisphere.
● Family Congiopodidae: several genera and species.
2 [usu. with modifier] any of a number of other marine fishes, especially one that grunts:
● a western Atlantic grunt (*Orthopristis chrysoptera*, family Pomadasyidae). ● Austral. a wrasse or groper (genera *Bodianus* and *Achoerodus*, family Labridae). Compare with HOGFISH.

pig-footed bandicoot ▶ noun an Australian bandicoot with toes that form a paired foot pad on the forelimbs, and a single foot pad on the hindlimbs. It is believed to be extinct.
● *Chaeropus ecaudatus*, family Peramelidae.

piggery ▶ noun (pl. **-ies**) **1** a farm where pigs are bred or kept.
■ a pigsty.
2 [mass noun] behaviour regarded as characteristic of pigs in greed or unpleasantness.

piggish ▶ adjective resembling a pig, especially in being unpleasant.
– DERIVATIVES **piggishly** adverb, **piggishness** noun.

Piggott /ˈpɪɡət/, Lester (Keith) (b.1935), English jockey. He was champion jockey nine times between 1960 and 1971 and again in 1981 and 1982; he won the Derby a record nine times.

piggy ▶ noun (pl. **-ies**) (used by or when talking to children) a pig or piglet.
▶ adjective resembling a pig, especially in features or appetite: *three pairs of little piggy eyes.*
– PHRASES **piggy** (also **pig**) **in the middle** chiefly Brit. a game in which two people attempt to throw a ball to each other without a third person in the middle catching it.
■ a person who is placed in an awkward situation between two others.

piggyback ▶ noun a ride on someone's back and shoulders.
▶ adverb on the back and shoulders of another person: *he had to carry him piggyback.*
■ on top of something else: *Duncan headed back with the car riding piggyback on his truck.*
▶ verb [with obj.] carry by or as if by means of a piggyback.
■ mount on or attach to (an existing object or system): *they have piggybacked their own networks on to the system.* ■ [no obj.] use existing work or an existing product as a basis or support: *we were piggybacking on their training program.*
– ORIGIN mid 16th cent. (as an adverb): although analysed by folk etymology in various ways from an early date, the word's origin remains obscure.

piggy bank ▶ noun a money box, especially one shaped like a pig.
■ figurative savings: *many people would dip into their piggy bank to pay their higher tax bills.*

pig-headed ▶ adjective stupidly obstinate.
– DERIVATIVES **pig-headedly** adverb, **pig-headedness** noun.

pightle /ˈpaɪt(ə)l/ ▶ noun dialect a small field or enclosure.

– ORIGIN Middle English: origin obscure, apparently diminutive.

pig-ignorant ▶ adjective informal extremely stupid or crude.

pig iron ▶ noun [mass noun] crude iron as first obtained from a smelting furnace, in the form of oblong blocks. Compare with PIG (in sense 2).

Pig Island Austral./NZ informal a nickname for New Zealand.
– ORIGIN said to be so named because of the pigs left on the island by Captain Cook.

pig-jump Austral. informal ▶ noun a jump made by a horse from all four legs.
▶ verb [no obj.] (of a horse) jump in this manner.

pig Latin ▶ noun [mass noun] a secret language formed from English by transferring the initial consonant or consonant cluster of each word to the end of the word and adding a vocalic syllable (usually /eɪ/): so *igpay atinlay.*

piglet ▶ noun a young pig.

pigman ▶ noun (pl. **-men**) a person who looks after pigs on a farm.

pigment ▶ noun the natural colouring matter of animal or plant tissue.
■ a substance used for colouring or painting, especially a dry powder, which when mixed with oil, water, or another medium constitutes a paint or ink.
▶ verb [with obj.] [usu. as adj. **pigmented**] colour (something) with or as if with pigment.
– DERIVATIVES **pigmentary** adjective.
– ORIGIN Middle English, from Latin *pigmentum*, from *pingere* 'to paint'. The verb dates from the early 20th cent.

pigmentation ▶ noun [mass noun] the natural colouring of animal or plant tissue.
■ the colouring of a person's skin, especially when abnormal or distinctive.

pigmy ▶ noun variant spelling of PYGMY.

pignut ▶ noun another term for EARTHNUT (in sense 1).

pig-out ▶ noun informal a bout of eating a large amount of food.

pigpen ▶ noun N. Amer. a pigsty.

Pigs, Bay of a bay on the SW coast of Cuba, scene of an unsuccessful attempt in 1961 by US-backed Cuban exiles to invade the country and overthrow the regime of Fidel Castro.

pigskin ▶ noun **1** the hide of a domestic pig.
■ [mass noun] leather made from this.
2 N. Amer. informal a football.

pig-sticker ▶ noun informal a long sharp knife or weapon.

pig-sticking ▶ noun [mass noun] the sport of hunting wild boar with a spear on horseback.

pigsty ▶ noun (pl. **-ies**) a pen or enclosure for a pig or pigs.
■ a very dirty or untidy house or room.

pigswill ▶ noun [mass noun] kitchen refuse and scraps fed to pigs.

pigtail ▶ noun **1** a lock of hair, plaited or loose, typically worn one either side of the head.
2 a short length of flexible braided wire connecting a stationary part to a moving part in an electrical device.
3 a thin twist of tobacco.
– DERIVATIVES **pigtailed** adjective.

pig-tailed macaque (also **pigtail macaque**) ▶ noun a forest-dwelling SE Asian macaque that has a brown coat with pale underparts, dark markings around the face, and a small piglike tail.
● *Macaca nemestrina*, family Cercopithecidae.

pigweed ▶ noun [mass noun] **1** an amaranth that grows as a weed or is used for fodder.
● Genus *Amaranthus*, family Amaranthaceae: several species, in particular *A. retroflexus* and *A. albus*.
2 North American term for FAT HEN.

pi-jaw ▶ noun [mass noun] informal, dated tediously moralizing talk.

pika /ˈpʌɪkə, ˈpiːkə/ ▶ noun a small mammal related to the rabbits, having rounded ears, short limbs, and a very small tail, found mainly in the mountains and deserts of Asia. Also called MOUSE HARE.
● Family Ochotonidae and genus *Ochotona*: many species, including the **collared pika** (*O. collaris*), of western North America.

– ORIGIN early 19th cent.: from Tungus *piika*.

pike[1] ▶ **noun** (pl. same) a long-bodied predatory freshwater fish with a pointed snout and large teeth, of both Eurasia and North America.
• Family Esocidae and genus *Esox*: five species, including the widespread **northern pike** (*E. lucius*).
■ used in names of other predatory fish with large teeth, e.g. **garpike**.
– ORIGIN Middle English: from **PIKE**[2] (because of the fish's pointed jaw).

pike[2] ▶ **noun** historical an infantry weapon with a pointed steel or iron head on a long wooden shaft.
■ N. English (in names of hills in the Lake District) a hill with a peaked top: *Scafell pike*. [ORIGIN: apparently of Scandinavian origin; compare with West Norwegian dialect *pīk* 'pointed mountain'.]
▶ **verb** [with obj.] historical kill or thrust (someone) through with a pike.
– ORIGIN early 16th cent.: from French *pique*, back-formation from *piquer* 'pierce', from *pic* 'pick, pike'; compare with Old English *pīc* 'point, prick' (of unknown origin).

pike[3] ▶ **noun** short for **TURNPIKE**.
– PHRASES **come down the pike** N. Amer. appear on the scene; come to notice.

pike[4] ▶ **noun** [often as modifier] a jackknife position in diving or gymnastics.
– ORIGIN 1920s: of unknown origin.

pike[5] ▶ **verb** [no obj.] (**pike on**) Austral./NZ informal withdraw from (a plan or agreement) because of over-cautiousness.
– ORIGIN late Middle English (as *pike oneself* 'take up a pilgrim's staff'): compare with Danish *pigge af* 'hasten off'. The current sense dates from the late 19th cent.

pikelet ▶ **noun** a thin kind of crumpet.
– ORIGIN late 18th cent.: from Welsh (*bara*) *pyglyd* 'pitchy (bread)'.

pikeman ▶ **noun** (pl. **-men**) historical the keeper of a turnpike.

pikeperch ▶ **noun** (pl. same) a predatory pike-like freshwater fish of the perch family, especially the zander.
• Genus *Stizostedion*, family Percidae: five species, including the sauger and the walleye.

piker ▶ **noun** informal, chiefly N. Amer. a gambler who makes only small bets.
■ a mean or cautious person.
– ORIGIN late 19th cent.: from the slang verb **PIKE**[5].

pikestaff ▶ **noun** historical the wooden shaft of a pike.
– PHRASES (**as**) **plain as a pikestaff** very obvious. ■ ordinary or unattractive in appearance. [ORIGIN: alteration of *as plain as a packstaff*, the staff being that of a pedlar, on which he rested his pack of wares.]
– ORIGIN late 16th cent.: from **PIKE**[2] + **STAFF**[1].

piki /ˈpiːki/ ▶ **noun** [mass noun] maize-meal bread in the form of very thin sheets, made by the Hopi Indians of the south-western US.
– ORIGIN Hopi.

pikkie /ˈpəki, ˈpɪki/ ▶ **noun** (pl. **-ies**) S. African informal a child.
■ a small object.
– ORIGIN Afrikaans, literally 'bantam or little chap', from Dutch dialect *piek* 'chicken', later also 'small child'.

Pik Pobedy /ˌpiːk pəˈbjɛdi/ a mountain in eastern Kyrgyzstan, situated close to the border with China. Rising to a height of 7,439 m (24,406 ft), it is the highest peak in the Tien Shan range.
– ORIGIN from Russian, literally 'Victory Peak'.

pilaf /pɪˈlaf/ (also **pilaff** or **pilau** /pɪˈlaʊ/, **pulao**) ▶ **noun** a Middle Eastern or Indian dish of rice or wheat, vegetables, and spices, typically having added meat or fish.
– ORIGIN from Turkish *pilâv*.

pilaster /pɪˈlastə/ ▶ **noun** a rectangular column, especially one projecting from a wall.
– DERIVATIVES **pilastered** adjective.
– ORIGIN late 16th cent.: from French *pilastre*, from Italian *pilastro* or medieval Latin *pilastrum*, from Latin *pila* 'pillar'.

Pilate /ˈpʌɪlət/, Pontius (died *c*.36 AD), Roman procurator of Judaea *c*.26–*c*.36. He is remembered for presiding at the trial of Jesus Christ and authorizing his crucifixion.

pilchard ▶ **noun** a small, edible, commercially valuable marine fish of the herring family.
• *Sardinops* and other genera, family Clupeidae: several species, including the European *Sardina pilchardus*. See also **SARDINE**[1].
– ORIGIN mid 16th cent.: of unknown origin.

pile[1] ▶ **noun** a heap of things laid or lying one on top of another: *he placed the books in a neat pile*.
■ informal a large amount of something: *the growing pile of work*. ■ a large imposing building or group of buildings: *a Victorian Gothic pile*. ■ a series of plates of dissimilar metals laid one on another alternately to produce an electric current. ■ short for **ATOMIC PILE**. ■ archaic a funeral pyre.
▶ **verb 1** [with obj. and adverbial] place (things) one on top of the other: *she piled all the groceries on the counter*.
■ (**be piled with**) be stacked or loaded with: *his in tray was piled high with papers*. ■ (**pile up/pile something up**) increase or cause to increase in quantity: [no obj.] *the work has piled up a bit* | [with obj.] *the debts he piled up*. ■ (**pile something on**) informal intensify or exaggerate something for effect: *you can pile on the guilt but my heart has turned to stone*.
2 [no obj.] (**pile into/out of**) (of a group of people) get into or out of (a vehicle) in a disorganized manner: *ten of us piled into the minibus*.
■ (**pile into**) (of a vehicle) crash into: *60 cars piled into each other on the M62*.
– PHRASES **make a** (or **one's**) **pile** informal make a lot of money. **pile arms** place a number of rifles (usually four) with their butts on the ground and the muzzles together. **pile it on** informal exaggerate the seriousness of a situation or of someone's behaviour to increase guilt or distress. **pile on the agony** informal exaggerate or aggravate a bad situation.
– ORIGIN late Middle English: from Old French, from Latin *pila* 'pillar, pier'.

pile[2] ▶ **noun 1** a heavy stake or post driven vertically into the bed of a river, soft ground, etc., to support the foundations of a superstructure.
2 Heraldry a triangular charge or ordinary formed by two lines meeting at an acute angle, usually pointing down from the top of the shield.
▶ **verb** [with obj.] strengthen or support (a structure) with piles.
– ORIGIN Old English *pīl* 'dart, arrow', also 'pointed stake', of Germanic origin; related to Dutch *pijl* and German *Pfeil*, from Latin *pilum* '(heavy) javelin'.

pile[3] ▶ **noun** [mass noun] the soft projecting surface of a carpet or a fabric such as velvet or flannel, consisting of many small threads.
– ORIGIN Middle English (in the sense 'downy feather'): from Latin *pilus* 'hair'. The current sense dates from the mid 16th cent.

pilea /ˈpʌɪlɪə/ ▶ **noun** a plant of the nettle family which lacks stinging hairs, native to warm regions and widely grown as an indoor plant.
• Genus *Pilea*, family Urticaceae.
– ORIGIN modern Latin, from Latin *pileus* 'felt cap'.

pileated woodpecker /ˈpʌɪlɪeɪtɪd/ ▶ **noun** a large North American woodpecker with mainly black plumage and a red cap and crest.
• *Dryocopus pileatus*, family Picidae.
– ORIGIN late 18th cent.: *pileated* from Latin *pileatus* 'capped', from *pileus* 'felt cap'.

piledriver ▶ **noun** a machine for driving piles into the ground.
■ Brit. informal a forceful act or thing: *the keeper pushed a Mick Tait piledriver round the post*.
– DERIVATIVES **piledriving** noun & adjective.

pile dwelling ▶ **noun** (in prehistoric times) a dwelling built on piles over a lake.

piles ▶ **plural noun** haemorrhoids.
– ORIGIN late Middle English: probably from Latin *pila* 'ball' (because of the globular form of external haemorrhoids).

pile-up ▶ **noun** informal **1** a crash involving several vehicles.
■ a confused mass of people fallen on top of one another, especially in a team game.
2 an accumulation of a specified thing: *a massive pile-up of data*.

pileus /ˈpʌɪlɪəs/ ▶ **noun** (pl. **pilei** /-lɪʌɪ/) Botany the cap of a mushroom or toadstool.
– ORIGIN mid 18th cent.: from Latin, literally 'felt cap'.

pilewort ▶ **noun** the lesser celandine, the bulbils of which are said to resemble haemorrhoids.
– ORIGIN late Middle English: from **PILES** (because of its reputed efficacy against piles) + **WORT**.

pilfer ▶ **verb** [with obj.] steal (things of little value).
– DERIVATIVES **pilferage** noun, **pilferer** noun.
– ORIGIN late Middle English (as a noun in the sense 'action of pilfering, something pilfered'): from Old French *pelfrer* 'to pillage', of unknown origin. Compare with **PELF**.

pilgrim ▶ **noun** a person who journeys to a sacred place for religious reasons.
■ chiefly poetic/literary a person whose life is compared to a journey. ■ a member of the Pilgrim Fathers.
▶ **verb** (**pilgrimed**, **pilgriming**) [no obj., with adverbial of direction] archaic travel or wander like a pilgrim.
– DERIVATIVES **pilgrimize** (also **-ise**) verb (archaic).
– ORIGIN Middle English: from Provençal *pelegrin*, from Latin *peregrinus* 'foreign' (see **PEREGRINE**).

pilgrimage ▶ **noun** a pilgrim's journey.
■ a journey to a place associated with someone or something well known or respected: *making a pilgrimage to the famous racing circuit*. ■ life viewed as a journey: *life's pilgrimage*.
▶ **verb** [no obj., with adverbial of direction] go on a pilgrimage.
– ORIGIN Middle English: from Provençal *pelegrinatge*, from *pelegrin* (see **PILGRIM**).

Pilgrim Fathers ▶ **plural noun** the pioneers of British colonization of North America. A group of 102 people led by English Puritans fleeing religious persecution sailed in the *Mayflower* and founded the colony of Plymouth, Massachusetts, in 1620.

Pilipino /ˌpɪlɪˈpiːnəʊ/ ▶ **noun** & **adjective** variant of **FILIPINO**.

pill[1] ▶ **noun** a small round mass of solid medicine for swallowing whole.
■ (**the Pill**) a contraceptive pill. ■ N. Amer. informal a tedious or unpleasant person. ■ informal (in some sports) a humorous term for a ball.
– PHRASES **a bitter pill** (**to swallow**) an unpleasant or painful necessity (to accept). **sugar** (or **sweeten**) **the pill** make an unpleasant or painful necessity more palatable.
– DERIVATIVES **pilular** adjective.
– ORIGIN late Middle English: ultimately from Latin *pilula* 'little ball', diminutive of *pila*; compare with Middle Dutch, Middle Low German *pille*.

pill[2] ▶ **verb** [no obj.] (of knitted fabric) form small balls of fluff on its surface.
– ORIGIN 1960s: from the noun *pill* denoting a small ball of fluff, extended sense of **PILL**[1].

pillage ▶ **verb** [with obj.] rob a (place) using violence, especially in wartime.
■ steal (something) using violence, especially in wartime: *artworks pillaged from churches and museums*.
▶ **noun** [mass noun] the action of pillaging a place or property, especially in war.
– DERIVATIVES **pillager** noun.
– ORIGIN late Middle English (as a noun): from Old French, from *piller* 'to plunder'.

pillar ▶ **noun** a tall vertical structure of stone, wood, or metal, used as a support for a building, or as an ornament or monument.
■ something shaped like such a structure: ***a pillar of** smoke*. ■ a solid mass of coal left to support the roof of a mine. ■ a person or thing regarded as reliably providing essential support for something: *he was **a pillar of** his local community*.
– PHRASES **from pillar to post** from one place to another in an unceremonious or fruitless manner: *the refugees have been pushed from pillar to post in that area*.
– DERIVATIVES **pillared** adjective, **pillaret** noun.
– ORIGIN Middle English: from Anglo-Norman French *piler*, based on Latin *pila* 'pillar'.

pillar box ▶ **noun** (in the UK) a large red cylindrical public postbox.

pillar-box red ▶ **noun** [mass noun] Brit. a bright red colour, like that in which pillar boxes are painted.

pillar rose ▶ **noun** a climbing rose suitable for training on an upright.

Pillars of Hercules an ancient name for two promontories on either side of the Strait of Gibraltar (the Rock of Gibraltar and Mount Acho in Ceuta), held by legend to have been parted by the arm of Hercules.

pill beetle ▶ **noun** a small convex beetle which is able to feign death by retracting its legs and contracting into a ball.
• Family Byrrhidae: several genera.

pillbox ▶ **noun** a small shallow cylindrical box for holding pills.
■ a hat of a similar shape. ■ a small enclosed, partly underground, concrete fort used as an outpost.

pill bug ▶ noun another term for PILL WOODLOUSE.

pillion ▶ noun a seat for a passenger behind a motorcyclist.
■ historical a woman's light saddle. ■ historical a cushion attached to the back of a saddle for an additional passenger.
– PHRASES **ride pillion** travel seated behind a motorcyclist.
– ORIGIN late 15th cent. (denoting a light saddle): from Scottish Gaelic *pillean*, Irish *pillín* 'small cushion', diminutive of *pell*, from Latin *pellis* 'skin'.

pilliwinks /ˈpɪlɪwɪŋks/ ▶ plural noun historical an instrument of torture used for squeezing the fingers.
– ORIGIN late Middle English *pyrwykes*, *pyrewinkes*, of unknown origin.

pillock ▶ noun Brit. informal a stupid person.
– ORIGIN mid 16th cent.: variant of archaic *pillicock* 'penis', the early sense of *pillock* in northern English.

pillory historical ▶ noun (pl. **-ies**) a wooden framework with holes for the head and hands, in which an offender was imprisoned and exposed to public abuse.
▶ verb (**-ies, -ied**) [with obj.] put (someone) in the pillory.
■ figurative attack or ridicule publicly: *he found himself pilloried by members of his own party.*
– ORIGIN Middle English: from Old French *pilori*, probably from Provençal *espilori* (associated by some with a Catalan word meaning 'peephole', of uncertain origin).

pillow ▶ noun a rectangular cloth bag stuffed with feathers, foam rubber, or other soft materials, used to support the head when lying or sleeping.
■ a piece of wood or metal used as a support; a block or bearing. ■ short for LACE PILLOW.
▶ verb [with obj.] rest (one's head) as if on a pillow.
■ poetic/literary serve as a pillow for.
– DERIVATIVES **pillowy** adjective.
– ORIGIN Old English *pyle*, *pylu*, of West Germanic origin; related to Dutch *peluw* and German *Pfühl*, based on Latin *pulvinus* 'cushion'.

pillow book ▶ noun (in Japanese classical literature) a type of private journal or diary.

pillowcase ▶ noun a removable cloth cover for a pillow.

pillow fight ▶ noun a mock fight using pillows.

pillow lace ▶ noun [mass noun] lace made by hand using a lace pillow.

pillow lava ▶ noun [mass noun] lava which has solidified as rounded masses, characteristic of eruption under water.

pillow sham ▶ noun N. Amer. a decorative pillowcase for covering a pillow when it is not in use.

pillowslip ▶ noun a pillowcase.

pillow talk ▶ noun [mass noun] intimate conversation in bed.

pill-popper ▶ noun informal a person who takes pills freely.
– DERIVATIVES **pill-popping** noun.

pill-pusher ▶ noun informal a person who resorts too readily to advocating the use of medicine to cure illness rather than considering other treatments.

pill woodlouse ▶ noun a woodlouse with a thick cuticle, which is able to roll up into a ball when threatened. Also called PILL BUG.
● Genus *Armadillidium*, order Isopoda.

pillwort ▶ noun a creeping grass-like aquatic fern which has slender stem-like shoots with small globular spore-producing bodies at their bases, growing on the muddy margins of ponds and lakes in western Europe.
● *Pilularia globulifera*, family Marsileaceae.

pilocarpine /ˌpʌɪlə(ʊ)ˈkɑːpiːn/ ▶ noun [mass noun] Chemistry a volatile alkaloid obtained from jaborandi leaves, used to contract the pupils and to relieve pressure in the eye in glaucoma patients.
– ORIGIN late 19th cent.: from modern Latin *Pilocarpus* (genus name of the jaborandi) + -INE⁴.

pilose /ˈpʌɪləʊz/ (also **pilous**) ▶ adjective Botany & Zoology covered with long soft hairs.
– DERIVATIVES **pilosity** noun.
– ORIGIN mid 18th cent.: from Latin *pilosus*, from *pilus* 'hair'.

pilot ▶ noun 1 a person who operates the flying controls of an aircraft.
■ a person with expert local knowledge qualified to take charge of a ship entering or leaving a harbour; a

steersman. ■ a navigational handbook for use at sea.
■ informal a jockey. ■ archaic a guide or leader. ■ [often as modifier] Telecommunications an unmodulated reference signal transmitted with another signal for the purposes of control or synchronization.
2 a television programme made to test audience reaction with a view to the production of a series.
3 another term for COWCATCHER.
▶ adjective [attrib.] done as an experiment or test before introducing something more widely: *a pilot scheme for training workers.*
▶ verb (**piloted, piloting**) [with obj.] 1 act as a pilot of (an aircraft or ship).
■ [with obj. and adverbial of direction] guide; steer: *the task of piloting the economy out of recession.*
2 test (a scheme, project, etc.) before introducing it more widely.
– DERIVATIVES **pilotage** noun, **pilotless** adjective.
– ORIGIN early 16th cent. (denoting a person who steers a ship): from French *pilote*, from medieval Latin *pilotus*, an alteration of *pedota*, based on Greek *pēdon* 'oar', (plural) 'rudder'.

pilot balloon ▶ noun a small meteorological balloon used to track air currents.

pilot bird ▶ noun a brown ground-dwelling Australian songbird, noted for its habit of accompanying superb lyrebirds to feed on disturbed insects.
● *Pycnoptilus floccosus*, family Acanthizidae.

pilot biscuit ▶ noun North American term for SHIP'S BISCUIT.

pilot chute ▶ noun a small parachute used to bring the main one into operation.

pilot cloth ▶ noun [mass noun] thick blue woollen cloth, used to make seamen's coats.

pilotfish ▶ noun (pl. same or **-fishes**) a fish of warm seas that is often seen swimming close to large fish such as sharks and sometimes turtles and boats.
● *Naucrates ductor*, family Carangidae.

pilot hole ▶ noun a small hole drilled ahead of a full-sized hole as a guide.

pilot house ▶ noun another term for WHEELHOUSE (in sense 1).

pilot jacket ▶ noun another term for PEA JACKET.

pilot light ▶ noun 1 a small gas burner kept alight permanently to light a larger burner when needed, especially on a gas cooker or boiler.
2 an electric indicator light or control light.

pilot officer ▶ noun the lowest rank of officer in the RAF, above warrant officer and below flying officer.

pilot whale ▶ noun a toothed whale that has black skin with a grey anchor-shaped marking on the chin, a low dorsal fin, and a square bulbous head. Also called BLACKFISH.
● Genus *Globicephala*, family Delphinidae: the long-finned *G. melas* of subtropical waters, and the short-finned *G. macrorhyncus* of temperate waters.

pilous /ˈpʌɪləs/ ▶ adjective another term for PILOSE.

Pils /pɪlz, -s/ ▶ noun [mass noun] a type of lager beer similar to Pilsner.
– ORIGIN 1960s: abbreviation of PILSNER.

Pilsen /ˈpɪls(ə)n/ an industrial city in the western part of the Czech Republic; pop. 173,130 (1991). Czech name PLZEŇ.

Pilsner /ˈpɪlznə, ˈpɪls-/ (also **Pilsener**) ▶ noun [mass noun] a lager beer with a strong hop flavour, originally brewed at Pilsen (Plzeň) in the Czech Republic.

Piltdown man /ˈpɪltdaʊn/ ▶ noun a fraudulent fossil composed of a human cranium and an ape jaw, allegedly discovered near Lewes in East Sussex and presented in 1912 as a genuine hominid of the early Pleistocene, but shown to be a hoax in 1953.
– ORIGIN *Piltdown*, the name of a village in Sussex.

PIM ▶ abbreviation for personal information manager.

Pima /ˈpiːmə/ ▶ noun (pl. same or **Pimas**) 1 a member of an American Indian people living chiefly along the Gila and Salt rivers in Arizona and in northern Mexico.
2 [mass noun] the Uto-Aztecan language of this people and the Papago.
▶ adjective of or relating to this people or their language.
– ORIGIN Spanish, shortening of *Pimahito*, from Pima *pimahaitu* 'nothing'.

pimento /pɪˈmɛntəʊ/ ▶ noun (pl. **-os**) 1 variant spelling of PIMIENTO.

2 chiefly W. Indian another term for ALLSPICE (in sense 2).
– ORIGIN late 17th cent.: from Spanish *pimiento* (see PIMIENTO).

pi-meson ▶ noun another term for PION.

pimiento /ˌpɪmɪˈɛntəʊ, pɪmˈjɛn-/ (also **pimento**) ▶ noun (pl. **-os**) a red sweet pepper.
– ORIGIN mid 17th cent.: from Spanish, from medieval Latin *pigmentum* 'spice', from Latin, 'pigment'.

pimp ▶ noun 1 a man who controls prostitutes and arranges clients for them, taking a percentage of their earnings in return.
2 Austral./NZ informal a telltale or informer.
▶ verb [no obj.] 1 [often as noun **pimping**] act as a pimp.
■ [with obj.] provide (someone) as a prostitute.
2 Austral./NZ (**pimp on**) inform on.
– ORIGIN late 16th cent.: of unknown origin.

pimpernel /ˈpɪmpənɛl/ ▶ noun a small European plant of the primrose family, with creeping stems and flat five-petalled flowers.
● Genera *Anagallis* and *Lysimachia*, family Primulaceae: several species, in particular the **scarlet pimpernel**.
– ORIGIN late Middle English (denoting the great burnet and the salad burnet): from Old French *pimpernelle*, based on Latin *piper* 'pepper' (because of the resemblance of the burnet's fruit to a peppercorn).

pimping ▶ adjective archaic small or insignificant.
– ORIGIN late 17th cent.: of unknown origin.

pimple ▶ noun a small hard inflamed spot on the skin.
– DERIVATIVES **pimpled** adjective, **pimply** adjective.
– ORIGIN Middle English: related to Old English *piplian* 'break out in pustules'.

pimpmobile ▶ noun US informal a large ostentatious car, in a style associated with pimps.

PIN (also **PIN number**) ▶ abbreviation for personal identification number.

pin ▶ noun 1 a small piece of metal or wood for fastening or attaching things, in particular:
■ a thin piece of metal with a sharp point at one end and a round head at the other, used for fastening pieces of cloth, paper, etc. ■ a small brooch or badge.
■ Medicine a steel rod used to join the ends of fractured bones while they heal. ■ a metal peg that holds down the activating lever of a hand grenade, preventing its explosion. ■ short for HAIRPIN. ■ Music a peg round which one string of a musical instrument is fastened.
2 a short piece of wood or metal for various purposes, in particular:
■ a skittle in bowling. ■ a metal projection from a plug or an integrated circuit which makes an electrical connection with a socket or another part of a circuit.
■ Golf a stick with a flag placed in a hole to mark its position.
3 (**pins**) informal legs: *she was very nimble on her pins.*
4 Chess an attack on a piece or pawn which is thereby pinned.
5 Brit. historical a half-firkin cask for beer.
▶ verb (**pinned, pinning**) [with obj. and adverbial] attach with a pin or pins: *pin a note on the door.*
■ fasten (something) with a pin or pins in a specified position: *her hair was pinned back.* ■ (**pin something on**) fix blame or responsibility for something on (someone). ■ hold someone firmly in a specified position so they are unable to move: *she was standing pinned against the door.* ■ [with obj.] transfix (something) with a pin or other pointed instrument: *an enormous butterfly pinned by a heartless collector.* ■ [with obj.] Chess hinder or prevent (a piece or pawn) from moving because of the danger to a more valuable piece standing behind it along the line of an attack.
– PHRASES (**as**) **clean** (or **neat**) **as a new pin** extremely clean and neat. **for two pins I'd** (or **she'd** etc.) — used to indicate that one is very tempted to do something, especially out of annoyance. **hear a pin drop** used to describe absolute silence or stillness. **on pins and needles** in an agitated state of suspense. **pin one's colours to the mast** see MAST¹. **pin one's ears back** listen carefully. **pin one's hopes** (or **faith**) **on** rely heavily on: *ministers were pinning their hopes on a big-spending Christmas.*
– ORIGIN late Old English *pinn*, of West Germanic origin; related to Dutch *pin* 'pin, peg', from Latin *pinna* 'point, tip, edge'.
▶ **pin someone down** restrict the actions or movement of an enemy by firing at them. ■ force someone to be specific and make their intentions

clear.
pin something down define something precisely.

pina colada /ˌpiːnə kəˈlɑːdə/ ▶ **noun** a cocktail made with rum, pineapple juice, and coconut.
– ORIGIN from Spanish *piña colada*, literally 'strained pineapple'.

pinafore ▶ **noun** (also **pinafore dress**) a collarless sleeveless dress worn over a blouse or jumper.
■ Brit. a woman's loose sleeveless garment, typically full length and worn over clothes to keep them clean.
– ORIGIN late 18th cent.: from **PIN** + **AFORE** (because the term originally denoted an apron with a bib pinned on the front of a dress).

Pinang variant spelling of **PENANG**.

Pinatubo, Mount /ˌpɪnəˈtuːbəʊ/ a volcano on the island of Luzon, in the Philippines. It erupted in 1991, killing more than 300 people and destroying the homes of more than 200,000.

pinball ▶ **noun** [mass noun] a game in which small metal balls are shot across a sloping board and score points by striking various targets.

pinboard ▶ **noun** a board covered with cork and fixed to a wall so that messages and pictures can be pinned on to it for display.

pince-nez /pãsˈneɪ/ ▶ **noun** [treated as sing. or pl.] a pair of eyeglasses with a nose clip instead of earpieces.
– ORIGIN late 19th cent.: from French, literally '(that) pinches (the) nose'.

pincer ▶ **noun** (usu. **pincers**) (also **a pair of pincers**) a tool made of two pieces of metal bearing blunt concave jaws that are arranged like the blades of scissors, used for gripping and pulling things.
■ a front claw of a lobster, crab, or similar crustacean.
– ORIGIN Middle English: from Anglo-Norman French, from Old French *pincier* 'to pinch'.

pincer movement ▶ **noun** a movement by two separate bodies of troops converging on the enemy.

pincette /pɪnˈsɛt, pãˈsɛt/ ▶ **noun** a small pair of pincers; tweezers.
– ORIGIN mid 16th cent.: from French, diminutive of *pince* 'pair of pincers'.

pinch ▶ **verb** [with obj.] **1** grip (the skin of a part of someone's body) tightly and sharply between finger and thumb: *she pinched his cheek.*
■ grip the skin of a part of the body of (someone) in such a way: *Rosa pinched her hard.* ■ (of a shoe) hurt (a foot) by being too tight. ■ compress (the lips), especially with worry or tension: *Aunt Rose* **pinched** *her thin lips* **together**. ■ remove (a bud, leaves, etc.) to encourage bushy growth: **pinch out** *tips of shoots regularly.*
2 [no obj.] live in a frugal way: *if I* **scraped and pinched** *a bit, I might manage.*
3 informal arrest (someone): *I was pinched for dangerous driving last month.*
■ informal, chiefly Brit. steal: *he pinched a handful of sweets.*
4 Sailing sail (a boat) so close to the wind that the sails begin to lose power.
▶ **noun** an act of gripping the skin of someone's body between finger and thumb: *he gave her a gentle pinch.*
■ an amount of an ingredient that can be held between fingers and thumb: *add a* **pinch of** *salt.*
2 informal an arrest.
■ an act of theft or plagiarism.
3 Baseball a critical point in the game.
– PHRASES **at** (or N. Amer. **in**) **a pinch** if absolutely necessary. **feel the pinch** experience hardship, especially financial.
– ORIGIN Middle English (as a verb): from an Old Northern French variant of Old French *pincier* 'to pinch'.

pinchbeck ▶ **noun** [mass noun] an alloy of copper and zinc resembling gold, used in watchmaking and cheap jewellery.
▶ **adjective** appearing valuable, but actually cheap or tawdry.
– ORIGIN mid 18th cent.: named after Christopher *Pinchbeck* (died 1732), English watchmaker.

pinched ▶ **adjective** **1** tense and pale from cold, worry, or hunger.
2 (of a person) hurt by financial hardship.

pinch effect ▶ **noun** [mass noun] Physics the constriction of a plasma through which a large electric current is flowing, caused by the attractive force of the current's own magnetic field.

pinch-hit ▶ **verb** [no obj.] Baseball bat instead of another, typically at a critical point in the game.
■ N. Amer. informal act as a substitute for someone, especially in an emergency.
– DERIVATIVES **pinch-hitter** noun.

pinchpenny ▶ **noun** (pl. **-ies**) [usu. as modifier] a miserly person.

pinch-run ▶ **verb** [no obj.] Baseball substitute for another as a base-runner, typically at a critical point in the game.
– DERIVATIVES **pinch-runner** noun.

pin curl ▶ **noun** a curl which has been held by a hairpin while setting.

pincushion ▶ **noun** **1** a small pad for holding pins.
■ (also **pincushion distortion**) [mass noun] a form of optical distortion in which straight lines along the edge of a screen or a lens bulge towards the centre.
2 (also **pincushion protea**) S. African an African shrub or tree related to the proteas, with rounded flower heads that resemble pincushions.
● Genus *Leucospermum*, family Proteaceae.

Pindar /ˈpɪndə/ (c.518–c.438 BC), Greek lyric poet. He is famous for his odes (the *Epinikia*), which celebrate victories in athletic contests at Olympia and elsewhere and relate them to religious and moral themes.
– DERIVATIVES **Pindaric** /pɪnˈdarɪk/ adjective.

Pindus Mountains /ˈpɪndəs/ a range of mountains in west central Greece, stretching from the border with Albania southwards to the Gulf of Corinth. The highest peak is Mount Smolikas, which rises to 2,637 m (8,136 ft). Greek name **PÍNDHOS** /ˈpinðɔs/.

pine[1] ▶ **noun** **1** (also **pine tree**) an evergreen coniferous tree which has clusters of long needle-shaped leaves. Many kinds are grown for the soft timber, which is widely used for furniture and pulp, or for tar and turpentine. Compare with **FIR**.
● Genus *Pinus*, family Pinaceae: many species, including the **Scots pine** and **stone pine**.
■ used in names of coniferous trees of other families, e.g. **Chile pine**. ■ used in names of unrelated plants that resemble the pines in some way, e.g. **ground pine**, **screw pine**. ■ [as modifier] having the scent of pine needles: *a pine pot-pourri.*
2 informal a pineapple.
– DERIVATIVES **pinery** noun.
– ORIGIN Old English, from Latin *pinus*, reinforced in Middle English by Old French *pin*.

pine[2] ▶ **verb** [no obj.] suffer a mental and physical decline, especially because of a broken heart: *she thinks I am* **pining away** *from love.*
■ (**pine for**) miss and long for the return of.
– ORIGIN Old English *pīnian* '(cause to) suffer', of Germanic origin; related to Dutch *pijnen*, German *peinen* 'experience pain', also to obsolete *pine* 'punishment'; ultimately based on Latin *poena* 'punishment'.

pineal /ˈpɪnɪəl, ˈpʌɪ-/ (also **pineal gland**, **pineal body**) ▶ **noun** a pea-sized conical mass of tissue behind the third ventricle of the brain, secreting a hormone-like substance in some mammals.
– ORIGIN late 17th cent.: from French *pinéal*, from Latin *pinea* 'pine cone'. The anatomical term refers to the shape of the gland.

pineal eye ▶ **noun** Zoology (in some reptiles and lower vertebrates) an eye-like structure on the top of the head, covered by almost transparent skin and derived from or linked to the pineal body.

pineapple ▶ **noun** **1** a large juicy tropical fruit consisting of aromatic edible yellow flesh surrounded by a tough segmented skin and topped with a tuft of stiff leaves.
2 the widely cultivated tropical American plant that bears this fruit. It is low-growing, with a spiral of spiny sword-shaped leaves on a thick stem.
● *Ananas comosus*, family Bromeliaceae.
3 informal a hand grenade.
– PHRASES **the rough end of the pineapple** Austral./NZ informal a situation in which someone receives unfair or harsh treatment.
– ORIGIN late Middle English (denoting a pine cone): from **PINE**[1] + **APPLE**. The word was applied to the fruit in the mid 17th cent., because of its resemblance to a pine cone.

pineapple weed ▶ **noun** [mass noun] a small strongly aromatic mayweed with flowers that lack ray florets and resemble tiny pineapples.
● Genus *Matricaria*, family Compositae: the European *M. matricarioides* and the North American *M. discoidea*.

pine beauty ▶ **noun** a brown European moth whose caterpillars feed on pine needles and are a serious pest of plantations.
● *Panolis flammea*, family Noctuidae.

pine cone ▶ **noun** the conical or rounded woody fruit of a pine tree, with scales which open to release the seeds.

pine marten ▶ **noun** an arboreal weasel-like mammal that has a dark brown coat with a yellowish throat and a bushy tail, native to northern Eurasia.
● *Martes martes*, family Mustelidae.

pinene /ˈpʌɪniːn/ ▶ **noun** [mass noun] Chemistry a colourless flammable liquid present in turpentine, juniper oil, and other natural extracts.
● A bicyclic terpene; chem. formula: $C_{10}H_{16}$; four isomers, especially **α-pinene**, the main constituent of turpentine.
– ORIGIN late 19th cent.: from Latin *pinus* 'pine' + **-ENE**.

pine nut ▶ **noun** the edible seed of various pine trees.

Pinero /pɪˈnɪərəʊ, -ˈnɛːrəʊ/, Sir Arthur Wing (1855–1934), English dramatist and actor. Notable works: *The Second Mrs Tanqueray* (1893).

pinesap ▶ **noun** N. Amer. a woodland plant related to wintergreen, lacking chlorophyll and bearing one or more waxy bell-shaped flowers.
● Two species in the family Monotropaceae: the violet-scented **sweet pinesap** (*Monotropsis odorata*), and the yellow bird's-nest.

pine snake ▶ **noun** a large harmless North American snake with dark markings. When disturbed it hisses loudly and vibrates its tail.
● *Pituophis melanoleucus*, family Colubridae.

Pine Tree State informal name for **MAINE**.

pinetum /pʌɪˈniːtəm/ ▶ **noun** (pl. **pineta** /-tə/) a plantation of pine trees or other conifers for scientific or ornamental purposes.
– ORIGIN mid 19th cent.: from Latin, from *pinus* 'pine'.

pine vole ▶ **noun** a vole with dense mole-like fur, found chiefly in montane forests in North America and Eurasia.
● Genus *Pitymys*, family Muridae: many species.

piney ▶ **adjective** variant spelling of **PINY**.

pin feather ▶ **noun** Ornithology an immature feather, before the veins have expanded and while the shaft is full of fluid.

pinfold historical ▶ **noun** a pound for stray animals.
▶ **verb** [with obj.] confine (a stray animal) in such a pound.
– ORIGIN late Old English *pundfald*, from a base shared by **POND** and **POUND**[3] + **FOLD**[2].

ping ▶ **noun** an abrupt high-pitched ringing sound.
▶ **verb** **1** [no obj.] make such a sound: *the doorbell pinged.*
■ [with obj.] cause (something) to make a such a sound.
2 [with obj.] informal (of a racehorse) jump (a fence) well.
■ (of a racehorse) leave (the starting stalls) swiftly.
3 US another term for **PINK**[3].
– ORIGIN mid 19th cent.: imitative.

pinger ▶ **noun** a device that transmits short high-pitched signals at brief intervals for purposes of detection, measurement, or identification.
■ Brit. a timer that gives off a high-pitched noise after a preset period of time, used chiefly in cooking.

pingo /ˈpɪŋgəʊ/ ▶ **noun** (pl. **-os**) Geology a dome-shaped mound consisting of a layer of soil over a large core of ice, occurring in permafrost areas.
– ORIGIN 1920s: from Inuit *pinguq* 'nunatak'.

ping-pong ▶ **noun** informal term for **TABLE TENNIS**.
– ORIGIN early 20th cent.: imitative of the sound of a bat striking a ball.

pinguid /ˈpɪŋgwɪd/ ▶ **adjective** formal of the nature of or resembling fat; oily or greasy.
– DERIVATIVES **pinguidity** noun.
– ORIGIN mid 17th cent.: from Latin *pinguis* 'fat' + **-ID**[1].

pinguin /ˈpɪŋgwɪn/ (also **pingwing** /ˈpɪŋwɪŋ/) ▶ **noun** a large prickly plant related to the pineapple, native to tropical America and the Caribbean. Its fruit is edible but contains enzymes that can irritate the throat.
● *Bromelia pinguin*, family Bromeliaceae.
– ORIGIN late 17th cent.: of unknown origin.

pinhead ▶ **noun** **1** the flattened head of a pin.
■ [often as modifier] a very small rounded object: *pinhead dots.*
2 informal a stupid or foolish person.

pinheaded ▶ **adjective** informal stupid; foolish.

– DERIVATIVES **pinheadedness** noun.

pin-high ▶ adjective Golf (of a ball) at the same distance from the tee as the hole, but off to one side.

pinhole ▶ noun a very small hole.

pinhole borer ▶ noun the larva of an ambrosia beetle, which makes minute round holes in timber.

pinhole camera ▶ noun a camera with a pinhole aperture and no lens.

pinion[1] /ˈpɪnjən/ ▶ noun the outer part of a bird's wing including the flight feathers.
■ poetic/literary a bird's wing as used in flight.
▶ verb [with obj.] **1** tie or hold the arms or legs of (someone): *he was pinioned to the ground.*
■ bind (the arms or legs) of someone.
2 cut off the pinion of (a wing or bird) to prevent flight.
– ORIGIN late Middle English: from Old French *pignon*, based on Latin *pinna, penna* 'feather'.

pinion[2] /ˈpɪnjən/ ▶ noun a small cogwheel or spindle engaging with a large cogwheel.
– ORIGIN mid 17th cent.: from French *pignon*, alteration of obsolete *pignol*, from Latin *pinea* 'pine cone', from *pinus* 'pine'.

pink[1] ▶ adjective **1** of a colour intermediate between red and white, as of coral or salmon: *her healthy pink cheeks | bright pink lipstick.*
■ (of wine) rosé.
2 informal, often derogatory having or showing left-wing tendencies: *pale pink politics.*
3 of or associated with homosexuals: *a boom in the pink economy.*
▶ noun **1** [mass noun] pink colour or pigment.
■ pink clothes or material: *the gorgeous little blonde in pink.* ■ (also **hunting pink**) the red clothing or material worn by fox-hunters.
2 a pink thing, in particular:
■ the pink ball in snooker. ■ a rosé wine.
3 (**the pink of**) the best condition or degree: *the economy is not in the pink of health.*
4 informal, often derogatory a person with left-wing tendencies. See also **PINKO**.
– PHRASES **in the pink** informal in extremely good health and spirits. **turn** (or **go**) **pink** blush.
– DERIVATIVES **pinkish** adjective, **pinkly** adverb, **pinkness** noun, **pinky** adjective.
– ORIGIN mid 17th cent.: from **PINK**[2], the early use of the adjective being to describe the colour of the flowers of this plant.

pink[2] ▶ noun a herbaceous Eurasian plant with sweet-smelling pink or white flowers and slender, typically grey-green leaves.
● Genus *Dianthus*, family Caryophyllaceae (the **pink family**). This family includes the campions, chickweeds, stitchworts, and the cultivated carnations. See also **CLOVE**[1] (sense 3).
– ORIGIN late 16th cent.: perhaps short for *pink eye*, literally 'small or half-shut eye'; compare with the synonymous French word *oeillet*, literally 'little eye'.

pink[3] ▶ verb [with obj.] **1** cut a scalloped or zigzag edge on: [as adj. **pinked**] *a bonnet with pinked edging.*
■ rare pierce or nick (someone) slightly with a weapon or missile. ■ Austral./NZ shear (a sheep) so closely that the skin shows.
2 archaic decorate: *April pinked the earth with flowers.*
– ORIGIN early 16th cent. (in the sense 'pierce or nick slightly'): compare with Low German *pinken* 'strike, peck'.

pink[4] ▶ verb [no obj.] Brit. (of a vehicle engine) make a series of rattling sounds as a result of over-rapid combustion of the fuel–air mixture in the cylinders.
– ORIGIN early 20th cent.: imitative.

pink[5] ▶ noun historical a small square-rigged sailing ship, typically with a narrow, overhanging stern.
– ORIGIN late 15th cent.: from Middle Dutch *pin(c)ke*, of unknown ultimate origin; compare with Spanish *pinque* and Italian *pinco*.

pink[6] ▶ noun [mass noun] dated a yellowish lake pigment made by combining vegetable colouring matter with a white base.
– ORIGIN mid 17th cent.: of unknown origin.

pink-collar ▶ adjective of or relating to work traditionally associated with women.

pink elephants ▶ plural noun informal hallucinations supposedly typical of those experienced by a person who is drunk.

Pinkerton, Allan (1819–84), Scottish-born American detective. In 1850 he established the first American private detective agency.

pink-eye[1] ▶ noun [mass noun] **1** a viral disease of horses, symptoms of which include fever, abortion, and redness of the eyes.
● The virus belongs to the genus *Arterivirus*.
2 conjunctivitis in humans and some livestock.

pink-eye[2] (also **pink-hi**) ▶ noun Austral. another term for **WALKABOUT** (as used of an Aboriginal).
■ (in extended use) a holiday; a festivity.
– ORIGIN from Aboriginal *pinkayi*, from *pinka* 'hunting'.

pink fir apple ▶ noun a potato of a pink-skinned knobbly variety which is chiefly used in salads.

pink gin ▶ noun Brit. gin flavoured with angostura bitters.

pinkie[1] ▶ noun informal the little finger.
– ORIGIN early 19th cent.: partly from Dutch *pink* 'the little finger', reinforced by **PINK**[1].

pinkie[2] ▶ noun (pl. **-ies**) [mass noun] Austral. **1** cheap or home-made wine. [ORIGIN: originally British slang.]
2 a derogatory term used by black people for a white person.
3 (usu. **pinkies**) the maggot of the greenbottle fly, used as fishing bait.
– ORIGIN late 19th cent.: from **PINK**[2], of obscure origin.

pinking shears (also **pinking scissors**) ▶ plural noun shears with a serrated blade, used to cut a zigzag edge in fabric to prevent it fraying.

pink noise ▶ noun [mass noun] Physics random noise having equal energy per octave, and so having more low-frequency components than white noise.

pinko ▶ noun (pl. **-os** or **-oes**) informal, derogatory, chiefly N. Amer. a person with left-wing or liberal views.

pink pound ▶ noun (**the pink pound**) the perceived buying power of homosexuals as a group.

pink salmon ▶ noun another term for **HUMPBACK** (in sense 2).
■ [mass noun] the pale pink flesh of the humpback salmon used as food.

pink slip N. Amer. informal ▶ noun a notice of dismissal from employment.
▶ verb (**pink-slip**) [with obj.] dismiss (someone) from employment.

Pinkster /ˈpɪŋ(k)stə/ ▶ noun US dialect Whitsuntide.
– ORIGIN mid 18th cent.: from Dutch, 'Pentecost', from celebrations in areas of former Dutch influence, such as New York.

pin money ▶ noun [mass noun] a small sum of money for spending on inessentials.
■ historical an allowance to a woman for dress and other personal expenses from her husband.
– ORIGIN late 17th cent.: from **PIN** in the sense 'decorative clasp for the hair or a garment' + **MONEY**.

pinna /ˈpɪnə/ ▶ noun (pl. **pinnae** /-niː/) **1** Anatomy & Zoology the external part of the ear in humans and other mammals; the auricle.
2 Botany a primary division of a pinnate leaf, especially of a fern.
3 Zoology any of a number of animal structures resembling fins or wings.
– ORIGIN late 18th cent.: modern Latin, from a variant of Latin *penna* 'feather, wing, fin'.

pinnace /ˈpɪnɪs/ ▶ noun chiefly historical a small boat, typically with sails and/or several oars, forming part of the equipment of a warship or other large vessel.
– ORIGIN mid 16th cent.: from French *pinace*, probably based on Latin *pinus* 'pine' (see **PINE**[1]); compare with Italian *pinaccia* and Spanish *pinaza*.

pinnacle ▶ noun a high pointed piece of rock.
■ a small pointed turret built as an ornament on a roof. ■ the most successful point; the culmination: *he had reached the pinnacle of his career.*
▶ verb [with obj.] poetic/literary set on or as if on a pinnacle.
■ form the culminating point or example of.
– DERIVATIVES **pinnacled** adjective.
– ORIGIN Middle English: from Old French, from late Latin *pinnaculum*, diminutive of *pinna* 'wing, point'.

pinnae plural form of **PINNA**.

pinnate ▶ adjective Botany (of a compound leaf) having leaflets arranged on either side of the stem, typically in pairs opposite each other.
■ Zoology (especially of an invertebrate animal) having branches, tentacles, etc., on each side of an axis, like the vanes of a feather.

– DERIVATIVES **pinnated** adjective, **pinnately** adverb, **pinnation** /-ˈneɪʃ(ə)n/ noun.
– ORIGIN early 18th cent.: from Latin *pinnatus* 'feathered', from *pinna, penna* (see **PINNA**).

pinnatifid /pɪˈneɪtɪfɪd, -ˈnatɪ-/ ▶ adjective Botany (of a leaf) pinnately divided, but not all the way down to the central axis.
– ORIGIN mid 18th cent.: from modern Latin *pinnatifidus*, from Latin *pinnatus* 'feathered' + *fid-* 'cleft' (from the verb *findere*).

pinni- /ˈpɪnɪ/ ▶ combining form relating to wings or fins: *pinniped.*
– ORIGIN from Latin *pinna, penna* 'wing, fin'.

Pinnipedia /ˌpɪnɪˈpiːdɪə/ Zoology an order of carnivorous aquatic mammals which comprises the seals, sea lions, and walrus. They are distinguished by their flipper-like limbs.
● Order Pinnipedia: three families.
– DERIVATIVES **pinniped** noun & adjective.
– ORIGIN modern Latin (plural), from Latin *pinna* 'wing, fin' + *pes, ped-* foot.

pinnule /ˈpɪnjuːl/ ▶ noun Botany a secondary division of a pinnate leaf, especially of a fern.
■ Zoology a part or organ like a small wing or fin, especially a side branch on the arm of a crinoid.
– ORIGIN late 16th cent. (denoting one of the sights of an astrolabe): from Latin *pinnula* 'small wing', diminutive of *pinna*.

PIN number ▶ noun see **PIN**.

pinny ▶ noun (pl. **-ies**) informal a pinafore.
– ORIGIN mid 19th cent.: abbreviation.

Pinochet /ˈpɪnəʃeɪ/, Augusto (b.1915), Chilean general and statesman, President 1974–90; full name *Augusto Pinochet Ugarte*. Having masterminded the military coup which overthrew President Allende in 1973, he imposed a military dictatorship until forced to call elections, giving way to a democratically elected President in 1990.

pinochle /ˈpiːnɒk(ə)l/ ▶ noun [mass noun] a North American card game for two or more players using a 48-card pack consisting of two of each card from nine to ace, the object being to score points for various combinations and to win tricks.
■ the combination of queen of spades and jack of diamonds in this game.
– ORIGIN mid 19th cent.: of unknown origin.

pinocytosis /ˌpiːnəʊsʌɪˈtəʊsɪs, ˌpɪnəʊ-, ˌpʌɪnəʊ-/ ▶ noun [mass noun] Biology the ingestion of liquid into a cell by the budding of small vesicles from the cell membrane.
– ORIGIN late 19th cent.: from Greek *pino* 'drink' + *-cytosis* on the pattern of *phagocytosis*.

pinole /piːˈnəʊleɪ, -li/ ▶ noun [mass noun] US flour made from parched cornflour mixed with sweet flour made of mesquite beans, sugar, and spice.
– ORIGIN mid 19th cent.: from Latin American Spanish, from Nahuatl *pinolli*.

piñon /pɪˈnjɒn, ˈpɪnjən/ (also **pinyon** or **piñon pine**) ▶ noun a small pine tree with edible seeds, native to Mexico and the south-western US.
● *Pinus cembroides*, family Pinaceae.
■ (also **piñon nut**) a pine nut obtained from this tree.
– ORIGIN mid 19th cent.: from Spanish, from Latin *pinea* 'pine cone'.

Pinot /ˈpiːnəʊ/ ▶ noun [mass noun] any of several varieties of wine grape, especially the chief varieties **Pinot Noir**, a black grape, and **Pinot Blanc**, a white grape.
■ a wine made from these grapes.
– ORIGIN variant of earlier *Pineau*, diminutive of *pin* 'pine' (because of the shape of the grape cluster).

pinotage /ˈpɪnə(ʊ)tɑːʒ/ ▶ noun [mass noun] a variety of red wine grape grown in South Africa, produced by crossing Pinot Noir and other varieties.
■ red wine made from this grape.
– ORIGIN blend of *Pinot* (*Noir*) and *Hermitage*, names of types of grape.

pinout ▶ noun Electronics a diagram showing the arrangement of pins on an integrated circuit and their functions.

pinpoint ▶ noun a tiny dot or point: *a pinpoint of light from a torch.*
▶ adjective [attrib.] absolutely precise; to the finest degree: *this weapon fired shells with pinpoint accuracy.*
■ tiny: *a pinpoint hole.*
▶ verb [with obj.] find or locate exactly: *one flare had pinpointed the target | figurative it is difficult to pinpoint the source of his life's inspiration.*

pinprick ▶ **noun** a prick caused by a pin.
■ a cause of minor irritation.

pins and needles ▶ **plural noun** a tingling sensation in a limb recovering from numbness.

pinspot ▶ **noun** a small powerful spotlight for sharp illumination of a very small area.

pinstripe ▶ **noun** a very narrow stripe in cloth, especially of the type used for formal suits.
■ a pinstripe suit.
– DERIVATIVES **pinstriped** adjective.

pint (abbrev.: **pt**) ▶ **noun** a unit of liquid or dry capacity equal to one eighth of a gallon, in Britain equal to 0.568 litre and in the US equal to 0.473 litre (for liquid measure) or 0.551 litre (for dry measure):
■ Brit. informal a pint of beer: *pop in for a pint on the way home.* ■ Brit. a pint of milk. ■ Brit. a measure of shellfish, being the amount containable in a pint mug.
– ORIGIN late Middle English: from Old French *pinte*, of unknown origin.

pinta ▶ **noun** Brit. informal a pint of milk.
– ORIGIN 1950s: representing a pronunciation of *pint of.*

pintado petrel /pɪnˈtɑːdəʊ/ ▶ **noun** a common petrel of southern oceans, having black plumage with white markings.
● *Daption capense*, family Procellariidae.
– ORIGIN early 17th cent.: from Portuguese and Spanish *pintado* 'guineafowl' + **PETREL**.

pintail ▶ **noun** a mainly migratory duck with a pointed tail.
● Genus *Anas*, family Anatidae: three species, in particular the **northern pintail** (*A. acuta*) of Eurasia and North America, the male of which has boldly marked plumage and two long tail streamers.
■ informal any of a number of other birds with long pointed tails, especially (US) a grouse.

Pinter /ˈpɪntə/, Harold (b.1930), English dramatist, actor, and director. His plays are associated with the Theatre of the Absurd and are typically marked by a sense of menace. Notable plays: *The Birthday Party* (1958), *The Caretaker* (1960), and *Party Time* (1991).

pintle /ˈpɪnt(ə)l/ ▶ **noun** a pin or bolt on which a rudder or other part turns.
– ORIGIN Old English *pintel* 'penis', perhaps a diminutive; compare with Dutch *pint* and German *Pint* 'penis', of unknown ultimate origin.

pinto /ˈpɪntəʊ/ N. Amer. ▶ **adjective** piebald.
▶ **noun** (pl. **-os**) a piebald horse.
– ORIGIN mid 19th cent.: from Spanish, literally 'mottled', based on Latin *pictus*, past participle of *pingere* 'to paint'.

pinto bean ▶ **noun** a medium-sized speckled variety of kidney bean.
– ORIGIN early 20th cent.: *pinto* from **PINTO**, because of the mottled seed of this variety of bean.

pint pot ▶ **noun** a beer glass or mug that holds a pint, especially one made of pewter.

pint-sized ▶ **adjective** informal (especially of a person) very small.

pin-tuck ▶ **noun** a very narrow ornamental tuck.

pin-up ▶ **noun** a poster showing a famous or attractive person, designed to be displayed on a wall.
■ a person shown in such a poster.

pinwheel ▶ **noun** a small Catherine-wheel firework.
■ something shaped or rotating like such a firework.
▶ **verb** [no obj.] spin or rotate like a pinwheel.

pinworm ▶ **noun** a small nematode worm which is an internal parasite of vertebrates.
● Family Oxyuridae, class Phasmida, including *Enterobius vermicularis* (in humans) and *Oxyuris equi* (in horses).

piny (also **piney**) ▶ **adjective** of, like, or full of pines.

Pinyin /pɪnˈjɪn/ ▶ **noun** [mass noun] the standard system of romanized spelling for transliterating Chinese.
– ORIGIN 1960s: from Chinese *pīn-yīn*, literally 'spell-sound'.

pinyon ▶ **noun** variant spelling of **PIÑON**.

piolet /pjəʊˈleɪ/ ▶ **noun** Climbing an ice pick.
– ORIGIN mid 19th cent.: from French dialect, literally 'little pick', diminutive of *piolo*; related to *pioche* 'pickaxe'.

pion /ˈpʌɪɒn/ ▶ **noun** Physics a meson having a mass approximately 270 times that of an electron. Also called **PI-MESON**.
– DERIVATIVES **pionic** adjective.
– ORIGIN 1950s: from **PI**[1] (the letter used as a symbol for the particle) + **-ON**.

Pioneer a series of American space probes launched between 1958 and 1973, two of which provided the first clear pictures of Jupiter and Saturn (1973–79).

pioneer ▶ **noun** a person who is among the first to explore or settle a new country or area.
■ a person who is among the first to research and develop a new area of knowledge or activity: *a famous pioneer of birth control.* ■ (in the former USSR and other communist countries) a member of a movement for children below the age of sixteen that aimed to foster communist ideals. ■ a member of an infantry group preparing roads or terrain for the main body of troops.
▶ **verb** [with obj.] develop or be the first to use or apply (a new method, area of knowledge, or activity): *he pioneered the use of television in lessons.*
■ open up (a road or terrain) as a pioneer.
– ORIGIN early 16th cent. (as a military term denoting a member of the infantry): from French *pionnier* 'foot soldier, pioneer', Old French *paonier*, from *paon*, from Latin *pedo*, *pedon-* (see **PAWN**[1]).

pioneering ▶ **adjective** involving new ideas or methods: *his pioneering work on consciousness.*

pious ▶ **adjective** devoutly religious.
■ making a hypocritical display of virtue: *there'll be no pious words said over her.* ■ [attrib.] (of a hope) sincere but unlikely to be fulfilled. ■ archaic dutiful or loyal, especially towards one's parents.
– DERIVATIVES **piously** adverb, **piousness** noun.
– ORIGIN late Middle English: from Latin *pius* 'dutiful, pious' + **-OUS**.

pious fraud ▶ **noun** a deception intended to benefit those deceived, especially to strengthen religious belief.

pip[1] ▶ **noun** a small hard seed in a fruit.
■ S. African the stone of soft fruits such as peaches and plums.
– PHRASES **squeeze someone until the pips squeak** Brit. informal extract the maximum amount of money from someone.
– DERIVATIVES **pipless** adjective.
– ORIGIN late 18th cent.: abbreviation of **PIPPIN**.

pip[2] ▶ **noun** (usu. **the pips**) Brit. a short high-pitched sound used especially to indicate the time on the radio or to instruct a caller using a public telephone to insert more money.
– ORIGIN early 20th cent.: imitative.

pip[3] ▶ **noun** a small shape or symbol, in particular:
■ Brit. a star (1–3 according to rank) on the shoulder of an army officer's uniform. ■ any of the spots on a playing card, dice, or domino. ■ an image of an object on a radar screen.
– ORIGIN late 16th cent. (originally *peep*, denoting each of the dots on playing cards, dice, and dominoes): of unknown origin.

pip[4] ▶ **noun** [mass noun] a disease of poultry or other birds causing thick mucus in the throat and white scale on the tongue.
– PHRASES **give someone the pip** informal, dated make someone angry or depressed.
– ORIGIN late Middle English: from Middle Dutch *pippe*, probably from an alteration of Latin *pituita* 'slime'. In the late 15th cent. the word came to be applied humorously to unspecified human diseases, and later to ill humour.

pip[5] Brit. informal ▶ **verb** (**pipped**, **pipping**) [with obj.] (usu. **be pipped**) defeat by a small margin or at the last moment: *you were just pipped for the prize.*
■ dated hit or wound (someone) with a gunshot.
– PHRASES **pip someone at** (or **to**) **the post** defeat someone at the last moment.
– ORIGIN late 19th cent.: from **PIP**[1] or **PIP**[3].

pip[6] ▶ **verb** (**pipped**, **pipping**) [with obj.] (of a young bird) crack (the shell of the egg) when hatching.
– ORIGIN late 19th cent.: perhaps of imitative origin.

pipa /pɪˈpɑː, ˈpʌɪpə, ˈpɪpə/ ▶ **noun** another term for **SURINAME TOAD**.
– ORIGIN early 18th cent.: probably from Galibi.

pipal /ˈpiːp(ə)l/ ▶ **noun** variant spelling of **PEEPUL**.

pipe ▶ **noun 1** a tube of metal, plastic, or other material used to convey water, gas, oil, or other fluid substances.
■ a cylindrical vein of ore or rock, especially one in which diamonds are found. ■ a cavity in cast metal. ■ informal a duct, vessel, or tubular structure in the body, or in an animal or plant.
2 a narrow tube made from wood, clay, etc. with a bowl at one end containing burning tobacco, the smoke from which is drawn into the mouth.
■ a quantity of tobacco held by this.
3 a wind instrument consisting of a single tube with holes along its length that are covered by the fingers to produce different notes.
■ (usu. **pipes**) bagpipes. ■ (**pipes**) a set of pipes joined together, as in pan pipes. ■ a tube by which sound is produced in an organ. ■ [in sing.] a high-pitched cry or song, especially of a bird. ■ a boatswain's whistle.
4 a cask for wine, especially as a measure equal to two hogsheads, usually equivalent to 105 gallons (about 477 litres).
▶ **verb 1** [with obj. and adverbial of direction] convey (water, gas, oil, or other fluid substances) through a pipe or pipes: *water from the lakes is piped to Manchester.*
■ transmit (music, a radio or television programme, signal, etc.) by wire or cable.
2 [with obj.] play (a tune) on a pipe or pipes.
■ [no obj.] (of a bird) sing in a high or shrill voice. ■ [with direct speech] say something in a high, shrill voice: *'No, miss,' piped Lucy.* ■ [with obj. and adverbial of direction] play a pipe or pipes as a ceremonial accompaniment to the arrival or departure of (someone): *the Duke was piped on board.* ■ [with obj. and adverbial] use a boatswain's whistle to summon (the crew) to work or a meal: *the hands were piped to breakfast.*
3 [with obj.] decorate (clothing or soft furnishings) with a thin cord covered in fabric.
■ put (a decorative line or pattern) on a cake or similar dish using cream, icing, etc.
4 [with obj.] propagate (a pink or similar plant) by taking a cutting at the joint of a stem.
– PHRASES **put that in one's pipe and smoke it** informal used to indicate that someone should accept what one has said, even if it is unwelcome.
– DERIVATIVES **pipeful** noun (pl. **-fuls**), **pipeless** adjective, **pipy** adjective.
– ORIGIN Old English *pīpe* 'musical tube', *pīpian* 'play a pipe', of Germanic origin; related to Dutch *pijp* and German *Pfeife*, based on Latin *pipare* 'to peep, chirp', reinforced in Middle English by Old French *piper* 'to chirp, squeak'.
▶ **pipe someone away** (or **down**) Nautical dismiss someone from duty.
pipe something away Nautical give a signal for a boat to start.
pipe down [often in imperative] informal stop talking; be less noisy.
pipe up say something suddenly.

pipe band ▶ **noun** a band, especially a military one, consisting of bagpipe players, drummers, and a pipe major.

pipe berth (Brit. also **pipe cot**) ▶ **noun** a collapsible bed with a frame of metal pipes, used on a boat.

pipe bomb ▶ **noun** a home-made bomb, the components of which are contained in a pipe.

pipeclay ▶ **noun** [mass noun] a fine white clay, used especially for making tobacco pipes or for whitening leather.
▶ **verb** [with obj.] whiten (leather) with such clay.

pipe-cleaner ▶ **noun** a piece of wire covered with fibre used to clean a tobacco pipe.

piped music ▶ **noun** [mass noun] pre-recorded background music played through loudspeakers in a public place.

pipe dream ▶ **noun** an unattainable or fanciful hope or scheme.
– ORIGIN late 19th cent.: referring to a dream experienced when smoking an opium pipe.

pipefish ▶ **noun** (pl. same or **-fishes**) a narrow elongated chiefly marine fish with segmented bony armour beneath the skin and a long tubular snout. The male typically has a brood pouch in which the eggs develop.
● *Syngnathus* and other genera, family Syngnathidae: numerous species.

pipe jacking ▶ **noun** [mass noun] a method of laying underground pipes without digging a trench, in which the pipes are assembled in an access shaft and then pushed into position by a hydraulic jack.

pipeline ▶ **noun** a long pipe, typically underground, for conveying oil, gas, etc. over long distances.
■ figurative a channel supplying goods or information: *the biggest heroin pipeline in history.* ■ (in surfing) the hollow formed by the breaking of a very large wave. ■ Computing a linear sequence of specialized modules used for pipelining.
▶ **verb** [with obj. and adverbial of direction] convey (a substance) by a pipeline.
■ [with obj.] [often as adj. **pipelined**] Computing design or

execute (a computer or instruction) using the technique of pipelining.

– PHRASES **in the pipeline** in the process of being developed.

pipelining ▶ noun [mass noun] **1** the laying of pipelines.

■ transportation by means of pipelines.

2 Computing a form of computer organization in which successive steps of an instruction sequence are executed in turn by a sequence of modules able to operate concurrently, so that another instruction can be begun before the previous one is finished.

pipe major ▶ noun an NCO commanding regimental pipes and drums.

pip emma ▶ adverb & noun Brit., dated informal term for **P.M.**

– ORIGIN First World War: signallers' name for these letters.

pipe-opener ▶ noun Brit. informal a spell of exercise taken as a warm-up.

■ an event or item introducing a sequence or series.

pipe organ ▶ noun Music an organ using pipes instead of or as well as reeds.

Piper, John (1903–92), English painter and decorative designer. He is best known for his watercolours and aquatints of buildings and for his stained glass in Coventry and Llandaff cathedrals.

piper ▶ noun **1** a bagpipe player.

2 a person who plays a pipe, especially an itinerant musician.

– ORIGIN Old English *pīpere*.

pipe-rack ▶ noun a rack for holding tobacco pipes.

Piper Alpha an oil platform in the North Sea off the coast of Scotland, which in July 1988 was destroyed by an explosion with the loss of 167 lives.

piperazine /prˈpɛrəziːn, ˌpʌɪ-/ ▶ noun [mass noun] Chemistry a synthetic crystalline compound with basic properties, sometimes used as an anthelmintic and insecticide.

● A heterocyclic compound; chem. formula: $C_4H_{10}N_2$.

– ORIGIN late 19th cent.: from **PIPERIDINE** + **AZINE**.

piperidine /prˈpɛrɪdiːn, ˌpʌɪ-/ ▶ noun [mass noun] Chemistry a peppery-smelling liquid formed by the reduction of pyridine.

● Chem. formula: $C_5H_{11}N$.

– ORIGIN mid 19th cent.: from Latin *piper* 'pepper' + **-IDE** + **-INE**[4].

pipe roll ▶ noun the annual records of the British Exchequer from the 12th to the 19th century.

– ORIGIN probably so named because subsidiary documents were rolled in pipe form.

pipe snake ▶ noun any of a number of slender tropical burrowing snakes, in particular:

● a South American snake marked with bold red and black stripes (*Anilius scytale*, the only member of the family Aniliidae). ● an Asian snake which displays its bright under-tail coloration when alarmed (genus *Cylindrophis*, family Uropeltidae).

pipe-stem ▶ noun the shaft of a tobacco pipe.

pipe-stone ▶ noun [mass noun] hard red clay used by North American Indians for tobacco pipes.

pipette /prˈpɛt/ ▶ noun a slender tube attached to or incorporating a bulb, for transferring or measuring out small quantities of liquid, especially in a laboratory.

▶ verb [with obj. and adverbial of direction] pour, convey, or draw off using a pipette.

– ORIGIN mid 19th cent.: from French, literally 'little pipe', diminutive of *pipe*.

pipework ▶ noun [mass noun] pipes that make up a network in a house, heating system, etc.

pipewort ▶ noun an aquatic or marsh plant with leafless stems bearing heads of inconspicuous flowers, native to western Ireland, the Hebrides, and North America.

● *Eriocaulon aquaticum*, family Eriocaulaceae.

pipi[1] /ˈpiːpi/ ▶ noun (pl. same or **pipis**) either of two edible marine bivalve molluscs native to New Zealand.

● *Amphidesma australe* (family Amphidesmatidae) and *Chione stutchburyi* (family Veneridae).

– ORIGIN mid 19th cent.: from Maori.

pipi[2] /ˈpiːpiː/ ▶ noun variant spelling of **PEE-PEE**.

piping ▶ noun [mass noun] **1** lengths of pipe made of metal, plastic, or other materials.

2 ornamentation on food consisting of lines of icing, cream, etc.

■ thin cord covered in fabric, used to decorate clothing or soft furnishings and reinforce seams.

3 the action or art of playing a pipe or pipes.

4 [count noun] a cutting of a pink or similar plant taken at a joint.

▶ adjective [attrib.] (of a voice or sound) high-pitched.

piping hot ▶ adjective (of food or water) very hot.

– ORIGIN *piping*, because of the whistling sound made by very hot liquid or food.

pipistrelle /ˌpɪpɪˈstrɛl, ˈpɪp-/ (also **pipistrelle bat**) ▶ noun a small insectivorous Old World bat with jerky, erratic flight.

● Genus *Pipistrellus*, family Vespertilionidae: numerous species, including *P. pipistrellus*, which is the commonest bat in Eurasia.

– ORIGIN late 18th cent.: from French, from Italian *pipistrello*, from Latin *vespertilio(n-)* 'bat', from *vesper* 'evening'.

pipit /ˈpɪpɪt/ ▶ noun a mainly ground-dwelling songbird of open country, typically having brown streaky plumage.

● Family Motacillidae: three genera, in particular *Anthus*, and many species, e.g. the meadow pipit.

– ORIGIN mid 18th cent.: probably imitative.

pipkin ▶ noun a small earthenware pot or pan.

– ORIGIN mid 16th cent.: of unknown origin.

pippin ▶ noun a red and yellow dessert apple.

■ an apple grown from seed. ■ informal, chiefly US an excellent person or thing.

– ORIGIN Middle English: from Old French *pepin*, of unknown ultimate origin.

pip pip ▶ exclamation informal, dated goodbye.

– ORIGIN early 20th cent.: imitative, probably of the repeated short blasts on the horn of a motor car or bicycle.

pipsissewa /pɪpˈsɪsɪwə/ ▶ noun a North American plant of the wintergreen family, with whorled evergreen leaves.

● *Chimaphila umbellata*, family Pyrolaceae.

■ [mass noun] a preparation of the leaves of this plant, used as a diuretic and tonic.

– ORIGIN late 18th cent.: from Abnaki, literally 'flower of the woods'.

pipsqueak ▶ noun informal a person considered to be insignificant, especially because they are small or young.

– ORIGIN early 20th cent.: symbolic and imitative.

piquant /ˈpiːk(ə)nt, -kɒnt/ ▶ adjective having a pleasantly sharp taste or appetizing flavour.

■ pleasantly stimulating or exciting to the mind.

– DERIVATIVES **piquancy** noun, **piquantly** adverb.

– ORIGIN early 16th cent. (in the sense 'severe, bitter'): from French, literally 'stinging, pricking', present participle of *piquer*.

pique[1] /piːk/ ▶ noun [mass noun] a feeling of irritation or resentment resulting from a slight, especially to one's pride: *he left in a fit of pique.*

▶ verb (**piques, piqued, piquing**) **1** [with obj.] stimulate (interest or curiosity).

2 (**be piqued**) feel irritated or resentful: *she was piqued by his curtness.*

3 (**pique oneself**) archaic pride oneself.

– ORIGIN mid 16th cent. (denoting animosity between two or more people): from French *piquer* 'prick, irritate'.

pique[2] /piːk/ ▶ noun (in piquet) the scoring of 30 points on declarations and play before one's opponent scores anything. Compare with **REPIQUE**.

▶ verb (**piques, piqued, piquing**) [with obj.] score a pique against (one's opponent).

– ORIGIN mid 17th cent.: from French *pic*, from the Old French sense 'stabbing blow', of unknown ultimate origin.

piqué /ˈpiːkeɪ/ ▶ noun [mass noun] stiff fabric, typically cotton, woven in a strongly ribbed or raised pattern.

– ORIGIN mid 19th cent.: from French, literally 'backstitched', past participle of *piquer*.

piquet[1] /prˈkɛt/ ▶ noun [mass noun] a trick-taking card game for two players, using a 32-card pack consisting of the seven to the ace only.

– ORIGIN mid 17th cent.: from French, of unknown origin.

piquet[2] ▶ noun variant spelling of **PICKET** (in sense 2).

PIR ▶ abbreviation for passive infrared (denoting a type of sensor).

pir /pɪə/ ▶ noun a Muslim saint or holy man.

– ORIGIN from Persian *pīr* 'old man'.

piracy ▶ noun [mass noun] the practice of attacking and robbing ships at sea.

■ a similar practice in other contexts, especially hijacking: *air piracy.* ■ the unauthorized use or reproduction of another's work: *software piracy.*

– ORIGIN mid 16th cent.: via medieval Latin from Greek *pirateia*, from *peiratēs* (see **PIRATE**).

Piraeus /pʌɪˈriːəs, pɪˈreɪəs/ the chief port of Athens, situated on the Saronic Gulf 8 km (5 miles) SW of the city; pop. 182,670 (1991). Greek name **Piraiévs** or **Piraiéus** /ˌpiːrɛˈɛfs/.

Pirandello /ˌpɪrənˈdɛləʊ/, Luigi (1867–1936), Italian dramatist and novelist. His plays, including *Six Characters in Search of an Author* (1921) and *Henry IV* (1922), challenged the conventions of naturalism. Notable novels: *The Outcast* (1901) and *The Late Mattia Pascal* (1904). Nobel Prize for Literature (1934).

Piranesi /ˌpɪrəˈneɪzi/, Giovanni Battista (1720–78), Italian engraver. Notable works: *Prisons* (1745–61).

piranha /pɪˈrɑːnə, -njə/ ▶ noun a deep-bodied South American freshwater fish that typically lives in shoals and has very sharp teeth that are used to tear flesh from prey. It has a reputation as a fearsome predator.

● *Serrosalmus* and other genera, family Characidae: several species.

– ORIGIN mid 18th cent.: via Portuguese from Tupi *pirá* 'fish' + *sainha* 'tooth'.

pirate ▶ noun a person who attacks and robs ships at sea.

■ a person who appropriates or reproduces the work of another for profit without permission, usually in contravention of patent or copyright: [as modifier] *pirate recordings.* ■ a person or organization that broadcasts radio or television programmes without official authorization: [as modifier] *a pirate radio station.*

▶ verb [with obj.] **1** dated rob or plunder (a ship).

2 [often as adj. **pirated**] use or reproduce (another's work) for profit without permission, usually in contravention of patent or copyright: *he sold pirated tapes of Hollywood blockbusters.*

– DERIVATIVES **piratic** adjective, **piratical** adjective, **piratically** adverb.

– ORIGIN Middle English: from Latin *pirata*, from Greek *peiratēs*, from *peirein* 'to attempt, attack' (from *peira* 'an attempt').

piriform ▶ adjective variant spelling of **PYRIFORM**.

pirimicarb /prˈrɪmɪkɑːb/ ▶ noun [mass noun] a synthetic compound used as a pesticide, especially against aphids.

● A heterocyclic compound; chem. formula: $C_{11}H_{18}N_4O_2$.

– ORIGIN late 20th cent.: from *pirimi-* (alteration of **PYRIMIDINE**) + *carb*(amate).

piripiri /ˈpɪrɪˌpɪri/ (also **pirri-pirri burr**) ▶ noun (pl. **piripiris**) a New Zealand plant of the rose family, with prickly burrs.

● Genus *Acaena*, family Rosaceae: several species, in particular *A. anserinifolia*.

– ORIGIN mid 19th cent.: from Maori.

piri-piri /ˈpɪrɪˌpɪri/ ▶ noun [mass noun] a very hot sauce made with red chilli peppers.

– ORIGIN Ronga (a Bantu language of southern Mozambique), literally 'pepper'.

pirk /pəːk/ ▶ noun a metal weight fitted with a hook, used as a lure for sea fishing.

pirog /prˈrɒg/ ▶ noun (pl. **pirogi** /-gi/ or **pirogen** /-g(ə)n/) a large Russian pie.

– ORIGIN Russian.

pirogi /pəˈrəʊgi/ ▶ noun (pl. **pirogies**) N. Amer. a dough dumpling stuffed with a filling such as potato or cheese, typically served with onions or sour cream.

– ORIGIN from Polish *pieróg* or Ukrainian *pyrih*.

pirogue /prˈrəʊg/ ▶ noun a long narrow canoe made from a single tree trunk, especially in Central America and the Caribbean.

– ORIGIN early 17th cent.: from French, probably from Galibi.

piroplasmosis /ˌpʌɪrə(ʊ)plazˈməʊsɪs/ ▶ noun another term for **BABESIOSIS**.

piroshki /prˈrɒʃki/ (also **pirozhki** /-ʒki/) ▶ plural noun small Russian savoury pastries or patties, filled with meat or fish and rice.

– ORIGIN from Russian *pirozhki*, plural of *pirozhok*, diminutive of *pirog* (see **PIROG**).

pirouette /ˌpɪrʊˈɛt/ ▶ noun chiefly Ballet an act of spinning on one foot, typically with the raised foot touching the knee of the supporting leg.

■ a movement performed in advanced dressage and

classical riding, in which the horse makes a circle by pivoting on a hind leg, while cantering.
▶ **verb** [no obj.] perform a pirouette.
– ORIGIN mid 17th cent.: from French, literally 'spinning top', of unknown ultimate origin.

pirri-pirri burr ▶ **noun** see PIRIPIRI.

Pisa /ˈpiːzə/ a city in northern Italy, in Tuscany, on the River Arno; pop. 101,500 (1990). It is noted for the 'Leaning Tower of Pisa', a circular bell tower which leans about 5 m (17 ft) from the perpendicular over its height of 55 m (181 ft)

pis aller /piːz ˈaleɪ, French piz ale/ ▶ **noun** a course of action followed as a last resort.
– ORIGIN French, from *pis* 'worse' + *aller* 'go'.

Pisan, Christine de, see DE PISAN.

Pisano[1] /pɪˈsɑːnəʊ/, Andrea (c.1290–c.1348) and Nino, his son (died c.1368), Italian sculptors. Andrea created the earliest pair of bronze doors for the baptistery at Florence (completed 1336). Nino was one of the earliest to specialize in free-standing life-size figures.

Pisano[2] /pɪˈsɑːnəʊ/ two Italian sculptors, **Nicola** (c.1220–c.1278) and his son **Giovanni** (c.1250–c.1314). Nicola's work departed from medieval conventions and signalled a revival of interest in classical sculpture. His most famous works are the pulpits in the baptistery at Pisa and in Siena cathedral. Giovanni's works include the richly decorated facade of Siena cathedral.

piscary /ˈpɪskəri/ ▶ **noun** (in phrase **common of piscary**) Brit., chiefly historical the right of fishing in another's water.
– ORIGIN late 15th cent.: from medieval Latin *piscaria* 'fishing rights', neuter plural of Latin *piscarius* 'relating to fishing', from *piscis* 'fish'.

piscatorial /ˌpɪskəˈtɔːrɪəl/ ▶ **adjective** formal of or concerning fishermen or fishing.
– ORIGIN early 19th cent.: from Latin *piscatorius* 'relating to fishing' (from *piscator* 'fisherman', from *piscis* 'fish') + -AL.

piscatory /ˈpɪskət(ə)ri/ ▶ **adjective** another term for PISCATORIAL.

Pisces /ˈpaɪsiːz, ˈpɪskiːz/ **1** Astronomy a large constellation (the Fish or Fishes), said to represent a pair of fishes tied together by their tails.
■ [as genitive **Piscium** /ˈpaɪsɪəm, ˈpɪsɪəm/] used with preceding letter or numeral to designate a star in this constellation: *the star Alpha Piscium*.
2 Astrology the twelfth sign of the zodiac, which the sun enters about 20 February.
■ (**a Pisces**) (pl. same) a person born when the sun is in this sign.
– DERIVATIVES **Piscean** /ˈpaɪsɪən/ noun & adjective (only in sense 2).
– ORIGIN Latin, plural of *piscis* 'fish'.

pisciculture /ˈpɪsɪˌkʌltʃə/ ▶ **noun** [mass noun] the controlled breeding and rearing of fish.
– DERIVATIVES **piscicultural** adjective, **pisciculturist** noun.
– ORIGIN mid 19th cent.: from Latin *piscis* 'fish' + CULTURE, on the pattern of words such as *agriculture*.

piscina /pɪˈsiːnə, pɪˈsaɪnə/ ▶ **noun** (pl. **piscinas** or **piscinae** /-niː/) **1** a stone basin near the altar in Catholic and pre-Reformation churches for draining water used in the Mass.
2 (in ancient Roman architecture) a pool or pond for bathing or swimming.
– ORIGIN late 16th cent. (in sense 2): from Latin, literally 'fish pond', from *piscis* 'fish'; sense 1 was found in medieval Latin.

piscine /ˈpɪsaɪn/ ▶ **adjective** of or concerning fish.
– ORIGIN late 18th cent.: from Latin *piscis* 'fish' + -INE[1].

Piscis Austrinus /ˌpaɪsɪs ɒˈstraɪnəs/ (also **Piscis Australis** /ɒˈstreɪlɪs/) Astronomy a southern constellation (the Southern Fish), south of Aquarius and Capricornus. It contains the bright star Fomalhaut.
■ [as genitive **Piscis Austrini** /ɒˈstraɪnaɪ/] used with preceding letter or numeral to designate a star in this constellation: *the star Gamma Piscis Austrini*.
– ORIGIN Latin.

piscivorous /pɪˈsɪv(ə)rəs/ ▶ **adjective** Zoology (of an animal) feeding on fish.
– DERIVATIVES **piscivore** noun.
– ORIGIN mid 17th cent.: from Latin *piscis* 'fish' + -VOROUS.

pisco /ˈpɪskəʊ/ ▶ **noun** [mass noun] a white brandy made in Peru from muscat grapes.
– ORIGIN named after a port in Peru.

pisé /ˈpiːzeɪ/ ▶ **noun** [mass noun] building material of stiff clay or earth, forced between boards which are removed as it hardens.
– ORIGIN late 18th cent.: French, literally 'pounded', past participle of *piser*.

pish ▶ **exclamation** dated used to express annoyance, impatience, or disgust.
– ORIGIN natural utterance: first recorded in English in the late 16th cent.

pishogue /pɪˈʃəʊɡ/ (also **pishrogue** /pɪˈʃrəʊɡ/) ▶ **noun** [mass noun] Irish the power or skill of sorcery.
■ [count noun] a fairy or sorcerer. ■ [count noun] an incredible or invented story.
– ORIGIN early 19th cent.: from Irish *piseog* 'witchcraft'.

Pishpek /pɪʃˈpɛk/ former name (until 1926) for BISHKEK.

Pisidia /paɪˈsɪdɪə/ an ancient region of Asia Minor, between Pamphylia and Phrygia. It was incorporated into the Roman province of Galatia in 25 BC.
– DERIVATIVES **Pisidian** adjective & noun.

pisiform /ˈpaɪsɪfɔːm, ˈpɪzɪ-/ (also **pisiform bone**) ▶ **noun** a small rounded carpal bone situated where the palm of the hand meets the outer edge of the wrist and articulating with the triquetral.
– ORIGIN mid 18th cent.: from modern Latin *pisiformis* 'pea-shaped', from *pisum* 'pea' + *forma* 'shape'.

Pisistratus /paɪˈsɪstrətəs/ (also **Peisistratus**) (c.600–c.527 BC), tyrant of Athens. He reduced aristocratic power in rural Attica and promoted the financial prosperity and cultural pre-eminence of Athens.

pismire /ˈpɪsmaɪə/ ▶ **noun** archaic an ant.
– ORIGIN Middle English: from PISS (alluding to the smell of an anthill) + obsolete *mire* 'ant'.

pisolite /ˈpɪzəlaɪt, ˈpaɪsə-/ ▶ **noun** [mass noun] Geology a sedimentary rock, especially limestone, made up of small pea-shaped pieces.
– DERIVATIVES **pisolitic** adjective.
– ORIGIN early 19th cent.: from modern Latin *pisolithus* (see PISOLITH) + -LITE.

pisolith /ˈpɪzəlɪθ, ˈpaɪsə-/ ▶ **noun** Geology any of the component pieces of which pisolite consists.
– ORIGIN late 18th cent.: from modern Latin *pisolithus*, from Greek *pisos* 'pea'.

piss vulgar slang ▶ **verb** [no obj.] urinate.
■ [with obj.] wet with urine. ■ [with obj.] discharge (something, especially blood) when urinating. ■ (**piss oneself**) wet one's clothing by accidentally or involuntarily urinating (often used figuratively to indicate that one has lost control of oneself through fear, amusement, excitement, etc.). ■ (**piss down/piss with rain**) rain heavily.
▶ **noun** [mass noun] urine.
■ [in sing.] an act of urinating.
– PHRASES **be** (or **go**) **on the piss** Brit. be engaged in (or go on) a heavy drinking session. **not have a pot to piss in** N. Amer. be very poor. **a piece of piss** Brit. a very easy thing to do. **piss in the wind** do something that is ineffective or a waste of time. **take the piss** (**out of someone/thing**) Brit. mock someone or something.
– ORIGIN Middle English: from Old French *pisser*, probably of imitative origin.
▶ **piss about/around** Brit. waste time on silly or unimportant things.
piss something away waste something, especially money.
piss off [usu. in imperative] go away (usually used to angrily dismiss someone).
piss someone off annoy someone.
piss on/over show complete contempt for.
piss something up spoil or ruin something.

pissabed ▶ **noun** the dandelion.
– ORIGIN late 16th cent.: from the verb PISS (because of its diuretic properties) + ABED, suggested by French *pissenlit*.

pissaladière /ˌpɪsaləˈdjɛː/ ▶ **noun** a Provençal open tart resembling pizza, typically made with onions, anchovies, and black olives.
– ORIGIN French, from Provençal *pissaladiero*, from *pissala* 'salt fish'.

piss and vinegar ▶ **noun** [mass noun] vulgar slang aggressive energy.

pissant /ˈpɪsant/ US vulgar slang ▶ **noun** an insignificant or contemptible person or thing.
▶ **adjective** worthless; contemptible.
– ORIGIN mid 17th cent.: from the noun PISS + -ANT.

Pissarro /pɪˈsɑːrəʊ/, Camille (1830–1903), French painter and graphic artist. He was a leading figure of the Impressionist movement, typically painting landscapes and cityscapes. He also experimented with pointillism in the 1880s.

piss artist ▶ **noun** Brit. vulgar slang a drunkard.
■ a person who wastes time by behaving foolishly.

pissed vulgar slang ▶ **adjective** **1** (also **pissed up**) Brit. drunk.
2 (**pissed off**) (N. Amer. also **pissed**) very annoyed.
– PHRASES **as pissed as a newt** (or **fart**) Brit. very drunk.

pisser ▶ **noun** vulgar slang **1** a person who urinates.
■ a toilet.
2 [in sing.] used to refer to an annoying or disappointing event or circumstance.

pisshead ▶ **noun** informal a drunkard.

piss-hole ▶ **noun** vulgar slang a squalid place.

pissing ▶ **adjective** [attrib.] vulgar slang **1** (of rain) heavy.
2 used to express annoyance or contempt.

pissoir /piːˈswɑː, ˈpiːswɑː, French piswaʀ/ ▶ **noun** a public urinal.
– ORIGIN French.

piss-poor ▶ **adjective** vulgar slang of a very low standard.

pisspot ▶ **noun** vulgar slang a chamber pot.

piss-take ▶ **noun** Brit. vulgar slang an act of mockery.
– DERIVATIVES **piss-taker** noun, **piss-taking** noun.

piss-up ▶ **noun** Brit. vulgar slang a heavy drinking session.

pissy ▶ **adjective** vulgar slang **1** of, relating to, or suggestive of urine.
■ inferior; contemptible.
2 chiefly US arrogantly aggressive and argumentative.

pistachio /pɪˈstɑːʃɪəʊ, pɪˈstatʃəʊ/ ▶ **noun** (pl. **-os**) **1** (also **pistachio nut**) the edible pale green seed of an Asian tree.
■ (also **pistachio green**) [mass noun] a pale green colour.
2 the evergreen tree which produces this nut, with small brownish-green flowers and oval reddish fruit. It is widely cultivated, especially around the Mediterranean and in the US.
● *Pistacia vera*, family Anacardiaceae.
– ORIGIN late Middle English *pistace*, from Old French, superseded in the 16th cent. by forms from Italian *pistaccio*, via Latin from Greek *pistakion*, from Old Persian.

pistacite /ˈpɪstəsaɪt/ ▶ **noun** [mass noun] a green iron-rich variety of epidote.
– ORIGIN early 19th cent.: from German *Pistazit*, from Latin *pistacia* 'pistachio' (because of its colour) + -ITE[1].

piste /piːst/ ▶ **noun** a ski run of compacted snow.
– ORIGIN French, literally 'racetrack'.

piste-basher ▶ **noun** informal a machine which compacts and levels the snow on ski runs.
■ a person who enjoys skiing on pistes.

pisteur /piːˈstəː/ ▶ **noun** a person employed to prepare the snow on a piste.
– ORIGIN French.

pistil /ˈpɪstɪl/ ▶ **noun** Botany the female organs of a flower, comprising the stigma, style, and ovary.
– ORIGIN early 18th cent.: from French *pistile* or Latin *pistillum* 'pestle'.

pistillate /ˈpɪstɪlət/ ▶ **adjective** Botany (of a plant or flower) having pistils but no stamens. Compare with STAMINATE.

pistol ▶ **noun** a small firearm designed to be held in one hand.
▶ **verb** (**pistolled**, **pistolling**; US **pistoled**, **pistoling**) [with obj.] dated shoot (someone) with a pistol.
– ORIGIN mid 16th cent.: from obsolete French *pistole*, from German *Pistole*, from Czech *pišt'ala*, of which the original meaning was 'whistle', hence 'a firearm' by the resemblance in shape.

pistole /pɪˈstəʊl/ ▶ **noun** any of various gold coins used in Europe or Scotland in the 17th and 18th centuries.
– ORIGIN late 16th cent.: from French, abbreviation of *pistolet*, in the same sense, of uncertain ultimate origin.

pistoleer /ˌpɪstəˈlɪə/ ▶ **noun** archaic a soldier armed with a pistol.

pistolero /ˌpɪstəˈlɛːrəʊ/ ▶ **noun** (pl. **-os** /-əs, -əʊz/) (in Spain and Spanish-speaking areas) a gunman or gangster.
– ORIGIN Spanish.

pistol grip ▶ **noun** a handle shaped like the butt of a pistol.

pistol shot ▶ **noun** a shot fired from a pistol.
■ [mass noun] the range of a pistol. ■ [with adj.] a person who shows a specified degree of skill in shooting with a pistol.

pistol-whip ▶ **verb** [with obj.] hit or beat (someone) with the butt of a pistol.

piston /ˈpɪst(ə)n/ ▶ **noun** a disc or short cylinder fitting closely within a tube in which it moves up and down against a liquid or gas, used in an internal-combustion engine to derive motion, or in a pump to impart motion.
■ a valve in a brass musical instrument in the form of a piston, depressed to alter the pitch of a note.
– ORIGIN early 18th cent.: from French, from Italian *pistone*, variant of *pestone* 'large pestle', augmentative of *pestello* 'pestle'.

piston corer ▶ **noun** Geology a piston-driven cylindrical device for taking samples of material from the seabed.

piston engine ▶ **noun** an engine, especially in an aircraft, in which power is derived from cylinders and pistons rather than a turbine.
– DERIVATIVES **piston-engined** adjective.

piston ring ▶ **noun** a ring on a piston sealing the gap between the piston and the cylinder wall.

piston rod ▶ **noun** a rod or crankshaft attached to a piston to drive a wheel or to impart motion.

pistou /ˈpiːstuː/ ▶ **noun** [mass noun] sauce or paste made chiefly from crushed basil, garlic, and cheese, used especially in Provençal dishes.
■ a thick vegetable soup made with this.
– ORIGIN Provençal.

pit[1] ▶ **noun 1** a large hole in the ground.
■ a large deep hole from which stones or minerals are dug. ■ a coal mine. ■ a sunken enclosure in which certain animals are kept in captivity: [in combination] *a bear pit*. ■ short for *orchestra pit* (see **ORCHESTRA**). ■ a sunken area in a workshop floor allowing access to a car's underside. ■ figurative a low or wretched psychological state: *the service remains in a pit of despair*. ■ (**the pit**) poetic/literary hell.
2 an area reserved or enclosed for a specific activity, in particular:
■ an area at the side of a track where racing cars are serviced and refuelled. ■ a part of the floor of an exchange in which a particular stock or commodity is traded, typically by open outcry. ■ chiefly historical an enclosure in which animals are made to fight. ■ (**the pit**) Brit. dated the seating at the back of the stalls of a theatre.
3 a hollow or indentation in a surface.
■ a small indentation left on the skin after smallpox, acne, or other diseases; a pockmark.
4 Brit. informal a person's bed.
▶ **verb** (**pitted**, **pitting**) [with obj.] **1** (**pit someone/thing against**) set someone or something in conflict or competition with: *a chance to pit herself against him*.
■ historical set an animal to fight against (another animal) for sport. [ORIGIN: because formerly set against each other in a 'pit' or enclosure.]
2 make a hollow or indentation in the surface of: *rain poured down, pitting the bare earth*.
■ [no obj.] sink in or contract so as to form a pit or hollow.
3 [no obj.] drive a racing car into the pits for fuel or maintenance.
– PHRASES **be the pits** informal be extremely bad or the worst of its kind. **dig a pit for** try to trap. **the pit of one's** (or **the**) **stomach** an ill-defined region of the lower abdomen regarded as the seat of strong feelings, especially anxiety.
– ORIGIN Old English *pytt*, of West Germanic origin; related to Dutch *put* and German *Pfütze*, based on Latin *puteus* 'well, shaft'.

pit[2] chiefly N. Amer. ▶ **noun** the stone of a fruit.
▶ **verb** (**pitted**, **pitting**) [with obj.] remove the pit from (fruit).
– ORIGIN mid 19th cent.: apparently from Dutch; related to **PITH**.

pita ▶ **noun** chiefly N. Amer. variant spelling of **PITTA**[1].

pitahaya /ˌpɪtəˈhʌɪə/ ▶ **noun** any tall cactus of Mexico and the south-western US, in particular the saguaro.
■ the edible fruit of such cacti.
– ORIGIN late 18th cent.: from Spanish, from Haitian Creole.

pit-a-pat (also **pitapat**) ▶ **adverb** with a sound like quick light steps or taps.
▶ **noun** [in sing.] a sound of this kind.
– ORIGIN early 16th cent.: imitative of alternating sounds.

pit boss ▶ **noun** informal, chiefly US an employee in a casino in charge of gaming tables.

pit bull (in full **pit bull terrier**) ▶ **noun** a dog of an American variety of bull terrier, noted for its ferocity.

Pitcairn Islands /ˈpɪtkɛːn/ a British dependency comprising a group of volcanic islands in the South Pacific, east of French Polynesia. The colony's only settlement is Adamstown, on Pitcairn Island, the chief island of the group; pop. 54 (1995). Pitcairn Island was discovered in 1767, and remained uninhabited until settled in 1790 by mutineers from HMS *Bounty*.
– ORIGIN named after the midshipman who first sighted the islands.

pitch[1] ▶ **noun 1** Brit. an area of ground marked out or used for play in an outdoor team game.
■ used in reference to the time a sports player spends playing as opposed to doing other things: *off the pitch he has a reputation as an easy-going character*. ■ Cricket the strip of ground between the two sets of stumps.
2 [mass noun] the quality of a sound governed by the rate of vibrations producing it; the degree of highness or lowness of a tone: *a car engine seems to change pitch downwards as the vehicle passes you*.
■ a standard degree of highness or lowness used in performance: *the guitars were strung and tuned to pitch*. See also **CONCERT PITCH**.
3 [mass noun] the steepness of a slope, especially of a roof.
■ [count noun] Climbing a section of a climb, especially a steep one. ■ the height to which a hawk soars before swooping on its prey.
4 [in sing.] the level of intensity of something: *he brought the machine to a high pitch of development*.
■ (**a pitch of**) a very high degree of: *rousing herself to a pitch of indignation*.
5 Baseball a delivery of the ball by the pitcher.
■ (also **pitch of the ball**) Cricket the spot where the ball bounces when bowled. ■ (also **pitch shot**) Golf a high approach shot on to the green.
6 a form of words used when trying to persuade someone to buy or accept something: *he put over a very strong sales pitch*.
7 Brit. a place where a street vendor or performer stations themselves or sets up a stall.
8 [mass noun] a swaying or oscillation of a ship, aircraft, or vehicle around a horizontal axis perpendicular to the direction of motion.
9 [mass noun] technical the distance between successive corresponding points or lines, for example between the teeth of a cogwheel.
■ a measure of the angle of the blades of a screw propeller, equal to the distance forward a blade would move in one revolution if it exerted no thrust on the medium. ■ the density of typed or printed characters on a line, typically expressed as numbers of characters per inch.
▶ **verb 1** [with obj. and adverbial] set (one's voice or a piece of music) at a particular pitch: *you've pitched the melody very high*.
■ express at a particular level of difficulty: *he should pitch his talk at a suitable level for the age group*. ■ set (a charge) at a particular level: *if they pitch fares too high they could drive away passengers*. ■ aim (a product) at a particular section of the market: *the machine is being pitched at banks*.
2 [with obj. and adverbial of direction] throw or fling roughly or casually: *he crumpled the page up and pitched it into the fireplace*.
■ [no obj., with adverbial of direction] fall heavily, especially headlong: *she pitched forward into blackness*.
3 [with obj.] Baseball throw (the ball) for the batter to try and hit.
■ Cricket (of a bowler) cause (the ball) to strike the ground at a specified point: *all too often you pitch the ball short*. ■ Golf hit (the ball) on to the green with a pitch shot. ■ [no obj.] Cricket & Golf (of the ball) strike the ground in a particular spot.
4 [no obj.] make a bid to obtain a contract or other business: *they were pitching for an account*.
5 [with obj.] set up and fix in a definite position: *we pitched camp for the night*.
■ Cricket fix (the stumps) in the ground and place the bails in preparation for play.
6 [no obj.] (of a moving ship, aircraft, or vehicle) rock or oscillate around a lateral axis, so that the front moves up and down: *the little steamer pressed on, pitching gently*.
■ (of a vehicle) move with a vigorous jogging motion: *a Land Rover came pitching round the hillside*.
7 [with obj.] cause (a roof) to slope downwards from the ridge: *the roof was pitched at an angle of 75 degrees* | [as adj. **pitched**] *a pitched roof*.
■ [no obj.] slope downwards: *the ravine pitches down to the creek*.
8 [with obj.] pave (a road) with stones.
9 [with obj.] (in brewing) add yeast to (wort) to induce fermentation.
– PHRASES **make a pitch** make a bid to obtain a contract or other business.
– ORIGIN Middle English (as a verb in the senses 'thrust (something pointed) into the ground') and 'fall headlong': perhaps related to Old English *picung* 'stigmata', of unknown ultimate origin. The sense development is obscure.
▶ **pitch someone/thing against** informal pit someone or something against.
pitch in informal vigorously join in to help with a task or activity. ■ join in a fight or dispute.
pitch into informal vigorously tackle or begin to deal with. ■ forcefully assault.
pitch up informal turn up; arrive.
pitch something up (or **pitch up**) Cricket bowl a ball so that it bounces near the batsman.

pitch[2] ▶ **noun** [mass noun] a sticky resinous black or dark brown substance semi-liquid when hot, hard when cold, obtained by distilling tar or turpentine and used for waterproofing.
■ any of various similar substances, such as asphalt or bitumen.
▶ **verb** [with obj.] archaic or W. Indian cover, coat, or smear with pitch.
– ORIGIN Old English *pic* (noun), *pician* (verb), of Germanic origin; related to Dutch *pek* and German *Pech*; based on Latin *pix*, *pic-*.

pitch and putt ▶ **noun** [mass noun] a form of golf played on a miniature course in which the green can be reached in one stroke from the tee.

pitch and run ▶ **noun** Golf a pitch shot with a lower trajectory and no backspin, so that the ball runs forward on landing.

pitch-and-toss ▶ **noun** [mass noun] a gambling game in which the player who manages to throw a coin closest to a mark gets to toss all the coins, winning those that land with the head up.

pitch bend ▶ **noun** [mass noun] a facility in a synthesizer that enables the player to change the pitch of the note played by a small amount.

pitch-black (also **pitch-dark**) ▶ **adjective** completely dark.
– DERIVATIVES **pitch-blackness** noun.

pitchblende /ˈpɪtʃblɛnd/ ▶ **noun** [mass noun] a form of the mineral uraninite occurring in brown or black pitch-like masses and containing radium.
– ORIGIN late 18th cent.: from German *Pechblende*, from *Pech* 'pitch' + *Blende* (see **BLENDE**).

pitch circle ▶ **noun** Mechanics an imaginary circle concentric to a toothed wheel, along which the pitch of the teeth is measured.

pitch control ▶ **noun** [mass noun] **1** control of the pitch of a helicopter's rotors or an aircraft's propellers.
2 control of the pitching motion of an aircraft.

pitched battle ▶ **noun** a relatively static battle fought between large formations of troops.
■ a violent confrontation involving large numbers of people.

pitcher[1] ▶ **noun** Brit. a large earthenware container, with one or two handles and a lip, for holding liquids.
■ N. Amer. a jug. ■ the contents of such containers: *a pitcher of water*. ■ (**pitchers**) broken pottery crushed and reused. ■ the modified leaf of a pitcher plant.
– DERIVATIVES **pitcherful** noun (pl. **-fuls**).
– ORIGIN Middle English: from Old French *pichier* 'pot', based on late Latin *picarium*.

pitcher[2] /ˈpɪtʃə/ ▶ **noun 1** Baseball the player who delivers the ball to the batter.
2 a stone used for paving.

pitcher plant ▶ **noun** a plant with a deep pitcher-shaped pouch that contains fluid into which insects are attracted and drowned. Nutrients are then absorbed from their bodies by the plant.

p

• Three families, in particular Sarraceniaceae (New World) and Nepenthaceae (Old World): many species, including the purple-flowered *Sarracenia purpurea*, naturalized in Ireland.

pitchfork ▶ noun a farm tool with a long handle and two sharp metal prongs, used especially for lifting hay.
▶ verb [with obj. and adverbial of direction] lift with a pitchfork.
▪ figurative thrust (someone) suddenly into an unexpected and difficult situation.
– ORIGIN late Middle English: from earlier *pickfork*, influenced by the verb **PITCH**[1] (because the tool is used for 'pitching' or throwing sheaves on to a stack).

pitchman ▶ noun (pl. **-men** /-mɛn/) N. Amer. informal a person delivering a sales pitch.

pitchout ▶ noun **1** Baseball a pitch thrown intentionally beyond the reach of the batter to allow the catcher a clear throw at an advancing base-runner.
2 American Football a lateral pass, especially from the quarterback to a running back.

pitch pine ▶ noun a pine tree with hard, heavy, resinous timber that is used in building, especially the longleaf pine of North America.

pitch-pipe ▶ noun Music a small pipe blown to set the pitch for singing or tuning an instrument.

pitchpole ▶ verb [no obj.] dialect somersault.
▪ Nautical (of a boat) be overturned so that its stern pitches forward over its bows.
▶ noun dialect a somersault.
– ORIGIN mid 17th cent. (as a noun): from the verb **PITCH**[1] + **POLL**.

pitchstone ▶ noun [mass noun] Geology a dull vitreous rock resembling hardened pitch, formed by weathering of obsidian.

pitchy ▶ adjective (**pitchier**, **pitchiest**) of, like, or as dark as pitch.

piteous ▶ adjective deserving or arousing pity.
– DERIVATIVES **piteously** adverb, **piteousness** noun.
– ORIGIN Middle English: from Old French *piteus*, from Latin *pietas* 'piety, pity' (see **PIETY**).

pitfall ▶ noun a hidden or unsuspected danger or difficulty.
▪ a covered pit for use as a trap.

pith ▶ noun [mass noun] **1** soft or spongy tissue in plants or animals, in particular:
▪ spongy white tissue lining the rind of oranges, lemons, and other citrus fruits. ▪ Botany the spongy cellular tissue in the stems and branches of many higher plants. ▪ archaic spinal marrow.
2 figurative the essence of something: *the pith and core of socialism.*
3 figurative vigorous and concise expression: *he writes with a combination of pith and exactitude.*
▶ verb [with obj.] **1** dated, chiefly figurative remove the pith from.
2 rare pierce or sever the spinal cord of (an animal) so as to kill or immobilize it.
– DERIVATIVES **pithless** adjective.
– ORIGIN Old English *pitha*, of West Germanic origin.

pithead ▶ noun the top of a mineshaft.
▪ the area surrounding this.

Pithecanthropus /ˌpɪθɪˈkanθrəpəs/ ▶ noun a former genus name applied to some fossil hominids found in Java in 1891. See **JAVA MAN**.
– ORIGIN late 19th cent.: modern Latin, from Greek *pithēkos* 'ape' + *anthrōpos* 'man'.

pith helmet ▶ noun a lightweight sun helmet made from the dried pith of the sola or a similar tropical plant.

pithivier /ˌpɪtɪˈvjeɪ/ ▶ noun a tart consisting of puff pastry filled with almond cream.
– ORIGIN from French *Pithiviers*, the name of a small town in the department of the Loiret.

pithos /ˈpɪθɒs/ ▶ noun (pl. **pithoi** /-θɔɪ/) Archaeology a large earthenware storage jar.
– ORIGIN Greek.

pithy ▶ adjective (**pithier**, **pithiest**) **1** (of a fruit or plant) containing much pith.
2 (of language or style) terse and vigorously expressive.
– DERIVATIVES **pithily** adverb, **pithiness** noun.

pitiable ▶ adjective deserving or arousing pity.
▪ contemptibly poor or small.
– DERIVATIVES **pitiableness** noun, **pitiably** adverb.
– ORIGIN late Middle English: from Old French *piteable*, from *piteer* 'to pity'.

pitiful ▶ adjective deserving or arousing pity.
▪ very small or poor; inadequate. ▪ archaic compassionate.
– DERIVATIVES **pitifully** adverb, **pitifulness** noun.

pitiless ▶ adjective showing no pity; cruel.
▪ (especially of weather) unrelentingly harsh.
– DERIVATIVES **pitilessly** adverb, **pitilessness** noun.

Pitman, Sir Isaac (1813–97), English inventor of a shorthand system, published as *Stenographic Sound Hand* (1837). Pitman shorthand is still widely used in the UK and elsewhere.

pitman ▶ noun **1** (pl. **-men**) a coal miner.
2 N. Amer. (pl. **-mans**) a connecting rod in machinery.

piton /ˈpiːtɒn/ ▶ noun a peg or spike driven into a rock or crack to support a climber or a rope.
▪ (**the Pitons**) two conical mountains in St Lucia in the Caribbean. Reaching a height of 798 m (2,618 ft) and 750 m (2,461 ft), they rise up out of the sea just off the SW coast of the island.
– ORIGIN late 19th cent.: from French, literally 'eye bolt'.

pitot tube /ˈpiːtəʊ/ (also **pitot**) ▶ noun an open-ended right-angled tube pointing in opposition to the flow of a fluid and used to measure pressure.
▪ (also **pitot-static tube**, **pitot head**) a device consisting of a pitot tube inside or adjacent to a parallel tube closed at the end but with holes along its length, the pressure difference between them being a measure of the relative velocity of the fluid, or the airspeed of an aircraft.
– ORIGIN late 19th cent.: named after Henri *Pitot* (1695–1771), French physicist.

pitpan ▶ noun a flat-bottomed boat made from a hollowed tree trunk, used in Central America.
– ORIGIN late 18th cent.: from Miskito *pitban* 'boat'.

pit pony ▶ noun Brit. historical a pony that hauled loads in a coal mine.

pit prop ▶ noun a large wooden beam used to support the roof of a coal mine.

pit saw ▶ noun historical a large saw with handles at the top and bottom, used in a vertical position by two men, one standing above the timber to be cut, the other in a pit below it.

pit stop ▶ noun Motor Racing a stop at a pit for servicing and refuelling, especially during a race.
▪ informal a brief rest, especially during a journey.
▪ informal a place where one takes such a rest.

Pitt the name of two British statesmen:
▪ **William**, 1st Earl of Chatham (1708–78); known as **Pitt the Elder**. As Secretary of State (effectively Prime Minister), he headed coalition governments 1756–61 and 1766–8. He brought the Seven Years War to an end in 1763 and also masterminded the conquest of French possessions overseas, particularly in Canada and India.
▪ **William** (1759–1806), Prime Minister 1783–1801 and 1804–6, the son of Pitt the Elder; known as **Pitt the Younger**. The youngest-ever Prime Minister, he introduced financial reforms to reduce the national debt.

pitta[1] /ˈpɪtə/ (also **pitta bread**, chiefly N. Amer. **pita**) ▶ noun [mass noun] flat hollow unleavened bread which can be split open to hold a filling.
– ORIGIN modern Greek, literally 'cake or pie'; compare with Turkish *pide*, in a similar sense.

pitta[2] /ˈpɪtə/ ▶ noun a small ground-dwelling thrush-like bird with brightly coloured plumage and a very short tail, found in the Old World tropics.
• Family Pittidae and genus *Pitta*: many species.
– ORIGIN mid 19th cent.: from Telugu *piṭṭa* '(young) bird'.

pittance ▶ noun **1** [usu. in sing.] a very small or inadequate amount of money paid to someone as an allowance or wage.
2 historical a pious bequest to a religious house or order to provide extra food and wine at particular festivals, or on the anniversary of the benefactor's death.
– ORIGIN Middle English: from Old French *pitance*, from medieval Latin *pitantia*, from Latin *pietas* 'pity'.

pitted ▶ adjective **1** having a hollow or indentation on the surface: *his jowled and pitted face.*
2 (of a fruit) having had the stone removed.

pitter-patter ▶ noun a sound as of quick light steps or taps.
▶ adverb with this sound: *footsteps that go pitter-patter.*
– ORIGIN late Middle English: reduplication (expressing rhythmic repetition) of the verb **PATTER**[1].

Pitti /ˈpɪti/ an art gallery and museum in Florence, housed in the Pitti Palace (built 1440–*c.*1549). Its contents include masterpieces from the Medici collections and Gobelin tapestries.

Pitt Island see **CHATHAM ISLANDS**.

pittosporum /pɪˈtɒsp(ə)rəm/ ▶ noun an evergreen shrub or small tree that typically has small fragrant flowers and is chiefly native to Australasia.
• Genus *Pittosporum*, family Pittosporaceae.
– ORIGIN modern Latin, from Greek *pitta* 'pitch' (because of the resinous pulp around the seeds) + *sporos* 'seed'.

Pitt-Rivers, Augustus Henry Lane Fox (1827–1900), English archaeologist and anthropologist. He developed a new scientific approach to archaeology. His collection of weapons and artefacts from different cultures formed the basis of the ethnological museum in Oxford which bears his name.

Pittsburgh /ˈpɪtsbəːg/ an industrial city in SW Pennsylvania, at the junction of the Allegheny and Monongahela Rivers; pop. 369,880 (1990).

pituitary /pɪˈtjuːɪt(ə)ri/ ▶ noun (pl. **-ies**) (in full **pituitary gland** or **pituitary body**) the major endocrine gland, a pea-sized body attached to the base of the brain that is important in controlling growth and development and the functioning of the other endocrine glands. Also called **HYPOPHYSIS**.
▶ adjective of or relating to this gland.
– ORIGIN early 17th cent.: from Latin *pituitarius* 'secreting phlegm', from *pituita* 'phlegm'.

pit viper ▶ noun a venomous snake of a group distinguished by visible sensory pits on the head which can detect prey by heat. They are found in both America and Asia.
• Subfamily Crotalinae, family Viperidae: numerous genera and species, including the rattlesnakes.

pity ▶ noun (pl. **-ies**) **1** [mass noun] the feeling of sorrow and compassion caused by the sufferings and misfortunes of others: *her voice was full of pity.*
2 [in sing.] a cause for regret or disappointment: *what a pity we can't be friends.*
▶ verb (**-ies**, **-ied**) [with obj.] feel sorrow for the misfortunes of: *Clare didn't know whether to envy or pity them* | [as adj. **pitying**] *he gave her a pitying look.*
– PHRASES **for pity's sake** informal used to express impatience or make an urgent appeal. **more's the pity** informal used to express regret about a fact that has just been stated. **take** (or **have**) **pity** show compassion: *the old couple* ***took pity on*** *him and gave him food.*
– DERIVATIVES **pityingly** adverb.
– ORIGIN Middle English (also in the sense 'clemency, mildness'): from Old French *pite* 'compassion', from Latin *pietas* 'piety'; compare with **PIETY**.

pityriasis /ˌpɪtɪˈrʌɪəsɪs/ ▶ noun [mass noun] [with modifier] Medicine a skin disease characterized by the shedding of fine flaky scales.
– ORIGIN late 17th cent.: modern Latin, from Greek *pituriasis* 'scurf', from *pituron* 'bran'.

più mosso /pjuː ˈmɒsəʊ/ ▶ adverb & adjective Music (especially as a direction) more quickly.
– ORIGIN Italian.

Pius XII /ˈpʌɪəs/ (1876–1958), pope 1939–58; born *Eugenio Pacelli*. He upheld the neutrality of the Roman Catholic Church during the Second World War, and was criticized after the war for failing to condemn Nazi atrocities.

pivot ▶ noun the central point, pin, or shaft on which a mechanism turns or oscillates.
▪ [usu. in sing.] a person or thing that plays a central part in an activity or organization: *the* ***pivot of*** *community life was the chapel.* ▪ the man or men about whom a body of troops wheels. ▪ (also **pivotman**) chiefly N. Amer. a player in a central position in a team sport. ▪ Basketball a movement in which the player holding the ball may move in any direction with one foot, while keeping the other (the pivot foot) in contact with the floor.
▶ verb (**pivoted**, **pivoting**) [no obj.] turn on or as if on a pivot: *the axles* ***pivoted about*** *the motors* | *he swung round,* ***pivoting on*** *his heel.*
▪ (**pivot on**) figurative depend on: *the government's reaction pivoted on the response of the Prime Minister.* ▪ [with obj.] provide (a mechanism) with a pivot; fix (a mechanism) on a pivot: [as adj. **pivoted**] *a pivoted bracket.*
– DERIVATIVES **pivotability** noun, **pivotable** adjective.

– ORIGIN late Middle English: from French, probably from the root of dialect *pue* 'tooth of a comb' and Spanish *pu(y)a* 'point'. The verb dates from the mid 19th cent.

pivotal ▶ **adjective** of crucial importance in relation to the development or success of something else: *play a pivotal role in the transitional process.*
▪fixed on or as if on a pivot: *a sliding or pivotal motion.*

pix[1] ▶ **plural noun** informal pictures, especially photographs.
– ORIGIN 1930s: pluralized abbreviation.

pix[2] ▶ **noun** variant spelling of **PYX**.

pixel /ˈpɪks(ə)l, -sɛl/ ▶ **noun** Electronics a minute area of illumination on a display screen, one of many from which an image is composed.
– ORIGIN 1960s: abbreviation of *picture element* (compare with **PIX**[1]).

pixelate /ˈpɪksəleɪt/ (also **pixellate** or **pixilate**) ▶ **verb** [with obj.] divide (an image) into pixels, typically for display or storage in a digital format.
▪display an image of (someone or something) on television as a small number of large pixels, typically in order to disguise someone's identity.
– DERIVATIVES **pixelation** noun.

Pixelvision ▶ **noun** [mass noun] a film-making system (originally designed for children) which uses a low-resolution video camera to record images.

pixie (also **pixy**) ▶ **noun** (pl. **-ies**) a supernatural being in folklore and children's stories, typically portrayed as small and human-like in form, with pointed ears and a pointed hat.
– DERIVATIVES **pixieish** adjective.
– ORIGIN mid 17th cent.: of unknown origin.

pixie hat (also **pixie hood**) ▶ **noun** a child's hat with a pointed crown.

pixilate ▶ **verb** variant spelling of **PIXELATE**.

pixilated (also **pixillated**) ▶ **adjective** crazy; confused.
▪informal, dated drunk.
– ORIGIN mid 19th cent.: variant of *pixie-led*, literally 'led astray by pixies', figuratively 'confused', or from **PIXIE**, on the pattern of words such as *elated* and *emulated*.

pixilation (also **pixillation**) ▶ **noun** [mass noun] **1** a technique used in film whereby the movements of real people are filmed or edited in such a way that they appear to move like artificial animations.
2 the state of being crazy, confused, or drunk.
3 variant spelling of **PIXELATION** (see **PIXELATE**).

Pizan, Christine de, see **DE PISAN**.

Pizarro /pɪˈzɑːrəʊ/, Francisco (*c.*1478–1541), Spanish conquistador. He defeated the Inca empire and in 1533 set up a puppet monarchy at Cuzco, building his own capital at Lima (1535), where he was assassinated.

pizza /ˈpiːtsə, ˈpɪtsə/ ▶ **noun** a dish of Italian origin, consisting of a flat, round base of dough baked with a topping of tomatoes and cheese, typically with added meat, fish, or vegetables.
– ORIGIN Italian, literally 'pie'.

pizza box ▶ **noun** a computer casing which is not very tall and has a square cross section.

pizzazz (also **pizazz** or **pzazz**) ▶ **noun** [mass noun] informal an attractive combination of vitality and glamour: *a summer collection with pizzazz.*
– ORIGIN said to have been invented by Diana Vreeland, fashion editor of *Harper's Bazaar* in the 1930s.

pizzeria /ˌpiːtsəˈriːə, ˈpɪtsə-/ ▶ **noun** a place where pizzas are made or sold; a pizza restaurant.
– ORIGIN Italian.

pizzicato /ˌpɪtsɪˈkɑːtəʊ/ Music ▶ **adverb** (often as a direction) plucking the strings of a violin or other stringed instrument with one's finger.
▶ **adjective** performed in this way.
▶ **noun** (pl. **pizzicatos** or **pizzicati** /-ti/) [mass noun] this technique of playing.
▪[count noun] a note or passage played in this way.
– ORIGIN Italian, literally 'pinched, twitched', past participle of *pizzicare*, based on *pizza* 'point, edge'.

pizzle ▶ **noun** chiefly Austral. or archaic the penis of an animal, especially a bull, formerly used for flogging people.
– ORIGIN late 15th cent.: from Low German *pēsel* or Flemish *pezel* (diminutives of Middle Low German *pēse* and Middle Dutch *pēze*).

PK ▶ **abbreviation for** ▪ Pakistan (international vehicle registration). ▪ psychokinesis.

pK ▶ **noun** Chemistry a figure expressing the acidity or alkalinity of a solution of a weak electrolyte in a similar way to pH, equal to $-\log_{10} K$ where K is the dissociation (or ionization) constant of the electrolyte.
– ORIGIN from *p* as in *pH* and *K* representing a constant.

pk ▶ **abbreviation for** ▪ (also **Pk**) park. ▪ peak. ▪ peck(s).

PKU ▶ **abbreviation for** phenylketonuria.

PL ▶ **abbreviation for** ▪ Poland (international vehicle registration). ▪ Computing programming language.

pl. ▶ **abbreviation for** ▪ (also **Pl.**) place: *3 Palmerston Pl., Edinburgh.* ▪ plate (referring to illustrations in a book). ▪ chiefly Military platoon. ▪ Grammar plural.

PLA ▶ **abbreviation for** ▪ People's Liberation Army. ▪ (in the UK) Port of London Authority.

placable /ˈplakəb(ə)l/ ▶ **adjective** archaic easily calmed; gentle and forgiving.
– DERIVATIVES **placability** noun, **placably** adverb.
– ORIGIN late Middle English (in the sense 'pleasing, agreeable'): from Old French, or from Latin *placabilis*, from *placare* 'appease'.

placard /ˈplakɑːd/ ▶ **noun** a printed or handwritten notice or sign for public display, either fixed to a wall or carried during a demonstration.
▶ **verb** /also plaˈkɑːd/ [with obj.] cover with notices: *they were placarding the town with posters.*
– ORIGIN late 15th cent. (denoting a warrant or licence): from Old French *placquart*, from *plaquier* 'to plaster, lay flat', from Middle Dutch *placken*. The current sense of the verb dates from the early 19th cent.

placate /pləˈkeɪt, ˈplakeɪt, ˈpleɪ-/ ▶ **verb** [with obj.] make (someone) less angry or hostile: *they attempted to placate the students with promises.*
– DERIVATIVES **placatingly** adverb, **placation** noun, **placatory** adjective.
– ORIGIN late 17th cent.: from Latin *placat-* 'appeased', from the verb *placare*.

place ▶ **noun 1** a particular position or point in space: *there were still some remote places in the world | the monastery was a peaceful place.*
▪used to refer to an area already identified (giving an impression of informality): *we head to a disco—the place is pandemonium.* ▪a particular point on a larger surface or in a larger object or area: *he lashed out and cut the policeman's hand in three places.* ▪a building or area used for a specified purpose or activity: *the town has many excellent eating places.* ▪ informal a person's home: *what about dinner at my place?* ▪a point in a book or other text reached by a reader at a particular time: *I must have lost my place in the script.*
2 a portion of space occupied by someone: *he was watching from his place across the room.*
▪a portion of space available or designated for someone: *they hurried to their places at the table.* ▪a vacancy or available position: *she won a place to study German at university.* ▪ [mass noun] the regular or proper position of something: *lay each slab* **in place**. ▪ [often with negative] somewhere where it is appropriate or prudent for someone to be or for something to occur: *that street at that time was* **no place for** *a lady.* ▪a chance to be accepted or to be of use: *the policy left no place for individual initiative.* ▪a person's rank or status: *occupation structures a person's place in society.* ▪ [usu. with negative] a right or privilege resulting from someone's role or position: *I'm sure she has a story to tell, but it's* **not my place** *to ask.* ▪ the role played by or importance attached to someone or something in a particular context: *the place of computers in improving office efficiency varies between companies.*
3 a position in a sequence, in particular:
▪a position in a sporting contest: *his score was good enough to leave him in ninth place.* ▪ Brit. any of the first three or sometimes four positions in a race (used especially of the second, third, or fourth positions). ▪ N. Amer. the second position, especially in a horse race. ▪ the degree of priority given to something: *accurate reportage* **takes second place** *to lurid detail.* ▪ the position of a figure in a series indicated in decimal or similar notation, especially one after the decimal point: *calculate the ratios* **to** *one* **decimal place**.
4 [in place names] a square or short street: *the lecture theatre is in New Burlington Place.*
▪a country house with its grounds.
▶ **verb** [with obj.] **1** [with obj. and adverbial] put in a particular position: *a newspaper had been placed beside my plate.*
▪cause to be in a particular situation: *enemy officers were placed under arrest | you are not placing yourself under any obligation.* ▪ used to express the attitude someone has towards someone or something: *I am not able to place any trust in you.* ▪ **(be placed)** used to indicate the degree of advantage or convenience enjoyed by someone or something as a result of their position or circumstances: [with infinitive] *the company is well placed to seize the opportunity.*
2 [with obj.] find a home or employment for: *the children were placed with foster-parents | the agency had placed 3,000 people in work.*
▪dispose of (something, especially shares) by selling to a customer. ▪ arrange for the recognition and implementation of (an order, bet, etc.): *they placed a contract for three boats.* ▪ order or obtain a connection for (a telephone call) through an operator.
3 [with obj. and adverbial] identify or classify as being of a specified type or as holding a specified position in a sequence or hierarchy: *a survey placed the company 13th for achievement.*
▪[with obj.] [usu. with negative] remember where one has seen or how one comes to recognize (someone or something): *she eventually said she couldn't place him.* ▪ **(be placed)** Brit. achieve a specified position in a race: *he was placed eleventh in the long individual race.* ▪ [no obj.] be among the first three or four in a race (or the first three in the US).
4 [with obj.] Rugby & American Football score (a goal) by a place kick.
– PHRASES **give place to** be succeeded or replaced by. **go places** informal visit places; travel. ▪ be increasingly successful. **in place 1** working or ready to work; established. **2** N. Amer. on the spot; not travelling any distance. **in place of** instead of. **keep someone in his** (or **her**) **place** keep someone from becoming presumptuous. **out of place** not in the proper position; disarranged. ▪ in a setting where one is or feels inappropriate or incongruous. **place in the sun** a position of favour or advantage. **put oneself in someone's place** consider a situation from someone's point of view. **put someone in his** (or **her**) **place** deflate or humiliate someone regarded as being presumptuous. **take place** occur. **take one's place** take up the physical position or status in society that is correct or due for one. **take the place of** replace.
– DERIVATIVES **placeless** adjective.
– ORIGIN Middle English: from Old French, from an alteration of Latin *platea* 'open space', from Greek *plateia (hodos)* 'broad (way)'.

place-bet ▶ **noun** (in the UK) a bet on a horse to win a place in a race, usually first, second, or third.
▪(in the US) a bet on a horse to come first or second.

placebo /pləˈsiːbəʊ/ ▶ **noun** (pl. **-os**) a pill, medicine, or procedure prescribed more for the psychological benefit to the patient of being given a prescription than for any physiological effect.
▪a substance that has no therapeutic effect, used as a control in testing new drugs. ▪ figurative a measure designed merely to calm or please someone.
– ORIGIN late 18th cent.: from Latin, literally 'I shall be acceptable or pleasing', from *placere* 'to please'.

placebo effect ▶ **noun** a beneficial effect produced by a placebo drug or treatment, which cannot be attributed to the properties of the placebo itself, and must therefore be due to the patient's belief in that treatment.

place brick ▶ **noun** a brick which has been imperfectly fired due to being on the outward side of the kiln.

place card ▶ **noun** a card bearing a person's name and used to mark their place at a dining or meeting table.

placeholder ▶ **noun 1** Mathematics a significant zero in the decimal representation of a number.
▪a symbol or piece of text used in a mathematical expression or in an instruction in a computer program to denote a missing quantity or operator.
2 Linguistics an element of a sentence that is required by syntactic constraints but carries little or no semantic information, for example the word *it* as a subject in *it is a pity that she left*, where the true subject is *that she left*.

place kick American Football, Rugby, & Soccer ▶ **noun** a kick made after the ball is first placed on the ground.
▶ **verb (place-kick)** [no obj.] [often as noun **place-kicking**] take such a kick.
– DERIVATIVES **place-kicker** noun.

placeman ▶ **noun** (pl. **-men**) Brit. derogatory a person appointed to a position, especially in government

p

service, for personal profit and as a reward for political support.

place mat ▶ **noun** a small mat underneath a person's dining plate, used to protect the table from the heat of the plate and food.

placement ▶ **noun** [mass noun] the action of putting someone or something in a particular place or the fact of being placed: *the proper placement of microphones.*
■ the action of finding a home, employment, or school for someone: *a baby put up for adoption may wait up to three years or more for placement* | [count noun] *a placement in a special school.* ■ the temporary posting of someone in a workplace to enable them to gain work experience: *students spend one year on industrial placement* | [count noun] *teaching practice placements.*

place name ▶ **noun** the name of a geographical location, such as a town, lake, or a range of hills.

placenta /plə'sɛntə/ ▶ **noun** (pl. **placentae** /-tiː/ or **placentas**) **1** a flattened circular organ in the uterus of pregnant eutherian mammals, nourishing and maintaining the fetus through the umbilical cord.

> The placenta consists of vascular tissue in which oxygen and nutrients can pass from the mother's blood into that of the fetus, and waste products can pass in the reverse direction. The placenta is expelled from the uterus at the birth of the fetus, when it is often called the afterbirth. Marsupials and monotremes do not develop placentas.

2 Botany (in flowers) part of the ovary wall to which the ovules are attached.
– ORIGIN late 17th cent.: from Latin, from Greek *plakous, plakount-* 'flat cake', based on *plax, plak-* 'flat plate'.

placental ▶ **adjective** of or relating to a placenta.
■ Zoology relating to or denoting mammals that possess a placenta; eutherian.
▶ **noun** Zoology a placental mammal. See **EUTHERIA**.

placental abruption ▶ **noun** see **ABRUPTION**.

placenta praevia /'priːvɪə/ (US **placenta previa**) ▶ **noun** [mass noun] Medicine a condition in which the placenta partially or wholly blocks the neck of the uterus, so interfering with normal delivery of a baby.
– ORIGIN early 19th cent.: from **PLACENTA** and Latin *praevia* 'going before', feminine of *praevius*.

placentation /ˌplas(ə)n'teɪʃ(ə)n/ ▶ **noun** [mass noun] Anatomy & Zoology the formation or arrangement of a placenta or placentae in a woman's or female animal's uterus.
■ Botany the arrangement of the placenta or placentae in the ovary of a flower.

placer[1] ▶ **noun** [often as modifier] a deposit of sand or gravel in the bed of a river or lake, containing particles of valuable minerals: *placer gold deposits.*
– ORIGIN early 19th cent.: from Latin American Spanish, literally 'deposit, shoal'; related to *placel* 'sandbank', from *plaza* 'a place'.

placer[2] ▶ **noun** **1** [with modifier] a person or animal gaining a specified position in a competition or race: *last year's fifth placer had a good run.*
2 a person who positions, sets, or arranges something: *he was a shrewd placer of the ball.*
■ a person who puts the material ready for firing in a pottery kiln.
3 Brit. informal a dealer in stolen goods.

place setting ▶ **noun** a complete set of crockery and cutlery provided for one person at a meal.

placet /'pleɪsɛt/ ▶ **noun** Brit. an affirmative vote in a church or university assembly.
– ORIGIN Latin, literally 'it pleases'.

place value ▶ **noun** the numerical value that a digit has by virtue of its position in a number.

placid ▶ **adjective** (of a person or animal) not easily upset or excited: *this horse has a placid nature.*
■ (especially of a place or stretch of water) calm and peaceful, with little movement or activity: *the placid waters of a small lake.*
– DERIVATIVES **placidity** noun, **placidly** adverb.
– ORIGIN early 17th cent.: from French *placide*, from Latin *placidus*, from *placere* 'to please'.

Placidyl /'plasɪdɪl/ ▶ **noun** [mass noun] N. Amer. trademark a short-acting sedative and hypnotic drug used to treat insomnia.

placing ▶ **noun** **1** an instance of being placed, in particular:
■ (usu. **placings**) a ranking one is given during or after a sports race or other competition. ■ a post that is found for a job-seeker.
2 [mass noun] the action of putting something in position or the fact of being positioned.
3 [mass noun] the action of making an order.
4 a sale or new issue of a large quantity of shares.

placket ▶ **noun** an opening or slit in a garment, covering fastenings or for access to a pocket, or the flap of fabric under such an opening.
– ORIGIN early 17th cent.: variant of **PLACARD** in an obsolete sense 'garment worn under an open coat or gown'.

placoderm /'plakə(ʊ)dəːm/ ▶ **noun** a fossil fish of the Devonian period, having the front part of the body encased in broad flat bony plates.
• Class Placodermi: several orders.
– ORIGIN mid 19th cent.: from Greek *plax, plak-* 'flat plate' + *derma* 'skin'.

placodont /'plakə(ʊ)dɒnt/ ▶ **noun** a fossil marine shellfish-eating reptile of the Triassic period, having short flat grinding palatal teeth and sometimes a turtle-like shell.
• Suborder Placodontia, superorder Sauropterygia: several families and genera, including *Placodus.*
– ORIGIN late 19th cent.: from Greek *plax, plak-* 'flat plate' + *odous, odont-* 'tooth'.

placoid /'plakɔɪd/ ▶ **adjective** Zoology (of fish scales) tooth-like, being made of dentine with a pointed backward projection of enamel, as in sharks and rays. Compare with **CTENOID** and **GANOID**.
– ORIGIN mid 19th cent.: from Greek *plax, plak-* 'flat plate' + **-OID**.

Placozoa /ˌplakə'zəʊə/ Zoology a minor phylum that contains a single minute marine invertebrate (*Trichoplax adhaerens*), which has a flattened body with two cell layers and is the simplest known metazoan.
– ORIGIN modern Latin (plural), from Greek *plakos* 'flat' + *zōia* 'animals'.

plafond /pla'fɔ̃(d)/ ▶ **noun** an ornately decorated ceiling.
■ a painting or decoration on a ceiling.
– ORIGIN French, from *plat* 'flat' + *fond* 'bottom, base'.

plagal /'pleɪg(ə)l/ ▶ **adjective** Music (of a church mode) containing notes between the dominant and the note an octave higher. Compare with **AUTHENTIC**.
– ORIGIN late 16th cent.: from medieval Latin *plagalis*, from *plaga* 'plagal mode', from Latin *plagius*, from medieval Greek *plagios* (*hēchos*) 'plagal (mode)', from Greek *plagos* 'side'.

plagal cadence ▶ **noun** Music a cadence in which the chord of the subdominant immediately precedes that of the tonic.

plage ▶ **noun** **1** /plɑːʒ/ dated a beach by the sea, especially at a fashionable resort.
2 /pleɪdʒ/ Astronomy an unusually bright region on the sun.
– ORIGIN late 19th cent.: from French.

plagiarism ▶ **noun** [mass noun] the practice of taking someone else's work or ideas and passing them off as one's own.
– DERIVATIVES **plagiarist** noun, **plagiaristic** adjective.
– ORIGIN early 17th cent.: from Latin *plagiarius* 'kidnapper' (from *plagium* 'a kidnapping', from Greek *plagion*) + **-ISM**.

plagiarize /'pleɪdʒərʌɪz/ (also **-ise**) ▶ **verb** [with obj.] take (the work or an idea of someone else) and pass it off as one's own.
■ copy from (someone) in such a way.
– DERIVATIVES **plagiarizer** noun.

plagio- /'pleɪdʒɪəʊ, 'plagɪəʊ/ ▶ **combining form** oblique: *plagioclase.*
– ORIGIN from Greek *plagios* 'slanting', from *plagos* 'side'.

plagioclase /'pleɪdʒɪə(ʊ)kleɪz, 'plagɪəʊ-/ (also **plagioclase feldspar**) ▶ **noun** [mass noun] a form of feldspar consisting of aluminosilicates of sodium and/or calcium, common in igneous rocks and typically white.
– ORIGIN mid 19th cent.: from **PLAGIO-** 'oblique' + Greek *klasis* 'cleavage' (because originally characterized as having two cleavages at an oblique angle).

plague ▶ **noun** [mass noun] a contagious bacterial disease characterized by fever and delirium, typically with the formation of buboes (see **BUBONIC PLAGUE**) and sometimes infection of the lungs (**pneumonic plague**):
■ [count noun] a contagious disease that spreads rapidly and kills many people. ■ [count noun] an unusually large number of insects or animals infesting a place and causing damage: *a* **plague of** *fleas.* ■ [in sing.] a thing causing trouble or irritation: *staff theft is usually the* **plague of** *restaurants.* ■ [in sing.] archaic used as a curse or an expression of despair or disgust: *a plague on all their houses!* [ORIGIN: in recent use echoing Shakespeare's *Romeo and Juliet* (III. i. 94).]
▶ **verb** (**plagues, plagued, plaguing**) [with obj.] cause continual trouble or distress to: *he has been plagued by ill health* | *the problems that plagued the company.*
■ pester or harass (someone) continually: *he was* **plaguing** *her* **with** *questions.*
– ORIGIN late Middle English: Latin *plaga* 'stroke, wound', probably from Greek (Doric dialect) *plaga*, from a base meaning 'strike'.

plaguy /'pleɪgi/ (also **plaguey**) ▶ **adjective** [attrib.] informal troublesome; annoying.

plaice ▶ **noun** (pl. same) a North Atlantic flatfish which is a commercially important food fish.
• Two species in the family Pleuronectidae: the European *Pleuronectes platessa*, often found in very shallow water, and the American *Hippoglossoides platessoides*, found in deeper waters.
– ORIGIN Middle English: from Old French *plaiz*, from late Latin *platessa*, from Greek *platus* 'broad'.

plaid /plad/ ▶ **noun** [mass noun] chequered or tartan twilled cloth, typically made of wool.
■ [count noun] a long piece of such cloth worn over the shoulder as part of Scottish Highland dress.
– DERIVATIVES **plaided** adjective.
– ORIGIN early 16th cent.: from Scottish Gaelic *plaide* 'blanket', of unknown ultimate origin.

Plaid Cymru /plʌɪd 'kʌmri/ the Welsh Nationalist party, founded in 1925 and dedicated to seeking autonomy for Wales. It won its first parliamentary seat in 1966, and since 1974 has maintained a small number of representatives in Parliament.
– ORIGIN Welsh, 'party of Wales'.

plain[1] ▶ **adjective** **1** not decorated or elaborate; simple or ordinary in character: *good plain food* | *everyone dined at a plain wooden table.*
■ without a pattern; in only one colour: *a plain fabric.* ■ bearing no indication as to contents or affiliation: *donations can be put in a plain envelope.* ■ (of paper) without lines. ■ (of a person) having no pretensions; not remarkable or special: *a plain, honest man with no nonsense about him.* ■ [attrib.] (of a person) without a special title or status: *for years he was just plain Bill.*
2 easy to perceive or understand; clear: *the advantages were* **plain to see** | *it was* **plain** *that something was very wrong.*
■ [attrib.] (of written or spoken usage) clearly expressed, without the use of technical or abstruse terms: *written* **in plain English**. ■ not using concealment or deception; frank: *he recalled her plain speaking.*
3 (of a woman or girl) not beautiful or attractive: *the dark-haired, rather plain woman.*
4 [attrib.] sheer; simple (used for emphasis): *the main problem is* **just plain** *exhaustion.*
5 (of a knitting stitch) made by putting the needle through the front of the stitch from left to right. Compare with **PURL**[1].
▶ **adverb** informal **1** [as submodifier] used for emphasis: *perhaps the youth was just plain stupid.*
2 clearly; unequivocally: *I'm finished with you, I'll* **tell** *you* **plain**.
▶ **noun** a large area of flat land with few trees.
– PHRASES **as plain as the nose on one's face** informal very obvious. **plain and simple** informal used to emphasize the statement preceding or following. **plain as day** informal very clearly.
– DERIVATIVES **plainness** noun.
– ORIGIN Middle English: from Old French *plain*, from Latin *planus*, from a base meaning 'flat'.

plain[2] ▶ **verb** [no obj.] archaic mourn; lament.
■ complain. ■ emit a mournful or plaintive sound.
– ORIGIN Middle English: from Old French *plaindre*, from Latin *plangere* 'to lament'.

plain card ▶ **noun** a playing card that is neither a trump nor a court card.

plainchant ▶ **noun** another term for **PLAINSONG**.

plain chocolate ▶ **noun** [mass noun] Brit. dark, slightly bitter, chocolate without added milk.

plain clothes ▶ **plural noun** ordinary clothes rather than uniform, especially when worn as a disguise by police officers.
▶ **adjective** [attrib.] (especially of a police officer) wearing such clothes.

plain cook ▶ **noun** Brit. a person competent in simple English cooking.

plain dealing ▶ **noun** [mass noun] honest and straightforward behaviour towards others.

plain flour ▶ **noun** [mass noun] Brit. flour that does not contain a raising agent.

plain hunting ▶ **noun** another term for **HUNTING** (in sense 2).

plainly ▶ **adverb 1** [as submodifier] able to be perceived easily: *the lake was plainly visible.*
■ [sentence adverb] used to state one's belief that something is obviously or undeniably true: *her mother was plainly anxious to leave.* ■ in a frank and direct way; unequivocally: *let me speak plainly.*
2 in a style that is simple and without decoration: *the restaurant was plainly furnished.*

plain-paper ▶ **adjective** denoting a fax or other device that does not require special paper to print on.

Plain People ▶ **plural noun** US the Amish, the Mennonites, and the Dunkers, three strict Christian sects emphasizing a simple way of life.

plain sailing ▶ **noun** [mass noun] [often with negative] used to describe a process or activity which goes well and is easy and uncomplicated: *teambuilding was not all plain sailing.*
– ORIGIN mid 18th cent.: probably a popular use of *plane sailing*, denoting the practice of determining a ship's position on the theory that it is moving on a plane.

plain sawing ▶ **noun** [mass noun] the method or action of sawing timber tangential to the growth rings, so that the rings make angles of less than 45° with the faces of the boards produced.

plain service ▶ **noun** a church service without music.

Plains Indian ▶ **noun** a member of any of various North American Indian peoples who formerly inhabited the Great Plains area.

Although a few of the Plains Indian peoples were sedentary farmers, most, including the Blackfoot, Cheyenne, and Comanche, were nomadic buffalo hunters, who gathered in tribes during the summer and dispersed into family groups in the winter.

plainsman ▶ **noun** (pl. **-men**) a person who lives on a plain, especially a frontiersman who lived on the Great Plains of North America.

Plains of Abraham a plateau beside the city of Quebec, overlooking the St Lawrence River. It was the scene in 1759 of a battle in which the British army under General Wolfe, having scaled the heights above the city under cover of darkness, surprised and defeated the French. The battle led to British control over Canada.

plainsong ▶ **noun** [mass noun] unaccompanied church music sung in unison in medieval modes and in free rhythm corresponding to the accentuation of the words, which are taken from the liturgy. Compare with **GREGORIAN CHANT**.
– ORIGIN late Middle English: translating Latin *cantus planus*.

plain-spoken ▶ **adjective** outspoken; blunt.

plain suit ▶ **noun** (in bridge and whist) a suit that is not trumps.

plains-wanderer ▶ **noun** a short-tailed quail-like bird found in the sparse grasslands of SE Australia.
• *Pedionomus torquatus*, the only member of the family Pedionomidae.

plaint ▶ **noun** Law, Brit. an accusation; a charge.
■ chiefly poetic/literary a complaint; a lamentation.
– ORIGIN Middle English: from Old French *plainte*, feminine past participle of *plaindre* 'complain', or from Old French *plaint*, from Latin *planctus* 'beating of the breast'.

plain text ▶ **noun** [mass noun] text that is not written in code.

plaintiff ▶ **noun** Law a person who brings a case against another in a court of law. Compare with **DEFENDANT**.
– ORIGIN late Middle English: from Old French *plaintif* 'plaintive' (used as a noun). The *-f* ending has come down through Law French; the word was originally the same as *plaintive*.

plain tiger ▶ **noun** a migratory African butterfly related to the monarch, with orange, white, and black wing markings.
• *Danaus chrysippus*, subfamily Danainae, family Nymphalidae.

plain tile ▶ **noun** a kind of flat tile used in roofing.

plain time ▶ **noun** [mass noun] Brit. working time paid for at the normal rate rather than overtime.

plaintive ▶ **adjective** sounding sad and mournful: *a plaintive cry.*
– DERIVATIVES **plaintively** adverb, **plaintiveness** noun.
– ORIGIN late Middle English: from Old French *plaintif, -ive*, from *plainte* 'lamentation' (see **PLAINT**).

plain weave ▶ **noun** [mass noun] a style of weave in which the weft alternates over and under the warp.

plait ▶ **noun** Brit. a single length of hair, straw, rope, or other material made up of three or more interlaced strands.
■ archaic term for **PLEAT**.
▶ **verb** [with obj.] form (hair, straw, rope, or other material) into a plait or plaits.
■ make (something) by forming material into a plait or plaits.
– ORIGIN late Middle English: from Old French *pleit* 'a fold', based on Latin *plicare* 'to fold'. The word was formerly often pronounced like 'plate'; since late Middle English there has been an alternative spelling *plat*, to which the current pronunciation corresponds.

plan ▶ **noun 1** a detailed proposal for doing or achieving something: *the UN peace plan.*
■ [with modifier] a scheme for the regular payment of contributions towards a pension, savings account, or insurance policy: *a personal pension plan.*
2 (usu. **plans**) an intention or decision about what one is going to do: *I have no plans to retire.*
3 a detailed diagram, drawing, or program, in particular:
■ a fairly large-scale map of a town or district: *a street plan.* ■ a drawing or diagram made by projection on a horizontal plane, especially one showing the layout of a building or one floor of a building. Compare with **ELEVATION** (in sense 3). ■ a diagram showing how something will be arranged: *look at the seating plan.* ■ (in the Methodist Church) a document listing the preachers for all the services in a circuit during a given period.
▶ **verb** (**planned**, **planning**) [with obj.] **1** decide on and arrange in advance: *they were planning a trip to Egypt* | [with infinitive] *he plans to fly on Wednesday* | [no obj.] *we* **plan on** *getting married in the near future.*
■ [no obj.] make preparations for an anticipated event or time: *we have to* **plan for** *the future.*
2 design or make a plan of (something to be made or built): *they were planning a garden.*
– PHRASES **someone's** (or **the**) **best plan** a person's (or the) most sensible course of action. **go according to plan** happen as one arranged or intended. **make a plan** S. African devise a way of overcoming difficulties. **plan of action** (or **campaign** or **attack**) an organized programme of measures to be taken in order to achieve a goal.
– ORIGIN late 17th cent.: from French, from earlier *plant* 'ground plan, plane surface', influenced in sense by Italian *pianta* 'plan of building'. Compare with **PLANT**.

planar /ˈpleɪnə/ ▶ **adjective** Mathematics of, relating to, or in the form of a plane: *planar surfaces.*

planarian /pləˈnɛːrɪən/ ▶ **noun** a free-living flatworm which has a three-branched intestine and a tubular pharynx, typically located halfway down the body.
• Order Tricladida, class Turbellaria: *Planaria* and other genera.
– ORIGIN mid 19th cent.: from modern Latin *Planaria* (feminine of Latin *planarius* 'lying flat') + **-IAN**.

planation /pləˈneɪʃ(ə)n/ ▶ **noun** [mass noun] the levelling of a landscape by erosion.
– ORIGIN late 19th cent.: from **PLANE**[1] + **-ATION**.

planche /plɑːntʃ, plɑːnʃ/ ▶ **noun** (in gymnastics) a position in which the body is held parallel with the ground by the arms, performed on the parallel bars, rings, or floor.
– ORIGIN early 20th cent.: French, literally 'plank'.

planchet /ˈplɑn(t)ʃɪt/ ▶ **noun** a plain metal disc from which a coin is made.
– ORIGIN early 17th cent.: diminutive of earlier *planch* 'slab of metal', from Old French *planche* 'plank, slab'.

planchette /plɑːnˈʃɛt/ ▶ **noun** a small board supported on castors, typically heart-shaped and fitted with a vertical pencil, used for automatic writing and in seances.
– ORIGIN mid 19th cent.: from French, literally 'small plank', diminutive of *planche*.

Planck /plaŋk/, Max (Karl Ernst Ludwig) (1858–1947), German theoretical physicist who founded quantum theory, announcing the radiation law named after him in 1900. Nobel Prize for Physics (1918).

Planck's constant (also **Planck constant**) Physics a fundamental constant, equal to the energy of a quantum of electromagnetic radiation divided by its frequency, with a value of 6.626×10^{-34} joules.

Planck's law Physics a law, forming the basis of quantum theory, which states that electromagnetic radiation from heated bodies is not emitted as a continuous flow but is made up of discrete units or quanta of energy, the size of which involve a fundamental physical constant (Planck's constant).

plane[1] ▶ **noun 1** a flat surface on which a straight line joining any two points on it would wholly lie: *the horizontal plane.*
■ an imaginary flat surface through or joining material objects: *the planets orbit the sun in roughly the same plane.* ■ (**plane of**) a flat or level surface of a material object: *the plane of his forehead.* ■ a flat surface producing lift by the action of air or water over and under it.
2 a level of existence, thought, or development: *everything is connected on the spiritual plane.*
▶ **adjective** [attrib.] completely level or flat.
■ of or relating to only two-dimensional surfaces or magnitudes: *plane and solid geometry.*
▶ **verb** [no obj., with adverbial of direction] (of a bird or an airborne object) soar without moving the wings; glide: *a bird planed down towards the water below.*
■ [no obj.] (of a boat, surfboard, etc.) skim over the surface of water as a result of lift produced hydrodynamically.
– ORIGIN early 17th cent.: from Latin *planum* 'flat surface', neuter of the adjective *planus* 'plain'. The adjective was suggested by French *plan(e)* 'flat'. The word was introduced to differentiate the geometrical senses, previously expressed by **PLAIN**[1], from the latter's other meanings.

plane[2] ▶ **noun** an aeroplane.
▶ **verb** [no obj., with adverbial of direction] rare travel in an aeroplane.
– ORIGIN early 20th cent.: shortened form.

plane[3] ▶ **noun** a tool consisting of a block with a projecting steel blade, used to smooth a wooden or other surface by paring shavings from it.
▶ **verb** [with obj.] smooth (wood or other material) with a plane.
■ [with obj. and adverbial] reduce or remove (redundant material) with a plane: *high areas can be* **planed down**.
■ archaic make smooth or level.
– ORIGIN Middle English: from a variant of obsolete French *plaine* 'planing instrument', from late Latin *plana* (in the same sense), from Latin *planare* 'make level', from *planus* 'plain, level'.

plane[4] (also **plane tree**) ▶ **noun** a tall spreading tree of the northern hemisphere, with maple-like leaves and bark which peels in uneven patches.
• Genus *Platanus*, family Platanaceae. See also **LONDON PLANE**, **CHINAR**.
– ORIGIN late Middle English: from Old French, from Latin *platanus*, from Greek *platanos*, from *platus* 'broad'.

plane polarization ▶ **noun** [mass noun] a process restricting the vibrations of electromagnetic radiation, especially light, to one direction.
– DERIVATIVES **plane-polarized** adjective.

planer ▶ **noun** another term for **PLANE**[3].

planesman ▶ **noun** (pl. **-men**) a person who operates the hydroplanes on a submarine.

planet ▶ **noun** a celestial body moving in an elliptical orbit round a star.
■ (**the planet**) the earth: *no generation has the right to pollute the planet.* ■ chiefly Astrology & historical a celestial body distinguished from the fixed stars by having an apparent motion of its own (including the moon and sun), especially with reference to its supposed influence on people and events.

The nine planets of the solar system are either gas giants—Jupiter, Saturn, Uranus, and Neptune—or smaller rocky bodies—Mercury, Venus, Earth, Mars, and Pluto. The minor planets or asteroids orbit mainly between the orbits of Mars and Jupiter.

– PHRASES **what planet are you on?** Brit. informal used to indicate that someone is out of touch with reality.
– DERIVATIVES **planetologist** noun, **planetology** noun.
– ORIGIN Middle English: from Old French *planete*,

from late Latin *planeta*, *planetes*, from Greek *planētēs* 'wanderer, planet', from *planan* 'wander'.

plane table ▶ **noun** a surveying instrument used for direct plotting in the field, with a circular drawing board and pivoted alidade.

planetarium /ˌplanɪˈtɛːrɪəm/ ▶ **noun** (pl. **planetariums** or **planetaria** /-rɪə/) **1** a domed building in which images of stars, planets, and constellations are projected for public entertainment or education.
■ a device used to project such images.
2 another term for **ORRERY**.
– ORIGIN mid 18th cent.: modern Latin, from Latin *planetarius* 'relating to the planets'.

planetary ▶ **adjective** of, relating, or belonging to a planet or planets.
■ of or relating to the earth as a planet.
– ORIGIN late 16th cent.: from late Latin *planetarius* 'relating to the planets' (recorded only as a noun meaning 'astrologer'), from *planeta* 'planet'.

planetary gear (also **planetary wheel**) ▶ **noun** another term for **PLANET GEAR**.

planetary nebula ▶ **noun** Astronomy a ring-shaped nebula formed by an expanding shell of gas round an ageing star.

planetesimal /ˌplanɪˈtɛsɪm(ə)l/ Astronomy ▶ **noun** a minute planet; a body which could come together with many others under gravitation to form a planet.
▶ **adjective** [attrib.] denoting or relating to such bodies.
– ORIGIN early 20th cent.: from **PLANET**, on the pattern of *infinitesimal*.

planetfall ▶ **noun** [mass noun] (chiefly in science fiction) a landing or arrival on a planet after a journey through space.

planet gear (also **planet wheel**) ▶ **noun** see **SUN-AND-PLANET GEAR**.

planetoid ▶ **noun** another term for **ASTEROID**.

planform ▶ **noun** the shape or outline of an aircraft wing as projected upon a horizontal plane.

plangent /ˈplan(d)ʒ(ə)nt/ ▶ **adjective** chiefly poetic/literary (of a sound) loud, reverberating, and often melancholy.
– DERIVATIVES **plangency** noun, **plangently** adverb.
– ORIGIN early 19th cent.: from Latin *plangent-* 'lamenting', from the verb *plangere*.

planification /ˌplanɪfɪˈkeɪʃ(ə)n/ ▶ **noun** [mass noun] the management of resources according to a plan of economic or political development.
– ORIGIN 1950s: from French *planifier* 'to plan' (see **-FICATION**).

planigale /ˈplanɪgeɪl, ˌplanɪˈgeɪli/ ▶ **noun** a very small mouse-like carnivorous marsupial with a long tail, native to Australia and New Guinea.
• Genus *Planigale*, family Dasyuridae: several species.
– ORIGIN 1940s: modern Latin, from Latin *planus* 'flat' (referring to the flat skull of the marsupial), on the pattern of *phascogale*.

planigraphy /pləˈnɪgrəfi/ ▶ **noun** [mass noun] Medicine the process of obtaining a visual representation of a plane section through living tissue, by such techniques as tomography, ultrasonography, etc.
– ORIGIN 1930s: from Dutch *planigraphie*, from Latin *planus* 'flat, level' + Greek *-graphia* (see **-GRAPHY**).

planimeter /pləˈnɪmɪtə/ ▶ **noun** an instrument for mechanically measuring the area of a plane figure.
– DERIVATIVES **planimetric** adjective, **planimetrically** adverb, **planimetry** noun.
– ORIGIN mid 19th cent.: from French *planimètre*, from Latin *planus* 'level' + *-mètre* '(instrument) measuring'.

planish /ˈplanɪʃ/ ▶ **verb** [with obj.] flatten (sheet metal) with a smooth-faced hammer or between rollers.
– DERIVATIVES **planisher** noun.
– ORIGIN late Middle English (in the sense 'make level'): from obsolete French *planiss-*, lengthened stem of *planir* 'to smooth', from *plain* 'smooth, level'.

planisphere /ˈplanɪsfɪə/ ▶ **noun** a map formed by the projection of a sphere or part of a sphere on a plane, especially an adjustable circular star map that shows the appearance of the heavens at a specific time and place.
– DERIVATIVES **planispheric** /-ˈsfɛrɪk/ adjective.
– ORIGIN late Middle English *planisperie*, from medieval Latin *planisphaerium*, from Latin *planus* 'level' + *sphaera* 'sphere'; later influenced by French *planisphère*.

plank ▶ **noun 1** a long, thin, flat piece of timber, used especially in building and flooring.
2 a fundamental point of a political or other programme: *the central plank of the bill is the curb on industrial polluters.*
▶ **verb** [with obj.] **1** make, provide, or cover with planks: [as adj. **planked**] *the planked wooden steps.*
2 informal, chiefly N. Amer. & Irish put or set (something) down forcefully or abruptly: *he planked the glasses in front of him.*
■ (**plank oneself down**) sit down in a hurried or undignified way.
3 Scottish hide (something): *he had planked £1,000 under the mattress.* [ORIGIN: alteration of the verb **PLANT**.]
– PHRASES **walk the plank** (formerly) be forced by pirates to walk blindfold along a plank over the side of a ship to one's death in the sea. ■ informal lose one's job or position.
– ORIGIN Middle English: from Old Northern French *planke*, from late Latin *planca* 'board', feminine (used as a noun) of *plancus* 'flat-footed'.

plank bed ▶ **noun** a bed consisting of wooden boards, typically a prison bed without a mattress.

planking ▶ **noun** [mass noun] planks collectively, especially when used for flooring or as part of a boat.

plankton /ˈplaŋ(k)t(ə)n, -tɒn/ ▶ **noun** [mass noun] the small and microscopic organisms drifting or floating in the sea or fresh water, consisting chiefly of diatoms, protozoans, small crustaceans, and the eggs and larval stages of larger animals. Many animals are adapted to feed on plankton, especially by filtering the water. Compare with **NEKTON**.
– DERIVATIVES **planktic** adjective, **planktonic** adjective.
– ORIGIN late 19th cent.: from German, from Greek *planktos* 'wandering', from the base of *plazein* 'wander'.

planned economy ▶ **noun** an economy in which production, investment, prices, and incomes are determined centrally by the government.

planned obsolescence ▶ **noun** [mass noun] a policy of producing consumer goods that rapidly become obsolete and so require replacing, achieved by frequent changes in design, termination of the supply of spare parts, and the use of non-durable materials.

planner ▶ **noun 1** a person who makes plans.
■ a person who controls or plans urban development: *city planners.*
2 [usu. with modifier] a list or chart with information that is an aid to planning: *my day planner.*

planning ▶ **noun** [mass noun] the process of making plans for something.
■ [often as modifier] the control of urban development by a local government authority, from which a licence must be obtained to build a new property or change an existing one: *planning applications.*

planning blight ▶ **noun** [mass noun] the reduction of economic activity or property values in a particular area resulting from expected or possible future development or restriction of development.

planning gain ▶ **noun** [mass noun] provision by a developer to include in a proposal projects beneficial to a community in exchange for permission for a commercially promising but potentially unacceptable development.

planning permission ▶ **noun** [mass noun] Brit. formal permission from a local authority for the erection or alteration of buildings or similar development.

plano- /ˈpleɪnəʊ/ ▶ **combining form** level; flat: *planoconvex* | *planometer.*
– ORIGIN from Latin *planus* 'flat'.

planoconcave ▶ **adjective** (of a lens) with one surface plane and the opposite one concave.

planoconvex ▶ **adjective** (of a lens) with one surface plane and the opposite one convex.

planographic ▶ **adjective** Printing relating to or denoting a printing process in which the printing surface is flat, as in lithography.
– DERIVATIVES **planography** noun.

planometer /pləˈnɒmɪtə/ ▶ **noun** a flat plate, typically of cast iron, used in metalwork as a standard gauge for plane surfaces.

plant ▶ **noun 1** a living organism of the kind exemplified by trees, shrubs, herbs, grasses, ferns, and mosses, typically growing in a permanent site, absorbing water and inorganic substances through their roots, and synthesizing nutrients in their leaves by photosynthesis using the green pigment chlorophyll.
■ a small organism of this kind, as distinct from a shrub or tree: *garden plants.*

> Plants differ from animals in lacking specialized sense organs, having no capacity for voluntary movement, having cell walls, and growing to suit their surroundings rather than having a fixed body plan.

2 a place where an industrial or manufacturing process takes place: *a giant car plant.*
■ [mass noun] machinery used in an industrial or manufacturing process: *inadequate investment in new plant.*
3 a person placed in a group as a spy or informer: *we thought he was a CIA plant spreading disinformation.*
■ a thing put among someone's belongings to incriminate or compromise them.
4 Snooker a shot in which the cue ball is made to strike one of two touching or nearly touching balls with the result that the second is potted.
▶ **verb** [with obj.] **1** place (a seed, bulb, or plant) in the ground so that it can grow.
■ place a seed, bulb, or plant in (a place) to grow: *the garden is planted with herbs.* ■ (**plant something out**) place a plant in the ground out of doors so it can grow, especially after growing it from seed in an indoor environment. ■ informal bury (someone).
2 [with obj. and adverbial of place] place or fix in a specified position: *she planted a kiss on his cheek.*
■ (**plant oneself**) position oneself: *she planted herself on the arm of his chair.* ■ establish (an idea) in someone's mind: *the seed of doubt is planted in his mind.* ■ secretly place (a bomb that is set to go off at a later time). ■ put or hide (something) among someone's belongings to compromise or incriminate the owner: *he planted cannabis on him to extort a bribe.* ■ send (someone) to join a group or organization to act as a spy or informer. ■ found or establish (a colony, city, or community). ■ deposit (young fish, spawn, oysters, etc.) in a river or lake.
– PHRASES **have** (or **keep**) **one's feet firmly planted on the ground** be (or remain) level-headed and sensible.
– DERIVATIVES **plantable** adjective, **plantlet** noun, **plant-like** adjective.
– ORIGIN Old English *plante* 'seedling', *plantian* (verb), from Latin *planta* 'sprout, cutting' (later influenced by French *plante*) and *plantare* 'plant, fix in a place'.

Plantagenet /planˈtadʒɪnɪt/ ▶ **adjective** of or relating to the English royal dynasty which held the throne from the accession of Henry II in 1154 until the death of Richard III in 1485.
▶ **noun** a member of this dynasty.
– ORIGIN from Latin *planta genista* 'sprig of broom', said to be worn as a crest by and given as a nickname to Geoffrey, count of Anjou, the father of Henry II.

plantain[1] /ˈplantɪn, -teɪn/ ▶ **noun** a low-growing plant which typically has a rosette of leaves and a slender green flower spike, occurring widely as a weed of lawns.
• Genus *Plantago*, family Plantaginaceae: many species.
– ORIGIN late Middle English: from Old French, from Latin *plantago*, *plantagin-*, from *planta* 'sole of the foot' (because of its broad prostrate leaves).

plantain[2] /ˈplantɪn, -teɪn/ ▶ **noun 1** a banana containing high levels of starch and little sugar, which is harvested green and widely used as a cooked vegetable in the tropics.
2 the plant which bears this fruit.
• *Musa* × *paradisiaca*, family Musaceae.
– ORIGIN mid 16th cent.: from Spanish *plá(n)tano*, probably by assimilation of a South American word to the Spanish *plá(n)tano* 'plane tree'.

plantain-eater ▶ **noun** an African bird of the turaco family, especially a grey one with a long tail.
• Family Musophagidae, in particular two species in the genus *Crinifer*.

plantain lily ▶ **noun** another term for **HOSTA**.

plantar /ˈplantə/ ▶ **adjective** Anatomy of or relating to the sole of the foot.
– ORIGIN early 18th cent.: from Latin *plantaris*, from *planta* 'sole'.

plantation ▶ **noun** [often with modifier] an estate on which crops such as coffee, sugar, and tobacco are grown.
■ an area in which trees have been planted, especially for commercial purposes. ■ [mass noun] (often

Plantation) colonization or the settlement of emigrants, especially of English and then Scottish families in Ireland in the 16th–17th centuries under government sponsorship. ■ historical a colony.
– ORIGIN late Middle English (denoting the action of planting seeds): from Latin *plantatio(n-)*, from the verb *plantare* 'to plant'.

plantation song ▶ **noun** a song of the kind formerly sung by black slaves on American plantations.

planter ▶ **noun 1** [often with modifier] a manager or owner of a plantation: *sugar planters*.
2 a decorative container in which plants are grown.
3 a machine or person that plants seeds, bulbs, etc.

planter's punch ▶ **noun** a cocktail containing rum.

plant geography ▶ **noun** another term for **PHYTOGEOGRAPHY**.

plant hopper ▶ **noun** a small widely distributed plant-sucking bug that leaps when disturbed. Some kinds are pests of rice and sugar cane.
● Delphacidae and other families, suborder Homoptera.

plantigrade /ˈplantɪɡreɪd/ ▶ **adjective** (of a mammal) walking on the soles of the feet, like a human or a bear. Compare with **DIGITIGRADE**.
– ORIGIN mid 19th cent.: from French, from modern Latin *plantigradus*, from Latin *planta* 'sole' + *-gradus* '-walking'.

plant louse ▶ **noun** a small bug that infests plants and feeds on the sap or tender shoots, especially an aphid.
● Several families in the series Sternorrhyncha, suborder Homoptera. See also **JUMPING PLANT LOUSE**.

plantocracy /plɑːnˈtɒkrəsi/ ▶ **noun** (pl. **-ies**) a population of planters regarded as the dominant class, especially in the West Indies.

plantsman ▶ **noun** (pl. **-men**) an expert in garden plants and gardening.

plantswoman ▶ **noun** (pl. **-women**) a female expert in garden plants and gardening.

planula /ˈplanjʊlə/ ▶ **noun** (pl. **planulae** /-liː/) Zoology a free-swimming coelenterate larva with a flattened, ciliated, solid body.
– ORIGIN late 19th cent.: modern Latin, diminutive of Latin *planus* 'plane, flat'.

plan view ▶ **noun** a view of an object as projected on a horizontal plane.

plaque /plak, plɑːk/ ▶ **noun 1** an ornamental tablet, typically of metal, porcelain, or wood, that is fixed to a wall or other surface in commemoration of a person or event.
■ a flat counter used in gambling.
2 [mass noun] a sticky deposit on teeth in which bacteria proliferate.
3 Medicine a small, distinct, typically raised patch or region resulting from local damage or deposition of material, such as a fatty deposit on an artery wall in atherosclerosis or a site of localized damage of brain tissue in Alzheimer's disease.
■ Microbiology a clear area in a cell culture caused by the inhibition of growth or destruction of cells by an agent such as a virus.
– DERIVATIVES **plaquette** /plaˈkɛt/ noun.
– ORIGIN mid 19th cent.: from French, from Dutch *plak* 'tablet', from *plakken* 'to stick'.

plash[1] poetic/literary ▶ **noun** [in sing.] a sound produced by liquid striking something or being struck.
■ a pool or puddle.
▶ **verb** [no obj.] splash: *grey curtains of rain plashed down.*
■ [with obj.] strike the surface of (water) with a splashing sound.
– DERIVATIVES **plashy** adjective.
– ORIGIN early 16th cent.: probably imitative.

plash[2] ▶ **verb** [with obj.] archaic bend down and interweave (branches and twigs) to form a hedge.
■ make or renew (a hedge) in this way.
– ORIGIN late 15th cent.: from Old French *plaissier*, based on Latin *plectere* 'to plait'. Compare with **PLEACH**.

plasma /ˈplazmə/ (also **plasm** /ˈplaz(ə)m/) ▶ **noun** [mass noun] **1** the colourless fluid part of blood, lymph, or milk, in which corpuscles or fat globules are suspended.
■ this substance taken from donors or donated blood for administering in transfusions.
2 an ionized gas consisting of positive ions and free electrons in proportions resulting in more or less no overall electric charge, typically at low pressures (as in the upper atmosphere and in fluorescent lamps) or at very high temperatures (as in stars and nuclear fusion reactors).
■ an analogous substance consisting of mobile charged particles (such as a molten salt or the electrons within a metal).
3 a bright green, translucent variety of quartz used in mosaic and for other decorative purposes.
4 another term for **CYTOPLASM** or **PROTOPLASM**.
– DERIVATIVES **plasmatic** adjective, **plasmic** adjective.
– ORIGIN early 18th cent. (in the sense 'mould, shape'): from late Latin, literally 'mould', from Greek *plasma*, from *plassein* 'to shape'.

plasma cell ▶ **noun** Physiology a fully differentiated B-lymphocyte (white blood cell) which produces a single type of antibody.

plasmalemma /ˈplazməˌlɛmə/ ▶ **noun** Biology a plasma membrane which bounds a cell, especially one immediately within the wall of a plant cell.
– DERIVATIVES **plasmalemmal** adjective.
– ORIGIN 1920s: from **PLASMA** + Greek *lemma* 'rind'.

plasma membrane ▶ **noun** Biology a microscopic membrane of lipids and proteins which forms the external boundary of the cytoplasm of a cell or encloses a vacuole, and regulates the passage of molecules in and out of the cytoplasm.

plasmapause ▶ **noun** Astronomy the outer limit of a plasmasphere, marked by a sudden change in plasma density.

plasmapheresis /ˌplazməˈfɛrɪsɪs, -fəˈriːsɪs/ ▶ **noun** [mass noun] Medicine a method of removing blood plasma from the body by withdrawing blood, separating it into plasma and cells, and transfusing the cells back into the bloodstream. It is performed especially to remove antibodies in treating autoimmune conditions.
– ORIGIN 1920s: from **PLASMA** + Greek *aphairesis* 'taking away' (from *apo-* 'from' + *hairein* 'take').

plasma sheet ▶ **noun** Astronomy a layer of plasma in the magnetotail of the earth (or another planet), lying in the equatorial plane beyond the plasmapause, with two divergent branches that reach the earth at polar latitudes.

plasmasphere ▶ **noun** Astronomy the roughly toroidal region surrounding and thought to rotate with the earth (or another planet) at latitudes away from the poles, containing a relatively dense plasma of low-energy electrons and protons.

plasmid /ˈplazmɪd/ ▶ **noun** Biology a genetic structure in a cell that can replicate independently of the chromosomes, typically a small circular DNA strand in the cytoplasm of a bacterium or protozoan. Plasmids are much used in the laboratory manipulation of genes. Compare with **EPISOME**.
– ORIGIN 1950s: from **PLASMA** + **-ID**[2].

plasmin /ˈplazmɪn/ ▶ **noun** [mass noun] Biochemistry an enzyme, formed in the blood in some circumstances, which destroys blood clots by attacking fibrin.
– ORIGIN mid 19th cent.: from French *plasmine*, from late Latin *plasma* 'mould, image'.

plasminogen /plazˈmɪnədʒ(ə)n/ ▶ **noun** [mass noun] Biochemistry the inactive precursor of the enzyme plasmin, present in blood.

plasmodesma /ˌplazmə(ʊ)ˈdɛzmə/ ▶ **noun** (pl. **plasmodesmata** /-mətə/) Botany a narrow thread of cytoplasm that passes through the cell walls of adjacent plant cells and allows communication between them.
– ORIGIN early 20th cent.: from German *Plasmodesma*, from late Latin *plasma* 'mould, formation' + Greek *desma* 'bond, fetter'.

plasmodium /plazˈməʊdɪəm/ ▶ **noun** (pl. **plasmodia** /-dɪə/) **1** a parasitic protozoan of a genus which includes those causing malaria.
● Genus *Plasmodium*, phylum Sporozoa.
2 Biology a form within the life cycle of some simple organisms such as slime moulds, typically consisting of a mass of naked protoplasm containing many nuclei.
– DERIVATIVES **plasmodial** adjective.
– ORIGIN late 19th cent.: modern Latin, based on late Latin *plasma* 'mould, formation'.

plasmolyse /ˈplazməlʌɪz/ (US **plasmolyze**) ▶ **verb** [with obj.] Botany subject to plasmolysis.

plasmolysis /plazˈmɒlɪsɪs/ ▶ **noun** [mass noun] Botany contraction of the protoplast of a plant cell as a result of loss of water from the cell.
– ORIGIN late 19th cent.: modern Latin, from *plasmo-* 'consisting of protoplasm' (from late Latin *plasma* 'mould, formation') + Greek *lusis* 'loosening' (because of the separation of the plasma membrane from the cell wall).

plasmon /ˈplazmɒn/ ▶ **noun** Physics a quantum or quasiparticle associated with a local collective oscillation of charge density.
– ORIGIN 1950s: from **PLASMA** + **-ON**.

Plassey /ˈplasi/ a village in NE India, in West Bengal, north-west of Calcutta. It was the scene in 1757 of a battle in which a small British army under Robert Clive defeated the forces of the nawab of Bengal, establishing British supremacy in Bengal.

plasteel /ˈplastiːl/ ▶ **noun** [mass noun] (in science fiction) an ultra-strong non-metallic material.
– ORIGIN 1970s: blend of **PLASTIC** and **STEEL**.

plaster ▶ **noun** [mass noun] **1** a soft mixture of lime with sand or cement and water for spreading on walls, ceilings, or other structures to form a smooth hard surface when dried.
■ (also **plaster of Paris**) a hard white substance made by the addition of water to powdered and partly dehydrated gypsum, used for holding broken bones in place and making sculptures and casts. ■ the powder from which such a substance is made.
2 (also **sticking plaster**) an adhesive strip of material for covering cuts and wounds.
■ dated a bandage on which a poultice or liniment is spread for application. See **MUSTARD PLASTER**.
▶ **verb** [with obj.] cover (a wall, ceiling, or other structure) with plaster.
■ (**plaster something with/in**) coat or cover something with (a substance), especially to an extent considered excessive: *a face plastered in heavy make-up*. ■ [with obj. and adverbial] make (hair) lie flat by applying a liquid to it: *his hair was plastered down with water.* ■ apply a plaster cast or medical plaster to (a part of the body). ■ (**plaster something with**) cover a surface with (large numbers of pictures or posters): *the shop's windows are plastered with posters.* ■ (**plaster something over**) present a story or picture conspicuously and sensationally in (a newspaper or magazine): *her story was plastered all over the December issue.* ■ informal, dated bomb or shell (a target) heavily.
– DERIVATIVES **plastery** adjective.
– ORIGIN Old English, denoting a bandage spread with a curative substance, from medieval Latin *plastrum* (shortening of Latin *emplastrum*, from Greek *emplastron* 'daub, salve'), later reinforced by the Old French noun *plastre*. Sense 1 dates from late Middle English.

plasterboard ▶ **noun** [mass noun] board made of plaster set between two sheets of paper, used especially to form or line the inner walls of houses.

plaster cast ▶ **noun** see **CAST**[1] (sense 1).

plastered ▶ **adjective 1** informal very drunk: *I went out and got totally plastered.*
2 covered with or made of plaster.

plasterer ▶ **noun** a person whose job it is to apply plaster to walls, ceilings, or other structures.

plaster of Paris ▶ **noun** see **PLASTER** (sense 1).

plaster saint ▶ **noun** a person who makes a show of being without moral faults or human weakness, especially in a hypocritical way.

plasterwork ▶ **noun** [mass noun] plaster as part of the interior of a building, especially covering the surface of a wall or formed into decorative shapes and patterns.

plastic ▶ **noun** [mass noun] a synthetic material made from a wide range of organic polymers such as polyethylene, PVC, nylon, etc., that can be moulded into shape while soft, and then set into a rigid or slightly elastic form.
■ informal credit cards or other types of plastic card that can be used as money: *he pays with cash instead of with plastic.*
▶ **adjective 1** made of plastic: *plastic bags.*
■ looking or tasting artificial: *long-distance flights with their plastic food | she smiled a little plastic smile.*
2 (of substances or materials) easily shaped or moulded: *rendering the material more plastic.*
■ (in art) of or relating to moulding or modelling in three dimensions, or to produce three-dimensional effects. ■ (in science and technology) of or relating to the permanent deformation of a solid without fracture by the temporary application of force. ■ offering scope for creativity: *the writer is drawn to words as a plastic medium.* ■ Biology exhibiting

p

adaptability to change or variety in the environment.
– DERIVATIVES **plastically** adverb.
– ORIGIN mid 17th cent. (in the sense 'characteristic of moulding'): from French *plastique* or Latin *plasticus*, from Greek *plastikos*, from *plassein* 'to mould'.

plastic arts ▶ plural noun art forms that involve modelling or moulding, such as sculpture and ceramics, or art involving the representation of solid objects with three-dimensional effects.

plastic bomb ▶ noun a bomb containing plastic explosive.

plastic bullet ▶ noun a bullet made of PVC or another plastic material, typically used by security and police forces for riot control.

plastic explosive ▶ noun [mass noun] a putty-like explosive capable of being moulded by hand.

plasticine (also **Plasticine**) ▶ noun [mass noun] trademark a soft modelling material, used especially by children.
– ORIGIN late 19th cent.: from the adjective **PLASTIC** + **-INE**[4].

plasticity ▶ noun [mass noun] the quality of being easily shaped or moulded.
■ Biology the adaptability of an organism to changes in its environment or differences between its various habitats.

plasticize ▶ verb [with obj.] [often as adj. **plasticized**] make plastic or mouldable, especially by the addition of a plasticizer.
■ treat or make with plastic: *plasticized cotton*.
– DERIVATIVES **plasticization** noun.

plasticizer ▶ noun a substance (typically a solvent) added to a synthetic resin to produce or promote plasticity and flexibility and to reduce brittleness.

plasticky ▶ adjective resembling plastic.
■ seeming artificial or of inferior quality.

plastic surgery ▶ noun [mass noun] the process of reconstructing or repairing parts of the body by the transfer of tissue, either in the treatment of injury or for cosmetic reasons.
– DERIVATIVES **plastic surgeon** noun.

plastic wood ▶ noun [mass noun] a mouldable material which hardens to resemble wood and is used for filling cracks in wood.

plastic wrap ▶ noun North American term for **CLING FILM**.

plastid /'plastɪd/ ▶ noun Botany any of a class of small organelles in the cytoplasm of plant cells, containing pigment or food.
– ORIGIN late 19th cent.: from German, based on Greek *plastos* 'shaped'.

plastique /pla'sti:k/ ▶ noun [mass noun] plastic explosive.
– ORIGIN mid 20th cent.: French, literally 'plastic' (adjective used as a noun).

plastisol /'plastɪsɒl/ ▶ noun a liquid substance which can be converted into a solid plastic simply by heating, consisting of particles of synthetic resin dispersed in a non-volatile liquid.
– ORIGIN 1940s: from the noun **PLASTIC** + **SOL**[2].

plastron /'plastrən/ ▶ noun **1** a large pad worn by a fencer to protect the chest.
■ a lancer's breast covering of facings material.
2 an ornamental front of a women's bodice or shirt consisting of colourful material with lace or embroidery, fashionable in the late 19th century.
■ a man's starched shirt front without pleats.
3 Zoology the part of a tortoise's or turtle's shell forming the underside.
■ a similar ventral plate in some invertebrate animals. ■ Entomology (in an aquatic insect) a patch of cuticle covered with hairs which retain a thin layer of air that acts like a gill for breathing under water.
– DERIVATIVES **plastral** adjective.
– ORIGIN early 16th cent.: from French, from Italian *piastrone*, augmentative of *piastra* 'breastplate', from Latin *emplastrum* 'a plaster' (see **PLASTER**).

-plasty ▶ combining form moulding, grafting, or formation of a specified part, especially a part of the body: *rhinoplasty*.
– ORIGIN based on Greek *plastos* 'formed, moulded'.

plat[1] N. Amer. ▶ noun a plot of land.
■ a map or plan of an area of land showing actual or proposed features.
▶ verb [with obj.] plan out or make a map of (an area of land, especially a proposed site for construction).
– ORIGIN late Middle English: variant of the noun **PLOT** in the sense 'piece of ground'. The current verb sense dates from the early 18th cent.

plat[2] ▶ noun & verb variant spelling of **PLAIT**.

Plataea, Battle of /plə'ti:ə/ a battle in 479 BC, during the Persian Wars, in which the Persian forces were defeated by the Greeks near the city of Plataea in Boeotia.

platan /'plat(ə)n/ ▶ noun poetic/literary a plane tree.
– ORIGIN late Middle English: via Latin from Greek *platanos* 'plane tree'.

platanna /plə'tanə/ ▶ noun South African term for **CLAWED TOAD**.
– ORIGIN mid 19th cent.: from Afrikaans, apparently from Dutch *plat* 'flat' + *-hander*, literally 'handed one'.

plat du jour /ˌplɑ: d(j)u: 'ʒʊə, French pla dy ʒuʀ/ ▶ noun (pl. **plats du jour** pronunc. same) a dish specially prepared by a restaurant on a particular day, in addition to the usual menu.
– ORIGIN French, literally 'dish of the day'.

plate ▶ noun **1** a flat dish, typically circular and made of china, from which food is eaten or served.
■ an amount of food on such a dish: *a plate of spaghetti*. ■ a similar dish, typically made of metal or wood, passed round a church congregation in order to collect donations of money. ■ N. Amer. a main course of a meal, served on one plate: *he recommended the roast beef plate*. ■ Austral./NZ a plate of food contributed by a guest to a social gathering: *he was invited to a party and asked to bring a plate*. ■ Biology a shallow glass dish on which a culture of cells or micro-organisms may be grown. ■ [mass noun] dishes, bowls, cups, and other utensils made of gold, silver, or other metal. [ORIGIN: from Old French *vaisselle en plate* 'dishes and plates made of a single piece of metal'.] ■ a silver or gold dish or trophy awarded as a prize in a race or competition: *she lifted the plate in victory*. ■ [in names] a race or competition in which such a prize is awarded: *the final of the Ladies' Plate at Henley*.
2 a thin, flat sheet or strip of metal or other material, typically one used to join or strengthen things or forming part of a machine: *he underwent surgery to have a steel plate put into his leg*.
■ a small, flat piece of metal or other material bearing a name or inscription and attached to a door or other object: *a discreet brass plate announced William Marsden, RA*. ■ (usu. **plates**) short for **NUMBER PLATE**. ■ Botany & Zoology a thin, flat organic structure or formation: *the fused bony plates protect the tortoise's soft parts*. ■ Geology each of the several rigid pieces of the earth's lithosphere which together make up the earth's surface. (See also **PLATE TECTONICS**.) ■ Baseball short for **HOME PLATE**. ■ a horizontal timber laid along the top of a wall to support the ends of joists or rafters. ■ a light horseshoe for a racehorse.
3 a sheet of metal, plastic, or some other material bearing an image of type or illustrations from which multiple copies are printed.
■ a printed photograph, picture, or illustration, especially one on superior-quality paper in a book. ■ a thin sheet of metal, glass, or other substance coated with a light-sensitive film on which an image is formed, used in larger or older types of camera.
4 a thin piece of plastic moulded to the shape of a person's mouth and gums, to which artificial teeth or another orthodontic appliance are attached.
■ informal a complete denture or orthodontic appliance.
5 a thin piece of metal that acts as an electrode in a capacitor, battery, or cell.
■ N. Amer. the anode of a thermionic valve.
▶ verb [with obj.] **1** cover (a metal object) with a thin coating or film of a different metal.
■ cover (an object) with plates of metal for decoration, protection, or strength.
2 serve or arrange (food) on a plate or plates before a meal: *overcooked vegetables won't look appetizing, no matter how they are plated*.
3 Baseball score or cause to score (a run or runs).
4 Biology inoculate (cells or infective material) on to a culture plate, especially with the object of isolating a particular strain of micro-organisms or estimating viable cell numbers.
– PHRASES **on a plate** informal used to indicate that someone has achieved something with little or no effort. **on one's plate** chiefly Brit. occupying one's time or energy: *you've got a lot on your plate at the moment*. **plates of meat** rhyming slang a person's feet.
– DERIVATIVES **plateful** noun (pl. **-fuls**), **plateless** adjective, **plater** noun.
– ORIGIN Middle English (denoting a flat, thin sheet, usually of metal): from Old French, from medieval Latin *plata* 'plate armour', based on Greek *platus* 'flat'. Sense 1 represents Old French *plat* 'platter, large dish', also 'dish of meat', noun use of Old French *plat* 'flat'.

Plate, River /pleɪt/ a wide estuary on the Atlantic coast of South America at the border between Argentina and Uruguay, formed by the confluence of the Rivers Paraná and Uruguay. The cities of Buenos Aires and Montevideo lie on its shores. In 1939 it was the scene of a naval battle in which the British defeated the Germans. Spanish name **Río de la Plata**.
– ORIGIN *Plate* from Spanish *plata* 'silver', exported from the region in the Spanish colonial period.

plate armour ▶ noun [mass noun] protective armour of metal plates, especially as worn in medieval times by mounted knights.

plateau /'platəʊ/ ▶ noun (pl. **plateaux** /-təʊz/ or **plateaus**) an area of fairly level high ground.
■ figurative a state of little or no change following a period of activity or progress: *the peace process had reached a plateau*. ■ [as modifier] denoting a group of American Indian peoples of the high plains of western Canada and the US, including the Nez Percé.
▶ verb (**plateaus**, **plateaued**, **plateauing**) [no obj.] reach a state of little or no change after a time of activity or progress: *the industry's problems have plateaued out*.
– ORIGIN late 18th cent.: from French, from Old French *platel*, diminutive of *plat* 'level'.

plate glass ▶ noun [mass noun] [often as modifier] thick fine-quality glass, typically used for shop windows and doors and originally cast in plates.

platelayer ▶ noun Brit. a person employed in laying and maintaining railway track.

platelet ▶ noun Physiology a small colourless disc-shaped cell fragment without a nucleus, found in large numbers in blood and involved in clotting. Also called **THROMBOCYTE**.

platemaker ▶ noun a person or machine that makes printing plates.

platen /'plat(ə)n/ ▶ noun **1** the plate in a small letterpress printing press which presses the paper against the type.
2 the cylindrical roller in a typewriter against which the paper is held.
– ORIGIN late 16th cent.: from French *platine* 'flat piece' from *plat* 'flat'.

plate number ▶ noun a serial number in the margin of a plate from which postage stamps are printed.

plate rack ▶ noun Brit. a rack in which plates are stored or placed to drain after being washed.

plateresque /ˌplatə'rɛsk/ ▶ adjective (especially of Spanish architecture) richly ornamented in a style suggesting silverware.
– ORIGIN late 19th cent.: from Spanish *plateresco*, from *platero* 'silversmith', from *plata* 'silver'.

plate tectonics ▶ plural noun [treated as sing.] a theory explaining the structure of the earth's crust and many associated phenomena as resulting from the interaction of rigid lithospheric plates which move slowly over the underlying mantle.

plate tracery ▶ noun [mass noun] Architecture tracery with perforations in otherwise continuous stone.

platform ▶ noun **1** a raised level surface on which people or things can stand: *there are viewing platforms where visitors may gape at the chasm*.
■ a raised floor or stage used by public speakers or performers so that they can be seen by their audience: *earning her living on the concert platform*. ■ a raised structure along the side of a railway track where passengers get on and off trains at a station. ■ chiefly Brit. the raised floor area at the entrance to a bus. ■ a raised structure standing in the sea from which oil or gas wells can be drilled or regulated. ■ [usu. with modifier] a raised structure or orbiting satellite from which rockets or missiles may be launched. ■ Computing a standard for the hardware of a computer system, which determines what kinds of software it can run.
2 [usu. in sing.] the declared policy of a political party or group: *seeking election on a platform of low taxes*.
■ an opportunity to voice one's views or initiate action: *the forum will provide a platform for discussion of communication issues*.
3 (**platforms**) shoes with very thick soles: *chunky platforms* | [as modifier] *yellow platform shoes*.

– ORIGIN mid 16th cent.: from French *plateforme* 'ground plan', literally 'flat shape'.

platformer ▶**noun** informal term for **PLATFORM GAME**.

platform game ▶**noun** a type of video game featuring two-dimensional graphics where the player controls a character jumping or climbing between solid platforms at different positions on the screen.

platform ticket ▶**noun** Brit. historical a ticket allowing a non-traveller access to a railway station platform.

Plath /plaθ/, Sylvia (1932–63), American poet, wife of Ted Hughes. Her work is notable for its treatment of extreme and painful states of mind. In 1963 she committed suicide. Notable works: *Ariel* (poems, 1965) and *The Bell Jar* (novel, 1963).

plating ▶**noun** [mass noun] **1** a thin coating of gold, silver, or other metal.
■the process of applying such a layer.
2 an outer covering of broad, flattish sections, typically of metal: *the tractors carried steel plating for protection.*
3 the process of knitting two yarns together so that each yarn appears mainly on one side of the finished piece.
4 the racing of horses in which the prize for the winner is a plate.

platinize /ˈplatɪnʌɪz/ (also **-ise**) ▶**verb** [with obj.] [usu. as adj. **platinized**] coat (something) with platinum.
– DERIVATIVES **platinization** noun.

platinoid /ˈplatɪnɔɪd/ ▶**noun** [mass noun] an alloy of copper with zinc, nickel, and sometimes tungsten, used for its high electrical resistance.

platinum /ˈplatɪnəm/ ▶**noun** [mass noun] a precious silvery-white metal, the chemical element of atomic number 78. It was first encountered by the Spanish in South America in the 16th century, and is used in jewellery, electrical contacts, laboratory equipment, and industrial catalysts. (Symbol: **Pt**)
■[as modifier] greyish-white or silvery like platinum: *a platinum wig.*
– PHRASES **go platinum** (of a recording) achieve sales meriting a platinum disc.
– ORIGIN early 19th cent.: alteration of earlier *platina*, from Spanish, diminutive of *plata* 'silver'.

platinum black ▶**noun** [mass noun] platinum in the form of a finely divided black powder, used as a catalyst and absorbent for gases.

platinum blonde ▶**noun** a woman with silvery-blonde hair.
▶**adjective** (of a woman's hair) silvery-blonde.

platinum disc ▶**noun** a framed platinum disc awarded to a recording artist or group for sales of a record exceeding a specified high figure.

platinum metals ▶**plural noun** Chemistry the six metals platinum, palladium, ruthenium, osmium, rhodium, and iridium, which have similar properties and tend to occur together in nature.

platitude /ˈplatɪtjuːd/ ▶**noun** a remark or statement, especially one with a moral content, that has been used too often to be interesting or thoughtful: *she began uttering liberal platitudes.*
– DERIVATIVES **platitudinize** (also **-ise**) verb, **platitudinous** adjective.
– ORIGIN early 19th cent.: from French, from *plat* 'flat'.

Plato /ˈpleɪtəʊ/ (*c.*429–*c.*347 BC), Greek philosopher.

A disciple of Socrates and the teacher of Aristotle, he founded the Academy in Athens. An integral part of his thought is the theory of 'ideas' or 'forms', in which abstract entities or **universals** are contrasted with their objects or **particulars** in the material world. His philosophical writings are presented in the form of dialogues, with Socrates as the principal speaker; they include the *Symposium* and the *Timaeus*. Plato's political theories appear in the *Republic*, in which he explored the nature and structure of a just society.

Platonic /pləˈtɒnɪk/ ▶**adjective** of or associated with the Greek philosopher Plato or his ideas.
■(**platonic**) (of love or friendship) intimate and affectionate but not sexual: *their relationship is purely platonic.* ■ (**platonic**) confined to words, theories, or ideals, and not leading to practical action.
– DERIVATIVES **platonically** adverb.
– ORIGIN mid 16th cent.: via Latin from Greek *Platōnikos*, from *Platōn* 'Plato'.

Platonic solid (also **Platonic body**) ▶**noun** one of five regular solids (a tetrahedron, cube, octahedron, dodecahedron, or icosahedron).

Platonism /ˈpleɪt(ə)nɪz(ə)m/ ▶**noun** [mass noun] the philosophy of Plato or his followers. See **PLATO**.
■any of various revivals of Platonic doctrines or related ideas, especially Neoplatonism and Cambridge Platonism (a 17th-century attempt to reconcile Christianity with humanism and science). ■ the theory that numbers or other abstract objects are objective, timeless entities, independent of the physical world and of the symbols used to represent them.
– DERIVATIVES **Platonist** noun.

platoon ▶**noun** a subdivision of a company of soldiers, usually forming a tactical unit that is commanded by a subaltern or lieutenant and divided into three sections.
■a group of people acting together: *platoons of sharp lawyers.* ■ [as modifier] (in South Africa) denoting a school or schooling system in which two separate sets of teachers and pupils use the same buildings, one in the morning and one in the afternoon.
▶**verb** [with obj.] (in South Africa) apply the platoon system to (a school).
– ORIGIN mid 17th cent.: from French *peloton* 'platoon', literally 'small ball', diminutive of *pelote*.

Plattdeutsch /ˈplatdɔɪtʃ/ ▶**noun** & **adjective** another term for **LOW GERMAN**.
– ORIGIN German, from Dutch *Platduits*, from *plat* 'flat, low' + *Duits* 'German'.

platteland /ˈplatəland/ S. African ▶**noun** [mass noun] remote country districts.
▶**adjective** belonging to or characteristic of remote country districts; rustic.
– DERIVATIVES **plattelander** noun.
– ORIGIN Afrikaans, literally 'flat land'.

platter ▶**noun 1** a large flat dish or plate, typically made of metal or wood, for serving food.
■a quantity of food served on such a dish: *huge platters of cooked meat.* ■ a meal or selection of food placed on a platter, especially one served in a restaurant: *dinner was a bowl of soup and a cold platter.*
2 something shaped like such a dish or plate, in particular:
■informal, dated a gramophone record. ■ the rotating metal disc forming the turntable of a record player. ■ Computing a rigid rotating disk on which data is stored in a disk drive; a hard disk (considered as a physical object).
– PHRASES **on a (silver) platter** informal used to indicate that someone receives or achieves something with little or no effort.
– ORIGIN Middle English: from Anglo-Norman French *plater*, from *plat* 'large dish' (see **PLATE**).

platy /ˈplati/ ▶**noun** (pl. **-ies**) a small live-bearing freshwater fish of Central America, which is popular in aquaria.
● Genus *Xiphophorus*, family Poeciliidae: several species, in particular *X. maculatus*, which has been bred in a wide variety of colours.
– ORIGIN early 20th cent.: colloquial abbreviation of modern Latin *Platypoecilus* (former genus name), from Greek *platus* 'broad' + *poikilos* 'variegated'.

platy- ▶**combining form** broad; flat: *platypus.*
– ORIGIN from Greek *platus* 'broad, flat'.

Platyhelminthes /ˌplatɪhɛlˈmɪnθiːz/ Zoology a phylum of invertebrates that comprises the flatworms.
– DERIVATIVES **platyhelminth** /ˌplatɪˈhɛlmɪnθ/ noun.
– ORIGIN modern Latin (plural), from **PLATY-** 'flat' + Greek *helminth* 'worm'.

platykurtic /ˌplatɪˈkəːtɪk/ ▶**noun** Statistics (of a frequency distribution or its graphical representation) having less kurtosis than the normal distribution. Compare with **LEPTOKURTIC**, **MESOKURTIC**.
– DERIVATIVES **platykurtosis** noun.
– ORIGIN early 20th cent.: from **PLATY-** 'broad, flat' + Greek *kurtos* 'bulging' + **-IC**.

platypus /ˈplatɪpəs/ ▶**noun** (pl. **platypuses**) a semiaquatic egg-laying mammal which frequents lakes and streams in eastern Australia. It has a sensitive pliable bill shaped like that of a duck, webbed feet with venomous spurs, and dense fur. Also called **DUCKBILL** or **DUCK-BILLED PLATYPUS**.
● *Ornithorhynchus anatinus*, the only member of the family Ornithorhynchidae, order Monotremata.
– ORIGIN late 18th cent.: modern Latin, from Greek *platupous* 'flat-footed', from *platus* 'flat' + *pous* 'foot'.

platyrrhine /ˈplatɪrʌɪn/ Zoology ▶**adjective** of or relating to primates of a group that comprises the New World monkeys, marmosets, and tamarins. They are distinguished by having nostrils that are far apart and directed forwards or sideways, and typically have a prehensile tail. Compare with **CATARRHINE**.
▶**noun** a platyrrhine primate.
● Infraorder Platyrrhini, order Primates: families Cebidae and Callitrichidae.
– ORIGIN mid 19th cent.: from **PLATY-** 'flat' + Greek *rhis, rhin-* 'nose' + **-INE**[1].

platysma /pləˈtɪzmə/ ▶**noun** (pl. **platysmas** or **platysmata** /-mətə/) Anatomy a broad sheet of muscle fibres extending from the collar bone to the angle of the jaw.
– ORIGIN late 17th cent.: modern Latin, from Greek *platusma* 'flat piece, plate'.

plaudits /ˈplɔːdɪts/ ▶**plural noun** praise: *the network has received plaudits for its sports coverage.*
■the applause of an audience: *the plaudits for the winner died down.*
– ORIGIN early 17th cent.: *plaudit* shortened from Latin *plaudite* 'applaud!' (said by Roman actors at the end of a play), imperative plural of *plaudere*.

plausible ▶**adjective** (of an argument or statement) seeming reasonable or probable: *a plausible explanation | it seems plausible that one of two things may happen.*
■(of a person) skilled at producing persuasive arguments, especially ones intended to deceive: *a plausible liar.*
– DERIVATIVES **plausibility** noun, **plausibly** adverb.
– ORIGIN mid 16th cent. (also in the sense 'deserving applause or approval'): from Latin *plausibilis*, from *plaus-* 'applauded', from the verb *plaudere*.

Plautus /ˈplɔːtəs/, Titus Maccius (*c.*250–184 BC), Roman comic dramatist. His plays, such as *Rudens*, are modelled on Greek New Comedy.

play ▶**verb 1** [no obj.] engage in activity for enjoyment and recreation rather than a serious or practical purpose: *the children were playing by a pool | her friends were **playing with** their dolls.*
■[with obj.] engage in (a game or activity) for enjoyment: *I want to play Snakes and Ladders.* ■ amuse oneself by engaging in imaginative pretence: *the boys were **playing at** soldiers.* ■ (**play at**) engage in without proper seriousness or understanding: *you cannot play at being a Christian.* ■ (**play with**) treat inconsiderately for one's own amusement: *she likes to play with people's emotions.* ■ (**play with**) handle without skill so as to damage or prevent from working: *has somebody been playing with these taps?* ■ [with negative or in questions] (**be playing at**) used to convey one's irritation at someone's actions or one's failure to understand their motives: *what on earth do you think you're playing at?*
2 [with obj.] take part in (a sport) on a regular basis: *I play squash and badminton.*
■participate in (a sporting match or contest). ■ compete against (another player or team) in a sporting match: *the team will play France on Wednesday.* ■ [no obj.] [usu. with negative] figurative be cooperative: *he needs financial backing, but the building societies won't play.* ■ [no obj.] be part of a team, especially in a specified position, in a sporting contest: *he played in goal.* ■ strike (a ball) or execute (a stroke) in a game. ■ [no obj., with adverbial] (of a cricket ground) be in such condition as to have a specified effect on play. ■ assign to take part in a match, especially in a specified position: *the manager played his strongest side of the season.* ■ move (a piece) or display (a playing card) in one's turn in a game: *he played his queen.* ■ bet or gamble at or on: *he didn't gamble or play the ponies.*
3 [with obj.] represent (a character) in a theatrical performance or a film: *early in her career she played Ophelia.*
■[no obj.] perform in a film or theatrical production: *he was proud to be playing opposite a famous actor.* ■ put on or take part in (a theatrical performance, film, or concert): *the show was one of the best we ever played.* ■ give a dramatic performance at (a particular theatre or place). ■ behave as though one were (a specified type of person): *the skipper played the innocent, but smuggled goods were found on his vessel.* ■ (**play someone for**) treat someone as being of (a specified type): *don't imagine you can play me for a fool.* ■ (**play a trick/joke on**) behave in a deceptive or teasing way towards.
4 [with obj.] perform on (a musical instrument).
■possess the skill of performing upon (a musical instrument): *he taught himself to play the violin.* ■ produce (notes) from a musical instrument; perform (a piece of music): *they played a violin sonata.* ■ make (a record, record player, radio, etc.) produce sounds. ■ [no obj.] (of a musical instrument, record, record player, etc.) produce sounds: *somewhere within,*

p

a harp was playing. ■ [with obj. and adverbial of direction] accompany (someone) with music as they are moving in a specified direction: *the bagpipes played them out of the dining room.*
5 [no obj.] move lightly and quickly, so as to appear and disappear; flicker: *a smile played about her lips.*
■ (of a fountain or similar source of water) emit a stream of gently moving water.
6 [with obj.] allow (a fish) to exhaust itself pulling against a line before reeling it in.
▶ **noun** [mass noun] **1** activity engaged in for enjoyment and recreation, especially by children: *a child* ***at play*** *may use a stick as an aeroplane.*
■ behaviour or speech that is not intended seriously: *I flinched, but only* ***in play.*** ■ [as modifier] designed to be used in games of pretence; not real: *play families are arranged in play houses.*
2 the conducting of a sporting match: *rain wrecked the second day's play.*
■ the action or manner of engaging in a sport or game: *he maintained the same rhythm of play throughout the game.* ■ the status of the ball in a game as being available to be played according to the rules: *the ball was put in play.* ■ figurative the state of being active, operative, or effective: *luck* ***comes into play.*** ■ [count noun] a move or manoeuvre in a sport or game: *the best play is to lead the 3 of Clubs.* ■ archaic gambling.
3 [count noun] a dramatic work for the stage or to be broadcast: *the actors put on a new play.*
4 the space in or through which a mechanism can or does move: *the steering rack was loose, and there was a little play.*
■ figurative scope or freedom to act or operate: *our policy allows the market to have freer play.* ■ light and constantly changing movement: *the artist exploits the play of light across the surface.*
– PHRASES **make a play for** informal attempt to attract or attain. **make (great) play of** (or **with**) draw attention to in an ostentatious manner, typically to gain prestige or advantage: *the company made great play of their recent growth in profits.* **make play with** treat frivolously. **not playing with a full deck** see **DECK**. **play ball** see **BALL**[1]. **play both ends against the middle** keep one's options open by supporting or favouring opposing sides. **play something by ear** perform music without having to read from a score. ■ **(play it by ear)** informal proceed instinctively according to results and circumstances rather than according to rules or a plan. **play by the rules** follow what is generally held to be the correct line of behaviour. **play one's cards close to one's chest** see **CHEST**. **play one's cards right** (or **well**) see **CARD**[1]. **play ducks and drakes with** see **DUCKS AND DRAKES**. **play fair** observe principles of justice; avoid cheating. **play someone false** prove treacherous or deceitful towards someone. **play fast and loose** behave irresponsibly or immorally. **play favourites** chiefly N. Amer. show favouritism towards someone or something. **play the field** see **FIELD**. **play for time** use specious excuses or unnecessary manoeuvres to gain time. **play the game** see **GAME**[1]. **play God** see **GOD**. **play havoc with** see **HAVOC**. **play hell** see **HELL**. **play hookey** see **HOOKEY**. **play a** (or **one's**) **hunch** make an instinctive choice. **play oneself in** Brit. become accustomed to the circumstances and conditions of a game or activity. **play into someone's hands** act in such a way as unintentionally to give someone an advantage. **play it cool** informal make an effort to be or appear to be calm and unemotional. **play the market** speculate in stocks. **a play on words** a pun. **play** (or **play it**) **safe** (or **for safety**) take precautions; avoid risks. **play to the gallery** see **GALLERY**. **play truant** see **TRUANT**. **play with oneself** informal masturbate. **play with fire** take foolish risks.
– DERIVATIVES **playability** noun, **playable** adjective.
– ORIGIN Old English *pleg(i)an* 'to exercise', *plega* 'brisk movement', related to Middle Dutch *pleien* 'leap for joy, dance'.
▶ **play about** (or **around**) behave in a casual, foolish, or irresponsible way: *you shouldn't* ***play around with*** *a child's future.* ■ informal (of a married person) have a love affair.
play along perform a piece of music at the same time as it is playing on a tape or record. ■ pretend to cooperate: *she had to play along and be polite.*
play someone along informal deceive or mislead someone over a period of time.
play away Brit. play a sports fixture on an opponent's ground. ■ informal (of a married person) have a love affair.
play something back play sounds that one has recently recorded, especially to monitor recording quality.
play something down represent something as being less important than it in fact is: *he tried to play down the seriousness of his illness.*
play someone off bring people into conflict or competition for one's own advantage: *top footballers were able to* ***play*** *clubs* ***off against*** *each other to gain higher pay.*
play off (of two teams or competitors) play an extra match to decide a draw or tie.
play on exploit (a weak or vulnerable point in someone): *he played on his opponent's nerves.*
play someone out (usu. **be played out**) drain someone of strength or life.
play something out act the whole of a drama; enact a scene or role.
play up 1 Brit. informal fail to function properly. **2** Brit. put all one's energy into a game.
play someone up (of a part of the body or an illness) cause pain or discomfort to someone.
play something up emphasize the extent or importance of something: *the mystery surrounding his death was played up by the media.*
play up to humour or flatter, especially to win favour.

playa /'plʌɪə/ ▶ **noun** an area of flat, dried-up land, especially a desert basin from which water evaporates quickly.
– ORIGIN mid 19th cent.: from Spanish, literally 'beach', from late Latin *plagia*.

play-act ▶ **verb** [no obj.] act in a play.
■ [with obj.] act (a scene, role, etc.). ■ [usu. as noun **play-acting**] engage in histrionic pretence: *the defender indulged in some play-acting after tumbling to the ground.*
– DERIVATIVES **play-actor** noun.

playback ▶ **noun** [mass noun] the reproduction of previously recorded sounds or moving images.

playbill ▶ **noun** a poster announcing a theatrical performance.
■ N. Amer. a theatre programme.

playboy ▶ **noun** a wealthy man who spends his time enjoying himself, especially one who behaves irresponsibly or is sexually promiscuous.

play-by-play ▶ **noun** N. Amer. a detailed running commentary on a sporting contest.

play centre ▶ **noun** a place separate from school where children can play under supervision.
■ chiefly NZ a pre-school playgroup.

play dough ▶ **noun** [mass noun] modelling clay for children, typically made at home out of flour, water, and salt.

playdown ▶ **noun** chiefly Canadian & Scottish a game or match forming part of a tournament or competition.

Player, Gary (b.1936), South African golfer. He has won numerous championships including the British Open (1959; 1968; 1974), the Masters (1961; 1974; 1978), and the PGA (1962; 1972).

player ▶ **noun 1** a person taking part in a sport or game: *a tennis player.*
■ a person or body that is involved and influential in an area or activity: *the country's isolationism made it a secondary player in world political events.*
2 [usu. with modifier] a person who plays a musical instrument: *a guitar player.*
■ a device for playing records, compact discs, cassettes, etc.
3 an actor.

player-manager ▶ **noun** a person who both plays in a sports team and manages it.

player-piano ▶ **noun** a piano fitted with an apparatus enabling it to be played automatically.

Playfair, John (1748–1819), Scottish mathematician and geologist. A friend of James Hutton, he summarized the latter's views for a wider readership in his *Illustrations of the Huttonian Theory of the Earth* (1802).

playfellow ▶ **noun** a playmate.

playful ▶ **adjective** fond of games and amusement; light-hearted.
■ intended for one's own or others' amusement rather than seriously: *he gave me a playful punch on the arm.* ■ giving or expressing pleasure and amusement: *the ballet accents the playful use of movement.*
– DERIVATIVES **playfully** adverb, **playfulness** noun.

playground ▶ **noun** an outdoor area provided for children to play on, especially at a school or public park.
■ a place where a particular group of people choose to enjoy themselves: *the mountains are* ***a playground for*** *hang-gliders.*

playgroup ▶ **noun** Brit. a regular meeting of a group of pre-school children at a particular place, organized by parents for their children to take part in supervised creative and social play.

playhouse ▶ **noun 1** (also **Playhouse**) a theatre.
2 a toy house for children to play in.

playing card ▶ **noun** each of a set of rectangular pieces of card or other material with an identical pattern on one side and different numbers and symbols on the other, used to play various games, some involving gambling. A standard pack contains 52 cards divided into four suits.

playing field ▶ **noun** a field used for outdoor team games.
– PHRASES **a level playing field** see **LEVEL**.

playlet ▶ **noun** a short play or dramatic piece.

playlist ▶ **noun** a list of recorded songs or pieces of music chosen to be broadcast on a radio show or by a particular radio station.
▶ **verb** [with obj.] place (a song or piece of music) on such a list.

playmaker ▶ **noun** a player in a team game who leads attacks or brings other players on the same side into a position from which they could score.
– DERIVATIVES **playmaking** noun.

playmate ▶ **noun 1** a friend with whom a child plays.
2 used euphemistically to refer to a person's lover.

play-off ▶ **noun** an additional match played to decide the outcome of a contest.

playpen ▶ **noun** a small portable enclosure in which a baby or small child can play safely.

play-play S. African informal ▶ **adjective** [attrib.] not genuine; make-believe: *they're at the age when they want more than a play-play watch.*
▶ **verb** [no obj.] engage in make-believe: [with clause] *I could play-play I was a beach boy.*

playroom ▶ **noun** a room in a house that is set aside for children to play in.

playscheme ▶ **noun** a local project or scheme providing recreational facilities and activities for children for a certain period of time, typically during the school holidays.

playschool ▶ **noun** a playgroup.

playsuit ▶ **noun** an all-in-one stretchy garment for a baby or very young child, covering the body, arms, and legs.
■ a women's all-in-one garment, or matching set of garments.

play therapy ▶ **noun** [mass noun] therapy in which emotionally disturbed children are encouraged to act out their fantasies and express their feelings through play, aided by a therapist's interpretations.
– DERIVATIVES **play therapist** noun.

plaything ▶ **noun** a toy.
■ figurative a person treated as amusing but unimportant by someone else: *she was the mistress and plaything of a wealthy businessman.*

playwright ▶ **noun** a person who writes plays.

playwriting ▶ **noun** [mass noun] the activity or process of writing plays.

plaza ▶ **noun 1** a public square, marketplace, or similar open space in a built-up area.
2 N. Amer. a shopping centre.
– ORIGIN late 17th cent.: from Spanish, literally 'place'.

plc (also **PLC**) Brit. ▶ **abbreviation for** public limited company.

plea ▶ **noun 1** a request made in an urgent and emotional manner: *he made a dramatic plea for disarmament.*
■ a claim that a circumstance means that one should not be blamed for or should not be forced to do something: *her plea of a headache was not entirely false.*
2 Law a formal statement by or on behalf of a defendant or prisoner, stating guilt or innocence in response to a charge, offering an allegation of fact, or claiming that a point of law should apply: *he changed his plea to not guilty.*
– PHRASES **plea of tender** Law a plea that the

defendant has always been ready to satisfy the plaintiff's claim and now brings the sum into court.
– ORIGIN Middle English (in the sense 'lawsuit'): from Old French *plait, plaid* 'agreement, discussion', from Latin *placitum* 'a decree', neuter past participle of *placere* 'to please'.

plea-bargaining ▶ **noun** [mass noun] Law an arrangement between prosecutor and defendant of an agreement whereby the defendant pleads guilty to a lesser charge in the expectation of leniency.
– DERIVATIVES **plea-bargain** verb, **plea bargain** noun.

pleach /pliːtʃ/ ▶ **verb** [with obj.] [usu. as adj. **pleached**] entwine or interlace (tree branches) to form a hedge or provide cover for an outdoor walkway: *an avenue of pleached limes.*
– ORIGIN late Middle English: from an Old French variant of *plaissier* (see **PLASH**[2]).

plead ▶ **verb** (past and past participle **pleaded** or N. Amer., Scottish, or dialect **pled**) **1** [reporting verb] make an emotional appeal: [no obj.] *she **pleaded with** them not to gag the boy* | [with direct speech] *'Don't go,' she pleaded* | [with infinitive] *Anne pleaded to go with her.*
2 [with obj.] present and argue for (a position), especially in court or in another public context.
■ [no obj.] Law address a court as an advocate on behalf of a party. ■ [no obj., with complement] Law state formally in court whether one is guilty or not guilty of the offence with which one is charged: *the youth pleaded guilty to murdering the girl.* ■ Law invoke (a reason or a point of law) as an accusation or defence: *on trial for attempted murder, she pleaded self-defence.* ■ offer or present as an excuse for doing or not doing something: *he pleaded family commitments as a reason for not attending.*
– DERIVATIVES **pleader** noun, **pleadingly** adverb.
– ORIGIN Middle English (in the sense 'to wrangle'): from Old French *plaidier* 'go to law', from *plaid* 'discussion' (see **PLEA**).

USAGE In a law court a person can **plead guilty** or **plead not guilty**. The phrase **plead innocent** is not a technical legal term, although it is commonly found in general use.

pleadable ▶ **adjective** Law able to be offered as a formal plea in court.

pleading ▶ **noun 1** [mass noun] the action of making an emotional or earnest appeal to someone: *he ignored her pleading.*
2 (usu. **pleadings**) Law a formal statement of the cause of an action or defence.

pleasance ▶ **noun** a secluded enclosure or part of a garden, especially one attached to a large house.
– ORIGIN Middle English (in the sense 'pleasure'): from Old French *plaisance*, from *plaisant* 'pleasing' (see **PLEASANT**).

pleasant ▶ **adjective** (**pleasanter, pleasantest**) giving a sense of happy satisfaction or enjoyment: *a very pleasant evening* | *what a pleasant surprise!*
■ (of a person or their manner) friendly and considerate; likeable: *they found him pleasant and cooperative.*
– DERIVATIVES **pleasantly** adverb, **pleasantness** noun.
– ORIGIN Middle English (in the sense 'pleasing'): from Old French *plaisant* 'pleasing', from the verb *plaisir* (see **PLEASE**).

pleasantry ▶ **noun** (pl. **-ies**) (usu. **pleasantries**) an inconsequential remark made as part of a polite conversation: *after an exchange of pleasantries, I proceeded to outline a plan.*
■ a mild joke: *he laughed at his own pleasantry.*
– ORIGIN late 16th cent.: from French *plaisanterie*, from Old French *plaisant* 'pleasing' (see **PLEASANT**).

please ▶ **verb** [with obj.] **1** cause to feel happy and satisfied: *he arranged a fishing trip to please his son* | [with obj. and infinitive] *it **pleased** him to be seen with someone in the news.*
■ [no obj.] give satisfaction: *she was quiet and eager to please.* ■ satisfy aesthetically: [as adj. **pleasing**] *the pleasing austerity of the surroundings.*
2 (**please oneself**) take only one's own wishes into consideration in deciding how to act or proceed: *this is the first time in ages that I can just please myself.*
■ [no obj.] wish or desire to do something: *feel free to wander around **as you please**.* ■ (**it pleases, pleased,** etc., **someone to do something**) dated it is someone's choice to do something: *instead of attending the meeting, it pleased him to go off hunting.*
▶ **adverb** used in polite requests or questions: *please address letters to the Editor* | *what type of fish is this, please?*
■ used to add urgency and emotion to a request: *please, please come home!* ■ used to agree politely to a request: *'May I ring you at home?' 'Please do.'* ■ used in polite or emphatic acceptance of an offer: *'Would you like a drink?' 'Yes, please.'* ■ used to ask someone to stop doing something of which the speaker disapproves: *Rita, please—people are looking.*
– PHRASES **as —— as you please** informal used to emphasize the manner in which someone does something, especially when this is seen as surprising: *she walked forward as calm as you please.* **if you please 1** used in polite requests: *follow me, if you please.* **2** used to express indignation at something perceived as unreasonable: *she wants me to make fifty cakes in time for the festival, if you please!* **please yourself** used to express indifference, especially when someone does not cooperate or behave as expected: *'I can manage on my own.' 'Please yourself.'*
– DERIVATIVES **pleasingly** adverb.
– ORIGIN Middle English: from Old French *plaisir* 'to please', from Latin *placere*.

pleased ▶ **adjective** feeling or showing pleasure and satisfaction, especially at an event or a situation: *both girls were **pleased with** their new hairstyles* | *he seemed really **pleased that** she was there* | *a pleased smile.*
■ [with infinitive] willing or glad to do something: *we will be pleased to provide an independent appraisal.* ■ (**pleased with oneself**) proud of one's achievements, especially excessively so; self-satisfied.
– PHRASES **(as) pleased as Punch** see **PUNCH**[4]. **pleased to meet you** said on being introduced to someone: *'This is my wife.' 'Pleased to meet you.'*

pleasurable ▶ **adjective** pleasing; enjoyable.
– DERIVATIVES **pleasurableness** noun, **pleasurably** adverb.
– ORIGIN late 16th cent.: from **PLEASURE**, on the pattern of *comfortable*.

pleasure ▶ **noun** [mass noun] a feeling of happy satisfaction and enjoyment: *she smiled with pleasure at being praised.*
■ enjoyment and entertainment, contrasted with things done out of necessity: *she had not travelled for pleasure for a long time.* ■ [count noun] an event or activity from which one derives enjoyment: *the car makes driving in the city a pleasure.* ■ sensual gratification: *the touch of his fingers gave her such pleasure.*
▶ **adjective** [attrib.] used or intended for entertainment rather than business: *pleasure boats.*
▶ **verb** [with obj.] give sexual enjoyment or satisfaction to: *tell me what will pleasure you.*
■ [no obj.] (**pleasure in**) derive enjoyment from: *risky verbal exchanges that the pair might pleasure in.*
– PHRASES **at Her** (or **His**) **Majesty's pleasure** detained in a British prison. **at someone's pleasure** as and when someone wishes: *the landlord could terminate the agreement at his pleasure.* **have the pleasure of something** (or **of doing something**) used in formal requests and descriptions: *he asked if he might have the pleasure of taking her to lunch.* **my pleasure** used as a polite reply to thanks. **take pleasure in** derive happiness or enjoyment from: *they take a perverse pleasure in causing trouble.* **what's your pleasure?** what would you like? (used especially when offering someone a choice): *'What's your pleasure?' 'A cappuccino, please.'* **with pleasure** gladly (used to express polite agreement or acceptance).
– ORIGIN late Middle English: from Old French *plaisir* 'to please' (used as a noun). The second syllable was altered under the influence of abstract nouns ending in *-ure*, such as *measure*.

pleasure principle ▶ **noun** Psychoanalysis the instinctive drive to seek pleasure and avoid pain, expressed by the id as a basic motivating force which reduces psychic tension.

pleat ▶ **noun** a double or multiple fold in a garment or other item made of cloth, held by stitching the top or side.
▶ **verb** [with obj.] fold into pleats: *she was absently pleating her skirt between her fingers* | [as adj. **pleated**] *a short pleated skirt.*
– ORIGIN late Middle English: a variant of **PLAIT**. The written form of the word became obsolete between *c.*1700 and the end of the 19th cent.

pleb ▶ **noun** (usu. **plebs**) derogatory an ordinary person, especially one from the lower social classes.
– DERIVATIVES **plebby** adjective.

plebe /pliːb/ ▶ **noun** US informal a newly entered cadet or freshman, especially at a military or naval academy.
– ORIGIN early 17th cent.: perhaps an abbreviation of **PLEBEIAN**.

plebeian /plɪˈbiːən/ ▶ **noun** (in ancient Rome) a commoner.
■ a member of the lower social classes.
▶ **adjective** of or belonging to the commoners of ancient Rome.
■ of or belonging to the lower social classes. ■ lacking in refinement: *he is a man of plebeian tastes.*
– ORIGIN mid 16th cent.: from Latin *plebeius* (from *plebs, pleb-* 'the common people') + **-AN**.

plebiscite /ˈplɛbɪsʌɪt, -sɪt/ ▶ **noun 1** the direct vote of all the members of an electorate on an important public question such as a change in the constitution.
■ Roman History a law enacted by the plebeians' assembly.
– DERIVATIVES **plebiscitary** /-ˈbɪsɪt(ə)ri/ adjective.
– ORIGIN mid 16th cent. (referring to Roman history): from French *plébiscite*, from Latin *plebiscitum*, from *plebs, pleb-* 'the common people' + *scitum* 'decree' (from *sciscere* 'vote for'). The sense 'direct vote of the whole electorate' dates from the mid 19th cent.

Plecoptera /plɪˈkɒptərə/ Entomology an order of insects that comprises the stoneflies.
■ [as plural noun **plecoptera**] insects of this order; stoneflies.
– DERIVATIVES **plecopteran** noun & adjective.
– ORIGIN modern Latin (plural), from Greek *plekos* 'wickerwork' (from *plekein* 'to plait') + *pteron* 'wing'.

plectrum /ˈplɛktrəm/ ▶ **noun** (pl. **plectrums** or **plectra** /-trə/) a thin flat piece of plastic, tortoiseshell, or other slightly flexible material held by or worn on the fingers and used to pluck the strings of a musical instrument such as a guitar.
■ the corresponding mechanical part which plucks the strings of an instrument such as a harpsichord.
– ORIGIN late Middle English: via Latin from Greek *plēktron* 'something with which to strike', from *plēssein* 'to strike'.

pled North American, Scottish, or dialect past participle of **PLEAD**.

pledge ▶ **noun 1** a solemn promise or undertaking: [with infinitive] *the conference ended with a joint pledge to limit pollution.*
■ a promise of a donation to charity: *appeals for emergency relief met with pledges totalling only $450,000,000.* ■ (**the pledge**) a solemn undertaking to abstain from alcohol: *she persuaded Arthur to **take the pledge**.*
2 Law a thing that is given as security for the fulfilment of a contract or the payment of a debt and is liable to forfeiture in the event of failure.
■ a thing given as a token of love, favour, or loyalty.
3 archaic the drinking of a person's health; a toast.
▶ **verb 1** [with obj. and infinitive] commit (a person or organization) by a solemn promise: *the government pledged itself to deal with environmental problems.*
■ [with clause] formally declare or promise that something is or will be the case: *the Prime Minister pledged that there would be no increase in VAT.* ■ [no obj., with infinitive] solemnly undertake to do something: *they pledged to continue the campaign for funding.* ■ [with obj.] undertake formally to give: *Japan pledged $100 million in humanitarian aid.*
2 [with obj.] Law give as security on a loan: *the creditor to whom the land is pledged.*
3 [with obj.] archaic drink to the health of.
– PHRASES **pledge one's troth** see **TROTH**.
– DERIVATIVES **pledger** noun, **pledgor** noun (Law).
– ORIGIN Middle English (denoting a person acting as surety for another): from Old French *plege*, from medieval Latin *plebium*, perhaps related to the Germanic base of **PLIGHT**[1].

pledgee ▶ **noun** a person to whom a pledge is given.

Pledge of Allegiance (in the US) a solemn oath of loyalty to the United States, declaimed as part of flag-saluting ceremonies.

pledget /ˈplɛdʒɪt/ ▶ **noun** a small wad of lint or other soft material used to stop up a wound or an opening in the body.
– ORIGIN mid 16th cent.: of unknown origin.

pleiad /ˈplʌɪəd/ ▶ **noun** poetic/literary an outstanding group of seven people or things.
– ORIGIN early 17th cent.: from **PLEIADES**.

a **cat** | ɑː **arm** | ɛ **bed** | ɛː **hair** | ə **ago** | əː **her** | ɪ **sit** | i **cosy** | iː **see** | ɒ **hot** | ɔː **saw** | ʌ **run** | ʊ **put** | uː **too** | ʌɪ **my** | aʊ **how** | eɪ **day** | əʊ **no** | ɪə **near** | ɔɪ **boy** | ʊə **poor** | ʌɪə **fire** | aʊə **sour**

Pleiades /ˈplʌɪədiːz/ **1** Greek Mythology the seven daughters of the Titan Atlas and the Oceanid Pleione, who were pursued by the hunter Orion until Zeus changed them into a cluster of stars.
2 Astronomy a well-known open cluster of stars in the constellation Taurus. Six (or more) stars are visible to the naked eye but there are actually some five hundred present, formed very recently in stellar terms. Also called **SEVEN SISTERS**.
– ORIGIN via Latin from Greek.

plein-air /plɛn ˈɛː, French plɛn ɛʀ/ ▶ **adjective** [attrib.] denoting or in the manner of a 19th-century style of painting outdoors, or with a strong sense of the open air, which became a central feature of French Impressionism.
– ORIGIN from French *en plein air* 'in the open air'.

pleiotropy /plʌɪˈɒtrəpi/ ▶ **noun** [mass noun] Genetics the production by a single gene of two or more apparently unrelated effects.
– DERIVATIVES **pleiotropic** /-ˈtrəʊpɪk, -ˈtrɒpɪk/ adjective, **pleiotropism** noun.
– ORIGIN 1930s: from Greek *pleiōn* 'more' + *tropē* 'turning'.

Pleistocene /ˈplʌɪstəsiːn/ ▶ **adjective** Geology of, relating to, or denoting the first epoch of the Quaternary period, between the Pliocene and Holocene epochs.
■ [as noun **the Pleistocene**] the Pleistocene epoch or the system of deposits laid down during it.

The Pleistocene epoch lasted from 1,640,000 to about 10,000 years ago. It was marked by great fluctuations in temperature that caused the ice ages, with glacial periods followed by warmer interglacial periods. Several forms of fossil human, leading up to modern humans, appeared during this epoch.

– ORIGIN mid 19th cent.: from Greek *pleistos* 'most' + *kainos* 'new'.

plenary /ˈpliːnəri/ ▶ **adjective** **1** unqualified; absolute: *crusaders were offered a plenary indulgence by the Pope.*
2 (of a meeting) to be attended by all participants at a conference or assembly, who otherwise meet in smaller groups: *a plenary session of the European Parliament.*
▶ **noun** a meeting or session of this type.
– ORIGIN late Middle English: from late Latin *plenarius* 'complete', from *plenus* 'full'.

plenipotentiary /ˌplɛnɪpəˈtɛnʃ(ə)ri/ ▶ **noun** (pl. **-ies**) a person, especially a diplomat, invested with the full power of independent action on behalf of their government, typically in a foreign country.
▶ **adjective** having full power to take independent action: [postpositive] *a minister plenipotentiary.*
■ (of power) absolute.
– ORIGIN mid 17th cent.: from medieval Latin *plenipotentiarius*, from *plenus* 'full' + *potentia* 'power'.

plenitude ▶ **noun** an abundance: *an ancient Celtic god thought to bring **a plenitude of** wealth or food.*
■ [mass noun] the condition of being full or complete: *the plenitude of the pope's powers.*
– ORIGIN late Middle English: from Old French, from late Latin *plenitudo*, from *plenus* 'full'.

plenteous ▶ **adjective** poetic/literary plentiful.
– DERIVATIVES **plenteously** adverb, **plenteousness** noun.
– ORIGIN Middle English: from Old French *plentivous*, from *plentif, -ive*, from *plente* 'plenty'. Compare with **BOUNTEOUS**.

plentiful ▶ **adjective** existing in or yielding great quantities; abundant: *coal is cheap and plentiful.*
– DERIVATIVES **plentifully** adverb, **plentifulness** noun.

plentitude ▶ **noun** rare term for **PLENITUDE**.

plenty ▶ **pronoun** a large or sufficient amount or quantity; more than enough: *I would have **plenty of** time to get home before my parents arrived | you'll have plenty to keep you busy | there are shops **in plenty** |* [as determiner] informal or dialect *there was plenty room.*
▶ **noun** [mass noun] a situation in which food and other necessities are available in sufficiently large quantities: *such natural phenomena as famine and plenty.*
▶ **adverb** [usu. as submodifier] informal used to emphasize the degree of something: *she has **plenty more** ideas.*
– ORIGIN Middle English (in the sense 'fullness, perfection'): from Old French *plente*, from Latin *plenitas*, from *plenus* 'full'.

Plenty, Bay of a region of North Island, New Zealand, extending around the bay of the same name. The port of Tauranga is situated on it.

plenum /ˈpliːnəm/ ▶ **noun** **1** an assembly of all the members of a group or committee. [ORIGIN: influenced by Russian *plenum* 'plenary session'.]
2 Physics a space completely filled with matter, or the whole of space so regarded.
– ORIGIN late 17th cent.: from Latin, literally 'full space', neuter of *plenus* 'full'.

pleo- ▶ **combining form** having more than the usual or expected number: *pleocytosis.*
– ORIGIN from Greek *pleōn* 'more'.

pleochroic /ˌpliːə(ʊ)ˈkrəʊɪk/ ▶ **adjective** (of a crystal) absorbing different wavelengths of light differently depending on the direction of incidence of the rays or their plane of polarization, often resulting in the appearance of different colours according to the direction of view.
– DERIVATIVES **pleochroism** noun.
– ORIGIN mid 19th cent.: from **PLEO-** 'more' + *khrōs* 'colour' + **-IC**.

pleocytosis /ˌpliːə(ʊ)sʌɪˈtəʊsɪs/ ▶ **noun** [mass noun] Medicine the presence of an abnormally large number of lymphocytes in the cerebrospinal fluid.

pleomorphism /ˌpliːə(ʊ)ˈmɔːfɪz(ə)m/ ▶ **noun** [mass noun] the occurrence of more than one distinct form of a natural object, such as a crystalline substance, a virus, the cells in a tumour, or an organism at different stages of the life cycle.
– DERIVATIVES **pleomorphic** adjective.
– ORIGIN mid 19th cent.: from Greek *pleiōn* 'more' + *morphē* 'form' + **-ISM**.

pleonasm /ˈpliːə(ʊ)ˌnaz(ə)m/ ▶ **noun** [mass noun] the use of more words than are necessary to convey meaning (e.g. *see with one's eyes*), either as a fault of style or for emphasis.
– DERIVATIVES **pleonastic** adjective, **pleonastically** adverb.
– ORIGIN mid 16th cent.: via late Latin from Greek *pleonasmos*, from *pleonazein* 'be superfluous'.

pleopod /ˈpliːə(ʊ)pɒd/ ▶ **noun** Zoology a forked swimming limb of a crustacean, five pairs of which are typically attached to the abdomen. Also called **SWIMMERET**.
– ORIGIN mid 19th cent.: from Greek *plein* 'swim, sail' + *pous, pod-* 'foot'.

pleroma /plɪˈrəʊmə/ ▶ **noun** [in sing.] **1** (in Gnosticism) the spiritual universe as the abode of God and of the totality of the divine powers and emanations.
2 (in Christian theology) the totality or fullness of the Godhead which dwells in Christ.
– DERIVATIVES **pleromatic** adjective.
– ORIGIN mid 18th cent.: from Greek *plērōma* 'that which fills', from *plēroun* 'make full', from *plērēs* 'full'.

plesiosaur /ˈpliːsɪəsɔː, ˈpliːz-/ ▶ **noun** a large fossil marine reptile of the Mesozoic era, with a broad flat body, large paddle-like limbs, and typically a long flexible neck and small head.
• Infraorder Plesiosauria, superorder Sauropterygia: several families, including Plesiosauridae.
– ORIGIN mid 19th cent.: from modern Latin *Plesiosaurus*, from Greek *plēsios* 'near' + *sauros* 'lizard'.

plessor /ˈplɛsə/ ▶ **noun** variant spelling of **PLEXOR**.

plethora /ˈplɛθ(ə)rə/ ▶ **noun** (**a plethora of**) an excess of (something): *a plethora of committees and subcommittees.*
■ Medicine an excess of a bodily fluid, particularly blood.
– DERIVATIVES **plethoric** /ˈplɛθ(ə)rɪk, plɪˈθɒrɪk/ adjective (archaic or Medicine).
– ORIGIN mid 16th cent. (in the medical sense): via late Latin from Greek *plēthōrē*, from *plēthein* 'be full'.

plethysmograph /plɪˈθɪzməgrɑːf/ ▶ **noun** Medicine an instrument for recording and measuring variation in the volume of a part of the body, especially as caused by changes in blood pressure.
– DERIVATIVES **plethysmographic** adjective.
– ORIGIN late 19th cent.: from Greek *plēthusmos* 'enlargement' (based on *plēthus* 'fullness') + **-GRAPH**.

pleura[1] /ˈplʊərə/ ▶ **noun** (pl. **pleurae** /-riː/) **1** each of a pair of serous membranes lining the thorax and enveloping the lungs in humans and other mammals.
2 Zoology a lateral part in an animal body or structure. Compare with **PLEURON**.
– DERIVATIVES **pleural** adjective.
– ORIGIN late Middle English: via medieval Latin from Greek, literally 'side of the body, rib'.

pleura[2] plural form of **PLEURON**.

pleurisy /ˈplʊərɪsi/ ▶ **noun** [mass noun] Medicine inflammation of the pleurae, which impairs their lubricating function and causes pain when breathing. It is caused by pneumonia and other diseases of the chest or abdomen.
– DERIVATIVES **pleuritic** adjective.
– ORIGIN late Middle English: from Old French *pleurisie*, from late Latin *pleurisis*, alteration of earlier Latin *pleuritis*, from Greek *pleura* 'side of the body, rib'.

pleuro- ▶ **combining form** of or relating to the pleura or pleurae: *pleuropneumonia.*
– ORIGIN from Greek *pleura* 'side', *pleuron* 'rib'.

pleurodynia /ˌplʊərə(ʊ)dɪˈniːə/ ▶ **noun** [mass noun] Medicine severe pain in the muscles between the ribs or in the diaphragm.
– ORIGIN early 19th cent.: from **PLEURO-** 'of the pleura' + Greek *odunē* 'pain'.

pleuron /ˈplʊərɒn/ ▶ **noun** (pl. **pleura** /-rə/) Zoology the side wall of each segment of the body of an arthropod.
– ORIGIN early 18th cent.: from Greek, literally 'side of the body, rib'.

pleuropneumonia ▶ **noun** [mass noun] pneumonia complicated with pleurisy.

Pleven /ˈplɛv(ə)n/ an industrial town in northern Bulgaria, north-east of Sofia; pop. 168,000 (1990). An important fortress town and trading centre of the Ottoman Empire, it was taken from the Turks by the Russians in the Russo-Turkish War of 1877, after a siege of 143 days.

plew /pluː/ ▶ **noun** Canadian historical a beaver skin, used as a standard unit of value in the fur trade.
– ORIGIN mid 19th cent.: from Canadian French *pélu* 'hairy', from French *poil* 'hair, bristle'.

plexiglas /ˈplɛksɪglɑːs/ (also **Plexiglas**) ▶ **noun** [mass noun] trademark, chiefly N. Amer. a solid transparent plastic made of polymethyl methacrylate (the same material as perspex or lucite).
– ORIGIN 1930s: from Greek *plēxis* 'percussion' + **GLASS**.

plexor /ˈplɛksə/ (also **plessor**) ▶ **noun** a small hammer with a rubber head used to test reflexes and in medical percussion.
– ORIGIN mid 19th cent.: formed irregularly from Greek *plēxis* 'percussion' (from *plēssein* 'to strike') + **-OR**[1].

plexus ▶ **noun** (pl. same or **plexuses**) Anatomy a network of nerves or vessels in the body.
■ an intricate network or web-like formation.
– DERIVATIVES **plexiform** adjective.
– ORIGIN late 17th cent.: from Latin, literally 'plaited formation', past participle of *plectere* 'to plait'.

pliable ▶ **adjective** easily bent; flexible: *quality leather is pliable and will not crack.*
■ figurative easily influenced: *pliable teenage minds.*
– DERIVATIVES **pliability** noun, **pliably** adverb.
– ORIGIN late Middle English: from French, from *plier* 'to bend' (see **PLY**[1]).

pliant ▶ **adjective** pliable: *pliant willow stems |* figurative *a more pliant prime minister.*
– DERIVATIVES **pliancy** noun, **pliantly** adverb.
– ORIGIN Middle English: from Old French, literally 'bending', present participle of *plier.*

plica /ˈplɪkə, ˈplʌɪkə/ ▶ **noun** **1** (pl. **plicae** /-kiː/ or **plicas**) Anatomy a fold or ridge of tissue.
■ Botany a small lobe between the petals of a flower.
2 [mass noun] Medicine a densely matted condition of the hair.
– ORIGIN mid 17th cent.: modern Latin, from medieval Latin, 'fold', from *plicare* 'to fold'.

plicate /ˈplʌɪkət, ˈplʌɪkeɪt/ ▶ **adjective** Biology & Geology folded, crumpled, or corrugated.
– DERIVATIVES **plicated** /plɪˈkeɪtɪd/ adjective.
– ORIGIN mid 18th cent.: from Latin *plicatus* 'folded', past participle of *plicare.*

plication ▶ **noun** a fold or corrugation.
■ [mass noun] the manner of folding or condition of being folded.
– ORIGIN late Middle English: via Old French from medieval Latin *plicatio(n-)*, from Latin *plicare* 'to fold'.

plié /ˈpliːeɪ/ Ballet ▶ **noun** a movement in which a dancer bends the knees and straightens them again, usually with the feet turned right out and heels firmly on the ground.
▶ **verb** [no obj.] perform a plié.
– ORIGIN French, literally 'bent', past participle of *plier* (see also **PLY**[1]).

pliers (also **a pair of pliers**) ▶ **plural noun** pincers with parallel, flat, and typically serrated surfaces, used chiefly for gripping small objects or bending wire.
– ORIGIN mid 16th cent.: from dialect *ply* 'bend', from French *plier* 'to bend', from Latin *plicare* 'to fold'.

plight[1] ▶ **noun** a dangerous, difficult, or otherwise unfortunate situation: *we must direct our efforts towards relieving the plight of children living in poverty.*
– ORIGIN Middle English: from Anglo-Norman French *plit* 'fold'. The *-gh-* spelling is by association with **PLIGHT**[2].

plight[2] ▶ **verb** [with obj.] archaic pledge or promise solemnly (one's faith or loyalty).
■ (**be plighted to**) be engaged to be married to.
– PHRASES **plight one's troth** see **TROTH**.
– ORIGIN Old English *plihtan* 'endanger', of Germanic origin; related to Dutch *plicht* and German *Pflicht* 'duty'. The current sense is recorded only from Middle English, but is probably original, in view of the related Germanic words.

plimsoll (also **plimsole**) ▶ **noun** Brit. a light rubber-soled canvas shoe, worn especially for sports.
– ORIGIN late 19th cent.: probably from the resemblance of the side of the sole to a **PLIMSOLL LINE**.

Plimsoll line (also **Plimsoll mark**) ▶ **noun** a marking on a ship's side showing the limit of legal submersion when loaded with cargo under various sea conditions.
– ORIGIN named after Samuel *Plimsoll* (1824–98), the English politician whose agitation in the 1870s resulted in the Merchant Shipping Act of 1876, ending the practice of sending to sea overloaded and heavily insured old ships, from which the owners profited if they sank.

Plinian /ˈplɪnɪən/ ▶ **adjective** Geology relating to or denoting a type of volcanic eruption in which a narrow stream of gas and ash is violently ejected from a vent to a height of several miles.
– ORIGIN mid 17th cent.: from Italian *pliniano*, with reference to the eruption of Vesuvius in AD 79, in which Pliny the Elder died.

plink ▶ **verb** [no obj.] emit a short, sharp, metallic or ringing sound.
■ play a musical instrument in such a way as to produce such sounds. ■ [with obj.] chiefly US shoot at (a target) casually.
▶ **noun** a short, sharp, metallic or ringing sound.
– DERIVATIVES **plinky** adjective.
– ORIGIN 1940s: imitative.

plinth ▶ **noun** a heavy base supporting a statue or vase.
■ Architecture the lower square slab at the base of a column.
– ORIGIN late 16th cent.: from Latin *plinthus*, from Greek *plinthos* 'tile, brick, squared stone'. The Latin form was in early use in English.

Pliny[1] /ˈplɪni/ (23–79), Roman statesman and scholar; Latin name *Gaius Plinius Secundus*; known as **Pliny the Elder**. His *Natural History* (77) is a vast encyclopedia of the natural and human worlds. He died while observing the eruption of Vesuvius.

Pliny[2] /ˈplɪni/ (*c.*61–*c.*112), Roman senator and writer, nephew of Pliny the Elder; Latin name *Gaius Plinius Caecilius Secundus*; known as **Pliny the Younger**. He is noted for his books of letters which deal with both public and private affairs and which include a description of the eruption of Vesuvius in 79.

Pliocene /ˈplʌɪə(ʊ)siːn/ ▶ **adjective** Geology of, relating to, or denoting the last epoch of the Tertiary period, between the Miocene and Pleistocene epochs.
■ [as noun **the Pliocene**] the Pliocene epoch or the system of rocks deposited during it.

> The Pliocene epoch lasted from 5.2 to 1.64 million years ago. Temperatures were falling at this time and many mammals were becoming extinct. The first hominids, including *Australopithecus* and *Homo habilis*, appeared.

– ORIGIN mid 19th cent.: from Greek *pleiōn* 'more' + *kainos* 'new'.

Plio-Pleistocene ▶ **adjective** Geology of, relating to, or linking the Pliocene and Pleistocene epochs or rock systems together.
■ [as noun **the Plio-Pleistocene**] the Pliocene and Pleistocene epochs together or the system of rocks deposited during them.

pliosaur /ˈplʌɪəsɔː/ ▶ **noun** a plesiosaur with a short neck, large head, and massive toothed jaws.
• Family Pliosauridae, infraorder Plesiosauria: several genera, including *Pliosaurus*.
– ORIGIN mid 19th cent.: from modern Latin *Pliosaurus* (genus name), from Greek *pleiōn* 'more' + *sauros* 'lizard' (because of its greater similarity to a lizard than the ichthyosaur).

plissé /ˈpliːseɪ/ ▶ **adjective** (of fabric) treated to give a permanent puckered or crinkled effect.
▶ **noun** [mass noun] material treated in this way.
– ORIGIN late 19th cent.: French, literally 'pleated', past participle of *plisser*.

PLO ▶ **abbreviation for** Palestine Liberation Organization.

plock ▶ **verb** [no obj.] make a short, low, clicking sound.
▶ **noun** a sound of this kind.
– ORIGIN 1930s: imitative.

plod ▶ **verb** (**plodded**, **plodding**) [no obj., with adverbial of direction] walk doggedly and slowly with heavy steps: *we plodded back up the hill* | figurative *talks on a new constitution have plodded on.*
■ work slowly and perseveringly at a dull task: *we were plodding through a textbook.*
▶ **noun 1** a slow, heavy walk: *he settled down to a steady plod.*
2 (also **PC Plod**) Brit. informal a police officer. [ORIGIN: with allusion to Mr *Plod* the Policeman in Enid Blyton's *Noddy* stories for children.]
– DERIVATIVES **plodder** noun.
– ORIGIN mid 16th cent.: probably symbolic of a heavy gait.

plodding ▶ **adjective** slow-moving and unexciting: *a plodding comedy drama.*
■ (of a person) thorough and hard-working but lacking in imagination or intelligence.
– DERIVATIVES **ploddingly** adverb.

-ploid ▶ **combining form** Biology denoting the number of sets of chromosomes in a cell: *triploid.*
– ORIGIN based on (*ha*)*ploid* and (*di*)*ploid*.

ploidy /ˈplɔɪdi/ ▶ **noun** [mass noun] Genetics the number of sets of chromosomes in a cell, or in the cells of an organism.
– ORIGIN 1940s: from words such as (*di*)*ploidy* and (*poly*)*ploidy*.

Ploieşti /plɔɪˈɛʃt/ an oil-refining city in central Romania, north of Bucharest; pop. 254,300 (1993).

plongeur /plɒ̃ˈʒəː/ ▶ **noun** a person employed to wash dishes and carry out other menial tasks in a restaurant or hotel.
– ORIGIN French, literally 'person who plunges'.

plonk[1] informal ▶ **verb 1** [with obj. and adverbial of place] set down heavily or carelessly: *she plonked her glass on the table.*
■ (**plonk oneself**) sit down heavily and without ceremony: *he plonked himself down on the sofa.*
2 [no obj.] play on a musical instrument laboriously or unskilfully: *people plonking around on expensive instruments.*
▶ **noun** a sound as of something being set down heavily: *he sat down with a plonk.*
– ORIGIN late 19th cent. (originally dialect): imitative; compare with **PLUNK**.

plonk[2] ▶ **noun** [mass noun] Brit. informal cheap wine of inferior quality.
– ORIGIN 1930s (originally Australian): probably an alteration of *blanc* in French *vin blanc* 'white wine'.

plonker ▶ **noun** Brit. informal **1** a foolish or inept person.
2 a man's penis.
– ORIGIN mid 19th cent. (as a dialect word meaning 'something large of its kind'): from the verb **PLONK**[1] + **-ER**[1].

plook /pluːk/ ▶ **noun** Scottish a spot or pimple.
– ORIGIN Middle English: of unknown origin.

plop ▶ **noun** a short sound as of a small, solid object dropping into water without a splash.
▶ **verb** (**plopped**, **plopping**) fall or cause to fall with such a sound: [no obj.] *the stone plopped into the pond* | [with obj.] *she plopped a sugar cube into the cup.*
■ (**plop oneself down**) sit or lie down gently but clumsily: *he plopped himself down on the nearest chair.*
– ORIGIN early 19th cent.: imitative.

plosion /ˈpləʊʒ(ə)n/ ▶ **noun** [mass noun] Phonetics the sudden release of air in the pronunciation of a plosive consonant.
– ORIGIN early 20th cent.: shortening of **EXPLOSION**.

plosive /ˈpləʊsɪv, -z-/ Phonetics ▶ **adjective** denoting a consonant that is produced by stopping the airflow using the lips, teeth, or palate, followed by a sudden release of air.
▶ **noun** a plosive speech sound. The basic plosives in English are *t*, *k*, and *p* (voiceless) and *d*, *g*, and *b* (voiced).
– ORIGIN late 19th cent.: shortening of **EXPLOSIVE**.

plot ▶ **noun 1** a plan made in secret by a group of people to do something illegal or harmful: [with infinitive] *there's a plot to overthrow the government.*
2 the main events of a play, novel, film, or similar work, devised and presented by the writer as an interrelated sequence.
3 a small piece of ground marked out for a purpose such as building or gardening: *a vegetable plot.*
4 a graph showing the relation between two variables.
■ chiefly US a diagram, chart, or map.
▶ **verb** (**plotted**, **plotting**) [with obj.] **1** secretly make plans to carry out (an illegal or harmful action): *the two men are serving sentences for plotting a bomb campaign* | [no obj.] *brother* ***plots against*** *brother.*
2 devise the sequence of events in (a play, novel, film, or similar work).
3 mark (a route or position) on a chart: *he started to plot lines of ancient sites.*
■ mark out or allocate (points) on a graph. ■ make (a curve) by marking out a number of such points. ■ illustrate by use of a graph: *it is possible to plot fairly closely the rate at which recruitment of girls increased.*
– PHRASES **lose the plot** informal lose one's ability to understand or cope with what is happening: *many people believe that he is feeling the strain or has lost the plot.* **the plot thickens** see **THICKEN**.
– DERIVATIVES **plotless** adjective, **plotter** noun.
– ORIGIN late Old English (in sense 3 of the noun), of unknown origin. The sense 'secret plan', dating from the late 16th cent., is associated with Old French *complot* 'dense crowd, secret project', the same term being used occasionally in English from the mid 16th cent. Compare with **PLAT**[1].

Plotinus /plə'tʌɪnəs/ (*c.*205–70), philosopher, probably of Roman descent. He was the founder and leading exponent of Neoplatonism; his writings were published after his death by his pupil Porphyry.

plot ratio ▶ **noun** a ratio representing the density of building in a specified area of land.

Plott (also **Plott hound**) ▶ **noun** a hunting dog of a breed developed from German stock by the Plott family of North Carolina. It has a smooth dark brown coat and large drooping ears.

plotty ▶ **adjective** informal (of a novel, play, or film) having an excessively elaborate or complicated plot.

plotz ▶ **verb** [no obj.] N. Amer. informal collapse or be beside oneself with frustration, annoyance, or other strong emotion: *lots of directors plotz while making their films.*
– ORIGIN 1960s: from Yiddish *platsen*, literally 'to burst', from Middle High German *platzen*.

plough (US **plow**) ▶ **noun 1** a large farming implement with one or more blades fixed in a frame, drawn by a tractor or by animals and used for cutting furrows in the soil and turning it over, especially to prepare for the planting of seeds.
■ [mass noun] land where the earth has been turned using such an implement: *she saw a brown strip of plough.* ■ chiefly N. Amer. a snowplough.
2 (**the Plough**) a prominent formation of seven stars in the constellation Ursa Major (the Great Bear), containing the Pointers that indicate the direction to the Pole Star. Also called **BIG DIPPER** (in North America), **CHARLES'S WAIN** (formerly, in Britain).
▶ **verb** [with obj.] **1** turn up the earth of (an area of land) with a plough, especially before sowing: *the fields had all been* ***ploughed up*** | [as adj. **ploughed**] *a ploughed field.*
■ cut (a furrow or line) with or as if with a plough: *icebergs have ploughed furrows on the seabed.* ■ (of a ship or boat) travel through (an area of water): *cruise liners plough the long-sailed routes.* ■ (**plough something up**) unearth something while using a plough: *some day someone will plough up the bomb and lose a leg.*
2 [no obj., with adverbial of direction] (especially of a vehicle) move in a fast and uncontrolled manner: *the car ploughed into the side of a van.*
■ advance or progress laboriously or forcibly: *they ploughed their way through deep snow* | *the students are ploughing through a set of grammar exercises.* ■ (**plough**

p

on) continue steadily despite difficulties or warnings to stop: *he ploughed on, trying to outline his plans.* **3** chiefly N. Amer. clear snow from (a road) using a snowplough. **4** Brit. informal, dated fail (an examination).

– PHRASES **plough a lonely** (or **one's own**) **furrow** follow a course of action in which one is isolated or in which one can act independently. **put** (or **set**) **one's hand to the plough** embark on a task. [ORIGIN: with biblical allusion to Luke 9:62.]

– DERIVATIVES **ploughable** adjective, **plougher** noun.

– ORIGIN late Old English *plōh*, of Germanic origin; related to Dutch *ploeg* and German *Pflug*. The spelling *plough* became common in England in the 18th cent.; earlier (16th–17th cents) the noun was normally spelled *plough*, the verb *plow*.

▶ **plough something in/back** plough grass or other material into the soil to enrich it. ■ invest money in a business or reinvest profits in the enterprise producing them.

ploughland (US **plowland**) ▶ **noun** [mass noun] land that is ploughed for growing crops; arable land. ■ [count noun] a measure of land used in the northern and eastern counties of England after the Norman conquest, based on the area able to be ploughed in a year by a team of eight oxen.

ploughman (US **plowman**) ▶ **noun** (pl. **-men**) a person who uses a plough.

ploughman's lunch ▶ **noun** Brit. a meal of bread and cheese, typically with pickle and salad.

ploughman's spikenard ▶ **noun** a European plant of the daisy family, with purple and yellow flower heads.
● *Inula conyzae*, family Compositae.

Plough Monday ▶ **noun** the first Monday after Epiphany, formerly marked by popular festivals or observances in some regions.

– ORIGIN from the custom of dragging a plough through the streets to mark the beginning of the ploughing season.

plough pan ▶ **noun** a compacted layer in cultivated soil resulting from repeated ploughing.

ploughshare (US **plowshare**) ▶ **noun** the main cutting blade of a plough, behind the coulter.

– ORIGIN late Middle English: from **PLOUGH** + Old English *scær, scear* 'ploughshare' (related to **SHEAR**).

Plovdiv /ˈplɒvdɪf/ an industrial and commercial city in southern Bulgaria; pop. 379,080 (1990). Known to the ancient Greeks as Philippopolis and to the Romans as Trimontium, it assumed its present name after the First World War.

plover /ˈplʌvə/ ▶ **noun** a short-billed gregarious wading bird, typically found by water but sometimes frequenting grassland, tundra, and mountains.
● Family Charadriidae (the **plover family**): several genera and numerous species, especially the **ringed plovers** (*Charadrius*), **grey** and **golden plovers** (*Pluvialis*), and lapwings (*Vanellus*).
■ used in names of similar birds in other families, e.g. **crab plover**.

– ORIGIN Middle English: from Anglo-Norman French, based on Latin *pluvia* 'rain'.

plow ▶ **noun** & **verb** US spelling of **PLOUGH**.

ploy ▶ **noun** a cunning plan or action designed to turn a situation to one's own advantage: *the president has dismissed the referendum as a ploy to buy time.* ■ an activity done for amusement: *the craft is a pleasant ploy during the holiday season.*

– ORIGIN late 17th cent. (originally Scots and northern English in the sense 'pastime'): of unknown origin. The notion of 'a calculated plan' dates from the 1950s.

PLP ▶ **abbreviation for** (in the UK) Parliamentary Labour Party.

PLR ▶ **abbreviation for** (in the UK) Public Lending Right.

pluck ▶ **verb** [with obj.] take hold of (something) and quickly remove it from its place: *she plucked a blade of grass* | *he plucked a tape from the shelf.* ■ catch hold of and pull quickly: *she plucked his sleeve* | [no obj.] *brambles* ***plucked at*** *her jeans.* ■ quickly or suddenly remove someone from a dangerous or unpleasant situation: *the baby was plucked from a grim orphanage.* ■ pull the feathers from (a bird's carcass) to prepare it for cooking. ■ pull some of the hairs from (one's eyebrows) to make them look neater. ■ sound (a musical instrument or its strings) with one's finger or a plectrum.

▶ **noun** [mass noun] **1** spirited and determined courage. **2** the heart, liver, and lungs of an animal as food.

– DERIVATIVES **plucker** noun [usu. in combination] *a goose-plucker.*

– ORIGIN late Old English *ploccian, pluccian*, of Germanic origin; related to Flemish *plokken*; probably from the base of Old French *(es)peluchier* 'to pluck'. Sense 1 of the noun is originally boxers' slang.

▶ **pluck up courage** see **COURAGE**.

plucky ▶ **adjective** (**pluckier, pluckiest**) having or showing determined courage in the face of difficulties.

– DERIVATIVES **pluckily** adverb, **pluckiness** noun.

plug ▶ **noun 1** a piece of solid material fitting tightly into a hole and blocking it up: *somewhere in the pipes there is a plug of ice blocking the flow.* ■ a circular piece of metal, rubber, or plastic used to stop the plughole of a bath or basin and keep the water in it. ■ N. Amer. informal a baby's dummy. ■ a mass of solidified lava filling the neck of a volcano. ■ (in gardening) a young plant or clump of grass with a small mass of soil protecting its roots, for planting out. **2** a device for making an electrical connection, especially between an appliance and the mains, consisting of an insulated casing with metal pins that fit into holes in a socket. ■ a socket into which such a device can be fitted. ■ short for **SPARK PLUG**. **3** informal a piece of publicity promoting a product, event, or establishment: *he threw in a plug, boasting that the restaurant offered many entrées for under $5.* **4** a piece of tobacco cut from a larger cake for chewing. ■ [mass noun] (also **plug tobacco**) tobacco in large cakes designed to be cut for chewing. **5** Fishing a lure with one or more hooks attached. **6** short for **FIREPLUG**. **7** N. Amer. informal a tired or old horse.

▶ **verb** (**plugged, plugging**) [with obj.] **1** block or fill in (a hole or cavity): *trucks arrived loaded with gravel to plug the hole and clear the road* | figurative *the new sanctions are meant to plug the gaps in the trade embargo.* ■ insert (something) into an opening so as to fill it: *the baby plugged his thumb into his mouth.* **2** informal mention (a product, event, or establishment) publicly in order to promote it: *during the show he plugged his new record.* **3** informal shoot or hit (someone or something). **4** [no obj., with adverbial] informal proceed steadily and laboriously with a journey or task: *during the years of poverty, he* ***plugged away at*** *his writing.*

– DERIVATIVES **plugger** noun.

– ORIGIN early 17th cent.: from Middle Dutch and Middle Low German *plugge*, of unknown ultimate origin.

▶ **plug something in** connect an electrical appliance to the mains by inserting a plug in a socket.
plug into (of an electrical appliance) be connected to another appliance by a lead inserted in a socket. ■ gain or have access to a system of computerized information: *we plug into the research facilities available at the institute.* ■ figurative become knowledgeable about and involved with: *the good thing about this job is that I'm plugged into what's going on.*

Plug and Play ▶ **noun** a standard for the connection of peripherals to personal computers, whereby a device only needs to be connected to a computer in order to be configured to work perfectly, without any action by the user.

plugboard ▶ **noun** a board containing several sockets into which plugs may be inserted to interconnect electric circuits, telephone lines, or computer components, by means of short lengths of wire.

plug-compatible ▶ **adjective** relating to or denoting computing equipment which is compatible with devices or systems produced by different manufacturers, to the extent that it can be plugged in and operated successfully.

▶ **noun** a piece of computing equipment designed in this way.

plug flow ▶ **noun** [mass noun] Geology & Physics the flow of a body of ice or viscous fluid with no shearing between adjacent layers; idealized flow without any mixing of particles of fluid.

plug fuse ▶ **noun** a fuse designed to be pushed into a socket in a panel or board.

plug gauge ▶ **noun** a gauge in the form of a plug, used for measuring the diameter of a hole.

plughole ▶ **noun** Brit. a hole at the lowest point of a bath, basin, or sink, down which waste water drains away and which can be stopped with a plug.

– PHRASES **go down the plughole** informal be unsuccessful, lost, or wasted: *the company went down the plughole.*

plug-in ▶ **adjective** able to be connected by means of a plug: *a plug-in kettle.* ■ Computing (of a module or software) able to be added to a system to give extra features or functions: *a plug-in graphics card.*

▶ **noun 1** Computing a module or software of this kind. **2** Canadian an electric socket in a car park or garage for plugging in the block heater of a vehicle to prevent the engine from freezing.

plug-ugly informal, chiefly N. Amer. ▶ **noun** (pl. **-ies**) a thug or villain.

▶ **adjective** (of a person) very ugly.

– ORIGIN by association with the verb **PLUG** in the informal sense 'hit with the fist'.

plum ▶ **noun 1** an oval fleshy fruit which is purple, reddish, or yellow when ripe and contains a flattish pointed stone. ■ [usu. with modifier] W. Indian a small edible fruit from any of a number of trees. **2** (also **plum tree**) the deciduous tree which bears plums.
● Several species in the genus *Prunus*, family Rosaceae, in particular *P. domestica*.
3 [mass noun] a reddish-purple colour: [as modifier] *a plum blazer.* **4** [usu. as modifier] informal a thing, typically a job, considered to be highly desirable: *he landed a plum assistant producer's job.*

▶ **adverb** chiefly US variant spelling of **PLUMB**[1]: *the helicopter crashed plum on the cabins.*

– PHRASES **have a plum in one's mouth** Brit. have an accent thought typical of the English upper classes. **like a ripe plum** (or **ripe plums**) used to convey that something can be obtained with little or no effort: *the country is likely to fall into the enemy's hands like a ripe plum.*

– ORIGIN Old English *plūme*, from medieval Latin *pruna*, from Latin *prunum* (see **PRUNE**[1]).

plumage /ˈpluːmɪdʒ/ ▶ **noun** [mass noun] a bird's feathers collectively.

– DERIVATIVES **plumaged** adjective [usu. in combination] *a grey-plumaged bird.*

– ORIGIN late Middle English: from Old French, from *plume* 'feather'.

plumb[1] ▶ **verb** [with obj.] **1** measure (the depth of a body of water). ■ [no obj., with adverbial] (of water) be of a specified depth: *at its deepest the lake scarcely plumbed seven feet.* ■ explore or experience fully or to extremes: *she had* ***plumbed the depths of*** *depravity.* **2** test (an upright surface) to determine the vertical.

▶ **noun** a ball of lead or other heavy object attached to the end of a line for finding the depth of water or determining the vertical on an upright surface.

▶ **adverb 1** informal exactly: *trading opportunities plumb in the centre of central Europe.* ■ [as submodifier] N. Amer. to a very high degree; extremely: *they must both be plumb crazy.* ■ [as submodifier] N. Amer. completely: *the transmission was plumb worn out.* **2** archaic vertically: *drapery fell from their human forms plumb down.*

▶ **adjective** vertical: *ensure that the skirting is straight and plumb.* ■ Cricket (of the wicket) level; true.

– PHRASES **out of plumb** not exactly vertical: *the towers are inclined, from four to ten feet out of plumb.*

– ORIGIN Middle English (originally in the sense 'sounding lead'): via Old French from Latin *plumbum* 'lead'.

plumb[2] ▶ **verb** [with obj.] (**plumb something in**) install an appliance such as a bath, toilet, or washing machine and connect to water and drainage pipes. ■ install and connect water and drainage pipes in (a building or room): *the kitchen is* ***plumbed for*** *a washing machine.*

– ORIGIN late 19th cent. (in the sense 'work as a plumber'): back-formation from **PLUMBER**.

plumbago /plʌmˈbeɪgəʊ/ ▶ **noun** (pl. **-os**) **1** old-fashioned term for **GRAPHITE**. [ORIGIN: early 17th cent. (denoting an ore such as galena containing

lead): from Latin, from *plumbum* 'lead'. The sense 'graphite' arose through its use for pencil leads.]
2 an evergreen flowering shrub or climber which is widely distributed in warm regions and grown elsewhere as a greenhouse or indoor plant. Also called **LEADWORT**. [ORIGIN: named from the colour of the flowers.]
• Genus *Plumbago*, family Plumbaginaceae.

plumbate /ˈplʌmbeɪt/ ▶ **noun** Chemistry a salt in which the anion contains both lead and oxygen, especially one of the anion PbO_3^{2-}.
– ORIGIN mid 19th cent.: from Latin *plumbum* 'lead' + **-ATE**[1].

plumb bob ▶ **noun** a bob of lead or other heavy material forming the weight of a plumb line.

plumbeous /ˈplʌmbɪəs/ ▶ **adjective** chiefly Ornithology of the dull grey colour of lead.
– ORIGIN late 16th cent.: from Latin *plumbeus* 'leaden' (from *plumbum* 'lead') + **-OUS**.

plumber ▶ **noun** a person who fits and repairs the pipes, fittings, and other apparatus of water supply, sanitation, or heating systems.
– ORIGIN late Middle English (originally denoting a person dealing in and working with lead): from Old French *plommier*, from Latin *plumbarius*, from *plumbum* 'lead'.

plumber's snake ▶ **noun** see **SNAKE**.

plumbic /ˈplʌmbɪk/ ▶ **adjective** Chemistry of lead with a valency of four; of lead (IV). Compare with **PLUMBOUS**.
■ Medicine caused by the presence of lead.
– ORIGIN late 18th cent.: from Latin *plumbum* 'lead' + **-IC**.

plumbing ▶ **noun** [mass noun] the system of pipes, tanks, fittings, and other apparatus required for the water supply, heating, and sanitation in a building.
■ the work of installing and maintaining such a system. ■ informal used as a humorous euphemism for the excretory tracts and urinary system: *I'd never discuss my plumbing with ladies.*

plumbism /ˈplʌmbɪz(ə)m/ ▶ **noun** technical term for **LEAD POISONING**.

plumbless /ˈplʌmlɪs/ ▶ **adjective** poetic/literary (of a body of water) extremely deep.

plumb line ▶ **noun** a line with a plumb attached to it, used for finding the depth of water or determining the vertical on an upright surface.

plumbous /ˈplʌmbəs/ ▶ **adjective** Chemistry of lead with a valency of two; of lead (II). Compare with **PLUMBIC**.
– ORIGIN late 17th cent.: from Latin *plumbosus* 'full of lead'.

plumb rule ▶ **noun** a plumb line attached to a board, used by builders and surveyors.

plum cake ▶ **noun** chiefly Brit. a cake containing raisins, currants, or other dried fruit.

plum duff ▶ **noun** a rich, spiced suet pudding made with raisins or currants.

plume ▶ **noun** a long, soft feather or arrangement of feathers used by a bird for display or worn by a person for ornament: *a hat with a jaunty ostrich plume.*
■ Zoology a part of an animal's body that resembles a feather: *the antennae are divided into large feathery plumes.* ■ a long cloud of smoke or vapour resembling a feather as it spreads from its point of origin: *as he spoke, the word was accompanied by a white plume of breath.* ■ a mass of material, typically a pollutant, spreading from a source: *a radioactive plume.* ■ (also **mantle plume**) Geology a localized column of hotter magma rising by convection in the mantle, believed to cause volcanic activity in locations away from plate margins.
▶ **verb 1** [no obj.] spread out in a shape resembling a feather: *smoke plumed from the chimneys.*
■ [with obj.] decorate with or as if with feathers: [as adj. **plumed**] *rain began to beat down on my plumed cap.*
2 (**plume oneself**) chiefly archaic (of a bird) preen itself.
■ figurative feel a great sense of self-satisfaction about something: *she* **plumed herself on** *being cosmopolitan.*
– DERIVATIVES **plumeless** adjective, **plume-like** adjective, **plumery** noun.
– ORIGIN late Middle English: from Old French, from Latin *pluma* 'down'.

plumed serpent ▶ **noun** a mythical creature depicted as part bird, part snake, in particular Quetzalcóatl, a god of the Toltec and Aztec civilizations having this form.

plume moth ▶ **noun** a small slender long-legged moth with narrow wings divided into feathery plumes. At rest the wings are rolled and held out sideways, giving the moth the shape of a letter T.
• Family Pterophoridae: several genera.

plumeria /pluːˈmɪərɪə/ ▶ **noun** a fragrant flowering tropical tree of a genus which includes frangipani.
• Genus *Plumeria*, family Apocynaceae.
– ORIGIN modern Latin, named after Charles *Plumier* (1646–1704), French botanist.

plummet ▶ **verb** (**plummeted**, **plummeting**) [no obj.] fall or drop straight down at high speed: *a climber was killed when he plummeted 300 feet down an icy gully.*
■ decrease rapidly in value or amount: *hardware sales plummeted.*
▶ **noun 1** a steep and rapid fall or drop.
2 a plumb or plumb line.
– ORIGIN late Middle English (as a noun): from Old French *plommet* 'small sounding lead', diminutive of *plomb* 'lead'. The current verb sense dates from the 1930s.

plummy ▶ **adjective** (**plummier**, **plummiest**)
1 resembling a plum in taste, scent, or colour: *cosy reds and plummy blues.*
2 Brit. informal (of a person's voice) having an accent thought typical of the English upper classes.
3 Brit. informal choice; highly desirable: *there are some plummy roles for the taking here.*

plumose /pluːˈməʊs, ˈpluːməʊs, -z/ ▶ **adjective** chiefly Biology having many fine filaments or branches which give a feathery appearance.
– ORIGIN mid 18th cent.: from Latin *plumosus* 'full of down or feathers', from *pluma* 'down'.

plumose anemone ▶ **noun** a sea anemone with numerous slender feathery tentacles.
• Genus *Metridium*, order Actiniaria.

plump[1] ▶ **adjective** having a full rounded shape: *the berries were plump and sweet.*
■ rather fat.
▶ **verb** [with obj.] shake or pat (a cushion or pillow) to adjust its stuffing and make it rounded and soft: *she* **plumped up** *her pillows.*
■ [no obj.] (**plump up**) become rounder and fatter: *stew the dried fruits gently until they plump up.*
– DERIVATIVES **plumpish** adjective, **plumply** adverb, **plumpness** noun, **plumpy** adjective.
– ORIGIN late 15th cent. (in the sense 'blunt, forthright'): related to Middle Dutch *plomp*, Middle Low German *plump*, *plomp* 'blunt, obtuse, blockish'. The sense has become appreciative, perhaps by association with **PLUM**.

plump[2] ▶ **verb 1** [with obj. and adverbial of place] set down heavily or unceremoniously: *she plumped her bag on the table.*
■ (**plump oneself**) sit down in this way: *she plumped herself down in the nearest seat* | [no obj.] *he plumped down on the bench beside me.*
2 [no obj.] (**plump for**) decide definitely in favour of (one of two or more possibilities): *offered a choice of drinks, he plumped for brandy.*
▶ **noun** archaic an abrupt plunge; a heavy fall.
▶ **adverb** informal **1** with a sudden or heavy fall: *she sat down plump on the bed.*
2 dated directly and bluntly: *he must tell her plump and plain that he was on the dole.*
– ORIGIN late Middle English: related to Middle Low German *plumpen*, Middle Dutch *plompen* 'fall into water', probably of imitative origin.

plum pox ▶ **noun** [mass noun] an aphid-borne virus disease of plum trees characterized by yellow blotches on the leaves and pockets of dead tissue in the fruit.

plum pudding ▶ **noun** a rich boiled suet pudding containing raisins, currants, and spices.
– ORIGIN early 18th cent.: so named because the pudding was originally made with plums, the word *plum* being retained later to denote 'raisin' which became a substituted ingredient.

plum tomato ▶ **noun** a tomato of an Italian variety which is large and shaped like a plum, typically used in cooking rather than eaten raw.

plumule /ˈpluːmjuːl/ ▶ **noun 1** Botany the rudimentary shoot or stem of an embryo plant.
2 Ornithology a bird's down feather, numbers of which form an insulating layer under the contour feathers.
– ORIGIN early 18th cent.: from French *plumule* or Latin *plumula* 'small feather', diminutive of *pluma* 'down'.

plumy ▶ **adjective** (**plumier**, **plumiest**) resembling or decorated with feathers.

plunder ▶ **verb** [with obj.] steal goods from (a place or person), typically using force and in a time of war or civil disorder: *looters moved into the disaster area to plunder shops.*
■ steal (goods) in such a way. ■ take material from (artistic or academic work) for one's own purposes: *we shall plunder related sciences to assist our research.*
▶ **noun** [mass noun] the violent and dishonest acquisition of property: *the commander refused to maintain his troops through pillage and plunder.*
■ property acquired illegally and violently: *the army sacked the city and carried off huge quantities of plunder.*
– DERIVATIVES **plunderer** noun.
– ORIGIN mid 17th cent.: from German *plündern*, literally 'rob of household goods', from Middle High German *plunder* 'household effects'. Early use of the verb was with reference to the Thirty Years War (reflecting German usage); on the outbreak of the Civil War in 1642, the word and activity were associated with the forces under Prince Rupert.

plunge ▶ **verb 1** [no obj., with adverbial] jump or dive quickly and energetically: *our little daughters whooped as they* **plunged into** *the sea.*
■ fall suddenly and uncontrollably: *a car swerved to avoid a bus and plunged into a ravine.* ■ embark impetuously on a speech or course of action: *he came to a decision, and plunged on before he had time to reconsider it.* ■ suffer a rapid decrease in value: *shares in the company plunged 18p on news that profits had fallen.* ■ (of a ship) pitch: *the ship plunged through the 20-foot seas.*
2 [with obj. and adverbial] push or thrust quickly: *he plunged his hands into his pockets.*
■ put (something) in liquid so as to immerse it completely: *to peel fruit, cover with boiling water and then plunge them into iced water.* ■ (often **be plunged into**) suddenly bring into a specified condition or state: *for a moment the scene was illuminated, then it was plunged back into darkness.* ■ [with obj.] sink (a plant or a pot containing a plant) in the ground.
▶ **noun** an act of jumping or diving into water: *fanatics went straight from the hot room to take a cold plunge.*
■ a swift and drastic fall in value or amount: *the central bank declared a 76% plunge in its profits.*
– PHRASES **take the plunge** informal commit oneself to a course of action about which one is nervous.
– ORIGIN late Middle English: from Old French *plungier* 'thrust down', based on Latin *plumbum* 'lead, plummet'.

plunge bed ▶ **noun** a flower bed, typically containing peat or other moisture-retaining materials, in which plants in pots can be sunk.

plunge pool ▶ **noun 1** a deep basin excavated at the foot of a waterfall by the action of the falling water.
2 a small, deep swimming pool, typically one filled with cold water and used to refresh or invigorate the body after a sauna.

plunger ▶ **noun 1** a part of a device or mechanism that works with a plunging or thrusting movement.
■ a device consisting of a rubber cup on a long handle, used to clear blocked pipes by means of suction.
2 informal a person who gambles or spends money recklessly.

plunk informal ▶ **verb 1** [no obj.] play a keyboard or plucked stringed instrument, especially in an unexpressive way.
2 [with obj.] US hit (someone) abruptly.
3 [with obj. and adverbial] chiefly N. Amer. set down heavily or abruptly: *she plunked her pack on top of the bar.*
■ (**plunk something down**) pay a sum of money: *I plunked down $24.95 for the new paperback edition.*
▶ **noun 1** the sound made by abruptly plucking a string of a stringed instrument.
2 US a heavy blow.
3 N. Amer. an act of setting something down heavily.
– ORIGIN early 19th cent.: probably imitative.

pluperfect ▶ **adjective** Grammar (of a tense) denoting an action completed prior to some past point of time specified or implied, formed in English by *had* and the past participle, as in *he had gone by then.*
▶ **noun** the pluperfect tense.
– ORIGIN late 15th cent.: from modern Latin *plusperfectum*, from Latin (*tempus praeteritum*) *plus quam perfectum* '(past tense) more than perfect'.

p

plural ▶ **adjective** more than one in number: *the meanings of the text are plural.*
■ Grammar (of a word or form) denoting more than one, or (in languages with dual number) more than two: *[postpositive] the first person plural.*
▶ **noun 1** Grammar a plural word or form.
■ [in sing.] the plural number: *the verb is in the plural.*
2 S. African formerly used as a joking or ironical way of referring to a black person: *these men have been running the affairs of us plurals for thirty years.* [ORIGIN: ironically (mocking official terminology), from *Department of Plural Relations and Development.*]
– DERIVATIVES **plurally** adverb.
– ORIGIN late Middle English: from Old French *plurel* or Latin *pluralis*, from *plus, plur-* 'more'.

pluralism ▶ **noun** [mass noun] **1** a condition or system in which two or more states, groups, principles, sources of authority, etc., coexist.
■ a political theory or system of power-sharing among a number of political parties. ■ a theory or system of devolution and autonomy for individual bodies in preference to monolithic state control. ■ a form of society in which the members of minority groups maintain their independent cultural traditions. ■ Philosophy a theory or system that recognizes more than one ultimate principle. Compare with **MONISM**.
2 the practice of holding more than one office or church benefice at a time.
– DERIVATIVES **pluralist** noun & adjective, **pluralistic** adjective, **pluralistically** adverb.

plurality ▶ **noun** (pl. **-ies**) **1** [mass noun] the fact or state of being plural: *some languages add an extra syllable to mark plurality.*
■ [in sing.] a large number of people or things: *a plurality of critical approaches.*
2 US the number of votes cast for a candidate who receives more than any other but does not receive an absolute majority.
■ the number by which this exceeds the number of votes cast for the candidate placed second.
3 chiefly historical another term for **PLURALISM** (in sense 2).
– ORIGIN late Middle English: from Old French *pluralite*, from late Latin *pluralitas*, from Latin *pluralis* 'relating to more than one' (see **PLURAL**).

pluralize (also **-ise**) ▶ **verb** [with obj.] **1** cause to become more numerous.
■ cause to be made up of several different elements.
2 give a plural form to (a word).
– DERIVATIVES **pluralization** noun.

plural society ▶ **noun** a society composed of different ethnic groups or cultural traditions, or in the political structure of which ethnic or cultural differences are reflected.

plural voting ▶ **noun** [mass noun] the system or practice of casting more than one vote, or of voting in more than one constituency.

pluri- ▶ **combining form** several: *pluripotent.*
– ORIGIN from Latin *plus, plur-* 'more', *plures* 'several'.

pluripotent /ˌplʊərɪˈpəʊt(ə)nt/ ▶ **adjective** Biology (of an immature or stem cell) capable of giving rise to several different cell types.
– ORIGIN 1940s: from **PLURI-** 'several' + Latin *potent-* 'being able' (see **POTENT**[1]).

plus ▶ **preposition 1** with the addition of: *two plus four is six | he was awarded the full amount plus interest.*
■ informal together with: *all apartments have a small kitchen plus private bathroom.*
2 (of temperature) above zero: *the temperature is frequently plus 35 degrees C at midday.*
▶ **adjective 1** [postpositive] (after a number or amount) at least: *companies put losses at $500,000 plus.*
■ (after a grade) rather better than: *B plus.*
2 (before a number) above zero; positive: *plus 60 degrees centigrade.*
3 having a positive electric charge.
▶ **noun 1** short for **PLUS SIGN**.
■ a mathematical operation of addition.
2 an advantage: *knowing the language is a decided plus | [as modifier] on the plus side, the staff are enthusiastic and good-natured.*
▶ **conjunction** informal furthermore; also: *it's packed full of medical advice, plus it keeps you informed about the latest research.*
– ORIGIN mid 16th cent.: from Latin, literally 'more'.

plus ça change /ˌpluː sa ˈʃɒ̃ʒ, French ply sa ʃɑ̃ʒ/ ▶ **exclamation** used to express resigned acknowledgement of the fundamental immutability of human nature and institutions.
– ORIGIN French, from *plus ça change, plus c'est la même chose* 'the more it changes, the more it stays the same'.

plus fours ▶ **plural noun** dated baggy knickerbockers reaching below the knee, worn by men for hunting and golf.
– ORIGIN 1920s: so named because the overhang at the knee requires an extra four inches of material.

plush ▶ **noun** [mass noun] a rich fabric of silk, cotton, wool, or a combination of these, with a long, soft nap: *[as modifier] deep-buttoned plush upholstery.*
▶ **adjective** informal richly luxurious and expensive: *a plush Mayfair flat.*
– DERIVATIVES **plushly** adverb, **plushness** noun, **plushy (plushier, plushiest)** adjective.
– ORIGIN late 16th cent.: from obsolete French *pluche*, contraction of *peluche*, from Old French *peluchier* 'to pluck', based on Latin *pilus* 'hair'. The sense 'luxurious' dates from the 1920s.

plush velvet ▶ **noun** [mass noun] a kind of plush with a short, soft, dense nap, resembling velvet.

plus-minus ▶ **noun** [often as modifier] Ice Hockey a running total used as an indication of a player's effectiveness, calculated by adding one for each goal scored by the player's team in even-strength play while the player is on the ice, and subtracting one for each goal conceded.
▶ **adverb** S. African more or less; roughly: *it was plus-minus 8.30 a.m.*

plus sign ▶ **noun** the symbol +, indicating addition or a positive value.

plus twos ▶ **plural noun** dated a shorter version of plus fours.

Plutarch /ˈpluːtɑːk/ (c.46–c.120), Greek biographer and philosopher; Latin name *Lucius Mestrius Plutarchus*. He is chiefly known for *Parallel Lives*, a collection of biographies of prominent Greeks and Romans.

pluteus /ˈpluːtɪəs/ ▶ **noun** (pl. **plutei** /ˈpluːtɪʌɪ/) Zoology the planktonic larva of some echinoderms, being somewhat triangular with lateral projections.
– ORIGIN late 19th cent.: from Latin, literally 'barrier' (with reference to its shape).

Pluto 1 Greek Mythology the god of the underworld. Also called **HADES**.
2 Astronomy the most remote known planet of the solar system, ninth in order from the sun, discovered in 1930 by Clyde Tombaugh.

> Pluto usually orbits beyond Neptune at an average distance of 5,900 million km from the sun, though its orbit is so eccentric that at perihelion it is closer to the sun than Neptune (as in 1979–99). Pluto is smaller than earth's moon (diameter about 2,250 km), but it was discovered in 1978 to have its own satellite (Charon), which is so large that the pair should properly be regarded as a double planet.

– ORIGIN via Latin from *Ploutōn*, the Greek name of the god of the underworld.

plutocracy /pluːˈtɒkrəsi/ ▶ **noun** (pl. **-ies**) [mass noun] government by the wealthy.
■ [count noun] a state or society governed in this way. ■ [count noun] an elite or ruling class whose power derives from their wealth.
– DERIVATIVES **plutocratic** adjective, **plutocratically** adverb.
– ORIGIN mid 17th cent.: from Greek *ploutokratia*, from *ploutos* 'wealth' + *kratos* 'strength, authority'.

plutocrat ▶ **noun** often derogatory a person whose power derives from their wealth.

pluton /ˈpluːt(ə)n/ ▶ **noun** Geology a body of intrusive igneous rock.
– ORIGIN 1930s: back-formation from **PLUTONIC**.

Plutonian ▶ **adjective 1** of or associated with the underworld.
2 of or relating to the planet Pluto.

plutonic ▶ **adjective 1** Geology relating to or denoting igneous rock formed by solidification at considerable depth beneath the earth's surface.
2 (**Plutonic**) relating to the underworld or the god Pluto.

plutonism ▶ **noun** [mass noun] Geology the formation of intrusive igneous rocks by solidification of magma beneath the earth's surface.
■ (**Plutonism**) historical the theory (now accepted) that rocks such as granite were formed by solidification from the molten state, as proposed by James Hutton and others, rather than by precipitation from the sea. Compare with **NEPTUNISM**.
– DERIVATIVES **Plutonist** noun & adjective (historical).

plutonium ▶ **noun** [mass noun] the chemical element of atomic number 94, a dense silvery radioactive metal of the actinide series, used as a fuel in nuclear reactors and as an explosive in nuclear fission weapons. Plutonium only occurs in trace amounts in nature but is manufactured in nuclear reactors from uranium-238. (Symbol: **Pu**)
– ORIGIN 1940s: from Greek 'Pluto', on the pattern of *neptunium*, being the next planet beyond Neptune.

pluvial chiefly Geology ▶ **adjective** relating to or characterized by rainfall.
▶ **noun** a period marked by increased rainfall.
– ORIGIN mid 17th cent.: from Latin *pluvialis*, from *pluvia* 'rain'.

Pluviose /ˈpluːvɪəʊs/ (also **Pluviôse** /French plyvjoz/) ▶ **noun** the fifth month of the French Republican calendar (1793–1805), originally running from 20 January to 18 February.
– ORIGIN French *Pluviôse*, from Latin *pluviosus* 'relating to rain'.

ply[1] ▶ **noun** (pl. **-ies**) **1** a thickness or layer of a folded or laminated material.
■ [usu. in combination] a strand of yarn or rope. ■ the number of multiple layers or strands of which something is made: *the yarn can be any ply from two to eight.*
2 short for **PLYWOOD**.
3 [mass noun] (in game theory) the number of levels at which branching occurs in a tree of possible outcomes, typically corresponding to the number of moves ahead (in chess strictly half-moves ahead) considered by a computer program.
■ [count noun] a half-move (i.e. one player's move) in computer chess.
– ORIGIN late Middle English (in the sense 'fold'): from French *pli* 'fold', from the verb *plier*, from Latin *plicare* 'to fold'.

ply[2] ▶ **verb** (**-ies**, **-ied**) [with obj.] **1** work with (a tool), especially one requiring steady, rhythmic movements: *a tailor delicately plying his needle.*
■ work steadily at (one's business or trade); conduct.
2 [no obj., with adverbial of direction] (of a vessel or vehicle) travel regularly over a route, typically for commercial purposes: *ferries ply across a strait to the island.*
■ [with obj.] travel over (a route) in this way: *the fleet has plied the Bristol Channel since Victorian times.*
3 (**ply someone with**) provide someone with (food or drink) in a continuous or insistent way: *she plied me with tea and scones.*
■ direct (numerous questions) at someone.
– PHRASES **ply for hire** search for or be available for customers to hire.
– ORIGIN late Middle English: shortening of **APPLY**.

Plymouth /ˈplɪməθ/ **1** a port and naval base in SW England, on the Devon coast; pop. 238,800 (1991). In 1620 it was the scene of the Pilgrim Fathers' departure to North America in the *Mayflower.*
■ a shipping forecast area covering the English Channel roughly between the meridians of the Scilly Isles in the west and Start Point in the east.
2 a town in SE Massachusetts, on the Atlantic coast; pop. 40,290 (1986). The site in 1620 of the landing of the Pilgrim Fathers, it was the earliest permanent European settlement in New England.
3 the capital of the island of Montserrat in the Caribbean; pop. 3,500 (1991). It was abandoned following the eruption of the Soufrière Hills volcano from 1995.

Plymouth Brethren a strict Calvinistic religious body formed at Plymouth in Devon *c.*1830, having no formal creed and no official order of ministers. Its teaching emphasizes an expected millennium and members renounce many secular occupations, allowing only those compatible with New Testament standards.

Plymouth Rock[1] a granite boulder at Plymouth, Massachusetts, on to which the Pilgrim Fathers are said to have stepped from the *Mayflower.*

Plymouth Rock[2] ▶ **noun** a chicken of a large domestic breed of American origin, having grey plumage with blackish stripes, and a yellow beak, legs, and feet.

ply rating ▶ **noun** a number indicating the strength of a tyre casing.
– ORIGIN 1950s: formerly referring to the number of cord plies in a casing.

plywood ▶ **noun** [mass noun] a type of strong thin wooden board consisting of two or more layers glued and pressed together with the direction of the grain alternating.

Plzeň /pl'zɛɲ/ Czech name for **PILSEN**.

PM ▶ abbreviation for ■ post-mortem. ■ Prime Minister. ■ Provost Marshal.

Pm ▶ symbol for the chemical element promethium.

p.m. ▶ abbreviation after noon, used after times of day between noon and midnight not expressed using the 24-hour clock: *at 3.30 p.m.*
– ORIGIN from Latin *post meridiem*.

PMG ▶ abbreviation for ■ Paymaster General. ■ Postmaster General.

PMS ▶ abbreviation for premenstrual syndrome.

PMT chiefly Brit. ▶ abbreviation for premenstrual tension.

PNdB ▶ abbreviation for perceived noise decibel(s).

pneuma /'njuːmə/ ▶ noun Philosophy (in Stoic thought) the vital spirit, soul, or creative force of a person.
– ORIGIN Greek, literally 'that which is breathed or blown'.

pneumatic ▶ adjective containing or operated by air or gas under pressure.
■ Zoology (chiefly of cavities in the bones of birds) containing air. ■ informal (of a woman) having large breasts.
▶ noun (usu. **pneumatics**) an item of pneumatic equipment.
– DERIVATIVES **pneumatically** adverb, **pneumaticity** noun.
– ORIGIN mid 17th cent.: from French *pneumatique* or Latin *pneumaticus*, from Greek *pneumatikos*, from *pneuma* 'wind', from *pnein* 'breathe'.

pneumatic drill ▶ noun a large, heavy mechanical drill driven by compressed air, used for breaking up a hard surface such as a road.

pneumatics ▶ plural noun [treated as sing.] the branch of physics or technology concerned with the mechanical properties of gases.

pneumatic trough ▶ noun Chemistry a shallow liquid-filled container with which gases can be collected by displacing liquid from a jar inverted in the trough.

pneumatique /,njuːmə'tiːk, French pnɔmatik/ ▶ noun (pl. same or **pneumatiques**) (in Paris) a system of conveying mail along tubes by air pressure.
■ a message conveyed in this way.
– ORIGIN French.

pneumato- /'njuːmətəʊ/ ▶ combining form **1** of or containing air: *pneumatophore.*
2 relating to the spirit: *pneumatology.*
– ORIGIN from Greek *pneuma, pneumat-* 'wind, breath, spirit'.

pneumatology ▶ noun [mass noun] the branch of Christian theology concerned with the Holy Ghost and other spiritual concepts.
– DERIVATIVES **pneumatological** adjective.

pneumatolysis /,njuːmə'tɒlɪsɪs/ ▶ noun [mass noun] Geology the chemical alteration of rocks and the formation of minerals by the action of hot magmatic gases and vapours.
– DERIVATIVES **pneumatolytic** adjective.

pneumatophore /'njuːmətəfɔː/ ▶ noun **1** Zoology the gas-filled float of some colonial coelenterates, such as the Portuguese man-of-war.
2 Botany (in mangroves and other swamp plants) an aerial root specialized for gaseous exchange.

pneumo- ▶ combining form **1** of or relating to the lungs: *pneumogastric.*
2 of or relating to the presence of air or gas: *pneumothorax.*
– ORIGIN sense 1 from Greek *pneumōn* 'lung'; sense 2 from Greek *pneuma* 'air'.

pneumococcus /,njuːmə(ʊ)'kɒkəs/ ▶ noun (pl. **pneumococci** /-'kɒk(s)ʌɪ, -'kɒk(s)iː/) a bacterium associated with pneumonia and some forms of meningitis.
● *Streptococcus pneumoniae*, a Gram-positive diplococcus.
– DERIVATIVES **pneumococcal** adjective.

pneumoconiosis /,njuːmə(ʊ)kəʊnɪ'əʊsɪs/ ▶ noun [mass noun] Medicine a disease of the lungs due to inhalation of dust, characterized by inflammation, coughing, and fibrosis.
– ORIGIN late 19th cent.: from **PNEUMO-** 'relating to the lungs' + Greek *konis* 'dust' + **-OSIS**.

pneumocystis /,njuːmə(ʊ)'sɪstɪs/ ▶ noun [mass noun] Medicine a parasitic protozoan that can cause fatal pneumonia in people affected with immunodeficiency disease.
● *Pneumocystis carinii*, phylum Sporozoa.

pneumoencephalography /,njuːməʊɛnsɛfə'lɒɡrəfi, -kɛf-/ ▶ noun [mass noun] Medicine a radiographic technique (now largely superseded) for examining the brain. It involved displacing the cerebrospinal fluid in the ventricles of the brain by air or oxygen, which served as a contrast medium.
– DERIVATIVES **pneumoencephalographic** adjective.

pneumogastric ▶ adjective of or relating to the lungs and stomach.

pneumonectomy /,njuːmə(ʊ)'nɛktəmi/ ▶ noun (pl. **-ies**) [mass noun] surgical removal of a lung or part of a lung.

pneumonia /njuː'məʊnɪə/ ▶ noun [mass noun] lung inflammation caused by bacterial or viral infection, in which the air sacs fill with pus and may become solid. Inflammation may affect both lungs (**double pneumonia**) or only one (**single pneumonia**).
– DERIVATIVES **pneumonic** adjective.
– ORIGIN early 17th cent.: via Latin from Greek, from *pneumōn* 'lung'.

pneumonic plague ▶ noun see **PLAGUE**.

pneumonitis /,njuːmə(ʊ)'nʌɪtɪs/ ▶ noun [mass noun] Medicine inflammation of the walls of the alveoli (air sacs) in the lungs, usually caused by a virus.

pneumonoultramicroscopicsilico-volcanoconiosis ▶ noun [mass noun] an artificial long word said to mean a lung disease caused by inhaling very fine ash and sand dust.

pneumotachograph ▶ noun an apparatus for recording the rate of airflow during breathing.

pneumothorax ▶ noun [mass noun] Medicine the presence of air or gas in the cavity between the lungs and the chest wall, causing collapse of the lung.

PNG ▶ abbreviation for Papua New Guinea.

p-n junction ▶ noun Electronics a boundary between p-type and n-type material in a semiconductor device, functioning as a rectifier.

PNP ▶ adjective Electronics denoting a semiconductor device in which an *n*-type region is sandwiched between two *p*-type regions.
▶ abbreviation for (in computing) Plug and Play.

Pnyx /pnɪks/ the public place of assembly in ancient Athens, a semicircular level cut out of the side of a small hill west of the Acropolis.
– ORIGIN from Greek *pnux*.

PO ▶ abbreviation for ■ Petty Officer. ■ Pilot Officer. ■ postal order. ■ Post Office.

Po[1] /pəʊ/ a river in northern Italy. Italy's longest river, it rises in the Alps near the border with France and flows 668 km (415 miles) eastwards to the Adriatic.

Po[2] ▶ symbol for the chemical element polonium.

po /pəʊ/ ▶ noun (pl. **-os**) Brit. informal a chamber pot.
– ORIGIN late 19th cent.: from French *pot de chambre* 'chamber pot'.

po' /pɔː/ ▶ adjective US short for **POOR**, used to represent dialectal speech.

POA ▶ abbreviation for (in the UK) Prison Officers' Association.

poach[1] ▶ verb [with obj.] cook (an egg) without its shell in or over boiling water.
■ cook by simmering in a small amount of liquid.
– ORIGIN late Middle English: from Old French *pochier*, earlier in the sense 'enclose in a bag', from *poche* 'bag, pocket'.

poach[2] ▶ verb [with obj.] **1** illegally hunt or catch (game or fish) on land that is not one's own or in contravention of official protection.
■ take or acquire in an unfair or clandestine way: *employers risk having their newly trained workers poached by other firms.* ■ [no obj.] (in ball games) take a shot that a partner or teammate would have expected to take.
2 (of an animal) trample or cut up (turf) with its hoofs.
■ [no obj.] (of land) become sodden by being trampled.
– PHRASES **poach on someone's territory** encroach on someone else's rights.
– ORIGIN early 16th cent. (in the sense 'push roughly together'): apparently related to **POKE**[1]; sense 1 is perhaps partly from French *pocher* 'enclose in a bag' (see **POACH**[1]).

poached egg fungus ▶ noun another term for **PORCELAIN FUNGUS**.

poacher[1] ▶ noun [usu. with modifier] a pan for cooking eggs or other food by poaching: *an egg poacher.*

poacher[2] ▶ noun a person who hunts or catches game or fish illegally.
– PHRASES **poacher turned gamekeeper** someone who now protects the interests they previously attacked.

poacher[3] ▶ noun a small spiny fish which has an armour of overlapping plates and lives chiefly in cooler coastal waters.
● Family Agonidae: several genera and species.

poblano /pɒ'blɑːnəʊ/ ▶ noun a large dark green chilli pepper of a mild-flavoured variety.
– ORIGIN Spanish.

po'boy ▶ noun another term for **POOR BOY**.

Pocahontas /,pɒkə'hɒntəs/ (c.1595–1617), American Indian princess, daughter of an Algonquian chief in Virginia. According to an English colonist, Pocahontas rescued him from death at the hands of her father. In 1613 she was seized as a hostage by the English and she later married another colonist, John Rolfe.

pochard /'pəʊtʃəd, 'pɒ-/ ▶ noun (pl. same or **pochards**) a diving duck, the male of which typically has a reddish-brown head and a black breast.
● Genera *Aythya* and *Netta*, family Anatidae: five species, in particular the common *A. ferina* of Eurasia.
– ORIGIN mid 16th cent.: of unknown origin.

pochette /pɒ'ʃɛt/ ▶ noun a woman's small handbag shaped like an envelope.
– ORIGIN late 19th cent.: from French, literally 'small pocket', diminutive of *poche*.

pocho /'pɒtʃəʊ/ informal, often derogatory ▶ noun (pl. **-os**) a US citizen of Mexican origin; a culturally Americanized Mexican.
▶ adjective denoting or relating to such a person.
– ORIGIN via Mexican Spanish from Spanish, literally 'discoloured, pale'.

pock ▶ noun a pockmark.
– DERIVATIVES **pocked** adjective, **pocky** adjective (archaic).
– ORIGIN Old English *poc* 'pustule', of Germanic origin; related to Dutch *pok* and German *Pocke*. Compare with **POX**.

pocket ▶ noun **1** a small bag sewn into or on clothing so as to form part of it, used for carrying small articles.
■ a pouch-like compartment providing separate storage space, for example in a suitcase or car door. ■ S. African a narrow sack in which agricultural produce is sold, used as a measure for trading. ■ an opening at the corner or on the side of a billiard table into which balls are struck. ■ informal a person's financial resources: *the food was all priced to suit the hard-up airman's pocket.*
2 a small patch of something: *some of the gardens still had pockets of dirty snow in them.*
■ a small, isolated group or area: *there were pockets of disaffection in parts of the country.*
▶ adjective [attrib.] of a suitable size for carrying in a pocket: *a pocket German dictionary.*
■ on a small scale: *a 6,000 acre pocket paradise.*
▶ verb (**pocketed, pocketing**) [with obj.] put into one's pocket: *she watched him lock up and pocket the key.*
■ take or receive (money or other valuables) for oneself, especially dishonestly: *local politicians were found to have been pocketing the proceeds of fund-raisers.* ■ Billiards & Snooker drive (a ball) into a pocket. ■ enclose as though in a pocket: *the fillings can be pocketed in a pitta bread.* ■ suppress (one's feelings) and proceed despite them: *they were prepared to pocket their pride.*
– PHRASES **in pocket** having enough money or money to spare; having gained in a transaction. ■ (of money) gained by someone from a transaction. **in someone's pocket 1** dependent on someone financially and therefore under their influence. **2** very close to and closely involved with someone: *I'm tired of villages where everyone lives in everyone else's pocket.* **out of pocket** having lost money in a transaction. ■ **out-of-pocket** [as modifier] (of an expense or cost) paid for directly rather than being put on account or charged to some other person or organization. **pay out of pocket** US pay for something with one's own money, rather than from a particular fund or account. **put one's hand in one's pocket** spend or provide one's own money.
– DERIVATIVES **pocketable** adjective, **pocketful** (pl. **-fuls**) noun, **pocketless** adjective.
– ORIGIN Middle English (in the sense 'bag, sack', also used as a measure of quantity): from Anglo-

Norman French *poket(e)*, diminutive of *poke* 'pouch'. The verb dates from the late 16th cent. Compare with POKE².

pocket battleship ▶ noun any of a class of cruisers with large-calibre guns, operated by the German navy in the Second World War.

pocketbook ▶ noun 1 Brit. a notebook.
■ (**pocket book**) N. Amer. a paperback or other small or cheap edition of a book.
2 US a wallet, purse, or handbag.
■ N. Amer. one's financial resources: *they provide packages for every taste and every pocketbook.*

pocket borough ▶ noun (in the UK) a borough in which the election of political representatives was controlled by one person or family. Such boroughs were abolished by the Reform Acts of 1832 and 1867.

pocket gopher ▶ noun see GOPHER (sense 1).

pocket knife ▶ noun a penknife.

pocket money ▶ noun [mass noun] Brit. a small amount of money given to a child by their parents, typically on a regular basis.
■ a small amount of money suitable for minor expenses.

pocket mouse ▶ noun a small nocturnal rodent with large cheek pouches for carrying food, native to the deserts of North and Central America.
● Genus *Perognathus*, family Heteromyidae: several species.

pocket veto ▶ noun an indirect veto of a legislative bill by the US President or a state governor by retaining the bill unsigned until it is too late for it to be dealt with during the legislative session.

pocket watch ▶ noun a watch on a chain, intended to be carried in the pocket of a jacket or waistcoat.

pockmark ▶ noun a pitted scar or mark on the skin left by a pustule or spot.
■ a scar, mark, or pitted area disfiguring a surface.
▶ verb [with obj.] (usu. **be pockmarked**) cover or disfigure with such marks: *the area is pockmarked by gravel pits* | [as adj.] **pockmarked** *a pockmarked face.*

poco /ˈpəʊkəʊ/ ▶ adverb Music (in directions) a little; rather: *poco adagio.*
– ORIGIN Italian.

Pocomania /ˌpəʊkə(ʊ)ˈmeɪnɪə/ ▶ noun [mass noun] a Jamaican folk religion combining revivalism with ancestor worship and spirit possession.
– ORIGIN 1930s: probably a Hispanicized form of a local word, the second element being interpreted as -MANIA.

pod¹ ▶ noun 1 an elongated seed vessel of a leguminous plant such as the pea, splitting open on both sides when ripe.
■ the egg case of a locust. ■ Geology a body of rock or sediment whose length greatly exceeds its other dimensions. ■ a narrow-necked purse net for catching eels.
2 [often with modifier] a detachable or self-contained unit on an aircraft, spacecraft, vehicle, or vessel, having a particular function: *the torpedo's sensor pod contains a television camera.*
▶ verb (**podded, podding**) 1 [no obj.] (of a plant) bear or form pods: *the peas have failed to pod.*
2 [with obj.] remove (peas or beans) from their pods prior to cooking.
– PHRASES **in pod** informal, dated pregnant.
– ORIGIN late 17th cent.: back-formation from dialect *podware, podder* 'field crops', of unknown origin.

pod² ▶ noun a small herd or school of marine animals, especially whales.
– ORIGIN mid 19th cent. (originally US): of unknown origin.

podagra /pəˈdagrə, ˈpɒdəgrə/ ▶ noun [mass noun] Medicine gout of the foot, especially the big toe.
– DERIVATIVES **podagral** adjective, **podagric** adjective, **podagrous** adjective.
– ORIGIN Middle English: from Latin, from Greek *pous, pod-* 'foot' + *agra* 'seizure'.

podge ▶ noun informal a short, fat person.
■ [mass noun] excess weight; fat: *pregnancy podge.*
– ORIGIN mid 19th cent.: of unknown origin.

podger ▶ noun a short bar of iron or steel used as a lever, especially for tightening a box spanner.

Podgorica /ˌpɒdˈgɔːrɪtsə/ the capital of Montenegro; pop. 117,875 (1991). It was under Turkish rule from 1474 until 1878. Between 1946 and 1993 it was named Titograd in honour of Marshal Tito.

podgy ▶ adjective (**podgier, podgiest**) Brit. informal (of a person or part of their body) rather fat; chubby: *he put a podgy arm round Alan's shoulders.*
– DERIVATIVES **podginess** noun.

podiatry /pə(ʊ)ˈdʌɪətri/ ▶ noun another term for CHIROPODY.
– DERIVATIVES **podiatrist** noun.
– ORIGIN early 20th cent.: from Greek *pous, pod-* 'foot' + *iatros* 'physician'.

podium /ˈpəʊdɪəm/ ▶ noun (pl. **podiums** or **podia** /-dɪə/) a small platform on which a person may stand to be seen by an audience, as when making a speech or conducting an orchestra.
■ N. Amer. a lectern. ■ a continuous projecting base or pedestal under a building. ■ a projecting lower structure around the base of a tower block. ■ a raised platform surrounding the arena in an ancient amphitheatre.
– ORIGIN mid 18th cent.: via Latin from Greek *podion*, diminutive of *pous, pod-* 'foot'.

podocarp /ˈpəʊdə(ʊ)kɑːp/ ▶ noun a coniferous tree or shrub that is chiefly native to the southern hemisphere, widely grown as an ornamental or timber tree.
● Genus *Podocarpus*, family Podocarpaceae.
– ORIGIN mid 19th cent.: from modern Latin *Podocarpus*, from Greek *pous, pod-* 'foot' + *karpos* 'fruit'.

Podolsk /pəˈdɒlsk/ an industrial city in Russia, south of Moscow; pop. 209,000 (1990).

Podunk /ˈpəʊdʌŋk/ ▶ noun [usu. as modifier] US informal a hypothetical small town regarded as typically dull or insignificant.
– ORIGIN mid 19th cent.: a place name of southern New England, of Algonquian origin.

podzol /ˈpɒdzɒl/ (also **podsol** /-sɒl/) ▶ noun Soil Science an infertile acidic soil having an ash-like subsurface layer (from which minerals have been leached) and a lower dark stratum, occurring typically under temperate coniferous woodland.
– DERIVATIVES **podzolic** adjective, **podzolization** noun, **podzolize** (also **-ise**) verb.
– ORIGIN early 20th cent.: from Russian, from *pod* 'under' + *zola* 'ashes'.

Poe /pəʊ/, Edgar Allan (1809–49), American short-story writer, poet, and critic. His fiction and poetry are Gothic in style and characterized by their exploration of the macabre and the grotesque. Notable works: 'The Fall of the House of Usher' (short story, 1840); 'The Murders in the Rue Morgue' (detective story, 1841); 'The Raven' (poem, 1845).

poem ▶ noun a piece of writing in which the expression of thoughts and feelings or the description of places and events is given intensity by particular attention to diction (sometimes involving rhyme), rhythm (sometimes involving metrical composition), and imagery.
■ something which arouses strong emotions because of its beauty: *she was a poem in the flesh.*
– ORIGIN late 15th cent.: from French *poème* or Latin *poema*, from Greek *poēma*, early variant of *poiēma* 'fiction, poem', from *poiein* 'create'.

poenskop /ˈpɒnzkɒp, ˈpʊns-, ˈpuːnz-, ˈpuːns-/ ▶ noun (pl. same) S. African a large South African sea bream of shallow waters, which typically has a fleshy bump on the snout.
● *Cymatoceps* and other genera, family Sparidae.
– ORIGIN Afrikaans, from South African Dutch, probably from Dutch *pots* 'bump' + *kop* 'head'.

poesy /ˈpəʊɪzi, -si/ ▶ noun [mass noun] archaic or poetic/literary poetry.
■ the art or composition of poetry.
– ORIGIN late Middle English: from Old French *poesie*, via Latin from Greek *poēsis*, variant of *poiēsis* 'making, poetry', from *poiein* 'create'.

poet ▶ noun a person who writes poems.
■ a person possessing special powers of imagination or expression.
– ORIGIN Middle English: from Old French *poete*, via Latin from Greek *poētēs*, variant of *poiētēs* 'maker, poet', from *poiein* 'create'.

poetaster /ˈpəʊɪtastə/ ▶ noun a person who writes inferior poetry.
– ORIGIN late 16th cent.: modern Latin, from Latin *poeta* 'poet' + -ASTER.

poète maudit /ˌpəʊɛt məʊˈdiː/ ▶ noun (pl. **poètes maudits**) a poet who is insufficiently appreciated by their contemporaries.

– ORIGIN French, literally 'cursed poet'.

poetess ▶ noun a female poet.

poetic ▶ adjective of, relating to, or used in poetry: *the muse is a poetic convention.*
■ written in verse rather than prose: *a poetic drama.* ■ having an imaginative or sensitively emotional style of expression: *the orchestral playing was colourful and poetic.*
– DERIVATIVES **poetical** adjective, **poetically** adverb.
– ORIGIN mid 16th cent.: from French *poétique*, from Latin *poeticus* 'poetic, relating to poets', from Greek *po(i)ētikos*, from *po(i)ētēs* (see POET).

poeticize (also **-ise**) ▶ verb [with obj.] make poetic in character.
■ [no obj.] write or speak poetically.
– DERIVATIVES **poeticism** noun.

poetic justice ▶ noun [mass noun] the fact of experiencing a fitting or deserved retribution for one's actions.

poetic licence ▶ noun [mass noun] the freedom to depart from the facts of a matter or from the conventional rules of language when speaking or writing in order to create an effect.

poetics ▶ plural noun [treated as sing.] the art of writing poetry.
■ the study of linguistic techniques in poetry and literature.

poetize (also **-ise**) ▶ verb [no obj.] dated write or speak in verse or in a poetic style.
■ [with obj.] represent in poetic form.

Poet Laureate ▶ noun (pl. **Poets Laureate**) an eminent poet appointed as a member of the British royal household.

> The first Poet Laureate in the modern sense was Ben Jonson, but the title became established with the appointment of John Dryden in 1668. The Poet Laureate was formerly expected to write poems for state occasions, but since Victorian times the post has carried no specific duties. Since 1999 the post has been held by Andrew Motion.

poetry ▶ noun [mass noun] literary work in which special intensity is given to the expression of feelings and ideas by the use of distinctive style and rhythm; poems collectively or as a genre of literature: *he is chiefly famous for his love poetry.*
■ a quality of beauty and intensity of emotion regarded as characteristic of poems: *poetry and fire are nicely balanced in the music.* ■ something regarded as comparable to poetry in its beauty: *the music department is housed in a building which is pure poetry.*
– ORIGIN late Middle English: from medieval Latin *poetria*, from Latin *poeta* 'poet'. In early use the word sometimes referred to creative literature in general.

Poets' Corner part of Westminster Abbey where several poets are buried or commemorated.

po-faced ▶ adjective Brit. humourless and disapproving: *don't be so po-faced about everything.*
– ORIGIN 1930s: perhaps from PO, influenced by *poker-faced.*

pogey /ˈpəʊgi/ ▶ noun [mass noun] Canadian informal unemployment or welfare benefit: *so you want me to end up on pogey?*
– ORIGIN late 19th cent.: of unknown origin.

pogo ▶ noun (also **pogo stick**) (pl. **-os**) a toy for jumping about on, consisting of a long, spring-loaded pole with a handle at the top and rests for a person's feet near the bottom.
▶ verb (**-oes, -oed**) [no obj.] informal jump up and down as if on such a toy, typically as a form of dancing to certain types of rock music, especially punk.
– ORIGIN 1920s: of unknown origin.

Pogonophora /ˌpəʊgəˈnɒfərə/ Zoology a small phylum of long deep-sea worms which live in upright tubes of protein and chitin. They lack mouths and guts, subsisting mainly on the products of symbiotic bacteria.
– DERIVATIVES **pogonophoran** noun & adjective.
– ORIGIN modern Latin (plural), from Greek *pōgōn* 'beard' + *pherein* 'to bear'.

pogrom /ˈpɒgrəm, -grɒm, pəˈgrɒm/ ▶ noun an organized massacre of a particular ethnic group, in particular that of Jews in Russia or eastern Europe.
– ORIGIN early 20th cent.: from Russian, literally 'devastation', from *gromit'* 'destroy by the use of violence'.

Po Hai /pəʊ ˈhʌɪ/ variant of BO HAI.

pohutukawa /pə(ʊ)ˌhuːtəˈkɑːwə/ ▶ noun an evergreen New Zealand tree of the myrtle family, which bears crimson flowers in December and

January. Also called **CHRISTMAS TREE** or **FIRE TREE** in New Zealand.
• *Metrosideros excelsa*, family Myrtaceae.
– ORIGIN mid 19th cent.: from Maori.

poi¹ /pɔɪ/ ▶ **noun** [mass noun] a Hawaiian dish made from the fermented root of the taro which has been baked and pounded to a paste.
– ORIGIN of Polynesian origin.

poi² /pɔɪ/ ▶ **noun** (pl. same or **pois**) a small light ball of woven flax, swung rhythmically on the end of a string in Maori action songs and dances.
– ORIGIN Maori.

poignant /ˈpɔɪnjənt/ ▶ **adjective** evoking a keen sense of sadness or regret: *a poignant reminder of the passing of time.*
■ archaic sharp or pungent in taste or smell.
– DERIVATIVES **poignance** noun, **poignancy** noun, **poignantly** adverb.
– ORIGIN late Middle English: from Old French, literally 'pricking', present participle of *poindre*, from Latin *pungere* 'to prick'.

poikilitic /ˌpɔɪkɪˈlɪtɪk/ ▶ **adjective** Geology relating to or denoting the texture of an igneous rock in which small crystals of one mineral occur within crystals of another.
– ORIGIN mid 19th cent.: from Greek *poikilos* 'variegated' + **-ITE¹** + **-IC**.

poikilo- ▶ **combining form** variegated: *poikiloblastic.*
■ variable: *poikilotherm.*
– ORIGIN from Greek *poikilos* 'variegated, varied'.

poikiloblastic /ˌpɔɪkɪlə(ʊ)ˈblastɪk/ ▶ **adjective** Geology relating to or denoting the texture of a metamorphic rock in which small crystals of an original mineral occur within crystals of its metamorphic product.

poikilotherm /ˈpɔɪkɪlə(ʊ)ˌθəːm/ ▶ **noun** Zoology an organism that cannot regulate its body temperature except by behavioural means such as basking or burrowing. Often contrasted with **HOMEOTHERM**.
– DERIVATIVES **poikilothermal** adjective, **poikilothermic** adjective, **poikilothermy** noun.

poilu /pwʌˈluː, French pwaly/ ▶ **noun** historical, informal an infantry soldier in the French army, especially one who fought in the First World War.
– ORIGIN French, literally 'hairy', by extension 'brave', whiskers being associated with virility.

Poincaré /ˈpwãkareɪ, French pwɛ̃kaʀe/, Jules-Henri (1854–1912), French mathematician and philosopher of science, who transformed celestial mechanics and was one of the pioneers of algebraic topology. He proposed a relativistic philosophy which implied the absolute velocity of light, which nothing could exceed.

Poincaré map ▶ **noun** Mathematics & Physics a representation of the phase space of a dynamic system, indicating all possible trajectories.
■ (also **Poincaré section**) the intersection of this representation with a given line, plane, etc.

poinciana /ˌpɔɪnsɪˈɑːnə/ ▶ **noun** a tropical tree of the pea family, with showy red or red and yellow flowers.
• Genera *Caesalpinia* and *Delonix* (formerly *Poinciana*), family Leguminosae: several species, including the flamboyant.
– ORIGIN mid 18th cent.: modern Latin, named after M. de Poinci, a 17th-cent. governor of the Antilles.

poind /pɔɪnd, pɪnd/ ▶ **verb** [with obj.] Scots Law distrain or impound (a person's goods).
■ subject (someone) to such action.
– ORIGIN late Middle English: variant of dialect *pind* 'impound'.

poinsettia /ˌpɔɪnˈsɛtɪə/ ▶ **noun** a small Mexican shrub with large showy scarlet bracts surrounding the small yellow flowers, popular as a house plant at Christmas.
• *Euphorbia* (formerly *Poinsettia*) *pulcherrima*, family Euphorbiaceae.
– ORIGIN mid 19th cent.: modern Latin, named after Joel R. *Poinsett* (1779–1851), American diplomat and amateur botanist.

point /pɔɪnt/ ▶ **noun 1** the tapered, sharp end of a tool, weapon, or other object: *the point of his dagger | a pencil point.*
■ Archaeology a pointed flake or blade, especially one that has been worked. ■ Ballet another term for **POINTE**. ■ Boxing the tip of a person's chin as a spot for a blow. ■ the prong of a deer's antler.
2 a dot or other punctuation mark, in particular a full stop.
■ a decimal point: *fifty-five point nine.* ■ a dot or small stroke used in Semitic languages to indicate vowels or distinguish particular consonants. ■ a very small dot or mark on a surface: *the sky was studded with points of light.*
3 a particular spot, place, or position in an area or on a map, object, or surface: *turn left at the point where you see a sign to Appleford | the furthermost point of the gallery | the check-in point.*
■ a particular moment in time or stage in a process: *from this point onwards the teacher was completely won over.* ■ (usu. **the point**) the critical or decisive moment: *when it came to the point he would probably do what was expected of him.* ■ (**the point of**) the verge or brink of (doing or being something): *she was* ***on the point of*** *leaving.* ■ [usu. with modifier] a stage or level at which a change of state occurs: *local kennels are full to bursting point.* ■ [with modifier] Brit. a socket in a wall for connecting a device to an electrical supply or communications network: *a power point.* ■ (in geometry) something having position but not spatial extent, magnitude, dimension, or direction, for example the intersection of two lines.
4 a single item or detail in an extended discussion, list, or text: *the main points of the Edinburgh agreement.*
■ an argument or idea put forward by a person in discussion: *he* ***made the point that*** *economic regulation involves controls on pricing.* ■ an interesting or convincing idea: *you must admit he does have a point.* ■ (usu. **the point**) the significant or essential element of what is intended or being discussed: *it took her a long time to* ***come to the point****.* ■ [in sing.] [usu. with negative or in questions] advantage or purpose that can be gained from doing something: *there was* ***no point in*** *denying the truth |* ***what's the point of*** *having things I don't need?* ■ [mass noun] relevance or effectiveness. ■ a distinctive feature or characteristic, typically a good one, of a person or thing: *the film had its points.*
5 (in sports and games) a mark or unit of scoring awarded for success or performance: *he kicked a penalty goal to put Bangor eight points ahead.*
■ a unit used in measuring value, achievement, or extent: *the shares index was down seven points.* ■ an advantage or success in an argument or discussion: *she smiled, assuming she had* ***won her point****.* ■ a unit of credit towards an award or benefit: *points were allocated according to the inadequacy of the existing accommodation.* ■ a percentage of the profits from a film or recording offered to certain people involved in its production. ■ (**point of**) (in piquet) the longest suit in a player's hand, containing a specified number of up to eight cards. ■ a unit of weight (2 mg) for diamonds. ■ a unit of varying value, used in quoting the price of stocks, bonds, or futures. ■ Bridge a value assigned to certain cards (4 points for an ace, 3 for a king, 2 for a queen, and 1 for a jack, sometimes with extra points for long or short suits) by a player in assessing the strength of their hand.
6 each of thirty-two directions marked at equal distances round a compass.
■ the corresponding direction towards the horizon. ■ the angular interval between two successive points of a compass, i.e. one eighth of a right angle (11° 15'). ■ (**points ——**) unspecified places considered in terms of their direction from a specified place: *they headed down Highway 401 to Ontario and points west.*
7 a narrow piece of land jutting out into the sea: *the boat came round the point |* [in names] *Blakeney Point.*
8 (usu. **points**) Brit. a junction of two railway lines, with a pair of linked tapering rails that can be moved laterally to allow a train to pass from one line to the other.
9 Printing a unit of measurement for type sizes and spacing (in the UK and US 0.351 mm, in Europe 0.376 mm).
10 Cricket a fielding position on the off side near the batsman.
■ a fielder at this position. ■ Ice Hockey either of two areas to the left and right of the net, just inside the blue line where it meets the boards.
11 (usu. **points**) each of a set of electrical contacts in the distributor of a motor vehicle.
12 a small leading party of an advanced guard of troops.
■ [mass noun] chiefly N. Amer. the position at the head of a column or wedge of troops: *he* ***walked point*** *and I took the tail.* ■ chiefly N. Amer. short for **POINT MAN**.
13 (usu. **points**) the extremities of an animal, typically a horse or cat, such as the face, paws, and tail of a Siamese cat.
14 Hunting a spot to which a straight run is made.
■ a run of this type: *our fox* ***made his point*** *to Moorhill.*
15 (usu. **points**) historical a tagged piece of ribbon or cord used for lacing a garment or attaching a hose to a doublet.
16 a short piece of cord at the lower edge of a sail for tying up a reef.
17 [mass noun] the action or position of a dog in pointing: *a bird dog* ***on point****.*
18 Music an important phrase or subject, especially in a contrapuntal composition.
▶ **verb 1** [no obj.] direct someone's attention to the position or direction of something, typically by extending one's finger: *the lads were nudging each other and* ***pointing at*** *me.*
■ [with adverbial of direction] indicate a particular time, direction, or reading: *a sign pointing left.* ■ [with obj.] direct or aim (something) at someone or something: *he* ***pointed*** *the torch beam* ***at*** *the floor.* ■ [with adverbial of direction] face or be turned in a particular direction: *two of its toes point forward and two point back.* ■ [with adverbial] cite or put forward a fact or situation as evidence of something: *he points to several factors supporting this conclusion.* ■ (**point to**) (of a situation) be evidence or an indication that (something) is likely to happen or be the case: *everything pointed to an eastern attack.* ■ [with obj.] (of a dog) indicate the presence of (game) by acting as pointer. ■ [with obj.] chiefly Ballet extend (the toes or feet) by tensing the foot and ankle so as to form a point.
2 [with obj.] give force or emphasis to (words or actions): *he wouldn't miss the opportunity to point a moral.*
■ (**point something up**) reveal the true nature or importance of something: *he did so much to point up their plight in the 1960s.*
3 [with obj.] fill in or repair the joints of (brickwork, a brick structure, or tiling) with smoothly finished mortar or cement.
4 [with obj.] give a sharp, tapered point to: *he twisted and pointed his moustache.*
5 [with obj.] insert points in (written Hebrew).
■ mark (Psalms) with signs for chanting.
– PHRASES **at all points** in every part or respect. **beside the point** irrelevant. **case in point** an instance or example that illustrates what is being discussed: *the 'green revolution' in agriculture is a good case in point.* **in point of fact** see **FACT**. **make one's point** put across a proposition clearly and convincingly. **make a point of** make a special and noticeable effort to do (a specified thing): *she made a point of taking a walk each day.* **off the point** irrelevant. **point the finger** openly accuse someone or apportion blame. **the point of no return** the point in a journey or enterprise at which it becomes essential or more practical to continue to the end. **point of sailing** a sailing boat's heading in relation to the wind. **score points** deliberately make oneself appear superior to someone else by making clever remarks: *she was constantly trying to think of ways to* ***score points off*** *him.* **take someone's point** chiefly Brit. accept the validity of someone's idea or argument. **to the point** relevant: *his evidence was brief and to the point.* **up to a point** to some extent but not completely. **win on points** Boxing win by scoring more points than one's opponent (as awarded by the judges and/or the referee) rather than by a knockout.
– ORIGIN Middle English: the noun partly from Old French *point*, from Latin *punctum* 'something that is pricked', giving rise to the senses 'unit, mark, point in space or time'; partly from Old French *pointe*, from Latin *puncta* 'pricking', giving rise to the senses 'sharp tip, promontory'. The verb is from Old French *pointer*, and in some senses from the English noun.
▶ **point something out** direct someone's gaze or attention towards something, especially by extending one's finger. ■ [reporting verb] say something to make someone aware of a fact or circumstance: [with clause] *she pointed out that his van had been in the car park all day |* [with direct speech] *'Most of the people round here are very poor,' I pointed out.*

point-and-click ▶ **adjective** Computing (of an interface) giving the user the ability to initiate tasks by using a mouse to move a cursor over an area of the screen and clicking on it.
▶ **verb** [no obj.] use a mouse in such a way.

point-and-shoot ▶ **adjective** Photography of, relating to, or denoting an automatic camera which, when it is pointed at a subject and the shutter release is pressed, will take a properly exposed and focused photograph.

point bar ▶ **noun** Geology an alluvial deposit that

p

forms by accretion inside an expanding loop of a river.

point-blank ▶ adjective & adverb (of a shot, bullet, or other missile) fired from very close to its target.
■[as adj.] (of the range of a shot, bullet, or missile) so close as to allow no possibility of missing. ■(of a statement or question) blunt and direct; without explanation or qualification: [as adv.] *he refuses point-blank to be photographed or give interviews.*
– ORIGIN late 16th cent.: probably from **POINT** + **BLANK** in the contemporaneous sense 'white spot in the centre of a target'.

point blanket ▶ noun Canadian a type of Hudson's Bay blanket with distinctive markings or points woven in to indicate weight.

point break ▶ noun (in surfing) a type of wave characteristic of a coast with a headland.

point charge ▶ noun chiefly Physics an electric charge regarded as concentrated in a mathematical point, without spatial extent.

point contact ▶ noun Electronics the contact of a metal point with the surface of a semiconductor so as to form a rectifying junction.

point d'appui /ˌpwã daˈpwiː, French pwɛ̃ dapɥi/ ▶ noun (pl. **points d'appui**) a support or prop.
– ORIGIN French, literally 'point of support'.

point duty ▶ noun [mass noun] Brit. the duties of a police officer or other official stationed at a junction to control traffic.

pointe /pwãt/ ▶ noun (pl. pronounced same) Ballet the tips of the toes.
■(also **pointe work**) [mass noun] dance performed on the tips of the toes.
– PHRASES **on** (or **en**) **pointe** on the tips of the toes.
– ORIGIN French, literally 'tip'.

Pointe-à-Pitre /ˌpwãtaˈpiːtr(ə)/ the chief port and commercial capital of the French island of Guadeloupe in the Caribbean; pop. 26,000 (1994).

pointed ▶ adjective **1** having a sharpened or tapered tip or end: *his face tapers to a pointed chin.*
2 (of a remark or look) expressing criticism in a direct and unambiguous way.
– DERIVATIVES **pointedly** adverb (only in sense 2), **pointedness** noun.

pointed arch ▶ noun an arch with a pointed crown, characteristic of Gothic architecture.

pointelle /ˌpɔɪnˈtɛl/ (also trademark **Pointelle**) ▶ noun [mass noun] a type of knitwear or woollen fabric with small eyelet holes that create a lacy effect.
– ORIGIN 1950s: probably from *point* in the sense 'lace made entirely with a needle' + the French diminutive suffix *-elle*.

Pointe-Noire /pwãtˈnwɑː/ the chief seaport of the Congo, an oil terminal on the Atlantic coast; pop. 576,200 (1995).

pointer ▶ noun **1** a long thin piece of metal on a scale or dial which moves to indicate a figure or position.
■a rod used for pointing to features on a map or chart. ■a hint as to what might happen in the future: *the figures were a* ***pointer*** *to gradual economic recovery.* ■a small piece of advice; a tip: *here are some* ***pointers*** *on how to go about the task.* ■Computing another term for **CURSOR**. ■Computing a variable whose value is the address of another variable; a link.
2 a dog of a breed that on scenting game stands rigid looking towards it.

Pointers (**the Pointers**) Astronomy (in the northern hemisphere) two stars of the Plough or Big Dipper in Ursa Major, through which a line points nearly to the Pole Star.
■(in the southern hemisphere) two stars in the Constellation Crux, through which a line points nearly to the south celestial pole.

point estimate ▶ noun Statistics a single value given as an estimate of a parameter of a population. Compare with **INTERVAL ESTIMATE**.

pointe work ▶ noun see **POINTE**.

point group ▶ noun Crystallography any of the 32 sets of symmetry operations which can be used to characterize three-dimensional lattices and are the basis of the system of crystal classes.

point guard ▶ noun Basketball the player who directs the team's offence.

pointillism /ˈpwantɪlɪz(ə)m/ ▶ noun [mass noun] a technique of neo-Impressionist painting using tiny dots of various pure colours, which become blended in the viewer's eye. It was developed by Seurat with the aim of producing a greater degree of luminosity and brilliance of colour.
– DERIVATIVES **pointillist** noun & adjective, **pointillistic** adjective.
– ORIGIN early 20th cent.: from French *pointillisme*, from *pointiller* 'mark with dots'.

pointing ▶ noun [mass noun] cement or mortar used to fill the joints of brickwork, especially when added externally to a wall to improve its appearance and weatherproofing.
■the process of adding such cement or mortar.

pointing device ▶ noun Computing a generic term for any device (e.g. a graphics tablet, mouse, stylus, or trackball) used to control the movement of a cursor on a computer screen.

point lace ▶ noun [mass noun] lace made with a needle on a parchment pattern.

pointless ▶ adjective **1** having little or no sense, use, or purpose: *speculating like this is a pointless exercise* | [with infinitive] *it's pointless to plan too far ahead.*
2 (of a contest or competitor) without a point scored: *they are bottom of the league and pointless.*
– DERIVATIVES **pointlessly** adverb, **pointlessness** noun.

point man ▶ noun the soldier at the head of a patrol; the leader of an armed force.
■chiefly N. Amer. (especially in a political context) a person at the forefront of an activity or endeavour.

point mutation ▶ noun Genetics a mutation affecting only one or very few nucleotides in a gene sequence.

point of departure ▶ noun the starting point of a line of thought or course of action; an initial assumption: *historians took Lenin's ideas as their point of departure.*

point of honour ▶ noun an action or circumstance that affects one's reputation or conscience: *he languished in jail refusing, as a point of honour, to talk.*

point of order ▶ noun a query in a formal debate or meeting as to whether correct procedure is being followed.

point of view ▶ noun a particular attitude or way of considering a matter: *I'm trying to get Matthew to change his point of view.*
■(in fictional writing) the narrator's position in relation to the story being told: *this story is told from a child's point of view.* ■the position from which something or someone is observed.

point source ▶ noun Physics a source of energy, such as light or sound, which can be regarded as having negligible dimensions.

point spread ▶ noun **1** N. Amer. a forecast of the number of points constituting the margin by which a stronger team is expected to defeat a weaker one, used for betting purposes.
2 Physics & Physiology the spread of energy from a point source, especially with respect to light coming into an optical instrument or eye.

points system (also **point system**) ▶ noun a system for distributing or allocating resources or for ranking or evaluating candidates or claimants on the basis of points allocated or accumulated.

point-to-point ▶ noun (pl. **point-to-points**) an amateur steeplechase for horses used in hunting, over a set cross-country course.
▶ adjective (of a route or journey) from one place to the next without stopping or changing; direct.
■(of a telecommunication or computer link) directly from the sender to the receiver.
– DERIVATIVES **point-to-pointer** noun, **point-to-pointing** noun.

pointy ▶ adjective (**pointier**, **pointiest**) informal having a pointed tip or end: *pointy ears.*

pointy-headed ▶ adjective N. Amer. informal, chiefly derogatory expert; intellectual: *some pointy-headed college professor.*
– ORIGIN by association with **EGGHEAD**.

poise[1] ▶ noun [mass noun] **1** graceful and elegant bearing in a person: *poise and good deportment can be cultivated.*
■composure and dignity of manner: *at least he had a moment to think, to recover his poise.*
2 archaic balance; equilibrium.
▶ verb be or cause to be balanced or suspended: [no obj.] *he poised motionless on his toes* | [with obj.] figurative *the world was poised between peace and war.*
■(**be poised**) (of a person or organization) be ready and prepared to do something: [with infinitive] *teachers are poised to resume their attack on government school tests.*
– ORIGIN late Middle English (in the sense 'weight'): from Old French *pois, peis* (noun), *peser* (verb), from an alteration of Latin *pensum* 'weight', from the verb *pendere* 'weigh'. From the early senses of 'weight' and 'measure of weight' arose the notion of 'equal weight, balance', leading to the extended senses 'composure' and 'elegant bearing'.

poise[2] ▶ noun Physics a unit of dynamic viscosity, such that a tangential force of one dyne per square centimetre causes a velocity change one centimetre per second between two parallel planes separated by one centimetre in a liquid.
– ORIGIN early 20th cent.: from the name of Jean L. M. *Poiseuille* (1799–1869), French physician.

poised ▶ adjective having a composed and self-assured manner.
■having a graceful and elegant bearing.

Poiseuille flow /pwaˈzəːi/ ▶ noun [mass noun] Physics laminar or streamline flow of an incompressible viscous fluid, especially through a long narrow cylinder.
– ORIGIN 1940s: named after Jean L. M. *Poiseuille* (1799–1869), French physician.

poisha /ˈpɔɪʃə/ ▶ noun (pl. same) a monetary unit of Bangladesh, equal to one hundredth of a taka.
– ORIGIN Bengali, alteration of **PAISA**.

poison ▶ noun [mass noun] a substance that when introduced into or absorbed by a living organism causes death or injury, especially one that kills by rapid action even in a small quantity.
■Chemistry a substance that reduces the activity of a catalyst. ■Physics an additive or impurity in a nuclear reactor that slows a reaction by absorbing neutrons. ■a person, idea, action, or situation that is considered to have a destructive or corrupting effect or influence: *the late 1930s, when Nazism was spreading its poison.*
▶ verb [with obj.] administer poison to (a person or animal), either deliberately or accidentally: *he tried to poison his wife* | [as noun **poisoning**] *symptoms of poisoning may include nausea, diarrhoea, and vomiting.*
■adulterate or contaminate (food or drink) with poison. ■[usu. as adj. **poisoned**] treat (a weapon or missile) with poison in order to augment its lethal effect. ■(of a dangerous substance) kill or cause to become very ill: *swans are being poisoned by lead from anglers' lines.* ■contaminate or pollute (an area, the air, or water). ■figurative prove harmful or destructive to: *his disgust had poisoned his attitude toward everyone.* ■Chemistry (of a substance) reduce the activity of (a catalyst).
– PHRASES **what's your poison?** informal used to ask someone what they would like to drink.
– DERIVATIVES **poisoner** noun.
– ORIGIN Middle English (denoting a harmful medicinal draught): from Old French *poison* 'magic potion', from Latin *potio(n-)* 'potion', related to *potare* 'to drink'.

poison-arrow frog ▶ noun a small slender tropical American frog which is typically brightly coloured. The skin of these frogs secretes a virulent poison, which is used by American Indians to coat their arrows.
• Family Dendrobatidae: several genera and numerous species.

poisoned chalice ▶ noun an assignment, award, or honour which is likely to prove a disadvantage or source of problems to the recipient: *many thought the new minister had been handed a poisoned chalice.*

poison gas ▶ noun [mass noun] poisonous gas or vapour, used especially to disable an enemy in warfare.

poison ivy ▶ noun a North American climbing plant which secretes an irritant oil from its leaves that can cause dermatitis.
• *Rhus radicans*, family Anacardiaceae.

poison oak ▶ noun a North American climbing shrub related to poison ivy and having similar properties.
• *Rhus toxicodendron*, family Anacardiaceae.

poisonous ▶ adjective (of an animal or insect) producing poison as a means of attacking enemies or prey: *a poisonous snake.*
■(of a plant or substance) causing or capable of causing death or illness if taken into the body: *poisonous chemicals.* ■figurative extremely unpleasant or malicious: *there was a poisonous atmosphere at the office.*
– DERIVATIVES **poisonously** adverb.

poison pen letter ▶ noun an anonymous letter that is libellous, abusive, or malicious.

poison pill ▶ noun Finance a tactic used by a company threatened with an unwelcome takeover bid to make itself unattractive to the bidder.

Poisson /ˈpwʌsɒ̃/, Siméon-Denis (1781–1840), French mathematical physicist. His major contributions were in probability theory, in which he greatly improved Laplace's work and developed several concepts that are now named after him.

Poisson distribution /ˈpwʌsɒ̃/ ▶ noun Statistics a discrete frequency distribution which gives the probability of a number of independent events occurring in a fixed time.

Poisson's ratio ▶ noun Physics the ratio of the proportional decrease in a lateral measurement to the proportional increase in length in a sample of material that is elastically stretched.

Poitier /ˈpwʌtɪeɪ/, Sidney (b.1924), American actor and film director, the first black American actor to achieve superstar status. Notable films: *Lilies of the Field* (1963, for which he won an Oscar) and *In the Heat of the Night* (1967).

Poitiers /ˈpwʌtɪeɪ/ a city in west central France, the chief town of Poitou-Charentes region and capital of the former province of Poitou; pop. 82,500 (1990).

Poitou /ˈpwatuː/ a former province of west central France, now united with Charente to form the region of Poitou-Charentes. Formerly part of Aquitaine, it was held by the French and English in succession until it was finally united with France at the end of the Hundred Years War.

Poitou-Charentes /ˌpwatuːʃaˈrɒ̃t, French pwatuʃaʀɑ̃t/ a region of western France, on the Bay of Biscay, centred on Poitiers.

poke[1] ▶ verb [with obj.] jab or prod (someone or something), especially with one's finger: *he poked Benny in the ribs and pointed* | [no obj.] *they sniffed, felt, and* ***poked at*** *everything they bought.*
■ [with obj. and adverbial of direction] jab (one's finger) at someone or into something: *keep adding water until you can comfortably poke your finger into the soil.* ■ prod and stir (a fire) with a poker to make it burn more fiercely. ■ make (a hole) in something by prodding or jabbing at it. ■ [with obj. and adverbial of direction] thrust (something, such as one's head) in a particular direction: *I poked my head around the door to see what was going on* | *she poked her tongue out.* ■ [no obj., with adverbial] protrude and be or become visible: *she had wisps of grey hair poking out from under her bonnet.* ■ vulgar slang (of a man) have sexual intercourse with (a woman).
▶ noun **1** an act of poking someone or something: *she gave the fire a poke.*
■ (**a poke round/around**) informal a look or search around a place. ■ vulgar slang an act of sexual intercourse.
2 [mass noun] informal power or acceleration in a car: *I expect you'd prefer something with a bit more poke.*
3 (usu. **POKE**) Computing a statement or function in BASIC for altering the contents of a specified memory location. Compare with **PEEK** (in sense 2).
4 (also **poke bonnet**) a woman's bonnet with a projecting brim or front, popular especially in the early 19th century.
– PHRASES **poke fun at** tease or make fun of. **poke one's nose into** informal take an intrusive interest in. **take a poke at someone** informal hit or punch someone. ■ criticize someone.
– ORIGIN Middle English: origin uncertain; compare with Middle Dutch and Middle Low German *poken*, of unknown ultimate origin. The noun dates from the late 18th cent.
▶ **poke about/around** look around a place, typically in search of something.

poke[2] ▶ noun chiefly Scottish a bag or small sack: *he fished out a poke of crisps from under the counter.*
■ N. Amer. informal a purse or wallet.
– PHRASES **a pig in a poke** see **PIG**.
– ORIGIN Middle English: from Old Northern French *poke*, variant of Old French *poche* 'pocket'. Compare with **POUCH**.

poke[3] ▶ noun **1** another term for **POKEWEED**.
2 (**Indian poke**) a North American plant of the lily family with a poisonous black rhizome and tall sprays of yellow-green flowers.
• *Veratrum viride*, family Liliaceae.
– ORIGIN early 18th cent.: from Algonquian *poughkone* (see **PUCCOON**).

poke-check ▶ verb [with obj.] Ice Hockey poke the puck off the stick of (an opposing player).

poker[1] ▶ noun a metal rod with a handle, used for prodding and stirring an open fire.

poker[2] ▶ noun [mass noun] a card game played by two or more people who bet on the value of the hands dealt to them. A player wins the pool either by having the highest combination at the showdown or by forcing all opponents to concede without a showing of the hand, sometimes by means of bluff.
– ORIGIN mid 19th cent.: of US origin; perhaps related to German *pochen* 'to brag', *Pochspiel* 'bragging game'.

poker dice ▶ plural noun dice with card designs (from nine to ace) on the faces instead of spots.
■ [mass noun] a dice game in which the thrower aims for combinations of several dice similar to winning hands in poker.

poker-face ▶ noun an impassive expression that hides one's true feelings.
■ a person with such an expression.
– DERIVATIVES **poker-faced** adjective.

pokerwork ▶ noun British term for **PYROGRAPHY**.

pokeweed ▶ noun [mass noun] a North American plant with red stems, spikes of cream flowers, and purple berries. Also called **POKE**[3].
• *Phytolacca americana*, family Phytolaccaceae.
– ORIGIN early 18th cent.: *poke* from Algonquian *poughkone*.

pokey ▶ noun (usu. **the pokey**) informal, chiefly N. Amer. prison.
– ORIGIN early 20th cent.: alteration of **POGEY** (an early sense being 'hostel for the needy'), perhaps influenced by **POKY**.

poky (also **pokey**) ▶ adjective (**pokier**, **pokiest**) **1** (of a room or building) uncomfortably small and cramped: *five of us shared the poky little room.*
2 informal (especially of a car) having considerable power or acceleration.
3 N. Amer. annoyingly slow: *his speech was poky, like he was a little simple.*
– DERIVATIVES **pokily** adverb, **pokiness** noun.
– ORIGIN mid 19th cent. (in the sense 'concerned with petty matters'): from **POKE**[1] (in contemporaneous sense 'confine') + **-Y**[1].

pol ▶ noun informal, chiefly N. Amer. a politician.

Polack /ˈpəʊlak/ (also **polack**) derogatory, chiefly N. Amer.
▶ noun a person from Poland or of Polish descent.
▶ adjective of Polish origin or descent.
– ORIGIN late 16th cent.: from Polish *Polak*.

Poland a country in central Europe with a coastline on the Baltic Sea; pop. 38,183,160 (1990); official language, Polish; capital, Warsaw. Polish name **POLSKA**.

First united as a nation in the 11th century, Poland became a dominant power in the region in the 16th century but thereafter suffered severely from the rise of Russian, Swedish, Prussian, and Austrian power, being partitioned in the late 18th century. Poland regained full independence (as a republic) after the First World War. Its invasion by German forces in 1939 precipitated the Second World War, from which it eventually emerged as a communist state under Soviet domination. In the 1980s the rise of the independent trade union movement Solidarity eventually led to the end of communist rule (1989).

Polanski /pəˈlanski/, Roman (b.1933), French film director, of Polish descent. His second wife, the actress **Sharon Tate** (1943–69), was one of the victims of a multiple murder by followers of the cult leader Charles Manson. Notable films: *Rosemary's Baby* (1968) and *Chinatown* (1974).

polar ▶ adjective **1** of or relating to the North or South Pole: *the polar regions.*
■ (of an animal or plant) living in the north or south polar region. ■ Astronomy of or relating to the poles of a celestial body. ■ Astronomy of or relating to a celestial pole. ■ Geometry of or relating to the poles of a sphere. See **POLE**[2]. ■ Biology of or relating to the poles of a cell, organ, or part.
2 Physics & Chemistry having electrical or magnetic polarity.
■ (of a liquid, especially a solvent) consisting of molecules with a dipole moment. ■ (of a solid) ionic.
3 directly opposite in character or tendency: *depression and its polar opposite, mania.*
▶ noun **1** Geometry the straight line joining the two points at which tangents from a fixed point touch a conic section.
2 Astronomy a variable binary star which emits strongly polarized light, one component being a strongly magnetic white dwarf.
– ORIGIN mid 16th cent.: from medieval Latin *polaris* 'heavenly', from Latin *polus* 'end of an axis' (see **POLE**[2]).

polar axis ▶ noun Astronomy the axis of an equatorially mounted telescope which is at right angles to the declination axis and parallel to the earth's axis of rotation, about which the telescope is turned to follow the apparent movement of celestial objects resulting from the earth's rotation.

polar bear ▶ noun a large white arctic bear which lives mainly on the pack ice. It is a powerful swimmer and feeds chiefly on seals.
• *Thalarctos maritimus*, family Ursidae.

polar body ▶ noun Biology each of the small cells which bud off from an oocyte at the two meiotic divisions and do not develop into ova.

polar cap ▶ noun Astronomy a region of ice or other frozen matter surrounding a pole of a planet.

polar coordinates ▶ plural noun Geometry a pair of coordinates locating the position of a point in a plane, the first being the length of the straight line (*r*) connecting the point to the origin, and the second the angle (*θ*) made by this line with a fixed line.
■ the coordinates in a three-dimensional extension of this system.

polar curve ▶ noun Geometry a curve drawn on polar coordinates around a fixed point, as in a polar diagram.

polar diagram ▶ noun chiefly Physics & Electronics a diagram in which a point of origin is surrounded by a curve whose radius at any given point is proportional to the magnitude of some property measured in the direction of that point. Polar diagrams are often used to depict the directional sensitivity of aerials and microphones.

polar distance ▶ noun Geometry the angular distance of a point on a sphere from the nearest pole.

polarimeter /ˌpəʊləˈrɪmɪtə/ ▶ noun an instrument for measuring the polarization of light, and especially (in chemical analysis) for determining the effect of a substance in rotating the plane of polarization of light.
– DERIVATIVES **polarimetric** adjective, **polarimetry** noun.
– ORIGIN mid 19th cent.: from medieval Latin *polaris* 'polar' + **-METER**.

Polaris /pəˈlɑːrɪs/ **1** Astronomy the Pole Star.
2 a type of submarine-launched ballistic missile designed to carry nuclear warheads, formerly in service with the US and British navies.
– ORIGIN mid 19th cent.: from medieval Latin *polaris* 'heavenly', from Latin *polus* 'end of an axis'.

polariscope /pəˈlarɪskəʊp/ ▶ noun another term for **POLARIMETER**.
– DERIVATIVES **polariscopic** adjective.
– ORIGIN early 19th cent.: from medieval Latin *polaris* 'polar' + **-SCOPE**.

polarity ▶ noun (pl. **-ies**) [mass noun] the property of having poles or being polar: *it exhibits polarity when presented to a magnetic needle.*
■ the relative orientation of poles; the direction of a magnetic or electric field: *the magnetic field peaks in strength immediately after switching polarity.* ■ the state of having two opposite or contradictory tendencies, opinions, or aspects: *the polarity between male and female* | [count noun] *the cold war's neat polarities can hardly be carried on.* ■ Biology the tendency of living organisms or parts to develop with distinct anterior and posterior (or uppermost and lowermost) ends, or to grow or orientate in a particular direction.

polarity therapy ▶ noun [mass noun] a system of treatment used in alternative medicine, intended to restore a balanced distribution of the body's energy, and incorporating manipulation, exercise, and dietary restrictions.

polarize (also **-ise**) ▶ verb **1** [with obj.] Physics restrict the vibrations of (a transverse wave, especially light) wholly or partially to one direction: [as adj. **polarizing**] *a polarizing microscope.*
2 [with obj.] Physics cause (something) to acquire polarity: *the electrode is polarized in aqueous solution.*
3 divide or cause to divide into two sharply contrasting groups or sets of opinions or beliefs: [no obj.] *the cultural sphere has* ***polarized into*** *two competing*

p

ideological positions | [with obj.] *Vietnam polarized political opinion.*
– DERIVATIVES **polarizable** adjective, **polarization** noun, **polarizer** noun.

polarizing filter ▶ **noun** a photographic or optical filter that polarizes the light passing through it, used chiefly for reducing reflections and improving contrast. Two polarizing filters are often used together, such that rotation of one of them results in a neutral density filter of variable density.

polarography /ˌpəʊləˈrɒɡrəfi/ ▶ **noun** [mass noun] Chemistry a method of analysis in which a sample is subjected to electrolysis using a special electrode and a range of applied voltages, a plot of current against voltage showing steps corresponding to particular chemical species and proportional to their concentration.
– DERIVATIVES **polarographic** adjective.
– ORIGIN 1930s: from *polarization* (see **POLARIZE**) + **-GRAPHY**.

Polaroid ▶ **noun** trademark **1** [mass noun] material in thin plastic sheets that produces a high degree of plane polarization in light passing through it.
■ (**Polaroids**) sunglasses with lenses made from such material.
2 a photograph taken with a Polaroid camera.
▶ **adjective** Photography denoting a type of camera with internal processing that produces a finished print rapidly after each exposure.
■ denoting film for or a photograph taken with such a camera: *a small Polaroid snapshot.*
– ORIGIN 1930s: from **POLARIZE** + **-OID**.

polar orbit ▶ **noun** a satellite orbit that passes over polar regions, especially one whose plane contains the polar axis.

polar star ▶ **noun** Astronomy a star at or close to a celestial pole, especially the Pole Star.

polar wandering ▶ **noun** [mass noun] the slow erratic movement of the earth's poles relative to the continents throughout geological time, due largely to continental drift.

polder /ˈpəʊldə/ ▶ **noun** a piece of low-lying land reclaimed from the sea or a river and protected by dykes, especially in the Netherlands.
– ORIGIN early 17th cent.: from Dutch, from Middle Dutch *polre*.

Pole ▶ **noun** a native or national of Poland, or a person of Polish descent.
– ORIGIN via German from Polish *Polanie*, literally 'field-dwellers', from *pole* 'field'.

pole[1] ▶ **noun 1** a long, slender, rounded piece of wood or metal, typically used with one end placed in the ground as a support for something: *a tent pole.*
■ Athletics a long, slender, flexible rod of wood or fibreglass used by a competitor in pole-vaulting. ■ a young tree with a straight slender trunk and no lower branches. ■ short for **SKI POLE**. ■ a wooden shaft fitted to the front of a cart or carriage drawn by animals and attached to their yokes or collars. ■ a simple fishing rod.
2 historical, chiefly Brit. another term for **PERCH**[3] (in sense 1).
■ (also **square pole**) another term for **PERCH**[3] (in sense 2).
▶ **verb** [with obj.] propel (a boat) by pushing a pole against the bottom of a river, canal, or lake.
– PHRASES **under bare poles** Sailing with no sail set. **up the pole** informal **1** Brit. mad: *taxes can be enough to drive you up the pole.* **2** chiefly Irish pregnant.
– ORIGIN late Old English *pāl* (in early use without reference to thickness or length), of Germanic origin; related to Dutch *paal* and German *Pfahl*, based on Latin *palus* 'stake'.

pole[2] ▶ **noun** either of the two locations (**North Pole** or **South Pole**) on the surface of the earth (or of a celestial object) which are the northern and southern ends of the axis of rotation. See also **MAGNETIC POLE**.
■ Geometry either of the two points at which the axis of a circle cuts the surface of a sphere. ■ Geometry a fixed point to which other points or lines are referred, e.g. the origin of polar coordinates or the point of which a line or curve is a polar. ■ Biology an extremity of the main axis of a cell, organ, or part. ■ each of the two opposite points on the surface of a magnet at which magnetic forces are strongest. ■ figurative one of two opposed or contradictory principles or ideas: *Miriam and Rebecca represent two poles in the argument about transracial adoption.*
– PHRASES **be poles apart** have nothing in common.
– DERIVATIVES **poleward** adjective, **polewards** adjective & adverb.
– ORIGIN late Middle English: from Latin *polus* 'end of an axis', from Greek *polos* 'pivot, axis, sky'.

pole[3] ▶ **noun** short for **POLE POSITION**.

poleaxe (US also **poleax**) ▶ **noun** another term for **BATTLEAXE** (in sense 1).
■ a short-handled axe with a spike at the back, formerly used in naval warfare for boarding, resisting boarders, and cutting ropes. ■ a butcher's axe with a hammer head at the back, used to slaughter animals.
▶ **verb** [with obj.] hit, kill, or knock down with or as if with a poleaxe.
■ (often **be poleaxed**) cause great shock to (someone): *I was poleaxed by this revelation.*
– ORIGIN Middle English: related to Middle Dutch *pol(l)aex*, Middle Low German *pol(l)exe* (see **POLL**, **AXE**). The change in the first syllable was due to association with **POLE**[1]; the first element *poll-* may have referred to a special head of the axe or to the head of an enemy.

pole barn ▶ **noun** a farm building which has sides consisting of poles covered with wire mesh.

pole bean ▶ **noun** N. Amer. a climbing bean.

polecat ▶ **noun** a weasel-like Eurasian mammal with mainly dark brown fur and a darker mask across the eyes, noted for its fetid smell.
• Genus *Mustela*, family Mustelidae: three species, in particular the **European polecat** (*M. putorius*), which is the probable ancestor of the domestic ferret.
■ North American term for **SKUNK**.
– ORIGIN Middle English: perhaps from Old French *pole* 'chicken' + **CAT**[1].

polecat-ferret ▶ **noun** a domestic ferret of a variety that has the darker colouring of the wild polecat.

pole lathe ▶ **noun** an ancient form of lathe operated by a treadle, in which the work is turned by a cord passing round it and rotated back by the action of a springy pole or sapling attached to the top end.

polemic /pəˈlɛmɪk/ ▶ **noun** a strong verbal or written attack on someone or something: *his polemic against the cultural relativism of the Sixties* | [mass noun] *a writer of feminist polemic.*
■ (usu. **polemics**) the art or practice of engaging in controversial debate or dispute: *the history of science has become embroiled in religious polemics.*
▶ **adjective** another term for **POLEMICAL**.
– DERIVATIVES **polemicist** noun, **polemicize** (also **-ise**) verb.
– ORIGIN mid 17th cent.: via medieval Latin from Greek *polemikos*, from *polemos* 'war'.

polemical ▶ **adjective** of, relating to, or involving strongly critical, controversial, or disputatious writing or speech: *a polemical essay.*
– DERIVATIVES **polemically** adverb.

polenta /pəˈlɛntə/ ▶ **noun** [mass noun] maize flour as used in Italian cookery; cornmeal.
■ a paste or dough made from this flour, which is boiled and typically then fried or baked.
– ORIGIN late 16th cent.: Italian, from Latin, 'pearl barley' (a sense of *polenta* in Old English).

pole piece ▶ **noun** Physics a mass of iron forming the end of an electromagnet, through which the lines of magnetic force are concentrated and directed.

pole position ▶ **noun** the most favourable position at the start of a motor race.
■ figurative a leading or dominant position: *a company boasting the pole position in the communications business.*
– ORIGIN 1950s: from a 19th-cent. use of *pole* in horse racing, denoting the starting position next to the inside boundary fence.

Pole Star Astronomy a fairly bright star located within one degree of the celestial north pole, in the constellation Ursa Minor. It is a double star, the bright component of which is a cepheid variable. Also called **NORTH STAR**, **POLARIS**.
■ (**pole star**) [as noun] figurative a thing or principle that guides or attracts people: *the shop is a pole star for both actual and armchair travellers.*

pole vault ▶ **noun** [mass noun] (**the pole vault**) an athletic event in which competitors attempt to vault over a high bar with the end of an extremely long flexible pole held in the hands and used to give extra spring.
■ [count noun] a vault performed in this way.
▶ **verb** (**pole-vault**) [no obj.] perform a pole vault.
– DERIVATIVES **pole-vaulter** noun.

police ▶ **noun** [treated as pl.] (usu. **the police**) the civil force of a state, responsible for the prevention and detection of crime and the maintenance of public order.
■ members of a police force: *there are fewer women police than men.* ■ [with adj. or noun modifier] an organization engaged in the enforcement of official regulations in a specified domain: *transport police.*
▶ **verb** [with obj.] [often as noun **policing**] (of a police force) have the duty of maintaining law and order in or for (an area or event).
■ enforce regulations or an agreement in (a particular area or domain): *a UN resolution to use military force to police the no-fly zone.* ■ enforce the provisions of (a law, agreement, or treaty): *the regulations will be policed by factory inspectors.*
– ORIGIN late 15th cent. (in the sense 'public order'): from French, from medieval Latin *politia* 'citizenship, government' (see **POLICY**[1]). Current senses date from the early 19th cent.

police constable ▶ **noun** see **CONSTABLE**.

police dog ▶ **noun** a dog, especially an Alsatian, trained for use in police work.

police force ▶ **noun** an organized body of police officers responsible for a country, district, or town.

policeman ▶ **noun** (pl. **-men**) a male member of a police force.

policeman's helmet ▶ **noun** the Himalayan balsam. See **BALSAM** (sense 2).

Police Motu ▶ **noun** see **MOTU**.

police officer ▶ **noun** a policeman or policewoman.

police procedural ▶ **noun** a crime novel in which the emphasis is on the procedures used by the police in solving the crime.

police record ▶ **noun** (usu. **police records**) a dossier kept by the police on all people convicted of crime.
■ (**a police record**) a personal history which includes some conviction for crime: *a well-known character with a police record.*

police state ▶ **noun** a totalitarian state controlled by a political police force that secretly supervises the citizens' activities.

police station ▶ **noun** the office or headquarters of a local police force.

policewoman ▶ **noun** (pl. **-women**) a female member of a police force.

policier /ˌpɒlɪˈsjeɪ, French pɔlisje/ ▶ **noun** a film based on a police novel, portraying crime and its detection by police.
– ORIGIN French, from *roman policier* 'detective novel'.

policy[1] ▶ **noun** (pl. **-ies**) a course or principle of action adopted or proposed by a government, party, business, or individual: *the government's controversial economic policies* | [mass noun] *it is not company policy to dispense with our older workers.*
■ [mass noun] archaic prudent or expedient conduct or action: *a course of policy and wisdom.*
– ORIGIN late Middle English: from Old French *policie* 'civil administration', via Latin from Greek *politeia* 'citizenship', from *politēs* 'citizen', from *polis* 'city'.

policy[2] ▶ **noun** (pl. **-ies**) a contract of insurance: *they took out a joint policy.*
– ORIGIN mid 16th cent.: from French *police* 'bill of lading, contract of insurance', from Provençal *poliss(i)a*, probably from medieval Latin *apodissa*, *apodixa*, based on Greek *apodeixis* 'evidence, proof', from *apodeiknunai* 'demonstrate, show'.

policyholder ▶ **noun** a person or group in whose name an insurance policy is held.

polio ▶ **noun** short for **POLIOMYELITIS**.

poliomyelitis /ˌpəʊlɪəʊmʌɪəˈlʌɪtɪs, ˌpɒlɪəʊ-/ ▶ **noun** [mass noun] Medicine an infectious viral disease that affects the central nervous system and can cause temporary or permanent paralysis.
– ORIGIN late 19th cent.: modern Latin, from Greek *polios* 'grey' + *muelos* 'marrow'.

poliovirus ▶ **noun** Medicine any of a group of enteroviruses including those that cause poliomyelitis.

polis[1] /ˈpəʊlɪs, ˈpɒlɪs/ ▶ **noun** Scottish and Irish form of **POLICE**.

polis[2] /ˈpɒlɪs/ ▶ **noun** (pl. **poleis**) a city state in

ancient Greece, especially as considered in its ideal form for philosophical purposes.
– ORIGIN Greek.

Polisario /ˌpɒlɪˈsɑːrɪəʊ/ (also **Polisario Front**) ▶ **noun** an independence movement in Western (formerly Spanish) Sahara, formed in 1973.
– ORIGIN Spanish acronym, from *Frente Popular para la Liberación de Sagnia el-Hamra y Río de Oro* 'Popular Front for the Liberation of Sagnia el-Hamra and Rio de Oro'.

Polish /ˈpəʊlɪʃ/ ▶ **adjective** of or relating to Poland, its inhabitants, or their language.
▶ **noun** [mass noun] the Western Slavic language of Poland, spoken by some 38 million people.

polish /ˈpɒlɪʃ/ ▶ **verb** [with obj.] make the surface of (something) smooth and shiny by rubbing it: *behind the bar the steward polished glasses busily.*
■ improve, refine, or add the finishing touches to: *he's got to **polish up** his French for his job.*
▶ **noun** [mass noun] a substance used to give something a smooth and shiny surface when rubbed in: *a tin of shoe polish.*
■ [in sing.] an act of rubbing something to give it a shiny surface: *I could give the wardrobe a polish.* ■ smoothness or glossiness produced by rubbing or friction: *the machine refines the shape of the stone and gives it polish.* ■ refinement or elegance in a person or thing: *you can't expect a country GP to have much polish.*
– DERIVATIVES **polishable** adjective, **polisher** noun.
– ORIGIN Middle English: from Old French *poliss-*, lengthened stem of *polir* 'to polish', from Latin *polire*.
▶ **polish something off** finish or consume something quickly: *they polished off most of the sausages.*

Polish Corridor a former region of Poland which extended northwards to the Baltic coast and separated East Prussia from the rest of Germany, granted to Poland after the First World War to ensure Polish access to the coast. Its annexation by Germany in 1939, with the German occupation of the rest of Poland, precipitated the Second World War. After the war the area was restored to Poland.

polished ▶ **adjective** shiny as a result of being rubbed: *a polished mahogany table.*
■ accomplished and skilful: *his polished performance in the film.* ■ refined, sophisticated, or elegant: *he was polished and charming.* ■ (of rice) having had the outer husk removed during milling.

Polish notation ▶ **noun** [mass noun] Logic & Computing a system of formula notation without brackets or special punctuation, frequently used to represent the order in which arithmetical operations are performed in many computers and calculators. In the usual form (**reverse Polish notation**), operators follow rather than precede their operands.

politburo /ˈpɒlɪtˌbjʊərəʊ/ ▶ **noun** (pl. **-os**) the principal policy-making committee of a communist party.
■ (**Politburo**) this committee in the former USSR, founded in 1917. Also called (1952–66) the **PRESIDIUM**.
– ORIGIN from Russian *politbyuro*, from *polit(icheskoe) byuro* 'political bureau'.

polite ▶ **adjective** (**politer**, **politest**) having or showing behaviour that is respectful and considerate of other people: *they thought she was wrong but were too polite to say so.*
■ [attrib.] of or relating to people who regard themselves as more cultured and refined than others: *the picture outraged polite society.*
– DERIVATIVES **politely** adverb, **politeness** noun.
– ORIGIN late Middle English (in the Latin sense): from Latin *politus* 'polished, made smooth', past participle of *polire*.

politesse /ˌpɒlɪˈtɛs/ ▶ **noun** [mass noun] formal politeness or etiquette.
– ORIGIN early 18th cent.: French, from Italian *politezza, pulitezza*, from *pulito* 'polite'.

politic ▶ **adjective** (of an action) seeming sensible and judicious in the circumstances: [with infinitive] *I did not think it politic to express my reservations.*
■ (also **politick**) archaic (of a person) prudent and sagacious.
▶ **verb** (**politicked**, **politicking**) [no obj.] [often as noun **politicking**] often derogatory engage in political activity: *the cumbersome bureaucracy and politicking of the European Community.*
– DERIVATIVES **politicly** adverb (rare).
– ORIGIN late Middle English: from Old French *politique* 'political', via Latin from Greek *politikos*, from *politēs* 'citizen', from *polis* 'city'.

political ▶ **adjective** of or relating to the state, the government, or the public affairs of a country: *a period of political and economic stability.*
■ of or relating to the ideas or strategies of a particular party or group in politics: *a decision taken for purely political reasons.* ■ interested in or active in politics: *I'm not very political.* ■ motivated or caused by a person's beliefs or actions concerning politics: *a political crime.* ■ chiefly derogatory relating to, affecting, or acting according to the interests of status or authority within an organization rather than matters of principle.
– DERIVATIVES **politically** adverb.

political asylum ▶ **noun** see **ASYLUM**.

political commissar ▶ **noun** a person responsible for political education and organization in a military unit in China.

political correctness (also **political correctitude**) ▶ **noun** [mass noun] the avoidance of forms of expression or action that are perceived to exclude, marginalize, or insult groups of people who are socially disadvantaged or discriminated against.

political economy ▶ **noun** [mass noun] dated economics as a branch of knowledge or academic discipline.
– DERIVATIVES **political economist** noun.

political geography ▶ **noun** [mass noun] the branch of geography that deals with the boundaries, divisions, and possessions of states.

politically correct (or **incorrect**) ▶ **adjective** exhibiting (or failing to exhibit) political correctness: *it is not politically correct to laugh at speech impediments.*

political offence ▶ **noun** Law an offence regarded as justifiable or deserving of special consideration because of its political motivation.

political prisoner ▶ **noun** a person imprisoned for their political beliefs or actions.

political refugee ▶ **noun** a refugee from an oppressive government.

political science ▶ **noun** [mass noun] the branch of knowledge that deals with the state and systems of government; the scientific analysis of political activity and behaviour.
– DERIVATIVES **political scientist** noun.

politician ▶ **noun** a person who is professionally involved in politics, especially as a holder of or a candidate for an elected office.
■ chiefly US a person who acts in a manipulative and devious way, typically to gain advancement within an organization.

politicize (also **-ise**) ▶ **verb** [with obj.] [often as adj. **politicized**] cause (an activity or event) to become political in character: *wage bargaining in the public sector became more politicized.*
■ make (someone) politically aware, especially by persuading them of the truth of views considered radical: *we successfully politicized a generation of women.* ■ [no obj.] engage in or talk about politics.
– DERIVATIVES **politicization** noun.

politick ▶ **adjective** archaic spelling of **POLITIC**.

politico ▶ **noun** (pl. **-os**) informal, chiefly derogatory a politician or person with strong political views.
– ORIGIN Spanish and Italian, 'politic' or 'political person'.

politico- ▶ **combining form** politically: *politico-ethical.*
■ political and ...: *politico-economic.*
– ORIGIN from Greek *politikos* 'civic, political'.

politics ▶ **plural noun** [usu. treated as sing.] the activities associated with the governance of a country or area, especially the debate or conflict between individuals or parties having or hoping to achieve power: *the Communist Party was a major force in French politics | thereafter he dropped out of active politics.*
■ the activities of governments concerning the political relations between states: *in the conduct of global politics, economic status must be backed by military capacity.* ■ the academic study of government and the state: [as modifier] *a politics lecturer.* ■ activities within an organization which are aimed at improving someone's status or position and are typically considered to be devious or divisive: *I didn't want to become embroiled in yet another discussion of office politics and personalities.* ■ a particular set of political beliefs or principles: *people do not buy their paper purely for its politics.* ■ (often **the politics of**) the assumptions or principles relating to or inherent in a sphere, theory, or activity, especially when concerned with power and status in a society: *the politics of gender.*
– PHRASES **play politics** act for political or personal gain rather than from principle.

polity /ˈpɒlɪti/ ▶ **noun** (pl. **-ies**) a form or process of civil government or constitution.
■ an organized society; a state as a political entity.
– ORIGIN mid 16th cent.: from obsolete French *politie*, via Latin from Greek *politeia* 'citizenship, government', from *politēs* 'citizen', from *polis* 'city'.

polje /ˈpɒljə/ ▶ **noun** Geology a flat-floored depression in a karstic region, especially in Slovenia, with steep enclosing walls and a covering of alluvium.
– ORIGIN late 19th cent.: from Serbo-Croat.

Polk /pəʊk/, James Knox (1795–1849), American Democratic statesman, 11th President of the US 1845–9. His term of office resulted in major territorial additions to the US: Texas was admitted to the Union in 1845 and conflict with Mexico resulted in the annexation of California and the south-west two years later.

polka /ˈpɒlkə, ˈpəʊlkə/ ▶ **noun** a lively dance of Bohemian origin in duple time.
■ a piece of music for this dance or in its rhythm.
▶ **verb** (**polkas**, **polkaed** or **polka'd**, **polkaing**) [no obj.] dance the polka.
– ORIGIN mid 19th cent.: via French and German from Czech *půlka* 'half-step', from *půl* 'half'.

polka dot ▶ **noun** one of a number of large round dots repeated to form a regular pattern on fabric: [as modifier] *a red and white polka-dot shirt.*
– DERIVATIVES **polka-dotted** adjective.

poll /pəʊl/ ▶ **noun** **1** (often **the polls**) the process of voting in an election: *the country went to the polls on March 10.*
■ a record of the number of votes cast in an election: *the ruling party won 24 seats, narrowly topping the poll.* ■ (**the polls**) the places where votes are cast in an election: *the polls have only just closed.* ■ short for **OPINION POLL**.
2 dialect a person's head.
■ the part of the head on which hair grows; the scalp.
3 a hornless animal, especially one of a breed of hornless cattle. See also **RED POLL**.
▶ **verb** [with obj.] **1** (often **be polled**) record the opinion or vote of: *over half of those polled do not believe the prime minister usually tells the truth.*
■ [no obj., with adverbial] (of a candidate in an election) receive a specified number of votes: *the Green candidate polled 3.6 per cent.* ■ Telecommunications & Computing check the status of (a measuring device, part of a computer, or a node in a network), especially as part of a repeated cycle.
2 cut the horns off (an animal, especially a young cow).
■ archaic cut off the top of (a tree or plant), typically to encourage further growth; pollard.
– DERIVATIVES **pollee** /pəʊˈliː/ noun (in sense 1 of the verb).
– ORIGIN Middle English (in the sense 'head'): perhaps of Low German origin. The original sense was 'head', and hence 'an individual person among a number', from which developed the sense 'number of people ascertained by counting of heads' and then 'counting of heads or of votes' (17th cent.).

pollack /ˈpɒlək/ (also **pollock**) ▶ **noun** (pl. same or **pollacks**) an edible greenish-brown fish of the cod family, with a protruding lower jaw. Found in the NE Atlantic, it is popular with anglers.
• *Pollachius pollachius*, family Gadidae.
– ORIGIN late Middle English: perhaps of Celtic origin.

Pollaiuolo /ˌpɒlʌɪˈwəʊləʊ/, Antonio (*c.*1432–98) and Piero (1443–96), Italian sculptors, painters, and engravers. Both brothers worked on the monuments to Popes Sixtus IV and Innocent VIII in St Peter's, and Antonio is particularly known for his realistic depiction of the human form.

pollan /ˈpɒlən/ ▶ **noun** an Arctic cisco (fish) of a variety which occurs in Irish lakes.
– ORIGIN early 18th cent.: from Irish *pollán*, perhaps based on *poll* 'pool'.

pollard /ˈpɒləd/ ▶ **verb** [with obj.] [often as adj. **pollarded**] cut off the top and branches of (a tree) to encourage new growth at the top.
▶ **noun** **1** a tree whose top and branches have been cut off for this reason.

2 archaic an animal, e.g. a sheep or deer, that has lost its horns or cast its antlers.
– ORIGIN early 17th cent.: from the verb POLL + -ARD.

polled /pəʊld/ ▶ **adjective** (of cattle, sheep, or goats) lacking horns, either naturally or because they have been removed.

pollen ▶ **noun** [mass noun] a fine powdery substance, typically yellow, consisting of microscopic grains discharged from the male part of a flower or from a male cone. Each grain contains a male gamete that can fertilize the female ovule, to which pollen is transported by the wind, insects, or other animals.
– ORIGIN mid 18th cent.: from Latin, literally 'fine powder'.

pollen analysis ▶ **noun** [mass noun] the analysis of samples of pollen to determine the species present; palynology.

pollen basket ▶ **noun** Entomology a flattened area fringed with hairs on the hind leg of a social bee, used for carrying pollen. Also called CORBICULA.

pollen count ▶ **noun** an index of the amount of pollen in the air, published chiefly for the benefit of those allergic to it.

pollen grain ▶ **noun** each of the microscopic particles, typically single cells, of which pollen is composed. Pollen grains have a tough coat which has a form characteristic of the plant producing it.

pollen tube ▶ **noun** Botany a hollow tube which develops from a pollen grain when deposited on the stigma of a flower. It penetrates the style and conveys the male gametes to the ovule.

pollen zone ▶ **noun** a characteristic assemblage of pollen obtained by pollen analysis. Each zone (denoted by a Roman numeral) corresponds to one of the climatic stages of the late-glacial and postglacial periods.

pollex /ˈpɒlɛks/ ▶ **noun** (pl. **pollices** /-lɪsiːz/) Anatomy & Zoology the innermost digit of a forelimb, especially the thumb in primates.
– ORIGIN mid 19th cent.: from Latin, literally 'thumb or big toe'.

pollie ▶ **noun** variant spelling of POLLY.

pollinate ▶ **verb** [with obj.] convey pollen to or deposit pollen on (a stigma, ovule, flower, or plant) and so allow fertilization.
– DERIVATIVES **pollination** noun, **pollinator** noun.
– ORIGIN late 19th cent.: from Latin pollen, pollin- 'pollen' + -ATE³.

polling booth ▶ **noun** Brit. a compartment with one open side in which one voter at a time stands to mark their ballot paper.

polling day ▶ **noun** the day of a local or general election.

polling station (N. Amer. also **polling place**) ▶ **noun** a building where voting takes place during an election, typically one that normally has another function, such as a school.

pollinium /pəˈlɪnɪəm/ ▶ **noun** (pl. **pollinia** /pəˈlɪnɪə/) Botany a coherent mass of pollen grains that is the product of each anther lobe of some flowers, especially orchids. Single or paired pollinia are often attached to, and carried by, pollinating insects.
– ORIGIN mid 19th cent.: modern Latin, from Latin pollen, pollin- 'pollen'.

polliwog (also **pollywog**) chiefly N. Amer. ▶ **noun** a tadpole.
– ORIGIN late Middle English (earlier as pollywiggle): from POLL in the sense 'head' + the verb WIGGLE.

pollo /ˈpɒləʊ/ ▶ **noun** [mass noun] chicken (as used in the names of Italian, Spanish, or Mexican dishes).
– ORIGIN Spanish and Italian.

Pollock, (Paul) Jackson (1912–56), American painter. He was a leading figure in the abstract expressionist movement and from 1947 became the chief exponent of the style known as action painting, whereby he poured, splashed, or dripped paint on to the canvas.

pollock ▶ **noun 1** North American term for SAITHE.
2 variant spelling of POLLACK.

pollster /ˈpəʊlstə/ ▶ **noun** a person who conducts or analyses opinion polls.

poll tax ▶ **noun** [mass noun] a tax levied on every adult, without reference to their income or resources.
■ informal term for COMMUNITY CHARGE.

pollute ▶ **verb** [with obj.] contaminate (water, air, or a place) with harmful or poisonous substances: the explosion polluted the town with dioxin | [as adj. **polluted**] the Mersey is one of Europe's most polluted rivers.
■ figurative defile; corrupt: a society polluted by racism.
– DERIVATIVES **pollutant** adjective & noun, **polluter** noun.
– ORIGIN late Middle English: from Latin pollut- 'soiled, defiled', from the verb polluere, based on the root of lutum 'mud'.

pollution ▶ **noun** [mass noun] the presence in or introduction into the environment of a substance or thing which has harmful or poisonous effects: the level of pollution in the air is rising.
– ORIGIN late Middle English: from Latin pollutio(n-), from the verb polluere (see POLLUTE).

Pollux /ˈpɒləks/ **1** Greek Mythology the twin brother of Castor. Also called POLYDEUCES. See DIOSCURI.
2 Astronomy the brightest star in the constellation Gemini, close to Castor.
– ORIGIN Latin.

polly (also **pollie**) ▶ **noun** (pl. **-ies**) Austral. informal a politician.
– ORIGIN 1960s: abbreviation.

Pollyanna ▶ **noun** an excessively cheerful or optimistic person.
– DERIVATIVES **Pollyannaish** adjective, **Pollyannaism** noun.
– ORIGIN early 20th cent.: the name of the optimistic heroine created by Eleanor Hodgman Porter (1868–1920), American author of children's stories.

pollywog ▶ **noun** variant spelling of POLLIWOG.

Polo, Marco, see MARCO POLO.

polo ▶ **noun** [mass noun] a game of Eastern origin resembling hockey, played on horseback with a long-handled mallet.
– ORIGIN late 19th cent.: from Balti, 'ball'.

poloidal /pəˈlɔɪd(ə)l/ ▶ **adjective** Physics relating to or denoting a magnetic field associated with a toroidal electric field, in which each line of force is confined to a radial or meridian plane.
– ORIGIN 1940s: from POLAR, on the pattern of toroidal.

polonaise /ˌpɒləˈneɪz/ ▶ **noun 1** a slow dance of Polish origin in triple time, consisting chiefly of an intricate march or procession.
■ a piece of music for this dance or in its rhythm.
2 historical a woman's dress with a tight bodice and a skirt open from the waist downwards, looped up to show a decorative underskirt.
▶ **adjective** (of a dish, especially a vegetable dish) garnished with chopped hard-boiled egg yolk, breadcrumbs, and parsley.
– ORIGIN mid 18th cent.: from French, feminine of polonais 'Polish', from medieval Latin Polonia 'Poland'.

polo neck ▶ **noun** Brit. a high, close-fitting, turned-over collar on a garment, typically a sweater.
■ a sweater with a neck of this type.
– DERIVATIVES **polo-necked** adjective.

polonium /pəˈləʊnɪəm/ ▶ **noun** [mass noun] the chemical element of atomic number 84, a radioactive metal occurring in nature only as a product of radioactive decay of uranium. (Symbol: **Po**)
– ORIGIN late 19th cent.: modern Latin, from medieval Latin Polonia 'Poland' (the native country of Marie Curie, the element's co-discoverer).

Polonnaruwa /ˌpɒlɒˈnɑːrʊwə/ a town in NE Sri Lanka; pop. 11,600 (1981). Succeeding Anuradhapura in the 8th century as the capital of Ceylon, it became an important Buddhist centre in the 12th century. It was subsequently deserted until a modern town was built in the 20th century.

polony /pəˈləʊni/ ▶ **noun** (pl. **-ies**) Brit. another term for BOLOGNA.
– ORIGIN mid 18th cent.: apparently an alteration of BOLOGNA.

polo pony ▶ **noun** a horse used in playing polo, typically bred for speed and agility.

polo shirt ▶ **noun** a casual short-sleeved cotton shirt with a collar and several buttons at the neck.

polo stick ▶ **noun** a long-handled mallet used for playing polo.

Pol Pot /pɒl ˈpɒt/ (c.1925–98), Cambodian communist leader of the Khmer Rouge, Prime Minister 1976–9; born Saloth Sar. During his regime the Khmer Rouge embarked on a brutal reconstruction programme in which many millions of Cambodians were killed. Overthrown in 1979, Pol Pot led the Khmer Rouge in a guerrilla war against the new Vietnamese-backed government until his official retirement in 1985.

Polska /ˈpɒlska/ Polish name for POLAND.

Poltava /pɒlˈtɑːvə/ a city in east central Ukraine; pop. 317,000 (1990).

poltergeist /ˈpɒltəɡʌɪst/ ▶ **noun** a ghost or other supernatural being supposedly responsible for physical disturbances such as making loud noises and throwing objects about.
– ORIGIN mid 19th cent.: from German Poltergeist, from poltern 'create a disturbance' + Geist 'ghost'.

Poltoratsk /ˌpɒltəˈrɑːtsk/ former name (1919–27) for ASHGABAT.

poltroon /pɒlˈtruːn/ ▶ **noun** archaic or poetic/literary an utter coward.
– DERIVATIVES **poltroonery** noun.
– ORIGIN early 16th cent.: from French poltron, from Italian poltrone, perhaps from poltro 'sluggard'.

poly ▶ **noun** (pl. **polys**) informal short for:
■ polyester. ■ Brit. polytechnic. ■ polythene.

poly- ▶ **combining form** many; much: polyandry | polychrome.
■ Chemistry denoting the presence of many atoms or groups of a particular kind in a molecule: polycarbonate.
– ORIGIN from Greek polus 'much', polloi 'many'.

polyacetylene /ˌpɒlɪəˈsɛtɪliːn/ ▶ **noun** [mass noun] Chemistry a black, electrically conducting solid which is a hydrocarbon polymer containing chains of carbon atoms joined by alternate double and single bonds.

polyacrylamide /ˌpɒlɪəˈkrɪləmʌɪd/ ▶ **noun** [mass noun] a synthetic resin made by polymerizing acrylamide, especially a water-soluble polymer used to form or stabilize gels and as a thickening or clarifying agent.

polyadic /ˌpɒlɪˈadɪk/ ▶ **adjective** involving three or more quantities, elements, or individuals.
– ORIGIN early 20th cent.: from POLY- 'many', on the pattern of words such as dyadic, monadic.

polyamide /ˌpɒlɪˈeɪmʌɪd, -ˈam-/ ▶ **noun** [mass noun] a synthetic polymer of a type made by the linkage of an amino group of one molecule and a carboxylic acid group of another, including many synthetic fibres such as nylon.

polyandry /ˈpɒlɪandri/ ▶ **noun** [mass noun] polygamy in which a woman has more than one husband. Compare with POLYGYNY.
■ Zoology a pattern of mating in which a female animal has more than one male mate.
– DERIVATIVES **polyandrous** adjective.
– ORIGIN late 17th cent.: from POLY- 'many' + Greek anēr- 'male'.

polyanthus /ˌpɒlɪˈanθəs/ ▶ **noun** (pl. same) a herbaceous flowering plant which is a complex hybrid between the wild primrose and primulas, cultivated in Europe since the 17th century.
● Primula × polyantha, family Primulaceae.
– ORIGIN early 18th cent.: modern Latin, from POLY- 'many' + Greek anthos 'flower'.

polyatomic ▶ **adjective** consisting of many atoms.

Polybius /pəˈlɪbɪəs/ (c.200–c.118 BC), Greek historian. His forty books of Histories (only partially extant) chronicled the rise of the Roman Empire from 220 to 146 BC.

polycarbonate ▶ **noun** [mass noun] a synthetic resin in which the polymer units are linked through carbonate groups, including many moulding materials and films.

Polycarp, St /ˈpɒlɪkɑːp/ (c.69–c.155), Greek bishop of Smyrna in Asia Minor. The leading Christian figure in Smyrna, he was arrested during a pagan festival, refused to recant his faith, and was burnt to death. Feast day, 23 February.

Polychaeta /ˌpɒlɪˈkiːtə/ Zoology a class of marine annelid worms which comprises the bristle worms.
– DERIVATIVES **polychaete** /ˈpɒlɪkiːt/ noun.
– ORIGIN modern Latin (plural), from Greek polu- 'many' + khaitē 'mane' (taken to mean 'bristle').

polychlorinated biphenyl (abbrev: PCB)
▶ **noun** Chemistry any of a class of toxic aromatic compounds, often formed as waste in industrial

processes, whose molecules contain two benzene rings in which hydrogen atoms have been replaced by chlorine atoms.

polychromatic ▶ adjective of two or more or of varying colours; multicoloured.
  ■ Physics (of light or other radiation) of a number of wavelengths or frequencies.
  – DERIVATIVES **polychromatism** noun.

polychrome ▶ adjective painted, printed, or decorated in several colours.
  ▶ noun [mass noun] varied colouring.
  ■ [count noun] a work of art in several colours, especially a statue.
  ▶ verb [with obj.] [usu. as adj. **polychromed**] execute or decorate (a work of art) in several colours.
  – ORIGIN early 19th cent.: from French, from Greek *polukhrōmos*, from *polu-* 'many' + *khrōma* 'colour'.

polychromy /ˈpɒlɪkrəʊmi/ ▶ noun [mass noun] the art of painting in several colours, especially as applied to ancient pottery, sculpture, and architecture.

polyclinic ▶ noun a clinic (typically one independent of a hospital) where both general and specialist examinations and treatments are available to outpatients.

Polyclitus /ˌpɒlɪˈklʌɪtəs/ (5th century BC), Greek sculptor, known for his statues of idealized male athletes. Two Roman copies of his works survive, the *Doryphoros* (spear-bearer) and the *Diadumenos* (youth fastening a band round his head).

polyclonal /ˌpɒlɪˈkləʊn(ə)l/ ▶ adjective Medicine & Biology consisting of or derived from many clones.

polycotton ▶ noun [mass noun] fabric made from a mixture of cotton and polyester fibre.

polycrystalline ▶ adjective (of a metal or other solid) consisting of many crystalline parts that are randomly oriented with respect to each other.

polyculture ▶ noun [mass noun] the simultaneous cultivation or exploitation of several crops or kinds of animals.

polycyclic /ˌpɒlɪˈsʌɪklɪk, -ˈsɪk-/ ▶ adjective of, relating to, or resulting from many cycles.
  ■ Chemistry (of an organic compound) having several rings of atoms in the molecule. ■ Geology (of a landform or deposit) having undergone two or more cycles of erosion and deposition.

polycystic ▶ adjective Medicine characterized by multiple cysts.

polycythaemia /ˌpɒlɪsʌɪˈθiːmɪə/ (US **polycythemia**) ▶ noun [mass noun] Medicine an abnormally increased concentration of haemoglobin in the blood, either through reduction of plasma volume or increase in red cell numbers. It may be a primary disease of unknown cause, or a secondary condition linked to respiratory or circulatory disorder or cancer.
  – ORIGIN mid 19th cent.: from modern Latin, from **POLY-** 'many' + **-CYTE** 'cell' + **HAEMO-** 'blood' + **-IA**[1].

polydactyly /ˌpɒlɪˈdaktɪli/ ▶ noun [mass noun] a condition in which a person or animal has more than five fingers or toes on one, or on each, hand or foot.
  – DERIVATIVES **polydactyl** adjective & noun.
  – ORIGIN late 19th cent.: from Greek *poludaktulos* (from *polu-* 'many' + *daktulos* 'finger') + **-Y**[3].

Polydeuces /ˌpɒlɪˈdjuːsiːz/ another name for **POLLUX** (in sense 1).

polydipsia /ˌpɒlɪˈdɪpsɪə/ ▶ noun [mass noun] Medicine abnormally great thirst as a symptom of disease (such as diabetes) or psychological disturbance.
  – ORIGIN mid 17th cent.: from Greek *poludipsios* 'very thirsty', *poludipsos* 'causing great thirst', based on *dipsa* 'thirst'.

polyelectrolyte /ˌpɒlɪˈlɛktrəlʌɪt/ ▶ noun Chemistry a polymer which has several ionizable groups along the molecule, especially any of those used for coagulating and flocculating particles during water treatment or for making electrophoretic gels.

polyembryony /ˌpɒlɪˈɛmbrɪəni/ ▶ noun [mass noun] Biology the formation of more than one embryo from a single fertilized ovum or in a single seed.
  – DERIVATIVES **polyembryonic** adjective.

polyene /ˈpɒlijiːn/ ▶ noun Chemistry a hydrocarbon with several carbon–carbon double bonds, especially one having a chain of conjugated single and double bonds.

polyester ▶ noun [mass noun] a synthetic resin in which the polymer units are linked by ester groups,

used chiefly to make synthetic textile fibres (e.g. Terylene).

polyethnic ▶ adjective belonging to, comprising or containing many ethnic groups.
  – DERIVATIVES **polyethnicity** noun.

polyethylene /ˌpɒlɪˈɛθɪliːn/ ▶ noun another term for **POLYTHENE**.

polyethylene glycol ▶ noun [mass noun] a synthetic resin made by polymerizing ethylene glycol, in particular any of a series of water-soluble oligomers and polymers used chiefly as solvents or waxes.

polyethylene terephthalate /ˌtɛrəfˈθaleɪt/ (abbrev.: **PET**) ▶ noun [mass noun] a synthetic resin made by copolymerizing ethylene glycol and terephthalic acid, widely used to make polyester fibres.

Polyfilla ▶ noun [mass noun] trademark a type of plaster used to make minor building repairs, such as filling small holes.

polygamous ▶ adjective practising, relating to, or involving polygamy: *polygamous societies*.
  ■ Zoology (of an animal) typically having more than one mate. ■ Botany (of a plant) bearing some flowers with stamens only, some with pistils only, and some with both, on the same or different plants.
  – DERIVATIVES **polygamously** adverb.
  – ORIGIN early 17th cent.: from Greek *polugamos* (from *polu-* 'much, often' + *-gamos* 'marrying') + **-OUS**.

polygamy ▶ noun [mass noun] the practice or custom of having more than one wife or husband at the same time.
  ■ Zoology a pattern of mating in which an animal has more than one mate of the opposite sex.
  – DERIVATIVES **polygamist** noun.
  – ORIGIN late 16th cent.: from French *polygamie*, via late Latin from Greek *polugamia*, from *polugamos* 'often marrying'.

polygene ▶ noun Genetics a gene whose individual effect on a phenotype is too small to be observed, but which can act together with others to produce observable variation.
  – ORIGIN 1940s: back-formation from **POLYGENIC**.

polygenesis /ˌpɒlɪˈdʒɛnɪsɪs/ ▶ noun [mass noun] origination from several independent sources, in particular:
  ■ Biology the hypothetical origination of a race or species from a number of independent stocks. Compare with **POLYGENY**. ■ the hypothetical origination of language or of a surname from a number of independent sources in different places at different times.

polygenetic ▶ adjective of or relating to polygenesis; having more than one origin or source.
  ■ Geology denoting or originating from a volcano that has erupted several times.
  – DERIVATIVES **polygenetically** adverb.

polygenic /ˌpɒlɪˈdʒɛnɪk/ ▶ adjective Genetics of, relating to, or determined by polygenes.
  – DERIVATIVES **polygenically** adverb.
  – ORIGIN 1940s: from Greek *polugenēs* 'of many kinds' + **-IC**.

polygenism /pəˈlɪdʒɪnɪz(ə)m/ ▶ noun [mass noun] the doctrine of polygeny.
  – DERIVATIVES **polygenist** noun & adjective.

polygeny /pəˈlɪdʒ(ə)ni/ ▶ noun [mass noun] the theory (not now generally held) that humans evolved from several independent pairs of ancestors. Compare with **POLYGENESIS**.

polyglot /ˈpɒlɪglɒt/ ▶ adjective knowing or using several languages: *a polyglot career woman*.
  ■ (of a book) having the text translated into several languages: *polyglot and bilingual technical dictionaries*.
  ▶ noun a person who knows and is able to use several languages.
  – ORIGIN mid 17th cent.: from French *polyglotte*, from Greek *poluglōttos*, from *polu-* 'many' + *glōtta* 'tongue'.

polygon /ˈpɒlɪg(ə)n/ ▶ noun Geometry a plane figure with at least three straight sides and angles, and typically five or more.
  – DERIVATIVES **polygonal** adjective.
  – ORIGIN late 16th cent.: via late Latin from Greek *polugōnon*, neuter (used as a noun) of *polugōnos* 'many-angled'.

polygon of forces ▶ noun Physics a polygon that represents by the length and direction of its sides all the forces acting on a body or point.

polygonum /pəˈlɪg(ə)nəm/ ▶ noun a plant of a genus that includes knotgrass and knotweed, some of which are weeds and some are garden ornamentals.
  ● Genus *Polygonum*, family Polygonaceae.
  – ORIGIN modern Latin, from Greek *polu-* 'many' + *gonu* 'knee, joint' (because of the swollen joints sheathed by stipules).

polygraph ▶ noun a machine designed to detect and record changes in physiological characteristics, such as a person's pulse and breathing rates, used especially as a lie detector.
  ■ a lie-detector test carried out with a machine of this type.
  – DERIVATIVES **polygraphic** adjective.

polygyne ▶ adjective Entomology (of a social insect) having more than one egg-laying queen in each colony.

polygyny /pəˈlɪdʒɪni/ ▶ noun [mass noun] polygamy in which a man has more than one wife. Compare with **POLYANDRY**.
  ■ Zoology a pattern of mating in which a male animal has more than one female mate.
  – DERIVATIVES **polygynous** /pəˈlɪdʒɪnəs/ adjective.
  – ORIGIN late 18th cent.: from **POLY-** 'many' + Greek *gunē* 'woman'.

polyhedron /ˌpɒlɪˈhiːdrən, -ˈhɛd-/ ▶ noun (pl. **polyhedra** /-drə/ or **polyhedrons**) Geometry a solid figure with many plane faces, typically more than six.
  – DERIVATIVES **polyhedral** adjective, **polyhedric** adjective.
  – ORIGIN late 16th cent.: from Greek *poluedron*, neuter (used as a noun) of *poluedros* 'many-sided'.

polyhistor /ˌpɒlɪˈhɪstə/ ▶ noun another term for **POLYMATH**.
  – ORIGIN late 16th cent.: from Greek *poluistōr* 'very learned', from *polu-* 'much, very' + *histōr* 'wise man'.

Polyhymnia /ˌpɒlɪˈhɪmnɪə/ Greek & Roman Mythology the Muse of the art of mime.
  – ORIGIN via Latin from Greek, literally 'she of the many hymns'.

polyimide /ˌpɒlɪˈɪmʌɪd/ ▶ noun [mass noun] a synthetic resin in which the polymer units are linked by imide groups, used chiefly for heat-resistant films and coatings.

polymath /ˈpɒlɪmaθ/ ▶ noun a person of wide-ranging knowledge or learning.
  – DERIVATIVES **polymathic** adjective, **polymathy** /pəˈlɪməθi/ noun.
  – ORIGIN early 17th cent.: from Greek *polumathēs* 'having learned much', from *polu-* 'much' + the stem of *manthanein* 'learn'.

polymer /ˈpɒlɪmə/ ▶ noun Chemistry a substance which has a molecular structure built up chiefly or completely from a large number of similar units bonded together, e.g. many synthetic organic materials used as plastics and resins.
  – DERIVATIVES **polymeric** adjective.
  – ORIGIN mid 19th cent.: from German, from Greek *polumeros* 'having many parts', from *polu-* 'many' + *meros* 'a share'.

polymerase /ˈpɒlɪməreɪz, pəˈlɪməreɪz/ ▶ noun Biochemistry an enzyme which brings about the formation of a particular polymer, especially DNA or RNA.

polymerize (also **-ise**) ▶ verb Chemistry combine or cause to combine to form a polymer.
  – DERIVATIVES **polymerizable** adjective, **polymerization** noun.

polymerous /pəˈlɪm(ə)rəs/ ▶ adjective Biology having or consisting of many parts.

polymetallic ▶ adjective chiefly Geology containing or involving several metals or their ores.

polymethyl methacrylate /ˌpɒlɪˌmiːθʌɪl mɪˈθakrɪlət, -ˌmɛθ-, -ˈθɪl/ ▶ noun [mass noun] a glassy synthetic resin obtained by polymerizing methyl methacrylate, used to make perspex, plexiglas, and lucite.

polymict /ˈpɒlɪmɪkt/ ▶ adjective Geology (of a conglomerate) consisting of fragments of several different rock types.
  – ORIGIN 1950s: from **POLY-** 'much' + Greek *miktos* 'mixed'.

polymorph ▶ noun an organism or inorganic object or material which takes various forms.
  ■ Physiology a polymorphonuclear leucocyte.

– ORIGIN early 19th cent.: from Greek *polumorphos*, from *polu-* 'many' + *morphē* 'form'.

polymorphism ▶ *noun* [mass noun] the occurrence of something in several different forms, in particular:
■Biology the occurrence of different forms among the members of a population or colony, or in the life cycle of an individual organism. ■ Genetics the presence of genetic variation within a population, upon which natural selection can operate. ■ Computing a feature of a programming language that allows routines to use variables of different types at different times.
– DERIVATIVES **polymorphic** adjective, **polymorphous** adjective.

polymorphonuclear /ˌpɒlɪˌmɔːfə(ʊ)ˈnjuːklɪə/ ▶ *adjective* Physiology (of a leucocyte) having a nucleus with several lobes and a cytoplasm that contains granules, as in an eosinophil or basophil.

polymorphous perversity ▶ *noun* [mass noun] Psychology a generalized sexual desire that can be excited and gratified in many ways, normal in young children but unusual in adults.
– DERIVATIVES **polymorphously perverse** adjective.

polymyositis /ˌpɒlɪmaɪə(ʊ)ˈsaɪtɪs/ ▶ *noun* [mass noun] Medicine a condition marked by inflammation and degeneration of skeletal muscle throughout the body.

polymyxin /ˌpɒlɪˈmɪksɪn/ ▶ *noun* Medicine any of a group of polypeptide antibiotics that are active chiefly against Gram-negative bacteria.
● Polymyxins are obtained from soil bacteria of the genus *Bacillus*, in particular *B. polymyxa*.
– ORIGIN 1940s: from modern Latin *polymyxa*, from Greek *polu-* 'much' + *muxa* 'slime' + -IN[1].

Polynesia /ˌpɒlɪˈniːzɪə, -ˈniːʒə/ a region of the central Pacific, lying to the east of Micronesia and Melanesia and containing the easternmost of the three great groups of Pacific islands, including Hawaii, the Marquesas Islands, Samoa, the Cook Islands, and French Polynesia.
– ORIGIN from POLY- 'many' + Greek *nēsos* 'island'.

Polynesian ▶ *adjective* of or relating to Polynesia, its people, or their languages.
▶ *noun* **1** a native or inhabitant of Polynesia, or a person of Polynesian descent.
2 [mass noun] a group of Austronesian languages spoken in Polynesia, including Maori, Hawaiian, and Samoan.

polyneuritis /ˌpɒlɪnjʊəˈraɪtɪs/ ▶ *noun* [mass noun] Medicine any disorder that affects the peripheral nerves collectively.
– DERIVATIVES **polyneuritic** adjective.

polyneuropathy /ˌpɒlɪnjʊəˈrɒpəθi/ ▶ *noun* [mass noun] Medicine a general degeneration of peripheral nerves that spreads towards the centre of the body.

polynomial /ˌpɒlɪˈnəʊmɪəl/ ▶ *adjective* consisting of several terms.
■Mathematics of, relating to, or denoting a polynomial or polynomials.
▶ *noun* Mathematics an expression of more than two algebraic terms, especially the sum of several terms that contain different powers of the same variable(s).
■Biology a Latin name with more than two parts.
– ORIGIN late 17th cent.: from POLY- 'many', on the pattern of *multinomial*.

polynomial time ▶ *noun* [mass noun] Computing the time required for a computer to solve a problem, where this time is a simple polynomial function of the size of the input.

polynuclear ▶ *adjective* Chemistry (of a complex) containing more than one metal atom.
■(of a compound) polycyclic.

polynucleotide ▶ *noun* Biochemistry a linear polymer whose molecule is composed of many nucleotide units, constituting a section of a nucleic acid molecule.

polynya /pə(ʊ)ˈlɪnjə/ ▶ *noun* a stretch of open water surrounded by ice, especially in Arctic seas.
– ORIGIN mid 19th cent.: from Russian, from the base of *pole* 'field'.

polyoma virus /ˌpɒlɪˈəʊmə/ ▶ *noun* Medicine any of a group of papovaviruses that are usually endemic in their host species without causing disease but which can cause tumours when injected into other species.

polyp /ˈpɒlɪp/ ▶ *noun* **1** Zoology a solitary or colonial sedentary form of a coelenterate such as a sea anemone, typically having a columnar body with the mouth uppermost surrounded by a ring of tentacles. In some species, polyps are a phase in the life cycle which alternates with a medusoid phase. Compare with MEDUSA.
2 Medicine a small growth, usually benign and with a stalk, protruding from a mucous membrane.
– DERIVATIVES **polypous** adjective (only in sense 2).
– ORIGIN late Middle English (in sense 2): from Old French *polipe*, from Latin *polypus* (see POLYPUS). Sense 1 dates from the mid 18th cent.

polypary /ˈpɒlɪp(ə)ri/ ▶ *noun* (pl. **-ies**) Zoology the common stem or skeletal support of a colony of polyps, to which the individual zooids are attached.
– ORIGIN mid 18th cent.: from modern Latin *polyparium*, from Latin *polypus* (see POLYPUS).

polypeptide ▶ *noun* Biochemistry a linear organic polymer consisting of a large number of amino-acid residues bonded together in a chain, forming part of (or the whole of) a protein molecule.
– ORIGIN early 20th cent.: from POLY- 'many' + PEPTONE + -IDE.

polyphagous /pəˈlɪfəgəs/ ▶ *adjective* Zoology (of an animal) able to feed on various kinds of food.
– ORIGIN early 19th cent.: from Greek *poluphagos* 'eating to excess' + -OUS.

polyphase ▶ *adjective* consisting of or occurring in a number of separate stages.
■(of an electrical device or circuit) designed to supply or use simultaneously several alternating currents of the same voltage and frequency but with different phases.
– DERIVATIVES **polyphasic** adjective.

Polyphemus /ˌpɒlɪˈfiːməs/ Greek Mythology a Cyclops who trapped Odysseus and some of his companions in a cave, from which they escaped by putting out his one eye while he slept. In another story Polyphemus loved the sea nymph Galatea, and in jealousy killed his rival Acis.

polyphenol /ˌpɒlɪˈfiːnɒl/ ▶ *noun* Chemistry a compound containing more than one phenolic hydroxyl group.

polyphonic ▶ *adjective* producing many sounds simultaneously; many-voiced.
■Music (especially of vocal music) in two or more parts each having a melody of its own; contrapuntal. Compare with HOMOPHONIC. ■ Music (of an instrument) capable of producing more than one note at a time.
– DERIVATIVES **polyphonically** adverb.
– ORIGIN late 18th cent.: from Greek *poluphōnos* (from *polu-* 'many' + *phōnē* 'voice, sound') + -IC.

polyphony /pəˈlɪf(ə)ni/ ▶ *noun* (pl. **-ies**) [mass noun] Music the style of simultaneously combining a number of parts, each forming an individual melody and harmonizing with each other.
■[count noun] a composition written, played, or sung in this style. ■(on an electronic keyboard or synthesizer) the number of notes or voices that can be played simultaneously without loss.
– DERIVATIVES **polyphonist** noun, **polyphonous** adjective.
– ORIGIN early 19th cent.: from Greek *poluphōnia*, from *polu-* 'many' + *phōnē* 'sound'.

polyphosphate ▶ *noun* Chemistry a salt or ester of an oxyacid with two or more phosphorus atoms in its anion, especially any of a number used chiefly as detergents or food additives.

polyphyletic /ˌpɒlɪfʌɪˈlɛtɪk/ ▶ *adjective* Biology (of a group of organisms) derived from more than one common evolutionary ancestor or ancestral group and therefore not suitable for placing in the same taxon.

polypi plural form of POLYPUS.

polyploid /ˈpɒlɪplɔɪd/ Biology ▶ *adjective* (of a cell or nucleus) containing more than two homologous sets of chromosomes.
■(of an organism or species) composed of polyploid cells.
▶ *noun* a polyploid organism, variety, or species.
– DERIVATIVES **polyploidy** noun.

polypod ▶ *adjective* Zoology having many feet or foot-like appendages, especially denoting a phase of insect larval development characterized by a segmented abdomen with rudimentary or functional appendages.
– ORIGIN mid 18th cent. (as a noun denoting an animal having many feet): from French *polypode* 'many-footed', from Greek *polupous, polupod-*, from *polu-* 'many' + *pous, pod-* 'foot'.

polypody /ˈpɒlɪpəʊdi/ ▶ *noun* (pl. **-ies**) a widely distributed fern which has stout scaly creeping rhizomes and remains green during the winter, growing on trees, walls, and stones, especially in limestone areas.
● Genus *Polypodium*, family Polypodiaceae: several species, in particular the **common polypody** (*P. vulgare*).
– ORIGIN late Middle English: via Latin from Greek *polupodion*, denoting a kind of fern, from *polu-* 'many' + *pous, pod-* 'foot'.

polypoid /ˈpɒlɪpɔɪd/ ▶ *adjective* **1** Zoology of, relating to, or resembling a polyp or hydra.
■of, relating to, or denoting the polyp stage in the life cycle of a coelenterate. Also called HYDROID. Compare with MEDUSOID.
2 Medicine (of a growth) resembling or in the form of a polyp.

polypore /ˈpɒlɪpɔː/ ▶ *noun* a bracket fungus in which the spores are expelled through fine pores on the underside.
● Several families in the order Aphyllophorales, class Hymenomycetes, in particular Polyporaceae, which includes the **beech polypore** (*Piptoporus* (formerly *Polyporus*) *betulinus*).

polyposis /ˌpɒlɪˈpəʊsɪs/ ▶ *noun* [mass noun] Medicine a condition characterized by the presence of numerous internal polyps, especially a hereditary disease (**familial adenomatous polyposis**) which affects the colon and in which the polyps may become malignant.

polypropylene /ˌpɒlɪˈprəʊpɪliːn/ ▶ *noun* [mass noun] a synthetic resin which is a polymer of propylene, used chiefly for films, fibres, or moulding materials.

polyptych /ˈpɒlɪptɪk/ ▶ *noun* a painting, typically an altarpiece, consisting of more than three leaves or panels joined by hinges or folds.
– ORIGIN mid 19th cent.: from late Latin *polyptycha* (neuter plural) 'registers', from Greek *poluptukhos* 'having many folds', from *polu-* 'many' + *ptukhē* 'fold'.

polypus /ˈpɒlɪpəs/ ▶ *noun* (pl. **polypi** /-pʌɪ/) archaic or technical term for POLYP.
– ORIGIN late Middle English: via Latin from a variant of Greek *polupous* 'cuttlefish, polyp', from *polu-* 'many' + *pous, pod-* 'foot'.

polyrhythm ▶ *noun* Music a rhythm which makes use of two or more different rhythms simultaneously.
– DERIVATIVES **polyrhythmic** adjective.

polyribosome /ˌpɒlɪˈrʌɪbəsəʊm/ ▶ *noun* another term for POLYSOME.

polysaccharide ▶ *noun* Biochemistry a carbohydrate (e.g. starch, cellulose, or glycogen) whose molecules consist of a number of sugar molecules bonded together.

polysemy /ˈpɒlɪsiːmi, pəˈlɪsɪmi/ ▶ *noun* [mass noun] Linguistics the coexistence of many possible meanings for a word or phrase.
– DERIVATIVES **polysemic** adjective, **polysemous** adjective.
– ORIGIN early 20th cent.: from POLY- 'many' + Greek *sēma* 'sign'.

polysome /ˈpɒlɪsəʊm/ ▶ *noun* Biology a cluster of ribosomes held together by a strand of messenger RNA which each is translating.

polystyrene /ˌpɒlɪˈstʌɪriːn/ ▶ *noun* [mass noun] a synthetic resin which is a polymer of styrene, used chiefly as lightweight rigid foams and films.

polysulphide (US **polysulfide**) ▶ *noun* Chemistry a compound containing two or more sulphur atoms bonded together as an anion or group.
■a synthetic rubber or other polymer in which the units are linked through such groups.

polysyllabic ▶ *adjective* (of a word) having more than one syllable.
■using or characterized by words of many syllables: *polysyllabic jargon*.
– DERIVATIVES **polysyllabically** adverb.

polysyllable ▶ *noun* a polysyllabic word.

polysymptomatic ▶ *adjective* (of a disease condition or a person or animal) involving or exhibiting many symptoms.

polysynthetic ▶ *adjective* denoting or relating to a language characterized by complex words consisting of several morphemes, in which a single word may function as a whole sentence. Many American Indian languages are polysynthetic.

polytechnic ▶ noun an institution of higher education offering courses at degree level or below, especially in vocational subjects.
– ORIGIN early 19th cent.: from French *polytechnique*, from Greek *polutekhnos*, from *polu-* 'many' + *tekhnē* 'art'.

USAGE In Britain the term **polytechnic** has largely dropped out of use. This is because of the changes whereby in 1989 British polytechnics gained autonomy from local education authorities and in 1992 were able to call themselves **universities**.

polytene /ˈpɒlɪtiːn/ ▶ adjective Genetics relating to or denoting a giant chromosome which is composed of many parallel copies of the genetic material, as found in *Drosophila* fruit flies where they are much used in genetic research.
– ORIGIN 1930s: from POLY- 'many' + *-tene* (from Greek *tainia* 'band, ribbon') denoting stages of the first meiotic division.

polytetrafluoroethylene /ˌpɒlɪˌtetrəˌflʊərəʊˈɛθɪliːn, -ˌflɔː-/ ▶ noun [mass noun] a tough translucent synthetic resin made by polymerizing tetrafluoroethylene, chiefly used to make seals and bearings and to coat non-stick cooking utensils.

polytheism /ˈpɒlɪˌθiːɪz(ə)m/ ▶ noun [mass noun] the belief in or worship of more than one god.
– DERIVATIVES **polytheist** noun, **polytheistic** adjective.
– ORIGIN early 17th cent.: from French *polythéisme*, from Greek *polutheos* 'of many gods', from *polu-* 'many' + *theos* 'god'.

polythene ▶ noun [mass noun] chiefly Brit. a tough, light flexible synthetic resin made by polymerizing ethylene, chiefly used for plastic bags, food containers, and other packaging.
– ORIGIN 1930s: contraction of POLYETHYLENE.

polythetic /ˌpɒlɪˈθɛtɪk/ ▶ adjective relating to or sharing a number of characteristics which occur commonly in members of a group or class, but none of which is essential for membership of that group or class.
– ORIGIN 1960s: from POLY- 'many' + Greek *thetos* 'placed, arranged' + -IC.

polytonality ▶ noun [mass noun] the simultaneous use of two or more keys in a musical composition.
– DERIVATIVES **polytonal** adjective.

polytunnel ▶ noun an elongated polythene-covered frame under which seedlings or other plants are grown outdoors.

polytype ▶ noun Crystallography any of a number of forms of a crystalline substance which differ only in one of the dimensions of the unit cell.
– DERIVATIVES **polytypic** adjective, **polytypism** noun.

polyunsaturated ▶ adjective Chemistry (of an organic compound, especially a fat or oil molecule) containing several double or triple bonds between carbon atoms.

polyunsaturates ▶ plural noun polyunsaturated fats or fatty acids.

polyurethane /ˌpɒlɪˈjʊərɪθeɪn/ ▶ noun [mass noun] a synthetic resin in which the polymer units are linked by urethane groups, used chiefly as constituents of paints, varnishes, adhesives, and foams.
▶ verb [with obj.] [usu. as adj. **polyurethaned**] coat or protect with paint or varnish of this kind.

polyuria /ˌpɒlɪˈjʊərɪə/ ▶ noun [mass noun] Medicine production of abnormally large volumes of dilute urine. Compare with DIURESIS.
– DERIVATIVES **polyuric** adjective.

polyvalent /ˌpɒlɪˈveɪl(ə)nt/ ▶ adjective Chemistry having a valency of three or more.
■Medicine having the property of counteracting several related poisons or affording immunity against different strains of a micro-organism. ■ Medicine another term for MULTIVALENT. ■ figurative having many different functions, forms, or facets: *as emotion, love is polyvalent.*

polyvinyl /ˌpɒlɪˈvaɪn(ə)l/ ▶ adjective [attrib.] denoting materials or objects made from polymers of vinyl compounds.

polyvinyl acetate ▶ noun [mass noun] a synthetic resin made by polymerizing vinyl acetate, used chiefly in paints and adhesives.

polyvinyl chloride ▶ noun [mass noun] a tough

chemically resistant synthetic resin made by polymerizing vinyl chloride and used for a wide variety of products including pipes, flooring, and sheeting.

polyvinylpyrrolidone /ˌpɒlɪˌvaɪn(ə)lpɪˈrɒlɪdəʊn/ ▶ noun [mass noun] Chemistry a water-soluble polymer of vinyl pyrrolidone, used as a synthetic blood plasma substitute and in the cosmetic, drug, and food-processing industries.

Polyzoa /ˌpɒlɪˈzəʊə/ Zoology another term for BRYOZOA.
– DERIVATIVES **polyzoan** noun & adjective.
– ORIGIN modern Latin (plural), from POLY- 'many' + *zōion* 'animal'.

Pom ▶ noun 1 short for POMERANIAN.
2 short for POMMY.

poma /ˈpəʊmə/ ▶ noun trademark a ski lift in which a pole attached to a moving cable pulls each skier uphill on their skis.
– ORIGIN 1950s: named after Jan *Pomagalski* (died 1969), its Polish inventor.

pomace /ˈpʌmɪs/ ▶ noun [mass noun] (especially in cider-making) the pulpy residue remaining after fruit has been crushed in order to extract its juice.
■the pulpy matter remaining after some other substance has been pressed or crushed, for example castor oil seeds after the oil has been extracted.
– ORIGIN late 16th cent.: apparently from medieval Latin *pomacium* 'cider', from Latin *pomum* 'apple'.

pomade /pəˈmeɪd, -ˈmɑːd/ dated ▶ noun [mass noun] a scented ointment applied to the hair or scalp.
▶verb [with obj.] [often as adj. **pomaded**] apply pomade to.
– ORIGIN mid 16th cent.: from French *pommade*, based on Latin *pomum* 'apple' (from which it was originally made).

Pomak /ˈpəʊmak/ ▶ noun a Muslim Bulgarian.
– ORIGIN Bulgarian.

pomander /pəˈmandə, ˈpɒməndə/ ▶ noun a ball or perforated container of sweet-smelling substances such as herbs and spices, placed in a cupboard or room to perfume the air or (formerly) carried as a supposed protection against infection.
■a piece of fruit, typically an orange, studded with cloves and hung in a wardrobe by a ribbon for a similar purpose.
– ORIGIN late 15th cent.: from Old French *pome d'embre*, from medieval Latin *pomum de ambra* 'apple of ambergris'.

pomarine skua /ˈpɒmərʌɪn/ ▶ noun a large Arctic-breeding skua, having dark brown plumage with (in some birds) pale underparts.
● *Stercorarius pomarinus*, family Stercorariidae. North American name: **pomarine jaeger**.
– ORIGIN mid 19th cent.: *pomarine* from French *pomarin*, from Greek *pōma* 'cover, lid' + *rhis, rhin-* 'nose' (because the bird's nostrils are partly covered by a cere).

pomatum /pəˈmeɪtəm/ ▶ noun & verb another term for POMADE.
– ORIGIN mid 16th cent.: modern Latin, from Latin *pomum* 'apple'.

pombe /ˈpɒmbeɪ/ ▶ noun [mass noun] (in Central and East Africa) a fermented drink made from various kinds of grain and fruit.
– ORIGIN Kiswahili.

pome /pəʊm/ ▶ noun Botany a fruit consisting of a fleshy enlarged receptacle and a tough central core containing the seeds, e.g. an apple, pear, or quince.
– ORIGIN late Middle English: from Old French, based on Latin *poma*, plural of *pomum* 'apple'.

pomegranate /ˈpɒmɪɡranɪt/ ▶ noun 1 an orange-sized fruit with a tough golden-orange outer skin and sweet red gelatinous flesh containing many seeds.
2 the tree that bears this fruit, which is native to North Africa and western Asia and has long been cultivated.
● *Punica granatum*, family Punicaceae.
– ORIGIN Middle English: from Old French *pome grenate*, from *pome* 'apple' + *grenate* 'pomegranate' (from Latin (*malum*) *granatum* '(apple) having many seeds', from *granum* 'seed').

pomelo /ˈpɒmɪləʊ, ˈpʌm-/ (also **pummelo**) ▶ noun (pl. -os) 1 the largest of the citrus fruits, with a thick yellow skin and bitter pulp which resembles grapefruit in flavour. Also called SHADDOCK.
2 the tree which bears this fruit.
● *Citrus maxima*, family Rutaceae.
– ORIGIN mid 19th cent.: of unknown origin.

Pomerania /ˌpɒməˈreɪnɪə/ a region of northern Europe, extending along the south shore of the Baltic Sea between Stralsund in NE Germany and the Vistula in Poland. The region was controlled variously by Germany, Poland, the Holy Roman Empire, Prussia, and Sweden, until the larger part was restored to Poland in 1945, the western portion becoming a part of the German state of Mecklenburg-West Pomerania.

Pomeranian ▶ noun a small dog of a breed with long silky hair, a pointed muzzle, and pricked ears.

Pomerol /ˈpɒmərɒl/ ▶ noun [mass noun] a red Bordeaux wine produced in Pomerol, a region in the Gironde, France.

pomfret /ˈpɒmfrɪt/ ▶ noun a deep-bodied fish of open seas, which typically has scales on the dorsal and anal fins.
● Family Bramidae: several genera and species, including the edible *Brama brama* of the North Atlantic (also called **RAY'S BREAM**).
– ORIGIN early 18th cent.: apparently from Portuguese *pampo*.

pomfret cake /ˈpɒmfrɪt, ˈpʌm-/ ▶ noun archaic variant of PONTEFRACT CAKE.

pomiculture /ˈpəʊmɪˌkʌltʃə/ ▶ noun [mass noun] fruit-growing.
– ORIGIN late 19th cent.: from Latin *pomum* 'fruit' + CULTURE, on the pattern of words such as *agriculture*.

pommel /ˈpʌm(ə)l/ ▶ noun 1 a rounded knob on the end of the handle of a sword, dagger, or old-fashioned gun.
2 the upward curving or projecting part of a saddle in front of the rider.
▶verb (**pommelled, pommelling**; US **pommeled, pommeling**) another term for PUMMEL.
– ORIGIN Middle English (denoting a ball or finial at the top point of a tower, corner of an altar, etc.): from Old French *pomel*, from a diminutive of Latin *pomum* 'fruit, apple'.

pommel horse ▶ noun a vaulting horse fitted with a pair of curved handgrips, used for a gymnastic exercise consisting of swings of the legs and body.

pommes frites /pɒm friːt/ ▶ plural noun (especially in recipes or on menus) fried potato chips.
– ORIGIN French, from *pommes de terre frites*, literally 'fried potatoes'.

Pommy (also **Pommie**) ▶ noun (pl. -ies) Austral./NZ informal, derogatory a British person.
– ORIGIN early 20th cent.: of unknown origin; said by some to be short for *pomegranate*, as a near rhyme to *immigrant*, but evidence is lacking.

po-mo informal ▶ abbreviation for postmodern.

pomology /pəˈmɒlədʒi/ ▶ noun [mass noun] the science of fruit-growing.
– DERIVATIVES **pomological** adjective, **pomologist** noun.
– ORIGIN early 19th cent.: from Latin *pomum* 'fruit' + -LOGY.

pomp ▶ noun [mass noun] ceremony and splendid display, especially at a public event: *St Paul's was perfectly adapted to pomp and circumstance.*
■(**pomps**) archaic ostentatious boastfulness or vanity: *the pomps and vanities of this world.*
– ORIGIN Middle English: from Old French *pompe*, via Latin from Greek *pompē* 'procession, pomp', from *pempein* 'send'.

Pompadour /ˈpɒmpədʊə/, Jeanne Antoinette Poisson, Marquise de (1721–64), French noblewoman; known as **Madame de Pompadour**. In 1744 she became the mistress of Louis XV, gaining considerable influence at court, but she later became unpopular as a result of her interference in political affairs.

pompadour /ˈpɒmpədʊə/ ▶ noun US a men's hairstyle in which the hair is combed back from the forehead without a parting.
■a woman's hairstyle in which the hair is turned back off the forehead in a roll.
▶verb [with obj.] [usu. as adj. **pompadoured**] US arrange (hair) in a pompadour.
– ORIGIN late 19th cent.: named after Madame de POMPADOUR.

pompano /ˈpɒmpənəʊ/ ▶ noun (pl. -os) 1 an edible butterfish that lives in shoals along the west coast of North America.
● *Peprilus simillimus*, family Stromateidae.
2 another term for JACK[1] (in sense 11).

– ORIGIN late 18th cent.: from Spanish *pámpano*, perhaps from *pámpana* 'vine leaf', because of its shape.

Pompeii /pɒmˈpeɪɪ/ an ancient city in western Italy, south-east of Naples. The city was buried by an eruption of Mount Vesuvius in 79 AD; excavations of the site began in 1748, revealing well-preserved remains of buildings, mosaics, furniture, and the personal possessions of the city's inhabitants.

Pompey /ˈpɒmpɪ/ (106–48 BC), Roman general and statesman; Latin name *Gnaeus Pompeius Magnus*; known as **Pompey the Great**. He founded the First Triumvirate, but later quarrelled with Caesar, who defeated him at the battle of Pharsalus. He then fled to Egypt, where he was murdered.

Pompidou /ˈpɒmpɪduː/, Georges (Jean Raymond) (1911–74), French statesman, Prime Minister 1962–8 and President 1969–74. He was instrumental in ending the conflict in Algeria between French forces and nationalist guerrillas.

Pompidou Centre a modern art gallery, exhibition centre, and concert hall in Paris, designed by Sir Richard Rogers and the Italian architect Renzo Piano (b.1937) and opened in 1977. Also called **BEAUBOURG CENTRE**.

pompier /ˈpɒmpɪə/ ▶ noun (pl. pronounced same) an artist regarded as painting in an academic, imitative, and vulgarly neoclassical style.
– ORIGIN mid 19th cent.: from French, literally 'fireman', said to derive from the similarity between firemen's helmets and those worn by the Greek gods and heroes depicted by late Classical artists.

pompom (also **pompon**) ▶ noun a small woollen ball attached to a garment, especially a hat, for decoration.
■ a dahlia, chrysanthemum, or aster with small tightly clustered petals.
– ORIGIN mid 18th cent.: French *pompon*, of unknown origin.

pom-pom ▶ noun Brit. an automatic quick-firing two-pounder cannon of the Second World War period, typically mounted on a ship and used against aircraft.
– ORIGIN late 19th cent.: imitative of the sound of the discharge.

pompous ▶ adjective affectedly and irritatingly grand, solemn, or self-important: *a pompous ass who pretends he knows everything.*
■ archaic characterized by pomp or splendour: *there were many processions and other pompous shows.*
– DERIVATIVES **pomposity** noun, **pompously** adverb, **pompousness** noun.
– ORIGIN late Middle English: from Old French *pompeux* 'full of grandeur', from late Latin *pomposus*, from *pompa* 'pomp'.

'pon ▶ preposition short for **UPON**, especially in poetic use or to represent dialect.

ponce Brit. informal ▶ noun a man who lives off a prostitute's earnings.
■ derogatory an effeminate man.
▶ verb [no obj.] live off a prostitute's earnings.
■ [with obj.] ask for or obtain (something to which one is not strictly entitled): *I ponced a ciggie off her.*
▶ **ponce about/around** behave in a ridiculous, ineffective, or posturing way: *I ponced around in front of the mirror.*
ponce something up make overly elaborate and unnecessary changes to something in an attempt to improve it.
– ORIGIN late 19th cent.: perhaps from the verb **POUNCE**[1].

Ponce de León /ˌpɒnseɪ də leɪˈɒn, Spanish ˌponθe de leˈon, ˌponse/, Juan (*c.*1460–1521), Spanish explorer. He accompanied Columbus on his second voyage to the New World in 1493, became governor of Puerto Rico (1510–12), and landed on the coast of Florida in 1513, claiming the area for Spain.

poncey (also **poncy**) ▶ adjective Brit. informal considered to be pretentious or affected: *a poncey wine bar.*

poncho ▶ noun (pl. **-os**) a garment of a type originally worn in South America, made of a thick piece of woollen cloth with a slit in the middle for the head.
– ORIGIN early 18th cent.: from South American Spanish, from Araucanian.

pond ▶ noun a fairly small body of still water formed naturally or by artificial means. ·

■ **(the pond)** informal the Atlantic ocean: *he's relatively unknown on this side of the pond.*
▶ verb [with obj.] hold back or dam up (flowing water or another liquid) to form a small lake.
■ [no obj.] (of flowing water or other liquids) form such a lake.
– ORIGIN Middle English: alteration of **POUND**[3], commonly used in dialect in the same sense.

ponder ▶ verb [with obj.] think about (something) carefully, especially before making a decision or reaching a conclusion: *I pondered the question of what clothes to wear for the occasion* | [no obj.] *she sat pondering over her problem.*
– DERIVATIVES **ponderation** noun (rare).
– ORIGIN Middle English (in the sense 'appraise, judge the worth of'): from Old French *ponderer* 'consider', from Latin *ponderare* 'weigh, reflect on', from *pondus, ponder-* 'weight'.

ponderable ▶ adjective poetic/literary having appreciable weight or significance.
– DERIVATIVES **ponderability** noun.
– ORIGIN mid 17th cent.: from late Latin *ponderabilis*, from *ponderare* 'weigh, reflect on' (see **PONDER**).

ponderal index /ˈpɒnd(ə)r(ə)l/ ▶ noun Medicine an index of weight in relation to height or length.
– ORIGIN early 17th cent.: *ponderal* from Latin *pondus, ponder-* 'weight' + **AL**.

ponderosa /ˌpɒndəˈrəʊzə, -sə/ (also **ponderosa pine**) ▶ noun a tall slender North American pine tree, planted for timber and as an ornamental.
● *Pinus ponderosa*, family Pinaceae.
– ORIGIN late 19th cent.: feminine of Latin *ponderosus* 'massive, ponderous', used as a specific epithet in *Pinus ponderosa.*

ponderous ▶ adjective slow and clumsy because of great weight: *her footsteps were heavy and ponderous.*
■ dull, laborious, or excessively solemn: *Liz could hardly restrain herself from finishing all his ponderous sentences.*
– DERIVATIVES **ponderosity** noun, **ponderously** adverb, **ponderousness** noun.
– ORIGIN late Middle English: via French from Latin *ponderosus*, from *pondus, ponder-* 'weight'.

Pondicherry /ˌpɒndɪˈtʃɛri/ a Union Territory of SE India, on the Coromandel Coast, formed from several former French territories and incorporated into India in 1954.
■ its capital city; pop. 202,650 (1991).

pond life ▶ noun [mass noun] the animals, especially the invertebrates, that live in ponds or stagnant water.

pondok /ˈpɒndɒk/ (also **pondokkie**) ▶ noun (pl. **pondoks** or **pondokkies**) S. African a rough shelter made of scraps of wood, cardboard, or corrugated iron.
– ORIGIN Afrikaans, probably from Malay.

pond scum ▶ noun [mass noun] N. Amer. a mass of algae forming a green film on the surface of stagnant water.
■ informal a person or thing perceived as worthless or contemptible.

pond skater ▶ noun a slender predatory bug which moves quickly across the surface film of water, using its front legs for catching prey. Called **WATER STRIDER** in North America.
● Family Gerridae, suborder Heteroptera: *Gerris* and other genera, and many species, in particular the common European *G. lacustris*.

pond snail ▶ noun an aquatic European snail with a brown conical shell, living typically in fresh water.
● Genus *Limnaea*, family Limnaeidae.

pond terrapin (also **European pond terrapin**) ▶ noun a terrapin with a dark shell that is typically patterned with yellow, native to Europe, western Asia, and NW Africa.
● *Emys orbicularis*, family Emydidae.

pond turtle ▶ noun a freshwater turtle that lives in ponds, especially the pond terrapin.

pondweed ▶ noun [mass noun] a submerged aquatic plant that grows in still or running water and sometimes has floating leaves. See also **CANADIAN PONDWEED**.
● Genus *Potamogeton*, family Potamogetonaceae.

pone /pəʊn/ (also **corn pone** or **pone bread**) [mass noun] US unleavened maize bread in the form of flat oval cakes or loaves, originally as prepared with water by North American Indians and cooked in hot ashes.
– ORIGIN Algonquian, 'bread'.

pong Brit. informal ▶ noun a strong, unpleasant smell.
▶ verb [no obj.] smell strongly and unpleasantly.
– DERIVATIVES **pongy** adjective.
– ORIGIN early 20th cent.: of unknown origin.

ponga /ˈpʌŋə/ (also **punga**) ▶ noun NZ a tree fern found in forests throughout New Zealand. Also called **SILVER FERN**.
● *Cyathea dealbata*, family Cyatheaceae.
– ORIGIN mid 19th cent.: from Maori.

pongal /ˈpʌŋɡ(ə)l/ ▶ noun the Tamil New Year festival, celebrated by the cooking of new rice.
■ [mass noun] a southern Indian dish of rice cooked with various herbs and spices.
– ORIGIN from Tamil *poṅkal*, literally 'boiling, swelling' (with reference to the cooking process of rice).

pongee /pʌnˈdʒiː, pɒn-/ ▶ noun [mass noun] a soft and typically unbleached type of Chinese plain-woven fabric, originally made from threads of raw silk and now also from other fibres such as cotton which are usually mercerized.
– ORIGIN early 18th cent.: from Chinese (Mandarin dialect) *běnjī* literally 'own loom' or *běnzhì* literally 'home-woven'.

pongid /ˈpɒn(d)ʒɪd/ ▶ noun Zoology a primate of a family (Pongidae) which comprises the great apes. See also **HOMINID**.
– ORIGIN 1950s: from modern Latin *Pongidae* (plural), from the genus name *Pongo* (see **PONGO**).

pongo ▶ noun (pl. **-os**) Brit. military slang a soldier (used especially by members of the Royal Navy or RAF).
– ORIGIN early 20th cent.: originally from Congolese *mpongo*, used as a term in zoology to refer to the gorilla and other apes.

poniard /ˈpɒnjəd/ ▶ noun historical a small, slim dagger.
– ORIGIN mid 16th cent.: from French *poignard*, based on Latin *pugnus* 'fist'.

pons /pɒnz/ (in full **pons Varolii** /vəˈrəʊlɪaɪ/) ▶ noun (pl. **pontes** /ˈpɒntiːz/) Anatomy the part of the brainstem that links the medulla oblongata and the thalamus.
– ORIGIN late 17th cent.: from Latin, literally 'bridge', (in full) 'bridge of Varolius', named after C. Varoli (1543–75), Italian anatomist.

pons asinorum /ˌasɪˈnɔːrəm/ ▶ noun the point at which many learners fail, especially a theory or formula that is difficult to grasp.
– ORIGIN mid 18th cent.: Latin, literally 'bridge of asses', term taken from the fifth proposition of the first book of Euclid.

pont /pɒnt/ ▶ noun S. African a flat-bottomed ferry worked on cables or ropes.
– ORIGIN Dutch.

Ponte, Lorenzo Da, see **DA PONTE**.

Pontefract cake /ˈpɒntɪfrakt/ ▶ noun Brit. a flat, round liquorice sweet.
– ORIGIN mid 19th cent.: named after *Pontefract* (earlier *Pomfret*), a town in Yorkshire where the sweets were first made.

pontes plural form of **PONS**.

Pontiac fever /ˈpɒntɪak/ ▶ noun [mass noun] Medicine a mild systemic disease with symptoms resembling influenza, probably caused by a legionella infection.
– ORIGIN 1960s: named after *Pontiac*, Michigan, US, where the first major outbreak was recorded.

Pontianak /ˌpɒntɪˈɑːnak/ a seaport in Indonesia, on the west coast of Borneo at the delta of the Kapuas River; pop. 304,770 (1980).

Pontic ▶ adjective of or relating to ancient Pontus.

pontifex /ˈpɒntɪfɛks/ ▶ noun (pl. **pontifices** /-ˈtɪfɪsiːz/) (in ancient Rome) a member of the principal college of priests.
– ORIGIN Latin, from *pons, pont-* 'bridge' + *-fex* from *facere* 'make'.

Pontifex Maximus /ˈmaksɪməs/ ▶ noun (in ancient Rome) the head of the principal college of priests.
■ (in the Roman Catholic Church) a title of the Pope.
– ORIGIN *Maximus*, superlative of Latin *magnus* 'great'.

pontiff (also **sovereign** or **supreme pontiff**) ▶ noun the Pope.
– ORIGIN late 17th cent.: from French *pontife*, from Latin *pontifex* (see **PONTIFEX**).

pontifical /pɒnˈtɪfɪk(ə)l/ ▶ adjective **1** (in the Roman

Catholic Church) of or relating to a pontiff: *a pontifical commission.*
2 characterized by a pompous and superior air of infallibility: *such explanations were greeted with pontifical disdain.*
▶**noun** rare (in the Roman Catholic Church) an office book of the Western Church containing rites to be performed by the Pope or bishops.
■(**pontificals**) the vestments and insignia of a bishop, cardinal, or abbot: *a bishop in full pontificals.*
– DERIVATIVES **pontifically** adverb.
– ORIGIN late Middle English: from Latin *pontificalis*, from *pontifex* (see **PONTIFEX**).

pontifical Mass ▶**noun** (in the Roman Catholic Church) a High Mass celebrated by a cardinal or bishop.

pontificate ▶**verb** /pɒnˈtɪfɪkeɪt/ [no obj.] **1** (in the Roman Catholic Church) officiate as bishop, especially at Mass.
2 express one's opinions in a way considered annoyingly pompous and dogmatic: *he was pontificating about art and history.*
▶**noun** /pɒnˈtɪfɪkət/ (also **Pontificate**) (in the Roman Catholic Church) the office of pope or bishop.
■the period of such an office: *Pope Gregory VIII enjoyed only a ten-week pontificate.*
– ORIGIN late Middle English (as a noun): from Latin *pontificatus*, from *pontifex* (see **PONTIFEX**). The verb dates from the early 19th cent.

pontifices plural form of **PONTIFEX**.

pontil /ˈpɒntɪl/ (also **punty**) ▶**noun** (in glass-making) an iron rod used to hold or shape soft glass.
– ORIGIN mid 19th cent.: from French, apparently from Italian *pontello* 'small point', diminutive of *punto*.

pontine /ˈpɒntʌɪn/ ▶**adjective** Anatomy of, relating to, or affecting the pons of the brain.
– ORIGIN late 19th cent.: from Latin *pons, pont-* 'bridge' + **-INE**[1].

Pontine Marshes /ˈpɒntʌɪn/ an area of marshland in western Italy, on the Tyrrhenian coast south of Rome. It became infested with malaria in ancient Roman times, and it was not until 1928 that an extensive scheme to drain the marshes was begun. Several new towns have since been built in the region, which is now a productive agricultural area. Italian name **AGRO PONTINO**.

Pont l'Évêque /ˌpɔ̃ ləˈvɛk/ ▶**noun** [mass noun] a kind of creamy soft cheese made originally at Pont l'Évêque in Normandy, France.

pontoon[1] /pɒnˈtuːn/ ▶**noun** [mass noun] Brit. the card game blackjack or vingt-et-un.
■[count noun] a hand of two cards totalling 21 in this game.
– ORIGIN early 20th cent.: probably an alteration of *vingt-et-un* 'twenty-one'.

pontoon[2] /pɒnˈtuːn/ ▶**noun** a flat-bottomed boat or hollow metal cylinder used with others to support a temporary bridge or floating landing stage.
■a bridge or landing stage supported by pontoons. ■a large flat-bottomed barge or lighter equipped with cranes and tackle for careening ships and salvage work. ■either of two floats fitted to an aircraft to enable it to land on water.
– ORIGIN late 17th cent.: from French *ponton*, from Latin *ponto, ponton-*, from *pons, pont-* 'bridge'.

Pontormo /pɒnˈtɔːməʊ/, Jacopo da (1494–1557), Italian painter, whose use of dynamic composition, anatomical exaggeration, and bright colours placed him at the forefront of early mannerism.

Pontus /ˈpɒntəs/ an ancient region of northern Asia Minor, on the Black Sea coast north of Cappadocia. It reached its height between 120 and 63 BC under Mithridates VI, when it dominated the whole of Asia Minor; by the end of the 1st century BC it had been defeated by Rome and absorbed into the Roman Empire.

pony ▶**noun** (pl. **-ies**) **1** a horse of a small breed, especially one below 15 hands (or 14 hands 2 inches).
■(**the ponies**) informal, chiefly N. Amer. racehorses: *he had been playing the ponies on the side.*
2 informal a small drinking glass or the drink contained in it: *a pony of vodka.*
3 Brit. informal twenty-five pounds sterling.
– ORIGIN mid 17th cent.: probably from French *poulenet* 'small foal', diminutive of *poulain*, from late Latin *pullanus*, from Latin *pullus* 'young animal'.

Pony Express (in the US) a system of mail delivery operating from 1860–1 between St Joseph in Missouri and Sacramento in California, using continuous relays of horse riders.

ponytail ▶**noun** a hairstyle in which the hair is drawn back and tied at the back of the head, causing it to hang down like a pony's tail.
– DERIVATIVES **ponytailed** adjective.

pony-trekking ▶**noun** [mass noun] Brit. the activity of riding across country on a pony or horse for pleasure, typically as a holiday activity.
– DERIVATIVES **pony-trekker** noun.

Ponzi scheme /ˈpɒnzi/ ▶**noun** a form of fraud in which belief in the success of a non-existent enterprise is fostered by the payment of quick returns to the first investors from money invested by later investors.
– ORIGIN named after Charles Ponzi (died 1949), who carried out such a fraud (1919–20).

poo ▶**exclamation, noun, & verb** variant spelling of **POOH**.

pooch[1] ▶**noun** informal a dog.
– ORIGIN 1920s: of unknown origin.

pooch[2] ▶**verb** US informal protrude or cause to protrude: [no obj.] *a dress that made her stomach pooch out even more than usual.*
– ORIGIN mid 17th cent.: from the noun **POUCH**.

poodle ▶**noun** a dog of a breed with a curly coat that is usually clipped.
■Brit. a person or organization considered to be servile or obsequious: *the council is being made a poodle of central government.*
▶**verb** [no obj., with adverbial of direction] Brit. informal move or travel in a leisurely manner: *the chap who just wants to poodle along the road at 50 mph.*
– ORIGIN early 19th cent.: from German *Pudel(hund)*, from Low German *pud(d)eln* 'splash in water' (the poodle being a water-dog).

poodlefaker ▶**noun** Brit. informal, dated a man who habitually chooses to socialize with women.

poof[1] /pʊf, puːf/ (also **pouf**) ▶**noun** Brit. informal, derogatory an effeminate or homosexual man.
– DERIVATIVES **poofy** adjective.
– ORIGIN mid 19th cent.: perhaps an alteration of the archaic noun *puff* in the sense 'braggart'.

poof[2] /pʊf/ (also **pouf**) ▶**exclamation 1** used to convey the suddenness with which someone or something disappears: *once you've used it, poof—it's gone.*
2 used to express contemptuous dismissal: *'Oh, poof!' said Will. 'You say that every year.'*
– ORIGIN early 19th cent.: symbolic.

poofter /ˈpʊftə, ˈpuː-/ ▶**noun** another term for **POOF**[1].
– ORIGIN early 20th cent.: extended form.

pooh (also **poo**) informal ▶**exclamation** used to express disgust at an unpleasant smell.
■used to express impatience or contempt: *Oh pooh! Don't be such a spoilsport.*
▶**noun** [mass noun] excrement.
■[in sing.] an act of defecating.
▶**verb** [no obj.] defecate.
– ORIGIN natural exclamation: first recorded in English in the late 16th cent.

pooh-bah /puːˈbɑː/ ▶**noun** a person having much influence or holding many offices at the same time, especially one perceived as pompously self-important.
– ORIGIN from the name of a character in W. S. Gilbert's *The Mikado* (1885).

pooh-pooh ▶**verb** [with obj.] informal dismiss (an idea or suggestion) as being foolish or impractical.
– ORIGIN late 18th cent.: reduplication of **POOH**.

Poohsticks ▶**noun** [mass noun] a game in which each player throws a stick over the upstream side of a bridge into a stream or river, the winner being the person whose stick emerges first from under the bridge.
– ORIGIN 1920s: from Winnie-the-*Pooh*, the name of a toy bear in the children's books of A. A. Milne.

pooja ▶**noun** variant spelling of **PUJA**.

pooka /ˈpuːkə/ ▶**noun** (in Irish mythology) a hobgoblin.
– ORIGIN from Irish *púca*.

pool[1] ▶**noun** a small area of still water, typically one formed naturally.
■a small, shallow patch of liquid lying on a surface: *a pool of blood* | figurative *the lamps cast pools of light on the wet streets.* ■a swimming pool. ■a deep place in a river.
▶**verb** [no obj.] (of water or another liquid) form a pool on the ground or another surface: *the oil pooled behind the quay walls, escaping slowly into the river.*
■(of blood) accumulate in parts of the venous system.
– ORIGIN Old English *pōl*, of West Germanic origin; related to Dutch *poel* and German *Pfuhl*.

pool[2] ▶**noun 1** a supply of vehicles or goods available for use when needed: *a car pool.*
■a group of people available for work when required: *the typing pool.* ■a group of people considered as a resource: *a nationwide pool of promising high-school students.* ■an arrangement, illegal in many countries, between competing parties to fix prices or rates and share business in order to eliminate competition. ■a common fund into which all contributors pay and from which financial backing is provided: *big public investment pools.* ■a source of common funding for speculative operations on financial markets: *a huge pool of risk capital.* ■a group of contestants who compete against each other in a tournament for the right to advance to the next round. ■the collective amount of players' stakes in gambling or sweepstakes; a kitty. ■(usu. **the pools**) another term for **FOOTBALL POOL**.
2 [mass noun] a game played on a small billiard table using two sets of seven coloured and numbered balls together with one black ball and a white cue ball, with the aim of pocketing all one's own balls and then the black.
▶**verb** [with obj.] **1** (of two or more people or organizations) put (money or other assets) into a common fund: *they entered a contract to pool any gains and invest them profitably.*
■share (things) in common, for the benefit of all those involved: [as noun **pooling**] *a pooling of ideas.*
2 Austral. informal implicate or inform on. [ORIGIN: early 20th cent.: special use of *pool* 'to share'.]
– ORIGIN late 17th cent. (originally denoting a game of cards having a pool): from French *poule* in the sense 'stake, kitty', associated with **POOL**[1].

Poole a port and resort town on the south coast of England, just west of Bournemouth; pop. 130,900 (1991).

poolroom ▶**noun** N. Amer. **1** a place for playing pool.
2 a betting shop.

poolside ▶**noun** the area adjoining a swimming pool: [as modifier] *the poolside bar.*
▶**adverb** chiefly N. Amer. towards or beside a swimming pool: *she and her parents lounged poolside.*

poon[1] ▶**noun** Austral. informal a simple or foolish person.
– ORIGIN 1940s: from Sinhalese *pūna*.

poon[2] ▶**verb** [no obj.] (**poon up**) Austral. informal dress in such a way as to attract attention, typically with sexual success in view.
– ORIGIN 1940s: of unknown origin.

poon[3] ▶**noun** short for **POONTANG**.

Poona /ˈpuːnə/ (also **Pune**) an industrial city in Maharashtra, western India, in the hills south-east of Bombay; pop. 1,560,000 (1991). It was a military and administrative centre under British rule.

poontang /ˈpuːntaŋ/ (also **poon**) ▶**noun** [mass noun] N. Amer. vulgar slang sexual activity.
■a woman or women regarded solely in terms of potential sexual gratification.
– ORIGIN 1920s: alteration of French *putain* 'prostitute'.

poop[1] ▶**noun** (also **poop deck**) the aftermost and highest deck of a ship, especially in a sailing ship where it typically forms the roof of a cabin in the stern.
▶**verb** [with obj.] (usu. **be pooped**) (of a wave) break over the stern of (a ship), sometimes causing it to capsize.
– ORIGIN late Middle English: from Old French *pupe*, from a variant of Latin *puppis* 'stern'.

poop[2] ▶**verb** [with obj.] N. Amer. informal (usu. **be pooped**) exhaust: *I was pooped and just flopped into bed.*
▶**poop out** stop functioning.
– ORIGIN 1930s: of unknown origin.

poop[3] N. Amer. informal ▶**noun** [mass noun] excrement.
▶**verb** [no obj.] defecate.
– ORIGIN early 18th cent.: imitative.

poop[4] ▶**noun** [mass noun] informal, chiefly N. Amer. up-to-date or inside information.
– ORIGIN 1940s: of unknown origin.

poop[5] ▶**noun** informal, chiefly N. Amer. a stupid or ineffectual person.

– DERIVATIVES **poopy** adjective.
– ORIGIN early 20th cent.: perhaps a shortening of **NINCOMPOOP**.

pooper scooper (also **poop scoop**) ▶ noun an implement for clearing up dog excrement.

poor ▶ adjective **1** lacking sufficient money to live at a standard considered comfortable or normal in a society: *people who were too poor to afford a telephone* | [as noun **the poor**] *the gap between the rich and the poor has widened.*
▪(of a place) inhabited by people without sufficient money: *Deptford is a poor area.*
2 worse than is usual, expected, or desirable; of a low or inferior standard or quality: *her work was poor* | *many people are eating a very poor diet.*
▪[predic.] (**poor in**) deficient or lacking in: *the water is poor in nutrients.* ▪ dated used ironically to deprecate something belonging to or offered by oneself: *he is, in my poor opinion, a more handsome young man.*
3 [attrib.] (of a person) considered to be deserving of pity or sympathy: *they enquired after poor Dorothy's broken hip.*
– PHRASES **(as) poor as a church mouse** (or **as church mice**) extremely poor. **poor little rich boy** (or **girl**) a wealthy young person whose money brings them no contentment (often used as an expression of mock sympathy). **the poor man's ——** an inferior or cheaper substitute for the thing specified: *corduroy has always been the poor man's velvet.* **poor relation** a person or thing that is considered inferior or subordinate to others of the same type or group: *for many years radio has been* **the** *poor relation of* the *media.* **take a poor view of** regard with disfavour or disapproval.
– ORIGIN Middle English: from Old French *poure*, from Latin *pauper*.

poor box ▶ noun historical a collection box, especially one in a church, for gifts of money or other articles towards the relief of the poor.

poor boy (also **poor-boy sandwich**) ▶ noun US a large oval sandwich filled with a range of simple but substantial ingredients.

Poor Clare ▶ noun a member of an order of Franciscan nuns founded by St Clare of Assisi in *c.*1212.

poorhouse ▶ noun Brit. another term for **WORKHOUSE**.

Poor Law ▶ noun Brit. historical a law relating to the support of the poor. Originally the responsibility of the parish, the relief and employment of the poor passed over to the workhouses in 1834. In the early 20th century the Poor Law was replaced by schemes of social security.

poorly ▶ adverb in a way or at a level which is considered inadequate: *schools that were performing poorly* | [as submodifier] *a poorly attended church.*
▪with insufficient money or resources: *he lived as poorly as his peasant parishioners.*
▶ adjective chiefly Brit. unwell: *she looked poorly.*

poor man's orchid ▶ noun another term for **SCHIZANTHUS**.

poor man's weather glass ▶ noun the scarlet pimpernel.
– ORIGIN mid 19th cent.: so named because its flowers close before rain.

poor-me-one ▶ noun W. Indian the common potto (bird), which has a nocturnal call consisting of five descending notes.
▪a small anteater, which is wrongly thought to make this call.
– ORIGIN imitative of its call.

poor-mouth ▶ verb informal **1** [with obj.] N. Amer. & Irish talk disparagingly about.
2 [no obj.] N. Amer. claim to be poor.

poorness ▶ noun [mass noun] the state of lacking or being deficient in some desirable quality or constituent: *the poorness of the food.*

poor rate ▶ noun historical a local tax levied by a parish to finance the relief or support of the poor.

poor relief ▶ noun [mass noun] historical financial assistance given to the poor from state or local community funds.

poor-spirited ▶ adjective archaic timid; cowardly.

poort /ˈpʊə(r)t/ ▶ noun [often in place names] S. African a narrow pass through mountains.
– ORIGIN South African Dutch, 'passage', from Dutch *poort* 'gate'.

poor white ▶ noun derogatory a member of a group of white people regarded as socially inferior, especially one living in the southern US.
▪(in South Africa) a member of the poorest section of the Afrikaans-speaking white population.

poorwill ▶ noun a small nightjar found mainly in central and western North America.
• Three genera in the family Caprimulgidae: four species, in particular the **common poorwill** (*Phalaenoptilus nuttallii*), which hibernates in cold weather.
– ORIGIN late 19th cent.: imitative of its call.

poot ▶ verb [with obj.] informal use a pooter to collect (insects).
– ORIGIN late 20th cent.: back-formation from **POOTER**.

pooter ▶ noun chiefly Entomology a suction bottle for collecting small insects and other invertebrates, having one tube through which they are drawn into the bottle and another, protected by muslin or gauze, which is sucked.
– ORIGIN 1930s: said to be from the name of William *Poos* (1891–1987), American entomologist.

pootle ▶ verb [no obj., with adverbial of direction] Brit. informal move or travel in a leisurely manner: *they were pootling down a canal in their new boat.*
– ORIGIN 1970s: blend of the verbs **POODLE** and **TOOTLE**.

POP ▶ abbreviation for ▪(also **PoP**) (in computing) point of presence, denoting equipment that acts as access to the Internet. ▪(in the UK) Post Office Preferred, used to specify the size of envelopes and other items.

pop[1] ▶ verb (**popped**, **popping**) **1** [no obj.] make a sudden, sharp, explosive sound: *corks popped, glasses tinkled, and delicate canapés were served.*
▪[with obj.] cause (something) to burst, making such a sound: *some teenagers were popping balloons with darts.* ▪(of a person's ears) make a small popping sound within their head as pressure is equalized, typically because of a change of altitude. ▪[with obj.] heat (popcorn or another foodstuff) until it bursts open, making such a sound. ▪[no obj.] (of popcorn or another foodstuff) burst open in such a way. ▪(of a person's eyes) bulge or appear to bulge when opened wide, especially as an indication of surprise.
2 [no obj., with adverbial of direction] go somewhere, typically for a short time and often without notice: *she popped in to see if she could help.*
▪[with obj. and adverbial of direction] put or move (something) somewhere quickly: *she popped a pen into the pocket of her white dress.*
3 [with obj.] informal take or inject (a drug).
4 [with obj.] Brit. informal pawn (something).
▶ noun **1** a sudden sharp explosive sound: *at first there were just a few pops, perhaps from pistols.*
2 [mass noun] informal, dated or US a sweet fizzy drink such as lemonade.
3 (also **pop fly** or **pop-up**) Baseball a ball hit high in the air but not far from the home plate, providing an easy catch.
▶ adverb with a sudden explosive sound: *the champagne went pop.*
– PHRASES **—— a pop** N. Amer. informal costing a specified amount per item: *those swimsuits she wears are $50 a pop.* **have** (or **take**) **a pop at** informal attack physically or verbally. **make someone's eyes pop** (or US **pop out**) informal cause great astonishment to someone. **pop one's clogs** Brit. informal die. **pop the question** informal propose marriage.
– ORIGIN late Middle English (in the senses 'a blow, knock' and 'to strike'): imitative.
▶ **pop off** informal die.
pop up 1 appear or occur suddenly and unexpectedly: *these memories can pop up from time to time.* **2** Cricket (of a cricket ball) rise sharply off the pitch.

pop[2] ▶ adjective [attrib.] **1** of or relating to commercial popular music: *a pop star* | *a pop group.*
2 often derogatory (especially of a technical, scientific, or academic subject) made accessible to the general public; popularized: *pop psychology.*
▶ noun (also **pop music**) [mass noun] commercial popular music, in particular accessible, tuneful music of a kind popular since the 1950s and sometimes contrasted with rock, soul, or other forms of popular music.
▪[count noun] dated a pop record or song.
– ORIGIN late 19th cent.: abbreviation of **POPULAR**.

pop[3] ▶ noun chiefly US informal term for **FATHER**.
– ORIGIN mid 19th cent.: abbreviation of **POPPA**.

pop. ▶ abbreviation for population.

popadom (also **popadum**) ▶ noun variant spellings of **POPPADOM**.

pop art ▶ noun [mass noun] art based on modern popular culture and the mass media, especially as a critical or ironic comment on traditional fine art values.

> The term is applied specifically to the works, largely from the mid 1950s and 1960s, of a group of artists including Andy Warhol, Roy Lichtenstein, Jasper Johns, and Peter Blake, who used images from comic books, advertisements, consumer products, television, and cinema.

popcorn ▶ noun [mass noun] maize of a variety with hard kernels that swell up and burst open with a pop when heated.
▪these kernels when popped, typically buttered and eaten as a snack.

pop culture ▶ noun [mass noun] commercial culture based on popular taste.

Pope, Alexander (1688–1744), English poet. A major figure of the Augustan age, he is famous for his caustic wit and metrical skill, in particular his use of the heroic couplet. Notable works: *The Rape of the Lock* (1712; enlarged 1714); *An Essay on Man* (1733–4).

pope[1] ▶ noun **1** (usu. **the Pope**) the Bishop of Rome as head of the Roman Catholic Church.
▪the head of the Coptic Church, the Bishop or Patriarch of Alexandria.
2 another term for **RUFFE**.
– PHRASES **Is the Pope (a) Catholic?** informal used to indicate that something is blatantly obvious: *Did he bet that day? Is the Pope Catholic?*
– DERIVATIVES **popedom** noun.
– ORIGIN Old English, via ecclesiastical Latin from ecclesiastical Greek *papas* 'bishop, patriarch', variant of Greek *pappas* 'father'.

pope[2] ▶ noun a parish priest of the Orthodox Church in Russia and the Balkans.
– ORIGIN mid 17th cent.: from Russian *pop*, from Old Church Slavonic *popŭ*.

Pope Joan (according to a legend widely believed in the Middle Ages) a woman in male disguise who (*c.*1100) became a distinguished scholar and then pope, reigned for more than two years, and died after giving birth to a child during a procession.

Popemobile ▶ noun informal a bulletproof vehicle with a raised viewing area, used by the Pope on official visits.

popery ▶ noun [mass noun] derogatory, chiefly archaic the doctrines, practices, and ceremonies associated with the Pope or the papal system; Roman Catholicism.

pope's eye ▶ noun Scottish an edible lymph gland surrounded with fat in a sheep's leg.

pop-eyed ▶ adjective informal (of a person) having bulging eyes.
▪(of a person) having their eyes wide open, typically in surprise or fear.

pop festival ▶ noun a large, outdoor event, typically lasting several days, at which popular music is performed.

pop fly ▶ noun Baseball see **POP**[1].

popgun ▶ noun a child's toy gun which shoots a harmless pellet or cork.
▪a small, inefficient, or antiquated gun.

pop-hole ▶ noun a hole in a fence or divider through which animals can pass, especially one allowing poultry access to the outside or allowing piglets access to the sow.

popinjay /ˈpɒpɪndʒeɪ/ ▶ noun **1** dated a vain or conceited person, especially one who dresses or behaves extravagantly.
2 archaic a parrot.
– ORIGIN Middle English: from Old French *papingay*, via Spanish from Arabic *babbaġā*. The change in the ending was due to association with **JAY**.

popish ▶ adjective derogatory Roman Catholic.
– DERIVATIVES **popishly** adverb.

Popish Plot a fictitious Jesuit plot concocted by Titus Oates in 1678, involving a plan to kill Charles II, massacre Protestants, and put the Catholic Duke of York on the English throne. The 'discovery' of the plot led to widespread panic and the execution of about thirty-five Catholics.

poplar ▶ noun **1** a tall, fast-growing tree of north temperate regions, widely grown in shelter belts and for timber and pulp.
• Genus *Populus*, family Salicaceae: many species, including

the North American cottonwoods and the balm of Gilead poplars.
2 (**yellow poplar**) North American term for **TULIP TREE**.
– ORIGIN Middle English: from Old French *poplier*, from Latin *populus* 'poplar'.

poplin ▶ noun [mass noun] a plain-woven fabric, typically a very lightweight cotton, with a corded surface.
– ORIGIN early 18th cent.: from obsolete French *papeline*, perhaps from Italian *papalina* (feminine) 'papal', referring to the town of Avignon (residence of popes in exile (1309–77), and site of papal property), where it was first made.

popliteal /pɒˈplɪtɪəl, ˌpɒplɪˈtiːəl/ ▶ adjective Anatomy relating to or situated in the hollow at the back of the knee.
– ORIGIN early 18th cent.: from modern Latin *popliteus* (from Latin *poples*, *poplit-* 'ham, hough') + **-AL**.

pop music ▶ noun fuller form of **POP**².

Popocatépetl /ˌpɒpəˈkatəˌpɛt(ə)l, -ˌkatəˈpɛt(ə)l/ an active volcano in Mexico, south-east of Mexico City, which rises to 5,452 m (17,700 ft).

pop-out ▶ noun Baseball, an act of being put out by a caught fly ball.
▶ adjective N. Amer. denoting something designed or made so that it is easily removable for use: *a pop-out panel*.

popover ▶ noun N. Amer. a very light cake made from a thin batter, which rises to form a hollow shell when baked.

poppa ▶ noun N. Amer. informal term for **FATHER**.
– ORIGIN late 19th cent.: alteration of **PAPA**.

poppadom /ˈpɒpədəm/ (also **poppadum** or **poppadam**) ▶ noun (in Indian cookery) a large, circular piece of thin, spiced bread made from ground lentils and fried in oil.
– ORIGIN from Tamil *pappaḍam*.

Popper, Sir Karl Raimund (1902–94), Austrian-born British philosopher. In *The Logic of Scientific Discovery* (1934) he argued that scientific hypotheses can never be finally confirmed as true, but are tested by attempts to falsify them. In *The Open Society and its Enemies* (1945) he criticizes the historicist social theories of Plato, Hegel, and Marx.

popper ▶ noun a thing that makes a popping sound, in particular:
■ Brit. informal a press stud. ■ informal a small vial of amyl nitrite used for inhalation which makes a popping sound when opened. ■ (in fishing) an artificial lure which makes a popping sound when moved over the surface of the water. ■ N. Amer. a utensil for popping corn.

poppet ▶ noun **1** Brit. informal an endearingly sweet or pretty child or young girl (often used as an affectionate form of address): *'Here you are, poppet,' the nurse said.*
2 chiefly historical a small figure of a human being used in sorcery and witchcraft.
3 (also **poppet valve**) Engineering a mushroom-shaped valve with a flat end piece that is lifted in and out of an opening by an axial rod.
– ORIGIN late Middle English: based on Latin *pup(p)a* 'girl, doll'. Compare with **PUPPET**.

poppet-head ▶ noun Brit. the frame at the top of a mineshaft, supporting pulleys for the ropes used in hoisting.

popping crease ▶ noun Cricket a line four feet (1.22 metres) in front of and parallel to the line of the stumps, within which the batsman must keep the bat or one foot grounded to avoid the risk of being stumped or run out.
– ORIGIN late 18th cent.: from the verb **POP**¹, perhaps in the obsolete sense 'strike'.

popple archaic ▶ verb [no obj.] (of water) flow in a tumbling or rippling way.
▶ noun [in sing.] a rolling or rippling of water.
– DERIVATIVES **popply** adjective.
– ORIGIN late Middle English: probably from Middle Dutch *popelen* 'to murmur', of imitative origin.

poppy¹ ▶ noun a herbaceous plant with showy flowers, milky sap, and rounded seed capsules. Many poppies contain alkaloids and are a source of drugs such as morphine and codeine.
● *Papaver* and other genera, family Papaveraceae (the **poppy family**): many species, including the wild red-flowered **corn poppy** (*P. rhoeas*). The poppy family also includes the corydalis, greater celandine, and bloodroot.
– DERIVATIVES **poppied** adjective.
– ORIGIN Old English *popig*, *papæg*, from a medieval Latin alteration of Latin *papaver*.

poppy² ▶ adjective (of popular music) tuneful and immediately appealing: *catchy, poppy tunes*.

poppycock ▶ noun [mass noun] informal nonsense.
– ORIGIN mid 19th cent.: from Dutch dialect *pappekak*, from *pap* 'soft' + *kak* 'dung'.

Poppy Day ▶ noun Brit. another name for **REMEMBRANCE SUNDAY**.

poppy head ▶ noun **1** the seed capsule of a poppy.
2 an ornamental top on the end of a church pew.

pop rivet ▶ noun a tubular rivet that is inserted into a hole and clinched by the withdrawing of a central rod, used where only one side of the work is accessible.
▶ verb (**pop-rivet**) (**-riveted**, **-riveting**) [with obj.] secure or fasten with pop rivets.

pop shop ▶ noun Brit. informal, dated a pawnbroker's shop.

Popsicle ▶ noun N. Amer. trademark an ice lolly.
– ORIGIN 1920s: fanciful formation.

popsock ▶ noun a type of nylon stocking with an elasticated top, reaching to the wearer's knee.

popster ▶ noun informal a pop musician.

popsy (also **popsie**) ▶ noun (pl. **-ies**) informal, chiefly Brit. an attractive young woman.
– ORIGIN mid 19th cent.: alteration of **POPPET**.

pop-top ▶ noun North American term for **RING PULL**: [as modifier] *a pop-top beer can*.

populace /ˈpɒpjʊləs/ ▶ noun [treated as sing. or pl.] the people living in a particular country or area: *the party misjudged the mood of the populace*.
– ORIGIN late 16th cent.: from French, from Italian *popolaccio* 'common people', from *popolo* 'people' + the pejorative suffix *-accio*.

popular ▶ adjective **1** liked, admired, or enjoyed by many people or by a particular person or group: *she was one of the most popular girls in the school | these cheeses are very popular in Europe.*
2 [attrib.] (of cultural activities or products) intended for or suited to the taste, understanding, or means of the general public rather than specialists or intellectuals: *editorials accusing the government of wanting to gag the popular press.*
■ (of a belief or attitude) held by the majority of the general public: *many adult cats, contrary to popular opinion, actively dislike milk.*
3 [attrib.] (of political activity) of or carried on by the people as a whole rather than restricted to politicians or political parties: *a popular revolt against colonial rule.*
– DERIVATIVES **popularism** noun.
– ORIGIN late Middle English (in the sense 'prevalent among the general public'): from Latin *popularis*, from *populus* 'people'. sense 1 dates from the early 17th cent.

popular etymology ▶ noun another term for **FOLK ETYMOLOGY**.

popular front ▶ noun a party or coalition representing left-wing elements, in particular (**the Popular Front**) an alliance of communist, radical, and socialist elements formed and gaining some power in countries such as France and Spain in the 1930s.

popularity ▶ noun [mass noun] the state or condition of being liked, admired, or supported by many people: *he was forced to step down as mayor despite his popularity with the voters.*

popularize (also **-ise**) ▶ verb [with obj.] cause (something) to become generally liked: *his books have done much to popularize the sport.*
■ make (something technical, scientific, or academic) accessible or interesting to the general public by presenting it in a readily understandable form: *they are skilled at popularizing the technical aspects of genetics.*
– DERIVATIVES **popularization** noun, **popularizer** noun.

popularly ▶ adverb by many or most people; generally: *advancing age is popularly associated with a declining capacity to work.*
■ (of a term, name, or title) in informal, common, or non-specialist use: *the community charge (popularly known as the poll tax).* ■ (of a politician or government) chosen by the majority of the voters; democratically: *a popularly elected Parliament.*

popular music ▶ noun [mass noun] music appealing to the popular taste, including rock and pop and also soul, reggae, rap, and dance music.

populate ▶ verb [with obj.] (usu. **be populated**) form the population of (a town, area, or country): *the island is populated by scarcely 40,000 people |* [as adj., with submodifier] (**populated**) *a densely populated area.*
■ figurative fill or be present in (a place, environment, or domain): *the spirit of the book and the characters who populate its pages.* ■ cause people to settle in (an area or place): *Finland pursues a policy designed to populate its Russian borders.*
– ORIGIN late 16th cent.: from medieval Latin *populat-* 'supplied with people', from the verb *populare*, from *populus* 'people'.

population ▶ noun all the inhabitants of a particular town, area, or country: *the island has a population of about 78,000.*
■ [with adj. or noun modifier] a particular section, group, or type of people or animals living in an area or country: *measures to speed up integration of the country's immigrant population.* ■ [mass noun] [with adj.] the specified extent or degree to which an area is or has been populated: *areas of sparse population.* ■ [mass noun] the action of populating an area. ■ Biology a community of animals, plants, or humans among whose members interbreeding occurs. ■ Statistics a finite or infinite collection of items under consideration. ■ Astronomy each of three groups (designated I, II, and III) into which stars can be approximately divided on the basis of their manner of formation.
– ORIGIN late 16th cent. (denoting an inhabited place): from late Latin *populatio(n-)*, from the verb *populare*, from *populus* 'people'.

population group ▶ noun (in South Africa during the apartheid era) the official term for an ethnic group.

population inversion ▶ noun see **INVERSION** (sense 1).

populist ▶ noun a member or adherent of a political party seeking to represent the interests of ordinary people. [ORIGIN: originally referring to a party formed in the US in 1892.]
■ a person who holds, or who is concerned with, the views of ordinary people.
▶ adjective of or relating to a populist or populists: *a populist leader.*
– DERIVATIVES **populism** noun, **populistic** adjective.
– ORIGIN late 19th cent.: from Latin *populus* 'people' + **-IST**.

populous ▶ adjective having a large population; densely populated.
– DERIVATIVES **populously** adverb, **populousness** noun.
– ORIGIN late Middle English: from late Latin *populosus*, from *populus* 'people'.

pop-up ▶ adjective [attrib.] (of a book or greetings card) containing folded cut-out pictures that rise up to form a three-dimensional scene or figure when the page is turned.
■ (of an electric toaster) operating so as to push up a piece of toast quickly when it is ready. ■ Computing (of a menu or other utility) able to be superimposed on the screen being worked on and suppressed rapidly.
▶ noun **1** a pop-up picture in a book.
■ a book containing such pictures.
2 Baseball see **POP**¹ (sense 3).
3 Computing a pop-up menu or other utility.

porangi /ˈpɔːraŋi/ ▶ adjective NZ informal mad; crazy.
– ORIGIN Maori.

porbeagle /ˈpɔːbiːg(ə)l/ ▶ noun a large active shark which is found chiefly in the open seas of the North Atlantic and in the Mediterranean. Also called **MACKEREL SHARK**.
● *Lamna nasus*, family Lamnidae.
– ORIGIN mid 18th cent.: from Cornish dialect, perhaps from Cornish *porth* 'harbour, cove' + *bugel* 'shepherd'.

porcelain /ˈpɔːs(ə)lɪn/ ▶ noun [mass noun] a white vitrified translucent ceramic; china. See also **HARD-PASTE**, **SOFT-PASTE**.
■ [count noun] (usu. **porcelains**) articles made of this. ■ such articles collectively: *a collection of Chinese porcelain.*
– DERIVATIVES **porcellanous** /pɔːˈsɛlənəs/ adjective.
– ORIGIN mid 16th cent.: from French *porcelaine*, from Italian *porcellana* 'cowrie shell', hence 'chinaware' (from its resemblance to the dense polished shells).

porcelain clay ▶ noun another term for **KAOLIN**.

porcelain crab ▶ noun a marine crablike

crustacean with long antennae, related to the hermit crabs.
● *Porcellana* and other genera, superfamily Galatheoidea.
– ORIGIN mid 19th cent.: so named because of its smooth and polished shell.

porcelain fungus ▶ noun a common edible Eurasian mushroom which is white and covered with a slimy fluid, growing on beech trees. Also called **POACHED EGG FUNGUS**.
● *Oudemansiella mucida*, family Tricholomataceae, class Hymenomycetes.

porch ▶ noun a covered shelter projecting in front of the entrance of a building.
■ N. Amer. a veranda.
– DERIVATIVES **porched** adjective, **porchless** adjective.
– ORIGIN Middle English: from Old French *porche*, from Latin *porticus* 'colonnade', from *porta* 'passage'.

porcine /ˈpɔːsʌɪn/ ▶ adjective of, affecting, or resembling a pig or pigs: *his flushed, porcine features*.
– ORIGIN mid 17th cent.: from French *porcin* or Latin *porcinus*, from *porcus* 'pig'.

porcini /pɔːˈtʃiːni/ ▶ noun (pl. same) chiefly N. Amer. the cep (a wild mushroom), especially as an item on a menu.
– ORIGIN Italian, literally 'little pigs'.

porcupine ▶ noun a large rodent with defensive spines or quills on the body and tail.
● Suborder Hystricomorpha: families Hystricidae (three Old World genera) and Erethizontidae (four New World genera).
– ORIGIN late Middle English: from Old French *porc espin*, from Provençal *porc espi(n)*, from Latin *porcus* 'pig' + *spina* 'thorn'.

porcupine fish ▶ noun a tropical marine fish which has a parrot-like beak and is covered with sharp spines. It inflates itself like a balloon when threatened.
● Family Diodontidae: three genera and several species, including the widely distributed *Diodon hystrix*. See also **BURRFISH**.

pore[1] ▶ noun chiefly Biology a minute opening in a surface, especially the skin or integument of an organism, through which gases, liquids, or microscopic particles may pass.
– ORIGIN late Middle English: from Old French, via Latin from Greek *poros* 'passage, pore'.

pore[2] ▶ verb [no obj.] **(pore over/through)** be absorbed in the reading or study of: *Marjorie and Heather spent hours poring over cookery books*.
■ archaic think intently; ponder: *when he has thought and* **pored on** *it*.
– ORIGIN Middle English: perhaps related to **PEER**[1].

pore water ▶ noun [mass noun] Geology water contained in pores in soil or rock.

porgy /ˈpɔːɡi/ ▶ noun (pl. **-ies**) a deep-bodied fish related to the sea breams, which is typically silvery but sometimes changes to a blotched pattern. It usually lives in warm coastal waters.
● *Calamus* and other genera, family Sparidae: many species.
– ORIGIN mid 17th cent.: alteration of Spanish and Portuguese *pargo*.

Pori /ˈpɔːri/ an industrial port in SW Finland, on the Gulf of Bothnia; pop. 76,360 (1990).

Porifera /pəˈrɪf(ə)rə/ Zoology a phylum of aquatic invertebrate animals that comprises the sponges.
– DERIVATIVES **poriferan** adjective & noun.
– ORIGIN modern Latin (plural), from Latin *porus* 'pore' + *-fer* 'bearing'.

porin /ˈpɔːrɪn/ ▶ noun Biochemistry any of a class of proteins whose molecules can form channels (large enough to allow the passage of small ions and molecules) through cellular membranes.
– ORIGIN 1970s: from Greek *poros* 'pore' + **-IN**[1].

pork ▶ noun [mass noun] **1** the flesh of a pig used as food, especially when uncured.
2 short for **PORK BARREL**.
▶ verb [with obj.] vulgar slang, chiefly US (of a man) have sexual intercourse with.
– ORIGIN Middle English: from Old French *porc*, from Latin *porcus* 'pig'.

pork barrel ▶ noun [in sing.] N. Amer. informal used in reference to the use of government funds for projects designed to please voters or legislators and win votes.
– DERIVATIVES **pork-barrelling** noun.
– ORIGIN figuratively, from the use of such a barrel by farmers, to keep a reserve supply of meat.

porker ▶ noun a pig raised for food.
■ a young fattened pig. ■ informal, derogatory a fat person.

porkling ▶ noun a young or small pig; a piglet.

pork pie ▶ noun a raised pie made with minced, cooked pork, typically eaten cold.

pork-pie hat ▶ noun a hat with a flat crown and a brim turned up all round.

pork scratchings ▶ plural noun see **SCRATCHINGS**.

porky[1] ▶ adjective (**porkier**, **porkiest**) **1** informal (of a person or part of their body) fleshy or fat.
2 of or resembling pork.
▶ noun (pl. **-ies**) (also **porky-pie**) Brit. rhyming slang a lie: *you've been telling porkies*.

porky[2] ▶ noun (pl. **-ies**) US informal a porcupine.

porn (also **porno**) informal ▶ noun [mass noun] pornography.
▶ adjective pornographic.
– ORIGIN 1950s: abbreviation.

pornography ▶ noun [mass noun] printed or visual material containing the explicit description or display of sexual organs or activity, intended to stimulate erotic rather than aesthetic or emotional feelings.
– DERIVATIVES **pornographer** noun, **pornographic** adjective, **pornographically** adverb.
– ORIGIN mid 19th cent.: from Greek *pornographos* 'writing about prostitutes', from *pornē* 'prostitute' + *graphein* 'write'.

porous ▶ adjective (of a rock or other material) having minute interstices through which liquid or air may pass.
■ figurative not retentive or secure: *he ran through a porous home defence to score easily*.
– DERIVATIVES **porosity** noun, **porousness** noun.
– ORIGIN late Middle English: from Old French *poreux*, based on Latin *porus* 'pore'.

porphyria /pɔːˈfɪrɪə/ ▶ noun [mass noun] Medicine a rare hereditary disease in which there is abnormal metabolism of the blood pigment haemoglobin. Porphyrins are excreted in the urine, which becomes dark; other symptoms include mental disturbances and extreme sensitivity of the skin to light.
– ORIGIN 1920s: modern Latin, from **PORPHYRIN**.

porphyrin /ˈpɔːfɪrɪn/ ▶ noun Biochemistry any of a class of pigments (including haem and chlorophyll) whose molecules contain a flat ring of four linked heterocyclic groups, sometimes with a central metal atom.
– ORIGIN early 20th cent.: from Greek *porphura* 'purple' + **-IN**[1].

porphyritic /ˌpɔːfɪˈrɪtɪk/ ▶ adjective Geology relating to or denoting a rock texture containing distinct crystals or crystalline particles embedded in a compact groundmass.

porphyroblast /ˈpɔːfɪrə(ʊ)blast/ ▶ noun Geology a larger recrystallized grain occurring in a finer groundmass in a metamorphic rock.
– DERIVATIVES **porphyroblastic** adjective.

Porphyry /ˈpɔːfɪri/ (*c.*232–303), Neoplatonist philosopher; born *Malchus*. He was a pupil of Plotinus, whose works he edited after the latter's death.

porphyry /ˈpɔːfɪri/ ▶ noun (pl. **-ies**) [mass noun] a hard igneous rock containing crystals of feldspar in a fine-grained, typically reddish groundmass.
– ORIGIN late Middle English: via medieval Latin from Greek *porphuritēs*, from *porphura* 'purple'.

porpoise /ˈpɔːpəs, -pɔɪs/ ▶ noun a small toothed whale with a low triangular dorsal fin and a blunt rounded snout.
● Family Phocoenidae: three genera and several species, in particular the **common** (or **harbour**) **porpoise** (*Phocoena phocoena*), of the North Atlantic and North Pacific.
▶ verb [no obj.] move through the water like a porpoise, alternately rising above it and submerging: *the boat began to porpoise badly*.
– ORIGIN Middle English: from Old French *porpois*, based on Latin *porcus* 'pig' + *piscis* 'fish', rendering earlier *porcus marinus* 'sea hog'.

porridge ▶ noun [mass noun] **1** a dish consisting of oatmeal or another meal or cereal boiled in water or milk.
2 Brit. informal time spent in prison: *I'm sweating it out* **doing porridge**.
– DERIVATIVES **porridgy** adjective.
– ORIGIN mid 16th cent. (denoting soup thickened with barley): alteration of **POTTAGE**. Sense 2 dates from the 1950s.

porringer /ˈpɒrɪn(d)ʒə/ ▶ noun historical a small bowl, typically with a handle, used for soup, stew, or similar dishes.
– ORIGIN late Middle English (earlier as *potager* and *pottinger*): from Old French *potager*, from *potage* 'contents of a pot'.

porro prism /ˈpɒrəʊ/ (also **Porro prism**) ▶ noun a reflecting prism in which the light is reflected on two 45° surfaces and returned parallel to the incoming beam. Compare with **ROOF PRISM**.
■ **(porro prisms)** (also **porro-prism binoculars**) a pair of binoculars using two such prisms at right angles, resulting in a conventional instrument with objective lenses that are further apart than the eyepieces.

Porsche /pɔːʃ, German ˈpɔrʃə/, Ferdinand (1875–1952), Austrian car designer. In 1934 he designed the Volkswagen ('people's car'), while his name has since become famous for the high-performance sports and racing cars produced by his company, originally to his designs.

Porsenna /pɔːˈsɛnə/ (also **Porsena** /ˈpɔːsɪnə/), Lars (6th century BC), a legendary Etruscan chieftain, king of the town of Clusium. Summoned by Tarquinius Superbus after the latter's overthrow and exile from Rome, Porsenna subsequently laid siege to the city, but did not succeed in capturing it.

port[1] ▶ noun a town or city with a harbour where ships load or unload, especially one where customs officers are stationed.
■ a harbour: [as modifier] *extensions to Belfast's port facilities*. ■ (also **inland port**) an inland town or city whose connection to the coast by a canal or other body of water enables it to act as a port.
– PHRASES **any port in a storm** proverb in adverse circumstances one welcomes any source of relief or escape. **port of entry** a harbour or airport by which people and goods may enter a country.
– ORIGIN Old English, from Latin *portus* 'haven, harbour', reinforced in Middle English by Old French.

port[2] (also **port wine**) ▶ noun [mass noun] a strong, sweet, dark red (occasionally brown or white) fortified wine, originally from Portugal, typically drunk as a dessert wine.
– ORIGIN shortened form of **OPORTO**, a major port from which the wine is shipped.

port[3] ▶ noun the side of a ship or aircraft that is on the left when one is facing forward. The opposite of **STARBOARD**.
▶ verb [with obj.] turn (a ship or its helm) to port.
– ORIGIN mid 16th cent.: probably originally the side turned towards the port.

port[4] ▶ noun an aperture or opening, in particular:
■ Electronics a socket in a computer network into which a device can be plugged. ■ an opening for the passage of steam, liquid, or gas: *loss of fuel from the exhaust port*. ■ (also **gun port**) an opening in the body of an aircraft or in a wall or armoured vehicle through which a gun may be fired. ■ a porthole. ■ an opening in the side of a ship for boarding or loading. ■ chiefly Scottish a gate or gateway, especially into a walled city.
– ORIGIN Old English (in the sense 'gateway'), from Latin *porta* 'gate'; reinforced in Middle English by Old French *porte*. The later sense 'opening in the side of a ship' led to the general sense 'aperture'.

port[5] ▶ verb **1** [with obj. and adverbial of direction] Computing transfer (software) from one system or machine to another: *the software can be ported to an IBM RS/6000*.
2 [with obj.] [often in imperative] Military carry (a rifle or other weapon) diagonally across and close to the body with the barrel or blade near the left shoulder: *Detail! For inspection—port arms!*
▶ noun [mass noun] **1** Military the position required by an order to port a rifle or other weapon: *Parker had his rifle* **at the port**.
2 poetic/literary a person's carriage or bearing: *she has the proud port of a princess*.
3 Computing a transfer of software from one system or machine to another.
– PHRASES **at port arms** Military in the position adopted when given a command to port one's weapon.
– ORIGIN Middle English (in sense 2 of the noun): from Old French *port* 'bearing, gait', from the verb *porter*, from Latin *portare* 'carry'. The verb (from French *porter*) dates from the mid 16th cent.

port[6] ▶ noun Austral. informal a suitcase or travelling bag: *she packed her ports and walked out*.

p

– ORIGIN early 20th cent.: abbreviation of **PORTMANTEAU**.

porta- ▶ **combining form** denoting something that is movable or portable, often used as part of a proprietary name: *Portaloo* | *Portakabin*.
– ORIGIN from **PORTABLE**.

portable ▶ **adjective** able to be easily carried or moved, especially because being of a lighter and smaller version than usual: *a portable television*.
■ Computing (of software) able to be transferred from one machine or system to another. ■ (of a loan or pension) capable of being transferred or adapted in altered circumstances.
▶ **noun** a version of something, such as a small lightweight television or computer, that can be easily carried.
■ N. Amer. a small transportable building used as a classroom.
– DERIVATIVES **portability** noun, **portably** adverb.
– ORIGIN late Middle English: from Old French *portable*, from late Latin *portabilis*, from Latin *portare* 'carry'.

portage /ˈpɔːtɪdʒ/ ▶ **noun** [mass noun] the carrying of a boat or its cargo between two navigable waters: *the return journey was made much simpler by portage*.
■ [count noun] a place at which this is necessary: *a portage over the weir*. ■ archaic the action of carrying or transporting something.
▶ **verb** [with obj.] carry (a boat or its cargo) between navigable waters: *we portaged everything here*.
■ [no obj., with adverbial] (of a boat) be carried between or across unnavigable waters: *the cataracts meant that boats had to portage on to the Lualaba*.
– ORIGIN late Middle English: from French, from *porter* 'carry'. The sense relating to carrying between navigable waters dates from the late 17th cent.

Portakabin ▶ **noun** Brit. trademark a small, portable building, used as a temporary office, classroom, etc.
– ORIGIN 1960s: blend of **PORTABLE** and an alteration of **CABIN**.

portal[1] ▶ **noun** a doorway, gate, or other entrance, especially a large and elaborate one.
– ORIGIN late Middle English: from Old French, from medieval Latin *portale*, neuter (used as a noun) of *portalis* 'like a gate', from Latin *porta* 'door, gate'.

portal[2] ▶ **adjective** [attrib.] Anatomy of or relating to an opening in an organ through which major blood vessels pass, especially the transverse fissure of the liver.
– ORIGIN mid 19th cent.: from modern Latin *portalis*, from Latin *porta* 'gate'.

portal frame ▶ **noun** Engineering a rigid structural frame consisting essentially of two uprights connected at the top by a third member.

Portaloo ▶ **noun** Brit. trademark a portable building containing a toilet.

portal system ▶ **noun** Anatomy the system of blood vessels consisting of the hepatic portal vein with its tributaries and branches.
■ any system of blood vessels which has a capillary network at each end.

portal vein (in full **hepatic portal vein**) ▶ **noun** Anatomy a vein conveying blood to the liver from the spleen, stomach, pancreas, and intestines.

portamento /ˌpɔːtəˈmɛntəʊ/ ▶ **noun** (pl. **portamentos** or **portamenti** /-ti/) Music **1** a slide from one note to another, especially in singing or playing the violin.
■ [mass noun] this as a technique or style.
2 [mass noun] piano playing in a manner intermediate between legato and staccato: [as modifier] *a portamento style*.
– ORIGIN Italian, literally 'carrying'.

Porta Potti (also **Portapotti** or **Porta potty**) ▶ **noun** trademark, chiefly N. Amer. a portable building containing a toilet.
■ a chemical toilet, or one connected to a holding tank, in a vehicle or small boat or aircraft.

Port Arthur former name (1898–1905) for **LUSHUN**.

Portastudio ▶ **noun** (pl. **-os**) trademark a portable multi-track recording and mixing desk.

portative organ ▶ **noun** chiefly historical a small portable pipe organ.
– ORIGIN early 16th cent. (as a compound): *portative* from Old French *portatif, -ive*, apparently an alteration of *portatil*, based on Latin *portare* 'carry'.

Port-au-Prince /ˌpɔːtəʊˈprɪns, French pɔʀtoprɛ̃s/ the capital of Haiti, a port on the west coast; pop. 1,255,080 (est. 1992). Founded by the French in 1749, it became capital of the new republic in 1806.

Port Blair a port on the southern tip of South Andaman Island in the Bay of Bengal; pop. 74,810 (1991). It is the capital of the Andaman and Nicobar Islands.

portcullis ▶ **noun** a strong, heavy grating that can be lowered down grooves on each side of a gateway to block it.
– DERIVATIVES **portcullised** adjective.
– ORIGIN Middle English: from Old French *porte coleice* 'sliding door', from *porte* 'door' (from Latin *porta*) + *coleice* 'sliding' (feminine of *couleis*, from Latin *colare* 'to filter').

port de bras /ˌpɔː də ˈbrɑː/ ▶ **noun** (pl. **ports de bras** pronunc. same) chiefly Ballet an act or manner of moving and posing the arms.
■ an exercise designed to develop graceful movement and disposition of the arms, typically involving a bend accompanied by arm movement.
– ORIGIN French, literally 'bearing of (the) arms'.

Port de France former name for **NOUMÉA**.

Porte /pɔːt/ (in full **the Sublime** or **Ottoman Porte**) historical the Ottoman court at Constantinople.
– ORIGIN early 17th cent.: from French *la Sublime Porte* 'the exalted gate', translation of the Turkish title of the central office of the Ottoman government.

porte cochère /ˌpɔːt kɒˈʃɛː/ ▶ **noun** Architecture a covered entrance large enough for vehicles to pass through, typically opening into a courtyard.
■ N. Amer. a porch where vehicles stop to set down passengers.
– ORIGIN late 17th cent.: French, literally 'coach gateway'.

Port Elizabeth a port in South Africa, on the coast of the province of Eastern Cape; pop. 853,200 (1991). Settled by the British in 1820, it is now a motor-manufacturing city and beach resort.

portend ▶ **verb** [with obj.] be a sign or warning that (something, especially something momentous or calamitous) is likely to happen: *the eclipses portend some major events*.
– ORIGIN late Middle English: from Latin *portendere*, based on *pro-* 'forth' + *tendere* 'stretch'.

portent /ˈpɔːtɛnt, -t(ə)nt/ ▶ **noun 1** a sign or warning that something, especially something momentous or calamitous, is likely to happen: *many birds are regarded as being portents of death*.
■ [mass noun] future significance: *an omen of grave portent for the tribe*.
2 archaic an exceptional or wonderful person or thing: *what portent can be greater than a pious notary?*
– ORIGIN late 16th cent.: from Latin *portentum* 'omen, token', from the verb *portendere* (see **PORTEND**).

portentous ▶ **adjective** of or like a portent: *the envelope and its portentous contents*.
■ done in a pompously or overly solemn manner so as to impress: *the author's portentous moralizings*.
– DERIVATIVES **portentously** adverb, **portentousness** noun.

Porter[1], Cole (1892–1964), American songwriter. Notable songs: 'Let's Do It', 'Night and Day', and 'Begin the Beguine' and the musicals *Anything Goes* (1934) and *Kiss me, Kate* (1948).

Porter[2], Katherine Anne (1890–1980), American short-story writer and novelist. Notable works: *Pale Horse, Pale Rider* (short stories, 1939), *Ship of Fools* (novel, 1962), and *Collected Short Stories* (1965).

Porter[3], Peter (Neville Frederick) (b.1929), Australian poet, resident chiefly in England since 1951.

porter[1] ▶ **noun 1** a person employed to carry luggage and other loads. especially in a railway station, airport, hotel, or market.
■ (also **hospital porter**) a hospital employee who moves equipment or patients. ■ a person employed to carry supplies on a mountaineering expedition. ■ N. Amer. a sleeping-car attendant.
2 [mass noun] dark brown bitter beer brewed from malt partly charred or browned by drying at a high temperature. [ORIGIN: originally made as a drink for porters.]
– ORIGIN Middle English: from Old French *porteour*, from medieval Latin *portator*, from Latin *portare* 'carry'.

porter[2] ▶ **noun** Brit. an employee in charge of the entrance of a hotel, block of flats, college, or other large building.
– ORIGIN Middle English: from Old French *portier*, from late Latin *portarius*, from *porta* 'gate, door'.

porterage ▶ **noun** [mass noun] the work of carrying luggage, supplies, or other materials, done by porters or labourers.

porterhouse ▶ **noun** historical, chiefly N. Amer. an establishment at which porter and sometimes steaks were served.
– ORIGIN mid 18th cent.: from sense 2 of **PORTER**[1] + **HOUSE**.

porterhouse steak ▶ **noun** a thick steak cut from the thick end of a sirloin.

porter's knot ▶ **noun** historical a double shoulder pad and forehead loop used for carrying loads.

Port Étienne /eɪˈtjɛn/ former name for **NOUADHIBOU**.

portfire ▶ **noun** historical a hand-held fuse used for firing cannons, igniting explosives in mining, etc.
– ORIGIN mid 17th cent.: partial Anglicization of French *porte-feu*, from *porter* 'carry' + *feu* 'fire'.

portfolio ▶ **noun** (pl. **-os**) **1** a large, thin, flat case for loose sheets of paper such as drawings or maps.
■ a set of pieces of creative work collected by someone to display their skills, especially to a potential employer. ■ a varied set of photographs of a model or actor intended to be shown to a potential employer.
2 a range of investments held by a person or organization: *a portfolio of insured municipal securities*.
■ a range of products or services offered by an organization, especially when considered as a business asset: *an unrivalled portfolio of quality brands*.
3 the position and duties of a Minister or Secretary of State: *he took on the Foreign Affairs portfolio*.
– ORIGIN early 18th cent.: from Italian *portafogli*, from *portare* 'carry' + *foglio* 'leaf' (from Latin *folium*).

Port-Gentil /ˌpɔːʒɒnˈtiː/ the principal port of Gabon, on the Atlantic coast south of Libreville; pop. 75,800 (1992).

Port Harcourt /ˈhɑːkɔːt/ a port in SE Nigeria, on the Gulf of Guinea at the eastern edge of the Niger delta; pop. 371,000 (1991).

Port Hedland a seaport on the NW coast of Western Australia; pop. 13,600 (est. 1987).

porthole ▶ **noun** a small window on the outside of a ship or aircraft.
■ historical an opening for firing a cannon through.

portico /ˈpɔːtɪkəʊ/ ▶ **noun** (pl. **-oes** or **-os**) a structure consisting of a roof supported by columns at regular intervals, typically attached as a porch to a building.
– ORIGIN early 17th cent.: from Italian, from Latin *porticus* 'porch'.

portière /ˌpɔːtiˈɛː/ ▶ **noun** a curtain hung over a door or doorway.
– ORIGIN mid 19th cent.: French, from *porte* 'door', from Latin *porta* 'gate, door'.

Porţile de Fier /porˌtsiːlɛ dɛ ˈfjɛr/ Romanian name for **IRON GATE**.

portion ▶ **noun** a part of a whole; an amount, section, or piece of something: *a portion of the jetty still stands* | *he could repeat large portions of Shakespeare*.
■ a part of something divided between two or more people; a share: *she wanted the right to decide how her portion of the allowance should be spent*. ■ an amount of food suitable for or served to one person: *a portion of ice cream* | *burger joints offering huge portions*. ■ Law the part or share of an estate given or descending by law to an heir. ■ archaic a person's future as allotted by fate; one's destiny or lot: *what will be my portion?* ■ (also **marriage portion**) archaic a dowry given to a bride at her marriage.
▶ **verb** [with obj.] (usu. **be portioned**) divide (something) into shares to be distributed among two or more people: *for centuries meadowland with common hay rights was portioned out*.
■ [usu. as adj., with submodifier] (**portioned**) serve (food) in an amount suitable for one person: *generously portioned lunches*. ■ archaic give a dowry to (a bride at her marriage): *my parents will portion me most handsomely*.
– ORIGIN Middle English: from Old French *porcion*, from Latin *portio(n-)*, from the phrase *pro portione* 'in proportion'.

portionless ▶ **adjective** archaic (of a woman) without a dowry.

Port Jackson willow ▶ **noun** either of two

Australian acacias which were introduced into South Africa where they have become naturalized.
• Genus *Acacia*, family Leguminosae: *A. longifolia* and *A. cyanophylla*, which is a useful sand-binding tree.
– ORIGIN mid 19th cent.: named after the harbour of Sydney, Australia.

Portland 1 an industrial port in NW Oregon, on the Willamette river near its confluence with the Columbia River; pop. 437,320 (1990). It is the largest city in Oregon.
2 a shipping forecast area covering the English Channel roughly between the meridians of Start Point in the west and Poole in the east, taking its name from the Isle of Portland.

Portland, Isle of a rocky limestone peninsula on the south coast of England, in Dorset. Its southernmost tip is known as the Bill of Portland or Portland Bill. The peninsula is quarried for its fine building stone.

Portland cement ▶ **noun** [mass noun] cement manufactured from chalk and clay which hardens under water and when hard resembles Portland stone in colour.

Portland stone ▶ **noun** [mass noun] limestone from the Isle of Portland in Dorset, highly prized as a building material.

Portland vase a dark blue Roman glass vase with white decoration, dating from around the 1st century AD. Acquired in the 18th century by the Duchess of Portland, it is now in the British Museum.

Portlaoise /pɔːtˈliːʃ/ (also **Portlaoighise**) the county town of Laois in the Republic of Ireland; pop. 9,500 (est. 1990). It is the site of a top-security prison.

Port Louis /ˈluːɪs, ˈluːi/ the capital of Mauritius, a port on the NW coast; pop. 143,510 (est. 1993).

portly ▶ **adjective** (**portlier**, **portliest**) **1** (especially of a man) having a stout body; rather fat.
2 archaic of a stately or dignified appearance and manner: *he was a man of portly presence.*
– DERIVATIVES **portliness** noun.
– ORIGIN late 15th cent.: from **PORT**[5] in the sense 'bearing' + **-LY**[1].

Port Mahon another name for **MAHON**.

portmanteau /pɔːtˈmantəʊ/ ▶ **noun** (pl. **portmanteaus** or **portmanteaux** /-əʊz/) a large travelling bag, typically made of stiff leather and opening into two equal parts.
▪[as modifier] consisting of or combining two or more separable aspects or qualities: *a portmanteau movie composed of excerpts from his most famous films.*
– ORIGIN mid 16th cent.: from French *portemanteau*, from *porter* 'carry' + *manteau* 'mantle'.

portmanteau word ▶ **noun** a word blending the sounds and combining the meanings of two others, for example *motel* or *brunch*.
– ORIGIN *portmanteau* coined, in this sense, by Lewis Carroll in *Through the Looking Glass* (1871).

Port Moresby /ˈmɔːzbi/ the capital of Papua New Guinea, situated on the south coast of the island of New Guinea, on the Coral Sea; pop. 193,240 (1990).

Port Natal former name (until 1835) for **DURBAN**.

Porto /ˈportu/ Portuguese name for **OPORTO**.

Pôrto Alegre /ˌpɔːtuː əˈlɛgreɪ/ a major port and commercial city in SE Brazil, capital of the state of Rio Grande do Sul; pop. 1,263,400 (1991). It is situated on the Lagoa dos Patos, a lagoon separated from the Atlantic by a sandy peninsula.

portobello /ˌpɔːtəˈbɛləʊ/ (also **portobello mushroom**) ▶ **noun** a large mature mushroom with an open flat cap.

port of call ▶ **noun** a place where a ship stops on a voyage.
▪any of a number of places that a person visits in succession: *his last port of call that morning was Angela's solicitor* | figurative *if you 're serious about spreadsheeting, then this package must be your first port of call.*

Port of London Authority the corporate body controlling the London harbour and docks.

Port-of-Spain the capital of Trinidad and Tobago, a port on the NW coast of the island of Trinidad; pop. 46,000 (1990).

portolan /ˈpɔːtəlan/ (also **portolano** /ˌpɔːtəˈlɑːnəʊ/) ▶ **noun** (pl. **portolans** or **portolanos**) historical a book of sailing directions with charts and descriptions of harbours and coasts.
– ORIGIN mid 19th cent.: from Italian *portolano*, from *porto* 'harbour'.

Porto Novo /ˌpɔːtəʊ ˈnəʊvəʊ/ the capital of Benin, a port on the Gulf of Guinea close to the border with Nigeria; pop. 179,140 (1992). It was a centre of the Portuguese slave trade.

Pôrto Velho /ˌpɔːtuː ˈvɛlju:/ a town in western Brazil, capital of the state of Rondônia; pop. 286,000 (1991).

Port Petrovsk /pɪˈtrɒfsk/ former name (until 1922) for **MAKHACHKALA**.

Port Pirie /ˈpɪri/ a port on the coast of South Australia, on the Spencer Gulf north of Adelaide; pop. 15,160 (est. 1987).

portrait ▶ **noun 1** a painting, drawing, photograph, or engraving of a person, especially one depicting only the face or head and shoulders.
▪a representation or impression of someone or something in language or on film or television: *the writer builds up a full and fascinating portrait of a community.*
2 [as modifier] (of a page, book, or illustration, or the manner in which it is set or printed) higher than it is wide. Compare with **LANDSCAPE** (sense 2).
– DERIVATIVES **portraitist** noun (only in sense 1).
– ORIGIN mid 16th cent.: from French, past participle (used as a noun) of Old French *portraire* 'portray'.

portraiture ▶ **noun** [mass noun] the art of painting or taking portraits.
▪graphic and detailed description, especially of a person: *it's part murder mystery and part portraiture through poetry.* ▪ [count noun] formal a portrait.
– ORIGIN late Middle English: from Old French, from *portrait* (see **PORTRAIT**).

portray ▶ **verb** [with obj.] depict (someone or something) in a work of art or literature: *the ineffectual Oxbridge dons portrayed by Evelyn Waugh.*
▪(of an actor) represent or play the part of (someone) in a film or play: *he chose Trevor Howard to portray Captain Bligh.* ▪ [with obj. and adverbial] describe (someone or something) in a particular way: *the book **portrayed** him **as** a self-serving careerist.*
– DERIVATIVES **portrayable** adjective, **portrayal** noun, **portrayer** noun.
– ORIGIN Middle English: from Old French *portraire*, based on *traire* 'to draw', from an alteration of Latin *trahere*.

Port Said /sʌɪd/ a port in Egypt, on the Mediterranean coast at the north end of the Suez Canal; pop. 461,000 (est. 1990). It was founded in 1859 at the start of the construction of the Suez Canal.

Port Salut /ˌpɔː saˈluː/ ▶ **noun** [mass noun] a pale, mild type of cheese.
– ORIGIN named after the Trappist monastery in France, where it was first produced.

Portsmouth a port and naval base on the south coast of England, a unitary council formerly in Hampshire; pop. 174,700 (1991). The naval dockyard was established there in 1496.

Port Stanley another name for **STANLEY**[1].

Port Sudan the chief port of Sudan, on the Red Sea; pop. 206,700 (1983).

Port Sunlight a village on the south bank of the Mersey. Founded and built in the 1880s by Viscount Leverhulme, it provided model housing for the employees of his 'Sunlight' soap factory.

Portugal /ˈpɔːtjʊg(ə)l, ˈpɔːtʃʊ-/ a country occupying the western part of the Iberian peninsula in SW Europe; pop. 10,393,000 (est. 1991); official language, Portuguese; capital, Lisbon.

The country was linked with Spain until it became an independent kingdom in the 12th century. In the 15th and 16th centuries it emerged as one of the leading European colonial powers. Portugal became a republic in 1911, after the expulsion of the monarchy. A long period of dictatorship by Antonio Salazar (Prime Minister 1932–68), and his successor Marcello Caetano (1906–80) was ended in 1974 by a military coup, which led to Portugal's rapid withdrawal from its African colonies and eventually to democratic reform. Portugal became a member of the EC in 1986.

Portuguese /ˌpɔːtjʊˈgiːz, -tʃʊ-/ ▶ **adjective** of or relating to Portugal or its people or language.
▶ **noun** (pl. same) **1** a native or national of Portugal, or a person of Portuguese descent.
2 [mass noun] the language of Portugal and Brazil, a Romance language spoken by about 160 million people.
– ORIGIN from Portuguese *portuguez*, from medieval Latin *portugalensis*.

Portuguese man-of-war ▶ **noun** a floating colonial coelenterate with a number of polyps and a conspicuous float. It bears long tentacles which are able to inflict painful stings and occurs chiefly in warm seas.
• *Physalia physalis*, order Siphonophora, class Hydrozoa.

Port Vila another name for **VILA**.

port watch ▶ **noun** see **WATCH** (sense 2).

port wine ▶ **noun** see **PORT**[2].

port wine stain ▶ **noun** a kind of large, deep red birthmark, a persistent haemangioma or naevus, typically on the face.

POS ▶ **abbreviation for** point of sale.

posada /pəˈsɑːdə/ ▶ **noun** (in Spanish-speaking countries) a hotel or inn.
– ORIGIN Spanish, from *posar* 'to lodge'.

pose[1] ▶ **verb 1** [with obj.] present or constitute (a problem, danger, or difficulty): *the sheer number of visitors is posing a threat to the area.*
▪raise (a question or matter for consideration): *a statement which posed more questions than it answered.*
2 [no obj.] assume a particular attitude or position in order to be photographed, painted, or drawn: *the prime minister posed for photographers.*
▪[with obj.] place (someone) in a particular attitude or position in order to be photographed, painted, or drawn: *he posed her on the sofa.* ▪ (**pose as**) set oneself up as or pretend to be (someone or something): *a man posing as a customer* | figurative *whitewashed chicken coops which posed as villas.* ▪ behave affectedly in order to impress others: *some people like to drive kit cars, but most just like to pose in them.*
▶ **noun** a particular way of standing or sitting, usually adopted for effect or in order to be photographed, painted, or drawn: *photographs of boxers in ferocious poses.*
▪a particular way of behaving adopted in order to give others a false impression: *the man dropped his pose of amiability.* ▪ an affected way of behaving adopted in order to impress others.
– ORIGIN Middle English: from Old French *poser* (verb), from late Latin *pausare* 'to pause', which replaced Latin *ponere* 'to place'. The noun dates from the early 19th cent.

pose[2] ▶ **verb** [with obj.] archaic puzzle or perplex (someone) with a question or problem: *we have thus posed the mathematician and the historian.*
– ORIGIN early 16th cent.: shortening of obsolete *appose*, from Old French *aposer*, variant of *opposer* 'oppose'.

Poseidon /pəˈsʌɪd(ə)n/ Greek Mythology the god of the sea, water, earthquakes, and horses, son of Cronus and Rhea and brother of Zeus. He is often depicted with a trident in his hand. Roman equivalent **NEPTUNE**.

Posen /ˈpoːzn/ German name for **POZNAŃ**.

poser[1] ▶ **noun** a person who acts in an affected manner in order to impress others.

poser[2] ▶ **noun** a difficult or perplexing question or problem.

poseur /pəʊˈzəː/ ▶ **noun** another term for **POSER**[1].
– ORIGIN French, from *poser* 'to place'.

poseuse /pəʊˈzəːz/ ▶ **noun** humorous a female poser.
– ORIGIN French, feminine of *poseur* (see **POSEUR**).

posey (also **posy**) ▶ **adjective** informal (of a person or their behaviour) affected and attempting to impress others; pretentious.

posh informal ▶ **adjective** elegant or stylishly luxurious: *a posh Munich hotel* | *I'll have to look posh.*
▪chiefly Brit. typical of or belonging to the upper class of society: *she had a posh accent.*
▶ **adverb** Brit. in an upper-class way: *trying to talk posh.*
▶ **noun** [mass noun] Brit. the quality or state of being elegant, stylish, or upper class: *we finally bought a colour TV, which seemed the height of posh.*
– DERIVATIVES **poshly** adverb, **poshness** noun.
– ORIGIN early 20th cent.: perhaps from slang *posh*, denoting a dandy. There is no evidence to support the folk etymology that *posh* is formed from the initials of *port out starboard home* (referring to the practice of using the more comfortable accommodation, out of the heat of the sun, on ships between England and India).
▶ **posh something up** Brit. smarten something up: *the sealing wax with which she poshed up Muriel's dancing shoes.*

posho[1] ▶ **noun** Brit. informal an upper-class person.

posho² ▶ **noun** [mass noun] (in East Africa) daily rations consisting typically of maize or rice, given to soldiers or in payment for menial work.
– ORIGIN Kiswahili, literally 'daily rations'.

posing pouch ▶ **noun** a man's garment covering only the genitals.

posit /ˈpɒzɪt/ ▶ **verb** (**posited**, **positing**) **1** [with obj.] assume as a fact; put forward as a basis of argument: *the Confucian view posits a perfectible human nature* | [with clause] *he posited that the world economy is a system with its own particular equilibrium.*
■ (**posit something on**) base something on the truth of (a particular assumption): *these plots are posited on a false premise about women's nature as inferior.*
2 [with obj. and adverbial] put in position; place: *the Professor posits Cohen in his second category of poets.*
▶ **noun** Philosophy a statement which is made on the assumption that it will prove to be true.
– ORIGIN mid 17th cent.: from Latin *posit-* 'placed', from the verb *ponere*.

positif /ˈpɒzɪtɪf/ ▶ **noun** Music (in some organs) a separate division of stops with its own manual, similar to a choir organ.
– ORIGIN French.

position ▶ **noun** **1** a place where someone or something is located or has been put: *the distress call had given the ship's position* | *Mrs Snell had taken up her position on the bottom step of the stairs.*
■ [mass noun] the location where someone or something should be; the correct place: *the lid was put* ***into position*** *and screwed down* | *make sure that no slates have slipped* ***out of position.*** ■ (often **positions**) a place where part of a military force is posted for strategic purposes: *the guns were shelling the German positions.*
2 a particular way in which someone or something is placed or arranged: *he moved himself into a reclining position* | [mass noun] *cramp forced her to change position.*
■ the configuration of the pieces and pawns on the board at any point in a game of chess. ■ Music a particular location of the hand on the fingerboard of a stringed instrument: *be familiar with the first six positions across the four strings.* ■ Music the arrangement of the constituent notes of a chord.
3 a situation or set of circumstances, especially one that affects one's power to act: *the company's financial position is grim* | [with infinitive] *we felt we were not in a position to judge the merits of the case.*
■ [mass noun] the state of being placed where one has an advantage over one's rivals in a competitive situation: *sleek motor launches jostled for position.* ■ a person's place or rank in relation to others, especially in a competitive situation: *he made up ground to finish in second position.* ■ [mass noun] high rank or social standing: *a woman of supposed wealth and position.* ■ a job: *she retired from her position as marketing director.*
4 a person's particular point of view or attitude towards something: *the official US* ***position on*** *Palestine.*
5 an investor's net holdings in one or more markets at a particular time; the status of an individual or institutional trader's open contracts: *traders were covering short positions.*
6 Logic a proposition laid down or asserted; a tenet or assertion.
▶ **verb** [with obj. and adverbial] put or arrange (someone or something) in a particular place or way: *he pulled out a chair and positioned it between them* | *she positioned herself on a bench.*
■ promote (a product, service, or business) within a particular sector of a market, or as the fulfilment of that sector's specific requirements: *a comprehensive development plan which will* ***position*** *the city* ***as*** *a major economic force in the region.* ■ [with adj. and adverbial] figurative portray or regard (someone) as a particular type of person: *I had* ***positioned*** *her* ***as*** *my antagonist.*
– ORIGIN late Middle English: from Old French, from Latin *positio(n-)*, from *ponere* 'to place'. The current sense of the verb dates from the early 19th cent.

positional ▶ **adjective** of, relating to, or determined by position: *United will be forced to make several positional changes.*
– DERIVATIVES **positionally** adverb.

positional goods ▶ **plural noun** Economics goods which are in limited supply and which become more sought after and relatively more expensive as material prosperity increases.

positioner ▶ **noun** a device for moving an object into position and automatically keeping it there.

position paper ▶ **noun** (in business and politics) a written report outlining someone's attitude or intentions regarding a particular matter.

positive ▶ **adjective** **1** consisting in or characterized by the presence or possession of features or qualities rather than their absence.
■ (of a statement or decision) expressing or implying affirmation, agreement, or permission: *the company received a positive response from investors.* ■ (of the results of a test or experiment) indicating the presence of something: *three players who had tested positive for cocaine use.* ■ constructive in intention or attitude: *there needs to be a positive approach to young offenders.* ■ showing optimism and confidence: *I hope you will be feeling very positive about your chances of success.* ■ showing pleasing progress, gain, or improvement: *the election result will have a positive effect because it will restore people's confidence.*
2 with no possibility of doubt; clear and definite: *he made a positive identification of a glossy ibis.*
■ convinced or confident in one's opinion; certain: *'You are sure it was the same man?' 'Positive!' said George* | [with clause] *I am positive that he is not coming back.* ■ [attrib.] informal downright; complete (used for emphasis): *it's a positive delight to see you.*
3 of, containing, producing, or denoting an electric charge opposite to that carried by electrons.
4 (of a photographic image) showing lights and shades or colours true to the original.
5 Grammar (of an adjective or adverb) expressing a quality in its basic, primary degree. Contrasted with **COMPARATIVE** and **SUPERLATIVE**.
6 chiefly Philosophy dealing only with matters of fact and experience; not speculative or theoretical. Compare with **POSITIVISM** (sense 1).
7 (of a quantity) greater than zero.
8 Astrology of, relating to, or denoting any of the air or fire signs, considered active in nature.
▶ **noun** **1** a good, affirmative, or constructive quality or attribute: *take your weaknesses and translate them into positives* | *to manage your way out of recession, accentuate* ***the positive.***
2 a photographic image showing lights and shades or colours true to the original, especially one printed from a negative.
3 a result of a test or experiment indicating the presence of something: *let us look at the distribution of those positives.*
4 [mass noun] the part of an electric circuit that is at a higher electrical potential than another point designated as having zero electrical potential.
5 Grammar an adjective or adverb in the positive degree.
6 Music another term for **POSITIF**.
7 a number greater than zero.
– DERIVATIVES **positiveness** noun, **positivity** noun.
– ORIGIN late Middle English: from Old French *positif, -ive* or Latin *positivus*, from *posit-* 'placed', from the verb *ponere*. The original sense referred to laws as being formally 'laid down', which gave rise to the sense 'explicitly laid down and admitting no question', hence 'very sure, convinced'.

positive discrimination ▶ **noun** [mass noun] Brit. (in the context of the allocation of resources or employment) the practice or policy of favouring individuals belonging to groups which suffer discrimination.

positive feedback ▶ **noun** [mass noun] chiefly Biology the enhancing or amplification of an effect by its own influence on the process which gives rise to it.
■ Electronics the return of part of an output signal to the input, which is in phase with it, so that the amplifier gain is increased and often the output is distorted.

positive geotropism ▶ **noun** [mass noun] Botany the tendency of roots to grow downwards.

positive law ▶ **noun** [mass noun] statutes which have been laid down by a legislature, court, or other human institution and can take whatever form the authors want. Compare with **NATURAL LAW**.

positive logic ▶ **noun** [mass noun] a method using electrical signals to represent binary digits, in which the positive signal is taken to represent 1 and the negative signal 0.

positively ▶ **adverb** in a positive way, in particular:
■ with certainty; so as to leave no room for doubt: *experts could not positively identify the voices.* ■ [as submodifier] used to emphasize that something is the case, even though it may seem surprising or unlikely: *some of the diets may be positively dangerous.*

positive organ ▶ **noun** chiefly historical a large but movable pipe organ. Compare with **PORTATIVE ORGAN**.
– ORIGIN early 18th cent.: *positive* in the sense 'adapted to be placed in position'.

positive pole ▶ **noun** Physics a north-seeking pole of a magnet.

positive prescription ▶ **noun** see **PRESCRIPTION** (sense 3).

positive pressure ▶ **noun** [mass noun] air or gas pressure greater than that of the atmosphere, as used e.g. in the artificial ventilation of the lungs.

positive sign ▶ **noun** Mathematics another term for **PLUS SIGN**.

positive vetting ▶ **noun** [mass noun] Brit. a process of exhaustive inquiry into the background and character of a candidate for a Civil Service post that involves access to secret material.

positivism ▶ **noun** [mass noun] Philosophy **1** a philosophical system which holds that every rationally justifiable assertion can be scientifically verified or is capable of logical or mathematical proof, and which therefore rejects metaphysics and theism. [ORIGIN: from French *positivisme*, coined by the French philosopher Auguste **COMTE**.]
■ a humanistic religious system founded on this. ■ another term for **LOGICAL POSITIVISM**.
2 the theory that laws are to be understood as social rules, valid because they are enacted by authority or derive logically from existing decisions, and that ideal or moral considerations (e.g. that a rule is unjust) should not limit the scope or operation of the law.
– DERIVATIVES **positivist** noun & adjective, **positivistic** adjective, **positivistically** adverb.

positron /ˈpɒzɪtrɒn/ ▶ **noun** Physics a subatomic particle with the same mass as an electron and a numerically equal but positive charge.
– ORIGIN 1930s: from **POSITIVE** + **-TRON**.

Posix /ˈpɒsɪks/ ▶ **noun** [mass noun] Computing a set of formal descriptions that provide a standard for the design of operating systems, especially ones which are compatible with Unix.
– ORIGIN 1980s: from the initial letters of *portable operating system* + *-ix* suggested by **UNIX**.

posology /pəˈsɒlədʒi/ ▶ **noun** [mass noun] rare the part of medicine concerned with dosage.
– DERIVATIVES **posological** adjective.
– ORIGIN early 19th cent.: from French *posologie*, from Greek *posos* 'how much' + *-logia* (see **-LOGY**).

poss ▶ **abbreviation for** possible: *if poss* | *as soon as poss.*

posse /ˈpɒsi/ ▶ **noun** US historical a body of men summoned by a sheriff to enforce the law.
■ (also **posse comitatus** /ˌkɒmɪˈteɪtəs/) Brit. historical the body of men above the age of fifteen in a county (excluding peers, the clergy, or the infirm), whom the sheriff could summon to repress a riot or for other purposes. [ORIGIN: *comitatus* from medieval Latin, 'of the county'.] ■ informal a group of people who have a common characteristic, occupation, or purpose: *tea was handed round by* ***a posse of*** *mothers.* ■ informal a gang of black youths, especially Jamaicans, involved in (usually drug-related) crime. ■ informal a group of people who socialize together, especially to go to clubs or raves.
– ORIGIN mid 17th cent.: from medieval Latin, literally 'power', from Latin *posse* 'be able'.

possess ▶ **verb** [with obj.] **1** have as belonging to one; own: *I do not possess a television set.*
■ Law have possession of as distinct from ownership: *a two-year suspended sentence for possessing cocaine.* ■ have as an ability, quality, or characteristic: *he did not possess a sense of humour* | (**be possessed of**) *a fading blonde possessed of a powerful soprano voice.* ■ (**possess oneself of**) archaic take for one's own: *all that the plaintiffs did was to possess themselves of the securities.*
2 (usu. **be possessed**) (of a demon or spirit, especially an evil one) have complete power over (someone) and be manifested through their speech or actions: *she was possessed by the Devil.*
■ (of an emotion, idea, etc.) dominate the mind of; have an overpowering influence on: *I was possessed by a desire to tell her everything.*
3 chiefly poetic/literary have sexual intercourse with (a woman).
4 archaic maintain (oneself or one's mind or soul) in a state or condition of patience or quiet: *I tried to* ***possess*** *my soul* ***in*** *patience and to forget how hungry I was.* [ORIGIN: often with biblical allusion to Luke 21:19, the proper sense ('gain your souls') being misunderstood.]
– PHRASES **what possessed you?** used to express

surprise at an action regarded as extremely unwise: *what possessed you to come here?*

– ORIGIN late Middle English: from Old French *possesser*, from Latin *possess-* 'occupied, held', from the verb *possidere*, from *potis* 'able, capable' + *sedere* 'sit'.

possession ▶ **noun 1** [mass noun] the state of having, owning, or controlling something: *are you **in possession of** any items over £500 in value?* | *he had **taken possession of** one of the sofas* | *the book **came into my possession**.*
■Law visible power or control over something, as distinct from lawful ownership; holding or occupancy as distinct from ownership: *the landlord wishes to **gain possession of** the accommodation* | *they were imprisoned for possession of explosives.* ■ informal the state of possessing an illegal drug: *they're charged with possession.* ■ (in soccer, rugby, and other ball games) temporary control of the ball by a particular player or team: *the ball hit a defender and Brown's quick reaction put him **in possession**.*
2 (usu. **possessions**) an item of property; something belonging to one: *I was alone with no money or possessions* | *that photograph was Bert's most precious possession.*
■a territory or country controlled or governed by another: *France's former colonial possessions.*
3 [mass noun] the state of being controlled by a demon or spirit: *they said prayers to protect the people inside the hall from demonic possession.*
■the state of being completely under the influence of an idea or emotion: *fear **took possession of** my soul.*

– DERIVATIVES **possessionless** adjective.

– ORIGIN Middle English: from Old French, from Latin *possessio(n-)*, from the verb *possidere* (see **POSSESS**).

possession order ▶ **noun** chiefly Brit. an order made by a court directing that possession of a property be given to the owner or other claimant.

possessive ▶ **adjective 1** demanding someone's total attention and love: *as soon as she'd been out with a guy a few times, he'd get possessive* | *she was **possessive of** our eldest son.*
■showing a desire to own things and an unwillingness to share what one already owns: *young children are proud and **possessive of** their own property.*
2 Grammar relating to or denoting the case of nouns and pronouns expressing possession. [ORIGIN: from Latin *possessivus*, translation of Greek *ktētikē (ptōsis)* 'possessive (case)'.]
▶ **noun** Grammar a possessive word or form.
■(**the possessive**) the possessive case.

– DERIVATIVES **possessively** adverb, **possessiveness** noun.

possessive determiner ▶ **noun** Grammar a determiner indicating possession, for example *my, your, her, their.*

possessive pronoun ▶ **noun** Grammar a pronoun indicating possession, for example *mine, yours, hers, theirs.*

possessor ▶ **noun** a person who owns something or has a particular quality: *his father was the possessor of a considerable fortune.*
■Law a person who takes, occupies, or holds something without necessarily having ownership, or as distinguished from the owner.

– DERIVATIVES **possessory** adjective.

posset /ˈpɒsɪt/ ▶ **noun** historical a drink made of hot milk curdled with ale, wine, or other alcoholic liquor and typically flavoured with spices, drunk as a delicacy or as a remedy for colds.
▶ **verb** (**possetted, possetting**) [no obj.] (of a baby) regurgitate curdled milk.

– ORIGIN late Middle English: of unknown origin. The verb is first recorded in English dialect in the late 19th cent.

possibility ▶ **noun** (pl. **-ies**) a thing that may happen or be the case: *relegation remains a distinct possibility* | [with clause] *there was always the possibility that he might be turned down.*
■[mass noun] the state or fact of being likely or possible; likelihood: *there is **no possibility of** any government achieving this level of expenditure.* ■ a thing that may be chosen or done out of several possible alternatives: *one possibility is to allow all firms to participate* | *there are three possibilities for obtaining extra money.* ■ (**possibilities**) unspecified qualities of a promising nature; potential: *the house was old but it had possibilities.*

– ORIGIN late Middle English: from Old French *possibilite*, from late Latin *possibilitas*, from *possibilis* 'able to be done' (see **POSSIBLE**).

possible ▶ **adjective** able to be done; within the power or capacity of someone or something: *surely it's not **possible for** a man to live so long?* | *what are the possible alternatives?* | *contact me **as soon as possible*** | *I'd like the report this afternoon, **if possible**.*
■able to happen although not certain to; denoting a fact, event, or situation that may or may not occur or be so: *a new theory emerged about the possible cause of the plane crash* | [with clause] *it is possible that he will have to return to hospital.* ■ [attrib.] able to be or become; potential: *he was a possible future customer.* ■ [with superlative] having as much or as little of a specified quality as can be achieved: *children need the best education possible* | *the shortest possible route.* ■ [attrib.] (of a number or score) as high as is achievable in a test, competition, or game: *the team have now taken just three points from a possible twelve.*
▶ **noun** a person or thing that has the potential to become or do something, especially a potential candidate for a job or membership of a team: *I have marked five possibles with an asterisk.*
■(**the possible**) that which is likely or achievable: *they were living right at the edge of the possible.* ■ the highest possible score, especially in a shooting competition: *Mickey scored the possible.*

– ORIGIN late Middle English: from Old French, or from Latin *possibilis*, from *posse* 'be able'.

possibly ▶ **adverb 1** [sentence adverb] perhaps (used to indicate doubt or hesitancy): *he found himself alone, possibly the only surviving officer.*
■[with modal] used in polite requests: *could you possibly pour me another cup of tea?*
2 [usu. with modal] in accordance with what is likely or achievable, in particular:
■used to emphasize that one feels strongly that something is difficult, surprising, or bewildering: *what can you possibly mean?* ■ used to emphasize that someone has or will put all their effort into something: *be as noisy as you possibly can.*

possum ▶ **noun** a tree-dwelling Australasian marsupial that typically has a prehensile tail.
● Four families, especially Petauridae: many species, including the ringtails.
■N. Amer. informal an opossum.

– PHRASES **play possum 1** pretend to be asleep or unconscious when threatened. **2** feign ignorance.

– ORIGIN early 17th cent.: shortening of **OPOSSUM**.

post[1] ▶ **noun** a long, sturdy piece of timber or metal set upright in the ground and used to support something or as a marker: *follow the blue posts until the track meets a forestry road.*
■a goalpost: *Robertson, at the near post, headed wide.* ■ (**the post**) a starting post or winning post.
▶ **verb** [with obj.] (often **be posted**) display (a notice) in a public place: *a curt notice had been posted on the door* | *the exam results were **posted up**.*
■announce or publish (something, especially a financial result): *the company posted a £460,000 loss.* ■ (of a player or team) achieve or record (a particular score or result): *Smith and Lamb posted a century partnership.* ■ [with obj. and complement] publish the name of (a member of the armed forces) as missing or dead: *a whole troop had been posted missing.* ■ Computing make (information) available on the Internet. ■ put notices on or in: *we have posted all the bars.*

– PHRASES **go** (or **come**) **to post** (of a racehorse) start a race.

– ORIGIN Old English, from Latin *postis* 'doorpost', later 'rod, beam', probably reinforced in Middle English by Old French *post* 'pillar, beam' and Middle Dutch, Middle Low German *post* 'doorpost'.

▶ **post up** Basketball play in a position near the basket, along the side of the key.

post[2] ▶ **noun 1** [mass noun] chiefly Brit. the official service or system that delivers letters and parcels: *winners will be notified by post* | *the tickets are in the post.*
■letters and parcels delivered: *she was opening her post.* ■ [in sing.] a single collection or delivery of letters or parcels: *entries must be received no later than first post on Friday 14th June.* ■ used in names of newspapers: *the Washington Post.*
2 historical one of a series of couriers who carried mail on horseback between fixed stages.
■archaic a person or vehicle that carries mail.
▶ **verb 1** [with obj.] chiefly Brit. send (a letter or parcel) via the postal system: *I've just been to post a letter* | *post off your order form today.*
2 [with obj.] (in bookkeeping) enter (an item) in a ledger: *post the transaction in the second column.*
■complete (a ledger) in this way.
3 [no obj., with adverbial] historical travel with relays of horses: *we posted in an open carriage.*
■[with adverbial of direction] archaic travel with haste; hurry: *he comes posting up the street.*
▶ **adverb** archaic with haste: *come now, come post.*

– PHRASES **keep someone posted** keep someone informed of the latest developments or news.

– ORIGIN early 16th cent. (in sense 2 of the noun): from French *poste*, from Italian *posta*, from a contraction of Latin *posita*, feminine past participle of *ponere* 'to place'.

post[3] ▶ **noun 1** a position of paid employment; a job: *he resigned from the post of Foreign Minister* | *a teaching post.*
2 a place where someone is on duty or where a particular activity is carried out: *a shift worker asleep at his post* | *a customs post.*
■a place where a soldier, guard, or police officer is stationed or which they patrol: *he gave the two armed men orders not to leave their posts* | *a command post.* ■ N. Amer. a force stationed at a permanent position or camp; a garrison. ■ US a local group in an organization of military veterans.
3 historical the status or rank of full-grade captain in the Royal Navy: *Captain Miller was **made post** in 1796.*
▶ **verb** [with obj. and adverbial] (usu. **be posted**) send (someone) to a particular place to take up an appointment: *he was posted to Washington as military attaché.*
■station (someone, especially a soldier, guard, or police officer) in a particular place: *a guard was posted at the entrance.*

– ORIGIN mid 16th cent.: from French *poste*, from Italian *posto*, from a contraction of popular Latin *positum*, neuter past participle of *ponere* 'to place'.

post- ▶ **prefix** after in time or order: *post-date* | *post-operative.*

– ORIGIN from Latin *post* 'after, behind'.

postage ▶ **noun** [mass noun] the sending or conveying of letters and parcels by post: *proof of postage is required.*
■the amount required to send a letter or parcel by post: *the prices given here include postage and packing.*

postage due ▶ **noun** [mass noun] the balance of postage not prepaid.
■[count noun] a special postage stamp indicating postage still to be paid on a letter or parcel.

postage meter ▶ **noun** N. Amer. a franking machine.

postage stamp ▶ **noun** a small adhesive piece of paper of specified value issued by a national Post Office to be affixed to a letter or parcel to indicate the amount of postage paid.

postal ▶ **adjective** [attrib.] of or relating to the post: *the London postal area* | *postal services.*
■chiefly Brit. done by post: *a postal ballot* | *a postal survey.*
▶ **noun** US informal a postcard.

– DERIVATIVES **postally** adverb.

– ORIGIN mid 19th cent.: from French, from *poste* 'postal service'.

postal card ▶ **noun** US term for **POSTCARD**.

postal code ▶ **noun** another term for **POSTCODE**.

postal note ▶ **noun** Australian and NZ term for **POSTAL ORDER**.

postal order ▶ **noun** Brit. an order for payment of a specified sum to a named payee, issued by the Post Office.

postal vote ▶ **noun** a vote sent in by post rather than cast in person.

post-and-beam ▶ **adjective** (of a building or a method of construction) having or using a framework of upright and horizontal beams.

postbag ▶ **noun** British term for **MAILBAG**.

post-bellum /ˈbɛləm/ ▶ **adjective** occurring or existing after a war, in particular the American Civil War.

– ORIGIN late 19th cent.: from Latin *post* 'after' + *bellum* 'war'.

postbox ▶ **noun** a box with a slot into which post is placed for collection by the post office.
■British term for **MAILBOX**.

post captain ▶ **noun** historical a Royal Navy officer holding the full rank of captain, as opposed to a commander with the courtesy title of captain.

postcard ▶ **noun** a card for sending a message by post without an envelope, typically having a photograph or other illustration on one side.

post-chaise /(t)ʃeɪz/ ▶ **noun** (pl. **post-chaises**

pronunc. same) historical a horse-drawn carriage used for transporting passengers or mail, especially in the 18th and early 19th centuries.
– ORIGIN late 17th cent.: from **POST**[2] + **CHAISE** in the sense 'horse-drawn carriage'.

post-classical ▶ **adjective** of or relating to a time after the classical period of any language, art, or culture, in particular the classical period of ancient Greek and Latin culture.

postcode ▶ **noun** Brit. a group of numbers or letters and numbers which are added to a postal address to assist the sorting of mail.
– DERIVATIVES **postcoded** adjective.

post-coital ▶ **adjective** occurring or done after sexual intercourse: *post-coital contraception.*
– DERIVATIVES **post-coitally** adverb.

post-date ▶ **verb** [with obj.] **1** [usu. as adj. **post-dated**] affix or assign a date later than the actual one to (a document or event): *a post-dated cheque.*
2 occur or come at a later date than: *Stonehenge was presumed to post-date these structures.*

postdoc ▶ **noun** informal a person engaged in postdoctoral research.
■ [mass noun] postdoctoral research.

postdoctoral ▶ **adjective** of, relating to, or denoting research undertaken after the completion of doctoral research: *a postdoctoral fellowship.*

poster ▶ **noun 1** a large printed picture used for decoration.
■ a large printed picture, notice, or advertisement displayed in a public place: [as modifier] *a poster campaign.*
2 Computing someone who sends a message to a newsgroup.

poste restante /pəʊst ˈrɛst(ə)nt/ ▶ **noun** Brit. written on a letter as an indication that it should be kept at a specified post office until collected by the addressee.
■ the department in a post office keeping such letters.
– ORIGIN mid 18th cent.: from French, literally 'mail remaining'.

posterior ▶ **adjective 1** technical, chiefly Anatomy further back in position; of or nearer the rear or hind end, especially of the body or a part of it: *the posterior part of the gut | a basal body situated just* **posterior to** *the nucleus.* The opposite of **ANTERIOR**.
■ Medicine relating to or denoting presentation of a fetus in which the rear or caudal end is nearest the cervix and emerges first at birth: *a posterior labour.*
2 formal coming after in time or order; later: *a date posterior to the first Reform Bill.*
▶ **noun** humorous a person's buttocks.
– DERIVATIVES **posteriority** noun, **posteriorly** adverb.
– ORIGIN early 16th cent. (as a plural noun denoting descendants): from Latin, comparative of *posterus* 'following', from *post* 'after'.

posterior probability ▶ **noun** the statistical probability that a hypothesis is true calculated in the light of relevant observations.

posterity ▶ **noun** [mass noun] all future generations of people: *the victims' names are recorded for posterity.*
■ [in sing.] archaic the descendants of a person: *God offered Abraham a posterity like the stars of heaven.*
– ORIGIN late Middle English: from Old French *posterite*, from Latin *posteritas*, from *posterus* 'following'.

posterize /ˈpəʊstərʌɪz/ (also **posterise**) ▶ **verb** [with obj.] print or display (a photograph or other image) using only a small number of different tones.
– DERIVATIVES **posterization** noun.

postern /ˈpɒst(ə)n, ˈpəʊst-/ ▶ **noun** a back or side entrance: [as modifier] *a small postern door.*
– ORIGIN Middle English: from Old French *posterne*, alteration of *posterle*, from late Latin *posterula*, diminutive of *posterus* 'following'.

poster paint ▶ **noun** [mass noun] an opaque paint with a water-soluble binder, used for posters and children's paintings.

post exchange (abbrev.: **PX**) ▶ **noun** a shop at a US military camp, selling food, clothing, and other items.

postface ▶ **noun** a brief explanatory comment or note at the end of a book or other piece of writing.

post-feminist ▶ **adjective** coming after the feminism of the 1960s and subsequent decades, in particular moving beyond or rejecting some of the ideas of feminism as out of date.
▶ **noun** a person who rejects some feminist ideas for this reason.
– DERIVATIVES **post-feminism** noun.

postfix ▶ **verb** [with obj.] (usu. **be postfixed**) Biology treat (a biological substance or specimen) with a second fixative.

post-Fordism ▶ **noun** [mass noun] the theory that modern industrial production should change from the large-scale mass-production methods pioneered by Henry Ford towards the use of small flexible manufacturing units.
– DERIVATIVES **post-Fordist** noun & adjective.

post-free ▶ **adjective** & **adverb** Brit. carried by post free of charge to the customer.

postfrontal ▶ **noun** Zoology a bone behind the orbit of the eye in some vertebrates.

postglacial ▶ **adjective** Geology of or relating to the period since the last (Weichsel or Devensian) glaciation, from the sudden rise in temperature that marks the beginning of the Flandrian about 10,000 years ago. Compare with **LATE-GLACIAL**.
■ [as noun **the postglacial**] the postglacial period.

postgrad ▶ **adjective** & **noun** informal short for **POSTGRADUATE**.

postgraduate ▶ **adjective** of, relating to, or denoting a course of study undertaken after completing a first degree: *a postgraduate degree.*
▶ **noun** a student engaged in such a course of study.

post-haste ▶ **adverb** with great speed or immediacy: *she would go post-haste to England.*
– ORIGIN mid 16th cent.: from the direction 'haste, post, haste', formerly given on letters.

post hoc /ˈhɒk/ ▶ **adjective** occurring or done after the event, especially with reference to the fallacious assumption that the occurrence or action in question has a logical relationship with the event it follows: *this rhetoric offers a post hoc justification for the changes.*
▶ **adverb** after the event.
– ORIGIN Latin, literally 'after this'.

post horn ▶ **noun** historical a valveless horn used to signal the arrival or departure of a mounted courier or mail coach.

posthumous /ˈpɒstjʊməs/ ▶ **adjective** occurring, awarded, or appearing after the death of the originator: *he was awarded a posthumous Military Cross | a posthumous collection of his articles.*
■ (of a child) born after the death of its father.
– DERIVATIVES **posthumously** adverb.
– ORIGIN early 17th cent.: from Latin *postumus* 'last' (superlative from *post* 'after'), in late Latin spelled *posth-* by association with *humus* 'ground'.

posthypnotic ▶ **adjective** relating to or denoting the giving of ideas or instructions to a subject under hypnosis that are intended to affect behaviour after the hypnotic trance ends: *posthypnotic suggestion.*

postie ▶ **noun** Brit. informal a postman or postwoman.
– ORIGIN late 19th cent.: abbreviation.

postil /ˈpɒstɪl/ ▶ **noun** archaic a marginal note or comment, especially on a biblical text.
■ a commentary, homily, or book of homilies.
– ORIGIN late Middle English: from Old French *postille*, from medieval Latin *postilla*, perhaps from Latin *post illa (verba)* 'after those words', written as a direction to a scribe.

postilion /pɒˈstɪlɪən/ (also **postillion**) ▶ **noun** a person who rides the leading nearside (left-hand side) horse of a team or pair drawing a coach or carriage, especially when there is no coachman.
– ORIGIN mid 16th cent. (in the sense 'forerunner acting as guide to the post-horse rider'): from French *postillon*, from Italian *postiglione* 'post-boy', from *posta* (see **POST**[2]).

post-Impressionism ▶ **noun** [mass noun] the work or style of a varied group of late 19th-century and early 20th-century artists including Van Gogh, Gauguin, and Cézanne. They reacted against the naturalism of the Impressionists to explore colour, line, and form, and the emotional response of the artist, a concern which led to the development of expressionism.
– DERIVATIVES **post-Impressionist** noun & adjective, **post-Impressionistic** adjective.

post-industrial ▶ **adjective** of or relating to an economy which no longer relies on heavy industry: *a post-industrial society.*
– DERIVATIVES **post-industrialism** noun.

posting ▶ **noun** chiefly Brit. an appointment to a job, especially one abroad or in the armed forces: *he requested a posting to Japan | an overseas posting.*
■ the location of such an appointment: *Norway was an attractive posting because of its quality of life.*

Post-it (also **Post-it note**) ▶ **noun** trademark a piece of paper with an adhesive strip on one side, designed to be stuck prominently to an object or surface and easily removed when necessary.

postlapsarian /ˌpəʊstlapˈsɛːrɪən/ ▶ **adjective** Theology or poetic/literary occurring or existing after the Fall of Man.
– ORIGIN mid 18th cent.: from **POST-** 'occurring after', on the pattern of *sublapsarian.*

postlude ▶ **noun** Music a concluding piece of music.
■ a written or spoken epilogue; an afterword.
– ORIGIN mid 19th cent.: from **POST-** 'later, after', on the pattern of *prelude.*

postman ▶ **noun** (pl. **-men**) Brit. a person who is employed to deliver or collect letters and parcels.

postman's knock ▶ **noun** Brit. a game, played especially by children, in which imaginary letters are delivered in exchange for kisses.

postmark ▶ **noun** an official mark stamped on a letter or other postal package, giving the place, date, and time of posting, and serving to cancel the postage stamp: *the package had a York postmark.*
▶ **verb** [with obj.] (usu. **be postmarked**) stamp (a letter or other postal package) officially with such a mark: [with obj. and complement] *the letter was postmarked New York.*

postmaster ▶ **noun** a man in charge of a post office.

postmaster general ▶ **noun** the head of a country's postal service (abolished in the UK as an office in 1969).

post-matric ▶ **noun** (in South Africa) a thirteenth year of schooling, after the school-leaving examination has been taken: [as modifier] *post-matric courses.*
■ (also **post-matriculant**) a student in this year.

post mill ▶ **noun** chiefly historical a windmill supported by a post on which it pivots to catch the wind.

postmillennial /ˌpəʊs(t)mɪˈlɛnɪəl/ ▶ **adjective** (especially in Christian doctrine) following the millennium.

postmillennialism ▶ **noun** [mass noun] (among fundamentalist Christians) the doctrine that the Second Coming of Christ will be the culmination of the prophesied millennium of blessedness.
– DERIVATIVES **postmillennialist** noun.

postmistress ▶ **noun** a woman in charge of a post office.

postmodernism ▶ **noun** [mass noun] a late 20th-century style and concept in the arts, architecture, and criticism, which represents a departure from modernism and has at its heart a general distrust of grand theories and ideologies as well as a problematical relationship with any notion of 'art'.

> Typical features include a deliberate mixing of different artistic styles and media, the self-conscious use of earlier styles and conventions, and often the incorporation of images relating to the consumerism and mass communication of late 20th-century post-industrial society. Postmodernist architecture was pioneered by Robert Venturi; the AT&T skyscraper in New York (completed in 1984) is a prime example of the style. Influential literary critics include Jean Baudrillard and Jean-François Lyotard.

– DERIVATIVES **postmodern** adjective, **postmodernist** noun & adjective, **postmodernity** noun.

postmodify ▶ **verb** (**-modifies**, **-modified**) [with obj.] Grammar modify the sense of (a noun or other word) by being placed after it.
– DERIVATIVES **postmodification** noun, **postmodifier** noun.

post-mortem ▶ **noun** (also **post-mortem examination**) an examination of a dead body to determine the cause of death.
■ an analysis or discussion of an event held soon after it has occurred, especially in order to determine why it was a failure: *an election post-mortem on why the party lost.*
▶ **adjective** [attrib.] of or relating to a post-mortem: *a post-mortem report.*
■ happening after death: *post-mortem changes in his body* | [as adv.] *assessment of morphology in nerves taken post-mortem.*
– ORIGIN mid 18th cent.: from Latin, literally 'after death'.

p

postmultiply ▶ verb (-ies, -ied) [with obj.] Mathematics multiply (a vector, matrix, or element of a group) non-commutatively by a following factor.
– DERIVATIVES **postmultiplication** noun.

post-natal ▶ adjective of, relating to, characteristic of, or denoting the period after childbirth: *post-natal care*.
– DERIVATIVES **post-natally** adverb.

post-natal depression ▶ noun [mass noun] depression suffered by a mother following childbirth, typically arising from the combination of hormonal changes, psychological adjustment to motherhood, and fatigue.

postnuptial ▶ adjective occurring in or relating to the period after marriage.
■ Zoology occurring in or relating to the period after the mating season of an animal.

post-obit ▶ adjective archaic taking effect after death.
– ORIGIN mid 18th cent.: from Latin *post obitum*, from *post* 'after' + *obitus* 'decease' (from *obire* 'to die').

post office ▶ noun 1 the public department or corporation responsible for postal services and (in some countries) telecommunications.
■ a building where postal business is carried on.
2 US term for **POSTMAN'S KNOCK**.

post office box ▶ noun a numbered box in a post office assigned to a person or organization, where letters for them are kept until called for.

post-op ▶ abbreviation for post-operative.

post-operative ▶ adjective during, relating to, or denoting the period following a surgical operation: *post-operative care*.

postorbital chiefly Zoology ▶ adjective [attrib.] situated at the back of the orbit or eye socket, in particular denoting a process of the frontal bone which in some reptiles forms a separate bone.
▶ noun a postorbital bone.

post-paid ▶ adjective & adverb (with reference to a letter or parcel) on which postage has already been paid: [as adj.] *use the post-paid envelope provided*.

post-partum /ˈpɑːtəm/ ▶ adjective Medicine & Veterinary Medicine following childbirth or the birth of young.
– ORIGIN mid 19th cent.: from Latin *post partum* 'after childbirth'.

postpone ▶ verb [with obj.] cause or arrange for (something) to take place at a time later than that first scheduled: *the visit had to be postponed for some time* | [with present participle] *he postponed implementing the scheme until industry and business were consulted*.
– DERIVATIVES **postponable** adjective, **postponement** noun, **postponer** noun.
– ORIGIN late 15th cent.: from Latin *postponere*, from *post* 'after' + *ponere* 'to place'.

postpose ▶ verb [with obj.] Grammar place (a modifying word or morpheme) after the word that it modifies.
– ORIGIN late 16th cent. (in the sense 'place later or lower'): from French *postposer*, from *post-* 'after' + *poser* 'to place'. The current sense dates from the 1920s.

postposition ▶ noun Grammar a word or morpheme placed after the word it governs, for example *-ward* in *homeward*.
– DERIVATIVES **postpositional** adjective.
– ORIGIN mid 19th cent.: from **PREPOSITION**, by substitution of the prefix **POST-** for *pre-*.

postpositive ▶ adjective (of a word) placed after or as a suffix on the word that it relates to.
▶ noun a postpositive word.
– DERIVATIVES **postpositively** adverb.

postprandial ▶ adjective formal or humorous during or relating to the period after dinner or lunch: *we were jolted from our postprandial torpor*.
■ Medicine occurring after a meal.
– ORIGIN early 19th cent.: from **POST-** 'after' + Latin *prandium* 'a meal' + **-AL**.

post-production ▶ noun [mass noun] [often as modifier] work done on a film or recording after filming or recording has taken place: *post-production editing*.

post room ▶ noun Brit. the department of a company that deals with incoming and outgoing mail.

postscript ▶ noun an additional remark at the end of a letter, after the signature and introduced by 'PS': *he added a postscript: 'Leaving tomorrow'*.
■ an additional statement or action which provides further information on or a sequel to something: *as a postscript to this, Paul did finally marry*.

– ORIGIN mid 16th cent.: from Latin *postscriptum*, neuter past participle (used as a noun) of *postscribere* 'write under, add', from *post* 'after, later' + *scribere* 'write'.

postseason ▶ adjective chiefly N. Amer. (of a sporting fixture or other event) taking place after the end of the regular season.
▶ noun the period following the regular season.
■ a game or competition held during this period.

post-structuralism ▶ noun [mass noun] an extension and critique of structuralism, especially as used in critical textual analysis.

Emerging in French intellectual life in the late 1960s and early 1970s, post-structuralism embraced Jacques Derrida's deconstructionism and the later work of Roland Barthes, the psychoanalytic theories of Jacques Lacan and Julia Kristeva (b.1941), the historical critiques of Michel Foucault, and the writings of Jean-François Lyotard and Jean Baudrillard. It departed from the claims to objectivity and comprehensiveness made by structuralism and emphasized instead plurality and deferral of meaning, rejecting the fixed binary oppositions of structuralism and the validity of authorial authority.

– DERIVATIVES **post-structural** adjective, **post-structuralist** noun & adjective.

post-synch ▶ verb [with obj.] add a sound recording to (film or video footage) at a later time.

post-tax ▶ adjective (of income or profits) remaining after the deduction of taxes.

post-tension ▶ verb [with obj.] strengthen (reinforced concrete) by applying tension to the reinforcing rods after the concrete has set.

post town ▶ noun Brit. a town having a main branch of the Post Office or its own postcode.

post-traumatic stress disorder ▶ noun [mass noun] Medicine a condition of persistent mental and emotional stress occurring as a result of injury or severe psychological shock, typically involving disturbance of sleep and constant vivid recall of the experience, with dulled responses to others and to the outside world.

postulant /ˈpɒstjʊl(ə)nt/ ▶ noun a candidate, especially one seeking admission into a religious order.
– ORIGIN mid 18th cent.: from French *postulant* or Latin *postulant-* 'asking', from the verb *postulare* (see **POSTULATE**).

postulate ▶ verb /ˈpɒstjʊleɪt/ [with obj.] 1 suggest or assume the existence, fact, or truth of (something) as a basis for reasoning, discussion, or belief: *his theory postulated a rotatory movement for hurricanes* | [with clause] *he postulated that the environmentalists might have a case*.
2 (in ecclesiastical law) nominate or elect (someone) to an ecclesiastical office subject to the sanction of a higher authority.
▶ noun /ˈpɒstjʊlət/ formal a thing suggested or assumed as true as the basis for reasoning, discussion, or belief: *perhaps the postulate of Babylonian influence on Greek astronomy is incorrect*.
■ Mathematics an assumption used as a basis for mathematical reasoning.
– DERIVATIVES **postulation** noun.
– ORIGIN late Middle English (in sense 2): from Latin *postulat-* 'asked', from the verb *postulare*.

postulator ▶ noun 1 a person who postulates something.
2 a person who presents a case for the canonization or beatification of someone in the Roman Catholic Church.

posture ▶ noun a position of a person's body when standing or sitting: *he stood in a flamboyant posture with his hands on his hips* | [mass noun] *good posture will protect your spine*.
■ Zoology a particular pose adopted by a bird or other animal, interpreted as a signal of a specific pattern of behaviour. ■ figurative a particular way of dealing with or considering something; an approach or attitude: *trade unions adopted a more militant posture in wage negotiations*. ■ figurative a particular way of behaving that is intended to convey a false impression; a pose: *despite pulling back its missiles, the government maintained a defiant posture for home consumption*.
▶ verb 1 [no obj.] [often as noun **posturing**] behave in a way that is intended to impress or mislead others: *a masking of fear with macho posturing*.
■ [with obj.] adopt (a certain attitude) so as to impress or mislead: *the companies may posture regret, but they have a vested interest in increasing Third World sales*.
2 [with obj. and adverbial] archaic place (someone) in a

particular attitude or pose: *and still these two were postured motionless*.
– DERIVATIVES **postural** adjective, **posturer** noun.
– ORIGIN late 16th cent. (denoting the relative position of one thing to another): from French, from Italian *postura*, from Latin *positura* 'position', from *posit-* 'placed', from the verb *ponere*.

postviral syndrome (also **postviral fatigue syndrome**) ▶ noun [mass noun] myalgic encephalomyelitis following a viral infection.

postvocalic ▶ adjective (of a speech sound) occurring immediately after a vowel.

post-war ▶ adjective occurring or existing after a war (especially the Second World War): *post-war Britain* | *post-war reconstruction*.

postwoman ▶ noun (pl. -women) a woman who is employed to deliver or collect letters and parcels.

posy[1] ▶ noun (pl. -ies) 1 a small bunch of flowers.
2 archaic a short motto or line of verse inscribed inside a ring.
– ORIGIN late Middle English (in sense 2): contraction of **POESY**.

posy[2] ▶ adjective variant spelling of **POSEY**.

pot[1] ▶ noun 1 a container, typically rounded or cylindrical and of ceramic ware or metal, used for storage or cooking: *clay pots for keeping water cool in summer* | *a cooking pot*.
■ short for **TEAPOT**, **FLOWERPOT**, and **CHAMBER POT**. ■ a container for holding drink, especially beer. ■ the contents of any of such containers: *a pot of coffee*.
2 (**the pot**) the total sum of the bets made on a round in poker, brag, etc.: *Jim raked in half the pot*.
■ all the money contributed by a group of people for a particular purpose: *in insurance, everybody puts money into the pot used to pay claims*.
3 informal a prize in a sporting contest, especially a silver cup.
4 informal a pot belly.
5 informal an engine cylinder.
6 Billiards & Snooker a shot in which a player strikes a ball into a pocket.
▶ verb (**potted**, **potting**) [with obj.] 1 plant in a flowerpot: *pot individual cuttings as soon as you see new young leaves*.
■ (**pot a plant on**) transplant a plant from a smaller flowerpot to a larger one. ■ (**pot a plant up**) transplant a seedling into a flowerpot.
2 preserve (food, especially meat or fish) in a sealed pot or jar: *venison can be potted in the same way as tongue*.
3 Billiards & Snooker strike (a ball) into a pocket: *he failed to pot a red at close range*.
4 informal hit or kill (someone or something) by shooting: *he was shot in the eye as neighbours potted clay pigeons*.
■ informal succeed in obtaining (something desirable); win: *do you fancy potting a fine trophy?*
5 (often **be potted**) Brit. sit (a young child) on a chamber pot.
6 [no obj.] make articles from earthenware or baked clay: *why not paint or pot in the sun this winter?*
7 encapsulate (an electrical component or circuit) in a liquid insulating material, typically a synthetic resin, which sets solid.
– PHRASES **for the pot** for food or cooking: *at the age of fifteen weeks the snails are ready for the pot*. **go to pot** informal deteriorate through neglect: *the foundry was allowed to go to pot in the seventies*. **the pot calling the kettle black** used to convey that the criticisms a person is aiming at someone else could equally well apply to themselves. **pot of gold** see **GOLD**. **pots of money** informal a very large amount of money. **put someone's pot on** Austral./NZ informal inform on a person. **shit** (or **piss**) **or get off the pot** vulgar slang used to convey that someone should stop wasting time and get on with something. **a watched pot never boils** proverb time seems to drag endlessly when you're waiting anxiously for something to happen.
– DERIVATIVES **potful** noun (pl. -fuls).
– ORIGIN late Old English *pott*, probably reinforced in Middle English by Old French *pot*; of unknown ultimate origin (compare with late Latin *potus* 'drinking cup'). Current senses of the verb date from the early 17th cent.

pot[2] ▶ noun [mass noun] informal cannabis.
– ORIGIN 1930s: probably from Mexican Spanish *potiguaya* 'cannabis leaves'.

pot[3] ▶ noun (chiefly in rugby) an attempt to score a goal with a kick.

▶verb (**potted**, **potting**) [with obj.] score (a goal).
– ORIGIN 1950s: abbreviation of **POTSHOT**.

pot⁴ ▶noun short for **POTENTIOMETER** (in sense 2).

potable /ˈpəʊtəb(ə)l/ ▶adjective formal safe to drink; drinkable: there is no supply of potable water available.
– DERIVATIVES **potability** noun.
– ORIGIN late Middle English: from French potable, from late Latin potabilis, from Latin potare 'to drink'.

potage /pɒˈtɑːʒ/ ▶noun [mass noun] thick soup.
– ORIGIN mid 16th cent.: from French. Compare with **POTTAGE**.

potager /ˈpɒtədʒə/ ▶noun a kitchen garden.
– ORIGIN mid 17th cent.: from French jardin potager 'garden providing vegetables for the pot'.

potamology /ˌpɒtəˈmɒlədʒi/ ▶noun [mass noun] Geography the study of rivers.
– ORIGIN early 19th cent.: from Greek potamos 'river' + -LOGY.

potash ▶noun [mass noun] an alkaline potassium compound, especially potassium carbonate or hydroxide.
– ORIGIN early 17th cent.: from pot-ashes, from obsolete Dutch potasschen, originally obtained by leaching vegetable ashes and evaporating the solution in iron pots.

potash alum ▶noun see **ALUM**.

potassium /pəˈtasɪəm/ ▶noun [mass noun] the chemical element of atomic number 19, a soft silvery-white reactive metal of the alkali-metal group. (Symbol: **K**)
– DERIVATIVES **potassic** adjective (Mineralogy).
– ORIGIN early 19th cent.: from **POTASH** (earlier potass, from French potasse) + -IUM.

potassium–argon dating ▶noun [mass noun] Geology a method of dating rocks from the relative proportions of radioactive potassium-40 and its decay product, argon-40.

potassium hydroxide ▶noun [mass noun] a strongly alkaline white deliquescent compound used in many industrial processes, e.g. soap manufacture.
● Chem. formula: KOH.

potassium nitrate ▶noun [mass noun] a white crystalline salt which occurs naturally in nitre and is used in preserving meat and as a constituent of gunpowder.
● Chem. formula: KNO_3.

potation /pəʊˈteɪʃ(ə)n/ ▶noun archaic or humorous a drink.
■ [mass noun] the action of drinking something, especially alcohol: you did rather abstain from potation. ■ (often **potations**) a drinking bout.
– ORIGIN late Middle English: from Old French, from Latin potatio(n-), from potare 'to drink'.

potato ▶noun 1 a starchy plant tuber which is one of the most important food crops, cooked and eaten as a vegetable: roasted potatoes | [mass noun] mashed potato | [as modifier] leek and potato soup.
2 the plant of the nightshade family which produces these tubers on underground runners.
● Solanum tuberosum, family Solanaceae. It was first cultivated in the Andes about 1,800 years ago and was introduced to Europe in c.1570.
3 Brit. informal a large hole in a sock or stocking, especially one in the heel.
– ORIGIN mid 16th cent.: from Spanish patata, variant of Taino batata 'sweet potato'. The English word originally denoted the sweet potato and gained its current sense in the late 16th cent.

potato blight ▶noun [mass noun] a destructive fungal disease of potatoes resulting in dry brown rot of the tubers.
● **Early blight** is caused by Alternaria solani (subdivision Deuteromycotina), and **late blight** is caused by Phytophthora infestans (subdivision Mastigomycotina).

potato chip ▶noun see **CHIP** (sense 2).

potato crisp ▶noun see **CRISP**.

potato pancake ▶noun a small flat cake of grated potatoes mixed with flour and egg and fried.

potato salad ▶noun [mass noun] a side dish consisting of cold cooked potato chopped and mixed with mayonnaise and seasonings.

potato vine ▶noun a semi-evergreen climbing plant with pale blue or white flowers, related to the potato and native to South and Central America.
● Solanum jasminoides, family Solanaceae.

pot-au-feu /ˌpɒtəʊˈfəː/ ▶noun a French soup of meat, typically boiled beef, and vegetables cooked in a large pot.
– ORIGIN French, literally 'pot on the fire'.

Potawatomi /ˌpɒtəˈwɒtəmi/ ▶noun (pl. same or **Potawatomis**) 1 a member of an American Indian people inhabiting the Great Lakes region, principally in Michigan and Wisconsin.
2 [mass noun] the Algonquian language of this people, now with few speakers.
▶adjective of or relating to this people or their language.
– ORIGIN the name in Ojibwa.

pot-bellied stove ▶noun a small bulbous-sided wood-burning stove.

pot belly ▶noun a large, protruding, rotund stomach.
– DERIVATIVES **pot-bellied** adjective.

potboiler ▶noun informal a book, painting, or recording produced merely to make the writer or artist a living by catering to popular taste.

pot-bound ▶adjective (of a plant) having roots which fill the flowerpot, leaving no room for them to expand.

potch (also **potch opal**) ▶noun [mass noun] opal which has no play of colour and is of no value.
– ORIGIN late 19th cent.: of unknown origin.

pot cheese ▶noun [mass noun] US a coarse type of cottage cheese.

poteen /pɒˈtiːn/ (also **potheen**) ▶noun [mass noun] chiefly Irish alcohol made illicitly, typically from potatoes.
– ORIGIN early 19th cent.: from Irish (fuisce) poitín 'little pot (of whiskey)', diminutive of pota 'pot'.

Potemkin¹ /pəˈtɛmkɪn/ a battleship whose crew mutinied in the Russian Revolution of 1905 when in the Black Sea, bombarding Odessa before seeking asylum in Romania. The incident persuaded the tsar to agree to a measure of reform.

Potemkin² /pəˈtɛmkɪn/ ▶adjective informal having a false or deceptive appearance, especially one presented for the purpose of propaganda: it is a Potemkin party; there is little behind the impressive parliamentary group seen on television.
– ORIGIN 1930s: from Grigori Aleksandrovich Potyomkin (often transliterated Potemkin), a favourite of Empress Catherine II of Russia, who reputedly gave the order for sham villages to be built for the empress's tour of the Crimea in 1787.

potency ▶noun (pl. **-ies**) [mass noun] 1 power or influence: a myth of enormous potency | the unexpected potency of the rum punch.
■ [count noun] (in homeopathy) the number of times a remedy has been diluted and succussed, taken as a measure of the strength of the effect it will produce: she was given a low potency twice daily. ■ Genetics the extent of the contribution of an allele towards the production of a phenotypic characteristic. ■ Biology a capacity in embryonic tissue for developing into a particular specialized tissue or organ.
2 a male's ability to achieve an erection or to reach orgasm: the myth of declining sexual potency with increasing age.

potent¹ ▶adjective 1 having great power, influence, or effect: thrones were potent symbols of authority | a potent drug | a potent argument.
2 (of a male) able to achieve an erection or to reach an orgasm.
– DERIVATIVES **potence** noun, **potently** adverb.
– ORIGIN late Middle English: from Latin potent- 'being powerful, being able', from the verb posse.

potent² Heraldry ▶adjective [postpositive] 1 formed of crutch-shaped pieces; (especially of a cross) having a straight bar across the end of each extremity.
2 of the fur called potent (as a tincture).
▶noun [mass noun] fur resembling vair, but with the alternating pieces T-shaped.
– ORIGIN late Middle English (denoting a crutch): alteration of Old French potence 'crutch', from Latin potentia 'power' (in medieval Latin 'crutch'), from potent- (see **POTENT¹**).

potentate ▶noun a monarch or ruler, especially an autocratic one.
– ORIGIN late Middle English: from Latin potentatus 'dominion', from potent- 'being able or powerful' (see **POTENT¹**).

potential ▶adjective [attrib.] having or showing the capacity to become or develop into something in the future: a two-pronged campaign to woo potential customers.
▶noun 1 [mass noun] latent qualities or abilities that may be developed and lead to future success or usefulness: a young broadcaster with great potential | [count noun] the potentials of the technology were never wholly controllable.
■ (often **potential for/to do something**) the possibility of something happening or of someone doing something in the future: the crane operator's clear view reduces the potential for accidents | pesticides with the potential to cause cancer.
2 Physics the quantity determining the energy of mass in a gravitational field or of charge in an electric field.
– DERIVATIVES **potentiality** noun, **potentialize** (also -**ise**) verb, **potentially** adverb [as submodifier] potentially dangerous products.
– ORIGIN late Middle English: from late Latin potentialis, from potentia 'power', from potent- 'being able' (see **POTENT¹**). The noun dates from the early 19th cent.

potential barrier ▶noun Physics a region within a force field in which the potential is significantly higher than at points either side of it, so that a particle requires energy to pass through it.

potential difference ▶noun Physics the difference of electrical potential between two points.

potential divider ▶noun another term for **VOLTAGE DIVIDER**.

potential energy ▶noun [mass noun] Physics the energy possessed by a body by virtue of its position relative to others, stresses within itself, electric charge, and other factors. Compare with **KINETIC ENERGY**.

potential well ▶noun Physics a region in a field of force, in particular the region in which an atomic nucleus is situated, in which the potential is significantly lower than at points immediately outside it, so that a particle in it is likely to remain there unless it gains a relatively large amount of energy.

potentiate /pə(ʊ)ˈtɛnʃɪeɪt/ ▶verb [with obj.] technical increase the power, effect, or likelihood of (something, especially a drug or physiological reaction): the glucose will potentiate intestinal absorption of sodium.
– ORIGIN early 19th cent.: from **POTENT¹**, on the pattern of substantiate.

potentiation ▶noun [mass noun] Physiology the increase in strength of nerve impulses along pathways which have been used previously, either short-term or long-term.

potentilla /ˌpəʊt(ə)nˈtɪlə/ ▶noun a plant of a genus that includes the cinquefoils, especially (in gardening) a small shrub with yellow or red flowers.
● Genus Potentilla, family Rosaceae: many species.
– ORIGIN modern Latin, based on Latin potent- 'being powerful' (with reference to its herbal qualities) + the diminutive suffix -illa.

potentiometer /pə(ʊ)ˌtɛnʃɪˈɒmɪtə/ ▶noun 1 an instrument for measuring an electromotive force by balancing it against the potential difference produced by passing a known current through a known variable resistance.
2 a variable resistor with a third adjustable terminal. The potential at the third terminal can be adjusted to give any fraction of the potential across the ends of the resistor.

potentiometry ▶noun [mass noun] Chemistry the measurement of electrical potential as a technique in chemical analysis.
– DERIVATIVES **potentiometric** adjective.

potentize (also -**ise**) ▶verb [with obj.] rare make stronger or more potent.
■ make (a homeopathic medicine) more powerful by diluting and shaking it.
– DERIVATIVES **potentization** noun.

Potenza /pəˈtɛnzə/ a market town in southern Italy, capital of Basilicata region; pop. 68,500 (1990).

pothead ▶noun informal a person who smokes cannabis.

potheen /pɒˈtʃiːn/ ▶noun chiefly Irish variant spelling of **POTEEN**.

pother /ˈpɒðə/ ▶noun [in sing.] poetic/literary a commotion or fuss: what a pother you make!
– ORIGIN late 16th cent.: of unknown origin.

pot-herb ▶noun any herb grown for culinary use.

pot holder ▶ **noun** N. Amer. a piece of quilted or thick fabric for handling hot dishes and pans.

pothole ▶ **noun** a deep natural underground cave formed by the erosion of rock, especially by the action of water.
■ a deep circular hole in a river bed formed by the erosion of the rock by the rotation of stones in an eddy. ■ a depression or hollow in a road surface caused by wear or subsidence. ■ (also **pothole lake**) N. Amer. a pond formed by a natural hollow in the ground in which water has collected.
▶ **verb** [no obj.] [often as noun **potholing**] Brit. explore underground potholes as a pastime: *they went potholing in the Pennines.*
– DERIVATIVES **potholed** adjective, **potholer** noun.
– ORIGIN early 19th cent.: from Middle English *pot* 'pit' (perhaps of Scandinavian origin) + **HOLE**.

pot-hook ▶ **noun** **1** chiefly historical a hook used for hanging a pot over a hearth or for lifting a hot pot. **2** dated a curved stroke in handwriting, especially as made by children learning to write.

pot-house ▶ **noun** dated a small tavern.

pot-hunter ▶ **noun** chiefly archaic a person who hunts solely to achieve a kill, rather than as a sport.
■ a person who takes part in a contest merely for the sake of the prize.

potion ▶ **noun** a liquid with healing, magical, or poisonous properties: *a love potion.*
– ORIGIN Middle English: from Old French, from Latin *potio(n-)* 'drink, poisonous draught', related to *potare* 'to drink'.

Potiphar /'pɒtɪfə/ (in the Bible) an Egyptian officer whose wife tried to seduce Joseph and then falsely accused him of attempting to rape her (Gen. 39).

potjie /'pɔɪki, 'pʊɪki/ ▶ **noun** (pl. **-ies**) S. African a lidded, almost spherical, cast-iron pot for use over an open fire.
■ (also **potjiekos**) [mass noun] a stew cooked in such a pot: *the seafood potjie was a winner.*
– ORIGIN Afrikaans, literally 'little pot'.

potlatch ▶ **noun** (among North American Indian peoples of the northwest coast) an opulent ceremonial feast at which possessions are given away or destroyed to display wealth or enhance prestige.
▶ **verb** [no obj.] hold such a feast or ceremony.
– ORIGIN Chinook Jargon, from Nootka *p'ačitl* 'make a gift at a potlatch'.

pot liquor ▶ **noun** [mass noun] chiefly US liquor in which meat, fish, or vegetables have been boiled; stock.

pot luck ▶ **noun** used in reference to a situation in which one must take a chance that whatever is available will prove to be good or acceptable: *he could* **take pot luck** *in a town not noted for its restaurants.*
■ (usu. **potluck**) a meal or party to which each of the guests contributes a dish: [as modifier] *a potluck supper.*

potman ▶ **noun** (pl. **-men** /'pɒtmɛn/) dated a man who serves drinks in a public house or bar.

Potomac /pə'təʊmək/ a river of the eastern US, which rises in the Appalachian Mountains in West Virginia and flows about 459 km (285 miles) through Washington DC into Chesapeake Bay on the Atlantic coast.

potoo /pə'tu:/ ▶ **noun** a nocturnal insectivorous bird resembling a large nightjar, which mimics a dead branch when alarmed and is found in tropical America.
● Genus *Nyctibius* and family Nyctibiidae: five species, in particular the **common potoo** (*N. griseus*).
– ORIGIN mid 19th cent.: from Jamaican creole, from Twi, of imitative origin.

potoroo /ˌpɒtə'ru:/ ▶ **noun** a small nocturnal rat-kangaroo with long hindlimbs and typically a hopping gait, native to Australia.
● Genus *Potorous*, family Potoroidae: three species.
– ORIGIN late 18th cent.: probably from Dharuk *badaru*.

Potosí /ˌpɒtəʊ'si:/ a city in southern Bolivia; pop. 112,290 (1992). Situated at an altitude of about 4,205 m (13,780 ft), it is one of the highest cities in the world.

pot pie ▶ **noun** chiefly N. Amer. **1** a savoury pie baked in a deep dish, typically with a top crust only. **2** a stew with dumplings.

pot plant ▶ **noun** chiefly Brit. a plant grown or suitable for growing in a flowerpot, especially indoors.

pot-pourri /pəʊ'pʊəri, -'ri:, pɒt'pʊəri/ ▶ **noun** (pl. **pot-pourris**) [mass noun] a mixture of dried petals and spices placed in a bowl or small sack to perfume clothing or a room.
■ a mixture of things, especially a musical or literary medley: *he played* **a pot-pourri of** *tunes from Gilbert and Sullivan.*
– ORIGIN early 17th cent. (denoting a stew made of different kinds of meat): from French, literally 'rotten pot'.

potrero /pɒ'trɛːrəʊ/ ▶ **noun** (pl. **-os**) (in the south-western US and South America) a paddock or pasture for horses or cattle.
– ORIGIN mid 19th cent.: from Spanish, from *potro* 'colt, pony'.

pot roast ▶ **noun** a piece of meat cooked slowly in a covered dish.
▶ **verb** (**pot-roast**) [with obj.] cook (a piece of meat) slowly in a covered dish.

Potsdam /'pɒtsdam/ a city in eastern Germany, the capital of Brandenburg, situated just south-west of Berlin on the Havel River; pop. 95,000 (est. 1990). It is the site of the rococo Sans Souci palace built for Frederick II between 1745 and 1747.

Potsdam Conference a meeting held in Potsdam in the summer of 1945 between US, Soviet, and British leaders, which established principles for the Allied occupation of Germany following the end of the Second World War.

potsherd /'pɒtʃəːd/ ▶ **noun** a broken piece of ceramic material, especially one found on an archaeological site.

potshot ▶ **noun** a shot aimed unexpectedly or at random at someone or something with no chance of self-defence: *a sniper took a potshot at him.*
■ figurative a criticism, especially a random or unfounded one: *the show takes wickedly funny potshots at as many movies as it can muster.* ■ a shot at a game bird or other animal purely to kill it for food, without regard to the rules of the sport.
– ORIGIN mid 19th cent.: originally a *shot* at an animal intended for the *pot*, i.e. for food, rather than for display (which would require skilled shooting).

pot still ▶ **noun** a still to which heat is applied directly and not by means of a steam jacket.

pottage ▶ **noun** [mass noun] archaic soup or stew.
– PHRASES **sell something for a mess of pottage** sell something for a ridiculously small amount. [ORIGIN: with biblical allusion to the story of Esau who sold his birthright (Gen. 25:31).]
– ORIGIN Middle English (as *potage*): from Old French *potage* 'that which is put into a pot'. Compare with **POTAGE** and **PORRIDGE**.

potted ▶ **adjective** **1** (of a plant) planted or grown in a flowerpot and usually kept indoors: *an array of exotic potted palms.*
■ (of food, especially meat or fish) preserved in a sealed pot or jar: *potted shrimps.* ■ (of a literary work or descriptive account) put into a short and easily assimilable form: *a potted history of the band's career.* ■ (of an electrical component or circuit) encapsulated in insulating material.
2 [predic.] N. Amer. informal intoxicated by drink or drugs, especially cannabis: *a party where everybody was pretty potted.*

Potter[1], Dennis (Christopher George) (1935–94), English television dramatist. His series use popular songs to contrast the humdrum or painful realities of everyday life with the imagination's capacity for hope and self-delusion. Notable works: *Brimstone and Treacle* (play, 1976) and the series *Pennies from Heaven* (1978) and *The Singing Detective* (1986).

Potter[2], (Helen) Beatrix (1866–1943), English writer for children. She is known for her series of animal stories, illustrated with her own delicate watercolours, which began with *The Tale of Peter Rabbit* (first published privately in 1900).

potter[1] (N. Amer. **putter**) ▶ **verb** [no obj.] occupy oneself in a desultory but pleasant manner, doing a number of small tasks or not concentrating on anything particular: *I'm quite happy just to* **potter about** *by myself here.*
■ [with adverbial of direction] move or go in a casual, unhurried way: *I might potter into Nice for the day.*
▶ **noun** [in sing.] an idle but pleasant look around something; a desultory stroll: *an afternoon's potter through the rooms and possessions of the rich.*
– DERIVATIVES **potterer** noun.
– ORIGIN mid 16th cent. (in the sense 'poke repeatedly'): frequentative of dialect *pote* 'to push, kick, or poke' of unknown origin.

potter[2] ▶ **noun** a person who makes ceramic ware.
– ORIGIN late Old English *pottere* (see **POT**[1], **-ER**[1]).

potter's field ▶ **noun** historical a burial place for paupers and strangers.
– ORIGIN with biblical allusion to Matt. 27:7.

potter's wheel ▶ **noun** a horizontal revolving disc on which wet clay is shaped into pots or other round ceramic objects.

potter wasp ▶ **noun** a solitary wasp which builds a flask-shaped nest of mud into which it seals an egg and a supply of food for the larva.
● Genus *Eumenes*, family Eumenidae: many species, including *E. coarctatus* of European heathland.

pottery ▶ **noun** (pl. **-ies**) [mass noun] pots, dishes, and other articles made of earthenware or baked clay. Pottery can be broadly divided into earthenware, porcelain, and stoneware.
■ the craft or profession of making such ware: *courses include drawing, painting, and pottery.* ■ [count noun] a factory or workshop where such ware is made. ■ (**the Potteries**) the area around Stoke-on-Trent, Staffordshire, where the English pottery industry is based.
– ORIGIN Middle English: from Old French *poterie*, from *potier* 'a potter'.

potting compost ▶ **noun** [mass noun] a mixture of loam, peat, sand, and nutrients, used as a growing medium for plants in containers.

potting shed ▶ **noun** a shed which is used for potting plants and in which plants and garden tools and supplies are stored.

pottle ▶ **noun** **1** Brit. archaic a small punnet or carton for strawberries or other fruit.
■ NZ a small cardboard or plastic container of food: *a* **pottle of** *apricot yogurt.*
2 archaic a measure for liquids equal to a half gallon.
■ a pot or container holding this.
– ORIGIN Middle English (in sense 2): from Old French *potel* 'little pot', diminutive of *pot*.

potto /'pɒtəʊ/ (also **potto gibbon**) ▶ **noun** (pl. **-os**) a small nocturnal slow-moving primate with a short tail, living in dense vegetation in the tropical forests of Africa.
● *Perodicticus potto*, family Lorisidae, suborder Prosimii.
– ORIGIN early 18th cent.: perhaps from Guinea dialect.

Pott's fracture ▶ **noun** a fracture of the lower end of the fibula, usually involving a dislocation of the ankle.
– ORIGIN mid 19th cent.: named after Sir Percivall Pott (1713–88), English surgeon.

potty[1] ▶ **adjective** (**pottier**, **pottiest**) informal, chiefly Brit. **1** foolish; crazy: *he felt she really had gone potty.*
■ [predic.] extremely enthusiastic about or fond of someone or something: *I'm* **potty about** *my two sons.*
2 [attrib.] insignificant or feeble: *that* **potty little** *motor mower.*
– DERIVATIVES **pottiness** noun.
– ORIGIN mid 19th cent.: of unknown origin.

potty[2] ▶ **noun** (pl. **-ies**) informal a bowl used by small children as a toilet.

potty-train ▶ **verb** [with obj.] train (a small child) to use a potty.

pot-valiant ▶ **adjective** archaic (of a person) courageous as a result of being drunk.
– DERIVATIVES **pot-valour** noun.

pouch ▶ **noun** **1** a small bag or other flexible receptacle, typically carried in a pocket or attached to a belt: *a tobacco pouch | webbing with pouches for stun grenades.*
■ a lockable bag for mail or dispatches.
2 a pocket-like abdominal receptacle in which marsupials carry their young during lactation.
■ any of a number of similar animal structures, such as those in the cheeks of rodents.
3 (often **pouches**) a baggy area of skin underneath a person's eyes, usually seen as a sign of fatigue or illness: *he had deep pouches under his dark eyes.*
▶ **verb** [with obj.] **1** put into a pouch: *he stopped, pouched his tickets, and plodded on.*
■ informal take possession of: *he pouched his fifth first prize by beating Higginson in the final.* ■ Cricket catch (the ball): *Hick pouched his fourth catch with ease.*
2 make (part of a garment) hang like a pouch: *the muslin is lightly pouched over the belt.*
– DERIVATIVES **pouched** adjective, **pouchy** adjective.
– ORIGIN Middle English (as a noun): from Old

Northern French *pouche*, variant of Old French *poche* 'bag'. Compare with **POKE**².

pouchong /puːˈ(t)ʃɒŋ/ ▶ noun [mass noun] a kind of China tea made by fermenting the withered leaves only briefly, typically scented with rose petals.
– ORIGIN Chinese.

pouf¹ ▶ noun variant spelling of **POOF**¹, **POUFFE**.
▶ exclamation variant spelling of **POOF**².

pouf² ▶ noun a dress or part of a dress in which a large mass of material has been gathered so that it stands away from the body: [as modifier] *a dress with a pouf skirt*.
■ a bouffant hairstyle: *he grew his hair out in a sort of pouf*.
– ORIGIN early 19th cent. (denoting an elaborate female head-dress fashionable at the time): from French, of imitative origin.

pouffe /puːf/ (also **pouf**) ▶ noun a cushioned footstool or low seat with no back.
– ORIGIN late 19th cent.: from French *pouf*, of imitative origin.

poui /ˈpuːi/ ▶ noun (pl. same or **pouis**) a Caribbean and tropical American tree with trumpet-shaped flowers, grown as an ornamental and valued for its timber.
● Genus *Tabebuia*, family Bignoniaceae.
– ORIGIN mid 19th cent.: a local word in Trinidad.

Poulenc /ˈpuːlãk, French pulɛ̃k/, Francis (Jean Marcel) (1899–1963), French composer. He was a member of Les Six. His work is characterized by lyricism as well as the use of idioms of popular music such as jazz. His work includes songs and the ballet *Les Biches* (1923).

poult¹ /pəʊlt/ ▶ noun Farming a young domestic chicken, turkey, pheasant, or other fowl being raised for food.
– ORIGIN late Middle English: contraction of **PULLET**.

poult² /puːlt, pɒlt/ (also **poult-de-soie** /ˌpuːdəˈswɑː/) ▶ noun [mass noun] a fine corded silk or taffeta, typically coloured and used as a dress fabric.
– ORIGIN 1930s: from French *poult-de-soie*, from *poult* (of unknown origin) + *de soie* 'of silk'.

poulterer ▶ noun Brit. a dealer in poultry and, typically, game.
– ORIGIN late 16th cent.: from archaic *poulter*, in the same sense, from Old French *pouletier*.

poultice /ˈpəʊltɪs/ ▶ noun a soft moist mass of material, typically of plant material or flour, applied to the body to relieve soreness and inflammation and kept in place with a cloth.
▶ verb [with obj.] apply a poultice to: *he poulticed the wound*.
– ORIGIN late Middle English: from Latin *pultes* (plural), from *puls*, *pult-* 'pottage, pap'.

poultry /ˈpəʊltri/ ▶ noun [mass noun] domestic fowl, such as chickens, turkeys, ducks, and geese.
– ORIGIN Middle English: from Old French *pouletrie*, from *poulet* 'pullet'.

pounce¹ ▶ verb [no obj.] (of an animal or bird of prey) spring or swoop suddenly so as to catch prey: *as he watched, a mink pounced on the vole* | *she looked like a vulture waiting to pounce*.
■ (of a person) spring forward suddenly so as to attack or seize someone or something: *the gang pounced on him and knocked him to the ground*. ■ figurative take sudden decisive action so as to grasp an opportunity: *he pounced after the break to give the United the goal they deserved*. ■ figurative notice and take swift and eager advantage of a mistake, remark, or sign of weakness: *the paper pounced on her admission that she is still a member of CND*.
▶ noun 1 a sudden swoop or spring. 2 archaic a bird's claw.
– DERIVATIVES **pouncer** noun.
– ORIGIN late Middle English (as a noun denoting a tool for stamping or punching): origin obscure, perhaps from **PUNCHEON**¹. The noun sense 'a bird's claw' arose in the late 15th cent. and gave rise to the verb (late 17th cent.).

pounce² ▶ noun [mass noun] a fine resinous powder formerly used to prevent ink from spreading on unglazed paper or to prepare parchment to receive writing.
■ powdered charcoal or other fine powder dusted over a perforated pattern to transfer the design to the object beneath.
▶ verb [with obj.] **1** smooth down by rubbing with pounce or pumice.
2 transfer (a design) by the use of pounce.
– DERIVATIVES **pouncer** noun.

– ORIGIN late 16th cent. (as a verb): from French *poncer*, based on Latin *pumex* 'pumice'.

pouncet-box /ˈpaʊnsɪt/ ▶ noun archaic a small box with a perforated lid used for holding perfume.
– ORIGIN late 16th cent.: perhaps originally erroneously from *pounced* (= perforated) *box*.

Pound, Ezra (Weston Loomis) (1885–1972), American poet and critic, resident in Europe 1908–45. Initially associated with imagism, he later developed a highly eclectic poetic voice, drawing on a vast range of classical and other references and establishing a reputation as a modernist poet. Notable works: *Hugh Selwyn Mauberley* (1920) and *Cantos* (series, 1917–70).

pound¹ ▶ noun **1** (abbrev.: **lb**) a unit of weight equal to 16 oz. avoirdupois (0.4536 kg), or 12 oz. troy (0.3732 kg).
2 (also **pound sterling** (pl. **pounds sterling**)) the basic monetary unit of the UK, equal to 100 pence.
■ another term for **PUNT**⁴. ■ the basic monetary unit of several Middle Eastern countries, equal to 100 piastres. ■ the basic monetary unit of Cyprus, equal to 100 cents. ■ a monetary unit of the Sudan, equal to one tenth of a dinar.
– PHRASES **one's pound of flesh** something one is strictly or legally entitled to, but which it is ruthless or inhuman to demand. [ORIGIN: with allusion to Shakespeare's *Merchant of Venice*.]
– ORIGIN Old English *pund*, of Germanic origin; related to Dutch *pond* and German *Pfund*, from Latin (*libra*) *pondo*, denoting a Roman 'pound weight' of 12 ounces.

pound² ▶ verb [with obj.] strike or hit heavily and repeatedly: *Patrick pounded the couch with his fists* | *US gunships pounded the capital* | [no obj.] *pounding on the door, she shouted at the top of her voice*.
■ crush or grind (something) into a powder or paste by beating it with an instrument such as a pestle: *pound the cloves with salt and pepper until smooth*. ■ [no obj.] beat, throb, or vibrate with a strong regular rhythm: *her heart was pounding*. ■ [no obj., with adverbial of direction] walk or run with heavy steps: *I heard him pounding along the gangway*. ■ walk along (somewhere) repeatedly or at length: *he saw a little figure in a tracksuit pounding the pavement towards him*. ■ informal defeat (an opponent) in a resounding way: [with obj. and complement] *he pounded the unseeded American 6-2 7-5 7-5*.
– PHRASES **pound the beat** (of a police officer) patrol an allocated route or area.
▶ **pound something out** type something with heavy keystrokes: *an old typewriter on which she pounded out her poems*. ■ produce music by striking an instrument heavily and repeatedly: *the women pounded out a ringing tattoo on several oil drums*.
– ORIGIN Old English *pūnian*; related to Dutch *puin*, Low German *pün* '(building) rubbish'.

pound³ ▶ noun a place where stray animals, especially dogs, may be officially taken and kept until claimed by their owners.
■ a place where illegally parked motor vehicles removed by the police are kept until their owners pay a fine in order to reclaim them. ■ archaic a place of confinement; a trap or prison.
▶ verb [with obj.] archaic shut (an animal) in a pound.
– ORIGIN late Middle English (earlier in compounds): of uncertain origin. Early use referred to an enclosure for the detention of stray or trespassing cattle.

poundage ▶ noun **1** Brit. a payment of a particular amount per pound sterling of the sum involved in a transaction.
■ a percentage of the total earnings of a business, paid as wages.
2 [mass noun] weight, especially when regarded as excessive: *reduce excess poundage without risking overexertion*.

poundal /ˈpaʊnd(ə)l/ ▶ noun Physics a unit of force equal to that required to give a mass of one pound an acceleration of one foot per second per second.
– ORIGIN late 19th cent.: from **POUND**¹ + the suffix *-al*, perhaps suggested by **QUINTAL**.

pound cake ▶ noun a rich cake containing a pound, or equal weights, of each chief ingredient.

pound coin ▶ noun a coin worth one pound sterling.

pounder ▶ noun [usu. in combination] **1** a person or thing weighing a specified number of pounds: *Sloan set a blue-shark record with a 184-pounder*.

■ a gun designed to fire a shell weighing a specified number of pounds.
2 a person or thing that pounds something: *he's direct, but not abrasive, not a desk-pounder*.

pounding ▶ noun [mass noun] repeated and heavy striking or hitting of someone or something: *the pounding of the surf on a sandy beach* | [count noun] figurative *shares took a pounding last week*.
■ [count noun] informal a resounding defeat: *injury-hit Australia look set for further poundings*.

pound lock ▶ noun fuller term for **LOCK**¹ (in sense 2).
– ORIGIN late 18th cent.: *pound* from **POUND**³, in the sense 'body of still water, pond'.

pound note ▶ noun a banknote worth one pound sterling, now replaced by the pound coin in England and Wales.

pound sign ▶ noun the sign '£', representing a pound sterling.
■ North American term for **HASH**³.

pound sterling ▶ noun see **POUND**¹ (sense 2).

pour ▶ verb [no obj., with adverbial of direction] (especially of a liquid) flow rapidly in a steady stream: *water poured off the roof* | figurative *words poured from his mouth*.
■ [with obj. and adverbial of direction] cause (a liquid) to flow from a container in a steady stream by holding the container at an angle: *she poured a little whisky into a glass*. ■ [with obj.] serve (a drink) in this way: *she poured out a cup of tea* | [with two objs] *Harry poured her a drink*. ■ [no obj.] (of rain) fall heavily: *the storm clouds gathered and the rain poured down* | *it's pouring with rain*. ■ (of people or things) come or go in a steady stream and in large numbers: *letters poured in*. ■ [with obj.] (**pour something into**) donate something, especially money, to (a particular enterprise or project) in copious amounts: *Belgium has been pouring money into the company*. ■ [with obj.] (**pour something out**) express one's feelings or thoughts in a full and unrestrained way: *in his letters, Edward poured out his hopes*. ■ (**pour oneself into**) humorous dress oneself in (a tight-fitting piece of clothing): *I poured myself into a short Lycra skirt*.
– PHRASES **it never rains but it pours** proverb misfortunes or difficult situations tend to follow each other in rapid succession or to arrive all at the same time. **pour cold water on** see **COLD**. **pour it on** N. Amer. informal progress or work quickly or with all one's energy. **pour oil on troubled waters** try to settle a disagreement or dispute with words intended to placate or pacify those involved. **pour scorn on** see **SCORN**.
– DERIVATIVES **pourable** adjective, **pourer** noun.
– ORIGIN Middle English: of unknown origin.

pourboire /pʊəˈbwɑː/ ▶ noun a gratuity; a tip.
– ORIGIN French, from *pour boire* literally '(money) for drinking'.

pousada /pəʊˈsɑːdə/ ▶ noun (in Portugal) an inn or hotel, especially one of a chain of hotels administered by the state.
– ORIGIN Portuguese, literally 'resting place'.

pousse-cafe /ˌpuːskaˈfeɪ/ ▶ noun (pl. pronounced same) a glass of various liqueurs or cordials poured in successive layers, taken immediately after coffee.
– ORIGIN from French *pousse-café*, literally 'push coffee'.

Poussin /ˈpuːsã, French pusɛ̃/, Nicolas (1594–1665), French painter. He is regarded as the chief representative of French classicism and a master of the grand manner. His subject matter included biblical scenes (*The Adoration of the Golden Calf*, c.1635), classical mythology (*Et in Arcadia Ego*, c.1655), and historical landscapes.

poussin /ˈpuːsã/ ▶ noun a chicken killed young for eating.
– ORIGIN French.

pout¹ ▶ verb [no obj.] push one's lips or one's bottom lip forward as an expression of petulant annoyance or in order to make oneself look sexually attractive: *she lounged on the steps, pouting* | [with obj.] *he shrugged and pouted his lips*.
■ (of a person's lips) be pushed forward in such a way: *her lips pouted provocatively*.
▶ noun a pouting expression: *his lower lip protruded in a sulky pout*.
– DERIVATIVES **poutingly** adverb, **pouty** adjective.
– ORIGIN Middle English (as a verb): perhaps from the base of Swedish dialect *puta* 'be inflated'. Compare with **POUT**².

pout² ▶ noun **1** another term for **BIB**¹ (in sense 2).

2 North American term for **EELPOUT**.
– ORIGIN Old English *pūta* (only in *ǣlepūta* 'eelpout'); related to Dutch *puit* 'frog, chub', *puitaal* 'eelpout', and perhaps to **POUT**[1].

pouter ▶ noun a kind of pigeon able to inflate its crop considerably.

pouting ▶ noun another term for **BIB**[1] (in sense 2).

POV ▶ abbreviation for point of view.

poverty ▶ noun [mass noun] the state of being extremely poor: *thousands of families are living in abject poverty.*
▪ the state of being inferior in quality or insufficient in amount: *the poverty of her imagination.* ▪ the renunciation of the right to individual ownership of property as part of a religious vow.
– ORIGIN Middle English: from Old French *poverte*, from Latin *paupertas*, from *pauper* 'poor'.

poverty line ▶ noun the estimated minimum level of income needed to secure the necessities of life.

poverty-stricken ▶ adjective extremely poor: *thousands of poverty-stricken people.*

poverty trap ▶ noun Brit. a situation in which an increase in someone's income is offset by a consequent loss of state benefits, leaving them no better off.

povidone iodine /ˈpɒvɪdəʊn/ ▶ noun [mass noun] Medicine a brown powder used as an antiseptic for external application, consisting of a complex of polyvinylpyrrolidone and iodine.
– ORIGIN 1950s: *povidone*, contraction of **POLYVINYLPYRROLIDONE**.

POW ▶ abbreviation for prisoner of war.

pow ▶ exclamation expressing the sound of a blow or explosion: *Pow! Bombs went off on six beaches at once.*
– ORIGIN late 19th cent. (originally US): imitative.

powan /ˈpəʊən/ ▶ noun a widely distributed freshwater whitefish of lakes and rivers in northern Eurasia, especially one of a variety occurring only in two Scottish lochs.
• *Coregonus lavaretus*, family Salmonidae. See also **GWYNIAD**, **SCHELLY**.
– ORIGIN mid 17th cent.: Scots variant of **POLLAN**.

powder ▶ noun [mass noun] fine dry particles produced by the grinding, crushing, or disintegration of a solid substance: *when the powder is mixed with water it becomes a creamy white paste* | *cocoa powder* | [in sing.] *crush the poppy seeds to a powder.*
▪ (also **face powder**) a cosmetic in this form designed to be applied to a person's face with a brush or soft pad. ▪ [count noun] dated a medicine or drug in this form, usually designed to be dissolved in a liquid. ▪ (also **powder snow**) loose, dry, newly fallen snow: [as modifier] *powder skiing.* ▪ short for **GUNPOWDER** (in sense 1).
▶ verb [with obj.] **1** apply powder to (the face or body): *she powdered her face and put on a dab of perfume.*
▪ sprinkle or cover (a surface) with powder or a powdery substance: *broken glass powdered the floor* | figurative *high cheekbones powdered with freckles.*
2 reduce (a substance) to a powder by drying or crushing it: *then the rose petals are dried and powdered* | [as adj. **powdered**] *powdered milk.*
– PHRASES **keep one's powder dry** remain cautious and ready for a possible emergency. **powder one's nose** (of a woman) go to the toilet (used as a euphemism). **take a powder** N. Amer. informal depart quickly, especially in order to avoid a difficult situation.
– ORIGIN Middle English: from Old French *poudre*, from Latin *pulvis*, *pulver-* 'dust'.

powder blue ▶ noun [mass noun] a soft, pale blue: [as modifier] *a powder-blue jumpsuit.*

powder-coat ▶ verb [with obj.] cover (an object) with a polyester or epoxy powder, which is then heated to fuse into a protective layer.

powdered sugar ▶ noun North American term for **ICING SUGAR**.

powder flask ▶ noun historical a small container with a nozzle for carrying and dispersing gunpowder.

powder horn ▶ noun historical the horn of an ox, cow, or similar animal used to hold gunpowder, with the wide end filled in and a nozzle at the pointed end.

powder hound ▶ noun informal a person who enjoys skiing on powder snow.

powder keg ▶ noun a barrel of gunpowder.
▪ figurative a dangerous or volatile political situation: *the place had been a powder keg since the uprising.*

powder metallurgy ▶ noun [mass noun] the production and working of metals as fine powders which can be pressed and sintered to form objects.

powder monkey ▶ noun historical a boy employed on a sailing warship to carry powder to the guns.
▪ N. Amer. a person who works with explosives.

powder-post beetle ▶ noun a small brown beetle whose wood-boring larvae reduce wood to a very fine powder.
• Family Lyctidae: several genera.

powder puff ▶ noun a soft pad for applying powder to the skin, especially the face.
▪ informal a person or thing regarded as ineffectual: [as modifier] *a powder-puff bowler.*

powder room ▶ noun used euphemistically to refer to a women's toilet in a public building.

powder snow ▶ noun see **POWDER**.

powdery ▶ adjective consisting of or resembling powder: *powdery snow.*
▪ covered with powder: *her pale powdery cheeks.*

powdery mildew ▶ noun [mass noun] mildew on a plant which is marked by a white floury covering consisting of conidia. Compare with **DOWNY MILDEW**.
• Family Erysiphaceae, subdivision Ascomycotina.

Powell[1] /ˈpəʊəl/, Anthony (Dymoke) (1905–2000), English novelist. He is best known for his sequence of twelve novels *A Dance to the Music of Time* (1951–75), a satirical portrayal of the English upper middle classes between the two World Wars.

Powell[2] /ˈpaʊəl/, (John) Enoch (1912–98), British Conservative and Ulster Unionist politician, noted for his condemnation of multiracial immigration into Britain and his opposition to British entry into the Common Market.

Powell[3] /ˈpaʊəl/, Michael (Latham) (1905–90), English film director, producer, and scriptwriter. He founded The Archers Company with the Hungarian scriptwriter **Emeric Pressburger** (1902–88); their films included *The Red Shoes* (1948) and *The Tales of Hoffman* (1951).

power ▶ noun [mass noun] **1** the ability to do something or act in a particular way, especially as a faculty or quality: *the power of speech* | [with infinitive] *the power to raise the dead* | (**powers**) *his powers of concentration.*
2 the capacity or ability to direct or influence the behaviour of others or the course of events: *the idea that men should have power over women* | *she had me under her power.*
▪ political or social authority or control, especially that exercised by a government: *the party had been in power for eight years* | [as modifier] *a power struggle.* ▪ [count noun] a right or authority that is given or delegated to a person or body: *police do not have the power to stop and search* | *emergency powers.* ▪ the military strength of a state: *the sea power of Venice.* ▪ [count noun] a state or country, especially one viewed in terms of its international influence and military strength: *a great colonial power.* ▪ [count noun] a person or organization that is strong or influential within a particular context: *he was a power in the university.* ▪ [count noun] a supernatural being, deity, or force: *the powers of darkness.* ▪ (**powers**) (in traditional Christian angelology) the sixth highest order of the ninefold celestial hierarchy. ▪ [as modifier] informal denoting something associated with people that hold authority and influence, especially in the context of business or politics: *power dressing.* ▪ [with modifier] used in the names of movements aiming to enhance the status of a specified group: *gay power.*
3 physical strength and force exerted by something or someone: *the power of the storm.*
▪ capacity or performance of an engine or other device: *he applied full power.* ▪ the capacity of something to affect the emotions or intellect strongly: *the lyrical power of his prose.* ▪ [as modifier] denoting a sports player, team, or style of play that makes use of power rather than finesse: *a power pitcher.* ▪ the magnifying capacity of a lens.
4 energy that is produced by mechanical, electrical, or other means and used to operate a device: *generating power from waste* | [as modifier] *power cables.*
▪ electrical energy supplied to an area, building, etc.: *the power went off.* ▪ [as modifier] driven by such energy: *a power drill.* ▪ Physics the rate of doing work, measured in watts or less frequently horse power.
5 Mathematics the product obtained when a number is multiplied by itself a certain number of times: *2 to the power of 4 equals 16.*
6 (**a power of**) chiefly dialect a large number or amount of something: *there's a power of difference between farming now and when I was a lad.*
▶ verb **1** [with obj.] supply (a device) with mechanical or electrical energy: *the car is powered by a fuel-injected 3.0-litre engine* | [as adj., in combination **-powered**] *a nuclear-powered submarine.*
▪ (**power something up/down**) switch a device on or off: *the officer powered up the fighter's radar.*
2 [no obj., with adverbial of direction] move or travel with great speed or force: *he powered round a bend.*
▪ [with obj. and adverbial of direction] direct (something, especially a ball) with great force: *Nicholas powered a header into the net.*
– PHRASES **do someone/thing a power of good** informal be very beneficial to someone or something. **in the power of** under the control of. **more power to your elbow!** Brit. said to encourage someone or express approval of their actions. **power behind the throne** a person who exerts authority or influence without having formal status. **the powers that be** the authorities. [ORIGIN: with biblical allusion to Rom. 13:1.]
– ORIGIN Middle English: from Anglo-Norman French *poeir*, from an alteration of Latin *posse* 'be able'.

power-assisted ▶ adjective (especially of steering or brakes in a motor vehicle) using an inanimate source of power to assist manual operation.

power base ▶ noun a source of authority, influence, or support, especially in politics or negotiations: *the party's power base was confined to one province.*

power bloc (also **block**) ▶ noun an association of groups, especially nations, having a common interest and acting as a single political force.

powerboat ▶ noun a fast motor boat designed for racing or recreation.

power broker ▶ noun a person who deliberately affects the distribution of political or economic power by exerting influence or by intrigue.
– DERIVATIVES **power-broking** noun & adjective.

power cut ▶ noun a temporary withdrawal or failure of an electrical power supply.

power dive ▶ noun a steep dive of an aircraft with the engines providing thrust.
▶ verb (**power-dive**) [no obj.] perform a power dive.

power factor ▶ noun the ratio of the actual electrical power dissipated by an a.c. circuit to the product of the r.m.s. values of current and voltage. The difference between the two is caused by reactance in the circuit and represents power that does no useful work.

power forward ▶ noun Basketball a large forward who plays in the low post and typically has good shot-blocking and rebounding skills.

powerful ▶ adjective having great power or strength: *a fast, powerful car* | *computers are now more compact and powerful.*
▪ (of a person, organization, or country) having control and influence over people and events: *the world's most powerful nation.* ▪ having a strong effect on people's feelings or thoughts: *his photomontages are powerful anti-war images.*
▶ adverb [as submodifier] chiefly dialect very: *walking is powerful hot work.*
– DERIVATIVES **powerfully** adverb, **powerfulness** noun.

powerhouse ▶ noun a person or thing of great energy, strength, or power.
▪ dated or US another term for **POWER STATION**.

power law ▶ noun Mathematics a relationship between two quantities such that one is proportional to a fixed power of the other.

powerless ▶ adjective [often with infinitive] without ability, influence, or power: *troops were powerless to stop last night's shooting.*
– DERIVATIVES **powerlessly** adverb, **powerlessness** noun.

powerlifting ▶ noun [mass noun] a form of competitive weightlifting in which contestants attempt three types of lift in a set sequence.
– DERIVATIVES **powerlifter** noun.

power line ▶ noun a cable carrying electrical power, especially one supported by pylons or poles.

power of attorney ▶ noun [mass noun] Law the

p

authority to act for another person in specified or all legal or financial matters.
■[count noun] a legal document giving such authority to someone.

power pack ▶**noun** a self-contained and typically transportable unit which stores and supplies electrical power.
■a transformer for converting an alternating current (from the mains) to a direct current at a different (usually lower) voltage.

power plant ▶**noun** another term for **POWER STATION**.
■an engine or other apparatus which provides power for a machine, building, etc.

power play ▶**noun** [mass noun] **1** tactics exhibiting or intended to increase a person's power or influence: *the sexual power play of their relationship* | [count noun] *the petty power plays of showbiz.*
■the use of physical strength to defeat one's opponent in a sport through sheer force.
2 tactics in a team sport involving the concentration of players at a particular point.
■[count noun] Ice Hockey a temporary situation in which a team has a numerical advantage over its opponents because one or more players is serving a penalty.

power politics ▶**plural noun** [treated as sing. or pl.] political action by a person or group which makes use of or is intended to increase their power or influence.

power series ▶**noun** Mathematics an infinite series of the form $\Sigma a_n x^n$ (where n is a positive integer).
■a generalization of this for more than one variable.

power-sharing ▶**noun** [mass noun] a policy agreed between political parties or within a coalition to share responsibility for decision-making and political action.

power shovel ▶**noun** a mechanical excavator.

power shower ▶**noun** a shower bath using an electric pump to produce a high-pressure spray.

power slide ▶**noun** a deliberate controlled skid in a vehicle, usually done in order to turn corners at high speed.

power spectrum ▶**noun** Physics the distribution of the energy of a waveform among its different frequency components.
– DERIVATIVES **power spectral** adjective.

power station ▶**noun** an installation where electrical power is generated for distribution.

power steering ▶**noun** [mass noun] power-assisted steering.

power stroke ▶**noun** the stage of the cycle of an internal-combustion engine in which the piston is driven outward by the expansion of gases.

power take-off ▶**noun** a device which transfers mechanical power from an engine to another piece of equipment, especially on a tractor or similar vehicle.

power train ▶**noun** the mechanism that transmits the drive from the engine of a vehicle to its axle.
■this mechanism, the engine, and the axle considered collectively.

power-up ▶**noun** [mass noun] the action of switching on an electrical device, especially a computer.
■[count noun] (in a computer game) a bonus which a player can collect and which gives their character an advantage such as more strength or firepower.

power user ▶**noun** Computing a user who needs products having the most features and the fastest performance.

Powhatan /ˈpaʊətan/ ▶**noun** (pl. same or **Powhatans**) **1** a member of an American Indian people of eastern Virginia.
2 [mass noun] the extinct Algonquian language of this people.
▶**adjective** of or relating to this people or their language.
– ORIGIN Virginia Algonquian.

powwow ▶**noun** a North American Indian ceremony involving feasting and dancing.
■a conference or meeting for discussion, especially among friends or colleagues.
▶**verb** [no obj.] informal hold a powwow; confer: *news squads powwowed nervously.*
– ORIGIN early 17th cent.: from Narragansett *powah, powwaw* 'magician' (literally 'he dreams').

Powys /ˈpəʊɪs, ˈpaʊ-/ a county of east central Wales, on the border with England, formed in 1974 from the former counties of Montgomeryshire, Radnorshire, and most of Breconshire; administrative centre, Llandrindod Wells.
■a former Welsh kingdom. At its most powerful in the early 12th century, Powys was conquered by the English in 1284.

pox ▶**noun** any of several viral diseases producing a rash of pimples that become pus-filled and leave pockmarks on healing.
■(**the pox**) informal syphilis. ■(**the pox**) historical smallpox.
– PHRASES **a pox on** archaic used to express anger or intense irritation with someone or something: *a pox on both their houses!*
– ORIGIN late Middle English: alteration of *pocks*, plural of **POCK**.

poxvirus ▶**noun** Medicine any of a group of large DNA viruses that cause smallpox and similar infectious diseases in vertebrates.

poxy ▶**adjective** (**poxier, poxiest**) informal, chiefly Brit. insignificant; worthless (used as a general term of abuse): *they've won one poxy trophy.*

Pozidriv /ˈpɒzɪdrʌɪv/ (US **Poz-i-Driv**) ▶**noun** trademark a type of cross-head screwdriver with a smaller ridge bisecting each quarter of the cross.

Poznań /ˈpoznaɲ/ a city in NW Poland; pop. 590,100 (1990). An area of German colonization since the 13th century, it was under German control almost continuously until the First World War, and was overrun by the Germans again in 1939. It was severely damaged during the Second World War. German name **POSEN**.

Pozsony /Hungarian ˈpoʒoɲ/ Hungarian name for **BRATISLAVA**.

pozzolana /ˌpɒtsəˈlɑːnə/ ▶**noun** [mass noun] a type of volcanic ash used for mortar or for cement that sets under water.
– ORIGIN early 18th cent.: from Italian, from *pozz(u)olana* '(earth) of *Pozzuoli*', a town near Naples.

pp ▶**abbreviation for** ■(**pp.**) pages: *pp. 71–73.* ■(also **p.p.**) per procurationem (used when signing a letter on someone else's behalf). [ORIGIN: Latin.] ■Music pianissimo.

USAGE The traditional way to use **pp** when signing a letter on someone else's behalf is to place **pp** before one's own name rather than before the name of the other person. This is because the original Latin phrase **per procurationem** means 'through the agency of'. However, **pp** is now often taken to mean 'on behalf of' and is placed before the name of the person who has not signed, and this has become standard practice in many offices.

PPARC ▶**abbreviation for** (in the UK) Particle Physics and Astronomy Research Council.

PPE ▶**abbreviation for** philosophy, politics, and economics (a degree course at Oxford University).

ppi Computing ▶**abbreviation for** pixels per inch, a measure of the resolution of display screens, scanners, and printers.

ppm ▶**abbreviation for** ■part(s) per million: *water containing 1 ppm fluoride.* ■Computing page(s) per minute, a measure of the speed of printers.

PPP ▶**abbreviation for** ■Pakistan People's Party. ■(in computing) point to point protocol, which allows data conforming to the Internet protocol IP to be handled on a serial line. ■purchasing power parity (a way of measuring what an amount of money will buy in different countries).

PPS ▶**abbreviation for** ■additional postscript: *PS Those photos are ghastly! PPS Can I have your other address?* ■Brit. Parliamentary Private Secretary.

PPU ▶**abbreviation for** Peace Pledge Union.

PPV ▶**abbreviation for** pay-per-view, a system in which television viewers are charged for the length of time that they watch programmes.

PR ▶**abbreviation for** ■proportional representation. ■public relations. ■N. Amer. Puerto Rico.

Pr ▶**symbol for** the chemical element praseodymium.

pr ▶**abbreviation for** ■pair: *patterned gloves, £7.99/pr.* ■archaic per: *$6 pr day.*

PRA ▶**abbreviation for** progressive retinal atrophy (a disease afflicting dogs).

practicable ▶**adjective** able to be done or put into practice successfully: *the measures will be put into effect as soon as is reasonably practicable.*
■able to be used; useful: *signal processing can let you transform a signal into a practicable form.*
– DERIVATIVES **practicability** noun, **practicably** adverb.
– ORIGIN mid 17th cent.: from French *praticable*, from *pratiquer* 'put into practice'.

practical ▶**adjective 1** of or concerned with the actual doing or use of something rather than with theory and ideas: *there are two obvious practical applications of the research.*
■(of an idea, plan, or method) likely to succeed or be effective in real circumstances; feasible: *neither of these strategies are practical for smaller businesses.* ■suitable for a particular purpose: *a practical, stylish kitchen.* ■(of a person) sensible and realistic in their approach to a situation or problem: *I'm merely being practical—we must find a ground-floor flat.* ■(of a person) skilled at manual tasks: *Steve'll fix it—he's quite practical.*
2 so nearly the case that it can be regarded as so; virtual: *it was a practical certainty that he would try to raise more money.*
▶**noun** Brit. an examination or lesson in which theories and procedures learned are applied to the actual making of something or the conducting of experiments.
– ORIGIN late 16th cent.: from archaic *practic* 'practical' (from Old French *practique*, via late Latin from Greek *praktikos* 'concerned with action', from *prattein* 'do, act') + **-AL**.

practicality ▶**noun** (pl. **-ies**) **1** [mass noun] the quality or state of being practical: *there are still major doubts about the practicality of the proposal.*
2 (**practicalities**) the aspects of a situation that involve the actual doing or experience of something rather than theories or ideas: *the practicalities of living at sea.*

practical joke ▶**noun** a trick played on someone in order to make them look foolish and to amuse others.
– DERIVATIVES **practical joker** noun.

practically ▶**adverb 1** virtually; almost: *the strike lasted practically a fortnight* | *the place was practically empty.*
2 in a practical manner.
■[sentence adverb] in practical terms: *the law isn't unreasonable or practically inconvenient.*

practical nurse ▶**noun** (in North America) a nurse who has completed a training course of a lower standard than a registered nurse, especially one who is licensed by the state to perform certain duties (a **licensed practical nurse**).

practice ▶**noun** [mass noun] **1** the actual application or use of an idea, belief, or method as opposed to theories about such application or use: *the principles and practice of teaching* | *he* **put** *his self-defence training* **into practice** *by helping police arrest the armed robber.*
■the customary, habitual, or expected procedure or way of doing of something: *current nursing practice* | [count noun] *modern child-rearing practices.* ■the carrying out or exercise of a profession, especially that of a doctor or lawyer: *he abandoned medical practice for the Church.* ■[count noun] the business or premises of a doctor or lawyer: *Dr Apps has a practice in Neasham Road.* ■an established method of legal procedure.
2 repeated exercise in or performance of an activity or skill so as to acquire or maintain proficiency in it: *it must have taken a lot of practice to become so fluent.*
■[count noun] a period of time spent doing this: *daily choir practices.*
▶**verb** US spelling of **PRACTISE**.
– PHRASES **in practice** in reality (used to refer to what actually happens as opposed to what is meant or believed to happen): *in theory this method is ideal—in practice it is unrealistic.* ■currently proficient in a particular activity or skill as a result of repeated exercise or performance of it. **out of practice** not currently proficient in a particular activity or skill through not having exercised or performed it for some time: *he was out of practice at interrogation.* **practice makes perfect** used to convey that regular exercise of an activity or skill is the way to become proficient in it, especially when encouraging someone to persist in it.
– ORIGIN late Middle English: from **PRACTISE**, on the pattern of pairs such as *advise, advice.*

practician ▶**noun** archaic a person who practises a profession or occupation, especially a practical one; a practitioner.
– ORIGIN late 15th cent.: from Old French *practicien*, from *practique* 'practical' (see **PRACTICAL**).

practicum /ˈpraktɪkəm/ ▶**noun** (pl. **practicums**) chiefly N. Amer. a practical section of a course of study.

p

– ORIGIN early 20th cent.: from late Latin, neuter of *practicus* 'practical'.

practise (US **practice**) ▶ **verb** [with obj.] **1** perform (an activity) or exercise (a skill) repeatedly or regularly in order to improve or maintain one's proficiency: *I need to practise my French* | [no obj.] *they were practising for the Olympics.*
2 carry out or perform (a particular activity, method, or custom) habitually or regularly: *we still practise some of these rituals today.*
■ actively pursue or be engaged in (a particular profession or occupation): *he began to practise law* | [no obj.] *he practised as a barrister* | [as adj. **practising**] *a practising architect.* ■ observe the teaching and rules of (a particular religion): *non-Muslims were free to practise their religion* | [as adj. **practising**] *a practising Roman Catholic.* ■ [no obj.] archaic scheme or plot for an evil purpose: *what a tangled web we weave when we first practise to deceive.*
– PHRASES **practise what one preaches** do what one advises others to do.
– DERIVATIVES **practiser** noun.
– ORIGIN late Middle English: from Old French *practiser* or medieval Latin *practizare*, alteration of *practicare* 'perform, carry out', from *practica* 'practice', from Greek *praktikē*, feminine (used as a noun), of *praktikos* (see **PRACTICAL**).

practised (US **practiced**) ▶ **adjective** expert, typically as the result of much experience: *admiring the dress with a practised eye* | *the waiter was* ***practised at*** *disrupting moments of intimacy.*

practitioner ▶ **noun** a person actively engaged in an art, discipline, or profession, especially medicine: *patients are treated by skilled practitioners.*
– ORIGIN mid 16th cent.: extension of obsolete *practitian*, variant of **PRACTICIAN**.

prad ▶ **noun** informal, chiefly Austral. a horse.
– ORIGIN late 18th cent.: altered form of Dutch *paard* 'horse'.

Prader–Willi syndrome /ˌprɑːdəˈvɪli/ ▶ **noun** [mass noun] a rare congenital disorder characterized by mental handicap, growth abnormalities, and obsessive eating, caused especially by the absence of certain genes normally present on the copy of chromosome 15 inherited from the father.
– ORIGIN 1960s: named after Andrea *Prader* (born 1919) and Heinrich *Willi* (born 1900), Swiss paediatricians.

Prado /ˈprɑːdəʊ/ the Spanish national art gallery in Madrid, established in 1818.

prae- ▶ **prefix** (used especially in words regarded as Latin or relating to Roman antiquity) equivalent to **PRE-**.
– ORIGIN from Latin.

praecipe /ˈpriːsɪpi/ ▶ **noun** Law an order requesting a writ or other legal document.
■ historical a writ demanding action or an explanation of non-action.
– ORIGIN Latin (the first word of the writ), imperative of *praecipere* 'enjoin, command'. See also **PRECEPT**.

praemunire /ˌpriːmjuːˈnʌɪri/ ▶ **noun** [mass noun] historical the offence of asserting or maintaining papal jurisdiction in England.
■ [count noun] a writ charging a sheriff to summon a person accused of this offence.
– ORIGIN late Middle English: from medieval Latin, 'forewarn', from Latin *praemonere*, from *prae* 'beforehand' + *monere* 'warn'. The term comes from *praemunire facias* 'that you warn (a person to appear)', part of the wording in the writ.

praenomen /priːˈnəʊmɛn/ ▶ **noun** an ancient Roman's first or personal name, for example *Marcus* Tullius Cicero.
– ORIGIN Latin, from *prae* 'before' + *nomen* 'name'.

praepostor /prɪˈpɒstə/ (also **prepostor**) ▶ **noun** Brit. (at some public schools) a prefect or monitor.
– ORIGIN mid 18th cent.: from *praepostor*, alteration of Latin *praepositus* 'head, chief', past participle of *praeponere* 'set over', from *prae* 'ahead' + *ponere* 'to place'.

Praesepe /prʌɪˈsiːpi/ Astronomy a large open cluster of stars in the constellation Cancer; the Beehive.
– ORIGIN Latin, literally 'manger, hive'.

praesidium ▶ **noun** variant spelling of **PRESIDIUM**.

praetor /ˈpriːtə, -tɔː/ (US also **pretor**) ▶ **noun** Roman History each of two ancient Roman magistrates ranking below consul.
– DERIVATIVES **praetorial** adjective, **praetorship** noun.
– ORIGIN from Latin *praetor*, perhaps from *prae* 'before' + *it-* 'gone' (from the verb *ire*).

praetorian (US also **pretorian**) ▶ **adjective** Roman History of or having the powers of a praetor.
▶ **noun** a man of praetorian rank.

praetorian guard ▶ **noun** Roman History the bodyguard of the Roman emperor.

pragmatic ▶ **adjective** dealing with things sensibly and realistically in a way that is based on practical rather than theoretical considerations: *a pragmatic approach to politics.*
■ relating to philosophical or political pragmatism.
■ Linguistics of or relating to pragmatics.
– DERIVATIVES **pragmatically** adverb.
– ORIGIN late 16th cent. (in the senses 'busy, interfering, conceited'): via Latin from Greek *pragmatikos* 'relating to fact', from *pragma* 'deed' (from the stem of *prattein* 'do'). The current sense dates from the mid 19th cent.

pragmatics ▶ **plural noun** [usu. treated as sing.] the branch of linguistics dealing with language in use and the contexts in which it is used, including such matters as deixis, turn taking in conversation, text organization, presupposition, and implicature.

pragmatic sanction ▶ **noun** historical an imperial or royal ordinance or decree that has the force of law.
■ **(Pragmatic Sanction)** a document drafted in 1717 by the Emperor Charles VI providing for his daughter Maria Theresa to succeed to all his territories should he die without a son. Opposition to it led to the War of the Austrian Succession on Charles's death in 1740.
– ORIGIN translating Law Latin *pragmatica sanctio*.

pragmatism ▶ **noun** [mass noun] **1** a pragmatic attitude or policy: *ideology was tempered with pragmatism.*
2 Philosophy an approach that assesses the truth of meaning of theories or beliefs in terms of the success of their practical application.
– DERIVATIVES **pragmatist** noun, **pragmatistic** adjective.
– ORIGIN mid 19th cent.: from Greek *pragma*, *pragmat-* 'deed' (see **PRAGMATIC**) + **-ISM**.

Prague /prɑːg/ the capital of the Czech Republic, in the north-east on the River Vltava; pop. 1,212,000 (1991). Czech name **PRAHA**.

Prague was the capital of Czechoslovakia from 1918 until the partition of 1993. The capital of Bohemia from the 14th century, it was the scene of much religious conflict. In 1618 Protestant citizens threw Catholic officials from the windows of Hradčany Castle, an event, known as the **Defenestration of Prague**, which contributed to the outbreak of the Thirty Years War.

Prague School a group of linguists established in Prague in 1926 who developed distinctive feature theory in phonology and communicative dynamism in language teaching. Leading members were Nikolai Trubetzkoy (1890–1938) and Roman Jakobson.

Prague Spring a brief period of liberalization in Czechoslovakia, ending in August 1968, during which a programme of political, economic, and cultural reform was initiated.

Praha /ˈpraha/ Czech name for **PRAGUE**.

prahu /ˈprɑːuː/ ▶ **noun** variant spelling of **PROA**.

Praia /ˈprʌɪə/ the capital of the Cape Verde Islands, a port on the island of São Tiago; pop. 62,000 (1990).

Prairial /ˈprɛːrɪəl, French prɛʀjal/ ▶ **noun** the ninth month of the French Republican calendar (1793–1805), originally running from 20 May to 18 June.
– ORIGIN French, from *prairie* 'meadow'.

prairie ▶ **noun 1** a large open area of grassland, especially in North America.
2 (**Prairie**) [often as modifier] a steam locomotive of 2–6–2 wheel arrangement.
– ORIGIN late 18th cent.: from French, from Old French *praerie*, from Latin *pratum* 'meadow'.

prairie chicken (also **prairie hen**) ▶ **noun** a large North American grouse found on the prairies, the male being noted for the display dance in which it inflates two orange neck pouches and makes a booming sound.
● Genus *Tympanuchus*, family Tetraonidae: two species, in particular the **greater prairie chicken** (*T. cupido*).

prairie dog ▶ **noun** a gregarious ground squirrel that lives in interconnected burrows which may cover many hectares, native to the grasslands of North America.
● Genus *Cynomys*, family Sciuridae: several species.

prairie oyster ▶ **noun 1** a drink made with a raw egg and seasoning, drunk as a cure for a hangover.
2 (**prairie oysters**) chiefly N. Amer. the testicles of a calf cooked and served as food.

prairie schooner ▶ **noun** N. Amer. a covered wagon used by the 19th-century pioneers in crossing the North American prairies.

Prairie State informal name for **ILLINOIS**.

prairie wolf ▶ **noun** North American term for **COYOTE**.

prairie wool ▶ **noun** [mass noun] Canadian the natural grassy plant cover of prairie land.

praise ▶ **verb** [with obj.] express warm approval or admiration of: *we can't praise Chris enough—he did a brilliant job.*
■ express one's respect and gratitude towards (a deity), especially in song: *we praise God for past blessings.*
▶ **noun** [mass noun] the expression of approval or admiration for someone or something: *the audience was full of praise for the whole production.*
■ the expression of respect and gratitude as an act of worship: *give praise to God.*
– PHRASES **praise be** archaic used as an expression of relief, joy, or gratitude. **sing the praises of** express enthusiastic approval or admiration of (someone or something): *Uncle Felix never stopped singing her praises.*
– DERIVATIVES **praiseful** adjective.
– ORIGIN Middle English (also in the sense 'set a price on, attach value to'): from Old French *preisier* 'to prize, praise', from late Latin *pretiare*, from Latin *pretium* 'price'. Compare with **PRIZE**[1].

praiser ▶ **noun** S. African another term for **IMBONGI**.

praiseworthy ▶ **adjective** deserving approval and admiration: *the government's praiseworthy efforts.*
– DERIVATIVES **praiseworthily** adverb, **praiseworthiness** noun.

prajna /ˈprʌʒnə/ ▶ **noun** [mass noun] Buddhism direct insight into the truth taught by the Buddha, as a faculty required to attain enlightenment.
– ORIGIN from Sanskrit *prajñā*.

Prakrit /ˈprɑːkrɪt/ ▶ **noun** any of the ancient or medieval vernacular dialects of north and central India which existed alongside or were derived from Sanskrit.
– ORIGIN from Sanskrit *prākṛta* 'unrefined, natural'. Compare with **SANSKRIT**.

praline /ˈprɑːliːn/ ▶ **noun** [mass noun] a smooth, sweet substance made by boiling nuts in sugar and grinding the mixture, used especially as a filling for chocolates.
■ [count noun] a chocolate filled with praline.
– ORIGIN early 18th cent.: from French, named after Marshal de Plessis-*Praslin* (1598–1675), the French soldier whose cook invented it.

pralltriller /ˈpralˌtrɪlə/ ▶ **noun** a musical ornament consisting of one rapid alternation of the written note with the note immediately above it.
– ORIGIN mid 19th cent.: from German, from *prallen* 'rebound' + *Triller* 'a trill'.

pram[1] /pram/ ▶ **noun** Brit. a four-wheeled carriage for a baby, pushed by a person on foot.
– ORIGIN late 19th cent.: contracted abbreviation of **PERAMBULATOR**.

pram[2] /prɑːm, pram/ ▶ **noun** a flat-bottomed sailing boat.
■ US a small flat-bottomed rowing boat for fishing.
– ORIGIN late Middle English: from Middle Dutch *prame*, Middle Low German *prāme*, perhaps from Czech *prám* 'raft'.

prana /ˈprɑːnə/ ▶ **noun** [mass noun] Hinduism breath, considered as a life-giving force.
– ORIGIN Sanskrit.

pranam /prəːˈnɑːm/ ▶ **noun** [mass noun] (in the Indian subcontinent) a respectful greeting made by putting one's palms together and often touching the feet of the person greeted: *she joined her palms* ***in pranam.***
– ORIGIN from Hindi *praṇām*.

pranayama /ˌprɑːnʌˈjɑːmɑː/ ▶ **noun** [mass noun] (in yoga) the regulation of the breath through certain techniques and exercises.
– ORIGIN Sanskrit, from *prāṇa* 'breath' + *āyāma* 'restraint'.

prance ▶ **verb** [no obj., with adverbial of direction] (of a horse) move with high springy steps: *the pony was prancing around the paddock.*

p

■(of a person) walk or move around with ostentatious, exaggerated movements: *she pranced around the lounge impersonating her favourite pop stars.*
▶ **noun** an act or instance of prancing.
– DERIVATIVES **prancer** noun.
– ORIGIN late Middle English (as a verb): of unknown origin.

prandial /ˈprandɪəl/ ▶ **adjective** [attrib.] formal, often humorous during or relating to dinner or lunch.
■Medicine during or relating to the eating of food.
– ORIGIN early 19th cent.: from Latin *prandium* 'meal' + **-AL**.

Prandtl /ˈprant(ə)l/, Ludwig (1875–1953), German physicist. He established the existence of the boundary layer and made important studies on streamlining.

Prandtl number ▶ **noun** Physics a dimensionless parameter used in calculations of heat transfer between a moving fluid and a solid body, equal to $c_p v/k$, where c_p is the heat capacity per unit volume of the fluid, v its kinematic viscosity, and k its thermal conductivity.

prang Brit. informal ▶ **verb** [with obj.] crash (a motor vehicle or aircraft).
■dated bomb (a target) successfully from the air.
▶ **noun** a crash involving a motor vehicle or aircraft.
■dated a bombing raid.
– ORIGIN 1940s: imitative.

prank ▶ **noun** a practical joke or mischievous act.
– DERIVATIVES **prankish** adjective, **prankishness** noun.
– ORIGIN early 16th cent. (denoting a wicked deed): of unknown origin.

prankster ▶ **noun** a person fond of playing pranks.

prasad /prʌˈsɑːd/ ▶ **noun** Hinduism a devotional offering made to a god, typically consisting of food that is later shared among devotees.
– ORIGIN from Sanskrit *prasāda* 'clearness, kindness, grace'.

prase /preɪz/ ▶ **noun** [mass noun] a translucent leek-green variety of quartz.
– ORIGIN late 18th cent.: from French, via Latin from Greek *prasios* 'leek-green', from *prason* 'leek'.

praseodymium /ˌpreɪzɪə(ʊ)ˈdɪmɪəm/ ▶ **noun** [mass noun] the chemical element of atomic number 59, a soft silvery-white metal of the lanthanide series. (Symbol: **Pr**)
– ORIGIN late 19th cent.: modern Latin, from German *Praseodym*, from Greek *prasios* 'leek-green' (because of its green salts) + German *Didym* 'didymium'.

prat ▶ **noun** informal **1** Brit. an incompetent, stupid, or foolish person; an idiot.
2 a person's buttocks.
– ORIGIN mid 16th cent. (in sense 2): of unknown origin. Sense 1 dates from the 1960s.

prate ▶ **verb** [no obj.] talk foolishly or at tedious length about something: *I sat in my pew and heard him prate on for at least an hour and a half.*
– DERIVATIVES **prater** noun (rare).
– ORIGIN late Middle English: from Middle Dutch, Middle Low German *praten*, probably of imitative origin.

pratfall ▶ **noun** informal a fall on to one's buttocks: *she took a* **pratfall** *into a dessert trolley.*
■a stupid and humiliating action: *the first political pratfalls of the new administration.*

pratie /ˈpreɪti/ ▶ **noun** chiefly Irish a potato.
– ORIGIN late 18th cent.: from Irish *prátaí*, plural of *práta*.

pratincole /ˈpratɪŋkəʊl/ ▶ **noun** a long-winged fork-tailed insectivorous bird related to the plovers, resembling a swallow in flight and typically living near water.
• Genus *Glareola* (and *Stiltia*), family Glareolidae: several species, in particular *G. pratincola* of Africa and the Mediterranean.
– ORIGIN late 18th cent.: from modern Latin *pratincola*, from Latin *pratum* 'meadow' + *incola* 'inhabitant'.

pratique /ˈpratiːk/ ▶ **noun** [mass noun] historical permission granted to a ship to have dealings with a port, given after quarantine or on showing a clean bill of health.
– ORIGIN early 17th cent.: from French, literally 'practice', via Italian from medieval Latin *practica*, feminine (used as a noun) of *practicus* 'practical'.

Prato /ˈprɑːtəʊ/ a city in northern Italy, north-west of Florence; pop. 166,690 (1990).

prattle ▶ **verb** [no obj.] talk at length in a foolish or inconsequential way: *she began to* **prattle on** *about her visit to the dentist.*
▶ **noun** [mass noun] foolish or inconsequential talk: *do you intend to keep up this childish prattle?*
– DERIVATIVES **prattler** noun.
– ORIGIN mid 16th cent.: from Middle Low German *pratelen*, from *praten* (see **PRATE**).

prau ▶ **noun** variant spelling of **PROA**.

Pravda /ˈprɑːvdə/ a Russian daily newspaper, founded in 1912 and from 1918 to 1991 the official organ of the Soviet Communist Party.
– ORIGIN Russian, literally 'truth'.

prawn ▶ **noun** a marine crustacean which resembles a large shrimp.
• *Leander* and other genera, class Malacostraca. See also **DUBLIN BAY PRAWN, KING PRAWN**.
– PHRASES **don't come the raw prawn with me** see **RAW**.
– ORIGIN late Middle English: of unknown origin.

prawn cracker ▶ **noun** (in Chinese cooking) a light crisp made from rice or tapioca flour with prawn flavouring which puffs up when deep-fried.

prawner ▶ **noun** a boat used for fishing for prawns.
– DERIVATIVES **prawning** noun.

praxis /ˈpraksɪs/ ▶ **noun** [mass noun] formal practice, as distinguished from theory: *the divorce between theory and praxis of Marxism which ensued under Stalinism.*
■accepted practice or custom: *patterns of Christian praxis in church and society.*
– ORIGIN late 16th cent.: via medieval Latin from Greek, literally 'doing', from *prattein* 'do'.

Praxiteles /prakˈsɪtəliːz/ (mid 4th century BC), Athenian sculptor. Only one of his works, *Hermes Carrying the Infant Dionysus*, survives. He is also noted for a statue of Aphrodite, of which there are only Roman copies.

pray ▶ **verb** [no obj.] address a solemn request or expression of thanks to a deity or other object of worship: *the whole family are praying for Michael* | [with obj.] *pray God this is true.*
■wish or hope strongly for a particular outcome or situation: *after several days of rain, we were praying for sun* | [with clause] *I prayed that James wouldn't notice.*
▶ **adverb** formal or archaic used as a preface to polite requests or instructions: *pray continue.*
■used as a way of adding ironic or sarcastic emphasis to a question: *and what, pray, was the purpose of that?*
– ORIGIN Middle English (in the sense 'ask earnestly'): from Old French *preier*, from late Latin *precare*, alteration of Latin *precari* 'entreat'.

prayer /prɛː/ ▶ **noun** a solemn request for help or expression of thanks addressed to God or an object of worship: *I'll say a prayer for him* | [mass noun] *the peace of God is ours through prayer.*
■(**prayers**) a religious service, especially a regular one, at which people gather in order to pray together: *500 people were detained as they attended Friday prayers.* ■ an earnest hope or wish: *it is our prayer that the current progress on human rights will be sustained.*
– PHRASES **not have a prayer** informal have no chance at all of succeeding at something: *he doesn't have a prayer of toppling Tyson.*
– ORIGIN Middle English: from Old French *preiere*, based on Latin *precarius* 'obtained by entreaty', from *prex, prec-* 'prayer'.

prayer bead ▶ **noun** a bead which is or has been on a string of beads used in prayer.

prayer book ▶ **noun** a book containing the forms of prayer regularly used in Christian worship, especially a Book of Common Prayer.

prayer flag ▶ **noun** (especially in Tibetan Buddhism) a flag on which prayers are inscribed.

prayerful ▶ **adjective** (of an action or event) characterized by or expressive of prayer: *reflect last thing at night as a prayerful self-examination.*
■(of a person) given to praying; devout.
– DERIVATIVES **prayerfully** adverb, **prayerfulness** noun.

prayer mat (also **prayer rug**) ▶ **noun** a small carpet used by Muslims for kneeling on when praying.

Prayer of Manasses /məˈnasiːz/ a book of the Apocrypha consisting of a penitential prayer put into the mouth of Manasseh, king of Judah.

prayer plant ▶ **noun** a Brazilian plant with variegated leaves which are erect at night but lie flat during the day, grown as a house plant.
• *Maranta leuconeura*, family Marantaceae.

prayer shawl ▶ **noun** Judaism another term for **TALLITH**.

prayer stick ▶ **noun** a stick decorated with feathers, used by various American Indian peoples in their religious ceremonies.

prayer wheel ▶ **noun** a small revolving cylinder inscribed with or containing prayers, a revolution of which symbolizes the repetition of a prayer, used by Tibetan Buddhists.

praying mantis ▶ **noun** see **MANTIS**.

praziquantel /ˌprazɪˈkwantəl, ˌpreɪzɪˈkwɒntəl/ ▶ **noun** [mass noun] Medicine a synthetic anthelmintic drug used in the treatment of schistosomiasis and other infestations of humans and animals with parasitic trematodes or cestodes.
– ORIGIN 1970s: from *p(y)razi(ne)* + *-quantel* (perhaps from elements of **QUINOLINE** and **ANTHELMINTIC**).

pre- ▶ **prefix** before (in time, place, order, degree, or importance): *pre-adolescent* | *precaution* | *precede.*
– ORIGIN from Latin *prae-*.

preach ▶ **verb** [no obj.] deliver a sermon or religious address to an assembled group of people, typically in church: *he preached to a large congregation* | [with obj.] *our pastor will preach the sermon.*
■[with obj.] publicly proclaim or teach (a religious message or belief): *a Church that preaches the good news of Jesus.* ■ [with obj.] earnestly advocate (a belief or course of action): *my parents have always preached toleration and moderation.* ■ give moral advice to someone in an annoying or pompously self-righteous way: *viewers want to be entertained, not preached at.*
– PHRASES **preach to the converted** advocate something to people who already share one's convictions about its merits or importance.
– ORIGIN Middle English: from Old French *prechier*, from Latin *praedicare* 'proclaim', in ecclesiastical Latin 'preach', from *prae* 'before' + *dicare* 'declare'.

preacher ▶ **noun** a person who preaches, especially a minister of religion.
– ORIGIN Middle English: from Old French *precheor*, from ecclesiastical Latin *praedicator*, from the verb *praedicare* (see **PREACH**).

preachify ▶ **verb** (**-ies, -ied**) [no obj.] informal preach or moralize tediously: [as adj. **preachifying**] *I'm not an admirer of paternalistic, preachifying Christianity.*

preachment ▶ **noun** [mass noun] dogmatic instruction and exhortation: *successful leadership is a process of persuasion rather than preachment.*
– ORIGIN Middle English: from Old French *prechement*, from late Latin *praedicamentum*.

preachy ▶ **adjective** (**preachier, preachiest**) informal having or revealing a tendency to give moral advice in a tedious or self-righteous way: *his patriotic pictures had a preachy tone.*
– DERIVATIVES **preachiness** noun.

pre-adapt ▶ **verb** [with obj.] Biology adapt (an organism or part of an organism) for life in conditions it has yet to encounter: *the insulation of marine mammals in temperate seas pre-adapts them for polar seas.*
– DERIVATIVES **pre-adaptation** noun.

pre-adolescent ▶ **adjective** (of a child) having nearly reached adolescence.
■of or relating to the two or three years preceding adolescence: *Mozart's pre-adolescent sonatas.*
▶ **noun** a pre-adolescent child.
– DERIVATIVES **pre-adolescence** noun.

pre-agricultural ▶ **adjective** denoting a people, tribe, or culture that has not developed agriculture as a means of subsistence.

pre-Aids ▶ **adjective** following infection with HIV but before the full development of Aids: *pre-Aids patients.*
■before the recognition of Aids as a disease: *we are dealing with an era that was pre-Aids.*

preamble /priːˈamb(ə)l, ˈpriː-/ ▶ **noun** a preliminary or preparatory statement; an introduction: *he could tell that what she said was by way of a preamble* | [mass noun] *I gave him the bad news without preamble.*
■Law the introductory part of a statute or deed, stating its purpose, aims, and justification.
– DERIVATIVES **preambular** adjective (formal).
– ORIGIN late Middle English: from Old French *preambule*, from medieval Latin *praeambulum*, from late Latin *praeambulus* 'going before'.

preamp ▶ **noun** short for **PREAMPLIFIER**.

preamplifier ▶ **noun** an electronic device that amplifies a very weak signal, for example from a

p

microphone or pickup, and transmits it to a main amplifier.

pre-arrange ▶ verb [with obj.] [usu. as adj. **pre-arranged**] arrange or agree upon (something) in advance: *did she have a pre-arranged meeting?*
– DERIVATIVES **pre-arrangement** noun.

Preb. ▶ abbreviation for Prebendary.

pre-baiting ▶ noun [mass noun] the practice of accustoming vermin or fish to harmless bait, so that they will take poisoned or hooked bait more readily.

prebend /ˈprɛb(ə)nd/ ▶ noun historical the portion of the revenues of a cathedral or collegiate church formerly granted to a canon or member of the chapter as his stipend.
■ the property from which such a stipend was derived. ■ the tenure of this as a benefice. ■ another term for **PREBENDARY**.
– ORIGIN late Middle English: from Old French *prebende*, from late Latin *praebenda* 'things to be supplied, pension', neuter plural gerundive of Latin *praebere* 'to grant', from *prae* 'before' + *habere* 'hold, have'.

prebendal /prɪˈbɛnd(ə)l/ ▶ adjective of or relating to a prebend or a prebendary: *the prebendal manor.*

prebendary /ˈprɛb(ə)nd(ə)ri/ ▶ noun (pl. **-ies**) an honorary canon.
■ historical a canon of a cathedral or collegiate church whose income originally came from a prebend.
– DERIVATIVES **prebendaryship** noun.
– ORIGIN late Middle English: from medieval Latin *praebendarius*, from late Latin *praebenda* 'pension' (see **PREBEND**).

prebiotic ▶ adjective existing or occurring before the emergence of life.

pre-book ▶ verb [with obj.] [usu. as adj. **pre-booked**] book (something) in advance: *a pre-booked hotel reservation* | [as noun **pre-booking**] *pre-booking is essential.*
– DERIVATIVES **pre-bookable** adjective.

Preboreal /priːˈbɔːrɪəl/ ▶ adjective Geology of, relating to, or denoting the first climatic stage of the postglacial period in northern Europe, between the Younger Dryas and Boreal stages (about 10,000 to 9,000 years ago). The stage was marked by a rapid spread of birch and pine forests.
■ [as noun **the Preboreal**] the Preboreal climatic stage.

Precambrian /priːˈkambrɪən/ ▶ adjective Geology of, relating to, or denoting the earliest aeon, preceding the Cambrian period and the Phanerozoic aeon. Compare with **CRYPTOZOIC**.
■ [as noun **the Precambrian**] the Precambrian aeon or the system of rocks deposited during it.

The Precambrian extended from the origin of the earth (believed to have been about 4,600 million years ago) to about 570 million years ago, representing nearly ninety per cent of geological time. The oldest known Precambrian rocks have been dated to about 3,800 million years old, and the earliest living organisms date from the latter part of the aeon. The Precambrian is now replaced in formal stratigraphic schemes by the Archaean, Proterozoic, and (in some schemes) Priscoan aeons.

precancerous ▶ adjective Medicine (of a cell or medical condition) likely to develop into cancer if untreated: *precancerous skin lesions.*

precarious ▶ adjective **1** not securely held or in position; dangerously likely to fall or collapse: *a precarious ladder.*
2 dependent on chance; uncertain: *she made a precarious living by writing.*
– DERIVATIVES **precariously** adverb, **precariousness** noun.
– ORIGIN mid 17th cent.: from Latin *precarius* 'obtained by entreaty' (from *prex, prec-* 'prayer') + **-OUS**.

precast ▶ verb (past and past participle **precast**) [with obj.] [usu. as adj. **precast**] cast (an object or material, typically concrete) in its final shape before positioning: *precast concrete beams.*

precatory /ˈprɛkət(ə)ri/ ▶ adjective formal of, relating to, or expressing a wish or request.
■ Law (in a will) expressing a wish or intention of the testator: *a trust can be left in precatory words.*
– ORIGIN mid 17th cent.: from late Latin *precatorius*, from *precat-* 'prayed', from the verb *precari.*

precaution ▶ noun a measure taken in advance to prevent something dangerous, unpleasant, or inconvenient from happening: *he had **taken the precaution** of seeking legal advice.*

■ (**precautions**) informal used euphemistically to refer to contraception: *we never **took precautions**.*
– DERIVATIVES **precautionary** adjective.
– ORIGIN late 16th cent. (in the sense 'prudent foresight'): from French *précaution*, from late Latin *praecautio(n-)*, from Latin *praecavere*, from *prae* 'before' + *cavere* 'take heed, beware of'.

precede ▶ verb [with obj.] come before (something) in time: *a gun battle had preceded the explosions.*
■ come before in order or position: *take time to read the chapters that precede the recipes* | [as adj. **preceding**] *the preceding pages.* ■ go in front or ahead of: *he let her precede him through the gate.* ■ (**precede something with**) preface or introduce something with: *he preceded the book with a collection of poems.*
– ORIGIN late Middle English: from Old French *preceder*, from Latin *praecedere*, from *prae* 'before' + *cedere* 'go'.

precedence /ˈprɛsɪd(ə)ns, ˈpriː-, prɪˈsiːd(ə)ns/ ▶ noun [mass noun] the condition of being considered more important than someone or something else; priority in importance, order, or rank: *his desire for power soon **took precedence over** any other consideration.*
■ the order to be ceremonially observed by people of different rank, according to an acknowledged or legally determined system: *quarrels over precedence among the Bonaparte family marred the coronation.*

precedent ▶ noun /ˈprɛsɪd(ə)nt/ an earlier event or action that is regarded as an example or guide to be considered in subsequent similar circumstances: *there are substantial precedents for using interactive media in training* | [mass noun] *breaking with all precedent.*
■ Law a previous case or legal decision that may be or (**binding precedent**) must be followed in subsequent similar cases: *we hope to **set a legal precedent** to protect hundreds of miles of green lanes.*
▶ adjective /prɪˈsiːd(ə)nt, ˈprɛsɪ-/ preceding in time, order, or importance: *a precedent case.*
– ORIGIN late Middle English: from Old French, literally 'preceding'.

precentor /prɪˈsɛntə/ ▶ noun a person who leads a congregation in its singing or (in a synagogue) prayers.
■ a minor canon who administers the musical life of a cathedral.
– DERIVATIVES **precent** verb, **precentorship** noun.
– ORIGIN early 17th cent.: from French *précenteur* or Latin *praecentor*, from *praecent-* 'sung before', from the verb *praecinere*, from *prae* 'before' + *canere* 'sing'.

precept /ˈpriːsɛpt/ ▶ noun **1** a general rule intended to regulate behaviour or thought: *moral precepts* | *the legal precept of being innocent until proven guilty* | [mass noun] *children learn far more by example than by precept.*
2 a writ or warrant: *the Commissioner issued precepts requiring the companies to provide information.*
■ Brit. an order issued by one local authority to another specifying the rate of tax to be charged on its behalf. ■ Brit. this rate, or the tax itself.
– DERIVATIVES **preceptive** adjective.
– ORIGIN late Middle English: from Latin *praeceptum*, neuter past participle of *praecipere* 'warn, instruct', from *prae* 'before' + *capere* 'take'.

preceptor /prɪˈsɛptə/ ▶ noun a teacher or instructor.
– DERIVATIVES **preceptorial** /ˌpriːsɛpˈtɔːrɪəl/ adjective, **preceptorship** noun.
– ORIGIN late Middle English: from Latin *praeceptor*, from *praecept-* 'warned, instructed', from the verb *praecipere* (see **PRECEPT**).

precession ▶ noun [mass noun] Physics the slow movement of the axis of a spinning body around another axis due to a torque (such as gravitational influence) acting to change the direction of the first axis. It is seen in the circle slowly traced out by the pole of a spinning gyroscope.
– DERIVATIVES **precess** verb, **precessional** adjective.
– ORIGIN late 16th cent. (as a term in astronomy, referring to the **PRECESSION OF THE EQUINOXES**): from late Latin *praecessio(n-)*, from *praecedere* 'go before' (see **PRECEDE**).

precession of the equinoxes ▶ noun [mass noun] Astronomy the slow retrograde motion of equinoctial points along the ecliptic.
■ the resulting earlier occurrence of equinoxes in each successive sidereal year.

As the earth rotates about its axis it responds to the gravitational attraction of the sun upon its equatorial bulge, so that its axis of rotation describes a circle in the sky, with a period of about 26,000 years. The precession of the equinoxes was discovered by Hipparchus in c.125 BC, when the vernal equinox was in Aries.

pre-Christian ▶ adjective of or relating to a time before Christ or the advent of Christianity: *the pre-Christian world.*

precinct /ˈpriːsɪŋ(k)t/ ▶ noun **1** (usu. **precincts**) the area within the walls or perceived boundaries of a particular building or place: *a former MP who still works in the precincts of the House* | figurative *beyond the precincts of my own family I am quite inhibited.*
■ an enclosed or clearly defined area of ground around a cathedral, church, or college.
2 Brit. an area in a town designated for specific or restricted use, especially one which is closed to traffic: *a pedestrian precinct.*
3 N. Amer. a district of a city or town as defined for police purposes.
■ the police station situated in such a subdivision. ■ an electoral district of a city or town served by a single polling station.
– ORIGIN late Middle English (denoting an administrative district): from medieval Latin *praecinctum*, neuter past participle (used as a noun) of *praecingere* 'encircle', from *prae* 'before' + *cingere* 'gird'.

preciosity /ˌprɛʃɪˈɒsɪti/ ▶ noun [mass noun] over-refinement in art, music, or language, especially in the choice of words.
– ORIGIN mid 19th cent.: suggested by French *préciosité*, a sense derived from Molière's *Les Précieuses Ridicules* (1659), a comedy in which ladies frequenting the literary salons of Paris were satirized.

precious ▶ adjective **1** (of an object, substance, or resource) of great value; not to be wasted or treated carelessly: *precious works of art* | *my time's precious.*
■ greatly loved or treasured by someone: *look after my daughter—she's very precious to me.* ■ [attrib.] informal used to express the speaker's contempt for someone or something greatly valued by another person: *you and your precious schedule—you've got to lighten up!* ■ [attrib.] informal used for emphasis, often in an ironic context: *a precious lot you know about dogs!*
2 derogatory affectedly concerned with elegant or refined behaviour, language, or manners: *his exaggerated, precious manner.*
▶ noun used as a term of address to a beloved person: *don't be frightened, my precious.*
– PHRASES **precious little/few** extremely little or few (used for emphasis): *police still know precious little about the dead man.*
– DERIVATIVES **preciously** adverb, **preciousness** noun.
– ORIGIN Middle English: from Old French *precios*, from Latin *pretiosus* 'of great value', from *pretium* 'price'.

precious coral ▶ noun another term for **RED CORAL**.

precious metals ▶ plural noun gold, silver, and platinum.

precious stone ▶ noun a highly attractive and valuable piece of mineral, used especially in jewellery; a gemstone.

precipice ▶ noun a very steep rock face or cliff, especially a tall one: *we swerved toward the edge of the precipice.*
– ORIGIN late 16th cent. (denoting a headlong fall): from French *précipice* or Latin *praecipitium* 'abrupt descent', from *praeceps, praecip(it)-* 'steep, headlong'.

precipitancy ▶ noun [mass noun] rashness or suddenness of action: *matters were taken out of his control by the precipitancy of his commander.*

precipitant ▶ noun a cause of a particular action or event: *the immediate precipitants of the conflict were a succession of undisciplined actions.*
■ chiefly Psychology a cause or stimulus which precipitates a particular condition: *depression may be a precipitant in many cases.* ■ Chemistry a substance that causes the precipitation of a specified substance: *a protein precipitant.*
– DERIVATIVES **precipitance** noun.
– ORIGIN early 17th cent.: from obsolete French *précipitant* 'precipitating', present participle of *précipiter.*

precipitate ▶ verb /prɪˈsɪpɪteɪt/ [with obj.] **1** cause (an event or situation, typically one that is bad or undesirable) to happen suddenly, unexpectedly, or prematurely: *the incident precipitated a political crisis.*
■ [with obj. and adverbial of direction] cause to move suddenly and with force: *suddenly the ladder broke, precipitating them down into a heap.* ■ (**precipitate someone/thing into**) send someone or something suddenly into a

particular state or condition: *they were precipitated into a conflict for which they were quite unprepared.*
2 (usu. **be precipitated**) Chemistry cause (a substance) to be deposited in solid form from a solution.
■cause (drops of moisture or particles of dust) to be deposited from the atmosphere or from a vapour or suspension.
▶**adjective** /prɪˈsɪpɪtət/ done, made, or acting suddenly or without careful consideration: *I must apologize for my staff—their actions were precipitate.*
■(of an event or situation) occurring suddenly or abruptly: *a precipitate decline in Labour fortunes.*
▶**noun** /prɪˈsɪpɪtət, -teɪt/ Chemistry a substance precipitated from a solution. [ORIGIN: from modern Latin *praecipitatum*.]
– DERIVATIVES **precipitable** adjective, **precipitately** adverb, **precipitateness** /prɪˈsɪpɪtətnɪs/ noun.
– ORIGIN early 16th cent.: from Latin *praecipitat-* 'thrown headlong', from the verb *praecipitare*, from *praeceps, praecip(it)-* 'headlong', from *prae* 'before' + *caput* 'head'. The original sense of the verb was 'hurl down, send violently'; hence 'cause to move rapidly', which gave rise to sense 1 (early 17th cent.).

precipitation ▶**noun** [mass noun] **1** Chemistry the action or process of precipitating a substance from a solution.
2 rain, snow, sleet, or hail that falls to or condenses on the ground.
3 archaic the fact or quality of acting suddenly and rashly: *Cora was already regretting her precipitation.*
– ORIGIN late Middle English (denoting the action of falling or throwing down): from Latin *praecipitatio(n-)*, from *praecipitare* 'throw down or headlong' (see **PRECIPITATE**).

precipitator ▶**noun** an apparatus for causing precipitation, especially a device for removing dust from a gas.

precipitin /prɪˈsɪpɪtɪn/ ▶**noun** Biochemistry an antibody that produces a visible precipitate when it reacts with its antigen.
– ORIGIN early 20th cent.: from the verb **PRECIPITATE** + **-IN**[1].

precipitous /prɪˈsɪpɪtəs/ ▶**adjective 1** dangerously high or steep: *the track skirted a precipitous drop.*
■(of a change to a worse situation or condition) sudden and dramatic: *a precipitous slide in the government's popularity.*
2 (of an action) done suddenly and without careful consideration: *precipitous intervention.*
– DERIVATIVES **precipitously** adverb, **precipitousness** noun.
– ORIGIN mid 17th cent.: from obsolete French *précipiteux*, from Latin *praeceps, praecip(it)-* 'steep, headlong' (see **PRECIPITATE**).

precis /ˈpreɪsiː/ ▶**noun** (pl. same /-siːz/) a summary or abstract of a text or speech.
▶**verb** (**precises** /-siːz/, **precised** /-siːd/, **precising** /-siːɪŋ/) [with obj.] make a precis of (a text or speech).
– ORIGIN mid 18th cent.: from French *précis*, literally 'precise' (adjective used as a noun).

precise ▶**adjective** marked by exactness and accuracy of expression or detail: *precise directions* | *I want as precise a time of death as I can get.*
■(of a person) exact, accurate, and careful about details: *the director was precise with his camera positions.* ■ [attrib.] used to emphasize that one is referring to an exact and particular thing: *at that precise moment the car stopped.*
– PHRASES **to be precise** used to indicate that one is now giving more exact or detailed information: *there were not many—five, to be precise.*
– DERIVATIVES **preciseness** noun.
– ORIGIN late Middle English: from Old French *precis*, from Latin *praecis-* 'cut short', from the verb *praecidere*, from *prae* 'in advance' + *caedere* 'to cut'.

precisely ▶**adverb** in exact terms; without vagueness: *the guidelines are precisely defined.*
■exactly (used to emphasize the complete accuracy or truth of a statement): *at 2.00 precisely, the phone rang* | *kids will love it precisely because it will irritate their parents.* ■used as a reply to assert emphatic agreement with or confirmation of a statement: *'You mean it was a conspiracy?' 'Precisely.'*

precisian /prɪˈsɪʒ(ə)n/ ▶**noun** chiefly archaic a person who is rigidly precise or punctilious, especially as regards religious rules.
– DERIVATIVES **precisianism** noun.

precision ▶**noun** [mass noun] the quality, condition, or fact of being exact and accurate: *the deal was planned and executed with military precision.*
■[as modifier] marked by or adapted for accuracy and exactness: *a precision instrument.* ■ technical refinement in a measurement, calculation, or specification, especially as represented by the number of digits given: *this has brought an unprecedented degree of precision to the business of dating rocks* | [count noun] *a precision of six decimal figures.* Compare with **ACCURACY**.
– ORIGIN mid 18th cent.: from French *précision* or Latin *praecisio(n-)*, from *praecidere* 'cut off' (see **PRECISE**).

pre-classical ▶**adjective** of or relating to a time before a period regarded as classical, especially in music, literature, or ancient history.

preclinical ▶**adjective** Medicine relating to or denoting a stage preceding a clinical stage, in particular:
■relating to or denoting the first, chiefly theoretical, stage of a medical education: *preclinical students.* ■ relating to or denoting the stage in a disease prior to the appearance of symptoms that make a diagnosis possible. ■ relating to or denoting the stage of drug testing that precedes the clinical stage.

preclude ▶**verb** [with obj.] prevent from happening; make impossible: *the secret nature of his work precluded official recognition.*
■(**preclude someone from**) (of a situation or condition) prevent someone from doing something: *his difficulties preclude him from leading a normal life.*
– DERIVATIVES **preclusion** noun, **preclusive** adjective.
– ORIGIN late 15th cent. (in the sense 'bar (a route or passage)'): from Latin *praecludere*, from *prae* 'before' + *claudere* 'to shut'.

precocial /prɪˈkəʊʃ(ə)l/ Zoology ▶**adjective** (of a young bird or other animal) hatched or born in an advanced state and able to feed itself almost immediately. Also called **NIDIFUGOUS**. Often contrasted with **ALTRICIAL**.
■(of a particular species) having such young.
▶**noun** a precocial bird.
– ORIGIN late 19th cent.: from modern Latin *Praecoces* (the name of a former division of birds, plural of Latin *praecox* 'mature before its time') + **-IAL**.

precocious ▶**adjective** (of a child) having developed certain abilities or inclinations at an earlier age than usual: *he was a precocious, solitary boy.*
■(of behaviour or ability) indicative of such development: *a precocious talent for computing.* ■ (of a plant) flowering or fruiting earlier than usual.
– DERIVATIVES **precociously** adverb, **precociousness** noun, **precocity** noun.
– ORIGIN mid 17th cent.: from Latin *praecox, praecoc-* (from *praecoquere* 'ripen fully', from *prae* 'before' + *coquere* 'to cook') + **-IOUS**.

precognition ▶**noun 1** [mass noun] foreknowledge of an event, especially of a paranormal kind.
2 Law, chiefly Scottish the preliminary examination of witnesses, especially to decide whether there is ground for a trial.
– DERIVATIVES **precognitive** adjective (in sense 1).
– ORIGIN late Middle English: from late Latin *praecognitio(n-)*, based on Latin *cognoscere* 'know'.

precoital ▶**adjective** occurring before or as a preliminary to sexual intercourse.
– DERIVATIVES **precoitally** adverb.

pre-Columbian ▶**adjective** of or relating to the history and cultures of the Americas before the arrival of Columbus in 1492.

preconceived ▶**adjective** (of an idea or opinion) formed before having the evidence for its truth or usefulness: *the same set of facts can be tailored to fit any preconceived belief.*

preconception ▶**noun** a preconceived idea or prejudice.

preconcert /ˌpriːkənˈsəːt/ ▶**verb** [with obj.] archaic arrange or organize (something) in advance: [as adj. **preconcerted**] *a preconcerted signal.*

precondition ▶**noun** a condition that must be fulfilled before other things can happen or be done: *a precondition for peace.*
▶**verb** [with obj.] **1** (usu. **be preconditioned**) condition (an action) to happen in a certain way: *enquiries are always preconditioned by cultural assumptions.*
■condition or influence (a person or animal) by exposing them to stimuli or information prior to the relevant behavioural situation: [with obj. and infinitive] *the anthropologist is not preconditioned to interact with those he studies* | [as noun **preconditioning**] *the protective effect of preconditioning.*
2 bring (something) into the desired state for use: [as adj. **preconditioned**] *preconditioned paper.*

preconize /ˈpriːkənʌɪz/ (also **-ise**) ▶**verb** [with obj.] rare proclaim or commend publicly.
■(of the Pope) publicly approve the appointment of (a bishop).
– DERIVATIVES **preconization** noun.
– ORIGIN late Middle English: from medieval Latin *praeconizare*, from Latin *praeco(n-)* 'herald'.

pre-Conquest ▶**adjective** occurring or existing before the Norman conquest of England.

preconscious ▶**adjective** Psychoanalysis of or associated with a part of the mind below the level of immediate conscious awareness, from which memories and emotions that have not been repressed can be recalled: *beliefs and values which are on a preconscious level.*
▶**noun** (**one's/the preconscious**) Psychology the part of the mind in which preconscious thoughts or memories reside.
– DERIVATIVES **preconsciousness** noun.

pre-cook ▶**verb** [with obj.] cook in advance: [as adj. **pre-cooked**] *a pre-cooked pastry case.*

pre-cool ▶**verb** [with obj.] cool in advance: [as adj. **pre-cooled**] *clean, pre-cooled glass slides.*

precordium /priːˈkɔːdɪəm/ ▶**noun** Anatomy the region of the thorax immediately in front of or over the heart.
– DERIVATIVES **precordial** adjective.
– ORIGIN late 19th cent.: singular of Latin *praecordia* 'diaphragm, entrails'.

precursor ▶**noun** a person or thing that comes before another of the same kind; a forerunner: *a three-stringed precursor of the violin* | [as modifier] *precursor cells.*
■a substance from which another is formed, especially by metabolic reaction: *pepsinogen is the inactive precursor of pepsin.*
– ORIGIN late Middle English: from Latin *praecursor*, from *praecurs-* 'preceded', from *praecurrere*, from *prae* 'beforehand' + *currere* 'to run'.

precursory ▶**adjective** preceding something in time, development, or position; preliminary: *precursory seismic activity.*
– ORIGIN late 16th cent.: from Latin *praecursorius*, from *praecurs-* 'preceded' (see **PRECURSOR**).

pre-cut ▶**verb** [with obj.] [usu. as adj. **pre-cut**] cut into the desired shape or sections in advance: *pre-cut pieces of cloth.*

predacious /prɪˈdeɪʃəs/ (also **predaceous**) ▶**adjective** (of an animal) predatory: *predacious insects.*
– DERIVATIVES **predaciousness** noun, **predacity** noun.
– ORIGIN early 18th cent.: from Latin *praeda* 'booty' + **-ACIOUS**.

pre-date ▶**verb** [with obj.] exist or occur at a date earlier than (something): *here parish boundaries seem clearly to pre-date Roman roads.*

predation /prɪˈdeɪʃ(ə)n/ ▶**noun** [mass noun] Zoology the preying of one animal on others: *an effective defence against predation.*
– ORIGIN late 15th cent. (in the Latin sense): from Latin *praedatio(n-)* 'taking of booty', from the verb *praedari* 'seize as plunder', from *praeda* 'booty'. The current sense dates from the 1930s.

predator ▶**noun** an animal that naturally preys on others: *wolves are major predators of small mammals*
■figurative a rapacious, exploitative person or group: *predators prey on pensioners.* ■ figurative a company that tries to take over another.
– ORIGIN 1920s: from Latin *praedator* 'plunderer', from *praedat-* 'seized as plunder', from the verb *praedari* (see **PREDATION**).

predatory ▶**adjective** relating to or denoting an animal or animals preying naturally on others: *predatory birds.*
■figurative seeking to exploit or oppress others: *in pubs she always felt at the mercy of predatory men.*
– DERIVATIVES **predatorily** adverb, **predatoriness** noun.
– ORIGIN late 16th cent. (in the sense 'relating to plundering'): from Latin *praedatorius*, from *praedator* 'plunderer' (see **PREDATOR**).

predatory pricing ▶**noun** [mass noun] the pricing of goods or services at such a low level that other firms cannot compete and are forced to leave the market.

predecease formal ▶ **verb** [with obj.] die before (another person, typically someone related by blood or marriage): *his second wife predeceased him.*
▶ **noun** a death preceding that of another person.

predecessor ▶ **noun** a person who held a job or office before the current holder: *the new President's foreign policy is very similar to that of his predecessor.*
■ a thing that has been followed or replaced by another: *the chapel was built in 1864 on the site of its predecessor.*
– ORIGIN late Middle English: from late Latin *praedecessor*, from Latin *prae* 'beforehand' + *decessor* 'retiring officer' (from *decedere* 'depart').

predefined ▶ **adjective** defined, limited, or established in advance: *the terms are keyed in as predefined codes.*

predella /prɪˈdɛlə/ ▶ **noun 1** a step or platform on which an altar is placed.
2 a raised shelf above an altar.
■ a painting or sculpture on this, typically forming an appendage to an altarpiece.
– ORIGIN mid 19th cent.: from Italian, literally 'stool'.

predestinarian /prɪˌdɛstɪˈnɛːrɪən/ ▶ **noun** a person who believes in the doctrine of predestination.
▶ **adjective** upholding, affirming, or relating to the doctrine of predestination.

predestinate ▶ **verb** /priːˈdɛstɪneɪt/ [with obj.] predestine.
▶ **adjective** /priːˈdɛstɪnət/ predestined.
– ORIGIN late Middle English: from ecclesiastical Latin *praedestinat-* 'made firm beforehand', from the verb *praedestinare*, from *prae* 'in advance' + *destinare* 'establish'.

predestination ▶ **noun** [mass noun] (as a doctrine in Christian theology) the divine foreordaining of all that will happen, especially with regard to the salvation of some and not others. It has been particularly associated with the teachings of St Augustine of Hippo and of Calvin.
– ORIGIN Middle English: from ecclesiastical Latin *praedestinatio(n-)*, from *praedestinare* 'make firm beforehand' (see **PREDESTINATE**).

predestine ▶ **verb** [with obj.] (usu. **be predestined**) (of God) destine (someone) for a particular fate or purpose: *Calvinists believed that every person was predestined by God to go to heaven or to hell.*
■ determine (an outcome or course of events) in advance by divine will or fate: *she was certain that fate was with her and everything was predestined* | [as adj. **predestined**] *our predestined end.*
– ORIGIN late Middle English: from Old French *predestiner* or ecclesiastical Latin *praedestinare* (see **PREDESTINATE**).

p

predetermine ▶ **verb** [with obj.] establish or decide in advance: *closed questions almost predetermine the response given* | [as adj. **predetermined**] *a predetermined level of spending.*
■ (usu. **be predetermined**) predestine (an outcome or course of events): *a strong sense that life had been predetermined.*
– DERIVATIVES **predeterminable** adjective, **predetermination** adjective, **predetermination** noun.
– ORIGIN early 17th cent.: from late Latin *praedeterminare*, from *prae* 'beforehand' + *determinare* 'limit, settle'.

predeterminer ▶ **noun** Grammar a word or phrase that occurs before a determiner, typically quantifying the noun phrase, for example *both* or *a lot of*.

predial /ˈpriːdɪəl/ ▶ **adjective** archaic of, relating to, or consisting of land or farming: *political or predial sources of discontent.*
■ historical relating to or denoting a slave or tenant attached to farms or the land: *predial service.* ■ historical (of a tithe) consisting of agricultural produce.
▶ **noun** historical a predial slave.
– ORIGIN late Middle English: from medieval Latin *praedialis*, from Latin *praedium* 'farm'.

predicable /ˈprɛdɪkəb(ə)l/ ▶ **adjective** that may be predicated or affirmed.
▶ **noun** a thing that is predicable.
■ (usu. **predicables**) (in Aristotelian logic) each of the classes to which predicates belong, usually listed as: genus, species, difference, property, and accident.
– DERIVATIVES **predicability** noun.
– ORIGIN mid 16th cent.: from medieval Latin *praedicabilis* 'able to be affirmed', from Latin *praedicare* 'declare' (see **PREDICATE**).

predicament ▶ **noun 1** a difficult, unpleasant, or embarrassing situation: *the club's financial predicament.*
2 Philosophy, archaic (in Aristotelian logic) each of the ten 'categories', often listed as: substance or being, quantity, quality, relation, place, time, posture, having or possession, action, and passion.
– ORIGIN late Middle English (in sense 2): from late Latin *praedicamentum* 'something predicated' (rendering Greek *katēgoria* 'category'), from Latin *praedicare* (see **PREDICATE**). From the sense 'category' arose the sense 'state of being, condition'; hence 'unpleasant situation'.

predicant /ˈprɛdɪk(ə)nt/ ▶ **adjective** archaic (especially of the religious order of the Dominicans) characterized by preaching.
▶ **noun 1** archaic a preacher, especially a Dominican friar.
2 S. African variant spelling of **PREDIKANT**.
– ORIGIN late 16th cent.: from Latin *praedicant-* 'declaring', from the verb *praedicare*, in ecclesiastical Latin meaning 'preach'.

predicate ▶ **noun** /ˈprɛdɪkət/ Grammar the part of a sentence or clause containing a verb and stating something about the subject (e.g. *went home* in *John went home*).
■ Logic something which is affirmed or denied concerning an argument of a proposition.
▶ **verb** /ˈprɛdɪkeɪt/ [with obj.] **1** Grammar & Logic state, affirm, or assert (something) about the subject of a sentence or an argument of a proposition: *a word which predicates something about its subject* | *aggression is* ***predicated of*** *those who act aggressively.*
2 (**predicate something on/upon**) found or base something on: *the theory of structure on which later chemistry was predicated.*
– DERIVATIVES **predication** noun.
– ORIGIN late Middle English (as a noun): from Latin *praedicatum* 'something declared', neuter of *praedicatus* 'declared, proclaimed', past participle of the verb *praedicare*, from *prae* 'beforehand' + *dicare* 'make known'.

predicate calculus ▶ **noun** [mass noun] the branch of symbolic logic that deals with propositions containing predicates, names, and quantifiers.

predicative /prɪˈdɪkətɪv/ ▶ **adjective 1** Grammar (of an adjective or noun) forming or contained in the predicate, as *old* in *the dog is old* (but not in *the old dog*) and *house* in *there is a large house*. Contrasted with **ATTRIBUTIVE**.
■ denoting a use of the verb *to be* to assert something about the subject.
2 Logic acting as a predicate.
– DERIVATIVES **predicatively** adverb.
– ORIGIN mid 19th cent.: from Latin *praedicativus*, from *praedicat-* 'declared' (in medieval Latin 'predicated'), from the verb *praedicare* (see **PREDICATE**).

predicator /ˈprɛdɪkeɪtə/ ▶ **noun** (in systemic grammar) a verb phrase considered as a constituent of clause structure, along with subject, object, and adjunct.

predict ▶ **verb** [with obj.] say or estimate that (a specified thing) will happen in the future or will be a consequence of something: *it is too early to predict a result* | [with clause] *he predicts that the trend will continue* | [as adj. **predicted**] *the predicted growth in road traffic.*
– DERIVATIVES **predictor** noun.
– ORIGIN early 17th cent.: from Latin *praedict-* 'made known beforehand, declared', from the verb *praedicere*, from *prae-* 'beforehand' + *dicere* 'say'.

predictable ▶ **adjective** able to be predicted: *the market is volatile and never predictable.*
■ chiefly derogatory behaving or occurring in a way that is expected: *how very predictable you can be at times.*
– DERIVATIVES **predictability** noun, **predictably** adverb [sentence adverb] *predictably, Margaret found an excuse to interrupt him* | [as submodifier] *a predictably hostile response.*

prediction ▶ **noun** a thing predicted; a forecast: *a prediction that economic growth would resume.*
■ [mass noun] the action of predicting something: *the prediction of future behaviour.*
– ORIGIN mid 16th cent.: from Latin *praedictio(n-)*, from *praedicere* 'make known beforehand' (see **PREDICT**).

predictive ▶ **adjective** relating to or having the effect of predicting an event or result: *predictive accuracy* | *rules are not* ***predictive of*** *behaviour.*
– DERIVATIVES **predictively** adverb.

predigest ▶ **verb** (of an animal) treat (food) by a process similar to digestion in order to make it more digestible when subsequently eaten.
■ figurative make (language or ideas) easier to understand or appreciate, typically by simplification.
– DERIVATIVES **predigestion** noun.

predikant /ˌprɛdɪˈkant, ˌprɪədə-/ (also **predicant**) ▶ **noun** S. African a minister of the Dutch Reformed Church.
– ORIGIN Dutch, from ecclesiastical Latin *praedicare* 'preach'.

predilection /ˌpriːdɪˈlɛkʃ(ə)n/ ▶ **noun** a preference or special liking for something; a bias in favour of something: *your* ***predilection for*** *pretty girls.*
– ORIGIN mid 18th cent.: from French *prédilection*, from Latin *praedilect-* 'preferred', from the verb *praediligere*, from *prae* 'in advance' + *diligere* 'to select'.

predispose ▶ **verb** [with obj.] (**predispose someone to/to do something**) make someone liable or inclined to a specified attitude, action, or condition: *lack of exercise may predispose an individual to high blood pressure.*

predisposition ▶ **noun** a liability or tendency to suffer from a particular condition, hold a particular attitude, or act in a particular way: *a child may inherit a* ***predisposition to*** *schizophrenia* | [mass noun] *genetic predisposition.*

prednisolone /prɛdˈnɪsələʊn/ ▶ **noun** [mass noun] Medicine a synthetic steroid with similar properties and uses to those of prednisone, of which it is a reduced derivative.
– ORIGIN 1950s: from **PREDNISONE**, with the insertion of **-OL**.

prednisone /ˈprɛdnɪzəʊn/ ▶ **noun** [mass noun] Medicine a synthetic drug similar to cortisone, used to relieve rheumatic and allergic conditions and to treat leukaemia.
– ORIGIN 1950s: perhaps from *pre(gnane)* (a synthetic hydrocarbon) + *d(ie)n(e)* + *(cort)isone*.

predominance ▶ **noun** [mass noun] the state or condition of being greater in number or amount: *the demographic predominance of the Muslims* | [in sing.] *there is a predominance of female teachers.*
■ the possession or exertion of control or power: *an area of Soviet predominance.*

predominant ▶ **adjective** present as the strongest or main element: *its predominant colour was white.*
■ having or exerting control or power: *the predominant political forces.*
– ORIGIN mid 16th cent.: from Old French, from medieval Latin *predominant-* 'predominating', from the verb *predominari* (see **PREDOMINATE**).

predominantly ▶ **adverb** mainly; for the most part: [sentence adverb] *it is predominantly a coastal bird* | [as submodifier] *predominantly Russian areas.*

predominate ▶ **verb** [no obj.] be the strongest or main element; be greater in number or amount: *small-scale producers predominate in the south.*
■ have or exert control or power: *private interest was not allowed to* ***predominate over*** *the public good.*
– ORIGIN late 16th cent.: from medieval Latin *predominat-* 'predominated', from the verb *predominari* (see **PRE-**, **DOMINATE**).

predominately ▶ **adverb** another term for **PREDOMINANTLY**.

predoom ▶ **verb** [with obj.] poetic/literary condemn or determine the fate of (someone or something) in advance: *he was predoomed by the decrees of heaven.*

predynastic /ˌpriːdɪˈnastɪk, -dʌɪ-/ ▶ **adjective** of or relating to a period before the normally recognized dynasties, especially in ancient Egypt before about 3000 BC.

pre-echo ▶ **noun** (pl. **-oes**) **1** a faint copy heard just before an actual sound in a recording, caused by the accidental transfer of signals.
2 a foreshadowing: *one can detect pre-echoes of both the later works.*
▶ **verb** [with obj.] foreshadow: *these three sonatas all pre-echo things to come.*

pre-eclampsia ▶ **noun** [mass noun] a condition in pregnancy characterized by high blood pressure, sometimes with fluid retention and proteinuria.
– DERIVATIVES **pre-eclamptic** adjective & noun.

pre-elect ▶ **verb** [with obj.] (at Oxford and Cambridge Universities) elect (someone) to a post before the time they take up the appointment: *she was pre-elected to a junior research fellowship.*

pre-embryo ▶ **noun** technical a human embryo or fertilized ovum in the first fourteen days after fertilization, before implantation in the womb has occurred.
– DERIVATIVES **pre-embryonic** adjective.

preemie /ˈpriːmi/ ▶ **noun** (pl. **-ies**) N. Amer. informal a baby born prematurely.
– ORIGIN 1920s (as *premy*): from **PREMATURE** + **-IE**.

pre-eminent ▶ **adjective** surpassing all others; very distinguished in some way: *the world's pre-eminent expert on asbestos.*
– DERIVATIVES **pre-eminence** noun.
– ORIGIN late Middle English: from Latin *praeeminent-* 'towering above, excelling', from the verb *praeeminere*, from *prae* 'before' + *eminere* 'stand out'.

pre-eminently ▶ **adverb** [sentence adverb] above all; in particular: *the nineteenth century was pre-eminently the Railway Age.*

pre-empt ▶ **verb** [with obj.] **1** take action in order to prevent (an anticipated event) happening; forestall: *the government pre-empted a coup attempt.*
■act in advance of (someone) in order to prevent them doing something: *it looked as if she'd ask him more, but Parr pre-empted her.* ■ N. Amer. (of a broadcast) interrupt or replace (a scheduled programme): *the violence pre-empted regular programming.*
2 acquire or appropriate (something) in advance: *many tables were already pre-empted by family parties.*
■N. Amer. take (something, especially public land) for oneself so as to have the right of pre-emption.
3 [no obj.] Bridge make a pre-emptive bid.
▶ **noun** Bridge a pre-emptive bid.
– DERIVATIVES **pre-emptor** noun.
– ORIGIN mid 19th cent.: back-formation from **PRE-EMPTION**.

pre-emption ▶ **noun** [mass noun] **1** the purchase of goods or shares by one person or party before the opportunity is offered to others: *the commission had the right of pre-emption.*
■historical, chiefly N. Amer. & Austral. the right to purchase public land in this way.
2 the action of pre-empting or forestalling, especially of making a pre-emptive attack: *damaging retaliation for any attempt at pre-emption.*
■N. Amer. the interruption or replacement of a scheduled radio or television programme.
– ORIGIN early 17th cent.: from medieval Latin *praeemptio(n-)*, from the verb *praeemere*, from *prae* 'in advance' + *emere* 'buy'.

pre-emptive ▶ **adjective** serving or intended to pre-empt or forestall something, especially to prevent attack by disabling the enemy: *pre-emptive action* | *a pre-emptive strike.*
■relating to the purchase of goods or shares by one person or party before the opportunity is offered to others: *pre-emptive rights.* ■ Bridge denoting a bid, typically an opening bid, intended to be so high that it prevents or interferes with effective bidding by the opponents.

preen ▶ **verb** [no obj.] (of a bird) tidy and clean its feathers with its beak: *reed buntings preened at the pool's edge* | [with obj.] *the pigeon preened her feathers.*
■(of a person) devote effort to making oneself look attractive and then admire one's appearance: *adolescents preening in their bedroom mirrors.* ■ (**preen oneself**) congratulate or pride oneself: *he's busy preening himself on acquiring such a pretty girlfriend.*
– DERIVATIVES **preener** noun.
– ORIGIN late Middle English: apparently a variant of obsolete *prune* (based on Latin *ungere* 'anoint'), in the same sense, associated with Scots and northern English dialect *preen* 'pierce, pin' (because of the 'pricking' action of the bird's beak).

preen gland ▶ **noun** Ornithology (on a bird) a gland at the base of the tail, which produces the oil used in preening.

pre-establish ▶ **verb** [with obj.] [usu. as adj. **pre-established**] establish (something) in advance: *he had no pre-established plan.*

pre-exist ▶ **verb** [no obj.] [usu. as adj. **pre-existing**] exist at or from an earlier time: *a pre-existing contractual obligation.*
■[with obj.] exist at or from an earlier time than (something): *demons who pre-existed the Great Flood.*
– DERIVATIVES **pre-existence** noun, **pre-existent** adjective.

pre-exposure ▶ **noun** previous or premature exposure to something.
▶ **adjective** occurring or existing before exposure, especially exposure to a disease or infection: *pre-exposure vaccination.*

pref. ▶ **abbreviation for**
■preface. ■ preference (with reference to preference shares). ■ preferred (with reference to a preferred share).

prefab ▶ **noun** informal a prefabricated building.
– ORIGIN 1930s: abbreviation.

prefabricate ▶ **verb** [with obj.] [usu. as adj. **prefabricated**] manufacture sections of (a building or piece of furniture) to enable quick or easy assembly on site: *prefabricated homes.*
– DERIVATIVES **prefabrication** noun.

preface /ˈprɛfəs/ ▶ **noun** an introduction to a book, typically stating its subject, scope, or aims.
■the introduction or preliminary part of a speech or event. ■ Christian Church the introduction to the central part of the Eucharist, historically forming the first part of the canon or prayer of consecration. In the Western Church it comes between the Sursum Corda and the Sanctus and varies with the season.
▶ **verb** [with obj.] provide (a book) with a preface: *the book is prefaced by a quotation from William Faulkner.*
■(**preface something with/by**) introduce or begin (a speech or event) with or by doing something: *it is important to preface the debate with a general comment.*
– DERIVATIVES **prefatory** /ˈprɛfət(ə)ri/ adjective.
– ORIGIN late Middle English: via Old French from medieval Latin *praefatia*, alteration of Latin *praefatio(n-)* 'words spoken beforehand', from the verb *praefari*, from *prae* 'before' + *fari* 'speak'.

prefect ▶ **noun** **1** chiefly Brit. a senior pupil in some schools authorized to enforce discipline.
2 a chief officer, magistrate, or regional governor in certain countries: *the prefect of police.*
■a senior magistrate or governor in the ancient Roman world: *Avitus was prefect of Gaul from AD 439.*
– DERIVATIVES **prefectoral** adjective, **prefectorial** adjective.
– ORIGIN late Middle English (in sense 2): from Old French, from Latin *praefectus*, past participle of *praeficere* 'set in authority over', from *prae* 'before' + *facere* 'make'. Sense 1 dates from the early 19th cent.

prefecture ▶ **noun** a district under the government of a prefect.
■a prefect's office or tenure. ■ the official residence or headquarters of a prefect.
– DERIVATIVES **prefectural** adjective.
– ORIGIN late Middle English: from Latin *praefectura*, from *praefectus* '(person) set in authority over' (see **PREFECT**).

prefer ▶ **verb** (**preferred**, **preferring**) [with obj.] **1** like (one thing or person) better than another or others; tend to choose: *I prefer Venice* **to** *Rome* | [with infinitive] *I would prefer to discuss the matter in private* | [with clause] *Val would presumably prefer that you didn't get arrested* | [as adj. **preferred**] *his preferred candidate.*
2 formal submit (a charge or a piece of information) for consideration: *the police will prefer charges.*
3 archaic promote or advance (someone) to a prestigious position: *he was* **preferred to** *the post.*
– ORIGIN late Middle English: from Old French *preferer*, from Latin *praeferre*, from *prae* 'before' + *ferre* 'to bear, carry'.

preferable ▶ **adjective** more desirable or suitable: *lower interest rates were* **preferable to** *higher ones.*
– DERIVATIVES **preferability** noun.

preferably ▶ **adverb** [sentence adverb] ideally; if possible: *he would like a place of his own, preferably outside the town.*

preference ▶ **noun** **1** a greater liking for one alternative over another or others: **a preference for** *long walks and tennis over jogging* | [mass noun] *he chose a clock* **in preference to** *a watch.*
■a thing preferred: *nearly 40 per cent named acid house as their musical preference.* ■ [mass noun] favour shown to one person or thing over another or others: *preference is given to those who make a donation.*
2 Law a prior right or precedence, especially in connection with the payment of debts: *debts owed to the community should be accorded a preference.*
– ORIGIN late Middle English (in the sense 'promotion'): from Old French, from medieval Latin *praeferentia*, from Latin *praeferre* 'carry in front' (see **PREFER**).

preference share (or **stock**) (US **preferred share** or **stock**) ▶ **noun** a share which entitles the holder to a fixed dividend, whose payment takes priority over that of ordinary share dividends.

preferential ▶ **adjective** of or involving preference or partiality; constituting a favour or privilege: *preferential interest rates may be offered to employees.*
■(of regulations or rates) favouring particular countries: *preferential trade terms.* ■ (of voting or an election) in which the voter puts candidates in order of preference. ■ (of a creditor) having a claim on the receipt of payment from a debtor which will be met before those of other creditors.
– DERIVATIVES **preferentially** adverb.
– ORIGIN mid 19th cent.: from **PREFERENCE**, on the pattern of *differential*.

preferment ▶ **noun** [mass noun] promotion or appointment to a position or office: *after ordination, preferment was fast* | [count noun] *most of her ministers owed their first preferment to her.*

preferred share ▶ **noun** US term for **PREFERENCE SHARE**.

prefetch Computing ▶ **verb** /priːˈfɛtʃ/ [with obj.] transfer (data) from main memory to temporary storage in readiness for later use.
▶ **noun** /ˈpriːfɛtʃ/ a process involving such a transfer.

prefigure ▶ **verb** [with obj.] **1** be an early indication or version of (something): *the Hussite movement prefigured the Reformation.*
2 archaic imagine beforehand: *she had prefigured her small pilgrimage as made in solitude.*
– DERIVATIVES **prefiguration** noun, **prefigurative** adjective, **prefigurement** noun.
– ORIGIN late Middle English: from ecclesiastical Latin *praefigurare* 'represent beforehand', from *prae* 'before' + *figurare* 'to form, fashion'.

prefix ▶ **noun** a word, letter, or number placed before another: *the Institute was granted the prefix 'Royal' in 1961.*
■an element placed at the beginning of a word to adjust or qualify its meaning (e.g. *ex-*, *non-*, *re-*) or (in some languages) as an inflection. ■ a title placed before a name (e.g. *Mr*).
▶ **verb** [with obj.] add (something) at the beginning as a prefix or introduction: *a preface is* **prefixed to** *the book.*
■add a prefix or introduction to (something): *all three-digit numbers will now be* **prefixed by** *580.*
– DERIVATIVES **prefixation** noun.
– ORIGIN mid 16th cent. (as a verb): from Old French *prefixer*, from Latin *praefixus* 'fixed in front', from the verb *praefigere*, from *prae* 'before' + *figere* 'to fix'. The noun is from modern Latin *praefixum*, neuter (used as a noun) of *praefixus*, and dates from the mid 17th cent.

preflight ▶ **adjective** occurring before a flight in an aircraft: *our detailed preflight briefing.*

prefocus ▶ **adjective** [attrib.] relating to or denoting a light bulb which is designed so that its beam is focused automatically when it is fitted inside a lamp, especially a vehicle headlamp.

preform ▶ **verb** [with obj.] [usu. as adj. **preformed**] form (something) beforehand: *a preformed pool.*

preformation ▶ **noun** [mass noun] the action or process of preforming something.
■Biology, historical the theory, now discarded, that an embryo develops from a complete miniature version of the organism. Often contrasted with **EPIGENESIS**.
– DERIVATIVES **preformationist** noun & adjective.

prefrontal ▶ **adjective** [attrib.] **1** Anatomy in or relating to the foremost part of the frontal lobe of the brain: *the prefrontal cortex.*
2 Zoology relating to or denoting a bone in front of the eye socket in some lower vertebrates (equivalent to part of the human ethmoid bone).
▶ **noun** Zoology a prefrontal bone.

pregenital ▶ **adjective** **1** Psychoanalysis relating to psychosexual development before the genital phase.
2 Zoology situated in front of the genital region.

preggers ▶ **adjective** [predic.] informal pregnant.

preglacial ▶ **adjective** of, relating to, or denoting a time before a glacial period.

pregnable ▶ **adjective** vulnerable to attack; not impregnable: *the fort's pregnable approaches.*
– ORIGIN late Middle English: from Old French *prenable*, literally 'takable', from Latin *prehendere* 'seize'. The *g* was sometimes written in French, perhaps indicating palatal *n*, but has come to be pronounced as a separate sound in English.

pregnancy ▶ **noun** (pl. **-ies**) [mass noun] the condition or period of being pregnant: *the first weeks of pregnancy.*

p

■[count noun] a case or situation of being pregnant: *a straightforward pregnancy.*

pregnant ▶ adjective 1 (of a woman or female animal) having a child or young developing in the uterus: *a pregnant woman | she was heavily pregnant with her second child.*
■having been in such a condition for a specified time: *she was six months pregnant.*
2 full of meaning; significant or suggestive: *a pregnant pause | a development pregnant with implications.*
– DERIVATIVES **pregnantly** adverb.
– ORIGIN late Middle English: from Latin *praegnant-*, probably from *prae* 'before' + the base of *gnasci* 'be born'.

preheat ▶ verb [with obj.] heat (something, especially an oven or grill) beforehand: *preheat the oven to 200°C.*

prehensile /prɪˈhɛnsʌɪl/ ▶ adjective (chiefly of an animal's limb or tail) capable of grasping.
– DERIVATIVES **prehensility** noun.
– ORIGIN late 18th cent.: from French *préhensile*, from Latin *prehens-* 'grasped', from the verb *prehendere*, from *prae* 'before' + *hendere* 'to grasp'.

prehension ▶ noun [mass noun] 1 Zoology & Psychology the action of grasping or seizing.
2 Philosophy an interaction of a subject with an event or entity which involves perception but not necessarily cognition.
– ORIGIN early 19th cent.: from Latin *prehensio(n-)*, from *prehendere* 'to grasp'.

prehistoric ▶ adjective of, relating to, or denoting the period before written records: *prehistoric man.*
■informal very old, primitive, or out of date: *my dad's electric typewriter was a prehistoric machine.*
– DERIVATIVES **prehistorian** noun, **prehistorically** adverb.
– ORIGIN mid 19th cent.: from French *préhistorique* (see **PRE-**, **HISTORIC**).

prehistory ▶ noun [mass noun] the period of time before written records: *myths that stretch back into prehistory.*
■the events or conditions leading up to a particular occurrence or phenomenon: *the prehistory of capitalism.*

prehuman ▶ adjective of, relating to, or denoting the time before the appearance of human beings, especially the evolutionary stage immediately preceding the development of modern humans.
▶ noun a precursor of the human species.

pre-ignition ▶ noun [mass noun] the premature combustion of the fuel–air mixture in an internal-combustion engine.

pre-industrial ▶ adjective of or relating to a time before industrialization: *a pre-industrial society.*

pre-install ▶ verb another term for **PRELOAD**.

prejudge ▶ verb [with obj.] form a judgement on (an issue or person) prematurely and without having adequate information: *it is wrong to prejudge an issue on the basis of speculation.*
– DERIVATIVES **prejudgement** (also **prejudgment**) noun.

prejudice ▶ noun [mass noun] 1 preconceived opinion that is not based on reason or actual experience: *English prejudice against foreigners* | [count noun] *anti-Jewish prejudices.*
■dislike, hostility, or unjust behaviour formed on such a basis: *accusations of racial prejudice.*
2 chiefly Law harm or injury that results or may result from some action or judgement: *prejudice resulting from delay in the institution of the proceedings.*
▶ verb [with obj.] 1 give rise to prejudice in (someone); make biased: *the statement might prejudice the jury.*
2 chiefly Law cause harm to (a state of affairs): *delay is likely to prejudice the child's welfare.*
– PHRASES **without prejudice** Law without detriment to any existing right or claim: *the payment was made without any prejudice to her claim.*
– ORIGIN Middle English (in sense 2 of the noun): from Old French, from Latin *praejudicium*, from *prae* 'in advance' + *judicium* 'judgement'.

prejudiced ▶ adjective having or showing a dislike or distrust that is derived from prejudice; bigoted: *people are prejudiced against us | prejudiced views.*

prejudicial ▶ adjective harmful to someone or something; detrimental: *the proposals were considered prejudicial to the city centre.*
– DERIVATIVES **prejudicially** adverb.

– ORIGIN late Middle English: from Old French *prejudiciel*, from *prejudice* (see **PREJUDICE**).

prelacy /ˈprɛləsi/ ▶ noun (pl. **-ies**) [mass noun] chiefly archaic the government of the Christian Church by clerics of high social rank and power.
■[count noun] the office or rank of a prelate. ■ (**the prelacy**) prelates collectively.
– ORIGIN Middle English: from Anglo-Norman French *prelacie*, from medieval Latin *prelatia*, from *praelatus* (see **PRELATE**).

prelapsarian /ˌpriːlapˈsɛːrɪən/ ▶ adjective Theology or poetic/literary characteristic of the time before the Fall of Man; innocent and unspoilt: *a prelapsarian Eden of astonishing plenitude.*
– ORIGIN late 19th cent.: from **PRE-** 'before', on the pattern of *sublapsarian.*

prelate /ˈprɛlət/ ▶ noun formal or historical a bishop or other high ecclesiastical dignitary.
– DERIVATIVES **prelatic** /prɪˈlatɪk/ adjective, **prelatical** /prɪˈlatɪk(ə)l/ adjective.
– ORIGIN Middle English: from Old French *prelat*, from medieval Latin *praelatus* 'civil dignitary', past participle (used as a noun) of Latin *praeferre* 'carry before', also 'place before in esteem'.

prelature ▶ noun the office, rank, or sphere of authority of a prelate.
■(**the prelature**) prelates collectively.
– ORIGIN early 17th cent.: from French *prélature*, from medieval Latin *praelatura*, from *praelatus* 'civil dignitary' (see **PRELATE**).

prelim /ˈpriːlɪm, prɪˈlɪm/ ▶ noun informal 1 an event which precedes or prepares for another, in particular:
■a preliminary examination, especially at a university. ■ a preliminary round in a sporting competition: *the prelims of the 400-meter free relay.*
2 (**prelims**) the pages preceding the main text of a book, including the title, contents, and preface.
– ORIGIN late 19th cent.: abbreviation of **PRELIMINARY**.

preliminary ▶ adjective denoting an action or event preceding or done in preparation for something fuller or more important: *preliminary talks | the discussions were seen as preliminary to the policy paper.*
▶ noun (pl. **-ies**) an action or event preceding or preparing for something fuller or more important: *the bombardment was resumed as a preliminary to an infantry attack.*
■(**preliminaries**) business or talk, especially of a formulaic or polite nature, taking place before an action or event: *she began speaking, without preliminaries.* ■ a preliminary round in a sporting competition. ■ (**preliminaries**) fuller form of *prelims* (see **PRELIM** (sense 2)).
– PHRASES **preliminary to** preparatory to; in advance of.
– DERIVATIVES **preliminarily** adverb.
– ORIGIN mid 17th cent.: from modern Latin *praeliminaris* or French *préliminaire*, from Latin *prae* 'before' + *limen, limin-* 'threshold'.

prelingually deaf ▶ adjective deaf from birth or from a time in infancy before the development of the ability to speak.

prelinguistic ▶ adjective of or at a stage before the development of language (by the human species) or the acquisition of speech (by a child).

preliterate ▶ adjective of, relating to, or denoting a society or culture that has not developed the use of writing.

preload ▶ verb /priːˈləʊd/ [with obj.] load beforehand: *the camera comes preloaded with a 24-exposure film.*
■give (a mechanical component) an internal load independent of any working load, typically in order to reduce distortion or noise in operation.
▶ noun [mass noun] something loaded or applied as a load beforehand.

prelude /ˈprɛljuːd/ ▶ noun 1 an action or event serving as an introduction to something more important: *education cannot simply be a prelude to a career.*
2 an introductory piece of music, most commonly an orchestral opening to an act of an opera, the first movement of a suite, or a piece preceding a fugue.
■a short piece of music of a similar style, especially for the piano. ■ the introductory part of a poem or other literary work.
▶ verb [with obj.] serve as a prelude or introduction to: *the bombardment preluded an all-out final attack.*

– DERIVATIVES **preludial** adjective.
– ORIGIN mid 16th cent.: from French *prélude*, from medieval Latin *praeludium*, from Latin *praeludere* 'play beforehand', from *prae* 'before' + *ludere* 'to play'.

premarital ▶ adjective occurring or existing before marriage: *premarital sex.*
– DERIVATIVES **premaritally** adverb.

premaster ▶ verb [with obj.] Computing make a master copy of (data) on a hard disk before writing it to a CD-ROM.

premature ▶ adjective occurring or done before the usual or proper time; too early: *the sun can cause premature ageing* | [with infinitive] *it would be premature to do so at this stage.*
■(of a baby) born before the end of the full term of gestation, especially three or more weeks before.
– DERIVATIVES **prematurely** adverb [as submodifier] *prematurely grey hair,* **prematurity** noun.
– ORIGIN late Middle English (in the sense 'ripe, mature'): from Latin *praematurus* 'very early', from *prae* 'before' + *maturus* 'ripe'.

premaxillary ▶ adjective Anatomy situated in front of the maxilla.

pre-med ▶ noun 1 chiefly N. Amer. a program of premedical studies.
■a student on such a course.
2 short for **PRE-MEDICATION**.
▶ adjective short for **PREMEDICAL**.

premedical ▶ adjective of, relating to, or engaged in study in preparation for medical school.

pre-medication ▶ noun [mass noun] medication which is given in preparation for an operation or other treatment.

premeditate ▶ verb [with obj.] [usu. as adj. **premeditated**] think out or plan (an action, especially a crime) beforehand: *premeditated murder.*
– DERIVATIVES **premeditation** noun.
– ORIGIN mid 16th cent.: from Latin *praemeditat-* 'thought out before', from the verb *praemeditari*, from *prae* 'before' + *meditari* 'meditate'.

premenopausal /priːˌmɛnəˈpɔːz(ə)l/ ▶ adjective of or in the period of a woman's life immediately preceding the menopause.

premenstrual /priːˈmɛnstruəl/ ▶ adjective of, occurring, or experienced before menstruation: *premenstrual tension.*
– DERIVATIVES **premenstrually** adverb.

premenstrual syndrome (abbrev.: **PMS**) ▶ noun [mass noun] any of a complex of symptoms (including emotional tension and fluid retention) experienced by some women in the days immediately before menstruation.

premier /ˈprɛmɪə, ˈpriː-/ ▶ adjective [attrib.] first in importance, order, or position; leading: *Germany's premier rock band | the premier league.*
■of earliest creation: *he holds the premier barony in the UK—created in 1269.*
▶ noun a Prime Minister or other head of government.
■(in Australia and Canada) the chief minister of a government of a state or province.
– ORIGIN late 15th cent.: from Old French, 'first', from Latin *primarius* 'principal'.

premier cru /ˌprɛmɪə ˈkruː, French prəmje kry/ ▶ noun (pl. **premiers crus** pronunc. same) (chiefly in French official classifications) a wine of a superior grade, or the vineyard that produces it. Compare with **GRAND CRU**.
– ORIGIN French, literally 'first growth'.

premiere /ˈprɛmɪɛː/ ▶ noun the first performance of a musical or theatrical work or the first showing of a film.
▶ verb [with obj.] give the first performance of: *his first stage play was premiered at the Birmingham Repertory Theatre.*
■[no obj.] (of a musical or theatrical work or a film) have its first performance: *the show premiered in New York this week.*
– ORIGIN late 19th cent.: French *première*, feminine of *premier* 'first' (see **PREMIER**).

premier grand cru /ˌprɛmɪə ˌgrɒ̃(d) ˈkruː, French prəmje grɑ̃ kry/ ▶ noun (pl. **premier grand crus**) S. African a dry white wine, especially a blended one.
– ORIGIN French, literally 'first great growth'.

premiership ▶ noun [mass noun] 1 the office or position of a Prime Minister or other head of government.

2 (**the Premiership**) the top division of professional soccer in England.

premillennial ▶**adjective** existing or occurring before a new millennium.
■Christian Theology relating to or believing in premillennialism.

premillennialism ▶**noun** [mass noun] (among Christian fundamentalists) the doctrine that the prophesied millennium of blessedness will begin with the imminent Second Coming of Christ.
– DERIVATIVES **premillennialist** noun.

Preminger /ˈprɛmɪndʒə/, Otto (Ludwig) (1906–86), Austrian-born American film director. Notable productions: *The Moon is Blue* (1953), *The Man with the Golden Arm* (1955), and *Bonjour Tristesse* (1959).

premise ▶**noun** /ˈprɛmɪs/ (Brit. also **premiss**) Logic a previous statement or proposition from which another is inferred or follows as a conclusion: *if the premise is true, then the conclusion must be true.*
■an assertion or proposition which forms the basis for a work or theory: *the fundamental premise of the report.*
▶**verb** /prɪˈmʌɪz/ [with obj.] (**premise something on/upon**) base an argument, theory, or undertaking on: *the reforms were premised on our findings.*
■state or presuppose (something) as a premise: [with clause] *one school of thought premised that the cosmos is indestructible.* ■archaic state by way of introduction: [with clause] *I will premise generally that I hate lecturing.*
– ORIGIN late Middle English: from Old French *premisse*, from medieval Latin *praemissa (propositio)* '(proposition) set in front', from Latin *praemittere*, from *prae* 'before' + *mittere* 'send'.

premises ▶**plural noun** a house or building, together with its land and outbuildings, occupied by a business or considered in an official context: *business premises | supplying alcoholic liquor for consumption **on the premises**.*

premium ▶**noun** (pl. **premiums**) **1** an amount to be paid for a contract of insurance.
2 a sum added to an ordinary price or charge: *customers are reluctant to pay a premium for organic fruit.*
■a sum added to interest or wages; a bonus. ■[as modifier] relating to or denoting a commodity or product of superior quality and therefore a higher price: *premium lagers.* ■Stock Exchange the amount by which the price of a share or other security exceeds its issue price, its nominal value, or the value of the assets it represents: *the shares jumped to a 70 per cent premium on the first day.*
3 something given as a reward, prize, or incentive: *the Society of Arts awarded him a premium.*
– PHRASES **at a premium 1** scarce and in demand: *space was at a premium.* **2** above the usual or nominal price: *touts sell the tickets at a premium.* **put** (or **place**) **a premium on** regard or treat as particularly valuable or important: *he put a premium on peace and stability.*
– ORIGIN early 17th cent. (in the sense 'reward, prize'): from Latin *praemium* 'booty, reward', from *prae* 'before' + *emere* 'buy, take'.

Premium Bond (also **Premium Savings Bond**) ▶**noun** (in the UK) a government security that offers no interest or capital gain but is entered in regular draws for cash prizes.

premix ▶**verb** [with obj.] mix in advance: *I premix all my colours.*
▶**noun** a mixture that is provided already mixed, in particular:
■a ready-mixed feed for cattle or horses. ■a preparation of the dry components of a building material such as concrete or plaster.

premodify ▶**verb** (**-modifies**, **-modified**) [with obj.] Grammar modify the sense of (a noun or other word) by being placed before it.
– DERIVATIVES **premodification** noun, **premodifier** noun.

premolar ▶**noun** a tooth situated between the canine and the molar teeth. An adult human normally has eight, two in each jaw on each side.

premonition /ˌprɛməˈnɪʃ(ə)n, ˌpriː-/ ▶**noun** a strong feeling that something is about to happen, especially something unpleasant: *he had a **premonition of** imminent disaster.*
– DERIVATIVES **premonitory** adjective.
– ORIGIN mid 16th cent. (in the sense 'advance warning'): from French *prémonition*, from late Latin *praemonitio(n-)*, from Latin *praemonere*, from *prae* 'before' + *monere* 'warn'.

Premonstratensian /ˌpriːmɒnstrəˈtɛnsɪən/ ▶**noun** a member of an order of regular canons founded at Prémontré in France in 1120, or of the corresponding order of nuns. Also called **NORBERTINE**.
▶**adjective** of or relating to the Premonstratensians.
– ORIGIN from medieval Latin *Praemonstratensis*, from *Praemonstratus* (literally 'foreshown'), the Latin name of the abbey of Prémontré, so named because the site was prophetically pointed out by the order's founder, St Norbert.

premorbid ▶**adjective** Medicine & Psychiatry preceding the occurrence of symptoms of disease or disorder.

premotor ▶**adjective** [attrib.] Anatomy relating to or denoting the anterior part of the motor cortex in the frontal lobe of the brain, which is concerned with coordinating voluntary movement.

premultiply ▶**verb** (**-ies**, **-ied**) [with obj.] Mathematics multiply (a vector, matrix, or element of a group) non-commutatively by a preceding factor.
– DERIVATIVES **premultiplication** noun.

prenatal ▶**adjective** before birth; during or relating to pregnancy; antenatal: *prenatal development.*
– DERIVATIVES **prenatally** adverb.

pre-need ▶**adjective** denoting a scheme in which one pays in advance for a service or facility.

prenominal ▶**adjective** Grammar (of a word or part of speech) preceding a noun.
– DERIVATIVES **prenominally** adverb.
– ORIGIN mid 17th cent.: from Latin *praenomen, praenomin-* 'first name' + **-AL**.

prentice ▶**noun** & **verb** archaic term for **APPRENTICE**.
– DERIVATIVES **prenticeship** noun.

prenup ▶**noun** N. Amer. informal a prenuptial agreement.
– ORIGIN 1990s: abbreviation.

prenuptial ▶**adjective** existing or occurring before marriage: *prenuptial pregnancy.*
■Zoology existing or occurring before mating.

prenuptial agreement ▶**noun** chiefly N. Amer. an agreement made by a couple before they marry concerning the ownership of their respective assets should the marriage fail.

preoccupation ▶**noun** [mass noun] the state or condition of being preoccupied or engrossed with something: *his **preoccupation with** politics.*
■[count noun] a subject or matter that engrosses someone: *their main preoccupation was how to feed their families.*
– ORIGIN late 16th cent. (first used in rhetoric in the sense 'anticipating and meeting objections beforehand'): from Latin *praeoccupatio(n-)*, from *praeoccupare* 'seize beforehand' (see **PREOCCUPY**).

preoccupy ▶**verb** (**-ies**, **-ied**) [with obj.] (of a matter or subject) dominate or engross the mind of (someone) to the exclusion of other thoughts: *his mother was **preoccupied with** paying the bills* | [as adj. **preoccupied**] *she seemed a bit preoccupied.*
– ORIGIN mid 16th cent.: from **PRE-** + **OCCUPY**, suggested by Latin *praeoccupare* 'seize beforehand'.

preocular ▶**adjective** in front of the eye.

pre-op informal ▶**adjective** short for **PREOPERATIVE**.
▶**noun** a tranquillizing injection or other treatment administered in preparation for a surgical operation.

preoperative ▶**adjective** denoting, administered in, or occurring in the period before a surgical operation.
– DERIVATIVES **preoperatively** adverb.

preorbital ▶**adjective** chiefly Zoology situated in front of the orbit or eye socket.

preordain ▶**verb** [with obj.] (usu. **be preordained**) decide or determine (an outcome or course of action) beforehand: *you might think the company's success was preordained* | [as adj. **preordained**] *a divinely preordained plan of creation.*

pre-owned ▶**adjective** chiefly N. Amer. second-hand.

prep[1] ▶**noun** informal **1** [mass noun] Brit. (especially in an independent school) school work that is set to be done outside lessons.
■a period when this is done. ■[as modifier] relating to education in a preparatory school: *the prep department.*
2 N. Amer. a student in a preparatory school.
– ORIGIN mid 19th cent.: abbreviation of **PREPARATION**.

prep[2] N. Amer. informal ▶**verb** (**prepped**, **prepping**) [with obj.] prepare (something); make ready: *scores of volunteers help prep the food.*
■[no obj.] N. Amer. prepare oneself for an event: *to prep for his role he trimmed his unruly locks.*
▶**noun** [mass noun] preparation: *I do the prep* | [as modifier] *I had virtually no prep time.*
– ORIGIN 1920s: abbreviation of **PREPARE** or **PREPARATION**.

prep. ▶**abbreviation** for preposition.

pre-pack (also **pre-package**) ▶**verb** [with obj.] [usu. as adj. **pre-packed**] pack or wrap (goods, especially food) on the site of production or before sale: *pre-packed salmon steaks.*

prepaid past and past participle of **PREPAY**.

preparation ▶**noun** [mass noun] the action or process of making ready or being made ready for use or consideration: *the preparation of a draft contract | the project is **in preparation**.*
■[count noun] (usu. **preparations**) something done to get ready for an event or undertaking: *she continued her **preparations for** the party.* ■[count noun] a substance that is specially made up and usually sold, especially a medicine or food. ■[count noun] a specimen that has been prepared for scientific or medical examination: *a microscope preparation.* ■Brit. dated fuller form of **PREP**[1] (in sense 1). ■Music (in conventional harmony) the sounding of the discordant note in a chord in the preceding chord where it is not discordant, lessening the effect of the discord.
– ORIGIN late Middle English: via Old French from Latin *praeparatio(n-)*, from *praeparare* 'make ready before' (see **PREPARE**).

preparative ▶**adjective** preparatory.
▶**noun** a thing which acts as a preparation: *schools where parents send children as a preparative for worldly success.*
– DERIVATIVES **preparatively** adverb.

preparatory ▶**adjective** serving as or carrying out preparation for a task or undertaking: *more preparatory work is needed.*
■Brit. relating to education in a preparatory school: *preparatory schooling.*
– PHRASES **preparatory to** as a preparation for: *she applied her make-up preparatory to leaving.*
– ORIGIN late Middle English: from late Latin *praeparatorius*, from *praeparat-* 'made ready beforehand', from the verb *praeparare* (see **PREPARE**).

preparatory school ▶**noun 1** Brit. a private school for pupils between the ages of seven and thirteen.
2 N. Amer. a private school that prepares pupils for college or university.

prepare ▶**verb** [with obj.] **1** make (something) ready for use or consideration: *prepare a brief summary of the article.*
■make (food or a meal) ready for cooking or eating: *she was busy preparing lunch.* ■make (someone) ready or able to do or deal with something: *schools should **prepare** children **for** life | by this time I was **prepared for** anything.* ■[no obj.] make oneself ready to do or deal with something: *she took time off to **prepare for** her exams* | [with infinitive] *school-leavers preparing to start degree courses.* ■(**be prepared to do something**) be willing to do something: *I wasn't prepared to go along with that.* ■make (a chemical product) by a reaction or series of reactions.
2 Music (in conventional harmony) lead up to (a discord) by means of preparation.
– DERIVATIVES **preparer** noun.
– ORIGIN late Middle English: from French *préparer* or Latin *praeparare*, from *prae* 'before' + *parare* 'make ready'.

preparedness ▶**noun** [mass noun] a state of readiness, especially for war: *the country maintained a high level of military preparedness.*

prepared piano ▶**noun** a piano with objects placed on or between the strings, or some strings retuned, to produce an unusual tonal effect.

prepay ▶**verb** (past and past participle **prepaid**) [with obj.] [usu. as adj. **prepaid**] pay for in advance: *prepaid holidays.*
■[as adj. **prepaid**] (of an envelope or address label) supplied with the postage already paid for contents up to a certain weight.
– DERIVATIVES **prepayable** adjective, **prepayment** noun.

prepense /prɪˈpɛns/ ▶**adjective** [usu. postpositive] chiefly Law, dated deliberate; intentional: *malice prepense.*
– DERIVATIVES **prepensely** adverb.

P

– ORIGIN early 18th cent.: alteration of *prepensed*, past participle of obsolete *prepense*, from Old French *purpenser*, from *por-* 'beforehand' + *penser* 'think'. The prefix *pre-* was substituted to emphasize the notion of 'beforehand'.

pre-plan ▶ **verb** [with obj.] [usu. as adj. **pre-planned**] plan in advance: *a pre-planned route.*

prepolymer ▶ **noun** Chemistry a substance which represents an intermediate stage in polymerization, and can be usefully manipulated before polymerization is completed.

preponderance ▶ **noun** [mass noun] the quality or fact of being greater in number, quantity, or importance: *the preponderance of women among older people* | [count noun] *a preponderance of lower-paid jobs.*

preponderant ▶ **adjective** predominant in influence, number, or importance: *the preponderant influence of the US within the alliance.*
– DERIVATIVES **preponderantly** adverb.
– ORIGIN late Middle English: from Latin *preponderant-* 'weighing more', from the verb *praeponderare* (see **PREPONDERATE**).

preponderate ▶ **verb** [no obj.] be greater in number, influence, or importance: *the advantages **preponderate over** this apparent disadvantage.*
– ORIGIN early 17th cent. (in the sense 'weigh more, have greater intellectual weight'): from Latin *praeponderat-* 'of greater weight', from the verb *praeponderare*, from *prae* 'before' + *ponderare* 'weigh, consider'.

prepone /priːˈpəʊn/ ▶ **verb** [with obj.] Indian bring (something) forward to an earlier date or time: *the publication date has been preponed from July to June.*
– ORIGIN 1970s: from **PRE-** + **POSTPONE**.

prepose ▶ **verb** [with obj.] Linguistics place (an element or word) in front of another.
– ORIGIN late 15th cent. (in the sense 'place in authority'): from French *préposer*, suggested by Latin *praeponere* 'put before'.

preposition /ˌprɛpəˈzɪʃ(ə)n/ ▶ **noun** Grammar a word governing, and usually preceding, a noun or pronoun and expressing a relation to another word or element in the clause, as in 'the man *on* the platform', 'she arrived *after* dinner', 'what did you do it *for*?'.
– DERIVATIVES **prepositional** adjective, **prepositionally** adverb.
– ORIGIN late Middle English: from Latin *praepositio(n-)*, from the verb *praeponere*, from *prae* 'before' + *ponere* 'to place'.

USAGE There is a traditional view, first set forth by the 17th-century poet and dramatist John Dryden, that it is incorrect to put a preposition at the end of a sentence, as in *where do you come **from**?* or *she's not a writer I've ever come **across**.* The rule was formulated on the basis that, since in Latin a preposition cannot come after the word it governs or is linked with, the same should be true of English. The problem is that English is not like Latin in this respect, and in many cases (particularly in questions and with phrasal verbs) the attempt to move the preposition produces awkward, unnatural-sounding results. Winston Churchill famously objected to the rule, saying *'This is the sort of English **up with** which I will not **put**.'* In standard English the placing of a preposition at the end of a sentence is widely accepted, provided the use sounds natural and the meaning is clear.

prepositional object ▶ **noun** Grammar a noun phrase governed by a preposition.

prepositive /priːˈpɒzɪtɪv/ ▶ **adjective** Grammar (of a word, particle, etc.) placed in front of the word that it governs or modifies.
– ORIGIN late 16th cent.: from late Latin *praepositivus* (see **PRE-**, **POSITIVE**).

prepossessing ▶ **adjective** [often with negative] attractive or appealing in appearance: *he was not a prepossessing sight.*
– DERIVATIVES **prepossession** noun.

preposterous ▶ **adjective** contrary to reason or common sense; utterly absurd or ridiculous: *a preposterous suggestion.*
– DERIVATIVES **preposterously** adverb, **preposterousness** noun.
– ORIGIN mid 16th cent.: from Latin *praeposterus* 'reversed, absurd' (from *prae* 'before' + *posterus* 'coming after') + **-OUS**.

prepostor ▶ **noun** variant spelling of **PRAEPOSTOR**.

prepotent ▶ **adjective** greater than others in power or influence.
■ (of a breeding animal) showing great effectiveness in transmitting hereditary characteristics to its offspring.
– DERIVATIVES **prepotence** noun, **prepotency** noun.
– ORIGIN late Middle English: from Latin *praepotent-* 'having greater power', from *prae* 'before, ahead' + *posse* 'be able'.

preppy (also **preppie**) informal, chiefly US ▶ **noun** (pl. **-ies**) a pupil or graduate of an expensive preparatory school or a person resembling such a pupil in dress or appearance.
▶ **adjective** (**preppier**, **preppiest**) of or typical of such a person, especially with reference to their style of dress: *the preppy look.*
– ORIGIN early 20th cent.: from **PREP SCHOOL** + **-Y**[2].

preprandial ▶ **adjective** formal or humorous done or taken before dinner: *a preprandial glass of sherry.*
■ Medicine before a main meal: *urine testing results in the preprandial state.*
– ORIGIN early 19th cent.: from **PRE-** 'before' + Latin *prandium* 'a meal' + **-AL**.

prepreg ▶ **noun** a fibrous material pre-impregnated with a particular synthetic resin, used in making reinforced plastics.
– ORIGIN 1950s: from **PRE-** 'before' + *(im)preg(nated)*.

pre-press ▶ **adjective** of or relating to composition, page layout, and other work done on a publication before it is actually printed.

pre-print ▶ **verb** [with obj.] [usu. as adj. **pre-printed**] print (something) in advance: *a pre-printed form.*
▶ **noun** something which is printed in advance, especially a part of a work printed and issued before general publication of that work.

pre-process ▶ **verb** [with obj.] subject (data) to preliminary processing.

pre-processor ▶ **noun** a computer program that modifies data to conform with the input requirements of another program.

pre-production ▶ **noun** [mass noun] work done on a product, especially a film or broadcast programme, before full-scale production begins: [as modifier] *the pre-production script.*

pre-program ▶ **verb** [with obj.] [usu. as adj. **pre-programmed**] program (a computer or other electronic device) in advance for ease of use: *a pre-programmed function key.*
■ program (something) into a computer or other electronic device before use: *pre-programmed messages.*

prep school ▶ **noun** another term for **PREPARATORY SCHOOL**.

pre-pubertal ▶ **adjective** another term for **PRE-PUBESCENT**.
– DERIVATIVES **pre-puberty** noun.

pre-pubescent ▶ **adjective** relating to or in the period preceding puberty: *a pre-pubescent girl.*
▶ **noun** a pre-pubescent boy or girl.
– DERIVATIVES **pre-pubescence** noun.

pre-publication ▶ **adjective** issued or occurring before publication: *pre-publication censorship.*
▶ **noun** [mass noun] publication in advance.

prepuce /ˈpriːpjuːs/ ▶ **noun** Anatomy **1** technical term for **FORESKIN**.
2 the fold of skin surrounding the clitoris.
– DERIVATIVES **preputial** adjective.
– ORIGIN late Middle English: from French *prépuce*, from Latin *praeputium*.

pre-qualify ▶ **verb** [no obj.] qualify in advance to take part in a sporting event: [as adj. **pre-qualifying**] *players who fail at the pre-qualifying stage.*

prequel /ˈpriːkw(ə)l/ ▶ **noun** a story or film containing events which precede those of an existing work: *the film is **a prequel to** the cult TV series.*
– ORIGIN 1970s: from **PRE-** 'before' + **SEQUEL**.

Pre-Raphaelite /priːˈrafəlʌɪt/ ▶ **noun** a member of a group of English 19th-century artists, including Holman Hunt, Millais, and D. G. Rossetti, who consciously sought to emulate the simplicity and sincerity of the work of Italian artists from before the time of Raphael.

Seven young English artists and writers founded the **Pre-Raphaelite Brotherhood** in 1848 as a reaction against the slick sentimentality and academic convention of much Victorian art. Their work is characterized by strong line and colour, naturalistic detail, and often biblical or literary subjects. The group began to disperse in the 1850s, and the term became applied to the rather different later work of Rossetti, and that of Burne-Jones and William Morris, in which a romantic and decorative depiction of classical and medieval themes had come to predominate.

▶ **adjective** of or relating to the Pre-Raphaelites.
■ of a style or appearance associated with the later Pre-Raphaelites or especially with the women they frequently used as models, with long, thick, wavy auburn hair, pale skin, and a fey demeanour.
– DERIVATIVES **Pre-Raphaelitism** noun.

pre-record ▶ **verb** [with obj.] [often as adj. **pre-recorded**] record (sound or film) in advance: *a pre-recorded talk.*
■ record sound on (a tape) beforehand.

preregistration ▶ **noun** [mass noun] **1** [as modifier] relating to or denoting the period of a doctor's training between qualification and registration: *the preregistration year.*
2 the action of registering or being registered in advance: *members are entitled to free preregistration.*

pre-release ▶ **adjective** of, relating to, or denoting a record, film, or other product that has not yet been generally released: *a pre-release version of the software.*
■ of or relating to the period before the release of a suspect or prisoner.
▶ **noun** a film, record, or other product given restricted availability before being generally released.

prerequisite /priːˈrɛkwɪzɪt/ ▶ **noun** a thing that is required as a prior condition for something else to happen or exist: *sponsorship is not **a prerequisite for** any of our courses.*
▶ **adjective** required as a prior condition: *the student must have the prerequisite skills.*

prerogative /prɪˈrɒgətɪv/ ▶ **noun** a right or privilege exclusive to a particular individual or class: *owning a motor car was still the prerogative of the rich.*
■ (also **royal prerogative**) [mass noun] the right of the sovereign, which in British law is theoretically subject to no restriction. ■ a faculty or property distinguishing a person or class: *it's not a female prerogative to feel insecure.*
▶ **adjective** [attrib.] Law, Brit. arising from the prerogative of the Crown (usually delegated to the government or the judiciary) and based in common law rather than statutory law: *the monarch retained the formal prerogative power to appoint the Prime Minister.*
– ORIGIN late Middle English: via Old French from Latin *praerogativa* '(the verdict of) the political division which was chosen to vote first in the assembly', feminine (used as noun) of *praerogativus* 'asked first', from *prae* 'before' + *rogare* 'ask'.

prerogative court ▶ **noun** historical (in the UK) either of two ecclesiastical courts at Canterbury and York formerly responsible for the probate of wills involving property in more than one diocese.

prerogative of mercy ▶ **noun** [mass noun] the right and power of a sovereign, state president, or other supreme authority to commute a death sentence, to change the mode of execution, or to pardon an offender.

pre-Roman ▶ **adjective** of or relating to a period before the rise or dominance of ancient Rome, or before the conquest of a particular region by the ancient Romans: *the Celtic kingdoms of pre-Roman Britain.*

Pres. ▶ **abbreviation for** President.

presage /ˈprɛsɪdʒ/ ▶ **verb** /also prɪˈseɪdʒ/ [with obj.] (of an event) be a sign or warning that (something, typically something bad) will happen: *the heavy clouds above the moorland presaged snow.*
■ archaic (of a person) predict: *lands he could measure, terms and tides presage.*
▶ **noun** a sign or warning that something, typically something bad, will happen; an omen or portent: *the fever was a sombre presage of his final illness.*
■ archaic a feeling of presentiment or foreboding: *he had a strong presage that he had only a very short time to live.*
– DERIVATIVES **presager** noun (archaic).
– ORIGIN late Middle English (as a noun): via French from Latin *praesagium*, from *praesagire* 'forebode', from *prae* 'before' + *sagire* 'perceive keenly'.

presbyopia /ˌprɛzbɪˈəʊpɪə/ ▶ **noun** [mass noun] long-sightedness caused by loss of elasticity of the lens of the eye, occurring typically in middle and old age.
– DERIVATIVES **presbyopic** adjective.
– ORIGIN late 18th cent.: modern Latin, from Greek *presbus* 'old man' + *ōps*, *ōp-* 'eye'.

presbyter /ˈprɛzbɪtə/ ▶ **noun** historical an elder or minister of the Christian Church.
■ formal (in presbyterian Churches) an elder. ■ formal (in

episcopal Churches) a minister of the second order, under the authority of a bishop; a priest.
– DERIVATIVES **presbyteral** /-ˈbɪt(ə)r(ə)l/ adjective, **presbyterate** noun, **presbyterial** adjective, **presbytership** noun.
– ORIGIN late 16th cent.: via ecclesiastical Latin from Greek *presbuteros* 'elder' (used in the New Testament to denote an elder of the early church), comparative of *presbus* 'old (man)'.

Presbyterian /ˌprɛzbɪˈtɪərɪən/ ▶ **adjective** of, relating to, or denoting a Christian Church or denomination governed by elders according to the principles of Presbyterianism.
▶ **noun** a member of a Presbyterian Church.
■ an advocate of the Presbyterian system.
– ORIGIN mid 17th cent.: from ecclesiastical Latin *presbyterium* (see **PRESBYTERY**) + **-AN**.

Presbyterianism ▶ **noun** [mass noun] a form of Protestant Church government in which the Church is administered locally by the minister with a group of elected elders of equal rank, and regionally and nationally by representative courts of ministers and elders.

> Presbyterianism was first introduced in Geneva in 1541 under John Calvin, in the belief that it best represented the pattern of the early church. There are now many Presbyterian Churches (often called Reformed Churches) worldwide, notably in the Netherlands and Scotland and in countries with which they have historic links (including the United States and Northern Ireland). They typically subscribe (more or less strictly) to the Westminster Confession.

presbytery /ˈprɛzbɪt(ə)ri/ ▶ **noun** (pl. **-ies**) **1** [treated as sing. or pl.] a body of Church elders and ministers, especially (in Presbyterian Churches) an administrative body (court) representing all the local congregations of a district.
■ a district represented by such a body of elders and ministers.
2 the house of a Roman Catholic parish priest.
3 chiefly Architecture the eastern part of a church chancel beyond the choir; the sanctuary.
– ORIGIN late Middle English (in sense 3): from Old French *presbiterie*, via ecclesiastical Latin from Greek *presbuterion*, from *presbuteros* (see **PRESBYTER**).

pre-school ▶ **adjective** [attrib.] of or relating to the time before a child is old enough to go to school: *a pre-school playgroup*.
■ (of a child) under the age at which compulsory schooling begins.
▶ **noun** a nursery school: *she goes to pre-school*.
– DERIVATIVES **pre-schooler** noun.

prescient /ˈprɛsɪənt/ ▶ **adjective** having or showing knowledge of events before they take place: *a prescient warning*.
– DERIVATIVES **prescience** noun, **presciently** adverb.
– ORIGIN early 17th cent.: from Latin *praescient-* 'knowing beforehand', from the verb *praescire*, from *prae* 'before' + *scire* 'know'.

pre-scientific ▶ **adjective** of or relating to the time before the development of modern science or the application of scientific method.

prescind /prɪˈsɪnd/ ▶ **verb** [no obj.] (**prescind from**) formal leave out of consideration: *we have prescinded from many vexing issues*.
■ [with obj.] cut off or separate from something: *his is an idea entirely prescinded from all of the others*.
– ORIGIN mid 17th cent. (in the sense 'cut off abruptly or prematurely'): from Latin *praescindere*, from *prae* 'before' + *scindere* 'to cut'.

prescribe ▶ **verb** [with obj.] (of a medical practitioner) advise and authorize the use of (a medicine or treatment) for someone, especially in writing: *Dr Greene prescribed magnesium sulphate* | [with two objs] *he was prescribed a course of antibiotics*.
■ recommend (a substance or action) as something beneficial: *marriage is often prescribed as a universal remedy*. ■ state authoritatively or as a rule that (an action or procedure) should be carried out: *rules prescribing five acts for a play are purely arbitrary* | [as adj. **prescribed**] *doing things in the prescribed manner*.
– DERIVATIVES **prescriber** noun.
– ORIGIN late Middle English (in the sense 'confine within bounds', also as a legal term meaning 'claim by prescription'): from Latin *praescribere* 'direct in writing', from *prae* 'before' + *scribere* 'write'.

> **USAGE** The verbs **prescribe** and **proscribe** do not have the same meaning. **Prescribe** is a much commoner word (occurring around 15 times more often than **proscribe** in the British National Corpus) and means either 'issue a medical prescription' or 'recommend with authority', as in *the doctor* ***prescribed*** *antibiotics*. **Proscribe**, on the other hand, is a formal word meaning 'condemn or forbid', as in *gambling was strictly* ***proscribed*** *by the authorities*.

prescript /ˈpriːskrɪpt/ ▶ **noun** formal or dated an ordinance, law, or command.
– ORIGIN mid 16th cent.: from Latin *praescriptum* 'something directed in writing', neuter past participle of *praescribere* (see **PRESCRIBE**).

prescription ▶ **noun 1** an instruction written by a medical practitioner that authorizes a patient to be issued with a medicine or treatment: *he scribbled a prescription for tranquillizers* | [mass noun] *the lotion is available* ***on prescription*** | [as modifier] *prescription drugs*.
■ [mass noun] the action of prescribing a medicine or treatment: *the unnecessary prescription of antibiotics*. ■ a medicine or remedy that is prescribed: *I've got to pick up my prescription from the chemist's*.
2 a recommendation that is authoritatively put forward: *effective prescriptions for sustaining rural communities*.
■ [mass noun] the authoritative recommendation of an action or procedure: *rather than prescription there would be guidance*.
3 (also **positive prescription**) Law the establishment of a claim founded on the basis of a long or indefinite period of uninterrupted use or of long-standing custom.
– ORIGIN late Middle English (as a legal term): via Old French from Latin *praescriptio(n-)*, from the verb *praescribere* (see **PRESCRIBE**). Sense 1 dates from the late 16th cent.

prescriptive ▶ **adjective 1** of or relating to the imposition or enforcement of a rule or method: *these guidelines are not intended to be prescriptive*.
■ Linguistics attempting to impose rules of correct usage on the users of a language: *a prescriptive grammar book*. Often contrasted with **DESCRIPTIVE**.
2 (of a right, title, or institution) having become legally established or accepted by long usage or the passage of time: *a prescriptive right of way*.
■ archaic established by long-standing custom or usage: *his regular score at the bar and his prescriptive corner at the winter's fireside*.
– DERIVATIVES **prescriptively** adverb, **prescriptiveness** noun, **prescriptivism** noun, **prescriptivist** noun & adjective.
– ORIGIN mid 18th cent.: from late Latin *praescriptivus* 'relating to a legal exception', from *praescript-* 'directed in writing', from the verb *praescribere* (see **PRESCRIBE**).

preseason ▶ **adjective** (of a sporting fixture) taking place before the regular season.
▶ **noun** [in sing.] the period of time before the regular season.

pre-select ▶ **verb** [with obj.] select or set in advance: *four British swimmers pre-selected for the Olympics*.
– DERIVATIVES **pre-selection** noun, **pre-selective** adjective.

pre-selector ▶ **noun** a device for selecting a mechanical or electrical operation in advance of its execution.

presence ▶ **noun** [mass noun] the state or fact of existing, occurring, or being present in a place or thing: *my presence in the flat made her happy* | *the presence of chlorine in the atmosphere* | *the memorial was unveiled* ***in the presence of*** *24 veterans*.
■ [count noun] a person or thing that exists or is present in a place but is not seen: *the monks became aware of a strange presence*. ■ [in sing.] a group of people, especially soldiers or police, stationed in a particular place: *the USA would maintain a presence in the Indian Ocean region*. ■ the impressive manner or appearance of a person: *Richard was not a big man but his presence was overwhelming* | [in sing.] *he has a real physical presence*.
– PHRASES **make one's presence felt** have a strong and obvious effect or influence on others or on a situation. **presence of mind** the ability to remain calm and take quick, sensible action: *he had the presence of mind to record the scene on video*.
– ORIGIN Middle English: via Old French from Latin *praesentia* 'being at hand', from the verb *praeesse* (see **PRESENT**[1]).

presence chamber ▶ **noun** a room, especially one in a palace, in which a monarch or other distinguished person receives visitors.

presenile /priːˈsiːnʌɪl/ ▶ **adjective** occurring in or characteristic of the period of life preceding old age: *Alzheimer's disease is a form of presenile dementia*.

present[1] /ˈprɛz(ə)nt/ ▶ **adjective 1** [predic.] (of a person) in a particular place: *a doctor must be present at the ringside* | *the speech caused embarrassment to all those present*.
■ (often **present in**) (of a thing) existing or occurring in a place or thing: *organic molecules are present in comets*.
2 [attrib.] existing or occurring now: *she did not expect to find herself in her present situation*.
■ now being considered or discussed: *the present article cannot answer every question*. ■ Grammar (of a tense or participle) expressing an action now going on or habitually performed, or a condition now existing.
▶ **noun** [in sing.] (usu. **the present**) the period of time now occurring: *they are happy and at peace, refusing to think beyond the present*.
■ Grammar a present tense: *the verbs are all in the present*. See also **HISTORIC PRESENT**.
– PHRASES **all present and correct** used to indicate that not a single thing or person is missing. **at present** now: *membership at present stands at about 5,000*. **for the present** for now; temporarily. (**there is**) **no time like the present** used to suggest that something should be done now rather than later: *'When do you want me to leave?' 'No time like the present.'* **present company excepted** excluding those who are here now. **these presents** Law, formal this document: *the premises outlined in red on the Plan annexed to these presents*.
– ORIGIN Middle English: via Old French from Latin *praesent-* 'being at hand', present participle of *praeesse*, from *prae* 'before' + *esse* 'be'.

present[2] /prɪˈzɛnt/ ▶ **verb** [with obj.] **1** (**present something to**) give something to (someone) formally or ceremonially: *the duke presented certificates to the men*.
■ (**present someone with**) give someone (something) in such a way: *my pupils presented me with some flowers*. ■ show or offer (something) for others to scrutinize or consider: *he stopped and presented his passport*. ■ formally introduce (someone) to someone else: *may I present my wife?* ■ (**present someone to**) (in church use) recommend an ordained minister to a bishop for institution to (a benefice). ■ proffer (compliments or good wishes) in a formal manner: *may I present the greetings of my master?* ■ formally deliver (a cheque or bill) for acceptance or payment: *a cheque presented by Mr Jackson was returned by the bank*. ■ Law bring (a complaint, petition, or evidence) formally to the notice of a court. ■ (of a company or producer) put (a show or exhibition) before the public. ■ introduce or announce the various items of (a television or radio show) as a participant: *the Late Show was presented by Cynthia Rose*.
2 bring about or be the cause of (a problem or difficulty): *this should not present much difficulty*.
■ exhibit (a particular state or appearance) to others: *the EC presented a united front over the crisis*. ■ represent (someone) to others in a particular way, typically one that is false or exaggerated: *the prime minister* ***presented himself as*** *a radical figure*. ■ (**present oneself**) come forward into the presence of another or others, especially for a formal occasion; appear: *he failed to present himself in court*. ■ (**present itself**) (of an opportunity or idea) occur and be available for use or exploitation: *when a favourable opportunity presented itself he would submit his proposition*. ■ [no obj.] (**present with**) Medicine (of a patient) come forward for or undergo initial medical examination for a particular condition or symptom: *the patient presented with mild clinical encephalopathy*. ■ [no obj.] Medicine (of a part of a fetus) be directed towards the cervix during labour. ■ [no obj.] Medicine (of an illness) manifest itself.
3 hold out or aim (a firearm) at something so as to be ready to fire: *they were to present their rifles, take aim, and fire*.
▶ **noun** (**the present**) the position of a firearm when aimed or held ready to be aimed, especially the position from which a rifle is fired.
– PHRASES **present arms** hold a rifle vertically in front of the body as a salute.
– ORIGIN Middle English: from Old French *presenter*, from Latin *praesentare* 'place before' (in medieval Latin 'present as a gift'), from *praesent-* 'being at hand' (see **PRESENT**[1]).

present[3] /ˈprɛz(ə)nt/ ▶ **noun** a thing given to someone as a gift: *a Christmas present*.

p

– PHRASES **make a present of** give as a gift: *he had made a present of a hacienda to the president.*
– ORIGIN Middle English: from Old French, originally in the phrase *mettre une chose en present à quelqu'un* 'put a thing into the presence of a person'.

presentable ▶ **adjective** clean, smart, or decent enough to be seen in public: *I did my best to make myself look presentable.*
– DERIVATIVES **presentability** noun, **presentably** adverb.

presentation ▶ **noun** [mass noun] **1** the proffering or giving of something to someone, especially as part of a formal ceremony: *the presentation of certificates to new members* | [count noun] *the Lord Lieutenant made the presentations.*
■ the manner or style in which something is given, offered, or displayed: *the presentation of foods is designed to stimulate your appetite.* ■ a formal introduction of someone, especially at court. ■ the official submission of something for consideration in a law court: *the presentation of the bankruptcy petition.* ■ chiefly historical the action or right of formally proposing a candidate for a church benefice or other position: *the Earl of Pembroke offered Herbert the presentation of the living of Bremerton.* ■ [count noun] a demonstration or display of a product or idea: *a sales presentation.* ■ [count noun] an exhibition or theatrical performance.
2 Medicine the position of a fetus in relation to the cervix at the time of delivery: *breech presentation.*
■ the coming forward of a patient for initial examination and diagnosis: *all patients in this group were symptomatic at initial presentation.*
3 (**Presentation of Christ**) another term for **CANDLEMAS**.
– DERIVATIVES **presentational** adjective, **presentationally** adverb.
– ORIGIN late Middle English: via Old French from late Latin *praesentatio(n-)*, from Latin *praesentare* 'place before' (see **PRESENT**[2]).

presentative ▶ **adjective** historical (of a benefice) to which a patron has the right of presentation.
– ORIGIN mid 16th cent.: probably from medieval Latin, based on Latin *praesentare* (see **PRESENT**[2]).

present-day ▶ **adjective** [attrib.] of or relating to the current period of time: *present-day technological developments.*

presentee ▶ **noun** a person nominated or recommended for an office or position, especially a church living.
– ORIGIN late 15th cent.: from Anglo-Norman French, literally 'presented', from the verb *presenter* (see **PRESENT**[2]).

presenteeism ▶ **noun** [mass noun] the practice of being present at one's place of work for more hours than is required by one's terms of employment.

presenter ▶ **noun** a person who introduces and appears in a television or radio programme.

presentient /prɪˈsɛnʃ(ə)nt, -ˈzɛn-/ ▶ **adjective** rare having a presentiment.
– ORIGIN early 19th cent.: from Latin *praesentient-* 'perceiving beforehand', from the verb *praesentire*, from *prae* 'before' + *sentire* 'to feel'.

presentiment /prɪˈzɛntɪm(ə)nt, -ˈsɛn-/ ▶ **noun** an intuitive feeling about the future, especially one of foreboding: *a presentiment of disaster.*
– ORIGIN early 18th cent.: from obsolete French *présentiment.*

presentism ▶ **noun** [mass noun] uncritical adherence to present-day attitudes, especially the tendency to interpret past events in terms of modern values and concepts.
– DERIVATIVES **presentist** adjective.

presently ▶ **adverb** **1** after a short time; soon: *this will be examined in more detail presently.*
2 at the present time; now: *there are presently 1,128 people on the waiting list*

presentment /prɪˈzɛntm(ə)nt/ ▶ **noun** Law, chiefly historical a formal presentation of information to a court, especially by a sworn jury regarding an offence or other matter.
– ORIGIN Middle English: from Old French *presentement*, from *presenter* 'place before' (see **PRESENT**[2]).

present participle ▶ **noun** Grammar the form of a verb, ending in *-ing* in English, which is used in forming continuous tenses, e.g. in *I'm thinking*, alone in non-finite clauses, e.g. in *sitting here, I haven't a care in the world*, as a noun, e.g. in *good thinking*, and as an adjective, e.g. in *running water.*

present value (also **net present value**) ▶ **noun** Finance the value in the present of a sum of money, in contrast to some future value it will have when it has been invested at compound interest.

preservation ▶ **noun** [mass noun] the action of preserving something: *the preservation of the city's green spaces* | *food preservation.*
■ the state of being preserved, especially to a specified degree: *in a fine state of preservation.*
– ORIGIN late Middle English: via Old French from medieval Latin *praeservatio(n-)*, from late Latin *praeservare* 'to keep' (see **PRESERVE**).

preservationist ▶ **noun** a supporter or advocate of the preservation of something, especially of historic buildings and artefacts.

preservation order ▶ **noun** chiefly Brit. a legal obligation laid on an owner to preserve a building of historic interest, or to conserve trees and natural habitat regarded as contributing amenity value to the environment.

preservative ▶ **noun** a substance used to preserve foodstuffs, wood, or other materials against decay.
▶ **adjective** acting to preserve something: *the preservative effects of freezing.*
– ORIGIN late Middle English: via Old French from medieval Latin *praeservativus*, from late Latin *praeservat-* 'kept', from the verb *praeservare* (see **PRESERVE**).

preserve ▶ **verb** [with obj.] maintain (something) in its original or existing state: *all records of the past were zealously preserved* | [as adj. **preserved**] *a magnificently preserved monastery.*
■ retain (a condition or state of affairs): *a fight to preserve local democracy.* ■ maintain or keep alive (a memory or quality): *the film has preserved all the qualities of the novel.* ■ keep safe from harm or injury: *a place for preserving endangered species.* ■ treat or refrigerate (food) to prevent its decomposition or fermentation. ■ prepare (fruit) for long-term storage by boiling it with sugar: [as adj. **preserved**] *those sweet preserved fruits associated with Cremona.* ■ keep (game or an area where game is found) undisturbed to allow private hunting or shooting.
▶ **noun** **1** [mass noun] a foodstuff made with fruit preserved in sugar, such as jam or marmalade: *a jar of cherry preserve* | [count noun] *home-made preserves.*
2 a sphere of activity regarded as being reserved for a particular person or group: *the civil service became **the preserve of** the educated middle class.*
3 a place where game is protected and kept for private hunting or shooting.
– DERIVATIVES **preservable** adjective, **preserver** noun.
– ORIGIN late Middle English (in the sense 'keep safe from harm'): from Old French *preserver*, from late Latin *praeservare*, from *prae-* 'before, in advance' + *servare* 'to keep'.

pre-service ▶ **adjective** of or relating to the period before a person takes a job that requires training, especially in teaching: *pre-service training.*

preset ▶ **verb** (**presetting**; past and past participle **preset**) [with obj.] [usu. as adj. **preset**] set or adjust (a value that controls the operation of a device) in advance of its use: *the water is heated quickly to a preset temperature.*
▶ **noun** a control on electronic equipment that is set or adjusted beforehand to facilitate use.

pre-shrunk ▶ **adjective** (of a fabric or garment) having undergone a shrinking process during manufacture to prevent further shrinking in use.
– DERIVATIVES **pre-shrink** verb.

preside ▶ **verb** [no obj.] **1** be in the position of authority in a meeting or gathering: *the prime minister will preside at an emergency cabinet meeting* | [as adj. **presiding**] *the sentence imposed by the presiding judge.*
■ (**preside over**) be in charge of (a place or situation): *the Home Secretary has presided over the worst crime figures the country has known.*
2 (**preside at**) play (a musical instrument, especially a keyboard instrument) at a public gathering.
– ORIGIN early 17th cent.: from French *présider*, from Latin *praesidere*, from *prae* 'before' + *sedere* 'sit'.

presidency ▶ **noun** (pl. **-ies**) the office of president: *the presidency of the United States.*
■ the period of this: *the liberal climate that existed during Carter's presidency.* ■ Christian Church the role of the priest or minister who conducts a Eucharist.
– ORIGIN late 16th cent.: from medieval Latin *praesidentia*, from *praesidere* 'sit before' (see **PRESIDE**).

president ▶ **noun** **1** the elected head of a republican state: *the Irish president* | [as title] *President Khrushchev.*
■ the head of a society, council, or other organization: *the president of the European Community.* ■ the head of certain colleges. ■ N. Amer. the head of a university. ■ N. Amer. the head of a company.
2 Christian Church the celebrant at a Eucharist.
– DERIVATIVES **presidential** adjective, **presidentially** adverb, **presidentship** noun (archaic).
– ORIGIN late Middle English: via Old French from Latin *praesident-* 'sitting before' (see **PRESIDE**).

president-elect ▶ **noun** (pl. **presidents-elect**) a person who has been elected president but has not yet taken up office.

Presidential Medal of Freedom ▶ **noun** (in the US) a medal constituting the highest award that can be given to a civilian in peacetime.

presiding officer ▶ **noun** an official in charge of a polling station at an election.

presidio /prɛˈsɪdɪəʊ/ ▶ **noun** (pl. **-os**) (in Spain and Spanish America) a fortified military settlement.
– ORIGIN Spanish, from Latin *praesidium* 'garrison'.

presidium /prɪˈsɪdɪəm, -ˈzɪ-/ (also **praesidium**) ▶ **noun** a standing executive committee in a communist country.
■ (**Presidium**) the committee of this type in the former USSR, which functioned as the legislative authority when the Supreme Soviet was not sitting.
– ORIGIN 1920s: from Russian *prezidium*, from Latin *praesidium* 'protection, garrison' (see **PRESIDE**).

Presley, Elvis (Aaron) (1935–77), American rock-and-roll and pop singer. He was the dominant personality of early rock and roll with songs such as 'Heartbreak Hotel' and 'Blue Suede Shoes' (both 1956). He also made a number of films, including *King Creole* (1958).

Presocratic /ˌpriːsəˈkratɪk/ ▶ **adjective** of, relating to, or denoting the speculative philosophers active in the ancient Greek world in the 6th and 5th centuries BC (before the time of Socrates), who attempted to find rational explanations for natural phenomena. They included Parmenides, Anaxagoras, Empedocles, and Heraclitus.
▶ **noun** a Presocratic philosopher.

press[1] ▶ **verb** **1** move or cause to move into a position of contact with something by exerting continuous physical force: [with obj. and adverbial of direction] *he pressed his face to the glass* | [no obj., with adverbial of direction] *her body pressed against his.*
■ [with obj.] exert continuous physical force on (something), typically in order to operate a device or machine: *he pressed a button and the doors slid open.* ■ [with obj.] squeeze (someone's arm or hand) as a sign of affection. ■ [no obj., with adverbial of direction] move in a specified direction by pushing: *the mob was still pressing forward.* ■ figurative (of an enemy or opponent) attack persistently and fiercely: [no obj.] *their enemies pressed in on all sides* | [with obj.] *two assailants were pressing Agrippa.* ■ [no obj.] (**press on/ahead**) figurative continue in one's action: *he stubbornly **pressed on** with his work.* ■ [with obj.] Weightlifting raise (a specified weight) by first lifting it to shoulder height and then gradually pushing it upwards above the head.
2 [with obj.] apply pressure to (something) to flatten, shape, or smooth it, typically by ironing: *she pressed her nicest blouse* | [as adj. **pressed**] *immaculately pressed trousers.*
■ apply pressure to (a flower or leaf) between sheets of paper in order to dry and preserve it. ■ extract (juice or oil) by crushing or squeezing fruit, vegetables, etc.: [as adj. **pressed**] *freshly pressed orange juice.* ■ squeeze or crush (fruit, vegetables, etc.) to extract the juice or oil. ■ manufacture (something, especially a gramophone record) by moulding under pressure.
3 [with obj.] forcefully put forward (an opinion, claim, or course of action): *Rose did not press the point.*
■ make strong efforts to persuade or force (someone) to do or provide something: *when I **pressed** him **for** precise figures he evaded the subject* | [with infinitive] *the marketing directors were pressed to justify their expenditure* | [no obj.] *they continued to **press for** changes in legislation.* ■ [no obj.] Golf try too hard to achieve distance with a shot, at the risk of inaccuracy. ■ (**press something on/upon**) insist that (someone) accepts an offer or gift: *he pressed dinner invitations on her.* ■ [no obj.] (of

p

something, especially time) be in short supply and so demand immediate action. ■(**be pressed**) have barely enough of something, especially time: *I'm terribly **pressed** for time.* ■(**be pressed to do something**) have difficulty doing or achieving something: *they may be **hard pressed** to keep their promise.*

▶**noun 1** a device for applying pressure to something in order to flatten or shape it or to extract juice or oil: *a flower press | a wine press.*

■a machine that applies pressure to a workpiece by means of a tool, in order to punch shapes.

2 a printing press.

■[often in names] a business that prints or publishes books: *the Clarendon Press.* ■[mass noun] the process of printing: *the book is ready to **go to press**.*

3 (**the press**) [treated as sing. or pl.] newspapers or journalists viewed collectively: *the press was notified* | [as modifier] *press coverage.*

■[mass noun] coverage in newspapers and magazines: *there's no point in demonstrating if you don't get any press* | [in sing.] *the government has had a bad press for years.*

4 an act of pressing something: *the system summons medical help at the press of a button | these clothes could do with a press.*

■[in sing.] a closely packed crowd or mass of people or things: *among the press of cars he saw a taxi.* ■ dated pressure of business. ■ Weightlifting an act of raising a weight up to shoulder height and then gradually pushing it upwards above the head. ■ Basketball any of various forms of close guarding by the defending team.

5 chiefly Irish & Scottish a large cupboard for clothes, books, and other items, typically in a recess.

– PHRASES **press charges** see **CHARGE**. **press something home** see **HOME**. **press (the) flesh** informal, chiefly N. Amer. (of a celebrity or politician) greet people by shaking hands.

– ORIGIN Middle English: from Old French *presse* (noun), *presser* (verb), from Latin *pressare* 'keep pressing', frequentative of *premere*.

press[2] ▶**verb** [with obj.] (**press someone/thing into**) put (someone or something) to a specified use, especially as a temporary or makeshift measure: *many of these stones have been pressed into service as gateposts.*

■historical force (a man) to enlist in the army or navy.

▶**noun** historical a forcible enlistment of men, especially for the navy.

– ORIGIN late 16th cent.: alteration (by association with **PRESS**[1]) of obsolete *prest* 'pay given on enlistment, enlistment by such payment', from Old French *prest* 'loan, advance pay', based on Latin *praestare* 'provide'.

press agent ▶**noun** a person employed to organize advertising and publicity in the press on behalf of an organization or well-known person.

pressboard ▶**noun** [mass noun] chiefly N. Amer. a hard, dense kind of board with a smooth finish, typically made from wood or textile pulp or laminated waste paper, and used as an electrical insulator and for making light furniture.

press box ▶**noun** an area reserved for journalists at a sports event.

Pressburg /ˈprɛsbʊrk/ German name for **BRATISLAVA**.

press-button ▶**noun** Brit. another term for **PUSH-BUTTON**.

press card ▶**noun** an official authorization carried by a reporter, especially one that gives admission to an event.

press conference ▶**noun** an interview given to journalists by a prominent person in order to make an announcement or answer questions.

Press Council ▶**noun** a body established in the UK in 1953 to raise and maintain professional standards among journalists.

press cutting ▶**noun** a paragraph or short article cut out of a newspaper or magazine.

presser foot ▶**noun** the footplate of a sewing machine which holds the material down on to the part which feeds it under the needle.

press fit ▶**noun** an interference fit between two parts in which one is forced under pressure into a slightly smaller hole in the other.

– DERIVATIVES **press-fitted** adjective.

press gallery ▶**noun** a place reserved for journalists observing the proceedings in a parliament or law court.

press gang ▶**noun** historical a body of men employed to enlist men forcibly into service in the army or navy.

▶**verb** [with obj.] (**press-gang**) chiefly historical forcibly enlist (someone) into service in the army or navy.

■(**press-gang someone into**) force someone to do something: *we press-ganged Simon into playing.*

pressie ▶**noun** variant spelling of **PREZZIE**.

pressing ▶**adjective** (of a problem, need, or situation) requiring quick or immediate action or attention: *inflation was the most pressing problem.*

■(of an engagement or activity) important and requiring one's attendance or presence: *he had some pressing business in Scotland.* ■(of an invitation) strongly expressed.

▶**noun** a thing made by the application of force or weight, especially a record.

■a series of such things made at one time: *the EP sold out its first pressing in one day.* ■an act or instance of applying force or weight to something: *pure-grade olive oil is the product of the second or third pressings.*

– DERIVATIVES **pressingly** adverb.

pressman ▶**noun** (pl. **-men**) **1** chiefly Brit. a journalist.

2 a person who operates a printing press.

pressmark ▶**noun** Brit. (especially in older libraries) a mark on a library book indicating its location.

pressor ▶**adjective** [attrib.] Physiology producing an increase in blood pressure by stimulating constriction of the blood vessels: *a pressor response.*

press release ▶**noun** an official statement issued to newspapers giving information on a particular matter.

press stud ▶**noun** Brit. a small fastener on clothing, engaged by pressing its two halves together.

press time ▶**noun** the moment when a magazine or other publication goes to press.

press-up ▶**noun** Brit. an exercise in which a person lies facing the floor and, keeping their back straight, raises their body by pressing down on their hands.

pressure ▶**noun** [mass noun] **1** the continuous physical force exerted on or against an object by something in contact with it: *the slight extra pressure he applied to her hand.*

■[count noun] the force per unit area exerted by a fluid against a surface with which it is in contact: *gas can be fed to the turbines at a pressure of around 250 psi.*

2 the use of persuasion, influence, or intimidation to make someone do something: *back-benchers put pressure on the government to provide safeguards* | [count noun] *the many pressures on girls to worry about their looks.*

■the influence or effect of someone or something: *oil prices came under some downwards pressure.* ■the feeling of stressful urgency caused by the necessity of doing or achieving something, especially with limited time: *he resigned due to pressure of work* | [count noun] *some offenders might find prison a refuge against the pressures of the outside world.*

▶**verb** [with obj.] attempt to persuade or coerce (someone) into doing something: *it might now be possible to **pressure** him **into** resigning* | [with obj. and infinitive] *she pressured her son to accept a job offer from the bank.*

– ORIGIN late Middle English: from Old French, from Latin *pressura*, from *press-* 'pressed', from the verb *premere* (see **PRESS**[1]).

pressure cooker ▶**noun** an airtight pot in which food can be cooked quickly under steam pressure.

– DERIVATIVES **pressure-cook** verb.

pressure group ▶**noun** a group that tries to influence public policy in the interest of a particular cause: *an environmental pressure group.*

pressure hull ▶**noun** the inner hull of a submarine, in which approximately normal pressure is maintained when the vessel is submerged.

pressure lamp ▶**noun** a portable oil or paraffin lamp in which the fuel is forced up into the mantle or burner by air pressure in the reservoir, which can be increased by pumping with a plunger.

pressure point ▶**noun** a point on the surface of the body sensitive to pressure.

■a point where an artery can be pressed against a bone to inhibit bleeding. ■a place in which trouble or difficulty is likely to be found: *Tottenham was a pressure point for racial tension.*

pressure suit ▶**noun** an inflatable suit that protects the wearer against low pressure, for example when flying at a high altitude.

pressure vessel ▶**noun** a container designed to hold material at high pressures.

■an enclosed structure containing a nuclear reactor core immersed in pressurized coolant.

pressurize (also **-ise**) ▶**verb** [with obj.] **1** produce or maintain raised pressure artificially in (a gas or its container): *the mixture was pressurized to 1,900 atmospheres* | [as adj. **pressurized**] *a pressurized can.*

■maintain a tolerable atmospheric pressure in (an aircraft cabin) at a high altitude: [as adj. **pressurized**] *a pressurized cabin.*

2 [with obj.] attempt to persuade or coerce (someone) into doing something: *the protests were an attempt to **pressurize** the government **into** bringing an end to the violence* | [with obj. and infinitive] *people had been pressurized to vote.*

– DERIVATIVES **pressurization** noun.

pressurized-water reactor (abbrev.: **PWR**) ▶**noun** a nuclear reactor in which the fuel is uranium oxide clad in zircaloy and the coolant and moderator is water at high pressure so that it does not boil at the operating temperature of the reactor.

presswork ▶**noun** [mass noun] **1** the shaping of metal by pressing or drawing it into a shaped hollow die.

2 the process of using a printing press.

■printed matter, especially with regard to its quality.

Prester John /ˈprɛstə/ a legendary medieval Christian king of Asia, said to have defeated the Muslims and to be destined to bring help to the Holy Land.

– ORIGIN Middle English: from Old French *prestre Jehan*, from medieval Latin *presbyter Johannes* 'priest John'.

prestidigitation /ˌprɛstɪˌdɪdʒɪˈteɪʃ(ə)n/ ▶**noun** [mass noun] formal magic tricks performed as entertainment.

– DERIVATIVES **prestidigitator** noun.

– ORIGIN mid 19th cent.: from French, from *preste* 'nimble' + Latin *digitus* 'finger' + **-ATION**.

prestige ▶**noun** [mass noun] widespread respect and admiration felt for someone or something on the basis of a perception of their achievements or quality: *he experienced a tremendous increase in prestige following his victory.*

■[as modifier] denoting something that arouses such respect or admiration: *prestige diplomatic posts.*

– DERIVATIVES **prestigeful** adjective.

– ORIGIN mid 17th cent. (in the sense 'illusion, conjuring trick'): from French, literally 'illusion, glamour', from late Latin *praestigium* 'illusion', from Latin *praestigiae* (plural) 'conjuring tricks'. The transference of meaning occurred by way of the sense 'dazzling influence, glamour', at first depreciatory.

prestige pricing ▶**noun** [mass noun] the practice of pricing goods at a high level in order to give the appearance of quality.

prestigious ▶**adjective** inspiring respect and admiration; having high status: *a prestigious academic post.*

– DERIVATIVES **prestigiously** adverb, **prestigiousness** noun.

– ORIGIN mid 16th cent. (in the sense 'practising legerdemain'): from late Latin *praestigiosus*, from *praestigiae* 'conjuring tricks'. The current sense dates from the early 20th cent.

prestissimo /prɛˈstɪsɪməʊ/ Music ▶**adverb** & **adjective** (especially as a direction) in a very quick tempo.

▶**noun** (pl. **-os**) a movement or passage marked to be performed in a very quick tempo.

– ORIGIN Italian, superlative of *presto* 'quick, quickly' (see **PRESTO**).

presto ▶**adverb** & **adjective** Music (especially as a direction) in a quick tempo.

▶**noun** (pl. **-os**) Music a movement or passage marked to be performed in a quick tempo.

▶**exclamation** another way of saying **HEY PRESTO**.

– ORIGIN Italian, 'quick, quickly', from late Latin *praestus* 'ready', from Latin *praesto* 'at hand'.

Preston a city in NW England, the administrative centre of Lancashire, on the River Ribble; pop. 126,200 (1991). It was the site in the 18th century of the first English cotton mills.

Prestonpans, Battle of /ˌprɛstənˈpanz/ a battle in 1745 near the town of Prestonpans just east of Edinburgh, the first major engagement of the Jacobite uprising of 1745–6. The Jacobites routed the Hanoverians, leaving the way clear for Charles Edward Stuart's subsequent invasion of England.

prestressed ▶ **adjective** strengthened by the application of stress during manufacture, especially (of concrete) by means of rods or wires inserted under tension before the material is set.
– DERIVATIVES **prestressing** noun.

Prestwick a town to the south of Glasgow in South Ayrshire, SW Scotland, the site of an international airport; pop. 14,052 (1989).

presumably ▶ **adverb** [sentence adverb] used to convey that what is asserted is very likely though not known for certain: *it was not yet ten o'clock, so presumably the boys were still at the pub.*

presume ▶ **verb** **1** [with clause] suppose that something is the case on the basis of probability: *I presumed that the man had been escorted from the building* | [with obj. and complement] *the two men were presumed dead when the wreck of their boat was found.*
■ take for granted that something exists or is the case: *the argument presumes that only one person can do the work* | [with obj.] *the task demands skills which cannot be presumed and therefore require proper training.*
2 [no obj., with infinitive] be audacious enough to do something: *kindly don't presume to issue me orders in my own house.*
■ [no obj.] make unjustified demands; take liberties: *forgive me if I have presumed.* ■ [no obj.] (**presume on/upon**) unjustifiably regard (something) as entitling one to privileges: *she knew he regarded her as his protegée, but was determined not to presume on that.*
– DERIVATIVES **presumable** adjective.
– ORIGIN late Middle English: from Old French *presumer*, from Latin *praesumere* 'anticipate' (in late Latin 'take for granted'), from *prae* 'before' + *sumere* 'take'.

presuming ▶ **adjective** archaic presumptuous.
– DERIVATIVES **presumingly** adverb.

presumption ▶ **noun** **1** an act or instance of taking something to be true or adopting a particular attitude towards something, especially at the start of a chain of argument or action: *the* ***presumption of*** *guilt has changed to a presumption of innocence.*
■ an idea that is taken to be true, and often used as the basis for other ideas, although it is not known for certain: *underlying presumptions about human nature.* ■ chiefly Law an attitude adopted in law or as a matter of policy towards an action or proposal in the absence of acceptable reasons to the contrary: *the planning policy shows a general* ***presumption in favour of*** *development.*
2 [mass noun] behaviour perceived as arrogant, disrespectful, and transgressing the limits of what is permitted or appropriate: *he lifted her off the ground and she was enraged at his presumption.*
– ORIGIN Middle English: from Old French *presumpcion*, from Latin *praesumptio(n)* 'anticipation', from the verb *praesumere* (see **PRESUME**).

presumptive ▶ **adjective** of the nature of a presumption; presumed in the absence of further information: *a presumptive diagnosis.*
■ Law giving grounds for the inference of a fact or of the appropriate interpretation of the law. ■ another term for **PRESUMPTUOUS**.
– DERIVATIVES **presumptively** adverb.
– ORIGIN late Middle English: from French *présomptif, -ive*, from late Latin *praesumptivus*, from *praesumpt-* 'taken before', from the verb *praesumere* (see **PRESUME**).

presumptuous ▶ **adjective** (of a person or their behaviour) failing to observe the limits of what is permitted or appropriate: *I hope I won't be considered presumptuous if I offer some advice.*
– DERIVATIVES **presumptuously** adverb, **presumptuousness** noun.
– ORIGIN Middle English: from Old French *presumptueux*, from late Latin *praesumptuosus*, variant of *praesumptiosus* 'full of boldness', from *praesumptio* (see **PRESUMPTION**).

presuppose ▶ **verb** [with obj.] (of an action, process, or argument) require as a precondition of possibility or coherence: *his relationships did not permit the degree of self-revelation that true intimacy presupposes.*
■ [with clause] tacitly assume at the beginning of a line of argument or course of action that something is the case: *your argument presupposes that it does not matter who is in power.*
– ORIGIN late Middle English: from Old French *presupposer*, suggested by medieval Latin *praesupponere*, from *prae* 'before' + *supponere* 'place under' (see **SUPPOSE**).

presupposition ▶ **noun** a thing tacitly assumed beforehand at the beginning of a line of argument or course of action: *images that challenge presuppositions about feminine handiwork.*
■ [mass noun] the action or state of presupposing or being presupposed.
– ORIGIN mid 16th cent.: from medieval Latin *praesuppositio(n-)*, from the verb *praesupponere* (see **PRESUPPOSE**).

presynaptic /ˌpriːsɪˈnaptɪk/ ▶ **adjective** Physiology relating to or denoting a nerve cell that releases a transmitter substance into a synapse during transmission of an impulse.
– DERIVATIVES **presynaptically** adverb.

prêt-à-porter /ˌprɛtəˈpɔːteɪ/ ▶ **adjective** (of designer clothes) sold ready-to-wear as opposed to made to measure.
▶ **noun** [mass noun] designer clothes sold ready-to-wear.
– ORIGIN French, literally 'ready to wear'.

pre-tax ▶ **adjective** (of income or profits) considered or calculated before the deduction of taxes: *pre-tax profits rose 23 per cent.*

pre-teen ▶ **adjective** [attrib.] of or relating to a child just under the age of thirteen.
▶ **noun** a child of such an age.

pretence (US **pretense**) ▶ **noun** **1** an attempt to make something that is not the case appear true: *his anger is masked by a pretence that all is well* | [mass noun] *they have finally abandoned their secrecy and pretence.*
■ a false display of feelings, attitudes, or intentions: *he asked me questions without any pretence at politeness.* ■ [mass noun] the practice of inventing imaginary situations in play: *before the age of two, children start to engage in pretence.* ■ [mass noun] affected and ostentatious speech and behaviour.
2 (**pretence to**) a claim, especially a false or ambitious one: *he was quick to disclaim any pretence to superiority.*
– ORIGIN late Middle English: from Anglo-Norman French *pretense*, based on medieval Latin *pretensus* 'pretended', alteration of Latin *praetentus*, from the verb *praetendere* (see **PRETEND**).

pretend ▶ **verb** **1** [with clause or infinitive] speak and act so as to make it appear that something is the case when in fact it is not: *I closed my eyes and pretended I was asleep* | *she turned the pages and pretended to read.*
■ engage in a game or fantasy which involves supposing something that is not the case to be so: *children pretending to be grown-ups.* ■ [with obj.] give the appearance of feeling or possessing (an emotion or quality); simulate: *she pretended a greater surprise than she felt.*
2 [no obj.] (**pretend to**) lay claim to (a quality or title): *he cannot pretend to sophistication.*
▶ **adjective** [attrib.] informal not really what it is represented as being; used in a game or deception: *the children are pouring out pretend tea for the dolls.*
– ORIGIN late Middle English: from Latin *praetendere* 'stretch forth, claim', from *prae* 'before' + *tendere* 'stretch'. The adjective dates from the early 20th cent.

pretender ▶ **noun** a person who claims or aspires to a title or position: *the* ***pretender to*** *the throne.*

pretense ▶ **noun** US spelling of **PRETENCE**.

pretension ▶ **noun** **1** (**pretension to**) a claim or the assertion of a claim to something: *his pretensions to the imperial inheritance* | [mass noun] *all that we cannot tolerate is pretension to infallibility.*
■ (often **pretensions**) an aspiration or claim to a certain status or quality: *another ageing rocker with literary pretensions.*
2 [mass noun] the use of affectation to impress; ostentatiousness: *he spoke simply, without pretension.*
– ORIGIN late Middle English: from medieval Latin *praetensio(n-)*, from *praetens-* 'alleged', from the verb *praetendere* (see **PRETEND**).

pre-tension ▶ **verb** [with obj.] apply tension to (an object) before some other process or event: *the safety system pre-tensions the seat belts.*
■ strengthen (reinforced concrete) by applying tension to the reinforcing rods before the concrete has set.

pre-tensioner ▶ **noun** a device designed to pull a seat belt tight in an accident.

pretentious ▶ **adjective** attempting to impress by affecting greater importance, talent, culture, etc., than is actually possessed: *a pretentious literary device.*
– DERIVATIVES **pretentiously** adverb, **pretentiousness** noun.
– ORIGIN mid 19th cent.: from French *prétentieux*, from *prétention* (see **PRETENSION**).

preter- /ˈpriːtə/ ▶ **combining form** more than: *preternatural.*
– ORIGIN from Latin *praeter* 'past, beyond'.

preterite /ˈprɛt(ə)rɪt/ (US also **preterit**) Grammar
▶ **adjective** expressing a past action or state.
▶ **noun** a simple past tense or form.
– ORIGIN Middle English (in the sense 'bygone, former'): from Latin *praeteritus* 'gone by', past participle of *praeterire*, from *praeter* 'past, beyond' + *ire* 'go'.

preterition /ˌpriːtəˈrɪʃ(ə)n/ ▶ **noun** [mass noun] the action of passing over or disregarding a matter, especially the rhetorical technique of making summary mention of something by professing to omit it.
– ORIGIN late 16th cent.: from late Latin *praeteritio(n-)*, from *praeterire* 'pass, go by'.

preterm Medicine ▶ **adjective** born or occurring after a pregnancy significantly shorter than normal, especially after no more than 37 weeks of pregnancy: *babies born during preterm labour.*
▶ **adverb** after a short pregnancy; prematurely: *babies born preterm are likely to lack surfactant in the lungs.*

pretermit /ˌpriːtəˈmɪt/ ▶ **verb** (**pretermitted**, **pretermitting**) [with obj.] archaic **1** omit to do or mention: *some points of conduct we advisedly pretermit.*
2 abandon (a custom or continuous action) for a time: *the pleasant musical evenings were now entirely pretermitted.*
– DERIVATIVES **pretermission** /-ˈmɪʃ(ə)n/ noun.
– ORIGIN late 15th cent.: from Latin *praetermittere*, from *praeter* 'past, beyond' + *mittere* 'let go'.

preternatural /ˌpriːtəˈnatʃ(ə)r(ə)l/ (also **praeternatural**) ▶ **adjective** beyond what is normal or natural: *autumn had arrived with preternatural speed.*
– DERIVATIVES **preternaturalism** noun, **preternaturally** adverb.

pretext ▶ **noun** a reason given in justification of a course of action that is not the real reason: *the rebels had the perfect pretext for making their move.*
– PHRASES **on** (or **under**) **the pretext** giving the specified reason as one's justification: *he called round* ***on the pretext of*** *asking after her mother.*
– ORIGIN early 16th cent.: from Latin *praetextus* 'outward display', from the verb *praetexere* 'to disguise', from *prae* 'before' + *texere* 'weave'.

Pretoria /prɪˈtɔːrɪə/ the administrative capital of South Africa; pop. 1,080,180 (1991). It was founded in 1855 by Marthinus Wessel Pretorius (1819–1901), the first President of the South African Republic, and named after his father Andries.

Pretoria-Witwatersrand-Vereeniging /fəˈriːnɪkɪŋ/ former name (until 1995) for **GAUTENG**.

pretreat ▶ **verb** [with obj.] treat (something) with a chemical before use.
– DERIVATIVES **pretreatment** noun.

prettify ▶ **verb** (**-ies**, **-ied**) [with obj.] make (someone or something) appear superficially pretty or attractive: *nothing has been done to prettify the site.*
– DERIVATIVES **prettification** noun, **prettifier** noun.

pretty ▶ **adjective** (**prettier**, **prettiest**) attractive in a delicate way without being truly beautiful or handsome: *a pretty little girl with an engaging grin.*
■ [attrib.] informal used ironically in expressions of annoyance or disgust: *he led me a pretty dance.*
▶ **adverb** [as submodifier] informal to a moderately high degree; fairly: *he looked pretty fit for his age.*
▶ **noun** (pl. **-ies**) informal an attractive thing, typically a pleasing but unnecessary accessory: *he buys her lots of pretties—bangles and rings and things.*
■ used to refer in a condescending way to an attractive person: *six pretties in sequined leotards.*
▶ **verb** (**-ies**, **-ied**) [with obj.] make pretty or attractive: *she'll be all* ***prettied up*** *and ready to go in an hour.*
– PHRASES **pretty much** (or **nearly** or **well**) informal very nearly: *the case is pretty well over.* **a pretty penny** informal a large sum of money. **pretty please** used as an emphatic or wheedling form of request. **be sitting pretty** informal be in an advantageous position or situation: *if she could get sponsors, she would be sitting pretty.*
– DERIVATIVES **prettily** adverb, **prettiness** noun, **prettyish** adjective.

p

– ORIGIN Old English *prættig*; related to Middle Dutch *pertich* 'brisk, clever', obsolete Dutch *prettig* 'humorous, sporty', from a West Germanic base meaning 'trick'. The sense development 'deceitful, cunning, clever, skilful, admirable, pleasing, nice' has parallels in adjectives such as *canny, fine, nice,* etc.

pretty boy ▶ **noun** informal, often derogatory a foppish or effeminate man.

pretty-face wallaby ▶ **noun** another term for **WHIPTAIL WALLABY**.

pretzel /ˈprɛts(ə)l/ chiefly N. Amer. ▶ **noun** a crisp biscuit baked in the form of a knot or stick and flavoured with salt.
▶ **verb** (**pretzeled**, **pretzeling**) [with obj.] twist, bend, or contort: *he found the snake pretzeled into a tangle of knots.*
– ORIGIN mid 19th cent.: from German *Pretzel*.

prevail ▶ **verb** [no obj.] prove more powerful than opposing forces; be victorious: *it is hard for logic to* ***prevail over*** *emotion.*
■ be widespread in a particular area at a particular time; be current: *a leisured friendly atmosphere prevailed among the crowds* | [as adj. **prevailing**] *the prevailing political culture.* ■ (**prevail on/upon**) persuade (someone) to do something: *she was prevailed upon to give an account of her work.*
– DERIVATIVES **prevailingly** adverb.
– ORIGIN late Middle English: from Latin *praevalere* 'have greater power', from *prae* 'before' + *valere* 'have power'.

prevailing wind ▶ **noun** a wind from the direction that is predominant or most usual at a particular place or season.

prevalent /ˈprɛv(ə)l(ə)nt/ ▶ **adjective** widespread in a particular area at a particular time: *the social ills prevalent in society today.*
■ archaic predominant; powerful.
– DERIVATIVES **prevalence** noun, **prevalently** adverb.
– ORIGIN late 16th cent.: from Latin *praevalent-* 'having greater power', from the verb *praevalere* (see **PREVAIL**).

prevaricate /prɪˈvarɪkeɪt/ ▶ **verb** [no obj.] speak or act in an evasive way: *he seemed to prevaricate when journalists asked pointed questions.*
– DERIVATIVES **prevarication** noun, **prevaricator** noun.
– ORIGIN mid 16th cent. (in the sense 'go astray, transgress'): from Latin *praevaricat-* 'walked crookedly, deviated', from the verb *praevaricari*, from *prae* 'before' + *varicari* 'straddle' (from *varus* 'bent, knock-kneed').

USAGE The verbs **prevaricate** and **procrastinate** have similar but not identical meanings. **Prevaricate** means 'act or speak in an evasive way', as in *he* ***prevaricated*** *at the mention of money.* **Procrastinate**, on the other hand, means 'put off doing something', as in *the Western powers will* ***procrastinate*** *until it is too late.* The meanings are closely related—if someone prevaricates they often also procrastinate—and this can give rise to confusion in use. In around 50 per cent of the citations in the Oxford Reading Programme for **prevaricate** the meaning could be either 'act evasively' or 'put off doing something', or both, as for example in *they may* ***prevaricate*** *before facing the brutal truth.*

prevenient /prɪˈviːnɪənt/ ▶ **adjective** formal preceding in time or order: antecedent.
– ORIGIN early 17th cent.: from Latin *praevenient-* 'coming before', from the verb *praevenire*, from *prae* 'before' + *venire* 'come'.

prevent ▶ **verb** [with obj.] **1** keep (something) from happening or arising: *action must be taken to prevent further accidents.*
■ make (someone or something) unable to do something: *opposition parties were* ***prevented*** *by riot police* ***from*** *joining the demonstration.*
2 archaic (of God) go before (someone) with spiritual guidance and help.
– DERIVATIVES **preventability** noun, **preventable** (also **preventible**) adjective.
– ORIGIN late Middle English (in the sense 'act in anticipation of'): from Latin *praevent-* 'preceded, hindered', from the verb *praevenire*, from *prae* 'before' + *venire* 'come'.

preventative ▶ **adjective** & **noun** another term for **PREVENTIVE**.
– DERIVATIVES **preventatively** adverb.

preventer ▶ **noun** a person or thing that prevents something: *effective as preventers of further infection.*
■ Sailing an extra line or wire rigged to support a piece of rigging under strain, or to hold the boom and prevent it from gybing.

prevention ▶ **noun** [mass noun] the action of stopping something from happening or arising: *crime prevention* | *the treatment and prevention of Aids.*
– PHRASES **prevention is better than cure** proverb it's easier to stop something happening in the first place than to repair the damage after it has happened.

preventive ▶ **adjective** designed to keep something undesirable such as illness, harm, or accidents from occurring: *preventive medicine.*
▶ **noun** a medicine or other treatment designed to stop disease or ill health from occurring.
– DERIVATIVES **preventively** adverb.

preventive detention ▶ **noun** [mass noun] Law the imprisonment of a person with the aim of preventing them from committing further offences or of maintaining public order.

preverbal ▶ **adjective 1** existing or occurring before the development of speech: *preverbal communication.*
2 Grammar occurring before a verb: *preverbal particles.*

preview ▶ **noun** an inspection or viewing of something before it is bought or becomes generally known and available: *you can get a* ***sneak preview*** *of the pictures on sale.*
■ a showing of a film, play, exhibition, etc., before its official opening. ■ a short item shown in a cinema as publicity for a forthcoming film; a trailer. ■ a commentary on or appraisal of a forthcoming film, play, book, etc., based on an advance viewing. ■ Computing a facility for inspecting the appearance of a document prepared on a word processor before it is printed.
▶ **verb** [with obj.] display (a product, film, play, etc.) before it officially goes on sale or opens to the public: *the company will preview an enhanced version of its database.*
■ see or inspect (something) before it is used or becomes generally available: *the teacher should preview teaching aids to ensure that they are at the right level.* ■ comment on or appraise (a forthcoming event) in advance: *next week we'll be previewing the new season.*

Previn /ˈprɛvɪn/, André (George) (b.1929), German-born American conductor, pianist, and composer. He is most famous as a conductor, notably with the London Symphony Orchestra (1968–79), the Pittsburgh Symphony Orchestra (1976–86), and the Royal Philharmonic Orchestra (1987–91).

previous ▶ **adjective 1** [attrib.] existing or occurring before in time or order: *she looked tired after her exertions of the previous evening* | *tickets will be sold on the same basis as in previous years.*
2 informal over-hasty in acting or drawing a conclusion: *I admit I may have been a bit previous.*
– PHRASES **previous to** before: *the month previous to publication* | *he seemed to have been in good health previous to the fatal injury.*
– DERIVATIVES **previously** adverb.
– ORIGIN early 17th cent.: from Latin *praevius* 'going before' (from *prae* 'before' + *via* 'way') + **-OUS**.

previous question ▶ **noun** (in parliamentary procedure) a motion to decide whether to vote on a main question, moved before the main question itself is put.

previse /prɪˈvʌɪz/ ▶ **verb** [with obj.] poetic/literary foresee or predict (an event): *he had intelligence to previse the possible future.*
– DERIVATIVES **prevision** noun, **previsional** adjective.
– ORIGIN late 16th cent.: from Latin *praevis-* 'foreseen, anticipated', from the verb *praevidere*, from *prae* 'before' + *videre* 'to see'.

prevocalic /ˌpriːvəˈkalɪk/ ▶ **adjective** occurring immediately before a vowel.
– DERIVATIVES **prevocalically** adverb.

pre-vocational ▶ **adjective** given or performed as preparation for vocational training.

Prévost d'Exiles /ˌpreɪvəʊ dɛgˈziːl, French prevo dɛkzil/, Antoine-François (1696–1763), French novelist; known as **Abbé Prévost**. A Benedictine monk and priest, he is remembered for his novel *Manon Lescaut* (1731), which inspired operas by Jules Massenet and Puccini.

pre-war ▶ **adjective** existing, occurring, or built before a war: *the pre-war years.*

pre-wash ▶ **noun** a preliminary wash, especially one performed as part of a cycle in an automatic washing machine.
■ a substance applied as a treatment before washing.
▶ **verb** [with obj.] give a preliminary wash to (a garment), typically before putting it on sale.

prewire ▶ **verb** [with obj.] wire (something requiring electrical circuitry) in advance of usual installation: *we prewired the building.*

prexy (also **prex**) ▶ **noun** (pl. **-ies**) US informal a president, especially the president of a college or society.
– ORIGIN early 19th cent. (as *prex*): college slang.

prey ▶ **noun** [mass noun] an animal that is hunted and killed by another for food: *the kestrel is ready to pounce on unsuspecting prey.*
■ a person or thing easily injured or taken advantage of: *he was* ***easy prey*** *for the two con men.* ■ a person who is vulnerable to distressing emotions or beliefs: *the settlers become* ***prey to*** *nameless fears.* ■ archaic plunder or (in biblical use) a prize.
▶ **verb** [no obj.] (**prey on/upon**) hunt and kill for food: *small birds that prey on insect pests.*
■ take advantage of; exploit or injure: *this is a mean type of theft by ruthless people preying on the elderly.* ■ cause constant trouble and distress to: *the problem had begun to* ***prey on my mind.***
– PHRASES **fall prey to** be hunted and killed by: *small rodents fell prey to domestic cats.* ■ be vulnerable to or overcome by: *he would often fall prey to melancholy.*
– DERIVATIVES **preyer** noun.
– ORIGIN Middle English (also denoting plunder taken in war): the noun from Old French *preie*, from Latin *praeda* 'booty', the verb from Old French *preier*, based on Latin *praedari* 'seize as plunder', from *praeda*.

Prez, Josquin des, see **DES PREZ**.

prez ▶ **noun** informal term for **PRESIDENT**.

prezzie (also **pressie**) ▶ **noun** Brit. informal a present.
– ORIGIN 1930s (as *presee*): abbreviation.

prial /ˈprʌɪəl/ ▶ **noun** (in card games) a set of three cards of the same denomination.
– ORIGIN early 19th cent.: alteration of *pair royal*.

Priam /ˈprʌɪam/ Greek Mythology the king of Troy at the time of its destruction by the Greeks under Agamemnon. The father of Paris and Hector and husband of Hecuba, he was slain by Neoptolemus, son of Achilles.

priapic /prʌɪˈapɪk/ ▶ **adjective** of, relating to, or resembling a phallus: *priapic carvings.*
■ of or relating to male sexuality and sexual activity: *the spirit of these pages is downright priapic.* ■ Medicine (of a man) having a persistently erect penis.
– ORIGIN late 18th cent.: from *Priapos* (see **PRIAPISM**) + **-IC**.

priapism /ˈprʌɪəpɪz(ə)m/ ▶ **noun** [mass noun] Medicine persistent and painful erection of the penis.
– ORIGIN late Middle English: via late Latin from Greek *priapismos*, from *priapizein* 'be lewd', from *Priapos* (see **PRIAPUS**).

Priapulida /ˌprʌɪəˈpjʊlɪdə/ Zoology a small phylum of burrowing worm-like marine invertebrates which have a thick body, a large eversible proboscis, and a terminal tail.
– DERIVATIVES **priapulid** /prʌɪˈapjʊlɪd/ noun & adjective.
– ORIGIN modern Latin (plural), from *Priapulus* (genus name), diminutive of **PRIAPUS**.

Priapus /prʌɪˈeɪpəs/ Greek Mythology a god of fertility, whose cult spread to Greece (and, later, Italy) from Turkey after Alexander's conquests. He was also a god of gardens and the patron of seafarers and shepherds.

Pribilof Islands /ˈprɪbɪlɒf/ a group of four islands in the Bering Sea, off the coast of SW Alaska. First visited in 1786 by the Russian explorer Gavriil Loginovich Pribylov (d.1796), they came into US possession after the purchase of Alaska in 1867.

Price, Vincent (1911–93), American actor, best known for his performances in a series of films based on stories by Edgar Allan Poe.

price ▶ **noun** the amount of money expected, required, or given in payment for something: *land could be sold for a high price* | [mass noun] *a wide selection of tools varying in price.*
■ figurative an unwelcome experience, event, or action involved as a condition of achieving a desired end: *the price of their success was an entire day spent in discussion.* ■ the odds in betting. ■ [mass noun] archaic value; worth: *the parable of the pearl of great price.*
▶ **verb** [with obj.] (often **be priced**) decide the amount required as payment for (something offered for sale): *the watches in this range are* ***priced at*** *£14.50.*

p

– PHRASES **at any price** no matter what expense, sacrifice, or difficulty is involved: *they wanted peace at any price.* **at a price** requiring great expense or involving unwelcome consequences: *his generosity comes at a price.* **beyond** (or **without**) **price** so valuable that no price can be stated. **a price on someone's head** a reward offered for someone's capture or death. **price oneself out of the market** become unable to compete commercially. **put a price on** determine the value of: *you can't put a price on what she has to offer.* **what price —?** **1** used to ask what has become of something or to suggest that something has or would become worthless: *what price justice if he were allowed to go free?* **2** used to make a suggestion or ask about the likelihood of its being fulfilled: *what price cricket at the Olympics?*

– ORIGIN Middle English: the noun from Old French *pris*, from Latin *pretium* 'value, reward'; the verb, a variant (by assimilation to the noun) of earlier *prise* 'estimate the value of' (see **PRIZE**[1]). Compare with **PRAISE**.

price control ▶ noun a government regulation establishing a maximum price to be charged for specified goods and services, especially during periods of war or inflation.

price discrimination ▶ noun [mass noun] the action of selling the same product at different prices to different buyers, in order to maximize sales and profits.

price-earnings ratio (also **price-earnings multiple**) ▶ noun Finance the current market price of a company share divided by the earnings per share of the company.

price elasticity ▶ noun [mass noun] Economics a measure of the effect of a price change or a change in the quantity supplied on the demand for a product or service.

price leadership ▶ noun [mass noun] Economics the setting of prices in a market by a dominant company, which is followed by others in the same market.

priceless ▶ adjective so precious that its value cannot be determined: *priceless works of art.*
■ informal used to express great and usually affectionate amusement: *darling, you're priceless!*

– DERIVATIVES **pricelessly** adverb, **pricelessness** noun.

price lining ▶ noun [mass noun] the sale of a related range of products at different prices, each representing a distinct level of quality.

price point ▶ noun a point on a scale of possible prices at which something might be marketed.

price relative ▶ noun the ratio of the price of something at one time to its price at another.

price ring ▶ noun a group of traders or companies acting illegally to fix a minimum retail price for their competing products, thus forming a cartel.

price-sensitive ▶ adjective denoting a product whose sales are greatly influenced by the price.
■ (of information) likely to affect share prices if it were made public.

price support ▶ noun [mass noun] Economics government assistance in maintaining the levels of market prices regardless of supply or demand.

price system ▶ noun an economic system in which prices are determined by market forces.

price tag ▶ noun the label on an item for sale, showing its price.
■ figurative the cost of a company, enterprise, or undertaking: *a $400 billion price tag was put on the venture.*

price-taker ▶ noun Economics a company that must accept the prevailing prices in the market of its products, its own transactions being unable to affect the market price.

pricey (also **pricy**) ▶ adjective (**pricier**, **priciest**) informal expensive: *boutiques selling pricey clothes.*

– DERIVATIVES **priciness** noun.

prick ▶ verb [with obj.] **1** make a small hole in (something) with a sharp point; pierce slightly: *prick the potatoes all over with a fork.*
■ [no obj.] feel a sensation as though a sharp point were sticking into one: *she felt her scalp prick and her palms were damp.* ■ (of tears) cause the sensation of imminent weeping in (a person's eyes): *tears of disappointment were pricking her eyelids.* ■ [no obj.] (of a person's eyes) experience such a sensation. ■ cause mental or emotional discomfort to: *her conscience pricked her as she told the lie.* ■ arouse or provoke to action: *the police were pricked into action by the horrifying sight.*
2 (usu. **be pricked**) (especially of a horse or dog) make (the ears) stand erect when on the alert: *the dog's tail was wagging and her ears were pricked.*

▶ noun **1** an act of piercing something with a fine, sharp point: *the pin prick had produced a drop of blood.*
■ a small hole or mark made by piercing something with a fine, sharp point. ■ a sharp pain caused by being pierced with a fine point. ■ a sudden feeling of distress, anxiety, or some other unpleasant emotion: *she felt a prick of resentment.* ■ archaic a goad for oxen.
2 vulgar slang a man's penis.
■ a man regarded as stupid, unpleasant, or contemptible.

– PHRASES **kick against the pricks** hurt oneself by persisting in useless resistance or protest. [ORIGIN: with biblical allusion to Acts 9:5.] **prick up one's ears** (especially of a horse or dog) make the ears stand erect when on the alert. ■ (of a person) become suddenly attentive: **a spare prick at a wedding** Brit. vulgar slang a person who is out of place or has no role in a particular situation.

– DERIVATIVES **pricker** noun.

– ORIGIN Old English *pricca* (noun), *prician* (verb), probably of West Germanic origin and related to Low German and Dutch *prik* (noun), *prikken* (verb).

▶ **prick something out** **1** draw a picture or pattern by making small holes in a surface: *he pricked out a rough design with his dagger.* ■ decorate a surface in this way. **2** plant seedlings in small holes made in the earth: *he was in the garden pricking out marigolds.*

pricket ▶ noun **1** a male fallow deer in its second year, having straight, unbranched horns.
2 historical a spike for holding a candle.

– ORIGIN late Middle English: from **PRICK** + **-ET**[1].

prickle ▶ noun a short, slender, sharp-pointed outgrowth on the bark or epidermis of a plant; a small thorn: *the prickles of the gorse bushes.*
■ a small spine or pointed outgrowth on the skin of certain animals. ■ a tingling sensation on someone's skin, typically caused by strong emotion: *Kathleen felt a prickle of excitement.*

▶ verb [no obj.] (of a person's skin or a part of the body) experience a tingling sensation, especially as a result of strong emotion: *the sound made her skin prickle with horror.*
■ [with obj.] cause a tingling or mildly painful sensation in: *I hate the way the fibres prickle your skin.* ■ (of a person) react defensively or angrily to something: *she prickled at the implication that she had led a soft and protected life.*

– ORIGIN Old English *pricel* 'instrument for pricking, sensation of being pricked'; related to Middle Dutch *prickel*, from the Germanic base of **PRICK**. The verb is partly a diminutive of the verb **PRICK**.

prickleback ▶ noun a long slender fish with a spiny dorsal fin running the length of the body. It lives in cooler seas of the northern hemisphere, typically in shallow inshore waters.
• Family Stichaeidae: many genera and species.

prickly ▶ adjective (**pricklier**, **prickliest**) **1** covered in prickles: *masses of prickly brambles.*
■ resembling or feeling like prickles: *his hair was prickly and short.* ■ having or causing a tingling or itching sensation: *a dress that was prickly round the neck | my skin feels prickly.*
2 (of a person) ready to take offence.
■ liable to cause someone to take offence: *this is a prickly subject.*

– DERIVATIVES **prickliness** noun.

prickly ash ▶ noun a spiny North American shrub or tree with prickly branches and bark that can be used medicinally.
• Genus *Zanthoxylum*, family Rutaceae: the northern *Z. americanum* and the southern *Z. clava-herculis* (also called **HERCULES' CLUB**).
■ [mass noun] a medicinal preparation of the bark of these trees.

prickly heat ▶ noun [mass noun] an itchy inflammation of the skin, typically with a rash of small vesicles, common in hot moist weather especially in infants, obese people, and Europeans in tropical climates. Also called **MILIARIA**.

prickly pear ▶ noun a cactus with jointed stems and oval flattened segments, having barbed bristles and large pear-shaped, prickly fruits.
• Genus *Opuntia*, family Cactaceae: several species, in particular *O. ficus-indica*, which is cultivated for its fruit and has become naturalized in the Mediterranean.
■ the edible orange or red fruit of this plant.

prickly poppy ▶ noun a Central American plant with prickly leaves and large scented yellow flowers. It has become a weed in many tropical regions, but is cultivated in cooler regions as an ornamental.
• *Argemone mexicana*, family Papaveraceae.

prick-teaser (also **prick-tease**) ▶ noun vulgar slang another term for **COCK-TEASER**.

pricy ▶ adjective variant spelling of **PRICEY**.

pride ▶ noun **1** [mass noun] a feeling of deep pleasure or satisfaction derived from one's own achievements, the achievements of those with whom one is closely associated, or from qualities or possessions that are widely admired: *the team were bursting with pride after recording a sensational victory | a woman who* **takes** *great* **pride in** *her appearance.*
■ the consciousness of one's own dignity: *he swallowed his pride and asked for help.* ■ the quality of having an excessively high opinion of oneself or one's importance: *the worst sin in a ruler was pride.* ■ a person or thing that is the object or source of a feeling or deep pleasure or satisfaction: *the pride of the village is the swimming pool.* ■ poetic/literary the best state or condition of something; the prime: *in the* **pride** *of youth.*
2 a group of lions forming a social unit.

▶ verb (**pride oneself on/upon**) be especially proud of a particular quality or skill: *she'd always prided herself on her ability to deal with a crisis.*

– PHRASES **one's pride and joy** a person or thing of which one is very proud and which is a source of great pleasure: *the car was his pride and joy.* **pride goes** (or **comes**) **before a fall** proverb if you're too conceited or self-important, something will happen to make you look foolish. **pride of place** the most prominent or important position among a group of things: *the certificate has pride of place on my wall.*

– DERIVATIVES **prideful** adjective, **pridefully** adverb.

– ORIGIN late Old English *prȳde* 'excessive self-esteem', variant of *prȳtu*, *prȳte*, from *prūd* (see **PROUD**).

pride of India ▶ noun any of a number of Asian trees which are cultivated as ornamentals, in particular:
• the chinaberry. • a yellow-flowered tree which has become naturalized in parts of southern Europe (*Koelreuteria paniculata*, family Sapindaceae).

Pride's Purge the exclusion or arrest of about 140 members of parliament likely to vote against a trial of the captive Charles I by soldiers under the command of Colonel Thomas Pride (d.1658) in December 1648. Following the purge, the remaining members, known as the Rump Parliament, voted for the trial which resulted in Charles's execution.

prie-dieu /priːˈdjəː/ ▶ noun (pl. **prie-dieux** pronunc. same) a piece of furniture for use during prayer, consisting of a kneeling surface and a narrow upright front with a rest for the elbows or for books.

– ORIGIN mid 18th cent.: French, literally 'pray God'.

priest ▶ noun **1** an ordained minister of the Catholic, Orthodox, or Anglican Church having the authority to perform certain rites and administer certain sacraments.
■ a person who performs religious ceremonies and duties in a non-Christian religion.
2 a mallet used to kill fish caught when angling. [ORIGIN: with allusion to the priest's function in performing the last rites.]

▶ verb [with obj.] (usu. **be priested**) formal ordain to the priesthood.

– DERIVATIVES **priestlike** adjective.

– ORIGIN Old English *prēost*, of Germanic origin; related to Dutch *priester*, German *Priester*, based on ecclesiastical Latin *presbyter* 'elder' (see **PRESBYTER**).

priestcraft ▶ noun [mass noun] often derogatory the knowledge and work of a priest.

priestess ▶ noun a female priest of a non-Christian religion.

priesthood ▶ noun [mass noun] (often **the priesthood**) the office or position of a priest.
■ priests in general.

priest-in-charge ▶ noun (pl. **priests-in-charge**) (in the Anglican Church) an ordained minister who has charge of a parish but has not been formally appointed as its incumbent.

Priestley[1], J. B. (1894–1984), English novelist,

dramatist, and critic; full name *John Boynton Priestley*. Notable works: *The Good Companions* (1929), a picaresque novel, and the mystery drama *An Inspector Calls* (1947).

Priestley², Joseph (1733–1804), English scientist and theologian. Priestley was the author of about 150 books, mostly theological or educational. His chief work was on the chemistry of gases, in which his most significant discovery was of 'dephlogisticated air' (oxygen) in 1774; he demonstrated that it was important to animal life, and that plants give off this gas in sunlight.

priestly ▶ **adjective** of, relating to, or befitting a priest or priests: *performing priestly duties.*
– DERIVATIVES **priestliness** noun.
– ORIGIN Old English *prēostlic* (see **PRIEST**, **-LY¹**).

priest's hole ▶ **noun** historical a hiding place for a Roman Catholic priest during times of religious persecution.

prig ▶ **noun** a self-righteously moralistic person who behaves as if they are superior to others.
– DERIVATIVES **priggery** noun, **priggish** adjective, **priggishly** adverb, **priggishness** noun.
– ORIGIN mid 16th cent.: of unknown origin. The earliest sense was 'tinker' or 'petty thief', whence 'disliked person', especially 'someone who is affectedly and self-consciously precise' (late 17th cent.).

prill ▶ **noun** a pellet or solid globule of a substance formed by the congealing of a liquid during an industrial process.
– DERIVATIVES **prilled** adjective.
– ORIGIN late 18th cent. (as a term in copper mining, denoting rich copper ore remaining after removal of low-grade material): of unknown origin.

prim ▶ **adjective** (**primmer**, **primmest**) stiffly formal and respectable; feeling or showing disapproval of anything regarded as improper: *a very prim and proper lady.*
▶ **verb** (**primmed**, **primming**) [with obj.] purse (the mouth or lips) into a prim expression: *Laurie **primmed up** his mouth.*
– DERIVATIVES **primly** adverb, **primness** noun.
– ORIGIN late 17th cent. (as a verb): probably ultimately from Old French *prin*, Provençal *prim* 'excellent, delicate', from Latin *primus* 'first'.

prima ballerina /ˈpriːmə/ ▶ **noun** the chief female dancer in a ballet or ballet company.
– ORIGIN late 19th cent.: Italian, literally 'first ballerina'.

primacy /ˈprʌɪməsi/ ▶ **noun** [mass noun] **1** the fact of being primary, pre-eminent, or more important: *London's primacy as a financial centre.*
2 the office, period of office, or authority of a primate of the Church.
3 [usu. as modifier] Psychology the fact of an item having been presented earlier to the subject (especially as increasing its likelihood of being remembered): *the **primacy effect** is thought to reflect recall from a long-term memory store.*
– ORIGIN late Middle English: from Old French *primatie*, from medieval Latin *primatia*, from Latin *primas*, *primat-* 'of the first rank' (see **PRIMATE¹**).

prima donna ▶ **noun** the chief female singer in an opera or opera company.
■ a very temperamental person with an inflated view of their own talent or importance.
– DERIVATIVES **prima donna-ish** adjective.
– ORIGIN late 18th cent.: Italian, literally 'first lady'.

primaeval ▶ **adjective** variant spelling of **PRIMEVAL**.

prima facie /ˌprʌɪmə ˈfeɪʃiː/ ▶ **adjective** & **adverb** Law based on the first impression; accepted as correct until proved otherwise: [as adj.] *a prima facie case of professional misconduct* | [as adv.] *the original lessee prima facie remains liable for the payment of the rent.*
– ORIGIN Latin, from *primus* 'first' + *facies* 'face'.

primal /ˈprʌɪm(ə)l/ ▶ **adjective** fundamental; essential: *for me, writing is a primal urge.*
■ relating to an early stage in evolutionary development; primeval: *primal hunting societies.*
■ Psychology of, relating to, or denoting the needs, fears, or behaviour that are postulated (especially in Freudian theory) to form the origins of emotional life: *he preys on people's primal fears.* See also **PRIMAL SCENE**.
– DERIVATIVES **primally** adverb.
– ORIGIN early 17th cent.: from medieval Latin *primalis*, from Latin *primus* 'first'.

primal father ▶ **noun** Anthropology & Psychoanalysis a male authority figure, identified (especially in Freudian theory) with the dominant male of the primal horde.

primal horde ▶ **noun** Anthropology (in Freudian theory) a hypothetical patriarchal unit of prehistoric human social organization.

primal scene ▶ **noun** Psychology (in Freudian theory) the occasion on which a child becomes aware of its parents' sexual intercourse, the timing of which is thought to be crucial in determining predisposition to future neuroses.

primal scream ▶ **noun** a release of intense basic frustration, anger, and aggression, especially that rediscovered by means of primal therapy.

primal therapy ▶ **noun** [mass noun] a form of psychotherapy which focuses on a patient's earliest emotional experiences and encourages verbal expression of childhood suffering, typically using an empty chair or other prop to represent a parent towards whom anger is directed.

primaquine /ˈprʌɪməkwiːn, ˈpriːmə-/ ▶ **noun** [mass noun] Medicine a synthetic compound derived from quinoline used in the treatment of malaria.
– ORIGIN 1940s: apparently from Latin *prima* (feminine of *primus* 'first') + *quin(olin)e*

primarily /ˈprʌɪm(ə)rɪli, prʌɪˈmɛr-/ ▶ **adverb** for the most part; mainly: *around 80 per cent of personal computers are used primarily for word processing.*

primary ▶ **adjective** **1** of chief importance; principal: *the government's primary aim is to see significant reductions in unemployment.*
2 earliest in time or order of development: *the country was in the primary stage of socialism.*
■ not derived from, caused by, or based on anything else: *the research involved the use of primary source materials in national and local archives.*
3 of or relating to education for children between the ages of about five and eleven: *a primary teacher.*
4 Biology & Medicine belonging to or directly derived from the first stage of development or growth: *a primary bone tumour.*
5 (**Primary**) Geology former term for **PALAEOZOIC**.
6 relating to or denoting the input side of a device using electromagnetic induction, especially in a transformer.
7 Chemistry (of an organic compound) having its functional group located on a carbon atom which is bonded to no more than one other carbon atom.
■ (chiefly of amines) derived from ammonia by replacement of one hydrogen atom by an organic group.
▶ **noun** (pl. **-ies**) **1** (also **primary election**) (in the US) a preliminary election to appoint delegates to a party conference or to select the candidates for a principal, especially presidential, election.
2 short for:
■ Brit. a primary school. ■ a primary colour. ■ Ornithology a primary feather. ■ a primary coil or winding in an electrical transformer.
3 Astronomy the body orbited by a smaller satellite or companion.
4 (**the Primary**) Geology, dated the Primary or Palaeozoic era.
– ORIGIN late Middle English (in the sense 'original, not derivative'): from Latin *primarius*, from *primus* 'first'. The noun uses date from the 18th cent.

primary care (also **primary health care**) ▶ **noun** [mass noun] health care provided in the community for people making an initial approach to a medical practitioner or clinic for advice or treatment.

primary cell ▶ **noun** an electric cell that produces current by an irreversible chemical reaction.

primary colour ▶ **noun** any of a group of colours from which all other colours can be obtained by mixing.

> The primary colours for pigments are red, blue, and yellow. The primary additive colours for light are red, green, and blue; the primary subtractive colours (which give the primary additive colours when subtracted from white light) are magenta, cyan, and yellow.

primary evidence ▶ **noun** [mass noun] Law evidence, such as the original of a document, that by its nature does not suggest that better evidence is available.
■ first-hand historical evidence about an event rather than that based on other sources.

primary feather ▶ **noun** any of the largest flight feathers in a bird's wing, growing from the manus.

primary group ▶ **noun** Sociology a group held together by relationships formed by family and environmental associations, regarded as basic to social life and culture.

primary industry ▶ **noun** [mass noun] Economics industry, such as mining, agriculture, or forestry, that is concerned with obtaining or providing natural raw materials for conversion into commodities and products for the consumer.

primary planet ▶ **noun** a planet that directly orbits the sun.

primary poverty ▶ **noun** [mass noun] Economics effective poverty due to insufficiency of means rather than waste, inefficiency, or some other drain on resources.

primary process ▶ **noun** Psychoanalysis an unconscious thought process arising from the pleasure principle, such as condensation or displacement, which is irrational and not subject to compulsion.

primary production ▶ **noun** [mass noun] the production of raw materials for industry.

primary qualities ▶ **plural noun** Philosophy properties or qualities, such as size, motion, shape, number, etc., belonging to physical matter independently of an observer.
■ the four original qualities of matter (hot, cold, wet, and dry) recognized by Aristotle, from which other qualities were held to derive.

primary school ▶ **noun** Brit. a school where young children are taught, especially those below the age of 11.
■ N. Amer. a grade school, especially one covering the first three or four grades and sometimes kindergarten.

primary sector ▶ **noun** Economics the sector of the economy concerned with or relating to primary industry.

primary structure ▶ **noun** **1** Biochemistry the characteristic sequence of amino acids forming a protein or polypeptide chain, considered as the most basic element of its structure.
2 Aeronautics the parts of an aircraft whose failure would seriously endanger safety.

primary treatment ▶ **noun** [mass noun] the sedimentation and removal of most suspended matter from sewage effluent.

primate¹ /ˈprʌɪmeɪt, -mət/ ▶ **noun** Christian Church the chief bishop or archbishop of a province: *Cardinal Glemp, the primate of Poland.*
– DERIVATIVES **primatial** /-ˈmeɪʃ(ə)l/ adjective.
– ORIGIN Middle English: from Old French *primat*, from Latin *primas*, *primat-* 'of the first rank', from *primus* 'first'.

primate² /ˈprʌɪmeɪt/ ▶ **noun** Zoology a mammal of an order that includes the lemurs, bushbabies, tarsiers, marmosets, monkeys, apes, and humans. They are distinguished by having hands, hand-like feet, and forward-facing eyes, and are typically agile tree-dwellers.
• Order Primates: several families.
– ORIGIN late 19th cent.: from Latin *primas*, *primat-* 'of the first rank' (see **PRIMATE¹**).

Primate of All England ▶ **noun** a title of the Archbishop of Canterbury.

Primate of All Ireland ▶ **noun** a title of both the Catholic and Anglican Archbishops of Armagh.

Primate of England ▶ **noun** a title of the Archbishop of York.

primatology /ˌprʌɪməˈtɒlədʒi/ ▶ **noun** [mass noun] the branch of zoology that deals with primates.
– DERIVATIVES **primatological** adjective, **primatologist** noun.

primavera /ˌpriːməˈvɛːrə/ ▶ **noun** [mass noun] the hard, light-coloured timber of a Central American tree.
• The tree is *Cybistax donnellsmithii*, family Bignoniaceae.
▶ **adjective** [postpositive] (of a pasta dish) made with lightly sautéed spring vegetables: *house specialities include linguine primavera.*
– ORIGIN late 19th cent.: from Spanish, denoting the season of spring, from Latin *primus* 'first, earliest' + *ver* 'spring' (alluding to the tree's early flowering).

prime¹ ▶ **adjective** **1** of first importance; main: *a nurse's prime concern is the well-being of the patient.*
■ from which another thing may derive or proceed: *Diogenes' conclusion that air is the prime matter.*
2 [attrib.] of the best possible quality; excellent: *a prime site in the centre of Glasgow* | *prime cuts of meat.*
■ having all the expected or typical characteristics of

P

something: *the novel is a prime example of the genre.* ■ most suitable or likely: *it's the prime contender for dance single of the year.*
3 Mathematics (of a number) divisible only by itself and unity (e.g. 2, 3, 5, 7, 11).
■ [predic.] (of two or more numbers in relation to each other) having no common factor but unity.
▶ **noun 1** [in sing.] a state or time of greatest strength, vigour, or success in a person's life: *you're in the prime of life | he wasn't elderly, but clearly past his prime.*
■ archaic the beginning or first period of something: *the prime of the world.*
2 Christian Church a service forming part of the Divine Office of the Western Church, traditionally said (or chanted) at the first hour of the day (i.e. 6 a.m.), but now little used.
■ archaic this time of day.
3 a prime number.
4 Printing a symbol (′) written after a letter or symbol as a distinguishing mark or after a figure as a symbol for minutes or feet.
5 Fencing the first of eight parrying positions, used to protect the upper inside of the body, with the sword hand at head height in pronation and the tip of the blade pointing downwards. [ORIGIN: French.]
6 a special section in a cycle race, attracting a special prize.
7 short for **PRIME RATE**.
– DERIVATIVES **primeness** noun.
– ORIGIN Old English *prīm* (in sense 2 of the noun), from Latin *prima (hora)* 'first (hour)', reinforced in Middle English by Old French *prime*; the adjective dates from late Middle English, via Old French from Latin *primus* 'first'.

prime² ▶ **verb** [with obj.] **1** make (something) ready for use or action, in particular:
■ prepare (a firearm or explosive device) for firing or detonation. ■ cover (wood, canvas, or metal) with a preparatory coat of paint in order to prevent the absorption of subsequent layers of paint. ■ pour or spray liquid into (a pump) before starting in order to seal the moving parts and facilitate its operation. ■ inject extra fuel into (the cylinder or carburettor of an internal-combustion engine) in order to facilitate starting. ■ [no obj.] (of a steam engine or its boiler) mix water with the steam being passed into the cylinder. ■ Biology & Medicine induce a susceptibility or proclivity in (an animal, person, or tissue): *artificial milk can prime the baby's body for future allergic reactions.* ■ Biochemistry serve as a starting material for (a polymerization process).
2 prepare (someone) for a situation or task, typically by supplying them with relevant information: [with obj. and infinitive] *the sentries had been primed to admit him without challenge.*
– PHRASES **prime the pump** stimulate or support the growth or success of something by supplying it with money: *the money was intended to prime the community care pump.*
– ORIGIN early 16th cent. (in the sense 'fill, load'): origin uncertain; probably based on Latin *primus* 'first', since the sense expressed is a 'first' operation prior to something else.

prime cost ▶ **noun** the direct cost of a commodity in terms of the materials and labour involved in its production, excluding fixed costs.

prime lens ▶ **noun** Photography a lens of fixed focal length.

prime meridian ▶ **noun** a planet's meridian adopted as the zero of longitude.

prime minister ▶ **noun** the head of an elected government; the principal minister of a sovereign or state.

> In current use, the terms *Premier* and *Prime Minister* refer to the same office in Britain, but in Canada and Australia the government of a province or state is headed by a Premier, that of the federal government by a Prime Minister. In countries such as France, where the President has an executive function, the Prime Minister is in a subordinate position.

prime mover ▶ **noun** a person who is chiefly responsible for the creation or execution of a plan or project.
■ an initial natural or mechanical source of motive power.

primer¹ ▶ **noun** [mass noun] a substance used as a preparatory coat on previously unpainted wood, metal, or canvas, especially to prevent the absorption of subsequent layers of paint or the development of rust.
■ a cap or cylinder containing a compound which responds to friction or an electrical impulse and ignites the charge in a cartridge or explosive. ■ a small pump for pumping fuel to prime an internal-combustion engine, especially in an aircraft. ■ Biochemistry a molecule that serves as a starting material for a polymerization process.

primer² ▶ **noun** an elementary textbook that serves as an introduction to a subject of study or is used for teaching children to read.
– ORIGIN late Middle English: from medieval Latin *primarius (liber)* 'primary (book)' and *primarium (manuale)* 'primary (manual)'.

prime rate ▶ **noun** the lowest rate of interest at which money may be borrowed commercially.

prime rib ▶ **noun** N. Amer. a roast or steak cut from the seven ribs immediately before the loin.

prime time ▶ **noun** the time at which a radio or television audience is expected to be at its highest: *the show is networked at prime time.*

primeur /priːˈməː/ ▶ **noun 1** (**primeurs**) fruit or vegetables grown to be available very early in the season.
2 (also **Primeur**) newly produced wines which have recently been made available.
– ORIGIN French, literally 'newness'.

primeval /prʌɪˈmiːv(ə)l/ (also **primaeval**) ▶ **adjective** of the earliest ages in the history of the world: *mile after mile of primeval forest.*
■ (of feelings or actions) based on primitive instinct; raw and elementary: *a primeval desire.*
– DERIVATIVES **primevally** adverb.
– ORIGIN mid 17th cent.: from Latin *primaevus* (from *primus* 'first' + *aevum* 'age') + **-AL**.

primeval soup ▶ **noun** another term for **PRIMORDIAL SOUP**.

prime vertical ▶ **noun** Astronomy a great circle in the celestial sphere passing through the zenith and the east and west points of the horizon.

primigravida /ˌpriːmɪˈɡravɪdə, ˌprʌɪm-/ ▶ **noun** (pl. **primigravidae** /-diː/) Medicine a woman who is pregnant for the first time.
– ORIGIN late 19th cent.: modern Latin (feminine), from Latin *primus* 'first' + *gravidus* 'pregnant' (see **GRAVID**).

priming ▶ **noun** [mass noun] a substance which prepares something for use or action, in particular:
■ another term for **PRIMER¹**. ■ gunpowder placed in the pan of a firearm to ignite a charge.

primipara /prʌɪˈmɪp(ə)rə/ ▶ **noun** (pl. **primiparae** /-riː/) Medicine a woman who is giving birth for the first time.
– DERIVATIVES **primiparous** adjective.
– ORIGIN mid 19th cent.: modern Latin (feminine), from *primus* 'first' + *-parus* 'bringing forth' (from the verb *parere*).

primitive ▶ **adjective 1** relating to, denoting, or preserving the character of an early stage in the evolutionary or historical development of something: *primitive mammals | Primitive Germanic.*
■ relating to or denoting a preliterate, non-industrial society or culture characterized by simple social and economic organization: *primitive people.* ■ having a quality or style that offers an extremely basic level of comfort, convenience, or efficiency: *the accommodation at the camp was a bit primitive.* ■ (of behaviour, thought, or emotion) apparently originating in unconscious needs or desires and unaffected by objective reasoning: *the primitive responses we share with many animals.* ■ of or denoting a simple, direct style of art that deliberately rejects sophisticated artistic techniques.
2 not developed or derived from anything else: *primitive material of the universe.*
■ Linguistics denoting a word, base, or root from which another is historically derived. ■ Mathematics (of an algebraic or geometric expression) from which another is derived, or which is not itself derived from another.
3 Biology (of a part or structure) in the first or early stage of formation or growth; rudimentary. See also **PRIMITIVE STREAK**.
▶ **noun 1** a person belonging to a preliterate, non-industrial society or culture.
2 a pre-Renaissance painter.
■ a modern painter who imitates the pre-Renaissance style. ■ an artist employing a simple, naive style that deliberately rejects subtlety or conventional techniques. ■ a painting by a primitive artist, or an object in a primitive style.
3 Linguistics a word, base, or root from which another is historically derived.
■ Mathematics an algebraic or geometric expression from which another is derived; a curve of which another is the polar or reciprocal. ■ Computing a simple operation or procedure of a limited set from which complex operations or procedures may be constructed, especially a simple geometric shape which may be generated in computer graphics by such an operation or procedure.
– DERIVATIVES **primitively** adverb, **primitiveness** noun.
– ORIGIN late Middle English (in the sense 'original, not derivative'): from Old French *primitif, -ive*, from Latin *primitivus* 'first of its kind', from *primus* 'first'.

primitive cell ▶ **noun** Crystallography the smallest possible unit cell of a lattice, having lattice points at each of its eight vertices only.

Primitive Church ▶ **noun** the Christian Church in its earliest times.

Primitive Methodist ▶ **noun** historical a member of a society of Methodists which was formed in 1811 and joined the united Methodist Church in 1932.

primitive streak ▶ **noun** Embryology the faint streak which is the earliest trace of the embryo in the fertilized ovum of a higher vertebrate.

primitivism ▶ **noun** [mass noun] **1** a belief in the value of what is simple and unsophisticated, expressed as a philosophy of life or through art or literature.
2 unsophisticated behaviour that is unaffected by objective reasoning.
– DERIVATIVES **primitivist** noun & adjective.

primo /ˈpriːməʊ/ ▶ **noun** (pl. **-os**) Music the leading or upper part in a duet.
▶ **adjective** N. Amer. informal of top quality or importance: *the primo team in the land.*
– ORIGIN mid 18th cent.: Italian, literally 'first'.

Primo de Rivera /ˌpriːməʊ deɪ rɪˈvɛːrə, Spanish ˌprimo ðe riˈβera/, Miguel (1870–1930), Spanish general and statesman, head of state 1923–30. He assumed dictatorial powers after leading a military coup. His son, **José Antonio Primo de Rivera** (1903–36), founded the Falange in 1933 and was executed by Republicans in the Spanish Civil War.

primogenitor /ˌprʌɪmə(ʊ)ˈdʒɛnɪtə/ ▶ **noun** an ancestor, especially the earliest ancestor of a people; a progenitor.
– ORIGIN mid 17th cent.: variant of **PROGENITOR**, on the pattern of *primogeniture*.

primogeniture /ˌprʌɪmə(ʊ)ˈdʒɛnɪtʃə/ ▶ **noun** [mass noun] the state of being the firstborn child.
■ (also **right of primogeniture**) the right of succession belonging to the firstborn child, especially the feudal rule by which the whole real estate of an intestate passed to the eldest son.
– DERIVATIVES **primogenital** adjective, **primogenitary** adjective.
– ORIGIN early 17th cent.: from medieval Latin *primogenitura*, from Latin *primo* 'first' + *genitura* 'geniture'.

primordial /prʌɪˈmɔːdɪəl/ ▶ **adjective** existing at or from the beginning of time; primeval: *the primordial oceans.*
■ (especially of a state or quality) basic and fundamental: *the primordial needs of the masses.* ■ Biology (of a cell, part, or tissue) in the earliest stage of development.
– DERIVATIVES **primordiality** noun, **primordially** adverb.
– ORIGIN late Middle English: from late Latin *primordialis* 'first of all', from *primordius* 'original' (see **PRIMORDIUM**).

primordial soup ▶ **noun** [mass noun] a solution rich in organic compounds in the primitive oceans of the earth, from which life is thought to have originated.

primordium /prʌɪˈmɔːdɪəm/ ▶ **noun** (pl. **primordia** /-dɪə/) Biology an organ, structure, or tissue in the earliest stage of development.
– ORIGIN late 19th cent.: from Latin, neuter of *primordius* 'original', from *primus* 'first' + *ordiri* 'begin'.

Primorsky /priːˈmɔːski/ a krai (administrative territory) in the far south-east of Siberian Russia, between the Sea of Japan and the Chinese border; capital, Vladivostok.

primo uomo /ˌpriːməʊ ˈwəʊməʊ, Italian ˌprimo ˈwɔmo/ ▶ **noun** (pl. **primi uomi** or **primo uomos**) the principal male singer in an opera or opera company.

– ORIGIN Italian, literally 'first man'.

primp ▶ verb [with obj.] spend time making minor adjustments to (one's hair, make-up, or clothes).
– ORIGIN late 16th cent.: related to PRIM.

primrose ▶ noun a European plant of woodland and hedgerows, which produces pale yellow flowers in the early spring.
● *Primula vulgaris*, family Primulaceae (the **primrose family**). This family also includes the cowslip, pimpernels, and cyclamens.
■ (also **primrose yellow**) [mass noun] a pale yellow colour.
– PHRASES **primrose path** the pursuit of pleasure, especially when it is seen to bring disastrous consequences: *blithely unaware of his doom, he continued down his primrose path.* [ORIGIN: with allusion to Shakespeare's *Hamlet* I. iii. 50.]
– ORIGIN late Middle English: compare with Old French *primerose* and medieval Latin *prima rosa*, literally 'first rose'.

Primrose League a political association, formed in memory of Benjamin Disraeli (whose favourite flower was reputedly the primrose) in 1883, to promote and sustain the principles of Conservatism as represented by him.

primula /ˈprɪmjʊlə/ ▶ noun a plant of a genus that includes primroses, cowslips, and polyanthuses. Many kinds are cultivated as ornamentals, bearing flowers in a wide variety of colours in the spring.
● Genus *Primula*, family Primulaceae.
– ORIGIN modern Latin, feminine of *primulus*, diminutive of *primus* 'first'.

primulaceous ▶ adjective Botany of, relating to, or denoting plants of the primrose family (Primulaceae).
– ORIGIN mid 19th cent.: from modern Latin *Primulaceae* (plural), based on medieval Latin *primula* (see PRIMULA), + -OUS.

primum mobile /ˌpraɪməm ˈməʊbɪleɪ, ˌpriːməm ˈməʊbɪli/ ▶ noun 1 the central or most important source of motion or action.
2 (in the medieval version of the Ptolemaic system) an outer sphere supposed to move round the earth in 24 hours carrying the inner spheres with it.
– ORIGIN from medieval Latin, literally 'first moving thing'.

Primus /ˈpraɪməs/ ▶ noun trademark a brand of portable cooking stove that burns vaporized oil.

primus /ˈpraɪməs/ ▶ noun the presiding bishop of the Scottish Episcopal Church, elected by the bishops from among their number.
– ORIGIN late 16th cent.: from Latin, literally 'first'.

primus inter pares /ˌpriːməs ɪntə ˈpɑːriːz, ˌpraɪməs/ ▶ noun a first among equals; the senior or representative member of a group.
– ORIGIN Latin.

prince ▶ noun the son of a monarch.
■ a close male relative of a monarch, especially a son's son. ■ a male royal ruler of a small state, actually, nominally, or originally subject to a king or emperor. ■ (in France, Germany and other European countries) a nobleman, usually ranking next below a duke. ■ (**prince of/among**) a man or thing regarded as outstanding or excellent in a particular sphere or group: *arctic char is a prince among fishes.*
– PHRASES **prince of the blood** a man who is a prince by right of his royal descent.
– DERIVATIVES **princedom** noun.
– ORIGIN Middle English: via Old French from Latin *princeps, princip-* 'first, chief, sovereign', from *primus* 'first' + *capere* 'take'.

Prince Albert, Prince Charles, etc. see ALBERT, PRINCE; CHARLES, PRINCE, etc.

Prince Charming a fairy-tale hero in *King Charming* or *Prince Charming* by James Robinson Planché (1796–1880). The name was later adopted for the hero of various fairy-tale pantomimes.
■ [as noun] (also **a Prince Charming**) an ideal male lover who is both handsome and of admirable character.
– ORIGIN partial translation of French *Roi Charmant*, literally 'King Charming'.

prince consort ▶ noun the husband of a reigning female sovereign who is himself a prince.

Prince Edward Island an island in the Gulf of St Lawrence, in eastern Canada, the country's smallest province; capital, Charlottetown. Explored by Jacques Cartier in 1534 and colonized by the French, it was ceded to the British in 1763. It became a province of Canada in 1873.

princeling ▶ noun chiefly derogatory the ruler of a small principality or domain.
■ a young prince.

princely ▶ adjective of or held by a prince: *the princely states of India | princely authority.*
■ sumptuous and splendid: *princely accommodation.* ■ (of a sum of money) large or generous (often used ironically): *she's paying a princely sum.*
– DERIVATIVES **princeliness** noun.

Prince of Darkness ▶ noun a name for the Devil.

Prince of Peace ▶ noun a title given to Jesus Christ (in allusion to Isa. 9:6).

prince of the blood ▶ noun see PRINCE.

Prince of the Church ▶ noun historical a dignitary in the Church, especially a wealthy or influential cardinal or bishop.

Prince of Wales ▶ noun a title traditionally granted to the heir apparent to the British throne (usually the eldest son of the sovereign) since Edward I of England gave the title to his son in 1301 after the conquest of Wales.

Prince of Wales check ▶ noun [usu. as modifier] a large check pattern: *a Prince of Wales check suit.*

Prince of Wales' feathers ▶ plural noun a plume of three ostrich feathers, first adopted as a crest by the eldest son of Edward III, Edward Plantagenet, the Black Prince.

Prince of Wales Island 1 an island in the Canadian Arctic, in the Northwest Territories to the east of Victoria Island.
2 former name for PENANG.

Prince Regent ▶ noun a prince who acts as regent, in particular the title of the future George IV, who was regent from 1811 until he became king in 1820.

prince royal ▶ noun the eldest son of a reigning monarch.

Prince Rupert's drop ▶ noun a pear-shaped bubble of glass with a long tail, made by dropping melted glass into water. Prince Rupert's drops have the property, due to internal strain, of disintegrating explosively when the tail is broken off or the surface scratched.
– ORIGIN late 17th cent.: so named because introduced to England by Prince *Rupert* of Germany.

Prince Rupert's Land another name for RUPERT'S LAND.

prince's feather ▶ noun a tall South American plant with upright brush-like spikes of small red flowers.
● *Amaranthus hypochondriacus*, family Amaranthaceae.

Princes in the Tower the young sons of Edward IV, namely Edward, Prince of Wales (b.1470) and Richard, Duke of York (b.1472), supposedly murdered in the Tower of London in or shortly after 1483. They were taken to the Tower of London by their uncle (the future Richard III) and are generally assumed to have been murdered, but whether at the instigation of Richard III or of another is not known; two skeletons discovered in 1674 are thought to have been those of the princes.

princess ▶ noun the daughter of a monarch.
■ a close female relative of monarch, especially a son's daughter. ■ the wife or widow of a prince. ■ the female ruler of a small state, actually, nominally, or originally subject to a king or emperor. ■ (**princess of/among**) a woman or thing regarded as pre-eminent in a particular sphere or group: *the princess of American politics.* ■ N. Amer. a spoilt or arrogant young woman. ■ informal a form of address used by a man to a girl or woman: *is something the matter, princess?*
– PHRASES **princess of the blood** a woman who is a princess by right of her royal descent.
– ORIGIN late Middle English: from Old French *princesse*, from *prince* (see PRINCE).

Princess Anne, Princess Margaret, etc. see ANNE, PRINCESS; MARGARET, PRINCESS, etc.

princesse lointaine /prãˌsɛs lwaˈtɛn/ ▶ noun (pl. **princesses lointaines**) poetic/literary an ideal but unattainable woman.
– ORIGIN French, literally 'distant princess', from the title of a play by E. ROSTAND, based on a theme in troubadour poetry.

Princess Regent ▶ noun a princess who acts as regent.
■ the wife of a Prince Regent.

Princess Royal ▶ noun the eldest daughter of a

reigning monarch (especially as a title conferred by the British monarch).

Princeton University /ˈprɪnstən/ a university at Princeton in New Jersey, one of the most prestigious in the US. It was founded in 1746.

principal ▶ adjective [attrib.] **1** first in order of importance; main: *the country's principal cities.*
2 (of money) denoting an original sum invested or lent: *the principal amount of your investment.*
▶ noun **1** the person with the highest authority or most important position in an organization, institution, or group: *a design consultancy whose principal is based in San Francisco.*
■ the head of a school, college, or other educational institution. ■ the leading performer in a concert, play, ballet, or opera. ■ Music the leading player in each section of an orchestra. ■ (in certain professions) a fully qualified practitioner. ■ (in the UK) a senior civil servant in charge of a particular section.
2 [mass noun] a sum of money lent or invested on which interest is paid: *the winners are paid from the interest without even touching the principal.*
3 a person for whom another acts as an agent or representative: *stockbrokers in Tokyo act as agents rather than as principals.*
■ Law the person directly responsible for a crime. ■ historical each of the combatants in a duel.
3 a main rafter supporting purlins.
4 an organ stop sounding a main register of open flue pipes typically an octave above the diapason.
– DERIVATIVES **principalship** noun.
– ORIGIN Middle English: via Old French from Latin *principalis* 'first, original', from *princeps, princip-* 'first, chief'.

> USAGE On the confusion of **principal** and **principle**, see usage at PRINCIPLE.

principal axis ▶ noun Physics each of three mutually perpendicular axes in a body about which the moment of inertia is at a maximum.
■ another term for OPTICAL AXIS.

principal boy ▶ noun Brit. the leading male role in a pantomime, especially when played by a woman.

principal component analysis ▶ noun [mass noun] Statistics a method of analysis which involves finding the linear combination of a set of variables that has maximum variance and removing its effect, repeating this successively.

principal diagonal ▶ noun Mathematics the set of elements of a matrix that lie on the line joining the top left corner to the bottom right corner.

principal girl ▶ noun Brit. the leading female role in a pantomime.

principal in the first degree ▶ noun Law a person who is directly responsible for a crime as its actual perpetrator.

principal in the second degree ▶ noun Law a person who is directly responsible for a crime as aiding in its perpetration.

principality ▶ noun (pl. -ies) **1** a state ruled by a prince.
■ (the Principality) Brit. Wales.
2 (principalities) (in traditional Christian angelology) the fifth highest order of the ninefold celestial hierarchy.
– ORIGIN Middle English (denoting the rank of a prince): from Old French *principalite*, from late Latin *principalitas*, from Latin *principalis* 'first, original' (see PRINCIPAL).

principally ▶ adverb [sentence adverb] for the most part; chiefly: *he was principally a landscape painter.*

principal parts ▶ plural noun Grammar the forms of a verb from which all other inflected forms can be deduced, for example *swim, swam, swum.*

principate /ˈprɪnsɪpət/ ▶ noun the rule of the early Roman emperors, during which some features of republican government were retained.
– ORIGIN late Middle English (denoting a principality): from Latin *principatus* 'first place', from *princeps, princip-* 'first, chief' (see PRINCE). The current sense dates from the mid 19th cent.

principe /ˈprɪntʃɪpeɪ/ ▶ noun (pl. **principi** /ˈprɪntʃɪpi/) (in Italy) a prince.
– ORIGIN Italian, from Latin *princeps, princip-* 'first, chief' (see PRINCE).

principessa /ˌprɪntʃɪˈpɛsə/ ▶ noun (pl. **principesse** /ˌprɪntʃɪˈpɛseɪ/) (in Italy) a princess.

– ORIGIN Italian, from medieval Latin *principissa*, from Latin *princeps, princip-* (see **PRINCE**).

principle ▶ **noun** **1** a fundamental truth or proposition that serves as the foundation for a system of belief or behaviour or for a chain of reasoning: *the basic principles of Christianity.*
▪ (usu. **principles**) a rule or belief governing one's personal behaviour: *struggling to be true to their own principles* | [mass noun] *she resigned over a matter of principle.* ▪ [mass noun] morally correct behaviour and attitudes: *a man of principle.* ▪ a general scientific theorem or law that has numerous special applications across a wide field. ▪ a natural law forming the basis for the construction or working of a machine: *these machines all operate on the same general principle.*
2 a fundamental source or basis of something: *the first principle of all things was water.*
▪ a fundamental quality or attribute determining the nature of something; an essence: *the combination of male and female principles.* ▪ [with adj.] Chemistry an active or characteristic constituent of a substance, obtained by simple analysis or separation: *the active principle of Spanish fly.*
– PHRASES **in principle** as a general idea or plan, although the details are not yet established or clear: *the government agreed in principle to a peace plan that included a ceasefire.* ▪ used to indicate that although something is theoretically possible, in reality it may not actually happen: *in principle, the banks are entitled to withdraw these loans when necessary.* **on principle** because of or in order to demonstrate one's adherence to a particular belief: *he refused, on principle, to pay the fine.*
– ORIGIN late Middle English: from Old French, from Latin *principium* 'source', *principia* (plural) 'foundations', from *princeps, princip-* 'first, chief'.

USAGE The words **principle** and **principal** are pronounced in the same way but they do not have the same meaning. **Principle** is normally used as a noun meaning 'a fundamental basis of a system of thought or belief', as in *this is one of the basic* ***principles*** *of democracy.* **Principal**, on the other hand, is normally an adjective meaning 'main or most important', as in *one of the country's* ***principal*** *cities.* **Principal** can also be a noun, where it is used to refer to the most senior or most important person in an organization or other group: *the deputy* ***principal***. The spelling of **principal** when **principle** is meant, and of **principle** when **principal** is meant are quite common mistakes: around 5 per cent of citations for **principle** and **principal** on the British National Corpus represent one of these errors.

principled ▶ **adjective** **1** (of a person or their behaviour) acting in accordance with morality and showing recognition of right and wrong: *a principled politician.*
2 (of a system or method) based on a given set of rules: *a coherent and principled approach.*

principle of parsimony ▶ **noun** see **PARSIMONY**.

prink ▶ **verb** (**prink oneself**) spend time making minor adjustments to one's appearance: *women were prinking themselves in front of the looking glass.*
– ORIGIN late 16th cent.: probably related to archaic *prank* 'dress or adorn in a showy manner'; related to Middle Low German *prank* 'pomp', Dutch *pronk* 'finery'.

print ▶ **verb** [with obj.] (often **be printed**) **1** produce (books, newspapers, magazines, etc.), especially in large quantities, by a mechanical process involving the transfer of text or designs to paper: *a thousand copies of the book were printed.*
▪ produce (text or a picture) in such a way: *the words had been printed in dark, inky type.* ▪ (of a newspaper or magazine) publish (a piece of writing) within its pages: *the article was printed in the first edition.* ▪ (of a publisher or printer) arrange for (a book, manuscript, etc.) to be reproduced in large quantities: *in 1923 he printed Yeats' 'Biographical Fragments'.* ▪ produce a paper copy of (information stored on a computer): *the results of a search can be* ***printed out.*** ▪ produce (a photographic print) from a negative: *any make of film can be developed and printed.* ▪ write (text) clearly without joining the letters together: *print your name and address on the back of the cheque.*
2 mark (a surface, typically a textile or a garment) with a coloured design or pattern: *a delicate fabric* ***printed with*** *roses.*
▪ transfer (a coloured design or pattern) to a surface: *patterns of birds, flowers, and trees were printed on the cotton.* ▪ make (a mark or indentation) on a surface or in a soft substance by pressing something on to it: *he printed a mark on her soft skin.* ▪ mark or indent (the surface of a soft substance) in such a way: *we printed the butter with carved wooden butter moulds.* ▪ figurative fix (something) firmly or indelibly in someone's mind: *his face, with its clearly drawn features, was* ***printed on*** *her memory.*
▶ **noun** **1** [mass noun] the text appearing in a book, newspaper, or other printed publication, especially with reference to its size, form, or style: *she forced herself to concentrate on the tiny print* | *bold print.*
▪ the state of being available in published form: *the news will never* ***get into print.*** ▪ (usu. **the prints**) informal a newspaper: *the report's contents were widely summarized in the public prints.* ▪ [as modifier] of or relating to the printing industry or the printed media: *the print unions* | *a print worker.*
2 an indentation or mark left on a surface or soft substance by pressure, especially that of a foot or hand: *there were paw prints everywhere.*
▪ (**prints**) fingerprints: *the FBI matched the prints to those of the Las Vegas drug suspect.*
3 a picture or design printed from a block or plate or copied from a painting by photography: *the walls were hung with sporting prints.*
▪ a photograph printed on paper from a negative or transparency. ▪ a copy of a motion picture on film, especially a particular version of it.
4 a piece of fabric or clothing with a decorative coloured pattern or design printed on it: *light summer prints* | [as modifier] *a floral print dress.*
▪ such a pattern or design.
– PHRASES **appear in print** (of an author) have one's work published. **in print** **1** (of a book) available from the publisher: *he was surprised to find it was still in print.* **2** in printed or published form: *she did not live to see her work in print.* **out of print** (of a book) no longer available from the publisher: *the title I want is out of print.* **the printed word** language or ideas as expressed in books, newspapers, or other publications, especially when contrasted with their expression in speech.
– ORIGIN Middle English (denoting the impression made by a stamp or seal): from Old French *preinte* 'pressed', feminine past participle of *preindre*, from Latin *premere* 'to press'.

printability ▶ **noun** [mass noun] the ability of paper to take print: *the paper's printability and porosity.*

printable ▶ **adjective** suitable or fit to be printed or published: *break photographs up into printable form* | *few people had a good, or even printable, word for him.*
▪ Computing (of text) able to be printed: *the file is printable.*

printed circuit ▶ **noun** an electronic circuit consisting of thin strips of a conducting material such as copper, which have been etched from a layer fixed to a flat insulating sheet called a **printed circuit board**, and to which integrated circuits and other components are attached.

printer ▶ **noun** a person whose job or business is commercial printing.
▪ a machine for printing text or pictures on to paper, especially one linked to a computer.

printer's devil ▶ **noun** historical a person, typically a young boy serving as an apprentice, who ran errands in a printing office.

printer's mark ▶ **noun** a logo serving as a printer's trademark.

printery ▶ **noun** (pl. **-ies**) a printing works.

printhead ▶ **noun** Computing a component in a printer that assembles and holds the characters and from which the images of the characters are transferred to the printing medium.

printing ▶ **noun** [mass noun] the production of books, newspapers, or other printed material: *the invention of printing* | [as modifier] *the printing industry.*
▪ [count noun] a single impression of a book: *the second printing was ready just after Christmas.* ▪ handwriting in which the letters are written separately rather than being joined together.

printing press ▶ **noun** a machine for printing text or pictures from type or plates.

printing works ▶ **noun** [treated as sing. or pl.] a factory where the printing of newspapers, books, and other materials takes place.

printmaker ▶ **noun** a person who makes pictures or designs by printing them from specially prepared plates or blocks.
– DERIVATIVES **printmaking** noun.

printout ▶ **noun** Computing a page or set of pages of printed material obtained from a computer's printer.

print queue ▶ **noun** Computing a series of print jobs waiting to use a printer.

print run ▶ **noun** the number of copies of a book, magazine, etc. printed at one time.

print through ▶ **noun** [mass noun] the accidental transfer of recorded signals to adjacent layers in a reel of magnetic tape.

printworks ▶ **noun** [treated as sing. or pl.] a factory where the printing of textiles takes place.

prion[1] /ˈprʌɪən/ ▶ **noun** a small petrel of southern seas, having a wide bill fringed with comb-like plates for feeding on planktonic crustaceans.
• Genus *Pachyptila*, family Procellariidae: six species.
– ORIGIN mid 19th cent.: modern Latin (former genus name), from Greek *priōn* 'a saw' (referring to its saw-like bill).

prion[2] /ˈpriːɒn/ ▶ **noun** Microbiology a protein particle that is believed to be the cause of brain diseases such as BSE, scrapie, and CJD. Prions are not visible microscopically, contain no nucleic acid, and are highly resistant to destruction. Compare with **VIRINO**.
– ORIGIN 1980s: by rearrangement of elements from *pro(teinaceous) in(fectious particle).*

prior[1] ▶ **adjective** [attrib.] existing or coming before in time, order, or importance: *he has a prior engagement this evening.*
▶ **noun** N. Amer. informal a previous criminal conviction: *he had no juvenile record, no priors.*
– PHRASES **prior to** before a particular time or event: *she visited me on the day prior to her death.*
– ORIGIN early 18th cent.: from Latin, literally 'former, elder', related to *prae* 'before'.

prior[2] ▶ **noun** the male head of a house or group of houses of certain religious orders, in particular:
▪ the man next in rank below an abbot. ▪ the head of a house of friars.
– DERIVATIVES **priorate** noun, **priorship** noun.
– ORIGIN late Old English, from a medieval Latin noun use of Latin *prior* 'elder, former' (see **PRIOR**[1]).

prior charge ▶ **noun** Finance a class of stock or capital on which claims for payment take precedence over the claims of ordinary stock or capital.

prioress ▶ **noun** a woman who is head of a house of certain orders of nuns.
▪ the woman who is next in rank below an abbess.

prioritize (also **-ise**) ▶ **verb** [with obj.] designate or treat (something) as more important than other things: *the department has failed to prioritize safety within the oil industry.*
▪ determine the order for dealing with (a series of items or tasks) according to their relative importance: *age affects the way people prioritize their goals* | [no obj.] *do you enjoy a challenge—are you able to prioritize?*
– DERIVATIVES **prioritization** noun.

priority ▶ **noun** (pl. **-ies**) a thing that is regarded as more important than others: *housework didn't figure high on her list of priorities.*
▪ [mass noun] the fact or condition of being regarded or treated as more important: *the safety of the country* ***takes priority over*** *any other matter.* ▪ [mass noun] the right to proceed before other traffic: *priority is given to traffic already on the roundabout.*
– ORIGIN late Middle English (denoting precedence in time or rank): from Old French *priorite*, from medieval Latin *prioritas*, from Latin *prior* 'former' (see **PRIOR**[1]).

prior probability ▶ **noun** Statistics a probability as assessed before making reference to certain relevant observations, especially subjectively or on the assumption that all possible outcomes be given the same probability.

priory ▶ **noun** (pl. **-ies**) a small monastery or nunnery that is governed by a prior or prioress.
– ORIGIN Middle English: from Anglo-Norman French *priorie*, medieval Latin *prioria*, from Latin *prior* 'elder, superior' (see **PRIOR**[2]).

Pripyat /ˈpriːpjət/ (also **Pripet** /-pət/) a river of NW Ukraine and southern Belarus, which rises in Ukraine near the border with Poland and flows some 710 km (440 miles) eastwards through the Pripyat Marshes to join the River Dnieper north of Kiev.

Priscian /ˈprɪʃɪən/ (6th century AD), Byzantine grammarian; full name *Priscianus Caesariensis.* His *Grammatical Institutions* became one of the standard Latin grammatical works in the Middle Ages.

Priscoan /prɪˈskəʊən, ˈprɪ-/ ▶ **adjective** Geology of, relating to, or denoting the aeon that (in some schemes) constitutes the earliest part of the Precambrian, preceding the Archaean aeon. It extended from the origin of the earth to about 4,000 million years ago, and has left no identifiable rocks.

■ [as noun **the Priscoan**] the Priscoan aeon.
– ORIGIN formed irregularly from Latin *priscus* 'ancient' + -AN.

prise (US **prize**) ▶ **verb** [with obj. and adverbial of direction] use force in order to move or open (something) or to separate (something) from something else: *using a screwdriver, he prised open the window.*

■ (**prise something out of/from**) obtain something from (someone) with effort or difficulty: *I got the loan, though I had to prise it out of him.*
– ORIGIN late 17th cent.: from dialect *prise* 'lever', from Old French *prise* 'grasp, taking hold'. Compare with PRY[2].

prism /ˈprɪz(ə)m/ ▶ **noun** Geometry a solid geometric figure whose two ends are similar, equal, and parallel rectilinear figures, and whose sides are parallelograms.

■ Optics a glass or other transparent object in this form, especially one that is triangular with refracting surfaces at an acute angle with each other and that separates white light into a spectrum of colours. ■ used figuratively with reference to the clarification or distortion afforded by a particular viewpoint: *the prism of science.*
– ORIGIN late 16th cent.: via late Latin from Greek *prisma* 'thing sawn', from *prizein* 'to saw'.

prismatic /prɪzˈmatɪk/ ▶ **adjective** of, relating to, or having the form of a prism or prisms: *a prismatic structure.*

■ (of colours) formed, separated, or distributed by an optical prism or something acting as one: *a flash of prismatic light on the edge of the glass.* ■ (of colours) varied and brilliant: *a hundred prismatic tints.* ■ (of an instrument) incorporating a prism or prisms: *a prismatic compass.*
– DERIVATIVES **prismatically** adverb.
– ORIGIN early 18th cent.: from French *prismatique*, from Greek *prisma* 'thing sawn' (see PRISM).

prismatic layer ▶ **noun** Zoology the middle layer of the shell of a mollusc, consisting of crystalline calcite or aragonite.

prismoid /ˈprɪzmɔɪd/ ▶ **noun** Geometry a body like a prism, in which the end faces have the same number of sides but are not equal.

prison ▶ **noun** a building to which people are legally committed as a punishment for crimes they have committed or while awaiting trial: *he died in prison | both men were sent to prison.*

■ [mass noun] confinement in such a building.
▶ **verb** (**prisoned**, **prisoning**) [with obj.] poetic/literary imprison: *the young man prisoned behind the doors.*
– ORIGIN late Old English, from Old French *prisun*, from Latin *prensio(n-)*, variant of *prehensio(n-)* 'laying hold of', from the verb *prehendere*.

prison camp ▶ **noun** a camp where prisoners of war or political prisoners are kept under guard.

prisoner ▶ **noun** a person legally committed to prison as a punishment for crimes they have committed or while awaiting trial.

■ a person captured and kept confined by an enemy, opponent, or criminal: *she may have been held prisoner before being killed | 200 rebels were taken prisoner.* ■ figurative a person who is or perceives themselves to be confined or trapped by a situation or set of circumstances: *he's become a prisoner of the publicity he's generated.*
– PHRASES **take no prisoners** be ruthlessly aggressive or uncompromising in the pursuit of one's objectives.
– ORIGIN late Middle English: from Old French *prisonier*, from *prison* (see PRISON).

prisoner of conscience ▶ **noun** a person who has been put in prison for holding political or religious views that are not tolerated in the state in which they live.

prisoner of state (also **state prisoner**) ▶ **noun** a person confined on the authority of the state for political reasons.

prisoner of war (abbrev.: **POW**) ▶ **noun** a person who has been captured and imprisoned by the enemy in war.

prisoner's base ▶ **noun** [mass noun] a chasing game played by two groups of children each occupying a distinct base or home.

prisoner's dilemma ▶ **noun** (in game theory) a situation in which two players each have two options whose outcome depends crucially on the simultaneous choice made by the other, often formulated in terms of two prisoners separately deciding whether to confess to a crime.

prissy ▶ **adjective** (**prissier**, **prissiest**) (of a person or their manner) fussily and excessively respectable: *a middle-class family with two prissy children.*
– DERIVATIVES **prissily** adverb, **prissiness** noun.
– ORIGIN late 19th cent.: perhaps a blend of PRIM and SISSY.

Priština /ˈpriːʃtɪnə/ a city in southern Serbia, the capital of the autonomous province of Kosovo; pop. 108,000 (1991). The capital of medieval Serbia, it was under Turkish control from 1389 until 1912.

pristine /ˈprɪstiːn, -stʌɪn/ ▶ **adjective** in its original condition; unspoilt: *pristine copies of an early magazine.*

■ clean and fresh as if new; spotless: *a pristine white shirt.*
– ORIGIN mid 16th cent. (in the sense 'original, former, primitive and undeveloped'): from Latin *pristinus* 'former'. The senses 'unspoilt' and 'spotless' date from the 1920s.

Pritchett /ˈprɪtʃɪt/, Sir V. S. (1900–97), English writer and critic; full name *Victor Sawdon Pritchett*. He is chiefly remembered for his short stories.

prithee /ˈprɪðiː/ ▶ **exclamation** archaic please (used to convey a polite request): *prithee, Jack, answer me honestly.*
– ORIGIN late 16th cent.: abbreviation of *I pray thee.*

privacy /ˈprɪvəsi, ˈprʌɪ-/ ▶ **noun** [mass noun] the state or condition of being free from being observed or disturbed by other people: *she returned to the privacy of her own home.*

■ the state of being free from public attention: *a law to restrict newspapers' freedom to invade people's privacy.*

private ▶ **adjective 1** belonging to or for the use of one particular person or group of people only: *all bedrooms have private facilities | his private plane.*

■ (of a situation, activity, or gathering) affecting or involving only a particular person or group of people: *a small private service in the chapel.* ■ (of thoughts and feelings) not to be shared with or revealed to others: *she felt awkward at intruding on private grief.* ■ (of a person) not choosing to share their thoughts and feelings with others: *he was a very private man.* ■ (of a meeting or discussion) involving only a small number of people and dealing with matters that are not to be disclosed to others: *this is a private conversation.* ■ (of a place) quiet and free from people who may interrupt: *can we go somewhere a little more private?* ■ [predic.] (especially of two people) alone and undisturbed by others: *we can phone from the library—we'll be private in there.*
2 (of a person) having no official or public role or position: *the paintings were sold to a private collector.*

■ not connected with one's work or official position: *the president was visiting China in a private capacity.*
3 (of a service or industry) provided or owned by an individual or an independent, commercial company rather than the state: *research projects carried out by private industry.*

■ of or relating to a system of education or medical treatment conducted outside the state system and charging fees to the individuals who make use of it: *private education | if I could afford it I'd go private.* ■ of, relating to, or denoting a transaction between individuals and not involving commercial organizations: *it was a private sale—no estate agent's commission.*
▶ **noun 1** the lowest rank in the army, below lance corporal or private first class.
2 (**privates**) informal short for PRIVATE PARTS.
– PHRASES **in private** with no one else present: *I've got to talk to you in private.*
– ORIGIN late Middle English (originally denoting a person not acting in an official capacity): from Latin *privatus* 'withdrawn from public life', a use of the past participle of *privare* 'bereave, deprive', from *privus* 'single, individual'.

private bill ▶ **noun** a legislative bill affecting the interests only of a particular body or individual.

private company ▶ **noun** Brit. a company whose shares may not be offered to the public for sale and which operates under legal requirements less strict than those for a public company.

private detective (also **private investigator**) ▶ **noun** a freelance detective who carries out covert investigations on behalf of private clients.

private enterprise ▶ **noun** [mass noun] business or industry that is managed by independent companies or private individuals rather than being controlled by the state.

privateer /ˌprʌɪvəˈtɪə/ ▶ **noun 1** chiefly historical an armed ship owned and officered by private individuals holding a government commission and authorized for use in war, especially in the capture of merchant shipping.

■ a commander or crew member of such a ship, often regarded as a pirate.
2 an advocate or exponent of private enterprise.
3 Motor Racing a competitor who races as a private individual rather than as a member of a team.
– DERIVATIVES **privateering** noun.
– ORIGIN mid 17th cent.: from PRIVATE, on the pattern of *volunteer.*

privateersman ▶ **noun** (pl. **-men**) historical a commander or crew member of a privateer.

private eye ▶ **noun** informal a private detective.

private first class ▶ **noun** a rank in the US army, above private and below corporal.

private income ▶ **noun** another term for UNEARNED INCOME.

private investigator ▶ **noun** another term for PRIVATE DETECTIVE.

private key ▶ **noun** see PUBLIC KEY.

private language ▶ **noun** Philosophy a language which cannot in principle be communicated to another person.

private law ▶ **noun** [mass noun] a branch of the law that deals with the relations between individuals or institutions, rather than relations between these and the state.

private life ▶ **noun** a person's personal relationships, interests, etc., as distinct from their public or professional life.

privately ▶ **adverb** in a private way, manner, or capacity: *I must insist we speak privately | their children were privately educated.*

■ [often sentence adverb] used to refer to a situation in which someone's thoughts and feelings are not disclosed to others: *privately, Robert considered that she was overreacting.*

private means ▶ **plural noun** Brit. income from investments, property, or inheritance, as opposed to earned income or state benefit.

private member ▶ **noun** (in the UK, Canada, Australia, and New Zealand) a member of a parliament who is not a minister or does not hold government office.

private member's bill ▶ **noun** (in the UK, Canada, Australia, and New Zealand) a legislative bill that is introduced by a private Member of Parliament and is not part of a government's planned legislation. Such bills rarely become law.

private nuisance ▶ **noun** Law see NUISANCE.

private parts ▶ **plural noun** used euphemistically to refer to a person's genitals.

private practice ▶ **noun** [mass noun] the work of a professional practitioner such as a doctor or lawyer who is self-employed.

■ Brit. medical practice that is not part of the National Health Service.

private press ▶ **noun** a printing establishment operated on a small scale by a private person or group, in which the emphasis is on quality and individuality rather than profit.

private school ▶ **noun 1** Brit. an independent school supported wholly by the payment of fees.
2 N. Amer. a school supported by a private organization or private individuals rather than by the state.

private secretary ▶ **noun 1** a secretary who deals with the personal and confidential concerns of a businessman, businesswoman, or public figure.
2 a civil servant acting as an aide to a senior government official.

private sector ▶ **noun** the part of the national economy that is not under direct state control.

private soldier ▶ **noun** a soldier of the lowest rank.

■ US a soldier of this type who is not a recruit.

private treaty ▶ **noun** [mass noun] the agreement for

the sale of a property at a price negotiated directly between the vendor and purchaser or their agents.

private view ▶ noun an event attended by invited guests at which an art exhibition may be seen before it is opened to the public.

private war ▶ noun **1** a feud between people or families that is conducted without regard to the law.
2 hostilities against members of another state that take place without government sanction.

privation /prʌɪˈveɪʃ(ə)n/ ▶ noun [mass noun] a state in which things that are essential for human well-being such as food and warmth are scarce or lacking: *years of rationing and privation* | [count noun] *the **privations of** life at the front.*
■ formal the loss or absence of a quality or attribute that is normally present: *cold is the privation of heat.*
– ORIGIN Middle English: from Latin *privatio(n-)*, from *privat-* 'deprived', from the verb *privare* (see **PRIVATE**).

privatism /ˈprʌɪvətɪz(ə)m/ ▶ noun [mass noun] a tendency to be concerned with ideas or issues only in so far as they affect one as an individual.

privative /ˈprɪvətɪv/ ▶ adjective (of an action or state) marked by the absence, removal, or loss of some quality or attribute that is normally present.
■ (of a statement or term) denoting the absence or loss of an attribute or quality: *parliament may insert a privative clause to achieve this result.* ■ Grammar (of a particle or affix) expressing absence or negation, for example the Greek *a-*, meaning 'not', in *atypical*.
– ORIGIN late 16th cent.: from Latin *privativus* 'denoting privation', from *privat-* 'deprived' (see **PRIVATION**).

privatize (also **-ise**) ▶ verb [with obj.] transfer (a business, industry, or service) from public to private ownership and control: *they were opposed to plans to privatize electricity and water.*
– DERIVATIVES **privatization** noun, **privatizer** noun.

privet /ˈprɪvɪt/ ▶ noun a shrub of the olive family, with small white heavily scented flowers and poisonous black berries.
● Genus *Ligustrum*, family Oleaceae: several species, in particular the evergreen *L. ovalifolium*, often used as hedging in towns.
– ORIGIN mid 16th cent.: of unknown origin.

privilege ▶ noun a special right, advantage, or immunity granted or available only to a particular person or group of people: *education is a right, not a privilege* | [mass noun] *he has been accustomed all his life to wealth and privilege.*
■ something regarded as a rare opportunity and bringing particular pleasure: *I had the privilege of giving the Sir George Brown memorial lecture.* ■ (also **absolute privilege**) (especially in a parliamentary context) the right to say or write something without the risk of incurring punishment or legal action for defamation. ■ the right of a lawyer or official to refuse to divulge confidential information. ■ chiefly historical a grant to an individual, corporation, or place of special rights or immunities, especially in the form of a franchise or monopoly.
▶ verb [with obj.] formal grant a privilege or privileges to: *English inheritance law privileged the eldest son.*
■ (usu. **be privileged from**) exempt (someone) from a liability or obligation to which others are subject: *barristers are privileged from arrest going to, coming from, and abiding in court.*
– ORIGIN Middle English: via Old French from Latin *privilegium* 'bill or law affecting an individual', from *privus* 'private' + *lex*, *leg-* 'law'.

privileged ▶ adjective having special rights, advantages, or immunities: *in the nineteenth century only a privileged few had the vote.*
■ [with infinitive] having the rare opportunity to do something that brings particular pleasure: *I felt I had been privileged to compete in such a race.* ■ (of information) legally protected from being made public: *the ombudsman's reports are privileged.*

privity /ˈprɪvɪti/ ▶ noun (pl. **-ies**) Law a relation between two parties that is recognized by law, such as that of blood, lease, or service: *the parties no longer have privity with each other.*
– ORIGIN Middle English (in the sense 'secrecy, intimacy'): from Old French *privete*, from medieval Latin *privitas*, from Latin *privus* 'private'.

privity of contract ▶ noun [mass noun] Law the relation between the parties in a contract which entitles them to sue each other but prevents a third party from doing so.

privy ▶ adjective [predic.] (**privy to**) sharing in the knowledge of (something secret or private): *he was no longer privy to her innermost thoughts.*
■ archaic hidden; secret: *a privy place.*
▶ noun (pl. **-ies**) **1** a toilet located in a small shed outside a house or other building.
2 Law a person having a part or interest in any action, matter, or thing.
– DERIVATIVES **privily** adverb.
– ORIGIN Middle English (originally in the sense 'belonging to one's own private circle'): from Old French *prive* 'private' (also used as a noun meaning 'private place' and 'familiar friend'), from Latin *privatus* 'withdrawn from public life' (see **PRIVATE**).

privy chamber ▶ noun a private apartment in a royal residence.

Privy Council ▶ noun a body of advisers appointed by a sovereign or a Governor General (now chiefly on an honorary basis and including present and former government ministers).
■ chiefly historical a sovereign's or Governor General's private counsellors.

> In Britain, the Privy Council originated in the council of the Norman kings. A select body of officials met regularly with the sovereign to carry on everyday government, known from the 14th century as the Privy (= 'private') Council. In the 18th century the importance of the cabinet, a smaller group drawn from the Privy Council, increased and the full Privy Council's functions became chiefly formal.

privy counsellor (also **privy councillor**) ▶ noun a member of a Privy Council.

privy purse ▶ noun (in the UK) an allowance from the public revenue for the monarch's private expenses.

privy seal ▶ noun (in the UK) a seal affixed to documents that are afterwards to pass the Great Seal or that do not require it.

Prix de Rome /ˌpriː də ˈrəʊm, French pʀi də ʀɔm/ ▶ noun (pl. **Prixs de Rome**) a prize awarded annually by the French government in a competition for artists, sculptors, architects, and musicians.
– ORIGIN French, literally 'prize of Rome', because the winner of the first prize in each category is funded for a period of study in Rome.

prix fixe /ˈfiks, French pʀi fiks/ ▶ noun a meal consisting of several courses served at a total fixed price.
– ORIGIN French, literally 'fixed price'.

Prix Goncourt /gɒ̃ˈkʊə, gɔ̃kuʀ/ ▶ noun an award given annually for a work of French literature. See **GONCOURT**.

prize[1] ▶ noun a thing given as a reward to the winner of a competition or race or in recognition of another outstanding achievement: *Britain's most prestigious prize for contemporary art.*
■ a thing, especially an amount of money or a valuable object, that can be won in a lottery or other game of chance: *the star prize in the charity raffle* | [as modifier] *prize money.* ■ something of great value that is worth struggling to achieve: *the prize will be victory in the general election.* ■ chiefly historical an enemy ship captured during the course of naval warfare. [ORIGIN: late Middle English: from Old French *prise* 'taking, booty', from *prendre* 'take'.]
▶ adjective [attrib.] (especially of something entered in a competition) having been or likely to be awarded a prize: *prize onions* | *a prize bull.*
■ denoting something for which a prize is awarded: *a prize crossword.* ■ excellent of its kind; outstanding: *a prize example of how well organic farming can function.* ■ complete; utter: *you must think I'm a prize idiot.*
▶ verb [with obj.] (often **be prized**) value extremely highly: *the berries were prized for their healing properties* | [as adj. **prized**] *the bicycle was her most prized possession.*
– PHRASES (**there are**) **no prizes for guessing** used to convey that something is obvious: *there's no prizes for guessing what you two have been up to!*
– ORIGIN Middle English: the noun, a variant of **PRICE**; the verb (originally in the sense 'estimate the value of') from Old French *pris-*, stem of *preisier* 'to praise, appraise' (see **PRAISE**).

prize[2] ▶ verb US spelling of **PRISE**.

prize court ▶ noun a naval court that adjudicates on the distribution of ships and property captured in the course of naval warfare.

prizefight ▶ noun a boxing match, typically an unlicensed one, fought for prize money.
– DERIVATIVES **prizefighter** noun, **prizefighting** noun.

prize-giving ▶ noun Brit. a ceremonial event at which prizes are awarded, especially one held at a school.

prizeman ▶ noun (pl. **-men**) a winner of a prize, especially an academic one.

prize ring ▶ noun a ring used for prizefighting.
■ (**the prize ring**) the practice of prizefighting; boxing.

prizewinner ▶ noun a winner of a prize.
– DERIVATIVES **prize-winning** adjective.

PRO ▶ abbreviation for ■ Public Record Office. ■ public relations officer.

pro[1] ▶ noun (pl. **-os**) informal **1** a professional, especially in sport: *a tennis pro.*
2 a prostitute.
▶ adjective (of a person or an event) professional: *a pro golfer.*
– ORIGIN mid 19th cent.: abbreviation.

pro[2] ▶ noun (pl. **-os**) (usu. **pros**) an advantage of something or an argument in favour of a course of action: *the **pros and cons** of share ownership.*
▶ preposition & adverb in favour of: [as prep.] *they were pro the virtues of individualism.*
– ORIGIN late Middle English (as a noun): from Latin, literally 'for, on behalf of'.

pro-[1] ▶ prefix **1** favouring; supporting: *pro-choice.*
2 acting as a substitute or deputy for: *proconsul.*
3 denoting motion forwards, out, or away: *proceed* | *propel* | *prostrate.*
– ORIGIN from Latin *pro* 'in front of, on behalf of, instead of, on account of'.

pro-[2] ▶ prefix before in time, place, order, etc.: *proactive* | *prothalamium.*
– ORIGIN from Greek *pro* 'before'.

proa /ˈprəʊə/ (also **prau** or **prahu**) ▶ noun a type of sailing boat originating in Malaysia and Indonesia that may be sailed with either end at the front, typically having a large triangular sail and an outrigger.
– ORIGIN late 16th cent.: from Malay *perahu*.

proactive ▶ adjective (of a person, policy, or action) creating or controlling a situation by causing something to happen rather than responding to it after it has happened: *be proactive in identifying and preventing potential problems.*
– DERIVATIVES **proaction** noun, **proactively** adverb, **proactivity** noun.
– ORIGIN 1930s: from **PRO-**[2] (denoting earlier occurrence), on the pattern of *reactive*.

proactive interference (also **proactive inhibition**) ▶ noun [mass noun] Psychology the tendency of previously learned material to hinder subsequent learning.

pro-am ▶ adjective (of a sports event) involving both professionals and amateurs: *a pro-am golf tournament.*
▶ noun an event of this type.

prob ▶ noun informal a problem: *there's no prob.*
– ORIGIN 1930s: abbreviation.

probabilistic ▶ adjective based on or adapted to a theory of probability; subject to or involving chance variation: *the main approaches are either rule-based or probabilistic.*

probability ▶ noun (pl. **-ies**) [mass noun] the extent to which something is probable; the likelihood of something happening or being the case: *the rain will make the probability of their arrival even greater.*
■ [count noun] a probable event: *for a time revolution was a strong probability.* ■ [count noun] the most probable thing: *the probability is that it will be phased in over a number of years.* ■ Mathematics the extent to which an event is likely to occur, measured by the ratio of the favourable cases to the whole number of cases possible: *the area under the curve represents probability* | [count noun] *a probability of 0.5.*
– PHRASES **in all probability** used to convey that something is very likely: *he would in all probability make himself known.*
– ORIGIN late Middle English: from Latin *probabilitas*, from *probabilis* 'provable, credible' (see **PROBABLE**).

probability density function ▶ noun Statistics a function of a continuous random variable, whose integral across an interval gives the probability that the value of the variable lies within the same interval.

probability distribution ▶ noun Statistics a function of a discrete variable whose integral over any interval is the probability that the variate specified by it will lie within that interval.

probability theory ▶ noun [mass noun] the branch

of mathematics that deals with quantities having random distributions.

probable ▸ adjective [often with clause] likely to be the case or to happen: *it is probable that the economic situation will deteriorate further* | *the probable consequences of his action.*
▸ noun **1** a person who is likely to become or do something, especially one who is likely to be chosen for a team: *Merson and Wright are probables.*
2 an aircraft recorded as likely to have been shot down.
– ORIGIN late Middle English (in the sense 'worthy of belief'): via Old French from Latin *probabilis*, from *probare* 'to test, demonstrate'.

probable cause ▸ noun [mass noun] Law, chiefly US reasonable grounds (for making a search, preferring a charge, etc.).

probably ▸ adverb [sentence adverb] almost certainly; as far as one knows or can tell: *she would probably never see him again* | *'A bomb, do you think?' 'Probably.'*

proband /ˈprəʊband/ ▸ noun a person serving as the starting point for the genetic study of a family (used especially in medicine and psychiatry).
– ORIGIN 1920s: from Latin *probandus* 'to be proved', gerundive of *probare* 'to test'.

probang /ˈprəʊbaŋ/ ▸ noun Medicine a strip of flexible material with a sponge or tuft at the end, used to remove an object from the throat or apply medication to it.
– ORIGIN mid 17th cent. (named *provang* by its inventor): perhaps an alteration suggested by **PROBE**.

probate ▸ noun [mass noun] the official proving of a will: *the house has been valued for probate* | [as modifier] *a probate court.*
▪ [count noun] a verified copy of a will with a certificate as handed to the executors.
▸ verb [with obj.] N. Amer. establish the validity of (a will).
– ORIGIN late Middle English: from Latin *probatum* 'something proved', neuter past participle of *probare* 'to test, prove'.

probation ▸ noun [mass noun] Law the release of an offender from detention, subject to a period of good behaviour under supervision: *I went to court and was put on probation.*
▪ the process of testing or observing the character or abilities of a person in a certain role, for example a new employee: *for an initial period of probation your line manager will closely monitor your progress.*
– DERIVATIVES **probationary** adjective.
– ORIGIN late Middle English (denoting testing, investigation, or examination): from Old French *probacion*, from Latin *probatio(n-)*, from *probare* 'to test, prove' (see **PROVE**). The legal use dates from the late 19th cent.

probationer ▸ noun a person who is serving a probationary or trial period in a job or position to which they are newly appointed (such as a new teacher, nurse, or police constable).
▪ an offender on probation.

probation officer ▸ noun a person appointed to supervise offenders who are on probation.

probative /ˈprəʊbətɪv/ ▸ adjective chiefly Law having the quality or function of proving or demonstrating something; affording proof or evidence: *it places the probative burden on the defendant.*
– ORIGIN late Middle English (describing something that serves as a test): from Latin *probativus*, from *probat-* 'proved', from the verb *probare* (see **PROVE**).

probe ▸ noun a blunt-ended surgical instrument used for exploring a wound or part of the body.
▪ a small device, especially an electrode, used for measuring, testing, or obtaining information. ▪ a projecting device for engaging in a drogue, either on an aircraft for use in in-flight refuelling or on a spacecraft for use in docking with another craft. ▪ (also **space probe**) an unmanned exploratory spacecraft designed to transmit information about its environment. ▪ an investigation into a crime or other matter: *a probe into the maritime industry by the FBI.*
▸ verb [with obj.] physically explore or examine (something) with the hands or an instrument: *hands probed his body from top to bottom.*
▪ [no obj.] seek to uncover information about someone or something: *Beth had secured his promise that he would never probe into her past* | [with obj.] *police are probing a nightwatchman's murder.*
– DERIVATIVES **prober** noun, **probingly** adverb.

– ORIGIN late Middle English (as a noun): from late Latin *proba* 'proof' (in medieval Latin 'examination'), from Latin *probare* 'to test'. The verb dates from the mid 17th cent.

probenecid /prəʊˈbɛnɪsɪd/ ▸ noun [mass noun] Medicine a synthetic sulphur-containing compound which promotes increased excretion of uric acid and is used to treat gout.
– ORIGIN 1950s: from *pro(pyl)* + *ben(zoic)* + *-e-* + *(a)cid*.

probit /ˈprɒbɪt/ ▸ noun Statistics a unit of probability based on deviation from the mean of a standard distribution.
– ORIGIN 1930s: from *prob(ability un)it*.

probity /ˈprəʊbɪti, ˈprɒb-/ ▸ noun [mass noun] formal the quality of having strong moral principles; honesty and decency: *financial probity.*
– ORIGIN late Middle English: from Latin *probitas*, from *probus* 'good'.

problem ▸ noun **1** a matter or situation regarded as unwelcome or harmful and needing to be dealt with and overcome: *they have financial problems* | *mental health problems.*
▪ a thing that is difficult to achieve or accomplish: *motivation of staff can also be a problem.*
2 Physics & Mathematics an inquiry starting from given conditions to investigate or demonstrate a fact, result, or law.
▪ Geometry a proposition in which something has to be constructed. Compare with **THEOREM**. ▪ (in various games, especially chess) an arrangement of pieces in which the solver has to achieve a specified result.
– PHRASES **have a problem with** disagree with or have an objection to: *I have no problem with shopping on Sundays.* **no problem** used to express one's agreement or acquiescence: *'Can you come over here right away?' 'No problem.'* **that's your** (or **his**, or **her**, etc.) **problem** used to express one's lack of interest in or sympathy with the problems or misfortunes of another person: *he'd made a mistake but that was his problem.*
– ORIGIN late Middle English (originally denoting a riddle or a question for academic discussion): from Old French *probleme*, via Latin from Greek *problēma*, from *proballein* 'put forth', from *pro* 'before' + *ballein* 'to throw'.

problematic ▸ adjective constituting or presenting a problem or difficulty: *the situation was problematic for teachers.*
▸ noun a thing that constitutes a problem or difficulty: *the problematics of artificial intelligence.*
– DERIVATIVES **problematical** adjective, **problematically** adverb.
– ORIGIN early 17th cent.: via French from late Latin *problematicus*, from Greek *problēmatikos*, from *problēma* (see **PROBLEM**).

problematize (also **-ise**) ▸ verb [with obj.] make into or regard as a problem requiring a solution: *he problematized the concept of history.*
– DERIVATIVES **problematization** noun.

problem child ▸ noun a child with behavioural or other difficulties.

pro bono publico /prəʊ ˌbɒnəʊ ˈpʊblɪkəʊ, ˌbəʊnəʊ ˈpʌblɪkəʊ/ ▸ adverb & adjective for the public good: [as adv.] *the burden they carried pro bono publico.*
▪ (usu. **pro bono**) chiefly N. Amer. denoting work undertaken for the public good without charge, especially legal work for a client on low income: [as adv.] *the attorneys are representing him pro bono* | [as adj.] *providing pro bono legal services.*
– ORIGIN Latin.

Proboscidea /ˌprɒbəˈsɪdɪə/ Zoology an order of large mammals that comprises the elephants and their extinct relatives. They are distinguished by the possession of a trunk and tusks.
– DERIVATIVES **proboscidean** (also **proboscidian**) noun & adjective.
– ORIGIN modern Latin (plural), from **PROBOSCIS**.

proboscis /prəˈbɒsɪs/ ▸ noun (pl. **probosces** /-siːz/, **proboscides** /-sɪdiːz/, or **proboscises**) the nose of a mammal, especially when it is long and mobile such as the trunk of an elephant or the snout of a tapir.
▪ Entomology (in many insects) an elongated sucking mouthpart that is typically tubular and flexible. ▪ Zoology (in some worms) an extensible tubular sucking organ.
– ORIGIN early 17th cent.: via Latin from Greek *proboskis* 'means of obtaining food', from *pro* 'before' + *boskein* '(cause to) feed'.

proboscis monkey ▸ noun a leaf-eating monkey

native to the forests of Borneo, the male of which is twice the weight of the female and has a large pendulous nose.
● *Nasalis larvatus*, family Cercopithecidae.

proboscis worm ▸ noun another term for **RIBBON WORM**.

procaine /ˈprəʊkeɪn/ ▸ noun [mass noun] a synthetic compound derived from benzoic acid, used as a local anaesthetic, especially in dentistry.
– ORIGIN early 20th cent.: from **PRO-**[1] (denoting substitution) + *-caine* (from **COCAINE**).

procaine penicillin ▸ noun [mass noun] Medicine a slow-acting antibiotic made from a salt of procaine and a form of penicillin.

procaryote ▸ noun variant spelling of **PROKARYOTE**.

procedure ▸ noun an established or official way of doing something: *the police are now reviewing procedures* | [mass noun] *rules of procedure.*
▪ a series of actions conducted in a certain order or manner: *the standard procedure for informing new employees about conditions of work.* ▪ a surgical operation: *the procedure is carried out under general anaesthetic.* ▪ Computing another term for **SUBROUTINE**.
– DERIVATIVES **procedural** adjective, **procedurally** adverb.
– ORIGIN late 16th cent.: from French *procédure*, from *procéder* (see **PROCEED**).

proceed ▸ verb [no obj.] begin a course of action: *the consortium could proceed with the plan.*
▪ [no obj., with adverbial of direction] move forward, especially after reaching a certain point: *from the High Street, proceed over Magdalen Bridge.* ▪ [with infinitive] do something as a natural or seemingly inevitable next step: *opposite the front door was a staircase which I proceeded to climb.* ▪ Law start a lawsuit against someone: *he may still be able to proceed against the contractor under the common law negligence rules.* ▪ (of an action) be started: *negotiations must proceed without delay.* ▪ (of an action) be carried on or continued: *as the excavation proceeds the visible layers can be recorded and studied.* ▪ Brit. dated advance to a higher rank, status, or education: *he did not proceed to university in his seventeenth year.* ▪ originate from: *his claim that all power proceeded from God.*
– ORIGIN late Middle English: from Old French *proceder*, from Latin *procedere*, from *pro-* 'forward' + *cedere* 'go'.

proceedings ▸ plural noun an event or a series of activities involving a formal or set procedure: *you complete a form to start proceedings.*
▪ Law action taken in a court to settle a dispute: *criminal proceedings were brought against him.* ▪ a published report of a set of meetings or a conference.

proceeds ▸ plural noun money obtained from an event or activity: *proceeds from the event will go to aid the work of the charity.*
– ORIGIN early 17th cent.: plural of the obsolete noun *proceed*, in the same sense, earlier meaning 'procedure'.

process[1] /ˈprəʊsɛs/ ▸ noun **1** a series of actions or steps taken in order to achieve a particular end: *military operations could jeopardize the peace process.*
▪ a natural or involuntary series of changes: *the ageing process.* ▪ a systematic series of mechanized or chemical operations that are performed in order to produce or manufacture something: *the modern block printer needs to accommodate all the traditional factory processes in one shop.* ▪ [as modifier] Printing relating to or denoting printing using ink in three colours (cyan, magenta, and yellow) and black to produce a complete range of colour: *process inks.*
2 Law a summons or writ requiring a person to appear in court.
3 Biology & Anatomy a natural appendage or outgrowth on or in an organism, such as a protuberance on a bone.
▸ verb perform a series of mechanical or chemical operations on (something) in order to change or preserve it: *the various stages in processing the wool.*
▪ Computing operate on (data) by means of a program. ▪ deal with (someone) using an official and established procedure: *the immigration authorities who processed him.*
– PHRASES **be in the process of doing something** be continuing with an action already started: *a hurricane that was in the process of devastating South Carolina.* **in the process** as an unintended part of a course of action: *she would make him pay for this, even if she killed herself in the process.* **in process of time** as time goes on.

– DERIVATIVES **processable** adjective.

– ORIGIN Middle English: from Old French *proces*, from Latin *processus* 'progression, course', from the verb *procedere* (see **PROCEED**). Current senses of the verb date from the late 19th cent.

process² /prəˈsɛs/ ▶ **verb** [no obj., with adverbial of direction] walk or march in procession: *they processed down the aisle.*

– ORIGIN early 19th cent.: back-formation from **PROCESSION**.

process engineering ▶ **noun** [mass noun] the branch of engineering that is concerned with industrial processes, especially continuous ones such as the production of petrochemicals.

– DERIVATIVES **process engineer** noun.

procession ▶ **noun 1** a number of people or vehicles moving forward in an orderly fashion, especially as part of a ceremony or festival: *a funeral procession.*
▪[mass noun] the action of moving forward in such a way: *the fully robed civic dignitaries walk **in procession**.* ▪ a race in which the competitors finish well spaced out as if in a procession. ▪ figurative a relentless succession of people or things: *magistrates complain that they see **a procession of** recidivist minor offenders.*
2 [mass noun] Theology the emanation of the Holy Spirit.

– ORIGIN late Old English, via Old French from Latin *processio(n-)*, from *procedere* 'move forward' (see **PROCEED**).

processional ▶ **adjective** of, for, or used in a religious or ceremonial procession: *a processional cross.*
▶ **noun** a book containing litanies and hymns for use in religious processions.

processionary ▶ **noun** (also **processionary moth**) (pl. **-ies**) a greyish moth whose caterpillars live communally in silken tents in trees, marching out at night in single file or broader processions to feed, causing substantial damage to trees.
● Family Thaumetopoeidae: several species, in particular the European **pine processionary** (*Thaumetopoea pityocampa*).
▪(also **processionary caterpillar**) the larva of this moth.

processor ▶ **noun** a machine that processes something: *the processor overexposed the film.*
▪Computing another term for **CENTRAL PROCESSING UNIT**. ▪ short for **FOOD PROCESSOR**.

process server ▶ **noun** a sheriff's officer who serves writs; a bailiff.

processual /prəˈsɛsjʊəl/ ▶ **adjective** relating to or involving the study of processes rather than discrete events.

process water ▶ **noun** [mass noun] water used in an industrial process.

procès-verbal /ˌprɒseɪvəːˈbɑːl/ ▶ **noun** (pl. **procès-verbaux** /-ˈbəʊ/) a written report of proceedings.
▪a written statement of facts in support of a charge.

– ORIGIN mid 17th cent.: French.

prochlorperazine /ˌprəʊklɔːˈpɛrəziːn/ ▶ **noun** [mass noun] Medicine a synthetic compound derived from phenothiazine, used as a tranquillizer.

– ORIGIN 1950s: from *pro(pyl)* + *chlor(ine)* + *(pi)perazine*.

pro-choice ▶ **adjective** advocating the legal right of a woman to choose whether or not she will have an abortion: *a pro-choice demonstration.*

– DERIVATIVES **pro-choicer** noun.

proclaim ▶ **verb** [with clause] announce officially or publicly: *the joint manifesto proclaimed that imperialism would be the coalition's chief objective* | [with obj.] *army commanders proclaimed a state of emergency.*
▪declare (something one considers important) with due emphasis: *she proclaimed that what I had said was untrue* | [with obj. and infinitive] *he proclaimed the car to be in sound condition.* ▪ [with obj. and complement] declare officially or publicly to be: *he **proclaimed** King James III **as** King of England.* ▪ [with obj.] demonstrate or indicate clearly: *his high, intelligent forehead proclaimed a strength of mind that was almost tangible* | [with obj. and complement] *he had a rolling gait that proclaimed him a man of the sea.*

– DERIVATIVES **proclaimer** noun, **proclamatory** adjective.

– ORIGIN late Middle English *proclame*, from Latin *proclamare* 'cry out', from *pro-* 'forth' + *clamare* 'to shout'. The change in the second syllable was due to association with the verb **CLAIM**.

proclamation ▶ **noun** a public or official announcement, especially one dealing with a matter of great importance: *the issuing by the monarch of a proclamation dissolving Parliament.*
▪[mass noun] the public or official announcement of such a matter: *the government restricted the use of water by proclamation.* ▪ a clear declaration of something: *they often make proclamations about their heterosexuality.*

– ORIGIN late Middle English: via Old French from Latin *proclamatio(n-)*, from *proclamare* 'shout out' (see **PROCLAIM**).

proclitic /prə(ʊ)ˈklɪtɪk/ Linguistics ▶ **noun** a word pronounced with so little emphasis that it is shortened and forms part of the following word, e.g. *at* in *at home*. Compare with **ENCLITIC**.
▶ **adjective** being or relating to such a word.

– DERIVATIVES **proclitically** adverb.

– ORIGIN mid 19th cent.: from modern Latin *procliticus* (from Greek *proklinein* 'lean forward'), on the pattern of late Latin *encliticus* (see **ENCLITIC**).

proclivity /prəˈklɪvɪti/ ▶ **noun** (pl. **-ies**) a tendency to choose or do something regularly; an inclination or predisposition towards a particular thing: *a **proclivity for** hard work.*

– ORIGIN late 16th cent.: from Latin *proclivitas*, from *proclivis* 'inclined', from *pro-* 'forward, down' + *clivus* 'slope'.

Procne /ˈprɒkni/ Greek Mythology the sister of Philomel.

procoagulant /ˌprəʊkəʊˈagjʊl(ə)nt/ Biochemistry ▶ **adjective** relating to or denoting substances that promote the conversion in the blood of the inactive protein prothrombin to the clotting enzyme thrombin.
▶ **noun** a substance of this kind.

Proconsul /prəʊˈkɒns(ə)l/ ▶ **noun** a fossil hominoid primate found in Lower Miocene deposits in East Africa, one of the last common ancestors of both humans and the great apes.
● Genus *Proconsul*, family Pongidae.

proconsul /prəʊˈkɒns(ə)l/ ▶ **noun 1** a governor of a province in ancient Rome, having much of the authority of a consul.
2 a governor or deputy consul of a modern colony.

– DERIVATIVES **proconsular** adjective, **proconsulate** noun, **proconsulship** noun.

– ORIGIN from Latin *pro consule* '(one acting) for the consul'.

Procopius /prəˈkəʊpɪəs/ (*c.*500–*c.*562), Byzantine historian, born in Caesarea in Palestine. He accompanied Justinian's general Belisarius on his campaigns between 527 and 540. His principal works are the *History of the Wars of Justinian* and *On Justinian's Buildings*.

procrastinate /prə(ʊ)ˈkrastɪneɪt/ ▶ **verb** [no obj.] delay or postpone action; put off doing something: *the temptation will be to procrastinate until the power struggle plays itself out.*

– DERIVATIVES **procrastination** noun, **procrastinator** noun, **procrastinatory** adjective.

– ORIGIN late 16th cent.: from Latin *procrastinat-* 'deferred till the morning', from the verb *procrastinare*, from *pro-* 'forward' + *crastinus* 'belonging to tomorrow' (from *cras* 'tomorrow').

USAGE On the difference between **procrastinate** and **prevaricate**, see **usage** at **PREVARICATE**.

procreate ▶ **verb** [no obj.] (of people or animals) produce young; reproduce: *species that procreate by copulation.*

– DERIVATIVES **procreant** adjective (archaic), **procreation** noun, **procreative** adjective, **procreator** noun.

– ORIGIN late Middle English: from Latin *procreat-* 'generated, brought forth', from the verb *procreare*, from *pro-* 'forth' + *creare* 'create'.

Procrustean /prə(ʊ)ˈkrʌstɪən/ ▶ **adjective** (especially of a framework or system) enforcing uniformity or conformity without regard to natural variation or individuality: *a fixed Procrustean rule.*

– ORIGIN mid 19th cent.: from the name **PROCRUSTES** + **-AN**.

Procrustes /prəʊˈkrʌstiːz/ Greek Mythology a robber who forced travellers to lie on a bed and made them fit it by stretching their limbs or cutting off the appropriate length of leg. Theseus killed him in like manner.

– ORIGIN from Greek *prokroustēs*, literally 'stretcher', from *prokrouein* 'beat out'.

proctitis /prɒkˈtʌɪtɪs/ ▶ **noun** [mass noun] Medicine inflammation of the rectum and anus.

– ORIGIN early 19th cent.: from Greek *prōktos* 'anus' + **-ITIS**.

proctology /prɒkˈtɒlədʒi/ ▶ **noun** [mass noun] the branch of medicine concerned with the anus and rectum.

– DERIVATIVES **proctological** adjective, **proctologist** noun.

– ORIGIN late 19th cent.: from Greek *prōktos* 'anus' + **-LOGY**.

proctor ▶ **noun 1** Brit. an officer (usually one of two) at certain universities, appointed annually and having mainly disciplinary functions.
2 N. Amer. an invigilator at a university or college examination.
3 (in the Church of England) an elected representative of the clergy in the convocation of Canterbury or York.
▪historical a qualified practitioner of law in ecclesiastical and certain other courts. See also **QUEEN'S PROCTOR**.

– DERIVATIVES **proctorial** adjective, **proctorship** noun.

– ORIGIN late Middle English: contraction of **PROCURATOR**.

proctoscope /ˈprɒktəskəʊp/ ▶ **noun** a medical instrument with an integral lamp for examining the anus and lower part of the rectum or carrying out minor medical procedures.

– DERIVATIVES **proctoscopy** noun.

– ORIGIN late 19th cent.: from Greek *prōktos* 'anus' + **-SCOPE**.

procumbent /prə(ʊ)ˈkʌmb(ə)nt/ ▶ **adjective** Botany (of a plant or stem) growing along the ground without throwing out roots.

– ORIGIN mid 17th cent.: from Latin *procumbent-* 'falling forwards', from the verb *procumbere*, from *pro-* 'forwards, down' + a verb related to *cubare* 'to lie'.

procuracy /prəˈkjʊərəsi/ ▶ **noun** (pl. **-ies**) the position or office of a procurator.

procuration ▶ **noun** [mass noun] Law, dated the appointment, authority, or action of an attorney.
▪archaic the action of procuring or obtaining something.

– ORIGIN late Middle English: via Old French from Latin *procuratio(n-)*, from *procurare* 'attend to, take care of' (see **PROCURE**).

procurator /ˈprɒkjʊreɪtə/ ▶ **noun** Law an agent representing others in a court of law in countries retaining Roman civil law.
▪(in Scotland) a lawyer practising before the lower courts. ▪ historical a treasury officer in a province of the Roman Empire.

– DERIVATIVES **procuratorial** adjective, **procuratorship** noun.

– ORIGIN Middle English (denoting a steward): from Old French *procuratour* or Latin *procurator* 'administrator, finance agent', from *procurat-* 'taken care of', from the verb *procurare* (see **PROCURE**).

procurator fiscal ▶ **noun** (in Scotland) a local coroner and public prosecutor.

procure ▶ **verb** [with obj.] **1** obtain (something), especially with care or effort: *food procured for the rebels* | [with two objs] *he persuaded a friend to procure him a ticket.*
▪obtain (someone) as a prostitute for another person: *men who haunted railway stations to procure young girls for immoral purposes.*
2 [with obj. and infinitive] Law persuade or cause (someone) to do something: *he procured his wife to sign the mandate for the joint account.*
▪archaic or Law cause (something) to happen: *he was charged with procuring the deaths of the Earl of Lancaster and other nobles.*

– DERIVATIVES **procurable** adjective, **procurement** noun.

– ORIGIN Middle English: from Old French *procurer*, from Latin *procurare* 'take care of, manage', from *pro-* 'on behalf of' + *curare* 'see to'.

procurement ▶ **noun** [mass noun] the action of obtaining or procuring something: *financial assistance for the procurement of legal advice* | [count noun] *the company's procurements from foreign firms.*
▪the action or occupation of acquiring military equipment and supplies: *defence procurement.*

procurer ▶ **noun 1** a person who obtains a woman as a prostitute for another person.
2 Law a person who causes someone to do something or something to happen.

– ORIGIN late Middle English (denoting a steward): from Anglo-Norman French *procurour*, from Latin *procurator* (see **PROCURATOR**). Sense 1 dates from the mid 17th cent.

procuress ▶ **noun** a female procurer.

Procyon /ˈprəʊsɪən/ Astronomy the eighth brightest star in the sky, and the brightest in the constellation Canis Minor.
– ORIGIN Greek, literally 'before the dog' (because it rises before Sirius, the Dog Star).

procyonid /ˌprəʊsɪˈɒnɪd, -ˈsʌɪ-/ ▶ **noun** Zoology a mammal of the raccoon family (Procyonidae).
– ORIGIN early 20th cent.: from modern Latin *Procyonidae* (plural), from the genus name *Procyon* (see **PROCYON**).

Prod ▶ **noun** informal, offensive (especially in Ireland) a Protestant.
– ORIGIN 1940s: abbreviation representing a pronunciation.

prod ▶ **verb** (**prodded**, **prodding**) [with obj.] poke (someone) with a finger, foot, or pointed object: *he prodded her in the ribs to stop her snoring* | [no obj.] *he took up a fork and* ***prodded at*** *the food.*
■ stimulate or persuade (someone who is reluctant or slow) to do something: *he has been trying to* ***prod*** *the White House* ***into*** *launching an anti-poverty programme.*
▶ **noun 1** a poke with a finger, foot, or pointed object: *he gave the wire netting an experimental prod.*
■ an act of stimulating or reminding someone to do something: *you need a gentle prod to remind you that life is only what you make it.*
2 a pointed implement, typically one discharging an electric current and used as a goad: *a cattle prod.*
– PHRASES **on the prod** N. Amer. informal looking for trouble: *a gangster on the prod.*
– DERIVATIVES **prodder** noun.
– ORIGIN mid 16th cent. (as a verb): perhaps symbolic of a short poking movement, or a blend of **POKE**[1] and dialect *brod* 'to goad, prod'. The noun dates from the mid 18th cent.

Proddie (also **Proddy**) ▶ **noun** (pl. **-ies**) informal, offensive (especially in Ireland) a Protestant.

pro Deo /prəʊ ˈdeɪəʊ/ ▶ **adjective** & **adverb** Law, S. African (with reference to legal representation of someone accused of a capital offence and unable to afford counsel) with legal costs paid by the state at the instruction of the court: [as adv.] *the counsel defended him pro Deo* | [as adj.] *pro Deo counsel.*
■ free of charge: [as adv.] *who'd work pro Deo in this day and age?*
– ORIGIN Latin, literally 'for God'.

prodigal ▶ **adjective 1** spending money or resources freely and recklessly; wastefully extravagant: *prodigal habits die hard.*
2 having or giving something on a lavish scale: *the dessert was crunchy with brown sugar and prodigal with whipped cream.*
▶ **noun** a person who spends money in a recklessly extravagant way.
■ (also **prodigal son** or **daughter**) a person who leaves home and behaves in such a way, but later makes a repentant return. [ORIGIN: with biblical allusion to the parable in Luke 15:11–32.]
– DERIVATIVES **prodigality** noun, **prodigally** adverb.
– ORIGIN late Middle English: from late Latin *prodigalis*, from Latin *prodigus* 'lavish'.

prodigious /prəˈdɪdʒəs/ ▶ **adjective 1** remarkably or impressively great in extent, size, or degree: *the stove consumed a prodigious amount of fuel.*
2 archaic unnatural or abnormal: *rumours of prodigious happenings, such as monstrous births.*
– DERIVATIVES **prodigiously** adverb, **prodigiousness** noun.
– ORIGIN late 15th cent. (in the sense 'portentous'): from Latin *prodigiosus*, from *prodigium* 'portent' (see **PRODIGY**).

prodigy ▶ **noun** (pl. **-ies**) [often with modifier] a person, especially a young one, endowed with exceptional qualities or abilities: *a Russian pianist who was a child prodigy in his day.*
■ an impressive or outstanding example of a particular quality: *Germany seemed* ***a prodigy of*** *industrial discipline.* ■ an amazing or unusual thing, especially one out of the ordinary course of nature: *omens and prodigies abound in Livy's work.*
– ORIGIN late 15th cent. (denoting something extraordinary considered to be an omen): from Latin *prodigium* 'portent'.

prodromal /prəʊˈdrəʊm(ə)l/ ▶ **adjective** Medicine relating to or denoting the period between the appearance of initial symptoms and the full development of a rash or fever.

prodrome /ˈprəʊdrəʊm, ˈprɒdrəʊm/ ▶ **noun** Medicine an early symptom indicating the onset of a disease or illness.
– DERIVATIVES **prodromic** /prə(ʊ)ˈdrɒmɪk/ adjective.
– ORIGIN early 17th cent.: from French, from modern Latin *prodromus*, from Greek *prodromos* 'precursor', from *pro* 'before' + *dromos* 'running'.

prodrug ▶ **noun** a biologically inactive compound which can be metabolized in the body to produce a drug.

produce ▶ **verb** [with obj.] **1** make or manufacture from components or raw materials: *the company have just produced a luxury version of the aircraft.*
■ (of a region, country, or process) yield, grow, or supply: *the vineyards in the Val d'Or produce excellent wines.* ■ create or form (something) as part of a physical, biological, or chemical process: *the plant produces blue flowers in late autumn.* ■ make (something) using creative or mental skills: *the garden where the artist produced many of his flower paintings.*
2 cause (a particular result or situation) to happen or come into existence: *no conventional drugs had produced any significant change.*
3 show or provide (something) for consideration, inspection, or use: *he produced a sheet of paper from his pocket.*
4 administer the financial and managerial aspects of (a film or broadcast) or the staging of (a play, opera, etc.).
■ supervise the making of a (musical recording), especially by determining the overall sound.
5 Geometry, dated extend or continue (a line): *one side of the triangle was produced.*
▶ **noun** [mass noun] things that have been produced or grown, especially by farming: *dairy produce.*
■ the result of something, especially a person's work or efforts: *the work was in some degree the produce of their joint efforts.*
– DERIVATIVES **producibility** noun, **producible** adjective.
– ORIGIN late Middle English (in sense 3 of the verb): from Latin *producere*, from *pro-* 'forward' + *ducere* 'to lead'. Current noun senses date from the late 17th cent.

producer ▶ **noun 1** a person, company, or country that makes, grows, or supplies goods or commodities for sale: *an oil producer.*
■ a person or thing that makes or causes something: *the mould is the producer of the toxin aflatoxin.*
2 a person responsible for the financial and managerial aspects of making of a film or broadcast or for staging a play, opera, etc.
■ a person who supervises the making of a musical recording, especially by determining the overall sound.

producer gas ▶ **noun** [mass noun] a low-grade fuel gas consisting largely of nitrogen and carbon monoxide, formed by passing air, or air and steam, through red-hot carbon.

product ▶ **noun 1** an article or substance that is manufactured or refined for sale: *marketing products and services* | *dairy products.*
■ a substance produced during a natural, chemical, or manufacturing process: *waste products.* ■ a thing or person that is the result of an action or process: *her perpetual suntan was the product of a solarium.* ■ a person whose character and identity have been formed by a particular period or situation: *an ageing academic who is a product of the 1960s.* ■ [mass noun] commercially manufactured articles, especially recordings, viewed collectively: *too much product of too little quality.*
2 Mathematics a quantity obtained by multiplying quantities together, or from an analogous algebraic operation.
– ORIGIN late Middle English (as a mathematical term): from Latin *productum* 'something produced', neuter past participle (used as a noun) of *producere* 'bring forth' (see **PRODUCE**).

product differentiation ▶ **noun** [mass noun] Economics the marketing of generally similar products with minor variations that are used by consumers when making a choice.

production ▶ **noun** [mass noun] **1** the action of making or manufacturing from components or raw materials, or the process of being so manufactured: *banning the production of chemical weapons* | *it is no longer* ***in production.***
■ the harvesting or refinement of something natural: *non-intensive methods of food production.* ■ the total amount of something that is manufactured, harvested, or refined: *steel production had peaked in 1974.* ■ the creation or formation of something as part of a physical, biological, or chemical process: *excess production of collagen by the liver.* ■ [as modifier] denoting a car or other vehicle which has been been manufactured in large numbers.
2 the provision of something for consideration, inspection, or use: *members are entitled to a discount* ***on production of*** *their membership card.*
3 the process of or financial and administrative management involved in making a film, play, or record: *the film was still* ***in production*** | [as modifier] *a production company.*
■ [count noun] a film, record, or play, especially when viewed in terms of its making or staging: *this production updates the play and sets it in the sixties.* ■ [in sing.] the overall sound of a musical recording; the way a record is produced: *the record's production is gloriously relaxed.*
– PHRASES **make a production of** do (something) in an unnecessarily elaborate or complicated way.
– ORIGIN late Middle English: via Old French from Latin *productio(n-)*, from *producere* 'bring forth' (see **PRODUCE**).

production line ▶ **noun** an arrangement in a factory in which a thing being manufactured is passed through a set linear sequence of mechanical or manual operations.

production number ▶ **noun** a spectacular musical item, typically including song and dance and involving all or most of the cast, in a theatrical show or film.

production platform ▶ **noun** a platform which houses equipment necessary to keep an oil or gas field in production, with facilities for temporarily storing the output of several wells.

productive ▶ **adjective** producing or able to produce large amounts of goods, crops, or other commodities: *the most productive employees.*
■ relating to or engaged in the production of goods, crops, or other commodities: *the country's productive capacity.* ■ achieving or producing a significant amount or result: *a long and productive career* | *the therapy sessions became more productive.* ■ [predic.] (**productive of**) producing or giving rise to: *the hotel was not productive of amusing company.* ■ Linguistics (of a morpheme or other linguistic unit) currently used in forming new words or expressions: *many suffixes are common and productive.* ■ Medicine (of a cough) that raises mucus from the respiratory tract.
– DERIVATIVES **productively** adverb, **productiveness** noun.
– ORIGIN early 17th cent.: from French *productif, -ive* or late Latin *productivus*, from *product-* 'brought forth', from the verb *producere* (see **PRODUCE**).

productivity ▶ **noun** [mass noun] the state or quality of producing something, especially crops: *the long-term productivity of land* | *agricultural productivity.*
■ the effectiveness of productive effort, especially in industry, as measured in terms of the rate of output per unit of input: *workers have boosted productivity by 30 per cent.* ■ Ecology the rate of production of new biomass by an individual, population, or community; the fertility or capacity of a given habitat or area: *nutrient-rich waters with high primary productivity.*

product liability ▶ **noun** [mass noun] the legal liability a manufacturer or trader incurs for producing or selling a faulty product.

product placement ▶ **noun** [mass noun] a practice in which manufacturers of goods or providers of a service gain exposure for their products by paying for them to be featured in films and television programmes.

proem /ˈprəʊɪm/ ▶ **noun** formal a preface or preamble to a book or speech.
– DERIVATIVES **proemial** /-ˈiːmɪəl/ adjective.
– ORIGIN late Middle English: from Old French *proeme*, via Latin from Greek *prooimion* 'prelude', from *pro* 'before' + *oimē* 'song'.

proenzyme ▶ **noun** Biochemistry a biologically inactive substance which is metabolized into an enzyme.

pro-European ▶ **adjective** (of a person, attitude, or policy) favouring or supporting closer links with the European Union.
▶ **noun** a person who favours or supports closer links with the European Union.

Prof. ▶ **abbreviation for** professor: [as title] *Prof. Smith.*

prof ▶ **noun** informal a professor.

p

– ORIGIN mid 19th cent.: abbreviation.

pro-family ▶ adjective chiefly US promoting family life and traditional moral values.

profane /prəˈfeɪn/ ▶ adjective **1** not relating or devoted to that which is sacred or biblical; secular rather than religious: *a talk that tackled topics both sacred and profane.*
■ (of a person) not initiated into religious rites or any esoteric knowledge: *he was an agnostic, a profane man.* **2** (of a person or their behaviour) not respectful of orthodox religious practice; irreverent: *a profane person might be tempted to violate the tomb.*
■ (of language) blasphemous or obscene.
▶ verb [with obj.] treat (something sacred) with irreverence or disrespect: *it was a serious matter to profane a tomb.*
– DERIVATIVES **profanation** noun, **profanely** adverb, **profaneness** noun, **profaner** noun.
– ORIGIN late Middle English (in the sense 'heathen'): from Old French *prophane*, from Latin *profanus* 'outside the temple, not sacred', from *pro-* (from Latin *pro* 'before') + *fanum* 'temple'.

profanity /prəˈfanɪti/ ▶ noun (pl. **-ies**) [mass noun] blasphemous or obscene language: *an outburst of profanity.*
■ [count noun] a swear word; an oath. ■ irreligious or irreverent behaviour.
– ORIGIN mid 16th cent.: from late Latin *profanitas*, from Latin *profanus* 'not sacred' (see **PROFANE**).

proferens /prəˈfɛrɛnz/ ▶ noun (pl. **proferentes** /ˌprɒfəˈrɛntiːz/) Law the party which proposes or adduces a contract or a condition in a contract.
– ORIGIN Latin, literally 'uttering'.

profess ▶ verb [with obj.] **1** claim openly but often falsely that one has (a quality or feeling): *he had professed his love for her only to walk away without a backward glance* | [with infinitive] *I don't profess to be an expert* | [with complement] (**profess oneself**) *he professed himself amazed at the boy's ability.* **2** affirm one's faith in or allegiance to (a religion or set of beliefs): *a people professing Christianity.*
■ (**be professed**) be received into a religious order under vows: *she entered St Margaret's Convent, and was professed in 1943.* **3** dated or humorous teach (a subject) as a professor: *a professor—what does he profess?* **4** archaic have or claim knowledge or skill in (a subject or accomplishment): *though knowing little of the arts I professed, he proved a natural adept.*
– ORIGIN Middle English (as *be professed* 'be received into a religious order'): from Latin *profess-* 'declared publicly', from the verb *profiteri*, from *pro-* 'before' + *fateri* 'confess'.

professed ▶ adjective **1** (of a quality, feeling, or belief) claimed or asserted openly but often falsely: *for all her professed populism, she was seen as remote from ordinary people.* **2** (of a person) self-acknowledged or openly declared to be: *a professed and conforming Anglican.*
■ (of a monk or nun) having taken the vows of a religious order. ■ archaic claiming to be qualified as a particular specialist; professional.

professedly ▶ adverb [sentence adverb] ostensibly; apparently (used in reference to something claimed or asserted, possibly falsely): *restrictions professedly designed to stop the use of political propaganda.*

profession ▶ noun **1** a paid occupation, especially one that involves prolonged training and a formal qualification: *his chosen profession of teaching* | *a barrister by profession.*
■ [treated as sing. or pl.] a body of people engaged in a particular profession: *the profession is divided on the issue.* **2** an open but often false declaration or claim: *a profession of allegiance.*
■ a declaration of belief in a religion. ■ the declaration or vows made on entering a religious order. ■ [mass noun] the ceremony or fact of being professed in a religious order: *after profession she taught in Maidenhead.*
– PHRASES **the oldest profession** humorous the practice of working as a prostitute.
– ORIGIN Middle English (denoting the vow made on entering a religious order): via Old French from Latin *professio(n-)*, from *profiteri* 'declare publicly' (see **PROFESS**). Sense 1 derives from the notion of an occupation that one 'professes' to be skilled in.

professional ▶ adjective **1** [attrib.] of, relating to, or belonging to a profession: *young professional people.* **2** (of a person) engaged in a specified activity as one's main paid occupation rather than as a pastime: *a professional boxer.*
■ having or showing the skill appropriate to a professional person; competent or skilful: *their music is both memorable and professional.* ■ worthy of or appropriate to a professional person: *his professional expertise.* ■ informal, derogatory denoting a person who persistently makes a feature of a particular activity or attribute: *a professional gloom-monger.*
▶ noun a person engaged or qualified in a profession: *professionals such as lawyers and surveyors.*
■ a person engaged in a specified activity, especially a sport or branch of the performing arts, as a main paid occupation rather than as a pastime. ■ a person competent or skilled in a particular activity: *she was a real professional on stage.*
– DERIVATIVES **professionally** adverb.

professional foul ▶ noun (especially in soccer) a deliberate foul to deny an opponent an advantageous position.

professionalism ▶ noun [mass noun] the competence or skill expected of a professional: *the key to quality and efficiency is professionalism.*
■ the practising of an activity, especially a sport, by professional rather than amateur players: *the trend towards professionalism.*

professionalize (also **-ise**) ▶ verb [with obj.] give (an occupation, activity, or group) professional qualities, typically by increasing training or raising required qualifications: *attempts to professionalize the police are resisted by many.*
– DERIVATIVES **professionalization** noun.

professor ▶ noun **1** a university academic of the highest rank; the holder of a university chair.
■ N. Amer. a university teacher. **2** a person who affirms a faith in or allegiance to something: *the professors of true religion.*
– DERIVATIVES **professorate** noun, **professorial** adjective, **professorially** adverb, **professoriate** noun, **professorship** noun.
– ORIGIN late Middle English: from Latin *professor*, from *profess-* 'declared publicly', from the verb *profiteri* (see **PROFESS**).

proffer ▶ verb [with obj.] hold out (something) to someone for acceptance; offer: *he proffered his resignation.*
▶ noun poetic/literary an offer or proposal.
– ORIGIN Middle English: from Anglo-Norman French *proffrir*, from Latin *pro-* 'before' + *offerre* 'to offer'.

proficient ▶ adjective competent or skilled in doing or using something: *I was proficient at my job* | *she felt reasonably proficient in Italian.*
– DERIVATIVES **proficiency** noun, **proficiently** adverb.
– ORIGIN late 16th cent.: from Latin *proficient-* 'advancing', from the verb *proficere*, from *pro-* 'on behalf of' + *facere* 'do, make'.

profile ▶ noun **1** an outline of something, especially a person's face, as seen from one side: *the man turned and she caught his profile.*
■ a drawing or other representation of such an outline. ■ a vertical cross section of a structure: *skilfully made vessels with an S-shaped profile.* ■ Geography an outline of part of the earth's surface, e.g. the course of a river, as seen in a vertical section. ■ a flat outline piece of scenery on stage. ■ a graphical or other representation of information relating to particular characteristics of something, recorded in quantified form: *a sleep profile for someone on a shift system.* ■ a short article giving a description of a person or organization, especially a public figure: *a profile of a Texas tycoon.* **2** [in sing.] the extent to which a person or organization attracts public notice or comment: *raising the profile of women in industry.*
▶ verb [with obj.] **1** describe (a person or organization, especially a public figure) in a short article: *he was to profile a back-bench MP.* **2** (usu. **be profiled**) represent in outline from one side: *he was standing motionless, profiled on the far side of the swimming pool.*
■ (**be profiled**) have a specified shape or appearance in outline: *a proud bird profiled like a phoenix.* ■ shape (something), especially by means of a tool guided by a template: [as adj.] **profiled** *profiled and plain tiles.*
– PHRASES **in profile** (in reference to someone's face) as seen from one side: *a photograph of Leon in profile.*
– DERIVATIVES **profiler** noun.
– ORIGIN mid 17th cent.: from obsolete Italian *profilo*, from the verb *profilare*, from *pro-* 'forth' + *filare* 'to spin', formerly 'draw a line' (from Latin *filare*, from *filum* 'thread').

profile component ▶ noun an attainment target in a particular subject, forming part of a general assessment of a pupil.

profiling ▶ noun [mass noun] the recording and analysis of a person's psychological and behavioural characteristics, so as to assess or predict their capabilities in a certain sphere or to assist in identifying a particular subgroup of people.

profit ▶ noun a financial gain, especially the difference between the amount earned and the amount spent in buying, operating, or producing something: *record pre-tax profits* | [mass noun] *his eyes brightened at the prospect of profit.*
■ [mass noun] advantage; benefit: *there's no profit in screaming at referees from the bench.*
▶ verb (**profited**, **profiting**) [no obj.] obtain a financial advantage or benefit, especially from an investment: *the only people to profit from the entire episode were the lawyers.*
■ obtain an advantage or benefit: *not all children would profit from this kind of schooling.* ■ [with obj.] be beneficial to: *it would profit us to change our plans.*
– PHRASES **at a profit** making more money than is spent buying, operating, or producing something: *doing up houses and selling them at a profit.*
– ORIGIN Middle English (in the sense 'advantage, benefit'): from Old French, from Latin *profectus* 'progress, profit', from *proficere* 'to advance', from *pro-* 'on behalf of' + *facere* 'do'. The verb is from Old French *profiter*.

profitable ▶ adjective **1** (of a business or activity) yielding profit or financial gain. **2** beneficial; useful: *he'd had a profitable day.*
– DERIVATIVES **profitability** noun, **profitably** adverb.
– ORIGIN Middle English: from Old French, from the verb *profiter* (see **PROFIT**).

profit and loss account (abbrev.: **P & L**) ▶ noun an account in the books of an organization to which incomes and gains are credited and expenses and losses debited, so as to show the net profit or loss over a given period.
■ a financial statement showing a company's net profit or loss in a given period.

profit centre ▶ noun a part of an organization with assignable revenues and costs and hence ascertainable profitability.

profiteer ▶ verb [no obj.] make or seek to make an excessive or unfair profit, especially illegally or in a black market: [as noun **profiteering**] *seven food merchants were charged with profiteering.*
▶ noun a person who profiteers: *a war profiteer.*

profiterole ▶ noun a small ball of soft, sweet choux pastry filled with cream and covered with chocolate sauce, served as a dessert.
– ORIGIN French, diminutive of *profit* 'profit'.

profitless ▶ adjective without benefit or advantage; pointless: *a long and profitless public row.*

profit margin ▶ noun the amount by which revenue from sales exceeds costs in a business.

profit-sharing ▶ noun [mass noun] a system in which the people who work for a company receive a direct share of the profits.

profit-taking ▶ noun [mass noun] the sale of securities that have risen in price.

profligate /ˈprɒflɪɡət/ ▶ adjective recklessly extravagant or wasteful in the use of resources: *profligate consumers of energy.*
■ licentious; dissolute: *he succumbed to drink and a profligate lifestyle.*
▶ noun a licentious, dissolute person.
– DERIVATIVES **profligacy** noun, **profligately** adverb.
– ORIGIN mid 16th cent. (in the sense 'overthrown, routed'): from Latin *profligatus* 'dissolute', past participle of *profligare* 'overthrow, ruin', from *pro-* 'forward, down' + *fligere* 'strike down'.

pro-form ▶ noun Linguistics a word or lexical unit which is dependent for its meaning on reference to some other part of the context, for example a pronoun or the verb *do* in *she likes chocolate and so do I.*

pro forma /prəʊ ˈfɔːmə/ ▶ adverb as a matter of form or politeness: *he nodded to him pro forma.*
▶ adjective done or produced as a matter of form: *pro forma reports.*
■ [attrib.] denoting a standard document or form, especially an invoice sent in advance of or with goods supplied. ■ [attrib.] (of a financial statement) showing potential or expected income, costs, assets,

or liabilities, especially in relation to some planned or expected act or situation.

▶**noun** a standard document or form or financial statement of such a type.

– ORIGIN early 16th cent.: from Latin.

profound ▶**adjective** (**profounder**, **profoundest**) **1** (of a state, quality, or emotion) very great or intense: *profound social changes | profound feelings of disquiet.*

■(of a disease or disability) very severe; deep-seated: *a case of profound liver failure.*

2 (of a person or statement) having or showing great knowledge or insight: *a profound philosopher.*

■(of a subject or thought) demanding deep study or thought: *expressing profound truths in simple language.*

3 archaic at, from, or extending to a great depth; very deep: *he opened the door with a profound bow.*

▶**noun** (**the profound**) poetic/literary the vast depth of the ocean or of the mind.

– DERIVATIVES **profoundly** adverb [as submodifier] *a profoundly disturbing experience*, **profoundness** noun.

– ORIGIN Middle English: from Old French *profund*, from Latin *profundus* 'deep', from Latin *pro* 'before' + *fundus* 'bottom'. The word was used earliest in the sense 'showing deep insight'.

Profumo /prəˈfjuːməʊ/, John (Dennis) (b.1915), British Conservative politician. In 1960 he was appointed Secretary of State for War under Harold Macmillan. Three years later news broke of his relationship with the mistress of a Soviet diplomat, Christine Keeler, raising fears of a security breach and precipitating his resignation.

profundity ▶**noun** (pl. **-ies**) [mass noun] deep insight; great depth of knowledge or thought: *the simplicity and profundity of the message.*

■great depth or intensity of a state, quality, or emotion: *the profundity of her misery.* ■[count noun] a statement or idea that shows great knowledge or insight.

profuse ▶**adjective** (especially of something offered or discharged) exuberantly plentiful; abundant: *I offered my profuse apologies.*

■archaic (of a person) lavish; extravagant: *they are profuse in hospitality.*

– DERIVATIVES **profusely** adverb, **profuseness** noun.

– ORIGIN late Middle English (in the sense 'extravagant'): from Latin *profusus* 'lavish, spread out', past participle of *profundere*, from *pro-* 'forth' + *fundere* 'pour'.

profusion ▶**noun** [in sing.] an abundance or large quantity of something: *a rich **profusion of** wild flowers* | [mass noun] *the beautiful pink foxgloves growing **in profusion** among the ferns.*

– ORIGIN mid 16th cent.: via French from Latin *profusio(n-)*, from *profundere* 'pour out'. Early use expressed the senses 'extravagance', 'squandering', and 'waste'.

prog informal ▶**noun** a television or radio programme: *he's the star of a new prog.*

▶**adjective** [attrib.] (of rock music) progressive: *prog rock bands.*

– ORIGIN 1950s: abbreviation.

progenitive ▶**adjective** formal having the quality of producing offspring; reproductive power.

progenitor /prə(ʊ)ˈdʒɛnɪtə/ ▶**noun** a person or thing from which a person, animal, or plant is descended or originates; an ancestor or parent: *his sons and daughters were the progenitors of many of Scotland's leading noble families.*

■a person who originates an artistic, political, or intellectual movement: *the progenitor of modern jazz.*

– DERIVATIVES **progenitorial** adjective.

– ORIGIN late Middle English: from Old French *progeniteur*, from Latin *progenitor*, from *progenit-* 'begotten', from the verb *progignere*, from *pro-* 'forward' + *gignere* 'beget'.

progeniture /prə(ʊ)ˈdʒɛnɪtʃə/ ▶**noun** [mass noun] formal the production of offspring; procreation.

■young; offspring.

– ORIGIN late 15th cent.: from *progenit-* 'begotten' (from the verb *progignere*) + **-URE**.

progeny /ˈprɒdʒ(ə)ni/ ▶**noun** [treated as sing. or pl.] a descendant or the descendants of a person, animal, or plant; offspring: *the progeny of mixed marriages.*

– ORIGIN Middle English: from Old French *progenie*, from Latin *progenies*, from *progignere* 'beget' (see **PROGENITOR**).

progeria /prə(ʊ)ˈdʒɪərɪə/ ▶**noun** [mass noun] Medicine a rare syndrome in children characterized by physical symptoms suggestive of premature old age.

– ORIGIN early 20th cent.: modern Latin, from Greek *progērōs* 'prematurely old'.

progesterone /prəˈdʒɛstərəʊn/ ▶**noun** [mass noun] Biochemistry a steroid hormone released by the corpus luteum that stimulates the uterus to prepare for pregnancy.

– ORIGIN 1930s: blend of **PROGESTIN** and the German synonym *Luteosteron* (from **CORPUS LUTEUM** + **STEROL**).

progestin /prə(ʊ)ˈdʒɛstɪn/ ▶**noun** Biochemistry another term for **PROGESTOGEN**.

progestogen /prə(ʊ)ˈdʒɛstədʒ(ə)n/ ▶**noun** Biochemistry a natural or synthetic steroid hormone, such as progesterone, that maintains pregnancy and prevents further ovulation during pregnancy.

– ORIGIN 1940s: from **PROGESTIN** + **-GEN**.

proglottid /prəʊˈglɒtɪd/ ▶**noun** Zoology each segment in the strobila of a tapeworm, containing a complete sexually mature reproductive system.

– ORIGIN late 19th cent.: from Greek *proglōssis*, *proglōssid-* 'point of the tongue', based on *glōssa*, *glōtta* 'tongue' (because of its shape).

prognathous /prɒgˈneɪθəs, ˈprɒgnəθəs/ ▶**adjective** (especially of a person) having a projecting lower jaw or chin.

■(of a jaw or chin) projecting.

– DERIVATIVES **prognathic** /prɒgˈnaθɪk/ adjective, **prognathism** noun.

– ORIGIN mid 19th cent.: from **PRO-**[2] 'before' + Greek *gnathos* 'jaw' + **-OUS**.

prognosis /prɒgˈnəʊsɪs/ ▶**noun** (pl. **prognoses** /-siːz/) the likely course of a disease or ailment: *the disease has a poor prognosis.*

■a forecast of the likely course of a disease or ailment: *it is very difficult to make an accurate prognosis.* ■a forecast of the likely outcome of a situation: *gloomy prognoses about overpopulation.*

– ORIGIN mid 17th cent.: via late Latin from Greek *prognōsis*, from *pro-* 'before' + *gignōskein* 'know'.

prognostic /prɒgˈnɒstɪk/ ▶**adjective** serving to predict the likely outcome of a disease or ailment; of or relating to a medical prognosis.

▶**noun** archaic an advance indication or portent of a future event: *a pale moon and watery sun are known as prognostics of rain.*

– DERIVATIVES **prognostically** adverb.

– ORIGIN late Middle English: from Latin *prognosticus* from Greek *prognōstikos*, from *prognōsis* (see **PROGNOSIS**).

prognosticate ▶**verb** [with obj.] foretell or prophesy (an event in the future): *the economists were prognosticating financial Armageddon.*

– DERIVATIVES **prognosticator** noun, **prognosticatory** adjective.

– ORIGIN late Middle English: from medieval Latin *prognosticat-*, from the verb *prognosticare* 'make a prediction' (see **PROGNOSTIC**).

prognostication ▶**noun** [mass noun] the action of foretelling or prophesying future events: *an unprecedented amount of soul-searching and prognostication.*

■[count noun] a prophecy: *these gloomy prognostications proved to be unfounded.*

– ORIGIN late Middle English: from Old French *prognosticacion*, from medieval Latin *prognosticatio(n-)*, from the verb *prognosticare* (see **PROGNOSTICATE**).

prograde /ˈprəʊgreɪd/ ▶**adjective** **1** Astronomy (of planetary motion) proceeding from west to east; direct. The opposite of **RETROGRADE**.

2 Geology (of a metamorphic change) resulting from an increase in temperature or pressure.

▶**verb** [no obj.] Geology (of a beach or coastline) advance towards the sea as a result of the accumulation of water-borne sediment.

– DERIVATIVES **progradation** noun.

– ORIGIN early 20th cent. (as a verb): from **PRO-**[1] 'forwards' + **RETROGRADE**.

program ▶**noun** & **verb** US spelling of **PROGRAMME** (also widely used in computing contexts).

programmatic ▶**adjective** of the nature of or according to a programme, schedule, or method: *a programmatic approach to change.*

■of the nature of programme music.

– DERIVATIVES **programmatically** adverb.

programme (US **program**) ▶**noun** **1** a planned series of future events, items, or performances: *a weekly programme of films | the programme includes Dvorak's New World symphony.*

■a set of related measures, events, or activities with a particular long-term aim: *the British nuclear power programme.*

2 a sheet or booklet giving details of items or performers at an event or performance: *a theatre programme.*

3 a presentation or item on radio or television, especially one broadcast regularly between stated times: *a nature programme.*

■dated a radio or television service or station providing a regular succession of programmes on a particular frequency; a channel.

4 (**program**) a series of coded software instructions to control the operation of a computer or other machine.

▶**verb** (**programmed**, **programming**; US **programed**, **programing**) [with obj.] **1** (**program**) provide (a computer or other machine) with coded instructions for the automatic performance of a particular task: *it is a simple matter to program the computer to recognize such symbols.*

■input (instructions for the automatic performance of a task) into a computer or other machine: *simply **program in** your desired volume level.* ■(often **be programmed**) figurative cause (a person or animal) to behave in a predetermined way: *all members of a particular species are **programmed to** build nests in the same way.*

2 arrange according to a plan or schedule: *we learn how to programme our own lives consciously.*

■schedule (an item) within a framework: *the next stage of the treaty is programmed for next year.* ■US broadcast (an item): *the station does not program enough contemporary works.*

– PHRASES **get with the program** [often in imperative] N. Amer. informal do what is expected of one; adopt the prevailing viewpoint.

– DERIVATIVES **programmability** noun, **programmable** adjective.

– ORIGIN early 17th cent. (in the sense 'written notice'): via late Latin from Greek *programma*, from *prographein* 'write publicly', from *pro* 'before' + *graphein* 'write'.

programmed cell death ▶**noun** less technical term for **APOPTOSIS**.

programmed learning ▶**noun** [mass noun] a teaching method in which information is broken into simple sections on which pupils are able to test themselves.

programme evaluation and review technique (abbrev.: **PERT**) ▶**noun** a network analysis technique which is used to determine the time it will take to complete a complex process.

programme music ▶**noun** [mass noun] music that is intended to evoke images or convey the impression of events. Compare with **ABSOLUTE MUSIC**.

programmer ▶**noun** a person who writes computer programs.

■a device that automatically controls the operation of something in accordance with a prescribed programme.

programme trading ▶**noun** [mass noun] the simultaneous purchase and sale of many different stocks, or of stocks and related futures contracts, with the use of a computer program to exploit price differences in different markets.

programming ▶**noun** [mass noun] **1** the action or process of writing computer programs.

■figurative predetermined behaviour: *men and women are the playthings of programming.*

2 the action or process of scheduling something, especially radio or television programmes: *the programming of shows.*

■radio or television programmes that are scheduled or broadcast: *the station is to expand its late-night programming.*

progress ▶**noun** [mass noun] forward or onward movement towards a destination: *the darkness did not stop my progress | they failed to **make** any progress up the narrow estuary.*

■advance or development towards a better, more complete, or more modern condition: *we are **making progress** towards equal rights.* ■[count noun] Brit. archaic a state journey or official tour, especially by royalty.

▶**verb** [no obj.] move forward or onward in space or time: *as the century progressed the quality of telescopes improved.*

■advance or develop towards a better, more complete,

or more modern state: *work on the pond is progressing.* ■ [with obj.] cause (a task or undertaking) to make regular progress: *I cannot predict how quickly we can progress the matter.* ■ [with obj.] [usu. as adj. **progressed**] Astrology calculate the position of (a planet) or of all the planets and coordinates of (a chart) according to the technique of progression.

– PHRASES **in progress** in the course of being done or carried out: *a meeting was in progress.*

– ORIGIN late Middle English (as a noun): from Latin *progressus* 'an advance', from the verb *progredi*, from *pro-* 'forward' + *gradi* 'to walk'. The verb became obsolete in British English use at the end of the 17th cent. and was readopted from American English in the early 19th cent.

progress chaser ▶ **noun** a person in an organization who is responsible for checking that work is done efficiently and to schedule.

progression ▶ **noun** a movement or development towards a destination or a more advanced state, especially gradually or in stages: *the normal progression from junior to senior status* | [mass noun] *their mode of progression through the forest.*
■ a succession; a series: *counting the twenty-four hours in a single progression from midnight.* ■ Music a passage or movement from one note or chord to another: *a blues progression.* ■ Mathematics short for **ARITHMETIC PROGRESSION**, **GEOMETRIC PROGRESSION**, or **HARMONIC PROGRESSION**. ■ Astrology a predictive technique in which the daily movement of the planets, starting from the day of birth, represents a year in the subject's life.

– DERIVATIVES **progressional** adjective.

– ORIGIN late Middle English: from Old French, from Latin *progressio(n-)*, from the verb *progredi* (see **PROGRESS**).

progressionist chiefly historical ▶ **noun** **1** Biology a supporter of the theory that all life forms gradually progress or evolve to a higher form.
2 an advocate of or believer in political or social progress.
▶ **adjective** Biology (of a person or theory) supporting or based on the theory that all life forms progress or evolve to a higher form: *progressionist evolutionists.*

progressive ▶ **adjective** **1** happening or developing gradually or in stages; proceeding step by step: *a progressive decline in popularity.*
■ (of a disease or ailment) increasing in severity or extent: *progressive liver failure.* ■ (of taxation or a tax) increasing as a proportion of the sum taxed as that sum increases: *steeply progressive income taxes.* ■ (of a card game or dance) involving a series of sections for which participants successively change place or relative position. ■ archaic engaging in or constituting forward motion.
2 (of a group, person, or idea) favouring or implementing social reform or new, liberal ideas: *a relatively progressive Minister of Education.*
■ favouring or promoting change or innovation: *the most progressive art school in Britain.* ■ relating to or denoting a style of rock music popular especially in the 1970s and characterized by classical influences, the use of keyboard instruments, and lengthy compositions.
3 Grammar denoting an aspect or tense of a verb that expresses an action in progress, e.g. *am writing, was writing.* Also called **CONTINUOUS**.
▶ **noun** **1** a person advocating or implementing social reform or new, liberal ideas.
2 Grammar a progressive tense or aspect: *the present progressive.*
3 (also **progressive proof**) (usu. **progressives**) Printing each of a set of proofs of colour work, showing all the colours separately and the cumulative effect of overprinting them.

– DERIVATIVES **progressively** adverb, **progressiveness** noun, **progressivism** noun, **progressivist** noun & adjective.

– ORIGIN early 17th cent.: from French *progressif, -ive* or medieval Latin *progressivus*, from *progress-* 'gone forward', from the verb *progredi* (see **PROGRESS**).

Progressive Conservative Party a Canadian political party advocating free trade and holding moderate views on social policies. Founded in the mid 19th century but operating under its present name since 1942, the party was in power 1984–93 under Brian Mulroney.

proguanil /prəʊˈgwɑːnɪl/ ▶ **noun** [mass noun] Medicine a bitter-tasting synthetic compound derived from biguanide, used in the prevention and treatment of malaria.

– ORIGIN 1940s: from *pro(pyl)* + *(bi)guan(ide)* (a crystalline base) + **-IL**.

pro hac vice /ˌprəʊ hɑːk ˈvʌɪsi/ ▶ **adverb** for or on this occasion only.

– ORIGIN Latin.

prohibit ▶ **verb** (**prohibited**, **prohibiting**) [with obj.] formally forbid (something) by law, rule, or other authority: *laws prohibiting cruelty to animals.*
■ (**prohibit someone/thing from doing something**) formally forbid a person or group from doing something: *he is prohibited from being a director.* ■ (of a fact or situation) prevent (something); make impossible: *the budget agreement had prohibited any tax cuts.*

– DERIVATIVES **prohibiter** noun, **prohibitor** noun, **prohibitory** adjective.

– ORIGIN late Middle English: from Latin *prohibit-* 'kept in check', from the verb *prohibere*, from *pro-* 'in front' + *habere* 'to hold'.

prohibited degrees ▶ **plural noun** another term for ***the forbidden degrees*** (see **FORBID**).

prohibition /ˌprəʊhɪˈbɪʃ(ə)n, prəʊɪ-/ ▶ **noun** **1** [mass noun] the action of forbidding something, especially by law: *they argue that prohibition of drugs will always fail.*
■ [count noun] a law or regulation forbidding something: *those who favour prohibitions on insider dealing.* ■ [count noun] English Law a writ from a superior court forbidding an inferior court from proceeding in a suit deemed to be beyond its cognizance.
2 (**Prohibition**) [mass noun] the prevention by law of the manufacture and sale of alcohol, especially in the US between 1920 and 1933.

– DERIVATIVES **prohibitionary** adjective, **Prohibitionist** noun.

– ORIGIN late Middle English: from Old French, from Latin *prohibitio(n-)*, from *prohibere* 'keep in check' (see **PROHIBIT**).

prohibitive ▶ **adjective** **1** (of a price or charge) excessively high; difficult or impossible to pay: *the costs involved were prohibitive* | *prohibitive interest rates.*
2 (especially of a law or rule) forbidding or restricting something: *prohibitive legislation.*
■ (of a condition or situation) preventing someone from doing something: *a wind over force 5 is prohibitive.*

– DERIVATIVES **prohibitively** adverb, **prohibitiveness** noun.

– ORIGIN late Middle English (in sense 2): from French *prohibitif, -ive* or Latin *prohibitivus*, from *prohibit-* 'kept in check', from the verb *prohibere* (see **PROHIBIT**).

proinsulin ▶ **noun** [mass noun] Biochemistry a substance produced by the pancreas which is converted to insulin.

project ▶ **noun** **1** an individual or collaborative enterprise that is carefully planned and designed to achieve a particular aim: *a research project* | *a nationwide project to encourage business development.*
■ a piece of school or college work in which a student undertakes their own research and submits the results for assessment: *a history project.* ■ a proposed or planned undertaking: *the novel undermines its own stated project of telling a story.*
2 (also **housing project**) N. Amer. a government-subsidized estate or block of homes with relatively low rents.
▶ **verb** [with obj.] **1** (usu. **be projected**) estimate or forecast (something) on the basis of present trends: *spending was projected at £72,900 million.*
■ [often as adj. **projected**] plan (a scheme or undertaking): *a projected exhibition of contemporary art.*
2 [no obj.] extend outwards beyond something else; protrude: *I noticed a slip of paper projecting from the book* | [as adj. **projecting**] *a projecting bay window.*
3 [with obj. and adverbial of direction] throw or cause to move forward or outward: *seeds are projected from the tree.*
■ cause (light, shadow, or an image) to fall on a surface: *the one light projected shadows on the wall.* ■ cause (a sound, especially the voice) to be heard at a distance: *being audible depends on your ability to project your voice.* ■ imagine (oneself, a situation, etc.) as having moved to a different place or time: *people may be projecting the present into the past.*
4 present or promote (a particular view or image): *he strives to project an image of youth.*
■ present (someone or something) in a way intended to create a favourable impression: *the scheme was projected as a public service.* ■ display (an emotion or quality) in one's behaviour: *everyone would be amazed that a young girl could project such depths of emotion.* ■ (**project something on to**) transfer or attribute an emotion or desire to (another person), especially unconsciously: *men may sometimes project their own fears on to women.*
5 Geometry draw straight lines from a centre of or parallel lines through every point of (a given figure) to produce a corresponding figure on a surface or a line by intersecting the surface.
■ draw (such lines). ■ produce (such a corresponding figure).
6 make a projection of (the earth, sky, etc.) on a plane surface.

– ORIGIN late Middle English (in the sense 'preliminary design, tabulated statement'): from Latin *projectum* 'something prominent', neuter past participle of *proicere* 'throw forth', from *pro-* 'forth' + *jacere* 'to throw'. Early senses of the verb were 'plan, devise' and 'cause to move forward'.

projectile ▶ **noun** a missile designed to be fired from a rocket or gun.
■ an object propelled through the air, especially one thrown as a weapon: *they tried to shield Johnson from the projectiles that were being thrown.*
▶ **adjective** [attrib.] of or relating to such a missile or object: *a projectile weapon.*
■ impelled with great force.

– ORIGIN mid 17th cent.: modern Latin, from *project-* 'thrown forth', from the verb *proicere* (see **PROJECT**).

projection ▶ **noun** **1** an estimate or forecast of a future situation or trend based on a study of present ones: *plans based on projections of slow but positive growth* | [mass noun] *population projection is essential for planning.*
2 [mass noun] the presentation of an image on a surface, especially a cinema screen: *quality illustrations for overhead projection.*
■ [count noun] an image projected in such a way: *the band use stage projections featuring moon shots.* ■ the ability to make a sound, especially the voice, heard at a distance: *I taught him voice projection.*
3 [mass noun] the presentation or promotion of someone or something in a particular way: *the legal profession's projection of an image of altruism.*
■ [count noun] a mental image viewed as reality: *monsters can be understood as mental projections of mankind's fears.* ■ the unconscious transfer of one's own desires or emotions to another person: *we protect the self by a number of defence mechanisms, including repression and projection.*
4 a thing that extends outwards from something else: *the chipboard covered all the sharp projections.*
5 [mass noun] Geometry the action of projecting a figure.
6 [mass noun] the representation on a plane surface of any part of the surface of the earth or a celestial sphere.
■ (also **map projection**) [count noun] a method by which such representation may be done.

– DERIVATIVES **projectionist** noun (in sense 2).

– ORIGIN mid 16th cent. (in sense 6): from Latin *projectio(n-)*, from *proicere* 'throw forth' (see **PROJECT**).

projection television ▶ **noun** a large television receiver in which the image is projected optically on to a large viewing screen.

projective ▶ **adjective** **1** Geometry relating to or derived by projection: *projective transformations.*
■ (of a property of a figure) unchanged by projection.
2 Psychology relating to the unconscious transfer of one's own desires or emotions to another person: *the projective contents of wish fantasies.*
■ relating to or exploiting the unconscious expression or introduction of one's impressions or feelings.

– DERIVATIVES **projectively** adverb.

projective geometry ▶ **noun** [mass noun] the study of the projective properties of geometric figures.

projective test ▶ **noun** a psychological test in which words, images, or situations are presented to a person and the responses analysed for unconscious expression of elements of personality that they reveal.

projector ▶ **noun** **1** an object that is used to project rays of light, especially an apparatus with a system of lenses for projecting slides or film on to a screen.
2 archaic a person who plans and sets up a project or enterprise.
■ a promoter of a dubious or fraudulent enterprise.

prokaryote /prəʊˈkarɪəʊt, -ɒt/ (also **procaryote**)

▶ **noun** Biology a microscopic single-celled organism which has neither a distinct nucleus with a membrane nor other specialized organelles, including the bacteria and cyanobacteria. Compare with **EUKARYOTE**.
– DERIVATIVES **prokaryotic** adjective.
– ORIGIN 1960s: from **PRO-**[2] 'before' + Greek *karuon* 'nut, kernel' + *-ote* as in **ZYGOTE**.

Prokofiev /prəˈkɒfɪɛf/, Sergei (Sergeevich) (1891–1953), Russian composer. Notable works include seven symphonies, the opera *The Love for Three Oranges* (1919), the *Lieutenant Kijé* suite (1934), the ballet music for *Romeo and Juliet* (1935–6), and *Peter and the Wolf* (1936), a young person's guide to the orchestra.

Prokopyevsk /prəˈkɒpjɛfsk/ a coal-mining city in southern Russia, in the Kuznets Basin industrial region to the south of Kemerovo; pop. 274,000 (1990).

prolactin /prəʊˈlaktɪn/ ▶ **noun** [mass noun] Biochemistry a hormone released from the anterior pituitary gland that stimulates milk production after childbirth.
– ORIGIN 1930s: from **PRO-**[2] 'before' + **LACTATION**.

prolapse ▶ **noun** /ˈprəʊlaps, prəˈlaps/ a slipping forward or down of one of the parts or organs of the body: *a rectal prolapse*.
■ a prolapsed part or organ, especially a uterus or rectum.
▶ **verb** /prəʊˈlaps/ [no obj.] [usu. as adj. **prolapsed**] (of a part or organ of the body) slip forward or down: *a prolapsed uterus*.
– ORIGIN mid 18th cent.: from Latin *prolaps-* 'slipped forward', from the verb *prolabi*, from *pro-* 'forward, down' + *labi* 'to slip'.

prolapsus /prəʊˈlapsəs/ ▶ **noun** [mass noun] technical term for **PROLAPSE**.
– ORIGIN late 18th cent.: modern Latin, from late Latin, literally 'fall'.

prolate /ˈprəʊleɪt/ ▶ **adjective** Geometry (of a spheroid) lengthened in the direction of a polar diameter. Often contrasted with **OBLATE**[2].
– ORIGIN late 17th cent.: from Latin *prolatus* 'carried forward', past participle of *proferre* 'prolong', from *pro-* 'forward' + *ferre* 'carry'.

prole informal, derogatory ▶ **noun** a member of the working class; a worker.
▶ **adjective** working class: *prole soldiers*.
– ORIGIN late 19th cent.: abbreviation of **PROLETARIAT**.

proleg ▶ **noun** Entomology a fleshy abdominal limb of a caterpillar or similar insect larva.

prolegomenon /ˌprəʊlɪˈɡɒmɪnən/ ▶ **noun** (pl. **prolegomena**) a critical or discursive introduction to a book.
– DERIVATIVES **prolegomenous** adjective.
– ORIGIN mid 17th cent.: via Latin from Greek, passive present participle (neuter) of *prolegein* 'say beforehand', from *pro* 'before' + *legein* 'say'.

prolepsis /prəʊˈlɛpsɪs, -ˈliːpsɪs/ ▶ **noun** (pl. **prolepses** /-siːz/) [mass noun] **1** Rhetoric the anticipation and answering of possible objections in rhetorical speech.
■ poetic/literary anticipation.
2 the representation of a thing as existing before it actually does or did so, as in *he was a dead man when he entered*.
– DERIVATIVES **proleptic** adjective.
– ORIGIN late Middle English (as a term in rhetoric): via late Latin from Greek *prolēpsis*, from *prolambanein* 'anticipate', from *pro* 'before' + *lambanein* 'take'.

proletarian /ˌprəʊlɪˈtɛːrɪən/ ▶ **adjective** of or relating to the proletariat: *a proletarian ideology*.
▶ **noun** a member of the proletariat.
– DERIVATIVES **proletarianism** noun, **proletarianization** (also **-isation**) noun, **proletarianize** (also **-ise**) verb.
– ORIGIN mid 17th cent.: from Latin *proletarius* (from *proles* 'offspring'), denoting a person having no wealth in property, who only served the state by producing offspring, + **-AN**.

proletariat (also archaic **proletariate**) ▶ **noun** [treated as sing. or pl.] workers or working-class people, regarded collectively (often used with reference to Marxism): *the growth of the industrial proletariat*.
■ the lowest class of citizens in ancient Rome.
– ORIGIN mid 19th cent.: from French *prolétariat*, from Latin *proletarius* (see **PROLETARIAN**).

pro-life ▶ **adjective** opposing abortion and euthanasia: *she is a pro-life activist*.
– DERIVATIVES **pro-lifer** noun.

proliferate /prəˈlɪfəreɪt/ ▶ **verb** [no obj.] increase rapidly in numbers; multiply: *the science-fiction magazines which proliferated in the 1920s*.
■ (of a cell, structure, or organism) reproduce rapidly: *the Mediterranean faces an ecological disaster if the seaweed continues to proliferate at its present rate*. ■ [with obj.] cause (cells, tissue, structures, etc.) to reproduce rapidly: *electromagnetic radiation can only proliferate cancers already present*. ■ [with obj.] produce (something) in large or increasing quantities: *the promise of new technology proliferating options on every hand*
– DERIVATIVES **proliferative** adjective, **proliferator** noun.
– ORIGIN late 19th cent.: back-formation from **PROLIFERATION**.

proliferation ▶ **noun** [mass noun] rapid increase in numbers: *a continuing threat of nuclear proliferation*.
■ rapid reproduction of a cell, part, or organism: *we attempted to measure cell proliferation*. ■ [in sing.] a large number of something: *stress levels are high, forcing upon them* ***a proliferation of*** *ailments*.
– ORIGIN mid 19th cent.: from French *prolifération*, from *prolifère* 'proliferous'.

proliferous ▶ **adjective** Biology (of a plant) producing buds or side shoots from a flower or other terminal part.
■ (of a plant or invertebrate) propagating or multiplying by means of buds or offsets.
– ORIGIN mid 17th cent.: from Latin *proles* 'offspring' + **-FEROUS**.

prolific ▶ **adjective** **1** (of a plant, animal, or person) producing much fruit or foliage or many offspring: *in captivity tigers are prolific breeders*.
■ (of an artist, author, or composer) producing many works: *he was a prolific composer of operas*. ■ (of a sports player) high-scoring: *a prolific goalscorer*.
2 present in large numbers or quantities; plentiful: *mahogany was once prolific in the tropical forests*.
■ (of a river, area, or season of the year) characterized by plentiful wildlife or produce: *the prolific rivers and lakes around Galway*.
– DERIVATIVES **prolificacy** noun, **prolifically** adverb, **prolificness** noun.
– ORIGIN mid 17th cent.: from medieval Latin *prolificus*, from Latin *proles* 'offspring' (see **PROLIFEROUS**).

proline /ˈprəʊliːn/ ▶ **noun** [mass noun] Biochemistry an amino acid which is a constituent of most proteins, especially collagen.
• A heterocyclic compound; chem. formula: $C_5H_9NO_2$.
– ORIGIN early 20th cent.: contraction of the chemical name *p(yr)rol(id)ine*-2-carboxylic acid.

prolix /ˈprəʊlɪks, prəˈlɪks/ ▶ **adjective** (of speech or writing) using or containing too many words; tediously lengthy: *he found the narrative too prolix and discursive*.
– DERIVATIVES **prolixity** noun, **prolixly** adverb.
– ORIGIN late Middle English: from Old French *prolixe* or Latin *prolixus* 'poured forth, extended', from *pro-* 'outward' + *liquere* 'be liquid'.

prolocutor /ˈprəʊləˌkjuːtə, ˈprɒl-, prə(ʊ)ˈlɒkjʊtə/ ▶ **noun** **1** a chairperson of the lower house of convocation in a province of the Church of England.
2 archaic or formal a spokesman.
– ORIGIN late Middle English (in sense 2): from Latin, from *prolocut-* 'spoken out', from the verb *proloqui*, from *pro-* 'before' + *loqui* 'speak'.

Prolog /ˈprəʊlɒɡ/ ▶ **noun** [mass noun] Computing a high-level computer programming language first devised for artificial intelligence applications.
– ORIGIN 1970s: from the first elements of **PROGRAMMING** and **LOGIC**.

prologue (US **prolog**) ▶ **noun** a separate introductory section of a literary or musical work: *the suppressed prologue to* Women in Love.
■ an event or action that leads to another event or situation: *the events from 1945 to 1956 provided the* ***prologue to*** *the post-imperial era*. ■ (in professional cycling) a short preliminary time trial held before a race to establish a leader. ■ the actor who delivers the prologue in a play.
– ORIGIN Middle English: from Old French, via Latin from Greek *prologos*, from *pro-* 'before' + *logos* 'saying'.

prolong ▶ **verb** [with obj.] extend the duration of: *an idea which prolonged the life of the engine by many years*.
■ (usu. **be prolonged**) rare extend in spatial length: *the line of his lips was prolonged in a short red scar*.
– DERIVATIVES **prolongation** noun, **prolonger** noun.
– ORIGIN late Middle English: from Old French *prolonguer*, from late Latin *prolongare*, from *pro-* 'forward, onward' + *longus* 'long'.

prolonged ▶ **adjective** continuing for a long time or longer than usual; lengthy: *the region suffered a prolonged drought*.
– DERIVATIVES **prolongedly** adverb.

prolusion /prəˈl(j)uːʒ(ə)n/ ▶ **noun** archaic or formal a preliminary action or event; a prelude.
■ a preliminary essay or article.
– ORIGIN early 17th cent.: from Latin *prolusio(n-)*, from *prolus-* 'practised beforehand', from the verb *proludere*, from *pro* 'before' + *ludere* 'to play'.

prom ▶ **noun** informal **1** Brit. short for **PROMENADE** (in sense 1): *she took a short cut along the prom*.
2 (also **Prom**) Brit. short for **PROMENADE CONCERT**: *the last night of the Proms*.
3 N. Amer. a formal dance, especially one held by a class in high school or college at the end of a year.

promenade /ˌprɒməˈnɑːd, -ˈneɪd, ˈprɒm-/ ▶ **noun** **1** a paved public walk, typically one along the seafront at a resort.
■ a leisurely walk, or sometimes a ride or drive, typically one taken in a public place so as to meet or be seen by others: *the admiring glances of strangers when she went on a promenade with Jules*. ■ (in country dancing) a movement in which couples follow one another in a given direction, each couple having both hands joined.
2 N. Amer. archaic term for **PROM** (in sense 3).
▶ **verb** [no obj.] take a leisurely walk, ride, or drive in public, especially to meet or be seen by others: *women who promenaded in the Bois de Boulogne*.
■ [with obj.] take such a walk through (a place): *people began to promenade the streets*. ■ [with obj.] dated escort (someone) about a place, especially so as to be seen by others: *the governor of Utah promenades the daughter of the Maryland governor*.
– ORIGIN mid 16th cent. (denoting a leisurely walk in public): from French, from *se promener* 'to walk', reflexive of *promener* 'take for a walk'.

promenade concert ▶ **noun** Brit. a concert of classical music at which a part of the audience stands in an area without seating, for which tickets are sold at a reduced price. The most famous series of such concerts is the annual BBC Promenade Concerts (known as **the Proms**), instituted by Sir Henry Wood in 1895 and held since the Second World War chiefly in the Albert Hall in London.

promenade deck ▶ **noun** an upper deck on a passenger ship for the use of passengers who wish to enjoy the open air.

promenader ▶ **noun** a person who takes a leisurely walk, ride, or drive in public.
■ Brit. a person attending a promenade concert and choosing to stand in the area without seating.

promethazine /prə(ʊ)ˈmɛθəziːn/ ▶ **noun** [mass noun] Medicine a synthetic antihistamine drug derived from phenothiazine, used chiefly to treat the symptoms of allergies and motion sickness.
– ORIGIN 1950s: from *pro(pyl)* + *(di)meth(ylamine)*, a colourless gas + *(phenothi)azine*.

Prometheus /prəˈmiːθɪəs/ Greek Mythology a demigod, one of the Titans, who was worshipped by craftsmen. When Zeus hid fire away from man Prometheus stole it by trickery and returned it to earth. As punishment Zeus chained him to a rock where an eagle fed each day on his liver, which grew again each night; he was rescued by Hercules.
– DERIVATIVES **Promethean** adjective.

promethium /prəˈmiːθɪəm/ ▶ **noun** [mass noun] the chemical element of atomic number 61, a radioactive metal of the lanthanide series. It was first produced artificially in a nuclear reactor and occurs in nature in traces as a product of uranium fission. (Symbol: **Pm**)
– ORIGIN 1940s: modern Latin, from the name of the Titan **PROMETHEUS**.

prominence ▶ **noun** [mass noun] **1** the state of being important or famous: *Bridget Riley* ***came to prominence*** *as an artist in the 1960s* | [in sing.] *the commission gave the case a prominence which it might otherwise have escaped*.
2 the fact or condition of standing out from something by physically projecting or being particularly noticeable: *radiographs showed*

enlargement of the right heart with prominence of the pulmonary outflow tract.
■[count noun] a thing that projects from something, especially a projecting feature of the landscape or a protuberance on a part of the body: *the steep, rocky prominence resembled a snow-capped mountain.* ■ [count noun] Astronomy a stream of incandescent gas projecting above the sun's chromosphere.
– ORIGIN late 16th cent. (denoting something that juts out): from obsolete French, from Latin *prominentia* 'jutting out', from the verb *prominere* (see **PROMINENT**).

prominent ▶ **adjective 1** important; famous: *she was a prominent member of the city council.*
2 projecting from something; protuberant: *a man with big, prominent eyes like a lobster's.*
■situated so as to catch the attention; noticeable: *the new housing estates are prominent landmarks.*
▶**noun** (also **prominent moth**) a stout drab-coloured moth with tufts on the forewings which stick up while at rest, and the caterpillars of which typically have fleshy growths on the back.
• Family Notodontidae: many species.
– DERIVATIVES **prominency** noun, **prominently** adverb.
– ORIGIN late Middle English (in the sense 'projecting'): from Latin *prominent-* 'jutting out', from the verb *prominere*. Compare with **EMINENT**.

prominenti /ˌprɒmɪˈnɛnti/ ▶ **plural noun** distinguished or eminent people: *a restaurant which attracted the prominenti.*
– ORIGIN Italian, from *prominente* 'prominent'.

promiscuous /prəˈmɪskjʊəs/ ▶ **adjective 1** (of a person) having many sexual relationships, especially transient ones: *she's a wild, promiscuous, good-time girl.*
■(of sexual behaviour or a society) characterized by such relationships: *they ran wild, indulging in promiscuous sex and experimenting with drugs.*
2 demonstrating or implying an undiscriminating or unselective approach; indiscriminate or casual: *the city fathers were promiscuous with their honours.*
■consisting of a wide range of different things: *Americans are free to pick and choose from a promiscuous array of values and behaviour.*
– DERIVATIVES **promiscuity** noun, **promiscuously** adverb, **promiscuousness** noun.
– ORIGIN early 17th cent.: from Latin *promiscuus* 'indiscriminate', (based on *miscere* 'to mix') + **-OUS**. The early sense was 'consisting of elements mixed together', giving rise to 'indiscriminate' and 'undiscriminating', whence the notion of 'casual'.

promise ▶ **noun** a declaration or assurance that one will do a particular thing or that guarantees that a particular thing will happen: *what happened to all those firm promises of support?* | [with clause] *he took my fax number with the promise that he would send me a drawing* | [with infinitive] *I did not keep my promise to go home early.*
■[mass noun] the quality of potential excellence: *he showed great promise even as a junior officer.* ■ [in sing.] an indication that something specified is expected or likely to occur: *there was a promise of peace in a land that had endured the threat of war for six months.*
▶**verb 1** [reporting verb] assure someone that one will definitely do, give, or arrange something; undertake or declare that something will happen: [with infinitive] *he promised to forward my mail* | [with clause] *she made him promise that he wouldn't do it again* | [with direct speech] *'I'll bring it straight back,' she promised* | [with two objs] *he promised her the job.*
■[with obj.] (usu. **be promised**) archaic pledge (someone, especially a woman) to marry someone else; betroth: *I've been promised to him for years.*
2 [with obj.] give good grounds for expecting (a particular occurrence or situation): *forthcoming concerts promise a feast of music from around the world* | [with infinitive] *it promised to be a night that all present would long remember.*
■(of a person, publication, institution, etc.) announce (something) as being expected to happen: *China yesterday promised a record summer grain harvest* | [with two objs] *we're promised more winter weather tonight.* ■ (**promise oneself**) contemplate the pleasant expectation of: *he tidied up the sitting room, promising himself an early night.*
– PHRASES **I promise** (or **I promise you**) informal used for emphasis, especially so as to reassure, encourage, or threaten someone: *oh, I'm not joking, I promise you.* **on a promise** informal (of a person) confidently assured of something, especially of having sexual intercourse with someone: *a shop where Tom and I are on a promise with the girls serving there.* **promise (someone) the earth** (or **moon**) make extravagant promises to someone that are unlikely to be fulfilled: *interactive technology titillates, promises the earth but delivers nothing.* **promises, promises** informal used to indicate that the speaker is sceptical about someone's stated intention to do something.
– DERIVATIVES **promiser** noun.
– ORIGIN late Middle English: from Latin *promissum* 'something promised', neuter past participle of *promittere* 'put forth, promise', from *pro-* 'forward' + *mittere* 'send'.

promised land ▶ **noun** (**the Promised Land**) (in the Bible) the land of Canaan, that was promised to Abraham and his descendants (Gen. 12:7).
■(**the promised land**) a place or situation in which someone expects to find great happiness: *Italy is the promised land for any musician.*

promisee ▶ **noun** Law a person to whom a promise is made.

promising ▶ **adjective** showing signs of future success: *a promising film actor* | *a promising start to the season.*
– DERIVATIVES **promisingly** adverb.

promisor ▶ **noun** Law a person who makes a promise.

promissory /ˈprɒmɪs(ə)ri/ ▶ **adjective** chiefly Law conveying or implying a promise: *statements that are promissory in nature* | *promissory words.*
■archaic indicative of something to come; full of promise: *the glow of evening is* **promissory of** *the splendid days to come.*
– ORIGIN late Middle English: from medieval Latin *promissorius*, from *promiss-* 'promised', from the verb *promittere* (see **PROMISE**).

promissory note ▶ **noun** a signed document containing a written promise to pay a stated sum to a specified person or the bearer at a specified date or on demand.

prommer ▶ **noun** Brit. informal a person attending a promenade concert and choosing to stand in the area without seating; a promenader.

promo /ˈprəʊməʊ/ informal ▶ **noun** (pl. **-os**) a piece of publicity or advertising, especially in the form of a short film or video: *a trade promo* | [as modifier] *a promo video.*
– ORIGIN 1960s: abbreviation of **PROMOTION**.

promontory /ˈprɒm(ə)nt(ə)ri/ ▶ **noun** (pl. **-ies**) a point of high land that juts out into the sea or a large lake; a headland: *a rocky promontory.*
■Anatomy a prominence or protuberance on an organ or other structure in the body.
– ORIGIN mid 16th cent.: from Latin *promontorium*, variant (influenced by *mons, mont-* 'mountain') of *promunturium*.

promote ▶ **verb** [with obj.] **1** further the progress of (something, especially a cause, venture, or aim); support or actively encourage: *some regulation is still required to promote competition.*
■give publicity to (a product, organization, or venture) so as to increase sales or public awareness: *they are using famous personalities to promote the library nationally.* ■attempt to ensure the passing of (a private Act of Parliament): *the government of the day would not be promoting the bill.* ■ Chemistry act as a promoter of (a catalyst).
2 (often **be promoted**) advance or raise (someone) to a higher position or rank: *she was* **promoted to** *General Manager* | [with obj. and complement] *he was promoted Wing Commander while he was recovering from his injuries.*
■transfer (a sports team) to a higher division of a league: *they were promoted from the Third Division last season.* ■ Chess exchange (a pawn) for a more powerful piece of the same colour, typically a queen, as part of the move in which it reaches the opponent's end of the board. ■ Bridge enable (a relatively low card) to win a trick by playing off the higher ones first.
– DERIVATIVES **promotability** noun, **promotable** adjective, **promotive** adjective.
– ORIGIN late Middle English: from Latin *promot-* 'moved forward', from the verb *promovere*, from *pro-* 'forward, onward' + *movere* 'to move'.

promoter ▶ **noun** a person or thing that promotes something, in particular:
■a person or company that finances or organizes a sporting event or theatrical production: *a boxing promoter.* ■ (also **company promoter**) a person involved in setting up and funding a new company. ■ a supporter of a cause or aim: *Mitterrand was a fierce promoter of European integration.* ■ (also **promotor**) Chemistry an additive that increases the activity of a catalyst. ■ Biology a region of a DNA molecule which forms the site at which transcription of a gene starts.
– ORIGIN late Middle English: from Anglo-Norman French *promotour*, from medieval Latin *promotor* (see **PROMOTE**).

promotion ▶ **noun** [mass noun] **1** activity that supports or provides active encouragement for the furtherance of a cause, venture, or aim: *GPs have a vital role to play in health promotion.*
■the publicization of a product, organization, or venture so as to increase sales or public awareness. ■ [count noun] a publicity campaign for a particular product, organization, or venture: *the paper is reaping the rewards of a series of promotions.* ■ [often as modifier] (**promotions**) the activity or business of organizing such publicity or campaigns: *she's the promotions manager for EMI.* ■ [count noun] a sporting event, especially a series of boxing matches, staged for profit: *a boxing promotion.* ■ Chemistry the action of promoting a catalyst.
2 the action of raising someone to a higher position or rank or the fact of being so raised: *majors designated for* **promotion to** *lieutenant colonel* | [count noun] *a promotion to Divisional Sales Director.*
■the transfer of a sports team to a higher division of a league: *they won promotion last season.*
– ORIGIN late Middle English (in sense 2): via Old French from Latin *promotio(n-)*, from *promovere* 'move forward' (see **PROMOTE**).

promotional ▶ **adjective** of or relating to the publicizing of a product, organization, or venture so as to increase sales or public awareness: *she was on a promotional tour for her books.*

prompt ▶ **verb** [with obj.] **1** (of an event or fact) cause or bring about (an action or feeling): *the growing public expenditure bill has prompted a review of spending.*
■(**prompt someone to/to do something**) cause (someone) to take a course of action: *a demonstration by around 20,000 people prompted the government to step up security.*
2 assist or encourage (a hesitating speaker) to say something: [with direct speech] *'And the picture?' he prompted.*
■supply a forgotten word or line to (an actor) during the performance of a play. ■ Computing (of a computer) request input from (a user).
▶**noun 1** an act of assisting or encouraging a hesitating speaker: *with barely a prompt, Barbara talked on.*
■the word or phrase spoken as a reminder to an actor of a forgotten word or line. ■ Computing a word or symbol on a VDU screen to show that the system is waiting for input. ■ another term for **PROMPTER**.
2 the time limit for the payment of an account, stated on a prompt-note.
▶**adjective** done without delay; immediate: *the owner would have died but for the prompt action of two ambulancemen.*
■(of a person) acting without delay: *the fans were prompt and courteous in complying with police requests.* ■ (of goods) for immediate delivery and payment.
▶**adverb** Brit. exactly (with reference to a specified time): *the man set off at three-thirty prompt.*
– DERIVATIVES **promptitude** noun, **promptly** adverb, **promptness** noun.
– ORIGIN Middle English (as a verb): based on Old French *prompt* or Latin *promptus* 'brought to light', also 'prepared, ready', past participle of *promere* 'to produce', from *pro-* 'out, forth' + *emere* 'take'.

prompt book ▶ **noun** an annotated copy of a play for the use of a prompter during a performance.

prompt box ▶ **noun** an area in a theatre in which a prompter sits, located in front of the footlights beneath the stage.

prompter ▶ **noun** a person seated out of sight of the audience who supplies a forgotten word or line to an actor during the performance of a play.

prompting ▶ **noun** [mass noun] the action of saying something to persuade, encourage, or remind someone to do or say something: *after some prompting, the defendant gave the police his name.*

prompt-note ▶ **noun** a note sent to a customer as a reminder of payment due.

prompt side ▶ **noun** the side of the stage where the prompter sits, usually to the actor's left in the UK and to the actor's right in the US.

promulgate /ˈprɒm(ə)lgeɪt/ ▶ **verb** [with obj.] promote or make widely known (an idea or cause): *these*

p

objectives have to be promulgated within the organization.
■put (a law or decree) into effect by official proclamation: *in January 1852 the new Constitution was promulgated.*
– DERIVATIVES **promulgation** noun, **promulgator** noun.
– ORIGIN mid 16th cent.: from Latin *promulgat-* 'exposed to public view', from the verb *promulgare*, from *pro-* 'out, publicly' + *mulgere* 'cause to come forth' (literally 'to milk').

promulge /prəˈmʌldʒ/ ▶verb archaic variant of **PROMULGATE**.
– ORIGIN late 15th cent.: from Latin *promulgare*.

pronaos /prəʊˈneɪɒs/ ▶noun (pl. **pronaoi** /-ˈneɪɔɪ/) a vestibule at the front of a classical temple, enclosed by a portico and projecting side walls.
– ORIGIN via Latin from Greek *pronaos* 'hall of a temple', from *pro* 'before' + *naos* 'temple'.

pronate /ˈprəʊneɪt/ ▶verb [with obj.] technical put or hold (a hand, foot, or limb) with the palm or sole turned downwards: [as adj. **pronated**] *a pronated foot.* Compare with **SUPINATE**.
– DERIVATIVES **pronation** noun.
– ORIGIN mid 19th cent.: back-formation from *pronation*, based on Latin *pronus* 'leaning forward'.

pronator ▶noun Anatomy a muscle whose contraction produces or assists in the pronation of a limb or part of a limb.
■any of several specific muscles in the forearm.

prone ▶adjective **1** [predic.] (**prone to/to do something**) likely or liable to suffer from, do, or experience something, typically something regrettable or unwelcome: *years of logging had left the mountains prone to mudslides | he is prone to jump to conclusions.*
2 lying flat, especially face downwards or on the stomach: *I was lying prone on a foam mattress | a prone position.*
■technical denoting the position of the forearm with the palm of the hand facing downwards.
3 archaic with a downward slope or direction.
– DERIVATIVES **proneness** noun.
– ORIGIN late Middle English: from Latin *pronus* 'leaning forward', from *pro* 'forwards'.

prong ▶noun each of two or more projecting pointed parts at the end of a fork.
■a projecting part on various other devices: *a small rubber brush with large prongs.* ■ figurative each of the separate parts of an attack or operation: *the three main prongs of the new government's program.* ■ vulgar slang a man's penis.
▶verb [with obj.] pierce or stab with a fork: *he passed his fork to the right hand to prong the meat.*
– DERIVATIVES **pronged** adjective [in combination] *a three-pronged attack.*
– ORIGIN late 15th cent. (denoting a forked implement): perhaps related to Middle Low German *prange* 'pinching instrument'. The verb dates from the mid 19th cent.

pronghorn (also **prong-horned antelope**) ▶noun a deer-like North American mammal with a stocky body, long slim legs, and black horns that are shed and regrown annually.
• *Antilocapra americana*, the only member of the family Antilocapridae.

pronk ▶verb [no obj.] (of a springbok or other antelope) leap in the air with an arched back and stiff legs, typically as a form of display or when threatened.
– ORIGIN late 19th cent.: from Afrikaans, literally, 'show off', from Dutch *pronken* 'to strut'.

pronominal /prəʊˈnɒmɪn(ə)l/ ▶adjective of, relating to, or serving as a pronoun: *a pronominal form.*
– DERIVATIVES **pronominalization** (also **-isation**) noun, **pronominalize** (also **-ise**) verb, **pronominally** adverb.
– ORIGIN mid 17th cent.: from late Latin *pronominalis* 'belonging to a pronoun', from Latin *pronomen* (see **PRONOUN**).

pronoun ▶noun a word that can function as a noun phrase used by itself and that refers either to the participants in the discourse (e.g. *I, you*) or to someone or something mentioned elsewhere in the discourse (e.g. *she, it, this*).
– ORIGIN late Middle English: from **PRO-**[1] 'on behalf of', + **NOUN**, suggested by French *pronom*, Latin *pronomen* (from *pro-* 'for, in place of' + *nomen* 'name').

pronounce ▶verb [with obj.] **1** make the sound of (a word or part of a word), typically in the correct or a particular way: *Gerry pronounced the hero's name 'Cahoolin' | a refugee whose name no one could pronounce.*
2 declare or announce, typically formally or solemnly: *allow history to pronounce the verdict* | [with complement] *she was pronounced dead at the scene* | [with clause] *Asquith pronounced that this was the right course.*
■[no obj.] (**pronounce on**) pass judgement or make a decision on: *the Secretary of State will shortly pronounce on alternative measures.*
– DERIVATIVES **pronounceability** noun, **pronounceable** adjective, **pronouncement** noun, **pronouncer** noun.
– ORIGIN late Middle English: from Old French *pronuncier*, from Latin *pronuntiare*, from *pro-* 'out, forth' + *nuntiare* 'announce' (from *nuntius* 'messenger').

pronounced ▶adjective very noticeable or marked; conspicuous: *he had a pronounced squint.*
– DERIVATIVES **pronouncedly** adverb.

pronto ▶adverb informal promptly; quickly: *put it in the refrigerator, pronto.*
– ORIGIN early 20th cent.: from Spanish, from Latin *promptus* (see **PROMPT**).

Prontosil /ˈprɒntəsɪl/ ▶noun [mass noun] Medicine, historical the first sulphonamide antibiotic, a reddish-brown crystalline pigment formerly used to treat a range of infections.
– ORIGIN 1930s: from German, an invented proprietary name.

pronucleus /prəʊˈnjuːklɪəs/ ▶noun (pl. **pronuclei**) Biology either of a pair of gametic nuclei, in the stage following meiosis but before their fusion leads to the formation of the nucleus of the zygote.
– DERIVATIVES **pronuclear** adjective.

pronunciamento /prəˌnʌnsɪəˈmɛntəʊ/ ▶noun (pl. **-os**) (especially in Spain and Spanish-speaking countries) a political manifesto or proclamation.
– ORIGIN Spanish *pronunciamiento*, from *pronunciar* 'pronounce'.

pronunciation ▶noun [mass noun] the way in which a word is pronounced: *spelling does not determine pronunciation* | [count noun] *similar pronunciations are heard in Ulster.*
– ORIGIN late Middle English: from Latin *pronuntiatio(n-)*, from the verb *pronuntiare* (see **PRONOUNCE**).

USAGE The word **pronunciation** is often pronounced, by analogy with **pronounce**, as if the second syllable rhymed with **bounce**. This is not correct in standard English: the standard pronunciation, /prəˌnʌnsɪˈeɪʃ(ə)n/, has the second syllable rhyming with **dunce**. The correct spelling is **pronunciation**, never **pronounciation**.

pro-nuncio /prəʊˈnʌnsɪəʊ, -ʃɪəʊ/ ▶noun (pl. **-os**) a papal ambassador to a country that does not accord the Pope's ambassador automatic precedence over other ambassadors.
– ORIGIN 1960s: from Italian *pro-nunzio*, from *pro-* 'before' + *nunzio* 'nuncio'.

proof ▶noun **1** [mass noun] evidence or argument establishing or helping to establish a fact or the truth of a statement: *you will be asked to give proof of your identity* | [count noun] *this is not a proof for the existence of God.*
■Law the spoken or written evidence in a trial. ■ the action or process of establishing the truth of a statement: *it shifts the onus of proof in convictions from the police to the public.* ■ [count noun] archaic a test or trial. ■ [count noun] a series of stages in the resolution of a mathematical or philosophical problem. ■ [count noun] Scots Law a trial or a civil case before a judge without a jury.
2 a trial print of something, in particular:
■Printing a trial impression of a page, taken from type or film and used for making corrections before final printing. ■ a trial photographic print made for initial selection. ■ each of a number of impressions from an engraved plate, especially (in commercial printing) of a limited number before the ordinary issue is printed and before an inscription or signature is added. ■ a specially struck specimen coin with a polished or frosted finish.
3 [mass noun] the strength of distilled alcoholic liquor, relative to proof spirit taken as a standard of 100: [in combination] *powerful 132-proof rum.*
▶adjective **1** able to withstand something damaging; resistant: *the marine battle armour was **proof against** most weapons* | [in combination] *the system comes with idiot-proof instructions.*
2 [attrib.] denoting a trial impression of a page or printed work: *a proof copy is sent up for checking.*
▶verb [with obj.] **1** make (fabric) waterproof: [as adj. **proofed**] *the flysheet is made from proofed nylon.*
2 make a proof of (a printed work, engraving, etc.): [as noun **proofing**] *proofing could be done on a low-cost printer.*
■proof-read (a text): *a book about dinosaurs was being proofed by the publisher.*
3 N. Amer. activate (yeast) by the addition of liquid.
■knead (dough) until light and smooth. ■ [no obj.] (of dough) prove: *shape into a baguette and let proof for a few minutes.*
– PHRASES **the proof of the pudding is in the eating** proverb the real value of something can be judged only from practical experience or results and not from appearance or theory.
– ORIGIN Middle English *preve*, from Old French *proeve*, from late Latin *proba*, from Latin *probare* 'to test, prove'. The change of vowel in late Middle English was due to the influence of **PROVE**. Current sense of the verb date from the late 19th cent.

proof positive ▶noun [mass noun] evidence taken to be final or absolute proof of the existence of something: *he still needs proof positive of her love.*

proof-read ▶verb [with obj.] read (printer's proofs or other written or printed material) and mark any errors.
– DERIVATIVES **proof-reader** noun.

proof sheet ▶noun Printing a page of proofed text; a proof.

proof spirit ▶noun [mass noun] a mixture of alcohol and water containing (in the UK) 57.1 per cent alcohol by volume or (in the US) 50 per cent alcohol by volume, used as a standard of strength of distilled alcoholic liquor.

proof-text ▶noun a passage of the Bible to which appeal is made in support of an argument or position in theology.

prop[1] ▶noun **1** a pole or beam used as a support or to keep something in position, typically one that is not an integral part of the thing supported: *he looked around for a prop or a wedge to pin the door open.*
■figurative a person or thing that is a major source of support or assistance: *the second institutional prop of conservative Spain was the army.* ■ Grammar a word used to fill a syntactic role without any specific meaning of its own, for example *it* in *it is raining.* ■ (also **prop forward**) Rugby a forward at either end of the front row of a scrum.
2 chiefly Austral. a sudden stop made by a horse when going at speed.
▶verb (**propped**, **propping**) **1** [with obj. and adverbial of place] position something underneath (someone or something) for support: *she propped her chin in the palm of her right hand.*
■position (someone or something) more or less upright by leaning them against something else: *a jug of milk with a note propped against it | she propped the picture up on the mantlepiece.* ■ use an object to keep (something) in position: *he found that the door to the office was **propped open**.*
2 [no obj.] chiefly Austral. (of an animal, especially a horse) come to a dead stop with the forelegs rigid.
– PHRASES **prop up the bar** informal spend a considerable time drinking in a public house.
– ORIGIN late Middle English: probably from Middle Dutch *proppe* 'support (for vines)'.
▶**prop someone/thing up** provide support or assistance for someone or something that would otherwise fail or decline: *the government spent £3 billion in an attempt to prop up the pound.*

prop[2] ▶noun (usu. **props**) a portable object other than furniture or costumes used on the set of a play or film.
■(**props**) [treated as sing.] informal, dated a property man or mistress.
– ORIGIN mid 19th cent.: abbreviation of **PROPERTY**.

prop[3] ▶noun informal an aircraft propeller.
– ORIGIN early 20th cent.: abbreviation.

prop. ▶abbreviation for ■ proposition. ■ proprietor.

propaedeutic /ˌprəʊpɪˈdjuːtɪk/ ▶adjective formal (of an area of study) serving as a preliminary instruction or as an introduction to further study.
– DERIVATIVES **propaedeutical** adjective.
– ORIGIN late 18th cent.: from **PRO-**[2] 'before' + Greek *paideutikos* 'of or for teaching', suggested by Greek *propaideuein* 'teach beforehand'.

p

propaganda ▶**noun 1** [mass noun] chiefly derogatory information, especially of a biased or misleading nature, used to promote or publicize a particular political cause or point of view: *he was charged with distributing enemy propaganda.*
■the dissemination of such information as a political strategy: *the party's leaders believed that a long period of education and propaganda would be necessary .*
2 (**Propaganda**) a committee of cardinals of the Roman Catholic Church responsible for foreign missions, founded in 1622 by Pope Gregory XV.
– ORIGIN Italian, from modern Latin *congregatio de propaganda fide* 'congregation for propagation of the faith' (see sense 2). Sense 1 dates from the early 20th cent.

propagandist chiefly derogatory ▶**noun** a person who promotes or publicizes a particular organization or cause: *a highly persuasive political propagandist.*
▶**adjective** consisting of or spreading propaganda: *propagandist films.*
– DERIVATIVES **propagandism** noun, **propagandistic** adjective, **propagandistically** adverb.

propagandize (also **-ise**) ▶**verb** [no obj.] chiefly derogatory promote or publicize a particular cause, organization, or view, especially in a biased or misleading way: *abolitionist leaders had not specifically* ***propagandized for*** *emancipation.*
■[with obj.] (often **be propagandized**) attempt to influence (someone) in such a way: *people who have to be emotionalized and propagandized by logical arguments.*

propagate ▶**verb** [with obj.] **1** breed specimens of (a plant, animal, etc.) by natural processes from the parent stock: *try propagating your own house plants from cuttings.*
■[no obj.] (of a plant, animal, etc.) reproduce in such a way: *the plant propagates freely from stem cuttings.* ■cause (something) to increase in number or amount: *operational error includes those errors propagated during the digitizing process.*
2 spread and promote (an idea, theory, knowledge, etc.) widely: *the French propagated the idea that the English were violent and gluttonous drunkards.*
3 [with obj. and adverbial of direction] transmit (motion, light, sound, etc.) in a particular direction or through a medium: *electromagnetic effects can be propagated at a finite velocity only through material substances* | [as adj. **propagated**] *a propagated electrical signal.*
■[no obj.] (of motion, light, sound, etc.) be transmitted or travel in such a way: *a hydraulic fracture is generally expected to propagate in a vertical plane.*
– DERIVATIVES **propagation** noun, **propagative** adjective.
– ORIGIN late Middle English: from Latin *propagat-* 'multiplied from layers or shoots', from the verb *propagare*; related to *propago* 'young shoot' (from a base meaning 'fix').

propagator ▶**noun 1** a covered, typically electrically heated, container filled with earth or compost, used for germinating or raising seedlings.
2 a person who spreads and promotes an idea, theory, or branch of knowledge: *a propagator of the doctrine.*

propagule /ˈprɒpəɡjuːl/ ▶**noun** Botany a vegetative structure that can become detached from a plant and give rise to a new plant, e.g. a bud, sucker, or spore.
– ORIGIN mid 19th cent.: from modern Latin *propagulum* 'small shoot', diminutive of *propago* 'shoot, runner'.

propane /ˈprəʊpeɪn/ ▶**noun** [mass noun] Chemistry a flammable hydrocarbon gas of the alkane series, present in natural gas and used as bottled fuel.
●Chem. formula: C_3H_8.
– ORIGIN mid 19th cent.: from **PROPIONIC ACID** + **-ANE**[2].

propanoic acid /ˌprəʊpəˈnəʊɪk/ ▶**noun** Chemistry another term for **PROPIONIC ACID**.
– DERIVATIVES **propanoate** /prəˈpanəʊeɪt/ noun.

propanol /ˈprəʊpənɒl/ ▶**noun** [mass noun] Chemistry each of two isomeric liquid alcohols used as solvents; propyl alcohol.
●Chem. formula: $CH_3CH_2CH_2OH$ (**1-propanol**, **propan-1-ol**) and $CH_3CH(OH)CH_3$ (**2-propanol**, **propan-2-ol**).
– ORIGIN late 19th cent.: from **PROPANE** + **-OL**.

propanone /ˈprəʊpənəʊn/ ▶**noun** Chemistry another term for **ACETONE**.

propel ▶**verb** (**propelled**, **propelling**) [with obj.] drive, push, or cause to move in a particular direction, typically forwards: *the boat is propelled by using a very long paddle* | [as adj., in combination **-propelled**] *a rocket-propelled grenade launcher.*
■[with obj. and adverbial of direction] figurative spur or drive into a particular situation: *fear propelled her out of her stillness.*
– ORIGIN late Middle English (in the sense 'expel, drive out'): from Latin *propellere*, from *pro-* 'forward' + *pellere* 'to drive'.

propellant ▶**noun** a thing or substance that causes something to move or be driven forwards or outwards, in particular:
■an inert fluid, liquefied under pressure, in which the active contents of an aerosol are dispersed. ■an explosive that fires bullets from a firearm. ■a substance used as a reagent in a rocket engine to provide thrust.
▶**adjective** another term for **PROPELLENT**.
– ORIGIN mid 17th cent.: originally from Latin *propellent-* 'driving ahead (of oneself)', from the verb *propellere*, later from **PROPEL**.

propellent ▶**adjective** capable of driving, pushing, or moving something in a particular direction: *propellent gases.*

propeller ▶**noun** a mechanical device for propelling a boat or aircraft, consisting of a revolving shaft with two or more broad, angled blades attached to it.

propeller-head ▶**noun** informal a person who has an obsessive interest in computers or technology.
– ORIGIN 1980s: probably with reference to a beanie hat with a propeller on top, popularized by science-fiction enthusiasts.

propeller shaft ▶**noun** a shaft transmitting power from an engine to a propeller or to the wheels of a motor vehicle.

propeller turbine ▶**noun** another term for **TURBOPROP**.

propelling pencil ▶**noun** a pencil with a plastic or metal case and a thin replaceable lead that may be extended as the point is worn away by twisting the outer casing.

propene /ˈprəʊpiːn/ ▶**noun** Chemistry another term for **PROPYLENE**.
– ORIGIN mid 19th cent.: blend of **PROPANE** and **ALKENE**.

propenoic acid /ˌprəʊpəˈnəʊɪk/ ▶**noun** systematic chemical name for **ACRYLIC ACID**.
– DERIVATIVES **propenoate** noun.

propensity ▶**noun** (pl. **-ies**) an inclination or natural tendency to behave in a particular way: *she has* ***a propensity for*** *breaking plates* | [with infinitive] *their innate propensity to attack one another.*
– ORIGIN late 16th cent.: from archaic *propense* (from Latin *propensus* 'inclined', past participle of *propendere*, from *pro-* 'forward, down' + *pendere* 'hang') + **-ITY**.

proper ▶**adjective 1** [attrib.] truly what something is said or regarded to be; genuine: *she's never had a proper job* | *a proper meal.*
■[postpositive] strictly so called; in its true form: *after this event, three countries will progress to the World Cup proper.* ■informal, chiefly Brit. used as an intensifier, especially in derogatory contexts: *a* ***proper little*** *do-gooder, aren't I?*
2 [attrib.] of the required type; suitable or appropriate: *an artist needs the proper tools.*
■according to what is correct or prescribed for a particular situation or thing: *they had not followed the proper procedures.* ■according to or respecting recognized social standards or conventions; respectable, especially excessively so: *her parents' view of what was* ***proper for*** *a well-bred girl* | *a very prim and proper Swiss lady.*
3 [predic.] (**proper to**) belonging or relating exclusively or distinctively to; particular to: *the two elephant types proper to Africa and to southern Asia.*
■(of a psalm, lesson, prayer, etc.) appointed for a particular day, occasion, or season. ■archaic belonging to oneself or itself; own: *to judge with my proper eyes.*
4 [usu. postpositive] Heraldry in the natural colours.
5 archaic or dialect (of a person) good-looking: *he is a proper youth!*
6 Mathematics denoting a subset or subgroup that does not constitute the entire set or group, especially one that has more than one element.
▶**adverb** Brit. informal or dialect satisfactorily or correctly: *my eyes were all blurry and I couldn't see proper.*
■thoroughly: *he blotted his copybook* ***good and proper.***
▶**noun** the part of a church service that varies with the season or feast.
– DERIVATIVES **properness** noun.
– ORIGIN Middle English: from Old French *propre*, from Latin *proprius* 'one's own, special'.

properdin /prəʊˈpəːdɪn/ ▶**noun** [mass noun] Biochemistry a protein present in the blood, involved in the body's response to certain kinds of infection.
– ORIGIN 1950s: from **PRO-**[2] 'before' + Latin *perdere* 'destroy' + **-IN**[1].

proper fraction ▶**noun** a fraction that is less than one, with the numerator less than the denominator.

properly ▶**adverb 1** correctly or satisfactorily: *ensuring the work is carried out properly* | *a properly drafted agreement.*
■appropriately for the circumstances; suitably; respectably: *I'm trying to get my mother to behave properly.* ■[sentence adverb] in the strict sense; exactly: *algebra is,* ***properly speaking****, the analysis of equations.*
2 [usu. as submodifier] informal, chiefly Brit. thoroughly; completely: *on the first day she felt properly well, Millie sat out on the front steps.*

proper motion ▶**noun** [mass noun] Astronomy the part of the apparent motion of a fixed star that is due to its actual movement in space relative to the sun.

proper noun (also **proper name**) ▶**noun** a name used for an individual person, place, or organization, spelled with an initial capital letter, e.g. *Jane*, *London*, and *Oxfam*. Often contrasted with **COMMON NOUN**.

propertied ▶**adjective** (of a person or group) owning property and land, especially in large amounts: *a propertied country gentleman.*

Propertius /prəˈpəːʃəs/, Sextus (*c.*50–*c.*16 BC), Roman poet. His four books of elegies are largely concerned with his love affair with a woman whom he called Cynthia.

property ▶**noun** (pl. **-ies**) **1** [mass noun] a thing or things belonging to someone; possessions collectively: *she wanted Oliver and his property out of her flat* | *the stolen property was not recovered.*
■a building or buildings and the land belonging to it or them: *he's expanding now, buying property* | [count noun] *the renovation of council properties.* ■(**properties**) shares or investments in property. ■Law the right to the possession, use, or disposal of something; ownership: *rights of property.* ■old-fashioned term for **PROP**[2].
2 an attribute, quality, or characteristic of something: *the property of heat to expand metal at uniform rates.*
– ORIGIN Middle English: from an Anglo-Norman French variant of Old French *propriete*, from Latin *proprietas*, from *proprius* 'one's own, particular' (see **PROPER**).

property man ▶**noun** dated a man in charge of theatrical props.

property mistress ▶**noun** dated a woman in charge of theatrical props.

property qualification ▶**noun** chiefly historical a qualification for office or for the exercise of a right, especially the right to vote, based on the ownership of property.

prop forward ▶**noun** see **PROP**[1] (sense 1).

prophage /ˈprəʊfeɪdʒ/ ▶**noun** Microbiology the genetic material of a bacteriophage, incorporated into the genome of a bacterium and able to produce phages if specifically activated.
– ORIGIN 1950s: from **PRO-**[2] 'before' + **PHAGE**.

prophase ▶**noun** [mass noun] Biology the first stage of cell division, before metaphase, during which the chromosomes become visible as paired chromatids and the nuclear envelope disappears. The first prophase of meiosis includes the reduction division.
– ORIGIN late 19th cent.: from **PRO-**[2] 'before' + **PHASE**.

prophecy /ˈprɒfɪsi/ ▶**noun** (pl. **-ies**) a prediction of what will happen in the future: *a bleak prophecy of war and ruin.*
■[mass noun] the faculty, function, or practice of prophesying: *the gift of prophecy.*
– ORIGIN Middle English: from Old French *profecie*, via late Latin from Greek *prophēteia*, from *prophētēs* (see **PROPHET**).

prophesy /ˈprɒfɪsʌɪ/ ▶**verb** (**-ies**, **-ied**) [with obj.] say that (a specified thing) will happen in the future: *Jacques was prophesying a bumper harvest* | [with clause]

the papers prophesied that he would resign after the weekend.
■[no obj.] speak or write by divine inspiration; act as a prophet: *when a man prophesies, it is because the Spirit of the Lord comes upon him.*
– DERIVATIVES **prophesier** noun.
– ORIGIN Middle English: from Old French *profecier*, from *profecie* (see **PROPHECY**). The differentiation of the spellings *prophesy* and *prophecy* as verb and noun was not established until after 1700.

prophet ▶ **noun 1** a person regarded as an inspired teacher or proclaimer of the will of God: *the Old Testament prophet, Jeremiah.*
■(**the Prophet**) (among Muslims) Muhammad. ■ (**the Prophet**) (among Mormons) Joseph Smith or one of his successors. ■ a person who advocates or speaks in a visionary way about a new belief, cause, or theory: *he was a prophet of revolutionary socialism.* ■ a person who predicts, or claims to be able to predict, what will happen in the future: *the prime minister ignored the **prophets of** financial **doom**.*
2 (**the Prophets**) the prophetic writings of the Old Testament or Hebrew scriptures, in particular:
■(in Christian use) the books of Isaiah, Jeremiah, Ezekiel, Daniel, and the twelve minor prophets. ■ (in Jewish use) one of the three canonical divisions of the Hebrew Bible, distinguished from the Law and the Hagiographa, and comprising the books of Joshua, Judges, Samuel, Kings, Jeremiah, Ezekiel, Isaiah, and the twelve minor prophets.
– PHRASES **a prophet is not without honour save in his own country** proverb a person's gifts and talents are rarely appreciated by those close to him. [ORIGIN: with biblical allusion to Matt. 13:57.]
– DERIVATIVES **prophethood** noun.
– ORIGIN Middle English: from Old French *prophete*, via Latin from Greek *prophētēs* 'spokesman', from *pro* 'before' + *phētēs* 'speaker' (from *phēnai* 'speak').

prophetess ▶ **noun** a female prophet.

prophetic /prəˈfɛtɪk/ ▶ **adjective 1** accurately describing or predicting what will happen in the future: *his warnings proved prophetic.*
2 of, relating to, or characteristic of a prophet or prophecy: *the prophetic books of the Old Testament.*
– DERIVATIVES **prophetical** adjective, **prophetically** adverb.
– ORIGIN late 15th cent.: from French *prophétique* or late Latin *propheticus*, from Greek *prophētikos* 'predicting' (see **PROPHET**).

prophylactic /ˌprɒfɪˈlaktɪk/ ▶ **adjective** intended to prevent disease: *prophylactic measures.*
▶ **noun** a medicine or course of action used to prevent disease: *I took malaria prophylactics.*
■chiefly N. Amer. a condom.
– DERIVATIVES **prophylactically** adverb.
– ORIGIN late 16th cent.: from French *prophylactique*, from Greek *prophulaktikos*, from *pro* 'before' + *phulassein* 'to guard'.

prophylaxis /ˌprɒfɪˈlaksɪs/ ▶ **noun** [mass noun] action taken to prevent disease, especially by specified means or against a specified disease: *the treatment and prophylaxis of angina pectoris.*
– ORIGIN mid 19th cent.: modern Latin, from **PRO-**[2] 'before' + Greek *phulaxis* 'act of guarding'.

propinquity /prəˈpɪŋkwɪti/ ▶ **noun** [mass noun] **1** the state of being close to someone or something; proximity: *he kept his distance as though afraid propinquity might lead him into temptation.*
2 technical close kinship.
– ORIGIN late Middle English: from Old French *propinquité*, from Latin *propinquitas*, from *propinquus* 'near', from *prope* 'near to'.

propionibacterium /ˌprəʊpɪˌɒnɪbakˈtɪərɪəm/ ▶ **noun** (pl. **propionibacteria** /-rɪə/) a bacterium which metabolizes carbohydrate, some kinds being involved in the fermentation of dairy products and the aetiology of acne.
● Genus *Propionibacterium*; Gram-positive rods.
– ORIGIN modern Latin, from *propionic* (see **PROPIONIC ACID**) + **BACTERIUM**.

propionic acid /ˌprəʊpɪˈɒnɪk/ ▶ **noun** [mass noun] Chemistry a colourless pungent liquid organic acid produced in some forms of fermentation and used for inhibiting the growth of mould in bread.
● Alternative name: **propanoic acid**; chem. formula: C_2H_5COOH.
– DERIVATIVES **propionate** /ˈprəʊpɪəneɪt/ noun.
– ORIGIN mid 19th cent.: *propionic* from French *propionique*, from Greek *pro* 'before' + *piōn* 'fat', it being the first member of the fatty acid series to form fats.

propitiate /prəˈpɪʃɪeɪt/ ▶ **verb** [with obj.] win or regain the favour of (a god, spirit, or person) by doing something that pleases them: *the pagans thought it was important to propitiate the gods with sacrifices.*
– DERIVATIVES **propitiator** noun, **propitiatory** adjective.
– ORIGIN late 16th cent.: from Latin *propitiat-* 'made favourable', from the verb *propitiare*, from *propitius* 'favourable, gracious' (see **PROPITIOUS**).

propitiation ▶ **noun** [mass noun] the action of propitiating or appeasing a god, spirit, or person: *he lifted his hands in propitiation.*
■atonement, especially that of Christ.
– ORIGIN late Middle English: from late Latin *propitiatio(n-)*, from the verb *propitiare* (see **PROPITIATE**).

propitious /prəˈpɪʃəs/ ▶ **adjective** giving or indicating a good chance of success; favourable: *the timing for such a meeting seemed propitious.*
■archaic favourably disposed towards someone: *there were points on which they did not agree, moments in which she did not seem propitious.*
– DERIVATIVES **propitiously** adverb, **propitiousness** noun.
– ORIGIN late Middle English: from Old French *propicieus* or Latin *propitius* 'favourable, gracious'.

prop jet ▶ **noun** a turboprop aircraft or engine.

propolis /ˈprɒp(ə)lɪs/ ▶ **noun** [mass noun] a red or brown resinous substance collected by honeybees from tree buds, used by them to fill crevices and to fix and varnish honeycombs.
– ORIGIN early 17th cent.: via Latin from Greek *propolis* 'suburb', also 'bee glue', from *pro* 'before' + *polis* 'city'.

proponent /prəˈpəʊnənt/ ▶ **noun** a person who advocates a theory, proposal, or project: *a collection of essays by both critics and proponents of graphology.*
– ORIGIN late 16th cent.: from Latin *proponent-* 'putting forth', from the verb *proponere* (see **PROPOUND**).

Propontis /prəˈpɒntɪs/ ancient name for the Sea of Marmara (see **MARMARA, SEA OF**).

proportion ▶ **noun** a part, share, or number considered in comparative relation to a whole: *the proportion of greenhouse gases in the atmosphere is rising.*
■the relationship of one thing to another in terms of quantity, size, or number; the ratio: *the **proportion of** examination **to** coursework | the bleach can be diluted with water in the proportion one part bleach to ten parts water.* ■ (**proportions**) the comparative measurements or size of different parts of a whole: *the view of what constitutes perfect bodily proportions changes from one generation to the next.* ■ (**proportions**) dimensions; size: *the room, despite its ample proportions, seemed too small for him.* ■ [mass noun] the correct, attractive, or ideal relationship in size or shape between one thing and another or between the parts of a whole: *perceptions of colour, form, harmony, and proportion.*
▶ **verb** [with obj.] formal adjust or regulate (something) so that it has a particular or suitable relationship to something else: *a life after death in which happiness can be **proportioned to** virtue.*
– PHRASES **in proportion** according to a particular relationship in size, amount, or degree: *the pension was docked **in proportion to** earnings.* ■ in comparison with; in relation to: *the cuckoo's eggs are unusually small **in proportion to** its size.* ■ in the correct or appropriate relation to the size, shape, or position of other things: *her figure was completely in proportion.* ■ correctly or realistically regarded in terms of relative importance or seriousness: *the problem of hooliganism has to be **kept in proportion**.* **out of proportion** in the wrong relation to the size, shape, or position of other things: *the sculpture seemed **out of proportion to** its surroundings.* ■ greater or more serious than is necessary or appropriate: *the award was **out of all proportion to** the alleged libel.* ■ wrongly or unrealistically regarded in terms of relative importance or seriousness. **sense of proportion** the ability to judge the relative importance or seriousness of things.
– DERIVATIVES **proportionless** adjective.
– ORIGIN late Middle English: from Old French, from Latin *proportio(n-)*, from *pro portione* 'in respect of (its or a person's) share'.

proportionable ▶ **adjective** archaic term for **PROPORTIONAL**.
– DERIVATIVES **proportionably** adverb.

proportional ▶ **adjective** corresponding in size or amount to something else: *the punishment should be **proportional to** the crime.*
■Mathematics (of a variable quantity) having a constant ratio to another quantity.
– DERIVATIVES **proportionality** noun, **proportionally** adverb.
– ORIGIN late Middle English: from late Latin *proportionalis*, from *proportio(n-)* (see **PROPORTION**).

proportional counter ▶ **noun** Physics an ionization chamber in which the operating voltage is large enough to produce amplification but not so large that the output pulse ceases to be proportional to the initial ionization.

proportional representation (abbrev.: **PR**) ▶ **noun** [mass noun] an electoral system in which parties gain seats in proportion to the number of votes cast for them.

proportionate ▶ **adjective** another term for **PROPORTIONAL**.
– DERIVATIVES **proportionately** adverb.

proportioned ▶ **adjective** [with submodifier] having dimensions or a comparative relationship of parts of a specified type: *she was tall and perfectly proportioned.*

proposal ▶ **noun 1** a plan or suggestion, especially a formal or written one, put forward for consideration or discussion by others: *a set of **proposals for** a major new high-speed rail link.*
■the action of putting forward such a plan or suggestion: *the proposal of a flexible school-leaving age.*
2 an offer of marriage.

propose ▶ **verb 1** [with obj.] put forward (an idea or plan) for consideration or discussion by others: *he proposed a new nine-point peace plan* | [with infinitive] *he proposed to attend the meeting* | [with clause] *I proposed that the government should retain a 51 per cent stake in the company.*
■nominate (someone) for an elected office or as a member of a society: *Roy Thomson was proposed as chairman.* ■ put forward (a motion) to a legislature or committee: *the government put its slim majority to the test by proposing a vote of confidence.*
2 [no obj.] make an offer of marriage to someone: *I have already **proposed to** Sarah.*
– PHRASES **propose marriage** make an offer of marriage to someone. **propose a toast** (or **propose someone's health**) ask a group of people at a social occasion to drink to the health and happiness of a specified person: *the Lord Mayor **proposed a toast to** the Queen.*
– DERIVATIVES **proposer** noun.
– ORIGIN Middle English: from Old French *proposer*, from Latin *proponere* (see **PROPONENT**), but influenced by Latin *propositus* 'put or set forth' and Old French *poser* 'to place'.

proposition ▶ **noun 1** a statement or assertion that expresses a judgement or opinion: *the proposition that high taxation is undesirable.*
■Logic a statement that expresses a concept that can be true or false. ■ Mathematics a formal statement of a theorem or problem, typically including the demonstration.
2 a suggested scheme or plan of action, especially in a business context: *he put a detailed investment proposition to me.*
■US a constitutional proposal; a bill. ■ informal an offer of sexual intercourse made to a person with whom one is not sexually involved, especially one that is made in an unsubtle or offensive way.
3 [with adj.] a project, task, or idea considered in terms of its likely success or difficulty, especially in a commercial context: *a paper that has lost half its readers is unlikely to be an attractive proposition.*
■a person considered in terms of the likely success or difficulty of one's dealings with them: *Brian's a far better bloke as a long-term proposition.*
▶ **verb** [with obj.] informal make a suggestion of sexual intercourse to (someone with whom one is not sexually involved), especially in an unsubtle or offensive way: *she had been propositioned at the party by a subeditor with bad breath.*
■make an offer or suggestion to (someone): *I was propositioned by the editor about becoming film critic of the paper.*
– DERIVATIVES **propositional** adjective (chiefly Logic).
– ORIGIN Middle English: from Old French, from Latin *propositio(n-)*, from the verb *proponere* (see **PROPOUND**). The verb dates from the 1920s.

propositional attitude ▶ **noun** Philosophy the relation that a person has with a proposition, such as having an opinion concerning it or responding emotionally to it.

propositional calculus ▶ noun [mass noun] the branch of symbolic logic that deals with propositions and the relations between them, without examination of their content.

propound /prə'paʊnd/ ▶ verb [with obj.] put forward (an idea, theory, or point of view) for consideration by others: *he began to propound the idea of a 'social monarchy' as an alternative to Franco*.
– DERIVATIVES **propounder** noun.
– ORIGIN mid 16th cent.: alteration of archaic *propone*, from Latin *proponere* 'set forth', from *pro-* 'forward' + *ponere* 'put'. The addition of the final *-d* can be compared with that in *expound* and *compound*.

propoxyphene /prəʊ'pɒksɪfiːn/ ▶ noun [mass noun] Medicine a synthetic compound chemically related to methadone, used as a mild narcotic analgesic.
– ORIGIN 1950s: from **PROPYL** + **OXY-** + *-phene* (from **PHENYL**).

propranolol /prəʊ'pranəlɒl/ ▶ noun [mass noun] Medicine a synthetic compound which acts as a beta blocker and is used mainly in the treatment of cardiac arrhythmia.
● Chemical formula: $C_{16}H_{21}NO_2$
– ORIGIN 1960s: from *pro(pyl)* + *pr(op)anol*, with the reduplication of *-ol*.

proprietary ▶ adjective of or relating to an owner or ownership: *the company has a proprietary right to the property*.
■ (of a product) marketed under and protected by a registered trade name: *proprietary brands of insecticide*. ■ behaving as if one was the owner of someone or something: *he looked about him with a proprietary air*.
– ORIGIN late Middle English (as a noun denoting a member of a religious order who held property): from late Latin *proprietarius* 'proprietor', from *proprietas* (see **PROPERTY**).

proprietary name (also **proprietary term**) ▶ noun a name of a product or service registered by its owner as a trademark and not usable by others without permission.

proprietor ▶ noun the owner of a business.
■ a holder of property.
– DERIVATIVES **proprietorial** adjective, **proprietorially** adverb, **proprietorship** noun.

proprietress ▶ noun a female proprietor.

propriety ▶ noun (pl. **-ies**) [mass noun] the state or quality of conforming to conventionally accepted standards of behaviour or morals: *he always behaved with the utmost propriety*.
■ (**proprieties**) the details or rules of behaviour conventionally considered to be correct: *she's a great one for the proprieties*. ■ the condition of being right, appropriate, or fitting: *they questioned the propriety of certain investments made by the council*.
– ORIGIN late Middle English (in the sense 'peculiarity, essential quality'): from Old French *propriete*, from Latin *proprietas* (see **PROPERTY**).

proprioceptive /ˌprəʊprɪə(ʊ)'sɛptɪv/ ▶ adjective Physiology relating to stimuli that are produced and perceived within an organism, especially those connected with the position and movement of the body. Compare with **EXTEROCEPTIVE** and **INTEROCEPTIVE**.
– DERIVATIVES **proprioception** noun, **proprioceptively** adverb.
– ORIGIN early 20th cent.: from Latin *proprius* 'own' + **RECEPTIVE**.

proprioceptor /ˌprəʊprɪə(ʊ)'sɛptə/ ▶ noun Physiology a sensory receptor which receives stimuli from within the body, especially one that responds to position and movement.
– ORIGIN early 20th cent.: from Latin *proprius* 'own' + **RECEPTOR**.

propshaft ▶ noun a propeller shaft, especially of a motor vehicle.

proptosis /prɒp'təʊsɪs/ ▶ noun [mass noun] Medicine abnormal protrusion or displacement of an eye or other body part.
– ORIGIN late 17th cent.: via late Latin from Greek *proptōsis*, from *pro* 'before' + *piptein* 'to fall'.

propulsion ▶ noun [mass noun] the action of driving or pushing forward: *they dive and use their wings for propulsion under water*.
– DERIVATIVES **propulsive** adjective.
– ORIGIN early 17th cent. (in the sense 'expulsion'):

from medieval Latin *propulsio(n-)*, from Latin *propellere* 'drive before (oneself)'.

propulsor ▶ noun a ducted propeller which can be swivelled to give forward, upward, or downward flight to an airship.

prop wash ▶ noun a current of water or air created by the action of a propeller or rotor.

propyl /'prəʊpʌɪl, -pɪl/ ▶ noun [as modifier] Chemistry of or denoting the alkyl radical —C_3H_7, derived from propane. Compare with **ISOPROPYL**.

propyla plural form of **PROPYLON**.

propylaeum /ˌprɒpɪ'liːəm/ ▶ noun (pl. **propylaea** /-'liːə/) the structure forming the entrance to a temple.
■ (**the Propylaeum**) the entrance to the Acropolis at Athens.
– ORIGIN via Latin from Greek *propulaion*, neuter (used as a noun) of *propulaios* 'before the gate', from *pro* 'before' + *pulē* 'gate'.

propylene /'prəʊpɪliːn/ ▶ noun [mass noun] Chemistry a gaseous hydrocarbon of the alkene series, made by cracking alkanes.
● Alternative name: **propene**; chem. formula: C_3H_6.

propylene glycol ▶ noun [mass noun] Chemistry a liquid alcohol which is used as a solvent, in antifreeze, and in the food, plastics, and perfume industries.
● Chem. formula: $C_3H_6(OH)_2$: two isomers.

propylon /'prɒpɪlɒn/ ▶ noun (pl. **propylons** or **propyla** /-lə/) another term for **PROPYLAEUM**.
– ORIGIN mid 19th cent.: via Latin from Greek *propulon*, from *pro* 'before' + *pulē* 'gate'.

pro rata /prəʊ 'rɑːtə, 'reɪtə/ ▶ adjective proportional: *as the pound has fallen costs have risen on a pro rata basis*.
▶ adverb proportionally: *their fees will rise pro rata with salaries*.
– ORIGIN late 16th cent.: Latin, literally 'according to the rate'.

prorate /prəʊ'reɪt, 'prəʊ-/ ▶ verb [with obj.] (usu. **be prorated**) chiefly N. Amer. allocate, distribute, or assess pro rata: *bonuses are prorated over the life of a player's contract*.
– DERIVATIVES **proration** noun.

prorogue /prə'rəʊg/ ▶ verb (**prorogues**, **prorogued**, **proroguing**) [with obj.] discontinue a session of (a parliament or other legislative assembly) without dissolving it: *James prorogued this Parliament, never to call another one*.
■ [no obj.] (of such an assembly) be discontinued in this way: *the House was all set to prorogue*.
– DERIVATIVES **prorogation** /-rə'geɪʃ(ə)n/ noun.
– ORIGIN late Middle English: from Old French *proroger*, from Latin *prorogare* 'prolong, extend', from *pro-* 'in front of, publicly' + *rogare* 'ask'.

prosaic /prə(ʊ)'zeɪɪk/ ▶ adjective having the style or diction of prose; lacking poetic beauty: *prosaic language can't convey the experience*.
■ commonplace; unromantic: *the masses were too preoccupied by prosaic day-to-day concerns*.
– DERIVATIVES **prosaically** adverb, **prosaicness** noun.
– ORIGIN late 16th cent. (as a noun denoting a prose writer): from late Latin *prosaicus*, from Latin *prosa* 'straightforward (discourse)' (see **PROSE**). Current senses of the adjective date from the mid 18th cent.

prosaist /'prəʊzeɪɪst/ ▶ noun 1 a person who writes in prose.
2 a prosaic person.
– DERIVATIVES **prosaism** noun.
– ORIGIN early 19th cent.: from French *prosaïste*, from Latin *prosa* 'straightforward (discourse)' (see **PROSE**).

prosauropod /prəʊ'sɔːrəpɒd, -'saʊr-/ ▶ noun an elongated partly bipedal herbivorous dinosaur of the late Triassic and early Jurassic periods, related to the ancestors of sauropods.
● Infraorder Prosauropoda, suborder Sauropodomorpha, order Saurischia.
– ORIGIN 1950s: from **PRO-²** 'before in time' + **SAUROPOD**.

proscenium /prə(ʊ)'siːnɪəm/ ▶ noun (pl. **prosceniums** or **proscenia** /-nɪə/) the part of a theatre stage in front of the curtain.
■ short for **PROSCENIUM ARCH**. ■ the stage of an ancient theatre.
– ORIGIN early 17th cent.: via Latin from Greek *proskēnion*, from *pro* 'before' + *skēnē* 'stage'.

proscenium arch ▶ noun an arch framing the opening between the stage and the auditorium in some theatres.

prosciutto /prə'ʃuːtəʊ/ ▶ noun [mass noun] raw cured Italian ham, eaten especially in thin slices as an hors d'oeuvre.
– ORIGIN Italian.

proscribe ▶ verb [with obj.] forbid, especially by law: *strikes remained proscribed in the armed forces*.
■ denounce or condemn: *certain customary practices which the Catholic Church proscribed, such as polygyny*. ■ historical outlaw (someone).
– DERIVATIVES **proscription** noun, **proscriptive** adjective.
– ORIGIN late Middle English (in the sense 'to outlaw'): from Latin *proscribere*, from *pro-* 'in front of' + *scribere* 'write'.

> **USAGE** Proscribe does not have the same meaning as prescribe: see usage at **PRESCRIBE**.

prose ▶ noun [mass noun] **1** written or spoken language in its ordinary form, without metrical structure: *a short story in prose* | [as modifier] *a prose passage*.
■ [count noun] a passage of this, especially for translation into a foreign language. ■ figurative plain or dull writing, discourse, or expression: *closely typed in best office prose*.
2 another term for **SEQUENCE** (in sense 4).
▶ verb **1** [no obj.] talk tediously: *prosing on about female beauty*.
2 [with obj.] dated compose or convert in or into prose.
– DERIVATIVES **proser** noun.
– ORIGIN Middle English: via Old French from Latin *prosa* (*oratio*) 'straightforward (discourse)', feminine of *prosus*, earlier *prorsus* 'direct'.

prosector /prə(ʊ)'sɛktə/ ▶ noun chiefly N. Amer. a person who dissects dead bodies for examination or anatomical demonstration.
– ORIGIN mid 19th cent.: from late Latin, literally 'anatomist', based on Latin *secare* 'to cut', perhaps via French *prosecteur*.

prosecute ▶ verb [with obj.] **1** institute legal proceedings against (a person or organization): *they were prosecuted for obstructing the highway*.
■ institute legal proceedings in respect of (a claim or offence): *the state's attorney's office seemed to decide that this was a case worth prosecuting* | [no obj.] *the company didn't prosecute because of his age*. ■ [no obj.] (of a barrister or other lawyer) conduct the case against the party being accused or sued in a lawsuit: *Mr Antonis Georges, prosecuting, told the court they were specimen charges*.
2 continue with (a course of action) with a view to its completion: *a serious threat to the government's ability to prosecute the war*.
■ archaic carry on (a trade or pursuit): *waiting for permission to prosecute my craft*.
– DERIVATIVES **prosecutable** adjective.
– ORIGIN late Middle English (in sense 2): from Latin *prosecut-* 'pursued, accompanied', from the verb *prosequi*, from *pro-* 'onward' + *sequi* 'follow'.

prosecution ▶ noun [mass noun] **1** the institution and conducting of legal proceedings against someone in respect of a criminal charge: *the organizers are facing prosecution for noise nuisance* | [count noun] *they lacked the funds to embark on private prosecutions*.
■ (**the prosecution**) [treated as sing. or pl.] the party instituting or conducting legal proceedings against someone in a lawsuit: *the main witness for the prosecution*.
2 the continuation of a course of action with a view to its completion: *the BBC's prosecution of its commercial ends*.
– ORIGIN mid 16th cent. (in sense 2): from Old French, or from late Latin *prosecutio(n-)*, from *prosequi* 'pursue, accompany' (see **PROSECUTE**).

prosecutor ▶ noun a person, especially a public official, who institutes legal proceedings against someone.
■ a barrister or other lawyer who conducts the case against a defendant in a criminal court.
– DERIVATIVES **prosecutorial** adjective.

proselyte /'prɒsɪlʌɪt/ ▶ noun a person who has converted from one opinion, religion, or party to another, especially recently.
■ a Gentile who has converted to Judaism.
▶ verb US term for **PROSELYTIZE**.
– DERIVATIVES **proselytism** /-lɪtɪz(ə)m/ noun.
– ORIGIN late Middle English: via late Latin from

Greek *prosēluthos* 'stranger, convert', from *prosēluth-*, past stem of *proserkhesthai* 'approach'.

proselytize /ˈprɒsɪlɪtʌɪz/ (also **-ise**) ▶ **verb** [with obj.] convert or attempt to convert (someone) from one religion, belief, or opinion to another: *the programme did have a tremendous evangelical effect, proselytizing many* | [no obj.] *proselytizing for converts* | [as noun **proselytizing**] *no amount of proselytizing was going to change their minds.*
■advocate or promote (a belief or course of action): *Davis wanted to share his concept and proselytize his ideas.*
– DERIVATIVES **proselytizer** noun.

prosencephalon /ˌprɒsɛnˈsɛfəlɒn, -ˈkɛf-/ ▶ **noun** another term for **FOREBRAIN**.
– ORIGIN mid 19th cent.: from Greek *prosō* 'forwards' + *enkephalos* 'brain'.

prosenchyma /prɒˈsɛŋkɪmə/ ▶ **noun** [mass noun] Biology a plant tissue consisting of elongated cells with interpenetrating tapering ends, occurring especially in vascular tissue.
– DERIVATIVES **prosenchymatous** /ˌprɒsɛŋˈkɪmətəs/ adjective.
– ORIGIN mid 19th cent.: from Greek *pros* 'toward' + *enkhuma* 'infusion', on the pattern of *parenchyma*.

prose poem ▶ **noun** a piece of imaginative poetic writing in prose.
– DERIVATIVES **prose poetry** noun.

Proserpina /prəˈsəːpɪnə/ (also **Proserpine** /-pɪni/) Roman Mythology Roman name for **PERSEPHONE**.

pro shop ▶ **noun** a retail outlet at a golf club, typically run by the resident professional, where golfing equipment can be purchased or repaired.

prosimian /prəʊˈsɪmɪən/ Zoology ▶ **noun** a primitive primate of a group that includes the lemurs, lorises, bushbabies, and tarsiers.
● Suborder Prosimii, order Primates: several families.
▶**adjective** of or relating to the prosimians. Compare with **SIMIAN**.
– ORIGIN late 19th cent.: from **PRO-**[2] 'before' + **SIMIAN**.

prosit /ˈprəʊzɪt/ ▶ **exclamation** an expression used in drinking a person's health.
– ORIGIN German, from Latin, literally 'may it benefit'.

Prosobranchia /ˌprɒsə(ʊ)ˈbraŋkɪə/ Zoology a group of molluscs which includes the limpets, abalones, and many terrestrial and aquatic snails. They all have a shell, and many have an operculum.
● Subclass Prosobranchia, class Gastropoda.
– DERIVATIVES **prosobranch** /ˈprɒsəbraŋk/ noun.
– ORIGIN modern Latin (plural), from Greek *prosō* 'forwards' + *brankhia* 'gills'.

prosocial ▶ **adjective** Psychology relating to or denoting behaviour which is positive, helpful, and intended to promote social acceptance and friendship.

prosodic analysis /prəˈsɒdɪk/ ▶ **noun** [mass noun] Linguistics analysis of a language based on its patterns of stress and intonation in different contexts. In systemic grammar, prosodic analysis is regarded as an essential foundation for the analysis of syntax and meaning.

prosody /ˈprɒsədi/ ▶ **noun** [mass noun] the patterns of rhythm and sound used in poetry: *the translator is not obliged to reproduce the prosody of the original.*
■the theory or study of these patterns, or the rules governing them. ■the patterns of stress and intonation in a language: *the salience of prosody in child language acquisition* | [count noun] *early English prosodies.*
– DERIVATIVES **prosodic** adjective, **prosodist** noun.
– ORIGIN late 15th cent.: from Latin *prosodia* 'accent of a syllable', from Greek *prosōidia* 'song sung to music, tone of a syllable', from *pros* 'towards' + *ōidē* 'song'.

prosoma /prə(ʊ)ˈsəʊmə/ ▶ **noun** another term for **CEPHALOTHORAX**.
– ORIGIN late 19th cent.: from **PRO-**[2] 'before' + Greek *sōma* 'body'.

prosopagnosia /ˌprɒsə(ʊ)pagˈnəʊsɪə, -ˈnəʊzɪə/ ▶ **noun** [mass noun] Psychiatry an inability to recognize the faces of familiar people, typically as a result of damage to the brain.
– ORIGIN 1950s: modern Latin, from Greek *prosōpon* 'face' + *agnōsia* 'ignorance'.

prosopography /ˌprɒsə(ʊ)ˈpɒgrəfi/ ▶ **noun** (pl. **-ies**) a description of a person's appearance, personality, social and family connections, career, etc., or a collection of such descriptions.
■[mass noun] the study of such descriptions, especially in Roman history.
– DERIVATIVES **prosopographer** noun, **prosopographical** /-pəˈgrafɪk(ə)l/ adjective.
– ORIGIN 1920s: from modern Latin *prosopographia*, from Greek *prosōpon* 'face, person' + *-graphia* 'writing'.

prosopopoeia /ˌprɒsəpəˈpiːə/ ▶ **noun** [mass noun] **1** a figure of speech in which an abstract thing is personified.
2 a figure of speech in which an imagined or absent person or thing is represented as speaking.
– ORIGIN mid 16th cent.: via Latin from Greek *prosōpopoiia*, from *prosōpon* 'person' + *poiein* 'to make'.

prospect ▶ **noun** **1** [mass noun] the possibility or likelihood of some future event occurring: *there was no prospect of a reconciliation* | [count noun] *some training which offered a prospect of continuous employment.*
■[in sing.] a mental picture of a future or anticipated event: *this presents a disturbing prospect of one party government.* ■(usu. **prospects**) chances or opportunities for success or wealth: *the poor prospects for the steel industry.*
2 a person regarded as a potential customer or subscriber to something: *clients deemed likely prospects for active party membership.*
■a person regarded as likely to succeed, especially in a sporting event: *Norwich's unbeaten heavyweight prospect.* ■a place likely to yield mineral deposits.
3 an extensive view of landscape: *a viewpoint commanding a magnificent prospect of the estuary.*
▶**verb** [no obj.] search for mineral deposits in a place, especially by means of experimental drilling and excavation: *the company is also* **prospecting for** *gold.*
■(**prospect for**) figurative look out for; search for: *the responsibilities of salespeople to prospect for customers.*
– DERIVATIVES **prospectless** adjective, **prospector** noun.
– ORIGIN late Middle English (as a noun denoting the action of looking towards a distant object): from Latin *prospectus* 'view', from *prospicere* 'look forward', from *pro-* 'forward' + *specere* 'to look'. Early use, referring to a view of landscape, gave rise to the meaning 'mental picture' (mid 16th cent.), whence 'anticipated event'.

prospective ▶ **adjective** [attrib.] (of a person) expected or expecting to be something particular in the future: *she showed a prospective buyer around the house.*
■likely to happen at a future date; concerned with or applying to the future: *a meeting to discuss prospective changes in government legislation.*
– DERIVATIVES **prospectively** adverb, **prospectiveness** noun.
– ORIGIN late 16th cent. (in the sense 'looking forward, having foresight'): from obsolete French *prospectif, -ive* or late Latin *prospectivus*, from Latin *prospectus* 'view' (see **PROSPECT**).

prospectus ▶ **noun** (pl. **prospectuses**) a printed booklet advertising a school or university to potential parents or students or giving details of a share offer for the benefit of investors.
– ORIGIN mid 18th cent.: from Latin, literally 'view, prospect', from the verb *prospicere*, from *pro-* 'forward' + *specere* 'to look'.

prosper ▶ **verb** [no obj.] succeed in material terms; be financially successful: *his business prospered* | *the state plans to prosper from free trade with the United States.*
■flourish physically; grow strong and healthy: *areas where grey squirrels cannot prosper.* ■[with obj.] make successful: *God has wonderfully prospered this nation.*
– ORIGIN late Middle English: from Old French *prosperer*, from Latin *prosperare*, from *prosperus* 'doing well'.

prosperity ▶ **noun** [mass noun] the state of being prosperous: *a long period of prosperity.*
– ORIGIN Middle English: from Old French *prosperite*, from Latin *prosperitas*, from *prosperus* 'doing well'.

prosperous ▶ **adjective** successful in material terms; flourishing financially: *prosperous middle-class professionals.*
■bringing wealth and success: *we wish you a Merry Christmas and a prosperous New Year.*
– DERIVATIVES **prosperously** adverb, **prosperousness** noun.
– ORIGIN late Middle English: from Old French *prospereus*, from Latin *prosperus* 'doing well'.

Prost /prɒst/, Alain (b.1955), French motor-racing driver. He won the Formula One world championship in 1985, 1986, 1989, and 1993, after which he retired from racing.

prostacyclin /ˌprɒstəˈsʌɪklɪn/ ▶ **noun** [mass noun] Biochemistry a compound of the prostaglandin type produced in arterial walls, which functions as an anticoagulant and vasodilator.
– ORIGIN 1970s: from **PROSTAGLANDIN** + **CYCLIC** + **-IN**[1].

prostaglandin /ˌprɒstəˈglandɪn/ ▶ **noun** Biochemistry any of a group of compounds with varying hormone-like effects, notably the promotion of uterine contractions. They are cyclic fatty acids.
– ORIGIN 1930s: from **PROSTATE** + **GLAND**[1] + **-IN**[1].

prostate (also **prostate gland**) ▶ **noun** a gland surrounding the neck of the bladder in male mammals and releasing a fluid component of semen.
– DERIVATIVES **prostatic** adjective.
– ORIGIN mid 17th cent.: via French from modern Latin *prostata*, from Greek *prostatēs* 'one that stands before', from *pro* 'before' + *statos* 'standing'.

prostatectomy /ˌprɒstəˈtɛktəmi/ ▶ **noun** (pl. **-ies**) a surgical operation to remove all or part of the prostate gland.

prostate-specific antigen ▶ **noun** [mass noun] Medicine an antigenic enzyme released in the prostate and found in abnormally high concentrations in the blood of men with prostate cancer.

prostatitis /ˌprɒsteɪˈtʌɪtɪs/ ▶ **noun** [mass noun] Medicine inflammation of the prostate gland.

prosthesis /prɒsˈθiːsɪs, ˈprɒsθɪˌsɪs/ ▶ **noun** (pl. **prostheses** /-siːz/) **1** an artificial body part, such as a leg, a heart, or a breast implant: *his upper jaw was removed and a prosthesis was fitted.*
2 the addition of a letter or syllable at the beginning of a word, as in Spanish *escuela* derived from Latin *scola*.
– DERIVATIVES **prosthetic** /-ˈθɛtɪk/ adjective, **prosthetically** adverb.
– ORIGIN mid 16th cent. (in sense 2): via late Latin from Greek *prosthesis*, from *prostithenai*, from *pros* 'in addition' + *tithenai* 'to place'.

prosthetic group ▶ **noun** Biochemistry a non-protein group forming part of or combined with a protein.

prosthetics /prɒsˈθɛtɪks/ ▶ **plural noun** artificial body parts; prostheses.
■pieces of flexible material applied to actors' faces to transform their appearance. ■[treated as sing.] the branch of surgery concerned with the making and fitting of artificial body parts.

prosthetist /ˈprɒsθɪtɪst/ ▶ **noun** a specialist in prosthetics.

prosthodontics /ˌprɒsθəˈdɒntɪks/ ▶ **plural noun** [treated as sing.] the branch of dentistry concerned with the design, manufacture, and fitting of artificial replacements for teeth and other parts of the mouth.
– DERIVATIVES **prosthodontist** noun.
– ORIGIN 1940s: from **PROSTHESIS**, on the pattern of *orthodontics*.

prostitute ▶ **noun** a person, typically a woman, who engages in sexual activity for payment.
■figurative a person who misuses their talents or who sacrifices their self-respect for the sake of personal or financial gain: *the careerist political prostitutes.*
▶**verb** [with obj.] offer (someone, typically a woman) for sexual activity in exchange for payment: *although she was paid £15 to join a man at his table, she never* **prostituted herself**.
■figurative put (oneself or one's talents) to an unworthy or corrupt use or purpose for the sake of personal or financial gain: *his willingness to prostitute himself to the worst instincts of the electorate.*
– DERIVATIVES **prostitutor** noun.
– ORIGIN mid 16th cent. (as a verb): from Latin *prostitut-* 'exposed publicly, offered for sale', from the verb *prostituere*, from *pro-* 'before' + *statuere* 'set up, place'.

prostitution ▶ **noun** [mass noun] the practice or occupation of engaging in sexual activity with someone for payment.
■figurative the unworthy or corrupt use of one's talents for the sake of personal or financial gain.

prostrate ▶ **adjective** /ˈprɒstreɪt/ lying stretched out on the ground with one's face downwards.
■[predic.] figurative completely overcome or helpless, especially with distress or exhaustion: *his wife was*

prostrate with shock. ■ Botany growing along the ground.

▶ **verb** /prɒˈstreɪt/ [with obj.] (**prostrate oneself**) throw oneself flat on the ground so as to be lying face downwards, especially in reverence or submission: *she prostrated herself on the bare floor of the church.*
■ (often **be prostrated**) (of distress, exhaustion, or illness) reduce (someone) to extreme physical weakness: *she was so prostrated by migraine that she could scarcely totter up the stairs to bed.*

– DERIVATIVES **prostration** noun.

– ORIGIN Middle English: from Latin *prostratus* 'thrown down', past participle of *prosternere*, from *pro-* 'before' + *sternere* 'lay flat'.

prostyle /ˈprəʊstʌɪl/ ▶ **noun** Architecture a portico with a maximum of four columns.

– ORIGIN late 17th cent.: from Latin *prostylos* '(building) having pillars in front', from Greek *pro* 'before' + *stulos* 'column'.

prosy /ˈprəʊzi/ ▶ **adjective** (**prosier**, **prosiest**) (especially of speech or writing) showing no imagination; commonplace or dull.

– DERIVATIVES **prosily** adverb, **prosiness** noun.

prot- ▶ **combining form** variant spelling of **PROTO-** before a vowel (as in *protamine*).

protactinium /ˌprəʊtakˈtɪnɪəm/ ▶ **noun** [mass noun] the chemical element of atomic number 91, a radioactive metal of the actinide series, occurring in small amounts as a product of the natural decay of uranium. (Symbol: **Pa**)

– ORIGIN early 20th cent.: from **PROTO-** 'original, earlier' + **ACTINIUM**, so named because one of its isotopes decays to form actinium.

protagonist ▶ **noun** the leading character or one of the major characters in a drama, film, novel, or other fictional text.
■ the main figure or one of the most prominent figures in a real situation: *in this colonial struggle the main protagonists were Great Britain and France.* ■ an advocate or champion of a particular cause or idea: *a strenuous protagonist of the new agricultural policy.*

– ORIGIN late 17th cent.: from Greek *prōtagōnistēs*, from *prōtos* 'first in importance' + *agōnistēs* 'actor'.

USAGE The first sense of **protagonist**, as originally used in connection with ancient Greek drama, is 'the main character in a play'. In the early 20th century a new sense arose meaning 'a supporter of a cause', as in *a strenuous **protagonist** of the new agricultural policy.* This new sense probably arose by analogy with **antagonist**, the **pro-** in **protagonist** being interpreted as meaning 'in favour of'. In fact, the **prot-** in **protagonist** derives from the Greek root meaning 'first'. For this reason some traditionalists regard the newer use as incorrect, although it is now widely accepted in standard English.

protamine /ˈprəʊtəmiːn/ ▶ **noun** Biochemistry any of a group of simple proteins found combined with nucleic acids, especially in fish sperm.

– ORIGIN late 19th cent.: from **PROTO-** 'original' + **AMINE**.

protandrous /prəʊˈtandrəs/ ▶ **adjective** Botany & Zoology (of a hermaphrodite flower or animal) having the male reproductive organs come to maturity before the female. The opposite of **PROTOGYNOUS**.

– DERIVATIVES **protandry** noun.

protanope /ˈprəʊt(ə)nəʊp/ ▶ **noun** a person suffering from protanopia.

protanopia /ˌprəʊtəˈnəʊpɪə/ ▶ **noun** [mass noun] colour blindness resulting from insensitivity to red light, causing confusion of greens, reds, and yellows. It is hereditary, and is the commonest form of colour blindness. Also called **DALTONISM**. Compare with **DEUTERANOPIA**, **TRITANOPIA**.

– ORIGIN early 20th cent.: from **PROTO-** 'original' (red being regarded as the first component of colour vision) + **AN-**[1] 'lacking' + **-OPIA**.

pro tanto /prəʊ ˈtantəʊ/ ▶ **adjective** & **adverb** to such an extent; to that extent.

– ORIGIN Latin, literally 'for so much'.

protasis /ˈprɒtəsɪs/ ▶ **noun** (pl. **protases** /-siːz/) Grammar the clause expressing the condition in a conditional sentence (e.g. *if you asked me* in *if you asked me I would agree*). Often contrasted with **APODOSIS**.

– ORIGIN late 16th cent.: via Latin from Greek *protasis* 'proposition', from *pro* 'before' + *teinein* 'to stretch'.

protea /ˈprəʊtɪə/ ▶ **noun** an evergreen shrub or small tree with large nectar-rich cone-like flower heads surrounded by brightly coloured bracts, chiefly native to South Africa.
● Genus *Protea*, family Proteaceae: many species, including *P. repens*, which was formerly used as a source of sweet syrup.

– ORIGIN modern Latin, from **PROTEUS**, with reference to the many species of the genus.

protean /ˈprəʊtɪən, prəʊˈtiːən/ ▶ **adjective** tending or able to change frequently or easily: *it is difficult to comprehend the whole of this protean subject.*
■ able to do many different things; versatile: *protean thinkers who scan the horizons of work and society.*

– ORIGIN late 16th cent.: from **PROTEUS** + **-AN**.

protease /ˈprəʊtɪeɪz/ ▶ **noun** Biochemistry an enzyme which breaks down proteins and peptides.

– ORIGIN early 20th cent.: from **PROTEIN** + **-ASE**.

protect ▶ **verb** [with obj.] keep safe from harm or injury: *he tried to **protect** Kelly **from** the attack* | [no obj.] *use a sunscreen that **protects against** both UVA and UVB.*
■ [often as adj. **protected**] aim to preserve (a threatened plant or animal species) by legislating against collecting or hunting. ■ [often as adj. **protected**] restrict by law access to or development of (land) so as to preserve its natural state: *logging is continuing in protected areas in violation of an international agreement.* ■ (often **be protected**) (of an insurance policy) promise to pay (someone) an agreed amount in the event of loss, injury, fire, theft, or other misfortune: *in the event of your death, your family will be protected against any financial problems that may arise.* ■ Economics shield (a domestic industry) from competition by imposing import duties on foreign goods. ■ Computing restrict access to or use of (data or a memory location): *security products are designed to **protect** information **from** unauthorized access.* ■ provide funds to meet (a bill of exchange or commercial draft).

– DERIVATIVES **protectable** adjective.

– ORIGIN late Middle English: from Latin *protect-* 'covered in front', from the verb *protegere*, from *pro-* 'in front' + *tegere* 'to cover'.

protectant ▶ **noun** a substance that provides protection, e.g. against disease or ultraviolet radiation.

protection ▶ **noun** [mass noun] the action of protecting someone or something, or the state of being protected: *the B vitamins give protection against infection* | *his son was put under police protection.*
■ a person or thing that prevents someone or something from suffering harm or injury: *the castle was built as protection against the Saxons* | [in sing.] *a protection against the evil eye.* ■ the cover provided by an insurance policy. ■ (usu. **protections**) a legal or other formal measure intended to preserve civil liberties and rights. ■ [count noun] a document guaranteeing immunity from harm to the person specified in it. ■ the practice of paying money to criminals so as to prevent them from attacking oneself or one's property: [as modifier] *a protection racket.* ■ (also **protection money**) the money so paid, especially on a regular basis. ■ Climbing the number and quality of running belays or other equipment employed to safeguard a pitch. ■ archaic used euphemistically to refer to the keeping of a mistress by her lover in a separate establishment: *she was living **under his lordship's protection** at Gloucester Gate.*

– ORIGIN Middle English: from Old French, from late Latin *protectio(n-)*, from *protegere* 'cover in front' (see **PROTECT**).

protectionism ▶ **noun** [mass noun] Economics the theory or practice of shielding a country's domestic industries from foreign competition by taxing imports.

– DERIVATIVES **protectionist** noun & adjective.

protective ▶ **adjective** capable of or intended to protect someone or something: *protective gloves are worn to minimize injury.*
■ having or showing a strong wish to keep someone or something safe from harm: *I felt protective towards her* | *Marco wrapped a protective arm around her shoulder.* ■ Economics of or relating to the protection of domestic industries from foreign competition: *protective tariffs.*

▶ **noun** Brit. a thing that protects someone or something: *an effectual protective against the midge.*
■ dated a condom.

– DERIVATIVES **protectively** adverb, **protectiveness** noun.

protective colouring (also **protective coloration**) ▶ **noun** [mass noun] colouring that disguises or camouflages a plant or animal.

protective custody ▶ **noun** [mass noun] the detention of a person for their own protection.

protector ▶ **noun** **1** a person who protects or defends someone or something: *a stalwart protector of civic rectitude.*
2 [often with modifier] a thing that protects someone or something from injury: *ear protectors.*
3 (usu. **Protector**) historical a regent in charge of a kingdom during the minority, absence, or incapacity of the sovereign.
■ (also **Lord Protector of the Commonwealth**) the title of the head of state in England during the later period of the Commonwealth between 1653 and 1659, first Oliver Cromwell (1653–8), then his son Richard (1658–9).

– DERIVATIVES **protectoral** adjective, **protectorship** noun.

protectorate ▶ **noun** **1** a state that is controlled and protected by another.
■ the relationship between a state of this kind and the one that controls it: *a French protectorate had been established over Tunis.*
2 (usu. **Protectorate**) historical the position or period of office of a Protector, especially that in England of Oliver and Richard Cromwell.

protectress ▶ **noun** a female protector.

protégé /ˈprɒtɪʒeɪ, -tɛʒeɪ, ˈprəʊ-/ ▶ **noun** a person who is guided and supported by an older and more experienced or influential person: *Ruskin submitted his protégé's name for election.*

– ORIGIN late 18th cent.: French, literally 'protected', past participle of *protéger*, from Latin *protegere* 'cover in front' (see **PROTECT**).

protégée /ˈprɒtɪʒeɪ, -tɛʒeɪ, ˈprəʊ-/ ▶ **noun** a female protégé.

protein ▶ **noun** any of a class of nitrogenous organic compounds which have large molecules composed of one or more long chains of amino acids and are an essential part of all living organisms, especially as structural components of body tissues such as muscle, hair, collagen, etc., and as enzymes and antibodies.
■ [mass noun] such substances collectively, especially as a dietary component: *a diet high in protein.*

– DERIVATIVES **proteinaceous** adjective.

– ORIGIN mid 19th cent.: from French *protéine*, German *Protein*, from Greek *prōteios* 'primary', from *prōtos* 'first'.

proteinase /ˈprəʊtiːneɪz/ ▶ **noun** another term for **ENDOPEPTIDASE**.

proteinuria /ˌprəʊtiːˈnjʊərɪə/ ▶ **noun** [mass noun] Medicine the presence of abnormal quantities of protein in the urine, which may indicate damage to the kidneys.

pro tem /prəʊ ˈtɛm/ ▶ **adverb** & **adjective** for the time being: [as adv.] *a printer which Marisa could use pro tem* | [as adj.] *a pro tem committee.*

– ORIGIN abbreviation of Latin *pro tempore*.

proteoglycan /ˌprəʊtɪəʊˈglʌɪkan/ ▶ **noun** Biochemistry a compound consisting of a protein bonded to mucopolysaccharide groups, present especially in connective tissue.

proteolysis /ˌprəʊtɪˈɒlɪsɪs/ ▶ **noun** [mass noun] Biochemistry the breakdown of proteins or peptides into amino acids by the action of enzymes.

– DERIVATIVES **proteolytic** adjective, **proteolytically** adverb.

– ORIGIN late 19th cent.: modern Latin, from **PROTEIN** + **-LYSIS**.

Proterozoic /ˌprəʊt(ə)rəˈzəʊɪk/ ▶ **adjective** Geology of, relating to, or denoting the aeon that constitutes the later part of the Precambrian, between the Archaean aeon and the Cambrian period, in which the earliest forms of life evolved.
■ [as noun **the Proterozoic**] the Proterozoic aeon or the system of rocks deposited during it.

The Proterozoic lasted from about 2,500 to 570 million years ago. For millions of years only bacteria and single-celled organisms existed, and the early invertebrates that followed were soft-bodied and rarely left any trace in the form of fossils.

– ORIGIN early 20th cent.: from Greek *proteros* 'former' + *zōē* 'life', *zōos* 'living' + **-IC**.

protest ▶ **noun** **1** a statement or action expressing disapproval of or objection to something: *the British team lodged an official protest* | [mass noun] *two senior scientists resigned **in protest**.*
■ an organized public demonstration expressing strong objection to a policy or course of action adopted by those in authority: [as modifier] *a protest march.*
2 Law a written declaration, typically by a notary

public, that a bill has been presented and payment or acceptance refused.

▶**verb 1** [no obj.] express an objection to what someone has said or done: *she wouldn't let him pay and he didn't protest too much.*

■publicly demonstrate strong objection to a policy or course of action adopted by those in authority: *doctors and patients* ***protested against*** *plans to cut services at the hospital.* ■ [with obj.] N. Amer. publicly demonstrate such objection to (a policy or course of action): *the workers were protesting economic measures enacted a week earlier.*

2 [reporting verb] declare (something) firmly and emphatically in the face of stated or implied doubt or in response to an accusation: [with direct speech] *'I'm not being coy!' Lucy protested* | [with obj.] *she has always protested her innocence.*

3 [with obj.] Law write or obtain a protest in regard to (a bill).

– PHRASES **under protest** after expressing one's objection or reluctance; unwillingly: *'I'm only here under protest,' Jenna said shortly.*

– DERIVATIVES **protester** noun, **protestingly** adverb, **protestor** noun.

– ORIGIN late Middle English (as a verb in the sense 'make a solemn declaration'): from Old French *protester*, from Latin *protestari*, from *pro-* 'forth, publicly' + *testari* 'assert' (from *testis* 'witness').

Protestant /ˈprɒtɪst(ə)nt/ ▶**noun** a member or follower of any of the Western Christian Churches that are separate from the Roman Catholic Church in accordance with the principles of the Reformation, including the Baptist, Presbyterian, and Lutheran Churches.

> Protestants are so called after the declaration (*protestatio*) of Martin Luther and his supporters dissenting from the decision of the Diet of Spires (1529), which reaffirmed the edict of the Diet of Worms against the Reformation. All Protestants reject the authority of the papacy, both religious and political, and find authority in the text of the Bible, made available to all in vernacular translation.

▶**adjective** of, relating to, or belonging to any of the Protestant Churches.

– DERIVATIVES **Protestantization** (also **-isation**) noun, **Protestantize** (also **-ise**) verb.

– ORIGIN mid 16th cent.: via German or French from Latin *protestant-* 'protesting', from Latin *protestari* (see **PROTEST**).

Protestant ascendancy ▶**noun** historical the domination by the Anglo-Irish Protestant minority in Ireland, especially in the 18th and 19th centuries.

Protestant ethic (also **Protestant work ethic**) ▶**noun** the view that a person's duty and responsibility is to achieve success through hard work and thrift.

– ORIGIN translating German *die protestantische Ethik*, coined (1904) by the economist Max Weber in his thesis on the relationship between the teachings of Calvin and the rise of capitalism.

Protestantism ▶**noun** [mass noun] the faith, practice, and church order of the Protestant Churches.

■adherence to the forms of Christian doctrine which are generally regarded as Protestant rather than Catholic or Eastern Orthodox.

protestation /ˌprɒtɪˈsteɪʃ(ə)n/ ▶**noun** an emphatic declaration that something is or is not the case: *her protestations of innocence were in vain* | [mass noun] *no amount of protestation to the contrary made any difference.*

■an objection or protest: *he was warned by the referee for his loud protestations.*

– ORIGIN Middle English: from Old French, from late Latin *protestatio(n-)*, from *protestari* 'to protest' (see **PROTEST**).

Proteus /ˈprəʊtɪəs/ **1** Greek Mythology a minor sea god who had the power of prophecy but who would assume different shapes to avoid answering questions.

2 Astronomy a satellite of Neptune, the sixth closest to the planet, discovered by the Voyager 2 space probe in 1989 (diameter 400 km).

proteus /ˈprəʊtɪəs/ ▶**noun 1** a bacterium found in the intestines of animals and in the soil.

● Genus *Proteus*; motile Gram-negative rods.

2 another term for **OLM**.

– ORIGIN early 19th cent.: from **PROTEUS**.

prothalamium /ˌprəʊθəˈleɪmɪəm/ ▶**noun** (pl. **prothalamia** /-mɪə/) poetic/literary a song or poem celebrating a forthcoming wedding.

– ORIGIN late 16th cent.: from *Prothalamion*, the title of a poem by Spenser, on the pattern of *epithalamium*.

prothallus /prəʊˈθaləs/ ▶**noun** (pl. **prothalli** /-lʌɪ, -liː/) Botany the gametophyte of ferns and related plants.

– DERIVATIVES **prothallial** adjective.

– ORIGIN mid 19th cent.: modern Latin, from **PRO-**[2] 'before, earlier' + Greek *thallos* 'green shoot'.

prothesis /ˈprɒθɪsɪs/ ▶**noun** (pl. **protheses** /-siːz/) **1** [mass noun] Christian Church (especially in the Orthodox Church) the action of placing the Eucharistic elements on the credence table.

■[count noun] a credence table. ■ [count noun] the part of a church where the credence table stands.

2 another term for **PROSTHESIS** (in sense 2).

– DERIVATIVES **prothetic** adjective.

– ORIGIN late 16th cent. (in sense 2): from Greek, 'placing before or in public view', from *pro* 'before' + *thesis* 'placing'.

prothonotary /ˌprəʊθəˈnəʊt(ə)ri, prəˈθɒnə-/ ▶**noun** variant spelling of **PROTONOTARY**.

prothonotary warbler ▶**noun** a North American warbler, the male of which has a golden-yellow head, breast, and underparts.

● *Protonotaria citrea*, family Parulidae.

– ORIGIN late 18th cent.: named with reference to the saffron colour of the robes worn by clerks to the Pope (see **PROTONOTARY APOSTOLIC**).

prothorax ▶**noun** Entomology the anterior segment of the thorax of an insect, not bearing any wings.

– DERIVATIVES **prothoracic** adjective.

prothrombin /prəʊˈθrɒmbɪn/ ▶**noun** [mass noun] Biochemistry a protein present in blood plasma which is converted into active thrombin during coagulation.

Protista /prəʊˈtɪstə/ Biology a kingdom or large grouping that comprises mostly single-celled organisms such as the protozoa, simple algae and fungi, slime moulds, and (formerly) the bacteria. They are now divided among up to thirty phyla, and some have both plant and animal characteristics.

– DERIVATIVES **protist** /ˈprəʊtɪst/ noun, **protistan** adjective & noun, **protistology** noun.

– ORIGIN modern Latin (plural), from Greek *prōtista*, neuter plural of *prōtistos* 'very first', superlative of *prōtos* 'first'.

protium /ˈprəʊtɪəm/ ▶**noun** [mass noun] Chemistry the common, stable isotope of hydrogen, as distinct from deuterium and tritium.

– ORIGIN 1930s: modern Latin, from Greek *prōtos* 'first'.

Proto /ˈprəʊtəʊ/ ▶**noun** S. African trademark a breathing apparatus which filters out toxic gases and supplies oxygen to the wearer during underground rescue operations.

proto- (usu. **prot-** before a vowel) ▶**combining form** original; primitive: *prototherian* | *prototype.*

■first; anterior; relating to a precursor: *protomartyr* | *protozoon.*

– ORIGIN from Greek *prōtos* 'first'.

protoceratops /ˌprəʊtə(ʊ)ˈsɛrətɒps/ ▶**noun** a small quadrupedal dinosaur of the late Cretaceous period, having a bony frill above the neck and probably ancestral to triceratops. The remains of many individuals and their eggs have been found in Mongolia.

● Genus *Protoceratops*, infraorder Ceratopsia, order Ornithischia.

protocol ▶**noun 1** [mass noun] the official procedure or system of rules governing affairs of state or diplomatic occasions: *protocol forbids the prince from making any public statement in his defence.*

■the accepted or established code of procedure or behaviour in any group, organization, or situation: *what is the protocol at a smart lunch if one's neighbour dozes off during the speeches?* ■ [count noun] Computing a set of rules governing the exchange or transmission of data electronically between devices.

2 the original draft of a diplomatic document, especially of the terms of a treaty agreed to in conference and signed by the parties.

■an amendment or addition to a treaty or convention: *a protocol to the treaty allowed for this Danish referendum.*

3 a formal or official record of scientific experimental observations.

■a procedure for carrying out a scientific experiment or a course of medical treatment.

– ORIGIN late Middle English (denoting the original minute of an agreement, forming the legal authority for future dealings relating to it): from Old French *prothocole*, via medieval Latin from Greek *prōtokollon* 'first page, flyleaf', from *prōtos* 'first' + *kolla* 'glue'. Sense 1 derives from French *protocole*, the collection of set forms of etiquette to be observed by the French head of state, and the name of the government department responsible for this (in the 19th cent.).

Protoctista /ˌprəʊtɒkˈtɪstə/ Biology a kingdom or large grouping that is either synonymous with the Protista or equivalent to the Protista together with their multicellular descendants.

– DERIVATIVES **protoctist** noun.

– ORIGIN modern Latin (plural), based on Greek *prōtos* 'first'.

protogalaxy ▶**noun** (pl. **-ies**) Astronomy a vast mass of gas from which a galaxy is thought to develop.

– DERIVATIVES **protogalactic** adjective.

Proto-Germanic ▶**noun** see **GERMANIC**.

protogynous /prəʊˈtɒdʒɪnəs/ ▶**adjective** Botany & Zoology (of a hermaphrodite flower or animal) having the female reproductive organs come to maturity before the male. The opposite of **PROTANDROUS**.

– DERIVATIVES **protogyny** noun.

protohuman Anthropology ▶**noun** a hypothetical prehistoric primate, resembling humans and thought to be their ancestor, whose profile has been compiled mainly from fossil evidence.

▶**adjective** relating to or denoting such a primate.

Proto-Indo-European ▶**noun** [mass noun] the lost language from which all Indo-European languages derive. See **INDO-EUROPEAN**.

▶**adjective** of or relating to this language.

protolanguage ▶**noun** a hypothetical lost parent language from which actual languages are derived.

protomartyr ▶**noun** the first martyr for a cause, especially the first Christian martyr, St Stephen.

proton /ˈprəʊtɒn/ ▶**noun** Physics a stable subatomic particle occurring in all atomic nuclei, with a positive electric charge equal in magnitude to that of an electron.

> The mass of the proton is 1,836 times greater than that of the electron. The atoms of each chemical element have a characteristic number of protons in the nucleus; this is known as the atomic number. The common isotope of hydrogen has a nucleus consisting of a single proton.

– DERIVATIVES **protonic** adjective.

– ORIGIN 1920s: from Greek, neuter of *prōtos* 'first'.

protonate /ˈprəʊt(ə)neɪt/ ▶**verb** [with obj.] (often **be protonated**) Chemistry transfer a proton to (a molecule, group, or atom) which forms a coordinate bond to the proton.

– DERIVATIVES **protonation** noun.

protonotary /ˌprəʊtəˈnəʊt(ə)ri, prəˈtɒnət(ə)ri/ (also **prothonotary**) ▶**noun** (pl. **-ies**) chiefly historical a chief clerk in some law courts, originally in the Byzantine court.

– ORIGIN late Middle English: via medieval Latin from late Greek *prōtonotarios*, from *prōtos* 'first' + *notarios* 'notary'.

Protonotary Apostolic (also **Protonotary Apostolical**) ▶**noun** a member of the Roman Catholic college of prelates who register papal acts and direct the canonization of saints.

protopathic /ˌprəʊtə(ʊ)ˈpaθɪk/ ▶**adjective** Physiology relating to or denoting those sensory nerve fibres of the skin which are capable of discriminating only between relatively coarse stimuli, chiefly heat, cold, and pain. Often contrasted with **EPICRITIC**.

– ORIGIN mid 19th cent.: from **PROTO-** 'primitive' + Greek *pathos* 'suffering, feeling' + **-IC**.

protoplasm /ˈprəʊtə(ʊ)ˌplaz(ə)m/ ▶**noun** [mass noun] Biology the colourless material comprising the living part of a cell, including the cytoplasm, nucleus, and other organelles.

– DERIVATIVES **protoplasmic** adjective.

– ORIGIN mid 19th cent.: from Greek *prōtoplasma* (see **PROTO-**, **PLASMA**).

protoplast /ˈprəʊtə(ʊ)plast, -plɑːst/ ▶**noun** chiefly Botany the protoplasm of a living plant or bacterial cell whose cell wall has been removed.

– ORIGIN late 19th cent.: from Greek *prōtoplastos* 'first formed', from *prōtos* 'first' + *plassein* 'to mould'.

protopodite /prəʊˈtɒpədʌɪt/ (also **protopod** /ˈprəʊtə(ʊ)pɒd/) ▶**noun** Zoology the basal segments of

p

the biramous limb or appendage of a crustacean. Compare with **ENDOPODITE, EXOPODITE.**
– ORIGIN late 19th cent.: from **PROTO-** 'early, original' + Greek *pous, pod-* 'foot' + **-ITE**[1].

protostar ▶ **noun** Astronomy a contracting mass of gas which represents an early stage in the formation of a star, before nucleosynthesis has begun.

protostome /'prəʊtə(ʊ)stəʊm/ ▶ **noun** Zoology a multicellular organism whose mouth develops from a primary embryonic opening, such as an annelid, mollusc, or arthropod.
– ORIGIN 1950s: from **PROTO-** 'primitive' + Greek *stoma* 'mouth'.

Prototheria /ˌprəʊtə(ʊ)'θɪərɪə/ Zoology a group of mammals that comprises the monotremes and their extinct relatives. Compare with **THERIA.**
• Subclass Prototheria, class Mammalia.
– DERIVATIVES **prototherian** noun & adjective.
– ORIGIN modern Latin (plural), from **PROTO-** 'first, original' + Greek *thēr* 'wild beast'.

prototype ▶ **noun** a first or preliminary model of something, especially a machine, from which other forms are developed or copied: *the firm is testing a prototype of the weapon.*
■ a typical example of something: *he was married to the prototype of an ideal parson's wife.* ■ the archetypal example of a class of living organisms, astronomical objects, or other items: *these objects are the prototypes of a category of rapidly spinning neutron stars.* ■ a building, vehicle, or other object which acts as a pattern for a full-scale model. ■ Electronics a basic filter network with specified cut-off frequencies, from which other networks may be derived to obtain sharper cut-offs, constancy of characteristic impedance with frequency, etc.
▶ **verb** [with obj.] make a prototype of (a product).
– DERIVATIVES **prototypal** adjective, **prototypic** adjective, **prototypical** adjective, **prototypically** adverb.
– ORIGIN late 16th cent. (denoting the original of which something else is a copy or derivative): via French or late Latin from Greek *prōtotupos* (see **PROTO-, TYPE**).

Protozoa /ˌprəʊtə'zəʊə/ Zoology a phylum or grouping of phyla which comprises the single-celled microscopic animals, which include amoebas, flagellates, ciliates, sporozoans, and many other forms. They are now usually treated as a number of phyla belonging to the kingdom Protista.
■ [as plural noun **protozoa**] organisms of this group.
– DERIVATIVES **protozoal** adjective, **protozoan** noun & adjective, **protozoic** adjective, **protozoon** noun.
– ORIGIN modern Latin (plural), from **PROTO-** 'first' + Greek *zōion* 'animal'.

protract ▶ **verb** [with obj.] prolong: *he had certainly taken his time, even protracting the process.*
– ORIGIN mid 16th cent.: from Latin *protract-* 'prolonged', from the verb *protrahere*, from *pro-* 'out' + *trahere* 'to draw'.

protracted ▶ **adjective** lasting for a long time or longer than expected or usual: *a protracted and bitter dispute.*
– DERIVATIVES **protractedly** adverb, **protractedness** noun.

protractile /prə'traktʌɪl, -tɪl/ ▶ **adjective** another term for **PROTRUSIBLE.**

protraction ▶ **noun** [mass noun] **1** the action of prolonging something or the state of being prolonged: *the protraction of the war.*
2 the action of extending a part of the body.
– ORIGIN mid 16th cent.: from French, or from late Latin *protractio(n-)*, from *protrahere* 'prolong' (see **PROTRACT**).

protractor ▶ **noun 1** an instrument for measuring angles, typically in the form of a flat semicircle marked with degrees along the curved edge.
2 (also **protractor muscle**) chiefly Zoology a muscle serving to extend a part of the body. Compare with **RETRACTOR.**

protrude ▶ **verb** [no obj., with adverbial of direction] extend beyond or above a surface: *something like a fin protruded from the water.*
■ [with obj.] (of an animal) cause (a body part) to do this.
– DERIVATIVES **protrusion** noun, **protrusive** adjective.
– ORIGIN early 17th cent. (in the sense 'thrust (something) forward or onward'): from Latin *protrudere*, from *pro-* 'forward, out' + *trudere* 'to thrust'.

protrusible ▶ **adjective** Zoology (of a body part, such as the jaws of a fish) capable of being protruded or extended.
– ORIGIN mid 19th cent.: from Latin *protrus-* 'extended or thrust forward' (from the verb *protrudere*) + **-IBLE.**

protuberance /prə'tju:b(ə)r(ə)ns/ ▶ **noun** a thing that protrudes from something else: *some dinosaurs evolved protuberances on top of their heads.*
■ [mass noun] the fact or state of protruding: *the large size and protuberance of the incisors.*

protuberant ▶ **adjective** protruding; bulging: *his protuberant eyes fluttered open.*
– ORIGIN mid 17th cent.: from late Latin *protuberant-* 'swelling out', from the verb *protuberare*, from *pro-* 'forward, out' + *tuber* 'bump'.

Protura /prə(ʊ)'tjʊərə/ Entomology an order of minute white wingless insects with slender bodies. They lack eyes and antennae, using the first pair of legs as sensory organs.
• Order Protura, subclass Apterygota, class Insecta (or Hexapoda).
– DERIVATIVES **proturan** noun & adjective.
– ORIGIN modern Latin (plural), from Greek *prōtos* 'first, primitive'.

proud ▶ **adjective 1** feeling deep pleasure or satisfaction as a result of one's own achievements, qualities, or possessions or those of someone with whom one is closely associated: *a proud grandma of three boys | she got nine passes and he was so* **proud of** *her.*
■ (of an event, achievement, etc.) causing someone to feel this way: *we have a proud history of innovation.* ■ having or showing a consciousness of one's own dignity: *I was too proud to go home.* ■ having or showing a high or excessively high opinion of oneself or one's importance: *he was a proud, arrogant man.* ■ imposing; splendid: *bulrushes emerge tall and proud from the middle of the pond.*
2 [predic.] Brit. slightly projecting from a surface: *when the brake is engaged, the lever does not stand* **proud of** *the horizontal.*
■ [attrib.] (of flesh) overgrown round a healing wound.
– PHRASES **do someone proud** informal act in a way that gives someone cause to feel pleased or satisfied: *they did themselves proud in a game which sent the fans home happy.* ■ treat someone very well, typically by lavishly feeding or entertaining them.
– DERIVATIVES **proudly** adverb, **proudness** noun.
– ORIGIN late Old English *prūt, prūd* 'having a high opinion of one's own worth', from Old French *prud* 'valiant', based on Latin *prodesse* 'be of value'. The phrase *proud flesh* dates back to late Middle English, but the sense 'slightly projecting' is first recorded in English dialect of the 19th cent.

proud-hearted ▶ **adjective** arrogant.

Proudhon /'pru:dɒ̃, French pʀydɔ̃/, Pierre Joseph (1809–65), French social philosopher and journalist. His pamphlet *What is Property?* (1840) argues that property, in the sense of the exploitation of one person's labour by another, is theft.

Proust[1] /pru:st/, Joseph Louis (1754–1826), French analytical chemist. He proposed the law of constant proportions, demonstrating that any pure sample of a chemical compound (such as an oxide of a metal) always contains the same elements in fixed proportions.

Proust[2] /pru:st/, Marcel (1871–1922), French novelist, essayist, and critic. He devoted much of his life to writing his novel *À la recherche du temps perdu* (published in seven sections between 1913 and 1927). Its central theme is the recovery of the lost past and the releasing of its creative energies through the stimulation of unconscious memory.
– DERIVATIVES **Proustian** adjective.

Prout /praʊt/, William (1785–1850), English chemist and biochemist. He developed the hypothesis that hydrogen is the primary substance from which all other elements are formed, which although incorrect stimulated research in atomic theory.

Prov. ▶ **abbreviation for** ■ Proverbs (in biblical references). ■ chiefly Canadian Province or Provincial.

prove /pru:v/ ▶ **verb** (past participle **proved** or **proven** /'pru:v(ə)n, 'prəʊ-/) **1** [with obj.] demonstrate the truth or existence of (something) by evidence or argument: *the concept is difficult to prove* | [as adj. **proven**] *a proven ability to work hard.*
■ [with obj. and complement] demonstrate by evidence or argument (someone or something) to be: *if they are proved guilty we won't trade with them.* ■ Law establish the genuineness and validity of (a will). ■ [no obj., with complement] be seen or found to be: *the scheme has proved a great success.* ■ (**prove oneself**) demonstrate one's abilities or courage. ■ [with obj.] rare test the accuracy of (a mathematical calculation). ■ subject (a gun) to a testing process.
2 [no obj.] (of bread dough) become aerated by the action of yeast; rise. [ORIGIN: from Northamptonshire dialect.]
– PHRASES **not proven** Scots Law a verdict that there is insufficient evidence to establish guilt or innocence.
– DERIVATIVES **provability** noun, **provable** adjective, **provably** adverb.
– ORIGIN Middle English: from Old French *prover*, from Latin *probare* 'test, approve, demonstrate', from *probus* 'good'.

USAGE For complex historical reasons, **prove** developed two past participles: **proved** and **proven**. Both are correct and can be used more or less interchangeably (*this hasn't been* **proved** *yet; this hasn't been* **proven** *yet*). In British English **proved** is more common, with the exception that **proven** is always used when the word is an adjective coming before the noun: *a* **proven** *talent*, not *a* **proved** *talent.*

provenance /'prɒv(ə)nəns/ ▶ **noun** [mass noun] the place of origin or earliest known history of something: *an orange rug of Iranian provenance.*
■ [count noun] the beginning of something's existence; something's origin: *they try to understand the whole universe, its provenance and fate.* ■ [count noun] a record of ownership of a work of art or an antique, used as a guide to authenticity or quality: *the manuscript has a distinguished provenance.*
– ORIGIN late 18th cent.: from French, from the verb *provenir* 'come or stem from', from Latin *provenire*, from *pro-* 'forth' + *venire* 'come'.

Provençal /ˌprɒvɒ̃'sɑ:l, French pʀɔvɑ̃sal/ ▶ **adjective** of, relating to, or denoting Provence or its people or language.
▶ **noun 1** a native or inhabitant of Provence.
2 [mass noun] the language of Provence.

Provençal is a Romance language closely related to French, Italian, and Catalan; it is sometimes called *langue d'oc* (or Occitan), though strictly speaking it is one dialect of this. In the 12th–14th centuries it was the language of the troubadours and cultured speakers of southern France, but the spread of the northern dialects of French led to its decline.

– ORIGIN French, from Latin *provincialis* 'provincial'.

provençale /ˌprɒvɒ̃'sɑ:l/ ▶ **adjective** [postpositive] denoting a dish cooked in a sauce made with tomatoes, garlic, and olive oil: *chicken provençale.*
– ORIGIN from French *à la provençale* 'in the Provençal style'.

Provence /prɒ'vɒ̃s, French pʀɔvɑ̃s/ a former province of SE France, on the Mediterranean coast east of the Rhône. Settled by the Greeks in the 6th century BC, the area around Marseilles became, in the 1st century BC, part of the Roman colony of Gaul. It was united with France in 1481 and is now part of the region of Provence-Alpes-Côte d'Azur.
– ORIGIN from Latin *provincia* 'province', a colloquial name for southern Gaul, the first Roman province to be established outside Italy.

Provence-Alpes-Côte d'Azur /alp ˌkəʊt da'zjʊə, French alp kot dazyʀ/ a mountainous region of SE France, on the border with Italy and including the French Riviera.

provender /'prɒvɪndə/ ▶ **noun** [mass noun] often humorous food.
■ dated animal fodder.
– ORIGIN Middle English: from Old French *provendre*, based on an alteration of Latin *praebenda* 'things to be supplied' (see **PREBEND**).

provenience /prə'vi:nɪəns/ ▶ **noun** US term for **PROVENANCE.**

proventriculus /ˌprəʊvɛn'trɪkjʊləs/ ▶ **noun** (pl. **proventriculi**) Zoology the narrow glandular first region of a bird's stomach between the crop and the gizzard.
■ the thick-walled muscular expansion of the oesophagus above the stomach of crustaceans and insects.
– ORIGIN mid 19th cent.: from **PRO-**[2] 'before' + Latin *ventriculus* 'small belly', diminutive of *venter, ventr-* 'belly'.

proverb ▶ **noun** a short pithy saying in general use, stating a general truth or piece of advice.
– ORIGIN Middle English: from Old French *proverbe*,

from Latin *proverbium*, from *pro-* '(put) forth' + *verbum* 'word'.

proverbial ▶ **adjective** (of a word or phrase) referred to in a proverb or idiom: *I'm going to stick out like the proverbial sore thumb.*
■ [as noun] used, often euphemistically, to stand for a word or phrase that is normally part of a proverb or idiom but is not actually uttered: *one word out of line, and the proverbial hits the fan.* ■ well known, especially so as to be stereotypical: *the Welsh people, whose hospitality is proverbial.*
– DERIVATIVES **proverbiality** noun, **proverbially** adverb.
– ORIGIN late Middle English: from Latin *proverbialis*, from *proverbium* (see **PROVERB**).

Proverbs (also **Book of Proverbs**) a book of the Bible containing maxims attributed mainly to Solomon.

pro-vice-chancellor ▶ **noun** an assistant or deputy vice-chancellor of a university.

provide ▶ **verb 1** [with obj.] make available for use; supply: *these clubs provide a much appreciated service for this area.*
■ (**provide someone with**) equip or supply someone with (something useful or necessary): *we were provided with a map of the area.* ■ present or yield (something useful): *neither will provide answers to these problems.*
2 [no obj.] (**provide for**) make adequate preparation for (a possible event): *new qualifications must provide for changes in technology.*
■ supply sufficient money to ensure the maintenance of (someone): *Emma was handsomely provided for in Frannie's will.* ■ (of a law) enable or allow (something to be done).
3 [with clause] stipulate in a will or other legal document: *the order should be varied to provide that there would be no contact with the father.*
4 (**provide someone to**) Christian Church, historical appoint an incumbent to (a benefice).
– ORIGIN late Middle English (also in the sense 'prepare to do, get ready'): from Latin *providere* 'foresee, attend to', from *pro-* 'before' + *videre* 'to see'.

provided ▶ **conjunction** on the condition or understanding that: *cutting corners was acceptable, provided that you could get away with it.*

Providence the state capital of Rhode Island, a port on the Atlantic coast; pop. 160,730 (1990). It was founded in 1636 as a haven for religious dissenters.

providence ▶ **noun** [mass noun] the protective care of God or of nature as a spiritual power: *they found their trust in divine providence to be a source of comfort.*
■ (**Providence**) God or nature as providing such care: *I live out my life as Providence decrees.* ■ timely preparation for future eventualities: *it was considered a duty to encourage providence.*
– ORIGIN late Middle English: from Old French, from Latin *providentia*, from *providere* 'foresee, attend to' (see **PROVIDE**).

provident ▶ **adjective** making or indicative of timely preparation for the future: *she had learned to be provident.*
– DERIVATIVES **providently** adverb.
– ORIGIN late Middle English: from Latin *provident-* 'foreseeing, attending to', from the verb *providere* (see **PROVIDE**).

providential ▶ **adjective 1** occurring at a favourable time; opportune: *his appearance had seemed more than just providential.*
2 involving divine foresight or interference.
– DERIVATIVES **providentially** adverb.
– ORIGIN mid 17th cent.: from **PROVIDENCE**, on the pattern of *evidential*.

Provident Society ▶ **noun** Brit. another term for **FRIENDLY SOCIETY**.

provider ▶ **noun** a person or thing that provides something: *a leading provider of personal financial services.*
■ a breadwinner.

providing ▶ **conjunction** on the condition or understanding that: *we have the team which can win the league, providing we avoid bad injuries.*

Provie /ˈprəʊvi, ˈprɒvi/ ▶ **noun** informal another term for **PROVO**.

province ▶ **noun 1** a principal administrative division of a country or empire: *Chengdu, capital of Sichuan province.*
■ (**the Province**) Brit. Northern Ireland. ■ Christian Church a district under an archbishop or a metropolitan. ■ Roman History a territory outside Italy under a Roman governor. ■ (**the provinces**) the whole of a country outside the capital, especially when regarded as lacking in sophistication or culture: *I made my way home to the dreary provinces by train.*
2 (**one's province**) an area of special knowledge, interest, or responsibility: *she knew little about wine—that had been her father's province.*
– ORIGIN late Middle English: from Old French, from Latin *provincia* 'charge, province', of uncertain ultimate origin.

provincial ▶ **adjective 1** of or concerning a province of a country or empire: *provincial elections.*
2 of or concerning the regions outside the capital city of a country: *scenes of violence were reported in provincial towns.*
■ unsophisticated or narrow-minded, especially when considered as typical of such regions.
▶ **noun 1** an inhabitant of a province of a country or empire.
■ (**provincials**) (in Canada) sporting contests held between teams representing the country's administrative divisions.
2 an inhabitant of the regions outside the capital city of a country, especially when regarded as unsophisticated or narrow-minded.
■ (**provincials**) Brit. local newspapers, as contrasted with national ones.
3 Christian Church the head or chief of a province or of a religious order in a province.
– DERIVATIVES **provinciality** noun, **provincialization** noun, **provincially** adverb.
– ORIGIN late Middle English: from Old French, from Latin *provincialis* 'belonging to a province' (see **PROVINCE**).

provincialism ▶ **noun** [mass noun] **1** the way of life or mode of thought characteristic of the regions outside the capital city of a country, especially when regarded as unsophisticated or narrow-minded.
■ narrow-mindedness, insularity, or lack of sophistication: *the myopic provincialism of women's studies.*
2 concern for one's own area or region at the expense of national or supranational unity.
3 [count noun] a word or phrase peculiar to a local area.
4 the degree to which plant or animal communities are restricted to particular areas.
– DERIVATIVES **provincialist** noun & adjective.

provirus /prəʊˈvʌɪrəs/ ▶ **noun** Microbiology the genetic material of a virus as incorporated into, and able to replicate with, the genome of a host cell.
– DERIVATIVES **proviral** adjective.

provision ▶ **noun** [mass noun] **1** the action of providing or supplying something for use: *new contracts for the provision of services.*
■ (**provision for/against**) financial or other arrangements for future eventualities or requirements: *farmers have been slow to **make provision** for their retirement.* ■ [count noun] an amount set aside out of profits in the accounts of an organization for a known liability, especially a bad debt or the diminution in value of an asset.
2 an amount or thing supplied or provided: *changing levels of transport provision.*
■ (**provisions**) supplies of food, drink, or equipment, especially for a journey.
3 [count noun] a condition or requirement in a legal document: *the first private prosecution **under the provisions** of the 1989 Water Act.*
4 Christian Church, historical an appointment to a benefice, especially directly by the Pope rather than by the patron, and originally before it became vacant.
▶ **verb 1** [with obj.] supply with food, drink, or equipment, especially for a journey.
2 [no obj.] set aside an amount in an organization's accounts for a known liability: *financial institutions have to **provision against** loan losses.*
– DERIVATIVES **provisioner** noun.
– ORIGIN late Middle English (also in the sense 'foresight'): via Old French from Latin *provisio(n-)*, from *providere* 'foresee, attend to' (see **PROVIDE**). The verb dates from the early 19th cent.

provisional ▶ **adjective 1** arranged or existing for the present, possibly to be changed later: *a provisional government | provisional bookings.*
■ Brit. (of a driving licence) to be obtained before starting to learn to drive and upgraded to a full licence on passing a driving test. ■ (of a stamp) put into circulation temporarily, usually owing to the unavailability of the definitive issue.
2 (**Provisional**) [attrib.] of or relating to the unofficial wings of the IRA and Sinn Fein established in 1969 and advocating terrorism.
▶ **noun 1** a provisional licence or stamp.
2 (**Provisional**) a member of the Provisional wings of the IRA or Sinn Fein.
– DERIVATIVES **provisionality** noun, **provisionally** adverb.

proviso /prəˈvʌɪzəʊ/ ▶ **noun** (pl. **-os**) a condition attached to an agreement: *he let his house **with the proviso that** his own staff should remain to run it.*
– ORIGIN late Middle English: from the medieval Latin phrase *proviso (quod)* 'it being provided (that)', from Latin *providere* 'foresee, provide'.

provisor ▶ **noun 1** (in the Roman Catholic Church) a deputy of a bishop or archbishop.
2 Christian Church, historical the holder of a provision.
– ORIGIN late Middle English: from Anglo-Norman French *provisour*, from Latin *provisor*, from *provis-* 'provided' (see **PROVISION**).

provisory ▶ **adjective 1** rare subject to a proviso; conditional.
2 another term for **PROVISIONAL** (in sense 1).
– ORIGIN early 17th cent.: from French *provisoire* or medieval Latin *provisorius*, from *provis-* 'foreseen, attended to', from the verb *providere* (see **PROVIDE**).

provitamin ▶ **noun** Biochemistry a substance which is converted into a vitamin within an organism.

Provo /ˈprəʊvəʊ/ ▶ **noun** (pl. **-os**) informal term for **PROVISIONAL** (in sense 2).

provocation ▶ **noun** [mass noun] **1** action or speech that makes someone annoyed or angry, especially deliberately: *you should remain calm and not respond to provocation | he burst into tears **at the slightest provocation.***
■ Law action or speech held to be likely to prompt physical retaliation: *the assault had taken place **under provocation.***
2 the action of arousing sexual desire or interest, especially deliberately: *walking with deliberate provocation, she struck a pose, then giggled.*
3 Medicine testing to elicit a particular response or reflex: *twenty patients had a high increase of serum gastrin after provocation with secretin.*
– ORIGIN late Middle English: from Old French, from Latin *provocatio(n-)*, from the verb *provocare* (see **PROVOKE**).

provocative ▶ **adjective** causing annoyance, anger, or another strong reaction, especially deliberately: *a provocative article | his provocative remarks on race.*
■ arousing sexual desire or interest, especially deliberately.
– DERIVATIVES **provocatively** adverb, **provocativeness** noun.
– ORIGIN late Middle English: from Old French *provocatif, -ive*, from late Latin *provocativus*, from *provocat-* 'called forth, challenged', from the verb *provocare* (see **PROVOKE**).

provoke ▶ **verb** [with obj.] stimulate or give rise to (a reaction or emotion, typically a strong or unwelcome one) in someone: *the decision provoked a storm of protest from civil rights organizations |* [as adj., in combination **-provoking**] *anxiety-provoking situations.*
■ stimulate or incite (someone) to do or feel something, especially by arousing anger in them: *a teacher can **provoke** you **into** working harder.* ■ deliberately make (someone) annoyed or angry: *Rachel refused to be provoked.*
– DERIVATIVES **provokable** adjective, **provoker** noun, **provokingly** adverb.
– ORIGIN late Middle English (also in the sense 'invoke, summon'): from Old French *provoquer*, from Latin *provocare* 'challenge', from *pro-* 'forth' + *vocare* 'to call'.

provolone /ˌprɒvəˈləʊneɪ, -ˈləʊni/ ▶ **noun** [mass noun] an Italian soft smoked cheese made from cow's milk and having a mellow flavour.
– ORIGIN Italian, from *provola* 'buffalo's milk cheese'.

provost /ˈprɒvəst/ ▶ **noun 1** Brit. the head of certain university colleges, especially at Oxford or Cambridge, and public schools.
■ N. Amer. a senior administrative officer in certain universities.
2 Scottish term for **MAYOR**. See also **LORD PROVOST**.
3 the head of a chapter in a cathedral.
■ the Protestant minister of the principal church of a

p

town or district in Germany and certain other European countries. ■ historical the head of a Christian community. [ORIGIN: translating German *Propst*, Dutch *proost*, etc.]

4 short for **PROVOST MARSHAL**.

5 historical the chief magistrate of a French or other European town.

– DERIVATIVES **provostship** noun.

– ORIGIN late Old English *profost* 'head of a chapter, prior', reinforced in Middle English by Anglo-Norman French *provost*, from medieval Latin *propositus*, synonym of Latin *praepositus* 'head, chief' (see **PRAEPOSTOR**).

provost guard ▶ noun US a detachment of soldiers acting as military police under the command of a provost marshal.

provost marshal ▶ noun the head of military police in camp or on active service.
 ■ (in the Royal Navy) a senior commissioned officer in the Regulatory Branch or Naval Dockyard Port.

prow /praʊ/ ▶ noun the pointed front part of a ship; the bow.
 ■ the pointed or projecting front part of something such as a car or building.

– ORIGIN mid 16th cent.: from Old French *proue*, from Provençal *proa*, probably via Latin from Greek *prōira*, from a base represented by Latin *pro* 'in front'.

prowess ▶ noun [mass noun] **1** skill or expertise in a particular activity or field: *his prowess as a fisherman | her culinary prowess.*
 2 bravery in battle.

– ORIGIN Middle English (in sense 2): from Old French *proesce*, from *prou* 'valiant'. Sense 1 dates from the early 20th cent.

prowfish /ˈpraʊfɪʃ/ ▶ noun (pl. same or **-fishes**) any of a number of marine fishes that typically have dark spots and a dorsal fin extending the length of the body:
 ● a scaleless Australian fish that has a deep head and tapers towards the tail (family Pataecidae: several genera). ● a fish of the North Pacific (*Zaprora silenus*, the only member of the family Zaproridae).

prowl ▶ verb [with obj.] (of a person or animal) move about (a place) in search of or as if in search of prey: *black bears prowl the canyons.*
 ■ [no obj., with adverbial] (of a person or animal) move stealthily or restlessly as or like a hunter: *David had been prowling about in the garden, waiting for her car.*
 ▶ noun an act of prowling: *I met her once on one of my off-duty bookshop prowls.*
 – PHRASES **on the prowl** (of a person or animal) moving about in search of or as if in search of prey.
 – ORIGIN late Middle English: of unknown origin.

prowl car ▶ noun US a police squad car.

prowler ▶ noun a person who moves stealthily about or loiters near a place with a view to committing a crime.

prox. ▶ abbreviation for proximo.

prox. acc. ▶ abbreviation for proxime accessit.

proxemics /prɒkˈsiːmɪks/ ▶ plural noun [treated as sing.] the branch of knowledge that deals with the amount of space that people feel it necessary to set between themselves and others.

– ORIGIN 1960s: from **PROXIMITY**, on the pattern of words such as *phonemics*.

Proxima Centauri /ˌprɒksɪmə senˈtɔːraɪ/ Astronomy a faint red dwarf star associated with the bright binary star Alpha Centauri. It is the closest known star to the solar system (distance 4.24 light years).

– ORIGIN Latin, 'nearest (star) of Centaurus'.

proximal ▶ adjective Anatomy situated nearer to the centre of the body or the point of attachment: *the proximal end of the forearm.* The opposite of **DISTAL**.
 ■ Geology relating to or denoting an area close to a centre of a geological process such as sedimentation or volcanism.

– DERIVATIVES **proximally** adverb.

– ORIGIN early 19th cent. (as a term in anatomy and zoology): from Latin *proximus* 'nearest' + **-AL**. In geology, usage dates from the 1940s.

proximate ▶ adjective **1** (especially of a cause of something) closest in relationship; immediate.
 ■ closest in space or time: *the failure of the proximate military power to lend assistance.*
 2 nearly accurate; approximate: *he would try to change her speech into proximate ladylikeness.*

– DERIVATIVES **proximately** adverb, **proximation** noun.

– ORIGIN late 16th cent.: from Latin *proximatus*,

'drawn near', past participle of *proximare*, from *proximus* 'nearest'.

proxime accessit /ˌprɒksɪmeɪ akˈsɛsɪt, -mi/ ▶ noun used to name the person who comes second in an examination or is runner-up for an award: *winner: J. W. Wright; proxime accessit: T. G. Broadbent.*

– ORIGIN Latin, literally 'came very near' .

proximity ▶ noun [mass noun] nearness in space, time, or relationship: *do not operate microphones in close proximity to television sets.*

– ORIGIN late 15th cent.: from French *proximité*, from Latin *proximitas*, from *proximus* 'nearest'.

proximity fuse ▶ noun an electronic detonator that causes a projectile to explode when it comes within a preset distance of its target.

proximo /ˈprɒksɪməʊ/ ▶ adjective [postpositive] dated of next month: *he must be in Edinburgh on 1st proximo.*

– ORIGIN from Latin *proximo mense* 'in the next month'.

proxy ▶ noun (pl. **-ies**) **1** [mass noun] the authority to represent someone else, especially in voting or marrying: *Britons overseas may register to vote by proxy.*
 ■ [count noun] a person authorized to act on behalf of another. ■ [count noun] a document authorizing a person to vote on another's behalf.
 2 a figure that can be used to represent the value of something in a calculation: *the use of a US wealth measure as a proxy for the true worldwide measure.*

– ORIGIN late Middle English: contraction of **PROCURACY**.

proxy war ▶ noun a war instigated by a major power which does not itself become involved.

Prozac /ˈprəʊzak/ ▶ noun trademark for **FLUOXETINE**.

– ORIGIN 1980s: an invented name.

prozone /ˈprəʊzəʊn/ ▶ noun [mass noun] Immunology (in testing for antigens) the range of relative quantities of precipitin (or agglutinin) and antigen within which any precipitation (or agglutination) is inhibited by the predominance of one component.

– ORIGIN early 20th cent.: from **PRO-**[2] before + (*agglutination*) *zone*.

PRS ▶ abbreviation for ■ Performing Rights Society. ■ (in the UK) President of the Royal Society.

prude ▶ noun a person who is or claims to be easily shocked by matters relating to sex or nudity.

– DERIVATIVES **prudery** noun, **prudish** adjective, **prudishly** adverb, **prudishness** noun.

– ORIGIN early 18th cent.: from French, back-formation from *prudefemme*, feminine of *prud'homme* 'good man and true', from *prou* 'worthy'.

prudent ▶ adjective acting with or showing care and thought for the future: *no prudent money manager would authorize a loan without first knowing its purpose.*

– DERIVATIVES **prudence** noun, **prudently** adverb.

– ORIGIN late Middle English: from Old French, or from Latin *prudent-*, contraction of *provident-* 'foreseeing, attending to' (see **PROVIDENT**).

prudential ▶ adjective involving or showing care and forethought, typically in business.

– DERIVATIVES **prudentially** adverb.

– ORIGIN late Middle English: from **PRUDENT**, on the pattern of words such as *evidential*.

Prudhoe Bay /ˈpruːdəʊ/ an inlet of the Arctic Ocean on the north coast of Alaska. It is a major centre of Alaskan oil production.

pruinose /ˈpruːɪnəʊs, -z/ ▶ adjective chiefly Botany (of a surface, such as that of a grape) covered with white powdery granules; frosted in appearance.

– ORIGIN early 19th cent.: from Latin *pruinosus*, from *pruina* 'hoar frost'.

prune[1] ▶ noun a plum preserved by drying and having a black, wrinkled appearance: *stewed prunes.*
 ■ informal an unpleasant or disagreeable person: *he was a good leader, but a right miserable old prune.*

– ORIGIN Middle English: from Old French, via Latin from Greek *prou(m)non* 'plum'.

prune[2] ▶ verb [with obj.] trim (a tree, shrub, or bush) by cutting away dead or overgrown branches or stems, especially to increase fruitfulness and growth.
 ■ cut away (a branch or stem) in this way: *prune back the branches.* ■ reduce the extent of (something) by removing superfluous or unwanted parts: *the cabinet is zealous to prune expenditure.* ■ remove (superfluous

or unwanted parts) from something: *Eliot deliberately pruned away details.*
 ▶ noun [in sing.] an instance of trimming a tree, shrub, or bush.

– DERIVATIVES **pruner** noun.

– ORIGIN late 15th cent. (in the sense 'abbreviate'): from Old French *pro(o)ignier*, possibly based on Latin *rotundus* 'round'.

prunella[1] /pruːˈnɛlə/ ▶ noun a plant of a genus that includes self-heal. Several kinds are cultivated as ground cover and rockery plants.
 ● Genus *Prunella*, family Labiatae.

– ORIGIN modern Latin, literally 'quinsy', in medieval Latin *brunella*, diminutive of *brunus* 'brown', denoting a disease causing a brown coating on the tongue. Self-heal was a reputed cure for the disease.

prunella[2] /pruːˈnɛlə/ ▶ noun [mass noun] a strong silk or worsted fabric used formerly for barristers' gowns and the uppers of women's shoes.

– ORIGIN mid 17th cent.: perhaps from French *prunelle* 'sloe' (because of its dark colour).

pruning hook ▶ noun a cutting tool used for pruning, consisting of a hooked blade on a long handle.

pruning knife ▶ noun a knife specifically designed for pruning, typically having a sharp, slightly curved blade and a hooked end.

prunus /ˈpruːnəs/ ▶ noun a tree or shrub of a large genus that includes many varieties grown for their spring blossom (cherry and almond) or for their fruit (plum, peach, and apricot).
 ● Genus *Prunus*, family Rosaceae.

– ORIGIN modern Latin, from Latin, literally 'plum tree'.

prurient /ˈprʊərɪənt/ ▶ adjective having or encouraging an excessive interest in sexual matters: *she'd been the subject of much prurient curiosity.*

– DERIVATIVES **prurience** noun, **pruriency** noun, **pruriently** adverb.

– ORIGIN late 16th cent. (in the sense 'having a mental itching'): from Latin *prurient-* 'itching, longing' and 'being wanton', from the verb *prurire*.

prurigo /prʊəˈraɪgəʊ/ ▶ noun [mass noun] Medicine a chronic skin disease causing severe itching.

– DERIVATIVES **pruriginous** /prʊəˈrɪdʒɪnəs/ adjective.

– ORIGIN mid 17th cent.: from Latin, from *prurire* 'to itch'.

pruritus /prʊəˈraɪtəs/ ▶ noun [mass noun] Medicine severe itching of the skin, as a symptom of various ailments.

– DERIVATIVES **pruritic** adjective.

– ORIGIN mid 17th cent.: from Latin, 'itching' (see **PRURIGO**).

prusik /ˈprʌsɪk/ Climbing ▶ noun [mass noun] a method of ascending or descending a rope by means of two loops, each attached to it by a special knot tightening when weight is applied and slackening when it is removed, enabling the loop to be moved along the rope.
 ■ (also **prusik knot**) [count noun] a sliding knot that locks under pressure enabling a person to climb in this way.
 ▶ verb (**prusiked**, **prusiking**) [no obj.] [usu. as noun **prusiking**] climb using this method.

– ORIGIN 1930s: from the name of Karl *Prusik*, the Austrian mountaineer who devised this method of climbing.

Prussia a former kingdom of Germany. Originally a small country on the SE shores of the Baltic, under Frederick the Great it became a major European power covering much of modern NE Germany and Poland. After the Franco-Prussian War of 1870–1 it became the centre of Bismarck's new German Empire, but following Germany's defeat in the First World War the Prussian monarchy was abolished.

– DERIVATIVES **Prussian** adjective & noun.

Prussian blue ▶ noun [mass noun] a deep blue pigment used in painting and dyeing, made from or in imitation of ferric ferrocyanide.
 ■ the deep blue colour of this pigment.

prussic acid /ˈprʌsɪk/ ▶ noun old-fashioned term for **HYDROCYANIC ACID**.

– DERIVATIVES **prussiate** noun.

– ORIGIN late 18th cent.: *prussic* from French *prussique* 'relating to Prussian blue'.

Prut /pruːt/ (also **Pruth**) a river of SE Europe, which rises in the Carpathian Mountains in southern Ukraine and flows south-east for 850 km (530 miles), joining the Danube near Galaţi in Romania. For much of its course it forms the border between Romania and Moldova.

pry[1] ▶ verb (**-ies**, **-ied**) [no obj.] enquire too inquisitively into a person's private affairs: *I'm sick of you* **prying into** *my personal life* | [as adj. **prying**] *she felt there was no place where she could escape from the prying eyes.*
– DERIVATIVES **pryingly** adverb.
– ORIGIN Middle English (in the sense 'peer inquisitively'): of unknown origin.

pry[2] ▶ verb (**-ies**, **-ied**) chiefly N. Amer. another term for **PRISE**: *prying open the door* | *he pried his left leg free.*
– ORIGIN early 19th cent.: from the verb **PRISE**, interpreted as *pries*, third person singular of the present tense.

pry bar ▶ noun N. Amer. a small, flattish iron bar used in the same way as a crowbar.

prytany /'prɪtəni/ ▶ noun (pl. **-ies**) (in ancient Greece) each of the ten divisions of the Athenian Council of Five Hundred.
■ a period of five weeks for which each division presided in turn.
– ORIGIN from Greek *prutaneia*, from *prutanis* 'prince, ruler'.

Przewalski's horse /ˌpəˈʒɜːˈvalski/ ▶ noun a stocky wild Mongolian horse with a dun-coloured coat and a dark brown erect mane, now extinct in the wild. It is the only true wild horse, and is the ancestor of the domestic horse.
● *Equus ferus*, family Equidae.
– ORIGIN late 19th cent.: named after Nikolai M. *Przheval'sky* (1839–88), Russian explorer.

PS ▶ abbreviation for ■ Police Sergeant. ■ postscript. ■ private secretary. ■ (in the theatre) prompt side.

Ps. (pl. **Pss.**) ▶ abbreviation for Psalm or Psalms.

psalm /sɑːm/ (also **Psalm**) ▶ noun a sacred song or hymn, in particular any of those contained in the biblical Book of Psalms and used in Christian and Jewish worship: *a delightful setting of Psalm 150.*
■ (**the Psalms** or **the Book of Psalms**) a book of the Bible comprising a collection of religious verses, sung or recited in both Jewish and Christian worship. Many are traditionally ascribed to King David.
– DERIVATIVES **psalmic** adjective.
– ORIGIN Old English (p)*sealm*, via ecclesiastical Latin from Greek *psalmos* 'song sung to harp music', from *psallein* 'to pluck'.

psalm book ▶ noun a book containing psalms, especially with metrical settings for worship.

psalmist ▶ noun the author or composer of a psalm, especially of any of the biblical Psalms.
– ORIGIN late 15th cent.: from late Latin *psalmista*, from *psalmus* 'song sung to harp music' (see **PSALM**).

psalmody /'sɑːmədi, 'salm-/ ▶ noun [mass noun] the singing of psalms or similar sacred canticles, especially in public worship.
■ psalms arranged for singing: *these books offer a useful collection of psalmody.*
– DERIVATIVES **psalmodic** adjective, **psalmodist** noun.
– ORIGIN Middle English: via late Latin from Greek *psalmōidia* 'singing to a harp', from *psalmos* (see **PSALM**) + *ōidē* 'song'.

psalter /'sɔːltə, 'sɒl-/ ▶ noun (**the psalter**) the Book of Psalms.
■ a copy of the biblical Psalms, especially for liturgical use.
– ORIGIN Old English (p)*saltere*, via Latin *psalterium* from Greek *psaltērion* 'stringed instrument'.

psalterium /sɔːl'tɪərɪəm, sɒl-/ ▶ noun another term for **OMASUM**.
– ORIGIN mid 19th cent.: from Latin, literally 'psalter' (see **PSALTER**), because of its many folds of tissue, resembling pages of a book.

psaltery /'sɔːlt(ə)ri, 'sɒl-/ ▶ noun (pl. **-ies**) an ancient and medieval musical instrument like a dulcimer but played by plucking the strings with the fingers or a plectrum.
– ORIGIN Middle English *sautrie*, from Old French *sauterie*, from Latin *psalterium* (see **PSALTER**).

PSBR Brit. ▶ abbreviation for public-sector borrowing requirement.

psephology /sɛˈfɒlədʒi, sɪ-/ ▶ noun [mass noun] the statistical study of elections and trends in voting.
– DERIVATIVES **psephological** adjective, **psephologically** adverb, **psephologist** noun.
– ORIGIN 1950s: from Greek *psēphos* 'pebble, vote' + **-LOGY**.

pseud /sjuːd/ informal ▶ adjective intellectually or socially pretentious.
▶ noun a pretentious person; a poseur.
– ORIGIN 1960s: abbreviation of **PSEUDO**.

pseud- ▶ combining form variant spelling of **PSEUDO-** reduced before a vowel (as in *pseudepigrapha*).

pseudepigrapha /ˌsjuːdɪˈpɪɡrəfə/ ▶ plural noun spurious or pseudonymous writings, especially Jewish writings ascribed to various biblical patriarchs and prophets but composed within approximately 200 years of the birth of Christ.
– DERIVATIVES **pseudepigraphal** adjective, **pseudepigraphic** adjective.
– ORIGIN late 17th cent.: neuter plural of Greek *pseudepigraphos* 'with false title' (see **PSEUDO-**, **EPIGRAPH**).

pseudo /'sjuːdəʊ/ ▶ adjective not genuine; sham: *we are talking about real journalists and not the pseudo kind.*
■ pretentious; insincere: *the show's pseudo, with just one memorable song.*
▶ noun (pl. **-os**) a pretentious or insincere person.
– ORIGIN late Middle English: independent use of **PSEUDO-**.

pseudo- (also **pseud-** before a vowel) ▶ combining form **1** supposed or purporting to be but not really so; false; not genuine: *pseudonym | pseudoscience.*
2 resembling or imitating: *pseudo-hallucination.*
– ORIGIN from Greek *pseudēs* 'false', *pseudos* 'falsehood'.

pseudobulb ▶ noun Botany a bulb-like enlargement of the stem in many orchids, especially tropical and epiphytic ones.

pseudocarp ▶ noun technical term for **FALSE FRUIT**.
– ORIGIN mid 19th cent.: from **PSEUDO-** 'false' + Greek *karpos* 'fruit'.

pseudocholinesterase /ˌsjuːdəʊˌkəʊlɪˈnɛstəreɪz/ ▶ noun [mass noun] Biochemistry an enzyme present in the blood and certain organs which hydrolyses acetylcholine more slowly than acetylcholinesterase.

pseudo-classical ▶ adjective having a false or spurious classical style.

pseudo-cleft Grammar ▶ noun a sentence which resembles a cleft sentence by conveying emphasis or politeness through the use of a relative clause, such as *what we want is* representing *we want.*
▶ adjective relating to or denoting a sentence of this kind.

pseudocode ▶ noun [mass noun] Computing a notation resembling a simplified programming language, used in program design.

pseudocopulation /ˌsjuːdəʊˌkɒpjʊˈleɪʃ(ə)n/ ▶ noun [mass noun] Biology attempted copulation by a male insect with a flower (especially an orchid) that resembles the female, carrying pollen to it in the process.

pseudocyesis /ˌsjuːdəʊsaɪˈiːsɪs/ ▶ noun technical term for **PHANTOM PREGNANCY**.
– ORIGIN mid 19th cent.: from **PSEUDO-** 'false' + Greek *kuēsis* 'conception'.

pseudocyst ▶ noun Medicine a fluid-filled cavity resembling a cyst but lacking a wall or lining.

Pseudo-Dionysius (6th century AD), the unidentified author of important theological works formerly attributed to Dionysius the Areopagite.

pseudoextinction ▶ noun [mass noun] Palaeontology the apparent extinction of a group of organisms of which modified descendant forms survive.

pseudogene ▶ noun Genetics a section of a chromosome that is an imperfect copy of a functional gene.

pseudohermaphroditism /ˌsjuːdəʊhɜːˈmafrədɪtɪz(ə)m/ ▶ noun [mass noun] Medicine the condition in which an individual of one sex has external genitalia superficially resembling those of the other sex.

pseudomembrane ▶ noun Medicine a layer of exudate resembling a membrane, formed on the surface of the skin or of a mucous membrane, especially the conjunctiva.

– DERIVATIVES **pseudomembranous** adjective.

pseudomonas /ˌsjuːdə(ʊ)ˈməʊnəs, sjuːˈdɒmənəs/ ▶ noun Microbiology a bacterium which occurs in soil and detritus, including a number that are pathogens of plants or animals.
● Genus *Pseudomonas*; aerobic Gram-negative bacteria.
– ORIGIN modern Latin, from **PSEUDO-** 'false' + *monas* 'monad'.

pseudomorph /'sjuːdə(ʊ)mɔːf/ Crystallography ▶ noun a crystal consisting of one mineral but having the form of another.
▶ verb [with obj.] replace (another substance) to form a pseudomorph.
– DERIVATIVES **pseudomorphic** adjective, **pseudomorphism** noun, **pseudomorphous** adjective.
– ORIGIN mid 19th cent.: from **PSEUDO-** 'false' + Greek *morphē* 'form'.

pseudonym /'sjuːdənɪm/ ▶ noun a fictitious name, especially one used by an author.
– ORIGIN mid 19th cent.: from French *pseudonyme*, from Greek *pseudōnymos*, from *pseudēs* 'false' + *onoma* 'name'.

pseudonymous /sjuːˈdɒnɪməs/ ▶ adjective writing or written under a false name.
– DERIVATIVES **pseudonymity** /-'nɪmɪti/ noun, **pseudonymously** adverb.

pseudopod /'sjuːdə(ʊ)pɒd/ ▶ noun another term for **PSEUDOPODIUM**.

pseudopodium /ˌsjuːdə(ʊ)ˈpəʊdɪəm/ ▶ noun (pl. **pseudopodia** /-dɪə/) Biology a temporary protrusion of the surface of an amoeboid cell for movement and feeding.
– ORIGIN mid 19th cent.: modern Latin, from **PSEUDO-** + **PODIUM**.

pseudopregnancy ▶ noun (pl. **-ies**) another term for **PHANTOM PREGNANCY**.

pseudorabies /ˌsjuːdəʊˈreɪbiːz/ ▶ noun [mass noun] Veterinary Medicine an infectious herpesvirus disease of the central nervous system in domestic animals that causes convulsions and intense itching and is usually fatal.

pseudorandom ▶ adjective (of a number, a sequence of numbers, or any digital data) satisfying one or more statistical tests for randomness but produced by a definite mathematical procedure.
– DERIVATIVES **pseudorandomly** adverb.

pseudoscience ▶ noun a collection of beliefs or practices mistakenly regarded as being based on scientific method.
– DERIVATIVES **pseudoscientific** adjective, **pseudoscientist** noun.

pseudoscorpion ▶ noun another term for **FALSE SCORPION**.

pseudouridine /ˌsjuːdəʊˈjʊərɪdiːn/ ▶ noun [mass noun] Biochemistry a nucleoside present in transfer RNA and differing from uridine in having the sugar residue attached at a carbon atom instead of nitrogen.

pshaw /pʃɔː, ʃɔː/ dated or humorous ▶ exclamation an expression of contempt or impatience: *'Poison? Pshaw! The very idea!'*
▶ verb [no obj.] utter such an exclamation: *when I suggested that free trade might dilute Canadian culture, he pshawed.*
– ORIGIN natural exclamation: first recorded in English in the late 17th cent.

psi /psaɪ, saɪ/ ▶ noun **1** the twenty-third letter of the Greek alphabet (Ψ, ψ), transliterated as 'ps'.
■ (**Psi**) [followed by Latin genitive] Astronomy the twenty-third star in a constellation: *Psi Aquarii.*
2 [mass noun] supposed parapsychological or psychic faculties or phenomena.
– ORIGIN Greek.

p.s.i. ▶ abbreviation for pounds per square inch.

psilocybin /ˌsaɪlə(ʊ)ˈsaɪbɪn/ ▶ noun [mass noun] Chemistry a hallucinogenic compound of the alkaloid class, found in the liberty cap and related toadstools.
– ORIGIN 1950s: from modern Latin *Psilocybe* (genus name), from Greek *psilos* 'bald' + *kubē* 'head'.

psionic /saɪˈɒnɪk/ ▶ adjective relating to or denoting the practical use of psychic powers or paranormal phenomena: *psionic communication.*
– DERIVATIVES **psionically** adverb.
– ORIGIN 1950s: from **PSI**, on the pattern of *electronic*.

psittacine /'sɪtəkʌɪn, -sɪn/ ▶ adjective Ornithology of, relating to, or denoting birds of the parrot family: *psittacine beak and feather disease.*
■ parrot-like (especially referring to parrots' ability to

copy human speech): *issues are thought through in a distinctive way, rather than by psittacine repetition.*
▶ **noun** Ornithology a bird of the parrot family.
– ORIGIN late 19th cent.: from Latin *psittacinus* 'of a parrot', from *psittacus*, from Greek *psittakos* 'parrot'.

psittacosaurus /sɪˈtakəsɔːrəs/ ▶ **noun** a partly bipedal herbivorous dinosaur of the mid Cretaceous period, having a parrot-like beak and probably ancestral to other ceratopsians.
• Genus *Psittacosaurus*, infraorder Ceratopsia, order Ornithischia.
– ORIGIN modern Latin, from Greek *psittakos* 'parrot' + *sauros* 'lizard'.

psittacosis /ˌsɪtəˈkəʊsɪs/ ▶ **noun** [mass noun] a contagious disease of birds, caused by chlamydiae and transmissible (especially from parrots) to human beings as a form of pneumonia.
– ORIGIN late 19th cent.: from Latin *psittacus* 'parrot' + **-OSIS**.

psoas /ˈsəʊəs/ (also **psoas major**) ▶ **noun** Anatomy each of a pair of large muscles which run from the lumbar spine through the groin on either side and, with the iliacus, flex the hip. A second muscle, the **psoas minor**, has a similar action but is often absent.
– ORIGIN late 17th cent.: from Greek, accusative plural of *psoa*, interpreted as singular.

psocid /ˈsəʊkɪd, -sɪd/ ▶ **noun** Entomology a small or minute insect of an order that includes the booklice. Many psocids are wingless and somewhat resemble lice or aphids, and most live on bark and among foliage.
• Order Psocoptera: many families, including the large family Psocidae.
– ORIGIN late 19th cent.: from modern Latin *Psocidae* (plural), from *Psocus* (genus name), from Greek *psōkhein* 'to grind'.

Psocoptera /sə(ʊ)ˈkɒptərə/ Entomology an order of insects that comprises the booklice and other psocids.
– DERIVATIVES **psocopteran** noun & adjective.
– ORIGIN modern Latin (plural), from *Psocus* (genus name) + *pteron* 'wing'.

psoralen /ˈsɔːrəlɛn/ ▶ **noun** [mass noun] Chemistry a compound present in certain plants which is used in perfumery and (in combination with ultraviolet light) to treat psoriasis and other skin disorders.
• A tricyclic lactone; chem. formula: $C_{11}H_6O_3$.
– ORIGIN 1930s: from modern Latin *Psoralea* (former genus name), from Greek *psōraleos* 'itchy' (from *psōra* 'itch') + the suffix *-en* (compare with **-ENE**).

psoriasis /sɒˈrʌɪəsɪs/ ▶ **noun** [mass noun] Medicine a skin disease marked by red, itchy, scaly patches.
– DERIVATIVES **psoriatic** /ˌsɔːrɪˈatɪk/ adjective.
– ORIGIN late 17th cent.: modern Latin, from Greek *psōriasis*, from *psōrian* 'have an itch', from *psōra* 'itch'.

p

psst ▶ **exclamation** used to attract someone's attention surreptitiously: *Psst! Want to know a secret?*
– ORIGIN 1920s: imitative.

PST ▶ **abbreviation for** Pacific Standard Time (see **PACIFIC TIME**).

PSV Brit. ▶ **abbreviation for** public service vehicle.

psych /sʌɪk/ (also **psyche**) ▶ **verb 1** [with obj.] informal mentally prepare (someone) for a testing task or occasion: *we had to **psych** ourselves **up** for the race.*
■ subject (someone) to psychological investigation or psychotherapy.
2 (usu. **psyche**) [no obj.] Bridge make a psychic bid.
▶ **noun 1** informal short for **PSYCHIATRIST** or **PSYCHOLOGIST**.
■ [mass noun] short for **PSYCHIATRY** or **PSYCHOLOGY**.
2 (usu. **psyche**) Bridge a psychic bid.
▶ **adjective** [attrib.] informal **1** short for **PSYCHIATRIC**.
2 short for **PSYCHEDELIC**: *a rare old psych album.*
▶ **psych someone out** informal intimidate an opponent or rival by appearing very confident or aggressive: *we won't be **psyched out** of beating them.*
psych something out informal analyse something in psychological terms.

Psyche /ˈsʌɪki/ Greek Mythology a Hellenistic personification of the soul as female, or sometimes as a butterfly. The allegory of Psyche's love for Cupid is told in *The Golden Ass* by Apuleius.

psyche[1] /ˈsʌɪki/ ▶ **noun** the human soul, mind, or spirit: *I will never really fathom the female psyche.*
– ORIGIN mid 17th cent.: via Latin from Greek *psukhē* 'breath, life, soul'.

psyche[2] /sʌɪk/ ▶ **verb**, **noun**, & **adjective** variant spelling of **PSYCH**.

psychedelia /ˌsʌɪkəˈdiːlɪə/ ▶ **noun** [mass noun] music, culture, or art based on the experiences produced by psychedelic drugs.
– ORIGIN 1960s: back-formation from **PSYCHEDELIC**.

psychedelic /ˌsʌɪkəˈdɛlɪk, -ˈdiːlɪk/ ▶ **adjective** relating to or denoting drugs (especially LSD) that produce hallucinations and apparent expansion of consciousness.
■ relating to or denoting a style of rock music originating in the mid 1960s, characterized by musical experimentation and drug-related lyrics. ■ denoting or having an intense, vivid colour or a swirling abstract pattern: *a psychedelic T-shirt.*
▶ **noun** a psychedelic drug.
– DERIVATIVES **psychedelically** adverb.
– ORIGIN 1950s: formed irregularly from **PSYCHE**[1] + Greek *dēlos* 'clear, manifest' + **-IC**.

psychiatric /ˌsʌɪkɪˈatrɪk/ ▶ **adjective** of or relating to mental illness or its treatment: *a psychiatric disorder.*
– DERIVATIVES **psychiatrically** adverb.

psychiatrist ▶ **noun** a medical practitioner specializing in the diagnosis and treatment of mental illness.

psychiatry /sʌɪˈkʌɪətri/ ▶ **noun** [mass noun] the study and treatment of mental illness, emotional disturbance, and abnormal behaviour.
– ORIGIN mid 19th cent.: from Greek *psukhē* 'soul, mind' + *iatreia* 'healing' (from *iatros* 'healer').

psychic /ˈsʌɪkɪk/ ▶ **adjective 1** relating to or denoting faculties or phenomena that are apparently inexplicable by natural laws, especially involving telepathy or clairvoyance: *psychic powers.*
■ (of a person) appearing or considered to have powers of telepathy or clairvoyance: *I could sense it—I must be psychic.*
2 of or relating to the soul or mind: *he dulled his psychic pain with gin.*
3 Bridge denoting a bid that deliberately misrepresents the bidder's hand, in order to mislead the opponents.
▶ **noun** a person considered or claiming to have psychic powers; a medium.
■ (**psychics**) [treated as sing. or pl.] the study of psychic phenomena.
– DERIVATIVES **psychical** adjective (usu. in sense 1), **psychically** adverb, **psychism** noun (only in sense 1).
– ORIGIN early 19th cent.: from Greek *psukhikos* (see **PSYCHE**[1]).

psychic income ▶ **noun** [mass noun] Economics the non-monetary or non-material satisfactions that accompany an occupation or economic activity.

psycho informal ▶ **noun** (pl. **-os**) a psychopath.
▶ **adjective** psychopathic.
– ORIGIN 1930s: abbreviation.

psycho- ▶ **combining form** relating to the mind or psychology: *psychobabble | psychometrics.*
– ORIGIN from Greek *psukhē* 'breath, soul, mind'.

psychoacoustics ▶ **plural noun** [treated as sing.] the branch of psychology concerned with the perception of sound and its physiological effects.
– DERIVATIVES **psychoacoustic** adjective.

psychoactive ▶ **adjective** (chiefly of a drug) affecting the mind.

psychoanalysis ▶ **noun** [mass noun] a system of psychological theory and therapy which aims to treat mental disorders by investigating the interaction of conscious and unconscious elements in the mind and bringing repressed fears and conflicts into the conscious mind by techniques such as dream interpretation and free association.
– DERIVATIVES **psychoanalyse** (US **psychoanalyze**) verb, **psychoanalytic** adjective, **psychoanalytical** adjective, **psychoanalytically** adverb.

psychoanalyst ▶ **noun** a person who practises psychoanalysis.

psychobabble ▶ **noun** [mass noun] informal, derogatory jargon used in popular psychology.

psychobiology ▶ **noun** [mass noun] the branch of science that deals with the biological basis of behaviour and mental phenomena.
– DERIVATIVES **psychobiological** adjective, **psychobiologist** noun.

psychodrama ▶ **noun 1** [mass noun] a form of psychotherapy in which patients act out events from their past.
2 a play, film, or novel in which psychological elements are the main interest.
■ [mass noun] the genre to which such works belong.

psychodynamics ▶ **plural noun** [treated as sing.] the interrelation of the unconscious and conscious mental and emotional forces that determine personality and motivation.
■ the branch of psychology that deals with this.
– DERIVATIVES **psychodynamic** adjective, **psychodynamically** adverb.

psychogenesis /ˌsʌɪkə(ʊ)ˈdʒɛnɪsɪs/ ▶ **noun** [in sing.] the psychological cause to which a mental illness or behavioural disturbance may be attributed (as distinct from a physical cause).

psychogenic /ˌsʌɪkə(ʊ)ˈdʒɛnɪk/ ▶ **adjective** having a psychological origin or cause rather than a physical one: *psychogenic ill health.*

psychogeriatrics ▶ **plural noun** [treated as sing.] the branch of health care concerned with mental illness and disturbance in elderly people, particularly those who have suffered distress as a result of moving into an institution.
– DERIVATIVES **psychogeriatric** adjective, **psychogeriatrician** noun.

psychographics ▶ **plural noun** [treated as sing.] the study and classification of people according to their attitudes, aspirations, and other psychological criteria, especially in market research.
– DERIVATIVES **psychographic** adjective.

psychohistory ▶ **noun** (pl. **-ies**) [mass noun] the interpretation of historical events with the aid of psychological theory.
■ [count noun] a work that interprets historical events in such a way: *this psychohistory of postmodernity focuses on the changing image of California.* ■ [count noun] a psychological history of an individual.
– DERIVATIVES **psychohistorian** noun, **psychohistorical** adjective.

psychokinesis /ˌsʌɪkəʊkɪˈniːsɪs, -kʌɪ-/ ▶ **noun** [mass noun] the supposed ability to move objects by mental effort alone.
– DERIVATIVES **psychokinetic** adjective.

psycholinguistics ▶ **plural noun** [treated as sing.] the study of the relationships between linguistic behaviour and psychological processes, including the process of language acquisition.
– DERIVATIVES **psycholinguist** noun, **psycholinguistic** adjective.

psychologese /sʌɪˌkɒləˈdʒiːz/ ▶ **noun** [mass noun] informal psychological jargon or technical terms used for effect.

psychological ▶ **adjective** of, affecting, or arising in the mind; related to the mental and emotional state of a person: *the victim had sustained physical and psychological damage.*
■ of or relating to psychology: *psychological research.* ■ (of an ailment or problem) having a mental rather than a physical cause: *it was concluded that her pain was psychological.*
– DERIVATIVES **psychologically** adverb.

psychological block ▶ **noun** another term for **MENTAL BLOCK**.

psychological moment ▶ **noun** [in sing.] the moment at which something will or would have the greatest psychological effect: *there was a psychological moment when they might have accepted the report.*

psychological warfare ▶ **noun** [mass noun] actions intended to reduce an opponent's morale.

psychologism ▶ **noun** [mass noun] Philosophy a tendency to interpret events or arguments in subjective terms, or to exaggerate the relevance of psychological factors.

psychologist ▶ **noun** an expert or specialist in psychology.

psychologize (also **-ise**) ▶ **verb** [with obj.] analyse or regard in psychological terms.
■ [no obj.] theorize or speculate concerning psychology.

psychology ▶ **noun** [mass noun] the scientific study of the human mind and its functions, especially those affecting behaviour in a given context.
■ [in sing.] the mental characteristics or attitude of a person or group: *the psychology of child-killers.* ■ [in sing.] the mental factors governing a situation or activity: *the psychology of interpersonal relationships.*
– ORIGIN late 17th cent.: from modern Latin *psychologia* (see **PSYCHO-**, **-LOGY**).

psychometric /ˌsʌɪkə(ʊ)ˈmɛtrɪk/ ▶ **adjective** of, relating to, or deriving from psychometry or psychometrics.
– DERIVATIVES **psychometrically** adverb.

psychometrics ▶ **plural noun** [treated as sing.] the science of measuring mental capacities and processes.

psychometry /sʌɪˈkɒmɪtri/ ▶ **noun** [mass noun] **1** the supposed ability to discover facts about an event or person by touching inanimate objects associated with them.
2 another term for **PSYCHOMETRICS**.
– DERIVATIVES **psychometrist** noun.

psychomotor ▶ **adjective** [attrib.] of or relating to the origination of movement in conscious mental activity.

psychoneuroimmunology /ˌsʌɪkə(ʊ)ˌnjʊərəʊˌɪmjʊˈnɒlədʒi/ ▶ **noun** [mass noun] Medicine the study of the effect of the mind on health and resistance to disease.

psychoneurosis ▶ **noun** another term for **NEUROSIS**.

psychopath ▶ **noun** a person suffering from chronic mental disorder with abnormal or violent social behaviour.
– DERIVATIVES **psychopathic** adjective, **psychopathically** adverb.

psychopathology ▶ **noun** [mass noun] the scientific study of mental disorders.
■ features of people's mental health considered collectively: *ageism, family discord and psychopathology all play their part in abuse.* ■ mental or behavioural disorder: *she showed evidence of genuine psychopathology.*
– DERIVATIVES **psychopathological** adjective, **psychopathologist** noun.

psychopathy /sʌɪˈkɒpəθi/ ▶ **noun** [mass noun] mental illness or disorder.

psychopharmacology ▶ **noun** [mass noun] the branch of psychology concerned with the effects of drugs on the mind and behaviour.
– DERIVATIVES **psychopharmacological** adjective, **psychopharmacologist** noun.

psychophysics ▶ **plural noun** [treated as sing.] the branch of psychology that deals with the relations between physical stimuli and mental phenomena.
– DERIVATIVES **psychophysical** adjective.

psychophysiology ▶ **noun** [mass noun] Psychology the study of the relationship between physiological and psychological phenomena.
■ the way in which the mind and body interact.
– DERIVATIVES **psychophysiological** adjective, **psychophysiologist** noun.

psychopomp /ˈsʌɪkə(ʊ)pɒmp/ (also **psychopompos**) ▶ **noun** (in Greek mythology) a guide of souls to the place of the dead.
■ the spiritual guide of a living person's soul.
– ORIGIN from Greek *psukhopompos*, from *psukhē* 'soul' + *pompos* 'conductor'.

psychosexual ▶ **adjective** of or involving the psychological aspects of the sexual impulse.
– DERIVATIVES **psychosexually** adverb.

psychosis /sʌɪˈkəʊsɪs/ ▶ **noun** (pl. **psychoses** /-siːz/) a severe mental disorder in which thought and emotions are so impaired that contact is lost with external reality.
– ORIGIN mid 19th cent.: from Greek *psukhōsis* 'animation', from *psukhoō* 'I give life to', from *psukhē* 'soul, mind'.

psychosocial ▶ **adjective** of or relating to the interrelation of social factors and individual thought and behaviour.
– DERIVATIVES **psychosocially** adverb.

psychosomatic /ˌsʌɪkə(ʊ)səˈmatɪk/ ▶ **adjective** (of a physical illness or other condition) caused or aggravated by a mental factor such as internal conflict or stress: *her doctor was convinced that most of Edith's problems were psychosomatic.*
■ of or relating to the interaction of mind and body.
– DERIVATIVES **psychosomatically** adverb.

psychosurgery ▶ **noun** [mass noun] brain surgery, such as leucotomy, used to treat mental illness.
– DERIVATIVES **psychosurgical** adjective.

psychosynthesis ▶ **noun** [mass noun] Psychoanalysis the integration of separated elements of the psyche or personality.

psychotherapy ▶ **noun** [mass noun] the treatment of mental disorder by psychological rather than medical means.
– DERIVATIVES **psychotherapeutic** adjective, **psychotherapist** noun.

psychotic /sʌɪˈkɒtɪk/ ▶ **adjective** of, denoting, or suffering from a psychosis: *a psychotic disturbance.*
▶ **noun** a person suffering from a psychosis.
– DERIVATIVES **psychotically** adverb.

psychotomimetic /sʌɪˌkɒtə(ʊ)mɪˈmɛtɪk/ ▶ **adjective** relating to or denoting drugs which are capable of producing an effect on the mind similar to a psychotic state.
▶ **noun** a drug of this kind.

psychotronic /ˌsʌɪkə(ʊ)ˈtrɒnɪk/ ▶ **adjective** **1** denoting or relating to a genre of films typically with a science fiction, horror, or fantasy theme and which were made on a low budget or poorly received by critics. [ORIGIN: 1980s: coined in this sense by Michael Weldon, who edited a weekly New York guide to the best and worst films on local television.]
2 of or relating to psychotronics.

psychotronics ▶ **plural noun** [treated as sing.] a particular branch of parapsychology which supposes an energy or force to emanate from living organisms and affect matter.
– ORIGIN 1970s: from **PSYCHO-**, on the pattern of *electronics.*

psychotropic /ˌsʌɪkə(ʊ)ˈtrəʊpɪk, ˌsʌɪkə(ʊ)ˈtrɒpɪk/ ▶ **adjective** relating to or denoting drugs that affect a person's mental state.
▶ **noun** a drug of this kind.

psychrometer /sʌɪˈkrɒmɪtə/ ▶ **noun** a hygrometer consisting of wet and dry-bulb thermometers, the difference in the two thermometer readings being used to determine atmospheric humidity.
– ORIGIN early 18th cent.: from Greek *psukhros* 'cold' + **-METER**.

psyllid /ˈsɪlɪd/ ▶ **noun** Entomology a minute insect of a family (Psyllidae) that comprises the jumping plant lice.
– ORIGIN late 19th cent.: from modern Latin *Psyllidae* (plural), from Greek *psulla* 'flea'.

psyllium /ˈsɪlɪəm/ ▶ **noun** a leafy-stemmed Eurasian plantain, the seeds of which are used as a laxative and as a bulking agent in the treatment of obesity.
● *Plantago psafra*, family Plantaginaceae.
– ORIGIN mid 16th cent.: via Latin from Greek *psullion*, from *psulla* 'flea' (because the seeds resemble fleas).

PT ▶ **abbreviation for** physical training.

Pt ▶ **abbreviation for** ■ Part: *Pt 1 of the Consumer Protection Act 1987.* ■ (**pt**) pint. ■ (in scoring) point. ■ Printing point (as a unit of measurement): *12 pt type.* ■ (**Pt.**) Point (on maps): *Pt. Cloates.* ■ (**pt**) (denoting a side of a ship or aircraft) port.
▶ **symbol for** the chemical element platinum.

PTA ▶ **abbreviation for** ■ parent–teacher association. ■ (in the UK) Passenger Transport Authority, a local body responsible for operating public transport in a particular region.

Ptah /tɑː/ ▶ Egyptian Mythology an ancient deity of Memphis, creator of the universe, god of artisans, and husband of Sekhmet. He became one of the chief deities of Egypt, and was identified by the Greeks with Hephaestus.

ptarmigan /ˈtɑːmɪg(ə)n/ ▶ **noun** a northern grouse of mountainous and Arctic regions, with feathered legs and feet and plumage that typically changes to white in winter.
● Genus *Lagopus*, family Tetraonidae: two species, in particular the (**rock**) **ptarmigan** (*L. mutus*) of Eurasia and North America.
– ORIGIN late 16th cent.: from Scottish Gaelic *tàrmachan*. The spelling with *p-* was introduced later, suggested by Greek words starting with *pt-*.

PTE ▶ **abbreviation for** (in the UK) Passenger Transport Executive, a local body responsible for implementing public transport policy in a particular region.

Pte ▶ **abbreviation for** Private (in the army).

pteranodon /tɛˈranədɒn/ ▶ **noun** a large tailless pterosaur of the Cretaceous period, with a long toothless beak, a long bony crest, and a wingspan of up to 7 m.
● Genus *Pteranodon*, family Pteranodontidae, order Pterosauria.
– ORIGIN modern Latin, from Greek *pteron* 'wing' + *an-* 'without' + *odous, odont-* 'tooth'.

pteridology /ˌtɛrɪˈdɒlədʒi/ ▶ **noun** [mass noun] the study of ferns and related plants.
– DERIVATIVES **pteridological** adjective, **pteridologist** noun.
– ORIGIN mid 19th cent.: from Greek *pteris, pterid-* 'fern' + **-LOGY**.

Pteridophyta /ˌtɛrɪdə(ʊ)ˈfʌɪtə/ ▶ Botany a division of flowerless green plants that comprises the ferns and their relatives.
● Division Pteridophyta: classes Filicopsida (ferns), Sphenopsida (horsetails), and Lycopsida (clubmosses).
– DERIVATIVES **pteridophyte** /ˈtɛrɪdə(ʊ)fʌɪt/ noun.
– ORIGIN from modern Latin (plural), from Greek *pteris, pterid-* 'fern' + *phuton* 'plant'.

pteridosperm /ˈtɛrɪdəʊspəːm/ ▶ **noun** a fossil plant which is intermediate between the ferns and seed-bearing plants, dying out in the Triassic period. Also called **SEED FERN**.
● Formerly placed in their own taxon (class Pteridospermeae), but now included with the gymnosperms.
– ORIGIN early 20th cent.: from modern Latin *pteridospermeae*, from Greek *pteris, pterid-* 'fern'.

ptero- /ˈtɛrəʊ/ ▶ **combining form** relating to wings; having wings: *pterosaur.*
– ORIGIN from Greek *pteron* 'feather, wing'.

pterobranch /ˈtɛrə(ʊ)braŋk/ ▶ **noun** Zoology a minute tube-dwelling colonial acorn worm found chiefly in deep water.
● Class Pterobranchia, phylum Hemichordata.

pterodactyl /ˌtɛrəˈdaktɪl/ ▶ **noun** a pterosaur of the late Jurassic period, with a long slender head and neck and a very short tail.
● Family Pterodactylidae, order Pterosauria: several genera, including *Pterodactylus.*
■ (in general use) any pterosaur.
– ORIGIN early 19th cent.: from modern Latin *Pterodactylus* (genus name), from Greek *pteron* 'wing' + *daktulos* 'finger'.

pteropod /ˈtɛrəpɒd/ ▶ **noun** Zoology a sea butterfly.
– ORIGIN mid 19th cent.: from modern Latin *Pteropoda* (plural), from Greek *pteron* 'wing' + Greek *pous, pod-* 'foot'.

pterosaur /ˈtɛrəsɔː/ ▶ **noun** a fossil warm-blooded flying reptile of the Jurassic and Cretaceous periods, with membranous wings supported by a greatly lengthened fourth finger, and probably covered with fur.
● Order Pterosauria, subdivision Archosauria: several families, including pterodactyls, pteranodons, etc.
– ORIGIN mid 19th cent.: from modern Latin *Pterosauria* (plural), from Greek *pteron* 'wing' + *sauros* 'lizard'.

pteroylglutamic acid /ˌtɛrəʊʌɪlɡluːˈtamɪk, -rɔʊl-/ ▶ **noun** another term for **FOLIC ACID**.
– DERIVATIVES **pteroylglutamate** noun.
– ORIGIN 1940s: the initial element of *pteroylglutamic* is from Greek *pteron* 'wing', with reference to insect pigments.

pterygoid process /ˈtɛrɪɡɔɪd/ ▶ **noun** Anatomy each of a pair of projections from the sphenoid bone in the skull.
– ORIGIN early 18th cent.: from modern Latin *pterygoides* (plural), from Greek *pterux, pterug-* 'wing'.

Pterygota /ˌtɛrɪˈɡəʊtə/ ▶ Entomology a large group of insects that comprises those that have wings or winged ancestors, including the majority of modern species. Compare with **APTERYGOTA**.
● Subclass Pterygota, class Insecta (or Hexapoda): many orders.
– DERIVATIVES **pterygote** noun.
– ORIGIN modern Latin (plural), from Greek *pterugōtos* 'winged', from *pteron, pterug-* 'wing'.

PTFE ▶ **abbreviation for** polytetrafluoroethylene.

PTO ▶ **abbreviation for** ■ please turn over (written at the foot of a page to indicate that the text continues on the reverse). ■ (also **pto**) (in a tractor or other vehicle) power take-off.

Ptolemaic /ˌtɒləˈmeɪɪk/ ▶ **adjective** **1** of or relating to the Greek astronomer Ptolemy or his theories.
2 of or relating to the Ptolemies of Egypt (see **PTOLEMY**[1]).

Ptolemaic system (also **Ptolemaic theory**) ▶ **noun** Astronomy, historical the theory that the earth is the stationary centre of the universe, with the planets moving in epicyclic orbits within surrounding concentric spheres. Compare with **COPERNICAN SYSTEM**.

Ptolemy[1] /ˈtɒlɪmi/ the name of all the Macedonian

rulers of Egypt, a dynasty founded by Ptolemy, the close friend and general of Alexander the Great, who took charge of Egypt after the latter's death and declared himself king (Ptolemy I) in 304 BC. The dynasty ended with the death of Cleopatra in 30 BC.

Ptolemy² /ˈtɒlɪmi/ (2nd century) Greek astronomer and geographer. His teachings had enormous influence on medieval thought, the geocentric view of the cosmos being adopted as Christian doctrine until the late Renaissance. Ptolemy's *Geography*, giving lists of places with their longitudes and latitudes, was also a standard work for centuries, despite its inaccuracies.

ptomaine /ˈtəʊmeɪn/ ▶ noun Chemistry, dated any of a group of amine compounds of unpleasant taste and odour formed in putrefying animal and vegetable matter and formerly thought to cause food poisoning.
– ORIGIN late 19th cent.: from French *ptomaïne*, from Italian *ptomaina*, formed irregularly from Greek *ptōma* 'corpse'.

ptosis /ˈtəʊsɪs/ ▶ noun [mass noun] Medicine drooping of the upper eyelid due to paralysis or disease, or as a congenital condition.
– DERIVATIVES **ptotic** /ˈtəʊtɪk/ adjective.
– ORIGIN mid 18th cent.: from Greek *ptōsis*, from *piptein* 'to fall'.

P-trap ▶ noun a trap consisting of a U-bend with the upper part of its outlet arm bent horizontally.
– ORIGIN late 19th cent.: so named because of its shape.

PTSD ▶ abbreviation for post-traumatic stress disorder.

Pty Austral./NZ & S. African ▶ abbreviation for proprietary (used in the names of companies): *Apex Engineering Pty Ltd*.

ptyalin /ˈtʌɪəlɪn/ ▶ noun [mass noun] Biochemistry a form of amylase found in the saliva of humans and some other animals.
– ORIGIN mid 19th cent.: from Greek *ptualon* 'spittle' + -IN¹.

P-type ▶ adjective Electronics denoting a region in a semiconductor in which electrical conduction is due chiefly to the movement of positive holes. Compare with N-TYPE.

Pu ▶ symbol for the chemical element plutonium.

pub Brit. ▶ noun an establishment for the sale of beer and other (alcoholic and non-alcoholic) drinks, sometimes also serving food, to be consumed on the premises.
■ Austral. a hotel.
▶ verb [no obj.] [usu. as noun **pubbing**] informal frequent pubs.
– ORIGIN mid 19th cent.: abbreviation of PUBLIC HOUSE.

pub. ▶ abbreviation for ■ publication(s). ■ published. ■ publisher.

pub crawl informal, chiefly Brit. ▶ noun a tour taking in several pubs or drinking places, with one or more drinks at each.
▶ verb [no obj.] (**pub-crawl**) go on a pub crawl.

pube /pjuːb/ ▶ noun informal a pubic hair.

puberty ▶ noun [mass noun] the period during which adolescents reach sexual maturity and become capable of reproduction.
– DERIVATIVES **pubertal** adjective.
– ORIGIN late Middle English: from Latin *pubertas*, from *puber* 'adult', related to *pubes* (see PUBES).

pubes ▶ noun **1** /ˈpjuːbiːz/ (pl. same) the lower part of the abdomen at the front of the pelvis, covered with hair from puberty.
2 /ˈpjuːbiːz/ plural form of PUBIS.
3 /pjuːbz/ informal plural form of PUBE.
– ORIGIN late 16th cent.: from Latin, 'pubic hair, groin, genitals'.

pubescence /pjʊˈbɛs(ə)ns/ ▶ noun [mass noun] **1** the time when puberty begins.
2 Botany & Zoology soft down on the leaves and stems of plants or on various parts of animals, especially insects.
– ORIGIN late Middle English: from French, or from medieval Latin *pubescentia*, from Latin *pubescent-* 'reaching puberty' (see PUBESCENT).

pubescent ▶ adjective **1** relating to or denoting a person at or approaching the age of puberty.
2 Botany & Zoology covered with short soft hair; downy.

▶ noun a person at or approaching the age of puberty.
– ORIGIN mid 17th cent.: from French, or from Latin *pubescent-* 'reaching puberty', from the verb *pubescere*.

pubic ▶ adjective [attrib.] of or relating to the pubes or pubis: *pubic hair*.

pubis /ˈpjuːbɪs/ ▶ noun (pl. **pubes** /-biːz/) either of a pair of bones forming the two sides of the pelvis.
– ORIGIN late 16th cent.: from Latin *os pubis* 'bone of the pubes'.

public ▶ adjective **1** of or concerning the people as a whole: *public concern* | *public affairs*.
■ open to or shared by all the people of an area or country: *a public library*. ■ of or provided by the state rather than an independent, commercial company: *public services*. ■ of or involved in the affairs of the community, especially in government or entertainment: *he was forced to withdraw from public life* | *a public figure*.
2 done, perceived, or existing in open view: *he wanted a public apology in the Wall Street Journal* | *we should talk somewhere less public*.
3 Brit. of, for, or acting for a university: *public examination results*.
▶ noun **1** (**the public**) [treated as sing. or pl.] ordinary people in general; the community: *the library is open to the public* | *the public has an informed choice*.
■ [with adj. or noun modifier] a section of the community having a particular interest or connection: *the reading public*. ■ (**one's public**) the people who watch or are interested in an artist, writer, or performer: *some famous last words to give my public*.
2 Brit. short for PUBLIC BAR or PUBLIC HOUSE.
– PHRASES **go public 1** become a public company. **2** reveal details about a previously private concern: *Bates went public with the news at a press conference*. **in public** in view of other people; where others are present: *men don't cry in public*. **the public eye** the state of being known or of interest to people in general, especially through the media: *the pressures of being constantly in the public eye*.
– ORIGIN late Middle English: from Old French, from Latin *publicus*, blend of *poplicus* 'of the people' (from *populus* 'people') and *pubes* 'adult').

public act ▶ noun an act of legislation affecting the public as a whole.

public address system ▶ noun a system of microphones, amplifiers, and loudspeakers used to amplify speech or music in a large building or at an outdoor gathering.

publican ▶ noun **1** Brit. a person who owns or manages a pub.
■ Austral. a person who owns or manages a hotel.
2 (in ancient Roman and biblical times) a collector or farmer of taxes: *publicans and sinners*.
– ORIGIN Middle English (in sense 2): from Old French *publicain*, from Latin *publicanus*, from *publicum* 'public revenue', neuter (used as a noun) of *publicus* 'of the people'. Sense 1 dates from the early 18th cent.

public analyst ▶ noun Brit. a health official who analyses food.

publication ▶ noun [mass noun] the preparation and issuing of a book, journal, or piece of music for public sale: *the publication of her first novel*.
■ [count noun] a book or journal issued for public sale: *scientific publications*. ■ the action of making something generally known: *the publication of April trade figures*.
– ORIGIN late Middle English (in the sense 'public announcement or declaration'): via Old French from Latin *publicatio(n-)*, from *publicare* 'make public' (see PUBLISH).

public bar ▶ noun Brit. the less expensive bar in a pub. Compare with LOUNGE BAR.

public bill ▶ noun a bill of legislation affecting the public as a whole.

public company ▶ noun a company whose shares are traded freely on a stock exchange.

public defender ▶ noun US Law a lawyer employed by the state in a criminal trial to represent a defendant who is unable to afford legal assistance.

public domain ▶ noun the state of belonging or being available to the public as a whole, especially through not being subject to copyright or other legal restrictions.

public enemy ▶ noun a notorious wanted criminal.
■ figurative a person or thing regarded as the greatest

threat to a group or community: *he identified inflation as public enemy number one*.

public good ▶ noun (usu. **public goods**) Economics a commodity or service that is provided without profit to all members of a society, either by the government or a private individual or organization.

public house ▶ noun formal term for PUB.

public interest immunity ▶ noun [mass noun] (in the UK and some Commonwealth countries) a principle by which the government can request that sensitive documents are not used as evidence in a trial, on the grounds that to do so would be against the public or national interest.

publicist ▶ noun **1** a person responsible for publicizing a product, person, or company.
2 dated a journalist, especially one concerned with current affairs.
■ archaic a writer or other person skilled in international law.
– DERIVATIVES **publicistic** adjective.
– ORIGIN late 18th cent.: from French *publiciste*, from Latin *(jus) publicum* 'public (law)'.

publicity ▶ noun [mass noun] notice or attention given to someone or something by the media: *the case attracted wide publicity in the press*.
■ the giving out of information about a product, person, or company for advertising or promotional purposes: [as modifier] *a publicity campaign*. ■ material or information used for such a purpose: *we distributed publicity from a stall in the marketplace*.
– ORIGIN late 18th cent.: from French *publicité*, from *public* 'public' (see PUBLIC).

publicity agent ▶ noun another term for PUBLICIST (in sense 1).

publicize (also **-ise**) ▶ verb [with obj.] make (something) widely known: *use the magazine to publicize human rights abuses*.
■ give out publicity about (a product, person, or company) for advertising or promotional purposes: *Judy had started to publicize books and celebrities*.

public key ▶ noun a cryptographic key that can be obtained and used by anyone to encrypt messages intended for a particular recipient, such that the encrypted messages can be deciphered only by using a second key that is known only to the recipient (the **private key**).

public law ▶ noun [mass noun] the law of relations between individuals and the state.

public lending right (abbrev.: PLR) ▶ noun [mass noun] (in the UK) the right of authors to receive payment when their books or other works are lent out by public libraries.

public limited company ▶ noun (in the UK) a company registered under the Companies Act (1980), with statutory minimum capital requirements and shares offered to the public subject to conditions of limited liability.

publicly ▶ adverb so as to be seen by other people; in public: *some weep publicly*.
■ [often sentence adverb] used in reference to views expressed to others and not necessarily genuinely felt: *publicly, officials criticized the resolution, but privately they thought it tolerable*. ■ by the state rather than an independent, commercial company: *a publicly owned company*.

public nuisance ▶ noun Brit. an act that is illegal because it interferes with the rights of the public generally.
■ informal an obnoxious or dangerous person or group of people.

public opinion ▶ noun [mass noun] views prevalent among the general public.

public orator ▶ noun see ORATOR.

public prosecutor ▶ noun a law officer who conducts criminal proceedings on behalf of the state or in the public interest. Compare with CROWN PROSECUTOR.

public purse ▶ noun the funds raised by a government by taxation or other means.

Public Record Office ▶ noun (in the UK) an institution where official archives are kept for public inspection.

public relations ▶ plural noun [also treated as sing.] the professional maintenance of a favourable public image by a company or other organization or a famous person.
■ the state of the relationship between a company or other organization or a famous person and the

public: *companies justify the cost in terms of improved public relations.*

public school ▶ **noun** **1** (in the UK) a private fee-paying secondary school, especially one for boarders.
2 (chiefly in North America) a school supported by public funds.
– ORIGIN late 16th cent.: from Latin *publica schola*, denoting a school maintained at the public expense; in England *public school* (a term recorded from 1580) originally denoted a grammar school under public management, founded for the benefit of the public (contrasting with *private school*, run for the profit of the proprietor); since the 19th cent. the term has been applied to the old endowed English grammar schools, and newer schools modelled on them, which have developed into fee-paying boarding schools.

public sector ▶ **noun** the part of an economy that is controlled by the state.

public servant ▶ **noun** a person who works for the state or for local government, such as a judge or teacher.

public spirit ▶ **noun** [mass noun] willingness to do things that help the public.
– DERIVATIVES **public-spirited** adjective, **public-spiritedly** adverb, **public-spiritedness** noun.

public transport (N. Amer. **public transportation**) ▶ **noun** [mass noun] buses, trains, trams, and occasionally other forms of transport that are available to the public, charge set fares, and run on fixed routes, especially if state-owned.

public utility ▶ **noun** an organization supplying the community with electricity, gas, water, or sewerage.

public works ▶ **plural noun** the work of building such things as roads, schools, and hospitals, carried out by the state for the community.

publish ▶ **verb** [with obj.] **1** (of an author or company) prepare and issue (a book, journal, or piece of music) for public sale: *we publish practical reference books* | [no obj.] *the pressures on researchers to publish.*
■ print (something) in a book or journal so as to make it generally known: *we pay £5 for every letter we publish.* ■ [usu. as adj. **published**] prepare and issue the works of (a particular writer): *a published author.* ■ formally announce or read (an edict or marriage banns).
2 Law communicate (a libel) to a third party.
– DERIVATIVES **publishable** adjective.
– ORIGIN Middle English (in the sense 'make generally known'): from the stem of Old French *puplier*, from Latin *publicare* 'make public', from *publicus* (see **PUBLIC**).

publisher ▶ **noun** (also **publishers**) a company or person that prepares and issues books, journals, or music for sale: *the publishers of* Vogue | *a commercial music publisher.*
■ chiefly N. Amer. a newspaper proprietor.

publishing ▶ **noun** [mass noun] the occupation or activity of preparing and issuing books, journals, and other material for sale: *she worked in publishing.*

Puccini /pʊˈtʃiːni/, Giacomo (1858–1924), Italian composer. Puccini's sense of the dramatic, gift for melody, and skilful use of the orchestra have contributed to his enduring popularity. Notable operas: *La Bohème* (1896), *Tosca* (1900), and *Madama Butterfly* (1904).

puccoon /pʌˈkuːn/ ▶ **noun** a North American plant which yields a pigment from which dye or medicinal products were formerly obtained.
● a yellow-flowered plant with slender leaves (genus *Lithospermum*, family Boraginaceae). ● (**red puccoon**) another term for **BLOODROOT** (in sense 1).
– ORIGIN early 17th cent.: from Algonquian *poughkone*.

puce /pjuːs/ ▶ **adjective** of a dark red or purple-brown colour: *his face was puce with rage and frustration.*
▶ **noun** [mass noun] a dark red or purple-brown colour.
– ORIGIN late 18th cent.: from French, literally 'flea(-colour)', from Latin *pulex, pulic-*.

Puck ▶ **noun** another name for **ROBIN GOODFELLOW**.
■ (**puck**) a mischievous or evil sprite.
– DERIVATIVES **puck-like** adjective.
– ORIGIN Old English *pūca*; it is unclear whether the word is of Celtic or Germanic origin.

puck ▶ **noun** **1** a black disc made of hard rubber, used in ice hockey.
2 Computing an input device similar to a mouse, but which is dragged across a mat which senses its position to move the cursor on the screen.
– ORIGIN late 19th cent.: of unknown origin.

pucka ▶ **adjective** variant spelling of **PUKKA**.

pucker ▶ **verb** [no obj.] (especially of a person's face or a facial feature) tightly gather or contract into wrinkles or small folds: *the child's face puckered, ready to cry* | *her brows puckered in a frown.*
■ [with obj.] cause to do this: *the baby stirred, **puckering up** its tiny face.*
▶ **noun** a tightly gathered wrinkle or small fold, especially on a person's face: *a pucker between his eyebrows.*
– DERIVATIVES **puckery** adjective.
– ORIGIN late 16th cent. (as a verb): probably frequentative, from the base of **POKE**[2] and **POCKET** (suggesting the formation of small purse-like gatherings).

puckish ▶ **adjective** playful, especially in a mischievous way: *a puckish sense of humour.*
– DERIVATIVES **puckishly** adverb, **puckishness** noun.

pud ▶ **noun** Brit. informal short for **PUDDING**.

pudding ▶ **noun** **1** a cooked sweet dish served after the main course of a meal: *a rice pudding* | [mass noun] *a good helping of pudding.*
■ [mass noun] chiefly Brit. the dessert course of a meal: *what's for pudding?* ■ N. Amer. a dessert with a soft or creamy consistency.
2 a sweet or savoury steamed dish made with suet and flour: *a steak and kidney pudding.*
■ the intestines of a pig or sheep stuffed with oatmeal, spices, and meat and boiled. See also **BLACK PUDDING**, **BLOOD PUDDING**. ■ informal a fat, dumpy, or stupid person: *away with you, you big pudding!*
– PHRASES **in the pudding club** Brit. informal pregnant.
– DERIVATIVES **puddingy** adjective.
– ORIGIN Middle English (denoting a sausage such as *black pudding*): apparently from Old French *boudin* 'black pudding', from Latin *botellus* 'sausage, small intestine'.

pudding basin ▶ **noun** a deep round bowl, used for mixing and cooking steamed puddings.
■ [as modifier] denoting a hairstyle cut or as if cut by inverting such a basin on a person's head and cutting away all the hair that sticks out under it.

pudding cloth ▶ **noun** a cloth used for tying up some puddings for boiling.

pudding face ▶ **noun** informal a large fat face.
– DERIVATIVES **pudding-faced** adjective.

pudding-head ▶ **noun** informal a stupid person.

puddingstone ▶ **noun** [mass noun] a conglomerate rock in which dark-coloured round pebbles contrast with a paler fine-grained matrix.

puddle ▶ **noun** **1** a small pool of liquid, especially of rainwater on the ground: *splashing through deep puddles* | figurative *a little puddle of light.*
2 [mass noun] clay and sand mixed with water and used as a watertight covering for embankments.
3 Rowing a circular patch of disturbed water made by the blade of an oar at each stroke.
▶ **verb** [with obj.] **1** wet or cover (a surface) with water, especially rainwater: *the cobbles under our feet were wet and puddled.*
■ [no obj.] (of liquid) form a small pool: *rivulets of water coursed down the panes, puddling on the sill.* ■ [no obj.] archaic dabble or wallow in mud or shallow water: *children are playing and puddling about in the dirt.* ■ [no obj.] (**puddle about/around**) informal occupy oneself in a disorganized or unproductive way: *the Internet is just the latest excuse for puddling around at work.*
2 line (a hole) with puddle.
■ knead (clay and sand) into puddle. ■ work (mixed water and clay) to separate gold or opal. ■ [usu. as noun **puddling**] chiefly historical stir (molten iron) with iron oxide in a furnace, to produce wrought iron by oxidizing carbon.
– DERIVATIVES **puddler** noun, **puddly** adjective.
– ORIGIN Middle English: diminutive of Old English *pudd* 'ditch, furrow'; compare with German dialect *Pfudel* 'pool'.

puddle jumper ▶ **noun** informal, chiefly N. Amer. a small light aeroplane which is fast and highly manoeuvrable and used for short trips.

puddysticks (also **pudsticks**) ▶ **adjective** [predic.] S. African informal (in children's use) very easy: *doing handstands is puddysticks.*
– ORIGIN of unknown origin.

pudendum /pjʊˈdɛndəm/ ▶ **noun** (pl. **pudenda** /-də/) (often **pudenda**) a person's external genitals, especially a woman's.
– DERIVATIVES **pudendal** adjective, **pudic** /ˈpjuːdɪk/ adjective.
– ORIGIN mid 17th cent.: from Latin *pudenda* (*membra*) '(parts) to be ashamed of', neuter plural of the gerundive of *pudere* 'be ashamed'.

pudeur /pjuːˈdəː, French pydœr/ ▶ **noun** [mass noun] a sense of shame or embarrassment, especially with regard to matters of a sexual or personal nature.
– ORIGIN mid 20th cent.: French, literally 'modesty'.

pudge ▶ **noun** [mass noun] N. Amer. informal fat on a person's body.
– ORIGIN early 19th cent. (denoting a fat person): of unknown origin; compare with **PODGE**.

pudgy ▶ **adjective** (**pudgier**, **pudgiest**) informal (of a person or part of their body) rather fat: *his pudgy fingers.*
– DERIVATIVES **pudgily** adverb, **pudginess** noun.

pudu /ˈpuːduː/ ▶ **noun** a very small and rare deer found in the lower Andes of South America.
● Genus *Pudu*, family Cervidae: two species.
– ORIGIN late 19th cent.: from Araucanian.

Puebla /ˈpwɛblə/ a state of south central Mexico.
■ its capital city; pop. 1,054,920 (1990). It lies at the edge of the central Mexican plateau at an altitude of 2,150 m (7,055 ft). Full name **PUEBLA DE ZARAGOZA** /deɪ ˌsarəˈɡɒsə/.

pueblo /ˈpwɛbləʊ/ ▶ **noun** (pl. **-os**) **1** a town or village in Spain, Latin America, or the south-western US, especially an American Indian settlement.
2 (**Pueblo**) (pl. same or **-os**) a member of any of various American Indian peoples, including the Hopi, occupying pueblo settlements chiefly in New Mexico and Arizona. Their prehistoric period is known as the Anasazi culture.
▶ **adjective** (**Pueblo**) of, relating to, or denoting the Pueblos or their culture.
– ORIGIN Spanish, literally 'people', from Latin *populus*.

puerile /ˈpjʊərʌɪl/ ▶ **adjective** childishly silly and trivial: *you're making puerile excuses.*
– DERIVATIVES **puerilely** adverb, **puerility** noun (pl. **-ies**).
– ORIGIN late 16th cent. (in the sense 'like a boy'): from French *puéril* or Latin *puerilis*, from *puer* 'boy'.

puerperal fever ▶ **noun** [mass noun] fever caused by uterine infection following childbirth.

puerperium /ˌpjuːəˈpɛrɪəm, ˌpjuːəˈpiːrɪəm/ ▶ **noun** [mass noun] Medicine the period of about six weeks after childbirth during which the mother's reproductive organs return to their original non-pregnant condition.
– DERIVATIVES **puerperal** adjective.
– ORIGIN early 17th cent.: from Latin, from *puerperus* 'parturient' (from *puer* 'child' + *-parus* 'bearing').

Puerto Cortés /ˌpwɛːtəʊ kɔːˈtɛz/ a port in NW Honduras, on the Caribbean coast at the mouth of the Ulua River; pop. 40,000 (1986).

Puerto Limón another name for **LIMÓN**.

Puerto Plata /ˈplɑːtə/ a resort town in the Dominican Republic, on the north coast; pop. 96,500 (1986).

Puerto Rico /ˈriːkəʊ/ an island of the Greater Antilles in the Caribbean; pop. 3,522,040 (1990); official languages, Spanish and English; capital, San Juan. One of the earliest Spanish settlements in the New World, it was ceded to the US in 1898 after the Spanish-American War, and in 1952 it became a commonwealth in voluntary association with the US, with full powers of local government.
– DERIVATIVES **Puerto Rican** adjective & noun.

Puerto Rico Trench an ocean trench extending in an east–west direction to the north of Puerto Rico and the Leeward Islands. It reaches a depth of 9,220 m (28,397 ft).

puff ▶ **noun** **1** a short, explosive burst of breath or wind: *a puff of wind swung the weathercock round.*
■ the sound of air or vapour escaping suddenly: *the whistle and puff of steam.* ■ a small quantity of vapour or smoke, emitted in one blast: *the fire breathed out **a puff of** blue smoke.* ■ an act of drawing quickly on a pipe, cigarette, or cigar: *he took a puff of his cigar.* ■ [mass noun] informal breath: *after a chase of over three miles he had finally run out of puff.*
2 [usu. with modifier or in combination] a light pastry case, typically one made of puff pastry, containing a sweet or savoury filling: *a jam puff.*
■ a gathered mass of material in a dress or other garment. ■ a rolled protuberant mass of hair. ■ a

p

powder puff. ■ N. Amer. an eiderdown: *the plump pillows and puffs with which the snowy beds were piled.*
3 informal a review of a work of art, book, or theatrical production, especially an excessively complimentary one: *the publishers sent him a copy of the book hoping for a puff.*
■ Brit. an advertisement, especially one exaggerating the value of the goods advertised.
▶ **verb** **1** [no obj.] breathe in repeated short gasps: *exercises that make you puff.*
■ [with adverbial] (of a person, engine, etc.) move with short, noisy breaths or bursts of air or steam: *the train came puffing in.* ■ smoke a pipe, cigarette, or cigar: *he puffed on his pipe contentedly.* ■ [with obj. and adverbial of direction] blow (dust, smoke, or a light object) in a specified direction with a quick breath or blast of air: *he puffed out smoke through his long cigarette holder.* ■ move through the air in short bursts: *his breath puffed out like white smoke.*
2 (**puff something out/up** or **puff out/up**) cause to swell or become swollen: [with obj.] *he suddenly sucked his stomach in and puffed his chest out* | [no obj.] *when he was in a temper, his cheeks puffed up and his eyes shrank.*
■ [with obj.] (usu. **be puffed up**) figurative cause to become conceited: *he was never puffed up about his writing.*
3 [with obj.] advertise with exaggerated or false praise: *publishers have puffed the book on the grounds that it contains new discoveries.*
– PHRASES **in all one's puff** informal, chiefly Brit. in one's whole life. **puff and blow** breathe in gasps during or after exertion.
– ORIGIN Middle English: imitative of the sound of a breath, perhaps from Old English *pyf* (noun), *pyffan* (verb).

puff adder ▶ **noun** a large, sluggish, mainly nocturnal African viper which inflates the upper part of its body and hisses loudly when under threat.
● *Bitis arietans*, family Viperidae.
■ North American term for **HOGNOSE SNAKE**.

puffback (also **puff-back shrike**) ▶ **noun** a small black-and-white African shrike, the male of which displays by puffing up the feathers of the lower back.
● Genus *Dryoscopus*, family Laniidae: several species, in particular *D. gambensis*.

puffball ▶ **noun** **1** a fungus that produces a spherical or pear-shaped fruiting body which ruptures when ripe to release a cloud of spores.
● Families Lycoperdaceae, class Gasteromycetes, in particular genus *Lycoperdon*. See also **GIANT PUFFBALL**.
2 a short full skirt gathered around the hemline to produce a soft puffy shape.

puffbird ▶ **noun** a stocky large-headed bird somewhat resembling a kingfisher, found in tropical American forests.
● Family Bucconidae: several genera and many species.

puffed ▶ **adjective** **1** [predic.] (also **puffed out**) out of breath: *he felt puffed after climbing to the top of the apartment block.*
2 (also **puffed up**) swollen: *symptoms include puffed eyelids.*
■ (of a sleeve or other part of a garment) gathered so as to have a rounded shape.

puffer ▶ **noun** **1** a person or thing that puffs, in particular:
■ informal a person who smokes. ■ chiefly Scottish a steamboat, especially a small coastal freighter. ■ informal an aerosol inhaler used for administering a drug for a condition such as asthma. ■ another term for **PUFF-PUFF**.
2 short for **PUFFERFISH**.

pufferfish ▶ **noun** (pl. same or **-fishes**) a stout-bodied marine or freshwater fish which typically has spiny skin and inflates itself like a balloon when threatened. It is sometimes used as food, but some parts are highly toxic.
● Family Tetraodontidae: several genera and many species, including the **common pufferfish** (*Tetraodon cutcutia*).

puffery ▶ **noun** [mass noun] chiefly US exaggerated or false praise.

puffin ▶ **noun** a hole-nesting auk of northern and Arctic waters, with a large head and a massive brightly coloured triangular bill.
● Genera *Fratercula* and *Lunda*, family Alcidae: three species, in particular the (**Atlantic**) **puffin** (*F. arctica*).
– ORIGIN Middle English (denoting the Manx shearwater): apparently from **PUFF** + **-ING**[3], with reference to the Manx shearwater's fat nestlings. The later use is a confusion, by association of nesting habits and habitat.

puffin crossing ▶ **noun** (in the UK) a pedestrian crossing with traffic lights which go green again only when no more pedestrians are detected on the crossing by infrared detectors and mats.
– ORIGIN 1990s: *puffin* from *p(edestrian) u(ser) f(riendly) in(telligent)*, respelled after the bird's name by analogy with *pelican crossing*.

puff pastry ▶ **noun** [mass noun] light flaky pastry, used for pie crusts, canapés, and sweet pastries.

puff piece ▶ **noun** N. Amer. informal a newspaper article or item on a television show using exaggerated praise to advertise or promote a celebrity, book, or event.

puff-puff ▶ **noun** Brit. a child's word for a steam engine or train.

puff sleeve ▶ **noun** a short sleeve gathered at the top and cuff and full in the middle.

puffy ▶ **adjective** (**puffier**, **puffiest**) **1** (especially of part of the body) unusually swollen and soft: *her eyes were puffy and full of tears.*
■ soft, rounded, and light: *small puffy clouds.* ■ (of a garment or part of a garment) padded or gathered to give a rounded shape: *a puffy blue ski-jacket.* ■ figurative (of a piece of writing) over-embellished and pompous: *prose at its most laboured and puffy.*
2 (of wind or breath) coming in short bursts: *his breath was puffy and fast.*
– DERIVATIVES **puffily** adverb, **puffiness** noun.

pug[1] ▶ **noun** **1** (also **pug dog**) a dog of a dwarf breed like a bulldog with a broad flat nose and deeply wrinkled face.
2 a small slender moth which rests with its wings stretched out to the sides.
● *Eupithecia* and other genera, family Geometridae.
– DERIVATIVES **puggish** adjective, **puggy** adjective.
– ORIGIN mid 18th cent. (in sense 1): perhaps of Low German origin. Sense 2 dates from the early 19th cent.

pug[2] ▶ **noun** [mass noun] loam or clay mixed and worked into a soft, plastic condition without air pockets for making bricks or pottery.
▶ **verb** (**pugged**, **pugging**) [with obj.] **1** [usu. as adj. **pugged**] prepare (clay) in this way, typically in a machine with rotating blades.
2 [usu. as noun **pugging**] pack (a space, typically the space under a floor) with pug, sawdust, or other material in order to deaden sound.
– ORIGIN early 19th cent.: of unknown origin.

pug[3] ▶ **noun** informal a boxer.
– ORIGIN mid 19th cent.: abbreviation of **PUGILIST**.

pug[4] ▶ **noun** the footprint of an animal: [as modifier] *I saw the pug marks of the tigress in the soft earth.*
▶ **verb** (**pugged**, **pugging**) [with obj.] track (an animal) by its footprints.
– ORIGIN mid 19th cent.: from Hindi *pag* 'footprint'.

pug dog ▶ **noun** another term for **PUG**[1] (in sense 1).

Puget Sound /ˈpjuːdʒɪt/ an inlet of the Pacific on the coast of Washington State in the US. It is linked to the ocean by the Strait of Juan de Fuca.
– ORIGIN named after Peter *Puget*, the aide of George Vancouver who explored it in 1792.

puggaree /ˈpʌg(ə)riː/ (also **pagri**) ▶ **noun** an Indian turban.
■ a thin muslin scarf tied round a sun helmet so as to hang down over the wearer's neck and shield it from the sun.
– ORIGIN from Hindi *pagṛī* 'turban'.

pugilist /ˈpjuːdʒɪlɪst/ ▶ **noun** dated or humorous a boxer, especially a professional one.
– DERIVATIVES **pugilism** noun, **pugilistic** adjective.
– ORIGIN mid 18th cent.: from Latin *pugil* 'boxer' + **-IST**.

Pugin /ˈpjuːdʒɪn/, Augustus Welby Northmore (1812–52), English architect, theorist, and designer. He believed that the Gothic style was the only proper architectural style because of its origins in medieval Christian society. He is known particularly for his work on the external detail and internal fittings for the Houses of Parliament, designed by Sir Charles Barry.

Puglia /ˈpulja/ Italian name for **APULIA**.

pug mill ▶ **noun** a machine for mixing and working clay and other materials into pug. (See **PUG**[2].)

pugnacious /pʌgˈneɪʃəs/ ▶ **adjective** eager or quick to argue, quarrel, or fight: *the increasingly pugnacious demeanour of right-wing politicians.*
■ having the appearance of a willing fighter: *the set of her pugnacious jaw.*
– DERIVATIVES **pugnaciously** adverb, **pugnacity** noun.
– ORIGIN mid 17th cent.: from Latin *pugnax, pugnac-* (from *pugnare* 'to fight', from *pugnus* 'fist') + **-IOUS**.

pug nose ▶ **noun** a short nose with an upturned tip.
– DERIVATIVES **pug-nosed** adjective.

Pugwash conferences /ˈpʌgwɒʃ/ a series of international conferences first held in Pugwash (a village in Nova Scotia) in 1957 by scientists to promote the peaceful application of scientific discoveries.

puha[1] /ˈpuːhɑː/ ▶ **noun** [mass noun] NZ the leaves of the sowthistle used as a vegetable.
– ORIGIN mid 19th cent.: from Maori.

puha[2] /ˈpuːhə/ ▶ **noun** [mass noun] (in American Indian religion) supernatural or spiritual power.

puisne /ˈpjuːni/ ▶ **adjective** [attrib.] Law (in the UK and some other countries) denoting a judge of a superior court inferior in rank to chief justices.
– ORIGIN late 16th cent. (as a noun, denoting a junior or inferior person): from Old French, from *puis* (from Latin *postea* 'afterwards') + *ne* 'born' (from Latin *natus*). Compare with **PUNY**.

puisne mortgage ▶ **noun** Law, chiefly Brit. a second or subsequent mortgage of unregistered land of which the title deeds are retained by a first mortgagee.

puissance /ˈpjuːɪs(ə)ns, ˈpwiː-, ˈpwɪ-/ ▶ **noun** **1** /also ˈpwiːsɒ̃s/ (**Puissance**) [in sing.] a competitive test of a horse's ability to jump large obstacles in showjumping.
2 [mass noun] archaic or poetic/literary great power, influence, or prowess.
– ORIGIN late Middle English (in sense 2): from Old French, 'power', from *puissant* 'having power' (see **PUISSANT**). Sense 1 dates from the 1950s.

puissant /ˈpjuːɪs(ə)nt, ˈpwiː-, ˈpwɪ-/ ▶ **adjective** archaic or poetic/literary having great power or influence.
– DERIVATIVES **puissantly** adverb.
– ORIGIN late Middle English: via Old French from Latin *posse* 'be able'.

puja /ˈpuːdʒɑː/ (also **pooja**) ▶ **noun** a Hindu ceremonial offering.
– ORIGIN from Sanskrit *pūjā* 'worship'.

pujari /pʊˈdʒɑːri/ ▶ **noun** (pl. **pujaris**) a Hindu priest.
– ORIGIN via Hindi from Sanskrit *pūjā* 'worship'.

puke informal ▶ **verb** vomit: [no obj.] *wild with shame at puking up like a baby* | [with obj.] *he puked up his pizza.*
▶ **noun** [mass noun] vomit.
– DERIVATIVES **pukey** adjective.
– ORIGIN late 16th cent.: probably imitative; first recorded as a verb in: 'At first the infant, mewling, and puking in the nurse's arms', in Shakespeare's *As you like it* (II. vii. 144).

pukeko /ˈpuːkɛkəʊ/ ▶ **noun** (pl. **-os**) NZ another term for **SWAMPHEN**.
– ORIGIN mid 19th cent.: from Maori.

pukka /ˈpʌkə/ (also **pukkah**) ▶ **adjective** genuine: *the more expensive brands are pukka natural mineral waters.*
■ of or appropriate to high or respectable society: *it wouldn't be considered the pukka thing to do.* ■ informal excellent: *'That Danny is totally gorgeous.' 'Yeah, pukka haircut.'*
– ORIGIN late 17th cent.: from Hindi *pakkā* 'cooked, ripe, substantial'.

puku /ˈpuːkuː/ ▶ **noun** (pl. **pukus**) an antelope with a shaggy golden-yellow coat and short thick horns, native to wetland areas of southern Africa.
● *Kobus vardonii*, family Bovidae.
– ORIGIN late 19th cent.: from Zulu *mpuku*.

pul /puːl/ ▶ **noun** (pl. **puls** or **puli**) a monetary unit of Afghanistan, equal to one hundredth of an afghani.
– ORIGIN Pashto, from Persian *pūl* 'copper coin'.

pula /ˈpʊlə/ ▶ **noun** (pl. same) the basic monetary unit of Botswana, equal to 100 thebe.
– ORIGIN Setswana, literally 'rain'.

pulao /pəˈlaʊ/ ▶ **noun** variant spelling of **PILAF**.

pulaski /pʊˈlaski/ ▶ **noun** (pl. **pulaskis**) chiefly US a hatchet with a head that forms an axe blade on one side and an adze on the other.
– ORIGIN 1920s: named after Edward C. *Pulaski* (1866–1931), the American forest ranger who designed it.

Pulau Seribu /ˌpuːlaʊ ˈsɛrɪbuː/ Indonesian name for **THOUSAND ISLANDS** (in sense 2).

pulchritude /ˈpʌlkrɪtjuːd/ ▶**noun** [mass noun] poetic/literary beauty.
– DERIVATIVES **pulchritudinous** adjective.
– ORIGIN late Middle English: from Latin *pulchritudo*, from *pulcher, pulchr-* 'beautiful'.

pule /pjuːl/ ▶**verb** [no obj.] [often as adj. **puling**] poetic/literary cry querulously or weakly: *she's no puling infant.*
– ORIGIN late Middle English (originally referring to a bird's cry): probably imitative; compare with French *piauler*, in the same sense.

puli /ˈpuːli/ ▶**noun** (pl. **pulik** /ˈpuːlɪk/) a sheepdog of a black, grey, or white breed with a long thick coat.
– ORIGIN mid 20th cent.: from Hungarian.

Pulitzer /ˈpʊlɪtsə/, Joseph (1847–1911), Hungarian-born American newspaper proprietor and editor. A pioneer of campaigning popular journalism, he owned a number of newspapers. He made provisions in his will for the establishment of the annual Pulitzer Prizes.

Pulitzer Prize ▶**noun** an award for an achievement in American journalism, literature, or music. There are thirteen made each year.

pull ▶**verb** [with obj.] **1** exert force on (someone or something), typically by taking hold of them, in order to move or try to move them towards oneself or the origin of the force: *he pulled the car door handle and began to get out* | [no obj.] *the little boy* **pulled at** *her skirt.*
■(of an animal or vehicle) be attached to the front and be the source of forward movement of (a vehicle): *the carriage was pulled by four horses.* ■ [with obj. and adverbial] take hold of and exert force on (something) so as to move it from a specified position or in a specified direction: *she pulled a handkerchief out of her pocket* | *he pulled on his boots* | *I pulled up some onions.* ■ informal bring out (a weapon) for use against someone: *it's not every day a young woman* **pulls** *a gun* **on** *a burglar.* ■ Brit. draw (beer) from a barrel to serve. ■ [no obj.] (**pull at/on**) inhale deeply while smoking (a pipe or cigarette). ■ damage (a muscle, ligament, etc.) by abnormal strain. ■ print (a proof). ■ Computing retrieve (an item of data) from the top of a stack.
2 [no obj., with adverbial] (of a vehicle or person) move steadily in a specified direction or to reach a specified point: *the bus was about to pull away* | *the boy pulled ahead and disappeared round the corner.*
■[with adverbial of direction] (**pull oneself**) move in a specified direction with effort, especially by taking hold of something and exerting force: *he pulled himself into the saddle.* ■ [no obj., with adverbial of direction] move one's body in a specified direction, especially against resistance: *she tried to pull away from him.* ■ [no obj.] (of an engine) exert propulsive force; deliver power: *the engine warmed up quickly and pulled well.* ■ [no obj.] work oars to cause a boat to move: *he* **pulled** *at the oars and the boat moved swiftly through the water.*
3 cause (someone) to patronize, buy, or show interest in something; attract: *tourist attractions which* **pull in** *millions of foreign visitors.*
■influence in favour of a particular course of action: *they are pulled in incompatible directions by external factors and their own beliefs.* ■ informal succeed in attracting sexually: *I used my sense of humour to pull girls.* ■ informal carry out or achieve (something requiring skill, luck, or planning): *the magazine pulled its trick of producing the right issue at the right time.*
4 informal cancel or withdraw (an entertainment or advertisement): *the gig was pulled at the first sign of difficulty.*
■N. Amer. withdraw (a player) from a game; disqualify. ■ arrest: *I don't enjoy driving and am never likely to get pulled for speeding.* ■ check the speed of (a horse), especially so as to make it lose a race.
5 strike (a ball) in a certain manner or direction, in particular:
■Cricket play (the ball) round to the leg side from the off. ■ Golf & Baseball strike (the ball) so that it travels to the left (or, with a left-handed player, the right).
6 [no obj.] American Football (of a lineman) withdraw from and cross behind the line of scrimmage to block opposing players and clear the way for a runner.
▶**noun 1** an act of taking hold of something and exerting force to draw it towards one: *give the hair a quick pull and it comes out by the roots.*
■a handle to hold while performing such an action: *the car didn't have external door handles, just pulls inside.* ■ a deep draught of a drink. ■ an act of sucking at a cigarette, cigar, or pipe: *he took a pull on his cheroot.* ■ [in sing.] an act of moving steadily or with effort: *a pull for ten minutes brought me to the summit.* ■ an injury to a muscle or ligament caused by abnormal strain: *he was ruled out of the game with a hamstring pull.* ■ a printer's proof.
2 [in sing.] a force drawing someone or something in a particular direction: *the pull of the water tore her away.*
■a powerful influence or compulsion: *the pull of her home town was a strong one.* ■ [count noun] something exerting an influence or attraction: *one of the pulls of urban life is the opportunity of finding employment.* ■ [mass noun] the condition of being able to exercise influence: *the team might be seeded because of their pull within soccer's international body.* ■ informal an attempt to attract someone sexually: *an eligible bachelor* **on the pull**.
3 (in cricket, golf, baseball, etc.) a pulling stroke.
– PHRASES **like pulling teeth** informal used to convey that something is extremely difficult to do: *it had been like pulling teeth to extract these two small items from Moore.* **pull a boner** see **BONER**. **pull a face** (or **faces**) see **FACE**. **pull a fast one** see **FAST**[1]. **pull someone's leg** deceive someone playfully; tease someone. **pull the other one (it's got bells on)** Brit. informal used to express a suspicion that one is being deceived or teased: *Your boat was sunk by a swordfish? Pull the other one!* **pull out all the stops** see **STOP**. **pull the plug** informal prevent something from happening or continuing: *the company* **pulled the plug on** *the deal because it was not satisfied with the terms.* **pull (one's) punches** [usu. with negative] be less forceful, severe, or violent than one could be: *a smooth-tongued critic who doesn't pull his punches.* **pull rank** see **RANK**[1]. **pull one's socks up** see **SOCK**. **pull strings** make use of one's influence and contacts to gain an advantage unofficially or unfairly. **pull the strings** be in control of events or of other people's actions. **pull together** cooperate in a task or undertaking. **pull oneself together** recover control of one's emotions. **pull someone/thing to pieces** see **PIECE**. **pull one's weight** do one's fair share of work. **pull wires** chiefly US another way of saying ***pull strings*** above. **pull the wool over someone's eyes** see **WOOL**.
– DERIVATIVES **puller** noun.
– ORIGIN Old English *pullian* 'pluck, snatch'; origin uncertain; the sense has developed from expressing a short sharp action to one of sustained force.
▶**pull back** (or **pull someone/thing back**) **1** retreat or cause troops to retreat from an area: *the pact called on the rival forces to pull back and allow a neutral force to take control.* ■ (**pull back**) withdraw from an undertaking: *the party pulled back from its only positive policy.* **2** improve or restore a team's position in a sporting contest: *Rovers pulled back to 4–3 with a goal two minutes from time* | *Scotland pulled the game back to 3–2.*
pull something down 1 demolish a building. **2** informal earn a sum of money: *he was pulling down sixty grand.*
pull in 1 (of a vehicle or its driver) move to the side of or off the road: *he pulled in at the kerb.* **2** (of a bus or train) arrive to take passengers.
pull someone/thing in 1 succeed in securing or obtaining something: *the party pulled in 10% of the vote.* ■ informal earn a sum of money: *you could pull in £100,000.* **2** informal arrest someone: *I'd pull him in for questioning.* **3** use reins to check a horse.
pull something off informal succeed in achieving or winning something difficult: *he pulled off a brilliant first round win.*
pull out 1 withdraw from an undertaking: *he was forced to* **pull out of** *the championship because of an injury.* ■ retreat or cause to retreat from an area: *the army pulled out, leaving the city in ruins* | (**pull someone out**) *the CIA had pulled its operatives out of Tripoli.* **2** (of a bus or train) leave with its passengers. **3** (of a vehicle or its driver) move out from the side of the road, or from its normal position in order to overtake: *as he turned the corner a police car pulled out in front of him.*
pull over (of a vehicle or its driver) move to the side of or off the road.
pull someone over cause a driver to pull off the road to be charged for a traffic offence: *he was pulled over for speeding.*
pull round chiefly Brit. recover from an illness.
pull through (or **pull someone/thing through**) get through or enable someone or something to get through an illness or other dangerous or difficult situation: *the illness is difficult to overcome, but we hope she'll pull through.*
pull up 1 (of a vehicle or its driver) come to a halt: *he pulled up outside the cottage.* **2** increase the altitude of an aircraft.
pull someone up cause someone to stop or pause; check someone: *the shock of his words* **pulled her up short**. ■ reprimand someone.

pull-apart ▶**adjective** [attrib.] (of a casing, cover, or container) made in sections that can be pulled apart.
■Geology denoting an area which has been ruptured or stretched by the tensional stresses of faulting.

pullback ▶**noun 1** an act of withdrawing troops. **2** a reduction in price or demand: *wait for pullbacks to buy international stocks.*

pull cord ▶**noun** a cord which operates a mechanism when pulled.

pull-down ▶**adjective** [attrib.] designed to be worked or made operable by being pulled down: *guests may be put up on folding or pull-down beds.*
■Computing (of a menu) appearing below a menu title only while selected. Compare with **DROP-DOWN**.
▶**noun** Computing a pull-down menu.

pullet ▶**noun** a young hen, especially one less than one year old.
– ORIGIN late Middle English: from Old French *poulet*, diminutive of *poule*, from the feminine of Latin *pullus* 'chicken, young animal'.

pulley ▶**noun** (pl. **-eys**) (also **pulley wheel**) a wheel with a grooved rim around which a cord passes, which acts to change the direction of a force applied to the cord and is chiefly used (typically in combination) to raise heavy weights.
■a wheel or drum fixed on a shaft and turned by a belt, used especially to increase speed or power.
▶**verb** (**-eys, -eyed**) [with obj.] hoist with a pulley.
– ORIGIN Middle English: from Old French *polie*, probably from a medieval Greek diminutive of *polos* 'pivot, axis'.

pulley block ▶**noun** a block or casing in which one or more pulleys are mounted.

pull hitter ▶**noun** Baseball a hitter who normally strikes the ball in the direction in which they follow through.

pull-in ▶**noun** chiefly Brit. an area at the side of the road where vehicles may pull off the road and stop.
■Brit. dated a roadside cafe.

pulling guard ▶**noun** American Football an offensive guard who pulls back from the line of scrimmage and runs toward the sideline to block for a runner.

Pullman ▶**noun** (pl. **Pullmans**) [usu. as modifier] a railway carriage affording special comfort, typically with a lounge interior and meals service at the passengers' seats: *a train of Pullman cars.*
■a train consisting of such carriages. ■ N. Amer. (also **Pullman case**) a large suitcase designed to fit under the seat in a Pullman carriage.
– ORIGIN mid 19th cent.: named after George M. *Pullman* (1831–97), its American designer.

pull-off ▶**adjective** [attrib.] designed to be pulled off: *a pull-off end cap.*
▶**noun** a lay-by.

pull-on ▶**adjective** [attrib.] (of a garment) designed to be put on without the need to undo any fastenings: *pull-on trousers with an elasticated waist.*
▶**noun** a garment of this type.

pull-out ▶**noun 1** a section of a magazine or newspaper that is designed to be detached and kept for rereading: *don't miss Monday's 8-page Games pull-out.*
2 a withdrawal, especially from military involvement or participation in a commercial venture.
▶**adjective** [attrib.] designed to be pulled out of the usual position: *a pull-out cutlery drawer.*
■(of a section of a magazine, newspaper, or other publication) designed to be detached and kept.

pullover ▶**noun** a knitted garment put on over the head and covering the top half of the body.

pull-quote ▶**noun** US a brief, attention-catching quotation, typically in a distinctive typeface, taken from the main text of an article and used as a sub-heading or graphic feature.

pull-tab ▶**noun 1** another term for **RING PULL**. **2** US a gambling card with a tab that can be pulled back to reveal a row or rows of symbols, with prizes for matching symbols.

pullulate /ˈpʌljʊleɪt/ ▶**verb** [no obj.] [often as adj. **pullulating**] breed or spread so as to become extremely common: *the pullulating family.*

■be very crowded; be full of life and activity: *the supertowers of our pullulating megalopolis.*
– DERIVATIVES **pullulation** noun.
– ORIGIN early 17th cent.: from Latin *pullulat-* 'sprouted', from the verb *pullulare*, from *pullulus*, diminutive of *pullus* 'young animal'.

pull-up ▶ noun **1** an exercise involving raising oneself with one's arms by pulling up against a horizontal bar fixed above one's head.
2 an act of pulling up; a sudden stop.
■Brit. dated a place for pulling up or stopping, especially a roadside cafe.

pulmonaria /ˌpʌlməˈnɛːrɪə/ ▶ noun a plant of a genus that includes lungwort.
● Genus *Pulmonaria*, family Boraginaceae.
– ORIGIN modern Latin, from medieval Latin *pulmonaria (herba)*, feminine (used as a noun) of Latin *pulmonarius* 'relating to the lungs' (from the belief in its efficacy in curing lung diseases).

pulmonary /ˈpʌlmən(ə)ri/ ▶ adjective [attrib.] of or relating to the lungs: *pulmonary blood flow.*
– ORIGIN mid 17th cent.: from Latin *pulmonarius*, from *pulmo*, *pulmon-* 'lung'.

pulmonary artery ▶ noun the artery carrying blood from the right ventricle of the heart to the lungs for oxygenation.

pulmonary tuberculosis ▶ noun see **TUBERCULOSIS**.

pulmonary vein ▶ noun a vein carrying oxygenated blood from the lungs to the left atrium of the heart.

Pulmonata /ˌpʌlməˈneɪtə/ Zoology a group of molluscs which includes the land snails and slugs and many freshwater snails. They have a modified mantle cavity which acts as a lung for breathing air.
● Subclass Pulmonata, class Gastropoda.
– DERIVATIVES **pulmonate** noun & adjective.
– ORIGIN modern Latin (plural), from Latin *pulmo*, *pulmon-* 'lung'.

pulmonic /pʌlˈmɒnɪk/ ▶ adjective another term for **PULMONARY**.

pulmonic airstream ▶ noun Phonetics the flow of air from the lungs under comparatively constant pressure, used in forming speech sounds. Contrasted with **VELARIC AIRSTREAM**.

pulp ▶ noun [mass noun] a soft, wet, shapeless mass of material: *boiling with soda will reduce your peas to pulp.*
■the soft fleshy part of a fruit. ■ a soft wet mass of fibres derived from rags or wood, used in papermaking. ■ vascular tissue filling the interior cavity and root canals of a tooth. ■ Mining pulverized ore mixed with water. ■ [usu. as modifier] figurative popular or sensational writing that is generally regarded as being of poor quality: *the story is a mix of pulp fiction and Greek tragedy.* [ORIGIN: formerly printed on rough paper.]
▶ verb [with obj.] crush into a soft, shapeless mass.
■withdraw (a publication) from the market and recycle the paper.
– PHRASES **beat** (or **smash**) **someone to a pulp** beat someone severely.
– DERIVATIVES **pulper** noun, **pulpiness** noun, **pulpy** adjective.
– ORIGIN late Middle English (denoting the soft fleshy part of fruit): from Latin *pulpa*. The verb dates from the mid 17th cent.

pulp cavity ▶ noun the space in the interior of a tooth which contains the pulp.

pulpit ▶ noun a raised enclosed platform in a church or chapel from which the preacher delivers a sermon.
■(**the pulpit**) religious teaching as expressed in sermons; preachers collectively: *the movies could rival the pulpit as an agency moulding the ideas of the mass public.* ■ a raised platform in the bows of a fishing boat or whaler. ■ a guard rail enclosing a small area at the bow of a yacht.
– ORIGIN Middle English: from Latin *pulpitum* 'scaffold, platform', in medieval Latin 'pulpit'.

pulpwood ▶ noun [mass noun] timber suitable for making into pulp.

pulque /ˈpʊlkeɪ, ˈpʊlki/ ▶ noun [mass noun] a Mexican alcoholic drink made by fermenting sap from the maguey.
– ORIGIN via American Spanish from Nahuatl *puliúhki* 'decomposed'.

pulsar /ˈpʌlsɑː/ ▶ noun Astronomy a celestial object, thought to be a rapidly rotating neutron star, that emits regular pulses of radio waves and other electromagnetic radiation at rates of up to one thousand pulses per second.
– ORIGIN from *puls(ating st)ar*, on the pattern of *quasar*.

pulsate /pʌlˈseɪt, ˈpʌlseɪt/ ▶ verb [no obj.] expand and contract with strong regular movements: *blood vessels throb and pulsate.*
■[often as adj. **pulsating**] produce a regular throbbing sensation or sound: *a pulsating headache.* ■ [usu. as adj. **pulsating**] be very exciting: *victory in a pulsating semi-final.*
– DERIVATIVES **pulsation** noun, **pulsator** noun, **pulsatory** /ˈpʌlsət(ə)ri/ adjective.
– ORIGIN late 18th cent.: from Latin *pulsat-* 'throbbed, pulsed', from the verb *pulsare*, frequentative of *pellere* 'to drive, beat'.

pulsatile /ˈpʌlsətʌɪl/ ▶ adjective chiefly Physiology pulsating; relating to pulsation: *pulsatile tinnitus.*
– ORIGIN late Middle English: from medieval Latin *pulsatilis* (in *vena pulsatilis* 'artery'), from the verb *pulsare* (see **PULSATE**).

pulsatilla /ˌpʌlsəˈtɪlə/ ▶ noun a plant of a genus that includes the pasque flower.
● Genus *Pulsatilla*, family Ranunculaceae.
– ORIGIN modern Latin, diminutive of *pulsatus* 'beaten about', expressing the notion 'small flower beaten by the wind'.

pulse[1] ▶ noun a rhythmical throbbing of the arteries as blood is propelled through them, typically as felt in the wrists or neck: *the doctor found a faint pulse.*
■the rate of this throbbing, used to ascertain the rate of someone's heartbeat and so their state of health or emotions: *the idea was enough to set my **pulse racing**.* ■ (usu. **pulses**) each successive throb of the arteries or heart. ■ a single vibration or short burst of sound, electric current, light, or other wave: *radio pulses* | [as modifier] *a pulse generator.* ■ a musical beat or other regular rhythm. ■ figurative the central point of energy and organization in an area or activity: *those close to the financial and economic pulse maintain that there have been fundamental changes.* ■ Biochemistry a measured amount of an isotopic label given to a culture of cells.
▶ verb [no obj.] throb rhythmically; pulsate: *a knot of muscles at the side of his jaw pulsed.*
■[with obj.] transmit in rhythmical beats: *the sun pulsed fire into her eyes.* ■ [with obj.] modulate (a wave or beam) so that it becomes a series of pulses. ■ [with obj.] apply a pulsed signal to (a device). ■ Biochemistry short for **PULSE-LABEL**.
– PHRASES **feel** (or **take**) **the pulse of** determine the heart rate of (someone) by feeling and timing the pulsation of an artery. ■ figurative ascertain the general mood or opinion of: *the conference will be an opportunity to feel the pulse of those working in the field.*
– DERIVATIVES **pulseless** adjective.
– ORIGIN late Middle English: from Latin *pulsus* 'beating', from *pellere* 'to drive, beat'.

pulse[2] ▶ noun (usu. **pulses**) the edible seeds of various leguminous plants, for example chickpeas, lentils, and beans.
■the plant or plants producing such seeds.
– ORIGIN Middle English: from Old French *pols*, from Latin *puls* 'porridge of meal or pulse'; related to **POLLEN**.

pulse code modulation (abbrev.: **PCM**) ▶ noun [mass noun] Electronics a pulse modulation technique in which the amplitude of an analogue signal is converted to a binary value represented as a series of pulses.

pulse dialling ▶ noun [mass noun] a method of telephone dialling in which each digit is transmitted as a corresponding number of electronic pulses, now being superseded by tone dialling.

pulse jet ▶ noun a type of jet engine in which combustion is intermittent, the ignition and expulsion of each charge of mixture causing the intake of a fresh charge.

pulse-label ▶ verb [with obj.] Biochemistry subject (cells in a culture) to a pulse of an isotopic label.

pulse modulation ▶ noun [mass noun] Electronics a type of modulation in which pulses are varied in some respect, such as width or amplitude, to represent the amplitude of a signal.

pultrude /pʊlˈtruːd, pʌl-/ ▶ verb [with obj.] [usu. as adj. **pultruded**] make (a reinforced plastic article) by drawing resin-coated glass fibres through a heated die.
– DERIVATIVES **pultrusion** noun.
– ORIGIN 1960s: from *pul(ling)* + **EXTRUDE**.

pulverize (also **-ise**) ▶ verb [with obj.] reduce to fine particles: *the brick of the villages was pulverized by the bombardment.*
■informal defeat utterly: *he had a winning car and pulverized the opposition.*
– DERIVATIVES **pulverizable** adjective, **pulverization** noun, **pulverizer** noun.
– ORIGIN late Middle English: from late Latin *pulverizare*, from *pulvis*, *pulver-* 'dust'.

pulverulent /pʌlˈvɛrʊl(ə)nt/ ▶ adjective archaic consisting of fine particles; powdery or crumbly.
– ORIGIN mid 17th cent.: from Latin *pulverulentus*, from *pulvis*, *pulver-* 'dust'.

pulvinus /pʌlˈvʌɪnəs/ ▶ noun (pl. **pulvini** /-nʌɪ/) Botany an enlarged section at the base of a leaf stalk in some plants, which is subject to changes of turgor leading to movements of the leaf or leaflet.
– ORIGIN mid 19th cent.: from Latin, literally 'cushion'.

puma ▶ noun a large American wild cat with a plain tawny to greyish coat, found from Canada to Patagonia. Also called **COUGAR**, **PANTHER**, and **MOUNTAIN LION** in North America.
● *Felis concolor*, family Felidae.
– ORIGIN late 18th cent.: via Spanish from Quechua.

pumice /ˈpʌmɪs/ ▶ noun [mass noun] a very light and porous volcanic rock formed when a gas-rich froth of glassy lava solidifies rapidly.
■(also **pumice stone**) [count noun] a piece of such rock used as an abrasive, especially for removing hard skin.
▶ verb [with obj.] rub with pumice to smooth or clean.
– DERIVATIVES **pumiceous** /pjuːˈmɪʃəs/ adjective.
– ORIGIN late Middle English: from Old French *pomis*, from a Latin dialect variant of *pumex*, *pumic-*. Compare with **POUNCE**[2].

pummel ▶ verb (**pummelled**, **pummelling**; US **pummeled**, **pummeling**) [with obj.] strike repeatedly, typically with the fists: *he felt like a boxer who had been pummelled mercilessly against the ropes.*
■N. Amer. informal criticize adversely: *he has been pummelled by the reviewers.*
– ORIGIN mid 16th cent.: variant of **POMMEL**.

pummelo ▶ noun variant spelling of **POMELO**.

pump[1] ▶ noun a mechanical device using suction or pressure to raise or move liquids, compress gases, or force air into inflatable objects such as tyres: *a petrol pump.*
■[in sing.] an instance of moving something or being moved by or as if by such a machine: *the pump of blood to her heart.* ■ [with modifier] Physiology an active transport mechanism in living cells by which specific ions are moved through the cell membrane against a concentration gradient: *the bacterium's sodium pump.* ■ US a pump-action shotgun.
▶ verb **1** [with obj. and adverbial of direction] force (liquid, gas, etc.) to move in a specified direction by or as if by means of a pump: *the blood is pumped around the body* | [no obj.] *if we pump long enough, we should bring the level up.*
■[no obj., with adverbial of direction] move in spurts as though driven by a pump: *blood was pumping from a wound in his shoulder.* ■ fill with something: *my veins had been **pumped full** of glucose.* ■ shoot (bullets) into a target. ■ (**pump something in/into**) informal invest a large sum of money in (something): *he pumped all his savings into building the boat.* ■ [with obj.] informal try to elicit information from (someone) by persistent questioning: *she began to **pump** her friend **for** details.*
2 [with obj.] move (something) vigorously up and down: *we had to pump the handle like mad.*
■[no obj.] move vigorously up and down or to and fro: *that's superb running—look at his legs pumping.* ■ apply and release (a brake pedal or lever) several times in quick succession, typically to prevent skidding.
– PHRASES **pump someone's hand** shake a person's hand vigorously. **pump iron** informal exercise with weights.
▶ **pump something up** inflate a tyre, balloon, etc. ■ informal increase something: *she needs to read and pump up her political grip.* ■ give inappropriate support and encouragement to: *we let them pump up our egos.*
– ORIGIN late Middle English (originally in nautical use): related to Dutch *pomp* 'ship's pump' (earlier in the sense 'wooden or metal conduit'), probably partly of imitative origin.

pump² ▶ noun a light shoe, in particular:
■ chiefly N. English a sports shoe; a plimsoll. ■ a light shoe for dancing. ■ N. Amer. a court shoe.
– ORIGIN mid 16th cent.: of unknown origin.

pump-action ▶ adjective [attrib.] **1** denoting a repeating firearm, typically a shotgun, in which a new round is brought from the magazine into the breech by a slide action in line with the barrel. **2** denoting an unpressurized spray dispenser for a liquid such as deodorant or frying oil that is worked by finger action rather than by internal pressure (as in an aerosol).

pumped (also **pumped up**) ▶ adjective informal, chiefly N. Amer. (of a person) stimulated or filled with enthusiasm or excitement: *I was so pumped that I overdid everything.*

pumper ▶ noun chiefly N. Amer. a fire engine that carries a hose and pumps water.

pumpernickel /ˈpʊmpəˌnɪk(ə)l, ˈpʌm-/ ▶ noun [mass noun] dark, dense German bread made from coarsely ground wholemeal rye.
– ORIGIN mid 18th cent.: transferred use of German *Pumpernickel* 'lout, bumpkin', of unknown ultimate origin.

pump gun ▶ noun a pump-action rifle with a tubular magazine.

pumpkin ▶ noun **1** a large rounded orange-yellow fruit with a thick rind and edible flesh, served as either a sweet or a savoury dish.
■ [mass noun] the flesh of this fruit, especially as food. ■ N. Amer. informal used as an affectionate term of address, especially to a child. **2** the plant of the gourd family which produces this fruit, having tendrils and large lobed leaves and native to warm regions of America.
● Genus *Cucurbita*, family Cucurbitaceae: several species, in particular *C. pepo*.
■ Brit. another term for SQUASH².
– ORIGIN late 17th cent.: alteration of earlier *pumpion*, from obsolete French *pompon*, via Latin from Greek *pepōn* 'large melon' (see PEPO).

pumpkinseed ▶ noun (pl. same or **pumpkinseeds**) a small, edible, brightly coloured freshwater fish of the sunfish family, native to North America. It is popular in aquaria and has been introduced into many European waters.
● *Lepomis gibbosus*, family Centrarchidae.

pump-priming ▶ noun [mass noun] **1** the introduction of fluid into a pump to prepare it for working. **2** the stimulation of economic activity by investment: [as modifier] *a pump-priming fund.*
– DERIVATIVES **pump-primer** noun.

pump room ▶ noun a room, building, or compartment in which pumps are housed or from which they are controlled.
■ a room at a spa where medicinal water is dispensed.

pun¹ ▶ noun a joke exploiting the different possible meanings of a word or the fact that there are words which sound alike but have different meanings: *the Railway Society reception was an informal party of people of all stations (excuse the pun) in life.*
▶ verb (**punned**, **punning**) [no obj.] (often as adj. **punning**) make a joke exploiting the different possible meanings of a word.
– DERIVATIVES **punningly** adverb, **punster** noun.
– ORIGIN mid 17th cent.: perhaps an abbreviation of obsolete *pundigrion*, as a fanciful alteration of PUNCTILIO.

pun² ▶ verb (**punned**, **punning**) [with obj.] Brit. consolidate (earth or rubble) by pounding it.
– DERIVATIVES **punner** noun.
– ORIGIN mid 16th cent.: dialect variant of POUND².

puna /ˈpuːnə/ ▶ noun **1** a high treeless plateau in the Peruvian Andes. **2** another term for ALTITUDE SICKNESS.
– ORIGIN via American Spanish from Quechua.

Punan /puːˈnɑːn/ ▶ noun (pl. same or **Punans**) **1** a member of any of various groups of Dayak peoples inhabiting parts of Borneo. **2** [mass noun] any of the related languages of these peoples, now with fewer than 4,000 speakers.
▶ adjective of or relating to these peoples or their languages.
– ORIGIN the name in Dayak.

punch¹ ▶ verb [with obj.] **1** strike with the fist: *he punched her in the face and ran off.*
■ drive with a blow from the fist: *he punched the ball into his own goal.*

2 press (a button or key on a machine).
■ (**punch something in/into**) enter information by this action. **3** N. Amer. drive (cattle) by prodding them with a stick.
▶ noun a blow with the fist.
■ [mass noun] informal the strength needed to deliver such a blow: *he has the punch to knock out anyone in his division.* ■ [in sing.] the power to impress or startle: *photos give their arguments an extra visual punch.*
– PHRASES **beat someone to the punch** informal anticipate or forestall someone's actions. **punch above one's weight** informal engage in an activity or contest perceived as being beyond one's capacity or abilities. **punch the (time) clock** N. Amer. (of an employee) clock in or out. ■ be employed in a conventional job with regular hours. **punch someone's lights out** see LIGHTS.
– DERIVATIVES **puncher** noun.
– ORIGIN late Middle English (as a verb in the sense 'puncture, prod'): variant of POUNCE¹.
▶ **punch in** (or **out**) N. Amer. (of an employee) clock in (or out).

punch² ▶ noun **1** a device or machine for making holes in materials such as paper, leather, metal, and plaster. **2** a tool or machine for impressing a design or stamping a die on a material.
▶ verb [with obj.] pierce a hole in (metal, paper, leather, etc.) with or as though with a punch.
■ pierce (a hole) with or as though with a punch.
– ORIGIN early 16th cent.: perhaps an abbreviation of PUNCHEON¹, or from the verb PUNCH¹.

punch³ ▶ noun [mass noun] a drink made from wine or spirits mixed with water, fruit juices, spices, etc., and typically served hot.
– ORIGIN mid 17th cent.: apparently from Sanskrit *pañca* 'five, five kinds of' (because the drink had five ingredients).

punch⁴ ▶ noun **1** (**Punch**) a grotesque, hook-nosed humpbacked buffoon, the chief male character of the Punch and Judy show. Punch is the English variant of a stock character derived ultimately from Italian *commedia dell'arte*. Also called PUNCHINELLO. **2** (in full **Suffolk punch**) a draught horse of a short-legged thickset breed.
– PHRASES **as pleased** (or **proud**) **as Punch** feeling great delight or pride. [ORIGIN: with allusion to the delight displayed by the character *Punch* of the PUNCH AND JUDY show.]
– ORIGIN mid 17th cent. (as a dialect term denoting a short, fat person): abbreviation of PUNCHINELLO.

Punch and Judy an English puppet show presented on the miniature stage of a tall collapsible booth traditionally covered with striped canvas. The show was probably introduced from the Continent in the 17th century. Punch is on the manipulator's right hand, remaining on stage all the time, while the left hand provides a series of characters—baby, wife (Judy), priest, doctor, policeman, hangman—for him to nag, beat, and finally kill.

punchbag ▶ noun Brit. a stuffed cylindrical bag suspended so it can be punched for exercise or training, especially by boxers.
■ a person on whom another person vents their anger.

punchball ▶ noun **1** Brit. a stuffed or inflated ball mounted on a stand or attached to the floor and ceiling, used for punching as exercise or training, especially by boxers. **2** [mass noun] US a team ball game in which a rubber ball is punched or headed.

punchboard ▶ noun N. Amer. a board with holes containing slips of paper which are punched out as a form of gambling, with the object of locating a winning slip.

punchbowl ▶ noun a bowl used for mixing and serving punch.
■ chiefly Brit. a deep round hollow in a hilly area.

punch-drunk ▶ adjective stupefied by or as if by a series of heavy blows.

punched card (also **punchcard**) ▶ noun a card perforated according to a code, for controlling the operation of a machine, formerly used to program computers.

punched tape ▶ noun a paper tape perforated according to a code, formerly used for conveying instructions or data to a data processor.

puncheon¹ /ˈpʌn(t)ʃ(ə)n/ ▶ noun **1** a short post, especially one used for supporting the roof in a coal mine.
■ US a rough board or other length of wood, used for flooring or building. **2** another term for PUNCH².
– ORIGIN Middle English: from Old French *poinchon*, probably based on Latin *punct-* 'punctured', from the verb *pungere*. Compare with the noun POUNCE¹.

puncheon² /ˈpʌn(t)ʃ(ə)n/ ▶ noun historical a large cask for liquids or other commodities holding from 72 to 120 gallons.
– ORIGIN late Middle English: from Old French *poinchon*, of uncertain origin although forms in Old French and English correspond to those of PUNCHEON¹.

Punchinello /ˌpʌn(t)ʃɪˈnɛləʊ/ ▶ noun (pl. **-os**) another name for PUNCH⁴ (in sense 1).
■ archaic a short, stout, comical-looking person.
– ORIGIN mid 17th cent.: alteration of Neapolitan dialect *Polecenella*, perhaps a diminutive of *pollecena* 'young turkey cock with a hooked beak', from *pulcino* 'chicken', from Latin *pullus*.

punching bag ▶ noun North American term for PUNCHBAG.

punchline ▶ noun the final phrase or sentence of a joke or story, providing the humour or some other crucial element.

punch press ▶ noun a press that is designed to drive a punch for shaping metal.

punch-up ▶ noun informal, chiefly Brit. a disorderly bout of fighting with the fists; a brawl.

punchy ▶ adjective (**punchier**, **punchiest**) having an immediate impact; forceful: *his style is journalistic, with short punchy sentences.*
– DERIVATIVES **punchily** adverb, **punchiness** noun.

puncta plural form of PUNCTUM.

punctae /ˈpʌŋ(k)tiː/ ▶ plural noun Biology minute rounded dots or spots of colour, or small elevations or depressions on a surface.
– ORIGIN modern Latin (plural).

punctate /ˈpʌŋ(k)teɪt/ ▶ adjective Biology studded with or denoting dots or tiny holes.
– DERIVATIVES **punctation** noun.
– ORIGIN mid 18th cent.: from Latin *punctum* 'point' + -ATE².

punctilio /pʌŋ(k)ˈtɪlɪəʊ/ ▶ noun (pl. **-os**) a fine or petty point of conduct or procedure.
– ORIGIN late 16th cent.: from Italian *puntiglio(n-)* and Spanish *puntillo*, diminutive of *punto* 'a point'.

punctilious /pʌŋ(k)ˈtɪlɪəs/ ▶ adjective showing great attention to detail or correct behaviour: *he was punctilious in providing every amenity for his guests.*
– DERIVATIVES **punctiliously** adverb, **punctiliousness** noun.
– ORIGIN mid 17th cent.: from French *pointilleux*, from *pointille*, from Italian *puntiglio* (see PUNCTILIO).

punctual /ˈpʌŋ(k)tʃʊəl, -tjʊəl/ ▶ adjective happening or doing something at the agreed or proper time: *he's the sort of man who's always punctual.*
■ Grammar denoting or relating to an action that takes place at a particular point in time. Contrasted with DURATIVE.
– DERIVATIVES **punctuality** noun, **punctually** adverb.
– ORIGIN late 17th cent.: from medieval Latin *punctualis*, from Latin *punctum* 'a point'.

punctuate /ˈpʌŋ(k)tʃʊeɪt, -tjʊ-/ ▶ verb [with obj.] **1** (often **be punctuated**) occur at intervals throughout (a continuing event or a place): *the country's history has been punctuated by coups.*
■ (**punctuate something with**) interrupt or intersperse (an activity) with: *she punctuates her conversation with snatches of song.* **2** insert punctuation marks in (text).
– ORIGIN mid 17th cent. (in the sense 'point out'): from medieval Latin *punctuat-* 'brought to a point', from the verb *punctuare*, from *punctum* 'a point'.

punctuated equilibrium ▶ noun [mass noun] Biology the hypothesis that evolutionary development is marked by isolated episodes of rapid speciation between long periods of little or no change.

punctuation ▶ noun [mass noun] **1** the marks, such as full stop, comma, and brackets, used in writing to separate sentences and their elements and to clarify meaning. **2** Biology rapid or sudden speciation, as suggested by the theory of punctuated equilibrium.

– DERIVATIVES **punctuational** adjective.
– ORIGIN mid 17th cent.: from medieval Latin *punctuatio(n-)*, from the verb *punctuare* (see **PUNCTUATE**).

punctuationist ▶ **noun** Biology a person who believes in or advocates the hypothesis of punctuated equilibrium.
– DERIVATIVES **punctuationalism** noun, **punctuationalist** adjective, **punctuationism** noun.

punctuation mark ▶ **noun** a mark, such as a full stop, comma, or question mark, used in writing to separate sentences and their elements and to clarify meaning.

punctum /ˈpʌŋ(k)təm/ ▶ **noun** (pl. **puncta** /-tə/) technical a small, distinct point.
■ Anatomy the opening of a tear duct.
– ORIGIN late 16th cent. (figuratively, denoting a point): from Latin, literally 'a point'.

puncture ▶ **noun** a small hole in a tyre resulting in an escape of air: *she was on her way home when she had a puncture.*
■ a small hole in something such as the skin, caused by a sharp object: [as modifier] *a puncture wound.*
▶ **verb** [with obj.] make such a hole in (something): *one of the knife blows had punctured a lung.*
■ [no obj.] sustain such a small hole: *the tyre had punctured and it would have to be replaced.* ■ figurative bring about a dramatic reversal in (mood or behaviour) resembling a sudden deflation or collapse: *the earlier mood of optimism was punctured.*
– ORIGIN late Middle English: from Latin *punctura*, from *punct-* 'pricked', from the verb *pungere*. The verb dates from the late 17th cent.

pundit /ˈpʌndɪt/ ▶ **noun 1** an expert in a particular subject or field who is frequently called upon to give their opinions about it to the public: *political pundits were tipping him for promotion.*
2 variant spelling of **PANDIT**.
– DERIVATIVES **punditry** noun (only in sense 1).
– ORIGIN from Sanskrit *paṇḍita* 'learned'.

Pune variant spelling of **POONA**.

punga /ˈpʌŋə/ ▶ **noun** variant spelling of **PONGA**.

pungent ▶ **adjective** having a sharply strong taste or smell: *the pungent smell of frying onions.*
■ (of comment, criticism, or humour) having a sharp and caustic quality.
– DERIVATIVES **pungency** noun, **pungently** adverb.
– ORIGIN late 16th cent. (in the sense 'very painful or distressing'): from Latin *pungent-* 'pricking', from the verb *pungere*.

Punic /ˈpjuːnɪk/ ▶ **adjective** of or relating to Carthage.
▶ **noun** [mass noun] the language of ancient Carthage, related to Phoenician.
– ORIGIN from Latin *Punicus* (earlier *Poenicus*), from *Poenus*, from Greek *Phoinix* 'Phoenician'.

Punic Wars three wars between Rome and Carthage, which led to the unquestioned dominance of Rome in the western Mediterranean.

In the first Punic War (264–241 BC), Rome secured Sicily from Carthage and established herself as a naval power; in the second (218–201 BC), the defeat of Hannibal (largely through the generalship of Fabius Cunctator and Scipio Africanus) put an end to Carthage's position as a Mediterranean power; the third (149–146 BC) ended in the total destruction of the city of Carthage.

punish ▶ **verb** [with obj.] inflict a penalty or sanction on (someone) as retribution for an offence, especially a transgression of a legal or moral code: *I have done wrong and I'm being **punished for** it.*
■ inflict a penalty or sanction on someone for (such an offence): *fraudulent acts would be punished by up to two years in prison.* ■ informal take advantage of and capitalize on (an opponent's mistake), especially in sport: *Australia punished Ireland's handling blunders and scored three tries.* ■ treat (someone) in an unfairly harsh way: *a rise in prescription charges would punish the poor.* ■ [usu. as adj. **punishing**] subject (someone or something) to severe and debilitating treatment: *the recession was having a punishing effect on our business.*
– DERIVATIVES **punishable** adjective, **punisher** noun, **punishingly** adverb.
– ORIGIN Middle English: from Old French *puniss-*, lengthened stem of *punir* 'punish', from Latin *punire*, from *poena* 'penalty'.

punishment ▶ **noun** [mass noun] the infliction or imposition of a penalty as retribution for an offence: *crime demands just punishment.*
■ the penalty inflicted: *she assisted her husband to escape **punishment for** the crime* | [count noun] *he approved of stiff punishments for criminals.* ■ informal rough treatment or handling inflicted on or suffered by a person or thing: *your machine can **take** a fair amount of **punishment** before falling to bits.*
– ORIGIN late Middle English: from Old French *punissement*, from the verb *punir* (see **PUNISH**).

punitive /ˈpjuːnɪtɪv/ ▶ **adjective** inflicting or intended as punishment: *he called for punitive measures against the Eastern bloc.*
■ (of a tax or other charge) extremely high: *a current punitive interest rate of 31.3%.*
– DERIVATIVES **punitively** adverb, **punitiveness** noun.
– ORIGIN early 17th cent.: from French *punitif, -ive* or medieval Latin *punitivus*, from Latin *punit-* 'punished', from the verb *punire* (see **PUNISH**).

punitive damages ▶ **plural noun** Law damages exceeding simple compensation and awarded to punish the defendant.

Punjab /pʌnˈdʒɑːb, ˈpʌndʒɑːb, pʊn-/ (also **the Punjab**) a region of NW India and Pakistan, a wide, fertile plain traversed by the Indus and the five tributaries which gave the region its name.
■ a province of Pakistan; capital, Lahore. ■ a state of India; capital, Chandigarh. Until 1966 the Punjab also encompassed what is now the state of Haryana.

The region became a centre of Sikhism in the 15th century and, after the capture of Lahore in 1799 by Ranjit Singh, a powerful Sikh kingdom. It was annexed by the British in 1849 and became a part of British India. In the partition of 1947 it was divided between Pakistan and India.

– ORIGIN from Hindi *panj* 'five' + *āb* 'waters'.

Punjabi /pʌnˈdʒɑːbi, pʊn-/ (also **Panjabi**) ▶ **noun** (pl. **Punjabis**) **1** a native or inhabitant of Punjab.
2 [mass noun] the Indic language of Punjab, spoken by over 50 million people.
3 (**punjabi**) a long kurta with cuffs and a bottom edge which is rounded up towards the seams.
▶ **adjective** of or relating to Punjab or its people or language.
– ORIGIN from Hindi *pājābī*.

punji stick /ˈpʌndʒi/ (also **punji stake**) ▶ **noun** a sharpened bamboo stake, typically one tipped with poison, set in a camouflaged hole in the ground as a means of defence, especially in SE Asia.
– ORIGIN late 19th cent.: *punji* probably of Tibeto-Burman origin.

punk ▶ **noun 1** informal, chiefly N. Amer. a worthless person (often used as a general term of abuse).
■ a criminal or hoodlum. ■ US (in prison slang) a passive male homosexual. ■ an inexperienced young person; a novice.
2 (also **punk rock**) [mass noun] a loud, fast-moving, and aggressive form of rock music, popular in the late 1970s.
■ (also **punk rocker**) [count noun] an admirer or player of such music, typically characterized by coloured spiked hair and clothing decorated with safety pins or zips.
3 [mass noun] chiefly N. Amer. soft, crumbly wood that has been attacked by fungus, widely used as tinder.
▶ **adjective 1** N. Amer. informal in poor or bad condition: *I felt too punk to eat.*
2 of or relating to punk rock and its associated subculture: *a punk band* | *a punk haircut.*
– DERIVATIVES **punkish** adjective, **punky** adjective.
– ORIGIN late 17th cent. (in sense 3): perhaps, in some senses, related to archaic *punk* 'prostitute', also to **SPUNK**.

punkah /ˈpʌŋkə, -kɑː/ ▶ **noun** chiefly historical (in India) a large cloth fan on a frame suspended from the ceiling, moved backwards and forwards by pulling on a cord.
■ Indian an electric fan.
– ORIGIN via Hindi from Sanskrit *pakṣaka*, from *pakṣa* 'wing'.

punker ▶ **noun** chiefly N. Amer. a punk rocker.

punkette ▶ **noun** a female punk rocker.
– ORIGIN 1980s: from **PUNK** + the feminine suffix **-ETTE**.

punnet ▶ **noun** Brit. a small light basket or other container for fruit or vegetables: *a punnet of strawberries.*
– ORIGIN early 19th cent.: perhaps a diminutive of dialect *pun* 'a pound'.

punt[1] /pʌnt/ ▶ **noun** a long, narrow, flat-bottomed boat, square at both ends and propelled with a long pole, used on inland waters chiefly for recreation.
▶ **verb** [no obj.] travel in such a boat.
■ [with obj.] convey in such a boat.
– ORIGIN Old English, from Latin *ponto*, denoting a flat-bottomed ferry boat; readopted in the early 16th cent. from Middle Low German *punte* or Middle Dutch *ponte* 'ferry boat', of the same origin.

punt[2] /pʌnt/ ▶ **verb** [no obj.] American Football & Rugby kick the ball after it has dropped from the hands and before it reaches the ground.
■ [with obj. and adverbial of direction] Soccer kick (the ball) a long distance upfield: *Leeds punted the ball back to them.*
▶ **noun** a kick of this kind.
– ORIGIN mid 19th cent.: probably from dialect *punt* 'push forcibly'. Compare with **BUNT**[3].

punt[3] /pʌnt/ ▶ **verb** [no obj.] (in some gambling card games) lay a stake against the bank.
■ Brit. informal bet or speculate on something: *investors are **punting on** a takeover.*
▶ **noun** informal, chiefly Brit. a bet: *those **taking a punt on** the company's success.*
– PHRASES **take** (or **have**) **a punt at** Austral./NZ informal attempt to do (something).
– ORIGIN early 18th cent.: from French *ponte* 'player against the bank', from Spanish *punto* 'a point'.

punt[4] /pʊnt/ ▶ **noun** (until the introduction of the euro in 2002) the basic monetary unit of the Republic of Ireland, equal to 100 pence.
– ORIGIN Irish, literally 'pound'.

Punta Arenas /ˌpʊntə əˈreɪnəs/ a port in southern Chile, on the Strait of Magellan; pop. 113,660 (1992).

punter ▶ **noun 1** informal, chiefly Brit. a person who gambles, places a bet, or makes a risky investment.
■ a customer or client, especially a member of an audience. ■ a prostitute's client. ■ the victim of a swindler or confidence trickster.
2 American Football & Rugby a player who punts.
3 a person who propels or travels in a punt.

punty /ˈpʌnti/ ▶ **noun** (pl. **-ies**) another term for **PONTIL**.

puny /ˈpjuːni/ ▶ **adjective** (**punier**, **puniest**) small and weak: *skeletal, white-faced, puny children.*
■ poor in quality, amount, or size: *the army was reduced to a puny 100,000 men.*
– DERIVATIVES **punily** adverb, **puniness** noun.
– ORIGIN mid 16th cent. (as a noun denoting a younger or more junior person): phonetic spelling of **PUISNE**.

pup ▶ **noun** a young dog.
■ a young wolf, seal, rat, or other mammal. ■ dated, chiefly Brit. a cheeky or arrogant boy or young man: *you saucy young pup!*
▶ **verb** (**pupped**, **pupping**) [no obj.] (of bitches and certain other female animals) give birth to young.
– PHRASES **in pup** (of a bitch) pregnant. **sell someone** (or **buy**) **a pup** Brit. informal swindle someone (or be swindled), especially by selling (or buying) something worthless.
– ORIGIN late 16th cent. (in the sense 'arrogant young man'): back-formation from **PUPPY**, interpreted as a diminutive.

pupa /ˈpjuːpə/ ▶ **noun** (pl. **pupae** /-piː/) an insect in its inactive immature form between larva and adult, e.g. a chrysalis.
– DERIVATIVES **pupal** adjective.
– ORIGIN late 18th cent.: modern Latin, from Latin *pupa* 'girl, doll'.

puparium /pjuːˈpɛːrɪəm/ ▶ **noun** (pl. **puparia** /-rɪə/) Entomology the hardened last larval skin which encloses the pupa in some insects, especially higher diptera.
■ a pupa enclosed in such a skin.
– ORIGIN early 19th cent.: modern Latin, from **PUPA**, on the pattern of words such as *herbarium*.

pupate ▶ **verb** [no obj.] (of a larva) become a pupa.
– DERIVATIVES **pupation** noun.

pupfish ▶ **noun** (pl. same or **-fishes**) a small fish found in fresh or brackish water in the deserts of the south-western US and northern Mexico.
• Genus *Cyprinodon*, family Cyprinodontidae: several species, some of which are confined to single pools.

pupil[1] ▶ **noun** a person who is taught by another, especially a schoolchild or student in relation to a teacher.
■ Brit. a trainee barrister.
– ORIGIN late Middle English (in the sense 'orphan, ward'): from Old French *pupille*, from Latin *pupillus* (diminutive of *pupus* 'boy') and *pupilla* (diminutive of *pupa* 'girl').

pupil[2] ▶ **noun** the dark circular opening in the centre of the iris of the eye, which varies in size to regulate the amount of light reaching the retina.

– DERIVATIVES **pupillary** adjective.
– ORIGIN late Middle English: from Old French *pupille* or Latin *pupilla*, diminutive of *pupa* 'doll' (so named from the tiny reflected images visible in the eye).

pupillage ▶ **noun** [mass noun] the state of being a pupil or student.
■ Law (in the UK) apprenticeship to a member of the Bar, which qualifies a barrister to practise independently.

pupil-master ▶ **noun** Brit. a barrister in charge of a trainee barrister.

pupiparous /pjuːˈpɪp(ə)rəs/ ▶ **adjective** Entomology (of certain flies, e.g. the tsetse) producing young which are already ready to pupate.
– ORIGIN early 19th cent.: from modern Latin *pupipara* (neuter plural of *pupiparus* 'bringing forth young') + **-OUS**.

puppet ▶ **noun** a movable model of a person or animal that is used in entertainment and is typically moved either by strings controlled from above or by a hand inside it.
■ figurative a person, party, or state under the control of another person, group, or power: *the new Shah began his reign as an Anglo-Soviet puppet.*
– DERIVATIVES **puppetry** noun.
– ORIGIN mid 16th cent. (denoting a doll): later form of **POPPET**, generally having a more unfavourable connotation.

puppeteer ▶ **noun** a person who works puppets.
– DERIVATIVES **puppeteering** noun.

Puppis /ˈpʌpɪs/ Astronomy a southern constellation (the Poop or Stern), lying partly in the Milky Way south of Canis Major and originally part of Argo.
■ [as genitive **Puppis**] used with preceding letter or numeral to designate a star in this constellation: *the star Zeta Puppis.*
– ORIGIN Latin.

puppy ▶ **noun** (pl. **-ies**) a young dog.
■ informal, dated a conceited or arrogant young man: *you ungrateful puppy.*
– DERIVATIVES **puppyhood** noun, **puppyish** adjective.
– ORIGIN late 15th cent. (denoting a lapdog): perhaps from Old French *poupee* 'doll, plaything'; compare with **PUPPET**, synonymous with dialect *puppy* (as in *puppy-show* 'puppet show').

puppy-dog ▶ **noun** a child's word for a puppy.
■ figurative a gentle or devotedly loyal person.

puppy fat ▶ **noun** [mass noun] fat on the body of a baby or child which disappears around adolescence.

puppy love ▶ **noun** [mass noun] intense but relatively shallow romantic attachment, typically associated with adolescents.

pup tent ▶ **noun** N. Amer. a small triangular tent, especially one for two people and without side walls.

pur- ▶ **prefix** equivalent to **PRO-**[1] (as in *purloin, pursue*).
– ORIGIN from Anglo-Norman French, from Latin *por-, pro-*.

Purana /pʊˈrɑːnə/ ▶ **noun** (usu. **Puranas**) any of a class of Sanskrit sacred writings on Hindu mythology and folklore of varying date and origin, the most ancient of which dates from the 4th century AD.
– DERIVATIVES **Puranic** adjective.
– ORIGIN from Sanskrit *purāṇa* 'ancient (legend)', from *purā* 'formerly'.

Purbeck marble /ˈpəːbɛk/ (also **Purbeck stone**) ▶ **noun** [mass noun] a hard limestone from Purbeck in Dorset, which is polished and used for decorative parts of buildings, fonts, and effigies.

purblind /ˈpəːblʌɪnd/ ▶ **adjective** having impaired or defective vision.
■ figurative slow or unable to understand; dim-witted.
– DERIVATIVES **purblindness** noun.
– ORIGIN Middle English (as two words in the sense 'completely blind'): from the adverb **PURE** 'utterly' (later assimilated to **PUR-**) + **BLIND**.

Purcell /pəːˈsɛl, ˈpəːs(ə)l/, Henry (1659–95), English composer. Organist for Westminster Abbey (1679–95), he composed choral odes and songs for royal occasions. His main interest was music for the theatre; he composed the first English opera *Dido and Aeneas* (1689) and the incidental music for many plays.

purchase ▶ **verb** [with obj.] **1** acquire (something) by paying for it; buy: *Mr Gill spotted the manuscript at a local auction and purchased it for £1,500.*
■ archaic obtain or achieve with effort or suffering: *the victory was purchased by the death of Rhiwallon.*
2 Nautical haul up (a rope, cable, or anchor) by means of a pulley or lever.
▶ **noun 1** [mass noun] the action of buying something: *the large number of videos currently available for purchase* | [count noun] *we carefully* **make** *our* **purchases** *after consulting each other.*
■ [count noun] a thing that has been bought: *she stowed her purchases in the car.* ■ Law the acquisition of property by one's personal action and not by inheritance. ■ archaic the annual rent or return from land.
2 [mass noun] firm contact or grip: *the horse's hooves fought for* **purchase on** *the slippery pavement* | [in sing.] *an attempt to gain a purchase on the soft earth.*
■ [count noun] a pulley or similar device for moving heavy objects.
– DERIVATIVES **purchasable** adjective, **purchaser** noun.
– ORIGIN Middle English: from Old French *pourchacier* 'seek to obtain or bring about', the earliest sense also in English, which soon gave rise to the senses 'gain' (hence, in nautical use, the notion of 'gaining' one portion of rope after another) and 'buy'.

purchase tax ▶ **noun** a tax added to the price of goods sold to consumers.

purdah /ˈpəːdə/ ▶ **noun** [mass noun] the practice among women in certain Muslim and Hindu societies of living in a separate room or behind a curtain, or of dressing in all-enveloping clothes, in order to stay out of the sight of men or strangers: *he never required them to observe purdah.*
■ the state of living in such a place or dressing in this way: *she was supposed to be* **in purdah** *upstairs.* ■ figurative isolation or hiding: *in the thirties and seventies, legs went into purdah.* ■ [count noun] a curtain used for screening off women in this way.
– ORIGIN early 19th cent.: from Urdu and Persian *parda* 'veil, curtain'.

pure ▶ **adjective** not mixed or adulterated with any other substance or material: *cars can run on pure alcohol* | *the jacket was pure wool.*
■ without any extraneous and unnecessary elements: *the romantic notion of pure art devoid of social responsibility.* ■ free of any contamination: *the pure, clear waters of Scotland.* ■ wholesome and untainted by immorality, especially that of a sexual nature: *our fondness for each other is pure and innocent.* ■ (of a sound) perfectly in tune and with a clear tone. ■ (of an animal or plant) of unmixed origin or descent: *the pure Charolais is white or light wheat in the coat.* ■ (of a subject of study) dealing with abstract concepts and not practical application: *a theoretical discipline such as pure physics.* Compare with **APPLIED**. ■ Phonetics (of a vowel) not joined with another to form a diphthong. ■ [attrib.] involving or containing nothing else but; sheer (used for emphasis): *a shout of pure anger* | *an outcome which may be a matter of pure chance.*
– PHRASES **pure and simple** and nothing else (used for emphasis): *it was revenge, pure and simple.*
– DERIVATIVES **pureness** noun.
– ORIGIN Middle English: from Old French *pur* 'pure', from Latin *purus*.

pure-bred ▶ **adjective** (of an animal) bred from parents of the same breed or variety.
▶ **noun** an animal of this kind.

pure culture ▶ **noun** Microbiology a culture in which only one strain or clone is present.

purée /ˈpjʊəreɪ/ ▶ **noun** [mass noun] a smooth cream of liquidized or crushed fruit or vegetables: *stir in the tomato purée.*
▶ **verb** (**purées**, **puréed**, **puréeing**) [with obj.] make a purée of (fruit or vegetables).
– ORIGIN early 18th cent.: French, literally 'purified', feminine past participle of *purer*.

pure line ▶ **noun** Biology an inbred line of genetic descent.

purely ▶ **adverb** in a pure manner: *act nobly, speak purely, and think charitably.*
■ entirely; exclusively: *the purpose of the meeting was purely to give information.*

pure mathematics ▶ **plural noun** see **MATHEMATICS**.

pure science ▶ **noun** a science depending on deductions from demonstrated truths, such as mathematics or logic, or studied without regard to practical applications.

purfle /ˈpəːf(ə)l/ ▶ **noun** an ornamental border, typically one inlaid on the back or belly of a violin.
■ archaic an ornamental or embroidered edge of a garment.
▶ **verb** [with obj.] [often as noun **purfling**] decorate (something) with an ornamental border.
– ORIGIN Middle English (as a verb): from Old French *porfil* (noun), *porfiler* (verb), based on Latin *pro* 'forward' + *filum* 'thread'.

purgation /pəːˈgeɪʃ(ə)n/ ▶ **noun** [mass noun] the purification or cleansing of someone or something: *the purgation by ritual violence of morbid social emotions.*
■ (in Catholic doctrine) the spiritual cleansing of a soul in purgatory. ■ historical the action of clearing oneself of accusation or suspicion by an oath or ordeal. ■ evacuation of the bowels brought about by laxatives.
– ORIGIN late Middle English: from Old French *purgacion*, from Latin *purgatio(n-)*, from *purgare* 'purify' (see **PURGE**).

purgative /ˈpəːgətɪv/ ▶ **adjective** strongly laxative in effect.
■ figurative having the effect of ridding someone of unwanted feelings or memories: *the purgative action of language.*
▶ **noun** a laxative.
■ figurative a thing that rids someone of unwanted feelings or memories: *confrontation would be a purgative.*
– ORIGIN late Middle English: from Old French *purgatif, -ive*, from late Latin *purgativus*, from *purgat-* 'purified', from the verb *purgare* (see **PURGE**).

purgatory /ˈpəːgət(ə)ri/ ▶ **noun** (pl. **-ies**) (in Catholic doctrine) a place or state of suffering inhabited by the souls of sinners who are expiating their sins before going to heaven.
■ [mass noun] mental anguish or suffering: *this was purgatory, worse than anything she'd faced in her life.*
▶ **adjective** archaic having the quality of cleansing or purifying: *infernal punishments are purgatory and medicinal.*
– DERIVATIVES **purgatorial** adjective.
– ORIGIN Middle English: from Anglo-Norman French *purgatorie* or medieval Latin *purgatorium*, neuter (used as a noun) of late Latin *purgatorius* 'purifying', from the verb *purgare* (see **PURGE**).

purge ▶ **verb** [with obj.] rid (someone) of an unwanted feeling, memory, or condition, typically giving a sense of cathartic release: *Bob had helped* **purge** *Martha* **of** *the terrible guilt that had haunted her.*
■ remove (an unwanted feeling, memory, or condition) in such a way. ■ remove (a group of people considered undesirable) from an organization or place, typically in an abrupt or violent manner: *he purged all but 26 of the central committee members.* ■ remove someone from (an organization or place) in such a way: *an opportunity to* **purge** *the party* **of** *unsatisfactory members.* ■ Law atone for or wipe out (contempt of court). ■ physically remove (something) completely: *a cold air blower* **purges** *residual solvents* **from** *the body.* ■ [no obj.] [often as noun **purging**] evacuate one's bowels, especially as a result of taking a laxative.
▶ **noun** an abrupt or violent removal of a group of people from an organization or place: *a purge of the ruling class is absolutely necessary* | *the Stalinist purges.*
■ dated a laxative.
– DERIVATIVES **purger** noun.
– ORIGIN Middle English (in the legal sense 'clear oneself of a charge'): from Old French *purgier*, from Latin *purgare* 'purify', from *purus* 'pure'.

puri /ˈpuːri/ ▶ **noun** (pl. **puris**) (in Indian cookery) a small, round, flat piece of bread made of unleavened wheat flour, deep-fried and served with meat or vegetables.
– ORIGIN via Hindi from Sanskrit *pūrikā*.

purify ▶ **verb** (**-ies**, **-ied**) [with obj.] remove contaminants from: *the filtration plant is able to purify 70 tons of water a day* | [as adj. **purified**] *purified linseed oil.*
■ make ceremonially clean: *a ritual bath to purify the soul.* ■ rid (something) of an unwanted element: *Mao's campaign to purify the Communist Party hierarchy.* ■ (**purify something from**) extract something from: *genomic DNA was purified from whole blood.*
– DERIVATIVES **purification** noun, **purificatory** adjective, **purifier** noun.
– ORIGIN Middle English: from Old French *purifier*, from Latin *purificare*, from *purus* 'pure'.

Purim /ˈpʊərɪm, pʊˈriːm/ ▶ **noun** a lesser Jewish festival held in spring (on the 14th or 15th day of Adar) to commemorate the defeat of Haman's plot

a cat | ɑː arm | ɛ bed | ɛː hair | ə ago | əː her | ɪ sit | i cosy | iː see | ɒ hot | ɔː saw | ʌ run | ʊ put | uː too | ʌɪ my | aʊ how | eɪ day | əʊ no | ɪə near | ɔɪ boy | ʊə poor | ʌɪə fire | aʊə sour

to massacre the Jews as recorded in the book of Esther.
– ORIGIN Hebrew, plural of *pūr*, explained in the book of Esther (3:7, 9:24) as meaning 'lot', with allusion to the casting of lots by Haman.

purine /ˈpjʊəriːn/ ▶ **noun** [mass noun] Chemistry a colourless crystalline compound with basic properties, forming uric acid on oxidation.
● A bicyclic compound; chem. formula: $C_5H_4N_4$.
■ (also **purine base**) [count noun] a substituted derivative of this, especially the bases adenine and guanine present in DNA.
– ORIGIN late 19th cent.: from German *Purin*, from Latin *purus* 'pure' + *uricum* 'uric acid' + **-INE**[4].

purism ▶ **noun** [mass noun] **1** scrupulous or exaggerated observance of or insistence on traditional rules or structures, especially in language or style.
2 (**Purism**) an early 20th-century artistic style and movement founded by Le Corbusier and the French painter Amédée Ozenfant (1886–1966) and emphasizing purity of geometric form. It arose out of a rejection of cubism and was characterized by a return to the representation of recognizable objects.

purist ▶ **noun 1** a person who insists on absolute adherence to traditional rules or structures, especially in language or style.
2 (**Purist**) an adherent of Purism.
– DERIVATIVES **puristic** adjective.
– ORIGIN early 18th cent.: from French *puriste*, from *pur* 'pure'.

puritan ▶ **noun** (**Puritan**) a member of a group of English Protestants of the late 16th and 17th centuries who regarded the Reformation of the Church under Elizabeth as incomplete and sought to simplify and regulate forms of worship.
■ a person with censorious moral beliefs, especially about pleasure and sex.
▶ **adjective** (usu. **Puritan**) of or relating to the Puritans.
■ having or displaying censorious moral beliefs, especially about pleasure and sex.
– DERIVATIVES **puritanism** (also **Puritanism**) noun.
– ORIGIN late 16th cent.: from late Latin *puritas* 'purity' + **-AN**.

puritanical ▶ **adjective** often derogatory practising or affecting strict religious or moral behaviour.
– DERIVATIVES **puritanically** adverb.

purity ▶ **noun** [mass noun] freedom from adulteration or contamination: *the purity of our our drinking water.*
■ freedom from immorality, especially of a sexual nature: *white is meant to represent purity and innocence.*
– ORIGIN Middle English: from Old French *purete*, later assimilated to late Latin *puritas*, from Latin *purus* 'pure'.

Purkinje cell /pəːˈkɪndʒi/ ▶ **noun** Anatomy a nerve cell of a large, branched type found in the cortex of the cerebellum.
– ORIGIN mid 19th cent.: named after Jan E. *Purkinje* (1787–1869), Bohemian physiologist.

purl[1] ▶ **adjective** [attrib.] denoting or relating to a knitting stitch made by putting the needle through the front of the stitch from right to left. Compare with **PLAIN**[1] (in sense 5).
▶ **noun** [mass noun] purl stitch.
▶ **verb** [with obj.] knit with a purl stitch: *knit one, purl one.*
– ORIGIN mid 17th cent. (as a noun): of uncertain origin.

purl[2] ▶ **verb** [no obj.] (of a stream or river) flow with a swirling motion and babbling sound.
▶ **noun** [in sing.] a motion or sound of this kind.
– ORIGIN early 16th cent. (denoting a small swirling stream): probably imitative; compare with Norwegian *purla* 'bubble up'.

purler ▶ **noun** Brit. informal a headlong fall: *the horse went a purler at the last fence.*
– ORIGIN mid 19th cent.: from dialect *purl* 'upset, overturn'.

purlieu /ˈpəːljuː/ ▶ **noun** (pl. **purlieus** or **purlieux**) (usu. **purlieus**) the area near or surrounding a place: *the photogenic purlieus of Cambridge.*
■ Brit. historical a tract on the border of a forest, especially one earlier included in it and still partly subject to forest laws. ■ figurative a person's usual haunts.
– ORIGIN late 15th cent. (denoting a tract on the border of a forest): probably an alteration (suggested by French *lieu* 'place') of Anglo-Norman French *puralee* 'a going round to settle the boundaries'.

purlin /ˈpəːlɪn/ ▶ **noun** a horizontal beam along the length of a roof, resting on principals and supporting the common rafters or boards.
– ORIGIN late Middle English: perhaps of French origin.

purloin /pəˈlɔɪn/ ▶ **verb** [with obj.] formal or humorous steal (something): *he must have managed to purloin a copy of the key.*
– DERIVATIVES **purloiner** noun.
– ORIGIN Middle English (in the sense 'put at a distance'): from Anglo-Norman French *purloigner* 'put away', from *pur-* 'forth' + *loign* 'far'.

puro /ˈpʊərəʊ/ ▶ **noun** (pl. **-os**) (in Spain and Spanish-speaking countries) a cigar.
– ORIGIN Spanish, literally 'pure'.

puromycin /ˌpjʊərə(ʊ)ˈmʌɪsɪn/ ▶ **noun** [mass noun] Medicine an antibiotic used to treat sleeping sickness and amoebic dysentery.
● This antibiotic is produced by the bacterium *Streptomyces alboniger.*
– ORIGIN 1950s: from **PURINE** + **-MYCIN**.

purple ▶ **noun** [mass noun] a colour intermediate between red and blue: *the painting was mostly in shades of blue and purple.*
■ purple clothing or material. ■ (also **Tyrian purple**) a crimson dye obtained from some molluscs, formerly used for fabric worn by an emperor or senior magistrate in ancient Rome or Byzantium. ■ (**the purple**) (in ancient Rome or Byzantium) clothing of this colour. ■ (**the purple**) (in ancient Rome) a position of rank, authority, or privilege: *he was too young to assume the purple.* ■ (**the purple**) the scarlet official dress of a cardinal.
▶ **adjective** of a colour intermediate between red and blue: *a faded purple T-shirt.*
▶ **verb** become or make purple in colour: [no obj.] *Edmund's cheeks purpled* | [with obj.] *the neon was purpling the horizon above the highway.*
– PHRASES **born in** (or **to**) **the purple** born into a reigning family or privileged class.
– DERIVATIVES **purpleness** noun, **purplish** adjective, **purply** adjective.
– ORIGIN Old English (describing the clothing of an emperor), alteration of *purpre*, from Latin *purpura* 'purple', from Greek *porphura*, denoting molluscs that yielded a crimson dye, also cloth dyed with this.

purple emperor ▶ **noun** a large European woodland butterfly that has iridescent purplish-black wings with white markings.
● *Apatura iris*, subfamily Apaturinae, family Nymphalidae.

purple gallinule ▶ **noun** another term for **SWAMPHEN**.
■ N. Amer. see **GALLINULE**.

purple heart ▶ **noun 1** (**Purple Heart**) (in the US) a decoration for those wounded or killed in action, established in 1782 and re-established in 1932.
2 a large tree of the rainforests of Central and South America, with dark purplish-brown timber which blackens on contact with water.
● Genus *Peltogyne*, family Leguminosae: several species, in particular *P. paniculata*.
3 Brit. informal a mauve-coloured heart-shaped stimulant tablet, especially of amphetamine.

purple passage ▶ **noun** an elaborate or excessively ornate passage in a literary composition.

purple patch ▶ **noun 1** informal a run of success or good luck: *people expect me to score in every game now I've hit a purple patch.*
2 another term for **PURPLE PASSAGE**.

purple prose ▶ **noun** [mass noun] prose that is too elaborate or ornate.

purple swamphen ▶ **noun** see **SWAMPHEN**.

purport ▶ **verb** /pəˈpɔːt/ [with infinitive] appear to be or do something, especially falsely: *she is not the person she purports to be.*
▶ **noun** /ˈpəːpɔːt/ [mass noun] the meaning or substance of something, typically a document or speech: *I do not understand the purport of your remarks.*
■ the purpose of a person or thing: *the purport of existence.*
– DERIVATIVES **purportedly** adverb.
– ORIGIN late Middle English (in the sense 'express, signify'): from Old French *purporter*, from medieval Latin *proportare*, from Latin *pro-* 'forth' + *portare* 'carry, bear'. The sense 'appear to be' dates from the late 18th cent.

purpose ▶ **noun** the reason for which something is done or created or for which something exists: *the purpose of the meeting is to appoint a trustee | the building is no longer needed for its original purpose.*
■ [mass noun] a person's sense of resolve or determination: *there was a new* ***sense of purpose*** *in her step as she set off.* ■ (usu. **purposes**) a particular requirement or consideration, typically one that is temporary or restricted in scope or extent: *state pensions are considered as earned income for tax purposes.*
▶ **verb** [with obj.] formal have as one's intention or objective: *God has allowed suffering, even purposed it.*
– PHRASES **on purpose** intentionally. **to no purpose** with no result or effect; pointlessly. **to the purpose** relevant or useful: *you may have heard something from them which is to the purpose.*
– ORIGIN Middle English: from Old French *porpos*, from the verb *porposer*, variant of *proposer* (see **PROPOSE**).

purpose-built ▶ **adjective** Brit. built for a particular purpose: *purpose-built accommodation for the elderly.*

purposeful ▶ **adjective** having or showing determination or resolve: *the purposeful stride of a great barrister.*
■ having a useful purpose: *purposeful activities.* ■ intentional: *if his sudden death was not accidental, it must have been purposeful.*
– DERIVATIVES **purposefully** adverb, **purposefulness** noun.

purposeless ▶ **adjective** done or made with no discernible point or purpose: *purposeless thuggery and vandalism.*
■ having no aim or plan: *his purposeless life.*
– DERIVATIVES **purposelessly** adverb, **purposelessness** noun.

purposely ▶ **adverb** on purpose; intentionally: *she had purposely made it difficult.*

purpose-made ▶ **adjective** Brit. made for a particular purpose: *purpose-made planting baskets.*

purposive ▶ **adjective** having, serving, or done with a purpose: *teaching is a purposive activity.*
– DERIVATIVES **purposively** adverb, **purposiveness** noun.

purpura /ˈpəːpjʊrə/ ▶ **noun** [mass noun] Medicine a rash of purple spots on the skin caused by internal bleeding from small blood vessels.
■ [with modifier] any of a number of diseases characterized by such a rash: *psychogenic purpura.*
– DERIVATIVES **purpuric** /-ˈpjʊərɪk/ adjective.
– ORIGIN mid 18th cent.: from Latin, from Greek *porphura* 'purple'.

purpure /ˈpəːpjʊə/ ▶ **noun** [mass noun] purple, as a heraldic tincture.
– ORIGIN Old English (in the sense 'purple garment'), from Latin *purpura* (see **PURPURA**), reinforced by Old French *purpre* and influenced by words ending in *-ure*.

purpurin /ˈpəːpjʊrɪn/ ▶ **noun** [mass noun] Chemistry a red dye originally extracted from madder and also prepared artificially by the oxidation of alizarin.
● An anthraquinone derivative; chem. formula: $C_{14}H_8O_5$.
– ORIGIN mid 19th cent.: from Latin *purpura* 'purple' + **-IN**[1].

purr ▶ **verb** [no obj.] (of a cat) make a low continuous vibratory sound expressing contentment.
■ (of a vehicle or machine) make such a sound when running smoothly at low speed. ■ [no obj., with adverbial of direction] (of a vehicle or engine) move smoothly while making such a sound: *a sleek blue BMW purred past him.* ■ speak in a low soft voice, especially when expressing contentment or acting seductively: [with direct speech] *'Would you like a coffee?' she purred.*
▶ **noun** a low continuous vibratory sound, typically that made by a cat or vehicle.
– ORIGIN early 17th cent.: imitative.

purse ▶ **noun** a small pouch of leather or plastic used for carrying money, typically by a woman.
■ N. Amer. a handbag. ■ the money possessed or available to a person or country: *institutions are funded from the same general purse.* ■ a sum of money given as a prize in a sporting contest, especially a boxing match.
▶ **verb** (with reference to the lips) pucker or contract, typically to express disapproval or irritation: [with obj.] *Marianne took a glance at her reflection and pursed her lips disgustedly* | [no obj.] *under stress his lips would purse slightly.*
– PHRASES **hold the purse strings** have control of expenditure. **tighten** (or **loosen**) **the purse strings** restrict (or increase) the amount of money available to be spent.
– ORIGIN late Old English, alteration of late Latin *bursa* 'purse', from Greek *bursa* 'hide, leather'. The

current verb sense (from the notion of drawing purse strings) dates from the early 17th cent.

purser ▶ noun an officer on a ship who keeps the accounts, especially the head steward on a passenger vessel.

purse seine /seɪn/ ▶ noun [usu. as modifier] a fishing net or seine which may be drawn into the shape of a bag, used for catching shoal fish.
– DERIVATIVES **purse-seiner** noun.

purslane /ˈpəːslən/ ▶ noun any of a number of small, typically fleshy-leaved plants which grow in damp or marshy habitats, in particular:
• (also **sea purslane**) an edible plant which grows in salt marshes (*Atriplex portulacoides*, family Chenopodiaceae).
• (also **pink purslane**) a small pink-flowered North American plant of damp places (genus *Claytonia*, family Portulacaceae).
– ORIGIN late Middle English: from Old French *porcelaine*, probably from Latin *porcil(l)aca*, variant of *portulaca*, influenced by French *porcelaine* 'porcelain'.

pursuance ▶ noun [mass noun] formal the carrying out of a plan or action: *you have a right to use public areas in the* ***pursuance of*** *your lawful hobby.*
▪ the action of trying to achieve something: *staff took industrial action in pursuance of a better deal.*

pursuant /pəˈsjuːənt/ ▶ adverb (**pursuant to**) formal in accordance with (a law or a legal document or resolution): *the local authority applied for care orders pursuant to section 31 of the Children Act 1989.*
▶ adjective archaic following; going in pursuit: *the pursuant lady.*
– DERIVATIVES **pursuantly** adverb.
– ORIGIN late Middle English *poursuiant* (as a noun in the sense 'prosecutor'): from Old French, 'pursuing', from the verb *poursuir*; later influenced in spelling by **PURSUE**.

pursue ▶ verb (**pursues**, **pursued**, **pursuing**) [with obj.] **1** follow (someone or something) in order to catch or attack them: *the officer pursued the van* | figurative *a heavily indebted businessman was being pursued by creditors.*
▪ seek to form a sexual relationship with (someone) in a persistent or predatory way: *Sophie was being pursued by a number of men.* ▪ seek to attain or accomplish (a goal), especially over a long period: *should people pursue their own happiness at the expense of others?* ▪ archaic or poetic/literary (of something unpleasant) persistently afflict (someone): *mercy lasts as long as sin pursues man.*
2 (of a person or way) continue or proceed along (a path or route): *the road pursued a straight course over the scrubland.*
▪ engage in (an activity or course of action): *Andrew was determined to pursue a computer career* | *the council decided not to pursue an appeal.* ▪ continue to investigate, explore, or discuss (a topic, idea, or argument): *we shall not pursue the matter any further.*
– DERIVATIVES **pursuable** adjective.
– ORIGIN Middle English (originally in the sense 'follow with enmity'): from Anglo-Norman French *pursuer*, from an alteration of Latin *prosequi* 'prosecute'.

pursuer ▶ noun a person or thing that pursues another.
▪ Scots Law a person who brings a case against another into court; a plaintiff.

pursuit ▶ noun **1** [mass noun] the action of following or pursuing someone or something: *the cat crouched in the grass* ***in pursuit of*** *a bird* | *those whose business is the pursuit of knowledge.*
▪ [count noun] a cycling race in which competitors set off from different parts of a track and attempt to overtake one another. ▪ Physiology the action of the eye in following a moving object.
2 [with adj. or noun modifier] (often **pursuits**) an activity of a specified kind, especially a recreational or sporting one: *a whole range of leisure pursuits.*
– PHRASES **give pursuit** (of a person, animal, or vehicle) start to chase another.
– ORIGIN late Middle English: from Anglo-Norman French *purseute* 'following after', from *pursuer* (see **PURSUE**). Early senses included 'persecution, annoyance' and in legal contexts 'petition, prosecution'.

pursuivant /ˈpəːsɪv(ə)nt/ ▶ noun **1** Brit. an officer of the College of Arms ranking below a herald. The four ordinary pursuivants are Rouge Croix, Bluemantle, Rouge Dragon, and Portcullis.
2 archaic a follower or attendant.
– ORIGIN late Middle English (denoting a junior heraldic officer): from Old French *pursivant*, present participle (used as a noun) of *pursivre* 'follow after'.

pursy ▶ adjective archaic **1** (especially of a horse) short of breath; asthmatic.
2 (of a person) fat.
– DERIVATIVES **pursiness** noun.
– ORIGIN late Middle English: reduction of Anglo-Norman French *porsif*, alteration of Old French *polsif*, from *polser* 'breathe with difficulty', from Latin *pulsare* 'set in violent motion'.

purulent /ˈpjʊərʊl(ə)nt/ ▶ adjective Medicine consisting of, containing, or discharging pus.
– ORIGIN late Middle English: from Latin *purulentus* 'festering', from *pus, pur-* (see **PUS**).

purvey ▶ verb [with obj.] provide or supply (food, drink, or other goods) as one's business: *shops purveying cooked food* | figurative *the majority of newspapers purvey a range of right-wing attitudes.*
– DERIVATIVES **purveyor** noun.
– ORIGIN Middle English: from Anglo-Norman French *purveier*, from Latin *providere* 'foresee, attend to' (see **PROVIDE**). Early senses included 'foresee', 'attend to in advance', and 'equip'.

purveyance ▶ noun [mass noun] the action of purveying something.
▪ Brit. historical the right of the sovereign to buy provisions and use horses and vehicles for a fixed price lower than the market value.
– ORIGIN Middle English (in the senses 'foresight' and 'pre-arrangement'): from Old French *porveance*, from Latin *providentia* 'foresight' (see **PROVIDENCE**).

purview ▶ noun [in sing.] the scope of the influence or concerns of something: *such a case might be within the purview of the legislation.*
▪ a range of experience or thought: *social taboos meant that little information was likely to come within the purview of women generally.*
– ORIGIN late Middle English: from Anglo-Norman French *purveu* 'foreseen', past participle of *purveier* (see **PURVEY**). Early use was as a legal term specifying the body of a statute following the words 'be it enacted …'.

pus ▶ noun [mass noun] a thick yellowish or greenish opaque liquid produced in infected tissue, consisting of dead white blood cells and bacteria with tissue debris and serum.
– ORIGIN late Middle English: from Latin.

Pusan /puːˈsan/ an industrial city and seaport on the SE coast of South Korea; pop. 3,797,570 (1990).

Pusey /ˈpjuːzi/, Edward Bouverie (1800–82), English theologian. In 1833, while professor of Hebrew at Oxford, he founded the Oxford Movement, and became its leader after the withdrawal of John Henry Newman (1841). His many writings include a series of *Tracts for the Times*.
– DERIVATIVES **Puseyism** noun, **Puseyite** noun.

push ▶ verb **1** [with obj. and adverbial] exert force on (someone or something), typically by setting one's hand against them, in order to move them away from oneself or the origin of the force: *she pushed her glass towards him* | *he pushed a card under the door* | [no obj.] *he* ***pushed at*** *the skylight, but it wouldn't budge.*
▪ [with obj.] hold and exert force on (something) so as to cause it to move in front of one: *a woman was pushing a pram.* ▪ move one's body or a part of it into a specified position, especially forcefully or with effort: *she pushed her hands into her pockets.* ▪ [with obj.] press (a part of a machine or other device): *the lift boy pushed the button for the twentieth floor.* ▪ figurative affect (something) so that it reaches a specified level or state: *they expect that the huge crop will push down prices.*
2 [no obj., with adverbial] move forward by using force to pass people or cause them to move aside: *she pushed her way through the crowded streets* | *he pushed past an old woman in his haste.*
▪ (of an army) advance over territory: *the guerrillas have pushed south to within 100 miles of the capital.* ▪ exert oneself to attain something or surpass others: *I was pushing hard until about 10 laps from the finish.* ▪ (**push for**) demand persistently: *the council continued to push for the better management of water resources.* ▪ [with obj.] compel or urge (someone) to do something, especially to work hard: *she believed he was pushing their daughter too hard.* ▪ (**be pushed**) informal have very little of something, especially time: *I'm a bit pushed for time at the moment.* ▪ (**be pushed to do something**) informal find it difficult to achieve something: *he will be pushed to retain the title as his form this season has been below par.* ▪ (**be pushing**) informal be nearly (a particular age): *she must be pushing forty, but she's still a good looker.*
3 [with obj.] informal promote the use, sale, or acceptance of: *the company is pushing a £500 asking price.*
▪ put forward (an argument or demand) with undue force or in too extreme a form: *he thought that the belief in individualism had been pushed too far.* ▪ sell (a narcotic drug) illegally.
4 [with obj.] Computing prepare (a stack) to receive a piece of data on the top.
▪ transfer (data) to the top of a stack.
5 [with obj.] Photography develop (a film) so as to compensate for deliberate underexposure.
▶ noun **1** an act of exerting force on someone or something in order to move them away from oneself: *he closed the door with a push.*
▪ an act of pressing a part of a machine or device: *the door locks at the push of a button.* ▪ figurative something which encourages or assists something else: *the fall in prices was given a push by official policy.*
2 a vigorous effort to do or obtain something: *many clubs are joining in the fund-raising push* | *he determined to make one last push for success.*
▪ a military attack in force: *the army was engaged in a push against guerrilla strongholds.* ▪ an advertising or promotional campaign: *TV ads will be accompanied by a colour press push.* ▪ [mass noun] forcefulness and enterprise: *an investor with the necessary money and push.* ▪ (**a push**) informal something that is hard to achieve: *we're managing on our own but it's a push.*
– PHRASES **at a push** Brit. informal if absolutely necessary; only with a certain degree of difficulty: *there's room for four people, or five at a push.* **get** (or **give someone**) **the push** (or **shove**) Brit. informal be dismissed (or dismiss someone) from a job. ▪ be rejected in (or end) a relationship. **push at** (or **against**) **an open door** have no difficulty in accomplishing a task. **push the boat out** see **BOAT**. **push someone's buttons** see **BUTTON**. **pushing up the daisies** see **DAISY**. **push one's luck** informal take a risk on the assumption that one will continue to be successful or in favour. **when push comes to shove** informal when one must commit oneself to an action or decision: *when push came to shove, I always stood up for him.*
▶ **push ahead** proceed with or continue a course of action or policy: *he promised to* ***push ahead with*** *economic reform.*
push along Brit. informal go away; depart.
push someone around (or **about**) informal treat someone roughly or inconsiderately.
push in go in front of people who are already queuing.
push off 1 use an oar, boathook, etc. to exert pressure so as to move a boat out from a bank. **2** informal go away.
push on continue on a journey: *the light was already fading, but she pushed on.*
push something through get a proposed measure completed or accepted quickly.
– ORIGIN Middle English (as a verb): from Old French *pousser*, from Latin *pulsare* 'to push, beat, pulse' (see **PULSE**[1]). The early sense was 'exert force on', giving rise later to 'make a strenuous effort, endeavour'.

pushbike ▶ noun Brit. informal a bicycle.

push-button ▶ noun [usu. as modifier] a button that is pushed to operate an electrical device: *a push-button telephone.*

pushcart ▶ noun a small handcart or barrow.

pushchair ▶ noun Brit. a folding chair on wheels, in which a baby or young child can be pushed along.

pusher ▶ noun **1** informal a person who sells illegal drugs.
2 a person or thing that pushes something: *the checkout trolley-pushers.*
▪ informal a forceful or pushy person: *she got things moving, she was a tremendous pusher.*

push fit ▶ noun a fit between two parts in which one is connected to the other by manually pushing or sliding them together:

pushful ▶ adjective arrogantly self-assertive; pushy.
– DERIVATIVES **pushfully** adverb, **pushfulness** noun.

Pushkin /ˈpʊʃkɪn/, Aleksandr (Sergeevich) (1799–1837), Russian poet, novelist, and dramatist. He wrote prolifically in many genres; his first success was the romantic narrative poem *Ruslan and Ludmilla* (1820). Other notable works include the verse novel *Eugene Onegin* (1833) and the blank-verse historical drama *Boris Godunov* (1831).

pushover ▶ noun **1** informal a person who is easy to

overcome or influence: *Colonel Moore was benevolent but no pushover.* ■ a thing that is very easily done: *this is going to be a pushover.* **2** (also **pushover try**) Rugby a try in which one side in a scrum pushes the ball over the opponents' goal line.

pushpin ▶ noun chiefly N. Amer. a drawing pin with a spherical or cylindrical head of coloured plastic.

pushpit ▶ noun a raised safety rail in the stern of a yacht.
– ORIGIN 1960s: humorous formation, suggested by **PULPIT**.

push processing ▶ noun [mass noun] Photography the development of film so as to compensate for deliberate underexposure, thereby increasing the effective film speed.

push-pull ▶ adjective [attrib.] operated by pushing and pulling. ■ Electronics having or involving two matched valves or transistors that operate 180 degrees out of phase, conducting alternately for increased output.

pushrod ▶ noun a rod operated by cams that opens and closes the valves in an internal-combustion engine.

push-start ▶ verb [with obj.] start (a motor vehicle) by pushing it in order to make the engine turn.
▶ noun an act of starting a motor vehicle in this way.

push technology ▶ noun [mass noun] Computing a service in which the user downloads software from a provider which then continually supplies information from the Internet in categories selected by the user.

Pushtu /ˈpʌʃtuː/ ▶ noun variant of **PASHTO**.

push-up ▶ noun chiefly N. Amer. another term for **PRESS-UP**.
▶ adjective denoting a padded or underwired bra or similar garment which gives uplift to the breasts.

pushy ▶ adjective (**pushier**, **pushiest**) excessively or unpleasantly self-assertive or ambitious.
– DERIVATIVES **pushily** adverb, **pushiness** noun.

pusillanimous /ˌpjuːsɪˈlanɪməs/ ▶ adjective showing a lack of courage or determination; timid.
– DERIVATIVES **pusillanimity** /-ləˈnɪmɪti/ noun, **pusillanimously** adverb.
– ORIGIN late Middle English: from ecclesiastical Latin *pusillanimis* (translating Greek *olugopsukhos*), from *pusillus* 'very small' + *animus* 'mind', + **-OUS**.

Puskas /ˈpʊʃkəs/, Ferenc (b.1927), Hungarian footballer. A striker, he came to prominence in the Hungarian national team of the early 1950s. In 1956 he went to play for Real Madrid, scoring four goals in their 1960 European Cup Final victory.

puss[1] ▶ noun informal a cat (especially as a form of address): *You naughty little puss!* ■ [usu. with modifier] a playful or coquettish girl or young woman: *a bubbly glamour puss from Mississippi.*
– ORIGIN early 16th cent.: probably from Middle Low German *pūs* (also *pūskatte*) or Dutch *poes*, of unknown origin.

puss[2] ▶ noun N. Amer. informal or Irish & Scottish a person's face or mouth.
– ORIGIN late 19th cent.: from Irish *pus* 'lip, mouth'.

puss moth ▶ noun a large furry greyish-white moth with darker markings. The boldly marked caterpillar rears up when threatened, waving whip-like appendages and spitting formic acid.
● *Cerura vinula*, family Notodontidae.

pussy ▶ noun (pl. **-ies**) **1** (also **pussy cat**) informal a cat.
2 vulgar slang a woman's genitals. ■ [mass noun] offensive women in general, considered sexually. ■ N. Amer. informal a weak, cowardly, or effeminate man.

pussyfoot ▶ verb [no obj., with adverbial] act in a cautious or non-committal way: *I realized I could no longer pussyfoot around.* ■ move stealthily or warily: *they make a great show of pussyfooting through the greenery.*
– DERIVATIVES **pussyfooter** noun.

pussy-whip ▶ verb [with obj.] [usu. as adj. **pussy-whipped**] vulgar slang henpeck (a man).

pussy willow ▶ noun a willow with soft fluffy yellow or silvery catkins that appear before the leaves. See also **SALLOW**[2] (sense 1).
● Genus *Salix*, family Salicaceae: several species, in particular (in the US) the glaucous willow (*S. discolor*), and (in Britain) the goat willow (*S. caprea*) and grey willow (*S. cinerea*).
– ORIGIN mid 19th cent.: originally a child's word,

because of the resemblance of the soft fluffy catkins to a cat's fur.

pustulate ▶ verb /ˈpʌstjʊleɪt/ [no obj.] form into pustules: [as adj. **pustulating**] *pustulating epidermal ulcers.*
▶ adjective /ˈpʌstjʊlət/ chiefly Biology having or covered with pustules: *the surface is coarsely pustulate.*
– DERIVATIVES **pustulation** noun.
– ORIGIN late Middle English (as an adjective): from late Latin *pustulatus*, past participle of *pustulare* 'to blister', from *pustula* 'pustule'.

pustule /ˈpʌstjuːl/ ▶ noun Medicine a small blister or pimple on the skin containing pus.
■ Biology a small raised spot or rounded swelling, especially one on a plant resulting from fungal infection.
– DERIVATIVES **pustular** adjective.
– ORIGIN late Middle English: from Latin *pustula*.

put ▶ verb (**putting**; past and past participle **put**) [with obj. and adverbial] **1** move to or place in a particular position: *Harry put down his cup* | *I put my hand out towards her* | *watch where you're putting your feet!* ■ cause (someone or something) to go to a particular place and remain there for a time: *India has put three experimental satellites into space.* ■ [no obj., with adverbial of direction] (of a ship) proceed in a particular direction: *she stepped into the boat and put out to sea.* ■ write or print (something) in a particular place: *they put my name on the cover page.* ■ [no obj., with adverbial of direction] US archaic (of a river) flow in a particular direction. **2** bring into a particular state or condition: *they tried to put me at ease* | *a large aid programme was put into practice* | *he is putting himself at risk.* ■ (**put oneself in**) imagine oneself in (a particular situation): *it was no use trying to put herself in his place.* ■ express (a thought or comment) in a particular way, form, or language: *to put it bluntly, he was not really divorced.* **3** (**put something on/on to**) cause (someone or something) to carry or be subject to something: *commentators put some of the blame on Congress* | *he defended his decision to put VAT on domestic fuel.* ■ assign a particular value, figure, or limit to: *it is very difficult to put a figure on the size of the budget.* ■ (**put something at**) estimate something to be (a particular amount): *estimates put the war's cost at £1 million a day.* **4** throw (a shot or weight) as an athletic sport: *she set a women's record by putting the shot 56' 7".*
▶ noun **1** a throw of the shot or weight.
2 Stock Exchange short for **PUT OPTION**.
– PHRASES **not know where to put oneself** informal feel deeply embarrassed. **put something behind one** get over a bad experience by distancing oneself from it: *they have tried to put their grief behind them and rebuild their lives.* **put the clocks back** (or **forward**) adjust clocks or watches backwards (or forwards) to take account of official changes in time. **put someone's eyes out** blind someone, typically in a violent way. **put one's hands together** applaud; clap: *I want you all to put your hands together for Barry.* **put one's hands up** raise one's hands in surrender. **put it** (or **oneself**) **about** Brit. informal be sexually promiscuous. **put it there** [in imperative] informal used to indicate that the speaker wishes to shake hands with someone in agreement or congratulation: *put it there Steven, we beat them, so we did.* **put it to** [with clause] make a statement or allegation to (someone) and challenge them to deny it: *I put it to him that he was just a political groupie.* **put one over on** informal deceive (someone) into accepting something false. **put up or shut up** informal justify oneself or remain silent: *they called for the minister to either put up or shut up.*
– ORIGIN Old English (recorded only in the verbal noun *putung*), of unknown origin; compare with dialect *pote* 'to push, thrust' (an early sense of the verb *put*).

▶ **put about** Nautical (of a ship) turn on the opposite tack.
put someone about chiefly Scottish & N. English upset or trouble someone.
put something about (often **be put about**) spread information or rumours.
put something across (or **over**) communicate something effectively.
put something aside 1 save money for future use. **2** forget or disregard something, typically a feeling or a past difference.
put someone away informal **1** (often **be put away**) confine someone in a prison or psychiatric hospital: *he deserves to be put away forever.* **2** (in sport)

defeat an opponent: *they wasted a chance to put the other team away.*
put something away 1 save money for future use. **2** informal consume food or drink in large quantities. **3** another way of saying *put something down* (in sense 3 below). **4** informal (in sport) dispatch or deal with a goal or shot.
put something back reschedule a planned event to a later time or date. ■ delay something: *greater public control may put back the modernization of the industry.*
put something by another way of saying *put something aside* (in sense 1 above).
put someone down 1 informal lower someone's self-esteem by criticizing them in front of others. **2** (of a vehicle or aircraft) stop to let someone get off: *driving back into town, he put them down near their homes.* **3** lay a baby down to sleep.
put something down 1 record something in writing: *he's putting a few thoughts down on paper.* ■ make a recording of a piece of music. **2** suppress a rebellion, coup, or riot by force. **3** (usu. **be put down**) kill an animal because it is sick, injured, or old. **4** pay a specified sum as a deposit: *he put a thousand down and paid the rest over six months.* **5** preserve or store food or wine for future use. **6** (also **put down**) land an aircraft.
put someone down as consider or judge someone or something to be: *I'd have put you down as a Vivaldi man.*
put someone down for enter someone's name on a list as wishing to do, join, or subscribe to (something): *he put his son down for Eton.*
put something down to attribute something to: *if I forget anything, put it down to old age.*
put someone forward recommend someone as a suitable candidate for a job or position: *he put me forward as head of publicity.*
put something forward submit a plan, proposal, or theory for consideration.
put in [with direct speech] interrupt in a conversation or discussion: *'But you're a sybarite, Roger,' put in Isobel.*
put in at/into (of a ship) enter (a port or harbour).
put someone in appoint someone to fulfil a particular role or job: *he was put in to rescue the company by the stockbrokers.* ■ Cricket make the opposing team take first innings.
put something in/into 1 present or submit something formally: *the airport had put in a claim for damages.* ■ (**put in for**) apply formally for: *Adam put in for six months' leave.* **2** devote time or effort to (something): *employed mothers put in the longest hours of all women.* **3** invest money or resources in.
put someone off 1 cancel or postpone an appointment with someone: *he'd put off Martin until nine o'clock.* **2** cause someone to lose interest or enthusiasm: *she wanted to be a nurse, but the thought of night shifts put her off.* ■ cause someone to feel dislike or distrust: *she had a coldness that just put me off.* **3** distract someone: *you're just trying to put me off my game.*
put something off postpone something: *they can't put off a decision much longer.*
put someone on (in team sports) send a player out to participate in an ongoing game.
put something on 1 place a garment, spectacles, or jewellery on part of one's body: *Juliet had put on a cotton dress.* ■ attach or apply something: *she put on fresh make-up.* **2** cause a device to operate: *shall I put the light on?* ■ start cooking something: *she was moaning that he hadn't put the dinner on.* ■ play recorded music or a video. **3** organize or present a play, exhibition, or event. ■ provide a public transport service: *so many people wanted to visit this spot that an extra train had to be put on.* **4** add a specified amount to (the cost of something): *the news put 12 pence on the share price.* ■ increase in body weight; become heavier by a specified amount: *she's given up her diet and put on 20 lb.* ■ Cricket (of batsmen) score a particular number of runs in a partnership: *Gooch and Broad put on 125 for the first wicket.* **5** assume a particular expression, accent, etc.: *he put on a lugubrious look.* ■ behave deceptively: *she doesn't feel she has to put on an act.* **6** bet a specified amount of money on: *he put £1,000 on the horse to win.*
put someone on to draw someone's attention to (someone or something useful, notable, or interesting): *Pike put me on to the Department's Legal Section.*
put out for informal, chiefly N. Amer. agree to have sexual

intercourse with (someone).
put someone out 1 cause someone trouble or inconvenience: *would it put you out too much to let her visit you for a couple of hours?* ■ (often **be put out**) upset or annoy someone: *he was not put out by the rebuff.* **2** (in sport) defeat a player or side and so cause them to be out of a competition. **3** make someone unconscious, typically by means of drugs or an anaesthetic.
put something out 1 extinguish something that is burning: *fire crews from Grangetown put out the blaze.* ■ turn off a light. **2** lay something out ready for use: *she put out glasses and paper napkins.* **3** issue or broadcast something: *a limited-edition single was put out to promote the album.* **4** dislocate a joint: *she fell off her horse and put her shoulder out.* **5** (of a company) allocate work to a contractor or freelancer to be done off the premises. **6** (of an engine or motor) produce a particular amount of power: *the non-turbo is expected to put out about 250bhp.*
put something over 1 another way of saying ***put something across*** above. **2** N. Amer. postpone something: *let's put the case over for a few weeks.*
put someone through 1 connect someone by telephone to another person or place: *put me **through to** the police office, please.* **2** subject someone to an unpleasant or demanding experience: *I hate Brian for what he put me through.* **3** pay for one's child to attend school or college.
put something through initiate something and see it through to a successful conclusion: *he put through a reform programme to try to save the regime.*
put someone to cause (inconvenience or difficulty) to someone: *I don't want to put you to any trouble.*
put something to 1 submit something to (someone) for consideration or attention: *we are making a takeover bid and putting an offer to the shareholders.* **2** devote something to (a particular use or purpose): *they put the land to productive use.* **3** couple an animal with (another of the opposite sex) for breeding.
put something together make something by assembling different parts or people: *he can take a clock apart and **put it back together** again | they decided to put a new band together.* ■ assemble things or people to make something: *a carpenter puts together shaped pieces of wood to make a table.*
put someone under another way of saying ***put someone out*** (in sense 3 above).
put up 1 offer or show (a particular degree of resistance, effort, or skill) in a fight or competitive situation: *he put up a brave fight.* **2** stay temporarily in accommodation other than one's own home: *we **put up at** a hotel in the city centre.*
put someone up 1 accommodate someone temporarily. **2** propose someone for election or adoption: *the party had put up a candidate in each constituency.*
put something up 1 construct or erect something: *I put up the tent and cooked a meal.* **2** raise one's hand to signal that one wishes to answer or ask a question. **3** display a notice, sign, or poster. ■ present a proposal, theory, or argument for discussion or consideration. ■ publish banns. **4** chiefly Brit. increase the cost of something: *I'm afraid I've got to put your rent up.* **5** provide money as backing for an enterprise: *the sponsors are putting up £5,000 for the event.* **6** (often **be put up for**) offer something for sale or auction. **7** cause game to rise from cover. **8** archaic return a sword to its sheath.
put upon informal [often as adj. **put-upon**] take advantage of (someone) by exploiting their good nature: *a put-upon drudge who slaved for her employer.*
put someone up to 1 informal encourage someone to do (something wrong or unwise): *Who else would play a trick like that on me? I expect Rose put him up to it.* **2** archaic inform someone about (something).
put up with tolerate; endure: *I'm too tired to put up with any nonsense.*

puta /ˈputa/ ▶ **noun** informal (in Spanish-speaking countries or parts of America) a prostitute or promiscuous woman.
– ORIGIN Spanish.

putamen /pjʊˈteɪmɛn/ ▶ **noun** (pl. **putamina** /-ˈteɪmɪnə/ or **putamens**) Anatomy the outer part of the lentiform nucleus of the brain.
– DERIVATIVES **putaminal** adjective.
– ORIGIN late 19th cent.: from Latin, literally 'shell remaining after pruning'.

put-and-take ▶ **adjective** [attrib.] denoting a system whereby waters are stocked with fish for anglers to catch.

putative /ˈpjuːtətɪv/ ▶ **adjective** [attrib.] generally considered or reputed to be: *the putative father of a boy of two.*
– DERIVATIVES **putatively** adverb.
– ORIGIN late Middle English: from Old French *putatif, -ive* or late Latin *putativus*, from Latin *putat-* 'thought', from the verb *putare*.

put-down ▶ **noun** informal a remark intended to humiliate or criticize someone.

Putin /ˈpuːtɪn/, Vladimir (b.1952), Russian statesman, President since 2000.

put-in ▶ **noun** Rugby an act or the right of putting the ball into a scrum.

putlog /ˈpʌtlɒg/ (also **putlock** /-lɒk/) ▶ **noun** a short horizontal pole projecting from a wall, on which scaffold floorboards rest.
– ORIGIN mid 17th cent.: of unknown origin.

put-off ▶ **noun** informal **1** an evasive reply. **2** an unpleasant or deterrent quality or feature.

put-on ▶ **noun** informal a deception; a hoax.

putonghua /puːˈtʊŋhwɑː/ ▶ **noun** [mass noun] the standard spoken form of modern Chinese, based on the dialect of Beijing.
– ORIGIN Chinese, literally 'common spoken language'.

put option ▶ **noun** Stock Exchange an option to sell assets at an agreed price on or before a particular date.

put-put /ˈpʌtpʌt/ ▶ **noun** & **verb** another term for **PUTTER**[2].
– ORIGIN early 20th cent.: imitative.

putrefaction ▶ **noun** [mass noun] the process of decay or rotting in a body or other organic matter.
– ORIGIN late Middle English: from Old French, or from late Latin *putrefactio(n-)*, from *putrefacere* 'make rotten' (see **PUTREFY**).

putrefactive ▶ **adjective** relating to or causing decay: *they were killed by the putrefactive bacteria.*

putrefy /ˈpjuːtrɪfʌɪ/ ▶ **verb** (**-ies**, **-ied**) [no obj.] (of a body or other organic matter) decay or rot and produce a fetid smell.
– ORIGIN late Middle English: via French from Latin *putrefacere*, from *puter, putr-* 'rotten'.

putrescent /pjuːˈtrɛs(ə)nt/ ▶ **adjective** undergoing the process of decay; rotting.
– DERIVATIVES **putrescence** noun.
– ORIGIN mid 18th cent.: from Latin *putrescent-* 'beginning to go rotten', inceptive of *putrere* 'to rot' (see **PUTRID**).

putrescible ▶ **adjective** liable to decay; subject to putrefaction: *putrescible domestic waste.*
▶ **noun** (usu. **putrescibles**) something that is liable to decay.

putrid ▶ **adjective** (of organic matter) decaying or rotting and emitting a fetid smell.
■ of or characteristic of rotting matter: *the putrid smells from the slaughterhouses.* ■ informal very unpleasant; repulsive: *the cocktail is a putrid pink colour.*
– DERIVATIVES **putridity** noun, **putridly** adverb, **putridness** noun.
– ORIGIN late Middle English: from Latin *putridus*, from *putrere* 'to rot', from *puter, putr-* 'rotten'.

putsch /pʊtʃ/ ▶ **noun** a violent attempt to overthrow a government; a coup.
– ORIGIN 1920s: from Swiss German, literally 'thrust, blow'.

putt /pʌt/ ▶ **verb** (**putted**, **putting**) [no obj.] try to hit a golf ball into a hole by striking it gently so that it rolls across the green.
▶ **noun** a stroke of this kind made in an attempt to hole the ball.
– ORIGIN mid 17th cent. (originally Scots): differentiated from **PUT**.

puttee /ˈpʌti/ ▶ **noun** a long strip of cloth wound spirally round the leg from ankle to knee for protection and support.
■ N. Amer. a leather legging.
– ORIGIN late 19th cent.: from Hindi *paṭṭī* 'band, bandage'.

putter[1] /ˈpʌtə/ ▶ **noun 1** a golf club designed for use in putting, typically with a flat-faced head. **2** [with adj.] a golfer considered in terms of their ability at putting: *you'll need to be a good putter to break par.*

putter[2] /ˈpʌtə/ ▶ **noun** the rapid intermittent sound of a small petrol engine: *the putter of an old aeroplane.*
▶ **verb** [no obj.] make such a sound: *I could hear the generator puttering away.*
■ [no obj., with adverbial of direction] move under the power of an engine that makes such a sound: *barges puttered slowly through the water.*
– ORIGIN 1940s: imitative.

putter[3] /ˈpʌtə/ ▶ **verb** North American term for **POTTER**[1].
– ORIGIN late 19th cent.: alteration.

putting green ▶ **noun** a smooth area of short grass surrounding a hole, either as part of a golf course or as a separate area for putting.

Puttnam /ˈpʌtnəm/, Sir David (Terence) (b.1941), English film producer. Puttnam produced *Chariots of Fire* (1981), which won four Oscars, *The Killing Fields* (1984), and *The Mission* (1986).

putto /ˈpʊtəʊ/ ▶ **noun** (pl. **putti** /-ti/) a representation of a naked child, especially a cherub or a cupid in Renaissance art.
– ORIGIN Italian, literally 'boy', from Latin *putus*.

putty[1] ▶ **noun** [mass noun] **1** a soft, malleable, greyish-yellow paste, made from whiting and raw linseed oil, that hardens after a few hours and is used chiefly for sealing glass panes in wooden window frames.
■ [usu. with modifier] any of a number of similar malleable substances used inside and outside buildings, e.g. **plumber's putty**, **lime putty**, or used for modelling or casting, e.g. **epoxy putty**.
2 a polishing powder, usually made from tin oxide, used in jewellery work.
▶ **verb** (**-ies**, **-ied**) [with obj.] seal or cover (something) with putty.
– PHRASES **be (like) putty in someone's hands** be easily manipulated or dominated by someone.
– ORIGIN mid 17th cent.: from French *potée*, literally 'potful', from *pot* 'pot'.

putty[2] ▶ **adjective** another term for **PUDDYSTICKS**.

put-up ▶ **adjective** [attrib.] arranged beforehand in order to deceive someone: *the whole thing could be a **put-up job** to get his wife over to Ireland.*

put-you-up (also **put-you-up bed**) ▶ **noun** Brit. a sofa or settee that can be converted into a bed.

putz /pʊts, pʌts/ N. Amer. informal ▶ **noun 1** a stupid or worthless person. **2** vulgar slang a man's penis.
▶ **verb** [no obj.] engage in inconsequential or unproductive activity: *too much **putzing around** up there would ruin them.*
– ORIGIN 1960s: Yiddish, literally 'penis'.

puzzle ▶ **verb** [with obj.] cause (someone) to feel confused because they cannot understand or make sense of something: *one remark he made puzzled me* | [as adj. **puzzling**] *that was the most puzzling aspect of the whole affair.*
■ [no obj.] think hard about something because one cannot understand or explain it: *she was still **puzzling over** this problem when she reached the office.* ■ (**puzzle something out**) solve or understand something by thinking hard.
▶ **noun** a game, toy, or problem designed to test ingenuity or knowledge.
■ short for ***jigsaw puzzle*** (see **JIGSAW**). ■ [usu. in sing.] a person or thing that is difficult to understand or explain; an enigma: *the meaning of the poem has always been a puzzle.*
– DERIVATIVES **puzzlement** noun, **puzzlingly** adverb.
– ORIGIN late 16th cent. (as a verb): of unknown origin.

puzzler ▶ **noun** a difficult question or problem.
■ a person who solves puzzles as a pastime. ■ informal a computer game in which the player must solve puzzles.

PVA ▶ **abbreviation for** polyvinyl acetate.

PVC ▶ **abbreviation for** polyvinyl chloride.

PVS Medicine ▶ **abbreviation for** ■ persistent vegetative state. ■ postviral (fatigue) syndrome (another term for **ME**).

Pvt. ▶ **abbreviation for** ■ (in the US army) private. ■ private (in company names).

PW ▶ **abbreviation for** policewoman.

p.w. ▶ **abbreviation for** per week.

PWA ▶ **abbreviation for** person with Aids.

PWR ▶ **abbreviation for** pressurized-water reactor.

PWV abbreviation for Pretoria–Witwatersrand–Vereeniging.

PX ▶ abbreviation for ■ Pedro Ximenez. ■ post exchange.

PY ▶ abbreviation for Paraguay (international vehicle registration).

pya /pjɑː/ ▶ noun a monetary unit of Burma (Myanmar), equal to one hundredth of a kyat.
– ORIGIN Burmese.

pyaemia /pʌɪˈiːmɪə/ (US **pyemia**) ▶ noun [mass noun] blood poisoning (septicaemia) caused by the spread in the bloodstream of pus-forming bacteria released from an abscess.
– DERIVATIVES **pyaemic** adjective.
– ORIGIN mid 19th cent.: modern Latin, from Greek *puon* 'pus' + *haima* 'blood'.

pycnocline /ˈpɪknə(ʊ)klʌɪn/ ▶ noun Geography a layer in an ocean or other body of water in which water density increases rapidly with depth.
– ORIGIN 1950s: from Greek *puknos* 'thick' + **CLINE**.

pye-dog /ˈpʌɪdɒɡ/ (also **pie-dog** or **pi-dog**) ▶ noun a stray mongrel, especially in Asia.
– ORIGIN mid 19th cent.: from Anglo-Indian *pye*, Hindi *pāhī* 'outsider' + **DOG**.

pyelitis /ˌpʌɪəˈlʌɪtɪs/ ▶ noun [mass noun] Medicine inflammation of the renal pelvis.
– ORIGIN mid 19th cent.: from Greek *puelos* 'trough, basin' + **-ITIS**.

pyelography /ˌpʌɪəˈlɒɡrəfi/ ▶ noun [mass noun] Medicine an X-ray technique for producing an image of the renal pelvis and urinary tract by the introduction of a radiopaque fluid. Also called **UROGRAPHY**.
– DERIVATIVES **pyelogram** noun.
– ORIGIN early 20th cent.: from Greek *puelos* 'trough, basin' + **-GRAPHY**.

pyelonephritis /ˌpʌɪələʊnɪˈfrʌɪtɪs/ ▶ noun [mass noun] Medicine inflammation of the substance of the kidney as a result of bacterial infection.
– DERIVATIVES **pyelonephritic** adjective.
– ORIGIN mid 19th cent.: from Greek *puelos* 'trough, basin' + **NEPHRITIS**.

pyemia ▶ noun US spelling of **PYAEMIA**.

pygidium /pʌɪˈdʒɪdɪəm, -ˈɡɪdɪəm/ ▶ noun (pl. **pygidia** /-ɪə/) Zoology the terminal part or hind segment of the body in certain invertebrates.
– ORIGIN mid 19th cent.: modern Latin, from Greek *pugē* 'rump'.

Pygmalion[1] /pɪɡˈmeɪlɪən/ Greek Mythology a king of Cyprus who fashioned an ivory statue of a beautiful woman and loved it so deeply that in answer to his prayer Aphrodite gave it life. The woman (at some point named Galatea) bore him a daughter, Paphos.

Pygmalion[2] /pɪɡˈmeɪlɪən/ a legendary king of Tyre, brother of Elissa (Dido), whose husband he killed in the hope of obtaining his fortune.

pygmy (also **pigmy**) ▶ noun (pl. **-ies**) a member of certain peoples of very short stature in equatorial Africa and parts of SE Asia.
■ chiefly derogatory a very small person, animal, or thing. ■ [usu. with adj.] an insignificant person, especially one who is deficient in a particular respect: *he regarded them as intellectual pigmies*.

Pygmies (e.g. the Mbuti and Twa peoples) are typically dark-skinned, nomadic hunter-gatherers with an average male height not above 150 cm (4 ft 11 in.). The term *Negrito* is also used in reference to such populations of SE Asia.

▶ adjective [attrib.] (of a person or thing) very small.
■ used in names of animals and plants that are much smaller than more typical kinds, e.g. **pygmy shrew**, **pygmy water lily**.
– DERIVATIVES **pygmean** adjective (archaic).
– ORIGIN late Middle English (originally in the plural, denoting a mythological race of small people): via Latin from Greek *pugmaios* 'dwarf', from *pugmē* 'the length measured from elbow to knuckles'.

pygmy chimpanzee ▶ noun another term for **BONOBO**.

pygmy owl ▶ noun a very small owl found in America and northern Eurasia.
● Genus *Glaucidium*, family Strigidae: several species.

pygmy possum ▶ noun a very small Australasian marsupial that feeds on insects and nectar, with hand-like feet and a prehensile tail.
● Family Burramyidae: two genera and five species.

pygmy shrew ▶ noun a shrew which is one of the smallest known mammals.
● Genus *Sorex*, family Soricidae: several species, in particular the Eurasian *S. minutus* and the American *S. hoyi*.

pygostyle /ˈpʌɪɡə(ʊ)stʌɪl/ ▶ noun Ornithology (in a bird) a triangular plate formed of the fused caudal vertebrae, typically supporting the tail feathers.
– ORIGIN late 19th cent.: from Greek *pugē* 'rump' + *stulos* 'column'.

pyinkado /ˈpjɪŋkədəʊ/ ▶ noun a southern Asian tree of the pea family, yielding hard durable timber which is used in heavy construction work.
● *Xylia dolabriformis*, family Leguminosae.
– ORIGIN mid 19th cent.: from Burmese.

pyjamas (US **pajamas**) ▶ plural noun a suit of loose trousers and jacket for sleeping in: *a pair of pyjamas* | [as modifier] (**pyjama**) *pyjama trousers*.
■ [in sing.] (**pyjama**) a pair of loose trousers tied by a drawstring around the waist, worn by both sexes in some Asian countries.
– ORIGIN early 19th cent.: from Urdu and Persian, from *pāy* 'leg' + *jāma* 'clothing'.

pyknic /ˈpɪknɪk/ ▶ adjective Anthropology of, relating to, or denoting a stocky physique with a rounded body and head, thickset trunk, and a tendency to fat.
– ORIGIN 1920s: from Greek *puknos* 'thick' + **-IC**. The word was first used by the German psychiatrist, Ernst Kretschmer (1888–1964), in his tripartite classification of human types (the other two being *asthenic* and *athletic*).

pylon ▶ noun an upright structure that is used for support or navigation, in particular:
■ (also **electricity pylon**) a tall tower-like structure used for carrying electricity cables high above the ground. ■ a pillar-like structure on the wing of an aircraft used for carrying an engine, weapon, fuel tank, or other load. ■ a tower or post marking a path for light aircraft, cars, or other vehicles, especially in racing. ■ a monumental gateway to an ancient Egyptian temple formed by two truncated pyramidal towers.
– ORIGIN mid 19th cent.: from Greek *pulōn*, from *pulē* 'gate'.

pyloric /pʌɪˈlɒrɪk/ ▶ adjective Anatomy & Medicine relating to or affecting the region where the stomach opens into the duodenum (small intestine): *pyloric stenosis*.

pylorus /pʌɪˈlɔːrəs/ ▶ noun (pl. **pylori** /-rʌɪ/) Anatomy the opening from the stomach into the duodenum.
– ORIGIN early 17th cent.: via late Latin from Greek *pulouros* 'gatekeeper', from *pulē* 'gate' + *ouros* 'warder'.

Pynchon /ˈpɪntʃən/, Thomas (Ruggles) (b.1937), American novelist. He is an elusive author who shuns public attention, while his works abandon the normal conventions of the novel. Notable works: *V* (1963), *The Crying of Lot 49* (1966), and *Gravity's Rainbow* (1972).

pyoderma /ˌpʌɪə(ʊ)ˈdəːmə/ ▶ noun [mass noun] Medicine a skin infection with formation of pus.
– ORIGIN 1930s: from Greek *puo-* (from *puon* 'pus') + *derma* 'skin'.

pyogenic /ˌpʌɪə(ʊ)ˈdʒɛnɪk/ ▶ adjective Medicine involving or relating to the production of pus.
– ORIGIN mid 19th cent.: from Greek *puo-* (from *puon* 'pus') + **-GENIC**.

Pyongyang /pjɒŋˈjaŋ/ the capital of North Korea; pop. 2,000,000 (1994). The oldest city on the Korean peninsula, it was first mentioned in records of 108 BC. It developed as an industrial city during the years of Japanese occupation, from 1910 to 1945.

pyorrhoea /ˌpʌɪəˈriːə/ (also **pyorrhoea alveolaris** US, **pyorrhea**) ▶ noun another term for **PERIODONTITIS**.
– ORIGIN early 19th cent.: from Greek *puo-* (from *puon* 'pus') + *rhoia* 'flux' (from *rhein* 'to flow').

pyracantha /ˌpʌɪrəˈkanθə/ ▶ noun a thorny evergreen Eurasian shrub with white flowers and bright red or yellow berries, which is a popular ornamental. Also called **FIRETHORN**.
● Genus *Pyracantha*, family Rosaceae.
– ORIGIN modern Latin, via Latin from Greek *purakantha*, the name of an unidentified plant, from *pur* 'fire' + *akantha* 'thorn'.

pyralid /pʌɪˈralɪd, -ˈreɪ-/ ▶ noun Entomology an insect of a family (Pyralidae) of small delicate moths with narrow forewings. The larvae of many species are pests of stored foodstuffs.
– ORIGIN late 19th cent.: from modern Latin *Pyralidae* (plural), based on Greek *puralis*, denoting a mythical fly said to live in fire.

pyramid /ˈpɪrəmɪd/ ▶ noun **1** a monumental structure with a square or triangular base and sloping sides that meet in a point at the top, especially one built of stone as a royal tomb in ancient Egypt.

Pyramids were built as tombs for Egyptian pharaohs from the 3rd dynasty (*c*.2649 BC) until *c*.1640 BC. The early step pyramid, with several levels and a flat top, developed into the true pyramid, such as the three largest at Giza near Cairo (**the Pyramids**, including the Great Pyramid of Cheops) which were one of the Seven Wonders of the World. Monuments of similar shape are associated with the Aztec and Maya civilizations of *c*.1200 BC–AD 750, and, like those in Egypt, were part of large ritual complexes.

2 an object, shape, or graph with such a form: *the pyramid of the Matterhorn*.
■ Geometry a polyhedron of which one face is a polygon of any number of sides, and the other faces are triangles with a common vertex: *a three-sided pyramid*. ■ a pile of things with such a form: *a pyramid of logs*. ■ a fruit tree trained in such a form. ■ (**pyramids**) a game played on a billiard table with fifteen coloured balls arranged in a triangle and a cue ball. ■ Anatomy a structure of more or less pyramidal form, especially in the brain or the renal medulla. ■ an organization or system that is structured with fewer people or things at each level as one approaches the top: *the lowest strata of the social pyramid*. ■ a system of financial growth achieved by a small initial investment, with subsequent investments being funded by using unrealized profits as collateral.
▶ verb [with obj.] chiefly N. Amer. heap or stack in the shape of a pyramid: *debt was pyramided on top of unrealistic debt in an orgy of speculation*.
■ achieve a substantial return on (money or property) after making a small initial investment.
– DERIVATIVES **pyramidal** /-ˈramɪd(ə)l/ adjective, **pyramidally** adverb, **pyramidical** /-ˈmɪdɪk(ə)l/ adjective, **pyramidically** adverb.
– ORIGIN late Middle English (in the geometrical sense): via Latin from Greek *puramis*, *puramid-*, of unknown ultimate origin.

pyramidal orchid ▶ noun a small orchid of calcareous grassland, with a conical spike of pinkish-purple flowers.
● *Anacamptis pyramidalis*, family Orchidaceae.

pyramid selling ▶ noun [mass noun] a system of selling goods in which agency rights are sold to an increasing number of distributors at successively lower levels.

Pyramus /ˈpɪrəməs/ Roman Mythology a Babylonian youth, lover of Thisbe.

Forbidden to marry by their parents, who were neighbours, the lovers conversed through a chink in a wall and agreed to meet at a tomb outside the city. There, Thisbe was frightened away by a lioness coming from its kill, and Pyramus, seeing her bloodstained cloak and supposing her dead, stabbed himself. Thisbe, finding his body when she returned, threw herself upon his sword.

pyrargyrite /pʌɪˈrɑːdʒɪrʌɪt/ ▶ noun [mass noun] a dark reddish-grey mineral consisting of a sulphide of silver and antimony.
– ORIGIN mid 19th cent.: from Greek *puro-* (from *pur* 'fire') + *arguros* 'silver' + **-ITE**[1].

pyre ▶ noun a heap of combustible material, especially one for burning a corpse as part of a funeral ceremony.
– ORIGIN mid 17th cent.: via Latin from Greek *pura*, from *pur* 'fire'.

pyrene /ˈpʌɪriːn/ ▶ noun [mass noun] Chemistry a crystalline aromatic hydrocarbon present in coal tar.
● A tetracyclic compound; chemical formula: $C_{16}H_{10}$.
– ORIGIN mid 19th cent.: from Greek *pur* 'fire' + **-ENE**.

Pyrenean mountain dog ▶ noun a large heavily built dog of a white breed, with a thick shaggy double coat.

Pyrenean sheepdog ▶ noun a sheepdog of a small fawn or grey long-coated breed, often with white markings.

Pyrenees /ˌpɪrəˈniːz/ a range of mountains extending along the border between France and Spain from the Atlantic coast to the Mediterranean. Its highest peak is the Pico de Aneto in northern Spain, which rises to a height of 3,404 m (11,168 ft).
– DERIVATIVES **Pyrenean** adjective.

pyrethrin /pʌɪˈriːθrɪn/ ▶ noun Chemistry any of a group of insecticidal compounds present in pyrethrum flowers.
– ORIGIN 1920s: from **PYRETHRUM** + **-IN**[1].

pyrethroid /pʌɪˈriːθrɔɪd/ ▶ noun Chemistry a pyrethrin or related insecticidal compound.

pyrethrum /pʌɪˈriːθrəm/ ▶ noun an aromatic plant

of the daisy family, typically having feathery foliage and brightly coloured flowers.
• Genus *Tanacetum* (formerly *Chrysanthemum* or *Pyrethrum*), family Compositae: several species, in particular *T. coccineum*, grown as an ornamental, and *T. cinerariifolium*, grown as a source of the insecticide pyrethrum.
■ [mass noun] an insecticide made from the dried flowers of these plants.
– ORIGIN Middle English (denoting pellitory): from Latin, from Greek *purethron* 'feverfew'. The current senses (based on the former genus name) date from the late 19th cent.

pyretic /pʌɪˈrɛtɪk, pɪ-/ ▶ **adjective** rare fevered, feverish, or inducing fever.
– ORIGIN early 18th cent. (as a medical term, now only in *antipyretic*): from modern Latin *pyreticus*, from Greek *puretos* 'fever'.

Pyrex ▶ **noun** [mass noun] [usu. as modifier] trademark a hard heat-resistant type of glass, typically used for ovenware: *a set of Pyrex dishes.*
– ORIGIN early 20th cent.: an invented word.

pyrexia /pʌɪˈrɛksɪə, pɪ-/ ▶ **noun** [mass noun] Medicine raised body temperature; fever.
– DERIVATIVES **pyrexial** adjective, **pyrexic** adjective.
– ORIGIN mid 18th cent.: modern Latin, from Greek *purexis*, from *puressein* 'be feverish', from *pur* 'fire'.

pyridine /ˈpɪrɪdiːn/ ▶ **noun** [mass noun] Chemistry a colourless volatile liquid with an unpleasant odour, present in coal tar and used chiefly as a solvent.
• A heteroaromatic compound; chem. formula: C_5H_5N.
– ORIGIN mid 19th cent.: from Greek *pur* 'fire' + **-IDE** + **-INE**[4].

pyridostigmine /ˌpɪrɪdə(ʊ)ˈstɪgmiːn/ ▶ **noun** [mass noun] Medicine a synthetic compound related to neostigmine, with similar but weaker and longer-acting effects.
– ORIGIN 1950s: blend of **PYRIDINE** and **NEOSTIGMINE**.

pyridoxal /ˌpɪrɪˈdɒksəl/ ▶ **noun** [mass noun] Biochemistry an oxidized derivative of pyridoxine which acts as a coenzyme in transamination and other processes.
– ORIGIN 1940s: from **PYRIDOXINE** + **-AL**.

pyridoxine /ˌpɪrɪˈdɒksɪn, -iːn/ ▶ **noun** [mass noun] Biochemistry a colourless weakly basic solid present chiefly in cereals, liver oils, and yeast, and important in the metabolism of unsaturated fatty acids. Also called **vitamin B_6**.
• An alcohol derived from pyridine; chem. formula: $C_8H_{11}NO_3$.
– ORIGIN 1930s: from *pyrid(ine)* + **OX-** 'oxygen' + **-INE**[4].

pyriform /ˈpɪrɪfɔːm/ (also **piriform**) ▶ **adjective** Anatomy & Biology pear-shaped: *the pyriform fossa.*
– ORIGIN mid 18th cent.: from modern Latin *pyriformis*, from *pyrum* (misspelling of *pirum* 'pear') + **-IFORM**.

pyrimethamine /ˌpɪrɪˈmɛθəmiːn/ ▶ **noun** [mass noun] Medicine a synthetic compound derived from pyrimidine, used to treat malaria.

pyrimidine /pɪˈrɪmɪdiːn/ ▶ **noun** [mass noun] Chemistry a colourless crystalline compound with basic properties.
• A heteroaromatic compound; chem. formula: $C_4H_4N_2$.
■ (also **pyrimidine base**) [count noun] a substituted derivative of this, especially the bases thymine and cytosine present in DNA.
– ORIGIN late 19th cent.: from German *Pyrimidin*, from **PYRIDINE**, with the insertion of *-im-* from **IMIDE**.

pyrites /pʌɪˈrʌɪtiːz/ (also **iron pyrites**; Mineralogy **pyrite**) ▶ **noun** [mass noun] a shiny yellow mineral consisting of iron disulphide and typically occurring as intersecting cubic crystals. See also **COPPER PYRITES**.
– DERIVATIVES **pyritic** adjective, **pyritization** (also **-isation**) noun, **pyritize** (also **-ise**) verb, **pyritous** adjective.
– ORIGIN late Middle English (denoting a mineral used for kindling fire): via Latin from Greek *puritēs* 'of fire', from *pur* 'fire'.

pyro ▶ **noun** (pl. **-os**) informal a pyromaniac.

pyro- ▶ **combining form 1** of or relating to fire: *pyromania.*
2 Chemistry & Mineralogy denoting a compound or mineral that is formed or affected by heat or has a fiery colour: *pyrophosphate | pyroxene.*
– ORIGIN from Greek *pur* 'fire'.

pyroclastic /ˌpʌɪrə(ʊ)ˈklastɪk/ Geology ▶ **adjective** relating to, consisting of, or denoting fragments of rock erupted by a volcano.
▶ **plural noun** (**pyroclastics**) pyroclastic fragments.
– DERIVATIVES **pyroclast** noun.

pyroclastic flow ▶ **noun** Geology a dense, destructive mass of very hot ash, lava fragments, and gases ejected explosively from a volcano and typically flowing at great speed.

pyroelectric ▶ **adjective** having the property of becoming electrically charged when heated.
■ of, relating to, or utilizing this property: *a pyroelectric detector.*
– DERIVATIVES **pyroelectricity** noun.

pyrogallol /ˌpʌɪrə(ʊ)ˈgalɒl/ ▶ **noun** [mass noun] Chemistry a weakly acid crystalline compound chiefly used as a developer in photography.
• Alternative name: **1,3,5-trihydroxybenzene**; chem. formula: $C_6H_3(OH)_3$.

pyrogen /ˈpʌɪrədʒ(ə)n/ ▶ **noun** Medicine a substance, typically produced by a bacterium, which produces fever when introduced or released into the blood.

pyrogenic ▶ **adjective** Medicine inducing fever.
■ caused or produced by combustion or the application of heat: *pyrogenic factors affecting the fluctuation of the forest–savannah boundary.*
– DERIVATIVES **pyrogenicity** noun.

pyrography /pʌɪˈrɒgrəfi/ ▶ **noun** [mass noun] the art or technique of decorating wood or leather by burning a design on the surface with a heated metallic point. Also called **POKERWORK** in Britain.

pyrolusite /ˌpʌɪrə(ʊ)ˈluːsʌɪt/ ▶ **noun** [mass noun] a black or dark grey mineral with a metallic lustre, consisting of manganese dioxide.
– ORIGIN early 19th cent.: from **PYRO-** 'fire, heat' + Greek *lousis* 'washing' (because of the mineral's use in decolourizing glass).

pyrolyse /ˈpʌɪrəlʌɪz/ (US **pyrolyze**) ▶ **verb** Chemistry make or become decomposed through heating to a high temperature.
– ORIGIN 1920s: from **PYROLYSIS**, on the pattern of *analyse.*

pyrolysis /pʌɪˈrɒlɪsɪs/ ▶ **noun** [mass noun] Chemistry decomposition brought about by high temperatures.
– DERIVATIVES **pyrolytic** adjective.

pyromania ▶ **noun** [mass noun] an obsessive desire to set fire to things.
– DERIVATIVES **pyromaniac** noun, **pyromaniacal** adjective, **pyromanic** adjective.

pyrometallurgy ▶ **noun** [mass noun] the branch of science and technology concerned with the use of high temperatures to extract and purify metals.
– DERIVATIVES **pyrometallurgical** adjective.

pyrometer /pʌɪˈrɒmɪtə/ ▶ **noun** an instrument for measuring high temperatures, especially in furnaces and kilns.
– DERIVATIVES **pyrometric** adjective, **pyrometrically** adverb, **pyrometry** noun.

pyrometric cone ▶ **noun** see **CONE** (sense 1).

pyromorphite /ˌpʌɪrə(ʊ)ˈmɔːfʌɪt/ ▶ **noun** [mass noun] a mineral consisting of a chloride and phosphate of lead, typically occurring as green, yellow, or brown crystals in the oxidized zones of lead deposits.
– ORIGIN early 19th cent.: from **PYRO-** 'fire, heat' + Greek *morphē* 'form' + **-ITE**[1].

pyrope /ˈpʌɪrəʊp/ (also **pyrope garnet**) ▶ **noun** [mass noun] a deep red variety of garnet.
– ORIGIN early 19th cent.: from German *Pyrop*, via Latin from Greek *purōpos* 'gold-bronze', literally 'fiery-eyed', from *pur* 'fire' + *ōps* 'eye'.

pyrophoric /ˌpʌɪrə(ʊ)ˈfɒrɪk/ ▶ **adjective** liable to ignite spontaneously on exposure to air.
■ (of an alloy) emitting sparks when scratched or struck.
– ORIGIN mid 19th cent.: from modern Latin *pyrophorus*, from Greek *purophoros* 'fire-bearing', from *pur* 'fire' + *pherein* 'to bear'.

pyrophosphoric acid /ˌpʌɪrə(ʊ)fɒsˈfɒrɪk/ ▶ **noun** [mass noun] Chemistry a glassy solid obtained by heating phosphoric acid.
• A tetrabasic acid; chem. formula: $H_4P_2O_7$.
– DERIVATIVES **pyrophosphate** noun.

pyrosis /pʌɪˈrəʊsɪs/ ▶ **noun** another term for **HEARTBURN**.
– ORIGIN late 18th cent.: modern Latin, from Greek *purōsis*, from *puroun* 'set on fire', from *pur* 'fire'.

pyrotechnic /ˌpʌɪrə(ʊ)ˈtɛknɪk/ ▶ **adjective** of or relating to fireworks: *the sun flickered in the carriage like a pyrotechnic display.*
■ brilliant or sensational: *his writing contains more pyrotechnic energy, more colour and action.*
– DERIVATIVES **pyrotechnical** adjective, **pyrotechnist** noun.
– ORIGIN early 19th cent.: from **PYRO-** 'fire' + Greek *tekhnē* 'art' + **-IC**.

pyrotechnics ▶ **plural noun** a firework display.
■ [usu. with adj. or noun modifier] a brilliant performance or display, especially of a specified skill: *he thrilled his audience with vocal pyrotechnics.* ■ [treated as sing.] the art of making or displaying fireworks.

pyrotechny ▶ **noun** [mass noun] historical the use of fire in alchemy.
■ another term for **PYROTECHNICS**.
– ORIGIN late 16th cent.: from French *pyrotechnie* or modern Latin *pyrotechnia*, from Greek *pur* + *tekhnē* 'art'.

pyroxene /pʌɪˈrɒksiːn/ ▶ **noun** any of a large class of rock-forming silicate minerals, generally containing calcium, magnesium, and iron and typically occurring as prismatic crystals.
– ORIGIN early 19th cent.: from **PYRO-** 'fire' + Greek *xenos* 'stranger' (because the mineral group was supposed alien to igneous rocks).

pyroxenite /pʌɪˈrɒksɪnʌɪt/ ▶ **noun** [mass noun] Geology a dark, greenish, granular intrusive igneous rock consisting chiefly of pyroxenes and olivine.
– ORIGIN mid 19th cent.: from **PYROXENE** + **-ITE**[1].

pyroxylin /pʌɪˈrɒksɪlɪn/ ▶ **noun** [mass noun] Chemistry a form of nitrocellulose which is less highly nitrated and is soluble in ether and alcohol.
– ORIGIN mid 19th cent.: from French *pyroxyline*, from Greek *pur* 'fire' + *xulon* 'wood'.

Pyrrha /ˈpɪrə/ Greek Mythology the wife of Deucalion.

pyrrhic[1] /ˈpɪrɪk/ ▶ **adjective** [attrib.] (of a victory) won at too great a cost to have been worthwhile for the victor.
– ORIGIN late 19th cent.: from the name **PYRRHUS** + **-IC**.

pyrrhic[2] /ˈpɪrɪk/ ▶ **noun** a metrical foot of two short or unaccented syllables.
▶ **adjective** written in or based on such a measure.
– ORIGIN early 17th cent.: via Latin from Greek *purrhikhios (pous)* 'pyrrhic (foot)', the metre of a song accompanying a war dance, named after *Purrhikhos*, inventor of the dance.

Pyrrho /ˈpɪrəʊ/ (*c.*365–*c.*270 BC), Greek philosopher, regarded as the founder of scepticism. He is credited with arguing that happiness comes from suspending judgement because certainty of knowledge is impossible.

Pyrrhonism /ˈpɪrənɪz(ə)m/ ▶ **noun** [mass noun] the philosophy of Pyrrho.
■ philosophic doubt; scepticism.
– DERIVATIVES **Pyrrhonist** noun & adjective.

pyrrhotite /ˈpɪrətʌɪt/ ▶ **noun** [mass noun] a reddish-bronze mineral consisting of iron sulphide, typically forming massive or granular deposits.
– ORIGIN mid 19th cent.: from Greek *purrhotēs* 'redness' + **-ITE**[1].

Pyrrhus /ˈpɪrəs/ (*c.*318–272 BC), king of Epirus *c.*307–272. After invading Italy in 280, he defeated the Romans at Asculum in 279, but sustained heavy losses; the term *pyrrhic victory* is named in allusion to this.

pyrrole /ˈpɪrəʊl/ ▶ **noun** [mass noun] Chemistry a weakly basic sweet-smelling liquid compound present in bone oil and coal tar.
• A heteroaromatic compound; chem. formula: C_4H_4NH.
– ORIGIN mid 19th cent.: from Greek *purrhos* 'reddish' + Latin *oleum* 'oil'.

pyrrolidine /pɪˈrɒlɪdiːn/ ▶ **noun** [mass noun] Chemistry a pungent liquid made by reduction of pyrrole.
• Chem. formula: C_4H_8NH.

pyrrolidone /pɪˈrɒlɪdəʊn/ ▶ **noun** [mass noun] Chemistry a colourless weakly basic solid which is a keto derivative of pyrrolidine.
• Chem. formula: C_4H_7NO.

pyruvic acid /pʌɪˈruːvɪk/ ▶ **noun** [mass noun] Biochemistry a yellowish organic acid which occurs as an intermediate in many metabolic processes, especially glycolysis.
• A keto acid; chem. formula: $CH_3COCOOH$.
– DERIVATIVES **pyruvate** noun.
– ORIGIN mid 19th cent.: from modern Latin *acidum pyruvicum*, from *acidum* 'acid' + *pyruvicum* based on **PYRO-** (denoting an acid) + Latin *uva* 'grape'.

Pythagoras /pʌɪˈθagərəs/ *c.*580–500 BC, Greek philosopher; known as **Pythagoras of Samos**. Pythagoras sought to interpret the entire physical

world in terms of numbers, and founded their systematic and mystical study; he is best known for the theorem of the right-angled triangle. His analysis of the courses of the sun, moon, and stars into circular motions was not set aside until the 17th century.
– DERIVATIVES **Pythagorean** /-ˌθagəˈriːən/ adjective & noun.

Pythagoras' theorem a theorem attributed to Pythagoras that the square on the hypotenuse of a right-angled triangle is equal in area to the sum of the squares on the other two sides.

Pythia /ˈpɪθɪə/ the priestess of Apollo at Delphi in ancient Greece. See **DELPHI**.
– DERIVATIVES **Pythian** adjective.
– ORIGIN from *Puthō*, a former name of Delphi.

Pythias /ˈpɪθɪas/ see **DAMON**.

python ▶ noun a large heavy-bodied non-venomous snake occurring throughout the Old World tropics, killing prey by constriction and asphyxiation.
● Family Pythonidae: genera *Python* (of Asia and Africa), and *Morelia* and *Aspidites* (of Australasia).

– DERIVATIVES **pythonic** adjective.
– ORIGIN late 16th cent. (in the Greek sense): via Latin from Greek *Puthōn*, the name of a huge serpent killed by Apollo. The current sense dates from the mid 19th cent.

Pythonesque ▶ adjective after the style of or resembling the absurdist or surrealist humour of *Monty Python's Flying Circus*, a British television comedy series (1969–74).

pythoness ▶ noun archaic a female soothsayer or conjuror of spirits.
– ORIGIN late Middle English: from Old French *phitonise*, from an alteration of late Latin *pythonissa*, based on Greek *puthōn* 'soothsaying demon'. Compare with **PYTHIA**.

pyuria /pʌɪˈjʊərɪə/ ▶ noun [mass noun] Medicine the presence of pus in the urine, typically from bacterial infection.
– ORIGIN early 19th cent.: from Greek *puon* 'pus' + **-URIA**.

pyx /pɪks/ ▶ noun **1** Christian Church the container in

which the consecrated bread of the Eucharist is kept.
2 (in the UK) a box at the Royal Mint in which specimen gold and silver coins are deposited to be tested annually at the **trial of the pyx** by members of the Goldsmiths' Company.
– ORIGIN late Middle English: from Latin *pyxis*, from Greek *puxis* 'box'.

pyxidium /pɪkˈsɪdɪəm/ ▶ noun (pl. **pyxidia** /-dɪə/) Botany a seed capsule that splits open so that the top comes off like the lid of a box.
– ORIGIN mid 19th cent.: modern Latin, from Greek *puxidion*, diminutive of *puxis* 'box'.

Pyxis /ˈpɪksɪs/ Astronomy a small and inconspicuous southern constellation (the Compass Box or Mariner's Compass), lying in the Milky Way between Vela and Puppis.
■ [as genitive **Pyxidis** /ˈpɪksɪdɪs/] used with preceding letter or numeral to designate a star in this constellation: *the star Alpha Pyxidis.*
– ORIGIN Latin.

pzazz ▶ noun variant spelling of **PIZZAZZ**.

Qq

Q¹ (also **q**) ▶ noun (pl. **Qs** or **Q's**) the seventeenth letter of the alphabet.
■ denoting the next after P in a set of items, categories, etc.
– PHRASES **mind ones Ps and Qs** see **MIND**.

Q² ▶ abbreviation for ■ quarter (used to refer to a specified quarter of the financial year): *we expect to have an exceptional Q4.* ■ queen (used especially in describing card games and recording moves in chess): *17. Qb4.* ■ question: *Q: What's the problem? A: I don't feel well.* ■ Theology denoting the hypothetical source of the passages shared by the gospels of Matthew and Luke, but not found in Mark. [ORIGIN: probably from German *Quelle* 'source'.]

q ▶ symbol for Physics electric charge.
– ORIGIN mid 19th cent.: initial letter of *quantity*.

QA ▶ abbreviation for quality assurance.

Qabalah ▶ noun variant spelling of **KABBALAH**.

Qabis variant spelling of **GABÈS**.

Qaddafi variant spelling of **GADDAFI**.

qanat /kəˈnɑːt/ (also **kanat**) ▶ noun (in the Middle East) a gently sloping underground channel or tunnel constructed to lead water from the interior of a hill to a village below.
– ORIGIN Persian, from Arabic *ḳanāt* 'reed, pipe, channel'.

Qaraghandy /ˈkarəˌgandɪ/ an industrial city in eastern Kazakhstan, at the centre of a major coal-mining region; pop. 613,000 (1990). Russian name **KARAGANDA**.

Qatar /kaˈtɑː, ˈkʌtə/ a sheikhdom occupying a peninsula on the west coast of the Persian Gulf; pop. 402,000 (est. 1991); official language, Arabic; capital, Doha. The country was a British protectorate from 1916 until 1971, when it became a sovereign independent state. Oil is the chief source of revenue.
– DERIVATIVES **Qatari** adjective & noun.

Qattara Depression /kəˈtɑːrə/ an extensive, low-lying, and largely impassable area of desert in NE Africa, to the west of Cairo, that falls to 133 m (436 ft) below sea level.

qawwali /kəˈvɑːli/ ▶ noun [mass noun] a style of Muslim devotional music now associated particularly with Sufis in Pakistan.
– ORIGIN from Arabic *qawwāli*, from *Qawwāl* 'loquacious', also 'singer'.

QB ▶ abbreviation for ■ American Football quarterback. ■ Law Queen's Bench.

QC ▶ abbreviation for ■ quality control. ■ Quebec (in official postal use). ■ Law Queen's Counsel.

QCD ▶ abbreviation for quantum chromodynamics.

Q-Celtic ▶ noun & adjective another term for **GOIDELIC**.
– ORIGIN *Q*, from the retention of the Indo-European *kw* sound as *q* or *c* in this group of languages.

QED ▶ abbreviation for ■ quantum electrodynamics. ■ quod erat demonstrandum.

Q fever ▶ noun [mass noun] an infectious fever caused by rickettsiae and transmitted to humans from cattle, sheep, and goats by unpasteurized milk.
– ORIGIN 1930s: from *Q* for *query* + **FEVER**.

qi /kiː/ ▶ noun variant spelling of **CHI²**.

qibla ▶ noun variant spelling of **KIBLAH**.

qigong /tʃiːˈgɒŋ/ ▶ noun [mass noun] a Chinese system of physical exercises and breathing control related to tai chi.
– ORIGIN Chinese.

Qin /tʃɪn/ (also **Ch'in**) a dynasty that ruled China 221–206 BC and was the first to establish rule over a united China. The construction of the Great Wall of China was begun during this period.

Qing /tʃɪŋ/ (also **Ch'ing**) a dynasty established by the Manchus that ruled China 1644–1912. Its overthrow in 1912 by Sun Yat-sen and his supporters ended imperial rule in China.

Qingdao /tʃɪŋˈdaʊ/ a port in eastern China, in Shandong province on the Yellow Sea coast; pop. 2,040,000 (1990).

Qinghai /tʃɪŋˈhʌɪ/ (also **Tsinghai**) a mountainous province in north central China; capital, Xining.

qintar /ˈkɪntɑː/ ▶ noun (pl. same, **qintars**, or **qindarka**) a monetary unit of Albania, equal to one hundredth of a lek.
– ORIGIN from Albanian *qindar*, from *qind* 'hundred'.

Qiqihar /ˌtʃiːtʃɪˈhɑː/ a port on the River Nen, in Heilongjiang province, NE China; pop. 1,370,000 (1990).

Qld ▶ abbreviation for Queensland.

QM ▶ abbreviation for Quartermaster.

QMG ▶ abbreviation for Quartermaster General.

QMS ▶ abbreviation for Quartermaster Sergeant.

Qom /kʊm/ (also **Qum** or **Kum**) a city in central Iran; pop. 780,450 (1994). It is a holy city and centre of learning among Shiite Muslims.

QPM ▶ abbreviation for (in the UK) Queen's Police Medal.

qr ▶ abbreviation for quarter(s).

Q-ship ▶ noun historical a merchant ship with concealed weapons, used by the British in the First and Second World Wars in an attempt to destroy submarines.
– ORIGIN First World War: from *Q* as a non-explicit symbol of the type of vessel + **SHIP**.

QSO ▶ abbreviation for quasi-stellar object, a quasar.

qt ▶ abbreviation for quart(s).

q.t. ▶ noun (in phrase **on the q.t.**) informal secretly; secret.
– ORIGIN late 19th cent.: abbreviation.

qua /kweɪ, kwɑː/ ▶ conjunction formal in the capacity of; as being: *shareholders qua members may be under obligations to the company.*
– ORIGIN Latin, ablative feminine singular of *qui* 'who'.

quack¹ ▶ noun [in sing.] the characteristic harsh sound made by a duck.
▶ verb [no obj.] (of a duck) make this sound.
■ informal talk loudly and foolishly.
– ORIGIN mid 16th cent. (as a verb): imitative.

quack² ▶ noun a person who dishonestly claims to have special knowledge and skill in some field, typically in medicine: [as modifier] *quack cures.*
■ Brit. informal a doctor.
– DERIVATIVES **quackery** noun, **quackish** adjective.
– ORIGIN mid 17th cent.: abbreviation of earlier

quacksalver, from Dutch, probably from obsolete *quacken* 'prattle' + *salf, zalf* (see **SALVE¹**).

quack grass ▶ noun North American term for **COUCH²**.
– ORIGIN early 19th cent.: *quack*, variant of *quick*, northern form of **QUITCH**.

quad ▶ noun **1** informal short for:
■ a quadrangle. ■ QUADRUPLET (in sense 1). ■ a quadriceps. ■ a quad bike. ■ quadraphony.
2 (in telephony) a group of four insulated conductors twisted together, usually forming two circuits. [ORIGIN: abbreviation of *quadraplex*.]
3 a radio aerial in the form of a square or rectangle broken in the middle of one side. [ORIGIN: abbreviation of **QUADRILATERAL**.]
4 a traditional roller skate. [ORIGIN: *quad*, with reference to the four wheels.]
5 Printing a small metal block in various sizes, lower than type height, used in letterpress printing for filling up short lines. [ORIGIN: abbreviation of the late 17th-cent. printing term *quadrat*.]
▶ adjective [attrib.] informal short for:
■ quadruple. ■ quadraphonic.

quad bike ▶ noun a motorcycle with four large tyres, typically used for racing.

quadplex ▶ noun another term for **QUADRAPLEX**.

quadragenarian /ˌkwɒdrədʒɪˈnɛːrɪən/ ▶ noun a person who is between 40 and 49 years old.
– ORIGIN mid 19th cent.: from late Latin *quadragenarius* (based on Latin *quadraginta* 'forty') + **-AN**.

Quadragesima /ˌkwɒdrəˈdʒɛsɪmə/ (also **Quadragesima Sunday**) ▶ noun the first Sunday in Lent.
– ORIGIN from ecclesiastical Latin, feminine of Latin *quadragesimus* 'fortieth', from *quadraginta* 'forty' (Lent lasting 40 days).

quadragesimal ▶ adjective [attrib.] archaic (of a fast, especially one in Lent) lasting forty days.
■ belonging or appropriate to the period of Lent.

quadraminium ▶ noun variant spelling of **QUADROMINIUM**.

quadrangle ▶ noun Geometry a four-sided plane figure, especially a square or rectangle.
■ a square or rectangular space or courtyard enclosed by buildings.
– ORIGIN late Middle English: from Old French, or from late Latin *quadrangulum* 'square', neuter of *quadrangulus*, from Latin 'four' + *angulus* 'corner, angle'.

quadrangular ▶ adjective (of an object or architectural structure) having four sides.
■ Brit. (of a sporting contest) involving four teams competing against each other.

quadrant ▶ noun technical each of four quarters of a circle.
■ each of four parts of a plane, sphere, space, or body divided by two lines or planes at right angles: *the right upper quadrant of the kidney.* ■ historical an instrument used for taking angular measurements of altitude in astronomy and navigation, typically consisting of a graduated quarter circle and a sighting mechanism. ■ a frame fixed to the head of a ship's rudder, to which the steering mechanism is attached. ■ a panel with slots through which a lever

q

is moved to orient or otherwise control a mechanism.
– DERIVATIVES **quadrantal** adjective.
– ORIGIN late Middle English (denoting the astronomical instrument): from Latin *quadrans*, *quadrant-* 'quarter', from *quattuor* 'four'.

Quadrantids /kwɒˈdrantɪdz/ Astronomy an annual meteor shower with a radiant in the constellation Boötes, reaching a peak about 3 January.
– ORIGIN from Latin *Quadrans Muralis* 'the Mural Quadrant', the name of a former constellation.

quadraphonic (also **quadrophonic**) ▶ adjective (of sound reproduction) transmitted through four channels.
– DERIVATIVES **quadraphonically** adverb, **quadraphonics** plural noun, **quadraphony** noun.
– ORIGIN 1960s: from **QUADRI-** 'four' + a shortened form of **STEREOPHONIC**.

quadraplex (also **quadriplex**) ▶ noun N. Amer. a building divided into four self-contained residences. Also called **QUADPLEX**.
– ORIGIN 1970s: from **QUADRI-** 'four', on the pattern of *duplex*.

quadrat /ˈkwɒdrət/ ▶ noun Ecology each of a number of small areas of habitat, typically of one square metre, selected at random to act as samples for assessing the local distribution of plants or animals.
■ a portable frame, typically with an internal grid, used to mark out such an area.
– ORIGIN early 20th cent.: variant of **QUADRATE**.

quadrate ▶ noun /ˈkwɒdrət/ **1** (also **quadrate bone**) Zoology (in the skull of a bird or reptile) a squarish bone with which the jaw articulates, thought to be homologous with the incus of the middle ear in mammals.
2 Anatomy another term for **QUADRATUS**.
▶ adjective /ˈkwɒdrət/ roughly square or rectangular.
▶ verb /kwɒˈdreɪt, ˈkwɒdreɪt/ archaic **1** [with obj.] make square.
2 conform or cause to conform.
– ORIGIN late Middle English (as an adjective): from Latin *quadrat-* 'made square', from the verb *quadrare*, from *quattuor* 'four'.

quadratic /kwɒˈdratɪk/ ▶ adjective Mathematics involving the second and no higher power of an unknown quantity or variable: *a quadratic equation*.
▶ noun a quadratic equation.
– ORIGIN mid 17th cent.: from French *quadratique* or modern Latin *quadraticus*, from *quadratus* 'made square', past participle of *quadrare* (see **QUADRATE**).

quadrature /ˈkwɒdrətʃə/ ▶ noun [mass noun]
1 Mathematics the process of constructing a square with an area equal to that of a circle, or of another figure bounded by a curve.
2 Astronomy the position of the moon or a planet when it is 90° from the sun as viewed from the earth.
3 Electronics a phase difference of 90 degrees between two waves of the same frequency, as in the colour difference signals of a television screen.
– ORIGIN mid 16th cent. (as a mathematical term): from Latin *quadratura* 'a square, squaring', from *quadrare* (see **QUADRATE**).

quadrature amplitude modulation ▶ noun [mass noun] Telecommunications a modulation system used in microwave and satellite communication, involving phase and amplitude modulation of a carrier wave.

quadratus /kwɒˈdreɪtəs/ ▶ noun (pl. **quadrati** /-tʌɪ/) Anatomy any of several roughly square or rectangular muscles, e.g. in the abdomen, thigh, and eye socket.
– ORIGIN mid 18th cent.: from Latin, literally 'made square'.

quadrennial /kwɒˈdrɛnɪəl/ ▶ adjective recurring every four years.
■ lasting for or relating to a period of four years.
– DERIVATIVES **quadrennially** adverb.
– ORIGIN mid 17th cent.: from **QUADRENNIUM** + **-AL**.

quadrennium /kwɒˈdrɛnɪəm/ ▶ noun (pl. **quadrennia** /-nɪə/ or **quadrenniums**) a specified period of four years.
– ORIGIN early 19th cent.: from Latin *quadriennium*, from *quadri-* 'four' + *annus* 'year'.

quadri- ▶ combining form four; having four: *quadriceps | quadriplegia*.
– ORIGIN from Latin, from *quattuor* 'four'.

quadric /ˈkwɒdrɪk/ Geometry ▶ adjective (of a surface

or curve) described by an equation of the second degree.
▶ noun a quadric surface or curve.
– ORIGIN mid 19th cent.: from Latin *quadra* 'square' + **-IC**.

quadriceps /ˈkwɒdrɪsɛps/ ▶ noun (pl. same) Anatomy the large muscle at the front of the thigh, which is divided into four distinct portions and acts to extend the leg.
– ORIGIN mid 16th cent.: from Latin, literally 'four-headed'.

quadrilateral ▶ noun a four-sided figure.
▶ adjective having four straight sides.
– ORIGIN mid 17th cent.: from late Latin *quadrilaterus* (from Latin *quadri-* 'four' + *latus*, *later-* 'side') + **-AL**.

quadrille¹ /kwɒˈdrɪl/ ▶ noun a square dance performed typically by four couples and containing five figures, each of which is a complete dance in itself.
■ a piece of music for this dance. ■ each of four groups of riders taking part in a tournament or carousel, distinguished by a special costume or colours. ■ a riding display.
– ORIGIN mid 18th cent.: from French from Spanish *cuadrilla* or Italian *quadriglia* 'troop, company', from *cuadra*, *quadra* 'square', based on Latin *quadrare* 'make square'.

quadrille² /kwɒˈdrɪl/ ▶ noun [mass noun] a trick-taking card game for four players using a pack of forty cards (i.e. one lacking eights, nines, and tens), fashionable in the 18th century.
– ORIGIN early 18th cent.: from French, perhaps from Spanish *cuartillo* (from *cuarto* 'fourth'). The change in the first syllable was due to association with **QUADRILLE**¹.

quadrille³ /kwɒˈdrɪl/ ▶ noun [mass noun] a ruled grid of small squares, especially on paper.
– ORIGIN late 19th cent.: from French *quadrillé*, from *quadrille* 'small square', from Spanish *cuadrillo* 'small block'.

quadrillion /kwɒˈdrɪljən/ ▶ cardinal number (pl. **quadrillions** or (with numeral) same) a thousand raised to the power of five (10^{15}).
■ dated, chiefly Brit. a thousand raised to the power of eight (10^{24}).
– DERIVATIVES **quadrillionth** ordinal number.
– ORIGIN late 17th cent.: from French, from *million*, by substitution of the prefix *quadri-* 'four' for the initial letters.

quadripartite /ˌkwɒdrɪˈpɑːtʌɪt/ ▶ adjective consisting of four parts.
■ shared by or involving four parties.
– ORIGIN late Middle English: from Latin *quadripartitus*, from *quadri-* 'four' + *partitus* 'divided'.

quadriplegia /ˌkwɒdrɪˈpliːdʒə/ ▶ noun [mass noun] Medicine paralysis of all four limbs; tetraplegia.
– DERIVATIVES **quadriplegic** adjective & noun.
– ORIGIN 1920s: from **QUADRI-** 'four' + a shortened form of **PARAPLEGIA**.

quadriplex ▶ noun variant spelling of **QUADRAPLEX**.

quadrivalent /ˌkwɒdrɪˈveɪl(ə)nt/ ▶ adjective Chemistry another term for **TETRAVALENT**.

quadrivium /kwɒˈdrɪvɪəm/ ▶ noun historical a medieval university course involving the 'mathematical arts' of arithmetic, geometry, astronomy, and music. Compare with **TRIVIUM**.
– ORIGIN Latin, literally 'the place where four roads meet' (in late Latin 'the four branches of mathematics'), from *quadri-* 'four' + *via* 'road'.

quadrominium /ˌkwɒdrəˈmɪnɪəm/ (also **quadraminium**) ▶ noun N. Amer. a condominium consisting of four apartments.
– ORIGIN 1970s: blend of **QUADRI-** 'four' and **CONDOMINIUM**.

quadroon /kwɒˈdruːn/ ▶ noun a person whose parents are a mulatto and a white person and who is therefore one-quarter black by descent.
– ORIGIN early 18th cent. (earlier as *quarteron*): via French from Spanish *cuarterón*, from *cuarto* 'quarter', from Latin *quartus*; later assimilated to words beginning with **QUADRI-**.

quadrophonic ▶ adjective variant spelling of **QUADRAPHONIC**.

quadrumanous /kwɒˈdruːmənəs, ˌkwɒdrʊˈmɑːnəs/ ▶ adjective Zoology, dated (of primates other than

humans) having all four feet modified as hands, i.e. having opposable digits.
– ORIGIN late 17th cent.: from modern Latin *Quadrumana* (former order name, neuter plural of *quadrumanus*, from *quadru-* 'four' + Latin *manus* 'hand') + **-OUS**.

quadruped /ˈkwɒdrʊpɛd/ ▶ noun an animal which has four feet, especially an ungulate mammal.
– DERIVATIVES **quadrupedal** /-ˈpiːd(ə)l, -ˈruːpɪd(ə)l/ adjective.
– ORIGIN mid 17th cent.: from French *quadrupède* or Latin *quadrupes*, *quadruped-*, from *quadru-* 'four' + *pes*, *ped-* 'foot'.

quadruple /ˈkwɒdrʊp(ə)l, kwɒˈdruːp(ə)l/ ▶ adjective [attrib.] consisting of four parts or elements: *a quadruple murder*.
■ consisting of four times as much or as many as usual: *a quadruple vodka*. ■ (of time in music) having four beats in a bar.
▶ verb increase or be increased fourfold: [no obj.] *oil prices quadrupled in the 1970s*.
▶ noun a quadruple thing, number, or amount.
– DERIVATIVES **quadruply** adverb.
– ORIGIN late Middle English (as a verb): via French from Latin *quadruplus*, from *quadru-* 'four' + *-plus* as in *duplus* (see **DUPLE**).

Quadruple Alliance a union or association between four powers or states, notably that formed in 1813 between Britain, Russia, Austria, and Prussia in order to defeat Napoleon and to maintain the international order established in Europe at the end of the Napoleonic Wars.

quadruplet /ˈkwɒdrʊplɪt, kwɒˈdruːplɪt/ ▶ noun
1 (usu. **quadruplets**) each of four children born at one birth.
2 Music a group of four notes to be performed in the time of three.
– ORIGIN late 18th cent.: from **QUADRUPLE**, on the pattern of *triplet*.

quadruplicate ▶ adjective /kwɒˈdruːplɪkət/ consisting of four parts or elements.
■ of which four copies are made.
▶ verb /kwɒˈdruːplɪkeɪt/ [with obj.] multiply (something) by four.
■ [usu. as adj. **quadruplicated**] make or provide in quadruplicate.
– PHRASES **in quadruplicate** in four identical copies.
– DERIVATIVES **quadruplication** noun.
– ORIGIN mid 17th cent.: from Latin *quadruplicat-* 'quadrupled', from the verb *quadruplicare*, from *quadruplex*, *quadruplic-* 'fourfold', from *quadru-* 'four' + *plicare* 'to fold'.

quadruplicity /ˌkwɒdrʊˈplɪsɪti/ ▶ noun [mass noun] the state of being fourfold or of forming a set of four.
■ [count noun] Astrology a group of four zodiacal signs of the same quality.

quadrupole /ˈkwɒdrʊpəʊl/ ▶ noun Physics a distribution of electric charge or magnetization consisting of four equal monopoles, or two equal dipoles, arranged close together with alternating polarity and operating as a unit.
■ a device using such an arrangement directed at one point to focus beams of subatomic particles.

quad-speed ▶ adjective Computing (of a CD-ROM drive) capable of revolving the CD-ROM at a speed of 920 rpm.

quaestor /ˈkwiːstə/ ▶ noun (in ancient Rome) any of a number of officials who had charge of public revenue and expenditure.
– DERIVATIVES **quaestorial** adjective, **quaestorship** noun.
– ORIGIN Latin, from an old form of *quaesit-* 'sought', from the verb *quaerere*.

quaff /kwɒf, kwɑːf/ ▶ verb [with obj.] drink (something, especially an alcoholic drink) heartily.
▶ noun informal, dated an alcoholic drink.
– DERIVATIVES **quaffable** adjective, **quaffer** noun.
– ORIGIN early 16th cent.: probably imitative of the sound of drinking.

quag /kwag, kwɒg/ ▶ noun archaic a marshy or boggy place.
– DERIVATIVES **quaggy** adjective.
– ORIGIN late 16th cent.: related to dialect *quag* 'shake, quiver'; probably symbolic, the *qu-* suggesting movement (as in *quake* and *quick*).

quagga /ˈkwagə/ ▶ noun an extinct South African

zebra that had a yellowish-brown coat with darker stripes, exterminated in 1883.
● *Equus quagga*, family Equidae; recent studies have shown that it was probably a variety of the common zebra.
– ORIGIN South African Dutch, probably from Khoikhoi, imitative of its braying.

quagmire /ˈkwagmʌɪə, ˈkwɒg-/ ▶ **noun** a soft boggy area of land that gives way underfoot: *torrential rain turned the building site into a quagmire.*
■ an awkward, complex, or hazardous situation: *a legal quagmire.*
– ORIGIN late 16th cent.: from **QUAG** + **MIRE**.

quahog /ˈkwɔːhɒg, ˈkwɑː-/ (also **quahaug** /-hɔːg/) ▶ **noun** N. Amer. a large, rounded edible clam of the Atlantic coast of North America. Also called **HARD CLAM**, **HARDSHELL CLAM**.
● *Venus mercenaria*, family Veneridae.
– ORIGIN mid 18th cent.: from Narragansett *poquaûhock*.

quaich /kweɪk, -x/ (also **quaigh**) ▶ **noun** Scottish a shallow drinking cup, typically made of wood and having two handles.
■ a trophy of similar design.
– ORIGIN mid 16th cent.: from Scottish Gaelic *cuach* 'cup'.

Quai d'Orsay /ˌkeɪ dɔːˈseɪ, French kɛ dɔʀsɛ/ a riverside street on the left bank of the Seine in Paris.
■ the French ministry of foreign affairs, which has its headquarters in this street.

quail[1] ▶ **noun** (pl. same or **quails**) **1** a small short-tailed Old World game bird resembling a tiny partridge, typically having brown camouflaged plumage.
● Family Phasianidae: three genera, in particular *Coturnix*, and several species, e.g. the widespread migratory **common quail** (*C. coturnix*).
2 a small or medium-sized New World game bird, the male of which has distinctive facial markings.
● Family Phasianidae (or Odontophoridae): several genera and many species, including the bobwhite.
– ORIGIN Middle English: from Old French *quaille*, from medieval Latin *coacula* (probably imitative of its call).

quail[2] ▶ **verb** [no obj.] feel or show fear or apprehension: *she quailed at his heartless words.*
– ORIGIN late Middle English (in the sense 'waste away, come to nothing'): of unknown origin.

quaint ▶ **adjective** attractively unusual or old-fashioned: *quaint country cottages* | *a quaint old custom.*
– DERIVATIVES **quaintly** adverb, **quaintness** noun.
– ORIGIN Middle English: from Old French *cointe*, from Latin *cognitus* 'ascertained', past participle of *cognoscere*. The original sense was 'wise, clever', also 'ingenious, cunningly devised', hence 'out of the ordinary' and the current sense (late 18th cent.).

quake ▶ **verb** [no obj.] (especially of the earth) shake or tremble: *the rumbling vibrations set the whole valley quaking.*
■ (of a person) shake or shudder with fear: *those words should have them* ***quaking in their boots.***
▶ **noun** informal an earthquake.
■ [usu. in sing.] an act of shaking or quaking.
– DERIVATIVES **quaky** adjective (**quakier**, **quakiest**).
– ORIGIN Old English *cwacian*.

Quaker ▶ **noun** a member of the Religious Society of Friends, a Christian movement founded by George Fox *c.*1650 and devoted to peaceful principles. Central to the Quakers' belief is the doctrine of the 'Inner Light', or sense of Christ's direct working in the soul. This has led them to reject both formal ministry and all set forms of worship.
– DERIVATIVES **Quakerish** adjective, **Quakerism** noun.
– ORIGIN from **QUAKE** + **-ER**[1], perhaps alluding to George Fox's direction to his followers to 'tremble at the name of the Lord', or from fits supposedly experienced by worshippers when moved by the Spirit. Compare with **SHAKER** (sense 2).

quaking grass ▶ **noun** [mass noun] a slender-stalked grass with oval or heart-shaped flower heads which tremble in the wind.
● Genus *Briza*, family Gramineae: several species, including *B. media*, which is sometimes cultivated as an ornamental.

quale /ˈkweɪli/ ▶ **noun** (pl. **qualia** /ˈkweɪlɪə/) (usu. **qualia**) Philosophy a quality or property as perceived or experienced by a person.
– ORIGIN late 17th cent.: from Latin, neuter of *qualis* 'of what kind'.

qualification ▶ **noun 1** a pass of an examination or an official completion of a course, especially one conferring status as a recognized practitioner of a profession or activity: *he left school at 16 with few qualifications.*
■ a quality or accomplishment that makes someone suitable for a particular job or activity: *only one qualification required—fabulous sense of humour.* ■ [mass noun] the action or fact of becoming qualified as a practitioner of a particular profession or activity: *an opportunity for student teachers to share experiences before qualification.* ■ a condition that must be fulfilled before a right can be acquired; an official requirement: *the five-year residency qualification for presidential candidates.*
2 [mass noun] the action or fact of qualifying or being eligible for something: *they need to beat Poland to ensure qualification for the World Cup finals.*
3 a statement or assertion that makes another less absolute: *this important qualification needs to be remembered when interpreting the results* | [mass noun] *I welcome without qualification the Minister's statement.*
■ Grammar the attribution of a quality to a word, especially a noun.
– DERIVATIVES **qualificatory** adjective.
– ORIGIN mid 16th cent.: from medieval Latin *qualificatio(n-)*, from the verb *qualificare* (see **QUALIFY**).

qualifier ▶ **noun 1** a person or team that qualifies for a competition or its final rounds.
■ a match or contest to decide which individuals or teams qualify for a competition or its final rounds.
2 Grammar a word or phrase, especially an adjective, used to attribute a quality to another word, especially a noun.
■ (in systemic grammar) a word or phrase added after a noun to qualify its meaning.

qualify ▶ **verb** (**-ies**, **-ied**) **1** [no obj.] be entitled to a particular benefit or privilege by fulfilling a necessary condition: *a pensioner who does not* ***qualify for*** *income support.*
■ become eligible for a competition or its final rounds, by reaching a certain standard or defeating a competitor: *England are in danger of failing to qualify* | [as noun modifier] (**qualifying**) *a World Cup qualifying game.* ■ be or make properly entitled to be classed in a particular way: [no obj.] *he* ***qualifies as*** *a genuine political refugee.*
2 [no obj.] become officially recognized as a practitioner of a particular profession or activity by satisfying the relevant conditions or requirements, typically by undertaking a course and passing examinations: *the training necessary to* ***qualify as*** *a solicitor* | *I've only just qualified.*
■ [with obj.] officially recognize or establish (someone) as a practitioner of a particular profession or activity: *the courses qualify you as an instructor of the sport* | [as adj. **qualified**] *qualified teachers.* ■ [with obj. and infinitive] make (someone) competent or knowledgeable enough to do something: *I'm not qualified to write on the subject.*
3 [with obj.] make (a statement or assertion) less absolute; add reservations to: *she felt obliged to qualify her first short answer* | [as adj. **qualified**] *it was given a qualified welcome.*
■ archaic make (something extreme or undesirable) less severe or extreme: *his sincere piety, his large heart alway qualify his errors.* ■ archaic alter the strength or flavour of (something, especially a liquid): *he qualified his mug of water with a plentiful infusion of the liquor.* ■ (**qualify something as**) archaic attribute a specified quality to something; describe something as: *the propositions have been qualified as heretical.* ■ [with obj.] Grammar (of a word or phrase) attribute a quality to (another word, especially a preceding noun).
– DERIVATIVES **qualifiable** adjective.
– ORIGIN late Middle English (in the sense 'describe in a particular way'): from French *qualifier*, from medieval Latin *qualificare*, from Latin *qualis* 'of what kind, of such a kind' (see **QUALITY**).

qualitative /ˈkwɒlɪtətɪv/ ▶ **adjective** relating to, measuring, or measured by the quality of something rather than its quantity: *a qualitative change in the undergraduate curriculum.* Often contrasted with **QUANTITATIVE**.
■ Grammar (of an adjective) describing the quality of something in size, appearance, value, etc. Such adjectives can be submodified by words such as *very* and have comparative and superlative forms. Contrasted with **CLASSIFYING**.
– DERIVATIVES **qualitatively** adverb.
– ORIGIN late Middle English: from late Latin *qualitativus*, from Latin *qualitas* (see **QUALITY**).

qualitative analysis ▶ **noun** [mass noun] Chemistry identification of the constituents, e.g. elements or functional groups, present in a substance.

quality ▶ **noun** (pl. **-ies**) **1** [mass noun] the standard of something as measured against other things of a similar kind; the degree of excellence of something: *an improvement in product quality* | [count noun] *people today enjoy a better quality of life.*
■ general excellence of standard or level: *a masterpiece for connoisseurs of quality* | [as modifier] *a wide choice of quality beers.* ■ (usu. **qualities**) short for **QUALITY PAPER**. ■ archaic high social standing: *commanding the admiration of people of quality.* ■ [treated as pl.] archaic people of high social standing: *he's dazed at being called on to speak before quality.*
2 a distinctive attribute or characteristic possessed by someone or something: *he shows strong leadership qualities* | *the plant's aphrodisiac qualities.*
■ Phonetics the distinguishing characteristic or characteristics of a speech sound. ■ Astrology any of three properties (cardinal, fixed, or mutable), representing types of movement, that a zodiacal sign can possess.
– ORIGIN Middle English (in the senses 'character, disposition' and 'particular property or feature'): from Old French *qualite*, from Latin *qualitas* (translating Greek *poiotēs*), from *qualis* 'of what kind, of such a kind'.

quality assurance ▶ **noun** [mass noun] the maintenance of a desired level of quality in a service or product, especially by means of attention to every stage of the process of delivery or production.

quality circle ▶ **noun** a group of employees who meet regularly to consider ways of resolving problems and improving production in their organization.

quality control ▶ **noun** [mass noun] a system of maintaining standards in manufactured products by testing a sample of the output against the specification.
– DERIVATIVES **quality controller** noun.

quality factor ▶ **noun** Physics a parameter of an oscillatory system or device, such as a laser, representing the degree to which it is undamped and hence expressing the relationship between stored energy and energy dissipation.
■ a figure expressing the ability of ionizing radiation to cause biological damage, relative to a standard dose of X-rays.

quality paper (also **quality newspaper**) ▶ **noun** Brit. a newspaper, typically a broadsheet, that is considered to deal seriously with issues and to have high editorial standards.

quality time ▶ **noun** [mass noun] time spent in giving another person one's undivided attention in order to strengthen a relationship, especially with reference to a working parent and their child or children.

qualm /kwɑːm, kwɔːm/ ▶ **noun** an uneasy feeling of doubt, worry, or fear, especially about one's own conduct; a misgiving: *military regimes generally* ***have no qualms about*** *controlling the press.*
■ a momentary faint or sick feeling.
– DERIVATIVES **qualmish** adjective.
– ORIGIN early 16th cent. (in the sense 'momentary sick feeling'): perhaps related to Old English *cw(e)alm* 'pain', of Germanic origin.

quamash /kwəˈmaʃ, ˈkwɒmaʃ/ ▶ **noun** variant spelling of **CAMAS**.

quandary /ˈkwɒnd(ə)ri/ ▶ **noun** (pl. **-ies**) a state of perplexity or uncertainty over what to do in a difficult situation: *Kate was* ***in a quandary.***
■ a difficult situation; a practical dilemma: *a legal quandary.*
– ORIGIN late 16th cent.: perhaps partly from Latin *quando* 'when'.

quandong /ˈkwɒndɒŋ, ˈkwan-/ ▶ **noun** either of two Australian trees:
● a small tree of the sandalwood family, which has round red fruit with an edible pulp and kernel (*Eucarya acuminata*, family Santalaceae). ● (also **blue quandong**) a large tree of the subtropical rainforest, which has blue berries (*Elaeocarpus grandis*, family Elaeocarpaceae).
– ORIGIN mid 19th cent.: from Wiradhuri.

quango /ˈkwaŋgəʊ/ ▶ **noun** (pl. **-os**) Brit., chiefly derogatory a semi-public administrative body outside the civil service but with financial support from and senior appointments made by the government.
– ORIGIN 1970s (originally US): acronym from *quasi* (or *quasi-autonomous*) *non-government(al) organization*.

Quant /kwɒnt/, Mary (b.1934), English fashion designer. She was a principal creator of the '1960s look', launching the miniskirt in 1966 and promoting bold colours and geometric designs. She was also one of the first to design for the ready-to-wear market.

quant[1] /kwɒnt/ ▶ noun informal a quantity analyst.
– ORIGIN late 20th cent.: abbreviation.

quant[2] /kwɒnt, kwant/ ▶ noun Brit. a pole for propelling a barge or punt, especially one with a prong at the bottom to prevent it sinking into the mud.
– ORIGIN late Middle English: perhaps from Latin contus, from Greek kontos 'boat pole'.

quanta plural form of QUANTUM.

quantal /'kwɒnt(ə)l/ ▶ adjective technical composed of discrete units; varying in steps rather than continuously: a quantal release of neurotransmitter.
 ■Physics of or relating to a quantum or quanta, or to quantum theory. ■ chiefly Physiology relating to or denoting an all-or-none response or state.
– DERIVATIVES **quantally** adverb.
– ORIGIN early 20th cent.: from QUANTUM + -AL.

quantic ▶ noun Mathematics a homogeneous function of two or more variables having rational or integral coefficients.
– ORIGIN mid 19th cent.: from Latin quantus 'how great, how much' + -IC.

quantifier ▶ noun Logic an expression (e.g. all, some) that indicates the scope of a term to which it is attached.
 ■Grammar a determiner or pronoun indicative of quantity (e.g. all, both).

quantify ▶ verb (-ies, -ied) [with obj.] 1 express or measure the quantity of: it is impossible to quantify the extent of the black economy.
 2 Logic define the application of (a term or proposition) by the use of all, some, etc., e.g. 'for all x if x is A then x is B'.
– DERIVATIVES **quantifiability** noun, **quantifiable** adjective, **quantification** noun.
– ORIGIN mid 16th cent.: from medieval Latin quantificare, from Latin quantus 'how much'.

quantile /'kwɒntʌɪl/ ▶ noun Statistics each of any set of values of a variate which divide a frequency distribution into equal groups, each containing the same fraction of the total population.
 ■any of the groups so produced, e.g. a quartile or percentile.
– ORIGIN 1940s: from Latin quantus 'how great, how much' + -ILE.

quantitate /'kwɒntɪteɪt/ ▶ verb [with obj.] Medicine & Biology determine the quantity or extent of (something in numerical terms); quantify.
– DERIVATIVES **quantitation** noun.
– ORIGIN 1960s: from QUANTITY + -ATE[3].

quantitative /'kwɒntɪˌtətɪv, -ˌteɪtɪv/ ▶ adjective relating to, measuring, or measured by the quantity of something rather than its quality: quantitative analysis. Often contrasted with QUALITATIVE.
 ■denoting or relating to verse whose metre is based on the length of syllables, as in Latin, as opposed to the stress, as in English.
– DERIVATIVES **quantitatively** adverb.
– ORIGIN late 16th cent. (in the sense 'having magnitude or spatial extent'): from medieval Latin quantitativus, from Latin quantitas (see QUANTITY).

quantitative analysis ▶ noun [mass noun] Chemistry measurement of the quantities of particular constituents present in a substance.

quantitative linguistics ▶ plural noun [treated as sing.] the comparative study of the frequency and distribution of words and syntactic structures in different texts.

quantitive ▶ adjective another term for QUANTITATIVE.
– DERIVATIVES **quantitively** adverb.

quantity ▶ noun (pl. -ies) [mass noun] 1 the amount or number of a material or immaterial thing not usually estimated by spatial measurement: the quantity and quality of the fruit can be controlled | [count noun] note down the sizes, colours, and quantities that you require.
 ■a certain, usually specified, amount or number of something: a small quantity of food | if taken in large quantities, the drug can result in liver failure. ■ (often quantities) a considerable number or amount of something: she was able to drink quantities of beer

without degenerating into giggles | [mass noun] many people like to buy in quantity.
 2 [mass noun] Phonetics the perceived length of a vowel sound or syllable.
 3 [mass noun] Mathematics & Physics a value or component that may be expressed in numbers.
 ■[count noun] the figure or symbol representing this.
– ORIGIN Middle English: from Old French quantite, from Latin quantitas (translating Greek posotēs), from quantus 'how great, how much'.

quantity surveyor ▶ noun Brit. a person who calculates the amount of materials needed for building work, and how much they will cost.

quantity theory (also **the quantity theory of money**) ▶ noun [mass noun] Economics the hypothesis that changes in prices correspond to changes in the monetary supply.

quantize (also **-ise**) ▶ verb [with obj.] 1 Physics form into quanta, in particular restrict the number of possible values of (a quantity) or states of (a system) so that certain variables can assume only certain discrete magnitudes.
 2 Electronics approximate (a continuously varying signal) by one whose amplitude is restricted to a prescribed set of values.
– DERIVATIVES **quantization** noun, **quantizer** noun (only in sense 2).

quantum /'kwɒntəm/ ▶ noun (pl. **quanta** /-tə/) 1 Physics a discrete quantity of energy proportional in magnitude to the frequency of the radiation it represents.
 ■an analogous discrete amount of any other physical quantity, such as momentum or electric charge. ■ Physiology the unit quantity of acetylcholine released at a neuromuscular junction by a single synaptic vesicle, contributing a discrete small voltage to the measured end-plate potential.
 2 a required or allowed amount, especially an amount of money legally payable in damages.
 ■a share or portion: each man has only a quantum of compassion.
– ORIGIN mid 16th cent. (in the general sense 'quantity'): from Latin, neuter of quantus (see QUANTITY). Sense 1 dates from the early 20th cent.

quantum chromodynamics (abbrev.: **QCD**) ▶ plural noun [treated as sing.] Physics a quantum field theory in which the strong interaction is described in terms of an interaction between quarks mediated by gluons, both quarks and gluons being assigned a quantum number called 'colour'.

quantum electrodynamics ▶ plural noun [treated as sing.] a quantum field theory that deals with the electromagnetic field and its interaction with electrically charged particles.

quantum field theory ▶ noun Physics a field theory that incorporates quantum mechanics and the principles of the theory of relativity.

quantum gravity ▶ noun [mass noun] Physics a theory that attempts to explain gravitational physics in terms of quantum mechanics.

quantum jump ▶ noun Physics an abrupt transition of an electron, atom, or molecule from one quantum state to another, with the absorption or emission of a quantum.
 ■another term for QUANTUM LEAP.

quantum leap ▶ noun a sudden large increase or advance: there has been a quantum leap in the quality of wines marketed in the UK.

quantum mechanics ▶ plural noun [treated as sing.] Physics the branch of mechanics that deals with the mathematical description of the motion and interaction of subatomic particles, incorporating the concepts of quantization of energy, wave–particle duality, the uncertainty principle, and the correspondence principle.
– DERIVATIVES **quantum-mechanical** adjective.

quantum meruit /ˌkwɒntəm 'mɛrʊɪt/ ▶ noun [mass noun] [usu. as modifier] Law a reasonable sum of money to be paid for services rendered or work done when the amount due is not stipulated in a legally enforceable contract.
– ORIGIN Latin, literally 'as much as he has deserved'.

quantum number ▶ noun Physics a number which occurs in the theoretical expression for the value of some quantized property of a subatomic particle, atom, or molecule and can only have certain integral or half-integral values.

quantum state ▶ noun Physics a state of a

quantized system which is described by a set of quantum numbers.

quantum theory ▶ noun [mass noun] Physics a theory of matter and energy based on the concept of quanta, especially quantum mechanics.

Quapaw /'kwɔːpɔː/ ▶ noun (pl. same or **Quapaws**) 1 a member of an American Indian people of the Arkansas River region, now living mainly in NE Oklahoma.
 2 [mass noun] the extinct Siouan language of this people.
▶ adjective of or relating to this people or their language.
– ORIGIN from Quapaw okáxpa, originally the name of a village.

quarantine ▶ noun [mass noun] a state, period, or place of isolation in which people or animals that have arrived from elsewhere or been exposed to infectious or contagious disease are placed: many animals die in quarantine.
▶ verb [with obj.] impose such isolation on (a person, animal, or place); put in quarantine.
– ORIGIN mid 17th cent.: from Italian quarantina 'forty days', from quaranta 'forty'.

quare /kwɛː/ ▶ adjective non-standard spelling of QUEER, used to represent Irish speech.

quark[1] /kwɑːk, kwɔːk/ ▶ noun Physics any of a number of subatomic particles carrying a fractional electric charge, postulated as building blocks of the hadrons. Quarks have not been directly observed but theoretical predictions based on their existence have been confirmed experimentally.
– ORIGIN 1960s: a word invented by Murray GELL-MANN. Originally quork, the term was changed by association with the line 'Three quarks for Muster Mark' in Joyce's Finnegans Wake (1939).

quark[2] /kwɑːk/ ▶ noun [mass noun] a type of low-fat curd cheese.
– ORIGIN 1930s: from German Quark 'curd, curds'.

quarrel[1] ▶ noun an angry argument or disagreement, typically between people who are usually on good terms: he made the mistake of picking a quarrel with John.
 ■[usu. with negative] a reason for disagreement with a person, group, or principle: we have no quarrel with the people of the country, only with the dictator.
▶ verb (**quarrelled**, **quarrelling**; US **quarreled**, **quarreling**) [no obj.] have an angry argument or disagreement: stop quarrelling with your sister.
 ■(quarrel with) take exception to or disagree with (something): some people quarrel with this approach. ■ [no obj.] W. Indian complain; scold: he will quarrel like hell if he see black pods on the trees.
– DERIVATIVES **quarreller** noun.
– ORIGIN Middle English (in the sense 'reason for disagreement with a person'): from Old French querele, from Latin querel(l)a 'complaint', from queri 'complain'.

quarrel[2] ▶ noun historical a short heavy square-headed arrow or bolt used in a crossbow or arbalest.
– ORIGIN Middle English: from Old French, based on late Latin quadrus 'square'. Compare with QUARRY[3].

quarrelsome ▶ adjective given to or characterized by quarrelling.
– DERIVATIVES **quarrelsomely** adverb, **quarrelsomeness** noun.

quarrion /'kwɒrɪən/ (also **quarrien**) ▶ noun Austral. another term for COCKATIEL.
– ORIGIN early 20th cent.: from Wiradhuri guwarraying.

quarry[1] ▶ noun (pl. -ies) a place, typically a large, deep pit, from which stone or other materials are or have been extracted.
▶ verb (-ies, -ied) [with obj.] extract (stone or other materials) from a quarry.
 ■cut into (rock or ground) to obtain stone or other materials.
– ORIGIN Middle English: from a variant of medieval Latin quareria, from Old French quarriere, based on Latin quadrum 'a square'. The verb dates from the late 18th cent.

quarry[2] ▶ noun (pl. -ies) an animal pursued by a hunter, hound, predatory mammal, or bird of prey.
 ■a thing or person that is chased or sought: the security police crossed the border in pursuit of their quarry.
– ORIGIN Middle English: from Old French cuiree, alteration, influenced by cuir 'leather' and curer 'clean, disembowel', of couree, based on Latin cor

'heart'. Originally the term denoted the parts of a deer that were placed on the hide and given as a reward to the hounds.

quarry[3] ▶ noun (pl. **-ies**) **1** a diamond-shaped pane of glass as used in lattice windows.
2 (also **quarry tile**) an unglazed floor tile.
– ORIGIN mid 16th cent. (in sense 2): alteration of QUARREL[2], which in late Middle English denoted a lattice windowpane.

quarryman ▶ noun (pl. **-men**) a worker in a quarry.

quart ▶ noun **1** a unit of liquid capacity equal to a quarter of a gallon or two pints, equivalent in Britain to approximately 1.13 litres and in US to approximately 0.94 litre.
■ N. Amer. a unit of dry capacity equivalent to approximately 1.10 litres.
2 /kɑːt/ (also **quarte** or **carte**) Fencing the fourth of eight parrying positions. [ORIGIN: French.]
3 (in piquet) a sequence of four cards of the same suit.
– PHRASES **you can't get a quart into a pint pot** Brit. proverb you cannot achieve the impossible.
– ORIGIN Middle English: from Old French *quarte*, from Latin *quarta* (*pars*) 'fourth (part)', from *quartus* 'fourth', from *quattuor* 'four'.

quartan /ˈkwɔːt(ə)n/ ▶ adjective [attrib.] Medicine denoting a mild form of malaria causing a fever that recurs every third day: *quartan fever.*
● Quartan malaria (or quartan ague) is caused by infection with *Plasmodium malariae*. Compare with TERTIAN.
– ORIGIN late Middle English: from Latin (*febris*) *quartana*, based on Latin *quartus* 'fourth' (because, by inclusive reckoning, the fever recurs every fourth day).

quarter ▶ noun **1** each of four equal or corresponding parts into which something is or can be divided: *she cut each apple into quarters | a page and a quarter | a quarter of a mile.*
■ a period of three months regarded as one fourth of a year, used especially in reference to financial transactions such as the payment of bills or a company's earnings: *the payment for each quarter's electricity is made in the next quarter.* ■ a period of fifteen minutes or a point of time marking the transition from one fifteen-minute period to the next: *he sat with his pint until a quarter past nine.* ■ a coin representing 25 cents, a quarter of a US or Canadian dollar. ■ each of the four parts into which an animal's or bird's carcass may be divided, each including a leg or wing. ■ (**quarters**) the haunches or hindquarters of a horse. ■ one fourth of a lunar month. ■ (in basketball, American football, and Australian Rules) each of four equal periods into which a game is divided. ■ chiefly US one of four terms into which a school or university year may be divided.
2 one fourth of a measure of weight, in particular:
■ one fourth of a pound weight (avoirdupois, equal to 4 ounces). ■ one fourth of a hundredweight (Brit. 28 lb or US 25 lb). ■ Brit. a grain measure equivalent to 8 bushels.
3 [usu. with adj. or noun] a part of a town or city having a specific character or use: *it is a beautiful port city with a fascinating medieval quarter.*
4 the direction of one of the points of the compass, especially as a direction from which the wind blows.
■ a particular but unspecified person, group of people, or area: *we have just had help from an unexpected quarter.* ■ either side of a ship aft of the beam: *he trained his glasses over the starboard quarter.*
5 (**quarters**) rooms or lodgings, especially those allocated to servicemen or to staff in domestic service: *they lived in RAF married quarters.*
6 [mass noun] pity or mercy shown towards an enemy or opponent who is in one's power: *the riot squad gave no quarter.*
7 Heraldry each of four or more roughly equal divisions of a shield separated by vertical and horizontal lines.
■ a square charge which covers the top left (dexter chief) quarter of the field.
▶ verb [with obj.] **1** divide into four equal or corresponding parts: *peel and quarter the bananas.*
■ historical cut (the body of an executed person) into four parts: *the plotters were hanged, drawn, and quartered.* ■ cut (a log) into quarters, and these into planks so as to show the grain well.
2 (**be quartered**) [with adverbial of place] be stationed or lodged in a specified place: *many were quartered in tents.*
■ (**quarter someone on**) impose someone on (another person) as a lodger: *you would have had her quartered on you forever.*
3 range over or traverse (an area) in every direction: *we watched a pair of kingfishers quartering the river looking for minnows.*
■ [no obj., with adverbial of direction] move at an angle; go in a diagonal or zigzag direction: *his young dog quartered back and forth in quick turns.*
4 Heraldry display (different coats of arms) in quarters of a shield, especially to show arms inherited from heiresses who have married into the bearer's family: *Edward III* ***quartered*** *the French royal arms* ***with*** *his own.*
■ divide (a shield) into four or more parts by vertical and horizontal lines.
– ORIGIN Middle English: from Old French *quartier*, from Latin *quartarius* 'fourth part of a measure', from *quartus* 'fourth', from *quattuor* 'four'.

quarterage ▶ noun archaic a sum paid or received quarterly.

quarterback ▶ noun American Football a player stationed behind the centre who directs a team's offensive play.
■ figurative N. Amer. a person who directs or coordinates an operation or project.
▶ verb [with obj.] American Football play as a quarterback for (a particular team).
■ figurative N. Amer. direct or coordinate (an operation or project).

quarter binding ▶ noun [mass noun] a type of bookbinding in which the spine is bound in one material (usually leather) and the rest of the cover in another.
– DERIVATIVES **quarter-bound** adjective.

quarter day ▶ noun Brit. each of four days fixed by custom as marking off the quarters of the year, on which some tenancies begin and end and quarterly payments of rent and other charges fall due.

quarterdeck ▶ noun the part of a ship's upper deck near the stern, traditionally reserved for officers.
■ the officers of a ship or the navy.

quarter-final ▶ noun a match or round of a knockout competition that precedes the semi-final.

Quarter Horse ▶ noun a horse of a small stocky breed noted for agility and speed over short distances. It is reputed to be the fastest breed of horse over distances of a quarter of a mile.

quarter-hour (also **quarter of an hour**) ▶ noun a period of 15 minutes.
■ a point of time 15 minutes before or after any hour.

quartering ▶ noun **1** (**quarterings**) Heraldry the coats of arms marshalled on a shield to denote the marriages into a family of the heiresses of others.
2 [mass noun] the provision of accommodation or lodgings, especially for troops.
3 [mass noun] the action of dividing something into four parts.

quarter-light ▶ noun Brit. a window in the side of a motor vehicle other than the main door window.

quarterly ▶ adjective **1** [attrib.] done, produced, or occurring once every quarter of a year: *a quarterly newsletter is distributed to members.*
2 Heraldry (of a shield or charge) divided into four (or occasionally more) subdivisions by vertical and horizontal lines.
▶ adverb **1** once every quarter of a year: *interest is paid quarterly.*
2 Heraldry in the four, or in two diagonally opposite, quarters of a shield. [ORIGIN: on the pattern of Old French *quartilé*.]
▶ noun (pl. **-ies**) a magazine or journal that is published four times a year.

quartermaster ▶ noun **1** a regimental officer, usually commissioned from the ranks, responsible for administering barracks, laying out the camp, and looking after supplies.
2 a naval petty officer with particular responsibility for steering and signals.

Quartermaster General ▶ noun (pl. **Quartermaster Generals**) the head of the army department in charge of the quartering and equipment of troops.

quartermaster sergeant ▶ noun a senior rank of non-commissioned officer in the army, above sergeant, employed on administrative duties.

quartern /ˈkwɔːt(ə)n/ ▶ noun Brit. archaic a quarter of a pint.
– ORIGIN Middle English (in the general sense 'a quarter'): from Old French *quart(e)ron*, from *quart(e)* (see QUART).

quartern loaf ▶ noun archaic a four-pound loaf.

quarter note ▶ noun Music, chiefly N. Amer. a crotchet.

quarter-pipe ▶ noun a ramp with a slightly convex surface, used by skateboarders, rollerbladers, or snowboarders to perform jumps and other manoeuvres.

quarter plate ▶ noun Brit. a photographic plate measuring 3¼ × 4¼ inches (*c.*8.3 × 10.8 cm).
■ a photograph reproduced from such a plate.

quarter-pounder ▶ noun a hamburger that weighs a quarter of a pound.

quarter-saw ▶ verb [with obj.] [usu. as adj. **quarter-sawn**] saw (a log) radially into quarters and then into boards.
■ produce (a board or a piece of furniture) using this technique.

quarter section ▶ noun N. Amer. a quarter of a square mile of land; 160 acres (approximately 64.7 hectares).

quarter sessions ▶ plural noun historical (in England, Wales, and Northern Ireland) a court of limited criminal and civil jurisdiction and of appeal, usually held quarterly in counties or boroughs, and replaced in 1972 by crown courts.

quarterstaff ▶ noun historical a stout pole 6–8 feet long, formerly used as a weapon.

quarter-tone ▶ noun Music half a semitone.

quartet (also **quartette**) ▶ noun a group of four people playing music or singing together.
■ a composition for such a group. ■ a set of four people or things.
– ORIGIN early 17th cent. (in the general sense 'set of four'): from French *quartette*, from Italian *quartetto*, from *quarto* 'fourth', from Latin *quartus*.

quartic /ˈkwɔːtɪk/ Mathematics ▶ adjective involving the fourth and no higher power of an unknown quantity or variable.
▶ noun a quartic equation, function, curve, or surface.
– ORIGIN mid 19th cent.: from Latin *quartus* 'fourth' + -IC.

quartier /ˈkɑːtɪeɪ, French kartje/ ▶ noun (pl. pronounced same) a district of a French city.
– ORIGIN French.

quartile /ˈkwɔːtʌɪl/ ▶ noun Statistics each of four equal groups into which a population can be divided according to the distribution of values of a particular variable.
■ each of the three values of the random variable which divide a population into four such groups.
– ORIGIN late 19th cent.: from medieval Latin *quartilis*, from Latin *quartus* 'fourth'.

quarto /ˈkwɔːtəʊ/ (abbrev.: **4to**) ▶ noun (pl. **-os**) [mass noun] Printing a size of book page resulting from folding each printed sheet into four leaves (eight pages).
■ [count noun] a book of this size. ■ a size of writing paper, 10 in. × 8 in. (254 × 203 mm).
– ORIGIN late 16th cent.: from Latin (*in*) *quarto* '(in) the fourth (of a sheet)', ablative of *quartus* 'fourth'.

quartz ▶ noun [mass noun] a hard mineral consisting of silica, found widely in igneous and metamorphic rocks and typically occurring as colourless or white hexagonal prisms. It is often coloured by impurities (as in amethyst, citrine, and cairngorm).
– ORIGIN mid 18th cent.: from German *Quarz*, from Polish dialect *kwardy*, corresponding to Czech *tvrdý* 'hard'.

quartz clock ▶ noun an electric clock in which the current is regulated and accuracy maintained by the regular vibrations of a quartz crystal.

quartz-halogen ▶ adjective (of a high-intensity electric lamp) using a quartz bulb containing the vapour of a halogen, usually iodine.

quartzite ▶ noun [mass noun] Geology an extremely compact, hard, granular rock consisting essentially of quartz. It often occurs as silicified sandstone, as in sarsen stones.

quartz lamp ▶ noun an electric lamp in which the envelope is made of quartz, which allows ultraviolet light to pass through it. It may be a bulb containing a halogen or a tube containing mercury vapour.

quartz watch ▶ noun a watch operated by vibrations of an electrically driven quartz crystal.

quasar /ˈkweɪzɑː, -sɑː/ ▶ noun Astronomy a massive and

q

extremely remote celestial object, emitting exceptionally large amounts of energy, which typically has a starlike image in a telescope. It has been suggested that quasars contain massive black holes and may represent a stage in the evolution of some galaxies.
– ORIGIN 1960s: contraction of *quasi-stellar*.

quash ▶ verb [with obj.] reject as invalid, especially by legal procedure: *his conviction was quashed on appeal*.
■ put an end to; suppress: *a hospital executive quashed rumours that nursing staff will lose jobs*.
– ORIGIN Middle English: from Old French *quasser* 'annul', from late Latin *cassare* (medieval Latin also *quassare*), from *cassus* 'null, void'. Compare with **SQUASH**[1].

quasi- /'kweɪzʌɪ, -sʌɪ, 'kwɑːzi/ ▶ combining form seemingly; apparently but not really: *quasi-American | quasi-scientific*.
■ being partly or almost: *quasicrystalline*.
– ORIGIN from Latin *quasi* 'as if, almost'.

quasi-contract ▶ noun an obligation of one party to another imposed by law independently of an agreement between the parties.
– DERIVATIVES **quasi-contractual** adjective.

quasicrystal ▶ noun Physics a locally regular aggregation of molecules resembling a crystal in certain properties (such as that of diffraction) but not having a consistent spatial periodicity.
– DERIVATIVES **quasicrystalline** adjective.

Quasimodo[1] /ˌkwɒzɪ'məʊdəʊ/ the name of the hunchback in Victor Hugo's novel *Notre-Dame de Paris* (1831).

Quasimodo[2] /kwaː'zɪmɒdəʊ/, Salvatore (1901–68), Italian poet, whose early work was influenced by French symbolism. His later work is more concerned with political and social issues. Nobel Prize for Literature (1959).

quasiparticle ▶ noun Physics a quantum of energy in a crystal lattice or other system of bodies which has momentum and position and can in some respects be regarded as a particle.

quassia /'kwɒʃə, 'kwɒʃɪə, 'kwɑːsɪə/ ▶ noun a South American shrub or small tree related to ailanthus.
● Genera *Quassia* and *Picrasma*, family Simaroubaceae: several species, in particular *Q. amara*.
■ [mass noun] the wood, bark, or root of this tree, yielding a bitter medicinal tonic, insecticide, and vermifuge.
– ORIGIN named after Graman *Quassi*, an 18th-cent Surinamese slave who discovered its medicinal properties in 1730.

quatercentenary /ˌkwatəsɛn'tiːnəri, -'tɛn-, ˌkweɪtə-/ ▶ noun (pl. -ies) the four-hundredth anniversary of a significant event.
▶ adjective of or relating to such an anniversary.
– ORIGIN late 19th cent.: from Latin *quater* 'four times' + **CENTENARY**.

quaternary /kwə'təːn(ə)ri/ ▶ adjective 1 fourth in order or rank; belonging to the fourth order.
2 (**Quaternary**) Geology of, relating to, or denoting the most recent period in the Cenozoic era, following the Tertiary period and comprising the Pleistocene and Holocene epochs.
3 Chemistry denoting an ammonium compound containing a cation of the form NR_4^+, where R represents organic groups or atoms other than hydrogen.
■ (of a carbon atom) bonded to four other carbon atoms.
▶ noun (**the Quaternary**) Geology the Quaternary period or the system of deposits laid down during it.

> The Quaternary began about 1,640,000 years ago and is still current. Humans and other mammals evolved into their present forms, and were strongly affected by the ice ages of the Pleistocene.

– ORIGIN late Middle English (as a noun denoting a set of four): from Latin *quaternarius*, from *quaterni* 'four at once', from *quater* 'four times', from *quattuor* 'four'.

quaternion /kwə'təːnɪən/ ▶ noun 1 Mathematics a complex number of the form $w + xi + yj + zk$, where w, x, y, z are real numbers and i, j, k are imaginary units that satisfy certain conditions.
2 rare a set of four people or things.
– ORIGIN mid 19th cent.: from late Latin *quaternio(n-)*, from Latin *quaterni* (see **QUATERNARY**).

quatorze /kə'tɔːz/ ▶ noun (in piquet) a set of four aces, kings, queens, jacks, or tens held in one hand.

– ORIGIN early 18th cent.: French, literally 'fourteen', from Latin *quattuordecim*.

quatrain /'kwɒtreɪn/ ▶ noun a stanza of four lines, especially one having alternate rhymes.
– ORIGIN late 16th cent.: from French, from *quatre* 'four'.

quatrefoil /'katrəfɔɪl/ ▶ noun an ornamental design of four lobes or leaves as used in architectural tracery, resembling a flower or clover leaf.
– ORIGIN late 15th cent.: from Anglo-Norman French, from Old French *quatre* 'four' + *foil* 'leaf'.

quattrocento /ˌkwatrə(ʊ)'tʃɛntəʊ/ ▶ noun (the **quattrocentro**) the 15th century as a period of Italian art or architecture.
– ORIGIN Italian, literally '400' (shortened from *milquattrocento* '1400'), used with reference to the years 1400–99.

quaver ▶ verb [no obj.] (of a person's voice) shake or tremble in speaking, typically through nervousness or emotion.
▶ noun 1 a shake or tremble in a person's voice.
2 Music, chiefly Brit. a note having the time value of an eighth of a semibreve or half a crotchet, represented by a large dot with a hooked stem. Also called **EIGHTH NOTE**.
– DERIVATIVES **quaveringly** adverb, **quavery** adjective.
– ORIGIN late Middle English (as a verb in the general sense 'tremble'): from dialect *quave* 'quake, tremble', probably from an Old English word related to **QUAKE**. The noun is first recorded (mid 16th cent.) as a musical term.

quay ▶ noun a stone or metal platform lying alongside or projecting into water for loading and unloading ships.
– DERIVATIVES **quayage** noun.
– ORIGIN late Middle English *key*, from Old French *kay*, of Celtic origin. The change of spelling in the late 17th cent. was influenced by the modern French spelling *quai*.

quayside ▶ noun a quay and the area around it.

Que. ▶ abbreviation for Quebec.

quean /kwiːn/ ▶ noun archaic an impudent or badly behaved girl or woman.
■ a prostitute.
– ORIGIN Old English *cwene* 'woman', of Germanic origin; related to Dutch *kween* 'barren cow', from an Indo-European root shared by Greek *gunē*.

queasy ▶ adjective (**queasier**, **queasiest**) nauseous; feeling sick: *in the morning he was still pale and queasy*.
■ inducing a feeling of nausea: *the queasy swell of the boat*. ■ figurative slightly nervous or worried about something.
– DERIVATIVES **queasily** adverb, **queasiness** noun.
– ORIGIN late Middle English *queisy*, *coisy* 'causing nausea', of uncertain origin; perhaps related to Old French *coisier* 'to hurt'.

Quebec /kwɪ'bɛk/ ▶ noun 1 a heavily forested province in eastern Canada; pop. 6,845,700 (1991). It was settled by the French in 1608, ceded to the British in 1763, and became one of the original four provinces in the Dominion of Canada in 1867. The majority of its residents are French-speaking and it is a focal point of the French-Canadian nationalist movement, which advocates independence for Quebec. French name **QUÉBEC** /kebɛk/.
■ (also **Quebec City**) its capital city, a port on the St Lawrence River; pop. 574,400 (1991). Founded in 1608, it is Canada's oldest city. It was captured from the French by a British force in 1759 after the battle of the Plains of Abraham, and became capital of Lower Canada (later Quebec) in 1791.
2 a code word representing the letter Q, used in radio communication.
– DERIVATIVES **Quebecker** (also **Quebecer**) noun.

quebracho /kɪ'brɑːtʃəʊ/ ▶ noun (pl. -os) a South American tree whose timber and bark are a rich source of tannin.
● Genera *Aspidosperma* (family Apocynaceae) and *Schinopsis* (family Anacardiaceae).
– ORIGIN late 19th cent.: from Spanish, from *quebrar* 'to break' + *hacha* 'axe'.

Quechua /'kɛtʃwə/ (also **Quecha** /'kɛtʃə/, **Quichua**) ▶ noun (pl. same or **Quechuas**) 1 a member of an American Indian people of Peru and parts of Bolivia, Chile, Colombia, and Ecuador.
2 [mass noun] the language or group of languages of this people, spoken by some 11 million people.
▶ adjective of or relating to this people or their language.

– DERIVATIVES **Quechuan** (also **Quechan**) adjective & noun.
– ORIGIN Spanish, from Quechua *ghechwa* 'temperate valleys'.

Queen, Ellery, American writer of detective novels; pseudonym of *Frederic Dannay* (1905–82) and *Manfred Lee* (1905–71). The novels feature a detective also called Ellery Queen.

queen ▶ noun 1 the female ruler of an independent state, especially one who inherits the position by right of birth.
■ (also **queen consort**) a king's wife. ■ a woman or thing regarded as excellent or outstanding of its kind: *the queen of the social columns | the Tourist's Guide to Islay, the Queen of the Hebrides*. ■ a woman or girl chosen to hold the most important position in a festival or event: *she's the official carnival queen*. ■ (**the Queen**) dated (in the UK) the national anthem when there is a female sovereign. ■ informal a man's wife or girlfriend.
2 the most powerful chess piece that each player has, able to move in any direction along a rank, file, or diagonal on which it stands.
3 a playing card bearing a representation of a queen, normally ranking next below a king and above a jack.
4 Entomology a reproductive female in a colony of social ants, bees, wasps, or termites.
5 an adult female cat that has not been spayed.
6 informal a male homosexual, typically one regarded as ostentatiously effeminate.
▶ verb [with obj.] **1** (**queen it over**) (of a woman) behave in an unpleasant and superior way towards.
2 Chess convert (a pawn) into a queen when it reaches the opponent's back rank on the board.
– DERIVATIVES **queendom** noun, **queen-like** adjective, **queenship** noun.
– ORIGIN Old English *cwēn*, of Germanic origin; related to **QUEAN**.

Queen Anne ▶ adjective denoting a style of English furniture or architecture characteristic of the early 18th century. The furniture is noted for its simple, proportioned style and for its cabriole legs and walnut veneer; the architecture is characterized by the use of red brick in simple, basically rectangular designs.

Queen Anne's Bounty ▶ noun [mass noun] historical duties called 'first fruits and tenths', payable originally to the Pope but made payable to the Crown by Henry VIII, and directed by Queen Anne in 1704 to be used to augment the livings of the poorer clergy.

Queen Anne's lace ▶ noun another term for **COW PARSLEY**.

queen bee ▶ noun the single reproductive female in a hive or colony of honeybees.
■ informal a woman who has a dominant or controlling position in a particular group or sphere.

queen cake ▶ noun a small, soft, typically heart-shaped currant cake.

Queen Charlotte Islands a group of more than 150 islands off the west coast of Canada, in British Columbia.

Queen City ▶ noun N. Amer. the pre-eminent city of a region.

queen consort ▶ noun see **QUEEN** (sense 1 of noun).

queen dowager ▶ noun the widow of a king.

queenfish ▶ noun (pl. same or **-fishes**) an edible marine fish, in particular:
● a popular sporting fish of the Indo-Pacific (*Chorinemus lysan*, family Carangidae). ● a drumfish of the Pacific coast of North America (*Seriphus politus*, family Sciaenidae).

queenie ▶ noun old-fashioned term for **QUEEN** (in sense 6).

Queen in Council ▶ noun (in the UK) the Privy Council as issuing Orders in Council or receiving petitions when the reigning monarch is a queen.

queenly ▶ adjective (**queenlier**, **queenliest**) fit for or appropriate to a queen.
– DERIVATIVES **queenliness** noun.

Queen Maud Land /mɔːd/ a part of Antarctica bordering the Atlantic Ocean, claimed since 1939 by Norway.
– ORIGIN named after *Queen Maud* of Norway (1869–1938).

queen mother ▶ **noun** the widow of a king and mother of the sovereign.

queen of puddings ▶ **noun** a pudding made with bread, jam, and meringue.

Queen of the May ▶ **noun** another term for **MAY QUEEN**.

queen post ▶ **noun** either of two upright timbers between the tie beam and principal rafters of a roof truss.

Queens a borough of New York City, at the western end of Long Island; pop. 1,951,600 (1990).

Queen's Award ▶ **noun** (in the UK) any of a number of annual awards given to firms for achievements in exporting goods or services or in advancing technology.

Queen's Bench (in full **Queen's Bench Division**) ▶ **noun** (in the UK) a division of the High Court of Justice.

Queensberry Rules /ˈkwiːnzb(ə)ri/ the standard rules of boxing, originally drawn up in 1867 to govern the sport in Britain.
■standard rules of polite or acceptable behaviour.
– ORIGIN late 19th cent.: named after John Sholto Douglas (1844–1900), 9th Marquess of *Queensberry*, who supervised the preparation of the rules.

queen's bishop ▶ **noun** Chess each player's bishop on the queen's side of the board at the start of a game.

Queen's bounty ▶ **noun** in the reign of a queen, the term for **KING'S BOUNTY**.

queen scallop ▶ **noun** a small edible European scallop.
● *Chlamys opercularis*, family Pectinidae.

Queen's Champion ▶ **noun** another term for **CHAMPION OF ENGLAND**.

Queen's colour ▶ **noun** (in the UK) a silk union flag carried by a particular regiment along with its regimental colour.

Queen's Counsel (abbrev.: **QC**) ▶ **noun** a senior barrister appointed on the recommendation of the Lord Chancellor.

Queen's County former name for **LAOIS**.

Queen's English ▶ **noun** [mass noun] (**the Queen's English**) the English language as written and spoken correctly by educated people in Britain.

Queen's evidence ▶ **noun** [mass noun] English Law evidence for the prosecution given by a participant in or accomplice to the crime being tried: *what happens if they* **turn Queen's evidence**?

Queen's Guide ▶ **noun** (in the UK) a Guide who has reached the highest rank of proficiency.

Queen's highway ▶ **noun** [mass noun] Brit. formal the public road network, regarded as being under royal protection.

queenside ▶ **noun** Chess the half of the board on which both queens stand at the start of a game (the left-hand side for White, right for Black).

queen-sized (also **queen-size**) ▶ **adjective** (especially of a commercial product) of a larger size than the standard but smaller than something that is king-sized: *queen-sized fitted sheets.*

queen's knight ▶ **noun** Chess each player's knight on the queen's side of the board at the start of a game.

Queensland a state comprising the NE part of Australia; pop. 2,921,700 (est. 1990); capital, Brisbane. Originally established in 1824 as a penal settlement, Queensland was constituted a separate colony in 1859, having previously formed part of New South Wales, and was federated with the other states of Australia in 1901.
– DERIVATIVES **Queenslander** noun.

Queensland blue ▶ **noun** Austral. **1** (also **Queensland blue heeler**) a cattle dog with a dark speckled body.
2 a pumpkin of a slaty-grey variety.

Queensland nut ▶ **noun** another term for **MACADAMIA**.

Queen's Messenger ▶ **noun** (in the UK) a courier in the diplomatic service, employed by the government to carry important official papers within Britain and abroad.

queen's pawn ▶ **noun** Chess the pawn occupying the square immediately in front of each player's queen at the start of a game.

Queen's Proctor ▶ **noun** Law (in the UK) an official who has the right to intervene in probate, divorce, and nullity cases when collusion or the suppression of facts is alleged.

queen's rook ▶ **noun** Chess each player's rook on the queen's side of the board at the start of a game.

Queen's Scout ▶ **noun** (in the UK) a Scout who has reached the highest standard of proficiency.

Queen's Speech ▶ **noun** (in the UK) a statement read by the sovereign at the opening of a new session of parliament, detailing the government's proposed legislative programme.

queensware ▶ **noun** [mass noun] a type of fine, cream-coloured Wedgwood pottery.
– ORIGIN mid 18th cent. (as *Queen's ware*): named in honour of Queen Charlotte (wife of George III), who had been presented with a set in 1765.

queer ▶ **adjective** **1** strange; odd: *she had a queer feeling that they were being watched.*
■[predic.] Brit. informal, dated slightly ill.
2 informal, offensive (of a man) homosexual.
▶ **noun** informal, offensive a homosexual man.
▶ **verb** [with obj.] informal spoil or ruin (an agreement, event, or situation): *Reg didn't want someone meddling and queering the deal at the last minute.*
– PHRASES **in Queer Street** Brit. informal, dated in difficulty, typically by being in debt. **queer someone's pitch** Brit. spoil someone's plans or chances of doing something, especially secretly or maliciously.
– DERIVATIVES **queerish** adjective, **queerly** adverb, **queerness** noun.
– ORIGIN early 16th cent.: considered to be from German *quer* 'oblique, perverse', but the origin is doubtful.

USAGE The word **queer** was first used to mean 'homosexual' in the early 20th century: it was originally, and usually still is, a deliberately offensive and aggressive term when used by heterosexual people. In recent years, however, gay people have taken the word **queer** and deliberately used it in place of **gay** or **homosexual**, in an attempt, by using the word positively, to deprive it of its negative power. This use of **queer** is now well established and widely used among gay people (especially as an adjective or noun modifier, as in *queer rights*; *queer bashing*) and at present exists alongside the other, deliberately offensive use.

quelea /ˈkwiːlɪə/ ▶ **noun** a brownish weaver bird found in Africa, the male of which has either a black face or a red head. Also called **DIOCH**.
● Genus *Quelea*, family Ploceidae: three species, in particular the **red-billed quelea** (*Q. quelea*), which occurs in huge numbers and is an important pest of crops.
– ORIGIN modern Latin, perhaps from medieval Latin *qualea* 'quail'.

quell ▶ **verb** [with obj.] put an end to (a rebellion or other disorder), typically by the use of force: *extra police were called to quell the disturbance.*
■subdue or silence someone: *Connor quelled him with a look.* ■ suppress (a feeling, especially an unpleasant one): *he spoke up again to quell any panic among the assembled youngsters.*
– DERIVATIVES **queller** noun.
– ORIGIN Old English *cwellan* 'kill', of Germanic origin; related to Dutch *kwellen* and German *quälen*.

quench ▶ **verb** [with obj.] **1** satisfy (one's thirst) by drinking.
■satisfy (a desire): *he only pursued her to quench an aching need.*
2 extinguish (a fire): *firemen hauled on hoses in a desperate bid to quench the flames.*
■stifle or suppress (a feeling): *fury rose in him, but he quenched it.* ■ dated reduce (someone) to silence: *she quenched Anne by a curt command to hold her tongue.* ■ rapidly cool (red-hot metal or other material), especially in cold water or oil. ■ Physics & Electronics suppress or damp (an effect such as luminescence, or an oscillation or discharge).
▶ **noun** an act of quenching something very hot.
– DERIVATIVES **quenchable** adjective, **quencher** noun (chiefly Physics & Metallurgy), **quenchless** adjective (poetic/literary).
– ORIGIN Old English *-cwencan* (in *acwencan* 'put out, extinguish'), of Germanic origin.

quenelle /kəˈnɛl/ ▶ **noun** (usu. **quenelles**) a small seasoned ball of pounded fish or meat.
– ORIGIN French, probably from Alsatian German *knödel*.

quercetin /ˈkwəːsɪtɪn/ ▶ **noun** [mass noun] Chemistry a yellow crystalline pigment present in plants, used as a food supplement to reduce allergic responses or boost immunity.
● A flavone derivative; chem. formula: $C_{15}H_{10}O_7$.
– ORIGIN mid 19th cent.: probably from Latin *quercetum* 'oak grove' (from *quercus* 'oak') + **-IN**[1].

Quercia, Jacopo della, see **DELLA QUERCIA**.

querencia /kɛˈrɛnθɪə, Spanish keˈrenθja, -sja/ ▶ **noun** the part of a bullring where the bull takes its stand.
■a person's or animal's home ground; a refuge.
– ORIGIN Spanish, literally 'lair, home ground', from *querer* 'desire, love', from Latin *quaerere* 'seek'.

Querétaro /kɛˈrɛtərəʊ/ a state of central Mexico.
■its capital city; pop. 454,050 (1990). In 1847 it was the scene of the signing of the treaty ending the US–Mexican war.

querist /ˈkwɪərɪst/ ▶ **noun** chiefly archaic a person who asks questions; a questioner.
– ORIGIN mid 17th cent.: from Latin *quaerere* 'ask' + **-IST**.

quern /kwəːn/ ▶ **noun** a simple hand mill for grinding corn, typically consisting of two circular stones, the upper of which is rotated or rubbed to and fro on the lower one.
– ORIGIN Old English *cweorn(e)*, of Germanic origin; related to Old Norse *kvern* and Dutch *kweern*.

quernstone ▶ **noun** chiefly Archaeology either of the two circular stones forming a quern, found at prehistoric sites from the Neolithic onwards.

querulous /ˈkwɛrʊləs, ˈkwɛrjʊləs/ ▶ **adjective** complaining in a rather petulant or whining manner: *she became querulous and demanding.*
– DERIVATIVES **querulously** adverb, **querulousness** noun.
– ORIGIN late 15th cent.: from late Latin *querulosus*, from Latin *querulus*, from *queri* 'complain'.

query ▶ **noun** (pl. **-ies**) a question, especially one addressed to an official or organization: *if you have any queries please telephone our office.*
■used in writing or speaking to question the accuracy of a following statement or to introduce a question.
■ chiefly Printing a question mark.
▶ **verb** (**-ies**, **-ied**) [reporting verb] ask a question about something, especially in order to express one's doubts about it or to check its validity or accuracy: [with clause] *many people queried whether any harm had been done* | [with obj.] *I rang the water company to query my bill* | [with direct speech] *'Why not?' he queried.*
■[with obj.] chiefly US put a question or questions to (someone): *when these officers were queried, they felt unhappy.*
– ORIGIN mid 17th cent.: Anglicized form of the Latin imperative *quaere!*, used in the 16th cent. in English as a verb in the sense 'inquire' and as a noun meaning 'query', from Latin *quaerere* 'ask, seek'.

query language ▶ **noun** [mass noun] Computing a language for the specification of procedures for the retrieval (and sometimes also modification) of information from a database.

quesadilla /ˌkeɪsəˈdiːljə, -ˈdiːjə/ ▶ **noun** a tortilla filled with cheese and heated.
– ORIGIN Spanish.

quest ▶ **noun** a long or arduous search for something: *the* **quest for** *a reliable vaccine has intensified.*
■(in medieval romance) an expedition made by a knight to accomplish a prescribed task.
▶ **verb** [no obj.] search for something: *he was a real scientist, questing after truth.*
■[with obj.] poetic/literary search for; seek out.
– DERIVATIVES **quester** (also **questor**) noun, **questingly** adverb.
– ORIGIN late Middle English: from Old French *queste* (noun), *quester* (verb), based on Latin *quaerere* 'ask, seek'. See also **INQUEST**.

question ▶ **noun** a sentence worded or expressed so as to elicit information: *we hope this leaflet has been helpful in answering your questions.*
■a doubt about the truth or validity of something: *there was no question that the West Indies were now the outstanding team in the world.* ■ [mass noun] the raising of a doubt about or objection to something: *Edward was the only one she obeyed* **without question** | *her loyalty is really* **beyond question**. ■ a matter forming the basis of a problem requiring resolution: *we have kept an eye on the question of political authority.* ■ a matter or concern depending on or involving a specified condition or thing: *it was not simply* **a question of** *age and hierarchy.*
▶ **verb** [with obj.] ask questions of (someone), especially in an official context: *four men were being questioned*

q

about the killings | [as noun **questioning**] *the young lieutenant escorted us to the barracks for questioning.*
▪feel or express doubt about; raise objections to: *members had questioned the cost of the scheme.*
– PHRASES **be a question of time** be certain to happen sooner or later. **bring something into question** raise an issue for further consideration or discussion: *technology had brought into question the whole future of work.* **come into question** become an issue for further consideration or discussion: *our Sunday Trading laws have come into question.* **in question 1** being considered or discussed: *on the day in question, there were several serious emergencies.* **2** in doubt: *all of the old certainties are in question.* **no question of** no possibility of. **out of the question** too impracticable or unlikely to merit discussion. **put the question** (in a formal debate or meeting) require supporters and opponents of a proposal to record their votes.
– DERIVATIVES **questioner** noun, **questioningly** adverb.
– ORIGIN late Middle English: from Old French *question* (noun), *questionner* (verb), from Latin *quaestio(n-)*, from *quaerere* 'ask, seek'.

questionable ▶ **adjective** doubtful as regards truth or quality: [with clause] *it is questionable whether any of these exceptions is genuine.*
▪not clearly in accordance with honesty, honour, or wisdom: *a few men of allegedly questionable character.*
– DERIVATIVES **questionability** noun, **questionableness** noun, **questionably** adverb.

questionary ▶ **noun** (pl. **-ies**) chiefly Medicine a questionnaire.
– ORIGIN late 19th cent.: from French *questionnaire* (see **QUESTIONNAIRE**).

question mark ▶ **noun** a punctuation mark (?) indicating a question.
▪figurative used to express doubt or uncertainty about something: *there's a question mark over his future.*

question master ▶ **noun** Brit. a person who presides over a quiz or panel game.

questionnaire /ˌkwɛstʃəˈnɛː, ˌkɛstjə-/ ▶ **noun** a set of printed or written questions with a choice of answers, devised for the purposes of a survey or statistical study.
– ORIGIN late 19th cent.: from French, from *questionner* 'to question'.

question time ▶ **noun** (in the UK) a period during parliamentary proceedings in the House of Commons when MPs may question ministers.

Quetta /ˈkwɛtə/ a city in western Pakistan, the capital of Baluchistan province; pop. 350,000 (est. 1991).

quetzal /ˈkɛts(ə)l, ˈkwɛt-/ ▶ **noun 1** a bird of the trogon family, with iridescent green plumage and typically red underparts, found in the forests of tropical America.
• Genus *Pharomachrus*, family Trogonidae: five species, especially the **resplendent quetzal** (*P. mocinno*), the male of which has very long tail coverts and was venerated by the Aztecs.
2 the basic monetary unit of Guatemala, equal to 100 centavos.
– ORIGIN early 19th cent. (in sense 1): from Spanish, from Aztec *quetzalli* 'brightly coloured tail feather'.

Quetzalcóatl /ˌkɛts(ə)lkəʊˈat(ə)l/ the plumed serpent god of the Toltec and Aztec civilizations.

quetzalcoatlus /ˌkwɛts(ə)lkəʊˈatləs/ ▶ **noun** a giant pterosaur of the late Cretaceous period, which was the largest ever flying animal with a wingspan of up to 15 m.
• Genus *Quetzalcoatlus*, family Azhdarchidae, order Pterosauria.
– ORIGIN modern Latin, from the name of the Aztec god **QUETZALCÓATL**.

queue ▶ **noun 1** a line or sequence of people or vehicles awaiting their turn to be attended to or to proceed.
▪Computing a list of data items, commands, etc., stored so as to be retrievable in a definite order, usually the order of insertion.
2 archaic a plait of hair worn at the back.
▶ **verb** (**queues**, **queued**, **queuing** or **queueing**) [no obj.] take one's place in a queue: *in the war they had queued for food* | [with infinitive] figurative *companies are queuing up to move to the bay.*
▪[with obj.] Computing arrange in a queue.
– ORIGIN late 16th cent. (as a heraldic term denoting the tail of an animal): from French, based on Latin *cauda* 'tail'. Compare with **CUE**[2]. Sense 1 dates from the mid 19th cent.

queue-jump ▶ **verb** [no obj.] Brit. move forward out of turn in a queue or waiting list.
– DERIVATIVES **queue-jumper** noun.

Quezon City /ˈkeɪzɒn/ a city on the island of Luzon in the northern Philippines; pop. 1,667,000 (1990). It was established in 1940 and from 1948 to 1976 it was the capital of the Philippines.
– ORIGIN named after Manuel Luis *Quezon* (1878–1944), the first President of the republic.

Qufu /tʃuːˈfuː/ a small town in Shandong province in eastern China, where Confucius was born in 551 BC and lived for much of his life.

quibble ▶ **noun 1** a slight objection or criticism: *the only quibble about this book is the price.*
2 a play on words; a pun.
▶ **verb** [no obj.] argue or raise objections about a trivial matter: *they are always quibbling about the amount they are prepared to pay.*
– DERIVATIVES **quibbler** noun, **quibblingly** adverb.
– ORIGIN early 17th cent. (in the sense 'play on words, pun'): diminutive of obsolete *quib* 'a petty objection', probably from Latin *quibus*, dative and ablative plural of *qui, quae, quod* 'who, what, which', frequently used in legal documents and so associated with subtle distinctions or verbal niceties.

Quiché /kiːˈtʃeɪ/ ▶ **noun** (pl. same or **Quichés**) **1** a member of a people inhabiting the western highlands of Guatemala.
2 [mass noun] the Mayan language of this people, with around 800,000 speakers.
▶ **adjective** of or relating to this people or their language.
– ORIGIN the name in Quiché.

quiche /kiːʃ/ ▶ **noun** a baked flan or tart with a savoury filling thickened with eggs, usually eaten cold.
– ORIGIN French, from Alsatian dialect *Küchen*; related to German *Kuchen* 'cake'.

Quichua /ˈkɪtʃwə/ ▶ **noun** & **adjective** variant spelling of **QUECHUA**.

quick ▶ **adjective 1** moving fast or doing something in a short time: *some children are particularly quick learners* | *I was much quicker than him and held him at bay for several laps* | [with infinitive] *he was always quick to point out her faults.*
▪lasting or taking a short time: *she took a quick look through the drawers* | *we went to the pub for a quick drink* ▪ happening with little or no delay; prompt: *children like to see quick results from their efforts.*
2 (of a person) prompt to understand, think, or learn; intelligent: *it was quick of him to spot the mistake.*
▪(of a person's eye or ear) keenly perceptive; alert. ▪ (of a person's temper) easily roused.
▶ **adverb** informal at a fast rate; quickly: *he'll find some place where he can make money quicker* | [as exclamation] *Get out, quick!*
▶ **noun 1** (**the quick**) the soft tender flesh below the growing part of a fingernail or toenail.
▪figurative the central or most sensitive part of someone or something.
2 [as plural noun **the quick**] archaic those who are living: *the quick and the dead.*
3 Cricket, informal a fast bowler.
– PHRASES **be quick off the mark** see **MARK**[1]. **cut someone to the quick** cause someone deep distress by a hurtful remark or action. **(as) quick as a flash** see **FLASH**[1]. **quick on the draw** see **DRAW**. **a quick one** informal a rapidly consumed alcoholic drink. **quick with child** archaic at a stage of pregnancy when movements of the fetus have been felt.
– DERIVATIVES **quickly** adverb, **quickness** noun.
– ORIGIN Old English *cwic, cwicu* 'alive, animated, alert', of Germanic origin; related to Dutch *kwiek* 'sprightly' and German *keck* 'saucy', from an Indo-European root shared by Latin *vivus* 'alive' and Greek *bios, zōē* 'life'.

quick and dirty ▶ **adjective** informal, chiefly US makeshift; done or produced hastily: *a quick and dirty synopsis of their work.*

quickbeam ▶ **noun** another term for **MOUNTAIN ASH** (in sense 1).
– ORIGIN Old English, apparently from **QUICK** (although the sense of the adjective is unclear) + **BEAM**.

quicken ▶ **verb 1** make or become faster or quicker: [with obj.] *she quickened her pace, desperate to escape* | [no obj.] *I felt my pulse quicken.*
2 [no obj.] spring to life; become animated: *her interest quickened* | [as adj. **quickening**] *he looked with quickening curiosity through the smoke.*
▪[with obj.] stimulate: *the coroner's words suddenly quickened his own memories.* ▪ [with obj.] give or restore life to: *on the third day after his death the human body of Jesus was quickened by the Spirit.* ▪ archaic (of a woman) reach a stage in pregnancy when movements of the fetus can be felt. ▪ archaic (of a fetus) begin to show signs of life. ▪ [with obj.] archaic make (a fire) burn brighter.

quick-fire ▶ **adjective** [attrib.] (especially of something said in dialogue or done in a sequence) unhesitating and rapid: *he scored quick-fire goals.*
▪(of a gun) able to fire shots in rapid succession.

quick fix ▶ **noun** a speedy solution to a problem, recognized as being inadequate in the long term.

quick-freeze ▶ **verb** [with obj.] freeze (food) rapidly so as to preserve its nutritional value.

quickie informal ▶ **noun 1** a thing done or made quickly or hastily, in particular:
▪a rapidly consumed alcoholic drink. ▪ a brief act of sexual intercourse.
2 Cricket a fast bowler.
▶ **adjective** done or made quickly: *his wife cooperated with a quickie divorce.*

quicklime ▶ **noun** see **LIME**[1].

quick march ▶ **noun** a brisk military march.
▶ **exclamation** a command to begin marching quickly.

quick-release ▶ **adjective** (of a device) designed for rapid release: *a quick-release button.*

quicksand ▶ **noun** [mass noun] (also **quicksands**) loose wet sand that yields easily to pressure and sucks in anything resting on or falling into it: *her arm was grabbed, and slowly she was pulled from the quicksand* | figurative *John found himself sinking fast in financial quicksand.*

quickset ▶ **noun** [mass noun] Brit. hedging, especially of hawthorn, grown from slips or cuttings.

quicksilver ▶ **noun** [mass noun] the liquid metal mercury.
▪used in similes and metaphors to describe something that moves or changes very quickly, or that is difficult to hold or contain: *his mood changed like quicksilver.*

quickstep ▶ **noun** a fast foxtrot in 4/4 time.
▶ **verb** (**-stepped**, **-stepping**) [no obj.] dance the quickstep.

quick-tempered ▶ **adjective** easily made angry.

quickthorn ▶ **noun** another term for **HAWTHORN**.

quick time ▶ **noun** [mass noun] Military marching that is conducted at about 120 paces per minute.

quick trick ▶ **noun** (usu. **quick tricks**) Bridge a card such as an ace (or a king in a suit where the ace is also held) that can normally be relied on to win a trick.

quick-witted ▶ **adjective** showing or characterized by an ability to think or respond quickly or effectively.
– DERIVATIVES **quick-wittedness** noun.

Quicunque vult /kwiːˈkʊŋkweɪ ˌvʊlt/ ▶ **noun** another term for **ATHANASIAN CREED**.
– ORIGIN from Latin *quicunque vult* (*salvus esse*) 'whosoever wishes (to be saved)', the opening words of the creed.

quid[1] ▶ **noun** (pl. same) Brit. informal one pound sterling: *we paid him four hundred quid.*
– PHRASES **not the full quid** Austral./NZ informal not very intelligent. **quids in** Brit. informal in a position where one has profited or is likely to profit from something.
– ORIGIN late 17th cent. (denoting a sovereign): of obscure origin.

quid[2] ▶ **noun** a lump of tobacco for chewing.
– ORIGIN early 18th cent.: variant of **CUD**.

quiddity /ˈkwɪdɪti/ ▶ **noun** (pl. **-ies**) [mass noun] chiefly Philosophy the inherent nature or essence of someone or something.
▪[count noun] a distinctive feature; a peculiarity: *his quirks and quiddities.*
– ORIGIN late Middle English: from medieval Latin *quidditas*, from Latin *quid* 'what'.

quidnunc /ˈkwɪdnʌŋk/ ▶ **noun** archaic an inquisitive and gossipy person.
– ORIGIN early 18th cent.: from Latin *quid nunc?* 'what now?'.

q

quid pro quo /ˌkwɪd prəʊ ˈkwəʊ/ ▶ **noun** (pl. **-os**) a favour or advantage granted in return for something: *the pardon was a quid pro quo for their help in releasing hostages.*
– ORIGIN mid 16th cent. (denoting a medicine substituted for another): Latin, 'something for something'.

quiescent /kwɪˈɛs(ə)nt, kwʌɪ-/ ▶ **adjective** in a state or period of inactivity or dormancy: *strikes were headed by groups of workers who had previously been quiescent | quiescent ulcerative colitis.*
– DERIVATIVES **quiescence** noun, **quiescently** adverb.
– ORIGIN mid 17th cent.: from Latin *quiescent-* 'being still', from the verb *quiescere*, from *quies* 'quiet'.

quiet ▶ **adjective** (**quieter**, **quietest**) **1** making little or no noise: *the car has a quiet, economical engine | I was as quiet as I could be, but he knew I was there.*
■(of a place, period of time, or situation) without much activity, disturbance, or excitement: *the street below was quiet, little traffic braving the snow.* ■ without being disturbed or interrupted: *all he wanted was a quiet drink.*
2 carried out discreetly, secretly, or with moderation: *we wanted a quiet wedding | I'll have a quiet word with him.*
■(of a person) tranquil and reserved by nature; not brash or forceful: *his quiet, middle-aged parents.* ■ [attrib.] expressed in a restrained or understated way: *Molly spoke with quiet confidence.* ■ (of a colour or garment) unobtrusive; not bright or showy.
▶ **noun** [mass noun] absence of noise or bustle; silence; calm: *the ringing of the telephone shattered the early morning quiet.*
■freedom from disturbance or interruption by others: *he understood her wish for **peace and quiet**.* ■ a peaceful or settled state of affairs in social or political life: *after several months of comparative quiet, the scandal re-erupted in August.*
▶ **verb** chiefly N. Amer. make or become silent, calm, or still: [with obj.] *there are ways of **quieting** kids **down** |* [no obj.] *the journalists **quieted down** as Judy stepped on to the dias.*
– PHRASES **do anything for a quiet life** see **LIFE**. **keep quiet** (or **keep someone quiet**) refrain or prevent someone from speaking or from disclosing something secret. **keep something quiet** (or **keep quiet about something**) refrain from disclosing information about something; keep something secret. **on the quiet** informal without anyone knowing or noticing; secretly or unobtrusively. **(as) quiet as the grave** see **GRAVE**[1]. **(as) quiet as a mouse** (or **lamb**) (of a person or animal) extremely quiet or docile.
– DERIVATIVES **quietly** adverb, **quietness** noun.
– ORIGIN Middle English (originally as a noun denoting peace as opposed to war): via Old French, based on Latin *quies, quiet-* 'repose, quiet'.

quieten ▶ **verb** chiefly Brit. make or become quiet and calm: [with obj.] *her mother was trying to quieten her |* [no obj.] *things seemed to have **quietened down**.*

quietism ▶ **noun** [mass noun] (in the Christian faith) devotional contemplation and abandonment of the will as a form of religious mysticism.
■calm acceptance of things as they are without attempts to resist or change them: *political quietism.*
– DERIVATIVES **quietist** noun & adjective, **quietistic** adjective.
– ORIGIN late 17th cent. (denoting the religious mysticism based on the teachings of the Spanish priest Miguel de Molinos (*c.*1640–97)): from Italian *quietismo*, based on Latin *quies, quiet-* 'quiet'.

quietude ▶ **noun** [mass noun] a state of stillness, calmness, and quiet in a person or place.
– ORIGIN late 16th cent.: from French *quiétude* or medieval Latin *quietudo*, from Latin *quietus* 'quiet'.

quietus /kwʌɪˈiːtəs/ ▶ **noun** (pl. **quietuses**) death or something that causes death, regarded as a release from life.
■archaic something that has a calming or soothing effect.
– ORIGIN late Middle English: abbreviation of medieval Latin *quietus est* 'he is quit' (see **QUIT**[1]), originally used as a form of receipt or discharge on payment of a debt.

quiff ▶ **noun** chiefly Brit. a piece of hair, especially on a man, brushed upwards and backwards from the forehead.
– ORIGIN late 19th cent. (originally denoting a lock of hair plastered down on the forehead, especially as worn by soldiers): of unknown origin.

quill ▶ **noun 1** (also **quill feather**) any of the main wing or tail feathers of a bird.
■the hollow shaft of a feather, especially the lower part or calamus that lacks barbs. ■ (also **quill pen**) a pen made from a main wing or tail feather of a large bird by pointing and slitting the end of the shaft.
2 an object in the form of a thin tube, in particular:
■the hollow sharp spines of a porcupine, hedgehog, or other spiny mammal. ■ (**quills**) another term for **PENNE**. ■ (**quills**) US informal, dated pan pipes.
▶ **verb** [with obj.] form (fabric) into small cylindrical folds.
– ORIGIN late Middle English (in the senses 'hollow stem' and 'shaft of a feather'): probably from Middle Low German *quiele*.

quilling ▶ **noun** a piece of quilled lace or other fabric used as a trim.
■[mass noun] N. Amer. a type of ornamental craftwork involving the shaping of paper, fabric, or glass into delicate pleats or folds.

quillwork ▶ **noun** [mass noun] a type of decoration for clothing and possessions characteristic of certain North American Indian peoples, using softened and dyed porcupine quills to make elaborate applied designs.

quillwort ▶ **noun** a plant related to the clubmosses, with a dense rosette of long slender leaves, the bases of which contain the spore-producing organs, occurring typically as a submerged aquatic.
● Genus *Isoetes*, family Isoetaceae, class Lycopsida.

quilt[1] ▶ **noun** a warm bed covering made of padding enclosed between layers of fabric and kept in place by lines of stitching, typically applied in a decorative design.
■a knitted or fabric bedspread with decorative stitching. ■ a layer of padding used for insulation.
▶ **verb** [with obj.] join together (layers of fabric or padding) with lines of stitching to form a bed covering, a warm garment, or for decorative effect.
– DERIVATIVES **quilter** noun.
– ORIGIN Middle English: from Old French *cuilte*, from Latin *culcita* 'mattress, cushion'.

quilt[2] ▶ **verb** [with obj.] Austral. informal punch (someone).
– ORIGIN mid 19th cent.: perhaps a transferred use of the verb **QUILT**[1] (with the association of quilting for protection).

quilted ▶ **adjective** (of a garment, bed covering, or sleeping bag) made of two layers of cloth filled with padding held in place by lines of stitching: *a blue quilted jacket.*
■(of an item of furniture) covered in padded fabric made in this way: *she sank on to the quilted bench.*

quilting ▶ **noun** [mass noun] the making of quilts as a craft or leisure activity.
■the work so produced; quilted material. ■ the pattern of stitching used for such work.

quim ▶ **noun** Brit. vulgar slang a woman's genitals.
– ORIGIN mid 18th cent.: of unknown origin.

quin ▶ **noun** informal, chiefly Brit. short for **QUINTUPLET**.

quinacridone /kwɪˈnakrɪdəʊn/ ▶ **noun** Chemistry any of a group of synthetic organic compounds whose molecules contain three benzene and two pyridine rings arranged alternately. They include a number of red to violet pigments.
– ORIGIN early 20th cent.: from *quin(oline)* + *acrid(ine)* + **-ONE**.

quinacrine /ˈkwɪnəkriːn, -krɪn/ ▶ **noun** [mass noun] Medicine a synthetic compound derived from acridine, used as an anthelmintic and antimalarial drug.
■(in full **quinacrine mustard**) Biochemistry a nitrogen mustard derived from this, used as a fluorescent stain for chromosomes.
– ORIGIN 1930s: blend of **QUININE** and **ACRIDINE**.

quinary /ˈkwʌɪnəri/ ▶ **adjective** of or relating to the number five, in particular:
■of the fifth order or rank. ■ Zoology, historical relating to or denoting a former system of classification in which the animal kingdom is divided into five subkingdoms, and each subkingdom into five classes.
– ORIGIN early 17th cent.: from Latin *quinarius*, from *quini* 'five at once, a set of five', from *quinque* 'five'.

quince ▶ **noun 1** a hard, acid pear-shaped fruit used in preserves or as flavouring.
2 the shrub or small tree which bears this fruit, native to western Asia.
● *Cydonia oblonga*, family Rosaceae.
■(**Japanese quince**) another term for **JAPONICA**.
– ORIGIN Middle English (originally a collective plural): from Old French *cooin*, from Latin (*malum*) *cotoneum*, variant of (*malum*) *cydonium* 'apple of *Cydonia* (= Chania, in Crete)'.

quincentenary /ˌkwɪnsɛnˈtiːn(ə)ri, -ˈtɛn-/ ▶ **noun** (pl. **-ies**) the five-hundredth anniversary of a significant event.
▶ **adjective** of or relating to such an anniversary.
– ORIGIN late 19th cent.: from Latin *quinque* 'five' + **CENTENARY**.

quincentennial ▶ **noun** & **adjective** another term for **QUINCENTENARY**.

Quincey, Thomas De, see **DE QUINCEY**.

quincunx /ˈkwɪnkʌŋks/ ▶ **noun** (pl. **quincunxes**) **1** an arrangement of five objects with four at the corners of a square or rectangle and the fifth at its centre, used for the five on a dice or playing card, and in planting trees.
2 [mass noun] Astrology an aspect of 150°, equivalent to five zodiacal signs.
– DERIVATIVES **quincuncial** adjective, **quincuncially** adverb.
– ORIGIN mid 17th cent.: from Latin, literally 'five twelfths', from *quinque* 'five' + *uncia* 'twelfth'.

Quine /kwʌɪn/, Willard Van Orman (b.1908), American philosopher and logician. A radical critic of modern empiricism, Quine took issue with the philosophy of language proposed by Rudolf Carnap, arguing that 'no statement is immune from revision' and that even the principles of logic themselves can be questioned and replaced. In *Word and Object* (1961) he held that there is no such thing as satisfactory translation.

quinella /kwɪˈnɛlə/ ▶ **noun** a bet in which the first two places in a race must be predicted, but not necessarily in the correct order. Compare with **PERFECTA**.
– ORIGIN 1940s (originally US): from Latin American Spanish *quiniela*.

quinidine /ˈkwɪnɪdiːn/ ▶ **noun** [mass noun] Medicine a compound obtained from cinchona bark and used to treat irregularities of heart rhythm. It is an isomer of quinine.
– ORIGIN mid 19th cent.: from Spanish *quina* 'cinchona bark' (from Quechua *kina* 'bark') + **-IDE** + **-INE**[4].

quinine /ˈkwɪniːn, kwɪˈniːn/ ▶ **noun** [mass noun] a bitter crystalline compound present in cinchona bark, used as a tonic and formerly as an antimalarial drug.
● An alkaloid; chem formula: $C_{20}H_{24}N_2O_2$.
– ORIGIN early 19th cent.: from Spanish *quina* 'cinchona bark' (from Quechua *kina* 'bark') + **-INE**[4].

quinoa /ˈkiːnəʊə, kwɪˈnəʊə/ ▶ **noun** [mass noun] a goosefoot found in the Andes, where it was widely cultivated for its edible starchy seeds prior to the introduction of Old World grains.
● *Chenopodium quinoa*, family Chenopodiaceae.
■the grain-like seeds of this plant, used as food and in the production of alcoholic drinks.
– ORIGIN early 17th cent.: Spanish spelling of Quechua *kinua, kinoa*.

quinoline /ˈkwɪnəliːn/ ▶ **noun** [mass noun] Chemistry a pungent oily liquid present in coal tar and bone oil.
● A heteroaromatic compound with fused benzene and pyridine rings; chem. formula: C_9H_7N.
– ORIGIN mid 19th cent.: from Spanish *quina* (see **QUININE**) + **-OL** + **-INE**[4].

quinone /ˈkwɪnəʊn, kwɪˈnəʊn/ ▶ **noun** [mass noun] Chemistry another term for 1,4-benzoquinone (see **BENZOQUINONE**).
■[count noun] any compound with the same ring structure as 1,4-benzoquinone.
– ORIGIN mid 19th cent.: from Spanish *quina* (see **QUININE**) + **-ONE**.

quinquagenarian /ˌkwɪŋkwədʒɪˈnɛːrɪən/ ▶ **noun** a person who is between 50 and 59 years old.
– ORIGIN early 19th cent.: from Latin *quinquagenarius* (based on *quinquaginti* 'fifty') + **-AN**.

Quinquagesima /ˌkwɪŋkwəˈdʒɛsɪmə/ (also **Quinquagesima Sunday**) ▶ **noun** the Sunday before the beginning of Lent.
– ORIGIN from medieval Latin, feminine of Latin *quinquagesimus* 'fiftieth', on the pattern of *Quadragesima* (because it is ten days before the forty penitential days of Lent).

quinque- ▶ **combining form** five; having five: *quinquevalent.*
– ORIGIN from Latin *quinque* 'five'.

q

quinquennial /kwɪŋˈkwɛnɪəl/ ▶ **adjective** recurring every five years.
▪ lasting for or relating to a period of five years.
– DERIVATIVES **quinquennially** adverb.
– ORIGIN late 15th cent. (in the sense 'lasting five years'): from Latin *quinquennis* (from *quinque* 'five' + *annus* 'year') + **-AL**.

quinquennium /kwɪŋˈkwɛnɪəm/ ▶ **noun** (pl. **quinquennia** /-nɪə/ or **quinquenniums**) a specified period of five years.
– ORIGIN early 17th cent.: from Latin, from *quinque* 'five' + *annus* 'year'.

quinquereme /ˈkwɪŋkwɪˌriːm/ ▶ **noun** an ancient Roman or Greek galley of a kind believed to have had three banks of oars, the oars in the top two banks being rowed by pairs of oarsmen and the oars in the bottom bank being rowed by single oarsmen.
– ORIGIN mid 16th cent.: from Latin *quinqueremis*, from *quinque* 'five' + *remus* 'oar'.

quinquevalent /ˌkwɪnkwɪˈveɪl(ə)nt/ ▶ **adjective** Chemistry another term for **PENTAVALENT**.

quinsy /ˈkwɪnzi/ ▶ **noun** [mass noun] inflammation of the throat, especially an abscess in the region of the tonsils.
– ORIGIN Middle English: from Old French *quinencie*, from medieval Latin *quinancia*, from Greek *kunankhē* 'canine quinsy', from *kun-* 'dog' + *ankhein* 'throttle'.

quint /kɪnt, kwɪnt/ ▶ **noun 1** (in piquet) a sequence of five cards of the same suit. A run of ace, king, queen, jack, and ten is a **quint major** and one of jack, ten, nine, eight, and seven a **quint minor**. [ORIGIN: late 17th cent.: from French, from Latin *quintus* 'fifth', from *quinque* 'five'.]
2 N. Amer. short for **QUINTUPLET**.

quinta /ˈkwɪntə, ˈkɪntə/ ▶ **noun** (in Spain, Portugal, and Latin America) a large house in the country or on the outskirts of a town.
▪ a country estate, in particular a wine-growing estate in Portugal.
– ORIGIN Spanish and Portuguese, from *quinta parte* 'fifth part' (originally referring to the amount of a farm's produce paid in rent).

quintain /ˈkwɪntɪn/ ▶ **noun** historical a post set up as a mark in tilting with a lance, typically with a sandbag attached that would swing round and strike an unsuccessful tilter.
▪ (**the quintain**) the medieval military exercise of tilting at such a post.
– ORIGIN late Middle English: from Old French *quintaine*, perhaps based on Latin *quintana*, a street in a Roman camp separating the fifth and sixth maniples, where military exercises were performed (from *quintus* 'fifth').

quintal /ˈkwɪnt(ə)l/ ▶ **noun** a unit of weight equal to a hundredweight (112 lb) or formerly, 100 lb.
▪ a unit of weight equal to 100 kg.
– ORIGIN late Middle English: via Old French from medieval Latin *quintale*, from Arabic *ḳinṭār*, based on Latin *centenarius* 'containing a hundred'.

Quintana Roo /kiːnˌtɑːnə ˈrəʊ/ a state of SE Mexico, on the Yucatán Peninsula; capital, Chetumal.

quinte /kɑ̃t/ ▶ **noun** Fencing the fifth of eight parrying positions.
– ORIGIN early 18th cent.: French, from Latin *quintus* 'fifth', from *quinque* 'five'.

quintessence /kwɪnˈtɛs(ə)ns/ ▶ **noun** the most perfect or typical example of a quality or class: *he was the quintessence of political professionalism.*
▪ the aspect of something regarded as the intrinsic and central constituent of its character: *we were all brought up to believe that advertising is the quintessence of marketing.* ▪ [count noun] a refined essence or extract of a substance. ▪ (in classical and medieval philosophy) a fifth substance in addition to the four elements, thought to compose the heavenly bodies and to be latent in all things.
– ORIGIN late Middle English (as a term in philosophy): via French from medieval Latin *quinta essentia* 'fifth essence'.

quintessential /ˌkwɪntɪˈsɛnʃ(ə)l/ ▶ **adjective** representing the most perfect or typical example of a quality or class: *he was the quintessential tough guy—strong, silent, and self-contained.*
– DERIVATIVES **quintessentially** adverb.

quintet ▶ **noun** a group of five people playing music or singing together.
▪ a musical composition for such a group. ▪ any group of five people or things: *a novel about a quintet of interrelated lovers.*
– ORIGIN late 18th cent.: from French *quintette* or Italian *quintetto*, from *quinto* 'fifth', from Latin *quintus*.

quintile /ˈkwɪntɪl, -ʌɪl/ ▶ **noun 1** Statistics any of five equal groups into which a population can be divided according to the distribution of values of a particular variable.
▪ each of the four values of the random variable which divide a population into five such groups.
2 [mass noun] Astrology an aspect of 72° (one fifth of a circle).
– ORIGIN early 17th cent.: from Latin *quintilis* (*mensis*) 'fifth month, July', from *quintus* 'fifth'.

Quintilian /kwɪnˈtɪlɪən/ (*c.*35–*c.*96 AD), Roman rhetorician; Latin name *Marcus Fabius Quintilianus*. He is best known for his *Education of an Orator*, a comprehensive treatment of the art of rhetoric and the training of an orator.

quintillion /kwɪnˈtɪljən/ ▶ **cardinal number** (pl. **quintillions** or (with numeral) same) a thousand raised to the power of six (10^{18}).
▪ dated, chiefly Brit. a million raised to the power of five (10^{30}).
– DERIVATIVES **quintillionth** ordinal number.
– ORIGIN late 17th cent.: from French, from *million*, by substitution of the prefix *quinti-* 'five' (from Latin *quintus* 'fifth') for the initial letters.

quintuple /ˈkwɪntjʊp(ə)l, kwɪnˈtjuːp(ə)l/ ▶ **adjective** [attrib.] consisting of five parts or things.
▪ five times as much or as many. ▪ (of time in music) having five beats in a bar.
▶ **verb** increase or cause to increase fivefold.
▶ **noun** a fivefold number or amount; a set of five.
– DERIVATIVES **quintuply** adverb.
– ORIGIN late 16th cent.: via French from medieval Latin *quintuplus*, from Latin *quintus* 'fifth' + *-plus* as in *duplus* (see **DUPLE**).

quintuplet /ˈkwɪntjʊˌplɪt, kwɪnˈtjuːplɪt/ ▶ **noun 1** (usu. **quintuplets**) each of five children born to the same mother at one birth.
2 Music a group of five notes to be performed in the time of three or four.
– ORIGIN late 19th cent.: from **QUINTUPLE**, on the pattern of words such as *triplet*.

quintuplicate ▶ **adjective** fivefold.
▪ of which five copies are made.
▶ **verb** [with obj.] multiply by five.
– PHRASES **in quintuplicate** in five identical copies.
▪ in groups of five.
– ORIGIN mid 17th cent.: from **QUINTUPLE**, on the pattern of words such as *quadruplicate*.

quip ▶ **noun** a witty remark.
▪ archaic a verbal equivocation.
▶ **verb** (**quipped**, **quipping**) [no obj.] make a witty remark: [with direct speech] *'Flattery will get you nowhere,' she quipped.*
– DERIVATIVES **quipster** noun.
– ORIGIN mid 16th cent.: perhaps from Latin *quippe* 'indeed, forsooth'.

quipu /ˈkiːpuː, ˈkwɪ-/ ▶ **noun** an ancient Inca device for recording information, consisting of variously coloured threads knotted in different ways.
– ORIGIN from Quechua *khipu* 'knot'.

quire /kwʌɪə/ ▶ **noun** four sheets of paper or parchment folded to form eight leaves, as in medieval manuscripts.
▪ any collection of leaves one within another in a manuscript or book. ▪ 25 (formerly 24) sheets of paper; one twentieth of a ream.
– ORIGIN Middle English: from Old French *quaier*, from Latin *quaterni* 'set of four'.

quirk ▶ **noun 1** a peculiar behavioural habit: *they accepted her attitude as one of her little quirks.*
▪ a strange chance occurrence: *a strange quirk of fate had led her to working for Nathan.* ▪ a sudden twist, turn, or curve: *wry humour put a slight quirk in his mouth.*
2 Architecture an acute hollow between convex or other mouldings.
▶ **verb** [no obj.] (of a person's mouth or eyebrow) move or twist suddenly, especially to express surprise or amusement.
▪ [with obj.] move or twist (one's mouth or eyebrow) in such a way.
– DERIVATIVES **quirkish** adjective.
– ORIGIN early 16th cent. (as a verb): of unknown origin. The early sense of the noun was 'subtle verbal twist, quibble', later 'unexpected twist'.

quirky ▶ **adjective** (**quirkier**, **quirkiest**) characterized by peculiar or unexpected traits: *her sense of humour was decidedly quirky.*
– DERIVATIVES **quirkily** adverb, **quirkiness** noun.

quirt /kwəːt/ ▶ **noun** a short-handled riding whip with a braided leather lash.
▶ **verb** [with obj.] hit with a whip of this kind.
– ORIGIN mid 19th cent. (originally US): from Spanish *cuerda* 'cord' (from Latin *chorda* 'cord') or from Mexican Spanish *cuarta* 'whip'.

quisling /ˈkwɪzlɪŋ/ ▶ **noun** a traitor who collaborates with an enemy force occupying their country.
– ORIGIN Second World War: from the name of Major Vidkun *Quisling* (1887–1945), the Norwegian army officer and diplomat who ruled Norway on behalf of the German occupying forces (1940–45).

quit[1] ▶ **verb** (**quitting**; past and past participle **quitted** or **quit**) **1** [with obj.] leave (a place), usually permanently: *hippies finally quit two sites in Hampshire last night.*
▪ [no obj.] (of a tenant) leave rented accommodation: *the landlord issued a notice to quit.* ▪ informal resign from (a job): *she quit her job in a pizza restaurant* | [no obj.] *he quit as manager of struggling Third Division City.* ▪ informal, chiefly N. Amer. stop or discontinue (an action or activity): *quit moaning!* | *I want to quit smoking.*
2 (**quit oneself**) [with adverbial] archaic behave in a specified way: *quit yourselves like men, and fight.*
▶ **adjective** [predic.] (**quit of**) rid of: *I want to be quit of him.*
– PHRASES **quit hold of** archaic let go of.
– ORIGIN Middle English (in the sense 'set free'): from Old French *quiter* (verb), *quite* (adjective), from Latin *quietus*, past participle of *quiescere* 'be still', from *quies* 'quiet'.

quit[2] ▶ **noun** [in combination] used in names of various small songbirds found in the Caribbean area, e.g. **bananaquit**, **grassquit**.
– ORIGIN mid 19th cent.: probably imitative.

quitch (also **quitch grass**) ▶ **noun** another term for **COUCH**[2].
– ORIGIN Old English *cwice*, of uncertain origin; perhaps related to **QUICK** (with reference to its vigorous growth).

quitclaim ▶ **noun** Law, historical & US a formal renunciation or relinquishing of a claim.

quite ▶ **adverb** [usu. as submodifier] **1** to the utmost or most absolute extent or degree; absolutely; completely: *it's quite out of the question* | *are you quite certain about this?* | *this is quite a different problem* | *I quite agree* | *quite frankly, I don't blame you.*
▪ US very; really (used as an intensifier): *'You've no intention of coming back?' 'I'm quite sorry, but no, I have not.'* ▪ W. Indian all the way: *dresses quite from Port of Spain.*
2 to a certain or fairly significant extent or degree; fairly: *it's quite warm outside* | *I was quite embarrassed, actually* | *she did quite well at school* | *he's quite an attractive man.*
▶ **exclamation** (also **quite so**) expressing agreement with or understanding of a remark or statement: *'I don't want to talk about that now.' 'Quite'.*
– PHRASES **not quite** not completely or entirely: *my hair's not quite dry* | *she hasn't quite got the hang of it yet.* **quite a ——** (also often ironic **quite the ——**) used to indicate that the specified person or thing is perceived as particularly notable, remarkable, or impressive: *quite a party, isn't it?* | *it's been quite a year* | *quite the little horsewoman, aren't you?* **quite a few** see **FEW**. **quite a lot** (or **a bit**) a considerable number or amount of something: *my job involves quite a lot of travel* | *he's quite a bit older than she is.* **quite some 1** a considerable amount of: *she hasn't been seen for quite some time.* **2** informal way of saying *quite a*. **quite something** see **SOMETHING**. **quite the thing** dated well, healthy, or normal: *I'm afraid Oliver isn't feeling quite the thing this morning.* ▪ socially acceptable: *it wouldn't be quite the thing to turn up in a raincoat and wellies.*
– ORIGIN Middle English: from the obsolete adjective *quite*, variant of **QUIT**[1].

Quito /ˈkiːtəʊ/ the capital of Ecuador; pop. 1,401,400 (est. 1995). It is situated in the Andes just south of the equator, at an altitude of 2,850 m (9,350 ft).

quit-rent ▶ **noun** historical a rent, typically a small one, paid by a freeholder or copyholder in lieu of services which might be required of them.

quits ▶ **adjective** [predic.] (of two people) on even terms, especially because a debt or score has been settled: *I think we're just about quits now, don't you?*
– PHRASES **call it quits** agree or acknowledge that

terms are now equal, especially on the settlement of a debt: *take this cheque and we'll call it quits.* ■ decide to abandon an activity or venture: *surely, after covering eleven wars, he could be forgiven for calling it quits?*
– ORIGIN late 15th cent. (in the sense 'freed from a liability or debt'): perhaps a colloquial abbreviation of medieval Latin *quittus*, from Latin *quietus*, used as a receipt (see **QUIETUS**).

quittance ▶ **noun** archaic or poetic/literary a release or discharge from a debt or obligation.
■ a document certifying this; a receipt.
– ORIGIN Middle English: from Old French *quitance*, from *quiter* 'to release' (see **QUIT**[1]).

quitter ▶ **noun** [usu. with negative] informal a person who gives up easily or does not have the courage or determination to finish a task.

quiver[1] ▶ **verb** [no obj.] tremble or shake with a slight rapid motion: *the tree's branches stopped quivering.*
■ (of a person, a part of their body, or their voice) tremble with sudden strong emotion: *Bertha's voice quivered with indignation.* ■ [with obj.] cause (something) to make a slight rapid motion: *the bird runs along in a zigzag path, quivering its wings.*
▶ **noun** a slight trembling movement or sound, especially one caused by a sudden strong emotion: *Meredith felt a quiver of fear.*
– DERIVATIVES **quiveringly** adverb, **quivery** adjective.
– ORIGIN Middle English: from Old English *cwifer* 'nimble, quick'. The initial *qu-* is probably symbolic of quick movement (as in *quaver* and *quick*).

quiver[2] ▶ **noun** an archer's portable case for holding arrows.
■ a set of surfboards of different lengths and shapes for use with different types of waves.
– PHRASES **an arrow in the quiver** one of a number of resources or strategies that can be drawn on or followed.
– ORIGIN Middle English: from Anglo-Norman French *quiveir*, of West Germanic origin; related to Dutch *koker* and German *Köcher*.

quiverful ▶ **noun** (pl. **-fuls**) the amount of arrows a quiver can hold.
■ Brit. humorous a large number of offspring. [ORIGIN: figuratively, with biblical allusion to Ps. 127:5.]
– ORIGIN mid 19th cent.: from **QUIVER**[2] + **-FUL**.

quiver tree ▶ **noun** a tropical aloe which forms a tree, the hollow branches of which were formerly used by the San (Bushmen) as quivers.
• *Aloe dichotoma*, family Liliaceae (or Aloaceae).

qui vive /kiː 'viːv/ ▶ **noun** (in phrase **on the qui vive**) on the alert or lookout: *duty requires the earnest liberal to spend most of his time on the qui vive for fascism.*
– ORIGIN late 16th cent.: from French, literally '(long) live who?', i.e. 'on whose side are you?', used as a sentry's challenge.

Quixote see **DON QUIXOTE**.

quixotic /kwɪk'sɒtɪk/ ▶ **adjective** exceedingly idealistic; unrealistic and impractical: *a vast and perhaps quixotic project.*
– DERIVATIVES **quixotically** adverb, **quixotism** /'kwɪksətɪz(ə)m/ noun, **quixotry** /'kwɪksətri/ noun.
– ORIGIN late 18th cent.: from **DON QUIXOTE** + **-IC**.

quiz[1] ▶ **noun** (pl. **quizzes**) a test of knowledge, especially as a competition between individuals or teams as a form of entertainment.
■ informal, chiefly Brit. an act of questioning someone, especially as part of a police investigation or a formal inquiry. ■ N. Amer. an informal written test or examination given to students.
▶ **verb** (**quizzes**, **quizzed**, **quizzing**) [with obj.] (often **be quizzed**) ask (someone) questions: *four men have been quizzed about the murder.*
■ N. Amer. give (a student or class) an informal written test or examination.
– ORIGIN mid 19th cent. (as a verb; originally US): possibly from **QUIZ**[2], influenced by **INQUISITIVE**.

quiz[2] archaic ▶ **verb** (**quizzes**, **quizzed**, **quizzing**) [with obj.] **1** look curiously or intently at (someone) through or as if through an eyeglass: *deep-set eyes quizzed her in the candlelight.*
2 make fun of: *he says there's a great deal of poetry in brewing beer, but of course he's only quizzing us.*
▶ **noun** (pl. **quizzes**) **1** a practical joke or hoax; a piece of banter or ridicule: *I am impatient to know if the whole be not one grand quiz.*
■ a person who ridicules another; a hoaxer or practical joker: *braving the ridicule with which it pleased the quizzes to asperse the husband chosen for her.*
2 a person who is odd or eccentric in character or appearance: *she means to marry that quiz for the sake of his thousands.*
– DERIVATIVES **quizzer** noun.
– ORIGIN late 18th cent.: sometimes said to have been invented by a Dublin theatre proprietor who, having made a bet that a nonsense word could be made known within 48 hours throughout the city, and that the public would give it a meaning, had the word written up on walls all over the city. There is no evidence to support this theory.

quizmaster ▶ **noun** Brit. a person who asks the questions and enforces the rules in a television or radio quiz programme.

quizzical ▶ **adjective** (of a person's expression or behaviour) indicating mild or amused puzzlement: *she gave me a quizzical look.*
■ rare causing mild amusement because of its oddness or strangeness.
– DERIVATIVES **quizzicality** noun, **quizzically** adverb, **quizzicalness** noun.

Qum variant spelling of **QOM**.

Qumran /kʊm'rɑːn/ a region on the western shore of the Dead Sea. The Dead Sea scrolls were found (1947–56) in caves at nearby Khirbet Qumran, the site of an ancient Jewish settlement.

quod /kwɒd/ ▶ **noun** Brit. informal, dated prison: *ten years in quod.*
– ORIGIN late 17th cent.: of unknown origin.

quod erat demonstrandum /kwɒd ˌɛrat dɛmən'strandəm/ (abbrev.: **QED**) ▶ used to convey that a fact or situation demonstrates the truth of one's theory or claim, especially to mark the conclusion of a formal proof.
– ORIGIN Latin, literally 'which was to be demonstrated'.

quodlibet /'kwɒdlɪbɛt/ ▶ **noun 1** archaic a topic for or exercise in philosophical or theological discussion.
2 poetic/literary a light-hearted medley of well-known tunes.
– DERIVATIVES **quodlibetarian** /-bɪ'tɛːrɪən/ noun.
– ORIGIN late Middle English: from Latin, from *quod* 'what' + *libet* 'it pleases'.

quoin /kɔɪn, kwɔɪn/ ▶ **noun 1** an external angle of a wall or building.
■ (also **quoin stone**) any of the stones or bricks forming such an angle; a cornerstone.
2 Printing a wedge or expanding mechanical device used for locking a letterpress forme into a chase.
3 a wedge for raising the level of a gun barrel or for keeping it from rolling.
▶ **verb** [with obj.] **1** provide (a wall) with quoins or corners.
2 Printing lock up (a forme) with a quoin.
– ORIGIN Middle English: variant of **COIN**, used earlier in the sense 'cornerstone' and 'wedge'.

quoining ▶ **noun** [mass noun] the stone or brick used to form a quoin of a wall or building.

quoit /kɔɪt, kwɔɪt/ ▶ **noun 1** a ring of iron, rope, or rubber thrown in a game to encircle or land as near as possible to an upright peg.
■ (**quoits**) [treated as sing.] a game consisting of aiming and throwing such rings. See also **DECK QUOITS**.
2 the flat covering stone of a dolmen.
■ [often in place names] the dolmen itself.
▶ **verb** [with obj. and adverbial of direction] archaic throw or propel like a quoit.
– ORIGIN late Middle English: probably of French origin.

quokka /'kwɒkə/ ▶ **noun** a small short-tailed wallaby with a short face, round ears on top of the head, and some tree-climbing ability, native to Western Australia.
• *Setonix brachyurus*, family Macropodidae.
– ORIGIN mid 19th cent.: from Nyungar *kwaka*.

quoll /kwɒl/ ▶ **noun** a catlike carnivorous marsupial with short legs and a white-spotted coat, native to the forests of Australia and New Guinea. Also called **DASYURE**, **NATIVE CAT**, **TIGER CAT**.
• Genus *Dasyurus*, family Dasyuridae: several species.
– ORIGIN late 18th cent.: from Guugu Yimidhirr (an Aboriginal language) *dhigul*.

quondam /'kwɒndəm, -dam/ ▶ **adjective** [attrib.] formal that once was; former: *quondam dissidents joined the establishment | its quondam popularity.*
– ORIGIN late 16th cent.: from Latin, 'formerly'.

Quonset /'kwɒnsɪt/ (also **Quonset hut**) ▶ **noun** N. Amer. trademark a building made of corrugated metal and having a semicircular cross section.
– ORIGIN Second World War: named after *Quonset* Point, Rhode Island, where such huts were first made.

quorate /'kwɔːrət, -reɪt/ ▶ **adjective** Brit. (of a meeting) attended by a quorum and so having valid proceedings.

Quorn /kwɔːn/ ▶ **noun** [mass noun] Brit. trademark a type of textured vegetable protein made from an edible fungus and used as a meat substitute.
– ORIGIN 1980s: the name of a former company in the Leicestershire village of Quorndon.

quorum /'kwɔːrəm/ ▶ **noun** (pl. **quorums**) the minimum number of members of an assembly or society that must be present at any of its meetings to make the proceedings of that meeting valid.
– ORIGIN late Middle English (referring to justices of the peace): used in commissions for committee members designated by the Latin *quorum vos … unum (duos, etc.) esse volumus* 'of whom we wish that you … be one (two, etc.)'.

quota ▶ **noun** a limited or fixed number or amount of people or things, in particular:
■ a limited quantity of a particular product which under official controls can be produced, exported, or imported: *the country may be exceeding its OPEC quota of 1,100,000 barrels of oil per day.* ■ a fixed share of something that a person or group is entitled to receive from a total. ■ a person's share of something that must be done: *they were arrested to help fill the quota of arrests the security police had to make during the crackdown.* ■ a fixed minimum or maximum number of a particular group of people allowed to do something, as immigrants to enter a country, workers to undertake a job, or students to enrol for a course: *the removal of entry quotas encouraged young people to enter universities.* ■ (in a system of proportional representation) the minimum number of votes required to elect a candidate. ■ figurative a person's share of a particular thing, quality, or attribute: *an Irishman with a double ration of blarney and a treble quota of charm.* ■ (also **diocesan quota**) (in the Anglican Church) the proportion of the funds of a parish contributed to the finances of the diocese.
– ORIGIN early 17th cent.: from medieval Latin *quota (pars)* 'how great (a part)', feminine of *quotus*, from *quot* 'how many'.

quotable ▶ **adjective** (of a person or remark) suitable for or worth quoting.
– DERIVATIVES **quotability** noun.

quota sample ▶ **noun** Statistics a sample taken from a stratified population by sampling until a pre-assigned quota in each stratum is represented.
– DERIVATIVES **quota sampling** noun.

quotation ▶ **noun 1** a group of words taken from a text or speech and repeated by someone other than the original author or speaker: *a quotation from Mark Twain | biblical quotations.*
■ a short musical passage or visual image taken from one piece of music or work of art and used in another. ■ [mass noun] the action of quoting from a text, speech, piece of music, or work of art: *a great argument with much quotation of Darwin.*
2 a formal statement setting out the estimated cost for a particular job or service: *ensure you receive a written quotation covering all aspects of the job.*
■ Stock Exchange a price offered by a market-maker for the sale or purchase of a stock or other security. ■ Stock Exchange a registration granted to a company enabling their shares to be officially listed and traded.
– ORIGIN mid 16th cent. (denoting a marginal reference to a passage of text): from medieval Latin *quotatio(n-)*, from the verb *quotare* (see **QUOTE**).

quotation mark ▶ **noun** each of a set of punctuation marks, single (' ') or double (" "), used either to mark the beginning and end of a title or quoted passage, or to indicate that a word or phrase is regarded as slang or jargon or is being discussed rather than used within the sentence.

quote ▶ **verb** [with obj.] **1** repeat or copy out (a group of words from a text or speech), typically with an indication that one is not the original author or speaker: *he **quoted** a passage **from** the Psalms* | [with direct speech] *'The stream mysterious glides beneath,' Melinda quoted* | [no obj.] *when we told her this she said, and I quote, 'Phooey!'*
■ repeat a passage from (a work or author) or statement by (someone): *the prime minister was **quoted as saying** that he would resist all attempts to 'sabotage' his government | he quoted Shakespeare, Goethe, and other poets.* ■ mention or refer to (someone or something) to provide evidence or authority for a statement, argument, or opinion: *they won't be here at all in three*

years' time—you can quote me on that. ■ (**quote someone/thing as**) put forward or describe someone or something as being: *heavy teaching loads are often quoted as a bad influence on research.*
2 give someone (the estimated price of a job or service): [with two objs] *a garage quoted him £30.*
■ (usu. **be quoted**) Stock Exchange give (a company) a quotation or listing on a stock exchange: *an organization that is quoted on the Stock Exchange.* ■ (**quote someone/thing at/as**) name at (specified odds): *he is quoted as 9–2 favourite to score the first goal of the match.*
▶ noun **1** a quotation from a text or speech: *a quote from Wordsworth.*
2 a quotation giving the estimated cost for a particular job or service: *quotes from different insurance companies.*
■ Stock Exchange a price offered by a market-maker for the sale or purchase of a stock or other security. ■ Stock Exchange a quotation or listing of a company on a stock exchange.
3 (**quotes**) quotation marks.
– PHRASES **quote —— unquote** informal used parenthetically when speaking to indicate the beginning and end (or just the beginning) of a statement or passage that one is repeating, especially to emphasize the speaker's detachment from or disagreement with the original.

– ORIGIN late Middle English: from medieval Latin *quotare*, from *quot* 'how many', or from medieval Latin *quota* (see **QUOTA**). The original sense was 'mark a book with numbers, or with marginal references', later 'give a reference by page or chapter', hence 'cite a text or person' (late 16th cent.).

quoth /kwəʊθ/ ▶ verb [with direct speech] archaic or humorous said (used only in first and third person singular before the subject): *'Ah,' quoth he, as soon as the bike started, 'a blown cylinder head gasket.'*
– ORIGIN Middle English: past tense of obsolete *quethe* 'say, declare', of Germanic origin.

quotidian /kwɒˈtɪdɪən, kwəʊ-/ ▶ adjective [attrib.] of or occurring every day; daily: *the car sped noisily off through the quotidian traffic.*
■ ordinary or everyday, especially when mundane: *his story is an achingly human one, mired in quotidian details.* ■ Medicine denoting the malignant form of malaria.
– ORIGIN Middle English: via Old French from Latin *quotidianus*, earlier *cotidianus*, from *cotidie* 'daily'.

quotient /ˈkwəʊʃ(ə)nt/ ▶ noun **1** Mathematics a result obtained by dividing one quantity by another.
2 [usu. with adj. or noun modifier] a degree or amount of a specified quality or characteristic: *the increase in Washington's cynicism quotient.*

– ORIGIN late Middle English: from Latin *quotiens* 'how many times' (from *quot* 'how many'), by confusion with participial forms ending in -*ens*, -*ent*-.

quo warranto /ˌkwəʊ wəˈrantəʊ/ ▶ noun Law, historical & US [usu. as modifier] a writ or legal action requiring a person to show by what warrant an office or franchise is held, claimed, or exercised.
– ORIGIN Law Latin, literally 'by what warrant'.

Qur'an /kɔˈrɑːn/ (also **Quran**) ▶ noun Arabic spelling of **KORAN**.

qursh /kʊəʃ/ ▶ noun (pl. same) a monetary unit of Saudi Arabia, equal to one twentieth of a rial.
– ORIGIN from Arabic *ḳirsh*, from Slavic *grossus*.

q.v. ▶ abbreviation used to direct a reader to another part of a book or article for further information.
– ORIGIN from Latin *quod vide*, literally 'which see'.

Qwaqwa /ˈkwakwə/ a former homeland established in South Africa for the South Sotho people, situated in the Drakensberg Mountains in Free State province.

qwerty /ˈkwɜːti/ ▶ adjective denoting the standard layout on English-language typewriters and keyboards, having q, w, e, r, t, and y as the first keys from the left on the top row of letters.

Rr

R¹ (also **r**) ▸ **noun** (pl. **Rs** or **R's**) the eighteenth letter of the alphabet.
- ■denoting the next after Q in a set of items, categories, etc.
- PHRASES **the R months** the months with R in their names (September to April), considered to be the season for eating oysters. **the three Rs** reading, writing, and arithmetic, regarded as the fundamentals of learning.

R² ▸ **abbreviation for** ■ rand: *a farm worth nearly R1,3 million*. ■ (in names of sports clubs) Rangers or Rovers. ■ Réaumur: *198.6 °R*. ■ Regina or Rex: *Elizabeth R*. ■ (also ®) registered as a trademark. ■ (in the US) Republican. ■ US (in film classification) restricted (denoting films restricted to viewers over seventeen years of age). ■ (on a gear shift) reverse. ■ (**R.**) River (chiefly on maps). ■ roentgen(s). ■ Romania (international vehicle registration). ■ rook (in recording moves in chess): *21.Rh4*. ■ Cricket (on scorecards) run(s).
▸ **symbol for** ■ Chemistry an unspecified alkyl or other organic radical or group. [ORIGIN: abbreviation of **RADICAL**.] ■ electrical resistance. ■ Chemistry the gas constant.

r ▸ **abbreviation for** ■ recto. ■ (giving position or direction) right: *l to r: Evan, Nic, and David*. ■ Law rule.
▸ **symbol for** ■ radius. ■ Statistics correlation coefficient.

RA ▸ **abbreviation for** ■ Argentina (international vehicle registration). [ORIGIN: from Spanish *República Argentina* 'Argentine Republic'.] ■ Astronomy right ascension. ■ (in the UK) Royal Academician. ■ (in the UK) Royal Academy. ■ (in the UK) Royal Artillery. ■ (in the UK) Rugby Association (in the names of rugby clubs).

Ra¹ /rɑː/ (also **Re**) Egyptian Mythology the sun god, the supreme Egyptian deity, worshipped as the creator of all life and typically portrayed with a falcon's head bearing the solar disc. From earliest times he was associated with the pharaoh.

Ra² ▸ **symbol for** the chemical element radium.

RAAF ▸ **abbreviation for** Royal Australian Air Force.

Rabat /rəˈbat/ the capital of Morocco, an industrial port on the Atlantic Coast; pop. 1,220,000 (1993). It was founded as a military fort in the 12th century by the Almohads.
- ORIGIN from Arabic *Ribat el-Fath* 'fort of victory'.

Rabaul /rəˈbaʊl/ the chief town and port of the island of New Britain, Papua New Guinea; pop. 17,020 (1990).

rabbet /ˈrabɪt/ ▸ **noun** & **verb** chiefly N. Amer. another term for **REBATE²**.
- ORIGIN late Middle English: from Old French *rabat* 'abatement, recess'.

rabbi /ˈrabʌɪ/ ▸ **noun** (pl. **rabbis**) a Jewish scholar or teacher, especially one who studies or teaches Jewish law.
- ■a person appointed as a Jewish religious leader.
- DERIVATIVES **rabbinate** /ˈrabɪnət/ noun.
- ORIGIN late Old English, via ecclesiastical Latin and Greek from Hebrew *rabbī* 'my master', from *ra<u>b</u>* 'master'.

rabbinic /rəˈbɪnɪk/ ▸ **adjective** [attrib.] of or relating to rabbis or to Jewish law or teachings.

- DERIVATIVES **rabbinical** adjective, **rabbinically** adverb.

rabbit ▸ **noun 1** a burrowing gregarious plant-eating mammal, with long ears, long hind legs, and a short tail.
- ● Family Leporidae: several genera and species, in particular the **European rabbit** (*Oryctolagus cuniculus*), which is often kept as a pet or raised for food.
- ■[mass noun] the flesh of the rabbit as food. ■ [mass noun] the fur of the rabbit. ■ North American term for **HARE**. ■ informal a poor performer in a sport or game, in particular (in cricket) a poor batsman. ■ US a runner who acts as pacesetter in the first laps of a race.
2 Brit. informal a conversation: *we had quite a heated rabbit about it*. [ORIGIN: from *rabbit and pork*, rhyming slang for 'talk'.]
▸ **verb** (**rabbited**, **rabbiting**) [no obj.] **1** [usu. as noun **rabbiting**] hunt rabbits: *locate the area where you can go rabbiting*.
2 Brit. informal talk at length, especially about trivial matters: *stop rabbiting on, will you, and go to bed!*
- PHRASES **breed like rabbits** informal reproduce prolifically. **pull** (or **bring**) **a rabbit out of the** (or **a**) **hat** used to describe an action that is fortuitous, and may involve sleight of hand or deception: *a rabbit has been pulled out of the political hat*.
- DERIVATIVES **rabbity** adjective.
- ORIGIN late Middle English: apparently from Old French (compare with French dialect *rabotte* 'young rabbit'), perhaps of Dutch origin (compare with Flemish *robbe*).

rabbitbrush (also **rabbitbush**) ▸ **noun** a North American shrub of the daisy family, which bears clusters of small yellow flowers.
- ● *Chrysothamnus nauseosus*, family Compositae.

rabbit-eared bandicoot (also **rabbit bandicoot**) ▸ **noun** a burrowing Australian bandicoot with long ears, long limbs, and a long furry tail. Also called **BILBY**.
- ● Family Thylacomyidae and genus *Macrotis*: two species, one of which is possibly extinct.

rabbit fever ▸ **noun** informal term for **TULARAEMIA**.

rabbitfish ▸ **noun** (pl. same or **-fishes**) **1** a blunt-nosed chimaera with rodent-like front teeth and a long thin tail, found in the NE Atlantic and around South Africa. Also called **RATFISH, RAT-TAIL**.
- ● *Chimaera monstrosa*, family Chimaeridae.
2 a fish with a blunt snout and rabbit-like jaws, found in inshore waters of the tropical Indo-Pacific, especially around reefs.
- ● Family Siganidae: several genera and species, in particular *Siganus oramin*.

rabbit food ▸ **noun** [mass noun] humorous salad, seen as insubstantial or tasteless.

rabbit punch ▸ **noun** a sharp chop with the edge of the hand to the back of the neck.

rabbit's foot ▸ **noun** the foot of a rabbit carried as a good luck charm.

rabbit warren ▸ **noun** see **WARREN**.

rabble ▸ **noun** a disorderly crowd; a mob: *he was met by a rabble of noisy, angry youths*.
- ■(**the rabble**) ordinary people, especially when regarded as socially inferior or uncouth.
- ORIGIN late Middle English (in the senses 'string of

meaningless words' and 'pack of animals'): perhaps related to dialect *rabble* 'to gabble'.

rabble-rouser ▸ **noun** a person who speaks with the intention of inflaming the emotions of a crowd of people, typically for political reasons.
- DERIVATIVES **rabble-rousing** adjective & noun.

Rabelais /ˈrabəleɪ, French ʀablɛ/, François (c.1494–1553), French satirist. His writings are noted for their earthy humour, their parody of medieval learning and literature, and their affirmation of humanist values. Notable works: *Pantagruel* (c.1532); *Gargantua* (1534).
- DERIVATIVES **Rabelaisian** /ˌrabəˈleɪzɪən/ adjective & noun.

rabi /ˈrʌbiː/ ▸ **noun** [mass noun] (in the Indian subcontinent) the grain crop sown in September and reaped in the spring.
- ORIGIN from Hindi *rabī*.

rabid /ˈrabɪd, ˈreɪ-/ ▸ **adjective 1** having or proceeding from an extreme or fanatical support of or belief in something: *a rabid feminist*.
2 (of an animal) affected with rabies.
- ■of or connected with rabies.
- DERIVATIVES **rabidity** /rəˈbɪdɪti/ noun, **rabidly** adverb, **rabidness** noun.
- ORIGIN early 17th cent. (in the sense 'furious, madly violent'): from Latin *rabidus*, from *rabere* 'to rave'.

rabies /ˈreɪbiːz, -ɪz/ ▸ **noun** [mass noun] a contagious and fatal viral disease of dogs and other mammals, transmissible through the saliva to humans and causing madness and convulsions. Also called **HYDROPHOBIA**.
- ORIGIN late 16th cent.: from Latin, from *rabere* 'rave'.

Rabin /rəˈbiːn/, Yitzhak (1922–95), Israeli statesman and military leader, Prime Minister 1974–7 and 1992–5. In 1993 he negotiated a PLO–Israeli peace accord with Yasser Arafat, for which he shared the 1994 Nobel Peace Prize with Arafat and Shimon Peres. He was assassinated by a Jewish extremist.

RAC ▸ **abbreviation for** ■ (in the UK) Royal Armoured Corps. ■ (in the UK) Royal Automobile Club.

raccoon /rəˈkuːn/ (also **racoon**) ▸ **noun** a greyish-brown American mammal which has a foxlike face with a black mask, a ringed tail, and the habit of washing its food in water.
- ● Genus *Procyon*, family Procyonidae (the **raccoon family**): two species, in particular the **common raccoon** (*P. lotor*), which often occurs in urban areas in North America. The raccoon family also includes the coati, kinkajou, cacomistle, and olingo.
- ■[mass noun] the fur of the raccoon.
- ORIGIN early 17th cent.: from Virginia Algonquian *aroughcun*.

raccoon dog ▸ **noun** a small wild dog of raccoon-like appearance, with a black facial mask and long brindled fur, native to the forests of south and east Asia.
- ● *Nyctereutes procyonoides*, family Canidae.

race¹ ▸ **noun 1** a competition between runners, horses, vehicles, boats, etc. to see which is the fastest in covering a set course: *Hill started from pole position and won the race*.
- ■(**the races**) a series of such competitions for horses or dogs, held at a fixed time on a set course. ■ [in sing.]

a situation in which individuals or groups compete to be first to achieve a particular objective: *the race for nuclear power*. ■ archaic the course of the sun or moon through the heavens.
2 a strong or rapid current flowing through a narrow channel in the sea or a river: *angling for tuna in turbulent tidal races.*
3 a groove, channel, or passage, in particular: ■ a water channel, especially one built to lead water to or from a point where its energy is utilized, as in a mill or mine. See also **MILL RACE**. ■ a smooth ring-shaped groove or guide in which a ball bearing or roller bearing runs. ■ a fenced passageway in a stockyard through which animals pass singly for branding, loading, washing, etc. ■ (in weaving) the channel along which the shuttle moves.
▶ verb **1** [no obj.] compete with another or others to see who is fastest at covering a set course or achieving an objective: *the vet took blood samples from the horses before they raced* | [with obj.] *two drivers raced each other through a housing estate.*
■ compete regularly in races as a sport or leisure activity: *next year, he raced again for the team.* ■ [with obj.] prepare and enter (an animal or vehicle) for races as a sport or leisure activity: *he raced his three horses simply for the fun of it.*
2 [no obj., with adverbial] move or progress swiftly or at full speed: *I raced into the house* | figurative *she spoke automatically, while her mind raced ahead.*
■ [no obj.] (of an engine or other machinery) operate at excessive speed: *the truck came to rest against a tree with its engine racing.* ■ [no obj.] (of a person's heart or pulse) beat faster than usual because of fear or excitement. ■ [with obj.] cause to move, progress, or operate swiftly or at excessive speed: *she'd driven like a madwoman, racing the engine and swerving around corners.*
– PHRASES **be in the race** [usu. with negative] Austral./NZ informal have a chance of success: *with you dressed up, none of us others will be in the race.* **a race against time** a situation in which something must be done before a particular point in time: *it was a race against time to reach shore before the dinghy sank.*
– ORIGIN late Old English, from Old Norse *rás* 'current'. It was originally a northern English word with the sense 'rapid forward movement', which gave rise to the senses 'contest of speed' (early 16th cent.) and 'channel, path' (i.e. the space traversed). The verb dates from the late 15th cent.

race² ▶ noun each of the major divisions of humankind, having distinct physical characteristics: *people of all races, colours, and creeds.*
■ a group of people sharing the same culture, history, language, etc.; an ethnic group: *we Scots were a bloodthirsty race then.* ■ [mass noun] the fact or condition of belonging to such a division or group; the qualities or characteristics associated with this: *people of mixed race.* ■ a group or set of people or things with a common feature or features: *some male firefighters still regarded women as a race apart.* ■ Biology a population within a species that is distinct in some way, especially a subspecies: *people have killed so many tigers that two races are probably extinct.* ■ (in non-technical use) each of the major divisions of living creatures: *a member of the human race* | *the race of birds.* ■ poetic/literary a group of people descended from a common ancestor: *a prince of the race of Solomon.* ■ [mass noun] archaic ancestry: *two coursers of ethereal race.*

Although ideas of race are centuries old, it was not until the 19th century, with the growth of interest in ethnology and physical anthropology, that attempts to systematize racial divisions were made. Ideas of supposed racial superiority and social Darwinism reached their culmination in Nazi ideology of the 1930s and gave pseudoscientific justification to policies and attitudes of discrimination, exploitation, slavery, and extermination. Theories of race asserting a link between racial type and intelligence are now discredited. Scientifically it is accepted as obvious that there are subdivisions of the human species, but it is also clear that genetic variation between individuals of the same race can be as great as that between members of different races.

– ORIGIN early 16th cent. (denoting a group with common features): via French from Italian *razza*, of unknown ultimate origin.

USAGE In recent years, the associations of **race** with the ideologies and theories that grew out of the work of 19th-century anthropologists and physiologists has led to the use of the word **race** itself becoming problematic. Although still used in general contexts, it is now often replaced by other words which are less emotionally charged, such as **people(s)** or **community**.

race³ ▶ noun dated a ginger root.
– ORIGIN late Middle English: from Old French *rais*, from Latin *radix, radic-* 'root'.

racecard ▶ noun a programme giving information

about the races scheduled for a particular race meeting.

racecourse ▶ noun a ground or track for horse or dog racing.

racehorse ▶ noun a horse bred, trained, and kept for racing.

racemate /ˈrasɪmeɪt/ ▶ noun Chemistry a racemic mixture.

raceme /ˈrasiːm, rəˈsiːm/ ▶ noun Botany a flower cluster with the separate flowers attached by short equal stalks at equal distances along a central stem. The flowers at the base of the central stem develop first. Compare with **CYME** and **SPIKE²**.
– ORIGIN late 18th cent.: from Latin *racemus* 'bunch of grapes'.

race meeting ▶ noun Brit. a sporting event consisting of a series of races, typically horse races, held at a particular course over one or more days.

race memory ▶ noun a supposedly inherited subconscious memory of events in human history or prehistory.

racemic /rəˈsiːmɪk, rəˈsɛmɪk/ ▶ adjective Chemistry composed of dextrorotatory and laevorotatory forms of a compound in equal proportion.
– DERIVATIVES **racemize** /ˈrasɪmʌɪz/ (also **-ise**) verb.
– ORIGIN early 19th cent. (in *racemic acid*): from French *racémique* 'derived from grape juice' (originally referring to tartaric acid in this) + **-IC**.

racemose /ˈrasɪməʊs, -z/ ▶ adjective Botany (of a flower cluster) taking the form of a raceme.
■ Anatomy (especially of compound glands) having the form of a cluster.
– ORIGIN late 17th cent.: from Latin *racemosus*, from *racemus* (see **RACEME**).

race music ▶ noun [mass noun] US dated music popular among or played by black people, especially jazz and blues.

racer ▶ noun **1** an animal or means of transport bred or designed especially for racing: *tall-masted ocean racers.*
■ a person who competes in races. ■ [as modifier] denoting an article of clothing that has a T-shaped back behind the shoulder blades to allow ease of movement in sporting activities.
2 a fast-moving, harmless, and typically slender-bodied snake.
● Several genera in the family Colubridae: genus *Coluber*, including the American *C. constrictor* and the European *C. gemonensis* (see also **WHIP SNAKE**), and the Asian genera *Ptyas* and *Argyrogena* (also called **RAT SNAKE**).
3 a circular horizontal rail along which the carriage or traversing platform of a heavy gun moves.

race relations ▶ plural noun relations between members or communities of different races within one country.

race riot ▶ noun a public outbreak of violence due to racial antagonism.

racerunner ▶ noun any of a number of fast-moving active lizards with longitudinal markings and a pointed snout, in particular:
● an American lizard (genus *Cnemidophorus*, family Teiidae). ● (**desert racerunner**) an East European lizard (*Eremias arguta*, family Lacertidae).

racetrack ▶ noun a racecourse.
■ a track for motor racing.

raceway ▶ noun chiefly N. Amer. **1** a track or channel along which something runs, in particular:
■ a water channel, especially an artificial one of running water in which fish are reared. ■ a groove or race in which bearings run. ■ a pipe or tubing enclosing electric wires.
2 a track for trotting, pacing, or harness racing.
■ a track for motor racing.

rachis /ˈreɪkɪs/ ▶ noun (pl. **rachides** /-kɪdiːz/) **1** Botany a stem of a plant, especially a grass, bearing flower stalks at short intervals.
■ the midrib of a compound leaf or frond.
2 Anatomy the vertebral column or the cord from which it develops.
3 Ornithology the shaft of a feather, especially the part bearing the barbs.
– ORIGIN late 18th cent.: modern Latin, from Greek *rhakhis* 'spine'. The English plural *-ides* is by false analogy.

rachitis /rəˈkʌɪtɪs/ ▶ noun old-fashioned medical term for **RICKETS**.
– DERIVATIVES **rachitic** /-ˈkɪtɪk/ adjective.

– ORIGIN early 18th cent.: modern Latin, from Greek *rhakhitis*, from *rhakhis* 'spine'.

Rachmaninov /rakˈmanɪnɒf/, Sergei (Vasilevich) (1873–1943), Russian composer and pianist, resident in the US from 1917. Part of the Russian romantic tradition, he is primarily known for his compositions for piano, including concertos and the Prelude in C sharp minor (1892).

Rachmanism /ˈrakmənɪz(ə)m/ ▶ noun [mass noun] Brit. the exploitation and intimidation of tenants by unscrupulous landlords.
– ORIGIN named after Peter *Rachman* (1919–62), a London landlord whose practices became notorious in the early 1960s.

racial ▶ adjective of or relating to race: *a racial minority.*
■ on the grounds of or connected with difference in race: *racial abuse.*
– DERIVATIVES **racially** adverb.

racialism ▶ noun another term for **RACISM**.
– DERIVATIVES **racialist** noun & adjective, **racialize** (also **-ise**) verb.

Racine /raˈsiːn, French ʀasin/, Jean (1639–99), French dramatist, the principal tragedian of the French classical period. Central to most of his tragedies is a perception of the blind folly of human passion, continually enslaved and unsatisfied. Notable works: *Andromaque* (1667) and *Phèdre* (1677).

racing ▶ noun [mass noun] short for **HORSE RACING**.
■ any sport that involves competing in races: *cycle racing* | *yacht racing.*
▶ adjective **1** moving swiftly: *he controlled his racing thoughts.*
2 (of a person) following horse racing: *Kevin was not a racing man.*

racing car ▶ noun a motor car built for racing on a prepared track.

racing demon ▶ noun [mass noun] a competitive version of the card game patience played simultaneously by a number of players.

racing driver ▶ noun a person who drives racing cars as a profession.

racism ▶ noun [mass noun] the belief that all members of each race possess characteristics, abilities, or qualities specific to that race, especially so as to distinguish it as inferior or superior to another race or races.
■ prejudice, discrimination, or antagonism directed against someone of a different race based on such a belief: *a programme to combat racism.*
– DERIVATIVES **racist** noun & adjective.

rack¹ ▶ noun **1** a framework, typically with rails, bars, hooks, or pegs, for holding or storing things: *a spice rack* | *a letter rack.*
■ an overhead shelf on a coach, train, or plane for stowing luggage. ■ a vertically barred frame for holding animal fodder: *a hay rack.* ■ N. Amer. a set of antlers. ■ N. Amer. informal a bed.
2 a cogged or toothed bar or rail engaging with a wheel or pinion, or using pegs to adjust the position of something: *a steering rack.*
3 (**the rack**) historical an instrument of torture consisting of a frame on which the victim was stretched by turning rollers to which the wrists and ankles were tied.
4 a triangular structure for positioning the balls in pool. Compare with **FRAME** (in sense 5).
■ a single game of pool.
5 a digital effects unit for a guitar or other instrument, typically giving many different sounds.
▶ verb [with obj.] **1** (also **wrack**) (often **be racked**) cause extreme physical or mental pain to; subject to extreme stress: *he was racked with guilt.*
■ historical torture (someone) on the rack.
2 [with obj. and adverbial of place] place in or on a rack: *the shoes were racked neatly beneath the dresses.*
■ [with obj.] put (pool balls) in a rack.
3 move by a rack and pinion.
4 chiefly archaic raise (rent) above a fair or normal amount. See also **RACK-RENT**.
■ oppress (a tenant) by exacting excessive rent.
– PHRASES **go to rack** (or **wrack**) **and ruin** gradually deteriorate in condition because of neglect: *fall into disrepair.* [ORIGIN: *rack* from Old English *wræc* 'vengeance'; related to **WREAK**.] **off the rack** North American term for *off the peg* (see **PEG**). **on the rack** suffering intense distress or strain. **rack** (or **wrack**)

one's brains (or **brain**) make a great effort to think of or remember something.
– ORIGIN Middle English: from Middle Dutch *rec*, Middle Low German *rek* 'horizontal bar or shelf', probably from *recken* 'to stretch, reach' (possibly the source of sense 1 of the verb).

USAGE The relationship between the forms **rack** and **wrack** is complicated. The most common noun sense of **rack** 'a framework for holding and storing things' is always spelled **rack**, never **wrack**. The figurative senses of the verb, deriving from the type of torture in which someone is stretched on a **rack**, can, however, be spelled either **rack** or **wrack**: thus ***racked*** *with guilt* or ***wracked*** *with guilt*; ***rack*** *your brains* or ***wrack*** *your brains*; *the bank was* ***racked*** *by internal division* or *the bank was* ***wracked*** *by internal division*. In addition, the phrase **rack and ruin** can also be spelled **wrack and ruin**. In the contexts mentioned here as having the variant **wrack**, **rack** is always the commoner spelling.

▶**rack something up** accumulate or achieve something, typically a score or amount: *Japan is racking up record trade surpluses with the United States.*

rack[2] ▶**noun** a horse's gait in which both hoofs on either side in turn are lifted almost simultaneously, and all four hoofs are off the ground together at certain moments.
▶**verb** [no obj., with adverbial of direction] (of a horse) move with such a gait.
▶**rack off** [in imperative] Austral./NZ informal go away.
– ORIGIN mid 16th cent.: of unknown origin.

rack[3] ▶**noun** a joint of meat, typically lamb, that includes the front ribs.
– ORIGIN late 16th cent.: of unknown origin.

rack[4] ▶**verb** [with obj.] draw off (wine, beer, etc.) from the sediment in the barrel: *the wine is* ***racked off*** *into large oak casks.*
– ORIGIN late 15th cent.: from Provençal *arracar*, from *raca* 'stems and husks of grapes, dregs'.

rack[5] ▶**noun** variant spelling of **WRACK**[3].
▶**verb** [no obj., with adverbial of direction] archaic (of a cloud) be driven before the wind.
– ORIGIN Middle English (denoting a rush or collision): probably of Scandinavian origin; compare with Norwegian and Swedish dialect *rak* 'wreckage', from *reka* 'to drive'.

rack-and-pinion ▶**adjective** [attrib.] denoting a mechanism (e.g. for a car steering system) using a fixed cogged or toothed bar or rail engaging with a smaller cog.

racket[1] (also **racquet**) ▶**noun** a bat with a round or oval frame strung with catgut, nylon, etc., used especially in tennis, badminton, and squash.
■chiefly N. Amer. a snowshoe resembling such a bat.
– ORIGIN early 16th cent.: from French *raquette* (see **RACKETS**).

racket[2] ▶**noun 1** [in sing.] a loud unpleasant noise; a din: *the kids were* ***making a racket.***
■archaic the noise and liveliness of fashionable society.
2 informal an illegal or dishonest scheme for obtaining money: *a protection racket.*
■a person's line of business or way of life: *I'm in the insurance racket.*
▶**verb** (**racketed**, **racketing**) [no obj., with adverbial] make a loud unpleasant noise: *trains racketed by.*
■(**racket about/around**) enjoy oneself socially; go in pursuit of pleasure or entertainment.
– DERIVATIVES **rackety** adjective.
– ORIGIN mid 16th cent.: perhaps imitative of clattering.

racketeer ▶**noun** a person who engages in dishonest and fraudulent business dealings.
– DERIVATIVES **racketeering** noun.

rackets ▶**plural noun** [treated as sing.] a ball game for two or four people played with rackets in a plain four-walled court, distinguished from squash in particular by the use of a solid, harder ball.
– ORIGIN late Middle English (also in the singular): from French *raquette*, via Italian from Arabic *rāḥa*, *rāḥat-* 'palm of the hand'.

racket-tail (also **racquet-tail**) ▶**noun** a South American hummingbird with long racket-shaped tail feathers.
• Genera *Ocreatus* and *Loddigesia*, family Trochilidae: two species.
■any of a number of other birds, in particular certain parrots, drongos, and motmots, with racket-shaped tails.

Rackham /ˈrakəm/, Arthur (1867–1939), English illustrator, noted for his illustrations of books such as the Grimm brothers' *Fairy Tales* (1900) and *Peter Pan* (1906).

rack mounting ▶**noun** [mass noun] [usu. as modifier] the use of standardized racks for supporting electrical or electronic equipment.
– DERIVATIVES **rack-mount** adjective, **rack-mounted** adjective.

rack railway ▶**noun** a railway with a toothed rail between the bearing rails which engages with a cogwheel under the locomotive, for very steep slopes.

rack rent ▶**noun** an extortionate or very high rent.
▶**verb** (**rack-rent**) [with obj.] dated exact an excessive or extortionate rent from (a tenant) or for (a property).
– DERIVATIVES **rack-renter** noun.
– ORIGIN late 16th cent. (as *rack-rented*): from the verb **RACK**[1] (in the sense 'cause stress') + the noun **RENT**[1].

raclette /raˈklɛt/ ▶**noun** [mass noun] a Swiss dish of melted cheese, typically eaten with potatoes.
– ORIGIN French, literally 'small scraper', referring to the practice of holding the cheese over the heat and scraping it on to a plate as it melts.

racon /ˈreɪkɒn/ ▶**noun** chiefly US a radar beacon that can be identified and located by its response to a specific radar signal.
– ORIGIN 1940s: blend of **RADAR** and **BEACON**.

raconteur /ˌrakɒnˈtəː/ ▶**noun** a person who tells anecdotes in a skilful and amusing way.
– ORIGIN early 19th cent.: French, from *raconter* 'relate, recount'.

raconteuse /ˌrakɒnˈtəːz/ ▶**noun** a female raconteur.
– ORIGIN mid 19th cent.: French, feminine of *raconteur* (see **RACONTEUR**).

racoon ▶**noun** variant spelling of **RACCOON**.

racquet ▶**noun** variant spelling of **RACKET**[1].

racy ▶**adjective** (**racier**, **raciest**) (of speech, writing, or behaviour) lively, entertaining, and typically mildly sexually titillating: *the novel was considered rather racy at the time.*
■(of a person or thing) showing vigour or spirit: *a racy fiddle.* ■(of a wine, flavour, etc.) having a characteristic quality in a high degree. ■(of a vehicle or animal) designed or bred to be suitable for racing: *the yacht is fast and racy.*
– DERIVATIVES **racily** adverb, **raciness** noun.

RAD ▶**abbreviation for** (in the UK) Royal Academy of Dance.

rad[1] ▶**abbreviation for** radian(s).

rad[2] ▶**noun** informal a political radical.
– ORIGIN early 19th cent.: abbreviation.

rad[3] ▶**noun** Physics a unit of absorbed dose of ionizing radiation, corresponding to the absorption of 0.01 joule per kilogram of absorbing material.
– ORIGIN early 20th cent.: acronym from *radiation absorbed dose.*

rad[4] ▶**adjective** informal, chiefly US excellent; impressive: *his style is so rad | a really rad game.*
– ORIGIN 1980s: probably an abbreviation of **RADICAL**.

rad[5] ▶**noun** short for **RADIATOR**.

RADA /ˈrɑːdə/ ▶**abbreviation for** (in the UK) Royal Academy of Dramatic Art.

radar ▶**noun** [mass noun] a system for detecting the presence, direction, distance, and speed of aircraft, ships, and other objects, by sending out pulses of high-frequency electromagnetic waves which are reflected off the object back to the source.
■[count noun] an apparatus used for this.
– ORIGIN 1940s: from *ra(dio) d(etection) a(nd) r(anging).*

radar gun ▶**noun** a hand-held device used by traffic police to estimate the speed of a passing vehicle.

radar trap ▶**noun** an area of road in which radar is used by the police to detect vehicles exceeding a speed limit.

RADC ▶**abbreviation for** (in the UK) Royal Army Dental Corps.

Radcliffe, Mrs Ann (1764–1823), English novelist, a leading exponent of the Gothic novel. Notable works: *The Mysteries of Udolpho* (1794) and *The Italian* (1797).

raddle ▶**noun** another term for **REDDLE**.
■[count noun] a block or stick of reddle.
▶**verb** [with obj.] colour (someone or something) with reddle.
– ORIGIN early 16th cent.: related to **RED**; compare with **RUDDLE**.

raddled ▶**adjective 1** (of a person or their face) showing signs of age or fatigue: *he's beginning to look quite raddled.*
2 coloured with or as if with raddle: *raddled sheep.*
– ORIGIN sense 1 from **RADDLE** in the sense 'rouge', by association with its exaggerated use in make-up.

Radha /ˈrɑːdɑː, ˈrɑːðɑː/ Hinduism the favourite mistress of the god Krishna, and an incarnation of Lakshmi.
– ORIGIN from Sanskrit, literally 'prosperity'.

Radhakrishnan /ˌrɑːdəˈkrɪʃnən/, Sir Sarvepalli (1888–1975), Indian philosopher and statesman, President 1962–7. He introduced classical Indian philosophy to the West through works such as *Indian Philosophy* (1923–7).

radial ▶**adjective 1** of or arranged like rays or the radii of a circle; diverging in lines from a common centre.
■(of a road or route) running directly from a town or city centre to an outlying district. ■(also **radial-ply**) denoting a tyre in which the layers of fabric have their cords running at right angles to the circumference of the tyre and the tread is strengthened by further layers round the circumference. ■denoting an internal-combustion engine with its cylinders fixed like the spokes of a wheel around a rotating crankshaft (a type used chiefly in aircraft).
2 Anatomy & Zoology of or relating to the radius.
▶**noun 1** a radial tyre.
2 a radial road.
3 Zoology a supporting ray in a fish's fin.
4 a radial engine.
– DERIVATIVES **radially** adverb.
– ORIGIN late 16th cent.: from medieval Latin *radialis*, from Latin *radius* (see **RADIUS**).

radial keratotomy ▶**noun** see **KERATOTOMY**.

radial symmetry ▶**noun** [mass noun] chiefly Biology symmetry about a central axis, as in a starfish or a tulip flower.

radial velocity ▶**noun** chiefly Astronomy the velocity of a star or other body along the line of sight of an observer.

radian /ˈreɪdɪən/ ▶**noun** Geometry a unit of angle, equal to an angle at the centre of a circle the arc of which is equal in length to the radius.

radiance ▶**noun** [mass noun] **1** light or heat as emitted or reflected by something: *the radiance of the sunset dwindled and died.*
■great joy or love, apparent in someone's expression or bearing: *the radiance of the bride's smile.* ■a glowing quality of the skin, especially as indicative of good health or youth.
2 Physics the flux of radiation emitted per unit solid angle in a given direction by a unit area of a source.

radiant ▶**adjective 1** sending out light; shining or glowing brightly: *a bird with radiant green and red plumage.*
■(of a person or their expression) clearly emanating great joy, love, or health: *she gave him a radiant smile.* ■(of an emotion or quality) emanating powerfully from someone or something; very intense or conspicuous: *he praised her radiant self-confidence.*
2 [attrib.] (of electromagnetic energy, especially heat) transmitted by radiation, rather than conduction or convection.
■(of an appliance) designed to emit such energy, especially for cooking or heating.
▶**noun** a point or object from which light or heat radiates, especially a heating element in an electric or gas heater.
■Astronomy a radiant point.
– DERIVATIVES **radiancy** noun, **radiantly** adverb.
– ORIGIN late Middle English: from Latin *radiant-* 'emitting rays', from the verb *radiare* (see **RADIATE**).

radiant point ▶**noun** a centre point from which rays or radii proceed.
■Astronomy the apparent focal point of a meteor shower.

radiate ▶**verb 1** [with obj.] emit (energy, especially light or heat) in the form of rays or waves: *the hot stars radiate energy.*
■[no obj., with adverbial of direction] (of light, heat, or other energy) be emitted in such a way: *the continual stream of energy which radiates from the sun.* ■(of a person) clearly emanate (a strong feeling or quality) through their expression or bearing: *she lifted her chin, radiating defiance.* ■(**radiate from**) (of a feeling or quality) emanate clearly from: *leadership and confidence radiate from her.*

2 [no obj., with adverbial of direction] diverge or spread from or as if from a central point: *he ran down one of the passages that radiated from the room.*
■ Biology (of an animal or plant group) evolve into a variety of forms adapted to new situations or ways of life.
▶ **adjective** rare having rays or parts proceeding from a centre; arranged in or having a radial pattern: *the radiate crown.*
– DERIVATIVES **radiative** adjective (only in sense 1).
– ORIGIN early 17th cent.: from Latin *radiat-* 'emitted in rays', from the verb *radiare*, from *radius* 'ray, spoke'.

radiated ▶ **adjective** [attrib.] **1** (of light, heat, or other energy) emitted by radiation.
2 used in names of animals with markings arranged like rays, e.g. **radiated tortoise**.

radiation ▶ **noun** [mass noun] **1** Physics the emission of energy as electromagnetic waves or as moving subatomic particles, especially high-energy particles which cause ionization.
■ the energy transmitted in this way.
2 chiefly Biology divergence out from a central point, in particular evolution from an ancestral animal or plant group into a variety of new forms.
– DERIVATIVES **radiational** adjective, **radiationally** adverb.
– ORIGIN late Middle English (denoting the action of sending out rays of light): from Latin *radiatio(n-)*, from *radiare* 'emit rays' (see RADIATE).

radiation belt ▶ **noun** Astronomy a region surrounding a planet where charged particles accumulate under the influence of the planet's magnetic field.

radiation chemistry ▶ **noun** [mass noun] the branch of chemistry concerned with the effects of radiation on matter.

radiation pattern ▶ **noun** Physics the directional variation in intensity of the radiation from an aerial or other source.

radiation sickness ▶ **noun** [mass noun] illness caused by exposure of the body to ionizing radiation, characterized by nausea, hair loss, diarrhoea, bleeding, and damage to the bone marrow and central nervous system.

radiation therapy (also **radiation treatment**) ▶ **noun** another term for RADIOTHERAPY.

radiator ▶ **noun** **1** a thing that radiates or emits light, heat, or sound.
■ a device for heating a room consisting of a metal case connected by pipes through which hot water is pumped by a central heating system. ■ a portable oil or electric heater resembling such a device.
2 an engine-cooling device in a motor vehicle or aircraft consisting of a bank of thin tubes in which circulating water is cooled by the surrounding air.

radiator grille ▶ **noun** a grille at the front of a motor vehicle allowing air to circulate to the radiator to cool it.

radical ▶ **adjective 1** (especially of change or action) relating to or affecting the fundamental nature of something; far-reaching or thorough: *a radical overhaul of the existing regulatory framework.*
■ forming an inherent or fundamental part of the nature of someone or something: *the assumption of radical differences between the mental attributes of literate and non-literate peoples.* ■ (of surgery or medical treatment) thorough and intended to be completely curative. ■ characterized by departure from tradition; innovative or progressive: *the city is known for its radical approach to transport policy.*
2 advocating thorough or complete political or social reform; representing or supporting an extreme or progressive section of a political party: *a radical American activist.*
■ (of a measure or policy) following or based on such principles. ■ Brit. historical belonging to an extreme section of the Liberal party during the 19th century.
3 of or relating to the root of something, in particular:
■ Mathematics of the root of a number or quantity. ■ denoting or relating to the roots of a word. ■ Music belonging to the root of a chord. ■ Botany of, or springing direct from, the root or stem base of a plant.
4 [usu. as exclamation] informal, chiefly US very good; excellent: *Okay, then. Seven o'clock. Radical!*
▶ **noun 1** a person who advocates thorough or complete political or social reform; a member of a political party or part of a party pursuing such aims.

2 Chemistry a group of atoms behaving as a unit in a number of compounds. See also FREE RADICAL.
[ORIGIN: early 19th cent.: from French.]
3 the root or base form of a word.
■ any of the basic set of approximately 214 Chinese characters constituting semantically or functionally significant elements in the composition of other characters and used as a means of classifying characters in dictionaries.
4 Mathematics a quantity forming or expressed as the root of another.
■ a radical sign.
– DERIVATIVES **radicalism** noun (only in sense 1 of the noun), **radically** adverb [as submodifier] *a radically different approach*, **radicalness** noun.
– ORIGIN late Middle English (in the senses 'forming the root' and 'inherent'): from late Latin *radicalis*, from Latin *radix, radic-* 'root'.

radical chic ▶ **noun** [mass noun] the fashionable affectation of radical left-wing views.
■ the dress, lifestyle, or people associated with this.
– ORIGIN 1970: coined by the American writer, Tom Wolfe.

radicalize (also **-ise**) ▶ **verb** [with obj.] cause (someone) to become an advocate of radical political or social reform: *some of those involved had been radicalized by the Vietnam War.*
■ initiate or introduce fundamental or far-reaching changes in: *the push to radicalize 16–19 science education.*
– DERIVATIVES **radicalization** noun.

radical sign ▶ **noun** Mathematics the sign √ which indicates the square root of the number following (or a higher root indicated by a preceding superscript numeral).

radicchio /raˈdiːkɪəʊ/ ▶ **noun** (pl. **-os**) chicory of a variety which has dark red leaves.
– ORIGIN Italian.

radices plural form of RADIX.

radicle /ˈradɪk(ə)l/ ▶ **noun** Botany the part of a plant embryo that develops into the primary root.
■ Anatomy a root-like subdivision of a nerve or vein.
– DERIVATIVES **radicular** adjective (Anatomy).
– ORIGIN late 17th cent.: from Latin *radicula*, diminutive of *radix, radic-* 'root'.

radii plural form of RADIUS.

radio ▶ **noun** (pl. **-os**) [mass noun] the transmission and reception of electromagnetic waves of radio frequency, especially those carrying sound messages: *cellular phones are linked by radio rather than wires.*
■ the activity or industry of broadcasting sound programmes to the public: *she has written much material for radio* | [as modifier] *a radio station.* ■ radio programmes: *we used to listen to a lot of radio.* ■ [count noun] an apparatus for receiving such programmes: *he switched the radio on.* ■ [count noun] an apparatus capable of both receiving and transmitting radio messages between individuals, ships, planes, etc.: *a ship-to-shore radio.* ■ [in names] a broadcasting station or channel: *Radio One.*
▶ **verb** (**-oes**, **-oed**) [no obj.] communicate or send a message by radio: *the pilot radioed for help.*
■ [with obj.] communicate with (a person or place) by radio: *we'll radio Athens right away.*
– ORIGIN early 20th cent.: abbreviation of RADIO-TELEPHONY.

radio- ▶ **combining form 1** denoting radio waves or broadcasting: *radio-controlled* | *radiogram.*
2 Physics connected with rays, radiation, or radioactivity: *radiogenic* | *radiograph.*
■ denoting artificially prepared radioisotopes of elements: *radio-cobalt.*
3 Anatomy belonging to the radius in conjunction with some other part: *radio-carpal.*
– ORIGIN from RADIO or RADIUS.

radioactive ▶ **adjective** emitting or relating to the emission of ionizing radiation or particles: *radioactive decay* | *the water was radioactive.*
– DERIVATIVES **radioactively** adverb.

radioactivity ▶ **noun** [mass noun] the emission of ionizing radiation or particles caused by the spontaneous disintegration of atomic nuclei.
■ radioactive substances, or the radiation emitted by these.

radio amateur ▶ **noun** a person whose hobby is picking up, and generally also transmitting, radio messages.

radio astronomy ▶ **noun** [mass noun] the branch of astronomy concerned with radio emissions from celestial objects.

radiobiology ▶ **noun** [mass noun] the branch of biology concerned with the effects of ionizing radiation on organisms and the application in biology of radiological techniques.
– DERIVATIVES **radiobiological** adjective, **radiobiologically** adverb, **radiobiologist** noun.

radio button ▶ **noun** Computing (in a graphical display) an icon representing one of a set of options, only one of which can be selected at any time.

radio car ▶ **noun** a car, especially a police car, equipped with a two-way radio.

radiocarbon ▶ **noun** [mass noun] Chemistry a radioactive isotope of carbon.

radiocarbon dating ▶ **noun** another term for CARBON DATING.

radiochemistry ▶ **noun** [mass noun] the branch of chemistry concerned with radioactive substances.
– DERIVATIVES **radiochemical** adjective, **radiochemist** noun.

radio-controlled ▶ **adjective** (especially of an electronic model toy) controllable from a distance by radio.

radio-element ▶ **noun** a radioactive element or isotope.

radio frequency ▶ **noun** a frequency or band of frequencies in the range 10^4 to 10^{11} or 10^{12} Hz, suitable for use in telecommunications.

radio galaxy ▶ **noun** a galaxy emitting radiation in the radio-frequency range of the electromagnetic spectrum.

radiogenic /ˌreɪdɪə(ʊ)ˈdʒɛnɪk, -ˈdʒiːn-/ ▶ **adjective**
1 produced by radioactivity: *a radiogenic isotope.*
2 well suited in style or subject for broadcasting by radio: *a radiogenic series.*
– DERIVATIVES **radiogenically** adverb.

radio-goniometer ▶ **noun** an instrument for finding direction using radio waves.

radiogram ▶ **noun 1** Brit. a combined radio and record player built into a cabinet with a speaker.
[ORIGIN: from RADIO- + GRAMOPHONE.]
2 another term for RADIOGRAPH.
3 a telegram sent by radio.

radiograph ▶ **noun** an image produced on a sensitive plate or film by X-rays, gamma rays, or similar radiation, and typically used in medical examination.
▶ **verb** [with obj.] produce an image of (something) on a sensitive plate or film by X-rays, gamma rays, or similar radiation.
– DERIVATIVES **radiographer** noun, **radiographic** adjective, **radiographically** adverb, **radiography** noun.

radio ham ▶ **noun** see HAM[2] (in sense 2).

radioimmunoassay ▶ **noun** Medicine a technique for determining antibody levels by introducing an antigen labelled with a radioisotope and measuring the subsequent radioactivity of the antibody component.

radioimmunology ▶ **noun** [mass noun] the use of radioactively labelled antigens and antibodies in medical and biological research.
– DERIVATIVES **radioimmunological** adjective, **radioimmunologically** adverb.

radioisotope ▶ **noun** Chemistry a radioactive isotope.
– DERIVATIVES **radioisotopic** adjective.

radiolaria /ˌreɪdɪə(ʊ)ˈlɛːrɪə/ ▶ **plural noun** Zoology radiolarians collectively.
– ORIGIN late 19th cent.: modern Latin (former order name), from late Latin *radiolus* 'faint ray', diminutive of *radius* 'ray'.

radiolarian Zoology ▶ **noun** a single-celled aquatic animal which has a spherical amoebalike body with a spiny skeleton of silica. Their skeletons can accumulate as a slimy deposit on the seabed.
● Three classes of the phylum Actinopoda, kingdom Protista (formerly subclass or order Radiolaria).
▶ **adjective** of, relating to, or formed from radiolarians.

radiology ▶ **noun** [mass noun] the science dealing with X-rays and other high-energy radiation, especially the use of such radiation for the diagnosis and treatment of disease.
– DERIVATIVES **radiologic** adjective, **radiological** adjective, **radiologically** adverb, **radiologist** noun.

radiolucent /ˌreɪdɪəʊ'luːsənt/ ▶ adjective transparent to X-rays.
– DERIVATIVES **radiolucency** noun.

radiometer /ˌreɪdɪ'ɒmɪtə/ ▶ noun an instrument for detecting or measuring the intensity or force of radiation.
– DERIVATIVES **radiometry** noun.

radiometric ▶ adjective Physics of or relating to the measurement of radioactivity.
– DERIVATIVES **radiometrically** adverb.

radiometric dating ▶ noun [mass noun] a method of dating geological specimens by determining the relative proportions of particular radioactive isotopes present in a sample.

radionics /ˌreɪdɪ'ɒnɪks/ ▶ plural noun [treated as sing.] a system of alternative medicine based on the supposition that detectable electromagnetic radiation emitted by living matter can be interpreted diagnostically and transmitted to treat illness at a distance by complex electrical instruments.
– ORIGIN 1940s: from **RADIO-** 'radiation', on the pattern of *electronics*.

radionuclide ▶ noun a radioactive nuclide.

radiopaque /ˌreɪdɪəʊ'peɪk/ (also **radio-opaque**) ▶ adjective (of a substance) opaque to X-rays or similar radiation.
– DERIVATIVES **radiopacity** noun.

radiophonic ▶ adjective of, relating to, or denoting sound, especially music, produced electronically.

radioscopy /ˌreɪdɪ'ɒskəpi/ ▶ noun [mass noun] Physics the examination by X-rays or similar radiation of objects opaque to light.
– DERIVATIVES **radioscopic** adjective.

radiosonde /ˈreɪdɪəʊˌsɒnd/ ▶ noun dated an instrument carried by balloon or other means to various levels of the atmosphere and transmitting measurements by radio.
– ORIGIN 1930s: from **RADIO-** (relating to broadcasting) + German *Sonde* 'probe'.

radio-telephony ▶ noun [mass noun] telephony using radio transmission.
– DERIVATIVES **radio-telephone** noun, **radio-telephonic** adjective.

radio telescope ▶ noun Astronomy an instrument used to detect radio emissions from the sky, whether from natural celestial objects or from artificial satellites.

radiotelex ▶ noun a telex sent by radio, typically from a ship to land.

radiotherapy ▶ noun [mass noun] the treatment of disease, especially cancer, using X-rays or similar forms of radiation.
– DERIVATIVES **radiotherapeutic** adjective, **radiotherapist** noun.

radio wave ▶ noun an electromagnetic wave of a frequency between about 10^4 and 10^{11} or 10^{12} Hz, as used for long-distance communication.

radish ▶ noun **1** a swollen pungent-tasting edible root, especially a variety which is small, spherical, and red, and eaten raw with salad. See also **MOOLI**. **2** the plant of the cabbage family which yields this root.
● *Raphanus sativus*, family Cruciferae.
– ORIGIN Old English *rædic*, from Latin *radix, radic-* 'root'.

radium /ˈreɪdɪəm/ ▶ noun [mass noun] the chemical element of atomic number 88, a rare radioactive metal of the alkaline earth series. It was formerly used as a source of radiation for radiotherapy. (Symbol: **Ra**)
– ORIGIN late 19th cent.: from Latin *radius* 'ray' + **-IUM**.

radium emanation ▶ noun archaic term for **RADON**.

radius /ˈreɪdɪəs/ ▶ noun (pl. **radii** /-dɪʌɪ/ or **radiuses**) **1** a straight line from the centre to the circumference of a circle or sphere.
■ a radial line from the focus to any point of a curve. ■ the length of the radius of a circle or sphere. ■ a specified distance from a centre in all directions: *there are plenty of local pubs within a two-mile radius.* **2** Anatomy the thicker and shorter of the two bones in the human forearm. Compare with **ULNA**.
■ Zoology the corresponding bone in a vertebrate's foreleg or a bird's wing. ■ Zoology (in an echinoderm or coelenterate) any of the primary axes of radial

symmetry. ■ Entomology any of the main veins in an insect's wing.
▶ verb (**radiused, radiusing**) [with obj.] [often as adj. **radiused**] give a rounded form to (a corner or edge).
– ORIGIN late 16th cent. (in sense 2): from Latin, literally 'staff, spoke, ray'.

radius of curvature ▶ noun Mathematics the radius of a circle which touches a curve at a given point and has the same tangent and curvature at that point.

radius vector ▶ noun Mathematics a line of variable length drawn from a fixed origin to a curve.
■ Astronomy such a line joining a satellite or other celestial object to its primary.

radix /ˈradɪks, 'reɪ-/ ▶ noun (pl. **radices** /-dɪsiː/) **1** Mathematics the base of a system of numeration. **2** formal a source or origin of something: *Judaism is the radix of Christianity.*
– ORIGIN early 17th cent. (in sense 2): from Latin, literally 'root'. Sense 1 dates from the late 18th cent.

Radnorshire /ˈradnəʃɪə, -ʃə/ a former county of eastern Wales. It became part of Powys in 1974.

Radom /ˈrɑːdɒm/ an industrial city in central Poland; pop. 228,490 (1990).

radome /ˈreɪdəʊm/ ▶ noun a dome or other structure protecting radar equipment and made from material transparent to radio waves, especially one on the outer surface of an aircraft.
– ORIGIN 1940s: blend of **RADAR** and **DOME**.

radon /ˈreɪdɒn/ ▶ noun [mass noun] the chemical element of atomic number 86, a rare radioactive gas belonging to the noble gas series. (Symbol: **Rn**)
– ORIGIN early 20th cent.: from **RADIUM**, on the pattern of *argon*.

radula /ˈradjʊlə/ ▶ noun (pl. **radulae** /-liː/) Zoology (in a mollusc) a rasp-like structure of tiny teeth used for scraping food particles off a surface and drawing them into the mouth.
– DERIVATIVES **radular** adjective.
– ORIGIN late 19th cent.: from Latin, literally 'scraper', from *radere* 'to scrape'.

radwaste /ˈradweɪst/ ▶ noun [mass noun] informal radioactive waste.

Raeburn /ˈreɪbəːn/, Sir Henry (1756–1823), Scottish portrait painter. The leading Scottish portraitist of his day, he depicted the local intelligentsia and Highland chieftains in a bold and distinctive style.

RAF ▶ abbreviation for (in the UK) Royal Air Force.

Rafferty's rules /ˈrafətɪz/ ▶ plural noun Austral./NZ informal no rules at all: *the campaign was fought according to Rafferty's rules.*
– ORIGIN 1920s: *Rafferty*, probably an English dialect alteration of **REFRACTORY**.

raffia ▶ noun a palm tree native to tropical Africa and Madagascar, with a short trunk and leaves which may be up to 18 m (60 feet) long.
● *Raphia ruffia*, family Palmae.
■ [mass noun] the fibre from these leaves, used for making items such as hats, baskets, and mats.
– ORIGIN early 18th cent.: from Malagasy.

raffinate /ˈrafɪneɪt/ ▶ noun Chemistry a liquid from which impurities have been removed by solvent extraction.
– ORIGIN 1920s: from French *raffiner* or German *raffinieren* 'refine' + **-ATE**[1].

raffinose /ˈrafɪnəʊz, -s/ ▶ noun [mass noun] Chemistry a sugar present in sugar beet, cotton seed, and many cereals. It is a trisaccharide containing glucose, galactose, and fructose units.
– ORIGIN late 19th cent.: from French *raffiner* 'refine' + **-OSE**[2].

raffish ▶ adjective unconventional and slightly disreputable, especially in an attractive manner: *his raffish air.*
– DERIVATIVES **raffishly** adverb, **raffishness** noun.
– ORIGIN early 19th cent.: from **RIFF-RAFF** + **-ISH**[1].

raffle[1] ▶ noun a means of raising money by selling numbered tickets, one or some of which are subsequently drawn at random, the holder or holders of such tickets winning a prize.
▶ verb [with obj.] (usu. **be raffled**) offer (something) as a prize in such a draw.
– ORIGIN late Middle English (denoting a kind of dice game): from Old French, of unknown origin. The current sense dates from the mid 18th cent.

raffle[2] ▶ noun [mass noun] dialect rubbish; refuse: *the raffle of the yard below.*
– ORIGIN late Middle English (in the sense 'rabble, riff-raff'): perhaps from Old French *ne rifle ne rafle* 'nothing at all'.

Raffles, Sir (Thomas) Stamford (1781–1826), British colonial administrator. As Lieutenant General of Sumatra he persuaded the East India Company to purchase the undeveloped island of Singapore (1819), undertaking much of the preliminary work for transforming it into an international port and centre of commerce.

rafflesia /rə'fliːʒɪə, -'zɪə/ ▶ noun a parasitic plant which lacks chlorophyll and bears a single very large flower which smells of carrion, native to Malaysia and Indonesia.
● Genus *Rafflesia*, family Rafflesiaceae: several species, including *R. arnoldii*, with flowers over 60 cm (2 ft) across.
– ORIGIN modern Latin, named after Sir T. Stamford **RAFFLES**.

Rafsanjani /ˌrafsan'dʒɑːni/, Ali Akbar Hashemi (b.1934), Iranian statesman and religious leader, President 1989–97. In 1978 he helped organize the mass demonstrations that led to the shah's overthrow. As leader of Iran he sought to improve the country's relations with the West.

raft[1] ▶ noun a flat buoyant structure of timber or other materials fastened together, used as a boat or floating platform.
■ a small inflatable rubber or plastic boat, especially one for use in emergencies. ■ a floating mass of fallen trees, vegetation, ice, or other material. ■ a dense flock of swimming birds or mammals: *great rafts of cormorants, often 5,000 strong.* ■ a layer of reinforced concrete forming the foundation of a building.
▶ verb **1** [no obj., with adverbial of direction] travel on or as if on a raft: *I have rafted along the Rio Grande.*
■ [with obj. and adverbial of direction] transport on a raft: *the stores were rafted ashore.* ■ (of an ice floe) be driven on top of or underneath another floe. ■ [with obj. and adverbial of direction] transport (timber) on water in the form of a raft.
2 [with obj.] bring or fasten together (a number of boats or other objects) side by side.
– ORIGIN late Middle English (in the sense 'beam, rafter'): from Old Norse *raptr* 'rafter'. The verb dates from the late 17th cent.

raft[2] ▶ noun a large amount of something: *a raft of government initiatives.*
– ORIGIN mid 19th cent.: alteration of dialect *raff* 'abundance' (perhaps of Scandinavian origin), by association with **RAFT**[1] in the sense 'floating mass'.

rafter[1] ▶ noun a beam forming part of the internal framework of a roof.
– ORIGIN Old English *ræfter*, of Germanic origin; related to **RAFT**[1].

rafter[2] ▶ noun a person who travels on a raft.
■ a person employed in rafting timber.

raftered ▶ adjective (of a room or ceiling) having exposed rafters.

rafting ▶ noun [mass noun] the sport or pastime of travelling down a river on a raft.

raftsman ▶ noun (pl. **-men**) a man who works on a raft.

raft spider ▶ noun a large European spider which frequents pools and swamps, reaching through the surface to capture insects, tadpoles, and sometimes small fish.
● Genus *Dolomedes*, family Pisauridae.

rag[1] /rag/ ▶ noun **1** a piece of old cloth, especially one torn from a larger piece, used typically for cleaning things: *he wiped his hands on an oily rag* | [mass noun] *a piece of rag.*
■ (**rags**) old or tattered clothes. ■ (**rags**) figurative the remnants of something: *she clung to the rags of her self-control.* ■ [with negative] archaic the smallest scrap of cloth or clothing: *not a rag of clothing has arrived to us this winter.*
2 informal a newspaper, typically one regarded as being of low quality: *the local rag.*
▶ verb [with obj.] give a decorative effect to (a painted surface) by applying paint, typically of a different colour, with a rag.
■ apply (paint) to a surface with a rag.
– PHRASES **be on the rag** informal, chiefly N. Amer. be menstruating. [ORIGIN: from *rag* in the sense 'sanitary towel'.] **chew the rag** see **CHEW. in rags** (of clothes) tattered and torn. ■ (of a person) wearing such clothes. **lose one's rag** informal lose

one's temper. **(from) rags to riches** used to describe a person's rise from a state of extreme poverty to one of great wealth: *it was the old rags-to-riches fantasy.*
– ORIGIN Middle English: probably a back-formation from RAGGED or RAGGY.

rag² /rag/ ▶ noun [mass noun] [usu. as modifier] Brit. a programme of stunts, parades, and other entertainments organized by students to raise money for charity: *rag week.*
■ [count noun] informal, dated a boisterous prank or practical joke.
▶ verb (**ragged, ragging**) [with obj.] **1** make fun of (someone) in a loud, boisterous manner. **2** rebuke severely. **3** Ice Hockey keep possession of (the puck) by skilful stick-handling and avoidance of opponents, so as to waste time.
▶ **rag on** N. Amer. informal **1** complain about or criticize continually. **2** make fun of; tease constantly.
– ORIGIN mid 18th cent.: of unknown origin.

rag³ /rag/ ▶ noun **1** a large coarse roofing slate. **2** (also **ragstone**) [mass noun] Brit. a hard coarse sedimentary rock that can be broken into thick slabs.
– ORIGIN late Middle English (in sense 2): of unknown origin; later associated with RAG¹.

rag⁴ /rag/ ▶ noun a ragtime composition or tune.
– ORIGIN late 19th cent.: perhaps from RAGGED; compare with RAGTIME.

rag⁵ /rɑːg/ ▶ noun variant of RAGA.

raga /ˈrɑːɡə, ˈrɑːɡɑː/ ▶ noun (in Indian music) a pattern of notes having characteristic intervals, rhythms, and embellishments, used as a basis for improvisation.
■ a piece using a particular raga.
– ORIGIN late 18th cent.: from Sanskrit, literally 'colour, musical tone'.

ragamuffin (also **raggamuffin**) ▶ noun **1** a person, typically a child, in ragged, dirty clothes. **2** an exponent or follower of ragga, typically one dressing in ragged clothes.
■ another term for RAGGA.
– ORIGIN Middle English: probably based on RAG¹, with a fanciful suffix.

rag-and-bone man ▶ noun Brit. an itinerant dealer in old clothes, furniture, and small, cheap second-hand items.

ragbag ▶ noun a bag in which scraps of fabric and old clothes are kept for use.
■ a miscellaneous collection of something: *a ragbag of reforms are now being discussed.* ■ informal a woman dressed in an untidy or scruffy way.

rag bolt ▶ noun a bolt with barbs to keep it tight when it has been driven in.

rag book ▶ noun Brit. a book for very small children made of strong cloth that cannot be torn.

rag doll ▶ noun a soft doll made from pieces of cloth.

rage ▶ noun **1** [mass noun] violent uncontrollable anger: *her face was distorted with rage* | [count noun] *she flew into a rage.*
■ figurative the violent action of a natural agency: *the rising rage of the sea.* ■ [in sing.] a vehement desire or passion: *a rage for absolute honesty informs much western art.* ■ (**the rage**) a widespread temporary enthusiasm or fashion: *video and computer games are all the rage.* ■ poetic/literary intense feeling, especially prophetic, poetic, or martial enthusiasm or ardour. **2** Austral./NZ informal a lively party.
▶ verb [no obj.] **1** feel or express violent uncontrollable anger: *he raged at the futility of it all* | [with direct speech] 'That's unfair!' Maggie raged.
■ [with adverbial] (of a natural agency or a conflict) continue violently or with great force: *the argument raged for days.* ■ [with adverbial of direction] (of an illness) spread very rapidly or uncontrollably: *the great cholera epidemic which raged across Europe in 1831.* ■ (of an emotion) have or reach a high degree of intensity: *she couldn't hide the fear that raged within her.* **2** Austral./NZ informal go out and enjoy oneself socially: *get ready to rage!*
– DERIVATIVES **rager** noun.
– ORIGIN Middle English (also in the sense 'madness'): from Old French *rage* (noun), *rager* (verb), from a variant of Latin *rabies* (see RABIES).

ragfish ▶ noun (pl. same or **-fishes**) a large fish of the North Pacific, the bones of which are mostly cartilaginous, causing the body to feel limp when held.

■ *Icosteus aenigmaticus*, the only member of the family Icosteidae.

ragga /ˈragə/ ▶ noun [mass noun] chiefly Brit. a style of dance music similar to dancehall in which a DJ improvises lyrics over a sampled or electronic backing track.
– ORIGIN 1990s: from RAGAMUFFIN, because of the style of clothing worn by its followers.

raggamuffin ▶ noun variant spelling of RAGAMUFFIN.

ragged /ˈraɡɪd/ ▶ adjective **1** (of cloth or clothes) old and torn.
■ (of a person) wearing such clothes: *a ragged child.* **2** having a rough, irregular, or uneven surface, edge, or outline: *a ragged coastline.*
■ lacking finish, smoothness, or uniformity: *the ragged discipline of the players.* ■ (of a sound) rough or uneven: *his breathing became ragged.* ■ (of an animal) having a rough, shaggy coat: *a pair of ragged ponies.* ■ Printing (especially of a right margin) uneven because the lines are unjustified. **3** suffering from exhaustion or stress: *he looked a little ragged, a little shadowy beneath the eyes.*
– PHRASES **run someone ragged** exhaust someone by making them undertake a lot of physical activity.
– DERIVATIVES **raggedly** adverb, **raggedness** noun.
– ORIGIN Middle English: of Scandinavian origin; compare with Old Norse *rǫgvathr* 'tufted' and Norwegian *ragget* 'shaggy'.

ragged robin ▶ noun a pink-flowered European campion of damp grassland, with divided petals that give it a tattered appearance.
● *Lychnis flos-cuculi*, family Caryophyllaceae.

raggedy ▶ adjective informal, chiefly N. Amer. scruffy; shabby.

raggedy-ass (also **raggedy-assed**) ▶ adjective [attrib.] N. Amer. informal shabby; miserably inadequate: *she finally sold that raggedy-ass house.*
■ (of a person) new and inexperienced.

raggle-taggle ▶ adjective untidy and scruffy.
– ORIGIN early 20th cent.: apparently a fanciful variant of RAGTAG.

raggy ▶ adjective (**-ier, -iest**) informal ragged: *his raggy clothes.*
– ORIGIN late Old English, of Scandinavian origin.

raghead ▶ noun N. Amer. informal, offensive a person who wears a turban.

ragi /ˈrɑːɡiː/ ▶ noun [mass noun] chiefly Indian another term for **finger millet** (see MILLET).
– ORIGIN from Sanskrit and Hindi *rāgī*, from Telugu.

raging ▶ adjective showing violent uncontrollable anger: *a raging bull.*
■ (of a natural agency) continuing with overpowering force: *the stream could become a raging torrent in wet weather.* ■ (of a feeling, illness, process, or activity) so powerful as to seem out of control: *her raging thirst.* ■ informal tremendous: *he had been a raging success in Spain.*

raglan ▶ adjective (of a sleeve) continuing in one piece up to the neck of a garment, without a shoulder seam.
■ (of a garment) having sleeves of this type.
▶ noun an overcoat with sleeves of this type.
– ORIGIN mid 19th cent.: named after Lord *Raglan* (1788–1855), a British commander in the Crimean War.

ragman ▶ noun (pl. **-men**) a person who collects or deals in rags, old clothes, and other items.

Ragnarök /ˈraɡnərɒk/ Scandinavian Mythology the final battle between the gods and the powers of evil, the Scandinavian equivalent of the *Götterdämmerung.*
– ORIGIN from Old Norse *ragnarǫkr* 'twilight of the gods'.

ragout /raˈɡuː/ ▶ noun a highly seasoned dish of meat cut into small pieces and stewed with vegetables.
– ORIGIN from French *ragoût*, from *ragoûter* 'revive the taste of'.

rag paper ▶ noun [mass noun] paper made from cotton, originally from cotton rags, but now from cotton linters.

ragpicker ▶ noun historical a person who collected and sold rags.

rag-roll ▶ verb [with obj.] create a striped or marbled effect on (a surface) by painting it with a rag crumpled up into a roll.

rag rug ▶ noun a rug made from small strips of

---

fabric hooked into or pushed through a base material such as hessian.

ragstone ▶ noun see RAG³ (sense 2).

ragtag ▶ adjective [attrib.] untidy, disorganized, or incongruously varied in character: *a ragtag group of idealists.*
▶ noun (also **ragtag and bobtail**) [in sing.] a group of people perceived as disreputable or undesirable.
– ORIGIN early 19th cent.: superseding earlier *tag-rag* and *tag and rag* (see RAG¹, TAG¹).

ragtime ▶ noun [mass noun] music characterized by a syncopated melodic line and regularly accented accompaniment, evolved by black American musicians in the 1890s and played especially on the piano.
▶ adjective informal, dated disorderly; disreputable: *a ragtime army.*
– ORIGIN probably from RAG⁴ (from the syncopation) + TIME.

ragtop ▶ noun a car with a convertible roof.

rag trade ▶ noun (**the rag trade**) informal the clothing or fashion industry.

raguly /ˈraɡjʊli/ ▶ adjective [usu. postpositive] Heraldry having an edge with oblique notches like a row of sawn-off branches.
– ORIGIN mid 17th cent.: perhaps from RAGGED, on the pattern of *nebuly.*

Ragusa /raˈɡuːza/ Italian name (until 1918) for DUBROVNIK.

ragweed ▶ noun [mass noun] a North American plant of the daisy family. Its tiny green flowers produce copious amounts of pollen, making it a major causative agent of hay fever in some areas.
● *Ambrosia artemisia*, family Compositae.

ragworm ▶ noun a predatory marine bristle worm which is frequently used as bait by fishermen.
■ Family Nereidae: several genera and species, especially *Nereis diversicolor.*

ragwort ▶ noun a yellow-flowered ragged-leaved European plant of the daisy family, which is a common weed of grazing land. It is toxic to livestock, especially when dried.
● Genus *Senecio*, family Compositae: several species, in particular *S. jacobaea.*

rah ▶ exclamation informal, chiefly N. Amer. a cheer of encouragement or approval.
– ORIGIN late 19th cent.: shortening of HURRAH.

Rahman see ABDUL RAHMAN, MUJIBUR RAHMAN.

rah-rah N. Amer. informal ▶ adjective marked by great or uncritical enthusiasm or excitement: *many players were turned off by his rah-rah style.*
▶ noun [mass noun] great or uncritical enthusiasm and excitement.
– ORIGIN early 20th cent.: reduplication of RAH.

rah-rah skirt ▶ noun a short skirt with layered flounces, of a kind typically worn by cheerleaders.

rai /rʌɪ/ ▶ noun [mass noun] a style of music fusing Arabic and Algerian folk elements with Western rock.
– ORIGIN 1980s: perhaps from Arabic *ha er-ray*, literally 'that's the thinking, here is the view', a phrase frequently found in the songs.

RAID ▶ abbreviation for redundant array of independent (or inexpensive) disks, a system for providing greater capacity, faster access, and security against data corruption by spreading the data across several disk drives.

raid ▶ noun a rapid surprise attack on an enemy by troops, aircraft, or other armed forces in warfare: *a bombing raid.*
■ a rapid surprise attack to commit a crime, especially to steal from business premises: *an early morning raid on a bank.* ■ a surprise visit by police to arrest suspected people or seize illicit goods. ■ Stock Exchange a hostile attempt to buy a major or controlling interest in the shares of a company.
▶ verb [with obj.] conduct a raid on: *officers raided thirty homes yesterday.*
■ quickly and illicitly take something from (a place): *she crept down the stairs to raid the larder.*
– DERIVATIVES **raider** noun.
– ORIGIN late Middle English (as a noun): Scots variant of ROAD in the early senses 'journey on horseback', 'foray'. The noun became rare from the end of the 16th cent. but was revived by Sir Walter Scott; the verb dates from the mid 19th cent.

rail¹ /reɪl/ ▶ noun **1** a bar or series of bars, typically

---

r

fixed on upright supports, serving as part of a fence or barrier or used to hang things on.
■(**the rails**) the inside boundary fence of a racecourse. ■ the edge of a surfboard or sailboard.
2 a steel bar or continuous line of bars laid on the ground as one of a pair forming a railway track: *the goods train left the rails.*
■[mass noun] [often as modifier] railways as a means of transport: *rail fares | travelling by rail.*
3 a horizontal piece in the frame of a panelled door or sash window. Compare with **STILE**[2].
4 Electronics a conductor which is maintained at a fixed potential and to which other parts of a circuit are connected.
▶**verb 1** [with obj.] provide or enclose (a space or place) with a rail or rails: *the altar is* ***railed off from*** *the nave.*
2 [with obj. and adverbial of direction] convey (goods) by rail: *perishables were trucked and railed into Manhattan.*
3 [no obj.] (in windsurfing) sail the board on its edge, so that it is at a sharp angle to the surface of the water.
– PHRASES **go off the rails** informal begin behaving in a strange, abnormal, or wildly uncontrolled way. **on the rails 1** informal behaving or functioning in a normal or regulated way: *he is determined to get the club* ***back on the rails.*** **2** (of a racehorse or jockey) in a position on the racetrack nearest the inside fence.
– DERIVATIVES **railage** noun, **railless** adjective.
– ORIGIN Middle English: from Old French *reille* 'iron rod', from Latin *regula* 'straight stick, rule'.

rail[2] ▶**verb** [no obj.] (**rail against/at/about**) complain or protest strongly and persistently about: *he railed at human fickleness.*
– DERIVATIVES **railer** noun.
– ORIGIN late Middle English: from French *railler*, from Provençal *ralhar* 'to jest', based on an alteration of Latin *rugire* 'to bellow'.

rail[3] ▶**noun** a secretive bird with drab grey and brown plumage, typically having a long bill and found in dense waterside vegetation.
● Family Rallidae (the **rail family**): several genera, especially *Rallus*, and numerous species. The rail family also includes the crakes, gallinules, moorhens, and coots.
– ORIGIN late Middle English: from Old Northern French *raille*, perhaps of imitative origin.

rail-babbler ▶**noun** a long-tailed songbird of the logrunner family, with bold blue, red-brown, and white plumage, found mainly in the forests of New Guinea.
● Genus *Ptilorrhoa* (and *Eupetes*), family Orthonychidae: four species.

rail bird ▶**noun** N. Amer. a spectator at a horse race, especially one who watches from the railings along the track.

railbus ▶**noun** a lightweight diesel or petrol-driven railway passenger vehicle, typically with four wheels.

railcar ▶**noun** Brit. a powered railway passenger vehicle designed to operate singly or as part of a multiple unit.
■(**rail car**) N. Amer. any railway carriage or wagon.

railcard ▶**noun** Brit. a pass entitling the holder to reduced rail fares on off-peak trains.

rail fence ▶**noun** chiefly N. Amer. a fence, typically a wooden one, made of posts and rails.

railhead ▶**noun** a point on a railway from which roads and other transport routes begin.
■the furthest point reached in constructing a railway.

railing ▶**noun** (usu. **railings**) a fence or barrier made of rails.

raillery /ˈreɪləri/ ▶**noun** [mass noun] good-humoured teasing.
– ORIGIN mid 17th cent.: from French *raillerie*, from *railler* 'to rail' (see **RAIL**[2]).

railman ▶**noun** (pl. **-men**) another term for **RAILWAYMAN**.

railroad ▶**noun** North American term for **RAILWAY**.
▶**verb 1** [with obj.] informal press (someone) into doing something by rushing or coercing them: *she hesitated, unwilling to be* ***railroaded into*** *a decision.*
■cause (a measure) to be passed or approved quickly by applying pressure: *the Bill had been* ***railroaded through*** *the House.* ■ N. Amer. send (someone) to prison without a fair trial or by means of false evidence.
2 [no obj.] [usu. as noun **railroading**] N. Amer. travel or work on the railways.

Railtrack an authority set up in the United Kingdom in 1994 to take responsibility for the infrastructure of the British railway system.

railway ▶**noun 1** a track or set of tracks made of steel rails along which passenger and goods trains run: [as modifier] *a railway line.*
■a set of tracks for other vehicles.
2 a system of such tracks with the trains, organization, and personnel required for its working: [in names] *Canadian National Railways.*

railwayman ▶**noun** (pl. **-men**) chiefly Brit. a man who works on a railway.

raiment /ˈreɪm(ə)nt/ ▶**noun** [mass noun] archaic or poetic/literary clothing: *ladies clothed in raiment bedecked with jewels.*
– ORIGIN late Middle English: shortening of obsolete *arrayment* 'dress, outfit'.

rain ▶**noun** [mass noun] the condensed moisture of the atmosphere falling visibly in separate drops: *the rain had not stopped for days | it's pouring with rain.*
■(**rains**) falls of rain: *the plants were washed away by some unusually heavy rains.* ■ [in sing.] a large or overwhelming quantity of things that fall or descend: *he fell under the* ***rain of*** *blows.*
▶**verb** [no obj.] (**it rains, it is raining**, etc.) rain falls: *it was beginning to rain.*
■poetic/literary (of the sky, the clouds, etc.) send down rain. ■ [with adverbial of direction] (of objects) fall in large or overwhelming quantities: *bombs rained down.* ■ [with obj.] (**it rains ——, it is raining ——**, etc.) used to convey that a specified thing is falling in large or overwhelming quantities: *it was just raining glass.* ■ [with obj. and adverbial of direction] send down in large or overwhelming quantities: *she rained blows on to him.*
– PHRASES **be as right as rain** (of a person) be perfectly fit and well. **it never rains but it pours** see **POUR**. **rain cats and dogs** rain very hard. [ORIGIN: origin uncertain; first recorded in 1738, used by Jonathan Swift, but the phrase *rain dogs and polecats* was used a century earlier in Richard Brome's *The City Witt.*] **rain on someone's parade** informal, chiefly N. Amer. prevent someone from enjoying an occasion or event; spoil someone's plans. (**come**) **rain or shine** whether it rains or not: *he runs six miles every morning, rain or shine.*
– DERIVATIVES **rainless** adjective.
▶**rain something off** (or N. Amer. **out**) (usu. **be rained off**) cause an event to be terminated or cancelled because of rain: *the match was rained off.*
– ORIGIN Old English *regn* (noun), *regnian* (verb), of Germanic origin; related to Dutch *regen* and German *Regen*.

rainbird ▶**noun** a bird that is said to foretell rain by its call, especially (in Britain) the green woodpecker or (in South Africa) a kind of coucal.

rainbow ▶**noun** an arch of colours formed in the sky in certain circumstances, and caused by the refraction and dispersion of the sun's light by rain or other water droplets in the atmosphere. The colours of the rainbow are generally said to be red, orange, yellow, green, blue, indigo, and violet.
■any display of the colours of the spectrum produced by dispersion of light. ■ a wide range or variety of related and typically colourful things: *a* ***rainbow of*** *medals decorated his chest.* ■ [as modifier] many-coloured: *a big rainbow packet of felt pens.* ■ short for **RAINBOW TROUT**.
– PHRASES **at the end of the rainbow** used to refer to something much sought after but impossible to attain. [ORIGIN: with allusion to the story of a crock of gold supposedly to be found by anyone reaching the end of a rainbow.] **chase rainbows** (or **a rainbow**) pursue an illusory goal.
– ORIGIN Old English *regnboga* (see **RAIN, BOW**[1]).

Rainbow Bridge a bridge of natural rock, the world's largest natural bridge, situated in southern Utah, just north of the border with Arizona. Its span is 86 m (278 ft).

rainbow coalition ▶**noun** (especially in the US) a political alliance of differing groups, typically one comprising minority peoples and other disadvantaged groups.

rainbowfish ▶**noun** (pl. same or **-fishes**) any of a number of small brightly coloured fish of warm waters, in particular:
● an Australian freshwater fish (genus *Melanotaenia*, family Melanotaenidae). ● (**Celebes rainbowfish**) a freshwater fish native to Sulawesi and popular in aquaria (*Telmatherina ladigesi*, family Atherinidae).

rainbow lorikeet (also **rainbow lory**) ▶**noun** a small vividly coloured Australasian parrot, found in many different races on SW Pacific islands.
● *Trichoglossus haematodus*, family Loridae (or Psittacidae).

rainbow trout ▶**noun** a large, partly migratory trout native to the Pacific seaboard of North America. It has been widely introduced elsewhere, both as a farmed food fish and as a sporting fish.
● *Onchorhynchus mykiss*, family Salmonidae.

rain check ▶**noun** N. Amer. a ticket given for later use when a sporting fixture or other outdoor event is interrupted or postponed by rain.
■a coupon issued to a customer by a shop, guaranteeing that a sale item which is out of stock may be purchased by that customer at a later date at the same reduced price.
– PHRASES **take a rain check** said when politely refusing an offer, with the implication that one may take it up at a later date.

raincoat ▶**noun** a long coat, typically having a belt, made from waterproofed or water-resistant fabric.

rain dance ▶**noun** a ritual dance to summon rain, as practised by some Pueblo Indians and other peoples.

raindrop ▶**noun** a single drop of rain.
– ORIGIN Old English *regndropa* (see **RAIN, DROP**).

rainfall ▶**noun** [mass noun] the fall of rain.
■the quantity of rain falling within a given area in a given time: *low rainfall.*

rainfast ▶**adjective** (of a chemical spray or other substance) not able to be washed away by rain.

rainfly ▶**noun** (pl. **-flies**) **1** N. Amer. the flysheet of a tent.
2 W. Indian a winged ant or termite, seen in numbers after rain.

rainforest ▶**noun** a luxuriant, dense forest rich in biodiversity, found typically in tropical areas with consistently heavy rainfall.

rain gauge ▶**noun** a device for collecting and measuring the amount of rain which falls.

Rainier, Mount /rəˈnɪə, ˈreɪnɪə/ a volcanic peak in the south-west of Washington State in the US. Rising to a height of 4,395 m (14,410 ft), it is the highest peak in the Cascade Range.

rainmaker ▶**noun** a person who attempts to cause rain to fall, either by rituals or by a scientific technique such as seeding clouds with crystals.
■N. Amer. informal a person who is highly successful, especially in business.
– DERIVATIVES **rainmaking** noun.

rainout ▶**noun** N. Amer. a cancellation or premature ending of an event because of rain.

rainproof ▶**adjective** (especially of a building or garment) impervious to rain: *a rainproof coat.*

rain scald ▶**noun** [mass noun] a skin disease of horses caused by infection with actinomycete bacteria, typically contracted in persistently rainy conditions.

rain shadow ▶**noun** a region having little rainfall because it is sheltered from prevailing rain-bearing winds by a range of hills.

rainstorm ▶**noun** a storm with heavy rain.

rainswept ▶**adjective** exposed to or frequently experiencing rain and wind: *the rainswept quayside.*

rain tree ▶**noun** a large tropical American tree which is widely planted as a street tree. It has grooved bark which typically supports epiphytic plants, and 'rain' is excreted by cicadas that live in the tree.
● *Albizia saman*, family Leguminosae.

rainwash ▶**noun** [mass noun] the washing away of soil or other loose material by rain.

rainwater ▶**noun** [mass noun] water that has fallen as or been obtained from rain.

rainworm ▶**noun 1** the earthworm, which often comes to the surface after rain.
2 a soil-dwelling nematode worm, the juveniles of which parasitize grasshoppers.
● *Mermis nigrescens*, class Aphasmida (or Adenophorea).

rainy ▶**adjective** (**rainier, rainiest**) (of weather, a period of time, or an area) having a great deal of rainfall: *a rainy afternoon.*
– PHRASES **a rainy day** used in reference to a possible time in the future when something, especially money, will be needed: *putting money by for a rainy day.*
– DERIVATIVES **raininess** noun.
– ORIGIN Old English *rēnig* (see **RAIN, -Y**[1]).

Raipur /raɪˈpʊə/ a city in central India, in Madhya Pradesh; pop. 438,000 (1991).

raise ▶**verb** [with obj.] **1** lift or move to a higher position or level: *she raised both arms above her head | his flag was raised over the city.*

■ lift or move to a vertical position; set upright: *Melody managed to raise him to his feet.* ■ construct or build (a structure): *a fence was being raised around the property.* ■ cause to rise or form: *the galloping horse raised a cloud of dust.* ■ bring to the surface (a ship that has sunk). ■ cause (bread) to rise, especially by the action of yeast. ■ [usu. as adj. **raised**] cause (pastry) to stand without support. ■ make a (nap) on cloth.

2 increase the amount, level, or strength of: *the bank raised interest rates | the aim was to raise awareness of the plight of the homeless.*

■ promote (someone) to a higher rank: *the king **raised** him **to** the title of Count Torre Bella.* ■ [usu. as noun **raising**] Linguistics (in transformational grammar) move (a noun phrase) out of a subordinate clause and into a main clause under certain conditions. ■ (**raise something to**) Mathematics multiply a quantity to (a specified power): *3 raised to the 7th power is 2,187.* ■ [with two objs] (in poker or brag) bet (a specified amount) more than (another player): *I'll raise you another hundred dollars.* ■ [with obj.] Bridge make a higher bid in the same suit as that bid by (one's partner). ■ [with obj.] increase (a bid) in this way.

3 cause to be heard, considered, or discussed: *doubts have been raised about the future of the reprocessing plant.*

■ cause to occur, appear, or be felt: *recent sightings have raised hopes that otters are making a return.* ■ generate (an invoice or other document).

4 collect, levy, or bring together (money or resources): *it is hoped that the event will raise £50,000.*

5 chiefly N. Amer. bring up (a child): *he was born and raised in San Francisco.*

■ breed or grow (animals or plants): *they raised pigs and kept a pony.*

6 bring (someone) back from death: *God **raised** Jesus **from the dead**.*

7 abandon or force an enemy to abandon (a siege, blockade, or embargo).

8 drive (an animal) from its lair: *the jack rabbit was only 250 yards from where he first raised it.*

■ cause (a ghost or spirit) to appear: figurative *the piece raises the ghosts of a number of twentieth-century art ideas.* ■ Brit. informal establish contact with (someone), especially by telephone or radio: *I raised him on the open line.* ■ (of someone at sea) come in sight of (land or another ship): *they raised the low coast by evening.*

9 Immunology stimulate production of (an antiserum, antibody, or other biologically active substance) against the appropriate target cell or substance.

▶ **noun 1** chiefly N. Amer. an increase in salary: *he wants a raise and some perks.*

2 (in poker or brag) an increase in a stake.

■ Bridge a higher bid in the suit that one's partner has bid.

3 [usu. with adj. or noun modifier] Weightlifting an act of lifting or raising a part of the body while holding a weight: *bent-over raises.*

– PHRASES **raise Cain** see **CAIN**. **raise the devil** informal make a noisy disturbance. **raise one's eyebrows** see **EYEBROW**. **raise one's glass** drink a toast: *I **raised my glass to** Susan.* **raise one's hand** strike or seem to be about to strike someone: *she **raised her hand to** me.* **raise one's hat** briefly remove one's hat as a gesture of courtesy or respect to someone. **raise hell** informal make a noisy disturbance. ■ complain vociferously: *he raised hell with real estate developers and polluters.* **raise hob** see **HOB**². **raise a laugh** make people laugh. **raise the roof** make or cause someone else to make a great deal of noise, especially through cheering: *when I finally scored the fans raised the roof.* **raise one's voice** speak more loudly. ■ begin to speak or sing.

– DERIVATIVES **raisable** adjective, **raiser** noun.

– ORIGIN Middle English: from Old Norse *reisa*; related to the verb **REAR**².

raised beach ▶ **noun** Geology a former beach now lying above water level owing to geological changes since its formation.

raised bog ▶ **noun** a peat bog in which growth is most rapid at the centre, giving it a domed shape.

raisin ▶ **noun** a partially dried grape.

– DERIVATIVES **raisiny** adjective.

– ORIGIN Middle English: from Old French, 'grape', from an alteration of Latin *racemus* 'grape bunch'.

raison d'état /ˌreɪzɒ̃ deɪˈtɑ, French rɛzɔ̃ deta/ ▶ **noun** (pl. **raisons d'état** pronunc. same) a purely political reason for action on the part of a ruler or government, especially where a departure from openness, justice, or honesty is involved.

– ORIGIN French, literally 'reason of state'.

raison d'être /ˌreɪzɒ̃ ˈdɛtrə, French rɛzɔ̃ dɛtʀ/ ▶ **noun** (pl. **raisons d'être** pronunc. same) the most important reason or purpose for someone or something's existence: *seeking to shock is the catwalk's raison d'être.*

– ORIGIN French, literally 'reason for being'.

raita /ˈrʌɪtə/ ▶ **noun** [mass noun] an Indian side dish of yogurt containing chopped cucumber or other vegetables, and spices.

– ORIGIN from Hindi *rāytā*.

Raj /rɑː(d)ʒ/ ▶ **noun** (**the Raj**) historical British sovereignty in India: *the last days of the Raj.*

■ (**raj**) [mass noun] Indian rule; government.

– ORIGIN from Hindi *rāj* 'reign'.

raja /ˈrɑːdʒɑː/ (also **rajah**) ▶ **noun** historical an Indian king or prince.

■ a title extended to petty dignitaries and nobles in India during the British Raj. ■ a title extended by the British to a Malay or Javanese ruler or chief.

– ORIGIN from Hindi *rājā*, Sanskrit *rājan* 'king'.

Rajasthan /ˌrɑːdʒəˈstɑːn/ a state in western India, on the Pakistani border; capital, Jaipur. The western part of the state consists largely of the Thar Desert and is sparsely populated.

– DERIVATIVES **Rajasthani** noun & adjective.

Rajasthan Canal former name for **INDIRA GANDHI CANAL**.

raja yoga ▶ **noun** [mass noun] a form of yoga intended to achieve control over the mind and emotions.

– ORIGIN from Sanskrit, from *rājan* 'king' + **YOGA**.

Rajkot /rɑːdʒˈkəʊt/ a city in Gujarat, western India; pop. 556,000 (1991).

Rajneesh /rʌdʒˈniːʃ/, Bhagwan Shree (1931–90), Indian guru; born *Chandra Mohan Jain*; known as **the Bhagwan** (Sanskrit, 'lord'). He founded an ashram in Poona, India, and a commune in Oregon, becoming notorious for his doctrine of communal therapy and salvation through free love. He was deported from the US in 1985 for immigration violations.

Rajput /ˈrɑːdʒpʊt/ ▶ **noun** a member of a Hindu military caste claiming Kshatriya descent.

– ORIGIN from Hindi *rājpūt*, from Sanskrit *rājan* 'king' + *putra* 'son'.

Rajputana /ˌrɑːdʒpʊˈtɑːnə/ an ancient region of India consisting of a collection of princely states ruled by dynasties. Following independence from Britain in 1947, they united to form the state of Rajasthan, parts also being incorporated into Gujarat and Madhya Pradesh.

Rajshahi /rɑːdʒˈʃɑːhi/ a port on the Ganges River in western Bangladesh; pop. 324,530 (1991).

Rajya Sabha /ˌrɑːdʒjə sʌˈbɑː/ the upper house of the Indian parliament. Compare with **LOK SABHA**.

– ORIGIN from Sanskrit *rājya* 'State' + *sabhā* 'council'.

rake¹ ▶ **noun** an implement consisting of a pole with a crossbar toothed like a comb at the end, or with several tines held together by a crosspiece, used especially for drawing together cut grass or smoothing loose soil or gravel.

■ a wheeled implement used for the same purposes. ■ a similar implement used for other purposes, e.g. by a croupier drawing in money at a gaming table. ■ [in sing.] an act of raking: *giving the lawn a rake.*

▶ **verb** [with obj.] collect, gather, or move with a rake or similar implement: *they started **raking up** hay.*

■ make (a stretch of ground) tidy or smooth with a rake: *I sometimes **rake over** the allotment.* ■ scratch or scrape (something, especially a person's flesh) with a long sweeping movement: *her fingers raked Bill's face.* ■ [with obj. and adverbial of direction] draw or drag (something) with a long sweeping movement: *she raked a comb through her hair.* ■ sweep (something) from end to end with gunfire, a look, or a beam of light: *the road was raked with machine-gun fire.* ■ [no obj., with adverbial of direction] move across something with a long sweeping movement: *his icy gaze raked mercilessly over Lissa's slender figure.* ■ [no obj., with adverbial] search or rummage through something: *he raked through his pockets and brought out a five-pound note.*

– PHRASES **rake and scrape** black English be extremely thrifty; scrimp and save. **rake over** (**old**) **coals** (or **rake over the ashes**) chiefly Brit. revive the memory of a past event which is best forgotten. (**as**) **thin as a rake** (of a person) very thin.

– DERIVATIVES **raker** noun.

– ORIGIN Old English *raca*, *racu*, of Germanic origin; related to Dutch *raak* and German *Rechen*, from a base meaning 'heap up'; the verb is partly from Old Norse *raka* 'to scrape, shave'.

▶ **rake something in** informal make a lot of money, typically very easily: *the shop's **raking it in** now.*

rake something up/over revive the memory of an incident or period of time that is best forgotten: *I have no desire to rake over the past.*

rake² ▶ **noun** a fashionable or wealthy man of dissolute or promiscuous habits.

– PHRASES **a rake's progress** a progressive deterioration, especially through self-indulgence. [ORIGIN: from the title of a series of engravings by Hogarth (1735).]

– ORIGIN mid 17th cent.: abbreviation of archaic *rakehell* in the same sense.

rake³ ▶ **verb** [with obj.] (often **be raked**) set (something, especially a stage or the floor of an auditorium) at a sloping angle.

■ [no obj.] (of a ship's mast or funnel) incline from the perpendicular towards the stern. ■ [no obj.] (of a ship's bow or stern) project at its upper part beyond the keel.

▶ **noun 1** [in sing.] the angle at which a thing slopes.

2 the angle of the edge or face of a cutting tool.

– ORIGIN early 17th cent.: probably related to German *ragen* 'to project', of unknown ultimate origin; compare with Swedish *raka*.

rake⁴ ▶ **noun** Brit. a number of railway carriages or wagons coupled together.

– ORIGIN early 20th cent. (originally Scots and northern English): from Old Norse *rák* 'stripe, streak', from an alteration of *rek-* 'to drive'. The word was in earlier use in the senses 'path, groove' and 'vein of ore'.

rake-off ▶ **noun** informal a commission or share of the profits from a deal, especially one that is disreputable.

rakhi /ˈrɑːki/ ▶ **noun** (pl. **rakhis**) a cotton bracelet, typically bearing elaborate ornamentation, given at Raksha Bandhan by a girl or woman to a brother or to a close male friend who must then treat and protect her as a sister.

– ORIGIN from Hindi *rākhī*.

raki /rəˈkiː, ˈraki/ ▶ **noun** [mass noun] a strong alcoholic spirit made in eastern Europe or the Middle East.

– ORIGIN from Turkish *rakı*.

raking light ▶ **noun** [mass noun] (in art or photography) bright light, usually beamed obliquely, used to reveal such things as texture and detail.

rakish¹ ▶ **adjective** having or displaying a dashing, jaunty, or slightly disreputable quality or appearance: *he had a rakish, debonair look.*

– DERIVATIVES **rakishly** adverb, **rakishness** noun.

rakish² ▶ **adjective** (especially of a boat or car) smart and fast-looking, with streamlined angles and curves.

– ORIGIN early 19th cent.: from the noun **RAKE**³ + **-ISH**¹.

Rákosi /ˈrɑːkɒʃi/, Mátyás (1892–1971), Hungarian Communist statesman, First Secretary of the Hungarian Socialist Workers' Party 1945–56 and Prime Minister 1952–3 and 1955–6. After the Communist seizure of power in 1945 he did much to establish a firmly Stalinist regime. He was ousted as Premier by the more liberal Imre Nagy in 1953.

Raksha Bandhan /ˌrʌkʃɑː ˈbʌnd(ə)n/ ▶ **noun** (in the Indian subcontinent) a popular festival of friendship occurring annually in August, during which a girl or woman gives cotton bracelets (rakhis) to brothers and close male friends.

raku /ˈrɑːkuː/ ▶ **noun** [mass noun] [usu. as modifier] a kind of lead-glazed Japanese earthenware, typically irregular in shape and used especially for the tea ceremony.

– ORIGIN Japanese, literally 'enjoyment'.

rale /rɑːl/ ▶ **noun** (usu. **rales**) Medicine an abnormal rattling sound heard when examining unhealthy lungs with a stethoscope.

– ORIGIN early 19th cent.: from French *râle*, from *râler* 'to rattle'.

Raleigh¹ /ˈrɑːli/ the state capital of North Carolina; pop. 207,950 (1990).

Raleigh² /ˈrɑːli, ˈrɔːli/ (also **Ralegh**), Sir Walter (*c.*1552–1618), English explorer, courtier, and writer. A favourite of Elizabeth I, he organized several voyages of exploration and colonization to the Americas, and introduced potato and tobacco plants to England. Imprisoned in 1603 by James I on a charge of conspiracy, he was released in 1616 to lead an expedition in search of El Dorado, but was executed on the original charge when he returned empty-handed.

rall. Music ▶ **abbreviation for** rallentando.

rallentando /ˌralən'tandəʊ/ Music ▶ **adverb** & **adjective** (especially as a direction) with a gradual decrease of speed.
▶ **noun** (pl. **rallentandos** or **rallentandi** /-di/) a gradual decrease in speed.
– ORIGIN Italian, literally 'slowing down', from the verb *rallentare*.

ralli car (also **ralli cart**) ▶ **noun** Brit. historical a light two-wheeled horse-drawn vehicle for four people.
– ORIGIN late 19th cent.: from *Ralli*, the name of the first purchaser of such a vehicle.

rally[1] ▶ **verb** (**-ies, -ied**) [no obj.] **1** (of troops) come together again in order to continue fighting after a defeat or dispersion: *De Montfort's troops rallied and drove back the king's infantry.*
■ [with obj.] bring together (forces) again in order to continue fighting: *the king escaped to Perth to rally his own forces.* ■ assemble in a mass meeting: *up to 50,000 people rallied in the city centre.* ■ come together in order to support a person or cause or for concerted action: [with infinitive] *colleagues **rallied round** to help Ann.* ■ [with obj.] bring together (forces or support) in such a way: *a series of meetings to rally support for the union.* ■ (of a person) recover their health, spirits, or poise: *she floundered for a moment, then rallied again.* ■ [with obj.] revive (a person or their health or spirits): *they rallied her with a drink.* ■ (of share, currency, or commodity prices) increase after a fall: *prices of metals such as aluminium and copper have rallied.*
2 drive in a rally.
▶ **noun** (pl. **-ies**) **1** a mass meeting of people making a political protest or showing support for a cause: *a rally attended by around 100,000 people.*
■ an open-air event for people who own a particular kind of vehicle: *a traction engine rally.*
2 a competition for motor vehicles in which they are driven a long distance over public roads or rough terrain, typically in several stages: [as modifier] *a rally driver.*
3 a quick or marked recovery after a reverse or a period of weakness: *the market staged a late rally.*
4 (in tennis and other racket sports) an extended exchange of strokes between players.
– DERIVATIVES **rallier** noun, **rallyist** noun (only in sense 2 of the noun).
– ORIGIN early 17th cent. (in the sense 'bring together again'): from French *rallier*, from *re-* 'again' + *allier* 'to ally'.

rally[2] ▶ **verb** (**-ies, -ied**) [with obj.] archaic subject (someone) to good-humoured ridicule; tease: *he rallied her on the length of her pigtail.*
– ORIGIN mid 17th cent.: from French *railler* 'to rib, tease' (see **RAIL**[2]).

rallycross ▶ **noun** [mass noun] Brit. a form of motor racing in which cars are driven in heats over a course including rough terrain and tarmac roads, but not public roads. Compare with **AUTOCROSS**.

rallying ▶ **noun** [mass noun] **1** [often as modifier] the action or process of coming together to support a person or cause or take concerted action: *a rallying cry.*
2 the sport or action of participating in a motor rally: *established names in international rallying.*

RAM ▶ **abbreviation for** ■ Computing random-access memory. ■ (in the UK) Royal Academy of Music.

ram ▶ **noun 1** an uncastrated male sheep.
■ (**the Ram**) the zodiacal sign or constellation Aries.
2 short for **BATTERING RAM**.
■ the falling weight of a piledriving machine. ■ historical a beak or other projecting part of the bow of a warship, for piercing the sides of other ships. ■ historical a warship with such a bow.
3 a hydraulic water-raising or lifting machine.
■ the piston of a hydrostatic press. ■ the plunger of a force pump.
▶ **verb** (**rammed, ramming**) [with obj. and adverbial of direction] roughly force (something) into place: *he rammed his stick into the ground.*
■ [with obj.] (of a vehicle or vessel) be driven violently into (something, typically another vehicle or vessel) in an attempt to stop or damage it: *their boat was rammed by a Japanese warship.* ■ [no obj., with adverbial] crash violently against something: *the stolen car rammed into the front of the house.* ■ [with obj.] [often as adj. **rammed**] beat (earth or the ground) with a heavy implement to make it hard and firm. ■ (**be rammed**) Brit. informal (of a place) be very full of people: *the club is rammed to the rafters every week.*
– PHRASES **ram something down someone's throat** see **THROAT**. **ram something home** see **HOME**.
– DERIVATIVES **rammer** noun.
– ORIGIN Old English *ram(m)*, of Germanic origin; related to Dutch *ram*.

Rama /'rɑːmə/ the hero of the Ramayana, husband of Sita. He is the Hindu model of the ideal man, the seventh incarnation of Vishnu, and is widely venerated, by some sects as the supreme god.

ramada /rə'mɑːdə/ ▶ **noun** US an arbour or porch.
– ORIGIN mid 19th cent.: from Spanish.

Ramadan /'ramədan, ˌramə'dan/ (also **Ramadhan** /-zan/) ▶ **noun** the ninth month of the Muslim year, during which strict fasting is observed from sunrise to sunset.
– ORIGIN from Arabic *ramaḍān*, from *ramaḍa* 'be hot'. The lunar reckoning of the Muslim calendar brings the fast eleven days earlier each year, eventually causing Ramadan to occur in any season; originally it was supposed to be in one of the hot months.

ram air ▶ **noun** [mass noun] technical air which is forced to enter a moving aperture, such as the air intake of an aircraft.

Ramakrishna /ˌrɑːmə'krɪʃnə/ (1836–86), Indian yogi and mystic; born *Gadadhar Chatterjee*. He condemned lust, money, and the caste system, preaching that all religions leading to the attainment of mystical experience are equally good and true.

Raman /'rɑːmən/, Sir Chandrasekhara Venkata (1888–1970), Indian physicist. He discovered the Raman effect, one of the most important proofs of the quantum theory of light. Nobel Prize for Physics (1930).

Raman effect ▶ **noun** [mass noun] Physics a change of wavelength exhibited by some of the radiation scattered in a medium. The effect is specific to the molecules which cause it, and so can be used in spectroscopic analysis. Compare with **RAYLEIGH SCATTERING**.

Ramanujan /rɑː'mɑːnʊdʒ(ə)n/, Srinivasa Aaiyangar (1887–1920), Indian mathematician. He made a number of original discoveries in number theory, especially, in collaboration with G. H. Hardy (1877–1947), a theorem concerning the partition of numbers into a sum of smaller integers.

Ramapithecus /ˌrɑːmə'pɪθɪkəs/ ▶ **noun** a fossil anthropoid ape of the Miocene epoch, known from remains found in SW Asia and East Africa, and probably ancestral to the orang-utan.
● Genus *Ramapithecus*, family Pongidae.
– ORIGIN modern Latin, from **RAMA** + Greek *pithēkos* 'ape'.

Ramayana /rɑː'mɑːjʌnə/ one of the two great Sanskrit epics of the Hindus, composed *c.*300 BC. It describes how Rama, aided by his brother and the monkey Hanuman, rescued his wife Sita from Ravana, the ten-headed demon king of Lanka.
– ORIGIN Sanskrit, literally 'exploits of Rama'.

Rambert /'rɒmbɛː/, Dame Marie (1888–1982), British ballet dancer, teacher, and director, born in Poland; born *Cyvia Rambam*. After moving to London in 1917 she formed and directed the Ballet Club, which became known as the Ballet Rambert in 1935.

ramble ▶ **verb** [no obj.] **1** walk for pleasure in the countryside, typically without a definite route.
■ (of a plant) put out long shoots and grow over walls or other plants.
2 talk or write at length in a confused or inconsequential way: *Willy **rambled on** about Norman archways.*
▶ **noun** a walk taken for pleasure in the countryside.
– ORIGIN late Middle English (as a verb in sense 2): probably related to Middle Dutch *rammelen*, used of animals in the sense 'wander about on heat', also to the noun **RAM**.

rambler ▶ **noun 1** a person who walks in the countryside for pleasure.
2 a straggling or climbing rose.

rambling ▶ **adjective 1** (of writing or speech) lengthy and confused or inconsequential.
2 (of a plant) putting out long shoots and growing over walls or other plants; climbing: *rambling roses.*
■ (of a building or path) spreading or winding irregularly in various directions: *a big old rambling house.* ■ (of a person) travelling from place to place; wandering.
▶ **noun** [mass noun] the activity of walking in the countryside for pleasure: [as modifier] *a rambling club.*
– DERIVATIVES **ramblingly** adverb.

Rambo /'rambəʊ/ ▶ **noun** an exceptionally tough, aggressive man.
– ORIGIN the name of the hero of David Morrell's novel *First Blood* (1972), popularized in the films *First Blood* (1982) and *Rambo: First Blood Part II* (1985).

Rambouillet /'rambəleɪ, 'rɒmbuːjeɪ/ ▶ **noun** (pl. pronounced same) a sheep of a hardy breed developed from the Spanish merino but bred elsewhere for its meat and its heavy fleece of fine wool.

rambunctious /ram'bʌŋ(k)ʃəs/ ▶ **adjective** informal, chiefly N. Amer. uncontrollably exuberant; boisterous.
– DERIVATIVES **rambunctiously** adverb, **rambunctiousness** noun.
– ORIGIN mid 19th cent.: of unknown origin.

rambutan /ram'b(j)uːt(ə)n/ ▶ **noun 1** a red, plum-sized tropical fruit with soft spines and a slightly acidic taste.
2 the Malaysian tree that bears this fruit.
● *Nephelium lappaceum*, family Sapindaceae.
– ORIGIN early 18th cent.: from Malay *rambūtan*, from *rambut* 'hair', with allusion to the fruit's spines.

RAMC ▶ **abbreviation for** (in the UK) Royal Army Medical Corps.

Rameau /'rɑːməʊ, French ʀamo/, Jean-Philippe (1683–1764), French composer, musical theorist, and organist. He is best known for his four volumes of harpsichord pieces (1706–41), which are noted for their bold harmonies and textural diversity.

ramekin /'ramɪkɪn, 'ramkɪn/ (also **ramekin dish**) ▶ **noun** a small dish for baking and serving an individual portion of food.
■ a quantity of food served in such a dish, in particular a small quantity of cheese baked with breadcrumbs, eggs, and seasoning.
– ORIGIN mid 17th cent.: from French *ramequin*, of Low German or Dutch origin; compare with obsolete Flemish *rameken* 'toasted bread'.

ramen /'rɑːmɛn/ ▶ **plural noun** (in oriental cuisine) quick-cooking noodles, typically served in a broth with meat and vegetables.
– ORIGIN Japanese, from Chinese *lā* 'to pull' + *miàn* 'noodles'.

Rameses /'ramɪsiːz/ variant spelling of **RAMSES**.

ramie /'rami/ ▶ **noun** [mass noun] **1** a vegetable fibre noted for its length and toughness.
■ cloth woven from this fibre.
2 the plant of the nettle family which yields this fibre, native to tropical Asia and cultivated elsewhere.
● *Boehmeria nivea*, family Urticaceae.
– ORIGIN mid 19th cent.: from Malay *rami*.

ramification ▶ **noun** (usu. **ramifications**) a consequence of an action or event, especially when complex or unwelcome: *any change is bound to have legal ramifications.*
■ a subdivision of a complex structure or process perceived as comparable to a tree's branches: *an extended family with its ramifications of neighbouring in-laws.* ■ [mass noun] formal or technical the action or state of ramifying or being ramified.
– ORIGIN mid 17th cent.: from French, from *ramifier* 'form branches' (see **RAMIFY**).

ramify /'ramɪfʌɪ/ ▶ **verb** (**-ies, -ied**) [no obj.] formal or technical form branches or offshoots; spread or branch out: *an elaborate system of canals was built, ramifying throughout the UK.*
■ [with obj.] [often as adj. **ramified**] cause to branch or spread out: *a ramified genealogical network.*
– ORIGIN late Middle English: from Old French *ramifier*, from medieval Latin *ramificare*, from Latin *ramus* 'branch'.

Ramillies, Battle of /'ramɪlɪz, French ʀamiji/ a battle in the War of the Spanish Succession which took place in 1706 near the village of Ramillies, north of Namur, in Belgium. The British army under General Marlborough defeated the French.

ramin /ra'miːn/ ▶ **noun** a hardwood tree of Malaysian swamp forests, which yields pale lightweight timber.
● *Gonystylus bancanus*, family Thymelaeaceae.
– ORIGIN mid 20th cent.: from Malay.

ramjet ▶ **noun** a type of jet engine in which the air

r

drawn in for combustion is compressed solely by the forward motion of the aircraft.

rammies /ˈramɪz/ ▶ **plural noun** Austral. & S. African informal trousers.
– ORIGIN early 20th cent.: perhaps from **RAMIE**.

rammy ▶ **noun** (pl. **-ies**) Scottish a quarrel or brawl.
– ORIGIN 1930s: perhaps from Scots *rammle* 'row, uproar', variant of **RAMBLE**.

Ramón y Cajal /raˌmɒn iː kaˈhɑːl/, Santiago (1852–1934), Spanish physician and histologist. He was a founder of the science of neurology, identifying the neuron as the fundamental unit of the nervous system. Nobel Prize for Physiology or Medicine (1906, shared with Camillo Golgi).

ramp ▶ **noun 1** a slope or inclined plane for joining two different levels, as at the entrance or between floors of a building: *a wheelchair ramp*.
■ a movable set of steps for entering or leaving an aircraft. ■ Brit. a transverse ridge in a road to control the speed of vehicles. ■ N. Amer. an inclined slip road leading on to or off a main road or motorway: *an exit ramp*.
2 an upward bend in a stair rail.
3 an electrical waveform in which the voltage increases or decreases linearly with time.
4 Brit. informal a swindle or racket, especially one involving a fraudulent increase of the price of a share. [ORIGIN: see sense 4 of the verb.]
▶ **verb 1** [with obj.] provide or build (something) with a ramp.
2 [no obj.] archaic (of an animal) rear up on its hind legs in a threatening posture.
■ [with adverbial of direction] rush about violently or uncontrollably. ■ [with adverbial of direction] (of a plant) grow or climb luxuriantly: *ivy ramped over the flower beds*.
3 [no obj.] (of an electrical waveform) increase or decrease voltage linearly with time.
4 [no obj.] [usu. as noun **ramping**] Brit. purchase shares or other securities in order to fraudulently raise their price. [ORIGIN: late 20th cent.: of unknown origin; a 19th-cent. slang use of the term was 'rob, swindle'.]
– ORIGIN Middle English (as a verb in the sense 'rear up', also used as a heraldic term): from Old French *ramper* 'creep, crawl', of unknown origin. Sense 1 of the noun dates from the late 18th cent.
▶ **ramp something up** (or **ramp up**) (especially in reference to the production of goods) increase or cause to increase in amount: *they ramped up production to meet booming demand*.

rampage ▶ **verb** /ramˈpeɪdʒ/ [no obj., with adverbial of direction] (especially of a large group of people) rush around in a violent and uncontrollable manner: *several thousand demonstrators rampaged through the city*.
▶ **noun** /ramˈpeɪdʒ, ˈrampeɪdʒ/ a period of violent and uncontrollable behaviour, typically involving a large group of people: *thugs* **went on the rampage** *and wrecked a classroom*.
– DERIVATIVES **rampager** noun.
– ORIGIN late 17th cent.: perhaps based on the verb **RAMP** and the noun **RAGE**.

rampageous ▶ **adjective** archaic boisterously or violently uncontrollable.

rampant ▶ **adjective 1** (especially of something unwelcome or unpleasant) flourishing or spreading unchecked: *political violence was rampant* | *rampant inflation*.
■ (of a person or activity) violent or unrestrained in action or performance: *rampant sex*. ■ (of a plant) lush in growth; luxuriant: *a rich soil soon becomes home to rampant weeds*.
2 [usu. postpositive] Heraldry (of an animal) represented standing on one hind foot with its forefeet in the air (typically in profile, facing the dexter side, with right hind foot and tail raised, unless otherwise specified): *two gold lions rampant*.
– DERIVATIVES **rampancy** noun, **rampantly** adverb.
– ORIGIN Middle English (as a heraldic term): from Old French, literally 'crawling', present participle of *ramper* (see **RAMP**). From the original use describing a wild animal, arose the sense 'fierce', whence the current notion of 'unrestrained'.

rampart ▶ **noun** (usu. **ramparts**) a defensive wall of a castle or walled city, having a broad top with a walkway and typically a stone parapet.
▶ **verb** [with obj.] (usu. **be ramparted**) rare fortify or surround with or as if with a rampart.
– ORIGIN late 16th cent.: from French *rempart*, from *remparer* 'fortify, take possession of again', based on Latin *ante* 'before' + *parare* 'prepare'.

rampion /ˈrampɪən/ ▶ **noun** a Eurasian plant of the bellflower family, some kinds of which have a root that can be eaten in salads:
• a Mediterranean plant with a long narrow spike of bluish flowers and a thick taproot (*Campanula rapunculus*, family Campanulaceae). • (**horned rampion**) a grassland plant with dense rounded flower heads of inward curving, typically blue, tubular flowers (genus *Phyteuma*, family Campanulaceae).
– ORIGIN late 16th cent.: from a variant of medieval Latin *rapuncium*; compare with German *Rapunzel* 'lamb's lettuce'.

ram raid ▶ **noun** a robbery in which a shop window is rammed with a vehicle and looted.
– DERIVATIVES **ram-raider** noun, **ram-raiding** noun.

ramrod ▶ **noun** a rod for ramming down the charge of a muzzle-loading firearm.
■ used in similes and metaphors to describe someone's erect or rigid posture: *he held himself ramrod straight*. ■ N. Amer. a foreman or manager, especially one who is a strict disciplinarian.
▶ **verb** (**ramrodded**, **ramrodding**) [with obj.] (**ramrod something through**) chiefly US force a proposed measure to be accepted or completed quickly: *they ramrodded through legislation voiding the court injunctions*.

Ramsay[1] /ˈramzi/, Allan (1713–84), Scottish portrait painter. His style is noted for its French rococo grace and sensitivity, particularly in his portraits of women.

Ramsay[2] /ˈramzi/, Sir William (1852–1916), Scottish chemist, discoverer of the noble gases. He first discovered argon, helium, and (with the help of **M. W. Travers**, 1872–1961) neon, krypton, and xenon, determing their atomic weights and places in the periodic table. In 1910, with Frederick Soddy and **Sir Robert Whytlaw-Gray** (1877–1958), he identified the last noble gas, radon. Nobel Prize for Chemistry (1904).

Ramses /ˈramsiːz/ (also **Rameses**) the name of eleven Egyptian pharaohs, notably:
■ Ramses II (died *c.*1225 BC), reigned *c.*1292–*c.*1225 BC; known as **Ramses the Great**. The third pharaoh of the 19th dynasty, he built vast monuments and statues, including the two rock temples at Abu Simbel.
■ Ramses III (died *c.*1167 BC), reigned *c.*1198–*c.*1167 BC. The second pharaoh of the 20th dynasty, he fought decisive battles against the Libyans and the Sea Peoples. After his death the power of Egypt declined.

Ramsey /ˈramzi/, Sir Alf (1920–99), English footballer and manager; full name *Alfred Ernest Ramsey*. He played as a defender for Southampton, Tottenham Hotspur, and England, and managed England from 1963 to 1974, winning the World Cup in 1966.

ramshackle ▶ **adjective** (especially of a house or vehicle) in a state of severe disrepair: *a ramshackle cottage*.
– ORIGIN early 19th cent. (originally dialect in the sense 'irregular, disorderly'): alteration of earlier *ramshackled*, altered form of obsolete *ransackled* 'ransacked'.

ramshorn snail /ˈramzhɔːn/ ▶ **noun** a plant-eating European freshwater snail which has a flat spiral shell.
• Family Planorbidae: several genera.

ramsons /ˈrams(ə)nz/ ▶ **plural noun** [usu. treated as sing.] a Eurasian woodland plant with broad shiny leaves and round heads of white flowers, producing a strong aroma of garlic. Also called **WILD GARLIC**.
• *Allium ursinum*, family Liliaceae (or Alliaceae).
– ORIGIN Old English *hramsan*, plural of *hramsa* 'wild garlic', later interpreted as singular.

ramus /ˈreɪməs/ ▶ **noun** (pl. **rami** /ˈreɪmʌɪ, ˈreɪmiː/)
1 Anatomy an arm or branch of a bone, in particular those of the ischium and pubes or of the jawbone.
■ a major branch of a nerve.
2 Zoology a structure in an invertebrate that has the form of a projecting arm, typically one of two or more that are conjoined or adjacent.
■ a barb of a feather.
– ORIGIN mid 17th cent.: from Latin, literally 'branch'.

RAN ▶ **abbreviation for** Royal Australian Navy.

ran past of **RUN**.

ranch ▶ **noun** a large farm, especially in the western US and Canada, where cattle or other animals are bred.
■ (also **ranch house**) N. Amer. a single-storey house.
▶ **verb** [no obj.] [often as noun **ranching**] run a ranch: *cattle ranching*.
■ [with obj.] [often as adj. **ranched**] breed (animals) on a ranch. ■ [with obj.] use (land) as a ranch.
– ORIGIN early 19th cent.: from Spanish *rancho* 'group of persons eating together'.

rancher ▶ **noun 1** a person who owns or runs a ranch.
2 N. Amer. a ranch house.

rancheria /ˌrɑːn(t)ʃəˈriːə/ ▶ **noun** (in Spanish America and the western US) a small Indian settlement.
– ORIGIN Spanish, from *rancho* (see **RANCH**).

ranchero /rɑːnˈtʃɛːrəʊ/ ▶ **noun** (pl. **-os**) chiefly US a person who farms or works on a ranch, especially in the south-western US and Mexico.
– ORIGIN Spanish, from *rancho* (see **RANCH**).

Ranchi /ˈrɑːntʃi/ a city in Bihar, NE India; pop. 598,000 (1991).

rancid ▶ **adjective** (of foods containing fat or oil) smelling or tasting unpleasant as a result of being old and stale.
– DERIVATIVES **rancidity** noun.
– ORIGIN early 17th cent.: from Latin *rancidus* 'stinking'.

rancour (US **rancor**) ▶ **noun** [mass noun] bitterness or resentfulness, especially when long standing: *he spoke without rancour*.
– DERIVATIVES **rancorous** adjective, **rancorously** adverb.
– ORIGIN Middle English: via Old French from late Latin *rancor* 'rankness', (in the Vulgate 'bitter grudge'), related to Latin *rancidus* 'stinking'.

Rand[1] /rand, rɑːnt/ (**the Rand**) another name for **WITWATERSRAND**.

Rand[2] /rand/, Ayn (1905–82), Russian-born American writer and philosopher; born *Alissa Rozenbaum*. She developed a philosophy of 'objectivism', arguing for 'rational self-interest', individualism, and laissez-faire capitalism, which she presented in both non-fiction works and novels. Notable novels: *The Fountainhead* (1943) and *Atlas Shrugged* (1957).

rand[1] /rand, rant/ ▶ **noun 1** the basic monetary unit of South Africa, equal to 100 cents. [ORIGIN: from *the Rand*, the name of a goldfield district near Johannesburg.]
2 S. African an area of high, sloping ground; a long rocky hillock. [ORIGIN: Afrikaans, literally 'edge'; related to **RAND**[2].]

rand[2] /rand/ ▶ **noun** a strip of leather placed under the back part of a shoe or boot to make it level before the lifts of the heel are attached.
– ORIGIN Old English (denoting a border): of Germanic origin; related to Dutch *rand* and German *Rand* 'edge'. The current sense dates from the late 16th cent.

R & B ▶ **abbreviation for** rhythm and blues.

R & D ▶ **abbreviation for** research and development.

Randers /ˈrɑːnəz/ a port of Denmark, on the Randers Fjord on the east coast of the Jutland peninsula; pop. 61,020 (1990).

random ▶ **adjective** made, done, happening, or chosen without method or conscious decision: *a random sample of 100 households*.
■ Statistics governed by or involving equal chances for each item. ■ (of masonry) with stones of irregular size and shape.
– PHRASES **at random** without method or conscious decision: *he opened the book at random*.
– DERIVATIVES **randomly** adverb, **randomness** noun.
– ORIGIN Middle English (in the sense 'impetuous headlong rush'): from Old French *randon* 'great speed', from *randir* 'gallop', from a Germanic root shared by **RAND**[2].

random access Computing ▶ **noun** [mass noun] the process of transferring information to or from memory in which every memory location can be accessed directly rather than being accessed in a fixed sequence: [as modifier] *random-access programming*.

random error ▶ **noun** Statistics an error in measurement caused by factors which vary from one measurement to another.

randomize (also **-ise**) ▶ **verb** [with obj.] [usu. as adj. **randomized**] technical make unpredictable, unsystematic, or random in order or arrangement; employ random selection or sampling in (an experiment or procedure).

– DERIVATIVES **randomization** noun.

random walk ▶ **noun** Physics the movements of an object or changes in a variable that follow no discernible pattern or trend.

R & R ▶ **abbreviation for** ■ informal rest and recreation. ■ Medicine rescue and resuscitation. ■ (also **R'n'R**) rock and roll.

Randstad /ˈrandstat/ a conurbation in the north-west of the Netherlands that stretches in a horseshoe shape from Dordrecht and Rotterdam round to Utrecht and Amersfoort via The Hague, Leiden, Haarlem, and Amsterdam. The majority of the people of the Netherlands live in this area.

randy ▶ **adjective** (**randier**, **randiest**) **1** informal, chiefly Brit. sexually aroused or excited.
2 Scottish archaic (of a person) having a rude, aggressive manner.
– DERIVATIVES **randily** adverb, **randiness** noun.
– ORIGIN mid 17th cent.: perhaps from obsolete *rand* 'rant, rave', from obsolete Dutch *randen* 'to rant'.

ranee /ˈrɑːniː/ ▶ **noun** archaic spelling of **RANI**.

Raney nickel /ˈreɪni/ ▶ **noun** [mass noun] Chemistry, trademark a form of nickel catalyst with a high surface area, used in organic hydrogenation reactions.
– ORIGIN 1930s: named after Murray *Raney* (1885–1966), American engineer.

rang past of **RING**[2].

rangatira /ˌraŋɡəˈtɪərə/ ▶ **noun** NZ a Maori chief or noble.
– ORIGIN Maori.

range ▶ **noun 1** the area of variation between upper and lower limits on a particular scale: *the cost is thought to be* ***in the range of*** *$1–5 million a day | it's outside my price range.*
■ a set of different things of the same general type: *the area offers a wide range of activities for the tourist.* ■ the scope of a person's knowledge or abilities: *in this film he gave some indication of his range.* ■ the compass of a person's voice or a musical instrument: *she was gifted with an incredible vocal range.* ■ the extent of time covered by something such as a forecast. See also **LONG-RANGE**, **SHORT-RANGE**. ■ the area or extent covered by or included in something: *an introductory guide to the range of debate this issue has generated.* ■ Mathematics the set of values that a given function can take as its argument varies.
2 [mass noun] the distance within which a person can see or hear: *something lurked just beyond her range of vision.*
■ the maximum distance at which a radio transmission can be effectively received: *planets within radio range of Earth.* ■ [count noun] the distance that can be covered by a vehicle or aircraft without refuelling: *the vans have a range of 125 miles.* ■ the maximum distance to which a gun will shoot or over which a missile will travel: *a duck came within range | [count noun] these rockets have a range of 30 to 40 miles.* ■ [count noun] the distance between a camera and the subject to be photographed.
3 a line or series of mountains or hills: *the coastal ranges of the north-west USA.*
■ (**ranges**) Austral./NZ mountainous or hilly country. ■ a row of buildings.
4 a large area of open land for grazing or hunting.
■ an area of land or sea used as a testing ground for military equipment. ■ an open or enclosed area with targets for shooting practice. ■ the area over which a thing, especially a plant or animal, is distributed.
5 a large cooking stove with burners or hotplates and one or more ovens, all of which are kept continually hot.
■ N. Amer. an electric or gas cooker with several burners.
6 [mass noun] archaic the direction or position in which something lies: *the range of the hills and valleys is nearly from north to south.*
▶ **verb 1** [no obj., with adverbial] vary or extend between specified limits: *patients whose ages ranged from 13 to 25 years.*
2 [with obj. and adverbial] (usu. **be ranged**) place or arrange in a row or rows or in a specified order or manner: *a table with half a dozen chairs ranged around it.*
■ (**range someone against** or **be ranged against**) place oneself or be placed in opposition to (a particular person or group): *Japan ranged herself against the European nations.* ■ [no obj., with adverbial of direction] run or extend in a line in a particular direction: *he regularly came to the benches that ranged along the path.* ■ [with obj.] Printing, Brit. align (type), especially at the ends of successive lines. ■ [no obj.] Printing, Brit. (of type) be aligned, especially at the ends of successive lines.
3 [no obj., with adverbial of direction] (of a person or animal) travel or wander over a wide area: *patrols ranged thousands of miles deep into enemy territory | [with obj.] nomadic tribesmen who ranged the windswept lands of the steppe.*
■ (of a person's eyes) pass from one person or thing to another: *his eyes* ***ranged over*** *them.* ■ (of something written or spoken) cover or embrace a wide number of different topics: *tutorials* ***ranged over*** *a variety of subjects.*
4 [no obj.] obtain the range of a target by adjustment after firing past it or short of it, or by the use of radar or laser equipment: *radar-type transmissions which appeared to be* ***ranging on*** *our convoys.*
■ [with adverbial] (of a projectile) cover a specified distance. ■ [with adverbial] (of a gun) send a projectile over a specified distance.
– PHRASES **at a range of** with a specified distance between one person or thing and another: *a bat can detect a moth at a range of less than 8 feet.*
– ORIGIN Middle English (in the sense 'line of people or animals'): from Old French *range* 'row, rank', from *rangier* 'put in order', from *rang* 'rank'. Early usage also included the notion of 'movement over an area'.

rangé /ˈrɒ̃ʒeɪ, rɒ̃ˈʒeɪ/ ▶ **adjective** rare (of a person or their lifestyle) orderly; settled.
– ORIGIN French, literally 'in order', past participle of *ranger.*

rangefinder ▶ **noun** an instrument for estimating the distance of an object, especially for use with a camera or gun.

rangeland ▶ **noun** [mass noun] (also **rangelands**) open country used for grazing or hunting animals.

Ranger a series of nine American moon probes launched between 1961 and 1965, the last three of which took many photographs before crashing into the moon.

ranger ▶ **noun 1** a keeper of a park, forest, or area of countryside.
2 a member of a body of armed men, in particular:
■ a mounted soldier. ■ US a commando.
3 (**Ranger** or **Ranger Guide**) Brit. a member of the senior branch of the Guides.
4 a person or thing that wanders or ranges over a particular area or domain: *rangers of the mountains.*

ranging pole (also **ranging rod**) ▶ **noun** Surveying a pole or rod used for setting a straight line.

rangoli /rʌŋˈəʊli/ ▶ **noun** [mass noun] traditional Indian decoration and patterns made with ground rice, particularly during festivals.
– ORIGIN from Marathi *rā̃golī.*

Rangoon /raŋˈɡuːn/ the capital of Burma (Myanmar), a port in the Irrawaddy delta; pop. 2,458,710 (1983). For centuries a Buddhist religious centre, it is the site of the Shwe Dagon Pagoda, built over 2,500 years ago. The modern city was established by the British in the mid 19th century and became capital in 1886. Burmese name **YANGON**.

rangy /ˈreɪn(d)ʒi/ ▶ **adjective** (**rangier**, **rangiest**) (of a person) tall and slim with long, slender limbs.

rani /ˈrɑːniː/ (also **ranee**) ▶ **noun** (pl. **ranis**) historical a Hindu queen, either by marriage to a raja or in her own right.
– ORIGIN from Hindi *rānī*, Sanskrit *rājñī*, feminine of *rājan* 'king'.

ranitidine /raˈnɪtɪdiːn, -ˈnʌɪt-/ ▶ **noun** [mass noun] Medicine a synthetic compound with antihistamine properties, used to treat ulcers and related conditions.
– ORIGIN 1970s: blend of **FURAN** and **NITRO-**, + **-IDE** + **-INE**[4].

Ranjit Singh /ˌrʌndʒɪt ˈsɪŋ/ (1780–1839), Indian maharaja, founder of the Sikh state of Punjab; known as the **Lion of the Punjab**. He proclaimed himself maharaja of Punjab in 1801, and went on to make it the most powerful state in India. Most of his territory was annexed by Britain after the Sikh Wars which followed his death.

Ranjitsinhji Vibhaji /ˌrʌndʒɪtˌsɪndʒɪ vɪˈbɑːdʒi/, Kumar Shri, Maharaja Jam Sahib of Navanagar (1872–1933), Indian cricketer and statesman. He scored a total of 72 centuries as a batsman for Sussex and England. In 1907 he succeeded his cousin as maharaja of the state of Navanagar.

Rank, J. Arthur, 1st Baron (1888–1972), English industrialist and film executive; full name *Joseph Arthur Rank*. In 1941 he founded the Rank Organization, a film production and distribution company that acquired control of the leading British studios and cinema chains in the 1940s and 1950s.

rank[1] ▶ **noun 1** a position in the hierarchy of the armed forces: *an army officer of fairly high rank | he was promoted to the rank of Captain.*
■ a position within the hierarchy of an organization or society: *only two cabinet members had held ministerial rank before.* ■ [mass noun] high social position: *persons of rank and breeding.* ■ Statistics a number specifying position in a numerically ordered series. ■ (in systemic grammar) the level of a linguistic unit or set of linguistic units in relation to other sets in the hierarchy.
2 a single line of soldiers or police officers drawn up abreast.
■ (**the ranks**) common soldiers as opposed to officers: *he was fined and* ***reduced to the ranks.*** See also **OTHER RANKS**. ■ (**ranks**) the people belonging to or constituting a group or class: *the ranks of Britain's unemployed.* ■ a regular row or line of things or people: *conifer plantations growing in serried ranks.* ■ Chess each of the eight rows of eight squares running from side to side across a chessboard. Compare with **FILE**[2]. ■ Brit. short for **TAXI RANK**.
3 Mathematics the value or the order of the largest non-zero determinant of a given matrix.
■ an analogous quantity in other kinds of group.
▶ **verb** [with obj. and adverbial] **1** give (someone or something) a rank or place within a grading system: *rank them in order of preference | [with obj. and complement] she is ranked number four in the world.*
■ [no obj., with adverbial] have a specified rank or place within a grading system: *he now ranks third in America.* ■ [with obj.] US take precedence over (someone) in respect to rank; outrank: *the Secretary of State ranks all the other members of the cabinet.*
2 arrange in a rank or ranks: *the tents were ranked in orderly rows.*
– PHRASES **break rank** (or **ranks**) (of soldiers or police officers) fail to remain in line. ■ figurative fail to maintain solidarity: *the government is prepared to* ***break ranks with*** *the Allied states.* **close ranks** (of soldiers or police officers) come closer together in a line. ■ figurative unite in order to defend common interests: *the family had always closed ranks in times of crisis.* **keep rank** (of soldiers or police officers) remain in line. **pull rank** take unfair advantage of one's seniority or privileged position. **rise through** (or **from**) **the ranks** (of a private or a non-commissioned officer) receive a commission. ■ advance in an organization by one's own efforts: *he rose through the ranks to become managing director.*
– ORIGIN Middle English: from Old French *ranc*, of Germanic origin; related to **RING**[1]. The early sense 'row of things' remains in modern usage in **TAXI RANK**.

rank[2] ▶ **adjective 1** (of vegetation) growing too thickly and coarsely.
2 (especially of air or water) having a foul or offensive smell.
3 [attrib.] (especially of something bad or deficient) complete and utter (used for emphasis): *rank stupidity | rank amateurs | a rank outsider.*
– DERIVATIVES **rankly** adverb, **rankness** noun.
– ORIGIN Old English *ranc* 'proud, rebellious, sturdy', also 'fully grown', of Germanic origin. An early sense 'luxuriant' gave rise to 'too luxuriant', whence the negative connotation of modern usage.

rank and file ▶ **noun** [treated as pl.] (**the rank and file**) the ordinary members of an organization as opposed to its leaders: *the rank and file of the Labour party | [as modifier] rank-and-file members.*
– ORIGIN referring to the 'ranks' and 'files' into which privates and non-commissioned officers form on parade.

rank correlation ▶ **noun** Statistics an assessment of the degree of correlation between two ways of assigning ranks to the members of a set.

ranker[1] ▶ **noun 1** chiefly Brit. a soldier in the ranks; a private.
■ a commissioned officer who has been in the ranks.
2 [in combination] a person or animal of a specified rank: *of the 26 top-rankers in humanities, 18 are girls.*

ranker[2] ▶ **noun** Soil Science a simple soil consisting of a layer of humus lying directly on an unaltered substrate such as bedrock, glacial drift, or volcanic ash.

r

– ORIGIN based on Austrian German *Rank* 'steep slope'.

ranking ▶ **noun** a position in a scale of achievement or status; a classification: *his world number-one ranking.*
■[mass noun] the action or process of giving a specified rank or place within a grading system: *the ranking of students.*
▶ **adjective** [in combination] having a specified position in a scale of achievement or status: *high-ranking army officers.*
■[attrib.] N. Amer. having a high position in such a scale: *two ranking PLO figures.*

rankle ▶ **verb** [no obj.] **1** archaic (of a wound or sore) continue to be painful; fester.
2 (of a comment, event, or fact) cause annoyance or resentment that persists: *the casual manner of his dismissal still rankles.*
■[with obj.] chiefly N. Amer. annoy or irritate (someone): *Lisa was rankled by his assertion.*
– ORIGIN Middle English: from Old French *rancler*, from *rancle, draoncle* 'festering sore', from an alteration of medieval Latin *dracunculus*, diminutive of *draco* 'serpent'.

rankshift ▶ **noun** (in systemic grammar) a use of a linguistic unit at a lower rank than the one to which it ordinarily belongs.
▶ **verb** (**be rankshifted**) (of a linguistic unit) be used at a lower rank.

Rann of Kutch see **KUTCH, RANN OF**.

ransack ▶ **verb** [with obj.] go hurriedly through (a place) stealing things and causing damage: *burglars ransacked her home.*
■search through (a place or receptacle) to find something, especially in such a way as to cause disorder and damage: *man has* **ransacked** *the planet* **for** *fuel.*
– DERIVATIVES **ransacker** noun.
– ORIGIN Middle English: from Old Norse *rannsaka*, from *rann* 'house' + a second element related to *sœkja* 'seek'.

Ransom, John Crowe (1888–1974), American poet and critic. With *The New Criticism* (1941) he started a school of criticism which rejected the Victorian emphasis on literature as a moral force and advocated a close analysis of textual structure in isolation from the social background of the text.

ransom ▶ **noun** a sum of money or other payment demanded or paid for the release of a prisoner.
■[mass noun] the holding or freeing of a prisoner in return for payment of such money: *the capture and ransom of the king.*
▶ **verb** [with obj.] obtain the release of (a prisoner) by making a payment demanded: *the lord was captured in war and had to be ransomed.*
■hold (a prisoner) and demand payment for their release: *an English force burnt the village and ransomed the inhabitants.* ■ release (a prisoner) after receiving payment.
– PHRASES **hold someone/thing to ransom** hold someone prisoner and demand payment for their release. ■ demand concessions from a person or organization by threatening damaging action. **a king's ransom** a huge amount of money; a fortune.
– ORIGIN Middle English: from Old French *ransoun* (noun), *ransouner* (verb), from Latin *redemptio(n-)* 'ransoming, releasing' (see **REDEMPTION**). Early use also occurred in theological contexts expressing 'deliverance' and 'atonement'.

Ransome, Arthur (Michell) (1884–1967), English novelist and journalist, best known for the children's classic *Swallows and Amazons* (1930).

rant ▶ **verb** [no obj.] speak or shout at length in a wild, impassioned way: *she was still* **ranting on** *about the unfairness of it all.*
▶ **noun** a spell of ranting; a tirade: *his rants against organized religion.*
– PHRASES **rant and rave** shout and complain angrily and at length.
– DERIVATIVES **rantingly** adverb.
– ORIGIN late 16th cent. (in the sense 'behave in a boisterous way'): from Dutch *ranten* 'talk nonsense, rave'.

ranter ▶ **noun 1** a person who rants.
2 (**Ranter**) a member of an antinomian Christian sect in England during the mid 17th century which denied the authority of scripture and clergy.
■(in the 19th century) a member of certain Nonconformist, in particular Methodist, groups.

ranunculaceous /rəˌnʌŋkjʊˈleɪʃəs/ ▶ **adjective** Botany of, relating to, or denoting plants of the buttercup family (Ranunculaceae).
– ORIGIN mid 19th cent.: from modern Latin *Ranunculaceae* (plural), based on Latin *ranunculus* 'little frog', + **-OUS**.

ranunculus /rəˈnʌŋkjʊləs/ ▶ **noun** (pl. **ranunculuses** or **ranunculi** /-lʌɪ, -liː/) a temperate plant of a genus that includes the buttercups and water crowfoots, typically having yellow or white bowl-shaped flowers and lobed or toothed leaves.
• Genus *Ranunculus*, family Ranunculaceae: many species, including several garden ornamentals.
– ORIGIN modern Latin, from Latin, literally 'little frog', diminutive of *rana*.

Ranvier's node ▶ **noun** see **NODE OF RANVIER**.

Rao /raʊ/, P. V. Narasimha (b.1921), Indian statesman, Prime Minister 1991–6; full name *Pamulaparti Venkata Narasimha Rao*.

RAOC ▶ **abbreviation for** (in the UK) Royal Army Ordnance Corps.

Raoult's law /ˈraʊlz, raˈuːlz, ˈraʊlts/ Chemistry a law stating that the freezing and boiling points of an ideal solution are respectively depressed and elevated relative to that of the pure solvent by an amount proportional to the mole fraction of solute.
■a law stating that the vapour pressure of an ideal solution is proportional to the mole fraction of solvent.
– ORIGIN late 19th cent.: named after François-Marie *Raoult* (1830–1901), French chemist.

rap[1] ▶ **verb** (**rapped, rapping**) **1** [with obj.] strike (a hard surface) with a series of rapid audible blows, especially in order to attract attention: *he stood up and rapped the table* | [no obj.] *she* **rapped** *angrily* **on** *the window.*
■strike (something) against a hard surface in such a way: *she rapped her stick on the floor.* ■ strike (someone or something) sharply with stick or similar implement: *she rapped my fingers with a ruler.* ■ informal rebuke or criticize sharply: *certain banks are to be rapped for delaying interest rate cuts.* ■ say sharply or suddenly: *the ambassador* **rapped out** *an order.*
2 [no obj.] informal, chiefly US talk or chat in an easy and familiar manner: *we could be here all night rapping about the finer points of spiritualism.*
3 [no obj.] perform rap music.
▶ **noun 1** a quick, sharp knock or blow: *there was a confident rap at the door.*
■informal a rebuke or criticism: *social services were smarting from an Ombudsman's rap.*
2 [mass noun] a type of popular music of US black origin in which words are recited rapidly and rhythmically over a pre-recorded, typically electronic instrumental backing.
■[count noun] a piece of music performed in this style, or the words themselves.
3 informal, chiefly US a talk or discussion, especially a lengthy or impromptu one: *dropping in after work for a rap over a beer.*
4 [usu. with adj. or noun modifier] informal, chiefly N. Amer. a criminal charge, especially of a specified kind: *he's just been acquitted on a murder rap.*
■a person or thing's reputation, typically a bad one: *there's no reason why drag queens should get a bad rap.*
– PHRASES **beat the rap** N. Amer. informal escape punishment for or be acquitted of a crime. **rap someone on** (or **over**) **the knuckles** rebuke or criticize someone. **take the rap** informal be punished or blamed, especially for something that is not one's fault or for which others are equally responsible.
– ORIGIN Middle English (originally in the senses 'severe blow with a weapon' and 'deliver a heavy blow'): probably imitative and of Scandinavian origin; compare with Swedish *rappa* 'beat, drub', also with **CLAP**[1] and **FLAP**.

rap[2] ▶ **noun** [in sing., with negative] the smallest amount (used to add emphasis to a statement): *he doesn't care a rap whether it's true or not.*
– ORIGIN early 19th cent.: from Irish *ropaire* 'robber'; used as the name of a counterfeit coin in 18th-cent Ireland.

rapacious /rəˈpeɪʃəs/ ▶ **adjective** aggressively greedy or grasping: *rapacious landlords.*
– DERIVATIVES **rapaciously** adverb, **rapaciousness** noun, **rapacity** noun.
– ORIGIN mid 17th cent.: from Latin *rapax, rapac-* (from *rapere* 'to snatch') + **-IOUS**.

RAPC ▶ **abbreviation for** (in the UK) Royal Army Pay Corps.

rape[1] ▶ **noun** [mass noun] the crime, committed by a man, of forcing another person to have sexual intercourse with the offender against their will, especially by threatening or using violence against them: *he denied two charges of attempted rape* | [count noun] *he had committed at least two rapes.*
■figurative the wanton destruction or spoiling of a place or area: *the rape of the Russian countryside.* ■ poetic/literary the abduction of a woman, especially for the purpose of having sexual intercourse with her: *the Rape of the Sabine Women.*
▶ **verb** [with obj.] (of a man) force (another person) to have sexual intercourse with him against their will, especially by threatening or using violence against them: *the woman was raped at knifepoint.*
■figurative spoil or destroy (a place): *timber men doubt the government's ability to ensure the forests are not raped.*
– DERIVATIVES **raper** noun chiefly US.
– ORIGIN late Middle English (originally denoting violent seizure of property, later carrying off a woman by force): from Anglo-Norman French *rap* (noun), *raper* (verb), from Latin *rapere* 'seize'.

rape[2] ▶ **noun** [mass noun] a plant of the cabbage family with bright yellow heavily scented flowers, especially a variety (**oilseed rape**) grown for its oil-rich seed and as stockfeed. Also called **COLE, COLZA**.
• Genus *Brassica*, family Cruciferae, in particular *B. napus* subsp. *oleifera*.
– ORIGIN late Middle English (originally denoting the turnip plant): from Latin *rapum, rapa* 'turnip'.

rape[3] ▶ **noun** historical (in the UK) any of the six ancient divisions of Sussex.
– ORIGIN Old English, variant of **ROPE**, with reference to the fencing-off of land.

rape[4] ▶ **noun** [mass noun] (often **rapes**) the stalks and skins of grapes left after winemaking, used in making vinegar.
– ORIGIN early 17th cent. (as *rape wine*): from French *râpe*, medieval Latin *raspa* 'bunch of grapes'.

rape crisis centre ▶ **noun** an agency offering advice and support to victims of violent sexual crime.

rape oil ▶ **noun** [mass noun] an oil obtained from rapeseed, used as a lubricant, in alternative fuels, and in foodstuffs.

rapeseed ▶ **noun** [mass noun] seeds of the rape plant, used chiefly for oil. See **RAPE**[2].

Raphael[1] /ˈrafeɪəl/ (in the Bible) one of the seven archangels in the apocryphal Book of Enoch. He is said to have 'healed' the earth when it was defiled by the sins of the fallen angels.

Raphael[2] /ˈrafeɪəl/ (1483–1520), Italian painter and architect; Italian name *Raffaello Sanzio*. Regarded as one of the greatest artists of the Renaissance, he is particularly noted for his madonnas, including his altarpiece the *Sistine Madonna* (*c.*1513).

raphe /ˈreɪfi/ ▶ **noun** (pl. **raphae** /ˈreɪfiː/) Anatomy & Biology a groove, ridge, or seam in an organ or tissue, typically marking the line where two halves fused in the embryo, in particular:
■the connecting ridge between the two halves of the medulla oblongata or the tegmentum of the midbrain. ■ Botany a longitudinal ridge on the side of certain ovules or seeds. ■ Botany a longitudinal groove in the valve of many diatoms.
– ORIGIN mid 18th cent.: modern Latin, from Greek *rhaphē* 'seam'.

raphide /ˈreɪfʌɪd/ ▶ **noun** Botany a needle-shaped crystal of calcium oxalate occurring in clusters within the tissues of certain plants.
– ORIGIN mid 19th cent.: via French from Greek *rhaphis, rhaphid-* 'needle'.

rapid ▶ **adjective** happening in a short time or at a great rate: *the country's rapid economic decline* | *they lost three wickets in rapid succession.*
■(of movement or activity) characterized by great speed: *his breathing was rapid and jerky.*
▶ **noun** (usu. **rapids**) a fast-flowing and turbulent part of the course of a river.
– DERIVATIVES **rapidity** noun, **rapidly** adverb, **rapidness** noun.
– ORIGIN mid 17th cent.: from Latin *rapidus*, from *rapere* 'take by force'.

rapid eye movement ▶ **noun** a jerky motion of a person's eyes occurring in REM sleep.

rapid-fire ▶ **adjective** another term for **QUICK-FIRE**.

rapid transit ▶ **noun** [mass noun] [usu. as modifier] a form of high-speed urban passenger transport such as an elevated railway system.

rapier ▶ noun a thin, light sharp-pointed sword used for thrusting.
■ [as modifier] (especially of speech or intelligence) quick and incisive: *rapier wit.*
– ORIGIN early 16th cent.: from French *rapière*, from *râpe* 'rasp, grater' (because the perforated hilt resembles a rasp or grater).

rapine /'rapʌɪn, -pɪn/ ▶ noun [mass noun] poetic/literary the violent seizure of someone's property.
– ORIGIN late Middle English: from Old French, or from Latin *rapina*, from *rapere* 'seize'.

rapist ▶ noun a man who commits rape.

rapparee /ˌrapə'riː/ ▶ noun a bandit or irregular soldier in Ireland in the 17th century.
– ORIGIN from Irish *rapaire* 'short pike'.

rappee /ra'piː/ ▶ noun [mass noun] a type of coarse snuff.
– ORIGIN mid 18th cent.: from French *(tabac) râpé* 'rasped (tobacco)'.

rappel /ra'pɛl/ ▶ noun & verb (**rappelled, rappelling**) another term for ABSEIL.
– ORIGIN 1930s: from French, literally 'a recalling', from *rappeler* in the sense 'bring back to oneself' (with reference to the rope manoeuvre).

rappen /'rap(ə)n/ ▶ noun (pl. same) a monetary unit in the German-speaking cantons of Switzerland and in Liechtenstein, equal to one hundredth of the Swiss franc.
– ORIGIN from German *Rappe* 'raven', with reference to the depiction of the head of a raven, on a medieval coin.

rapper ▶ noun a person that performs rap music.

rapport /ra'pɔː/ ▶ noun a close and harmonious relationship in which the people or groups concerned understand each other's feelings or ideas and communicate well: *she was able to establish a good rapport with the children* | [mass noun] *there was little rapport between them.*
– ORIGIN mid 17th cent.: French, from *rapporter* 'bring back'.

rapporteur /ˌrapɔː'təː/ ▶ noun a person who is appointed by an organization to report on the proceedings of its meetings: *the UN rapporteur.*
– ORIGIN late 18th cent.: French, from *rapporter* 'bring back'.

rapprochement /ra'prɒʃmɒ̃/ ▶ noun (especially in international relations) an establishment or resumption of harmonious relations: *there were signs of a growing rapprochement between the two countries.*
– ORIGIN French, from *rapprocher*, from *re-* (expressing intensive force) + *approcher* 'to approach'.

rapscallion /rap'skalɪən/ ▶ noun archaic or humorous a mischievous person.
– ORIGIN late 17th cent.: alteration of earlier *rascallion*, perhaps from RASCAL.

rap sheet ▶ noun informal, chiefly US a criminal record.

rapt ▶ adjective **1** completely fascinated by what one is seeing or hearing: *Oliver looked at her, rapt.*
■ indicating or characterized by such a state of fascination: *they listened with rapt attention.* ■ filled with an intense and pleasurable emotion; enraptured: *she shut her eyes and seemed rapt with desire.* ■ Austral. informal another term for WRAPPED.
2 archaic or poetic/literary having been carried away bodily or transported to heaven: *he was rapt on high.*
– DERIVATIVES **raptly** adverb, **raptness** noun.
– ORIGIN late Middle English (in the sense 'transported by religious feeling'): from Latin *raptus* 'seized', past participle of *rapere*.

raptor ▶ noun a bird of prey, e.g. an eagle, hawk, falcon, or owl.
■ informal a dromaeosaurid dinosaur, especially velociraptor or utahraptor. [ORIGIN: from VELOCIRAPTOR, a shortened form used originally by palaeontologists, popularized by the film *Jurassic Park* (1993).]
– ORIGIN late Middle English: from Latin, literally 'plunderer', from *rapt-* 'seized', from the verb *rapere*.

raptorial ▶ adjective chiefly Zoology (of a bird or other animal) predatory.
■ (of a limb or other organ) adapted for seizing prey.
– DERIVATIVES **raptorially** adverb.
– ORIGIN early 19th cent.: from Latin *raptor* 'plunderer' + -IAL.

rapture ▶ noun **1** [mass noun] a feeling of intense pleasure or joy: *Leonora listened with rapture.*
■ **(raptures)** expressions of intense pleasure or enthusiasm about something: *the tabloids went into raptures about her.*
2 (**the Rapture**) N. Amer. (according to some millenarian teaching) the transporting of believers to heaven at the second coming of Christ.
▶ verb [with obj.] (usu. **be raptured**) N. Amer. (according to some millenarian teaching) transport (a believer) from earth to heaven at the second coming of Christ.
– ORIGIN late 16th cent. (in the sense 'seizing and carrying off'): from obsolete French, or from medieval Latin *raptura* 'seizing', partly influenced by RAPT.

rapture of the deep ▶ noun informal term for NITROGEN NARCOSIS.

rapturous ▶ adjective characterized by, feeling, or expressing great pleasure or enthusiasm: *he was greeted with rapturous applause.*
– DERIVATIVES **rapturously** adverb, **rapturousness** noun.

rara avis /ˌrɛːrə 'eɪvɪs, ˌrɑːrə 'avɪs/ ▶ noun (pl. **rarae aves** /-riː, -viːz/) another term for RARE BIRD.
– ORIGIN Latin.

rare[1] ▶ adjective (**rarer, rarest**) (of an event, situation, or condition) not occurring very often: *a rare genetic disorder* | [with infinitive] *it's rare to meet someone who's content with their life.*
■ (of a thing) not found in large numbers and consequently of interest or value: *one of Britain's rarest birds, the honey buzzard.* ■ unusually good or remarkable: *he plays with rare strength and sensitivity.*
– DERIVATIVES **rareness** noun.
– ORIGIN late Middle English (in the sense 'widely spaced, infrequent'): from Latin *rarus.*

rare[2] ▶ adjective (**rarer, rarest**) (of meat, especially beef) lightly cooked, so that the inside is still red.
– ORIGIN late 18th cent.: variant of obsolete *rear* 'half-cooked' (used to refer to soft-boiled eggs, from the mid 17th to mid 19th cents).

rare bird ▶ noun an exceptional person or thing; a rarity: *the style is a rare bird in Brazilian music.*
– ORIGIN translating Latin *rara avis* (Juvenal's *Satires*, vi.165).

rarebit (also **Welsh rarebit**) ▶ noun [mass noun] a dish of melted and seasoned cheese on toast, sometimes with other ingredients.
– ORIGIN late 18th cent.: alteration of *rabbit* in WELSH RABBIT; the reason for the use of the term *rabbit* is unknown.

rare earth (also **rare earth element** or **rare earth metal**) ▶ noun Chemistry any of a group of chemically similar metallic elements comprising the lanthanide series and (usually) scandium and yttrium. They are not especially rare, but they tend to occur together in nature and are difficult to separate from one another.

raree-show /'rɛːriː/ ▶ noun archaic a form of entertainment, especially one carried in a box, such as a peep show.
– ORIGIN late 17th cent.: apparently representing *rare show*, as pronounced by Savoyard showmen.

rarefaction /ˌrɛːrɪ'fakʃ(ə)n/ ▶ noun [mass noun] diminution in the density of something, especially air or a gas.
■ Medicine the lessening of density of tissue, especially of nervous tissue or bone.
– ORIGIN early 17th cent.: from medieval Latin *rarefactio(n-)*, from the verb *rarefacere* 'grow thin, become rare'.

rarefied /'rɛːrɪfʌɪd/ ▶ adjective (of air, especially that at high altitudes) containing less oxygen than usual.
■ figurative esoterically distant from the lives and concerns of ordinary people: *debates about the nature of knowledge can seem very rarefied.*

rare gas ▶ noun another term for NOBLE GAS.

rarely ▶ adverb **1** not often; seldom: *I rarely drive above 50 mph.*
2 archaic unusually or remarkably well: *you can write rarely now, after all your schooling.*
■ to an unusual degree; exceptionally: [as submodifier] *the rarely fine Sheraton bookcase.*

raring ▶ adjective [with infinitive] informal very enthusiastic and eager to do something: *she was raring to get back to her work* | *I'll be ready and **raring** to go.*
– ORIGIN 1920s: present participle of *rare*, dialect variant of ROAR or REAR[2].

rarity ▶ noun (pl. **-ies**) [mass noun] the state or quality of being rare: *the rarity of the condition.*
■ [count noun] a thing that is rare, especially one having particular value as a result of this: *to take the morning off was a rarity.*
– ORIGIN late Middle English: from Latin *raritas*, from *rarus* 'far apart, infrequently found' (see RARE[1]).

Rarotonga /ˌrarə'tɒŋgə/ a mountainous island in the South Pacific, the chief island of the Cook Islands. Its chief town, Avarua, is the capital of the Cook Islands.
– DERIVATIVES **Rarotongan** noun & adjective.

Ras /rɑːs/ ▶ noun an Ethiopian king, prince, or feudal lord.
– ORIGIN from Amharic *rās* 'head'.

rasa /'rɑːsə/ ▶ noun [mass noun] Hinduism the essence or characteristic quality of something, in particular the flavour or juice of a foodstuff.
– ORIGIN Sanskrit, literally 'juice'.

Ras al Khaimah /ˌrɑːs al 'kʌɪmə/ one of the seven member states of the United Arab Emirates; pop. 144,400 (1995). It joined the United Arab Emirates in 1972, after the British withdrawal from the Persian Gulf.
■ its capital, a port on the Gulf; pop. 42,000 (1980).

rasam /'rʌsəm/ ▶ noun [mass noun] a thin, very spicy southern Indian soup served with other dishes, typically as a drink.
– ORIGIN Tamil.

rascal ▶ noun a mischievous or cheeky person or child (typically used in an affectionate way).
– DERIVATIVES **rascality** noun (pl. **-ies**), **rascally** adjective.
– ORIGIN Middle English (in the senses 'a mob' and 'member of the rabble'): from Old French *rascaille* 'rabble', of uncertain origin.

rascasse /ras'kas/ ▶ noun a small scorpionfish with brick-red skin and spiny fins, found chiefly in the Mediterranean and used as an ingredient of bouillabaisse.
● *Scorpaena scrofa*, family Scorpaenidae.
– ORIGIN 1920s: from French.

rase ▶ verb variant spelling of RAZE.

rasgulla /rʌs'gʊlə/ ▶ noun an Indian sweet consisting of a ball of paneer cooked in syrup.
– ORIGIN from Hindi *rasgullā*, from *ras* 'juice' + *gullā* 'ball'.

rash[1] ▶ adjective displaying or proceeding from a lack of careful consideration of the possible consequences of an action: *it would be extremely rash to make such an assumption* | *a rash decision.*
– DERIVATIVES **rashly** adverb, **rashness** noun.
– ORIGIN late Middle English (also in Scots and northern English in the sense 'nimble, eager'): of Germanic origin; related to German *rasch*.

rash[2] ▶ noun an area of reddening of a person's skin, sometimes with raised spots, appearing especially as a result of illness.
■ a series of things of the same type, especially when unpleasant or undesirable, occurring or appearing one after the other within a short space of time: *a rash of strikes by health-service workers.*
– ORIGIN early 18th cent.: probably related to Old French *rasche* 'eruptive sores, scurf'; compare with Italian *raschia* 'itch'.

rasher ▶ noun a thin slice of bacon.
– ORIGIN late 16th cent.: of unknown origin.

ras malai /'rʌs mʌˌlʌɪ/ ▶ noun [mass noun] an Indian sweet dish consisting of small, flat cakes of paneer in sweetened, thickened milk.
– ORIGIN from Hindi *ras* 'juice' and *malāī* 'cream'.

rasp ▶ noun **1** a coarse file or similar metal tool with a roughened surface for scraping, filing, or rubbing down objects of metal, wood, or other hard material.
2 [in sing.] a harsh, grating noise: *the rasp of the engine.*
▶ verb **1** [with obj.] scrape (something) with a rasp in order to make it smoother.
■ (of a rough surface or object) scrape (something, especially someone's skin) in a painful or unpleasant way. ■ (**rasp something away/off**) remove something by scraping it off.
2 [no obj.] make a harsh, grating noise: *my breath rasped in my throat.*
■ [with direct speech] say in a harsh, grating voice: *'Stay where you are!' he rasped.*
– DERIVATIVES **raspingly** adverb, **raspy** adjective.

– ORIGIN Middle English (as a verb): from Old French *rasper*, perhaps of Germanic origin.

raspberry ▶ **noun** **1** an edible soft fruit related to the blackberry, consisting of a cluster of reddish-pink drupelets.
2 the plant which yields this fruit, forming tall stiff prickly stems or 'canes'.
● *Rubus idaeus*, family Rosaceae; cultivars include the loganberry, tayberry, and veitchberry.
3 [mass noun] a deep reddish-pink colour like that of a ripe raspberry: [as modifier] *a raspberry tweed jacket.*
4 informal a sound made with the tongue and lips in order to express derision or contempt: *Clare* ***blew a raspberry*** *and stood up.* [ORIGIN: from *raspberry tart*, rhyming slang for 'fart'.]
– ORIGIN early 17th cent.: from dialect *rasp*, abbreviation of obsolete *raspis* 'raspberry' (also used as a collective), of unknown origin, + **BERRY**.

raspberry beetle ▶ **noun** a small yellowish-brown beetle which is a pest of raspberries. The adults feed on the flower buds and the larvae on the growing fruit.
● *Byturus tomentosus*, family *Byturidae*.

raspberry cane ▶ **noun** a cultivated raspberry plant.

rasper ▶ **noun** a person or thing that scrapes something with or as if with a rasp.
■ Hunting a high fence that is difficult to jump.

rasp fern ▶ **noun** a small robust fern with prickly toothed edges to the lobes, growing in woodland and rainforests in Australasia and Polynesia, typically in rocky crevices.
● Genus *Doodia*, family Blechnaceae.

Rasputin /ra'spjuːtɪn/, Grigori (Efimovich) (1871–1916), Russian monk. He came to exert great influence over Tsar Nicholas II and his family during the First World War; this influence, combined with his reputation for debauchery, steadily discredited the imperial family, and he was assassinated by a group loyal to the tsar.

rass /rɑːs/ ▶ **noun** black slang a person's buttocks.
■ a contemptible person.
– ORIGIN late 18th cent.: alteration of **ARSE**, perhaps partly from *your arse*.

rassle ▶ **verb** N. Amer. non-standard spelling of **WRESTLE**, representing a regional pronunciation.
– DERIVATIVES **rassler** noun.

Rasta /'rastə/ ▶ **noun** & **adjective** informal short for **RASTAFARIAN**.

Rastafari /ˌrastə'fɑːri/ ▶ **noun** [mass noun] [usu. as modifier] the Rastafarian movement.
– ORIGIN from *Ras Tafari*, the name by which Haile Selassie was known (1916–30).

Rastafarian /ˌrastə'fɑːrɪən, -'fɛːrɪən/ ▶ **adjective** of or relating to a religious movement of Jamaican origin holding that blacks are the chosen people. Rastafarians believe that Emperor Haile Selassie of Ethiopia was the Messiah, and that black people will eventually return to their African homeland.
▶ **noun** a member of the Rastafarian religious movement. Rastafarians have distinctive codes of behaviour and dress, including the wearing of dreadlocks, the smoking of cannabis, and the rejection of Western medicine, and they follow a diet that excludes pork, shellfish, and milk.
– DERIVATIVES **Rastafarianism** noun.

r

Rastaman /'rastəman/ ▶ **noun** (pl. **-men**) informal a male Rastafarian.

raster /'rastə/ ▶ **noun** a rectangular pattern of parallel scanning lines followed by the electron beam on a television screen or computer monitor.
– ORIGIN mid 20th cent.: from German *Raster*, literally 'screen', from Latin *rastrum* 'rake', from *ras-* 'scraped', from the verb *radere*.

raster image processor (abbrev.: **RIP**) ▶ **noun** Computing a device that rasterizes an image.

rasterize (also **-ise**) ▶ **verb** [with obj.] Computing convert (an image stored as an outline) into pixels that can be displayed on a screen or printed.
– DERIVATIVES **rasterization** noun, **rasterizer** noun.

Rastyapino /ra'stjɑːpɪnəʊ/ former name (1919–29) for **DZERZHINSK**.

rat ▶ **noun** **1** a rodent that resembles a large mouse, typically having a pointed snout and a long sparsely haired tail. Some kinds have become cosmopolitan and are sometimes responsible for transmitting diseases.
● Family Muridae: many genera, including *Rattus* (the Old World rats), and several hundred species.
2 informal a person regarded as despicable, especially a man who has been deceitful or disloyal.
■ an informer.
3 [with modifier] N. Amer. a person who is associated with or frequents a specified place: *a wharf rat.*
▶ **exclamation** (**rats**) informal used to express mild annoyance or irritation.
▶ **verb** (**ratted**, **ratting**) [no obj.] **1** [usu. as noun **ratting**] (of a person, dog, or cat) hunt or kill rats.
2 informal desert one's party, side, or cause.
▶ **rat on** (US also **rat someone out**) informal inform on (someone) to a person in a position of authority: *men will literally choose death over ratting out another prisoner.* ■ break (an agreement or promise): *he accused the government of ratting on an earlier pledge.*
– ORIGIN Old English *ræt*, probably of Romance origin; reinforced in Middle English by Old French *rat*. The verb dates from the early 19th cent.

rata /'rɑːtə/ ▶ **noun** a large New Zealand tree of the myrtle family, with crimson flowers and hard red timber.
● Genus *Metrosideros*, family Myrtaceae: several species, in particular *M. robusta*.
– ORIGIN late 18th cent.: from Maori.

ratable ▶ **adjective** variant spelling of **RATEABLE**.

ratafia /ˌratə'fɪə/ ▶ **noun** [mass noun] a liqueur flavoured with almonds or the kernels of peaches, apricots, or cherries.
■ (also **ratafia biscuit**) [count noun] an almond-flavoured biscuit like a small macaroon.
– ORIGIN late 17th cent.: from French; perhaps related to **TAFIA**.

ratamacue /'ratəməˌkjuː/ ▶ **noun** Music one of the basic patterns (rudiments) of drumming, consisting of a two-beat figure, the first beat of which is played as a triplet and preceded by two grace notes.
– ORIGIN 1940s: imitative.

Ratana /'rɑːtənə/, Tahupotiki Wiremu (1873–1939), Maori political and religious leader. He founded the Ratana Church (1920), a religious revival movement which aimed to unite all Maori people.

rataplan /ˌratə'plan/ ▶ **noun** [in sing.] a drumming or beating sound.
– ORIGIN mid 19th cent.: from French, of imitative origin.

rat-arsed ▶ **adjective** Brit. vulgar slang very drunk.

ratatat ▶ **noun** variant of **RAT-TAT**.

ratatouille /ˌratə'tuːi, -'twiː/ ▶ **noun** [mass noun] a vegetable dish consisting of onions, courgettes, tomatoes, aubergines, and peppers, fried and stewed in oil and sometimes served cold.
– ORIGIN a French dialect word.

ratbag ▶ **noun** Brit. informal an unpleasant or disliked person.

rat-bite fever ▶ **noun** Medicine a disease contracted from the bite of a rat which causes inflammation of the skin and fever or vomiting.
● This disease can be caused by either the bacterium *Spirillum minus* or the fungus *Streptobacillus moniliformis*.

ratchet ▶ **noun** a device consisting of a bar or wheel with a set of angled teeth in which a pawl, cog, or tooth engages, allowing motion in one direction only.
■ a bar or wheel which has such a set of teeth.
■ figurative a situation or process that is perceived to be deteriorating or changing steadily in a series of irreversible steps: *yet another turn in the ratchet of state control over local experimentation.*
▶ **verb** (**ratcheted**, **ratcheting**) [with obj.] operate by means of a ratchet.
■ (**ratchet something up/down**) figurative cause something to rise (or fall) as a step in what is perceived as a steady and irreversible process: *the Bank of Japan ratcheted up interest rates again.* ■ [no obj.] make a sound like a ratchet.
– ORIGIN mid 17th cent.: from French *rochet*, originally denoting a blunt lance head, later in the sense 'bobbin, ratchet'; related to the base of archaic *rock* 'quantity of wool on a distaff for spinning'.

rate[1] ▶ **noun** **1** a measure, quantity, or frequency, typically one measured against some other quantity or measure: *the crime rate in the first quarter of 1991 rose by 26 per cent.*
■ the speed with which something moves, happens, or changes: *your heart rate.*
2 a fixed price paid or charged for something, especially goods or services: *a £3.40 minimum hourly rate of pay | advertising rates.*
■ the amount of a charge or payment expressed as a percentage of some other amount, or as a basis of calculation: *you'll find our current interest rate very competitive.* ■ (usu. **rates**) (in the UK) a tax on land and buildings paid to the local authority by a business, and formerly also by occupants of private property (for whom it was replaced by the community charge and council tax).
▶ **verb** **1** [with obj.] assign a standard or value to (something) according to a particular scale: *they were asked to rate their ability at different driving manoeuvres* | [with obj. and complement] *the hotel, rated four star, had no hot water and no sink plugs.*
■ [with obj. and adverbial] assign a standard, optimal, or limiting rating to (a piece of equipment): *the average life of the new bulb is* ***rated at*** *approximately 500 hours.* ■ Brit. assess the value of (a property) for the purpose of levying a local tax.
2 [with obj. and adverbial] consider to be of a certain quality, standard, or rank: *Atkinson rates him as Europe's top defender* | [with obj. and complement] *the program has been rated a great success.*
■ [no obj., with adverbial] be regarded in a specified way: *Jeff still rates as one of the nicest people I have ever met.* ■ [with obj.] informal have a high opinion of; consider to be good: *Mike certainly rated her, goodness knows why.* ■ [with obj.] be worthy of; merit: *the ambassador rated a bulletproof car and a police escort.*
– PHRASES **at any rate** whatever happens or may have happened: *for the moment, at any rate, he was safe.* ■ used to indicate that one is correcting or clarifying a previous statement or emphasizing a following one: *the story, or at any rate, a public version of it, was known and remembered.* **at this** (or **that**) **rate** used to introduce the prediction of a particular unwelcome eventuality should things continue as they are or if a certain assumption is true: *at this rate, I won't have a job to go back to.*
– ORIGIN late Middle English (expressing a notion of 'estimated value'): from Old French, from medieval Latin *rata* (from Latin *pro rata parte* (or *portione*) 'according to the proportional share'), from *ratus* 'reckoned', past participle of *reri*.

rate[2] ▶ **verb** [with obj.] archaic scold (someone) angrily: *he rated the young man soundly for his want of respect.*
– ORIGIN late Middle English: of unknown origin.

rate[3] ▶ **verb** variant spelling of **RET**.

rateable (also **ratable**) ▶ **adjective** able to be rated or estimated.
– DERIVATIVES **rateability** noun, **rateably** adverb.

rateable value ▶ **noun** (in the UK) a value ascribed to a domestic or commercial building based on its size, location, and other factors, used to determine the rates payable by its owner.

rate-capping ▶ **noun** [mass noun] (formerly in the UK) the imposition of an upper limit on the rates leviable by a local authority.
– DERIVATIVES **rate-cap** verb.

rate card ▶ **noun** a table of charges for advertising.

rate constant ▶ **noun** Chemistry a coefficient of proportionality relating the rate of a chemical reaction at a given temperature to the concentration of reactant (in a unimolecular reaction) or to the product of the concentrations of reactants.

ratel /'reɪt(ə)l, 'rɑː-/ ▶ **noun** a badger-like mammal with a white or grey back and black underparts, native to Africa and Asia. In Africa it is attracted by the honeyguide bird to bee nests, which it breaks open to gain access to the grubs and honey. Also called **HONEY BADGER**.
● *Mellivora capensis*, family Mustelidae.
– ORIGIN late 18th cent.: from Afrikaans, of unknown ultimate origin.

rate of exchange ▶ **noun** another term for **EXCHANGE RATE**.

ratepayer ▶ **noun** **1** (in the UK) a person liable to pay rates.
2 N. Amer. a customer of a public utility.

ratfish ▶ **noun** (pl. same or **-fishes**) **1** a blunt-nosed chimaera with rodent-like front teeth and a long thin tail, found chiefly in cooler waters. See also **RABBITFISH**.
● Genera *Chimaera* and *Hydrolagus*, family Chimaeridae: several species, including *H. colliei* of the eastern North Pacific.
2 a long thin purplish edible fish which lives in shallow temperate waters of the Indo-Pacific where it burrows in the sand.

• *Gonorhynchus gonorhynchus*, the only member of the family Gonorhynchidae.

rath[1] /rɑːθ/ ▶ **noun** Archaeology (in Ireland) a strong circular earthen wall forming an enclosure and serving as a fort and residence for a tribal chief.
– ORIGIN Irish.

rath[2] /rʌθ/ ▶ **noun** Indian a chariot, especially one used to carry an idol in a ceremonial procession. See also **RATH YATRA**.
– ORIGIN Hindi.

Rathaus /ˈrathaʊs/ ▶ **noun** (pl. **Rathäuser**) a town hall in a German-speaking country.
– ORIGIN German, from *Rat* 'council' + *Haus* 'house'.

rathe /reɪð/ ▶ **adjective** archaic or poetic/literary (of a person or their actions) prompt and eager.
■ (of flowers or fruit) blooming or ripening early in the year.
– ORIGIN Old English *hræth*, *hræd*, of Germanic origin; perhaps related to the base of **RASH**[1].

rather ▶ **adverb 1** (**would rather**) used to indicate one's preference in a particular matter: *would you like some wine or would you rather stick to sherry?* | *she'd* **rather** *die* **than** *cause a scene* | [with clause] *I'd rather you didn't tell him* | *'You'd better ask her.' 'I'd rather not.'*
2 [as submodifier] to a certain or significant extent or degree: *she's been behaving rather strangely* | *he's rather an unpleasant man.*
■ used before verbs as a way of making the expression of a feeling or opinion less assertive: *I rather think he wants me to marry him* | *we were rather hoping you might do that for us.*
3 on the contrary (used to suggest that the opposite of what has just been implied or stated is the case): [sentence adverb] *There is no shortage of basic skills in the workplace. Rather, the problem is poor management.*
■ more precisely (used to modify or clarify something previously stated): *I walked,* **or rather** *limped, the two miles home.* ■ instead of; as opposed to: *she seemed indifferent* **rather than** *angry.*
▶ **exclamation** Brit. dated used to express emphatic affirmation, agreement, or acceptance: *'You are glad to be home, aren't you?' 'Rather!'*
– PHRASES **had rather** poetic/literary or archaic would rather: *I had rather not see him.* **rather you** (or **him** or **her** etc.) **than me** used to convey that one would be reluctant oneself to undertake a particular task or project undertaken by someone else: *'I'm picking him up after lunch.' 'Rather you than me.'*
– ORIGIN Old English *hrathor* 'earlier, sooner', comparative of *hræthe* 'without delay', from *hræth* 'prompt' (see **RATHE**).

rathe-ripe ▶ **adjective** archaic or poetic/literary (of fruits or grain) ripening early in the year.
■ (of a person) maturing early; physically or intellectually precocious.

Rathlin Island /ˈraθlɪn/ an island in the North Channel, off the north coast of Ireland.

rathole ▶ **noun 1** informal a cramped or squalid room or building.
2 N. Amer. informal used to refer to the waste of money or resources: *pouring our assets* **down the rathole** *of military expenditure.*
3 (in the oil industry) a shallow hole drilled near a well to accommodate the drill string joint when not in use.
■ a small hole drilled at the bottom of a larger hole.
▶ **verb** [with obj.] N. Amer. informal hide (money or goods), typically as part of a fraud or deception.

rathskeller /ˈrɑːtsˌkɛlə/ ▶ **noun** US a beer hall or restaurant in a basement.
– ORIGIN early 20th cent.: from obsolete German (now *Ratskeller*), from *Rathaus* 'town hall' + *Keller* 'cellar', denoting the place where beer and wine were sold.

rath yatra /ˈrʌθ ˌjɑːtrɑː/ ▶ **noun** Hinduism a ceremonial procession centred around a chariot carrying an idol, specifically the procession of the Juggernaut.
– ORIGIN via Hindi from Sanskrit *ratha* 'chariot' + *yātrā* from *yā* 'to travel'.

ratify ▶ **verb** (**-ies**, **-ied**) [with obj.] sign or give formal consent to (a treaty, contract, or agreement), making it officially valid.
– DERIVATIVES **ratifiable** adjective, **ratification** noun, **ratifier** noun.
– ORIGIN late Middle English: from Old French *ratifier*, from medieval Latin *ratificare*, from Latin *ratus* 'fixed' (see **RATE**[1]).

rating[1] ▶ **noun 1** a classification or ranking of someone or something based on a comparative assessment of their quality, standard, or performance: *the hotel regained its five-star rating.*
■ (**ratings**) the estimated audience size of a particular television or radio programme: *the soap's ratings have recently picked up.* ■ the value of a property or condition which is claimed to be standard, optimal, or limiting for a substance, material, or item of equipment: *fuel with a low octane rating.* ■ any of the classes into which racing yachts are assigned according to dimensions.
2 Brit. a non-commissioned sailor in the navy. [ORIGIN: so named from the position held by a sailor, recorded on a ship's books.]

rating[2] ▶ **noun** dated an angry reprimand.

ratio ▶ **noun** (pl. **-os**) the quantitative relation between two amounts showing the number of times one value contains or is contained within the other: *the ratio of men's jobs to women's is 8 to 1.*
– ORIGIN mid 17th cent.: from Latin, literally 'reckoning', from *rat-* 'reckoned', from the verb *reri*.

ratiocinate /ˌratɪˈɒsɪneɪt, ˌraʃɪ-/ ▶ **verb** [no obj.] formal form judgements by a process of logic; reason.
– DERIVATIVES **ratiocination** noun, **ratiocinative** adjective, **ratiocinator** noun.
– ORIGIN mid 17th cent.: from Latin *ratiocinat-* 'deliberated, calculated', from the verb *ratiocinari*, from *ratio* (see **RATIO**).

ratio decidendi /ˌdɛsɪˈdɛndiː/ ▶ **noun** (pl. **rationes decidendi** /ˌratɪˈəʊniːz/) Law the rule of law on which a judicial decision is based.
– ORIGIN Latin, literally 'reason for deciding'.

ration ▶ **noun** a fixed amount of a commodity officially allowed to each person during a time of shortage, as in wartime: *1947 saw the bread ration reduced on two occasions.*
■ (usu. **rations**) an amount of food supplied on a regular basis, especially to members of the armed forces during a war. ■ (**rations**) food; provisions: *their emergency rations ran out.* ■ figurative a fixed amount of a particular thing: *holidaymakers who like* **a** *generous* **ration of** *activity.*
▶ **verb** [with obj.] (usu. **be rationed**) allow each person to have only a fixed amount of (a particular commodity): *petrol was so strictly rationed that bikes were always in demand.*
■ (**ration someone to**) allow someone to have only (a fixed amount of a certain commodity): *the population was rationed to four litres of water per person per day.*
– PHRASES **come up** (or **be given**) **with the rations** military slang (of a medal) be awarded automatically and without regard to merit.
– ORIGIN early 18th cent.: from French, from Latin *ratio(n-)* 'reckoning, ratio'.

rational ▶ **adjective 1** based on or in accordance with reason or logic: *I'm sure there's a perfectly rational explanation.*
■ (of a person) able to think clearly, sensibly, and logically: *Ursula's upset—she's not being very rational.* ■ endowed with the capacity to reason: *man is a rational being.*
2 Mathematics (of a number, quantity, or expression) expressible, or containing quantities which are expressible, as a ratio of whole numbers. When expressed as a decimal, a rational number has a finite or recurring expansion.
– DERIVATIVES **rationality** noun, **rationally** adverb.
– ORIGIN late Middle English (in the sense 'having the ability to reason'): from Latin *rationalis*, from *ratio(n-)* 'reckoning, reason' (see **RATIO**).

rational dress ▶ **noun** [mass noun] a style of women's dress introduced in the late 19th century, characterized by the wearing of knickerbockers or bloomers in place of a skirt.

rationale /ˌraʃəˈnɑːl/ ▶ **noun** a set of reasons or a logical basis for a course of action or a particular belief: *he explained the rationale behind the change.*
– ORIGIN mid 17th cent.: modern Latin, neuter (used as a noun) of Latin *rationalis* 'endowed with reason' (see **RATIONAL**).

rational expectations hypothesis ▶ **noun** Economics the hypothesis that an economic agent will make full use of all available information when forming expectations, especially with regard to inflation, and not just past values of a particular variable. Compare with **ADAPTIVE EXPECTATIONS HYPOTHESIS**.

rationalism ▶ **noun** [mass noun] a belief or theory that opinions and actions should be based on reason and knowledge rather than on religious belief or emotional response: *scientific rationalism.*
■ Philosophy the theory that reason rather than experience is the foundation of certainty in knowledge. ■ Theology the practice of treating reason as the ultimate authority in religion.
– DERIVATIVES **rationalist** noun, **rationalistic** adjective, **rationalistically** adverb.

rationalize (also **-ise**) ▶ **verb** [with obj.] **1** attempt to explain or justify (one's own or another's behaviour or attitude) with logical, plausible reasons, even if these are not true or appropriate: *she couldn't rationalize her urge to return to the cottage.*
2 make (a company, process, or industry) more efficient by reorganizing it in such a way as to dispense with personnel or equipment perceived to be unnecessary: *if we rationalize production, will that mean redundancies?*
■ reorganize (a process or system) in such a way as to make it more logical and consistent: *Parliament should seek to rationalize the country's court structure.*
3 Mathematics convert (a function or expression) to a rational form.
– DERIVATIVES **rationalization** noun, **rationalizer** noun.

ratite /ˈratʌɪt/ Ornithology ▶ **adjective** (of a bird) having a flat breastbone without a keel, and so unable to fly. Contrasted with **CARINATE**.
▶ **noun** any of the mostly large, flightless birds with such a breastbone, i.e. the ostrich, rhea, emu, cassowary, and kiwi, together with the extinct moa and elephant bird.
– ORIGIN late 19th cent.: from Latin *ratis* 'raft' + **-ITE**[1].

rat-kangaroo ▶ **noun** a small rat-like Australian marsupial with long hindlimbs used for hopping.
• Family Potoroidae: several genera and species.

ratlines /ˈratlɪnz/ ▶ **plural noun** a series of small rope lines fastened across a sailing ship's shrouds like the rungs of a ladder, used for climbing the rigging.
– ORIGIN late Middle English: of unknown origin.

ratoon /rəˈtuːn/ ▶ **noun** a new shoot or sprout springing from the base of a crop plant, especially sugar cane, after cropping.
▶ **verb** [no obj.] (of sugar cane) produce ratoons.
■ [with obj.] cut down (a plant) to cause it to sprout in this way.
– ORIGIN mid 17th cent. (as a noun): from Spanish *retoño* 'a sprout'.

rat pack[1] ▶ **noun** informal a group of journalists and photographers perceived as aggressive or relentless in their pursuit of stories about celebrities.

rat pack[2] ▶ **noun** S. African informal a food pack issued by the army to men on duty away from base camp.

rat race ▶ **noun** informal a way of life in which people are caught up in a fiercely competitive struggle for wealth or power.

rat run ▶ **noun** Brit. informal a minor, typically residential street used by drivers during peak periods to avoid congestion on main roads.

ratsbane ▶ **noun** [mass noun] poetic/literary rat poison.

rat snake ▶ **noun** a harmless constricting snake that feeds on rats and other small mammals.
• Several genera and species in the family Colubridae: genus *Elaphe* of America, in particular *E. obsoleta*, and genera *Ptyas* and *Argyrogena* of Asia (also called **RACER**), in particular *P. mucosus*.

rat-tail ▶ **noun 1** (also **rat's tail**) a narrow hairless tail like that of a rat, or something that resembles one.
■ (**rat's tails**) Brit. informal hair hanging in lank, damp or greasy strands.
2 a fish with a long narrow tail, in particular:
■ another term for **GRENADIER** (in sense 2). ■ another term for **RABBITFISH** (in sense 1).
3 [mass noun] a design used in the manufacture of cutlery in which the handle of a knife, fork, or spoon is decorated with a moulding in the shape of a rat's tail: [as modifier] *the traditional English rat-tail design.*

rat-tailed maggot ▶ **noun** the aquatic larva of the drone fly, with a tail-like telescopic breathing tube that enables it to breathe air while submerged.

rattan /rəˈtan/ ▶ **noun 1** [mass noun] the thin pliable stems of a palm, used to make furniture.
■ [count noun] a length of such a stem used as a walking stick.
2 the tropical Old World climbing palm which yields this product, with long, spiny, jointed stems.
• Genus *Calamus*, family Palmae.
– ORIGIN mid 17th cent.: from Malay *rotan*, probably from *raut* 'pare, trim'.

r

rat-tat (also **rat-tat-tat**) ▶ **noun** a rapping sound (used especially in reference to a sequence of two or three knocks on a door or the sound of gunfire).
– ORIGIN late 17th cent.: imitative.

ratted ▶ **adjective** Brit. informal very drunk.

ratter ▶ **noun** a dog or other animal that is used for hunting rats.

Rattigan /ˈratɪɡ(ə)n/, Sir Terence (Mervyn) (1911–77), English dramatist. Notable plays: *The Winslow Boy* (1946) and *The Browning Version* (1948).

Rattle, Sir Simon (Denis) (b.1955), English conductor. He was principal conductor with the City of Birmingham Symphony Orchestra 1980–91, and is noted particularly for his interpretation of works by early 20th-century composers such as Mahler.

rattle ▶ **verb 1** [no obj.] make a rapid succession of short, sharp knocking sounds, typically as a result of being shaken and striking repeatedly against a hard surface or object: *there was a sound of bottles rattling as he stacked the crates.*
■ [with obj.] cause (something) to make such sounds: *he rattled some change in his pocket.* ■ [with adverbial of direction] (of a vehicle or its driver or passengers) move or travel somewhere while making such sounds: *trains rattled past at frequent intervals.* ■ (**rattle about/around in**) figurative be in or occupy (an unnecessarily or undesirably spacious room or building).
2 [with obj.] (often **be rattled**) informal cause (someone) to feel nervous, worried, or irritated: *she turned quickly, rattled by his presence.*
▶ **noun 1** a rapid succession of short, sharp, hard sounds: *the rattle of teacups on the tray.*
■ a gurgling sound in the throat of a dying person. ■ an act or instance of saying something in a rapid, continuous way. ■ archaic a person who talks incessantly in a lively or inane way.
2 a thing used to make a rapid succession of short, sharp sounds, in particular:
■ a baby's toy consisting of a container filled with small pellets, which makes a noise when shaken. ■ a wooden device that makes a loud noise when whirled around, formerly used by spectators at football matches. ■ the set of horny rings at the end of a rattlesnake's tail, shaken with a dry buzzing sound as a warning.
– PHRASES **rattle someone's cage** informal make someone feel angry or annoyed. **rattle sabres** threaten to take aggressive action. See also **SABRE-RATTLING**.
– DERIVATIVES **rattly** adjective.
– ORIGIN Middle English (as a verb): related to Middle Dutch and Low German *ratelen*, of imitative origin.
▶ **rattle something off** say, perform, or produce something quickly and effortlessly: *he rattled off some instructions.*
rattle on/away talk rapidly and at length, especially in an inane or boring way.

rattler ▶ **noun 1** a thing that rattles, especially an old or rickety vehicle.
2 N. Amer. informal a rattlesnake.

rattlesnake ▶ **noun** a heavy-bodied American pit viper with a series of horny rings on the tail that produce a characteristic rattling sound when vibrated as a warning.
• Genera *Crotalus* and *Sistrurus*, family Viperidae: several species.

rattletrap ▶ **noun** informal an old or rickety vehicle.

rattling ▶ **adjective 1** making a series of short, sharp knocking sounds: *a rattling old lift.*
2 informal, dated denoting something very good of its kind (used for emphasis): *a rattling good story.*

rat trap ▶ **noun** informal **1** an unpleasant or restricting situation that offers no prospect of improvement.
2 a shabby, squalid, or ramshackle building or establishment.

ratty ▶ **adjective** (**rattier**, **rattiest**) **1** resembling or characteristic of a rat: *his ratty eyes glittered.*
■ (of a place) infested with rats. ■ informal shabby, untidy, or in bad condition: *a ratty old armchair.*
2 [predic.] Brit. informal (of a person) bad-tempered and irritable: *I was a bit ratty with the children.*
– DERIVATIVES **rattily** adverb, **rattiness** noun.

raucous /ˈrɔːkəs/ ▶ **adjective** making or constituting a disturbingly harsh and loud noise: *raucous youths.*
– DERIVATIVES **raucously** adverb, **raucousness** noun.
– ORIGIN mid 18th cent.: from Latin *raucus* 'hoarse' + **-OUS**.

rauli /ˈraʊli/ ▶ **noun** a southern beech tree with showy autumn foliage, native to Chile and cultivated as an ornamental.
• *Nothofagus procera*, family Fagaceae.
– ORIGIN early 20th cent.: via American Spanish from Mapuche *ruili*.

raunch ▶ **noun** [mass noun] informal energetic earthiness; vulgarity: *the raunch of his first album.*
– ORIGIN 1960s: back-formation from **RAUNCHY**.

raunchy ▶ **adjective** (**raunchier**, **raunchiest**) informal **1** energetically earthy and sexually explicit: *a raunchy new novel.*
2 chiefly US (especially of a person or place) slovenly; grubby: *the restaurant's style is raunchy and the sanitation chancy.*
– DERIVATIVES **raunchily** adverb, **raunchiness** noun.
– ORIGIN 1930s: of unknown origin.

Rauschenberg /ˈraʊʃ(ə)nbəːɡ/, Robert (b.1925), American artist. His series of 'combine' paintings, such as *Charlene* (1954) and *Rebus* (1955), incorporate three-dimensional objects such as nails, rags, and bottles.

rauwolfia /raʊˈwɒlfɪə, raʊˈvɒlfɪə/ (also **rauvolfia**) ▶ **noun** a tropical shrub or small tree, some kinds of which are cultivated for the medicinal drugs which they yield.
• Genus *Rauwolfia* (or *Rauvolfia*), family Apocynaceae: many species, in particular the Indian snakeroot (*R. serpentina*), from which the drug reserpine is obtained.
– ORIGIN modern Latin, named after Leonhard *Rauwolf* (died 1596), German botanist.

rav /rɒv/ ▶ **noun** Judaism a rabbi, especially one who holds a position of authority or who acts as a personal mentor. [ORIGIN: partly via Yiddish.]
■ (**Rav**) (in orthodox Judaism) a title of respect and form of address preceding a personal name.
– ORIGIN from Hebrew and Aramaic *rab̲* 'master'.

ravage ▶ **verb** [with obj.] cause severe and extensive damage to: *fears that a war could ravage their country.*
▶ **noun** (**ravages**) the severely damaging or destructive effects of something: *his face had withstood* **the ravages of time**.
■ acts of destruction: *the ravages committed by man.*
– DERIVATIVES **ravager** noun.
– ORIGIN early 17th cent.: from French *ravager*, from earlier *ravage*, alteration of *ravine* 'rush of water'.

rave[1] ▶ **verb** [no obj.] **1** talk wildly or incoherently, as if one were delirious or mad: *Nancy's having hysterics and raving about a black ghost.*
■ address someone in an angry, uncontrolled way: [with direct speech] *'Never mind how he feels!' Melissa raved.*
2 speak or write about someone or something with great enthusiasm or admiration: *New York's theatre critics raved about the acting.*
3 informal, chiefly Brit. attend or take part in a rave party.
▶ **noun 1** informal, chiefly US an extremely enthusiastic recommendation or appraisal of someone or something: *the film has won raves from American reviewers* | [as modifier] *their recent tour received* **rave reviews**.
■ a person or thing that inspires intense and widely shared enthusiasm: *last year's fave raves are back for a live performance.* ■ Brit. informal, dated a passionate and usually transitory infatuation.
2 informal a lively party or gathering involving dancing and drinking: *their annual fancy-dress rave.*
■ chiefly Brit. a party or event attended by large numbers of young people, with dancing to fast, electronic music. ■ [mass noun] electronic dance music of the kind played at such events.
– ORIGIN Middle English (in the sense 'show signs of madness': probably from Old Northern French *raver*; related obscurely to (Middle) Low German *reven* 'be senseless, rave'.

rave[2] ▶ **noun** a rail of a cart.
■ (**raves**) a permanent or removable framework added to the sides of a cart to increase its capacity.
– ORIGIN mid 16th cent.: variant of the synonymous dialect word *rathe*, of unknown origin.

Ravel /raˈvɛl, French ravɛl/, Maurice (Joseph) (1875–1937), French composer. Noted for their colourful orchestration, his works have a distinctive tone and make use of unresolved dissonances. Notable works: *Daphnis and Chloë* (ballet) (1912); *Boléro* (orchestral work) (1928).

ravel ▶ **verb** (**ravelled**, **ravelling**; US **raveled**, **raveling**) [with obj.] **1** (**ravel something out**) untangle something: *Davy had finished ravelling out his herring net* | figurative *sleep ravelled out the tangles of his mind.*
2 confuse or complicate (a question or situation).
▶ **noun** rare a tangle, cluster, or knot: *a lovely yellow ravel of sunflowers.*
– ORIGIN late Middle English (in the sense 'entangle, confuse'): probably from Dutch *ravelen* 'fray out, tangle'.

ravelin /ˈravlɪn/ ▶ **noun** historical an outwork of fortifications, with two faces forming a salient angle, constructed beyond the main ditch and in front of the curtain.
– ORIGIN late 16th cent.: from French, from obsolete Italian *ravellino*, of unknown origin.

ravelling ▶ **noun** a thread from a woven or knitted fabric that has frayed or started to unravel.

raven[1] /ˈreɪv(ə)n/ ▶ **noun** a large heavily built crow with mainly black plumage, feeding chiefly on carrion.
• Genus *Corvus*, family Corvidae: several species, in particular the widespread all-black **common raven** (*C. corax*)
▶ **adjective** (especially of hair) of a glossy black colour.
– ORIGIN Old English *hræfn*, of Germanic origin; related to Dutch *raaf* and German *Rabe*.

raven[2] /ˈrav(ə)n/ ▶ **verb** [no obj.] archaic (of a ferocious wild animal) hunt for prey.
■ [with obj.] devour voraciously.
– ORIGIN late 15th cent. (in the sense 'take as spoil'): from Old French *raviner*, originally 'to ravage', based on Latin *rapina* 'pillage'.

ravening ▶ **adjective** (of a ferocious wild animal) extremely hungry and hunting for prey: *they turned on each other like ravening wolves.*

Ravenna /rəˈvɛnə/ a city near the Adriatic coast in NE central Italy; pop. 136,720 (1991). Ravenna became the capital of the Western Roman Empire in 402 and then of the Ostrogothic kingdom of Italy, afterwards serving as capital of Byzantine Italy. It is noted for its ancient mosaics dating from the early Christian period.

ravenous ▶ **adjective** extremely hungry.
■ (of hunger or need) very great; voracious: *a ravenous appetite.*
– DERIVATIVES **ravenously** adverb, **ravenousness** noun.
– ORIGIN late Middle English: from Old French *ravineus*, from *raviner* 'to ravage' (see **RAVEN**[2]).

raver ▶ **noun 1** informal a person who has an exciting and uninhibited social life.
■ Brit. a person who regularly goes to raves.
2 a person who talks wildly or incoherently, as if delirious or mad.

rave-up ▶ **noun** Brit. informal a lively, noisy party or gathering involving dancing and drinking.
■ N. Amer. informal a fast, loud, or danceable piece of pop music.

Ravi /ˈrʌvi/ a river in the north of the Indian subcontinent, one of the headwaters of the Indus, which rises in the Himalayas in Himachel Pradesh, NW India, and flows generally south-westwards into Pakistan, where it empties into the Chenab River just north of Multan. It is one of the five rivers that gave Punjab its name.

ravigote /ˈravɪɡɒt/ (also **ravigotte**) ▶ **noun** [mass noun] a mixture of chopped chervil, chives, tarragon, and shallots, used to give piquancy to a sauce or as a base for a herb butter.
– ORIGIN French, from *ravigoter* 'invigorate'.

ravin /ˈravɪn/ ▶ **noun** [mass noun] archaic or poetic/literary violent seizure of prey or property; plunder.
– ORIGIN Middle English: from Old French *ravine*, from Latin *rapina* 'pillage' (see **RAPINE**).

ravine /rəˈviːn/ ▶ **noun** a deep, narrow gorge with steep sides.
– DERIVATIVES **ravined** adjective.
– ORIGIN late 18th cent.: from French, 'violent rush (of water)' (see **RAVIN**).

raving ▶ **noun** (usu. **ravings**) wild, irrational, or incoherent talk: *the ravings of a madman.*
▶ **adjective** informal used to emphasize the bad or extreme quality of someone or something: *she'd never been a raving beauty* | [as submodifier] *have you gone raving mad?*

ravioli /ˌraviˈəʊli/ ▶ **plural noun** small pasta envelopes containing minced meat, cheese, or vegetables.
– ORIGIN Italian.

ravish ▶ **verb** [with obj.] **1** archaic seize and carry off (someone) by force.
■ dated (of a man) force (a woman or girl) to have sexual intercourse against their will.
2 (often **be ravished**) poetic/literary fill (someone) with intense delight; enrapture: *ravished by a sunny afternoon, she had agreed without even thinking.*
– DERIVATIVES **ravisher** noun, **ravishment** noun.
– ORIGIN Middle English: from Old French *raviss-*, lengthened stem of *ravir*, from an alteration of Latin *rapere* 'seize'.

ravishing ▶ **adjective** delightful; entrancing: *she looked ravishing.*
– DERIVATIVES **ravishingly** adverb.

raw ▶ **adjective 1** (of food) uncooked: *raw eggs | salsify can be eaten raw in salads or cooked.*
■ (of a material or substance) in its natural state; not yet processed or purified: *raw silk | raw sewage.* ■ (of information) not analysed, evaluated, or processed for use: *there were a number of errors in the raw data.* ■ (of the edge of a piece of cloth) not having a hem or selvedge. ■ (of a person) new to an activity or job and therefore lacking experience or skill: *they were replaced by* ***raw recruits.*** ■ S. African derogatory (of a black African) from a traditional tribal or rural culture.
2 (of a part of the body) red and painful, especially as the result of skin abrasion: *he scrubbed his hands until they were raw |* figurative *Fran's nerves were raw.*
3 (of the weather) bleak, cold, and damp: *a raw February night.*
4 (of an emotion or quality) strong and undisguised: *he exuded an air of raw, vibrant masculinity.*
■ frank and realistic in the depiction of unpleasant facts or situations: *a raw, uncompromising portrait.* ■ US informal (of language) coarse or crude, typically in relation to sexual matters.
– PHRASES **don't come the raw prawn with me** Austral. informal don't try and make me believe something that is not true; don't treat me like a fool. **in the raw 1** in its true state; not made to seem better or more palatable than it actually is: *he didn't much care for nature in the raw.* **2** informal (of a person) naked: *I slept in the raw.* **touch someone on the raw** upset someone by referring to a subject about which they are extremely sensitive.
– DERIVATIVES **rawish** adjective, **rawly** adverb, **rawness** noun.
– ORIGIN Old English *hrēaw*, of Germanic origin; related to Dutch *rauw* and German *roh*, from an Indo-European root shared by Greek *kreas* 'raw flesh'.

Rawalpindi /rɔːlˈpɪndi, ˌrɑːwəl-/ a city in Punjab province, northern Pakistan, in the foothills of the Himalayas; pop. 955,000 (est. 1991). A former military station, it was the interim capital of Pakistan, 1959–67, during the construction of Islamabad.

raw bar ▶ **noun** US a bar or counter which sells raw oysters and other seafood.

raw-boned ▶ **adjective** having a bony or gaunt physique.

rawhide ▶ **noun** [mass noun] stiff untanned leather.
■ [count noun] N. Amer. a whip or rope made of such leather.

Rawlplug /ˈrɔːlplʌg/ ▶ **noun** Brit. trademark a thin plastic or fibre sheath that is inserted into a hole in masonry in order to hold a screw.
– ORIGIN early 20th cent.: from *Rawlings* (the name of the engineers who introduced it) + **PLUG**.

Rawls /rɔːlz/, John (b.1921), American philosopher. His books *A Theory of Justice* (1971) and *Political Liberalism* (1993) consider the basic institutions of a just society as those chosen by rational people under conditions which ensure impartiality.

raw material ▶ **noun** the basic material from which a product is made.

raw sienna ▶ **noun** see **SIENNA**.

raw umber ▶ **noun** see **UMBER**.

Ray[1] /reɪ/, John (1627–1705), English naturalist. Ray was the first to classify flowering plants into monocotyledons and dicotyledons, and he established the species as the basic taxonomic unit. His systematic scheme was not improved upon until that of Linnaeus.

Ray[2] /reɪ/, Man (1890–1976), American photographer, painter, and film-maker; born *Emmanuel Rudnitsky.* A leading figure in the New York and European Dada movements, he is perhaps best known for his photograph the *Violin d'Ingres* (1924), which achieved the effect of making the back of a female nude resemble a violin.

Ray[3] /rʌɪ/, Satyajit (1921–92), Indian film director, the first to bring Indian films to the attention of Western audiences. Notable films: *Pather Panchali* (1955).

ray[1] ▶ **noun 1** each of the lines in which light (and heat) may seem to stream from the sun or any luminous body, or pass through a small opening: *a ray of sunlight came through the window.*
■ the straight line in which light or other electromagnetic radiation travels to a given point. ■ [with adj. or noun modifier] (**rays**) a specified form of non-luminous radiation: *water reflects and intensifies UV rays.* ■ Mathematics any of a set of straight lines passing through one point. ■ (**rays**) informal, chiefly N. Amer. sunlight considered in the context of sunbathing: ***catch some rays*** *on a secluded sandy beach.* ■ figurative an initial or slight indication of a positive or welcome quality in a time of difficulty or trouble: *if only I could see some* ***ray of*** *hope.*
2 a thing that is arranged radially, in particular:
■ Botany (in a composite flower head of the daisy family) an array of ray florets arranged radially around the central disc, forming the white part of the flower head of a daisy. ■ (also **fin ray**) Zoology each of the long slender bony supports in the fins of most bony fishes. ■ Zoology each radial arm of a starfish.
▶ **verb** [no obj., with adverbial of direction] spread from or as if from a central point: *delicate lines rayed out at each corner of her eyes.*
■ [with obj. and adverbial of direction] poetic/literary radiate (light): *the sun rays forth its natural light into the air.*
– PHRASES **ray of sunshine** informal a person or thing that brings happiness into the lives of others.
– DERIVATIVES **rayless** adjective (chiefly Botany).
– ORIGIN Middle English: from Old French *rai*, based on Latin *radius* 'spoke, ray'. The verb dates from the late 16th cent.

ray[2] ▶ **noun** a broad flat marine or freshwater fish with a cartilaginous skeleton, wing-like pectoral fins, and a long slender tail. Many rays have venomous spines or electric organs.
● Order Batiformes: several families, including Rajidae (the skates).
– ORIGIN Middle English: from Old French *raie*, from Latin *raia*.

ray[3] (also **re**) ▶ **noun** Music (in tonic sol-fa) the second note of a major scale.
■ the note D in the fixed-doh system.
– ORIGIN Middle English *re*, representing (as an arbitrary name for the note) the first syllable of *resonare*, taken from a Latin hymn (see **SOLMIZATION**).

ray blight ▶ **noun** [mass noun] a fungal disease of chrysanthemums which causes collapse and rotting of the leading shoot.
● The fungus is *Ascochyta chrysanthemi*, subdivision Deuteromycotina (or *Didymella chrysanthemi*, subdivision Ascomycotina).

rayed ▶ **adjective** [in combination] chiefly Biology having rays of a specified number or kind: *white-rayed daisies.*

ray-finned fish ▶ **noun** a fish of a large group having thin fins strengthened by slender rays, including all bony fishes apart from the coelacanth and lungfishes. Compare with **LOBE-FINNED FISH**, **TELEOST**.
● Subclass (or class) Actinopterygii: numerous orders.

ray floret ▶ **noun** Botany (in a composite flower head of the daisy family) any of a number of strap-shaped and typically sterile florets that form the ray. In plants such as dandelions the flower head is composed entirely of ray florets. Compare with **DISC FLORET**.

ray gun ▶ **noun** (in science fiction) a gun causing injury or damage by the emission of rays.

Rayleigh /ˈreɪli/, John William Strutt, 3rd Baron (1842–1919), English physicist. He established the electrical units of resistance, current, and electromotive force. With William Ramsay he discovered argon and other inert gases. Nobel Prize for Physics (1904).

Rayleigh number ▶ **noun** Physics a dimensionless parameter that is a measure of the instability of a layer of fluid due to differences of temperature and density at the top and bottom.

Rayleigh scattering ▶ **noun** [mass noun] Physics the scattering of light by particles in a medium, without change in wavelength. It accounts, for example, for the blue colour of the sky, since blue light is scattered slightly more efficiently than red. Compare with **RAMAN EFFECT**.

Rayleigh wave ▶ **noun** Physics an undulating wave that travels over the surface of a solid, especially of the ground in an earthquake, with a speed independent of wavelength, the motion of the particles being in ellipses.

Raynaud's disease /ˈreɪnəʊ/ (also **Raynaud's syndrome**) ▶ **noun** [mass noun] a disease characterized by spasm of the arteries in the extremities, especially the fingers (**Raynaud's phenomenon**). It is typically brought on by constant cold or vibration, and leads to pallor, pain, numbness, and in severe cases, gangrene.
– ORIGIN late 19th cent.: named after Maurice *Raynaud* (1834–81), French physician.

rayon ▶ **noun** [mass noun] a textile fibre made from regenerated cellulose (viscose).
■ fabric or cloth made from this fibre.
– ORIGIN 1920s: an arbitrary formation.

rayonnant /ˌreɪjɒˈnɒ̃, French ʀɛjɔnɑ̃/ ▶ **adjective** relating to or denoting a French style of Gothic architecture prevalent from *c.*1230 to *c.*1350, characterized by distinctive rose windows.
– ORIGIN French, literally 'radiating', from the pattern of radiating lights in the windows.

Ray's bream ▶ **noun** see **POMFRET**.
– ORIGIN mid 19th cent.: named after John **RAY** (1627–1705), English naturalist.

raze (also **rase**) ▶ **verb** [with obj.] (usu. **be razed**) completely destroy (a building, town, or other site): *villages were* ***razed to the ground.***
– ORIGIN Middle English (in the sense 'scratch, incise'): from Old French *raser* 'shave closely', from Latin *ras-* 'scraped', from the verb *radere*.

razoo /ˈrɑːzuː/ ▶ **noun** [with negative] Austral./NZ informal used to denote an imaginary coin of little value or a very small sum of money: *the lousy government never gave them a* ***brass razoo.***
– ORIGIN 1930s: of unknown origin.

razor ▶ **noun** an instrument with a sharp blade or combination of blades, used to remove unwanted hair from the face or body.
▶ **verb** [with obj.] cut with a razor.
■ [no obj.] (**razor through**) figurative cut through (something) as if with a razor: *draughts razored through the gaps.*
– ORIGIN Middle English: from Old French *rasor*, from *raser* 'shave closely' (see **RAZE**).

razorback ▶ **noun 1** (also **razorback hog**) a pig of a half-wild breed common in the southern US, with the back formed into a high narrow ridge.
2 (also **razorback ridge**) a steep-sided narrow ridge of land.

razorbill ▶ **noun** a black-and-white auk with a deep bill that is said to resemble a cut-throat razor, found in the North Atlantic and Baltic Sea.
● *Alca torda*, family Alcidae.

razor blade ▶ **noun** a blade used in a razor, typically a flat piece of metal with a sharp edge or edges used in a safety razor.

razor clam ▶ **noun** North American term for **RAZOR SHELL**.

razor cut ▶ **noun** a haircut effected with a razor, typically having a short or tapered style.
▶ **verb** (**razor-cut**) [with obj.] cut (hair) with a razor.

razor edge (also **razor's edge**) ▶ **noun** a sharp edge of a knife, axe, or similar implement.
■ figurative a state of sharp incisiveness: *he had honed his mind to a razor edge.* ■ (**the razor edge**) figurative the most advanced stage in the development of something; the cutting edge: *in 1960 jet planes were* ***the razor edge of*** *chic.* ■ another term for **ARÊTE**.
– DERIVATIVES **razor-edged** adjective.

razorfish ▶ **noun** (pl. same or **-fishes**) **1** a small fish of the Indo-Pacific, with a long flattened snout and a laterally compressed body encased in thin bony shields that meet to form a sharp ridge on the belly.
● Family Centriscidae: several genera and species, including *Aeoliscus strigatus*, which swims in a head-down vertical posture.
2 a small brightly coloured wrasse with a steeply sloping forehead, living chiefly in sandy coastal waters of the western Atlantic.
● Genus *Hemipteronotus*, family Labridae: several species.
3 another term for **RAZOR SHELL**.

razor grass ▶ **noun** [mass noun] W. Indian a tall sedge or

grass with leaf blades that have sharp cutting edges.
• Genera *Scleria* (family Cyperaceae) and *Paspalum* (family Gramineae): several species.

razor-sharp ▶ adjective extremely sharp: *razor-sharp teeth* | figurative *his razor-sharp mind.*

razor shell ▶ noun a burrowing bivalve mollusc with a long slender shell which resembles the handle of a cut-throat razor. Also called **JACKKNIFE CLAM** or **RAZOR CLAM** in North America.
• Family Solenidae: *Ensis* and other genera.

razor wire ▶ noun [mass noun] a metal wire or ribbon with sharp edges or studded with small sharp blades, used as a barrier to deter intruders.

razz informal, chiefly N. Amer. ▶ verb [with obj.] tease (someone) playfully.
▶ noun another term for **RASPBERRY** (in sense 4).
– ORIGIN early 20th cent.: from informal *razzberry*, alteration of **RASPBERRY**.

razzia /ˈrazɪə/ ▶ noun historical a hostile raid for purposes of conquest, plunder, and capture of slaves, especially one carried out by Moors in North Africa.
– ORIGIN mid 19th cent.: via French from Algerian Arabic *ġāziya* 'raid'.

razzle ▶ noun (in phrase **on the razzle**) informal out celebrating or enjoying oneself: *he's gone out on the razzle again.*
– ORIGIN early 20th cent.: abbreviation of **RAZZLE-DAZZLE**.

razzle-dazzle ▶ noun another term for **RAZZMATAZZ**.
– ORIGIN late 19th cent.: reduplication of **DAZZLE**.

razzmatazz (also **razzamatazz**) ▶ noun [mass noun] informal noisy, showy, and exciting activity and display designed to attract and impress: *the razzmatazz of a political campaign.*
– ORIGIN late 19th cent.: probably an alteration of **RAZZLE-DAZZLE**.

RB ▶ abbreviation for Botswana (international vehicle registration).
– ORIGIN from *Republic of Botswana*.

Rb ▶ symbol for the chemical element rubidium.

RBI Baseball ▶ abbreviation for run batted in (a run credited to the batter for enabling a runner to score during his play).

RC ▶ abbreviation for ■ (in cycling) racing club. ■ Red Cross. ■ reinforced concrete. ■ Electronics resistance/capacitance (or resistor/capacitor). ■ Roman Catholic.

RCA ▶ abbreviation for ■ Central African Republic (international vehicle registration). [ORIGIN: from French *République Centrafricaine*.] ■ (in the US) Radio Corporation of America. ■ (in the UK) Royal College of Art.

RCH ▶ abbreviation for Chile (international vehicle registration).
– ORIGIN from Spanish *República de Chile*.

RCM ▶ abbreviation for (in the UK) Royal College of Music.

RCMP ▶ abbreviation for Royal Canadian Mounted Police.

RCN ▶ abbreviation for (in the UK) Royal College of Nursing.

RCP ▶ abbreviation for (in the UK) Royal College of Physicians.

RCS ▶ abbreviation for ■ (in the UK) Royal College of Scientists. ■ (in the UK) Royal College of Surgeons. ■ (in the UK) Royal Corps of Signals.

RCVS ▶ abbreviation for (in the UK) Royal College of Veterinary Surgeons.

RD ▶ abbreviation for ■ Brit. refer to drawer (used by banks when suspending payment of a cheque). ■ (in the UK) Royal Naval Reserve Decoration.

Rd ▶ abbreviation for Road (used in street names).

RDA ▶ abbreviation for ■ recommended daily (or dietary) allowance, the quantity of a particular nutrient which should be consumed daily in order to maintain good health. ■ (in the UK) Regional Development Agency.

RDBMS Computing ▶ abbreviation for relational database management system.

RDC historical ▶ abbreviation for (in the UK) Rural District Council.

RDF ▶ abbreviation for ■ radio direction-finder (or -finding). ■ (in the US) rapid deployment force.

RDI ▶ abbreviation for recommended (or reference) daily intake, another term for **RDA**.

RDS ▶ abbreviation for ■ radio data system, in which a digital signal is transmitted with a normal radio signal to provide further data or control the receiver. ■ respiratory distress syndrome.

RDX ▶ noun [mass noun] a type of high explosive.
– ORIGIN 1940s: from *R(esearch) D(epartment) (E)x(plosive)*.

RE ▶ abbreviation for ■ religious education (as a school subject). ■ (in the UK) Royal Engineers.

Re¹ /reɪ/ variant spelling of **RA¹**.

Re² ▶ symbol for the chemical element rhenium.

re¹ /riː, reɪ/ ▶ preposition in the matter of (used typically as the first word in the heading of an official document or to introduce a reference in an official letter): *re: invoice 87.*
■ about; concerning: *I saw the deputy head re the incident.*
– ORIGIN Latin, ablative of *res* 'thing'.

USAGE It is often said that, strictly speaking, **re** should be used in headings and references, as in ***Re:** Ainsworth versus Chambers*, but not as a normal word meaning 'regarding', as in *thanks for your letter **re** TSB*. However, the evidence suggests that **re** is now widely used in the second context in official and semi-official contexts, and is now generally accepted. It is hard to see any compelling logical argument against using it as an ordinary English word in this way.

re² ▶ noun variant spelling of **RAY³**.

re- ▶ prefix **1** once more; afresh; anew: *reaccustom* | *reactivate.*
■ with return to a previous state: *restore* | *revert.*
2 (also **red-**) in return; mutually: *react* | *resemble.*
■ in opposition: *repel* | *resistance.*
3 behind or after: *relic* | *remain.*
■ in a withdrawn state: *recluse* | *reticent.* ■ back and away; down: *recede* | *relegation.*
4 with frequentative or intensive force: *refine* | *resound.*
5 with negative force: *recant.*
– ORIGIN from Latin *re-*, *red-* 'again, back'.

USAGE In modern English, the tendency is for words formed with prefixes such as **re-** to be unhyphenated: **restore, remain, reacquaint**. One general exception to this is when the word to which **re-** attaches begins with **e**: in this case a hyphen is often inserted for clarity: **re-examine, re-enter, re-enact**. A hyphen is sometimes also used where the word formed with the prefix would be identical to an already existing word: **re-cover** (meaning 'cover again', as in *we decided to **re-cover** the dining-room chairs*) not **recover** (meaning 'get better in health'). Similar guidelines apply to other prefixes such as **pre-**.

're informal ▶ abbreviation for are (usually after the pronouns you, we, and they): *we're a bit worried.*

reabsorb ▶ verb [with obj.] absorb (something) again.
– DERIVATIVES **reabsorption** noun.

reaccustom ▶ verb [with obj.] accustom (someone) to something again.

reach ▶ verb **1** [no obj., with adverbial of direction] stretch out an arm in a specified direction in order to touch or grasp something: *he reached over and turned off his bedside light.*
■ (**reach for**) make a movement with one's hand or arm in an attempt to touch or grasp (something): *Leith reached for the nearest folder.* ■ [with obj.] (**reach something out**) stretch out one's hand or arm: *he reached out a hand and touched her forehead.* ■ [with obj.] (**reach something down**) pick up something with one's hand stretched upwards and bring it down to a lower level: *she reached down another plate from the cupboard.* ■ [with two objs] hand (something) to (someone): *reach me those glasses.* ■ [no obj.] be able to touch something with an outstretched arm or leg: *I had to stand on tiptoe and even then I could hardly reach.*
2 [with obj.] arrive at; get as far as: *'Goodbye,' she said as they reached the door* | *the show is due to reach our screens early next year.*
■ [no obj.] W. Indian arrive: *just round that corner, by them mango trees, and we reach.* ■ attain or extend to (a specified point, level, or condition): *unemployment reached a peak in 1933* | [no obj.] *in its native habitat it will **reach to** about 6 m in height.* ■ succeed in achieving: *the intergovernmental conference reached agreement on the draft treaty.* ■ make contact or communicate with (someone) by telephone or other means: *I've been trying to reach you all morning.* ■ (of a broadcast or other communication) be received by: *television reached those parts of the electorate that other news sources could not.* ■ succeed in influencing or having an effect on: *he seeks opportunities to reach viewers without journalistic interference.*
3 [no obj.] Sailing sail with the wind blowing from the side, or from slightly behind the side, of the ship.
▶ noun **1** an act of reaching out with one's arm: *she made a reach for him.*
■ [in sing.] the distance to which someone can stretch out their hand (used especially of a boxer): *a giant, over six feet seven with a reach of over 81 inches.* ■ the extent or range of application, effect, or influence: *the diameter and the reach of the spark plug varies from engine to engine.* ■ the number of people who watch or listen to a particular broadcast or channel during a specified period: *the programme's daily reach is 400,000.*
2 (often **reaches**) a continuous extent of land or water, especially a stretch of river between two bends, or the part of a canal between locks: *the upper reaches of the Nile.*
3 Sailing a distance traversed in reaching.
– PHRASES **out of** (or **beyond**) **reach** outside the distance to which someone can stretch out their hand. ■ beyond the capacity of someone to attain or achieve something: *she thought university was out of her reach.* **within** (or **in**) **reach** inside the distance to which someone can stretch out their hand. ■ inside a distance that can be travelled: *a 1930s semi **within easy reach** of the centre of town.* ■ within the capacity of someone to attain or achieve something.
– DERIVATIVES **reachable** adjective.
– ORIGIN Old English *rǣcan*, of West Germanic origin; related to Dutch *reiken* and German *reichen*.

reacher ▶ noun **1** a thing which reaches, especially a device that enables a disabled or elderly person to pick up objects that are difficult to reach.
2 a kind of jib on a sailing ship.

reach-me-down Brit. informal, dated ▶ adjective [attrib.] (of a garment) ready-made or second-hand.
▶ noun a second-hand or ready-made garment.
■ (**reach-me-downs**) trousers.

reacquaint ▶ verb [with obj.] make (someone) acquainted or familiar with someone or something again: *he was able to **reacquaint himself with** an old school chum.*
– DERIVATIVES **reacquaintance** noun.

react ▶ verb [no obj.] respond or behave in a particular way in response to something: *company bosses have **reacted** angrily **to** the new council demands* | *the market reacted by falling a further 3.1%.*
■ (**react against**) respond with hostility, opposition, or a contrary course of action to: *they reacted against the elite art music of their time.* ■ (of a person) suffer from adverse physiological effects after ingesting, breathing, or touching a substance: *many babies react to soy-based formulas.* ■ Chemistry & Physics interact and undergo a chemical or physical change: *the sulphur in the coal **reacts with** the limestone during combustion.* ■ [with obj.] Chemistry cause (a substance) to undergo such a change by interacting with another substance. ■ Stock Exchange (of share prices) fall after rising.
– ORIGIN mid 17th cent.: from **RE-** (expressing intensive force or reversal) + **ACT**, originally suggested by medieval Latin *react-* 'done again', from the verb *reagere*.

reactance ▶ noun [mass noun] Physics the non-resistive component of impedance in an AC circuit, arising from the effect of inductance or capacitance or both and causing the current to be out of phase with the electromotive force causing it.

reactant ▶ noun Chemistry a substance that takes part in and undergoes change during a reaction.

reaction ▶ noun an action performed or a feeling experienced in response to a situation or event: *Carrie's immediate reaction was one of relief.*
■ (**reactions**) a person's ability to respond physically and mentally to external stimuli: *a skilled driver with quick reactions.* ■ an adverse physiological response to a substance that has been breathed in, ingested, or touched: *such allergic reactions as hay fever and asthma.* ■ a chemical process in which two or more substances act mutually on each other and are changed into different substances, or one substance changes into two or more other substances. ■ Physics an analogous transformation of atomic nuclei or other particles. ■ a mode of thinking or behaving that is deliberately different from previous modes of thought and behaviour: *the work of these painters was a **reaction against** fauvism.* ■ [mass noun] opposition to political or social progress or reform: *the institution is*

under threat from the forces of reaction. ■ [mass noun] Physics repulsion or resistance exerted in opposition to the impact or pressure of another body; a force equal and opposite to the force giving rise to it.
– DERIVATIVES **reactionist** noun & adjective.
– ORIGIN mid 17th cent.: from **REACT** + **-ION**, originally suggested by medieval Latin *reactio(n-)*, from *react-* 'done again' (see **REACT**).

reactionary ▶ **adjective** (of a person or a set of views) opposing political or social progress or reform.
▶ **noun** (pl. **-ies**) a person who holds such views.

reaction formation ▶ **noun** [mass noun] Psychoanalysis the tendency of a repressed wish or feeling to be expressed at a conscious level in a contrasting form.

reaction shot ▶ **noun** (in a film or video recording) a portrayal of a person's response to an event or to a statement made by another.

reactivate ▶ **verb** [with obj.] restore (something) to a state of activity; bring (something) back into action.
– DERIVATIVES **reactivation** noun.

reactive ▶ **adjective** showing a response to a stimulus: *pupils are reactive to light.*
■ acting in response to a situation rather than creating or controlling it: *a proactive rather than a reactive approach.* ■ having a tendency to react chemically: *nitrogen dioxide is a highly reactive gas.* ■ Physiology showing an immune response to a specific antigen. ■ (of a disease or illness) caused by a reaction to something: *reactive arthritis | reactive depression.* ■ Physics of or relating to reactance: *a reactive load.*

reactive inhibition ▶ **noun** [mass noun] Psychology the inhibiting effect of fatigue or boredom on the response to a stimulus and ability to learn.

reactivity ▶ **noun** [mass noun] the state or power of being reactive or the degree to which a thing is reactive.
■ the extent to which a nuclear reactor deviates from a steady state.

reactor ▶ **noun** **1** (also **nuclear reactor**) an apparatus or structure in which fissile material can be made to undergo a controlled, self-sustaining nuclear reaction with the consequent release of energy.
■ a container or apparatus in which substances are made to react chemically, especially one in an industrial plant.
2 Medicine a person who shows an immune response to a specific antigen or an adverse reaction to a drug or other substance.
3 Physics a coil or other component which provides reactance in a circuit.

read ▶ **verb** (past and past participle **read**) [with obj.] **1** look at and comprehend the meaning of (written or printed matter) by mentally interpreting the characters or symbols of which it is composed: *it's the best novel I've ever read | I never learned to read music | Emily* ***read over*** *her notes |* [no obj.] *I'll go to bed and read for a while.*
■ speak (the written or printed matter that one is reading) aloud, typically to another person: *the charges against him were* ***read out*** | [with two objs] *his mother read him a bedtime story |* [no obj.] *I'll read to you if you like.* ■ [no obj.] have the ability to look at and comprehend the meaning of written or printed matter: *only three of the girls could read and none could write.* ■ habitually read (a particular newspaper or journal). ■ discover (information) by reading it in a written or printed source: *he was arrested yesterday—I read it in the paper |* [no obj.] *I read about the course in a magazine.* ■ [as adj., with submodifier] (**read**) (of a person) knowledgeable and informed as a result of extensive reading: *Ada was* ***well read*** *in French and German literature.* ■ discern (a fact, emotion, or quality) in someone's eyes or expression: *she looked down, terrified that he would read fear on her face.* ■ understand or interpret the nature or significance of: *he didn't dare look away, in case this was read as a sign of weakness.* ■ [no obj., with adverbial] (of a piece of writing) convey a specified impression to the reader: *the brief note read like a cry for help.* ■ [no obj., with complement] (of a passage, text, or sign) contain or consist of specified words; have a certain wording: *the placard read 'We want justice'.* ■ used to indicate that a particular word in a text or passage is incorrect and that another should be substituted for it: *for madam read madman.* ■ proof-read (written or typeset material). ■ [no obj.] (**read for**) (of an actor) audition for (a part in a play or film). ■ present (a bill or other measure) before a legislative assembly. ■ (of a device) obtain data from (light or other input).
2 inspect and record the figure indicated on (a measuring instrument): *I've come to read the gas meter.*
■ [no obj., with complement] (of such an instrument) indicate a specified measurement or figure: *the thermometer read 0° C.*
3 chiefly Brit. study (an academic subject) at a university: *I'm reading English at Cambridge |* [no obj.] *he went to Manchester to* ***read for*** *a BA in Economics.*
4 (of a computer) copy or transfer (data).
■ [with obj. and adverbial] enter or extract (data) in an electronic storage device: *the commonest way of reading a file into the system.*
5 hear and understand the words of (someone speaking on a radio transmitter): *'Do you read me? Over.'*
▶ **noun** [usu. in sing.] chiefly Brit. a period or act of reading something: *I was having a quiet read of the newspaper.*
■ [with adj.] informal a book considered in terms of its readability: *the book is a thoroughly entertaining read.* ■ US a person's interpretation of something: *their* ***read on*** *the national situation may be correct.*
– PHRASES **read between the lines** look for or discover a meaning that is hidden or implied rather than explicitly stated. **read someone like a book** understand someone's thoughts and motives clearly or easily. **read someone's mind** (or **thoughts**) discern what someone is thinking. **read my lips** N. Amer. informal listen carefully (used to emphasize the importance of the speaker's words or the earnestness of their intent). **take something as read** assume something without the need for further discussion. **you wouldn't read about it** Austral./NZ informal used to express incredulity, disgust, or ruefulness.
– ORIGIN Old English *rǣdan*, of Germanic origin; related to Dutch *raden* and German *raten* 'advise, guess'. Early senses included 'advise' and 'interpret (a riddle or dream)' (see **REDE**).
▶ **read something back** read a message or piece of writing aloud so that its accuracy can be checked.
read something into attribute a meaning or significance to (something) that it may not in fact possess: *was I reading too much into his behaviour?*
read someone out of chiefly US formally expel someone from (an organization or body). [ORIGIN: with reference to the reading of the formal sentence of expulsion.]
read up on something (or **read something up**) acquire information about a particular subject by studying it intensively or systematically: *she spent the time reading up on antenatal care.*

readable ▶ **adjective** (of a text, script, or code) able to be read or deciphered; legible.
■ easy or enjoyable to read: *a marvellously readable book.*
– DERIVATIVES **readability** noun, **readably** adverb.

readdress ▶ **verb** [with obj.] **1** change the address written or printed on (a letter or parcel).
2 look at or attend to (an issue or problem) once again.

Reade, Charles (1814–84), English novelist and dramatist, remembered for his historical romance *The Cloister and the Hearth* (1861).

reader ▶ **noun** **1** a person who reads or who is fond of reading: *the books of Roald Dahl appeal to young readers | she's an avid reader.*
■ a person who reads a particular newspaper, magazine, or text: *Guardian readers.* ■ short for **LAY READER**. ■ a person entitled to use a particular library. ■ a person who reads and reports to a publisher or producer on the merits of manuscripts submitted for publication or production, or who provides critical comments on the text prior to publication. ■ short for ***proof-reader*** (see **PROOF-READ**).
2 a book containing extracts of a particular author's work or passages of text designed to give learners of a language practice in reading.
3 (**Reader**) Brit. a university lecturer of the highest grade below professor.
4 a machine for producing on a screen a magnified, readable image of any desired part of a microfiche or microfilm.
■ Computing a device or piece of software used for reading or obtaining data stored on tape, cards, or other media.
– ORIGIN Old English *rǣdere* 'interpreter of dreams, reader'.

readerly ▶ **adjective** of or relating to a reader: *he tries one's readerly patience to breaking point.*

readership ▶ **noun** **1** [treated as sing. or pl.] the readers of a newspaper, magazine, or book regarded collectively: *it has a readership of 100 million.*
2 (**Readership**) Brit. the position of Reader at a university.

readily ▶ **adverb** without hesitation or reluctance; willingly: *he readily admits that the new car surpasses its predecessors.*
■ without delay or difficulty; easily: [as submodifier] *transport is readily available.*

read-in ▶ **noun** [mass noun] Computing the input or entry of data to a computer or storage device.

readiness ▶ **noun** **1** [in sing.] [with infinitive] willingness to do something: *Spain had indicated a readiness to accept his terms.*
2 [mass noun] the state of being fully prepared for something: *your muscles tense* ***in readiness for*** *action.*
3 [mass noun] immediacy, quickness, or promptness: *quickness of hearing and readiness of speech were essential.*

Reading /ˈrɛdɪŋ/ a town in southern England, on the River Kennet near its junction with the Thames; pop. 122,600 (1991).

reading ▶ **noun** **1** [mass noun] the action or skill of reading written or printed matter silently or aloud: *suggestions for further reading |* [as modifier] *reading skills.*
■ written or printed matter that can be read: *his main reading was detective stories.* ■ [with adj.] used to convey the specified quality of such written or printed matter: *his file certainly* ***makes*** *interesting* ***reading.*** ■ [usu. with adj.] knowledge of literature: *a man of wide reading.* ■ the formal reading aloud of a legal document to an audience: *the reading of a will.* ■ [count noun] an occasion at which poetry or other pieces of literature are read aloud to an audience. ■ [count noun] a piece of literature or passage of scripture read aloud to a group of people: *readings from the Bible.*
2 an interpretation: *feminist readings of Goethe | his reading of the situation was justified.*
■ a form in which a given passage appears in a particular edition of a text.
3 a figure or amount shown by a meter or other measuring instrument: *radiation readings were taken every hour.*
4 a stage of debate in parliament through which a Bill must pass before it can become law: *the Bill returns to the House for its final reading next week.*

reading age ▶ **noun** a child's reading ability expressed with reference to an average age at which a comparable ability is found.

readjust ▶ **verb** [with obj.] set or adjust (something) again: *I readjusted the rear-view mirror.*
■ [no obj.] adjust or adapt to a changed environment or situation: [as adj. **readjusted**] *she wondered if she could ever become* ***readjusted to*** *this sort of life.*
– DERIVATIVES **readjustment** noun.

readmit ▶ **verb** (**readmitted**, **readmitting**) [with obj.] admit (someone) to a place or organization again: *they were readmitted to hospital.*
– DERIVATIVES **readmission** noun.

read-only memory (abbrev.: **ROM**) ▶ **noun** Computing memory read at high speed but not capable of being changed by program instructions.

readopt ▶ **verb** [with obj.] adopt (a physical position) again.
■ start to follow (a principle or course of action) again.
– DERIVATIVES **readoption** noun.

read-out ▶ **noun** a visual record or display of the output from a computer or scientific instrument.
■ [mass noun] the process of transferring or displaying such data.

read-through ▶ **noun** an initial rehearsal of a play at which actors read their parts from scripts.

re-advertise ▶ **verb** [with obj.] advertise (something, especially a job vacancy) again.
– DERIVATIVES **re-advertisement** noun.

read-write ▶ **adjective** Computing capable of reading existing data and accepting alterations or further input.

ready ▶ **adjective** (**readier**, **readiest**) **1** [predic.] in a suitable state for an activity, action, or situation; fully prepared: *are you ready, Carrie? | I began to* ***get ready for*** *bed |* [with infinitive] *she was about ready to leave.*
■ (of a thing) made suitable and available for immediate use: *dinner's ready! | could you have the list ready by this afternoon?* ■ (**ready with**) keen or quick to give: *every time I rang up, she was ready with some excuse.* ■ (**ready for**) in need of or having a desire for:

r

I expect you're ready for a drink | she always looks ready for a fight. ■ [with infinitive] eager, inclined, or willing to do something: *she is ready to die for her political convictions.* ■ [with infinitive] in such a condition as to be likely to do something: *by the time he arrived he was ready to drop.*

2 easily available or obtained; within reach: *there was a ready supply of drink | the murderer knew that the mallet would be* ***ready to hand.***

■ [attrib.] immediate, quick, or prompt: *those who have ready access to the arts | a girl with a ready smile.*

▶**noun** (pl. **-ies**) (**readies** or **the ready**) Brit. informal available money; cash.

▶**verb** (**-ies, -ied**) [with obj.] prepare (someone or something) for an activity or purpose: *the spare transformer was readied for shipment* | [with obj. and infinitive] *she had readied herself to speak first.*

– PHRASES **at the ready** prepared or available for immediate use: *the men walk with their guns at the ready.* **make ready** prepare: *they were told to* ***make ready for*** *the journey home.* **ready, steady, go** used to announce the beginning of a race.

– ORIGIN Middle English: from Old English *rǣde* (from a Germanic base meaning 'arrange, prepare'; related to Dutch *gereed*) + **-Y**[1].

ready-made ▶**adjective** (especially of products such as clothes and curtains) made to a standard size or specification rather than to order.

■ available straight away; not needing to be specially created or devised: *we have no ready-made answers.* ■ (of food) ready to be served without further preparation: *a ready-made Christmas cake.*

▶**noun** (usu. **ready-mades**) a ready-made article: *he smokes ready-mades now.*

■ a mass-produced article selected by an artist and displayed as a work of art.

ready meal ▶**noun** a meal sold in a pre-cooked form that only requires reheating.

ready-mix ▶**noun** [mass noun] ready-mixed concrete.

ready-mixed ▶**adjective** (especially of a mixture used in building or cooking) having some or all of the constituents already mixed together; commercially prepared.

ready money (also **ready cash**) ▶**noun** [mass noun] money in the form of cash that is immediately available.

ready reckoner ▶**noun** a book or table listing standard numerical calculations or other kinds of information presented formulaically.

ready-to-wear ▶**adjective** (of clothes) made for the general market and sold through shops rather than made to order for an individual customer.

reaffirm ▶**verb** [reporting verb] state again as a fact; assert again strongly: *the prime minister reaffirmed his commitment to the agreement* | [with clause] *he reaffirmed that it was essential to strengthen the rule of law.*

■ [with obj.] confirm the validity or correctness of (something previously established): *the election reaffirmed his position as leader.*

– DERIVATIVES **reaffirmation** noun.

reafforest ▶**verb** chiefly Brit. another term for **REFOREST**.

– DERIVATIVES **reafforestation** noun.

Reagan /ˈreɪɡ(ə)n/, Ronald (Wilson) (b.1911), American Republican statesman, 40th President of the US 1981–9. He was a Hollywood actor before entering politics. His presidency saw the launch of the Strategic Defense Initiative, cuts in taxes and social services budgets, and a record rise in the national budget deficit, as well as the Irangate scandal and the signing of an intermediate nuclear forces non-proliferation treaty, both in 1987.

– DERIVATIVES **Reaganism** noun, **Reaganite** adjective & noun.

reagent /rɪˈeɪdʒ(ə)nt/ ▶**noun** a substance or mixture for use in chemical analysis or other reactions.

reagent grade ▶**noun** [mass noun] Chemistry a grade of commercial chemicals of a high standard of purity suitable for use in chemical analysis.

reagin /rɪˈeɪdʒɪn/ ▶**noun** [mass noun] Immunology the antibody which is involved in allergic reactions, causing the release of histamine when it combines with antigen in tissue, and capable of producing sensitivity to the antigen when introduced into the skin of a normal individual.

■ the substance in the blood which is responsible for a positive response to the Wassermann test.

– DERIVATIVES **reaginic** adjective.

– ORIGIN early 20th cent.: coined in German from *reagieren* 'react'.

real[1] /riːl/ ▶**adjective 1** actually existing as a thing or occurring in fact; not imagined or supposed: *Julius Caesar was a real person | a story drawing on real events | her many illnesses, real and imaginary.*

■ used to emphasize the significance or seriousness of a situation or circumstance: *there is a real danger of civil war | the competitive threat from overseas is very real.* ■ Philosophy relating to something as it is, not merely as it may be described or distinguished.

2 (of a substance or thing) not imitation or artificial; genuine: *the earring was presumably real gold.*

■ true or actual: *his real name is James | this isn't my real reason for coming.* ■ [attrib.] (of a person or thing) rightly so called; proper: *he's my idea of a real man | Jamie is my only real friend.*

3 [attrib.] informal complete; utter (used for emphasis): *the tour turned out to be a real disaster.*

4 [attrib.] adjusted for changes in the value of money; assessed by purchasing power: *real incomes had fallen by 30 per cent | an increase* ***in real terms*** *of 11.6 per cent.*

5 Mathematics (of a number or quantity) having no imaginary part. See **IMAGINARY**.

6 Optics (of an image) of a kind in which the light that forms it actually passes through it; not virtual.

▶**adverb** [as submodifier] informal, chiefly N. Amer. really; very: *my head hurts real bad.*

– PHRASES **for real** informal used to assert that something is genuine or is actually the case: *I'm not playing games—this is for real!* ■ N. Amer. used in questions to express surprise or to question the truth or seriousness of what one has seen or heard: *are these guys for real?* **get real!** informal, chiefly N. Amer. used to convey that an idea or statement is foolish or overly idealistic: *You want teens to have committed sexual relationships? Get real!* **real live** humorous used to emphasize the existence of something, especially if it is surprising or unusual: *a real live detective had been at the factory.* **real money** informal money in a large or significant amount. **the real thing** informal a thing that is absolutely genuine or authentic: *you've never been in love before, so how can you be sure this is the real thing?*

– DERIVATIVES **realness** noun.

– ORIGIN late Middle English (as a legal term meaning 'relating to things, especially real property'): from Anglo-Norman French, from late Latin *realis*, from Latin *res* 'thing'.

real[2] /reɪˈɑːl/ ▶**noun** the basic monetary unit of Brazil since 1994, equal to 100 centavos.

■ a former coin and monetary unit of various Spanish-speaking countries.

– ORIGIN Spanish, literally 'royal' (adjective used as a noun).

real account ▶**noun** Finance an account dealing with the material assets of a business, such as its property.

real ale ▶**noun** [mass noun] chiefly Brit. cask-conditioned beer that is served traditionally, without additional gas pressure.

real estate ▶**noun** [mass noun] chiefly N. Amer. another term for **REAL PROPERTY**.

real estate agent ▶**noun** N. Amer. an estate agent.

– DERIVATIVES **real estate agency** noun.

realgar /rɪˈalɡə/ ▶**noun** [mass noun] a soft reddish mineral consisting of arsenic sulphide, formerly used as a pigment and in fireworks.

– ORIGIN late Middle English: via medieval Latin from Arabic *rahj al-ġār* 'arsenic', literally 'dust of the cave'.

realia /reɪˈɑːlɪə, rɪˈeɪlɪə/ ▶**noun** [mass noun] objects and material from everyday life used as teaching aids.

– ORIGIN 1950s: from late Latin, neuter plural (used as a noun) of *realis* 'relating to things' (see **REAL**[1]).

realign ▶**verb** [with obj.] change or restore to a different or former position or state: *they worked to relieve his shoulder pain and realign the joint | the president realigned his government to reflect the balance of parties.*

■ (**realign oneself with**) change one's position or attitude with regard to (a person, organization, or cause): *he wished to realign himself with Bagehot's more pessimistic position.*

– DERIVATIVES **realignment** noun.

realism ▶**noun** [mass noun] **1** the attitude or practice of accepting a situation as it is and being prepared to deal with it accordingly: *the summit was marked by a new mood of realism.*

■ the view that the subject matter of politics is political power, not matters of principle: *political realism is the oldest approach to global politics.* ■ the doctrine that the law is better understood by analysis of judges rather than the judgements given.

2 the quality or fact of representing a person, thing, or situation accurately or in a way that is true to life: *the traditional British soaps will stay because of their gritty realism.*

■ (in art and literature) the movement or style of representing familiar things as they actually are. Often contrasted with **IDEALISM** (in sense 1).

> While realism in art is often used in the same contexts as naturalism, implying a concern to depict or describe accurately and objectively, it also suggests a deliberate rejection of conventionally beautiful or appropriate subjects in favour of sincerity and a focus on simple and unidealized treatment of contemporary life. Specifically, the term is applied to a late 19th-century movement in French painting and literature represented by Gustave Courbet in the former and Balzac, Stendhal, and Flaubert in the latter.

3 Philosophy the doctrine that universals or abstract concepts have an objective or absolute existence. The theory that universals have their own reality is sometimes call **Platonic realism** because it was first outlined by Plato's doctrine of 'forms' or ideas. Often contrasted with **NOMINALISM**.

■ the doctrine that matter as the object of perception has real existence and is neither reducible to universal mind or spirit nor dependent on a perceiving agent. Often contrasted with **IDEALISM** (in sense 2).

– DERIVATIVES **realist** noun.

realistic ▶**adjective 1** having or showing a sensible and practical idea of what can be achieved or expected: *jobs are scarce at the moment, so you've got to be realistic | a more realistic figure was 20 per cent.*

2 representing familiar things in a way that is accurate or true to life: *a realistic human drama.*

– DERIVATIVES **realistically** adverb [sentence adverb] *realistically, there was little prospect of any improvement.*

reality ▶**noun** (pl. **-ies**) [mass noun] **1** the world or the state of things as they actually exist, as opposed to an idealistic or notional idea of them: *he refuses to face reality | Laura was losing touch with reality.*

■ [count noun] a thing that is actually experienced or seen, especially when this is grim or problematic: *the harsh* ***realities of*** *life in a farming community | the law ignores* ***the reality of*** *the situation.* ■ [count noun] a thing that exists in fact, having previously only existed in one's mind: *we want to make the dream a reality.* ■ the quality of being lifelike or resembling an original: *the reality of Marryat's detail.*

2 the state or quality of having existence or substance: *youth, when death has no reality.*

■ Philosophy existence that is absolute, self-sufficient, or objective, and not subject to human decisions or conventions.

– PHRASES **in reality** in actual fact (used to contrast a false idea of what is true or possible with one that is more accurate): *she had believed she could control these feelings, but in reality that was not so easy.* **the reality is ——** used to assert that the truth of a matter is not what one would think or expect: *the popular view of the Dobermann is of an aggressive guard dog—the reality is very different.*

– ORIGIN late 15th cent.: via French from medieval Latin *realitas*, from late Latin *realis* 'relating to things' (see **REAL**[1]).

reality check ▶**noun** [usu. in sing.] informal, chiefly N. Amer. an occasion on which one is reminded of the state of things in the real world.

reality principle ▶**noun** Psychoanalysis the control by the ego of the pleasure-seeking activity of the id in order to meet the demands of the external world.

reality testing ▶**noun** [mass noun] Psychology the objective evaluation of an emotion or thought against real life, as a faculty present in normal individuals but defective in psychotics.

realizable (also **-isable**) ▶**adjective 1** able to be achieved or made to happen: *such a dream, if it is realizable at all, is one for the far future.*

2 in or able to be converted into cash: *10 per cent of realizable assets.*

– DERIVATIVES **realizability** noun.

realization (also **realisation**) ▶**noun 1** [in sing.] an act of becoming fully aware of something as a fact: *there was a growing realization of the need to create common economic structures* | [mass noun] *realization dawned suddenly.*

2 [mass noun] the fulfilment or achievement of

something desired or anticipated: *he did not live to see the realization of his dream.*

■ [count noun] an actual, complete, or dramatic form given to a concept or work: *a perfect realization of Bartók's Second Violin Concerto on disc.* ■ Linguistics the way in which a particular linguistic feature is used in speech or writing on a particular occasion. ■ [count noun] Mathematics an instance or embodiment of an abstract group as the set of symmetry operations of some object or set. ■ [count noun] Statistics a particular series which might be generated by a specified random process.

3 [mass noun] the action of converting an asset into cash.

■ [count noun] a sale of goods: *auction realizations.*

realize (also **-ise**) ▶ **verb** [with obj.] **1** become fully aware of (something) as a fact; understand clearly: *he realized his mistake at once* | [with clause] *they realized that something was wrong* | *she had not realized how hungry she was.*

2 cause (something desired or anticipated) to happen: *our loans are helping small business realize their dreams* | *his worst fears have been realized.*

■ fulfil: *it is only now that she is beginning to realize her potential.*

3 (usu. **be realized**) give actual or physical form to: *the stage designs have been beautifully realized.*

■ use (a linguistic feature) in a particular spoken or written form. ■ Music add to or complete (a piece of music left sparsely notated by the composer).

4 make (money or a profit) from a transaction: *she realized a profit of $100,000.*

■ (of goods) be sold for (a specified price); fetch: *the drawings are expected to realize £500,000.* ■ convert (an asset) into cash: *he realized all the assets in her trust fund.*

– DERIVATIVES **realizer** noun.

– ORIGIN early 17th cent.: from **REAL**[1], on the pattern of French *réaliser.*

real life ▶ **noun** [mass noun] life as it is lived in reality, involving unwelcome as well as welcome experiences, as distinct from a fictional world: [as modifier] *real-life situations.*

real line ▶ **noun** Mathematics a notional line in which every real number is conceived of as represented by a point.

reallocate ▶ **verb** [with obj.] allocate in a different way.

– DERIVATIVES **reallocation** noun.

really ▶ **adverb 1** in actual fact, as opposed to what is said or imagined to be true or possible: *so what really happened?* | *they're not really my aunt and uncle* | [sentence adverb] *really, there are only three options.*

■ used to add strength, sincerity, or seriousness to a statement or opinion: *I really want to go* | *I'm sorry, Ruth, I really am* | *you really ought to tell her.* ■ seriously (used in questions and exclamations with an implied negative answer): *do you really expect me to believe that?*

2 [as submodifier] very; thoroughly: *I think she's really great* | *a really cold day* | *he writes really well.*

▶ **exclamation** used to express interest, surprise, or doubt: *'I've been working hard.' 'Really?'*

■ used to express mild protest: *really, Marjorie, you do jump to conclusions!* ■ chiefly US used to express agreement: *'It's a nightmare finding somewhere to live in this town.' 'Yeah, really.'*

– PHRASES **really and truly** used to emphasize the sincerity of a statement or opinion: *I sometimes wonder whether you really and truly love me.*

realm ▶ **noun** archaic, poetic/literary, or Law a kingdom: *the peers of the realm* | *the defence of the realm.*

■ a field or domain of activity or interest: *the realm of applied chemistry* | *it is beyond the realms of possibility.* ■ Zoology a primary biogeographical division of the earth's surface.

– ORIGIN Middle English *rewme*, from Old French *reaume*, from Latin *regimen* 'government' (see **REGIMEN**). The spelling with *-l-* (standard from *c.*1600) was influenced by Old French *reiel* 'royal'.

realo /ˈriːələʊ, reɪˈaləʊ/ ▶ **noun** (pl. **-os**) informal a member of the pragmatic, as opposed to the radical, wing of the Green movement. Often contrasted with **FUNDIE**.

– ORIGIN 1980s: from German, from *Realist* 'realist'.

realpolitik /reɪˈɑːlpɒlɪˌtiːk/ ▶ **noun** [mass noun] a system of politics or principles based on practical rather than moral or ideological considerations.

– ORIGIN early 20th cent.: from German *Realpolitik* 'practical politics'.

real presence ▶ **noun** Christian Theology the actual presence of Christ's body and blood in the Eucharistic elements.

real property ▶ **noun** [mass noun] Law property consisting of land or buildings. Compare with **PERSONAL PROPERTY**.

real tennis ▶ **noun** [mass noun] the original form of tennis, played with a solid ball on an enclosed court divided into equal but dissimilar halves, the service side (from which service is always delivered) and the hazard side (on which service is received). A similar game was played in monastery cloisters in the 11th century.

real time ▶ **noun** the actual time during which a process or event occurs.

■ [as modifier] Computing of or relating to a system in which input data is processed within milliseconds so that it is available virtually immediately as feedback to the process from which it is coming, e.g. in a missile guidance or airline booking system.

realtor /ˈrɪəltə/ ▶ **noun** N. Amer. a person who acts as an agent for the sale and purchase of buildings and land; an estate agent.

– ORIGIN early 20th cent.: from **REALTY** + **-OR**[1].

realty /ˈrɪəlti/ ▶ **noun** [mass noun] Law a person's real property. The opposite of **PERSONALTY**.

ream[1] ▶ **noun** 500 (formerly 480) sheets of paper.

■ a large quantity of something, typically paper or writing on paper: ***reams of** paper have been used to debate these questions.*

– ORIGIN late Middle English: from Old French *raime*, based on Arabic *rizma* 'bundle'.

ream[2] ▶ **verb** [with obj.] widen (a bore or hole) with a special tool.

■ widen a bore or hole in (a gun or other metal object) in such a way. ■ N. Amer. clear out or remove (material) from something. ■ N. Amer. vulgar slang have anal intercourse with (someone). ■ N. Amer. informal rebuke someone fiercely: *the agent was **reaming** him **out** for walking away from the deal.*

– PHRASES **ream someone's ass** (or **butt**) N. Amer. vulgar slang criticize or rebuke someone.

– ORIGIN early 19th cent.: of unknown origin.

reamer ▶ **noun** a tool for widening or finishing drilled holes.

■ an instrument for scraping the burrs off the inside of water pipes. ■ a blade for scraping the carbon layer from the inside of the bowl of a smoking pipe. ■ North American term for **LEMON-SQUEEZER**.

reanimate ▶ **verb** [with obj.] restore to life or consciousness; revive.

■ give fresh vigour or impetus to: *his personal dislike of the man was reanimated.*

– DERIVATIVES **reanimation** noun.

reap ▶ **verb** [with obj.] cut or gather (a crop or harvest): *large numbers of men were employed to reap the harvest* | figurative *in terms of science, the Apollo programme reaped a meagre harvest.*

■ harvest the crop from (a piece of land). ■ figurative receive (a reward or benefit) as a consequence of one's own or other people's actions: *the company is poised to reap the benefits of this investment.*

– PHRASES **reap the harvest** (or **fruits**) **of** suffer the results or consequences of: *critics believe we are now reaping the harvest of our permissive ways.* **you reap what you sow** proverb you eventually have to face up to the consequences of your actions.

– ORIGIN Old English *ripan, reopan*, of unknown origin.

reaper ▶ **noun** a person or machine that harvests a crop.

■ (**the Reaper**) short for **GRIM REAPER**.

reappear ▶ **verb** [no obj.] appear again: *her symptoms reappeared.*

– DERIVATIVES **reappearance** noun.

reapply ▶ **verb** (**-ies**, **-ied**) **1** [no obj.] make another application or request: *he was ordered to take a driving test before reapplying for a licence.*

2 [with obj.] apply (an existing rule or principle) in a different context.

3 [with obj.] spread (a substance) on a surface again: *reapply the sunscreen hourly.*

– DERIVATIVES **reapplication** noun.

reappoint ▶ **verb** [with obj.] appoint (someone) once again to a position they have previously held.

– DERIVATIVES **reappointment** noun.

reapportion ▶ **verb** [with obj.] assign or distribute (something) again or in a different way.

– DERIVATIVES **reapportionment** noun.

reappraise ▶ **verb** [with obj.] appraise or assess (something) again or in a different way: *it made me reappraise my attitudes.*

– DERIVATIVES **reappraisal** noun.

rear[1] ▶ **noun** [in sing.] the back part of something, especially a building or vehicle: *the kitchen door at the rear of the house.*

■ the space or position at the back of something or someone: *the field at the rear of the church.* ■ the hindmost part of an army, fleet, or line of people: *two blue policemen at the rear fell out of the formation.* ■ (also **rear end**) [count noun] informal a person's buttocks.

▶ **adjective** [attrib.] at the back: *the car's rear window.*

– PHRASES **bring up the rear** be at the very end of a line of people. ■ come last in a race or other contest. **take someone in rear** attack an army from behind.

– ORIGIN Middle English (first used as a military term): from Old French *rere*, based on Latin *retro* 'back'.

rear[2] ▶ **verb 1** [with obj.] (usu. **be reared**) bring up and care for (a child) until they are fully grown, especially in a particular manner or place: *Nigel was born and reared in Bath* | *I was reared on stories of coal and collieries.*

■ (of an animal) care for (its young) until they are fully grown. ■ breed and raise (animals): *the calves are reared for beef.* ■ grow or cultivate (plants): [as adj., in combination **-reared**] *laboratory-reared plantlets.*

2 [no obj.] (of a horse or other animal) raise itself upright on its hind legs: *the horse reared in terror.*

■ [with adverbial of place] (of a building, mountain, etc.) extend or appear to extend to a great height: *houses reared up on either side.* ■ [with obj.] archaic set (something) upright.

– PHRASES **rear one's head** raise one's head. ■ (**rear its head**) (of an unpleasant matter) emerge; present itself: *elitism is **rearing its ugly head** again.*

– DERIVATIVES **rearer** noun.

– ORIGIN Old English *rǣran* 'set upright, construct, elevate', of Germanic origin; related to **RAISE** (which has supplanted *rear* in many applications), also to **RISE**.

▶ **rear up** (of a person) show anger or irritation; go on the attack: *the press reared up in the wake of the bombings.*

rear admiral ▶ **noun** a rank of naval officer, above commodore and below vice admiral.

rear commodore ▶ **noun** an officer in a yacht club ranking below vice commodore.

rear echelon ▶ **noun** the section of an army concerned with administrative and supply duties.

rearguard ▶ **noun** the soldiers positioned at the rear of a body of troops, especially those protecting an army when it is in retreat.

■ a defensive or conservative element in an organization or community. ■ (in team sports) a defending player or players.

– ORIGIN late Middle English (denoting the rear part of an army): from Old French *rereguarde.*

rearguard action ▶ **noun** a defensive action carried out by a retreating army.

rear light (also **rear lamp**) ▶ **noun** chiefly Brit. a red light at the rear of a vehicle; a tail light.

rearm ▶ **verb** [with obj.] provide with a new supply of weapons: *his plan to rearm Germany.*

■ [no obj.] acquire or build up a new supply of weapons.

– DERIVATIVES **rearmament** noun.

rearmost ▶ **adjective** furthest back: *the rearmost door.*

rearrange ▶ **verb** [with obj.] move (something) into a more acceptable position or state: *she rearranged her skirt as she sat back in her chair.*

■ change (the position, time, or order of something): *he had rearranged his schedule.*

– DERIVATIVES **rearrangement** noun.

rearrest ▶ **verb** [with obj.] arrest (someone) again.

▶ **noun** an act of arresting someone again.

rear sight ▶ **noun** the sight nearest to the stock on a firearm.

rear-view mirror ▶ **noun** a small angled mirror fixed inside the windscreen of a motor vehicle enabling the driver to see the vehicle or road behind.

rearward ▶ **adjective** directed towards the back: *a slight rearward movement.* [ORIGIN: early 17th cent.: from **REAR**[1] + **-WARD**.]

▶ **adverb** (also **rearwards**) towards the back: *the engine nozzles point rearward.*

▶ **noun** (usu. **in/at/on the rearward**) archaic or poetic/literary

r

the part or position at the back of something. [ORIGIN: Middle English (denoting the rear part of an army): from Anglo-Norman French *rerewarde* 'rearguard'.]

rear-wheel drive ▶ noun [mass noun] a transmission system that provides power to the rear wheels of a motor vehicle: [as modifier] *a rear-wheel drive coupé.*

reascend ▶ verb [no obj.] ascend again or to a former position: *the fallen angel reascends to the upper air.*
– DERIVATIVES **reascension** noun.

reason ▶ noun **1** a cause, explanation, or justification for an action or event: *the minister resigned for personal reasons | it is hard to know for the simple reason that few records survive.*
■ [mass noun] good or obvious cause to do something: *we have reason to celebrate.* ■ Logic a premise of an argument in support of a belief, especially a minor premise when given after the conclusion.
2 [mass noun] the power of the mind to think, understand, and form judgements by a process of logic: *there is a close connection between reason and emotion.*
■ what is right, practical, or possible; common sense: *people are willing, within reason, to pay for schooling.* ■ (one's reason) one's sanity: *she is in danger of losing her reason.*
▶ verb [no obj.] think, understand, and form judgements by a process of logic: *humans do not reason entirely from facts |* [as noun **reasoning**] *the present chapter will outline the reasoning behind the review.*
■ [with obj.] (**reason something out**) find an answer to a problem by considering various possible solutions. ■ (**reason with**) persuade (someone) with rational argument: *I tried to reason with her, but without success.*
– PHRASES **beyond (all) reason** to a foolishly excessive degree: *he indulged Andrew beyond all reason.* **by reason of** formal because of: *persons who, by reason of age, are in need of care.* **for some reason** used to convey that one doesn't know the reason for a particular state of affairs, often with the implication that one finds it strange or surprising: *for some reason he likes you.* **listen to reason** be persuaded to act sensibly: *the child is usually too emotionally overwrought to listen to reason.* **theirs (or ours) not to reason why** used to suggest that it is not someone's (or one's) place to question a situation or system. [ORIGIN: with allusion to Tennyson's *Charge of the Light Brigade* (1854).] **reason of state** another term for RAISON D'ÉTAT. **(it) stands to reason** it is obvious or logical: *it stands to reason that if you can eradicate the fear the nervousness will subside.*
– DERIVATIVES **reasoner** noun, **reasonless** adjective (archaic).
– ORIGIN Middle English: from Old French *reisun* (noun), *raisoner* (verb), from a variant of Latin *ratio(n-)*, from the verb *reri* 'consider'.

USAGE **1** The construction **the reason why** ... has been objected to on the grounds that the subordinate clause should express a statement, using a *that*-clause, not imply a question with a *why*-clause: **the reason** (*that*) *I decided not to phone* rather than **the reason why** *I decided not to phone*.
2 An objection is also made to the construction **the reason** ... **is because**, as in *the reason I didn't phone is because my mother has been ill.* The objection is made on the grounds that either 'because' or 'the reason' is redundant; it is better to use the word **that** instead (*the reason I didn't phone is that* ...) or rephrase altogether (*I didn't phone because* ...).
Nevertheless, both the above usages are well established (nearly 20 per cent of relevant citations in the Oxford Reading Programme are for the construction **the reason** ... **is because**, for example) and, though more elegant phrasing can no doubt be found, they are generally accepted in standard English.

reasonable ▶ adjective **1** (of a person) having sound judgement; fair and sensible: *no reasonable person could have objected.*
■ based on good sense: *it seems a reasonable enough request | the guilt of a person on trial must be proved beyond reasonable doubt.* ■ archaic (of a person or animal) able to think, understand, or form judgements by a logical process: *man is by nature reasonable.*
2 as much as is appropriate or fair; moderate: *a police officer may use reasonable force to gain entry.*
■ fairly good; average: *the carpet is in reasonable condition.*

■ (of a price or product) not too expensive: *a restaurant serving excellent food at reasonable prices | they are lovely shoes and very reasonable.*
– DERIVATIVES **reasonableness** noun.
– ORIGIN Middle English: from Old French *raisonable*, suggested by Latin *rationabilis* 'rational', from *ratio* (see REASON).

reasonably ▶ adverb **1** in a fair and sensible way: *he began to talk calmly and reasonably about his future.*
■ by fair or sensible standards of judgement; rightly or justifiably: *a constable who reasonably believes a breach of the peace is about to take place |* [sentence adverb] *it was assumed, reasonably enough, that the murder had taken place by the pond.*
2 to a moderate or acceptable degree: fairly; quite: [as submodifier] *she played the piano reasonably well.*
■ inexpensively: *ski wear which looks good and is reasonably priced.*

reasoned ▶ adjective underpinned by logic or good sense: *a reasoned judgement.*

reasoned amendment ▶ noun (in the UK) an amendment to a parliamentary bill that seeks to prevent a further reading by proposing reasons for its alteration or rejection.

reassemble ▶ verb [no obj.] (of a group) gather together again: *after lunch the class reassembled.*
■ [with obj.] put (something) together again: *the trucks had to be reassembled on arrival.*
– DERIVATIVES **reassembly** noun.

reassert ▶ verb [with obj.] assert again: *he moved quickly to reassert his control.*
– DERIVATIVES **reassertion** noun.

reassess ▶ verb [with obj.] consider or assess again, especially while paying attention to new or different factors: *we have decided to reassess our timetable.*
– DERIVATIVES **reassessment** noun.

reassign ▶ verb [with obj.] appoint (someone) to a different post or task: *he had been reassigned to another post.*
■ allocate or distribute (work or resources) differently: *it ordered the ministries to reassign 10 per cent of the vehicles.*
– DERIVATIVES **reassignment** noun.

reassume ▶ verb [with obj.] take on or gain (something) again: *he reassumed the title of Governor General.*
– DERIVATIVES **reassumption** noun.

reassurance ▶ noun [mass noun] the action of removing someone's doubts or fears: *children need reassurance and praise.*
■ [count noun] a statement or comment that removes someone's doubts or fears: *we have been given reassurances that the water is safe to drink.*

reassure ▶ verb [with obj.] say or do something to remove the doubts and fears of someone: *he understood her feelings and tried to reassure her |* [with obj. and clause] *Joachim reassured him that he was needed |* [as adj. **reassuring**] *Gina gave her a reassuring smile.*
– DERIVATIVES **reassuringly** adverb.

reattach ▶ verb [with obj.] attach (something that has fallen or been taken off) in its former position.
– DERIVATIVES **reattachment** noun.

reattain ▶ verb [with obj.] attain (an objective or position) again.
– DERIVATIVES **reattainment** noun.

reattempt ▶ verb [with obj.] attempt to achieve or complete (something) again: *I reattempted entry.*

Réaumur scale /ˈreɪə(ʊ)ˌmjʊə/ ▶ noun an obsolete scale of temperature at which water freezes at 0° and boils at 80° under standard conditions.
– ORIGIN late 18th cent.: named after René A. F. de Réaumur (1683–1757), French naturalist.

reave /riːv/ ▶ verb (past and past participle **reft** /rɛft/) [no obj.] archaic carry out raids in order to plunder.
■ [with obj.] rob (a person or place) of something by force: *reft of a crown, he yet may share the feast.* ■ [with obj.] steal (something).
– DERIVATIVES **reaver** noun.
– ORIGIN Old English *rēafian*, of Germanic origin; related to Dutch *roven*, German *rauben*, also to ROB.

reawaken ▶ verb [with obj.] restore (a feeling or state): *his departure reawakened deep divisions within the party.*
■ [no obj.] (of a feeling or state) emerge again; return: *the sense of community started to reawaken in the 1970s.*

Reb¹ /rɛb/ ▶ noun a traditional Jewish title or form of address, corresponding to Sir, for a man who is not a rabbi (used preceding the forename or surname).

– ORIGIN Yiddish.

Reb² /rɛb/ (also **Johnny Reb**) ▶ noun US informal a Confederate soldier in the American Civil War.
– ORIGIN abbreviation of REBEL.

rebab /rɪˈbab/ ▶ noun a bowed or plucked stringed instrument of Arab origin, used especially in North Africa, the Middle East, and the Indian subcontinent.
– ORIGIN mid 18th cent.: from Arabic *rabāb*.

rebadge ▶ verb [with obj.] relaunch (a product) under a new name or logo.

rebar ▶ noun [mass noun] a steel reinforcing rod in concrete: *a piece of rebar.*

rebarbative /rɪˈbɑːbətɪv/ ▶ adjective formal unattractive and objectionable: *rebarbative modern buildings.*
– ORIGIN late 19th cent.: from French *rébarbatif, -ive*, from Old French *se rebarber* 'face each other 'beard to beard' aggressively', from *barbe* 'beard'.

rebase ▶ verb [with obj.] establish a new base level for (a tax level, price index, etc.).

rebate¹ /ˈriːbeɪt/ ▶ noun a partial refund to someone who has paid too much money for tax, rent, or a utility.
■ a deduction or discount on a sum of money due.
▶ verb [with obj.] pay back (such a sum of money).
– DERIVATIVES **rebatable** adjective.
– ORIGIN late Middle English (as a verb in the sense 'diminish (a sum or amount)'): from Anglo-Norman French *rebatre* 'beat back', also 'deduct'.

rebate² /ˈriːbeɪt/ ▶ noun a step-shaped recess cut along the edge or in the face of a piece of wood, typically forming a match to the edge or tongue of another piece: [as modifier] *a rebate joint.*
▶ verb (**rebated**, **rebating**) [with obj.] make a rebate in (a piece of wood).
■ [with obj. and adverbial] join or fix (a piece of wood) to another with a rebate: *the oak boarding was rebated in.*
– ORIGIN late 17th cent.: alteration of RABBET.

rebate plane ▶ noun a plane for making a rebate in a piece of wood.

rebbe /ˈrɛbə/ ▶ noun Judaism a rabbi, especially a religious leader of the Hasidic sect.
■ the chosen spiritual mentor of an individual.
– ORIGIN Yiddish, from Hebrew *rabbī* 'rabbi'.

rebbetzin /ˈrɛbɪtsɪn/ (also **rebbitzin**) ▶ noun Judaism the wife of a rabbi.
■ a female religious teacher.
– ORIGIN Yiddish, feminine of *rebbe* (see REBBE).

rebec /ˈriːbɛk/ (also **rebeck**) ▶ noun a medieval stringed instrument played with a bow, typically having three strings.
– ORIGIN late Middle English: from French, based on Arabic *rabāb*.

rebel ▶ noun /ˈrɛb(ə)l/ a person who rises in opposition or armed resistance against an established government or ruler: *Tory rebels |* [as modifier] *rebel forces.*
■ a person who resists authority, control, or convention.
▶ verb /rɪˈbɛl/ (**rebelled**, **rebelling**) [no obj.] rise in opposition or armed resistance to an established government or ruler: *the Earl of Pembroke subsequently rebelled against Henry III.*
■ (of a person) resist authority, control, or convention: *respect did not prevent children from rebelling against their parents.* ■ show or feel repugnance for or resistance to something: *as I came over the hill my legs rebelled—I could walk no further.*
– ORIGIN Middle English: from Old French *rebelle* (noun), *rebeller* (verb), from Latin *rebellis* (used originally with reference to a fresh declaration of war by the defeated), based on *bellum* 'war'.

rebellion ▶ noun an act of violent or open resistance to an established government or ruler: *the authorities put down a rebellion by landless colonials |* [mass noun] *Simon de Montfort rose in rebellion.*
■ [mass noun] the action or process of resisting authority, control, or convention: *an act of teenage rebellion.*
– ORIGIN Middle English: from Old French, from Latin *rebellio(n-)*, from *rebellis* (see REBEL).

rebellious ▶ adjective showing a desire to resist authority, control, or convention: *I became very rebellious and opted out.*
■ (of a person, city, or state) engaged in opposition or armed resistance to an established government or ruler: *the rebellious republics.* ■ (of a thing) not easily handled or kept in place: *he smoothed back a rebellious lock of hair.*

– DERIVATIVES **rebelliously** adverb, **rebelliousness** noun.

rebel yell ▶ noun US a shout or battle cry used by the Confederates during the American Civil War.

rebid ▶ verb (**rebidding**; past and past participle **rebid**) [no obj.] bid again: *it will be in an ideal position when it comes to rebidding for its franchise.*
▶ noun a further bid.

rebind ▶ verb (past and past participle **rebound**) [with obj.] give a new binding to (a book).

rebirth ▶ noun [mass noun] the process of being reincarnated or born again: *the endless cycle of birth, death, and rebirth.*
■ the action of reappearing or starting to flourish or increase after a decline; revival: *the rebirth of a defeated nation.*

rebirthing ▶ noun [mass noun] a form of therapy involving controlled breathing intended to simulate the trauma of being born.
– DERIVATIVES **rebirther** noun.

reblochon /ˈrəblɒʃɒ̃/ ▶ noun [mass noun] a kind of soft French cheese, made originally and chiefly in Savoy.
– ORIGIN French.

reboot ▶ verb [with obj.] boot (a computer system) again.
■ [no obj.] (of a computer system) be booted again.
▶ noun an act or instance of booting a computer system again.

rebore ▶ verb [with obj.] make a new boring in (the cylinders of an internal-combustion engine), typically in order to widen them.
▶ noun an act of reboring an engine's cylinders.
■ an engine with rebored cylinders.

reborn ▶ adjective brought back to life or activity: *Lake Erie station stands reborn as a four-star restaurant.*
■ having experienced a complete spiritual change: *a reborn Catholic.*

rebound[1] ▶ verb /rɪˈbaʊnd/ [no obj.] bounce back through the air after hitting a hard surface or object: *his shot hammered into the post and rebounded across the goal.*
■ [no obj.] recover in value, amount, or strength after a previous decrease or decline: *the Share Index rebounded to show a twenty-point gain.* ■ [no obj.] (**rebound on/upon**) (of an event or situation) have an unexpected adverse consequence for (someone, especially the person responsible for it): *Nicholas's tricks are rebounding on him.* ■ [no obj.] Basketball gain possession of a missed shot after it bounces off the backboard or basket rim.
▶ noun /ˈriːbaʊnd/ (in sporting contexts) a ball or shot that bounces back after striking a hard surface: *he blasted the rebound into the net.*
■ Basketball a recovery of possession of a missed shot. ■ an instance of increasing in value, amount, or strength after a previous decline: *they revealed a big rebound in profits for last year.* ■ [usu. as modifier] the recurrence of a medical condition, especially after withdrawal of medication: *rebound hypertension.*
– PHRASES **on the rebound** in the process of bouncing back after striking a hard surface. ■ while still affected by the emotional distress caused by the ending of a romantic or sexual relationship: *I was on the rebound when I met Jack.*
– ORIGIN late Middle English: from Old French *rebondir*, from *re-* 'back' + *bondir* 'bounce up'.

rebound[2] past and past participle of **REBIND**.

rebounder ▶ noun **1** a small circular trampoline used for exercising.
2 Basketball a player who rebounds the ball.

rebozo /rɪˈbəʊzəʊ/ ▶ noun (pl. **-os**) a long scarf covering the head and shoulders, traditionally worn by Spanish-American women.
– ORIGIN Spanish.

rebrand ▶ verb [with obj.] [usu. as noun **rebranding**] change the corporate image of (a company or organization).

rebreathe ▶ verb [with obj.] breathe in (exhaled air).

rebreather ▶ noun an aqualung in which the diver's exhaled breath is partially purified of carbon dioxide, mixed with more oxygen and then breathed again by the diver.

rebroadcast ▶ verb (past **rebroadcast** or **rebroadcasted**; past participle **rebroadcast**) [with obj.] broadcast or relay (a programme or signal) again.
▶ noun a repeated or relayed broadcast.
– DERIVATIVES **rebroadcaster** noun.

rebuff ▶ verb [with obj.] reject (someone or something) in an abrupt or ungracious manner: *I asked her to be my wife, and was rebuffed in no uncertain terms.*
▶ noun an abrupt or ungracious refusal or rejection of an offer, request, or friendly gesture: *any attempt to win her friendship was met with rebuffs.*
– ORIGIN late 16th cent.: from obsolete French *rebuffer* (verb), *rebuffe* (noun), from Italian *ri-* (expressing opposition) + *buffo* 'a gust, puff', of imitative origin.

rebuild ▶ verb (past and past participle **rebuilt**) [with obj.] build (something) again after it has been damaged or destroyed: *he rebuilt the cathedral church* | figurative *we try to help them rebuild their lives.*
▶ noun an instance of rebuilding something, especially a vehicle or other machine.
■ a thing that has been rebuilt, especially a vehicle or other machine.
– DERIVATIVES **rebuildable** adjective, **rebuilder** noun.

rebuke ▶ verb [with obj.] express sharp disapproval or criticism of (someone) because of their behaviour or actions: *she had* ***rebuked*** *him* ***for*** *drinking too much* | *the judge publicly rebuked the jury.*
▶ noun an expression of sharp disapproval or criticism: *he hadn't meant it as a rebuke, but Neil flinched.*
– DERIVATIVES **rebuker** noun, **rebukingly** adverb.
– ORIGIN Middle English (originally in the sense 'force back, repress'): from Anglo-Norman French and Old Northern French *rebuker*, from *re-* 'back, down' + *bukier* 'to beat' (originally 'cut down wood', from Old French *busche* 'log').

rebury ▶ verb (**-ies**, **-ied**) [with obj.] bury again.
– DERIVATIVES **reburial** noun.

rebus /ˈriːbəs/ ▶ noun (pl. **rebuses**) a puzzle in which words are represented by combinations of pictures and individual letters; for instance, *apex* might be represented by a picture of an ape followed by a letter X.
■ historical an ornamental device associated with a person to whose name it punningly alludes.
– ORIGIN early 17th cent.: from French *rébus*, from Latin *rebus*, ablative plural of *res* 'thing'.

rebut /rɪˈbʌt/ ▶ verb (**rebutted**, **rebutting**) [with obj.] **1** claim or prove that (evidence or an accusation) is false: *he had to rebut charges of acting for the convenience of his political friends.*
2 archaic drive back or repel (a person or attack).
– DERIVATIVES **rebuttable** adjective.
– ORIGIN Middle English (in the senses 'rebuke' and 'repulse'): from Anglo-Norman French *rebuter*, from Old French *re-* (expressing opposition) + *boter* 'to butt'. Sense 1 (originally a legal use) dates from the early 19th cent.

rebuttal ▶ noun a refutation or contradiction.
■ another term for **REBUTTER**.

rebutter ▶ noun Law, archaic a defendant's reply to the plaintiff's surrejoinder.
– ORIGIN mid 16th cent.: from Anglo-Norman French *rebuter* (from Old French *rebut* 'a reproach or rebuke').

REC ▶ abbreviation for (in the UK) Regional Electricity Company.

rec ▶ noun informal **1** Brit. a recreation ground.
2 N. Amer. recreation: [as modifier] *the rec centre.*
– ORIGIN 1920s: abbreviation.

recalcitrant /rɪˈkalsɪtr(ə)nt/ ▶ adjective having an obstinately uncooperative attitude towards authority or discipline: *a class of recalcitrant fifteen-year-olds.*
▶ noun a person with such an attitude.
– DERIVATIVES **recalcitrance** noun, **recalcitrantly** adverb.
– ORIGIN mid 19th cent.: from Latin *recalcitrant-* 'kicking out with the heels', from the verb *recalcitrare*, based on *calx*, *calc-* 'heel'.

recalculate ▶ verb [with obj.] calculate again, typically using different data.
– DERIVATIVES **recalculation** noun.

recalescence /ˌriːkəˈlɛs(ə)ns/ ▶ noun [mass noun] Metallurgy a temporary rise in temperature during cooling of a metal, caused by a change in crystal structure.
– DERIVATIVES **recalescent** adjective.
– ORIGIN late 19th cent.: from **RE-** 'again' + Latin *calescere* 'grow hot' + **-ENCE**.

recall /rɪˈkɔːl/ ▶ verb [with obj.] **1** bring (a fact, event, or situation) back into one's mind, especially so as to recount it to others; remember: *I can still vaguely recall being taken to the hospital* | [with direct speech] *'He was awfully fond of teasing people,' she recalled* | [with clause] *he recalled how he felt at the time.*
■ cause one to remember or think of: *the film's analysis of contemporary concerns recalls* The Big Chill. ■ (**recall someone/thing to**) bring the memory or thought of someone or something to (a person or their mind): *the smell of a blackcurrant bush has ever since recalled to me that evening.* ■ call up (stored computer data) for processing or display.
2 officially order (someone) to return to a place: *the Panamanian ambassador was recalled from Peru.*
■ select (a sports player) as a member of a team from which they have previously been dropped: *the Fulham defender has been* ***recalled to*** *the Welsh squad for the World Cup.* ■ (of a manufacturer) request all the purchasers of (a certain product) to return it, as the result of the discovery of a fault. ■ bring (someone) out of a state of inattention or reverie: *her action* ***recalled*** *him* ***to*** *the present.* ■ archaic revoke or annul (an action or decision).
▶ noun /also ˈriːkɔːl/ **1** an act or instance of officially recalling someone or something: *a recall of Parliament.*
■ N. Amer. the removal of an elected government official from office by a petition followed by voting.
2 [mass noun] the action or faculty of remembering something learned or experienced: *did he note the whole lot down, or did he have extraordinary recall?* | *people's understanding and subsequent recall of stories or events.*
■ the proportion of the number of relevant documents retrieved from a database in response to an enquiry.
– PHRASES **beyond recall** in such a way that restoration is impossible: *shopping developments have already blighted other parts of the city beyond recall*
– DERIVATIVES **recallable** adjective.
– ORIGIN late 16th cent. (as a verb): from **RE-** 'again' + **CALL**, suggested by Latin *revocare* or French *rappeler* 'call back'.

recant /rɪˈkant/ ▶ verb [no obj.] say that one no longer holds an opinion or belief, especially one considered heretical: *heretics were burned if they would not recant* | [with obj.] *Galileo was forced to recant his assertion that the earth orbited the sun.*
– DERIVATIVES **recantation** /ˌriːkanˈteɪʃ(ə)n/ noun, **recanter** noun.
– ORIGIN mid 16th cent.: from Latin *recantare* 'revoke', from *re-* (expressing reversal) + *cantare* 'sing, chant'.

recap informal ▶ verb (**recapped**, **recapping**) [with obj.] state again as a summary; recapitulate: *a way of recapping the story so far* | [no obj.] *to recap, the reason for distinguishing between these occupations was to show employment change.*
▶ noun a summary of what has been said; a recapitulation: *a quick recap of the idea and its main advantages.*
– ORIGIN 1950s: abbreviation.

recapitalize (also **-ise**) ▶ verb [with obj.] provide (a business) with more capital, especially by replacing debt with stock.
– DERIVATIVES **recapitalization** noun.

recapitulate /ˌriːkəˈpɪtjʊleɪt/ ▶ verb [with obj.] summarize and state again the main points of: *he began to recapitulate his argument with care.*
■ Biology repeat (an evolutionary or other process) during development and growth.
– DERIVATIVES **recapitulatory** adjective.
– ORIGIN late 16th cent.: from late Latin *recapitulat-* 'gone through heading by heading', from *re-* 'again' + *capitulum* 'chapter' (diminutive of *caput* 'head').

recapitulation /ˌriːkəpɪtjʊˈleɪʃ(ə)n/ ▶ noun an act or instance of summarizing and restating the main points of something: *his recapitulation of the argument.*
■ [mass noun] Biology the repetition of an evolutionary or other process during development or growth. ■ Music a part of a movement (especially one in sonata form) in which themes from the exposition are restated.

recaption ▶ noun [mass noun] Law the action of taking back, without legal process, property of one's own that has been wrongfully taken or withheld.
– ORIGIN mid 18th cent.: from Anglo-Latin *recaptio(n-)*, from *re-* 'back' + Latin *captio(n-)* 'taking'.

recapture ▶ verb [with obj.] capture (a person or animal that has escaped): *armed police have recaptured a prisoner who's been on the run for five days.*
■ recover (something previously captured by an enemy): *Edward I recaptured the castle.* ■ regain (something that has been lost): *Leeds failed to recapture the form which had swept them to the title.* ■ recreate or experience again (a past time, event, or feeling): *the*

programmes give viewers a chance to recapture their own childhoods.
▶**noun** [in sing.] an act of recapturing.

recast ▶**verb** (past and past participle **recast**) [with obj.] **1** give (a metal object) a different form by melting it down and reshaping it.
■present or organize in a different form or style: *his doctoral thesis has been recast for the general reader.*
2 allocate the parts in (a play or film) to different actors: *there were moves to recast the play.*

recce /ˈrɛki/ chiefly Brit. ▶**noun** informal term for **RECONNAISSANCE**.
▶**verb** (**recced**, **recceing**) informal term for **RECONNOITRE**.
– ORIGIN 1940s: abbreviation.

recd ▶**abbreviation for** received.

recede ▶**verb** [no obj.] go or move back or further away from a previous position: *the flood waters had receded | his footsteps receded down the corridor.*
■(of a quality, feeling, or possibility) gradually diminish: *the prospects of an early end to the war receded.* ■ (of a man's hair) cease to grow at the temples and above the forehead: *his dark hair was receding a little |* [as adj. **receding**] *a receding hairline.* ■ (of a man) begin to go bald in such a way: *Fred was receding a bit.* ■ [usu. as adj. **receding**] (of a facial feature) slope backwards: *a slightly receding chin.* ■ (**recede from**) archaic withdraw from (an undertaking, promise, or agreement).
– ORIGIN late 15th cent. (in the sense 'depart from (a usual state or standard)'): from Latin *recedere*, from *re-* 'back' + *cedere* 'go'.

receipt ▶**noun** **1** [mass noun] the action of receiving something or the fact of its being received: *I would be grateful if you would acknowledge receipt of this letter | families **in receipt of** supplementary benefit.*
■[count noun] a written or printed statement acknowledging that something has been paid for or that goods have been received. ■ (**receipts**) an amount of money received during a particular period by an organization or business: *box office receipts.*
2 archaic a recipe.
▶**verb** [with obj.] [usu. as adj. **receipted**] mark (a bill) as paid: *the receipted hotel bill.*
– ORIGIN late Middle English: from Anglo-Norman French *receite*, from medieval Latin *recepta* 'received', feminine past participle of Latin *recipere*. The *-p-* was inserted in imitation of the Latin spelling.

receivable ▶**adjective** able to be received.
▶**plural noun** (**receivables**) amounts owed to a business, regarded as assets.

receive ▶**verb** [with obj.] **1** be given, presented with, or paid (something): *the band will receive a £100,000 advance | she received her prize from the manager.*
■take delivery of (something sent or communicated): *he received fifty enquiries after advertising the job.* ■ chiefly Brit. buy or accept goods in the knowledge that they have been stolen: *he was deprived of his licence for receiving a stolen load of whisky.* ■ detect or pick up (broadcast signals): *Turkish television began to be received in Tashkent.* ■ form (an idea or impression) as a result of perception or experience: *the impression she received was one of unhurried leisure.* ■ (in tennis and similar games) be the player to whom the server serves (the ball). ■ eat or drink (the Eucharistic bread or wine): *he received Communion and left.* ■ consent to formally hear (an oath or confession): *he failed to find a magistrate to receive his oath.* ■ serve as a receptacle for: *the basin that receives your blood.*
2 suffer, experience, or be subject to (specified treatment): *the event received wide press coverage | he received an eight-year prison sentence | she received only cuts and bruises.*
■[with obj. and adverbial] (usu. **be received**) respond to (something) in a specified way: *her first poem was not well received.* ■ meet with (a specified response or reaction): *the rulings have received widespread acceptance.* ■ [as adj. **received**] widely accepted as authoritative or true: *the myths and received wisdom about the country's past.* ■ meet and have to withstand: *the landward slopes receive the full force of the wind.*
3 greet or welcome (a visitor) formally: *representatives of the club will be received by the Mayor.*
■be visited by: *she was not allowed to receive visitors.* ■ admit as a member: *hundreds of converts were **received into** the Church.* ■ provide space or accommodation for: *three lines are reserved for special vehicles, and the remaining lines receive the general rolling stock.*
– PHRASES **be at** (or **on**) **the receiving end** be the person to whom a telephone call is made. ■ informal be subjected to something unpleasant: *she found herself on the receiving end of a good deal of teasing.*
– ORIGIN Middle English: from Anglo-Norman French *receivre*, based on Latin *recipere*, from *re-* 'back' + *capere* 'take'.

received pronunciation (also **received standard**) ▶**noun** [mass noun] the standard form of British English pronunciation, based on educated speech in southern England, widely accepted as a standard elsewhere.

receiver ▶**noun** **1** the part of a telephone apparatus contained in the earpiece, in which electrical signals are converted into sounds.
■a complete telephone handset: *he picked up the receiver.* ■ a piece of radio or television apparatus that detects broadcast signals and converts them into visible or audible form: *a satellite receiver.*
2 a person who gets or accepts something that has been sent or given to them: *the receiver of a gift.*
■(in tennis and similar games) the player to whom the ball is served to begin play. ■ American Football a player who specializes in catching passes. ■ chiefly Brit. a person who buys or accepts stolen goods in the knowledge that they have been stolen.
3 (Brit. also **official receiver**) a person or company appointed by a court to manage the financial affairs of a business or person that has gone bankrupt: *the company is in the hands of the receivers.*
4 Chemistry a container for collecting the products of distillation, chromatography, or other process.
5 the part of a firearm which houses the action and to which the barrel and other parts are attached.

receivership ▶**noun** [mass noun] the state of being dealt with by an official receiver: *the company went **into receivership** last week.*

receiving line ▶**noun** a collection of people who gather in a row to greet guests as they arrive at a formal social event.

receiving order ▶**noun** Brit. a court order authorizing an official receiver to act in a case of bankruptcy (since 1986 superseded by a bankruptcy order).

recension /rɪˈsɛnʃ(ə)n/ ▶**noun** a revised edition of a text; an act of making a revised edition of a text.
– ORIGIN mid 17th cent. (in the sense 'survey, review'): from Latin *recensio(n-)*, from *recensere* 'revise', from *re-* 'again' + *censere* 'to review'.

recent ▶**adjective** **1** having happened, begun, or been done not long ago or not long before; belonging to a past period of time comparatively close to the present: *his recent visit to Britain | a recent edition of the newspaper.*
2 (**Recent**) Geology another term for **HOLOCENE**.
▶**noun** (**the Recent**) Geology the Holocene epoch.
– DERIVATIVES **recency** noun, **recently** adverb, **recentness** noun.
– ORIGIN late Middle English (in the sense 'fresh'): from Latin *recens, recent-* or French *récent*.

receptacle /rɪˈsɛptək(ə)l/ ▶**noun** **1** an object or space used to contain something: *fast-food receptacles.*
■chiefly Zoology an organ or structure which receives a secretion, eggs, sperm, etc.
2 Botany an enlarged area at the apex of a stem on which the parts of a flower or the florets of a flower head are inserted.
■a structure supporting the sexual organs in some algae, mosses, and liverworts.
– ORIGIN late Middle English: from Latin *receptaculum*, from *receptare* 'receive back', frequentative of *recipere* (see **RECEIVE**).

reception ▶**noun** **1** [mass noun] the action or process of receiving something sent, given, or inflicted: *sensation is not the passive reception of stimuli | the reception of the sacrament.*
■[count noun] the way in which a person or group of people reacts to someone or something: *the election budget got a stony reception in the City.* ■ the receiving of broadcast signals: *a microchip that will allow parents to block reception of violent programmes.* ■ the quality of this: *I had to put up with poor radio reception.* ■ the action of admitting someone to a place, group, or institution or the process of being admitted: *their reception into the Church.* ■ the formal or ceremonious welcoming of a guest: *his reception by the Prime Minister.* ■ [count noun] American Football an act of catching a pass.
2 a formal social occasion held to welcome someone or to celebrate a particular event: *a wedding reception.*
3 the area in a hotel, office, or other establishment where guests and visitors are greeted and dealt with: *wait for me downstairs **in reception** |* [as modifier] *the reception desk.*
4 [usu. as modifier] Brit. the first class in an infant school: *the reception class.*
– ORIGIN late Middle English: from Old French, or from Latin *receptio(n-)*, from the verb *recipere* (see **RECEIVE**).

reception centre ▶**noun** a hostel providing temporary accommodation for distressed people such as refugees, the homeless, and those with psychiatric difficulties.

receptionist ▶**noun** a person employed in an office, surgery, or other establishment to greet and deal with clients and visitors.
■Brit. a person employed in a hotel to receive guests and deal with their bookings.

reception order ▶**noun** Brit. an order authorizing the admission and detention of a patient in a psychiatric hospital.

reception room ▶**noun** a room in a hotel or other building used for functions such as parties and meetings.
■Brit. (chiefly in commercial use) a room in a private house suitable for entertaining visitors, especially a lounge or dining room.

receptive ▶**adjective** able or willing to receive something, especially signals or stimuli.
■willing to consider or accept new suggestions and ideas: *a receptive audience | the institution was **receptive to** new ideas.* ■ (of a female animal) ready to mate.
– DERIVATIVES **receptively** adverb, **receptiveness** noun, **receptivity** noun.

receptor /rɪˈsɛptə/ ▶**noun** Physiology an organ or cell able to respond to light, heat, or other external stimulus and transmit a signal to a sensory nerve.
■a region of tissue, or a molecule in a cell membrane, which responds specifically to a particular neurotransmitter, hormone, antigen, or other substance.
– ORIGIN early 20th cent.: coined in German from Latin *receptor*, from *recept-* 'taken back', from the verb *recipere* (see **RECEIVE**).

recess /rɪˈsɛs, ˈriːsɛs/ ▶**noun** **1** a small space created by building part of a wall further back from the rest: *a table set into a recess.*
■a hollow space inside something: *the concrete block has a recess in its base.* ■ (usu. **recesses**) a remote, secluded, or secret place: *the recesses of the silent pine forest |* figurative *the dark recesses of his soul.*
2 a period of time when the proceedings of a parliament, committee, court of law, or other official body are temporarily suspended: *talks resumed after a month's recess | Parliament was **in recess**.*
■chiefly N. Amer. a break between school classes: *the mid-morning recess.*
▶**verb** **1** [with obj.] [often as adj. **recessed**] attach (a fitment) by setting it back into the wall or surface to which it is fixed: *recessed ceiling lights.*
2 [no obj.] chiefly N. Amer. (of formal proceedings) be temporarily suspended: *the talks recessed at 2.15.*
■[with obj.] suspend (such proceedings) temporarily. ■ (of an official body) suspend its proceedings for a period of time.
– ORIGIN mid 16th cent. (in the sense 'withdrawal, departure'): from Latin *recessus*, from *recedere* 'go back' (see **RECEDE**). The verb dates from the early 19th cent.

recession ▶**noun** **1** a period of temporary economic decline during which trade and industrial activity are reduced, generally identified by a fall in GDP in two successive quarters.
2 [mass noun] chiefly Astronomy the action of receding; motion away from an observer.
– DERIVATIVES **recessionary** adjective.
– ORIGIN mid 17th cent.: from Latin *recessio(n-)*, from *recess-* 'gone back', from the verb *recedere* (see **RECEDE**).

recessional ▶**adjective** of or relating to an economic recession: *recessional times.*
■chiefly Astronomy relating to or denoting motion away from the observer. ■ Geology (of a moraine or other deposit) left during a pause in the retreat of a glacier or ice sheet.
▶**noun** a hymn sung while the clergy and choir process out of church at the end of a service.

recessive ▶**adjective** **1** Genetics relating to or denoting heritable characteristics controlled by genes which are expressed in offspring only when

inherited from both parents, i.e. when not masked by a dominant characteristic inherited from one parent. Often contrasted with **DOMINANT**.
■ Linguistics tending to fall into disuse.
2 undergoing an economic recession: *the recessive housing market.*
3 Phonetics (of the stress on a word or phrase) tending to fall on the first syllable.
▶ **noun** Genetics a recessive trait or gene.
– DERIVATIVES **recessively** adverb, **recessiveness** noun, **recessivity** noun.
– ORIGIN late 17th cent.: from **RECESS**, on the pattern of *excessive*.

Rechabite /ˈrɛkəbʌɪt/ ▶ **noun** (in the Bible) a member of an Israelite family, descended from Rechab, who refused to drink wine or live in houses (Jer. 35).
■ a member of the Independent Order of Rechabites, a benefit society of teetotallers, founded in 1835.

recharge ▶ **verb** [with obj.] restore an electric charge to (a battery or a battery-operated device) by connecting it to a device that draws power from another source of electricity: *he plugged his razor in to recharge it.*
■ [no obj.] (of a battery or battery-operated device) be refilled with electrical power in such a way: *the drill takes about three hours to recharge.* ■ refill (a cup, glass, or other container) with liquid. ■ [no obj.] be refilled: *the rate at which the aquifer recharges naturally.* ■ [no obj.] figurative (of a person) return to a normal state of mind or strength after a period of physical or mental exertion: *she needs a bit of time to recharge after giving so much of herself this morning.*
▶ **noun** [mass noun] the replenishment of an aquifer by the absorption of water.
– PHRASES **recharge one's batteries** regain one's strength and energy by resting and relaxing for a time.
– DERIVATIVES **rechargeable** adjective, **recharger** noun.

réchauffé /reɪˈʃəʊfeɪ/ ▶ **noun** a dish of warmed-up food left over from a previous meal.
– ORIGIN French, literally 'reheated', past participle of *réchauffer*.

recheck ▶ **verb** [with obj.] check or verify again: *switch off at once and recheck all the wiring.*
▶ **noun** an act of checking or verifying something again: *a recheck of the data.*

recherché /rəˈʃɛːʃeɪ/ ▶ **adjective** rare, exotic, or obscure: *a few linguistic terms are perhaps a bit recherché for the average readership.*
– ORIGIN French, literally 'carefully sought out', past participle of *rechercher*.

rechipping ▶ **noun** [mass noun] Brit. the practice of changing the electronic identification numbers of a stolen mobile phone so as to enable it to be reused.

rechristen ▶ **verb** [with obj. and complement] give a new name to: *the brewery rechristened the pub The Brown Trout.*

recidivist /rɪˈsɪdɪvɪst/ ▶ **noun** a convicted criminal who reoffends, especially repeatedly.
▶ **adjective** denoting such a person: *recidivist male prisoners | women are rarely recidivist.*
– DERIVATIVES **recidivism** noun, **recidivistic** adjective.
– ORIGIN late 19th cent.: from French *récidiviste*, from *récidiver* 'fall back', based on Latin *recidivus* 'falling back', from the verb *recidere*, from *re-* 'back' + *cadere* 'to fall'.

Recife /rəˈsiːfi/ a port on the Atlantic coast of NE Brazil, capital of the state of Pernambuco; pop. 1,298,230 (1991). Former name **PERNAMBUCO**.

recipe /ˈrɛsɪpi/ ▶ **noun** a set of instructions for preparing a particular dish, including a list of the ingredients required: *a traditional Yorkshire recipe.*
■ figurative something which is likely to lead to a particular outcome: *sky-high interest rates are **a recipe for** disaster.* ■ archaic a medical prescription.
– ORIGIN late Middle English: from Latin, literally 'receive!' (first used as an instruction in medical prescriptions), imperative of *recipere*.

recipe dish ▶ **noun** a dish of a type which would ordinarily require lengthy preparation, sold ready-made and requiring only to be heated before consumption.

recipient ▶ **noun** a person or thing that receives or is awarded something: *the recipient of the Nobel Peace Prize.*
▶ **adjective** [attrib.] receiving or capable or receiving something: *a recipient country.*
– DERIVATIVES **recipiency** noun.
– ORIGIN mid 16th cent.: from Latin *recipient-* 'receiving', from the verb *recipere*.

reciprocal /rɪˈsɪprək(ə)l/ ▶ **adjective 1** given, felt, or done in return: *she was hoping for some reciprocal comment or gesture.*
2 (of an agreement or obligation) bearing on or binding each of two parties equally: *the treaty is a bilateral commitment with reciprocal rights and duties.*
■ Grammar (of a pronoun or verb) expressing mutual action or relationship.
3 (of a course or bearing) differing from a given course or bearing by 180 degrees.
4 Mathematics (of a quantity or function) related to another so that their product is unity.
▶ **noun 1** technical a mathematical expression or function so related to another that their product is unity; the quantity obtained by dividing the number one by a given quantity.
2 Grammar a pronoun or verb expressing mutual action or relationship, e.g. *each other, fight*.
– DERIVATIVES **reciprocality** noun, **reciprocally** adverb.
– ORIGIN late 16th cent.: from Latin *reciprocus* (based on *re-* 'back' + *pro-* 'forward') + **-AL**.

reciprocal cross ▶ **noun** Genetics a pair of crosses between a male of one strain and a female of another, and vice versa.

reciprocate /rɪˈsɪprəkeɪt/ ▶ **verb 1** [with obj.] respond to (a gesture or action) by making a corresponding one: *the favour was reciprocated* | [no obj.] *perhaps I was expected to reciprocate with some remark of my own.*
■ experience the same (love, liking, or affection) for someone that has such feelings for oneself: *her passion for him was not reciprocated.*
2 [no obj.] [usu. as adj. **reciprocating**] (of a part of a machine) move backwards and forwards in a straight line: *a reciprocating blade.*
– DERIVATIVES **reciprocation** noun, **reciprocator** noun.
– ORIGIN late 16th cent.: from Latin *reciprocat-* 'moved backwards and forwards', from the verb *reciprocare*, from *reciprocus* (see **RECIPROCAL**).

reciprocating engine ▶ **noun** an engine in which one or more pistons move up and down in cylinders; a piston engine.

reciprocity /ˌrɛsɪˈprɒsɪti/ ▶ **noun** [mass noun] the practice of exchanging things with others for mutual benefit, especially privileges granted by one country or organization to another.
– ORIGIN mid 18th cent.: from French *réciprocité*, from *réciproque*, from Latin *reciprocus* 'moving backwards and forwards' (see **RECIPROCATE**).

reciprocity failure ▶ **noun** [mass noun] Photography deviation of an emulsion from the principle that the degree of darkening is constant for a given product of light intensity and exposure time, typically at very low or very high light intensities.

recirculate ▶ **verb** [with obj.] circulate again.
– DERIVATIVES **recirculation** noun.

recital ▶ **noun 1** the performance of a programme of music by a solo instrumentalist or singer or by a small group: *a piano recital.*
2 an enumeration or listing of connected names, facts, or elements; *a recital of their misfortunes.*
3 (usu. **recitals**) Law the part of a legal document that explains the purpose of the deed and gives factual information.
– DERIVATIVES **recitalist** noun.

recitative /ˌrɛsɪtəˈtiːv/ ▶ **noun** [mass noun] musical declamation of the kind usual in the narrative and dialogue parts of opera and oratorio, sung in the rhythm of ordinary speech with many words on the same note: *singing in recitative.*
– ORIGIN mid 17th cent.: from Italian *recitativo*, from Latin *recitare* 'to read out' (see **RECITE**).

recitativo /ˌrɛsɪtəˈtiːvəʊ/ ▶ **noun** (pl. **-os**) another term for **RECITATIVE**.
– ORIGIN Italian.

recite ▶ **verb** [with obj.] repeat aloud or declaim (a poem or passage) from memory before an audience: *we provided our own entertainment by singing and reciting poetry.*
■ state (names, facts, etc.) in order: *she recited the dates and names of kings and queens.*
– DERIVATIVES **recitation** noun, **reciter** noun.
– ORIGIN late Middle English (as a legal term in the sense 'state (a fact) in a document'): from Old French *reciter* or Latin *recitare* 'read out', from *re-* (expressing intensive force) + *citare* 'cite'.

reck ▶ **verb** [no obj.] [with negative or in questions] archaic pay heed to something: *ye **reck** not **of** lands or goods* | [with clause] *little recking where she was wandering* | [with obj.] *he recks not Syria, recks not Britain.*
■ (**it recks**) it is of importance: *what recks it?*
– ORIGIN Old English, of Germanic origin; compare with **RECKLESS**. The word became common in rhetorical and poetic language in the 19th cent.

reckless ▶ **adjective** (of a person or their actions) without thinking or caring about the consequences of an action: *reckless driving.*
– DERIVATIVES **recklessly** adverb, **recklessness** noun.
– ORIGIN Old English *recceléas*, from the Germanic base (meaning 'care') of **RECK**.

reckon ▶ **verb 1** [with obj.] establish by counting or calculation; calculate: *his debts were **reckoned at** £300,000 | the Byzantine year was reckoned from 1 September.*
■ (**reckon someone/thing among**) include in (a class or group): *the society can reckon among its members males of the royal blood.*
2 [with clause] informal conclude after calculation; be of the opinion: *he reckons that the army should pull out entirely | I reckon I can manage that.*
■ [with obj. and complement] (often **be reckoned**) consider or regard in a specified way: *it was generally reckoned a failure.* ■ [no obj.] (**reckon on/to**) informal have a specified view or opinion of: *'What do you reckon on this place?' she asked.* ■ [with obj.] Brit. informal rate highly: *I don't reckon his chances.*
3 [no obj.] (**reckon on**) rely on or be sure of doing, having, or dealing with: *they had reckoned on a day or two more of privacy.*
■ [with infinitive] informal expect to do a particular thing: *I reckon to get away by two-thirty.*
– PHRASES **a —— to be reckoned with** (or **to reckon with**) a thing or person of considerable importance or ability that is not to be ignored or underestimated: *the trade unions were a political force to be reckoned with.*
▶ **reckon with** (or **without**) **1** take (or fail to take) into account: *they hadn't reckoned with a visit from Eunice.* **2** (**reckon with**) archaic settle accounts with.
– ORIGIN Old English *(ge)recenian* 'recount, relate', of West Germanic origin; related to Dutch *rekenen* and German *rechnen* 'to count (up)'. Early senses included 'give an account of items received' and 'mention things in order', which gave rise to the notion of 'calculation' and hence of 'coming to a conclusion'.

reckoner ▶ **noun** a table or device designed to assist with calculation.

reckoning ▶ **noun** [mass noun] **1** the action or process of calculating or estimating something: *the sixth, or by another reckoning eleventh, Earl of Mar | the system of time reckoning in Babylon.*
■ a person's view, opinion, or judgement: *by ancient reckoning, bacteria are plants.* ■ [count noun] archaic a bill or account, or its settlement. ■ the avenging or punishing of past mistakes or misdeeds: *the fear of being brought to reckoning* | [count noun] *there will be a terrible reckoning.*
2 (**the reckoning**) contention for a place in a team or among the winners of a contest: *he has hit the sort of form which could thrust him **into the reckoning**.*

reclaim ▶ **verb** [with obj.] **1** retrieve or recover (something previously lost, given, or paid); obtain the return of: *you can reclaim £25 of the £435 deducted | when Dennis emerged I reclaimed my room.*
■ redeem (someone) from a state of vice; reform: *societies for reclaiming beggars and prostitutes.* ■ archaic tame or civilize (an animal or person).
2 bring (waste land or land formerly under water) under cultivation: *much of the Camargue has now been reclaimed* | [as adj. **reclaimed**] *reclaimed land.*
■ recover (material) for reuse; recycle: *a sufficient weight of plastic could easily be reclaimed.*
▶ **noun** [mass noun] the action or process of reclaiming or being reclaimed: *VAT reclaim.*
– DERIVATIVES **reclaimable** adjective, **reclaimer** noun, **reclamation** noun.
– ORIGIN Middle English (used in falconry in the sense 'recall'): from Old French *reclamer*, from Latin *reclamare* 'cry out against', from *re-* 'back' + *clamare* 'to shout'.

reclassify ▶ **verb** (**-ies**, **-ied**) [with obj.] (often **be reclassified**) assign to a different class or category:

r

what was previously tax relief may be reclassified as government expenditure.
■(in South Africa during the apartheid era) officially assign (someone) to a different legally defined ethnic group.
– DERIVATIVES **reclassification** noun.

recline ▶ **verb** [no obj.] lean or lie back in a relaxed position with the back supported: *she was reclining in a deckchair* | [as adj. **reclining**] *a reclining figure.*
■(of a seat) be able to have the back moved into a sloping position: *all the seats recline.* ■ [with obj.] move the back of (a seat) into a sloping position.
– DERIVATIVES **reclinable** adjective.
– ORIGIN late Middle English (in the sense 'cause to lean back'): from Old French *recliner* or Latin *reclinare* 'bend back, recline', from *re-* 'back' + *clinare* 'to bend'.

recliner ▶ **noun 1** a person who reclines.
2 an upholstered armchair that can be tilted backwards, especially one with a footrest that simultaneously extends from the front.

reclothe ▶ **verb** [with obj.] dress again, especially in different clothes: *she was ceremonially reclothed in a new robe.*

recluse /rɪˈkluːs/ ▶ **noun** a person who lives a solitary life and tends to avoid other people.
▶ **adjective** archaic favouring a solitary life.
– DERIVATIVES **reclusion** noun.
– ORIGIN Middle English: from Old French *reclus*, past participle of *reclure*, from Latin *recludere* 'enclose', from *re-* 'again' + *claudere* 'to shut'.

reclusive ▶ **adjective** avoiding the company of other people; solitary: *he led a reclusive life.*
– DERIVATIVES **reclusiveness** noun.

recode ▶ **verb** [with obj.] put (something, especially a computer program) into a different code.
■assign a different code to.

recognition ▶ **noun** [mass noun] the action or process of recognizing or being recognized, in particular:
■identification of a thing or person from previous encounters or knowledge: *she saw him pass by without a sign of recognition* | *methods of production have improved* ***out of all recognition.*** ■ acknowledgement of something's existence, validity, or legality: *the unions must receive proper recognition.* ■ appreciation or acclaim for an achievement, service, or ability: *his work was slow to gain recognition* | *she received the award* ***in recognition of*** *her courageous human rights work.* ■ (also **diplomatic recognition**) formal acknowledgement by a country that another political entity fulfils the conditions of statehood and is eligible to be dealt with as a member of the international community.
– DERIVATIVES **recognitory** adjective (rare).
– ORIGIN late 15th cent. (denoting the acknowledgement of a service): from Latin *recognitio(n-)*, from the verb *recognoscere* 'know again, recall to mind' (see **RECOGNIZE**).

recognizable (also **-isable**) ▶ **adjective** able to be recognized or identified from previous encounters or knowledge.
– DERIVATIVES **recognizability** noun, **recognizably** adverb.

recognizance /rɪˈkɒ(g)nɪz(ə)ns/ (also **recognisance**) ▶ **noun** Law a bond by which a person undertakes before a court or magistrate to observe some condition, especially to appear when summoned: *he was released* ***on his own recognizance*** *of £30,000.*
– ORIGIN Middle English: from Old French *reconissance*, from *reconnaistre* 'recognize'.

recognizant /rɪˈkɒgnɪz(ə)nt/ (also **recognisant**) ▶ **adjective** [predic.] (**recognizant of**) formal conscious or aware of (something, especially a favour).

recognize (also **-ise**) ▶ **verb** [with obj.] **1** identify (someone or something) from having encountered them before; know again: *I recognized her when her wig fell off* | *Julia hardly recognized Jill when they met.*
■identify from knowledge of appearance or character: *Pat is very good at recognizing wild flowers.* ■ (of a computer or other machine) automatically identify and respond correctly to (a sound, printed character, etc.).
2 acknowledge the existence, validity, or legality of: *the defence is recognized in British law* | *he was* ***recognized as*** *an international authority* | [with clause] *it is important to recognize that a variety of indirect forms of discrimination operate.*
■officially regard (a qualification) as valid or proper: *these qualifications are recognized by the Department of Education* | [as adj. **recognized**] *courses that lead to recognized qualifications.* ■ grant diplomatic recognition to (a country or government). ■ show official appreciation of; reward formally: *his work was recognized by an honorary degree from Glasgow University.* ■ (of a person presiding at a meeting or debate) call on (someone) to speak.
– DERIVATIVES **recognizer** noun.
– ORIGIN late Middle English (earliest attested as a term in Scots law): from Old French *reconniss-*, stem of *reconnaistre*, from Latin *recognoscere* 'know again, recall to mind', from *re-* 'again' + *cognoscere* 'learn'.

recoil ▶ **verb** [no obj.] suddenly spring or flinch back in fear, horror, or disgust: *he recoiled in horror.*
■feel fear, horror, or disgust at the thought or prospect of something; shrink mentally: *Ronni felt herself recoil at the very thought.* ■ (of a gun) move abruptly backwards as a reaction on firing a bullet, shell, or other missile. ■ rebound or spring back through force of impact or elasticity: *the muscle has the ability to recoil.* ■ (**recoil on/upon**) (of an action) have an adverse reactive effect on (the originator).
▶ **noun** [mass noun] the action of recoiling: *his body jerked with the recoil of the rifle.*
– DERIVATIVES **recoilless** adjective.
– ORIGIN Middle English (denoting the act of retreating): from Old French *reculer* 'move back', based on Latin *culus* 'buttocks'.

recollect[1] /ˌrɛkəˈlɛkt/ ▶ **verb** [with obj.] remember (something); call to mind: *he could not quite recollect the reason* | [with clause] *'Can you recollect how your brother reacted?'*
– ORIGIN early 16th cent. (in the sense 'gather'): from Latin *recollect-* 'gathered back', from the verb *recolligere*, from *re-* 'back' + *colligere* 'collect'.

recollect[2] /ˌriːkəˈlɛkt/ ▶ **verb** [with obj.] rare collect or gather together again.
■(**recollect oneself**) bring oneself back to a state of composure: *he had a look round, recollected himself, and prepared his mind for the day.*
– ORIGIN early 17th cent.: later form of **RECOLLECT**[1], from **RE-** 'once more' + the verb **COLLECT**[1].

recollection /ˌrɛkəˈlɛkʃ(ə)n/ ▶ **noun** [mass noun] the action or faculty of remembering or recollecting something: ***to the best of my recollection*** *no one ever had a bad word to say about him.*
■[count noun] a thing recollected; a memory: *a biography based on his wife's recollections.* ■ Philosophy (in Platonic thought) anamnesis.
– DERIVATIVES **recollective** adjective.
– ORIGIN late 16th cent. (denoting gathering things together again): from French or medieval Latin *recollectio(n-)*, from the verb *recolligere* 'gather again' (see **RECOLLECT**[1]).

Recollet /ˈrɛkəleɪ/ (also **Recollect** /ˈrɛkəlɛkt/) ▶ **noun** historical a member of a reformed branch of the Franciscan order, founded in France in the late 16th century.
– ORIGIN from French *récollet*, from medieval Latin *recollectus* 'gathered together', expressing a notion of concentration, and absorption in thought.

recolonize (also **-ise**) ▶ **verb** [with obj.] (chiefly of a plant or animal species) colonize (a region or habitat) again.
– DERIVATIVES **recolonization** noun.

recolour (US **recolor**) ▶ **verb** [with obj.] colour again or differently.

recombinant /rɪˈkɒmbɪnənt/ Genetics ▶ **adjective** [attrib.] of, relating to, or denoting an organism, cell, or genetic material formed by recombination.
▶ **noun** a recombinant organism, cell, or piece of genetic material.

recombination ▶ **noun** [mass noun] the process of recombining things.
■Genetics the rearrangement of genetic material, especially by crossing over in chromosomes or by the artificial joining of segments of DNA from different organisms.

recombine ▶ **verb** combine or cause to combine again or differently: [no obj.] *carbohydrates can recombine with oxygen* | [with obj.] *decompose the calculation into components and recombine them to find the solution.*

recommence ▶ **verb** begin or cause to begin again: [no obj.] *the war recommenced* | [with obj.] *it was agreed to recommence talks.*
– DERIVATIVES **recommencement** noun.

recommend ▶ **verb** [with obj.] **1** put forward (someone or something) with approval as being suitable for a particular purpose or role: *George had recommended some local architects* | *a book I* ***recommended to*** *a friend of mine.*
■advise or suggest (something) as a course of action: *some doctors recommend putting a board under the mattress* | [with clause] *the report recommended that criminal charges be brought.* ■ [with obj. and infinitive] advise (someone) to do something: *you are strongly recommended to seek professional advice.* ■ make (someone or something) appealing or desirable: *the house had much to recommend it.*
2 (**recommend someone/thing to**) archaic commend or entrust someone or something to (someone): *I devoutly recommended my spirit to its maker.*
– DERIVATIVES **recommendable** adjective, **recommendation** noun, **recommendatory** adjective, **recommender** noun.
– ORIGIN late Middle English (in sense 2): from medieval Latin *recommendare*, from Latin *re-* (expressing intensive force) + *commendare* 'commit to the care of'.

recommission ▶ **verb** [with obj.] commission again.

recommit ▶ **verb** (**recommitted**, **recommitting**) [with obj.] commit again.
■return (a motion, proposal, or parliamentary bill) to a committee for further consideration.
– DERIVATIVES **recommitment** noun, **recommittal** noun.

recompense /ˈrɛkəmpɛns/ ▶ **verb** [with obj.] make amends to (someone) for loss or harm suffered; compensate: *offenders should recompense their victims* | *he was recompensed for the wasted time.*
■pay or reward (someone) for effort or work: *he was handsomely recompensed.* ■ make amends to or reward someone for (loss, harm, or effort): *he thought his loyalty had been inadequately recompensed.* ■ archaic punish or reward (someone) appropriately for an action: *according to their doings will he recompense them.*
▶ **noun** [mass noun] compensation or reward given for loss or harm suffered or effort made: *substantial damages were paid* ***in recompense.***
■archaic restitution made or punishment inflicted for a wrong or injury.
– ORIGIN late Middle English: from Old French, from the verb *recompenser* 'do a favour to requite a loss', from late Latin *recompensare*, from Latin *re-* 'again' (also expressing intensive force) + *compensare* 'weigh one thing against another'.

recompose ▶ **verb** [with obj.] compose again or differently: *a marble panel recomposed from fragments.*
– DERIVATIVES **recomposition** noun.

recon /rɪˈkɒn/ informal, chiefly N. Amer. ▶ **noun** short for **RECONNAISSANCE.**
▶ **verb** (**reconned**, **reconning**) short for **RECONNOITRE.**

reconcile /ˈrɛk(ə)nsʌɪl/ ▶ **verb** [with obj.] (often **be reconciled**) restore friendly relations between: *she wanted to be* ***reconciled with*** *her father* | *the news reconciled us.*
■cause to coexist in harmony; make or show to be compatible: *the hope that Christianity and feminism could be reconciled* | *you may have to adjust your ideal to* ***reconcile*** *it* ***with*** *reality.* ■ make (one account) consistent with another, especially by allowing for transactions begun but not yet completed: *it is not necessary to reconcile the cost accounts to the financial accounts.* ■ settle (a quarrel): *advice on how to reconcile the conflict.* ■ (**reconcile someone to**) make someone accept (a disagreeable or unwelcome thing): *he was reconciled to leaving.*
– DERIVATIVES **reconcilability** noun, **reconcilable** adjective, **reconcilement** noun, **reconciler** noun, **reconciliation** noun, **reconciliatory** adjective.
– ORIGIN late Middle English: from Old French *reconcilier* or Latin *reconciliare*, from Latin *re-* 'back' (also expressing intensive force) + *conciliare* 'bring together'.

reconciliation statement ▶ **noun** a statement of account in which discrepancies are adjusted so that different accounts balance.

recondite /ˈrɛk(ə)ndʌɪt, rɪˈkɒn-/ ▶ **adjective** (of a subject or knowledge) little known; abstruse: *the book is full of recondite information.*
– ORIGIN mid 17th cent.: from Latin *reconditus* 'hidden, put away', past participle of *recondere*, from *re-* 'back' + *condere* 'put together, secrete'.

recondition ▶ **verb** [with obj.] condition again.
■Brit. overhaul or renovate (a vehicle engine or piece of equipment): *a ship was being reconditioned* | [as adj. **reconditioned**] *a reconditioned engine.*

reconfigure ▶ **verb** [with obj.] configure (something)

differently: *you don't have to reconfigure the modem each time you make a connection.*
– DERIVATIVES **reconfigurable** adjective, **reconfiguration** noun.

reconfirm ▶ **verb** [with obj.] confirm again.
– DERIVATIVES **reconfirmation** noun.

reconnaissance /rɪˈkɒnɪs(ə)ns/ ▶ **noun** [mass noun] military observation of a region to locate an enemy or ascertain strategic features: *an excellent aircraft for low-level reconnaissance* | [as modifier] *reconnaissance missions* | [count noun] *after a reconnaissance British forces took the island.*
■ preliminary surveying or research: *conducting client reconnaissance.*
– ORIGIN early 19th cent.: from French, from *reconnaître* 'recognize' (see **RECONNOITRE**).

reconnect ▶ **verb** [with obj.] connect back together: *surgeons had to reconnect tendons, nerves, and veins.*
– DERIVATIVES **reconnection** noun.

reconnoitre /ˌrɛkəˈnɔɪtə/ (US **reconnoiter**) ▶ **verb** [with obj.] make a military observation of (a region): *they reconnoitred the beach some weeks before the landing* | [no obj.] *the raiders were reconnoitring for further attacks.*
▶ **noun** informal an act of reconnoitring: *a nocturnal reconnoitre of the camp.*
– ORIGIN early 18th cent.: from obsolete French *reconnoître*, from Latin *recognoscere* 'know again' (see **RECOGNIZE**).

reconquer ▶ **verb** [with obj.] conquer again.
– DERIVATIVES **reconquest** noun.

reconsecrate ▶ **verb** [with obj.] consecrate (someone or something) again.
– DERIVATIVES **reconsecration** noun.

reconsider ▶ **verb** [with obj.] consider (something) again, especially for a possible change of decision regarding it: *they called on the US government to reconsider its policy* | [no obj.] *I beg you to reconsider.*
– DERIVATIVES **reconsideration** noun.

reconsign ▶ **verb** [with obj.] consign again or differently.
– DERIVATIVES **reconsignment** noun.

reconsolidate ▶ **verb** [with obj.] consolidate (something) again or anew.
– DERIVATIVES **reconsolidation** noun.

reconstitute ▶ **verb** [with obj.] build up again from parts; reconstruct.
■ change the form and organization of (an institution): *he reconstituted his cabinet.* ■ restore (something dried, especially food) to its original state by adding water to it: [as adj. **reconstituted**] *reconstituted milk.*
– DERIVATIVES **reconstitution** noun.

reconstruct ▶ **verb** [with obj.] build or form (something) again after it has been damaged or destroyed: *a small area of painted Roman plaster has been reconstructed.*
■ reorganize (something): *later emperors reconstructed the army.* ■ form an impression, model, or re-enactment of (a past event or thing) from the available evidence: *from copies of correspondence it is possible to reconstruct the broad sequence of events.*
– DERIVATIVES **reconstructable** (also **reconstructible**) adjective, **reconstructive** adjective, **reconstructor** noun.

reconstruction ▶ **noun** [mass noun] the action or process of reconstructing or being reconstructed: *the economic reconstruction of Russia* | [as modifier] *reconstruction work.*
■ [count noun] a thing that has been rebuilt after being damaged or destroyed: *comparison between the original and the reconstruction.* ■ [count noun] an impression, model, or re-enactment of a past event formed from the available evidence: *a reconstruction of the accident would be staged to try to discover the cause of the tragedy.* ■ (**the Reconstruction**) the period 1865–77 following the American Civil War, during which the Southern states of the Confederacy were controlled by federal government and social legislation, including the granting of new rights to black people, was introduced.

reconvene ▶ **verb** convene or cause to convene again, especially after a pause in proceedings: [no obj.] *parliament reconvenes on 1st June* | [with obj.] *it was agreed to reconvene the permanent commission.*

reconvert ▶ **verb** [with obj.] convert back to a former state.
– DERIVATIVES **reconversion** noun.

record ▶ **noun 1** a thing constituting a piece of evidence about the past, especially an account of an act or occurrence kept in writing or some other permanent form: *identification was made through dental records* | *a record of meter readings.*
■ (also **court record**) Law an official report of the proceedings and judgement in a court. ■ Computing a number of related items of information which are handled as a unit.
2 the sum of the past achievements or actions of a person or organization; a person or thing's previous conduct or performance: *the safety record at the airport is first class* | *the team preserved their unbeaten home record.*
■ short for **CRIMINAL RECORD**.
3 (especially in sport) the best performance or most remarkable event of its kind that has been officially measured and noted: *he held the world record for over a decade* | *he managed to beat the record* | [as modifier] *record profits.*
4 a thin plastic disc carrying recorded sound, especially music, in grooves on each surface, for reproduction by a record player.
■ a piece or collection of music reproduced on such a disc or on another medium, such as compact disc: *my favourite record* | [as modifier] *a record company.*
▶ **verb** [with obj.] **1** set down in writing or some other permanent form for later reference, especially officially: *they were asked to keep a diary and record everything they ate or drank* | [as adj. **recorded**] *levels of recorded crime.*
■ state or express publicly or officially; make an official record of: *the coroner recorded a verdict of accidental death.* ■ (of an instrument or observer) show or register (a measurement or result): *the temperature was the lowest recorded since 1926.* ■ achieve (a certain score or result): *they recorded their first win of the season.*
2 convert (sound or a broadcast) into permanent form for later reproduction: *they were recording a guitar recital.*
■ produce (a piece or collection of music or a programme) by such means: *they go into the studio next week to record their debut album.*
– PHRASES **for the record** so that the true facts are recorded or known: *for the record, I have never been to the flat.* **a matter of record** a thing that is established as a fact through being officially recorded. **off the record** not made as an official or attributable statement. **on record 1** (also **on the record**) used in reference to the making of an official or public statement: *I would like to* ***place on record*** *my sincere thanks.* **2** officially measured and noted: *it proved to be one of the warmest Decembers on record.* **3** recorded on tape and reproduced on a record or another sound medium: *the material works far better live than on record.* **put** (or **set**) **the record straight** give the true version of events that have been reported incorrectly; correct a misapprehension.
– DERIVATIVES **recordable** adjective.
– ORIGIN Middle English: from Old French *record* 'remembrance', from *recorder* 'bring to remembrance', from Latin *recordari* 'remember', based on *cor, cord-* 'heart'. The noun was earliest used in law to denote the fact of being written down as evidence. The verb originally meant 'narrate orally or in writing', also 'repeat so as to commit to memory'.

record-breaking ▶ **adjective** surpassing a record or best-ever achievement: *the fair attracted a record-breaking 10,678 visitors.*
– DERIVATIVES **record-breaker** noun.

recorded delivery ▶ **noun** Brit. a Post Office service in which the sender receives a certificate that a letter or parcel has been posted and the Post Office obtains a signature from the recipient as a record that it has been delivered.

recorder ▶ **noun 1** an apparatus for recording sound, pictures, or data, especially a tape recorder.
2 a person that keeps records: *a poet and recorder of rural and industrial life.*
3 (**Recorder**) (in England and Wales) a barrister appointed to serve as a part-time judge.
■ Brit. historical a judge in certain courts.
4 a simple woodwind instrument without keys, held vertically and played by blowing air through a shaped mouthpiece against a sharp edge.
– DERIVATIVES **recordership** noun (only in sense 3).
– ORIGIN late Middle English (denoting a kind of judge): from Anglo-Norman French *recordour*, from Old French *recorder* 'bring to remembrance'; partly reinforced by the verb **RECORD** (also used in the obsolete sense 'practise a tune': see sense 4).

recording angel ▶ **noun** an angel that is believed to register each person's good and bad actions.

recordist ▶ **noun** a person who makes recordings, especially of sound: *a sound recordist.*

record player ▶ **noun** an apparatus for reproducing sound from gramophone records, comprising a turntable that spins the record at a constant speed and a stylus that slides along in the groove and picks up the sound, together with an amplifier and a loudspeaker.

record type ▶ **noun** [mass noun] Printing a typeface including characters which reproduce the contractions or particular letter forms found in medieval manuscripts.

recount[1] /rɪˈkaʊnt/ ▶ **verb** [reporting verb] tell someone about something; give an account of an event or experience: [with obj.] *I recounted the tale to Steve* | [with clause] *he recounts how they often talked of politics.*
– ORIGIN late Middle English: from Old Northern French *reconter* 'tell again', based on Old French *counter* (see **COUNT**[1]).

recount[2] ▶ **verb** /riːˈkaʊnt/ [with obj.] count again.
▶ **noun** /ˈriːkaʊnt/ an act of counting something again, especially votes in an election.

recoup ▶ **verb** [with obj.] regain (something lost): *rains have helped recoup water levels.*
■ regain (money spent or lost), especially through subsequent profits: *oil companies are keen to recoup their investment.* ■ reimburse or compensate (someone) for money spent or lost. ■ Law deduct or keep back (part of a sum due). ■ regain (lost physical or mental resources): *sleep was what she needed to recoup her strength* | [no obj.] *he's just resting, recouping from the trial.*
– DERIVATIVES **recoupable** adjective, **recoupment** noun.
– ORIGIN early 17th cent. (as a legal term): from French *recouper* 'retrench, cut back', from *re-* 'back' + *couper* 'to cut'.

recourse ▶ **noun** [in sing.] a source of help in a difficult situation: *surgery may be the only recourse.*
■ [mass noun] (**recourse to**) the use of someone or something as a source of help in a difficult situation: *a means of solving disputes* ***without recourse to*** *courts of law* | *all three countries* ***had recourse to*** *the IMF for standby loans.* ■ [mass noun] the legal right to demand compensation or payment: *the bank* ***has recourse against*** *the exporter for losses incurred.*
– PHRASES **without recourse** Finance a formula used to disclaim responsibility for future non-payment, especially of a negotiable financial instrument.
– ORIGIN late Middle English (also in the sense 'running or flowing back'): from Old French *recours*, from Latin *recursus*, from *re-* 'back, again' + *cursus* 'course, running'.

recover ▶ **verb 1** [no obj.] return to a normal state of health, mind, or strength: *Neil is still* ***recovering from*** *shock* | *the economy has begun to recover.*
■ (**be recovered**) (of a person) be well again: *you'll be fully recovered before you know it.*
2 [with obj.] find or regain possession of (something stolen or lost): *police recovered a stolen video.*
■ regain control of (oneself or of a physical or mental state): *he recovered his balance and sped on* | *one hour later I had recovered consciousness.* ■ regain or secure (compensation) by means of a legal process or subsequent profits: *many companies recovered their costs within six months.* ■ make up for (a loss in position or time): *the French recovered the lead.* ■ remove or extract (an energy source or industrial chemical) for use, reuse, or waste treatment.
▶ **noun** (**the recover**) a defined position of a firearm forming part of a military drill: *bring the firelock* ***to the recover.***
– DERIVATIVES **recoverer** noun.
– ORIGIN Middle English (originally with reference to health): from Anglo-Norman French *recoverer*, from Latin *recuperare* 'get again'.

re-cover ▶ **verb** [with obj.] put a new cover or covering on: *the cost of re-covering the armchair.*

recoverable ▶ **adjective 1** (of something lost) able to be regained or retrieved.
■ (of compensation or money spent or lost) able to be regained or secured by means of a legal process or subsequent profits.
2 (of an energy source or a supply of it) able to be economically extracted from the ground or sea.
– DERIVATIVES **recoverability** noun.

recovery ▶ **noun** (pl. **-ies**) [mass noun] **1** a return to a

r

normal state of health, mind, or strength: *signs of recovery in the housing market* | [count noun] *it is hoped that Lawrence can **make a full recovery**.*
2 the action or process of regaining possession or control of something stolen or lost: *a team of salvage experts to ensure the recovery of family possessions* | *the recovery of his sight.*
■ the action of regaining or securing compensation or money lost or spent by means of a legal process or subsequent profits: *debt recovery.* ■ [count noun] an object or amount of money recovered: *the recoveries included gold jewellery.* ■ [usu. as modifier] the action of taking a vehicle or aircraft that has broken down or crashed to a place for repair: *a recovery vehicle.* ■ the process of removing or extracting an energy source or industrial chemical for use, reuse, or waste treatment. ■ (also **recovery shot**) [count noun] Golf a stroke bringing the ball from the rough or from a hazard back on to the fairway or the green. ■ [count noun] American Football an act of regaining a dropped ball. ■ (in rowing, cycling, or swimming) the action of returning the paddle, leg, or arm to its initial position ready to make a new stroke.
– PHRASES **in recovery** recovering from mental illness or drug addiction.
– ORIGIN late Middle English (denoting a means of restoration): from Anglo-Norman French *recoverie*, from *recovrer* 'get back'.

recovery position ▶ **noun** Brit. a position used in first aid to prevent choking in unconscious patients, in which the body is placed facing downwards and slightly to the side, supported by the bent limbs. Also called **SEMI-PRONE POSITION**.

recovery stock ▶ **noun** Finance a share that has fallen in price but is thought to have the potential of climbing back to its original level.

recovery time ▶ **noun** the time required for a material or piece of equipment to resume its former or usual condition following an action, such as the passage of a current through electrical equipment.

recreant /ˈrɛkrɪənt/ archaic ▶ **adjective** **1** cowardly: *what a recreant figure must he make.*
2 unfaithful to a belief; apostate.
▶ **noun** **1** a coward.
2 a person who is unfaithful to a belief; an apostate.
– DERIVATIVES **recreancy** noun, **recreantly** adverb.
– ORIGIN Middle English: from Old French, literally 'surrendering', present participle of *recroire*, from medieval Latin (*se*) *recredere* 'surrender (oneself)', from *re-* (expressing reversal) + *credere* 'entrust'.

recreate ▶ **verb** [with obj.] create again: *the door was now open to recreate a single German state.*
■ reproduce; re-enact: *he recreated Mallory's 1942 climb for TV.*

recreation[1] /ˌrɛkrɪˈeɪʃ(ə)n/ ▶ **noun** [mass noun] activity done for enjoyment when one is not working: *she rides for recreation* | [as modifier] *sport and recreation facilities* | [count noun] *his recreations included golf and rugby.*
– ORIGIN late Middle English (also in the sense 'mental or spiritual consolation'): via Old French from Latin *recreatio(n-)*, from *recreare* 'create again, renew'.

recreation[2] /ˌriːkrɪˈeɪʃ(ə)n/ ▶ **noun** [mass noun] the action or process of creating something again: *the periodic destruction and recreation of the universe.*
■ [count noun] a re-enactment or simulation of something.
– ORIGIN early 16th cent.: from **RE-** 'again' + **CREATION**.

recreational ▶ **adjective** relating to or denoting activity done for enjoyment when one is not working: *money to provide recreational facilities* | *recreational cycling in the countryside.*
■ relating to or denoting drugs taken on an occasional basis for enjoyment, especially when socializing: *recreational drug use.*
– DERIVATIVES **recreationally** adverb.

recreation ground ▶ **noun** Brit. a piece of public land used for sports and games.

recreation room ▶ **noun** a room in an institution or place of work in which people can relax and play games.
■ N. Amer. another term for **REC ROOM**.

recreative /ˈrɛkrɪˌeɪtɪv, ˌriːkrɪˈeɪtɪv/ ▶ **adjective** another term for **RECREATIONAL**.

recriminate /rɪˈkrɪmɪneɪt/ ▶ **verb** [no obj.] archaic make counter accusations: *his party would never recriminate, never return evil for evil.*
– ORIGIN early 17th cent.: from medieval Latin *recriminat-* 'accused in return', from the verb *recriminari*, from *re-* (expressing opposition) + *criminare* 'accuse' (from *crimen* 'crime').

recrimination ▶ **noun** (usu. **recriminations**) an accusation in response to one from someone else: *there are no tears, no recriminations* | [mass noun] *there was a period of bitter recrimination.*

recriminative ▶ **adjective** archaic term for **RECRIMINATORY**.

recriminatory ▶ **adjective** involving or of the nature of mutual or counter accusations.

rec room ▶ **noun** N. Amer. a room in a private house, especially in the basement, used for recreation and entertainment.

recross ▶ **verb** [with obj.] cross or pass over again.

recrudesce /ˌriːkruːˈdɛs, ˌrɛk-/ ▶ **verb** [no obj.] formal break out again; recur.
– DERIVATIVES **recrudescence** noun, **recrudescent** adjective.
– ORIGIN late 19th cent.: back-formation from *recrudescence* 'recurrence', from Latin *recrudescere* 'become raw again', from *re-* 'again' + *crudus* 'raw'.

recruit ▶ **verb** [with obj.] enlist (someone) in the armed forces: *we recruit our toughest soldiers from the desert tribes* | [no obj.] *the regiment was still actively recruiting.*
■ form (an army or other force) by enlisting new people. ■ enrol (someone) as a member or worker in an organization or as a supporter of a cause: *there are plans to recruit more staff later this year.* ■ [with obj. and infinitive] informal persuade (someone) to do or assist in doing something: *she recruited her children to help run the racket.*
▶ **noun** a person newly enlisted in the armed forces and not yet fully trained.
■ a new member or supporter of an organization or cause.
– DERIVATIVES **recruitable** adjective, **recruiter** noun.
– ORIGIN mid 17th cent. (in the senses 'fresh body of troops' and 'supplement the numbers in (a group)'): from obsolete French dialect *recrute*, based on Latin *recrescere* 'grow again', from *re-* 'again' + *crescere* 'grow'.

recruitment ▶ **noun** [mass noun] the action of enlisting new people in the armed forces.
■ the action of finding new people to join an organization or support a cause: *the recruitment of nurses.* ■ Ecology the increase in a natural population as progeny grow and immigrants arrive. ■ Physiology the incorporation into a tissue or region of cells from elsewhere in the body.

recrystallize (also **-ise**) ▶ **verb** form or cause to form crystals again.
– DERIVATIVES **recrystallization** noun.

recta plural form of **RECTUM**.

rectal ▶ **adjective** [attrib.] of, relating to, or affecting the rectum: *rectal cancer.*
– DERIVATIVES **rectally** adverb.

rectangle ▶ **noun** a plane figure with four straight sides and four right angles, especially one with unequal adjacent sides, in contrast to a square.
– ORIGIN late 16th cent.: from medieval Latin *rectangulum*, from late Latin *rectiangulum*, based on Latin *rectus* 'straight' + *angulus* 'an angle'.

rectangular ▶ **adjective** **1** denoting or shaped like a rectangle: *a neat rectangular area.*
■ (of a solid) having a base, section, or side shaped like a rectangle: *a rectangular prism.*
2 placed or having parts placed at right angles.
– DERIVATIVES **rectangularity** noun, **rectangularly** adverb.

rectangular coordinates ▶ **plural noun** a pair of coordinates measured along axes at right angles to one another.

rectangular hyperbola ▶ **noun** a hyperbola with rectangular asymptotes.

recti plural form of **RECTUS**.

rectified spirit ▶ **noun** [mass noun] (also **rectified spirits**) a mixture of ethanol (95.6 per cent) and water produced as an azeotrope by distillation.

rectifier ▶ **noun** an electrical device which converts an alternating current into a direct one by allowing a current to flow through it in one direction only.

rectify ▶ **verb** (**-ies, -ied**) [with obj.] **1** put (something) right; correct: *mistakes made now cannot be rectified later* | *efforts to rectify the situation.*
2 convert (alternating current) to direct current: [as adj. **rectified**] *rectified AC power systems.*
3 find a straight line equal in length to (a curve).
– DERIVATIVES **rectifiable** adjective, **rectification** noun.
– ORIGIN late Middle English: from Old French *rectifier*, from medieval Latin *rectificare*, from Latin *rectus* 'right'.

rectilinear /ˌrɛktɪˈlɪnɪə/ (also **rectilineal** /-nɪəl/) ▶ **adjective** contained by, consisting of, or moving in a straight line or lines: *a rectilinear waveform.*
■ Photography of or relating to a straight line or lines: *rectilinear distortion.* ■ Photography (of a wide-angle lens) corrected as much as possible, so that straight lines in the subject appear straight in the image.
– DERIVATIVES **rectilinearity** noun, **rectilinearly** adverb.
– ORIGIN mid 17th cent.: from late Latin *rectilineus* (from Latin *rectus* 'straight' + *linea* 'line') + **-AR**[1].

rectitude ▶ **noun** [mass noun] formal morally correct behaviour or thinking; righteousness: *Mattie is a model of rectitude.*
– ORIGIN late Middle English (denoting straightness): from Old French, from late Latin *rectitudo*, from Latin *rectus* 'right, straight'.

recto ▶ **noun** (pl. **-os**) a right-hand page of an open book, or the front of a loose document. Contrasted with **VERSO**.
– ORIGIN early 19th cent.: from Latin *recto (folio)* 'on the right (leaf)'.

rectocele /ˌrɛktə(ʊ)ˈsiːl/ ▶ **noun** Medicine a prolapse of the wall between the rectum and the vagina.
– ORIGIN mid 19th cent.: from **RECTUM** + **-CELE**.

rector ▶ **noun** **1** (in the Church of England) the incumbent of a parish where all tithes formerly passed to the incumbent. Compare with **VICAR**.
■ (in other Anglican Churches) a member of the clergy who has charge of a parish. ■ (in the Roman Catholic Church) a priest in charge of a church or of a religious institution.
2 the head of certain universities, colleges, and schools.
■ (in Scotland) an elected representative of students on a university's governing body.
– DERIVATIVES **rectorate** noun, **rectorial** adjective, **rectorship** noun.
– ORIGIN late Middle English: from Latin *rector* 'ruler', from *rect-* 'ruled', from the verb *regere*.

rectory ▶ **noun** (pl. **-ies**) a rector's house.
■ a Church of England benefice held by a rector.
– ORIGIN mid 16th cent.: from Old French *rectorie* or medieval Latin *rectoria*, from Latin *rector* (see **RECTOR**).

rectrices /ˈrɛktrɪsiːz/ ▶ **plural noun** (sing. **rectrix** /-trɪx/) Ornithology the larger feathers in a bird's tail, used for steering in flight. Compare with **REMIGES**.
– ORIGIN mid 18th cent.: from Latin, feminine plural of *rector* 'ruler, governor' (see **RECTOR**).

rectum ▶ **noun** (pl. **rectums** or **recta** /-tə/) the final section of the large intestine, terminating at the anus.
– ORIGIN mid 16th cent.: from Latin *rectum* (*intestinum*) 'straight (intestine)'.

rectus /ˈrɛktəs/ ▶ **noun** (pl. **recti** /-tʌɪ/) Anatomy any of several straight muscles, in particular:
■ (also **rectus abdominis** /abˈdɒmɪnɪs/) each of a pair of long flat muscles at the front of the abdomen, joining the sternum to the pubis and acting to bend the whole body forwards or sideways. ■ any of a number of muscles controlling the movement of the eyeball.
– ORIGIN early 18th cent.: from Latin, literally 'straight'.

reculer pour mieux sauter /rəˌkjuːleɪ pʊə mjəːˈsəʊteɪ, French rəkyle puʀ mjø sote/ ▶ used in reference to the use of a tactical withdrawal, or of an apparent setback, as a basis for further advance or success.
– ORIGIN French, literally 'draw back in order to make a better jump'.

recumbent /rɪˈkʌmb(ə)nt/ ▶ **adjective** (especially of a person or effigy) lying down: *recumbent statues.*
■ (of a plant) growing close to the ground: *recumbent shrubs.*
▶ **noun** a type of bicycle designed to be ridden lying almost flat on one's back.
– DERIVATIVES **recumbency** noun, **recumbently** adverb.

– ORIGIN mid 17th cent.: from Latin *recumbent-* 'reclining', from the verb *recumbere*, from *re-* 'back' + a verb related to *cubare* 'to lie'.

recuperate /rɪˈkuːpəreɪt/ ▶ **verb 1** [no obj.] recover from illness or exertion: *she has been* **recuperating from** *a shoulder wound at a clinic | Christmas is a time to recuperate.*
2 [with obj.] recover or regain (something lost or taken).
– DERIVATIVES **recuperable** adjective.
– ORIGIN mid 16th cent.: from Latin *recuperat-* 'regained', from the verb *recuperare*, from *re-* 'back' + *capere* 'take'.

recuperation ▶ **noun** [mass noun] **1** recovery from illness or exertion: *the human body has amazing powers of recuperation.*
2 the recovery or regaining of something: *the recuperation of the avant-garde for art.*
■ the action of a recuperator in imparting heat to incoming air or gaseous fuel from hot waste gases.

recuperative ▶ **adjective 1** having the effect of restoring health or strength.
2 of or relating to the action of a recuperator or a similar heat exchanger.

recuperator ▶ **noun** a form of heat exchanger in which hot waste gases from a furnace are conducted continuously along a system of flues where they impart heat to incoming air or gaseous fuel.

recur ▶ **verb** (**recurred**, **recurring**) [no obj.] occur again, periodically, or repeatedly: *when the symptoms recurred, the doctor diagnosed something different* | [as adj. **recurring**] *a recurring theme.*
■ (of a thought, image, or memory) come back to one's mind: *Oglethorpe's words kept recurring to him.* ■ (**recur to**) go back to (something) in thought or speech: *the book remained a favourite and she constantly recurred to it.*
– DERIVATIVES **recurrence** noun.
– ORIGIN Middle English (in the sense 'return to'): from Latin *recurrere*, from *re-* 'again, back' + *currere* 'run'.

recurrent ▶ **adjective 1** occurring often or repeatedly, especially (of a disease or symptom) recurring after apparent cure or remission: *she had a recurrent dream about falling | recurrent fever.*
2 Anatomy (of a nerve or blood vessel) turning back so as to reverse direction.
– DERIVATIVES **recurrently** adverb.
– ORIGIN late 16th cent. (in sense 2): from Latin *recurrent-* 'running back', from the verb *recurrere* (see **RECUR**).

recurring decimal ▶ **noun** a decimal fraction in which a figure or group of figures is repeated indefinitely, as in *0.666 …* or as in *1.851851851 …*

recursion /rɪˈkəːʃ(ə)n/ ▶ **noun** [mass noun] Mathematics & Linguistics the repeated application of a recursive procedure or definition.
■ [count noun] a recursive definition.
– ORIGIN 1930s: from late Latin *recursio(n-)*, from *recurrere* 'run back' (see **RECUR**).

recursion formula ▶ **noun** Mathematics an equation relating the value of a function for a given value of its argument (or arguments) to its values for other values of the argument(s).

recursive ▶ **adjective** characterized by recurrence or repetition, in particular:
■ Mathematics & Linguistics relating to or involving the repeated application of a rule, definition, or procedure to successive results. ■ Computing relating to or involving a program or routine of which a part requires the application of the whole, so that its explicit interpretation requires in general many successive executions.
– DERIVATIVES **recursively** adverb.
– ORIGIN late 18th cent. (in the general sense): from late Latin *recurs-* 'returned' (from the verb *recurrere* 'run back') + **-IVE**. Specific uses have arisen in the 20th cent.

recurve ▶ **verb** [no obj.] chiefly Biology bend backwards: [as adj. **recurved**] *large recurved tusks.*
▶ **noun** Archery a bow that curves forward at the ends, which straighten out under tension when the bow is drawn.
– DERIVATIVES **recurvature** noun.
– ORIGIN late 16th cent.: from Latin *recurvare* 'bend (something) back', from *re-* 'back' + *curvare* 'to bend'.

recusant /ˈrɛkjʊz(ə)nt/ ▶ **noun** a person who refuses to submit to an authority or to comply with a regulation.
■ chiefly historical a person who refused to attend services of the Church of England.
▶ **adjective** of or denoting a recusant.
– DERIVATIVES **recusance** noun, **recusancy** noun.
– ORIGIN mid 16th cent.: from Latin *recusant-* 'refusing', from the verb *recusare* (see **RECUSE**).

recuse /rɪˈkjuːz/ ▶ **verb** (**recuse oneself**) chiefly N. Amer. & S. African (of a judge) excuse oneself from a case because of a possible conflict of interest or lack of impartiality.
– DERIVATIVES **recusal** noun.
– ORIGIN late Middle English (in the sense 'reject', specifically 'object to (a judge) as prejudiced'): from Latin *recusare* 'to refuse', from *re-* (expressing opposition) + *causa* 'a cause'. The current sense dates from the early 19th cent.

recyclable ▶ **adjective** able to be recycled.
▶ **noun** a substance or object that can be recycled.
– DERIVATIVES **recyclability** noun.

recycle ▶ **verb** [with obj.] convert (waste) into reusable material: *car hulks were recycled into new steel* | [as adj. **recycled**] *goods made of recycled materials* | [as noun **recycling**] *a call for the recycling of all paper.*
■ return (material) to a previous stage in a cyclic process. ■ use again: *he reserves the right to recycle his own text.*
– DERIVATIVES **recycler** noun.

red ▶ **adjective** (**redder**, **reddest**) **1** of a colour at the end of the spectrum next to orange and opposite violet, as of blood, fire, or rubies: *her red lips | the sky was turning red outside.*
■ (of a person or their face or complexion) flushed or rosy, especially with embarrassment, anger, or a healthy glow: *there were some red faces in headquarters | he* **went bright red**. ■ (of a person's eyes) bloodshot or having pink rims, especially with tiredness or crying: *her eyes were red and swollen.* ■ (of hair or fur) of a reddish-brown colour. ■ dated, offensive (of a people) having or regarded as having reddish skin. ■ of or denoting the suits hearts and diamonds in a pack of cards. ■ (of wine) made from dark grapes and coloured by their skins. ■ denoting a red light or flag used as a signal to stop. ■ used to denote something forbidden, dangerous, or urgent: *the force went on* **red alert**. ■ (of a ski run) of the second highest level of difficulty, as indicated by coloured markers on the run. ■ Physics denoting one of three colours of quark.
2 (**Red**) informal, chiefly derogatory communist or socialist (used especially during the cold war with reference to the Soviet Union): *the Red Menace.* Contrasted with **WHITE** (in sense 3).
3 stained or covered with blood: *the red hands and sharp knives of the fishermen.*
■ archaic or poetic/literary involving bloodshed or violence: *red battle stamps his foot and nations feel the shock.*
4 (also **red-blanket**) S. African (of a Xhosa) coming from a traditional tribal culture. Contrasted with **SCHOOL**. [ORIGIN: with reference to the ochred blankets traditionally worn by the Xhosa people.]
▶ **noun 1** [mass noun] red colour or pigment: *colours range from yellow to deep red | their work is marked* **in red** *by the teacher* | [count noun] *the reds and browns of wood.*
■ red clothes or material: *she could not wear red.*
2 a red thing or person, in particular:
■ [mass noun] a red wine. ■ a red ball in snooker or billiards. ■ a red light.
3 (also **Red**) informal, chiefly derogatory a communist or socialist.
4 (**the red**) the situation of owing money to a bank because one has spent more than is in one's account: *the company* **was** *£4 million* **in the red**. [ORIGIN: from the conventional use of *red* to indicate debt items.]
– PHRASES **better dead than red** (or **better red than dead**) a cold-war slogan claiming that the prospect of nuclear war is preferable to that of a communist society (or vice versa). (**as**) **red as a beetroot** (N. Amer. **beet**) (of a person) red-faced, typically through embarrassment. **red in tooth and claw** involving savage or merciless conflict or competition: *nature, red in tooth and claw.* [ORIGIN: from Tennyson's *In Memoriam*.] **the red planet** a name for Mars. (**like**) **a red rag to a bull** an object, utterance, or act which is certain to provoke someone: *the refusal to discuss the central issue was like a red rag to a bull.* **reds under the bed** used during the cold war with reference to the feared presence and influence of communist sympathizers in a society. **see red** informal become very angry suddenly: *the mere thought of Piers with Nicole made her see red.*
– DERIVATIVES **reddish** adjective, **reddy** adjective, **redly** adverb, **redness** noun.
– ORIGIN Old English *rēad*, of Germanic origin; related to Dutch *rood* and German *rot*, from an Indo-European root shared by Latin *rufus*, *ruber*, Greek *eruthros*, and Sanskrit *rudhira* 'red'.

red- ▶ **prefix** variant spelling of **RE-** before a vowel (as in *redolent*).

redact /rɪˈdakt/ ▶ **verb** [with obj.] rare edit (text) for publication.
– DERIVATIVES **redactor** noun.
– ORIGIN mid 19th cent.: back-formation from **REDACTION**.

redaction ▶ **noun** [mass noun] the process of editing text for publication.
■ [count noun] a version of a text, such as a new edition or an abridged version.
– DERIVATIVES **redactional** adjective.
– ORIGIN late 18th cent.: from French *rédaction*, from late Latin *redactio(n-)*, from *redigere* 'bring back'.

red admiral ▶ **noun** a migratory butterfly which has dark wings marked with red bands and white spots.
• Genus *Vanessa*, subfamily Nymphalinae, family Nymphalidae: several species, in particular *V. atalanta*.

red algae ▶ **noun** a large group of algae that includes many seaweeds that are mainly red in colour. Some kinds yield useful products (agar, alginates) or are used as food (laver, dulse, carrageen).
• Division Rhodophyta (or phylum Rhodophyta, kingdom Protista).

redan /rɪˈdan/ ▶ **noun** an arrow-shaped embankment forming part of a fortification.
– ORIGIN late 17th cent.: from French, from *redent* 'notching (of a saw)', from *re-* 'again' (expressing repetition) + *dent* 'tooth'.

Red Army the army of the Soviet Union, formed after the Revolution of 1917. The name was officially dropped in 1946.
■ the army of China or some other Communist countries.

Red Army Faction a left-wing terrorist group in former West Germany, active from 1968 onwards. It was originally led by Andreas Baader (1943–77) and Ulrike Meinhof (1934–76). Also called **BAADER-MEINHOF GROUP**.

red arsenic ▶ **noun** another term for **REALGAR**.

redback (also **redback spider**) ▶ **noun** a highly venomous Australasian spider which is black with a bright red stripe down the back, closely related to the American black widow.
• *Latrodectus mactans hasseltii*, family Theridiidae.

red-backed vole ▶ **noun** a vole with a reddish-chestnut back, inhabiting the forest, scrub, and tundra regions of the northern hemisphere.
• Genus *Clethrionomys*, family Muridae: several species.

red-bait ▶ **verb** [with obj.] [often as noun **red-baiting**] N. Amer. informal harass or persecute (someone) on account of known or suspected communist sympathies.
▶ **noun** S. African a large sea squirt which is a popular bait with sea anglers.
• *Pyura stolonifera*, class Ascidiaceae.
– DERIVATIVES **red-baiter** noun.

red beds ▶ **plural noun** Geology sandstones or other sedimentary strata coloured red by haematite coating the grains.

red biddy ▶ **noun** [mass noun] Brit. informal, dated a mixture of cheap wine and methylated spirits.

red blood cell ▶ **noun** less technical term for **ERYTHROCYTE**.

red-blooded ▶ **adjective** (of a man) vigorous or virile, especially in having strong heterosexual appetites: *he was attracted to her, as any red-blooded male would be.*
– DERIVATIVES **red-bloodedness** noun.

redbone ▶ **noun** a dog with a red or red and tan coat of an American breed formerly used to hunt raccoons.

red book ▶ **noun** the title given to any of various official books of economic or political significance.
– ORIGIN *red* being the conventional colour of the binding of official books.

red box ▶ **noun** Brit. a box, typically covered with red leather, used by a Minister of State to hold official documents.

redbreast ▶ **noun** informal, chiefly Brit. a robin.

red-brick ▶ adjective built with red bricks.
■ (of a British university) founded in the late 19th or early 20th century.

Red Brigades an extreme left-wing terrorist organization based in Italy, which from the early 1970s was responsible for carrying out kidnappings, murders, and acts of sabotage.

redbud ▶ noun a North American tree of the pea family, with pink flowers that grow from the trunk, branches, and twigs.
● Genus *Cercis*, family Leguminosae.

redcap ▶ noun **1** Brit. informal a member of the military police.
2 N. Amer. a railway porter.

red card ▶ noun (in soccer and some other games) a red card shown by the referee to a player who is being sent off the field. Compare with **YELLOW CARD**.
▶ verb (**red-card**) [with obj.] (often **be red-carded**) (of a referee) send (a player) off the field by showing a red card.

red carpet ▶ noun a long, narrow red carpet laid on the ground for a distinguished visitor to walk along when arriving.
■ (**the red carpet**) used in reference to privileged treatment of a distinguished visitor: *they rolled out the red carpet for two special guests.*

red cedar ▶ noun either of two North American coniferous trees with reddish-brown bark:
● Two species in the family Cupressaceae: the **western red cedar** (*Thuja plicata*), which yields strong, lightweight timber and is cultivated in Europe, and the **eastern red cedar** (*Juniperus virginiana*), found chiefly in the eastern US.

red cell ▶ noun less technical term for **ERYTHROCYTE**.

red cent ▶ noun N. Amer. a one-cent coin.
■ [usu. with negative] the smallest amount of money: *some of the people don't deserve a single red cent.*
– ORIGIN early 19th cent.: so named because it was formerly made of copper.

red channel ▶ noun (at a customs area in an airport or port) the passage which should be taken by arriving passengers who have goods to declare.

redcoat ▶ noun **1** historical a British soldier.
2 (in the UK) an organizer and entertainer at a Butlin's holiday camp.
– ORIGIN early 16th cent. (in sense 1): so named because of the colour of the uniform. Sense 2 dates from the 1950s.

red coral (also **precious coral**) ▶ noun a branching pinkish-red horny coral which is used in jewellery.
● Genus *Corallium*, order Gorgonacea, class Anthozoa.

Red Crescent a national branch in Muslim countries of the International Movement of the Red Cross and the Red Crescent.

Red Cross the International Movement of the Red Cross and the Red Crescent, an international humanitarian organization bringing relief to victims of war or natural disaster. The Red Cross was set up in 1864 at the instigation of the Swiss philanthropist Henri Dunant (1828–1910) according to the Geneva Convention, and its headquarters are at Geneva.

redcurrant ▶ noun **1** a small, sweet red berry, chiefly used to make a jelly eaten as an accompaniment to turkey and other meats.
2 the shrub which produces this fruit, related to the blackcurrant.
● *Ribes rubrum*, family Grossulariaceae.

redd[1] ▶ verb (past and past participle **redd**) [with obj.] (**redd something up**) Scottish & Irish put something in order; tidy: *you take this baby while I redd the room up.*
– ORIGIN late Middle English (in the sense 'clear (space)'): perhaps related to **RID**.

redd[2] ▶ noun a hollow in a river bed made by a trout or salmon to spawn in.
– ORIGIN mid 17th cent. (originally Scots and northern English in the sense 'spawn'): of unknown origin.

red deer ▶ noun a deer with a rich red-brown summer coat that turns dull brownish-grey in winter, the male having large branched antlers. It is native to North America, Eurasia, and North Africa.
● *Cervus elaphus*, family Cervidae. Compare with **WAPITI**.

Red Delicious ▶ noun a widely grown dessert apple of a soft-fleshed red-skinned variety.

redden ▶ verb make or become red: [with obj.] *bare*

arms reddened by sun and wind | [no obj.] *the sky is reddening.*
■ [no obj.] (of a person) blush: *Lyn reddened at the description of herself.* ■ [no obj.] (of the eyes) become pink at the rims as a result of crying.

Redding, Otis (1941–67), American soul singer. 'Dock of the Bay', released after Redding's death in an air crash, became a number-one US hit in 1968.

Redditch an industrial town in west central England, in Worcestershire; pop. 76,900 (1991).

reddle ▶ noun [mass noun] a red pigment consisting of ochre.
– ORIGIN early 18th cent.: variant of **RUDDLE**.

red dog ▶ noun another term for **DHOLE**.

red duster ▶ noun Brit. informal term for **RED ENSIGN**.

red dwarf ▶ noun Astronomy a small, old, relatively cool star.

rede /riːd/ archaic ▶ noun [mass noun] advice or counsel given by one person to another: *what is your rede?*
▶ verb [with obj.] **1** advise (someone): [with obj. and infinitive] *therefore, my son, I rede thee stay at home.*
2 interpret (a riddle or dream).
– ORIGIN Old English *rǣd*, of Germanic origin; related to Dutch *raad*, German *Rat*. The verb is a variant of **READ**, of the same origin.

redecorate ▶ verb [with obj.] apply paint or wallpaper in (a room or building) again, typically differently.
– DERIVATIVES **redecoration** noun.

rededicate ▶ verb [with obj.] dedicate again: *the temple was rededicated as a Christian Church.*
– DERIVATIVES **rededication** noun.

redeem ▶ verb [with obj.] **1** compensate for the faults or bad aspects of (something): *a disappointing debate redeemed only by an outstanding speech* | [as adj. **redeeming**] *the splendid views are the one redeeming feature of the centre.*
■ (**redeem oneself**) do something that compensates for poor past performance or behaviour: *Australia redeemed themselves by dismissing India for 153.* ■ (of a person) atone or make amends for (error or evil): *the thief on the cross who by a single act redeemed a life of evil.* ■ save (someone) from sin, error, or evil: *he was a sinner, redeemed by the grace of God.*
2 gain or regain possession of (something) in exchange for payment: *his best suit had been redeemed from the pawnbrokers* | *statutes enabled state peasants to redeem their land.*
■ Finance repay (a stock, bond, or other instrument) at the maturity date. ■ exchange (a coupon, voucher, or trading stamp) for goods, a discount, or money. ■ pay the necessary money to clear (a debt): *owners were unable to redeem their mortgages.* ■ fulfil or carry out (a pledge or promise): *the party prepared to redeem the pledges of the past three years.* ■ archaic buy the freedom of.
– DERIVATIVES **redeemable** adjective.
– ORIGIN late Middle English (in the sense 'buy back'): from Old French *redimer* or Latin *redimere*, from *re-* 'back' + *emere* 'buy'.

redeemer ▶ noun a person who redeems someone or something.
■ (often **the Redeemer**) Christ.

redefine ▶ verb [with obj.] define again or differently: *the role of the Emperor was redefined.*
– DERIVATIVES **redefinition** noun.

redemption ▶ noun [mass noun] **1** the action of saving or being saved from sin, error, or evil: *God's plans for the redemption of his world.*
■ [in sing.] figurative a thing that saves someone from error or evil: *his marginalization from the Hollywood jungle proved to be his redemption.*
2 the action of regaining or gaining possession of something in exchange for payment, or clearing a debt.
■ archaic the action of buying one's freedom.
– PHRASES **beyond** (or **past**) **redemption** (of a person or thing) too bad to be improved or saved.
– ORIGIN late Middle English: from Old French, from Latin *redemptio(n-)*, from *redimere* 'buy back' (see **REDEEM**).

redemption yield ▶ noun Finance the yield of a stock calculated as a percentage of the redemption price with an adjustment made for any capital gain or loss which that price represents relative to the current price.

redemptive ▶ adjective acting to save someone from error or evil: *the healing power of redemptive love.*

red ensign ▶ noun a red flag with the Union Jack in the top corner next to the flagstaff, flown by British-registered ships.

redeploy ▶ verb [with obj.] assign (troops, employees, or resources) to a new place or task: *units concentrated in Buenos Aires would be redeployed to the provinces.*
– DERIVATIVES **redeployment** noun.

redesign ▶ verb [with obj.] design (something) again in a different way: *the front seats have been redesigned.*
▶ noun [mass noun] the action or process of redesigning something.

redetermine ▶ verb [with obj.] determine (something) again or differently.
– DERIVATIVES **redetermination** noun.

redevelop ▶ verb [with obj.] develop (something) again or differently.
■ construct new buildings in (an urban area), typically after demolishing the existing buildings: *plans to redevelop London's docklands.*
– DERIVATIVES **redeveloper** noun, **redevelopment** noun.

red-eye ▶ noun **1** [mass noun] the undesirable effect in flash photography of people appearing to have red eyes, caused by a reflection from the retina when the flash gun is too near the camera lens.
■ (also **red-eye flight**) [in sing.] informal, chiefly N. Amer. a flight on which a passenger cannot expect to get much sleep on account of the time of departure or arrival: *she caught the red-eye back to New York.*
2 a freshwater fish with red eyes, in particular:
■ Brit. a rudd. ■ US a rock bass.
3 [mass noun] US informal cheap whisky.
■ Canadian a drink made from tomato juice and beer.

red-eye gravy ▶ noun [mass noun] US gravy made by adding liquid to the fat from cooked ham.

red-faced ▶ adjective (of a person) having a red face, especially as a result of exertion, embarrassment, or shame: *Steve was left red-faced when a fan tried to rip his trousers off.*

red-figure ▶ noun [usu. as modifier] a type of ancient Greek pottery, originating in Athens in the late 6th century BC, in which figures are outlined and details added in black, and the background is then filled in with black to leave the figures in the red colour of the clay: *a red-figure vase.* Compare with **BLACK-FIGURE**.

redfish ▶ noun (pl. same or **-fishes**) **1** a bright red edible marine fish, in particular:
● a North Atlantic rockfish (genus *Sebastes*, family Scorpaenidae, in particular the commercially important *S. marinus*). ● the red drum of the western Atlantic, popular as a game fish (*Sciaenops ocellatus*, family Sciaenidae). ● a bottom-dwelling Australian fish (*Centroberyx affinis*, family Berycidae). Also called **NANNYGAI**.
2 Brit. a male salmon in the spawning season.

red fish ▶ noun [mass noun] fish with dark flesh, such as herring, mackerel, sardine, and pilchard. Compare with **WHITE FISH**.

red flag ▶ noun a red flag as the symbol of socialist revolution or a warning of danger.
■ (**the Red Flag**) the anthem of Britain's Labour Party, a socialist song with words written in 1889 by James Connell (1852–1929) and sung to the tune of the German song 'O Tannenbaum'.

red flannel hash ▶ noun [mass noun] US a type of hash made with beetroot.

Redford, (Charles) Robert (b.1936), American film actor and director. He made his name playing opposite Paul Newman in *Butch Cassidy and the Sundance Kid* (1969), co-starring again with him in *The Sting* (1973). Other notable films include *Ordinary People* (1980), for which he won an Oscar as director.

red fox ▶ noun a common fox with a reddish coat, native to both Eurasia and North America and living from the Arctic tundra to the centres of cities.
● *Vulpes vulpes*, family Canidae.

red giant ▶ noun Astronomy a very large star of high luminosity and low surface temperature. Red giants are thought to be in a late stage of evolution when no hydrogen remains in the core to fuel nuclear fusion.

red gold ▶ noun [mass noun] an alloy of gold and copper.

Redgrave[1] the name of a family of English actors, notably:
■ Sir Michael (Scudamore) (1908–85). A well-known

stage actor, he played numerous Shakespearean roles and also starred in films such as *The Browning Version* (1951) and *The Importance of Being Earnest* (1952).

■ **Vanessa** (b.1937), Sir Michael's eldest daughter. Her successful career in the theatre and cinema includes the films *Mary Queen of Scots* (1972), *Julia* (1976), for which she won an Oscar, and *Howard's End* (1992).

Redgrave[2], Sir Steven (Geoffrey) (b.1962), English rower. He won five consecutive Olympic gold medals between 1984 and 2000.

red–green ▶ adjective [attrib.] denoting colour blindness in which reds and greens are confused, either protanopia (daltonism) or deuteranopia.

red grouse ▶ noun a bird of a race of the willow grouse having entirely reddish-brown plumage, native only to the British Isles and familiar as a moorland game bird.
● *Lagopus lagopus scoticus*, family Phasianidae (or Tetraonidae).

Red Guard ▶ noun any of various radical or socialist groups, in particular an organized detachment of workers during the Russian Revolution of 1917 and a militant youth movement in China (1966–76) which carried out attacks on intellectuals and other disfavoured groups as part of Mao Zedong's Cultural Revolution.
■ a member of one of these groups.

red gum ▶ noun an Australian gum tree with smooth bark and hard dark red timber.
● Genera *Eucalyptus* (and *Angophora*), family Myrtaceae: many species, in particular the widespread **river red gum** (*E. camaldulensis*).
■ [mass noun] astringent reddish kino gum obtained from some of these trees, used for medicinal purposes and for tanning.

red hand ▶ noun the arms or badge of Ulster, a red left hand cut off squarely at the wrist. Also called **BLOODY HAND**.

red-handed ▶ adjective used to indicate that a person has been discovered in or just after the act of doing something wrong or illegal: *I caught him red-handed, stealing a wallet.*

red hat ▶ noun a cardinal's hat, especially as the symbol of a cardinal's office.

redhead ▶ noun 1 a person with reddish hair.
2 a North American diving duck with a reddish-brown head, related to the pochard.
● *Aythya americana*, family Anatidae.

red-headed ▶ adjective [attrib.] (of a person) having reddish-brown hair: *a red-headed man.*
■ used in names of birds, insects, and other animals with red heads, e.g. **red-headed woodpecker**.

red heat ▶ noun [mass noun] the temperature or state of something so hot that it emits red light.

red herring ▶ noun 1 a dried smoked herring, which is turned red by the smoke.
2 something, especially a clue, which is or is intended to be misleading or distracting: *the book is fast-paced, exciting, and full of red herrings.* [ORIGIN: so named from the practice of using the scent of red herring in training hounds.]

red-hot ▶ adjective 1 (of a substance) so hot as to glow red: *red-hot coals.*
■ very hot, especially too hot to touch.
2 extremely exciting or popular: *red-hot jazz.*
■ very passionate: *a red-hot lover.* ■ (of a favourite in a race or other contest) most strongly expected to win: *Ipswich Town are red-hot favourites for the championship.*

red-hot poker ▶ noun a South African plant with tall erect spikes of tubular flowers, the upper ones of which are typically red and the lower ones yellow.
● *Kniphofia uvaria*, family Liliaceae: many cultivars.

redial ▶ verb (**redialled**, **redialling**; US **redialed**, **redialing**) [with obj.] dial (a telephone number) again.
▶ noun (also **last number redial**) the facility on a telephone by which the number just dialled may be automatically redialled by pressing a single button.

redid past of **REDO**.

rediffusion ▶ noun [mass noun] Brit. the relaying of broadcast programmes, especially by cable from a central receiver.

Red Indian ▶ noun old-fashioned term for **AMERICAN INDIAN**.

USAGE The term **Red Indian**, first recorded in the early 19th century, has largely fallen out of use, associated as it is with an earlier period and the corresponding stereotypes of cowboys and Indians and the Wild West. If used today, the term may cause offence: the normal terms in use today are **American Indian** and **Native American** or, if appropriate, the name of the specific people (**Cherokee**, **Iroquois**, and so on).

redingote /ˈrɛdɪŋɡəʊt/ ▶ noun a woman's long coat with a cutaway or contrasting front.
– ORIGIN late 18th cent.: French, from English *riding coat*.

red ink ▶ noun [mass noun] chiefly N. Amer. used in reference to financial deficit or debt: *he voted for many of the projects that have left the state awash in red ink.*

redintegrate /rɛˈdɪntɪɡreɪt/ ▶ verb [with obj.] archaic restore (something) to a state of wholeness, unity, or perfection.
– DERIVATIVES **redintegration** noun, **redintegrative** adjective.
– ORIGIN late Middle English: from Latin *redintegrat-* 'made whole', from the verb *redintegrare*, from *re(d)-* 'again' + *integrare* 'restore'.

redirect ▶ verb [with obj.] direct (something) to a new or different place or purpose: *get the post office to redirect your mail* | *resources were redirected to a major project.*
– DERIVATIVES **redirection** noun.

rediscount Finance ▶ verb [with obj.] (of a central bank) discount (a bill of exchange or similar instrument) that has already been discounted by a commercial bank.
▶ noun [mass noun] the action of rediscounting something.

rediscover ▶ verb [with obj.] discover (something forgotten or ignored) again: *he was trying to rediscover his Gaelic roots.*
– DERIVATIVES **rediscovery** noun (pl. **-ies**).

redissolve ▶ verb dissolve or cause to dissolve again.
– DERIVATIVES **redissolution** noun.

redistribute ▶ verb [with obj.] distribute (something) differently or again, typically to achieve greater social equality: *their primary concern was to redistribute income from rich to poor.*
– DERIVATIVES **redistribution** noun, **redistributive** adjective.

redistributionist ▶ noun a person who advocates the redistribution of wealth.
▶ adjective of or relating to the belief that wealth should be redistributed: *redistributionist measures.*
– DERIVATIVES **redistributionism** noun.

redivide ▶ verb [with obj.] divide (something) again or differently.
– DERIVATIVES **redivision** noun.

redivivus /ˌrɛdɪˈviːvəs/ ▶ adjective [postpositive] poetic/literary come back to life; reborn: *one is tempted to think of Poussin as a sort of Titian redivivus.*
– ORIGIN late 16th cent.: from Latin, from *re(d)-* 'again' + *vivus* 'living'.

red kangaroo ▶ noun a large kangaroo of Australian grasslands, the male of which has a russet-red coat and the female (also called **BLUE FLYER**) typically a blue-grey coat.
● *Macropus rufus*, family Macropodidae.

red kite ▶ noun a bird of prey with reddish-brown plumage and a forked tail, found chiefly in Europe.
● *Milvus milvus*, family Accipitridae.

red lead ▶ noun [mass noun] a red form of lead oxide used as a pigment.

Red Leicester ▶ noun see **LEICESTER**[3].

red-letter day ▶ noun a day that is pleasantly noteworthy or memorable.
– ORIGIN early 18th cent.: from the practice of highlighting a festival in red on a calendar.

red light ▶ noun a red traffic light or similar signal that instructs moving vehicles to stop.

red-light district ▶ noun an area of a town or city containing many brothels, strip clubs, and other sex businesses.
– ORIGIN from the use of a red light as the sign of a brothel.

redline US informal ▶ verb [with obj.] 1 drive with (a car engine) at or above its rated maximum rpm: *both his engines were redlined now.*

---

2 refuse (a loan or insurance) to someone because they live in an area deemed to be a poor financial risk.
■ cancel (a project).
▶ noun the maximum number of revolutions per minute for a car engine.
– ORIGIN from the use of *red* as a limit marker, in sense 2 a limit marked out by ringing a section of a map.

red man ▶ noun offensive American Indian.

red meat ▶ noun [mass noun] meat that is red when raw, for example beef or lamb. Often contrasted with **WHITE MEAT**.

Redmond, John (Edward) (1856–1918), Irish politician, leader of the Irish Nationalist Party in the House of Commons 1891–1918. The Home Rule Bill of 1912 was introduced with his support, although it was never implemented because of the First World War.

red mullet ▶ noun an elongated fish with long barbels on the chin, living in warmer seas and widely valued as a food fish.
● Family Mullidae: several genera and many species, in particular *Mullus surmuletus* of the Mediterranean and East Atlantic.

redneck ▶ noun N. Amer. derogatory, informal a working-class white person from the southern US, especially a politically reactionary one: [as modifier] *redneck towns.*
– DERIVATIVES **rednecked** adjective.

redo ▶ verb (**redoes**; past **redid**; past participle **redone**) [with obj.] do (something) again or differently: *a whole day's work has to be redone.*
■ redecorate (a room or building): *the house is being redone exactly to suit his taste.*
▶ noun a redecoration of a room or building.

redolent /ˈrɛd(ə)l(ə)nt/ ▶ adjective 1 [predic.] (**redolent of/with**) strongly reminiscent or suggestive of (something): *names redolent of history and tradition.*
■ poetic/literary strongly smelling of (something): *the church was old, dark, and redolent of incense.*
2 archaic or poetic/literary fragrant or sweet-smelling: *a rich, inky, redolent wine.*
– DERIVATIVES **redolence** noun, **redolently** adverb.
– ORIGIN late Middle English (in the sense 'fragrant'): from Old French, or from Latin *redolent-* 'giving out a strong smell', from *re(d)-* 'back, again' + *olere* 'to smell'.

Redon /rəˈdɒ̃, French ʁədɔ̃/, Odilon (1840–1916), French painter and graphic artist. He was a leading exponent of symbolism and forerunner of surrealism, especially in his early charcoal drawings of fantastic or nightmarish subjects.

redouble ▶ verb [with obj.] make much greater, more intense, or more numerous: *we will redouble our efforts to reform agricultural policy.*
■ [no obj.] become greater or more intense or numerous: *pressure to solve the problem has redoubled.* ■ [no obj.] Bridge double a bid already doubled by an opponent.
▶ noun Bridge a call that doubles a bid already doubled by an opponent.
– ORIGIN late Middle English: from French *redoubler*, from *re-* 'again' + *doubler* 'to double'. The noun dates from the early 20th cent.

redoubt ▶ noun Military a temporary or supplementary fortification, typically square or polygonal and without flanking defences.
– ORIGIN early 17th cent.: from French *redoute*, from obsolete Italian *ridotta* and medieval Latin *reductus* 'refuge', from Latin *reducere* 'withdraw'. The *-b-* was added by association with **DOUBT**.

redoubtable ▶ adjective often humorous (of a person) formidable, especially as an opponent: *he was a redoubtable debater* | *the redoubtable ladies.*
– DERIVATIVES **redoubtably** adverb.
– ORIGIN late Middle English: from Old French *redoutable*, from *redouter* 'to fear', from *re-* (expressing intensive force) + *douter* 'to doubt'.

redound /rɪˈdaʊnd/ ▶ verb [no obj.] 1 (**redound to**) formal contribute greatly to (a person's credit or honour): *his latest diplomatic effort will redound to his credit.*
2 (**redound upon**) archaic come back upon; rebound on: *may his sin redound upon his head!* [ORIGIN: probably by association with **REBOUND**[1].]
– ORIGIN late Middle English (in the sense 'surge up, overflow'): from Old French *redonder*, from Latin *redundare* 'surge', from *re(d)-* 'again' + *unda* 'a wave'.

red-out ▶ noun a reddening of the vision resulting

---

from congestion of blood in the eyes when the body is accelerated downwards, sometimes followed by loss of consciousness.

redox /ˈriːdɒks, ˈrɛdɒks/ ▶**noun** [mass noun] [usu. as modifier] Chemistry a process in which one substance or molecule is reduced and another oxidized; oxidation and reduction considered together as complementary processes: *redox reactions involve electron transfer.*
– ORIGIN 1920s: blend.

red panda ▶**noun** a raccoon-like mammal with thick reddish-brown fur and a bushy tail, native to high bamboo forests from the Himalayas to southern China. Also called **LESSER PANDA**, **CAT-BEAR**.
• *Ailurus fulgens*; it is variously placed with the raccoons or bears, or in its own family (Ailurudae).

red pepper ▶**noun** the ripe red fruit of a sweet pepper.

red phosphorus ▶**noun** see **PHOSPHORUS**.

red pine ▶**noun** any of a number of coniferous trees which yield reddish timber, in particular:
• a North American pine (*Pinus resinosa*, family Pinaceae).
• NZ another term for **RIMU**.

redpoll /ˈrɛdpəʊl/ ▶**noun** **1** a mainly brown finch with a red forehead, related to the linnet and widespread in Eurasia and North America.
• *Acanthis flammea*, family Fringillidae; occurs in a number of races that were formerly regarded as separate species.
2 (**red poll**) an animal of a breed of red-haired polled cattle.

Red Power ▶**noun** [mass noun] N. Amer. a movement in support of rights and political power for American Indians: [as modifier] *the Red Power movement.*
– ORIGIN 1960s: suggested by **BLACK POWER**.

Red Queen hypothesis Biology the hypothesis that organisms are constantly struggling to keep up with one another in an evolutionary race between predator and prey species.
– ORIGIN late 20th cent.: named from a passage in Lewis Carroll's *Through the Looking Glass*, in which the Red Queen tells Alice that 'it takes all the running you can do to stay in the same place'.

redraft ▶**verb** [with obj.] draft (a document, text, or map) again in a different way: [as adj. **redrafted**] *I enclose a redrafted version.*
▶**noun** a document, text, or map which has been redrafted.

red rattle ▶**noun** a pink-flowered lousewort of marshy places, the seeds of which produce a rattling sound inside their capsule when ripe.
• *Pedicularis palustris*, family Scrophulariaceae.

redraw ▶**verb** (past **redrew**; past participle **redrawn**) [with obj.] draw or draw up again or differently: *the rota was redrawn.*

redress ▶**verb** [with obj.] remedy or set right (an undesirable or unfair situation): *the power to redress the grievances of our citizens.*
■archaic set upright again: *some ambitious Architect being called to redress a leaning Wall.*
▶**noun** [mass noun] remedy or compensation for a wrong or grievance: *those seeking redress for an infringement of public law rights.*
– PHRASES **redress the balance** take action to restore equality in a situation.
– DERIVATIVES **redressable** adjective, **redressal** noun, **redresser** noun.
– ORIGIN Middle English: the verb from Old French *redresser*; the noun via Anglo-Norman French *redresse*.

re-dress ▶**verb** [with obj.] dress (someone or something) again: *he re-dressed the wound.*

red ribbon ▶**noun** US an award given for coming second in a competition.

Red River **1** a river in SE Asia, which rises in southern China and flows 1,175 km (730 miles) generally south-eastwards through northern Vietnam to the Gulf of Tonkin. Chinese name **YUAN JIANG**; Vietnamese name **SONG HONG**.
2 a river in the southern US, a tributary of the Mississippi, which rises in northern Texas and flows 1,966 km (1,222 miles) generally south-eastwards, forming part of the border between Texas and Oklahoma, and enters the Mississippi in Louisiana. Also called **RED RIVER OF THE SOUTH**.
3 a river in the northern US and Canada, which rises in North Dakota and flows 877 km (545 miles) northwards, forming for most of its length the border between North Dakota and Minnesota, before entering Canada and emptying into Lake Winnipeg. Also called **RED RIVER OF THE NORTH**.

Red River cart ▶**noun** historical a strong two-wheeled cart formerly used on the Canadian prairies.

red river hog ▶**noun** another term for **BUSH PIG**.

red roan ▶**adjective** denoting an animal's coat consisting of bay or chestnut mixed with white or grey.
▶**noun** a red roan animal.

red rose ▶**noun** **1** the emblem of Lancashire or the Lancastrians.
2 the symbol of the British Labour Party.

red salmon ▶**noun** another term for **SOCKEYE**.
■[mass noun] the reddish-pink flesh of the sockeye salmon used as food.

red sandalwood ▶**noun** either of two SE Asian trees of the pea family which yield red timber.
• Two species in the family Leguminosae: *Pterocarpus santalinus*, from which a red dye is obtained, and *Adenanthera pavonina*, whose seeds were formerly used as weights by goldsmiths.

Red Sea a long, narrow landlocked sea separating Africa from the Arabian peninsula. It is linked to the Indian Ocean in the south by the Gulf of Aden and to the Mediterranean in the north by the Suez Canal.

red setter ▶**noun** less formal term for **IRISH SETTER**.

redshank ▶**noun** a large Eurasian sandpiper with long red legs and brown, grey, or blackish plumage.
• Genus *Tringa*, family Scolopacidae: two species, in particular *T. totanus*.

red shift ▶**noun** Astronomy the displacement of spectral lines towards longer wavelengths (the red end of the spectrum) in radiation from distant galaxies and celestial objects. This is interpreted as a Doppler shift which is proportional to the velocity of recession and thus to distance. Compare with **BLUE SHIFT**.

redshirt ▶**noun** US informal a college athlete who is withdrawn from university sporting events during one year in order to develop his skills and extend his period of eligibility by a further year at this level of competition.
▶**verb** [with obj.] (usu. **be redshirted**) US keep (an athlete) out of university competition for a year.
– ORIGIN from the red shirts worn by such athletes in practices with regular team members.

redskin ▶**noun** dated or offensive an American Indian.

red snapper ▶**noun** a reddish marine fish which is of commercial value as a food fish, in particular:
• a tropical fish of the snapper family (genus *Lutjanus*, family Lutjanidae). • a North Pacific rockfish (*Sebastes ruberrimus*, family Scorpaenidae).

red sorrel ▶**noun** see **SORREL**[1] (sense 2).

Red Square a large square in Moscow next to the Kremlin. In existence since the late 15th century, under Communism the square was the scene of great parades celebrating May Day and the October Revolution.

red squirrel ▶**noun** a small tree squirrel with a reddish coat:
• a Eurasian squirrel with distinctive ear tufts during the winter months and (in Britain) a whitish tail (*Sciurus vulgaris*, family Sciuridae). • a North American squirrel with a pale belly and a black line along the sides during the summer (*Tamiasciurus hudsonicus*, family Sciuridae).

red star ▶**noun** chiefly historical the emblem of some communist countries.

redstart ▶**noun** **1** a Eurasian and North African songbird related to the chats, having a reddish tail and underparts.
• *Phoenicurus* and other genera, family Turdidae: several species, in particular the widespread *P. phoenicurus*.
2 an American warbler, the male of which is black with either a red belly or orange markings.
• Genera *Setophaga* and *Myioborus*, family Parulidae: several species, in particular the **American redstart** (*S. ruticilla*).

red tabby ▶**noun** a cat with a reddish-orange coat striped or dappled in a deeper red. This is a technical term for the colouring commonly called ginger or marmalade.

red-tailed hawk ▶**noun** the commonest and most widespread buzzard of North and Central America, with a reddish tail.
• *Buteo jamaicensis*, family Accipitridae.

red tape ▶**noun** [mass noun] excessive bureaucracy or adherence to rules and formalities, especially in public business: *this law will just create more red tape.*
– ORIGIN early 18th cent.: so named because of the red or pink tape used to bind and secure official documents.

red tide ▶**noun** a discoloration of seawater caused by a bloom of toxic red dinoflagellates.

Red Tory ▶**noun** (in Canada) a member of a political group who, while maintaining some conservative principles, supports many liberal and socialist policies.

reduce ▶**verb** [with obj.] **1** make smaller or less in amount, degree, or size: *the need for businesses to reduce costs* | *the workforce has been reduced to some 6,100* | [as adj. **reduced**] *a reduced risk of coronary disease.*
■[no obj.] become smaller or less in size, amount, or degree: *the number of priority homeless cases has reduced slightly.* ■ boil (a sauce or other liquid) in cooking so that it becomes thicker and more concentrated. ■ [no obj.] chiefly N. Amer. (of a person) lose weight, typically by dieting: *by May she had reduced to 9 stone.* ■ archaic conquer (a place), in particular besiege and capture (a town or fortress). ■ Photography make (a negative or print) less dense. ■ Phonetics articulate (a speech sound) in a way requiring less muscular effort, giving rise in vowels to a more central articulatory position.
2 (**reduce someone/thing to**) bring someone or something to (a lower or weaker state, condition, or role): *she has been reduced to near poverty* | *the church was reduced to rubble.*
■(**be reduced to doing something**) (of a person) be forced by difficult circumstances into doing something desperate: *ordinary soldiers are reduced to begging.* ■ make someone helpless with (an expression of emotion, especially with hurt, shock, or amusement): *Olga was reduced to stunned silence.* ■ force into (obedience or submission): *he succeeds in reducing his grandees to due obedience.*
3 (**reduce something to**) change a substance to (a different or more basic form): *it is difficult to understand how lava could have been reduced to dust.*
■present a problem or subject in (a simplified form): *he reduces unimaginable statistics to manageable proportions.* ■ convert a fraction to (the form with the lowest terms).
4 Chemistry cause to combine chemically with hydrogen.
■undergo or cause to undergo a reaction in which electrons are gained from another substance or molecule. The opposite of **OXIDIZE**.
5 restore (a dislocated part) to its proper position by manipulation or surgery.
■remedy (a dislocation) in such a way.
– PHRASES **reduced circumstances** used euphemistically to refer to the state of being poor after being relatively wealthy: *a divorcee living in reduced circumstances.* **reduce someone to the ranks** demote a non-commissioned officer to an ordinary soldier.
– DERIVATIVES **reducer** noun.
– ORIGIN late Middle English: from Latin *reducere*, from *re-* 'back, again' + *ducere* 'bring, lead'. The original sense was 'bring back' (hence 'restore', now surviving in sense 5); this led to 'bring to a different state', then 'bring to a simpler or lower state' (hence sense 3); and finally 'diminish in size or amount' (sense 1, dating from the late 18th cent.).

reducible ▶**adjective** **1** [predic.] (of a subject or problem) capable of being simplified in presentation or analysis: *Shakespeare's major soliloquies are not* **reducible to** *categories.*
2 Mathematics (of a polynomial) able to be factorized into two or more polynomials of lower degree.
■(of a group) expressible as the direct product of two of its subgroups.
– DERIVATIVES **reducibility** noun.

reducing agent ▶**noun** Chemistry a substance that tends to bring about reduction by being oxidized and losing electrons.

reductant ▶**noun** Chemistry a reducing agent.

reductase /rɪˈdʌkteɪz/ ▶**noun** [usu. with modifier] Biochemistry an enzyme which promotes the chemical reduction of a specified substance.

reductio ad absurdum /rɪˌdʌktɪəʊ ad abˈsəːdəm/ ▶**noun** Philosophy a method of proving the falsity of a premise by showing that its logical consequence is absurd or contradictory.
– ORIGIN Latin, literally 'reduction to the absurd'.

reduction ▶**noun** [mass noun] **1** the action or fact of

making a specified thing smaller or less in amount, degree, or size: *talks on arms reduction* | [count noun] *there had been* ***a reduction in*** *the number of casualties.*
■[count noun] the amount by which something is made smaller, less, or lower in price: *special reductions on knitwear.* ■ the simplification of a subject or problem to a particular form in presentation or analysis: *the* ***reduction*** *of classical genetics* ***to*** *molecular biology.* ■ Mathematics the process of converting an amount from one denomination to a smaller one, or of bringing down a fraction to its lowest terms. ■ Biology the halving of the number of chromosomes per cell that occurs at one of the two anaphases of meiosis.
2 [count noun] a thing that is made smaller or less in size or amount, in particular:
■an arrangement of an orchestral score for piano or for a smaller group of performers. ■ a thick and concentrated liquid or sauce made by boiling. ■ a copy of a picture or photograph made on a smaller scale than the original.
3 the action of remedying a dislocation or fracture by returning the affected part of the body to its normal position.
4 Chemistry the process or result of reducing or being reduced.
5 Phonetics substitution of a sound which requires less muscular effort to articulate: *the process of vowel reduction.*
– ORIGIN late Middle English (denoting the action of bringing back): from Old French, or from Latin *reductio(n-)*, from *reducere* 'bring back, restore' (see **REDUCE**). The sense development was broadly similar to that of **REDUCE**; sense 1 dates from the late 17th cent.

reduction gear ▶ **noun** a system of gearwheels in which the driven shaft rotates more slowly than the driving shaft.

reductionism ▶ **noun** [mass noun] often derogatory the practice of analysing and describing a complex phenomenon, especially a mental, social, or biological phenomenon, in terms of phenomena which are held to represent a simpler or more fundamental level, especially when this is said to provide a sufficient explanation.
– DERIVATIVES **reductionist** noun & adjective, **reductionistic** adjective.

reductive ▶ **adjective 1** tending to present a subject or problem in a simplified form, especially one viewed as crude: *such a conclusion by itself would be reductive.*
■(with reference to art) minimal: *he combines his reductive abstract shapes with a rippled surface.*
2 of or relating to chemical reduction.
– DERIVATIVES **reductively** adverb, **reductiveness** noun.

reductivism ▶ **noun 1** another term for **MINIMALISM**.
2 another term for **REDUCTIONISM**.

redundancy ▶ **noun** (pl. **-ies**) [mass noun] the state of being no longer needed or useful: *the redundancy of 19th-century heavy plant machinery.*
■chiefly Brit. the state of being no longer in employment because there is no more work available: *the factory's workers face redundancy* | [count noun] *the car giant is expected to announce around 5,000 redundancies.* ■ Engineering the inclusion of extra components which are not strictly necessary to functioning, in case of failure in other components: *a high degree of redundancy is built into the machinery installation.*

redundant ▶ **adjective** no longer needed or useful; superfluous: *an appropriate use for a redundant church* | *many of the old skills had become redundant.*
■chiefly Brit. (of a person) no longer in employment because there is no more work available: *eight permanent staff* ***were made redundant.*** ■ (of words) able to be omitted without loss of meaning or function. ■ Engineering (of a component) not strictly necessary to functioning but included in case of failure in another component.
– DERIVATIVES **redundantly** adverb.
– ORIGIN late 16th cent. (in the sense 'abundant'): from Latin *redundant-* 'surging up', from the verb *redundare* (see **REDOUND**).

reduplicate ▶ **verb** [with obj.] repeat or copy so as to form another of the same kind: *the upper parts of the harmony may be reduplicated at the octave above.*
■repeat (a syllable or other linguistic element) exactly or with a slight change (e.g. *hurly-burly, see-saw*).
– DERIVATIVES **reduplication** noun, **reduplicative** adjective.
– ORIGIN late 16th cent.: from late Latin *reduplicat-*, 'doubled again', from the verb *reduplicare*, from *re-* 'again' + *duplicare* (see **DUPLICATE**).

redux /ˈriːdʌks/ ▶ **adjective** [postpositive] brought back; revived: *Damian has the veneer of the angry young man redux.*
– ORIGIN late 19th cent.: from Latin, from *reducere* 'bring back'.

redwater (also **redwater fever**) ▶ **noun** [mass noun] the disease babesiosis in cattle.

red wiggler ▶ **noun** N. Amer. another term for **REDWORM** (in sense 1).

redwing ▶ **noun 1** a small migratory thrush that breeds mainly in northern Europe, with red underwings showing in flight.
● *Turdus iliacus*, family Turdidae.
2 any of a number of other red-winged birds, especially the American red-winged blackbird.
● Several species, in particular *Agelaius phoeniceus*, family Icteridae.

red wolf ▶ **noun** a fairly small wolf with a cinnamon or tawny coloured coat, native to the south-eastern US but possibly extinct in the wild.
● *Canis rufus*, family Canidae.

redwood ▶ **noun** either of two giant conifers with thick fibrous bark, native to California and Oregon. They are the tallest known trees and are among the largest living organisms.
● Two species in the family Taxodiaceae: the **California** (or **coast**) **redwood** (*Sequoia sempervirens*), which can grow to a height of *c.*110 m (328 ft), and the **giant redwood**, giant sequoia, wellingtonia, or big tree (*Sequoiadendron giganteum*), which can reach a trunk diameter of 11 m (36 ft).
■used in names of other, chiefly tropical, trees with reddish timber, e.g. **Andaman redwood**.

redworm ▶ **noun 1** a red earthworm used in composting kitchen waste and as fishing bait.
● *Lumbricus rubellus*, family Lumbricidae.
2 a parasitic nematode worm occurring in the intestines of horses.
● Genus *Strongylus*, class Phasmida.

red zone ▶ **noun** a red sector on a gauge or dial corresponding to conditions that exceed safety limits: *ozone readings edged into the red zone.*
■a region that is dangerous or forbidden, or in which a particular activity is prohibited. ■ American Football the region between the opposing team's 20-yard line and goal line, which is a major focus of their attack strategy.

reebok ▶ **noun** variant spelling of **RHEBOK**.

re-echo ▶ **verb** (**-oes**, **-oed**) echo again or repeatedly: [no obj.] *Dawn's words re-echoed in her mind.*

Reed[1], Sir Carol (1906–76), English film director. His films include *Odd Man Out* (1947), *The Third Man* (1949), and the musical *Oliver!* (1968), for which he won an Oscar.

Reed[2], Walter (1851–1902), American physician. He headed a group that were responsible for identifying the mosquito *Aedes aegypti* as carrier of yellow fever. They showed that the agent responsible was a virus—the first to be recognized as the cause of a human disease.

reed ▶ **noun 1** a tall, slender-leaved plant of the grass family, which grows in water or on marshy ground.
● Genera *Phragmites* and *Arundo*, family Gramineae: several species, in particular the **common** (or **Norfolk**) **reed** (*P. australis*), which is used for thatching.
■used in names of similar plants growing in wet habitats, e.g. **bur-reed**. ■ a tall, thin, straight stalk of such a plant, used especially as material for thatching. ■ [mass noun] [often as modifier] such plants growing in a mass or used as material, especially for making thatch or household items: *a reed curtain* | *clumps of reed and grass.* ■ poetic/literary a rustic musical pipe made from such plants or from straw. ■ [mass noun] Brit. straw used for thatching.
2 a thing or person resembling or likened to such plants, in particular:
■a weak or impressionable person: *the jurors were mere* ***reeds in the wind.*** ■ poetic/literary an arrow. ■ a weaver's comb-like implement for separating the threads of the warp and correctly positioning the weft. ■ (**reeds**) a set of semi-cylindrical adjacent mouldings like reeds laid together.
3 a piece of thin cane or metal, sometimes doubled, which vibrates in a current of air to produce the sound of various musical instruments, as in the mouthpiece of a clarinet or oboe, at the base of some organ pipes, and as part of a set in the accordion and harmonium.
■a wind instrument played with a reed. ■ an organ stop with reed pipes.
4 an electrical contact used in a magnetically operated switch or relay.
– PHRASES **a broken reed** a weak or ineffectual person. (**as**) **slim as a reed** (of a person) very slim.
– ORIGIN Old English *hrēod*, of West Germanic origin; related to Dutch *riet* and German *Ried*.

reed bed ▶ **noun** an area of water or marshland dominated by reeds.

reedbuck (S. African also **rietbok**) ▶ **noun** an African antelope with a distinctive whistling call and high bouncing jumps.
● Genus *Redunca*, family Bovidae: three species.

reed bunting ▶ **noun** a Eurasian bunting that frequents reed beds and hedgerows, the male having a black head and white collar.
● *Emberiza schoeniclus*, family Emberizidae (subfamily Emberizinae).

reeded ▶ **adjective 1** shaped into or decorated with semi-cylindrical adjacent mouldings.
2 (of a wind instrument) having a reed or reeds: [in combination] *a double-reeded oboe.*

reeding ▶ **noun** a small semi-cylindrical moulding or ornamentation.
■[mass noun] the making of such mouldings.

re-edit ▶ **verb** (**re-edited**, **re-editing**) [with obj.] edit (a text or film) again in order to make changes in it.
– DERIVATIVES **re-edition** noun.

reedling (also **bearded reedling**) ▶ **noun** another term for **BEARDED TIT**.

reed mace ▶ **noun** another term for **BULRUSH** (in sense 1).

reed organ ▶ **noun** a keyboard instrument similar to a harmonium, in which air is drawn upwards past metal reeds.

reed pipe ▶ **noun** a simple wind instrument made from a reed or with the sound produced by a reed.
■an organ pipe with a reed.

reed stop ▶ **noun** an organ stop controlling reed pipes.

re-educate ▶ **verb** [with obj.] educate or train (someone) in order to change their beliefs or behaviour: *criminals are to be re-educated.*
– DERIVATIVES **re-education** noun.

reed warbler ▶ **noun** a Eurasian and African songbird with plain plumage, frequenting reed beds.
● Genus *Acrocephalus*, family Sylviidae: several species, in particular the common *A. scirpaceus*.

reedy ▶ **adjective** (**reedier**, **reediest**) **1** (of a voice, sound, or instrument) high and thin in tone: *Franco's reedy voice.*
2 (of water or land) full of or edged with reeds: *they swam in the reedy lake.*
3 (of a person) tall and thin: *a reedy twelve-year-old.*
– DERIVATIVES **reediness** noun.

reef[1] ▶ **noun** a ridge of jagged rock, coral, or sand just above or below the surface of the sea.
■a vein of ore in the earth, especially one containing gold.
– ORIGIN late 16th cent. (earlier as *riff*): from Middle Low German and Middle Dutch *rif, ref*, from Old Norse *rif*, literally 'rib', used in the same sense; compare with **REEF**[2].

reef[2] Sailing ▶ **noun** each of the several strips across a sail which can be taken in or rolled up to reduce the area exposed to the wind.
▶ **verb** [with obj.] take in one or more reefs of (a sail): *reefing the mainsail in strong winds.*
■shorten (a topmast or a bowsprit).
– ORIGIN Middle English: from Middle Dutch *reef, rif*, from Old Norse *rif*, literally 'rib', used in the same sense; compare with **REEF**[1].

reef-builder ▶ **noun** a marine organism, especially a coral, which builds reefs.
– DERIVATIVES **reef-building** noun.

reefer[1] ▶ **noun** informal a cannabis cigarette.
■[mass noun] cannabis.
– ORIGIN 1930s: perhaps related to Mexican Spanish *grifo* '(smoker of) cannabis'.

reefer[2] ▶ **noun 1** short for **REEFER JACKET**.
2 Sailing a person who reefs a sail.
■Nautical slang, archaic a midshipman.

reefer[3] ▶ **noun** informal a refrigerated lorry, railway wagon, or ship.
– ORIGIN early 20th cent.: abbreviation.

r

reefer jacket ▶ **noun** a thick close-fitting double-breasted jacket.

reef flat ▶ **noun** the horizontal upper surface of a coral reef.

reef knot ▶ **noun** a type of double knot which is made symmetrically to hold securely and cast off easily.

reefpoint ▶ **noun** Sailing each of several short pieces of rope attached to a sail to secure it when reefed.

reek ▶ **verb** [no obj.] smell strongly and unpleasantly; stink: *the yard* ***reeked of*** *wet straw and stale horse manure* | [as adj. **reeking**] *the reeking lavatories.*
■ figurative be suggestive of something unpleasant or disapproved of: *the speeches* ***reeked of*** *anti-Semitism.* ■ archaic give off smoke, steam, or fumes: *while temples crash, and towers in ashes reek.*
▶ **noun 1** [in sing.] a foul smell: *the reek of cattle dung.*
2 [mass noun] chiefly Scottish smoke.
– DERIVATIVES **reeky** adjective.
– ORIGIN Old English *rēocan* 'give out smoke or vapour', *rēc* (noun) 'smoke', of Germanic origin; related to Dutch *rieken* 'to smell', *rook* 'smoke', German *riechen* 'to smell', *Rauch* 'smoke'.

reel ▶ **noun 1** a cylinder on which film, wire, thread, or other flexible materials can be wound: *a cotton reel.*
■ a length of something wound on to such a device: *a* ***reel of*** *copper wire.* ■ a part of a film: *in the final reel he is transformed from unhinged sociopath into local hero.*
2 a lively Scottish or Irish folk dance.
■ a piece of music for such a dance, typically in simple or duple time.
▶ **verb 1** [with obj.] (**reel something in**) wind a line on to a reel by turning the reel.
■ bring something attached to a line, especially a fish, towards one by turning a reel and winding in the line: *he struck, and reeled in a good perch.*
2 [no obj.] lose one's balance and stagger or lurch violently: *he punched Connolly in the ear,* ***sending him reeling*** | *she reeled back against the van.*
■ feel very giddy, disorientated, or bewildered, typically as a result of an unexpected setback: *the Prime Minister was reeling from a savaging inflicted in the Commons* | *the unaccustomed intake of alcohol made my head reel.* ■ [with adverbial of direction] walk in a staggering or lurching manner, especially while drunk: *the two reeled out of the bar arm in arm.*
3 [no obj.] dance a reel.
– DERIVATIVES **reeler** noun.
– ORIGIN Old English *hrēol*, denoting a rotatory device on which spun thread is wound; of unknown origin.
▶ **reel something off** say or recite something very rapidly and without apparent effort: *she proceeded to reel off in rapid Italian the various dishes of the day.*

re-elect ▶ **verb** [with obj.] (usu. **be re-elected**) elect (someone) to a further term of office: *Wilson was re-elected in September 1974.*
– DERIVATIVES **re-election** noun.

re-eligible ▶ **adjective** eligible for re-election to a further term of office.

reel-to-reel ▶ **adjective** denoting a tape recorder in which the tape passes between two reels mounted separately rather than within a cassette, now generally superseded by cassette players except for professional use.

re-embark ▶ **verb** [no obj.] go on board ship again.
– DERIVATIVES **re-embarkation** noun.

re-emerge ▶ **verb** [no obj.] emerge again; come into sight or prominence once more: *nationalism has re-emerged in western Europe.*
– DERIVATIVES **re-emergence** noun, **re-emergent** adjective.

re-emphasize (also **-ise**) ▶ **verb** [with obj.] place emphasis on (something) again: *the latter document re-emphasized the need for a national curriculum.*
– DERIVATIVES **re-emphasis** noun.

re-enact ▶ **verb** [with obj.] **1** act out (a past event): *bombers were gathered together to re-enact the historic first air attack.*
2 bring (a law) into effect again when the original statute has been repealed.
– DERIVATIVES **re-enactment** noun.

re-engineer ▶ **verb** [with obj.] redesign (a device or machine).
■ [often as noun **re-engineering**] restructure (a company or part of its operations), especially by exploiting information technology.

re-enlist ▶ **verb** [no obj.] enlist again in the armed forces.
– DERIVATIVES **re-enlister** noun.

re-enter ▶ **verb** [with obj.] enter (something) again: *women who wish to re-enter the labour market.*
– DERIVATIVES **re-entrance** noun.

re-entrant ▶ **adjective** (of an angle) pointing inwards. The opposite of **SALIENT**.
■ having an inward-pointing angle or angles.
▶ **noun 1** a re-entrant angle.
■ an indentation or depression in terrain.
2 a person who has re-entered something, especially the labour force.

re-entry ▶ **noun** (pl. **-ies**) [mass noun] **1** the action or process of re-entering something: *programmes designed to prepare you for re-entry to the profession* | *she feared she would not be granted re-entry into Britain.*
■ the return of a spacecraft or missile into the earth's atmosphere.
2 Law the action of retaking or repossession.
3 [count noun] a visible duplication of part of the design for a postage stamp due to an inaccurate first impression.
■ a stamp displaying such a duplication.

re-equip ▶ **verb** (**re-equipped**, **re-equipping**) [with obj.] provide with new equipment: *the mill was re-equipped with modern machinery.*

re-erect ▶ **verb** [with obj.] (usu. **be re-erected**) erect (something, especially a building) again.
– DERIVATIVES **re-erection** noun.

re-establish /ˌriːɪˈstablɪʃ, ˌriːɛ-/ ▶ **verb** [with obj.] establish (something) again or anew: *this project will re-establish contact with students.*
– DERIVATIVES **re-establishment** noun.

re-evaluate ▶ **verb** [with obj.] evaluate again or differently: *fifteen patients were re-evaluated after six months* | *I began to re-evaluate my life.*
– DERIVATIVES **re-evaluation** noun.

reeve[1] ▶ **noun** chiefly historical a local official, in particular the chief magistrate of a town or district in Anglo-Saxon England.
■ Canadian the president of a village or town council.
– ORIGIN Old English *rēfa.*

reeve[2] ▶ **verb** (past and past participle **rove** or **reeved**) [with obj.] Nautical thread (a rope or rod) through a ring or other aperture: *one end of the new rope was* ***reeved through*** *the chain.*
■ fasten (a rope or block) in this way.
– ORIGIN early 17th cent.: probably from Dutch *reven* 'reef (a sail)' (see **REEF**[2]).

reeve[3] ▶ **noun** a female ruff. See **RUFF**[1] sense 4.
– ORIGIN early 17th cent.: variant of dialect *ree*, of unknown origin.

re-examine ▶ **verb** [with obj.] examine again or further: *I will have the body re-examined.*
■ Law examine (a witness) again, after cross-examination by the opposing counsel.
– DERIVATIVES **re-examination** noun.

re-export ▶ **verb** /ˌriːɪkˈspɔːt, -ɛk-/ [with obj.] export (imported goods), typically after they have undergone further processing or manufacture.
▶ **noun** /riːˈɛkspɔːt/ [mass noun] the action of re-exporting something.
■ [count noun] a thing that has or will be re-exported.
– DERIVATIVES **re-exportation** noun, **re-exporter** /ˌriːɪkˈspɔːtə, -ɛk-/ noun.

ref ▶ **noun** informal (in sports) a referee.
– ORIGIN late 19th cent.: abbreviation.

ref. ▶ **abbreviation for** ■ reference. ■ refer to.

reface ▶ **verb** [with obj.] put a new facing on (a building): *part of the tower was refaced with brick.*

refashion ▶ **verb** [with obj.] fashion (something) again or differently.

refection ▶ **noun** [mass noun] poetic/literary refreshment by food or drink.
■ [count noun] a meal, especially a light one. ■ Zoology the eating of partly digested faecal pellets, as practised by rabbits.
– ORIGIN Middle English: from Old French, from Latin *refectio(n-)*, from *reficere* 'renew' (see **REFECTORY**).

refectory ▶ **noun** (pl. **-ies**) a room used for communal meals, especially in an educational or religious institution.
– ORIGIN late Middle English: from late Latin *refectorium*, from Latin *reficere* 'refresh, renew', from *re-* 'back' + *facere* 'make'.

refectory table ▶ **noun** a long, narrow table.

refer /rɪˈfəː/ ▶ **verb** (**referred**, **referring**) **1** [no obj.] (**refer to**) mention or allude to: *the reports of the commission are often referred to in the media* | *the Royal Navy is* ***referred to as*** *the Senior Service.*
■ [with obj.] (**refer someone to**) direct the attention of someone to: *I refer my honourable friend to the reply that I gave some moments ago.* ■ (**refer to**) (of a word or phrase) describe or denote; have as a referent: *'God' refers to something that cannot be known.*
2 [with obj.] (**refer something to**) pass a matter to (another body, typically one with more authority or expertise) for a decision: *the prisoner may require the Secretary of State to refer his case to the Parole Board.*
■ send or direct (someone) to a medical specialist: *she was* ***referred to*** *a clinical psychologist for counselling.* ■ [no obj.] (**refer to**) read or otherwise use (a source of information) in order to ascertain something; consult: *I always refer to a dictionary when I come upon a new word.*
3 [with obj.] (**refer something to**) archaic trace or attribute something to (someone or something) as a cause or source: *the God to whom he habitually referred his highest inspirations.*
■ regard something as belonging to (a certain period, place, or class).
4 [with obj.] fail (a candidate in an examination).
– PHRASES **refer to drawer** Brit. a phrase used by banks when suspending payment of a cheque.
– DERIVATIVES **referable** /rɪˈfəːrəb(ə)l, ˈrɛf(ə)r-/ adjective, **referrer** noun.
– ORIGIN late Middle English: from Old French *referer* or Latin *referre* 'carry back', from *re-* 'back' + *ferre* 'bring'.

referee ▶ **noun 1** an official who watches a game or match closely to ensure that the rules are adhered to and (in some sports) to arbitrate on matters arising from the play.
2 a person willing to testify in writing about the character or ability of someone, especially an applicant for a job.
■ a person appointed to examine and assess for publication a scientific or other academic work.
▶ **verb** (**referees**, **refereed**, **refereeing**) [with obj.] officiate as referee at (a game or match): *he had refereed two of the first-round group matches.*

reference ▶ **noun** [mass noun] **1** the action of mentioning or alluding to something: *he* ***made reference to*** *the enormous power of the mass media* | [count noun] *references to Darwinism and evolution.*
■ [count noun] a mention or citation of a source of information in a book or article. ■ [count noun] a book or passage cited in such a way.
2 use of a source of information in order to ascertain something: *popular works of reference.*
■ the sending of a matter for decision or consideration to some authority: *the publishers reprinted and sold the work* ***without reference to*** *the author.*
3 [count noun] a letter from a previous employer testifying to someone's ability or reliability, used when applying for a new job.
▶ **verb** [with obj.] provide (a book or article) with citations of authorities: *each chapter is referenced, citing literature up to 1990.*
– PHRASES **for future reference** for use at a later date: *she lodged this idea in the back of her mind for future reference.* **terms of reference** the scope and limitations of an activity or area of knowledge: *the minister will present a plan outlining the inquiry's terms of reference.* **with** (or **in**) **reference to** in relation to; as regards: *war can only be explained with reference to complex social factors.*

reference book ▶ **noun 1** a book intended to be consulted for information on specific matters rather than read from beginning to end.
2 S. African historical another term for **PASS**[1] (in sense 3).

reference electrode ▶ **noun** Electronics an electrode having an accurately maintained potential, used as a reference for measurement by other electrodes.

reference frame ▶ **noun** see **FRAME OF REFERENCE**.

reference group ▶ **noun** a social group which a person takes as a standard in forming attitudes and behaviour.

reference library ▶ **noun** a library, typically one holding many reference books, in which the books are not for loan but may be read on site.

reference point ▶ **noun** a basis or standard for evaluation, assessment, or comparison; a criterion.

referendum /ˌrɛfəˈrɛndəm/ ▶ **noun** (pl. **referendums** or **referenda** /-də/) a general vote by the electorate

on a single political question which has been referred to them for a direct decision.
− ORIGIN mid 19th cent.: from Latin, gerund ('referring'), or neuter gerundive ('something to be brought back or referred') of *referre* (see **REFER**).

referent ▶ noun Linguistics the thing in the world that a word or phrase denotes or stands for: *'the Morning Star' and 'the Evening Star' have the same referent (the planet Venus)*.
− ORIGIN mid 19th cent.: from Latin *referent-* 'bringing back', from the verb *referre* (see **REFER**).

referential ▶ adjective **1** containing or of the nature of references or allusions.
2 Linguistics of or relating to a referent, in particular having the external world rather than a text or language as a referent.
− DERIVATIVES **referentiality** noun, **referentially** adverb.

referral ▶ noun an act of referring someone or something for consultation, review, or further action.
■ [mass noun] the directing of a patient to a medical specialist by a general physician. ■ a person whose case has been referred to a specialist doctor or a professional body.

referred pain ▶ noun [mass noun] Medicine pain felt in a part of the body other than its actual source.

reffo ▶ noun (pl. **-os**) Austral. informal, offensive a refugee from Europe, in particular one who left Germany or German-occupied Europe before the Second World War.

refill ▶ verb /riːˈfɪl/ [with obj.] fill (a container) again: *she paused and refilled her glass with wine before going on*.
■ [no obj.] (of a container) become full again: *the empty pool will rapidly refill from rain and snow*.
▶ noun /ˈriːfɪl/ an act of filling a container again, or a container, especially a glass, that is so filled: *the waitress appeared with refills*.
− DERIVATIVES **refillable** adjective.

refinance ▶ verb [with obj.] finance (something) again, typically with new loans at a lower rate of interest.

refine ▶ verb [with obj.] remove impurities or unwanted elements from (a substance), typically as part of an industrial process: *sugar was refined by boiling it in huge iron vats*.
■ improve (something) by making small changes, in particular make (an idea, theory, or method) more subtle and accurate: *ease of access to computers has refined analysis and presentation of data*.
− DERIVATIVES **refiner** noun.
− ORIGIN late 16th cent.: from **RE-** 'again' + the verb **FINE**[1], influenced by French *raffiner*.

refined ▶ adjective with impurities or unwanted elements having been removed by processing.
■ elegant and cultured in appearance, manner, or taste: *her voice was very low and refined*.

refinement ▶ noun [mass noun] the process of removing impurities or unwanted elements from a substance: *the refinement of uranium*.
■ the improvement or clarification of something by the making of small changes: *this gross figure needs considerable refinement* | [count noun] *recent refinements to production techniques*. ■ cultured elegance in behaviour or manner: *her carefully cultivated veneer of refinement*. ■ sophisticated and superior good taste: *the refinement of Hellenistic art*.

refinery ▶ noun (pl. **-ies**) an industrial installation where a substance is refined: *an oil refinery*.

refinish ▶ verb [with obj.] apply a new finish to (a surface or object).
▶ noun an act of refinishing a surface or object.

refit ▶ verb (**refitted**, **refitting**) [with obj.] replace or repair machinery, equipment, and fittings in (a ship, building, etc.): *a lucrative contract to refit a submarine fleet*.
▶ noun a restoration or repair of machinery, equipment, or fittings.

reflag ▶ verb (**reflagged**, **reflagging**) [with obj.] change the national registration of (a ship).

reflate ▶ verb [with obj.] expand the level of output of (an economy) by government stimulus, using either fiscal or monetary policy.
− DERIVATIVES **reflation** noun, **reflationary** noun.
− ORIGIN 1930s: from **RE-** 'again', on the pattern of *inflate*, *deflate*.

reflect ▶ verb **1** [with obj.] (of a surface or body) throw back (heat, light, or sound) without absorbing it: *when the sun's rays hit the Earth a lot of the heat is*

reflected back into space | [as adj. **reflected**] *his eyes gleamed in the reflected light*.
■ (of a mirror or shiny surface) show an image of: *he could see himself reflected in Keith's mirrored glasses*.
■ embody or represent (something) in a faithful or appropriate way: *shares are priced at a level that reflects a company's prospects* | *schools should reflect cultural differences*. ■ (of an action or situation) bring (credit or discredit) to the relevant parties: *the main contract is progressing well, which reflects great credit on those involved*. ■ [no obj.] (**reflect well/badly on**) bring about a good or bad impression of: *the incident reflects badly on the operating practices of the airlines*.
2 [no obj.] (**reflect on/upon**) think deeply or carefully about: *he reflected with sadness on the unhappiness of his marriage* | [with clause] *Charles reflected that maybe there was hope for the family after all*.
■ archaic make disparaging remarks about: *the clergy were strictly charged not to reflect on the Catholic religion in their discourses*.
− ORIGIN late Middle English: from Old French *reflecter* or Latin *reflectere*, from *re-* 'back' + *flectere* 'to bend'.

reflectance ▶ noun Physics the measure of the proportion of light or other radiation striking a surface which is reflected off it.

reflecting telescope ▶ noun a telescope in which a mirror is used to collect and focus light.

reflection ▶ noun **1** [mass noun] the throwing back by a body or surface of light, heat, or sound without absorbing it: *the reflection of light*.
■ [count noun] an amount of light, heat, or sound that is thrown back in such a way: *the reflections from the street lamps gave them just enough light*. ■ [count noun] an image seen in a mirror or shiny surface: *Marianne surveyed her reflection in the mirror*. ■ [count noun] a thing that is a consequence of or arises from something else: *a healthy skin is a reflection of good health in general*. ■ [in sing.] a thing bringing discredit to someone or something: *it was a sad reflection on society that because of his affliction he was picked on*. ■ [count noun] Mathematics the conceptual operation of inverting a system or event with respect to a plane, each element being transferred perpendicularly through the plane to a point the same distance the other side of it.
2 [mass noun] serious thought or consideration: *he doesn't get much time for reflection*.
■ [count noun] an idea about something, especially one that is written down or expressed: *reflections on human destiny and art*.
− ORIGIN late Middle English: from Old French *reflexion* or late Latin *reflexio(n-)*, from Latin *reflex-* 'bent back', from the verb *reflectere*.

reflection coefficient ▶ noun another term for **REFLECTANCE**.

reflective ▶ adjective **1** providing a reflection; capable of reflecting light or other radiation: *reflective glass* | *reflective clothing*.
■ produced by reflection: *a colourful reflective glow*.
2 relating to or characterized by deep thought; thoughtful: *a quiet, reflective, astute man*.
− DERIVATIVES **reflectively** adverb, **reflectiveness** noun.

reflectivity ▶ noun Physics the property of reflecting light or radiation, especially reflectance as measured independently of the thickness of a material.

reflectometer /ˌriːflɛkˈtɒmɪtə/ ▶ noun an instrument for measuring quantities associated with reflection, in particular (also **time domain reflectometer**) an instrument for locating discontinuities (e.g. faults in electric cables) by detecting and measuring reflected pulses of energy.
− DERIVATIVES **reflectometry** noun.

reflector ▶ noun a piece of glass or metal for reflecting light in a required direction, e.g. a red one on the back of a motor vehicle or bicycle.
■ an object or device which reflects radio waves, seismic vibrations, sound, or other waves. ■ a reflecting telescope.

reflet /rəˈfleɪ/ ▶ noun [mass noun] lustre or iridescence, especially on ceramics.
− ORIGIN French, literally 'reflection'.

reflex ▶ noun **1** an action that is performed without conscious thought as a response to a stimulus: *a newborn baby is equipped with basic reflexes*.
■ (**reflexes**) a person's ability to perform such actions: *he was saved by his superb reflexes*. ■ (in reflexology) a response in a part of the body to stimulation of a

corresponding point on the feet, hands, or head: [as modifier] *reflex points*.
2 a thing which is determined by and reproduces the essential features or qualities of something else: *politics was no more than a reflex of economics*.
■ a word formed by development from an earlier stage of a language. ■ archaic a reflected source of light: *the reflex from the window lit his face*.
▶ adjective **1** (of an action) performed without conscious thought as an automatic response to a stimulus: *sneezing is a reflex action*.
2 (of an angle) exceeding 180°.
■ archaic (of light) reflected. ■ archaic bent or turned backwards. ■ archaic (of a thought) directed or turned back upon the mind itself; introspective.
− DERIVATIVES **reflexly** adverb.
− ORIGIN early 16th cent. (as a noun denoting reflection): from Latin *reflexus* 'a bending back', from *reflectere* 'bend back' (see **REFLECT**).

reflex arc ▶ noun Physiology the nerve pathway involved in a reflex action including at its simplest a sensory nerve and a motor nerve with a synapse between.

reflex camera ▶ noun a camera with a ground-glass focusing screen on which the image is formed by a combination of lens and mirror, enabling the scene to be correctly composed and focused.

reflexible ▶ adjective chiefly technical capable of being reflected.
− DERIVATIVES **reflexibility** noun.

reflexion ▶ noun archaic spelling of **REFLECTION**.

reflexive ▶ adjective **1** Grammar denoting a pronoun that refers back to the subject of the clause in which it is used, e.g. *myself*, *themselves*.
■ (of a verb or clause) having a reflexive pronoun as its object (e.g. *wash oneself*).
2 Logic (of a relation) always holding between a term and itself.
3 (of a method or theory in the social sciences) taking account of itself or of the effect of the personality or presence of the researcher on what is being investigated.
4 (of an action) performed as a reflex, without conscious thought: *at concerts like this one standing ovations have become reflexive*.
▶ noun a reflexive word or form, especially a pronoun.
− DERIVATIVES **reflexively** adverb, **reflexiveness** noun, **reflexivity** noun.

reflexology ▶ noun [mass noun] **1** a system of massage used to relieve tension and treat illness, based on the theory that there are reflex points on the feet, hands, and head linked to every part of the body.
2 Psychology the scientific study of reflex action as it affects behaviour.
− DERIVATIVES **reflexologist** noun (usu. in sense 1).

refloat ▶ verb [with obj.] set (a grounded ship) afloat again.

reflow ▶ noun [mass noun] **1** Electronics a soldering technique in which surface-mount components are held in position on a circuit board using a paste containing solder which melts to form soldered joints when the circuit board is heated.
2 (in word processing) the action of rearranging text on a page having varied such features as type size, line length, and spacing.
▶ verb [with obj.] **1** Electronics attach (a surface-mount component) using the reflow technique.
2 (in word processing) rearrange (text) on a page having varied such features as type size, line length, and spacing.

refluent /ˈrɛflʊənt/ ▶ adjective poetic/literary flowing back; ebbing: *the refluent waters of the Mississippi*.
− DERIVATIVES **refluence** noun.
− ORIGIN late Middle English: from Latin *refluent-* 'flowing back', from the verb *refluere*, from *re-* 'back' + *fluere* 'to flow'.

reflux /ˈriːflʌks/ ▶ noun [mass noun] Chemistry the process of boiling a liquid so that any vapour is liquefied and returned to the stock.
■ technical the flowing back of a liquid, especially that of a fluid in the body.
▶ verb [no obj.] Chemistry boil or cause to boil in circumstances such that the vapour returns to the stock of liquid after condensing.
■ [no obj., with adverbial of direction] technical (of a liquid, especially a bodily fluid) flow back.

refocus ▶ verb (**refocused**, **refocusing** or **refocussed**, **refocussing**) [with obj.] adjust the focus of (a lens or one's eyes).

▪focus (attention or resources) on something new or different: *refocus attention on yourself through repeating your main points.*

reforest ▶**verb** [with obj.] replant with trees; cover again with forest: *a project to reforest the country's coastal areas.*
– DERIVATIVES **reforestation** noun.

reforge ▶**verb** [with obj.] forge (something) again or differently: *they wanted to reforge the identity of the nation.*

reform ▶**verb** [with obj.] **1** make changes in (something, typically a social, political, or economic institution or practice) in order to improve it: *the Bill will reform the health benefits system.* ▪bring about a change in (someone) so that they no longer behave in an immoral, criminal, or self-destructive manner: *the state has a duty to reform criminals* | [as adj. **reformed**] *I'm considered a **reformed** character these days.* ▪[no obj.] (of a person) change oneself in such a way: *it was only when his drunken behaviour led to blows that he started to reform.*
2 Chemistry subject (hydrocarbons) to a catalytic process in which straight-chain molecules are converted to branched forms for use as petrol.
▶**noun** [mass noun] the action or process of reforming an institution or practice: *the reform of the divorce laws* | [count noun] *economic reforms.*
– DERIVATIVES **reformable** adjective, **reformative** adjective, **reformer** noun.
– ORIGIN Middle English (as a verb in the senses 'restore (peace)' and 'bring back to the original condition'): from Old French *reformer* or Latin *reformare*, from *re-* 'back' + *formare* 'to form, shape'. The noun dates from the mid 17th cent.

re-form ▶**verb** form or cause to form again: [no obj.] *the clouds re-formed over the sun.*

Reform Act ▶**noun** an act framed to amend the system of parliamentary representation, especially those introduced in Britain during the 19th century.

The first Reform Act (1832) disenfranchised various rotten boroughs and lowered the property qualification, widening the electorate by about 50 per cent to include most of the male members of the upper middle class. The second (1867) doubled the electorate to about 2 million men by again lowering the property qualification, and the third (1884) increased it to about 5 million.

reformat ▶**verb** (**reformatted**, **reformatting**) [with obj.] chiefly Computing give a new format to; revise or represent in another format.

reformation ▶**noun 1** [mass noun] the action or process of reforming an institution or practice: *the reformation of the Senate.*
2 (**the Reformation**) a 16th-century movement for the reform of abuses in the Roman Church ending in the establishment of the Reformed and Protestant Churches.

The roots of the Reformation go back to the 14th-century attacks on the wealth and hierarchy of the Church made by groups such as the Lollards and the Hussites. But the Reformation is usually thought of as beginning in 1517 when Martin Luther issued ninety-five theses criticizing Church doctrine and practice. In Denmark, Norway, Sweden, Saxony, Hesse, and Brandenburg, supporters broke away and established Protestant Churches, while in Switzerland a separate movement was led by Zwingli and later Calvin.

– DERIVATIVES **reformational** adjective.
– ORIGIN late Middle English: from Latin *reformatio(n-)*, from *reformare* 'shape again' (see **REFORM**).

re-formation ▶**noun** [mass noun] the action or process of forming again.

reformatory /rɪˈfɔːmət(ə)ri/ ▶**noun** (pl. **-ies**) N. Amer. historical an institution to which young offenders are sent as an alternative to prison.
▶**adjective** tending or intended to produce reform.

Reformed Church ▶**noun** a Church that has accepted the principles of the Reformation, especially a Calvinist Church (as distinct from Lutheran).

reformist ▶**adjective** supporting or advancing gradual reform rather than abolition or revolution.
▶**noun** a person who advocates gradual reform rather than abolition or revolution.
– DERIVATIVES **reformism** noun.

Reform Judaism ▶**noun** [mass noun] a form of Judaism, initiated in Germany by the philosopher Moses Mendelssohn (1729–86), which has reformed or abandoned aspects of Orthodox Jewish worship and ritual in an attempt to adapt to modern changes in social, political, and cultural life.
– DERIVATIVES **Reform Jew** noun.

reform school ▶**noun** historical an institution to which young offenders were sent as an alternative to prison.

reformulate ▶**verb** [with obj.] formulate again or differently: *pupils benefit from the opportunity to reformulate their thinking in a helpful atmosphere.*
– DERIVATIVES **reformulation** noun.

refract ▶**verb** [with obj.] (usu. **be refracted**) (of water, air, or glass) make (a ray of light) change direction when it enters at an angle: *the rays of light are refracted by the material of the lens.* ▪measure the focusing characteristics of (an eye) or of the eyes of (someone).
– ORIGIN early 17th cent.: from Latin *refract-* 'broken up', from the verb *refringere*, from *re-* 'back' + *frangere* 'to break'.

refracting telescope ▶**noun** a telescope which uses a converging lens to collect the light.

refraction ▶**noun** [mass noun] Physics the fact or phenomenon of light, radio waves, etc., being deflected in passing obliquely through the interface between one medium and another or through a medium of varying density. ▪change in direction of propagation of any wave as a result of its travelling at different speeds at different points along the wave front. ▪measurement of the focusing characteristics of an eye or eyes.
– ORIGIN mid 17th cent.: from late Latin *refractio(n-)*, from *refringere* 'break up' (see **REFRACT**).

refractive ▶**adjective** of or involving refraction.
– DERIVATIVES **refractively** adverb.

refractive index ▶**noun** the ratio of the velocity of light in a vacuum to its velocity in a specified medium.

refractometer /ˌriːfrakˈtɒmɪtə/ ▶**noun** an instrument for measuring a refractive index.
– DERIVATIVES **refractometric** adjective, **refractometry** noun.

refractor ▶**noun** a lens or other object which causes refraction. ▪a refracting telescope.

refractory ▶**adjective** formal **1** stubborn or unmanageable: *his refractory pony.*
2 resistant to a process or stimulus: *some granules are refractory to secretory stimuli.* ▪Medicine (of a person, illness, or diseased tissue) not yielding to treatment: *healing of previously refractory ulcers.* ▪Medicine, rare (of a person or animal) resistant to infection. ▪technical (of a substance) resistant to heat; hard to melt or fuse.
▶**noun** (pl. **-ies**) technical a substance that is resistant to heat.
– DERIVATIVES **refractoriness** noun.
– ORIGIN early 17th cent.: alteration of obsolete *refractary*, from Latin *refractarius* 'stubborn' (see also **REFRACT**).

refractory period ▶**noun** Physiology a period immediately following stimulation during which a nerve or muscle is unresponsive to further stimulation.

refrain[1] ▶**verb** [no obj.] stop oneself from doing something: *she **refrained from** comment.*
– ORIGIN Middle English (in the sense 'restrain (a thought or feeling)'): from Old French *refrener*, from Latin *refrenare*, from *re-* (expressing intensive force) + *frenum* 'bridle'.

refrain[2] ▶**noun** a repeated line or number of lines in a poem or song, typically at the end of each verse. ▪the musical accompaniment for such a line or number of lines. ▪a comment or complaint that is often repeated: *'Poor Tom' had become the constant refrain of his friends.*
– ORIGIN late Middle English: from Old French, from *refraindre* 'break', based on Latin *refringere* 'break up' (because the refrain 'broke' the sequence).

refrangible ▶**adjective** able to be refracted.
– DERIVATIVES **refrangibility** noun.
– ORIGIN late 17th cent.: from modern Latin *refrangibilis*, from *refrangere* 'break up' (see **REFRACT**).

refreeze ▶**verb** (past **refroze**; past participle **refrozen**) make or become frozen again.

refresh ▶**verb** [with obj.] give new strength or energy to; reinvigorate: *the shower had refreshed her* | [as adj. **refreshed**] *I awoke feeling calm and refreshed.* ▪stimulate or jog (someone's memory) by checking or going over previous information: *he was able to refresh her memory on many points.* ▪revise or update (skills or knowledge): *short-term courses give nurses an opportunity to refresh their skills.* ▪Computing update the display on (a screen). ▪chiefly N. Amer. pour more (drink) for someone or refill (a container) with drink: *the tea is cold and the pot needs refreshing.* ▪place or keep (food) in cold water so as to cool or maintain freshness.
▶**noun** Computing an act or function of updating the display on a screen.
– ORIGIN late Middle English: from Old French *refreschier*, from *re-* 'back' + *fres(che)* 'fresh'.

refresher ▶**noun** a thing that refreshes, in particular: ▪[usu. as modifier] an activity that revises or updates one's skills or knowledge: *candidates take some refresher training before coming back.* ▪dated a drink. ▪Law, Brit. an extra fee payable to counsel in a prolonged case.

refresher course ▶**noun** a short course reviewing or updating previous studies or training connected with one's profession.

refreshing ▶**adjective** serving to refresh or reinvigorate someone: *a refreshing drink* | *the morning air was so refreshing.* ▪welcome or stimulating because new or different: *it **makes a refreshing change** to able to write about something nice* | *her directness is refreshing.*
– DERIVATIVES **refreshingly** adverb [as submodifier] *a refreshingly different concept* | [sentence adverb] *refreshingly, the party's current spokesman is very frank.*

refreshment ▶**noun 1** (usu. **refreshments**) a light snack or drink, especially one provided in a public place or at a public event: *light refreshments are available* | [mass noun] *an ample supply of liquid refreshment.*
2 [mass noun] the giving of fresh mental or physical strength or energy: *hobbies and holidays are for refreshment and recreation.*
– ORIGIN late Middle English (in sense 2): from Old French *refreschement*, from the verb *refreschier* (see **REFRESH**).

Refreshment Sunday ▶**noun** the fourth Sunday in Lent, traditionally a day when certain Lenten restrictions are lifted.

refried beans ▶**plural noun** pinto beans boiled and fried in advance and reheated when required, used especially in Mexican cooking.

refrigerant ▶**noun** a substance used for refrigeration.
▶**adjective** causing cooling or refrigeration.
– ORIGIN late 16th cent. (denoting a substance that cools or allays fever): from French *réfrigérant* or Latin *refrigerant-* 'making cool', from the verb *refrigerare* (see **REFRIGERATE**).

refrigerate ▶**verb** [with obj.] subject (food or drink) to cold in order to chill or preserve it, typically by placing it in a refrigerator: *refrigerate the dough for one hour.*
– DERIVATIVES **refrigeration** noun, **refrigeratory** adjective.
– ORIGIN late Middle English: from Latin *refrigerat-* 'made cool', from the verb *refrigerare*, from *re-* 'back' + *frigus, frigor-* 'cold'.

refrigerated ▶**adjective** (of food or drink) chilled, especially in a refrigerator: *sandwiches must be kept refrigerated in shops* | *refrigerated meat.* ▪(of a vehicle or container) used to keep or transport food or drink in a chilled condition.

refrigerator ▶**noun** an appliance or compartment which is artificially kept cool and used to store food and drink. Modern refrigerators generally make use of the cooling effect produced when a volatile liquid is forced to evaporate in a sealed system in which it can be condensed back to liquid outside the refrigerator.

refringent /rɪˈfrɪn(d)ʒ(ə)nt/ ▶**adjective** Physics refractive.
– DERIVATIVES **refringence** noun.
– ORIGIN late 18th cent.: from Latin *refringent-*, literally 'breaking again', from the verb *refringere*.

refroze past of **REFREEZE**.

refrozen past participle of **REFREEZE**.

reft past and past participle of **REAVE**.

refuel ▶**verb** (**refuelled**, **refuelling**; US **refueled**, **refueling**) [with obj.] supply (a vehicle) with more fuel: *the authorities agreed to refuel the plane.* ▪[no obj.] (of a vehicle) be supplied with more fuel.

refuge ▶ **noun** [mass noun] a condition of being safe or sheltered from pursuit, danger, or trouble: *he was forced to **take refuge in** the French embassy | I **sought refuge in** drink.*
■ [count noun] something providing such shelter: *the family came to be seen as a **refuge from** a harsh world.* ■ [count noun] an institution providing safe accommodation for women who have suffered violence from a husband or partner. ■ [count noun] Brit. a traffic island.
– ORIGIN late Middle English: from Old French, from Latin *refugium*, from Latin *re-* 'back' + *fugere* 'flee'.

refugee ▶ **noun** a person who has been forced to leave their country in order to escape war, persecution, or natural disaster: *refugees from Nazi persecution* | [as modifier] *a refugee camp.*
– ORIGIN late 17th cent.: from French *réfugié* 'gone in search of refuge', past participle of *(se) réfugier*, from *refuge* (see **REFUGE**).

refugium /rɪˈfjuːdʒɪəm/ ▶ **noun** (pl. **refugia** /-dʒɪə/) Biology an area in which a population of organisms can survive through a period of unfavourable conditions, especially glaciation.
– ORIGIN 1950s: from Latin, literally 'place of refuge'.

refulgent /rɪˈfʌldʒ(ə)nt/ ▶ **adjective** poetic/literary shining very brightly: *refulgent blue eyes.*
– DERIVATIVES **refulgence** noun, **refulgently** adverb.
– ORIGIN late 15th cent.: from Latin *refulgent-* 'shining out', from the verb *refulgere*, from *re-* (expressing intensive force) + *fulgere* 'to shine'.

refund ▶ **verb** /rɪˈfʌnd/ [with obj.] pay back (money), typically to a customer who is not satisfied with goods or services bought: *if you're not delighted with your purchase, we guarantee to refund your money in full.*
■ pay back money to (someone): *I'll refund you for the apples and any other damage.*
▶ **noun** /ˈriːfʌnd/ a repayment of a sum of money, typically to a dissatisfied customer: *you may be allowed to claim a refund of the VAT.*
– DERIVATIVES **refundable** adjective.
– ORIGIN late Middle English (in the senses 'pour back' and 'restore'): from Old French *refonder* or Latin *refundere*, from *re-* 'back' + *fundere* 'pour', later associated with the verb **FUND**. The noun dates from the mid 19th cent.

refurbish ▶ **verb** [with obj.] (usu. **be refurbished**) renovate and redecorate (a building): *the premises have been completely refurbished in our corporate style.*
– DERIVATIVES **refurbishment** noun.

refurnish ▶ **verb** [with obj.] (often **be refurnished**) furnish (a room or building) again or differently.

refusal ▶ **noun** [usu. with infinitive] an act of indicating or showing that one is not willing to do something: *their refusal to accept change* | [mass noun] *refusal to do military service was rife.*
■ an indication that one is not willing to accept or grant an offer or request: *an appeal against the refusal of a licence.* ■ an instance of a horse stopping short or running aside at a jump.

refuse[1] /rɪˈfjuːz/ ▶ **verb** [no obj., with infinitive] indicate or show that one is not willing to do something: *I refused to answer* | [no obj.] *he was severely beaten when he refused.*
■ [with obj.] indicate that one is not willing to accept or grant (something offered or requested): *she refused a cigarette* | [with two objs] *the old lady was refused admission to four hospitals.* ■ informal (of a thing) fail to perform a required action: *the car refused to start.* ■ [with obj.] dated decline to accept an offer of marriage from (someone): *he's so conceited he'd never believe anyone would refuse him.* ■ [with obj.] (of a horse) stop short or run aside at (a fence or other obstacle) instead of jumping it.
– DERIVATIVES **refuser** noun.
– ORIGIN Middle English: from Old French *refuser*, probably an alteration of Latin *recusare* 'to refuse', influenced by *refutare* 'refute'.

refuse[2] /ˈrɛfjuːs/ ▶ **noun** [mass noun] matter thrown away or rejected as worthless; rubbish: *heaps of refuse* | [as modifier] *refuse collection.*
– ORIGIN late Middle English : perhaps from Old French *refusé* 'refused', past participle of *refuser* (see **REFUSE**[1]).

refusenik /rɪˈfjuːznɪk/ ▶ **noun 1** a Jew in the former Soviet Union who was refused permission to emigrate to Israel.
2 a person who refuses to follow orders or obey the law, especially as a protest.
– ORIGIN 1970s: from **REFUSE**[1] + **-NIK**.

refute /rɪˈfjuːt/ ▶ **verb** [with obj.] prove (a statement or theory) to be wrong or false; disprove: *these claims have not been convincingly refuted.*
■ prove that (someone) is wrong. ■ deny or contradict (a statement or accusation) : *a spokesman totally refuted the allegation of bias.*
– DERIVATIVES **refutable** adjective, **refutal** noun (rare), **refutation** noun, **refuter** noun.
– ORIGIN mid 16th cent. : from Latin *refutare* 'repel, rebut'.

> **USAGE** The core meaning of **refute** is 'prove (a statement or theory) to be wrong', as in *attempts to **refute** Einstein's theory.* In the second half of the 20th century, a more general sense developed from the core one, meaning simply 'deny', as in *I absolutely **refute** the charges made against me.* Traditionalists object to the second use on the grounds that it is an unacceptable degradation of the language, but it is now widely accepted in standard English.

reg ▶ **noun** [usu. in combination] Brit. informal a vehicle's registration mark, especially the letter denoting the year of manufacture: *a B-reg lorry.*
– ORIGIN 1960s: abbreviation.

regain ▶ **verb** [with obj.] obtain possession or use of (something, typically something abstract) again after losing it: *she died without regaining consciousness | the tyrant was able to regain Sicily.*
■ reach (a place, position, or thing) again; get back to: *they were unable to regain their boats.*
– ORIGIN mid 16th cent.: from French *regagner* (see **RE-**, **GAIN**).

regal ▶ **adjective** of, resembling, or fit for a monarch, especially in being magnificent or dignified: *regal authority | her regal bearing.*
– DERIVATIVES **regally** adverb.
– ORIGIN late Middle English: from Old French, or from Latin *regalis*, from *rex*, *reg-* 'king'.

regale ▶ **verb** [with obj.] entertain or amuse (someone) with talk: *he **regaled** her **with** a colourful account of that afternoon's meeting.*
■ lavishly supply (someone) with food or drink: *he was regaled with excellent home cooking.*
– DERIVATIVES **regalement** noun (rare).
– ORIGIN mid 17th cent.: from French *régaler*, from *re-* (expressing intensive force) + Old French *gale* 'pleasure'.

regalia /rɪˈɡeɪlɪə/ ▶ **plural noun** [treated as sing. or pl.] the emblems or insignia of royalty, especially the crown, sceptre, and other ornaments used at a coronation.
■ the distinctive clothing worn and ornaments carried at formal occasions as an indication of status: *the Bishop of Florence **in full regalia**.*
– ORIGIN mid 16th cent. (in the sense 'royal powers'): from medieval Latin, literally 'royal privileges', from Latin, neuter plural of *regalis* 'regal'.

> **USAGE** The word **regalia** comes from Latin and is, technically speaking, the plural of *regalis*. However, in the way the word is used in English today it behaves as a collective noun, similar to words like **staff** or **government**. This means that it can be used with either a singular or plural verb (*the **regalia** of Russian tsardom **is** now displayed in the Kremlin* or *the **regalia** of Russian tsardom **are** now displayed in the Kremlin*), but it has no other singular form.

regalian ▶ **adjective** formal belonging or relating to a monarch; regal: *regalian rights.*
– ORIGIN early 19th cent.: from French *régalien*, from Latin *regalis* 'regal'.

regalism ▶ **noun** [mass noun] the doctrine of a sovereign's supremacy in ecclesiastical matters.
– DERIVATIVES **regalist** noun & adjective.

regality ▶ **noun** (pl. **-ies**) [mass noun] **1** the state of being a king or queen.
■ the demeanour or dignity appropriate to a king or queen: *Enid awaited her guests, radiating regality.*
2 historical (in Scotland) territorial jurisdiction granted by the king to a powerful subject.
■ [count noun] a territory subject to such jurisdiction.
3 [count noun] archaic a royal privilege.
– ORIGIN late Middle English: from Anglo-Norman French *regalite* or medieval Latin *regalitas*, from *regalis* 'royal' (see **REGAL**).

regard ▶ **verb** [with obj. and adverbial] consider or think of (someone or something) in a specified way: *she regarded London as her base | he was highly regarded by senators of both parties.*
■ gaze at steadily in a specified fashion: *Professor Ryker regarded him with a faint smile | Nuala regarded him unflinchingly.* ■ [with obj.] archaic pay attention to; heed: *he talk'd very wisely, but I regarded him not.* ■ [with obj.] archaic (of a thing) have relation to or connection with; concern: *if these things regarded only myself, I could stand it with composure.*
▶ **noun 1** [mass noun] attention to or concern for something: *the court must have **regard to** the principle of welfare | she rescued him without **regard for** herself.*
■ [count noun] high opinion; liking and respect; esteem: *she had a particular **regard for** Eliot.* ■ [in sing.] a gaze; a steady or significant look: *he shifted uneasily before their clear regard.*
2 (**regards**) best wishes (used to express friendliness in greetings, especially at the end of letters): *Regards, Yours sincerely, … | give her my regards.*
– PHRASES **as regards** concerning; in respect of: *as regards content, the programme will cover important current issues.* **in this** (or **that**) **regard** in connection with the point previously mentioned: *there was little incentive for them to be active in this regard.* **with** (or **in** or **having**) **regard to** as concerns; in respect of: *he made enquiries with regard to Beth.*
– ORIGIN Middle English: from Old French *regarder* 'to watch', from *re-* 'back' (also expressing intensive force) + *garder* 'to guard'.

regardant /rɪˈɡɑːd(ə)nt/ ▶ **adjective** [usu. postpositive] Heraldry looking backwards.
– ORIGIN late Middle English: from Anglo-Norman French and Old French, present participle of *regarder* 'look (again)'.

regardful ▶ **adjective** [predic.] (**regardful of**) formal paying attention to; mindful of: *Parker was not overly regardful of public opinion.*
– DERIVATIVES **regardfully** adverb.

regarding ▶ **preposition** in respect of; concerning: *your recent letter regarding the above proposal.*

regardless ▶ **adverb** without paying attention to the present situation; despite the prevailing circumstances: *they were determined to carry on regardless.*
– PHRASES **regardless of** without regard or consideration for: *the allowance is paid regardless of age or income.*
– DERIVATIVES **regardlessly** adverb, **regardlessness** noun.

regather ▶ **verb 1** [with obj.] collect or gather (something) again: *after 1910 the workers' movement regathered momentum.*
2 [no obj.] meet or come together again.

regatta ▶ **noun** a sporting event consisting of a series of boat or yacht races.
– ORIGIN early 17th cent.: from Italian (Venetian dialect), literally 'a fight, contest'.

regd ▶ **abbreviation for** registered.

regelate /ˌriːdʒɪˈleɪt/ ▶ **verb** [no obj.] technical (chiefly of pieces of ice thawed apart) freeze together again.
– DERIVATIVES **regelation** noun.
– ORIGIN mid 19th cent.: from **RE-** 'again' + Latin *gelat-* 'frozen' (from the verb *gelare*).

Régence /reɪˈʒɒ̃s, French reʒɑ̃s/ ▶ **adjective** relating to or denoting a style of costume, furniture, and interior decoration characteristic of the French Regency.
– ORIGIN French, 'Regency'.

regency /ˈriːdʒ(ə)nsi/ ▶ **noun** (pl. **-ies**) the office or period of government by a regent.
■ a commission acting as regent. ■ (**the Regency**) the particular period of a regency, especially (in Britain) from 1811 to 1820 and (in France) from 1715 to 1723.
▶ **adjective** (**Regency**) relating to or denoting British architecture, clothing, and furniture of the Regency or, more widely, of the late 18th and early 19th centuries. Regency style was contemporary with the Empire style and shares many of its features: elaborate and ornate, it is generally neoclassical, with a generous borrowing of Greek and Egyptian motifs.
– ORIGIN late Middle English: from medieval Latin *regentia*, from Latin *regent-* 'ruling' (see **REGENT**).

regenerate ▶ **verb** /rɪˈdʒɛnəreɪt/ [with obj.] (of a living organism) regrow (new tissue) to replace lost or injured tissue: *a crab in the process of regenerating a claw.*
■ [no obj.] (of an organ or tissue) regrow: *once destroyed, brain cells do not regenerate.* ■ bring into renewed existence; generate again: *the issue was regenerated last month.* ■ bring new and more vigorous life to (an area or institution), especially in economic terms; revive: *regenerating the inner cities.* ■ (especially in Christian use) give a new and higher spiritual nature to. ■ [usu. as adj. **regenerated**] Chemistry precipitate (a

r

natural polymer such as cellulose) in a different form following chemical processing, especially in the form of fibres.
▶ **adjective** /rɪˈdʒɛn(ə)rət/ reformed or reborn, especially in a spiritual or moral sense.
– DERIVATIVES **regenerator** noun.
– ORIGIN late Middle English (as an adjective): from Latin *regeneratus* 'created again', past participle of *regenerare*, from *re-* 'again' + *generare* 'create'. The verb dates from the mid 16th cent.

regeneration ▶ **noun** [mass noun] the action or process of regenerating or being regenerated, in particular the formation of new animal or plant tissue.
■ Electronics positive feedback. ■ Chemistry the action or process of regenerating polymer fibres.
– ORIGIN Middle English: from Latin *regeneratio(n-)*, from *regenerare* 'create again' (see **REGENERATE**).

regenerative ▶ **adjective** tending to or characterized by regeneration: *natural regenerative processes.*
■ denoting a method of braking in which energy is extracted from the parts braked, to be stored and reused.
– DERIVATIVES **regeneratively** adverb.

regent ▶ **noun 1** a person appointed to administer a state because the monarch is a minor or is absent or incapacitated.
2 N. Amer. a member of the governing body of a university or other academic institution.
▶ **adjective** [postpositive] acting as regent for a monarch: *the queen regent of Portugal.* See also **PRINCE REGENT**.
– ORIGIN late Middle English: from Old French, or from Latin *regent-* 'ruling', from the verb *regere.*

regent bowerbird ▶ **noun** an Australian bowerbird, the male of which has conspicuous black and gold plumage.
● *Sericulus chrysocephalus*, family Ptilonorhynchidae.

reggae /ˈrɛgeɪ/ ▶ **noun** [mass noun] a style of popular music with a strongly accented subsidiary beat, originating in Jamaica. Reggae evolved in the late 1960s from ska and other local variations on calypso and rhythm and blues, and became widely known in the 1970s through the work of Bob Marley; its lyrics are much influenced by Rastafarian ideas.
– ORIGIN perhaps related to Jamaican English *rege-rege* 'quarrel, row'.

Reggio di Calabria /ˌrɛdʒɪəʊ diː kəˈlabrɪə/ a port at the southern tip of the 'toe' of Italy, on the Strait of Messina, capital of Calabria region; pop. 183,440 (1991). The original settlement was founded about 720 BC by Greek colonists as Rhegion (Latin Rhegium).

reggo ▶ **noun** variant spelling of **REGO**.

regicide /ˈrɛdʒɪsʌɪd/ ▶ **noun** [mass noun] the action of killing a king.
■ [count noun] a person who kills or takes part in killing a king.
– DERIVATIVES **regicidal** adjective.
– ORIGIN mid 16th cent.: from Latin *rex, reg-* 'king' + **-CIDE**, probably suggested by French *régicide.*

Régie /reɪˈʒiː/ ▶ **noun** (in some European countries) a government department that controls an industry or service, historically one with complete control of the importation, manufacture, and taxation of tobacco, salt, and other resources.
– ORIGIN French, feminine past participle of *régir* 'to rule'.

regime /reɪˈʒiːm/ ▶ **noun 1** a government, especially an authoritarian one.
2 a system or planned way of doing things, especially one imposed from above: *detention centres with a very tough physical regime | a tax regime.*
■ a coordinated programme for the promotion or restoration of health; a regimen: *a low-calorie, low-fat regime.* ■ the conditions under which a scientific or industrial process occurs.
– ORIGIN late 15th cent. (in the sense 'regimen'): French *régime*, from Latin *regimen* 'rule' (see **REGIMEN**). Sense 1 dates from the late 18th cent. (with original reference to the Ancien Régime).

regimen /ˈrɛdʒɪmən/ ▶ **noun 1** a prescribed course of medical treatment, way of life, or diet for the promotion or restoration of health: *a regimen of one or two injections per day | a treatment regimen.*
2 archaic a system of government.
– ORIGIN late Middle English (denoting the action of governing): from Latin, from *regere* 'to rule'.

regiment ▶ **noun** /ˈrɛdʒɪm(ə)nt/ **1** a permanent unit of an army typically commanded by a lieutenant colonel and divided into several companies, squadrons, or batteries and often into two battalions: [in names] *the Royal Highland Regiment.*
■ an operational unit of artillery. ■ a large array or number of people or things: *the whole **regiment of** women MPs | a neat **regiment of** jars and bottles.*
2 [mass noun] archaic rule or government over a person, people, or country: *the powers of ecclesiastical regiment which none but the Church should wield.*
▶ **verb** /ˈrɛdʒɪmɛnt/ [with obj.] (usu. **be regimented**) **1** organize according to a strict, sometimes oppressive system or pattern: *every aspect of their life is strictly regimented* | [as adj. **regimented**] *the regimented environment of the ward.*
2 rare form (troops) into a regiment or regiments.
– DERIVATIVES **regimentation** noun.
– ORIGIN late Middle English (in the sense 'rule or government over a person, people, or country'): via Old French from late Latin *regimentum* 'rule', from *regere* 'to rule'.

regimental ▶ **adjective** of or relating to a regiment: *a regimental badge | regimental traditions.*
– DERIVATIVES **regimentally** adverb.

regimental colour ▶ **noun** (in the UK) a regimental standard in the form of a silk flag, carried by a particular regiment along with its Queen's colour.

regimentals ▶ **plural noun** military uniform, especially that of a particular regiment.

regimental sergeant major ▶ **noun** see **SERGEANT MAJOR** (sense 1).

Regina[1] /rɪˈdʒʌɪnə/ the capital of Saskatchewan, situated in the centre of the wheat-growing plains of south central Canada; pop. 179,180 (1991).

Regina[2] /rɪˈdʒʌɪnə/ ▶ **noun** the reigning queen (used following a name or in the titles of lawsuits, e.g. *Regina v. Jones*, the Crown versus Jones).
– ORIGIN Latin, literally 'queen'.

Regiomontanus /ˌrɛdʒɪəʊmɒnˈtɑːnəs/, Johannes (1436–76), German astronomer and mathematician; born *Johannes Müller.* Regiomontanus is considered the most important astronomer of the 15th century. He translated Ptolemy's *Mathematical Syntaxis* and wrote four monumental works on mathematics and astronomy.

region ▶ **noun** an area or division, especially part of a country or the world having definable characteristics but not always fixed boundaries: *one of the region's major employers | the equatorial regions | a major wine-producing region.*
■ an administrative district of a city or country. ■ (**the regions**) the parts of a country outside the capital or chief seat of government: *the promotion of investment in the regions.* ■ a part of the body, especially around or near an organ: *an unexpected clenching sensation in the region of her heart.* ■ figurative the sphere or realm of something: *his work takes craft and needlework into the region of folk art.*
– PHRASES **in the region of** approximately: *annual sales in the region of 30 million.*
– ORIGIN Middle English: from Old French, from Latin *regio(n-)* 'direction, district', from *regere* 'to rule, direct'.

regional ▶ **adjective** of, relating to, or characteristic of a region: *regional and local needs | regional variations.*
■ of or relating to the regions of a country rather than the capital: *a regional assembly | a regional accent.*
▶ **noun** (usu. **regionals**) a stamp, newspaper, or other thing produced or used in a particular region.
■ (**regionals**) N. Amer. a sporting contest involving competitors from a particular region.
– DERIVATIVES **regionally** adverb.

regionalism ▶ **noun 1** [mass noun] the theory or practice of regional rather than central systems of administration or economic, cultural, or political affiliation: *a strong expression of regionalism.*
2 a linguistic feature peculiar to a particular region and not part of the standard language of a country.
– DERIVATIVES **regionalist** noun & adjective.

regionalize (also **-ise**) ▶ **verb** [with obj.] [usu. as adj. **regionalized**] organize (a country, area, or enterprise) on a regional basis: *a regionalized system.*
– DERIVATIVES **regionalization** noun.

regional metamorphism ▶ **noun** [mass noun] Geology metamorphism affecting rocks over an extensive area as a result of the large-scale action of heat and pressure.

regisseur /ˌrɛʒɪˈsəː/ ▶ **noun** a person who stages a theatrical production, especially a ballet.
– ORIGIN from French *régisseur.*

register ▶ **noun 1** an official list or record, for example of births, marriages, and deaths, of shipping, or of professionally qualified people.
■ a book or record of attendance, for example of pupils in a class or school or guests in a hotel.
2 a particular part of the range of a voice or instrument: *his voice moved up a register | boy trebles singing in a high register.*
■ a sliding device controlling a set of organ pipes which share a tonal quality. ■ a set of organ pipes so controlled.
3 Linguistics a variety of a language or a level of usage, as determined by degree of formality and choice of vocabulary, pronunciation, and syntax, according to the communicative purpose, social context, and standing of the user.
4 [mass noun] Printing & Photography the exact correspondence of the position of colour components in a printed positive.
■ Printing the exact correspondence of the position of printed matter on the two sides of a leaf.
5 (in electronic devices) a location in a store of data, used for a specific purpose and with quick access time.
6 an adjustable plate for widening or narrowing an opening and regulating a draught, especially in a fire grate.
7 chiefly N. Amer. short for **CASH REGISTER**.
8 Art one of a number of bands or sections into which a design is divided.
▶ **verb** [with obj.] **1** enter or record in an official list as being in a particular category, having a particular eligibility or entitlement, or in keeping with a requirement: *the vessel is registered as British | his father was late in registering his birth* | [as adj. **registered**] *a registered charity.*
■ [no obj.] put one's name on an official list under such terms: *you must register for the tax.* ■ [no obj.] put one's name in a register as a guest in a hotel. ■ [no obj.] N. Amer. (of a couple to be married) have a list of wedding gifts compiled and kept at a shop for consultation by gift buyers. ■ entrust (a letter or parcel) to a post office for transmission by registered post: [as adj. **registered**] *a registered letter.* ■ express (an opinion or emotion): *I wish to register an objection.* ■ achieve (a certain score or result): *they registered their third consecutive draw.*
2 (of an instrument) detect and show (a reading) automatically: *the electroscope was too insensitive to register the tiny changes.*
■ [no obj., with complement] (of an event) give rise to a specified reading on an instrument: *the blast registered 5.4 on the Richter scale.* ■ [usu. with negative] properly notice or become aware of (something): *he had not even registered her presence.* ■ [no obj.] [usu. with negative] make an impression on a person's mind: *the content of her statement did not register.* ■ [no obj.] (of an emotion) show in a person's face or gestures: *nothing registered on their faces.* ■ indicate or convey (a feeling or emotion) by facial expression or gestures: *he did not register much surprise at this.*
3 Printing & Photography correspond or cause to correspond exactly in position: [no obj.] *they are adjusted until the impressions register.*
– DERIVATIVES **registrable** adjective.
– ORIGIN late Middle English: from Old French *regestre* or medieval Latin *regestrum, registrum*, alteration of *regestum*, singular of late Latin *regesta* 'things recorded', from *regerere* 'enter, record'.

registered nurse (abbrev.: **RN**) ▶ **noun** chiefly N. Amer. a fully trained nurse with an official state certificate of competence.
■ Brit. short for **STATE REGISTERED NURSE**.

registered post ▶ **noun** Brit. a postal procedure with special precautions for safety and for compensation in case of loss.

register office Brit. ▶ **noun** (in the UK) a local government building where civil marriages are conducted and births, marriages, and deaths are recorded with the issue of certificates.

USAGE The form **register office** is the official term, but **registry office** is the form which dominates in informal and non-official use.

register ton ▶ **noun** see **TON**[1] (sense 1).

registrant ▶ **noun** a person who registers.

registrar /ˈrɛdʒɪstrɑː, ˌrɛdʒɪˈstrɑː/ ▶ **noun 1** an official responsible for keeping a register or official records: *the registrar of births and deaths.*

■the chief administrative officer in a university. ■ (in the UK) the judicial and administrative officer of the High Court.
2 Brit. a middle-ranking hospital doctor undergoing training as a specialist.
– DERIVATIVES **registrarship** noun.
– ORIGIN late 17th cent.: from medieval Latin *registrarius*, from *registrum* (see **REGISTER**).

Registrar General ▶ **noun** a government official responsible for holding a population census.

registrary /ˈrɛdʒɪˌstr(ə)ri/ ▶ **noun** (pl. **-ies**) the chief administrative officer of Cambridge University.

registration ▶ **noun** [mass noun] the action or process of registering or of being registered: *the registration of births, marriages, and deaths* | [count noun] *the number of new private car registrations has increased.*
■(also **registration mark** or **registration number**) [count noun] Brit. the series of letters and figures identifying a motor vehicle, assigned on registration and displayed on a number plate: *her car registration is H53 UVO.* ■ the action or process of acquiring full British citizenship by a Commonwealth resident or a person of British descent. ■ Music a combination of stops used when playing the organ.
– ORIGIN mid 16th cent.: from medieval Latin *registratio(n-)*, based on Latin *regerere* 'enter, record' (see **REGISTER**).

registration document (also **vehicle registration document**) ▶ **noun** (in the UK) a document giving registered information about a vehicle, such as the owner's name, the date of its manufacture, and the engine and chassis numbers.

registration plate ▶ **noun** Brit. another term for **NUMBER PLATE**.

registry ▶ **noun** (pl. **-ies**) **1** a place or office where registers or records are kept.
2 [mass noun] registration.

registry office ▶ **noun** another term for **REGISTER OFFICE** (used in informal and non-official use).

Regius professor /ˈriːdʒɪəs/ ▶ **noun** (in the UK) the holder of a university chair founded by a sovereign (especially one at Oxford or Cambridge instituted by Henry VIII) or filled by Crown appointment.
– ORIGIN Latin *regius* 'royal', from *rex*, *reg-* 'king'.

reglaze ▶ **verb** [with obj.] glaze (a window) again.

reglet /ˈrɛglɪt/ ▶ **noun** **1** Printing a thin strip of wood or metal used to separate type.
2 Architecture a narrow strip used to separate mouldings or panels from one another.
– ORIGIN mid 17th cent.: from French *réglet*, diminutive of *règle* 'rule'.

regnal /ˈrɛgn(ə)l/ ▶ **adjective** [attrib.] of a reign or monarch.
– ORIGIN early 17th cent.: from Anglo-Latin *regnalis*, from Latin *regnum* 'kingdom'.

regnal year ▶ **noun** a year reckoned from the date or anniversary of a sovereign's accession.

regnant /ˈrɛgnənt/ ▶ **adjective** **1** [often postpositive] reigning; ruling: *a queen regnant.*
2 currently having the greatest influence; dominant: *the regnant belief.*
– ORIGIN early 17th cent.: from Latin *regnant-* 'reigning', from the verb *regnare*.

rego /ˈrɛdʒəʊ/ (also **reggo**) ▶ **noun** [often as modifier] Austral. informal a motor-vehicle registration.
– ORIGIN 1960s: abbreviation of **REGISTRATION** + the colloquial suffix **-O**.

regolith /ˈrɛg(ə)lɪθ/ ▶ **noun** [mass noun] Geology the layer of unconsolidated solid material covering the bedrock of a planet.
– ORIGIN late 19th cent.: from Greek *rhēgos* 'rug, blanket' + **-LITH**.

regorge ▶ **verb** [with obj.] archaic bring up again; disgorge.
■[no obj.] gush or flow back again.
– ORIGIN early 17th cent.: from French *regorger*, or from **RE-** 'again' + the verb **GORGE**.

regrade ▶ **verb** [with obj.] grade again or differently: [as noun **regrading**] *a demand for a regrading of pay levels.*

regress ▶ **verb** /rɪˈgrɛs/ **1** [no obj.] return to a former or less developed state: *they would not regress to pre-technological tribalism.*
■return mentally to a former stage of life or a supposed previous life, especially through hypnosis or mental illness: [no obj.] *she claims to be able to regress to the Roman era* | [with obj.] *I regressed Sylvia to early childhood.*
2 [with obj.] Statistics calculate the coefficient or coefficients of regression of (a variable) against or on another variable.
3 [no obj.] Astronomy move in a retrograde direction.
▶ **noun** /ˈriːgrɛs/ [mass noun] **1** the action of returning to a former or less developed state.
2 Philosophy a series of statements in which a logical procedure is continually reapplied to its own result without approaching a useful conclusion (e.g. defining something in terms of itself).
– ORIGIN late Middle English (as a noun): from Latin *regressus*, from *regredi* 'go back, return', from *re-* 'back' + *gradi* 'walk'.

regression ▶ **noun** [mass noun] **1** a return to a former or less developed state.
■a return to an earlier stage of life or a supposed previous life, especially through hypnosis or mental illness, or as a means of escaping present anxieties: [as modifier] *regression therapy.*
2 Statistics a measure of the relation between the mean value of one variable (e.g. output) and corresponding values of other variables (e.g. time and cost).

regressive ▶ **adjective** **1** becoming less advanced; returning to a former or less developed state: *the regressive, infantile wish for the perfect parent of early childhood.*
■of, relating to, or marked by psychological regression.
2 (of a tax) taking a proportionally greater amount from those on lower incomes.
3 Philosophy proceeding from effect to cause or from particular to universal.
– DERIVATIVES **regressively** adverb, **regressiveness** noun.

regret ▶ **verb** (**regretted**, **regretting**) [with obj.] feel sad, repentant, or disappointed over (something that has happened or been done, especially a loss or missed opportunity): *she immediately regretted her words* | [with clause] *I always regretted that I never trained.*
■used in polite formulas to express apology for or sadness over something bad or unpleasant: *any inconvenience to readers is regretted* | [with clause] *we regret that no tickets may be exchanged.* ■ archaic feel sorrow for the loss or absence of (something pleasant): *my home, when shall I cease to regret you!*
▶ **noun** [mass noun] a feeling of sadness, repentance, or disappointment over something that has happened or been done: *she expressed her regret at Virginia's death* | *he had to decline,* **to his regret**.
■(often **regrets**) an instance or cause of such a feeling: *she had few regrets in leaving the house.* ■ (often **one's regrets**) used in polite formulas to express apology for or sadness at an occurrence or an inability to accept an invitation: *please give your grandmother my regrets.*
– ORIGIN late Middle English: from Old French *regreter* 'bewail (the dead)', perhaps from the Germanic base of **GREET**[2].

regretful ▶ **adjective** feeling or showing regret: *he sounded regretful but pointed out that he had committed himself.*
– DERIVATIVES **regretfulness** noun.

regretfully ▶ **adverb** in a regretful manner.
■[sentence adverb] regrettably: *regretfully, mounting costs and diminishing traffic forced the line to close.*

> **USAGE** The adjectives **regretful** and **regrettable** are distinct in meaning: **regretful** means 'feeling or showing regret', as in *she shook her head with a **regretful** smile*, while **regrettable** means 'giving rise to regret; undesirable', as in *the loss of jobs is **regrettable***. The adverbs **regretfully** and **regrettably** have not, however, preserved the same distinction. **Regretfully** is used as a normal manner adverb to mean 'in a regretful manner', as in *he sighed **regretfully***, but it is also used as a sentence adverb meaning 'it is regrettable that', as in ***regretfully**, the trustees must turn down your request.* In this latter use it is synonymous with **regrettably**. Despite objections from traditionalists, this use is now well established (more than 30 per cent of citations in the British National Corpus for **regretfully** are in this disputed sense) and is included in most modern dictionaries without comment.

regrettable ▶ **adjective** (of conduct or an event) giving rise to regret; undesirable; unwelcome: *the loss of this number of jobs is regrettable* | *irresponsible and regrettable actions.*

regrettably ▶ **adverb** [sentence adverb] unfortunately (used to express apology for or sadness at something): *regrettably, last night's audience was a meagre one.*

> **USAGE** On the use of **regrettably** and **regretfully**, see usage at **REGRETFULLY**.

regroup ▶ **verb** [no obj.] (of troops) reassemble into organized groups, typically after being attacked or defeated: *their heroic resistance gave American forces time to regroup.*
■[with obj.] cause to reassemble in this way. ■ [with obj.] rearrange (something) into a new group or groups.
– DERIVATIVES **regroupment** noun.

regrow ▶ **verb** (past **regrew**; past participle **regrown**) grow or cause to grow again.
– DERIVATIVES **regrowth** noun.

regs informal ▶ **abbreviation for** ■ regulations.

Regt ▶ **abbreviation for** Regiment.

regulable ▶ **adjective** able to be regulated.

regular ▶ **adjective** **1** arranged in or constituting a constant or definite pattern, especially with the same space between individual instances: *plant the flags at regular intervals* | *a regular arrangement.*
■happening in such a pattern with the same time between individual instances; recurring at short uniform intervals: *a regular monthly check* | *her breathing became deeper, more regular.* ■ (of a person) doing the same thing or going to the same place with the same time between individual instances: *regular worshippers.* ■ (of a structure or arrangement) arranged in or constituting a symmetrical or harmonious pattern: *beautifully regular, heart-shaped leaves.* ■ (of a person) defecating or menstruating at predictable times.
2 done or happening frequently: *regular border clashes* | *parties were a fairly regular occurrence.*
■(of a person) doing the same thing or going to the same place frequently: *a regular visitor.*
3 conforming to or governed by an accepted standard of procedure or convention: *policies carried on by his ministers through regular channels* | *a regular job.*
■[attrib.] of or belonging to the permanent professional armed forces of a country: *a regular soldier.* ■ (of a person) properly trained or qualified and pursuing a full-time occupation: *a strong distrust of regular doctors.* ■ Christian Church subject to or bound by religious rule; belonging to a religious or monastic order: *the regular clergy.* Contrasted with **SECULAR** (sense 2). ■ informal, dated rightly so called; complete; absolute (used for emphasis): *this place is a regular fisherman's paradise.*
4 used, done, or happening on a habitual basis; usual; customary: *I couldn't get an appointment with my regular barber* | *our regular suppliers.*
■chiefly N. Amer. of a normal or ordinary kind; not special: *it's richer than regular pasta.* ■ (chiefly in commercial use) denoting merchandise, especially food or drink, of average, medium, or standard size: *a shake and regular fries.* ■ (in surfing and other board sports) with the left leg in front of the right on the board.
5 Grammar (of a word) following the normal pattern of inflection: *a regular verb.*
6 Geometry (of a figure) having all sides and all angles equal: *a regular polygon.*
■(of a solid) bounded by a number of equal figures.
7 Botany (of a flower) having radial symmetry.
▶ **noun** a regular customer or member, for example of a pub, shop, or team: *the absence of four first-team regulars.*
■a regular member of the armed forces. ■ Christian Church one of the regular clergy.
– PHRASES **keep regular hours** do the same thing, especially going to bed and getting up, at the same time each day.
– DERIVATIVES **regularly** adverb.
– ORIGIN late Middle English: from Old French *reguler*, from Latin *regularis*, from *regula* 'rule'.

regular canon ▶ **noun** see **CANON**[2].

regular guy ▶ **noun** N. Amer. informal an ordinary, uncomplicated, sociable man.

regularity ▶ **noun** (pl. **-ies**) [mass noun] the state or quality of being regular: *he came to see her with increasing regularity.*

regularize (also **-ise**) ▶ **verb** [with obj.] make (something) regular.
■establish (a hitherto temporary or provisional arrangement) on an official or correct basis: *immigrants applying to regularize their status as residents.*
– DERIVATIVES **regularization** noun.

regulate ▶ **verb** [with obj.] control or maintain the

r

rate or speed of (a machine or process) so that it operates properly: *a hormone which regulates metabolism and organ function.*
■control or supervise (something, especially a company or business activity) by means of rules and regulations: *the Code regulates the takeovers of all public companies.* ■set (a clock or other apparatus) according to an external standard.
– DERIVATIVES **regulative** adjective.
– ORIGIN late Middle English (in the sense 'control by rules'): from late Latin *regulat-* 'directed, regulated', from the verb *regulare*, from Latin *regula* 'rule'.

regulation ▶ **noun 1** a rule or directive made and maintained by an authority: *planning regulations.*
■[as modifier] in accordance with regulations; of the correct type: *regulation army footwear.* ■[as modifier] informal of a familiar or predictable type; formulaic; standardized: *a regulation Western parody.*
2 [mass noun] the action or process of regulating or being regulated: *the regulation of financial markets.*

regulator ▶ **noun** a person or thing that regulates something, in particular:
■a person or body that supervises a particular industry or business activity. ■a device for controlling the rate of working of machinery or for controlling fluid flow, in particular a handle controlling the supply of steam to the cylinders of a steam engine. ■a device for adjusting the balance of a clock or watch in order to regulate its speed.

regulatory ▶ **adjective** serving or intended to regulate something: *the existing legal and regulatory framework | regulatory enzymes.*

regulo /ˈrɛgjʊləʊ/ ▶ **noun** Brit. trademark used before a numeral to denote a setting on a temperature scale in a gas oven: *preheat the oven to 420° (regulo 7).*

Regulus /ˈrɛgjʊləs/ Astronomy the brightest star in the constellation Leo. It is a triple system of which the primary is a hot dwarf star.
– ORIGIN Latin, literally 'little king'.

regulus /ˈrɛgjʊləs/ ▶ **noun** (pl. **reguluses** or **reguli** /-lʌɪ, -liː/) **1** Chemistry, archaic a metallic form of a substance obtained by smelting or reduction.
2 a petty king or ruler.
– DERIVATIVES **reguline** /-lʌɪn/ adjective (only in sense 1).
– ORIGIN late 16th cent.: from Latin, diminutive of *rex, reg-* 'king'; originally in the phrase *regulus of antimony* (denoting metallic antimony), apparently so named because of its readiness to combine with gold.

regurgitate /rɪˈgəːdʒɪteɪt/ ▶ **verb** [with obj.] bring (swallowed food) up again to the mouth: *gulls regurgitate food for the chicks.*
■figurative repeat (information) without analysing or comprehending it: *facts which can then be regurgitated at examinations.*
– DERIVATIVES **regurgitation** noun.
– ORIGIN late 16th cent.: from medieval Latin *regurgitat-*, from the verb *regurgitare*, from Latin *re-* 'again, back' + *gurges, gurgit-* 'whirlpool'.

r

rehab /ˈriːhab/ informal ▶ **noun** [mass noun] rehabilitation: *Mark went into rehab two years ago.*
■[count noun] US a thing, especially a building, that has been rehabilitated or restored.
▶ **verb** (**rehabbed, rehabbing**) [with obj.] N. Amer. rehabilitate or restore: *they don't rehab you at all in jail | [as adj.* **rehabbed**] *newly rehabbed apartments for rent.*
– ORIGIN 1940s: abbreviation.

rehabilitate ▶ **verb** [with obj.] restore (someone) to health or normal life by training and therapy after imprisonment, addiction, or illness: *helping to rehabilitate former criminals.*
■restore (someone) to former privileges or reputation after a period of critical or official disfavour: *with the fall of the government many former dissidents were rehabilitated.* ■return (something, especially an environmental feature) to its former condition.
– DERIVATIVES **rehabilitation** noun, **rehabilitative** adjective.
– ORIGIN late 16th cent. (in the sense 'restore to former privileges'): from medieval Latin *rehabilitat-*, from the verb *rehabilitare* (see **RE-, HABILITATE**).

rehang ▶ **verb** /riːˈhaŋ/ (past and past participle **rehung**) [with obj.] hang (something) again or differently.
▶ **noun** /ˈriːhaŋ/ an act of rehanging works of art in a gallery.

rehash ▶ **verb** [with obj.] put (old ideas or material) into a new form without significant change or improvement: *he endlessly rehashes songs from his American era.*
■chiefly N. Amer. consider or discuss (something) at length after it has happened: *is it really necessary to rehash that trauma all over again?*
▶ **noun** a reuse of old ideas or material without significant change or improvement.

rehear ▶ **verb** (past and past participle **reheard**) hear or listen to again.
■Law hear (a case or plaintiff) in a court again: [as noun **rehearing**] *the parents produced fresh evidence and won a rehearing.*

rehearsal ▶ **noun** a practice or trial performance of a play or other work for later public performance: ***rehearsals for** the opera season.*
■[mass noun] the action or process of rehearsing: *I've had a fortnight **in rehearsal** | [as modifier] a rehearsal room.*

rehearse ▶ **verb** [with obj.] practise (a play, piece of music, or other work) for later public performance: *we were rehearsing a radio play | [no obj.] she was **rehearsing for** her world tour.*
■supervise (a performer or group) that is practising in this way: *he listened to Charlie rehearsing the band.* ■mentally prepare or recite (words one intends to say): *he had rehearsed a thousand fine phrases.* ■state (a list of points, especially those that have been made many times before); enumerate: *criticisms of factory farming have been rehearsed often enough.*
– DERIVATIVES **rehearser** noun.
– ORIGIN Middle English (in the sense 'repeat aloud'): from Old French *rehercier*, perhaps from *re-* 'again' + *hercer* 'to harrow', from *herse* 'harrow' (see **HEARSE**).

reheat ▶ **verb** [with obj.] heat (something, especially cooked food) again.
▶ **noun** [mass noun] the process of using the hot exhaust to burn extra fuel in a jet engine and produce extra power.
■[count noun] an afterburner.
– DERIVATIVES **reheater** noun.

reheel ▶ **verb** [with obj.] fit (a shoe) with a new heel.

Rehoboam /ˌriːəˈbəʊəm/, son of Solomon, king of ancient Israel *c.*930–*c.*915 BC. His reign witnessed the secession of the northern tribes and their establishment of a new kingdom under Jeroboam, leaving Rehoboam as the first king of Judah (1 Kings 11–14).

rehoboam ▶ **noun** a wine bottle of about six times the standard size.
– ORIGIN late 19th cent.: from the name **REHOBOAM**.

rehome ▶ **verb** [with obj.] (often **be rehomed**) find a new home for (a pet).

rehouse ▶ **verb** [with obj.] (usu. **be rehoused**) provide (someone) with new housing: *tenants will be rehoused in hotels until their homes are habitable.*

rehung past and past participle of **REHANG**.

rehydrate ▶ **verb** absorb or cause to absorb moisture after dehydration: [no obj.] *cubes of dried food which rehydrated in the mouth.*
– DERIVATIVES **rehydratable** adjective, **rehydration** noun.

Reich[1] /rʌɪk, -x, German raɪç/ the former German state, most often used to refer to the Third Reich, the Nazi regime from 1933 to 1945. The **First Reich** was considered to be the Holy Roman Empire, 962–1806, and the **Second Reich** the German Empire, 1871–1918, but neither of these terms are part of normal historical terminology.
– ORIGIN German, literally 'empire'.

Reich[2] /rʌɪx/, Steve (b.1936), American composer; full name *Stephen Michael Reich*. A leading minimalist, he uses the repetition of short phrases within a simple harmonic field. Influences include Balinese and West African music.

Reichsmark /ˈrʌɪxsˌmɑːk, ˈrʌɪks-, German ˈraɪçsˌmaːk/ ▶ **noun** the basic monetary unit of the Third Reich, replaced in 1948 by the Deutschmark.
– ORIGIN German.

Reichstag /ˈrʌɪxsˌtɑːg, ˈrʌɪks-/ the main legislature of the German state under the Second and Third Reichs.
■the building in which this met, badly damaged by fire on the Nazi accession to power in 1933.
– ORIGIN German, from *Reichs* 'of the empire' + *Tag* 'diet' (see **DIET**[2]).

reify /ˈriːɪfʌɪ, ˈreɪɪ-/ ▶ **verb** (**-ies, -ied**) [with obj.] formal make (something abstract) more concrete or real: *these instincts are, in man, reified as verbal constructs.*
– DERIVATIVES **reification** noun, **reificatory** adjective.
– ORIGIN mid 19th cent.: from Latin *res, re-* 'thing' + **-FY**.

reign ▶ **verb** [no obj.] hold royal office; rule as king or queen: *Queen Elizabeth **reigns over** the UK | figurative the Nashville sound will **reign supreme** once again.*
■[usu. as adj. **reigning**] (of a sports player or team) currently hold a particular title: *the reigning world champion.* ■(of a quality or condition) prevail; predominate: *confusion reigned.*
▶ **noun** the period during which a sovereign rules: *the original chapel was built in the reign of Charles I.*
■the period during which a sports player or team holds a specified title.
– ORIGIN Middle English: from Old French *reignier* 'to reign', *reigne* 'kingdom', from Latin *regnum*, related to *rex, reg-* 'king'.

USAGE The correct idiomatic phrase is **a free rein**, not **a free reign**; see **usage** at **REIN**.

reignite ▶ **verb** ignite or cause to ignite again: [no obj.] *oven burners automatically reignite if blown out.*

reign of terror ▶ **noun** a period of remorseless repression or bloodshed, in particular (**Reign of Terror**) the period of the Terror during the French Revolution.

reiki /ˈreɪki/ ▶ **noun** [mass noun] a healing technique based on the principle that the therapist can channel energy into the patient by means of touch, to activate the natural healing processes of the patient's body and restore physical and emotional well-being.
– ORIGIN Japanese, literally 'universal life energy'.

reimburse /ˌriːɪmˈbəːs/ ▶ **verb** [with obj.] (often **be reimbursed**) repay (a person who has spent or lost money): *the investors should be reimbursed for their losses.*
■repay (a sum of money that has been spent or lost): *they spend thousands of dollars which are not reimbursed by insurance.*
– DERIVATIVES **reimbursable** adjective, **reimbursement** noun.
– ORIGIN early 17th cent.: from **RE-** 'back, again' + obsolete *imburse* 'put in a purse', from medieval Latin *imbursare*, from *in-* 'into' + late Latin *bursa* 'purse'.

reimport ▶ **verb** [with obj.] import (goods processed or made from exported materials).
▶ **noun** [mass noun] the action of reimporting something.
■[count noun] a reimported item.
– DERIVATIVES **reimportation** noun.

reimpose ▶ **verb** [with obj.] impose (something, especially a law or regulation) again after a lapse.
– DERIVATIVES **reimposition** noun.

Reims /riːmz, French rɛ̃s/ (also **Rheims**) a city of northern France, chief town of Champagne-Ardenne region; pop. 185,160 (1990). It was the traditional coronation place of most French kings and is noted for its fine 13th-century Gothic cathedral.

rein ▶ **noun** (usu. **reins**) a long, narrow strap attached at one end to a horse's bit, typically used in pairs to guide or check a horse in riding or driving.
■a similar device used to restrain a young child.
■figurative the power to direct and control: *management is criticized for its unwillingness to let go of the reins of an organization and delegate routine tasks.*
▶ **verb** [with obj. and adverbial] cause (a horse) to stop or slow down by pulling on its reins: *he **reined in** his horse and waited for her.*
■cause (a horse) to change direction by pulling on its reins: *he reined the mare's head about and rode off.* ■keep under control; restrain: *with an effort, she **reined back** her impatience | critics noted the failure of the government to **rein in** public spending.*
– PHRASES **draw rein** Brit. stop one's horse. **(a) free rein** freedom of action or expression: *he was **given free rein** to work out his designs.* **keep a tight rein on** exercise strict control over; allow little freedom to: *her only chance of survival was to keep a tight rein on her feelings and words.*
– ORIGIN Middle English: from Old French *rene*, based on Latin *retinere* 'retain'.

USAGE The idiomatic phrase **a free rein**, which derives from the literal meaning of using reins to control a horse, is sometimes misinterpreted and written as **a free reign**. Around 15 per cent of the citations for the phrase in the British National Corpus use **reign** instead of **rein**.

reincarnate ▶ **verb** /ˌriːɪnˈkɑːneɪt/ [with obj.] (often **be reincarnated**) cause (someone) to undergo rebirth in another body: *a man may be reincarnated in animal form* | [as adj. **reincarnated**] *a reincarnated soul.*
■ [no obj.] (of a person) be reborn in this way: *they were afraid she would reincarnate as a vampire.*
▶ **adjective** /ˌriːɪnˈkɑːnət/ [usu. postpositive] reborn in another body: *he claims that the girl is his dead daughter reincarnate.*

reincarnation ▶ **noun** [mass noun] the rebirth of a soul in a new body.
■ [count noun] a person or animal in whom a particular soul is believed to have been reborn: *he is said to be **a reincarnation of** the Hindu god Vishnu.* ■ [count noun] figurative a new version or close match of something from the past: *the latest reincarnation of the hippie look.*

reincorporate ▶ **verb** [with obj.] make (something) a part of something else once more: *a campaign to reincorporate the visual arts into religious devotion.*
– DERIVATIVES **reincorporation** noun.

reindeer ▶ **noun** (pl. same or **reindeers**) a deer of the tundra and subarctic regions of Eurasia and North America, both sexes of which have large branching antlers. Most Eurasian reindeer are domesticated and used for drawing sledges and as a source of milk, flesh, and hide. Called **CARIBOU** in North America.
• *Rangifer tarandus*, family Cervidae.
– ORIGIN late Middle English: from Old Norse *hreindýri*, from *hreinn* 'reindeer' + *dýr* 'deer'.

reindeer moss ▶ **noun** a large branching bluish-grey lichen which grows in arctic and subarctic regions, sometimes providing the chief winter food of reindeer.
• *Cladonia rangiferina*, order Cladoniales.

reinfect ▶ **verb** [with obj.] (usu. **be reinfected**) cause to become infected again.
– DERIVATIVES **reinfection** noun.

reinforce ▶ **verb** [with obj.] strengthen or support, especially with additional personnel or material: *paratroopers were sent to reinforce the troops already in the area.*
■ strengthen (an existing feeling, idea, or habit): *various actions of the leaders so reinforced fears and suspicions that war became unavoidable.*
– DERIVATIVES **reinforcer** noun.
– ORIGIN late Middle English: from French *renforcer*, influenced by *inforce*, an obsolete spelling of **ENFORCE**; the sense of providing military support is probably from Italian *rinforzare*.

reinforced concrete ▶ **noun** [mass noun] concrete in which metal bars or wire is embedded to increase its tensile strength.

reinforcement ▶ **noun** [mass noun] the action or process of reinforcing or strengthening.
■ the process of encouraging or establishing a belief or pattern of behaviour, especially by encouragement or reward. ■ [count noun] (**reinforcements**) extra personnel sent to increase the strength of an army or similar force: *a small force would hold the position until reinforcements could be sent.* ■ the strengthening structure or material employed in reinforced concrete or plastic.

Reinhardt[1] /ˈrʌɪnhɑːt/, Django (1910–53), Belgian jazz guitarist; born *Jean Baptiste Reinhardt*. He became famous in Paris in the 1930s for his improvisational style, blending swing with influences from his gypsy background. In 1934, together with violinist Stephane Grappelli, he formed the Quintette du Hot Club de France.

Reinhardt[2] /ˈrʌɪnhɑːt/, Max (1873–1943), Austrian director and impresario; born *Max Goldmann*. He produced large-scale versions of such works as Sophocles' *Oedipus Rex* (1910), and helped establish the Salzburg Festival, with Richard Strauss and Hugo von Hofmannsthal.

reinsert ▶ **verb** [with obj.] place (something) back into its previous position.
– DERIVATIVES **reinsertion** noun.

reinstate ▶ **verb** [with obj.] (often **be reinstated**) restore (someone or something) to their former position or state: *the union threatened strike action if Owen was not reinstated.*
– DERIVATIVES **reinstatement** noun.

reinsure ▶ **verb** [with obj.] (of an insurer) transfer (all or part of a risk) to another insurer to provide protection against the risk of the first insurance.
– DERIVATIVES **reinsurance** noun, **reinsurer** noun.

reintegrate ▶ **verb** [with obj.] restore (elements regarded as disparate) to unity.
■ restore to a position as a part fitting easily into a larger whole: *it can be difficult for an offender to be **reintegrated into** the community.*
– DERIVATIVES **reintegration** noun.

reinter ▶ **verb** [with obj.] bury (a corpse) again, often in a different place to that of the first burial.
– DERIVATIVES **reinterment** noun.

reinterpret ▶ **verb** (**reinterpreted**, **reinterpreting**) [with obj.] (often **be reinterpreted**) interpret (something) in a new or different light.
– DERIVATIVES **reinterpretation** noun.

reintroduce ▶ **verb** [with obj.] bring (something, especially a law or system) into existence or effect again: *thirty-six states have reintroduced the death penalty.*
■ put (a species of animal or plant) back into a region where it formerly lived: *a scheme to reintroduce wolves to Yellowstone National Park.*
– DERIVATIVES **reintroduction** noun.

reinvent ▶ **verb** [with obj.] change (something) so much that it appears to be entirely new: *he brought opera to the masses and reinvented the waltz.*
■ (**reinvent oneself**) take up a radically new job or way of life: *the actor wants to reinvent himself as an independent movie mogul.*
– PHRASES **reinvent the wheel** waste a great deal of time or effort in creating something that already exists.
– DERIVATIVES **reinvention** noun.

reinvest ▶ **verb** [with obj.] put (the profit on a previous investment) back into the same scheme.
– DERIVATIVES **reinvestment** noun.

reinvigorate ▶ **verb** [with obj.] give new energy or strength to: *we are fully committed to reinvigorating the economy of the area.*
– DERIVATIVES **reinvigoration** noun.

reissue ▶ **verb** (**reissues**, **reissued**, **reissuing**) [with obj.] make a new supply or different form of (a product, especially a book or record) available for sale: *the book was reissued with a new epilogue.*
▶ **noun** a new issue of such a product.

reiterate ▶ **verb** [reporting verb] say something again or a number of times, typically for emphasis or clarity: [with clause] *she reiterated that the government would remain steadfast in its support* | [with direct speech] *'I just want to forget it all,' he reiterated* | [with obj.] *he reiterated the points made in his earlier speech.*
– DERIVATIVES **reiteration** noun, **reiterative** adjective.
– ORIGIN late Middle English (in the sense 'do (an action) repeatedly'): from Latin *reiterat-* 'gone over again', from the verb *reiterare*, from *re-* 'again' + *iterare* 'do a second time'.

Reiter's syndrome /ˈrʌɪtəz/ (also **Reiter's disease**) ▶ **noun** [mass noun] a medical condition typically affecting young men, characterized by arthritis, conjunctivitis, and urethritis, and caused by an unknown pathogen, possibly a chlamydia.
– ORIGIN 1920s: named after Hans *Reiter* (1881–1969), German bacteriologist.

Reith /riːθ/, John (Charles Walsham), 1st Baron (1889–1971), Scottish administrator and politician, first general manager (1922–7) and first director general (1927–38) of the BBC. He played a major part in the growth of the BBC and championed the moral and intellectual role of broadcasting in the community.

reive /riːv/ ▶ **verb** [no obj.] [usu. as noun **reiving**] chiefly Scottish another term for **REAVE**.
– DERIVATIVES **reiver** noun.
– ORIGIN Middle English: variant of **REAVE**; the usual spelling when referring to the historical practice of cattle-raiding on the Scottish Borders.

reject ▶ **verb** /rɪˈdʒɛkt/ [with obj.] dismiss as inadequate, inappropriate, or not to one's taste: *union negotiators rejected a 1.5 per cent pay award* | *these explanations of criminal behaviour have been rejected by sociologists.*
■ refuse to agree to (a request): *an application to hold a pop concert at the club was rejected.* ■ fail to show due affection or concern for (someone); rebuff: *she didn't want him to feel he had been rejected after his sister was born.* ■ Medicine show an immune response to (a transplanted organ or tissue) so that it fails to survive.
▶ **noun** /ˈriːdʒɛkt/ a person or thing dismissed as failing to meet standards or satisfy tastes: *some of the team's rejects have gone on to prove themselves in championships.*
■ an item sold cheaply because of minor flaws: [as modifier] *a row of reject Royal Worcester plates.*
– DERIVATIVES **rejection** noun, **rejective** adjective (rare), **rejector** noun.
– ORIGIN late Middle English: from Latin *reject-* 'thrown back', from the verb *reicere*, from *re-* 'back' + *jacere* 'to throw'.

rejectionist ▶ **noun** [often as modifier] a person who rejects a proposed policy, especially an Arab who refuses to accept a negotiated peace with Israel.

rejection slip ▶ **noun** a formal notice sent by an editor or publisher to an author with a rejected manuscript or typescript.

rejig chiefly Brit. ▶ **verb** (**rejigged**, **rejigging**) [with obj.] **1** organize (something) differently; rearrange: *the organizers scrambled frantically to rejig schedules.*
2 dated re-equip with machinery; refit.
▶ **noun** a reorganization: *a cabinet rejig.*

rejigger ▶ **verb** US term for **REJIG** (in sense 1).

rejoice ▶ **verb** [no obj.] feel or show great joy or delight: *he rejoiced when he saw his friend alive* | *he **rejoiced in** her spontaneity and directness* | [as noun **rejoicing**] *an occasion for rejoicing.*
■ (**rejoice in**) used ironically to draw attention to a strange characteristic, especially a name: *the guard rejoiced in the name of Blossom.* ■ [with obj.] archaic cause joy to: *I love to rejoice their poor Hearts at this season.*
– DERIVATIVES **rejoicer** noun, **rejoicingly** adverb.
– ORIGIN Middle English (in the sense 'cause joy to'): from Old French *rejoiss-*, lengthened stem of *rejoir*, from *re-* (expressing intensive force) + *joir* 'experience joy'.

rejoin[1] ▶ **verb** [with obj.] join together again; reunite: *the stone had been cracked and crudely rejoined.*
■ return to (a companion, organization, or route that one has left): *the soldiers were returning from leave to rejoin their unit.*

rejoin[2] ▶ **verb** [reporting verb] say something in answer to a remark, typically rudely or in a discouraging manner: [with clause] *Harry said that he longed for a bath and soft towels, to which his father rejoined that he was a gross materialist.*
– ORIGIN late Middle English (in the sense 'reply to a charge or pleading in a lawsuit'): from Old French *rejoindre*, from *re-* 'again' + *joindre* 'to join'.

rejoinder ▶ **noun** a reply, especially a sharp or witty one: *she would have made some cutting rejoinder but none came to mind.*
■ Law, dated a defendant's answer to the plaintiff's reply or replication.
– ORIGIN late Middle English: from Anglo-Norman French *rejoindre* (infinitive used as a noun) (see **REJOIN**[2]).

rejuvenate /rɪˈdʒuːvəneɪt/ ▶ **verb** [with obj.] make (someone or something) look or feel younger, fresher, or more lively: *a bid to rejuvenate the town centre* | [as adj. **rejuvenating**] *the rejuvenating effects of therapeutic clay.*
■ [often as adj. **rejuvenated**] restore (a river or stream) to a condition characteristic of a younger landscape.
– DERIVATIVES **rejuvenation** noun, **rejuvenator** noun.
– ORIGIN early 19th cent.: from **RE-** 'again' + Latin *juvenis* 'young' + **-ATE**[3], suggested by French *rajeunir*.

rejuvenescence /rɪˌdʒuːvəˈnɛsəns/ ▶ **noun** [mass noun] the renewal of youth or vitality.
■ Biology the reactivation of vegetative cells, resulting in regrowth from old or injured parts.
– DERIVATIVES **rejuvenescent** adjective.
– ORIGIN mid 17th cent.: from late Latin *rejuvenescere* (from Latin *re-* 'again' + *juvenis* 'young') + **-ENCE**.

rekey ▶ **verb** [with obj.] chiefly Computing enter (text or other data) again using a keyboard.

rekindle ▶ **verb** [with obj.] relight (a fire).
■ revive (something that has been lost): *he tried to rekindle their friendship* | *the photos rekindled memories.*

-rel ▶ **suffix** forming nouns with diminutive or derogatory force such as *cockerel*, *scoundrel*.
– ORIGIN from Old French *-erel(le)*.

relabel ▶ **verb** (**relabelled**, **relabelling**; US **relabeled**, **relabeling**) [with obj.] label (something) again or differently.

relaid past and past participle of **RELAY**[2].

relapse /rɪˈlaps/ ▶ **verb** [no obj.] (of someone suffering from a disease) suffer deterioration after a period of improvement.
■ (**relapse into**) return to (a less active or a worse state): *he relapsed into silence.*
▶ **noun** /also ˈriː-/ a deterioration in someone's state of health after a temporary improvement: *he suffered a relapse of schizophrenia after a car crash.*
– DERIVATIVES **relapser** noun.

r

– ORIGIN late Middle English: from Latin *relaps-* 'slipped back', from the verb *relabi*, from *re-* 'back' + *labi* 'to slip'. Early senses referred to a return to heresy or wrongdoing.

relapsing fever ▶ noun [mass noun] an infectious bacterial disease marked by recurrent fever.
● The disease is caused by spirochaetes of the genus *Borrelia*.

relate ▶ verb [with obj.] **1** give an account of (a sequence of events); narrate: *various versions of the chilling story have been related by the locals.*
2 (**be related**) be connected by blood or marriage: *he was related to my mother | people who are related.*
■ be causally connected: *high unemployment is related to high crime rates.* ■ (**relate something to**) discuss something in such a way as to indicate its connections with (something else): *the study examines social change within the city and relates it to wider developments in the country as a whole.* ■ [no obj.] (**relate to**) have reference to; concern: *the new legislation related to corporate activities.* ■ [no obj.] (**relate to**) feel sympathy with; identify with: *kids related to him because he was so anti-establishment.*
– DERIVATIVES **relatable** adjective.
– ORIGIN mid 16th cent.: from Latin *relat-* 'brought back', from the verb *referre* (see **REFER**).

related ▶ adjective belonging to the same family, group, or type; connected: *sleeping sickness and related diseases.*
■ [in combination] associated with the specified item or process, especially causally: *income-related benefits.*
– DERIVATIVES **relatedness** noun.

relater (also **relator**) ▶ noun a person who tells a story; a narrator.

relation ▶ noun **1** the way in which two or more concepts, objects, or people are connected; a thing's effect on or relevance to another: *questions about the relation between writing and reality | the size of the targets bore no relation to their importance.*
■ (**relations**) the way in which two or more people, countries, or organizations feel about and behave towards each other: *the improvement in relations between the two countries | the meetings helped cement Anglo-American relations.* ■ (**relations**) chiefly formal sexual intercourse: *he wanted an excuse to abandon sexual relations with her.*
2 a person who is connected by blood or marriage; a kinsman or kinswoman: *she was no relation at all, but he called her Aunt Nora.*
3 [mass noun] the action of telling a story.
– PHRASES **in relation to** in the context of; in connection with: *there is an ambiguity in the provisions in relation to children's hearings.*
– ORIGIN Middle English: from Old French, or from Latin *relatio(n-)*, from *referre* 'bring back' (see **RELATE**).

relational ▶ adjective concerning the way in which two or more people or things are connected.
– DERIVATIVES **relationally** adverb.

relational database ▶ noun Computing a database structured to recognize relations between stored items of information.

relationship ▶ noun the way in which two or more concepts, objects, or people are connected, or the state of being connected: *the study will assess the relationship between unemployment and political attitudes.*
■ the state of being connected by blood or marriage: *they can trace their relationship to a common ancestor.* ■ the way in which two or more people or organizations regard and behave towards each other: *the landlord–tenant relationship | she was proud of her good relationship with the domestic staff.* ■ an emotional and sexual association between two people: *she has a daughter from a previous relationship.*

relative /ˈrɛlətɪv/ ▶ adjective **1** considered in relation or in proportion to something else: *the relative effectiveness of the various mechanisms is not known.*
■ existing or possessing a specified characteristic only in comparison to something else; not absolute: *she went down the steps into the relative darkness of the dining room | the firms are relative newcomers to computers.*
2 Grammar denoting a pronoun, determiner, or adverb that refers to an expressed or implied antecedent and attaches a subordinate clause to it, e.g. *which, who.*
■ (of a clause) attached to an antecedent by a relative word.
3 Music (of major and minor keys) having the same key signature.
4 (of a service rank) corresponding in grade to another in a different service.

▶ noun **1** a person connected by blood or marriage: *much of my time is spent visiting relatives.*
■ a species related to another by common origin: *the plant is a relative of ivy.*
2 Grammar a relative pronoun, determiner, or adverb.
3 Philosophy a term, thing, or concept which is dependent on something else.
– PHRASES **relative to 1** in comparison with: *the figures suggest that girls are underachieving relative to boys.* ■ in terms of a connection to: *we must consider the location of the hospital relative to its catchment area.*
2 in connection with; concerning: *if you have any queries relative to payment, please contact us.*
– DERIVATIVES **relatival** /-ˈtʌɪv(ə)l/ adjective (only in sense 2 of the noun).
– ORIGIN late Middle English: from Old French *relatif, -ive*, from late Latin *relativus* 'having reference or relation' (see **RELATE**).

relative atomic mass ▶ noun Chemistry the ratio of the average mass of one atom of an element to one twelfth of the mass of an atom of carbon-12.

relative density ▶ noun Chemistry the ratio of the density of a substance to the density of a standard, usually water for a liquid or solid, and air for a gas.

relative humidity ▶ noun the amount of water vapour present in air expressed as a percentage of the amount needed for saturation at the same temperature.

relatively ▶ adverb [sentence adverb] in relation, comparison, or proportion to something else: *although Europe's economy was growing, it was falling behind relatively | it is perfectly simple, **relatively** **speaking**, to store a full catalogue entry on magnetic tape.*
■ [as submodifier] viewed in comparison with something else rather than absolutely; quite: *relatively affluent people | the site was cheap and relatively clean.*

relative molecular mass ▶ noun Chemistry the ratio of the average mass of one molecule of an element or compound to one twelfth of the mass of an atom of carbon-12.

relativism /ˈrɛlətɪvɪz(ə)m/ ▶ noun [mass noun] the doctrine that knowledge, truth, and morality exist in relation to culture, society, or historical context, and are not absolute.
– DERIVATIVES **relativist** noun.

relativistic ▶ adjective Physics accurately described only by the theory of relativity.
– DERIVATIVES **relativistically** adverb.

relativity ▶ noun [mass noun] **1** the absence of standards of absolute and universal application: *moral relativity.*
2 Physics the dependence of various physical phenomena on relative motion of the observer and the observed objects, especially regarding the nature and behaviour of light, space, time, and gravity.

The concept of relativity was set out in Einstein's **special theory of relativity**, published in 1905. This states that all motion is relative and that the velocity of light in a vacuum has a constant value which nothing can exceed. Among its consequences are the following: the mass of a body increases and its length (in the direction of motion) shortens as its speed increases; the time interval between two events occurring in a moving body appears greater to a stationary observer; and mass and energy are equivalent and interconvertible. Einstein's **general theory of relativity**, published in 1915, extended the theory to accelerated motion and gravitation, which was treated as a curvature of the space–time continuum. It predicted that light rays would be deflected, and shifted in wavelength, when passing through a substantial gravitational field, effects which have been experimentally confirmed.

relativize (also **-ise**) ▶ verb [with obj.] chiefly Linguistics & Philosophy make or treat as relative to or dependent on something else.
■ Physics treat (a phenomenon or concept) according to the principles of the theory of relativity.
– DERIVATIVES **relativization** noun.

relator ▶ noun **1** Law a person who brings a public law suit, typically in the name of the Attorney General, regarding the abuse of an office or franchise.
2 variant spelling of **RELATER**.

relaunch ▶ verb [with obj.] cause to start again with renewed vigour after a period of inactivity.
■ reintroduce (a product): *he relaunched the paper as a tabloid.*
▶ noun an instance of reintroducing or restarting something, especially a product.

relax ▶ verb make or become less tense or anxious: [no obj.] *he relaxed and smiled confidently* | [as adj.] **relaxing**] *a relaxing holiday.*
■ [no obj.] rest or engage in an enjoyable activity so as to become less tired or anxious: *the team relax with a lot of skiing.* ■ [with obj.] cause (a limb or muscle) to become less rigid: *relax the leg by bringing the knee towards the chest.* ■ [with obj.] make (a rule or restriction) less strict while not abolishing it: *the ministry relaxed some of the restrictions.*
– DERIVATIVES **relaxer** noun.
– ORIGIN late Middle English: from Latin *relaxare*, from *re-* (expressing intensive force) + *laxus* 'lax, loose'.

relaxant ▶ noun a drug used to promote relaxation or reduce tension: *a muscle relaxant.*
■ a thing having a relaxing effect: *sex can be a great relaxant.*
▶ adjective causing relaxation.

relaxation ▶ noun [mass noun] **1** the state of being free from tension and anxiety.
■ recreation or rest, especially after a period of work: *his favourite form of relaxation was reading detective novels.* ■ the loss of tension in a part of the body, especially in a muscle when it ceases to contract. ■ the action of making a rule or restriction less strict: *relaxation of censorship rules.*
2 Physics the restoration of equilibrium following disturbance.

relaxation oscillator ▶ noun Electronics an oscillator in which sharp, sometimes aperiodic oscillations result from the rapid discharge of a capacitor or inductance.

relaxed ▶ adjective free from tension and anxiety; at ease: *we were having a great time and feeling very relaxed | the relaxed and comfortable atmosphere of the hotel.*
■ (of a muscle or other body part) not tense.
– DERIVATIVES **relaxedly** adverb, **relaxedness** noun.

relaxin /rɪˈlaksɪn/ ▶ noun [mass noun] Biochemistry a hormone secreted by the placenta that causes the cervix to dilate and prepares the uterus for the action of oxytocin during labour.

relay¹ /ˈriːleɪ/ ▶ noun **1** a group of people or animals engaged in a task or activity for a fixed period of time and then replaced by a similar group: *the wagons were pulled by relays of horses | gangs of workers were sent in relays.*
■ [usu. as modifier] a race between teams of runners, each team member in turn covering part of the total distance: *a 550-metre relay race.*
2 an electrical device, typically incorporating an electromagnet, which is activated by a current or signal in one circuit to open or close another circuit.
3 a device to receive, reinforce, and retransmit a broadcast or programme.
■ a message or programme transmitted by such a device: *a relay of a performance live from the concert hall.*
▶ verb (also rɪˈleɪ) [with obj.] receive and pass on (information or a message): *she intended to relay everything she had learned.*
■ broadcast (something) by passing signals received from elsewhere through a transmitting station: *the speech was relayed live from the palace.*
– ORIGIN late Middle English (referring to the provision of fresh hounds on the track of a deer): from Old French *relai* (noun), *relayer* (verb), based on Latin *laxare* 'slacken'.

relay² /riːˈleɪ/ ▶ verb (past and past participle **relaid**) [with obj.] lay again or differently: *they plan to relay about half a mile of the track.*

relearn ▶ verb (past and past participle **relearned** or **relearnt**) [with obj.] learn (something) again: *I've been relearning my Latin and Greek.*

release ▶ verb [with obj.] **1** allow or enable to escape from confinement; set free: *the government announced that the prisoners would be released.*
■ remove restrictions or obligations from (someone or something) so that they become available for other activity: *the strategy would release forces for service in other areas.* ■ allow (information) to be generally available: *no details about the contents of the talks were released.* ■ make (a film or recording) available for general viewing or purchase: *nine singles and one album had been released.* ■ allow (something concentrated in a small area) to spread and work freely: *growth hormone is released into the blood during the first part of sleep.* ■ remove (part of a machine or appliance) from a fixed position, allowing something else to move or function: *he released the handbrake.* ■ allow (something) to return to its resting position

by ceasing to put pressure on it: *press the cap down and release.*
2 Law remit or discharge (a debt).
■surrender (a right). ■ make over (property or money) to another.
▶**noun** [mass noun] **1** the action or process of releasing or being released: *a campaign by the prisoner's mother resulted in his release.*
■the action of making a film, recording, or other product available for general viewing or purchase: *the film was withheld for two years before its release.* ■ [count noun] a film or other product issued for viewing or purchase: *his current album release has topped the charts for six months.* ■ [count noun] a press release. ■ [count noun] a handle or catch that releases part of a mechanism.
2 Law the action of releasing property, money, or a right to another.
■[count noun] a document effecting this.
– PHRASES **on release** (of a film) being generally shown; available for viewing: *the movie will be on release from Christmas.*
– DERIVATIVES **releasable** adjective, **releasee** noun (Law), **releaser** noun, **releasor** noun (Law).
– ORIGIN Middle English: from Old French *reles* (noun), *relesser* (verb), from Latin *relaxare* 'stretch out again, slacken' (see **RELAX**).

release agent ▶**noun** a substance applied to a surface, typically the surface of a mould or container, to prevent other substances from sticking to it.

releasing factor ▶**noun** Biochemistry a substance which, when secreted by the hypothalamus, promotes the release of a specified hormone from the anterior lobe of the pituitary gland.

relegate ▶**verb** [with obj.] consign or dismiss to an inferior rank or position: *they aim to prevent women from being* ***relegated to*** *a secondary role.*
■(usu. **be relegated**) Brit. transfer (a sports team) to a lower division of a league: *United were relegated to division two.*
– DERIVATIVES **relegation** noun.
– ORIGIN late Middle English (in the sense 'send into exile'): from Latin *relegat-* 'sent away, referred', from the verb *relegare*, from *re-* 'again' + *legare* 'send'.

relent ▶**verb** [no obj.] abandon or mitigate a harsh intention or cruel treatment: *she was going to refuse his request, but relented.*
■(especially of bad weather) become less severe or intense: *by evening the rain relented.*
– ORIGIN late Middle English (in the sense 'dissolve, melt'): based on Latin *re-* 'back' + *lentare* 'to bend' (from *lentus* 'flexible').

relentless ▶**adjective** never ending; oppressively constant: *the relentless heat of the desert.*
■harsh or inflexible: *a patient but relentless taskmaster.*
– DERIVATIVES **relentlessly** adverb, **relentlessness** noun.

relet ▶**verb** (**reletting**; past and past participle **relet**) [with obj.] chiefly Brit. let (a property) for a further period or to a new tenant.
▶**noun** an act of letting a property again.

relevant ▶**adjective** closely connected or appropriate to the matter in hand: *the candidate's experience is* ***relevant to*** *the job.*
– DERIVATIVES **relevance** noun, **relevancy** noun, **relevantly** adverb.
– ORIGIN early 16th cent. (as a Scots legal term meaning 'legally pertinent'): from medieval Latin *relevant-* 'raising up', from Latin *relevare*.

relevé /ˌrələˈveɪ/ ▶**noun 1** Ballet a movement in which the dancer rises on the tips of the toes.
2 Ecology each of a number of small plots of vegetation, analysed as a sample of a wider area.
– ORIGIN French, literally 'raised up'.

reliable ▶**adjective** consistently good in quality or performance; able to be trusted: *a reliable source of information.*
▶**noun** (usu. **reliables**) a person or thing with such trustworthy qualities: *the supporting cast includes old reliables like Mitchell.*
– DERIVATIVES **reliability** noun, **reliableness** noun, **reliably** adverb.

reliance ▶**noun** [mass noun] dependence on or trust in someone or something: *the farmer's* ***reliance on*** *pesticides.*
■[count noun] archaic a person or thing on which someone depends.
– DERIVATIVES **reliant** adjective.

relic ▶**noun** an object surviving from an earlier time, especially one of historical or sentimental interest.
■a part of a deceased holy person's body or belongings kept as an object of reverence. ■ an object, custom, or belief that has survived from an earlier time but is now outmoded: *individualized computer programming and time-sharing would become expensive relics.* ■ (**relics**) all that is left of something: *relics of a lost civilization.*
– ORIGIN Middle English: from Old French *relique* (originally plural), from Latin *reliquiae* (see **RELIQUIAE**).

relict /ˈrɛlɪkt/ ▶**noun 1** a thing which has survived from an earlier period or in a primitive form.
■an animal or plant that has survived while others of its group have become extinct, e.g. the coelacanth. ■ a species or community that formerly had a wider distribution but now survives in only a few localities such as refugia. [ORIGIN: early 20th cent.: from Latin *relictus* 'left behind', past participle of the verb *relinquere*.]
2 archaic a widow. [ORIGIN: late Middle English: from Old French *relicte* '(woman) left behind', from late Latin *relicta*, from the verb *relinquere*.]

relief ▶**noun** [mass noun] **1** a feeling of reassurance and relaxation following release from anxiety or distress: *much to her relief, she saw the door open.*
■[count noun] a cause of or occasion for such a feeling: *it was a relief to find somewhere to stay.* ■ the alleviation of pain, discomfort, or distress: *tablets for the relief of pain.* ■ (usu. **light relief**) a temporary break in a generally tense or tedious situation: *the comic characters aren't part of the plot but just light relief.*
2 assistance, especially in the form of food, clothing, or money, given to those in special need or difficulty: *raising money for famine relief* | [as modifier] *relief workers.*
■a remission of tax normally due: *employees who donate money to charity will receive tax relief.* ■ chiefly Law the redress of a hardship or grievance. ■ the action of raising the siege of a besieged town: *the relief of Mafeking.*
3 [usu. as modifier] a person or group of people replacing others who have been on duty: *the relief nurse was late.*
■Brit. an extra vehicle providing supplementary public transport at peak times or in emergencies.
4 the state of being very clearly visible or obvious due to being accentuated in some way: *the setting sun threw the snow-covered peaks* ***into relief.***
■a method of moulding, carving, or stamping in which the design stands out from the surface, to a greater (**high relief**) or lesser (**low relief**) extent. ■ [count noun] a piece of sculpture in relief. ■ a representation of relief given by an arrangement of line or colour or shading. ■ Geography difference in height from the surrounding terrain: *the sharp relief of many mountains.* [ORIGIN: via French from Italian *rilievo*, from *rilevare* 'raise', from Latin *relevare*.]
– PHRASES **in relief 1** Art carved, moulded, or stamped so as to stand out from the surface. **2** Baseball acting as a substitute pitcher. **on relief** chiefly N. Amer. receiving state assistance because of need.
– ORIGIN late Middle English: from Old French, from *relever* 'raise up, relieve', from Latin *relevare* 'raise again, alleviate'.

relief map ▶**noun** a map indicating hills and valleys by shading rather than by contour lines alone.
■a map model with elevations and depressions representing hills and valleys, typically on an exaggerated relative scale.

relief printing ▶**noun** [mass noun] printing from raised images, as in letterpress and flexography.

relief road ▶**noun** Brit. a road taking traffic around, rather than through, a congested urban area.

relieve ▶**verb** [with obj.] **1** cause (pain, distress, or difficulty) to become less severe or serious: *the drug was used to promote sleep and to relieve pain.*
■(usu. **be relieved**) cause (someone) to stop feeling distressed or anxious about something: *he was relieved by her change of tone.* ■ make less tedious or monotonous by the introduction of variety or of something striking or pleasing: *the bird's body is black, relieved only by white under the tail.*
2 release (someone) from duty by taking their place: *another signalman relieved him at 5.30.*
■bring military support for (a besieged place): *he dispatched an expedition to relieve the city.* ■ (**relieve oneself**) used as a formal or euphemistic expression for urination or defecation.
3 (**relieve someone of**) take (a burden) from someone: *he relieved her of her baggage.*
■free someone from (a tiresome responsibility): *she relieved me of the household chores.* ■ used euphemistically to indicate that someone has been deprived of something: *he was relieved of his world title.*
4 archaic make (something) stand out: *the twilight relieving in purple masses the foliage of the island.*
– PHRASES **relieve one's feelings** use strong language or vigorous behaviour when annoyed.
– DERIVATIVES **relievable** adjective, **relievedly** adverb, **reliever** noun.
– ORIGIN Middle English: from Old French *relever*, from Latin *relevare*, from *re-* (expressing intensive force) + *levare* 'raise' (from *levis* 'light').

relieving officer ▶**noun** historical an official appointed by a parish or union to administer relief to the poor.

relievo /rɪˈliːvəʊ/ (also **rilievo**) ▶**noun** (pl. **-os**) chiefly Art another term for **RELIEF** (in sense 4).
– ORIGIN Italian *rilievo*.

relight ▶**verb** (past and past participle **relighted** or **relit**) [with obj.] light (something) again: *he reached for the matches to relight his pipe.*

religio- /rɪˈlɪdʒɪəʊ/ ▶**combining form** religious and ...: *religio-political* | *religio-national.*
– ORIGIN from **RELIGION** or **RELIGIOUS**.

religion ▶**noun** [mass noun] the belief in and worship of a superhuman controlling power, especially a personal God or gods: *ideas about the relationship between science and religion.*
■details of belief as taught or discussed: *children should be taught religion in schools.* ■ [count noun] a particular system of faith and worship: *the world's great religions.* ■ [count noun] a pursuit or interest to which someone ascribes supreme importance: *consumerism is the new religion.*
– PHRASES **get religion** informal be converted to religious belief and practices.
– DERIVATIVES **religionless** adjective.
– ORIGIN Middle English (originally in the sense 'life under monastic vows'): from Old French, or from Latin *religio(n-)* 'obligation, bond, reverence', perhaps based on Latin *religare* 'to bind'.

religionism ▶**noun** [mass noun] excessive religious zeal.
– DERIVATIVES **religionist** noun.

religiose /rɪˈlɪdʒɪəʊs/ ▶**adjective** excessively religious.
– DERIVATIVES **religiosity** noun.
– ORIGIN mid 19th cent.: from Latin *religiosus*, from *religio* 'reverence, obligation'.

religious ▶**adjective 1** believing in and worshipping a superhuman controlling power or powers, especially a personal God or gods: *both men were deeply religious, intelligent, and moralistic.*
■(of a belief or practice) forming part of someone's thought about or worship of a divine being: *he has strong religious convictions.* ■ of or relating to the worship of or a doctrine concerning a divine being or beings: *religious music.* ■ belonging or relating to a monastic order or other group of people who are united by their practice of religion: *religious houses were built on ancient pagan sites.* ■ treated or regarded with a devotion and scrupulousness appropriate to worship: *I have a religious aversion to reading manuals.*
▶**noun** (pl. same) a person bound by monastic vows.
– DERIVATIVES **religiously** adverb, **religiousness** noun.
– ORIGIN Middle English: from Old French, from Latin *religiosus*, from *religio* 'reverence, obligation' (see **RELIGION**).

Religious Society of Friends official name for the Quakers (see **QUAKER**).

reline ▶**verb** [with obj.] replace the lining of: *the heavily brocaded drapes that she had relined.*
■attach a new backing canvas to (a painting).

relinquish ▶**verb** [with obj.] voluntarily cease to keep or claim; give up: *he relinquished his managerial role to become chief executive.*
– DERIVATIVES **relinquishment** noun.
– ORIGIN late Middle English: from Old French *relinquiss-*, lengthened stem of *relinquir*, from Latin *relinquere*, from *re-* (expressing intensive force) + *linquere* 'to leave'.

reliquary /ˈrɛlɪkwəri/ ▶**noun** (pl. **-ies**) a container for holy relics.
– ORIGIN mid 16th cent.: from French *reliquaire*, from Old French *relique* (see **RELIC**).

reliquiae /rɪˈlɪkwiː/ ▶**plural noun** remains.
■Geology fossil remains of animals or plants.
– ORIGIN mid 17th cent.: Latin, feminine plural (used

as a noun) of *reliquus* 'remaining', based on *linquere* 'to leave'.

relish ▶ noun **1** [mass noun] great enjoyment: *she swigged a mouthful of wine with relish.* ■ liking for or pleasurable anticipation of something: *I was appointed to a post for which I had little relish.* **2** a condiment eaten with plain food to add flavour, typically a piquant sauce or pickle. **3** archaic an appetizing flavour: *the tired glutton finds no relish in the sweetest meat.* ■ a distinctive taste or tinge: *the relish of wine.* ■ an attractive quality.
▶ verb [with obj.] **1** enjoy greatly: *he was relishing his moment of glory.* ■ be pleased by or about: *I don't relish the thought of waiting on an invalid for the next few months.* **2** archaic make pleasant to the taste; add relish to: *I have also a novel to relish my wine.*
– DERIVATIVES **relishable** adjective.
– ORIGIN Middle English: alteration of obsolete *reles*, from Old French *reles* 'remainder', from *relaisser* 'to release'. The early noun sense was 'odour, taste' giving rise to 'appetizing flavour, piquant taste' (mid 17th cent.), and hence sense 2 (late 18th cent.).

relive ▶ verb [with obj.] live through (an experience or feeling, especially an unpleasant one) again in one's imagination or memory: *he broke down sobbing as he relived the attack.*

relleno /rɛˈljɛɪnəʊ/ ▶ noun (pl. **-os**) short for **CHILE RELLENO**.

rellie (Austral. also **relo**) ▶ noun (pl. **-ies**) informal, chiefly Austral./NZ a relative.

reload ▶ verb [with obj.] load (something, especially a gun that has been fired) again: *he reloaded the chamber of the shotgun with fresh cartridges* | [no obj.] *Charlie reloaded and took aim.*

relocate ▶ verb [no obj.] move to a new place and establish one's home or business there: *sixty workers could face redundancy because the firm is relocating* | [with obj.] *distribution staff will be relocated to Holland.*
– DERIVATIVES **relocation** noun.

reluctance ▶ noun [mass noun] unwillingness or disinclination to do something: *she sensed his reluctance to continue.* ■ Physics the property of a magnetic circuit of opposing the passage of magnetic flux lines, equal to the ratio of the magnetomotive force to the magnetic flux.

reluctant ▶ adjective unwilling and hesitant; disinclined: [with infinitive] *she seemed reluctant to discuss the matter.*
– DERIVATIVES **reluctantly** adverb.
– ORIGIN mid 17th cent. (in the sense 'writhing, offering opposition'): from Latin *reluctant-* 'struggling against', from the verb *reluctari*, from *re-* (expressing intensive force) + *luctari* 'to struggle'.

relume /rɪˈl(j)uːm/ ▶ verb [with obj.] poetic/literary relight or rekindle (a light, flame, etc.): *Oceana stole from her place of concealment, and relumed the taper.*
– ORIGIN early 17th cent.: from **RE-** 'again' + **ILLUME**, partly suggested by French *rallumer*.

rely ▶ verb (**-ies**, **-ied**) [no obj.] (**rely on/upon**) depend on with full trust or confidence: *I know I can rely on your discretion.* ■ be dependent on: *the charity has to rely entirely on public donations.*
– ORIGIN Middle English: from Old French *relier* 'bind together', from Latin *religare*, from *re-* (expressing intensive force) + *ligare* 'bind'. The original sense was 'gather together', later 'turn to, associate with', whence 'depend upon with confidence'.

rem ▶ noun (pl. same) a unit of effective absorbed dose of ionizing radiation in human tissue, equivalent to one roentgen of X-rays.
– ORIGIN 1940s: acronym from *roentgen equivalent man*.

remade past and past participle of **REMAKE**.

remain ▶ verb [no obj.] continue to exist, especially after other similar or related people or things have ceased to exist: *a cloister is all that remains of the monastery.* ■ stay in the place that one has been occupying: *her husband remained at the flat in Regent's Park.* ■ [with complement] continue to possess a particular quality or fulfil a particular role: *he had remained alert the whole time.* ■ be left over after others or other parts have been completed, used, or dealt with: [as adj. **remaining**] *he would see out the remaining two years of his contract.*
– PHRASES **remain to be seen** used to express the

notion that something is not yet known or certain: *she has broken her leg, but it remains to be seen how badly.*
– ORIGIN late Middle English: from Old French *remain-*, stressed stem of *remanoir*, from Latin *remanere*, from *re-* (expressing intensive force) + *manere* 'to stay'.

remainder ▶ noun **1** a part, number, or quantity that is left over: *leave a few mushrooms for garnish and slice the remainder.* ■ a part that is still to come: *the remainder of the year.* ■ the number which is left over in a division in which one quantity does not exactly divide another. ■ a copy of a book left unsold when demand has fallen. **2** Law an interest in an estate that becomes effective in possession only when a prior interest (devised at the same time) ends.
▶ verb [with obj.] (often be **remaindered**) dispose of (a book left unsold) at a reduced price: *titles are being remaindered increasingly quickly to save on overheads.*
– ORIGIN late Middle English (in sense 2): from Anglo-Norman French, from Latin *remanere* (see **REMAIN**).

remains ▶ plural noun the parts left over after other parts have been removed, used, or destroyed: *the remains of a sandwich lunch were on the table.* ■ historical or archaeological relics: *Roman remains.* ■ a person's body after death.
– ORIGIN late Middle English (occasionally treated as singular): from Old French *remain*, from *remaindre*, from an informal form of Latin *remanere* (see **REMAIN**).

remake ▶ verb (past and past participle **remade**) [with obj.] make (something) again or differently: *the bed would be more comfortable if it were remade.*
▶ noun a film or piece of music that has been filmed or recorded again and re-released.

reman ▶ verb (**remanned**, **remanning**) [with obj.] **1** equip with new personnel. **2** poetic/literary make (someone) manly or courageous again.

remand Law ▶ verb [with obj.] place (a defendant) on bail or in custody, especially when a trial is adjourned: *a man was remanded in custody yesterday accused of the murders.*
▶ noun a committal to custody.
– PHRASES **on remand** in custody pending trial.
– ORIGIN late Middle English (as a verb in the sense 'send back again'): from late Latin *remandare*, from *re-* 'back' + *mandare* 'commit'. The noun dates from the late 18th cent.

remand centre ▶ noun (in the UK and Canada) an institution in which people accused of a crime are held in custody while awaiting trial.

remanent /ˈrɛmənənt/ ▶ adjective technical remaining; residual. ■ (of magnetism) remaining after the magnetizing field has been removed.
– DERIVATIVES **remanence** noun.
– ORIGIN late Middle English: from Latin *remanent-* 'remaining', from the verb *remanere*.

remap ▶ verb (**remapped**, **remapping**) [with obj.] Computing assign (a function) to a different key.

remark ▶ verb **1** [reporting verb] say something as a comment; mention: [with direct speech] *'Tom's looking peaky,' she remarked* | [with clause] *he remarked that he had some work to finish* | [no obj.] *the judges remarked on the high standard of the entries.* **2** [with obj.] regard with attention; notice: *he remarked the man's inflamed eyelids.*
▶ noun a written or spoken comment: *I decided to ignore his rude remarks.* ■ [mass noun] notice or comment: *the landscape, familiar since childhood, was not worthy of remark.*
– ORIGIN late 16th cent. (in sense 2): from French *remarquer* 'note again', from *re-* (expressing intensive force) + *marquer* 'to mark, note'.

re-mark ▶ verb [with obj.] mark (an examination paper or piece of academic work) again.
▶ noun [in sing.] an act of marking an examination or piece of academic work again.

remarkable ▶ adjective worthy of attention; striking: *a remarkable coincidence.*
– DERIVATIVES **remarkableness** noun, **remarkably** adverb [sentence adverb] *remarkably, they finished two weeks ahead of schedule* | [as submodifier] *the two boys got on remarkably well.*

– ORIGIN early 17th cent.: from French *remarquable*, from *remarquer* 'take note of' (see **REMARK**).

Remarque /rɪˈmɑːk/, Erich Maria (1898–1970), German-born American novelist. His first novel, *All Quiet on the Western Front* (1929), was a huge international success. All of his ten novels deal with the horror of war and its aftermath.

remarry ▶ verb (**-ies**, **-ied**) [no obj.] marry again.
– DERIVATIVES **remarriage** noun.

remaster ▶ verb [with obj.] make a new master of (a recording), typically in order to improve the sound quality: *all the tracks have been remastered from the original tapes.*

rematch ▶ noun a second match or game between two sports teams or players.

Rembrandt /ˈrɛmbrant/ (1606–69), Dutch painter; full name *Rembrandt Harmensz van Rijn*.

He made his name as a portrait painter with the *Anatomy Lesson of Dr Tulp* (1632). With his most celebrated painting, the *Night Watch* (1642), he used chiaroscuro to give his subjects a more spiritual and introspective quality, a departure which was to transform the Dutch portrait tradition. Rembrandt is especially identified with the series of more than sixty self-portraits painted from 1629 to 1669.

REME ▶ abbreviation for (in the British army) Royal Electrical and Mechanical Engineers.

remeasure ▶ verb [with obj.] measure (something) again.
– DERIVATIVES **remeasurement** noun.

remedial ▶ adjective giving or intended as a remedy or cure: *remedial surgery.* ■ provided or intended for children who are experiencing learning difficulties: *remedial education.*
– DERIVATIVES **remedially** adverb.
– ORIGIN mid 17th cent.: from late Latin *remedialis*, from Latin *remedium* 'cure, medicine' (see **REMEDY**).

remediation /rɪˌmiːdɪˈeɪʃ(ə)n/ ▶ noun [mass noun] the action of remedying something, in particular of reversing or stopping environmental damage. ■ the giving of remedial teaching or therapy.
– DERIVATIVES **remediate** verb.
– ORIGIN early 19th cent.: from Latin *remediatio(n-)*, from *remediare* 'heal, cure' (see **REMEDY**).

remedy ▶ noun (pl. **-ies**) **1** a medicine or treatment for a disease or injury: *herbal remedies for aches and pains.* ■ a means of counteracting or eliminating something undesirable: *shopping became a remedy for personal problems.* ■ a means of legal reparation: *compensation is available as a remedy against governmental institutions.* **2** the margin within which coins as minted may differ from the standard fineness and weight.
▶ verb (**-ies**, **-ied**) [with obj.] set right (an undesirable situation): *money will be given to remedy the poor funding of nurseries.*
– DERIVATIVES **remediable** adjective.
– ORIGIN Middle English: from Anglo-Norman French *remedie*, from Latin *remedium*, from *re-* 'back' (also expressing intensive force) + *mederi* 'heal'.

remember ▶ verb [with obj.] have in or be able to bring to one's mind an awareness of (someone or something that one has seen, known, or experienced in the past): *I remember the screech of the horn as the car came towards me* | *no one remembered his name.* ■ [with infinitive] do something that one has undertaken to do or that is necessary or advisable: *did you remember to post the letters?.* ■ [with clause] used to emphasize the importance of what is asserted: *you must remember that this is a secret.* ■ bear (someone) in mind by making them a gift or making provision for them: *he has remembered the boy in a codicil to his will.* ■ (**remember someone to**) convey greetings from one person to (another): *remember me to Charlie.* ■ pray for the success or well-being of: *the congress should be remembered in our prayers.* ■ (**remember oneself**) recover one's manners after a lapse.
– DERIVATIVES **rememberer** noun.
– ORIGIN Middle English: from Old French *remembrer*, from late Latin *rememorari* 'call to mind', from *re-* (expressing intensive force) + Latin *memor* 'mindful'.

remembrance ▶ noun [mass noun] the action of remembering something: *a flash of understanding or remembrance passed between them.* ■ the action of remembering the dead, especially in a ceremony: *I decided to sell poppies in remembrance of those who died.* ■ [count noun] a memory or recollection: *the remembrance of her visit came back with startling*

clarity. ▪ [count noun] a thing kept or given as a reminder or in commemoration of someone.
– ORIGIN Middle English: from Old French, from *remembrer* (see **REMEMBER**).

Remembrance Day ▶ noun **1** another term for **REMEMBRANCE SUNDAY**.
2 historical another term for **ARMISTICE DAY**.

remembrancer ▶ noun **1** a person with the job or responsibility of reminding others of something; a chronicler.
2 an official of the Court of Exchequer.

Remembrance Sunday ▶ noun (in the UK) the Sunday nearest 11 November, when those who were killed in the First and Second World Wars and later conflicts are commemorated. Also called **POPPY DAY**.

remex ▶ noun singular form of **REMIGES**.

remiges /ˈrɛmɪdʒiːz/ ▶ plural noun (sing. **remex** /ˈriːmɛks/) Ornithology flight feathers. Compare with **RECTRICES**.
– ORIGIN mid 18th cent.: from Latin, literally 'rowers', based on *remus* 'oar'.

remind ▶ verb [with obj.] cause (someone) to remember someone or something: *he would have forgotten the boy's birthday if you hadn't reminded him* | [with obj. and direct speech] *'You had an accident,' he reminded her.*
▪ (**remind someone of**) cause someone to think of (something) because of a resemblance or likeness: *his impassive, fierce stare reminded her of an owl.* ▪ bring something, especially a commitment or necessary course of action, to the attention of (someone): [with obj. and clause] *the barman reminded them that singing was not permitted* | [with obj. and infinitive] *she reminded me to be respectful.*
– ORIGIN mid 17th cent.: from **RE-** 'again' + the verb **MIND**, probably suggested by obsolete *rememorate*, in the same sense.

reminder ▶ noun a thing that causes someone to remember something: *the watch tower is a reminder of the days when an enemy might appear at any moment.*
▪ a message or communication designed to ensure that someone remembers something. ▪ a letter sent to remind someone of an obligation, especially to pay a bill.

remindful ▶ adjective acting as a reminder: *his humour is **remindful of** that of Max.*

remineralize (also **-ise**) ▶ verb [with obj.] restore the depleted mineral content of (a part of the body, especially the bones or teeth).
– DERIVATIVES **remineralization** noun.

reminisce /ˌrɛmɪˈnɪs/ ▶ verb [no obj.] indulge in enjoyable recollection of past events: *they reminisced about their summers abroad.*
– DERIVATIVES **reminiscer** noun.
– ORIGIN early 19th cent.: back-formation from **REMINISCENCE**.

reminiscence ▶ noun a story told about a past event remembered by the narrator: *his reminiscences of his early days in Parliament.*
▪ [mass noun] the enjoyable recollection of past events: *his story made me smile in reminiscence.* ▪ (**reminiscences**) a collection in literary form of incidents and experiences that someone remembers. ▪ a characteristic of one thing reminding or suggestive of another: *his first works are too full of reminiscences of earlier poetry.*
– DERIVATIVES **reminiscential** adjective (archaic).
– ORIGIN late 16th cent. (denoting the action of remembering): from late Latin *reminiscentia*, from Latin *reminisci* 'remember'.

reminiscent ▶ adjective tending to remind one of something: *the sights were **reminiscent of** my childhood.*
▪ suggesting something by resemblance: *her robes were vaguely **reminiscent of** military dress.* ▪ (of a person or their manner) absorbed in or suggesting absorption in memories: *her expression was wistful and reminiscent.*
– DERIVATIVES **reminiscently** adverb.
– ORIGIN mid 18th cent.: from Latin *reminiscent-* 'remembering', from the verb *reminisci*.

remise /rɪˈmiːz/ Fencing ▶ verb [no obj.] make a second thrust after the first has failed.
▶ noun a second thrust made after the first has failed.
– ORIGIN French, past participle of *remettre* 'put back'.

remiss /rɪˈmɪs/ ▶ adjective [predic.] lacking care or attention to duty; negligent: *the Home Office has been remiss about security devices.*
– DERIVATIVES **remissly** adverb, **remissness** noun.
– ORIGIN late Middle English: from Latin *remissus* 'slackened', past participle of *remittere*. The early senses were 'weakened in colour or consistency' and (in describing sound) 'faint, soft'.

remissible ▶ adjective (especially of sins) able to be pardoned.
– ORIGIN late 16th cent.: from French *rémissible* or late Latin *remissibilis*, from *remiss-* 'slackened', from the verb *remittere* (see **REMISS**).

remission ▶ noun [mass noun] the cancellation of a debt, charge, or penalty: *the scheme allows for the partial remission of tuition fees.*
▪ Brit. the reduction of a prison sentence, especially as a reward for good behaviour. ▪ a diminution of the seriousness or intensity of disease or pain; a temporary recovery: *ten out of twenty patients remained **in remission**.* ▪ formal forgiveness of sins.
– ORIGIN Middle English: from Old French, or from Latin *remissio(n-)*, from *remittere* 'send back, restore' (see **REMIT**).

remit ▶ verb /rɪˈmɪt/ (**remitted**, **remitting**) [with obj.]
1 cancel or refrain from exacting or inflicting (a debt or punishment): *the excess of the sentence over 12 months was remitted.*
▪ Theology pardon (a sin).
2 send (money) in payment or as a gift: *the income they remitted to their families.*
3 refer (a matter for decision) to some authority: *the request for an investigation was remitted to a special committee.*
▪ Law send back (a case) to a lower court. ▪ Law send (someone) from one tribunal to another for a trial or hearing. ▪ archaic consign again to a previous state: *thus his indiscretion remitted him to the nature of an ordinary person.*
4 rare postpone: *the movers refused Mr Tierney's request to remit the motion.*
▪ [no obj.] archaic diminish: *phobias may remit spontaneously without any treatment.*
▶ noun /ˈriːmɪt, rɪˈmɪt/ **1** the task or area of activity officially assigned to an individual or organization: *the committee was becoming caught up in issues that did not fall within its remit.*
2 an item referred to someone for consideration.
– DERIVATIVES **remittable** adjective, **remittal** noun, **remitter** noun.
– ORIGIN late Middle English: from Latin *remittere* 'send back, restore', from *re-* 'back' + *mittere* 'send'. The noun dates from the early 20th cent.

remittance ▶ noun a sum of money sent, especially by post, in payment for goods or services or as a gift.
▪ [mass noun] the action of sending money in such a way.

remittance man ▶ noun chiefly historical an emigrant supported or assisted by payments of money from home.

remittent ▶ adjective (of a fever) characterized by fluctuating body temperatures.
– ORIGIN late 17th cent.: from Latin *remittent-* 'sending back', from the verb *remittere* (see **REMIT**).

remix ▶ verb [with obj.] mix (something) again.
▪ produce a different version of (a musical recording) by altering the balance of the separate tracks.
▶ noun a different version of a musical recording produced in such a way.
– DERIVATIVES **remixer** noun.

remnant ▶ noun a small remaining quantity of something.
▪ a piece of cloth left when the greater part has been used or sold. ▪ a surviving trace: *a **remnant of** the past.* ▪ Christian Theology a small minority of people who will remain faithful to God and so be saved (in allusion to biblical prophecies concerning Israel).
▶ adjective [attrib.] remaining: *remnant strands of hair.*
– ORIGIN Middle English: contraction of obsolete *remenant* from Old French *remenant*, from *remenoir*, *remanoir* 'remain'.

remodel ▶ verb (**remodelled**, **remodelling**; US **remodeled**, **remodeling**) [with obj.] change the structure or form of (something, especially a building, policy, or procedure): *the station was remodelled and enlarged in 1927.*
▪ fashion or shape (a figure or object) again or differently: *she remodelled the head with careful fingers.*

remodeler ▶ noun N. Amer. a person who carries out structural alterations to an existing building, such as adding a new bathroom.

remodify ▶ verb (**-ies**, **-ied**) [with obj.] modify again.
– DERIVATIVES **remodification** noun.

remold ▶ verb US spelling of **REMOULD**.

remonetize (also **-ise**) ▶ verb [with obj.] rare restore (a metal) to its former position as legal tender.
– DERIVATIVES **remonetization** noun.

remonstrance /rɪˈmɒnstr(ə)ns/ ▶ noun a forcefully reproachful protest: *angry remonstrances in the Commons* | [mass noun] *he shut his ears to any remonstrance.*
▪ (**the Remonstrance**) a document drawn up in 1610 by the Arminians of the Dutch Reformed Church, presenting the differences between their doctrines and those of the strict Calvinists.
– ORIGIN late 16th cent. (in the sense 'evidence'): from Old French, or from medieval Latin *remonstrantia*, from *remonstrare* 'demonstrate, show' (see **REMONSTRATE**).

Remonstrant /rɪˈmɒnstrənt/ ▶ noun a member of the Arminian party in the Dutch Reformed Church.
– ORIGIN early 17th cent.: from medieval Latin *remonstrant-* 'demonstrating' (see also **REMONSTRANCE**).

remonstrate /ˈrɛmənstreɪt/ ▶ verb [no obj.] make a forcefully reproachful protest: *he turned angrily to **remonstrate with** Tommy* | [with direct speech] *'You don't mean that,' she remonstrated.*
– DERIVATIVES **remonstration** noun, **remonstrative** adjective, **remonstrator** noun.
– ORIGIN late 16th cent. (in the sense 'make plain'): from medieval Latin *remonstrat-* 'demonstrated', from the verb *remonstrare*, from *re-* (expressing intensive force) + *monstrare* 'to show'.

remontant /rɪˈmɒnt(ə)nt/ ▶ adjective (of a plant) blooming or producing a crop more than once a season.
▶ noun a remontant plant.
– ORIGIN late 19th cent.: from French, literally 'coming up again', from the verb *remonter*.

remora /ˈrɛmərə/ ▶ noun a slender marine fish which attaches itself to large fish by means of a sucker on top of the head. It generally feeds on the host's external parasites. Also called **SHARK-SUCKER**, **SUCKERFISH**.
• Family Echeneidae: several genera and species, in particular the widespread *Remora remora*.
– ORIGIN mid 16th cent.: from Latin, literally 'hindrance', from *re-* 'back' + *mora* 'delay' (because of the former belief that the fish slowed down ships).

remorse ▶ noun [mass noun] deep regret or guilt for a wrong committed: *they were filled with remorse and shame.*
– DERIVATIVES **remorseful** adjective, **remorsefully** adverb.
– ORIGIN late Middle English: from Old French *remors*, from medieval Latin *remorsus*, from Latin *remordere* 'vex', from *re-* (expressing intensive force) + *mordere* 'to bite'.

remorseless ▶ adjective without regret or guilt: *a remorseless killer.*
▪ (of something unpleasant) never ending or improving; relentless: *remorseless poverty.*
– DERIVATIVES **remorselessly** adverb, **remorselessness** noun.

r

remortgage ▶ verb [with obj.] take out another or a different kind of mortgage on (a property).
▶ noun a different or additional mortgage.

remote ▶ adjective (**remoter**, **remotest**) **1** (of a place) far away; distant: *I'd chosen a spot that looked as **remote from** any road as possible.*
▪ (of a place) situated far from the main centres of population in a country: *a remote Welsh valley.* ▪ (of an electronic device) operating or operated by means of radio or infrared signals. ▪ distant in time: *a golden age in the remote past.* ▪ distantly related: *a remote cousin.* ▪ having very little connection with or relationship to: *the theory seems rather intellectual and **remote from** everyday experience.* ▪ (of a person) aloof and unfriendly in manner: *this morning Maud again seemed remote and patronizing.* ▪ Computing denoting a device which can only be accessed by means of a network. Compare with **LOCAL**.
2 (of a chance or possibility) unlikely to occur: *chances of a genuine and lasting peace become even more remote.*
▶ noun a remote control device.
– DERIVATIVES **remoteness** noun.
– ORIGIN late Middle English (in the sense 'far apart'): from Latin *remotus* 'removed', past participle of *removere* (see **REMOVE**).

remote control ▶ noun [mass noun] control of a machine or apparatus from a distance by means of

signals transmitted from a radio or electronic device.
■(also **remote controller**) [count noun] a device that controls an apparatus, especially a television or video, in such a way.
– DERIVATIVES **remote-controlled** adjective.

remotely ▶ adverb **1** from a distance; without physical contact: *new electronic meters that can be read remotely* | *a new type of remotely controlled torpedo.*
2 [as submodifier] [usu. with negative] in the slightest degree: *he had never been remotely jealous.*

remote sensing ▶ noun [mass noun] the scanning of the earth by satellite or high-flying aircraft in order to obtain information about it.

remoulade /ˈrɛmʊlɑːd/ ▶ noun [mass noun] salad or seafood dressing made with hard-boiled egg yolks, oil, and vinegar, and flavoured with mustard, capers, and herbs.
– ORIGIN French *rémoulade*, from Italian *remolata*.

remould (US **remold**) ▶ verb /riːˈməʊld/ [with obj.] change or refashion the appearance, structure, or character of: *did the welfare state remould capitalism to give it a more human face?*
■Brit. put a new tread on (a worn tyre).
▶ noun /ˈriːməʊld/ a tyre that has been given a new tread.

remount ▶ verb /riːˈmaʊnt/ [with obj.] mount (something) again, in particular:
■get on (something) in order to ride it again: *she went to remount her horse* | [no obj.] *Glenda remounted and rode stylishly through the gates.* ■ attach to a new frame or setting: *remount the best photos in glass-fronted mounts.* ■ produce (a play or exhibition) again. ■ organize and embark on (a significant course of action) again: *the raid was remounted in August.*
▶ noun /ˈriːmaʊnt/ a fresh horse for a rider.
■historical a supply of fresh horses for a regiment.

removal ▶ noun [mass noun] the action of removing someone or something, in particular:
■the taking away of something unwanted: *the removal of the brain tumour.* ■ the abolition of something: *the removal of all legal barriers to the free movement of goods.* ■ [usu. as modifier] chiefly Brit. the transfer of furniture and other contents when moving house: *removal men.* ■ the dismissal of someone from a job or office. ■ S. African historical the forcing of individuals or communities to leave their place of residence, especially to move to ethnically homogeneous rural settlements. ■(also **removal of remains**) Irish the formal procedure of taking a body from the house to the church for the funeral service.

removalist ▶ noun Austral. a person or firm engaged in household or business removals.

remove ▶ verb [with obj.] take away (something unwanted or unnecessary) from the position it occupies: *she sat down to remove her make-up.*
■take (something) from a place in order to take it to another location: *Customs officials also* ***removed*** *documents* ***from*** *the premises.* ■ eliminate or get rid of (someone or something): *they* ***removed*** *hundreds of thousands of needy youngsters* ***from*** *the benefit system.* ■ take off (clothing): *he sat down on the ground and quickly removed his shoes and socks.* ■ abolish: *exchange controls have finally been removed.* ■ dismiss from a job or office: *he was* ***removed from*** *his position as teacher.* ■ [no obj.] (**remove to**) dated change one's home or place of residence by moving to (another place or area): *he removed to Wales and began afresh.* ■ S. African historical compel (someone) by law to move to another area: *a man is removed to the tribal district of his forbears.* ■ (**be removed**) be very different from: *an explanation which is far* ***removed from*** *the truth.* ■ [as adj. **removed**] separated by a particular number of steps of descent: *his second cousin once removed.*
▶ noun **1** a degree of remoteness or separation: ***at this remove****, the whole incident seems insane.*
2 (also **Remove**) a form or division in some British schools: *a member of the Fifth Remove.*
– DERIVATIVES **removability** noun, **removable** adjective, **remover** noun.
– ORIGIN Middle English (as a verb): from the Old French stem *remov-*, from Latin *removere*, from *re-* 'back' + *movere* 'to move'.

REM sleep ▶ noun [mass noun] a kind of sleep that occurs at intervals during the night and is characterized by rapid eye movements, more dreaming and bodily movement, and faster pulse and breathing.

remuage /ˌrɛmjʊˈɑːʒ, French rəmɥaʒ/ ▶ noun [mass noun] the periodic turning or shaking of bottled wine, especially champagne, to move sediment towards the cork.
– ORIGIN French, literally 'moving about'.

remuda /rəˈmuːdə/ ▶ noun N. Amer. a herd of horses that have been saddle-broken, from which ranch hands choose their mounts for the day.
– ORIGIN late 19th cent.: via American Spanish, from Spanish, literally 'exchange, replacement'.

remunerate /rɪˈmjuːnəreɪt/ ▶ verb [with obj.] pay (someone) for services rendered or work done: *they should be remunerated fairly for their work.*
– DERIVATIVES **remunerative** adjective.
– ORIGIN early 16th cent.: from Latin *remunerat-* 'rewarded, recompensed', from the verb *remunerari*, from *re-* (expressing intensive force) + *munus, muner-* 'gift'.

remuneration ▶ noun [mass noun] money paid for work or a service.

Remus /ˈriːməs/ Roman Mythology the twin brother of Romulus.

REN ▶ abbreviation for ringer equivalent number, a measure of the load a device will place on a telephone line. The maximum REN allowed on a single line is usually limited by telephone companies.

Renaissance /rɪˈneɪs(ə)ns, -ɒ̃s/ the revival of art and literature under the influence of classical models in the 14th–16th centuries.
■the culture and style of art and architecture developed during this era. ■ [as noun **a renaissance**] a revival of or renewed interest in something: *cinema-going is enjoying something of a renaissance.*

> The Renaissance is generally regarded as beginning in Florence, where there was a revival of interest in classical antiquity. Important early figures are the writers Petrarch, Dante, and Boccaccio and the painter Giotto. Music flourished, from madrigals to the polyphonic masses of Palestrina, with a wide variety of instruments such as viols and lutes. The period from the end of the 15th century has become known as the High Renaissance, when Venice and Rome began to share Florence's importance and Raphael, Leonardo da Vinci, and Michelangelo were active. Renaissance thinking spread to the rest of Europe from the early 16th century, and was influential for the next hundred years.

– ORIGIN from French *renaissance*, from *re-* 'back, again' + *naissance* 'birth' (from Latin *nascentia*, from *nasci* 'be born').

Renaissance man ▶ noun a person with many talents or interests, especially in the humanities.

renal /ˈriːn(ə)l/ ▶ adjective technical of or relating to the kidneys: *renal failure.*
– ORIGIN mid 17th cent.: from French *rénal*, from late Latin *renalis*, from Latin *renes* 'kidneys'.

renal calculus ▶ noun another term for **KIDNEY STONE**.

renal pelvis ▶ noun see **PELVIS** (sense 2).

renal tubule ▶ noun another term for **KIDNEY TUBULE**.

rename ▶ verb [with obj. and complement] give a new name to (someone or something): *after independence Celebes was renamed Sulawesi.*

Renan /rəˈnɒ̃, French rənɑ̃/, (Joseph) Ernest (1823–92), French historian, theologian, and philosopher. He provoked a controversy with the publication of his *Life of Jesus* (1863), which rejected the supernatural element in Jesus' life.

renascence /rɪˈnas(ə)ns, -ˈneɪ-/ ▶ noun formal the revival of something that has been dormant: *the renascence of poetry as an oral art.*
■another term for **RENAISSANCE**.

renascent ▶ adjective becoming active or popular again: *renascent fascism.*
– ORIGIN early 18th cent.: from Latin *renascent-* 'being born again', from the verb *renasci*, from *re-* 'back, again' + *nasci* 'be born'.

Renault[1] /ˈrɛnəʊ, French rəno/, Louis (1877–1944), French engineer and motor manufacturer. He and his brothers established the Renault company in 1898, manufacturing racing cars, and later industrial and agricultural machinery and military technology.

Renault[2] /ˈrɛnəʊ/, Mary (1905–83), British novelist, resident in South Africa from 1948; pseudonym of *Mary Challans*. She wrote historical novels set in the ancient world, notably a trilogy dealing with Alexander the Great (1970–81).

rencontre /rɛnˈkɒntə/ ▶ noun archaic variant spelling of **RENCOUNTER**.
– ORIGIN early 17th cent.: French.

rencounter /rɛnˈkaʊntə/ archaic ▶ noun a chance meeting with someone.
■a battle, skirmish, or duel.
▶ verb [with obj.] meet by chance: *I wonder who those fellows were we rencountered last night.*
– ORIGIN early 16th cent.: from French *rencontre* (noun), *rencontrer* 'meet face to face'.

rend ▶ verb (past and past participle **rent**) [with obj.] tear (something) into two or more pieces: *snapping teeth that would rend human flesh to shreds* | figurative *the speculation and confusion which was rending the civilized world.*
■[with obj. and adverbial of direction] archaic wrench (something) violently: *he rent the branch out of the tree.* ■ poetic/literary cause great emotional pain to (a person or their heart): *you tell me this in order to make me able to betray you without rending my heart.*
– PHRASES **rend the air** poetic/literary sound piercingly: *a shrill scream rent the air.* **rend one's garments** (or **hair**) tear one's clothes (or wrench some of one's hair out) as a sign of extreme grief of distress.
– ORIGIN Old English *rendan*; related to Middle Low German *rende*.

Rendell /ˈrɛnd(ə)l/, Ruth (Barbara) (b.1930), English writer of detective fiction and thrillers. She is noted for her psychological crime novels and her character Chief Inspector Wexford; she also writes under the pseudonym of Barbara Vine.

render ▶ verb [with obj.] **1** provide (a service): *money serves as a reward for services rendered.*
■give (help): *Mrs Evans would* ***render*** *assistance* ***to*** *those she thought were in real need.* ■ submit or present for inspection or consideration: *he would render income tax returns at the end of the year.* ■ poetic/literary hand over: *he will* ***render up*** *his immortal soul.* ■ deliver (a verdict or judgement): *the jury's finding amounted to the clearest verdict yet rendered upon the scandal.*
2 [with obj. and complement] cause to be or become; make: *the rains rendered his escape impossible.*
3 represent or depict artistically: *the eyes and the cheeks are exceptionally well rendered.*
■translate: *the phrase was* ***rendered into*** *English.* ■ Music perform (a piece): *a soprano solo reverently rendered by Linda Howie.* ■ Computing process (an outline image) using colour and shading in order to make it appear solid and three-dimensional.
4 melt down (fat), typically in order to clarify it: *the fat was being cut up and rendered for lard.*
■process (the carcass of an animal) in order to extract proteins, fats, and other usable parts: [as adj. **rendered**] *the rendered down remains of sheep.*
5 cover (stone or brick) with a coat of plaster: *external walls will be rendered and tiled.*
▶ noun [mass noun] a first coat of plaster applied to a brick or stone surface.
– DERIVATIVES **renderer** noun.
– ORIGIN late Middle English: from Old French *rendre*, from an alteration of Latin *reddere* 'give back', from *re-* 'back' + *dare* 'give'. The earliest senses were 'recite', 'translate', and 'give back' (hence 'represent' and 'perform'); 'hand over' (hence 'give (help)' and 'submit for consideration'); 'cause to be'; and 'melt down'.

rendering ▶ noun **1** a performance of a piece of music or drama: *a lively rendering of 'Ilkley Moor'.*
■a translation: *a literal rendering of an idiom.* ■ [mass noun] Computing the processing of an outline image using colour and shading to make it appear solid and three-dimensional.
2 [mass noun] the action of applying plaster to a wall.
■the coating applied in such a way.
3 [mass noun] formal the action of giving, yielding, or surrendering something: *the rendering of church dues.*

render-set ▶ verb [with obj.] plaster (a wall) with two coats.
▶ noun [mass noun] plastering consisting of two coats.
▶ adjective (of plastering) consisting of two coats.

rendezvous /ˈrɒndɪvuː, -deɪvuː/ ▶ noun (pl. same /-vuːz/) a meeting at an agreed time and place, typically between two people.
■a place used for such a meeting. ■ a place, typically a bar or restaurant, that is used as a popular meeting place. ■ a meeting up of troops, ships, or aircraft at an agreed time and place. ■ a pre-arranged meeting between spacecraft in space.
▶ verb (**rendezvouses** /-vuːz/, **rendezvoused** /-vuːd/, **rendezvousing** /-vuːɪŋ/) [no obj.] meet at an agreed time and place: *I* ***rendezvoused with*** *Bea as planned.*
– ORIGIN late 16th cent.: from French *rendez-vous!* 'present yourselves!', imperative of *se rendre*.

rendition ▶ noun a performance or interpretation,

especially of a dramatic role or piece of music: *a wonderful rendition of 'Nessun Dorma'.*
■ a visual representation or reproduction: *a pen-and-ink rendition of Mars with his sword drawn.* ■ a translation or transliteration.
– ORIGIN early 17th cent.: from obsolete French, from *rendre* 'give back, render'.

rendzina /rɛn(d)ˈziːnə/ ▶ **noun** Soil Science a fertile lime-rich soil with dark humus above a pale soft calcareous layer, typical of grassland on chalk or limestone.
– ORIGIN 1920s: via Russian from Polish *rędzina*.

renegade /ˈrɛnɪɡeɪd/ ▶ **noun** a person who deserts and betrays an organization, country, or set of principles.
■ archaic a person who abandons religion; an apostate. ■ a person who behaves in a rebelliously unconventional manner.
▶ **adjective** having treacherously changed allegiance: *a renegade bodyguard.*
■ archaic having abandoned one's religious beliefs: *a renegade monk.*
▶ **verb** [no obj.] archaic become a renegade: *Johnson had renegaded from the Confederacy.*
– ORIGIN late 15th cent.: from Spanish *renegado*, from medieval Latin *renegatus* 'renounced', past participle (used as a noun) of *renegare*, from *re-* (expressing intensive force) + Latin *negare* 'deny'.

renegado /ˌrɛnɪˈɡeɪdəʊ/ ▶ **noun** (pl. **-oes**) archaic term for **RENEGADE**.
– ORIGIN Spanish.

renege /rɪˈneɪɡ, rɪˈniːɡ/ (also **renegue**) ▶ **verb** [no obj.] go back on a promise, undertaking, or contract: *the government had* **reneged on** *its election promises.*
■ another term for **REVOKE** (in sense 2). ■ [with obj.] archaic renounce or abandon (someone or something): *we fought for the royal Stuarts that reneged us against the Williamites.*
– DERIVATIVES **reneger** noun.
– ORIGIN mid 16th cent. (in the sense 'desert (especially a faith or a person)'): from medieval Latin *renegare*, from Latin *re-* (expressing intensive force) + *negare* 'deny'.

renegotiate ▶ **verb** [with obj.] negotiate (something) again in order to change the original agreed terms: *the parties will renegotiate the price.*
– DERIVATIVES **renegotiable** adjective, **renegotiation** noun.

renew ▶ **verb** [with obj.] resume (an activity) after an interruption: *the parents renewed their campaign to save the school.*
■ re-establish (a relationship): *he had renewed an acquaintance with MacAlister.* ■ repeat (an action or statement): *detectives renewed their appeal for those in the area at the time to contact them.* ■ give fresh life or strength to: [as adj. **renewed**] *she would face the future with renewed determination.* ■ extend for a further period the validity of (a licence, subscription, or contract): *her contract had not been renewed.* ■ replace (something that is broken or worn out): *check the joints—they may well need renewing.*
– DERIVATIVES **renewer** noun.

renewable ▶ **adjective** capable of being renewed: *the 30-day truce is renewable by mutual agreement.*
■ (of energy or its source) not depleted when used: *a shift away from fossil fuels to renewable energy.*
▶ **noun** (usu. **renewables**) a source of energy that is not depleted by use, such as water, wind, or solar power.
– DERIVATIVES **renewability** noun.

renewal ▶ **noun** [mass noun] the action of extending the period of validity of a licence, subscription, or contract: *the contracts came up for renewal* | [count noun] *a renewal of his passport.*
■ [count noun] an instance of resuming an activity or state after an interruption: *a renewal of hostilities.* ■ the replacing or repair of something that is worn out, run-down, or broken: *the need for urban renewal.* ■ (among charismatic Christians) the state or process of being made spiritually new in the Holy Spirit.

Renfrewshire /ˈrɛnfruːʃɪə, -ʃə/ an administrative region and former county of west central Scotland, on the Firth of Clyde, divided into **Renfrewshire** and **East Renfrewshire**.

renga /ˈrɛŋɡə/ ▶ **noun** (pl. same or **rengas**) a Japanese poem in the form of a tanka (or series of tanka), with the first three lines composed by one person and the second two by another.
– ORIGIN Japanese, from *ren* 'linking' + *ga* (from *ka* 'poetry').

reniform /ˈriːnɪfɔːm/ ▶ **adjective** chiefly Mineralogy & Botany kidney-shaped.
– ORIGIN mid 18th cent.: from Latin *ren* 'kidney' + **-IFORM**.

renin /ˈriːnɪn/ ▶ **noun** [mass noun] Biochemistry an enzyme secreted by and stored in the kidneys which promotes the production of the protein angiotensin.
– ORIGIN late 19th cent.: from Latin *ren* 'kidney' + **-IN**[1].

renminbi /ˈrɛnmɪnbi/ ▶ **noun** (pl. same) the national currency of the People's Republic of China, introduced in 1948.
– ORIGIN from Chinese *rénmínbì*, from *rénmín* 'people' + *bì* 'currency'.

Rennes /rɛn, French ʀɛn/ an industrial city in NW France; pop. 203,530 (1990). It was established as the capital of a Celtic tribe, the Redones, from whom it derives its name, later becoming the capital of the ancient kingdom of Brittany.

rennet /ˈrɛnɪt/ ▶ **noun** [mass noun] curdled milk from the stomach of an unweaned calf, containing rennin and used in curdling milk for cheese.
■ any preparation containing rennin.
– ORIGIN late 15th cent.: probably related to **RUN**.

Rennie, John (1761–1821), Scottish civil engineer. He is best known as the designer of the London and East India Docks (built *c.*1800), and Waterloo Bridge, Southwark Bridge, and London Bridge (1811–31).

rennin /ˈrɛnɪn/ ▶ **noun** [mass noun] an enzyme secreted into the stomach of unweaned mammals causing the curdling of milk.
– ORIGIN late 19th cent.: from **RENNET** + **-IN**[1].

Reno /ˈriːnəʊ/ a city in western Nevada; pop. 133,850 (1990). It is noted as a gambling resort and for its liberal laws enabling quick marriages and divorces.

Renoir[1] /rəˈnwɑː, ˈrɛnwɑː, French ʀənwaʀ/, Jean (1894–1979), French film director, son of Auguste Renoir. He is famous for films including *La Grande illusion* (1937) and *La Règle du jeu* (1939).

Renoir[2] /rəˈnwɑː, ˈrɛnwɑː, French ʀənwaʀ/, (Pierre) Auguste (1841–1919), French painter. An early Impressionist, he developed a style characterized by light, fresh colours and indistinct, subtle outlines. Notable works: *Les Grandes baigneuses* (1884–7).

renominate ▶ **verb** [with obj.] nominate (someone) for a further term of office.
– DERIVATIVES **renomination** noun.

renormalization (also **-isation**) ▶ **noun** [mass noun] Physics a method used in quantum mechanics in which unwanted infinities are removed from the solutions of equations by redefining parameters such as the mass and charge of subatomic particles.
– DERIVATIVES **renormalize** verb.

renosterbos /rɛˈnɒstəbɒs/ (also **rhenosterbos**) ▶ **noun** S. African a grey-leaved, evergreen southern African shrub of the daisy family.
• *Elytropappus rhinocerotis*, family Compositae.
– ORIGIN early 19th cent.: from Afrikaans, from *renoster* 'rhinoceros' + *bos* 'bush'.

renounce ▶ **verb** [with obj.] formally declare one's abandonment of (a claim, right, or possession): *Isabella offered to renounce her son's claim to the French Crown.*
■ refuse to recognize or abide by any longer: *these agreements were renounced after the fall of the Tsarist regime.* ■ declare that one will no longer engage in or support: *they renounced the armed struggle.* ■ reject and stop using or consuming: *he renounced drugs and alcohol completely.* ■ [no obj.] Law refuse or resign a right or position, especially one as an heir or trustee: *there will be forms enabling the allottee to renounce.*
– PHRASES **renounce the world** completely withdraw from society or material affairs in order to lead a life considered to be more spiritually fulfilling.
– DERIVATIVES **renounceable** adjective, **renouncement** noun, **renouncer** noun.
– ORIGIN late Middle English: from Old French *renoncer*, from Latin *renuntiare* 'protest against', from *re-* (expressing reversal) + *nuntiare* 'announce'.

renovate /ˈrɛnəveɪt/ ▶ **verb** [with obj.] restore (something old, especially a building) to a good state of repair: *the old school has been tastefully renovated as a private house.*
■ archaic refresh; reinvigorate: *a little warm nourishment renovated him for a short time.*
– DERIVATIVES **renovation** noun, **renovator** noun.
– ORIGIN early 16th cent.: from Latin *renovat-* 'made new again', from the verb *renovare*, from *re-* 'back, again' + *novus* 'new'.

renown ▶ **noun** [mass noun] the condition of being known or talked about by many people; fame: *authors of great renown.*
– ORIGIN Middle English: from Anglo-Norman French *renoun*, from Old French *renomer* 'make famous', from *re-* (expressing intensive force) + *nomer* 'to name', from Latin *nominare*.

renowned ▶ **adjective** known or talked about by many people; famous: *Britain is* **renowned for** *its love of animals.*

rent[1] ▶ **noun** [mass noun] a tenant's regular payment to a landlord for the use of property or land.
■ a sum paid for the hire of equipment.
▶ **verb** [with obj.] pay someone for the use of (something, typically property, land, or a car): *they rented a house together in Sussex* | [as adj. **rented**] *a rented apartment.*
■ (of an owner) let someone use (something) in return for payment: *he purchased a large tract of land and* **rented out** *most of it to local farmers.* ■ [no obj.] chiefly N. Amer. be let or hired out at a specified rate: *skis or snowboards* **rent for** *$60–80 for six days.*
– PHRASES **for rent** available to be rented.
– ORIGIN Middle English: from Old French *rente*, from a root shared by **RENDER**.

rent[2] ▶ **noun** a large tear in a piece of fabric.
■ an opening or gap resembling such a tear: *they stared at the rents in the clouds.*
– ORIGIN mid 16th cent.: from obsolete *rent* 'pull to pieces, lacerate', variant of **REND**.

rent[3] past and past participle of **REND**.

rent-a- ▶ **combining form** often humorous denoting availability for hire of a specified thing: *rent-a-car* | *rent-a-crowd.*

rentable ▶ **adjective** available or suitable for renting: *rentable office space.*
– DERIVATIVES **rentability** noun.

rental ▶ **noun** an amount paid or received as rent.
■ [mass noun] the action of renting something: *the office was on weekly* **rental**. ■ N. Amer. a rented house or car.
▶ **adjective** of, relating to, or available for rent: *rental accommodation.*
– ORIGIN late Middle English: from Anglo-Norman French, or from Anglo-Latin *rentale*, from Old French *rente* (see **RENT**[1]).

rental library ▶ **noun** US a library which rents books and other material for a fee.

rent boy ▶ **noun** Brit. informal a young male prostitute.

renter ▶ **noun 1** a person who rents a flat, a car, or other object.
2 (in the UK) a person who distributes cinema films.
3 Brit. informal a male prostitute.
4 US a rented car or video cassette.

rent-free ▶ **adjective** & **adverb** with exemption from rent: [as adj.] *rent-free periods* | [as adv.] *you could live in the cottage rent-free.*

rentier /ˈrɒntɪeɪ, French rɑ̃tje/ ▶ **noun** a person living on income from property or investments.
– ORIGIN French, from *rente* 'dividend'.

rent party ▶ **noun** US a party held to raise money to pay rent by charging guests for attendance.

rent roll ▶ **noun** a register of a landlord's lands and buildings with the rents due from them.
■ a landlord's total income from rent.

rent table ▶ **noun** an 18th-century office table.

renumber ▶ **verb** [with obj.] change the number or numbers assigned to (something).

renunciation ▶ **noun** [mass noun] the formal rejection of something, typically a belief, claim, or course of action: *the life of the Spirit required renunciation of marriage* | [count noun] *a renunciation of violence.*
■ Law a document expressing renunciation.
– DERIVATIVES **renunciant** noun & adjective.
– ORIGIN late Middle English: from late Latin *renuntiatio(n-)*, from Latin *renuntiare* 'protest against' (see **RENOUNCE**).

renvers /ˈrɛnvəs/ (also **renverse**) ▶ **noun** a movement performed in dressage, in which the horse moves parallel to the side of the arena, with its hindquarters carried closer to the wall than its shoulders and its body curved away from the centre.
– ORIGIN French.

r

renvoi /ˈrɒ̃vwʌ/ ▶ **noun** [mass noun] Law the action or process of referring a case or dispute to the jurisdiction of another country.
– ORIGIN late 19th cent.: French, from *renvoyer* 'send back'.

reoccupy ▶ **verb** (**-ies**, **-ied**) [with obj.] occupy (a place or position) again: *the English reoccupied the border counties.*
– DERIVATIVES **reoccupation** noun.

reoccur ▶ **verb** (**reoccurred**, **reoccurring**) [no obj.] occur again or repeatedly: *ulcers tend to reoccur after treatment has stopped.*
– DERIVATIVES **reoccurrence** noun.

reoffend ▶ **verb** [no obj.] commit a further offence: *people who reoffend while on bail.*
– DERIVATIVES **reoffender** noun.

reopen ▶ **verb** [with obj.] open again: *after being renovated it was reopened to the public* | [no obj.] *the trial reopens on 6 March.*

reorder ▶ **verb** [with obj.] **1** request (something) to be made, supplied, or served again: *reps reorder any titles which fall below the agreed number.*
2 arrange (something) again: *he fixed his bed and reordered his books.*
▶ **noun** a renewed or repeated order for goods.

reorg ▶ **noun** informal a reorganization.

reorganize (also **-ise**) ▶ **verb** [with obj.] change the way in which (something) is organized: *we have to reorganize the entire workload* | [no obj.] *the company reorganized into fewer key areas.*
– DERIVATIVES **reorganization** noun, **reorganizer** noun.

reorient /riːˈɔːrɪɛnt, -ˈɒr-/ ▶ **verb** [with obj.] change the focus or direction of: *the will is dislodged from false values and reoriented towards God.*
■ (**reorient oneself**) find one's position again in relation to one's surroundings: *slowly they advanced, stopping every so often and then reorienting themselves.*
– DERIVATIVES **reorientate** verb, **reorientation** noun.

reovirus /ˈriːə(ʊ),vʌɪrəs/ ▶ **noun** any of a group of RNA viruses that are sometimes associated with respiratory and enteric infection.
– ORIGIN mid 20th cent.: from the initial letters of *respiratory, enteric*, and *orphan* (referring to a virus not identified with a particular disease) + **VIRUS**.

Rep. ▶ **abbreviation** for ■ (in the US Congress) Representative. ■ Republic. ■ US a Republican.

rep[1] informal ▶ **noun** a representative: *a union rep.*
■ a sales representative.
▶ **verb** (**repped**, **repping**) [no obj.] act as a sales representative for a company or product: *at eighteen she was working for her dad, repping on the road.*
– ORIGIN late 19th cent.: abbreviation.

rep[2] ▶ **noun** [mass noun] informal repertory: *once, when I was in rep, I learned Iago in three days.*
■ [count noun] a repertory theatre or company.
– ORIGIN 1920s: abbreviation.

rep[3] (also **repp**) ▶ **noun** [mass noun] a fabric with a ribbed surface, used in curtains and upholstery.
– ORIGIN mid 19th cent.: from French *reps*, of unknown ultimate origin.

rep[4] ▶ **noun** N. Amer. informal short for **REPUTATION**: *I don't know why caffeine's suddenly got such a bad rep.*

rep[5] ▶ **noun** (in bodybuilding) a repetition of a set of exercises.
▶ **verb** [with obj.] (in knitting patterns) repeat (stitches or part of a design): *rep the last row.*
– ORIGIN 1950s: abbreviation.

repack ▶ **verb** [with obj.] pack (a suitcase or bag) again.

repackage ▶ **verb** [with obj.] package again or differently: *excess stock may be given to charities or repackaged.*
■ present in a new way: *the commission has repackaged its ideas.*

repaginate ▶ **verb** [with obj.] renumber the pages of (a book, magazine, or other printed item).
– DERIVATIVES **repagination** noun.

repaid past and past participle of **REPAY**.

repaint ▶ **verb** [with obj.] cover the surface of (something) with a new coat of paint.
▶ **noun** [in sing.] an act of painting something again.

repair[1] ▶ **verb** [with obj.] fix or mend (a thing suffering from damage or a fault): *faulty electrical appliances should be repaired by an electrician.*
■ make good (such damage) by fixing or repairing it: *an operation to repair damage to his neck.* ■ put right (a damaged relationship or unwelcome situation): *the new government moved quickly to repair relations with the USA.*
▶ **noun** [mass noun] the action of fixing or mending something: *the truck was* ***beyond repair*** | [count noun] *the abandoned house they bought needs repairs.*
■ [count noun] a result of such fixing or mending: *a coat of French polish was brushed over the repair.* ■ the relative physical condition of an object: *the existing hospital is* ***in a bad state of repair.***
– DERIVATIVES **repairable** adjective, **repairer** noun.
– ORIGIN late Middle English: from Old French *reparer*, from Latin *reparare*, from *re-* 'back' + *parare* 'make ready'.

repair[2] ▶ **verb** [no obj.] (**repair to**) formal or humorous go to (a place), especially in company: *we repaired to the tranquillity of a nearby cafe.*
▶ **noun** [mass noun] archaic frequent or habitual visiting of a place: *she exhorted repair to the church.*
■ [count noun] a place which is frequently visited or occupied: *the repairs of wild beasts.*
– ORIGIN Middle English: from Old French *repairer*, from late Latin *repatriare* 'return to one's country' (see **REPATRIATE**).

repairman ▶ **noun** (pl. **-men**) a person who repairs vehicles, machinery, or appliances.

repaper ▶ **verb** [with obj.] apply new wallpaper to (a wall or room).

reparable /ˈrɛp(ə)rəb(ə)l/ ▶ **adjective** (especially of an injury or loss) possible to rectify or repair.
– ORIGIN late 16th cent.: from French *réparable*, from Latin *reparabilis*, from *reparare* 'make ready again' (see **REPAIR**[1]).

reparation /,rɛpəˈreɪʃ(ə)n/ ▶ **noun** [mass noun] **1** the making of amends for a wrong one has done, by paying money to or otherwise helping those who have been wronged: *the courts required a convicted offender to* ***make financial reparation to*** *his victim.*
■ (**reparations**) the compensation for war damage paid by a defeated state.
2 archaic the action of repairing something: *the old hall was pulled down to avoid the cost of reparation.*
– DERIVATIVES **reparative** /ˈrɛp(ə)rətɪv, rɪˈparətɪv/ adjective.
– ORIGIN late Middle English: from Old French, from late Latin *reparatio(n-)*, from *reparare* 'make ready again' (see **REPAIR**[1]).

repartee /,rɛpɑːˈtiː/ ▶ **noun** [mass noun] conversation or speech characterized by quick, witty comments or replies.
– ORIGIN mid 17th cent.: from French *repartie* 'replied promptly', feminine past participle of *repartir*, from *re-* 'again' + *partir* 'set off'.

repartition ▶ **verb** [with obj.] partition or divide (something) again.

repass ▶ **verb** [no obj.] pass again, especially on the way back.
– ORIGIN late Middle English: from Old French *repasser*.

repast /rɪˈpɑːst/ ▶ **noun** formal a meal: *a sumptuous repast.*
– ORIGIN late Middle English: from Old French, based on late Latin *repascere*, from *re-* (expressing intensive force) + *pascere* 'to feed'.

repat /ˈriːpat, riːˈpat/ ▶ **noun** Brit. informal, dated a person who has been repatriated.
– ORIGIN 1940s: abbreviation.

repatriate /riːˈpatrɪeɪt, -ˈpeɪ-/ ▶ **verb** [with obj.] send (someone) back to their own country: *the government sought to repatriate thousands of Albanian refugees.*
■ send or bring (money) back to one's own country: *foreign firms would be permitted to repatriate all profits.*
▶ **noun** a person who has been repatriated.
– DERIVATIVES **repatriation** noun.
– ORIGIN early 17th cent.: from late Latin *repatriat-* 'returned to one's country', from the verb *repatriare*, from *re-* 'back' + Latin *patria* 'native land'.

repay ▶ **verb** (past and past participle **repaid**) [with obj.] pay back (a loan, debt, or sum of money): *the loans were to be repaid over a 20-year period.*
■ pay back money borrowed from (someone): *most of his fortune had been spent repaying creditors.* ■ do or give something as recompense for (a favour or kindness received): *the manager has given me another chance and I'm desperate to repay that faith.* ■ be well worth subjecting to (a specified action): *these sites would repay more detailed investigation.*
– DERIVATIVES **repayable** adjective, **repayment** noun.
– ORIGIN late Middle English: from Old French *repaier*.

repayment mortgage ▶ **noun** a mortgage in which the borrower repays the capital and interest together in fixed instalments over a fixed period.

repeal ▶ **verb** [with obj.] revoke or annul (a law or act of parliament): *the legislation was repealed five months later.*
▶ **noun** [mass noun] the action of revoking or annulling a law or act of parliament: *the House voted in favour of repeal.*
– DERIVATIVES **repealable** adjective.
– ORIGIN late Middle English: from Anglo-Norman French *repeler*, from Old French *re-* (expressing reversal) + *apeler* 'to call, appeal'.

repeat ▶ **verb** **1** [reporting verb] say again something one has already said: [with direct speech] *'Are you hurt?' he repeated* | [with obj.] *Billy repeated his question* | [with clause] *the landlady repeated that she was being very lenient with him.*
■ say again (something said or written by someone else): *he repeated the words after me* | [with clause] *she repeated what I'd said.* ■ (**repeat oneself**) say or do the same thing again. ■ used for emphasis: *force was not—repeat, not—to be used.*
2 [with obj.] do (something) again, either once or a number of times: *earlier experiments were to be repeated on a far larger scale* | [as adj. **repeated**] *there were repeated attempts to negotiate.*
■ broadcast (a television or radio programme) again. ■ undertake (a course or period or instruction) again: *Mark had to repeat first and second grades.* ■ (**repeat itself**) occur again in the same way or form: *I don't intend to let history repeat itself.* ■ [no obj.] US illegally vote more than once in an election. ■ [no obj.] N. Amer. attain a particular success or achievement again, especially by winning a championship for the second consecutive time: *the first team in nineteen years to repeat as NBA champions.* ■ [with obj.] (of a watch or clock) strike (the last hour or quarter) over again when required.
3 [no obj.] (of food) be tasted intermittently for some time after being swallowed as a result of belching or indigestion: *it sat rather uncomfortably on my stomach and* ***repeated on*** *me for hours.*
▶ **noun** an action, event, or other thing that occurs or is done again: *the final will be a repeat of last year.*
■ a repeated broadcast of a television or radio programme. ■ [as modifier] occurring, done, or used more than once: *a repeat prescription.* ■ a consignment of goods similar to one already received. ■ a decorative pattern which is repeated uniformly over a surface. ■ Music a passage intended to be repeated. ■ a mark indicating this.
– DERIVATIVES **repeatability** noun, **repeatable** adjective, **repeatedly** adverb.
– ORIGIN late Middle English: from Old French *repeter*, from Latin *repetere*, from *re-* 'back' + *petere* 'seek'.

repeater ▶ **noun** a person or thing that repeats something, in particular:
■ a firearm which fires several shots without reloading. ■ a watch or clock which repeats its last strike when required. ■ a device for the automatic retransmission or amplification of an electrically transmitted message. ■ a railway signal indicating the state of another that is out of sight.

repeat fee ▶ **noun** a fee paid to a radio or television artist each time their performance is rebroadcast.

repeating ▶ **adjective** **1** (of a firearm) capable of firing several shots in succession without reloading.
2 (of a pattern) recurring uniformly over a surface.

repeating decimal ▶ **noun** a recurring decimal.

repêchage /ˈrɛpəʃɑːʒ/ ▶ **noun** (in rowing and other sports) a contest in which the runners-up in the eliminating heats compete for a place in the final.
– ORIGIN early 20th cent.: French, from *repêcher* 'fish out, rescue'.

repel ▶ **verb** (**repelled**, **repelling**) [with obj.] **1** drive or force (an attack or attacker) back or away: *government units sought to repel the rebels.*
■ [with obj.] (of a magnetic pole or electric field) force (something similarly magnetized or charged) away from itself: *electrically charged objects attract or repel one another* | [no obj.] *like poles repel and unlike poles attract.* ■ (of a substance) resist mixing with or be impervious to (another substance): *boots with good-quality leather uppers to repel moisture.*
2 be repulsive or distasteful to: *she was repelled by the permanent smell of drink on his breath.*
3 formal refuse to accept (something, especially an argument or theory): *the alleged right of lien led by the bankrupt's solicitor was repelled.*

– DERIVATIVES **repeller** noun.
– ORIGIN late Middle English: from Latin *repellere*, from *re-* 'back' + *pellere* 'to drive'.

repellent (also **repellant**) ▶ **adjective 1** [often in combination] able to repel a particular thing; impervious to a particular substance: *water-repellent nylon.*
2 causing disgust or distaste: *the idea was slightly **repellent to** her.*
▶ **noun 1** a substance that dissuades particular insects or other pests from approaching or settling: *a flea repellent.*
2 a substance used to treat something, especially fabric or stone, so as to make it impervious to water: *treat brick with a silicone water repellent.*
– DERIVATIVES **repellence** noun, **repellency** noun, **repellently** adverb.
– ORIGIN mid 17th cent.: from Latin *repellent-* 'driving back', from the verb *repellere* (see **REPEL**).

repent ▶ **verb** [no obj.] feel or express sincere regret or remorse about one's wrongdoing or sin: *the Padre urged his listeners to repent* | *he **repented of** his action.*
■ [with obj.] view or think of (an action or omission) with deep regret or remorse: *Marian came to repent her hasty judgement.* ■ (**repent oneself**) archaic feel regret or penitence about: *I repent me of all I did.*
– DERIVATIVES **repentance** noun, **repentant** adjective, **repenter** noun.
– ORIGIN Middle English: from Old French *repentir*, from *re-* (expressing intensive force) + *pentir* (based on Latin *paenitere* 'cause to repent').

repeople ▶ **verb** [with obj.] repopulate (a place).

repercussion ▶ **noun 1** (usu. **repercussions**) an unintended consequence occurring some time after an event or action, especially an unwelcome one: *the move would have grave repercussions for the entire region.*
2 archaic the recoil of something after impact.
3 archaic an echo or reverberation.
– DERIVATIVES **repercussive** adjective.
– ORIGIN late Middle English (as a medical term meaning 'repressing of infection'): from Old French, or from Latin *repercussio(n-)*, from *repercutere* 'cause to rebound, push back', from *re-* 'back, again' + *percutere* 'to strike'. The early sense 'driving back, rebounding' (mid 16th cent.) gave rise later to 'blow given in return', hence sense 1 (early 20th cent.).

repertoire /ˈrɛpətwɑː/ ▶ **noun** a stock of plays, dances, or items that a company or a performer knows or is prepared to perform.
■ the whole body of items which are regularly performed: *the mainstream concert repertoire.* ■ a stock of skills or types of behaviour that a person habitually uses: *his repertoire of threats, stares, and denigratory gestures.*
– ORIGIN mid 19th cent.: from French *répertoire*, from late Latin *repertorium* (see **REPERTORY**).

repertory /ˈrɛpət(ə)ri/ ▶ **noun** (pl. **-ies**) **1** [mass noun] the performance of various plays, operas, or ballets by a company at regular short intervals: [as modifier] *a repertory actor.*
■ repertory theatres regarded collectively. ■ [count noun] a repertory company.
2 another term for **REPERTOIRE**.
■ a repository or collection, especially of information or retrievable examples.
– ORIGIN mid 16th cent. (denoting an index or catalogue): from late Latin *repertorium*, from Latin *repert-* 'found, discovered', from the verb *reperire*. Sense 1 (arising from the fact that a company has a 'repertory' of pieces for performance) dates from the late 19th cent.

repertory company ▶ **noun** a theatrical company that performs plays from its repertoire for regular, short periods of time, moving on from one play to another.

repetend /ˈrɛpɪtɛnd, ˌrɛpɪˈtɛnd/ ▶ **noun** Mathematics the repeating figure or figures of a recurring decimal fraction.
■ formal a recurring word or phrase; a refrain.
– ORIGIN early 18th cent.: from Latin *repetendum* 'something to be repeated', neuter gerundive of *repetere* (see **REPEAT**).

répétiteur /rɛˌpɛtɪˈtəː/ ▶ **noun** a tutor or coach of ballet dancers or musicians, especially opera singers.
– ORIGIN French.

repetition ▶ **noun** [mass noun] the action of repeating something that has already been said or written: *her comments are worthy of repetition* | [count noun] *a repetition of his reply to the delegation.*
■ [often with negative] the recurrence of an action or event: *there was to be no repetition of the interwar years* | [count noun] *I didn't want a repetition of the scene in my office that morning.* ■ [count noun] a thing repeated: *the geometric repetitions of Islamic art.* ■ [count noun] a training exercise which is repeated, especially a series of repeated raisings and lowerings of the weight in weight training. ■ Music the repeating of a passage or note. ■ [count noun] archaic a piece set by a teacher to be learned by heart and recited.
– DERIVATIVES **repetitional** adjective.
– ORIGIN late Middle English: from Old French *repeticion* or Latin *repetitio(n-)*, from *repetere* (see **REPEAT**).

repetitious ▶ **adjective** another term for **REPETITIVE**.
– DERIVATIVES **repetitiously** adverb, **repetitiousness** noun.

repetitive ▶ **adjective** containing or characterized by repetition, especially when unnecessary or tiresome: *a repetitive task.*
– DERIVATIVES **repetitively** adverb, **repetitiveness** noun.

repetitive strain injury (abbrev.: **RSI**) ▶ **noun** [mass noun] a condition in which the prolonged performance of repetitive actions, typically with the hands, causes pain or impairment of function in the tendons and muscles involved.

rephrase ▶ **verb** [with obj.] express (an idea or question) in an alternative way, especially with the purpose of changing the detail or perspective of the original idea or question: *rephrase the statement so that it is clear.*

repine ▶ **verb** [no obj.] poetic/literary feel or express discontent; fret: *you mustn't let yourself repine.*
– ORIGIN early 16th cent.: from **RE-** 'again' + the verb **PINE**[2], on the pattern of *repent*.

repique /rɪˈpiːk/ ▶ **noun** (in piquet) the scoring of 30 points on declarations alone before beginning to play. Compare with **PIQUE**[2].
▶ **verb** (**repiques, repiqued, repiquing**) [with obj.] score a repique against (one's opponent).
– ORIGIN mid 17th cent.: from French *repic*; compare with Italian *ripicco*.

replace ▶ **verb** [with obj.] **1** take the place of: *Ian's smile was replaced by a frown.*
■ provide or find a substitute for (something that is broken, old, or inoperative): *the light bulb needs replacing.* ■ fill the role of (someone or something) with a substitute: *the government dismissed 3,000 of its customs inspectors, replacing them with new recruits.*
2 put (something) back in a previous place or position: *he drained his glass and replaced it on the bar.*
– DERIVATIVES **replacer** noun.

replaceable ▶ **adjective** able to be replaced: *a knife with a replaceable blade.*
■ Chemistry denoting those hydrogen atoms in an acid which can be displaced by metal atoms when forming salts.

replacement ▶ **noun** [mass noun] the action or process of replacing someone or something: *the replacement of religion by poetry* | [count noun] *a hip replacement.*
■ a person or thing that takes the place of another.

replacement therapy ▶ **noun** [mass noun] Medicine treatment aimed at making up a deficit of a substance normally present in the body.

replan ▶ **verb** (**replanned, replanning**) [with obj.] plan (something, especially the layout of buildings or cities) differently or again.

replant ▶ **verb** [with obj.] plant (a tree or plant which has been dug up) again, especially when transferring it to a larger pot or new site.
■ provide (an area) with new plants or trees: *38 per cent of ancient woodland has been replanted with conifers.*

replay ▶ **verb** [with obj.] **1** play back (a recording on tape, video, or film): *he could stop the tape and replay it whenever he wished.*
■ figurative repeat (something, especially an event or sequence of events): *she replayed in her mind every detail of the night before.*
2 play (a match) again to decide a winner after the original encounter ended in a draw or contentious result.
▶ **noun 1** [mass noun] the playing again of a section of a recording, especially so as to be able to watch an incident more closely: *clouds can be studied in speeded-up replay* | [count noun] *the umpire studied TV replays.*
■ figurative an occurrence which closely follows the pattern of a previous event: *a replay of the Suarez case.*
2 a replayed match.

replenish ▶ **verb** [with obj.] fill (something) up again: *he replenished Justin's glass with mineral water.*
■ restore (a stock or supply of something) to the former level or condition: *all creatures need sleep to replenish their energies.*
– DERIVATIVES **replenisher** noun, **replenishment** noun.
– ORIGIN late Middle English (in the sense 'supply abundantly'): from Old French *repleniss-*, lengthened stem of *replenir*, from *re-* 'again' (also expressing intensive force) + *plenir* 'fill' (from Latin *plenus* 'full').

replete /rɪˈpliːt/ ▶ **adjective** [predic.] filled or well-supplied with something: *sensational popular fiction, **replete with** adultery and sudden death.*
■ very full of or sated by food: *I went out into the sun-drenched streets again, replete and relaxed.*
– DERIVATIVES **repletion** noun.
– ORIGIN late Middle English: from Old French *replet(e)* or Latin *repletus* 'filled up', past participle of *replere*, from *re-* 'back, again' + *plere* 'fill'.

replevin /rɪˈplɛvɪn/ ▶ **noun** [mass noun] Law a procedure whereby seized goods may be provisionally restored to their owner pending the outcome of an action to determine the rights of the parties concerned.
■ [count noun] an action arising from such a process.
– ORIGIN late Middle English: from Anglo-Norman French, from Old French *replevir* 'recover' (see **REPLEVY**).

replevy /rɪˈplɛvi/ ▶ **verb** (**-ies, -ied**) [with obj.] Law recover (seized goods) by replevin.
– ORIGIN mid 16th cent.: from Old French *replevir* 'recover'; apparently related to **PLEDGE**.

replica ▶ **noun** an exact copy or model of something, especially one on a smaller scale: *a replica of the Empire State Building.*
■ a duplicate of an original artistic work.
– ORIGIN mid 18th cent. (as a musical term in the sense 'a repeat'): from Italian, from *replicare* 'to reply'.

replicase /ˈrɛplɪkeɪz/ ▶ **noun** [mass noun] Biochemistry an enzyme which catalyses the synthesis of a complementary RNA molecule using an RNA template.
– ORIGIN 1960s: from the verb **REPLICATE** + **-ASE**.

replicate ▶ **verb** /ˈrɛplɪkeɪt/ [with obj.] make an exact copy of; reproduce: *it might be impractical to replicate eastern culture in the west.*
■ (**replicate itself**) (of genetic material or a living organism) reproduce or give rise to a copy of itself: *interleukin-16 prevents the virus from replicating itself* | [no obj.] *an enzyme which HIV needs in order to replicate.* ■ repeat (a scientific experiment or trial) to obtain a consistent result: *these findings have been replicated by Metzger and Antes.*
▶ **adjective** /ˈrɛplɪkət/ [attrib.] of the nature of a copy: *a replicate Earth.*
■ of the nature of a repetition of a scientific experiment or trial: *the variation of replicate measurements.*
▶ **noun** /ˈrɛplɪkət/ **1** a close or exact copy; a replica.
■ a repetition of an experimental test or procedure.
2 Music a tone one or more octaves above or below the given tone.
– DERIVATIVES **replicability** /ˌrɛplɪkəˈbɪlɪti/ noun, **replicable** /ˈrɛplɪkəb(ə)l/ adjective.
– ORIGIN late Middle English (in the sense 'repeat'): from Latin *replicat-*, from the verb *replicare*, from *re-* 'back, again' + *plicare* 'to fold'. The current senses date from the late 19th cent.

replication ▶ **noun 1** [mass noun] the action of copying or reproducing something.
■ [count noun] a copy: *a twentieth-century building would be cheaper than a replication of what was there before.* ■ the repetition of a scientific experiment or trial to obtain a consistent result. ■ the process by which genetic material or a living organism gives rise to a copy of itself: *HIV replication* | [count noun] *a crucial step in cold virus replications.*
2 Law, dated a plaintiff's reply to the defendant's plea.
– ORIGIN late Middle English: from Old French *replicacion*, from Latin *replicatio(n-)*, from *replicare* 'fold back, repeat', later 'make a reply' (see **REPLICATE**).

replicative ▶ **adjective** Biology relating to or

involving the replication of genetic material or living organisms.

replicator ▶ noun a thing which replicates or copies something.
- ■ Biology a structural gene at which replication of a specific replicon is believed to be initiated.

replicon /ˈrɛplɪkɒn/ ▶ noun Biology a nucleic acid molecule, or part of one, which replicates as a unit, beginning at a specific site within it.
– ORIGIN 1960s: from **REPLICATION** + **-ON**.

reply ▶ verb (**-ies, -ied**) [reporting verb] say something in response to something someone has said: [no obj.] *he was gone before we could* **reply to** *his last remark* | [with clause] *she replied that she had been sound asleep* | [with direct speech] *'I'm OK—just leave me alone,' he replied.*
- ■ [no obj.] write back to someone one has received a letter from: *she replied with a long letter the next day.* ■ [no obj.] respond by a similar action or gesture: *they* **replied to** *the shelling with a heavy mortar attack on the area.*
▶ noun (pl. **-ies**) a verbal or written answer: *I received a reply from the firm's managing director* | *'No,' was the curt reply.*
- ■ [mass noun] the action of answering someone or something: *I am writing* **in reply** *to your letter of 1 June.* ■ a response in the form of a gesture, action, or expression: *Clough scored the first goal and Speed hit a late reply.* ■ Law a plaintiff's response to the defendant's plea.
– DERIVATIVES **replier** noun.
– ORIGIN late Middle English (as a verb): from Old French *replier*, from Latin *replicare* 'repeat', later 'make a reply' (see **REPLICATE**).

reply coupon ▶ noun a coupon used for prepaying the postage for the reply to a letter sent to another country.

reply-paid ▶ adjective (of an envelope or card) for which the addressee will pay the postage.
- ■ historical (of a telegram) with the cost of a reply prepaid by the sender.

repmobile ▶ noun informal, derogatory a mid range saloon car, typically used as a company car.

repo /ˈriːpəʊ/ informal ▶ noun (pl. **-os**) **1** another term for **REPURCHASE AGREEMENT**. [ORIGIN: 1960s: abbreviation.]
2 N. Amer. a car or other item which has been repossessed.
▶ verb (**repo's, repo'd**) [with obj.] US repossess (a car or other item) when a buyer defaults on payments. [ORIGIN: 1970s: abbreviation.]

repoint ▶ verb [with obj.] fill in or repair the joints of (brickwork) again.

repolish ▶ verb [with obj.] polish (something) again.

repo man ▶ noun N. Amer. informal a person employed to repossess goods for which a purchaser has defaulted on payment.

repopulate ▶ verb [with obj.] introduce a population into a (previously occupied area or country): *the area was repopulated largely by Russians.*
– DERIVATIVES **repopulation** noun.

report ▶ verb **1** [reporting verb] give a spoken or written account of something that one has observed, heard, done, or investigated: [with obj.] *the minister reported a decline in milk and meat production* | [with clause] *police reported that the flood waters were abating* | [no obj.] *the teacher should* **report on** *the child's progress.*
- ■ [no obj.] cover an event or subject as a journalist or a reporter: *the press* **reported on** *Republican sex scandals* | [with clause] *the Egyptian news agency reported that a coup attempt had taken place* | [with obj.] *The Times reported a secret programme by the country to build nuclear warheads.* ■ (**be reported**) used to indicate that something has been stated, although one cannot confirm its accuracy: [with infinitive] *hoaxers are reported to be hacking into airline frequencies to impersonate air traffic controllers* | [as adj. **reported**] *a reported £50,000 in debt.* ■ [with obj.] make a formal statement or complaint about (someone or something) to the necessary authority: *undisclosed illegalities are* **reported to** *the company's directors* | [with obj. and complement] *eight Yorkshire Terriers have been reported missing in the last month.* ■ [with obj.] Brit. (of a parliamentary committee chairman) formally announce that the committee has dealt with (a bill): *the Chairman shall report the Bill to the House.* See also **report a bill out** below.
2 [no obj.] present oneself formally as having arrived at a particular place or as ready to do something: *you are instructed to* **report to** *Administration Shed Fourteen immediately, Captain.*
3 [no obj.] (**report to**) be responsible to (a superior or supervisor): *the officers now report to the Russian president, not the Politburo.*
▶ noun **1** an account given of a particular matter, especially in the form of an official document, after thorough investigation or consideration by an appointed person or body: *the chairman's annual report.*
- ■ a spoken or written description of an event or situation, especially one intended for publication or broadcasting in the media: *press reports suggested that the government was still using secret police to help maintain public order.* ■ Brit. a teacher's written assessment of a pupil's work, progress, and conduct, issued at the end of a term or school year. ■ Law a detailed formal account of a case heard in a court, giving the main points in the judgement, especially as prepared for publication. ■ a piece of information that is unsupported by firm evidence and that the speaker feels may or may not be true: *reports were circulating that the chairman was about to resign.* ■ [mass noun] dated rumour: *report has it that the beetles have now virtually disappeared.* ■ [mass noun] archaic the way in which someone or something is regarded; reputation: *whatsoever things are lovely and of good report.*
2 a sudden loud noise of or like an explosion or gunfire.
– PHRASES **on report 1** Brit. during the report stage of a bill in the House of Commons or House of Lords. **2** (especially of a prisoner or member of the armed forces) on a disciplinary charge.
– DERIVATIVES **reportable** adjective.
– ORIGIN late Middle English: from Old French *reporter* (verb), *report* (noun), from Latin *reportare* 'bring back', from *re-* 'back' + *portare* 'carry'. The sense 'give an account' gave rise to 'submit a formal report', hence 'inform an authority of one's presence' (sense 2, mid 19th cent.) and 'be accountable (to a superior)' (sense 3, late 19th cent.).

report back (or **report something back**) **1** deliver a spoken or written account of something one has been asked to do or investigate: *the deadpan voice of a police officer* **reporting back to** *his superior* | *every movement I made was reported back to him.* **2** return to work or duty after a period of absence.
report a bill out US (of a committee of Congress) return a bill to the legislative body for action.

reportage /ˌrɛpɔːˈtɑːʒ, rɪˈpɔːtɪdʒ/ ▶ noun [mass noun] the reporting of news, for the press and the broadcasting media: *extensive reportage of elections.*
- ■ factual presentation in a book or other text, especially when this adopts a journalistic style.
– ORIGIN early 17th cent.: French, from Old French *reporter* 'carry back' (see **REPORT**).

report card ▶ noun chiefly N. Amer. a teacher's written assessment of a pupil's work, progress, and conduct, sent home to a parent or guardian.
- ■ an evaluation of performance: *Democrat legislators fared poorly in a recent report card.*

reportedly ▶ adverb [sentence adverb] according to what some say (used to express the speaker's belief that the information given is not necessarily true): *he was in El Salvador, reportedly on his way to Texas.*

reported speech ▶ noun [mass noun] a speaker's words reported in subordinate clauses governed by a reporting verb, with the required changes of person and tense (e.g. *he said that he would go*, based on *I will go*). Also called **INDIRECT SPEECH**. Contrasted with **DIRECT SPEECH**.

reporter ▶ noun a person who reports, especially one employed to report news or conduct interviews for newspapers or broadcasts.

reporting verb ▶ noun a verb belonging to a class of verbs conveying the action of speaking and used with both direct and reported speech. Reporting verbs may also be used with a direct object and with an infinitive construction.

reportorial /ˌrɛpɔːˈtɔːrɪəl/ ▶ adjective N. Amer. of or characteristic of newspaper reporters: *reportorial ambition and curiosity.*
– DERIVATIVES **reportorially** adverb.
– ORIGIN mid 19th cent.: from **REPORTER**, on the pattern of *editorial.*

report stage ▶ noun (in the UK and Canada) the stage in the process of a bill becoming law at which it is debated in the House of Commons or House of Lords after it is reported.

repose¹ /rɪˈpəʊz/ ▶ noun [mass noun] temporary rest from activity, excitement, or exertion, especially sleep or the rest given by sleep: *in repose her face looked relaxed.*
- ■ a state of peace: *the repose of the soul of the dead man.* ■ composure: *he had lost none of his grace or his repose.* ■ Art harmonious arrangement of colours and forms, providing a restful visual effect.
▶ verb [no obj., with adverbial of place] be lying, situated, or kept in a particular place: *the diamond now reposes in the Louvre.*
- ■ lie down in rest: *how sweetly he would repose in the four-poster bed.* ■ [with obj.] poetic/literary (**repose something on/in**) lay something to rest in or on (something): *I'll go to him, and repose our distresses on his friendly bosom.* ■ [with obj.] archaic give rest to: *he halted to repose his way-worn soldiers.*
– DERIVATIVES **reposeful** adjective, **reposefully** adverb.
– ORIGIN late Middle English: from Old French *repos* (noun), *reposer* (verb), from late Latin *repausare*, from *re-* (expressing intensive force) + *pausare* 'to pause'.

repose² /rɪˈpəʊz/ ▶ verb [with obj.] (**repose something in**) place something, especially one's confidence or trust, in: *we have never betrayed the trust that you have reposed in us.*
– DERIVATIVES **reposal** noun (rare).
– ORIGIN late Middle English (in the sense 'put back in the same position'): from **RE-** 'again' + the verb **POSE¹**, suggested by Latin *reponere* 'replace', from *re-* (expressing intensive force) + *ponere* 'to place'.

reposition ▶ verb [with obj.] place in a different position; adjust or alter the position of: *try repositioning the thermostat in another room.*

repository /rɪˈpɒzɪt(ə)ri/ ▶ noun (pl. **-ies**) a place, building, or receptacle where things are or may be stored: *a deep repository for nuclear waste.*
- ■ a place in which something, especially a natural resource, has accumulated or where it is found in significant quantities: *accessible repositories of water.* ■ a person or thing regarded as a store of information or in which something abstract is held to exist or be found: *his mind was a rich repository of the past.*
– ORIGIN late 15th cent.: from Old French *repositoire* or Latin *repositorium*, from *reposit-* 'placed back', from the verb *reponere* (see **REPOSE²**).

repossess ▶ verb [with obj.] retake possession of (something) when a buyer defaults on payments: *565 homes were repossessed for non-payment of mortgages.*
– DERIVATIVES **repossession** noun.

repossessor ▶ noun chiefly US a person hired by a credit company to repossess an item when the buyer defaults on payments.

repot ▶ verb (**repotted, repotting**) [with obj.] put (a plant) in another pot, especially a larger one.

repoussé /rəˈpuːseɪ/ ▶ adjective (of metalwork) hammered into relief from the reverse side.
▶ noun [mass noun] ornamental metalwork fashioned in this way.
– ORIGIN mid 19th cent.: French, literally 'pushed back', past participle of *repousser*, from *re-* (expressing intensive force) + *pousser* 'to push'.

repp ▶ noun variant spelling of **REP³**.

repr. ▶ abbreviation for reprint or reprinted.

reprehend /ˌrɛprɪˈhɛnd/ ▶ verb [with obj.] reprimand: *a recklessness which cannot be too severely reprehended.*
– DERIVATIVES **reprehension** noun.
– ORIGIN Middle English: from Latin *reprehendere* 'seize, check, rebuke', from *re-* (expressing intensive force) + *prehendere* 'seize'.

reprehensible ▶ adjective deserving censure or condemnation: *his complacency and reprehensible laxity.*
– DERIVATIVES **reprehensibility** noun, **reprehensibly** adverb.
– ORIGIN late Middle English: from late Latin *reprehensibilis*, from *reprehens-* 'rebuked', from the verb *reprehendere* (see **REPREHEND**).

represent ▶ verb [with obj.] **1** be entitled or appointed to act or speak for (someone), especially in an official capacity: *for purposes of litigation, an infant can and must be represented by an adult.*
- ■ (of a competitor) participate in a sports event or other competition on behalf of (one's club, town, region, or country): *Wade represented Great Britain.* ■ be an elected Member of Parliament or member of a legislature for (a particular constituency, party, or group): *she became the first woman to represent a South Wales mining valley.* ■ (usu. **be represented**) act as a substitute for (someone), especially on an official or

ceremonial occasion: *the Duke of Edinburgh was represented by the Countess Mountbatten.*
2 constitute; amount to: *this figure represents eleven per cent of the company's total sales.*
■be a specimen or example of; typify: *twenty parents, picked to represent a cross section of Scottish life.* ■ **(be represented)** (of a group or type of person or thing) be present or found in something, especially to a particular degree: *abstraction is well represented in this exhibition.*
3 depict (a particular subject) in a picture or other work of art: *santos are small wooden figures representing saints.*
■[with obj. and adverbial or infinitive] describe or depict (someone or something) as being of a certain nature; portray in a particular way: *the young were consistently represented as being in need of protection.* ■ (of a sign or symbol) have a particular signification; stand for: *numbers 1–15 represent the red balls.* ■ be a symbol or embodiment of (a particular quality or thing): *the three heads of Cerberus represent the past, present, and future.* ■ play the part of (someone) in a theatrical production.
4 formal state or point out (something) clearly: *it was represented to him that she would be an unsuitable wife.*
■[with clause] allege; claim: *the vendors have represented that such information is accurate.*
– DERIVATIVES **representability** noun, **representable** adjective.
– ORIGIN late Middle English: from Old French *representer* or Latin *repraesentare*, from *re-* (expressing intensive force) + *praesentare* 'to present'.

re-present ▶verb [with obj.] present (something) again, especially for further consideration or in an altered form: *I will re-present Eikmeyer's model here.*
■present (a cheque or bill) again for payment.
– DERIVATIVES **re-presentation** noun.

representation ▶noun [mass noun] **1** the action of speaking or acting on behalf of someone or the state of being so represented: *asylum-seekers should be guaranteed good legal advice and representation.*
2 the description or portrayal of someone or something in a particular way or as being of a certain nature: *the representation of women in newspapers.*
■the depiction of someone or something in a picture or other work of art: *Picasso is striving for some absolute representation of reality.* ■ [count noun] a thing, especially a picture or model, that depicts a likeness or reproduction of someone or something: *a striking representation of a vase of flowers.* ■ (in some theories of perception) a mental state or concept regarded as corresponding to a thing perceived.
3 **(representations)** formal statements made to a higher authority, especially so as to communicate an opinion or register a protest: *the Law Society will make representations to the Lord Chancellor.*
■[count noun] a statement or allegation: *any buyer was relying on a representation that the tapes were genuine.*
– ORIGIN late Middle English (in the sense 'image, likeness'): from Old French *representation* or Latin *repraesentatio(n-)*, from *repraesentare* 'bring before, exhibit' (see **REPRESENT**).

representational ▶adjective of, relating to, or characterized by representation: *representational democracy.*
■relating to or denoting art which aims to depict the physical appearance of things. Contrasted with **ABSTRACT**.

representationalism /ˌrɛprɪzɛnˈteɪʃ(ə)n(ə)lɪz(ə)m/ ▶noun [mass noun] **1** the practice or advocacy of representational art.
2 Philosophy another term for **REPRESENTATIONISM**.
– DERIVATIVES **representationalist** adjective & noun.

representationism ▶noun [mass noun] Philosophy the doctrine that thought is the manipulation of mental representations which (somehow) correspond to external states or objects.
– DERIVATIVES **representationist** noun.

representative ▶adjective **1** typical of a class, group, or body of opinion: *Churchill was not properly representative of influential opinion in Britain.*
■containing typical examples of many or all types: *a representative sample of young people in Scotland.*
2 (of a legislative or deliberative assembly) consisting of people chosen to act and speak on behalf of a wider group.
■(of a government or political system) based on representation of the people by such deputies: *free elections and representative democracy.*
3 serving as a portrayal or symbol of something: *the show would be more **representative of** how women really are.*
■(of art) representational: *the bust involves a high degree of representative abstraction.*
4 Philosophy of or relating to mental representation.
▶noun **1** a person chosen or appointed to act or speak for another or others, in particular:
■an agent of a firm who travels to potential clients to sell its products. ■ an employee of a travel company who lives in a resort and looks after the needs of its holidaymakers. ■ a person chosen or elected to speak and act on behalf of others in a legislative assembly or deliberative body. ■ a delegate who attends a conference, negotiations, legal hearing, etc., so as to represent the interests of another person or group. ■ a person who takes the place of another on a ceremonial or official occasion.
2 an example of a class or group: *fossil representatives of lampreys and hagfishes.*
– DERIVATIVES **representatively** adverb, **representativeness** noun.

Representatives, House of the lower house of the US Congress and some other legislatures.

repress ▶verb [with obj.] subdue (someone or something) by force: *the uprisings were repressed.*
■restrain or prevent (the expression of a feeling): *Isabel couldn't repress a sharp cry of fear.* ■ suppress (a thought, feeling, or desire) in oneself so that it becomes or remains unconscious: *the thought that he had killed his brother was so terrible that he repressed it.* ■ inhibit the natural development or self-expression of (someone or something): *too much bureaucracy represses creativity.* ■ Biology prevent the transcription of (a gene).
– DERIVATIVES **represser** noun, **repressible** adjective, **repression** noun.
– ORIGIN Middle English (in the sense 'keep back (something objectionable)'): from Latin *repress-* 'pressed back, checked', from the verb *reprimere*, from *re-* 'back' + *premere* 'to press'.

repressed ▶adjective restrained, inhibited, or oppressed: *repressed indigenous groups* | *repressed energy.*
■(of a thought, feeling, or desire) kept suppressed and unconscious in one's mind: *repressed homosexuality.* ■ having or characterized by a large number of thoughts, feelings, or desires, especially sexual ones, which are suppressed in this way: *a very repressed, almost Victorian, household.*

repressive ▶adjective (especially of a social or political system) inhibiting or restraining the freedom of a person or group of people: *a repressive regime.*
■inhibiting or preventing the awareness of certain thoughts or feelings: *a repressive moral code.*
– DERIVATIVES **repressively** adverb, **repressiveness** noun.

repressor ▶noun Biochemistry a substance which acts on an operon to inhibit enzyme synthesis.

reprieve ▶verb [with obj.] cancel or postpone the punishment of (someone, especially someone condemned to death): *under the new regime, prisoners under sentence of death were reprieved.*
■abandon or postpone plans to close or put an end to (something): *the threatened pits could be reprieved.*
▶noun a cancellation or postponement of a punishment.
■a temporary escape from an undesirable fate or unpleasant situation: *a mother who faced eviction has been given a reprieve.*
– ORIGIN late 15th cent. (as the past participle *repryed*): from Anglo-Norman French *repris*, past participle of *reprendre*, from Latin *re-* 'back' + *prehendere* 'seize'. The insertion of *-v-* (16th cent.) remains unexplained. Sense development has undergone a reversal, from the early meaning 'send back to prison', via 'postpone (a legal process)', to the current sense 'rescue from impending punishment'.

reprimand /ˈrɛprɪmɑːnd/ ▶noun a rebuke, especially an official one.
▶verb [with obj.] rebuke (someone), especially officially: *officials were dismissed or reprimanded for poor work.*
– ORIGIN mid 17th cent.: from French *réprimande*, via Spanish from Latin *reprimenda*, 'things to be held in check', neuter plural gerundive of *reprimere* (see **REPRESS**).

reprint ▶verb [with obj.] print again or in a different form: *the story has been reprinted at intervals ever since it first appeared.*
▶noun an act of printing more copies of a work.
■a copy of a book or other material that has been reprinted. ■ an offprint.
– DERIVATIVES **reprinter** noun.

reprisal ▶noun an act of retaliation: *three youths died in the reprisals which followed* | [mass noun] *the threat of reprisal.*
■[mass noun] historical the forcible seizure of a foreign subject or their goods as an act of retaliation.
– ORIGIN late Middle English: from Anglo-Norman French *reprisaille*, from medieval Latin *reprisalia* (neuter plural), based on Latin *repraehens-* 'seized', from the verb *repraehendere* (see **REPREHEND**). The current sense dates from the early 18th cent.

reprise /rɪˈpriːz/ ▶noun a repeated passage in music.
■a repetition or further performance of something: *a stale reprise of past polemic.*
▶verb [with obj.] repeat (a piece of music or a performance).
– ORIGIN early 18th cent.: French, literally 'taken up again', feminine past participle of *reprendre* (see **REPRIEVE**).

repro ▶noun (pl. **-os**) [usu. as modifier] informal **1** a reproduction or copy, particularly of a piece of furniture: *a Georgian repro cabinet.*
2 [mass noun] the action or process of copying a document or image: *a repro house.*
– ORIGIN 1940s: abbreviation.

reproach ▶verb [with obj.] address (someone) in such a way as to express disapproval or disappointment: *critics of the administration **reproached** the president **for** his failure to tackle the deficiency* | [with direct speech] *'You know that isn't true,' he reproached her.*
■**(reproach someone with)** accuse someone of: *his wife reproached him with cowardice.* ■ archaic censure or rebuke (an offence).
▶noun [mass noun] the expression of disapproval or disappointment: *he gave her a look of reproach* | [count noun] *a farrago of warnings and pained reproaches.*
■**(a reproach to)** a thing that makes the failings of someone or something else more apparent: *his elegance is a living reproach to our slovenly habits.* ■ **(Reproaches)** (in the Roman Catholic Church) a set of antiphons and responses for Good Friday representing the reproaches of Christ to his people.
– PHRASES **above** (or **beyond**) **reproach** such that no criticism can be made; perfect.
– DERIVATIVES **reproachable** adjective, **reproacher** noun, **reproachingly** adverb.
– ORIGIN Middle English: from Old French *reprochier* (verb), from a base meaning 'bring back close', based on Latin *prope* 'near'.

reproachful ▶adjective expressing disapproval or disappointment: *she gave him a reproachful look.*
– DERIVATIVES **reproachfully** adverb, **reproachfulness** noun.

reprobate /ˈrɛprəbeɪt/ ▶noun an unprincipled person (often used humorously or affectionately).
■Christian Theology, archaic (in Calvinism) a sinner who is not of the elect and is predestined to damnation.
▶adjective unprincipled (often used as a humorous or affectionate reproach): *a long-missed old reprobate drinking comrade.*
■Christian Theology, archaic (in Calvinism) predestined to damnation.
▶verb [with obj.] archaic express or feel disapproval of: *his neighbours reprobated his method of proceeding.*
– DERIVATIVES **reprobation** noun.
– ORIGIN late Middle English (as a verb): from Latin *reprobat-* 'disapproved', from the verb *reprobare*, from *re-* (expressing reversal) + *probare* 'approve'.

reprocess ▶verb [with obj.] process (something, especially spent nuclear fuel) again or differently, typically in order to reuse it: *the costs of reprocessing radioactive waste.*

reproduce ▶verb [with obj.] produce again: *a concert performance cannot reproduce all the subtleties of a recording.*
■produce a copy or representation of: *his works are reproduced on postcards and posters.* ■ create something very similar to (something else), especially in a different medium or context: *the problems are difficult to reproduce in the laboratory.* ■ (of an organism) produce offspring by a sexual or asexual process: *bacteria normally divide and **reproduce themselves** every twenty minutes* | [no obj.] *an individual needs to avoid being eaten until it has reproduced.* ■ [no obj., with adverbial] be copied with a specified degree of success: *you'll be amazed to see how well half-tones reproduce.*
– DERIVATIVES **reproducer** noun, **reproducibility** noun, **reproducible** adjective, **reproducibly** adverb.

reproduction ▶noun [mass noun] the action or

r

process of making a copy of something: *the cost of colour reproduction in publication is high.*
■ the production of offspring by a sexual or asexual process. ■ [count noun] a copy of a work of art, especially a print or photograph of a painting. ■ [as modifier] made to imitate the style of an earlier period or of a particular artist or craftsman: *reproduction French classical beds.* ■ the quality of reproduced sound: *the design was changed to allow louder reproduction.*
– DERIVATIVES **reproductive** adjective, **reproductively** adverb, **reproductiveness** noun.

reprogram (also **reprogramme**) ▶ verb (**reprogrammed**, **reprogramming**; US also **reprogramed**, **reprograming**) [with obj.] program (a computer or something likened to one) again or differently.
– DERIVATIVES **reprogrammable** adjective.

reprographics ▶ plural noun [treated as sing.] reprography.

reprography /rɪˈprɒɡrəfi/ ▶ noun [mass noun] the science and practice of copying and reproducing documents and graphic material.
– DERIVATIVES **reprographer** noun, **reprographic** adjective.
– ORIGIN 1960s: from **REPRODUCE** + **-GRAPHY**.

reproof[1] /rɪˈpruːf/ ▶ noun an expression of blame or disapproval: *she welcomed him with a mild reproof for leaving her alone* | [mass noun] *a look of reproof.*
– ORIGIN Middle English: from Old French *reprove*, from *reprover* 'reprove'. Early senses included 'ignominy, personal shame' and 'scorn'.

reproof[2] /riːˈpruːf/ ▶ verb [with obj.] **1** Brit. render (a coat or other garment) waterproof again.
2 make a fresh proof of (printed matter).

reprove ▶ verb [with obj.] reprimand someone: *he was reproved for obscenity* | [with direct speech] *'Don't be childish, Hilary,' he reproved mildly* | [as adj. **reproving**] *a reproving glance.*
– DERIVATIVES **reprovable** adjective, **reprover** noun, **reprovingly** adverb.
– ORIGIN Middle English (also in the senses 'reject' and 'censure'): from Old French *reprover*, from late Latin *reprobare* 'disapprove' (see **REPROBATE**).

reptile ▶ noun **1** a cold-blooded vertebrate animal of a class that includes snakes, lizards, crocodiles, turtles, and tortoises. They are distinguished by having a dry scaly skin, and typically laying soft-shelled eggs on land.
• Class Reptilia: orders Chelonia (turtles and tortoises), Squamata (snakes and lizards), Rhynchocephalia (the tuatara), and Crocodylia (crocodilians). Among several extinct groups are the dinosaurs, pterosaurs, and ichthyosaurs.
2 informal a person regarded with loathing and contempt.
▶ adjective [attrib.] belonging to a reptile or to the class of reptiles: *reptile eggs.*
– DERIVATIVES **reptilian** adjective & noun.
– ORIGIN late Middle English: from late Latin, neuter of *reptilis*, from Latin *rept-* 'crawled', from the verb *repere.*

Repton /ˈrɛpt(ə)n/, Humphry (1752–1818), English landscape gardener. His parks were carefully informal after the model of Capability Brown. Important designs include the park at Cobham in Kent (*c.*1789–*c.*1793).

republic ▶ noun a state in which supreme power is held by the people and their elected representatives, and which has an elected or nominated president rather than a monarch.
■ archaic, figurative a community or group with a certain equality between its members.
– ORIGIN late 16th cent.: from French *république*, from Latin *respublica*, from *res* 'concern' + *publicus* 'of the people, public'.

republican ▶ adjective (of a form of government, constitution, etc.) belonging to, or characteristic of a republic.
■ advocating or supporting republican government: *the republican movement.*
▶ noun **1** a person advocating or supporting republican government.
2 (**Republican**) (in the US) a member or supporter of the Republican Party.
3 an advocate of a united Ireland.
– DERIVATIVES **republicanism** noun.

Republican Party one of the two main US political parties (the other being the Democratic Party), favouring a right-wing stance, limited central government and tough, interventionist foreign policy. It was formed in 1854 in support of the anti-slavery movement preceding the Civil War.

Republic Day ▶ noun the day on which the foundation of a republic is commemorated, in particular (in India) 26 January.

republish ▶ verb [with obj.] (often **be republished**) publish (a text) again, especially in a new edition.
– DERIVATIVES **republication** noun.

repudiate /rɪˈpjuːdɪeɪt/ ▶ verb [with obj.] refuse to accept or be associated with: *she has repudiated policies associated with previous party leaders.*
■ deny the truth or validity of: *the minister repudiated allegations of human rights abuses.* ■ chiefly Law refuse to fulfil or discharge (an agreement, obligation, or debt): *breach of a condition gives the other party the right to repudiate a contract.* ■ (especially in the past or in non-Christian religions) divorce (one's wife).
– DERIVATIVES **repudiation** noun, **repudiator** noun.
– ORIGIN late Middle English (originally an adjective in the sense 'divorced'): from Latin *repudiatus* 'divorced, cast off', from *repudium* 'divorce'.

repudiatory /rɪˈpjuːdɪəˌt(ə)ri/ ▶ adjective Law relating to or constituting repudiation of a contract: *a repudiatory breach of the partnership agreement.*

repugnance /rɪˈpʌɡnəns/ ▶ noun [mass noun] intense disgust: *our growing repugnance at the bleeding carcasses.*
– ORIGIN late Middle English (in the sense 'opposition'): from Old French *repugnance* or Latin *repugnantia*, from *repugnare* 'oppose', from *re-* (expressing opposition) + *pugnare* 'to fight'.

repugnancy ▶ noun [mass noun] inconsistency or incompatibility of ideas or statements.

repugnant ▶ adjective **1** extremely distasteful; unacceptable: *the thought of going back into the fog was* ***repugnant to*** *him.*
2 [predic.] (**repugnant to**) in conflict with; incompatible with: *a by-law must not be repugnant to the general law of the country.*
■ archaic or poetic/literary given to stubborn resistance.
– DERIVATIVES **repugnantly** adverb.
– ORIGIN late Middle English (in the sense 'offering resistance'): from Old French *repugnant* or Latin *repugnant-* 'opposing', from the verb *repugnare* (see **REPUGNANCE**).

repulse ▶ verb [with obj.] **1** drive back (an attack or attacking enemy) by force: *rioters tried to storm Interior Ministry buildings but were repulsed by police.*
■ fail to welcome (friendly advances or the person making them); rebuff: *she left, feeling hurt because she had been repulsed.* ■ refuse to accept (an offer): *his bid for the company was repulsed.*
2 (usu. **be repulsed**) cause (someone) to feel intense distaste and aversion: *audiences at early screenings of the film were repulsed by its brutality.*
▶ noun [mass noun] the action of driving back an attacking force or of being driven back: *the repulse of the invaders.*
■ [count noun] a discouraging response to friendly advances: *his evasion of her scheme had been another repulse.*
– ORIGIN late Middle English: from Latin *repuls-* 'driven back', from the verb *repellere* (see **REPEL**).

repulsion ▶ noun [mass noun] **1** a feeling of intense distaste or disgust: *people talk about the case with a mixture of fascination and repulsion.*
2 Physics a force under the influence of which objects tend to move away from each other, e.g. through having the same magnetic polarity or electric charge.

repulsive ▶ adjective **1** arousing intense distaste or disgust: *a repulsive smell.*
■ archaic lacking friendliness or sympathy.
2 of or relating to repulsion between physical objects.
– DERIVATIVES **repulsively** adverb, **repulsiveness** noun.

repurchase ▶ verb [with obj.] buy (something) back.
▶ noun [mass noun] the action of buying something back.

repurchase agreement ▶ noun Finance a contract in which the vendor of a security agrees to repurchase it from the buyer at an agreed price.

reputable ▶ adjective having a good reputation: *a reputable company.*
– DERIVATIVES **reputably** adverb.
– ORIGIN early 17th cent.: from obsolete French, or from medieval Latin *reputabilis*, from Latin *reputare* 'reflect upon' (see **REPUTE**).

reputation ▶ noun the beliefs or opinions that are generally held about someone or something: *his reputation was tarnished by allegations that he had taken bribes.*
■ a widespread belief that someone or something has a particular habit or characteristic: *his knowledge of his subject earned him a reputation as an expert.*
– ORIGIN Middle English: from Latin *reputatio(n-)*, from *reputare* 'think over' (see **REPUTE**).

repute ▶ noun [mass noun] the opinion generally held of someone or something; the state of being generally regarded in a particular way: *pollution could bring the authority's name into bad repute.*
■ the state of being highly thought of; fame: *chefs of international repute.*
▶ verb (**be reputed**) be generally said or believed to do something or to have particular characteristics: *he was reputed to have a fabulous house.*
■ [usu. as adj. **reputed**] be generally said or believed to exist or be of a particular type, despite not being so: *this area gave the lie to the reputed flatness of the country.* ■ [usu. as adj. **reputed**] be widely known and well thought of: *intensive training with reputed coaches.*
– DERIVATIVES **reputedly** adverb.
– ORIGIN late Middle English: from Old French *reputer* or Latin *reputare* 'think over', from *re-* (expressing intensive force) + *putare* 'think'.

request ▶ noun an act of asking politely or formally for something: *a* ***request for*** *information* | *the club's excursion was postponed* ***at the request of*** *some of the members.*
■ a thing that is asked for: *to have our ideas taken seriously is surely a reasonable request.* ■ an instruction to a computer to provide information or perform another function. ■ a tune or song played on a radio programme, in some instances accompanied by a personal message, in response to a letter or call asking for it. ■ [mass noun] archaic the state of being sought after: *human intelligence, which is in constant request in a family.*
▶ verb [with obj.] politely or formally ask for: *he received the information he had requested* | [with clause] *the chairman requested that the reports be considered.*
■ [with infinitive] politely ask (someone) to do something: *the letter requested him to report to London immediately.*
– PHRASES **by** (or **on**) **request** in response to an expressed wish.
– DERIVATIVES **requester** noun.
– ORIGIN Middle English: from Old French *requeste* (noun), based on Latin *requirere* (see **REQUIRE**).

request programme ▶ noun a radio programme consisting of music requested by the listeners.

request stop ▶ noun Brit. a bus stop at which the bus halts only if requested by a passenger or if hailed.

requiem /ˈrɛkwɪəm, -ɪɛm/ ▶ noun (especially in the Roman Catholic Church) a Mass for the repose of the souls of the dead.
■ a musical composition setting parts of such a Mass, or of a similar character. ■ an act or token of remembrance: *he designed the epic as a requiem for his wife.*
– ORIGIN Middle English: from Latin (first word of the Mass), accusative of *requies* 'rest'.

requiem shark ▶ noun a migratory, live-bearing shark of warm seas, sometimes also found in brackish or fresh water.
• Family Carcharhinidae: many species, including the tiger shark, blue shark, and tope.
– ORIGIN mid 17th cent.: from obsolete French *requiem*, variant of *requin* 'shark', influenced by **REQUIEM**.

requiescat /ˌrɛkwɪˈɛskat/ ▶ noun a wish or prayer for the repose of a dead person.
– ORIGIN Latin, from *requiescat in pace* (see **RIP**[1]).

requinto /rɛˈkɪntəʊ/ ▶ noun (pl. **-os**) (in Spanish-speaking countries) a small guitar, typically tuned a fifth higher than a standard guitar.
– ORIGIN Spanish, literally 'second fifth subtracted from a quantity'.

require ▶ verb [with obj.] need for a particular purpose; depend on for success or survival: *three patients required operations.*
■ cause to be necessary: *it would have required much research to produce a comprehensive list.* ■ specify as compulsory: *the minimum car insurance required by law.* ■ [with obj. and infinitive] (of someone in authority) instruct or expect (someone) to do something: *you will be required to attend for cross-examination.* ■ (**require something of**) regard an action, ability, or quality as due from (someone) by virtue of their position: *the care and diligence required of him as a*

trustee. ■ wish to have: *please indicate how many tickets you require.*
– DERIVATIVES **requirement** noun, **requirer** noun.
– ORIGIN late Middle English: from Old French *requere*, from Latin *requirere*, from *re-* (expressing intensive force) + *quaerere* 'seek'.

requisite /ˈrɛkwɪzɪt/ ▶ **adjective** made necessary by particular circumstances or regulations: *the application will not be processed until the requisite fee is paid.*
▶ **noun** a thing that is necessary for the achievement of a specified end: *she believed privacy to be a* ***requisite for*** *a peaceful life.*
– DERIVATIVES **requisitely** adverb.
– ORIGIN late Middle English: from Latin *requisitus* 'searched for, deemed necessary', past participle of *requirere* (see **REQUIRE**).

requisition /ˌrɛkwɪˈzɪʃ(ə)n/ ▶ **noun** an official order laying claim to the use of property or materials: *I had to make various requisitions for staff and accommodation.*
■ a formal written demand that some duty should be performed or something be put into operation. ■ (also **requisition on title**) Law a demand to the vendor of a property for the official search relating to the title. ■ [mass noun] the appropriation of goods, especially for military or public use.
▶ **verb** [with obj.] demand the use or supply of, especially by official order and for military or public use: *the government had assumed powers to requisition cereal products at fixed prices.*
■ demand the performance or occurrence of: *one of the stakeholders has requisitioned an extraordinary general meeting.*
– DERIVATIVES **requisitioner** noun.
– ORIGIN late Middle English (as a noun in the sense 'request, demand'): from Old French, or from Latin *requisitio(n-)*, from *requirere* 'search for' (see **REQUIRE**). The verb dates from the mid 19th cent.

requite /rɪˈkwʌɪt/ ▶ **verb** [with obj.] formal make appropriate return for (a favour or service); reward: *they are quick to requite a kindness.*
■ avenge or retaliate for (an injury or wrong). ■ return a favour to (someone): *to win enough to requite my friends.* ■ respond to (love or affection); return: *she did not requite his love.*
– DERIVATIVES **requital** noun.
– ORIGIN early 16th cent.: from **RE-** 'back' + obsolete *quite*, variant of the verb **QUIT**[1].

reran past of **RERUN**.

reread ▶ **verb** (past and past participle **reread**) [with obj.] read (a text) again: *I reread the poem.*
▶ **noun** [in sing.] an act or instance of reading something again.
– DERIVATIVES **rereadable** adjective.

re-record ▶ **verb** [with obj.] record (sound, especially music) again.

reredos /ˈrɪədɒs/ ▶ **noun** (pl. same) Christian Church an ornamental screen covering the wall at the back of an altar.
– ORIGIN late Middle English: from Anglo-Norman French, from Old French *areredos*, from *arere* 'behind' + *dos* 'back'.

re-release ▶ **verb** [with obj.] release (a recording or film) again: *he is re-releasing his 1983 hit single.*
▶ **noun** [mass noun] the action of releasing a recording or film again: *the long awaited re-release of my favourite film.*
■ [count noun] a recording or film which is released for a second or subsequent time.

re-roof ▶ **verb** [with obj.] provide (a building) with a new or substantially repaired roof.

re-route ▶ **verb** [with obj.] send (someone or something) by or along a different route: *the police had re-routed the march.*

rerun ▶ **verb** (**rerunning**; past **reran**; past participle **rerun**) [with obj.] show or perform (something, especially a film or programme) again: *she can stop the video and rerun a short sequence.*
▶ **noun** an event, competition, or programme which is run again.

resale ▶ **noun** [mass noun] the sale of a thing previously bought.
– DERIVATIVES **resaleable** (also **resalable**) adjective.

resale price maintenance ▶ **noun** [mass noun] Brit. an agreement between a manufacturer and a wholesaler or retailer not to sell a product below a specified price. Also called **RETAIL PRICE MAINTENANCE**.

resat past and past participle of **RESIT**.

reschedule ▶ **verb** [with obj.] change the time of (a planned event): *the concert has been rescheduled for September.*
■ arrange a new scheme of repayments of (a debt).

rescind /rɪˈsɪnd/ ▶ **verb** [with obj.] revoke, cancel, or repeal (a law, order, or agreement): *the government eventually rescinded the directive.*
– DERIVATIVES **rescindable** adjective.
– ORIGIN mid 16th cent.: from Latin *rescindere*, from *re-* (expressing intensive force) + *scindere* 'to divide, split'.

rescission /rɪˈsɪʒ(ə)n/ ▶ **noun** [mass noun] formal the revocation, cancellation, or repeal of a law, order, or agreement.
– ORIGIN mid 17th cent.: from late Latin *rescissio(n-)*, from *resciss-*, 'split again', from the verb *rescindere* (see **RESCIND**).

rescript /ˈriːskrɪpt/ ▶ **noun** an official edict or announcement.
■ historical a Roman emperor's written reply to an appeal for guidance, especially on a legal point. ■ the Pope's decision on a question of Roman Catholic doctrine or papal law.
– ORIGIN late Middle English (denoting a papal decision): from Latin *rescriptum*, neuter past participle of *rescribere* 'write back', from *re-* 'back' + *scribere* 'write'.

rescue ▶ **verb** (**rescues**, **rescued**, **rescuing**) [with obj.] save (someone) from a dangerous or distressing situation: *firemen were called out to rescue a man trapped in the river.*
■ informal keep from being lost or abandoned; retrieve: *he got out of his chair to rescue his cup of coffee.*
▶ **noun** an act of saving or being saved from danger or distress: *he* ***came to our rescue*** *with a loan of £100.*
■ [as modifier] denoting the emergency excavation of archaeological sites threatened by imminent building or road development.
– DERIVATIVES **rescuable** adjective, **rescuer** noun.
– ORIGIN Middle English: from Old French *rescoure* from Latin *re-* (expressing intensive force) + *excutere* 'shake out, discard'.

reseal ▶ **verb** [with obj.] seal (something) again.
– DERIVATIVES **resealable** adjective.

research /rɪˈsəːtʃ, ˈriːsəːtʃ/ ▶ **noun** [mass noun] the systematic investigation into and study of materials and sources in order to establish facts and reach new conclusions: *we are fighting meningitis by raising money for medical research.*
■ (**researches**) acts or periods of such investigation: *his pathological researches were included in official reports.* ■ [as modifier] engaged in or intended for use in such investigation and discovery: *a research student | a research paper.*
▶ **verb** [with obj.] investigate systematically: *the author spent 25 years researching the Tsar's life* | [no obj.] *the team have been* ***researching into*** *flora and fauna.*
■ discover facts by investigation for use in (a book, programme, etc.): *I was in New York researching my novel* | [as adj., with submodifier] (**researched**) *this is a well-researched and readable account.*
– DERIVATIVES **researchable** adjective, **researcher** noun.
– ORIGIN late 16th cent.: from obsolete French *recerche* (noun), *recercher* (verb), from Old French *re-* (expressing intensive force) + *cerchier* 'to search'.

USAGE The traditional pronunciation in British English puts the stress on the second syllable, **-search**. In US English the stress is reversed and comes on the **re-**. The US pronunciation is becoming more common in British English and, while some traditionalists view it as incorrect, it is now generally accepted as a standard variant of British English.

research and development ▶ **noun** [mass noun] (in industry) work directed towards the innovation, introduction, and improvement of products and processes.

reseat ▶ **verb** [with obj.] **1** cause (someone) to sit down again after they have risen: *he reseated himself in his armchair.*
■ cause to sit in a new position: *we reseated the orchestra for each variation.* ■ realign or repair (a tap, valve, or other object) in order to fit it into its correct position.
2 equip with new seats: *the coaches were reseated last year to increase capacity.*

réseau /ˈreɪzəʊ/ ▶ **noun** (pl. **réseaux** pronounced same) a network or grid.
■ a plain net ground used in lacemaking. ■ a reference marking pattern on a photograph, used in astronomy and surveying. ■ a spy or intelligence network, especially in the French resistance movement during the German occupation.
– ORIGIN late 16th cent. (as a term in lacemaking): French, literally 'net, web'.

resect /rɪˈsɛkt/ ▶ **verb** [with obj.] [often as adj. **resected**] Surgery cut out (tissue or part of an organ): *a small piece of resected colon.*
– DERIVATIVES **resectable** adjective, **resection** noun, **resectional** adjective, **resectionist** noun.
– ORIGIN mid 17th cent. (in the sense 'remove, cut away'): from Latin *resect-* 'cut off', from the verb *resecare*, from *re-* 'back' + *secare* 'to cut'.

reseda /ˈrɛsɪdə, rɪˈsiːdə/ ▶ **noun** **1** a plant of the genus *Reseda* (family Resedaceae), especially (in gardening) a mignonette.
2 /also ˈrɛz-/ the pale green colour of mignonette flowers.
▶ **adjective** pale green.
– ORIGIN mid 18th cent.: from Latin, interpreted in the sense 'assuage!', imperative of *resedare*, with reference to its supposed curative powers.

reseed ▶ **verb** [with obj.] sow (an area of land) with seed, especially grass seed, again.

reselect ▶ **verb** [with obj.] (usu. **be reselected**) select (someone or something) again or differently: *he was reselected as candidate for Sunderland South.*
– DERIVATIVES **reselection** noun.

resell ▶ **verb** (past and past participle **resold**) [with obj.] sell (something one has bought) to someone else: *products can be resold on the black market for huge profits.*
– DERIVATIVES **reseller** noun.

resemblance ▶ **noun** [mass noun] the state of resembling or being alike: *they* ***bear*** *some* ***resemblance to*** *Italian figurines.*
■ [count noun] a way in which two or more things are alike: *the physical resemblances between humans and apes.*
– DERIVATIVES **resemblant** adjective.
– ORIGIN Middle English: from Anglo-Norman French, from the verb *resembler* (see **RESEMBLE**).

resemble ▶ **verb** [with obj.] have qualities or features, especially those of appearance, in common with (someone or something); look or seem like: *some people resemble their dogs | they seemed to* ***resemble each other*** *closely.*
– DERIVATIVES **resembler** noun (rare).
– ORIGIN Middle English: from Old French *resembler*, based on Latin *similare* (from *similis* 'like').

resent ▶ **verb** [with obj.] feel bitterness or indignation at (a circumstance, action, or person): *she resented the fact that I had children.*
– ORIGIN late 16th cent.: from obsolete French *resentir*, from *re-* (expressing intensive force) + *sentir* 'feel' (from Latin *sentire*). The early sense was 'experience (an emotion or sensation)', later 'feel deeply', giving rise to 'feel aggrieved by'.

resentful ▶ **adjective** feeling or expressing bitterness or indignation at having been treated unfairly: *he was angry and* ***resentful of*** *their intrusion.*
– DERIVATIVES **resentfully** adverb, **resentfulness** noun.

resentment ▶ **noun** [mass noun] bitter indignation at having been treated unfairly: *his* ***resentment at*** *being demoted* | [count noun] *some people harbour resentments going back many years.*
– ORIGIN early 17th cent.: from Italian *risentimento* or French *ressentiment*, from obsolete French *resentir* (see **RESENT**).

reserpine /rɪˈsəːpiːn/ ▶ **noun** [mass noun] Medicine a compound of the alkaloid class obtained from Indian snakeroot and other plants and used in the treatment of hypertension.
– ORIGIN 1950s: from the modern Latin species name *R(auwolfia) serp(entina)*, named after Leonhard *Rauwolf* (see **RAUWOLFIA**), + **-INE**[4].

reservation ▶ **noun** **1** [mass noun] the action of reserving something: *the reservation of positions for non-Americans.*
■ [count noun] an arrangement whereby something, especially a seat or room, is booked or reserved for a particular person: *do you have a reservation?* ■ [count noun] an area of land set aside for occupation by North American Indians or Australian Aboriginals. ■ [count noun] Law a right or interest retained in an estate being conveyed. ■ (in church use) the practice of retaining a portion of the consecrated elements

r

after Mass for communion of the sick or as a focus for devotion.

2 a qualification to an expression of agreement or approval; a doubt: *some generals voiced reservations about making air strikes.*

3 (in the Roman Catholic Church) the action of a superior of reserving to himself the power of absolution.

■a right reserved to the Pope of nomination to a vacant benefice.

– ORIGIN late Middle English (denoting the Pope's right of nomination to a benefice): from Old French, or from late Latin *reservatio(n-)*, from *reservare* 'keep back' (see **RESERVE**).

reserve ▶ verb [with obj.] refrain from using or disposing of (something); retain for future use: *roll out half the dough and reserve the other half.*

■arrange for (a room, seat, ticket, etc.) to be kept for the use of a particular person and not given to anyone else: *a place was reserved for her in the front row.* ■ retain or hold (an entitlement to something), especially by formal or legal stipulation: [with obj. and infinitive] *the editor reserves the right to edit letters.* ■ refrain from delivering (a judgement or decision) immediately or without due consideration or evidence: *I'll reserve my views on his ability until he's played again.* ■ (**reserve something for**) use or engage in something only in or at (a particular circumstance or time): *Japanese food has been presented as expensive and reserved for special occasions.* ■ (in church use) retain (a portion of the consecrated elements) after Mass for communion of the sick or as a focus for devotion.

▶ noun **1** (often **reserves**) a supply of a commodity not needed for immediate use but available if required: *Australia has major coal, gas, and uranium reserves.*

■a force or body of troops withheld from action to reinforce or protect others, or additional to the regular forces and available in an emergency. ■ a member of the military reserve. ■ an extra player chosen to be a possible substitute in a team. ■ (**the reserves**) the second-choice team. ■ funds kept available by a bank, company, or government: *foreign exchange reserves.* ■ a part of a company's profits added to capital rather than paid as a dividend.

2 a place set aside for special use, in particular:

■an area designated as a habitat for a native people. ■ a protected area for wildlife.

3 [mass noun] a lack of warmth or openness in manner or expression: *she smiled and some of her natural reserve melted.*

■qualification or doubt attached to some statement or claim: *she trusted him **without reserve**.*

4 short for **RESERVE PRICE**.

5 (in the decoration of ceramics or textiles) an area which still has the original colour of the material or the colour of the background.

– PHRASES **in reserve** unused and available if required: *the platoon which had been kept in reserve.*

– DERIVATIVES **reservable** adjective, **reserver** noun.

– ORIGIN Middle English: from Old French *reserver*, from Latin *reservare* 'keep back', from *re-* 'back' + *servare* 'to keep'.

re-serve ▶ verb [no obj.] (in various sports) serve again.

reserve bank ▶ noun **1** (in the US) a regional bank operating under and implementing the policies of the Federal Reserve.

2 Austral./NZ a central bank.

reserve currency ▶ noun a strong currency widely used in international trade that a central bank is prepared to hold as part of its foreign exchange reserves.

reserved ▶ adjective **1** slow to reveal emotion or opinions: *he is a reserved, almost taciturn man.*

2 kept specially for a particular person: *a reserved seat.*

– DERIVATIVES **reservedly** adverb, **reservedness** noun.

reserved occupation ▶ noun Brit. an occupation from which a person will not be taken for military service.

reserved word ▶ noun Computing a word in a programming language which has a fixed meaning and cannot be redefined by the programmer.

reserve grade ▶ noun Austral. (in sport) a second division.

reserve price ▶ noun the price stipulated as the lowest acceptable by the seller for an item sold at auction.

reservist ▶ noun a member of the military reserve forces.

reservoir ▶ noun a large natural or artificial lake used as a source of water supply.

■a supply or source of something: *Scotland has always had a fine reservoir of comic talent.* ■ [usu. with modifier] a place where fluid collects, especially in rock strata or in the body. ■ a receptacle or part of a machine designed to hold fluid. ■ Medicine a population, tissue, etc. which is chronically infested with the causative agent of a disease and can act as a source of further infection.

– ORIGIN mid 17th cent.: from French *réservoir*, from *réserver* 'to reserve, keep'.

reset ▶ verb (**resetting**; past and past participle **reset**) [with obj.] set again or differently: *I must reset the alarm.*

■Electronics cause (a binary device) to enter the state representing the numeral 0.

– DERIVATIVES **resettability** noun, **resettable** adjective.

resettle ▶ verb settle or cause to settle in a different place: [with obj.] *they offered to resettle 300,000 refugees* | [no obj.] *144,000 East Germans had resettled in West Germany.*

– DERIVATIVES **resettlement** noun.

res gestae /reɪz ˈɡɛstaɪ, riːz ˈdʒɛstiː/ ▶ plural noun Law the events, circumstances, remarks, etc. which relate to a particular case, especially as constituting admissible evidence in a court of law.

– ORIGIN Latin, literally 'things done'.

reshape ▶ verb [with obj.] shape or form (something) differently or again: *the decrees will thoroughly reshape Poland's economy.*

reshuffle ▶ verb [with obj.] interchange the positions of (government ministers, members of a team, etc.): *the president was forced to reshuffle his cabinet.*

■put in a new order; rearrange: *genetic constituents are constantly reshuffled into individual organisms.*

▶ noun an act of reorganizing or rearranging something: *he was brought into the government in the last reshuffle.*

reside ▶ verb [no obj., with adverbial of place] have one's permanent home in a particular place: *people who work in the city actually reside in neighbouring towns.*

■be situated: *the paintings now reside on the walls of a restaurant.* ■ (of power or a right) belong by right to a person or body: *legislative powers reside with the Federal Assembly.* ■ (of a quality) be present or inherent in something: *the meaning of an utterance does not wholly reside in the semantic meaning.*

– ORIGIN late Middle English (in the sense 'be in residence as an official'): probably a back-formation from **RESIDENT**, influenced by French *résider* or Latin *residere* 'remain', from *re-* 'back' + *sedere* 'sit'.

residence ▶ noun a person's house, especially a large and impressive one.

■the official house of a government minister or other public and official figure. ■ [mass noun] the fact of living in a particular place: *Rome was his main place of residence.*

– PHRASES **in residence** living in or occupying a particular place: *the guests in residence at the hotel.* ■ (**—— in residence**) a person with a particular occupation (especially an artist or writer) paid to work in a college or other institution. **take up residence** start living in a particular place.

– ORIGIN late Middle English (denoting the fact of living in a place): from Old French, or from medieval Latin *residentia*, from Latin *residere* 'remain' (see **RESIDE**).

residence time ▶ noun technical the average length of time during which a substance, a portion of material, or an object is in a given location or condition, such as adsorption or suspension.

residency ▶ noun (pl. **-ies**) **1** [mass noun] the fact of living in a place: *a government ruling confirmed the returning refugees' right to residency.*

■[count noun] a residential post held by a writer, musician, or artist, typically for teaching purposes. ■ [count noun] Brit. a musician's regular engagement at a club or other venue.

2 historical the official residence of the Governor General's representative or other government agent, especially at the court of an Indian state.

■a group or organization of intelligence agents in a foreign country.

3 N. Amer. a period of specialized medical training in a hospital; the position of a resident.

resident ▶ noun **1** a person who lives somewhere permanently or on a long-term basis.

■a bird, butterfly, or other animal of a species that does not migrate. ■ Brit. a guest in a hotel who stays for one or more nights. ■ US a person who boards at a boarding school. ■ historical a British government agent in any semi-independent state, especially the Governor General's agent at the court of an Indian state. ■ an intelligence agent in a foreign country.

2 N. Amer. a medical graduate engaged in specialized practice under supervision in a hospital.

▶ adjective living somewhere on a long-term basis: *he has been resident in Brazil for a long time.*

■having quarters on the premises of one's work: *resident farm workers.* ■ attached to and working regularly for a particular institution: *the film studio needed a resident historian.* ■ (of a bird, butterfly or other animal) non-migratory; remaining in an area throughout the year. ■ (of a computer program, file, etc.) immediately available in computer memory, rather than having to be loaded from elsewhere.

– DERIVATIVES **residentship** (historical) noun.

– ORIGIN Middle English: from Latin *resident-* 'remaining', from the verb *residere* (see **RESIDE**).

resident commissioner ▶ noun a delegate elected to represent Puerto Rico in the US House of Representatives. They are able to speak in the House and serve on committees, but may not vote.

residential ▶ adjective designed for people to live in: *private residential and nursing homes.*

■providing accommodation in addition to other services: *a residential sixth-form college.* ■ occupied by private houses: *quieter traffic in residential areas.* ■ concerning or relating to residence: *land has been diverted from residential use.*

– DERIVATIVES **residentially** adverb.

residential school ▶ noun a boarding school.

■(in Canada) a government-supported boarding school for children from small or scattered Indian and Inuit communities.

residentiary ▶ adjective (of canons) required to live officially in a cathedral or collegiate church.

■relating to or involving residence in an establishment or place.

▶ noun (pl. **-ies**) a residentiary canon.

– ORIGIN early 16th cent. (as a noun): from medieval Latin *residentiarius*, from Latin *resident-* 'remaining' (see **RESIDENT**).

residua plural form of **RESIDUUM**.

residual ▶ adjective remaining after the greater part or quantity has gone: *the withdrawal of residual occupying forces.*

■(of a quantity) left after other things have been subtracted: *residual income after tax and mortgage payments.* ■ (of a physical state or property) remaining after the removal of or present in the absence of a causative agent: *residual stenosis.* ■ (of an experimental or arithmetical error) not accounted for or eliminated. ■ (of a soil or other deposit) formed in situ by weathering.

▶ noun a quantity remaining after other things have been subtracted or allowed for.

■a difference between a value measured in a scientific experiment and the theoretical or true value. ■ a royalty paid to a performer, writer, etc. for a repeat of a play, television show, etc. ■ Geology a portion of rocky or high ground remaining after erosion. ■ the resale value of a new car or other item at a specified time after purchase, expressed as a percentage of its purchase price.

– DERIVATIVES **residually** adverb.

residual current ▶ noun an electric current which flows briefly in a circuit after the voltage is reduced to zero, due to the momentum of the charge carriers.

residual current device ▶ noun a current-activated circuit-breaker used as a safety device for mains-operated electrical tools and appliances.

residual stress ▶ noun [mass noun] Physics the stress present in an object in the absence of any external load or force.

residuary ▶ adjective technical residual.

■Law of or relating to the residue of an estate: *a residuary legatee.*

– ORIGIN early 18th cent.: from **RESIDUUM** + **-ARY**[1].

residue /ˈrɛzɪdjuː/ ▶ noun a small amount of something that remains after the main part has gone or been taken or used.

■Law the part of an estate that is left after the payment of charges, debts, and bequests. ■ a substance that remains after a process such as combustion or evaporation.

– ORIGIN late Middle English: from Old French

residu, from Latin *residuum* 'something remaining' (see **RESIDUUM**).

residuum /rɪˈzɪdjʊəm/ ▶ **noun** (pl. **residua** /-djʊə/) technical a substance or thing that remains or is left behind, in particular:
■a chemical residue. ■ Sociology a class of society that is unemployed and without privileges or opportunities.
– ORIGIN late 17th cent.: from Latin, neuter of *residuus* 'remaining', from the verb *residere*.

resign ▶ **verb 1** [no obj.] voluntarily leave a job or other position: *he **resigned from** the government in protest at the policy.*
■[with obj.] give up (an office, power, privilege, etc.): *four deputies resigned their seats.* ■ [no obj.] Chess end a game by conceding defeat without being checkmated: *he lost his Queen and resigned in 45 moves.*
2 (**be resigned**) accept that something undesirable cannot be avoided: *he seems **resigned to** a shortened career | she **resigned herself to** a lengthy session.*
■archaic surrender oneself to another's guidance: *he vows to resign himself to her direction.*
– DERIVATIVES **resignedly** adverb, **resignedness** noun, **resigner** noun.
– ORIGIN late Middle English: from Old French *resigner*, from Latin *resignare* 'unseal, cancel', from *re-* 'back' + *signare* 'sign, seal'.

re-sign ▶ **verb** [with obj.] sign (a document) again.
■engage (a sports player) to play for a team for a further period. ■ [no obj.] (of a sports player) commit oneself to play for a team for a further period.

resignal ▶ **verb** (**resignalled**, **resignalling**; US **resignaled**, **resignaling**) [with obj.] [often as noun **resignalling**] equip (a railway line) with new signal equipment.

resignation ▶ **noun 1** an act of retiring or giving up a position: *he announced his resignation.*
■a document conveying someone's intention of retiring: *I'm thinking of handing in my resignation.* ■ Chess an act of ending a game by conceding defeat without being checkmated.
2 [mass noun] the acceptance of something undesirable but inevitable: *a shrug of resignation.*
– ORIGIN late Middle English: via Old French from medieval Latin *resignatio(n-)*, from *resignare* 'unseal, cancel' (see **RESIGN**).

resile /rɪˈzʌɪl/ ▶ **verb** [no obj.] formal abandon a position or a course of action: *can he **resile from** the agreement?*
– ORIGIN early 16th cent.: from obsolete French *resilir* or Latin *resilire* 'to recoil', from *re-* 'back' + *salire* 'to jump'.

resilient ▶ **adjective** (of a substance or object) able to recoil or spring back into shape after bending, stretching, or being compressed.
■(of a person or animal) able to withstand or recover quickly from difficult conditions: *the fish are **resilient to** most infections.*
– DERIVATIVES **resilience** noun, **resiliency** noun, **resiliently** adverb.
– ORIGIN mid 17th cent.: from Latin *resilient-* 'leaping back', from the verb *resilire* (see **RESILE**).

resilin /ˈrɛzɪlɪn/ ▶ **noun** [mass noun] Biochemistry an elastic material formed of cross-linked protein chains, found in insect cuticles, especially in the hinges and ligaments of wings.
– ORIGIN 1960s: from Latin *resilire* 'leap back, recoil' + **-IN**[1].

resin /ˈrɛzɪn/ ▶ **noun** [mass noun] a sticky flammable organic substance, insoluble in water, exuded by some trees and other plants (notably fir and pine). Compare with **GUM**[1] (in sense 1).
■(also **synthetic resin**) [count noun] a solid or liquid synthetic organic polymer used as the basis of plastics, adhesives, varnishes, or other products.
▶ **verb** (**resined**, **resining**) [with obj.] [usu. as adj. **resined**] rub or treat with resin: *resined canvas.*
– DERIVATIVES **resinous** adjective.
– ORIGIN late Middle English: from Latin *resina*; related to Greek *rhētinē* 'pine resin'. Compare with **ROSIN**.

resinate ▶ **verb** /ˈrɛzɪneɪt/ [with obj.] impregnate or flavour with resin: [as adj. **resinated**] *resinated white wine.*
▶ **noun** /ˈrɛzɪnət/ Chemistry a salt of an acid derived from resin.

res ipsa loquitur /ˌreɪz ˌɪpsə ˈlɒkwɪtə/ ▶ **noun** Law the principle that the occurrence of an accident implies negligence.
– ORIGIN Latin, literally 'the matter speaks for itself'.

resist ▶ **verb** [with obj.] withstand the action or effect of: *antibodies help us to resist infection.*
■try to prevent by action or argument: *we will continue to resist changes to the treaty.* ■ succeed in ignoring the attraction of (something wrong or unwise): *I couldn't resist buying the blouse.* ■ [no obj.] struggle against someone or something: *without giving her time to resist, he dragged her off her feet.*
▶ **noun** a resistant substance applied as a coating to protect a surface during some process, for example to prevent dye or glaze adhering.
– DERIVATIVES **resister** noun, **resistibility** noun, **resistible** adjective.
– ORIGIN late Middle English: from Old French *resister* or Latin *resistere*, from *re-* (expressing opposition) + *sistere* 'stop' (reduplication of *stare* 'to stand'). The current sense of the noun dates from the mid 19th cent.

resistance ▶ **noun 1** [mass noun] the refusal to accept or comply with something; the attempt to prevent something by action or argument: *she **put up no resistance to** being led away.*
■armed or violent opposition: *government forces were unable to crush guerrilla-style resistance.* ■ (also **resistance movement**) [in sing.] a secret organization resisting authority, especially in an occupied country. ■ (**the Resistance**) the underground movement formed in France during the Second World War to fight the German occupying forces and the Vichy government. Also called **MAQUIS**. ■ the impeding, slowing, or stopping effect exerted by one material thing on another: *air resistance would need to be reduced by streamlining.*
2 the ability not to be affected by something, especially adversely: *some of us have a lower resistance to cold than others.*
■[mass noun] Medicine & Biology lack of sensitivity to a drug, insecticide, etc., especially as a result of continued exposure or genetic change.
3 the degree to which a substance or device opposes the passage of an electric current, causing energy dissipation. By Ohm's law resistance (measured in ohms) is equal to the voltage divided by the current.
■[count noun] a resistor or other circuit component which opposes the passage of an electric current.
– PHRASES **the line** (or **path**) **of least resistance** an option avoiding difficulty or unpleasantness; the easiest course of action.
– ORIGIN late Middle English: from French *résistance*, from late Latin *resistentia*, from the verb *resistere* 'hold back' (see **RESIST**).

resistance thermometer ▶ **noun** Physics an instrument used to measure a change in temperature by its effect on the electrical resistance of a platinum or other metal wire.

resistant ▶ **adjective** offering resistance to something or someone: *some of the old churches are **resistant to** change* | [in combination] *a water-resistant adhesive.*

résistant /ˌreɪzɪˈstɒ̃, French rezistɑ̃/ ▶ **noun** (pl. pronounced same) a member of the French Resistance movement in the Second World War.
– ORIGIN French, literally 'resisting' (adjective used as a noun).

resistive /rɪˈzɪstɪv/ ▶ **adjective** technical able to withstand the action or effect of something.
■Physics of or concerning electrical resistance.

resistivity /ˌrɪzɪˈstɪvɪti/ ▶ **noun** [mass noun] Physics a measure of the resisting power of a specified material to the flow of an electric current.

resistivity surveying ▶ **noun** [mass noun] the measurement of the current passing between electrodes embedded in the ground at a series of positions over a given area, in order to locate buried structural features by their differing resistivity.

resistless ▶ **adjective** archaic powerful and irresistible: *a resistless impulse.*
■powerless to resist the effect of someone or something; unresisting.
– DERIVATIVES **resistlessly** adverb.

resistor ▶ **noun** Physics a device having resistance to the passage of an electric current.

resit Brit. ▶ **verb** (**resitting**; past and past participle **resat**) [with obj.] take (an examination) again after failing: *she is resitting her maths GCSE* | [no obj.] *many candidates' progress is disrupted because they have to resit.*
▶ **noun** an examination held specifically to enable candidates to do this.

resite ▶ **verb** [with obj.] place or situate in a different place: *they want the statue to be resited in the national headquarters.*

resize ▶ **verb** [with obj.] alter the size of (something, especially a computer window or image).

res judicata /reɪz ˌdʒuːdɪˈkɑːtə/ ▶ **noun** (pl. **res judicatae** /ˌdʒuːdɪˈkɑːtʌɪ, ˌdʒuːdɪˈkɑːtiː/) Law a matter that has been adjudicated by a competent court and may not be pursued further by the same parties.
– ORIGIN Latin, literally 'judged matter'.

reskill ▶ **verb** [with obj.] teach (a person, especially an unemployed person) new skills.

reskin ▶ **verb** (**reskinned**, **reskinning**) [with obj.] replace or repair the skin of (an aircraft or motor vehicle).

Resnais /rəˈneɪ, French rənɛ/, Alain (b.1922), French film director. One of the foremost directors of the *nouvelle vague*, he used experimental techniques to explore memory and time. Notable films: *Hiroshima mon amour* (1959) and *L'Année dernière à Marienbad* (1961).

resold past and past participle of **RESELL**.

resoluble /rɪˈzɒljʊb(ə)l/ ▶ **adjective** archaic able to be resolved.
– ORIGIN early 17th cent.: from French *résoluble* or late Latin *resolubilis*, based on Latin *solvere* 'release, loosen'.

re-soluble ▶ **adjective** able to dissolve or be dissolved again: *the re-soluble nature of the paint.*

resolute /ˈrɛzəluːt/ ▶ **adjective** admirably purposeful, determined, and unwavering: *she was resolute and unswerving.*
– DERIVATIVES **resolutely** adverb, **resoluteness** noun.
– ORIGIN late Middle English (in the sense 'paid', describing a rent): from Latin *resolutus* 'loosened, released, paid', past participle of *resolvere* (see **RESOLVE**).

resolution ▶ **noun 1** a firm decision to do or not to do something: *she kept her resolution not to see Anne any more | a New Year's resolution.*
■a formal expression of opinion or intention agreed on by a legislative body, committee, or other formal meeting, typicallyafter taking a vote: *the conference passed two resolutions.* ■ [mass noun] the quality of being determined or resolute: *he handled the last British actions of the war with resolution.*
2 [mass noun] the action of solving a problem, dispute, or contentious matter: *the peaceful resolution of all disputes* | [count noun] *a successful resolution to the problem.*
■Music the passing of a discord into a concord during the course of changing harmony. ■ Medicine the disappearance of inflammation, or of any symptom or condition.
3 [mass noun] chiefly Chemistry the process of reducing or separating something into constituent parts or components.
■Physics the replacing of a single force or other vector quantity by two or more jointly equivalent to it. ■ the conversion of something abstract into another form. ■ Prosody the substitution of two short syllables for one long one.
3 the smallest interval measurable by a scientific (especially optical) instrument; the resolving power.
■the degree of detail visible in a photographic or television image.
– ORIGIN late Middle English: from Latin *resolutio(n-)*, from *resolvere* 'loosen, release' (see **RESOLVE**).

resolutive /ˈrɛzəluːtɪv/ ▶ **adjective** formal or archaic having the power or ability to dissolve or dispel something.
– ORIGIN late Middle English: from medieval Latin *resolutivus*, from *resolut-* 'released', from the verb *resolvere* (see **RESOLVE**).

resolve ▶ **verb 1** [with obj.] settle or find a solution to (a problem, dispute, or contentious matter): *the firm aims to resolve problems within 30 days.*
■[with obj.] Medicine cause (a symptom or condition) to disperse, subside, or heal: *endoscopic biliary drainage can rapidly resolve jaundice.* ■ [no obj.] (of a symptom or condition) disperse, subside, or heal: *symptoms resolved after a median of four weeks.* ■ [no obj.] Music (of a discord) lead into a concord during the course of harmonic change. ■ [with obj.] Music cause (a discord) to pass into a concord.
2 [no obj.] decide firmly on a course of action: [with infinitive] *she resolved to ring Dana as soon as she got home.*

r

■ [with clause] (of a legislative body, committee, or other formal meeting) make a decision by a formal vote: *the government resolved that the retail prices of a list of non-essential goods would be freed* | [with infinitive] *the conference resolved to support an alliance.*
3 chiefly Chemistry separate or cause to be separated into constituent parts or components.
■ [with obj.] (**resolve something into**) reduce a subject, statement, etc. by mental analysis into (separate elements or a more elementary form): *the ability to resolve facts into their legal categories.* ■ [no obj.] (of something seen at a distance) turn into a different form when seen more clearly: *the orange light* ***resolved itself*** *into four roadwork lanterns.* ■ [with obj.] (of optical or photographic equipment) separate or distinguish between (closely adjacent objects): *Hubble was able to resolve six variable stars in M31.* ■ [with obj.] separately distinguish (peaks in a graph or spectrum). ■ [with obj.] Physics analyse (a force or velocity) into components acting in particular directions.
▶ **noun** [mass noun] firm determination to do something: *she received information that strengthened her resolve* | [count noun] *she intended to stick to her initial resolve.*
■ [count noun] US a formal resolution by a legislative body or public meeting.
– DERIVATIVES **resolvability** noun, **resolvable** adjective, **resolver** noun.
– ORIGIN late Middle English (in the senses 'dissolve, disintegrate' and 'solve (a problem)'): from Latin *resolvere*, from *re-* (expressing intensive force) + *solvere* 'loosen'.

resolved ▶ **adjective** [predic., with infinitive] firmly determined to do something: *Constance was resolved not to cry.*
– DERIVATIVES **resolvedly** adverb.

resolvent Mathematics ▶ **adjective** denoting an equation, function, or expression that is introduced in order to reach or complete a solution.
▶ **noun** an equation, function, or expression of this type.

resolving power ▶ **noun** [mass noun] the ability of an optical instrument or type of film to separate or distinguish small or closely adjacent images.

resonance ▶ **noun** [mass noun] the quality in a sound of being deep, full, and reverberating: *the resonance of his voice.*
■ figurative the ability to evoke or suggest images, memories, and emotions: *the concepts lose their emotional resonance.* ■ Physics the reinforcement or prolongation of sound by reflection from a surface or by the synchronous vibration of a neighbouring object. ■ Mechanics the condition in which an object or system is subjected to an oscillating force having a frequency close to its own natural frequency. ■ the condition in which an electric circuit or device produces the largest possible response to an applied oscillating signal, especially when its inductive and its capacitative reactances are balanced. ■ [count noun] Physics a short-lived subatomic particle that is an excited state of a more stable particle. ■ Astronomy the occurrence of a simple ratio between the periods of revolution of two bodies about a single primary. ■ Chemistry the state attributed to certain molecules of having a structure which cannot adequately be represented by a single structural formula but is a composite of two or more structures of higher energy.
– ORIGIN late Middle English: from Old French, from Latin *resonantia* 'echo', from *resonare* 'resound' (see **RESONANT**).

resonant ▶ **adjective** (of sound) deep, clear, and continuing to sound or ring: *a full-throated and resonant guffaw.*
■ technical of, relating to, or bringing about resonance in a circuit, atom, or other object. ■ (of a room, musical instrument, or hollow body) tending to reinforce or prolong sounds, especially by synchronous vibration. ■ (of a colour) enhancing or enriching another colour or colours by contrast. ■ [predic.] (**resonant with**) (of a place) filled or resounding with (the sound of something): *alpine valleys resonant with the sound of church bells.* ■ figurative having the ability to evoke or suggest enduring images, memories, or emotions: *the prints are* ***resonant with*** *traditions of Russian folk art and story.*
– DERIVATIVES **resonantly** adverb.
– ORIGIN late 16th cent.: from French *résonnant* or Latin *resonant-* 'resounding', from the verb *resonare*, from *re-* (expressing intensive force) + *sonare* 'to sound'.

resonate ▶ **verb** [no obj.] produce or be filled with a deep, full, reverberating sound: *the sound of the siren resonated across the harbour.*
■ figurative evoke or suggest images, memories, and emotions: *the words* ***resonate with*** *so many different meanings.* ■ chiefly US (of an idea or action) meet with someone's agreement: *the judge's ruling resonated among many of the women.* ■ technical produce electrical or mechanical resonance: *the crystal resonates at 16 MHz.*
– ORIGIN late 19th cent.: from Latin *resonat-* 'resounded', from the verb *resonare* (see **RESOUND**).

resonator ▶ **noun** an apparatus that increases the resonance of a sound, especially a hollow part of a musical instrument.
■ a musical or scientific instrument responding to a single sound or note, used for detecting it when it occurs in combination with other sounds. ■ Physics a device that displays electrical resonance, especially one used for the detection of radio waves. ■ Physics a hollow enclosure with conducting walls capable of containing electromagnetic fields having particular frequencies of oscillation and exchanging electrical energy with them, used to detect or amplify microwaves.

resorb /rɪˈsɔːb/ ▶ **verb** [with obj.] technical absorb (something) again: *the ability to resorb valuable solutes from the urine.*
■ Physiology remove (cells, or a tissue or structure) by gradual breakdown into its component materials and dispersal in the circulation: *bone tissue will be resorbed.*
– ORIGIN mid 17th cent.: from Latin *resorbere*, from *re-* (expressing intensive force) + *sorbere* 'absorb'.

resorcinol /rɪˈzɔːsɪnɒl/ ▶ **noun** [mass noun] Chemistry a crystalline compound originally obtained from galbanum resin, used in the production of dyes, resins, and cosmetics.
• Alternative name: **1,3-dihydroxybenzene**; chem. formula: $C_6H_4(OH)_2$.
– ORIGIN late 19th cent.: from the earlier term *resorcin* + **-OL**.

resorption /rɪˈzɔːpʃ(ə)n, -ˈsɔːp-/ ▶ **noun** [mass noun] the process or action by which something is reabsorbed: *the resorption of water.*
■ Physiology the absorption into the circulation of cells or tissue: *bone resorption.*
– DERIVATIVES **resorptive** adjective.
– ORIGIN early 19th cent.: from **RESORB**, on the pattern of the pair *absorb, absorption.*

resort ▶ **noun 1** a place that is a popular destination for holidays or recreation, or which is frequented for a particular purpose: *a seaside resort* | *a health resort.*
■ [mass noun] archaic the tendency of a place to be frequented by many people: *places of public resort.*
2 [mass noun] the action of turning to and adopting a strategy or course of action, especially a disagreeable or undesirable one, so as to resolve a difficult situation: *Germany and Italy tried to resolve their economic and social failures by* ***resort to*** *fascism.*
■ [in sing.] a strategy or course of action that may be adopted in a difficult situation: *her only resort is a private operation.*
▶ **verb** [no obj.] (**resort to**) **1** turn to and adopt (a strategy or course of action, especially a disagreeable or undesirable one) so as to resolve a difficult situation: *the duke was prepared to resort to force if negotiation failed.*
2 formal go often or in large numbers to: *local authorities have a duty to provide adequate sites for gypsies 'residing in or resorting to' their areas.*
– PHRASES **as a first** (or **last** or **final**) **resort** before anything else is attempted (or when all else has failed). **in the last resort** ultimately: *in the last resort what really moves us is our personal convictions.* [ORIGIN: suggested by French *en dernier ressort.*]
– DERIVATIVES **resorter** noun.
– ORIGIN late Middle English (denoting something one can turn to for assistance): from Old French *resortir*, from *re-* 'again' + *sortir* 'come or go out'. The sense 'place frequently visited' dates from the mid 18th cent.

re-sort ▶ **verb** [with obj.] sort (something) again or differently.

resound /rɪˈzaʊnd/ ▶ **verb** [no obj., with adverbial] (of a sound, voice, etc.) fill a place with sound; be loud enough to echo: *another scream resounded through the school.*
■ (of a place) be filled or echo with a particular sound or sounds: *the office* ***resounds with*** *the metronomic clicking of keyboards.* ■ figurative (of fame, a person's reputation, etc.) be much talked of: *whatever they do in the Nineties will not resound in the way that their earlier achievements did.* ■ [with obj.] poetic/literary sing (the praises) of: *Horace resounds the praises of Italy.* ■ [with obj.] poetic/literary (of a place) re-echo (a sound): *cliffs, woods, and caves, her viewless steps resound.*
– ORIGIN late Middle English: from **RE-** 'again' + the verb **SOUND**[1], suggested by Old French *resoner* or Latin *resonare* 'sound again'.

resounding ▶ **adjective 1** (of a sound) loud enough to reverberate: *a resounding smack across the face.*
2 [attrib.] unmistakable; emphatic: *the evening was a resounding success.*
– DERIVATIVES **resoundingly** adverb.

resource /rɪˈsɔːs, rɪˈzɔːs/ ▶ **noun 1** (usu. **resources**) a stock or supply of money, materials, staff, and other assets that can be drawn on by a person or organization in order to function effectively: *local authorities complained that they lacked resources.*
■ (**resources**) a country's collective means of supporting itself or becoming wealthier, as represented by its reserves of minerals, land, and other assets. ■ (**resources**) N. Amer. available assets.
2 an action or strategy which may be adopted in adverse circumstances: *sometimes anger is the only resource left in a situation like this.*
■ (**resources**) one's personal attributes and capabilities regarded as able to help or sustain one in adverse circumstances: *we had been left very much to our own resources.* ■ [mass noun] the ability to find quick and clever ways to overcome difficulties: *a man of resource.* ■ a teaching aid. ■ [mass noun] archaic the possibility of aid or assistance: *the flower of the French army was lost* ***without resource.***
3 archaic a leisure occupation.
▶ **verb** [with obj.] provide (a person or organization) with materials, money, staff, and other assets necessary for effective operation: *a strategy which ensures that primary health care workers are adequately resourced.*
– DERIVATIVES **resourceless** adjective, **resourcelessness** noun.
– ORIGIN early 17th cent.: from obsolete French *ressourse*, feminine past participle (used as a noun) of Old French dialect *resourdre* 'rise again, recover' (based on Latin *surgere* 'to rise').

resourceful ▶ **adjective** having the ability to find quick and clever ways to overcome difficulties.
– DERIVATIVES **resourcefully** adverb, **resourcefulness** noun.

respect ▶ **noun 1** [mass noun] a feeling of deep admiration for someone or something elicited by their abilities, qualities, or achievements: *the director had a lot of* ***respect for*** *Douglas as an actor.*
■ the state of being admired in such a way: *his first chance in over fifteen years to regain respect in the business.* ■ due regard for the feelings, wishes, rights, or traditions of others: ***respect for*** *human rights.* ■ (**respects**) a person's polite greetings: *give my respects to their Excellencies.* ■ informal compliments (used to express the speaker's approval of someone or something): *respect to KISS FM for taking on board the Somethin' Else project.*
2 a particular aspect, point, or detail: *the government's record* ***in this respect*** *is a mixed one.*
▶ **verb** [with obj.] admire (someone or something) deeply, as a result of their abilities, qualities, or achievements: *she was respected by everyone she worked with* | [as adj. **respected**] *a respected academic.*
■ have due regard for the feelings, wishes, rights, or traditions of: *I respected his views.* ■ avoid harming or interfering with: *it is incumbent upon all hill users to respect the environment.* ■ agree to recognize and abide by (a legal requirement): *the crown and its ministers ought to respect the ordinary law.*
– PHRASES **in respect of** (or **with respect to**) as regards; with reference to: *the two groups were similar with respect to age, sex, and diagnoses.* **in respect that** because. **pay one's respects, pay one's last respects** see **PAY**[1]. **with** (or **with all due**) **respect** used as a polite formula preceding, and intended to mitigate the effect of, an expression of disagreement or criticism: *with all due respect, Father, I think you've got to be more broad-minded these days.*
– ORIGIN late Middle English: from Latin *respectus*, from the verb *respicere* 'look back at, regard', from *re-* 'back' + *specere* 'look at'.

respectability ▶ **noun** [mass noun] the state or quality of being proper, correct, and socially acceptable: *provincial notions of respectability.*
■ the state or quality of being accepted as valid or important within a particular field: *scientific respectability.*

respectable ▶ **adjective 1** regarded by society to be

good, proper, or correct: *they thought the stage no life for a respectable lady.*

■(of a person's appearance, clothes, or behaviour) decent or presentable: *a perfectly respectable pair of pyjamas!*

2 of some merit or importance: *a respectable botanical text.*

■adequate or acceptable in number, size, or amount: *America's GDP grew by a respectable 2.6 per cent.*

– DERIVATIVES **respectably** adverb [as submodifier] *an architecture of respectably high standards.*

respecter ▶ **noun** [usu. with negative] a person who has a high regard for someone or something: *he was no respecter of the female sex.*

– PHRASES **be no respecter of persons** treat everyone in the same way, without being influenced by their status or wealth.

respectful ▶ **adjective** feeling or showing deference and respect: *they sit in respectful silence.*

– DERIVATIVES **respectfully** adverb, **respectfulness** noun.

respecting ▶ **preposition** dated or formal with reference or regard to: *he began to have serious worries respecting his car.*

respective ▶ **adjective** [attrib.] belonging or relating separately to each of two or more people or things: *they chatted about their respective childhoods.*

– ORIGIN late Middle English (in the sense 'relative, comparative'): from medieval Latin *respectivus*, from *respect-* 'regarded, considered', from the verb *respicere* (see **RESPECT**), reinforced by French *respectif, -ive.*

respectively ▶ **adverb** separately or individually and in the order already mentioned (used when enumerating two or more items or facts that refer back to a previous statement): *they received sentences of one year and eight months respectively.*

respell ▶ **verb** (past and past participle **respelled** or chiefly Brit. **respelt**) [with obj.] spell (a word) again or differently, especially phonetically in order to indicate its pronunciation.

Respighi /rɛ'spiːgi/, Ottorino (1879–1936), Italian composer. He is best known for his suites the *Fountains of Rome* (1917) and the *Pines of Rome* (1924), based on the poems of Gabriele d'Annunzio.

respirable /'rɛsp(ə)rəb(ə)l, rɪ'spʌɪ-/ ▶ **adjective** (of the air or a gas) able or fit to be breathed.

■(of particles in the air) able to be breathed in: *woodworking can create quantities of fine respirable dust.*

– ORIGIN late 18th cent.: from French *respirable* or late Latin *respirabilis*, from *respirare* 'breathe out' (see **RESPIRE**).

respirate /'rɛspɪreɪt/ ▶ **verb** [with obj.] Medicine & Biology assist (a person or animal) to breathe by means of artificial respiration.

– ORIGIN mid 17th cent.: back-formation from **RESPIRATION**.

respiration ▶ **noun** [mass noun] the action of breathing: *opiates affect respiration.*

■[count noun] chiefly Medicine a single breath. ■ Biology a process in living organisms involving the production of energy, typically with the intake of oxygen and the release of carbon dioxide from the oxidation of complex organic substances.

– ORIGIN late Middle English: from Latin *respiratio(n-)*, from *respirare* 'breathe out' (see **RESPIRE**).

respirator ▶ **noun** an apparatus worn over the mouth and nose or the entire face to prevent the inhalation of dust, smoke, or other noxious substances.

■an apparatus used to induce artificial respiration.

respiratory /rɪ'spɪrət(ə)ri, 'rɛsp(ə)rət(ə)ri, rɪ'spʌɪ-/ ▶ **adjective** of, relating to, or affecting respiration or the organs of respiration: *respiratory disease.*

respiratory distress syndrome ▶ **noun** another term for **HYALINE MEMBRANE DISEASE**.

respiratory pigment ▶ **noun** Biochemistry a substance (such as haemoglobin or haemocyanin) with a molecule consisting of protein with a pigmented prosthetic group, involved in the physiological transport of oxygen or electrons.

respiratory quotient ▶ **noun** Physiology the ratio of the volume of carbon dioxide evolved to that of oxygen consumed by an organism, tissue, or cell in a given time.

respiratory syncytial virus ▶ **noun** Medicine a paramyxovirus which causes disease of the respiratory tract. It is a major cause of bronchiolitis and pneumonia in young children, and may be a contributing factor in cot death.

respiratory tract ▶ **noun** the passage formed by the mouth, nose, throat, and lungs, through which air passes during breathing.

respiratory tree ▶ **noun** Zoology a branched respiratory organ in the body cavity of sea cucumbers.

respire ▶ **verb** [no obj.] breathe: *he lay back, respiring deeply* | [with obj.] *a country where fresh air seems impossible to respire.*

■(of a plant) carry out respiration, especially at night when photosynthesis has ceased. ■ poetic/literary recover hope, courage, or strength after a time of difficulty: *the archduke, newly respiring from so long a war.*

– ORIGIN late Middle English: from Old French *respirer* or Latin *respirare* 'breathe out', from *re-* 'again' + *spirare* 'breathe'.

respirometer ▶ **noun** Biology a device which measures the rate of consumption of oxygen by a living organism or organic system.

■Medicine an instrument for measuring the air capacity of the lungs.

respite /'rɛspʌɪt, -spɪt/ ▶ **noun** [mass noun] a short period of rest or relief from something difficult or unpleasant: *the refugee encampments will provide some* ***respite from*** *the suffering* | [in sing.] *a brief* ***respite from*** *a dire food shortage.*

■a short delay permitted before an unpleasant obligation is met or a punishment is carried out.

▶ **verb** [with obj.] rare postpone (a sentence, obligation, etc.): *the execution was only respited a few months.*

■archaic grant a delay or extension of time to; reprieve from death or execution: *some poor criminal ... from the gibbet or the wheel, respited for a day.*

– ORIGIN Middle English: from Old French *respit*, from Latin *respectus* 'refuge, consideration'.

respite care ▶ **noun** [mass noun] temporary institutional care of a dependent elderly, ill, or handicapped person, providing relief for their usual carers.

resplendent /rɪ'splɛnd(ə)nt/ ▶ **adjective** attractive and impressive through being richly colourful or sumptuous: *she was* ***resplendent in*** *a sea-green dress.*

– DERIVATIVES **resplendence** noun, **resplendency** noun, **resplendently** adverb.

– ORIGIN late Middle English: from Latin *resplendent-* 'shining out', from the verb *resplendere*, from *re-* (expressing intensive force) + *splendere* 'to glitter'.

respond ▶ **verb** [reporting verb] say something in reply: [no obj.] *she could not get Robert to* ***respond to*** *her words* | [with clause] *he responded that it would not be feasible* | [with direct speech] *'It's not part of my job,' Belinda responded.*

■(of a congregation) say or sing the response in reply to a priest. ■ [no obj.] (of a person) act or behave in reaction to someone or something: *she turned her head,* ***responding to*** *his grin with a smile.* ■ react quickly or positively to a stimulus or treatment: *his back injury has failed to respond to treatment.* ■ [with obj.] Bridge make (a bid) in answer to one's partner's preceding bid.

▶ **noun 1** Architecture a half-pillar or half-pier attached to a wall to support an arch, especially at the end of an arcade.

2 (in church use) a responsory; a response to a versicle.

– DERIVATIVES **respondence** noun (archaic), **respondency** noun (archaic), **responder** noun.

– ORIGIN late Middle English (in the noun senses): from Old French, from *respondre* 'to answer', from Latin *respondere*, from *re-* 'again' + *spondere* 'to pledge'. The verb dates from the mid 16th cent.

respondent ▶ **noun 1** a defendant in a lawsuit, especially one in an appeal or divorce case.

2 a person who replies to something, especially one supplying information for a survey or questionnaire or responding to an advertisement.

▶ **adjective** [attrib.] **1** in the position of defendant in a lawsuit: *the respondent defendant.*

2 replying to something, especially a survey or questionnaire: *the respondent firms in the survey.*

3 Psychology involving or denoting a response, especially a conditioned reflex, to a specific stimulus.

– ORIGIN early 16th cent. (in sense 2 of the noun): from Latin *respondent-* 'answering, offering in return', from the verb *respondere* (see **RESPOND**).

responsa plural form of **RESPONSUM**.

response ▶ **noun** a verbal or written answer: *without waiting for a response, she returned to her newspaper* | [mass noun] *we received 400 applications* ***in response to*** *one job ad.*

■a written or verbal answer to a question in a test, questionnaire, survey, etc. ■ a reaction to something: *an extended, jazzy piano solo drew the biggest* ***response from*** *the crowd* | [mass noun] *an Honours degree course in Japanese has been established* ***in response to*** *an increasing demand.* ■ Psychology & Physiology an excitation of a nerve impulse caused by a change or event; a physical reaction to a specific stimulus or situation. ■ the way in which a mechanical or electrical device responds to a stimulus or range of stimuli. ■ (usu. **responses**) a part of a religious liturgy said or sung by a congregation in answer to a minister or cantor. ■ Bridge a bid made in answer to one's partner's preceding bid.

– ORIGIN Middle English: from Old French *respons* or Latin *responsum* 'something offered in return', neuter past participle of *respondere* (see **RESPOND**).

response time ▶ **noun** the length of time taken for a person or system to react to a given stimulus or event.

■Electronics the time taken for a circuit or measuring device, when subjected to a change in input signal, to change its state by a specified fraction of its total response to that change.

response variable ▶ **noun** another term for **DEPENDENT VARIABLE**.

responsibility ▶ **noun** (pl. **-ies**) [mass noun] the state or fact of having a duty to deal with something or of having control over someone: *women bear children and* ***take responsibility for*** *childcare.*

■the state or fact of being accountable or to blame for something: *the group has claimed responsibility for a string of murders.* ■ the opportunity or ability to act independently and take decisions without authorization: *we would expect individuals lower down the organization to take on more responsibility.* ■ [count noun] (often **responsibilities**) a thing which one is required to do as part of a job, role, or legal obligation: *he will take over the responsibilities of Overseas Director.* ■ [in sing.] (**responsibility to/towards**) a moral obligation to behave correctly towards or in respect of: *individuals have a responsibility to control personal behaviour.*

– PHRASES **on one's own responsibility** without authorization.

responsible ▶ **adjective** [predic.] having an obligation to do something, or having control over or care for someone, as part of one's job or role: *the cabinet minister* ***responsible for*** *Education.*

■being the primary cause of something and so able to be blamed or credited for it: *Gooch was responsible for 198 of his side's 542 runs.* ■ [attrib.] (of a job or position) involving important duties, independent decision-making, or control over others. ■ [predic.] (**responsible to**) having to report to (a superior or someone in authority) and be answerable to them for one's actions: *the Prime Minister and cabinet are responsible to Parliament.* ■ capable of being trusted: *a responsible adult.* ■ morally accountable for one's behaviour: *the progressive emergence of the child as a responsible being.*

– DERIVATIVES **responsibleness** noun, **responsibly** adverb.

– ORIGIN late 16th cent. (in the sense 'answering to, corresponding'): from obsolete French *responsible*, from Latin *respons-* 'answered, offered in return', from the verb *respondere* (see **RESPOND**).

responsive ▶ **adjective 1** reacting quickly and positively: *a flexible service that is* ***responsive to*** *changing social and economic patterns.*

■responding readily and with interest or enthusiasm: *our most enthusiastic and responsive students.*

2 answering: *I'm distracted by a nibble on my line: I jig it several times, but there is no responsive tug.*

■(of a section of liturgy) using responses.

– DERIVATIVES **responsively** adverb, **responsiveness** noun.

responsorial /ˌrɪspɒn'sɔːrɪəl/ ▶ **adjective** (of a psalm or liturgical chant) recited in parts with a congregational response between each part.

responsory /rɪ'spɒns(ə)ri/ ▶ **noun** (pl. **-ies**) (in the Christian Church) an anthem said or sung by a soloist and choir after a lesson.

– ORIGIN late Middle English: from late Latin *responsorium*, from Latin *respons-* 'answered' from the verb *respondere* (see **RESPOND**).

responsum /rɪ'spɒnsəm/ ▶ **noun** (pl. **responsa**

r

/rɪˈspɒnsə/) a written reply by a rabbi or Talmudic scholar to an inquiry on some matter of Jewish law.
– ORIGIN Latin, literally 'reply'.

respray ▶ **verb** /riːˈspreɪ/ [with obj.] spray (something, especially a vehicle) with a new coat of paint.
▶ **noun** /ˈriːspreɪ/ [in sing.] an instance of respraying something.

res publica /reɪz ˈpʊblɪkə, ˈpʌblɪkə/ ▶ **noun** the state, republic, or commonwealth.
– ORIGIN Latin, literally 'public matter'.

ressentiment /rəˈsɒ̃tɪmɒ̃/ ▶ **noun** [mass noun] a psychological state resulting from suppressed feelings of envy and hatred which cannot be satisfied.
– ORIGIN via German (used by Nietzsche in this sense) from French *ressentiment* 'feeling'.

rest[1] ▶ **verb** [no obj.] **1** cease work or movement in order to relax, refresh oneself, or recover strength: *he needed to rest after the feverish activity* | *I'm going to* **rest up** *before travelling to England.*
■ [with obj.] allow to be inactive in order to regain strength, health, or energy: *her friend read to her while she rested her eyes.* ■ (**be resting**) Brit. used euphemistically by actors to indicate that they are out of work. ■ [with obj.] leave (a player) out of a team temporarily: *both men were rested for the cup final.* ■ (of a dead person or body) lie buried: *the king's body rested in his tomb.* ■ (of a problem or subject) be left without further investigation, discussion, or treatment: *the council has urged the planning committee not to allow the matter to rest.* ■ [with obj.] allow (land) to lie fallow: *the field should be grazed or rested.* ■ N. Amer. conclude the case for the prosecution or the defence in a law case: *the prosecution rests.* See also ***rest one's case*** below.
2 [no obj., with adverbial of place] be placed or supported so as to stay in a specified position: *her elbow was resting on the arm of the sofa.*
■ [with obj. and adverbial of place] place (something) so that it is supported in a specified position: *he rested a hand on her shoulder.* ■ (**rest on/upon**) (of a look) alight or be steadily directed on: *his eyes rested briefly on the boy.* ■ (**rest on/upon**) be based on or grounded in; depend on: *the country's security rested on its alliances.* ■ [with obj.] (**rest something in/on**) place hope, trust, or confidence on or in: *she rested her hopes in her attorney.* ■ belong or be located at a specified place or with a specified person: *ultimate control rested with the founders.*
▶ **noun 1** an instance or period of relaxing or ceasing to engage in strenuous or stressful activity: *you look as though you need a rest* | [mass noun] *a couple of days of complete rest.*
■ [mass noun] refreshment through sleep: *she curled up in a corner to get some rest.* ■ [mass noun] a motionless state: *the car accelerates rapidly from rest.* ■ Music an interval of silence of a specified duration. ■ Music the sign denoting such an interval. ■ a pause in elocution. ■ a caesura in verse. ■ [in place names] a place where people can stay: *the Travellers Rest inn.*
2 [in combination] an object that is used to support something: *a chin-rest* | *a shoulder-rest.*
■ a support or hook for a telephone receiver when not in use. ■ a support for a cue in billiards or snooker.
– PHRASES **at rest** not moving or exerting oneself. ■ not agitated or troubled; tranquil: *he felt at rest, the tension gone.* ■ dead and buried. **come to rest** stop moving; settle: *the lift came to rest at the first floor.* **give it a rest** informal used to ask someone to stop doing something or talking about something that the speaker finds irritating or tedious. **no rest for the wicked** see **WICKED**. **put** (or **set**) **someone's mind** (or **doubts** or **fears**) **at rest** relieve someone of anxiety or uncertainty; reassure someone. **rest one's case** conclude one's presentation of evidence and arguments in a lawsuit. ■ humorous said to show that one believes one has presented sufficient evidence for one's views. **rest on one's laurels** see **LAUREL**. **rest** (or **God rest**) **his** (or **her**) **soul** used to express a wish that God should grant someone's soul peace.
– ORIGIN Old English *ræst, rest* (noun), *ræstan, restan* (verb), of Germanic origin, from a root meaning 'league' or 'mile' (referring to a distance after which one rests).

rest[2] ▶ **noun 1** [in sing.] the remaining part of something: *what do you want to do for the rest of your life?* | *I'll tell you the rest tomorrow night.*
■ [treated as pl.] the remaining people or things; the others: *the rest of us were experienced skiers.* ■ Anatomy a small, detached portion of an organ or tissue.
2 a rally in real tennis.
▶ **verb** [no obj., with complement] remain or be left in a specified condition: *you can rest assured she will do everything she can to help her.*
– PHRASES **and (all) the rest (of it)** and everything else that might be mentioned or that one could expect: *it's all very well to talk about natural affection and love and the rest of it.* **for the rest** as far as other matters are concerned; apart from that. **the rest is history** see **HISTORY**.
– ORIGIN late Middle English: from Old French *reste* (noun), *rester* (verb), from Latin *restare* 'remain', from *re-* 'back' + *stare* 'to stand'.

restage ▶ **verb** [with obj.] present (a performance or public event) again or differently.

restart ▶ **verb** start again: [no obj.] *the talks will restart in September* | [with obj.] *he tried to restart his stalled car.*
▶ **noun** [in sing.] a new start or beginning.

restate ▶ **verb** [with obj.] state (something) again or differently, especially more clearly or convincingly: *he restated his opposition to abortion.*
– DERIVATIVES **restatement** noun.

restaurant /ˈrɛst(ə)rɒnt, -r(ə)nt, -rɒ̃/ ▶ **noun** a place where people pay to sit and eat meals that are cooked and served on the premises.
– ORIGIN early 19th cent.: from French, from *restaurer* 'provide food for' (literally 'restore to a former state').

restaurant car ▶ **noun** a dining car.

restaurateur /ˌrɛst(ə)rəˈtəː, ˌrɛstɒr-/ ▶ **noun** a person who owns and manages a restaurant.
– ORIGIN late 18th cent.: French, from the verb *restaurer* (see **RESTAURANT**).

> **USAGE** The word **restaurateur** is taken directly from the French form. A common misspelling is **restauranteur**, found in 20 per cent of citations for this word on the British National Corpus.

rest cure ▶ **noun** a period spent in inactivity or leisure with the intention of improving one's physical or mental health.

rest day ▶ **noun** a day spent in rest, especially as an interlude between periods of work or activity.
■ another term for **DAY OF REST**.

restenosis /ˌriːstɛˈnəʊsɪs/ ▶ **noun** [mass noun] Medicine the recurrence of abnormal narrowing of an artery or valve after corrective surgery.
– ORIGIN 1950s: from **RE-** 'again' + **STENOSIS**.

rest frame ▶ **noun** Physics a frame of reference relative to which a given body is at rest.

restful ▶ **adjective** having a quiet and soothing quality: *the rooms were cool and restful.*
– DERIVATIVES **restfully** adverb, **restfulness** noun.

restharrow ▶ **noun** a sticky Old World plant of the pea family, which has pink flowers and creeping woody stems with spines.
• Genus *Ononis*, family Leguminosae.
– ORIGIN mid 16th cent.: from obsolete *rest* 'stop, arrest' + **HARROW** (because the tough stems impeded the progress of a harrow).

rest home ▶ **noun** a residential institution where old or frail people are cared for.

rest house ▶ **noun** (in parts of Asia and Africa) a house or small hotel offering accommodation for travellers.

resting place ▶ **noun** a place in which a person or animal is able to rest for a short period, especially during a journey.
■ used in reference to the grave or death: *he would share her* **final resting place** *in the cemetery.*

resting potential ▶ **noun** Physiology the electrical potential of a neuron or other excitable cell relative to its surroundings when not stimulated or involved in passage of an impulse.

restitutio in integrum /rɛstɪˌtjuːtɪəʊ ɪn ɪnˈtɛɡrəm/ ▶ **noun** [mass noun] Law restoration of an injured party to the situation which would have prevailed had no injury been sustained; restoration to the original or pre-contractual position.
– ORIGIN Latin, literally 'restoration to the whole (i.e. uninjured) state'.

restitution ▶ **noun** [mass noun] **1** the restoration of something lost or stolen to its proper owner: *the ANC had demanded the restitution of land seized from blacks.*
2 recompense for injury or loss: *he was ordered to pay £6,000 in restitution.*
3 the restoration of something to its original state: *restitution of the damaged mucosa.*
■ Physics the resumption of an object's original shape or position through elastic recoil.
– DERIVATIVES **restitutive** adjective.
– ORIGIN Middle English: from Old French, or from Latin *restitutio(n-)*, from *restituere* 'restore', from *re-* 'again' + *statuere* 'establish'.

restive ▶ **adjective** (of a person) unable to keep still or silent and becoming increasingly difficult to control, especially because of impatience, dissatisfaction, or boredom.
■ (of a horse) refusing to advance, stubbornly standing still or moving backwards or sideways.
– DERIVATIVES **restively** adverb, **restiveness** noun.
– ORIGIN late 16th cent.: from Old French *restif, -ive*, from Latin *restare* 'remain'. The original sense, 'inclined to remain still, inert', has undergone a reversal; the association with the refractory movements of a horse gave rise to the current sense 'fidgety, restless'.

restless ▶ **adjective** (of a person or animal) unable to rest or relax as a result of anxiety or boredom: *the audience grew restless and inattentive.*
■ offering no physical or emotional rest; involving constant activity or motion: *a restless night.*
– DERIVATIVES **restlessly** adverb, **restlessness** noun.
– ORIGIN Old English *restlēas* (see **REST**[1], **-LESS**).

rest mass ▶ **noun** Physics the mass of a body when at rest.

restock ▶ **verb** [with obj.] replenish (a store) with fresh stock or supplies: *work began at once to restock the fishery.*

restoration ▶ **noun** [mass noun] **1** the action of returning something to a former owner, place, or condition: *the restoration of Andrew's sight.*
■ the process of repairing or renovating a building, work of art, vehicle, etc., so as to restore it to its original condition: *the altar paintings seem in need of restoration.* ■ the reinstatement of a previous practice, right, custom, or situation: *the restoration of capital punishment.* ■ [count noun] Dentistry a structure provided to replace or repair dental tissue so as to restore its form and function, such as a filling, crown, or bridge. ■ [count noun] a model or drawing representing the supposed original form of an extinct animal, ruined building, etc.
2 the return of a hereditary monarch to a throne, a head of state to government, or a regime to power.
■ (**the Restoration**) the re-establishment of Charles II as King of England in 1660. After the death of Oliver Cromwell in 1658, his son Richard (1626–1712) proved incapable of maintaining the Protectorate, and General Monck organized the king's return from exile. ■ (**Restoration**) [usu. as modifier] the period following this, especially with regard to its literature or architecture: *Restoration drama.* ■ (**the Restoration**) the restoration of the Bourbon monarchy in France in 1814, following the fall of Napoleon. Louis XVIII was recalled from exile by Talleyrand.
– ORIGIN late 15th cent. (denoting the action of restoring to a former state): partly from Old French, partly an alteration of obsolete *restauration* (from late Latin *restauratio(n-)*, from the verb *restaurare*), suggested by **RESTORE**.

Restoration comedy ▶ **noun** [mass noun] a style of drama which flourished in London after the Restoration in 1660, typically having a complicated plot marked by wit, cynicism, and licentiousness. Principal exponents include William Congreve, William Wycherley, George Farquhar, and Sir John Vanbrugh.

restorationism ▶ **noun** [mass noun] a charismatic Christian movement seeking to restore the beliefs and practices of the early Church.
– DERIVATIVES **restorationist** noun & adjective.

restorative ▶ **adjective** having the ability to restore health, strength, or a feeling of well-being: *the restorative power of long walks.*
■ Surgery & Dentistry relating to or concerned with the restoration of form or function to a damaged tooth or other part of the body.
▶ **noun** something, especially a medicine or drink, that restores health, strength, or well-being.
– DERIVATIVES **restoratively** adverb.
– ORIGIN late Middle English: from an Old French variant of *restauratif, -ive*, from *restorer* (see **RESTORE**).

restore ▶ **verb** [with obj.] bring back (a previous right, practice, custom, or situation); reinstate: *the government restored confidence in the housing market.*
■ return (someone or something) to a former

condition, place, or position: *the effort to* **restore** *him* **to** *office isn't working.* ■ repair or renovate (a building, work of art, vehicle, etc.) so as to return it to its original condition: *the building has been lovingly restored.* ■ give (something previously stolen, taken away, or lost) back to the original owner or recipient: *the government will* **restore** *land and property* **to** *those who lost it through confiscation.*

– DERIVATIVES **restorable** adjective, **restorer** noun.

– ORIGIN Middle English: from Old French *restorer*, from Latin *restaurare* 'rebuild, restore'.

restrain ▶ **verb** [with obj.] prevent (someone or something) from doing something; keep under control or within limits: *he had to be* **restrained from** *walking out of the meeting* | [as adj. **restraining**] *Cara put a restraining hand on his arm.*

■ prevent oneself from displaying or giving way to (a strong urge or emotion: *Amiss had to restrain his impatience.* ■ deprive (someone) of freedom of movement or personal liberty: *leg cuffs are used in the US for restraining and transporting extremely violent and dangerous criminals.* ■ (of a seat belt) hold (a person or part of their body) down and back while in a vehicle seat.

– DERIVATIVES **restrainable** adjective, **restrainer** noun.

– ORIGIN Middle English: from Old French *restreign-*, stem of *restreindre*, from Latin *restringere*, from *re-* 'back' + *stringere* 'to tie, pull tight'.

restrained ▶ **adjective** characterized by reserve or moderation; unemotional or dispassionate: *he had restrained manners.*

■ (of colour, clothes, decoration, etc.) understated and subtle; not excessively showy or ornate. ■ kept under control; prevented from freedom of movement or action: *a patch of land turned into a restrained wilderness.* ■ (of a person) held down and back in a vehicle seat by a seat belt.

– DERIVATIVES **restrainedly** adverb.

restraint ▶ **noun 1** (often **restraints**) a measure or condition that keeps someone or something under control or within limits: *decisions are made within the financial restraints of the budget.*

■ [mass noun] the action of keeping someone or something under control. ■ [mass noun] deprivation or restriction of personal liberty or freedom of movement: *he remained aggressive and required physical restraint.* ■ a device which limits or prevents freedom of movement: *car safety restraints.*

2 [mass noun] unemotional, dispassionate, or moderate behaviour; self-control: *he urged the protestors to exercise restraint.*

■ understatement, especially of artistic expression: *with strings and piano, all restraint vanished.*

– ORIGIN late Middle English: from Old French *restreinte*, feminine past participle of *restreindre* 'hold back' (see **RESTRAIN**).

restraint of trade ▶ **noun** [mass noun] Law action that interferes with free competition in a market.

■ [count noun] a clause in a contract that restricts a person's right to carry on their trade or profession.

restrict ▶ **verb** [with obj.] put a limit on; keep under control: *some roads may have to be closed at peak times to restrict the number of visitors.*

■ deprive (someone or something) of freedom of movement or action: *cities can* **restrict** *groups of protesters* **from** *gathering on a residential street.* ■ (**restrict someone to**) limit someone to only doing or having (a particular thing) or staying in (a particular place): *I shall restrict myself to a single example.* ■ (**restrict something to**) limit something, especially an activity, to (a particular place, time, or category of people): *the Zoological Gardens were at first restricted to members and their guests.* ■ withhold (information) from general circulation or disclosure: *at first the Americans tried to restrict news of their involvement in Vietnam.*

– ORIGIN mid 16th cent.: from Latin *restrict-* 'confined, bound fast', from the verb *restringere* (see **RESTRAIN**).

restricted ▶ **adjective** [attrib.] limited in extent, number, scope, or action: *Western scientists had only restricted access to the site.*

■ (of a document or information) for limited circulation and not to be revealed to the public for reasons of national security. ■ Biology (of a virus) unable to reproduce at its normal rate in certain hosts. ■ Biochemistry (of DNA) subject to degradation by a restriction enzyme.

– DERIVATIVES **restrictedly** adverb, **restrictedness** noun.

restricted area ▶ **noun** an area in which activity is restricted in a number of ways, in particular:

■ Brit. an area in which there is a speed limit for vehicles. ■ N. Amer. an area which unauthorized people are not allowed to enter.

restriction ▶ **noun** (often **restrictions**) a limiting condition or measure, especially a legal one: *planning restrictions on commercial development.*

■ [mass noun] the limitation or control of someone or something, or the state of being limited or restricted: *the restriction of local government power.*

– DERIVATIVES **restrictionism** noun, **restrictionist** adjective & noun.

– ORIGIN late Middle English: from Old French, or from Latin *restrictio(n-)*, from *restringere* 'bind fast, confine' (see **RESTRICT**).

restriction enzyme (also **restriction endonuclease**) ▶ **noun** Biochemistry an enzyme produced chiefly by certain bacteria, that has the property of cleaving DNA molecules at or near a specific sequence of bases.

restriction fragment ▶ **noun** Biochemistry a fragment of a DNA molecule that has been cleaved by a restriction enzyme.

restriction fragment length polymorphism ▶ **noun** Genetics a variation in the length of restriction fragments produced by a given restriction enzyme in a sample of DNA. Such variation is used in forensic investigations and to map hereditary disease.

restrictive ▶ **adjective 1** imposing restrictions or limitations on someone's activities or freedom: *a web of restrictive regulations.*

2 Grammar (of a relative clause or descriptive phrase) serving to specify the particular instance or instances being mentioned.

– DERIVATIVES **restrictively** adverb, **restrictiveness** noun.

> **USAGE** What is the difference between *the books which were on the table once belonged to my aunt* and *the books, which were on the table, once belonged to my aunt*? In the first sentence the speaker uses the relative clause to pick out a subset of books (the ones on the table) and imply a contrast with some other set of books. In the second sentence the size of the set of books referred to is unaffected by the relative clause; the speaker merely offers the additional information that they happen to be on the table.
> This distinction is between **restrictive** and **non-restrictive** relative clauses. In writing, a non-restrictive relative clause is set off within commas, while in speech the difference is expressed by a difference in intonation. Ignorance of the distinction can lead to unintentionally comic effects: for example, strictly speaking, the relative clause in *if you are in need of assistance, please ask any member of staff who will be pleased to help* implies contrast with another set of staff who will not be pleased to help. A comma is needed before **who**.

restrictive covenant ▶ **noun** Law a covenant imposing a restriction on the use of land so that the value and enjoyment of adjoining land will be preserved.

restrictive practice ▶ **noun** Brit. an arrangement by a group of workers to limit output or restrict the entry of new workers in order to protect their own interests.

■ an arrangement in industry or trade that restricts or controls competition between firms.

restring ▶ **verb** (past and past participle **restrung**) [with obj.] **1** fit new or different strings to (a musical instrument or sports racket).

2 thread (objects such as beads) on a new string.

restroom ▶ **noun 1** Brit. a room, especially in a public building, for people to relax or recover in.

2 chiefly N. Amer. a toilet in a public building.

restructure ▶ **verb** [with obj.] organize differently: *a plan to strengthen and restructure the EC.*

■ Finance convert (the debt of a business in difficulty) into another kind of debt, typically one that is repayable at a later time.

restudy ▶ **verb** (**-ies**, **-ied**) [with obj.] study (something) again.

▶ **noun** an instance of studying something again.

restyle ▶ **verb** [with obj.] **1** rearrange or remake in a new shape or layout: *Nick restyled Rebecca's hair.*

2 give a new designation to: [with obj. and complement] *BR's Network SouthEast division has restyled the branch the Lovejoy Line.*

▶ **noun** an instance of reshaping or rearranging something.

■ a new shape or arrangement.

resubmit ▶ **verb** [with obj.] submit (something, such as a plan, application, or resignation) again.

– DERIVATIVES **resubmission** noun.

result ▶ **noun** a consequence, effect, or outcome of something: *the tower collapsed* **as a result of** *safety violations.*

■ an item of information obtained by experiment or some other scientific method; a quantity or formula obtained by calculation. ■ (often **results**) a final score, mark, or placing in a sporting event or examination. ■ (often **results**) a satisfactory or favourable outcome of an undertaking or contest: *determination and persistence guarantee results.* ■ (usu. **results**) the outcome of a business's trading over a given period, expressed as a statement of profit or loss: *oil companies have reported markedly better results.*

▶ **verb** [no obj.] occur or follow as the consequence of something: *government unpopularity* **resulting from** *the state of the economy* | [as adj. **resulting**] *talk of a general election and the resulting political uncertainty.*

■ (**result in**) have (a specified end or outcome): *talks in July had resulted in stalemate.*

– PHRASES **without result** in vain: *Denny had inquired about getting work, without result.*

– ORIGIN late Middle English (as a verb): from medieval Latin *resultare* 'to result', earlier in the sense 'spring back', from *re-* (expressing intensive force) + *saltare* (frequentative of *salire* 'to jump'). The noun dates from the early 17th cent.

resultant ▶ **adjective** [attrib.] occurring or produced as a result or consequence of something: *restructuring and the resultant cost savings.*

▶ **noun** technical a force, velocity, or other vector quantity which is equivalent to the combined effect of two or more component vectors acting at the same point.

– ORIGIN mid 17th cent. (in the adjectival sense): from Latin *resultant-* 'springing back', from the verb *resultare* (see **RESULT**). The noun sense dates from the early 19th cent.

resultative Grammar ▶ **adjective** expressing, indicating, or relating to the outcome of an action.

▶ **noun** a resultative verb, conjunction, or clause.

resume ▶ **verb** [with obj.] begin to do or pursue (something) again after a pause or interruption: *a day later normal service was resumed.*

■ [no obj.] begin to be done, pursued, or used again after a pause or interruption: *hostilities had ceased and normal life had resumed.* ■ [no obj.] begin speaking again after a pause or interruption: *he sipped at the glass of water on the lectern and then resumed* | [with direct speech] *'As for Joe,' the Major resumed, 'I can't promise anything.'* ■ take, pick up, or put on again; return to the use of: *the judge resumed his seat.*

▶ **noun** N. Amer. variant spelling of **RÉSUMÉ** (in sense 2).

– DERIVATIVES **resumable** adjective, **resumption** noun.

– ORIGIN late Middle English: from Old French *resumer* or Latin *resumere*, from *re-* 'back' + *sumere* 'take'.

resumé /ˈrɛzjʊmeɪ/ ▶ **noun 1** a summary: *I gave him a quick résumé of events.*

2 N. Amer. a curriculum vitae.

– ORIGIN early 19th cent.: French *résumé*, literally 'resumed', past participle (used as a noun) of *résumer*.

resumptive ▶ **adjective** Grammar indicating resumption of a topic having previous reference.

resupinate /rɪˈsuːpɪneɪt, -ˈsjuː-/ ▶ **adjective** Botany (of a leaf, flower, fruiting body, etc.) upside down.

– DERIVATIVES **resupination** noun.

– ORIGIN late 18th cent.: from Latin *resupinatus* 'bent back', past participle of *resupinare*, based on *supinus* 'lying on the back'.

resupply ▶ **verb** (**-ies**, **-ied**) [with obj.] provide with a fresh supply: *he planned to use 216 Squadron to resupply his force.*

■ [no obj.] take on or acquire a fresh supply: *phase two envisaged a period to regroup and resupply.*

▶ **noun** an act or resupplying something or being resupplied.

resurface ▶ **verb 1** [with obj.] put a new coating on or reform (a surface such as a road, a floor, or ice).

2 [no obj.] come back up to the surface: *he resurfaced beside the boat.*

■ arise or become evident again: *serious concerns about the welfare of animals eventually resurfaced.* ■ (of a person) come out of hiding or obscurity: *he resurfaced under a false identity in Australia.*

resurgence ▶ **noun** [in sing.] an increase or revival

after a period of little activity, popularity, or occurrence: *a resurgence of interest in religion.*

resurgent ▶ **adjective** increasing or reviving after a period of little activity, popularity, or occurrence: *resurgent nationalism.*
– ORIGIN early 19th cent. (earlier as a noun): from Latin *resurgent-* 'rising again', from the verb *resurgere*, from *re-* 'again' + *surgere* 'to rise'.

resurrect ▶ **verb** [with obj.] restore (a dead person) to life: *he queried whether Jesus was indeed resurrected.*
■ revive the practice, use, or memory of (something); bring new vigour to: *the deal collapsed and has yet to be resurrected.*
– ORIGIN late 18th cent.: back-formation from **RESURRECTION**.

resurrection ▶ **noun** [mass noun] the action or fact of resurrecting or being resurrected: *the story of the resurrection of Osiris.*
■ (**the Resurrection**) (in Christian belief) Christ's rising from the dead. ■ (**the Resurrection**) (in Christian belief) the rising of the dead at the Last Judgement. ■ the revitalization or revival of something: *the resurrection of the country under a charismatic leader* | [count noun] *resurrections of long-forgotten scandals.*
– ORIGIN Middle English: from Old French, from late Latin *resurrectio(n-)*, from the verb *resurgere* 'rise again' (see **RESURGENT**).

resurrection man ▶ **noun** historical a person who illicitly retrieved corpses for dissection from rivers, scenes of disaster, or burial grounds.

resurrection plant ▶ **noun** any of a number of plants which are able to survive drought, typically folding up when dry and unfolding when moistened, in particular:
• a fern of tropical and warm-temperate America (*Polypodium polypodioides*, family Polypodiaceae). • a Californian clubmoss (*Selaginella lepidophylla*, family Selaginellaceae). • the Rose of Jericho.

resurvey ▶ **verb** [with obj.] survey (a district) again.
■ redraw (a map) after surveying a district again. ■ study or investigate again: *the same people surveyed in 1992 will be resurveyed periodically.*
▶ **noun** an act of surveying a district or studying something again.

resuscitate /rɪˈsʌsɪteɪt/ ▶ **verb** [with obj.] revive (someone) from unconsciousness or apparent death: *an ambulance crew tried to resuscitate him.*
■ figurative make (something such as an idea or enterprise) active or vigorous again: *measures to resuscitate the ailing Japanese economy.*
– DERIVATIVES **resuscitation** noun, **resuscitative** adjective, **resuscitator** noun.
– ORIGIN early 16th cent.: from Latin *resuscitat-* 'raised again', from the verb *resuscitare*, from *re-* 'back' + *suscitare* 'raise'.

ret /rɛt/ (also **rate**) ▶ **verb** (**retted**, **retting**) [with obj.] soak (flax or hemp) in water to soften it.
– ORIGIN late Middle English: related to Dutch *reten*, also to **ROT**.

ret. ▶ **abbreviation for** retired.

retable /rɪˈteɪb(ə)l/ (also **retablo** /rɪˈtɑːbləʊ/) ▶ **noun** (pl. **retables** or **retablos**) a frame or shelf enclosing decorated panels or revered objects above and behind an altar.
■ a painting or other image in such a position.
– ORIGIN early 19th cent.: from French *rétable*, from Spanish *retablo*, from medieval Latin *retrotabulum* 'rear table', from Latin *retro* 'backwards' + *tabula* 'table'.

retail /ˈriːteɪl/ ▶ **noun** [mass noun] the sale of goods to the public in relatively small quantities for use or consumption rather than for resale: [as modifier] *the product's retail price.*
▶ **adverb** being sold in such a way: *it is not yet available retail.*
▶ **verb** /also rɪˈteɪl/ [with obj.] **1** sell (goods) to the public in such a way: *the difficulties in retailing the new products.*
■ [no obj.] (**retail at/for**) (of goods) be sold in this way for (a specified price): *the product retails for around £20.*
2 recount or relate details of (a story or event) to others: *his inimitable way of retailing a diverting anecdote.*
– DERIVATIVES **retailer** noun.
– ORIGIN late Middle English: from an Anglo-Norman French use of Old French *retaille* 'a piece cut off', from *retaillier*, from *re-* (expressing intensive force) + *tailler* 'to cut'.

retail price index (abbrev.: **RPI**) ▶ **noun** (in the UK) an index of the variation in the prices of retail goods and other items.

retail price maintenance ▶ **noun** another term for **RESALE PRICE MAINTENANCE**.

retain ▶ **verb** continue to have (something); keep possession of: *Labour retained the seat* | *built in 1830, the house retains many of its original features.*
■ not abolish, discard, or alter: *the rights of defendants must be retained.* ■ keep in one's memory: *I retained a few French words and phrases.* ■ absorb and continue to hold (a substance): *limestone is known to retain water.* ■ [often as adj. **retaining**] keep (something) in place; hold fixed: *remove the retaining bar.* ■ keep (someone) engaged in one's service: *he has been retained as a freelance.* ■ secure the services of (a person, especially a barrister) with a preliminary payment: *retain a barrister to handle the client's business.*
– DERIVATIVES **retainability** noun, **retainable** adjective, **retainment** noun.
– ORIGIN late Middle English: via Anglo-Norman French from Old French *retenir*, from Latin *retinere*, from *re-* 'back' + *tenere* 'hold'.

retainer ▶ **noun 1** a thing that holds something in place: *a guitar string retainer.*
■ an appliance for keeping a loose tooth or orthodontic prosthesis in place.
2 a fee paid in advance to someone, especially a barrister, in order to secure or keep their services when required.
■ Brit. a reduced rent paid to retain accommodation during a period of non-occupancy.
3 a servant or follower of a noble or wealthy person, especially one that has worked for a person or family for a long time.

retaining fee ▶ **noun** another term for **RETAINER** (in sense 2).

retaining wall ▶ **noun** a wall that holds back earth or water on one side of it.

retake ▶ **verb** (past **retook**; past participle **retaken**) [with obj.] take again, in particular:
■ take (a test or examination) again after a failure or irregularity: *Dawn had to retake her driving test.* ■ recapture: *in 799 the Moors retook Barcelona.* ■ regain possession of (something left or lost): *he retook the world driver's championship.*
▶ **noun** a thing that is retaken, especially a test or examination.
■ an instance of filming a scene or recording a piece of music again.

retaliate /rɪˈtalɪeɪt/ ▶ **verb** [no obj.] make an attack or assault in return for a similar attack: *the blow stung and she retaliated immediately.*
■ [with obj.] archaic repay (an injury or insult) in kind: *they used their abilities to retaliate the injury.*
– DERIVATIVES **retaliation** noun, **retaliative** adjective, **retaliator** noun, **retaliatory** adjective.
– ORIGIN early 17th cent.: from Latin *retaliat-* 'returned in kind', from the verb *retaliare*, from *re-* 'back' + *talis* 'such'.

retard ▶ **verb** /rɪˈtɑːd/ [with obj.] delay or hold back in terms of progress, development, or accomplishment: *his progress was retarded by his limp.*
▶ **noun** /ˈriːtɑːd/ offensive a mentally handicapped person (often used as a general term of abuse).
– PHRASES **in retard** Brit. formal behind or late in terms of development or progress: *I was **in retard of** them in real knowledge.*
– DERIVATIVES **retardation** noun, **retarder** noun, **retardment** noun (rare).
– ORIGIN late 15th cent.: from French *retarder*, from Latin *retardare*, from *re-* 'back' + *tardus* 'slow'.

retardant ▶ **adjective** [in combination] (chiefly of a synthetic or treated fabric or substance) not readily susceptible to fire: *fire-retardant polymers.*
▶ **noun** a fabric or substance that prevents or inhibits something, especially the outbreak of fire.
– DERIVATIVES **retardancy** noun.

retardataire /rɪˌtɑːdəˈtɛː/ ▶ **adjective** (of a work of art or architecture) executed in an earlier or outdated style.
– ORIGIN French.

retardate /rɪˈtɑːdeɪt/ ▶ **noun** N. Amer., dated or offensive a mentally handicapped person.
– ORIGIN 1950s: from Latin *retardat-* 'slowed down', from the verb *retardare* (see **RETARD**).

retarded ▶ **adjective** less advanced in mental, physical, or social development than is usual for one's age.

retch ▶ **verb** [no obj.] make the sound and movement of vomiting.
■ vomit.
▶ **noun** a movement or sound of vomiting.
– ORIGIN mid 19th cent.: variant of dialect *reach*, from a Germanic base meaning 'spittle'.

retd (also **ret.**) ▶ **abbreviation for** retired (used after the name of a retired armed forces officer or in recording that a sports player retired from a game).

rete /ˈriːti/ ▶ **noun** (pl. **retia** /-tɪə, -ʃɪə/) Anatomy an elaborate network of blood vessels or nerve cells.
– ORIGIN mid 16th cent.: from Latin *rete* 'net'.

retell ▶ **verb** (past and past participle **retold**) [with obj.] tell (a story) again or differently: *Walker retells the history of the world from the black perspective.*

retention ▶ **noun** [mass noun] the continued possession, use, or control of something: *the retention of direct control by central government.*
■ the fact of keeping something in one's memory: *the children's retention of facts.* ■ the action of absorbing and continuing to hold a substance: *the soil's retention of moisture.* ■ failure to eliminate a substance from the body: *eating too much salt can lead to fluid retention.*
– ORIGIN late Middle English (denoting the power to retain something): from Old French, from Latin *retentio(n-)*, from *retinere* 'hold back' (see **RETAIN**).

retentive ▶ **adjective 1** (of a person's memory) having the ability to remember facts and impressions easily.
2 (of a substance) able to absorb and hold moisture.
■ chiefly Medicine serving to keep something in place.
– DERIVATIVES **retentively** adverb, **retentiveness** noun.
– ORIGIN late Middle English: from Old French *retentif, -ive* or medieval Latin *retentivus*, from *retent-* 'held back', from the verb *retinere* (see **RETAIN**).

retentivity ▶ **noun** (pl. **-ies**) Physics the ability of a substance to retain or resist magnetization, frequently measured as the strength of the magnetic field that remains in a sample after removal of an inducing field.

retexture ▶ **verb** [with obj.] treat (material or a garment) so as to restore firmness to its texture.

rethink ▶ **verb** (past and past participle **rethought**) [with obj.] think again about (something such as a policy or course of action), especially in order to make changes to it: *the Government were forced to rethink their plans* | [no obj.] *I've had to rethink.*
▶ **noun** [in sing.] a reassessment of something, especially one that results in changes being made: *a last-minute rethink of their tactics.*

Rethymnon /ˈrɛθɪmnɒn/ a port on the north coast of Crete; pop. 17,700 (1981). Greek name **RÉTHIMNON** /ˈrɛθimnɔn/.

retia plural form of **RETE**.

retiarius /ˌrɛtɪˈɑːrɪəs, -ˈɛːrɪəs/ ▶ **noun** (pl. **retiarii** /-rɪʌɪ, -rɪiː/) an ancient Roman gladiator who used a net to trap his opponent.
– ORIGIN Latin, from *rete* 'net'.

reticent /ˈrɛtɪs(ə)nt/ ▶ **adjective** not revealing one's thoughts or feelings readily: *she was extremely reticent about her personal affairs.*
– DERIVATIVES **reticence** noun, **reticently** adverb.
– ORIGIN mid 19th cent.: from Latin *reticent-* 'remaining silent', from the verb *reticere*, from *re-* (expressing intensive force) + *tacere* 'be silent'.

reticle /ˈrɛtɪk(ə)l/ ▶ **noun** North American term for **GRATICULE**.
– ORIGIN mid 18th cent.: from Latin *reticulum* 'net'.

reticula plural form of **RETICULUM**.

reticular formation (also **reticular activating system**) ▶ **noun** Anatomy a diffuse network of nerve pathways in the brainstem connecting the spinal cord, cerebrum, and cerebellum, and mediating the overall level of consciousness.

reticulate ▶ **verb** /rɪˈtɪkjʊleɪt/ [with obj.] rare divide or mark (something) in such a way as to resemble a net or network: *the numerous canals and branches of the river reticulate the flat alluvial plain.*
▶ **adjective** /rɪˈtɪkjʊlət/ chiefly Botany & Zoology reticulated.
– ORIGIN mid 17th cent.: from Latin *reticulatus* 'reticulated', from *reticulum* (see **RETICULUM**).

reticulated ▶ **adjective** [attrib.] constructed, arranged, or marked like a net or network: *a pinafore of a finely reticulated pattern.*
■ (of porcelain) having a pattern of interlacing lines, especially of pierced work, forming a net or web. ■ Architecture relating to or denoting a style of

decorated tracery characterized by circular shapes drawn at top and bottom into ogees, resulting in a net-like framework. ■ divided into small squares or sections: *a ranch-style brick home set among reticulated grounds.*

reticulated python ▶ **noun** a very large Asian python patterned with dark patches outlined in black. It is the longest snake at up to 11 m.
• *Python reticulatus*, family Pythonidae.

reticulation ▶ **noun** [mass noun] a pattern or arrangement of interlacing lines resembling a net: *the fish should have a blue back with white reticulation.*
■ [count noun] chiefly Austral./NZ a network of pipes used in irrigation and water supply. ■ Photography the formation of a network of wrinkles or cracks in a photographic emulsion.

reticule /ˈrɛtɪkjuːl/ ▶ **noun 1** chiefly historical a woman's small handbag, typically having a drawstring and decorated with embroidery or beading.
2 variant spelling of **RETICLE**.
– ORIGIN early 18th cent.: from French *réticule*, from Latin *reticulum* (see **RETICULUM**).

reticulin /rɪˈtɪkjʊlɪn/ ▶ **noun** [mass noun] Biochemistry a structural protein resembling collagen, present in connective tissue as a network of fine fibres, especially around muscle and nerve fibres.
– ORIGIN late 19th cent.: from *reticular* (see **RETICULUM**) + **-IN**[1].

reticulocyte /rɪˈtɪkjʊlə(ʊ)sʌɪt/ ▶ **noun** Physiology an immature red blood cell without a nucleus, having a granular or reticulated appearance when suitably stained.
– ORIGIN 1920s: from **RETICULATED** + **-CYTE**.

reticuloendothelial /rɪˌtɪkjʊləʊɛndə(ʊ)ˈθiːlɪəl/ ▶ **adjective** [attrib.] Physiology relating to or denoting a diverse system of fixed and circulating phagocytic cells (macrophages and monocytes) involved in the immune response. They are spread throughout the body, and are especially common in the liver, spleen, and lymphatic system. Also called **LYMPHORETICULAR**.
– ORIGIN 1920s: from **RETICULUM** + *endothelial* (see **ENDOTHELIUM**).

reticuloendotheliosis /rɪˌtɪkjʊləʊɛndə(ʊ)ˈθiːlɪəʊsɪs/ ▶ **noun** [mass noun] Medicine overgrowth of some part of the reticuloendothelial system, causing isolated swelling of the bone marrow and in severe cases the destruction of the bones of the skull.

Reticulum /rɪˈtɪkjʊləm/ Astronomy a small southern constellation (the Net), between Dorado and Hydrus.
■ [as genitive **Reticuli** /rɪˈtɪkjʊlʌɪ/] used with preceding letter or numeral to designate a star in this constellation: *the star Beta Reticuli.*
– ORIGIN Latin, diminutive of *rete* 'net'.

reticulum /rɪˈtɪkjʊləm/ ▶ **noun** (pl. **reticula** /-lə/) **1** a fine network or net-like structure. See also **ENDOPLASMIC RETICULUM**.
2 Zoology the second stomach of a ruminant, having a honeycomb-like structure, receiving food from the rumen and passing it to the omasum.
– DERIVATIVES **reticular** adjective.
– ORIGIN mid 17th cent.: from Latin, diminutive of *rete* 'net'.

retie ▶ **verb** (**retying**) [with obj.] tie (something) again.

retiform /ˈriːtɪfɔːm, ˈrɛtɪ-/ ▶ **adjective** rare net-like.
– ORIGIN late 17th cent.: from Latin *rete* 'net' + **-IFORM**.

re-time ▶ **verb** [with obj.] set a different time for: *management would have re-timed jobs and cut the piece rates.*

retina /ˈrɛtɪnə/ ▶ **noun** (pl. **retinas** or **retinae** /-niː/) a layer at the back of the eyeball that contains cells sensitive to light, which trigger nerve impulses that pass via the optic nerve to the brain, where a visual image is formed.
– DERIVATIVES **retinal** adjective.
– ORIGIN late Middle English: from medieval Latin, from Latin *rete* 'net'.

retinitis /ˌrɛtɪˈnʌɪtɪs/ ▶ **noun** [mass noun] Medicine inflammation of the retina of the eye.

retinitis pigmentosa /ˌpɪgmɛnˈtəʊsə/ ▶ **noun** [mass noun] Medicine a chronic hereditary eye disease characterized by black pigmentation and gradual degeneration of the retina.
– ORIGIN mid 19th cent.: *pigmentosa*, feminine of Latin *pigmentosus*, from *pigmentum* 'pigment'.

retinoblastoma /ˌrɛtɪnəʊblaˈstəʊmə/ ▶ **noun** [mass noun] Medicine a rare malignant tumour of the retina, affecting young children.

retinoid /ˈrɛtɪnɔɪd/ ▶ **noun** Biochemistry any of a group of compounds having effects in the body like those of vitamin A.

retinol /ˈrɛtɪnɒl/ ▶ **noun** [mass noun] Biochemistry a yellow compound found in green and yellow vegetables, egg yolk, and fish-liver oil. It is essential for growth and vision in dim light. Also called **VITAMIN A**.
• A carotenoid alcohol; chem. formula: $C_{20}H_{29}OH$.
– ORIGIN 1960s: from **RETINA** + **-OL**.

retinopathy /ˌrɛtɪˈnɒpəθi/ ▶ **noun** [mass noun] Medicine disease of the retina which results in impairment or loss of vision.

retinotopic /ˌrɛtɪnə(ʊ)ˈtɒpɪk/ ▶ **adjective** Physiology relating to or preserving the spatial relations of the sensory receptors of the retina.
– DERIVATIVES **retinotopically** adverb.

retinue /ˈrɛtɪnjuː/ ▶ **noun** a group of advisers, assistants, or others accompanying an important person.
– ORIGIN late Middle English: from Old French *retenue*, feminine past participle (used as a noun) of *retenir* 'keep back, retain'.

retiral /rɪˈtʌɪr(ə)l/ ▶ **noun** (in Scotland) a person's retirement from a job or office.

retire ▶ **verb 1** [no obj.] leave one's job and cease to work, typically upon reaching the normal age for leaving service: *he retired from the Navy in 1966.*
■ [with obj.] compel (an employee) to leave their job, especially before they have reached such an age: *the Home Office retired him.* ■ (of a sports player) cease to play competitively: *he retired from football several years ago.* ■ (of a sports player) withdraw from a race or match, typically as a result of accident or injury: *he was forced to retire with a damaged oil tank* | [with complement] *Stewart retired hurt.* ■ [with obj.] Baseball put out (a batter); cause (a side) to end a turn at bat: *Dopson retired twelve batters in a row.* ■ [with obj.] Economics withdraw (a bill or note) from circulation or currency. ■ Finance pay off or cancel (a debt): *the debt is to be retired from state gaming-tax receipts.*
2 withdraw to or from a particular place: *she retired into the bathroom with her toothbrush.*
■ (of a military force) retreat from an enemy or an attacking position: *lack of numbers compelled the British force to retire.* ■ [with obj.] order (a military force) to retreat: *the general retired all his troops.* ■ (of a jury) leave the courtroom to decide the verdict of a trial. ■ go to bed: *everyone retired early that night.*
– DERIVATIVES **retirer** noun.
– ORIGIN mid 16th cent. (in the sense 'withdraw (to a place of safety or seclusion)'): from French *retirer*, from *re-* 'back' + *tirer* 'draw'.

retiré /rəˈtɪəreɪ/ ▶ **noun** (pl. pronounced same) Ballet a movement in which one leg is raised at right angles to the body until the toe is in line with the knee of the supporting leg.
– ORIGIN French, literally 'drawn back'.

retired ▶ **adjective 1** [attrib.] having left one's job and ceased to work: *a retired headmaster.*
2 archaic (of a place) quiet and secluded; not seen or frequented by many people: *this retired corner of the world.*
■ (of a person's way of life) quiet and involving little contact with other people. ■ (of a person) reserved; uncommunicative.
– DERIVATIVES **retiredness** noun (archaic).

retirement ▶ **noun** [mass noun] **1** the action or fact of leaving one's job and ceasing to work: *a man nearing retirement* | [count noun] *the library has seen a large number of retirements this year.*
■ the period of one's life after leaving one's job and ceasing to work: *he spent much of his retirement travelling in Europe.* ■ the action or fact of ceasing to play a sport competitively.
2 the withdrawal of a jury from the courtroom to decide their verdict.
■ [count noun] the period of time during which a jury decides their verdict: *a three-hour retirement.*
3 seclusion: *he lived in retirement in Kent.*
■ [count noun] archaic a secluded or private place: *Exmouth, where he has a sweet country retirement.*

retirement home ▶ **noun** a house or flat in which a person lives in old age, especially one in a group or block designed for the needs of old people.
■ an institution for elderly people needing care.

retirement pension ▶ **noun** Brit. a pension paid by the state to retired people above a certain age.

retiring ▶ **adjective** shy and fond of being on one's own: *a retiring, acquiescent woman.*
– DERIVATIVES **retiringly** adverb.

retitle ▶ **verb** [with obj.] (usu. **be retitled**) give a different title to.

retold past and past participle of **RETELL**.

retook past of **RETAKE**.

retool ▶ **verb** [with obj.] equip (a factory) with new or adapted tools.
■ chiefly N. Amer. adapt or alter (someone or something) to make them more useful or suitable: *he likes to retool the old stories to make them relevant for today's kids.* ■ [no obj.] adapt or prepare oneself for something: *perhaps one can even* **retool for** *the afterlife.*

retort[1] ▶ **verb 1** [reporting verb] say something in answer to a remark or accusation, typically in a sharp, angry, or wittily incisive manner: [with direct speech] *'No need to be rude,' retorted Isabel* | [with clause] *he retorted that this was nonsense* | [no obj.] *I resisted the urge to retort.*
2 [with obj.] archaic repay (an insult or injury): *it was now his time to retort the humiliation.*
■ turn (an insult or accusation) back on the person who has issued it: *he was resolute to retort the charge of treason on his foes.* ■ use (an opponent's argument) against them: *the answer they make to us may very easily be retorted.*
▶ **noun** a sharp, angry, or wittily incisive reply to a remark: *she opened her mouth to make a suitably cutting retort.*
– ORIGIN late 15th cent. (in the sense 'hurl back (an accusation or insult)'): from Latin *retort-* 'twisted back, cast back', from the verb *retorquere*, from *re-* 'in return' + *torquere* 'to twist'.

retort[2] ▶ **noun** a container or furnace for carrying out a chemical process on a large or industrial scale.
■ historical a glass container with a long neck, used in distilling liquids and other chemical operations.
▶ **verb** [with obj.] heat in a retort in order to separate or purify: *the raw shale is retorted at four crude oil works.*
– ORIGIN early 17th cent.: from French *retorte*, from medieval Latin *retorta*, feminine past participle of *retorquere* 'twist back' (with reference to the long recurved neck of the laboratory container).

retouch ▶ **verb** [with obj.] improve or repair (a painting, photograph, or other image) by making slight additions or alterations.
– DERIVATIVES **retoucher** noun.
– ORIGIN late 17th cent.: probably from French *retoucher*.

retrace ▶ **verb** [with obj.] go back over (the same route that one has just taken): *he began to* **retrace his steps** *to the station car park.*
■ discover and follow (a route or course taken by someone else): *I've tried to retrace some of her movements.* ■ trace (something) back to its source or beginning: *I wanted to retrace a particular evolutionary pathway.*
– ORIGIN late 17th cent.: from French *retracer*.

retract ▶ **verb** [with obj.] draw or pull (something) back or back in: *she retracted her hand as if she'd been burnt.*
■ withdraw (a statement or accusation) as untrue or unjustified: *he retracted his allegations.* ■ withdraw or go back on (an undertaking or promise): *the parish council was forced to retract a previous resolution.* ■ (of an animal) draw (a part of itself) back into its body: *the cat retracted her claws.* ■ draw (the undercarriage or the wheels) up into the body of an aircraft. ■ [no obj.] be drawn back into something: *the tentacle retracted quickly.*
– DERIVATIVES **retractable** adjective, **retraction** noun, **retractive** adjective.
– ORIGIN late Middle English: from Latin *retract-* 'drawn back', from the verb *retrahere* (from *re-* 'back' + *trahere* 'drag'); the senses 'withdraw (a statement)' and 'go back on' via Old French from *retractare* 'reconsider' (based on *trahere* 'drag').

retractile /rɪˈtraktʌɪl/ ▶ **adjective** Zoology capable of being retracted: *a long retractile proboscis.*
– DERIVATIVES **retractility** noun.
– ORIGIN late 18th cent.: from **RETRACT**, on the pattern of *contractile*.

retractor ▶ **noun** a device for retracting something: *seat belts with automatic retractors.*
■ (also **retractor muscle**) chiefly Zoology a muscle serving to retract a part of the body. Compare with **PROTRACTOR**.

retrain ▶ **verb** [with obj.] teach (someone) new skills, especially so that they can do a different job.

■[no obj.] learn new skills, especially so as to be able to do a different job: *a workforce which is willing to retrain.*

retranslate /ˌriːtransˈleɪt, -trɑːns-, -nz-/ ▶**verb** [with obj.] translate again.
– DERIVATIVES **retranslation** noun.

retransmit /ˌriːtranzˈmɪt, -trɑːnz-, -ns-/ ▶**verb** (**retransmitted, retransmitting**) [with obj.] transmit (data, a radio signal, or a broadcast programme) again or on to another receiver.
– DERIVATIVES **retransmission** /-ˈmɪʃ(ə)n/ noun.

retread ▶**verb 1** (past **retrod**; past participle **retrodden**) [with obj.] go back over (a path or one's steps): *they never retread the same ground.*
2 (past and past participle **retreaded**) [with obj.] put a new tread on (a worn tyre).
▶**noun** a tyre that has been given a new tread; a remould.
■informal a person retrained for new work or recalled for service. ■ informal a superficially altered version of an original: *a retread of the 30s romantic comedy.*

retreat ▶**verb** [no obj.] (of an army) withdraw from enemy forces as a result of their superior power or after a defeat: *the French retreated in disarray.*
■move back or withdraw, especially so as to remove oneself from a difficult or uncomfortable situation: *it becomes so hot that the lizards retreat into the shade* | [as adj. **retreating**] *the sound of retreating footsteps.* ■ withdraw to a quiet or secluded place: *after the funeral he retreated to Scotland.* ■ (of an expanse of ice or water) become smaller in size or extent: *a series of trenches which filled with water when the ice retreated.* ■ change one's decisions, plans, or attitude, especially as a result of criticism from others: *his proposals were clearly unreasonable and he was soon forced to retreat.* ■ (of shares) decline in value: [with complement] *shares retreated 32p to 653p.* ■ [with obj.] Chess move (a piece) back from a forward or threatened position on the board.
▶**noun 1** an act of moving back or withdrawing: *a speedy retreat* | [mass noun] *the army was **in retreat**.*
■an act of changing one's decisions, plans, or attitude, especially as a result of criticism from others: *the trade unions made a retreat from their earlier position.* ■ a decline in the value of shares.
2 a signal for a military force to withdraw: *the bugle sounded a retreat.*
■[mass noun] a military musical ceremony carried out at sunset, originating in the playing of drums and bugles to tell soldiers to return to camp for the night.
3 a quiet or secluded place in which one can rest and relax: *their country retreat in Ireland.*
■a period of seclusion for the purposes of prayer and meditation: *the bishop is away on his annual retreat* | [mass noun] *before his ordination he **went into retreat**.*
– PHRASES **beat a retreat** see **BEAT**.
– ORIGIN late Middle English: from Old French *retret* (noun), *retraiter* (verb), from Latin *retrahere* 'pull back' (see **RETRACT**).

retrench ▶**verb** [no obj.] (of a company, government, or individual) reduce costs or spending in response to economic difficulty: *as a result of the recession the company retrenched* | [with obj.] *if people are forced to retrench their expenditure trade will suffer.*
■[with obj.] chiefly Austral. make (an employee) redundant: *if there are excess staff they should be retrenched.* ■ [with obj.] formal reduce or diminish (something) in extent or quantity: *fortune had retrenched her once abundant gifts.*
– DERIVATIVES **retrenchment** noun.
– ORIGIN late 16th cent. (in the now formal usage): from obsolete French *retrencher*, variant of *retrancher*, from *re-* (expressing reversal) + *trancher* 'to cut, slice'.

retrial ▶**noun** Law a second or further trial.

retribution ▶**noun** [mass noun] punishment that is considered to be morally right and fully deserved: *settlers drove the Navajo out of Arizona **in retribution for** their raids.*
– DERIVATIVES **retributive** /rɪˈtrɪbjʊtɪv/ adjective, **retributory** /rɪˈtrɪbjʊt(ə)ri/ adjective.
– ORIGIN late Middle English (also in the sense 'recompense for merit or a service'): from late Latin *retributio(n-)*, from *retribut-* 'assigned again', from the verb *retribuere*, from *re-* 'back' + *tribuere* 'assign'.

retrieval ▶**noun** [mass noun] the process of getting something back from somewhere: *the investigation was completed after the retrieval of plane wreckage.*
■the obtaining or consulting of material stored in a computer system.

retrieve ▶**verb** [with obj.] get (something) back; regain possession of: *I was sent to retrieve the balls from his garden.*
■pick (something) up: *Steven stooped and retrieved his hat.* ■ (of a dog) find and bring back (game that has been shot). ■ bring (something) back into one's mind: *the police hope to encourage him to retrieve forgotten memories.* ■ find or extract (information stored in a computer). ■ put right or improve (an unwelcome situation): *he made one last desperate attempt to retrieve the situation.* ■ [no obj.] reel or bring in a fishing line.
▶**noun 1** an act of retrieving something, especially game that has been shot.
■an act of reeling or drawing in a fishing line.
2 [mass noun] archaic the possibility of recovery: *he ruined himself **beyond retrieve**.*
– DERIVATIVES **retrievability** noun, **retrievable** adjective.
– ORIGIN late Middle English (in the sense 'find lost game', said of a hunting dog): from Old French *retroeve-*, stressed stem of *retrover* 'find again'.

retriever ▶**noun 1** a dog of a breed used for retrieving game.
2 a person who retrieves something.

retro[1] ▶**adjective** imitative of a style, fashion, or design from the recent past: *retro 60s fashions.*
▶**noun** [mass noun] clothes or music whose style or design are imitative of those of the recent past: *a look which mixes Italian casual wear and American retro.*
– ORIGIN 1960s: from French *rétro*, abbreviation of *rétrograde* 'retrograde'.

retro[2] ▶**noun** (pl. **-os**) short for **RETROROCKET**.

retro- ▶**combining form 1** denoting action that is directed backwards or is reciprocal: *retrocede* | *retroject.*
2 denoting location behind: *retrosternal* | *retrochoir.*
– ORIGIN from Latin *retro* 'backwards'.

retroactive ▶**adjective** (especially of legislation) taking effect from a date in the past: *a big retroactive tax increase.*
– DERIVATIVES **retroaction** noun, **retroactively** adverb, **retroactivity** noun.

retroactive interference (also **retroactive inhibition**) ▶**noun** [mass noun] Psychology the tendency of later learning to hinder the memory of previously learned material.

retrobulbar /ˌrɛtrəʊˈbʌlbə/ ▶**adjective** [attrib.] Anatomy & Medicine situated or occurring behind the eyeball: *a retrobulbar abscess.*

retrocede /ˌrɛtrə(ʊ)ˈsiːd/ ▶**verb** [with obj.] rare cede (territory) back again: *the British colony of Hong Kong, retroceded to China.*
– DERIVATIVES **retrocession** noun.
– ORIGIN early 19th cent.: from French *rétrocéder.*

retrochoir /ˈrɛtrəʊˌkwʌɪə/ ▶**noun** the interior of a cathedral or large church behind the high altar.
– ORIGIN mid 19th cent.: from medieval Latin *retrochorus* (see **RETRO-, CHOIR**).

retrod past of **RETREAD** (in sense 1).

retrodden past participle of **RETREAD** (in sense 1).

retrodiction /ˌrɛtrə(ʊ)ˈdɪkʃ(ə)n/ ▶**noun** [mass noun] the explanation or interpretation of past actions or events inferred from the laws that are assumed to have governed them.

retrofit /ˈrɛtrəʊfɪt/ ▶**verb** (**retrofitted, retrofitting**) [with obj.] add (a component or accessory) to something that did not have it when manufactured: *motorists who retrofit catalysts to older cars.*
■provide (something) with a component or accessory not fitted to it during manufacture: *buses have been retrofitted with easy-access features.*
▶**noun** an act of adding a component or accessory to something that did not have it when manufactured.
■a component or accessory added to something after manufacture.
– ORIGIN 1950s: blend of **RETROACTIVE** and **REFIT**.

retroflex /ˈrɛtrə(ʊ)flɛks/ (also **retroflexed**) ▶**adjective** Anatomy & Medicine turned backwards: *a retroflexed endoscope.*
■Phonetics pronounced with the tip of the tongue curled up towards the hard palate: *the retroflex /r/.*
– DERIVATIVES **retroflexion** noun.
– ORIGIN late 18th cent.: from Latin *retroflex-* 'bent backwards', from the verb *retroflectere*, from *retro* 'backwards' + *flectere* 'to bend'.

retrogradation /ˌrɛtrəʊgrəˈdeɪʃ(ə)n/ ▶**noun** [mass noun] Astronomy & Astrology the apparent temporary reverse motion of a planet (from east to west), resulting from the relative orbital progress of the earth and the planet.
■the orbiting or rotation of a planet or planetary satellite in a reverse direction from that normal in the solar system.
– ORIGIN mid 16th cent.: from late Latin *retrogradation-* (see **RETRO-, GRADATION**).

retrograde ▶**adjective 1** directed or moving backwards: *a retrograde flow.*
■reverting to an earlier and inferior condition: *to go back on the progress that has been made would be a retrograde step.* ■ (of the order of something) reversed; inverse: *the retrograde form of these inscriptions.* ■ (of amnesia) involving the period immediately preceding the causal event. ■ Geology (of a metamorphic change) resulting from a decrease in temperature or pressure. ■ Astronomy & Astrology (of the apparent motion of a planet) in a reverse direction from normal (from east to west), resulting from the relative orbital progress of the earth and the planet. The opposite of **PROGRADE**. ■ Astronomy (of the orbit or rotation of a planet or planetary satellite) in a reverse direction from that normal in the solar system.
▶**noun** rare a degenerate person.
▶**verb** [no obj.] **1** archaic go back in position or time: *our history must retrograde for the space of a few pages.*
■revert to an earlier and usually inferior condition: *people cannot habitually trample on law and justice without retrograding toward barbarism.*
2 Astronomy show retrogradation: *all the planets will at some time appear to retrograde.*
– DERIVATIVES **retrogradely** adverb (rare).
– ORIGIN late Middle English (as a term in astronomy): from Latin *retrogradus*, from *retro* 'backwards' + *gradus* 'step' (from *gradi* 'to walk').

retrogress /ˌrɛtrə(ʊ)ˈgrɛs/ ▶**verb** [no obj.] go back to an earlier state, typically a worse one: *she retrogressed to the starting point of her rehabilitation.*
– ORIGIN early 19th cent.: from **RETRO-** 'back', on the pattern of the verb *progress.*

retrogression ▶**noun** [mass noun] **1** the process of returning to an earlier state, typically a worse one: *a kind of extreme retrogression to 19th-century attitudes.*
2 Astronomy another term for **RETROGRADATION**.
– DERIVATIVES **retrogressive** adjective.
– ORIGIN mid 17th cent.: from **RETRO-** 'backwards', on the pattern of *progression.*

retroject /ˌrɛtrə(ʊ)ˈdʒɛkt/ ▶**verb** [with obj.] rare project backwards: *the rabbinic interpretation is retrojected into the biblical text.*
– ORIGIN mid 19th cent.: from **RETRO-** 'backwards', on the pattern of the verb *project.*

retrolental fibroplasia /ˌrɛtrəʊˌlɛnt(ə)l ˌfʌɪbrəʊˈpleɪzɪə/ ▶**noun** [mass noun] Medicine abnormal proliferation of fibrous tissue immediately behind the lens of the eye, leading to blindness. It affected many premature babies in the 1950s, owing to the excessive administration of oxygen.

retroperitoneal /ˌrɛtrəʊˌpɛrɪtəˈniːəl/ ▶**adjective** Anatomy & Medicine situated or occurring behind the peritoneum.

retroreflector ▶**noun** a device which reflects light back along the incident path, irrespective of the angle of incidence.
– DERIVATIVES **retroreflective** adjective.

retrorocket ▶**noun** a small auxiliary rocket on a spacecraft or missile, fired in the direction of travel to slow the craft down, for example, when landing on the surface of a planet.

retrorse /rɪˈtrɔːs/ ▶**adjective** Biology turned or pointing backwards: *retrorse spines.*
– ORIGIN early 19th cent.: from Latin *retrorsus*, contraction of *retroversus*, from *retro* 'backwards' + *versus* 'turned' (past participle of *vertere*).

retrospect ▶**noun** a survey or review of a past course of events or period of time.
– PHRASES **in retrospect** when looking back on a past event or situation; with hindsight: *perhaps, in retrospect, I shouldn't have gone.*
– ORIGIN early 17th cent.: from **RETRO-** 'back', on the pattern of the noun *prospect.*

retrospection ▶**noun** [mass noun] the action of looking back on or reviewing past events or situations, especially those in one's own life: *he was disinclined to indulge in retrospection.*
– ORIGIN mid 17th cent.: probably from **RETROSPECT** (used as a verb).

retrospective ▶**adjective** looking back on or

dealing with past events or situations: *our survey was retrospective.*
■(of an exhibition or compilation) showing the development of an artist's work over a period of time. ■(of a statute or legal decision) taking effect from a date in the past: *retrospective pay awards.*
▶**noun** an exhibition or compilation showing the development of the work of a particular artist over a period of time: *a Georgia O'Keeffe retrospective.*
– DERIVATIVES **retrospectively** adverb.

retrosternal /ˌrɛtrə(ʊ)'stəːn(ə)l/ ▶**adjective** Anatomy & Medicine behind the breastbone.

retrotransposon /ˌrɛtrəʊtrans'pəʊzɒn, -trɑːns-, -tranz-/ ▶**noun** Genetics a transposon whose sequence shows homology with that of a retrovirus.

retroussé /rə'truːseɪ/ ▶**adjective** (of a person's nose) turned up at the tip in an attractive way.
– ORIGIN early 19th cent.: French, literally 'tucked up', past participle of *retrousser.*

retroverted /'rɛtrəvəːt/ ▶**adjective** Anatomy (of the uterus) tilted abnormally backwards.
– DERIVATIVES **retroversion** noun.
– ORIGIN late 18th cent.: from Latin *retrovertere* 'turn backwards' + **-ED**².

Retrovir /'rɛtrə(ʊ)vɪə/ ▶**noun** trademark for **ZIDOVUDINE**.
– ORIGIN 1980s: abbreviation of **RETROVIRUS**.

retrovirus /'rɛtrəʊˌvʌɪrəs/ ▶**noun** Biology any of a group of RNA viruses which insert a DNA copy of their genome into the host cell in order to replicate, e.g. HIV.
– ORIGIN 1970s: modern Latin, from the initial letters of *reverse transcriptase* + **VIRUS**.

retry ▶**verb** (**-ies**, **-ied**) **1** [with obj.] Law try (a defendant or case) again.
2 [no obj.] Computing re-enter a command, especially differently because one has made an error the first time.
■(of a system) transmit data again because the first attempt was unsuccessful.
▶**noun** an instance of re-entering a command or retransmitting data.

retsina /rɛt'siːnə/ ▶**noun** [mass noun] a Greek white or rosé wine flavoured with resin.
– ORIGIN modern Greek.

retune ▶**verb** [with obj.] tune (something) again or differently, in particular:
■put (a musical instrument) back in tune or alter its pitch. ■tune (a radio, television, or other piece of electronic equipment) to a different frequency.

returf ▶**verb** [with obj.] Brit. cover (ground) or replace (a lawn or sports field) with new turf.

return ▶**verb 1** [no obj.] come or go back to a place or person: *he* ***returned to*** *America in the late autumn.*
■(**return to**) go back to (a particular state or activity): *Owen had returned to full health.* ■(**return to**) divert one's attention back to (something): *he returned to his newspaper.* ■(especially of a feeling) come back or reoccur after a period of absence: *her appetite had returned.* ■Golf play the last nine holes in a round of eighteen holes: *McAllister went out in 43 and returned in 32.*
2 [with obj.] give, put, or send (something) back to a place or person: *complete the application form and* ***return it to*** *this address.*
■feel, say, or do (the same feeling, action, etc.) in response: *she returned his kiss.* ■(in tennis and other sports) hit or send (the ball) back to an opponent. ■American Football intercept (a pass, kick, or fumble by the opposing team) and run upfield with the ball. ■(of a judge or jury) state or present (a verdict) in response to a formal request. ■Bridge lead (a card, especially one of a suit led earlier by one's partner) after taking a trick. ■Architecture continue (a wall) in a changed direction, especially at right angles.
3 [with obj.] yield or make (a profit): *the company returned a profit of £4.3 million.*
4 [with obj.] (of an electorate) elect (a person or party) to office: *the city of Glasgow returned eleven Labour MPs.*
▶**noun 1** an act of coming or going back to a place or activity: *he celebrated his safe return from the war* | [as modifier] *a return flight.*
■[in sing.] an act of going back to an earlier state or condition: *the designer advocated a return to elegance.* ■[mass noun] the action of giving, sending, or putting something back: *the tape is ready to despatch to you on return of the documents.* ■(in tennis and other sports) a stroke played in response to a serve or other stroke by one's opponent. ■a thing which has been given or sent back, especially an unwanted ticket for a sporting event or play. ■(also **return ticket**) chiefly Brit. a ticket which allows someone to travel to a place and back again. See also **DAY RETURN**. ■an electrical conductor bringing a current back to its source. ■(also **return match** or **game**) a second contest between the same opponents.
2 (often **returns**) a profit from an investment: *product areas are being developed to produce maximum returns.*
■[mass noun] a good rate of return.
3 an official report or statement submitted in response to a formal demand: *census returns.*
■Law an endorsement or report by a court officer or sheriff on a writ.
4 [mass noun] election to office: *I campaigned for the return of forty-four MPs.*
■[count noun] a returning officer's announcement of such an event: *falsification of the election return.*
5 (also **carriage return**) a mechanism or key on a typewriter that returns the carriage to a fixed position for the start of a new line.
■(also **return key**) a key pressed on a computer keyboard to simulate a carriage return in a word-processing program, or to indicate the end of a command or data string.
6 Architecture a part receding from the line of the front, for example the side of a house or of a window opening.
– PHRASES **by return** (**of post**) Brit. in the next available mail delivery to the sender. **in return** as a response, exchange, or reward for something: *he leaves the house to his sister in return for her kindness.* **many happy returns** (**of the day**) used as a greeting to someone on their birthday. **return thanks** Brit. express thanks, especially in a grace at a meal or in response to a toast or condolence.
– DERIVATIVES **returnable** adjective, **returner** noun.
– ORIGIN Middle English: the verb from Old French *returner*, from Latin *re-* 'back' + *tornare* 'to turn'; the noun via Anglo-Norman French.

return crease ▶**noun** Cricket each of two lines on either side of the wicket, at right angles to the bowling and popping creases, between which the bowler must deliver the ball.

returnee ▶**noun** a person who returns, in particular:
■a refugee returning from abroad. ■a person returning to work, especially after bringing up a family.

returning officer ▶**noun** (in the UK, Canada, Australia, and New Zealand) the official in each constituency or electorate who conducts an election and announces the result.

retying present participle of **RETIE**.

retype ▶**verb** [with obj.] type (text) again on a typewriter or computer, especially to correct errors.

Reuben /'ruːbɪn/ (in the Bible) a Hebrew patriarch, eldest son of Jacob and Leah (Gen. 29:32).
■the tribe of Israel traditionally descended from him.

reunify ▶**verb** (**-ies**, **-ied**) [with obj.] restore political unity to (a place or group, especially a divided territory): *communist insurgents had effectively reunified the country.*
– DERIVATIVES **reunification** noun.

Réunion /riː'juːnjən, -nɪən, French reynjɔ̃/ a volcanically active, subtropical island in the Indian Ocean east of Madagascar, one of the Mascarene Islands; pop. 596,700 (1990); capital, Saint-Denis. A French possession since 1638, the island became an administrative region of France in 1974.

reunion ▶**noun** an instance of two or more people coming together again after a period of separation: *she had a tearful reunion with her parents.*
■a social gathering attended by members of a certain group of people who have not seen each other for some time: *a school reunion.* ■[mass noun] the act or process of being brought together again as a unified whole: *the reunion of East and West Germany.*
– ORIGIN early 17th cent.: from French *réunion* or Anglo-Latin *reunio(n-)*, from Latin *reunire* 'unite'.

reunite ▶**verb** come together or cause to come together again after a period of separation or disunity: [no obj.] *the three friends reunited in 1959* | [with obj.] *Stephanie was* ***reunited with*** *her parents.*

reupholster ▶**verb** [with obj.] upholster with new materials, especially with a different covering fabric: *the bed was reupholstered in chintz.*
– DERIVATIVES **reupholstery** noun.

reuse ▶**verb** /riː'juːz/ [with obj.] use again or more than once: *the tape could be magnetically erased and reused.*
▶**noun** /riː'juːs/ [mass noun] the action of using something again: *the ballast was cleaned ready for reuse.*
– DERIVATIVES **reusable** adjective.

Reuter /'rɔɪtə/, Paul Julius, Baron von (1816–99), German pioneer of telegraphy and news reporting; born *Israel Beer Josaphat.* He founded the news agency Reuters.

Reuters /'rɔɪtəz/ an international news agency founded in London in 1851 by Paul Julius Reuter. The agency pioneered the use of telegraphy, building up a service used today by newspapers and radio and television stations in most countries.

reutilize (also **-ise**) ▶**verb** [with obj.] utilize again or for a different purpose.
– DERIVATIVES **reutilization** noun.

Rev. ▶**abbreviation for** ■the book of Revelation (in biblical references). ■(as the title of a priest) Reverend.

rev informal ▶**noun** (usu. **revs**) a revolution of an engine per minute: *an engine speed of 1,750 revs.*
■an act of increasing the speed of revolution of a vehicle's engine by pressing the accelerator, especially while the clutch is disengaged.
▶**verb** (**revved**, **revving**) [with obj.] increase the running speed of (an engine) or the engine speed of (a vehicle) by pressing the accelerator, especially while the clutch is disengaged: *he got into the car,* ***revved up*** *the engine and drove off* | [no obj.] *I* ***revved up*** *enthusiastically.*
■[no obj.] (of an engine or vehicle) operate with increasing speed when the accelerator is pressed, especially while the clutch is disengaged: *he could hear the sound of an engine revving nearby* | figurative *he's* ***revving up*** *for next week's World Cup game.*
– ORIGIN early 20th cent.: abbreviation of **REVOLUTION**.

revaccinate ▶**verb** [with obj.] vaccinate again for the same disease.
– DERIVATIVES **revaccination** noun.

revalue ▶**verb** (**revalues**, **revalued**, **revaluing**) [with obj.] assess the value of (something) again.
■Economics adjust the value of (a currency) in relation to other currencies.
– DERIVATIVES **revaluation** noun.

revamp ▶**verb** [with obj.] give new and improved form, structure, or appearance to: *an attempt to revamp the museum's image* | [as adj. **revamped**] *a revamped magazine.*
▶**noun** [usu. in sing.] an act of improving the form, structure, or appearance of something.
■a new and improved version: *the show was a revamp of an old idea.*

revanche /rə'vɑ̃ʃ/ ▶**noun** [mass noun] the policy of a nation to seek the return of lost territory.
– ORIGIN French, literally 'revenge'.

revanchism /rɪ'van(t)ʃɪz(ə)m/ ▶**noun** [mass noun] a policy of seeking to retaliate, especially to recover lost territory.
– DERIVATIVES **revanchist** adjective & noun.
– ORIGIN 1950s: from French *revanche* (see **REVANCHE**) + **-ISM**. The form *revanchist* dates from the 1920s.

revarnish ▶**verb** [with obj.] varnish (something) again.

rev counter ▶**noun** an instrument that measures and displays the rate of revolutions of an engine.

Revd ▶**abbreviation for** (as the title of a priest) Reverend.

reveal¹ ▶**verb** [with obj.] make (previously unknown or secret information) known to others: *Brenda was forced to reveal Robbie's whereabouts* | [with clause] *he revealed that he and his children had received death threats.*
■cause or allow (something) to be seen: *the clouds were breaking up to reveal a clear blue sky.* ■make (something) known to humans by divine or supernatural means: *the truth revealed at the Incarnation.*
– DERIVATIVES **revealable** adjective, **revealer** noun.
– ORIGIN late Middle English: from Old French *reveler* or Latin *revelare*, from *re-* 'again' (expressing reversal) + *velum* 'veil'.

reveal² ▶**noun** either side surface of an aperture in a wall for a door or window.
– ORIGIN late 17th cent.: from obsolete *revale* 'to lower', from Old French *revaler*, from *re-* 'back' + *avaler* 'go down, sink'.

revealed religion ▶**noun** [mass noun] religion based on divine revelation rather than reason.

revealing ▶ **adjective** making interesting or significant information known, especially about a person's attitude or character: *a revealing radio interview.*
■(of an item of clothing) allowing more of the wearer's body to be seen than is usual: *a very revealing dress.*
– DERIVATIVES **revealingly** adverb.

revegetate ▶ **verb** [with obj.] produce a new growth of vegetation on (disturbed or barren ground): *each spring we revegetate acre after acre with pine seedlings* | [no obj.] *a quarter of the area had revegetated.*
– DERIVATIVES **revegetation** noun.

reveille /rɪˈvali/ ▶ **noun** [in sing.] a signal sounded especially on a bugle or drum to wake personnel in the armed forces.
– ORIGIN mid 17th cent.: from French *réveillez!* 'wake up!', imperative plural of *réveiller*, based on Latin *vigilare* 'keep watch'.

réveillon /ˌrɛveɪˈjɒ̃, French ʀevɛjɔ̃/ ▶ **noun** (usu. **Le Réveillon**) (in France and French-speaking countries) a night-time celebration, especially a feast traditionally held after midnight on Christmas morning.
– ORIGIN French, from *réveiller* 'awaken'.

revel ▶ **verb** (**revelled**, **revelling**; US **reveled**, **reveling**) [no obj.] engage in lively and noisy festivities, especially those which involve drinking and dancing: [as noun **revelling**] *a night of drunken revelling.*
■(**revel in**) get great pleasure from (a situation or experience): *Bill said he was secretly revelling in his new-found fame.*
▶ **noun** (**revels**) lively and noisy festivities, especially those which involve drinking and dancing.
– DERIVATIVES **reveller** noun.
– ORIGIN late Middle English: from Old French *reveler* 'rise up in rebellion', from Latin *rebellare* 'to rebel'.

revelation ▶ **noun** **1** a surprising and previously unknown fact, especially one that is made known in a dramatic way: *revelations about his personal life.*
■[mass noun] the making known of something that was previously secret or unknown: *the revelation of an alleged plot to assassinate the king.* ■ used to emphasize the surprising or remarkable quality of someone or something: *seeing them play at international level was a revelation.*
2 [mass noun] the divine or supernatural disclosure to humans of something relating to human existence or the world: *an attempt to reconcile Darwinian theories with biblical revelation* | [count noun] *a divine revelation.*
■(**Revelation** or informal **Revelations**) (in full **the Revelation of St John the Divine**) the last book of the New Testament, recounting a divine revelation of the future to St John.
– DERIVATIVES **revelational** adjective.
– ORIGIN Middle English (in the theological sense): from Old French, or from late Latin *revelatio(n-)*, from *revelare* 'lay bare' (see **REVEAL**[1]). Sense 1 dates from the mid 19th cent.

revelationist ▶ **noun** a believer in divine revelation.

revelatory /ˌrɛvəˈleɪt(ə)ri, ˈrɛv(ə)lət(ə)ri/ ▶ **adjective** revealing something hitherto unknown: *an invigorating and revelatory performance.*

revelry ▶ **noun** (pl. **-ies**) [mass noun] (also **revelries**) lively and noisy festivities, especially when these involve drinking a large amount of alcohol: *sounds of revelry issued into the night* | *New Year revelries.*

revenant /ˈrɛv(ə)nənt/ ▶ **noun** a person who has returned, especially supposedly from the dead.
– ORIGIN early 19th cent.: French, literally 'coming back', present participle (used as a noun) of *revenir.*

revenge ▶ **noun** [mass noun] the action of inflicting hurt or harm on someone for an injury or wrong suffered at their hands: *other spurned wives have taken public revenge on their husbands.*
■the desire to inflict such retribution: *it was difficult not to be overwhelmed with feelings of hate and revenge.* ■ (in sporting contexts) the defeat of a person or team by whom one was beaten in a previous encounter: *Zimbabwe snatched the game 18–16, but the Spanish had their revenge later.*
▶ **verb** (**revenge oneself** or **be revenged**) chiefly archaic or poetic/literary inflict hurt or harm on someone for an injury or wrong done to oneself: *I'll be revenged on the whole pack of you.*
■[with obj.] inflict such retribution on behalf of (someone else): *it's a pity he chose that way to revenge his sister.* ■ inflict retribution for (a wrong or injury done to oneself or another): *her brother was slain, and she revenged his death.*
– PHRASES **revenge is a dish best served** (or **eaten**) **cold** proverb vengeance is often more satisfying if it is not exacted immediately.
– DERIVATIVES **revenger** noun (poetic/literary).
– ORIGIN late Middle English: from Old French *revencher*, from late Latin *revindicare*, from *re-* (expressing intensive force) + *vindicare* 'claim, avenge'.

revengeful ▶ **adjective** eager for revenge.
– DERIVATIVES **revengefully** adverb, **revengefulness** noun.

revenge tragedy ▶ **noun** [mass noun] a style of drama, popular in England during the late 16th and 17th centuries, in which the basic plot was a quest for vengeance and which typically featured scenes of carnage and mutilation. Examples of the genre include Thomas Kyd's *The Spanish Tragedy* (1592) and John Webster's *The Duchess Of Malfi* (1623).

revenue ▶ **noun** [mass noun] income, especially when of a company or organization and of a substantial nature.
■a state's annual income from which public expenses are met. ■ (**revenues**) items or amounts constituting such income: *the government's tax revenues.* ■ (often **the revenue**) the department of the civil service collecting such income. See also **INLAND REVENUE**.
– ORIGIN late Middle English: from Old French *revenu(e)* 'returned', past participle (used as a noun) of *revenir*, from Latin *revenire* 'return', from *re-* 'back' + *venire* 'come'.

revenue tariff ▶ **noun** a tariff imposed principally to raise government revenue rather than to protect domestic industries.

reverb /ˈriːvəːb, rɪˈvəːb/ ▶ **noun** [mass noun] an effect whereby the sound produced by an amplifier or an amplified musical instrument is made to reverberate slightly.
■[count noun] a device for producing such an effect.
– ORIGIN 1960s: abbreviation.

reverberate ▶ **verb** [no obj., usu. with adverbial] (of a loud noise) be repeated several times as an echo: *her deep booming laugh reverberated around the room.*
■(of a place) appear to vibrate or be disturbed because of a loud noise: *the hall reverberated with gaiety and laughter.* ■ [with obj.] archaic return or re-echo (a sound): *oft did the cliffs reverberate the sound.* ■ have continuing and serious effects: *the statements by the professor reverberated through the Capitol.*
– DERIVATIVES **reverberant** adjective, **reverberantly** adverb, **reverberation** noun, **reverberative** adjective, **reverberator** noun, **reverberatory** adjective.
– ORIGIN late 15th cent. (in the sense 'drive or beat back'): from Latin *reverberat-* 'struck again', from the verb *reverberare*, from *re-* 'back' + *verberare* 'to lash' (from *verbera* (plural) 'scourge').

reverberatory furnace ▶ **noun** a furnace in which the roof and walls are heated by flames and radiate heat on to material in the centre of the furnace.

Revere /rɪˈvɪə/, Paul (1735–1818), American patriot. In 1775 he rode from Boston to Lexington to warn fellow American revolutionaries of the approach of British troops.

revere /rɪˈvɪə/ ▶ **verb** [with obj.] (often **be revered**) feel deep respect or admiration for (something): *Cézanne's still lifes were revered by his contemporaries*
– ORIGIN mid 17th cent.: from French *révérer* or Latin *revereri*, from *re-* (expressing intensive force) + *vereri* 'to fear'.

reverence ▶ **noun** [mass noun] deep respect for someone or something: *rituals showed honour and reverence for the dead.*
■[count noun] archaic a gesture indicative of such respect; a bow or curtsy: *the messenger made his reverence.* ■ (**His/Your Reverence**) a title given to a member of the clergy, especially a priest in Ireland, or used in addressing them.
▶ **verb** [with obj.] regard or treat with deep respect: *the many divine beings reverenced by Hindu tradition.*
– ORIGIN Middle English: from Old French, from Latin *reverentia*, from *revereri* 'stand in awe of' (see **REVERE**).

reverend ▶ **adjective** used as a title or form of address to members of the clergy: *the Reverend Pat Tilly.*
▶ **noun** informal a clergyman.
– ORIGIN late Middle English: from Old French, or from Latin *reverendus* 'person to be revered', gerundive of *revereri* (see **REVERE**).

USAGE As a title **Reverend** is used for members of the clergy; the traditionally correct form of address is *the* **Reverend** *James Smith or the* **Reverend** *J. Smith*, rather than **Reverend** *Smith* or simply **Reverend**. Other words are prefixed in titles of more senior clergy: bishops are **Right Reverend**, archbishops are **Most Reverend**, and deans are **Very Reverend**.

Reverend Mother ▶ **noun** the title of the Mother Superior of a convent.

reverent ▶ **adjective** feeling or showing deep and solemn respect: *a reverent silence.*
– DERIVATIVES **reverently** adverb.
– ORIGIN late Middle English: from Latin *reverent-* 'revering', from the verb *revereri* (see **REVERE**).

reverential ▶ **adjective** of the nature of, due to, or characterized by reverence: *their names are always mentioned in reverential tones.*
– DERIVATIVES **reverentially** adverb.

reverie /ˈrɛv(ə)ri/ ▶ **noun** a state of being pleasantly lost in one's thoughts; a daydream: *a knock on the door broke her reverie* | [mass noun] *I slipped into reverie.*
■Music an instrumental piece suggesting a dreamy or musing state. ■ archaic a fanciful or impractical idea or theory.
– ORIGIN early 17th cent.: from obsolete French *resverie*, from Old French *reverie* 'rejoicing, revelry', from *rever* 'be delirious', of unknown ultimate origin.

revers /rɪˈvɪə/ ▶ **noun** (pl. same /-ˈvɪəz/) the turned-back edge of a garment revealing the undersurface, especially at the lapel.
– ORIGIN mid 19th cent.: from French, literally 'reverse'.

reversal ▶ **noun** a change to an opposite direction, position, or course of action: *a dramatic reversal in population decline in the Alps* | [mass noun] *the reversal of tidal currents.*
■Law an annulment of a judgement, sentence, or decree made by a lower court or authority: *a reversal by the House of Lords of the Court of Appeal's decision.* ■ an adverse change of fortune: *the champions suffered a League reversal at Gloucester last month.* ■ [mass noun] Photography direct production of a positive image from an exposed film or plate; direct reproduction of a positive or negative image.
– ORIGIN late 15th cent. (as a legal term): from the verb **REVERSE** + **-AL**.

reversal film ▶ **noun** [mass noun] Photography film that gives a positive image directly when processed, used chiefly for making transparencies.

reverse /rɪˈvəːs/ ▶ **verb** [no obj.] move backwards: *the lorry reversed into the back of a bus.*
■[with obj.] cause (a vehicle) to move backwards: *I got in the car, reversed it and drove it up the drive.* ■ [with obj.] turn (something) the other way round or up or inside out: [as adj. **reversed**] *a reversed S-shape.* ■ [with obj.] make (something) the opposite of what it was: *the damage done to the ozone layer may be reversed.* ■ [with obj.] exchange (the position or function) of two people or things: *the experimenter and the subject reversed roles and the experiment was repeated.* ■ [with obj.] Law revoke or annul (a judgement, sentence, or decree made by a lower court or authority): *the court reversed his conviction.* ■ (of an engine) work in a contrary direction: *the ship's engines reversed and cut out altogether.* ■ [with obj.] Printing make (type or a design) appear as white in a block of solid colour or a half-tone: *their press ads had a headline reversed out of the illustration.*
▶ **adjective** [attrib.] going in or turned towards the direction opposite to that previously stated: *the trend appears to be going in the reverse direction.*
■operating, behaving, or ordered in a way contrary or opposite to that which is usual or expected: *here are the results in reverse order.* ■ Electronics (of a voltage applied to a semiconductor junction) in the direction which does not allow significant current to flow. ■ Geology denoting a fault or faulting in which a relative downward movement occurred in the strata situated on the underside of the fault plane.
▶ **noun** **1** a complete change of direction or action: *the gall actuates a reverse of photosynthesis.*
■[mass noun] reverse gear on a motor vehicle; the position of a gear lever or selector corresponding to this. See also ***in reverse*** below. ■ (**the reverse**) the opposite or contrary to that previously stated: *he didn't feel homesick—quite the reverse.* ■ an adverse change of fortune; a setback or defeat: *United suffered their heaviest reverse of the season.* ■ American Football a play in which a player reverses the direction of attack by

passing the ball to a teammate moving in the opposite direction.
2 the opposite side or face to the observer: *the address is given on the reverse of this leaflet.*
▪a left-hand page of an open book, or the back of a loose document. ▪ the side of a coin or medal bearing the value or secondary design. ▪ the design or inscription on this side. See also **OBVERSE** (sense 1).
– PHRASES **in** (or **into**) **reverse** (of a motor vehicle) in reverse gear so as to travel backwards: *he put the Cadillac into reverse.* ▪ in the opposite direction or manner from usual: *a similar ride next year will do the route in reverse.* **reverse arms** hold a rifle with the butt upwards, typically as a drill movement at a military or state funeral. **reverse the charges** chiefly Brit. make the recipient of a telephone call responsible for payment.
– DERIVATIVES **reversely** adverb, **reverser** noun.
– ORIGIN Middle English: from Old French *revers, reverse* (nouns), *reverser* (verb), from Latin *reversus* 'turned back', past participle of *revertere*, from *re-* 'back' + *vertere* 'to turn'.

reverse-charge ▶ **adjective** chiefly Brit. (of a telephone call) for which the recipient pays.

reverse discrimination ▶ **noun** another term for **POSITIVE DISCRIMINATION**.

reverse engineering ▶ **noun** [mass noun] the reproduction of another manufacturer's product following detailed examination of its construction or composition.

reverse gear ▶ **noun** a gear used to make a vehicle or piece of machinery move or work backwards.

reverse osmosis ▶ **noun** [mass noun] Chemistry a process by which a solvent passes through a porous membrane in the direction opposite to that for natural osmosis when subjected to a hydrostatic pressure greater than the osmotic pressure.

reverse Polish notation ▶ **noun** see **POLISH NOTATION**.

reverse takeover ▶ **noun** a takeover of a public company by a smaller company.

reverse transcriptase ▶ **noun** see **TRANSCRIPTASE**.

reverse transcription ▶ **noun** [mass noun] Biochemistry the reverse of normal transcription, occurring in some RNA viruses, in which a sequence of nucleotides is copied from an RNA template during the synthesis of a molecule of DNA.

reversible ▶ **adjective** able to be reversed, in particular:
▪(of a garment, fabric, or bedlinen) faced on both sides so as to be worn or used with either outside. ▪ able to be turned the other way round: *a reversible pushchair seat.* ▪(of the effects of a process or condition) capable of being reversed so that the previous state or situation is restored: *potentially reversible forms of renal failure.* ▪ Chemistry (of a reaction) occurring together with its converse, and so yielding an equilibrium mixture of reactants and products. ▪ Physics (of a change or process) capable of complete and detailed reversal, especially denoting or undergoing an ideal change in which a system is in thermodynamic equilibrium at all times. ▪ Chemistry (of a colloid) capable of being changed from a gel into a sol by a reversal of the treatment which turns the sol into a gel.
– DERIVATIVES **reversibility** noun, **reversibly** adverb.

reversing light ▶ **noun** Brit. a white light at the rear of a vehicle that comes on when the vehicle is reversing.

reversion /rɪˈvəːʃ(ə)n/ ▶ **noun 1** [mass noun] a return to a previous state, practice, or belief: *there was some reversion to polytheism* | [in sing.] ***a reversion to** the two-party system.*
▪Biology the action of reverting to a former or ancestral type.
2 [mass noun] Law the right, especially of the original owner or their heirs, to possess or succeed to property on the death of the present possessor or at the end of a lease: *the reversion of property.*
▪[count noun] a property to which someone has such a right. ▪ the right of succession to an office or post after the death or retirement of the holder: *he was given a promise of **the reversion of** Boraston's job.*
3 a sum payable on a person's death, especially by way of life insurance.
4 (also **reversion disease**) [mass noun] an incurable disease of the blackcurrant transmitted by the blackcurrant gall mite.
– DERIVATIVES **reversionary** adjective (only in senses 2 and 3).
– ORIGIN late Middle English (denoting the action of returning to or from a place): from Old French, or from Latin *reversio(n-)*, from *revertere* 'turn back' (see **REVERSE**).

reversionary bonus ▶ **noun** a sum added to the amount of an insurance policy payable at the maturation of the policy or the death of the person insured.

reversioner ▶ **noun** Law a person who possesses the reversion to a property or privilege.

revert ▶ **verb** [no obj.] (**revert to**) return to (a previous state, condition, practice, etc.): *he reverted to his native language.*
▪return to (a previous topic): *he ignored her words by reverting to the former subject.* ▪ Biology return to (a former or ancestral type): *it is impossible that a fishlike mammal will actually revert to being a true fish.* ▪ Law (of property) return or pass to (the original owner) by reversion. ▪ [with obj.] archaic turn (one's eyes or steps) back: *on reverting our eyes, every step presented some new and admirable scene.*
– DERIVATIVES **reverter** noun (Law).
– ORIGIN Middle English: from Old French *revertir* or Latin *revertere* 'turn back'. Early senses included 'recover consciousness', 'return to a position', and 'return to a person (after estrangement)'.

revertant Biology ▶ **adjective** (of a cell, organism, or strain) having reverted to the normal type from a mutant or abnormal form.
▶ **noun** a cell, organism, or strain of this type.

revet /rɪˈvɛt/ ▶ **verb** (**revetted**, **revetting**) [with obj.] [usu. as adj. **revetted**] face (a rampart, wall, etc.) with masonry, especially in fortification: *sandbagged and revetted trenches.*
– ORIGIN early 19th cent.: from French *revêtir*, from late Latin *revestire*, from *re-* 'again' + *vestire* 'clothe' (from *vestis* 'clothing').

revetment /rɪˈvɛtm(ə)nt/ ▶ **noun** (especially in fortification) a retaining wall or facing of masonry or other material, supporting or protecting a rampart, wall, etc.
▪a barricade of earth or sandbags set up to provide protection from blast or to prevent aircraft from overrunning when landing.
– ORIGIN late 18th cent.: from French *revêtement*, from the verb *revêtir* (see **REVET**).

review ▶ **noun 1** a formal assessment or examination of something with the possibility or intention of instituting change if necessary: *a comprehensive review of UK defence policy* | [mass noun] *all areas of the company will come under review.*
▪a critical appraisal of a book, play, film, exhibition, etc. published in a newspaper or magazine. ▪ [often in names] a periodical publication with critical articles on current events, the arts, etc. ▪ Law a reconsideration of a judgement, sentence, etc. by a higher court or authority: *a review of her sentence* | [mass noun] *his case comes up for review in January.* Compare with **JUDICIAL REVIEW**. ▪ a retrospective survey or report on past events: *the Director General's end-of-year review.* ▪ a survey or evaluation of a particular subject: *a review of recent developments in multicultural education.*
2 a ceremonial display and formal inspection of military or naval forces, typically by a sovereign, commander-in-chief, or high-ranking visitor.
3 a facility for playing a tape recording during a fast wind or rewind, so that it can be stopped when a particular point is reached.
▶ **verb** [with obj.] **1** examine or assess (something) formally with the possibility or intention of instituting change if necessary: *the Home Secretary was called on to review Britain's gun laws.*
▪write a critical appraisal of (a book, play, film, etc.) for publication in a newspaper or magazine: *I reviewed his first novel.* ▪ Law submit (a sentence, case, etc.) for reconsideration by a higher court or authority: *the Attorney General asked the court to review the sentence.* ▪ make a retrospective assessment or survey of (past events): *ministers will meet to review progress on conventional arms negotiations in March.* ▪ survey or evaluate (a particular subject): *in the next chapter we review a number of recent empirical studies.*
2 (of a sovereign, commander-in-chief, or high-ranking visitor) make a ceremonial and formal inspection of (military or naval forces).
3 view or inspect visually for a second time or again: *all slides were then reviewed by one pathologist.*
– DERIVATIVES **reviewable** adjective, **reviewal** noun.
– ORIGIN late Middle English (as a noun denoting a formal inspection of military or naval forces): from obsolete French *reveue*, from *revoir* 'see again'.

reviewer ▶ **noun** a person who writes critical appraisals of books, plays, films, etc. for publication.
▪a person who formally assesses or examines something with a view to changing it if necessary: *a rent reviewer.*

revile ▶ **verb** [with obj.] (usu. **be reviled**) criticize in an abusive or angrily insulting manner: *he was now reviled by the party that he had helped to lead.*
– DERIVATIVES **revilement** noun, **reviler** noun.
– ORIGIN Middle English: from Old French *reviler*, based on *vil* 'vile'.

revise ▶ **verb 1** [with obj.] reconsider and alter (something) in the light of further evidence: *he had cause to revise his opinion a moment after expressing it.*
▪re-examine and make alterations to (written or printed matter): *the book was published in 1960 and revised in 1968* | [as adj. **revised**] *a revised edition.* ▪ alter so as to make more efficient or realistic: [as adj. **revised**] *the revised finance and administrative groups.*
2 [no obj.] Brit. reread work done previously to improve one's knowledge of a subject, typically to prepare for an examination: *students frantically revising for exams* | [with obj.] *revise your lecture notes on the topic.*
▶ **noun** Printing a proof including corrections made in an earlier proof.
– DERIVATIVES **revisable** adjective, **revisal** noun, **reviser** noun, **revisory** adjective.
– ORIGIN mid 16th cent. (in the sense 'look again or repeatedly (at)'): from French *réviser* 'look at', or Latin *revisere* 'look at again', from *re-* 'again' + *visere* (intensive form of *videre* 'to see').

Revised Standard Version (abbrev.: **RSV**) ▶ **noun** a modern English translation of the Bible, published 1946–57 and based on the American Standard Version of 1901.

Revised Version (abbrev.: **RV**) ▶ **noun** an English translation of the Bible published in 1881–95 and based on the Authorized Version.

revision ▶ **noun** [mass noun] the action of revising: *the scheme needs drastic revision.*
▪[count noun] a revised edition or form of something.
– DERIVATIVES **revisionary** adjective.

revisionism ▶ **noun** [mass noun] often derogatory a policy of revision or modification, especially of Marxism on evolutionary socialist (rather than revolutionary) or pluralist principles.
▪the theory or practice of revising one's attitude to a previously accepted situation or point of view.
– DERIVATIVES **revisionist** noun & adjective.

revisit ▶ **verb** (**revisited**, **revisiting**) [with obj.] come back to or visit again: *he'll revisit old friends* | [as adj. **revisited**] [postpositive] *the battle of Edgehill revisited.*

revitalize (also **-ise**) ▶ **verb** [with obj.] imbue (something) with new life and vitality: *a package of spending cuts to revitalize the economy.*
– DERIVATIVES **revitalization** noun.

revival ▶ **noun** an improvement in the condition or strength of something: *a revival in the fortunes of the party* | *an economic revival.*
▪an instance of something becoming popular, active, or important again: *cross-country skiing is enjoying a revival.* ▪ a new production of an old play or similar work. ▪ a reawakening of religious fervour, especially by means of a series of evangelistic meetings: *the revivals of the nineteenth century* | [mass noun] *a wave of religious revival.* ▪ a restoration to bodily or mental vigour, to life or consciousness, or to sporting success: *the thunder and lightning affected his revival in the third round.*

revivalism ▶ **noun** [mass noun] belief in or the promotion of a revival of religious fervour.
▪a tendency or desire to revive a former custom or practice: *Seventies revivalism.*
– DERIVATIVES **revivalist** noun & adjective, **revivalistic** adjective.

revive ▶ **verb** [with obj.] restore to life or consciousness: *both men collapsed, but were revived.*
▪[no obj.] regain life, consciousness, or strength: *she was beginning to revive from her faint.* ▪ give new strength or energy to: *the cool, refreshing water revived us all.* ▪ restore interest in or the popularity of: *many pagan traditions continue or are being revived.* ▪ improve the position or condition of: *the paper made panicky attempts to revive falling sales.*

r

– DERIVATIVES **revivable** adjective.
– ORIGIN late Middle English: from Old French *revivre* or late Latin *revivere*, from Latin *re-* 'back' + *vivere* 'live'.

reviver ▶ **noun** a person or thing that revives something: *the famous poet and reviver of classical literature.*
■ a preparation used for restoring a faded colour, polish, or lustre. ■ informal, chiefly Brit. a stimulating drink.

revivify /rɪˈvɪvɪfʌɪ/ ▶ **verb** (**-ies**, **-ied**) [with obj.] give new life or vigour to: *they revivified a wine industry that had all but vanished.*
– DERIVATIVES **revivification** noun.
– ORIGIN late 17th cent.: from French *revivifier* or late Latin *revivificare* (see **RE-**, **VIVIFY**).

revocable /ˈrɛvəkəb(ə)l/ ▶ **adjective** capable of being revoked or cancelled: *a revocable settlement.*
– DERIVATIVES **revocability** noun.

revoke ▶ **verb 1** [with obj.] put an end to the validity or operation of (a decree, decision, or promise): *the men appealed and the sentence was revoked.*
2 [no obj.] (in bridge, whist, and other card games) fail to follow suit despite being able to do so.
– DERIVATIVES **revocation** noun, **revocatory** adjective, **revoker** noun.
– ORIGIN late Middle English: from Old French *revoquer* or Latin *revocare*, from *re-* 'back' + *vocare* 'to call'.

revolt ▶ **verb 1** [no obj.] rise in rebellion: *the Iceni revolted and had to be suppressed.*
■ refuse to acknowledge someone or something as having authority: *voters may revolt when they realize the cost of the measures.* ■ [as adj. **revolted**] archaic having rebelled or revolted: *the emperor was leading an expedition against the revolted Bretons.*
2 [with obj.] (often **be revolted**) cause to feel disgust: *he was revolted by the stench that greeted him* | [as adj. **revolting**] *revolting green scum.*
■ [no obj.] archaic feel strong disgust: *'tis just the main assumption reason most revolts at.*
▶ **noun** an attempt to put an end to the authority of a person or body by rebelling: *a country-wide **revolt against** the central government* | [mass noun] *the peasants rose in revolt.*
■ a refusal to continue to obey or conform: *a revolt over tax increases.*
– DERIVATIVES **revoltingly** adverb.
– ORIGIN mid 16th cent.: from French *révolte* (noun), *révolter* (verb), from Italian *rivoltare*, based on Latin *revolvere* 'roll back' (see **REVOLVE**).

revolute /ˈrɛvəl(j)uːt/ ▶ **adjective** Botany (especially of the edge of a leaf) curved or curled back.
– ORIGIN mid 18th cent.: from Latin *revolutus* 'unrolled', past participle of *revolvere* (see **REVOLVE**).

revolution ▶ **noun 1** a forcible overthrow of a government or social order, in favour of a new system.
■ (often **the Revolution**) (in Marxism) the class struggle which is expected to lead to political change and the triumph of communism. ■ a dramatic and wide-reaching change in the way something works or is organized or in people's ideas about it: *marketing underwent a revolution.*
2 an instance of revolving: *one revolution a second.*
■ [mass noun] motion in orbit or a circular course or round an axis or centre. ■ the single completion of an orbit or rotation.
– DERIVATIVES **revolutionism** noun, **revolutionist** noun.
– ORIGIN late Middle English: from Old French, or from late Latin *revolutio(n-)*, from *revolvere* 'roll back' (see **REVOLVE**).

revolutionary ▶ **adjective** engaged in or promoting political revolution: *the revolutionary army.*
■ (**Revolutionary**) of or relating to a particular revolution, especially the War of American Independence. ■ involving or causing a complete or dramatic change: *a revolutionary new drug.*
▶ **noun** (pl. **-ies**) a person who works for or engages in political revolution.

Revolutionary Tribunal a court established in Paris in October 1793 to try political opponents of the French Revolution. There was no right of appeal and from June 1794 the only penalty was death.

revolutionize (also **-ise**) ▶ **verb** [with obj.] change (something) radically or fundamentally: *this fabulous new theory will revolutionize the whole of science.*

Revolutions of 1848 a series of revolts against monarchical rule in Europe during 1848.

They sprang from a shared background of autocratic government, lack of representation for the middle classes, economic grievances, and growing nationalism. Revolution occurred first in France, and in the German and Italian states there were uprisings and demonstrations; in Austria rioting caused the flight of the emperor. All of the revolutions ended in failure and repression, but some of the liberal reforms gained as a result survived.

revolve ▶ **verb** [no obj.] move in a circle on a central axis: *overhead, the fan revolved slowly.*
■ (**revolve about/around**) move in a circular orbit around: *the earth revolves around the sun.* ■ (**revolve around**) treat as the most important point or element: *her life revolved around her husband.* ■ [with obj.] consider (something) repeatedly and from different angles: *her mind revolved the possibilities.*
– ORIGIN late Middle English (in the senses 'turn (the eyes) back', 'restore', 'consider'): from Latin *revolvere*, from *re-* 'back' (also expressing intensive force) + *volvere* 'roll'.

revolver ▶ **noun 1** a pistol with revolving chambers enabling several shots to be fired without reloading.
2 an agreement to provide revolving credit.

revolving credit ▶ **noun** [mass noun] credit that is automatically renewed as debts are paid off.

revolving door ▶ **noun** an entrance to a large building in which four partitions turn about a central axis.
■ used to refer to a situation in which the same events or problems recur in a continuous cycle: *many patients are trapped in a revolving door of admission, discharge, and readmission.* ■ [usu. as modifier] a place or organization that people tend to enter and leave very quickly: *the newsroom became a revolving-door workplace.* ■ chiefly US used to refer to a situation in which someone moves from an influential government position to a position in a private company, or vice versa.

revolving fund ▶ **noun** a fund that is continually replenished as withdrawals are made.

revue /rɪˈvjuː/ ▶ **noun** a light theatrical entertainment consisting of a series of short sketches, songs, and dances, typically dealing satirically with topical issues.
– ORIGIN French, literally 'review'.

revulsion ▶ **noun** [mass noun] **1** a sense of disgust and loathing: *news of the attack will be met with sorrow and revulsion.*
2 Medicine, chiefly historical the drawing of disease or blood congestion from one part of the body to another, e.g. by counterirritation.
– ORIGIN mid 16th cent. (in sense 2): from French, or from Latin *revulsio(n-)*, from *revuls-* 'torn out', from the verb *revellere* (from *re-* 'back' + *vellere* 'pull'). Sense 1 dates from the early 19th cent.

reward ▶ **noun** a thing given in recognition of service, effort, or achievement: *the holiday was a reward for 40 years' service with the company* | figurative *the emotional rewards of being a carer.*
■ a fair return for good or bad behaviour: *a slap on the face was his reward for his cheek.* ■ a sum offered for the detection of a criminal, the restoration of lost property, or the giving of information.
▶ **verb** [with obj.] make a gift of something to (someone) in recognition of their services, efforts, or achievements: *the engineer who supervised the work was **rewarded with** the MBE.*
■ show one's appreciation of (an action or quality) by making a gift: *an effective organization recognizes and rewards creativity and initiative.* ■ (**be rewarded**) receive what one deserves: *their hard work was rewarded by the winning of a five-year contract.*
– PHRASES **go to one's reward** used euphemistically to indicate that someone has died.
– DERIVATIVES **rewardless** adjective.
– ORIGIN Middle English: from Anglo-Norman French, variant of Old French *reguard* 'regard, heed', also an early sense of the English word.

rewarding ▶ **adjective** providing satisfaction; gratifying: *skiing can be hugely rewarding.*
– DERIVATIVES **rewardingly** adverb.

rewarewa /ˈreɪwəˌreɪwə/ ▶ **noun** a tall red-flowered tree native to New Zealand, which yields decorative timber used for cabinetmaking.
• *Knightia excelsa*, family Proteaceae.
– ORIGIN mid 19th cent.: from Maori.

rewash ▶ **verb** [with obj.] (often **be rewashed**) wash (something) again.

reweigh ▶ **verb** [with obj.] weigh (something) again.

rewind ▶ **verb** (past and past participle **rewound**) [with obj.] wind (a film or tape) back to the beginning.
■ [no obj.] (of a tape or film) wind back to the beginning.
▶ **noun** a mechanism for rewinding a film or tape.
– DERIVATIVES **rewinder** noun.

rewire ▶ **verb** [with obj.] provide (an appliance, building, or vehicle) with new electric wiring.
▶ **noun** [in sing.] an installation of new wiring.
– DERIVATIVES **rewirable** adjective.

reword ▶ **verb** put (something) into different words: *there is a sound reason for rewording that clause.*

rework ▶ **verb** [with obj.] (often **be reworked**) make changes to something, especially in order to make it more up to date: *he reworked the orchestral score for two pianos* | [as noun **reworking**] *a reworking of the Sherwood Forest legend.*

rewound past and past participle of **REWIND**.

rewrap ▶ **verb** (**rewrapped**, **rewrapping**) [with obj.] wrap (something) again or differently.

rewritable ▶ **adjective** Computing (of a storage device) supporting overwriting of previously recorded data.

rewrite ▶ **verb** (past **rewrote**; past participle **rewritten**) [with obj.] write (something) again so as to alter or improve it: *the songs may have to be rewritten* | [no obj.] *he began rewriting, adding more and more layers.*
▶ **noun** an instance of writing of something again so as to alter or improve it.
■ a piece of text that has been altered or improved in such a way.
– PHRASES **rewrite history** select or interpret events from the past in a way that suits one's own particular purposes. **rewrite the record books** (of a sports player) break a record or several records.

Rex[1] ▶ **noun** the reigning king (used following a name or in the titles of lawsuits, e.g. *Rex v. Jones*: the Crown versus Jones).
– ORIGIN Latin, literally 'king'.

Rex[2] ▶ **noun** a cat of a breed with curly fur, which lacks guard hairs.
– ORIGIN 1960s: from Latin, literally 'king'.

Rexine /ˈrɛksiːn/ ▶ **noun** [mass noun] Brit. trademark an artificial leather, used in upholstery and bookbinding.
– ORIGIN early 20th cent.: of unknown origin.

Reye's syndrome /ˈreɪz, ˈrʌɪz/ ▶ **noun** [mass noun] a life-threatening metabolic disorder in young children, of uncertain cause but sometimes precipitated by aspirin and involving encephalitis and liver failure.
– ORIGIN 1960s: named after Ralph D. K. *Reye* (1912–78), Australian paediatrician.

Reykjavik /ˈreɪkjəvɪk, -viːk/ the capital of Iceland, a port on the west coast; pop. 97,570 (1990).
– ORIGIN from Icelandic *rejkja* 'smoky', referring to the steam from its many hot springs.

Reynard /ˈrɛnɑːd, ˈreɪ-/ ▶ **noun** poetic/literary a name for a fox.
– ORIGIN from Old French *renart*; the spelling was influenced by Middle Dutch *Reynaerd*.

Reynolds[1] /ˈrɛn(ə)ldz/, Albert (b.1933), Irish Fianna Fáil statesman, Taoiseach (Prime Minister) 1992–4. He was involved with John Major in drafting the 'Downing Street Declaration' (1993), intended as the basis of a peace initiative in Northern Ireland.

Reynolds[2] /ˈrɛn(ə)ldz/, Sir Joshua (1723–92), English painter. The first president of the Royal Academy (1768), he sought to raise portraiture to the status of historical painting by adapting poses and settings from classical statues and Renaissance paintings.

Reynolds number ▶ **noun** Physics a dimensionless number used in fluid mechanics to indicate whether fluid flow past a body or in a duct is steady or turbulent.
• This is evaluated as $\rho \upsilon d/\mu$, where *d* is a diameter or other characteristic length of the system, υ is a typical speed, ρ is the fluid density, and μ is the viscosity of the fluid. The **magnetic Reynolds number** is an analogous number used in the description of the dynamic behaviour of a magnetized plasma.
– ORIGIN early 20th cent.: named after Osborne *Reynolds* (1842–1912), English physicist.

Reynolds stress ▶ **noun** Physics the net rate of transfer of momentum across a surface in a fluid resulting from turbulence in the fluid.
– ORIGIN 1940s: named after Osborne *Reynolds* (see **REYNOLDS NUMBER**).

r

Reza Shah /ˌreɪzə ˈʃɑː/ see **Pahlavi**[1].

Rf ▶ symbol for the chemical element rutherfordium.

r.f. ▶ abbreviation for radio frequency.

RFA ▶ abbreviation for (in the UK) Royal Fleet Auxiliary.

RFC ▶ abbreviation for ■ (in computing) request for comment, a document circulated on the Internet which forms the basis of a technical standard. ■ historical Royal Flying Corps. ■ Rugby Football Club.

RFP chiefly N. Amer. ▶ abbreviation for request for proposal, a detailed specification of goods or services required by an organization, sent to potential contractors or suppliers.

RGS ▶ abbreviation for Royal Geographical Society.

Rh ▶ abbreviation for rhesus (factor).
▶ symbol for the chemical element rhodium.

r.h. ▶ abbreviation for right hand.

RHA ▶ abbreviation for ■ (in the UK) regional health authority. ■ (in the UK) Royal Horse Artillery.

rhabdom /ˈrabdəʊm/ (also **rhabdome**) ▶ noun Zoology a translucent cylinder forming part of the light-sensitive receptor in the eye of an arthropod.
– origin late 19th cent.: from late Greek *rhabdōma*, from *rhabdos* 'rod'.

rhabdomancy /ˈrabdəˌmansi/ ▶ noun [mass noun] formal dowsing with a rod or stick.
– origin mid 17th cent.: from Greek *rhabdomanteia*, from *rhabdos* 'rod'.

rhabdomyolysis /ˌrabdə(ʊ)mʌɪˈɒlɪsɪs/ ▶ noun [mass noun] Medicine the destruction of striated muscle cells; (especially in horses) azoturia.
– origin 1950s: from Greek *rhabdos* 'rod' + MYO- + -LYSIS.

rhabdomyosarcoma /ˌrabdə(ʊ)ˌmʌɪə(ʊ)sɑːˈkəʊmə/ ▶ noun (pl. **rhabdomyosarcomas** or **rhabdomyosarcomata** /-ˈmətə/) Medicine a rare malignant tumour involving striated muscle tissue.
– origin late 19th cent.: from Greek *rhabdos* 'rod' + MYO- + SARCOMA.

Rhadamanthine /ˌradəˈmanθʌɪn/ ▶ adjective poetic/literary showing stern and inflexible judgement.
– origin mid 17th cent.: from RHADAMANTHUS + -INE[1].

Rhadamanthus /ˌradəˈmanθəs/ Greek Mythology the son of Zeus and Europa, and brother of Minos, who, as a ruler and judge in the underworld, was renowned for his justice.

Rhaeto-Romance /ˌriːtə(ʊ)rəʊˈmans/ (also **Rhaeto-Romanic** /-ˈmanɪk/) ▶ adjective of, relating to, or denoting the Romance dialects spoken in parts of SE Switzerland, NE Italy, and Tyrol, especially Romansh and Ladin. The group also includes Friulian.
▶ noun [mass noun] any of these dialects.
– origin from Latin *Rhaetia* 'of Rhaetia' (the name of a Roman province in the Alps) + ROMANCE.

rhamnose /ˈramnəʊz, -s/ ▶ noun [mass noun] Chemistry a sugar of the hexose class which occurs widely in plants, especially in berries of the common buckthorn.
– origin late 19th cent.: from modern Latin *Rhamnus* (genus name) + -OSE[2].

rhapsode /ˈrapsəʊd/ ▶ noun a person who recites epic poems, especially one of a group in ancient Greece whose profession it was to recite the Homeric poems.
– origin from Greek *rhapsōidos*, from *rhapsōidia* (see RHAPSODY).

rhapsodist ▶ noun 1 a person who rhapsodizes.
2 another term for RHAPSODE.

rhapsodize (also **-ise**) ▶ verb [no obj.] speak or write about someone or something with great enthusiasm and delight: *he began to rhapsodize about Gaby's beauty and charm.*

rhapsody ▶ noun (pl. **-ies**) 1 an effusively enthusiastic or ecstatic expression of feeling: *rhapsodies of praise.*
■ Music a free instrumental composition in one extended movement, typically one that is emotional or exuberant in character.
2 (in ancient Greece) an epic poem, or part of it, of a suitable length for recitation at one time.
– derivatives **rhapsodic** adjective.
– origin mid 16th cent. (in sense 2): via Latin from Greek *rhapsōidia*, from *rhaptein* 'to stitch' + *ōidē* 'song, ode'.

rhatany /ˈratəni/ ▶ noun 1 [mass noun] an astringent extract of the root of a South American shrub, used in medicine.
2 the partially parasitic South American shrub which yields this root, which is also used as a source of dye.
● Genus *Krameria*, family Krameriaceae.
– origin early 19th cent.: from modern Latin *rhatania*, via Portuguese and Spanish from Quechua *ratánya*.

RHD ▶ abbreviation for right-hand drive.

Rhea /ˈriːə/ 1 Greek Mythology one of the Titans, wife of Cronus and mother of Zeus, Demeter, Poseidon, Hera, and Hades. Frightened of betrayal by their children, Cronus ate them; Rhea rescued Zeus from this fate by hiding him and giving Cronus a stone wrapped in blankets instead.
2 Astronomy a satellite of Saturn, the fourteenth closest to the planet, discovered by Cassini in 1672 (diameter 1,530 km).

rhea /ˈriːə/ ▶ noun a large flightless bird of South American grasslands, resembling a small ostrich with greyish-brown plumage.
● Family Rheidae: two species, *Rhea americana* and *Pterocnemia pennata*.
– origin early 19th cent.: modern Latin (genus name), from the name of the Titan RHEA.

rhebok /ˈriːbɒk/ (also **reebok**, **grey rhebok**, or **rhebuck**) ▶ noun a small South African antelope with a woolly brownish-grey coat, a long slender neck, and short straight horns.
● *Pelea capreolus*, family Bovidae.
– origin late 18th cent.: from Dutch *reebok* 'roebuck'.

Rheims variant spelling of REIMS.

Rhein /raɪn/ German name for RHINE.

Rheinland /ˈraɪnlant/ German name for RHINELAND.

Rheinland-Pfalz /ˌraɪnlant'pfalts/ German name for RHINELAND-PALATINATE.

rheme /riːm/ ▶ noun Linguistics the part of a clause that gives information about the theme. Compare with FOCUS and THEME.
– origin late 19th cent.: from Greek *rhēma* 'that which is said'.

Rhenish /ˈrɛnɪʃ/ ▶ adjective of the Rhine and the regions adjoining it.
▶ noun [mass noun] wine from this area.
– origin late Middle English: from Anglo-Norman French *reneis*, from a medieval Latin alteration of Latin *Rhenanus*, from *Rhenus* 'Rhine'.

rhenium /ˈriːnɪəm/ ▶ noun [mass noun] the chemical element of atomic number 75, a rare silvery-white metal which occurs in trace amounts in ores of molybdenum and other metals. (Symbol: **Re**)
– origin 1920s: modern Latin, from *Rhenus*, Latin name of the river RHINE.

rhenosterbos /rɛˈnɒstəbɒs/ (also **rhenosterbosch**) ▶ noun variant spelling of RENOSTERBOS.

rheology /rɪˈɒlədʒi/ ▶ noun [mass noun] the branch of physics that deals with the deformation and flow of matter, especially the non-Newtonian flow of liquids and the plastic flow of solids.
– derivatives **rheological** adjective, **rheologist** noun.
– origin 1920s: from Greek *rheos* 'stream' + -LOGY.

rheostat /ˈriːəstat/ ▶ noun an electrical instrument used to control a current by varying the resistance.
– derivatives **rheostatic** adjective.
– origin mid 19th cent.: from Greek *rheos* 'stream' + -STAT.

rhesus baby /ˈriːsəs/ ▶ noun an infant suffering from haemolytic disease of the newborn.
– origin 1960s: see RHESUS FACTOR.

rhesus factor ▶ noun [in sing.] an antigen occurring on the red blood cells of many humans (around 85 per cent) and some other primates. It is particularly important as a cause of haemolytic disease of the newborn and of incompatibility in blood transfusions.
– origin 1940s: *rhesus* from RHESUS MONKEY, in which the antigen was first observed.

rhesus monkey (also **rhesus macaque**) ▶ noun a small brown macaque with red skin on the face and rump, native to southern Asia. It is often kept in captivity and is widely used in medical research.
● *Macaca mulatta*, family Cercopithecidae.
– origin early 19th cent.: modern Latin *rhesus*, arbitrary use of Latin *Rhesus* (from Greek *Rhēsos*, the name of a mythical king of Thrace).

rhesus negative ▶ adjective lacking the rhesus factor.

rhesus positive ▶ adjective having the rhesus factor.

rhetor /ˈriːtə/ ▶ noun (in ancient Greece and Rome) a teacher of rhetoric.
■ an orator.
– origin via Latin from Greek *rhētōr*.

rhetoric /ˈrɛtərɪk/ ▶ noun [mass noun] the art of effective or persuasive speaking or writing, especially the exploitation of figures of speech and other compositional techniques.
■ language designed to have a persuasive or impressive effect on its audience, but which is often regarded as lacking in sincerity or meaningful content: *all we have from the Opposition is empty rhetoric.*
– origin Middle English: from Old French *rethorique*, via Latin from Greek *rhētorikē (tekhnē)* '(art) of rhetoric', from *rhētōr* 'rhetor'.

rhetorical /rɪˈtɒrɪk(ə)l/ ▶ adjective of, relating to, or concerned with the art of rhetoric: *repetition is a common rhetorical device.*
■ expressed in terms intended to persuade or impress: *the rhetorical commitment of the government to give priority to primary education.* ■ (of a question) asked in order to produce an effect or to make a statement rather than to elicit information.
– derivatives **rhetorically** adverb.
– origin late Middle English (first used in the sense 'eloquently expressed'): via Latin from Greek *rhētorikos* (from *rhētōr* 'rhetor') + -AL.

rhetorician ▶ noun an expert in formal rhetoric.
■ a speaker whose words are primarily intended to impress or persuade.
– origin late Middle English: from Old French *rethoricien*, from *rhetorique* (see RHETORIC).

rheum /ruːm/ ▶ noun [mass noun] chiefly poetic/literary a watery fluid that collects in or drips from the nose or eyes.
– origin late Middle English: from Old French *reume*, via Latin from Greek *rheuma* 'stream' (from *rhein* 'to flow').

rheumatic /rʊˈmatɪk/ ▶ adjective of, relating to, or caused by rheumatism: *rheumatic pains.*
■ (of a person or part of the body) suffering from or affected by rheumatism.
▶ noun a person suffering from rheumatism.
– derivatives **rheumatically** adverb, **rheumaticky** adjective (informal).
– origin late Middle English (originally referring to infection characterized by rheum): from Old French *reumatique*, or via Latin from Greek *rheumatikos*, from *rheuma* 'bodily humour, flow' (see RHEUM).

rheumatic fever ▶ noun [mass noun] a non-contagious acute fever marked by inflammation and pain in the joints. It chiefly affects young people and is caused by a streptococcal infection.

rheumatics ▶ plural noun [usu. treated as sing.] informal rheumatism; rheumatic pains.

rheumatism ▶ noun [mass noun] any disease marked by inflammation and pain in the joints, muscles, or fibrous tissue, especially rheumatoid arthritis.
– origin late 17th cent.: from French *rhumatisme*, or via Latin from Greek *rheumatismos*, from *rheumatizein* 'to snuffle', from *rheuma* 'stream': the disease was originally supposed to be caused by the internal flow of 'watery' humours.

rheumatoid /ˈruːmətɔɪd/ ▶ adjective Medicine relating to, affected by, or resembling rheumatism.

rheumatoid arthritis ▶ noun [mass noun] a chronic progressive disease causing inflammation in the joints and resulting in painful deformity and immobility, especially in the fingers, wrists, feet, and ankles. Compare with OSTEOARTHRITIS.

rheumatoid factor ▶ noun Medicine any of a group of autoantibodies which are present in the blood of many people with rheumatoid arthritis.

rheumatology /ˌruːmə'tɒlədʒi/ ▶ noun [mass noun] Medicine the study of rheumatism, arthritis, and other disorders of the joints, muscles, and ligaments.
– derivatives **rheumatological** adjective, **rheumatologist** noun.

rheumy ▶ adjective (especially of the eyes) full of rheum; watery.

rhinal /ˈrʌɪn(ə)l/ ▶ adjective Anatomy of or relating to the nose or the olfactory part of the brain.
– origin mid 19th cent.: from Greek *rhis, rhin-* 'nose' + -AL.

Rhine /raɪn/ a river in western Europe which rises in the Swiss Alps and flows for 1,320 km (820 miles) to the North Sea, forming the German–Swiss border, before flowing through Germany and the Netherlands. German name **RHEIN**; French name **RHIN** /rɛ̃/.

Rhineland the region of western Germany through which the Rhine flows, especially the part to the west of the river. German name **RHEINLAND** /'raɪnlant/.

Rhineland-Palatinate a state of western Germany; capital, Mainz. German name **RHEINLAND-PFALZ**.

rhinestone ▶ noun an imitation diamond, used in cheap jewellery and to decorate clothes.
– ORIGIN late 19th cent.: translating French *caillou du Rhin*, literally 'pebble of the Rhine'.

rhinitis /raɪ'naɪtɪs, rɪ-/ ▶ noun [mass noun] Medicine inflammation of the mucous membrane of the nose, caused by a virus infection (e.g. the common cold) or by an allergic reaction (e.g. hay fever).

rhino ▶ noun (pl. same or **-os**) informal a rhinoceros.
– ORIGIN late 19th cent.: abbreviation.

rhino- ▶ combining form of or relating to the nose: *rhinoplasty*.
– ORIGIN from Greek *rhis, rhin-* 'nose'.

rhinoceros /raɪ'nɒs(ə)rəs/ ▶ noun (pl. same or **rhinoceroses**) a large, heavily built plant-eating mammal with one or two horns on the nose and thick folded skin, native to Africa and South Asia. All kinds have become endangered through hunting.
● Family Rhinocerotidae: four genera and five species.
– DERIVATIVES **rhinocerotic** /raɪ,nɒsə'rɒtɪk/ adjective.
– ORIGIN Middle English: via Latin from Greek *rhinokerōs*, from *rhis, rhin-* 'nose' + *keras* 'horn'.

rhinoceros beetle ▶ noun a very large mainly tropical beetle, the male of which has a curved horn extending from the head and typically another from the thorax. In some parts of Asia males are put to fight as a spectator sport.
● Several genera and species in the family Scarabaeidae, including the South Asian *Oryctes rhinoceros*, which is a serious pest of cocoa palms.

rhinoceros bird ▶ noun another term for **OXPECKER**.

rhinoceros horn ▶ noun [mass noun] a mass of keratinized fibres that comprises the horn of a rhinoceros, reputed in Eastern medicine to have medicinal or aphrodisiac powers.

rhinoceros hornbill ▶ noun a large SE Asian hornbill with black-and-white plumage and an upturned casque.
● *Buceros rhinoceros*, family Bucerotidae.

rhinoplasty /'raɪnə(ʊ),plasti/ ▶ noun (pl. **-ies**) [mass noun] plastic surgery performed on the nose.
– DERIVATIVES **rhinoplastic** adjective.

rhinovirus /'raɪnəʊ,vaɪrəs/ ▶ noun Medicine any of a group of picornaviruses including those which cause some forms of the common cold.

rhizo- ▶ combining form Botany relating to a root or roots: *rhizomorph*.
– ORIGIN from Greek *rhiza* 'root'.

rhizobium /raɪ'zəʊbɪəm/ ▶ noun a nitrogen-fixing bacterium that is common in the soil, especially in the root nodules of leguminous plants.
● Genus *Rhizobium*; Gram-negative rods.
– ORIGIN 1920s: modern Latin, from **RHIZO-** 'root' + Greek *bios* 'life'.

rhizoctonia /,raɪzɒk'təʊnɪə/ ▶ noun [mass noun] a common soil fungus that sometimes causes plant diseases such as damping off, foot rot, and eyespot.
● Genus *Rhizoctonia*, subdivision Deuteromycotina, in particular *R. solani*.
– ORIGIN late 19th cent.: modern Latin (genus name), from Greek *rhiza* 'root' + *ktonos* 'murder'.

rhizoid /'raɪzɔɪd/ ▶ noun Botany a filamentous outgrowth or root hair on the underside of the thallus in some lower plants, especially mosses and liverworts, serving both to anchor the plant and (in terrestrial forms) to conduct water.
– DERIVATIVES **rhizoidal** adjective.

rhizome /'raɪzəʊm/ ▶ noun Botany a continuously growing horizontal underground stem which puts out lateral shoots and adventitious roots at intervals. Compare with **BULB** (in sense 1), **CORM**.
– ORIGIN mid 19th cent.: from Greek *rhizōma*, from *rhizousthai* 'take root', based on *rhiza* 'root'.

rhizomorph /'raɪzə(ʊ)mɔːf/ ▶ noun Botany a root-like aggregation of hyphae in certain fungi.

Rhizopoda /,raɪzə'pəʊdə, raɪ'zɒpədə/ Zoology a phylum of single-celled animals which includes the amoebas and their relatives, which have extensible pseudopodia.
– DERIVATIVES **rhizopod** noun.
– ORIGIN modern Latin (plural), from **RHIZO-** 'root' + Greek *pous, pod-* 'foot'.

rhizosphere /'raɪzə(ʊ),sfɪə/ ▶ noun Ecology the region of soil in the vicinity of plant roots in which the chemistry and microbiology is influenced by their growth, respiration, and nutrient exchange.

rho /rəʊ/ ▶ noun the seventeenth letter of the Greek alphabet (**P**, **ρ**), transliterated as 'r' or (when written with a rough breathing) 'rh'.
■ (**Rho**) [followed by Latin genitive] Astronomy the seventeenth star in a constellation: *Rho Cassiopeiae*.
▶ symbol for ■ (ρ) density. ■ (ρ) Spearman's correlation coefficient.
– ORIGIN Greek.

rhodamine /'rəʊdəmiːn/ ▶ noun Chemistry any of a number of synthetic dyes derived from xanthene, used to colour textiles.
– ORIGIN late 19th cent.: from **RHODO-** 'rose-coloured' + **AMINE**.

Rhode Island /rəʊd/ a state in the north-eastern US, on the Atlantic coast; pop. 1,003,460 (1990); capital, Providence. Settled from England in the 17th century, it was one of the original thirteen states of the Union (1776) and is the smallest and most densely populated.
– DERIVATIVES **Rhode Islander** noun.

Rhode Island Red ▶ noun a bird of a breed of reddish-black domestic chicken, originally from America.

Rhodes¹ /rəʊdz/ a Greek island in the SE Aegean, off the Turkish coast, the largest of the Dodecanese and the most easterly island in the Aegean; pop. 98,450 (1991). Greek name **RÓDHOS**.
■ its capital, a port on the northernmost tip; pop. 42,400 (1991). It was founded *c*.408 BC and was the site of the Colossus of Rhodes.

Rhodes² /rəʊdz/, Cecil (John) (1853–1902), British-born South African statesman, Prime Minister of Cape Colony 1890–6. He expanded British territory in southern Africa, annexing Bechuanaland (now Botswana) in 1884 and developing Rhodesia from 1889. By 1890 he had acquired 90 per cent of the world's production of diamonds.

Rhodes³ /rəʊdz/, Wilfred (1877–1973), English cricketer. An all-rounder, he played for Yorkshire and for England, scoring almost 40,000 runs during this time and taking a record 4,187 first-class wickets.

Rhodesia /rəʊ'diːʃə, -'diːʒə/ the former name of a large territory in central southern Africa which was divided into Northern Rhodesia (now Zambia) and Southern Rhodesia (now Zimbabwe).

The region was developed by Cecil Rhodes through the British South Africa Company, which administered it until Southern Rhodesia became a self-governing British colony in 1923 and Northern Rhodesia a British protectorate in 1924. From 1953 to 1963 Northern and Southern Rhodesia were united with Nyasaland (now Malawi) to form the Federation of Rhodesia and Nyasaland. The name Rhodesia was adopted by Southern Rhodesia when Northern Rhodesia left the Federation in 1963 to become the independent republic of Zambia; Rhodesia became independent Zimbabwe in 1979.

– DERIVATIVES **Rhodesian** adjective & noun.

Rhodesian ridgeback ▶ noun a dog of a breed having a short light brown coat and a ridge of hair along the middle of the back, growing in the opposite direction to the rest of the coat.

Rhodes Scholarship ▶ noun any of several scholarships awarded annually and tenable at Oxford University by students from certain Commonwealth countries, the United States, and Germany.
– DERIVATIVES **Rhodes Scholar** noun.
– ORIGIN named after Cecil *Rhodes* (see **RHODES²**), who founded the scholarships in 1902.

rhodium /'rəʊdɪəm/ ▶ noun [mass noun] the chemical element of atomic number 45, a hard silvery-white metal of the transition series, typically occurring in association with platinum. (Symbol: **Rh**)
– ORIGIN early 19th cent.: modern Latin, from Greek *rhodon* 'rose' (from the colour of the solution of its salts).

rhodo- ▶ combining form chiefly Mineralogy & Chemistry rose-coloured: *rhodochrosite*.
– ORIGIN from Greek *rhodon* 'rose'.

rhodochrosite /,rəʊdə(ʊ)'krəʊsʌɪt/ ▶ noun [mass noun] a mineral consisting of manganese carbonate, typically occurring as pink, brown, or grey rhombohedral crystals.
– ORIGIN mid 19th cent.: from Greek *rhodokhrōs* 'rose-coloured' + **-ITE¹**.

rhododendron /,rəʊdə'dɛndr(ə)n/ ▶ noun a shrub or small tree of the heather family, with large clusters of bell-shaped flowers and typically with large evergreen leaves, widely grown as an ornamental.
● Genus *Rhododendron*, family Ericaceae: many cultivars.
– ORIGIN via Latin from Greek, from *rhodon* 'rose' + *dendron* 'tree'.

rhodonite /'rəʊd(ə)nʌɪt/ ▶ noun [mass noun] a brownish or rose-pink mineral consisting of a silicate of manganese and other elements.
– ORIGIN early 19th cent.: from Greek *rhodon* 'rose' + **-ITE¹**.

Rhodope Mountains /'rɒdəpi/ a mountain system in the Balkans, SE Europe, on the frontier between Bulgaria and Greece, rising to a height of over 2,000 m (6,600 ft) and including the Rila Mountains in the north-west.

Rhodophyta /,rəʊdə(ʊ)'fʌɪtə/ Botany a division of lower plants that comprises the red algae.
– DERIVATIVES **rhodophyte** noun.
– ORIGIN modern Latin (plural), from **RHODO-** 'rose-coloured' + Greek *phuta* 'plants'.

rhodopsin /rə(ʊ)'dɒpsɪn/ ▶ noun another term for **VISUAL PURPLE**.
– ORIGIN late 19th cent.: from Greek *rhodon* 'rose' + *opsis* 'sight' + **-IN¹**.

rhodora /rə(ʊ)'dɔːrə/ ▶ noun a pink-flowered North American shrub of the heather family.
● *Rhododendron canadense*, family Ericaceae.
– ORIGIN late 18th cent.: modern Latin (former genus name), based on Greek *rhodon* 'rose'.

rhomb /rɒm(b)/ ▶ noun a rhombohedral crystal.
■ a rhombus.
– DERIVATIVES **rhombic** adjective.
– ORIGIN early 19th cent.: from Latin *rhombus* (see **RHOMBUS**).

rhombencephalon /,rɒmbɛn'sɛf(ə)lɒn, -'kɛf-/ ▶ noun Anatomy another term for **HINDBRAIN**.
– ORIGIN late 19th cent.: from **RHOMB** + **ENCEPHALON**.

rhombi plural form of **RHOMBUS**.

rhombohedral /,rɒmbə(ʊ)'hiːdr(ə)l/ ▶ adjective (chiefly of a crystal) shaped like a rhombohedron.

rhombohedron /,rɒmbə(ʊ)'hiːdr(ə)n, -'hɛd-/ ▶ noun (pl. **rhombohedra** /-drə/ or **rhombohedrons**) a solid figure whose faces are six equal rhombuses.
■ a crystal or other solid object of this form.
– ORIGIN mid 19th cent.: from **RHOMBUS** + **-HEDRON**, on the pattern of words such as *polyhedron*.

rhomboid /'rɒmbɔɪd/ ▶ adjective having or resembling the shape of a rhombus.
▶ noun **1** a quadrilateral of which only the opposite sides and angles are equal.
2 (also **rhomboid muscle**) another term for **RHOMBOIDEUS**.
– DERIVATIVES **rhomboidal** adjective.
– ORIGIN late 16th cent. (as a noun): from French *rhomboïde*, or via late Latin from Greek *rhomboeidēs*, from *rhombos* (see **RHOMBUS**).

rhomboideus /rɒm'bɔɪdɪəs/ ▶ noun (pl. **rhomboidei** /-dɪʌɪ/) Anatomy a muscle connecting the shoulder blade to the vertebrae.
– ORIGIN mid 19th cent.: modern Latin, from *rhomboideus (musculus)* (see **RHOMBOID**).

Rhombozoa /,rɒmbə(ʊ)'zəʊə/ Zoology a minor phylum of mesozoan worms which are parasites in the kidneys of cephalopod molluscs.
– DERIVATIVES **rhombozoan** noun & adjective.
– ORIGIN modern Latin (plural), from Greek *rhombos* 'rhombus' + *zōia* 'animals'.

rhombus /'rɒmbəs/ ▶ noun (pl. **rhombuses** or **rhombi** /-bʌɪ/) Geometry a parallelogram with oblique angles and equal sides.
– ORIGIN mid 16th cent.: via Latin from Greek *rhombos*.

Rhondda /'rɒndə/ an urbanized district of South Wales, which extends along the valleys of the

Rivers Rhondda Fawr and Rhondda Fach. It was formerly noted as a coal-mining area.

Rhône /rəʊn/ a river in SW Europe which rises in the Swiss Alps and flows 812 km (505 miles), through Lake Geneva into France, then to Lyons, Avignon, and the Mediterranean west of Marseilles, where it forms a wide delta that includes the Camargue.

Rhône-Alpes /rəʊnˈalp/ a region of SE France, extending from the Rhône valley to the borders with Switzerland and Italy and including much of the former duchy of Savoy.

rhotacization /ˌrəʊtəsʌɪˈzeɪʃ(ə)n/ (also **-isation**) ▶ **noun** [mass noun] Phonetics pronunciation of a vowel to reflect a following *r* in the orthography, as for example in American English *farm*, *bird*.
– DERIVATIVES **rhotacized** adjective.
– ORIGIN 1970s: from *rhotacize* (from Greek *rhōtakizein*) + **-ATION**.

rhotic /ˈrəʊtɪk/ ▶ **adjective** Phonetics of, relating to, or denoting a dialect or variety of English (e.g. in America and SW England) in which *r* is pronounced before a consonant (as in *hard*) and at the ends of words (as in *far*).
– DERIVATIVES **rhoticity** /rəʊˈtɪsɪti/ noun.
– ORIGIN 1960s: from Greek *rhōt-*, stem of *rho* (see **RHO**) + **-IC**.

RHS ▶ **abbreviation for** ■ Royal Historical Society. ■ Royal Horticultural Society. ■ Royal Humane Society.

rhubarb ▶ **noun** [mass noun] **1** the thick leaf stalks of a cultivated plant of the dock family, which are reddish or green and eaten as a fruit after cooking.
2 the large-leaved Eurasian plant which produces these stalks.
● *Rheum rhaponticum* (or *rhabarbarum*), family Polygonaceae.
■ used in names of other plants of this genus, several of which are used medicinally, e.g. **Chinese rhubarb**.
3 Brit. informal the noise made by a group of actors to give the impression of indistinct background conversation or to represent the noise of a crowd, especially by the random repetition of the word 'rhubarb' with different intonations.
■ nonsense: *it was all rhubarb, about me, about her daughter, about art*. ■ [count noun] N. Amer. informal a heated dispute.
– ORIGIN late Middle English (denoting the rootstock of other plants of this genus used medicinally): from Old French *reubarbe*, from a shortening of medieval Latin *rheubarbarum*, alteration (by association with *rheum* 'rhubarb') of *rhabarbarum* 'foreign rhubarb', from Greek *rha* (also meaning 'rhubarb') + *barbaros* 'foreign'.

Rhum /rʌm/ (also **Rum**) an island in the Inner Hebrides, to the south of Skye. In 1957 it was designated a nature reserve.

rhumb /rʌm/ ▶ **noun** Nautical **1** (also **rhumb line**) an imaginary line on the earth's surface cutting all meridians at the same angle, used as the standard method of plotting a ship's course on a chart.
2 any of the 32 points of the compass.
– ORIGIN late 16th cent.: from French *rumb* (earlier *ryn* (*de vent*) 'point of the compass'), probably from Dutch *ruim* 'space, room'. The spelling change was due to association with Latin *rhombus* (see **RHOMBUS**).

rhumba ▶ **noun** variant spelling of **RUMBA**.

rhyme ▶ **noun** [mass noun] correspondence of sound between words or the endings of words, especially when these are used at the ends of lines of poetry.
■ [count noun] a short poem in which the sound of the word or syllable at the end of each line corresponds with that at the end of another. ■ poetry or verse marked by such correspondence of sound: *the clues were written in rhyme*. ■ [count noun] a word that has the same sound as another.
▶ **verb** [no obj.] (of a word, syllable, or line) have or end with a sound that corresponds to another: *balloon rhymes with moon* | [as adj. **rhyming**] *rhyming couplets*.
■ (of a poem or song) be composed of lines that end in words or syllables with sounds that correspond with those at the ends of other lines: *the poem would have been better if it rhymed*. ■ [with obj.] (**rhyme something with**) put a word together with (another word that has a corresponding sound), as when writing poetry: *I'm not sure about rhyming perestroika with balalaika*. ■ poetic/literary compose verse or poetry: *Musa rhymed and sang*.
– PHRASES **rhyme or reason** [with negative] logical explanation or reason: *without rhyme or reason his mood changed*.
– DERIVATIVES **rhymer** noun, **rhymist** noun (archaic).
– ORIGIN Middle English *rime*, from Old French, from medieval Latin *rithmus*, via Latin from Greek *rhuthmos* (see **RHYTHM**). The current spelling was introduced in the early 17th cent. under the influence of *rhythm*.

rhyme scheme ▶ **noun** the ordered pattern of rhymes at the ends of the lines of a poem or verse.

rhymester ▶ **noun** a person who composes rhymes, especially simple ones.

rhyming slang ▶ **noun** [mass noun] a type of slang that replaces words with rhyming words or phrases, typically with the rhyming element omitted. For example *butcher's*, short for *butcher's hook*, means 'look' in Cockney rhyming slang.

rhynchosaur /ˈrɪŋkə(ʊ)sɔː/ ▶ **noun** a tusked herbivorous reptile of the Triassic period.
● Order Rhynchosauria, subclass Diapsida.
– ORIGIN mid 19th cent.: from modern Latin *Rhynchosaurus* (genus name), from Greek *rhunkos* 'snout' + *sauros* 'lizard'.

rhynchosporium /ˌrɪŋkə(ʊ)ˈspɔːrɪəm/ ▶ **noun** a fungus which causes barley and rye leaf blotch.
● Genus *Rhynchosporium*, subdivision Deuteromycotina.
■ [mass noun] a disease caused by such a fungus.
– ORIGIN modern Latin, from Greek *rhunkos* 'snout, beak' (because of the shape of the fungus) + **SPORE**.

rhyolite /ˈrʌɪəlʌɪt/ ▶ **noun** [mass noun] Geology a pale fine-grained volcanic rock of granitic composition, typically porphyritic in texture.
– ORIGIN mid 19th cent.: from German *Rhyolit*, from Greek *rhuax* 'lava stream' + *lithos* 'stone'.

Rhys /riːs/, Jean (1890–1979), British novelist and short-story writer, born in Dominica; pseudonym of *Ella Gwendolen Rees Williams*. Her novels include *Good Morning, Midnight* (1939) and *Wide Sargasso Sea* (1966).

rhythm /ˈrɪð(ə)m/ ▶ **noun** a strong, regular repeated pattern of movement or sound: *Ruth listened to the rhythm of his breathing*.
■ [mass noun] the systematic arrangement of musical sounds, principally according to duration and periodical stress. ■ a particular type of pattern formed by such arrangement: *guitar melodies with deep African rhythms*. ■ [mass noun] a person's natural feeling for such arrangement: *they've got no rhythm*. ■ [mass noun] the measured flow of words and phrases in verse or prose as determined by the relation of long and short or stressed and unstressed syllables. ■ a regularly recurring sequence of events, actions, or processes: *the twice daily rhythms of the tides*. ■ Art a harmonious sequence or correlation of colours or elements.
– DERIVATIVES **rhythmless** adjective.
– ORIGIN mid 16th cent. (also originally in the sense 'rhyme'): from French *rhythme*, or via Latin from Greek *rhuthmos* (related to *rhein* 'to flow').

rhythm and blues (abbrev.: **R & B**) ▶ **noun** [mass noun] a form of popular music of US black origin which arose during the 1940s from blues, with the addition of driving rhythms taken from jazz. It was an immediate precursor of rock and roll.

rhythm guitar ▶ **noun** [mass noun] a guitar part in a piece of pop music consisting of the chord sequences of a song or melody.

rhythmic ▶ **adjective** having or relating to rhythm: *a rhythmic dance*.
■ occurring regularly: *there are rhythmic changes in our bodies*.
– DERIVATIVES **rhythmical** adjective, **rhythmically** adverb.
– ORIGIN early 17th cent.: from French *rhythmique* or via Latin from Greek *rhuthmikos*, from *rhuthmos* (see **RHYTHM**).

rhythmic gymnastics ▶ **plural noun** [usu. treated as sing.] a form of gymnastics emphasizing dance-like rhythmic routines, typically accentuated by the use of ribbons or hoops.
– DERIVATIVES **rhythmic gymnast** noun.

rhythmicity ▶ **noun** [mass noun] rhythmical quality or character: *the nursery rhymes' rhythmicity makes them particularly easy to learn*.

rhythm method ▶ **noun** a method of avoiding conception favoured by the Roman Catholic Church, by which sexual intercourse is restricted to the times of a woman's menstrual cycle when ovulation is least likely to occur.

rhythm section ▶ **noun** the part of a pop or jazz group supplying the rhythm, generally regarded as consisting of bass and drums and sometimes piano or guitar.

rhyton /ˈrʌɪtɒn, ˈrɪtɒn/ ▶ **noun** (pl. **rhytons** or **rhyta** /ˈrʌɪtə, ˈrɪtə/) a type of drinking container used in ancient Greece, typically having the form of an animal's head or a horn, with the hole for drinking from located at the lower or pointed end.
– ORIGIN from Greek *rhuton*, neuter of *rhutos* 'flowing'; related to *rhein* 'to flow'.

RI ▶ **abbreviation for** ■ Indonesia (international vehicle registration). [ORIGIN: from Bahasa Indonesia *Républik Indonésia*.] ■ Rex et Imperator (King and Emperor) or Regina et Imperatrix (Queen and Empress). [ORIGIN: Latin.] ■ Rhode Island (in official postal use). ■ Royal Institute or Institution.

RIA ▶ **abbreviation for** ■ radioimmunoassay. ■ Royal Irish Academy.

ria /ˈriːə/ ▶ **noun** Geography a long narrow inlet formed by the partial submergence of a river valley.
– ORIGIN late 19th cent.: from Spanish *ría* 'estuary'.

rial /ˈriːɑːl/ (also **riyal**) ▶ **noun** **1** the basic monetary unit of Iran and Oman, equal to 100 dinars in Iran and 100 baiza in Oman.
2 (usu. **riyal**) the basic monetary unit of Saudi Arabia, Qatar, and Yemen, equal to 100 halala in Saudi Arabia, 100 dirhams in Qatar, and 100 fils in Yemen.
– ORIGIN via Persian from Arabic *riyāl*, from Spanish *real* 'royal'.

Rialto /rɪˈaltəʊ/ an island in Venice, containing the old mercantile quarter of medieval Venice. The Rialto Bridge, completed in 1591, crosses the Grand Canal between Rialto and San Marco islands.

RIB ▶ **noun** a small open boat with a fibreglass hull and inflatable rubber sides.
– ORIGIN acronym from *rigid inflatable boat*.

rib ▶ **noun** **1** each of a series of slender curved bones articulated in pairs to the spine (twelve pairs in humans), protecting the thoracic cavity and its organs.
■ a rib of an animal with meat adhering to it used as food; a joint or cut from the ribs of an animal.
2 a long raised piece of stronger or thicker material across a surface or through a structure, and typically serving to support or strengthen it, in particular:
■ Architecture a curved member supporting a vault or defining its form. ■ any of the curved transverse struts of metal or timber in a ship, extending up from the keel and forming part of the framework of the hull. ■ each of the curved pieces of wood forming the body of a lute or the sides of a violin. ■ each of the hinged rods supporting the fabric of an umbrella. ■ Aeronautics a structural member in an aerofoil, extending back from the leading edge and serving to define the contour of the aerofoil. ■ a vein of a leaf (especially the midrib) or an insect's wing. ■ a ridge of rock or land. ■ [mass noun] Knitting a combination of alternate plain and purl stitches producing a ridged, slightly elastic fabric, used especially for the cuffs and bottom edges of jumpers.
▶ **verb** (**ribbed**, **ribbing**) [with obj.] **1** (usu. **be ribbed**) mark with or form into raised bands or ridges: *the road ahead was ribbed with furrows of slush*.
2 informal tease good-naturedly: *the first time I appeared in the outfit I was ribbed mercilessly*.
– DERIVATIVES **ribless** adjective.
– ORIGIN Old English *rib*, *ribb* (noun), of Germanic origin; related to Dutch *rib(be)* and German *Rippe*. Sense 1 of the verb dates from the mid 16th cent.; the sense 'tease' was originally a US slang usage meaning 'to fool, dupe' (1930s).

RIBA ▶ **abbreviation for** Royal Institute of British Architects.

ribald /ˈrɪb(ə)ld, ˈrʌɪbɔːld/ ▶ **adjective** referring to sexual matters in an amusingly rude or irreverent way: *a ribald comment*.
– ORIGIN Middle English (as a noun denoting a lowly retainer or a licentious or irreverent person): from Old French *ribauld*, from *riber* 'indulge in licentious pleasures', from a Germanic base meaning 'prostitute'.

ribaldry ▶ **noun** [mass noun] ribald talk or behaviour.

riband /ˈrɪb(ə)nd/ ▶ **noun** archaic a ribbon.
– ORIGIN Middle English: from Old French *riban*, probably from a Germanic compound of the noun **BAND**[1].

ribbed ▶ **adjective** (especially of a fabric or garment) having a pattern of raised bands: *a ribbed cashmere sweater.*
■Architecture (of a vault or other structure) strengthened with ribs.

Ribbentrop /ˈrɪb(ə)ntrɒp/, Joachim von (1893–1946), German Nazi politician. As Foreign Minister (1938–45) he signed the non-aggression pact with the Soviet Union (1939). He was convicted as a war criminal in the Nuremberg trials and hanged.

ribber ▶ **noun** an attachment on a knitting machine for producing rib.

ribbie /ˈrɪbi/ ▶ **noun** (pl. **-ies**) Baseball, informal a run batted in. See **RBI**.
– ORIGIN mid 20th cent.: elaboration of **RBI**.

ribbing ▶ **noun** [mass noun] **1** a rib-like structure or pattern, especially a band of knitting in rib.
2 informal good-natured teasing.

ribbon ▶ **noun** a long, narrow strip of fabric, used especially for tying something or for decoration: *the tiny pink ribbons in her hair* | [mass noun] *cut four lengths of ribbon.*
■a strip of fabric of a special colour or design awarded as a prize or worn to indicate the holding of an honour, especially a small multicoloured piece of ribbon worn in place of the medal it represents. ■(**ribbons**) figurative prizes; honours: *in the Silk Cup trophy class Mullins stayed **in the ribbons**.* ■a long, narrow strip of something: *slice the peppers into ribbons lengthways.* ■a narrow band of impregnated material wound on a spool and forming the inking agent in some typewriters and computer printers.
▶ **verb** [no obj., with adverbial of direction] extend or move in a long narrow strip like a ribbon: *miles of concrete ribboned behind the bus.*
– PHRASES **cut a** (or **the**) **ribbon** perform an opening ceremony, typically by formally cutting a ribbon across the entrance to somewhere. **cut** (or **tear**) **something to ribbons** cut (or tear) something so badly that only ragged strips remain. ■figurative damage something severely: *the country has seen its economy torn to ribbons by recession.*
– DERIVATIVES **ribboned** adjective.
– ORIGIN early 16th cent.: variant of **RIBAND**. The French spelling *ruban* was also frequent in the 16th–18th cents.

ribbon cable ▶ **noun** a cable for transmitting electronic signals consisting of several insulated wires connected together to form a flat ribbon.

ribbon development ▶ **noun** [mass noun] Brit. the building of houses along a main road, especially one leading out of a town or village.

ribbonfish ▶ **noun** (pl. same or **-fishes**) any of a number of long slender fishes which typically have a dorsal fin running the length of the body, in particular:
• a fish of the dealfish family (Trachipteridae). • a fish of the cutlassfish family (Trichiuridae). • another term for **OARFISH**.

ribbon-grass ▶ **noun** another term for **TAPE-GRASS**.

ribbon worm ▶ **noun** a chiefly aquatic worm with an elongated, unsegmented, flattened body that is typically brightly coloured and tangled in knots, and a long proboscis for catching food.
• Phylum Nemertea: two classes.

ribby ▶ **adjective** having prominent ribs: *ribby, bony-rumped, horned cattle.*

ribcage ▶ **noun** the bony frame formed by the ribs round the chest.

Ribera /rɪˈbɛːrə/, José (or Jusepe) de (*c.*1591–1652), Spanish painter and etcher, resident in Italy from 1616; known as **Lo Spagnoletto** ('the little Spaniard'). He is best known for his religious and genre paintings, for example the *Martyrdom of St Bartholomew* (*c.*1630).

rib-eye ▶ **noun** [usu. as modifier] a cut of beef from the outer side of the ribs: *a rib-eye steak.*

ribitol /ˈrʌɪbɪtɒl, ˈrɪb-/ ▶ **noun** [mass noun] Chemistry a colourless crystalline compound which is formed by reduction of ribose and occurs in certain plants.
• An alcohol; chem. formula: $HOCH_2(CHOH)_3CH_2OH$.
– ORIGIN 1940s: from **RIBOSE** + **-ITE**[1] + **-OL**.

riboflavin /ˌrʌɪbə(ʊ)ˈfleɪvɪn/ ▶ **noun** [mass noun] Biochemistry a yellow vitamin of the B complex which is essential for metabolic energy production. It is present in many foods, especially milk, liver, eggs, and green vegetables, and is also synthesized by the intestinal flora. Also called ***vitamin*** B_2.
– ORIGIN 1930s: from **RIBOSE** + Latin *flavus* 'yellow' + **-IN**[1].

ribonuclease /ˌrʌɪbə(ʊ)ˈnjuːklɪeɪz/ ▶ **noun** another term for **RNASE**.

ribonucleic acid /ˌrʌɪbə(ʊ)njuːˈkleɪɪk, -ˈkliːɪk/ ▶ **noun** see **RNA**.
– ORIGIN 1930s: *ribonucleic* from **RIBOSE** + **NUCLEIC ACID**.

ribose /ˈrʌɪbəʊz, -s/ ▶ **noun** [mass noun] Chemistry a sugar of the pentose class which occurs widely in nature as a constituent of nucleosides and several vitamins and enzymes.
– ORIGIN late 19th cent.: arbitrary alteration of **ARABINOSE**, a related sugar.

ribosome /ˈrʌɪbə(ʊ)səʊm/ ▶ **noun** Biochemistry a minute particle consisting of RNA and associated proteins found in large numbers in the cytoplasm of living cells. They bind messenger RNA and transfer RNA to synthesize polypeptides and proteins.
– DERIVATIVES **ribosomal** adjective.
– ORIGIN 1950s: from **RIBONUCLEIC ACID** + **-SOME**[3].

ribozyme /ˈrʌɪbə(ʊ)zʌɪm/ ▶ **noun** Biochemistry an RNA molecule capable of acting as an enzyme.
– ORIGIN 1980s: blend of **RIBONUCLEIC ACID** and **ENZYME**.

rib-tickler ▶ **noun** informal a very amusing joke or story.
– DERIVATIVES **rib-tickling** adjective, **rib-ticklingly** adverb.

ribulose /ˈrʌɪbjʊləʊz, -s/ ▶ **noun** [mass noun] Chemistry a sugar of the pentose class which is an important intermediate in carbohydrate metabolism and photosynthesis.
– ORIGIN 1930s: from **RIBOSE** + *-ulose*.

ribwort (also **ribwort plantain**) ▶ **noun** a Eurasian plantain with erect ribbed leaves and a rounded flower spike.
• *Plantago lanceolata*, family Plantaginaceae.

Ricard /ˈriːkɑː/ ▶ **noun** [mass noun] trademark an aniseed-flavoured aperitif.
– ORIGIN the name of the manufacturers.

Ricardian /rɪˈkɑːdiən/ ▶ **adjective** of or relating to the time of any of three kings of England, Richard I, II, and III.
■of or holding the view that Richard III was a just king who was misrepresented by Shakespeare and other writers.
▶ **noun** a contemporary or supporter of Richard III.
– DERIVATIVES **Ricardianism** noun.
– ORIGIN from medieval Latin *Ricardus* 'Richard' + **-IAN**.

Ricci tensor /ˈriːtʃi/ ▶ **noun** Mathematics a set of components that describes part of the curvature of space-time. It is a symmetric second-order tensor.
– ORIGIN 1920s: named after Curbastro G. Ricci (1853–1925), Italian mathematician.

Rice, Sir Tim (b.1944), English lyricist and entertainer; full name *Timothy Miles Bindon Rice*. Together with Andrew Lloyd Webber he co-wrote a number of hit musicals, including *Joseph and the Amazing Technicolor Dreamcoat* (1968), *Jesus Christ Superstar* (1971), and *Evita* (1978). He has also won two Oscars for best original film song (1992 and 1994).

rice ▶ **noun** [mass noun] a swamp grass which is widely cultivated as a source of food, especially in Asia.
• *Oryza sativa*, family Gramineae. **African rice** belongs to the related species *O. glaberrima*, whereas the so-called **wild rice** is not a true rice at all.
■the grains of this cereal used as food.

> Rice provides the staple diet of half the world's population and is second only to wheat in terms of total output. Rice seedlings are usually planted in flooded fields or paddies, so that terraces are necessary on hillsides and a reliable source of water is essential.

▶ **verb** [with obj.] N. Amer. force (cooked potatoes or other vegetables) through a sieve or ricer.
– ORIGIN Middle English: from Old French *ris*, from Italian *riso*, from Greek *oruza*.

rice bowl ▶ **noun** a dish from which rice is eaten.
■an area in which abundant quantities of rice are grown.

rice burner ▶ **noun** US derogatory a Japanese motorcycle.

ricepaper ▶ **noun** [mass noun] thin translucent edible paper made from the flattened and dried pith of a shrub, used in painting (especially oriental) and in baking biscuits and cakes.
• This paper is obtained from the Chinese plant *Tetrapanax papyriferus* (family Araliaceae) or from the Indo-Pacific plant *Scaevola sericea* (family Goodeniaceae).

ricer ▶ **noun** N. Amer. a utensil with small holes through which boiled potatoes or other soft food can be pushed to form particles of a similar size to grains of rice.

rice rat ▶ **noun** a nocturnal rat that typically lives in marshy or damp areas, native to America, the Caribbean, and the Galapagos Islands.
• *Oryzomys* and other genera, family Muridae: numerous species.

ricercar /ˌriːtʃəˈkɑː, ˈriːtʃəˌkɑː/ (also **ricercare** /ˌriːtʃəˈkɑːreɪ, -ri/) ▶ **noun** (pl. **ricercars** or **ricercari**) Music an elaborate contrapuntal instrumental composition in fugal or canonic style, typically of the 16th to 18th centuries.
– ORIGIN from Italian *ricercare* 'search out'.

Rich, Buddy (1917–87), American jazz drummer and bandleader; born *Bernard Rich*. He played for bandleaders such as Artie Shaw and Tommy Dorsey, and formed his own band in 1946.

rich ▶ **adjective 1** having a great deal of money or assets; wealthy: *most of these artists are already quite rich* | [as plural noun **the rich**] *every day the split between the rich and the poor widens.*
■(of a country or region) having valuable natural resources or a successful economy. ■of expensive materials or workmanship; demonstrating wealth: *rich mahogany furniture.* ■generating wealth; valuable: *not all footballers enjoy rich rewards from the game.*
2 plentiful; abundant: *China's rich and diverse mammalian fauna.*
■having (a particular thing) in large amounts: *many vegetables and fruits are **rich in** antioxidant vitamins* | [in combination] *a protein rich diet.* ■(of food) containing a large amount of fat, spices, sugar, etc.: *dishes with wonderfully rich sauces.* ■(of drink) full-bodied: *a rich and hoppy best bitter.* ■(of the mixture in an internal-combustion engine) containing a high proportion of fuel. ■(of a colour or sound) pleasantly deep and strong: *his rich bass voice.* ■(of a smell or taste) pleasantly smooth and mellow: *basmati rice has a rich aroma.* ■figurative interesting because full of diversity or complexity: *what a full, rich life you lead!*
3 producing a large quantity of something: *novels have always been a rich source of material for the film industry.*
■(of soil or a piece of land) having the properties necessary to produce fertile growth. ■(of a mine or mineral deposit) yielding a large quantity or proportion of precious metal.
4 informal (of a remark) causing ironic amusement or indignation: *these comments are **a bit rich** coming from a woman with no money worries.*
– DERIVATIVES **richness** noun.
– ORIGIN Old English *rīce* 'powerful, wealthy', of Germanic origin, related to Dutch *rijk* and German *reich*; ultimately from Celtic; reinforced in Middle English by Old French *riche* 'rich, powerful'.

-rich ▶ **combining form** containing a large amount of something specified: *lime-rich* | *protein-rich.*

Richard[1] the name of three kings of England:
■**Richard I** (1157–99), son of Henry II, reigned 1189–99; known as **Richard Coeur de Lion** or **Richard the Lionheart**. He led the Third Crusade, defeating Saladin at Arsuf (1191), but failing to capture Jerusalem. Returning home, he was held hostage by the Holy Roman emperor Henry VI until being released in 1194 on payment of a huge ransom.
■**Richard II** (1367–1400), son of the Black Prince, reigned 1377–99. Following his minority, he executed or banished most of his former opponents. His confiscation of his uncle John of Gaunt's estate on the latter's death provoked Henry Bolingbroke's return from exile to overthrow him.
■**Richard III** (1452–85), brother of Edward IV, reigned 1483–5. He served as Protector to his nephew Edward V, who, after two months, was declared illegitimate and subsequently disappeared. Richard's brief rule ended at Bosworth Field, where he was defeated by Henry Tudor and killed.

Richard[2], Sir Cliff (b.1940), British pop singer, born in India; born *Harry Roger Webb*. With his group the Drifters (later called the Shadows), he recorded such songs as 'Living Doll' (1959). Since the 1970s he has combined a successful solo pop career with evangelism.

Richards[1], Sir Gordon (1904–86), English jockey. He was champion jockey twenty-six times between 1925 and 1953.

Richards[2], I. A. (1893–1979), English literary critic and poet; full name *Ivor Armstrong Richards*. He emphasized the importance of close textual study, and praised irony, ambiguity, and allusiveness. Notable works: *Practical Criticism* (1929).

Richards[3], Viv (b.1952), West Indian cricketer; full name *Isaac Vivian Alexander Richards*. He captained the West Indian team from 1985 until 1991, and scored over 6,000 runs during his test career.

Richardson[1], Sir Ralph (David) (1902–83), English actor. He played many Shakespearean roles as well as leading parts in plays including Harold Pinter's *No Man's Land* (1975) and films including *Oh! What a Lovely War* (1969).

Richardson[2], Samuel (1689–1761), English novelist. His first novel *Pamela* (1740–1), entirely in the form of letters and journals, popularized the epistolary novel. He experimented further with the genre in *Clarissa Harlowe* (1747–8).

Richard the Lionheart /ˈlʌɪənhɑːt/, Richard I of England (see **RICHARD**[1]).

Richelieu /ˈriːʃ(ə)ljəː/, French ʀiʃəljø/, Armand Jean du Plessis, duc de (1585–1642), French cardinal and statesman. As chief minister of Louis XIII (1624–42) he dominated French government. In 1635 he established the Académie française.

richen ▶ **verb** [with obj.] make richer: *a town richened by several auto-assembly plants.*

riches ▶ **plural noun** material wealth: *riches beyond their wildest dreams.*
■ valuable natural resources: *the riches of the world's waters* | figurative *the riches of the Serbian oral tradition.*
– ORIGIN Middle English: variant (later interpreted as a plural form) of archaic *richesse*, from Old French *richeise* (from *riche* 'rich').

Richler /ˈrɪtʃlə/, Mordecai (b.1931), Canadian writer. His best-known novel is probably *The Apprenticeship of Duddy Kravitz* (1959).

richly ▶ **adverb** in an elaborate, generous, or plentiful way: *she was richly dressed in the height of fashion* | *Levkas and its neighbouring islands reward explorers richly.*
■ [as submodifier] fully (used especially to indicate that someone or something merits a particular thing): *give your family a richly deserved holiday.*

Richmond /ˈrɪtʃmənd/ **1** a town in northern England, on the River Swale in North Yorkshire; pop. 7,600 (1981).
2 a residential borough of Greater London, situated on the Thames. It contains Hampton Court Palace and the Royal Botanic Gardens at Kew. Full name **RICHMOND-UPON-THAMES**.
3 the state capital of Virginia, a port on the James River; pop. 203,060 (1990). During the American Civil War it was the Confederate capital from July 1861 until its capture in 1865.

Richter scale /ˈrɪktə/ ▶ **noun** Geology a numerical scale for expressing the magnitude of an earthquake on the basis of seismograph oscillations. The more destructive earthquakes typically have magnitudes between about 5.5 and 8.9; it is a logarithmic scale and a difference of one represents an approximate thirtyfold difference in magnitude.
– ORIGIN 1930s: named after Charles F. *Richter* (1900–85), American geologist.

Richthofen /ˈrɪxtˌhəʊv(ə)n, German ˈrɪçtˌhoːfn/, Manfred, Freiherr von (1882–1918), German fighter pilot; known as **the Red Baron**. He joined a fighter squadron in 1915, flying a distinctive bright red aircraft. He was eventually shot down after destroying eighty enemy planes.

ricin /ˈrʌɪsɪn, ˈrɪsɪn/ ▶ **noun** [mass noun] Chemistry a highly toxic protein obtained from the pressed seeds of the castor oil plant.
– ORIGIN late 19th cent.: from modern Latin *Ricinus communis* (denoting the castor oil plant) + **-IN**[1].

rick[1] ▶ **noun** a stack of hay, corn, straw, or similar, especially one formerly built into a regular shape and thatched.
■ N. Amer. a pile of firewood somewhat smaller than a cord. ■ N. Amer. a set of shelving for storing barrels.
▶ **verb** [with obj.] form into a rick or ricks; stack: *the nine cords of good spruce wood* **ricked up** *in the back yard.*
– ORIGIN Old English *hrēac*, of Germanic origin; related to Dutch *rook*.

rick[2] ▶ **noun** a slight sprain or strain, especially in a person's neck or back.
▶ **verb** [with obj.] strain (one's neck or back) slightly.
– ORIGIN late 18th cent. (as a verb): of dialect origin.

rickets /ˈrɪkɪts/ ▶ **noun** [mass noun] [treated as sing. or pl.] Medicine a disease of children caused by vitamin D deficiency, characterized by imperfect calcification, softening, and distortion of the bones typically resulting in bow legs.
– ORIGIN mid 17th cent.: perhaps an alteration of Greek *rhakhitis* (see **RACHITIS**).

rickettsia /rɪˈkɛtsɪə/ ▶ **noun** (pl. **rickettsiae** /-ɪiː/ or **rickettsias**) any of a group of very small bacteria that include the causative agents of typhus and various other febrile diseases in humans. Like viruses, many of them can only grow inside living cells, and they are frequently transmitted by mites, ticks, or lice.
• Genus *Rickettsia*, order Rickettsiales; Gram-negative rods.
– DERIVATIVES **rickettsial** adjective.
– ORIGIN modern Latin, named after Howard Taylor *Ricketts* (1871–1910), American pathologist.

rickety ▶ **adjective** **1** (of a structure or piece of equipment) poorly made and likely to collapse: *we went carefully up the rickety stairs* | figurative *a rickety banking system.*
2 (of a person) suffering from rickets.
– DERIVATIVES **ricketiness** noun.
– ORIGIN late 17th cent.: from **RICKETS** + **-Y**[1].

rickey ▶ **noun** (pl. **-eys**) N. Amer. a drink consisting of a spirit, typically gin, mixed with lime or lemon juice, carbonated water, and ice.
– ORIGIN late 19th cent.: probably from the surname *Rickey*.

rickle ▶ **noun** Scottish, Irish, & N. English a loosely piled heap of something: *a rickle of bones.*
– ORIGIN late 15th cent.: perhaps from Norwegian dialect *rikl*, or from **RICK**[1].

rickrack ▶ **noun** [mass noun] braided trimming in a zigzag pattern, used as decoration on clothes.
– ORIGIN late 19th cent.: of unknown origin.

rickshaw ▶ **noun** a light two-wheeled hooded vehicle drawn by one or more people, chiefly used in Asian countries.
■ a similar vehicle like a three-wheeled bicycle, having a seat for passengers behind the driver.
– ORIGIN late 19th cent.: abbreviation of **JINRICKSHA**.

RICO ▶ **abbreviation for** (in the US) Racketeer Influenced and Corrupt Organizations Act.

ricochet /ˈrɪkəʃeɪ, -ʃɛt/ ▶ **noun** a shot or hit that rebounds one or more times off a surface.
■ [mass noun] the action or movement of a bullet, shell, or other projectile when rebounding in such a way.
▶ **verb** (**ricocheted** /-ʃeɪd/, **ricocheting** /-ʃeɪɪŋ/ or **ricochetted** /-ʃɛtɪd/, **ricochetting** /-ʃɛtɪŋ/) [no obj., with adverbial of direction] (of a bullet, shell, or other projectile) rebound one or more times off a surface: *a bullet ricocheted off a nearby wall.*
■ [with obj. and adverbial of direction] cause to rebound in such a way: *they fired off a couple of rounds, ricocheting the bullets against a wall.* ■ figurative move or appear to move with a series of such rebounds: *the sound ricocheted around the hall.*
– ORIGIN mid 18th cent.: from French, of unknown origin.

ricotta /rɪˈkɒtə/ ▶ **noun** [mass noun] a soft white unsalted Italian cheese.
– ORIGIN Italian, literally 'recooked, cooked twice'.

RICS ▶ **abbreviation for** (in the UK) Royal Institution of Chartered Surveyors.

rictus /ˈrɪktəs/ ▶ **noun** a fixed grimace or grin.
– DERIVATIVES **rictal** adjective.
– ORIGIN early 19th cent.: from Latin, literally 'open mouth', from *rict-* 'gaped', from the verb *ringi*.

rid ▶ **verb** (**ridding**; past and past participle **rid** or archaic **ridded**) [with obj.] (**rid someone/thing of**) make someone or something free of (a troublesome or unwanted person or thing): *we now have the greatest chance ever to rid the world of nuclear weapons.*
■ (**be rid of**) be freed or relieved from: *she couldn't wait to be rid of us.*
– PHRASES **be well rid of** be in a better state for having removed or disposed of (a troublesome or unwanted person or thing). **get rid of** take action so as to be free of (a troublesome or unwanted person or thing).
– ORIGIN Middle English: from Old Norse *rythja*. The original sense 'to clear' described clearing land of trees and undergrowth; this gave rise to 'free from rubbish or encumbrances', later becoming generalized.

riddance ▶ **noun** [mass noun] the action of getting rid of a troublesome or unwanted person or thing.
– PHRASES **good riddance** said to express relief at being free of a troublesome or unwanted person or thing.

ridden past participle of **RIDE**.

riddle[1] ▶ **noun** a question or statement intentionally phrased so as to require ingenuity in ascertaining its answer or meaning, typically presented as a game.
■ a person, event, or fact that is difficult to understand or explain: *the riddle of her death.*
▶ **verb** [no obj.] archaic speak in or pose riddles: *he who knows not how to riddle.*
■ [with two objs] solve or explain (a riddle) to (someone): *riddle me this then.*
– PHRASES **talk** (or **speak**) **in riddles** express oneself in an ambiguous or puzzling manner.
– DERIVATIVES **riddler** noun.
– ORIGIN Old English *rǣdels, rǣdelse* 'opinion, conjecture, riddle'; related to Dutch *raadsel*, German *Rätsel*, also to **READ**.

riddle[2] ▶ **verb** [with obj.] **1** (usu. **be riddled**) make many holes in (someone or something), especially with gunshot: *his car was riddled by sniper fire.*
■ fill or permeate (someone or something), especially with something unpleasant or undesirable: *the existing law is* **riddled with** *loopholes.*
2 pass (a substance) through a large coarse sieve: *for final potting, the soil mixture is not riddled.*
■ remove ashes or other unwanted material from (something, especially a fire or stove) in such a way.
▶ **noun** a large coarse sieve, especially one used for separating ashes from cinders or sand from gravel.
– ORIGIN late Old English *hriddel*, of Germanic origin; from an Indo-European root shared by Latin *cribrum* 'sieve', *cernere* 'separate', and Greek *krinein* 'decide'.

riddling ▶ **adjective** speaking or expressed in riddles; enigmatic: *the riddling sphinx.*
– DERIVATIVES **riddlingly** adverb.

ride ▶ **verb** (past **rode**; past participle **ridden**) [with obj.] **1** sit on and control the movement of (an animal, especially a horse), typically as a recreation or sport: *Diana went to watch him ride his horse* | [no obj.] *I haven't ridden much since the accident.*
■ [no obj., with adverbial] travel on a horse or other animal: *we* **rode on** *horseback* | *some of the officers were riding back.* ■ sit on and control (a bicycle or motorcycle) for recreation or as a means of transport: *he rode a Harley Davidson across the United States.* ■ [no obj.] (**ride in/on**) travel in or on (a vehicle) as a passenger: *I started riding on the buses.* ■ chiefly N. Amer. travel in (a vehicle) or on (a public transport system) as a passenger: *she rides the bus across 42nd Street.* ■ go through or over (an area) on horseback, a bicycle, etc.: *ride the full length of the Ridgeway.* ■ compete in (a race) on horseback or on a bicycle or motorcycle: *I rode a good race.* ■ N. Amer. travel up or down in (a lift): *the astronauts rode elevators to the launch pad* | [no obj.] *we ride up in the elevator, chatting lightly.* ■ S. African transport (goods): *neighbours rode loads of prickly pear to feed their animals.* ■ [no obj., with adverbial or complement] (of a vehicle, animal, racetrack, etc.) be of a particular character for riding on or in: *the Metro rode as well as some cars of twice the price.* ■ informal transport (someone) in a vehicle: *the taxi driver who rode Kale into the airport not long ago.*
2 [with obj.] be carried or supported by (something with a great deal of momentum): *a stream of young surfers fighting the elements to ride the waves* | figurative *the fund rode the growth boom in the 1980s.*
■ [no obj.] project or overlap: *when two lithospheric plates collide, one tends to* **ride over** *the other.* ■ [no obj.] (of a vessel) sail or float: *a large cedar barque* **rode at anchor**. ■ [no obj., with adverbial of place] float or seem to float: *the moon was riding high in the sky.* ■ yield to (a blow) so as to reduce its impact: *Harrison drew back his jaw as if riding the blow.* ■ vulgar slang have sexual intercourse with. ■ (of a supernatural being) take spiritual possession of (someone). ■ N. Amer. annoy, pester, or tease: *if you don't give all the kids a chance to play, the parents ride you.*
3 (**be ridden**) be full of or dominated by: *you must not think him ridden with angst* | [as adj., in combination **-ridden**] *the crime-ridden streets.*
▶ **noun** **1** a journey made on horseback, on a bicycle or motorcycle, or in a vehicle: *I hitched a ride* | figurative *investors have had a bumpy ride.*
■ N. Amer. a person giving someone a lift in their vehicle: *their ride into town had dropped them off near the bridge.* ■ US informal a motor vehicle. ■ the quality of comfort or smoothness offered by a vehicle while

it is being driven, as perceived by the driver or passenger: *the ride is comfortable, though there is a slight roll when cornering.* ■ a path, typically one through woods, for horse riding. ■ Canadian a demonstration of horse riding as an entertainment.

2 a roller coaster, roundabout, or other amusement ridden at a fair or amusement park.

3 vulgar slang an act of sexual intercourse.

■ a sexually attractive person.

4 (also **ride cymbal**) a cymbal used for keeping up a continuous rhythm.

– PHRASES **be riding for a fall** informal be acting in a reckless or arrogant way that invites defeat or failure. **for the ride** for pleasure or interest, rather than any serious purpose: *Chris didn't fit in with the rest of them, but was thrilled to be along for the ride.* **let something ride** take no immediate action over something. **ride herd on** N. Amer. keep watch over: *a man to ride herd on this frenetically paced enterprise.* **ride high** be successful: *the economy will be riding high on the top of the next boom.* **ride the pine** (or **bench**) N. Amer. informal (of an athlete) sit on the sidelines rather than participate in a game or event. **ride the rods** (or **rails**) Canadian, informal ride on a freight train surreptitiously without paying. **ride roughshod over** carry out one's own plans or wishes with arrogant disregard for (others or their wishes): *he rode roughshod over everyone else's opinions.* —— **rides again** used to indicate that someone or something has reappeared unexpectedly and with new vigour. **ride shotgun** chiefly N. Amer. travel as a guard in the seat next to the driver of a vehicle. ■ ride in the passenger seat of a vehicle. ■ figurative act as a protector: The Times *found itself to be riding shotgun for the Red Army.* **ride to hounds** chiefly Brit. go fox-hunting on horseback. **a rough** (or **easy**) **ride** a difficult (or easy) time doing something: *the prime minister was given a rough ride by left-wing MPs yesterday.* **take someone for a ride** informal deceive or cheat someone.

– DERIVATIVES **rideable** (also **ridable**) adjective.

– ORIGIN Old English *rīdan*, of Germanic origin; related to Dutch *rijden* and German *reiten*.

▶ **ride someone down** trample or overtake someone while on horseback.

ride on depend on: *there is a great deal of money riding on the results of these studies.*

ride something out come safely through something, especially a storm or a period of danger or difficulty: *the fleet had* **ridden out** *the storm.*

ride up (of a garment) gradually work or move upwards out of its proper position: *her skirt had ridden up.*

ride-off ▶ **noun** N. Amer. (in a riding competition) a round held to resolve a tie or determine qualifiers for a later stage; a jump-off.

ride-on ▶ **adjective** (especially of a lawnmower) on which one rides while operating it.

▶ **noun 1** a lawnmower of this type.

2 chiefly N. Amer. a toy car that a child can sit in and move by pedals, battery power, etc.

rider ▶ **noun 1** a person who is riding or who can ride a horse, bicycle, motorcycle, or snowboard.

2 a condition or proviso added to something already said or decreed: *one* **rider to** *the deal—if the hurricane heads north, we run for shelter.*

■ Brit. an addition or amendment to a bill at its third reading. ■ Brit. a recommendation or comment added by the jury to a judicial verdict.

3 a small weight positioned on the beam of a balance for fine adjustment.

– DERIVATIVES **riderless** adjective.

– ORIGIN late Old English *rīdere* 'mounted warrior, knight' (see **RIDE**, **-ER**[1]).

ridership ▶ **noun** [mass noun] chiefly N. Amer. the number of passengers using a particular form of public transport.

ridge ▶ **noun** a long narrow hilltop, mountain range, or watershed: *the North-East ridge of Everest.*

■ the line or edge formed where the two sloping sides of a roof meet at the top. ■ Meteorology an elongated region of high barometric pressure. ■ a narrow raised band running along or across a surface: *buff your nails in order to smooth ridges.* ■ a raised strip of arable land, especially (in medieval open fields) one of a set separated by furrows.

▶ **verb** [with obj.] [often as adj. **ridged**] mark with or form into narrow raised bands: *the ridged sand of the beach.*

■ [no obj.] (of a surface) form into or rise up as a narrow raised band: *the crust of the earth ridged.* ■ form (arable land) into raised strips separated by furrows: *a field ploughed in narrow stetches that are* **ridged up** *slightly.*

– DERIVATIVES **ridgy** adjective.

– ORIGIN Old English *hrycg* 'spine, crest', of Germanic origin; related to Dutch *rug* and German *Rücken* 'back'.

ridgeback ▶ **noun** short for **RHODESIAN RIDGEBACK**.

ridge piece (also **ridge tree**) ▶ **noun** a horizontal beam along the ridge of a roof, into which the rafters are fastened.

ridge pole ▶ **noun 1** the horizontal pole of a long tent.

2 another term for **RIDGE PIECE**.

ridge runner ▶ **noun** US informal a mountain farmer of the Southern states of the US.

ridge tent ▶ **noun** a tent having a central ridge supported by a pole or frame at each end.

ridge tile ▶ **noun** a semicircular or curved tile used in making a roof ridge.

ridgeway ▶ **noun** a road or track along a ridge, especially (**the Ridgeway**) a prehistoric trackway following the ridge of the downs in Wiltshire and Berkshire, in southern England.

ridicule ▶ **noun** [mass noun] the subjection of someone or something to mockery and derision: *he is held up as* **an object of ridicule**.

▶ **verb** [with obj.] subject (someone or something) to mockery and derision: *his theory was ridiculed and dismissed.*

– ORIGIN late 17th cent.: from French, or from Latin *ridiculum*, neuter (used as a noun) of *ridiculus* 'laughable', from *ridere* 'to laugh'.

ridiculous ▶ **adjective** deserving or inviting derision or mockery; absurd: *that ridiculous tartan cap.*

– DERIVATIVES **ridiculousness** noun.

– ORIGIN mid 16th cent.: from Latin *ridiculosus*, from *ridiculus* 'laughable' (see **RIDICULE**).

ridiculously ▶ **adverb** so as to invite mockery or derision; absurdly: [sentence adverb] *ridiculously, I felt like crying.*

■ [as submodifier] so as to cause surprise or disbelief: *it had been ridiculously easy to track him down.*

riding[1] ▶ **noun** [mass noun] the sport or activity of riding horses.

■ [count noun] a path for horse riding, typically one through woods.

riding[2] ▶ **noun 1** (usu. **the East/North/West Riding**) one of three former administrative divisions of Yorkshire.

2 an electoral district of Canada.

– ORIGIN Old English *trithing*, from Old Norse *thrithjungr* 'third part', from *thrithi* 'third'. The initial *th-* was lost due to assimilation with the preceding *-t* of *East*, *West*, or with the *-th* of *North*.

riding crop ▶ **noun** a short flexible whip with a loop for the hand, used in riding horses.

riding habit ▶ **noun** a woman's riding dress, consisting of a skirt worn with a double-breasted jacket.

riding light ▶ **noun** a light shown by a ship at anchor.

Ridley, Nicholas (*c.*1500–55), English Protestant bishop and martyr. He was appointed bishop of Rochester (1547) and then of London (1550). He opposed the Catholic policies of Mary I, for which he was burnt at the stake in Oxford.

ridley (also **ridley turtle**) ▶ **noun** (pl. **-eys**) a small turtle of tropical seas.

● Genus *Lepidochelys*, family Cheloniidae: **Kemp's ridley** (*L. kempi*) of the Atlantic, and the larger **olive ridley** (*L. olivacea*) of the Pacific.

– ORIGIN 1940s: of unknown origin.

Rie /riː/, Lucie (1902–95), Austrian-born British potter. Her pottery and stoneware were admired for their precise simple shapes and varied subtle glazes.

riebeckite /ˈriːbɛkʌɪt/ ▶ **noun** [mass noun] a dark blue or black mineral of the amphibole group, occurring chiefly in alkaline igneous rocks or as blue asbestos (crocidolite).

– ORIGIN late 19th cent.: from the name of Emil *Riebeck* (died 1885), German explorer, + **-ITE**[1].

Riefenstahl /ˈriːf(ə)nˌʃtɑːl/, Leni (b.1902), German film-maker and photographer; full name *Bertha Helene Amalie Riefenstahl*. She is chiefly known for *Triumph of the Will* (1934), a depiction of the 1934 Nuremberg Nazi Party rallies. Though she was not working for the Nazi Party, outside Germany her work was regarded as Nazi propaganda.

Riel /riːˈɛl/, Louis (1844–85), Canadian political leader. He led the rebellion of the Metis at Red River Settlement in 1869, later forming a provisional government and negotiating terms for the union of Manitoba with Canada. He was executed for treason after leading a further rebellion.

riel /ˈriːəl/ ▶ **noun** the basic monetary unit of Cambodia, equal to 100 sen.

– ORIGIN Khmer.

riem /rɪm, riːm/ (also **riempie** /ˈrɪmpi, riːmpi/) ▶ **noun** (pl. **riems** or **riempies**) S. African a strip of rawhide or worked leather, used as a rope or in making chairs and other furniture.

– ORIGIN Dutch.

Riemann /ˈriːmən, German ˈriːman/, (Georg Friedrich) Bernhard (1826–66), German mathematician. He founded Riemannian geometry, which is of fundamental importance to both mathematics and physics. The *Riemann hypothesis*, about the complex numbers which are roots of a certain transcendental equation, remains an unsolved problem.

Riemannian geometry /riːˈmanɪən/ ▶ **noun** [mass noun] a form of differential non-Euclidean geometry developed by Riemann, used to describe curved space. It provided Einstein with a mathematical basis for his general theory of relativity.

Riesling /ˈriːzlɪŋ, ˈriːs-/ ▶ **noun** [mass noun] a variety of wine grape grown in Germany, Austria, and elsewhere.

■ a dry white wine made from this grape.

– ORIGIN German.

rietbok /ˈriːtbɒk/ ▶ **noun** S. African another term for **REEDBUCK**.

– ORIGIN South African Dutch.

rifampicin /rɪˈfampɪsɪn/ (also **rifampin**) ▶ **noun** [mass noun] Medicine a reddish-brown antibiotic used chiefly to treat tuberculosis and leprosy.

● The antibiotic is obtained from the bacterium *Nocardia mediterranei*.

– ORIGIN 1960s: from *rifamycin* (an antibiotic first isolated from the bacterium *Streptomyces mediterranei*) + the insertion of *pi-* from **PIPERAZINE**.

rife ▶ **adjective** [predic.] (especially of something undesirable or harmful) of common occurrence; widespread: *male chauvinism was rife in medicine in those days.*

■ (**rife with**) full of: *the streets were rife with rumour and fear.*

▶ **adverb** in an unchecked or widespread manner: *speculation* **ran rife** *that he was an arms dealer.*

– DERIVATIVES **rifeness** noun.

– ORIGIN late Old English *rȳfe*, probably from Old Norse *rīfr* 'acceptable'.

riff ▶ **noun** (in popular music and jazz) a short repeated phrase, frequently played over changing chords or harmonies or used as a background to a solo improvisation: *a brilliant guitar riff.*

▶ **verb** [no obj.] play such phrases: *the other horns would be riffing behind him.*

– ORIGIN 1930s: abbreviation of the noun **RIFFLE**.

riffle ▶ **verb** [no obj.] turn over something, especially the pages of a book, quickly and casually: *he* **riffled through** *the pages* | [with obj.] *she opened a book with her thumbnail and riffled the pages.*

■ (**riffle through**) search quickly through (something), especially so as to cause disorder: *she riffled through her leather handbag.* ■ [with obj.] disturb the surface of; ruffle: *there was a slight breeze that riffled her hair.* ■ [with obj.] shuffle (playing cards) by flicking up and releasing the corners or sides of two piles of cards so that they intermingle and may be slid together to form a single pile.

▶ **noun 1** [usu. in sing.] a quick or casual leaf or search through something.

■ the rustle of paper being leafed through in such a way. ■ a shuffle performed by riffling playing cards.

2 chiefly N. Amer. a rocky or shallow part of a stream or river where the water flows brokenly.

■ a patch of waves or ripples.

– ORIGIN late 18th cent. (in sense 2): perhaps from a variant of the verb **RUFFLE**, influenced by **RIPPLE**.

riffler ▶ **noun** a narrow elongated tool with a curved file surface at each end, used in filing concave surfaces.

– ORIGIN late 18th cent.: from French *rifloir*, from Old French *rifler* 'to scrape'.

riff-raff ▶ noun [mass noun] disreputable or undesirable people.
– ORIGIN late 15th cent. (as *riff and raff*): from Old French *rif et raf* 'one and all, every bit', of Germanic origin.

rifle¹ ▶ noun a gun, especially one fired from shoulder level, having a long spirally grooved barrel intended to make a bullet spin and thereby have greater accuracy over a long distance.
■(**rifles**) troops armed with rifles: [in names] *the Burma Rifles.*
▶ verb **1** [with obj.] [usu. as adj. **rifled**] make spiral grooves in (a gun or its barrel or bore) to make a bullet spin and thereby have greater accuracy over a long distance: *a line of replacement rifled barrels.*
2 [with obj. and adverbial of direction] hit or kick (a ball) hard and straight: *Ferguson rifled home his fourth goal of the season.* [ORIGIN: 1940s: from *rifle* 'gun', suggestive of explosive speed; compare with the verb *shoot*.]
– ORIGIN mid 17th cent.: from French *rifler* 'graze, scratch', of Germanic origin. The earliest noun usage was in *rifle gun*, which had 'rifles' or spiral grooves cut into the inside of the barrel.

rifle² ▶ verb [no obj.] search through something in a hurried way in order to find or steal something: *she rifled through the cassette tapes* | [with obj.] *she rifled the house for money for him.*
■[with obj.] steal: *the Lieutenant's servant rifled the dead man's possessions.*
– ORIGIN Middle English: from Old French *rifler* 'graze, plunder', of Germanic origin.

rifle bird ▶ noun a bird of paradise, the male of which has mainly velvety-black plumage and a display call that sounds like a whistling bullet.
● Genus *Ptiloris*, family Paradisaeidae: three species.

rifle green ▶ noun [mass noun] a dark olive-green colour, like that of the uniform of a private in a British army rifle regiment.

rifleman ▶ noun (pl. **-men**) **1** a soldier armed with a rifle, especially a private in a rifle regiment.
2 a very small, short-tailed, greenish-yellow songbird which feeds on insects on tree bark, native to New Zealand. [ORIGIN: perhaps so named from a comparison between its plumage and an early military uniform.]
● *Acanthisitta chloris*, family Xenicidae.

rifle microphone ▶ noun a type of gun microphone with several parallel tubes of different lengths in front of the diaphragm to enhance its directional focus.

rifle range ▶ noun a place for practising shooting with rifles.
■an attraction at a fairground in which people fire rifles at targets in order to win prizes.

riflescope ▶ noun informal a telescopic sight on a rifle.

rifle shot ▶ noun a shot fired from a rifle.
■[mass noun] the range of a rifle: *the schooner had escaped out of rifle shot.* ■[with adj.] a person who is able to fire a rifle with a particular degree of skill: *he was an excellent rifle shot.*

rifling /ˈrʌɪflɪŋ/ ▶ noun [mass noun] the arrangement of spiral grooves on the inside of a rifle barrel.

Rif Mountains /rɪf/ (also **Er Rif**) a mountain range of northern Morocco, running parallel to the Mediterranean for about 290 km (180 miles) eastwards from Tangier. Rising to over 2,250 m (7,000 ft), it forms a westward extension of the Atlas Mountains.

rift ▶ noun a crack, split, or break in something: *the wind had torn open a rift in the clouds.*
■Geology a major fault separating blocks of the earth's surface; a rift valley. ■figurative a serious break in friendly relations: *the **rift between** the two branches of the legal profession.*
▶ verb [no obj.] chiefly Geology form fissures, cracks, or breaks, especially through large-scale faulting; move apart: *a fragment of continental crust which rifted away from eastern Australia* | [as noun **rifting**] *active rifting in south-western Mexico.*
■[with obj.] [usu. as adj. **rifted**] tear or force (something) apart: *the nascent rifted margins of the Red Sea.*
– ORIGIN Middle English: of Scandinavian origin; compare with Norwegian and Danish *rift* 'cleft, chink'.

rift valley ▶ noun a large elongated depression with steep walls formed by the downward

displacement of a block of the earth's surface between nearly parallel faults or fault systems.
■(**Rift Valley**) see GREAT RIFT VALLEY.

rig¹ ▶ verb (**rigged, rigging**) [with obj.] make (a sailing boat) ready for sailing by providing it with sails and rigging: *the catamaran will be rigged as a ketch* | [as adj., in combination **-rigged**] *a gaff-rigged cutter.*
■assemble and adjust (the equipment of a sailing boat, aircraft, etc.) to make it ready for operation: *most sails are kept ready rigged.* ■ set up (equipment or a device or structure), typically hastily or as a makeshift: *he had **rigged up** a sort of tent* | [with obj. and infinitive] *the power plant of the lifeboat had been rigged to explode.* ■ provide (someone) with clothes of a particular style or type: *a cavalry regiment **rigged out** in green and gold.*
▶ noun **1** the particular way in which a sailing boat's masts, sails, and rigging are arranged: *the yacht will emerge from the yard with her original rig.*
■the sail, mast, and boom of a windsurfer.
2 an apparatus, device, or piece of equipment designed for a particular purpose: *a lighting rig.*
■an oil rig or drilling rig. ■(in CB and short-wave radio) a transmitter and receiver. ■a particular type of construction for fishing tackle that bears the bait and hook.
3 a person's costume, outfit, or style of dress: *the rig of the American Army Air Corps.*
4 chiefly N. Amer. & Austral. a lorry; a semi-trailer.
– PHRASES (**in**) **full rig** informal (wearing) smart or ceremonial clothes.
– ORIGIN late 15th cent. (in nautical use): perhaps of Scandinavian origin: compare with Norwegian *rigga* 'bind or wrap up'. The noun dates from the early 19th cent.

rig² ▶ verb (**rigged, rigging**) [with obj.] manage or conduct (something) fraudulently so as to produce a result or situation to a particular person's advantage: *the results of the elections had been rigged* | [as noun, in combination **-rigging**] *charges of vote-rigging.*
■cause an artificial rise or fall in prices in (a market, especially the stock market) with a view to personal profit: *he accused games firms of rigging the market.*
▶ noun archaic a trick or way of swindling someone.
– ORIGIN late 18th cent. (in the noun sense): of unknown origin; the verb is related to the noun.

Riga /ˈriːɡə/ a port on the Baltic Sea, capital of Latvia; pop. 915,000 (1990).

rigadoon /ˌrɪɡəˈduːn/ ▶ noun a lively dance for couples, in duple or quadruple time, of Provençal origin.
– ORIGIN late 17th cent.: from French *rigaudon*, perhaps named after its inventor, said to be a dance teacher called *Rigaud*.

rigatoni /ˌrɪɡəˈtəʊni/ ▶ plural noun pasta in the form of short hollow fluted tubes.
– ORIGIN Italian.

Rigel /ˈrʌɪdʒəl, ˈrʌɪɡ(ə)l/ Astronomy the seventh brightest star in the sky, and the brightest in the constellation Orion. It is a blue supergiant nearly sixty thousand times as luminous as our sun.
– ORIGIN from Arabic *rijl* 'foot (of Orion)'.

rigger¹ ▶ noun **1** [in combination] a ship rigged in a particular way: *a square-rigger.*
2 a person who rigs or attends to the rigging of a sailing ship, aircraft, or parachute.
■a person who erects and maintains scaffolding, lifting tackle, cranes, etc. ■ a person who works on or helps construct an oil rig.
3 (also **rigger brush**) an artist's long-haired sable brush.
4 an outrigger carrying a rowlock on a racing rowing boat.

rigger² ▶ noun a person who fraudulently manipulates something so as to produce a result or situation to their advantage.

rigging ▶ noun [mass noun] **1** the system of ropes or chains employed to support a ship's masts (**standing rigging**) and to control or set the yards and sails (**running rigging**).
■the action of providing a sailing ship with sails, stays, and braces.
2 the ropes and wires supporting the structure of an airship, biplane, hang-glider, or parachute.
■the system of cables and fittings controlling the flight surfaces and engines of an aircraft. ■the action of assembling and adjusting such rigging.

right ▶ adjective **1** morally good, justified, or acceptable: *I hope we're doing the right thing* | [with infinitive] *you were quite right to criticize him.*

2 true or correct as a fact: *I'm not sure I know the right answer* | *her theories were proved right.*
■[predic.] correct in one's opinion or judgement: *she was right about Tom having no money.* ■used as an interrogative at the end of a statement as a way of inviting agreement, approval, or confirmation: *you went to see Angie on Monday, right?* ■ according to what is correct for a particular situation or thing: *is this the right way to the cottage?* | *you're not holding it the right way up.* ■ the best or most suitable of a number of possible choices for a particular purpose or occasion: *he was clearly the right man for the job* | *I was waiting for the right moment to ask him.* ■ socially fashionable or important: *he was seen at all the right places.* ■ [predic.] in a satisfactory, sound, or normal state or condition: *that sausage doesn't smell right* | *if only I could have helped put matters right.*
3 denoting or worn on the side of a person's body which is towards the east when they are facing north: *my right elbow* | *her right shoe.*
■denoting the corresponding side of any other object: *the right edge of the field.* ■ on this side from the point of view of a spectator.
4 [attrib.] informal, chiefly Brit. complete; absolute (used for emphasis, typically in derogatory contexts): *I felt a right idiot.*
5 of or relating to a person or political party or grouping favouring conservative views: *are you politically right, left, or centre?*
▶ adverb **1** [with prep. phr.] to the furthest or most complete extent or degree (used for emphasis): *the car spun right off the track* | *I'm right out of ideas.*
■exactly; directly (used to emphasize the precise location or time of something): *Harriet was standing right behind her.* ■ informal immediately; without delaying or hesitating: *I'll be right back.* ■ [as submodifier] dialect or archaic very: *it's right spooky in there!*
2 correctly: *he had guessed right.*
■in the required or necessary way; properly; satisfactorily: *nothing's going right for me this season.*
3 on or to the right side: *turn right off the B1269.*
▶ noun **1** [mass noun] that which is morally correct, just, or honourable: *she doesn't understand the difference between right and wrong* | [count noun] *the rights and wrongs of the matter.*
2 a moral or legal entitlement to have or obtain something or to act in a certain way: [with infinitive] *she had every right to be angry* | *you're quite **within your rights** to ask for your money back* | [mass noun] *there is no right of appeal against the decision.*
■(**rights**) the authority to perform, publish, film, or televise a particular work, event, etc.: *they sold the paperback rights.*
3 (**the right**) the right-hand part, side, or direction: *take the first turning on the right* | (**one's right**) *she seated me on her right.*
■(in football or a similar sport) the right-hand half of the field when facing the opponent's goal. ■ the right wing of an army. ■ a right turn: *he made a right in Dorchester Avenue.* ■ a road or entrance on the right: *take the first right over the stream.* ■ (especially in the context of boxing) a person's right fist. ■ a blow given with this: *the young copper swung a terrific right.*
4 (often **the Right**) [treated as sing. or pl.] a grouping or political party favouring conservative views and supporting capitalist economic principles.
■the section of a group or political party adhering particularly strongly to such views. [ORIGIN: see RIGHT WING.]
▶ verb [with obj.] restore to a normal or upright position: *we righted the capsized dinghy.*
■restore to a normal or correct condition or situation: *righting the economy demanded major cuts in defence spending.* ■ redress or rectify (a wrong or mistaken action): *she was determined to right the wrongs done to her father.* ■ (usu. **be righted**) archaic make reparation to (someone) for a wrong done to them: *we'll see you righted.*
▶ exclamation informal used to indicate one's agreement with a suggestion or to acknowledge a statement or order: *'Barry's here.' 'Oh, right'* | *right you are, sir.*
■used as a filler in speech or as a way of confirming that someone is listening to or understanding what one is saying: *and I didn't think any more of it, right, but Mum said I should take him to a doctor.* ■ used to introduce an utterance, exhortation, or suggestion: *right, let's have a drink.*
– PHRASES **bang** (or N. Amer. **dead**) **to rights** informal (of a criminal) with positive proof of guilt: *we've got you bang to rights handling stolen property.* **be in the right** be morally or legally justified in one's views, actions, or decisions. **by rights** if things had happened or been done fairly or correctly: *by rights, he should not be playing next week.* **do right by** treat

(someone) fairly. **in one's own right** as a result of one's own claims, qualifications, or efforts, rather than an association with someone else: *he was already established as a poet in his own right.* **(not) in one's right mind** (not) sane. **not right in the head** informal (of a person) not completely sane. **(as) of right** (or **by right**) as a result of having a moral or legal claim or entitlement: *the state will be obliged to provide health care and education as of right.* **put** (or **set**) **someone right 1** restore someone to health. **2** make someone understand the true facts of a situation. **put** (or **set**) **something to rights** restore something to its correct or normal state or condition. **(as) right as rain** informal (of a person) feeling completely well or healthy, typically after an illness or minor accident. **right** (or **straight**) **away** (or informal **off**) immediately. **right enough** informal certainly; undeniably: *your record's bad right enough.* **right on** informal used as an expression of strong support, approval, or encouragement. See also **RIGHT-ON**. **a right one** Brit. informal a silly or foolish person. **she's** (or **she'll be**) **right** Austral. informal that will be all right; don't worry. **too right** informal used to express one's enthusiastic agreement with a statement.

– DERIVATIVES **rightable** adjective, **righter** noun, **rightish** adjective, **rightness** noun.

– ORIGIN Old English *riht* (adjective and noun), *rihtan* (verb), *rihte* (adverb), of Germanic origin; related to Latin *rectus* 'ruled', from an Indo-European root denoting movement in a straight line.

right about (also **right about-face**) ▶ **noun** Military a right turn continued through 180° so as to face in the opposite direction: [as exclamation] *By twos—right about—march!*

right angle ▶ **noun** an angle of 90°, as in a corner of a square, or formed by dividing a circle into quarters.

– PHRASES **at right angles** (or **a right angle**) **to** forming an angle of 90° with (something): *hold the brush at right angles to the surface.*

right-angled ▶ **adjective** containing or being a right angle: *a right-angled triangle.*

right ascension (abbrev.: **RA**) ▶ **noun** Astronomy the distance of a point east of the First Point of Aries, measured along the celestial equator and expressed in hours, minutes, and seconds. Compare with **DECLINATION** and **CELESTIAL LONGITUDE**.

right back ▶ **noun** a defender in soccer or field hockey who plays primarily in a position on the right of the field.

Right Bank a district of the city of Paris, situated on the right bank of the River Seine, to the north of the river. The area contains the Champs Élysées and the Louvre.

right bank ▶ **noun** the bank of a river, on the right as one faces downstream.

right brain ▶ **noun** [mass noun] the right-hand side of the human brain, which is believed to be associated with creative thought and the emotions.

righten ▶ **verb** [with obj.] archaic make (something) right, correct, or straight: *thy stubborn mind will not be rightened.*

righteous /ˈrʌɪtʃəs/ ▶ **adjective** morally right or justifiable: *feelings of righteous indignation about pay and conditions.*

– DERIVATIVES **righteously** adverb, **righteousness** noun.

– ORIGIN Old English *rihtwīs*, from *riht* 'right' + *wīs* 'manner, state, condition'. The change in the ending in the 16th cent. was due to association with words such as *bounteous*.

right field ▶ **noun** Baseball the part of the outfield to the right of the batter when facing the pitcher: *a ball hit to right field.*

right-footed ▶ **adjective** (of a person) using the right foot more naturally than the left.
▪(of a kick) done with the right foot.

rightful ▶ **adjective** [attrib.] having a legitimate right to property, position, or status: *the rightful owner of the jewels.*
▪legitimately claimed; fitting: *they are determined to take their rightful place in a new South Africa.*

– DERIVATIVES **rightfully** adverb, **rightfulness** noun.

– ORIGIN Old English *rihtful* 'upright, righteous' (see **RIGHT**, **-FUL**). The notion of 'legitimacy' dates from Middle English.

right hand ▶ **noun** the hand of a person's right side.
▪the region or direction on the right side of a person or thing: *a great wall loomed above the street on the right hand.* ▪the most important position next to someone: *the place of honour at his host's right hand.* ▪an efficient or indispensable assistant: *she could have helped him, been her father's right hand.* ▪(in South Africa) the most important (in traditional Zulu society) or second most important (in traditional Xhosa society) branch of a family, especially a royal one.
▶ **adjective** [attrib.] on or towards the right side of a person or thing: *the top right-hand corner.*
▪done with or using the right hand: *wild right-hand punches.* ▪(in South Africa) of or relating to the most senior (in traditional Zulu society) or second (in traditional Xhosa society) wife of a chief.

right-hand drive ▶ **noun** [mass noun] a motor-vehicle steering system with the steering wheel and other controls fitted on the right side, designed for use in countries where vehicles drive on the left side of the road.
▪[count noun] a vehicle with steering of this type.

right-handed ▶ **adjective 1** (of a person) using the right hand more naturally than the left: *a right-handed golfer.*
▪(of a tool or item of equipment) made to be used with the right hand: *a right-handed guitar.* ▪made or done with the right hand: *right-handed batting.*
2 going towards or turning to the right, in particular:
▪(of a screw) advanced by turning clockwise. ▪Biology (of a spiral shell or helix) dextral. ▪(of a racecourse) turning clockwise.
▶ **adverb** with the right hand: *Jackson bats right-handed.*

– DERIVATIVES **right-handedly** adverb, **right-handedness** noun.

right-hander ▶ **noun 1** a right-handed person.
▪a blow struck with the right hand.
2 a corner on a road or racing track that bends to the right.

right-hand man ▶ **noun** an indispensable helper or chief assistant.

Right Honourable ▶ **noun** Brit. a title given to certain high officials such as Privy Counsellors and government ministers.

rightism ▶ **noun** [mass noun] the political views or policies of the right.

– DERIVATIVES **rightist** noun & adjective.

rightly ▶ **adverb** correctly: *if I remember rightly, she never gives interviews.*
▪with good reason: *the delicious cuisine for which her country was rightly famous.* ▪in accordance with justice or what is morally right: *the key rightly belonged to Craig.*

right-minded ▶ **adjective** having sound views and principles.

rightmost ▶ **adjective** [attrib.] situated furthest to the right.

righto (also **righty-ho**) ▶ **exclamation** Brit. informal expressing agreement or assent: *'Coming to pick up the kids?' 'Righto.'*

right of abode ▶ **noun** [mass noun] chiefly Brit. a person's right to take up residence or remain resident in a country.

right of common ▶ **noun** see **COMMON** (sense 4).

right of primogeniture ▶ **noun** see **PRIMOGENITURE**.

right of search ▶ **noun** [mass noun] the right of a ship of a belligerent state to stop and search a neutral merchant vessel for prohibited goods.

right of way ▶ **noun** [mass noun] **1** the legal right, established by usage or grant, to pass along a specific route through grounds or property belonging to another.
▪[count noun] a path or thoroughfare subject to such a right.
2 the legal right of a pedestrian, rider, or driver to proceed with precedence over other road users at a particular point.
▪the right of a ship, boat, or aircraft to proceed with precedence over others in a particular situation.
3 N. Amer. the right to build and operate a railway line, road, or utility on land belonging to another.
▪[count noun] the land on which a railway line, road, or utility is built.

right-on ▶ **adjective** often derogatory in keeping with fashionable liberal or left-wing opinions and values: *the right-on music press.*

Right Reverend ▶ **noun** a title given to a bishop.

right side ▶ **noun** the side of something, especially a garment or fabric, intended to be uppermost or foremost; the better or usable side of something.

– PHRASES **on the right side of** on the safe, appropriate, or desirable side of: *her portrayal of his neurotic wife falls just on the right side of caricature.* ▪in a position to be viewed with favour by: *he hasn't always remained on the right side of the law.* ▪somewhat less than (a specified age): *she's on the right side of forty.* **right side out** with the side intended to be seen or used uppermost: *turn the skirt right side out.*

rights issue ▶ **noun** an issue of shares offered at a special price by a company to its existing shareholders in proportion to their holding of old shares.

rightsize ▶ **verb** [with obj.] chiefly US convert (something) to an appropriate or optimum size: *organizations are beginning to rightsize computer systems to suit themselves.*
▪reduce the size of (a company or organization) by shedding staff.

rights of man ▶ **plural noun** rights held to be justifiably belonging to any person; human rights. The phrase is associated with the Declaration of the Rights of Man and of the Citizen, adopted by the French National Assembly in 1789 and used as a preface to the French Constitution of 1791.

right-thinking ▶ **adjective** right-minded.

right-to-life ▶ **adjective** another term for **PRO-LIFE**.

– DERIVATIVES **right-to-lifer** noun.

right-to-work ▶ **adjective** chiefly US relating to or promoting a worker's right not to be required to join a trade union: *Kansas is a right-to-work state.*

right triangle ▶ **noun** N. Amer. a right-angled triangle.

right turn ▶ **noun** a turn that brings a person's front to face the way their right side did before: *take a right turn into Barracks Lane.*

rightward ▶ **adverb** (also **rightwards**) towards the right: *the military regime drifted rightwards.*
▶ **adjective** going towards or situated on the right: *the rock face is climbed via a rightward curving crack.*

right whale ▶ **noun** a baleen whale with a large head and a deeply curved jaw, of Arctic and temperate waters.
• Family Balaenidae: two genera and three species, in particular *Balaena glacialis*, which has distinctive patches of callosities on the snout. See also **BOWHEAD**.

right wing ▶ **noun** (**the right wing**) **1** the conservative or reactionary section of a political party or system. [ORIGIN: with reference to the National Assembly in France (1789–91), where the nobles sat to the president's right and the commons to the left.]
2 the right side of a team on the field in soccer, rugby, and field hockey: *he reverted to his normal position on the right wing.*
▪the right side of an army.
▶ **adjective 1** conservative or reactionary: *a right-wing Republican senator.*
2 of or relating to the right wing in football or similar sports: *a right-wing cross.*

– DERIVATIVES **right-winger** noun.

righty ▶ **noun** (pl. **-ies**) N. Amer. informal **1** a right-handed person.
2 a person who supports or is involved in right-wing politics.

righty-ho ▶ **exclamation** variant spelling of **RIGHTO**.

rigid ▶ **adjective** unable to bend or be forced out of shape; not flexible: *a seat of rigid orange plastic.*
▪(of a person or part of their body) stiff and unmoving, especially as a result of shock or fear: *his face grew rigid with fear.* ▪figurative not able to be changed or adapted: *teachers are being asked to unlearn rigid rules for labelling children.* ▪figurative (of a person or their behaviour) not adaptable in outlook, belief, or response: *the College had not wanted to be too rigid in imposing teaching methods.*
▶ **noun** a lorry which is not articulated.

– DERIVATIVES **rigidify** verb, **rigidity** noun, **rigidly** adverb, **rigidness** noun.

– ORIGIN late Middle English: from Latin *rigidus*, from *rigere* 'be stiff'.

rigid designator ▶ **noun** Philosophy a term that identifies the same object or individual in every possible world.

Rigil Kentaurus /ˌrʌɪdʒɪl kɛnˈtɔːrəs/ (also **Rigil Kent**) Astronomy the star Alpha Centauri.
– ORIGIN Arabic, literally 'the foot of the Centaur'.

rigmarole /ˈrɪgmərəʊl/ ▶ **noun** [usu. in sing.] a lengthy and complicated procedure: *he went through the rigmarole of securing the front door.*
■ a long, rambling story or statement.
– ORIGIN mid 18th cent.: apparently an alteration of *ragman roll*, originally denoting a legal document recording a list of offences.

rigor[1] /ˈrɪgɔː, ˈrʌɪgɔː, -gə/ ▶ **noun** Medicine a sudden feeling of cold with shivering accompanied by a rise in temperature, often with copious sweating, especially at the onset or height of a fever.
■ short for **RIGOR MORTIS**.
– ORIGIN late Middle English: from Latin, literally 'stiffness', from *rigere* 'be stiff'.

rigor[2] ▶ **noun** US spelling of **RIGOUR**.

rigorism ▶ **noun** [mass noun] extreme strictness in interpreting or enforcing a law, precept, or principle.
■ the Roman Catholic doctrine that in doubtful cases of conscience the strict course is always to be followed.
– DERIVATIVES **rigorist** noun & adjective.

rigor mortis /ˈmɔːtɪs/ ▶ **noun** [mass noun] Medicine stiffening of the joints and muscles of a body a few hours after death, usually lasting from one to four days.
– ORIGIN mid 19th cent.: from Latin, literally 'stiffness of death'.

rigorous ▶ **adjective** extremely thorough, exhaustive, or accurate: *the rigorous testing of consumer products.*
■ (of a rule, system, etc.) strictly applied or adhered to: *rigorous controls on mergers.* ■ (of a person) adhering strictly or inflexibly to a belief, opinion, or way of doing something: *a rigorous teetotaller.* ■ (of an activity) physically demanding: *my exercise regime is a little more rigorous than most.* ■ (of the weather or climate) harsh: *Scotland has a more rigorous climate than England.*
– DERIVATIVES **rigorously** adverb, **rigorousness** noun.
– ORIGIN late Middle English: from Old French *rigorous* or late Latin *rigorosus*, from *rigor* 'stiffness' (see **RIGOR**[1]).

rigour (US **rigor**) ▶ **noun** [mass noun] the quality of being extremely thorough, exhaustive, or accurate: *his analysis is lacking in rigour.*
■ severity or strictness: *the full rigour of the law.* ■ (**rigours**) demanding, difficult, or extreme conditions: *the rigours of a harsh winter.*
– ORIGIN late Middle English: from Old French *rigour* from Latin *rigor* 'stiffness'.

rig-out ▶ **noun** informal, chiefly Brit. an outfit of clothes.

Rig Veda /rɪg ˈveɪdə, ˈviːdə/ Hinduism the oldest and principal of the Vedas, composed in the 2nd millennium BC and containing a collection of hymns in early Sanskrit. See **VEDA**.
– ORIGIN from Sanskrit *ṛgveda*, from *ṛc* '(sacred) stanza' + *veda* '(sacred) knowledge'.

Rijeka /riːˈɛkə/ a port on the Adriatic coast of Croatia; pop. 167,900 (1991). Italian name **FIUME**.

Rijksmuseum /ˈrʌɪksmuːˌzeɪəm/ the national art gallery of the Netherlands, in Amsterdam. It contains the most representative collection of Dutch art in the world.

rijsttafel /ˈrʌɪstˌtɑːf(ə)l/ ▶ **noun** [mass noun] a meal of SE Asian food consisting of a selection of spiced rice dishes.
– ORIGIN Dutch, from *rijst* 'rice' + *tafel* 'table'.

rikishi /ˈrɪkɪʃi/ ▶ **noun** (pl. same) a sumo wrestler.
– ORIGIN Japanese, from *riki* 'strength' + *shi* 'warrior'.

Riksmål /ˈriːksmɔːl/ ▶ **noun** another term for **BOKMÅL**.
– ORIGIN Norwegian, from *rike* 'state, nation' + *mål* 'language'.

Rila Mountains /ˈriːlə/ a range of mountains in western Bulgaria, forming the westernmost extent of the Rhodope Mountains. It is the highest range in Bulgaria, rising to a height of 2,925 m (9,596 ft) at Mount Musala.

rile ▶ **verb** [with obj.] **1** informal make (someone) annoyed or irritated: *he has been riled by suggestions that his Arsenal future is in doubt | he's getting you all* **riled up**.
2 N. Amer. make (water) turbulent or muddy.
– ORIGIN early 19th cent.: variant of **ROIL**.

Riley[1] ▶ **noun** (in phrase **the life of Riley**) informal a luxurious or carefree existence.
– ORIGIN early 20th cent.: of unknown origin.

Riley[2], Bridget (Louise) (b.1931), English painter. A leading exponent of op art, she worked with flat patterns to create optical illusions of light and movement. Notable paintings: *Fall* (1963).

rilievo /rɪˈljeɪvəʊ/ ▶ **noun** variant spelling of **RELIEVO**.

Rilke /ˈrɪlkə/, Rainer Maria (1875–1926), Austrian poet, born in Bohemia; pseudonym of *René Karl Wilhelm Josef Maria Rilke*. His conception of art as a quasi-religious vocation culminated in his best-known works, the *Duino Elegies* and *Sonnets to Orpheus* (both 1923).

rill /rɪl/ ▶ **noun** a small stream.
■ a shallow channel cut in the surface of soil or rocks by running water. ■ variant spelling of **RILLE**.
– ORIGIN mid 16th cent.: probably of Low German origin.

rille /rɪl/ (also **rill**) ▶ **noun** Astronomy a fissure or narrow channel on the moon's surface.
– ORIGIN mid 19th cent.: from German (see **RILL**).

rillettes /ˈriːjɛt/ ▶ **plural noun** pâté made of minced pork or other light meat, seasoned and combined with fat.
– ORIGIN French, diminutive (plural) of Old French *rille* 'strip of pork'.

RIM ▶ **abbreviation for** Mauritania (international vehicle registration).
– ORIGIN from French *République Islamique de Mauritanie*.

rim[1] ▶ **noun** the upper or outer edge of an object, typically something circular or approximately circular: *a china egg cup with a gold rim.*
■ (also **wheel rim**) the outer edge of a wheel, on which the tyre is fitted. ■ (often **rims**) the part of a spectacle frame surrounding the lenses. ■ a limit or boundary of something: *the outer rim of the solar system.* ■ an encircling stain or deposit: *a thick rim of suds.*
▶ **verb** (**rimmed**, **rimming**) [with obj.] form or act as an outer edge or rim for: *a huge lake rimmed by glaciers* | [as adj., in combination **-rimmed**] *steel-rimmed glasses.*
■ (usu. **be rimmed**) mark with an encircling stain or deposit: *his collar was rimmed with dirt.*
– DERIVATIVES **rimless** adjective.
– ORIGIN Old English *rima* 'a border, coast'; compare with Old Norse *rimi* 'ridge, strip of land' (the only known cognate).

rim[2] ▶ **verb** (**rimmed**, **rimming**) [with obj.] vulgar slang lick or suck the anus of (someone) as a means of sexual stimulation.

Rimbaud /ˈrambəʊ, French rɛ̃bo/, (Jean Nicholas) Arthur (1854–91), French poet. Known for poems such as 'Le Bateau ivre' (1871) and the collection of symbolist prose poems *Une Saison en enfer* (1873), and for his stormy relationship with Paul Verlaine, he stopped writing at about the age of 20 and spent the rest of his life travelling.

rim brake ▶ **noun** a brake acting on the rim of a wheel.

rime[1] /rʌɪm/ ▶ **noun** (also **rime ice**) [mass noun] frost formed on cold objects by the rapid freezing of water vapour in cloud or fog.
■ poetic/literary hoar frost.
▶ **verb** [with obj.] poetic/literary cover (an object) with hoar frost: *he does not brush away the frost that rimes his beard.*
– ORIGIN Old English *hrīm*, of Germanic origin; related to Dutch *rijm*. The word became rare in Middle English but was revived in literary use at the end of the 18th cent.

rime[2] ▶ **noun & verb** archaic spelling of **RHYME**.

rimfire ▶ **adjective** [attrib.] (of a cartridge) having the primer around the edge of the base.
■ (of a rifle) adapted for such cartridges.

Rimini /ˈrɪmɪni/ a port and resort on the Adriatic coast of NE Italy; pop. 130,900 (1990).

rimland ▶ **noun** [mass noun] (also **rimlands**) a peripheral region with political or strategic significance.

rim lock ▶ **noun** a lock that is fitted to the surface of a door with a matching box fitted into the door jamb.

Rimmon /ˈrɪmən/ (in the Bible) a deity worshipped in ancient Damascus (2 Kings 5: 18).

rimrock ▶ **noun** [mass noun] chiefly N. Amer. an outcrop of resistant rock forming a margin to a gravel deposit, especially one forming a cliff at the edge of a plateau.

rim-shot ▶ **noun** a drum stroke in which the stick strikes the rim and the head of the drum simultaneously.

Rimsky-Korsakov /ˌrɪmskɪˈkɔːsəkɒf/, Nikolai (Andreevich) (1844–1908), Russian composer. He achieved fame with his orchestral suite *Scheherazade* (1888) and his many operas drawing on Russian and Slavic folk tales.

rimu /ˈriːmuː/ ▶ **noun** a tall coniferous tree with dark brown flaking bark, which is the chief native softwood tree of New Zealand. The timber is used for furniture and interior fittings. Also called **RED PINE**.
• *Dacrydium cupressinum*, family Podocarpaceae.
– ORIGIN mid 19th cent.: from Maori.

rimy /ˈrʌɪmi/ ▶ **adjective** (**rimier**, **rimiest**) poetic/literary covered with frost.

rind ▶ **noun** [mass noun] the tough outer layer of something, in particular:
■ the tough outer skin of certain fruit, especially citrus fruit. ■ the hard outer edge of cheese or bacon, usually removed before eating. ■ the bark of a tree or plant. ■ the hard outer layer of a rhizomorph or other part of a fungus. ■ the skin or blubber of a whale.
▶ **verb** [with obj.] strip the bark from (a tree).
– DERIVATIVES **rinded** adjective [in combination] *yellow-rinded lemons*, **rindless** adjective.
– ORIGIN Old English *rind(e)* 'bark of a tree'; related to Dutch *run* and German *Rinde*, of unknown origin.

rinderpest /ˈrɪndəpɛst/ ▶ **noun** [mass noun] Veterinary Medicine an infectious disease of ruminants, especially cattle, caused by a paramyxovirus. It is characterized by fever, dysentery, and inflammation of the mucous membranes. Also called **CATTLE PLAGUE**.
– PHRASES **before** (or **since**) **the rinderpest** S. African a long time ago (or for a very long time). [ORIGIN: referring to the 1896 epidemic, treated as a landmark.]
– ORIGIN mid 19th cent.: from German, from *Rinder* 'cattle' + *Pest* 'plague'.

ring[1] ▶ **noun 1** a small circular band, typically of precious metal and often set with one or more gemstones, worn on a finger as an ornament or a token of marriage, engagement, or authority.
■ a circular band of any material: *fried onion rings.* ■ (also **leg ring**) Ornithology, Brit. an aluminium strip secured round a bird's leg to identify it. ■ Astronomy a thin band or disc of rock and ice particles round a planet. ■ a circular marking or pattern: *black rings round her eyes.* ■ short for **TREE RING**. ■ short for **RING ROAD**. ■ a flat circular device forming part of a gas or electric hob, providing heat from below and used for cooking. See also **GAS RING**. ■ [usu. as modifier] Archaeology a circular prehistoric earthwork, typically consisting of a bank and ditch: *a ring ditch.* ■ vulgar slang a person's anus.
2 an enclosed space, typically surrounded by seating for spectators, in which a sport, performance, or show takes place: *a circus ring.*
■ a roped enclosure for boxing or wrestling. ■ (**the ring**) the profession, sport, or institution of boxing.
3 a group of people or things arranged in a circle: *he pointed to the ring of trees.*
■ (**in a ring**) arranged or grouped in a circle: *everyone sat in a ring, holding hands.* ■ [usu. with modifier] a group of people drawn together due to a shared interest or goal, especially one involving illegal or unscrupulous activity: *the police had been investigating the drug ring.* ■ Chemistry a number of atoms bonded together to form a closed loop in a molecule.
4 a circular or spiral course: *they were dancing energetically in a ring.*
5 Mathematics a set of elements with two binary operations, addition and multiplication, the second being distributive over the first and associative.
▶ **verb** [with obj.] **1** (often **be ringed**) surround (someone or something), especially for protection or containment: *the courthouse was ringed with police.*
■ form a line around the edge of (something circular): *dark shadows ringed his eyes.* ■ draw a circle round (something), especially so as to focus attention on it: *an area of Soho had been ringed in red.*
2 Ornithology, Brit. put an aluminium strip around the leg of (a bird) for subsequent identification.
■ put a circular band through the nose of (a bull, pig,

or other farm animal) to lead or otherwise control it.

3 [with obj.] informal fraudulently change the identity of (a motor vehicle), typically by changing its registration plate. [ORIGIN: 1960s: from an earlier slang use in the general sense 'exchange'.]

4 short for **RINGBARK**.

– PHRASES **hold the ring** monitor a dispute or conflict without becoming involved in it. **run** (or **make**) **rings round** (or **around**) **someone** informal outclass or outwit someone very easily. **throw one's hat in the ring** see **HAT**.

– DERIVATIVES **ringed** adjective [in combination] *the five-ringed Olympic emblem*, **ringless** adjective.

– ORIGIN Old English *hring*, of Germanic origin; related to Dutch *ring*, German *Ring*, also to the noun **RANK**[1].

ring[2] ▶ **verb** (past **rang**; past participle **rung**) **1** [no obj.] make a clear resonant or vibrating sound: *a shot* **rang out** | *a bell rang loudly* | [as noun **ringing**] *the ringing of fire alarms.*

■ [with obj.] cause (a bell or alarm) to make such a sound: *he walked up to the door and rang the bell.* ■ (of a telephone) produce a series of resonant or vibrating sounds to signal an incoming call: *the phone rang again as I replaced it.* ■ call for service or attention by sounding a bell: *Ruth, will you* **ring for** *some tea?* ■ (of a person's ears) be filled with a continuous buzzing or humming sound, especially as the after-effect of a blow or loud noise: *he yelled so loudly that my eardrums rang.* ■ (**ring with/to**) (of a place) resound or reverberate with (a sound or sounds): *the room rang with laughter.* ■ (**ring with**) figurative be filled or permeated with (a particular quality): *those whose names ring with ethnicity.* ■ [no obj., with complement] convey a specified impression or quality: *the author's honesty rings true.* ■ [with obj.] sound (the hour, a peal, etc.) on a bell or bells: *a bell ringing the hour.*

2 [with obj.] chiefly Brit. call by telephone: *I rang her this morning* | *Harriet* **rang** *Dorothy* **up** *next day* | [no obj.] *I tried to ring, but the lines to Moscow were engaged.*

▶ **noun** an act of causing a bell to sound, or the resonant sound caused by this: *there was a ring at the door.*

■ each of a series of resonant or vibrating sounds signalling an incoming telephone call. ■ [in sing.] Brit. informal a telephone call: *I'd better* **give her a ring** *tomorrow.* ■ [in sing.] a loud clear sound or tone: *the ring of sledgehammers on metal.* ■ [in sing.] a particular quality conveyed by something heard or expressed: *the song had a curious* **ring of** *nostalgia to it.* ■ a set of bells, especially church bells.

– PHRASES **ring a bell** see **BELL**[1]. **ring the changes** see **CHANGE**. **ring down** (or **up**) **the curtain** cause a theatre curtain to be lowered (or raised). ■ figurative mark the end (or the beginning) of an enterprise or event: *the sendoff* **rings down the curtain on** *a major chapter in television history.* **ring in one's ears** (or **head**) linger in the memory: *he left Washington with the president's praises ringing in his ears.* **ring the knell of** see **KNELL**. **ring off the hook** N. Amer. (of a telephone) be constantly ringing due to a large number of incoming calls.

– ORIGIN Old English *hringan*, of Germanic origin, perhaps imitative.

▶ **ring in** Brit. report or make contact, especially to or with one's place of work, by telephone: *every morning she coughed she rang in sick.*

ring someone/thing in (or **out**) usher someone or something in (or out) by or as if by ringing a bell: *the bells were beginning to ring out the old year.*

ring off Brit. end a telephone call by replacing the receiver.

ring round (or **around**) Brit. telephone (several people), typically to find something out or arrange something.

ring something up record an amount on a cash register. ■ figurative make, spend, or announce a particular amount in sales, profits, or losses.

ring-a-ring o' roses ▶ **noun** [mass noun] a singing game played by children, in which the players hold hands and dance in a circle, falling down at the end of the song.

– ORIGIN said to refer to the inflamed ('rose-coloured') ring of buboes, symptomatic of the plague; the final part of the game is symbolic of death.

ringbark ▶ **verb** [with obj.] remove a ring of bark from (a tree) in order to kill it or to check rapid growth and thereby improve fruit production.

ring bearer ▶ **noun** N. Amer. the person, typically a young boy, who ceremoniously bears the rings at a wedding.

ring binder ▶ **noun** a loose-leaf binder with ring-shaped clasps that can be opened to pass through holes in the paper.

ringbolt ▶ **noun** a bolt with a ring attached for fitting a rope to.

ringbone ▶ **noun** [mass noun] osteoarthritis of the pastern joint of a horse, causing swelling and lameness.

ring-bound ▶ **adjective** bound in a ring binder.

ring circuit ▶ **noun** an electric circuit serving a number of power points, with one fuse in the supply to the circuit.

ringcraft ▶ **noun** [mass noun] skill in conducting oneself in a boxing ring.

■ skill in performing a challenging activity in a public arena.

ringdove ▶ **noun** a dove or pigeon with a ring-like mark on the neck, in particular:

● Brit. the wood pigeon. ● N. Amer. a captive or feral African collared dove (*Streptopelia roseogrisea*, family Columbidae).

ring dyke ▶ **noun** Geology a dyke that is roughly circular in plan, formed by upwelling of magma in a conical or cylindrical fracture system.

ringed plover ▶ **noun** a small plover found chiefly in Eurasia, with white underparts and a black collar, breeding on sand or shingle beaches.

● Genus *Charadrius*, family Charadriidae : three species, in particular *Charadrius hiaticula*.

ringed seal ▶ **noun** a seal of arctic and subarctic waters, which has pale ring-shaped markings on the back and sides and a short muzzle.

● *Phoca hispida*, family Phocidae.

ringer[1] ▶ **noun 1** informal an athlete or horse fraudulently substituted for another in a competition or event.

■ a person's or thing's double, especially an impostor: *he's a* **ringer for** *the French actor Fernandel.* ■ a motor vehicle whose identity has been fraudulently changed by the substitution of a different registration plate.

2 a person who rings something, especially a bell-ringer.

■ a device for ringing a bell, especially on a telephone.

ringer[2] ▶ **noun 1** Austral./NZ a shearer with the highest tally of sheep shorn in a given period. [ORIGIN: late 19th cent.: special use of dialect *ringer* 'something exceptionally good'.]

2 Austral. a stockman, especially one employed in droving. [ORIGIN: early 20th cent.: from *ring* 'turn (a group of cattle) back on itself, work as a drover'.]

3 Ornithology, Brit. a person who rings birds for identification purposes.

Ringer's solution ▶ **noun** [mass noun] Biology a physiological saline solution that typically contains, in addition to sodium chloride, salts of potassium and calcium.

– ORIGIN late 19th cent.: named after Sydney *Ringer* (1834–1910), English physician.

ringette ▶ **noun** [mass noun] Canadian a game resembling ice hockey, played (especially by women and girls) with a straight stick and a rubber ring, and in which no intentional body contact is allowed.

ring fence ▶ **noun** a fence completely enclosing an estate, farm, or piece of land.

■ figurative an effective or comprehensive barrier, protection, or means of segregation.

▶ **verb** (**ring-fence**) [with obj.] enclose (a piece of land) with a ring fence.

■ figurative guard securely; protect: *senior civil servants are attempting to ring-fence their jobs.* ■ figurative guarantee that (funds allocated for a particular purpose) will not be spent on anything else: *the government failed to ring-fence the money provided to schools.*

ring finger ▶ **noun** the finger next to the little finger, especially of the left hand, on which the wedding ring is worn.

ring flash ▶ **noun** Photography a circular electronic flash tube that fits round a camera lens to give shadowless lighting of a subject near the lens, especially for macrophotography.

ring fort ▶ **noun** Archaeology a prehistoric earthwork, especially an Iron Age hill fort, defended by circular ramparts and ditches.

ringgit /ˈrɪŋɡɪt/ ▶ **noun** (pl. same or **ringgits**) the basic monetary unit of Malaysia, equivalent to 100 hundred sen.

– ORIGIN Malay.

ringhals /ˈrɪŋhals/ ▶ **noun** variant spelling of **RINKHALS**.

ringing ▶ **adjective** [attrib.] having or emitting a clear resonant sound: *a ringing voice.*

■ figurative (of a statement) forceful and unequivocal: *the Russian leader received a ringing declaration of support.*

– DERIVATIVES **ringingly** adverb.

ringing tone ▶ **noun** a sound heard by a telephone caller when the number dialled is being rung.

ringleader ▶ **noun** a person who initiates or leads an illicit or illegal activity.

ringlet ▶ **noun 1** a lock of hair hanging in a corkscrew-shaped curl.

2 a brown butterfly which has wings bearing eyespots that are typically highlighted by a paler colour.

● *Aphantopus*, *Erebia*, and other genera in the subfamily Satyrinae, family Nymphalidae: several species, in particular the common Eurasian *A. hyperantus*.

– DERIVATIVES **ringletted** (also **ringleted**) adjective, **ringlety** adjective.

ring main ▶ **noun** Brit. **1** an electrical supply serving a series of consumers and returning to the original source, so that each consumer has an alternative path in the event of a failure.

■ another term for **RING CIRCUIT**.

2 an arrangement of pipes forming a closed loop into which steam, water, or sewage may be fed and whose points of draw-off are supplied by flow from two directions.

ringmaster ▶ **noun** the person directing a circus performance.

ring modulator ▶ **noun** an electronic circuit, especially in a musical instrument, that incorporates a closed loop of four diodes and can be used for the balanced mixing and modulation of signals.

ringneck ▶ **noun** any of a number of ring-necked birds, in particular:

● a common pheasant of a variety having a white neck ring. ● Austral. a green parrot with a yellow collar (genus *Barnardius*, family Psittacidae: two species). ● N. Amer. a ring-necked duck (*Aythya collaris*, family Anatidae).

ring-necked ▶ **adjective** used in names of birds and reptiles with a band or bands of colour round the neck, e.g. **ring-necked parakeet**.

ring ouzel (also **ring ousel**) ▶ **noun** a European thrush that resembles a blackbird with a white crescent across the breast, inhabiting upland moors and mountainous country.

● *Turdus torquatus*, family Turdidae.

ring pull ▶ **noun** a ring on a can that is pulled to break the seal in order to open it.

ring road ▶ **noun** a bypass encircling a town.

ringside ▶ **noun** [often as modifier] the area immediately beside a boxing ring or circus ring: *a ringside judge.*

– DERIVATIVES **ringsider** noun.

ringside seat ▶ **noun** a seat immediately adjacent to a boxing ring.

■ figurative an advantageous position from which to observe or monitor something.

ring spanner ▶ **noun** a spanner in which the jaws form a ring with internal serrations which fit completely around a nut, putting pressure on all its faces.

ringster ▶ **noun** N. Amer. archaic a member of a political or price-fixing ring.

ringtail ▶ **noun 1** any of a number of mammals or birds having a tail marked with a ring or rings, in particular:

■ a ring-tailed cat or lemur. ■ a female hen harrier or related harrier. ■ a golden eagle up to its third year.

2 (also **ringtail** or **ring-tailed possum**) a nocturnal tree-dwelling Australian possum that habitually curls its prehensile tail into a ring or spiral.

● Genus *Pseudocheirus* and other genera, family Petauridae: several species, in particular the **common ringtail** (*P. peregrinus*), of southern Australia and Tasmania.

ring-tailed ▶ **adjective** used in names of mammals and birds that have the tail banded in contrasting colours, e.g. **ring-tailed lemur**, or curled at the end, e.g. **ring-tailed possum**.

ring-tailed cat ▶ **noun** a nocturnal raccoon-like mammal with a dark-ringed tail, found in North America. Also called **RINGTAIL**, **CACOMISTLE**.

● *Bassariscus astutus*, family Procyonidae.

ring-tailed lemur ▶ **noun** a gregarious lemur

with a grey coat, black rings around the eyes, and distinctive black-and-white banding on the tail.
• *Lemur catta*, family Lemuridae.

ringwork ▶ **noun** Archaeology the circular entrenchment of a minor medieval castle, especially a fortified Norman manor.

ringworm ▶ **noun** [mass noun] a contagious itching skin disease occurring in small circular patches, caused by any of a number of fungi and affecting chiefly the scalp or the feet. The commonest form is athlete's foot. Also called **TINEA**.

rink ▶ **noun** (also **ice rink**) an enclosed area of ice for skating, ice hockey, or curling, especially one artificially prepared.
■ (also **roller rink**) a smooth enclosed floor of wood or asphalt for roller skating. ■ a building containing either of these. ■ (also **bowling rink**) the strip of a bowling green used for playing a match. ■ a team in curling or bowls.
– ORIGIN late Middle English (originally Scots in the sense jousting-ground): perhaps originally from Old French *renc* 'rank'.

rinkhals /ˈrɪŋkhals/ (also **ringhals**) ▶ **noun** a large nocturnal spitting cobra of southern Africa, with one or two white rings across the throat.
• *Hemachatus haemachatus*, family Elapidae.
– ORIGIN late 18th cent.: from Afrikaans *rinkhals*, from *ring* 'ring' + *hals* 'neck'.

rink rat ▶ **noun** N. Amer. informal **1** a young person who spends time around an ice-hockey rink in the hope of meeting players, watching practice, and spending time on the ice.
2 a synthetic broom used in the game of curling.

rinky-dink ▶ **adjective** informal, chiefly N. Amer. old-fashioned, amateurish, or shoddy: *the fifty-third issue of the quarterly looked just as rinky-dink as the first.*
– ORIGIN late 19th cent.: of unknown origin.

Rinpoche /ˈrɪnpɒtʃeɪ/ ▶ **noun** a religious teacher held in high regard among Tibetan Buddhists (often used as an honorific title).
– ORIGIN Tibetan, literally 'precious jewel'.

rinse ▶ **verb** [with obj.] wash (something) with clean water to remove soap, detergent, dirt, or impurities: *always rinse your hair thoroughly* | [no obj.] *drain the beans and rinse well.*
■ wash (something) quickly, especially without soap: *Rose* ***rinsed out*** *a tumbler.* ■ clean (one's mouth) by swilling round and then emitting a mouthful of water or mouthwash: *Karen* ***rinsed*** *her mouth* ***out***. ■ [with obj. and adverbial] remove (soap, detergent, dirt, or impurities) by washing with clean water: *the conditioning mousse doesn't have to be* ***rinsed out*** | [no obj.] *rub salt on to rough areas of skin, then* ***rinse off***.
▶ **noun 1** an act of rinsing something: *I gave my hands a quick rinse.*
2 an antiseptic solution for cleansing the mouth.
3 a preparation for conditioning or temporarily tinting the hair.
– DERIVATIVES **rinser** noun.
– ORIGIN Middle English (as a verb): from Old French *rincer*, of unknown ultimate origin.

Rio Branco /ˌriːuː ˈbraŋkuː/ a city in western Brazil, capital of the state of Acre; pop. 197,000 (1990).

Rio de Janeiro /ˌriːəʊ də dʒəˈnɪərəʊ/ a state of eastern Brazil, on the Atlantic coast.
■ (also **Rio**) its capital; pop. 5,480,770 (1991). The chief port of Brazil, it was the country's capital from 1763 until 1960, when it was replaced by Brasilia.

Río de la Plata /ˌrrio ðe la ˈplata/ Spanish name for the River Plate (see **PLATE, RIVER**).

Río de Oro /ˌriːəʊ deɪ ˈɔːrəʊ/ an arid region on the Atlantic coast of NW Africa, forming the southern part of Western Sahara. It was united with Saguia el Hamra in 1958 to form the province of Spanish Sahara (now Western Sahara).

Rio Grande /ˌriːəʊ ˈgrand, ˈgrandi/ a river of North America which rises in the Rocky Mountains of SW Colorado and flows 3,030 km (1,880 miles) generally south-eastwards to the Gulf of Mexico, forming the US–Mexico frontier from El Paso to the sea.

Rio Grande do Norte /ˌriːuː ˌgrandi duː ˈnɔːti/ a state of NE Brazil, on the Atlantic coast; capital, Natal.

Rio Grande do Sul /ˌriːuː ˌgrandi duː ˈsʊl/ a state of Brazil, situated on the Atlantic coast at the southern tip of the country, on the border with Uruguay; capital, Pôrto Alegre.

Rioja /rɪˈɒhə, rɪˈɒkə/ ▶ **noun** [mass noun] a wine produced in La Rioja, Spain.

Rio Muni /ˌriːəʊ ˈmuːni/ the part of Equatorial Guinea that lies on the mainland of West Africa. Its chief town is Bata.

Rio Negro /ˌriːəʊ ˈneɪgrəʊ, ˈnɛg-/ a river of South America, which rises as the Guainia in eastern Colombia and flows for about 2,255 km (1,400 miles) through NW Brazil before joining the Amazon near Manaus.

riot ▶ **noun 1** a violent disturbance of the peace by a crowd: *riots broke out in the capital* | [mass noun] *he was convicted on charges of riot and assault.*
■ [as modifier] concerned with or used in the suppression of such disturbances: *riot police.* ■ figurative an uproar: *the film's sex scenes caused a riot in Cannes.* ■ figurative an outburst of uncontrolled feelings: ***a riot of*** *emotions raged through Fabia.* ■ [mass noun] archaic uncontrolled revelry; rowdy behaviour.
2 [in sing.] an impressively large or varied display of something: *the garden was* ***a riot of*** *colour.*
3 [in sing.] informal a highly amusing or entertaining person or thing: *everyone thought she was a riot.*
▶ **verb** [no obj.] take part in a violent public disturbance: *students rioted in Paris* | [as noun **rioting**] *a night of rioting.*
■ figurative behave in an unrestrained way: *another set of emotions rioted through him.* ■ archaic act in a dissipated way: *an unrepentant prodigal son, rioting off to far countries.*
– PHRASES **run riot** behave in a violent and unrestrained way. ■ (of a mental faculty or emotion) function or be expressed without restraint: *her imagination ran riot.* ■ proliferate or spread uncontrollably: *traditional prejudices were allowed to run riot.*
– DERIVATIVES **rioter** noun.
– ORIGIN Middle English (originally in the sense 'dissolute living'): from Old French *riote* 'debate', from *rioter* 'to quarrel', of unknown ultimate origin.

Riot Act an Act passed by the British government in 1715 and repealed in 1967, designed to prevent civil disorder. The Act made it a felony for an assembly of more than twelve people to refuse to disperse after being ordered to do so and having been read a specified portion of the Act by lawful authority.
– PHRASES **read the Riot Act** give someone a strong warning that they must improve their behaviour.

riot gear ▶ **noun** [mass noun] protective clothing and equipment worn by police or prison officers in situations of crowd violence.

riot girl (also **riot grrrl**) ▶ **noun** a member of a movement of young feminists expressing their resistance to the sexual harassment and exploitation of women, especially through aggressive punk-style rock music.

riotous ▶ **adjective** marked by or involving public disorder: *a riotous crowd.*
■ characterized by wild and uncontrolled behaviour: *a riotous party.* ■ having a vivid, varied appearance: *a riotous display of bright red, green, and yellow vegetables.*
– DERIVATIVES **riotously** adverb, **riotousness** noun.
– ORIGIN Middle English (in the sense 'troublesome'): from Old French, from *riote* (see **RIOT**).

RIP[1] ▶ **abbreviation for** rest in peace (used on graves).
– ORIGIN from Latin *requiescat* (or, in the plural, *requiescant*) *in pace.*

RIP[2] /rɪp/ ▶ **noun** a raster image processor.
▶ **verb** (usu. **rip**) (**ripped**, **ripping**) [with obj.] rasterize (an image): *once you are happy with the image, you can rip it out.*
– ORIGIN 1970s: abbreviation.

rip[1] ▶ **verb** (**ripped**, **ripping**) **1** [with obj. and adverbial of direction] tear or pull (something) quickly or forcibly away from something or someone: *a fan tried to rip his trousers* ***off*** *during a show* | figurative *countries ripped apart by fighting.*
■ [with obj.] make a long tear or cut in: *you've ripped my jacket* | [as adj. **ripped**] *ripped jeans.* ■ make (a hole) by force: *the truck was struck by lightning and had a hole ripped out of its roof.* ■ [no obj.] come violently apart; tear: *the skirt of her frock ripped.*
2 [no obj., with adverbial of direction] move forcefully and rapidly: *fire* ***ripped through*** *her bungalow.*
▶ **noun 1** a long tear or cut.
■ [in sing.] an act of tearing something forcibly.
2 N. Amer. a fraud or swindle; a rip-off.
– PHRASES **let rip** informal do something or proceed vigorously or without restraint: *the brass sections let rip with sheer gusto.* ■ express oneself vehemently or angrily. **let something rip** informal allow something, especially a vehicle, to go at full speed. ■ allow something to happen forcefully or without interference: *once she started a tirade, it was best to let it rip.* ■ utter or express something forcefully and noisily: *when I passed the exam I let rip a 'yippee'.*
– ORIGIN late Middle English (as a verb): of unknown origin; compare with the verb **REAP**. The noun dates from the early 18th cent.
▶ **rip into** informal make a vehement verbal attack on: *he ripped into me just for going into the caravan.*
rip someone off informal cheat someone, especially financially.
rip something off informal steal: *they have ripped off £6.7 billion.* ■ copy; plagiarize: *the film is a shameless collection of ideas ripped off from other movies.*
rip something up tear something violently into small pieces so as to destroy it.

rip[2] ▶ **noun** a stretch of fast-flowing and rough water in the sea or in a river, caused by the meeting of currents.
■ short for **RIP CURRENT**.
– ORIGIN late 18th cent.: perhaps related to **RIP**[1].

rip[3] ▶ **noun** dated **1** a dissolute immoral person, especially a man: *'Where is that old rip?' a deep voice shouted.*
■ a mischievous person, especially a child.
2 a worthless horse.
– ORIGIN late 18th cent.: perhaps from *rep*, abbreviation of **REPROBATE**.

riparian /rʌɪˈpɛːrɪən/ ▶ **adjective** chiefly Law of, relating to, or situated on the banks of a river: *all the riparian states must sign an agreement.*
■ Ecology of or relating to wetlands adjacent to rivers and streams.
– ORIGIN mid 19th cent.: from Latin *riparius* (from *ripa* 'bank') + **-AN**.

ripcord ▶ **noun** a cord that is pulled to open a parachute.

rip current ▶ **noun** an intermittent strong surface current flowing seaward from the shore.

ripe ▶ **adjective** (of fruit or grain) developed to the point of readiness for harvesting and eating.
■ (of a cheese or wine) fully matured. ■ (of a smell or flavour) rich, intense, or pungent: *rich, ripe flavours emanate from this wine.* ■ (of a female fish or insect) ready to lay eggs or spawn. ■ [predic.] (**ripe for**) arrived at the fitting stage or time for (a particular action or purpose): *land ripe for development.* ■ [predic.] (**ripe with**) full of: *a population ripe with discontent.* ■ [attrib.] (of a person's age) advanced: *she lived to a ripe old age.* ■ informal (of a person's language) beyond the bounds of propriety; coarse.
– PHRASES **the time is ripe** a suitable time has arrived: *the time was ripe to talk about peace.*
– DERIVATIVES **ripely** adverb, **ripeness** noun.
– ORIGIN Old English *rīpe*, of West Germanic origin; related to Dutch *rijp* and German *reif*.

ripen ▶ **verb** become or make ripe: [no obj.] *honeydew melons ripen slowly* | [with obj.] *for ease of harvesting, the fruit is ripened to order.*

ripieno /ˌrɪpɪˈeɪnəʊ/ ▶ **noun** (pl. **ripienos** or **ripieni** /-ni/) [usu. as modifier] Music the body of instruments accompanying the concertino in baroque concerto music: *the concertino is accompanied by ripieno strings.*
– ORIGIN early 18th cent. (in the sense 'supplementary'): from Italian, from *ri-* 'again' + *pieno* 'full'.

rip-off ▶ **noun** informal a fraud or swindle, especially something that is grossly overpriced: *designer label clothes are just expensive rip-offs.*
■ an inferior imitation of something: *rip-offs of all the latest styles.*

riposte /rɪˈpɒst/ ▶ **noun 1** a quick clever reply to an insult or criticism.
2 a quick return thrust in fencing.
▶ **verb 1** [with direct speech] make a quick clever reply to an insult or criticism: *'You've got a strange sense of honour,' Grant riposted.*
2 [no obj.] make a quick return thrust in fencing.
– ORIGIN early 18th cent.: from French *risposte* (noun), *risposter* (verb), from Italian *risposta* 'response'.

ripper ▶ **noun 1** a tool that is used to tear or break something.
■ a murderer who mutilates victims' bodies.
2 informal a thing that is particularly admirable or excellent: *a* ***ripper of a*** *gig* | [as modifier] *everyone had a ripper time.*

■ a good snowboarder.

ripping ▶ **adjective** Brit. informal, dated splendid; excellent: *she's going to have a ripping time.*
– DERIVATIVES **rippingly** adverb.

ripple ▶ **noun 1** a small wave or series of waves on the surface of water, especially as caused by a slight breeze or an object dropping into it.
■ a thing resembling such a wave or series of waves in appearance or movement: *the sand undulated and was ridged with ripples.* ■ a gentle rising and falling sound, especially of laughter or conversation, that spreads through a group of people: *a ripple of laughter ran around the room.* ■ a particular feeling or effect that spreads through or to someone or something: *his words set off a ripple of excitement within her.* ■ Physics a wave on a fluid surface, the restoring force for which is provided by surface tension rather than gravity, and which consequently has a wavelength shorter than that corresponding to the minimum speed of propagation. ■ [mass noun] small periodic, usually undesirable, variations in electrical voltage superposed on a direct voltage or on an alternating voltage of lower frequency.
2 [mass noun] a type of ice cream with wavy lines of coloured flavoured syrup running through it: *a family block of raspberry ripple.*
▶ **verb** [no obj.] (of water) form or flow with small waves on the surface: *the Mediterranean rippled and sparkled* | [as adj. **rippling**] *the rippling waters.*
■ [with obj.] cause (the surface of water) to form small waves: *a cool wind rippled the surface of the estuary.* ■ move or cause to move in a way resembling such waves: [no obj.] *fields of grain rippling in the wind* | [with obj.] *which film star once rippled his biceps in Belfast?* ■ [no obj., with adverbial of direction] (of a sound or feeling) spread through a person, group, or place: *applause **rippled around** the tables.*
– DERIVATIVES **ripplet** noun, **ripply** adjective.
– ORIGIN late 17th cent. (as a verb): of unknown origin.

ripple effect ▶ **noun** the continuing and spreading results of an event or action.

ripple marks ▶ **plural noun** a system of parallel wavy ridges and furrows left on sand, mud, or rock by the action of water or wind.

riprap N. Amer. ▶ **noun** [mass noun] loose stone used to form a foundation for a breakwater or other structure.
▶ **verb** (**riprapped**, **riprapping**) [with obj.] strengthen with such a structure.
– ORIGIN mid 19th cent. (originally US): reduplication of **RAP**[1].

rip-roaring ▶ **adjective** [attrib.] full of energy and vigour: *a rip-roaring derby match.*
– DERIVATIVES **rip-roaringly** adverb.

ripsaw ▶ **noun** a coarse saw for cutting wood along the grain.

ripsnorting ▶ **adjective** [attrib.] informal showing great vigour or intensity: *a ripsnorting editorial.*
– DERIVATIVES **ripsnorter** noun, **ripsnortingly** adverb.

r

ripstop ▶ **noun** [mass noun] nylon fabric that is woven so that a tear will not spread.

rip tide ▶ **noun** another term for **RIP**[2].
■ figurative an experience of conflicting psychological forces.

Rip Van Winkle the hero of a story in Washington Irving's *Sketch Book* (1819–20), who fell asleep in the Catskill Mountains and awoke after twenty years to find the world completely changed.

RISC ▶ **noun** [usu. as modifier] Computing a computer based on a processor or processors designed to perform a limited set of operations extremely quickly.
■ [mass noun] computing using this kind of computer.
– ORIGIN 1980s: acronym from *reduced instruction set computer* (or *computing*).

rise ▶ **verb** (past **rose**; past participle **risen**) [no obj.] **1** move from a lower position to a higher one; come or go up: *the tiny aircraft rose from the ground.*
■ (of the sun, moon, or another celestial body) appear above the horizon: *the sun had just risen.* ■ (of a fish) come to the surface of water: *a fish rose and was hooked and landed.* ■ (of a voice) become higher in pitch: *my voice rose an octave or two as I screamed.* ■ reach a higher position in society or one's profession: *the officer was a man of great courage who had **risen from the ranks**.* ■ (**rise above**) succeed in not being limited or constrained by (a restrictive environment or situation): *he struggled to rise above his humble background.* ■ (**rise above**) be superior to: *I try to rise above prejudice.*
2 get up from lying, sitting, or kneeling: *she pushed back her chair and rose.*
■ get out of bed, especially in the morning: *I rose and got dressed.* ■ chiefly Brit. (of a meeting or a session of a court) adjourn: *the judge's remark heralded the signal for the court to rise.* ■ be restored to life: *your sister has **risen from** the dead.* ■ (of a wind) start to blow or to blow more strongly: *the wind continued to rise.* ■ (of a river) have its source: *the Euphrates rises in Turkey.* ■ cease to be submissive, obedient, or peaceful: *the activists urged militant factions to **rise up**.* ■ (**rise to**) (of a person) react with annoyance or argument to (provocation): *he didn't rise to my teasing.* ■ (**rise to**) find the strength or ability to respond adequately to (a challenging situation): *many participants in the race had never sailed before, but they rose to the challenge.*
3 (of land or a feature following the contours of the land) incline upwards; become higher: *the moorlands rise and fall in gentle folds.*
■ (of a building, mountain, or other high object or structure) be much taller than the surrounding landscape: *the cliff rose more than a hundred feet above us.* ■ (of someone's hair) stand on end: *he felt the hairs rise on the back of his neck.* ■ (of a building) undergo construction from the foundations: *rows of two-storey houses are slowly rising.* ■ (of dough) swell by the action of yeast: *leave the dough in a warm place to rise.* ■ (of a bump, blister, or weal) appear as a swelling on the skin: *blisters rose on his burned hand.* ■ (of a person's stomach) become nauseated: *Fabio's stomach **rose at** the foul bedding.*
4 increase in number, size, amount, or quality: *land prices had risen.*
■ (of the sea, a river, or other body of water) increase in height to a particular level, typically through tidal action or flooding: *the river level rose so high the work had to be abandoned* | figurative *the **rising tide of** crime.* ■ (of an emotion) develop and become more intense: *he felt a tide of resentment rising in him.* ■ (of a sound) become louder; be audible above other sounds: *her voice rose above the clamour.* ■ (of a person's mood) become more cheerful: *her spirits rose as they left the ugly city behind.* ■ (of the colour in a person's face) become deeper, especially as a result of embarrassment: *he was teasing her, and she could feel her colour rising.* ■ (of a barometer or other measuring instrument) give a higher reading.
5 (**rising**) approaching (a specified age): *she was thirty-nine rising forty.*
▶ **noun 1** an upward movement; an instance of becoming higher: *the bird has a display flight of steep flapping rises.*
■ an act of a fish moving to the surface to take a fly or bait. ■ an increase in sound or pitch: *the rise and fall of his voice.* ■ an instance of social, commercial, or political advancement: *few models have had such a meteoric rise.* ■ an upward slope or hill. ■ the vertical height of a step, arch, or incline. ■ another term for **RISER** (in sense 2).
2 an increase in amount, extent, size, or number: *local people are worried by the rise in crime.*
■ Brit. an increase in salary or wages.
3 [in sing.] a source; an origin: *it was here that the brook had its rise.*
– PHRASES **get** (or **take**) **a rise out of** informal provoke an angry or irritated response from (someone), especially by teasing. **on the rise** becoming greater or more numerous; increasing: *prices were on the rise.* ■ becoming more successful: *young stars on the rise.* **rise and shine** [usu. in imperative] informal get out of bed smartly; wake up. **rise to the bait** see **BAIT**. **rise with the sun** (or **lark**) get up early in the morning. **someone's star is rising** someone is becoming more successful or popular.
– ORIGIN Old English *rīsan* 'make an attack', 'wake, get out of bed', of Germanic origin; related to Dutch *rijzen* and German *reisen*.

riser ▶ **noun 1** [with adj.] a person who habitually gets out of bed at a particular time of the morning: *late risers always exasperate early risers.*
2 a vertical section between the treads of a staircase.
3 a vertical pipe for the upward flow of liquid or gas.
4 a low platform on a stage or in an auditorium, used to give greater prominence to a speaker or performer.
5 a strip of webbing joining the harness and the rigging lines of a parachute or paraglider.

rise time ▶ **noun** Electronics the time required for a pulse to rise from 10 per cent to 90 per cent of its steady value.

rishi /ˈrɪʃi/ ▶ **noun** (pl. **rishis**) a Hindu sage or saint.
– ORIGIN from Sanskrit *ṛṣi*.

risible /ˈrɪzɪb(ə)l/ ▶ **adjective** such as to provoke laughter: *a risible scene of lovemaking in a tent.*
■ rare (of a person) having the faculty or power of laughing; inclined to laugh.
– DERIVATIVES **risibility** noun, **risibly** adverb.
– ORIGIN mid 16th cent. (in the sense 'inclined to laughter'): from late Latin *risibilis*, from Latin *ris-* 'laughed', from the verb *ridere*.

rising ▶ **adjective** [postpositive] Heraldry (of a bird) depicted with the wings open but not fully displayed, as if preparing for flight.
▶ **noun** an armed protest against authority; a revolt.

rising damp ▶ **noun** [mass noun] Brit. moisture absorbed from the ground into a wall.

rising main ▶ **noun** Brit. a vertical pipe that rises from the ground to supply mains water to a building.
■ the vertical pipe of a water pump.

rising sign ▶ **noun** Astrology an ascendant sign.

risk ▶ **noun** a situation involving exposure to danger: *flouting the law was too much of a risk* | [mass noun] *all outdoor activities carry an element of risk.*
■ [in sing.] the possibility that something unpleasant or unwelcome will happen: ***reduce the risk of** heart disease* | [as modifier] *smoking is a risk factor for cot death.* ■ [usu. in sing.] [with adj.] a person or thing regarded as likely to turn out well or badly, as specified, in a particular context or respect: *Western banks regarded Romania as a good risk.* ■ [with modifier] a person or thing regarded as a threat to something in need of protection: *she's a security risk.* ■ [with modifier] a thing regarded as likely to result in a specified danger: *gloss paint can burn strongly and pose a fire risk.* ■ (usu. **risks**) a possibility of harm or damage against which something is insured. ■ [mass noun] the possibility of financial loss: [as modifier] *project finance is essentially an exercise in risk management.*
▶ **verb** [with obj.] expose (someone or something valued) to danger, harm, or loss: *he risked his life to save his dog.*
■ act or fail to act in such a way as to bring about the possibility of (an unpleasant or unwelcome event): *coal producers must sharpen up or risk losing half their business.* ■ incur the chance of unfortunate consequences by engaging in (an action): *he was far too intelligent to risk attempting to deceive him.*
– PHRASES **at risk** exposed to harm or danger: *23 million people in Africa are **at risk from** starvation.* **at one's** (**own**) **risk** used to indicate that if harm befalls a person or their possessions through their actions, it is their own responsibility: *they undertook the adventure at their own risk.* **at the risk of doing something** although there is the possibility of something unpleasant resulting: *at the risk of boring people to tears, I repeat the most important rule in painting.* **at risk to oneself** (or **something**) with the possibility of endangering oneself or something: *he visited prisons at considerable risk to his health.* **risk one's neck** put one's life in danger. **run the risk** (or **run risks**) expose oneself to the possibility of something unpleasant occurring: *she preferred not to **run the risk of** encountering his sister.* **take a risk** (or **take risks**) proceed in the knowledge that there is a chance of something unpleasant occurring.
– ORIGIN mid 17th cent.: from French *risque* (noun), *risquer* (verb), from Italian *risco* 'danger' and *rischiare* 'run into danger'.

risk capital ▶ **noun** another term for **VENTURE CAPITAL**.

risky ▶ **adjective** (**riskier**, **riskiest**) **1** full of the possibility of danger, failure, or loss: *it was much too risky to try to disarm him.*
2 risqué: *their risky patter made the guests laugh.*
– DERIVATIVES **riskily** adverb, **riskiness** noun.

Risorgimento /rɪˌsɔːdʒɪˈmɛntəʊ/ a movement for the unification and independence of Italy, which was achieved in 1870.

The restoration of repressive regimes after the Napoleonic Wars led to revolts in Naples and Piedmont (1821) and Bologna (1831). With French aid, the Austrians were driven out of northern Italy by 1859, and the south was won over by Garibaldi. Voting resulted in the acceptance of Victor Emmanuel II as the first king of a united Italy in 1861.

– ORIGIN Italian, literally 'resurrection'.

risotto /rɪˈzɒtəʊ/ ▶ **noun** (pl. **-os**) an Italian dish of rice cooked in stock with ingredients such as vegetables and meat or seafood.
– ORIGIN Italian, from *riso* 'rice'.

risqué /rɪˈskeɪ, ˈrɪskeɪ, ˈriːskeɪ/ ▶ **adjective** slightly

b **b**ut | d **d**og | f **f**ew | g **g**et | h **h**e | j **y**es | k **c**at | l **l**eg | m **m**an | n **n**o | p **p**en | r **r**ed | s **s**it | t **t**op | v **v**oice | w **w**e | z **z**oo | ʃ **sh**e | ʒ deci**si**on | θ **th**in | ð **th**is | ŋ ri**ng** | x lo**ch** | tʃ **ch**ip | dʒ **j**ar

indecent and liable to shock, especially by being sexually suggestive: *his risqué humour.*
– ORIGIN mid 19th cent.: French, past participle of *risquer* 'to risk'.

Riss /rɪs/ ▶ **noun** [usu. as modifier] Geology the penultimate Pleistocene glaciation in the Alps, possibly corresponding to the Saale of northern Europe.
■ the system of deposits laid down at this time.
– ORIGIN early 20th cent.: from the name of a tributary of the River Danube in Germany.

rissole ▶ **noun** a compressed mixture of meat and spices, coated in breadcrumbs and fried.
– ORIGIN early 18th cent.: from French, from Old French dialect *ruissole*, from a feminine form of late Latin *russeolus* 'reddish', from Latin *russus* 'red'.

Risso's dolphin /ˈrɪsəʊz/ ▶ **noun** a grey dolphin which has a rounded snout with no beak, and long black flippers, living mainly in temperate seas. Also called **GRAMPUS**.
● *Grampus griseus*, family Delphinidae.
– ORIGIN late 19th cent.: named after Giovanni A. *Risso* (1777–1845), Italian naturalist.

ristorante /ˌrɪstɒˈranteɪ, -ti/ ▶ **noun** (pl. **ristoranti** /-ti/) an Italian restaurant.
– ORIGIN Italian.

rit. Music ▶ **abbreviation for** ■ ritardando. ■ ritenuto.

Ritalin /ˈrɪtəlɪn/ ▶ **noun** trademark for **METHYLPHENIDATE**.

ritardando /ˌrɪtɑːˈdandəʊ/ ▶ **adverb**, **adjective**, & **noun** (pl. **ritardandos** or **ritardandi** /-di/) Music another term for **RALLENTANDO**.
– ORIGIN Italian.

rite ▶ **noun** a religious or other solemn ceremony or act.
■ a body of customary observances characteristic of a Church or a part of it: *the Byzantine rite.* ■ a social custom, practice, or conventional act: *the British family Christmas rite.*
– PHRASES **rite of passage** a ceremony or event marking an important stage in someone's life, especially birth, initiation, marriage, and death.
– ORIGIN Middle English: from Latin *ritus* '(religious) usage'.

rite de passage /ˌriːt də paˈsɑːʒ/ ▶ **noun** (pl. **rites de passage** pronunc. same) another term for ***rite of passage*** (see **RITE**).
– ORIGIN French.

ritenuto /ˌrɪtɛˈn(j)uːtəʊ/ Music ▶ **adverb** & **adjective** (especially as a direction) with an immediate reduction of speed.
▶ **noun** (pl. **ritenutos** or **ritenuti** /-ti/) an immediate reduction of speed.
– ORIGIN Italian, literally 'retained, restrained'.

ritornello /ˌrɪtɔːˈnɛləʊ/ ▶ **noun** (pl. **ritornellos** or **ritornelli** /-li/) Music a short instrumental refrain or interlude in a vocal work.
– ORIGIN Italian, diminutive of *ritorno* 'return'.

ritual ▶ **noun** a religious or solemn ceremony consisting of a series of actions performed according to a prescribed order: *the ancient rituals of Christian worship* | [mass noun] *the role of ritual in religion.*
■ a prescribed order of performing such a ceremony, especially one characteristic of a particular religion or Church. ■ a series of actions or type of behaviour regularly and invariably followed by someone: *her visits to Joy became a ritual.*
▶ **adjective** [attrib.] of, relating to, or done as a religious or solemn rite: *ritual burial.*
■ (of an action) arising from convention or habit: *the players gathered for the ritual pre-match huddle.* ■ S. African (of a murder) committed in order to obtain body parts for use in the making of muti.
– DERIVATIVES **ritually** adverb.
– ORIGIN late 16th cent. (as an adjective): from Latin *ritualis*, from *ritus* (see **RITE**).

ritual abuse (also **satanic abuse**) ▶ **noun** [mass noun] the alleged sexual abuse or murder of people, especially children, supposedly committed as part of satanic rituals.

ritualism ▶ **noun** [mass noun] the regular observance or practice of ritual, especially when excessive or without regard to its function.
– DERIVATIVES **ritualist** noun, **ritualistic** adjective, **ritualistically** adverb.

ritualization (also **-isation**) ▶ **noun** [mass noun] the action or process of ritualizing something, in particular:
■ the formalization of certain actions expressing a particular emotion or state of mind, whether abnormally (as in obsessive-compulsive disorder) or as part of the symbolism of religion or culture. ■ Zoology the evolutionary process by which an action or behaviour pattern in an animal loses its original function but is retained for its role in display or other social interaction.

ritualize (also **-ise**) ▶ **verb** [with obj.] [usu. as adj. **ritualized**] make (something) into a ritual by following a pattern of actions or behaviour: *interpreting football hooliganism as a ritualized expression of aggression.*
■ Zoology cause (an action or behaviour pattern) to undergo ritualization.

ritz ▶ **noun** [mass noun] informal, chiefly N. Amer. ostentatious luxury and glamour: *removed from all the ritz and glitz.*
– PHRASES **put on the ritz** make a show of luxury or extravagance.
– ORIGIN early 20th cent.: from *Ritz*, a name associated with luxury hotels. from César Ritz (1850–1918), a Swiss hotel owner.

ritzy ▶ **adjective** (**ritzier**, **ritziest**) informal expensively stylish: *the ritzy Plaza Hotel.*
– DERIVATIVES **ritzily** adverb, **ritziness** noun.

rival ▶ **noun** a person or thing competing with another for the same objective or for superiority in the same field of activity: *he has no serious rival for the job* | [as modifier] *gun battles between rival gangs.*
■ [with negative] a person or thing that equals another in quality: *she has no rivals as a female rock singer.*
▶ **verb** (**rivalled**, **rivalling**; US **rivaled**, **rivaling**) [with obj.] compete for superiority with; be or seem to be equal or comparable to: *the efficiency of the Bavarians **rivals that of** the Viennese.*
– ORIGIN late 16th cent.: from Latin *rivalis*, originally in the sense 'person using the same stream as another', from *rivus* 'stream'.

rivalrous ▶ **adjective** prone to or subject to rivalry: *rivalrous presidential aspirants.*

rivalry ▶ **noun** (pl. **-ies**) [mass noun] competition for the same objective or for superiority in the same field: *commercial rivalry* | [count noun] *ethnic rivalries.*

rive /rʌɪv/ ▶ **verb** (past **rived**; past participle **riven** /ˈrɪv(ə)n/) (usu. **be riven**) split or tear apart violently: *the party was riven by disagreements over Europe* | figurative *he was **riven with** guilt.*
■ archaic split or crack (wood or stone): *the wood was **riven with** deep cracks.* ■ [no obj.] archaic (of wood or stone) split or crack: *I started to chop furiously, the dry wood riving and splintering under the axe.*
– ORIGIN Middle English: from Old Norse *rífa*, of unknown ultimate origin.

river ▶ **noun** a large natural stream of water flowing in a channel to the sea, a lake, or another such stream.
■ a large quantity of a flowing substance: *great **rivers of** molten lava* | figurative *the trickle of disclosures has grown into a river of revelations.* ■ used in names of animals and plants living in or associated with rivers, e.g. **river dolphin**, **river birch**.
– PHRASES **sell someone down the river** informal betray someone, especially so as to benefit oneself. [ORIGIN: earlier referring to the sale of a troublesome slave to the owner of a sugar-cane plantation on the lower Mississippi, where conditions were relatively harsher.] **up the river** informal, chiefly N. Amer. to or in prison. [ORIGIN: with allusion to Sing Sing prison, situated up the Hudson River from the city of New York.]
– DERIVATIVES **rivered** adjective, **riverless** adjective.
– ORIGIN Middle English: from Anglo-Norman French, based on Latin *riparius*, from *ripa* 'bank of a river'.

Rivera /rɪˈvɛːrə, Spanish riˈβera/, Diego (1886–1957), Mexican painter. He inspired a revival of fresco painting in Latin America and the US. His largest mural is a history of Mexico for the National Palace in Mexico City (unfinished, 1929–57).

river blindness ▶ **noun** [mass noun] a tropical skin disease caused by a parasitic filarial worm, transmitted by the bite of blackflies (*Simulium damnosum*) which breed in fast-flowing rivers. The larvae of the parasite can migrate into the eye and cause blindness. Also called **ONCHOCERCIASIS**.
● The worm is *Onchocerca volvulus*, class Phasmida.

river capture ▶ **noun** [mass noun] Geology the natural diversion of the headwaters of one stream into the channel of another, typically resulting from rapid headward erosion by the latter stream.

river dolphin ▶ **noun** a solitary dolphin with a long slender beak, a small dorsal fin, and very poor eyesight. It lives in rivers and coastal waters of South America, India, and China, using echolocation to find its prey.
● Family Platanistidae: four genera and species.

riverine /ˈrɪvərʌɪn/ ▶ **adjective** technical or poetic/literary of, relating to, or situated on a river or riverbank; riparian: *a riverine village.*

riverscape ▶ **noun** a picturesque view or prospect of a river.
■ a painting of a river or riverside scene.

Riverside a city in southern California, situated in the centre of an orange-growing region; pop. 226,505 (1990).

riverside ▶ **noun** [often as modifier] the ground along a riverbank: *a riverside car park.*

rivet /ˈrɪvɪt/ ▶ **noun** a short metal pin or bolt for holding together two plates of metal, its headless end being beaten out or pressed down when in place.
▶ **verb** (**riveted**, **riveting**) [with obj.] join or fasten (plates of metal) with a rivet or rivets: *the linings are bonded, not riveted, to the brake shoes for longer wear.*
■ fix (someone or something) so as to make them incapable of movement: *the grip on her arm was firm enough to **rivet her to the spot**.* ■ attract and completely engross (someone): *he was riveted by the newsreels shown on television* | [as adj. **riveting**] *a riveting story.* ■ (usu. **be riveted**) direct (one's eyes or attention) intently: *all eyes **were riveted on** him.*
– DERIVATIVES **riveter** noun, **rivetingly** adverb.
– ORIGIN Middle English: from Old French, from *river* 'fix, clinch', of unknown ultimate origin.

riviera /ˌrɪvɪˈɛːrə/ ▶ **noun** a coastal region with a subtropical climate and vegetation.
■ (**the Riviera**) part of the Mediterranean coastal region of southern France and northern Italy, extending from Cannes to La Spezia, famous for its beauty, mild climate, and fashionable resorts.
– ORIGIN mid 18th cent.: from Italian, literally 'seashore'.

rivière /ˌrɪvɪˈɛː/ ▶ **noun** a necklace of gems that increase in size towards a large central stone, typically consisting of more than one string.
– ORIGIN late 19th cent.: French, literally 'river'.

Rivne /ˈrɪvnə/ an industrial city in western Ukraine north-east of Lviv; pop. 232,900 (1990). Russian name **ROVNO**.

rivulet /ˈrɪvjʊlɪt/ ▶ **noun 1** a very small stream: *sweat ran in rivulets down his back.*
2 a brownish European moth with white markings, occurring in rough grassland.
● *Perizoma affinitatum*, family Geometridae.
– ORIGIN late 16th cent.: alteration of obsolete *riveret* (from French, literally 'small river'), perhaps suggested by Italian *rivoletto*, diminutive of *rivolo*, based on Latin *rivus* 'stream'.

rivulus /ˈrɪvjʊləs/ ▶ **noun** a small tropical American killifish of fresh and brackish water.
● Genus *Rivulus*, family Cyprinodontidae: several species, many of which are spotted.
– ORIGIN modern Latin, from Latin, literally 'small stream'.

Riyadh /riːˈɑːd/ the capital of Saudi Arabia; pop. 2,000,000 (est. 1988). It is situated on a high plateau in the centre of the country.

riyal ▶ **noun** variant spelling of **RIAL**.

RKO a US film production and distribution company founded in 1928, which produced classic films such as *King Kong* (1933) and *Citizen Kane* (1941). It ceased film production in 1953.
– ORIGIN abbreviation of *Radio-Keith-Orpheum*, from a merger of Radio Corporation of America (RCA) with the *Keith* and *Orpheum* cinema chains.

RL ▶ **abbreviation for** ■ rugby league. ■ Lebanon (international vehicle registration). [ORIGIN: from *Republic of Lebanon*.]

rly ▶ **abbreviation for** railway.

RM ▶ **abbreviation for** ■ Madagascar (international vehicle registration). [ORIGIN: from French *République de Madagascar*.] ■ (in the UK) Royal Mail. ■ (in the UK) Royal Marines.

rm ▶ **abbreviation for** room.

RMA ▶ **abbreviation for** Royal Military Academy.

RMM ▶ **abbreviation for** Mali (international vehicle registration).

RMP ▶ **abbreviation for** Royal Military Police.

r.m.s. Mathematics ▶ abbreviation for root mean square.

RMT ▶ abbreviation for (in the UK) National Union of Rail, Maritime, and Transport Workers. It was formed in 1990 by a merger of the National Union of Railwaymen and National Union of Seamen.

RN ▶ abbreviation for ■ Niger (international vehicle registration). [ORIGIN: from French *République du Niger*.] ■ (chiefly in North America) Registered Nurse. ■ (in the UK) **ROYAL NAVY**.

Rn ▶ symbol for the chemical element radon.

RNA ▶ noun [mass noun] Biochemistry ribonucleic acid, a nucleic acid present in all living cells. Its principal role is to act as a messenger carrying instructions from DNA for controlling the synthesis of proteins, although in some viruses RNA rather than DNA carries the genetic information.

RNAS ▶ abbreviation for (in the UK) Royal Naval Air Station.

RNase ▶ noun [mass noun] Biochemistry an enzyme which promotes the breakdown of RNA into oligonucleotides and smaller molecules.
– ORIGIN 1950s: from **RNA** + **-ASE**.

RNA virus ▶ noun a virus in which the genetic information is stored in the form of RNA (as opposed to DNA).

RNLI ▶ abbreviation for (in the UK) Royal National Lifeboat Institution.

RNZAF ▶ abbreviation for Royal New Zealand Air Force.

RNZN ▶ abbreviation for Royal New Zealand Navy.

roach[1] ▶ noun (pl. same) an edible Eurasian freshwater fish of the carp family, popular with anglers. It can hybridize with related fishes, notably rudd and bream.
● *Rutilus rutilus*, family Cyprinidae.
– ORIGIN Middle English: from Old French *roche*, of unknown ultimate origin.

roach[2] ▶ noun informal **1** chiefly N. Amer. a cockroach. [ORIGIN: mid 19th cent.: shortened form.] **2** a roll of card or paper that forms the butt of a cannabis cigarette. [ORIGIN: 1930s: of unknown origin.]

roach[3] ▶ noun Sailing a curved part of a fore-and-aft sail extending beyond a straight line between its corners, especially on the leech side.
– ORIGIN late 18th cent.: of unknown origin.

roach clip ▶ noun informal, chiefly N. Amer. a clip for holding the base of a cannabis cigarette.

roached ▶ adjective chiefly US **1** (especially of an animal's back) having an upward curve. **2** (of a person's hair) brushed upwards or forwards into a roll. ■ (of a horse's mane) clipped or trimmed short so that the hair stands on end.

road ▶ noun **1** a wide way leading from one place to another, especially one with a specially prepared surface which vehicles can use. ■ the part of such a way intended for vehicles, especially in contrast to a verge or pavement. ■ [with modifier] historical a regular trade route for a particular commodity: *the Silk Road across Asia to the West.* ■ Mining an underground passage or gallery in a mine. ■ N. Amer. a railroad. ■ Brit. a railway track, especially as clear (or otherwise) for a train to proceed: *they waited for a clear road at Hellifield Junction.* **2** figurative a series of events or a course of action that will lead to a particular outcome: *he's well on the road to recovery.* ■ a particular course or direction taken or followed: *the low road of apathy and alienation.* **3** [often in place names] (usu. **roads**) a partly sheltered stretch of water near the shore in which ships can ride at anchor: *Boston Roads.*
– PHRASES **by road** in or on a road vehicle. **down the road** informal, chiefly N. Amer. in the future. **the end of the road** see **END. hit the road** see **HIT. in (or out of) the** (or **one's**) **road** [often in imperative] informal in (or out of) someone's way. **one for the road** informal a final drink, especially an alcoholic one, before leaving for home. **on the road 1** on a long journey or series of journeys, especially as part of one's job as a sales representative or a performer. ■ (of a person) without a permanent home and moving from place to place. **2** (of a car) in use; able to be driven. ■ (often **on-the-road**) (of or with reference to the price of a motor vehicle) including the cost of licence plates, tax, etc., so the vehicle is fully ready for use on public roads: *we found on-the-road prices*

from £5,780 to £6,151. **a road to nowhere** see **NOWHERE. take to the road** (or **take the road**) set out on a journey or series of journeys.
– DERIVATIVES **roadless** adjective.
– ORIGIN Old English *rād* 'journey on horseback', 'foray'; of Germanic origin; related to the verb **RIDE**.

roadbed ▶ noun the material laid down to form a road. ■ N. Amer. the part of a road on which vehicles travel. ■ another term for **TRACKBED**.

road bike ▶ noun **1** a motorcycle that meets the legal requirements for use on ordinary roads. **2** a bicycle that is only suitable for use on ordinary roads.

roadblock ▶ noun a barrier or barricade on a road, especially one set up by the authorities to stop and examine traffic.

road car ▶ noun a car that meets the legal requirements for use on ordinary roads, especially a race car adapted for road use.

road fund ▶ noun Brit. historical a fund for the construction and maintenance of roads and bridges.

road fund licence ▶ noun Brit. a disc displayed on a vehicle certifying payment of road tax.

road-going ▶ adjective (of a car) meeting legal requirements for use on ordinary roads.

road hog ▶ noun informal a motorist who drives recklessly or inconsiderately, making it difficult for others to pass.

roadholding ▶ noun [mass noun] the ability of a vehicle to remain stable when moving, especially when cornering at high speeds.

roadhouse ▶ noun an inn or club on a country road.

road hump ▶ noun another term for **SLEEPING POLICEMAN**.

roadie informal ▶ noun a person employed by a touring band of musicians to set up and maintain equipment.
▶ verb [no obj.] work as such a person.

road kill ▶ noun chiefly N. Amer. a killing of an animal on the road by a vehicle. ■ [mass noun] animals killed in such a way.

roadman ▶ noun (pl. **-men**) **1** Brit. archaic a man employed to repair or maintain roads. **2** Cycling a cyclist who specializes in long-distance road racing.

road manager ▶ noun the organizer and supervisor of a musicians' tour.

road map ▶ noun a map, especially one designed for motorists, showing the roads of a country or area.

road metal ▶ noun see **METAL** (sense 2).

road movie ▶ noun a film of a genre in which the main character is travelling, either in flight or on a journey of self-discovery.

road noise ▶ noun [mass noun] noise resulting from the movement of a vehicle's tyres over the road surface.

road pricing ▶ noun [mass noun] the practice of charging motorists to use busy roads at certain times, especially to relieve congestion in urban areas.

road rage ▶ noun [mass noun] violent anger caused by the stress and frustration involved in driving a motor vehicle in difficult conditions.

roadroller ▶ noun a motor vehicle with a heavy roller, used in road-making.

roadrunner ▶ noun a slender fast-running bird of the cuckoo family, found chiefly in arid country from the southern US to Central America.
● Genus *Geococcyx*, family Cuculidae: two species, in particular the (**greater**) **roadrunner** (*G. californianus*).

road sense ▶ noun [mass noun] Brit. a person's capacity for safe behaviour on the road, especially in traffic.

roadshow ▶ noun a radio or television programme broadcast on location, especially each of a series done from different venues. ■ a touring political or promotional campaign. ■ a touring show of performers, especially pop musicians.

roadside ▶ noun [often as modifier] the strip of land beside a road: *roadside cafes.*

road sign ▶ noun a sign giving information or instructions to road users.

roadstead ▶ noun another term for **ROAD** (in sense 3).
– ORIGIN mid 16th cent.: from **ROAD** + obsolete *stead* 'a place'.

roadster ▶ noun an open-top motor car with two seats. ■ a bicycle designed for use on the road. ■ historical a horse for use on the road.

road tax ▶ noun [mass noun] Brit. a periodic tax payable on motor vehicles using public roads.

road test ▶ noun a test of the performance of a vehicle or engine on the road. ■ figurative a test of equipment carried out in working conditions. ■ another term for **DRIVING TEST**.
▶ verb (**road-test**) [with obj.] test (a vehicle or engine) on the road. ■ figurative try out (something) in working conditions for review or prior to purchase or release: *we road-tested a new laptop computer.*

Road Town the capital of the British Virgin Islands, situated on the island of Tortola; pop. 6,330 (1991).

road train ▶ noun chiefly Austral. a large lorry pulling one or more trailers.

roadway ▶ noun a road. ■ the part of a road intended for vehicles, in contrast to the pavement or verge. ■ the part of a bridge or railway used by traffic.

roadwork ▶ noun [mass noun] **1** [usu. as modifier] Brit. work done in building or repairing roads: *roadwork delays.* ■ (**roadworks**) repairs to roads or to utilities under roads. **2** athletic exercise or training involving running on roads. ■ time spent travelling while working or on tour. ■ training or travelling with animals (especially horses) on roads.

roadworthy ▶ adjective (of a motor vehicle or bicycle) fit to be used on the road.
– DERIVATIVES **roadworthiness** noun.

roam ▶ verb [no obj., with adverbial of direction] move about or travel aimlessly or unsystematically, especially over a wide area: *tigers once roamed over most of Asia* | [as adj.] *roaming elephants.* ■ [with obj.] travel unsystematically over, through, or about (a place): *gangs of youths roamed the streets unopposed.* ■ (of a person's eyes or hands) pass lightly over something without stopping: *her eyes roamed over the chattering women* | [with obj.] *he let his eyes roam her face.* ■ [no obj.] (of a person's mind or thoughts) drift along without dwelling on anything in particular: *he let his mind roam as he walked.* ■ [with obj.] move from site to site on (the Internet); browse.
▶ noun [in sing.] an aimless walk.
– DERIVATIVES **roamer** noun.
– ORIGIN Middle English: of unknown origin.

roan[1] ▶ adjective denoting an animal, especially a horse or cow, having a coat of a main colour thickly interspersed with hairs of another colour, typically bay, chestnut, or black mixed with white.
▶ noun [usu. with modifier] an animal with such a coat: *a blue roan.*
– ORIGIN mid 16th cent.: from Old French, of unknown origin.

roan[2] ▶ noun [mass noun] soft flexible leather made from sheepskin, used in bookbinding as a substitute for morocco.
– ORIGIN early 19th cent.: perhaps from *Roan*, the old name of the French town of **ROUEN**.

roan antelope ▶ noun an African antelope with black-and-white facial markings, a mane of stiff hair, and large backwardly curving horns.
● *Hippotragus equinus*, family Bovidae.

roar ▶ noun a full, deep, prolonged cry uttered by a lion or other large wild animal. ■ a loud and deep sound uttered by a person or crowd, generally as an expression of pain, anger, or approval: *he gave a roar of rage.* ■ a loud outburst of laughter. ■ a very loud, prolonged sound made by something inanimate, such as a natural force, an engine, or traffic: *the roar of the sea.*
▶ verb **1** [no obj.] (of a lion or other large wild animal) utter a full, deep, prolonged cry. ■ (of something inanimate) make a very loud, deep, prolonged sound: *a huge fire roared in the grate.* ■ (of a person or crowd) utter a loud, deep, prolonged sound, typically because of anger, pain, or

excitement: *Manfred roared with rage.* ■ [with obj.] utter or express in a loud tone: *the crowd roared its approval* | [with direct speech] *'Get out of my way!' he roared.* ■ [with obj. and adverbial] (of a crowd) encourage (someone) to do something by loud shouts or cheering: *Damon Hill will be* ***roared on*** *this weekend by a huge home crowd.* ■ laugh loudly: *Shirley roared in amusement.* ■ (of a horse) make a loud noise in breathing as a symptom of disease of the larynx.

2 [no obj., with adverbial] (especially of a vehicle) move at high speed making a loud prolonged sound: *a car roared past.* ■ proceed, act, or happen fast and decisively or conspicuously: *Swindon roared back with two goals.*

– DERIVATIVES **roarer** noun.

– ORIGIN Old English *rārian* (verb), imitative of a deep prolonged cry, of West Germanic origin; related to German *röhren*. The noun dates from late Middle English.

roaring ▶ **adjective** [attrib.] **1** (of a person, crowd, or animal) making a loud and deep sound, especially as an expression of pain, anger, or approval: *he was greeted everywhere with roaring crowds.* ■ (of something inanimate, especially a natural phenomenon) making a loud, deep, or harsh prolonged sound: *a swollen, roaring river.* ■ (of a fire) burning fiercely and noisily. ■ chiefly archaic behaving or living in a noisy riotous manner: *he's a kind of Norwegian roaring boy.* ■ (of a period of time) characterized by optimism, buoyancy, or excitement: *the Roaring Eighties.*

2 informal very obviously or unequivocally the thing mentioned (used for emphasis): *the final week of* Hamlet *was a* ***roaring success*** | [as submodifier] *two roaring drunk firemen.*

– PHRASES **do a roaring trade** (or **business**) informal do very good business.

– DERIVATIVES **roaringly** adverb.

roaring forties (**the roaring forties**) stormy ocean tracts between latitudes 40° and 50° south.

roaring twenties ▶ **plural noun** (**the roaring twenties**) informal the decade 1920–29 (with reference to its post-war buoyancy).

roast ▶ **verb** [with obj.] cook (food, especially meat) by prolonged exposure to heat in an oven or over a fire: *she was going to roast a leg of mutton for Sunday dinner* | [as adj. **roasted**] *roasted chestnuts.* ■ [no obj.] (of food) be cooked in such a way: *she checked the meat roasting in the oven for lunch.* ■ process (a foodstuff, metal ore, etc.) by subjecting it to intense heat: *decaffeinated coffee beans are roasted and ground.* ■ make (someone or something) very warm, especially by exposure to the heat of the sun or a fire: *the fire was hot enough to roast anyone who stood close to it.* ■ [no obj.] become very hot: *Jessica could feel her face begin to roast.* ■ torture by exposure to fire or great heat: *a fresco of St. Catherine being roasted on a wheel.* ■ criticize or reprimand severely: *if you waste his time he'll roast you.*

▶ **adjective** [attrib.] (of food) having been cooked in an oven or over an open fire: *a plate of cold roast beef.*

▶ **noun** a joint of meat that has been roasted or that is intended for roasting: *carving the Sunday roast.* ■ a dish or meal of roasted food. ■ [mass noun] the process of roasting something, especially coffee, or the result of this. ■ [with adj.] a particular type of roasted coffee: *continental roasts.* ■ an outdoor party at which meat, especially of a particular type, is roasted: *Harold put on a terrific pig roast.*

– ORIGIN Middle English: from Old French *rostir*, of West Germanic origin.

roaster ▶ **noun** a container, oven, furnace, or apparatus for roasting something. ■ a person or company that processes coffee beans. ■ a foodstuff that is particularly suitable for roasting, especially a chicken.

roasting ▶ **adjective** [attrib.] (of a container) used for roasting food: *a roasting tin.* ■ (of food) undergoing roasting: *roasting coffee.* ■ informal very hot and dry: *a roasting day in London.*

▶ **noun** [mass noun] the action of cooking something in an oven or over an open fire. ■ [in sing.] informal a severe criticism or reprimand: *banks are to get a roasting from the Treasury.*

rob ▶ **verb** (**robbed**, **robbing**) [with obj.] take property unlawfully from (a person or place) by force or threat of force: *he tried, with three others, to rob a bank* | *she was* ***robbed of*** *her handbag* | [no obj.] *he was convicted of assault with intent to rob.* ■ (usu. **be robbed**) informal overcharge (someone) for something: *Bob thinks my suit cost £70, and even then he thinks I was robbed.* ■ informal or dialect steal: *he accused her of robbing the cream out of his chocolate eclair.* ■ deprive (someone or something) of something needed, deserved, or significant: *poor health has* ***robbed*** *her* ***of*** *a normal social life.* ■ Soccer deprive (an opposing player) of the ball: *Hughes robbed Vonk yards inside the City half.*

– PHRASES **rob Peter to pay Paul** take something away from one person to pay another, leaving the former at a disadvantage; discharge one debt only to incur another. [ORIGIN: probably with reference to the saints and apostles *Peter* and *Paul*; the allusion is uncertain, the phrase often showing variations such as 'unclothe Peter and clothe Paul', 'borrow from Peter …', etc.]

– ORIGIN Middle English: from Old French *rober*, of Germanic origin; related to the verb **REAVE**.

Robbe-Grillet /rɒbˈɡriːeɪ, French ʀɔbɡʀijɛ/, Alain (b.1922), French novelist. His first novel, *The Erasers* (1953), was an early example of the *nouveau roman*. He also wrote essays and screenplays.

Robben Island /ˈrɒb(ə)n/ a small island off the coast of South Africa, near Cape Town. It is the site of a prison which was formerly used for the detention of political prisoners, including Nelson Mandela.

robber ▶ **noun** a person who commits robbery.

– ORIGIN Middle English: from Anglo-Norman French and Old French *robere*, from the verb *rober* (see **ROB**).

robber baron ▶ **noun** a ruthless and unscrupulous plutocrat.

– ORIGIN originally denoting a feudal lord who engaged in plundering.

robber crab ▶ **noun** a large terrestrial crablike crustacean which climbs coconut palms to feed on the nuts, found on islands in the Indo-Pacific area. Also called **COCONUT CRAB**.

● *Birgus latro*, family Paguridae.

robber fly ▶ **noun** a large powerful predatory fly which darts out and grabs insect prey on the wing.

● Family Asilidae: many genera.

robbery ▶ **noun** (pl. **-ies**) [mass noun] the action of robbing a person or place: *he was involved in drugs, violence, extortion, and robbery* | [count noun] *an armed robbery.* ■ informal unashamed swindling or overcharging.

– ORIGIN Middle English: from Anglo-Norman French and Old French *roberie*, from the verb *rober* (see **ROB**).

Robbia see **DELLA ROBBIA**.

Robbins[1], Harold (1916–97), American novelist, author of best-sellers such as *The Carpetbaggers* (1961) and *The Betsy* (1971).

Robbins[2], Jerome (1918–98), American ballet dancer and choreographer. He choreographed a number of successful musicals, including *The King and I* (1951), *West Side Story* (1957), and *Fiddler on the Roof* (1964).

robe ▶ **noun** **1** a long, loose outer garment reaching to the ankles. ■ (often **robes**) such a garment worn, especially on formal or ceremonial occasions, as an indication of the wearer's rank, office, or profession. ■ a dressing gown or bathrobe.

2 N. Amer. a lap robe.

▶ **verb** [with obj.] [usu. as adj. **robed**] clothe in a long, loose outer garment: *a circle of robed figures* | [in combination] *a white-robed Bedouin.* ■ [no obj.] put on robes, especially for a formal or ceremonial occasion: *I went into the vestry and robed for the Mass.*

– ORIGIN Middle English: from Old French, from the Germanic base (in the sense 'booty') of **ROB** (because clothing was an important component of booty).

Robert the name of three kings of Scotland:

■ **Robert I** (1274–1329), reigned 1306–29; known as **Robert the Bruce**. He campaigned against Edward I, and defeated Edward II at Bannockburn (1314). He re-established Scotland as a separate kingdom, negotiating the Treaty of Northampton (1328).

■ **Robert II** (1316–90), grandson of Robert the Bruce, reigned 1371–90. He was steward of Scotland from 1326 to 1371, and the first of the Stuart line.

■ **Robert III** (c.1337–1406), son of Robert II, reigned 1390–1406; born *John*. An accident made him physically disabled, resulting in a power struggle among members of his family.

Roberts, Frederick Sleigh, 1st Earl Roberts of Kandahar (1832–1914), British Field Marshal. He helped suppress the Indian Mutiny of 1857–8, secured victory at Kandahar (1880), ending the Second Afghan War, and planned the successful march on the Boer capital of Pretoria (1900) during the Second Boer War.

Robertsonian /ˌrɒbətˈsəʊnɪən/ ▶ **adjective** Genetics denoting a chromosome with a central centromere formed from two chromosomes having non-central centromeres. ■ (of a karyotypic change or translocation) brought about by this process.

– ORIGIN 1950s: from the name of William R. B. *Robertson* (1881–1941), American biologist, + **-IAN**.

Robert the Bruce see **ROBERT**.

Robeson /ˈrəʊbs(ə)n/, Paul (Bustill) (1898–1976), American singer and actor. His singing of 'Ol' Man River' in the musical *Showboat* (1927) established his international reputation. His black activism and Communist sympathies led to ostracism in the 1950s.

Robespierre /ˈrəʊbzpjɛː, French ʀɔbɛspjɛʀ/, Maximilien François Marie Isidore de (1758–94), French revolutionary. As leader of the radical Jacobins in the National Assembly he backed the execution of Louis XVI, implemented a purge of the Girondists, and initiated the Terror, but the following year he fell from favour and was guillotined.

Robey, Sir George (1869–1954), English comedian and actor; born *George Edward Wade*. He performed in music halls and films.

robin ▶ **noun** **1** a small Old World thrush related to the chats, typically having a brown back with red on the breast or other colourful markings.

● *Erithacus* and other genera, family Turdidae: numerous species, e.g. the familiar **European robin** or redbreast (*E. rubecula*), which has an orange-red face and breast.

2 [usu. with adj. or noun modifier] any of a number of other birds that resemble the European robin, especially in having a red breast:

● a large New World thrush that typically has a reddish breast (genus *Turdus*, family Turdidae), in particular the **American robin** (*T. migratorius*). ● Austral./NZ a small songbird related to the flycatchers, with a red, pink, yellow, or white breast (family Eopsaltridae, in particular genus *Petroica*). ● see **PEKIN ROBIN**.

– ORIGIN mid 16th cent.: from Old French, pet form of the given name *Robert*.

robin-chat ▶ **noun** an African chat with a mainly dark back and orange underparts.

● Genus *Cossypha* (and *Pseudocossyphus*), family Turdidae: several species.

Robin Goodfellow a mischievous sprite or goblin believed, especially in the 16th and 17th centuries, to haunt the English countryside. Also called **PUCK**[2].

robing room ▶ **noun** a room where holders of ceremonial office put on official robes.

Robin Hood a semi-legendary English medieval outlaw, reputed to have robbed the rich and helped the poor. Although he is generally associated with Sherwood Forest in Nottinghamshire, it seems likely that the real Robin Hood operated in Yorkshire in the early 13th century. ■ [as noun **a Robin Hood**] a person considered to be taking from the wealthy and giving to the poor.

robinia /rəˈbɪnɪə/ ▶ **noun** a North American tree or shrub of a genus that includes the false acacia.

● Genus *Robinia*, family Leguminosae.

– ORIGIN modern Latin, named after Jean and Vespasien *Robin*, 17th-cent. French gardeners to the royal family in Paris.

robin's-egg (also **robin's-egg blue** or **robin-egg**) ▶ **noun** [mass noun] N. Amer. a greenish-blue colour.

Robinson[1], Edward G. (1893–1972), Romanian-born American actor; born *Emanuel Goldenberg*. He appeared in a number of gangster films in the 1930s, starting with *Little Caesar* (1930).

Robinson[2], (William) Heath (1872–1944), English cartoonist and illustrator. He lampooned the machine age by inventing absurdly complicated 'Heath Robinson contraptions' to perform elementary or ridiculous actions.

Robinson[3], Mary (Terese Winifred) (b.1944), Irish Labour stateswoman, President 1990–7. She became Ireland's first woman President, noted for her platform of religious toleration and her liberal attitude.

Robinson[4], Smokey (b.1940), American soul singer and songwriter; born *William Robinson*. He is known for a series of successes with his group the Miracles, such as 'Tracks of my Tears' (1965).

r

Robinson[5], Sugar Ray (1920–89), American boxer; born *Walker Smith*. He was world welterweight champion and seven times middleweight champion.

Robinson Crusoe /ˈkruːsəʊ/ the hero of Daniel Defoe's novel *Robinson Crusoe* (1719), who survives a shipwreck and lives on a desert island.

robin's pincushion ▶ **noun** another term for **BEDEGUAR**.

robot /ˈrəʊbɒt/ ▶ **noun** a machine capable of carrying out a complex series of actions automatically, especially one programmable by a computer.
■ (especially in science fiction) a machine resembling a human being and able to replicate certain human movements and functions automatically. ■ used in similes and metaphors to refer to a person who behaves in a mechanical or unemotional manner: *terminally bored tour guides chattering like robots*. ■ S. African a set of automatic traffic lights.
– ORIGIN from Czech, from *robota* 'forced labour'. The term was coined in K. Čapek's play *R.U.R.* 'Rossum's Universal Robots' (1920).

robotic /rə(ʊ)ˈbɒtɪk/ ▶ **adjective** of or relating to robots: *a robotic device for performing surgery*.
■ (of a person) mechanical, stiff, or unemotional.
– DERIVATIVES **robotically** adverb.

robotics ▶ **plural noun** [treated as sing.] the branch of technology that deals with the design, construction, operation, and application of robots.

robotize (also **-ise**) ▶ **verb** [with obj.] [usu. as adj. **robotized**] convert (a production system, factory, etc.) to operation by robots.
– DERIVATIVES **robotization** noun.

Rob Roy[1] (1671–1734), Scottish outlaw; born *Robert Macgregor*. His reputation as a Scottish Robin Hood was exaggerated in Sir Walter Scott's novel of the same name (1817).

Rob Roy[2] ▶ **noun** a cocktail made of Scotch whisky and vermouth.

Robsart /ˈrɒbsɑːt/, Amy (1532–60), English noblewoman, wife of Robert Dudley, Earl of Leicester. Her mysterious death aroused suspicions that her husband had had her killed so that he could be free to marry Queen Elizabeth I.

Robson /ˈrɒbs(ə)n/, Dame Flora (1902–84), English actress. She was noted for her performance as the Empress Elizabeth in *Catherine the Great* (1934), and later for her many character roles.

robust ▶ **adjective** (**robuster**, **robustest**) (of a person, animal, or plant) strong and healthy; vigorous: *the Caplan family are a robust, healthy lot*.
■ (of an object) sturdy in construction: *a robust metal cabinet*. ■ (of a process or system, especially an economic one) able to withstand or overcome adverse conditions: *California's robust property market*. ■ (of an intellectual approach or the person taking or expressing it) not perturbed by or attending to subtleties or difficulties; uncompromising and forceful: *Russians are robust and avoid circumlocution* | *he took quite a robust view of my case*. ■ (of action) involving physical force or energy: *a robust game of rugby*. ■ (of wine or food) strong and rich in flavour or smell.
– DERIVATIVES **robustly** adverb, **robustness** noun.
– ORIGIN mid 16th cent.: from Latin *robustus* 'firm and hard', from *robus*, earlier form of *robur* 'oak, strength'.

robusta ▶ **noun 1** [mass noun] coffee or coffee beans from a widely grown kind of coffee plant. Beans of this variety are often used in the manufacture of instant coffee.
2 the tropical West African bush that produces these beans.
● *Coffea canephora* (formerly *robusta*), family Rubiaceae. See also **ARABICA**.
– ORIGIN early 20th cent.: modern Latin, feminine of Latin *robustus* 'robust'.

ROC historical ▶ **abbreviation for** (in the UK) Royal Observer Corps.

roc ▶ **noun** a gigantic mythological bird described in the Arabian Nights.
– ORIGIN late 16th cent.: ultimately from Persian *ruk*.

rocaille /rə(ʊ)ˈkʌɪ/ ▶ **noun 1** [mass noun] an 18th-century artistic or architectural style of decoration characterized by elaborate ornamentation with pebbles and shells, typical of grottos and fountains.
2 (**rocailles**) tiny beads; seed beads.
– ORIGIN French, from *roc* 'rock'.

rocambole /ˈrɒk(ə)mbəʊl/ ▶ **noun** a Eurasian plant that is closely related to garlic and is sometimes used as a flavouring.
● *Allium scorodoprasum*, family Liliaceae (or Alliaceae).
– ORIGIN late 17th cent.: from French, from German *Rockenbolle*.

ROCE Finance ▶ **abbreviation for** return on capital employed.

Roche limit /rəʊʃ/ (also **Roche's limit**) ▶ **noun** Astronomy the closest distance from the centre of a planet that a satellite can approach without being pulled apart by the planet's gravitational field.
– ORIGIN late 19th cent.: named after Edouard Albert *Roche* (1820–83), French mathematician.

roche moutonnée /ˌrɒʃ muːˈtɒneɪ/ ▶ **noun** (pl. **roches moutonnées** pronunc. same) Geology a small bare outcrop of rock shaped by glacial erosion, with one side smooth and gently sloping and the other steep, rough, and irregular.
– ORIGIN mid 19th cent.: French, literally 'fleecy rock'.

Rochester[1] /ˈrɒtʃɪstə/ **1** a town on the Medway estuary south-east of London; pop. 24,400 (1981).
2 a city in NW New York State, on Lake Ontario; pop. 231,640 (1990).

Rochester[2] /ˈrɒtʃɪstə/, John Wilmot, 2nd Earl of (1647–80), English poet and courtier. Infamous for his dissolute life at the court of Charles II, he wrote sexually explicit love poems and verse satires.

rochet /ˈrɒtʃɪt/ ▶ **noun** Christian Church a vestment resembling a surplice, used chiefly by bishops and abbots.
– ORIGIN Middle English: from Old French, a diminutive from a Germanic base shared by German *Rock* 'coat'.

rock[1] ▶ **noun 1** [mass noun] the solid mineral material forming part of the surface of the earth and other similar planets, exposed on the surface or underlying the soil.
■ [count noun] a mass of such material projecting above the earth's surface or out of the sea: *there are dangerous rocks around the island*. ■ [count noun] Geology any natural material, hard or soft (e.g. clay), having a distinctive mineral composition. ■ (**the Rock**) Gibraltar. ■ (**the Rock**) informal name for **NEWFOUNDLAND**[1].
2 a large piece of such material which has become detached from a cliff or mountain; a boulder: *the stream flowed through a jumble of rocks*.
■ a stone of any size, especially one small enough to be picked up and used as a projectile. ■ [mass noun] Brit. a kind of hard confectionery in the form of cylindrical peppermint-flavoured sticks. ■ informal a precious stone, especially a diamond. ■ informal a small piece of crack cocaine. ■ (**rocks**) vulgar slang a man's testicles.
3 used in similes and metaphors to refer to someone or something that is extremely strong, reliable, or hard: *the Irish scrum has been as solid as a rock*.
■ (usu. **rocks**) (especially with allusion to shipwrecks) a source of danger or destruction: *the new system is heading for the rocks*.
4 (**rocks**) US informal, dated money.
– PHRASES **between a rock and a hard place** informal in a situation where one is faced with two equally difficult alternatives. **get one's rocks off** vulgar slang have an orgasm. ■ obtain pleasure or satisfaction. **on the rocks** informal **1** (of a relationship or enterprise) experiencing difficulties and likely to fail. **2** (of a drink) served undiluted and with ice cubes.
– DERIVATIVES **rockless** adjective, **rock-like** adjective.
– ORIGIN Middle English: from Old French *rocque*, from medieval Latin *rocca*, of unknown ultimate origin.

rock[2] ▶ **verb 1** [with obj.] cause (someone or something) to move gently to and fro or from side to side: *she rocked the baby in her arms*.
■ [no obj.] move in such a way: *the vase rocked back and forth on its base* | [as adj. **rocking**] *the rocking movement of the boat*. ■ (with reference to a building or region) shake or cause to shake or vibrate, especially because of an impact, earthquake, or explosion: [with obj.] *a terrorist blast rocked a Tube station* | [no obj.] *the building began to rock on its foundations*. ■ cause great shock or distress to (someone or something), especially so as to weaken or destabilize them or it: *diplomatic upheavals that rocked the British Empire*.
2 [no obj.] informal dance to or play rock music.
■ figurative (of a place) have an atmosphere of excitement or much social activity: *the new town really rocks* | [as adj. **rocking**] *a rocking resort*.
▶ **noun 1** [mass noun] rock music: [as modifier] *a rock star*.
■ rock and roll.
2 [in sing.] a gentle movement to and fro or from side to side: *she placed the baby in the cot and gave it a rock*.
– PHRASES **rock the boat** see **BOAT**.
– ORIGIN late Old English *roccian*, probably from a Germanic base meaning 'remove, move'; related to Dutch *rukken* 'jerk, tug' and German *rücken* 'move'. The noun dates from the early 19th cent.
▶ **rock out** informal perform rock music loudly and vigorously. ■ enjoy oneself in an enthusiastic and uninhibited way, especially by dancing to rock music.

rockabilly ▶ **noun** [mass noun] a type of popular music, originating in the south-eastern US in the 1950s, combining elements of rock and roll and country music.
– ORIGIN 1950s: blend of **ROCK AND ROLL** and **HILLBILLY**.

Rockall a rocky islet in the North Atlantic, about 400 km (250 miles) north-west of Ireland. It was formally annexed by Britain in 1955 but has since become the subject of territorial dispute between Britain, Denmark, Iceland, and Ireland.
■ a shipping forecast area in the NE Atlantic, containing the islet of Rockall near its northern boundary.

rock and roll (also **rock 'n' roll**) ▶ **noun** [mass noun] a type of popular dance music originating in the 1950s, characterized by a heavy beat and simple melodies. Rock and roll was an amalgam of black rhythm and blues and white country music, usually based around a twelve-bar structure and an instrumentation of guitar, double bass, and drums.
– DERIVATIVES **rock and roller** noun.

rock bass ▶ **noun** a red-eyed North American freshwater fish of the sunfish family, found chiefly in rocky streams. Also called **RED-EYE**.
● *Ambloplites rupestris*, family Centrarchidae.

rock borer ▶ **noun** any of a number of burrowing bivalve molluscs which bore into rock and other hard materials, in particular:
● a mussel with a cigar shaped shell, occurring in warm seas (genus *Lithophaga*, family Mytilidae). ● a clam with an oval to oblong shell (genus *Hiatella*, family Hiatellidae).

rock-bottom ▶ **adjective** at the lowest possible level: *rock-bottom prices*.
■ fundamental: *a pure, rock-bottom kind of realism*.
▶ **noun** (**rock bottom**) the lowest possible level: *the morale of Britain's family doctors was **at rock bottom***.

rock-bound ▶ **adjective** (of a coast or shore) rocky and inaccessible.

rockburst ▶ **noun** Mining a sudden, violent rupture or collapse of highly stressed rock in a mine.

rock cake ▶ **noun** chiefly Brit. a small currant cake with a hard rough surface.

rock candy ▶ **noun** [mass noun] N. Amer. a kind of hard confectionery typically made of masses of crystallized sugar.

rock climbing ▶ **noun** [mass noun] the sport or pastime of climbing rock faces, especially with the aid of ropes and special equipment.
– DERIVATIVES **rock climb** noun, **rock climber** noun.

rock cod ▶ **noun** any of a number of marine fishes that frequent rocky habitats, especially in Australian waters.
● Several species, chiefly in the families Scorpaenidae and Serranidae.

Rock Cornish (also **Rock Cornish hen** or **Rock Cornish game hen**) ▶ **noun** a stocky chicken of a breed which is kept for its meat.

rock cress ▶ **noun** another term for **ARABIS**.

rock-crusher ▶ **noun** a machine used to break down rocks.
■ Bridge, informal a very strong hand.

rock crystal ▶ **noun** [mass noun] transparent quartz, typically in the form of colourless hexagonal crystals.

rock cycle ▶ **noun** Geology an idealized cycle of processes undergone by rocks in the earth's crust, involving igneous intrusion, uplift, erosion, transportation, deposition as sedimentary rock, metamorphism, remelting, and further igneous intrusion.

rock dove ▶ **noun** a mainly grey Old World pigeon that frequents coastal and inland cliffs. It is the ancestor of domestic and feral pigeons.

● *Columba livia*, family Columbidae.

Rockefeller /ˈrɒkəfɛlə/, John D. (1839–1937), American industrialist and philanthropist; full name *John Davison Rockefeller*. By 1880 he exercised a virtual monopoly over oil refining in the US. Both he and his son, **John D. Rockefeller Jr** (1874–1960), established many philanthropic institutions.

rocker ▶ noun **1** a person who performs, dances to, or enjoys rock music, especially of a particular type: *a punk rocker*.
■ a rock song. ■ Brit. a young person, especially in the 1960s, belonging to a subculture characterized by leather clothing, riding motorcycles, and a liking for rock music. **2** a thing that rocks, in particular: ■ a rocking chair. ■ short for **ROCKER SWITCH**. ■ a rocking device forming part of a mechanism, especially one for controlling the positions of brushes in a dynamo. **3** a curved bar or similar support on which something such as a chair or cradle can rock. **4** [mass noun] the amount of curvature in the longitudinal contour of a boat or surfboard.
– PHRASES **off one's rocker** informal mad.

rocker arm ▶ noun a rocking lever in an engine, especially one in an internal-combustion engine which serves to work a valve and is operated by a pushrod from the camshaft.

rocker panel ▶ noun (in a motor vehicle) a panel forming part of the bodywork below the level of the passenger door.

rocker switch ▶ noun an electrical on/off switch incorporating a spring-loaded rocker.

rockery ▶ noun (pl. **-ies**) a heaped arrangement of rough stones with soil between them, planted with rock plants, especially alpines.

rocket¹ ▶ noun **1** a cylindrical projectile that can be propelled to a great height or distance by the combustion of its contents, used typically as a firework or signal.
■ (also **rocket engine** or **rocket motor**) an engine operating on the same principle, providing thrust as in a jet engine but without depending on the intake of air for combustion. ■ an elongated rocket-propelled missile or spacecraft. ■ used, especially in similes and comparisons, to refer to a person or thing that moves very fast or to an action that is done with great force: *she shot out of her chair like a rocket*. **2** [in sing.] Brit. informal a severe reprimand.
▶ verb (**rocketed**, **rocketing**) **1** [no obj.] (of an amount, price, etc.) increase very rapidly and suddenly: *sales of milk in supermarkets are rocketing* | [as adj. **rocketing**] *rocketing prices*.
■ [with adverbial of direction] move or progress very rapidly: *he rocketed to national stardom*. ■ [with obj. and adverbial] cause to move or progress very rapidly: *she showed the kind of form that rocketed her to the semi-finals last year*. **2** [with obj.] attack with rocket-propelled missiles: *the city was rocketed and bombed from the air*.
– PHRASES **rise like a rocket (and fall like a stick)** rise suddenly and dramatically (and subsequently fall in a similar manner).
– ORIGIN early 17th cent.: from French *roquette*, from Italian *rocchetto*, diminutive of *rocca* 'distaff (for spinning)', with reference to its cylindrical shape.

rocket² ▶ noun (also **garden rocket** or **salad rocket**) [mass noun] an edible Mediterranean plant of the cabbage family, sometimes eaten in salads. See also **ARUGULA**.
● *Eruca vesicaria* subsp. *sativa*, family Cruciferae.
■ used in names of other fast-growing plants of this family, e.g. **London rocket**, **sweet rocket**.
– ORIGIN late 15th cent.: from French *roquette*, from Italian *ruchetta*, diminutive of *ruca*, from Latin *eruca* 'downy-stemmed plant'.

rocketeer ▶ noun a person who works with space rockets; a rocket enthusiast.

rocketry ▶ noun [mass noun] the branch of science that deals with rockets and rocket propulsion.
■ the use of rockets.

rocket scientist ▶ noun [usu. with negative] informal, chiefly N. Amer. a very intelligent person: *he's a nice kid— maybe not a rocket scientist, but he should come out okay.*

rock face ▶ noun a bare vertical surface of natural rock.

rockfall ▶ noun a descent of loose rocks.
■ a mass of fallen rock.

rockfish ▶ noun (pl. same or **-fishes**) a marine fish of the scorpionfish family with a laterally

compressed body. It is generally a bottom-dweller in rocky areas and is frequently of sporting or commercial value.
● Genus *Sebastes*, family Scorpaenidae: numerous species.

rock flour ▶ noun [mass noun] finely powdered rock formed by glacial or other erosion.

rockfowl ▶ noun a long-necked crow-sized bird with a brightly coloured bare head, found in the forests of West Africa and nesting in caves. Also called **BALD CROW**.
● Genus *Picathartes*, family Picathartidae (or Timaliidae): two species.

rock garden ▶ noun an artificial mound or bank built of earth and stones, and planted with rock plants.
■ a garden in which rockeries are the chief feature.

Rockhampton a port on the Fitzroy River, in Queensland, NE Australia; pop. 55,790 (1991). It is the centre of Australia's largest beef-producing area.

rockhopper (also **rockhopper penguin**) ▶ noun a small penguin with a yellowish crest, breeding on subantarctic coastal cliffs which it ascends by hopping from rock to rock.
● *Eudyptes chrysocome*, family Spheniscidae.

rockhound ▶ noun informal, chiefly N. Amer. a geologist or amateur collector of mineral specimens.
– DERIVATIVES **rockhounding** noun.

rock hyrax ▶ noun an African hyrax that lives on rocky outcrops and cliffs and feeds mainly on grass. Also called **DASSIE**.
● Genus *Procavia* (and *Heterohyrax*), family Procaviidae: several species.

Rockies another name for the **ROCKY MOUNTAINS**.

rocking chair ▶ noun a chair mounted on rockers or springs, which can rock back and forth.

rocking horse ▶ noun a model of a horse mounted on rockers or springs for a child to sit on and rock to and fro.

rocking stone ▶ noun a boulder poised in such a way that it can be easily rocked.

rock jock ▶ noun US informal a mountaineer.

rockling ▶ noun a slender marine fish of the cod family, typically occurring in shallow water or tidal pools.
● Genera *Ciliata* and *Rhinonemus*, family Gadidae: several species.

rock lizard ▶ noun a small climbing lizard living in mountains and arid rocky habitats, in particular: ● a European and African lizard (genus *Lacerta*, family Lacertidae, including *L. saxicola*). ● (also **banded rock lizard**) a North American lizard (*Streptosaurus mearnsi*, family Iguanidae).

rock lobster ▶ noun another term for **SPINY LOBSTER**.

rock maple ▶ noun North American term for **SUGAR MAPLE**.

rock music ▶ noun [mass noun] a form of popular music which evolved from rock and roll and pop music during the mid and late 1960s. Harsher and often self-consciously more serious than that which had had gone before, it was initially characterized by musical experimentation and drug-related or anti-Establishment lyrics.
■ another term for **ROCK AND ROLL**.

rock 'n' roll ▶ noun variant spelling of **ROCK AND ROLL**.

Rock of Gibraltar see **GIBRALTAR**.

rock pigeon ▶ noun another term for **ROCK DOVE**.

rock pipit ▶ noun a dark-coloured pipit frequenting rocky shores in NW Europe.
● *Anthus petrosus*, family Motacillidae; formerly thought to be conspecific with the water pipit.

rock plant ▶ noun a plant that grows on or among rocks.

rock pool ▶ noun a pool of water among rocks, typically along a shoreline.

rock python ▶ noun a large dark-skinned constricting snake with paler markings and a distinctive pale mark on the crown.
● Genera *Python* and *Morelia*, family Pythonidae: several species, including *P. sebae* of Africa, *P. molurus* of Asia, and *M. amethistina* of Australia.

rock rabbit ▶ noun **1** South African term for **ROCK HYRAX**.
2 another term for **PIKA**.

rock-ribbed ▶ adjective N. Amer. resolute or

uncompromising, especially with respect to political allegiance: *rock-ribbed communists*.

rock rose ▶ noun a herbaceous or shrubby plant with rose-like flowers, native to temperate and warm regions. Also called **SUN ROSE**.
● Genera *Cistus* and *Helianthemum*, family Cistaceae.

rock salmon ▶ noun **1** a tropical snapper which occurs both in the sea and in rivers, valued for food and sport.
● *Lutjanus argentimaculatus*, family Lutjanidae: a.
2 [mass noun] Brit. dogfish or wolf fish as food.

rock salt ▶ noun [mass noun] common salt occurring naturally as a mineral; halite.

rock samphire ▶ noun see **SAMPHIRE**.

rockslide ▶ noun an avalanche of rock or other stony material.
■ a mass of stony material deposited by such an avalanche.

rock snake ▶ noun the Asian rock python.

rock solid ▶ adjective unlikely to change, fail, or collapse: *her love was rock solid*.

rocksteady ▶ noun [mass noun] an early form of reggae music originating in Jamaica in the 1960s, characterized by a slow tempo.

rock thrush ▶ noun an Old World thrush found in mountains and rocky habitats, with a grey or blue head and typically orange underparts.
● Genus *Monticola*, family Turdidae: several species, including the **blue rock thrush** (*M. solitarius*), the male of which is entirely slate-blue.

rockumentary ▶ noun informal a documentary about rock music and musicians.
– ORIGIN 1970s: from ROCK² + DOCUMENTARY.

rock wallaby ▶ noun an agile Australian wallaby that lives among cliffs and rocks, having feet with thick pads and fringes of stiff hair.
● Genus *Petrogale*, family Macropodidae: several species.

Rockwell, Norman (Percevel) (1894–1978), American illustrator. Known for his typically sentimental portraits of small-town American life, he was an illustrator for *Life* and the *Saturday Evening Post*.

rock wool ▶ noun [mass noun] inorganic material made into matted fibre used especially for insulation or soundproofing.

rocky¹ ▶ adjective (**rockier**, **rockiest**) consisting or formed of rock, especially when exposed to view: *a rocky crag above the village*.
■ full of rocks: *hillsides of dry, rocky soil*.
– PHRASES **the rocky road to ——** a difficult progression to something: *the rocky road to success*.
– DERIVATIVES **rockiness** noun.

rocky² ▶ adjective (**rockier**, **rockiest**) tending to rock or shake; unsteady.
■ figurative not stable or firm; full of problems: *the marriage seemingly got off to a rocky start*.
– DERIVATIVES **rockily** adverb, **rockiness** noun.

Rocky Mountain goat ▶ noun see **MOUNTAIN GOAT** (sense 1).

Rocky Mountains (also **the Rockies**) the chief mountain system of North America, which extends from the US–Mexico border to the Yukon Territory of northern Canada. It forms the Continental Divide. Several peaks rise to over 4,300 m (14,000 ft), the highest being Mount Elbert at 4,399 m (14,431 ft).

Rocky Mountain spotted fever ▶ noun see **SPOTTED FEVER**.

rococo /rəˈkəʊkəʊ/ ▶ adjective (of furniture or architecture) of or characterized by an elaborately ornamental late baroque style of decoration prevalent in 18th-century Continental Europe, with asymmetrical patterns involving motifs and scrollwork.
■ extravagantly or excessively ornate, especially (of music or literature) highly ornamented and florid.
▶ noun [mass noun] the rococo style of art, decoration, or architecture.
– ORIGIN mid 19th cent.: from French, humorous alteration of **ROCAILLE**.

rod ▶ noun **1** a thin straight bar, especially of wood or metal.
■ a wand or staff as a symbol of office, authority, or power. ■ a slender straight stick or shoot growing on or cut from a tree or bush. ■ a stick used for caning or flogging. ■ (**the rod**) the use of such a stick as punishment: *if you'd been my daughter, you'd have felt the rod*. ■ vulgar slang a man's penis.

2 a fishing rod.
■an angler.
3 historical, chiefly Brit. another term for **PERCH**³ (in sense 1).
■(also **square rod**) another term for **PERCH**³ (in sense 2).
4 US informal a pistol or revolver.
5 Anatomy a light-sensitive cell of one of the two types present in large numbers in the retina of the eye, responsible mainly for monochrome vision in poor light. Compare with **CONE** (in sense 3).
− PHRASES **kiss the rod** see **KISS**. **make a rod for one's own back** do something likely to cause difficulties for oneself later. **rule someone or something with a rod of iron** control or govern someone or something very strictly or harshly. **spare the rod and spoil the child** proverb if children are not physically punished when they do wrong their personal development will suffer.
− DERIVATIVES **rodless** adjective, **rodlet** noun, **rod-like** adjective.
− ORIGIN late Old English *rodd* 'slender shoot growing on or cut from a tree', also 'straight stick or bundle of twigs used to inflict punishment'; probably related to Old Norse *rudda* 'club'.

Roddenberry /ˈrɒd(ə)nˌbɛri/, Gene (1921–91), American television producer and scriptwriter; full name *Eugene Wesley Roddenberry*. He created and wrote many scripts for the TV science-fiction drama series *Star Trek*, first broadcast 1966–9.

Roddick, Anita (Lucia) (b.1943), English businesswoman. In 1976 she opened a shop selling cosmetics with an emphasis on environmentally conscious products. This developed into the Body Shop chain.

rode¹ past of **RIDE**.

rode² ▶ verb [no obj.] (of a woodcock) fly on a regular circuit in the evening as a territorial display, making sharp calls and grunts.
− ORIGIN mid 18th cent. (in the sense 'fly landwards in the evening'): of unknown origin.

rode³ ▶ noun Nautical, N. Amer. a rope, especially one securing an anchor or trawl.
− ORIGIN early 17th cent.: of unknown origin.

rodent ▶ noun a gnawing mammal of an order that includes rats, mice, squirrels, hamsters, porcupines, and their relatives, distinguished by strong constantly growing incisors and no canine teeth. They constitute the largest order of mammals.
● Order Rodentia: three suborders. See **SCIUROMORPHA**, **MYOMORPHA**, and **HYSTRICOMORPHA**.
▶ adjective **1** of or relating to mammals of this order. **2** Medicine see **RODENT ULCER**.
− ORIGIN mid 19th cent.: from Latin *rodent-* 'gnawing', from the verb *rodere*.

rodenticide /rəˈdɛntɪsʌɪd/ ▶ noun a poison used to kill rodents.

rodent ulcer ▶ noun Medicine a slow-growing malignant tumour of the face (basal cell carcinoma).

rodeo /ˈrəʊdɪəʊ, rəˈdeɪəʊ/ ▶ noun (pl. **-os**) **1** an exhibition or contest in which cowboys show their skill at riding broncos, roping calves, wrestling steers, etc.
■a similar exhibition or contest demonstrating other skills, such as motorcycle riding or canoeing.
2 a round-up of cattle on a ranch for branding, counting, etc.
■an enclosure for such a round-up.
▶ verb (**rodeoed, rodeoing**) [no obj.] compete in a rodeo.
− ORIGIN mid 19th cent.: from Spanish, from *rodear* 'go round', based on Latin *rotare* 'rotate'.

Rodgers, Richard (Charles) (1902–79), American composer. He worked with librettist **Lorenz Hart** (1895–1942) before collaborating with Oscar Hammerstein II on a succession of popular musicals, including *The Sound of Music* (1959).

rodgersia /rɒˈdʒəːzɪə/ ▶ noun an Asian plant which is sometimes cultivated for its attractive foliage.
● Genus *Rodgersia*, family Saxifragaceae.
− ORIGIN modern Latin, named after John *Rodgers* (1812–82), American admiral.

rodham /ˈrɒdəm/ ▶ noun (in the Fen district of East Anglia) a raised bank formed from silt deposits on the bed of a dry river course.
− ORIGIN mid 19th cent.: of unknown origin; other

spellings are recorded but *rodham* is preferred in local use.

Ródhos /ˈrɒðɒs/ Greek name for **RHODES**¹.

Rodin /ˈrəʊdæ̃, French rɔdɛ̃/, Auguste (1840–1917), French sculptor. He was chiefly concerned with the human form. Notable works: *The Thinker* (1880) and *The Kiss* (1886).

rodomontade /ˌrɒdə(ʊ)mɒnˈteɪd/ ▶ noun [mass noun] boastful or inflated talk or behaviour.
▶ verb [no obj.] archaic talk boastfully.
− ORIGIN early 17th cent.: from French, from obsolete Italian *rodomontada*, from Italian *rodomonte*, from the name of a boastful character in the medieval *Orlando* epics.

Roe, Sir (Edwin) Alliott Verdon (1877–1958), English engineer and aircraft designer. With his brother H. V. Roe he founded the Avro Company and built a number of planes, including the Avro 504 biplane of the First World War; in 1928 he formed the Saunders-Roe Company to design and manufacture flying boats.

roe¹ ▶ noun (also **hard roe**) [mass noun] the mass of eggs contained in the ovaries of a female fish or shellfish, especially when ripe and used as food; the full ovaries themselves.
■(soft roe) the ripe testes of a male fish, especially when used as food.
− ORIGIN late Middle English: related to Middle Low German, Middle Dutch *roge*.

roe² (also **roe deer**) ▶ noun (pl. same or **roes**) a small Eurasian deer which lacks a visible tail and has a reddish summer coat that turns greyish in winter.
● Genus *Capreolus*, family Cervidae: two species, in particular the **European roe deer** (*C. capreolus*).
− ORIGIN Old English *rā(ha)*, of Germanic origin; related to Dutch *ree* and German *Reh*.

roebuck ▶ noun a male roe deer.

Roedean an independent boarding school for girls, on the south coast of England east of Brighton. It was founded in 1885.

Roeg /rəʊg/, Nicholas (Jack) (b.1928), English film director. His work is often impressionistic, and uses cutting techniques to create disjointed narratives. Notable works: *Performance* (1970) and *The Man Who Fell to Earth* (1975).

roentgen /ˈrʌntjən, ˈrɜːnt-, ˈrɒnt-/ (abbrev.= **R**) ▶ noun a unit of ionizing radiation, the amount producing one electrostatic unit of positive or negative ionic charge in one cubic centimetre of air under standard conditions.
− ORIGIN 1920s: named after Wilhelm Conrad *Röntgen* (1845–1923), German physicist, discoverer of X-rays.

roentgenogram /ˈrʌntjənə(ʊ)gram, ˈrɜːnt-, ˈrɒnt-; -gənəʊ, -ʒənəʊ/ ▶ noun chiefly Medicine an X-ray photograph.

roentgenography /ˌrʌntjəˈnɒgrəfɪ, ˌrɜːnt-, ˌrɒnt-/ ▶ noun [mass noun] chiefly Medicine X-ray photography.
− DERIVATIVES **roentgenographic** adjective, **roentgenographically** adverb.

roentgenology /ˌrʌntjəˈnɒlədʒɪ, ˌrɜːnt-, ˌrɒnt-/ ▶ noun chiefly Medicine another term for **RADIOLOGY**.

roentgen rays ▶ plural noun dated X-rays.

Roeselare /ˈruːsəˌlɑːrə/ a town in NW Belgium, in the province of West Flanders; pop. 57,890 (1991). French name **ROULERS**.

rogan josh /ˌrəʊg(ə)n ˈdʒəʊʃ/ ▶ noun [mass noun] an Indian dish of curried meat, typically lamb, in a rich tomato-based sauce.
− ORIGIN from Urdu *rogan jōš*.

rogation /rə(ʊ)ˈgeɪʃ(ə)n/ ▶ noun [usu. as modifier] (in the Christian Church) a solemn supplication consisting of the litany of the saints chanted on the three days before Ascension Day: *Rogation Week*.
− ORIGIN late Middle English: from Latin *rogatio(n-)*, from *rogare* 'ask'.

Rogation Days (in the Western Christian Church) the three days before Ascension Day, traditionally marked by fasting and prayer, particularly for the blessing of the harvest (after the pattern of pre-Christian rituals).

Rogation Sunday ▶ noun the Sunday preceding the Rogation Days.

Rogationtide ▶ noun the period of the Rogation Days.

roger ▶ exclamation your message has been received

and understood (used in radio communication): *'Roger; we'll be with you in about ten minutes.'*
■informal used to express assent or understanding: *'Go light the stove.' 'Roger, Mister Bossman,' Frank replied.*
▶ verb [with obj.] Brit. vulgar slang have sexual intercourse with (a woman).
■[no obj.] have sexual intercourse.
− ORIGIN mid 16th cent.: from the given name *Roger*. The verb (dating from the early 18th cent.) is from an obsolete sense 'penis' of the noun.

Rogers¹, Ginger (1911–95), American actress and dancer; born *Virginia Katherine McMath*. She is known for her dancing partnership with Fred Astaire, during which she appeared in musicals including *Top Hat* (1935). Her solo acting career included the film *Kitty Foyle* (1940), for which she won an Oscar.

Rogers², Sir Richard (George) (b.1933), British architect, born in Italy. A leading exponent of high-tech architecture, his major works include the Pompidou Centre in Paris (1971–7), designed with the Italian architect Renzo Piano, and the Lloyd's Building in London (1986).

Roget /ˈrɒʒeɪ/, Peter Mark (1779–1869), English scholar. He worked as a physician but is remembered as the compiler of *Roget's Thesaurus of English Words and Phrases*, first published in 1852.

rogue ▶ noun **1** a dishonest or unprincipled man: *you are a rogue and an embezzler.*
■a person whose behaviour one disapproves of but who is nonetheless likeable or attractive (often used as a playful term of reproof): *Cenzo, you old rogue!*
2 [usu. as modifier] an elephant or other large wild animal driven away or living apart from the herd and having savage or destructive tendencies: *a rogue elephant.*
■a person or thing that behaves in an aberrant, faulty, or unpredictable way: *he hacked into data and ran rogue programs.* ■a horse inclined to shirk on the racecourse or when hunting. ■an inferior or defective specimen among many satisfactory ones, especially a seedling or plant deviating from the standard variety.
▶ verb [with obj.] remove inferior or defective plants or seedlings from (a crop).
− ORIGIN mid 16th cent. (denoting an idle vagrant): probably from Latin *rogare* 'beg, ask', and related to obsolete slang *roger* 'vagrant beggar' (many such cant terms were introduced towards the middle of the 16th cent.).

roguery ▶ noun (pl. **-ies**) [mass noun] conduct characteristic of a rogue, especially acts of dishonesty or playful mischief: *there has always been roguery associated with horse dealing.*

rogues' gallery ▶ noun informal a collection of photographs of known criminals, used by police to identify suspects.
■a collection of people or creatures notable for a certain shared quality or characteristic, typically a disreputable one: *a rogues' gallery of bureaucrats and cold-hearted advocates of 'progress'.*

roguish ▶ adjective characteristic of a dishonest or unprincipled person: *he led a roguish and uncertain existence.*
■playfully mischievous, especially in a way that is sexually attractive: *he gave her a roguish smile.*
− DERIVATIVES **roguishly** adverb, **roguishness** noun.

Rohypnol /rəʊˈhɪpnɒl/ ▶ noun [mass noun] trademark a powerful sedative drug of the benzodiazepine class.
− ORIGIN 1980s: invented name.

ROI Finance ▶ abbreviation for return on investment.

roil /rɔɪl/ ▶ verb **1** [with obj.] poetic/literary make (a liquid) turbid or muddy by disturbing the sediment: *winds roil these waters.*
■[no obj.] (of a liquid) move in a turbulent, swirling manner: *the sea roiled below her* | figurative *a kind of fear roiled in her.*
2 US word for **RILE** (in sense 1).
− ORIGIN late 16th cent.: perhaps from Old French *ruiler* 'mix mortar', from late Latin *regulare* 'regulate'.

roily ▶ adjective N. Amer. (chiefly of water) muddy; turbulent: *those waters were roily, high and muddy.*

roister /ˈrɔɪstə/ ▶ verb [no obj.] enjoy oneself or celebrate in a noisy or boisterous way: *workers from the refinery roistered in the bars.*
− DERIVATIVES **roisterer** noun, **roisterous** adjective.
− ORIGIN late 16th cent.: from obsolete *roister* 'roisterer', from French *rustre* 'ruffian', variant of *ruste*, from Latin *rusticus* 'rustic'.

ROK ▶ **abbreviation for** South Korea (international vehicle registration).
– ORIGIN from *Republic of Korea*.

Roland /ˈrəʊlənd/ the most famous of Charlemagne's paladins, hero of the *Chanson de Roland* (12th century). He is said to have become a friend of Oliver, another paladin, after engaging him in single combat in which neither won. Roland was killed at the Battle of Roncesvalles.
– PHRASES **a Roland for an Oliver** archaic an effective or adequate retort or response: *he had given Mrs Carr a Roland for her Oliver.*

role ▶ **noun** an actor's part in a play, film, etc.: *Dietrich's role as a wife in war-torn Paris.*
■ the function assumed or part played by a person or thing in a particular situation: *she greeted us all in her various roles of mother, friend, and daughter | religion plays a vital role in society.*
– ORIGIN early 17th cent.: from obsolete French *roule* 'roll', referring originally to the roll of paper on which the actor's part was written.

role model ▶ **noun** a person looked to by others as an example to be imitated.

role playing (also **role play**) ▶ **noun** [mass noun]
1 chiefly Psychology the acting out or performance of a particular role, either consciously (as a technique in psychotherapy or training) or unconsciously, in accordance with the perceived expectations of society as regards a person's behaviour in a particular context.
2 participation in a role-playing game.
– DERIVATIVES **role-play** verb, **role player** noun.

role-playing game ▶ **noun** a game in which players take on the roles of imaginary characters who engage in adventures, typically in a particular fantasy setting overseen by a referee.

role reversal ▶ **noun** a situation in which someone adopts a role the reverse of that which they normally assume in relation to someone else, who typically assumes their role in exchange.

Rolfing ▶ **noun** [mass noun] a massage technique aimed at the vertical realignment of the body, and therefore deep enough to release muscular tension at skeletal level, which can contribute to the relief of long-standing tension and neuroses.
– DERIVATIVES **Rolf** verb.
– ORIGIN 1970s: from the name of Ida P. Rolf (1897–1979), American physiotherapist, + **-ING**[1].

roll ▶ **verb 1** move or cause to move in a particular direction by turning over and over on an axis: [no obj., with adverbial of direction] *the car rolled down into a ditch* | [with obj. and adverbial of direction] *she rolled the ball across the floor.*
■ turn or cause to turn over to face a different direction: [no obj., with adverbial] *she rolled on to her side* | [with obj. and adverbial] *they rolled him over on to his back.* ■ [with obj.] turn (one's eyes) upwards, typically to show surprise or disapproval: *Sarah rolled her eyes.* ■ [with obj. and adverbial] make (something cylindrical) revolve between two surfaces: *Plummer rolled the glass between his hands.* ■ [no obj., with adverbial] (of a person or animal) lie down and turn over and over while remaining in the same place: *the buffalo rolled in the dust.* ■ [no obj.] (of a horse) lie on its back and kick about so as to keep its coat in good condition. ■ [no obj.] (of a moving ship, aircraft, or vehicle) rock or oscillate around an axis parallel to the direction of motion: *the ship pitched and rolled.* ■ [no obj., with adverbial] move along or from side to side unsteadily or uncontrollably: *they were rolling about with laughter.* ■ [with obj.] N. Amer. informal overturn (a vehicle): *he rolled his Mercedes in a 100 mph crash.* ■ [with obj.] throw (a die or dice). ■ [with obj.] obtain (a particular score) by doing this: *roll a 2, 3, or 12.*
2 [no obj., with adverbial of direction] (of a vehicle) move or run on wheels: *the van was rolling along the lane.*
■ [with obj. and adverbial of direction] move or push (a wheeled object): *Pat rolled the trolley to and fro.* ■ (**roll something up/down**) make a car window or a window blind move up or down by turning a handle. ■ (of time) elapse steadily: *the years rolled by.* ■ (of a drop of liquid) flow: *huge tears rolled down her cheeks.* ■ (**roll off**) (of a product) issue from (an assembly line or machine): *the first copies of the newspaper rolled off the presses.* ■ (of waves, smoke, cloud, or fog) move or flow forward with an undulating motion: *the fog rolled across the fields.* ■ [no obj. | usu. as adj. **rolling**] (of land) extend in gentle undulations: *the rolling countryside.* ■ [no obj.] (of credits for a film or television programme) be displayed as if moving on a roller up the screen. ■ [no obj.] (of a machine, device, or system) operate or begin operating: *the cameras started to roll.*

■ [with obj.] cause (a machine or device) to begin operating: *roll the camera.*
3 [with obj. and adverbial] turn (something flexible) over and over on itself to form a cylinder, tube, or ball: *she started to roll up her sleeping bag.*
■ (**roll something up**) fold the edge of a garment over on itself a number of times to shorten it: *she rolled up her sleeves to wash her hands.* ■ (**roll something down**) unfold the edge of a garment that has been turned up in this way: *my hands were too dirty to roll down my sleeves.* ■ [with obj.] make by forming material into a cylinder or ball: [with two objs] *Harry rolled himself a joint.* ■ [no obj., with adverbial] (of a person or animal) curl up tightly: *the shock made the hedgehog roll into a ball.*
4 [with obj. and adverbial] flatten (something) by passing a roller over it or by passing it between rollers: *roll out the dough on a floured surface.*
5 [no obj., with adverbial of direction] (of a loud, deep sound such as that of thunder or drums) reverberate: *the first peals of thunder rolled across the sky.*
■ [with obj.] pronounce (a consonant, typically an *r*) with a trill: *when he wanted to emphasize a point he rolled his rrrs.* ■ [with obj.] utter (a word or words) with a reverberating or vibratory effect: *he rolled the word around his mouth.* ■ (of words) flow effortlessly or mellifluously: *the names of his colleagues rolled off his lips.*
6 informal rob (someone, typically when they are intoxicated or asleep): *if you don't get drunk, you don't get rolled.*
▶ **noun 1** a cylinder formed by winding flexible material around a tube or by turning it over and over on itself without folding: *a roll of carpet.*
■ a cylindrical mass of something or a number of items arranged in a cylindrical shape: *a roll of mints.* ■ [with modifier] an item of food that is made by wrapping a flat sheet of pastry, cake, meat, or fish round a sweet or savoury filling: *salmon and rice rolls.* ■ N. Amer. & Austral. money, typically a quantity of banknotes rolled together: *I should eat out, enjoy the fat roll I'd taken out of my account.* ■ a roller for flattening something, especially one used to shape metal in a rolling mill.
2 a movement in which someone or something turns or is turned over on itself: *a roll of the dice | the ponies completed two rolls before getting back on their feet.*
■ a gymnastic exercise in which the body is rolled into a tucked position and turned in a forward or backward circle: *a forward roll.* ■ [mass noun] a swaying or oscillation of a ship, aircraft, or vehicle around an axis parallel to the direction of motion: *the car corners capably with a minimum of roll.* ■ [mass noun] undulation of the landscape: *hidden by the roll of the land was a refinery.*
3 a prolonged, deep, reverberating sound, typically made by thunder or a drum: *thunder exploded, roll after roll.*
■ Music one of the basic patterns (rudiments) of drumming, consisting of a sustained, rapid alternation of single or double strokes of each stick.
4 a very small loaf of bread, typically eaten with butter or a particular filling: *a bacon roll.*
5 an official list or register of names.
■ the total numbers on such a list: *a review of secondary schools to assess the effects of falling rolls.* ■ a document, typically an official record, in scroll form.
– PHRASES **a roll in the hay** (or **the sack**) informal an act of sexual intercourse. **be rolling** (**in money**) informal be very rich. **on a roll** informal experiencing a prolonged spell of success or good luck: *the organization is on a roll.* **rolled into one** (of characteristics drawn from different people or things) combined in one person or thing: *banks are several businesses rolled into one.* **rolling drunk** so drunk as to be swaying or staggering. **rolling in the aisles** informal (of an audience) laughing uncontrollably. **roll of honour** a list of people whose deeds or achievements are honoured. ■ a list of those who have died in battle. **roll one's own** informal make one's own cigarettes from loose tobacco. **roll up one's sleeves** prepare to fight or work. **roll with the punches** (of a boxer) move one's body away from an opponent's blows so as to lessen the impact. ■ figurative adapt oneself to adverse circumstances. **strike someone off the roll** Brit. debar a solicitor from practising as a penalty for dishonesty or other misconduct.
– DERIVATIVES **rollable** adjective.
– ORIGIN Middle English: from Old French *rolle* (noun), *roller* (verb), from Latin *rotulus* 'a roll', variant of *rotula* 'little wheel', diminutive of *rota*.
▶ **roll something back** reverse the progress or reduce the power or importance of something: *the strategy*

to roll back communism.

roll in informal be received in large amounts: *the money was rolling in.* ■ arrive at a place in a casual way, typically in spite of being late: *Steve rolled in about lunchtime.*

roll on [in imperative] informal used to indicate that one wants a particular time or event to come quickly: *roll on January!*

roll something on apply something with a roller: *roll on a decorative paint finish.*

roll something out officially launch or unveil a new product or service: *the firm rolled out its newest generation of supercomputers.*

roll something over Finance contrive or extend a particular financial arrangement: *this is not a good time for rolling over corporate debt.*

roll up informal arrive: *we rolled up at the same time.* ■ [in imperative] used to encourage passers-by to look at or participate in something, typically at a fairground: *roll up, roll up, for all the fun of the fair.* ■ informal roll a cigarette, especially a cannabis cigarette.

roll something up Military drive the flank of an enemy line back and round so that the line is shortened or surrounded.

Rolland /ˈrɒlɒ̃, French rɔlɑ̃/, Romain (1866–1944), French novelist, dramatist, and essayist. His interest in genius led to a number of biographies, and ultimately to *Jean-Christophe* (1904–12), a cycle of ten novels about a German composer. Nobel Prize for Literature (1915).

rollaway ▶ **noun** N. Amer. a bed fitted with wheels or castors, allowing it to be moved easily.

rollback ▶ **noun 1** chiefly US a reduction or decrease: *a 5 per cent rollback of personal income taxes.*
2 Computing the process of restoring a database or program to a previously defined state, typically to recover from an error.
▶ **verb** [with obj.] Computing restore (a database) to a previously defined state.

roll bar ▶ **noun** a metal bar running up the sides and across the top of a vehicle, especially one used in motor sport, strengthening its frame and protecting the occupants if the vehicle overturns.

roll cage ▶ **noun** a framework of reinforcements protecting a car's passenger cabin in the event that it should roll on to its roof.

roll-call ▶ **noun** the process of calling out a list of names to establish who is present.
■ figurative a list or group of people or things that are notable in some specified way: *a roll-call of young hopefuls.*

roll cast ▶ **noun** Fishing a cast in which the angler does not throw the line backwards.

rolled gold ▶ **noun** [mass noun] gold in the form of a thin coating applied to a baser metal by rolling.

rolled oats ▶ **plural noun** oats that have been husked and crushed.

roller[1] ▶ **noun 1** a cylinder that rotates about a central axis and is used in various machines and devices to move, flatten, or spread something.
■ an absorbent revolving cylinder attached to a handle, used to apply paint. ■ a small cylinder on which hair is rolled in order to produce curls. ■ (also **roller bandage**) a long surgical bandage rolled up for convenient application. ■ a long swelling wave that appears to roll steadily towards the shore. ■ [as modifier] of, relating to, or involving roller skates: *roller hockey.*
2 a brightly coloured crow-sized bird with predominantly blue plumage, having a characteristic tumbling display flight. [ORIGIN: late 17th cent.: from German *Roller*, from *rollen* 'to roll'.]
● Genera *Coracias* and *Eurystomus*, family Coraciidae: several species, especially the widespread **European roller** (*C. garrulus*). The Madagascan **cuckoo-roller** and **ground-rollers** are usually placed in separate families.
3 a bird of a breed of tumbler pigeon.
4 a bird of a breed of canary with a trilling song.
5 a broad surcingle, typically padded at the withers.

roller[2] ▶ **noun** Brit. informal a car made by Rolls-Royce.

rollerball ▶ **noun 1** a ballpoint pen using thinner ink than other ballpoints.
2 Computing an input device containing a ball which is moved with the fingers to control the cursor.

roller bearing ▶ **noun** a bearing similar to a ball bearing but using small cylindrical rollers instead of balls.
■ a roller used in such a bearing.

Rollerblade ▶ **noun** trademark an in-line skate.
▶ **verb** [no obj.] skate using Rollerblades.
– DERIVATIVES **rollerblader** noun.

roller blind ▶ **noun** a window blind fitted on a roller.

roller coaster ▶ **noun** a fairground attraction that consists of a light railway track which has many tight turns and steep slopes on which people ride in small fast open carriages.
■ figurative a thing that contains or goes through wild and unpredictable changes: *a terrific roller coaster of a book.*
▶ **verb** (**roller-coaster**) (also **roller-coast**) [no obj.] move, change, or occur in the dramatically changeable manner of a roller coaster: *the twentieth century fades behind us and history roller-coasters on.*

roller derby ▶ **noun** a type of speed-skating competition on roller skates.

roller rink ▶ **noun** see **RINK**.

roller skate ▶ **noun** each of a pair of boots or metal frames fitted to shoes with four or more small wheels, for gliding across a hard surface.
– DERIVATIVES **roller skater** noun.

roller skating ▶ **noun** [mass noun] skating on a hard surface other than ice, as a sport or a pastime.

roller towel ▶ **noun** a long towel with the ends joined and hung on a roller or one fed through a device from one roller holding the clean part to another holding the used part.

roll feed ▶ **noun** a feed mechanism supplying material in sheet form, e.g. paper, by means of rollers.

roll film ▶ **noun** [mass noun] photographic film with a protective lightproof backing paper wound on to a spool.

rollick ▶ **verb** [no obj.] rare act or behave in a jovial and exuberant fashion.
– ORIGIN early 19th cent.: probably dialect, perhaps a blend of **ROMP** and **FROLIC**.

rollicking[1] ▶ **adjective** [attrib.] exuberantly lively and amusing: *this is all good rollicking fun.*

rollicking[2] (also **rollocking**) ▶ **noun** [in sing.] Brit. informal a severe reprimand: *I've had a bit of a rollicking for not riding with more restraint.*

rolling hitch ▶ **noun** a kind of hitch used to attach a rope to a spar or larger rope.

rolling mill ▶ **noun** a factory or machine for rolling steel or other metal into sheets.

rolling pin ▶ **noun** a cylinder rolled over pastry or dough to flatten or shape it.

rolling stock ▶ **noun** [mass noun] locomotives, carriages, wagons, or other vehicles used on a railway.
■ US the road vehicles of a trucking company.

rolling stone ▶ **noun** a person who is unwilling to settle for long in one place.
– PHRASES **a rolling stone gathers no moss** proverb a person who does not settle in one place will not accumulate wealth or status, or responsibilities or commitments.

Rolling Stones an English rock group formed *c.*1962, featuring singer Mick Jagger and guitarist Keith Richards (b.1943). They became successful with a much-imitated rebel image and evolved a simple, derivative, yet distinctive style.

rolling strike ▶ **noun** a strike consisting of a coordinated series of consecutive limited strikes by small groups of workers.

roll-in roll-out ▶ **noun** [mass noun] Computing a method or the process of switching data or code between main and auxiliary memories in order to process several tasks simultaneously.

rollmop ▶ **noun** a rolled uncooked pickled herring fillet.
– ORIGIN early 20th cent.: from German *Rollmops*.

roll-neck ▶ **noun** a high loosely turned-over collar: [as modifier] *a black roll-neck sweater.*
■ a garment with such a collar.

rollocking ▶ **noun** variant spelling of **ROLLICKING**[2].

roll-off ▶ **noun** the smooth fall of response to zero at either end of the frequency range of a piece of audio equipment.

roll-on ▶ **adjective** [attrib.] (of deodorant or cosmetic) applied by means of a rotating ball in the neck of the container.
▶ **noun 1** a roll-on deodorant or cosmetic.
2 Brit. a light elastic corset.

roll-on roll-off ▶ **adjective** [attrib.] denoting a passenger ferry or other method of transport in which vehicles are driven directly on at the start of the voyage or journey and driven off at the end of it.

roll-out ▶ **noun 1** the unveiling of a new aircraft or spacecraft.
■ the official launch of a new product or service.
2 Aeronautics the stage of an aircraft's landing during which it travels along the runway while losing speed.
3 American Football a play in which a quarterback moves out toward the sideline before attempting to pass.

rollover ▶ **noun 1** Finance the extension or transfer of a debt or other financial arrangement.
■ (in a lottery) the accumulative carry-over of prize money to the following draw.
2 informal the overturning of a vehicle.
3 a facility on an electronic keyboard enabling one or several keystrokes to be registered correctly while another key is depressed.

Rolls, Charles Stewart (1877–1910), English motoring and aviation pioneer. He and Henry Royce formed the company Rolls-Royce Ltd in 1906. Rolls was the first Englishman to fly across the English Channel, and made the first double crossing in 1910 shortly before he was killed in an air crash. The Rolls-Royce company established its reputation with luxury cars such as the Silver Ghost and the Silver Shadow, and produced aircraft engines used in both world wars.

roll-top desk ▶ **noun** a writing desk with a semicircular flexible cover sliding in curved grooves.

roll-up ▶ **noun 1** (chiefly N. Amer. also **roll-your-own**) Brit. informal a hand-rolled cigarette.
2 Austral. informal an assembly or its turnout: *we should get a big roll-up.*
▶ **adjective** [attrib.] denoting something which can be rolled up: *roll-up panels.*
■ Finance denoting an investment fund in which returns are reinvested and tax liabilities can be reduced.

Rolodex /ˈrəʊlə(ʊ)dɛks/ ▶ **noun** N. Amer. trademark a type of desktop card index.

roly-poly ▶ **noun 1** (also **roly-poly pudding**) [mass noun] Brit. a pudding made of a sheet of suet pastry covered with jam or fruit, formed into a roll, and steamed or baked.
2 Austral. a bushy tumbleweed.
• Several species, in particular a saltwort (*Salsola kali*, family Chenopodiaceae), which is able to grow away from saline habitats.
▶ **adjective** (of a person) having a round, plump appearance: *a roly-poly young boy.*
– ORIGIN early 17th cent.: fanciful formation from the verb **ROLL**.

ROM Computing ▶ **abbreviation for** read-only memory.

Rom ▶ **noun** (pl. **Roma** /ˈrɒmə/) a gypsy, especially a man.
– ORIGIN mid 19th cent.: abbreviation of **ROMANY**.

Rom. ▶ **abbreviation for** Epistle to the Romans (in biblical references).

rom. ▶ **abbreviation for** roman (used as an instruction for a typesetter).

Roma /ˈroma/ Italian name for **ROME**.

Romaic /rə(ʊ)ˈmeɪɪk/ dated ▶ **adjective** of or relating to the vernacular language of modern Greece.
▶ **noun** [mass noun] this language.
– ORIGIN from modern Greek *romaiikos* 'Roman', used specifically of the eastern Roman Empire.

romaine /rə(ʊ)ˈmeɪn/ ▶ **noun** N. Amer. a cos lettuce.
– ORIGIN early 20th cent.: from French, feminine of *romain* 'Roman'.

romaji /ˈrəʊmədʒi/ ▶ **noun** [mass noun] a system of romanized spelling used to transliterate Japanese.
– ORIGIN early 20th cent.: from Japanese, from *rōma* 'Roman' + *ji* 'letter(s)'.

Roman ▶ **adjective 1** of or relating to ancient Rome or its empire or people: *an old Roman road.*
■ of or relating to medieval or modern Rome: *the Roman and Pisan lines of popes.*
2 dated short for **ROMAN CATHOLIC**: *the Roman Church's instructions to its clergy.*
3 denoting the alphabet (or any of the letters in it) used for writing Latin, English, and most European languages, developed in ancient Rome.
■ (**roman**) (of type) of a plain upright kind used in ordinary print, especially as distinguished from italic and Gothic.
▶ **noun 1** a citizen or soldier of the ancient Roman Republic or Empire.
■ a citizen of modern Rome.
2 dated a Roman Catholic.
3 (**roman**) [mass noun] roman type.
– ORIGIN Middle English: from Old French *Romain*, from Latin *Romanus*, from *Roma* 'Rome'.

roman (also **roman fish**) ▶ **noun** (pl. same or **romans**) S. African a red or pink South African sea bream.
• *Chrysoblephus* and other genera, family Sparidae: several species, in particular *C. laticeps*.
– ORIGIN late 18th cent.: from Afrikaans *rooi* 'red' + *man* 'man'.

roman-à-clef /ˌrəʊmɒ̃ɑːˈkleɪ, French ʀɔmɑ̃akle/ ▶ **noun** (pl. **romans-à-clef** pronunc. same) a novel in which real people or events appear with invented names.
– ORIGIN French, literally 'novel with a key'.

Roman baths ▶ **plural noun** a building containing a complex of rooms designed for bathing, relaxing, and socializing, as used in ancient Rome.

Roman blind ▶ **noun** a window blind made of fabric that draws up into pleats.

Roman Britain Britain during the period AD 43–410, when most of Britain was part of the Roman Empire.

The frontier of the Roman province of Britain was eventually established at Hadrian's Wall; the more northerly Antonine Wall was breached and abandoned (*c.*181). Roman settlers and traders built villas, and Roman towns including London (Londinium), York (Eboracum), Lincoln (Lindum Colonia), St Albans (Verulamium), and Colchester (Camulodunum) were established or developed.

Roman candle ▶ **noun** a firework giving off a series of flaming coloured balls and sparks.

Roman Catholic ▶ **adjective** of or relating to the Roman Catholic Church: *a Roman Catholic bishop.*
▶ **noun** a member of this Church.
– DERIVATIVES **Roman Catholicism** noun.
– ORIGIN late 16th cent.: translation of Latin (*Ecclesia*) *Romana Catholica* (*et Apostolica*) 'Roman Catholic (and Apostolic Church)'. It was apparently first used as a conciliatory term in place of the earlier *Roman*, *Romanist*, or *Romish*, considered derogatory.

Roman Catholic Church the part of the Christian Church which acknowledges the Pope as its head, especially as it has developed since the Reformation.

It is the largest Christian Church, dominant particularly in South America and southern Europe. Roman Catholicism differs from Protestantism in the importance it grants to tradition, ritual, and the authority of the Pope as successor to the Apostle St Peter, and especially in its doctrines of papal infallibility (formally defined in 1870) and of the Eucharist (transubstantiation), its celibate male priesthood, its emphasis on confession,and the veneration of the Virgin Mary and other saints. Much modern Roman Catholic thought and practice arises from scholastic theology and from the response to the Reformation made by the Council of Trent (1545–63). It became less rigid after the Second Vatican Council (1962–5), but its continuing opposition to divorce, abortion, and artificial contraception remains controversial.

Romance /rə(ʊ)ˈmans, ˈrəʊmans/ ▶ **noun** [mass noun] the group of Indo-European languages descended from Latin, principally French, Spanish, Portuguese, Italian, Catalan, Occitan, and Romanian.
▶ **adjective** of, relating to, or denoting this group of languages: *the Romance languages.*
– ORIGIN Middle English (originally denoting the vernacular language of France as opposed to Latin): from Old French *romanz*, based on Latin *Romanicus* 'Roman'.

romance /rə(ʊ)ˈmans, ˈrəʊmans/ ▶ **noun 1** [mass noun] a feeling of excitement and mystery associated with love: *I had a thirst for romance.*
■ love, especially when sentimental or idealized: *he asked her for a date and romance blossomed.* ■ [count noun] an exciting, enjoyable love affair, especially one that is not very serious or long-lasting: *a holiday romance.* ■ [count noun] a book or film dealing with love in a sentimental or idealized way: *light historical romances.* ■ a genre of fiction dealing with love in such a way: *wartime passion from the master of romance.*
2 [mass noun] a quality or feeling of mystery, excitement, and remoteness from everyday life: *the beauty and romance of the night.*
■ [count noun] a work of fiction dealing with events remote from real life.
3 a medieval tale dealing with a hero of chivalry, of

the kind common in the Romance languages: *the Arthurian romances.*
■[mass noun] the literary genre of such works.
4 Music a short informal piece.
▶**verb** [with obj.] **1** dated court; woo: *the wealthy estate owner romanced her.*
■informal seek the attention or custom of (someone), especially by use of flattery: *he is being romanced by the big boys in New York.* ■ [no obj.] engage in a love affair: *we start romancing.*
2 another term for **ROMANTICIZE**: *to a certain degree I am romancing the past.*
– ORIGIN Middle English: from **ROMANCE**, originally denoting a composition in the vernacular as opposed to works in Latin. Early use denoted vernacular verse on the theme of chivalry; the sense 'genre centred on romantic love' dates from the mid 17th cent.

romancer /rəʊˈmansə/ ▶**noun 1** a person prone to wild exaggeration or falsehood.
2 a writer of medieval romances.

Roman de la rose /ˌrəʊmɒ̃ də la ˈrəʊz, French rɔmɑ̃ də la ʀoz/ an extremely influential French poem of the 13th century, an allegorical romance embodying the aristocratic ethic of courtly love. It was composed by two different authors some forty years apart.
– ORIGIN French, literally 'romance of the rose'.

Roman Empire the empire established by Augustus in 27 BC and divided by Theodosius in AD 395 into the Western or Latin and Eastern or Greek Empire.

At its greatest extent Roman rule or influence extended from Armenia and Mesopotamia in the east to the Iberian peninsula in the west, and from the Rhine and Danube in the north to Egypt and provinces on the Mediterranean coast of North Africa. The empire was divided after the death of Theodosius I (AD 395) into the Western Empire and the Eastern or Byzantine Empire (centred on Constantinople). Peace was maintained largely by the substantial presence of the Roman army, and a degree of unity was achieved by an extensive network of roads, a single legal system, and a common language (Latin in the West, Greek in the East). Rome was sacked by the Visigoths under Alaric in 410, and the last emperor of the West, Romulus Augustulus, was deposed in 476. The Eastern Empire, which was stronger, lasted until 1453.

Romanesque /ˌrəʊməˈnɛsk/ ▶**adjective** of or relating to a style of architecture which prevailed in Europe *c.*900–1200, although sometimes dated back to the end of the Roman Empire (5th century).
▶**noun** [mass noun] Romanesque architecture.

Romanesque architecture is characterized by round arches and massive vaulting, and by heavy piers, columns, and walls with small windows. Although disseminated throughout western Europe, the style reached its fullest development in central and northern France; the equivalent style in England is usually called Norman.

– ORIGIN French, from *roman* 'romance'.

roman-fleuve /ˌrəʊmɒ̃ˈflə:v, French rɔmɑ̃flœv/ ▶**noun** (pl. **romans-fleuves** pronunc. same) a novel featuring the leisurely description of the lives of closely related people.
■a sequence of related, self-contained novels.
– ORIGIN French, literally 'river novel'.

Roman holiday ▶**noun** poetic/literary an occasion on which enjoyment or profit is derived from others' suffering or discomfort.
– ORIGIN early 19th cent.: from Byron's *Childe Harold*, originally with reference to a holiday given for a gladiatorial combat.

Romania /rəʊˈmeɪnɪə/ (also **Rumania**) a country in SE Europe with a coastline on the Black Sea; pop. 23,276,000 (est. 1991); official language, Romanian; capital, Bucharest.

In the Middle Ages the area consisted of the principalities of Wallachia and Moldavia, which were swallowed up by the Ottoman Empire in the 15th–16th centuries. The two principalities gained independence in 1878. After the Second World War, in which it supported Germany, Romania became a Communist state under Soviet domination. After 1974 the country pursued an increasingly independent course under the virtual dictatorship of Nicolae Ceaușescu. His regime collapsed in violent popular unrest in 1989 and a new democratic constitution was introduced.

Romanian (also **Rumanian**) ▶**adjective** of or relating to Romania or its people or language.
▶**noun 1** a native or national of Romania, or a person of Romanian descent.
2 [mass noun] the language of Romania, a Romance language influenced by the neighbouring Slavic languages. It is spoken by over 23 million people in Romania itself and by the majority of the population of Moldova.

Romanic /rə(ʊ)ˈmanɪk/ ▶**noun** & **adjective** less common term for **ROMANCE**.
– ORIGIN early 18th cent.: from Latin *Romanicus*, from *Romanus* 'Roman'.

Romanism ▶**noun** [mass noun] dated Roman Catholicism.

Romanist ▶**noun 1** an expert in or student of Roman antiquities or law, or of the Romance languages.
2 usu. derogatory a member or supporter of the Roman Catholic Church.
▶**adjective** usu. derogatory belonging or adhering to the Roman Catholic Church.

romanize /ˈrəʊmənʌɪz/ (also **-ise**) ▶**verb** [with obj.] **1** historical bring (something, especially a region or people) under Roman influence or authority: [as adj. **romanized**] *romanized buildings.*
2 make Roman Catholic in character: *he has Romanized the services of his church.*
3 put (text) into the Roman alphabet or into roman type: *Atatürk's decision to romanize the written language.*
– DERIVATIVES **romanization** noun.

Roman law ▶**noun** [mass noun] the law code of the ancient Romans forming the basis of civil law in many countries today.

Roman nose ▶**noun** a nose with a high bridge.

Roman numeral ▶**noun** any of the letters representing numbers in the Roman numerical system: I = 1, V = 5, X = 10, L = 50, C = 100, D = 500, M = 1,000. In this system a letter placed after another of greater value adds (thus XVI or xvi is 16), whereas a letter placed before another of greater value subtracts (thus XC is 90).

Romano /rə(ʊ)ˈmɑ:nəʊ/ ▶**noun** [mass noun] a strong-tasting hard cheese, originally made in Italy .
– ORIGIN Italian, literally 'Roman'.

Romano- /rə(ʊ)ˈmɑ:nəʊ/ ▶**combining form** Roman; Roman and …: *Romano-British.*

Romanov /rəʊˈmɑ:nɒf/ a dynasty that ruled in Russia from the accession of Michael Romanov (1596–1645) in 1613 until the overthrow of the last tsar, Nicholas II, in 1917.

Roman Republic the ancient Roman state from the expulsion of the Etruscan monarchs in 509 BC (see **TARQUINIUS**) until the assumption of power by Augustus (Octavian) in 27 BC.

The republic was dominated by a landed aristocracy, the patricians, who ruled through the advisory Senate and two annually elected chief magistrates or consuls; the plebeians or common people had their own representatives, the tribunes, who in time gained the power of veto over the other magistrates. During the life of the republic Rome came to dominate the rest of Italy and, following the Punic and Macedonian Wars, began to acquire extensive dominions in the Mediterranean and Asia Minor. Dissatisfaction with the Senate's control of government led to civil wars, which culminated in Julius Caesar's brief dictatorship. This established the principle of personal autocracy, and after Caesar's assassination another round of civil war ended with Octavian's assumption of authority.

Romans, Epistle to the a book of the New Testament, an epistle of St Paul to the Church at Rome.

Romansh /rə(ʊ)ˈmanʃ, -ˈmɑ:nʃ/ (also **Rumansh**) ▶**noun** [mass noun] the Rhaeto-Romance language spoken in the Swiss canton of Grisons by fewer than 30,000 people. It has several dialects, and is an official language of Switzerland.
▶**adjective** of or relating to this language.
– ORIGIN from Romansh *Roman(t)sch*, from medieval Latin *romanice* 'in the Romanic manner'.

Roman snail ▶**noun** another term for **EDIBLE SNAIL**.

romantic ▶**adjective 1** inclined towards or suggestive of the feeling of excitement and mystery associated with love: *a romantic candlelit dinner.*
■relating to love, especially in a sentimental or idealized way: *a romantic comedy.*
2 of, characterized by, or suggestive of an idealized view of reality: *a romantic attitude to the past | some romantic dream of country peace.*
3 (usu. **Romantic**) of, relating to, or denoting the artistic and literary movement of Romanticism: *the Romantic tradition.*
▶**noun** a person with romantic beliefs or attitudes: *I am an incurable romantic.*
■(usu. **Romantic**) a writer or artist of the Romantic movement.
– DERIVATIVES **romantically** adverb.
– ORIGIN mid 17th cent. (referring to the characteristics of romance in a narrative): from archaic *romaunt* 'tale of chivalry', from an Old French variant of *romanz* (see **ROMANCE**).

Romanticism ▶**noun** [mass noun] a movement in the arts and literature which originated in the late 18th century, emphasizing inspiration, subjectivity, and the primacy of the individual.

Romanticism was a reaction against the order and restraint of classicism and neoclassicism, and a rejection of the rationalism which characterized the Enlightenment. In music, the period embraces much of the 19th century, with composers including Schubert, Schumann, Liszt, and Wagner. Writers exemplifying the movement include Wordsworth, Coleridge, Byron, Shelley, and Keats; among romantic painters are such stylistically diverse artists as William Blake, J. M. W. Turner, Delacroix, and Goya.

romanticist ▶**noun** a writer, artist, or musician of the Romantic movement.
■a person who subscribes to the artistic movement or ideas of Romanticism.

romanticize (also **-ise**) ▶**verb** [with obj.] deal with or describe in an idealized or unrealistic fashion; make (something) seem better or more appealing than it really is: *the tendency to romanticize non-industrial societies* | [no obj.] *she was romanticizing about the past.*
– DERIVATIVES **romanticization** noun.

Romany /ˈrɒməni, ˈrəʊ-/ ▶**noun** (pl. **-ies**) **1** [mass noun] the language of the gypsies, which is an Indo-European language related to Hindi. It is spoken by a dispersed group of about 1 million people, and has many dialects.
2 a gypsy.
▶**adjective** of or relating to gypsies or their language.
– ORIGIN early 19th cent.: from Romany *Romani*, feminine and plural of the adjective *Romano*, from *Rom* 'man, husband' (see **ROM**).

Romberg /ˈrɒmbə:g/, Sigmund (1887–1951), Hungarian-born American composer. He wrote a succession of popular operettas, including *The Student Prince* (1924), *The Desert Song* (1926), and *New Moon* (1928).

Rome the capital of Italy and of the Lazio region, situated on the River Tiber about 25 km (16 miles) inland; pop. 2,791,350. Italian name **ROMA**.
■used allusively to refer to the Roman Catholic Church.

According to tradition the ancient city was founded by Romulus (after whom it is named) in 753 BC on the Palatine Hill; as it grew it spread to the other six hills of Rome (Aventine, Caelian, Capitoline, Esquiline, and Quirinal). Rome was ruled by kings until the expulsion of Tarquinius Superbus in 510 BC led to the establishment of the Roman Republic and the beginning of the Roman Empire. By the time of the empire's fall the city was overshadowed politically by Constantinople, but emerged as the seat of the papacy and as the spiritual capital of Western Christianity. In the 14th and 15th centuries Rome became a centre of the Renaissance. It remained under papal control, forming part of the Papal States, until 1871, when it was made the capital of a unified Italy.

– PHRASES **all roads lead to Rome** proverb there are many different ways of reaching the same goal or conclusion. **Rome was not built in a day** proverb a complex task is bound to take a long time and should not be rushed. **when in Rome** (**do as the Romans do**) proverb when abroad or in an unfamiliar environment you should adopt the customs or behaviour of those around you.

Rome, Treaty of a treaty setting up and defining the aims of the European Economic Community. It was signed at Rome on 25 March 1957 by France, West Germany, Italy, Belgium, the Netherlands, and Luxembourg.

Romeo /ˈrəʊmɪəʊ/ ▶**noun 1** (pl. **-os**) an attractive, passionate male seducer or lover.
2 a code word representing the letter R, used in radio communication.
– ORIGIN from the name of the hero of Shakespeare's romantic tragedy *Romeo and Juliet.*

romer /ˈrəʊmə/ ▶**noun** a small piece of plastic or card bearing perpendicularly aligned scales or (if transparent) a grid, used to determine the precise reference of a point within the grid printed on a map.
– ORIGIN 1930s: named after Carrol Romer (1883–1951), its British inventor.

Romish /ˈrəʊmɪʃ/ ▶ **adjective** chiefly derogatory Roman Catholic: *Romish ideas.*

Rommel /ˈrɒm(ə)l/, Erwin (1891–1944), German Field Marshal; known as **the Desert Fox**. As commander of the Afrika Korps he deployed a series of surprise manoeuvres and succeeded in capturing Tobruk (1942), but was defeated by Montgomery at El Alamein later that year. He was forced to commit suicide after being implicated in the officers' conspiracy against Hitler in 1944.

Romney /ˈrɒmni, ˈrʌmni/, George (1734–1802), English portrait painter. From the early 1780s he produced over fifty portraits of Lady Hamilton in historical costumes and poses.

Romney Marsh /ˈrɒmni, ˈrʌmni/ ▶ **noun** a sheep of a stocky long-woolled breed originally from Kent and now common in New Zealand.

romp ▶ **verb** [no obj.] (especially of a child or animal) play about roughly and energetically: *the noisy pack of children romped around the gardens.*
■[with adverbial] informal proceed without effort to achieve something: *Newcastle romped to victory.* ■ informal engage in sexual activity, especially illicitly: *a colleague stumbled on the couple romping in an office.*
▶**noun** a spell of rough, energetic play: *a romp in the snow.*
■a light-hearted film or other work: *an enjoyably gross sci-fi romp.* ■ informal an easy victory: *their UEFA Cup romp against the Luxembourg part-timers.* ■ informal a spell of sexual activity, especially an illicit one: *three-in-a-bed sex romps.*
▶**romp home** (or **in**) informal finish as the easy winner of a race or other contest: *a 33–1 'no-hoper' romped home.*
– ORIGIN early 18th cent.: perhaps an alteration of **RAMP**.

romper (also **romper suit**) ▶ **noun** (usu. **rompers**) a young child's one-piece outer garment.
■a similar item of clothing for adults, typically worn as overalls or as sports clothing.

Romulus /ˈrɒmjʊləs/ Roman Mythology the traditional founder of Rome, one of the twin sons of Mars by the Vestal Virgin Rhea Silvia. He and his brother Remus were abandoned at birth in a basket on the River Tiber but were found and suckled by a she-wolf and later brought up by a shepherd family.

Roncesvalles, Battle of /ˈrɒnsəval/ a battle which took place in 778 at a mountain pass in the Pyrenees, near the village of Roncesvalles in northern Spain. The rearguard of Charlemagne's army was attacked by the Basques and massacred. French name **RONCEVAUX** /ʀɔ̃svo/.

rondavel /rɒnˈdɑːv(ə)l/ ▶ **noun** S. African a traditional circular African dwelling with a conical thatched roof.
■a building based on the design of such a dwelling, used as a guest room, storeroom, or holiday cottage.
– ORIGIN from Afrikaans *rondawel*.

rond de jambe /ˌrɔ̃ də ˈʒɒmb/ ▶ **noun** (pl. **ronds de jambes** or **ronds de jambe**) Ballet a circular movement of the leg which can be performed on the ground or during a jump.
– ORIGIN French.

ronde /rɒnd/ ▶ **noun** a dance in which the dancers move in a circle.
– ORIGIN 1930s: French, feminine of *rond* 'round'.

rondeau /ˈrɒndəʊ/ ▶ **noun** (pl. **rondeaux** pronunc. same or /-əʊz/) a poem of ten or thirteen lines with only two rhymes throughout and with the opening words used twice as a refrain.
– ORIGIN early 16th cent.: French, later form of *rondel* (see **RONDEL**).

rondel /ˈrɒnd(ə)l/ ▶ **noun** a rondeau, especially one of three stanzas of thirteen or fourteen lines with a two line refrain.
– ORIGIN Middle English: from Old French, from *rond* 'round'; compare with **ROUNDEL**.

rondo /ˈrɒndəʊ/ ▶ **noun** (pl. **-os**) a musical form with a recurring leading theme, often found in the final movement of a sonata or concerto.
– ORIGIN late 18th cent.: Italian, from French *rondeau* (see **RONDEAU**).

Rondônia /rɒnˈdɒnjə/ a state of NW Brazil, on the border with Bolivia; capital, Pôrto Velho.

rone /rəʊn/ ▶ **noun** Scottish a gutter for carrying off rain from a roof.
– ORIGIN mid 18th cent.: of unknown origin.

rongo-rongo /ˌrɒŋgəʊˈrɒŋgəʊ/ ▶ **noun** [mass noun] Archaeology an ancient script of hieroglyphic signs found on wooden tablets on Easter Island. The symbols have not yet been deciphered, and may possibly date from the post-European period.
– ORIGIN early 20th cent.: a local word.

ronin /ˈrəʊnɪn/ ▶ **noun** (pl. same or **ronins**) historical (in feudal Japan) a wandering samurai who had no lord or master.
– ORIGIN Japanese.

ronquil /ˈrɒŋkɪl/ ▶ **noun** a slender bottom-dwelling fish that lives in cold coastal waters of the North Pacific.
● Family Bathymasteridae: several genera and species.
– ORIGIN late 19th cent.: from Spanish *ronquillo* 'slightly hoarse'.

Röntgen /ˈrʌntjən, ˈrɒntg(ə)n, German ˈrœntgn/, Wilhelm Conrad (1845–1923), German physicist, the discoverer of X-rays. He was a skilful experimenter and worked in a variety of areas as well as radiation. He was awarded the first Nobel Prize for Physics in 1901.

röntgen etc. ▶ **noun** variant spelling of **ROENTGEN** etc.

roo ▶ **noun** Austral. informal a kangaroo.
– ORIGIN early 20th cent.: shortened form.

roo bar ▶ **noun** Australian term for **BULL BAR**.

rood /ruːd/ ▶ **noun 1** a crucifix, especially one positioned above the rood screen of a church or on a beam over the entrance to the chancel.
2 historical, chiefly Brit. a measure of land area equal to a quarter of an acre (40 square perches, approximately 0.1012 hectare).
– ORIGIN Old English *rōd*; related to Dutch *roede* and German *Rute* 'rod'.

rood loft ▶ **noun** a gallery on top of the rood screen of a church.

rood screen ▶ **noun** a screen, typically of richly carved wood or stone, separating the nave from the chancel of a church. Rood screens are found throughout western Europe and date chiefly from the 14th–16th centuries.

roof ▶ **noun** (pl. **roofs**) the structure forming the upper covering of a building or vehicle.
■the top inner surface of a covered area or space; the ceiling: *the roof of the cave fell in.* ■ the upper limit or level of prices or wages: *starting salary £12,185, rising to a roof of £16,835.* ■ used to signify a house or other building, especially in the context of hospitality or shelter: *helping those without* **a roof over their heads** | *they slept* **under the same roof**.
▶**verb** [with obj.] (usu. **be roofed**) cover with a roof: *the yard had been roughly* **roofed over** *with corrugated iron.*
■function as the roof of: *fan vaults roof these magnificent buildings.*
– PHRASES **go through the roof** informal **1** (of prices or figures) reach extreme or unexpected heights. **2** another way of saying ***hit the roof***. **hit** (or **go through**) **the roof** informal suddenly become very angry. **raise the roof** see **RAISE**. **the roof of the world** a nickname given to the Himalayas.
– DERIVATIVES **roofless** adjective.
– ORIGIN Old English *hrōf*, of Germanic origin; related to Old Norse *hróf* 'boat shed', Dutch *roef* 'deckhouse'. English alone has the general sense 'covering of a house'; other Germanic languages use forms related to *thatch*.

roof bolt ▶ **noun** Mining a tensioned rod anchoring the roof of a working to the strata above.
– DERIVATIVES **roof-bolting** noun.

roofer ▶ **noun** a person who constructs or repairs roofs.

roof garden ▶ **noun** a garden on the flat roof of a building.

roofing ▶ **noun** [mass noun] material for constructing a building's roof: *a house with corrugated iron roofing.*
■the process of constructing a roof or roofs: *jobs such as roofing.*

roof light ▶ **noun** a window panel built into a roof to admit light.
■a small interior light on the ceiling of a motor vehicle. ■ a flashing warning light on the top of a police car or other emergency vehicle.

roofline ▶ **noun** the design or proportions of a vehicle's roof.

roof of the mouth ▶ **noun** the palate.

roof prism ▶ **noun** a reflecting prism in which the reflecting surface is in two parts that are angled like the two sides of a pitched roof. Compare with **PORRO PRISM**.
■(**roof prisms**) (also **roof-prism binoculars**) a pair of binoculars using two such prisms, resulting in an instrument with parallel sides and objective lenses that are the same distance apart as the eyepieces.

roof rack ▶ **noun** a framework for carrying luggage on the roof of a vehicle.

roof rat ▶ **noun** another term for **BLACK RAT**.

roofscape ▶ **noun** a scene or view of roofs, especially when considered in terms of its aesthetic appeal.

rooftop ▶ **noun** the outer surface of a building's roof.
– PHRASES **shout something from the rooftops** see **SHOUT**.

roof-tree ▶ **noun** the ridge piece of a roof.

rooibos /ˈrɔɪbɒs/ ▶ **noun** S. African **1** an evergreen South African shrub of the pea family, which has leaves that are sometimes used to make tea.
● Genus *Aspalathus*, family Leguminosae.
■(**rooibos tea**) [mass noun] an infusion of the leaves of this plant drunk as tea.
2 a tropical shrub or small tree with spikes of scented yellow flowers.
● Genus *Combretum*, family Combretaceae.
– ORIGIN early 20th cent.: from Afrikaans, literally 'red bush'.

rooigras /ˈrɔɪxras/ ▶ **noun** S. African a valuable southern African pasture grass which has a reddish tint in winter.
● *Themeda triandra*, family Poaceae.
– ORIGIN late 19th cent.: from Afrikaans, literally 'red grass'.

rooikat /ˈrɔɪkat/ ▶ **noun** South African term for **CARACAL**.
– ORIGIN late 18th cent.: from Afrikaans, literally 'red cat'.

rooinek /ˈrɔɪnɛk/ ▶ **noun** S. African informal, offensive an English person or an English-speaking South African (used chiefly by Afrikaners).
– ORIGIN Afrikaans, literally 'red-neck'.

rook[1] ▶ **noun** a gregarious Eurasian crow with black plumage and a bare face, nesting in colonies in treetops.
● *Corvus frugilegus*, family Corvidae.
▶**verb** [with obj.] informal take money from (someone) by cheating, defrauding, or overcharging them.
– ORIGIN Old English *hrōc*, probably imitative and of Germanic origin; related to Dutch *roek*.

rook[2] ▶ **noun** a chess piece, typically with its top in the shape of a battlement, that can move in any direction along a rank or file on which it stands. Each player starts the game with two rooks at opposite ends of the first rank. See also **CASTLE**.
– ORIGIN Middle English: from Old French *rock*, based on Arabic *rukk* (of which the sense remains uncertain).

rookery ▶ **noun** (pl. **-ies**) a breeding colony of rooks, typically seen as a collection of nests high in a clump of trees.
■a breeding colony of seabirds (especially penguins), seals, or turtles. ■ North American term for **HERONRY**. ■ figurative a dense collection of housing, especially in a slum area.

rookie ▶ **noun** informal a new recruit, especially in the army or police: [as modifier] *a rookie cop.*
■a member of a sports team in his or her first full season in that sport.
– ORIGIN late 19th cent.: perhaps an alteration of **RECRUIT**, influenced by **ROOK**[1].

rookoo /ˈruːkuː/ ▶ **noun** variant spelling of **ROUCOU**.

room /ruːm, rʊm/ ▶ **noun 1** [mass noun] space that can be occupied or where something can be done, especially viewed in terms of whether there is enough: *there's only room for a single bed in there* | [with infinitive] *she was trapped without room to move.*
■figurative opportunity or scope for something to happen or be done, especially without causing trouble or damage: *there is plenty of room for disagreement in this controversial area* | *there is* **room for improvement**.
2 a part or division of a building enclosed by walls, floor, and ceiling: *he wandered from room to room.*
■(**rooms**) a set of rooms, typically rented, in which a person, couple, or family live: *my rooms at Mrs Jenks's house.* ■ [in sing.] the people present in a room: *the whole room burst into an uproar of approval.*
▶**verb** [no obj.] chiefly US share a room or house or flat, especially a rented one at a college or similar institution: *I was rooming with my cousin.*

r

b **but** | d **dog** | f **few** | g **get** | h **he** | j **yes** | k **cat** | l **leg** | m **man** | n **no** | p **pen** | r **red** | s **sit** | t **top** | v **voice** | w **we** | z **zoo** | ʃ **she** | ʒ decision | θ **thin** | ð **this** | ŋ **ring** | x lo**ch** | tʃ **chip** | dʒ **jar**

■[with obj.] provide with a shared room or lodging: *they roomed us together.*

– PHRASES **make room** move aside or move something aside to allow someone to enter or pass or to clear space for something: *the secretary entered with the coffee tray and made room for it on the desk.* **no** (or **not**) **room to swing a cat** humorous used in reference to a very confined space. [ORIGIN: *cat* in the sense 'cat-o'-nine-tails'.] **smoke-filled room** used to refer to political bargaining or decision-making that is conducted privately by a small group of influential people rather than more openly or democratically.

– DERIVATIVES **roomed** adjective [in combination] *a four-roomed house*, **roomful** noun (pl. **-fuls**).

– ORIGIN Old English *rūm*, of Germanic origin; related to Dutch *ruim*, German *Raum*.

roomer ▶ noun N. Amer. a lodger occupying a room without board.

roomette ▶ noun N. Amer. **1** a private single compartment in a railway sleeping car.
2 a small bedroom for letting.

roomie ▶ noun N. Amer. informal a room-mate.

rooming house ▶ noun a lodging house.

room-mate ▶ noun a person occupying the same room as another.
■N. Amer. a person occupying the same room, flat, or house as another.

room service ▶ noun [mass noun] service provided in a hotel allowing guests to order food and drink to be brought to their rooms.

room temperature ▶ noun [mass noun] a comfortable ambient temperature, generally taken as about 20°C.

roomy ▶ adjective (**roomier**, **roomiest**) (especially of accommodation) having plenty of room; spacious.
– DERIVATIVES **roomily** adverb, **roominess** noun.

Rooney, Mickey (b.1920), American actor; born *Joseph Yule Jr.* He received Oscar nominations for his roles in *Babes in Arms* (1939) and *The Human Comedy* (1943).

Roosevelt[1] /ˈrəʊzəvɛlt/, (Anna) Eleanor (1884–1962), American humanitarian and diplomat. She was the niece of Theodore Roosevelt, and married Franklin D. Roosevelt in 1905. She was involved in a wide range of liberal causes; as chair of the UN Commission on Human Rights she helped draft the Declaration of Human Rights (1948).

Roosevelt[2] /ˈrəʊzəvɛlt/, Franklin D. (1882–1945), American Democratic statesman, 32nd President of the US 1933–45; full name *Franklin Delano Roosevelt*; known as **FDR**. His New Deal of 1933 helped to lift the US out of the Great Depression, and he played an important part in Allied policy during the Second World War. He was the only American President to be elected for a third term in office.

Roosevelt[3] /ˈrəʊzəvɛlt/, Theodore (1858–1919), American Republican statesman, 26th President of the US 1901–9; known as **Teddy Roosevelt**. He was noted for his antitrust laws and successfully engineered the American bid to build the Panama Canal (1904–14). He won the Nobel Peace Prize in 1906 for negotiating the end of the Russo-Japanese War.

roost[1] ▶ noun a place where birds regularly settle or congregate to rest at night, or where bats congregate to rest in the day.
▶ verb [no obj.] (of a bird or bat) settle or congregate for rest or sleep: *migrating martins and swallows were settling to roost.*
– PHRASES **curses, like chickens, come home to roost** proverb one's past mistakes or wrongdoings will eventually be the cause of present troubles: *for the overextended borrowers, the chickens have come home to roost.*
– ORIGIN Old English *hrōst*, related to Dutch *roest*; of unknown ultimate origin.

roost[2] ▶ noun (in the Orkneys and Shetlands) a tidal race.
– ORIGIN mid 17th cent.: from Old Norse *røst*.

rooster ▶ noun a male domestic fowl; a cock.

rooster tail ▶ noun N. Amer. informal the spray of water thrown up behind a speedboat or surfboard.

root[1] ▶ noun **1** the part of a plant which attaches it to the ground or to a support, typically underground, conveying water and nourishment to the rest of the plant via numerous branches and fibres: *cacti have deep and spreading roots | a tree root.*
■the persistent underground part of a plant, especially when fleshy and enlarged and used as a vegetable, e.g. a turnip or carrot. ■ any plant grown for such a root. ■ the embedded part of a bodily organ or structure such as a hair, tooth, or nail: *her hair was fairer at the roots.* ■ the part of a thing attaching it to a greater or more fundamental whole; the end or base: *a little lever near the root of the barrel.*
2 the basic cause, source, or origin of something: *money is the root of all evil | jealousy was at the root of it |* [as modifier] *the root cause of the problem.*
■the essential substance or nature of something: *matters at the heart and root of existence.* ■ (**roots**) family, ethnic, or cultural origins, especially as the reasons for one's long-standing emotional attachment to a place or community: *it's always nice to return to my roots.* ■ [as modifier] (**roots**) denoting or relating to something, especially music, from a particular ethnic or cultural origin, especially a non-Western one: *roots music.* ■ (in biblical use) a scion; a descendant: *the root of David.* ■ Linguistics a morpheme, not necessarily surviving as a word in itself, from which words have been made by the addition of prefixes or suffixes or by other modification: *many European words stem from this linguistic root |* [as modifier] *the root form of the word.* ■ (also **root note**) Music the fundamental note of a chord.
3 Mathematics a number or quantity that when multiplied by itself, typically a specified number of times, gives a specified number or quantity: *find the cube root of the result.*
■short for **SQUARE ROOT**. ■ a value of an unknown quantity satisfying a given equation: *the roots of the equation differ by an integer.*
4 Austral./NZ & Irish vulgar slang an act of sexual intercourse.
■[with adj.] a sexual partner of a specified nature or ability.
▶ verb [with obj.] **1** cause (a plant or cutting) to grow roots: *root your own cuttings from stock plants.*
■[no obj.] (of a plant or cutting) establish roots: *large trees had rooted in the canal bank.*
2 (usu. **be rooted**) establish deeply and firmly: *vegetarianism is* **rooted** *in Indian culture.*
■(**be rooted in**) have as an origin or cause: *the Latin* dubitare *is rooted in an Indo-European word.* ■ [with obj. and adverbial] [often as adj. **rooted**] cause (someone) to stand immobile through fear or amazement: *she found herself* **rooted to the spot** *in disbelief.*
3 [with obj.] Austral./NZ & Irish vulgar slang have sexual intercourse with.
■[with obj.] exhaust (someone) or frustrate their efforts.
– PHRASES **at root** basically; fundamentally: *it is a moral question at root.* **put down roots** (of a plant) begin to draw nourishment from the soil through its roots. ■ (of a person) begin to have a settled life in a particular place. **root and branch** used to express the thorough or radical nature of a process or operation: *root and branch reform of personal taxation.* **strike at the root** (or **roots**) **of** affect in a vital area with potentially destructive results: *the proposals struck at the roots of community life.* **take root** (of a plant) begin to grow and draw nourishment from the soil through its roots.
■ become fixed or established: *the idea had taken root in my mind.*
– DERIVATIVES **rootedness** noun, **rootlet** noun, **root-like** adjective, **rooty** adjective.
– ORIGIN late Old English *rōt*, from Old Norse *rót*; related to Latin *radix*, also to **WORT**.
▶ **root something out** (also **root something up**) dig or pull up a plant by the roots. ■ find and get rid of someone or something regarded as pernicious or dangerous: *a campaign to root out corruption.*

root[2] ▶ verb [no obj., with adverbial] (of an animal) turn up the ground with its snout in search of food: *stray dogs rooting around for bones and scraps.*
■search unsystematically through an untidy mass or area; rummage: *she was rooting through a pile of papers.*
■ [with obj.] (**root something out**) find or extract something by rummaging: *he managed to root out the cleaning kit.*
▶ noun [in sing.] an act of rooting: *I have a root through the open drawers.*
– ORIGIN Old English *wrōtan*, of Germanic origin; related to Old English *wrōt* 'snout', German *Rüssel* 'snout', and perhaps ultimately to Latin *rodere* 'gnaw'.
▶ **root for** informal support or hope for the success of (a person or group entering a contest or undertaking a challenge): *the whole of this club is rooting for him.*
root someone on N. Amer. informal cheer or spur someone on: *his mother rooted him on enthusiastically from ringside.*

root ball ▶ noun the mass formed by the roots of a plant and the soil surrounding them.

root beer ▶ noun [mass noun] N. Amer. an effervescent drink made from an extract of the roots and bark of certain plants.

root-bound ▶ adjective another term for **POT-BOUND**.

root canal ▶ noun the pulp-filled cavity in the root of a tooth.
■N. Amer. a procedure to replace infected pulp in a root canal with an inert material.

root cellar ▶ noun N. Amer. a domestic cellar used for storing root vegetables.

root crop ▶ noun a crop that is a root vegetable or other root, e.g. sugar beet.

root directory ▶ noun Computing the directory at the highest level of a hierarchy.

rooter ▶ noun N. Amer. informal a supporter or fan of a sports team or player.

root fly ▶ noun a dark slender fly whose larvae may cause serious damage to the roots of crops.
• Family Anthomyiidae: many genera and species, including the **cabbage root fly**.

root hair ▶ noun Botany each of a large number of elongated microscopic outgrowths from the outer layer of cells in a root, absorbing moisture and nutrients from the soil.

rootin'-tootin' ▶ adjective informal, chiefly N. Amer. brashly or boisterously enthusiastic: *their rootin'-tootin' summer adventures.*
– ORIGIN late 19th cent.: reduplication of *rooting* in the sense 'inquisitive', an early dialect sense of the compound.

root-knot ▶ noun [mass noun] a disease of cultivated flowers and vegetables caused by eelworm infestation, resulting in galls on the roots.
• The eelworms belong to the genus *Meloidogyne*, class Nematoda.

rootle ▶ verb Brit. informal term for **ROOT**[2].
– ORIGIN early 19th cent.: frequentative of **ROOT**[2].

rootless ▶ adjective **1** having no settled home or social or family ties: *a rootless nomad.*
2 (of a plant) not having roots: *a rootless flowering plant.*
– DERIVATIVES **rootlessness** noun.

root mean square ▶ noun Mathematics the square root of the arithmetic mean of the squares of a set of values.

root nodule ▶ noun see **NODULE** (sense 1).

root note ▶ noun see **ROOT**[1] (sense 2).

root run ▶ noun the space over which the roots of a plant extend.

root sign ▶ noun Mathematics another term for **RADICAL SIGN**.

rootstock ▶ noun a rhizome.
■a plant on to which another variety is grafted. ■ a primary form or source from which offshoots have arisen: *the rootstock of all post-Triassic ammonites.*

rootsy ▶ adjective informal (of music) uncommercialized and full-blooded, especially showing traditional or ethnic origins.

root vegetable ▶ noun the fleshy enlarged root of a plant used as a vegetable, e.g. a carrot, swede, or beetroot.

rope ▶ noun **1** a length of stout cord made by twisting together strands of hemp, sisal, flax, cotton, or similar material.
■N. Amer. a lasso. ■ (**the rope**) used in reference to execution by hanging: *executions by the rope continued well into the twentieth century.* ■ (**the ropes**) the ropes enclosing a boxing or wrestling ring.
2 a quantity of roughly spherical objects such as onions or pearls strung together: *a* **rope** *of pearls.*
3 (**the ropes**) informal used in reference to the established procedures in an organization or area of activity: *I want you to* **show her the ropes** *| new boys were expected to* **learn the ropes** *from the old hands.* [ORIGIN: mid 19th cent.: with reference to ropes used in sailing.]
▶ verb [with obj.] catch, fasten, or secure with rope: *the calves must be roped and led out of the stockade | the climbers were all roped together.*
■(**rope someone in/into**) persuade someone to take part in (an activity): *anyone who could play an instrument or sing in tune was roped in.* ■ (**rope something off**) enclose or separate an area with a

rope or tape: *police roped off the area of the find.* ■ [no obj.] Climbing (of a party of climbers) connect each other together with a rope: *we stopped at the foot of the Cavales Ridge and* **roped up**. ■ [no obj.] (**rope down/up**) Climbing climb down or up using a rope: *the party had been roping down a hanging glacier.*

– PHRASES **give a man enough rope** (or **plenty of rope**) **and he will hang himself** proverb given enough freedom of action a person will bring about their own downfall. **money for old rope** see **MONEY**. **on the rope** Climbing roped together: *the technique of moving together on the rope.* **on the ropes** Boxing forced against the ropes by the opponent's attack. ■ in state of near collapse or defeat: *behind the apparent success the company was on the ropes.* **a rope of sand** formal used in allusion to something providing only illusory security or coherence: *our union will become a mere rope of sand.*

– ORIGIN Old English *rāp*, of Germanic origin; related to Dutch *reep* and German *Reif*.

ropeable /ˈrəʊpəb(ə)l/ (also **ropable**) ▶ **adjective** [predic.] Austral./NZ informal angry; furious: *the idea of it gets him absolutely ropeable.*

– ORIGIN late 19th cent.: from the notion that the person requires to be restrained.

rope-a-dope ▶ **noun** [mass noun] US informal a boxing tactic of pretending to be trapped against the ropes, goading an opponent to throw tiring ineffective punches.

– ORIGIN 1970s: coined by Muhammad Ali, referring to a tactic in a boxing match with George Foreman.

rope ladder ▶ **noun** two long ropes connected by short crosspieces, typically made of wood or metal, used as a ladder.

ropemanship ▶ **noun** [mass noun] skill in walking on or climbing with ropes.

rope-moulding ▶ **noun** a moulding cut in an interweaving spiral in imitation of rope strands.

rope's end historical ▶ **noun** a short piece of rope used for flogging, especially on ships.

▶ **verb** (**rope's-end**) [with obj.] flog (someone) with a rope's end.

ropesight ▶ **noun** [mass noun] Bell-ringing skill in judging when to pull on a bell rope in change-ringing.

rope-walk ▶ **noun** historical a long piece of ground where ropes are made.

rope-walker ▶ **noun** dated a performer on a tightrope.

– DERIVATIVES **rope-walking** noun.

ropeway ▶ **noun** a transport system for materials or people, used especially in mines or mountainous areas, in which carriers are suspended from moving cables powered by a motor.

ropey ▶ **adjective** variant spelling of **ROPY**.

rope yarn ▶ **noun** [mass noun] material used for making the strands of rope.

roping ▶ **noun** [mass noun] **1** the action of catching or securing something with ropes: *calf roping.*

2 ropes collectively.

ropy (also **ropey**) ▶ **adjective** (**ropier**, **ropiest**) **1** resembling a rope in being long, strong, and fibrous or in forming viscous or gelatinous threads: *the ropy roots of the old tree.*

2 Brit. informal poor in quality or health; inferior: *a portrait by a pretty ropy artist.*

– DERIVATIVES **ropily** adverb, **ropiness** noun.

roque /rəʊk/ ▶ **noun** [mass noun] US a form of croquet played on a hard court surrounded by a bank.

– ORIGIN late 19th cent.: alteration of **ROQUET**.

Roquefort /ˈrɒkfɔː/ ▶ **noun** [mass noun] trademark a soft blue cheese made from ewes' milk. It is ripened in limestone caves and has a strong flavour.

– ORIGIN from the name of a village in southern France.

roquet /ˈrəʊkeɪ, -ki/ Croquet ▶ **verb** (**roqueted**, **roqueting**) [with obj.] strike (another ball) with one's own: *once you roquet a ball you can hit it where you please.*

▶ **noun** an act of roqueting.

– ORIGIN mid 19th cent.: apparently an arbitrary alteration of the verb **CROQUET**, originally used in the same sense.

roquette /rɒˈkɛt/ ▶ **noun** another term for **ROCKET**[2].

– ORIGIN French.

Roraima /rɔːˈrʌɪmə/ **1** a mountain in the Guiana Highlands of South America, situated at the junction of the borders of Venezuela, Brazil, and Guyana. Rising to 2,774 m (9,094 ft), it is the highest peak in the range.

2 a state of northern Brazil, on the borders with Venezuela and Guyana; capital, Boa Vista.

ro-ro Brit. ▶ **abbreviation for** roll-on roll-off.

– ORIGIN 1960s: abbreviation.

rorqual /ˈrɔːkw(ə)l/ ▶ **noun** a baleen whale of streamlined appearance with pleated skin on the underside.

● Family Balaenopteridae: two genera and six species, including the **common rorqual** (or fin whale).

– ORIGIN early 19th cent.: via French from Norwegian *røyrkval*, from Old Norse *reythr*, the specific name, + *hvalr* 'whale'.

Rorschach test /ˈrɔːʃɑːk/ ▶ **noun** Psychology a type of projective test used in psychoanalysis, in which a standard set of symmetrical ink blots of different shapes and colours is presented one by one to the subject, who is asked to describe what they suggest or resemble.

– ORIGIN 1920s: named after Hermann *Rorschach* (1884–1922), Swiss psychiatrist.

rort /rɔːt/ ▶ **noun** Austral. informal **1** [often with modifier] a fraudulent or dishonest act or practice: *a tax rort.*

2 a wild party.

– ORIGIN 1930s: back-formation from **RORTY**.

rorty ▶ **adjective** (**rortier**, **rortiest**) Brit. informal boisterous and high-spirited.

– ORIGIN mid 19th cent.: of unknown origin.

Rosa /ˈrəʊzə/, Salvator (1615–73), Italian painter and etcher. The picturesque and 'sublime' qualities of his landscapes, often peopled with bandits and containing scenes of violence in wild natural settings, were an important influence on the romantic art of the 18th and 19th centuries.

rosace /ˈrəʊzeɪs/ ▶ **noun** an ornamentation resembling a rose, in particular a rose window.

– ORIGIN mid 19th cent.: from French, from Latin *rosaceus* 'rose-like' (see **ROSACEOUS**).

rosacea /rəʊˈzeɪʃɪə/ (also **acne rosacea**) ▶ **noun** [mass noun] Medicine a condition in which certain facial blood vessels enlarge, giving the cheeks and nose a flushed appearance.

– ORIGIN late 19th cent.: from Latin, feminine of *rosaceus* in the sense 'rose-coloured'.

rosaceous /rəʊˈzeɪʃəs/ ▶ **adjective** Botany of, relating to, or denoting plants of the rose family (Rosaceae).

– ORIGIN mid 18th cent.: from modern Latin *Rosaceae* (based on Latin *rosa* 'rose') + **-OUS**.

rosaline /ˈrəʊzəliːn/ ▶ **noun** [mass noun] a variety of fine needlepoint or pillow lace.

– ORIGIN early 20th cent. (as *rosaline point*): probably from French.

rosaniline /rəʊˈzanɪliːn, -lɪn, -lʌɪn/ ▶ **noun** [mass noun] Chemistry a reddish-brown synthetic compound which is a base used in making a number of red dyes, notably fuchsin.

● A triphenylmethane derivative; chem. formula: $C_{20}H_{19}N_3$.

– ORIGIN mid 19th cent.: from **ROSE**[1] + **ANILINE**.

rosarian /rəʊˈzɛːrɪən/ ▶ **noun** a person who cultivates roses, especially as an occupation.

– ORIGIN mid 19th cent.: from Latin *rosarium* 'rose garden, rosary' + **-AN**.

Rosario /rəʊˈsɑːrɪəʊ/ an inland port on the Paraná River in east central Argentina; pop. 1,096,000 (1991).

rosarium /rəʊˈzɛːrɪəm/ ▶ **noun** (pl. **rosariums** or **rosaria**) formal a rose garden.

– ORIGIN mid 19th cent.: from Latin (see **ROSARY**).

rosary /ˈrəʊz(ə)ri/ ▶ **noun** (pl. **-ies**) (in the Roman Catholic Church) a form of devotion in which five (or fifteen) decades of Hail Marys are repeated, each decade preceded by an Our Father and followed by a Glory Be: *the congregation said the rosary.*

■ a string of beads for keeping count in such a devotion or in the devotions of some other religions, in Roman Catholic use 55 or 165 in number. ■ a book containing such a devotion.

– ORIGIN late Middle English (in the sense 'rose garden'): from Latin *rosarium* 'rose garden', based on *rosa* 'rose'.

Roscius /ˈrɒsɪəs, ˈrɒʃɪ-/ (d.62 BC), Roman actor; full name *Quintus Roscius Gallus*. Many notable English actors from the 16th century onwards were nicknamed in reference to his great skill.

roscoe /ˈrɒskəʊ/ ▶ **noun** US informal, dated a gun, especially a pistol or revolver.

– ORIGIN early 20th cent.: from the surname *Roscoe*.

Roscommon /rɒsˈkɒmən/ a county in the north central part of the Republic of Ireland, in the province of Connacht; pop. 51,880 (1991).

■ its county town; pop. 17,700 (1991).

rose[1] ▶ **noun 1** a prickly bush or shrub that typically bears red, pink, yellow, or white fragrant flowers, native to north temperate regions. Numerous hybrids and cultivars have been developed and are widely grown as ornamentals.

● Genus *Rosa*, family Rosaceae (the **rose family**). This large family includes most temperate fruits (apple, plum, peach, cherry, blackberry, strawberry) as well as the hawthorns, rowans, potentillas, avens, and lady's mantles.

■ the flower of such a plant: *he sent her a dozen red roses* | [as modifier] *a rose garden.* ■ used in names of other plants whose flowers resemble roses, e.g. **Christmas rose**, **rose of Sharon**. ■ used in similes and comparisons in reference to the rose flower's beauty or its typical rich red colour: *she looked as beautiful as a rose.* ■ [often with negative] (**roses**) used to express favourable circumstances or ease of success: *all is not roses in the firm today.*

2 a thing representing or resembling the flower, in particular:

■ a stylized representation of the flower in heraldry or decoration, typically with five petals (especially as a national emblem of England): *the Tudor rose.* ■ short for **COMPASS ROSE**. ■ short for **ROSE WINDOW**. ■ short for **ROSE DIAMOND**. ■ short for **CEILING ROSE**.

3 a perforated cap attached to a shower, the spout of a watering can, or the end of a hose to produce a spray.

4 [mass noun] a warm pink or light crimson colour: *the rose and gold of dawn* | [as modifier] *the 100% cotton range is available in* **rose pink** *and ocean blue* | [in combination] *leaves with* **rose-red** *margins.*

■ (usu. **roses**) used in reference to a rosy complexion, especially that of a young woman: *the fresh air will soon put the roses back in her cheeks.*

▶ **verb** [with obj.] poetic/literary make rosy: *a warm flush now rosed her hitherto blue cheeks.*

– PHRASES **a bed of roses** see **BED**. **come up roses** (of a situation) develop in a very favourable way: *new boyfriend, successful career—everything was coming up roses.* **come up** (or **out**) **smelling of roses** emerge from a difficult situation with reputation intact. **under the rose** archaic in confidence; under pledge of secrecy.

– DERIVATIVES **rose-like** adjective.

– ORIGIN Old English *rōse*, of Germanic origin, from Latin *rosa*; reinforced in Middle English by Old French *rose*.

rose[2] past of **RISE**.

rosé /ˈrəʊzeɪ/ ▶ **noun** [mass noun] any light pink wine, coloured by only brief contact with red grape skins.

– ORIGIN French, literally 'pink'.

roseapple ▶ **noun** a tropical evergreen tree cultivated for its foliage and fragrant fruit.

● Genus *Syzygium*, family Myrtaceae: several species, in particular the SE Asian *S. jambos*.

■ the spherical white rose-scented fruit of this tree.

roseate /ˈrəʊzɪət/ ▶ **adjective** rose-coloured: *the early, roseate light.*

■ used in names of birds with partly pink plumage, e.g. **roseate tern**, **roseate spoonbill**.

– ORIGIN late Middle English: from Latin *roseus* 'rosy' (from *rosa* 'rose') + **-ATE**[2].

Roseau /rəʊˈzəʊ/ the capital of Dominica in the Caribbean; pop. 15,860 (1991).

rosebay ▶ **noun 1** (also **rosebay willowherb**) a tall willowherb with pink flowers, native to north temperate regions and often spreading on burnt ground.

● *Epilobium* (or *Chamaenerion*) *angustifolium*, family Onagraceae.

2 N. Amer. a rhododendron.

● Genus *Rhododendron*, family Ericaceae: several species, in particular **Lapland rosebay** (*R. lapponicum*), a dwarf shrub of northern latitudes.

Rosebery /ˈrəʊzbəri/, Archibald Philip Primrose, 5th Earl of (1847–1929), British Liberal statesman, Prime Minister 1894–5.

rose bowl ▶ **noun** a bowl for displaying cut roses.

rose-breasted grosbeak ▶ **noun** a North American grosbeak, the male of which is black and white with a pinkish-red breast patch.

● *Pheucticus ludovicianus*, family Emberizidae (subfamily Cardinalinae).

rosebud ▶ **noun** an unopened flower of a rose.

■ Brit. dated a pretty young woman.

rose chafer ▶ **noun** a brilliant green or copper-

coloured day-flying chafer (beetle) which feeds on roses and other flowers. The larvae typically live in rotting timber.
● Genus *Cetonia*, family Scarabaeidae: several species, in particular the European *C. aurata*.

rose-coloured ▶ adjective of a warm pink colour: *rose-coloured silks*.
■used in reference to a naively optimistic or unfoundedly favourable viewpoint: *you are still seeing the profession through rose-coloured spectacles*.

rose-coloured starling ▶ noun a starling with a pink back and underparts, found from eastern Europe to central Asia and fond of feeding on locusts.
● *Sturnus roseus*, family Sturnidae.

rose comb ▶ noun a fleshy comb which lies flat on the head of certain breeds of domestic fowl.

rose-cut ▶ adjective (of a gem) cut in tiny triangular facets.

rose diamond ▶ noun a hemispherical diamond with the curved part cut in triangular facets.

rose engine (also **rose-engine lathe**) ▶ noun an appendage to a lathe for engraving curved patterns.

rosefinch ▶ noun an Asian finch found chiefly in mountainous areas, the male of which has predominantly pinkish-red plumage.
● *Carpodacus* and other genera, family Fringillidae: many species.

rosefish ▶ noun (pl. same or **-fishes**) N. Amer. the redfish of the North Atlantic (*Sebastes marinus*).

rose geranium ▶ noun a pink-flowered pelargonium with fragrant leaves.
● *Pelargonium graveolens*, family Geraniaceae.

rose hip ▶ noun see HIP².

rosella /rə(ʊ)ˈzɛlə/ ▶ noun **1** an Australian parakeet with vivid green, red, yellow, or blue plumage.
● Genus *Platycercus*, family Psittacidae: several species.
2 Austral. a sheep which is losing its wool (and said to resemble a rosella parakeet which has lost some of its feathers) and is therefore easy to shear.
– ORIGIN mid 19th cent.: alteration of *Rosehill*, New South Wales, where the bird was first found.

rose madder ▶ noun [mass noun] a pale shade of pink.

rosemaling /ˈrəʊsəˌmɑːlɪŋ, -ˌmɔːlɪŋ, -zə-/ ▶ noun [mass noun] chiefly US the art, originating in Norway, of painting wooden furniture and objects with flower motifs.
■painted flower motifs of this type.
– DERIVATIVES **rosemaled** adjective.
– ORIGIN 1940s: from Norwegian, literally 'rose painting'.

rose mallow ▶ noun an ornamental hibiscus.
● Genus *Hibiscus*, family Malvaceae, in particular *H. rosa-sinensis*.

rosemary ▶ noun [mass noun] an evergreen aromatic shrub of the mint family, native to southern Europe. The narrow leaves are used as a culinary herb, in perfumery, and as an emblem of remembrance.
● *Rosmarinus officinalis*, family Labiatae.
– ORIGIN Middle English *rosmarine*, based on Latin *ros marinus*, from *ros* 'dew' + *marinus* 'of the sea'. The spelling change was due to association with ROSE¹ and MARY¹.

rose of Jericho ▶ noun an annual desert plant whose dead branches fold inwards around the mature seeds forming a ball which is blown about, native to North Africa and the Middle East.
● *Anastatica hierochuntica*, family Cruciferae.

rose of Sharon ▶ noun a low shrub with dense foliage and large golden-yellow flowers, native to SE Europe and Asia Minor and widely cultivated for ground cover.
● *Hypericum calycinum*, family Guttiferae.
■(in biblical use) a flowering plant of unknown identity.

roseola /rə(ʊ)ˈziːələ/ ▶ noun [mass noun] Medicine a rose-coloured rash occurring in measles, typhoid fever, syphilis, and some other diseases.
■(in full **roseola infantum** /ɪnˈfantəm/) a disease of young children in which a fever is followed by a rash, caused by a herpesvirus.
– ORIGIN early 19th cent.: modern variant of RUBEOLA, from Latin *roseus* 'rose-coloured'.

rose-point ▶ noun [mass noun] point lace with a design of roses.

rose quartz ▶ noun [mass noun] a translucent pink variety of quartz.

roseroot ▶ noun a yellow-flowered stonecrop whose roots smell of roses when dried or bruised, native to north temperate regions.
● *Rhodiola rosea*, family Crassulaceae.

Roses, Wars of the see WARS OF THE ROSES.

Rose Theatre a theatre in Southwark, London, built in 1587. Many of Shakespeare's plays were performed there, some for the first time. Remains of the theatre, which was demolished *c.*1605, were uncovered in 1989.

rose-tinted ▶ adjective another term for ROSE-COLOURED.

Rosetta Stone /rəˈzɛtə/ an inscribed stone found near Rosetta on the western mouth of the Nile in 1799. Its text is written in three scripts: hieroglyphic, demotic, and Greek. The deciphering of the hieroglyphs by Jean-François Champollion in 1822 led to the interpretation of many other early records of Egyptian civilization.
■[as noun **a Rosetta stone**] a key to some previously undecipherable mystery or unattainable understanding: *zero point energy could be the Rosetta stone of physics*.

rosette ▶ noun **1** a rose-shaped decoration, typically made of ribbon, that is worn by supporters of a sports team or political party or awarded to winners of a competition.
2 a design, arrangement, or growth resembling a rose, in particular:
■Architecture a carved or moulded ornament resembling or representing a rose. ■ Biology a marking or group of markings resembling a rose. ■ a rose-like cluster of parts, especially a radiating arrangement of horizontally spreading leaves at the base of a low-growing plant. ■ a rose diamond.
– DERIVATIVES **rosetted** adjective.
– ORIGIN mid 18th cent.: from French, diminutive of *rose* (see ROSE¹).

rose water ▶ noun [mass noun] scented water made with rose petals, used as a perfume and formerly for medicinal and culinary purposes.

rose window ▶ noun a circular window with mullions or tracery radiating in a form suggestive of a rose.

rosewood ▶ noun **1** [mass noun] fragrant close-grained tropical timber with a distinctive fragrance, used particularly for making furniture and musical instruments.
2 the tree which produces this timber.
● Genus *Dalbergia*, family Leguminosae: several species, in particular *D. nigra* of Brazil.
■used in names of other trees which yield similar timber, e.g. **African rosewood**.

Rosh Hashana /ˌrɒʃ həˈʃɑːnə/ (also **Rosh Hashanah**) ▶ noun the Jewish New Year festival, held on the first (and sometimes the second) day of Tishri (in September). It is marked by the blowing of the shofar, and begins the ten days of penitence culminating in Yom Kippur.
– ORIGIN Hebrew, literally 'head (i.e. beginning) of the year'.

Roshi /ˈrəʊʃi/ ▶ noun (pl. **Roshis**) the spiritual leader of a community of Zen Buddhist monks.
– ORIGIN Japanese.

Rosicrucian /ˌrəʊzɪˈkruːʃ(ə)n/ ▶ noun a member of a secretive 17th- and 18th-century society devoted to the study of metaphysical, mystical, and alchemical lore. An anonymous pamphlet of 1614 about a mythical 15th-century knight called Christian Rosenkreuz is said to have launched the movement.
■a member of any of a number of later organizations deriving from this.
▶ adjective of or relating to the Rosicrucians.
– DERIVATIVES **Rosicrucianism** noun.
– ORIGIN from modern Latin *rosa crucis* (or *crux*), Latinization of German *Rosenkreuz*, + -IAN.

rosin /ˈrɒzɪn/ ▶ noun [mass noun] resin, especially the solid amber residue obtained after the distillation of crude turpentine oleoresin, or of naphtha extract from pine stumps. It is used in adhesives, varnishes, and inks and for treating the bows of stringed instruments.
▶ verb (**rosined**, **rosining**) [with obj.] rub (something, especially a violin bow or string) with rosin.
– DERIVATIVES **rosiny** adjective.

– ORIGIN Middle English: from medieval Latin *rosina*, from Latin *resina* (see RESIN).

Roskilde /ˈrɒskɪlə/ a port in Denmark, on the island of Zealand; pop. 49,080 (1990). It was the seat of Danish kings from *c.*1020 and the capital of Denmark until 1443.

rosolio /rə(ʊ)ˈzəʊlɪəʊ/ ▶ noun (pl. **-os**) [mass noun] a sweet cordial made in Italy from alcohol, raisins, sugar, rose petals, cloves, and cinnamon.
– ORIGIN Italian, from modern Latin *ros solis* 'dew of the sun'.

RoSPA /ˈrɒspə/ ▶ abbreviation for (in the UK) Royal Society for the Prevention of Accidents.

Ross¹, Diana (b.1944), American pop and soul singer. Originally the lead singer of the Supremes, she went on to become a successful solo artist. She received an Oscar for her role as Billie Holiday in the film *Lady Sings the Blues* (1973).

Ross², Sir James Clark (1800–62), British explorer. He discovered the north magnetic pole in 1831, and headed an expedition to the Antarctic from 1839 to 1843, in the course of which he discovered Ross Island, Ross Dependency, and the Ross Sea. He was the nephew of Sir John Ross.

Ross³, Sir John (1777–1856), British explorer. He led an expedition to Baffin Bay in 1818 and another in search of the North-West Passage between 1829 and 1833.

Ross⁴, Sir Ronald (1857–1932), British physician. Ross confirmed that the *Anopheles* mosquito transmitted malaria, and went on to elucidate the stages in the malarial parasite's life cycle. Nobel Prize for Physiology or Medicine (1902).

Ross and Cromarty a former county of northern Scotland, stretching from the Moray Firth to the North Minch. Since 1975 it has been part of Highland region.

Ross Dependency part of Antarctica administered by New Zealand, consisting of everything lying to the south of latitude 60° south between longitudes 150° and 160° west.
– ORIGIN named after J. C. Ross (see Ross²).

Rossellini /ˌrɒsəˈliːni/, Roberto (1906–77), Italian film director. He is known for his neo-realist films, particularly his quasi-documentary trilogy about the Second World War, *Open City* (1945).

Rossetti¹ /rəˈzɛti/, Christina (Georgina) (1830–94), English poet. She wrote much religious poetry (reflecting her High Anglican faith), love poetry, and children's verse. Notable works: *Goblin Market and Other Poems* (1862). She was the sister of Dante Gabriel Rossetti.

Rossetti² /rəˈzɛti/, Dante Gabriel (1828–82), English painter and poet; full name *Gabriel Charles Dante Rossetti*. A founder member of the Pre-Raphaelite brotherhood (1848), he is best known for his idealized images of women, including *Beata Beatrix* (*c.*1863) and *The Blessed Damozel* (1871–9). He was the brother of Christina Rossetti.

Rossini /rɒˈsiːni/, Gioacchino Antonio (1792–1868), Italian composer, one of the creators of Italian bel canto. He wrote over thirty operas, including *The Barber of Seville* (1816) and *William Tell* (1829).

Rosslare /rɒsˈlɛː/ a ferry port on the SE coast of the Republic of Ireland, in County Wexford.

Ross Sea a large arm of the Pacific forming a deep indentation in the coast of Antarctica.
– ORIGIN named after J. C. Ross (see Ross²).

Ross seal ▶ noun a small Antarctic seal with a short muzzle and large eyes, breeding on the pack ice.
● *Ommatophoca rossi*, family Phocidae.

Rostand /ˈrɒstɒ̃, French ʀɔstɑ̃/, Edmond (1868–1918), French dramatist and poet. He romanticized the life of the 17th-century soldier, duellist, and writer Cyrano de Bergerac in his poetic drama of that name (1897).

roster /ˈrɒstə, ˈrəʊst-/ ▶ noun a list or plan showing turns of duty or leave for individuals or groups in an organization: *next week's duty roster*.
■a list of members of a team or organization, in particular of sports players available for team selection.
▶ verb [with obj.] (usu. **be rostered**) place on or assign according to a duty roster: *the locomotive is rostered for service on Sunday*.
– ORIGIN early 18th cent. (originally denoting a list of duties and leave for military personnel): from

Dutch *rooster* 'list', earlier 'gridiron', from *roosten* 'to roast', with reference to its parallel lines.

Rostock /ˈrɒstɒk/ an industrial port on the Baltic coast of Germany; pop. 244,000 (1991).

Rostov /ˈrɒstɒv/ a port and industrial city in SW Russia, on the River Don near its point of entry into the Sea of Azov; pop. 1,025,000 (1990). The city is built around a fortress erected by the Turks in the 18th century. Full name **ROSTOV-ON-DON**.

rostra plural form of **ROSTRUM**.

rostral /ˈrɒstr(ə)l/ ▶ **adjective 1** Anatomy situated or occurring near the front end of the body, especially in the region of the nose and mouth or (in an embryo) near the hypophyseal region: *the rostral portion of the brain.*
2 Zoology of or on the rostrum: *in these snakes the rostral shield is enlarged and flattened.*
– DERIVATIVES **rostrally** adverb.
– ORIGIN early 19th cent.: from **ROSTRUM** + **-AL**.

rostrum /ˈrɒstrəm/ ▶ **noun** (pl. **rostra** /-trə/ or **rostrums**) **1** a raised platform on which a person stands to make a public speech, receive an award or medal, play music, or conduct an orchestra.
▪a similar platform for supporting a film or television camera.
2 chiefly Zoology a beak-like projection, especially a stiff snout or anterior prolongation of the head in an insect, crustacean, or cetacean.
– DERIVATIVES **rostrate** /-strət/ adjective (only in sense 2).
– ORIGIN mid 16th cent.: from Latin, literally 'beak' (from *rodere* 'gnaw'). The word was originally used (at first in the plural *rostra*) to denote part of the Forum in Rome, which was decorated with the beaks of captured galleys, and was used as a platform for public speakers.

Roswell /ˈrɒswɛl/ a town in New Mexico, the scene of a mysterious crash in July 1947. Controversy has surrounded claims by some investigators that the crashed object was a UFO.

rosy ▶ **adjective** (**rosier**, **rosiest**) **1** (especially of a person's skin) coloured like a pink or red rose, typically as an indication of health, youth, or embarrassment: *the memory had the power to make her cheeks turn rosy.*
2 promising or suggesting good fortune or happiness; hopeful: *the strategy has produced results beyond the most rosy forecasts.*
▪easy and pleasant: *life could never be rosy for them.*
– DERIVATIVES **rosily** adverb, **rosiness** noun.

rosy cross ▶ **noun** an equal-armed cross with a rose at its centre, the emblem of the Rosicrucians.

rosy finch ▶ **noun** a finch found in Asia and western North America, the male of which has pinkish underparts and rump.
• Genus *Leucosticte*, family Fringillidae: three species, in particular *L. arctoa*.

rosy pastor ▶ **noun** another term for **ROSE-COLOURED STARLING**.

rot ▶ **verb** (**rotted**, **rotting**) **1** [no obj.] (chiefly of animal or vegetable matter) decompose by the action of bacteria and fungi; decay: *the chalets were neglected and their woodwork was **rotting away**.*
▪[with obj.] cause to decay: *caries sets in at a weak point and spreads to rot the whole tooth.* ▪ figurative gradually deteriorate through lack of attention or opportunity: *he cannot understand the way the education system has been allowed to rot.*
2 [with obj.] Brit. informal, dated make fun of; tease: *has anybody been rotting you?*
▪[no obj.] talk or act without seriousness; joke.
▶ **noun** [mass noun] **1** the process of decaying: *the leaves were turning black with rot.*
▪rotten or decayed matter. ▪ (**the rot**) Brit. a process of deterioration; a decline in standards: *it was when they moved back to the family home that **the rot set in** | there is enough talent in the team to **stop the rot**.* ▪ [usu. with modifier] any of a number of fungal or bacterial diseases that cause tissue deterioration, especially in plants. ▪ (often **the rot**) liver rot in sheep.
2 informal nonsense; rubbish: *don't talk rot.*
▶ **exclamation** informal nonsense (used to express ridicule): *'Rot!' she said with caustic vehemence.*
– ORIGIN Old English *rotian* (verb), of Germanic origin; related to Dutch *rotten*; the noun (Middle English) may have come via Scandinavian.

rota ▶ **noun 1** chiefly Brit. a list showing when each of a number of people has to do a particular job: *a cleaning rota.* Compare with **ROSTER**.
2 (**the Rota**) the supreme ecclesiastical and secular court of the Roman Catholic Church.
– ORIGIN early 17th cent.: from Latin, literally 'wheel'.

rotamer /ˈrəʊtəmə/ ▶ **noun** Chemistry any of a number of isomers of a molecule which can be interconverted by rotation of part of the molecule about a particular bond.
– ORIGIN 1960s: from *rotational* (see **ROTATION**) + **-MER**.

Rotary (in full **Rotary International**) a worldwide charitable society of businessmen and women and professional people, formed in 1905.
– DERIVATIVES **Rotarian** noun & adjective.
– ORIGIN so named because members hosted events in rotation.

rotary ▶ **adjective** (of motion) revolving around a centre or axis; rotational: *a rotary motion.*
▪(of a thing) acting by means of rotation, especially (of a machine) operating through the rotation of some part: *a rotary mower.*
▶ **noun** (pl. **-ies**) **1** a rotary machine, engine, or device.
2 N. Amer. a traffic roundabout.
– ORIGIN mid 18th cent.: from medieval Latin *rotarius*, from *rota* 'wheel'.

Rotary club ▶ **noun** a local branch of Rotary.

rotary cutter ▶ **noun** a machine which produces veneer by rotating a log longitudinally against a blade.
– DERIVATIVES **rotary cutting** noun.

rotary engine ▶ **noun** an engine which produces rotary motion or which has a rotating part or parts, in particular:
▪an aircraft engine with a fixed crankshaft around which cylinders and propeller rotate. ▪ a Wankel engine.

rotary press ▶ **noun** a printing press that prints from a rotating cylindrical surface on to paper forced against it by another cylinder.

rotary wing ▶ **noun** [usu. as modifier] an aerofoil that rotates in an approximately horizontal plane, providing all or most of the lift in a helicopter or autogiro.

rotate /rə(ʊ)ˈteɪt/ ▶ **verb** [no obj.] move in a circle round an axis or centre: *the wheel continued to rotate* | [as adj. **rotating**] *a rotating drum.*
▪[with obj.] cause to move round an axis or in a circle: *the small directional side rockets rotated the craft.* ▪ pass to each member of a group in a regularly recurring order: *the job of chairing the meeting rotates.* ▪ [with obj.] grow (different crops) in succession on a particular piece of land to avoid exhausting the soil: *these crops were sometimes rotated with grass.* ▪ [with obj.] change the position of (tyres) on a motor vehicle to distribute wear.
– DERIVATIVES **rotatable** adjective, **rotative** /ˈrəʊtətɪv/ adjective, **rotatory** /ˈrəʊtət(ə)ri, -ˈteɪt(ə)ri/ adjective.
– ORIGIN late 17th cent.: from Latin *rotat-* 'turned in a circle', from the verb *rotare*, from *rota* 'wheel'.

rotation ▶ **noun** [mass noun] the action of rotating about an axis or centre: *the moon moves in the same direction as the earth's rotation* | [count noun] *several solar rotations.*
▪the passing of a privilege or responsibility from one member of a group to another in a regularly recurring succession: *it has become common for senior academics to act as heads of department **in rotation**.* ▪ (also **crop rotation**) the action or system of rotating crops. ▪ Forestry the cycle of planting, felling, and replanting. ▪ Mathematics the conceptual operation of turning a system about an axis. ▪ Mathematics another term for **CURL** (in sense 2).
– DERIVATIVES **rotational** adjective, **rotationally** adverb.
– ORIGIN mid 16th cent.: from Latin *rotatio(n-)*, from the verb *rotare* (see **ROTATE**).

rotator ▶ **noun** a thing which rotates or which causes something to rotate.
▪Anatomy a muscle whose contraction causes or assists in the rotation of a part of the body.

rotator cuff ▶ **noun** Anatomy, chiefly US a capsule with fused tendons that supports the arm at the shoulder joint.

rotavator /ˈrəʊtəveɪtə/ (also **rotovator**) ▶ **noun** trademark a machine with rotating blades for breaking up or tilling the soil.
– DERIVATIVES **rotavate** verb.
– ORIGIN 1930s: a blend of **ROTARY** + **CULTIVATOR**.

rotavirus /ˈrəʊtəˌvʌɪrəs/ ▶ **noun** Medicine any of a group of RNA viruses, some of which cause acute enteritis in humans.
– ORIGIN 1970s: modern Latin, from Latin *rota* 'wheel' + **VIRUS**.

ROTC ▶ **abbreviation for** (in the US) Reserve Officers' Training Corps.

rote ▶ **noun** [mass noun] mechanical or habitual repetition of something to be learned: *a poem learnt by rote in childhood* | [as modifier] ***rote learning**.*
– ORIGIN Middle English (also in the sense 'habit, custom'): of unknown origin.

rotenone /ˈrəʊtənəʊn/ ▶ **noun** [mass noun] Chemistry a toxic crystalline substance obtained from the roots of derris and related plants, widely used as an insecticide.
• A polycyclic ketone; chem. formula: $C_{23}H_{22}O_6$.
– ORIGIN 1920s: from Japanese *rotenon* (from *roten* 'derris') + **-ONE**.

rotgut ▶ **noun** informal poor-quality and potentially harmful alcoholic liquor.

Roth /rɒθ/, Philip (Milton) (b.1933), American novelist and short-story writer. He often writes about the complexity and diversity of contemporary American Jewish life. Notable works: *Portnoy's Complaint* (1969).

Rotherham /ˈrɒðərəm/ an industrial town in northern England, a unitary council formerly in Yorkshire; pop. 247,100 (1991).

Rothko /ˈrɒθkəʊ/, Mark (1903–70), American painter, born in Latvia; born *Marcus Rothkovich*. A leading figure in colour-field painting, he painted hazy and apparently floating rectangles of colour.

Rothschild /ˈrɒθsˌtʃʌɪld, ˈrɒθˌtʃʌɪld/, Meyer Amschel (1743–1812), German financier. He founded the Rothschild banking house in Frankfurt at the end of the 18th century.

roti /ˈrəʊti/ ▶ **noun** (pl. **rotis**) [mass noun] Indian bread, especially a flat round bread cooked on a griddle.
– ORIGIN from Hindi *roṭī*.

Rotifera /rəʊˈtɪf(ə)rə/ Zoology a small phylum of minute multicellular aquatic animals which have a characteristic wheel-like ciliated organ used in swimming and feeding.
– DERIVATIVES **rotifer** /ˈrəʊtɪfə/ noun.
– ORIGIN modern Latin (plural), from Latin *rota* 'wheel' + *ferre* 'to bear'.

rotisserie /rə(ʊ)ˈtɪs(ə)ri/ ▶ **noun 1** a restaurant specializing in roasted or barbecued meat.
2 a cooking appliance with a rotating spit for roasting and barbecuing meat.
– ORIGIN mid 19th cent.: from French *rôtisserie*, from *rôtir* 'to roast'.

rotogravure /ˌrəʊtə(ʊ)grəˈvjʊə/ ▶ **noun** [mass noun] a printing system using a rotary press with intaglio cylinders, typically running at high speed and used for long print runs of magazines and stamps.
▪[count noun] chiefly N. Amer. a sheet or magazine printed with this system, especially the colour magazine of a Sunday newspaper.
– ORIGIN early 20th cent.: from German *Rotogravur*, part of the name of a printing company.

rotor ▶ **noun** a rotary part of a machine or vehicle, in particular:
▪a hub with a number of radiating aerofoils that is rotated in an approximately horizontal plane to provide the lift for a rotary wing aircraft. ▪ the rotating assembly in a turbine, especially a wind turbine. ▪ the armature of an electric motor. ▪ (also **rotor arm**) the rotating part of the distributor of an internal-combustion engine which successively makes and breaks electrical contacts so that each spark plug fires in turn. ▪ the rotating container in a centrifuge. ▪ the rotary winder of a clockwork watch. ▪ Meteorology a large eddy in which the air circulates about a horizontal axis, especially in the lee of a mountain.
– ORIGIN early 20th cent.: formed irregularly from **ROTATOR**.

rotorcraft ▶ **noun** (pl. same) a rotary wing aircraft, such as a helicopter or autogiro.

Rotorua /ˌrəʊtəˈruːə/ a city and health resort on North Island, New Zealand, on the south-west shore of Lake Rotorua; pop. 53,700 (1991). It lies at the centre of a region of thermal springs and geysers.

rotoscope ▶ **noun** a device which projects and enlarges individual frames of filmed live action to permit them to be used to create cartoon animation and composite film sequences.

▪a computer application which combines live action and other images in a film.
▶**verb** [with obj.] transfer (an image from live action film) into another film sequence using a rotoscope.
– ORIGIN 1950s: origin obscure; perhaps the same word as 19th-cent. *rotascope*, denoting a kind of gyroscope.

rototiller /ˈrəʊtə(ʊ),tɪlə/ ▶**noun** trademark North American term for **ROTAVATOR**.
– DERIVATIVES **rototill** verb.

rotovator (also **Rotovator**) ▶**noun** variant spelling of **ROTAVATOR**.

rotten ▶**adjective** (**rottener**, **rottenest**) suffering from decay: *rotten eggs* | *the supporting beams were rotten.*
▪morally, socially, or politically corrupt: *he believed that the whole art business was rotten.* ▪ informal very bad: *she was a rotten cook.* ▪ informal extremely unpleasant: *it's rotten for you having to cope on your own.* ▪ [predic.] informal unwell: *she tried to tell me she felt rotten.*
▶**adverb** informal to an extreme degree; very much: *your mother said that I* ***spoiled*** *you* ***rotten*** | *we used to send him up* ***something rotten.***
– DERIVATIVES **rottenly** adverb, **rottenness** noun.
– ORIGIN Middle English: from Old Norse *rotinn*.

rotten borough ▶**noun** Brit. historical a borough that was able to elect an MP though having very few voters, the choice of MP typically being in the hands of one person or family.
– ORIGIN so named because the borough was found to have 'decayed' to the point of no longer having a constituency.

rottenstone ▶**noun** [mass noun] decomposed siliceous limestone used as a powder or paste for polishing metals.

rotter ▶**noun** informal, dated, chiefly Brit. a cruel, mean, or unkind person: *'You rotter!' I laughed.*

Rotterdam /ˈrɒtədam/ a city in the Netherlands, at the mouth of the River Meuse, 25 km (15 miles) inland from the North Sea; pop. 582,270 (1991). It is one of the world's largest ports and a major oil refinery, with extensive shipbuilding and petrochemical industries.

Rottweiler /ˈrɒtvʌɪlə, -wʌɪlə/ ▶**noun** a large powerful dog of a tall black-and-tan breed.
– ORIGIN early 20th cent.: German, from *Rottweil*, the name of a town in SW Germany.

rotund /rə(ʊ)ˈtʌnd/ ▶**adjective** (of a person) large and plump.
▪round or spherical: *huge stoves held great rotund cauldrons.* ▪ figurative (of speech or literary style) indulging in grandiloquent expression.
– DERIVATIVES **rotundity** noun, **rotundly** adverb.
– ORIGIN late 15th cent.: from Latin *rotundus*, from *rotare* 'rotate'.

rotunda ▶**noun** a round building or room, especially one with a dome.
– ORIGIN early 17th cent.: alteration of Italian *rotonda (camera)* 'round (chamber)', feminine of *rotondo* 'round' (see **ROTUND**).

Rouault /ˈruːəʊ, French rwo/, Georges (Henri) (1871–1958), French painter and engraver. Associated with expressionism, he used vivid colours and simplified forms enclosed in thick black outlines.

rouble /ˈruːb(ə)l/ (also **ruble**) ▶**noun** the basic monetary unit of Russia and some other former republics of the USSR, equal to 100 kopeks.
– ORIGIN via French from Russian *rubl'*.

roucou /ruːˈkuː/ (also **rookoo**) ▶**noun** West Indian term for **ANNATTO**.
– ORIGIN from Carib.

roué /ˈruːeɪ/ ▶**noun** a debauched man, especially an elderly one.
– ORIGIN early 19th cent.: French, literally 'broken on a wheel', referring to the instrument of torture thought to be deserved by such a person.

Rouen /ˈruːɒn, French rwɑ̃/ a port on the River Seine in NW France, chief town of Haute-Normandie; pop. 105,470 (1990). Rouen was in English possession from the time of the Norman Conquest until captured by the French in 1204, and again 1419–49; in 1431 Joan of Arc was tried and burnt at the stake there.

Rouen duck ▶**noun** a bird of a breed of large duck resembling the wild mallard in colouring.

rouge[1] /ruːʒ/ ▶**noun** [mass noun] a red powder or cream used as a cosmetic for colouring the cheeks or lips.
▪another term for **JEWELLER'S ROUGE**.
▶**verb** [with obj.] [often as adj. **rouged**] colour with rouge: *her brightly rouged cheeks.*
▪[no obj.] archaic apply rouge to one's cheeks.
– ORIGIN late Middle English (denoting the colour red): from French, 'red', from Latin *rubeus*. The cosmetic term dates from the mid 18th cent.

rouge[2] /ruː(d)ʒ/ ▶**noun** (in Canadian football) a single point awarded when the receiving team fails to run a kick out of its own end zone.
– ORIGIN late 19th cent.: of unknown origin.

rouget /ʀuʒɛ/ ▶**noun** French term for **RED MULLET**, used especially in cookery.
– ORIGIN French.

rough ▶**adjective 1** having an uneven or irregular surface; not smooth or level: *take a square of sandpaper, rough side out.*
▪(of ground or terrain) having many bumps or other obstacles; difficult to cross: *they had to carry the victim across the rough, stony ground.* ▪ not soft to the touch: *her skin felt dry and rough.* ▪ (of a voice) coming out with difficulty so as to sound harsh and rasping: *his voice was rough with barely suppressed fury.* ▪ (of wine or another alcoholic drink) sharp or harsh in taste. ▪ denoting the face of a tennis or squash racket on which the loops formed from the stringing process project (used as a call when the racket is spun to decide the right to serve first or to choose ends).
2 (of a person or their behaviour) not gentle; violent or boisterous: *pushchairs should be capable of withstanding rough treatment.*
▪(of an area or occasion) characterized by or notorious for the occurrence of violent behaviour: *the workmen hate going to the rough estates.* ▪ (of the sea) having large and dangerous waves: *the lifeboat crew braved rough seas to rescue a couple.* ▪ (of weather) wild and stormy. ▪ informal difficult and unpleasant: *the teachers gave me* ***a rough time*** *because my image didn't fit.* ▪ Brit. informal hard; severe: *the first day of a job is* ***rough on*** *everyone.* ▪ [as complement] informal unwell: *the altitude had hit her and she was feeling rough.* ▪ [as complement] informal depressed and anxious: *when he's feeling rough, he comes and talks things over to calm him down.*
3 not finished tidily or decoratively; plain and basic: *the customers sat at rough wooden tables.*
▪put together without the proper materials or skill; makeshift: *he had one arm in a rough sling.* ▪ (of hair or fur) not well cared for or tidy: *the creature's body was covered with rough hair.* ▪ lacking sophistication or refinement: *she took care of him in her rough, kindly way.* ▪ not worked out or correct in every detail: *he had a rough draft of his new novel.* ▪ (of stationery) used or designed to be used for making preliminary notes: *rough paper.*
▶**adverb** informal in a manner that lacks gentleness; harshly or violently: *treat 'em rough but treat 'em fair.*
▶**noun 1** chiefly Brit. a disreputable and violent person.
2 [mass noun] (on a golf course) longer grass around the fairway and the green: *his second shot was* ***in the rough*** *on the left.*
3 a preliminary sketch for a design: *I did a rough to work out the scale of the lettering.*
4 an uncut precious stone.
▶**verb** [with obj.] **1** work or shape (something) in a rough, preliminary fashion: *flat surfaces of wood are* ***roughed down.***
▪(**rough something out**) produce a preliminary and unfinished sketch or version of something: *the engineer roughed out a diagram on his notepad.* ▪ make uneven or ruffled: ***rough up*** *the icing with a palette knife* | *the water was roughed by the wind.*
2 (**rough it**) live in discomfort with only basic necessities: *she had had to rough it alone in digs.*
– PHRASES **bit of rough** informal a male sexual partner whose toughness or lack of sophistication is a source of attraction. **in the rough 1** in a natural state; without decoration or other treatment: *a diamond in the rough.* **2** in difficulties: *even before the recession hit, the project was in the rough.* **rough and ready** crude but effective: *a rough-and-ready estimating method.* ▪(of a person or place) unsophisticated or unrefined. **rough around the edges** having a few imperfections. **the rough edge** (or **side**) **of one's tongue** a scolding: *you two stop quarrelling or you'll get the rough edge of my tongue.* **rough edges** small imperfections in someone or something that is basically satisfactory. **rough justice** treatment that is not scrupulously fair or in accordance with the law. **rough passage** a journey over rough sea. ▪a difficult process of achieving something or of becoming successful: *the rough passage faced by the legislation.* **a rough ride** a difficult time or experience: *rebel shareholders are expected to give officials* ***a rough ride.*** **rough stuff** boisterous or violent behaviour. **sleep rough** Brit. sleep in uncomfortable conditions, typically out of doors. **take the rough with the smooth** accept the difficult or unpleasant aspects of life as well as the good.
– DERIVATIVES **roughish** adjective, **roughness** noun.
– ORIGIN Old English *rūh*, of West Germanic origin; related to Dutch *ruw* and German *rauh*.
▶**rough someone up** informal beat someone up.

roughage ▶**noun** [mass noun] fibrous indigestible material in vegetable foodstuffs which aids the passage of food and waste products through the gut.
▪Farming coarse, fibrous fodder.

rough and tumble ▶**noun** a situation without rules or organization; a free-for-all: *the rough and tumble of political life* | [as modifier] *the rough-and-tumble atmosphere of the dealing room.*
– ORIGIN early 19th cent.: originally boxing slang.

rough breathing ▶**noun** see **BREATHING** (sense 2).

roughcast ▶**noun** [mass noun] plaster of lime, cement, and gravel, used on outside walls.
▶**adjective 1** (of a building or part of a building) coated with roughcast: *a plain stone building, roughcast and whitewashed.*
2 (of a person) lacking refinement: *she thought of the roughcast yeomen she would meet.*
▶**verb** [with obj.] (usu. **be roughcast**) coat (a wall) with roughcast.

rough-coated ▶**adjective** (of a dog or other animal) having relatively coarse fur which does not lie flat: *a rough-coated Jack Russell.*

rough collie ▶**noun** a dog of a rough-coated breed of collie, typically black and white or black, white, and tan.

rough copy ▶**noun 1** a first draft of a piece of writing: *do a rough copy first.*
2 a copy of a picture showing only the essential features.

rough cut ▶**noun** the first version of a film after preliminary editing.
▶**verb** (**rough-cut**) [with obj.] cut (something) rapidly and without particular attention to quality or accuracy: *it would be best to rough-cut the boards to size with a portable saw.*

rough diamond ▶**noun** an uncut diamond.
▪a person who is generally of good character but lacks manners, education, or style.

rough-dry ▶**verb** [with obj.] dry (something) roughly or imperfectly: *she continued to rough-dry her hair.*

roughen ▶**verb** make or become rough: [with obj.] *the wind was roughening the surface of the river* | [no obj.] *his voice roughened.*

Rough Fell ▶**noun** a sheep of a large long-woolled breed found in the Pennine area of England.

rough grazing ▶**noun** [mass noun] uncultivated land used for grazing livestock.
▪[count noun] a piece of such land.

rough-hew ▶**verb** [with obj.] [usu. as adj. **rough-hewn**] shape (wood or stone) with a tool such as an axe without smoothing it off afterwards: *rough-hewn logs* | figurative *his broad, rough-hewn, Slavic features*
▪[as adj. **rough-hewn**] (of a person) uncultivated or uncouth.

rough hound ▶**noun** another term for **DOGFISH** (in sense 1).

rough house informal, chiefly US ▶**noun** a violent disturbance.
▶**verb** [no obj.] act in a boisterous, violent manner: *they rough-house on street corners.*
▪[with obj.] handle (someone) roughly or violently: *he had them rough-housed by his servants.*

roughie ▶**noun 1** dialect & Austral./NZ a hooligan.
▪Austral. an unfair or unreasonable act.
2 Austral. an outsider in a horse race.
3 variant spelling of **ROUGHY**.

roughing ▶**noun** [mass noun] Ice Hockey unnecessary or excessive use of force, for which a minor penalty may be assessed.

roughly ▶**adverb 1** in a manner lacking gentleness; harshly or violently: *the man picked me up roughly.*
2 in a manner lacking refinement and precision: *people were crouching over roughly built brick fireplaces.*
▪approximately: *this is a walk of roughly 13 miles* | [sentence adverb] *the narrative is,* ***roughly speaking,*** *contemporary with the earliest of the gospels.*

roughneck ▶ **noun** **1** informal a rough and uncouth person.
2 an oil rig worker.
▶ **verb** [no obj.] [usu. as noun **roughnecking**] work on an oil rig: *his savings from roughnecking are gone.*

rough-rider ▶ **noun** N. Amer. a person who rides horses a lot.
■ a person who breaks in or can ride unbroken horses.
■ (**Rough Rider**) a member of a volunteer cavalry force during the Spanish-American War.

roughshod ▶ **adjective** archaic (of a horse) having shoes with nail heads projecting to prevent slipping.
– PHRASES **ride roughshod over** see **RIDE**.

rough timber ▶ **noun** [mass noun] partly dressed timber, having only the branches removed.

rough tongue ▶ **noun** the habit of speaking rudely: *he was known as a jovial fellow but was not without a vicious temper and a rough tongue.*
– DERIVATIVES **rough-tongued** adjective.

rough trade ▶ **noun** [mass noun] informal male homosexual prostitution, especially when involving brutality or sadism.
■ people involved in prostitution of this type.

rough work ▶ **noun** [mass noun] **1** work done as a trial or as a basis for a final fair copy or finished product.
2 a task requiring physical effort and discomfort.

roughy /ˈrʌfi/ (also **roughie**) ▶ **noun** (pl. **-ies**) Austral.
1 a marine fish with a deep laterally compressed body and large rough-edged scales which become spiny on the belly.
• Family Trachichthyidae: several genera and species, including the small Australian *Trachichthys australis*, which occurs on rocky reefs.
2 another term for **RUFF**[2] (in sense 1).

rouille /ˈruːi/ ▶ **noun** [mass noun] a Provençal sauce made from pounded red chillies, garlic, breadcrumbs, and other ingredients blended with stock, typically added to bouillabaisse.
– ORIGIN French, literally 'rust', with reference to the colour.

roulade /ruːˈlɑːd/ ▶ **noun** **1** a dish cooked or served in the form of a roll, typically made from a flat piece of meat, fish, or sponge, spread with a soft filling and rolled up into a spiral.
2 a florid passage of runs in classical music for a solo virtuoso, especially one sung to one syllable.
– ORIGIN French, from *rouler* 'to roll'.

rouleau /ˈruːləʊ, ruːˈləʊ/ ▶ **noun** (pl. **rouleaux** or **rouleaus** /-əʊz/) **1** a cylindrical packet of coins.
2 a coil or roll of ribbon, knitted wool, or other material, especially used as trimming.
– ORIGIN late 17th cent.: French, from obsolete French *roule* 'a roll'.

roulement /ˈruːlmɒ̃/ ▶ **noun** [mass noun] Military movement of troops or equipment, especially for a short period of duty to relieve another force.
– ORIGIN early 20th cent.: French, literally 'rolling'.

Roulers /ʀulɛʀ/ French name for **ROESELARE**.

roulette ▶ **noun** **1** [mass noun] a gambling game in which a ball is dropped on to a revolving wheel with numbered compartments, the players betting on the number at which the ball comes to rest.
2 a tool or machine with a revolving toothed wheel, used in engraving or for making slit-shaped perforations between postage stamps.
▶ **verb** [with obj.] make slit-shaped perforations in (paper, especially sheets of postage stamps): *the pages are rouletted next to the binding.*
– ORIGIN mid 18th cent.: from French, diminutive of *rouelle* 'wheel', from late Latin *rotella*, diminutive of Latin *rota* 'wheel'.

Roumania /ruːˈmeɪnɪə/ old-fashioned variant of **ROMANIA**.

Roumanian /rʊˈmeɪnɪən/ ▶ **adjective** & **noun** old-fashioned variant of Romanian.

Roumelia variant spelling of **RUMELIA**.

round ▶ **adjective** **1** shaped like or approximately like a circle or cylinder: *she was seated at a small, round table.*
■ having a curved shape like part of the circumference of a circle: *round arches.* ■ (of a person's shoulders) bent forward from the line of the back.
2 shaped like or approximately like a sphere: *a round glass ball | the grapes are small and round.*
■ (of a person's body) plump. ■ having a curved surface with no sharp or jagged projections: *the boulders look round and smooth.* ■ figurative (of a voice) rich and mellow; not harsh.
3 [attrib.] (of a number) altered for convenience of expression or calculation, for example to the nearest whole number or multiple of ten or five: *the size of the fleet is given in round numbers.*
■ (of a number) convenient for calculation, typically through being a multiple of ten. ■ used to show that a figure has been completely and exactly reached: *the batsman made a round 100 | a round dozen.* ■ archaic (of a sum of money) considerable: *his business is worth a round sum to me.*
4 archaic (of a person or their manner of speaking) not omitting or disguising anything; frank and truthful: *she berated him in good round terms.*
▶ **noun** **1** a circular piece of a particular substance: *cut the pastry into rounds.*
■ a thick disc of beef cut from the haunch as a joint.
2 an act of visiting each of a number of people or places: *she **did the rounds of** her family to say goodbye | he **made the rounds of** the city's churches.*
■ a tour of inspection, typically repeated regularly, in which the safety or well-being of those visited is checked: *the doctor is just **making his rounds** in the wards.* ■ chiefly Brit. a journey along a fixed route delivering goods as part of one's job or a job involving such journeys: *I did a newspaper round.*
3 one of a sequence of sessions or groups of related actions or events, typically such that development or progress can be seen between one group and another: *the two sides held three rounds of talks.*
■ a division of a contest such as a boxing or wrestling match. ■ one of a succession of stages in a sporting contest or other competition, in each of which more candidates are eliminated: *the FA Cup first round.* ■ an act of playing all the holes in a golf course once: *Eileen enjoys the occasional **round of golf**.*
4 a regularly recurring sequence of activities or functions: *their lives were a **daily round** of housework and laundry.*
■ Music a song for three or more unaccompanied voices or parts, each singing the same theme but starting one after another, at the same pitch or in octaves; a simple canon. ■ a set of drinks bought for all the members of a group, typically as part of a sequence in which each member in turn buys such a set: *it's my round.*
5 a measured quantity or number of something, in particular:
■ Brit. a slice of bread: *two rounds of toast.* ■ Brit. the quantity of sandwiches made from two slices of bread. ■ the amount of ammunition needed to fire one shot. ■ Archery a fixed number of arrows shot from a fixed distance.
▶ **adverb** chiefly Brit. **1** with circular motion; so as to rotate or cause something to rotate: *she turned her glass **round and round**.*
■ so as to cover or take in the whole area surrounding a particular centre: *she paused to glance round admiringly at the décor.* ■ so as to reach everyone in a particular group or area: *he passed round a newspaper cutting.*
2 so as to rotate and face in the opposite direction: *he swung round to face her.*
■ so as to lead in another direction: *it was the last house before the road curved round.* ■ used in describing the position of something, typically with regard to the direction in which it is facing or its relation to other items. *the picture shows the pieces the wrong way round.*
■ used to describe a situation in terms of the relation between people, actions, or events: *it was he who was attacking her, not the other way round.*
3 so as to surround someone or something: *everyone crowded round | a pool with banks all the way round.*
■ figurative so as to give support and companionship: *if one girl is distraught the others will rally round.* ■ used in stating the girth of something: *the trunk is nine feet round.*
4 so as to reach a new place or position, typically by moving from one side of something to the other: *he made his way round to the back of the building | they went **the long way round** by the main road.*
■ used to convey an ability to navigate or orientate oneself: *I like pupils to **find** their own **way round**.*
■ informal used to convey the idea of visiting someone else: *why don't you come round to my flat?*
5 used to suggest idle and purposeless motion or activity: *he was driving round aimlessly.*
▶ **preposition** chiefly Brit. **1** on every side of (a focal point): *the area round the school | with shifting sands all round me.*
■ (of something abstract) having (the thing mentioned) as a focus: *the text is built round real practical examples.*
2 so as to encircle (someone or something), wholly or partially: *he wrapped the blanket round him.*
■ (of a person's arm or arms) partially encircling (another person) as part of a gesture of affection: *Angus put an arm round Flora and kissed her.*
3 following an approximately circular route past (a corner or obstacle): *a bus appeared round the corner.*
■ on the other side of (a corner or obstacle): *Steven parked the car round the corner.* ■ so as to hit (something) in passing: *if he didn't shut up he might get a clip round the ear.*
4 so as to cover or take in the whole area of (a place): *she went round the house and saw that all the windows were barred.*
▶ **verb** [with obj.] **1** pass and go round (something) so as to move on in a changed direction: *the ship rounded the cape and sailed north.*
2 alter (a number) to one less exact but more convenient for calculations: *we'll **round** the weight **up** to the nearest kilo | the committee **rounded down** the figure.*
3 give a round shape to: *a lathe that rounded chair legs.*
■ [no obj.] become circular in shape: *her eyes rounded in dismay.* ■ Phonetics pronounce (a vowel) with the lips narrowed and protruded.
– PHRASES **go the round** (or **rounds**) (of a story or joke) be passed on from person to person. **in the round 1** (of sculpture) standing free with all sides shown, rather than carved in relief against a ground. ■ figurative treated fully and thoroughly; with all aspects shown or considered: *to understand social phenomena one must see them in the round.* **2** (of a theatrical performance) with the audience placed on at least three sides of the stage. **round about 1** on all sides or in all directions; surrounding someone or something: *everything round about was covered with snow.* **2** at a point or time approximately equal to: *they arrived round about nine.* **round the bend** see **BEND**[1]. **round the twist** see **TWIST**.
– DERIVATIVES **roundish** adjective, **roundness** noun.
– ORIGIN Middle English: from the Old French stem *round-*, from a variant of Latin *rotundus* 'rotund'.

USAGE are **round** and **around** (as preposition and adverbial particle) interchangeable in all contexts? In many contexts in British English they are, as in *she put her arm **round** him*; *she put her arm **around** him.* There is, however, a general preference for **round** to be used for definite, specific movement (*she turned **round***; *a bus came **round** the corner*), while **around** tends to be used in contexts which are less definite (*she wandered **around** for ages*; *costing **around** £3,000*) or for abstract uses (*a rumour circulating **around** the cocktail bars*). In US English, the situation is different. The normal form in most contexts is **around**; **round** is generally regarded as informal or non-standard and is only standard in certain fixed expressions, as in *all year **round*** and *they went **round and round** in circles.*

▶ **round something off** make the edges or corners of something smooth: *round off the spars with a soft plastic fitting.* ■ complete something in a satisfying or suitable way: *a pint at the pub will round off the day nicely.*
round on make a sudden verbal attack on or unexpected retort to: *she rounded on me angrily.*
round something out make something more complete: *his father insisted he went to university to round out his education.*
round someone/thing up drive or collect a number of people or animals together for a particular purpose: *in the afternoon the cows are rounded up for milking.* ■ arrest a number of people.

roundabout ▶ **noun** **1** Brit. a road junction at which traffic moves in one direction round a central island to reach one of the roads converging on it.
2 Brit. a large revolving device in a playground, for children to ride on.
■ a merry-go-round.
▶ **adjective** not following a short direct route; circuitous: *we need to take a roundabout route to throw off any pursuit.*
■ not saying what is meant clearly and directly; circumlocutory: *in a roundabout way, he was fishing for information.*

round-arm ▶ **adjective** Cricket (of bowling) performed with an outward horizontal swing of the arm.

roundball ▶ **noun** US informal term for **BASKETBALL**.
– DERIVATIVES **roundballer** noun.

round brackets ▶ **plural noun** Brit. brackets of the form ( ).

round dance ▶ **noun** a folk dance in which the dancers form one large circle.
■ a ballroom dance such as a waltz or polka in which couples move in circles round the ballroom.

rounded ▶ **adjective 1** having a smooth, curved surface: *rounded grey hills.*
■ having a spherical shape: *its rounded, almost bulbous head.* ■ forming circular or elliptical shapes: *his writing was firm and rounded.* ■ Phonetics (of a vowel) pronounced with the lips narrowed and protruded.
2 well developed in all aspects; complete and balanced: *we should educate children to become rounded human beings.*

roundel /ˈraʊnd(ə)l/ ▶ **noun 1** a small disc, especially a decorative medallion.
■ a picture or pattern contained in a circle. ■ Heraldry a plain filled circle as a charge (often with a special name according to colour). ■ a circular identifying mark painted on military aircraft, as, for example, the red, white, and blue of the RAF.
2 a short poem consisting of three stanzas of three lines each, rhyming alternately, with the opening words repeated as a refrain after the first and third stanzas. The form, a variant of the rondeau, was developed by Swinburne.
– ORIGIN Middle English: from Old French *rondel*, from *ro(u)nd-* (see **ROUND**).

roundelay /ˈraʊndəleɪ/ ▶ **noun** poetic/literary a short simple song with a refrain.
■ a circle dance.
– ORIGIN late Middle English: from Old French *rondelet*, from *rondel* (see **RONDEL**). The change in the ending was due to association with the final syllable of **VIRELAY**.

rounder ▶ **noun** a complete run of a player through all the bases as a unit of scoring in rounders.

rounders ▶ **plural noun** [treated as sing.] a ball game played (chiefly in British schools) with a cylindrical wooden bat, in which players run round a circuit of bases after hitting the ball.

round game ▶ **noun** a game, typically a card game, for more than two players in which each player plays as an individual, not as part of a team.

round hand ▶ **noun** a style of handwriting in which the letters have clear rounded shapes.

Roundhead ▶ **noun** historical a member or supporter of the Parliamentary party in the English Civil War.
– ORIGIN so named because of the short-cropped hairstyle of the Puritans, who formed an important element in the party.

roundheel ▶ **noun** N. Amer. informal a promiscuous woman.
– DERIVATIVES **roundheeled** adjective.
– ORIGIN 1950s: with reference to worn-down heels, allowing the wearer to lean backwards.

roundhouse ▶ **noun 1** a railway locomotive maintenance shed built around a turntable.
2 informal a blow given with a wide sweep of the arm.
■ Baseball a slow, widely curving pitch. ■ a wide turn on a surfboard.
3 chiefly historical a cabin or set of cabins on the after part of the quarterdeck of a sailing ship.

roundhouse kick ▶ **noun** (chiefly in karate) a kick made with a wide sweep of the leg and rotation of the body.

roundly ▶ **adverb 1** in a vehement or emphatic manner: *the latest attacks have been roundly condemned by campaigners for peace.*
■ so thoroughly as to leave no doubt: *the army was roundly beaten.* ■ too plainly for politeness; bluntly: *she told him roundly to get to the point.*
2 so as to form a circular or roughly circular shape: *he was a middle-aged, roundly built man.*

round-nose ▶ **adjective 1** (of a tool) having the end rounded, so as to produce a rounded cut or surface or to prevent accidents or damage:
2 (of a bullet) having a rounded front end.
▶ **noun** a bullet with a rounded front end.
– DERIVATIVES **round-nosed** adjective.

round robin ▶ **noun 1** [often as modifier] a tournament in which each competitor plays in turn against every other: *a round-robin competition.*
2 a petition, especially one with signatures written in a circle to conceal the order of writing.

round shot ▶ **noun** [mass noun] historical ammunition in the form of cast-iron or steel spherical balls for firing from cannon.

round-shouldered ▶ **adjective** having the shoulders bent forward so that the back is rounded: *a round-shouldered slouch.*

roundsman ▶ **noun** (pl. **-men**) **1** Brit. a trader's employee who goes round delivering and taking orders: *a milk roundsman.*
2 US a police officer in charge of a patrol.
3 Austral. a journalist covering a specified subject.

Round Table ▶ **noun 1** the table at which King Arthur and his knights sat so that none should have precedence. It was first mentioned in 1155.
2 an international charitable association which holds discussions and undertakes community service, open to men between the ages of 18 and 40, typically from business and professional groups.
3 [often as modifier] (**round table**) an assembly for discussion, especially at a conference: *round-table talks.*

round trip ▶ **noun** a journey to one or more places and back again, especially by a route that does not cover the same ground twice.
■ [often as modifier] chiefly N. Amer. a journey to a place and back again, along the same route: *a round trip air fare.*

round turn ▶ **noun** a complete turn of a rope around another rope or an anchoring point.

round-up ▶ **noun** a systematic gathering together of people or things: *mass police round-ups and detentions.*
■ a summary of facts or events: *a news round-up every fifteen minutes.*

round window ▶ **noun** informal term for ***fenestra rotunda*** (see **FENESTRA**).

roundwood ▶ **noun** [mass noun] timber which is left as small logs, not sawn into planks or chopped for fuel, typically taken from near the tops of trees and used for furniture.

roundworm ▶ **noun** a nematode worm, especially a parasitic one found in the intestines of mammals.
● Many species in the class Phasmida, including the large *Ascaris lumbricoides* in humans.

roup[1] /raʊp/ chiefly Scottish & N. English ▶ **noun** an auction.
▶ **verb** [with obj.] (often **be rouped**) sell (something) by auction: *his effects were rouped.*
– ORIGIN Middle English (in the sense 'roar, croak'): of Scandinavian origin; compare with Old Norse *raupa* 'boast, brag'.

roup[2] /ruːp/ ▶ **noun** [mass noun] an infectious disease of poultry affecting the respiratory tract.
– DERIVATIVES **roupy** adjective.
– ORIGIN mid 16th cent.: of unknown origin.

rouse /raʊz/ ▶ **verb** [with obj.] bring out of sleep; awaken: *she was roused from a deep sleep by a hand on her shoulder.*
■ [no obj.] cease to sleep or to be inactive; wake up: *she roused, took off her eyepads, and looked around.* ■ startle out of inactivity; cause to become active: *once the enemy camp was roused, they would move on the castle | she'd just stay a few more minutes, then* ***rouse herself*** *and go back.* ■ startle (game) from a lair or cover. ■ cause to feel angry or excited: *the crowds were* ***roused to*** *fever pitch by the drama of the race.* ■ cause or give rise to (an emotion or feeling): *his evasiveness roused my curiosity.* ■ [with obj. and adverbial of direction] Nautical, archaic haul (something) vigorously in the specified direction: *rouse the cable out.* ■ stir (a liquid, especially beer while brewing): *rouse the beer as the hops are introduced.*
– DERIVATIVES **rousable** adjective, **rouser** noun.
– ORIGIN late Middle English (originally as a hawking and hunting term): probably from Anglo-Norman French, of unknown ultimate origin.

rouseabout ▶ **noun** Austral./NZ an unskilled labourer or odd jobber on a farm, especially in a shearing shed.
– ORIGIN mid 19th cent.: originally dialect in the sense 'rough bustling person', from the verb **ROUSE**.

rousette /rʊˈzɛt/ (also **rousette fruit bat**) ▶ **noun** a fruit bat that feeds mainly on nectar and pollen, forming very large colonies in caves from Africa to the Solomon Islands.
● Genus *Rousettus*, family Pteropodidae: several species.
– ORIGIN late 18th cent.: from French *roussette*, feminine of Old French *rousset* 'reddish', from *roux* 'red'.

rousing ▶ **adjective 1** exciting; stirring: *a rousing speech.*
2 archaic (of a fire) blazing strongly.
– DERIVATIVES **rousingly** adverb.

Rous sarcoma /raʊs/ ▶ **noun** a form of tumour, caused by an RNA virus, which affects birds, particularly poultry.
– ORIGIN early 20th cent.: named after Francis P. *Rous* (1879–1970), American physician.

Rousse variant spelling of **RUSE**.

Rousseau[1] /ˈruːsəʊ, French ruso/, Henri (Julien) (1844–1910), French painter; known as **le Douanier** ('customs officer'). After retiring as a customs official in 1893, he created bold and colourful paintings of fantastic dreams and exotic jungle landscapes, such as *Sleeping Gypsy* (1897) and *Tropical Storm with Tiger* (1891).

Rousseau[2] /ˈruːsəʊ, French ruso/, Jean-Jacques (1712–78), French philosopher and writer, born in Switzerland. He believed that civilization warps the fundamental goodness of human nature, but that the ill effects can be moderated by active participation in democratic consensual politics. Notable works: *Émile* (1762) and *The Social Contract* (1762).

Rousseau[3] /ˈruːsəʊ, French ruso/, (Pierre Étienne) Théodore (1812–67), French painter. A leading landscapist of the Barbizon School, his works typically depict the scenery and changing light effects of the forest of Fontainebleau, for example *Under the Birches, Evening* (1842–4).

Roussillon /ˈruːsɪjɒn, French rusijɔ̃/ a former province of southern France, on the border with Spain in the eastern Pyrenees, now part of Languedoc-Roussillon. Part of Spain until 1659, Roussillon retains many of its Spanish characteristics and traditions and Catalan is widely spoken.

roust /raʊst/ ▶ **verb** [with obj.] cause to get up or start moving; rouse: *I rousted him out of his bed with a cup of tea.*
■ N. Amer. informal treat roughly; harass: *the detectives who had rousted him the night of the murder.*
– ORIGIN mid 17th cent.: perhaps an alteration of **ROUSE**.

roustabout /ˈraʊstəbaʊt/ ▶ **noun** an unskilled or casual labourer.
■ a labourer on an oil rig. ■ N. Amer. a dock labourer or deckhand. ■ N. Amer. a circus labourer. ■ Austral. variant spelling of **ROUSEABOUT**.
– ORIGIN mid 19th cent.: from the verb **ROUST**.

rout[1] /raʊt/ ▶ **noun 1** a disorderly retreat of defeated troops: *the retreat degenerated into a rout* | [mass noun] *the army was in a state of demoralization verging on rout.*
■ a decisive defeat: *the party lost more than half their seats in the rout.*
2 Law, dated an assembly of people who have made a move towards committing an illegal act which would constitute an offence of riot.
■ archaic a disorderly or tumultuous crowd of people: *a rout of strangers ought not to be admitted.*
3 Brit. archaic a large evening party or reception.
▶ **verb** [with obj.] defeat and cause to retreat in disorder: *in a matter of minutes the attackers were routed.*
– PHRASES **put to rout** put to flight; defeat utterly: *I once put a gang to rout.*
– ORIGIN Middle English: ultimately based on Latin *ruptus* 'broken', from the verb *rumpere*; sense 1 and the verb (late 16th cent.) are from obsolete French *route*, probably from Italian *rotta* 'break-up of an army'; the other senses are via Anglo-Norman French *rute*.

rout[2] /raʊt/ ▶ **verb 1** [with obj.] cut a groove, or any pattern not extending to the edges, in (a wooden or metal surface): *you routed each plank all along its length.*
2 another term for **ROOT**[2].
■ find (someone or something), or force them from a place: *Simon routed him from the stable.*
– ORIGIN mid 16th cent. (in sense 2): alteration of the verb **ROOT**[2]. Sense 1 dates from the early 19th cent.

route /ruːt/ ▶ **noun** a way or course taken in getting from a starting point to a destination: *our route was via the Jerusalem road.*
■ the line of a road, path, railway, etc. ■ N. Amer. a round travelled in delivering, selling, or collecting goods. ■ a method or process leading to a specified result: *the many routes to a healthier diet will be described.*
▶ **verb** (**routeing** or **routing**) [with obj. and adverbial of direction] send or direct along a specified course: *all lines of communication were routed through London.*
– ORIGIN Middle English: from Old French *rute* 'road', from Latin *rupta* (*via*) 'broken (way)', feminine past participle of *rumpere*.

route man ▶**noun** North American term for **ROUNDSMAN** (in sense 1).

route march ▶**noun** a march for troops over a designated route, typically via roads or tracks.

Route One ▶**noun** [mass noun] Soccer, Brit. the use of a long kick upfield as an attacking tactic.
– ORIGIN from a phrase used in the 1960s television quiz show *Quizball*, in which questions (graded in difficulty) led to scoring a goal, *Route One* being the direct path.

router[1] /ˈraʊtə/ ▶**noun** a power tool with a shaped cutter, used in carpentry for making grooves for joints, decorative mouldings, etc.

router[2] /ˈruːtə/ ▶**noun** a device which forwards data packets to the appropriate parts of a computer network.

routier /ˈruːtɪeɪ, French rutje/ ▶**noun** (pl. pronounced same) **1** a member of a band of mercenaries in France in the late medieval period.
2 (in France) a long-distance lorry driver.
– ORIGIN French, from *route* 'road'.

routine ▶**noun** a sequence of actions regularly followed; a fixed programme: *I settled down into a routine of work and sleep* | [mass noun] *as a matter of routine a report will be sent to the director.*
■a set sequence in a performance such as a dance or comedy act: *he was trying to persuade her to have a tap routine in the play.* ■Computing a sequence of instructions for performing a task that forms a program or a distinct part of one.
▶**adjective** performed as part of a regular procedure rather than for a special reason: *the Ministry insisted that this was just a routine annual drill.*
▶**verb** [with obj.] rare organize according to a routine: *all had been routined with smoothness.*
– DERIVATIVES **routinely** adverb.
– ORIGIN late 17th cent. (denoting a regular course or procedure): from French, from *route* 'road' (see **ROUTE**).

routinism ▶**noun** [mass noun] archaic the prevalence or domination of routine.
– DERIVATIVES **routinist** noun & adjective.

routinize (also **-ise**) ▶**verb** [with obj.] (usu. **be routinized**) make (something) into a matter of routine; subject to a routine: *communication was routinized to ensure consistency of information.*
– DERIVATIVES **routinization** noun.

roux /ruː/ ▶**noun** (pl. same) Cookery a mixture of fat (especially butter) and flour used in making sauces.
– ORIGIN from French (*beurre*) *roux* 'browned (butter)'.

ROV ▶**abbreviation for** remotely operated vehicle.

Rovaniemi /ˈrəʊvəˌniəmi/ the principal town of Finnish Lapland; pop. 33,500 (1990).

rove[1] ▶**verb** [no obj., with adverbial of direction] travel constantly without a fixed destination; wander: *a quarter of a million refugees roved around the country.*
■[with obj.] wander over or through in such a way: *children roving the streets.* ■[usu. as adj. **roving**] travel for one's work, having no fixed base: *he trained as a roving reporter.* ■(of eyes) look in changing directions in order to see something thoroughly: *the policeman's eyes roved around the pub.*
▶**noun** [in sing.] chiefly US a journey, especially one with no specific destination; an act of wandering: *a new exhibit will electrify campuses on its national rove.*
– ORIGIN late 15th cent. (originally a term in archery in the sense 'shoot at a casual mark of undetermined range'): perhaps from dialect *rave* 'to stray', probably of Scandinavian origin.

rove[2] past of **REEVE**[2].

rove[3] ▶**noun** a sliver of cotton, wool, or other fibre, drawn out and slightly twisted, especially preparatory to spinning.
▶**verb** [with obj.] form (slivers of wool, cotton, or other fibre) into roves.
– ORIGIN late 18th cent.: of unknown origin.

rove[4] ▶**noun** a small metal plate or ring for a rivet to pass through and be clenched over, especially in boatbuilding.
– ORIGIN Middle English: from Old Norse *ró*, with the addition of parasitic *-v-*.

rove beetle ▶**noun** a long-bodied beetle with very short wing cases, typically found among decaying matter where it may scavenge or prey on other scavengers.
• Family Staphylinidae: numerous genera.

rover[1] ▶**noun 1** a person who spends their time wandering: *they became rovers who departed further and further from civilization.*
2 (in various sports) a player not restricted to a particular position on the field.
■Australian Rules one of the three players making up a ruck, typically one who is small, fast, and skilful at receiving the ball.
3 a vehicle for driving over rough terrain, especially one driven by remote control over extraterrestrial terrain.
4 Croquet a ball that has passed all the hoops but not pegged out.
■a player who has such a ball.
5 Archery a mark for long-distance shooting.
■a mark chosen at random and not at a determined range.
6 (**Rover** or **Rover Scout**) Brit. former term for **VENTURE SCOUT**.

rover[2] ▶**noun** archaic a sea robber; a pirate.
– ORIGIN Middle English: from Middle Low German, Middle Dutch *rōver*, from *rōven* 'rob'; related to **REAVE**.

rover[3] ▶**noun** a person or machine that makes roves of fibre (see **ROVE**[3]).

rover ticket ▶**noun** Brit. a ticket permitting unlimited travel on buses, trains, or other public transport in an area for a specified period.

roving ▶**noun** another term for **ROVE**[3].
■[mass noun] roves collectively.

roving commission ▶**noun** Brit. an authorization given to someone conducting an inquiry to travel as is necessary.

roving eye ▶**noun** [usu. in sing.] a tendency to flirt or be constantly looking to start a new sexual relationship: *if his wife wasn't around, he had a roving eye.*

Rovno /ˈrovnə/ Russian name for **RIVNE**.

row[1] /rəʊ/ ▶**noun** a number of people or things in a more or less straight line: *her villa stood in a row of similar ones.*
■a line of seats in a theatre: *they sat in the front row.* ■[often in place names] a street with a continuous line of houses along one or both of its sides: *he lives at 23 Saville Row.* ■a horizontal line of entries in a table. ■a complete line of stitches in knitting or crochet.
– PHRASES **a hard** (or **tough**) **row to hoe** a difficult task. **in a row** forming a line: *four chairs were set in a row.* ■informal in succession: *he jumped nineteen clear rounds in a row.*
– ORIGIN Old English *rāw*, of Germanic origin; related to Dutch *rij* and German *Reihe*.

row[2] /rəʊ/ ▶**verb** [with obj.] propel (a boat) with oars: *out in the bay a small figure was rowing a rubber dinghy.*
■[no obj., with adverbial of direction] travel by propelling a boat in this way: *we rowed down the river all day.* ■convey (a passenger) in a boat by propelling it with oars: *her father was rowing her across the lake.* ■[no obj.] engage in the sport of rowing, especially competitively: *he rowed for England* | [with complement] *he rowed stroke in the University Eight.*
▶**noun** [in sing.] a spell of rowing.
– DERIVATIVES **rower** noun.
– ORIGIN Old English *rōwan*, of Germanic origin; related to **RUDDER**; from an Indo-European root shared by Latin *remus* 'oar', Greek *eretmon* 'oar'.
▶**row someone down** overtake a team in a rowing race, especially a bumping race.
row someone out (usu. **be rowed out**) exhaust someone by rowing.
row over complete the course of a boat race with little effort, owing to the absence or inferiority of competitors.

row[3] /raʊ/ informal ▶**noun** chiefly Brit. a noisy acrimonious quarrel: *they had a row and she stormed out of the house.*
■a serious dispute: *the director is at the centre of a row over policy decisions.* ■a loud noise or uproar: *if he's at home he must have heard that row.* ■Brit. a severe reprimand: *I always got a row if I left food on my plate.*
▶**verb** [no obj.] have a quarrel: *they rowed about who would receive the money from the sale* | *she had rowed with her boyfriend the day before.*
■[with obj.] Brit. rebuke severely: *she was rowed for leaving her younger brother alone.*
– PHRASES **make** (or **kick up**) **a row** chiefly Brit. make a noise or commotion. ■make a vigorous protest.
– ORIGIN mid 18th cent.: of unknown origin.

rowan /ˈrəʊən, ˈraʊən/ (also **rowan tree**) ▶**noun** a small deciduous tree of the rose family, with compound leaves, white flowers, and red berries. Compare with **MOUNTAIN ASH**.
• Genus *Sorbus*, family Rosaceae: several species, in particular the European *S. aucuparia*, which is associated with much folklore.
– ORIGIN late 15th cent. (originally Scots and northern English): of Scandinavian origin; compare with Norwegian *rogn*.

rowboat ▶**noun** North American term for **ROWING BOAT**.

rowdy ▶**adjective** (**rowdier**, **rowdiest**) noisy and disorderly: *it was a rowdy but good-natured crowd.*
▶**noun** (pl. **-ies**) a noisy and disorderly person.
– DERIVATIVES **rowdily** adverb, **rowdiness** noun, **rowdyism** noun.
– ORIGIN early 19th cent. (originally US in the sense 'lawless backwoodsman'): of unknown origin.

Rowe, Nicholas (1674–1718), English dramatist. Notable works: *Tamerlane* (1701) and *The Fair Penitent* (1703).

rowel /ˈraʊ(ə)l/ ▶**noun** a spiked revolving disc at the end of a spur.
▶**verb** (**rowelled**, **rowelling**; US **roweled**, **roweling**) [with obj.] use a rowel to urge on (a horse): *he rowelled his horse on as fast as he could.*
– ORIGIN Middle English: from Old French *roel(e)*, from late Latin *rotella*, diminutive of Latin *rota* 'wheel'.

rowen /ˈraʊən/ ▶**noun** US a second growth of grass or hay in one season.
– ORIGIN Middle English: from an Old Northern French variant of Old French *regain* 'an increase'.

row house ▶**noun** N. Amer. a terrace house.

rowing ▶**noun** [mass noun] the sport or pastime of propelling a boat by means of oars.

> Racing takes place in narrow, light boats (**shells**), between single rowers (**scullers**) with two oars, or between crews of two, four, or eight people with one oar each; crews are often steered by a coxswain.

rowing boat ▶**noun** Brit. a small boat propelled by use of oars.

rowing machine ▶**noun** an exercise machine with oars and a sliding seat, for exercising the muscles used in rowing.

Rowlandson /ˈrəʊlən(d)s(ə)n/, Thomas (1756–1827), English painter, draughtsman, and caricaturist. Some of his watercolours and drawings feature in a series of books known as *The Tours of Dr Syntax* (1812–21).

rowlock /ˈrɒlək, ˈrʌlək/ ▶**noun** a fitting on the gunwale of a boat which serves as a fulcrum for an oar and keeps it in place.
– ORIGIN mid 18th cent.: alteration of **OARLOCK**, influenced by the verb **ROW**[2].

Rowntree /ˈraʊntriː/, a family of English business entrepreneurs and philanthropists. **Joseph** (1801–59) was a grocer who established several Quaker schools. His son **Henry Isaac** (1838–83) founded the family cocoa and chocolate manufacturing firm in York, while his brother **Joseph** (1836–1925) became Henry's business partner in 1869 and founded three Rowntree trusts (1904) to support research into social welfare and policy.

row vector ▶**noun** Mathematics a vector represented by a matrix consisting of a single row of elements.

Roxburghshire /ˈrɒksb(ə)rəʃɪə, -ʃə/ a former county of the Scottish Borders. Since 1975 it has been part of Borders region (now Scottish Borders).

royal ▶**adjective** having the status of a king or queen or a member of their family: *contributors included members of the royal family.*
■belonging to or carried out or exercised by a king or queen: *the royal palace* | *the coalition obtained royal approval for the appointment.* ■[attrib.] in the service or under the patronage of a king or queen: *a royal maid.* ■[attrib.] of a quality or size suitable for a king or queen; splendid: *a royal fortune.*
▶**noun 1** informal a member of the royal family.
2 short for **ROYAL SAIL** or **ROYAL MAST**.
3 short for **ROYAL STAG**.
4 (in full **metric royal**) [mass noun] a paper size, 636 × 480 mm.
■(in full **royal octavo**) a book size, 234 × 156 mm. ■(in full **royal quarto**) a book size, 312 × 237 mm.
5 Bell-ringing a system of change-ringing using ten bells.
– PHRASES **royal road to** a way of attaining or reaching something without trouble: *there is no royal road to teaching.*

– DERIVATIVES **royally** adverb.
– ORIGIN late Middle English: from Old French *roial*, from Latin *regalis* 'regal'.

Royal Academy of Arts (also **Royal Academy**) an institution established in London in 1768, whose purpose was to cultivate painting, sculpture, and architecture in Britain. Sir Joshua Reynolds was its first president and he instituted a highly influential series of annual lectures.

Royal Air Force (abbrev.: **RAF**) the British air force, formed in 1918 by amalgamation of the Royal Flying Corps (founded 1912) and the Royal Naval Air Service (founded 1914).

royal antelope ▶ noun a shy West African antelope with an arched back, short neck, and a red and brown coat with white underparts. It is the smallest known antelope.
● *Neotragus pygmaeus*, family Bovidae.

royal assent ▶ noun [mass noun] assent of the sovereign to a Bill which has been passed by Parliament, and which thus becomes an Act of Parliament. Royal assent by the sovereign (in person or through commissioners of the Crown) is required before a Bill (or a Measure passed by the General Synod of the Church of England) can come into force as law, but it has not been withheld since 1707.

royal blue ▶ noun [mass noun] a deep, vivid blue.

Royal British Legion (in the UK) an association for the charitable support of ex-servicemen and -women and their immediate dependants, formed in 1921.

royal burgh ▶ noun historical (in Scotland) a burgh holding a charter from the Crown.

Royal Canadian Mounted Police the national police force of Canada, founded in 1873 as the North West Mounted Police. A member of the force is informally called a **MOUNTIE**.

Royal Commission ▶ noun (in the UK) a commission of inquiry appointed by the Crown on the recommendation of the government.

royal demesne ▶ noun chiefly historical an area of land owned by the Crown.

royal duke ▶ noun a duke who is also a royal prince.

Royal Engineers the field engineering and construction corps of the British army.

royal fern ▶ noun a large pale green fern which has very long spreading fronds with widely spaced oblong lobes, occurring worldwide in wet habitats.
● *Osmunda regalis*, family Osmundaceae.

royal fish ▶ noun a whale, porpoise, or sturgeon caught near the British coast or cast ashore there. In these circumstances they belong to the Crown or, in the Duchy of Cornwall, to the Prince of Wales.

royal flush ▶ noun Poker a straight flush including ace, king, queen, jack, and ten all in the same suit, which is the hand of the highest possible value when wild cards are not in use.

Royal Gala ▶ noun a New Zealand dessert apple of a variety with red and yellow skin.
– ORIGIN 1960s: originally *Gala*, but renamed following a visit by Queen Elizabeth II, who was impressed by this variety.

Royal Greenwich Observatory the official astronomical institution of Great Britain. It was founded at Greenwich in London in 1675 by Charles II, and the old buildings now form part of the National Maritime Museum. The Observatory headquarters were moved to East Sussex in 1948 and to Cambridge in 1990.

royal icing ▶ noun [mass noun] chiefly Brit. hard white icing made from icing sugar and egg whites, typically used to decorate fruit cakes.

Royal Institution a British society founded in 1799 for the diffusion of scientific knowledge. It organizes educational events, promotes research, and maintains a museum, library, and information service.

royalist ▶ noun a person who supports the principle of monarchy or a particular monarchy.
■ a supporter of the King against Parliament in the English Civil War. ■ US a supporter of the British during the War of American Independence; a Tory.
▶ adjective giving support to the monarchy: *the paper claims to be royalist.*

■ (in the English Civil War) supporting the King against Parliament: *the royalist army.*
– DERIVATIVES **royalism** noun.

royal jelly ▶ noun [mass noun] a substance secreted by honeybee workers and fed by them to larvae which are being raised as potential queen bees.

Royal Leamington Spa official name for **LEAMINGTON SPA**.

Royal Marines a British armed service (part of the Royal Navy) founded in 1664, trained for service at sea, or on land under specific circumstances.

royal mast ▶ noun a section of a sailing ship's mast above the topgallant.

Royal Maundy ▶ noun see **MAUNDY**.

Royal Mint the establishment responsible for the manufacture of British coins. Set up in 1810 in London, it moved in 1968 to Llantrisant in South Wales.

Royal National Lifeboat Institution (abbrev.: **RNLI**) (in the UK) a voluntary organization formed in 1824 to operate an offshore rescue service with lifeboats.

Royal Navy (abbrev.: **RN**) the British navy. It was the most powerful navy in the world from the 17th century until the Second World War.

royal oak ▶ noun a sprig of oak worn on 29 May to commemorate the restoration of Charles II (1660), who hid in an oak after the battle of Worcester (1651).

royal palm ▶ noun a New World palm which is widely cultivated as an avenue tree.
● Genus *Roystonea*, family Palmae: several species, in particular *R. regia*.

royal plural ▶ noun another term for **ROYAL 'WE'**.

royal prerogative ▶ noun see **PREROGATIVE**.

royal purple ▶ noun [mass noun] a rich deep shade of purple.

royal sail ▶ noun a sail above a sailing ship's topgallant sail.

Royal Shakespeare Company (abbrev.: **RSC**) a British professional theatre company founded in 1961. It is based at Stratford and at the Barbican Centre in London.

Royal Society (in full **Royal Society of London**) the oldest and most prestigious scientific society in Britain. It was formed by followers of Francis Bacon to promote scientific discussion especially in the physical sciences, and received its charter from Charles II in 1662.

Royal Society for the Prevention of Cruelty to Animals (abbrev.: **RSPCA**) (in the UK) a charitable organization formed in 1824 to safeguard the welfare of animals.

Royal Society for the Protection of Birds (abbrev.: **RSPB**) (in the UK) a charitable organization founded in 1889 for the conservation of wild birds.

Royal Society of Arts (abbrev.: **RSA**) an institution established in London in 1754 whose original purpose was to forge a link between art and commerce following a decline in craftsmanship after the onset of the Industrial Revolution. It now holds examinations for a wide range of vocational and professional qualifications.

royal stag ▶ noun Brit. a red deer stag with a head of twelve or more points.

royal standard ▶ noun a banner bearing the royal coat of arms, flown in the presence of royalty.

royal tennis ▶ noun another term for **REAL TENNIS**.

Royal Tunbridge Wells official name for **TUNBRIDGE WELLS**.

royalty ▶ noun (pl. **-ies**) **1** [mass noun] people of royal blood or status: *diplomats, heads of state, and royalty shared tables at the banquet.*
■ a member of a royal family: *she swept by as if she were royalty.* ■ the status or power of a king or queen: *the brilliance of her clothes, her jewels, all revealed her royalty.*
2 a sum paid to a patentee for the use of a patent or to an author or composer for each copy of a book sold or for each public performance of a work.
3 a royal right (now especially over minerals) granted by the sovereign to an individual or corporation.
■ a payment made by a producer of minerals, oil, or natural gas to the owner of the site or of the mineral rights over it.

– ORIGIN late Middle English: from Old French *roialte*, from *roial* (see **ROYAL**). The sense 'royal right (especially over minerals)' (late 15th cent.) developed into the sense 'payment made by a mineral producer to the site owner' (mid 19th cent.), which was then transferred to payments for the use of patents and published materials.

Royal Victorian Chain (in the UK) an order founded by Edward VII in 1902 and conferred by the sovereign on special occasions.

Royal Victorian Order (in the UK) an order founded by Queen Victoria in 1896 and typically conferred for great service rendered to the sovereign.

> It has five classes of membership, which are: Knight or Dame Grand Cross of the Royal Victorian Order (GCVO), Knight or Dame Commander (KCVO/DCVO), Commander (CVO), Lieutenant (LVO), and Member (MVO).

royal warrant ▶ noun a warrant issued by the sovereign, in particular:
■ (**Royal Warrant**) one authorizing a company to display the royal arms, indicating that goods or services of quality are supplied to the sovereign or to a specified member of the royal family. ■ one establishing or conferring an award or decoration.

royal 'we' ▶ noun the use of 'we' instead of 'I' by a single person, as traditionally used by a sovereign.

Royal Worcester ▶ noun (trademark in the UK) see **WORCESTER**[2].

Royce, Sir (Frederick) Henry (1863–1933), English engine designer. He founded the company of Rolls-Royce Ltd with Charles Stewart Rolls in 1906, becoming famous as the designer of the Rolls-Royce Silver Ghost motor car and later also becoming known for his aircraft engines.

rozzer ▶ noun Brit. informal a police officer.
– ORIGIN late 19th cent.: of unknown origin.

RP ▶ abbreviation for received pronunciation.

RPG ▶ abbreviation for ■ report program generator, a high-level commercial computer programming language. ■ rocket-propelled grenade. ■ role-playing game.

RPI ▶ abbreviation for retail price index.

rpm ▶ abbreviation for ■ resale price maintenance. ■ revolutions per minute.

RPO ▶ abbreviation for Royal Philharmonic Orchestra.

rpt ▶ abbreviation for repeat.

RPV ▶ abbreviation for remotely piloted vehicle.

RR N. Amer. ▶ abbreviation for ■ railroad. ■ rural route.

-rrhoea ▶ combining form discharge; flow: *diarrhoea.*
– ORIGIN from Greek *rhoia* 'flow, flux'.

RRP Brit. ▶ abbreviation for recommended retail price.

RS ▶ abbreviation for ■ (in the US) received standard. ■ (in the UK) Royal Scots.

Rs. ▶ abbreviation for rupee(s).

RSA ▶ abbreviation for ■ Republic of South Africa. ■ Royal Scottish Academy; Royal Scottish Academician. ■ Royal Society of Arts.

RSC ▶ abbreviation for ■ Royal Shakespeare Company. ■ (in the UK) Royal Society of Chemistry.

RSE ▶ abbreviation for Royal Society of Edinburgh.

RSFSR historical ▶ abbreviation for Russian Soviet Federative Socialist Republic.

RSI ▶ abbreviation for repetitive strain injury.

RSJ ▶ abbreviation for rolled steel joist.

RSM ▶ abbreviation for ■ (in the British army) Regimental Sergeant Major. ■ San Marino (international vehicle registration). [ORIGIN: from Italian *Repubblica di San Marino*.]

RSNC ▶ abbreviation for (in the UK) Royal Society for Nature Conservation.

RSPB ▶ abbreviation for (in the UK) Royal Society for the Protection of Birds.

RSPCA ▶ abbreviation for (in the UK) Royal Society for the Prevention of Cruelty to Animals.

RSV ▶ abbreviation for Revised Standard Version (of the Bible).

RSVP ▶ abbreviation for répondez s'il vous plaît, please reply (used at the end of invitations to request a response).
– ORIGIN French.

RT ▶ abbreviation for ■ radio-telegraphy. ■ radio-telephony.

rt. ▶ abbreviation for right.

RTA Brit. ▶ abbreviation for road traffic accident.

RTF Computing ▶ **abbreviation for** rich text format, developed to allow the transfer of graphics and formatted text between different applications and operating systems.

RTFM Computing, informal ▶ **abbreviation for** read the fucking manual (used especially in electronic mail in reply to a question whose answer is patently obvious).

Rt Hon. Brit. ▶ **abbreviation for** Right Honourable.

Rt Revd (also **Rt Rev.**) ▶ **abbreviation for** Right Reverend.

RU ▶ **abbreviation for** ■ Burundi (international vehicle registration). [ORIGIN: from *Ruanda-Urundi* (now Rwanda and Burundi).] ■ rugby union.

Ru ▶ **symbol for** the chemical element ruthenium.

RU486 ▶ **noun** trademark for **MIFEPRISTONE**.

rub ▶ **verb** (**rubbed**, **rubbing**) [with obj.] move one's hand or a cloth repeatedly to and fro on the surface of (something) with firm pressure: *she rubbed her arm, where she had a large bruise* | [no obj.] *he* ***rubbed at*** *the earth on his jeans.*
■ [with obj. and adverbial of direction] move (one's hand, a cloth, or another object) over a surface in such a way: *he rubbed a finger round the rim of his mug.* ■ [with obj. and adverbial] cause (two things) to move to and fro against each other with a certain amount of pressure and friction: *many insects make noises by rubbing parts of their bodies together.* ■ [no obj., with adverbial] move to and fro over something while pressing or grinding against it: *the ice breaks into small floes that rub against each other.* ■ [no obj.] (of shoes or other hard items in contact with the skin) cause pain through friction: *badly fitting shoes can rub painfully.* ■ make dry, clean, or smooth with pressure from a hand, cloth, or other object: *she found a towel and began rubbing her hair* | [with obj. and complement] *she rubbed herself as dry as possible.* ■ [with obj. and adverbial] spread (ointment, polish, or a substance of similar consistency) over a surface with repeated movements of one's hand or a cloth: *she took out her suncream and rubbed some on her nose.* ■ (**rub something in/into/through**) work an ingredient into (a mixture) by breaking and blending it with firm movements of one's fingers: *sift the flour into a bowl and rub in the fat.* ■ reproduce the design of (a sepulchral brass or a stone) by rubbing paper laid on it with heelball or coloured chalk. ■ [no obj.] Bowls (of a bowl) be slowed or diverted by the unevenness of the ground.
▶ **noun 1** [usu. in sing.] an act of rubbing: *she pulled out a towel and gave her head a quick rub.*
■ an ointment designed to be rubbed on the skin to ease pain: *a muscle rub.*
2 (usu. **the rub**) a difficulty, especially one of central importance in a situation: *that was the rub—she had not cared enough.* [ORIGIN: from Shakespeare's *Hamlet* (III. i. 65).]
3 Bowls an inequality of the ground impeding or diverting a bowl; the diversion or hindering of a bowl by this.
– PHRASES **not have two —— to rub together** informal have none or hardly any of the specified item, especially money: *she doesn't have two farthings to rub together.* **rub one's hands** rub one's hands together to show keen satisfaction. **rub it in** (or **rub someone's nose in something**) informal emphatically draw someone's attention to an embarrassing or painful fact: *they don't just beat you, they rub it in.* **rub noses** rub one's nose against someone else's in greeting (especially as traditional among Maoris and some other peoples). **rub shoulders** (or US **elbows**) associate or come into contact with another person: *he rubbed shoulders with TV stars at the party.* **rub someone** (or Brit. **rub someone up**) **the wrong way** irritate or repel someone as by stroking a cat against the lie of its fur.
– ORIGIN Middle English (as a verb): perhaps from Low German *rubben*, of unknown ultimate origin. The noun dates from the late 16th cent.
▶ **rub along** Brit. informal cope or manage without undue difficulty: *they rub along because their overheads are so low.* ■ have a friendly but not intense relationship; get along together: *they liked each other and rubbed along quite well.*
rub something down dry, smooth, or clean something by rubbing. ■ rub the sweat from a horse or one's own body after exercise.
rub off be transferred by contact or association: *when parents are having a hard time, their tension can easily* ***rub off on*** *the kids.*
rub someone out informal, chiefly N. Amer. kill someone.
rub something out erase pencil marks with a rubber.
rub something up polish a metal or leather object.

Rub' al Khali /ˌrʊb al ˈkɑːli/ a vast desert in the Arabian peninsula, extending from central Saudi Arabia southwards to Yemen and eastwards to the United Arab Emirates and Oman. It is also known as the Great Sandy Desert and the Empty Quarter.

rubato /rʊˈbɑːtəʊ/ Music ▶ **noun** (pl. **rubatos** or **rubati** /-ti/) (also **tempo rubato**) the temporary disregarding of strict tempo to allow an expressive quickening or slackening, usually without altering the overall pace.
▶ **adjective** performed in this way.
– ORIGIN Italian, literally 'robbed'.

rubber[1] ▶ **noun** [mass noun] a tough elastic polymeric substance made from the latex of a tropical plant or synthetically.
■ [count noun] Brit. a piece of such material that is used for erasing pencil or ink marks: *a pencil with a rubber at the end.* ■ [count noun] N. Amer. informal a condom. ■ (**rubbers**) N. Amer. rubber boots; galoshes.
– DERIVATIVES **rubberiness** noun, **rubbery** adjective.
– ORIGIN mid 16th cent.: from the verb **RUB**[1] + **-ER**[1]. The original sense was 'an implement (such as a hard brush) used for rubbing and cleaning'. Because an early use of the elastic substance (previously known as **CAOUTCHOUC**) was to rub out pencil marks, *rubber* gained the sense 'eraser' in the late 18th cent. The sense was subsequently (mid 19th cent.) generalized to refer to the substance in any form or use, at first often differentiated as **INDIA RUBBER**.

rubber[2] ▶ **noun** a contest consisting of a series of successive matches (typically three or five) between the same sides or people in cricket, tennis, and other games.
■ Bridge a unit of play in which one side scores bonus points for winning the best of three games.
– ORIGIN late 16th cent.: of unknown origin; early use was as a term in bowls.

rubber band ▶ **noun** a loop of rubber for holding things together.

rubber boa ▶ **noun** a short snake with a stout shiny brown body that looks and feels like rubber, found in western North America.
● *Charina bottae*, family Boidae.

rubber bullet ▶ **noun** a large projectile made of rubber and shot from a firearm, used especially in riot control.

rubber cement ▶ **noun** [mass noun] a cement or adhesive containing rubber in a solvent.

rubber cheque ▶ **noun** informal, humorous a cheque that is returned unpaid.
– ORIGIN 1920s (originally US): by association with **BOUNCE**.

rubber chicken ▶ **noun** [mass noun] N. Amer. informal food consumed at social gatherings, especially at the events and dinners necessary for a public figure to attend.

rubber duck ▶ **noun** S. African informal an inflatable flat-bottomed rubber dinghy, typically motorized.
– DERIVATIVES **rubber ducker** noun.

rubberize (also **-ise**) ▶ **verb** [with obj.] [usu. as adj. **rubberized**] treat or coat (something) with rubber.

rubberneck informal ▶ **noun** a person who turns their head to stare at something in a foolish manner.
▶ **verb** [no obj.] stare in such a way: *a passer-by rubbernecking at the accident scene.*
– DERIVATIVES **rubbernecker** noun.

rubberoid ▶ **adjective** made of or resembling rubber.

rubber plant ▶ **noun 1** an evergreen tree of the fig family, which has large dark green shiny leaves and is widely cultivated as a house plant. Native to SE Asia, it was formerly grown as a source of rubber.
● *Ficus elastica*, family Moraceae.
2 another term for **RUBBER TREE**.

rubber solution ▶ **noun** [mass noun] a liquid that dries to a rubber-like material, used especially as an adhesive in mending rubber articles.

rubber stamp ▶ **noun** a hand-held device for inking and imprinting a message or design on a surface.
■ figurative a person or organization that approves the decisions of others, not having the power or ability to reject or alter them: *I hope we never get to the day judges dictate to juries so they become rubber stamps.* ■ an indication of such an approval.
▶ **verb** (**rubber-stamp**) [with obj.] approve automatically without proper consideration: *parliament merely rubber-stamped the decisions of the party.*

rubber tree ▶ **noun** a tree that produces the latex from which rubber is manufactured, native to the Amazonian rainforest and widely cultivated elsewhere.
● *Hevea brasiliensis*, family Euphorbiaceae.

rubbing ▶ **noun 1** [mass noun] the action of rubbing something: *dab at the stain—vigorous rubbing could damage the carpet.*
2 an impression of a design on brass or stone, made by rubbing on paper laid over it with coloured wax, pencil, chalk, etc.

rubbing alcohol ▶ **noun** [mass noun] denatured alcohol, typically perfumed, used as an antiseptic or in massage.

rubbing strake ▶ **noun** a protective strip running along a boat's side below the gunwale to prevent damage when coming alongside something.

rubbing strip ▶ **noun** a raised strip fitted to a vehicle to protect the bodywork.

rubbish ▶ **noun** [mass noun] chiefly Brit. waste material; refuse or litter: *householders may be charged for the removal of non-recyclable rubbish.*
■ material that is considered unimportant or valueless: *she had to sift through the rubbish in every drawer.* ■ absurd, nonsensical, or worthless talk or ideas: *critics said their work was* ***a load of rubbish*** | [as exclamation] *some MPs yelled 'Rubbish!'*
▶ **verb** [with obj.] Brit. informal criticize severely and reject as worthless: *he rubbished the idea of a European Community-wide carbon tax.*
▶ **adjective** Brit. informal very bad; worthless or useless: *people might say I was a rubbish manager* | *she was rubbish at maths.*
– DERIVATIVES **rubbishy** adjective.
– ORIGIN late Middle English: from Anglo-Norman French *rubbous*; perhaps related to Old French *robe* 'spoils'; compare with **RUBBLE**. The change in the ending was due to assocation with **-ISH**[1]. The verb (1950s) was originally Australian and New Zealand slang.

rubble ▶ **noun** [mass noun] waste or rough fragments of stone, brick, concrete, etc., especially as the debris from the demolition of buildings: *two buildings collapsed, trapping scores of people in the rubble.*
■ pieces of rough or undressed stone used in building walls, especially as filling for cavities.
– DERIVATIVES **rubbly** adjective.
– ORIGIN late Middle English: perhaps from an Anglo-Norman French alteration of Old French *robe* 'spoils'; compare with **RUBBISH**.

rubbled ▶ **adjective** covered in rubble or reduced to rubble.

rub board ▶ **noun 1** a board fitted with teeth, used for making drawn work from linen.
2 N. Amer. another term for **WASHBOARD** (in sense 2).

Rubbra /ˈrʌbrə/, (Charles) Edmund (1901–86), English composer and pianist. He wrote many songs and eleven symphonies.

rubby ▶ **noun** (pl. **-ies**) Canadian informal an alcoholic who habitually drinks rubbing alcohol.

rub-down ▶ **noun** an act of drying, smoothing down, or cleaning something by rubbing.

rube /ruːb/ ▶ **noun** N. Amer. informal a country bumpkin.
– ORIGIN late 19th cent.: abbreviation of the given name *Reuben*.

rubella /rʊˈbɛlə/ ▶ **noun** medical term for **GERMAN MEASLES**.
– ORIGIN late 19th cent.: modern Latin, neuter plural of Latin *rubellus* 'reddish'.

rubellite /ˈruːbəlʌɪt/ ▶ **noun** [mass noun] a red variety of tourmaline.
– ORIGIN late 18th cent.: from Latin *rubellus* 'reddish' + **-ITE**[1].

Rubens /ˈruːbənz/, Sir Peter Paul (1577–1640), Flemish painter. The foremost exponent of northern Baroque, he is best known for his portraits and mythological paintings featuring voluptuous female nudes, as in *Venus and Adonis* (*c.*1635).

rubeola /rʊˈbiːələ/ ▶ **noun** medical term for **MEASLES**.
– ORIGIN late 17th cent.: from medieval Latin,

diminutive (on the pattern of *variola*) of Latin *rubeus* 'red'.

rubescent /rʊˈbɛs(ə)nt/ ▶ **adjective** chiefly poetic/literary reddening; blushing.
– ORIGIN mid 18th cent.: from Latin *rubescent-* 'reddening', from the verb *rubescere*, from *ruber* 'red'.

Rubicon /ˈruːbɪk(ə)n, -kɒn/ a stream in NE Italy which marked the ancient boundary between Italy and Cisalpine Gaul. Julius Caesar led his army across it into Italy in 49 BC, breaking the law forbidding a general to lead an army out of his province, and so committing himself to war against the Senate and Pompey. The ensuing civil war resulted in victory for Caesar after three years.
■[as noun] a point of no return: *on the way to political union we are now **crossing the Rubicon**.*

rubicon ▶ **noun** (in piquet) an act of winning a game against an opponent whose total score is less than 100, in which case the loser's score is added to rather than subtracted from the winner's.
▶ **verb** (**rubiconed**, **rubiconing**) [with obj.] score a rubicon against (one's opponent).
– ORIGIN late 19th cent.: from **RUBICON**.

rubicund /ˈruːbɪk(ə)nd/ ▶ **adjective** (especially of someone's face) having a ruddy complexion; high-coloured.
– DERIVATIVES **rubicundity** /-ˈkʌndɪti/ noun.
– ORIGIN late Middle English (in the general sense 'red'): from Latin *rubicundus*, from *rubere* 'be red'.

rubidium /rʊˈbɪdɪəm/ ▶ **noun** [mass noun] the chemical element of atomic number 37, a rare soft silvery reactive metal of the alkali metal group. (Symbol: **Rb**)
– ORIGIN mid 19th cent.: modern Latin, from Latin *rubidus* 'red' (with reference to its spectral lines).

rubidium–strontium dating ▶ **noun** [mass noun] Geology a method of dating rocks from the relative proportions of rubidium-87 and its decay product, strontium-87.

rubiginous /rʊˈbɪdʒɪnəs/ ▶ **adjective** technical or poetic/literary rust-coloured.
– ORIGIN late 17th cent.: from Latin *rubigo*, *rubigin-* 'rust' + **-OUS**.

Rubik's cube /ˈruːbɪks/ ▶ **noun** trademark a puzzle in the form of a plastic cube covered with multicoloured squares, which the player attempts to twist and turn so that all the squares on each face are of the same colour.
– ORIGIN 1980s: named after Erno *Rubik* (born 1944), its Hungarian inventor.

Rubinstein[1] /ˈruːbɪnstʌɪn/, Anton (Grigorevich) (1829–94), Russian composer and pianist. In 1862 he founded the St Petersburg Conservatory and was its director 1862–7 and 1887–91. He composed symphonies, operas, songs, and piano music.

Rubinstein[2] /ˈruːbɪnstʌɪn/, Artur (1888–1982), Polish-born American pianist. He toured extensively in Europe and the US and among his many recordings are the complete works of Chopin.

Rubinstein[3] /ˈruːbɪnstʌɪn/, Helena (1870–1965), Polish-born beautician and businesswoman. Her American organization became an international cosmetics manufacturer and distributor.

rubisco /rʊˈbɪskəʊ/ ▶ **noun** [mass noun] Biochemistry an enzyme present in plant chloroplasts, involved in fixing atmospheric carbon dioxide during photosynthesis and in oxygenation of the resulting compound during photorespiration.
– ORIGIN 1980s: from *r(ib)u(lose)* + **BIS-** + *c(arb)o(xyl)*.

ruble ▶ **noun** variant spelling of **ROUBLE**.

rub of the green ▶ **noun** good fortune, especially as determining events in a sporting match: *we didn't **get the rub of the green**.*
■Golf any accidental or unpredictable influence on the course or position of the ball.

rubredoxin /ˌruːbrɪˈdɒksɪn/ ▶ **noun** Biochemistry any of a class of iron-containing proteins involved in electron transfer processes within living cells.
– ORIGIN 1960s: from Latin *ruber*, *rubr-* 'red' + **REDOX** + **-IN**[1].

rubric /ˈruːbrɪk/ ▶ **noun** a heading on a document.
■a set of instructions on an examination paper. ■a direction in a liturgical book as to how a church service should be conducted. ■a statement of purpose or function: *art of a purpose, not for its own sake, was his rubric.* ■a category: *party policies on matters falling **under the rubric of** law and order.*
– DERIVATIVES **rubrical** adjective.
– ORIGIN late Middle English *rubrish* (originally referring to a heading, section of text, etc. written in red for distinctiveness), from Old French *rubriche*, from Latin *rubrica* (*terra*) 'red (earth or ochre as writing material)', from the base of *rubeus* 'red'; the later spelling is influenced by the Latin form.

rubricate /ˈruːbrɪkeɪt/ ▶ **verb** chiefly historical add elaborate, typically red, capital letters or other decorations to (a manuscript).
– DERIVATIVES **rubrication** noun, **rubricator** noun.
– ORIGIN late 16th cent.: from Latin *rubricat-* 'marked in red', from the verb *rubricare*, from *rubrica* (see **RUBRIC**).

rub-up ▶ **noun** [in sing.] an act of polishing something.

ruby ▶ **noun** (pl. **-ies**) a precious stone consisting of corundum in colour varieties varying from deep crimson or purple to pale rose.
■[mass noun] an intense purplish-red colour: [as modifier] *the rich ruby liquid* | [in combination] *this wine has a youthful **ruby-red** colour.* ■ [mass noun] Printing an old type size equal to 5½ points (smaller than nonpareil and larger than pearl).
– ORIGIN Middle English: from Old French *rubi*, from medieval Latin *rubinus*, from the base of Latin *rubeus* 'red'.

ruby glass ▶ **noun** [mass noun] glass coloured red by the inclusion of specific impurities such as gold or metal oxides.

ruby port ▶ **noun** [mass noun] a deep red port, especially one matured in wood for only a few years and then fined.

ruby-tail (also **ruby-tail wasp**) ▶ **noun** a small metallic cuckoo wasp that is typically greenish-blue with an orange-red tip to the abdomen. Its larvae feed on the eggs and larvae of its host.
● Family Chrysididae: *Chrysis* and other genera, and many species, in particular *C. ignita*.

rubythroat ▶ **noun** a small thrush related to the robin, the male having a red throat and striped head, found from Siberia to China.
● Genus *Erithacus*, family Turdidae: three species.

ruby wedding (also **ruby wedding anniversary**) ▶ **noun** the fortieth anniversary of a wedding.

RUC ▶ **abbreviation for** Royal Ulster Constabulary.

ruche /ruːʃ/ ▶ **noun** a frill or pleat of fabric as decoration on a garment or soft furnishing.
– DERIVATIVES **ruched** adjective, **ruching** noun.
– ORIGIN early 19th cent.: from French, from medieval Latin *rusca* 'tree bark', of Celtic origin.

ruck[1] ▶ **noun** **1** Rugby a loose scrum formed around a player with the ball on the ground. Compare with **MAUL**.
■Australian Rules a group of three players who follow the play without fixed positions.
2 a tightly packed crowd of people: *Harry squeezed through the ruck to order another pint.*
■(**the ruck**) the mass of ordinary people or things: *education was the key to success, a way out of the ruck.*
▶ **verb** [no obj.] Rugby & Australian Rules take part in a ruck.
– ORIGIN Middle English (in the sense 'stack of fuel, heap'): apparently of Scandinavian origin; compare with Norwegian *ruke* 'heap of hay'.

ruck[2] ▶ **verb** [with obj.] compress or move (cloth or clothing) so that it forms a number of untidy folds or creases: *her skirt was **rucked up**.*
■[no obj.] (of cloth or clothing) form such folds of creases: *Eleanor's dress rucked up at the front.*
▶ **noun** a crease or wrinkle.
– ORIGIN late 18th cent. (as a noun): from Old Norse *hrukka*.

ruck[3] ▶ **noun** Brit. informal a quarrel or fight, especially a brawl involving several people.
– ORIGIN 1950s: perhaps a shortened form of **RUCTION** or **RUCKUS**.

ruckle ▶ **verb** & **noun** Brit. another term for **RUCK**[2].

rucksack /ˈrʌksak, ˈrʊk-/ ▶ **noun** a bag with shoulder straps which allow it to be carried on someone's back, typically made of a strong, waterproof material and widely used by hikers.
– ORIGIN mid 19th cent.: from German, from *rucken* (dialect variant of *Rücken* 'back') + *Sack* 'bag, sack'.

ruckus /ˈrʌkəs/ ▶ **noun** a row or commotion: *a child is raising a ruckus in class* | [mass noun] *there's enough ruckus over identity cards.*
– ORIGIN late 19th cent.: perhaps related to **RUCTION** and **RUMPUS**.

rucola /ˈruːkələ/ ▶ **noun** another term for **ARUGULA**.

ruction ▶ **noun** informal a disturbance or quarrel.
■(**ructions**) unpleasant reactions to or complaints about something: *if Mrs Salt catches her there'll be ructions.*
– ORIGIN early 19th cent.: of unknown origin.

rudaceous /rʊˈdeɪʃəs/ ▶ **adjective** Geology (of rock) composed of fragments of relatively large size (larger than sand grains).
– ORIGIN early 20th cent.: from Latin *rudus* 'rubble' + **-ACEOUS**.

rudbeckia /ruːdˈbɛkɪə, rʌd-/ ▶ **noun** a North American plant of the daisy family, with yellow or orange flowers and a dark cone-like centre.
● Genus *Rudbeckia*, family Compositae.
– ORIGIN modern Latin, named after Olaf *Rudbeck* (1660–1740), Swedish botanist.

rudd ▶ **noun** (pl. same) a European freshwater fish of the carp family with a silvery body and red fins.
● *Scardinius erythrophthalmus*, family Cyprinidae.
– ORIGIN early 16th cent.: apparently related to archaic *rud* 'red colour'.

rudder ▶ **noun** a flat piece hinged vertically near the stern of a boat or ship for steering.
■a vertical aerofoil pivoted from the tailplane of an aircraft, for controlling movement about the vertical axis. ■ [mass noun] application of a rudder in steering a boat, ship, or aircraft: *bring the aircraft to a stall and apply **full rudder*** | *a small amount of extra rudder.*
– ORIGIN Old English *rōther* 'paddle, oar', of West Germanic origin; related to Dutch *roer*, German *Ruder*, also to the verb **ROW**[2].

rudderless ▶ **adjective** lacking a rudder.
■lacking a clear sense of one's aims or principles: *today's leadership is rudderless.*

ruddle ▶ **noun** [mass noun] another term for **REDDLE**.
■a small block of reddle or a similar substance that is attached to the chest of a ram to mark the sheep that it tups.
– ORIGIN late Middle English: related to obsolete *rud* 'red colour' and **RED**; compare with **RADDLE**.

ruddy ▶ **adjective** (**ruddier**, **ruddiest**) **1** (of a person's face) having a healthy red colour: *a cheerful pipe-smoking man of ruddy complexion.*
■having a reddish colour: *the ruddy evening light.*
2 Brit. informal, dated used as a euphemism for 'bloody'.
▶ **verb** (**-ies**, **-ied**) [with obj.] make ruddy in colour: *a red flash ruddied the belly of a cloud.*
– DERIVATIVES **ruddily** adverb (rare), **ruddiness** noun.
– ORIGIN late Old English *rudig*, from the base of archaic *rud* 'red colour'; related to **RED**.

ruddy duck ▶ **noun** a New World stiff-tailed duck with a broad bill, naturalized in Britain, the male having mainly deep red-brown plumage and white cheeks.
● *Oxyura jamaicensis*, family Anatidae.

rude ▶ **adjective** **1** offensively impolite or ill-mannered: *she had **been rude to** her boss* | [with infinitive] *it's rude to ask a lady her age.*
■referring to a taboo subject such as sex in a way considered improper and offensive: *Graham giggled at every rude joke.* ■ [attrib.] having a startling abruptness: *the war came as a very **rude awakening**.*
2 [attrib.] chiefly Brit. vigorous or hearty: *Isabel had always been in **rude health**.*
3 dated roughly made or done; lacking subtlety or sophistication: *a rude coffin.*
■archaic ignorant and uneducated: *the new religion was first promulgated by rude men.*
– DERIVATIVES **rudely** adverb, **rudeness** noun, **rudery** noun.
– ORIGIN Middle English (in sense 3, also 'uncultured'): from Old French, from Latin *rudis* 'unwrought' (referring to handicraft), figuratively 'uncultivated'; related to *rudus* 'broken stone'.

rude boy ▶ **noun** (in Jamaica) a lawless urban youth who likes ska or reggae music.

ruderal /ˈruːd(ə)r(ə)l/ Botany ▶ **adjective** (of a plant) growing on waste ground or among rubbish.
▶ **noun** a plant growing on waste ground or among rubbish.
– ORIGIN mid 19th cent.: from modern Latin *ruderalis*, from Latin *rudera*, plural of *rudus* 'rubble'.

rudiment /ˈruːdɪm(ə)nt/ ▶ **noun** **1** (**the rudiments of**) the first principles of a subject: *she taught the girls the rudiments of reading and writing.*
■an elementary or primitive form of something: *the rudiments of a hot-water system.*
2 Biology an undeveloped or immature part or organ, especially a structure in an embryo or larva

which will develop into an organ, limb, etc.: *the fetal lung rudiment.*
3 Music a basic pattern used by drummers, such as the roll, the flam, and the paradiddle.
– ORIGIN mid 16th cent.: from French, or from Latin *rudimentum*, from *rudis* 'unwrought', on the pattern of *elementum* 'element'.

rudimentary /ˌruːdɪˈmɛnt(ə)ri/ ▶ **adjective** involving or limited to basic principles: *he received a rudimentary education.*
■ of or relating to an immature, undeveloped, or basic form: *a rudimentary stage of evolution.*
– DERIVATIVES **rudimentarily** adverb.

rudist /ˈruːdɪst/ (also **rudistid**) ▶ **noun** a cone-shaped fossil bivalve mollusc which formed colonies resembling reefs in the Cretaceous period.
• Superfamily Rudistacea, order Hippuritoida.
– ORIGIN late 19th cent.: from modern Latin *Rudista* (former group name), from Latin *rudis* 'rude'; for the variant spelling see **-ID**[3].

Rudolf, Lake former name (until 1979) for Lake Turkana (see **TURKANA, LAKE**).

Rudra /ˈrʊdrə/ Hinduism **1** (in the Rig Veda) a Vedic minor god, associated with the storm, father of the Maruts.
2 one of the names of **SHIVA**.

Rudras /ˈrʊdrəs/ another term for **MARUTS**.

rue[1] ▶ **verb** (**rues**, **rued**, **rueing** or **ruing**) [with obj.] bitterly regret (something one has done or allowed to happen) and wish it undone: *Ferguson will* ***rue the day*** *he turned down that offer | she might live to rue this impetuous decision.*
▶ **noun** [mass noun] archaic repentance; regret: *with rue my heart is laden.*
■ compassion; pity: *tears of pitying rue.*
– ORIGIN Old English *hrēow* 'repentance', *hrēowan* 'affect with contrition', of Germanic origin; related to Dutch *rouw* 'mourning' and German *Reue* 'remorse'.

rue[2] ▶ **noun** a perennial evergreen shrub with bitter strong-scented lobed leaves which are used in herbal medicine.
• *Ruta graveolens*, family Rutaceae.
■ used in names of other plants that resemble rue, especially in leaf shape, e.g. **goat's rue**, **meadow rue**, and **wall rue**.
– ORIGIN Middle English: from Old French, via Latin from Greek *rhutē*.

rueful ▶ **adjective** expressing sorrow or regret in a slightly humorous way: *she gave a rueful grin.*
– DERIVATIVES **ruefully** adverb, **ruefulness** noun.
– ORIGIN Middle English (also in the sense 'pitiable'): from the noun **RUE**[1] + **-FUL**.

ruff[1] ▶ **noun 1** a projecting starched frill worn round the neck, characteristic of Elizabethan and Jacobean costume.
2 a projecting or conspicuously coloured ring of feathers or hair round the neck of a bird or mammal.
3 a pigeon of a domestic breed with a ruff of feathers on its neck.
4 (pl. same or **ruffs**) a North Eurasian wading bird, the male of which has a large variously coloured ruff and ear tufts in the breeding season, used in display.
• *Philomachus pugnax*, family Scolopacidae; the female is called a **reeve**.
– DERIVATIVES **ruff-like** adjective.
– ORIGIN early 16th cent. (first used denoting a frill around a sleeve): probably from a variant of **ROUGH**.

ruff[2] ▶ **noun 1** (also **tommy ruff**) an edible marine fish of Australian inshore waters that is related to the Australian salmon. Also called **ROUGHY** in Australia.
• *Arripis georgianus*, family Arripidae.
2 variant spelling of **RUFFE**.
– ORIGIN late 19th cent.: from **RUFFE**.

ruff[3] ▶ **verb** [no obj.] (in bridge, whist, and similar card games) play a trump in a trick which was led in a different suit.
■ [with obj.] play a trump on (a card in another suit).
▶ **noun** an act of ruffing or opportunity to ruff.
– ORIGIN late 16th cent. (originally the name of a card game resembling whist): from Old French *rouffle*, a parallel formation to Italian *ronfa* (perhaps an alteration of *trionfo* 'a trump').

ruff[4] ▶ **noun** Music one of the basic patterns (rudiments) of drumming, consisting of a single note preceded by either two grace notes played with the other stick (**double-stroke ruff** or **drag**) or three grace notes played with alternating sticks (**four-stroke ruff**).
– ORIGIN late 17th cent.: probably imitative.

ruffe /rʌf/ (also **ruff**) ▶ **noun** a European freshwater fish of the perch family, with a greenish-brown back and yellow sides and underparts.
• *Gymnocephalus cernua*, family Percidae.
– ORIGIN late Middle English: probably from a variant of **ROUGH**.

ruffed grouse ▶ **noun** a North American woodland grouse which has a black ruff on the sides of the neck.
• *Bonasa umbellus*, family Tetraonidae (or Phasianidae).

ruffed lemur ▶ **noun** a lemur with a prominent muzzle and dense fur that forms a ruff around the neck, living in the Madagascan rainforest.
• *Varecia variegata*, family Lemuridae.

ruffian ▶ **noun** a violent person, especially one involved in crime.
– DERIVATIVES **ruffianism** noun, **ruffianly** adjective.
– ORIGIN late 15th cent.: from Old French *ruffian*, from Italian *ruffiano*, perhaps from dialect *rofia* 'scab, scurf', of Germanic origin.

ruffle ▶ **verb** [with obj.] **1** disorder or disarrange (someone's hair), typically by running one's hands through it: *he ruffled her hair affectionately.*
■ (of a bird) erect (its feathers) in anger or display: *they warbled incessantly, their throat feathers ruffled.* ■ disturb the smoothness or tranquillity of: *the evening breeze ruffled the surface of the pond in the yard.* ■ disconcert or upset the composure of (someone): *Lancaster had been ruffled by her questions.*
2 [usu. as adj. **ruffled**] ornament with or gather into a frill: *a blouse with a high ruffled neck.*
▶ **noun 1** an ornamental gathered or goffered frill of lace or other cloth on a garment, especially around the wrist or neck.
2 a vibrating drum beat.
– PHRASES **ruffle someone's feathers** cause someone to become annoyed or upset. **smooth someone's ruffled feathers** make someone less angry or irritated by using soothing words.
– ORIGIN Middle English (as a verb): of unknown origin. Current noun senses date from the late 17th cent.

rufiyaa /ˈruːfiːjɑː/ ▶ **noun** (pl. same) the basic monetary unit of the Maldives, equal to 100 laris.
– ORIGIN Maldivian.

rufous /ˈruːfəs/ ▶ **adjective** reddish brown in colour.
▶ **noun** [mass noun] a reddish-brown colour.
– ORIGIN late 18th cent.: from Latin *rufus* 'red, reddish' + **-OUS**.

rug ▶ **noun** a small carpet.
■ chiefly Brit. a thick woollen coverlet or wrap, used especially when travelling. ■ a shaped garment worn by horses for protection or warmth. ■ informal, chiefly N. Amer. a toupee or wig.
– PHRASES **pull the rug (from under someone)** abruptly withdraw support (from someone).
– ORIGIN mid 16th cent. (denoting a type of coarse woollen cloth): probably of Scandinavian origin; compare with Norwegian dialect *rugga* 'coverlet', Swedish *rugg* 'ruffled hair'; related to **RAG**[1]. The sense 'small carpet' dates from the early 19th cent.

Rugby /ˈrʌɡbi/ a town in central England, on the River Avon in Warwickshire; pop. 59,720 (1981). Rugby School was founded there in 1567.

rugby (also **rugby football**) ▶ **noun** [mass noun] a team game played with an oval ball that may be kicked, carried, and passed from hand to hand. Points are scored by grounding the ball behind the opponents' goal line (thereby scoring a try) or by kicking it between the two posts and over the crossbar of the opponents' goal. See also **RUGBY LEAGUE** and **RUGBY UNION**.
– ORIGIN mid 19th cent.: named after *Rugby* School (see **RUGBY**), where the game was first played.

rugby league ▶ **noun** [mass noun] a form of rugby played in teams of thirteen, originally by a group of northern English clubs which separated from rugby union in 1895. Besides having somewhat different rules, the game differed from rugby union in always allowing professionalism.

rugby union ▶ **noun** [mass noun] a form of rugby played in teams of fifteen. Unlike rugby league, the game was originally strictly amateur, being opened to professionalism only in 1995.

Rügen /ˈruːɡ(ə)n, German ˈryːɡn/ an island in the Baltic Sea off the north coast of Germany, to which it is linked by a causeway. It forms part of the state of Mecklenburg-West Pomerania.

rugged /ˈrʌɡɪd/ ▶ **adjective** (of ground or terrain) having a broken, rocky, and uneven surface: *a rugged coastline | the moors are very rugged in places.*
■ (of a machine or other manufactured object) strongly made and capable of withstanding rough handling: *the binoculars are compact, lightweight, and rugged.* ■ having or requiring toughness and determination: *a week of rugged, demanding adventure at an outdoor training centre.* ■ (of a man's face or looks) having attractively strong, rough-hewn features: *he was known for his rugged good looks.*
– DERIVATIVES **ruggedly** adverb, **ruggedness** noun.
– ORIGIN Middle English (in the sense 'shaggy', also (of a horse) 'rough-coated'): probably of Scandinavian origin; compare with Swedish *rugga* 'roughen', also with **RUG**.

ruggedized ▶ **adjective** chiefly US designed or improved to be hard-wearing or shock-resistant: *ruggedized computers suitable for use on the battlefield.*
– DERIVATIVES **ruggedization** noun.

rugger ▶ **noun** [mass noun] Brit. informal rugby.

rugger-bugger ▶ **noun** informal a boorish, aggressively masculine young man who is devoted to sport.
– ORIGIN 1970s (originally a South African usage): from **RUGGER** + *bugger* 'mate' (used freely and without sexual connotations in South African English).

rugola /ˈruːɡələ/ ▶ **noun** another term for **ARUGULA**.

rugosa /ruːˈɡəʊzə/ ▶ **noun** a SE Asian rose with dark green wrinkled leaves and deep pink flowers, widely used as a hedging plant.
• *Rosa rugosa*, family Rosaceae.
– ORIGIN late 19th cent.: feminine of Latin *rugosus* (see **RUGOSE**), used as a specific epithet.

rugose /ˈruːɡəʊs, rʊˈɡəʊs/ ▶ **adjective** chiefly Biology wrinkled; corrugated: *rugose corals.*
– DERIVATIVES **rugosity** noun.
– ORIGIN late Middle English: from Latin *rugosus*, from *ruga* 'wrinkle'.

rug rat ▶ **noun** N. Amer. informal a child.

Ruhr /rʊə, German ruːɐ̯/ a region of coal mining and heavy industry in North Rhine-Westphalia, western Germany. It is named after the River Ruhr, which flows through it, meeting the Rhine near Duisburg. The Ruhr was occupied by French troops 1923–4, after Germany defaulted on war reparation payments.

ruin ▶ **noun** [mass noun] the physical destruction or disintegration of something or the state of disintegrating or being destroyed: *a large white house* ***falling into*** *gentle* ***ruin.***
■ [count noun] the remains of a building, typically an old one, that has suffered much damage or disintegration: ***the ruins of*** *the castle | the church is a* ***ruin*** *now.* ■ the disastrous disintegration of someone's life: *the ruin and heartbreak wrought by alcohol, divorce, and violence.* ■ the cause of such disintegration: *they don't know how to say no, and that's been their ruin.* ■ the complete loss of one's money and other assets: *the financial cost could mean ruin.*
▶ **verb 1** [with obj.] reduce (a building or place) to a state of decay, collapse, or disintegration: [as adj. **ruined**] *a ruined castle.*
■ cause great and usually irreparable damage or harm to; have a disastrous effect on: *a noisy motorway has ruined village life.* ■ reduce to a state of poverty: *they were ruined by the highest interest rates this century.*
2 [no obj.] poetic/literary fall headlong or with a crash: *carriages go ruining over the brink from time to time.*
– PHRASES **in ruins** in a state of complete disorder or disintegration: *the economy was in ruins.*
– ORIGIN Middle English (in the sense 'collapse of a building'): from Old French *ruine*, from Latin *ruina*, from *ruere* 'to fall'.

ruination ▶ **noun** [mass noun] the action or fact of ruining someone or something or of being ruined: *commercial malpractice causes the ruination of thousands of people.*
■ the state of being ruined: *the headquarters fell into ruination.*
– ORIGIN mid 17th cent.: from obsolete *ruinate* + **-ION**.

ruin marble ▶ **noun** [mass noun] marble having irregular markings said to resemble the outline of ruins.

ruinous ▶ adjective **1** disastrous or destructive: *a ruinous effect on the environment.*
■costing far more than can be afforded: *the cost of their ransom might be ruinous.*
2 in ruins; dilapidated: *the castle is ruinous.*
– DERIVATIVES **ruinously** adverb, **ruinousness** noun.
– ORIGIN late Middle English (also in the sense 'falling down'): from Latin *ruinosus*, from *ruina* (see **RUIN**).

Ruisdael /'raʊsdɑːl, 'rɔɪz-, -deɪl/ (also **Ruysdael**), Jacob van (*c.*1628–82), Dutch landscape painter. Born in Haarlem, he painted the surrounding landscape from the mid 1640s until his move to Amsterdam in 1657.

Ruiz de Alarcón y Mendoza /rʊ,iːθ deɪ ,alɑː'kɒn iː mɛn,dəʊsə, Spanish ,rrwiθ de alar'kon i men,doθa, ,rrwis, men,dosa/, Juan (1580–1639), Spanish dramatist, born in Mexico City. His most famous play, the moral comedy *La Verdad sospechosa*, was the basis of Corneille's *Le Menteur* (1642).

Rukh /ruːx/ the nationalist movement which established the independence of the Ukraine in 1991.
– ORIGIN Ukrainian, 'people's movement'.

rukh /ruːk/ ▶ noun another term for **ROC**.
– ORIGIN from Hindi *rūkh*.

rule ▶ noun **1** one of a set of explicit or understood regulations or principles governing a person's conduct within a particular activity or sphere: *the rules of the game were understood | those who did* ***break the rules*** *would be dealt with swiftly.*
■a law or principle that operates within a particular sphere of knowledge, describing or prescribing what is possible or allowable: *the rules of grammar.* ■ a code of practice and discipline for a religious order or community: *the Rule of St Benedict.* ■ [mass noun] control of or dominion over an area or people: *the revolution brought an end to British rule.* ■ (**the rule**) the normal or customary state of things: *such accidents are the exception rather than the rule.*
2 a strip of wood or other rigid material used for measuring length or marking straight lines; a ruler.
■a thin printed line or dash.
3 (**Rules**) Austral. short for **AUSTRALIAN RULES**.
▶ verb **1** [with obj.] exercise ultimate power or authority over (an area and its people): *Latin America today is ruled by elected politicians* | [no obj.] *the period in which Spain* ***ruled over*** *Portugal.*
■(of a feeling) have a powerful and restricting influence on (a person's life): *her whole life seemed to be ruled by fear.* ■ [no obj.] be a dominant or powerful factor or force: [with complement] *the black market rules supreme.* ■ [with clause] pronounce authoritatively and legally to be the case: *an industrial tribunal ruled that he was unfairly dismissed from his job.* ■ Astrology (of a planet) have a particular influence over (a sign of the zodiac, house, aspect of life, etc.).
2 [with obj.] make parallel lines across (paper): [as adj. **ruled**] *a sheet of ruled paper.*
■make (a straight line) on paper with a ruler.
3 [no obj., with adverbial] (of a price or a traded commodity with regard to its price) have a specified general level or strength: *in the jutes section Indus and Pak Jute ruled firm.*
– PHRASES **as a rule** usually, but not always. **by rule** in a regular manner according to a particular set of rules: *stress is not predictable by rule and must be learned word by word.* **make it a rule to do something** have it as a habit or general principle to do something: *I make it a rule never to mix business with pleasure.* **rule of law** the restriction of the arbitrary exercise of power by subordinating it to well-defined and established laws. **rule of thumb** a broadly accurate guide or principle, based on experience or practice rather than theory. —— **rule** (or **rules**), **OK?** informal, humorous used to express one's enthusiasm for the specified person or thing. **rule the roost** be in complete control. **run the rule over** Brit. examine cursorily for correctness or adequacy.
– DERIVATIVES **ruleless** adjective.
– ORIGIN Middle English: from Old French *reule* (noun), *reuler* (verb), from late Latin *regulare*, from Latin *regula* 'straight stick'.
▶**rule something out** (or **in**) exclude (or include) something as a possibility: *the prime minister ruled out a November election.*

Rule 43 ▶ noun (in the UK) a prison regulation whereby prisoners, typically sex offenders, can be isolated or segregated for their own protection.

rule of the road ▶ noun a custom or law regulating the direction in which two vehicles (or riders or ships) should move to pass one another on meeting, or which should give way to the other, so as to avoid collision.

rule of three ▶ noun Mathematics, dated a method of finding a number in the same ratio to a given number as exists between two other given numbers.

ruler ▶ noun **1** a person exercising government or dominion.
■Astrology another term for **RULING PLANET**.
2 a straight strip or cylinder of plastic, wood, metal, or other rigid material, typically marked at regular intervals and used to draw straight lines or measure distances.
– DERIVATIVES **rulership** noun.

Rules Committee ▶ noun a house of a US federal or state legislature responsible for expediting the passage of bills.

ruling ▶ noun an authoritative decision or pronouncement, especially one made by a judge.
▶ adjective currently exercising authority or influence: *the ruling coalition.*

ruling elder ▶ noun a nominated or elected lay official of any of various Christian Churches, especially of a Presbyterian Church.

ruling passion ▶ noun an interest or concern that occupies a large part of someone's time and effort: *football remained their ruling passion.*

ruling planet ▶ noun Astrology a planet which is held to have a particular influence over a specific sign of the zodiac, house, aspect of life, etc.

Rum variant spelling of **RHUM**.

rum[1] ▶ noun [mass noun] an alcoholic spirit distilled from sugar-cane residues or molasses.
■N. Amer. intoxicating liquor.
– ORIGIN mid 17th cent.: perhaps an abbreviation of obsolete *rumbullion*, in the same sense.

rum[2] ▶ adjective (**rummer**, **rummest**) Brit. informal, dated odd; peculiar: *it's a rum business, certainly.*
– PHRASES **a rum go** dated a surprising occurrence or unforeseen turn of events.
– DERIVATIVES **rumly** adverb, **rumness** noun.
– ORIGIN late 18th cent.: of unknown origin.

Rumania /ruː'meɪnɪə/ variant spelling of **ROMANIA**.

Rumanian /rʊː'meɪnɪən/ ▶ adjective & noun variant spelling of **ROMANIAN**.

Rumansh /rʊ'manʃ, -'mɑːnʃ/ ▶ adjective & noun variant of **ROMANSH**.

rumba /'rʌmbə/ (also **rhumba**) ▶ noun a rhythmic dance with Spanish and African elements, originating in Cuba.
■a piece of music for this dance or in a similar style. ■ a ballroom dance imitative of this dance.
▶ verb (**rumbas**, **rumbaed** /-bəd/ or **rumba'd**, **rumbaing** /-bə(r)ɪŋ/) [no obj.] dance the rumba.
– ORIGIN 1920s: from Latin American Spanish.

rum baba ▶ noun see **BABA**[1].

rumble ▶ verb **1** [no obj.] make a continuous deep, resonant sound: *thunder rumbled, lightning flickered.*
■[with adverbial of direction] (especially of a large vehicle) move in the specified direction with such a sound: *heavy lorries rumbled through the streets.* ■ [with obj.] utter in a deep, resonant voice: *the man's low voice rumbled an instruction.* ■ (of a person's stomach) make a deep, resonant sound due to hunger. ■ (**rumble on**) figurative (of a dispute) continue in a persistent but low-key way: *the row over his banning rumbles on.*
2 [with obj.] Brit. informal discover (an illicit activity or its perpetrator): *it wouldn't need a genius to rumble my little game.*
3 [no obj.] US informal take part in a street fight between gangs or large groups.
▶ noun **1** a continuous deep, resonant sound like distant thunder: *the steady rumble of traffic* | figurative *rumbles of discontent.*
2 US informal a street fight between gangs or large groups.
– ORIGIN late Middle English: probably from Middle Dutch *rommelen*, *rummelen*, of imitative origin. Sense 2 of the verb may be a different word.

rumbler ▶ noun a person or thing that rumbles.
■a machine for peeling potatoes. ■ historical a round bell containing a small hard object placed inside to rattle, formerly used especially on horses' harnesses.

rumble seat ▶ noun N. Amer. an uncovered folding seat in the rear of a motor car.

rumble strip ▶ noun a series of raised strips across a road or along its edge, changing the noise a vehicle's tyres make on the surface and so warning drivers of speed restrictions or of the edge of the road.

rumbling ▶ noun a continuous deep, resonant sound: *the rumbling of wheels in the distance.*
■(often **rumblings**) an early indication or rumour of dissatisfaction or incipient change: *there are growing rumblings of discontent.*
▶ adjective making or constituting a deep resonant sound: *rumbling trams | a rumbling noise.*
■(of dissatisfaction or a dispute) continuing in a persistent but low-key way: *a rumbling dispute about changes to working conditions.*

rumbustious /rʌm'bʌstʃəs, -tɪəs/ ▶ adjective informal, chiefly Brit. boisterous or unruly.
– DERIVATIVES **rumbustiously** adverb, **rumbustiousness** noun.
– ORIGIN late 18th cent.: probably an alteration of archaic *robustious* 'boisterous, robust'.

rum butter ▶ noun [mass noun] a rich, sweet, hard rum-flavoured confection of butter and sugar, served especially as a sauce with mince pies or Christmas pudding.

rumdum /'rʌmdʌm/ ▶ noun N. Amer. informal a drunkard, especially a derelict alcoholic.
– ORIGIN late 19th cent.: from **RUM**[1] + **DUMB**.

Rumelia /ruː'miːlɪə/ (also **Roumelia**) the territories in Europe which formerly belonged to the Ottoman Empire, including Macedonia, Thrace, and Albania.
– ORIGIN from Turkish *Rumeli*, 'land of the Romans'.

rumen /'ruːmɛn/ ▶ noun (pl. **rumens** or **rumina** /-mɪnə/) Zoology the first stomach of a ruminant, which receives food or cud from the oesophagus, partly digests it with the aid of bacteria, and passes it to the reticulum.
– ORIGIN early 18th cent.: from Latin, literally 'throat'.

ruminant ▶ noun **1** an even-toed ungulate mammal that chews the cud regurgitated from its rumen. The ruminants comprise the cattle, sheep, antelopes, deer, giraffes, and their relatives.
• Suborder Ruminantia, order Artiodactyla: six families.
2 a contemplative person; a person given to meditation.
▶ adjective of or belonging to ruminants: *a ruminant protein ban.*
– ORIGIN mid 17th cent.: from Latin *ruminant-* 'chewing over again', from the verb *ruminari*, from *rumen* 'throat'(see **RUMEN**).

ruminate /'ruːmɪneɪt/ ▶ verb [no obj.] **1** think deeply about something: *we sat* ***ruminating on*** *the nature of existence.*
2 (of a ruminant) chew the cud.
– DERIVATIVES **rumination** noun, **ruminative** adjective, **ruminatively** adverb, **ruminator** noun.
– ORIGIN mid 16th cent.: from Latin *ruminat-* 'chewed over', from the verb *ruminari*.

rummage ▶ verb [no obj.] search unsystematically and untidily through a mass or receptacle: *he rummaged in his pocket for a handkerchief* | [with obj.] *he rummaged the drawer for his false teeth.*
■[with obj.] find (something) by searching in this way: *Mick* ***rummaged up*** *his skateboard.* ■ [with obj.] (of a customs officer) make a thorough search of (a vessel): *our brief was to rummage as many of the vessels as possible.*
▶ noun an unsystematic and untidy search through a mass or receptacle.
■a thorough search of a vessel by a customs officer.
– DERIVATIVES **rummager** noun.
– ORIGIN late 15th cent.: from Old French *arrumage*, from *arrumer* 'stow (in a hold)', from Middle Dutch *ruim* 'room'. In early use the word referred to the arranging of items such as casks in the hold of a ship, giving rise (early 17th cent.) to the verb sense 'make a search of (a vessel)'.

rummage sale ▶ noun chiefly N. Amer. a jumble sale.

rummer ▶ noun a large drinking glass.
– ORIGIN mid 17th cent.: of Low Dutch origin; related to Dutch *roemer*; the original meaning is perhaps 'Roman glass'.

rummy[1] ▶ noun [mass noun] a card game, sometimes played with two packs, in which the players try to form sets and sequences of cards.
– ORIGIN early 20th cent.: of unknown origin.

rummy[2] ▶ adjective (**rummier**, **rummiest**) another term for **RUM**[2].

rumour (US **rumor**) ▶ **noun** a currently circulating story or report of uncertain or doubtful truth: *they were investigating rumours of a massacre* | [mass noun] *rumour has it that he will take a year off.*
▶ **verb** (**be rumoured**) be circulated as an unverified account: [with clause] *it's rumoured that he lives on a houseboat* | [with infinitive] *she is rumoured to have gone into hiding.*
– ORIGIN late Middle English: from Old French *rumur*, from Latin *rumor* 'noise'.

rumour-monger ▶ **noun** derogatory a person who spreads rumours.
– DERIVATIVES **rumour-mongering** noun.

rump ▶ **noun 1** the hind part of the body of a mammal or the lower back of a bird.
■ chiefly humorous a person's buttocks.
2 a small or unimportant remnant of something originally larger: *once the profitable enterprises have been sold the unprofitable rump will be left.*
■ (**the Rump**) short for **RUMP PARLIAMENT**.
– DERIVATIVES **rumpless** adjective.
– ORIGIN late Middle English: probably of Scandinavian origin; compare with Danish and Norwegian *rumpe* 'backside'.

rumple ▶ **verb** [with obj.] [usu. as adj. **rumpled**] give a creased, ruffled, or dishevelled appearance to: *a rumpled bed.*
▶ **noun** [in sing.] an untidy state.
– DERIVATIVES **rumply** adjective.
– ORIGIN early 16th cent. (as a noun in the sense 'wrinkle'): from Middle Dutch *rompel*.

rumpot ▶ **noun** informal, chiefly N. Amer. an alcoholic.

Rump Parliament the part of the Long Parliament which continued to sit after Pride's Purge in 1648, and voted for the trial which resulted in the execution of Charles I.
– ORIGIN origin uncertain: said to derive from *The Bloody Rump*, the name of a paper written before the trial, the word being popularized after a speech by Major General Brown, given at a public assembly; also said to have been coined by Clem Walker in his *History of Independency* (1648), as a term for those strenuously opposing the king.

rumpsprung ▶ **adjective** informal (of furniture) baggy and worn in the seat: *a rumpsprung armchair.*

rump steak ▶ **noun** a cut of beef from the animal's rump.

rumpus ▶ **noun** (pl. **rumpuses**) [usu. in sing.] informal a noisy disturbance; a row: *he caused a rumpus with his flair for trouble-making.*
– ORIGIN mid 18th cent.: probably fanciful.

rumpus room ▶ **noun** N. Amer. & Austral./NZ a room for playing games, typically in the basement of a house.

rumpy pumpy ▶ **noun** [mass noun] informal, humorous sexual relations, especially when of a casual nature.
– ORIGIN 1960s: reduplication of **RUMP**.

run ▶ **verb** (**running**; past **ran** /ran/; past participle **run**)
1 [no obj.] move at a speed faster than a walk, never having both or all the feet on the ground at the same time: *the dog ran across the road* | *she ran the last few yards, breathing heavily* | *he hasn't paid for his drinks—run and catch him.*
■ run as a sport or for exercise: *I run every morning.* ■ (of an athlete or a racehorse) compete in a race: *she ran in the 200 metres.* | [with obj.] *Dave has run 42 marathons.* ■ [with obj.] enter (a racehorse) for a race. ■ Cricket (of a batsman) run from one wicket to the other in scoring or attempting to score a run. ■ [with obj.] W. Indian cause to run away; chase: *Ah went tuh eat the mangoes but the people run mih.* ■ (of hounds) chase or hunt their quarry. ■ (of a boat) sail straight and fast directly before the wind, especially in bad weather. ■ (of a migratory fish) go upriver from the sea in order to spawn.
2 [no obj.] move about in a hurried and hectic way: *I've spent the whole day running round after the kids.*
■ (**run to**) have rapid recourse to (someone) for support or help: *don't come running to me for a handout.*
3 pass or cause to pass quickly or smoothly in a particular direction: [no obj., with adverbial of direction] *the rumour ran through the pack of photographers* | [with obj. and adverbial of direction] *Helen ran her fingers through her hair.*
■ move or cause to move somewhere forcefully or with a particular result: [no obj., with adverbial of direction] *the tanker ran aground off the Shetland Islands* | [with obj. and adverbial of direction] *a woman ran a pushchair into the back of my legs.* ■ [with obj.] informal fail to stop at (a red traffic light). ■ [with obj.] chiefly N. Amer. navigate (rapids or a waterfall) in a boat. ■ extend or cause to extend in a particular direction: [no obj., with adverbial of direction] *cobbled streets run down to a tiny harbour* | [with obj. and adverbial of direction] *he ran a wire under the carpet.* ■ [no obj.] (**run in**) (of a quality or trait) be common or inherent in members of (a particular family), especially over several generations: *weight problems run in my family.* ■ [no obj.] pass into or reach a specified state or level: *inflation is running at 11 per cent* | [with complement] *the decision ran counter to previous government commitments.*
4 [no obj., with adverbial of direction] (of a liquid) flow in a specified direction: *a small river runs into the sea at one side of the castle.*
■ [with obj.] cause (a liquid) to flow: *she ran cold water into a basin.* ■ [with obj.] cause water to flow over (something): *I ran my hands under the tap.* ■ [with obj.] fill (a bath) with water: [with two objs] *I'll run you a nice hot bath.* ■ [no obj.] (**run with**) be covered or streaming with (a particular liquid): *his face was running with sweat.* ■ [no obj.] emit or exude a liquid: *she was weeping loudly and her nose was running.* ■ [no obj.] (of a solid substance) melt and become fluid: *it was so hot that the butter ran.* ■ [no obj.] (of the sea, the tide, or a river) rise higher or flow more quickly: *there was still a heavy sea running.* ■ [no obj.] (of dye or colour in fabric or paper) dissolve and spread when the fabric or paper becomes wet: *the red dye ran when the socks were washed.* ■ [no obj.] chiefly N. Amer. (of a stocking or pair of tights) develop a ladder.
5 [no obj.] (of a bus, train, ferry, or other form of transport) make a regular journey on a particular route: *buses run into town every half hour.*
■ [with obj.] put (a particular form of public transport) in service: *the group is drawing up plans to run trains on key routes.* ■ [with obj. and adverbial of direction] take (someone) somewhere in a car: *I'll run you home.*
6 [with obj.] be in charge of; manage: *Andrea runs her own catering business* | [as adj., in combination **-run**] *an attractive family-run hotel.*
■ [no obj., with adverbial] (of a system, organization, or plan) operate or proceed in a particular way: *everything's running according to plan.* ■ organize and make available for other people: *we decided to run a series of seminars.* ■ carry out (a test or procedure): *he asked the army to run tests on the anti nerve-gas pills.* ■ own, maintain, and use (a vehicle). ■ W. Indian provide: *the wait-and-see game continues until the government runs some ready cash.* ■ Austral./NZ provide pasture for (sheep or cattle); raise (livestock).
7 be in or cause to be in operation; function or cause to function: [no obj.] *the car runs on unleaded fuel* | [with obj.] *the modem must be run off a mains transformer.*
■ move or cause to move between the spools of a recording machine: [with obj.] *I ran the tape back* | [no obj.] *the tape has run through.*
8 [no obj.] continue or be valid or operative for a particular period of time: *the course ran for two days* | *this particular debate will run and run.*
■ [with adverbial or complement] happen or arrive at the specified time: *the programme was running fifteen minutes late.* ■ (of a play or exhibition) be staged or presented: *the play ran at Stratford last year.*
9 [no obj.] stand as a candidate in a political election: *he announced that he intended to run for President.*
■ [with obj.] (especially of a political party) sponsor (a candidate) in an election: *they ran their first independent candidate at the Bromley by-election.*
10 publish or be published in a newspaper or magazine: [with obj.] *the tabloid press ran the story* | [no obj.] *when the story ran, there was a big to-do.*
■ [no obj.] (of a story, argument, or piece of writing) have a specified wording or contents: *'Tapestries slashed!' ran the dramatic headline.*
12 [with obj.] bring (goods) into a country illegally and secretly; smuggle: *they run drugs for the cocaine cartels.*
13 [with two objs] N. Amer. (of an object or act) cost (someone) (a specified amount): *a new photocopier will run us about $1,300.*
▶ **noun 1** [usu. in sing.] an act or spell of running: *I usually go for a run in the morning* | *a cross-country run.*
■ a running pace: *Rory set off at a run.* ■ an opportunity or attempt to achieve something: *their absence means the Russians will have a clear run at the title.* ■ a preliminary test of the efficiency of a procedure or system: *if you are styling your hair yourself, have a practice run.* ■ an attempt to secure election to political office: *his run for the Republican nomination.* ■ an annual mass migration of fish up a river to spawn, or their return migration afterwards: *the annual salmon runs.*
2 a journey accomplished or route taken by a vehicle, aircraft, or boat, especially on a regular basis: *the London–Liverpool run.*
■ a short excursion made in a car: *we could take a run out to the country.* ■ the distance covered in a specified period, especially by a ship: *a record run of 398 miles from noon to noon.* ■ a short flight made by an aircraft on a straight and even course at a constant speed before or while dropping bombs.
3 Cricket a unit of scoring achieved by hitting the ball so that both batsmen are able to run between the wickets, or awarded in some other circumstances.
■ Baseball a point scored by the batter returning to the home plate after touching the other bases.
4 a continuous spell of a particular situation or condition: *he's had a run of bad luck.*
■ a continuous series of performances: *the play had a long run in the West End.* ■ a quantity or amount of something produced at one time: *a production run of only 150 cars.* ■ a continuous stretch or length of something: *long runs of copper piping.* ■ a rapid series of musical notes forming a scale. ■ a sequence of cards of the same suit.
5 (**a run on**) a widespread and sudden or continuous demand for (a particular currency or commodity): *there's been a big run on nostalgia toys this year.*
■ a sudden demand for repayment from a bank made by a large number of lenders: *growing nervousness among investors led to a run on some banks.*
6 (**the run of**) free and unrestricted use of or access to: *her cats were given the run of the house.*
7 (**the run**) [usu. with adj.] the average or usual type of person or thing: *she stood out from the general run of Tory women.*
■ the general tendency or trend of something: *quite against the run of play, Smith scored an early try.*
8 an enclosed area in which domestic animals or birds may run freely in the open: *a chicken run.*
■ [usu. with modifier] a track made or regularly used by a particular animal: *a badger run.* ■ a sloping snow-covered course or track used for skiing, bobsleighing, or tobogganing: *a ski run.* ■ Austral./NZ a large open stretch of land used for pasture or the raising of stock: *one of the richest cattle runs of the district.*
9 a ladder in stockings or tights.
10 a downward trickle of paint or a similar substance when applied too thickly.
11 a small stream or brook.
12 (**the runs**) informal diarrhoea.
13 Nautical the after part of a ship's bottom where it rises and narrows towards the stern.
– PHRASES **be run off one's feet** see **FOOT**. **come running** be eager to do what someone wants: *he had only to crook his finger and she would come running.* **give someone/thing a (good) run for their money** provide someone or something with challenging competition or opposition. **have a (good) run for one's money** derive reward or enjoyment in return for one's outlay or efforts. **on the run 1** trying to avoid being captured: *a criminal on the run from the FBI.* **2** while running: *he took a pass on the run.* ■ continuously active and busy: *I'm on the run every minute of the day.* **run before one can walk** attempt something difficult before one has grasped the basic skills. Compare with ***walk before one can run*** at **WALK**. **run a blockade** see **BLOCKADE**. **run dry** (of a well or river) cease to flow or have any water. ■ figurative (especially of a source of money or information) be completely used up: *municipal relief funds had long since run dry.* **run an errand** carry out an errand, typically on someone else's behalf. **(make a) run for it** attempt to escape someone or something by running away. **run foul** (or chiefly N. Amer. **afoul**) **of 1** Nautical collide or become entangled with (an obstacle or another vessel): *another ship ran foul of us.* **2** come into conflict with; go against: *the act may run foul of data protection legislation.* **run the gauntlet** see **GAUNTLET**[2]. **run someone close** almost defeat a person or team in a contest. **run high** see **HIGH**. **run oneself into the ground** see **GROUND**[1]. **run into the sand** come to nothing: *the peace initiative now seems to be running into the sand.* **run its course** see **COURSE**. **run low** (or **short**) become depleted: *supplies had run short.* ■ have too little of something: *we're running short of time.* **run a mile** see **MILE**. **run off at the mouth** N. Amer. informal talk excessively or indiscreetly. **run someone out of town** chiefly N. Amer. force someone to leave a place. **run rings round** see **RING**[1]. **run riot** see **RIOT**. **run the risk** (or **run risks**) see **RISK**. **run the show** informal dominate or be in charge of a project,

undertaking, or domain. **run a temperature** be suffering from a fever or high temperature. **run someone/thing to earth** (or **ground**) Hunting chase a quarry to its lair. ▪ find someone or something, typically after a long search. **run to ruin** archaic fall into disrepair; gradually deteriorate. **run to seed** see **SEED**. **run wild** see **WILD**. **you can't run with the hares and hunt with the hounds** proverb you can't be loyal to both sides in a conflict or dispute.
– DERIVATIVES **runnable** adjective.
– ORIGIN Old English *rinnan*, *irnan* (verb), of Germanic origin, probably reinforced in Middle English by Old Norse *rinna*, *renna*. The current form with *-u-* in the present tense is first recorded in the 16th cent.

USAGE On the use of verbs used with **and** instead of a 'to' infinitive, as in ***run and*** *fetch the paper*, see **usage** at **AND**.

▶**run across** meet or find by chance: *I just thought you might have run across him before.*
run after informal seek to acquire or attain; pursue persistently: *businesses which have spent years running after the baby boom market.* ▪ seek the company of (someone) with the aim of developing a romantic or sexual relationship with them.
run against archaic collide with (someone). ▪ happen to meet: *I ran against Flanagan the other day.*
run along [in imperative] informal go away (used typically to address a child): *run along now, there's a good girl.*
run around with (US also **run with**) informal associate habitually with (someone).
run at rush towards (someone) to attack or as if to attack them.
run away leave or escape from a place, person, or situation of danger: *children who* ***run away from*** *home normally go to London.* ▪ (also informal **run off**) leave one's home or current partner in order to establish a relationship with someone else: *he* ***ran off with*** *his wife's best friend | Fran, let's* ***run away together.*** ▪ try to avoid acknowledging or facing up to an unpleasant or difficult situation: *the government are* ***running away from*** *their responsibilities.*
run away with 1 (of one's imagination or emotions) work wildly, so as to overwhelm (one): *Susan's imagination was running away with her.* **2** accept (an idea) without thinking it through properly: *a lot of people ran away with the idea that they were pacifists.* **3** win (a competition or prize) easily: *Ipswich are running away with the championship.*
run something by (or **past**) tell (someone) about something, especially in order to ascertain their opinion or reaction.
run someone/thing down 1 (of a vehicle or its driver) hit a person or animal and knock them to the ground. ▪ (of a boat) collide with another vessel. **2** criticize someone or something unfairly or unkindly. **3** discover someone or something after a search: *she finally ran the professor down.*
run something down (or **run down**) reduce (or become reduced) in size, numbers, or resources: *the government were reviled for running down the welfare state | hardwood stocks in some countries are rapidly running down.* ▪ lose (or cause to lose) power; stop (or cause to stop) functioning: *the battery has run down.* ▪ gradually deteriorate (or cause to deteriorate) in quality or condition: *the property had been allowed to run down.*
run someone in informal arrest someone.
run something in Brit. prepare the engine of a new car for normal use by driving slowly, usually for a particular period of time. ▪ use something new in such a way as not to make maximum demands upon it: *whatever system you choose, you must run it in properly.*
run into 1 collide with: *he ran into a lamp post.* ▪ meet by chance: *I ran into Moira on the way home.* ▪ experience (a problem or difficult situation): *the bank ran into financial difficulties.* **2** reach (a level or amount): *debts running into millions of dollars.* **3** blend into or appear to coalesce with: *her words ran into each other.*
run off see *run away* above.
run off with informal steal: *the treasurer had run off with the pension funds.*
run something off 1 reproduce copies of a piece of writing on a machine. ▪ write or recite something quickly and with little effort. **2** drain liquid from a container: *run off the water that has been standing in the pipes.*
run on 1 continue without stopping; go on longer than is expected: *the story ran on for months.* ▪ talk incessantly. **2** (also **run upon**) (of a person's mind or a discussion) be preoccupied or concerned with (a particular subject): *my thoughts ran too much on death.* **3** Printing continue on the same line as the preceding matter.
run out 1 (of a supply of something) be used up: *our food is about to run out.* ▪ use up one's supply of something: *we've* ***run out of*** *petrol.* ▪ become no longer valid: *her contract runs out at the end of the year.* **2** (of rope) be paid out: *slowly, he let the cables run out.* **3** [with adverbial of direction] extend; project: *a row of buildings ran out to Whitehall Gate.* **4** [with complement] Brit. emerge from a contest in a specified position: *the team ran out 4–1 winners.*
run someone out Cricket dismiss a batsman by dislodging the bails with the ball while the batsman is still running between the wickets. ▪ (of a batsman) cause one's partner to be dismissed in this way by poor judgement.
run out on informal abandon (someone); cease to support or care for.
run over 1 (of a container or its contents) overflow: *the bath's running over.* **2** exceed (an expected limit): *the film ran over schedule and budget.*
run someone/thing over (of a vehicle or its driver) knock a person or animal down and pass over their body: *Anna accidentally ran over their cat.*
run something over see *run something through* below.
run through 1 be present in every part of; pervade: *a sense of personal loss runs through many of his lyrics.* **2** use or spend recklessly or rapidly: *her husband had long since run through her money.*
run someone/thing through stab a person or animal so as to kill them.
run something through (or **over**) discuss, read, or repeat something quickly or briefly: *I'll just run through the schedule for the weekend.* ▪ rehearse a performance or series of actions: *okay, let's run through Scene 3 again.*
run to 1 extend to or reach (a specified amount or size): *the document ran to almost 100 pages.* ▪ be enough to cover (a particular expense); have the financial resources for: *my income doesn't run to luxuries like taxis.* **2** (of a person) show a tendency to or inclination towards: *she was tall and running to fat.*
run something up 1 allow a debt or bill to accumulate quickly: *he ran up debts of $153,000.* ▪ achieve a particular score in a game or match: *they ran up 467 runs for the loss of eight wickets.* **2** make something quickly or hurriedly, especially a piece of clothing: *I'll run up a dress for you.* **3** raise a flag.
run up against experience or meet (a difficulty or problem): *the scheme has been dropped as it could run up against European regulations.*
run with 1 proceed with; accept: *we do lots of tests before we run with a product.* **2** see *run around with* above.

runabout ▶noun a small car or light aircraft, especially one used for short journeys.
▪ N. Amer. a small motor boat.

runaround informal ▶noun **1** (usu. **the runaround**) difficult or awkward treatment, especially in which someone is evasive or does not answer one's questions directly: *they are being* ***given the runaround*** *by the Defence Ministry.*
2 a runabout.

runaway ▶noun a person who has run away, especially from their family or an institution.
▪ [often as modifier] an animal or vehicle that is running out of control: *a runaway train.* ▪ [as modifier] denoting something happening or done very quickly, easily, or uncontrollably: *the runaway success of the book.*

runcible spoon /ˈrʌnsɪb(ə)l/ ▶noun a fork curved like a spoon, with three broad prongs, one of which has a sharpened outer edge for cutting.
– ORIGIN late 19th cent.: used by Edward Lear, perhaps suggested by late 16th-cent. *rouncival*, denoting a large variety of pea.

Runcorn /ˈrʌŋkɔːn/ an industrial town in NW England, on the River Mersey in Cheshire; pop. 64,600 (est. 1985). It was developed as a new town from 1964.

rundown ▶noun [usu. in sing.] **1** an analysis or summary of something by a knowledgeable person: *he gave his teammates* ***a rundown on*** *the opposition.*
2 a reduction in the productivity or activities of a company or institution: *a rundown in the business would be a devastating blow to the local economy.*
▶adjective (usu. **run-down**) **1** (especially of a building or area) in a poor or neglected state after having been prosperous: *a run-down Edwardian villa.*
▪ (of a company or industry) in a poor economic state.
2 [predic.] tired and rather unwell, especially through overwork: *feeling tired and generally run-down.*

rune /ruːn/ ▶noun a letter of an ancient Germanic alphabet, related to the Roman alphabet.
▪ a similar mark of mysterious or magic significance. ▪ (**runes**) small stones, pieces of bone, etc., bearing such marks, and used as divinatory symbols: *the casting of the runes.* ▪ a spell or incantation. ▪ a section of the Kalevala or of an ancient Scandinavian poem.

Runes were used by Scandinavians and Anglo-Saxons from about the 3rd century. They were formed mainly by modifying Roman or Greek characters to suit carving, and were used both in writing and in divination.

– PHRASES **read the runes** Brit. try to forecast the outcome of a situation by analysing all the significant factors involved.
– DERIVATIVES **runic** adjective.
– ORIGIN Old English *rūn* 'a secret, mystery'; not recorded between Middle English and the late 17th cent., when it was reintroduced under the influence of Old Norse *rúnir, rúnar* 'magic signs, hidden lore'.

rune stone ▶noun **1** a large stone carved with runes by ancient Scandinavians or Anglo-Saxons.
2 a small stone, piece of bone, etc., marked with a rune and used in divination.

run-flat ▶adjective [attrib.] relating to or denoting a kind of tyre which does not deflate after puncturing.
▶noun a tyre of this type.

rung[1] ▶noun **1** a horizontal support on a ladder for a person's foot.
▪ figurative a level in a hierarchical structure, especially a class or career structure: *we must ensure that the low-skilled do not get trapped on the bottom rung.*
2 a strengthening crosspiece in the structure of a chair.
– DERIVATIVES **runged** adjective, **rungless** adjective.
– ORIGIN Old English *hrung* (in sense 2); related to Dutch *rong* and German *Runge*.

rung[2] past participle of **RING**[2].

run-in ▶noun **1** [usu. in sing.] the approach to an action or event: *the final run-in to the World Cup.*
▪ the home stretch of a race course. ▪ a period during which an engine or other device is run in.
2 informal a disagreement or fight, especially with someone in an official position: *a run-in with armed police in Rio.*
▪ a collision: *a run-in with a parking meter.*

runlet ▶noun a small stream.

runnel ▶noun a gutter.
▪ a brook or rill. ▪ a small stream of a particular liquid: *a runnel of sweat.*
– ORIGIN late 16th cent. (denoting a brook or rill): variant of dialect *rindle*, influenced by the verb **RUN**.

runner ▶noun **1** a person that runs, especially in a specified way: *Mary was a fast runner.*
▪ a person who runs competitively as a sport or hobby: *a 400 metres runner.* ▪ a horse that runs in a particular race: *there were only four runners.* ▪ a vehicle or machine that operates in a satisfactory or specified way: *the van was a good and reliable runner.* ▪ a messenger, collector, or agent for a bank, bookmaker, or similar. ▪ an orderly in the army. ▪ Brit. informal a freelance antiques dealer. ▪ Brit. informal a contender for a job or position. ▪ Brit. informal an idea that has a chance of being accepted; a practical suggestion: *trying to determine whether a tax on books is a runner.* ▪ Cricket a person who runs between the wickets for an injured batsman.
2 [in combination] a person who smuggles specified goods into or out of a country or area: *a gun-runner.*
3 a rod, groove, or blade on which something slides.
▪ each of the long pieces on the underside of a sledge that forms the contact in sliding. ▪ (often **runners**) a roller for moving a heavy article. ▪ a ring capable of slipping or sliding along a strap or rod or through which something may be passed or drawn. ▪ Nautical a rope in a single block with one end round a tackle block and the other having a hook.
4 a shoot, typically leafless, which grows from the base of a plant along the surface of the ground and can take root at points along its length.

r

▪a plant that spreads by means of such shoots. ▪a twining plant.

5 a long, narrow rug or strip of carpet, especially for a hall or stairway.

6 (also **runner stone**) a revolving millstone.

7 archaic a police officer. See also **BOW STREET RUNNER**.

8 (also **runner duck**) see **INDIAN RUNNER**.

9 a fast-swimming fish of the jack family, occurring in tropical seas.

• Several species in the family Carangidae, in particular the colourfully striped **rainbow runner** (*Elagatis bipinnulata*) of warm seas worldwide, and the **blue runner** (*Caranx crysos*) of the western Atlantic.

– PHRASES **do a runner** Brit. informal leave hastily, especially to avoid paying for something or to escape from somewhere.

runner bean ▶ noun chiefly Brit. a Central American bean plant with scarlet flowers and very long flat edible pods. Also called **SCARLET RUNNER**.

• *Phaseolus coccineus*, family Leguminosae.

▪the pod and seed of this plant eaten as food.

runner-up ▶ noun (pl. **runners-up**) a competitor or team taking second place in a contest.

running ▶ noun [mass noun] **1** the action or movement of a runner: *his running tore United to shreds.*

▪the sport of racing on foot: *marathon running.*

2 the action of managing or operating something: *the day-to-day running of the office.*

▶ adjective **1** [attrib.] denoting something that runs, in particular:

▪(of water) flowing naturally or supplied to a building through pipes and taps: *hot and cold running water.* ▪(of a sore or a part of the body) exuding liquid or pus: *a running sore.* ▪continuous or recurring over a long period: *a running joke.* ▪done while running: *a running jump.*

2 [postpositive] consecutive; in succession: *he failed to produce an essay for the third week running.*

– PHRASES **in** (or **out of**) **the running** in (or no longer in) contention for an award, victory, or a place in a team: *he is in the running for an Oscar.* **make the running** set the pace in a race or activity. **take a running jump** [often as imperative] used when angrily rejecting or disagreeing with someone: *I hope you told that boss of yours to take a running jump.* **take up the running** take over as pacesetter in a race.

running back ▶ noun American Football an offensive player who specializes in carrying the ball.

running battle ▶ noun a military engagement which does not occur at a fixed location.

▪a confrontation which has gone on for a long time.

running belay ▶ noun Climbing a device attached to a rock face through which a climbing rope runs freely, acting as a pulley if the climber falls.

running-board ▶ noun a footboard extending along the side of a vehicle, typically found on early models of car.

running commentary ▶ noun a verbal description of events, given as they occur.

running dog ▶ noun **1** informal a servile follower, especially of a political system: *the running dogs of capitalism.* [ORIGIN: translating Chinese *zǒugǒu*.]

2 a dog bred to run, especially for racing or pulling a sled.

running fix ▶ noun a determination of one's position made by taking bearings at different times and allowing for the distance covered in the interval.

running gear ▶ noun [mass noun] the moving parts of a machine, especially the wheels, steering, and suspension of a vehicle.

▪the moving rope and tackle used in handling a boat.

running head (also **running headline**) ▶ noun a heading printed at the top of each page of a book or chapter.

running knot ▶ noun a knot that slips along the rope and changes the size of a noose.

running lights ▶ plural noun **1** another term for **NAVIGATION LIGHTS**.

2 small lights on a motor vehicle that remain illuminated while the vehicle is running.

running mate ▶ noun chiefly US **1** an election candidate for the lesser of two closely associated political offices.

2 a horse entered in a race in order to set the pace for another horse from the same stable, which is intended to win.

running pine ▶ noun N. Amer. a clubmoss which has a ground-hugging habit and propagates by means of runners.

• Genus *Lycopodium*, family Lycopodiaceae, in particular *L. clavatum*.

running repairs ▶ plural noun minor or temporary repairs carried out on machinery while it is in use.

running rigging ▶ noun see **RIGGING**[1] (sense 1).

running rope ▶ noun a rope that is able to move freely, especially through a pulley.

running stitch ▶ noun [mass noun] a simple needlework stitch consisting of a line of small even stitches which run back and forth through the cloth without overlapping.

running total ▶ noun a total that is continually adjusted to take account of further items.

runny ▶ adjective (**runnier**, **runniest**) **1** more liquid than is usual or expected: *the soufflé was hard on top and quite runny underneath.*

2 (of a person's nose) producing or discharging mucus; running.

Runnymede /ˈrʌnɪmiːd/ a meadow on the south bank of the Thames near Windsor. It is famous for its association with Magna Carta, which was signed by King John in 1215 there or nearby.

run-off ▶ noun **1** a further competition, election, race, etc., after a tie or inconclusive result.

2 [mass noun] the draining away of water (or substances carried in it) from the surface of an area of land, a building or structure, etc.

▪the water or other material that drains freely off the surface of something.

3 NZ a separate area of land where young animals are kept.

run-of-the-mill ▶ adjective lacking unusual or special aspects; ordinary: *a run-of-the-mill job.*

run-on ▶ adjective [attrib.] denoting a line of verse in which a sentence is continued without a pause beyond the end of a line, couplet, or stanza.

run-out ▶ noun **1** Cricket the dismissal of a batsman by being run out.

2 informal a short session of play, practice, or participation in sporting competition, especially at the beginning of a season or after a period of absence due to injury.

3 a slight error in a rotating tool, machine component, etc. such as being off-centre or not exactly round.

4 a length of time or stretch of ground over which something gradually ceases or is brought to an end or a halt: *the commission recommended abolition after a run-out of ten years.*

runt ▶ noun **1** a small pig or other animal, especially the smallest in a litter.

▪figurative an undersized or weak person.

2 a pigeon of a large domestic breed.

3 a small ox or cow, especially one of various Scottish Highland or Welsh breeds.

– DERIVATIVES **runty** adjective.

– ORIGIN early 16th cent. (in the sense 'old or decayed tree stump'): of unknown origin.

run-through ▶ noun **1** a rehearsal: *a run-through of the whole show.*

2 a brief outline or summary: *the textbooks provide a run-through of research findings.*

run-time Computing ▶ noun the length of time a program takes to run.

▪the time at which the program is run. ▪a cut-down version of a program that can be run but not changed: *you can distribute the run-time to your colleagues.*

▶ adjective (of software) in a reduced version that can be run but not changed.

run-up ▶ noun **1** the period preceding a notable event: *a programme aimed at lowering unemployment in the run-up to the next election.*

2 an act of running briefly to gain momentum before performing a jump in athletics, bowling in cricket, etc.

▪the strip of ground behind the wicket on which the bowler runs before bowling.

3 Golf a low approach shot that bounces and runs forward.

4 an act of running an engine or turbine to prepare it for use or to test it.

5 a marked rise in the value or level of something: *a sharp run-up of land and stock prices.*

runway ▶ noun **1** a strip of hard ground along which aircraft take off and land.

2 a raised gangway extending into the audience in a theatre or other public venue, especially as used for fashion shows.

3 an animal run, especially one made by small mammals in grass, under snow, etc.

4 an incline or chute down which logs are slid.

Runyon /ˈrʌnjən/, (Alfred) Damon (1884–1946), American author and journalist. His short stories about New York's underworld characters are written in a highly individual style with much use of colourful slang.

rupee /ruːˈpiː, rʊˈpiː/ ▶ noun the basic monetary unit of India, Pakistan, Sri Lanka, Nepal, Mauritius, and the Seychelles, equal to 100 paisa in India, Pakistan, and Nepal, and 100 cents in Sri Lanka, Mauritius, and the Seychelles.

– ORIGIN via Hindi from Sanskrit *rūpya* 'wrought silver'.

Rupert, Prince (1619–82), English Royalist general, son of Frederick V (elector of the Palatinate) and nephew of Charles I. The Royalist leader of cavalry, he initially won a series of victories, but was defeated by Parliamentarian forces at Marston Moor (1644) and Naseby (1645).

Rupert's Land (also **Prince Rupert's Land**) a historical region of northern and western Canada, roughly corresponding to what is now Manitoba, Saskatchewan, Yukon, Alberta, and the southern part of the Northwest Territories. It was originally granted in 1670 by Charles II to the Hudson's Bay Company and named after Prince Rupert, the first governor of the Company; it was purchased by Canada in 1870.

rupestrian /ruːˈpɛstrɪən/ ▶ adjective (of art) done on rock or cave walls.

– ORIGIN late 18th cent.: from modern Latin *rupestris* 'found on rocks' (from Latin *rupes* 'rock') + **-AN**.

rupiah /ruːˈpiːə/ ▶ noun the basic monetary unit of Indonesia, equal to 100 sen.

– ORIGIN Indonesian, from Hindi *rūpyah* (see **RUPEE**).

rupture ▶ verb [no obj.] (especially of a pipe or vessel, or bodily part such as an organ or membrane) break or burst suddenly: *if the main artery ruptures he could die.*

▪[with obj.] cause to break or burst suddenly and completely: *the impact ruptured both fuel tanks.* ▪[with obj.] suffer such a bursting of (a bodily part): *it was her first match since rupturing an Achilles tendon.* ▪(**be ruptured** or **rupture oneself**) suffer an abdominal hernia: *one of the boys was ruptured and needed to be fitted with a truss.* ▪[with obj.] figurative breach or disturb (a harmonious feeling or situation): *once trust and confidence has been ruptured it can be difficult to regain.*

▶ noun an instance of breaking or bursting suddenly and completely: *a small hairline crack could develop into a rupture* | [mass noun] *the patient died after rupture of an aneurysm.*

▪figurative a breach of a harmonious relationship: *the rupture with his father would never be healed.* ▪an abdominal hernia.

– ORIGIN late Middle English (as a noun): from Old French *rupture* or Latin *ruptura*, from *rumpere* 'to break'. The verb dates from the mid 18th cent.

rupturewort ▶ noun a small Old World plant of the pink family, which was formerly believed to cure hernia.

• *Herniaria glabra*, family Caryophyllaceae.

rural ▶ adjective in, relating to, or characteristic of the countryside rather than the town: *remote rural areas.*

– DERIVATIVES **ruralism** noun, **ruralist** noun, **rurality** noun, **ruralization** noun, **ruralize** (also **-ise**) verb, **rurally** adverb.

– ORIGIN late Middle English: from Old French, or from late Latin *ruralis*, from *rus*, *rur-* 'country'.

rural dean ▶ noun see **DEAN**[1] (sense 1).

rural district ▶ noun Brit. historical a group of country parishes governed by an elected council.

Rurik /ˈrʊərɪk/ (also **Ryurik**) ▶ noun a member of a dynasty that ruled Muscovy and much of Russia from the 9th century until the death of Fyodor, son of Ivan the Terrible, in 1598. It was reputedly founded by a Varangian chief who settled in Novgorod in 862.

▶ adjective of or relating to the Ruriks.

Ruritania /ˌrʊərɪˈteɪnɪə/ an imaginary kingdom in SE Europe used as a fictional background for the adventure novels of courtly intrigue and romance written by Anthony Hope (1863–1933).

– DERIVATIVES **Ruritanian** adjective & noun.

– ORIGIN from **RURAL**, on the pattern of *Lusitania*.

r

rusa /ˈruːsə/ (also **rusa deer**) ▶ **noun** an Indonesian deer with a brown coat and branched antlers.
• *Cervus timorensis*, family Cervidae.
– ORIGIN late 18th cent.: modern Latin (former genus name), from Malay.

rusbank /ˈrəsbaŋk/ ▶ **noun** (pl. **rusbanks** or **rusbanke**) S. African a long wooden settle, typically with back and seat made of woven leather thongs.
– ORIGIN Afrikaans, from *rus* 'rest' + *bank* 'bench'.

Ruse /ˈruːseɪ/ (also **Rousse**) an industrial city and the principal port of Bulgaria, on the Danube; pop. 209,760 (1990). Turkish during the Middle Ages, it was captured by Russia in 1877 and ceded to Bulgaria.

ruse /ruːz/ ▶ **noun** an action intended to deceive someone; a trick: *Emma tried to think of a ruse to get Paul out of the house.*
– ORIGIN late Middle English (as a hunting term): from Old French, from *ruser* 'use trickery', earlier 'drive back', perhaps based on Latin *rursus* 'backwards'.

rush[1] ▶ **verb 1** [no obj., with adverbial of direction] move with urgent haste: *Oliver rushed after her* | *I rushed outside and hailed a taxi.*
■ (of air or a liquid) flow strongly: *the water rushed in through the great oaken gates.* ■ [no obj.] act with great haste: *as soon as the campaign started they* **rushed into** *action* | [with infinitive] *shoppers rushed to buy computers.* ■ [with obj.] force (someone) to act hastily: *I don't want to* **rush** *you* **into** *something.* ■ [with obj. and adverbial of direction] take (someone) somewhere with great haste: *an ambulance was waiting to rush him to hospital.* ■ [with two objs] deliver (something) quickly to (someone): *we'll rush you a copy at once.* ■ (**rush something out**) produce and distribute something, or put something up for sale, very quickly: *a rewritten textbook was rushed out last autumn.* ■ [with obj.] deal with (something) hurriedly: *panic measures were* **rushed through** *parliament* | [as adj. **rushed**] *a rushed job.* ■ [with obj.] dash towards (someone or something) in an attempt to attack or capture them or it: *to rush the bank and fire willy-nilly could be disastrous for everyone.*
2 [with obj.] American Football advance towards (an opposing player, especially the quarterback).
■ [no obj.] gain a specified amount of ground by running forward with the ball: *he rushed for 100 yards on 22 carries.*
3 [with obj.] US entertain (a new student) in order to assess suitability for membership of a college fraternity or sorority.
■ (of a student) be entertained by (a college fraternity or sorority) in this way.
4 [with obj.] Brit. informal, dated overcharge (a customer).
▶ **noun 1** a sudden quick movement towards something, typically by a number of people: *there was a* **rush for** *the door.*
■ a flurry of hasty activity: *the pre-Christmas rush* | [as modifier] *a rush job.* ■ a sudden strong demand for a commodity: *there's been a* **rush on** *the Western News because of the murder.* ■ a sudden flow or flood: *she felt a rush of cold air.* ■ a sudden intense feeling: *Mark felt a rush of anger.* ■ a sudden thrill or feeling of euphoria such as experienced after taking certain drugs.
2 American Football an act of advancing forward, especially towards the quarterback.
3 (**rushes**) the first prints made of a film after a period of shooting.
– PHRASES **rush one's fences** Brit. act with undue haste. **a rush of blood** (**to the head**) a sudden attack of wild irrationality.
– DERIVATIVES **rusher** noun, **rushingly** adverb.
– ORIGIN late Middle English: from an Anglo-Norman French variant of Old French *ruser* 'drive back', an early sense of the word in English (see **RUSE**).

rush[2] ▶ **noun 1** a marsh or waterside plant with slender stem-like pith-filled leaves, widely distributed in temperate areas. Some kinds are used for matting, chair seats, and baskets, and some were formerly used for strewing on floors.
• Genus *Juncus*, family Juncaceae.
■ used in names of similar plants of wet habitats, e.g. **flowering rush**. ■ a stem of such a plant. ■ [mass noun] such plants used as a material.
2 archaic a thing of no value (used for emphasis): *not one of them is* **worth a rush**.
– DERIVATIVES **rushlike** adjective, **rushy** adjective.
– ORIGIN Old English *risc, rysc*, of Germanic origin.

Rushdie /ˈrʌʃdi, ˈrʊʃ-/, (Ahmed) Salman (b.1947), Indian-born British novelist. His work, chiefly associated with magic realism, includes *Midnight's Children* (Booker Prize, 1981) and *The Satanic Verses* (1988). The latter, regarded by Muslims as blasphemous, caused Ayatollah Khomeini to issue a fatwa in 1989 condemning Rushdie to death; in 1998 the Iranian government dissociated itself from the fatwa.

rush hour ▶ **noun** a time during each day when traffic is at its heaviest.

rushlight ▶ **noun** historical a candle made by dipping the pith of a rush in tallow.

Rushmore, Mount a mountain in the Black Hills of South Dakota, noted for its giant busts of four US Presidents—George Washington, Thomas Jefferson, Abraham Lincoln, and Theodore Roosevelt—carved (1927–41) under the direction of the sculptor Gutzon Borglum (1867–1941).

rus in urbe /ˌruːs ɪn ˈɜːbeɪ/ ▶ **noun** poetic/literary an illusion of countryside created by a building or garden within a city.
– ORIGIN Latin, literally 'country in the city'.

rusk ▶ **noun** a light, dry biscuit or piece of rebaked bread, especially one prepared for use as baby food.
■ [mass noun] rebaked bread used, for example, as extra filling for sausages, and formerly as rations at sea.
– ORIGIN late 16th cent.: from Spanish or Portuguese *rosca* 'twist, coil, roll of bread', of unknown ultimate origin.

Ruskin, John (1819–1900), English art and social critic. His prolific writings include attacks on Renaissance art in *The Stones of Venice* (1851–3), capitalism in 'The Political Economy of Art' (1857), and utilitarianism in *Unto This Last* (1860).

Russell[1], Bertrand (Arthur William), 3rd Earl Russell (1872–1970), British philosopher, mathematician, and social reformer. In *Principia Mathematica* (1910–13) he and A. N. Whitehead attempted to express all of mathematics in formal logic terms. He expounded logical atomism in *Our Knowledge of the External World* (1914) and neutral monism in *The Analysis of Mind* (1921). A conscientious objector during the First World War, he also campaigned for women's suffrage and against nuclear arms. Nobel Prize for Literature (1950).

Russell[2], George William (1867–1935), Irish poet and journalist. After the performance of his poetic drama *Deirdre* (1902) Russell became a leading figure in the Irish literary revival.

Russell[3], John, 1st Earl Russell (1792–1878), British Whig statesman, Prime Minister 1846–52 and 1865–6. He was responsible for introducing the Reform Bill of 1832 into Parliament and resigned his second premiership when his attempt to extend the franchise further was unsuccessful.

Russell[4], Ken (born Henry Kenneth Alfred Russell) (b.1927), English film director. Characterized by extravagant and extreme imagery, his films, for example *Women in Love* (1969), have often attracted controversy for their depiction of sex and violence.

Russell's paradox a logical paradox stated in terms of set theory, concerning the set of all sets that do not contain themselves as members, namely that the condition for it to contain itself is that it should not contain itself.
– ORIGIN 1920s: named after Bertrand *Russell* (see **RUSSELL**[1]).

Russell's viper ▶ **noun** a large venomous Asian snake which has a yellow-brown body with black markings.
• *Daboia* (or *Vipera*) *russelli*, family Viperidae.
– ORIGIN early 20th cent.: named after Patrick Russell (1727–1805), Scottish physician and naturalist.

russet ▶ **adjective 1** reddish brown in colour: *the russet bracken.*
2 archaic rustic; homely: *that terse and epigrammatic style, with its russet Saxon.*
▶ **noun 1** [mass noun] a reddish-brown colour: *the woods in autumn are a riot of russet and gold.*
2 a dessert apple of a variety with a slightly rough greenish-brown skin.
3 [mass noun] historical a coarse homespun reddish-brown or grey cloth used for simple clothing.
– DERIVATIVES **russety** adjective.
– ORIGIN Middle English: from an Anglo-Norman French variant of Old French *rousset*, diminutive of *rous* 'red', from Provençal *ros*, from Latin *russus* 'red'.

Russia /ˈrʌʃə/ a country in northern Asia and eastern Europe; pop. 148,930,000 (est. 1991); official language, Russian; capital, Moscow. Official name **RUSSIAN FEDERATION**.

> The modern state originated from the expansion of the principality of Muscovy into a great empire. Russia played an increasing role in Europe from the time of Peter the Great in the early 18th century. Following the overthrow of the tsar in the Russian Revolution of 1917, Russia became the largest of the constituent republics of the Soviet Union, with more than three quarters of the area and over half of the population. On the break-up of the Soviet Union and the collapse of Communist control in 1991, Russia emerged as an independent state and a founder member of the Commonwealth of Independent States.

Russia leather ▶ **noun** [mass noun] a durable leather made from calfskins and impregnated with birchbark oil, used for bookbinding.

Russian ▶ **adjective** of or relating to Russia, its people, or their language.
▶ **noun 1** a native or national of Russia.
■ a person of Russian descent. ■ historical (in general use) a national of the former Soviet Union.
2 [mass noun] the language of Russia, an Eastern Slavic language written in the Cyrillic alphabet and spoken by over 130 million people.
– DERIVATIVES **Russianization** noun, **Russianize** (also **-ise**) verb, **Russianness** noun.
– ORIGIN mid 16th cent.: from medieval Latin *Russianus*.

Russian ballet ▶ **noun** [mass noun] a style of ballet developed at the Russian Imperial Ballet Academy, popularized in the West by Sergei Diaghilev's Ballets Russes from 1909.

Russian Blue ▶ **noun** a cat of a breed with short greyish-blue fur, green eyes, and large pointed ears.

Russian boot ▶ **noun** a boot that loosely encloses the wearer's calf.

Russian Civil War a conflict fought in Russia (1918–21) after the Revolution, between the Bolshevik Red Army and the counter-revolutionary White Russians. The Bolsheviks were ultimately victorious, and the Union of Soviet Socialist Republics was established.

Russian doll ▶ **noun** each of a set of brightly painted hollow wooden dolls of varying sizes, designed to fit inside each other.

Russian Federation official name for **RUSSIA**.

Russian olive ▶ **noun** North American term for **OLEASTER**.

Russian Orthodox Church the national Church of Russia. See **ORTHODOX CHURCH**.

Russian Revolution the revolution in the Russian empire in 1917, in which the tsarist regime was overthrown and replaced by Bolshevik rule under Lenin.

> There were two phases to the Revolution: the first, in March (Old Style, February, whence **February Revolution**), was sparked off by food and fuel shortages during the First World War and began with strikes and riots in Petrograd (St Petersburg). The tsar abdicated, and a provisional government was set up. The second phase, in November 1917 (Old Style, October, whence **October Revolution**), was marked by the seizure of power by the Bolsheviks in a coup led by Lenin. After workers' councils or **soviets** took power in major cities, the new Soviet constitution was declared in 1918.

Russian Revolution of 1905 the uprising in Russia in 1905.

> Popular discontent, fuelled by heavy taxation and the country's defeat in the Russo-Japanese War, led to a peaceful demonstration in St Petersburg, which was fired on by troops. The crew of the battleship *Potemkin* mutinied and a soviet was formed in St Petersburg, prompting Tsar Nicholas II to make a number of short-lived concessions including the formation of an elected legislative body or Duma.

Russian roulette ▶ **noun** [mass noun] the practice of loading a bullet into one chamber of a revolver, spinning the cylinder, and then pulling the trigger while pointing the gun at one's own head.
■ figurative an activity that is potentially very dangerous.

Russian salad ▶ **noun** Brit. a salad of mixed diced vegetables with mayonnaise.

Russian tea ▶ **noun** [mass noun] tea laced with rum and typically served with lemon.

Russian thistle ▶ **noun** N. Amer. a prickly tumbleweed which is an inland form of saltwort. Native to Eurasia, it was accidentally introduced into North America, where it has become a pest.
• *Salsola pestifera*, family Chenopodiaceae.

Russian vine ▶ **noun** an Asian climbing plant of

the dock family, with long clusters of white or pink flowers, which is sometimes cultivated as a fast-growing screening plant.
• *Fallopia baldschuanica*, family Polygonaceae.

Russify /ˈrʌsɪfʌɪ/ ▶ **verb** (**-ies**, **-ied**) [with obj.] make Russian in character.
– DERIVATIVES **Russification** noun.

Russki /ˈrʌski/ (also **Russky**) ▶ **noun** (pl. **Russkis** or **Russkies**) informal, often offensive a Russian.
– ORIGIN mid 19th cent.: from Russian *russkiĭ* 'Russian', or from **RUSSIAN**, on the pattern of Russian surnames ending in *-skiĭ*.

Russo- ▶ **combining form** Russian; Russian and ...: *Russo-Japanese*.
■ relating to Russia.

Russo-Finnish War another term for **WINTER WAR**.

Russo-Japanese War a war between the Russian empire and Japan 1904–5, caused by territorial disputes in Manchuria and Korea. Russia suffered a series of humiliating defeats and the peace settlement gave Japan the ascendancy in the disputed region.

Russophile /ˈrʌsə(ʊ)fʌɪl/ ▶ **noun** a person who is friendly towards Russia or fond of Russia and things Russian, especially someone who is sympathetic to the political system and customs of the former Soviet Union.
– DERIVATIVES **Russophilia** noun.

Russophobe /ˈrʌsə(ʊ)fəʊb/ ▶ **noun** a person who feels an intense dislike towards Russia and things Russian, especially the political system or customs of the former Soviet Union.
– DERIVATIVES **Russophobia** noun.

Russo-Turkish Wars a series of wars between Russia and the Ottoman Empire, fought largely in the Balkans, the Crimea, and the Caucasus in the 19th century. The treaty ending the war of 1877–8 freed the nations of Romania, Serbia, and Bulgaria from Turkish rule.

russula /ˈrʌsələ/ ▶ **noun** a widespread woodland toadstool that typically has a brightly coloured flattened cap and a white stem and gills.
• Genus *Russula*, family Russulaceae, class Hymenomycetes: numerous species. See also **SICKENER** (sense 2).
– ORIGIN modern Latin, from Latin *russus* 'red' (because many, such as the sickener, have a red cap).

rust ▶ **noun** [mass noun] **1** a reddish- or yellowish-brown flaking coating of iron oxide that is formed on iron or steel by oxidation, especially in the presence of moisture.
■ figurative a state of deterioration or disrepair resulting from neglect or lack of use: *the MPs are here to scrape the rust off the derelict machinery of government.*
2 [usu. with adj. or noun modifier] a fungal disease of plants which results in reddish or brownish patches.
• The fungi belong to *Puccinia* and other genera, order Uredinales, class Teliomycetes.
3 a reddish-brown colour: [in combination] *his rust-coloured hair.*
▶ **verb** [no obj.] be affected with rust: *the blades had rusted away* | [as adj. **rusting**] *rusting machinery.*
■ figurative deteriorate through neglect or lack of use.
– DERIVATIVES **rustless** adjective.
– ORIGIN Old English *rūst*, of Germanic origin; related to Dutch *roest*, German *Rost*, also to **RED**.

rust belt ▶ **noun** [often as modifier] informal a part of a country considered to be characterized by declining industry, ageing factories, and a falling population, especially the American Midwest and NE states: *a rust-belt town.*

rust bucket ▶ **noun** informal, often humorous a car, ship, or other vehicle which is old and badly rusted.

rustic ▶ **adjective 1** having a simplicity and charm that is considered typical of the countryside: *a party of Morris dancers decked out in rustic costume.*
■ lacking the sophistication of the city; backward and provincial: *you are a rustic halfwit.*
2 constructed or made in a plain and simple fashion, in particular:
■ made of untrimmed branches or rough timber: *a rustic oak bench.* ■ Architecture with rough-hewn or roughened surface or with deeply sunk joints: *a rustic bridge.* ■ denoting freely formed lettering, especially a relatively informal style of handwritten Roman capital letter.
▶ **noun 1** often derogatory an unsophisticated country person.
2 a small brownish European moth.
• Several genera and species in the family Noctuidae.
– DERIVATIVES **rustically** adverb, **rusticity** noun.
– ORIGIN late Middle English (in the sense 'rural'): from Latin *rusticus*, from *rus* 'the country'.

rusticate /ˈrʌstɪkeɪt/ ▶ **verb 1** [with obj.] Brit. suspend (a student) from a university as a punishment (used chiefly at Oxford and Cambridge).
2 [no obj.] dated go to, live in, or spend time in the country.
3 [with obj.] fashion (masonry) in large blocks with sunk joints and a roughened surface.
– DERIVATIVES **rustication** noun.
– ORIGIN late 15th cent. (in the sense 'countrify'): from Latin *rusticat-* '(having) lived in the country', from the verb *rusticari*, from *rusticus* (see **RUSTIC**).

rustle ▶ **verb 1** [no obj.] make a soft, muffled crackling sound like that caused by the movement of dry leaves or paper: *she came closer, her skirt swaying and rustling.*
■ [with adverbial of direction] move with such sound: *a nurse rustled in with a syringe.* ■ [with obj.] move (something), causing it to make such a sound: *Dolly rustled the paper irritably.*
2 [with obj.] round up and steal (cattle, horses, or sheep).
3 [no obj.] N. Amer. informal move or act quickly or energetically; hustle: *rustle around the kitchen, see what there is.*
▶ **noun** [usu. in sing.] a soft, muffled crackling sound like that made by the movement of dry leaves or paper: *there was a rustle in the undergrowth behind her.*
– DERIVATIVES **rustler** noun (usu. in sense 2).
– ORIGIN late Middle English (as a verb): imitative; compare with Flemish *rijsselen* and Dutch *ritselen*. The noun dates from the mid 18th cent.
▶ **rustle something up** informal produce something quickly when it is needed: *see if you can rustle up a cup of tea for Paula and me, please.*

rustproof ▶ **adjective** (of metal or a metal object) not susceptible to corrosion by rust.
▶ **verb** [with obj.] make resistant to corrosion by rust.

rusty ▶ **adjective** (**rustier**, **rustiest**) **1** (of a metal object) affected by rust: *a rusty hinge.*
■ rust-coloured: *green grass turning a rusty brown.*
2 (of knowledge or a skill) impaired by lack of recent practice: *my typing is a little rusty.*
■ stiff with age or disuse: *it was my first race for three months and I felt a bit rusty.* ■ (of a voice) croaking: *her voice sounded rusty.*
– DERIVATIVES **rustily** adverb, **rustiness** noun.
– ORIGIN Old English *rūstig* (see **RUST**, **-Y**[1]).

rusty dusty ▶ **noun** black English a person's buttocks.
– ORIGIN late 16th cent. (in the sense 'dusty, fusty'): reduplication of **RUSTY**. The current transferred use dates from the 1950s.

rut[1] ▶ **noun** a long deep track made by the repeated passage of the wheels of vehicles.
■ figurative a habit or pattern of behaviour that has become dull and unproductive but is hard to change: *the EC was stuck* **in a rut** *and was losing its direction.*
– DERIVATIVES **rutted** adjective, **rutty** adjective.
– ORIGIN late 16th cent.: probably from Old French *rute* (see **ROUTE**).

rut[2] ▶ **noun** (**the rut**) an annual period of sexual activity in deer and some other mammals, during which the males fight each other for access to the females.
▶ **verb** (**rutted**, **rutting**) [no obj.] [often as adj. **rutting**] engage in such activity: *a rutting stag.*
– DERIVATIVES **ruttish** adjective.
– ORIGIN late Middle English: from Old French, from Latin *rugitus*, from *rugire* 'to roar'.

rutabaga /ˌruːtəˈbeɪɡə/ ▶ **noun** chiefly N. Amer. another term for **SWEDE** (in sense 1).
– ORIGIN late 18th cent.: from Swedish dialect *rotabagge*.

Ruth[1] a book of the Bible telling the story of Ruth, a Moabite woman, who married her deceased husband's kinsman Boaz and bore a son who became grandfather to King David.

Ruth[2], Babe (1895–1948), American baseball player; born *George Herman Ruth*. He played for the Boston Red Sox (1914–19) and the New York Yankees (1919–35), setting a record of 714 home runs which remained unbroken until 1974.

ruth ▶ **noun** [mass noun] archaic a feeling of pity, distress, or grief.
– ORIGIN Middle English: from the verb **RUE**[1], probably influenced by Old Norse *hrygth*.

Ruthenia /ruːˈθiːnɪə/ a region of central Europe on the southern slopes of the Carpathian Mountains, now forming the Transcarpathian region of western Ukraine.
– DERIVATIVES **Ruthenian** adjective & noun.
– ORIGIN named after the *Ruthenes* (from medieval Latin *Rutheni*), a Slavic people, ancestors of the Ukrainians.

ruthenium /rʊˈθiːnɪəm/ ▶ **noun** [mass noun] the chemical element of atomic number 44, a hard silvery-white metal of the transition series. (Symbol: **Ru**)
– ORIGIN mid 19th cent.: modern Latin, from medieval Latin *Ruthenia* (see **RUTHENIA**), so named because it was discovered in ores from the Urals.

ruther /ˈrʌðə/ ▶ **adverb** non-standard spelling of **RATHER**, used in representing black American dialectal speech: *I'd ruther walk.*

Rutherford[1] /ˈrʌðəfəd/, Sir Ernest, 1st Baron Rutherford of Nelson (1871–1937), New Zealand physicist, regarded as the founder of nuclear physics. As a result of his experiments on the scattering of alpha particles, he proposed that the positive charge in an atom, and virtually all its mass, is concentrated in a central nucleus. He also performed the first artificial transmutation of matter. Nobel Prize for Chemistry (1908).

Rutherford[2] /ˈrʌðəfəd/, Dame Margaret (1892–1972), English actress. Chiefly remembered for her roles as a formidable but jovial eccentric, she won an Oscar for *The VIPs* (1963).

rutherfordium /ˌrʌðəˈfɔːdɪəm/ ▶ **noun** [mass noun] the chemical element of atomic number 104, a very unstable element made by high-energy atomic collisions. (Symbol: **Rf**)
– ORIGIN 1960s: modern Latin, named after E. *Rutherford* (see **RUTHERFORD**[1]).

ruthless ▶ **adjective** having or showing no pity or compassion for others: *a ruthless manipulator.*
– DERIVATIVES **ruthlessly** adverb, **ruthlessness** noun.
– ORIGIN Middle English: from **RUTH** + **-LESS**.

rutilant /ˈruːtɪl(ə)nt/ ▶ **adjective** poetic/literary glowing or glittering with red or golden light: *rutilant gems.*
– ORIGIN late Middle English: from Latin *rutilant-* 'glowing red', from the verb *rutilare*, from *rutilus* 'reddish'.

rutile /ˈruːtɪl, ˈruːtʌɪl/ ▶ **noun** [mass noun] a black or reddish-brown mineral consisting of titanium dioxide, typically occurring as needle-like crystals.
– ORIGIN early 19th cent.: from French, or from German *Rutil*, from Latin *rutilus* 'reddish'.

rutin /ˈruːtɪn/ ▶ **noun** [mass noun] Chemistry a compound of the flavonoid class found in common rue, buckwheat, capers, and other plants, and sometimes taken as a dietary supplement.
– ORIGIN mid 19th cent.: from Latin *ruta* 'rue' + **-IN**[1].

Rutland /ˈrʌtlənd/ a county in the east Midlands, the smallest county in England; county town, Oakham. Between 1974 and 1997 it was part of Leicestershire.

Ruwenzori /ˌruːɛnˈzɔːri/ a mountain range in central Africa, on the Uganda–Zaire border between Lake Edward and Lake Albert, rising to 5,110 m (16,765 ft) at Margherita Peak on Mount Stanley. The range is generally thought to be the 'Mountains of the Moon' mentioned by Ptolemy, and as such the supposed source of the Nile.

Ruysdael variant spelling of **RUISDAEL**.

RV ▶ **abbreviation for** ■ N. Amer. recreational vehicle (especially a motorized caravan). ■ a rendezvous point. ■ Revised Version (of the Bible).

RWA ▶ **abbreviation for** Rwanda (international vehicle registration).

Rwanda /ruˈandə/ a landlocked country in central Africa, to the north of Burundi and the south of Uganda; pop. 7,403,000 (est. 1991); official languages, Rwanda (a Bantu language) and French; capital, Kigali. Official name **RWANDESE REPUBLIC**.

Inhabited largely by Hutu and Tutsi peoples, the area was claimed by Germany from 1890 and after the First World War became part of a Belgian trust territory. Rwanda became independent as a republic in 1962, shortly after the violent overthrow of the Tutsi monarchy by the majority Hutu people. In 1994 over 500,000 people, largely Tutsis, were slaughtered by predominantly Hutu supporters of the government, and over a million fled as refugees into Zaire (Democratic Republic of Congo) and neighbouring countries. The Tutsi-dominated Rwandan Patriotic Front took power as the new government.

– DERIVATIVES **Rwandan** adjective & noun, **Rwandese** adjective & noun.

Ry ▶ abbreviation for Railway.

-ry ▶ suffix a shortened form of **-ERY** (as in *devilry, rivalry*).

Ryazan /ˌrɪəˈzɑːn/ an industrial city in European Russia, situated to the south-east of Moscow; pop. 522,000 (1990).

Rybinsk /ˈrɪbɪnsk/ a city in NW Russia, a port on the River Volga; pop. 252,000 (1990). It was formerly known as Shcherbakov (1946–57) and, in honour of the former President of the Soviet Union, Yuri Andropov, as Andropov (1984–9).

Rydberg atom /ˈrɪdbəːɡ/ ▶ noun Physics an atom in a highly excited state in which one electron has almost sufficient energy to escape. Atoms, usually hydrogen atoms, in this **Rydberg state** are used in atomic research.
– ORIGIN named after J. R. *Rydberg* (see **RYDBERG CONSTANT**).

Rydberg constant Physics a constant, 1.097×10^7 m^{-1}, which appears in the formulae for the wave numbers of lines in atomic spectra and is a function of the rest mass and charge of the electron, the speed of light, and Planck's constant.
– ORIGIN early 20th cent.: named after Johannes R. *Rydberg* (1854–1919), Swedish physicist.

Ryder /ˈrʌɪdə/, Sue, Baroness Ryder of Warsaw and Cavendish (b.1923), English philanthropist. She co-founded an organization to care for former inmates of concentration camps, which expanded to provide homes for the mentally and physically disabled.

Ryder Cup a golf tournament held every two years and played between teams of male professionals from the US and Europe (originally Great Britain), first held in 1927.
– ORIGIN so named because the trophy was donated by Samuel *Ryder* (1859–1936), English seed merchant.

rye ▶ noun [mass noun] **1** a wheat-like cereal plant which tolerates poor soils and low temperatures.
● *Secale cereale*, family Gramineae.
■ grains of this, used mainly for making bread or whisky, and for fodder: [as modifier] *rye flour*.
2 (also **rye whisky**) whisky in which a significant amount of the grain used in distillation is fermented rye: *half a bottle of rye*.
3 chiefly N. Amer. short for **RYE BREAD**: *pastrami on rye*.
– ORIGIN Old English *ryge*, of Germanic origin; related to Dutch *rogge* and German *Roggen*.

rye bread ▶ noun [mass noun] bread made with rye flour, typically dark in colour and with a dense, chewy texture.

ryegrass ▶ noun [mass noun] a Eurasian grass which is a valuable fodder and lawn grass.
● Genus *Lolium*, family Gramineae: several species, in particular *L. perenne*.
– ORIGIN early 18th cent.: alteration of obsolete *ray-grass*, of unknown origin.

Ryle¹ /rʌɪl/, Gilbert (1900–76), English philosopher. In *The Concept of Mind* (1949) he attacks the mind-body dualism of Descartes. He was a cousin of the astronomer Sir Martin Ryle.

Ryle² /rʌɪl/, Sir Martin (1918–84), English astronomer. His demonstration that remote objects appeared to be different from closer ones helped to establish the big bang theory of the universe. Nobel Prize for Physics (1974). He was a cousin of the philosopher Gilbert Ryle.

ryokan /rɪˈəʊkan/ ▶ noun a traditional Japanese inn.
– ORIGIN Japanese.

ryot /ˈrʌɪət/ ▶ noun an Indian peasant or tenant farmer.
– ORIGIN from Urdu *raiyat*, from Arabic *raˈiyya* 'flock, subjects', from *raˈā* 'to pasture'.

Rysy /ˈrɪsi/ a peak in the Tatra Mountains rising to a height of 2,499 m (8,197 ft).

ryu /rɪˈuː/ ▶ noun (pl. same or **ryus**) a school or style in Japanese arts, especially in the martial arts.
– ORIGIN Japanese.

Ryukyu Islands /rɪˈuːkjuː/ a chain of islands in the western Pacific, stretching for about 960 km (600 miles) from the southern tip of the island of Kyushu, Japan, to Taiwan. Part of China in the 14th century, the archipelago was incorporated into Japan by 1879 and was held under US military control between 1945 and 1972.

Ryurik variant spelling of **RURIK**.

Ss

S¹ (also **s**) ▶ **noun** (pl. **Ss** or **S's**) **1** the nineteenth letter of the alphabet.
▪denoting the next after R in a set of items, categories, etc.
2 a shape like that of a capital S: [in combination] *an S-bend.*

S² ▶ **abbreviation for** ▪ (chiefly in Catholic use) Saint: *S Ignatius Loyola.* ▪ siemens. ▪ small (as a clothes size). ▪ South or Southern: 65° S. ▪ Biochemistry Svedberg unit(s). ▪ Sweden (international vehicle registration).
▶ **symbol for** ▪ the chemical element sulphur. ▪ Chemistry entropy.

s ▶ **abbreviation for** ▪ second(s). ▪ Law section (of an act). ▪ shilling(s). ▪ Grammar singular. ▪ Chemistry solid. ▪ (in genealogies) son(s). ▪ succeeded. ▪ Chemistry denoting electrons and orbitals possessing zero angular momentum and total symmetry: *s-electrons.* [ORIGIN: *s* from *sharp*, originally applied to lines in atomic spectra.]
▶ **symbol for** (in mathematical formulae) distance.

's /s, z after a vowel sound or voiced consonant/ informal ▶ **contraction of** ▪ is: *it's raining.* ▪ has: *she's gone.* ▪ us: *let's go.* ▪ does: *what's he do?*

's- /s, z before a voiced consonant/ ▶ **prefix** archaic (used chiefly in oaths) God's: *'sblood.*
– ORIGIN shortened form.

-s¹ /s, z after a vowel sound or voiced consonant/ ▶ **suffix** denoting the plurals of nouns (as in *apples, wagons,* etc.). Compare with **-ES¹**.
– ORIGIN Old English plural ending *-as.*

-s² /s, z after a vowel sound or voiced consonant/ ▶ **suffix** forming the third person singular of the present of verbs (as in *sews, vaunts,* etc.). Compare with **-ES²**.
– ORIGIN Old English dialect.

-s³ /s, z after a vowel sound or voiced consonant/ ▶ **suffix 1** forming adverbs such as *besides.*
2 forming possessive pronouns such as *hers, ours.*
– ORIGIN Old English *-es,* masculine and neuter genitive singular ending.

-s⁴ /s, z after a vowel sound or voiced consonant/ ▶ **suffix** forming nicknames or pet names: *ducks.*
– ORIGIN suggested by **-s¹**.

-'s¹ /s, z after a vowel sound or voiced consonant, iz after a sibilant/ ▶ **suffix** denoting possession in singular nouns, also in plural nouns not having a final *-s: the car's engine | Mrs Ross's son | the children's teacher.*
– ORIGIN Old English, masculine and neuter genitive singular ending.

-'s² /s, z after a vowel sound or voiced consonant, iz after a sibilant/ ▶ **suffix** denoting the plural of a letter or symbol: *T's | 9's.*

> **USAGE** In the formation of plurals of regular nouns, it is incorrect to use an apostrophe, e.g. *six pens* not *six pen's.*

SA ▶ **abbreviation for** ▪ Salvation Army. ▪ informal, dated sex appeal. ▪ South Africa. ▪ South America. ▪ South Australia. ▪ historical Sturmabteilung.

Saadi variant spelling of **SADI**.

saag /sɑːɡ/ (also **sag**) ▶ **noun** Indian term for **SPINACH**.
– ORIGIN from Hindi *sāg.*

Saale¹ /ˈsɑːlə/ a river of east central Germany. Rising in northern Bavaria near the border with the Czech Republic, it flows 425 km (265 miles) north to join the Elbe near Magdeburg.

Saale² /ˈzɑːlə/ ▶ **noun** [usu. as modifier] Geology the penultimate Pleistocene glaciation in northern Europe, corresponding to the Wolstonian of Britain (and possibly the Riss of the Alps).
▪the system of deposits laid down at this time.
– DERIVATIVES **Saalian** /ˈzɑːlɪən/ adjective & noun.
– ORIGIN 1930s: from **SAALE¹**.

Saanen /ˈsɑːnən/ ▶ **noun** a dairy goat of a white hornless breed, first developed in the region of Saanen in Switzerland.

Saar /sɑː/, German ˈzɑːɐ/ a river of western Europe. Rising in the Vosges mountains in eastern France, it flows 240 km (150 miles) northwards to join the Mosel River in Germany, just east of the border with Luxembourg. French name **SARRE**.
▪the Saarland.

Saarbrücken /sɑːˈbrʊkən, German ˌzɑːɐˈbrʏkn/ an industrial city in western Germany, the capital of Saarland, on the River Saar close to the border with France; pop. 361,600 (1991).

Saarland /ˈsɑːland, German ˈzɑːɐlant/ a state of western Germany, on the border with France; capital, Saarbrücken. Rich in coal and iron ore and historically dominated by France, the area was administered by the League of Nations from the end of the First World War until 1935; it became the tenth German state in 1957.

sab Brit. informal ▶ **noun** a hunt saboteur.
▶ **verb** (**sabbed, sabbing**) [no obj.] act as a hunt saboteur.
– ORIGIN 1970s: abbreviation of **SABOTEUR**.

Saba /ˈsɑːbə/ **1** an island in the Netherlands Antilles, in the Caribbean; pop. 1,130 (1992). The smallest island in the group, it is situated to the north-west of St Kitts.
2 an ancient kingdom in SW Arabia, famous for its trade in gold and spices; the biblical Sheba.

sabadilla /ˌsabəˈdɪlə/ ▶ **noun** a Mexican plant of the lily family, whose seeds contain veratrine.
● *Schoenocaulon officinale,* family Liliaceae.
▪[mass noun] a preparation of these seeds, used as an agricultural insecticide and in medicines.
– ORIGIN early 19th cent.: from Spanish *cebadilla,* diminutive of *cebada* 'barley'.

Sabaean /saˈbiːən/ ▶ **noun** a member of an ancient Semitic people who ruled Saba in SW Arabia until overrun by Persians and Arabs in the 6th century AD.
▶ **adjective** of or relating to this people.
– ORIGIN from Latin *Sabaeus* (from Greek *Sabaios*) + **-AN**.

Sabah /ˈsɑːbɑː/ a state of Malaysia, comprising the northern part of Borneo and some offshore islands; capital, Kota Kinabalu. A British protectorate from 1888, it joined Malaysia in 1963.

Sabaoth /ˈsabeɪɒθ, saˈbeɪɒθ/ ▶ **plural noun** archaic the hosts of heaven (in the biblical title 'Lord (God) of Sabaoth').
– ORIGIN via Latin from Greek *Sabaōth,* from Hebrew *ṣebā'ōṯ,* plural of *ṣābā* 'host (of heaven)'.

sabayon /ˈsabʌɪjɔ̃/ ▶ **noun** French term for **ZABAGLIONE**.

sabbatarian /ˌsabəˈtɛːrɪən/ ▶ **noun** a Christian who strictly observes Sunday as the sabbath.
▪a Jew who strictly observes the sabbath. ▪ a Christian belonging to a denomination or sect that observes Saturday as the sabbath.
▶ **adjective** relating to or upholding the observance of the sabbath.
– DERIVATIVES **sabbatarianism** noun.
– ORIGIN early 17th cent.: from late Latin *sabbatarius* (from Latin *sabbatum* 'sabbath') + **-AN**.

sabbath ▶ **noun 1** (often **the Sabbath**) a day of religious observance and abstinence from work, kept by Jews from Friday evening to Saturday evening, and by most Christians on Sunday.
2 (also **witches' sabbath**) a supposed annual midnight meeting of witches with the Devil.
– ORIGIN Old English, from Latin *sabbatum,* via Greek from Hebrew *šabbāt,* from *šābat* 'to rest'.

sabbatical /səˈbatɪk(ə)l/ ▶ **noun** a period of paid leave granted to a university teacher for study or travel, traditionally one year for every seven years worked: *she's away on sabbatical.*
▶ **adjective 1** of or relating to a sabbatical.
2 archaic of or appropriate to the sabbath.
– ORIGIN late 16th cent.: via late Latin from Greek *sabbatikos* 'of the sabbath' + **-AL**.

sabbatical year ▶ **noun 1** a year's sabbatical leave.
2 (in biblical times) a year observed every seventh year under the Mosaic law as a 'sabbath' during which the land was allowed to rest.

Sabellian¹ /səˈbɛlɪən/ ▶ **noun** a member of a group of Oscan-speaking peoples of ancient Italy, including the Sabines and Samnites.
▶ **adjective** of or relating to these peoples.
– ORIGIN from Latin *Sabellus* + **-IAN**.

Sabellian² /səˈbɛlɪən/ ▶ **adjective** of or relating to the teachings of Sabellius (*fl. c.*220 in North Africa), who developed a form of the modalist doctrine that the Father, Son, and Holy Spirit are not truly distinct but merely aspects of one divine being.
▶ **noun** a follower of the teachings of Sabellius.
– DERIVATIVES **Sabellianism** noun.

saber ▶ **noun** & **verb** US spelling of **SABRE**.

Sabian /ˈseɪbɪən/ ▶ **adjective** of or relating to a non-Muslim sect classed in the Koran with Jews, Christians, and Zoroastrians as having a faith revealed by the true God. It is not known who the original Sabians were, but the name was adopted by some groups in order to escape religious persecution by Muslims.
▶ **noun** a member of this sect.
– ORIGIN early 17th cent.: from Arabic *ṣābi* + **-AN**.

sabicu /ˌsabɪˈkuː/ ▶ **noun** a Caribbean tree of the pea family, with timber that resembles mahogany and is used chiefly in boatbuilding.
● *Lysiloma sabicu,* family Leguminosae.
– ORIGIN mid 19th cent.: from Cuban Spanish *sabicú.*

Sabine /ˈsabʌɪn/ ▶ **adjective** of, relating to, or denoting an ancient Oscan-speaking people of the central Apennines in Italy, north-east of Rome, who feature in early Roman legends and were incorporated into the Roman state in 290 BC.

b **b**ut | d **d**og | f **f**ew | g **g**et | h **h**e | j **y**es | k **c**at | l **l**eg | m **m**an | n **n**o | p **p**en | r **r**ed | s **s**it | t **t**op | v **v**oice | w **w**e | z **z**oo | ʃ **sh**e | ʒ deci**s**ion | θ **th**in | ð **th**is | ŋ ri**ng** | x lo**ch** | tʃ **ch**ip | dʒ **j**ar

▶ **noun** a member of this people.
– ORIGIN from Latin *Sabinus*.

Sabin vaccine /ˈseɪbɪn/ ▶ **noun** a vaccine against poliomyelitis containing attenuated virus and given by mouth.
– ORIGIN 1950s: named after Albert B. *Sabin* (1906–93), American virologist.

sabji /ˈsʌbdʒiː/ ▶ **noun** (pl. **sabjis**) Indian variant spelling of **SABZI**.

sabkha /ˈsabkə, -ə/ ▶ **noun** Geography an area of coastal flats subject to periodic flooding and evaporation which result in the accumulation of aeolian clays, evaporites, and salts, typically found in North Africa and Arabia.
– ORIGIN late 19th cent.: from Arabic *sabḳa* 'salt flat'.

sable¹ /ˈseɪb(ə)l/ ▶ **noun** a marten with a short tail and dark brown fur, native to Japan and Siberia and valued for its fur.
● *Martes zibellina*, family Mustelidae.
■ [mass noun] the fur of the sable.
– ORIGIN late Middle English: from Old French, in the sense 'sable fur', from medieval Latin *sabelum*, of Slavic origin.

sable² /ˈseɪb(ə)l/ ▶ **adjective** poetic/literary or Heraldry black.
▶ **noun 1** [mass noun] poetic/literary or Heraldry black.
■ (**sables**) archaic mourning garments.
2 (also **sable antelope**) a large African antelope with long curved horns, the male of which has a black coat and the female a russet coat, both having a white belly.
● *Hippotragus niger*, family Bovidae.
– ORIGIN Middle English: from Old French (as a heraldic term), generally taken to be identical with **SABLE¹**, although sable fur is dark brown.

sablefish ▶ **noun** (pl. same or **-fishes**) a large commercially important fish with a slaty-blue to black back, occurring throughout the North Pacific.
● *Anoplopoma fimbria*, family Anoplopomatidae.

sabot /ˈsabəʊ/ ▶ **noun 1** a kind of simple shoe, shaped and hollowed out from a single block of wood, traditionally worn by French and Breton peasants.
2 a device which ensures the correct positioning of a bullet or shell in the barrel of a gun, attached either to the projectile or inside the barrel and falling away as it leaves the muzzle.
3 a box from which cards are dealt at casinos in gambling games such as baccarat and chemin de fer. Also called **SHOE**.
– DERIVATIVES **saboted** /ˈsabəʊd/ adjective (only in sense 1).
– ORIGIN early 17th cent.: French, blend of *savate* 'shoe' and *botte* 'boot'.

sabotage /ˈsabətɑːʒ/ ▶ **verb** [with obj.] deliberately destroy, damage, or obstruct (something), especially for political or military advantage.
▶ **noun** [mass noun] the action of sabotaging something.
– ORIGIN early 20th cent.: from French, from *saboter* 'kick with sabots, wilfully destroy' (see **SABOT**).

saboteur /ˌsabəˈtəː/ ▶ **noun** a person who engages in sabotage.
– ORIGIN early 20th cent.: from French, from the verb *saboter* (see **SABOTAGE**).

sabra /ˈsabrə/ ▶ **noun** a Jew born in Israel (or before 1948 in Palestine).
– ORIGIN from modern Hebrew *ṣabbār* 'opuntia fruit' (opuntias being common in coastal regions of Israel).

Sabratha /ˈsabrəθə/ (also **Sabrata** /-brətə/) one of the three ancient cities of Tripolitania.

sabre /ˈseɪbə/ (US **saber**) ▶ **noun** a heavy cavalry sword with a curved blade and a single cutting edge.
■ a light fencing sword with a tapering, typically curved blade. ■ historical a cavalry soldier and horse.
▶ **verb** [with obj.] archaic cut down or wound with a sabre.
– ORIGIN late 17th cent.: from French, alteration of obsolete *sable*, from German *Sabel* (local variant of *Säbel*), from Hungarian *szablya*.

sabre-rattling ▶ **noun** [mass noun] the display or threat of military force.

sabre saw ▶ **noun** a portable electric jigsaw.

sabretache /ˈsabrətaʃ/ ▶ **noun** historical a flat satchel on long straps worn by some cavalry and horse artillery officers from the left of the waist-belt.
– ORIGIN early 19th cent.: from French, from

German *Säbeltasche*, from *Säbel* 'sabre' + *Tasche* 'pocket'.

sabretooth ▶ **noun 1** (also **sabre-toothed cat** or **tiger**) a large extinct carnivorous mammal of the cat family, with massive curved upper canine teeth.
● Several genera in the family Felidae, in particular *Smilodon* of the American Pleistocene and *Machairodus* of the Old World Pliocene.
2 a large extinct marsupial mammal with similar teeth, of the South American Pliocene.
● Genus *Thylacosmilus*, family Borhyaenidae.

sabreur /saˈbrəː/ ▶ **noun** a cavalryman or fencer using a sabre.
– ORIGIN French, from *sabrer* 'strike with a sabre'.

sabrewing ▶ **noun** a large tropical American hummingbird with a green back and long curved wings.
● Genus *Campylopterus*, family Trochilidae: several species.

sabzi /ˈsʌbziː/ (also **sabji** /ˈsʌbdʒiː/) ▶ **noun** (pl. **sabzis**) [mass noun] Indian vegetables, especially cooked vegetables.
– ORIGIN from Hindi *sabzī*.

SAC ▶ **abbreviation for** Senior Aircraftman.

sac /sak/ ▶ **noun** a hollow, flexible structure resembling a bag or pouch: *a fountain pen with an ink sac.*
■ a cavity enclosed by a membrane within a living organism, containing air, liquid, or solid structures. ■ the distended membrane surrounding a hernia, cyst, or tumour.
– DERIVATIVES **sac-like** adjective.
– ORIGIN mid 18th cent. (as a term in biology): from French *sac* or Latin *saccus* 'sack, bag'.

saccade /saˈkɑːd/ ▶ **noun** (usu. **saccades**) technical a rapid movement of the eye between fixation points.
– DERIVATIVES **saccadic** /saˈkadɪk/ adjective.
– ORIGIN early 18th cent.: from French, literally 'violent pull', from Old French *saquer* 'to pull'.

saccate /ˈsakeɪt/ ▶ **adjective** Botany dilated to form a sac.

saccharide /ˈsakərʌɪd/ ▶ **noun** Biochemistry another term for **SUGAR** (in sense 2).
– ORIGIN mid 19th cent.: from modern Latin *saccharum* 'sugar' + **-IDE**.

saccharin /ˈsakərɪn/ ▶ **noun** [mass noun] a sweet-tasting synthetic compound used in food and drink as a substitute for sugar.
● Alternative name: *o-sulphobenzoic imide*; chem. formula: $C_7H_5NO_3S$.
– ORIGIN late 19th cent.: from modern Latin *saccharum* 'sugar' + **-IN¹**.

saccharine /ˈsakərʌɪn, -ɪn, -iːn/ ▶ **adjective**
1 excessively sweet or sentimental.
2 dated relating to or containing sugar; sugary.
▶ **noun** another term for **SACCHARIN**.
– ORIGIN late 17th cent.: from modern Latin *saccharum* 'sugar' + **-INE¹**.

saccharo- ▶ **combining form** of or relating to sugar: *saccharometer*.
– ORIGIN via Latin from Greek *sakkharon* 'sugar'.

saccharometer /ˌsakəˈrɒmɪtə/ ▶ **noun** a hydrometer for estimating the sugar content of a solution.

saccharose /ˈsakərəʊz, -s/ ▶ **noun** Chemistry another term for **SUCROSE**.
– ORIGIN late 19th cent.: from modern Latin *saccharum* 'sugar' + **-OSE²**.

saccule /ˈsakjuːl/ ▶ **noun** Biology & Anatomy a small sac, pouch, or cyst.
■ another term for **SACCULUS**.
– DERIVATIVES **saccular** adjective, **sacculated** adjective, **sacculation** noun.
– ORIGIN mid 19th cent.: Anglicized form of Latin *sacculus* (see **SACCULUS**).

sacculus /ˈsakjʊləs/ ▶ **noun** Anatomy the smaller of the two fluid-filled sacs forming part of the labyrinth of the inner ear (the other being the utriculus). It contains a region of hair cells and otoliths which send signals to the brain concerning the orientation of the head.
■ another term for **SACCULE**.
– ORIGIN mid 18th cent.: from Latin, diminutive of *saccus* 'sack'.

sacerdotal /ˌsasəˈdəʊt(ə)l, ˌsakə-/ ▶ **adjective** relating to priests or the priesthood; priestly.
■ Theology relating to or denoting a doctrine which ascribes sacrificial functions and spiritual or supernatural powers to ordained priests.

– DERIVATIVES **sacerdotalism** noun.
– ORIGIN late Middle English: from Old French, or from Latin *sacerdotalis*, from *sacerdos*, *sacerdot-* 'priest'.

sachem /ˈseɪtʃəm, ˈsatʃəm/ ▶ **noun** (among some American Indian peoples) a chief.
■ N. Amer. informal a boss or leader.
– ORIGIN from Narragansett, 'chief, sagamore'.

Sachertorte /ˈzaxətɔːtə, German ˈzaxɐˌtɔrtə/ ▶ **noun** (pl. **Sachertorten** /-ˌtɔːt(ə)n, German -ˌtɔrtn/) a chocolate gateau with apricot jam filling and chocolate icing.
– ORIGIN German, from the name of Franz *Sacher*, the pastry chef who created it, + *Torte* 'tart, pastry'.

sachet /ˈsaʃeɪ/ ▶ **noun 1** chiefly Brit. a small sealed bag or packet containing a small quantity of something.
2 a small perfumed bag used to scent clothes.
■ [mass noun] archaic dried, scented material for use in scenting clothes.
– ORIGIN mid 19th cent. (in sense 2): from French, 'little bag', diminutive of *sac*, from Latin *saccus* 'sack, bag'.

Sachs /saks, zaks/, Hans (1494–1576), German poet and dramatist. Some of his poetry celebrated Luther and furthered the Protestant cause, while other pieces were comic verse dramas.

Sachsen /ˈzaksn/ German name for **SAXONY**.

Sachsen-Anhalt /ˌzaksnˈanhalt/ German name for **SAXONY-ANHALT**.

sack¹ ▶ **noun 1** a large bag made of a strong material such as hessian, thick paper, or plastic, used for storing and carrying goods.
■ the contents of such a bag or the amount it can contain: *a sack of flour.*
2 a loose, unfitted, or shapeless garment, in particular:
■ historical a woman's loose gown. ■ historical a decorative piece of dress material fastened to the shoulders of a woman's gown in loose pleats and forming a long train, fashionable in the 18th century.
3 (**the sack**) informal chiefly N. Amer. bed, especially as regarded as a place for sex.
4 (**the sack**) informal dismissal from employment: *he got the sack for swearing | they were given the sack.*
5 Baseball, informal a base.
6 American Football a tackle of a quarterback behind the line of scrimmage.
▶ **verb** [with obj.] **1** informal dismiss from employment: *any official found to be involved would be sacked on the spot.*
2 (**sack out**) informal, chiefly N. Amer. go to sleep or bed.
3 American Football tackle (a quarterback) behind the line of scrimmage.
4 rare put into a sack or sacks.
– PHRASES **hit the sack** informal go to bed. **a sack of potatoes** informal used in similes to refer to clumsiness, inertness, or unceremonious treatment of the person or thing in question: *he drags me in like a sack of potatoes.*
– DERIVATIVES **sackable** adjective, **sacklike** adjective.
– ORIGIN Old English *sacc*, from Latin *saccus* 'sack, sackcloth', from Greek *sakkos*, of Semitic origin. Sense 1 of the verb dates from the mid 19th cent.

sack² ▶ **verb** [with obj.] (chiefly in historical contexts) plunder and destroy (a captured town, building, or other place).
▶ **noun** the pillaging of a town or city.
– ORIGIN mid 16th cent.: from French *sac*, in the phrase *mettre à sac* 'put to sack', on the model of Italian *fare il sacco*, *mettere a sacco*, which perhaps originally referred to filling a sack with plunder.

sack³ ▶ **noun** [mass noun] historical a dry white wine formerly imported into Britain from Spain and the Canaries.
– ORIGIN early 16th cent.: from the phrase *wyne seck*, from French *vin sec* 'dry wine'.

sackbut /ˈsakbʌt/ ▶ **noun** an early form of trombone used in Renaissance music.
– ORIGIN late 15th cent.: from French *saquebute*, from obsolete *saqueboute* 'hook for pulling a man off a horse', from *saquer* 'to pull' + *bouter* 'to hit'.

sackcloth ▶ **noun** [mass noun] a very coarse, rough fabric woven from flax or hemp.
– PHRASES **sackcloth and ashes** used with allusion to the wearing of sackcloth and having ashes sprinkled on the head as a sign of penitence or mourning (Matt 11:21).

sack coat ▶ **noun** historical a loose-fitting coat hanging straight down from the shoulders, particularly as worn by men (sometimes as part of military uniform) in the 19th and early 20th centuries.

sack dress ▶ **noun** a woman's short loose unwaisted dress, originally fashionable in the 1950s.

sackful ▶ **noun** (pl. **-fuls**) the quantity of something held by a sack: *a sackful of rice.*

sacking ▶ **noun 1** an act of sacking someone or something.
2 [mass noun] coarse material for making sacks; sackcloth.

sack lunch ▶ **noun** N. Amer. informal a packed lunch.

sack race ▶ **noun** a race in which competitors, typically children, stand in sacks up to the waist or neck and jump forward.

sack suit ▶ **noun** chiefly N. Amer. a suit with a straight loose-fitting jacket.

Sackville-West, Vita (1892–1962), English novelist and poet; full name *Victoria Mary Sackville-West*. Her works include the novel *All Passion Spent* (1931). She is also known for the garden which she created at Sissinghurst in Kent and for her friendship with Virginia Woolf.

sacra plural form of **SACRUM**.

sacral /ˈseɪkr(ə)l, ˈsak-/ ▶ **adjective** [attrib.] **1** Anatomy of or relating to the sacrum.
2 Anthropology & Religion of, for, or relating to sacred rites or symbols: *sacral horns of a Minoan type.*
– DERIVATIVES **sacrality** noun (only in sense 2).

sacralize /ˈseɪkrəlʌɪz/ (also **-ise**) ▶ **verb** [with obj.] chiefly US imbue with or treat as having a sacred character or quality: *rural images that sacralize country life.*
– DERIVATIVES **sacralization** noun.

sacrament /ˈsakrəm(ə)nt/ ▶ **noun** a religious ceremony or act of the Christian Church which is regarded as an outward and visible sign of inward and spiritual divine grace, in particular:
▪(in the Roman Catholic and many Orthodox Churches) the seven rites of baptism, confirmation, the Eucharist, penance, anointing of the sick, ordination, and matrimony. ▪(among Protestants) baptism and the Eucharist. ▪(also **the Blessed Sacrament** or **the Holy Sacrament**) (in Catholic use) the consecrated elements of the Eucharist, especially the bread or Host: *he heard Mass and received the sacrament.* ▪a thing of mysterious and sacred significance; a religious symbol.
– ORIGIN Middle English: from Old French *sacrement*, from Latin *sacramentum* 'solemn oath' (from *sacrare* 'to hallow', from *sacer* 'sacred'), used in Christian Latin as a translation of Greek *mustērion* 'mystery'.

sacramental ▶ **adjective** relating to or constituting a sacrament or the sacraments.
▪attaching great importance to sacraments.
▶ **noun** an observance analogous to but not reckoned among the sacraments, such as the use of holy water or the sign of the cross.
– DERIVATIVES **sacramentalism** noun, **sacramentality** noun, **sacramentalize** (also **-ise**) verb, **sacramentally** adverb.

Sacramento /ˌsakrəˈmɛntəʊ/ **1** a river of northern California, which rises near the border with Oregon and flows some 611 km (380 miles) southwards to San Francisco Bay.
2 the state capital of California, situated on the Sacramento River to the north-east of San Francisco; pop. 369,365 (1990).

sacrament of reconciliation (also **sacrament of penance**) ▶ **noun** (chiefly in the Roman Catholic Church) the practice of private confession of sins to a priest and the receiving of absolution.

sacrarium /səˈkrɛːrɪəm/ ▶ **noun** (pl. **sacraria** /-rɪə/) the sanctuary of a church.
▪(in the Roman Catholic Church) a piscina. ▪(in the ancient Roman world) a shrine, in particular the room in a house containing the penates.
– ORIGIN Latin, from *sacer, sacr-* 'holy'.

sacré bleu /ˌsakreɪ ˈblɜː, French sakʀe blø/ ▶ **exclamation** a French expression of surprise, exasperation, or dismay.
– ORIGIN alteration of *sacré Dieu* 'holy God'.

sacred /ˈseɪkrɪd/ ▶ **adjective** connected with God (or the gods) or dedicated to a religious purpose and so deserving veneration: *sacred rites* | *the site at Eleusis is sacred to Demeter.*
▪religious rather than secular: *sacred music.* ▪(of writing or text) embodying the laws or doctrines of a religion: *a sacred Hindu text.* ▪regarded with great respect and reverence by a particular religion, group, or individual: *an animal* **sacred to** *Mexican culture.* ▪sacrosanct: *to a police officer nothing is sacred.*
– DERIVATIVES **sacredly** adverb, **sacredness** noun.
– ORIGIN late Middle English: past participle of archaic *sacre* 'consecrate', from Old French *sacrer*, from Latin *sacrare*, from *sacer, sacr-* 'holy'.

sacred bamboo ▶ **noun** another term for **NANDINA**.

Sacred College another term for **COLLEGE OF CARDINALS**.

sacred cow ▶ **noun** an idea, custom or institution held, especially unreasonably, to be above criticism (with reference to the Hindus' respect for the cow as a holy animal).

Sacred Heart ▶ **noun** an image representing the heart of Christ, used as an object of devotion among Roman Catholics.

sacred ibis ▶ **noun** a mainly white ibis with a bare black head and neck and black plumes over the lower back, native to Africa and the Middle East, and venerated by the ancient Egyptians.
• *Threskiornis aethiopicus*, family Threskiornithidae.

sacred lotus ▶ **noun** see **LOTUS** (sense 1).

sacred scarab ▶ **noun** see **SCARAB**.

sacrifice ▶ **noun** an act of slaughtering an animal or person or surrendering a possession as an offering to God or to a divine or supernatural figure: *they offer sacrifices to the spirits* | [mass noun] *the ancient laws of animal sacrifice.*
▪an animal, person, or object offered in this way. ▪an act of giving up something valued for the sake of something else regarded as more important or worthy: *we must all be prepared to* **make sacrifices**. ▪Christian Church Christ's offering of himself in the Crucifixion. ▪Christian Church the Eucharist regarded either (in Catholic terms) as a propitiatory offering of the body and blood of Christ or (in Protestant terms) as an act of thanksgiving. ▪Chess a move intended to allow the opponent to win a pawn or piece, for strategic or tactical reasons. ▪(also **sacrifice bunt** or **sacrifice fly**) Baseball a bunted or fly ball which puts the batter out but allows a base-runner to advance. ▪(also **sacrifice bid**) Bridge a bid made in the belief that it will be less costly to be defeated in the contract than to allow the opponents to make a contract.
▶ **verb** [with obj.] offer or kill as a religious sacrifice: *the goat was sacrificed at the shrine.*
▪give up (something important or valued) for the sake of other considerations: *working hard doesn't mean sacrificing your social life.* ▪Chess deliberately allow one's opponent to win (a pawn or piece). ▪Baseball advance (a base-runner) by a sacrifice. ▪[no obj.] Bridge make a sacrifice bid.
– ORIGIN Middle English: from Old French, from Latin *sacrificium*; related to *sacrificus* 'sacrificial', from *sacer* 'holy'.

sacrificial ▶ **adjective** of, relating to, or constituting a sacrifice: *an altar for sacrificial offerings.*
▪technical designed to be used up or destroyed in fulfilling a purpose or function.
– DERIVATIVES **sacrificially** adverb.

sacrilege /ˈsakrɪlɪdʒ/ ▶ **noun** [mass noun] violation or misuse of what is regarded as sacred: *putting ecclesiastical vestments to secular use was considered sacrilege.*
– DERIVATIVES **sacrilegious** adjective, **sacrilegiously** adverb.
– ORIGIN Middle English: via Old French from Latin *sacrilegium*, from *sacrilegus* 'stealer of sacred things', from *sacer, sacr-* 'sacred' + *legere* 'take possession of'.

sacring /ˈseɪkrɪŋ/ ▶ **noun** archaic or historical the consecration of a bishop, sovereign, or the Eucharistic elements.
– ORIGIN Middle English: from the obsolete verb *sacre* 'consecrate'.

sacring bell ▶ **noun** a bell rung in some Christian churches at certain points during the Mass or Eucharist, especially at the elevation of the consecrated elements.

sacrist /ˈsakrɪst, ˈseɪ-/ ▶ **noun** chiefly historical another term for **SACRISTAN**.

sacristan /ˈsakrɪstən/ ▶ **noun 1** a person in charge of a sacristy and its contents.
2 archaic the sexton of a parish church.
– ORIGIN Middle English: from medieval Latin *sacristanus*, based on Latin *sacer, sacr-* 'sacred'.

sacristy /ˈsakrɪsti/ ▶ **noun** (pl. **-ies**) a room in a church where a priest prepares for a service, and where vestments and other things used in worship are kept.
– ORIGIN late Middle English: from French *sacristie*, from medieval Latin *sacristia*, based on Latin *sacer, sacr-* 'sacred'.

sacro- /ˈseɪkrəʊ, ˈsakrəʊ-/ ▶ **combining form** of or relating to the sacrum: *sacroiliac.*
– ORIGIN from Latin (*os*) *sacrum* 'sacrum'.

sacroiliac /ˌseɪkrəʊˈɪlɪak, ˌsak-/ ▶ **adjective** Anatomy relating to the sacrum and the ilium.
▪denoting the rigid joint at the back of the pelvis between the sacrum and the ilium.

sacrosanct /ˈsakrə(ʊ)saŋ(k)t, ˈseɪk-/ ▶ **adjective** (especially of a principle, place, or routine) regarded as too important or valuable to be interfered with: *the individual's right to work has been upheld as sacrosanct.*
– DERIVATIVES **sacrosanctity** noun.
– ORIGIN late 15th cent.: from Latin *sacrosanctus*, from *sacro* 'by a sacred rite' (ablative of *sacrum*) + *sanctus* 'holy'.

sacrum /ˈseɪkrəm, ˈsak-/ ▶ **noun** (pl. **sacra** /-krə/ or **sacrums**) Anatomy a triangular bone in the lower back formed from fused vertebrae and situated between the two hip bones of the pelvis.
– ORIGIN mid 18th cent.: from Latin *os sacrum*, translation of Greek *hieron osteon* 'sacred bone' (from the belief that the soul resides in it).

SACW ▶ **abbreviation for** Senior Aircraftwoman.

SAD ▶ **abbreviation for** seasonal affective disorder.

sad ▶ **adjective** (**sadder, saddest**) **1** feeling or showing sorrow; unhappy: *I was sad and subdued* | *they looked at her with sad, anxious faces.*
▪causing or characterized by sorrow or regret; unfortunate and regrettable: *he told her the sad story of his life* | *a sad day for us all.*
2 informal pathetically inadequate or unfashionable: *sad people singing boating songs.*
3 (of dough) heavy through having failed to rise.
– PHRASES **sad to say** unfortunately, regrettably.
– DERIVATIVES **saddish** adjective, **sadness** noun.
– ORIGIN Old English *sæd* 'sated, weary', also 'weighty, dense', of Germanic origin; related to Dutch *zat* and German *satt*, from an Indo-European root shared by Latin *satis* 'enough'. The original meaning was replaced in Middle English by the senses 'steadfast, firm' and 'serious, sober', and later 'sorrowful'.

Sadat /saˈdat/, (Muhammad) Anwar al- (1918–81), Egyptian statesman, President 1970–81. Sadat worked to achieve peace in the Middle East, visiting Israel (1977) and attending talks with Menachim Begin at Camp David in 1978, the year they shared the Nobel Peace Prize. He was assassinated by members of the Islamic Jihad.

Saddam Hussein /saˈdam/ see **HUSSEIN**[3].

sadden ▶ **verb** [with obj.] (often **be saddened**) cause to feel sorrow; make unhappy: *he was greatly saddened by the death of his only son* | [with obj. and infinitive] *I was saddened to see their lack of commitment.*

saddle ▶ **noun 1** a seat fastened on the back of a horse or other animal for riding, typically made of leather and raised at the front and rear.
▪a seat on a bicycle or motorcycle.
2 something resembling a saddle in appearance, function, or position, in particular:
▪a low part of a ridge between two higher points or peaks. ▪Mathematics a low region of a curve between two high points, especially (in three dimensions) one representing the highest point of a curve in one direction and the lowest point in another direction. ▪the part of a draught horse's harness which supports the straps to which the shafts are attached. ▪a shaped support on which a cable, wire, or pipe rests. ▪a fireclay bar for supporting ceramic ware in a kiln.
3 a joint of meat consisting of the two loins.
▪the lower part of the back in a mammal or fowl, especially when distinct in shape or marking.
▶ **verb** [with obj.] put a saddle on (a horse): *he was in the stable* **saddling up** *his horse.*
▪(usu. **be saddled with**) burden (someone) with an onerous responsibility or task: *he's saddled with debts of $12 million.* ▪(of a trainer) enter (a horse) for a race.
– PHRASES **in the saddle** on horseback. ▪figurative in a position of control or responsibility.
– ORIGIN Old English *sadol, sadul*, of Germanic origin; related to Dutch *zadel* and German *Sattel*,

S

perhaps from an Indo-European root shared by Latin *sella* 'seat' and **SIT**.

saddleback ▶ noun **1** Architecture a tower roof which has two opposite gables connected by a pitched section.
2 a hill with a ridge along the top that dips in the middle.
3 a pig of a black breed with a white stripe across the back.
4 a New Zealand wattlebird with mainly black plumage, a reddish-brown back, and two small red wattles under the bill.
● *Creadion carunculatus*, family Callaeidae.
– DERIVATIVES **saddlebacked** adjective.

saddlebag ▶ noun each of a pair of bags attached behind the saddle on a horse, bicycle, or motorcycle.

saddle-bow ▶ noun chiefly archaic the pommel of a saddle, or a similar curved part behind the rider.

saddlebred ▶ noun a horse bred to have the gait of an American Saddle Horse.

saddlecloth ▶ noun a cloth laid on a horse's back under the saddle.

saddle horse ▶ noun **1** a wooden frame or stand on which saddles are cleaned or stored.
2 chiefly N. Amer. a horse kept for riding only.

saddler ▶ noun someone who makes, repairs, or deals in saddlery.

saddlery ▶ noun (pl. **-ies**) [mass noun] saddles, bridles, and other equipment for horses.
■ the making or repairing of such equipment. ■ [count noun] a saddler's business or premises.

saddle shoe ▶ noun an oxford shoe with a piece of leather in a contrasting colour stitched across the instep, typically black or brown on a white shoe.

saddle soap ▶ noun [mass noun] soft soap containing neat's-foot oil, used for cleaning leather.

saddle-sore ▶ noun a bruise or sore on a horse's back, caused by pressure or chafing of an ill-fitting saddle.
▶ adjective chafed by riding on a saddle.

saddle stitch ▶ noun a stitch of thread or a wire staple passed through the fold of a magazine or booklet.
■ [mass noun] (in needlework) a decorative stitch made with long stitches on the upper side of the cloth alternated with short stitches on the underside.
▶ verb (**saddle-stitch**) [with obj.] sew with such a stitch.

saddle tank ▶ noun a small steam locomotive with a water tank that fits over the top and sides of the boiler like a saddle.

saddle tree ▶ noun a frame around which a saddle is built.

saddo ▶ noun (pl. **-os**) Brit. informal a person perceived as contemptible or pathetically inadequate.
– ORIGIN 1990s: extension of **SAD**.

Sadducee /ˈsadjʊsiː/ ▶ noun a member of a Jewish sect or party of the time of Christ that denied the resurrection of the dead, the existence of spirits, and the obligation of oral tradition, emphasizing acceptance of the written Law alone. Compare with **PHARISEE**.
– DERIVATIVES **Saducean** /-ˈsiːən/ adjective.
– ORIGIN Old English *sadducēas* (plural), via late Latin from Greek *Saddoukaios*, from Hebrew *ṣĕḏōqī* in the sense 'descendant of Zadok' (2 Sam. 8:17).

Sade /saːd/, Donatien Alphonse François, Comte de (1740–1814), French writer and soldier; known as **the Marquis de Sade**. His career as a cavalry officer was interrupted by periods of imprisonment for cruelty and debauchery. While in prison he wrote a number of sexually explicit works, including *Les 120 Journées de Sodome* (1784) and *Justine* (1791).

sadhana /ˈsɑːðənɑː/ ▶ noun [mass noun] Indian disciplined and dedicated practice or learning, especially in religion or music.
– ORIGIN from Sanskrit *sādhanā* 'dedication to an aim', from *sādh* 'bring about'.

sadhu /ˈsɑːduː/ ▶ noun Indian a holy man, sage, or ascetic.
– ORIGIN Sanskrit.

Sadi /ˈsɑːdi/ (also **Saadi**) (c.1213–c.1291), Persian poet; born *Sheikh Muslih Addin*. His principal works were the collections known as the *Bustan* (1257) and the *Gulistan* (1258).

sadism ▶ noun [mass noun] the tendency to derive pleasure, especially sexual gratification, from inflicting pain, suffering, or humiliation on others.
■ (in general use) deliberate cruelty.
– DERIVATIVES **sadist** noun, **sadistic** adjective, **sadistically** adverb.
– ORIGIN late 19th cent.: from French *sadisme*, from the name of the Marquis de **SADE**.

Sadler's Wells Theatre /ˈsadləz/ a London theatre opened by Lilian Baylis in 1931, known for its ballet and opera companies.
– ORIGIN named after Thomas *Sadler*, who discovered a medicinal spring at the original site in 1683.

sadly ▶ adverb showing or feeling sadness: *he smiled sadly.*
■ [sentence adverb] it is a sad or regrettable fact that; unfortunately: *sadly, the forests of Sulawesi are now under threat.* ■ [as submodifier] to a regrettable extent; regrettably: *his schemes went sadly awry.*

sadomasochism /ˌseɪdəʊˈmasəkɪz(ə)m/ ▶ noun [mass noun] psychological tendency or sexual practice characterized by both sadism and masochism.
– DERIVATIVES **sadomasochist** noun, **sadomasochistic** adjective.

sad sack ▶ noun informal, chiefly US an inept blundering person.

sadza /ˈsadzə/ ▶ noun [mass noun] (in southern and east Africa) porridge made of ground maize or millet.
– ORIGIN Shona.

sae[1] Brit. ▶ abbreviation for stamped addressed envelope.

sae[2] /seɪ/ ▶ adverb non-standard spelling of **SO**[1], used in representing Scottish speech.

Safaqis /saˈfɑːkɪs/ another name for **SFAX**.

safari ▶ noun (pl. **safaris**) an expedition to observe or hunt animals in their natural habitat, especially in East Africa: *one week on safari.*
– ORIGIN late 19th cent.: from Kiswahili, from Arabic *safara* 'to travel'.

safari jacket ▶ noun a belted lightweight jacket, typically having short sleeves and four patch pockets.

safari park ▶ noun an area of parkland where wild animals are kept in the open and may be observed by visitors driving through.

safari suit ▶ noun a lightweight suit consisting of a safari jacket with matching trousers, shorts, or skirt.

safari supper ▶ noun a social occasion at which the different courses of a meal are eaten at different people's houses.

Safavid /ˈsafəvɪd/ ▶ noun a member of a dynasty which ruled Persia 1502–1736 and installed Shia rather than Sunni Islam as the state religion.
▶ adjective of or relating to this dynasty.
– ORIGIN from Arabic *safawī* 'descended from the ruler Sophy'.

safe ▶ adjective **1** [predic.] protected from or not exposed to danger or risk; not likely to be harmed or lost: *eggs remain in the damp sand, safe from marine predators* | *she felt safer with them than alone.*
■ not likely to cause or lead to harm or injury; not involving danger or risk: *we have to cross the river where it's safe for us to do so* | *a safe investment that produced regular income.* ■ (of a place) affording security or protection: *put it in a safe place.* ■ often derogatory cautious and unenterprising: *MacGregor would be a compromise, the safe choice.* ■ based on good reasons or evidence and not likely to be proved wrong: *the verdict is safe and satisfactory* | *his world, it's safe to say, will not fall apart.*
2 uninjured; with no harm done: *they had returned safe and sound* | *hopes of her safe return later faded.*
3 informal excellent (used to express approval or enthusiasm): *that shirt is real safe.*
▶ noun **1** a strong fireproof cabinet with a complex lock, used for the storage of valuables.
2 N. Amer. informal a condom.
– PHRASES **as safe as houses** see **HOUSE**. **in safe hands** see **HAND**. **safe in the knowledge that** used to indicate that one can do something without risk or worry on account of a specified fact: *they used to recruit hundreds a year, safe in the knowledge that many would leave.* **to be on the safe side** in order to have a margin of security against risks: *to be on the safe side, she had recorded everything.*
– DERIVATIVES **safely** adverb, **safeness** noun.
– ORIGIN Middle English (as an adjective): from Old French *sauf*, from Latin *salvus* 'uninjured'. The noun

is from the verb **SAVE**[1], later assimilated to the adjectival form.

safe area ▶ noun an area not liable to attack, especially one designated as such by the United Nations.

safe bet ▶ noun a bet that is certain to succeed.
■ a thing in which confidence can be placed regarding a future outcome.

safe-breaker (also **safe-blower** or **safe-cracker**) ▶ noun a person who breaks open and robs safes.

safe conduct ▶ noun [mass noun] immunity from arrest or harm when passing through an area.
■ [count noun] a document securing such a privilege.

safe deposit (also **safety deposit**) ▶ noun [usu. as modifier] a strongroom or safe in which valuables may be securely stored, typically within a bank or hotel: *a safe-deposit box.*

safeguard ▶ noun a measure, such as a law or procedure, designed to prevent something undesirable: *the charity called for tougher safeguards to protect Britain's remaining natural forests.*
▶ verb [with obj.] protect against something undesirable in this way: *a framework which safeguards employees from exploitation.*
– ORIGIN late Middle English (denoting protection or a safe conduct): from Old French *sauve garde*, from *sauve* 'safe' + *garde* 'guard'. Compare with **SAGGAR**.

safe haven ▶ noun a place of refuge or security.

safe house ▶ noun a house in a secret location, used by spies or criminals in hiding.

safe keeping ▶ noun [mass noun] preservation in a safe place: *she'd put her wedding ring in her purse for safe keeping.*

safelight ▶ noun a light with a coloured filter that can be used in a darkroom without affecting photosensitive film or paper.

safe period ▶ noun the time during and near a woman's menstrual period when conception is least likely.

safe seat ▶ noun a parliamentary seat that is likely to be retained in an election with a large majority.

safe sex ▶ noun [mass noun] sexual activity in which people take precautions to protect themselves against sexually transmitted diseases such as Aids.

safety ▶ noun (pl. **-ies**) **1** [mass noun] the condition of being protected from or unlikely to cause danger, risk, or injury: *they should leave for their own safety* | *the survivors were airlifted to safety.*
■ [as modifier] denoting something designed to prevent injury or damage: *a safety barrier* | *a safety helmet.* ■ [count noun] N. Amer. short for **SAFETY CATCH**. ■ [count noun] US informal a condom.
2 American Football a defensive back who plays in a deep position.
■ a play in which the ball is downed by the offence in their own end zone, scoring two points to the defence.
– PHRASES **safety first** used to advise caution. **there's safety in numbers** proverb being in a group of people makes you feel more confident or secure about taking action.
– ORIGIN Middle English: from Old French *sauvete*, from medieval Latin *salvitas*, from Latin *salvus* 'safe'.

safety belt ▶ noun a belt or strap securing a person to prevent injury, especially in a vehicle or aircraft.

safety boat ▶ noun an accompanying boat providing support in case of emergency, especially in water sports or competitive situations.

safety cage ▶ noun a framework of reinforced struts protecting a car's passenger cabin against crash damage.

safety catch ▶ noun a device that prevents a gun being fired or a machine being operated accidentally.

safety chain ▶ noun a chain fitted for security purposes, especially on a door, watch, or piece of jewellery.

safety-critical ▶ adjective designed or needing to be fail-safe for safety purposes.

safety curtain ▶ noun a fireproof curtain that can be lowered between the stage and the main part of a theatre to prevent the spread of fire.

safety deposit ▶ noun another term for **SAFE DEPOSIT**.

safety factor ▶ noun a margin of security against risks.

■technical the ratio of a material's strength to an expected strain.

safety film ▶ noun [mass noun] fire-resistant cinema film.

safety fuse ▶ noun **1** a protective electric fuse.
2 a fuse that burns at a constant slow rate, used for the controlled firing of a detonator.

safety glass ▶ noun **1** [mass noun] glass that has been toughened or laminated so that it is less likely to splinter when broken.
2 (**safety glasses**) toughened glasses or goggles for protecting the eyes when using power tools or industrial or laboratory equipment.

safety harness ▶ noun a system of belts or restraints to hold a person to prevent falling or injury.

safety lamp ▶ noun a miner's portable lamp with a flame which is protected, typically by wire gauze, to reduce the risk of explosion from ignited methane (firedamp). The first to be introduced, in the early 19th century, was the Davy lamp.

safety match ▶ noun a match igniting only when struck on a specially prepared surface, especially the side of a matchbox.

safety net ▶ noun a net placed to catch an acrobat or similar performer in case of a fall.
■figurative a safeguard against possible hardship or adversity: *a safety net for workers who lose their jobs.*

safety pin ▶ noun a pin with a point that is bent back to the head and is held in a guard when closed.

safety razor ▶ noun a razor with a guard to reduce the risk of cutting the skin.

safety valve ▶ noun a valve opening automatically to relieve excessive pressure, especially in a boiler.
■figurative a means of giving harmless vent to feelings of tension or stress.

safflower ▶ noun an orange-flowered thistle-like Eurasian plant with seeds that yield an edible oil and petals that were formerly used to produce a red or yellow dye.
● *Carthamus tinctorius,* family Compositae.
■(**safflower oil**) [mass noun] the edible oil obtained from the seeds of this plant.
– ORIGIN late Middle English: from Dutch *saffloer* or German *Saflor,* via Old French and Italian from Arabic *asfar* 'yellow'. The spelling has been influenced by **SAFFRON** and **FLOWER**.

saffron ▶ noun **1** [mass noun] an orange-yellow flavouring, food colouring, and dye made from the dried stigmas of a crocus: [as modifier] *saffron buns.*
■the orange-yellow colour of this.
2 (also **saffron crocus**) an autumn-flowering crocus with reddish-purple flowers, native to warmer regions of Eurasia. Enormous numbers of flowers are required to produce a small quantity of the large red stigmas used for the spice.
● *Crocus sativus,* family Iridaceae. See also **MEADOW SAFFRON**.
– DERIVATIVES **saffrony** adjective.
– ORIGIN Middle English: from Old French *safran,* based on Arabic *za'farān.*

safranine /'safrəniːn/ (also **safranin** /-nɪn/) ▶ noun Chemistry any of a large group of synthetic azo dyes, mainly red, used as biological stains.
– ORIGIN mid 19th cent. (denoting the yellow colouring matter in saffron): from French.

sag[1] ▶ verb (**sagged, sagging**) [no obj.] sink or subside gradually under weight or pressure or through lack of strength: *he closed his eyes and sagged against the wall.*
■hang down loosely or unevenly: *stockings which sagged at the knees.* ■ have a downward bulge or curve: *the bed sagged in the middle* ■ [as adj.] **sagging** *sagging shelves bearing rusty paint tins.* ■figurative decline to a lower level, usually temporarily: *exports are forging ahead while home sales sag.*
▶ noun a downward curve or bulge in a structure caused by weakness or excessive weight or pressure: *a sag in the middle necessitated a third set of wheels.*
■[mass noun] Geometry the amount of this, measured as the perpendicular distance from the middle of the curve to the straight line between the two supporting points. ■ figurative a decline, especially a temporary one.
– DERIVATIVES **saggy** adjective.
– ORIGIN late Middle English (as a verb): apparently related to Middle Low German *sacken,* Dutch *zakken* 'subside'.

sag[2] ▶ noun variant spelling of **SAAG**.

saga /'sɑːɡə/ ▶ noun a long story of heroic achievement, especially a medieval prose narrative in Old Norse or Old Icelandic: *a figure straight out of a Viking saga.*
■a long, involved story, account, or series of incidents: *launching into the saga of her engagement.*
– ORIGIN early 18th cent.: from Old Norse, literally 'narrative'; related to **SAW**[3].

saga boy ▶ noun informal, chiefly W. Indian a playboy.

sagacious /sə'ɡeɪʃəs/ ▶ adjective having or showing keen mental discernment and good judgement; shrewd: *they were sagacious enough to avoid any outright confrontation.*
– DERIVATIVES **sagaciously** adverb.
– ORIGIN early 17th cent.: from Latin *sagax, sagac-* 'wise' + **-IOUS**.

sagacity /sə'ɡasɪti/ ▶ noun [mass noun] the quality of being sagacious: *a man of great political sagacity.*

sagamore /'saɡəmɔː/ ▶ noun (among some American Indian peoples) a chief; a sachem.
– ORIGIN Eastern Abnaki.

Sagan[1] /'seɪɡ(ə)n/, Carl (Edward) (1934–96), American astronomer. Sagan showed that amino acids can be synthesized in an artificial primordial soup irradiated by ultraviolet light—a possible origin of life on the earth. He wrote several popular science books, and was co-producer of the television series *Cosmos* (1980).

Sagan[2] /sa'ɡɒ̃, French saɡɑ̃/, Françoise (b.1935), French novelist, dramatist, and short-story writer; pseudonym of *Françoise Quoirez.* She rose to fame with her first novel *Bonjour Tristesse* (1954); in this and subsequent novels she examined the transitory nature of love as experienced in brief liaisons.

saganaki /,saɡə'nɑːki/ ▶ noun [mass noun] a Greek dish consisting of breaded or floured cheese fried in butter, served as an appetizer.
– ORIGIN modern Greek, denoting a small two-handled frying pan, in which the dish is traditionally made.

sagbag ▶ noun a large beanbag used as a seat.

sage[1] ▶ noun [mass noun] **1** an aromatic plant with greyish-green leaves that are used as a culinary herb, native to southern Europe and the Mediterranean.
● *Salvia officinalis,* family Labiatae.
■used in names of similar aromatic plants of the mint family, e.g. **wood sage.**
2 (also **white sage**) either of two bushy North American plants with silvery-grey leaves:
● an aromatic plant which was formerly burnt by the Cheyenne for its cleansing properties and as an incense (*Artemisia ludoviciana,* family Compositae). ● a plant of the goosefoot family (*Krascheninnikovia lanata,* family Chenopodiaceae).
– ORIGIN Middle English: from Old French *sauge,* from Latin *salvia* 'healing plant', from *salvus* 'safe'.

sage[2] ▶ noun a profoundly wise man, especially one who features in ancient history or legend.
▶ adjective having, showing, or indicating profound wisdom: *they nodded in agreement with these sage remarks.*
– DERIVATIVES **sagely** adverb, **sageness** noun.
– ORIGIN Middle English (as an adjective): from Old French, from Latin *sapere* 'be wise'.

sagebrush ▶ noun [mass noun] a shrubby aromatic North American plant of the daisy family.
● Genus *Artemisia,* family Compositae: several species, in particular *A. tridentata.*
■scrub which is dominated by such shrubs, occurring chiefly in semi-arid regions of western North America.

Sagebrush State informal name for **NEVADA**.

sage Derby (also **sage Derby cheese**) ▶ noun [mass noun] a firm cheese made with an infusion of sage which flavours it and gives it a mottled green colour.

sage green ▶ noun [mass noun] a greyish-green colour like that of sage leaves.

sage grouse ▶ noun a large grouse of western North America, with long pointed tail feathers, noted for the male's courtship display in which air sacs are inflated to make a popping sound.
● *Centrocercus urophasianus,* family Tetraonidae (or Phasianidae).

saggar /'saɡə/ (also **sagger**) ▶ noun a protective fireclay box enclosing ceramic ware while it is being fired.

– ORIGIN mid 18th cent.: probably a contraction of the noun **SAFEGUARD**.

Sagitta /sə'dʒɪtə, -'ɡɪtə/ Astronomy a small northern constellation (the Arrow), lying in the Milky Way north of Aquila.
■[as genitive **Sagittae** /sə'dʒɪtiː, -'ɡɪtiː/] used with preceding letter or numeral to designate a star in this constellation: *the star Beta Sagittae.*
– ORIGIN Latin.

sagittal /'sadʒɪt(ə)l, sə'dʒɪt-/ Anatomy ▶ adjective **1** relating to or denoting the suture on top of the skull which runs between the parietal bones in a front to back direction.
2 of or in a plane parallel to this suture, especially that dividing the body into left and right halves.
– DERIVATIVES **sagitally** adverb.
– ORIGIN late Middle English: from medieval Latin *sagittalis,* from Latin *sagitta* 'arrow'.

sagittal crest ▶ noun Zoology (in many mammals) a bony ridge on the top of the skull to which the jaw muscles are attached.

Sagittarius /,sadʒɪ'tɛːrɪəs/ **1** Astronomy a large constellation (the Archer), said to represent a centaur carrying a bow and arrow. The centre of the Galaxy is situated within it.
■[as genitive **Sagittarii** /-'tɛːriːʌɪ/] used with preceding letter or numeral to designate a star in this constellation: *the star Mu Sagittarii.*
2 Astrology the ninth sign of the zodiac, which the sun enters about 22 November.
■(**a Sagittarius**) (pl. same) a person born when the sun is in this sign.
– DERIVATIVES **Sagittarian** noun & adjective (only in sense 2).
– ORIGIN Latin.

sagittate /'sadʒɪteɪt/ ▶ adjective Botany & Zoology shaped like an arrowhead.
– ORIGIN mid 18th cent.: from Latin *sagitta* 'arrow' + **-ATE**[2].

sago /'seɪɡəʊ/ ▶ noun (pl. **-os**) **1** [mass noun] edible starch which is obtained from a palm and is a staple food in parts of the tropics. The pith inside the trunk is scraped out, washed, and dried to produce a flour or processed to produce the granular sago used in the West.
■(also **sago pudding**) a sweet dish made from sago and milk.
2 (**sago palm**) the palm from which most sago is obtained, growing in freshwater swamps in SE Asia.
● *Metroxylon sagu,* family Palmae.
■any of a number of other palms or cycads which yield a similar starch.
– ORIGIN mid 16th cent.: from Malay *sagu* (originally via Portuguese).

saguaro /sə'ɡwɑːrəʊ, -'wɑː-/ (also **saguaro cactus**) ▶ noun (pl. **-os**) a giant cactus which can grow to 20 metres in height and whose branches are shaped like candelabra, native to the SW United States and Mexico. The edible fruit was formerly a source of food and drink.
● *Carnegiea gigantea,* family Cactaceae.
– ORIGIN mid 19th cent.: from Mexican Spanish.

Saguia el Hamra /sə,ɡiːə ɛl 'hamrə/ an intermittent river in the north of Western Sahara. It flows into the Atlantic west of La'youn.
■the region through which this river flows. A territory of Spain from 1934, it united with Río de Oro in 1958 to become a part of Spanish Sahara.

Saha /sɑː'hɑː/, Meghnad (1894–1956), Indian theoretical physicist. Saha worked on thermal ionization in stars and laid the foundations for modern astrophysics. He devised an equation expressing the relationship between ionization and temperature.

Sahara Desert /sə'hɑːrə/ (also **the Sahara**) a vast desert in North Africa, extending from the Atlantic in the west to the Red Sea in the east, and from the Mediterranean and the Atlas Mountains in the north to the Sahel in the south. The largest desert in the world, it covers an area of about 9,065,000 sq. km (3,500,000 sq. miles). In recent years it has been extending southwards into the Sahel.
– DERIVATIVES **Saharan** adjective.
– ORIGIN *Sahara* from Arabic *ṣaḥrā* 'desert'.

Sahel /sə'hɛl/ a vast semi-arid region of North Africa, to the south of the Sahara, which forms a transitional zone at the south of the desert and comprises the northern part of the region known as Sudan.
– DERIVATIVES **Sahelian** /-'hiːlɪən/ adjective & noun.

sahib /ˈsɑː(h)ɪb, sɑːb/ ▶ **noun** Indian a polite title or form of address for a man: *the Doctor Sahib.*
– ORIGIN Urdu, via Persian from Arabic *ṣāḥib* 'friend, lord'.

Sahin Line /saˈhɪn/ another term for **ATTILA LINE**.
– ORIGIN *Sahin*, the name of a town in Turkey.

sahitya /sɑːˈhɪtjəː/ ▶ **noun** [mass noun] Indian literature or lyrics.
– ORIGIN from Sanskrit *sāhitya*.

Sahiwal /ˈsɑːhɪvɑːl, -wɑːl/ ▶ **noun** an animal of a breed of cattle which originated in Pakistan but is now used in other tropical regions. Sahiwals have small horns and a hump on the back of the neck.
– ORIGIN early 20th cent.: from the name of a town in the central Punjab, Pakistan.

sai /sʌɪ/ ▶ **noun** (pl. same) a dagger with two sharp prongs curving outward from the hilt, originating in Okinawa and sometimes used in pairs in martial arts.
– ORIGIN Japanese.

Said /saˈiːd/, Edward W. (b.1935), American critic, born in Palestine; full name *Edward Wadi Said*. He came to public notice with *Orientalism* (1978), a study of Western attitudes towards Eastern culture. Other notable works: *Culture and Imperialism* (1993).

said past and past participle of **SAY**. ▶ **adjective** used in legal language or humorously to refer to someone or something already mentioned or named: *acting in pursuance of the said agreement.*

Saida /ˈsʌɪdə/ Arabic name for **SIDON**.

saiga /ˈseɪgə, ˈsʌɪgə/ (also **saiga antelope**) ▶ **noun** an Asian antelope which has a distinctive convex snout with the nostrils opening downwards, living in herds on the cold steppes.
• *Saiga tartarica*, family Bovidae.
– ORIGIN early 19th cent.: from Russian.

Saigon /sʌɪˈgɒn/ a city and port on the south coast of Vietnam; pop 3,015,700 (1992). It was the capital of the French colony established in Vietnam in the 19th century, becoming capital of South Vietnam in the partition of 1954. Official name (since 1975) **HO CHI MINH CITY**.

sail ▶ **noun 1** a piece of material extended on a mast to catch the wind and propel a boat or ship or other vessel: *all the sails were unfurled.*
■[mass noun] the use of sailing ships as a means of transport: *this led to bigger ships as steam replaced sail.* ■ [in sing.] a voyage or excursion in a ship, especially a sailing ship or boat: *they went for a sail.* ■ archaic a sailing ship: *sail ahoy!* ■ S. African a canvas sheet or tarpaulin. [ORIGIN: loan translation, based on Dutch *seil* 'tarpaulin'.]
2 something resembling a sail in shape or function, in particular:
■a wind-catching apparatus, typically one consisting of a set of boards, attached to the arm of a windmill. ■ the broad fin on the back of a sailfish or of some prehistoric reptiles. ■ a structure by which an animal is propelled across the surface of water by the wind, e.g. the float of a Portuguese man-of-war. ■ the conning tower of a submarine.
▶ **verb** [no obj.] **1** travel in a boat with sails, especially as a sport or recreation: *Ian took us out sailing on the lake.*
■[with adverbial] travel in a ship or boat using sails or engine power: *the ferry caught fire sailing between Caen and Portsmouth.* ■ [with adverbial] begin a voyage; leave a harbour: *the catamaran sails at 3:30.* ■ [with obj.] travel by ship on or across (a sea) or on (a route): *plastic ships could be sailing the oceans soon.* ■ [with obj. and adverbial of direction] navigate or control (a boat or ship): *I stole a small fishing boat and sailed it to the Delta.*
2 [with adverbial of direction] move smoothly and rapidly or in a stately or confident manner: *the ball sailed inside the right-hand post.*
■(**sail through**) informal succeed easily at (something, especially a test or examination): *Ali sailed through his exams.* ■ (**sail into**) informal attack physically or verbally with force.
– PHRASES **in** (or **under**) **full sail** with all the sails in position or fully spread: *a galleon in full sail.* **sail close to** (or **near**) **the wind** sail as nearly against the wind as possible. ■ figurative come close to breaking a rule or the law; behave or operate in a risky way. **take in sail** furl the sail or sails of a vessel. **under sail** with the sails hoisted: *at a speed of eight knots under sail.*
– DERIVATIVES **sailable** adjective, **sailed** adjective [in combination] *a black-sailed ship.*
– ORIGIN Old English *segel* (noun), *seglian* (verb), of Germanic origin; related to Dutch *zeil* and German *Segel* (nouns).

sailboard ▶ **noun** a board with a mast attached to it by a swivel joint, and a sail, used in windsurfing.
– DERIVATIVES **sailboarder** noun, **sailboarding** noun.

sailboat ▶ **noun** North American term for **SAILING BOAT**.

sailcloth ▶ **noun** [mass noun] canvas or other material used for making sails.
■a canvas-like fabric used for making durable weatherproof clothes.

sailer ▶ **noun** a sailing boat or ship of specified power or manner of sailing.

sailfin molly ▶ **noun** a small brightly coloured freshwater fish, the male of which has a long high dorsal fin. Native to North and Central America, it is popular in aquaria.
• Genus *Poecilia*, family Poeciliidae: *P. latipinna* and *P. velifera*.
– ORIGIN *sailfin* with reference to the dorsal fin + **MOLLY**.

sailfish ▶ **noun** (pl. same or **-fishes**) a fish with a high sail-like dorsal fin, in particular:
• an edible migratory billfish that is a prized game fish (genus *Istiophorus*, family Istiophoridae, in particular *I. platypterus*).
• (also **Celebes sailfish**) a small tropical freshwater fish of Sulawesi, popular in aquaria (*Telmatherina ladigesi*, family Atherinidae).

sail-fluke ▶ **noun** another term for **MEGRIM**².

sailing ▶ **noun** [mass noun] the action of sailing in a ship or boat: [as modifier] *a sailing club.*
■[count noun] a voyage made by a ferry or cruise ship, especially according to a planned schedule: *the company operates five sailings a day from Ramsgate to Dunkirk.* ■ [in sing.] an act of beginning a voyage or of leaving a harbour.

sailing boat ▶ **noun** chiefly Brit. a boat propelled by sails.

sailing master ▶ **noun** an officer responsible for the navigation of a ship or yacht.

sailing orders ▶ **plural noun** instructions to the captain of a vessel regarding such matters as time of departure and destination.

sailing ship ▶ **noun** a ship driven by sails.

sailmaker ▶ **noun** a person who makes, repairs, or alters sails as a profession.
– DERIVATIVES **sailmaking** noun.

sail-off ▶ **noun** a sailing contest used to decide the final result of a competition or championship.

sailor ▶ **noun** a person whose job it is to work as a member of the crew of a commercial or naval ship or boat, especially one who is below the rank of officer.
■[usu. with adj. or noun modifier] a person who goes sailing as a sport or recreation: *she was a keen sailor despite being confined to a wheelchair.* ■ (**a good/bad sailor**) a person who rarely (or often) becomes sick at sea in rough weather.
– DERIVATIVES **sailorly** adjective.
– ORIGIN mid 17th cent.: variant of obsolete *sailer*.

sailor collar ▶ **noun** a collar cut deep and square at the back, tapering to a V-neck at the front.

sailor hat ▶ **noun** another term for **BOATER** (in sense 1).

sailor suit ▶ **noun** a suit of blue and white material resembling the dress uniform of an ordinary seaman, especially as fashionable dress for young boys during the 19th century.

sail plan ▶ **noun** a scale diagram of the masts, spars, rigging, and sails of a sailing vessel.

sailplane ▶ **noun** a glider designed for sustained flight.

sainfoin /ˈseɪnfɔɪn, ˈsan-/ ▶ **noun** [mass noun] a pink-flowered plant of the pea family, which is native to Asia and grown widely for fodder.
• *Onobrychis viciifolia*, family Leguminosae.
– ORIGIN mid 17th cent.: from obsolete French *saintfoin*, from modern Latin *sanum foenum* 'wholesome hay' (with reference to its medicinal properties).

Sainsbury, John James (1844–1928), English grocer. He opened his first grocery store in London in 1875. After his death the business was continued by members of his family, developing into the large supermarket chain bearing the Sainsbury name.

saint /seɪnt, before a name usually s(ə)nt/ ▶ **noun 1** a person acknowledged as holy or virtuous and typically regarded as being in heaven after death.
■(in the Catholic and Orthodox Churches) a person formally recognized or canonized by the Church after death, who may be the object of veneration and prayers for intercession. ■ a person who is admired or venerated because of their virtue: *he was considered a living saint by recipients of his generosity.* ■ (in or alluding to biblical use) a Christian believer. ■ (**Saint**) a member of the Church of Jesus Christ of Latter-Day Saints; a Mormon.
2 (**Saint**) (abbrev.: **St** or **S**) used in titles of religious saints: *the epistles of Saint Paul | St Mary's Church.*
■used in place names or other dedications: *St Cross | St Malo.*
▶ **verb** [with obj.] formally recognize as a saint; canonize.
■[as adj. **sainted**] worthy of being a saint; very virtuous: *the story of his sainted sister Eileen.*
– PHRASES **my sainted aunt** see **AUNT**.
– DERIVATIVES **saintdom** noun, **sainthood** noun, **saintlike** adjective, **saintship** noun.
– ORIGIN Middle English, from Old French *seint*, from Latin *sanctus* 'holy', past participle of *sancire* 'consecrate'.

St Agnes, St Barnabas, etc. see **AGNES, ST**; **BARNABAS, ST**; etc.

St Albans /ˈɔːlbənz/ a city in Hertfordshire, in SE England; pop. 55,700 (1981). The city developed around an abbey, which was founded in Saxon times on the site of the martyrdom in the 3rd century of St Alban, a Christian Roman from the nearby Roman city of Verulamium.

St Andrews a town in east Scotland, in Fife, on the North Sea; pop. 14,050 (1991). It is noted for its university, founded in 1410, and its championship golf courses.

St Andrew's cross ▶ **noun** a diagonal or X-shaped cross, especially white on a blue background (as a national emblem of Scotland). Also called **SALTIRE**.

St Anthony cross (also **St Anthony's cross**) ▶ **noun** a T-shaped cross.

St Anthony's fire ▶ **noun 1** another term for **ERYSIPELAS**.
2 another term for **ERGOTISM**.

St Bartholomew's Day Massacre see **MASSACRE OF ST BARTHOLOMEW**.

St Bernard (also **St Bernard dog**) ▶ **noun** a very large dog of a breed originally kept to rescue travellers by the monks of the Hospice on the Great St Bernard.

St Bernard Pass either of two passes across the Alps in southern Europe. The **Great St Bernard Pass**, on the border between SW Switzerland and Italy, rises to 2,469 m (8,100 ft). The **Little St Bernard Pass**, on the French–Italian border south-east of Mont Blanc, rises to 2,188 m (7,178 ft).
– ORIGIN named after the hospices founded on their summits in the 11th century by the French monk *St Bernard*.

St Christopher and Nevis, Federation of official name for **ST KITTS AND NEVIS**.

St Croix /krɔɪ/ an island in the Caribbean, the largest of the US Virgin Islands; chief town, Christiansted. Purchased by Denmark in 1753, it was sold to the US in 1917.

St David's a small city near the coast of SW Wales, in Pembrokeshire; pop. 1,800 (1981). Its 12th-century cathedral houses the shrine of St David, the patron saint of Wales. Welsh name **TYDDEWI**.

Saint-Denis /ˌsãdəˈniː, French sɛ̃dəni/ **1** a municipality in France, now a northern suburb of Paris.
2 the capital of the French island of Réunion, a port on the north coast; pop. 121,670 (1990).

Sainte-Beuve /sãtˈbəːv, French sɛ̃tbœv/, Charles Augustin (1804–69), French critic and writer. In his criticism he concentrated on the influence of social and other factors in the development of character.

St Elmo's fire /ˈɛlməʊz/ ▶ **noun** [mass noun] a phenomenon in which a luminous electrical discharge appears on a ship or aircraft during a storm.
– ORIGIN regarded as a sign of protection given by St Elmo, the patron saint of sailors.

St Émilion /ˌsãt eɪˈmɪljɔ̃, French sɛ̃t emiljɔ̃/ a small town situated to the north of the Dordogne in SW France. It gives its name to a group of Bordeaux wines.

St-Étienne /ˌsãteɪˈtjɛn/ an industrial city in SE

S

central France, south-west of Lyons; pop. 201,570 (1990).

St Eustatius /juːˈsteɪʃəs/ a small volcanic island in the Caribbean, in the Netherlands Antilles; pop. 1,840 (1992).

Saint-Exupéry /ˌsætɪɡˈzuːpɛri, French sɛ̃tɛɡzypeʀi/, Antoine (Marie Roger de) (1900–44), French writer and aviator, best known for the fable *The Little Prince* (1943).

St George's the capital of Grenada in the Caribbean, a port in the south-west of the island; pop. 4,440 (1990).

St George's Channel a channel between Wales and Ireland, linking the Irish Sea with the Celtic Sea.

St George's cross ▸ noun a +-shaped cross, red on a white background (especially as a national emblem of England).

St George's mushroom ▸ noun a common European mushroom with a creamy-white cap and white gills, growing typically in rings and first appearing around St George's Day (April 23).
● *Tricholoma gambosum*, family Tricholomataceae, class Hymenomycetes.

St Gotthard Pass /ˈɡɒtɑːd/ a mountain pass in the Alps in southern Switzerland, situated at an altitude of 2,108 m (6,916 ft).
– ORIGIN named after a former chapel and hospice (14th cent.), dedicated to St Godehard or *Gotthard*, an 11th-cent. bishop of Hildesheim in Germany.

St Helena /hɪˈliːnə/ a solitary island in the South Atlantic, a British dependency; pop. 5,644 (1997); official language, English; capital, Jamestown. It was administered by the East India Company from 1659 until 1834, when it became a British colony. Ascension, Tristan da Cunha, and Gough Island are dependencies of St Helena. It is famous as the place of Napoleon's exile (1815–21) and death.
– DERIVATIVES **St Helenian** adjective & noun.
– ORIGIN so named when it was discovered by the Portuguese on the feast day of *St Helena*, 21 May, 1502.

St Helens an industrial town in NW England north-east of Liverpool; pop. 175,300 (1991).

St Helens, Mount an active volcano in SW Washington, in the Cascade Range, rising to 2,560 m (8,312 ft). A dramatic eruption in May 1980 reduced its height by several hundred metres and spread volcanic ash and debris over a large area.

St Helier /ˈhɛlɪə/ the capital of Jersey, situated on the south coast; pop. 28,120 (1991).

St James's Palace a royal palace in London, built by Henry VIII on the site of an earlier leper hospital dedicated to St James the Less.

St John 1 an island in the Caribbean, one of the three principal islands of the US Virgin Islands.
2 (usu. **Saint John**) a city in New Brunswick, eastern Canada, a port on the Bay of Fundy at the mouth of the St John River.

St John Ambulance a voluntary organization providing first aid, nursing, ambulance, and welfare services.

St John's 1 the capital of Antigua and Barbuda, situated on the NW coast of Antigua; pop. 21,510 (1991).
2 the capital of Newfoundland, a port on the SE coast of the island; pop. 121,030 (est. 1991); metropolitan area pop. 171,860.

St John's wort ▸ noun a herbaceous plant or shrub with distinctive yellow five-petalled flowers and paired oval leaves.
● Genus *Hypericum*, family Guttiferae: many species.
– ORIGIN so named because some species come into flower near the feast day of St John the Baptist (24 June).

St Kilda /ˈkɪldə/ a small island group of the Outer Hebrides, situated in the Atlantic 64 km (40 miles) west of Lewis and Harris. The islands are now uninhabited and are administered as a nature reserve.

St Kitts and Nevis a country in the Caribbean consisting of two adjoining islands of the Leeward Islands; pop. 40,620 (1991); languages, English (official), Creole; capital, Basseterre (on St Kitts). Official name **FEDERATION OF ST CHRISTOPHER AND NEVIS**.

St Kitts was visited in 1493 by Christopher Columbus. The islands were colonized by English settlers from 1623, becoming the first successful English colony in the West Indies. A self-governing union between St Kitts and Nevis (and briefly Anguilla) was created in 1967 and became a fully independent member of the Commonwealth in 1983.

– ORIGIN *St Kitts*, alteration (by settlers) of *St Christopher*, a name given to the island by Columbus; *Nevis* from Spanish *las nieves* 'the snows' (because of the 'snowy' clouds surrounding the peak).

Saint Laurent /ˌsɑ̃ lɔːˈrɒ̃, French sɛ̃ lɔʀɑ̃/, Yves (Mathieu) (b.1936), French couturier. He opened his own fashion house in 1962, later launching Rive Gauche boutiques to sell ready-to-wear garments and expanding the business to include perfumes.

St Lawrence River a river of North America, which flows for some 1,200 km (750 miles) from Lake Ontario along the border between Canada and the US to the Gulf of St Lawrence on the Atlantic coast.

St Lawrence Seaway a waterway in North America, which flows for 3,768 km (2,342 miles) through the Great Lakes and along the course of the St Lawrence River to the Atlantic. It is open along its entire length to ocean-going vessels.

St Leger /ˈlɛdʒə/ ▸ noun an annual flat horse race at Doncaster for three-year-olds, held in September.
– ORIGIN named after Colonel Barry *St Leger* (1737–89), who instituted the race in 1776.

St Louis a city and port in eastern Missouri, on the Mississippi just south of its confluence with the Missouri; pop. 396,685 (1990). Founded as a French fur-trading post, it passed to the US as part of the Louisiana Purchase.

St Louis encephalitis ▸ noun [mass noun] a form of viral encephalitis which can be fatal and is transmitted by mosquitoes.

St Lucia /ˈluːʃə/ a country in the Caribbean, one of the Windward Islands; pop. 133,310 (1991); languages, English (official), French Creole; capital, Castries.

First encountered by Europeans around 1500, St Lucia was settled by both French and British in the 17th century. Possession of the island was long disputed until France ceded it to Britain in 1814. Since 1979 it has been an independent state within the Commonwealth.

– DERIVATIVES **St Lucian** adjective & noun.

St Luke's summer ▸ noun Brit. a period of fine weather around 18 October (the saint's feast day).

saintly ▸ adjective (**saintlier**, **saintliest**) very holy or virtuous: *a truly saintly woman.*
■ of or relating to a saint: *a crypt for some saintly relic.*
– DERIVATIVES **saintliness** noun.

St Malo /sɑ̃ ˈmɑːləʊ/ a walled town and port on the north coast of Brittany, in NW France; pop. 49,270 (1990).

St Mark's Cathedral the cathedral church of Venice since 1807. It was built in the 9th century to house relics of St Mark, and rebuilt in the 11th century.

St Mark's fly ▸ noun a dark European fly which first appears around St Mark's Day (April 25th). It drifts slowly over low vegetation with the legs hanging down.
● *Bibio marci*, family Bibionidae.

St Martin /ˌsɑ̃ mɑːˈtɑ̃/ a small island in the Caribbean, one of the Leeward Islands; pop. 32,220 (1992). The southern section of the island is administered by the Dutch, forming part of the Netherlands Antilles; the larger northern part of the island is part of the French overseas department of Guadeloupe. Dutch name **SINT MAARTEN**.

St Martin's summer ▸ noun Brit., dated a period of fine weather around 11 November (the feast day of St Martin of Tours).

St Moritz /san ˈmɒrɪts, məˈrɪts/ a resort and winter-sports centre in SE Switzerland.

St-Nazaire /ˌsɑ̃naˈzɛː, French sɛ̃nazɛʀ/ a seaport and industrial town in NW France, on the Atlantic coast at the mouth of the Loire; pop. 66,090 (1990).

St Nicolas French name for **SINT-NIKLAAS** /sɛ̃ nikɔla/.

St Patrick's cabbage ▸ noun a European saxifrage with a rosette of long-stalked leaves and branching clusters of small white flowers.
● *Saxifraga spathularis*, family Saxifragaceae.

St Paul the state capital of Minnesota, situated on the Mississippi adjacent to Minneapolis, with which it forms the Twin Cities metropolitan area; pop. 272,235 (1990).

saintpaulia /ˌseɪntˈpɔːlɪə/ ▸ noun a plant of the genus *Saintpaulia* (family Gesneriaceae), especially (in gardening) an African violet.
– ORIGIN named after Baron W. von *Saint Paul* (1860–1910), the German explorer who discovered it.

St Paul's Cathedral a cathedral on Ludgate Hill, London, designed by Sir Christopher Wren and built between 1675 and 1711.

St Peter's Basilica a Roman Catholic basilica in the Vatican City. Built in the 16th century on the site of a structure erected by Constantine on the supposed site of St Peter's crucifixion, it is the largest Christian church.

St Petersburg /ˈpiːtəzbəːɡ/ 1 a city and seaport in NW Russia, situated on the delta of the River Neva, on the eastern shores of the Gulf of Finland; pop. 5,035,000 (1990). Former names **PETROGRAD** (1914–24) and **LENINGRAD** (1924–91).

Founded in 1703 by Peter the Great, St Petersburg was the capital of Russia from 1712 until the Russian Revolution. It was the scene in February and October 1917 of the events which triggered the Revolution. During the Second World War it was subjected by German and Finnish forces to a siege which lasted for more than two years (1941–4).

2 a resort city in western Florida, on the Gulf of Mexico; pop. 238,630 (1990).

St Peter's fish ▸ noun a fish with a dark mark near each pectoral fin, in particular a widely farmed cichlid of Africa and the Middle East (also called **TILAPIA**).
● *Sarotherodon galileus*, family Cichlidae. Alternative name: **Galilee cichlid**.
– ORIGIN with biblical allusion to Matt. 17:27.

St Pierre and Miquelon /sɑ̃ ˈpjɛː, ˈmiːklɒn/ a group of eight small islands in the North Atlantic, off the south coast of Newfoundland; pop. 6,390 (1990). An overseas territory of France, the islands form the last remaining French possession in North America.

St Pölten /ˈpɜːlt(ə)n/ a city in NE Austria, capital of the state of Lower Austria; pop. 50,025 (1991).

Saint-Saëns /ˈsæsɒ̃, French sɛ̃sɑ̃s/, (Charles) Camille (1835–1921), French composer, pianist, and organist. He is best known for his Third Symphony (1886), the symphonic poem *Danse macabre* (1874), and the *Carnaval des animaux* (1886).

saint's day ▸ noun a day on which a saint is particularly commemorated in the Christian Church.

Saint-Simon[1] /ˌsæsiːˈmɒ̃/, Claude-Henri de Rouvroy, Comte de (1760–1825), French social reformer and philosopher. Later claimed as the founder of French socialism, he argued that society should be organized by leaders of industry and given spiritual direction by scientists.

Saint-Simon[2] /ˌsæsiːˈmɒ̃/, Louis de Rouvroy, Duc de (1675–1755), French writer. He is best known for his *Mémoires*, a detailed record of court life between 1694 and 1723, in the reigns of Louis XIV and XV.

St Sophia /səˈfiːə, -ˈfʌɪə/ the key monument of Byzantine architecture, originally a church, at Istanbul. Built by order of Justinian and inaugurated in 537, it was converted into a mosque after the Turkish invasion of 1453. In 1935 Atatürk declared it a museum. Also called **HAGIA SOPHIA**, **SANTA SOPHIA**.

St Stephens a name for the House of Commons.
– ORIGIN from *St Stephen*, the name of the ancient chapel in Westminster, in which the House used to sit (1537–1834).

St Thomas an island in the Caribbean, the second largest of the US Virgin Islands, situated to the east of Puerto Rico; pop. 48,170 (1990); chief town, Charlotte Amalie. Settled by the Dutch in 1657, it passed nine years later to the Danes, who sold it to the US in 1917.

St Trinian's /ˈtrɪnɪənz/ a fictional girls' school invented by Ronald Searle in 1941, whose pupils are characterized by unruly behaviour, ungainly appearance, and unattractive school uniform.

St-Tropez /ˌsɑ̃trə(ʊ)ˈpeɪ/ a fishing port and resort on the Mediterranean coast of southern France, south-west of Cannes; pop. 5,790 (1990).

St Valentine's Day Massacre the shooting

on 14th February 1929 of seven members of the rival 'Bugsy' Moran's gang by some of Al Capone's men disguised as policemen.

St Vincent, Cape a headland in SW Portugal, which forms the south-westernmost tip of the country. It was the site of a sea battle in 1797 in which the British fleet under Admiral John Jervis defeated the Spanish. Portuguese name **SÃO VINCENTE**.

St Vincent and the Grenadines /ˈvɪns(ə)nt, ˈɡrɛnədiːnz/ an island state in the Windward Islands in the Caribbean, consisting of the mountainous island of St Vincent and some of the Grenadines; pop. 106,500 (1991); languages, English (official), English-based Creole; capital, Kingstown.

> The French, Dutch, and British all made attempts at settlements in the 18th century, and the islands finally fell to British possession in 1783. The state obtained full independence with a limited form of membership of the Commonwealth in 1979.

St Vitus's dance /ˈvʌɪtəsɪz/ ▶**noun** old-fashioned term for **SYDENHAM'S CHOREA**.
– ORIGIN so named because a visit to *St Vitus*'s shrine was believed to alleviate the disease.

Saipan /sʌɪˈpan/ the largest of the islands comprising the Northern Marianas in the western Pacific.

saith /sɛθ/ archaic third person singular present of **SAY**.

saithe /seɪθ/ ▶**noun** a commercially valuable food fish of the cod family, which occurs in the North Atlantic. Also called **COALFISH**, **COLEY**, and (in North America) **POLLOCK**.
• *Pollachius virens*, family Gadidae.
– ORIGIN mid 16th cent.: from Old Norse *seithr*.

Saiva /ˈsʌɪvə/ ▶**noun** a member of one of the main branches of modern Hinduism, devoted to the worship of the god Shiva as the supreme being. Compare with **VAISHNAVA**.
– DERIVATIVES **Saivite** noun & adjective.
– ORIGIN from Sanskrit *śaiva* 'sacred to Shiva'.

sakabula /ˌsakəˈbuːlə/ ▶**noun** S. African a widowbird of SE Africa, the mainly black male of which has a very long tail.
• *Euplectes progne*, family Ploceidae. Alternative name: **long-tailed widowbird.**
– ORIGIN late 19th cent.: from Xhosa *isakabula*.

Sakai /sɑːˈkʌɪ/ an industrial city in Japan, on Osaka Bay just south of the city of Osaka; pop. 807,860 (1990).

sake[1] /seɪk/ ▶**noun 1** (**for the sake of something** or **for something's sake**) for the purpose of; in the interest of; in order to achieve or preserve: *the couple moved to the coast for the sake of her health | for safety's sake, photographers are obliged to stand behind police lines.*
■used in phrases to comment on the speaker's purpose in choosing a particular way of wording a text or presenting an argument: *let us say, for the sake of argument, that the plotter and the assassin are one and the same person.* ■ (**for its own sake** or **something for something's sake** or **for the sake of it**) used to indicate something that is done as an end in itself rather than to achieve some other purpose: *new ideas amount to change for change's sake.*
2 (**for the sake of someone** or **for someone's sake**) out of consideration for or in order to help someone: *I felt I couldn't give up, for my own sake or the baby's | I have to make an effort for John's sake.*
■in order to please: *he'd do anything for me—even killed a man for my sake | I've spent a long time doing things for everybody's sake.*
3 (**for God's** or **goodness** etc. **sake**) used to express impatience, annoyance, urgency, or desperation: *'Oh, for God's sake!' snarled Dyson | where did you get it, for heaven's sake?*
– PHRASES **for old times' sake** in memory of former times; in acknowledgement of a shared past: *they sat in the back seats for old times' sake.*
– ORIGIN Old English *sacu* 'contention, crime', of Germanic origin; related to Dutch *zaak* and German *Sache*, from a base meaning 'affair, legal action, thing'. The phrase *for the sake of* may be from Old Norse.

sake[2] /ˈsɑːki, ˈsakeɪ/ ▶**noun** [mass noun] a Japanese alcoholic drink made from fermented rice, traditionally drunk warm in small porcelain cups.
– ORIGIN Japanese.

saker /ˈseɪkə/ ▶**noun 1** a large Eurasian falcon with a brown back and whitish head, used in falconry.
• *Falco cherrug*, family Falconidae.
2 an early form of cannon.
– ORIGIN late Middle English: from Old French *sacre*, from Arabic *ṣaḳr* 'falcon'.

Sakha, Republic of /ˈsɑːkə/ official name for **YAKUTIA**.

Sakhalin /ˌsakəˈliːn/ a large Russian island in the Sea of Okhotsk, situated off the coast of eastern Russia and separated from it by the Tartar Strait; capital, Yuzhno-Sakhalinsk. From 1905 to 1946 it was divided into the northern part, held by Russia, and the southern part (Karafuto), occupied by Japan.

Sakharov /ˈsakərɒf/, Andrei (Dmitrievich) (1921–89), Russian nuclear physicist and civil rights campaigner. Having helped to develop the Soviet hydrogen bomb, he campaigned against nuclear proliferation. He fought for reform and human rights in the USSR, for which he was awarded the Nobel Peace Prize in 1975 but was also sentenced to internal exile 1980–6.

Saki /ˈsɑːki/ (1870–1916), British short-story writer, born in Burma; pseudonym of *Hector Hugh Munro*. His stories encompass the satiric, comic, macabre, and supernatural, and frequently depict animals as agents seeking revenge on humankind.

saki /ˈsɑːki/ ▶**noun** (pl. **sakis**) a tropical American monkey with coarse fur and a long bushy non-prehensile tail.
• Genera *Pithecia* and *Chiropotes*, family Cebidae: several species.
– ORIGIN late 18th cent.: via French from Tupi *saui*.

sakkie-sakkie /ˌsakɪˈsaki/ ▶**noun** [mass noun] S. African a simple, rhythmical style of Afrikaner music and dance.
– ORIGIN Afrikaans, probably symbolic of the repetitive rhythm (also expressing disparagement).

Sakti ▶**noun** Hinduism variant spelling of **SHAKTI**.

sal /sɑːl/ ▶**noun** a North Indian tree which yields teak-like timber and dammar resin.
• *Shorea robusta*, family Dipterocarpaceae.
– ORIGIN late 18th cent.: from Hindi *sāl*.

salaam /səˈlɑːm/ ▶**exclamation** a common greeting in many Arabic-speaking and Muslim countries.
▶**noun** a gesture of greeting or respect, with or without a spoken salutation, typically consisting of a low bow of the head and body with the hand or fingers touching the forehead.
■(**salaams**) respectful compliments.
▶**verb** [no obj.] make a salaam.
– ORIGIN early 17th cent.: from Arabic *(al-)salām (ʿalaikum)* 'peace (be upon you)'.

salable ▶**adjective** variant spelling of **SALEABLE**.

salacious /səˈleɪʃəs/ ▶**adjective** (of writing, pictures, or talk) treating sexual matters in an indecent way and typically conveying undue interest in or enjoyment of the subject: *salacious stories.*
■lustful; lecherous: *his salacious grin faltered.*
– DERIVATIVES **salaciously** adverb, **salaciousness** noun, **salacity** noun (dated).
– ORIGIN mid 17th cent.: from Latin *salax, salac-* (from *salire* 'to leap') + **-IOUS**.

salad ▶**noun** a cold dish of various mixtures of raw or cooked vegetables, usually seasoned with oil, vinegar, or other dressing and sometimes accompanied by meat, fish, or other ingredients: *a green salad* | [mass noun] *bowls of salad.*
■[mass noun] [with modifier] a mixture containing a specified ingredient dressed with mayonnaise: *a red pepper filled with tuna salad.* ■ a vegetable suitable for eating raw.
– ORIGIN late Middle English: from Old French *salade*, from Provençal *salada*, based on Latin *sal* 'salt'.

salad cream ▶**noun** [mass noun] Brit. a creamy salad dressing resembling mayonnaise.

salad days ▶**plural noun** (**one's salad days**) the period when one is young and inexperienced.
■the peak or heyday of something.
– ORIGIN from Shakespeare's *Antony and Cleopatra* (I. v. 72).

salad dressing ▶**noun** see **DRESSING** (sense 1).

salade /səˈlɑːd/ ▶**noun** another term for **SALLET**.

Saladin /ˈsalədɪn/ (1137–93), sultan of Egypt and Syria 1174–93; Arabic name *Salah-ad-Din Yusuf ibn-Ayyub*. Saladin reconquered Jerusalem from the Christians in 1187, but he was defeated by Richard the Lionheart at Arsuf (1191). He earned a reputation not only for military skill but also for honesty and chivalry.

salal /səˈlal/ ▶**noun** a North American plant of the heather family, with clusters of pink or white flowers and edible purple-black berries.
• *Gaultheria shallon*, family Ericaceae.
– ORIGIN early 19th cent.: from Chinook Jargon *sallal*.

Salam /səˈlɑːm/, Abdus (1926–1996), Pakistani theoretical physicist. He independently developed a unified theory to explain electromagnetic interactions and the weak nuclear force. In 1979 he shared the Nobel Prize for Physics.

Salamanca /ˌsaləˈmaŋkə/ a city in western Spain, in Castilla-León; pop. 185,990 (1991).

salamander /ˈsaləˌmandə/ ▶**noun 1** a newt-like amphibian that typically has bright markings, once thought able to endure fire.
• Order Urodela: four families, in particular Salamandridae, and numerous species, including the **fire salamander**.
2 a mythical lizard-like creature said to live in fire or to be able to withstand its effects.
■an elemental spirit living in fire.
3 a metal plate heated and placed over food to brown it.
4 archaic a red-hot iron or poker.
– DERIVATIVES **salamandrine** /-ˈmandrɪn/ adjective.
– ORIGIN Middle English (in sense 2): from Old French *salamandre*, via Latin from Greek *salamandra*. Sense 1 dates from the early 17th cent.

salami /səˈlɑːmi/ ▶**noun** (pl. same or **salamis**) [mass noun] a type of highly seasoned sausage, originally from Italy, usually eaten cold in slices.
– ORIGIN Italian, plural of *salame*, from a late Latin word meaning 'to salt'.

Salamis /ˈsaləmɪs/ an island in the Saronic Gulf in Greece, to the west of Athens. The strait between the island and the mainland was the scene in 480 BC of a crushing defeat of the Persian fleet under Xerxes I by the Greeks under Themistocles.

sal ammoniac /ˌsal əˈməʊnɪak/ ▶**noun** old-fashioned term for **AMMONIUM CHLORIDE**.
– ORIGIN Middle English: from Latin *sal ammoniacus* 'salt of Ammon' (see **AMMONIACAL**).

Salang Pass /ˈsɑːlaŋ/ a high-altitude route across the Hindu Kush in Afghanistan. A road and tunnel were built by the Soviet Union during the 1960s to improve the supply route to Kabul.

salariat /səˈlɛːrɪət/ ▶**noun** (**the salariat**) salaried white-collar workers.
– ORIGIN early 20th cent.: from French, from *salaire* 'salary', on the pattern of *prolétariat* 'proletariat'.

salaried ▶**adjective** receiving or recompensed by a salary rather than a wage: *salaried employees | he was in salaried employment.*

salary ▶**noun** (pl. **-ies**) a fixed regular payment, typically paid on a monthly basis but often expressed as an annual sum, made by an employer to an employee, especially a professional or white-collar worker: *he received a salary of £19,000* | [as modifier] *a 15 per cent salary increase.* Compare with **WAGE**.
▶**verb** (**-ies, -ied**) [with obj.] archaic pay a salary to.
– ORIGIN Middle English: from Anglo-Norman French *salarie*, from Latin *salarium*, originally denoting a Roman soldier's allowance to buy salt, from *sal* 'salt'.

salaryman ▶**noun** (pl. **-men**) (especially in Japan) a white-collar worker.

salat /saˈlɑːt/ ▶**noun** [mass noun] the ritual prayer of Muslims, performed five times daily in a set form.
– ORIGIN Arabic, plural of *salāh* 'prayer, worship'.

Salazar /ˌsaləˈzɑː/, Antonio de Oliveira (1889–1970), Portuguese statesman, Prime Minister 1932–68. During his long premiership he ruled the country as a virtual dictator, enacting a new authoritarian constitution along Fascist lines. Salazar maintained Portugal's neutrality throughout the Spanish Civil War and the Second World War.

salbutamol /salˈbjuːtəmɒl/ ▶**noun** [mass noun] Medicine a synthetic compound related to aspirin, used as a bronchodilator in the treatment of asthma and other conditions involving constriction of the airways.
– ORIGIN 1960s: from *sal(icylic acid)* + *but(yl)* + *am(ine)* + **-OL**.

salchow /ˈsalkəʊ/ ▶**noun** a jump in figure skating from the backward inside edge of one skate to the

backward outside edge of the other, with one or more full turns in the air.
– ORIGIN early 20th cent.: named after Ulrich *Salchow* (1877–1949), Swedish skater.

sale ▶ **noun 1** [mass noun] the exchange of a commodity for money; the action of selling something: *we withdrew it from sale* | [count noun] *the sale has fallen through.*
■ (**sales**) a quantity or amount sold: *price cuts failed to boost sales.* ■ (**sales**) the activity or business of selling products: *director of sales and marketing.*
2 an event for the rapid disposal of goods at reduced prices for a period, especially at the end of a season: *a closing-down sale.*
■ [often with modifier] a public or charitable event at which goods are sold. ■ a public auction.
– PHRASES (**up**) **for sale** offered for purchase; to be bought: *cars for sale at reasonable prices.* **on sale** offered for purchase: *the November issue is on sale now.* ■ N. Amer. offered for purchase at a reduced price. **sale or return** [usu. as modifier] Brit. an arrangement by which a purchaser takes a quantity of goods with the right of returning surplus goods without payment: *booksellers normally order books on a sale-or-return basis.*
– ORIGIN late Old English *sala*, from Old Norse *sala*, of Germanic origin; related to **SELL**.

saleable (US also **salable**) ▶ **adjective** fit or able to be sold.
– DERIVATIVES **saleability** noun.

Salem /ˈseɪləm/ **1** the state capital of Oregon, situated on the Willamette river south-west of Portland; pop. 107,790 (1990).
2 a city and port in NE Massachusetts, on the Atlantic coast north of Boston; pop. 38,090 (1990). First settled in 1626, it was the scene in 1692 of a notorious series of witchcraft trials.
3 an industrial city in Tamil Nadu in southern India; pop. 364,000 (1991).

sale of work ▶ **noun** Brit. an event where goods made by members of a parish or other organization are sold, typically to raise funds for charity.

salep /ˈsaləp/ ▶ **noun** [mass noun] a starchy preparation of the dried tubers of various orchids, used as a thickener in cookery, and formerly in medicines and tonics.
– ORIGIN mid 18th cent.: from French, from Turkish *sālep*, from Arabic (*kuṣa-'ṯ-*) *ṯa'lab*, the name of an orchid (literally 'fox's testicles').

saleratus /ˌsaləˈreɪtəs/ ▶ **noun** [mass noun] US sodium bicarbonate (or sometimes potassium bicarbonate) as the main ingredient of baking powder.
– ORIGIN mid 19th cent.: from modern Latin *sal aeratus* 'aerated salt'.

sale ring ▶ **noun** Brit. an enclosure around which a circle of buyers stands at an auction to view livestock offered for sale.

Salerno /saˈlɛːnəʊ/, Italian saˈlɛrno/ a port on the west coast of Italy, on the Gulf of Salerno south-east of Naples; pop. 151,370 (1990).

saleroom ▶ **noun** chiefly Brit. a room in which items are sold at auction.

sales clerk ▶ **noun** N. Amer. a shop assistant.

sales engineer ▶ **noun** a salesperson with technical knowledge of the goods and their market.

salesgirl ▶ **noun** a female shop assistant.

Salesian /səˈliːzɪən, -ʒ(ə)n/ ▶ **adjective** of or relating to a Roman Catholic educational religious order founded near Turin in 1859 and named after St Francis de Sales.
▶ **noun** a member of this order.

salesman ▶ **noun** (pl. **-men**) a man whose job involves selling or promoting commercial products, either in a shop or visiting locations to get orders: *an insurance salesman.*
– DERIVATIVES **salesmanship** noun.

salesperson ▶ **noun** (pl. **-persons** or **-people**) a salesman or saleswoman (used as a neutral alternative).

salesroom ▶ **noun** another term for **SALEROOM**.
■ a showroom, especially one for cars.

saleswoman ▶ **noun** (pl. **-women**) a woman whose job involves selling or promoting commercial products.

Salford /ˈsɔːlfəd/ an industrial city in NW England, near Manchester; pop. 217,900 (1991).

Salian /ˈseɪlɪən/ ▶ **adjective** of or relating to the Salii, a 4th-century Frankish people living near the River IJssel, from whom the Merovingians were descended.
▶ **noun** a member of this people.

Salic /ˈsalɪk, ˈseɪ-/ ▶ **adjective** another term for **SALIAN**.

salicin /ˈsalɪsɪn/ ▶ **noun** [mass noun] Chemistry a bitter compound present in willow bark. It is a glucoside related to aspirin, and accounts for the ancient use of willow bark as a pain-relieving drug.
– ORIGIN mid 19th cent.: from French *salicine*, from Latin *salix*, *salic-* 'willow'.

salicional /səˈlɪʃ(ə)n(ə)l/ ▶ **noun** an organ stop with a soft reedy tone.
– ORIGIN mid 19th cent.: from German *Salicional*, from Latin *salix*, *salic-* 'willow' + the obscurely derived suffix *-ional*.

Salic law historical ▶ **noun 1** a law excluding females from dynastic succession, especially as the alleged fundamental law of the French monarchy.
2 a Frankish law book extant in Merovingian and Carolingian times.

salicylic acid /ˌsalɪˈsɪlɪk/ ▶ **noun** [mass noun] Chemistry a bitter compound present in certain plants. It is used as a fungicide and in the manufacture of aspirin and dyestuffs.
● Alternative name: *o*-**hydroxybenzoic acid**; chem. formula: $C_6H_4(OH)(COOH)$.
– DERIVATIVES **salicylate** /səˈlɪsɪleɪt/ noun.
– ORIGIN mid 19th cent.: *salicylic* from French *salicyle*, the radical of the acid, + **-IC**.

salient /ˈseɪlɪənt/ ▶ **adjective 1** most noticeable or important: *it succinctly covered all the salient points of the case.*
■ prominent; conspicuous: *it was always the salient object in my view.* ■ (of an angle) pointing outwards. The opposite of **RE-ENTRANT**.
2 [postpositive] Heraldry (of an animal) standing on its hind legs with the forepaws raised, as if leaping.
▶ **noun** a piece of land or section of fortification that juts out to form an angle.
■ an outward bulge in a line of military attack or defence.
– DERIVATIVES **salience** noun, **saliency** noun, **saliently** adverb.
– ORIGIN mid 16th cent. (as a heraldic term): from Latin *salient-* 'leaping', from the verb *salire*. The noun dates from the early 19th cent.

Salientia /ˌseɪlɪˈɛnʃɪə, -ˈɛnt-/ Zoology another term for **ANURA**.
– DERIVATIVES **salientian** noun & adjective.
– ORIGIN modern Latin (plural), from Latin *salire* 'to leap'.

Salieri /ˌsalɪˈɛːri/, Antonio (1750–1825), Italian composer. Salieri was hostile to Mozart and a rumour arose that he poisoned him, though the story is now thought to be without foundation.

salina /səˈlʌɪnə/ ▶ **noun** (chiefly in the Caribbean or South America) a salt pan, salt lake, or salt marsh.
– ORIGIN late 16th cent.: from Spanish, from medieval Latin, 'salt pit', in Latin *salinae* (plural) 'salt pans'.

saline /ˈseɪlʌɪn/ ▶ **adjective** containing or impregnated with salt: *saline alluvial soils.*
■ chiefly Medicine (of a solution) containing sodium chloride and/or a salt or salts of magnesium or another alkali metal.
▶ **noun** [mass noun] a solution of salt in water.
■ a saline solution used in medicine.
– DERIVATIVES **salinity** noun, **salinization** (also **-isation**) noun.
– ORIGIN late 15th cent.: from Latin *sal* 'salt' + **-INE**[1].

Salinger /ˈsalɪndʒə/, J. D. (b.1919), American novelist and short-story writer; full name *Jerome David Salinger*. He is best known for his colloquial novel of adolescence *The Catcher in the Rye* (1951).

salinometer /ˌsalɪˈnɒmɪtə/ ▶ **noun** an instrument for measuring the salinity of water.

Salisbury[1] /ˈsɔːlzb(ə)ri/ **1** a city in southern England, in Wiltshire; pop. 35,000 (1981). It is noted for its 13th-century cathedral, whose spire, at 123 m (404 ft), is the highest in England. Its diocese is known as Sarum, an old name for the city.
2 former name (until 1982) for **HARARE**.

Salisbury[2] /ˈsɔːlzb(ə)ri/, Robert Arthur Talbot Gascoigne-Cecil, 3rd Marquess of (1830–1903), British Conservative statesman, Prime Minister 1885–6, 1886–92, and 1895–1902. He supported the policies which resulted in the Second Boer War (1899–1902).

Salish /ˈseɪlɪʃ/ ▶ **noun** (pl. same) **1** a member of a group of American Indian peoples inhabiting areas of the north-western US and the west coast of Canada.
2 [mass noun] the group of related languages spoken by the Salish, now all extinct or nearly so.
▶ **adjective** of or relating to the Salish or their languages.
– DERIVATIVES **Salishan** adjective.
– ORIGIN a local name, literally 'Flatheads'.

saliva /səˈlʌɪvə/ ▶ **noun** [mass noun] watery liquid secreted into the mouth by glands, providing lubrication for chewing and swallowing, and aiding digestion.
– DERIVATIVES **salivary** /səˈlʌɪ-, ˈsalɪ-/ adjective.
– ORIGIN late Middle English: from Latin.

salivate /ˈsalɪveɪt/ ▶ **verb** [no obj.] secrete saliva, especially in anticipation of food.
■ figurative display great relish at the sight or prospect of something: *I was fairly **salivating at** the prospect of a $10 million loan.* ■ [with obj.] technical cause (a person or animal) to produce an unusually copious secretion of saliva.
– DERIVATIVES **salivation** noun.
– ORIGIN mid 17th cent.: from Latin *salivat-* '(having) produced saliva', from the verb *salivare*, from *saliva* (see **SALIVA**).

Salk /sɔːlk/, Jonas Edward (1914–95), American microbiologist. He developed the standard **Salk vaccine** against polio, using virus inactivated by formalin, in the early 1950s, and later became the director of the institute in San Diego that now bears his name.

sallee ▶ **noun** variant spelling of **SALLY**[3].

sallet /ˈsalɪt/ ▶ **noun** historical a light helmet with an outward curve extending over the back of the neck, worn as part of medieval armour.
– ORIGIN late Middle English: from French *salade*, based on Latin *caelare* 'engrave' (from *caelum* 'chisel').

sallow[1] ▶ **adjective** (**sallower**, **sallowest**) (of a person's face or complexion) of an unhealthy yellow or pale brown colour.
▶ **verb** [with obj.] rare make sallow.
– DERIVATIVES **sallowish** adjective, **sallowness** noun.
– ORIGIN Old English *salo* 'dusky', of Germanic origin; related to Old Norse *sǫlr* 'yellow', from a base meaning 'dirty'.

sallow[2] ▶ **noun 1** chiefly Brit. a willow tree, especially one of a low-growing or shrubby kind. Also called **PUSSY WILLOW**.
● Genus *Salix*, family Salicaceae: several species, in particular the **great sallow** (goat willow, *S. caprea*) and the **grey** (or **common**) **sallow** (grey willow, *S. cinerea*).
2 a European moth with dull yellow, orange, and brown patterned wings.
● Genus *Xanthia*, family Noctuidae: several species, in particular *X. icteritia*, whose larvae feed on sallow catkins.
– DERIVATIVES **sallowy** adjective.
– ORIGIN Old English *salh*, of Germanic origin; related to Old Norse *selja*, and Latin *salix* 'willow'.

Sallust /ˈsaləst/ (86–35 BC), Roman historian and politician; Latin name *Gaius Sallustius Crispus*. As a historian he was concerned with the political and moral decline of Rome after the fall of Carthage in 146 BC. His chief surviving works deal with the Catiline conspiracy and the Jugurthine War.

Sally (also **Sally Army**) ▶ **noun** (pl. **-ies**) Brit. informal the Salvation Army.
■ (usu. **Sallies**) a member of the Salvation Army.
– ORIGIN early 20th cent.: alteration of **SALVATION**.

sally[1] ▶ **noun** (pl. **-ies**) a sudden charge out of a besieged place against the enemy; a sortie.
■ a brief journey or sudden start into activity. ■ a witty or lively remark, especially one made as an attack or as a diversion in an argument; a retort.
▶ **verb** (**-ies**, **-ied**) [no obj., with adverbial of direction] make a military sortie: *they sallied out to harass the enemy.*
■ formal or humorous set out from a place to do something: *I made myself presentable and **sallied forth**.*
– ORIGIN late Middle English: from French *saillie*, feminine past participle (used as a noun) of *saillir* 'come or jut out', from Old French *salir* 'to leap', from Latin *salire*.

sally[2] ▶ **noun** (pl. **-ies**) the part of a bell rope that has coloured wool woven into it to provide a grip for the bell-ringer's hands.
– ORIGIN mid 17th cent. (denoting the first movement of a bell when set for ringing): perhaps from **SALLY**[1] in the sense 'leaping motion'.

sally[3] (also **sallee**) ▶ **noun** (pl. **sallies** or **sallees**) Austral. any of a number of acacias and eucalyptuses that resemble willows.
● Several species, including **white sally** (*Eucalyptus pauciflora*, family Myrtaceae).
– ORIGIN late 19th cent.: dialect variant of **SALLOW**[2].

Sally Lightfoot ▶ **noun** (pl. **Sally Lightfoots**) a common active crab of rocky shores in the Caribbean, Central America, and the Galapagos Islands.
● *Grapsus grapsus*, family Grapsidae.

Sally Lunn ▶ **noun** a sweet, light teacake, typically served hot.
– ORIGIN said to be from the name of a woman selling such cakes in Bath *c.*1800.

sally port ▶ **noun** a small exit point in a fortification for the passage of troops when making a sally.

salmagundi /ˌsalməˈɡʌndi/ ▶ **noun** (pl. **salmagundis**) a dish of chopped meat, anchovies, eggs, onions, and seasoning.
■ a general mixture; a miscellaneous collection.
– ORIGIN from French *salmigondis*, of unknown origin.

salmanazar /ˌsalməˈneɪzə/ ▶ **noun** a wine bottle of approximately twelve times the standard size.
– ORIGIN 1930s: named after *Shalmaneser*, a king of Assyria (2 Kings 17–18).

salmi /ˈsalmi/ ▶ **noun** (pl. **salmis**) a ragout or casserole of game stewed in a rich sauce: *a pheasant salmi.*
– ORIGIN French, abbreviation of *salmigondis* (see **SALMAGUNDI**).

salmon /ˈsamən/ ▶ **noun** (pl. same or (especially of types) **salmons**) **1** a large edible fish that is a popular sporting fish, much prized for its pink flesh. Salmon mature in the sea but migrate to freshwater streams to spawn.
● Family Salmonidae (the **salmon family**): the **Atlantic salmon** (*Salmo salar*), which sometimes returns to spawn two or three times, and five species of Pacific salmon (genus *Oncorhynchus*), which always die after spawning. The salmon family also includes trout, charr, whitefish, and their relatives.
■ [mass noun] the flesh of this fish as food.
2 [usu. with modifier] any of a number of fishes that resemble the true salmons, in particular:
● (**Australian salmon**) a large green and silver fish of Australasian inshore waters, popular as a game fish (*Arripis trutta*, family Arripidae). ● a prized food fish of the drum family (Sciaenidae), in particular the **Cape salmon** of the Indian Ocean (*Atractoscion aequidens*) and sea trouts of the western Atlantic (genus *Cynoscion*).
3 [mass noun] a pale pink colour.
– DERIVATIVES **salmony** adjective.
– ORIGIN Middle English *samoun*, from Anglo-Norman French *saumoun*, from Latin *salmo*, *salmon-*. The spelling with *-l-* is influenced by Latin.

salmon bass ▶ **noun** S. African another term for **KABELJOU**.

salmonberry ▶ **noun** (pl. **-ies**) a North American bramble which bears pink raspberry-like fruit.
● Genus *Rubus*, family Rosaceae: several species, in particular *R. spectabilis*.
■ the edible fruit of this plant.

salmonella /ˌsalməˈnɛlə/ ▶ **noun** (pl. **salmonellae** /-liː/) [mass noun] a bacterium that occurs mainly in the gut, especially a serotype causing food poisoning.
● Genus *Salmonella*: numerous serotypes; Gram-negative rods.
■ food poisoning caused by infection with a such a bacterium: *an outbreak of salmonella.*
– DERIVATIVES **salmonellosis** /-ˈləʊsɪs/ noun.
– ORIGIN modern Latin, named after Daniel E. *Salmon* (1850–1914), American veterinary surgeon.

salmonid /ˈsalmənɪd, salˈmɒnɪd/ ▶ **noun** Zoology a fish of the salmon family (Salmonidae).
– ORIGIN mid 19th cent.: from modern Latin *Salmonidae* (plural), based on Latin *salmo*, *salmon-* 'salmon' + **-ID**[2].

salmon ladder (also **salmon leap**) ▶ **noun** a series of natural steps in a cascade or steeply sloping river bed, or a similar arrangement incorporated into a dam, allowing salmon to pass upstream.

salmonoid Zoology ▶ **noun** a fish of a group that includes the salmon family together with the pikes, smelts, and argentines.
● Superfamily Salmonoidea: several families.
▶ **adjective** of or relating to fish of this group.

salmon trout ▶ **noun** a large trout or trout-like fish, in particular:
■ Brit. a sea trout. ■ N. Amer. a lake trout. ■ Austral. an Australian salmon.

Salome /səˈləʊmi/ (in the New Testament) the daughter of Herodias, who danced before her stepfather Herod Antipas. Given a choice of reward for her dancing, she asked for the head of St John the Baptist and thus caused him to be beheaded.

salon ▶ **noun** **1** an establishment where a hairdresser, beautician, or couturier conducts trade.
2 a reception room in a large house.
■ historical a regular social gathering of eminent people (especially writers and artists) at the house of a woman prominent in high society. ■ N. Amer. a meeting of intellectuals or other eminent people at the invitation of a celebrity or socialite.
3 (**Salon**) an annual exhibition of the work of living artists held by the Royal Academy of Painting and Sculpture in Paris, originally in the Salon d'Apollon in the Louvre in 1667.
– ORIGIN late 17th cent.: from French (see **SALOON**).

Salon des Refusés /ˌsalɒ̃ deɪ ˈrəfjuːzeɪ, French salɔ̃ de ʀəfyze/ an exhibition in Paris ordered by Napoleon III in 1863 to display pictures rejected by the Salon. The artists represented included Manet, Cézanne, Pissarro, and Whistler.
– ORIGIN French, literally 'exhibition of the rejected (works)'.

Salonica /səˈlɒnɪkə/ another name for **THESSALONÍKI**.

salon music ▶ **noun** [mass noun] often derogatory light classical music originally considered suitable for playing in a salon.

saloon ▶ **noun** **1** a public room or building used for a specified purpose: *a billiard saloon.*
■ (also **saloon bar**) Brit. another term for **LOUNGE BAR**. ■ N. Amer. historical or humorous a place where alcoholic drinks may be bought and drunk. ■ a large public room for use as a lounge on a ship. ■ (also **saloon car**) Brit. a luxurious railway carriage used as a lounge or restaurant or as private accommodation: *a dining saloon.*
2 (also **saloon car**) Brit. a motor car having a closed body and a closed boot separated from the part in which the driver and passengers sit.
– ORIGIN early 18th cent. (in the sense 'drawing room'): from French *salon*, from Italian *salone* 'large hall', augmentative of *sala* 'hall'.

saloon deck ▶ **noun** a deck on the same level as a ship's saloon, for the use of passengers.

saloon keeper ▶ **noun** N. Amer. a person who runs a bar; a bartender.

saloon pistol (also **saloon rifle**) ▶ **noun** a gun adapted for firing at short range.

Salop /ˈsaləp/ another name for **SHROPSHIRE**. It was the official name of the county 1974–80.
– DERIVATIVES **Salopian** /səˈləʊpɪən/ adjective & noun.
– ORIGIN abbreviation of Anglo-Norman French *Salopesberie*, a corruption of Old English *Scrobbesbyrig* 'Shrewsbury'.

salopettes /ˌsaləˈpɛts/ ▶ **plural noun** trousers with a high waist and shoulder straps, typically made of a padded fabric and worn for skiing.
– ORIGIN 1970s: from French *salopette* in the same sense + *-s* by analogy with such words as *trousers*.

salotto /saˈlɒtəʊ/ ▶ **noun** (pl. **salotti** /səˈlɒti/) (especially in Italy) a reception room.
– ORIGIN Italian, diminutive of *sala* 'hall'.

salp /salp/ ▶ **noun** a free-swimming marine invertebrate related to the sea squirts, with a transparent barrel-shaped body.
● Several genera in the class Thaliacea, subphylum Urochordata.
– ORIGIN mid 19th cent.: from French *salpe*, based on Greek *salpē* 'fish'.

salpicon /ˈsalpɪkɒn/ ▶ **noun** a mixture of finely chopped ingredients bound in a thick sauce and used as a filling or stuffing.
– ORIGIN via French from Spanish, from *salpicar* 'sprinkle (with salt)'.

salpiglossis /ˌsalpɪˈɡlɒsɪs/ ▶ **noun** a South American plant of the nightshade family, with brightly patterned funnel-shaped flowers.
● Genus *Salpiglossis*, family Solanaceae.
– ORIGIN modern Latin, formed irregularly from Greek *salpinx* 'trumpet' + *glōssa* 'tongue'.

salpingectomy /ˌsalpɪŋˈdʒɛktəmi/ ▶ **noun** (pl. **-ies**) [mass noun] surgical removal of the Fallopian tubes.

salpingitis /ˌsalpɪŋˈdʒʌɪtɪs/ ▶ **noun** [mass noun] Medicine inflammation of the Fallopian tubes.

salpingo- /ˈsalpɪŋɡəʊ/ (also **salping-** before a vowel) ▶ **combining form** relating to the Fallopian tubes: *salpingostomy.*
– ORIGIN from Greek *salpinx*, *salping-* 'trumpet'.

salpingostomy /ˌsalpɪŋˈɡɒstəmi/ ▶ **noun** [mass noun] surgical unblocking of a blocked Fallopian tube.

salsa /ˈsalsə/ ▶ **noun** [mass noun] **1** a type of Latin American dance music incorporating elements of jazz and rock.
■ [count noun] a dance performed to this music.
2 (especially in Latin American cookery) a spicy tomato sauce.
– ORIGIN Spanish, literally 'sauce', extended in American Spanish to denote the dance.

salsa verde /ˌsalsə ˈvəːdeɪ, ˈvəːdi/ ▶ **noun** [mass noun] **1** an Italian sauce made with olive oil, garlic, capers, anchovies, vinegar or lemon juice, and parsley.
2 a Mexican sauce of finely chopped onion, garlic, coriander, parsley, and hot peppers.
– ORIGIN Spanish, literally 'green sauce'.

salsify /ˈsalsɪfi/ ▶ **noun** [mass noun] an edible European plant of the daisy family, with a long root like that of a parsnip.
● *Tragopogon porrifolius*, family Compositae. See also **BLACK SALSIFY**.
■ the root of this plant used as a vegetable. Also called **VEGETABLE OYSTER**.
– ORIGIN late 17th cent.: from French *salsifis*, from obsolete Italian *salsefica*, of unknown ultimate origin.

SALT /sɔːlt, sɒlt/ ▶ **abbreviation for** Strategic Arms Limitation Talks.

salt /sɔːlt, sɒlt/ ▶ **noun** **1** (also **common salt**) [mass noun] a white crystalline substance which gives seawater its characteristic taste and is used for seasoning or preserving food.
● Alternative name: **sodium chloride**; chem. formula: NaCl.
■ poetic/literary something which adds freshness or piquancy: *he described danger as the salt of pleasure.* ■ [count noun] a salt cellar: *a turned beech salt.*
2 Chemistry any chemical compound formed from the reaction of an acid with a base, with all or part of the hydrogen of the acid replaced by a metal or other cation.
3 (usu. **old salt**) informal an experienced sailor.
▶ **adjective** [attrib.] **1** impregnated with, treated with, or tasting of salt: *salt water* | *salt beef.*
2 (of a plant) growing on the coast or in salt marshes.
▶ **verb** [with obj.] **1** [usu. as adj. **salted**] season or preserve with salt: *cook the carrots in boiling salted water.*
■ figurative make (something) piquant or more interesting: *there was good talk to salt the occasion.* ■ sprinkle (a road or path) with salt in order to melt snow or ice.
2 informal fraudulently make (a mine) appear to be a paying one by placing rich ore into it.
3 [as adj. **salted**] (of a horse) having developed a resistance to disease by surviving it.
– PHRASES **rub salt into the** (or **someone's**) **wound** make a painful experience even more painful for someone. **the salt of the earth** a person or group of people of great kindness, reliability, or honesty. [ORIGIN: with biblical allusion to Matt 5:13.] **sit below the salt** be of lower social standing or worth. [ORIGIN: from the former custom of placing a large salt cellar in the middle of a dining table with the host at one end.] **take something with a pinch** (or **grain**) **of salt** regard something as exaggerated; believe only part of something: *I take anything he says with a large pinch of salt.* **worth one's salt** good or competent at the job or profession specified: *any astrologer worth her salt would have predicted this.*
– DERIVATIVES **saltish** adjective, **saltless** adjective, **saltness** noun.
– ORIGIN Old English *sealt* (noun), *sealtan* (verb), of Germanic origin; related to Dutch *zout* and German *Salz* (nouns), from an Indo-European root shared by Latin *sal*, Greek *hals* 'salt'.
▶ **salt something away** informal secretly store or put by something, especially money.
salt something out cause soap to separate from lye by adding salt. ■ Chemistry cause an organic compound to separate from an aqueous solution by adding an electrolyte.

S

salt-and-pepper ▶ **adjective** another way of saying **PEPPER-AND-SALT**.

saltarello /ˌsaltəˈrɛləʊ/ ▶ **noun** (pl. **saltarellos** or **saltarelli** /-li/) an energetic Italian or Spanish dance for one couple, characterized by leaps and skips.
– ORIGIN early 18th cent.: Italian *salterello*, Spanish *saltarelo*, based on Latin *saltare* 'to dance'.

saltation /salˈteɪʃ(ə)n, sɔː-, sɒ-/ ▶ **noun** [mass noun] **1** Biology abrupt evolutionary change; sudden large-scale mutation.
2 Geology the transport of hard particles over an uneven surface in a turbulent flow of air or water.
3 archaic the action of leaping or dancing.
– DERIVATIVES **saltatory** /ˈsaltət(ə)ri, ˈsɔː-, ˈsɒ-/ adjective.
– ORIGIN early 17th cent. (in sense 3): from Latin *saltatio(n-)*, from *saltare* 'to dance', frequentative of *salire* 'to leap'.

saltatorial /ˌsaltəˈtɔːrɪəl, sɔː-, sɒ-/ ▶ **adjective** chiefly Entomology (especially of grasshoppers or their limbs) adapted for leaping.

saltbox ▶ **noun** N. Amer. a frame house having up to three storeys at the front and one fewer at the back with a steeply pitched roof.

salt bridge ▶ **noun** Chemistry **1** a tube containing an electrolyte (typically in the form of a gel), providing electrical contact between two solutions.
2 a link between electrically charged acidic and basic groups, especially on different parts of a large molecule such as a protein.

saltbush ▶ **noun** a salt-tolerant orache plant sometimes used in the reclamation of saline soils or to provide grazing in areas of salty soil.
• Genus *Atriplex*, family Chenopodiaceae: several species, in particular the Australian *A. vesicaria*.

salt cedar ▶ **noun** N. Amer. a European tamarisk with reddish-brown branches and feathery grey foliage.
• *Tamarix gallica*, family Tamaricaceae.

salt cellar ▶ **noun** a dish or container for storing salt, now typically a closed container with perforations in the lid for sprinkling.
■ informal a deep hollow that is sometimes evident above the collarbone.
– ORIGIN late Middle English: from **SALT** + obsolete *saler*, from Old French *salier* 'salt-box', from Latin *salarium* (see **SALARY**). The change in spelling of the second word was due to association with **CELLAR**.

salt chuck ▶ **noun** N. Amer. informal an inlet of the sea which flows into freshwater lakes or rivers.
■ the sea.

salt dome ▶ **noun** a dome-shaped structure in sedimentary rocks, formed where a large mass of salt has been forced upwards. Such structures often form traps for oil or natural gas.

salter ▶ **noun** historical a person dealing in or employed in the production of salt.
■ a person whose work involved the preservation of meat or fish in salt. ■ another term for **DRY-SALTER**.
– ORIGIN Old English *sealtere* (see **SALT**, **-ER**[1]).

saltern /ˈsɔːltən, ˈsɒ-/ ▶ **noun** a set of pools in which seawater is left to evaporate to make salt.
– ORIGIN Old English *sealtærn* 'salt building' (the original use denoting a salt works).

salt finger ▶ **noun** Oceanography one of several alternating columns of rising and descending water produced when a layer of water is overlain by a denser, saltier layer.
– DERIVATIVES **salt fingering** noun.

salt fish ▶ **noun** [mass noun] fish, especially cod, that has been preserved in salt.

salt flats ▶ **plural noun** areas of flat land covered with a layer of salt.

salt glaze ▶ **noun** Pottery a hard glaze with a pitted surface, produced on stoneware by adding salt to the kiln during firing.
– DERIVATIVES **salt-glazed** adjective, **salt glazing** noun.

salt horse ▶ **noun** [mass noun] Nautical slang, archaic salted beef.

Saltillo /salˈtiːjəʊ, -ˈtiːljəʊ/ a city in northern Mexico, capital of the state of Coahuila, situated in the Sierra Madre south-west of Monterrey; pop. 441,000.

saltimbocca /ˌsaltɪmˈbɒkə/ ▶ **noun** [mass noun] a dish consisting of rolled pieces of veal or poultry cooked with herbs, bacon, and other flavourings.
– ORIGIN Italian, literally 'leap into the mouth'.

saltine /sɔːlˈtiːn, sɒ-/ ▶ **noun** N. Amer. a thin crisp savoury biscuit sprinkled with salt.
– ORIGIN from **SALT** + **-INE**[4].

salting ▶ **noun** (usu. **saltings**) Brit. an area of coastal land that is regularly covered by the tide.

saltire /ˈsaltʌɪə, ˈsɔː-/ ▶ **noun** Heraldry a diagonal cross as a heraldic ordinary.
■ [as modifier] (of a design) incorporating a motif based on such a diagonal cross.
– DERIVATIVES **saltirewise** adverb.
– ORIGIN late Middle English: from Old French *saultoir* 'stirrup cord, stile, saltire', based on Latin *saltare* 'to dance'.

salt lake ▶ **noun** a lake of salt water.

Salt Lake City the capital of Utah, situated near the south-eastern shores of the Great Salt Lake; pop. 159,940 (1990). Founded in 1847 by Brigham Young, the city is the world headquarters of the Church of Latter-Day Saints (Mormons).

salt lick ▶ **noun** a place where animals go to lick salt from the ground.
■ a block of salt provided for animals to lick.

salt marsh ▶ **noun** an area of coastal grassland that is regularly flooded by seawater.

salt meadow ▶ **noun** chiefly N. Amer. a meadow that is subject to flooding by seawater; a salt marsh.

salt pan ▶ **noun** a shallow container or depression in the ground in which salt water evaporates to leave a deposit of salt.

saltpetre /sɔːltˈpiːtə, sɒ-/ (US **saltpeter**) ▶ **noun** another term for **POTASSIUM NITRATE**.
– ORIGIN late Middle English: from Old French *salpetre*, from medieval Latin *salpetra*, probably representing *sal petrae* 'salt of rock' (i.e. found as an encrustation). The change in the first element was due to association with **SALT**.

salt spoon ▶ **noun** a tiny spoon with a roundish deep bowl, used for serving oneself with salt.

saltus /ˈsaltəs/ ▶ **noun** poetic/literary a sudden transition; a breach of continuity.
– ORIGIN mid 17th cent.: from Latin, literally 'leap'.

saltwater ▶ **adjective** [attrib.] of or found in salt water; living in the sea: *saltwater fish*.

saltwater crocodile ▶ **noun** a large and dangerous crocodile occurring in estuaries and coastal waters from SW India to northern Australia.
• *Crocodylus porosus*, family Crocodylidae.

saltwort ▶ **noun** a plant of the goosefoot family, which typically grows in salt marshes. It is rich in alkali and its ashes were formerly used in soap-making.
• Genus *Salsola*, family Chenopodiaceae.

salty ▶ **adjective** (**saltier**, **saltiest**) tasting of, containing, or preserved with salt.
■ (of language or humour) down-to-earth; coarse. ■ informal tough; aggressive.
– DERIVATIVES **saltiness** noun.

salubrious /səˈluːbrɪəs/ ▶ **adjective** health-giving; healthy: *odours of far less salubrious origin*.
■ (of a place) pleasant; not run-down.
– DERIVATIVES **salubriously** adverb, **salubriousness** noun, **salubrity** noun.
– ORIGIN mid 16th cent.: from Latin *salubris* (from *salus* 'health') + **-OUS**.

saluki /səˈluːki/ ▶ **noun** (pl. **salukis**) a tall, swift, slender dog of a silky-coated breed with large drooping ears and fringed feet.
– ORIGIN early 19th cent.: from Arabic *salūḳī*.

salut /saˈluː/ ▶ **exclamation** used to express friendly feelings towards one's companions before drinking.
– ORIGIN French.

salutary /ˈsaljʊt(ə)ri/ ▶ **adjective** (especially with reference to something unwelcome or unpleasant) producing good effects; beneficial: *it failed to draw salutary lessons from Britain's loss of its colonies*.
■ archaic health-giving: *the salutary Atlantic air*.
– ORIGIN late Middle English (as a noun in the sense 'remedy'): from French *salutaire* or Latin *salutaris*, from *salus, salut-* 'health'.

salutation ▶ **noun** a gesture or utterance made as a greeting or acknowledgement of another's arrival or departure: *we greeted them but no one returned our salutations* | [mass noun] *he raised his glass* ***in salutation***.
■ a standard formula of words used in a letter to address the person being written to.
– DERIVATIVES **salutational** adjective.
– ORIGIN late Middle English: from Old French, or from Latin *salutatio(n-)*, from *salutare* 'pay one's respects to' (see **SALUTE**).

salutatorian /səˌljuːtəˈtɔːrɪən/ ▶ **noun** N. Amer. the student ranking second highest in a graduating class who delivers the salutatory.

salutatory /səˈljuːtət(ə)ri/ ▶ **adjective** chiefly N. Amer. (especially of an address) relating to or of the nature of a salutation.
▶ **noun** (pl. **-ies**) N. Amer. an address of welcome, especially one given as an oration by the student ranking second highest in a graduating class at a university or college.
– ORIGIN late 17th cent. (as an adjective): from Latin *salutatorius*, from *salutare* 'pay one's respects to' (see **SALUTE**).

salute ▶ **noun** a gesture of respect, homage, or polite recognition or acknowledgement, especially one made to or by a person when arriving or departing: *he raises his arms in a triumphant salute*.
■ a prescribed or specified movement, typically a raising of a hand to the head, made by a member of a military or similar force as a formal sign of respect or recognition. ■ [often with modifier] the discharge of a gun or guns as a formal or ceremonial sign of respect or celebration: *a twenty-one-gun salute*. ■ Fencing the formal performance of certain guards or other movements by fencers before engaging.
▶ **verb** [with obj.] make a formal salute to: *don't you usually salute a superior officer?* | [no obj.] *he clicked his heels and saluted*.
■ greet: *he saluted her with a smile*. ■ show or express admiration and respect for: *we salute a truly great photographer*. ■ [with obj. and complement] archaic hail (someone) as having a particular high office: *he was saluted king when he entered into Jerusalem*.
– PHRASES **take the salute** (of a senior officer in the armed forces or other person of importance) acknowledge formally a salute given by a body of troops marching past.
– DERIVATIVES **saluter** noun.
– ORIGIN late Middle English: from Latin *salutare* 'greet, pay one's respects to', from *salus, salut-* 'health, welfare, greeting'; the noun partly from Old French *salut*.

Salvador /ˈsalvədɔː/ a port on the Atlantic coast of eastern Brazil, capital of the state of Bahia; pop. 2,075,270 (1991). Founded in 1549, it was the capital of the Portuguese colony until 1763, when the seat of government was transferred to Rio de Janeiro. Former name **BAHIA**.

Salvadorean /ˌsalvəˈdɔːrɪən/ ▶ **adjective** of or relating to El Salvador.
▶ **noun** a native or inhabitant of El Salvador.

salvage ▶ **verb** [with obj.] rescue (a wrecked or disabled ship or its cargo) from loss at sea: *an emerald and gold cross was salvaged from the wreck*.
■ retrieve or preserve (something) from potential loss or adverse circumstances: *it was the only crumb of comfort he could* ***salvage from*** *the ordeal*.
▶ **noun** [mass noun] the rescue of a wrecked or disabled ship or its cargo from loss at sea: [as modifier] *a salvage operation was under way*.
■ the cargo saved from a wrecked or sunken ship: *salvage taken from a ship that had sunk in the river*. ■ the rescue of property or material from potential loss or destruction. ■ Law payment made or due to a person who has saved a ship or its cargo.
– DERIVATIVES **salvageable** adjective, **salvager** noun.
– ORIGIN mid 17th cent. (as a noun denoting payment for saving a ship or its cargo): from French, from medieval Latin *salvagium*, from Latin *salvare* 'to save'. The verb dates from the late 19th cent.

salvage yard ▶ **noun** N. Amer. a place where disused machinery is broken up.

Salvarsan /ˈsalvəsan/ ▶ **noun** Medicine, historical another term for **ARSPHENAMINE**.
– ORIGIN early 20th cent.: from German, from Latin *salvare* 'save' + German *Arsenik* 'arsenic' + **-AN**.

salvation ▶ **noun** [mass noun] Theology deliverance from sin and its consequences, believed by Christians to be brought about by faith in Christ.
■ preservation or deliverance from harm, ruin, or loss: *they try to sell it to us as economic salvation*. ■ (**one's salvation**) a source or means of being saved in this way: *his only salvation was to outfly the enemy*.
– ORIGIN Middle English: from Old French *salvacion*, from ecclesiastical Latin *salvation-* (from *salvare* 'to save'), translating Greek *sōtēria*.

Salvation Army (abbrev.: **SA**) a worldwide Christian evangelical organization on quasi-military lines. Established by William Booth, it is noted for its work with the poor and for its brass bands.

salvationist ▶ noun (**Salvationist**) a member of the Salvation Army.
▶ adjective of or relating to salvation.
■(**Salvationist**) of or relating to the Salvation Army.
– DERIVATIVES **salvationism** noun.

salve[1] ▶ noun an ointment used to promote healing of the skin or as protection.
■figurative something that is soothing or consoling for wounded feelings or an uneasy conscience: *the idea provided him with a salve for his guilt.*
▶ verb [with obj.] archaic apply salve to.
■figurative soothe (wounded pride or one's conscience): *charity salves our conscience.*
– ORIGIN Old English *sealfe* (noun), *sealfian* (verb), of Germanic origin; related to Dutch *zalf* and German *Salbe*.

salve[2] ▶ verb archaic term for **SALVAGE**.
– DERIVATIVES **salvable** adjective.
– ORIGIN early 18th cent.: back-formation from the noun **SALVAGE**.

salver ▶ noun a tray, typically one made of silver and used in formal circumstances.
– ORIGIN mid 17th cent.: from French *salve* 'tray for presenting food to the king', from Spanish *salva* 'sampling of food', from *salvar* 'make safe'.

Salve Regina /ˌsalveɪ rəˈdʒiːnə/ ▶ noun a Roman Catholic hymn or prayer said or sung after compline, and after the Divine Office from Trinity Sunday to Advent.
– ORIGIN the opening words in Latin, 'hail (holy) queen'.

salvia ▶ noun a widely distributed plant of the mint family, especially (in gardening) a bedding plant cultivated for its spikes of bright flowers.
■Genus *Salvia*, family Labiatae: many species, in particular the scarlet-flowered *S. splendens*.
– ORIGIN modern Latin, from Latin *salvia* 'sage'.

Salvo ▶ noun (pl. **-os**) Austral. informal a member of the Salvation Army.
– ORIGIN late 19th cent.: abbreviation of **SALVATION**.

salvo ▶ noun (pl. **-os** or **-oes**) a simultaneous discharge of artillery or other guns in a battle.
■a number of weapons released from one or more aircraft in quick succession. ■figurative a sudden, vigorous, or aggressive act or series of acts: *the pardons provoked a salvo of accusations.*
– ORIGIN late 16th cent. (earlier as *salve*): from French *salve*, Italian *salva* 'salutation'.

sal volatile /ˌsal vəˈlatɪli/ ▶ noun [mass noun] a scented solution of ammonium carbonate in alcohol, used as smelling salts.
– ORIGIN mid 17th cent.: modern Latin, literally 'volatile salt'.

salvor /ˈsalvə, ˈsalvɔː/ ▶ noun a person engaged in salvage of a ship or items lost at sea.

salwar /sʌlˈwaː/ (also **shalwar**) ▶ noun a pair of light, loose, pleated trousers tapering to a tight fit around the ankles, worn by women from the Indian subcontinent, typically with a kameez.
– ORIGIN from Persian and Urdu *šalwār*.

Salween /ˈsalwiːn, salˈwiːn/ a river of SE Asia, which rises in Tibet and flows for 2,400 km (1,500 miles) south-east and south through Burma to the Gulf of Martaban, an inlet of the Andaman Sea.

Salyut /saˈljuːt, ˈsaljuːt/ a series of seven Soviet manned orbiting space stations, launched between 1971 and 1982.
– ORIGIN Russian, used as a greeting; compare with French **SALUT**.

Salzburg /ˈsaltsbəːg, ˈsɔːlts-, German ˈzaltsbʊrk/ a city in western Austria, near the border with Germany, the capital of a state of the same name; pop 143,970 (1991). It is noted for its annual music festivals, one of which is dedicated to the composer Mozart, who was born in the city in 1756.

Salzgitter /ˈsaltsˌɡɪtə, ˈsɔːlts-, German ˈzaltsˌɡɪtɐ/ an industrial city in Germany, in Lower Saxony south-east of Hanover; pop. 115,380 (1991).

Salzkammergut /ˈsaltskaməˌɡuːt, ˈsɔːlts-, German ˈzaltskamɐˌɡuːt/ a resort area of lakes and mountains in the state of Salzburg in western Austria.

SAM ▶ abbreviation for surface-to-air missile.

Sam. ▶ abbreviation for Samuel (in biblical references).

samadhi /sʌˈmaːdi/ ▶ noun (pl. **samadhis**) [mass noun] Hinduism & Buddhism a state of intense concentration achieved through meditation. In yoga this is regarded as the final stage, at which union with the divine is reached (before or at death).
■Indian a tomb.
– ORIGIN from Sanskrit *samādhi* 'contemplation'.

saman /saˈmaːn/ (also **samaan, saman tree**) ▶ noun West Indian term for **RAIN TREE**.
– ORIGIN Latin American Spanish.

samango /saˈmaŋɡəʊ/ (also **samango monkey**) ▶ noun (pl. **-os**) S. African an African guenon which has blue-grey fur with black markings.
●*Cercopithecus mitis*, family Cercopithecidae. Alternative name: **diademed monkey**.
– ORIGIN late 19th cent.: a local African word.

Samar /ˈsaːmaː/ an island in the Philippines, situated to the south-east of Luzon. It is the third largest island of the group.

Samara /səˈmaːrə/ a city and river port in SW central Russia, situated on the Volga at its confluence with the River Samara; pop. 1,258,000 (1990). Former name (1935–91) **KUIBYSHEV**.

samara /ˈsamərə, səˈmaːrə/ ▶ noun Botany a winged nut or achene containing one seed, as in ash and maple.
– ORIGIN late 16th cent.: modern Latin, from Latin, denoting an elm seed.

Samaria /səˈmɛːrɪə/ 1 an ancient city of central Palestine, founded in the 9th century BC as the capital of the northern Hebrew kingdom of Israel. The ancient site is situated in the modern West Bank, north-west of Nablus.
2 the region of ancient Palestine around this city, between Galilee in the north and Judaea in the south.

Samarinda /ˌsaməˈrɪndə/ a city in Indonesia, in eastern Borneo; pop. 264,700 (1980).

Samaritan ▶ noun 1 (usu. **good Samaritan**) a charitable or helpful person (with reference to Luke 10:33).
2 a member of a people inhabiting Samaria in biblical times, or of the modern community claiming descent from them, adhering to a form of Judaism accepting only its own ancient version of the Pentateuch as Scripture.
3 [mass noun] the dialect of Aramaic formerly spoken in Samaria.
4 (the **Samaritans**) (in the UK) an organization which counsels the suicidal and others in distress, mainly through a telephone service.
■a member of such an organization.
▶ adjective of or relating to Samaria or the Samaritans.
– DERIVATIVES **Samaritanism** noun.
– ORIGIN from late Latin *Samaritanus*, from Greek *Samareitēs*, from *Samareia* 'Samaria'. The New Testament parable of the Good Samaritan reflects a proverbial hostility between Jews and Samaritans.

samarium /səˈmɛːrɪəm/ ▶ noun [mass noun] the chemical element of atomic number 62, a hard silvery-white metal of the lanthanide series. (Symbol: **Sm**)
– ORIGIN late 19th cent.: from *samar(skite)*, a mineral in which its spectrum was first observed (named after *Samarsky*, a 19th-cent. Russian official) + **-IUM**.

Samarkand /ˌsaməˈkand, ˈsaməkand/ (also **Samarqand**) a city in eastern Uzbekistan; pop. 369,900 (1990). One of the oldest cities of Asia, it was founded in the 3rd or 4th millennium BC. It grew to prominence as a prosperous centre of the silk trade, situated on the Silk Road, and in the 14th century became the capital of Tamerlane's Mongol empire.

Samarra /səˈmaːrə/ a city in Iraq, on the River Tigris north of Baghdad; pop. 62,000 (est. 1985).

Sama Veda /ˈsaːmə/ Hinduism one of the four Vedas, a collection of liturgical chants chanted aloud at the sacrifice. Its material is drawn largely from the Rig Veda. See **VEDA**.
– ORIGIN from Sanskrit *sāmaveda*, from *sāman* 'chant' and *veda* '(sacred) knowledge'.

samba /ˈsambə/ ▶ noun a Brazilian dance of African origin.
■a piece of music for this dance. ■a lively modern ballroom dance imitating this dance.
▶ verb (**sambas, sambaed** /-bəd/ or **samba'd, sambaing** /-bə(r)ɪŋ/) [no obj.] dance the samba.

– ORIGIN late 19th cent.: from Portuguese, of African origin.

sambal /ˈsambal/ ▶ noun (in oriental cookery) hot relish made with vegetables or fruit and spices.
– ORIGIN Malay.

sambar /ˈsambə/ ▶ noun a dark brown woodland deer with branched antlers, of southern Asia.
●*Cervus unicolor*, family Cervidae.
– ORIGIN late 17th cent.: from Hindi *sābar*, from Sanskrit *śambara*.

sambhar /ˈsaːmbaː/ ▶ noun [mass noun] a spicy south Indian dish consisting of lentils and vegetables.
– ORIGIN from Tamil *cāmpār*, via Marathi from Sanskrit *sambhāra* 'collection, materials'.

Sambo ▶ noun (pl. **-os** or **-oes**) 1 offensive a black person. [ORIGIN: early 18th cent.: perhaps from Fula *sambo* 'uncle'.]
2 (**sambo**) historical a person of mixed race, especially of black and Indian or black and European blood. [ORIGIN: mid 18th cent.: from American Spanish *zambo*, denoting a kind of yellow monkey.]

Sam Browne (also **Sam Browne belt**) ▶ noun a leather belt with a supporting strap that passes over the right shoulder, worn by army and police officers.
– ORIGIN early 20th cent.: named after Sir *Samuel J. Brown(e)* (1824–1901), the British military commander who invented it.

sambuca /samˈbuːkə/ ▶ noun [mass noun] an Italian aniseed-flavoured liqueur.
– ORIGIN Italian, from Latin *sambucus* 'elder tree'.

Samburu /samˈbʊruː/ ▶ noun (pl. same) 1 a member of a mainly pastoral people of northern Kenya.
2 [mass noun] the Nilotic language of this people.
▶ adjective of or relating to this people or their language.
– ORIGIN a local name.

same ▶ adjective (the **same**) 1 identical; not different; unchanged: *he's worked at the same place for quite a few years | I'm the same age as you are |* [with clause] *he put on the same costume that he had worn in Ottawa.*
■(this/that same) referring to a person or thing just mentioned: *that same year I went to Boston.*
2 of an identical type: *they all wore the same clothes.*
▶ pronoun 1 (the **same**) the same thing as something previously mentioned: *I'll resign and encourage everyone else to do the same.*
■people or things that are identical or share the same characteristics: *there are several brands and they're not all the same.*
2 (chiefly in formal or legal use) the person or thing just mentioned: *put the tailboard up and secure same with a length of wire.*
▶ adverb similarly; in the same way: *treating women the same as men | he gave me five dollars, same as usual.*
– PHRASES **all** (or **just**) **the same** in spite of this; nevertheless: *she knew they had meant it kindly, but it had hurt all the same.* ■ in any case; anyway: *thanks all the same, but I've something better to do.* **at the same time** 1 simultaneously. 2 on the other hand; nevertheless; yet: *it's a very creative place, but at the same time it's very relaxing.* **be all the same to** be unimportant to (someone) what happens: *it was all the same to me where it was being sold.* **by the same token** see **TOKEN**. **one and the same** the same person or thing (used for emphasis). **same again** another drink of the same kind as the last (said as a request or offer). **same difference** informal used to express the speaker's belief that two or more things are essentially the same, in spite of apparent differences. **same here** informal the same applies to me. (**the**) **same to you!** may you do or have the same thing (a response to a greeting or insult). **the very same** the same (used for emphasis, often to express surprise): *the very same people who practised all the rules are now the most sceptical.*
– DERIVATIVES **sameness** noun.
– ORIGIN Middle English: from Old Norse *sami*, from an Indo-European root shared by Sanskrit *sama*, Greek *homos*.

samey ▶ adjective (**samier, samiest**) Brit. informal lacking in variety; monotonous.
– DERIVATIVES **sameyness** noun.

samfu /ˈsamfuː/ ▶ noun a light suit consisting of a plain high-necked jacket and loose trousers, worn by women from China.

Samhain

– ORIGIN 1950s: from Chinese (Cantonese dialect) *shaam fòò*, from *shaam* 'coat' + *fòò* 'trousers'.

Samhain /saʊn, 'saʊın, 'sawın, Irish 'saʊn/ ▶ noun the first day of November, celebrated by the ancient Celts as a festival marking the beginning of winter and the Celtic new year.

– ORIGIN Irish, from Old Irish *samain*.

Sam Hill ▶ noun N. Amer. informal used in exclamations as a euphemism for 'hell': *what in Sam Hill is that?*

– ORIGIN mid 19th cent.: of unknown origin.

Sami /'saːmi, saːm/ ▶ plural noun the Lapps of northern Scandinavia.

– ORIGIN Lappish, of unknown origin.

USAGE **Sami** is the term by which the Lapps themselves prefer to be known. Its use is becoming increasingly common, although **Lapp** is still the main term in general use.

Samian /'seımıən/ ▶ noun a native or inhabitant of Samos.

▶ adjective of or relating to Samos.

Samian ware ▶ noun [mass noun] a type of fine, glossy, reddish-brown pottery widely made in the Roman Empire. Also called **TERRA SIGILLATA**.

samisen /'samısɛn/ (also **shamisen** /'ʃamısɛn/) ▶ noun a traditional Japanese three-stringed lute with a square body, played with a large plectrum.

– ORIGIN early 17th cent.: Japanese, from Chinese *san-hsien*, from *san* 'three' + *hsien* 'string'.

samite /'samʌɪt, seı-/ ▶ noun [mass noun] historical a rich silk fabric interwoven with gold and silver threads, used for dressmaking and decoration in the Middle Ages.

– ORIGIN Middle English: from Old French *samit*, via medieval Latin from medieval Greek *hexamiton*, from Greek *hexa-* 'six' + *mitos* 'thread'.

samizdat /'samızdat, ˌsamız'dat/ ▶ noun [mass noun] the clandestine copying and distribution of literature banned by the state, especially formerly in the communist countries of eastern Europe.

– ORIGIN 1960s: Russian, literally 'self-publishing house'.

Samnite /'samnʌɪt/ ▶ noun a member of an Oscan-speaking people of southern Italy in ancient times, who spent long periods at war with republican Rome in the 4th to 1st centuries BC.

▶ adjective of or relating to this people.

– ORIGIN from Latin *Samnites* (plural); related to *Sabinus* (see **SABINE**).

Samoa /səˈməʊə/ a group of islands in Polynesia, divided between American Samoa and the state of Samoa.

■ a country consisting of the western islands of Samoa; pop. 159,860 (1991); official languages, Samoan and English; capital, Apia.

Visited by the Dutch in the early 18th century, the islands were divided administratively in 1899 into American Samoa in the east and German Samoa in the west. After the First World War the nine western islands were mandated to New Zealand, and became an independent republic within the Commonwealth in 1962, as Western Samoa. The country became known as Samoa in 1997.

Samoan ▶ adjective of or relating to Samoa, its people, or their language.

▶ noun 1 a native or inhabitant of Samoa. 2 [mass noun] the Polynesian language of Samoa, which has over 300,000 speakers in Samoa, New Zealand, the US, and elsewhere.

Samos /'seımɒs/ a Greek island in the Aegean, situated close to the coast of western Turkey.

samosa /səˈməʊsə/ ▶ noun a triangular savoury pastry fried in ghee or oil, containing spiced vegetables or meat.

– ORIGIN from Persian and Urdu.

samovar /'saməvaː, ˌsamə'vaː/ ▶ noun a highly decorated tea urn used in Russia.

– ORIGIN Russian, literally 'self-boiler'.

Samoyed /'samɔɪɛd, ˌsamɔɪ'ɛd/ ▶ noun 1 a member of a group of mainly nomadic peoples of northern Siberia, who traditionally live as reindeer herders. 2 [mass noun] any of several Samoyedic (Uralic) languages of these peoples.

■ another term for **SAMOYEDIC**. 3 a dog of a white Arctic breed.

– ORIGIN from Russian *samoed*.

Samoyedic ▶ noun [mass noun] a group of Uralic languages of northern Siberia, of which the most widely spoken is Nenets.

▶ adjective of or relating to the Samoyeds or their languages.

samp ▶ noun [mass noun] US & S. African coarsely ground maize or porridge made from this.

– ORIGIN mid 17th cent.: from Algonquian *nasamp* 'softened by water'.

sampan /'sampan/ ▶ noun a small boat of a kind used in the Far East, typically with an oar or oars at the stern.

– ORIGIN early 17th cent.: from Chinese *san-ban*, from *san* 'three' + *ban* 'board'.

samphire /'samfʌɪə/ ▶ noun (also **rock samphire**) a European plant of the parsley family, which grows on rocks and cliffs by the sea. Its aromatic fleshy leaves were formerly used in pickles.

● *Crithmum maritimum*, family Umbelliferae.

■ used in names of other fleshy-leaved plants that grow near the sea, e.g. **golden samphire**.

– ORIGIN mid 16th cent. (earlier as *sampiere*): from French (*herbe de*) *Saint Pierre* 'St Peter('s herb)'.

sample ▶ noun a small part or quantity intended to show what the whole is like: *investigations involved analysing samples of handwriting.*

■ a specimen taken for scientific testing or analysis: *a urine sample.* ■ Statistics a portion drawn from a population, the study of which is intended to lead to statistical estimates of the attributes of the whole population. ■ a small amount of a food or other commodity, especially one given to a prospective customer. ■ a sound created by sampling.

▶ verb [with obj.] take a sample or samples of (something) for analysis: *bone marrow cells were sampled* | [as adj., with submodifier] (**sampled**) *a survey of two hundred randomly sampled households.*

■ try the qualities of (food or drink) by tasting it. ■ get a representative experience of: *sample some entertaining nights out in Liverpool.* ■ Electronics ascertain the momentary value of (an analogue signal) many times a second so as to convert the signal to digital form. ■ record or extract a small piece of music or sound digitally for reuse as part of a composition or song.

– ORIGIN Middle English (as a noun): from an Anglo-Norman French variant of Old French *essample* 'example'. Current senses of the verb date from the mid 18th cent.

sample bag ▶ noun another term for **SHOW BAG**.

sample point ▶ noun Statistics a single possible observed value of a variable.

sampler ▶ noun 1 a piece of embroidery worked in various stitches as a specimen of skill, typically containing the alphabet and some mottoes. 2 a representative collection or example of something: *the diversity of ace music on this sampler.* 3 a person or device that takes and analyses samples.

■ an electronic device for sampling music and sound.

– ORIGIN Middle English (denoting an example to be imitated): from Old French *essamplaire* 'exemplar'.

sample space ▶ noun Statistics the range of values of a random variable.

sampling ▶ noun [mass noun] 1 the taking of a sample or samples: *routine river sampling is carried out according to a schedule.*

■ [count noun] Statistics a sample. 2 the technique of digitally encoding music or sound and reusing it as part of a composition or recording.

sampling error ▶ noun [mass noun] Statistics error in a statistical analysis arising from the unrepresentativeness of the sample taken.

sampling frame ▶ noun Statistics a list of the items or people forming a population from which a sample is taken.

Sampras /'sampras/, Peter (b.1971), American tennis player. He was the youngest man ever to win the US Open, in 1990, and in 2000 won his seventh Wimbledon title, a record 13th grand slam win.

samsara /sʌm'saːrə/ ▶ noun Hinduism & Buddhism the material world.

■ [mass noun] the cycle of death and rebirth to which life in the material world is bound.

– DERIVATIVES **samsaric** adjective.

– ORIGIN from Sanskrit *saṃsāra*.

samskara /sʌm'skaːrə/ ▶ noun Hinduism a purificatory ceremony or rite marking a major event in one's life.

– ORIGIN from Sanskrit *saṃskāra* 'a making perfect, preparation'.

Samson an Israelite leader (probably 11th century BC) famous for his strength (Judges 13–16). He fell in love with Delilah and confided to her that his strength lay in his uncut hair. She betrayed him to the Philistines who cut off his hair and blinded him, but his hair grew again, and he pulled down the pillars of a house, destroying himself and a large gathering of Philistines.

Samson post ▶ noun a strong pillar fixed to a ship's deck to act as a support for a tackle or other equipment.

– ORIGIN late 16th cent. (denoting a kind of mousetrap): probably with biblical allusion to **SAMSON**.

Samuel (in the Bible) a Hebrew prophet who rallied the Israelites after their defeat by the Philistines and became their ruler.

■ either of two books of the Bible covering the history of ancient Israel from Samuel's birth to the end of the reign of David.

samurai /'sam(j)ʊrʌɪ/ ▶ noun (pl. same) historical a member of a powerful military caste in feudal Japan.

– ORIGIN Japanese.

San /saːn/ ▶ noun (pl. same) 1 a member of the aboriginal peoples of southern Africa commonly called Bushmen. See **BUSHMAN**. 2 [mass noun] the group of Khoisan languages spoken by these peoples.

■ any of these languages.

▶ adjective of or relating to the San or their languages.

– ORIGIN from Nama *sān* 'aboriginals, settlers'.

san ▶ noun informal term for **SANATORIUM**.

Sana'a /saˈnaː, 'saːnə/ (also **Sanaa**) the capital of Yemen; pop. 926,600 (est. 1993).

San Andreas fault /ˌsan anˈdreɪəs/ a fault line extending for some 965 km (600 miles) through the length of coastal California. Seismic activity is common along its course and is due to two crustal plates sliding past each other along the line of the fault.

San Antonio /san anˈtəʊnɪəʊ/ an industrial city in south central Texas; pop. 935,930 (1990). It is the site of the Alamo mission.

sanative /'sanətɪv/ ▶ adjective archaic conducive to physical or spiritual health and well-being; healing.

– ORIGIN late Middle English: from Old French *sanatif* or late Latin *sanativus*, from Latin *sanare* 'to cure'.

sanatorium /ˌsanəˈtɔːrɪəm/ ▶ noun (pl. **sanatoriums** or **sanatoria** /-rɪə/) an establishment for the medical treatment of people who are convalescing or have a chronic illness.

■ Brit. a room or building for sick children in a boarding school.

– ORIGIN mid 19th cent.: modern Latin, based on Latin *sanare* 'heal'.

Sancerre /sɒ̃ˈsɛː, French sɑ̃sɛʀ/ ▶ noun [mass noun] a light wine, typically white, produced in the part of France around Sancerre.

Sanchi /'saːntʃi/ the site in Madhya Pradesh of several well-preserved ancient Buddhist stupas.

Sancho Panza /ˌsantʃəʊ 'panzə/ the squire of Don Quixote. He is an uneducated peasant but has a store of proverbial wisdom, and is thus a foil to his master.

sancoche /saŋˈkɒtʃ, -kɒʃ, -kɒtʃi/ (also **sancocho** /-'kɒtʃəʊ/) ▶ noun [mass noun] (in South America and the Caribbean) a thick soup consisting of meat and root vegetables.

– ORIGIN from Latin American Spanish *sancocho* 'a stew'.

sanctify /'saŋ(k)tɪfʌɪ/ ▶ verb (**-ies**, **-ied**) [with obj.] set apart as or declare holy; consecrate: *a small Christian shrine was built to sanctify the site.*

■ (often **be sanctified**) make legitimate or binding by religious sanction: *they see their love sanctified by the sacrament of marriage.* ■ free from sin; purify. ■ (often **be sanctified**) figurative give the appearance of being right or good; legitimize: *they looked to royalty to sanctify their cause.*

– DERIVATIVES **sanctification** noun, **sanctifier** noun.

– ORIGIN late Middle English: from Old French *saintifier* (influenced later by *sanctifier*), from ecclesiastical Latin *sanctificare*, from Latin *sanctus* 'holy'.

sanctimonious /ˌsaŋ(k)tɪˈməʊnɪəs/ ▶ adjective derogatory making a show of being morally superior to other people: *what happened to all the sanctimonious talk about putting his family first?*

– DERIVATIVES **sanctimoniously** adverb, **sanctimoniousness** noun, **sanctimony** /ˈsaŋ(k)tɪməni/ noun.

– ORIGIN early 17th cent. (in the sense 'holy in character'): from Latin *sanctimonia* 'sanctity' (from *sanctus* 'holy') + **-OUS**.

sanction ▶ noun **1** a threatened penalty for disobeying a law or rule: *a range of sanctions aimed at deterring insider abuse.*
■(**sanctions**) measures taken by a state to coerce another to conform to an international agreement or norms of conduct, typically in the form of restrictions on trade or official sporting participation. ■ Ethics a consideration operating to enforce obedience to any rule of conduct.
2 [mass noun] official permission or approval for an action: *he appealed to the bishop for his sanction.*
■official confirmation or ratification of a law. ■ [count noun] Law, historical a law or decree, especially an ecclesiastical decree.
▶verb [with obj.] **1** (often **be sanctioned**) give official permission or approval for (an action): *the council will consider whether to sanction the operation.*
2 impose a sanction or penalty on.

– DERIVATIVES **sanctionable** adjective.

– ORIGIN late Middle English (as a noun denoting an ecclesiastical decree): from French, from Latin *sanctio(n-)*, from *sancire* 'ratify'. The verb dates from the late 18th cent.

sanctitude ▶ noun [mass noun] formal the state or quality of being holy, sacred, or saintly.

– ORIGIN late Middle English: from Latin *sanctitudo*, from *sanctus* 'holy'.

sanctity ▶ noun (pl. **-ies**) [mass noun] the state or quality of being holy, sacred, or saintly: *the site of the tomb was a place of sanctity for the ancient Egyptians.*
■ultimate importance and inviolability: *the sanctity of human life.*

– ORIGIN late Middle English (in the sense 'saintliness'): from Old French *saincte*, reinforced by Latin *sanctitas*, from *sanctus* 'holy'.

sanctuary ▶ noun (pl. **-ies**) **1** a place of refuge or safety: *people automatically sought a sanctuary in time of trouble* | [mass noun] *his sons* **took sanctuary** *in the church.*
■[mass noun] immunity from arrest: *he has been* **given sanctuary** *in the US Embassy in Beijing.*
2 [usu. with modifier] a nature reserve: *a bird sanctuary.*
■a place where injured or unwanted animals of a specified kind are cared for: *a donkey sanctuary.*
3 a holy place; a temple.
■the inmost recess or holiest part of a temple. ■ the part of the chancel of a church containing the high altar.

– ORIGIN Middle English (in sense 3): from Old French *sanctuaire*, from Latin *sanctuarium*, from *sanctus* 'holy'. The early sense 'a church or other sacred place where a fugitive was immune, by the law of the medieval Church, from arrest' gave rise to senses 1 and 2.

sanctuary lamp ▶ noun a candle or small light left lit in the sanctuary of a church, especially (in Catholic churches) a red lamp indicating the presence of the reserved Sacrament.

sanctum /ˈsaŋ(k)təm/ ▶ noun (pl. **sanctums**) a sacred place, especially a shrine within a temple or church.
■figurative a private place from which most people are excluded.

– ORIGIN late 16th cent.: from Latin, neuter of *sanctus* 'holy', from *sancire* 'consecrate'.

sanctum sanctorum /saŋ(k)ˈtɔːrəm/ ▶ noun (pl. **sancta sanctorum** or **sanctum sanctorums**) the holy of holies in the Jewish temple.

– ORIGIN late Middle English: Latin *sanctum* (see **SANCTUM**) + *sanctorum* 'of holy places', translating Hebrew *qōḏeš haqqŏḏāšîm* 'holy of holies'.

Sanctus /ˈsaŋ(k)təs/ ▶ noun Christian Church a hymn beginning *Sanctus, sanctus, sanctus* (Holy, holy, holy) forming a set part of the Mass.

– ORIGIN late Middle English: from Latin, literally 'holy'.

sanctus bell ▶ noun another term for **SACRING BELL**.

Sand /sɒ̃/, George (1804–76), French novelist; pseudonym of *Amandine-Aurore Lucille Dupin, Baronne Dudevant*. Her earlier novels, including *Lélia* (1833), portray women's struggles against conventional morals; she later wrote a number of pastoral novels, such as *La Mare au diable* (1846).

sand ▶ noun [mass noun] a loose granular substance, typically pale yellowish brown, resulting from the erosion of siliceous and other rocks and forming a major constituent of beaches, river beds, the seabed, and deserts.
■(**sands**) an expanse of sand, typically along a shore: [in place names] *Goodwin Sands.* ■ [count noun] a stratum of sandstone or compacted sand. ■ technical sediment whose particles are larger than silt (typically greater than 0.06 mm). ■ N. Amer. informal firmness of purpose: *no one has the sand to stand against him.* ■ a light yellow-brown colour like that of sand.
▶verb [with obj.] **1** smooth or polish with sandpaper or a mechanical sander: *mask off the area to be painted and* **sand** *it* **down** | [as noun **sanding**] *some recommend a light sanding between the second and third coats.*
2 sprinkle or overlay with sand, to give better purchase on a surface.

– PHRASES **drive** (or **run**) (**something**) **into the sand** come (or bring something) to a halt: *its privatization programme ran straight into the sand.* **the sands** (**of time**) **are running out** the allotted time is nearly at an end. [ORIGIN: with reference to the sand of an hourglass.]

– DERIVATIVES **sand-like** adjective.

– ORIGIN Old English, of Germanic origin; related to Dutch *zand* and German *Sand*.

sandal[1] ▶ noun a light shoe with either an openwork upper or straps attaching the sole to the foot.

– DERIVATIVES **sandalled** (US **sandaled**) adjective.

– ORIGIN late Middle English: via Latin from Greek *sandalion*, diminutive of *sandalon* 'wooden shoe', probably of Asiatic origin; compare with Persian *sandal*.

sandal[2] ▶ noun short for **SANDALWOOD**.

sandalwood ▶ noun (also **white sandalwood**) a widely cultivated Indian tree which yields fragrant timber and oil.
● *Santalum album*, family Santalaceae.
■[mass noun] a perfume or incense derived from this timber. ■ used in names of other trees which yield similar timber, e.g. **red sandalwood**.

– ORIGIN early 16th cent.: *sandal* from medieval Latin *sandalum* (based on Sanskrit *candana*) + **WOOD**.

Sandalwood Island another name for **SUMBA**.

sandarac /ˈsandərak/ (also **gum sandarac**) ▶ noun [mass noun] a gum resin obtained from the alerce (cypress) of Spain and North Africa, used in making varnish.

– ORIGIN late Middle English (denoting realgar): from Latin *sandaraca*, from Greek *sandarakē*, of Asiatic origin. The current sense dates from the mid 17th cent.

Sandawe /sanˈdɑːweɪ/ ▶ noun **1** (pl. same or **Sandawes**) a member of an indigenous people of Tanzania.
2 [mass noun] the Khoisan language of this people.
▶adjective of or relating to this people or their language.

sandbag ▶ noun a bag filled with sand, typically used for defensive purposes or as ballast in a boat.
▶verb (**-bagged**, **-bagging**) [with obj.] **1** [usu. as adj. **sandbagged**] barricade using sandbags: *boarded-up shopfronts and sandbagged doorways.*
2 hit or fell with or as if with a blow from a sandbag.
■N. Amer. coerce; bully.
3 [no obj.] deliberately underperform in a race or competition to gain an unfair advantage.

– DERIVATIVES **sandbagger** noun.

sandbank ▶ noun a deposit of sand forming a shallow area in the sea or a river.

sandbar ▶ noun a long, narrow sandbank, especially at the mouth of a river.

sand bath ▶ noun a container of heated sand, used in a laboratory to supply uniform heating.

sandblast ▶ verb [with obj.] roughen or clean (a surface) with a jet of sand driven by compressed air or steam.
▶noun such a jet of sand.

– DERIVATIVES **sandblaster** noun.

sandbox ▶ noun **1** a box containing sand, especially one kept on a train to hold sand for sprinkling on to slippery rails.
■historical a perforated container for sprinkling sand on to wet ink in order to dry it. ■ US term for **SANDPIT**.
2 (also **sandbox tree**) a tropical American tree whose seed cases were formerly used to hold sand for blotting ink.
● *Hura crepitans*, family Euphorbiaceae.

sandboy ▶ noun (in phrase (**as**) **happy as a sandboy**) extremely happy or carefree.

– ORIGIN probably originally denoting a boy hawking sand for sale.

sandcastle ▶ noun a model of a castle built out of sand, typically by children.

sand cat ▶ noun a small wild cat with a plain yellow to greyish coat, a dark-ringed tail, and large eyes, of the deserts of North Africa and SW Asia.
● *Felis margarita*, family Felidae.

sand cherry ▶ noun a dwarf North American wild cherry.
● Genus *Prunus*, family Rosaceae: two species.
■the fruit of this tree.

sand crab ▶ noun a crab which lives on or burrows in sand, especially one related to fiddler and ghost crabs.
● Genus *Uca*, family Ocypodidae.

sand crack ▶ noun a vertical fissure in the wall of a horse's hoof, originating at the top of the hoof.

sand dab ▶ noun a small flatfish which is found in the Pacific coastal waters of America.
● Genus *Citharichthys*, family Bothidae: several species.
■[mass noun] this fish as food. ■ another term for **WINDOWPANE** (in sense 2).

sand dollar ▶ noun a flattened sea urchin which lives partly buried in sand, feeding on detritus.
● Order Clypeasteroida, class Echinoidea.

sand eel ▶ noun a small elongated marine fish which lives in shallow waters of the northern hemisphere, often found burrowing in the sand.
● Family Ammodytidae: several genera and species, including the European *Ammodytes tobianus*.

sander ▶ noun a power tool used for smoothing a surface with sandpaper or other abrasive material.

sanderling /ˈsandəlɪŋ/ ▶ noun a small migratory sandpiper of northern Eurasia and Canada, typically seen running after receding waves on the beach.
● *Calidris alba*, family Scolopacidae.

– ORIGIN early 17th cent.: of unknown origin.

sanders /ˈsɑːndəz, ˈsan-/ (also **sanderswood**) ▶ noun [mass noun] the timber of the red sandalwood, from which a red dye is obtained.
● This timber is obtained from *Pterocarpus santalinus*, family Leguminosae.

– ORIGIN Middle English: from Old French *sandre*, variant of *sandle* 'sandalwood'.

sandesh /sʌnˈðeɪʃ/ ▶ noun [mass noun] an Indian sweet made from paneer and sugar and cut into squares.

– ORIGIN from Bengali *sandeś*.

sand filter ▶ noun a filter used in water purification and consisting of layers of sand arranged with coarseness of texture increasing downwards.

sandfish ▶ noun (pl. same or **-fishes**) **1** a small marine fish with fringed lips, which burrows in the sand, in particular:
● an elongated Australian fish (*Crapatulus arenarius*, family Leptoscopidae). ● a North Pacific fish (*Trichodon trichodon*, family Trichodontidae).
2 (**belted sandfish**) a small sea bass which lives only in shallow inshore waters around Florida.
● *Serranus subligarius*, family Serranidae.

sand flea ▶ noun **1** another term for **CHIGGER** (in sense 1).
2 another term for **SANDHOPPER**.

sandfly ▶ noun (pl. **-flies**) **1** a small hairy biting fly of tropical and subtropical regions, which transmits a number of diseases including leishmaniasis.
● Subfamily Phlebotominae, family Psychodidae: several genera, in particular *Phlebotomus*.
2 Austral. another term for **BLACKFLY** (in sense 2).

sand fox ▶ noun a small fox with long ears and a thick coat, living in desert and steppe areas from Morocco to Afghanistan.
● *Vulpes rueppellii*, family Canidae.

sandglass ▶ noun an hourglass measuring a fixed amount of time (not necessarily one hour).

Sandgroper ▶ noun Austral. informal a non-Aboriginal Western Australian.

– ORIGIN late 19th cent.: so named because of the large amount of sand in Western Australia.

sandgrouse ▶ noun (pl. same) a seed-eating ground-dwelling bird with brownish plumage, allied to the pigeons and found in the deserts and arid regions of the Old World.
● Family Pteroclididae, genera *Pterocles* and *Syrrhaptes*: several species.

sandhi /ˈsandi/ ▶ noun [mass noun] Grammar the process whereby the form of a word changes as a result of its position in an utterance (e.g. the change from *a* to *an* before a vowel).
– ORIGIN from Sanskrit *saṃdhi* 'putting together'.

sandhill crane ▶ noun a chiefly migratory North American crane with greyish plumage and a red crown.
● *Grus canadensis*, family Gruidae.

sandhog ▶ noun N. Amer. a person who does construction work underground or under water such as laying foundations or building a tunnel.

sandhopper ▶ noun a small crustacean of the seashore which typically lives among seaweed and leaps when disturbed. Also called **SAND FLEA**.
● *Orchestia* and other genera, order Amphipoda.

Sandhurst a training college at Camberley, Surrey, for officers for the British army. It was formed in 1946 from an amalgamation of the Royal Military College at Sandhurst in Berkshire and the Royal Military Academy at Woolwich, London. Official name **ROYAL MILITARY ACADEMY, SANDHURST**.

San Diego /ˌsan dɪˈeɪɡəʊ/ an industrial city and naval port on the Pacific coast of southern California, just north of the border with Mexico; pop. 1,110,550 (1990).

Sandinista /ˌsandɪˈniːstə/ ▶ noun a member of a left-wing Nicaraguan political organization, the Sandinista National Liberation Front (FSLN), which came to power in 1979 after overthrowing the dictator Anastasio Somoza. Opposed during most of their period of rule by the US-backed Contras, the Sandinistas were voted out of office in 1990.
– ORIGIN named after a similar organization founded by the nationalist leader Augusto César Sandino (1893–1934).

sand iron ▶ noun Golf a sand wedge.

sandiver /ˈsandɪvə/ ▶ noun [mass noun] a scum that forms on molten glass.
– ORIGIN late Middle English: apparently from Old French *suin de verre* 'exudation from glass', from *suer* 'to sweat' + *verre* 'glass'.

S & L ▶ abbreviation for savings and loan.

sand lance ▶ noun another term for **SAND EEL**.

sand lizard ▶ noun a small ground-dwelling Old World lizard favouring heathland or sandy areas.
● *Lacerta agilis* (of Eurasia), and genus *Pedioplanis* (of Africa), family Lacertidae.

sandlot ▶ noun N. Amer. a piece of unoccupied land used by children for games.
■ [as modifier] denoting or relating to sport played by amateurs: *sandlot baseball*.

sandman ▶ noun (**the sandman**) a fictional man supposed to make children sleep by sprinkling sand in their eyes.

sand martin ▶ noun a gregarious swallow-like bird with dark brown and white plumage, excavating nest holes in sandy banks and cliffs near water.
● Genus *Riparia*, family Hirundinidae: three species, in particular the widespread *R. riparia* (North American name: **bank swallow**).

sand painting ▶ noun [mass noun] an American Indian ceremonial art form using coloured sands, used especially in connection with healing ceremonies.
■ [count noun] an example of this art form.

sandpaper ▶ noun [mass noun] paper with sand or another abrasive stuck to it, used for smoothing or polishing woodwork or other surfaces.
■ used to refer to something that feels rough or has a very rough surface.
▶ verb [with obj.] smooth with sandpaper.
– DERIVATIVES **sandpapery** adjective.

sandpiper ▶ noun a wading bird with a long bill and typically long legs, nesting on the ground by water and frequenting coastal areas on migration.
● Family Scolopacidae (the **sandpiper family**): several genera, especially *Calidris*, *Tringa*, and *Actitis*, and numerous species. The sandpiper family also includes the godwits, curlews, redshanks, turnstones, phalaropes, woodcock, snipe, and ruff.

sandpit ▶ noun a quarry from which sand is excavated.
■ Brit. a shallow box or hollow in the ground, partly filled with sand for children to play in.

sand plover ▶ noun a migratory African and Asian plover, typically small in size and resembling a ringed plover without black on the breast.
● Genus *Charadrius*, family Charadriidae: several species.

Sandringham House /ˈsandrɪŋəm/ a country residence of the British royal family, north-east of King's Lynn in Norfolk.

sand shark ▶ noun a voracious brown-spotted shark of tropical Atlantic waters.
● *Odontaspis taurus*, family Odontaspididae.
■ any of a number of mainly harmless rays, dogfish, and sharks found in shallow coastal waters.

sandshoe ▶ noun chiefly Scottish & Austral. another term for **PLIMSOLL**.

sand stargazer ▶ noun see **STARGAZER** (sense 3).

sandstone ▶ noun [mass noun] sedimentary rock consisting of sand or quartz grains cemented together, typically red, yellow, or brown in colour.

sandstorm ▶ noun a strong wind carrying clouds of sand with it, especially in a desert.

sand table ▶ noun a relief model in sand used to explain military tactics and plan campaigns.

sandveld /ˈsandfelt/ ▶ noun [mass noun] S. African land characterized by dry, sandy soil.
– ORIGIN Afrikaans, from Dutch *zand* 'sand' + *veld* 'terrain'.

sand wasp ▶ noun a digger wasp that excavates its burrow in sandy soil and then catches prey with which to furnish it. Sand wasps typically have an abdomen with a very long and slender 'waist'.
● Subfamily Sphecinae, family Sphecidae: *Ammophila* and other genera.

sand wedge ▶ noun Golf a heavy, lofted iron with a flange on the bottom, used for hitting the ball out of sand.

sandwich /ˈsan(d)wɪdʒ, -wɪtʃ/ ▶ noun **1** an item of food consisting of two pieces of bread with meat, cheese, or other filling between them, eaten as a light meal: *a ham sandwich*.
■ [usu. with modifier] Brit. a sponge cake of two or more layers with jam or cream between. ■ something that is constructed like or has the form of a sandwich.
2 [as modifier] of or relating to a sandwich course.
▶ verb [with obj.] (usu. **be sandwiched between**) insert or squeeze (someone or something) between two other people or things, typically in a restricted space or so as to be uncomfortable: *the girl was sandwiched between two burly men in the back of the car*.
– PHRASES **the meat** (or **filling**) **in the sandwich** a person who is awkwardly caught between two opposing factions. **a sandwich** (or **two sandwiches**) **short of a picnic** see **SHORT**.
– ORIGIN mid 18th cent.: named after the 4th Earl of Sandwich (1718–92), an English nobleman said to have eaten food in this form so as not to leave the gaming table.

sandwich board ▶ noun a pair of advertisement boards connected by straps by which they are hung over a person's shoulders.

sandwich course ▶ noun Brit. a training course with alternate periods of formal instruction and practical experience.

sandwich generation ▶ noun chiefly US a generation of people, typically in their thirties or forties, responsible for bringing up their own children and for the care of their ageing parents.

Sandwich Islands former name for **HAWAII**.

sandwich tern ▶ noun a large crested tern found in both Europe and North and South America.
● *Thalasseus sandvicensis*, family Sternidae (or Laridae).
– ORIGIN late 18th cent.: named after *Sandwich*, a town in Kent.

sandwort ▶ noun a widely distributed low-growing plant of the pink family, typically having small white flowers and growing in dry sandy ground.
● *Arenaria* and other genera, family Caryophyllaceae.

sandy ▶ adjective (**sandier, sandiest**) **1** covered in or consisting mostly of sand: *pine woods and a fine sandy beach*.
2 (especially of hair) light yellowish brown.
– DERIVATIVES **sandiness** noun, **sandyish** adjective.
– ORIGIN Old English *sandig* (see **SAND, -Y¹**).

sand yacht ▶ noun a wind-driven three-wheeled vehicle with a sail, used for racing on beaches.

sandy blight ▶ noun [mass noun] Austral. an infection of the eyes, either conjunctivitis or trachoma, in which irritation is caused by granular inflammation of the eyelids.

sandy dog ▶ noun another term for **DOGFISH** (in sense 1).

sane ▶ adjective (of a person) of sound mind; not mad or mentally ill: *hard work kept me sane*.
■ (of an undertaking or manner) reasonable; sensible.
– DERIVATIVES **sanely** adverb, **saneness** noun.
– ORIGIN early 17th cent.: from Latin *sanus* 'healthy'.

Sanfilippo's syndrome /ˌsanfɪˈliːpəʊ/ ▶ noun [mass noun] Medicine a defect in metabolism similar to Hurler's syndrome.
– ORIGIN 1960s: named after Sylvester J. *Sanfilippo*, 20th-cent. American physician.

Sanforized /ˈsanfərʌɪzd/ (also **-ised**) ▶ adjective trademark (of cotton or other fabrics) pre-shrunk by a controlled compressive process; meeting certain standards of washing shrinkage.
– ORIGIN 1930s: from the name of *Sanford* L. Cluett (1874–1968), the American inventor of the process.

San Francisco /ˌsan franˈsɪskəʊ/ a city and seaport on the coast of California, situated on a peninsula between the Pacific and San Francisco Bay; pop. 723,960 (1990). The city suffered severe damage from an earthquake in 1906, and has been frequently shaken by less severe earthquakes since.
– DERIVATIVES **San Franciscan** noun & adjective.

sang past of **SING**.

sangam /ˈsʌŋɡʌm/ ▶ noun Indian a confluence of rivers, especially that of the Ganges and Jumna at Allahabad.
– ORIGIN from Sanskrit *saṃgama*.

sangar /ˈsaŋɡə/ (also **sanga**) ▶ noun a small protected structure used for observing or firing from, which is built up from the ground.
– ORIGIN mid 19th cent.: from Pashto, probably from Persian *sang* 'stone'.

sangaree /ˌsaŋɡəˈriː/ ▶ noun [mass noun] a cold drink of wine mixed with water and spices.
– ORIGIN from Spanish *sangría* (see **SANGRIA**).

sang-de-boeuf /ˌsɒ̃dəˈbəːf/ ▶ noun [mass noun] a deep red colour, typically found on old Chinese porcelain.
– ORIGIN French, literally 'ox blood'.

Sanger¹ /ˈsaŋə/, Frederick (b.1918), English biochemist. He determined the complete amino-acid sequence of insulin in 1955, and established the complete nucleotide sequence of a viral DNA in 1977. Nobel Prize for Chemistry (1958 and 1980).

Sanger² /ˈsaŋə/, Margaret (Higgins) (1883–1966), American birth-control campaigner. Her experiences as a nurse prompted her to distribute the pamphlet *Family Limitation* in 1914 and to found the first American birth-control clinic in 1916.

sangfroid /sɒ̃ˈfrwɑː/ ▶ noun [mass noun] composure or coolness as shown in danger or under trying circumstances.
– ORIGIN mid 18th cent.: from French *sang-froid*, literally 'cold blood'.

sangha /ˈsʌŋɡə/ ▶ noun the Buddhist monastic order, including monks, nuns, and novices.
– ORIGIN from Sanskrit *saṃgha* 'community'.

Sangiovese /ˌsandʒɪə(ʊ)ˈveɪzi/ ▶ noun [mass noun] a variety of black wine grape used in making Chianti and other Italian red wines.
■ a red wine made from this grape.
– ORIGIN Italian.

Sango /ˈsaŋɡəʊ/ ▶ noun [mass noun] a dialect of Ngbandi.
■ a lingua franca developed from this and related dialects, one of the national languages of the Central African Republic.
▶ adjective of or relating to this language.
– ORIGIN the name in Ngbandi.

sangoma /saŋˈɡɔːmə/ ▶ noun (in southern Africa) a traditional healer or diviner; a witch doctor.
– ORIGIN from Zulu *isangoma*.

sangrail /saŋˈɡreɪl/ (also **sangreal**) ▶ noun another term for **GRAIL**.
– ORIGIN late Middle English: from Old French *saint graal* 'Holy Grail'.

sangria /saŋˈɡriːə/ ▶ noun [mass noun] a Spanish drink of red wine mixed with lemonade, fruit, and spices.
– ORIGIN Spanish, literally 'bleeding'; compare with **SANGAREE**.

sanguinary /ˈsangwɪn(ə)ri/ ▶ adjective chiefly archaic involving or causing much bloodshed.
– ORIGIN Middle English (in the sense 'relating to blood'): from Latin *sanguinarius*, from *sanguis*, *sanguin-* 'blood'.

sanguine /ˈsangwɪn/ ▶ adjective **1** cheerfully optimistic: *they are not sanguine about the prospect.*
 ■ (in medieval science and medicine) of or having the constitution associated with the predominance of blood among the bodily humours, supposedly marked by a ruddy complexion and an optimistic disposition. ■ archaic (of the complexion) florid; ruddy. ■ archaic bloody or bloodthirsty.
 2 poetic/literary & Heraldry blood-red.
▶ noun [mass noun] a blood-red colour.
 ■ a deep red-brown crayon or pencil containing iron oxide. ■ Heraldry a blood-red stain used in blazoning.
– DERIVATIVES **sanguinely** adverb, **sanguineness** noun.
– ORIGIN Middle English: from Old French *sanguin(e)* 'blood red', from Latin *sanguineus* 'of blood', from *sanguis*, *sanguin-* 'blood'.

Sanhedrin /ˈsanɪdrɪn, sanˈhiːdrɪn, sanˈhɛdrɪn/ (also **Sanhedrim** /-rɪm/) the highest court of justice and the supreme council in ancient Jerusalem.
– ORIGIN from late Hebrew *sanhedrīn*, from Greek *sunedrion* 'council', from *sun-* 'with'+ *hedra* 'seat'.

sanicle /ˈsanɪk(ə)l/ ▶ noun a plant of the parsley family which has burr-like fruit.
 ● Genus *Sanicula*, family Umbelliferae: several species, in particular the Eurasian **wood sanicle** (*S. europaea*).
– ORIGIN late Middle English: via Old French from medieval Latin *sanicula*, perhaps from Latin *sanus* 'healthy'.

sanidine /ˈsanɪdiːn/ ▶ noun [mass noun] a glassy mineral of the alkali feldspar group, typically occurring as tabular crystals.
– ORIGIN early 19th cent.: from Greek *sanis*, *sanid-* 'board' + -INE⁴.

sanitarian ▶ noun chiefly archaic an official responsible for public health or a person in favour of public health reform.
– ORIGIN mid 19th cent.: from SANITARY + -IAN.

sanitarium /sanɪˈtɛːrɪəm/ ▶ noun (pl. **sanitariums** or **sanitaria** /-rɪə/) North American term for SANATORIUM.
– ORIGIN mid 19th cent.: pseudo-Latin, from Latin *sanitas* 'health'.

sanitary ▶ adjective of or relating to the conditions that affect hygiene and health, especially the supply of sewage facilities and clean drinking water: *a sanitary engineer.*
 ■ hygienic and clean: *the most convenient and sanitary way to get rid of food waste from your kitchen.*
– DERIVATIVES **sanitarily** adverb, **sanitariness** noun.
– ORIGIN mid 19th cent.: from French *sanitaire*, from Latin *sanitas* 'health', from *sanus* 'healthy'.

sanitary napkin ▶ noun see NAPKIN (sense 3).

sanitary protection ▶ noun [mass noun] sanitary towels and tampons, considered collectively.

sanitary towel (N. Amer. **sanitary napkin**) ▶ noun an absorbent pad worn by women to absorb menstrual blood.

sanitaryware ▶ noun [mass noun] toilet bowls, cisterns, and other fittings.

sanitation ▶ noun [mass noun] conditions relating to public health, especially the provision of clean drinking water and adequate sewage disposal.
– ORIGIN mid 19th cent.: formed irregularly from SANITARY.

sanitize (also **-ise**) ▶ verb [with obj.] make clean and hygienic: *new chemicals for sanitizing a pool.*
 ■ (usu. **be sanitized**) derogatory alter (something regarded as less acceptable) so as to make it more palatable: *old-established inns that have somehow avoided being bought over and sanitized by the big chains.*
– DERIVATIVES **sanitization** noun, **sanitizer** noun.

sanity ▶ noun [mass noun] the ability to think and behave in a normal and rational manner; sound mental health: *I began to doubt my own sanity.*
 ■ reasonable and rational behaviour.
– ORIGIN late Middle English (in the sense 'health'): from Latin *sanitas* 'health', from *sanus* 'healthy'. Current senses date from the early 17th cent.

sanjak /ˈsandʒak/ ▶ noun (in the Ottoman Empire) one of the several administrative districts into which a vilayet was divided.
– ORIGIN from Turkish *sancak*, literally 'banner'.

San Joaquin Valley fever /ˌsan wɑːˈkiːn/ ▶ noun North American term for COCCIDIOIDOMYCOSIS.

San Jose /həʊˈzeɪ/ a city in western California, situated to the south of San Francisco Bay; pop. 782,250 (1990).

San José /həʊˈzeɪ/ the capital and chief port of Costa Rica; pop. 318,765 (est. 1995).

San Juan /ˈhwɑːn/ the capital and chief port of Puerto Rico, on the north coast of the island; pop. 437,745 (1990).

sank past of SINK¹.

San Luis Potosí /san luːˌiːs ˌpɒtəʊˈsiː/ a state of central Mexico.
 ■ its capital; pop. 525,820 (1990).

San Marino /məˈriːnəʊ/ a republic forming a small enclave in Italy, near Rimini; pop. 22,680 (est. 1991); official language, Italian; capital, the town of San Marino. It is perhaps Europe's oldest state, claiming to have been independent almost continuously since its foundation in the 4th century.
– ORIGIN said to be named after *Marino*, a Dalmatian stonecutter who fled there to escape the persecution of Christians under Diocletian.

San Martín /mɑːˈtiːn/, José de (1778–1850), Argentinian soldier and statesman. Having assisted in the liberation of his country from Spanish rule (1812–13), he went on to aid in the liberation of Chile (1817–18) and Peru (1820–4).

sannyasi /sənˈjɑːsi/ (also **sanyasi** or **sannyasin**) ▶ noun (pl. same) a Hindu religious mendicant.
– ORIGIN based on Sanskrit *saṃnyāsin* 'laying aside, ascetic, from *saṃ* 'together' + *ni* 'down' + *as* 'throw'.

San Pedro Sula /ˌpɛdrəʊ ˈsuːlə/ a city in northern Honduras, near the Caribbean coast; pop. 325,900 (est. 1991).

sanpro ▶ noun short for SANITARY PROTECTION, especially in commercial language.

sans /sanz/ ▶ preposition poetic/literary or humorous without: *a picture of Maughan sans specs.*
– ORIGIN Middle English: from Old French *sanz*, from a variant of Latin *sine* 'without', influenced by Latin *absentia* 'in the absence of'.

sansa /ˈsansə/ ▶ noun another term for THUMB PIANO.
– ORIGIN based on Arabic *ṣanj* 'cymbal'.

San Salvador /ˈsalvədɔː, Spanish salβaˈðor/ the capital of El Salvador; pop. 1,522,120 (1992).

sans-culotte /ˌsan(z)kjʊˈlɒt, French sɑ̃kylɔt/ ▶ noun a lower-class Parisian republican in the French Revolution.
 ■ an extreme republican or revolutionary.
– DERIVATIVES **sans-culottism** noun.
– ORIGIN French, literally 'without knee breeches'.

San Sebastián /sɪˈbastɪən, Spanish seβasˈtjan/ a port and resort in northern Spain, situated on the Bay of Biscay close to the border with France; pop. 174,220 (1991).

sansei /ˈsanseɪ/ ▶ noun (pl. same) N. Amer. an American or Canadian whose grandparents were immigrants from Japan. Compare with NISEI and ISSEI.
– ORIGIN 1940s: Japanese, from *san* 'third' + *sei* 'generation'.

sansevieria /ˌsansɪˈvɪərɪə/ (also **sanseveria**) ▶ noun a plant of the genus *Sansevieria* in the agave family, especially (in gardening) mother-in-law's tongue.
– ORIGIN modern Latin, named after Raimondo di Sangro (1710–71), Prince of *Sanseviero* (now Sansevero), Italy.

Sanskrit /ˈsanskrɪt/ ▶ noun [mass noun] an ancient Indo-European language of India, in which the Hindu scriptures and classical Indian epic poems are written and from which many northern Indian (Indic) languages are derived.
▶ adjective of or relating to this language.

Sanskrit was spoken in India roughly 1200–400 BC, and continues in use as a language of religion and scholarship. It is written from left to right in the Devanagari script. The suggestion by Sir William Jones (1746–94) of its common origin with Latin and Greek was a major advance in the development of historical linguistics.

– DERIVATIVES **Sanskritic** adjective, **Sanskritist** noun.
– ORIGIN from Sanskrit *saṃskṛta* 'composed, elaborated', from *saṃ* 'together' + *kṛ* 'make' + past participle ending *-ta*.

Sansovino /ˌsansəˈviːnəʊ/, Jacopo Tatti (1486–1570), Italian sculptor and architect. He was city architect of Venice, where his buildings, including the

Palazzo Corner (1533) and St Mark's Library (begun 1536), show the development of classical architectural style for contemporary use.

sans serif /san ˈsɛrɪf/ (also **sanserif**) Printing ▶ noun [mass noun] a style of type without serifs.
▶ adjective without serifs.
– ORIGIN mid 19th cent.: apparently from French *sans* 'without' + SERIF.

sant /sʌnt/ ▶ noun Hinduism & Sikhism a saint.
– ORIGIN from Hindi *santah* 'venerable men'.

Santa Ana /ˌsantə ˈanə/ **1** a city in El Salvador, situated close to the border with Guatemala; pop. 202,340 (1992).
 2 a volcano in El Salvador, situated south-west of the city of Santa Ana. It rises to a height of 2,381 m (7,730 ft).
 3 a city in southern California, south-east of Los Angeles; pop. 293,740 (1990).

Santa Barbara a resort city in California, on the Pacific coast north-west of Los Angeles; pop. 85,570 (1990).

Santa Catarina /ˌkatəˈriːnə/ a state of southern Brazil, on the Atlantic coast; capital, Florianópolis.

Santa Claus (also informal **Santa**) another term for FATHER CHRISTMAS.
– ORIGIN originally a US usage, alteration of Dutch dialect *Sante Klaas* 'St Nicholas'.

Santa Cruz /kruːz, Spanish kruθ, krus/ **1** a city in the central region of Bolivia; pop. 694,610 (1992).
 2 a port and the chief city of the island of Tenerife, in the Canary Islands; pop. 191,970 (1991). Full name SANTA CRUZ DE TENERIFE.

Santa Fe /ˈfeɪ/ (also **Santa Fé**) **1** the state capital of New Mexico; pop. 55,860 (1990).
 2 a city in northern Argentina, on the Salado River near its confluence with the Paraná; pop. 395,000 (1991).

Santa Fé de Bogotá /ˌsantə feɪ deɪ bɒgəˈtɑː/ official name for BOGOTÁ.

Santali /sanˈtɑːli/ ▶ noun **1** (pl. same or **Santalis**) a member of an indigenous people of the NE of the Indian subcontinent.
 2 [mass noun] the Munda language of this people, with over 3 million speakers.
▶ adjective of or relating to this people or their language.

Santa Monica a resort city on the coast of SW California, situated on the west side of the Los Angeles conurbation; pop. 86,905 (1990).

Santander /ˌsantanˈdɛː/ a port in northern Spain, on the Bay of Biscay, capital of Cantabria; pop. 194,220 (1991).

Santa Sophia another name for ST SOPHIA.

Santayana /ˌsantɪˈjɑːnə/, George (1863–1952), Spanish philosopher and writer; born *Jorge Augustin Nicolás Ruiz de Santayana*. His works include *The Realms of Being* (1924), poetry, and the novel *The Last Puritan* (1935).

santeria /ˌsantɛˈriːə/ ▶ noun [mass noun] a pantheistic Afro-Cuban religious cult developed from the beliefs and customs of the Yoruba people and incorporating some elements of the Catholic religion.
– ORIGIN Spanish, literally 'holiness'.

santero /sanˈtɛːrəʊ/ ▶ noun (pl. **-os**) **1** (in Mexico and Spanish-speaking areas of the south-western US) a person who makes religious images.
 2 a priest of the santeria religious cult.
– ORIGIN Spanish.

Santiago /ˌsantɪˈɑːɡəʊ/ the capital of Chile, situated to the west of the Andes in the central part of the country; pop. 5,180,750 (1992).

Santiago de Compostela /deɪ ˌkɒmpɒˈstɛlə/ a city in NW Spain, capital in Galicia; pop. 105,530 (1991). The remains of St James the Great are said to have been brought there after his death; it is an important place of pilgrimage.

Santiago de Cuba /ˈkjuːbə/ a port on the coast of SE Cuba, the second largest city on the island; pop. 432,900 (est. 1992).

santim /ˈsantiːm/ ▶ noun a monetary unit of Latvia, equal to one hundredth of a lat.
– ORIGIN from Latvian *santims*, from French *centime* + the Latvian masculine ending *-s*.

santo /ˈsantəʊ/ ▶ noun (pl. **-os**) (in Mexico and Spanish-speaking areas of the south-western US) a

religious symbol, especially a wooden representation of a saint.
– ORIGIN Spanish or Italian.

Santo Domingo /ˌsantəʊ dəˈmɪŋɡəʊ/ the capital of the Dominican Republic, a port on the south coast; pop. 2,055,000 (est. 1991). From 1936 to 1961 it was called Ciudad Trujillo.

santolina /ˌsantəˈliːnə/ ▸ noun a plant of the genus *Santolina* in the daisy family, especially (in gardening) cotton lavender.
– ORIGIN modern Latin, perhaps an alteration of **SANTONICA**.

santon /ˈsantɒn/ ▸ noun (chiefly in Provence) a figurine adorning a representation of the manger in which Jesus was laid.
– ORIGIN French, from Spanish, from *santo* 'saint'.

santonica /sanˈtɒnɪkə/ ▸ noun [mass noun] the dried flower heads of a wormwood plant, containing the drug santonin.
● The plant is *Artemisia cina* (family Compositae) of Turkestan.
– ORIGIN mid 17th cent.: from Latin *Santonica (herba)* '(plant) of the Santoni', referring to a tribe of Aquitania (now **AQUITAINE**[1]).

santonin /ˈsantənɪn/ ▸ noun [mass noun] Chemistry a toxic crystalline compound present in santonica and related plants, used as an anthelmintic.
● Chem. formula: $C_{15}H_{18}O_3$.
– ORIGIN mid 19th cent.: from **SANTONICA** + **-IN**[1].

santoor /sʌnˈtʊə/ ▸ noun an Indian musical instrument like a dulcimer, played by striking with a pair of small, spoon-shaped wooden hammers.
– ORIGIN from Arabic *santīr*, alteration of Greek *psaltērion* 'psaltery'.

Santorini /ˌsantəˈriːni/ another name for **THERA**.

Santos /ˈsantɒs/ a port on the coast of Brazil, situated just south-east of São Paulo; pop. 428,920 (1991).

sanyasi ▸ noun variant spelling of **SANNYASI**.

São Francisco /ˌsaʊ franˈsɪskuː/ a river of eastern Brazil. It rises in Minas Gerais and flows for 3,200 km (1,990 miles) northwards then eastwards, meeting the Atlantic to the north of Aracajú.

São Luís /luːˈiːs/ a port in NE Brazil, on the Atlantic coast, capital of the state of Maranhão; pop. 695,000 (1990).

Saône /səʊn/ a river of eastern France, which rises in the Vosges mountains and flows 480 km (298 miles) south-west to join the Rhône at Lyons.

São Paulo /ˈpaʊluː/ a state of southern Brazil, on the Atlantic coast.
■ its capital city; pop. 9,700,110 (1990).

São Tomé and Príncipe /tɒˈmeɪ, ˈprɪnsɪpeɪ/ a country consisting of two main islands and several smaller ones in the Gulf of Guinea; pop. 120,000 (est. 1991); languages, Portuguese (official), Portuguese Creole; capital, São Tomé. The islands were settled by Portugal from 1493 and became an overseas province of that country. São Tomé and Príncipe became independent in 1975.

São Vincente /ˌsaʊ vɪnˈsent/ Portuguese name for Cape St Vincent (see **ST VINCENT, CAPE**).

sap[1] ▸ noun [mass noun] the fluid, chiefly water with dissolved sugars and mineral salts, which circulates in the vascular system of a plant.
■ figurative vigour or energy, especially sexual vitality: *the hot, heady days of youth when the sap was rising.*
▸ verb (**sapped, sapping**) [with obj.] gradually weaken or destroy (a person's strength or power): *our energy is being sapped by bureaucrats and politicians.*
■ (**sap someone of**) drain someone of (strength or power): *her illness had sapped her of energy and life.*
– DERIVATIVES **sapless** adjective.
– ORIGIN Old English *sæp*, probably of Germanic origin. The verb (dating from the mid 18th cent.) is often interpreted as a figurative use of the notion 'drain the sap from', but is derived originally from the verb **SAP**[2], in the sense 'undermine'.

sap[2] ▸ noun historical a tunnel or trench to conceal an assailant's approach to a fortified place.
▸ verb (**sapped, sapping**) [no obj.] historical dig a sap or saps.
■ [with obj.] archaic make insecure by removing the foundations of: *a crazy building, sapped and undermined by the rats.* ■ [with obj.] [often as noun **sapping**] Geography undercut by water or glacial action.
– ORIGIN late 16th cent. (as a verb in the sense 'dig a sap or covered trench'): from French *saper*, from Italian *zappare*, from *zappa* 'spade, spadework',

probably from Arabic *sarab* 'underground passage', or *sabora* 'probe a wound, explore'.

sap[3] ▸ noun informal, chiefly N. Amer. a foolish and gullible person: *He fell for it! What a sap!*
– ORIGIN early 19th cent.: abbreviation of dialect *sapskull* 'person with a head like sapwood', from **SAP**[1] (in the sense 'sapwood') + **SKULL**.

sap[4] N. Amer. informal ▸ noun a bludgeon or club.
▸ verb (**sapped, sapping**) [with obj.] hit with a bludgeon or club.
– ORIGIN late 19th cent. (as a noun): abbreviation of **SAPLING** (from which such a club was originally made).

sapele /səˈpiːli/ ▸ noun a large tropical African hardwood tree, with reddish-brown timber that resembles mahogany.
● Genus *Entandrophragma*, family Meliaceae.
– ORIGIN early 20th cent.: from the name of a port on the Benin River, Nigeria.

sap green ▸ noun [mass noun] a vivid yellowish-green pigment made from buckthorn berries.

saphenous /səˈfiːnəs/ ▸ adjective [attrib.] Anatomy relating to or denoting either of the two large superficial veins in the leg.
– ORIGIN mid 19th cent.: from medieval Latin *saphena* 'vein' + **-OUS**.

sapid /ˈsapɪd/ ▸ adjective chiefly N. Amer. having a strong, pleasant taste.
■ (of talk or writing) pleasant or interesting.
– DERIVATIVES **sapidity** /səˈpɪdɪti/ noun.
– ORIGIN early 17th cent.: from Latin *sapidus*, from *sapere* 'to taste'.

sapient /ˈseɪpɪənt/ ▸ adjective 1 formal wise, or attempting to appear wise.
■ (chiefly in science fiction) intelligent: *sapient life forms.*
2 of or relating to the human species (*Homo sapiens*): *our sapient ancestors of 40,000 years ago.*
▸ noun a human of the species *Homo sapiens*.
– DERIVATIVES **sapience** noun, **sapiently** adverb.
– ORIGIN late Middle English: from Old French, or from Latin *sapient-* 'being wise', from the verb *sapere*.

sapiential ▸ adjective poetic/literary of or relating to wisdom.
– ORIGIN late 15th cent.: from Old French, or from ecclesiastical Latin *sapientialis*, from Latin *sapientia* 'wisdom'.

Sapir /səˈpɪə/, Edward (1884–1939), German-born American linguistics scholar and anthropologist. One of the founders of American structural linguistics, he carried out important research on American Indian languages and linguistic theory.

Sapir–Whorf hypothesis /ˈwɔːf/ Linguistics a hypothesis, first advanced by Edward Sapir in 1929 and subsequently developed by Benjamin Whorf, that the structure of a language determines a native speaker's perception and categorization of experience.

sapling ▸ noun 1 a young tree, especially one with a slender trunk.
■ poetic/literary a young and slender or inexperienced person.
2 a greyhound in its first year.
– ORIGIN Middle English: from the noun **SAP**[1] + **-LING**.

sapodilla /ˌsapəˈdɪlə/ ▸ noun a large evergreen tropical American tree which has edible fruit and hard durable wood and yields chicle.
● *Manilkara zapota*, family Sapotaceae.
■ (also **sapodilla plum**) the sweet brownish bristly fruit of this tree.
– ORIGIN late 17th cent.: from Spanish *zapotillo*, diminutive of *zapote*, from Nahuatl *tzápotl*.

saponaceous /ˌsapəˈneɪʃəs/ ▸ adjective of, like, or containing soap; soapy.
– ORIGIN early 18th cent.: from modern Latin *saponaceus* (from Latin *sapo, sapon-* 'soap') + **-OUS**.

saponify /səˈpɒnɪfʌɪ/ ▸ verb (**-ies, -ied**) [with obj.] Chemistry turn (fat or oil) into soap by reaction with an alkali: [as adj. **saponified**] *saponified vegetable oils.*
■ convert (any ester) into an alcohol and a metal salt by alkaline hydrolysis.
– DERIVATIVES **saponifiable** adjective, **saponification** noun.
– ORIGIN early 19th cent.: from French *saponifier*, from Latin *sapo, sapon-* 'soap'.

saponin /ˈsapənɪn/ ▸ noun [mass noun] Chemistry a toxic compound which is present in soapwort and makes foam when shaken with water.
■ [count noun] any of the class of steroid and terpenoid glycosides typified by this, examples of which are used in detergents and foam fire extinguishers.
– ORIGIN mid 19th cent.: from French *saponine*, from Latin *sapo, sapon-* 'soap'.

sapper ▸ noun a military engineer who lays or detects and disarms mines.
■ Brit. a member of the Corps of Royal Engineers (especially as the official term for a private).
– ORIGIN early 17th cent.: from the verb **SAP**[2] + **-ER**[1].

sapphic /ˈsafɪk/ ▸ adjective 1 formal or humorous of or relating to lesbians or lesbianism: *sapphic lovers.*
2 (**Sapphic**) of or relating to Sappho or her poetry.
▸ plural noun (**sapphics**) verse in a metre associated with Sappho.
– ORIGIN early 16th cent. (in sense 2): from French *saphique*, via Latin from Greek *Sapphikos*, from *Sapphō* (see **SAPPHO**).

sapphire /ˈsafʌɪə/ ▸ noun 1 a transparent precious stone, typically blue, which is a variety of corundum (aluminium oxide): [as modifier] *a sapphire ring.*
■ [mass noun] a bright blue colour.
2 a small hummingbird with shining blue or violet colours in its plumage and a short tail.
● *Hylocharis* and other genera, family Trochilidae: several species.
– DERIVATIVES **sapphirine** /ˈsafɪrʌɪn/ adjective.
– ORIGIN Middle English: from Old French *safir*, via Latin from Greek *sappheiros*, probably denoting lapis lazuli.

sapphism /ˈsafɪz(ə)m/ ▸ noun [mass noun] formal or humorous lesbianism.
– ORIGIN late 19th cent.: from **SAPPHO** + **-ISM**.

Sappho /ˈsafəʊ/ (early 7th century BC), Greek lyric poet who lived on Lesbos. Many of her poems express her affection and love for women, and have given rise to her association with female homosexuality.

Sapporo /səˈpɒːrəʊ/ a city in northern Japan, capital of the island of Hokkaido; pop. 1,672,000 (1990).

sappy ▸ adjective (**sappier, sappiest**) 1 informal, chiefly N. Amer. over-sentimental; mawkish.
2 (of a plant) containing a lot of sap.
– DERIVATIVES **sappily** adverb, **sappiness** noun.

sapro- ▸ combining form Biology relating to putrefaction or decay: *saprogenic.*
– ORIGIN from Greek *sapros* 'putrid'.

saprogenic /ˌsaprə(ʊ)ˈdʒɛnɪk/ ▸ adjective Biology causing or produced by putrefaction or decay.

saprolegnia /ˌsaprə(ʊ)ˈlɛɡnɪə/ ▸ noun [mass noun] an aquatic fungus which can attack the bodies of fish and other aquatic animals.
● Genus *Saprolegnia*, subdivision Mastigomycotina.
– ORIGIN modern Latin, from **SAPRO-** 'of decay' + Greek *legnon* 'border'.

saprophagous /saˈprɒfəɡəs/ ▸ adjective Biology (of an organism) feeding on or obtaining nourishment from decaying organic matter.
– DERIVATIVES **saprophage** noun, **saprophagy** noun.

saprophyte /ˈsaprə(ʊ)fʌɪt/ ▸ noun Biology a plant, fungus, or micro-organism that lives on dead or decaying organic matter.
– DERIVATIVES **saprophytic** adjective, **saprophytically** adverb.

saprotroph /ˈsaprə(ʊ)trəʊf, -ˈtrɒf/ ▸ noun Biology an organism that feeds on or derives nourishment from decaying organic matter.
– DERIVATIVES **saprotrophic** adjective.
– ORIGIN back-formation from *saprotrophic*.

sapsucker ▸ noun an American woodpecker that pecks rows of small holes in trees and visits them for sap and insects.
● *Sphyrapicus*, family Picidae: four species.

sapwood ▸ noun [mass noun] the soft outer layers of recently formed wood between the heartwood and the bark, containing the functioning vascular tissue.

Saqqara /səˈkɑːrə/ a vast necropolis at the ancient Egyptian city of Memphis, with monuments dating from the 3rd millennium BC to the Graeco-Roman age, notably a step pyramid which is the first known building made entirely of stone (*c.*2650 BC).

SAR ▸ abbreviation for search and rescue, an emergency service involving the detection and rescue of those who have met with an accident or mishap in dangerous or isolated locations.

saraband /ˈsarəband/ (also **sarabande**) ▶ noun a slow, stately Spanish dance in triple time.
■ a piece of music written for such a dance.
– ORIGIN early 17th cent.: from French *sarabande*, from Spanish and Italian *zarabanda*.

Saracen /ˈsarəs(ə)n/ ▶ noun an Arab or Muslim, especially at the time of the Crusades.
■ a nomad of the Syrian and Arabian desert at the time of the Roman Empire.
– DERIVATIVES **Saracenic** adjective.
– ORIGIN Middle English, from Old French *sarrazin*, via late Latin from late Greek *Sarakēnos*, perhaps from Arabic *šarḳī* 'eastern'.

Saracen's head ▶ noun a conventionalized depiction of the head of a Saracen as a heraldic charge or inn sign.

Saragossa /ˌsarəˈɡɒsə/ a city in northern Spain, capital of Aragon, situated on the River Ebro; pop. 614,400 (1991). Spanish name **ZARAGOZA**.
– ORIGIN alteration of *Caesaraugusta*, the name given to the ancient settlement on the site, taken by the Romans in the 1st cent. BC.

Sarah (in the Bible) the wife of Abraham and mother of Isaac (Gen. 17:15 ff.).

Sarajevo /ˌsarəˈjeɪvəʊ/ the capital of Bosnia–Herzegovina; pop. 200,000 (est. 1993).

> Taken by the Austro-Hungarians in 1878, it became a centre of Slav opposition to Austrian rule. It was the scene in June 1914 of the assassination by a Bosnian Serb named Gavrilo Princip of Archduke Franz Ferdinand (1863–1914), the heir to the Austrian throne, an event which triggered the outbreak of the First World War. The city suffered severely from the ethnic conflicts following the break-up of Yugoslavia in 1991, and was besieged by Bosnian Serb forces in the surrounding mountains from 1992 to 1994.

Saran /səˈran/ (also **Saran Wrap**) ▶ noun N. Amer. trademark for **POLYVINYL CHLORIDE**, especially as cling film.
– ORIGIN 1940s: of unknown origin.

sarangi /səˈraŋɡi, saːˈrʌŋɡi/ ▶ noun (pl. **sarangis**) an Indian bowed musical instrument about two feet high, with three or four main strings and up to thirty-five sympathetic strings.
– ORIGIN from Hindi *sāraṅgī*.

Saransk /səˈransk/ a city in European Russia, capital of the autonomous republic of Mordvinia, situated to the south of Nizhni Novgorod; pop. 316,000 (1990).

sarape /sɛˈrɑːpeɪ/ ▶ noun variant spelling of **SERAPE**.

Saratoga, Battle of /ˌsarəˈtəʊɡə/ either of two battles fought in 1777 during the War of American Independence, near the modern city of Saratoga Springs in New York State. The British defeats are conventionally regarded as the turning point in the war in favour of the American side.

Saratov /səˈrɑːtɒf/ a city in SW central Russia, situated on the River Volga north of Volgograd; pop. 909,000 (1990).

Sarawak /səˈrɑːwək/ a state of Malaysia, comprising the north-western part of Borneo; capital, Kuching.

sarcasm ▶ noun [mass noun] the use of irony to mock or convey contempt: *she didn't like the note of sarcasm in his voice.*
– ORIGIN mid 16th cent.: from French *sarcasme*, or via late Latin from late Greek *sarkasmos*, from Greek *sarkazein* 'tear flesh', in late Greek 'gnash the teeth, speak bitterly' (from *sarx, sark-* 'flesh').

sarcastic ▶ adjective marked by or given to using irony in order to mock or convey contempt: *making sarcastic comments | I think they're being sarcastic.*
– DERIVATIVES **sarcastically** adverb.
– ORIGIN late 17th cent.: from French *sarcastique*, from *sarcasme* (see **SARCASM**), on the pattern of pairs such as *enthousiasme, enthousiastique*.

sarcenet ▶ noun variant spelling of **SARSENET**.

sarcococca /ˌsaːkəˈkɒksə/ ▶ noun a small East Asian winter-flowering shrub of the box family, with white or pink flowers and black or red berries.
● Genus *Sarcococca*, family Buxaceae.
– ORIGIN modern Latin, from Greek *sarx, sarc-* 'flesh' + *kokkos* 'berry'.

sarcoid /ˈsaːkɔɪd/ Medicine ▶ adjective [attrib.] relating to, denoting, or suffering from sarcoidosis.
▶ noun a granuloma of the type present in sarcoidosis.

■ [mass noun] the condition and symptoms of sarcoidosis: *tissues affected by sarcoid.*
– ORIGIN mid 19th cent. (in the sense 'resembling flesh'): from Greek *sarx, sark-* 'flesh' + **-OID**.

sarcoidosis /ˌsaːkɔɪˈdəʊsɪs/ ▶ noun [mass noun] a chronic disease of unknown cause characterized by the enlargement of lymph nodes in many parts of the body and the widespread appearance of granulomas derived from the reticuloendothelial system.

sarcolemma /ˌsaːkəʊˈlɛmə/ ▶ noun Physiology the fine transparent tubular sheath which envelops the fibres of skeletal muscles.
– DERIVATIVES **sarcolemmal** adjective.
– ORIGIN mid 19th cent.: from Greek *sarx, sark-* 'flesh' + *lemma* 'husk'.

sarcoma /saːˈkəʊmə/ ▶ noun (pl. **sarcomas** or **sarcomata** /-mətə/) Medicine a malignant tumour of connective or other non-epithelial tissue.
– DERIVATIVES **sarcomatosis** noun, **sarcomatous** adjective.
– ORIGIN early 19th cent.: modern Latin, from Greek *sarkōma*, from *sarkoun* 'become fleshy', from *sarx, sark-* 'flesh'.

sarcomere /ˈsaːkə(ʊ)mɪə/ ▶ noun Anatomy a structural unit of a myofibril in striated muscle, consisting of a dark band and the nearer half of each adjacent pale band.
– ORIGIN late 19th cent.: from Greek *sarx, sark-* 'flesh' + *meros* 'part'.

sarcophagus /saːˈkɒfəɡəs/ ▶ noun (pl. **sarcophagi** /-ɡʌɪ, -dʒʌɪ/) a stone coffin, typically adorned with a sculpture or inscription and associated with the ancient civilizations of Egypt, Rome, and Greece.
– ORIGIN late Middle English: via Latin from Greek *sarkophagos* 'flesh-consuming', from *sarx, sark-* 'flesh' + *-phagos* '-eating'.

sarcoplasm /ˈsaːkə(ʊ)plaz(ə)m/ ▶ noun [mass noun] Physiology the cytoplasm of striated muscle cells.
– DERIVATIVES **sarcoplasmic** adjective.
– ORIGIN late 19th cent.: from Greek *sarx, sark-* 'flesh' + **PLASMA**.

sarcoptic mange /saːˈkɒptɪk/ ▶ noun [mass noun] a form of mange caused by the itch mite and tending to affect chiefly the abdomen and hindquarters. Compare with **DEMODECTIC MANGE**.
– ORIGIN late 19th cent.: *sarcoptic* from the modern Latin genus name *Sarcoptes* (from Greek *sarx, sark-* 'flesh') + **-IC**.

sarcosine /ˈsaːkəsiːn/ ▶ noun [mass noun] Biochemistry a crystalline amino acid which occurs in the body as a product of the metabolism of creatine.
● Alternative name: *N-***methylglycine**; chem. formula: CH_3NHCH_2COOH.
– ORIGIN mid 19th cent.: from Greek *sarx, sark-* 'flesh' + **-INE**[4].

Sard /saːd/ ▶ adjective & noun another term for **SARDINIAN**.

sard /saːd/ ▶ noun [mass noun] a yellow or brownish-red variety of chalcedony.
– ORIGIN late Middle English: from French *sarde* or Latin *sarda*, from Greek *sardios*, probably from *Sardō* 'Sardinia'.

Sardanapalus /ˌsaːdəˈnapələs/ the name given by ancient Greek historians to the last king of Assyria (died before 600 BC), portrayed as being notorious for his wealth and sensuality. It may not represent a specific historical person.

sardar /ˈsədaː/ (also **sirdar**) ▶ noun chiefly Indian **1** a leader (often used as a proper name).
2 a Sikh (often used as a title or form of address).
– ORIGIN from Persian and Urdu *sar-dār*.

Sardegna /sarˈdeɲɲa/ Italian name for **SARDINIA**.

sardelle /saːˈdɛl/ ▶ noun a sardine, anchovy, or other small fish similarly prepared for eating.
– ORIGIN late 16th cent.: from Italian *sardella*, diminutive of *sarda* (see **SARDINE**[1]).

sardine[1] /saːˈdiːn/ ▶ noun **1** a young pilchard or other young or small herring-like fish.
2 (**sardines**) [treated as sing.] Brit. a children's game based on hide-and-seek, in which one child hides and the other children, as they find the hider, join him or her in the hiding place until just one child remains.
▶ verb [with obj.] informal pack closely together.
– PHRASES **packed like sardines** crowded very close together, as sardines are in tins.
– ORIGIN late Middle English: from French, or from

Latin *sardina*, from *sarda*, from Greek, probably from *Sardō* 'Sardinia'.

sardine[2] /saːˈdʌɪn/ ▶ noun another term for **SARDIUS**.
– ORIGIN late Middle English: via late Latin from Greek *sardinos*, variant of *sardios* (see **SARDIUS**).

Sardinia /saːˈdɪnɪə/ a large Italian island in the Mediterranean Sea to the west of Italy; pop. 1,664,370 (1990); capital, Cagliari. In 1720 it was joined with Savoy and Piedmont to form the kingdom of Sardinia; the kingdom formed the nucleus of the Risorgimento, becoming part of a unified Italy under Victor Emmanuel II of Sardinia in 1861. Italian name **SARDEGNA**.

Sardinian ▶ adjective of or relating to Sardinia, its people, or their language.
▶ noun **1** a native or inhabitant of Sardinia.
2 [mass noun] the Romance language of Sardinia, which has several distinct dialects.

Sardis /ˈsaːdɪs/ an ancient city of Asia Minor, the capital of Lydia, whose ruins lie near the west coast of modern Turkey, to the north-east of Izmir.

sardius /ˈsaːdɪəs/ ▶ noun a red precious stone mentioned in the Bible (e.g. Exod. 28:17) and in classical writings, probably ruby or carnelian.
– ORIGIN late Middle English: via late Latin from Greek *sardios*.

sardonic /saːˈdɒnɪk/ ▶ adjective grimly mocking or cynical: *Starkey attempted a sardonic smile.*
– DERIVATIVES **sardonically** adverb, **sardonicism** noun.
– ORIGIN mid 17th cent.: from French *sardonique*, earlier *sardonien*, via Latin from Greek *sardonios* 'of Sardinia', alteration of *sardanios*, used by Homer to describe bitter or scornful laughter.

sardonyx /ˈsaːdənɪks/ ▶ noun [mass noun] onyx in which white layers alternate with sard.
– ORIGIN Middle English: via Latin from Greek *sardonux*, probably from *sardios* 'sardius' + *onux* 'onyx'.

saree ▶ noun variant spelling of **SARI**.

sargasso /saːˈɡasəʊ/ (also **sargasso weed**) ▶ noun another term for **SARGASSUM**.
– ORIGIN late 16th cent.: from Portuguese *sargaço*, of unknown origin.

Sargasso Sea a region of the western Atlantic Ocean between the Azores and the Caribbean, so called because of the prevalence in it of floating sargasso seaweed. It is the breeding place of eels from the rivers of Europe and eastern North America, and is known for its usually calm conditions.

sargassum /saːˈɡasəm/ (also **sargassum weed**) ▶ noun [mass noun] a brown seaweed with berry-like air bladders, typically forming large floating masses.
● Genus *Sargassum*, class Phaeophyceae.
– ORIGIN modern Latin, from Portuguese *sargaço* (see **SARGASSO**).

sargassum fish ▶ noun a small toadfish which occurs worldwide, with a bizarre shape and intricate coloration to camouflage it among the floating sargassum weed that it frequents.
● *Histrio histrio*, family Antennariidae.

sarge ▶ noun informal sergeant.
– ORIGIN mid 19th cent.: abbreviation.

Sargent[1], John Singer (1856–1925), American painter. He is best known for his portraiture in a style noted for its bold brushwork. He was much in demand in Parisian circles, but following a scandal over the supposed eroticism of *Madame Gautreau* (1884) he moved to London.

Sargent[2], Sir (Henry) Malcolm (Watts) (1895–1967), English conductor and composer. In 1921 he made an acclaimed debut conducting his own *Impressions of a Windy Day*. He was responsible for the BBC Promenade Concerts from 1948.

Sargodha /səˈɡəʊdə/ a city in north central Pakistan; pop. 294,000 (1981).

Sargon /ˈsaːɡɒn/ (2334–2279 BC), the semi-legendary founder of the ancient kingdom of Akkad.

Sargon II /ˈsaːɡɒn/ (d.705 BC), king of Assyria 721–705. He was probably a son of Tiglath-pileser III and is famous for his conquest of cities in Syria and Palestine and transportation of many peoples, including Israelites.

sari /'sɑːri/ (also **saree**) ▶ noun (pl. **saris** or **sarees**) a garment consisting of a length of cotton or silk elaborately draped around the body, traditionally worn by women from the Indian subcontinent.
– ORIGIN late 18th cent.: from Hindi *sāṛī*.

sarin /'sɑːrɪn/ ▶ noun [mass noun] an organophosphorus nerve gas, developed in Germany during the Second World War.
– ORIGIN from German *Sarin*, of unknown origin.

Sark one of the Channel Islands, a small island lying to the east of Guernsey.

sark ▶ noun Scottish & N. English a shirt or chemise.
– ORIGIN Old English *serc*, of Germanic origin.

sarkar /sə'kɑː/ ▶ noun Indian a man who is in a position of authority, especially one who owns land worked by tenant farmers (often used as a form of address).
– ORIGIN from Persian and Urdu *sarkār*, from *sar* 'chief' + *kār* agent, doer.

sarking ▶ noun [mass noun] boarding or building felt fixed over the rafters of a roof before the tiles or slates are added.
– ORIGIN late Middle English (originally Scots and northern English): from **SARK** + **-ING**[1].

sarky ▶ adjective (**sarkier**, **sarkiest**) Brit. informal sarcastic.
– DERIVATIVES **sarkily** adverb, **sarkiness** noun.
– ORIGIN early 20th cent.: abbreviation.

Sarmatia /sɑː'meɪʃə/ an ancient region situated to the north of the Black Sea, extending originally from the Urals to the Don and inhabited by Slavic peoples.
– DERIVATIVES **Sarmatian** adjective & noun.

sarmie /'sɑːmi/ ▶ noun S. African informal a sandwich.

sarnie ▶ noun Brit. informal a sandwich.
– ORIGIN 1960s: probably representing a pronunciation of the first element of **SANDWICH**.

sarod /sə'rəʊd/ ▶ noun a lute used in classical North Indian music, with four main strings.
– ORIGIN Urdu, from Persian *surod* 'song, melody'.

sarong /sə'rɒŋ/ ▶ noun a garment consisting of a long piece of cloth worn wrapped round the body and tucked at the waist or under the armpits, traditionally worn in SE Asia and now also by women in the West.
– ORIGIN mid 19th cent.: Malay, literally 'sheath'.

Saronic Gulf /sə'rɒnɪk/ an inlet of the Aegean Sea on the coast of SE Greece. Athens and the port of Piraeus lie on its northern shores.

saros /'sɛːrɒs/ ▶ noun Astronomy a period of about 18 years between repetitions of solar and lunar eclipses.
– ORIGIN early 19th cent.: from Greek, from Babylonian *šār(u)* '3,600 (years)', the sense apparently based on a misinterpretation of the number.

sarpanch /'sʌrpʌntʃ/ ▶ noun Indian the head of a village or panchayat.
– ORIGIN from Urdu *sar-panch*, from *sar* 'head' + *panch* 'five'.

sarracenia /ˌsarə'siːnɪə/ ▶ noun a North American pitcher plant of marshy places, some kinds of which are cultivated as ornamentals.
● Genus *Sarracenia*, family Sarraceniaceae: several species, including the purple-flowered *S. purpurea*, which has become naturalized in Ireland.
– ORIGIN modern Latin, named after Michel *Sarrazin* (died 1734), Canadian botanist.

Sarre /sɑːr/ French name for **SAAR**.

sarrusophone /sə'rʌsəfəʊn/ ▶ noun a member of a family of wind instruments similar to saxophones but with a double reed like an oboe.
– ORIGIN late 19th cent.: from the name of W. *Sarrus*, the 19th-cent. French bandmaster who invented it, + **-PHONE**.

sarsaparilla /ˌsɑːs(ə)pə'rɪlə/ ▶ noun [mass noun] **1** a preparation of the dried rhizomes of various plants, especially smilax, used to flavour some drinks and medicines and formerly as a tonic.
■ a sweet drink flavoured with this.
2 the tropical American climbing plant from which these rhizomes are generally obtained.
● Genus *Smilax*, family Liliaceae: several species, in particular *S. regelii*, which is the chief source of commercial sarsaparilla.
– ORIGIN late 16th cent.: from Spanish *zarzaparilla*, from *zarza* 'bramble' + a diminutive of *parra* 'vine'.

sarsen /'sɑːs(ə)n/ (also **sarsen stone**) ▶ noun Geology a silicified sandstone boulder of a kind which occurs on the chalk downs of southern England. Such stones were used in constructing Stonehenge and other prehistoric monuments.
– ORIGIN late 17th cent.: probably a variant of **SARACEN**.

sarsenet /'sɑːsnɪt/ (also **sarcenet**) ▶ noun [mass noun] a fine soft silk fabric, used as a lining material and in dressmaking.
– ORIGIN late Middle English: from Anglo-Norman French *sarzinett*, perhaps a diminutive of *sarzin* 'Saracen', suggested by Old French *drap sarrasinois* 'Saracen cloth'.

Sarto /'sɑːtəʊ, Italian 'sarto/, Andrea del (1486–1531), Italian painter; born *Andrea d'Agnolo*. He worked chiefly in Florence, where his works include fresco cycles in the church of Santa Annunziata and the series of grisailles in the cloister of the Scalzi (1511–26).

sartorial /sɑː'tɔːrɪəl/ ▶ adjective [attrib.] of or relating to tailoring, clothes, or style of dress: *sartorial elegance*.
– DERIVATIVES **sartorially** adverb.
– ORIGIN early 19th cent.: from Latin *sartor* 'tailor' (from *sarcire* 'to patch') + **-IAL**.

sartorius /sɑː'tɔːrɪəs/ (also **sartorius muscle**) ▶ noun Anatomy a long, narrow muscle running obliquely across the front of each thigh from the hip bone to the inside of the leg below the knee.
– ORIGIN early 18th cent.: modern Latin, from Latin *sartor* 'tailor' (because the muscle is used when adopting a cross-legged position, earlier associated with a tailor's sewing posture).

Sartre /'sɑːtrə, French saʀtr/, Jean-Paul (1905–80), French philosopher, novelist, dramatist, and critic. A leading existentialist, he dealt in his work with the nature of human life and the structures of consciousness. He refused the Nobel Prize for Literature in 1964. Notable works: *Nausée* (novel, 1938), *Being and Nothingness* (treatise, 1943), and *Huis clos* (play, 1944).

Sarum /'sɛːrəm/ an old name for Salisbury, still used as the name of its diocese. See also **OLD SARUM**.
■ [as modifier] denoting the order of divine service used before the Reformation in the diocese of Salisbury and, by the 15th century, in most of England, Wales, and Ireland: *Sarum Use*.
– ORIGIN from medieval Latin, perhaps from an abbreviated form of Latin *Sarisburia* 'Salisbury'.

sarus crane /'sɛːrəs/ ▶ noun a large red-headed crane found from India to the Philippines.
● *Grus antigone*, family Gruidae.
– ORIGIN mid 19th cent.: *sarus* from Sanskrit *sārasa*.

sarvodaya /sɑː'vəʊdəjə/ ▶ noun [mass noun] Indian the economic and social development of the community as a whole, especially as advocated by Mahatma Gandhi.
– ORIGIN Sanskrit, from *sarva* 'all' + *udaya* 'prosperity'.

SAS ▶ abbreviation for Special Air Service.

sasanqua /sə'saŋkwə, -kə/ ▶ noun a Japanese camellia with fragrant white or pink flowers and seeds which yield tea oil.
● *Camellia sasanqua*, family Theaceae.
– ORIGIN mid 19th cent.: from Japanese *sasank(w)a*.

SASE N. Amer. ▶ abbreviation for self-addressed stamped envelope.

sash[1] ▶ noun a long strip or loop of cloth worn over one shoulder or round the waist, especially as part of a uniform or official dress.
– DERIVATIVES **sashed** adjective, **sashless** adjective.
– ORIGIN late 16th cent. (earlier as *shash*, denoting fine fabric twisted round the head as a turban): from Arabic *šāš* 'muslin, turban'.

sash[2] ▶ noun a frame holding the glass in a window, typically one of two sliding frames in a sash window.
– DERIVATIVES **sashed** adjective.
– ORIGIN late 17th cent.: alteration of **CHASSIS**, interpreted as plural.

sashay /sa'ʃeɪ/ ▶ verb [no obj.] informal, chiefly N. Amer. **1** [with adverbial of direction] walk in an ostentatious yet casual manner, typically with exaggerated movements of the hips and shoulders: *Louise was sashaying along in a long black satin dress*.
2 perform the sashay.
▶ noun (in American square dancing) a figure in which partners circle each other by taking sideways steps.
– ORIGIN mid 19th cent. (as a verb): alteration of **CHASSÉ**.

sash cord ▶ noun a strong cord attaching either of the sash weights of a sash window to a sash.

sash cramp ▶ noun a tool used for clamping the sashes of a window together during gluing.

sashimi /'saʃɪmi/ ▶ noun [mass noun] a Japanese dish of bite-sized pieces of raw fish eaten with soy sauce and horseradish paste: *tuna sashimi*.
– ORIGIN Japanese.

sash weight ▶ noun a weight attached by a cord to each side of the sash of a sash window to balance it at any height.

sash window ▶ noun a window with one or two sashes which can be slid vertically to make an opening.

sasin /'sasɪn/ ▶ noun another term for **BLACKBUCK**.
– ORIGIN mid 19th cent.: from Nepali.

sasine /'seɪsɪn/ ▶ noun [mass noun] Scots Law investment by registration of a deed transferring ownership of property.
■ [count noun] an act or record of such investment.
■ historical the conferring of possession of feudal property.
– ORIGIN mid 17th cent.: variant of **SEISIN**.

Sask. ▶ abbreviation for Saskatchewan.

Saskatchewan /sə'skatʃɪwən/ **1** a province of central Canada; pop. 994,000 (1991); capital, Regina.
2 a river of Canada. Rising in two headstreams in the Rocky Mountains, it flows eastwards for 596 km (370 miles) to Lake Winnipeg.

Saskatoon /ˌskə'tuːn/ an industrial city in south central Saskatchewan, situated in the Great Plains on the South Saskatchewan River; pop. 186,060 (1991).

Sasquatch /'saskwatʃ, -wɒtʃ/ ▶ noun another term for **BIGFOOT**.
– ORIGIN early 20th cent.: Salish.

sass N. Amer. informal ▶ noun [mass noun] impudence; cheek: *the kind of boy that wouldn't give you any sass*.
▶ verb [with obj.] be cheeky or rude to (someone): *we wouldn't have dreamed of sassing our parents*.
– ORIGIN mid 19th cent.: variant of **SAUCE**.

sassaby /sə'seɪbi/ ▶ noun variant spelling of **TSESSEBI**.

sassafras /'sasəfras/ ▶ noun **1** a deciduous North American tree with aromatic leaves and bark. The leaves are infused to make tea or ground into filé.
● *Sassafras albidum*, family Lauraceae.
■ [mass noun] an extract of the leaves or bark of this tree, used medicinally or in perfumery.
– ORIGIN late 16th cent.: from Spanish *sasafrás*, based on Latin *saxifraga* 'saxifrage'.

Sassanian /sa'seɪnɪən/ (also **Sassanid** /'sasənɪd/) ▶ adjective of or relating to a dynasty that ruled Persia from the early 3rd century AD until the Arab Muslim conquest of 651.
▶ noun a member of this dynasty.
– ORIGIN from *Sasan* (the name of the grandfather or father of Ardashir, the first Sassanian) + **-IAN**.

Sassenach /'sasənax, -nak/ Scottish & Irish, derogatory ▶ noun an English person.
▶ adjective English.
– ORIGIN early 18th cent. (as a noun): from Scottish Gaelic *Sasunnoch*, Irish *Sasanach*, from Latin *Saxones* 'Saxons'.

Sassoon[1] /sə'suːn/, Siegfried (Lorraine) (1886–1967), English poet and novelist. He is known for his starkly realistic poems written while serving in the First World War, expressing his contempt for war leaders as well as compassion for his comrades.

Sassoon[2] /sə'suːn/, Vidal (b.1928), English hairstylist. Opening a London salon in 1953, he introduced the cut and blow-dry.

sassy ▶ adjective (**sassier**, **sassiest**) informal, chiefly N. Amer. lively, bold, and full of spirit; cheeky.
– DERIVATIVES **sassily** adverb, **sassiness** noun.
– ORIGIN mid 19th cent.: variant of **SAUCY**.

sastra ▶ noun variant spelling of **SHASTRA**.

sastrugi /sa'struːgi/ ▶ plural noun parallel wave-like ridges caused by winds on the surface of hard snow, especially in polar regions.
– ORIGIN mid 19th cent.: from Russian *zastrugi* 'small ridges'.

SAT ▶ abbreviation for ■ trademark (in the US) Scholastic Aptitude Test, a test of a student's verbal and mathematical skills, used for admission to American colleges. ■ standard assessment task.

Sat. ▶ **abbreviation for** Saturday.

sat past and past participle of **SIT**.

satai ▶ **noun** variant spelling of **SATAY**.

Satan the Devil; Lucifer.
– ORIGIN Old English, via late Latin and Greek from Hebrew *śāṭān*, literally 'adversary', from *śāṭan* 'plot against'.

satang /'sataŋ/ ▶ **noun** (pl. same or **satangs**) a monetary unit of Thailand, equal to one hundredth of a baht.
– ORIGIN Thai, from Pali *sata* 'hundred'.

satanic ▶ **adjective** of or characteristic of Satan.
■ connected with Satanism: *a satanic cult.* ■ extremely evil or wicked.
– DERIVATIVES **satanically** adverb.

satanic abuse ▶ **noun** another term for **RITUAL ABUSE**.

satanism ▶ **noun** [mass noun] the worship of Satan, typically involving a travesty of Christian symbols and practices, such as placing a cross upside down.
– DERIVATIVES **satanist** noun & adjective.

satanize (also **-ise**) ▶ **verb** [with obj.] rare portray as satanic or evil.

satay /'sateɪ/ (also **satai** or **saté**) ▶ **noun** [mass noun] an Indonesian and Malaysian dish consisting of small pieces of meat grilled on a skewer and usually served with spiced sauce.
– ORIGIN from Malay *satai*, Indonesian *sate*.

SATB ▶ **abbreviation for** soprano, alto, tenor, and bass (used to describe the constitution of a choir or to specify the singing voices required for a particular piece of music).

satchel ▶ **noun** a bag carried on the shoulder by a long strap and closed by a flap, used especially for school books.
– ORIGIN Middle English: from Old French *sachel*, from Latin *saccellus* 'small bag'.

satchel charge ▶ **noun** an explosive on a board fitted with a rope or wire loop for carrying and attaching.

satcom (also **SATCOM**) ▶ **noun** [mass noun] satellite communications.
– ORIGIN late 20th cent.: blend.

sate[1] ▶ **verb** [with obj.] satisfy (a desire or an appetite) to the full: *sate your appetite at the resort's restaurant.*
■ supply (someone) with as much as or more of something than is desired or can be managed: *afterwards, sated and happy, they both slept.*
– DERIVATIVES **sateless** adjective (poetic/literary).
– ORIGIN early 17th cent.: probably an alteration of dialect *sade*, from Old English *sadian* 'become sated or weary' (related to **SAD**). The change in the final consonant was due to association with **SATIATE**.

sate[2] ▶ **verb** archaic spelling of **SAT**.

saté ▶ **noun** variant spelling of **SATAY**.

sateen /sa'tiːn/ ▶ **noun** [mass noun] a cotton fabric woven like satin with a glossy surface.
– ORIGIN late 19th cent.: alteration of **SATIN**, on the pattern of *velveteen*.

satellite ▶ **noun 1** (also **artificial satellite**) an artificial body placed in orbit round the earth or another planet in order to collect information or for communication.
■ [as modifier] transmitted by satellite; using or relating to satellite technology: *satellite broadcasting.* ■ [mass noun] satellite television: *a news service on satellite.*
2 Astronomy a celestial body orbiting the earth or another planet.
3 [usu. as modifier] something that is separated from or on the periphery of something else but is nevertheless dependent on or controlled by it: *satellite offices in London and New York.*
■ a small country or state politically or economically dependent on another. ■ a community or town dependent on a nearby larger town.
4 Biology a portion of the DNA of a genome with repeating base sequences and of different density from the main sequence.
– ORIGIN mid 16th cent. (in the sense 'follower, obsequious underling'): from French *satellite* or Latin *satelles, satellit-* 'attendant'.

satellite dish ▶ **noun** a bowl-shaped aerial with which signals are transmitted to or received from a communications satellite.

satellite feed ▶ **noun** a live broadcast via satellite forming part of another programme.

satellite television ▶ **noun** [mass noun] television broadcast using a satellite to relay signals to appropriately equipped customers in a particular area.

satellitium /ˌsatə'lɪtɪəm/ ▶ **noun** Astrology a grouping of several planets in a sign.

Sati /'sʌtiː/ Hinduism the wife of Shiva, reborn as Parvati. According to some accounts, she died by throwing herself into the sacred fire.

sati ▶ **noun** variant spelling of **SUTTEE**.

satiate /'seɪʃɪeɪt/ ▶ **verb** another term for **SATE**[1]: *he folded up his newspaper, his curiosity satiated.*
▶ **adjective** archaic satisfied to the full; satiated.
– DERIVATIVES **satiable** adjective (archaic), **satiation** noun.
– ORIGIN late Middle English: from Latin *satiatus*, past participle of *satiare*, from *satis* 'enough'.

Satie /'sati, 'saːti/, Erik (Alfred Leslie) (1866–1925), French avant-garde composer. He formed an irreverent avant-garde artistic set associated with Les Six, Dadaism, and surrealism. Notable works: *Gymnopédies* (1888).

satiety /sə'tʌɪɪti/ ▶ **noun** [mass noun] chiefly technical the feeling or state of being sated.
– ORIGIN mid 16th cent.: from Old French *saciete*, from Latin *satietas*, from *satis* 'enough'.

satiety centre ▶ **noun** Physiology an area of the brain situated in the hypothalamus and concerned with the regulation of food intake.

satin ▶ **noun** [mass noun] a smooth, glossy fabric, usually of silk, produced by a weave in which the threads of the warp are caught and looped by the weft only at certain intervals: [as modifier] *a blue satin dress.*
■ [as modifier] denoting or having a surface or finish resembling this fabric, produced on metal or other material: *an aluminium alloy with a black satin finish.*
▶ **verb** (**satined**, **satining**) [with obj.] give a smooth, glossy surface to: *it has been very carefully satined and waxed.*
▶ **adjective** smooth like satin: *a luxurious satin look.*
– DERIVATIVES **satinize** (also **-ise**) verb, **satiny** adjective.
– ORIGIN late Middle English: via Old French from Arabic *zaytūnī* 'of Tsinkiang', a town in China.

satinette /ˌsatɪ'nɛt, 'satɪnɪt/ (also **satinet**) ▶ **noun** [mass noun] a fabric with a similar finish to satin, made partly or wholly of cotton or synthetic fibre.

satin paper ▶ **noun** fine glossy paper, used for writing or printmaking.

satin spar ▶ **noun** [mass noun] a fibrous variety of gypsum.

satin stitch ▶ **noun** [mass noun] a long straight embroidery stitch, giving the appearance of satin.

satin walnut ▶ **noun** see **SWEET GUM**.

satin weave ▶ **noun** [mass noun] a method of weaving fabric in which either the warp or the weft predominates on the surface.

satinwood ▶ **noun 1** [mass noun] glossy yellowish timber from a tropical tree, valued for cabinetwork.
2 the tropical hardwood tree that produces this timber.
• Two species in the family Rutaceae: **Ceylon satinwood** (*Chloroxylon swietenia*), native to India and Sri Lanka, and **West Indian** (or **Jamaican**) **satinwood** (*Zanthoxylum flava*), native to the Caribbean, Bermuda, and southern Florida.
■ used in names of other trees which yield high-quality timber, e.g. **Nigerian satinwood**.

satire /'satʌɪə/ ▶ **noun** [mass noun] the use of humour, irony, exaggeration, or ridicule to expose and criticize people's stupidity or vices, particularly in the context of contemporary politics and other topical issues.
■ [count noun] a play, novel, film, or other work which uses satire: *a stinging **satire on** American politics.* ■ a genre of literature characterized by the use of satire. ■ [count noun] (in Latin literature) a literary miscellany, especially a poem ridiculing prevalent vices or follies.
– DERIVATIVES **satirist** noun.
– ORIGIN early 16th cent.: from French, or from Latin *satira*, later form of *satura* 'poetic medley'.

satiric /sə'tɪrɪk/ ▶ **adjective** another term for **SATIRICAL**.

satirical ▶ **adjective** containing or using satire: *a New York-based satirical magazine.*
■ (of a person or their behaviour) sarcastic, critical, and mocking another's weaknesses.
– DERIVATIVES **satirically** adverb.
– ORIGIN early 16th cent.: from late Latin *satiricus* (from *satira* 'poetic medley': see **SATIRE**) + **-AL**.

satirize /'satɪrʌɪz/ (also **-ise**) ▶ **verb** [with obj.] deride and criticize by means of satire: *the movie satirized the notion of national superiority.*
– DERIVATIVES **satirization** noun.

satisfaction ▶ **noun** [mass noun] fulfilment of one's wishes, expectations, or needs, or the pleasure derived from this: *I looked round with satisfaction | managing directors seeking greater job satisfaction.*
■ Law the payment of a debt or fulfilment of an obligation or claim: *in **full and final satisfaction** of the claim.* ■ [with negative] what is felt to be owed or due to one, especially in reparation of an injustice or wrong: *the work will come to a halt if the electricity and telephone people don't **get satisfaction**.* ■ Christian Theology Christ's atonement for sin. ■ historical the opportunity to defend one's honour in a duel: *I **demand** the **satisfaction** of a gentleman.*
– PHRASES **to one's satisfaction** so that one is satisfied: *some amendments were made, not entirely to his satisfaction.*
– ORIGIN Middle English: from Old French, or from Latin *satisfactio(n-)*, from *satisfacere* 'satisfy, content' (see **SATISFY**). The earliest recorded use referred to the last part of religious penance after 'contrition' and 'confession': this involved fulfilment of the observance required by the confessor, in contrast with the current meaning 'fulfilment of one's own expectations'.

satisfactory ▶ **adjective** fulfilling expectations or needs; acceptable, though not outstanding or perfect: *the brakes are satisfactory if not particularly powerful.*
■ (of a patient in a hospital) not deteriorating or likely to die. ■ Law (of evidence or a verdict) sufficient for the needs of the case: *the verdict is safe and satisfactory.*
– DERIVATIVES **satisfactorily** adverb, **satisfactoriness** noun.
– ORIGIN late Middle English (in the sense 'leading to the atonement of sin'): from Old French *satisfactoire* or medieval Latin *satisfactorius*, from Latin *satisfacere* 'to content' (see **SATISFY**). The current senses date from the mid 17th cent.

satisfice /'satɪsfʌɪs/ ▶ **verb** [no obj.] formal decide on and pursue a course of action that will satisfy the minimum requirements necessary to achieve a particular goal: *the tendency to satisfice rather than optimize goals.*
– ORIGIN mid 16th cent. (in the sense 'satisfy'): alteration of **SATISFY**, influenced by Latin *satisfacere*. The formal use dates from the 1950s.

satisfied ▶ **adjective** contented; pleased: *satisfied customers | she was very **satisfied with** the results.*

satisfy ▶ **verb** (**-ies**, **-ied**) [with obj.] meet the expectations, needs, or desires of (someone): *I have never been **satisfied with** my job |* [no obj.] *wealth, the promise of the eighties, has failed to satisfy.*
■ fulfil (a desire or need): *social services is trying to satisfy the needs of so many different groups.* ■ provide (someone) with adequate information or proof so that they are convinced about something: [with obj. and clause] *people need to be satisfied that the environmental assessments are accurate | the chief engineer **satisfied himself** that it was not a weapon.* ■ adequately meet or comply with (a condition, obligation, or demand): *the whole team is working flat out to satisfy demand.* ■ Mathematics (of a quantity) make (an equation) true. ■ pay off (a debt or creditor): *there was insufficient collateral to satisfy the loan.*
– PHRASES **satisfy the examiners** Brit. reach the standard required to pass an examination.
– DERIVATIVES **satisfiability** noun, **satisfiable** adjective.
– ORIGIN late Middle English: from Old French *satisfier*, formed irregularly from Latin *satisfacere* 'to content', from *satis* 'enough' + *facere* 'make'.

satisfying ▶ **adjective** giving fulfilment or the pleasure associated with this: *the work proved to be more satisfying than being a solicitor.*
– DERIVATIVES **satisfyingly** adverb.

satnav /'satnav/ ▶ **noun** [mass noun] navigation dependent on information received from satellites.
– ORIGIN 1970s: blend of **SATELLITE** and **NAVIGATION**.

satori /sə'tɔːri/ ▶ **noun** [mass noun] Buddhism sudden enlightenment: *the road that leads to satori.*
– ORIGIN Japanese, literally 'awakening'.

satrap /'satrap/ ▶ **noun** a provincial governor in the ancient Persian empire.
■ any subordinate or local ruler.

– ORIGIN late Middle English: from Old French *satrape* or Latin *satrapa*, based on Old Persian *kšathra-pāvan* 'country-protector'.

satrapy /ˈsatrəpi/ ▶ **noun** (pl. **-ies**) a province governed by a satrap.

satsang /ˈsatsaŋ, ˈsʌtsʌŋ/ ▶ **noun** Indian a spiritual discourse or sacred gathering.
– ORIGIN from Sanskrit *satsaṅga* 'association with good men'.

Satsuma /ˈsatsʊmə/ a former province of SW Japan. It comprised the major part of the south-western peninsula of Kyushu island, also known as the Satsuma Peninsula.

satsuma /satˈsuːmə/ ▶ **noun 1** a tangerine of a hardy loose-skinned variety, originally grown in Japan.
2 /also ˈsatsʊmə, -sjʊ-/ (**Satsuma** or **Satsuma ware**) [mass noun] Japanese pottery from Satsuma, ranging from simple 17th-century earthenware to later work made for export to Europe, often elaborately painted, with a crackled cream-coloured glaze.
– ORIGIN late 19th cent.: named after the province **SATSUMA**.

saturate ▶ **verb** /ˈsatʃəreɪt/ [with obj.] (usu. **be saturated**) cause (something) to become thoroughly soaked with water or other liquid so that no more can be absorbed: *the soil is saturated.*
■ cause (a substance) to combine with, dissolve, or hold the greatest possible quantity of another substance: *the groundwater is saturated with calcium hydroxide.* ■ magnetize or charge (a substance or device) fully. ■ Electronics put (a device) into a state in which no further increase in current is achievable. ■ (usu. **be saturated with**) figurative fill (something or someone) with something until no more can be held or absorbed: *they've become thoroughly saturated with powerful and seductive messages from the media.* ■ supply (a market) beyond the point at which the demand for a product is satisfied: *Japan's electronics industry began to saturate the world markets.* ■ overwhelm (an enemy target area) by concentrated bombing.
▶ **noun** /ˈsatʃərət/ (usu. **saturates**) a saturated fat.
▶ **adjective** /ˈsatʃərət/ poetic/literary saturated with moisture.
– DERIVATIVES **saturable** adjective (technical).
– ORIGIN late Middle English (as an adjective in the sense 'satisfied'): from Latin *saturat-* 'filled, glutted', from the verb *saturare*, from *satur* 'full'. The early sense of the verb (mid 16th cent.) was 'satisfy'; the noun dates from the 1950s.

saturated ▶ **adjective 1** holding as much water or moisture as can be absorbed; thoroughly soaked.
■ Chemistry (of a solution) containing the largest possible amount of a particular solute. ■ [often in combination] having or holding as much as can be absorbed of something: *the glitzy, media-saturated plasticity of Los Angeles.*
2 Chemistry (of an organic molecule) containing the greatest possible number of hydrogen atoms, without carbon–carbon double or triple bonds.
■ denoting fats containing a high proportion of fatty acid molecules without double bonds, considered to be less healthy in the diet than unsaturated fats.
3 (of colour) very bright, full, and free from an admixture of white: *intense and saturated colour.*

saturation ▶ **noun** [mass noun] the state or process that occurs when no more of something can be absorbed, combined with, or added.
■ Chemistry the degree or extent to which something is dissolved or absorbed compared with the maximum possible, usually expressed as a percentage. ■ [as modifier] to a very full extent, especially beyond the point regarded as necessary or desirable: *saturation bombing.* ■ (also **colour saturation**) (especially in photography) the intensity of a colour, expressed as the degree to which it differs from white.

saturation diving ▶ **noun** [mass noun] deep-sea diving in which the diver's bloodstream is saturated with helium or other suitable gas at the pressure of the surrounding water, so that the decompression time afterwards is independent of the duration of the dive.

saturation point ▶ **noun** [in sing.] Chemistry the stage at which no more of a substance can be absorbed into a vapour or dissolved into a solution.
■ figurative the stage beyond which no more of something can be absorbed or accepted.

Saturday ▶ **noun** the day of the week before Sunday and following Friday, and (together with Sunday) forming part of the weekend: *the match will be held* **on Saturday** | *the counter is closed on Saturdays and Sundays* | [as modifier] *Saturday night.*
▶ **adverb** chiefly N. Amer. on Saturday: *he made his first appearance Saturday.*
■ (**Saturdays**) on Saturdays; each Saturday: *they sleep late Saturdays.*
– ORIGIN Old English *Sætern(es)dæg*, translation of Latin *Saturni dies* 'day of Saturn'; compare with Dutch *zaterdag*.

Saturday night special ▶ **noun** informal, chiefly N. Amer. a cheap low-calibre pistol or revolver, easily obtained and concealed.

Saturn 1 Roman Mythology an ancient god, regarded as a god of agriculture. Greek equivalent **CRONUS**. [ORIGIN: from Latin *Saturnus*, perhaps from Etruscan.]
2 Astronomy the sixth planet from the sun in the solar system, circled by a system of broad flat rings.

Saturn orbits between Jupiter and Uranus at an average distance of 1,427 million km from the sun. It is a gas giant with an equatorial diameter of 120,000 km, with a conspicuous ring system extending out to a distance twice as great. The planet has a dense hydrogen-rich atmosphere, similar to that of Jupiter but with less distinct banding. There are at least eighteen satellites, the largest of which is Titan, and including small shepherd satellites that orbit close to two of the rings.

3 a series of American space rockets, of which the very large *Saturn V* was used as the launch vehicle for the Apollo missions of 1969–72.

Saturnalia /ˌsatəˈneɪlɪə/ ▶ **noun** [treated as sing. or pl.] the ancient Roman festival of Saturn in December, which was a period of general merrymaking and was the predecessor of Christmas.
■ (**saturnalia**) an occasion of wild revelry.
– DERIVATIVES **saturnalian** adjective.
– ORIGIN Latin, literally 'matters relating to Saturn', neuter plural of *Saturnalis*.

Saturnian ▶ **adjective 1** of or relating to the planet Saturn.
2 another term for **SATURNINE**.

saturniid /səˈtəːnɪɪd/ ▶ **noun** Entomology a silk moth of a family (Saturniidae) which includes the emperor moths and the giant Indian silk moths. They typically have prominent eyespots on the wings.
– ORIGIN late 19th cent.: from modern Latin *Saturniidae* (plural), from the genus name *Saturnia*.

saturnine /ˈsatənʌɪn/ ▶ **adjective** (of a person or their manner) slow and gloomy: *a saturnine temperament.*
■ (of a person or their features) dark in colouring and moody or mysterious: *his saturnine face and dark, watchful eyes.* ■ (of a place or an occasion) gloomy.
– DERIVATIVES **saturninely** adverb.
– ORIGIN late Middle English (as a term in astrology): from Old French *saturnin*, from medieval Latin *Saturninus* 'of Saturn' (identified with lead by the alchemists and associated with slowness and gloom by astrologers).

saturnism ▶ **noun** archaic term for **LEAD POISONING**.
– DERIVATIVES **saturnic** adjective.
– ORIGIN mid 19th cent.: from **SATURN** in the obsolete alchemical sense 'lead' + **-ISM**.

satyagraha /sʌˈtjɑːɡrəhɑː/ ▶ **noun** [mass noun] a policy of passive political resistance, especially that advocated by Mahatma Gandhi against British rule in India.
– ORIGIN Sanskrit, from *satya* 'truth' + *āgraha* 'obstinacy'.

satyr /ˈsatə/ ▶ **noun 1** Greek Mythology one of a class of lustful, drunken woodland gods. In Greek art they were represented as a man with a horse's ears and tail, but in Roman representations as a man with a goat's ears, tail, legs, and horns.
■ a man who has strong sexual desires.
2 a satyrid butterfly with chiefly dark brown wings.
• Tribes Satyrini (including the Eurasian genus *Satyrus*) and Euptychiini (the American **wood satyrs**), subfamily Satyrinae, family Nymphalidae.
– DERIVATIVES **satyric** adjective.
– ORIGIN late Middle English: from Old French *satyre*, or via Latin from Greek *saturos*.

satyriasis /ˌsatɪˈrʌɪəsɪs/ ▶ **noun** [mass noun] uncontrollable or excessive sexual desire in a man.
– ORIGIN late Middle English: via late Latin from Greek *saturiasis*, from *saturos* (see **SATYR**).

satyrid /səˈtɪrɪd/ ▶ **noun** Entomology a butterfly of a group which includes the browns, heaths, ringlets, and related species. They typically have brown wings with small eyespots and many live in woodland and breed on grasses. Also called **BROWN**.
• Subfamily Satyrinae, family Nymphalidae (formerly the family Satyridae).
– ORIGIN early 20th cent.: from modern Latin *Satyridae* (plural), from Latin *Satyrus* (see **SATYR**), used as a genus name.

sauce ▶ **noun** [mass noun] **1** thick liquid served with food, usually savoury dishes, to add moistness and flavour: *tomato sauce* | [count noun] *the cubes can be added to soups and sauces.*
■ N. Amer. stewed fruit, especially apples, eaten as dessert or used as a garnish.
2 (**the sauce**) informal, chiefly N. Amer. alcoholic drink: *she's been* **on the sauce** *for years.*
3 informal, chiefly Brit. impertinence; cheek.
▶ **verb** [with obj.] **1** (usu. **be sauced**) provide a sauce for (something); season with a sauce.
■ figurative make more interesting and exciting.
2 informal be rude or impudent to (someone).
– PHRASES **what's sauce for the goose is sauce for the gander** proverb what is appropriate in one case is also appropriate in the other case in question.
– DERIVATIVES **sauceless** adjective.
– ORIGIN Middle English: from Old French, based on Latin *salsus* 'salted', past participle of *salere* 'to salt', from *sal* 'salt'. Compare with **SALAD**.

sauce boat ▶ **noun** a long, narrow jug used for serving sauce.

sauced ▶ **adjective** informal, chiefly N. Amer. drunk.

sauce mousseline ▶ **noun** see **MOUSSELINE** (sense 3).

saucepan ▶ **noun** a deep cooking pan, typically round, made of metal, and with one long handle and a lid.
– DERIVATIVES **saucepanful** noun (pl. **-fuls**).

saucer ▶ **noun** a shallow dish, typically having a circular indentation in the centre, on which a cup is placed.
– PHRASES **have eyes like saucers** have one's eyes opened wide in amazement.
– DERIVATIVES **saucerful** noun (pl. **-fuls**), **saucerless** adjective.
– ORIGIN Middle English (denoting a condiment dish): from Old French *saussier(e)* 'sauce boat', probably suggested by late Latin *salsarium*.

saucer bug ▶ **noun** a disc-shaped predatory water bug which lives in muddy ponds and breathes by means of an air bubble around the body.
• *Ilyocoris cimicoides*, family Naucoridae, suborder Heteroptera.

saucier /ˈsəʊsɪeɪ/ ▶ **noun** a chef who prepares sauces.
– ORIGIN French.

saucisson /ˈsəʊsɪsɒ̃, French sosisɔ̃/ ▶ **noun** a large, thick French sausage, typically firm in texture and flavoured with herbs.
– ORIGIN French, literally 'large sausage'.

saucy ▶ **adjective** (**saucier**, **sauciest**) informal **1** chiefly Brit. sexually suggestive, typically in a way intended to be light-hearted and humorous.
2 chiefly N. Amer. (in favourable contexts) bold, lively, and full of spirit.
3 chiefly N. Amer. (of food) covered with sauce.
– DERIVATIVES **saucily** adverb, **sauciness** noun.
– ORIGIN early 16th cent. (in the sense 'savoury, flavoured with sauce'): from **SAUCE** + **-Y**[1].

saudade /saʊˈdɑːdə/ ▶ **noun** [mass noun] a feeling of longing, melancholy, or nostalgia that is supposedly characteristic of the Portuguese or Brazilian temperament.
– ORIGIN Portuguese.

Saudi /ˈsaʊdi, ˈsɔːdi/ ▶ **adjective** of or relating to Saudi Arabia or its ruling dynasty.
▶ **noun** (pl. **Saudis**) a citizen of Saudi Arabia, or a member of its ruling dynasty.
– ORIGIN from the name of Abdul-Aziz ibn *Saud* (1880–1953), first king of Saudi Arabia.

Saudi Arabia a country in SW Asia occupying most of the Arabian peninsula; pop. 15,431,000 (est. 1991); official language, Arabic; capital, Riyadh.

The birthplace of Islam in the 7th century, Saudi Arabia emerged from the Arab revolt against the Turks during the First World War to become an independent kingdom in 1932. Since the Second World War the economy has been revolutionized by the exploitation of the area's oil resources, and Saudi Arabia is the largest oil producer in the Middle East. It is ruled by the house of Saud along traditional Islamic lines.

– DERIVATIVES **Saudi Arabian** adjective & noun.

sauerbraten /ˈsaʊəˌbrɑːt(ə)n/ ▶ **noun** [mass noun] chiefly N. Amer. a dish of German origin consisting of beef that is marinaded in vinegar with

peppercorns, onions, and other seasonings before cooking.
– ORIGIN from German, from *sauer* 'sour' + *Braten* 'roast meat'.

sauerkraut /ˈsaʊəkraʊt/ ▶ **noun** [mass noun] a German dish of chopped pickled cabbage.
– ORIGIN from German, from *sauer* 'sour' + *Kraut* 'vegetable'.

sauger /ˈsɔːɡə/ ▶ **noun** a slender North American pikeperch with silver eyes, which is active at twilight and at night.
● *Stizostedion canadense*, family Percidae.
– ORIGIN late 19th cent.: of unknown origin.

Saul (in the Bible) the first king of Israel (11th century BC).

Saul of Tarsus see **PAUL, ST.**

Sault Sainte Marie /ˌsuː seɪnt məˈriː/ each of two North American river ports which face each other across the falls of the St Mary's River, between Lakes Superior and Huron. The northern port (pop. 72,822, 1991) lies in Ontario, Canada, while the southern port (pop. 14,700, 1990) is in the US state of Michigan.

Saumur /ˈsəʊmjʊə, French somyʀ/ ▶ **noun** [mass noun] a French white wine resembling champagne.
– ORIGIN from the name of a town in the department of Maine-et-Loire.

sauna /ˈsɔːnə/ ▶ **noun** a small room used as a hot-air or steam bath for cleaning and refreshing the body.
■ a session in such a room. ■ used in comparisons to refer to a very hot, humid place: *the restaurant is like a sauna despite open windows.*
– ORIGIN late 19th cent.: from Finnish.

saunf /sɔːf/ ▶ **noun** Indian term for **ANISEED**, often served in the Indian subcontinent after meals, mixed with sugar.
– ORIGIN from Hindi *saũph*.

saunter ▶ **verb** [no obj., with adverbial of direction] walk in a slow, relaxed manner, without hurry or effort: *Adam sauntered into the room.*
▶ **noun** a leisurely stroll: *a quiet saunter down the road.*
– DERIVATIVES **saunterer** noun.
– ORIGIN late Middle English (in the sense 'to muse, wonder'): of unknown origin. The current sense dates from the mid 17th cent.

-saur ▶ **combining form** forming names of reptiles, especially extinct ones: *ichthyosaur* | *stegosaur.*
– ORIGIN modern Latin, from Greek *sauros* 'lizard'; compare with **-SAURUS**, a suffix of modern Latin genus names.

Sauria /ˈsɔːrɪə/ Zoology former term for **LACERTILIA**.
– ORIGIN modern Latin (plural), from Greek *sauros* 'lizard'.

saurian /ˈsɔːrɪən/ ▶ **adjective** of or like a lizard.
▶ **noun** any large reptile, especially a dinosaur or other extinct form.
– ORIGIN early 19th cent.: from modern Latin *Sauria* (see **SAURIA**) + **-AN**.

saurischian /sɔːˈrɪskɪən, -ˈrɪʃɪən/ Palaeontology ▶ **adjective** of, relating to, or denoting dinosaurs of an order distinguished by having a pelvic structure resembling that of lizards. Compare with **ORNITHISCHIAN**.
▶ **noun** a saurischian dinosaur.
● Order Saurischia, superorder Dinosauria; comprises the carnivorous theropods and the herbivorous sauropods.
– ORIGIN late 19th cent.: from the modern Latin plural *Saurischia* (from Greek *sauros* 'lizard' + *iskhion* 'hip joint') + **-AN**.

sauropod /ˈsɔːrəpɒd, ˈsaʊr-/ ▶ **noun** a very large quadrupedal herbivorous dinosaur with a long neck and tail, small head, and massive limbs.
● Infraorder Sauropoda, suborder Sauropodomorpha, order Saurischia; e.g. apatosaurus, brachiosaurus, and diplodocus.
– ORIGIN late 19th cent.: from modern Latin *Sauropoda* (plural), from Greek *sauros* 'lizard' + *pous, pod-* 'foot'.

-saurus ▶ **combining form** forming genus names of reptiles, especially extinct ones: *stegosaurus.*
– ORIGIN modern Latin.

saury /ˈsɔːri/ ▶ **noun** (pl. **-ies**) a long slender-bodied edible marine fish with an elongated snout.
● Family Scomberesocidae: four genera and species, including *Scomberesox saurus* of the Atlantic (also called **SKIPPER**[2]), and *Cololabis saira* of the Pacific.
– ORIGIN late 18th cent.: perhaps via late Latin from Greek *sauros* 'horse mackerel'.

sausage ▶ **noun 1** a short cylindrical tube of minced pork, beef, or other meat encased in a skin, typically sold raw to be grilled or fried before eating.
■ [mass noun] a cylindrical tube of minced pork, beef, or other meat seasoned and cooked or preserved, sold mainly to be eaten cold in slices: *smoked German sausage.* ■ [usu. as modifier] used in references to the characteristic cylindrical shape of sausages: *mould into a sausage shape.*
2 Brit. used as an affectionate form of address, especially to a child: *'Silly sausage,' he teased.*
– PHRASES **not a sausage** Brit. informal nothing at all.
– ORIGIN late Middle English: from Old Northern French *saussiche*, from medieval Latin *salsicia*, from Latin *salsus* 'salted' (see **SAUCE**).

sausage dog ▶ **noun** informal British term for **DACHSHUND**.

sausage meat ▶ **noun** [mass noun] minced meat with spices and a binder such as cereal, used in sausages or as a stuffing.

sausage roll ▶ **noun** a tubular piece of sausage meat wrapped in pastry and baked.

sausage tree ▶ **noun** a tropical African tree with red bell-shaped flowers and large pendulous sausage-shaped fruits.
● *Kigelia pinnata*, family Bignoniaceae.

Saussure /səʊˈsjʊə, French sosyʀ/, Ferdinand de (1857–1913), Swiss linguistics scholar. He was one of the founders of modern linguistics and his work is fundamental to the development of structuralism. Saussure made a distinction between *langue* and *parole*, and stressed that linguistic study should focus on the former.

sauté /ˈsəʊteɪ/ ▶ **adjective** [attrib.] fried quickly in a little hot fat: *sauté potatoes.*
▶ **noun 1** a dish cooked in such a way.
2 Ballet a jump off both feet, landing in the same position.
▶ **verb** (**sautés**, **sautéed** or **sautéd**, **sautéing**) [with obj.] cook in such a way: *sauté the onions in the olive oil.*
– ORIGIN early 19th cent.: French, literally 'jumped', past participle of *sauter.*

Sauternes /sə(ʊ)ˈtəːn, French sotɛʀn/ ▶ **noun** [mass noun] a sweet white wine from Sauternes in the Bordeaux region of France.

sautoir /ˈsəʊtwɑː/ ▶ **noun** a long necklace consisting of a fine gold chain and typically set with jewels.
– ORIGIN 1930s: French, extended use of the original word which denoted a harness loop used as a stirrup for 'jumping' (from *sauter* 'to jump') into the saddle.

sauve qui peut /ˌsəʊv kiː ˈpəː/ ▶ **noun** archaic or poetic/literary a general stampede, panic, or disorder.
– ORIGIN French, literally 'save who can'.

Sauveterrian /səʊvˈtɛːrɪən/ ▶ **adjective** Archaeology of, relating to, or denoting an early Mesolithic culture of western Europe, especially France, dated to about 9,500–7,500 years ago.
■ [as noun **the Sauveterrian**] the Sauveterrian culture or period.
– ORIGIN 1940s: *Sauveterre*-la-Lémance, France, the type site, + **-IAN**.

Sauvignon /ˈsəʊvɪnjɒ̃/ (also **Sauvignon Blanc**) ▶ **noun** [mass noun] a variety of white wine grape.
■ a white wine made from this grape.
– ORIGIN French.

Savage, Michael Joseph (1872–1940), New Zealand Labour statesman, Prime Minister 1935–40. New Zealand's first Labour Prime Minister, he introduced many reforms, including social security legislation which he dubbed 'applied Christianity'.

savage ▶ **adjective** (of an animal or force of nature) fierce, violent, and uncontrolled: *he was attacked by a savage hound.*
■ cruel and vicious; aggressively hostile: *they launched a savage attack on the Budget.* ■ (chiefly in historical or literary contexts) primitive; uncivilized. ■ (of a place) wild-looking and inhospitable; uncultivated. ■ (of something bad or negative) very great; severe: *this would deal a savage blow to the government's fight.*
▶ **noun 1** (chiefly in historical or literary contexts) a member of a people regarded as primitive and uncivilized.
■ a brutal or vicious person: *the mother of one of the victims has described his assailants as savages.* ■ Heraldry a representation of a bearded and semi-naked man with a wreath of leaves.
▶ **verb** [with obj.] (especially of a dog or wild animal) attack ferociously and maul: *police are rounding up dogs after a girl was savaged.*
■ subject to a vicious verbal attack; criticize brutally: *he savaged the government for wasting billions in their failed bid to prop up the pound.*
– DERIVATIVES **savagely** adverb, **savageness** noun, **savagery** noun.
– ORIGIN Middle English: from Old French *sauvage* 'wild', from Latin *silvaticus* 'of the woods', from *silva* 'a wood'.

Savai'i /sɑːˈvʌɪi/ (also **Savaii**) a mountainous volcanic island in the SW Pacific, the largest of the Samoan islands.

SAVAK /ˈsavak/ ▶ **noun** the secret intelligence organization of Iran, established in 1957 and disbanded in 1979.
– ORIGIN acronym from *Sāzmān-i-Attalāt Va Amnīyat-i-Keshvar* 'National Security and Intelligence Organization'.

Savannah /səˈvanə/ a port in Georgia, just south of the border with South Carolina, on the Savannah River close to its outlet on the Atlantic; pop. 137,600 (1990).

savannah (also **savanna**) ▶ **noun** a grassy plain in tropical and subtropical regions, with few trees.
– ORIGIN mid 16th cent.: from Spanish *sabana*, from Taino *zavana.*

Savannakhet /ˌsavanəˈkɛt/ (also **Savannaket**) a town in southern Laos, on the Mekong River at the border with Thailand; pop. 50,700 (est. 1973).

savant /ˈsav(ə)nt, French savɑ̃/ ▶ **noun** a learned person, especially a distinguished scientist. See also **IDIOT SAVANT**.
– ORIGIN early 18th cent.: French, literally 'knowing (person)', present participle (used as a noun) of *savoir.*

savante /ˈsav(ə)nt, French savɑ̃t/ ▶ **noun** a female savant.
– ORIGIN mid 18th cent.: French, feminine of *savant* (see **SAVANT**).

savarin /ˈsavərɪn/ ▶ **noun** a light ring-shaped cake made with yeast and soaked in liqueur-flavoured syrup.
– ORIGIN named after Anthelme Brillat-*Savarin* (1755–1826), French gastronome.

savate /səˈvɑːt/ ▶ **noun** [mass noun] a French method of fighting in which feet and fists are used.
– ORIGIN French, originally denoting an ill-fitting shoe.

save[1] ▶ **verb** [with obj.] **1** keep safe or rescue (someone or something) from harm or danger: *they brought him in to help **save** the club **from** bankruptcy.*
■ prevent (someone) from dying: *the doctors did everything they could to save him.* ■ (in Christian use) preserve (a person's soul) from damnation. ■ keep (someone) in health (used in exclamations and formulaic expressions): *God save the Queen.*
2 keep and store up (something, especially money) for future use: *she had never been able to save much from her salary* | [no obj.] *you can **save up for** retirement in a number of ways.*
■ Computing keep (data) by moving a copy to a storage location: ***save** it **to** a new file.* ■ preserve (something) by not expending or using it: *save your strength till later.* ■ [in imperative] (**save it**) N. Amer. informal used to tell someone to stop talking: *save it, Joey—I'm in big trouble now.*
3 avoid the need to use up or spend (money, time, or other resources): ***save** £20 **on** a new camcorder* | [with two objs] *an efficient dishwasher would save them one year and three months at the sink.*
■ avoid, lessen, or guard against: *this approach saves wear and tear on the books* | [with two objs] *the statement was made to save the government some embarrassment.*
4 prevent an opponent from scoring (a goal or point) in a game or from winning (the game): *the powerful German saved three match points.*
■ Soccer (of a goalkeeper) stop (a shot) from entering the goal. ■ Baseball (of a relief pitcher) preserve (a winning position) gained by another pitcher.
▶ **noun** chiefly Soccer an act of preventing an opponent's scoring: *the keeper made a great save.*
■ Baseball an instance of a relief pitcher preserving a winning position gained by another pitcher.
– PHRASES **save one's breath** [often in imperative] not bother to say something because it is pointless. **save the day** (or **situation**) find or provide a solution to a difficulty or disaster. **save (someone's) face** see **FACE**. **save someone's life** prevent someone dying by taking specific action. ■ (**cannot do something to save one's life**) used to indicate that the person in question is completely incompetent at doing something:

S

Adrian couldn't draw to save his life. **save someone's skin** (or **neck** or **bacon**) rescue someone from danger or difficulty. **save the tide** Nautical, archaic get in and out of port while the tide lasts. **save someone the trouble** (or **bother**) avoid involving someone in useless or pointless effort: *write it down and save yourself the trouble of remembering.*
– DERIVATIVES **savable** (also **saveable**) adjective.
– ORIGIN Middle English: from Old French *sauver*, from late Latin *salvare*, from Latin *salvus* 'safe'. The noun dates from the late 19th cent.

save² ▶ **preposition** & **conjunction** formal or poetic/literary except; other than: *no one needed to know save herself* | *the kitchen was empty save for Boris.*
– ORIGIN Middle English: from Old French *sauf, sauve*, from Latin *salvo, salva* (ablative singular of *salvus* 'safe'), used in phrases such as *salvo jure, salva innocentia* 'with no violation of right or innocence'.

save-all ▶ **noun** a device for preventing waste.

save as you earn (abbrev.: **SAYE**) ▶ **noun** (in the UK) a method of saving money that carries certain tax privileges.

saveloy /ˈsavəlɔɪ/ ▶ **noun** Brit. a seasoned red pork sausage, dried and smoked and sold ready to eat.
– ORIGIN mid 19th cent.: alteration of obsolete French *cervelat*, from Italian *cervellata*; compare with **CERVELAT**.

saver ▶ **noun 1** a person who regularly saves money through a bank or recognized scheme.
2 [in combination] an object, action, or process that prevents a particular kind of resource from being used up or expended: *it is cheaper as well as a great space-saver.*
3 a travel fare offering reductions on the standard price: *a new saver from London to Edinburgh.*
4 Horse Racing, informal a hedging bet.

Savery /ˈseɪvəri/, Thomas (*c.*1650–1715), English engineer; known as **Captain Savery**. He patented an early steam engine that was later developed by Thomas Newcomen.

Save the Children Fund (in the UK) a charity founded in 1919 operating internationally to aid children. Princess Anne has been its president since 1971.

savin /ˈsavɪn/ ▶ **noun** a bushy Eurasian juniper which typically has horizontally spreading branches.
• *Juniperus sabina*, family Cupressaceae.
■ [mass noun] an extract obtained from this plant, formerly used as an abortifacient.
– ORIGIN Old English, from Old French *savine*, from Latin *sabina (herba)* 'Sabine (herb)'.

saving ▶ **noun 1** an economy of or reduction in money, time, or another resource: *this resulted in a considerable saving in development costs.*
2 (usu. **one's savings**) the money one has saved, especially through a bank or official scheme: *the agents were cheating them out of their life savings.*
3 Law a reservation; an exception.
▶ **adjective** [in combination] preventing waste of a particular resource: *an energy-saving light bulb.*
▶ **preposition 1** with the exception of; except.
2 archaic with due respect to.
– ORIGIN Middle English: from **SAVE¹**; the preposition probably from **SAVE²**, on the pattern of *touching*.

saving clause ▶ **noun** Law a clause in a contract or agreement containing an exemption from one or more of its conditions.

saving grace ▶ **noun** [mass noun] the redeeming grace of God.
■ [count noun] a redeeming quality or characteristic.

savings account ▶ **noun** a deposit account.

savings and loan (also **savings and loan association**) ▶ **noun** (in the US) an institution which accepts savings at interest and lends money to savers for house or other purchases.

savings bank ▶ **noun** a non-profit-making financial institution receiving small deposits at interest.

Savings Bond ▶ **noun 1** another term for **PREMIUM BOND**.
2 (in the US) a bond issued by the government and sold to the general public that yields variable interest.

savings certificate ▶ **noun** (in the UK) a document issued to savers by the government guaranteeing fixed interest for five years on a deposit.

savings ratio ▶ **noun** Economics the ratio of personal savings to disposable income in an economy.

savior ▶ **noun** US spelling of **SAVIOUR**.

saviour (US **savior**) ▶ **noun** a person who saves someone or something (especially a country or cause) from danger, and who is regarded with the veneration of a religious figure.
■ (**the/our Saviour**) (in Christianity) God or Jesus Christ as the redeemer of sin and saver of souls.
– ORIGIN Middle English: from Old French *sauveour*, from ecclesiastical Latin *salvator* (translating Greek *sōtēr*), from late Latin *salvare* 'to save'.

savoir faire /ˌsavwɑː ˈfɛː, French savwar fɛr/ ▶ **noun** [mass noun] the ability to act or speak appropriately in social situations.
– ORIGIN early 19th cent.: French, literally 'know how to do'.

Savonarola /ˌsavɒnəˈrəʊlə/, Girolamo (1452–98), Italian preacher and religious reformer. A Dominican monk and strict ascetic, he became popular for his passionate preaching against immorality and corruption. Savonarola became virtual ruler of Florence (1494–5) but in 1497 he was excommunicated and later executed as a heretic.

Savonlinna /ˌsɑːvɒnˈlɪnə/ a town in SE Finland; pop. 28,560 (1990).

Savonnerie carpet /ˈsavɒ̃ri/ ▶ **noun** a hand-knotted pile carpet, originally made in 17th-century Paris.
– ORIGIN late 19th cent.: French *savonnerie*, literally 'soap factory', referring to the original building on the site, converted to carpet manufacture.

savor ▶ **verb** & **noun** US spelling of **SAVOUR**.

savory¹ ▶ **noun** [mass noun] an aromatic plant of the mint family, used as a culinary herb.
• Genus *Satureja*, family Labiatae: several species, in particular the annual **summer savory** (*S. hortensis*), which is traditionally used with beans, and the coarser flavoured perennial **winter savory** (*S. montana*).
– ORIGIN Middle English: perhaps from Old English *sætherie*, or via Old French, from Latin *satureia*.

savory² ▶ **adjective** & **noun** US spelling of **SAVOURY**.

savour (US **savor**) ▶ **verb 1** [with obj.] taste (good food or drink) and enjoy it to the full: *gourmets will want to savour our game specialities.*
■ figurative enjoy or appreciate (something pleasant) to the full, especially by dwelling on it: *I wanted to savour every moment.*
2 [no obj.] (**savour of**) have a suggestion or trace of (something, especially something bad): *their genuflections savoured of superstition and popery.*
▶ **noun** [mass noun] a characteristic taste, flavour, or smell, especially a pleasant one: *the subtle savour of wood smoke.*
■ a suggestion or trace, especially of something bad.
– DERIVATIVES **savourless** adjective.
– ORIGIN Middle English: from Old French, from Latin *sapor*, from *sapere* 'to taste'.

savoury (US **savory**) ▶ **adjective 1** (of food) belonging to the category which is salty or spicy rather than sweet.
2 [usu. with negative] morally wholesome or acceptable: *everyone knew it was a front for less savoury operations.*
▶ **noun** (pl. **-ies**) chiefly Brit. a savoury snack.
– DERIVATIVES **savourily** adverb, **savouriness** noun.
– ORIGIN Middle English (in the sense 'pleasing to the sense of taste or smell'): from Old French *savoure* 'tasty, fragrant', based on Latin *sapor* 'taste'.

Savoy an area of SE France bordering on NW Italy, a former duchy ruled by the counts of Savoy from the 11th century. In 1720 Savoy was joined with Sardinia and Piedmont to form the kingdom of Sardinia, but in 1861, when Sardinia became part of a unified Italy, Savoy was ceded to France.
– DERIVATIVES **Savoyard** adjective & noun.

savoy (also **savoy cabbage**) ▶ **noun** a cabbage of a hardy variety with densely wrinkled leaves.
– ORIGIN late 16th cent.: from **SAVOY**.

Savu Sea /ˈsɑːvuː/ a part of the Indian Ocean which is encircled by the islands of Sumba, Flores, and Timor.

savvy informal, chiefly N. Amer. ▶ **noun** [mass noun] shrewdness and practical knowledge, especially in politics or business: *the corporate-finance bankers lacked the necessary political savvy.*
▶ **verb** (**-ies, -ied**) [with clause] know or understand: *Charley Force would savvy what to do about such a girl* | [no obj.] *I've been told, but I want to make sure. Savvy?*
▶ **adjective** (**savvier, savviest**) shrewd and knowledgeable in the realities of life.
– ORIGIN late 18th cent.: originally black and pidgin English imitating Spanish *sabe usted* 'you know'.

saw¹ ▶ **noun** a hand tool for cutting wood or other hard materials, typically with a long, thin serrated blade and operated using a backwards and forwards movement.
■ a mechanical power-driven tool for cutting which has a toothed rotating disc or moving band. ■ Zoology a serrated organ or part, such as the toothed snout of a sawfish.
▶ **verb** (past participle chiefly Brit. **sawn** or chiefly N. Amer. **sawed**) [with obj.] cut (something, especially wood or a tree) using a saw: *the top of each post is sawn off at railing height* | [no obj.] *thieves escaped undetected after sawing through iron bars on a basement window* | [as adj., in combination **-sawn**] *rough-sawn planks.*
■ make or form (something) using a saw: *the seats are sawn from well-seasoned elm planks.* ■ cut (something) as if with a saw, especially roughly or so as to leave rough or unfinished edges: *the woman who sawed off all my lovely hair.* ■ [no obj.] make rapid saw-like motions in cutting or in playing a stringed instrument: *he was sawing away energetically at the loaf.*
– DERIVATIVES **sawlike** adjective.
– ORIGIN Old English *saga*, of Germanic origin; related to Dutch *zaag*.
▶ **saw off** Canadian (of two or more people) compromise by making concessions to one another: *they sawed off over wages and security and concluded the deal.*

saw² past of **SEE¹**.

saw³ ▶ **noun** a proverb or maxim.
– ORIGIN Old English *sagu* 'a saying, speech', of Germanic origin; related to German *Sage*, also to **SAY** and **SAGA**.

sawbench ▶ **noun** a circular saw mounted under a bench so that the blade projects up through a slot.

sawbill ▶ **noun** another term for **MERGANSER**.

sawbones ▶ **noun** (pl. same) informal a doctor or surgeon.

sawbuck ▶ **noun** N. Amer. **1** a sawhorse.
2 informal a $10 note. [ORIGIN: by association of the X-shaped ends of a sawhorse with the Roman numeral X (= 10).]
– ORIGIN mid 19th cent.: from Dutch *zaagbok*, from *zaag* 'saw' + *bok* 'vaulting horse'.

saw doctor ▶ **noun** a specialist in the care and sharpening of saws.

sawdust ▶ **noun** [mass noun] powdery particles of wood produced by sawing.

saw-edged ▶ **adjective** with a jagged edge like a saw.

sawed-off ▶ **adjective** & **noun** North American term for **SAWN-OFF**.

sawfish ▶ **noun** (pl. same or **-fishes**) a large, tropical, mainly marine fish related to the rays, with an elongated flattened snout that bears large blunt teeth along each side.
• Family Pristidae: two genera, in particular *Pristis*, and several species.

sawfly ▶ **noun** (pl. **-flies**) an insect related to the wasps, with a saw-like egg-laying tube used to cut into plant tissue before depositing the eggs. The larvae resemble caterpillars and can be serious pests of crops and foliage.
• Suborder Symphyta, order Hymenoptera: many families.

saw frame ▶ **noun** a frame in which a saw blade is held taut.

saw gin ▶ **noun** Brit. another term for **COTTON GIN**.

sawgrass ▶ **noun** chiefly US a sedge with spiny-edged leaves.
• *Cladium*, family Cyperaceae: two species, in particular the North American *C. jamaicensis*, which is a dominant plant in the Florida everglades.

sawhorse ▶ **noun** N. Amer. a rack supporting wood for sawing.

sawlog ▶ **noun** a felled tree trunk suitable for cutting up into timber.

sawmill ▶ **noun** a factory in which logs are sawn into planks or boards by machine.

sawn past participle of **SAW¹**.

sawn-off (N. Amer. **sawed-off**) ▶ **adjective** [attrib.] (of a gun) having a specially shortened barrel to make handling easier and to give a wider field of fire.
■ informal (of an item of clothing) having been cut short.
■ US informal (of a person) short.
▶ **noun** a sawn-off shotgun.

saw palmetto ▶ **noun** a small palm with fan-shaped leaves that have sharply toothed stalks, native to the south-eastern US.
• Several species in the family Palmae, in particular *Serenoa repens*.

saw pit ▶ **noun** historical the pit in which the lower of two men working a pit saw stands.

saw set ▶ **noun** a tool for giving the teeth of a saw an alternating sideways inclination.

sawtooth (also **sawtoothed**) ▶ **adjective** shaped like the teeth of a saw with alternate steep and gentle slopes.
■(of a waveform) showing a slow linear rise and rapid linear fall or vice versa.

saw-whet owl ▶ **noun** a small North and Central American owl with a call that resembles the sound of a saw blade being sharpened.
• Genus *Aegolius*, family Strigidae: two species, in particular the North American *A. acadicus*.

saw-wort ▶ **noun** a plant of the daisy family, with purple flowers and serrated leaves, native to Eurasia and North Africa.
• *Serratula tinctoria*, family Compositae.

sawyer ▶ **noun** **1** a person who saws timber for a living.
2 US an uprooted tree floating in a river but held fast at one end. [ORIGIN: with allusion to the trapped log's movement backwards and forwards.]
3 a large longhorn beetle whose larvae bore tunnels in the wood of injured or recently felled trees, producing an audible chewing sound.
• Genus *Monochamus*, family Cerambycidae.
■NZ a large wingless bush cricket whose larvae bore in wood.
– ORIGIN Middle English (earlier as *sawer*): from the noun **SAW**[1] + **-YER**.

sax[1] ▶ **noun** informal a saxophone.
■a saxophone player.
– DERIVATIVES **saxist** noun.
– ORIGIN early 20th cent.: abbreviation.

sax[2] (also **zax**) ▶ **noun** a small axe used for cutting roof slates, with a point for making nail holes.
– ORIGIN Old English *seax* 'knife', of Germanic origin, from an Indo-European root meaning 'cut'.

saxe (also **saxe blue**) ▶ **noun** [mass noun] a light blue colour with a greyish tinge.
– ORIGIN mid 19th cent.: from French, literally 'Saxony', the source of a dye of this colour.

Saxe-Coburg-Gotha /saks,kəʊbəːg'gəʊtə, -'gəʊθə/ the name of the British royal house 1901–17. The name dates from the accession of Edward VII, whose father Prince Albert was a prince of the German duchy of Saxe-Coburg and Gotha.

saxhorn ▶ **noun** a member of a family of brass instruments with valves and a funnel-shaped mouthpiece, used mainly in military and brass bands.
– ORIGIN from the name of Charles J. *Sax* (1791–1865) and his son Antoine-Joseph 'Adolphe' *Sax* (1814–94), Belgian instrument-makers, + **HORN**.

saxifrage /'saksɪfreɪdʒ/ ▶ **noun** a low-growing plant of poor soils, bearing small white, yellow, or red flowers and forming rosettes of succulent leaves or hummocks of mossy leaves. Many are grown as alpines in rockeries.
• Genus *Saxifraga*, family Saxifragaceae.
– ORIGIN late Middle English: from Old French *saxifrage* or late Latin *saxifraga (herba)*, from Latin *saxum* 'rock' + *frangere* 'break'.

Saxon ▶ **noun** **1** a member of a people that inhabited parts of central and northern Germany from Roman times, many of whom conquered and settled in much of southern England in the 5th–6th centuries.
■a native of modern Saxony in Germany.
2 [mass noun] the language of the Saxons, in particular:
■(**Old Saxon**) the West Germanic language of the ancient Saxons. ■another term for **OLD ENGLISH**. ■ the Low German dialect of modern Saxony.
▶ **adjective** **1** of or relating to the Anglo-Saxons, their language (Old English), or their period of dominance in England (5th–11th centuries).
■relating to or denoting the style of early Romanesque architecture preceding the Norman in England.
2 of or relating to Saxony or the continental Saxons or their language.
– DERIVATIVES **Saxonize** (also **-ise**) verb.
– ORIGIN Middle English: from Old French, from late Latin and Greek *Saxones* (plural), of West Germanic origin; related to Old English *Seaxan, Seaxe* (plural), perhaps from the base of **SAX**[2].

Saxony /'saksəni/ a large region and former kingdom of Germany, including the modern states of Saxony in the south-east, Saxony-Anhalt in the centre, and Lower Saxony in the north-west. German name **SACHSEN**.
■a state of eastern Germany, on the upper reaches of the River Elbe; capital, Dresden.
– ORIGIN from late Latin *Saxonia*, from Latin *Saxo, Saxon-* (see **SAXON**).

saxony /'saks(ə)ni/ ▶ **noun** [mass noun] a fine kind of wool.
■a fine-quality cloth made from this kind of wool, chiefly used for making coats.
– ORIGIN mid 19th cent.: from **SAXONY**.

Saxony-Anhalt /,saksənɪ'anhalt/ a state of Germany, on the plains of the Elbe and the Saale Rivers; capital, Magdeburg. It corresponds to the former duchy of Anhalt and the central part of the former kingdom of Saxony. German name **SACHSEN-ANHALT**.

saxophone /'saksəfəʊn/ ▶ **noun** a member of a family of metal wind instruments with a reed like a clarinet, used especially in jazz and dance music.
– DERIVATIVES **saxophonic** /-'fɒnɪk/ adjective, **saxophonist** /sak'sɒf(ə)nɪst, 'saksə,fəʊnɪst/ noun.
– ORIGIN from the name of Adolphe *Sax* (see **SAXHORN**) + **-PHONE**.

say ▶ **verb** (**says**; past and past participle **said**) **1** [reporting verb] utter words so as to convey information, an opinion, a feeling or intention, or an instruction: [with direct speech] *'Thank you,' he said* | [with clause] *he said the fund stood at £100,000* | [with obj.] *our parents wouldn't believe a word we said* | [with infinitive] *he said to come early*.
■(of a text or a symbolic representation) convey specified information or instructions: [with clause] *the Act says such behaviour is an offence*. ■ [with obj.] enable a listener or reader to learn or understand something by conveying or revealing (information or ideas): *I don't want to say too much* | figurative *the film's title **says** it all*. ■ [with obj.] (of a clock or watch) indicate (a specified time): *the clock says ten past two*. ■ (**be said**) be asserted or reported (often used to avoid committing the speaker or writer to the truth of the assertion): [with infinitive] *they were said to be training freedom fighters* | [with clause] *it is said that she lived to over a hundred*. ■ [with obj.] (**say something for**) present a consideration in favour of or excusing (someone or something): *all I can say for him is that he's a better writer than some*. ■ [with obj.] utter the whole of (a speech or other set of words, typically one learned in advance): *the padre finished saying the Nunc Dimittis*.
2 [with clause] assume something in order to work out what its consequences would be; make a hypothesis: *let's say we pay in five thousand pounds in the first year*.
■used parenthetically to indicate that something is being suggested as possible or likely but not certain: *the form might include, say, a dozen questions*.
▶ **exclamation** N. Amer. informal used to express surprise or to draw attention to a remark or question: *say, did you notice any blood?*
▶ **noun** [in sing.] an opportunity for stating one's opinion or feelings: *the voters are entitled to **have their say** on the treaty*.
■an opportunity to influence developments and policy: *the assessor will **have a say** in how the money is spent* | [mass noun] *the households concerned would still **have** some **say** in what happened*.
– PHRASES **go without saying** be obvious: *it goes without saying that lay appointees must be selected with care*. [ORIGIN: translating French *(cela) va sans dire*.] **have something to say for oneself** contribute a specified amount to a conversation or discussion: *a dull girl with little to say for herself*. **how say you?** Law how do you find? (addressed to the jury when requesting its verdict). **I** (or **he**, **she**, etc.) **cannot** (or **could not**) **say** I (or he, she, etc.) do not know. **I'll say** informal used to express emphatic agreement: *'That was a good landing.' 'I'll say!'* **I must** (or **have to**) **say** I cannot refrain from saying (used to emphasize an opinion): *you have a nerve, I must say!* **I say!** Brit. dated used to express surprise or to draw attention to a remark: *I say, that's a bit much!* **I wouldn't say no** informal used to indicate that one would like something. **not to say** used to introduce a stronger alternative or addition to something already said: *it is easy to become sensitive, not to say paranoid*. **say no more** informal used to indicate that one understands what someone is trying to imply. **says I** (or **he**, **she** etc.) informal, chiefly Brit. used after direct speech in reporting someone's part in a conversation. **says you!** informal used in spoken English to express disagreement or disbelief: *'He's guilty.' 'Says you. I think he's innocent.'* **say when** informal said when helping someone to food or drink to instruct them to indicate when they have enough. **say the word** give permission or instructions to do something. **that is to say** used to introduce a clarification, interpretation, or correction of something already said. **there is no saying** it is impossible to know. **they say** it is rumoured. **to say nothing of** another way of saying ***not to mention*** (see **MENTION**). **what do** (or **would**) **you say** used to make a suggestion or offer: *what do you say to a glass of wine?* **when all is said and done** when everything is taken into account (used to indicate that one is making a generalized judgement about a situation). **you can say that again!** informal used in spoken English to express emphatic agreement. **you don't say** (or **you don't say so**)**!** informal used to express amazement or disbelief. **you** (or **you've**) **said it!** informal used to express the feeling that someone's words are true or appropriate.
– ORIGIN Old English *secgan*, of Germanic origin; related to Dutch *zeggen* and German *sagen*.
– DERIVATIVES **sayable** adjective, **sayer** noun [usu. in combination] *nay-sayers*.

SAYE ▶ **abbreviation for** save as you earn.

Sayers, Dorothy L. (1893–1957), English novelist and dramatist; full name *Dorothy Leigh Sayers*. She is chiefly known for her detective fiction featuring the amateur detective Lord Peter Wimsey; titles include *The Nine Tailors* (1934).

saying ▶ **noun** a short, pithy, commonly-known expression which generally offers advice or wisdom.
■(**sayings**) a collection of such expressions identified with a particular person, especially a political or religious leader.
– PHRASES **as** (or **so**) **the saying goes** (or **is**) used to introduce or append an expression, drawing attention to its status as a saying or as not part of one's normal language: *I am, as the saying goes, burnt out*.

sayonara /,sʌɪə'nɑːrə/ ▶ **exclamation** informal, chiefly US goodbye.
– ORIGIN Japanese.

Say's law /'seɪz/ Economics a law stating that supply creates its own demand.
– ORIGIN 1930s: named after Jean Baptiste *Say* (1767–1832), French economist.

say-so ▶ **noun** [in sing.] informal the power or act of deciding or allowing something: *no new employees come into the organization **without his say-so***.
■(usu. **on someone's say-so**) a person's arbitrary or unauthorized assertion or instruction: *I don't stop on the say-so of anybody's assistant*.

sayyid /'seɪjɪd, 'sʌɪɪd/ ▶ **noun** a Muslim claiming descent from Muhammad through Husayn, the prophet's younger grandson.
■a respectful Muslim form of address.
– ORIGIN Arabic, literally 'lord, prince'.

saz /saz/ ▶ **noun** a long-necked stringed instrument of the lute family, originating in the Ottoman Empire.
– ORIGIN late 19th cent.: from Turkish, from Persian *sāz* 'musical instrument'.

Sb ▶ **symbol for** the chemical element antimony.
– ORIGIN from Latin *stibium*.

SBA ▶ **abbreviation for** (in the US) Small Business Administration.

S-Bahn /'ɛsbɑːn/ ▶ **noun** (in some German cities) a fast urban railway line or system.
– ORIGIN German, abbreviation of *(Stadt) Schnellbahn* '(urban) fast railway'.

SBS ▶ **abbreviation for** Special Boat Service.

SC ▶ **abbreviation for** ■ South Carolina (in official postal use). ■ (in the UK) special constable.

Sc ▶ **symbol for** the chemical element scandium.

sc. ▶ **abbreviation** that is to say (used to introduce a word to be supplied or an explanation of an ambiguity).
– ORIGIN from **SCILICET**.

s.c. ▶ **abbreviation for** small capitals (used as an instruction for a typesetter).

S

scab ▶ **noun 1** a dry, rough protective crust that forms over a cut or wound during healing.
■ [mass noun] mange or a similar skin disease in animals. See also **SHEEP SCAB**. ■ [mass noun] [usu. with modifier] any of a number of fungal diseases of plants in which rough patches develop, especially on apples and potatoes.
2 figurative, informal a person or thing regarded with dislike and disgust.
■ derogatory a person who refuses to strike or join a trade union or who takes the place of a striking worker.
▶ **verb** (**scabbed, scabbing**) [no obj.] **1** [usu. as adj. **scabbed**] become encrusted or covered with a scab or scabs: *she rested her scabbed fingers on his arm.*
2 act or work as a scab.
■ [with obj.] Brit. informal scrounge.
– DERIVATIVES **scab-like** adjective.
– ORIGIN Middle English (as a noun): from Old Norse *skabb*; related to dialect *shab* (compare with **SHABBY**). The sense 'contemptible person' (dating from the late 16th cent.) was probably influenced by Middle Dutch *schabbe* 'slut'.

scabbard /ˈskabəd/ ▶ **noun** a sheath for the blade of a sword or dagger, typically made of leather or metal.
■ a sheath for a gun or other weapon or tool.
– ORIGIN Middle English: from Anglo-Norman French *escalberc*, from a Germanic compound of words meaning 'cut' (related to **SHEAR**) and 'protect' (related to the second element of **HAUBERK**).

scabbardfish ▶ **noun** (pl. same or **-fishes**) an elongated marine fish with heavy jaws and large teeth, which occurs mostly in the deeper waters of warm seas.
● Several genera and species in the family Trichiuridae, including the edible silvery-white *Lepidopus caudatus*.

scabby ▶ **adjective** (**scabbier, scabbiest**) **1** covered in scabs.
2 informal, chiefly Irish & Scottish (of a person) loathsome; despicable.
– DERIVATIVES **scabbiness** noun.

scabies /ˈskeɪbiːz/ ▶ **noun** [mass noun] a contagious skin disease marked by itching and small raised red spots, caused by the itch mite.
– ORIGIN late Middle English (denoting various skin diseases): from Latin, from *scabere* 'to scratch'. The current sense dates from the early 19th cent.

scabious /ˈskeɪbɪəs/ ▶ **noun** a plant of the teasel family, with pink, white, or (most commonly) blue pincushion-shaped flowers.
● *Scabiosa*, *Knautia*, and other genera, family Dipsacaceae: several species, including the **devil's bit scabious** (see **DEVIL'S BIT**).
▶ **adjective** affected with mange; scabby.
– ORIGIN late Middle English: based on Latin *scabiosus* 'rough, scabby'; the noun is from medieval Latin *scabiosa (herba)* 'rough, scabby (plant)', formerly regarded as a cure for skin disease (see **SCABIES**).

scablands ▶ **plural noun** Geology flat elevated land deeply scarred by channels of glacial or fluvioglacial origin and with poor soil and little vegetation, especially in the Columbia Plateau, Washington State, US.

S

scabrous /ˈskeɪbrəs, ˈskabrəs/ ▶ **adjective 1** rough and covered with, or as if with, scabs.
■ unpleasant; unattractive: *a scabrous Carnaby Street hovel.*
2 indecent; salacious: *scabrous details included being regularly seen with a mistress.*
– DERIVATIVES **scabrously** adverb, **scabrousness** noun.
– ORIGIN late 16th cent. (first used to describe an author's style as 'harsh, unmusical, unpolished'): from French *scabreux* or late Latin *scabrosus*, from Latin *scaber* 'rough'.

scad ▶ **noun** another term for **JACK**[1] (in sense 11) or **HORSE MACKEREL**.
– ORIGIN early 17th cent.: of unknown origin.

scads ▶ **plural noun** informal, chiefly N. Amer. a large number or quantity: *they raised* **scads of** *children.*
– ORIGIN mid 19th cent.: of unknown origin.

Scafell Pike /skɔːˈfɛl/ a mountain in the Lake District of NW England, in Cumbria. Rising to a height of 978 m (3,210 ft), it is the highest peak in England.

scaffold /ˈskafəʊld, -f(ə)ld/ ▶ **noun 1** a raised wooden platform used formerly for the public execution of criminals.
2 a structure made using scaffolding.
▶ **verb** [with obj.] attach scaffolding to (a building): [as adj. **scaffolded**] *the soot-black scaffolded structure.*
– DERIVATIVES **scaffolder** noun.
– ORIGIN Middle English (denoting a temporary platform from which to repair or erect a building): from Anglo-Norman French, from Old French *(e)schaffaut*, from the base of **CATAFALQUE**.

scaffolding ▶ **noun** [mass noun] a temporary structure on the outside of a building, made of wooden planks and metal poles, used by workmen while building, repairing, or cleaning the building.
■ the materials used in such a structure.

scag ▶ **noun** variant spelling of **SKAG**.

scagliola /skalˈjəʊlə/ ▶ **noun** [mass noun] imitation marble or other stone, made of plaster mixed with glue and dyes which is then painted or polished.
– ORIGIN mid 18th cent.: from Italian *scagliuola*, diminutive of *scaglia* 'a scale'.

scalable ▶ **adjective 1** able to be scaled or climbed.
2 able to be changed in size or scale: *scalable fonts.*
■ (of a computing process) able to be used or produced in a range of capabilities: *it is scalable across a range of systems.*
3 technical able to be measured or graded according to a scale.
– DERIVATIVES **scalability** noun.

scala media /ˌskeɪlə ˈmiːdɪə/ ▶ **noun** (pl. **scalae media** /ˌskeɪliː, ˌskeɪlʌɪ/) Anatomy the central duct of the cochlea in the inner ear, containing the sensory cells and separated from the scala tympani and scala vestibuli by membranes.
– ORIGIN late 19th cent.: from Latin, literally 'middle ladder'.

scalar /ˈskeɪlə/ Mathematics & Physics ▶ **adjective** (of a quantity) having only magnitude, not direction.
▶ **noun** a scalar quantity.
– ORIGIN mid 17th cent.: from Latin *scalaris*, from *scala* 'ladder' (see **SCALE**[3]).

scalar field ▶ **noun** Mathematics a function of a space whose value at each point is a scalar quantity.

scalariform /skəˈlarɪfɔːm/ ▶ **adjective** Botany (especially of the walls of water-conducting cells) having thickened bands arranged like the rungs of a ladder.
– ORIGIN mid 19th cent.: from Latin *scalaris* 'of a ladder' + **-IFORM**.

scalar product ▶ **noun** Mathematics a scalar function of two vectors, equal to the product of their magnitudes and the cosine of the angle between them. Also called **DOT PRODUCT**. Compare with **VECTOR PRODUCT**.
● Written as a.b or ab.

scala tympani /ˌskeɪlə tɪmˈpɑːni/ ▶ **noun** (pl. **scalae tympani** /ˌskeɪliː, ˌskeɪlʌɪ/) Anatomy the lower bony passage of the cochlea.
– ORIGIN early 18th cent.: from Latin, literally 'ladder of the tympanum'.

scala vestibuli /vɛˈstɪbjʊli/ ▶ **noun** (pl. **scalae vestibuli**) Anatomy the upper bony passage of the cochlea.
– ORIGIN early 18th cent.: from Latin, literally 'ladder of the vestibule'.

scalawag ▶ **noun** variant spelling of **SCALLYWAG**.

scald[1] ▶ **verb** [with obj.] injure with very hot liquid or steam: *the tea scalded his tongue.*
■ heat (milk or other liquid) to near boiling point. ■ immerse (something) briefly in boiling water for various purposes, such as to facilitate the removal of skin from fruit or to preserve meat. ■ archaic clean (a container) by rinsing with boiling water. ■ cause to feel a searing sensation like that of boiling water on skin: *she fought to stave off the hot tears scalding her eyes.*
▶ **noun** a burn or other injury caused by hot liquid or steam.
■ [mass noun] any of a number of plant diseases which produce a similar effect to that of scalding, especially a disease of fruit marked by browning and caused by excessive sunlight, bad storage conditions, or atmospheric pollution. See also **SUN SCALD**.
– PHRASES **like a scalded cat** at a very fast speed.
– ORIGIN Middle English (as a verb): from Anglo-Norman French *escalder*, from late Latin *excaldare*, from Latin *ex-* 'thoroughly' + *calidus* 'hot'. The noun dates from the early 17th cent.

scald[2] ▶ **noun** variant spelling of **SKALD**.

scaldfish ▶ **noun** (pl. same or **-fishes**) a small edible European flatfish of inshore waters, the fragile scales of which are easily scraped off, giving the appearance of a scald. Also called **MEGRIM**[2].
● *Arnoglossus laterna*, family Bothidae.

scalding ▶ **adjective** very hot; burning: *she took a sip of scalding tea* | [as submodifier] *the water was scalding hot.*
■ figurative intense and painful or distressing: *a scalding tirade of abuse.*

scale[1] ▶ **noun 1** each of the small, thin horny or bony plates protecting the skin of fish and reptiles, typically overlapping one another.
2 something resembling a fish scale in appearance or function, in particular:
■ a thick dry flake of skin. ■ a rudimentary leaf, feather, or bract. ■ each of numerous microscopic tile-like structures covering the wings of butterflies and moths.
3 [mass noun] a flaky deposit, in particular:
■ a white deposit formed in a kettle, boiler, etc. by the evaporation of water containing lime. ■ tartar formed on teeth. ■ a coating of oxide formed on heated metal.
▶ **verb 1** [with obj.] remove scale or scales from: *he scales the fish and removes the innards.*
■ remove tartar from (teeth) by scraping them.
2 [no obj.] [often as noun **scaling**] (especially of the skin) form scales: *moisturizers can ease off drying and scaling.*
■ come off in scales or thin pieces; flake off: *the paint was scaling from the brick walls.*
– PHRASES **the scales fall from someone's eyes** someone is no longer deceived. [ORIGIN: with biblical reference to Acts 9:18.]
– DERIVATIVES **scaled** adjective [often in combination] *a rough-scaled fish*, **scaleless** adjective, **scaler** noun.
– ORIGIN Middle English: shortening of Old French *escale*, from the Germanic base of **SCALE**[2].

scale[2] ▶ **noun** (usu. **scales**) an instrument for weighing, originally a simple balance (**a pair of scales**) but now usually a device with an electronic or other internal weighing mechanism.
■ (also **scale pan**) either of the dishes on a simple balance. ■ (**the Scales**) the zodiacal sign or constellation Libra. ■ S. African a large vessel for beer or other liquor; a measure for drink.
▶ **verb** weigh a specified weight: *some men scaled less than ninety pounds.*
– PHRASES **throw something on** (or **into**) **the scale** emphasize the relevance of something to one side of an argument or debate: *we should have thrown on the other scale all that was moderate in the Liberal Party as well.* **tip** (or **turn**) **the scales** see **TIP**[2].
– ORIGIN Middle English (in the sense 'drinking cup', surviving in South African English): from Old Norse *skál* 'bowl', of Germanic origin; related to Dutch *schaal*, German *Schale* 'bowl', also to English dialect *shale* 'dish'.

scale[3] ▶ **noun 1** a graduated range of values forming a standard system for measuring or grading something: *company employees have hit the top of their pay scales* | figurative *two men at opposite ends of* **the social scale**.
■ a series of marks at regular intervals in a line used in measuring something: *the mean delivery time is plotted against a scale on the right.* ■ a device having such a series of marks: *she read the exact distance off a scale.* ■ a rule determining the distances between such marks: *the vertical axis is given on a logarithmic scale.*
2 [in sing.] the relative size or extent of something: *no one foresaw the scale of the disaster* | *everything in the house is* **on a grand scale**.
■ [often as modifier] a ratio of size in a map, model, drawing, or plan: *a one-fifth scale model of a seven-storey building* | *an Ordnance map* **on a scale of** *1:2500.* ■ (in full **scale of notation**) Mathematics a system of numerical notation in which the value of a digit depends upon its position in the number, successive positions representing successive powers of a fixed base: *the conversion of the number to the binary scale.* ■ Photography the range of exposures over which a photographic material will give an acceptable variation in density.
3 Music an arrangement of the notes in any system of music in ascending or descending order of pitch: *the scale of C major.*
▶ **verb** [with obj.] **1** climb up or over (something high and steep): *thieves scaled an 8 ft high fence.*
2 represent in proportional dimensions; reduce or increase in size according to a common scale: [as adj. **scaled**] *scaled plans of the house.*
■ [no obj.] (of a quantity or property) be variable according to a particular scale.

3 N. Amer. estimate the amount of timber that will be produced from (a log or uncut tree).

– PHRASES **play** (or **sing** or **practise**) **scales** Music perform the notes of a scale as an exercise for the fingers or voice. **to scale** with a uniform reduction or enlargement: *it is hard to build models to scale from a drawing.* **in scale** (of a drawing or model) in proportion to the surroundings.

– DERIVATIVES **scaler** noun.

– ORIGIN late Middle English: from Latin *scala* 'ladder' (the verb via Old French *escaler* or medieval Latin *scalare* 'climb'), from the base of Latin *scandere* 'to climb'.

▶**scale something back** chiefly US reduce something in size, number, or extent: *in the short term, even scaling back defense costs money.*

scale something down (or **scale down**) reduce something (or be reduced) in size, number or extent: *manufacturing capacity has been scaled down | his whole income scaled down by 20 per cent.*

scale something up (or **scale up**) increase something (or be increased) in size or number: *one cannot suddenly scale up a laboratory procedure by a thousandfold.*

scale armour ▶**noun** [mass noun] historical armour consisting of small overlapping plates of metal, leather, or horn.

scale board ▶**noun** [mass noun] very thin wood used (especially formerly) in bookbinding, making hatboxes, and backing pictures.

scale insect ▶**noun** a small bug with a protective shield-like scale. It spends most of its life attached by its mouth to a single plant, sometimes occurring in such large numbers that it becomes a serious pest.

• Superfamily Coccoidea, suborder Homoptera: several families, in particular Coccidae.

scale leaf ▶**noun** Botany a small modified leaf, especially a colourless membranous one, such as on a rhizome or forming part of a bulb.

scalene /'skeɪliːn/ ▶**adjective** (of a triangle) having sides unequal in length.

▶**noun 1** (also **scalene muscle**) Anatomy another term for **SCALENUS**.

2 a scalene triangle.

– ORIGIN mid 17th cent.: via late Latin from Greek *skalēnos* 'unequal'; related to *skolios* 'bent'.

scalenus /skə'liːnəs/ ▶**noun** (pl. **scaleni** /-nʌɪ/) any of several muscles extending from the neck to the first and second ribs.

– ORIGIN early 18th cent.: modern Latin, from late Latin *scalenus* (*musculus*) 'unequal (muscle)' (see **SCALENE**).

scale of notation ▶**noun** see **SCALE**^{3} (sense 2).

scale-pan ▶**noun** see **SCALE**^{2}.

scale worm ▶**noun** a marine bristle worm with scales on the upper surface which have a protective function, and in some species are able to luminesce.

• Family Aphroditidae: *Aphrodite* and other genera. See also **SEA MOUSE**.

Scaliger^{1} /'skalɪdʒə/, Joseph Justus (1540–1609), French scholar, son of Julius Caesar Scaliger. His *De Emendatione Temporum* (1583) gave a more scientific foundation to the understanding of ancient chronology by comparing and revising the computations of time made by different civilizations, including those of the Babylonians and Egyptians.

Scaliger^{2} /'skalɪdʒə/, Julius Caesar (1484–1558), Italian-born French classical scholar and physician.

scaling ladder ▶**noun** historical a ladder used for climbing fortress walls in an attempt to break a siege or for firefighting.

scallion /'skalɪən/ ▶**noun** a long-necked onion with a small bulb, in particular a shallot or spring onion.

– ORIGIN late Middle English: from Anglo-Norman French *scaloun*, based on Latin *Ascalonia* (*caepa*) '(onion) of *Ascalon*', a port in ancient Palestine.

scallop /'skɒləp, 'skaləp/ ▶**noun 1** an edible bivalve mollusc with a ribbed fan-shaped shell. Scallops swim by rapidly opening and closing the shell valves.

• Family Pectinidae: *Chlamys*, *Pecten*, and other genera.

■short for **SCALLOP SHELL**. ■a small pan or dish shaped like a scallop shell and used for baking or serving food.

2 (usu. **scallops**) each of a series of convex rounded projections forming an ornamental edging cut in material or worked in lace or knitting in imitation of the edge of a scallop shell.

3 another term for **ESCALOPE**.

▶**verb** (**scalloped**, **scalloping**) **1** [with obj.] [usu. as adj. **scalloped**] ornament (an edge or material) with scallops: *a scalloped V-shaped neckline.*

■cut, shape, or arrange in the form of a scallop shell: *he leaned against the scalloped seat of the limousine.*

2 [no obj.] [usu. as noun **scalloping**] N. Amer. gather or dredge for scallops.

3 [with obj.] bake with milk or a sauce: [as adj. **scalloped**] *scalloped potatoes.*

– DERIVATIVES **scalloper** noun.

– ORIGIN Middle English: shortening of Old French *escalope*, probably of Germanic origin. The verb dates from the mid 18th cent.

scallop shell ▶**noun** a single valve from the shell of a scallop.

■historical a representation of this shell worn by a pilgrim as a souvenir of the shrine of St James at Santiago de Compostela in Spain.

scally ▶**noun** (pl. **-ies**) informal (in the north-west of England, especially Liverpool) a roguish self-assured young person, typically a man, who is boisterous, disruptive, or irresponsible.

– ORIGIN 1980s: abbreviation of **SCALLYWAG**.

scallywag (US also **scalawag**) ▶**noun** informal a person, typically a child, who behaves badly but in an amusingly mischievous rather than harmful way; a rascal.

■US a white Southerner who collaborated with northern Republicans during the post-Civil War reconstruction period.

– ORIGIN mid 19th cent.: of unknown origin.

scaloppine /ˌskalə'piːneɪ, -ni/ (also **scallopini**) ▶**plural noun** (in Italian cooking) thin, boneless slices of meat, typically veal, sautéed or fried.

– ORIGIN Italian, plural of *scaloppina*, diminutive of *scaloppa* 'envelope'.

scalp ▶**noun 1** the skin covering the head, excluding the face.

■historical the scalp with the hair belonging to it cut or torn away from an enemy's head as a battle trophy, especially by an American Indian. ■figurative used with reference to the defeat of an opponent: *in rugby Gloucester **claimed the scalp** of would-be champions Bath.* ■Scottish a bare rock projecting above surrounding water or vegetation.

▶**verb** [with obj.] historical take the scalp of (an enemy).

■informal punish severely: *if I ever heard anybody doing that I'd scalp them.* ■informal, chiefly N. Amer. resell (shares or tickets) at a large or quick profit.

– ORIGIN Middle English (denoting the skull or cranium): probably of Scandinavian origin.

scalpel ▶**noun** a knife with a small, sharp, sometimes detachable blade, as used by a surgeon.

– ORIGIN mid 18th cent.: from French, or from Latin *scalpellum*, diminutive of *scalprum* 'chisel', from *scalpere* 'to scratch'.

scalper ▶**noun** informal, chiefly N. Amer. a person who resells shares or tickets at a large or quick profit.

scalp lock ▶**noun** historical a long lock of hair left on the shaved head by a North American Indian as a challenge to enemies.

scaly ▶**adjective** (**scalier**, **scaliest**) covered in scales.

■(of skin) dry and flaking.

– DERIVATIVES **scaliness** noun.

scaly anteater ▶**noun** another term for **PANGOLIN**.

scalyfoot ▶**noun** (pl. **scalyfoots**) a snake-like Australian legless lizard with a prehensile tail and the hindlimb remnants visible as scaly flaps.

• Genus *Pygopus*, family Pygopodidae: two species, in particular the common *P. lepidopodus*.

scaly-tailed squirrel ▶**noun** a squirrel-like rodent with horny scales on the underside of the tail, native to west and central Africa.

• Family Anomaluridae: three genera and several species, in particular the **flightless scaly-tailed squirrel** (*Zenkerella insignis*); the remainder are all flying squirrels.

scam ▶**noun** informal a dishonest scheme; a fraud: [with modifier] *an insurance scam.*

▶**verb** (**scammed**, **scamming**) [with obj.] swindle: *a guy that scams old pensioners out of their savings.*

– DERIVATIVES **scammer** noun.

– ORIGIN 1960s: of unknown origin.

scammony /'skaməni/ ▶**noun** a plant of the convolvulus family, the dried roots of which yield a drastic purgative.

• Two species in the family Convolvulaceae: *Convolvulus scammonia* of Asia, and *Ipomoea orizabensis* of Mexico.

– ORIGIN Old English, from Old French *escamonie* or Latin *scammonia*, from Greek *skammōnia*.

scamp^{1} ▶**noun** informal a person, especially a child, who is mischievous in a likeable or amusing way.

■W. Indian a wicked or worthless person; a rogue.

– DERIVATIVES **scampish** adjective.

– ORIGIN mid 18th cent. (denoting a highwayman): from obsolete *scamp* 'rob on the highway', probably from Middle Dutch *schampen* 'slip away', from Old French *eschamper*. Early usage (still reflected in West Indian English) was derogatory.

scamp^{2} ▶**verb** [with obj.] dated do (something) in a perfunctory or inadequate way.

– ORIGIN mid 19th cent.: perhaps the same word as **SCAMP**^{1}, but associated in sense with the verb **SKIMP**.

scamper ▶**verb** [no obj., with adverbial of direction] (especially of a small animal or child) run with quick light steps, especially through fear or excitement: *he scampered in like an overgrown puppy.*

▶**noun** [in sing.] an act of scampering.

– ORIGIN late 17th cent. (in the sense 'run away'): probably from **SCAMP**^{2}.

scampi ▶**noun** [treated as sing. or pl.] Norway lobsters when prepared or cooked.

– ORIGIN Italian.

scan ▶**verb** (**scanned**, **scanning**) [with obj.] **1** look at all parts of (something) carefully in order to detect some feature: *he raised his binoculars to scan the coast.*

■look quickly but not very thoroughly through (a document or other text) in order to identify relevant information: *we scan the papers for news from the trouble spots* | [no obj.] *I **scanned through** the reference materials.* ■cause (a surface, object, or part of the body) to be traversed by a detector or an electromagnetic beam: *their brains are scanned so that researchers can monitor the progress of the disease.* ■[with obj. and adverbial] cause (a beam) to traverse across a surface or object: *we scanned the beam over a sector of 120°.* ■resolve (a picture) into its elements of light and shade in a pre-arranged pattern for the purposes of television transmission. ■convert (a document or picture) into digital form for storage or processing on a computer: *text and pictures can be **scanned into** the computer.*

2 analyse the metre of (a line of verse) by reading with the emphasis on its rhythm or by examining the pattern of feet or syllables.

■[no obj.] (of verse) conform to metrical principles.

▶**noun** an act of scanning someone or something: *a quick scan of the sports page.*

■a medical examination using a scanner: *a brain scan.* ■an image obtained by scanning or with a scanner: *you can't predict anything until he has seen the scan.*

– DERIVATIVES **scannable** adjective.

– ORIGIN late Middle English (as a verb in sense 2): from Latin *scandere* 'climb' (in late Latin 'scan (verses)'), by analogy with the raising and lowering of one's foot when marking rhythm. From 'analyse (metre)' arose the senses 'estimate the correctness of' and 'examine minutely', which led to 'look at searchingly' (late 18th cent.).

scandal ▶**noun** an action or event regarded as morally or legally wrong and causing general public outrage: *a bribery scandal involving one of his key supporters.*

■[mass noun] the outrage or anger caused by such an action or event: *divorce was cause for scandal in the island.* ■[mass noun] rumour or malicious gossip about such events or actions: *I know that you would want no scandal attached to her name.* ■[in sing.] a state of affairs regarded as wrong or reprehensible and causing general public outrage or anger: *it's a scandal that many older patients are dismissed as untreatable.*

– ORIGIN Middle English (in the sense 'discredit to religion (by the reprehensible behaviour of a religious person)'): from Old French *scandale*, from ecclesiastical Latin *scandalum* 'cause of offence', from Greek *skandalon* 'snare, stumbling block'.

scandalize (also **-ise**) ▶**verb** [with obj.] **1** shock or horrify (someone) by a real or imagined violation of propriety or morality: *their lack of manners scandalized their hosts.*

2 Sailing reduce the area of (a sail) by lowering the head or raising the boom. [ORIGIN: mid 19th cent.: alteration of obsolete *scantelize*, from *scantle* 'make small'.]

– ORIGIN late 15th cent. (in the sense 'make a public scandal of'): from French *scandaliser* or

S

ecclesiastical Latin *scandalizare*, from Greek *skandalizein*.

scandalmonger ▶ noun a person who stirs up public outrage towards someone or their actions by spreading rumours or malicious gossip.

scandalous ▶ adjective causing general public outrage by a perceived offence against morality or law: *a series of scandalous liaisons* | *a scandalous allegation*.
■(of a state of affairs) disgracefully bad, typically as a result of someone's negligence or irresponsibility: *a scandalous waste of ratepayers' money*.
– DERIVATIVES **scandalously** adverb, **scandalousness** noun.

scandal sheet ▶ noun derogatory a newspaper or magazine giving prominence to scandalous stories or gossip.

scandent /ˈskandənt/ ▶ adjective chiefly Palaeontology (especially of a graptolite) having a climbing habit.
– ORIGIN late 17th cent.: from Latin *scandent-* 'climbing', from the verb *scandere*.

Scandentia /skanˈdɛnʃə/ Zoology a small order of mammals which comprises the tree shrews.
– ORIGIN modern Latin (plural), from Latin *scandent-* 'climbing', from the verb *scandere*.

Scandinavia /ˌskandɪˈneɪvɪə/ a large peninsula in NW Europe, occupied by Norway and Sweden. It is bounded by the Arctic Ocean in the north, the Atlantic in the west, and the Baltic Sea in the south and east.
■a cultural region consisting of the countries of Norway, Sweden, and Denmark and sometimes also of Iceland, Finland, and the Faroe Islands.
– ORIGIN Latin.

Scandinavian ▶ adjective of or relating to Scandinavia, its people, or their languages.
▶ noun 1 a native or inhabitant of Scandinavia, or a person of Scandinavian descent.
2 [mass noun] the northern branch of the Germanic languages, comprising Danish, Norwegian, Swedish, Icelandic, and Faroese, all descended from Old Norse.

scandium /ˈskandɪəm/ ▶ noun [mass noun] the chemical element of atomic number 21, a soft silvery-white metal resembling the rare earth elements. (Symbol: **Sc**)
– ORIGIN late 19th cent.: modern Latin, from *Scandia*, contraction of *Scandinavia* (where minerals are found containing this element).

scanner ▶ noun a device for examining, reading, or monitoring something, in particular:
■Medicine a machine that examines the body through the use of radiation, ultrasound, or magnetic resonance imaging, as a diagnostic aid. ■ Electronics a device that scans documents and converts them into digital data.

scanning electron microscope (abbrev.: **SEM**) ▶ noun an electron microscope in which the surface of a specimen is scanned by a beam of electrons that are reflected to form an image.

scanning tunnelling microscope (abbrev.: **STM**) ▶ noun a high-resolution microscope using neither light nor an electron beam, but with an ultra-fine tip able to reveal atomic and molecular details of surfaces.

scansion /ˈskanʃ(ə)n/ ▶ noun [mass noun] the action of scanning a line of verse to determine its rhythm.
■the rhythm of a line of verse.
– ORIGIN mid 17th cent.: from Latin *scansio(n-)*, from *scandere* 'to climb'; compare with **SCAN**.

scant ▶ adjective barely sufficient or adequate: *companies with scant regard for the safety of future generations*.
■[attrib.] barely amounting to a specified number or quantity: *she weighed a scant two pounds*.
▶ verb [with obj.] chiefly N. Amer. provide grudgingly or in insufficient amounts: *he does not scant his attention to the later writings*.
■deal with inadequately; neglect: *the press regularly scants a host of issues relating to safety and health*.
– DERIVATIVES **scantly** adverb, **scantness** noun.
– ORIGIN Middle English: from Old Norse *skamt*, neuter of *skammr* 'short'.

scantling ▶ noun 1 a timber beam of small cross section.
■the size to which a piece of timber or stone is measured and cut.
2 (often **scantlings**) a set of standard dimensions for parts of a structure, especially in shipbuilding.

3 archaic a specimen, sample, or small amount of something.
– ORIGIN early 16th cent. (denoting prescribed size, or a set of standard dimensions): alteration of obsolete *scantillon* (from Old French *escantillon* 'sample'), by association with the suffix **-LING**.

scanty ▶ adjective (**scantier**, **scantiest**) small or insufficient in quantity or amount: *they paid whatever they could out of their scanty wages to their families*.
■(of clothing) revealing; skimpy: *the women looked cold in their scanty bodices*.
– DERIVATIVES **scantily** adverb, **scantiness** noun.
– ORIGIN late 16th cent.: from **SCANT** + **-Y**[1].

Scapa Flow /ˈskɑːpə, ˈskapə/ a strait in the Orkney Islands, Scotland. It was an important British naval base, especially in the First World War. The German High Seas Fleet was interned there after its surrender, and was scuttled in 1919 as an act of defiance against the terms of the Versailles peace settlement.

scape ▶ noun Entomology the basal segment of an insect's antenna, especially when it is enlarged and lengthened (as in a weevil).
– ORIGIN early 19th cent.: via Latin from Greek *skapos* 'rod'; related to **SCEPTRE**.

-scape ▶ combining form denoting a specified type of scene: *moonscape*.
– ORIGIN on the pattern of (*land*)*scape*.

scapegoat ▶ noun (in the Bible) a goat sent into the wilderness after the Jewish chief priest had symbolically laid the sins of the people upon it (Lev. 16).
■a person who is blamed for the wrongdoings, mistakes, or faults of others, especially for reasons of expediency.
▶ verb [with obj.] make a scapegoat of.
– ORIGIN mid 16th cent.: from archaic *scape* 'escape' + **GOAT**.

scapegrace ▶ noun archaic a mischievous or wayward person, especially a young person or child; a rascal.
– ORIGIN early 19th cent.: from *scape* (see **SCAPEGOAT**) + **GRACE**, literally denoting a person who escapes the grace of God.

scaphoid /ˈskafɔɪd/ ▶ noun Anatomy a large carpal bone articulating with the radius below the thumb.
– ORIGIN mid 18th cent. (in the sense 'boat-shaped'): from modern Latin *scaphoides*, from Greek *skaphoeidēs*, from *skaphos* 'boat'.

Scaphopoda /ˌskafəˈpəʊdə/ Zoology a class of molluscs that comprises the tusk shells.
– DERIVATIVES **scaphopod** noun.
– ORIGIN modern Latin (plural), from Greek *skaphē* 'boat' + *pous, pod-* 'foot'.

scapula /ˈskapjʊlə/ ▶ noun (pl. **scapulae** /-liː/ or **scapulas**) Anatomy technical term for **SHOULDER BLADE**.
– ORIGIN late 16th cent.: from late Latin, singular of Latin *scapulae* 'shoulder blades'.

scapular ▶ adjective Anatomy & Zoology of or relating to the shoulder or shoulder blade.
▶ noun 1 a short monastic cloak covering the shoulders.
■a symbol of affiliation to an ecclesiastical order, consisting of two strips of cloth hanging down the breast and back and joined across the shoulders.
2 Medicine a bandage passing over and around the shoulders.
3 Ornithology a scapular feather.
– ORIGIN late 15th cent. (in sense 1 of the noun): from late Latin *scapulare*, from *scapula* 'shoulder'. The adjective (late 17th cent.) and the later senses of the noun are from **SCAPULA** + **-AR**[1].

scapular feather ▶ noun Ornithology a feather covering the shoulder, growing above the region where the wing joins the body.

scapulary ▶ noun (pl. **-ies**) another term for **SCAPULAR** (in senses 1 and 3).
– ORIGIN Middle English: from an Anglo-Norman French variant of Old French *eschapeloyre*, based on late Latin *scapulare* (see **SCAPULAR**).

scapulimancy /ˈskapjʊlɪˌmansi/ ▶ noun [mass noun] Anthropology divination from the cracks in a burned animal shoulder blade, traditional among some North American hunting peoples.

scar ▶ noun 1 a mark left on the skin or within body tissue where a wound, burn, or sore has not healed

quite completely and fibrous connective tissue has developed: *a faint scar ran the length of his left cheek*.
■figurative a lasting effect of grief, fear, or other emotion left on a person's character by an unpleasant experience: *the attack has left mental scars on Terry and his family*. ■ a mark left on something following damage of some kind: *Max could see scars of the blast*. ■ a mark left at the point of separation of a leaf, frond, or other part from a plant.
2 a steep high cliff or rock outcrop, especially of limestone. [ORIGIN: Middle English: from Old Norse *sker* 'low reef'.]
▶ verb (**scarred**, **scarring**) [with obj.] (often **be scarred**) mark with a scar or scars: *he is likely to be scarred for life after injuries to his face, arms, and legs* | [as adj., in combination **-scarred**] *battle-scarred troops*.
■[no obj.] form or be marked with a scar.
– DERIVATIVES **scarless** adjective.
– ORIGIN late Middle English: from Old French *escharre*, via late Latin from Greek *eskhara* 'scab'.

scarab /ˈskarəb/ ▶ noun (also **sacred scarab**) a large dung beetle of the eastern Mediterranean area, regarded as sacred in ancient Egypt.
● *Scarabaeus sacer*, family Scarabaeidae (the **scarab family**). The scarab family also includes the smaller dung beetles and chafers, together with some very large tropical kinds such as Hercules, goliath, and rhinoceros beetles.
■an ancient Egyptian gem cut in the form of this beetle, sometimes depicted with the wings spread, and engraved with hieroglyphs on the flat underside. ■ any scarabaeid beetle.
– ORIGIN late 16th cent. (originally denoting a beetle of any kind): from Latin *scarabaeus*, from Greek *skarabeios*.

scarabaeid /ˌskarəˈbiːɪd/ ▶ noun Entomology a beetle of the scarab family (Scarabaeidae), typically having strong spiky forelegs for burrowing.
– ORIGIN mid 19th cent.: from modern Latin *Scarabaeidae* (plural), from Latin *scarabaeus* (see **SCARAB**).

scarabaeoid /ˌskarəˈbiːɔɪd/ ▶ noun Entomology a beetle of a large group that includes the scarabaeids, dor beetles, and stag beetles. Scarabaeoids include the largest known beetles, and are distinguished by having plate-like terminal segments in the antennae. Formerly called **LAMELLICORN**.
● Superfamily Scarabaeoidea (formerly Lamellicornia).
– ORIGIN late 19th cent.: from modern Latin *Scarabaeoidea* (plural), from Latin *scarabaeus* (see **SCARAB**).

scaramouch /ˈskarəmaʊtʃ, -muːtʃ/ ▶ noun archaic a boastful but cowardly person.
– ORIGIN mid 17th cent.: from Italian *Scaramuccia*, the name of a stock character in Italian farce, from *scaramuccia* 'skirmish'.

Scarborough /ˈskɑːbərə/ a fishing port and resort on the coast of North Yorkshire; pop. 38,000 (1981).

scarce ▶ adjective (especially of food, money, or some other resource) insufficient for the demand: *as raw materials became scarce, synthetics were developed*.
■occurring in small numbers or quantities; rare: *the freshwater shrimp becomes scarce in soft water*.
▶ adverb archaic scarcely: *a babe scarce two years old*.
– PHRASES **make oneself scarce** informal leave a place, especially so as to avoid a difficult situation.
– DERIVATIVES **scarceness** noun, **scarcity** noun.
– ORIGIN Middle English (in the sense 'restricted in quantity or size', also 'parsimonious'): from a shortening of Anglo-Norman *escars*, from a Romance word meaning 'plucked out, selected'.

scarcely ▶ adverb only just; almost not: *her voice is so low I can scarcely hear what she is saying*.
■only a very short time before: *she had scarcely dismounted before the door swung open*. ■ used to suggest that something is unlikely to be or certainly not the case: *they could scarcely all be wrong*.

scare /skɛː/ ▶ verb [with obj.] cause great fear or nervousness in; frighten: *the rapid questions were designed to scare her into blurting out the truth*.
■[with obj. and adverbial] drive or keep (someone) away by frightening them: *the ugly scenes scared the holiday crowds away*. ■ [no obj.] become scared: *I don't think I scare easily*.
▶ noun a sudden attack of fright: *gosh, that gave me a scare!*
■[usu. with modifier] a general feeling of anxiety or alarm about something: *bombs and bomb scares disrupted shopping*.
– DERIVATIVES **scarer** noun.

– ORIGIN Middle English: from Old Norse *skirra* 'frighten', from *skjarr* 'timid'.
▶**scare something up** informal, chiefly N. Amer. manage to find or obtain something: *for a price, the box office can usually scare up a pair of tickets.*

scarecrow ▶**noun** an object made to resemble a human figure, set up to scare birds away from a field where crops are growing.
■informal a person who is very badly dressed, odd-looking, or thin. ■ archaic an object of baseless fear.

scared ▶**adjective** fearful; frightened: *she's* ***scared stiff of*** *her dad* | [with clause] *I was scared I was going to kill myself* | [with infinitive] *he's scared to come to you and ask for help.*

scaredy-cat ▶**noun** informal a timid person.

scaremonger ▶**noun** a person who spreads frightening or ominous reports or rumours.
– DERIVATIVES **scaremongering** noun & adjective.

scare quotes ▶**plural noun** quotation marks placed round a word or phrase to draw attention to an unusual or arguably inaccurate use.

scare tactics ▶**plural noun** a strategy intended to influence public reaction by the exploitation of fear.

scarf[1] ▶**noun** (pl. **scarves** or **scarfs**) a length or square of fabric worn around the neck or head.
– DERIVATIVES **scarfed** (also **scarved**) adjective.
– ORIGIN mid 16th cent. (in the sense 'sash (around the waist or over the shoulder'): probably based on Old Northern French *escarpe*, probably identical with Old French *escharpe* 'pilgrim's scrip'.

scarf[2] ▶**verb** [with obj.] **1** join the ends of (two pieces of timber or metal) by bevelling or notching them so that they fit over or into each other.
2 make an incision in the blubber of (a whale).
▶**noun 1** a joint connecting two pieces of timber or metal in which the ends are bevelled or notched so that they fit over or into each other.
2 an incision made in the blubber of a whale.
– ORIGIN Middle English (as a noun): probably via Old French from Old Norse. The verb dates from the early 17th cent.

scarf[3] ▶**verb** [with obj.] N. Amer. informal eat or drink (something) hungrily or enthusiastically: *he scarfed down the waffles.*
– ORIGIN 1960s: variant of **SCOFF**[2].

scarf ring ▶**noun** a ring through which the ends or corners of a scarf are threaded in order to hold the scarf in position.

scarf-skin ▶**noun** [mass noun] archaic the thin outer layer of the skin; the epidermis.

scarifier /'skarɪfʌɪə, 'skɛːrɪ-/ ▶**noun** a tool with spikes or prongs used for breaking up matted vegetation in the surface of a lawn.
■a machine with spikes used for breaking up the surface of a road. ■ chiefly Austral. a machine with spikes or prongs used for loosening soil.

scarify[1] /'skarɪfʌɪ, 'skɛːrɪ-/ ▶**verb** (**-ies**, **-ied**) [with obj.] make cuts or scratches in (the surface of something), in particular:
■cut and remove debris from (a lawn) with a scarifier. ■ break up the surface of (soil or a road or pavement). ■ make shallow incisions in (the skin), especially as a medical procedure or traditional cosmetic practice: *she scarified the snakebite with a paring knife.* ■ figurative criticize severely and hurtfully.
– DERIVATIVES **scarification** noun.
– ORIGIN late Middle English: from Old French *scarifier*, via late Latin from Greek *skariphasthai* 'scratch an outline', from *skariphos* 'stylus'.

scarify[2] /'skɛːrɪfʌɪ/ ▶**verb** (**-ies**, **-ied**) [with obj.] [usu. as adj. **scarifying**] informal frighten: *a scarifying mix of extreme violence and absurdist humour.*
– ORIGIN late 18th cent.: formed irregularly from **SCARE**, perhaps on the pattern of *terrify*.

scarlatina /ˌskɑːlə'tiːnə/ (also **scarletina**) ▶**noun** another term for **SCARLET FEVER**.
– ORIGIN early 19th cent.: modern Latin, from Italian *scarlattina* (feminine), based on *scarlatto* 'scarlet'.

Scarlatti /skɑː'lati/ the name of two Italian composers. **(Pietro) Alessandro (Gaspare)** (1660–1725) was an important and prolific composer of operas which carried Italian opera through the baroque period and into the classical. His son **(Giuseppe) Domenico** (1685–1757) wrote over 550 sonatas for the harpsichord, and his work made an important contribution to the development of the sonata form.

scarlet ▶**adjective** of a brilliant red colour: *a mass of scarlet berries.*
▶**noun** [mass noun] a brilliant red colour: *papers lettered in scarlet and black.*
■clothes or material of this colour.
– ORIGIN Middle English (originally denoting any brightly coloured cloth): shortening of Old French *escarlate*, from medieval Latin *scarlata*, via Arabic and medieval Greek from late Latin *sigillatus* 'decorated with small images', from *sigillum* 'small image'.

scarlet elf cup ▶**noun** see **ELF CUP**.

scarlet fever ▶**noun** [mass noun] an infectious bacterial disease affecting especially children, and causing fever and a scarlet rash. It is caused by streptococci.

scarletina ▶**noun** variant spelling of **SCARLATINA**.

Scarlet Pimpernel the name assumed by the hero of a series of novels by Baroness Orczy. He was an English nobleman who rescued aristocrats during the French Revolution, always avoiding capture.

scarlet pimpernel ▶**noun** a small European plant with scarlet flowers that close in rainy or cloudy weather. Also called **POOR MAN'S WEATHER GLASS**.
● *Anagallis arvensis* subsp. *arvensis*, family Primulaceae.

scarlet runner ▶**noun** the runner bean.

scarlet tanager ▶**noun** a tanager of eastern North America, the breeding male of which is bright red with black wings and tail.
● *Piranga olivacea*, family Emberizidae (subfamily Thraupinae).

scarlet woman ▶**noun** a notoriously promiscuous or immoral woman.
– ORIGIN early 19th cent.: originally applied as a derogatory reference to the Roman Catholic Church, regarded as being devoted to showy ritual (Rev. 17).

scarp ▶**noun** a very steep bank or slope; an escarpment.
■the inner wall of a ditch in a fortification. Compare with **COUNTERSCARP**.
▶**verb** [with obj.] cut or erode (a slope or hillside) so that it becomes steep, perpendicular, or precipitous.
■provide (a ditch in a fortification) with a steep scarp and counterscarp.
– ORIGIN late 16th cent. (with reference to fortification): from Italian *scarpa*.

scarper ▶**verb** [no obj.] Brit. informal run away: *they left the stuff where it was and scarpered.*
– ORIGIN mid 19th cent.: probably from Italian *scappare* 'to escape', influenced by rhyming slang *Scapa Flow* 'go'.

scarp slope ▶**noun** a slope in the land that cuts across the underlying strata, especially the steeper slope of a cuesta. Often contrasted with **DIP SLOPE**.

Scart (also **SCART**) ▶**noun** a 21-pin socket used to connect video equipment.
– ORIGIN 1980s: acronym from French *Syndicat des Constructeurs des Appareils Radiorécepteurs et Téléviseurs*, the committee which designed the connector.

scarves plural form of **SCARF**[1].

scary ▶**adjective** (**scarier**, **scariest**) informal frightening; causing fear: *a scary movie.*
■uncannily striking or surprising: *it was scary the way they bonded with each other.*
– DERIVATIVES **scarily** adverb, **scariness** noun.

scat[1] ▶**verb** (**scatted**, **scatting**) [no obj., usu. in imperative] informal go away; leave: *Scat! Leave me alone.*
– ORIGIN mid 19th cent.: perhaps an abbreviation of **SCATTER**, or perhaps from the sound of a hiss (used to drive an animal away) + *-cat*.

scat[2] (also **scat singing**) ▶**noun** [mass noun] improvised jazz singing in which the voice is used in imitation of an instrument.
▶**verb** (**scatted**, **scatting**) [no obj.] sing in such a way.
– ORIGIN 1920s: probably imitative.

scat[3] ▶**noun** [mass noun] droppings, especially those of carnivorous mammals.
– ORIGIN 1950s: from Greek *skōr*, *skat-* 'dung'.

scat[4] ▶**noun** a small deep-bodied silvery fish that lives in inshore and estuarine waters of the Indo-Pacific.
● Family Scatophagidae: several genera and species. See also **ARGUS** (sense 3).
– ORIGIN 1960s: abbreviation of modern Latin *Scatophagidae*, from Greek *skatophagos* 'dung-eating' (because the fish is often found beside sewage outlets).

Scatchard plot /'skatʃɑːd/ ▶**noun** Biochemistry a plot of the concentration of a solute absorbed by a protein, membrane, cell, etc., against its concentration in the surrounding medium.
– ORIGIN 1940s: named after George *Scatchard* (1892–1973), American physical chemist.

scathe /skeɪð/ archaic ▶**verb** [with obj. and usu. with negative] (usu. **be scathed**) harm; injure: *he was barely scathed.*
■poetic/literary damage or destroy by fire or lightning.
▶**noun** [mass noun] harm; injury.
– DERIVATIVES **scatheless** adjective.
– ORIGIN Middle English: from Old Norse *skathi* (noun), *skatha* (verb); related to Dutch and German *schaden* (verb).

scathing ▶**adjective** witheringly scornful; severely critical: *she launched* ***a scathing attack on*** *the Prime Minister.*
– DERIVATIVES **scathingly** adverb.

scatology /ska'tɒlədʒi/ ▶**noun** [mass noun] an interest in or preoccupation with excrement and excretion.
■obscene literature that is concerned with excrement and excretion.
– DERIVATIVES **scatological** adjective.
– ORIGIN late 19th cent.: from Greek *skōr*, *skat-* 'dung' + **-LOGY**.

scatophagous /ska'tɒfəgəs/ ▶**adjective** Zoology (of an insect or other animal) feeding on dung; coprophagous.
– ORIGIN late 19th cent.: from modern Latin *scatophagus* (from Greek *skatophagos* 'dung-eating') + **-OUS**.

scatter ▶**verb** [with obj.] throw in various random directions: ***scatter*** *the coconut* ***over*** *the icing* | *his family are hoping to scatter his ashes at sea.*
■(**be scattered**) [usu. with adverbial] occur or be found at intervals rather than all together: *there are many watermills scattered throughout the marshlands* | [as adj. **scattered**] *a scattered cliff-top community.* ■ (of a group of people or animals) separate and move off quickly in different directions: *the roar made the dogs scatter.* ■ [with obj.] cause (a group or people or animals) to act in such a way: *he charged across the foyer, scattering people.* ■ (usu. **be scattered with**) cover (a surface) with objects thrown or spread randomly over it: *sandy beaches scattered with driftwood.* ■ Physics deflect or diffuse (electromagnetic radiation or particles). ■ Baseball pitch (balls) effectively allowing several hits but little or no scoring.
▶**noun** a small, dispersed amount of something: ***a scatter of*** *boulders round the pothole mouth.*
■[mass noun] Statistics the degree to which repeated measurements or observations of a quantity differ. ■ [mass noun] Physics the scattering of light, other electromagnetic radiation, or particles.
– DERIVATIVES **scatterer** noun.
– ORIGIN Middle English (as a verb): probably a variant of **SHATTER**.

scatterbrain ▶**noun** a person who tends to be disorganized and lacking in concentration.
– DERIVATIVES **scatterbrained** adjective.

scatter cushion ▶**noun** a small cushion designed to be placed randomly so as to create a casual effect and to be moved as required.

scatter diagram (also **scatter plot**) ▶**noun** Statistics a graph in which the values of two variables are plotted along two axes, the pattern of the resulting points revealing any correlation present.

scattergram (also **scattergraph**) ▶**noun** another term for **SCATTER DIAGRAM**.

scattergun chiefly N. Amer. ▶**noun** a shotgun.
▶**adjective** another term for **SCATTERSHOT**.

scattering ▶**noun** [in sing.] an act of scattering something.
■a small, dispersed amount of something: *the scattering of freckles across her cheeks and forehead* . ■ [mass noun] Physics the process in which electromagnetic radiation or particles are deflected or diffused.

scattering angle ▶**noun** Physics the angle through which a scattered particle or beam is deflected.

scatter rug ▶**noun** a small decorative rug designed to be placed with a casual effect and moved as required.

scattershot ▶**adjective** chiefly N. Amer. denoting something that is broad but random and

S

haphazard in its range: *a scattershot collection of stories.*

scatty ▶ **adjective** (**scattier**, **scattiest**) informal absent-minded and disorganized.
– DERIVATIVES **scattily** adverb, **scattiness** noun.
– ORIGIN early 20th cent.: abbreviation of **SCATTERBRAINED**.

scaup /skɔːp/ ▶ **noun** a Eurasian, North American, and New Zealand diving duck, the male of which has a black head with a green or purple gloss.
• Genus *Aythya*, family Anatidae: three species, in particular the widespread (**greater**) **scaup** (*A. marila*), with a black breast and white sides.
– ORIGIN late 17th cent.: Scots variant of Scots and northern English *scalp* 'mussel-bed', a feeding ground of the duck.

scauper ▶ **noun** variant of **SCORP**.

scaur ▶ **noun** archaic spelling of **SCAR** (in sense 2).

scavenge /ˈskavɪn(d)ʒ/ ▶ **verb** [with obj.] search for and collect (anything usable) from discarded waste: *people sell junk* **scavenged from** *the garbage* | [no obj.] *the city dump where the squatters scavenge to survive.*
■ (of an animal) search for (carrion) as food. ■ search for discarded items or food in (a place): *the mink is still commonly seen scavenging the beaches of California.* ■ remove (combustion products) from an internal-combustion engine cylinder on the return stroke of the piston. ■ Chemistry combine with and remove (molecules, radicals, etc.) from a particular medium.
– ORIGIN mid 17th cent. (in the sense 'clean out (dirt)'): back-formation from **SCAVENGER**.

scavenger ▶ **noun** an animal that feeds on carrion, dead plant material, or refuse.
■ a person who searches for and collects discarded items. ■ Brit. archaic a person employed to clean the streets. ■ Chemistry a substance that reacts with and removes particular molecules, radicals, etc.
– ORIGIN mid 16th cent.: alteration of earlier *scavager*, from Anglo-Norman French *scawager*, from Old Northern French *escauwer* 'inspect', from Flemish *scauwen* 'to show'. The term originally denoted an officer who collected *scavage*, a toll on foreign merchants' goods offered for sale in a town, later a person who kept the streets clean.

scavenger cell ▶ **noun** another term for **PHAGOCYTE**.

scavenger hunt ▶ **noun** a game, typically played in an extensive outdoor area, in which participants have to collect a number of miscellaneous objects.

scazon /ˈskeɪz(ə)n, ˈska-/ ▶ **noun** Prosody a modification of the iambic trimeter, in which a spondee or trochee takes the place of the final iambus.
– ORIGIN late 17th cent.: via Latin from Greek *skazōn*, neuter present participle (used as a noun) of *skazein* 'to limp'.

ScD ▶ **abbreviation for** Doctor of Science.
– ORIGIN from Latin *scientiae doctor*.

SCE ▶ **abbreviation for** Scottish Certificate of Education.

scena /ˈʃeɪnə/ ▶ **noun** a scene in an opera.
■ an elaborate dramatic solo usually including recitative.
– ORIGIN Italian, from Latin, 'scene'.

scenario /sɪˈnɑːrɪəʊ/ ▶ **noun** (pl. **-os**) a written outline of a film, novel, or stage work giving details of the plot and individual scenes: *imagine the scenarios for four short stories.*
■ a postulated sequence or development of events: *a possible scenario is that he was attacked after opening the front door.* ■ a setting, in particular for a work of art or literature: *the scenario is World War Two.*
– ORIGIN late 19th cent.: from Italian, from Latin *scena* 'scene'.

scenarist /sɪˈnɑːrɪst/ ▶ **noun** a screenwriter.

scend /sɛnd/ (also **send**) archaic ▶ **noun** the push or surge created by a wave.
■ a pitching or surging movement in a boat.
▶ **verb** [no obj.] (of a vessel) pitch or surge up in a heavy sea.
– ORIGIN late 15th cent. (as a verb): alteration of **SEND**[1] or **DESCEND**. The noun dates from the early 18th cent.

scene ▶ **noun** **1** the place where an incident in real life or fiction occurs or occurred: *the emergency team were among the first* **on the scene** | *relatives left floral tributes* **at the scene of** *the crash.*
■ a place, with the people, objects, and events in it, regarded as having a particular character or making a particular impression: *a scene of carnage.* ■ a landscape: *thick snow had turned the scene outside into a picture postcard.* ■ an incident of a specified nature: *there had already been some scenes of violence.* ■ a place or representation of an incident: *scenes of 1930s America.* ■ [with adj. or noun modifier] a specified area of activity or interest: *one of the biggest draws on the Irish music scene.* ■ (usu. **the scene**) informal a social environment frequented predominantly by homosexuals: *I don't go out into the scene now.* ■ [usu. in sing.] a public display of emotion or anger: *she was loath to* **make a scene** *in the office.*
2 a sequence of continuous action in a play, film, opera, or book: *a scene from the classic movie Casablanca.*
■ a subdivision of an act of a play in which the time is continuous and the setting fixed and which does not usually involve a change of characters: *beginning at Act One, Scene One.* ■ [mass noun] [usu. as modifier] the pieces of scenery used in a play or opera: *scene changes.*
– PHRASES **behind the scenes** out of sight of the public at a theatre or organization. ■ figurative secretly: *diplomatic manoeuvres going on behind the scenes.* **change of scene** a move to different surroundings. **come** (or **appear** or **arrive**) **on the scene** arrive; appear. **hit the scene** informal way of saying ***come on the scene*** above. **make the scene** US way of saying ***come on the scene*** above. **not one's scene** informal not something one enjoys or is interested in: *as for that job you mention, not my scene.* **set the scene** describe a place or situation in which something is about to happen. ■ create the conditions for a future event: *she jumped a flawless round and* **set the scene for** *a hair-raising jump-off.*
– ORIGIN mid 16th cent. (denoting a subdivision of a play, or (a piece of) stage scenery): from Latin *scena*, from Greek *skēnē* 'tent, stage'.

scene dock ▶ **noun** a space in a theatre near the stage in which scenery is stored.

scene-of-crime (also **scenes-of-crime**) ▶ **adjective** Brit. belonging to, relating to, or denoting a civilian branch of the police force concerned with the collection of forensic evidence.

scenery ▶ **noun** [mass noun] the natural features of a landscape considered in terms of their appearance, especially when picturesque: *spectacular views of mountain scenery.*
■ the painted background used to represent natural features or other surroundings on a theatre stage or film set.
– PHRASES **change of scenery** another way of saying ***change of scene*** (see **SCENE**).
– ORIGIN mid 18th cent. (earlier as *scenary*): from Italian *scenario* (see **SCENARIO**). The change in the ending was due to association with **-ERY**.

scene-shifter ▶ **noun** chiefly Brit. a person who moves the scenery on a stage between the scenes of a play.
– DERIVATIVES **scene-shifting** noun.

scene-stealer ▶ **noun** a person or thing which takes more than their fair share of attention.

scenester /ˈsiːnstə/ ▶ **noun** informal, chiefly N. Amer. a person associated with or immersed in a particular fashionable cultural scene.

scenic ▶ **adjective** providing or relating to views of impressive or beautiful natural scenery: *the scenic route from Florence to Siena* | *scenic beauty.*
■ [attrib.] of or relating to theatrical scenery: *a scenic artist from the Royal Opera House.* ■ (of a picture) representing an incident: *the trend to scenic figural work.*
– DERIVATIVES **scenically** adverb.
– ORIGIN early 17th cent. (in the sense 'theatrical'): via Latin from Greek *skēnikos* 'of the stage', from *skēnē* (see **SCENE**).

scenic railway ▶ **noun** an attraction at a fair or in a park consisting of a miniature railway that runs past natural features and artificial scenery.

scenography ▶ **noun** [mass noun] the design and painting of theatrical scenery.
■ (in painting and drawing) the representation of objects in perspective.
– DERIVATIVES **scenographic** adjective.
– ORIGIN mid 17th cent.: from French *scénographie*, or via Latin from Greek *skēnographia* 'scene-painting', from *skēnē* (see **SCENE**).

scent ▶ **noun** a distinctive smell, especially one that is pleasant: *the scent of freshly cut hay.*
■ [mass noun] pleasant-smelling liquid worn on the skin; perfume: *she sprayed scent over her body.* ■ a trail indicated by the characteristic smell of an animal and perceptible to hounds or other animals: *the hound followed the scent.* ■ figurative a trail of evidence or other signs assisting someone in a search or investigation: *once their interest is aroused they follow the scent with sleuth-like pertinacity.* ■ [mass noun] archaic the faculty or sense of smell.
▶ **verb** [with obj.] **1** (usu. **be scented with**) impart a pleasant scent to: *a glass of tea scented with a local herb* | [as adj. **scented**] *scented soap.*
2 discern by the sense of smell: *a shark can scent blood from well over half a kilometre away.*
■ figurative sense the presence, existence, or imminence of: *the Premier scented victory last night.* ■ sniff (the air) for a scent: *the bull advanced, scenting the breeze at every step.*
– PHRASES **on the scent** in possession of a useful clue in a search or investigation. **put** (or **throw**) **someone off the scent** mislead someone in the course of a search or investigation.
– DERIVATIVES **scentless** adjective.
– ORIGIN late Middle English (denoting the sense of smell): from Old French *sentir* 'perceive, smell', from Latin *sentire*. The addition of *-c-* (in the 17th cent.) is unexplained.

scent gland ▶ **noun** an animal gland that secretes an odorous pheromone or defensive substance, especially one under the tail of a carnivorous mammal such as a civet or skunk.

scent mark ▶ **noun** (also **scent marking**) an odoriferous substance containing a pheromone that is deposited by a mammal from a scent gland or in the urine or faeces, typically on prominent objects in an area.
▶ **verb** (**scent-mark**) [no obj.] (of a mammal) deposit such a substance.

scepter ▶ **noun** US spelling of **SCEPTRE**.

sceptic (US **skeptic**) ▶ **noun** **1** a person inclined to question or doubt all accepted opinions.
■ a person who doubts the truth of Christianity and other religions; an atheist.
2 Philosophy an ancient or modern philosopher who denies the possibility of knowledge, or even rational belief, in some sphere.

> The leading ancient sceptic was Pyrrho, whose followers at the Academy vigorously opposed Stoicism. Modern sceptics have held diverse views: the most extreme have doubted whether any knowledge at all of the external world is possible (see **SOLIPSISM**), while others have questioned the existence of objects beyond our experience of them.

▶ **adjective** another term for **SCEPTICAL**.
– DERIVATIVES **scepticism** (US **skepticism**) noun.
– ORIGIN late 16th cent. (in sense 2): from French *sceptique*, or via Latin from Greek *skeptikos*, from *skepsis* 'inquiry, doubt'.

sceptical (US **skeptical**) ▶ **adjective** **1** not easily convinced; having doubts or reservations: *the public were deeply sceptical about some of the proposals.*
2 Philosophy relating to the theory that certain knowledge is impossible.
– DERIVATIVES **sceptically** (US **skeptically**) adverb.

sceptre (US **scepter**) ▶ **noun** an ornamented staff carried by rulers on ceremonial occasions as a symbol of sovereignty.
– DERIVATIVES **sceptred** adjective.
– ORIGIN Middle English: from Old French *ceptre*, via Latin from Greek *skēptron*, from *skēptein* (alteration of *skēptesthai*) 'lean on'.

sch. ▶ **abbreviation for** ■ scholar. ■ school. ■ schooner.

Schadenfreude /ˈʃɑːd(ə)nˌfrɔɪdə, German ˈʃaːdənˌfrɔydə/ ▶ **noun** [mass noun] pleasure derived by someone from another person's misfortune.
– ORIGIN German, from *Schaden* 'harm' + *Freude* 'joy'.

schappe /ʃap, ˈʃapə/ ▶ **noun** [mass noun] fabric or yarn made from waste silk.
– ORIGIN late 19th cent.: from German *Schappe* 'waste silk'.

schedule /ˈʃɛdjuːl, ˈskɛd-/ ▶ **noun** **1** a plan for carrying out a process or procedure, giving lists of intended events and times: *we have drawn up an engineering schedule.*
■ (usu. **one's schedule**) one's day-to-day plans or timetable: *take a moment out of your busy schedule.* ■ a timetable: *information on airline schedules.*
2 chiefly Law an appendix to a formal document or statute, especially as a list, table, or inventory.
3 (with reference to the British income tax system) any of the forms (named 'A', 'B', etc.) issued for completion and relating to the various classes into which taxable income is divided.
▶ **verb** [with obj.] (often **be scheduled**) **1** arrange or plan

(an event) to take place at a particular time: *the release of the single is scheduled for April.* ■make arrangements for (someone or something) to do something: [with obj. and infinitive] *he is scheduled to be released from prison this spring.* **2** Brit. include (a building) in a list for legal preservation or protection.

− PHRASES **to** (or **on** or **according to**) **schedule** on time; as planned or expected. **ahead of** (or **behind**) **schedule** earlier (or later) than planned or expected.

− DERIVATIVES **schedular** adjective.

− ORIGIN late Middle English (in the sense 'scroll, explanatory note, appendix'): from Old French *cedule*, from late Latin *schedula* 'slip of paper', diminutive of *scheda*, from Greek *skhedē* 'papyrus leaf'. The verb dates from the mid 19th cent.

scheduled ▶ adjective included in or planned according to a schedule: *the bus makes one scheduled thirty-minute stop.* ■(especially of an airline or flight) relating to or forming part of a regular service rather than specially chartered. ■ Brit. (of a building or other historic monument) included in a list for legal preservation and protection.

scheduled caste ▶ noun the official name given in India to the untouchable caste.

scheduled territories ▶ plural noun another term for STERLING AREA.

scheduled tribe ▶ noun (in India) a category of people officially regarded as socially disadvantaged.

scheduler ▶ noun a person or machine that organizes or maintains schedules. ■Computing a program that arranges jobs or a computer's operations into an appropriate sequence.

Scheele /ˈʃiːlə, ˈʃeɪlə/, Carl Wilhelm (1742–86), Swedish chemist. He discovered a number of substances including glycerol, chlorine, and oxygen.

scheelite /ˈʃiːlʌɪt/ ▶ noun [mass noun] a fluorescent mineral, white when pure, which consists of calcium tungstate and is an important ore of tungsten.

− ORIGIN mid 19th cent.: from the name of Karl W. *Scheele* (1742–86), Swedish chemist, + -ITE[1].

schefflera /ˈʃɛflərə/ ▶ noun an evergreen tropical or subtropical shrub or small tree which is widely grown as a pot plant for its decorative foliage. ●Genus *Schefflera*, family Araliaceae.

− ORIGIN modern Latin, named after J. C. *Scheffler*, 18th-cent. German botanist.

Scheherazade /ʃə,hɛrəˈzɑːd, -ˈzɑːdə/ the narrator of the *Arabian Nights.*

Scheldt /skɛlt, ʃɛlt/ a river of northern Europe. Rising in northern France, it flows 432 km (270 miles) through Belgium and the Netherlands to the North Sea. Also called SCHELDE /ˈskɛldə, ˈʃɛl-/; French name ESCAUT.

schelly /ˈskɛli/ (also **skelly**) ▶ noun a powan (fish) of a variety occurring only in three lakes in the English Lake District.

− ORIGIN mid 18th cent.: a local name.

schema /ˈskiːmə/ ▶ noun (pl. **schemata** /-mətə/ or **schemas**) technical a representation of a plan or theory in the form of an outline or model: *a schema of scientific reasoning.* ■ Logic a syllogistic figure. ■ (in Kantian philosophy) a conception of what is common to all members of a class; a general or essential type or form.

− ORIGIN late 18th cent. (as a term in philosophy): from Greek *skhēma* 'form, figure'.

schematic ▶ adjective (of a diagram or other representation) symbolic and simplified. ■(of thought, ideas, etc.) simplistic or formulaic in character, usually to an extent inappropriate to the complexities of the subject matter: *Freeman constructs a highly schematic reading of the play.* ▶ noun (in technical contexts) a schematic diagram, in particular of an electric or electronic circuit.

− DERIVATIVES **schematically** adverb.

schematism ▶ noun [mass noun] the arrangement or presentation of something according to a scheme or schema.

− ORIGIN early 17th cent.: from modern Latin *schematismus*, from Greek *skhēmatismos* 'assumption of a certain form', from *skhēma, skhēmat-* 'form'.

schematize (also **-ise**) ▶ verb [with obj.] arrange or represent in a schematic form.

− DERIVATIVES **schematization** noun.

scheme ▶ noun a large-scale systematic plan or arrangement for attaining some particular object or putting a particular idea into effect: *the occupational sick pay scheme.* ■a secret or underhand plan; a plot: *police uncovered a scheme to steal paintings worth more than $250,000.* ■ a particular ordered system or arrangement: *a classical rhyme scheme.* ▶ verb **1** [no obj.] make plans, especially in a devious way or with intent to do something illegal or wrong: [with infinitive] *he schemed to bring about the collapse of the government.* ■S. African informal think; suppose. **2** [with obj.] arrange according to a colour scheme.

− PHRASES **the scheme of things** a supposed or apparent overall system, within which everything has a place and in relation to which individual details are ultimately to be assessed: *in the overall scheme of things, we didn't do badly.*

− ORIGIN mid 16th cent. (denoting a figure of speech): from Latin *schema*, from Greek (see SCHEMA). An early sense was 'diagram of the position of celestial objects', giving rise to 'diagram, outline', whence the current senses. The unfavourable notion 'plot' arose in the mid 18th cent.

schemer ▶ noun a person who is involved in making secret or underhand plans.

scheming ▶ adjective given to or involved in making secret and underhand plans: *they had mean, scheming little minds.* ▶ noun [mass noun] the activity or practice of making such plans.

− DERIVATIVES **schemingly** adverb.

schemozzle ▶ noun variant spelling of SHEMOZZLE.

scherzando /skɛːtˈsandəʊ/ Music ▶ adverb & adjective (especially as a direction) in a playful manner.

− ORIGIN Italian, literally 'joking'.

scherzo /ˈskɛːtsəʊ/ ▶ noun (pl. **scherzos** or **scherzi** /-tsiː/) Music a vigorous, light, or playful composition, typically comprising a movement in a symphony or sonata.

− ORIGIN Italian, literally 'jest'.

Schiaparelli[1] /,skjapəˈrɛli/, Elsa (1896–1973), Italian-born French fashion designer.

Schiaparelli[2] /,skjapəˈrɛli/, Giovanni Virginio (1835–1910), Italian astronomer. He studied the nature of cometary tails, and observed Mars in detail.

Schick test /ʃɪk/ ▶ noun Medicine a test for previously acquired immunity to diphtheria, using an intradermal injection of diphtheria toxin.

− ORIGIN early 20th cent.: named after Bela *Schick* (1877–1967), Hungarian-born American paediatrician.

Schiele /ˈʃiːlə/, Egon (1890–1918), Austrian painter and draughtsman. His style is characterized by an aggressive linear energy and a neurotic intensity. Notable works: *The Cardinal and the Nun* (1912) and *Embrace* (1917).

Schiff base ▶ noun Chemistry an organic compound having the structure $R^1R^2C{=}NR^3$ (where $R^{1,2,3}$ are alkyl groups and R^1 may be hydrogen).

− ORIGIN late 19th cent.: named after Hugo *Schiff* (1834–1915), German chemist.

Schiff's reagent /ʃɪfs/ ▶ noun [mass noun] Chemistry an acid solution of fuchsin decolorized by sulphur dioxide or potassium metabisulphite, used in testing for aldehydes (which restore the magenta colour).

− ORIGIN late 19th cent.: see SCHIFF BASE.

Schiller /ˈʃɪlə, German ˈʃɪlɐ/, (Johann Christoph) Friedrich von (1759–1805), German dramatist, poet, historian, and critic. Initially influenced by the *Sturm und Drang* movement, he was later an important figure of the Enlightenment. His historical plays include the trilogy *Wallenstein* (1800), *Mary Stuart* (1800), and *William Tell* (1804). Among his best-known poems is 'Ode to Joy', which Beethoven set to music in his Ninth Symphony.

schilling /ˈʃɪlɪŋ/ ▶ noun (until the introduction of the euro in 2002) the basic monetary unit of Austria, equal to 100 groschen.

− ORIGIN from German *Schilling*; compare with SHILLING.

Schindler /ˈʃɪndlə, German ˈʃɪndlɐ/, Oskar (1908–74), German industrialist. He saved more than 1,200 Jews from concentration camps by employing

them first in his enamelware factory in Cracow and then in an armaments factory that he set up in Czechoslovakia in 1944.

schipperke /ˈskɪpəki, ˈʃɪp-, -kə/ ▶ noun a small black tailless dog of a breed with a ruff of fur round its neck.

− ORIGIN late 19th cent.: from Dutch dialect, literally 'little boatman', with reference to its use as a watchdog on barges.

schism /ˈsɪz(ə)m, ˈskɪz(ə)m/ ▶ noun a split or division between strongly opposed sections or parties, caused by differences in opinion or belief. ■the formal separation of a Church into two Churches or the secession of a group owing to doctrinal and other differences. See also GREAT SCHISM.

− ORIGIN late Middle English: from Old French *scisme*, via ecclesiastical Latin from Greek *skhisma* 'cleft', from *skhizein* 'to split'.

schismatic ▶ adjective of, characterized by, or favouring schism. ▶ noun chiefly historical (especially in the Christian Church) a person who promotes schism; an adherent of a schismatic group.

− DERIVATIVES **schismatically** adverb.

− ORIGIN late Middle English: from Old French *scismatique*, via ecclesiastical Latin from ecclesiastical Greek *skhismatikos*, from *skhisma* (see SCHISM).

schist /ʃɪst/ ▶ noun [mass noun] Geology a coarse-grained metamorphic rock which consists of layers of different minerals and can be split into thin irregular plates.

− ORIGIN late 18th cent.: from French *schiste*, via Latin from Greek *skhistos* 'split', from the base of *skhizein* 'cleave'.

schistose /ˈʃɪstəʊs/ ▶ adjective Geology (of metamorphic rock) having a laminar structure like that of schist.

− DERIVATIVES **schistosity** noun.

schistosome /ˈʃɪstə(ʊ)səʊm/ ▶ noun Zoology & Medicine a parasitic flatworm which needs two hosts to complete its life cycle. The immature form infests freshwater snails and the adult lives in the blood vessels of birds and mammals, causing bilharzia in humans. Also called BLOOD FLUKE. ●Genus *Schistosoma*, subclass Digenea, class Trematoda.

− ORIGIN early 20th cent.: from modern Latin *Schistosoma*, from Greek *skhistos* 'divided' + *sōma* 'body'.

schistosomiasis /,ʃɪstə(ʊ)səˈmʌɪəsɪs/ ▶ noun another term for BILHARZIA (the disease).

schizanthus /skɪtˈsanθəs/ ▶ noun a South American plant of the nightshade family, with irregularly lobed showy flowers marked with one or more contrasting colours. Also called POOR MAN'S ORCHID. ●Genus *Schizanthus*, family Solanaceae.

− ORIGIN modern Latin, from Greek *skhizein* 'to split' + *anthos* 'flower'.

schizo informal ▶ adjective (of a person or their behaviour) schizophrenic. ▶ noun (pl. **-os**) a schizophrenic.

− ORIGIN 1940s: abbreviation.

schizo- ▶ combining form divided; split: *schizocarp.* ■relating to schizophrenia: *schizotype.*

− ORIGIN from Greek *skhizein* 'to split'.

schizo-affective ▶ adjective (of a person or a mental condition) characterized by symptoms of both schizophrenia and manic-depressive psychosis.

schizocarp /ˈsʃʌɪzə(ʊ)kɑːp, ˈskɪts-/ ▶ noun Botany a dry fruit that splits into single-seeded parts when ripe.

schizogenous /ʃʌɪˈzɒdʒənəs, skɪts-/ ▶ adjective Botany (of an intercellular space in a plant) formed by the splitting of the common wall of contiguous cells.

− DERIVATIVES **schizogenic** adjective, **schizogeny** noun.

schizogony /ʃʌɪˈzɒɡəni, skɪts-/ ▶ noun [mass noun] Biology asexual reproduction by multiple fission, found in some protozoa, especially parasitic sporozoans.

− DERIVATIVES **schizogonous** adjective.

− ORIGIN late 19th cent.: from SCHIZO- 'divided' + Greek *-gonia* 'production'.

schizoid /ˈskɪtsɔɪd, ˈskɪdz-/ ▶ adjective Psychiatry denoting or having a personality type

S

characterized by emotional aloofness and solitary habits.
■informal (in general use) resembling schizophrenia in having inconsistent or contradictory elements; mad or crazy: *it's a frenzied, schizoid place.*
▶ **noun** a schizoid person.

schizont /ˈʃaɪzɒnt, ˈskɪ-/ ▶ **noun** Biology (in certain sporozoan protozoans) a cell that divides by schizogony to form daughter cells.
– ORIGIN early 20th cent.: from **SCHIZO-** 'divided' + **-ONT**.

schizophrenia /ˌskɪtsə(ʊ)ˈfriːnɪə/ ▶ **noun** [mass noun] a long-term mental disorder of a type involving a breakdown in the relation between thought, emotion, and behaviour, leading to faulty perception, inappropriate actions and feelings, withdrawal from reality and personal relationships into fantasy and delusion, and a sense of mental fragmentation.
■(in general use) a mentality or approach characterized by inconsistent or contradictory elements.
– DERIVATIVES **schizophrenic** /-ˈfrɛnɪk/ adjective & noun.
– ORIGIN early 20th cent.: modern Latin, from Greek *skhizein* 'to split' + *phrēn* 'mind'.

schizostylis /ˌʃaɪzə(ʊ)ˈstaɪlɪs, ˌskɪts-/ ▶ **noun** (pl. same) a plant of a genus that includes the Kaffir lily.
● Genus *Schizostylis*, family Iridaceae.
– ORIGIN modern Latin, from **SCHIZO-** 'divided' + Latin *stilus* 'style' (because of the split styles of the plant).

schizotype /ˈskɪtsəʊtaɪp/ ▶ **noun** a personality type in which mild symptoms of schizophrenia are present.
– DERIVATIVES **schizotypal** adjective, **schizotypy** noun.

Schlegel /ˈʃleɪɡ(ə)l/, August Wilhelm von (1767–1845), German romantic poet and critic, who was among the founders of art history and comparative philology.

schlemiel /ʃləˈmiːl/ ▶ **noun** N. Amer. informal a stupid, awkward, or unlucky person.
– ORIGIN late 19th cent.: from Yiddish *shlemiel.*

schlenter /ˈʃlɛntə/ S. African ▶ **adjective** not genuine; counterfeit.
▶ **noun** a fake diamond.
■an illegal or dishonest scheme. ■ a confidence trickster.
▶ **verb** [with obj.] informal achieve or acquire by underhand means: *I can always manage to schlenter a car.*
– ORIGIN from Dutch and Afrikaans *slenter* 'trick'. The *sch-* probably reflects Yiddish influence in the 19th cent. in diamond mining.

schlep /ʃlɛp/ (also **schlepp**) informal, chiefly N. Amer.
▶ **verb** (**schlepped**, **schlepping**) [with obj.] haul or carry (something heavy or awkward): *she schlepped her groceries home.*
■[no obj., with adverbial of direction] (of a person) go or move reluctantly or with effort: *I would have preferred not to schlep all the way over there to run an errand.*
▶ **noun 1** a tedious or difficult journey.
2 another term for **SCHLEPPER**.
– ORIGIN early 20th cent. (as a verb): from Yiddish *shlepn* 'drag', from Middle High German *sleppen.*

schlepper /ˈʃlɛpə/ ▶ **noun** N. Amer. informal an inept or stupid person.
– ORIGIN 1930s: Yiddish, from *shlepn* (see **SCHLEP**).

Schleswig /ˈʃlɛsvɪɡ, German ˈʃleːsvɪç/ a former Danish duchy, situated in the southern part of the Jutland peninsula. Taken by Prussia in 1866, it was incorporated with the neighbouring duchy of Holstein as the province of Schleswig-Holstein. The northern part of Schleswig was returned to Denmark in 1920 after a plebiscite held in accordance with the Treaty of Versailles.

Schleswig-Holstein /ˈhɒlstaɪn, German ˈhɔlʃtaɪn/ a state of NW Germany, occupying the southern part of the Jutland peninsula; capital, Kiel. It comprises the former duchies of Schleswig and Holstein.

Schlick /ʃlɪk/, Moritz (1882–1936), German philosopher and physicist, founder of the Vienna Circle. Notable works: *General Theory of Knowledge* (1918).

Schliemann /ˈʃliːman/, Heinrich (1822–90), German archaeologist. In 1871 he began excavating the mound of Hissarlik on the NE Aegean coast of

Turkey, where he discovered the remains of nine superimposed cities and identified the second-oldest as Homer's Troy, although it was later found to be pre-Homeric. He subsequently undertook excavations at Mycenae (1876).

schlieren /ˈʃlɪərən/ ▶ **plural noun** technical discernible layers in a transparent material that differ from the surrounding material in density or composition.
■Geology irregular streaks or masses in igneous rock that differ from the surrounding rock in texture or composition.
– ORIGIN late 19th cent.: from German *Schlieren*, plural of *Schliere* 'streak'.

schlock /ʃlɒk/ ▶ **noun** [mass noun] N. Amer. informal cheap or inferior goods or material; trash.
– DERIVATIVES **schlocky** adjective.
– ORIGIN early 20th cent.: apparently from Yiddish *shlak* 'an apoplectic stroke', *shlog* 'wretch, untidy person, apoplectic stroke'.

schlockmeister /ˈʃlɒkˌmaɪstə/ ▶ **noun** informal, chiefly N. Amer. a purveyor of cheap or trashy goods.
– ORIGIN early 20th cent.: from **SCHLOCK** + German *Meister* 'master'.

schloss /ʃlɒs/ ▶ **noun** (in Germany, Austria, or their former territories) a castle.
– ORIGIN early 20th cent.: from German *Schloss.*

schlub /ʃlʌb/ (also **shlub**) ▶ **noun** US informal a talentless, unattractive, or boorish person.
– ORIGIN 1960s: Yiddish *shlub*, perhaps from Polish *żłób.*

schlump /ʃlʌmp/ ▶ **noun** N. Amer. informal a slow, slovenly, or inept person.
– ORIGIN 1940s: apparently related to Yiddish *shlumperdik* 'dowdy' and German *Schlumpe* 'slattern'.

schmaltz /ʃmɔːlts, ʃmalts/ ▶ **noun** [mass noun] informal excessive sentimentality, especially in music or films.
– DERIVATIVES **schmaltzy** adjective (**schmaltzier**, **schmaltziest**).
– ORIGIN 1930s: from Yiddish *shmaltz*, from German *Schmalz* 'dripping, lard'.

schmatte /ˈʃmatə/ (also **shmatte**) ▶ **noun** US informal a rag; a ragged or shabby garment.
– ORIGIN 1970s: Yiddish *shmatte*, from Polish *szmata* 'rag'.

schmear /ʃmɪə/ (also **schmeer**, **shmeer**, or **shmear**) US informal ▶ **noun** a corrupt or underhand inducement; a bribe.
▶ **verb** [with obj.] flatter or ingratiate oneself with (someone): *he was constantly buying us drinks and schmearing us up.*
– PHRASES **the whole schmear** everything possible or available; every aspect of the situation: *I'm going for the whole schmear.*
– ORIGIN 1960s: from Yiddish *shmirn* 'flatter, grease'.

Schmidt–Cassegrain telescope /ˈʃmɪt-ˈkasɪɡreɪn/ ▶ **noun** a type of catadioptric telescope, using the correcting plate of a Schmidt telescope together with the secondary mirror and rear focus of a Cassegrain telescope.

Schmidt telescope (also **Schmidt camera**) ▶ **noun** a type of catadioptric telescope used solely for wide-angle astronomical photography, with a thin glass plate at the front to correct for spherical aberration. A curved photographic plate is placed at the prime focus inside the telescope.
– ORIGIN 1930s: named after Bernhard V. Schmidt (1879–1935), the German inventor.

Schmitt trigger ▶ **noun** Electronics a bistable circuit in which the output increases to a steady maximum when the input rises above a certain threshold, and decreases almost to zero when the input voltage falls below another threshold.
– ORIGIN 1940s: named after Otto H. Schmitt (born 1913), American electronics engineer.

schmo /ʃməʊ/ (also **shmo**) ▶ **noun** (pl. **-oes**) N. Amer. informal a fool.
– ORIGIN 1940s: alteration of **SCHMUCK**.

schmooze /ʃmuːz/ chiefly N. Amer. ▶ **verb** [no obj.] talk intimately and cosily; gossip.
■[with obj.] talk in such a way to (someone), typically in order to manipulate them.
▶ **noun** a long and intimate conversation.
– DERIVATIVES **schmoozer** noun, **schmoozy** adjective.
– ORIGIN late 19th cent. (as a verb): from Yiddish *shmuesn* 'converse, chat'.

schmuck /ʃmʌk/ ▶ **noun** N. Amer. informal a foolish or contemptible person.
– ORIGIN late 19th cent.: from Yiddish *shmok* 'penis'.

schnapps /ʃnaps/ ▶ **noun** [mass noun] a strong alcoholic drink resembling gin.
– ORIGIN from German *Schnaps*, literally 'dram of liquor', from Low German and Dutch *snaps* 'mouthful'.

schnauzer /ˈʃnaʊzə/ ▶ **noun** a dog of a German breed with a close wiry coat and heavy whiskers round the muzzle.
– ORIGIN early 20th cent.: from German, from *Schnauze* 'muzzle, snout'.

schnitzel /ˈʃnɪts(ə)l/ ▶ **noun** a thin slice of veal or other light meat, coated in breadcrumbs and fried.
– ORIGIN from German *Schnitzel*, literally 'slice'.

schnook /ʃnʊk/ ▶ **noun** US informal a fool.
– ORIGIN 1940s: perhaps from German *Schnucke* 'small sheep' or from Yiddish *shnuk* 'snout'.

schnorrer /ˈʃnɒrə, ˈʃnɔːrə/ ▶ **noun** informal, chiefly N. Amer. a beggar or scrounger; a layabout.
– ORIGIN late 19th cent.: from Yiddish *shnorrer*, variant of German *Schnurrer.*

schnozz /ʃnɒz/ (also **schnozzola**) ▶ **noun** N. Amer. informal a person's nose.
– ORIGIN 1940s: from Yiddish *shnoytz*, from German *Schnauze* 'snout'.

Schoenberg /ˈʃɜːnbɜːɡ/, Arnold (1874–1951), Austrian-born American composer and music theorist. His major contribution to modernism was the development of atonality and serialism. He introduced atonality into his second string quartet (1907–8), while *Serenade* (1923) is the first example of the technique of serialism.

scholar ▶ **noun** a specialist in a particular branch of study, especially the humanities; a distinguished academic: *a Hebrew scholar.*
■chiefly archaic a person who is highly educated or has an aptitude for study: *Mr Bell declares himself no scholar.*
■ a university student holding a scholarship. ■ archaic a student or pupil.
– ORIGIN Old English *scol(i)ere* 'schoolchild, student', from late Latin *scholaris*, from Latin *schola* (see **SCHOOL**¹).

scholarly ▶ **adjective** involving or relating to serious academic study: *scholarly journals | a scholarly career.*
■having or showing knowledge, learning, or devotion to academic pursuits: *a scholarly account of the period | an earnest, scholarly man.*
– DERIVATIVES **scholarliness** noun.

scholarship ▶ **noun 1** [mass noun] academic study or achievement; learning of a high level.
2 a grant or payment made to support a student's education, awarded on the basis of academic or other achievement.

scholar's mate ▶ **noun** see **MATE**².

scholastic ▶ **adjective 1** of or concerning schools and education: *scholastic achievement.*
■US of or relating to secondary schools.
2 Philosophy & Theology of, relating to, or characteristic of medieval scholasticism.
■typical of scholasticism in being pedantic or overly subtle.
▶ **noun 1** Philosophy & Theology, historical an adherent of scholasticism; a schoolman.
2 (in the Roman Catholic Church) a member of a religious order, especially the Society of Jesus, who is between the novitiate and the priesthood.
– DERIVATIVES **scholastically** adverb.
– ORIGIN late 16th cent. (in sense 2 of the adjective): via Latin from Greek *skholastikos* 'studious', from *skholazein* 'be at leisure to study', from *skholē* (see **SCHOOL**¹).

scholasticism /skəˈlastɪˌsɪz(ə)m/ ▶ **noun** [mass noun] the system of theology and philosophy taught in medieval European universities, based on Aristotelian logic and the writings of the early Christian Fathers and having a strong emphasis on tradition and dogma.
■narrow-minded insistence on traditional doctrine.

scholiast /ˈskəʊlɪast/ ▶ **noun** historical a commentator on ancient or classical literature.
– DERIVATIVES **scholiastic** adjective.
– ORIGIN late 16th cent.: from medieval Greek *skholiastēs*, from *skholiazein* 'write scholia' (see **SCHOLIUM**).

scholium /ˈskəʊlɪəm/ ▶ **noun** (pl. **scholia** /-lɪə/) historical

a marginal note or explanatory comment made by a scholiast.
– ORIGIN mid 16th cent.: modern Latin, from Greek *skholion*, from *skholē* 'learned discussion'.

school[1] ▶ noun **1** an institution for educating children: *Ryder's children did not go to school at all* | [as modifier] *school books*.
■ the buildings used by such an institution: *the cost of building a new school*. ■ [treated as pl.] the pupils and staff of a school: *the headmaster was addressing the whole school*. ■ [mass noun] a day's work at school; lessons: *school started at 7 a.m*. ■ [with adj.] figurative used to describe the type of circumstances in which someone was brought up: *I was brought up in a hard school and I don't forget it*.
2 any institution at which instruction is given in a particular discipline: *a dancing school*.
■ N. Amer. informal another term for **UNIVERSITY**. ■ a department or faculty of a university concerned with a particular subject of study: *the School of Dental Medicine*.
3 a group of people, particularly writers, artists, or philosophers, sharing the same or similar ideas, methods, or style: *the Frankfurt school of critical theory*.
■ [with adj. or noun modifier] a style, approach, or method of a specified character: *film-makers are tired of the skin-deep school of cinema*.
4 (**schools**) Brit. (at Oxford University) the hall in which final examinations are held.
■ the examinations themselves.
5 Brit. a group of people gambling together: *a poker school*.
■ a group of people drinking together in a bar and taking turns to buy the drinks.
▶ verb [with obj.] chiefly formal or N. Amer. send to school; educate: *Taverier was born in Paris and schooled in Lyon*.
■ train or discipline (someone) in a particular skill or activity: *he schooled her in horsemanship* | *it's important to school yourself to be good at exams*. ■ Riding train (a horse) on the flat or over fences.
▶ adjective S. African (of a Xhosa) educated and westernized. Contrasted with **RED** (in sense 4).
■ (of a name) of Western origin. [ORIGIN: with reference to the mission schools, which encouraged westernized dress, language, and behaviour.]
– PHRASES **leave school** finish one's education: *he left school at 16*. **of** (or **from**) **the old school** see **OLD SCHOOL**. **the school of hard knocks** see **KNOCK**. **school of thought** a particular way of thinking, especially one not followed by the speaker: *there is a school of thought that says 1960s office blocks should be refurbished as residential accommodation*.
– ORIGIN Old English *scōl, scolu*, via Latin from Greek *skholē* 'leisure, philosophy, lecture-place', reinforced in Middle English by Old French *escole*.

school[2] ▶ noun a large group of fish or sea mammals.
▶ verb [no obj.] (of fish or sea mammals) form a large group.
– ORIGIN late Middle English: from Middle Low German, Middle Dutch *schōle*, of West Germanic origin; related to Old English *scolu* 'troop'. Compare with **SHOAL**[1].

school age ▶ noun [mass noun] the age range of children normally attending school.

school board ▶ noun N. Amer. or historical a local board or authority responsible for the provision and maintenance of schools.

schoolboy ▶ noun a boy attending school.
■ [as modifier] characteristic of or associated with schoolboys, especially in being immature: *schoolboy humour*.

School Certificate ▶ noun a qualification achieved by taking public examinations of proficiency for secondary-school pupils. These examinations existed between 1917 and 1951 in England and Wales, and are current in New Zealand.
■ the examinations themselves.

schoolchild ▶ noun (pl. **-children**) a child attending school.

school colours ▶ plural noun see **COLOUR** (sense 4).

schooldays ▶ plural noun the period in someone's life when they attended school: *a close friend from their schooldays*.

school district ▶ noun N. Amer. a unit for the local administration of schools.

schooled ▶ adjective [often in combination] educated or trained in a specified activity or in a particular way: *a man well schooled in making money*.

schooler ▶ noun [in combination] chiefly US a pupil attending a school of the specified kind or being educated in the specified way: *a high-schooler*.

schoolfellow ▶ noun more formal term for **SCHOOLMATE**.

schoolgirl ▶ noun a girl attending school.
■ [as modifier] characteristic of or associated with schoolgirls, especially in being elementary: *schoolgirl French*.

schoolhouse ▶ noun a building used as a school, especially in a small community or village.
■ Brit., chiefly historical a private house adjoining a small school, lived in by the school's teacher.

schoolie ▶ noun Austral. & dialect a schoolteacher.
■ a school pupil.

schooling ▶ noun [mass noun] education received at school: *his parents paid for his schooling*.
■ Riding the training of a horse on the flat or over fences: [as modifier] *schooling fences*.

school inspector (also **schools inspector**) ▶ noun (in the UK) an official who reports on teaching standards in schools on behalf of Ofsted.

school-leaver ▶ noun Brit. a young person who is about to leave or has just left school.

school-leaving age ▶ noun Brit. the minimum age at which a young person may legally leave school.

schoolman ▶ noun (pl. **-men**) historical **1** a teacher in a university in medieval Europe.
2 a scholastic theologian.

schoolmarm ▶ noun chiefly US a schoolmistress (typically used with reference to a woman regarded as prim, strict, and brisk in manner).
– DERIVATIVES **schoolmarmish** adjective.

schoolmaster ▶ noun **1** a male teacher in a school.
2 an experienced horse that is used to train or give confidence to inexperienced riders or horses.
– DERIVATIVES **schoolmasterly** adjective.

schoolmastering ▶ noun [mass noun] dated the profession of a schoolmaster; teaching.

schoolmate ▶ noun informal a person who attends or attended the same school as oneself.

schoolmistress ▶ noun a female teacher in a school.

schoolmistressy ▶ adjective informal having characteristics commonly associated with schoolmistresses, especially those of formality and briskness: *her crisp, rather schoolmistressy manner*.

schoolroom ▶ noun a room used for lessons, especially the main classroom in a small school.
■ (**the schoolroom**) used to refer to school as an institution: *I was green as grass, straight out of the schoolroom*.

school ship ▶ noun a training ship.

schoolteacher ▶ noun a person who teaches in a school.
– DERIVATIVES **schoolteaching** noun.

school year ▶ noun the period in the year during which pupils attend school, from the beginning of the autumn term to the end of the summer term.

schooner /ˈskuːnə/ ▶ noun **1** a sailing ship with two or more masts, typically with the foremast smaller than the mainmast.
2 Brit. a glass for drinking a large measure of sherry.
■ N. Amer. & Austral. a tall beer glass.
– ORIGIN early 18th cent.: of unknown origin.

Schopenhauer /ˈʃəʊp(ə)n,haʊə, ˈʃɒp-/, Arthur (1788–1860), German philosopher. According to his philosophy, as expressed in *The World as Will and Idea*, the will is identified with ultimate reality and happiness is only achieved by abnegating the will (as desire).

schorl /ʃɔːl/ ▶ noun [mass noun] a black iron-rich variety of tourmaline.
– ORIGIN late 18th cent.: from German *Schörl*, of unknown origin.

schottische /ʃɒˈtiːʃ, ˈʃɒtɪʃ/ ▶ noun a slow polka.
– ORIGIN mid 19th cent.: from German *der schottische Tanz* 'the Scottish dance'.

Schottky barrier /ˈʃɒtki/ ▶ noun Electronics an electrostatic depletion layer formed at the junction of a metal and a semiconductor, which causes it to act as an electrical rectifier.
– ORIGIN 1940s: named after Walter *Schottky* (1886–1976), German physicist.

Schottky diode ▶ noun Electronics a solid-state diode having a metal-semiconductor junction, used in fast switching applications.
– ORIGIN 1960s: named after W. *Schottky* (see **SCHOTTKY BARRIER**).

Schottky effect ▶ noun [mass noun] Electronics the increase in thermionic emission from a solid surface due to the presence of an external electric field.
– ORIGIN 1920s: named after W. *Schottky* (see **SCHOTTKY BARRIER**).

Schreiner /ˈʃrʌɪnə/, Olive (Emilie Albertina) (1855–1920), South African novelist and feminist. Notable works: *The Story of an African Farm* (novel, 1883) and *Woman and Labour* (1911).

Schrödinger /ˈʃrəːdɪŋə/, Erwin (1887–1961), Austrian theoretical physicist. He founded the study of wave mechanics, deriving the equation whose roots define the energy levels of atoms. His general works influenced scientists of many different disciplines. Nobel Prize for Physics (1933).

Schrödinger equation Physics a differential equation which forms the basis of the quantum-mechanical description of matter in terms of the wave-like properties of particles in a field. Its solution is related to the probability density of a particle in space and time.

schtuck ▶ noun variant spelling of **SHTOOK**.

schtum /ʃtʊm/ ▶ adjective variant spelling of **SHTUM**.

schtup /ʃtʊp/ ▶ verb variant spelling of **SHTUP**.

Schubert /ˈʃuːbət/, Franz (1797–1828), Austrian composer. His music is associated with the romantic movement for its lyricism and emotional intensity, but belongs in formal terms to the classical age. His works include more than 600 songs, the 'Trout' piano quintet (1819), and nine symphonies.

Schulz /ʃʊlts/, Charles (1922–2000), American cartoonist. He is remembered as the creator of the 'Peanuts' comic strip, which featured a range of characters including the boy Charlie Brown and the dog Snoopy.

Schumacher /ˈʃuːmaxə/, E. F. (1911–77), German economist and conservationist; full name *Ernst Friedrich Schumacher*. His most famous work is *Small is Beautiful: Economics as if People Mattered* (1973), which argues that mass production needs to be replaced by smaller, more energy-efficient enterprises.

Schumann /ˈʃuːmən/, Robert (Alexander) (1810–56), German composer. He was a leading romantic composer, particularly noted for his songs (including settings of poems by Heinrich Heine and Robert Burns) and piano music. His other works include four symphonies and much chamber music. His wife **Clara** (1819–96) was a noted pianist and composer.

schuss /ʃʊs/ ▶ noun a straight downhill run on skis.
▶ verb [no obj.] make a straight downhill run on skis.
– ORIGIN 1930s: from German *Schuss*, literally 'shot'.

Schütz /ʃʊts/, Heinrich (1585–1672), German composer and organist. He is regarded as the first German baroque composer, and composed what is thought to have been the first German opera (*Dafne*, 1627; now lost).

schwa /ʃwɑː/ ▶ noun Phonetics the unstressed central vowel (as in *a* mom*e*nt *a*go), represented by the symbol /ə/ in the International Phonetic Alphabet.
– ORIGIN late 19th cent.: from German, from Hebrew *šĕwā*.

Schwaben /ˈʃvɑːbn/ German name for **SWABIA**.

Schwäbisch Gmünd /ˌʃvɛɪbɪʃ gˈ(ə)mʊnt, German ˌʃvɛːbɪʃ ˈgmʏnt/ a city in SW Germany, situated to the east of Stuttgart; pop. 56,400 (1983).

Schwann /ʃvan, ʃvɒn/, Theodor Ambrose Hubert (1810–82), German physiologist. He showed that animals (as well as plants) are made up of individual cells and that the egg begins life as a single cell. He is best known for discovering the cells forming the myelin sheaths of nerve fibres (Schwann cells).

Schwarzenegger /ˈʃwɔːtsə,nɛgə/, Arnold (b.1947), Austrian-born American actor, noted for his action roles, for instance in *The Terminator* (1984).

Schwarzkopf /ˈʃvɑːtskɒpf/, Dame (Olga Maria) Elisabeth (Friederike) (b.1915), German operatic soprano. She is especially famous for her roles in works by Richard Strauss, such as *Der Rosenkavalier*.

Schwarzschild black hole /ˈʃvɑːtsʃiːlt, ˈʃwɔːtstʃʌɪld/ ▶ **noun** Physics a black hole of a kind supposed to result from the complete gravitational collapse of an electrically neutral and non-rotating body, having a physical singularity at the centre to which infalling matter inevitably proceeds and at which the curvature of space–time is infinite. A **Schwarzschild radius** is the radius of the boundary of a hole of this type.
– ORIGIN named after Karl *Schwarzschild* (1873–1916), German astronomer.

Schwarzwald /ˈʃvartsvalt/ German name for **BLACK FOREST**.

Schweinfurt /ˈʃvʌɪnfʊət/ a city in western Germany; pop. 54,520 (1991). It became part of Bavaria in 1803.

Schweitzer /ˈʃwʌɪtsə, ˈʃvʌɪ-/, Albert (1875–1965), German theologian, musician, and medical missionary, born in Alsace. In 1913 he qualified as a doctor and went as a missionary to Gabon, where he established a hospital. Nobel Peace Prize (1952).

Schweiz /ʃvaɪts/ German name for **SWITZERLAND**.

Schwerin /ʃvɛˈriːn/ a city in NE Germany, capital of Mecklenburg-West Pomerania, situated on the south-western shores of Lake Schwerin; pop. 125,960 (1991).

Schwyz /ʃviːts/ a city in central Switzerland, situated to the east of Lake Lucerne, the capital of a canton of the same name; pop. 12,530 (1990). The canton was one of the three original cantons of the Swiss Confederation, to which it gave its name.

sciaenid /sʌɪˈiːnɪd/ ▶ **noun** Zoology a fish of the drum family (Sciaenidae), whose members are mainly marine and important for food or sport.
– ORIGIN early 20th cent.: from modern Latin *Sciaenidae* (plural), from the genus name *Sciaena*, from Greek *skiaina*, denoting a kind of fish.

sciagraphy /sʌɪˈagrəfi/ (also **skiagraphy**) ▶ **noun** [mass noun] the use of shading and the projection of shadows to show perspective in architectural or technical drawing.
– DERIVATIVES **sciagram** noun, **sciagraph** noun & verb, **sciagraphic** adjective.
– ORIGIN late 16th cent.: from French *sciagraphie*, via Latin from Greek *skiagraphia*, from *skia* 'shadow'.

sciamachy /sʌɪˈaməki/ ▶ **noun** [mass noun] archaic sham fighting for exercise or practice.
■ argument or conflict with an imaginary opponent.
– ORIGIN early 17th cent.: from Greek *skiamakhia*, from *skia* 'shadow' + *-makhia* '-fighting'.

sciatic /sʌɪˈatɪk/ ▶ **adjective** of or relating to the hip.
■ of or affecting the sciatic nerve. ■ suffering from or liable to sciatica.
– DERIVATIVES **sciatically** adverb.
– ORIGIN early 16th cent. (as a noun denoting sciatica): from French *sciatique*, via late Latin from Greek *iskhiadikos* 'relating to the hips, subject to sciatica', from *iskhion* 'hip joint'.

sciatica ▶ **noun** [mass noun] pain affecting the back, hip, and outer side of the leg, caused by compression of a spinal nerve root in the lower back, often owing to degeneration of an intervertebral disc.
– ORIGIN late Middle English: from late Latin *sciatica (passio)* '(affliction) of sciatica', feminine of *sciaticus*, from Greek *iskhiadikos* (see **SCIATIC**).

sciatic nerve ▶ **noun** Anatomy a major nerve extending from the lower end of the spinal cord down the back of the thigh, and dividing above the knee joint. It is the nerve with the largest diameter in the human body.

SCID ▶ **abbreviation for** severe combined immune deficiency, a rare genetic disorder in which affected children have no resistance to disease and must be kept isolated from infection from birth.

science ▶ **noun** [mass noun] the intellectual and practical activity encompassing the systematic study of the structure and behaviour of the physical and natural world through observation and experiment: *the world of science and technology.*
■ a particular area of this: *veterinary science* | [count noun] *the agricultural sciences.* ■ a systematically organized body of knowledge on a particular subject: *the science of criminology.* ■ archaic knowledge of any kind.
– ORIGIN Middle English (denoting knowledge): from Old French, from Latin *scientia*, from *scire* 'know'.

science fiction (abbrev.: **SF**) ▶ **noun** [mass noun] fiction based on imagined future scientific or technological advances and major social or environmental changes, frequently portraying space or time travel and life on other planets.

Science Museum a national museum of science, technology, and industry in South Kensington, London.

science park ▶ **noun** an area devoted to scientific research or the development of science-based or technological industries.

scienter /sʌɪˈɛntə/ ▶ **noun** [mass noun] Law the fact of an act having been done knowingly, especially as grounds for civil damages.
– ORIGIN Latin, from *scire* know.

sciential /sʌɪˈɛnʃ(ə)l/ ▶ **adjective** archaic concerning or having knowledge.
– ORIGIN late Middle English: from late Latin *scientialis*, from *scientia* 'knowledge' (see **SCIENCE**).

scientific ▶ **adjective** based on or characterized by the methods and principles of science: *the scientific study of earthquakes.*
■ relating to or used in science: *scientific instruments.*
■ informal systematic; methodical: *how many people buy food in an organized, scientific way?*
– DERIVATIVES **scientifically** adverb, **scientificity** noun.
– ORIGIN late 16th cent.: from French *scientifique* or late Latin *scientificus* 'producing knowledge', from *scientia* (see **SCIENCE**). Early use described the liberal arts as opposed to the 'mechanic' arts (i.e. arts requiring manual skill).

scientific management ▶ **noun** [mass noun] management of a business, industry, or economy, according to principles of efficiency derived from experiments in methods of work and production, especially from time-and-motion studies.

scientific method ▶ **noun** a method of procedure that has characterized natural science since the 17th century, consisting in systematic observation, measurement, and experiment, and the formulation, testing, and modification of hypotheses.

scientific misconduct ▶ **noun** [mass noun] action which wilfully compromises the integrity of scientific research, such as plagiarism or the falsification or fabrication of data.

scientism ▶ **noun** [mass noun] rare thought or expression regarded as characteristic of scientists.
■ excessive belief in the power of scientific knowledge and techniques.
– DERIVATIVES **scientistic** adjective.

scientist ▶ **noun** a person who is studying or has expert knowledge of one or more of the natural or physical sciences.

Scientology ▶ **noun** [mass noun] trademark a religious system based on the seeking of self-knowledge and spiritual fulfilment through graded courses of study and training. It was founded by American science-fiction writer L. Ron Hubbard (1911–86) in 1955.
– DERIVATIVES **Scientologist** noun.
– ORIGIN from Latin *scientia* 'knowledge' + **-LOGY**.

sci-fi ▶ **noun** informal short for **SCIENCE FICTION**.

scilicet /ˈsʌɪlɪsɛt, ˈskiːlɪkɛt/ ▶ **adverb** that is to say; namely (introducing a word to be supplied or an explanation of an ambiguity).
– ORIGIN Latin, from *scire licet* 'one is permitted to know'.

scilla /ˈsɪlə/ ▶ **noun** a plant of the lily family which typically bears small blue star- or bell-shaped flowers and glossy strap-like leaves, native to Eurasia and temperate Africa.
• Genus *Scilla*, family Liliaceae.
– ORIGIN modern Latin, from Latin *scilla* 'sea onion', from Greek *skilla*.

Scilly Isles /ˈsɪli/ (also **Isles of Scilly** or **the Scillies** /ˈsɪlɪz/) a group of about 140 small islands (of which five are inhabited) off the south-western tip of England; pop. 2,900 (1991); capital, Hugh Town (on St Mary's).
– DERIVATIVES **Scillonian** adjective & noun.

scimitar /ˈsɪmɪtə/ ▶ **noun** a short sword with a curved blade that broadens towards the point, used originally in Eastern countries.
– ORIGIN mid 16th cent.: from French *cimeterre* or Italian *scimitarra*, of unknown origin.

scimitarbill ▶ **noun** a long-tailed East African bird with a long slender downcurved bill and mainly black plumage with a purple gloss.
• Genus *Rhinopomastus* (or *Pheoniculus*), family Phoeniculidae: two species. Alternative name: **scimitar-billed wood-hoopoe**.

scimitar oryx (also **scimitar-horned oryx**) ▶ **noun** an oryx with scimitar-shaped horns, now living only along the southern edge of the Sahara.
• *Oryx dammah*, family Bovidae.

scintigram /ˈsɪntɪgram/ ▶ **noun** Medicine an image of an internal part of the body produced by scintigraphy.
– ORIGIN 1950s: from **SCINTILLATION** + **-GRAM**[1].

scintigraphy /sɪnˈtɪgrəfi/ ▶ **noun** [mass noun] Medicine a technique in which a scintillation counter or similar detector is used with a radioactive tracer to obtain an image of a bodily organ or a record of its functioning.
– DERIVATIVES **scintigraphic** adjective.
– ORIGIN 1950s: from **SCINTILLATION** + **-GRAPHY**.

scintilla /sɪnˈtɪlə/ ▶ **noun** [in sing.] a tiny trace or spark of a specified quality or feeling: ***a scintilla of doubt.***
– ORIGIN late 17th cent.: from Latin.

scintillate /ˈsɪntɪleɪt/ ▶ **verb** [no obj.] emit flashes of light; sparkle.
■ Physics fluoresce momentarily when struck by a charged particle or photon.
– DERIVATIVES **scintillant** adjective & noun.
– ORIGIN early 17th cent.: from Latin *scintillat-* 'sparkled', from the verb *scintillare*, from *scintilla* 'spark'.

scintillating ▶ **adjective** sparkling or shining brightly: *the scintillating sun.*
■ brilliantly and excitingly clever or skilful: *the audience loved his scintillating wit* | *the team produced a scintillating second-half performance.*
– DERIVATIVES **scintillatingly** adverb.

scintillation ▶ **noun** a flash or sparkle of light: *scintillations of diamond-hard light.*
■ [mass noun] the process or state of emitting flashes of light. ■ Physics a small flash of visible or ultraviolet light emitted by fluorescence in a phosphor when struck by a charged particle or high-energy photon.
■ [mass noun] Astronomy the twinkling of the stars, caused by the earth's atmosphere diffracting starlight unevenly.

scintillator ▶ **noun** Physics a material that fluoresces when struck by a charged particle or high-energy photon.
■ a detector for charged particles and gamma rays in which scintillations produced in a phosphor are detected and amplified by a photomultiplier, giving an electrical output signal.

scintiscan ▶ **noun** Medicine another term for **SCINTIGRAM**.
– ORIGIN 1960s: from **SCINTILLATION** + **SCAN**.

sciolist /ˈsʌɪəlɪst/ ▶ **noun** archaic a person who pretends to be knowledgeable and well informed.
– DERIVATIVES **sciolism** noun, **sciolistic** adjective.
– ORIGIN early 17th cent.: from late Latin *sciolus* (diminutive of Latin *scius* 'knowing', from *scire* 'know') + **-IST**.

scion /ˈsʌɪən/ ▶ **noun 1** (US also **cion**) a young shoot or twig of a plant, especially one cut for grafting or rooting.
2 a descendant of a notable family or one with a long lineage: *he was the scion of a wealthy family.*
– ORIGIN Middle English: from Old French *ciun* 'shoot, twig', of unknown origin.

Scipio Aemilianus /ˌskɪpɪəʊ iːˌmɪlɪˈɑːnəs/ (*c.*185–129 BC), Roman general and politician; full name *Publius Cornelius Scipio Aemilianus Africanus Minor*, adoptive grandson of Scipio Africanus. He achieved distinction in the siege of Carthage (146) during the third Punic War and in his campaign in Spain (133).

Scipio Africanus /ˌafrɪˈkɑːnəs/ (236–*c.*184 BC), Roman general and politician; full name *Publius Cornelius Scipio Africanus Major*. He was successful in concluding the second Punic War, firstly by the defeat of the Carthaginians in Spain in 206 and then by the defeat of Hannibal in Africa in 202.

scire facias /ˌsʌɪriː ˈfeɪʃɪas/ ▶ **noun** US Law a writ requiring a person to show why a judgement regarding a record or patent should not be enforced or annulled.
– ORIGIN Latin, literally 'let (the person) know'.

scirocco ▶ **noun** variant spelling of **SIROCCO**.

S

scirrhus /ˈsɪrəs, ˈskɪ-/ ▶ **noun** (pl. **scirrhi** /-rʌɪ/) Medicine a carcinoma that is hard to the touch.
– DERIVATIVES **scirrhous** adjective.
– ORIGIN late Middle English: modern Latin, from Greek *skirros*, from *skiros* 'hard'.

scissel /ˈsɪs(ə)l/ ▶ **noun** [mass noun] clippings and strips of waste metal produced during the manufacture of coins.
– ORIGIN early 17th cent.: from French *cisaille*, from *cisailler* 'clip with shears'.

scissile /ˈsɪsʌɪl, -sɪl/ ▶ **adjective** chiefly Biochemistry (of a chemical bond) readily undergoing scission.
– ORIGIN early 17th cent.: from Latin *scissilis*, from *sciss-* 'cut, divided', from the verb *scindere*.

scission /ˈsɪʃ(ə)n/ ▶ **noun** [mass noun] technical the action or state of cutting or being cut, in particular:
■ chiefly Biochemistry breakage of a chemical bond, especially one in a long chain molecule so that two smaller chains result. ■ [count noun] a division or split between people or parties; a schism.
– ORIGIN late Middle English: from Old French, or from late Latin *scissio(n-)*, from *scindere* 'cut, cleave'.

scissor ▶ **verb 1** [with obj. and adverbial] cut (something) with scissors: *pages scissored out of a magazine.*
2 [with obj.] move (one's legs) move back and forth in a way resembling the action of scissors: *he was still hanging on, scissoring his legs uselessly.*
■ [no obj.] (of a person's legs) move in such a way.
▶ **noun** see **SCISSORS**.
– ORIGIN early 17th cent.: from **SCISSORS**.

scissorbill ▶ **noun** another term for **SKIMMER** (in sense 2).

scissor hold (also **scissors hold**) ▶ **noun** Wrestling a hold in which the head or other part of the opponent's body is gripped between the legs which are then locked at the instep or ankles to apply pressure.

scissor kick (also **scissors kick**) ▶ **noun** (in various sports, particularly swimming and soccer) a kick in which the legs make a sharp snapping movement like that of a pair of scissors.

scissor lift ▶ **noun** a surface raised or lowered by the closing or opening of crossed supports pivoted like the two halves of a pair of scissors.

scissors (also **a pair of scissors**) ▶ **plural noun** an instrument used for cutting cloth, paper, and other material, consisting of two blades laid one on top of the other and fastened in the middle so as to allow them to be opened and closed by a thumb and finger inserted through rings on the end of their handles.
■ (also **scissor**) [as modifier] denoting an action in which two things cross each other or open and close like the blades of a pair of scissors: *as the fish swims the tail lobes open and close in a slight scissor action.* ■ Rugby a tactical move in which a player running diagonally takes the ball from a teammate and changes the direction of the attack, or feints to do so.
– ORIGIN late Middle English: from Old French *cisoires*, from late Latin *cisoria*, plural of *cisorium* 'cutting instrument', from *cis-*, variant of *caes-*, stem of *caedere* 'to cut'. The spelling with *sc-* (16th cent.) was by association with the Latin stem *sciss-* 'cut'.

scissors and paste ▶ **noun** & **verb** another term for **CUT AND PASTE**.

scissortail ▶ **noun 1** (also **scissor-tailed flycatcher**) a tyrant flycatcher with a very long forked tail, found in the southern US and noted for its spectacular aerial display.
• *Tyrannus forficatus*, family Tyrannidae.
2 (also **scissors-tail**) a small SE Asian freshwater fish with a deeply forked tail
• *Rasbora trilineata*, family Cyprinidae.

Sciuromorpha /skɪˌʊərə(ʊ)ˈmɔːfə/ Zoology a major division of the rodents that comprises the squirrels, prairie dogs, and marmots.
• Suborder Sciuromorpha, order Rodentia.
– ORIGIN modern Latin (plural), from Greek *skiouros* (from *skia* 'shadow' + *oura* 'tail') + *morphē* 'form'.

sclera /ˈsklɪərə/ ▶ **noun** Anatomy the white outer layer of the eyeball. At the front of the eye it is continuous with the cornea.
– DERIVATIVES **scleral** adjective.
– ORIGIN late 19th cent.: modern Latin, from Greek *sklēros* 'hard'.

Scleractinia /ˌsklɛrakˈtɪnɪə/ Zoology an order of coelenterates that comprises the stony corals. Also called **MADREPORARIA**.
– DERIVATIVES **scleractinian** noun & adjective.
– ORIGIN modern Latin (plural), from Greek *sklēros* 'hard' + *aktis, aktin-* 'ray'.

sclerenchyma /sklɪəˈrɛŋkɪmə, sklə-/ ▶ **noun** [mass noun] Botany strengthening tissue in a plant, formed from cells with thickened, typically lignified, walls.
– DERIVATIVES **sclerenchymatous** adjective.
– ORIGIN mid 19th cent.: modern Latin, from Greek *sklēros* 'hard' + *enkhuma* 'infusion', on the pattern of *parenchyma*.

sclerite /ˈsklɪərʌɪt, ˈsklɛ-/ ▶ **noun** Zoology a component section of an exoskeleton, especially each of the plates forming the skeleton of an arthropod.
– ORIGIN mid 19th cent.: from Greek *sklēros* 'hard' + **-ITE**[1].

scleritis /sklɪəˈrʌɪtɪs, sklə-/ ▶ **noun** [mass noun] Medicine inflammation of the sclera of the eye.

sclero- /ˈsklɪərəʊ/ ▶ **combining form** hard; hardened; hardening: *scleroderma* | *sclerotherapy.*
– ORIGIN from Greek *sklēros* 'hard'.

scleroderma /ˌsklɪərəˈdəːmə/ ▶ **noun** [mass noun] Medicine a chronic hardening and contraction of the skin and connective tissue, either locally or throughout the body.

sclerophyll /ˈsklɪərəfɪl, ˈsklɛ-/ ▶ **noun** Botany a woody plant with evergreen leaves that are tough and thick in order to reduce water loss.
– DERIVATIVES **sclerophyllous** /-ˈrɒfɪləs/ adjective.
– ORIGIN early 20th cent.: from Greek *sklēros* 'hard' + *phullon* 'leaf'.

scleroprotein /ˌsklɪərə(ʊ)ˈprəʊtiːn, ˌsklɛ-/ ▶ **noun** Biochemistry an insoluble structural protein such as keratin, collagen, or elastin.

Scleroscope /ˈsklɪərəskəʊp, ˈsklɛ-/ ▶ **noun** (trademark in the US) an instrument for determining the hardness of materials by measuring the height of rebound of a small diamond-tipped hammer dropped on to the material from a standard height.

sclerosed /sklɪəˈrəʊst, sklə-, ˈsklɪə-/ ▶ **adjective** Medicine (especially of blood vessels) affected by sclerosis.

sclerosing cholangitis /sklɪəˈrəʊsɪŋ ˌkɒlanˈɡʌɪtɪs, sklə-/ ▶ **noun** [mass noun] Medicine a complication of ulcerative colitis in which the bile ducts develop irregularities and narrowing.
– ORIGIN 1980s: *sclerosing* from the verb *sclerose* (back-formation from **SCLEROSED**); *cholangitis* from Greek *kholē* 'bile' + *angeion* 'vessel' + **-ITIS**.

sclerosis /sklɪəˈrəʊsɪs, sklə-/ ▶ **noun** [mass noun] Medicine abnormal hardening of body tissue.
■ (in full **multiple sclerosis**) a chronic, typically progressive disease involving damage to the sheaths of nerve cells in the brain and spinal cord, whose symptoms may include numbness, impairment of speech and of muscular coordination, blurred vision, and severe fatigue. Also called **DISSEMINATED SCLEROSIS**. ■ figurative excessive resistance to change: *the challenge was to avoid institutional sclerosis.*
– ORIGIN late Middle English (originally denoting a hard external tumour): via medieval Latin from Greek *sklērōsis*, from *sklēroun* 'harden'.

sclerotherapy /ˌsklɪərə(ʊ)ˈθɛrəpi, ˌsklɛ-/ ▶ **noun** [mass noun] Medicine the treatment of varicose blood vessels by the injection of an irritant which causes inflammation, coagulation of blood, and narrowing of the blood vessel wall.

sclerotic /sklɪəˈrɒtɪk, sklə-/ ▶ **adjective 1** Medicine of or having sclerosis.
■ figurative becoming rigid and unresponsive; losing the ability to adapt: *sclerotic management.*
2 Anatomy of or relating to the sclera.
▶ **noun** another term for **SCLERA**.

sclerotin /ˈsklɪərətɪn, ˈsklɛ-/ ▶ **noun** [mass noun] Biochemistry a structural protein which forms the cuticles of insects and is hardened and darkened by a natural tanning process in which protein chains are cross-linked by quinone groups.
– ORIGIN 1940s: from **SCLERO-** 'hardened', on the pattern of such words as *keratin.*

sclerotium /sklɪəˈrəʊtɪəm, sklə-/ ▶ **noun** (pl. **sclerotia** /-tɪə/) Botany the hard dark resting body of certain fungi, consisting of a mass of hyphal threads, capable of remaining dormant for long periods.
– ORIGIN mid 19th cent.: modern Latin (former genus name), from Greek *sklēros* 'hard'.

sclerotized /ˈsklɪərətʌɪzd, ˈsklɛ-/ (also **-ised**) ▶ **adjective** Entomology (of an insect's body, or part of one) hardened by conversion into sclerotin.
– DERIVATIVES **sclerotization** noun.

sclerotome /ˈsklɪərə(ʊ)təʊm, ˈsklɛ-/ ▶ **noun 1** Embryology the part of each somite in a vertebrate embryo giving rise to bone or other skeletal tissue. Compare with **DERMATOME, MYOTOME**.

sclerous /ˈsklɪərəs/ ▶ **adjective** (of tissue) hardened or bony.
– ORIGIN mid 19th cent.: from Greek *sklēros* 'hard' + **-OUS**.

SCM (in the UK) ▶ **abbreviation for** ■ State Certified Midwife. ■ Student Christian Movement.

scoff[1] ▶ **verb** [no obj.] speak to someone or about something in a scornfully derisive or mocking way: *Patrick professed to scoff at soppy love scenes in films* | [with direct speech] *'You, a scientist?' he scoffed.*
▶ **noun** an expression of scornful derision.
■ archaic an object of ridicule: *his army was the scoff of all Europe.*
– DERIVATIVES **scoffer** noun, **scoffingly** adverb.
– ORIGIN Middle English (first used as a noun in the sense 'mockery, scorn'): perhaps of Scandinavian origin.

scoff[2] informal, chiefly Brit. ▶ **verb** [with obj.] eat (something) quickly and greedily: *he can scoff a cannelloni faster than you can drink a pint.*
▶ **noun** [mass noun] food.
– ORIGIN late 18th cent. (as a verb): originally a variant of Scots and dialect *scaff*. The noun is from Afrikaans *schoff*, representing Dutch *schoft* 'quarter of a day', (by extension) 'meal'.

scofflaw ▶ **noun** N. Amer. informal a person who flouts the law, especially by failing to comply with a law that is difficult to enforce effectively.

scold ▶ **verb** [with obj.] remonstrate with or rebuke (someone) angrily: *Mum took Anna away, scolding her for her bad behaviour.*
▶ **noun** archaic a woman who nags or grumbles constantly.
– DERIVATIVES **scolder** noun.
– ORIGIN Middle English (as a noun): probably from Old Norse *skáld* 'skald'.

scold's bridle ▶ **noun** another term for **BRANKS**.

scolex /ˈskəʊlɛks/ ▶ **noun** (pl. **scolices** /-lɪsiːz/) Zoology the anterior end of a tapeworm, bearing suckers and hooks for attachment.
– ORIGIN mid 19th cent.: modern Latin, from Greek *skōlēx* 'worm'.

scoliosis /ˌskɒlɪˈəʊsɪs, ˌskəʊ-/ ▶ **noun** [mass noun] Medicine abnormal lateral curvature of the spine.
– DERIVATIVES **scoliotic** adjective.
– ORIGIN early 18th cent.: modern Latin, from Greek, from *skolios* 'bent'.

scollop ▶ **noun** & **verb** archaic spelling of **SCALLOP**.

scombroid /ˈskɒmbrɔɪd/ Zoology ▶ **noun** a fish of the mackerel family, or one of a larger group that also includes the barracudas and billfishes.
• Family Scombridae or suborder Scombroidei.
▶ **adjective** of or relating to fish of this family or group.
– ORIGIN mid 19th cent.: from modern Latin *Scombroidea* (superfamily name), from Greek *skombros*, denoting a tuna or mackerel.

sconce[1] ▶ **noun** a candle holder that is attached to a wall with an ornamental bracket.
■ a flaming torch or candle secured in such a candle holder.
– ORIGIN late Middle English (originally denoting a portable lantern with a screen to protect the flame): shortening of Old French *esconse* 'lantern', or from medieval Latin *sconsa*, from Latin *absconsa (laterna)* 'dark (lantern)' (i.e. a lantern with a device for concealing the light), from *abscondere* 'to hide'.

sconce[2] ▶ **noun** archaic a small fort or earthwork defending a ford, pass, or castle gate.
■ a shelter or screen serving as protection from fire or the weather.
– ORIGIN late Middle English: from Dutch *schans* 'brushwood', from Middle High German *schanze*. The earliest recorded sense 'screen, interior partition' derives perhaps from **SCONCE**[1]; the later senses date from the late 16th cent.

Scone /skuːn/ an ancient Scottish settlement to the north of Perth, where the kings of medieval Scotland were crowned on the Stone of Destiny.

scone /skɒn, skəʊn/ ▶ **noun** a small unsweetened or lightly sweetened cake made from flour, fat, and milk and sometimes having added fruit, typically served with butter.

– ORIGIN early 16th cent. (originally Scots): perhaps from Middle Dutch *schoon(broot)* 'fine (bread)'.

USAGE There are two possible pronunciations of the word **scone**: the first rhymes with **gone** and the second rhymes with **tone**. In US English the pronunciation rhyming with **tone** is more common. In British English, the two pronunciations traditionally have different regional and class associations. The first pronunciation tends to be associated with the north of England, and the northern working class, while the second is associated with the south and the middle class. In modern British English, however, it has become fashionable among certain middle-class people to adopt the first pronunciation.

scoop ▶ **noun 1** a utensil resembling a spoon, with a long handle and a deep bowl, used for removing powdered, granulated, or semi-solid substances (such as ice cream) from a container.
■ a short-handled deep shovel used for moving grain, coal, etc. ■ a moving bowl-shaped part of a digging machine, dredger, or other mechanism into which material is gathered. ■ a long-handled spoon-like surgical instrument. ■ a quantity taken up by a scoop: *an apple pie with **scoops of** ice cream on top.*
2 informal a piece of news published by a newspaper or broadcast by a television or radio station in advance of its rivals.
■ (**the scoop**) N. Amer. the latest information about something.
3 an exaggerated upward slide or portamento in singing.
▶ **verb 1** [with obj. and adverbial] pick up and move (something) with a scoop: *Philip began to scoop grain into his polythene bag.*
■ create (a hollow or hole) with or as if with a scoop: *a hole was **scooped out** in the floor of the dwelling.* ■ pick up (someone or something) in a swift, fluid movement: *he laughed and **scooped** her **up** in his arms.*
2 [with obj.] informal publish a news story before (a rival reporter, newspaper, or radio or television station).
■ win (an amount of money, a prize, or a trophy).
3 [no obj.] (in singing) preface notes with an exaggerated upward slide or portamento.
– DERIVATIVES **scooper** noun, **scoopful** noun.
– ORIGIN Middle English (originally denoting a utensil for pouring liquids): from Middle Dutch, Middle Low German *schōpe* 'waterwheel bucket'; from a West Germanic base meaning 'draw water'; related to the verb **SHAPE**.

scoop neck ▶ **noun** a deeply curved wide neckline on a garment.

scoop net ▶ **noun** a fishing net on a long handle used for reaching to the bottom of a river or other shallow water.

scoosh Scottish, informal ▶ **verb** [with obj.] squirt or splash (liquid).
▶ **noun** a splash or squirt of liquid.
■ [mass noun] a fizzy drink such as lemonade.
– ORIGIN imitative.

scoot ▶ **verb** [no obj.] informal go or leave somewhere quickly: *they scooted off on their bikes.*
– ORIGIN mid 18th cent.: of unknown origin.

scooter ▶ **noun** (also **motor scooter**) a light two-wheeled open motor vehicle on which the driver sits over an enclosed engine with their legs together and their feet resting on a floorboard.
■ [often with modifier] any small, light, vehicle able to travel quickly across water, ice, or snow. ■ a child's toy consisting of a footboard mounted on two wheels and a long steering handle, propelled by resting one foot on the footboard and pushing the other against the ground.
▶ **verb** [no obj.] travel or ride on a scooter.
– DERIVATIVES **scooterist** noun.

scope[1] ▶ **noun** [mass noun] the extent of the area or subject matter that something deals with or to which it is relevant: *we widened the scope of our investigation | such questions go well beyond the scope of this book.*
■ the opportunity or possibility to do or deal with something: *the **scope for** major change is always limited by political realities.* ■ archaic a purpose, end, or intention: *Plato even maintains religion to be the chief aim and scope of human life.* ■ Nautical the length of cable extended when a ship rides at anchor. ■ Linguistics & Logic the number of terms or arguments affected by an operator such as a quantifier or conjunction.
– ORIGIN mid 16th cent. (in the sense 'target for shooting at'): from Italian *scopo* 'aim', from Greek *skopos* 'target', from *skeptesthai* 'look out'.

scope[2] informal ▶ **noun** a telescope, microscope, or other device having a name ending in *-scope*.
▶ **verb** [with obj.] N. Amer. informal look at carefully; scan: *they watched him scoping the room, looking for Michael.*
■ assess; weigh up: *they'd **scoped out** their market.*
– ORIGIN early 17th cent. (as a noun): shortened form. The verb dates from the 1970s.

-scope ▶ **combining form** denoting an instrument for observing, viewing, or examining: *microscope | telescope.*
– DERIVATIVES **-scopic** combining form in corresponding adjectives.
– ORIGIN from modern Latin *-scopium*, from Greek *skopein* 'look at'.

scopolamine /skəˈpɒləmiːn/ ▶ **noun** another term for **HYOSCINE**.
– ORIGIN late 19th cent.: from *Scopolia* (genus name of the plants yielding it) + **AMINE**.

scops owl /skɒps/ ▶ **noun** a small owl with distinctive ear tufts, found in Europe, Africa, and Asia.
• Genus *Otus*, family Strigidae: many species, in particular the widespread **Eurasian scops owl** (*O. scops*).
– ORIGIN early 18th cent.: *scops* from modern Latin *Scops* (former genus name), from Greek *skōps*.

-scopy ▶ **combining form** indicating viewing, observation, or examination, typically with an instrument having a name ending in *-scope*: *endoscopy | microscopy.*
– ORIGIN from Greek *skopia* 'observation', from *skopein* 'examine, look at'.

scorbutic /skɔːˈbjuːtɪk/ ▶ **adjective** relating to or affected with scurvy. See also **ANTISCORBUTIC**.
– ORIGIN mid 17th cent.: from modern Latin *scorbuticus*, from medieval Latin *scorbutus* 'scurvy', perhaps from Middle Low German *schorbūk* (from *schoren* 'to break' + *būk* 'belly').

scorch ▶ **verb 1** [with obj.] burn the surface of (something) with flame or heat: *surrounding houses were scorched by heat from the blast.*
■ [no obj.] become burnt when exposed to heat or a flame: *the meat had scorched.* ■ [often as adj. **scorched**] (of the heat of the sun) cause (vegetation or a place) to become dried out and lifeless: *a desolate, scorched landscape.*
2 [no obj., with adverbial of direction] informal (of a person or vehicle) move very fast: *a sports car scorching along the expressway.*
▶ **noun** [mass noun] the burning or charring of the surface of something: [as modifier] *a scorch mark.*
■ Botany a form of plant necrosis, typically of fungal origin, marked by browning of leaf margins.
– ORIGIN Middle English (as a verb): perhaps related to Old Norse *skorpna* 'be shrivelled'.

scorched earth policy ▶ **noun** a military strategy of burning or destroying crops or other resources that might be of use to an invading enemy force.
■ figurative a strategy that involves taking extreme action: *a lawyer renowned for his scorched earth policy in matrimonial cases.*

scorcher ▶ **noun** [usu. in sing.] informal **1** a day or period of very hot weather: *next week could be a real scorcher.*
2 Brit. a remarkable or extreme example of something, in particular:
■ a very powerfully struck shot or kick. ■ sensational book or film. ■ a violent argument. ■ dated a person who drives or cycles very fast.

scorching ▶ **adjective** very hot: *the scorching July sun.*
■ (of criticism) harsh; severe. ■ informal very fast: *she set a scorching pace.*
– DERIVATIVES **scorchingly** adverb.

scordatura /skɔːdəˈtjʊərə/ ▶ **noun** [mass noun] Music the technique of altering the normal tuning of a stringed instrument to produce particular effects.
– ORIGIN late 19th cent.: Italian, from *scordare* 'be out of tune'.

score ▶ **noun 1** the number of points, goals, runs, etc. achieved in a game: *the final score was 4–3 to Royston.*
■ the number of points, goals, runs, etc. achieved by an individual player or a team in a game: *his highest score of the season.* ■ informal an act of gaining a goal or point in a game. ■ a rating or grade, such as a mark achieved in a test: *an IQ score of 161.* ■ (**the score**) informal the state of affairs; the real facts about the present situation: *'What's wrong Simon? What's the score?'* ■ informal an act of buying illegal drugs. ■ informal the proceeds of a crime.
2 (pl. same) a group or set of twenty or about twenty: *a score of men lost their lives in the battle | Doyle's success brought imitators **by the score**.*
■ (**scores of**) a large amount or number of something: *he sent scores of enthusiastic letters to friends.*
3 a written representation of a musical composition showing all the vocal and instrumental parts arranged one below the other.
■ the music composed for a film or play.
4 a notch or line cut or scratched into a surface.
■ historical a running account kept by marks against a customer's name, typically in a public house.
▶ **verb** [with obj.] **1** gain (a point, goal, run, etc.) in a competitive game: *McCartney scored a fine goal | [no obj.] Wilson outstripped his marker to score.*
■ decide on the score to be awarded to (a competitor). ■ gain (a number of points) for a competitor; be worth: *a yes answer scores ten points.* ■ decide on the scores to be awarded in (a match or competition). ■ [no obj.] record the score during a game; act as scorer. ■ Baseball cause (a teammate) to score. ■ informal secure (a success or an advantage): *the band scored a hit single.* ■ [no obj.] informal be successful: [with complement] *his new movie scored big.* ■ informal buy or acquire (something, typically illegal drugs): *Sally had scored some acid.* ■ [no obj.] informal succeed in attracting a sexual partner, typically for a casual encounter.
2 orchestrate or arrange (a piece of music), typically for a specified instrument or instruments: *the Quartet Suite was scored for flute, violin, viola da gamba, and continuo.*
■ compose the music for (a film or play).
3 cut or scratch a notch or line on (a surface): *score the card until you cut through.*
■ historical record (a total owed) by making marks against a customer's name: *a slate on which the old man **scored up** vast accounts.* ■ Medicine & Biology examine (experimentally treated cells, bacterial colonies, etc.), making a record of the number showing a particular character.
– PHRASES **keep (the) score** register the score of a game as it is made. **know the score** informal be aware of the essential facts about a situation. **on the score of** Brit. because of: *power-driven hedge trimmers tend to get a bad press on the score of danger.* **on that** (or **this**) **score** so far as that (or this) is concerned: *my priority was to blend new faces into the team and we have succeeded on that score.* **score points** outdo another person, especially in an argument. **score points off** another way of saying ***score off*** below. **settle** (or **pay**) **a** (or **the**) **score 1** take revenge on someone for something damaging that they have done in the past. **2** dated pay off a debt or other obligation.
– DERIVATIVES **scoreless** adjective.
– ORIGIN late Old English *scoru* 'set of twenty', from Old Norse *skor* 'notch, tally, twenty', of Germanic origin; related to **SHEAR**. The verb (late Middle English) is from Old Norse *skora* 'make an incision'.
▶ **score off** Brit. informal outdo or humiliate, especially in an argument.
score something out/through delete text by drawing a line through it.

scoreboard ▶ **noun** a large board on which the score in a game or match is displayed.

scorebox ▶ **noun** Cricket a room or hut in which the official scorers work and on which the score is displayed for spectators.

scorecard (also **scoresheet** or **scorebook**) ▶ **noun** (in sport) a card, sheet, or book in which scores are entered.

score draw ▶ **noun** a draw in soccer in which goals have been scored, especially as distinguished from a no-score draw in football pools.

scoreline ▶ **noun** the number of points or goals scored in a match; the score.
– ORIGIN 1960s: extension of the original use denoting a line in a newspaper giving the score in a sports contest.

scorer ▶ **noun 1** a person who scores goals, points, etc. in a game.
2 a person who keeps a record of the score in a game.

scoria /ˈskɔːrɪə/ ▶ **noun** (pl. **scoriae** /-riː/) [mass noun] basaltic lava ejected as fragments from a volcano, typically with a frothy texture.
■ slag separated from molten metal during smelting.
– DERIVATIVES **scoriaceous** /-ˈeɪʃəs/ adjective.
– ORIGIN late Middle English (denoting slag from molten metal): via Latin from Greek *skōria* 'refuse', from *skōr* 'dung'. The geological term dates from the late 18th cent.

scorn ▶ **noun** [mass noun] the feeling or belief that someone or something is worthless or despicable; contempt: *I do not wish to become the object of scorn* | [in sing.] *a general* **scorn** *for human life.*
■[in sing.] archaic a person viewed with such feeling: *a scandal and a scorn to all who look on thee.* ■ [count noun] archaic a statement or gesture indicating such feeling.
▶ **verb** [with obj.] feel or express contempt or derision for: *the minister scorned Labour's attempt to woo voters.*
■reject (something) in a contemptuous way: *a letter scorning his offer of intimacy.* ■ [no obj., with infinitive] refuse to do something because one is too proud: *at her lowest ebb, she would have scorned to stoop to such tactics.*
– PHRASES **pour scorn on** speak with contempt or mockery of. **think scorn of** Brit. archaic view with contempt.
– DERIVATIVES **scorner** noun (rare).
– ORIGIN Middle English: shortening of Old French *escarn* (noun), *escharnir* (verb), of Germanic origin.

scornful ▶ **adjective** feeling or expressing contempt or derision: *the opposition were* **scornful** *of the Prime Minister's proposal* | *scornful laughter.*
– DERIVATIVES **scornfully** adverb, **scornfulness** noun.

scorp (also **scorper** or **scauper**) ▶ **noun** a drawknife with a circular blade and a single handle, used to scoop out wood when carving or engraving.
– ORIGIN mid 19th cent. (as *scorper*), based on Latin *scalper* 'knife'.

Scorpio Astrology the eighth sign of the zodiac (the Scorpion), which the sun enters about 23 October.
■(**a Scorpio**) (pl. **-os**) a person born when the sun is in this sign.
– DERIVATIVES **Scorpian** noun & adjective.
– ORIGIN Latin.

scorpioid ▶ **adjective** Zoology of, relating to, or resembling a scorpion.
■Botany (of a flower cluster) curled up at the end, and uncurling as the flowers develop.
– ORIGIN mid 19th cent.: from Greek *skorpioeidēs*, from *skorpios* 'scorpion'.

scorpion ▶ **noun** a terrestrial arachnid which has lobster-like pincers and a poisonous sting at the end of its jointed tail, which it can hold curved over the back. Most kinds live in tropical and subtropical areas.
• Order Scorpiones.
■used in names of other arachnids and insects resembling a scorpion, e.g. **false scorpion**, **water scorpion**. ■ (**the Scorpion**) the zodiacal sign Scorpio or the constellation Scorpius. ■ (**scorpions**) poetic/literary a whip with metal points. [ORIGIN: with allusion to 1 Kings 12:11.]
– ORIGIN Middle English: via Old French from Latin *scorpio(n-)*, based on Greek *skorpios* 'scorpion'.

scorpionfish ▶ **noun** (pl. same or **-fishes**) a chiefly bottom-dwelling marine fish which is typically red in colour and has spines on the head that are sometimes venomous.
• Family Scorpaenidae: many genera and numerous species, including the redfishes and rockfishes.

scorpion fly ▶ **noun** a slender predatory insect with membranous wings, long legs, and a downward-pointing beak. The terminal swollen section of the male's abdomen is carried curved up like a scorpion's sting.
• Order Mecoptera: several families, in particular Panorpidae.

scorpion senna ▶ **noun** a yellow-flowered southern European plant of the pea family.
• *Coronilla emerus*, family Leguminosae.

Scorpius /ˈskɔːpɪəs/ Astronomy a large constellation (the Scorpion). It contains the red giant Antares.
■[as genitive **Scorpii** /ˈskɔːpɪiː/] used with preceding letter or numeral to designate a star in this constellation: *the star Theta Scorpii.*
– ORIGIN Latin.

Scorsese /skɔːˈseɪzi/, Martin (b.1942), American film director. Notable works: *Mean Streets* (1973), *Taxi Driver* (1976), and *The Last Temptation of Christ* (1988).

scorzonera /ˌskɔːzə(ʊ)ˈnɪərə/ ▶ **noun** a plant of the daisy family with tapering purple-brown edible roots. Also called **BLACK SALSIFY**, **VIPER'S GRASS**.
• *Scorzonera hispanica*, family Compositae.
■[mass noun] the root of this plant used as a vegetable.
– ORIGIN early 17th cent.: from Italian, from *scorzone*, from an alteration of medieval Latin *curtio(n-)* 'venomous snake' (against whose venom the plant may have been regarded as an antidote).

Scot ▶ **noun** a native of Scotland or a person of Scottish descent.
■a member of a Gaelic people that migrated from Ireland to Scotland around the late 5th century.
– ORIGIN Old English *Scottas* (plural), from late Latin *Scottus*, of unknown ultimate origin.

USAGE On the different uses of **Scot**, **Scottish**, and **Scotch**, see **usage** at **SCOTTISH**.

Scot. ▶ **abbreviation for** Scotland. ■ Scottish.

scot ▶ **noun** archaic a payment corresponding to a modern tax, rate, or other assessed contribution.
– PHRASES **scot and lot** historical a tax levied by a municipal corporation on its members.
– ORIGIN late Old English, from Old Norse *skot* 'a shot', reinforced by Old French *escot*, of Germanic origin; related to **SHOT**[1].

Scotch ▶ **adjective** old-fashioned term for **SCOTTISH**.
▶ **noun 1** short for **SCOTCH WHISKY**.
2 [as plural noun **the Scotch**] dated the people of Scotland.
3 [mass noun] dated the form of English spoken in Scotland.
– ORIGIN late 16th cent.: contraction of **SCOTTISH**.

USAGE The use of **Scotch** to mean 'of or relating to Scotland or its people' is disliked by Scottish people and is now uncommon in modern English. It survives in a number of fixed expressions, such as ***Scotch** egg* and ***Scotch** whisky*. For more details, see **usage** at **SCOTTISH**.

scotch[1] ▶ **verb 1** [with obj.] decisively put an end to: *a spokesman has scotched the rumours.*
■archaic render (something regarded as dangerous) temporarily harmless: *feudal power in France was scotched, though far from killed.*
2 [with obj. and adverbial] wedge (someone or something) somewhere: *he soon scotched himself against a wall.*
■[with obj.] archaic prevent (a wheel or other rolling object) from moving or slipping by placing a wedge underneath.
▶ **noun** archaic a wedge placed under a wheel or other rolling object to prevent it moving or slipping.
– ORIGIN early 17th cent. (as a noun): of unknown origin; perhaps related to **SKATE**[1]. The sense 'render temporarily harmless' is based on an emendation of Shakespeare's *Macbeth* III. ii. 13 as 'We have scotch'd the snake, not kill'd it', originally understood as a use of **SCOTCH**[2]; the sense 'put an end to' (early 19th cent.) results from the influence on this of the notion of wedging or blocking something so as to render it inoperative.

scotch[2] ▶ **verb** [with obj.] archaic cut or score the skin or surface of.
▶ **noun** archaic a cut or score in skin or another surface.
– ORIGIN late Middle English: of unknown origin.

Scotch argus ▶ **noun** a brown Eurasian grassland butterfly marked with orange and a chain of eyespots near the wing margins, found chiefly in upland areas.
• *Erebia aethiops*, subfamily Satyrinae, family Nymphalidae.

Scotch bonnet (also **Scotch bonnet pepper**) ▶ **noun** W. Indian & N. Amer. a small chilli pepper which is the hottest variety available. Also called **HABANERO** in North America.

Scotch broth ▶ **noun** [mass noun] a traditional Scottish soup made from beef or mutton stock with pearl barley and vegetables.

Scotch cap ▶ **noun** another term for **BONNET** (the Scots type in sense 1).

Scotch catch ▶ **noun** another term for **SCOTCH SNAP**.

Scotch egg ▶ **noun** a hard-boiled egg enclosed in sausage meat, rolled in breadcrumbs, and fried.

Scotch fir ▶ **noun** old-fashioned term for **SCOTS PINE**.

Scotchgard ▶ **noun** [mass noun] trademark a preparation for giving a waterproof grease- and stain-resistant finish to textiles, leather, and other materials, based on organofluorine compounds.
▶ **verb** [with obj.] treat with such a substance.

Scotch glue ▶ **noun** [mass noun] an adhesive made from hide and other animal products, formerly used in carpentry.

Scotch kale ▶ **noun** [mass noun] kale of a variety with purplish leaves.

Scotchlite ▶ **noun** [mass noun] trademark a light-reflecting material containing a layer of minute glass lenses.

Scotchman ▶ **noun** (pl. **-men**) dated a Scotsman.

Scotch mist ▶ **noun** [mass noun] a thick drizzly mist of a kind common in the Scottish Highlands.
■Brit. used sarcastically to imply that a person has failed to understand or see something obvious: *what do you think this is? Scotch mist?*

Scotch pancake ▶ **noun** another term for **DROP SCONE**.

Scotch snap (also **Scotch catch**) ▶ **noun** Music a rhythmic feature in which a dotted note is preceded by a stressed shorter note, characteristic of strathspeys.

Scotch tape trademark, chiefly N. Amer. ▶ **noun** [mass noun] transparent adhesive tape.
▶ **verb** (**Scotch-tape**) [with obj. and adverbial] stick with transparent adhesive tape.

Scotch whisky ▶ **noun** [mass noun] whisky distilled in Scotland, especially from malted barley.

Scotchwoman ▶ **noun** (pl. **-women**) dated a Scotswoman.

scoter /ˈskəʊtə/ ▶ **noun** (pl. same or **scoters**) a northern diving duck that winters off the coast, the male of which has mainly black plumage.
• Genus *Melanitta*, family Anatidae: three species.
– ORIGIN late 17th cent.: of unknown origin.

scot-free ▶ **adverb** without suffering any punishment or injury: *the people who kidnapped you will get off scot-free.*
– ORIGIN from the early sense 'not subject to the payment of scot.'

scotia /ˈskəʊʃə/ ▶ **noun** (chiefly in classical architecture) a concave moulding, especially at the base of a column.
– ORIGIN mid 16th cent.: via Latin from Greek *skotia*, from *skotos* 'darkness', with reference to the shadow produced.

Scoticism ▶ **noun** variant spelling of **SCOTTICISM**.

Scoticize ▶ **verb** variant spelling of **SCOTTICIZE**.

Scotland a country forming the northernmost part of Great Britain and of the United Kingdom; pop. 4,957,300 (1991); capital, Edinburgh.

Scotland was settled by Celtic peoples during the Bronze and early Iron Age. An independent country in the Middle Ages, it was amalgamated with England as a result of the union of the Crowns in 1603 and of the Parliaments in 1707. The distinctive Celtic society of the Highlands, based on clans, was destroyed in the aftermath of the Jacobite uprisings of 1715 and 1745–6 and the Highland clearances of the 18th and 19th centuries. In 1997 the Scots voted in favour of the establishment of a devolved parliament with tax-raising powers, which was inaugurated in 2000.

Scotland Yard the headquarters of the London Metropolitan Police, situated from 1829 to 1890 in Great Scotland Yard off Whitehall, from 1890 until 1967 in New Scotland Yard on the Thames Embankment, and from 1967 in New Scotland Yard, Westminster.
■used to allude to the Criminal Investigation Department of the London Metropolitan Police force.

scotoma /skɒˈtəʊmə, skə(ʊ)-/ ▶ **noun** (pl. **scotomas** or **scotomata** /-mətə/) Medicine a partial loss of vision or blind spot in an otherwise normal visual field.
– ORIGIN mid 16th cent. (denoting dizziness and dim vision): via late Latin from Greek *skotōma*, from *skotoun* 'darken', from *skotos* 'darkness'.

scotopic /skə(ʊ)ˈtɒpɪk/ ▶ **adjective** Physiology relating to or denoting vision in dim light, believed to involve chiefly the rods of the retina. Often contrasted with **PHOTOPIC**.
– ORIGIN early 20th cent.: from Greek *skotos* 'darkness' + **-OPIA** + **-IC**.

Scots ▶ **adjective** another term for **SCOTTISH**: *Scots law* | [postpositive] *a pound Scots.* [ORIGIN: northern variant, originally as *Scottis*.]
▶ **noun 1** plural form of **SCOT**.
2 [mass noun] the form of English used in Scotland.

USAGE On the use of **Scots**, **Scottish**, and **Scotch**, see **usage** at **SCOTTISH**.

Scotsman ▶ **noun** (pl. **-men**) a male native or national of Scotland or a man of Scottish descent.

Scots pine ▶ **noun** a Eurasian pine tree which is extensively planted for its timber (deal) and other products. It is the dominant tree of the old Caledonian pine forest of the Scottish Highlands.
• *Pinus sylvestris*, family Pinaceae.

Scotswoman ▶ **noun** (pl. **-women**) a female native or national of Scotland or a woman of Scots descent.

Scott[1] two English architects. Sir George Gilbert

S

(1811–78) designed the Albert Memorial in London (1863–72), which exemplifies the Gothic style that he favoured. His grandson **Sir Giles Gilbert** (1880–1960) is best known for the Gothic Anglican cathedral in Liverpool (begun in 1904, completed in 1978).

Scott², Sir Peter (Markham) (1909–89), English naturalist and artist, son of Sir Robert Scott. In 1946 he founded the Wildfowl Trust at Slimbridge in Gloucestershire.

Scott³, Ridley (b.1939), English film director. Notable works: *Alien* (1979), *Blade Runner* (1982), and *Thelma and Louise* (1991).

Scott⁴, Sir Robert (Falcon) (1868–1912), English explorer and naval officer, father of Sir Peter Scott. In 1910–12 Scott and four companions made a journey to the South Pole by sled, arriving there in January 1912 to discover that Roald Amundsen had beaten them by a month. Scott and his companions died on the journey back to base.

Scott⁵, Sir Walter (1771–1832), Scottish novelist and poet. He established the form of the historical novel in Britain and was influential in his treatment of rural themes and use of regional speech. Notable novels: *Waverley* (1814), *Ivanhoe* (1819), and *Kenilworth* (1821).

Scotticism /ˈskɒtɪsɪz(ə)m/ (also **Scoticism**) ▶ **noun** a characteristically Scottish phrase, word, or idiom.
– ORIGIN early 18th cent.: from late Latin *Scot(t)icus* + **-ISM**.

Scotticize /ˈskɒtɪsʌɪz/ (also **Scoticize** or **-ise**) ▶ **verb** [with obj.] rare make Scottish in character.

Scottie ▶ **noun** informal **1** (also **Scottie dog**) a Scottish terrier.
2 used as a nickname for a Scotsman.

Scottish ▶ **adjective** of or relating to Scotland or its people: *the Scottish Highlands* | *Scottish dancing.*
▶ **noun** [as plural noun **the Scottish**] the people of Scotland. See also **SCOTS**.
– DERIVATIVES **Scottishness** noun.

USAGE The terms **Scottish**, **Scot**, **Scots**, and **Scotch** are all variants of the same word. They have had different histories, however, and in modern English they have developed different uses and connotations. The normal everyday word used to mean 'of or relating to Scotland or its people' is **Scottish**, as in ***Scottish** people*; ***Scottish** hills*; ***Scottish** Gaelic*; or *she's English, not **Scottish***. The normal, neutral word for 'a person from Scotland' is **Scot**, along with **Scotsman**, **Scotswoman**, and the plural form **the Scots** (or, less commonly, **the Scottish**). The word **Scotch**, meaning either 'of or relating to Scotland' or 'a person/the people from Scotland', was widely used in the past by Scottish writers such as Robert Burns and Sir Walter Scott. In the 20th century it has become less common; it is disliked by many Scottish people (as being an 'English' invention) and is now regarded as old-fashioned in most contexts. It survives in certain fixed phrases, as for example ***Scotch** broth*, ***Scotch** mist*, and ***Scotch** whisky*.
Scots is used, like **Scottish**, as an adjective meaning 'of or relating to Scotland'. However, it tends to be used in a narrower sense to refer specifically to the form of English spoken and used in Scotland, as in *a **Scots** accent* or *the **Scots** word for 'night'*.

Scottish Blackface ▶ **noun** a long-coated sheep of a hardy breed developed in upland areas of northern Britain, with black legs and muzzle.

Scottish Borders an administrative region of southern Scotland; administrative centre, Melrose.

Scottish Nationalist ▶ **noun** a member or supporter of Scottish nationalism or of the Scottish National Party.

Scottish National Party (abbrev.: **SNP**) a political party formed in 1934, which seeks autonomous government for Scotland. It won its first parliamentary seat in 1945, and has since maintained a small group of MPs.

Scottish terrier ▶ **noun** a small terrier of a rough-haired short-legged breed.

scoundrel ▶ **noun** a dishonest or unscrupulous person; a rogue.
– DERIVATIVES **scoundrelism** noun, **scoundrelly** adjective.
– ORIGIN late 16th cent.: of unknown origin.

scour¹ ▶ **verb 1** [with obj.] clean or brighten the surface of (something) by rubbing it hard, typically with an abrasive or detergent: *she scoured the cooker* | *I was **scouring out** the pans.*
■ remove (dirt or unwanted matter) by rubbing in such a way: *use an electric toothbrush to **scour off** plaque.* ■ (of water or a watercourse) make (a channel or pool) by flowing quickly over something and removing soil or rock: *a stream came crashing through a narrow cavern to **scour out** a round pool below.*
2 [no obj.] (of livestock) suffer from diarrhoea.
■ [with obj.] archaic administer a strong purgative to.
▶ **noun** [mass noun] **1** the action of scouring or the state of being scoured, especially by swift-flowing water.
■ [in sing.] an act of rubbing something hard to clean or brighten it: *give the floor a good scour.*
2 (also **scours**) diarrhoea in livestock, especially cattle and pigs.
– DERIVATIVES **scourer** noun.
– ORIGIN Middle English: from Middle Dutch, Middle Low German *schüren*, from Old French *escurer*, from late Latin *excurare* 'clean (off)', from *ex-* 'away' + *curare* 'to clean'.

scour² ▶ **verb** [with obj.] subject (a place, text, etc.) to a thorough search in order to locate something: *David **scoured** each newspaper **for** an article on the murder.*
■ [no obj., with adverbial of direction] move rapidly in a particular direction, especially in search or pursuit of someone or something: *he scoured up the ladder.*
– ORIGIN late Middle English: related to obsolete *scour* 'moving hastily', of unknown origin.

scourge ▶ **noun 1** historical a whip used as an instrument of punishment.
2 a person or thing that causes great trouble or suffering: *the scourge of mass unemployment.*
▶ **verb** [with obj.] **1** historical whip (someone) as a punishment.
2 cause great suffering to: *political methods used to scourge and oppress workers.*
– DERIVATIVES **scourger** noun (historical).
– ORIGIN Middle English: shortening of Old French *escorge* (noun), *escorgier* (verb), from Latin *ex-* 'thoroughly' + *corrigia* 'thong, whip'.

scouring rush ▶ **noun** a horsetail with a very rough ridged stem, formerly used for scouring and polishing.
● Genus *Equisetum*, family Equisetaceae, in particular *E. hyemale*.

Scouse /skaʊs/ Brit. informal ▶ **noun 1** [mass noun] the dialect or accent of people from Liverpool.
2 short for **SCOUSER**.
▶ **adjective** of or relating to Liverpool: *a Scouse accent.*
– ORIGIN mid 19th cent.: abbreviation of **LOBSCOUSE**.

Scouser ▶ **noun** Brit. informal a person from Liverpool.

scout¹ ▶ **noun 1** a soldier or other person sent out ahead of a main force so as to gather information about the enemy's position, strength, or movements.
■ a ship or aircraft employed for reconnaissance, especially a small fast aircraft. ■ short for **TALENT SCOUT**. ■ (also **scout bee**) a honeybee that searches for a new site for a swarm to settle or for a new food source. ■ [usu. in sing.] an instance of gathering information, especially by reconnoitring an area: *I returned from a lengthy scout round the area.*
2 (also **Scout** or **Boy Scout**) a member of the Scout Association.
3 a domestic worker at a college at Oxford University.
4 informal, dated a man or boy: *I've got nothing against old Adrian—he's a **good scout**.*
▶ **verb** [no obj.] make a search for someone or something in various places: *I was sent to **scout around** for a place to park the camper* | *we **scouted for** clues.*
■ (especially of a soldier) go ahead of a main force so as to gather information about an enemy's position, strength, or movements. ■ [with obj.] explore or examine (a place or area of business) so as to gather information about it: *American companies are keen to **scout out** business opportunities.* ■ look for suitably talented people for recruitment to one's own organization or sports team: *Butcher has been scouting for United.*
– PHRASES **Scout's honour** the oath taken by a Scout. ■ informal used to indicate that one has the same honourable standards associated with Scouts, and so will stand by a promise or tell the truth.
– DERIVATIVES **scouter** noun.
– ORIGIN late Middle English (as a verb): from Old French *escouter* 'listen', earlier *ascolter*, from Latin *auscultare*. Sense 3 (early 18th cent.) is of uncertain origin.

scout² ▶ **verb** [with obj.] rare reject (a proposal or idea) with scorn.
– ORIGIN early 17th cent.: of Scandinavian origin; compare with Old Norse *skúta*, *skúti* 'a taunt'.

Scout Association a worldwide youth organization founded for boys in 1908 by Lord Baden-Powell with the aim of developing their character by training them in self-sufficiency and survival techniques in the outdoors. Called the Boy Scouts until 1967, the Scout Association admitted girls as members from 1990.

scout car ▶ **noun** chiefly US a fast armoured vehicle used for military reconnaissance and liaison.

Scouter ▶ **noun** an adult leader in the Scout Association.

scouting ▶ **noun** [mass noun] **1** the action of gathering information about enemy forces or an area.
■ the activity of a talent scout.
2 (also **Scouting**) the characteristic activity and occupation of a Scout; the Scout movement.

Scoutmaster ▶ **noun** a man in charge of a group of Scouts.

scow /skaʊ/ ▶ **noun** a wide-beamed sailing dinghy.
■ chiefly US a flat-bottomed boat used for transporting cargo to and from ships in harbour.
– ORIGIN mid 17th cent.: from Dutch *schouw* 'ferry boat'.

scowl ▶ **noun** an angry or bad-tempered expression.
▶ **verb** [no obj.] frown in an angry or bad-tempered way: *she **scowled at** him defiantly.*
– DERIVATIVES **scowler** noun.
– ORIGIN late Middle English (as a verb): probably of Scandinavian origin; compare with Danish *skule* 'scowl'. The noun dates from the early 16th cent.

SCPO ▶ **abbreviation for** Senior Chief Petty Officer.

SCPS ▶ **abbreviation for** (in the UK) Society of Civil and Public Servants.

SCR Brit. ▶ **abbreviation for** Senior Common (or Combination) Room.

scrabble ▶ **verb** [no obj.] scratch or grope around with one's fingers to find, collect, or hold on to something: *she scrabbled at the grassy slope, desperate for purchase.*
■ (of an animal) scratch at something with its claws: *a lonely dog was scrabbling at the door.* ■ [with adverbial of direction] scramble or crawl quickly: *lizards scrabbling across the walls.* ■ make great efforts to get somewhere or achieve something: *I had to scrabble around to find my college place through Clearing.*
▶ **noun 1** [in sing.] an act of scratching or scrambling for something: *he heard the scrabble of claws behind him.*
■ a struggle to get somewhere or achieve something: *a scrabble among the salesmen to avoid going to the bottom of the heap.*
2 (**Scrabble**) [mass noun] trademark a game in which players build up words on a board from small lettered squares or tiles.
– ORIGIN mid 16th cent. (in the sense 'make marks at random, scrawl'): from Middle Dutch *schrabbelen*, frequentative of *schrabben* 'to scrape'. The noun sense 'struggle to achieve something' is originally a North American usage dating from the late 18th cent.

scrag ▶ **verb** (**scragged**, **scragging**) [with obj.] informal, chiefly Brit. handle roughly; beat up.
■ Rugby grasp (an opponent) by placing an arm around the neck. ■ archaic or US kill by strangling or hanging. ■ US kill; murder.
▶ **noun 1** an unattractively thin person or animal.
2 archaic, informal a person's neck.
– ORIGIN mid 16th cent. (as a noun): perhaps an alteration of Scots and northern English *crag* 'neck'. The verb (mid 18th cent.) developed the sense 'handle roughly' from the early use 'hang, strangle'.

scrag-end ▶ **noun** [mass noun] Brit. the inferior end of a neck of mutton.

scraggy ▶ **adjective** (**scraggier**, **scraggiest**) (of a person or animal) thin and bony.
■ (also chiefly N. Amer. **scraggly**) ragged, thin, or untidy in form or appearance: *an old man with a scraggy beard.*
– DERIVATIVES **scraggily** adverb, **scragginess** noun.

scram ▶ **verb** (**scrammed**, **scramming**) [no obj., usu. in imperative] informal go away from or get out of somewhere quickly: *get out of here, you miserable wretches—scram!*

b **b**ut | d **d**og | f **f**ew | g **g**et | h **h**e | j **y**es | k **c**at | l **l**eg | m **m**an | n **n**o | p **p**en | r **r**ed | s **s**it | t **t**op | v **v**oice | w **w**e | z **z**oo | ʃ **sh**e | ʒ de**c**ision | θ **th**in | ð **th**is | ŋ ri**ng** | x lo**ch** | tʃ **ch**ip | dʒ **j**ar

– ORIGIN early 20th cent.: probably from the verb **SCRAMBLE**.

scramasax /ˈskramәsaks/ ▶ **noun** a large knife with a single-edged blade found among the grave goods in many Anglo-Saxon burials. Such knives were used in hunting and fighting.
– ORIGIN mid 19th cent.: of Germanic origin.

scramble ▶ **verb 1** [no obj., with adverbial of direction] make one's way quickly or awkwardly up a steep gradient or over rough ground by using one's hands as well as one's feet: *we scrambled over the damp boulders.*
■ move hurriedly or clumsily from or into a particular place or position: *she scrambled out of the car | I tried to scramble to my feet.* ■ (**scramble into**) put (clothes) on hurriedly: *Robbie scrambled into jeans and a T-shirt.* ■ [with obj.] informal perform (an action) or achieve (a result) hurriedly, clumsily, or with difficulty: *Cork scrambled a 1–0 win over Monaghan.* ■ [with infinitive] struggle or compete with others for something in an eager or uncontrolled and undignified way: *firms scrambled to win public-sector contracts.* ■ [with obj.] (often **be scrambled**) order (a fighter aircraft or its pilot) to take off immediately in an emergency or for action. ■ [no obj.] (of a fighter aircraft or its pilot) take off in such a way. ■ [no obj.] American Football (of a quarterback) run with the ball behind the line of scrimmage, avoiding tackles.
2 [with obj.] make (something) jumbled or muddled: *maybe the alcohol has scrambled his brains.*
■ cook (eggs) by beating them with a little liquid and then cooking and stirring them gently. ■ make (a broadcast transmission or telephone conversation) unintelligible unless received by an appropriate decoding device: [as adj. **scrambled**] *scrambled phone discussions.*
▶ **noun** [usu. in sing.] **1** a difficult or hurried clamber up or over something: *an undignified scramble over the wall.*
■ a mountain walk up steep terrain involving the use of one's hands. ■ Brit. a motorcycle race over rough and hilly ground. ■ an eager or uncontrolled and undignified struggle with others to obtain or achieve something: *I lost Tommy in the* ***scramble for*** *a seat.* ■ an emergency take-off by fighter aircraft.
2 a disordered mixture of things: *an enciphering machine produced a scramble of the letters of the alphabet.*
– ORIGIN late 16th cent.: imitative; compare with the dialect words *scamble* 'stumble' and *cramble* 'crawl'.

scrambled egg ▶ **noun** [mass noun] **1** (also **scrambled eggs**) a dish of eggs prepared by beating them with a little liquid and then cooking and stirring gently.
2 informal gold braid on a military officer's cap.

scrambler ▶ **noun 1** a device for scrambling a broadcast transmission or telephone conversation.
2 a person who walks over steep, mountainous terrain as a pastime.
■ Brit. a motorcycle for racing over rough and hilly ground. ■ a plant with long slender stems supported by other plants. ■ American Football a quarterback noted for scrambling.

scrambling ▶ **noun** [mass noun] **1** the action of scrambling up or over rough or steep ground, especially as a leisure activity.
■ the sport of racing motorcycles over rough and hilly ground.
2 the alteration of the speech frequency of a telephone conversation or broadcast transmission so as to make it unintelligible without a decoding device.

scramjet ▶ **noun** Aeronautics a ramjet in which combustion takes place in a stream of gas moving at supersonic speed.
– ORIGIN 1960s: from *s(upersonic)* + *c(ombustion)* + **RAMJET**.

scran ▶ **noun** [mass noun] dialect food.
– ORIGIN early 18th cent. (denoting a bill at an inn): of unknown origin.

Scranton an industrial city in NE Pennsylvania; pop. 81,805 (1990).
– ORIGIN named after the *Scranton* family who established a steelworks on the site in 1840, around which the city developed.

scrap[1] ▶ **noun 1** a small piece or amount of something, especially one that is left over after the greater part has been used: *I scribbled her address on* ***a scrap of*** *paper |* ***scraps of*** *information.*
■ (**scraps**) bits of uneaten food left after a meal, especially when fed to animals: *he filled Sammy's bowls with fresh water and scraps.* ■ used to emphasize the lack or smallness of something: *there was not* ***a scrap of*** *aggression in him | every* ***scrap of*** *green land is up for grabs by development.* ■ informal a small person or animal, especially one regarded with affection or sympathy: *poor little scrap, she's too hot in that tight coat.* ■ a particularly small thing of its kind: *she was wearing a short black skirt and a tiny scrap of a top.*
2 (also **scrap metal**) [mass noun] discarded metal for reprocessing: *the steamer was eventually sold for scrap.*
■ [often as modifier] any waste articles or discarded material, especially that which can be put to another purpose: *we're burning scrap lumber.*
▶ **verb** (**scrapped**, **scrapping**) [with obj.] (often **be scrapped**) discard or remove from service (a redundant, old, or inoperative vehicle, vessel, or machine), especially so as to convert it to scrap metal: *a bold decision was taken to scrap existing plant.*
■ abolish or cancel (something, especially a plan, policy, or law) which is now regarded as unnecessary, unwanted, or unsuitable: *the chairman scrapped plans to buy the stadium himself.*
– ORIGIN late Middle English (as a plural noun denoting fragments of uneaten food): from Old Norse *skrap* 'scraps'; related to *skrapa* 'to scrape'. The verb dates from the late 19th cent.

scrap[2] informal ▶ **noun** a fight or quarrel, especially a minor or spontaneous one.
▶ **verb** (**scrapped**, **scrapping**) [no obj.] engage in such a fight or quarrel.
■ compete fiercely: *the two drivers scrapped for the lead.*
– DERIVATIVES **scrapper** noun.
– ORIGIN late 17th cent. (as a noun in the sense 'sinister plot, scheme'): perhaps from the noun **SCRAPE**.

scrapbook ▶ **noun** a book of blank pages for sticking cuttings, drawings, or pictures in.

scrape ▶ **verb 1** [with obj.] drag or pull a hard or sharp implement across (a surface or object) so as to remove dirt or other matter: *remove the green tops from the carrots and scrape them |* [with obj. and complement] *we scraped the dishes clean.*
■ [with obj. and adverbial] use a sharp or hard implement to remove (dirt or unwanted matter) from something: *she scraped the mud off her shoes.* ■ [with obj. and adverbial] apply (a hard or sharp implement) in this way: *he scraped the long-bladed razor across the stubble on his cheek.* ■ make (a hollow) by scraping away soil or rock: *he found a ditch, scraped a hole, and put the bag in it.*
2 rub or cause to rub by accident against a rough or hard surface, causing damage or injury: [no obj.] *he smashed into the wall and felt his teeth* ***scrape against*** *the plaster |* [with obj.] *she reversed in a reckless sweep, scraping the Range Rover.*
■ [with obj.] draw or move (something) along or over something else, making a harsh noise: *she* ***scraped back*** *her chair and stood up.* ■ [no obj.] move with or make such a sound: *she lifted the gate to prevent it scraping along the ground.* ■ [no obj.] humorous play a violin tunelessly: *Olivia was scraping away at her violin.* ■ [with obj.] (**scrape something back**) draw one's hair tightly back off the forehead: *her hair was* ***scraped back into*** *a bun.* ■ [with obj. and adverbial] Brit. spread (butter or margarine) thinly over bread.
3 [with obj.] just manage to achieve; accomplish with great effort or difficulty: *for some years he* ***scraped a living*** *as a tutor.*
■ (**scrape something together/up**) collect or accumulate something with difficulty: *they could hardly scrape up enough money for one ticket, let alone two.* ■ [no obj.] try to save as much money as possible; economize: *they had scrimped and scraped and saved for years.* ■ [no obj.] (**scrape by/along**) manage to live with difficulty: *she has to* ***scrape by on*** *Social Security.* ■ [no obj., with adverbial] narrowly pass by or through something: *there was only just room to* ***scrape through*** *between the tree and the edge of the stream.* ■ [no obj., with adverbial] barely manage to succeed in a particular undertaking: *Bowden* ***scraped in*** *with 180 votes at the last election | he* ***scraped through*** *the entrance exam.*
▶ **noun 1** an act or sound of scraping: *he heard the scrape of his mother's key in the lock.*
■ an injury or mark caused by scraping: *there was a long, shallow scrape on his shin.* ■ a place where soil has been scraped away, especially a shallow hollow formed in the ground by a bird during a courtship display or for nesting. ■ Medicine, informal a procedure of dilatation of the cervix and curettage of the uterus, or the result of this. ■ [in sing.] Brit. a thinly applied layer of butter or margarine on bread: *when making sandwiches, use only the thinnest scrape of fat.* ■ archaic an obsequious bow in which one foot is drawn backwards along the ground.
2 informal an embarrassing or difficult predicament caused by one's own unwise behaviour: *he'd been in worse scrapes than this before now.*
– PHRASES **scrape acquaintance with** dated contrive to get to know. **scrape the barrel** (or **the bottom of the barrel**) informal be reduced to using things or people of the poorest quality because there is nothing else available.
– ORIGIN Old English *scrapian* 'scratch with the fingernails', of Germanic origin, reinforced in Middle English by Old Norse *skrapa* or Middle Dutch *schrapen* 'to scratch'.

scraper ▶ **noun** a tool or device used for scraping, especially for removing dirt, paint, or other unwanted matter from a surface.
■ Archaeology a prehistoric flint implement with a sharpened edge used for scraping material such as hide or wood.

scraperboard ▶ **noun** [mass noun] Brit. cardboard or board with a blackened surface which can be scraped off for making white line drawings.

scrap heap ▶ **noun** a pile of discarded materials or articles: *cars on a scrap heap |* figurative *it should be consigned to the scrap heap of technological history.*

scrapie ▶ **noun** [mass noun] a disease of sheep involving the central nervous system, characterized by a lack of coordination causing affected animals to rub against trees and other objects for support, and thought to be caused by a virus-like agent such as a prion.
– ORIGIN early 20th cent.: from the verb **SCRAPE** + **-IE**.

scraping ▶ **noun** [mass noun] the action or sound of something scraping or being scraped: *the scraping of the spoon in the bowl |* [in sing.] *there was a scraping of chairs.*
■ [count noun] (usu. **scrapings**) a small amount of something that has been obtained by scraping it from a surface: *I got some scrapings from under the girl's fingernails.*

scrap merchant ▶ **noun** a person who deals in scrap metal or other waste articles.

scrap metal ▶ **noun** another term for **SCRAP**[1] (sense 2).

scrap paper ▶ **noun** [mass noun] odd bits of paper, used for making rough notes.

scrapple ▶ **noun** [mass noun] US scraps of pork or other meat stewed with maize meal and shaped into large cakes.
– ORIGIN mid 19th cent.: diminutive of the noun **SCRAP**[1].

scrappy ▶ **adjective** (**scrappier**, **scrappiest**) **1** consisting of disorganized, untidy, or incomplete parts: *scrappy lecture notes piled up unread.* [ORIGIN: mid 19th cent.: derivative of **SCRAP**[1].]
2 N. Amer. informal determined, argumentative, or pugnacious: *he had a scrappy New York temperament.* [ORIGIN: late 19th cent.: derivative of **SCRAP**[2].]
– DERIVATIVES **scrappily** adverb, **scrappiness** noun.

scrapyard ▶ **noun** Brit. a place where scrap is collected before being discarded, reused, or recycled.

scratch ▶ **verb 1** [with obj.] score or mark the surface of (something) with a sharp or pointed object: *the car's paintwork was battered and scratched |* [no obj.] *he scratched at a stain on his jacket.*
■ make a long, narrow superficial wound in the skin of: *her arms were scratched by the thorns | I scratched myself on the tree.* ■ rub (a part of one's body) with one's fingernails to relieve itching: *Jessica lifted her sunglasses and scratched her nose.* ■ [with obj. and adverbial] make (a mark or hole) by scoring a surface with a sharp or pointed object: *I found two names scratched on one of the windowpanes.* ■ write (something) hurriedly or awkwardly: *pass me my writing things—I'll scratch a few letters before I get up.* ■ [with obj. and adverbial] remove (something) from something else by pulling a sharp implement over it: *he scratched away the plaster.* ■ [no obj.] make a rasping or grating noise by scraping something over a hard surface: *the dog scratched to be let in |* [as noun **scratching**] *there was a sound of scratching behind the wall.* ■ [no obj.] [often as noun **scratching**] play a record using the scratch technique (see sense 1 of the noun below.) ■ [no obj.] (of a bird or mammal, especially a chicken) rake the ground with the beak or claws in search of food. ■ [no obj.] (**scratch for**) search for (someone or something that is hard to locate or find): *he's still* ***scratching around for*** *a woman to share his life.* ■ accomplish (something) with great effort or difficulty: *Tabitha wondered how long the woman had been* ***scratching a living*** *on the waterways.* ■ [no obj.] (**scratch along**) make a living with difficulty: *many architects now scratch along doing loft conversions.*

2 [with obj.] cancel or strike out (writing) with a pen or pencil: *the name of Dr McNab was **scratched out** and that of Dr Dunstaple substituted.*
■ withdraw (a competitor) from a competition: *Jolie's Halo was **scratched from** a minor stakes race at Monmouth Park.* ■ [no obj.] (of a competitor) withdraw from a competition: *due to a knee injury she was forced to **scratch from** the race.* ■ cancel or abandon (an undertaking or project): *banks seem prepared to scratch stabilization charges.*
▶**noun 1** a mark or wound made by scratching: *the scratches on her arm were throbbing* | [as modifier] *scratch marks on the window.*
■ [in sing.] informal a slight or insignificant wound or injury: *it's nothing—just a scratch.* ■ [in sing.] an act or spell of scratching oneself to relieve itching: *he gave his scalp a good scratch.* ■ a rasping or grating noise produced by something rubbing against a hard surface: *the scratch of a match lighting a cigarette.* ■ [mass noun] a rough hiss, caused by the friction of the stylus in the groove, heard when a record is played. ■ [mass noun] a technique, used especially in rap music, of stopping a record by hand and moving it back and forwards to give a rhythmic scratching effect.
2 [mass noun] the starting point in a handicap for a competitor receiving no odds. [ORIGIN: originally denoting a boundary or starting line for sports competitors.]
■ Golf a handicap of zero, indicating that a player is good enough to achieve par on a course.
3 [mass noun] informal money: *he was working to get some scratch together.*
▶**adjective** [attrib.] **1** assembled or made from whatever is available, and so unlikely to be of the highest quality: *City were fielding a scratch squad.*
2 (of a sports competitor or event) with no handicap given.
– PHRASES **from scratch** from the very beginning, especially without utilizing or relying on any previous work for assistance: *he built his own computer company from scratch.* **scratch a —— and find a ——** used to suggest that an investigation of someone or something soon reveals their true nature: *they believe that if you scratch a homophobe, you'll probably find a racist.* **scratch one's head** informal think hard in order to find a solution to something. ■ feel or express bewilderment. **scratch the surface 1** deal with a matter only in the most superficial way: *research has only scratched the surface of the paranormal.* **2** initiate the briefest investigation to discover something concealed: *they have a boring image but scratch the surface and it's fascinating.* **up to scratch** up to the required standard; satisfactory: *her German was not up to scratch.* **you scratch my back and I'll scratch yours** proverb if you do me a favour, I'll return it.
– DERIVATIVES **scratcher** noun.
– ORIGIN late Middle English: probably a blend of the synonymous dialect words *scrat* and *cratch*, both of uncertain origin; compare with Middle Low German *kratsen* and Old High German *krazzōn*.

scratchboard ▶**noun** another term for **SCRAPERBOARD**.

scratch card ▶**noun** a card with a section or sections coated in an opaque waxy substance which may be scraped away to reveal a symbol indicating whether a prize has been won in a competition.

scratch coat ▶**noun** N. Amer. a rough coating of plaster scratched before it is quite dry to ensure the adherence of the next coat.

scratchings (also **pork scratchings**) ▶**plural noun** Brit. crisp pieces of pork fat left after rendering lard, eaten as a snack.

scratch pad ▶**noun** chiefly N. Amer. a notepad.
■ Computing a small, fast memory for the temporary storage of data.

scratchplate ▶**noun** a plastic or metal plate attached to the front of a guitar to protect it from being scratched by the pick.

scratch video ▶**noun** a video made by mixing together short clips into a single film with a synchronized soundtrack.

scratchy ▶**adjective** (**scratchier**, **scratchiest**) (especially of a fabric or garment) having a rough, uncomfortable texture and tending to cause itching or discomfort.
■ (of a voice or sound) rough; grating: *she dropped her voice to a scratchy whisper.* ■ (of a record) making a crackling or rough sound because of scratches on the surface. ■ (of writing or a drawing) done with quick and jagged strokes: *a scratchy ink sketch of a man on horseback.* ■ bad-tempered or irritable: *she was a little abrupt and scratchy.*
– DERIVATIVES **scratchily** adverb, **scratchiness** noun.

scrawl ▶**verb** [with obj.] write (something) in a hurried, careless way: *Charlie scrawled his signature* | [no obj.] *he was scrawling on the back of a used envelope.*
▶**noun** an example of hurried, careless writing: *the page was covered in scrawls and doodles* | [mass noun] *reams and reams of handwritten scrawl.*
■ a note or message written in this way: *Duncan read the scrawl, then passed it to her.*
– DERIVATIVES **scrawly** adjective.
– ORIGIN early 17th cent.: apparently an alteration of the verb **CRAWL**, perhaps influenced by obsolete *scrawl* 'sprawl'.

scrawny ▶**adjective** (**scrawnier**, **scrawniest**) (of a person or animal) unattractively thin and bony.
■ (of vegetation) meagre or stunted.
– DERIVATIVES **scrawniness** noun.
– ORIGIN mid 19th cent.: variant of dialect *scranny*; compare with archaic *scrannel* 'weak, feeble' (referring to sound).

scream ▶**verb** [no obj.] give a long, loud, piercing cry or cries expressing extreme emotion or pain: *they could hear him screaming in pain* | [as adj. **screaming**] *a harassed mum with a screaming child.*
■ [reporting verb] cry something in a high-pitched, frenzied way: [no obj.] *I ran to the house screaming for help* | [with direct speech] *'Get out!' he screamed* | [with obj.] *he screamed abuse down the phone.* ■ urgently and vociferously call attention to one's views or feelings, especially ones of anger or distress: [with clause] *his supporters scream that he is being done an injustice* | figurative *the creative side of me is screaming out for attention.* ■ informal, dated turn informer. ■ make a loud, high-pitched sound: *sirens were screaming from all over the city.* ■ [no obj., with adverbial of direction] move very rapidly with or as if with such a sound: *a shell screamed overhead.*
▶**noun** a long, loud, piercing cry expressing extreme emotion or pain: *they were awakened by screams for help.*
■ a high-pitched cry made by an animal: *the screams of the seagulls.* ■ a loud, piercing sound: *the scream of a falling bomb.* ■ [in sing.] informal an irresistibly funny person, thing, or situation: *the movie's a scream.*
– ORIGIN Middle English: origin uncertain; perhaps from Middle Dutch.

screamer ▶**noun 1** a person or thing that makes a screaming sound.
2 informal a thing remarkable for speed or impact: *he won a screamer of a 500 cc final.*
■ an extremely fast ball or shot: *he sent two screamers past the Oxford goalkeeper.* ■ chiefly US a sensational or very large headline: *his death caused a front-page screamer.* ■ dated a thing that causes screams of laughter.
3 a large goose-like South American waterbird with a short bill, a sharp bony spur on each wing, and a harsh honking call.
● Family Anhimidae: two genera and three species.

screamingly ▶**adverb** [as submodifier] to a very great extent; extremely: *a screamingly dull daily routine.*

scree ▶**noun** [mass noun] a mass of small loose stones that form or cover a slope on a mountain.
■ [count noun] a slope covered with such stones.
– ORIGIN early 18th cent.: probably a back-formation from the plural *screes*, from Old Norse *skritha* 'landslip'; related to *skrítha* 'glide'.

screech ▶**verb** [no obj.] (of a person or animal) give a loud, harsh, piercing cry: *she hit her brother, causing him to screech with pain.*
■ make a loud, harsh, squealing sound: [as adj. **screeching**] *she brought the car to a screeching halt.* ■ [no obj., with adverbial of direction] move rapidly with such a sound: *the van screeched round a bend at speed.*
▶**noun** a loud, harsh, piercing cry.
■ a loud, harsh, squealing sound: *a screech of brakes.*
– DERIVATIVES **screecher** noun, **screechy** adjective (**screechier**, **screechiest**).
– ORIGIN mid 16th cent.: alteration of archaic *scritch*, of imitative origin.

screech beetle ▶**noun** an oval convex water beetle with large eyes, which lives in muddy pools. When held it squeaks by rubbing the tip of the abdomen against the wing cases.
● *Hygrobia hermanni*, family Hygrobiidae.

screech owl ▶**noun** an owl with a screeching call:
● a small American owl related to the scops owls (genus *Otus*, family Strigidae: in particular *Otus asio*). ● Brit. another term for **BARN OWL**.

screed ▶**noun 1** a long speech or piece of writing, typically one regarded as tedious.
2 [mass noun] a levelled layer of material (e.g. cement) applied to a floor or other surface.
■ [count noun] a strip of plaster or other material placed on a surface as a guide to thickness.
– ORIGIN Middle English: probably a variant of the noun **SHRED**. The early sense was 'fragment cut from a main piece', then 'torn strip, tatter', whence (via the notion of a long roll or list) sense 1.

screeding ▶**noun** [mass noun] a levelled layer of material (e.g. cement) applied to a floor or other surface.

screel /skriːl/ ▶**verb** [no obj.] chiefly Scottish & W. Indian utter or emit a high-pitched or a discordant cry or sound; screech.
– ORIGIN late 19th cent.: of imitative origin, or related to the verb **SKIRL**.

screen ▶**noun 1** a fixed or movable upright partition used to divide a room, give shelter from draughts, heat, or light, or to provide concealment or privacy.
■ a thing providing concealment or protection: *his jeep was discreetly parked behind a screen of trees* | figurative *the article is using science as a screen for unexamined prejudice.* ■ Military a detachment of troops or ships detailed to cover the movements of the main body. ■ [often with modifier] Architecture a partition of carved wood or stone separating the nave of a church from the chancel, choir, or sanctuary. See also **ROOD SCREEN**. ■ a windscreen of a motor vehicle: *a branch whipped across the screen and tore off one of the wipers.* ■ a frame with fine wire netting used in a window or doorway to keep out mosquitoes and other flying insects. ■ a part of an electrical or other instrument which protects it from or prevents it causing electromagnetic interference. ■ Electronics (also **screen grid**) a grid placed between the control grid and the anode of a valve to reduce the capacitance between these electrodes.
2 the surface of a cathode ray tube or similar electronic device, especially that of a television, VDU, or monitor, on which images and data are displayed.
■ a blank, typically white or silver surface on which a photographic image is projected: *two historical swashbucklers are due to fill cinema screens this year.* ■ (**the screen**) films or television; the film industry: *she's a star of the track as well as the screen.* ■ the data or images displayed on a computer screen: *pressing the F1 key at any time will display a help screen.* ■ Photography a flat piece of ground glass on which the image formed by a camera lens is focused.
3 Printing a transparent finely ruled plate or film used in half-tone reproduction.
4 [in sing.] a system of checking a person or thing for the presence or absence of something, especially a disease: *services offered by the centre include a health screen for people who have just joined the company.*
5 a large sieve or riddle, especially one for sorting substances such as grain or coal into different sizes.
▶**verb** [with obj.] **1** conceal, protect, or shelter (someone or something) with a screen or something forming a screen: *her hair swung across to screen her face* | *a high hedge screened all of the front from passers-by.*
■ (**screen something off**) separate something from something else with or as if with a screen: *an area had been screened off as a waiting room.* ■ protect (someone) from something dangerous or unpleasant: *in my country a man of my rank would be screened completely from any risk of attack.* ■ prevent from causing or protect from electromagnetic interference: *ensure that your microphone leads are properly screened from hum pickup.*
2 show (a film or video) or broadcast (a television programme): *the show is to be screened by the BBC later this year.*
3 test (a person or substance) for the presence or absence of a disease: *outpatients were **screened for** cervical cancer.*
■ check on or investigate (someone), typically to ascertain whether they are suitable for or can be trusted in a particular situation or job: *all prospective presidential candidates would have to screened by a pre-selection committee.* ■ evaluate or analyse (something) for its suitability for a particular purpose or application: *only one per cent of rainforest plants have been **screened for** medical use.* ■ (**screen someone/thing out**) exclude someone or something after such evaluation or investigation: *only those refugees who are screened out are sent back to Vietnam.*
4 pass (a substance such as grain or coal) through a

large sieve or screen, especially so as to sort it into different sizes.

5 Printing project (a photograph or other image) through a transparent ruled plate so as to be able to reproduce it as a half-tone.

− DERIVATIVES **screenable** adjective, **screener** noun, **screenful** noun.

− ORIGIN Middle English: shortening of Old Northern French *escren*, of Germanic origin.

screen door ▸ noun the outer door of a pair, used for protection against insects, weather, etc.

screen dump ▸ noun the process or an instance of causing what is displayed on a VDU screen to be printed out.
■ a resulting printout.

screening ▸ noun **1** a showing of a film, video, or television programme.
2 [mass noun] the evaluation or investigation of something as part of a methodical survey, to assess suitability for a particular role or purpose.
■ the testing of a person or group of people for the presence of a disease or other condition: *prenatal screening for Down's syndrome*.
3 (**screenings**) refuse separated by sieving grain.

screen pass ▸ noun American Football a forward pass to a player protected by a screen of blockers.

screenplay ▸ noun the script of a film, including acting instructions and scene directions.

screen-print ▸ verb [with obj.] [often as adj. **screen-printed**] force ink or metal on to (a surface) through a prepared screen of fine material so as to create a picture or pattern.
▸ noun (**screen print**) a picture or design produced by screen-printing.

screen saver ▸ noun Computing a program which, after a set time, replaces an unchanging screen display with a moving image to prevent damage to the phosphor.

screenshot ▸ noun Computing a photograph of the display on a computer screen to demonstrate the operation of a program.

screen test ▸ noun a filmed test to ascertain whether an actor is suitable for a film role.
▸ verb (**screen-test**) [with obj.] give such a test to (an actor).

screen time ▸ noun [mass noun] the time allotted to or occupied by a production, subject, etc., on film or television.

screenwash ▸ noun [mass noun] a mixture of water, detergents, and sometimes antifreeze used to clean the windscreens of vehicles.

screenwriter ▸ noun a person who writes a screenplay.

− DERIVATIVES **screenwriting** noun.

screw ▸ noun **1** a short, slender, sharp-pointed metal pin with a raised helical thread running around it and a slotted head, used to join things together by being rotated so that it pierces wood or other material and is held tightly in place.
■ a cylinder with a helical ridge or thread running round the outside (a **male screw**) that can be turned to seal an opening, apply pressure, adjust position, etc., especially one fitting into a corresponding internal groove or thread (a **female screw**). ■ historical (**the screws**) an instrument of torture acting in this way. ■ (also **screw propeller**) a ship's or aircraft's propeller (considered as acting like a screw in moving through water or air).
2 an act of turning a screw or other object having a thread.
■ [mass noun] Billiards & Snooker, Brit. backspin given to the cue ball by hitting it below centre, intended to make it move backwards after striking the object ball. ■ [count noun] Brit. a small twisted-up piece of paper, typically containing a substance such as salt or tobacco.
3 informal a prisoner's derogatory term for a warder.
4 [in sing.] vulgar slang an act of sexual intercourse.
■ [with adj.] a sexual partner of a specified ability.
5 [in sing.] Brit. informal, dated an amount of salary or wages: *he's offered me the job with a jolly good screw.*
6 Brit. archaic, informal a mean or miserly person.
7 Brit. informal a worn-out horse.
▸ verb **1** [with obj. and adverbial] fasten or tighten with a screw or screws: *screw the hinge to your new door.*
■ rotate (something) so as to fit it into or on to a surface or object by means of a spiral thread: *Philip screwed the top on the flask.* ■ [no obj., with adverbial] (of an object) be attached or removed by being rotated in this way: *a connector which screws on to the gas cylinder.*

■ (**screw something around/round**) turn one's head or body round sharply: *he screwed his head around to try and find the enemy.*
2 [with obj.] (usu. **be screwed**) informal cheat or swindle (someone), especially by charging them too much for something: *if you do what they tell you, you're screwed* | *the loss of advertising contracts will amount to more than the few quid that they're trying to screw us for.*
■ (**screw something out of**) extort or force something, especially money, from (someone) by putting them under strong pressure: *your grandmother screwed cash out of him for ten years.*
3 [with obj.] vulgar slang have sexual intercourse with.
■ [no obj.] (of a couple) have sexual intercourse. ■ [in imperative] informal used to express anger or contempt.
4 [with obj.] impart spin or curl to (a ball or shot).
■ [no obj.] Billiards & Snooker, Brit. play a shot with screw.
− PHRASES **have one's head screwed on** (**the right way**) informal have common sense. **have a screw loose** informal be slightly eccentric or mentally disturbed. **put the screws on** informal exert strong psychological pressure on (someone) so as to intimidate them into doing something. **a turn of the screw** informal an additional degree of pressure or hardship added to a situation that is already extremely difficult to bear. **turn** (or **tighten**) **the screw** (or **screws**) informal exert strong pressure on someone.
− DERIVATIVES **screwable** adjective, **screwer** noun.
− ORIGIN late Middle English (as a noun): from Old French *escroue* 'female screw, nut', from Latin *scrofa*, literally 'sow', later 'screw'. The early sense of the verb was 'contort (the features), twist around' (late 16th cent.).

screw around 1 vulgar slang have many different sexual partners. **2** informal fool about.
screw someone over informal treat someone unfairly; cheat or swindle someone.
screw up 1 (of the muscles of one's face or around one's eyes) contract, typically so as to express emotion or because or bright light. **2** informal, chiefly N. Amer. completely mismanage or mishandle a situation: *I'm sorry, Susan, I screwed up.*
screw someone up informal cause someone to be emotionally or mentally disturbed: *this job can really screw you up.*
screw something up 1 crush a piece of paper or fabric into a tight mass. ■ tense the muscles of one's face or around one's eyes, typically so as to register an emotion or because of bright light. **2** informal cause something to fail or go wrong: *why are you trying to screw up your life?* **3** summon up one's courage: *now Stephen had to screw up his courage and confess.*

screwball chiefly N. Amer. ▸ noun **1** Baseball a ball pitched with reverse spin as compared to a curve ball.
2 informal a crazy or eccentric person.
▸ adjective informal crazy; absurd.
■ relating to or denoting a style of fast-moving comedy film involving eccentric characters or ridiculous situations.
− DERIVATIVES **screwballer** noun (only in sense 1 of the noun).

screw cap ▸ noun a round cap or lid that can be screwed on to a bottle or jar.
− DERIVATIVES **screw-capped** adjective.

screw coupling ▸ noun a female screw with threads at both ends for joining lengths of pipes or rods.

screw-down ▸ adjective adapted or designed to be closed by screwing: *the flex is held by a screw-down bar.*

screwdriver ▸ noun **1** a tool with a flattened or cross-shaped tip that fits into the head of a screw to turn it.
2 a cocktail made from vodka and orange juice.

screwed ▸ adjective **1** (of a bolt or other device) having a helical ridge or thread running around the outside.
2 (of paper or fabric) crumpled or crushed into a ball: *the litter included screwed bags and used tickets.*
■ [predic.] archaic, informal drunk.

screwed-up ▸ adjective **1** informal (of a person) emotionally disturbed; neurotic: *the screwed-up children of wealthy parents.*
■ (of an event or a situation) spoiled by being badly managed or carried out: *that was the most screwed-up audition.*

2 [attrib.] (of paper or fabric) crumpled or crushed into a ball: *a screwed-up paper bag.*
■ (of a person's face or eyes) crumpled, especially because of worry or effort.

screw eye ▸ noun a screw with a loop for passing a cord through, instead of a slotted head.

screwgate (also **screwgate karabiner**) ▸ noun Climbing a type of lockable karabiner.

screw gear ▸ noun a gear consisting of an endless screw with a cogwheel or pinion.

screw hook ▸ noun a hook with a point and thread for fastening it to woodwork.

screw-in ▸ adjective adapted or designed to be attached by screwing into something.

screw jack ▸ noun a vehicle jack worked by a screw device.

screw-on ▸ adjective [attrib.] adapted or designed to be attached by screwing on to something.

screw pine ▸ noun another term for PANDANUS.

screw plate ▸ noun a steel plate with threaded holes for making male screws.

screw propeller ▸ noun see SCREW (sense 1).

screw tap ▸ noun a tool for making female screws.

screw thread ▸ noun see THREAD (sense 3).

screw top ▸ noun a round cap or lid that can be screwed on to a bottle or jar.
− DERIVATIVES **screw-topped** adjective.

screw-up ▸ noun informal, chiefly N. Amer. a situation that has been completely mismanaged or mishandled: *a massive bureaucratic screw-up.*

screw valve ▸ noun a stopcock opened and shut by a screw.

screw worm ▸ noun **1** a worm gear or other mechanical device bearing a screw.
2 a large American blowfly larva which enters the wounds of mammals and sometimes humans, developing under the skin and often causing death. The adult fly is called the **screw-worm fly**.
● *Cochliomyia* (or *Callitroga*) *hominivorax*, family Calliphoridae.

screwy ▸ adjective (**screwier**, **screwiest**) informal, chiefly N. Amer. rather odd or eccentric.
− DERIVATIVES **screwiness** noun.

Scriabin /skrɪˈɑːbɪn/ (also **Skryabin**), Aleksandr (Nikolaevich) (1872–1915), Russian composer and pianist. Notable works: *The Divine Poem* (symphony, 1903) and *Prometheus: The Poem of Fire* (symphonic poem, 1909–10).

scribble[1] ▸ verb [with obj.] write or draw (something) carelessly or hurriedly: *he took the clipboard and scribbled something illegible* | [as adj. **scribbled**] *scribbled notes* | [no obj.] *hastily he scribbled in the margin.*
■ [no obj.] informal write for a living or as a hobby: *they scribbled, potted, and painted.*
▸ noun a piece of writing or a picture produced in this way: *illegible scribbles* | [mass noun] *the postman would never be able to decipher your scribble.*
− DERIVATIVES **scribbly** adjective.
− ORIGIN late Middle English: from medieval Latin *scribillare*, diminutive of Latin *scribere* 'write'.

scribble[2] ▸ verb [with obj.] [often as noun **scribbling**] card (wool, cotton, etc.) coarsely.
− ORIGIN late 17th cent.: probably from Low German; compare with German *schrubbeln* (in the same sense), frequentative of Low German *schrubben* 'to scrub'.

scribbler ▸ noun informal a person who writes for a living or as a hobby.

scribe ▸ noun **1** historical a person who copies out documents, especially one employed to do this before printing was invented.
■ informal, often humorous a writer, especially a journalist.
2 (also **Scribe**) Jewish History an ancient Jewish record-keeper or, later, a professional theologian and jurist.
3 (also **scribe awl**) a pointed instrument used for making marks on wood, bricks, etc., to guide a saw or in signwriting.
▸ verb [with obj.] **1** chiefly poetic/literary write: *he scribed a note that he passed to Dan.*
2 mark with a pointed instrument.
− DERIVATIVES **scribal** adjective.
− ORIGIN Middle English (in sense 2 of the noun): from Latin *scriba*, from *scribere* 'write'. The verb was first used in the sense 'write down'; in sense 2 it is perhaps partly a shortening of DESCRIBE.

scriber ▸ noun another term for SCRIBE (in sense 3).

scrim ▶ **noun** [mass noun] strong, coarse fabric, chiefly used for heavy-duty lining or upholstery.
■ [count noun] Theatre a piece of gauze cloth that appears opaque until lit from behind, used as a screen or backcloth. ■ [count noun] a similar heatproof cloth put over film or television lamps to diffuse the light. ■ [count noun] chiefly US a thing that conceals or obscures something: *a thin scrim of fog covered the island.*
– ORIGIN late 18th cent.: of unknown origin.

scrimmage ▶ **noun 1** a confused struggle or fight.
2 [mass noun] American Football a sequence of play beginning with the placing of the ball on the ground with its longest axis at right angles to the goal line.
■ [count noun] chiefly American Football a session in which teams practice by playing a simulated game.
▶ **verb** [no obj.] chiefly American Football engage in a scrimmage.
■ [with obj.] put (the ball) into a scrimmage.
– DERIVATIVES **scrimmager** noun.
– ORIGIN late Middle English: alteration of dialect *scrimish*, variant of the noun **SKIRMISH**.

scrimp ▶ **verb** [no obj.] be thrifty or parsimonious; economize: *I have* **scrimped and saved** *to give you a good education.*
– ORIGIN mid 18th cent. (in the sense 'keep short of (food)'): from Scots *scrimp* 'meagre'; perhaps related to **SHRIMP**.

scrimshander /ˈskrɪmˌʃandə/ ▶ **verb** [with obj.] another term for **SCRIMSHAW**.
▶ **noun** a person who makes scrimshaws.
– ORIGIN mid 19th cent.: from a variant of **SCRIMSHAW** + **-ER**[1].

scrimshank /ˈskrɪmʃaŋk/ ▶ **verb** [no obj.] Brit. informal (especially of a person in the armed services) shirk one's duty.
– DERIVATIVES **scrimshanker** noun.
– ORIGIN late 19th cent.: of unknown origin.

scrimshaw ▶ **verb** [with obj.] adorn (shells, ivory, or other materials) with carved or coloured designs.
▶ **noun** a piece of work done in such a way.
– ORIGIN early 19th cent.: of unknown origin; perhaps influenced by the surname *Scrimshaw*.

scrip[1] ▶ **noun 1** a provisional certificate of money subscribed to a bank or company, entitling the holder to a formal certificate and dividends.
■ [mass noun] such certificates collectively. ■ (also **scrip issue** or **dividend**) Finance an issue of additional shares to shareholders in proportion to the shares already held.
2 (also **land scrip**) N. Amer. a certificate entitling the holder to acquire possession of certain portions of public land.
3 [mass noun] US historical paper money in amounts of less than a dollar.
– ORIGIN mid 18th cent.: abbreviation of *subscription receipt*.

scrip[2] ▶ **noun** historical a small bag or pouch, typically one carried by a pilgrim, shepherd, or beggar.
– ORIGIN Middle English: probably a shortening of Old French *escrepe* 'purse'.

scrip[3] ▶ **noun** another term for **SCRIPT**[2].

scripophily /skrɪˈpɒfɪli/ ▶ **noun** [mass noun] the collection of old bond and share certificates as a pursuit or hobby.
■ such articles collectively.
– DERIVATIVES **scripophilist** noun.
– ORIGIN 1970s: from **SCRIP**[1] + **-PHILY**.

script[1] ▶ **noun 1** [mass noun] handwriting as distinct from print; written characters: *her neat, tidy script.*
■ printed type imitating handwriting. ■ [with adj.] writing using a particular alphabet: *Russian script.*
2 the written text of a play, film, or broadcast.
■ Computing an automated series of instructions carried out in a specific order. ■ Psychology the social role or behaviour appropriate to particular situations that an individual absorbs through cultural influences and association with others.
3 Brit. a candidate's written answers in an examination.
▶ **verb** [with obj.] write a script for (a play, film, or broadcast).
– ORIGIN late Middle English (in the sense 'something written'): shortening of Old French *escript*, from Latin *scriptum*, neuter past participle (used as a noun) of *scribere* 'write'.

script[2] ▶ **noun** informal a doctor's prescription.

scriptorial ▶ **adjective** rare of or relating to writing.

scriptorium /skrɪpˈtɔːrɪəm/ ▶ **noun** (pl. **scriptoria** /-rɪə/ or **scriptoriums**) chiefly historical a room set apart for writing, especially one in a monastery where manuscripts were copied.
– ORIGIN late 18th cent.: from medieval Latin, from Latin *script-* 'written', from the verb *scribere*.

scriptural ▶ **adjective** of, from, or relating to the Bible: *scriptural quotations from Genesis.*
– DERIVATIVES **scripturally** adverb.
– ORIGIN mid 17th cent.: from late Latin *scripturalis*, from Latin *scriptura* 'writings' (see **SCRIPTURE**).

scripture /ˈskrɪptʃə/ ▶ **noun** [mass noun] (also **scriptures**) the sacred writings of Christianity contained in the Bible: *passages of scripture | the fundamental teachings of the scriptures.*
■ the sacred writings of another religion.
– ORIGIN Middle English: from Latin *scriptura* 'writings', from *script-* 'written', from the verb *scribere*.

scriptwriter ▶ **noun** a person who writes a script for a play, film, or broadcast.
– DERIVATIVES **scriptwriting** noun.

scrivener /ˈskrɪv(ə)nə/ ▶ **noun** historical **1** a clerk, scribe, or notary.
2 a person who invested money at interest for clients and lent funds to those who wanted to raise money on security.
– ORIGIN Middle English (in sense 1): shortening of Old French *escrivein*, from Latin *scriba* (see **SCRIBE**). Sense 2 dates from the early 17th cent.

scrod /skrɒd/ ▶ **noun** N. Amer. a young cod, haddock, or similar fish, especially one prepared for cooking.
– ORIGIN mid 19th cent.: of unknown origin.

scrofula /ˈskrɒfjʊlə/ ▶ **noun** [mass noun] chiefly historical a disease with glandular swellings, probably a form of tuberculosis. Also formerly called **KING'S EVIL**.
– DERIVATIVES **scrofulous** adjective.
– ORIGIN late Middle English: from medieval Latin, diminutive of Latin *scrofa* 'breeding sow' (said to be subject to the disease).

scroggin ▶ **noun** [mass noun] NZ a mixture of dried fruit, nuts, and other food eaten as a snack by hikers.
– ORIGIN 1940s: of unknown origin.

scroll ▶ **noun 1** a roll of parchment or paper for writing or painting on.
■ an ancient book or document on such a roll. ■ an ornamental design or carving resembling a partly unrolled scroll of parchment, e.g. on the capital of a column, or at the end of a stringed instrument. ■ Art & Heraldry a depiction of a narrow ribbon bearing a motto or inscription.
2 [mass noun] [usu. as modifier] the facility which moves a display on a VDU screen in order to view new material.
▶ **verb 1** [no obj., with adverbial] move displayed text or graphics in a particular direction on a computer screen in order to view different parts of them: *she scrolled through her file.*
■ (of displayed text or graphics) move up, down, or across a computer screen.
2 [with obj.] cause to move like paper rolling or unrolling: *the wind* **scrolled back** *the uppermost layer of loose dust.*
– DERIVATIVES **scrollable** adjective.
– ORIGIN late Middle English: alteration of obsolete *scrow* 'roll', shortening of **ESCROW**.

scroll bar ▶ **noun** a long thin section at the edge of a computer display by which material can be scrolled using a mouse.

scrolled ▶ **adjective** having an ornamental design or carving resembling a scroll of parchment.

scroller ▶ **noun 1** a computer game in which the background scrolls past at a constant rate.
2 another term for **SCROLL SAW**.

scrolling ▶ **noun** [mass noun] the action of moving displayed text or graphics up or down on a computer screen in order to view different parts of them.
▶ **adjective** [attrib.] (of an ornamental design or carving) made to resemble a partly unrolled scroll of parchment.

scroll saw ▶ **noun** a narrow-bladed saw for cutting decorative spiral lines or patterns.

scrollwork ▶ **noun** [mass noun] decoration consisting of spiral lines or patterns, especially as cut by a scroll saw.

scrooch ▶ **verb** [no obj.] informal crouch; bend.
– ORIGIN mid 19th cent. (originally US): dialect variant of US *scrouge* 'squeeze, crowd', perhaps reinforced by the verb **CROUCH**.

Scrooge, Ebenezer, a miserly curmudgeon in Charles Dickens's novel *A Christmas Carol* (1843).
■ [as noun **a Scrooge**] a person who is mean with money.

scrotum /ˈskrəʊtəm/ ▶ **noun** (pl. **scrota** /-tə/ or **scrotums**) a pouch of skin containing the testicles.
– DERIVATIVES **scrotal** adjective.
– ORIGIN late 16th cent.: from Latin.

scrounge informal ▶ **verb** [with obj.] seek to obtain (something, typically food or money) at the expense or through the generosity of others or by stealth: *he had managed to scrounge a free meal | [no obj.] we didn't* **scrounge off** *the social security.*
▶ **noun** [in sing.] an act of seeking to obtain something in such a way.
– PHRASES **on the scrounge** Brit. engaged in such activity.
– ORIGIN early 20th cent.: variant of dialect *scrunge* 'steal'.

scrounger ▶ **noun** informal, derogatory a person who borrows from or lives off others.

scrub[1] ▶ **verb** (**scrubbed**, **scrubbing**) [with obj.] **1** rub (someone or something) hard so as to clean them, typically with a brush and water: *he had to scrub the floor | she was* **scrubbing** *herself* **down** *at the sink | [no obj.] she* **scrubbed** *furiously* **at** *the plates.*
■ (**scrub something away/off**) remove dirt by rubbing hard: *it took ages to scrub off the muck.* ■ [no obj.] (**scrub up**) thoroughly clean one's hands and arms, especially before performing surgery: *the doctor scrubbed up and donned a protective gown.* ■ informal cancel or abandon (something): *opposition leaders suggested she should scrub the trip to China.* ■ use water to remove impurities from (gas or vapour). ■ [no obj.] (of a rider) rub the arms and legs urgently on a horse's neck and flanks to urge it to move faster.
2 Motor Racing (of a driver) allow (a tyre) to slide or scrape across the road surface so as to reduce speed.
■ [no obj.] (of tyres) slide or scrape across the road surface when reducing speed. ■ (of a driver) reduce (speed) by allowing the tyres to slide or scrape across the road surface.
▶ **noun 1** an act of scrubbing something or someone: *give the floor a good scrub.*
2 a semi-abrasive cosmetic lotion applied to the face or body in order to cleanse the skin.
3 (**scrubs**) special hygienic clothing worn by surgeons during operations.
– ORIGIN late 16th cent.: probably from Middle Low German, Middle Dutch *schrobben*, *schrubben*.
▶ **scrub round** Brit. informal avoid or disregard (something): *you must just forget, dear—scrub round it.*

scrub[2] ▶ **noun 1** [mass noun] vegetation consisting mainly of brushwood or stunted forest growth.
■ (also **scrubs**) land covered with such vegetation.
2 [as modifier] denoting a shrubby or small form of a plant: *scrub apple trees.*
■ N. Amer. denoting an animal of inferior breed or physique: *a scrub bull.*
3 informal an insignificant or contemptible person.
■ N. Amer. a sports team or player not among the best or most skilled. ■ short for **SCRUBBER** (in sense 2).
4 [mass noun] N. Amer. an informal team game played by children in a public area.
– DERIVATIVES **scrubby** adjective.
– ORIGIN late Middle English (in the sense 'stunted tree'): variant of **SHRUB**[1].

scrubber ▶ **noun 1** a brush or other object used to clean something.
■ a person who cleans something. ■ an apparatus using water or a solution for purifying gases or vapours.
2 derogatory, chiefly Brit. a sexually promiscuous woman.
3 Austral./NZ an animal which lives in the scrub.
■ informal a person of unkempt appearance.

scrub-bird ▶ **noun** a secretive Australian songbird with mainly brown plumage and a long tail, now rare.
● Family Atrichornithidae and genus *Atrichornis*: two species.

scrubfowl ▶ **noun** a small megapode with a short tail, typically having brown and grey plumage.
● Genera *Megapodius* and *Eulipoa*, family Megapodiidae: several species.

scrubland ▶ **noun** [mass noun] (also **scrublands**) land consisting of scrub vegetation.

scrub nurse ▶ **noun** a nurse who assists a surgeon by performing certain minor duties during a surgical operation.

scrub oak ▶ noun N. Amer. a shrubby dwarf oak which forms thickets.
● Genus *Quercus*, family Fagaceae: several species, in particular *Q. ilicifolia*.

scrub suit ▶ noun N. Amer. a garment worn by surgeons and other theatre staff while performing or assisting at an operation.

scrub-turkey ▶ noun another term for BRUSH-TURKEY.

scrub typhus ▶ noun [mass noun] a rickettsial disease transmitted to humans by mites and found in parts of east Asia. Also called TSUTSUGAMUSHI DISEASE.

scrub wallaby ▶ noun another term for PADEMELON.

scruff¹ ▶ noun the back of a person's or animal's neck: *he grabbed him by the scruff of his neck*.
▶ verb [with obj.] grasp (an animal) by the scruff of its neck.
– ORIGIN late 18th cent.: alteration of dialect *scuff*, of obscure origin.

scruff² ▶ noun Brit. informal a person with a dirty or untidy appearance.
– ORIGIN early 16th cent. (in the sense 'scurf'): variant of SCURF. The word came to mean 'worthless thing', whence the current sense (mid 19th cent.).

scruffy ▶ adjective (**scruffier**, **scruffiest**) shabby and untidy or dirty: *a teenager in scruffy jeans and a baggy T-shirt*.
– DERIVATIVES **scruffily** adverb, **scruffiness** noun.

scrum ▶ noun Rugby an ordered formation of players, used to restart play, in which the forwards of a team form up with arms interlocked and heads down, and push forward against a similar group from the opposing side. The ball is thrown into the scrum and the players try to gain possession of it by kicking it backwards towards their own side.
■ Brit. informal a disorderly crowd of people or things: *there was quite a scrum of people at the bar*.
▶ verb (**scrummed**, **scrumming**) [no obj.] Rugby form or take part in a scrum.
■ informal jostle; crowd: *everyone was scrumming around behind him*.
– ORIGIN late 19th cent.: abbreviation of SCRUMMAGE.

scrum half ▶ noun Rugby a halfback who puts the ball into the scrum and stands ready to receive it again.

scrummage ▶ noun & verb another term for SCRUM.
– DERIVATIVES **scrummager** noun.
– ORIGIN early 19th cent.: variant of SCRIMMAGE.

scrummy ▶ adjective (**scrummier**, **scrummiest**) informal delicious.
– ORIGIN early 20th cent.: from SCRUMPTIOUS + -Y¹.

scrump ▶ verb [with obj.] Brit. informal steal (fruit) from an orchard or garden.
– ORIGIN mid 19th cent.: from dialect *scrump* 'withered apple'.

scrumple ▶ verb [with obj.] Brit. crumple (paper or cloth): *she scrumpled it up and tossed it into the waste-paper basket*.
– ORIGIN early 16th cent.: alteration of CRUMPLE.

scrumptious ▶ adjective informal (of food) extremely appetizing or delicious.
■ (of a person) very attractive.
– DERIVATIVES **scrumptiously** adverb, **scrumptiousness** noun.
– ORIGIN mid 19th cent.: of unknown origin.

scrumpy ▶ noun [mass noun] Brit. rough strong cider, especially as made in the West Country of England.
– ORIGIN early 20th cent.: from dialect *scrump* 'withered apple'.

scrunch ▶ verb [no obj.] make a loud crunching noise: *crisp yellow leaves scrunched satisfyingly underfoot*.
■ [with obj. and adverbial] crush or squeeze (something) into a compact mass: *Flora scrunched the handkerchief into a ball*. ■ [no obj., with adverbial] become crushed or squeezed in such a way: *their faces scrunch up with concentration*. ■ [with obj.] style (hair) by squeezing or crushing it in the hands to give a tousled look.
▶ noun [in sing.] a loud crunching noise: *Charlotte heard the scrunch of boots on gravel*.
– ORIGIN late 18th cent. (in the sense 'eat or bite noisily'): probably imitative; compare with CRUNCH.

scrunch-dry ▶ verb [with obj.] dry (hair) while scrunching it to give a tousled look.

scrunchy ▶ adjective making a loud crunching noise when crushed or compressed: *scrunchy snow*.
▶ noun (also **scrunchie**) (pl. **-ies**) a circular band of fabric-covered elastic used for fastening the hair.

scruple ▶ noun 1 (usu. **scruples**) a feeling of doubt or hesitation with regard to the morality or propriety of a course of action: *I had no scruples about eavesdropping* | [mass noun] *without scruple, politicians use fear as a persuasion weapon*.
2 historical a unit of weight equal to 20 grains used by apothecaries.
■ archaic a very small amount of something, especially a quality.
▶ verb [no obj., with infinitive] [usu. with negative] hesitate or be reluctant to do something that one thinks may be wrong: *she doesn't scruple to ask her parents for money*.
– ORIGIN late Middle English: from French *scrupule* or Latin *scrupulus*, from *scrupus*, literally 'rough pebble', (figuratively) 'anxiety'.

scrupulous ▶ adjective (of a person or process) diligent, thorough, and extremely attentive to details: *the research has been carried out with scrupulous attention to detail*.
■ very concerned to avoid doing wrong: *she's too scrupulous to have an affair with a married man*.
– DERIVATIVES **scrupulosity** noun, **scrupulously** adverb [as submodifier] *she was scrupulously polite*, **scrupulousness** noun.
– ORIGIN late Middle English (in the sense 'troubled with doubts'): from French *scrupuleux* or Latin *scrupulosus*, from *scrupulus* (see SCRUPLE).

scrutator /skru:ˈteɪtə/ ▶ noun a person whose official duty it is to examine or investigate something.
■ historical a university official responsible for examining votes at university elections and announcing the result.
– ORIGIN late 16th cent.: from Latin, from *scrutari* 'search, examine'.

scrutineer ▶ noun a person who examines or inspects something closely and thoroughly.
■ chiefly Brit. a person who supervises the conduct of an election or competition.

scrutinize (also **-ise**) ▶ verb [with obj.] examine or inspect closely and thoroughly: *customers were warned to scrutinize the small print*.
– DERIVATIVES **scrutinization** noun, **scrutinizer** noun.

scrutiny ▶ noun (pl. **-ies**) [mass noun] critical observation or examination: *every aspect of local government was placed under scrutiny*.
– ORIGIN late Middle English: from Latin *scrutinium*, from *scrutari* 'to search' (originally 'sort rubbish', from *scruta* 'rubbish'). Early use referred to the taking of individual votes in an election procedure.

scry /skraɪ/ ▶ verb (**-ies**, **-ied**) [no obj.] foretell the future using a crystal ball or other reflective object or surface.
– DERIVATIVES **scryer** noun.
– ORIGIN early 16th cent.: shortening of DESCRY.

SCSI Computing ▶ abbreviation for small computer system interface, a bus standard for connecting computers and their peripherals together.

scuba /ˈskuːbə, ˈskjuːbə/ ▶ noun an aqualung.
■ [mass noun] scuba-diving.
– ORIGIN 1950s: acronym from *self-contained underwater breathing apparatus*.

scuba-diving ▶ noun [mass noun] the sport or pastime of swimming underwater using a scuba.
– DERIVATIVES **scuba-dive** verb, **scuba-diver** noun.

scud ▶ verb (**scudded**, **scudding**) **1** [no obj., with adverbial of direction] move fast in a straight line because or as if driven by the wind: *we lie watching the clouds scudding across the sky* | *three small ships were scudding before a brisk breeze*.
2 [with obj.] chiefly Scottish slap, beat, or spank: *she scudded me across the head*.
▶ noun chiefly poetic/literary a formation of vapoury clouds driven fast by the wind.
■ a mass of wind-blown spray. ■ a driving shower of rain or snow; a gust. ■ [mass noun] the action of moving fast in a straight line when driven by the wind: *the scud of the clouds before the wind*.
– ORIGIN mid 16th cent. (as a verb): perhaps an alteration of the noun SCUT¹, thus reflecting the sense 'race like a hare'.

scudo /ˈskuːdəʊ/ ▶ noun (pl. **scudi** /-di/) historical a coin, typically made of silver, formerly used in various Italian states.
– ORIGIN Italian, from Latin *scutum* 'shield'.

scuff ▶ verb [with obj.] scrape or brush the surface of (a shoe or other object) against something: *I accidentally scuffed the heel of one shoe on a paving stone*.
■ mark (a surface) by scraping or brushing it, especially with one's shoes: *the lino on the floor was scuffed*. ■ [no obj.] (of an object or surface) become marked by scraping or brushing: *for kids who play rough, shoes that won't scuff*. ■ drag (one's feet or heels) when walking: *he scuffed his feet boyishly*. ■ [no obj., with adverbial of direction] walk in such a way: *she scuffed along in her carpet slippers*.
▶ noun a mark made by scraping or grazing a surface or object: *dark colours don't show scuffs*.
– ORIGIN early 18th cent.: perhaps of imitative origin.

scuffle ▶ noun **1** a short, confused fight or struggle at close quarters: *there were minor scuffles with police*.
2 an act or sound of moving in a hurried, confused, or shuffling manner: *he heard the scuffle of feet*.
▶ verb [no obj.] **1** engage in a short, confused fight or struggle at close quarters: *the teacher noticed two pupils scuffling in the corridor*.
2 [with adverbial of direction] move in a hurried, confused, or awkward way, making a rustling or shuffling sound: *a drenched woman scuffled through the doorway*.
■ [with obj.] (of an animal or person) move (something) in a scrambling or confused manner: *the rabbit struggled free, scuffling his front paws*.
– ORIGIN late 16th cent. (as a verb): probably of Scandinavian origin; compare with Swedish *skuffa* 'to push'; related to SHOVE and SHUFFLE.

scull¹ ▶ noun each of a pair of small oars used by a single rower.
■ an oar placed over the stern of a boat to propel it by a side to side motion, reversing the blade at each turn. ■ a light, narrow boat propelled with a scull or a pair of sculls. ■ (**sculls**) a race between boats in which each participant uses a pair of oars.
▶ verb [no obj.] propel a boat with sculls.
■ [with obj. and adverbial of direction] transport (someone) in a boat propelled with sculls. ■ [no obj., with adverbial of direction] (of an aquatic animal) propel itself with fins or flippers.
– ORIGIN Middle English: of unknown origin.

scull² ▶ noun Canadian a large group of fish which has migrated from the open sea to inshore waters.
■ the season when this happens.
– ORIGIN variant of SCHOOL².

scullcap ▶ noun variant spelling of SKULLCAP (in sense 3).

sculler /ˈskʌlə/ ▶ noun a person who sculls a boat.
■ a boat propelled with a scull or pair of sculls.

scullery /ˈskʌl(ə)ri/ ▶ noun (pl. **-ies**) a small kitchen or room at the back of a house used for washing dishes and other dirty household work.
– ORIGIN late Middle English (denoting the department of a household concerned with kitchen utensils): from Old French *escuelerie*, from *escuele* 'dish', from Latin *scutella* 'salver', diminutive of *scutra* 'wooden platter'.

scullion ▶ noun archaic a servant assigned the most menial kitchen tasks.
– ORIGIN late 15th cent.: of unknown origin but perhaps influenced by SCULLERY.

sculpin /ˈskʌlpɪn/ ▶ noun a chiefly marine fish of the northern hemisphere, with a broad flattened head and spiny scales and fins.
● Cottidae and related families: many genera and numerous species, including the bullheads.
– ORIGIN late 17th cent.: perhaps from obsolete *scorpene*, via Latin from Greek *skorpaina*, denoting a kind of fish.

sculpt (also **sculp**) ▶ verb [with obj.] create or represent (something) by carving, casting, or other shaping techniques: *sculpting human figures from ivory* | [no obj.] *she was teaching him how to sculpt*.
– ORIGIN mid 19th cent.: from French *sculpter*, from *sculpteur* 'sculptor'; later regarded as a back-formation from SCULPTOR or SCULPTURE.

Sculptor /ˈskʌlptə/ ▶ noun Astronomy a faint southern constellation (the Sculptor or Sculptor's Workshop), between Grus and Cetus.
■ [as genitive **Sculptoris** /-ˈtɔːrɪs/] used with preceding letter or numeral to designate a star in this constellation: *the star Delta Sculptoris*.
– ORIGIN Latin.

sculptor ▶ noun an artist who makes sculptures.
– ORIGIN mid 17th cent.: from Latin, from *sculpt-* 'hollowed out', from the verb *sculpere*.

sculptress ▶ noun a female artist who makes sculptures.

sculptural ▶ adjective of, relating to, or resembling sculpture: *sculptural decoration* | *sculptural works*.
– DERIVATIVES **sculpturally** adverb.

sculpture ▶ noun [mass noun] the art of making two- or three-dimensional representative or abstract forms, especially by carving stone or wood or by casting metal or plaster.
▪[count noun] a work of such a kind: *a bronze sculpture* | [mass noun] *a collection of sculpture*. ▪Zoology & Botany raised or sunken patterns or texture on the surface of a shell, pollen grain, cuticle, or other biological specimen.
▶ verb [with obj.] make or represent (a form) by carving, casting, or other shaping techniques: *the choir stalls were each carefully sculptured*.
▪form, shape, or mark as if by sculpture, especially with strong, smooth curves: [as adj. **sculptured**] *he had an aquiline nose and sculptured lips*.
– ORIGIN late Middle English: from Latin *sculptura*, from *sculpere* 'carve'.

sculpturesque ▶ adjective old-fashioned term for SCULPTURAL.

sculpturing ▶ noun [mass noun] the action of forming or shaping something by or as if by sculpture: *the gadget is great for blow-drying, sculpturing, and moulding*.
▪the shape produced in such a way: *the mountain's graceful sculpturing*. ▪Zoology & Botany sculpture: *the external sculpturing consists of a series of corrugations*.

scum ▶ noun [mass noun] a layer of dirt or froth on the surface of a liquid: *green scum found on stagnant pools*.
▪informal a worthless or contemptible person or group of people: *you drug dealers are **the scum of the earth***.
▶ verb (**scummed**, **scumming**) [with obj.] form a layer of dirt or froth on (a liquid): *litter scummed the surface of the water*.
▪[no obj.] (of a liquid) become covered with a layer of dirt or froth: *the lagoon scummed over*.
– DERIVATIVES **scummy** adjective (**scummier**, **scummiest**).
– ORIGIN Middle English: from Middle Low German, Middle Dutch *schūm*, of Germanic origin.

scumbag ▶ noun informal a contemptible or objectionable person.

scumble /ˈskʌmb(ə)l/ Art ▶ verb [with obj.] modify (a painting or colour) by applying a very thin coat of opaque paint to give a softer or duller effect.
▪modify (a drawing) in a similar way with light shading in pencil or charcoal.
▶ noun a thin, opaque coat of paint or layer of shading applied to give a softer or duller effect.
▪the effect produced by adding such a coat or layer.
– ORIGIN late 17th cent. (as a verb): perhaps a frequentative of the verb SCUM.

scuncheon /ˈskʌn(t)ʃ(ə)n/ ▶ noun the inside face of a door jamb or window frame.
– ORIGIN Middle English: shortening of Old French *escoinson*, based on *coin* 'corner'.

scunge ▶ noun Austral./NZ informal a disagreeable person.
– ORIGIN early 19th cent. (originally Scots in the sense 'scrounger'): of unknown origin; compare with the verb SCROUNGE.

scungille /skʊnˈdʒiːleɪ, -li/ (also **scungile**) ▶ noun (pl. **scungilli** /-li/) a mollusc (especially with reference to its meat eaten as a delicacy).
– ORIGIN from Italian dialect *scunciglio*, probably an alteration of Italian *conchiglia* 'seashell'.

scungy ▶ adjective (**scungier**, **scungiest**) Austral./NZ informal dirty and disagreeable.

scunner chiefly Scottish ▶ noun a strong dislike: *why have you a scunner against Esme?*
▪a source of irritation or strong dislike.
▶ verb [no obj.] feel disgust or strong dislike.
– ORIGIN late Middle English (first used in the sense 'shrink back with fear'): of unknown origin.

Scunthorpe /ˈskʌnθɔːp/ an industrial town in NE England, in North Lincolnshire; pop. 60,500 (1991).

scup ▶ noun (pl. same) a common porgy (fish) with faint dark vertical bars, occurring off the coasts of the northwest Atlantic.
• *Stenotomus chrysops*, family Sparidae.
– ORIGIN mid 19th cent.: from Narragansett *mishcup*, from *mishe* 'big' + *cuppi* 'close together' (because of the shape of the scales).

scupper[1] ▶ noun (usu. **scuppers**) a hole in a ship's side to carry water overboard from the deck.
▪an outlet in the side of a building for draining water.
– ORIGIN late Middle English: perhaps via Anglo-Norman French from Old French *escopir* 'to spit'; compare with German *Speigatt*, literally 'spit hole'.

scupper[2] ▶ verb [with obj.] chiefly Brit. sink (a ship or its crew) deliberately.
▪informal prevent from working or succeeding; thwart: *plans for a bypass were scuppered by a public inquiry*.
– ORIGIN late 19th cent. (as military slang in the sense 'kill, especially in an ambush'): of unknown origin. The sense 'sink' dates from the 1970s.

scuppernong /ˈskʌpəˌnɒŋ/ ▶ noun [mass noun] a variety of the muscadine grape native to the basin of the Scuppernong River in North Carolina.
▪(often **scuppernong wine**) wine made from this grape.

scurf ▶ noun [mass noun] flakes on the surface of the skin that form as fresh skin develops below, occurring especially as dandruff.
▪a similar flaky deposit on any surface, especially one on a plant resulting from a fungal infection.
– DERIVATIVES **scurfy** adjective.
– ORIGIN late Old English *sceorf*, from the base of *sceorfan* 'gnaw', *sceorfian* 'cut to shreds'.

scurrilous /ˈskʌrɪləs/ ▶ adjective making or spreading scandalous claims about someone with the intention of damaging their reputation: *a scurrilous attack on his integrity*.
▪humorously insulting: *a very funny collection of bawdy and scurrilous writings*.
– DERIVATIVES **scurrility** noun (pl. **-ies**), **scurrilously** adverb, **scurrilousness** noun.
– ORIGIN late 16th cent.: from French *scurrile* or Latin *scurrilus* (from *scurra* 'buffoon') + -OUS.

scurry ▶ verb (**-ies**, **-ied**) [no obj., with adverbial of direction] (of a person or small animal) move hurriedly with short quick steps: *pedestrians scurried for cover*.
▶ noun [in sing.] a situation of hurried and confused movement: *I was in such a scurry*.
▪a flurry of rain or snow.
– ORIGIN early 19th cent.: abbreviation of *hurry-scurry*, reduplication of HURRY.

scurvy ▶ noun [mass noun] a disease caused by a deficiency of vitamin C, characterized by swollen bleeding gums and the opening of previously healed wounds, which particularly affected poorly nourished sailors until the end of the 18th century.
▶ adjective (**scurvier**, **scurviest**) [attrib.] archaic worthless or contemptible: *that was a scurvy trick*.
– DERIVATIVES **scurvily** adverb.
– ORIGIN late Middle English (as an adjective meaning 'scurfy'): from SCURF + -Y[1]. The noun use (mid 16th cent.) is by association with French *scorbut* (see SCORBUTIC).

scurvy grass ▶ noun [mass noun] a small cress-like European plant with fleshy tar-flavoured leaves, growing near the sea. It is rich in vitamin C and was formerly eaten, especially by sailors, to prevent scurvy.
• Genus *Cochlearia*, family Cruciferae: several species, in particular *C. officinalis*.

scut[1] ▶ noun the short tail of a hare, rabbit, or deer.
– ORIGIN late Middle English: of unknown origin; compare with obsolete *scut* 'short', also 'shorten'.

scut[2] ▶ noun informal, chiefly Irish a person perceived as foolish, contemptible, or objectionable.
– ORIGIN late 19th cent.: of unknown origin.

scuta plural form of SCUTUM.

scutage /ˈskjuːtɪdʒ/ ▶ noun [mass noun] (in a feudal society) money paid by a vassal to his lord in lieu of military service.
– ORIGIN late Middle English: from medieval Latin *scutagium*, from Latin *scutum* 'shield'.

Scutari /skuːˈtɑːri/ **1** a former name for Üsküdar near Istanbul, site of a British army hospital in which Florence Nightingale worked during the Crimean War.
2 /skuˈtari/ Italian name for SHKODËR.

scutch /skʌtʃ/ ▶ verb [with obj.] dress (fibrous material, especially retted flax) by beating it.
– DERIVATIVES **scutcher** noun.
– ORIGIN mid 18th cent.: from obsolete French *escoucher*, from Latin *excutere* 'shake out'.

scutcheon ▶ noun archaic spelling of ESCUTCHEON.

scute /skjuːt/ ▶ noun Zoology a thickened horny or bony plate on a turtle's shell or on the back of a crocodile, stegosaurus, etc.

scutellum /skjʊˈtɛləm/ ▶ noun (pl. **scutella** /-lə/) Botany & Zoology a small shield-like structure, in particular:
▪a modified cotyledon in the embryo of a grass seed. ▪the third dorsal sclerite in each thoracic segment of an insect.
– DERIVATIVES **scutellar** adjective.
– ORIGIN mid 18th cent.: modern Latin, diminutive of Latin *scutum* 'shield'.

scutter chiefly Brit. ▶ verb [no obj., with adverbial of direction] (especially of a small animal) move hurriedly with short steps: *a little dog scuttered up from the cabin*.
▶ noun [in sing.] an act or sound of scuttering.
– ORIGIN late 18th cent.: perhaps an alteration of the verb SCUTTLE[2].

scuttle[1] ▶ noun **1** a metal container with a sloping hinged lid and a handle, used to fetch and store coal for a domestic fire.
▪the amount of coal held in such a container: *carrying endless **scuttles of** coal up from the cellar*.
2 Brit. the part of a car's bodywork between the windscreen and the bonnet.
– ORIGIN late Old English *scutel* 'dish, platter', from Old Norse *skutill*, from Latin *scutella* 'dish'.

scuttle[2] ▶ verb [no obj., with adverbial of direction] run hurriedly or furtively with short quick steps: *a mouse scuttled across the floor*.
▶ noun [in sing.] an act or sound of scuttling: *I heard the scuttle of rats across the room*.
– ORIGIN late 15th cent.: compare with dialect *scuddle*, frequentative of SCUD.

scuttle[3] ▶ verb [with obj.] sink (one's own ship) deliberately by holing it or opening its seacocks to let water in.
▪deliberately cause (a scheme) to fail: *some of the stockholders are threatening to scuttle the deal*.
▶ noun an opening with a lid in a ship's deck or side.
– ORIGIN late 15th cent. (as a noun): perhaps from Old French *escoutille*, from the Spanish diminutive *escotilla* 'hatchway'. The verb dates from the mid 17th cent.

scuttlebutt ▶ noun [mass noun] informal, chiefly US rumour; gossip: *the scuttlebutt had it that he was a government spy*.
– ORIGIN early 19th cent. (denoting a water butt on the deck of a ship, providing drinking water): from *scuttled butt*.

Scutum /ˈskjuːtəm/ Astronomy a small constellation near the celestial equator (the Shield), lying in the Milky Way between Aquila and Serpens.
▪[as genitive **Scuti** /ˈskjuːtiː/] used with preceding letter or numeral to designate a star in this constellation: *the star Beta Scuti*.
– ORIGIN Latin.

scutum /ˈskjuːtəm/ ▶ noun (pl. **scuta** /-tə/) Zoology another term for SCUTE.
▪Entomology the second dorsal sclerite in each thoracic segment of an insect.
– ORIGIN late 18th cent.: from Latin, literally 'oblong shield'.

scutwork ▶ noun [mass noun] informal, chiefly US tedious, menial work.
– ORIGIN 1970s: of unknown origin; compare with SCUT[2].

scuzz ▶ noun [mass noun] informal, chiefly N. Amer. something regarded as disgusting, sordid, or disreputable.
▪[count noun] a disreputable or unpleasant person.
– DERIVATIVES **scuzzy** adjective.
– ORIGIN 1960s: probably an informal abbreviation of DISGUSTING.

scuzzball (also **scuzzbag**) ▶ noun informal, chiefly N. Amer. a despicable or disgusting person.

Scylla /ˈsɪlə/ Greek Mythology a female sea monster who devoured sailors when they tried to navigate the narrow channel between her cave and the whirlpool Charybdis. In later legend Scylla was a dangerous rock, located on the Italian side of the Strait of Messina.
– PHRASES **Scylla and Charybdis** used to refer to a situation involving two dangers in which an attempt to avoid one increases the risk from the other.

scyphistoma /sʌɪˈfɪstəmə, skʌɪ-, skɪ-/ ▶ noun (pl.

scyphistomae /-miː/ or **scyphistomas** Zoology the fixed polyp-like stage in the life cycle of a jellyfish, which reproduces asexually by budding (strobilation).
– ORIGIN late 19th cent.: from Latin *scyphus* 'cup' + Greek *stoma* 'mouth'.

Scyphozoa /ˌsaɪfəˈzəʊə, ˌskaɪf-, ˌskɪf-/ Zoology a class of marine coelenterates which comprises the jellyfishes.
– DERIVATIVES **scyphozoan** noun & adjective.
– ORIGIN modern Latin (plural), from Greek *skuphos* 'drinking cup' + Greek *zōion* 'animal'.

scythe ▶ noun a tool used for cutting crops such as grass or corn, with a long curved blade at the end of a long pole attached to one or two short handles.
▶ verb [with obj.] cut with a scythe.
■ [no obj., with adverbial] move through or penetrate something rapidly and forcefully: *attacking players can scythe through defences.*
– ORIGIN Old English *sīthe*, of Germanic origin; related to Dutch *zeis* and German *Sense*.

Scythia /ˈsɪðɪə/ an ancient region of SE Europe and Asia. The Scythian empire, which existed between the 8th and 2nd centuries BC, was centred on the northern shores of the Black Sea and extended from southern Russia to the borders of Persia.
– DERIVATIVES **Scythian** adjective & noun.

SD ▶ abbreviation for ■ South Dakota (in official postal use). ■ Swaziland (international vehicle registration).

S. Dak. ▶ abbreviation for South Dakota.

SDI ▶ abbreviation for Strategic Defense Initiative.

SDLP ▶ abbreviation for (in Northern Ireland) Social Democratic and Labour Party.

SDP ▶ abbreviation for (in the UK) Social Democratic Party.

SDR ▶ abbreviation for special drawing right (from the International Monetary Fund).

SE ▶ abbreviation for south-east or south-eastern.

Se ▶ symbol for the chemical element selenium.

se- ▶ prefix in words adopted from Latin originally meaning 'apart' (as in *separate*) or meaning 'without' (as in *secure*).
– ORIGIN from Latin *se-*, from the earlier preposition and adverb *se*.

SEA ▶ abbreviation for Single European Act.

sea ▶ noun (often **the sea**) the expanse of salt water that covers most of the earth's surface and surrounds its land masses: *a ban on dumping radioactive wastes in the sea* | [mass noun] *rocky bays lapped by vivid blue sea* | [as modifier] *a sea view.*
■ [often in place names] a roughly definable area of this: *the Black Sea.* ■ [in place names] a large lake: *the Sea of Galilee.* ■ [mass noun] used to refer to waves as opposed to calm sea: *there was still some sea running.* ■ **(seas)** large waves: *the lifeboat met seas of thirty-five feet head-on.* ■ [count noun] figurative a vast expanse or quantity of something: *she scanned the sea of faces for Stephen.*
– PHRASES **at sea** sailing on the sea. ■ (also **all at sea**) confused or unable to decide what to do: *he feels at sea with economics.* **by sea** by means of a ship or ships: *other army units were sent by sea.* **go to sea** set out on a voyage. ■ become a sailor in a navy or a merchant navy. **on the sea** situated on the coast. **put (out) to sea** leave land on a voyage.
– ORIGIN Old English *sǣ*, of Germanic origin; related to Dutch *zee* and German *See*.

sea anchor ▶ noun an object dragged in the water behind a boat in order to keep its bows pointing into the waves or to lessen leeway.

sea anemone ▶ noun a sedentary marine coelenterate with a columnar body which bears a ring of stinging tentacles around the mouth.
● Order Actiniaria, class Anthozoa.

sea-angel ▶ noun an angel shark.

seabag ▶ noun chiefly N. Amer. a sailor's travelling bag or trunk.

sea bass ▶ noun any of a number of marine fishes that are related to or resemble the common perch, in particular:
● a mainly tropical fish of a large family (Serranidae, the **sea bass family**), especially one of the genus *Centropristis*; the sea bass family also includes the groupers. ● (**white sea bass**) a large game fish of the Pacific coast of North America (*Cynoscion nobilis*, family Sciaenidae).

seabed ▶ noun the ground under the sea; the ocean floor.

Seabee ▶ noun a member of one of the construction battalions of the Civil Engineer Corps of the US Navy.
– ORIGIN representing a pronunciation of the letters *CB* (from *construction battalion*).

seabird ▶ noun a bird that frequents the sea or coast.

sea biscuit ▶ noun 1 another term for SHIP'S BISCUIT.
2 another term for SAND DOLLAR.

seaboard ▶ noun a region bordering the sea; the coastline: *the eastern seaboard of the United States.*

sea boat ▶ noun [usu. with adj.] a boat or ship considered in terms of its ability to cope with conditions at sea.

Seaborg /ˈsiːbɔːɡ/, Glenn (Theodore) (1912–99), American nuclear chemist. During 1940–58 Seaborg and his colleagues produced nine of the transuranic elements (plutonium to nobelium) in a cyclotron. Seaborg and his early collaborator Edwin McMillan (1907–91) shared the Nobel Prize for Chemistry in 1951.

seaborgium /siːˈbɔːɡɪəm/ ▶ noun [mass noun] the chemical element of atomic number 106, a very unstable element made by high-energy atomic collisions. (Symbol: **Sg**)
– ORIGIN modern Latin, named after G. *Seaborg* (see SEABORG).

seaborne ▶ adjective transported or travelling by sea: *seaborne trade.*

sea bream ▶ noun a deep-bodied marine fish that resembles the freshwater bream, in particular:
● Several genera and species in the family Sparidae (the **sea bream family**), in particular the **red sea bream** (*Pagellus bogaraveo*), which is fished commercially, and the **black sea bream** (*Spondyliosoma cantharus*), a popular angling fish; the sea bream family also includes the porgies. ● a fish of Australasian coastal waters, with a purple back and silver underside (*Seriolella brama*, family Centrolophidae). Also called WAREHOU in New Zealand.

sea breeze ▶ noun a breeze blowing towards the land from the sea, especially during the day owing to the relative warmth of the land.

sea buckthorn ▶ noun a bushy Eurasian shrub or small tree which typically grows on sandy coasts. It bears orange berries and some plants are spiny.
● *Hippophae rhamnoides*, family Elaeagnaceae.

sea butterfly ▶ noun a small mollusc with wing-like extensions to its body which it uses for swimming.
● Orders Thecosomata (with shells) and Gymnosomata (lacking shells), class Gastropoda.

sea captain ▶ noun a person who commands a ship, especially a merchant ship.

SeaCat ▶ noun trademark a large, high-speed catamaran used as a passenger and car ferry on short sea crossings.

sea change ▶ noun a profound or notable transformation.
– ORIGIN from Shakespeare's *Tempest* (I. ii. 403).

sea chest ▶ noun a sailor's storage chest.

sea coal ▶ noun [mass noun] archaic mineral coal, as distinct from other types of coal such as charcoal.

seacock ▶ noun a valve sealing off an opening through a ship's hull below or near to the waterline (e.g. one connecting a ship's sewage system to the sea).

sea cow ▶ noun a sirenian, especially a manatee.

sea cucumber ▶ noun an echinoderm which has a thick worm-like body with tentacles around the mouth. They typically have rows of tube feet along the body and breathe by means of a respiratory tree.
● Class Holothuroidea.

Sea Dayak ▶ noun another term for the IBAN people.
– ORIGIN so named because of their involvement in coastal raids on the neighbouring Land Dayaks.

sea dog ▶ noun 1 informal an old or experienced sailor.
2 Heraldry a mythical beast like a dog with fins, webbed feet, and a scaly tail.

sea duck ▶ noun any of a number of ducks that frequent the sea, especially the eiders, scoters, and long-tailed duck.
● Tribes Somateriini (and Mergini), family Anatidae: several genera.

sea eagle ▶ noun a large Eurasian fish-eating eagle that frequents coasts and wetlands.
● Genus *Haliaeetus*, family Accipitridae: several species, in particular the widespread **white-tailed sea eagle** (*H. albicilla*), recently re-introduced to Scotland.

sea egg ▶ noun a sea urchin.

sea elephant ▶ noun another term for ELEPHANT SEAL.

sea fan ▶ noun a horny coral with a vertical tree- or fan-like skeleton, living chiefly in warmer seas.
● *Gorgonis* and other genera, order Gorgonacea.

seafaring ▶ adjective (of a person) travelling by sea, especially regularly.
▶ noun [mass noun] the practice of travelling by sea, especially regularly.
– DERIVATIVES **seafarer** noun.

sea-floor spreading ▶ noun [mass noun] Geology the formation of fresh areas of oceanic crust which occurs through the upwelling of magma at mid ocean ridges and its subsequent outward movement on either side.

seafood ▶ noun [mass noun] shellfish and sea fish, served as food.

sea fret ▶ noun see FRET⁴.

seafront ▶ noun [usu. in sing.] the part of a coastal town next to and directly facing the sea.

sea-girt ▶ adjective poetic/literary surrounded by sea.

seagoing ▶ adjective [attrib.] (of a ship) suitable or designed for voyages on the sea.
■ characterized by or relating to travelling by sea, especially habitually: *a seagoing life.*

sea gooseberry ▶ noun a common comb jelly with a spherical body bearing two long retractile branching tentacles, typically occurring in swarms.
● *Pleurobrachia pileus*, class Tentaculata.

sea grape ▶ noun a salt-resistant tree of the dock family, bearing grape-like bunches of edible purple fruit and found on the Atlantic coasts of tropical America.
● *Coccoloba uvifera*, family Polygonaceae.
■ the fruit of this tree.

seagrass ▶ noun [mass noun] a grass-like plant that lives in or close to the sea, especially eelgrass.
● Genera *Cymodocea* (family Cymodoceaceae), *Zostera* (family Zosteraceae), and others.

sea green ▶ adjective of a pale bluish green colour.

seagull ▶ noun a popular name for a gull.

sea hare ▶ noun a large sea slug which has a minute internal shell and lateral extensions to the foot. Most species can swim, and many secrete distasteful chemicals to deter predators.
● *Aplysia* and other genera, order Anaspidea, class Gastropoda.

sea heath ▶ noun a small woody creeping plant of European salt marshes, bearing a superficial resemblance to heather.
● *Frankenia laevis*, family Frankeniaceae.

sea holly ▶ noun a spiny-leaved plant of the parsley family, with metallic blue teasel-like flowers, growing in sandy places by the sea and native to Europe.
● *Eryngium maritimum*, family Umbelliferae. See also ERYNGIUM.

sea horse ▶ noun 1 a small marine fish with segmented bony armour, an upright posture, a curled prehensile tail, a tubular snout, and a head and neck suggestive of a horse. The male has a brood pouch in which the eggs develop.
● Genus *Hippocampus*, family Syngnathidae: many species, including the European *H. ramulosus*.
2 a mythical creature with a horse's head and fish's tail.

sea-island cotton ▶ noun [mass noun] a fine-quality long-stapled cotton grown on islands off the southern US.

seakale ▶ noun [mass noun] a maritime Eurasian plant of the cabbage family, sometimes cultivated for its edible young shoots.
● *Crambe maritima*, family Cruciferae.

seakeeping ▶ noun [mass noun] [usu. as modifier] the ability of a vessel to withstand rough conditions at sea.

sea-kindly ▶ adjective (of a ship) easy to handle at sea.
– DERIVATIVES **sea-kindliness** noun.

sea krait ▶ noun a venomous sea snake with a compressed tail, occurring in tropical coastal

S

waters of the eastern Indian Ocean and western Pacific, coming ashore to bask and breed.
• Genus *Laticauda*, family Elapidae: two species.

seal[1] ▶ **noun** **1** a device or substance that is used to join two things together so as to prevent them coming apart or to prevent anything passing between them: *attach a draught seal to the door itself.*
■ [in sing.] the state or fact of being joined or rendered impervious by such a substance or device: *many fittings have tapered threads for a better seal.* ■ the water standing in the trap of a drain to prevent foul air from rising, considered in terms of its depth.
2 a piece of wax, lead, or other material with an individual design stamped into it, attached to a document to show that it has come from the person who claims to have issued it.
■ a design embossed in paper for this purpose. ■ an engraved device used for stamping a design that authenticates a document. ■ figurative a thing regarded as a confirmation or guarantee of something: *the monarchy is the seal of the unbroached integrity of the Isles.* ■ a decorative adhesive stamp. ■ (**the seal**) (also **the seal of confession** or **the seal of the confessional**) the obligation on a priest not to divulge anything said during confession: *I was told under the seal.*
▶ **verb** [with obj.] fasten or close securely: *he folded it, sealed the envelope, and walked to the postbox.*
■ (**seal something in**) prevent something from escaping by closing a container or opening. ■ (**seal something off**) isolate an area by preventing or monitoring entrance to and exit from it: *anti-terrorist squad officers sealed off the area to search for possible bombs.* ■ apply a non-porous coating to (a surface) to make it impervious: *the pine boarding should be sealed with polyurethane.* ■ fry (food) briefly in hot fat to prevent it losing too much of its moisture during subsequent cooking: *heat the oil and seal the lamb on both sides.* ■ fix a piece of wax or lead stamped with a design to (a document) to authenticate it. ■ conclude, establish, or secure (something) definitively, excluding the possibility of reversal or loss: *to seal the deal he offered Thornton a place on the board of the nascent company.*
– PHRASES **my** (or **his** etc.) **lips are sealed** used to convey that one will not discuss or reveal something. **put** (or **set**) **the seal on** give the final authorization to: *the UN envoy hopes to set the seal on a lasting peace.* ■ provide or constitute the final confirmatory or conclusive factor: *the rain set the seal on his depression.* **seal someone's** (or **something's**) **fate** irrevocably determine or cause a bad or unpleasant outcome for someone (or something). **set** (or **put**) **one's seal to** (or **on**) mark with one's distinctive character: *it was the Stewart dynasty which most markedly set its seal on the place.*
– DERIVATIVES **sealable** adjective.
– ORIGIN Middle English (in sense 2): from Old French *seel* (noun), *seeler* (verb), from Latin *sigillum* 'small picture', diminutive of *signum* 'a sign'.

seal[2] ▶ **noun** a fish-eating aquatic mammal with a streamlined body and feet developed as flippers, returning to land to breed or rest.
• Families Phocidae (the **true seals**) and Otariidae (the **eared seals**, including the fur seals and sea lions). The latter have external ear flaps and are able to sit upright, and the males are much larger than the females.
■ another term for **SEALSKIN**.
▶ **verb** [no obj.] [usu. as noun **sealing**] hunt for seals.
– ORIGIN Old English *seolh*, of Germanic origin.

sea lane ▶ **noun** a route at sea designated for use or regularly used by shipping.

sealant ▶ **noun** [mass noun] material used for sealing something so as to make it airtight or watertight.

sea lavender ▶ **noun** a chiefly maritime plant with small pink or lilac funnel-shaped flowers. Several kinds are cultivated and some are used as everlasting flowers.
• Genus *Limonium* (formerly *Statice*), family Plumbaginaceae.

sea lawyer ▶ **noun** informal an eloquently and obstinately argumentative person.

sealed-beam ▶ **adjective** denoting a vehicle headlamp with a sealed unit consisting of the light source, reflector, and lens.

sealed book ▶ **noun** archaic term for **CLOSED BOOK**.

sealed orders ▶ **plural noun** Military orders for procedure which are not to be opened before a specified time.

sea legs ▶ **plural noun** (**one's sea legs**) a person's ability to keep their balance and not feel seasick when on board a moving ship.

sea lemon ▶ **noun** a yellowish sea slug.
• *Archidoris* and other genera, order Nudibranchia, class Gastropoda.

sealer[1] ▶ **noun** **1** [usu. with modifier] a device or substance used to seal something, especially with a hermetic or an impervious seal.
2 (also **sealer jar**) Canadian a jar with a hermetic seal designed to preserve food such as fruit, pickles, and jams.

sealer[2] ▶ **noun** a ship or person engaged in hunting seals.

sea lettuce ▶ **noun** [mass noun] an edible seaweed with green fronds that resemble lettuce leaves.
• *Ulva lactuca*, division Chlorophyta.

sea level ▶ **noun** the level of the sea's surface, used in reckoning the height of geographical features such as hills and as a barometric standard: *it is only 500 feet above sea level.* Compare with **MEAN SEA LEVEL**.

sealift ▶ **noun** a large-scale transportation of troops, supplies, and equipment by sea.

sea lily ▶ **noun** a sedentary marine echinoderm which has a small body on a long jointed stalk, with feather-like arms to trap food.
• Class Crinoidea.

sealing wax ▶ **noun** [mass noun] a mixture of shellac and rosin with turpentine and pigment, softened by heating and used to make seals.

sea lion ▶ **noun** **1** an eared seal occurring mainly on Pacific coasts, the large male of which has a mane on the neck and shoulders.
• Five genera and species in the family Otariidae.
2 Heraldry a mythical beast formed of a lion's head and foreparts and a fish's tail.

sea loch ▶ **noun** see **LOCH**.

Sea Lord ▶ **noun** either of two senior officers in the Royal Navy (**First Sea Lord**, **Second Sea Lord**) serving originally as members of the Admiralty Board (now of the Ministry of Defence).

sealpoint ▶ **noun** a dark brown marking on the fur of the head, tail, and paws of a Siamese cat.
■ a cat with such markings.

seal ring ▶ **noun** chiefly historical a finger ring with a seal for impressing sealing wax.

sealskin ▶ **noun** [mass noun] [often as modifier] the skin or prepared fur of a seal, especially when made into a garment.

seals of office ▶ **plural noun** (in the UK) engraved seals held during tenure of an official position, especially that of Lord Chancellor or Secretary of State, and symbolizing the office held.

sealstone ▶ **noun** a gemstone bearing an engraved device for use as a seal.

seal-top ▶ **adjective** (of a spoon) having a flat design resembling an embossed seal at the end of its handle.
▶ **noun** a spoon with such a handle.

Sealyham /ˈsiːlɪəm/ (in full **Sealyham terrier**) ▶ **noun** a terrier of a wire-haired short-legged breed.
– ORIGIN late 19th cent.: from *Sealyham*, the name of a village in SW Wales, where the dog was first bred.

seam ▶ **noun** **1** a line where two pieces of fabric are sewn together in a garment or other article.
■ a line where the edges of two pieces of wood, wallpaper, or another material touch each other. ■ a long thin indentation or scar: *the track cleaves a seam through corn.*
2 an underground layer of a mineral such as coal or gold.
■ figurative a supply of something valuable: *Sunderland have a rich seam of experienced players.* ■ figurative an element of a particular characteristic: *there is a seam of despondency in Stipe's words.*
▶ **verb** **1** join with a seam: *it can be used for seaming garments.*
2 [usu. as adj. **seamed**] make a long narrow indentation in: *men in middle age have seamed faces.*
– PHRASES **bursting** (or **bulging**) **at the seams** informal (of a place or building) full to overflowing. **come** (or **fall**) **apart at the seams** informal (of a person or system) be in a very poor condition and near to collapse: *the attitude of the airport guard was symptomatic of a system falling apart at the seams.*
– ORIGIN Old English *sēam*, of Germanic origin; related to Dutch *zoom* and German *Saum*.

seaman ▶ **noun** (pl. **-men**) a person who works as a sailor, especially one below the rank of officer.
■ the lowest rank in the US navy, below petty officer.
■ [with adj.] a person regarded in terms of their ability to captain or crew a boat or ship: *he's the best seaman on the coast.*
– DERIVATIVES **seamanlike** adjective, **seamanly** adjective.
– ORIGIN Old English *sǣman* (see **SEA**, **MAN**).

seamanship ▶ **noun** [mass noun] the skill, techniques, or practice of handling a ship or boat at sea.

seamark ▶ **noun** a conspicuous object distinguishable at sea, serving to guide or warn sailors in navigation.

sea mat ▶ **noun** a bryozoan, especially one which forms mat-like encrustations on underwater objects.
• *Membranipora* and other genera, class Gymnolaemata.

seam bowler ▶ **noun** Cricket a bowler, generally fast, who makes the ball deviate by bouncing on its seam.
– DERIVATIVES **seam bowling** noun.

seamer ▶ **noun** **1** Cricket another term for **SEAM BOWLER**.
■ a ball which deviates by bouncing on its seam.
2 a person who seams garments.

seamfree ▶ **adjective** (of tights or stockings) having no seams up the backs of the legs.
■ (of underclothing, especially a bra) having no obvious seams so as to provide a smooth contour under close-fitting clothing.

sea mile ▶ **noun** a unit of distance equal to a minute of arc of a great circle and varying (because the earth is not a perfect sphere) between approximately 2,014 yards (1,842 metres) at the equator and 2,035 yards (1,861 metres) at the pole. Compare with **NAUTICAL MILE**.

seamless ▶ **adjective** (of a fabric or surface) smooth and without seams or obvious joins: *seamless stockings* | figurative *a seamless service between health and social care.*
– DERIVATIVES **seamlessly** adverb.

sea-moth ▶ **noun** a small fish with bony plates covering the body and large pectoral fins which spread out horizontally like wings. It lives in the warmer waters of the Indo-Pacific.
• Family Pegasidae: several genera and species, including the widely distributed *Eurypegasus draconis*.

seamount ▶ **noun** a submarine mountain.

sea mouse ▶ **noun** a large marine bristle worm with a stout oval body which bears matted fur-like iridescent chaetae.
• Genus *Aphrodite*, class Polychaeta.

seamstress ▶ **noun** a woman who sews, especially one who earns her living by sewing.
– ORIGIN late 16th cent.: from archaic *seamster*, *sempster* 'tailor, seamstress' + **-ESS**[1].

seamy ▶ **adjective** (**seamier**, **seamiest**) sordid and disreputable: *a seamy sex scandal.*
– DERIVATIVES **seaminess** noun.

Seanad /ˈʃanəð, -d, Irish ˈʃanəd/ (also **Seanad Eireann** /ˈɛːrən, Irish ˈeːrʲənʲ/) the upper House of Parliament in the Republic of Ireland, composed of sixty members, of whom eleven are nominated by the Taoiseach and forty-nine are elected by institutions.
– ORIGIN Irish, 'senate (of Ireland)'.

seance /ˈseɪɒns, -ɒ̃s, -ɑːns/ ▶ **noun** a meeting at which people attempt to make contact with the dead, especially through the agency of a medium.
– ORIGIN late 18th cent.: French *séance*, from Old French *seoir*, from Latin *sedere* 'sit'.

sea nettle ▶ **noun** a jellyfish with tentacles that can sting bathers.
• *Chrysaora* and other genera, class Scyphozoa.

Sea of Azov, Sea of Galilee, etc. see **AZOV, SEA OF**; **GALILEE, SEA OF**, etc.

sea otter ▶ **noun** an entirely aquatic marine otter of North Pacific coasts, formerly hunted for its dense fur. It is noted for its habit of floating on its back with a stone balanced on the abdomen, in order to crack open bivalve molluscs.
• *Enhydra lutris*, family Mustelidae.

sea pen ▶ **noun** a marine coelenterate related to the corals, forming a feather-shaped colony with a horny or calcareous skeleton.
• Order Pennatulacea, class Anthozoa.

Sea Peoples any or all of the groups of invaders, of uncertain identity, who encroached on Egypt and the eastern Mediterranean by land and sea in the late 13th century BC. The Egyptians were successful in driving them away, but some, including the Philistines, settled in Palestine. Also called **PEOPLES OF THE SEA**.

sea perch ▶ **noun** any of a number of marine fishes which typically have a long-based dorsal fin and which are popular as sporting fish, in particular:
● a fish of the snapper family (Lutjanidae: several genera). ● a surfperch.

sea pink ▶ **noun** another term for **THRIFT** (in sense 2).

seaplane ▶ **noun** an aircraft with floats or skis instead of wheels, designed to land on and take off from water.

seaport ▶ **noun** a town or city with a harbour for seagoing ships.

sea potato ▶ **noun** a yellowish-brown European heart urchin.
● *Echinocardium cordatum*, class Echinoidea.

sea power ▶ **noun** [mass noun] a country's naval strength, especially as a weapon of war.

SEAQ ▶ **abbreviation for** (in the UK) Stock Exchange Automated Quotations (the computer system on which dealers trade shares and seek or provide price quotations on the London Stock Exchange).

seaquake ▶ **noun** a sudden disturbance of the sea caused by a submarine eruption or earthquake.

sear ▶ **verb** [with obj.] burn or scorch the surface of (something) with a sudden, intense heat: *the water got so hot that it seared our lips* | figurative *a sharp pang of disappointment seared her.*
■ [no obj., with adverbial of direction] (of pain) be experienced as a sudden, burning sensation: *a crushing pain seared through his chest.* ■ brown (food) quickly at a high temperature so that it will retain its juices in subsequent cooking: [as adj. **seared**] *seared chicken livers.* ■ archaic cause to wither. ■ archaic make (someone's conscience, heart, or feelings) insensitive.
▶ **adjective** (also **sere**) poetic/literary (especially of plants) withered.
– ORIGIN Old English *sēar* (adjective), *sēarian* (verb), of Germanic origin.

search ▶ **verb** [no obj.] try to find something by looking or otherwise seeking carefully and thoroughly: *I searched among the rocks, but there was nothing* | *Daniel is then able to* ***search out*** *the most advantageous mortgage* | *Hugh will be* ***searching for*** *the truth.*
■ [with obj.] examine (a place, vehicle, or person) thoroughly in order to find something or someone: *she searched the house from top to bottom* | *the guards searched him for weapons.* ■ [as adj. **searching**] scrutinizing thoroughly, especially in a disconcerting way: *you have to ask yourselves some searching questions.*
▶ **noun** an act of searching for someone or something: *the police carried out a thorough search of the premises* | *he plans to go to the Himalayas* ***in search of*** *a yeti.*
■ (usu. **searches**) Law an investigation of public records to find if a property is subject to any liabilities or encumbrances.
– PHRASES **search me!** informal I do not know (used for emphasis).
– DERIVATIVES **searchable** adjective, **searcher** noun, **searchingly** adverb.
– ORIGIN Middle English: from Old French *cerchier* (verb), from late Latin *circare* 'go round', from Latin *circus* 'circle'.

search coil ▶ **noun** Physics a flat coil of insulated wire connected to a galvanometer, used for finding the strength of a magnetic field from the current induced in the coil when it is quickly turned over or withdrawn.

search engine ▶ **noun** Computing a program for the retrieval of data, files, or documents from a database or network, especially the Internet.

searchlight ▶ **noun** a powerful outdoor electric light with a concentrated beam that can be turned in the required direction.

search party ▶ **noun** a group of people organized to look for someone or something that is lost.

search warrant ▶ **noun** a legal document authorizing a police officer or other official to enter and search premises.

searing ▶ **adjective** extremely hot or intense: *the searing heat of the sun* | *a searing pain.*
■ severely critical: *a searing indictment of the government's performance.*

Searle /səːl/, Ronald (William Fordham) (b.1920), English artist and cartoonist, famous for creating the schoolgirls of St Trinian's.

sea robin ▶ **noun** a gurnard (fish), especially one of warm seas which has wing-like pectoral fins that are brightly coloured.
● Family Triglidae: several genera and many species.

sea room ▶ **noun** [mass noun] clear space at sea for a ship to turn or manoeuvre in.

Sears Tower /sɪəz/ a skyscraper in Chicago, the tallest building in the world when it was completed in 1973. It is 443 m (1,454 ft) high and has 110 floors.

sea-run ▶ **adjective** N. Amer. (of a migratory fish, especially a trout) having returned to the sea after spawning.

sea salt ▶ **noun** [mass noun] salt produced by the evaporation of seawater.

seascape ▶ **noun** a view of an expanse of sea.
■ a picture of such a view.

Sea Scout ▶ **noun** (especially in the UK) a member of the maritime branch of the Scout Association.

sea serpent ▶ **noun** a legendary serpent-like sea monster.

sea shanty ▶ **noun** see **SHANTY**[2].

seashell ▶ **noun** the shell of a marine mollusc.

seashore ▶ **noun** (usu. **the seashore**) an area of sandy, stony, or rocky land bordering and level with the sea.
■ Law the land between high- and low-water marks.

seasick ▶ **adjective** suffering from sickness or nausea caused by the motion of a ship at sea.
– DERIVATIVES **seasickness** noun.

seaside ▶ **noun** (usu. **the seaside**) a place by the sea, especially a beach area or holiday resort.

sea slater ▶ **noun** a common shore-dwelling crustacean which is related to the woodlouse.
● *Ligia oceanica*, order Isopoda.

sea slug ▶ **noun** a shell-less marine mollusc which is typically brightly coloured, with external gills and a number of appendages on the upper surface.
● Order Nudibranchia, class Gastropoda.

sea snail ▶ **noun 1** a marine mollusc, especially one with a spiral shell.
● Subclass Prosobranchia, class Gastropoda.
2 another term for **SNAILFISH**.

sea snake ▶ **noun** a venomous marine snake with a flattened tail, which lives in the warm coastal waters of the Indian and Pacific oceans and does not come on to land.
● Subfamily Hydrophiinae, family Elapidae: several genera and species, including the **yellow-bellied sea snake** (*Pelamis platurus*), the only species found in the open ocean.

season ▶ **noun** each of the four divisions of the year (spring, summer, autumn, and winter) marked by particular weather patterns and daylight hours, resulting from the earth's changing position with regard to the sun.
■ a period of the year characterized by a particular climatic feature or marked by a particular activity, event, or festivity: *the rainy season* | *the season for gathering pine needles.* ■ a fixed time in the year when a particular sporting activity is pursued: *the English cricket season is almost upon us.* ■ the time of year when a particular fruit, vegetable, or other food is plentiful and in good condition: *the pies are made with fruit that is* ***in season*** | *new season's lamb.* ■ a period when a female mammal is ready to mate: *this system of communication works very well, especially when a female is* ***in season.*** ■ (**the season**) a time of year traditionally adopted by the English upper classes for a series of fashionable social events. ■ archaic a proper or suitable time: *to everything there is a season.* ■ archaic an indefinite or unspecified period of time; a while: *this most beautiful soul; who walked with me for a season in this world.*
▶ **verb** [with obj.] **1** add salt, herbs, pepper, or other spices to (food): *season the soup to taste with salt and pepper* | [as adj. **seasoned**] *seasoned flour.*
■ add a quality or feature to (something), especially so as to make it more lively or exciting: *his conversation is seasoned liberally with exclamation points and punch lines.*
2 make (wood) suitable for use as timber by adjusting its moisture content to that of the environment in which it will be used: [as adj. **seasoned**] *it was made from seasoned, untreated oak.*
■ [as adj. **seasoned**] accustomed to particular conditions; experienced: *she is a seasoned traveller.*
– PHRASES **for all seasons** suitable in or appropriate for every kind of weather: *a coat for all seasons.* ■ adaptable to any circumstance: *a singer for all seasons.* **season's greetings** used as an expression of goodwill at Christmas or the New Year.
– ORIGIN Middle English: from Old French *seson*, from Latin *satio(n-)* 'sowing', later 'time of sowing', from the root of *serere* 'to sow'.

seasonable ▶ **adjective 1** usual for or appropriate to a particular season of the year: *seasonable temperatures*
2 archaic coming at the right time or meeting the needs of the occasion; opportune.
– DERIVATIVES **seasonability** noun, **seasonableness** noun, **seasonably** adverb.

seasonal ▶ **adjective** of, relating to, or characteristic of a particular season of the year: *a selection of seasonal fresh fruit.*
■ fluctuating or restricted according to the season or time of year: *there are companies whose markets are seasonal* | *seasonal rainfall.*
– DERIVATIVES **seasonality** noun, **seasonally** adverb.

seasonal affective disorder ▶ **noun** [mass noun] depression associated with late autumn and winter and thought to be caused by a lack of light.

seasoning ▶ **noun** [mass noun] **1** salt, herbs, or spices added to food to enhance the flavour.
2 the process of adjusting the moisture content of wood to make it more suitable for use as timber.

season ticket ▶ **noun** a ticket for a period of travel or a series of events which costs less than purchasing several separate tickets.

sea spider ▶ **noun** a spider-like marine arachnid which has a narrow segmented body with a minute abdomen and long legs.
● Class Pycnogonida.

sea squill ▶ **noun** see **SQUILL** (sense 1).

sea squirt ▶ **noun** a marine tunicate which has a bag-like body with orifices through which water flows into and out of a central pharynx.
● Class Ascidiacea, subphylum Urochordata.

sea stack ▶ **noun** see **STACK** (sense 2).

sea star ▶ **noun** a starfish.

sea state ▶ **noun** the degree of turbulence at sea, generally measured on a scale of 0 to 9 according to average wave height.

seat ▶ **noun 1** a thing made or used for sitting on, such as a chair or stool.
■ the roughly horizontal part of a chair, on which one's weight rests directly. ■ a sitting place for a passenger in a vehicle or for a member of an audience: *we have a fairly small theatre with about 1,300 seats.* ■ chiefly Brit. a place in an elected parliament or council: *he lost his seat in the 1997 election.* ■ Brit. a parliamentary constituency: *a safe Labour seat in the North-East.* ■ a site or location of something specified: *Parliament House was the seat of the Scots Parliament until the Union with England.* ■ short for **COUNTRY SEAT**. ■ a part of a machine that supports or guides another part.
2 a person's buttocks.
■ the part of a garment that covers the buttocks. ■ a manner of sitting on a horse: *he's got the worst seat on a horse of anyone I've ever seen.*
▶ **verb** [with obj.] arrange for (someone) to sit somewhere: *Owen seated his guests in the draughty baronial hall.*
■ (**seat oneself** or **be seated**) sit down: *she invited them to be seated* | [as adj. **seated**] *a dummy in a seated position.* ■ (of a place such as a theatre or restaurant) have seats for (a specified number of people): *a large tent that seats 100 to 150 people.* ■ [with obj. and adverbial of place] fit in position: *upper boulders were simply seated in the interstices below.*
– PHRASES **take one's seat** sit down, typically in a seat assigned to one. ■ start to take part in the business of an assembly after being elected.
– DERIVATIVES **seatless** adjective.
– ORIGIN Middle English (as a noun): from Old Norse *sæti*, from the Germanic base of **SIT**. The verb dates from the late 16th cent.

seat belt ▶ **noun** a belt used to secure someone in the seat of a motor vehicle or aircraft.

-seater ▶ **combining form** denoting a vehicle, sofa, or building with a specified number of seats: *a six-seater.*

seating ▶ **noun** [mass noun] the seats with which a building or room is provided: *the restaurant has seating for 80.*

SEATO ▶ **abbreviation for** South-East Asia Treaty Organization.

S

sea trout ▶ **noun** **1** Brit. a European brown trout of a salmon-like migratory race. Also called **SALMON TROUT**.
● *Salmo trutta trutta*, family Salmonidae.
2 [with modifier] N. Amer. a trout-like marine fish of the drum family occurring in the western Atlantic.
● Genus *Cynoscion*, family Sciaenidae: several species, including the weakfish.

Seattle /sɪˈat(ə)l/ a port and industrial city in the state of Washington, on the eastern shores of Puget Sound; pop. 516,260 (1990). First settled in 1852, it is now the largest city in the north-western US.

sea turtle ▶ **noun** see **TURTLE** (sense 1).

sea urchin ▶ **noun** a marine echinoderm which has a spherical or flattened shell covered in mobile spines, with a mouth on the underside and calcareous jaws.
● Class Echinoidea.

sea wall ▶ **noun** a wall or embankment erected to prevent the sea encroaching on or eroding an area of land.

seaward ▶ **adverb** (also **seawards**) towards the sea: *after about a mile they turned seaward.*
▶ **adjective** going or pointing towards the sea: *there was a seaward movement of water on the bottom.*
■ nearer or nearest to the sea: *the seaward end of the village.*
▶ **noun** [in sing.] the side that faces or is nearer to the sea: *breakwaters were extended further* ***to seaward.***

sea wasp ▶ **noun** a box jelly which can inflict a dangerous sting.

seaway ▶ **noun** **1** an inland waterway capable of accommodating seagoing ships.
■ a natural channel connecting two areas of sea. ■ a route across the sea used by ships.
2 [in sing.] a rough sea in which to sail: *with the engine mounted amidship, the boat pitches less* ***in a seaway.***

seaweed ▶ **noun** [mass noun] large algae growing in the sea or on rocks below the high-water mark.

sea wolf ▶ **noun** another term for **WOLF FISH**.

seaworthy ▶ **adjective** (of a boat) in a good enough condition to sail on the sea.
– DERIVATIVES **seaworthiness** noun.

sebaceous /sɪˈbeɪʃəs/ ▶ **adjective** technical of or relating to oil or fat.
■ of or relating to a sebaceous gland or its secretion.
– ORIGIN early 18th cent.: from Latin *sebaceus* (from *sebum* 'tallow') + **-OUS**.

sebaceous cyst ▶ **noun** a swelling in the skin arising in a sebaceous gland, typically filled with yellowish sebum. Also called **WEN**[1].

sebaceous gland ▶ **noun** a small gland in the skin which secretes a lubricating oily matter (sebum) into the hair follicles to lubricate the skin and hair.

Sebastian, St /sɪˈbastɪən/ (late 3rd century), Roman martyr. According to legend he was a soldier who was shot by archers on the orders of Diocletian, but who recovered, confronted the emperor, and was then clubbed to death. Feast day, 20 January.

Sebastopol /sɪˈbastəp(ə)l, -pɒl/ a fortress and naval base in Ukraine, near the southern tip of the Crimea; pop. 361,000 (1990). The focal point of military operations during the Crimean War, it fell to Anglo-French forces in September 1855 after a year-long siege. Ukrainian and Russian name **SEVASTOPOL**.

Sebat /ˈsiːbat/ (also **Shebat**, **Shevat**) ▶ **noun** (in the Jewish calendar) the fifth month of the civil and eleventh of the religious year, usually coinciding with parts of January and February.
– ORIGIN from Hebrew *šĕbaṭ*.

seborrhoea /ˌsɛbəˈriːə/ (US **seborrhea**) ▶ **noun** [mass noun] Medicine excessive discharge of sebum from the sebaceous glands.
– DERIVATIVES **seborrhoeic** adjective.
– ORIGIN late 19th cent.: from **SEBUM** + **-RRHOEA**.

sebum /ˈsiːbəm/ ▶ **noun** [mass noun] an oily secretion of the sebaceous glands.
– ORIGIN late 19th cent.: modern Latin, from Latin *sebum* 'grease'.

SEC ▶ **abbreviation for** Securities and Exchange Commission, a US governmental agency which monitors trading in securities and company takeovers.

Sec. ▶ **abbreviation for** secretary.

sec[1] ▶ **abbreviation for** secant.

sec[2] ▶ **noun** (**a sec**) informal a second; a very short space of time: *stay put, I'll be back in a sec.*
– ORIGIN late 19th cent.: abbreviation.

sec[3] ▶ **adjective** (of wine) dry.
– ORIGIN French, from Latin *siccus*.

sec. ▶ **abbreviation for** second(s).

SECAM /ˈsiːkam/ ▶ **noun** [mass noun] the television broadcasting system used in France and eastern Europe.
– ORIGIN from French *séquentiel couleur à mémoire* (so named because the colour information is transmitted in sequential blocks to a memory in the receiver).

secant /ˈsiːk(ə)nt, ˈsɛk-/ ▶ **noun** **1** (abbrev.: **sec.**) Mathematics the ratio of the hypotenuse to the shorter side adjacent to an acute angle (in a right-angled triangle); the reciprocal of a cosine.
2 Geometry a straight line that cuts a curve in two or more parts.
– ORIGIN late 16th cent.; from French *sécante*, based on Latin *secare* 'to cut'.

secateurs /ˌsɛkəˈtəːz, ˈsɛkətəːz/ ▶ **plural noun** (also a **pair of secateurs**) chiefly Brit. a pair of pruning clippers for use with one hand.
– ORIGIN mid 19th cent.: plural of French *sécateur* 'cutter', formed irregularly from Latin *secare* 'to cut'.

Secchi disc /ˈsɛki/ ▶ **noun** an opaque disc, typically white, used to gauge the transparency of water by measuring the depth—known as the **Secchi depth**—at which the disc ceases to be visible from the surface.
– ORIGIN early 20th cent.: named after Angelo *Secchi* (1818–78), Italian astronomer.

secco /ˈsɛkəʊ/ (also **fresco secco**) ▶ **noun** [mass noun] the technique of painting on dry plaster with pigments mixed in water.
– ORIGIN mid 19th cent.: from Italian, literally 'dry', from Latin *siccus*.

secede /sɪˈsiːd/ ▶ **verb** [no obj.] withdraw formally from membership of a federal union, an alliance, or a political or religious organization: *the kingdom of Belgium* ***seceded from*** *the Netherlands in 1830.*
– DERIVATIVES **seceder** noun.
– ORIGIN early 18th cent.: from Latin *secedere*, from *se-* 'apart' + *cedere* 'go'.

Secernentea /ˌsɪsəːˈnɛntɪə/ Zoology another term for **PHASMIDA** (in sense 2).
– ORIGIN modern Latin (plural), from Latin *secernent-* 'separating', from the verb *secernere*.

secession /sɪˈsɛʃ(ə)n/ ▶ **noun** [mass noun] the action of withdrawing formally from membership of a federation or body, especially a political state: *the republics want* ***secession from*** *the union.*
■ (**the Secession**) historical the withdrawal of eleven Southern states from the US Union in 1860, leading to the Civil War. ■ (**the Secession**) variant of **SEZESSION**.
– DERIVATIVES **secessional** adjective, **secessionism** noun, **secessionist** noun.
– ORIGIN mid 16th cent. (denoting the withdrawal of plebeians from ancient Rome in order to compel the patricians to redress their grievances): from French *sécession* or Latin *secessio(n-)*, from *secedere* 'go apart' (see **SECEDE**).

Sechuana /sɛˈtʃwɑːnə/ dated ▶ **noun** & **adjective** variant spelling of **SETSWANA**.

Seckel /ˈsɛk(ə)l/ ▶ **noun** a pear of a small sweet juicy brownish-red variety, grown chiefly in the US.
– ORIGIN early 19th cent.: from the surname of an early grower.

seclude ▶ **verb** [with obj.] keep (someone) away from other people: *I secluded myself up here for a life of study and meditation.*
– ORIGIN late Middle English (in the sense 'obstruct access to'): from Latin *secludere*, from *se-* 'apart' + *claudere* 'to shut'.

secluded ▶ **adjective** (of a place) not seen or visited by many people; sheltered and private: *the gardens are quiet and secluded.*

seclusion ▶ **noun** [mass noun] the state of being private and away from other people: *they enjoyed ten days of peace and seclusion.*
■ [count noun] archaic a sheltered or private place.
– DERIVATIVES **seclusive** adjective.
– ORIGIN early 17th cent.: from medieval Latin *seclusio(n-)*, from *secludere* 'shut off' (see **SECLUDE**).

Seconal /ˈsɛk(ə)nal, -(ə)l/ ▶ **noun** [mass noun] trademark a barbiturate drug used as a sedative and hypnotic.
– ORIGIN 1930s: blend of **SECONDARY** and **ALLYL**.

second[1] /ˈsɛk(ə)nd/ ▶ **ordinal number** **1** constituting number two in a sequence; coming after the first in time or order; 2nd: *he married for a second time | Herbert was the second of their six children.*
■ secondly (used to introduce a second point or reason): *second, they are lightly regulated; and third, they do business with non-resident clients.* ■ Music an interval spanning two consecutive notes in a diatonic scale. ■ the note which is higher by this interval than the tonic of a diatonic scale or root of a chord. ■ the second in a sequence of a vehicle's gears: *he took the corner in second.* ■ Baseball second base. ■ chiefly Brit. the second form of a school or college. ■ (**seconds**) informal a second course or second helping of food at a meal. ■ denoting someone or something regarded as comparable to or reminiscent of a better-known predecessor: *a fear that the conflict would turn into a second Vietnam.*
2 subordinate or inferior in position, rank, or importance: *it was* ***second only to*** *Copenhagen among Baltic ports | he is a writer first and a scientist second.*
■ additional to that already existing, used, or possessed: *a second home | French as a second language.* ■ the second finisher or position in a race or competition: *he finished second.* ■ Brit. a place in the second grade in an examination, especially for a degree. ■ Music performing a lower or subordinate of two or more parts for the same instrument or voice: *the second violins.* ■ (**seconds**) goods of an inferior quality. ■ (**the seconds**) the reserve team of a sports club. ■ coarse flour, or bread made from it.
3 an assistant, in particular:
■ an attendant assisting a combatant in a duel or boxing match. ■ a Cub or Brownie chosen by their pack to assist the Sixer and replace them when they are absent.
▶ **verb** [with obj.] formally support or endorse (a nomination or resolution or its proposer) as a necessary preliminary to adoption or further discussion: *Bridgeman seconded Maxwell's motion calling for the reform.*
■ express agreement with: *her view is seconded by most Indian leaders today.* ■ archaic support; back up: *so well was he seconded by the multitude of labourers at his command.*
– PHRASES **in the second place** as a second consideration or point. **second to none** the best, worst, fastest, etc.
– DERIVATIVES **seconder** noun.
– ORIGIN Middle English: via Old French from Latin *secundus* 'following, second', from the base of *sequi* 'follow'. The verb dates from the late 16th cent.

second[2] /ˈsɛk(ə)nd/ ▶ **noun** **1** (abbrev.: **s**) a sixtieth of a minute of time, which as the SI unit of time is defined in terms of the natural periodicity of the radiation of a caesium-133 atom. (Symbol: ″)
■ informal a very short time: *his eyes met Charlotte's for a second.*
2 (also **arc second** or **second of arc**) a sixtieth of a minute of angular distance. (Symbol: ″)
– ORIGIN late Middle English: from medieval Latin *secunda (minuta)* 'second (minute)', feminine (used as a noun) of *secundus*, referring to the 'second' operation of dividing an hour by sixty.

second[3] /sɪˈkɒnd/ ▶ **verb** [with obj.] Brit. transfer (a military officer or other official or worker) temporarily to other employment or another position: *I was* ***seconded to*** *a public relations unit.*
– DERIVATIVES **secondee** /-ˈdiː/ noun.
– ORIGIN early 19th cent.: from French *en second* 'in the second rank (of officers)'.

second Adam ▶ **noun** (**the second Adam**) (in Christian thought) Jesus Christ.
– ORIGIN with biblical allusion to 1 Cor. 15: 45–47.

Second Adar see **ADAR**.

Second Advent ▶ **noun** another term for **SECOND COMING**.

secondary ▶ **adjective** **1** coming after, less important than, or resulting from someone or something else that is primary: *luck plays a role, but it's ultimately* ***secondary to*** *local knowledge.*
■ of or relating to education for children from the age of eleven to sixteen or eighteen: *a secondary school.* ■ having a reversible chemical reaction and therefore able to store energy. ■ relating to or denoting the output side of a device using electromagnetic induction, especially in a transformer.
2 (**Secondary**) Geology former term for **MESOZOIC**.

3 Chemistry (of an organic compound) having its functional group located on a carbon atom which is bonded to two other carbon atoms.
■(chiefly of amines) derived from ammonia by replacement of two hydrogen atoms by organic groups.
▶noun (pl. **-ies**) **1** short for:
■Brit. a secondary school. ■ Ornithology a secondary feather. ■ a secondary coil or winding in an electrical transformer.
2 (the Secondary) Geology, dated the Secondary or Mesozoic era.
– DERIVATIVES **secondarily** adverb, **secondariness** noun.
– ORIGIN late Middle English: from Latin *secundarius* 'of the second quality or class', from *secundus* (see **SECOND**[1]).

secondary articulation ▶noun Phonetics an additional feature in the pronunciation of a consonant (besides the actual place of articulation), such as palatalization or lip-rounding.

secondary colour ▶noun a colour resulting from the mixing of two primary colours.

secondary evidence ▶noun [mass noun] Law something, in particular documentation, which confirms the existence of unavailable primary evidence.

secondary feather ▶noun any of the flight feathers growing from the second joint of a bird's wing.

secondary industry ▶noun [mass noun] Economics industry that converts the raw materials provided by primary industry into commodities and products for the consumer; manufacturing industry.

secondary modern school ▶noun historical a secondary school of a kind offering a general education to children not selected for grammar or technical schools.

secondary picketing ▶noun [mass noun] Brit. picketing by strikers of the premises of a firm that trades with their employer but is not otherwise involved in the dispute in question.

secondary planet ▶noun a satellite of a planet.

secondary process ▶noun Psychoanalysis a thought process connecting the preconscious and conscious, governed by the reality principle and reflecting the decision-making and problem-solving activity of the ego.

secondary sector ▶noun Economics the sector of the economy concerned with ⌐or relating to secondary industry.

secondary sexual characteristics ▶plural noun physical characteristics developed at puberty which distinguish between the sexes but are not involved in reproduction.

secondary smoke ▶noun [mass noun] smoke inhaled involuntarily from tobacco being smoked by others.

secondary smoking ▶noun another term for **PASSIVE SMOKING**.

secondary structure ▶noun Biochemistry the local three-dimensional structure of sheets, helices, or other forms adopted by a polynucleotide or polypeptide chain, due to electrostatic attraction between neighbouring residues.

secondary thickening ▶noun [mass noun] Botany (in the stem or root of a woody plant) the increase in girth resulting from the formation of new woody tissue by the cambium.

secondary treatment ▶noun [mass noun] the further treatment of sewage effluent by biological methods following sedimentation.

second ballot ▶noun a further ballot held to confirm the selection of a candidate where a previous ballot did not yield an absolute majority.

second best ▶adjective next after the best: *his second-best suit.*
▶noun a less adequate or less desirable alternative: *he would have to settle for second best.*
– PHRASES **come off second best** be defeated in a competition.

Second Boer War see **BOER WARS**.

second cause ▶noun Logic a cause that is itself caused.

second chamber ▶noun the upper house of a parliament with two chambers.

second childhood ▶noun a period in someone's adult life when they act as a child, either for fun or as a consequence of reduced mental capabilities.

second class ▶noun [in sing.] a set of people or things grouped together as the second best.
■[mass noun] the second-best accommodation in an aircraft, train, or ship. ■ Brit. the second-highest division in the results of the examinations for a university degree: *he obtained a second class in modern history.*
▶adjective & adverb of the second-best quality or in the second division: [as adj.] *until 1914 women were thought of as second-class citizens.*
■of or relating to the second-best accommodation in an aircraft, train, or ship: [as adj.] *I want second-class tickets* | [as adv.] *they don't fly second-class.* ■ of or relating to a class of mail having lower priority than first-class mail: [as adj.] *second-class postage stamps.* ■ (in North America) denoting a class of mail which includes newspapers and periodicals. ■ [as adj.] Brit. of or relating to the second-highest division in a university examination: *a respectable second-class degree.*

Second Coming ▶noun Christian Theology the prophesied return of Christ to Earth at the Last Judgement.

second cousin ▶noun see **COUSIN**.

second-cut ▶adjective another term for **CROSS-CUT**.

second-degree ▶adjective [attrib.] **1** Medicine denoting burns that cause blistering but not permanent scars.
2 Law, chiefly N. Amer. denoting a category of a crime, especially murder, that is less serious than a first-degree crime.

seconde /səˈkɒd/ ▶noun Fencing the second of eight parrying positions.
– ORIGIN early 18th cent.: from French, feminine of *second* 'second'.

Second Empire the imperial government in France of Napoleon III, 1852–70.
■this period in France.

second-generation ▶adjective **1** denoting the offspring of parents who have immigrated to a particular country: *she was a second-generation American.*
2 of a more advanced stage of technology than previous models or systems.

second-guess ▶verb [with obj.] **1** anticipate or predict (someone's actions or thoughts) by guesswork: *he had to second-guess what the environmental regulations would be in five years' time.*
2 judge or criticize (someone) with hindsight: *the prime minister was willing to second-guess senior ministers in public.*

second-hand ▶adjective **1** (of goods) having had a previous owner; not new: *a second-hand car.*
■[attrib.] denoting a shop where such goods can be bought: *a second-hand bookshop.*
2 (of information or experience) accepted on another's authority and not from original investigation: *second-hand knowledge of her country.*
▶adverb **1** on the basis that something has had a previous owner: *tips on the pitfalls to avoid when buying second-hand.*
2 on the basis of what others have said; indirectly: *I was discounting anything I heard second-hand.*
– PHRASES **at second hand** by hearsay rather than direct observation or experience.

second hand ▶noun an extra hand in some watches and clocks which moves round to indicate the seconds.

second-hand smoke ▶noun North American term for **SECONDARY SMOKE**.

second honeymoon ▶noun a romantic holiday taken by a couple who have been married for some time.

second in command ▶noun the officer next in authority to the commanding or chief officer.

second intention ▶noun [mass noun] Medicine the healing of a wound in which the edges do not meet, and new epithelium must form across granulation tissue: *healing by second intention.*

Second International see **INTERNATIONAL** (sense 2 of the noun).

Second Isaiah another name for **DEUTERO-ISAIAH**.

second lieutenant ▶noun a rank of officer in the army and the US air force, above warrant officer or chief warrant officer and below lieutenant or first lieutenant.

second line ▶noun anything used or held in reserve as support, replacement, or reinforcement, in particular:
■[usu. as modifier] a medical treatment or therapy used in support of another, or as a more drastic measure if the primary treatment is ineffective. ■ a battle line behind the front line to support it and make good its losses. ■ [as modifier] ranking second in strength, effectiveness, ability, or value: *the clutch of second-line US computer manufacturers.* ■ [as modifier] denoting shares that are not traded on the main stock exchange and are not subject to the same degree of regulation.

secondly ▶adverb in the second place (used to introduce a second point or reason): *he was presented first of all as a hopelessly unqualified candidate and, secondly, as an extremist.*

second master ▶noun a deputy headmaster.

second mate ▶noun another term for **SECOND OFFICER**.

secondment ▶noun [mass noun] the temporary transfer of an official or worker to another position or employment: *the banker spent two years on secondment to the Department of Industry.*

second messenger ▶noun Physiology a substance whose release within a cell is promoted by a hormone and which brings about a response by the cell.

second mortgage ▶noun a mortgage taken out on a property that is already mortgaged.

second name ▶noun Brit. a surname.

second nature ▶noun [mass noun] a characteristic or habit in someone that appears to be instinctive because that person has behaved in a particular way so often: *deceit was becoming second nature to her.*

secondo /sɪˈkɒndəʊ/ ▶noun (pl. **secondi** /-di/) Music the second or lower part in a duet.
– ORIGIN Italian.

second officer ▶noun an assistant mate on a merchant ship.

second person ▶noun see **PERSON** (sense 2).

second position ▶noun **1** Ballet a posture in which the feet form a straight line, being turned out to either side with the heels separated by the distance of a small step.
■a position of the arms in which they are held out to each side of the body, curving forwards and slightly upwards.
2 Music a position of the left hand on the fingerboard of a stringed instrument nearer to the bridge than the first position, enabling a higher-pitched set of notes to be played.

second-rate ▶adjective of mediocre or inferior quality: *a second-rate theatre.*
– DERIVATIVES **second-rater** noun.

second reading ▶noun a second presentation of a bill to a legislative assembly, in the UK to approve its general principles and in the US to debate committee reports.

Second Reich see **REICH**[1].

Second Republic the republican regime in France from the deposition of King Louis Philippe (1848) to the beginning of the Second Empire (1852).

second sight ▶noun [mass noun] the supposed ability to perceive future or distant events; clairvoyance.
– DERIVATIVES **second-sighted** adjective.

second strike ▶noun a retaliatory attack conducted with weapons designed to withstand an initial nuclear attack (a 'first strike').

second string ▶noun an alternative resource or course of action in case another one fails.

second teeth ▶plural noun the set of permanent teeth that replace the milk teeth in humans and other mammals.

second thoughts (US also **second thought**) ▶plural noun a change of opinion or resolve reached after considering something again. **on second thoughts, perhaps he was right.**

second wind ▶noun [in sing.] a person's ability to breathe freely during exercise, after having been out of breath.
■a new strength or energy to continue something that

is an effort: *she gained a second wind during the campaign and turned the opinion polls around.*

Second World ▶ noun the former communist block consisting of the Soviet Union and some countries in eastern Europe.

Second World War a war (1939–45) in which the Axis Powers (Germany, Italy, and Japan) were defeated by an alliance eventually including the United Kingdom and its dominions, the Soviet Union, and the United States.

Hitler's invasion of Poland in September 1939 led Great Britain and France to declare war on Germany. Germany defeated and occupied France the following year and soon overran much of Europe. Italy joined the war in 1940, and the US and Japan entered following the Japanese attack on the US fleet at Pearl Harbor. Italy surrendered in 1943 and the Allies launched a full-scale invasion in Normandy in June 1944. The war in Europe ended when Germany surrendered in May 1945; Japan surrendered after the US dropped atom bombs on Hiroshima and Nagasaki in August 1945. An estimated 55 million people were killed during the war, including a much higher proportion of civilians than in the First World War.

secrecy ▶ noun [mass noun] the action of keeping something secret or the state of being kept secret: *the bidding is conducted in secrecy.*
– ORIGIN late Middle English: from **SECRET**, probably on the pattern of *privacy*.

secret ▶ adjective not known or seen or not meant to be known or seen by others: *how did you guess I'd got a secret plan? | the resupply effort was probably kept secret from Congress.*
  ■ [attrib.] not meant to be known as such by others: *a secret drinker.* ■ fond of or good at keeping things about oneself unknown: *he can be the most secret man.*
▶ noun something that is kept or meant to be kept unknown or unseen by others: *a state secret | at first I tried to keep it a secret from my wife.*
  ■ something that is not properly understood; a mystery: *I'm not trying to explain the secrets of the universe in this book.* ■ a valid but not commonly known or recognized method of achieving or maintaining something: *the secret of a happy marriage is compromise.* ■ a prayer said by the priest in a low voice after the offertory in a Roman Catholic Mass.
– PHRASES **be in (on) the secret** be among the small number of people who know something. **in secret** without others knowing. **make no secret of something** make something perfectly clear.
– DERIVATIVES **secretly** adverb.
– ORIGIN late Middle English: from Old French, from Latin *secretus* (adjective) 'separate, set apart', from the verb *secernere*, from *se-* 'apart' + *cernere* 'sift'.

secret agent ▶ noun a spy acting for a country.

secretagogue /sɪˈkriːtəɡɒɡ/ ▶ noun Physiology a substance which promotes secretion.
– ORIGIN early 20th cent.: from **SECRETE**[1] + Greek *agōgos* 'leading'.

secretaire /ˌsɛkrɪˈtɛː/ ▶ noun a small writing desk; an escritoire.
– ORIGIN late 18th cent.: from French *secrétaire*, literally 'secretary'.

secretariat /ˌsɛkrɪˈtɛːrɪət/ ▶ noun a permanent administrative office or department, especially a governmental one.
  ■ [treated as sing. or pl.] the staff working in such an office.
– ORIGIN early 19th cent.: from French *secrétariat*, from medieval Latin *secretariatus*, from *secretarius* (see **SECRETARY**).

secretary ▶ noun (pl. **-ies**) a person employed by an individual or in an office to assist with correspondence, keep records, make appointments, and carry out similar tasks.
  ■ an official of a society or other organization who conducts its correspondence and keeps its records. ■ the principal assistant of a UK government minister or ambassador: [as title] *Chief Secretary to the Treasury.*
– DERIVATIVES **secretarial** adjective, **secretaryship** noun.
– ORIGIN late Middle English (originally in the sense 'person entrusted with a secret'): from late Latin *secretarius* 'confidential officer', from Latin *secretum* 'secret', neuter of *secretus* (see **SECRET**).

secretary bird ▶ noun a slender long-legged African bird of prey that feeds on snakes, having a crest likened to a quill pen stuck behind the ear.
  ● *Sagittarius serpentarius*, the only member of the family Sagittariidae.

Secretary General ▶ noun (pl. **Secretaries General**) a title given to the principal administrator of some organizations.

Secretary of State ▶ noun 1 (in the UK) the head of a major government department.
2 (in the US) the head of the State Department, responsible for foreign affairs.
3 (in Canada) a government minister responsible for a specific area within a department.

secret ballot ▶ noun a ballot in which votes are cast in secret.

secrete[1] /sɪˈkriːt/ ▶ verb [with obj.] (of a cell, gland, or organ) produce and discharge (a substance): *insulin is secreted in response to rising levels of glucose in the blood.*
– DERIVATIVES **secretor** noun, **secretory** adjective.
– ORIGIN early 18th cent.: back-formation from **SECRETION**.

secrete[2] /sɪˈkriːt/ ▶ verb [with obj.] conceal; hide: *the assets had been secreted in Swiss bank accounts.*
– ORIGIN mid 18th cent.: alteration of the obsolete verb *secret* 'keep secret'.

secretin /sɪˈkriːtɪn/ ▶ noun [mass noun] Biochemistry a hormone released into the bloodstream by the duodenum (especially in response to acidity) to stimulate secretion by the liver and pancreas.
– ORIGIN early 20th cent.: from **SECRETION** + **-IN**[1].

Secret Intelligence Service (abbrev.: **SIS**) official name for **MI6**.

secretion ▶ noun [mass noun] a process by which substances are produced and discharged from a cell, gland, or organ for a particular function in the organism or for excretion.
  ■ [count noun] a substance discharged in such a way.
– ORIGIN mid 17th cent.: from French *sécrétion* or Latin *secretio(n-)* 'separation', from *secret-* 'moved apart', from the verb *secernere*.

secretive ▶ adjective (of a person or an organization) inclined to conceal feelings and intentions or not to disclose information: *she was very secretive about her past.*
  ■ (of a state or activity) characterized by the concealment of intentions and information: *secretive deals.* ■ (of a person's expression or manner) having an enigmatic or conspiratorial quality: *a secretive smile.*
– DERIVATIVES **secretively** adverb, **secretiveness** noun.
– ORIGIN mid 19th cent.: back-formation from *secretiveness*, suggested by French *secrétivité*, from *secret* 'secret'.

secret list ▶ noun a register of research work or developments on sensitive military projects, the details of which may not be disclosed for reasons of national security.

secret police ▶ noun [treated as pl.] a police force working in secret against a government's political opponents.

secret service ▶ noun 1 a government department concerned with espionage.
2 (**Secret Service**) (in the US) a branch of the Treasury Department dealing with counterfeiting and providing protection for the President.

secret society ▶ noun an organization whose members are sworn to secrecy about its activities.

sect ▶ noun a group of people with somewhat different religious beliefs (typically regarded as heretical) from those of a larger group to which they belong.
  ■ often derogatory a group that has separated from an established Church; a nonconformist Church. ■ a philosophical or political group, especially one regarded as extreme or dangerous.
– ORIGIN Middle English: from Old French *secte* or Latin *secta*, literally 'following', hence 'faction, party', from the stem of *sequi* 'follow'.

sect. ▶ abbreviation for section.

sectarian ▶ adjective denoting or concerning a sect or sects: *among the sectarian offshoots of Ismailism were the Druze of Lebanon.*
  ■ (of an action) carried out on the grounds of membership of a sect, denomination, or other group: *they are believed to be responsible for the recent sectarian killings of Catholics.* ■ rigidly following the doctrines of a sect or other group: *the sectarian Bolshevism advocated by Moscow.*
▶ noun a member of a sect.
  ■ a person who rigidly follows the doctrines of a sect or other group.
– DERIVATIVES **sectarianism** noun, **sectarianize** (also **-ise**) verb.

– ORIGIN mid 17th cent.: from **SECTARY** + **-AN**, reinforced by **SECT**.

sectary /ˈsɛktəri/ ▶ noun (pl. **-ies**) a member of a religious or political sect.
– ORIGIN mid 16th cent.: from modern Latin *sectarius* 'schismatic', from medieval Latin *sectarius* 'adherent', from Latin *secta* (see **SECT**).

section ▶ noun 1 any of the more or less distinct parts into which something is or may be divided or from which it is made up.
  ■ a relatively distinct part of a book, newspaper, statute, or other document. ■ N. Amer. a measure of land, equal to one square mile. ■ chiefly US a particular district of a town.
2 a distinct group within a larger body of people or things: *the non-parliamentary section of the party.*
  ■ a group of players of a family of instruments within an orchestra: *the brass section.* ■ [in names] a specified military unit: *a GHQ Signals Section.* ■ a subdivision of an army platoon. ■ Biology a secondary taxonomic category, especially a subgenus.
3 [mass noun] the cutting of a solid by or along a plane.
  ■ the shape resulting from cutting a solid along a plane. ■ [count noun] a representation of the internal structure of something as if it has been cut through vertically or horizontally. ■ [count noun] Surgery a separation by cutting. ■ [count noun] Biology a thin slice of plant or animal tissue prepared for microscopic examination.
▶ verb [with obj.] 1 divide into sections: *she began to section the grapefruit.*
  ■ (**section something off**) separate an area from a larger one: *parts of the curved balcony had been sectioned off with wrought-iron grilles.* ■ Biology cut (animal or plant tissue) into thin slices for microscopic examination. ■ Surgery divide by cutting: *it is common veterinary practice to section the nerves to the hoof of a limping horse.*
2 (often **be sectioned**) Brit. commit (someone) compulsorily to a psychiatric hospital in accordance with a section of a mental health act: *should she be sectioned and forced back into hospital?*
– DERIVATIVES **sectioned** adjective [often in combination] *a square-sectioned iron peg.*
– ORIGIN late Middle English (as a noun): from French *section* or Latin *sectio(n-)*, from *secare* 'to cut'. The verb dates from the early 19th cent.

sectional ▶ adjective of or relating to a section or subdivision of a larger whole: *a sectional championship.*
  ■ of or relating to a section or group within a community: *the chairman of the commission looked on sectional interests as a danger to the common good.* ■ of or relating to a view of the structure of an object in section: *sectional drawings.* ■ made or supplied in sections: *sectional sills, made from more than one piece of timber.*
▶ noun N. Amer. a sofa made in sections that can be used separately as chairs.
– DERIVATIVES **sectionalize** (also **-ise**) verb, **sectionally** adverb.

sectionalism ▶ noun [mass noun] restriction of interest to a narrow sphere; undue concern with local interests or petty distinctions at the expense of general well-being.
– DERIVATIVES **sectionalist** noun & adjective.

section house ▶ noun chiefly Brit. a building providing residential accommodation for unmarried police officers.

section mark ▶ noun a sign (§) used as a reference mark or to indicate a section of a book.

sector ▶ noun 1 an area or portion that is distinct from others.
  ■ a distinct part or branch of a nation's economy or society or of a sphere of activity such as education. ■ Military a subdivision of an area for military operations. ■ Computing a subdivision of a track on a magnetic disk.
2 the plane figure enclosed by two radii of a circle or ellipse and the arc between them.
3 a mathematical instrument consisting of two arms hinged at one end and marked with sines, tangents, etc. for making diagrams.
– DERIVATIVES **sectoral** adjective.
– ORIGIN late 16th cent. (in senses 2 and 3): from late Latin, a technical use of Latin *sector* 'cutter', from *sect-* 'cut off', from the verb *secare*.

sectorial /sɛkˈtɔːrɪəl/ ▶ adjective 1 of or like a sector: *sectorial boundaries.*
2 Zoology denoting a carnassial tooth, or a similar cutting tooth in mammals other than carnivores.

secular /ˈsɛkjʊlə/ ▶ **adjective 1** denoting attitudes, activities, or other things that have no religious or spiritual basis: *secular buildings | secular attitudes to death.* Contrasted with **SACRED**.
2 Christian Church (of clergy) not subject to or bound by religious rule; not belonging to or living in a monastic or other order. Contrasted with **REGULAR**.
3 Astronomy of or denoting slow changes in the motion of the sun or planets.
4 Economics (of a fluctuation or trend) occurring or persisting over an indefinitely long period: *there is evidence that the slump is not cyclical but secular.*
5 occurring once every century or similarly long period (used especially in reference to celebratory games in ancient Rome).
▶ **noun** a secular priest.
– DERIVATIVES **secularism** noun, **secularist** noun, **secularity** noun, **secularization** noun, **secularize** (also **-ise**) verb, **secularly** adverb.
– ORIGIN Middle English: senses 1 and 2 from Old French *seculer*, from Latin *saecularis*, from *saeculum* 'generation, age', used in Christian Latin to mean 'the world' (as opposed to the Church); senses 3, 4, and 5 (early 19th cent.) from Latin *saecularis* 'relating to an age or period'.

secular arm ▶ **noun** (**the secular arm**) the legal authority of the civil power as invoked by the Church to punish offenders.

secular humanism ▶ **noun** [mass noun] liberalism, with regard in particular to the belief that religion should not be taught or practised within a publicly funded education system.
– DERIVATIVES **secular humanist** noun.

secund /sɪˈkʌnd/ ▶ **adjective** Botany arranged on one side only (such as the flowers of lily of the valley).
– DERIVATIVES **secundly** adverb.
– ORIGIN late 18th cent.: from Latin *secundus* (see **SECOND**[1]).

secure ▶ **adjective** fixed or fastened so as not to give way, become loose, or be lost: *check to ensure that all nuts and bolts are secure.*
■ not subject to threat; certain to remain or continue safe and unharmed: *they are working to ensure that their market share remains* ***secure against*** *competition.* ■ protected against attack or other criminal activity: *the official said that no airport could be totally secure.* ■ (of a place of detention) having provisions against the escape of inmates: *a secure unit for young offenders.* ■ feeling safe, stable, and free from fear or anxiety: *everyone needs to have a home and to feel secure and wanted.* ■ [predic.] (**secure of**) dated feeling no doubts about attaining; certain to achieve: *she remained poised and complacent, secure of admiration.*
▶ **verb** [with obj.] fix or attach (something) firmly so that it cannot be moved or lost: *pins* ***secure*** *the handle* ***to*** *the main body.*
■ make (a door or container) hard to open; fasten or lock: *doors are likely to be well secured at night.* ■ protect against threats; make safe: *the government is concerned to* ***secure*** *the economy* ***against*** *too much foreign ownership.* ■ succeed in obtaining (something), especially with difficulty: *the division secured a major contract.* ■ seek to guarantee repayment of (a loan) by having a right to take possession of an asset in the event of non-payment: *a loan* ***secured on*** *your home.* ■ Surgery compress (a blood vessel) to prevent bleeding.
– PHRASES **secure arms** Military hold a rifle with the muzzle downward and the lock in the armpit to guard it from rain.
– DERIVATIVES **securable** adjective, **securely** adverb, **securement** noun.
– ORIGIN mid 16th cent. (in the sense 'feeling no apprehension'): from Latin *securus*, from *se-* 'without' + *cura* 'care'.

Securitate /sɪˌkjʊərɪˈtɑːteɪ/ the internal security force of Romania, set up in 1948 and officially disbanded during the revolution of December 1989.
– ORIGIN Romanian, 'Security'.

securitize (also **-ise**) ▶ **verb** [with obj.] [often as adj. **securitized**] convert (an asset, especially a loan) into marketable securities, typically for the purpose of raising cash by selling them to other investors: *the use of securitized debt as a major source of corporate finance.*
– DERIVATIVES **securitization** noun.

security ▶ **noun** (pl. **-ies**) **1** [mass noun] the state of being free from danger or threat: *the system is designed to provide maximum* ***security against*** *toxic spills | job security.*
■ the safety of a state or organization against criminal activity such as terrorism, theft, or espionage: *a matter of national security.* ■ procedures followed or measures taken to ensure such safety: *amid tight security the presidents met in the Colombian resort.* ■ the state of feeling safe, stable, and free from fear or anxiety: *this man could give the emotional security she needed.*
2 a thing deposited or pledged as a guarantee of the fulfilment of an undertaking or the repayment of a loan, to be forfeited in case of default.
3 (often **securities**) a certificate attesting credit, the ownership of stocks or bonds, or the right to ownership connected with tradable derivatives.
– PHRASES **on security of something** using something as a guarantee.
– ORIGIN late Middle English: from Old French *securite* or Latin *securitas*, from *securus* 'free from care' (see **SECURE**).

security blanket ▶ **noun 1** a blanket or other familiar object which is a comfort to someone, typically a child.
2 Brit. an official sanction imposed on information in order to maintain complete secrecy about something.

security check ▶ **noun** a verification of the identity and trustworthiness of someone such as a government employee, in order to maintain security.
■ a search of an area or of a person and their baggage for concealed weapons or bombs.

Security Council a permanent body of the United Nations seeking to maintain peace and security. It consists of fifteen members, of which five (China, France, the UK, the US, and Russia) are permanent and have the power of veto. The other members are elected for two-year terms.

security guard ▶ **noun** a person employed to protect something, especially a building, against intruders or damage.

security risk ▶ **noun** a person or situation which poses a possible threat to the security of something.

Security Service official name for **MI5**.

securocrat /səˈkjʊərə(ʊ)krat/ ▶ **noun** S. African a military or police officer who holds an influential position in the government; an advocate of the close involvement of military and police officers in government.
– ORIGIN blend of **SECURITY** and **BUREAUCRAT**.

sedan /sɪˈdan/ ▶ **noun 1** (also **sedan chair**) chiefly historical an enclosed chair for conveying one person, carried between horizontal poles by two porters.
2 chiefly N. Amer. a motor car for four or more people.
– ORIGIN perhaps an alteration of an Italian dialect word, based on Latin *sella* 'saddle', from *sedere* 'sit'.

Sedan, Battle of /sɪˈdan/ a battle fought in 1870 near the town of Sedan in NE France, in which the Prussian army defeated a smaller French army under Napoleon III, opening the way for a Prussian advance on Paris and marking the end of the French Second Empire.

sedate[1] ▶ **adjective** calm, dignified, and unhurried: *in the old days, business was carried on at a rather more sedate pace.*
■ quiet and rather dull: *sedate suburban domesticity.*
– DERIVATIVES **sedately** adverb, **sedateness** noun.
– ORIGIN late Middle English (originally as a medical term meaning 'not sore or painful', also 'calm, tranquil'): from Latin *sedatus*, past participle of *sedare* 'settle', from *sedere* 'sit'.

sedate[2] ▶ **verb** [with obj.] calm (someone) or make them sleep by administering a sedative drug: *she was heavily sedated.*
– ORIGIN 1960s: back-formation from **SEDATION**.

sedation ▶ **noun** [mass noun] the administering of a sedative drug to produce a state of calm or sleep: *he was distraught with grief and* ***under sedation.***
– ORIGIN mid 16th cent.: from French *sédation* or Latin *sedatio(n-)*, from *sedare* 'settle' (see **SEDATE**[1]).

sedative ▶ **adjective** promoting calm or inducing sleep: *the seeds have a sedative effect.*
▶ **noun** a drug taken for its calming or sleep-inducing effect.
– ORIGIN late Middle English: from Old French *sedatif* or medieval Latin *sedativus*, from Latin *sedat-* 'settled', from the verb *sedare* (see **SEDATE**[1]).

sedentary /ˈsɛd(ə)nt(ə)ri/ ▶ **adjective** (of a person) tending to spend much time seated; somewhat inactive.
■ (of work or a way of life) characterized by much sitting and little physical exercise. ■ (of a position) sitting; seated. ■ Zoology & Anthropology inhabiting the same locality throughout life; not migratory or nomadic. ■ Zoology (of an animal) sessile.
– DERIVATIVES **sedentarily** adverb, **sedentariness** noun.
– ORIGIN late 16th cent. (in the sense 'not migratory'): from French *sédentaire* or Latin *sedentarius*, from *sedere* 'sit'.

Seder /ˈseɪdə/ ▶ **noun** a Jewish ritual service and ceremonial dinner for the first night or first two nights of Passover.
– ORIGIN from Hebrew *sēḏer* 'order, procedure'.

sederunt /sɪˈdɪərənt, -ˈdɛː-/ ▶ **noun** (in Scotland) a sitting of an ecclesiastical assembly or other body.
– ORIGIN early 17th cent.: from Latin, literally '(the following persons) sat', from *sedere* 'sit'.

sedge ▶ **noun** a grass-like plant with triangular stems and inconspicuous flowers, growing typically in wet ground. Sedges are widely distributed throughout temperate and cold regions.
● Family Cyperaceae: *Carex* and other genera.
– DERIVATIVES **sedgy** adjective.
– ORIGIN Old English *secg*, of Germanic origin, from an Indo-European root shared by Latin *secare* 'to cut'.

Sedgemoor, Battle of /ˈsɛdʒmʊə, -mɔː/ a battle fought in 1685 on the plain of Sedgemoor in Somerset. The forces of the rebel Duke of Monmouth, who had landed in Dorset as champion of the Protestant cause and pretender to the throne, were decisively defeated by James II's troops.

sedge warbler ▶ **noun** a common migratory Eurasian songbird with streaky brown plumage, frequenting marshes and reed beds.
● *Acrocephalus schoenobaenus*, family Sylviidae.

Sedgwick /ˈsɛdʒwɪk/, Adam (1785–1873), English geologist. He specialized in the fossil record of rocks from North Wales, assigning the oldest of these to a period that he named the Cambrian.

sedilia /sɪˈdɪlɪə/ ▶ **plural noun** (sing. **sedile** /sɪˈdʌɪli/) a group of stone seats for clergy in the south chancel wall of a church, usually three in number and often canopied and decorated.
– ORIGIN late 18th cent.: from Latin, 'seat', from *sedere* 'sit'.

sediment ▶ **noun** [mass noun] matter that settles to the bottom of a liquid; dregs.
■ Geology particulate matter that is carried by water or wind and deposited on the surface of the land or the seabed, and may in time become consolidated into rock.
▶ **verb** [no obj.] settle as sediment.
■ (of a liquid) deposit a sediment. ■ [with obj.] deposit (something) as a sediment: *the DNA was sedimented by centrifugation* | [as adj. **sedimented**] *sedimented waste.*
– DERIVATIVES **sedimentation** noun.
– ORIGIN mid 16th cent.: from French *sédiment* or Latin *sedimentum* 'settling', from *sedere* 'sit'.

sedimentary ▶ **adjective** of or relating to sediment.
■ Geology (of rock) that has formed from sediment deposited by water or air.

sedimentation coefficient (also **sedimentation constant**) ▶ **noun** Biochemistry a quantity related to the size of a microscopic particle, equal to the terminal outward velocity of the particle when centrifuged in a fluid medium divided by the centrifugal force acting on it, expressed in units of time.

sedition ▶ **noun** [mass noun] conduct or speech inciting people to rebel against the authority of a state or monarch.
– ORIGIN late Middle English (in the sense 'violent strife'): from Old French, or from Latin *seditio(n-)*, from *sed-* 'apart' + *itio(n-)* 'going' (from the verb *ire*).

seditious ▶ **adjective** inciting or causing people to rebel against the authority of a state or monarch: *the letter was declared seditious.*
– DERIVATIVES **seditiously** adverb.
– ORIGIN late Middle English: from Old French *seditieux* or Latin *seditiosus*, from *seditio* 'mutinous separation' (see **SEDITION**).

seditious libel ▶ **noun** Law a published statement which is seditious.
■ [mass noun] the action or crime of publishing such a statement.

S

seduce ▶ **verb** [with obj.] attract (someone) to a belief or into a course of action that is inadvisable or foolhardy: *they should not be* **seduced into** *thinking that their success ruled out the possibility of a relapse.*
■ entice into sexual activity. ■ attract powerfully: *the melody seduces the ear with warm string tones.*
– DERIVATIVES **seducer** noun, **seducible** adjective.
– ORIGIN late 15th cent. (originally in the sense 'persuade (someone) to abandon their duty'): from Latin *seducere*, from *se-* 'away, apart' + *ducere* 'to lead'.

seduction ▶ **noun** [mass noun] the action of seducing someone: *if seduction doesn't work, she can play on his sympathy* | [count noun] *she was planning a seduction.*
■ [count noun] (often **seductions**) a tempting or attractive thing: *the seductions of the mainland.*
– ORIGIN early 16th cent.: from French *séduction* or Latin *seductio(n-)*, from *seducere* 'draw aside' (see **SEDUCE**).

seductive ▶ **adjective** tempting and attractive; enticing: *a seductive voice.*
– DERIVATIVES **seductively** adverb, **seductiveness** noun.
– ORIGIN mid 18th cent.: from **SEDUCTION**, on the pattern of pairs such as *induction, inductive.*

seductress ▶ **noun** a woman who seduces someone, especially one who entices a man into sexual activity.
– ORIGIN early 19th cent.: from obsolete *seductor* 'male seducer', from *seducere* (see **SEDUCE**).

sedulous /ˈsɛdjʊləs/ ▶ **adjective** (of a person or action) showing dedication and diligence: *he watched himself with the most sedulous care.*
– DERIVATIVES **sedulity** /sɪˈdjuːlɪti/ noun, **sedulously** adverb, **sedulousness** noun.
– ORIGIN mid 16th cent.: from Latin *sedulus* 'zealous' + **-OUS**.

sedum /ˈsiːdəm/ ▶ **noun** a widely distributed fleshy-leaved plant with small star-shaped yellow, pink, or white flowers, grown as an ornamental.
● Genus *Sedum*, family Crassulaceae: many species, including the stonecrops.
– ORIGIN from modern Latin, denoting a houseleek.

see[1] ▶ **verb** (**sees, seeing**; past **saw**; past participle **seen**) [with obj.] **1** perceive with the eyes; discern visually: *in the distance she could see the blue sea* | [no obj.] *Andrew couldn't see out of his left eye* | figurative *I can't* **see into** *the future.*
■ [with clause] be or become aware of something from observation or from a written or other visual source: *I see from your appraisal report that you have asked for training.* ■ be a spectator of (a film, game, or other entertainment); watch: *I went to see King Lear at the Old Vic.* ■ visit (a place) for the first time: *see Alaska in style.* ■ [in imperative] refer to (a specified source) for further information (used as a direction in a text): *elements are usually classified as metals or non-metals (see chapter 11).* ■ experience or witness (an event or situation): *I shall not live to see it* | [with obj. and complement] *I can't bear to see you so unhappy.* ■ be the time or setting of (something): *the 1970s saw the beginning of a technological revolution.* ■ observe without being able to affect: *they see their rights being taken away.* ■ (**see something in**) find good or attractive qualities in (someone): *I don't know what I see in you.*
2 discern or deduce mentally after reflection or from information; understand: *I can't see any other way to treat it* | [with clause] *I saw that perhaps he was right* | *she could see what Rhoda meant.*
■ [with clause] ascertain after inquiring, considering, or discovering an outcome: *I'll go along to the club and see if I can get a game.* ■ [with obj. and adverbial] regard in a specified way: *he saw himself as a good teacher* | *you and I see things differently.* ■ foresee; view or predict as a possibility: *I can't see him earning any more anywhere else.* ■ used to ascertain or express comprehension, agreement, or continued attention, or to emphasize that an earlier prediction was correct: *it has to be the answer, don't you see?* | *see, I told you I'd come.*
3 meet (someone one knows) socially or by chance: *I went to see Caroline* | *I saw Colin last night.*
■ meet regularly as a boyfriend or girlfriend: *some guy she was seeing was messing her around.* ■ consult (a specialist or professional): *you may need to see a solicitor.* ■ give an interview or consultation to (someone): *the doctor will see you now.*
4 [with obj. and adverbial of direction] escort or conduct (someone) to a specified place: *don't bother seeing me out.*
■ [no obj.] (**see to**) attend to; provide for the wants of: *I'll see to Dad's tea.* ■ [no obj.] ensure: *Lucy saw to it that everyone got enough to eat and drink* | [with clause] *see that no harm comes to him.*
5 (in poker or brag) equal the bet of (an opponent) and require them to reveal their cards in order to determine who has won the hand.
– PHRASES **as far as I can see** to the best of my understanding or belief. **as I see it** in my opinion. **be seeing things** see **THING**. **(I'll) be seeing you** another way of saying ***see you***. **have seen better days** have declined from former prosperity or good condition: *this part of South London has seen better days.* **have seen it all before** be very worldly or very familiar with a particular situation. **let me see** said as an appeal for time to think before speaking: *Let me see, how old is he now?* **see a man about a dog** humorous said euphemistically when leaving to go to the toilet or keep an undisclosed appointment. **see eye to eye**, **see fit**, etc. see **EYE**, **FIT**[1], etc. **see here!** said to give emphasis to a statement or command or to express a protest: *now see here, you're going to get it back for me!* **see one's way clear to do** (or **doing**) **something** find that it is possible or convenient to do something (often used in polite requests). **see someone coming** recognize a person who can be fooled or deceived. **see something coming** foresee or be prepared for an event, typically an unpleasant one. **see someone damned first** Brit. informal said when refusing categorically and with hostility to do what a person wants. **see someone right** Brit. informal make sure that a person is appropriately rewarded or looked after. **see sense** (or **reason**) realize that one is wrong and start acting sensibly. **see the back of** Brit. informal be rid of (an unwanted person or thing): *we were always glad to see the back of her.* **see you (later)** informal said when parting from someone. **we'll see about that** said when angrily contradicting or challenging a claim or assertion: *Oh, you think it's funny, do you? We'll see about that!*
– DERIVATIVES **seeable** adjective.
– ORIGIN Old English *sēon*, of Germanic origin; related to Dutch *zien* and German *sehen*, perhaps from an Indo-European root shared by Latin *sequi* 'follow'.
▶ **see about** attend to; deal with: *he had gone to see about a job he had heard of.*
see after chiefly US or archaic take care of; look after.
see something of spend a specified amount of time with (someone) socially: *we saw a lot of the Bakers.* ■ spend some time in (a place): *I want to see something of those countries.*
see someone off 1 accompany a person who is leaving to their point of departure: *they came to the station to see him off.* **2** Brit. repel an invader or intruder: *the dogs saw them off in no time.* ■ informal deal with the threat posed by; get the better of: *they saw off Cambridge in the FA Cup.*
see someone out Brit. (of an article) last longer than the remainder of someone's life: *no point in fixing the gate, it'll see me out.*
see something out Brit. come to the end of a period of time or undertaking: *I could well see out my career in Italy.*
see over tour and examine (a building or site): *Bridget asked if he'd like to see over the house.*
see through not be deceived by; detect the true nature of: *he can see through her lies and deceptions.*
see someone through support a person for the duration of a difficult time.
see something through persist with an undertaking until it is completed.

see[2] ▶ **noun** the place in which a cathedral church stands, identified as the seat of authority of a bishop or archbishop.
– ORIGIN Middle English: from Anglo-Norman French *sed*, from Latin *sedes* 'seat', from *sedere* 'sit'.

seed ▶ **noun 1** a flowering plant's unit of reproduction, capable of developing into another such plant.
■ [mass noun] a quantity of these: *grass seed* | *you can grow artichokes from seed.* ■ figurative the cause or latent beginning of a feeling, process, or condition: *the conversation sowed a tiny seed of doubt in his mind.* ■ [mass noun] archaic (chiefly in biblical use) a person's offspring or descendants. ■ [mass noun] a man's semen. ■ (also **seed crystal**) a small crystal introduced into a liquid to act as a nucleus for crystallization. ■ a small container for radioactive material placed in body tissue during radiotherapy.
2 any of a number of stronger competitors in a sports tournament who have been assigned a specified position in an ordered list with the aim of ensuring that they do not play each other in the early rounds: *he knocked the top seed out of the championships.*
▶ **verb 1** [with obj.] sow (land) with seeds: *the shoreline is seeded with a special grass.*
■ sow (a particular kind of seed) on or in the ground. ■ figurative cause (something) to begin to develop or grow: *his interest in public service was seeded when he was a child.* ■ place a crystal or crystalline substance in (something) in order to cause crystallization or condensation (especially in a cloud to produce rain).
2 [no obj.] (of a plant) produce or drop seeds: *mulches encourage many plants to seed freely.*
■ (**seed itself**) (of a plant) reproduce itself by means of its own seeds: *feverfew will seed itself readily.*
3 [with obj.] remove the seeds from (vegetables or fruit): *stem and seed the chillies.*
4 [with obj.] give (a competitor) the status of seed in a tournament: [with obj. and complement] *Jeff Tarango, seeded five, was defeated by fellow American Todd Witsken.*
– PHRASES **go** (or **run**) **to seed** (of a plant) cease flowering as the seeds develop. ■ deteriorate in condition, strength, or efficiency: *Mark knows he has allowed himself to go to seed.*
– ORIGIN Old English *sǣd*, of Germanic origin; related to Dutch *zaad*, German *Saat*, also to the verb **sow**[1].

seedbed ▶ **noun** a bed of fine soil in which seedlings are germinated.

seed cake ▶ **noun** [mass noun] cake containing caraway seeds as flavouring.

seed capital ▶ **noun** see **SEED MONEY**.

seed coat ▶ **noun** Botany the protective outer coat of a seed.

seedcorn ▶ **noun** [mass noun] good-quality corn kept for seed.
■ figurative Brit. assets set aside for the generation of profit or other benefit in the future.

seedeater ▶ **noun** a finch or related songbird that feeds mainly on seeds, in particular:
● a small American bunting (genus *Sporophila*, subfamily Emberizinae, family Emberizidae). ● an African finch related to the canary (genus *Serinus*, family Fringillidae).

seeded ▶ **adjective 1** [in combination] (of a plant or fruit) having a seed or seeds of a specified kind or number: *a single-seeded fruit.*
■ (of land or an area of ground) having been sown with seed: *seeded lawns.* ■ Heraldry (of a flower) having seeds of a specified tincture.
2 (of a fruit or vegetable) having had the seeds removed: *seeded, chopped tomatoes.*
3 given the status of seed in a sports tournament: *Italy is one of the eight seeded teams.*

seeder ▶ **noun 1** a machine for sowing seed mechanically.
2 a plant that produces seeds in a particular way or under particular conditions: [in combination] *a beautiful, hardy annual self-seeder.*

seed fern ▶ **noun** another term for **PTERIDOSPERM**.

seed head ▶ **noun** a flower head in seed.

seed leaf ▶ **noun** Botany a cotyledon.

seedless ▶ **adjective** denoting a fruit that has no seeds: *seedless grapes.*

seedling ▶ **noun** a young plant, especially one raised from seed and not from a cutting.

seed-lip ▶ **noun** chiefly historical a basket for holding seed, used when sowing by hand.

seed money ▶ **noun** [mass noun] money allocated to initiate a project.

seed pearl ▶ **noun** a very small pearl.

seed plot ▶ **noun** old-fashioned term for **SEEDBED**.

seed potato ▶ **noun** a potato that is planted and used for the production of seeds.

seedsman ▶ **noun** (pl. **-men**) a person who deals in seeds as a profession.

seed-snipe ▶ **noun** a South American bird resembling a small partridge, with mainly brown plumage.
● Family Thinocoridae: two genera and four species.

seed time ▶ **noun** the sowing season.

seedy ▶ **adjective** (**seedier, seediest**) **1** sordid and disreputable: *his seedy affair with a soft-porn starlet.*
■ shabby and squalid: *an increasingly seedy and dilapidated property.*
2 dated unwell: *she felt weak and seedy.*
– DERIVATIVES **seedily** adverb, **seediness** noun.

Seeger /ˈsiːɡə/, Pete (b.1919), American folk

S

musician and songwriter. Seeger was a prominent figure in the American folk revival. Notable songs: 'If I Had a Hammer' (*c.*1949) and 'Where Have All the Flowers Gone?' (1956).

seeing ▶ **conjunction** because; since: *seeing that I'm awake, I might as well come with you.*

▶ **noun** [mass noun] the action of seeing someone or something.

■Astronomy the quality of observed images as determined by atmospheric conditions.

– PHRASES **seeing is believing** proverb you need to see something before you can accept that it really exists or occurs.

Seeing Eye dog ▶ **noun** trademark, chiefly N. Amer. a guide dog trained to lead the blind.

seek ▶ **verb** (past and past participle **sought**) [with obj.] attempt to find (something): *they came here to seek shelter from biting winter winds.*

■attempt or desire to obtain or achieve (something): *the new regime sought his extradition* | [no obj., with infinitive] *her parents had never sought to interfere with her freedom.* ■ ask for (something) from someone: *he* **sought** *help* **from** *the police.* ■ (**seek someone/thing out**) search for and find someone or something: *it's his job to seek out new customers.* ■ archaic go to (a place): *I sought my bedroom each night to brood over it.*

– PHRASES **seek dead** Brit. used to instruct a retriever to go and look for game that has been shot. **seek one's fortune** travel somewhere in the hope of achieving wealth and success. **to seek** archaic lacking; not yet found: *the end she knew, the means were to seek.* ■ (**far to seek**) out of reach; a long way off.

– DERIVATIVES **seeker** noun [often in combination] *a pleasure-seeker* | *a job-seeker.*

– ORIGIN Old English *sēcan*, of Germanic origin; related to Dutch *zieken* and German *suchen*, from an Indo-European root shared by Latin *sagire* 'perceive by scent'.

seek time ▶ **noun** Computing the time taken for a disk drive to locate the area on the disk where the data to be read is stored.

seel /siːl/ ▶ **verb** [with obj.] archaic close (a person's eyes); prevent (someone) from seeing: *the wise Gods seel our eyes in our own filth.*

– ORIGIN late 15th cent. (originally a term in falconry meaning 'stitch shut the eyelids of (a hawk)'): from French *ciller*, or medieval Latin *ciliare*, from Latin *cilium* 'eyelid'.

seem ▶ **verb** [no obj.] give the impression or sensation of being something or having a particular quality: [with complement] *Dawn seemed annoyed* | [with infinitive] *there seems to be plenty to eat* | [with clause] *it seemed that he was determined to oppose her.*

■[with infinitive] used to make a statement or description of one's thoughts, feelings, or actions less assertive or forceful: *I seem to remember giving you very precise instructions.* ■ (**cannot seem to do something**) be unable to do something, despite having tried: *he couldn't seem to remember his lines.* ■ [with clause] (**it seems** or **it would seem**) used to suggest in a cautious, guarded, or polite way that something is true or a fact: *it would seem that he has been fooling us all.*

– ORIGIN Middle English (also in the sense 'suit, befit, be appropriate'): from Old Norse *sœma* 'to honour', from *sœmr* 'fitting'.

seeming ▶ **adjective** appearing to be real or true, but not necessarily being so; apparent: *Ellen's seeming indifference to the woman's fate.*

■[in combination] giving the impression of having a specified quality: *an angry-seeming man.*

▶ **noun** [mass noun] poetic/literary the outward appearance or aspect of someone or something, especially when considered as deceptive or as distinguished from reality: *that dissidence between inward reality and outward seeming.*

seemingly ▶ **adverb** so as to give the impression of having a certain quality; apparently: *a seemingly competent and well-organized person.*

■[sentence adverb] according to the facts as one knows them; as far as one knows: *it's touch and go, seemingly, and she's asking for you.*

seemly ▶ **adjective** conforming to accepted notions of propriety or good taste; decorous: *I felt it was not seemly to observe too closely.*

– DERIVATIVES **seemliness** noun.

– ORIGIN Middle English: from Old Norse *sœmiligr*, from *sœmr* 'fitting' (see **SEEM**).

seen past participle of **SEE**[1].

See of Rome ▶ **noun** another term for **HOLY SEE**.

seep ▶ **verb** [no obj., with adverbial of direction] (of a liquid) flow or leak slowly through porous material or small holes: *water began to seep through the soles of his boots.*

▶ **noun** N. Amer. a place where petroleum or water oozes slowly out of the ground.

– ORIGIN late 18th cent.: perhaps a dialect form of Old English *sīpian* 'to soak'.

seepage ▶ **noun** [mass noun] the slow escape of a liquid or gas through porous material or small holes.

■the quantity of liquid or gas that seeps out.

seer[1] /ˈsiːə, sɪə/ ▶ **noun 1** a person of supposed supernatural insight who sees visions of the future.

■an expert who provides forecasts of the economic or political future: *our seers have grown gloomier about prospects for growth.*

2 [usu. in combination] chiefly archaic a person who sees something specified: *a seer of the future* | *ghost-seers.*

– ORIGIN Middle English: from **SEE**[1] + **-ER**[1].

seer[2] /sɪə/ ▶ **noun** (in the Indian subcontinent) a varying unit of weight (about one kilogram) or liquid measure (about one litre).

– ORIGIN from Hindi *ser.*

seersucker ▶ **noun** [mass noun] a printed cotton or synthetic fabric that has a surface consisting of puckered and flat sections, typically in a striped pattern.

– ORIGIN early 18th cent.: from Persian *šir o šakar*, literally 'milk and sugar', (by transference) 'striped cotton garment'.

see-saw ▶ **noun** a long plank balanced in the middle on a fixed support, on each end of which children sit and swing up and down by pushing the ground alternately with their feet.

■figurative a situation characterized by rapid, repeated changes from one state or condition to another: *the emotional see-saw of a first love affair* | [as modifier] *see-saw interest rates.*

▶ **verb** [no obj.] change rapidly and repeatedly from one position, situation, or condition to another and back again: *the market see-sawed as rumours spread of an imminent cabinet reshuffle.*

■[with obj.] cause (something) to move back and forth or up and down rapidly and repeatedly: *Sybil see-sawed the car back and forth.*

– ORIGIN mid 17th cent. (originally used by sawyers as a rhythmical refrain): reduplication of the verb **SAW**[1] (symbolic of the sawing motion).

seethe ▶ **verb** [no obj.] (of a liquid) bubble up as a result of being boiled: *the brew foamed and seethed.*

■[with obj.] archaic cook (food) by boiling it in a liquid: *others were cut into joints and seethed in cauldrons made of the animal's own skins.* ■ (of a river or the sea) foam as if it were boiling; be turbulent: *the grey ocean seethed.* ■ [no obj.] (of a person) be filled with intense but unexpressed anger: *inwardly he was seething at the slight to his authority.* ■ (of a place) be crowded with people or things moving about in a rapid or hectic way: *the entire cellar was* **seething with** *spiders* | *the village* **seethed with** *life.* ■ [with adverbial of direction] (of a crowd of people) move in a rapid or hectic way: *we cascaded down the stairs and seethed across the station* | [as adj. **seething**] *the seething mass of commuters.*

– ORIGIN Old English *sēothan* 'make or keep boiling', of Germanic origin; related to Dutch *zieden.*

see-through ▶ **adjective** (especially of clothing) translucent: *this shirt's a bit see-through when it's wet.*

Sefer /ˈseɪfə/ ▶ **noun** (pl. **Sifrei**) Judaism a book of Hebrew religious literature.

■(usu. **Sefer Torah** /ˈtɔːrə, ˈtəʊrə/) a scroll containing the Torah or Pentateuch.

– ORIGIN from Hebrew *sēper tōrāh* 'book of (the) Law'.

segment /ˈsɛgm(ə)nt/ ▶ **noun 1** each of the parts into which something is or may be divided.

■a portion of time allocated to a particular broadcast item on radio or television. ■ a separate broadcast item, typically one of a number that make up a particular programme. ■ Phonetics the smallest distinct part of a spoken utterance, especially with regard to vowel and consonant sounds rather than stress or intonation. ■ Zoology each of the series of similar anatomical units of which the body and appendages of some animals are composed, such as the visible rings of an earthworm's body.

2 Geometry a part of a figure cut off by a line or plane intersecting it, in particular:

■the part of a circle enclosed between an arc and a chord. ■ the part of a line included between two points. ■ the part of a sphere cut off by any plane not passing through the centre.

▶ **verb** /usually sɛgˈmɛnt/ [with obj.] divide (something) into separate parts or sections: *the unemployed are segmented into two groups.*

■[no obj.] divide into separate parts or sections: *the market is beginning to segment into a number of well-defined categories.* ■ [no obj.] Embryology (of a cell) undergo cleavage; divide into many cells.

– DERIVATIVES **segmentary** adjective, **segmentation** noun.

– ORIGIN late 16th cent. (as a term in geometry): from Latin *segmentum*, from *secare* 'to cut'. The verb dates from the mid 19th cent.

segmental ▶ **adjective 1** composed of separate parts or sections.

■Phonetics denoting or relating to the division of speech into segments.

2 Architecture denoting or of the form of an arch the curved part of which forms a shallow arc of a circle, less than a semicircle.

– DERIVATIVES **segmentalization** noun, **segmentalize** (also **-ise**) verb, **segmentally** adverb.

segmented /ˈsɛgm(ə)ntɪd, sɛgˈmɛntɪd/ ▶ **adjective** consisting of or divided into segments: *segmented labour markets.*

■Zoology (of an animal's body or appendage) formed of a longitudinal series of similar parts.

Segovia[1] /sɪˈgəʊvɪə, Spanish seˈɣoβja/ a city in north central Spain, north-east of Madrid; pop. 58,060 (1991). Taken by the Moors in the 8th century, it was reclaimed by the king of Castile, Alfonso VI (d.1109), in 1079.

Segovia[2] /sɪˈgəʊvɪə, Spanish seˈɣoβja/, Andrés (1893–1987), Spanish guitarist and composer. He was largely responsible for the revival of the classical guitar, elevating it to use as a concert instrument and making a large number of transcriptions of classical music to increase the repertoire of the instrument.

segregate[1] /ˈsɛgrɪgeɪt/ ▶ **verb** [with obj.] (usu. **be segregated**) set apart from the rest or from each other; isolate or divide: *handicapped people should not be segregated from the rest of society.*

■separate or divide (people, activities, or institutions) along racial, sexual, or religious lines: *blacks were segregated in churches, schools, and colleges* | [as adj. **segregated**] *segregated education systems.* ■ [no obj.] Genetics (of pairs of alleles) be separated at meiosis and transmitted independently via separate gametes.

– DERIVATIVES **segregable** adjective, **segregative** adjective.

– ORIGIN mid 16th cent.: from Latin *segregat-* 'separated from the flock', from the verb *segregare*, from *se-* 'apart' + *grex, greg-* 'flock'.

segregate[2] /ˈsɛgrɪgət/ ▶ **noun 1** Genetics an allele that has undergone segregation.

2 Botany a species within an aggregate.

– ORIGIN late 19th cent.: from Latin *segregatus* 'separate, isolated', past participle of *segregare* (see **SEGREGATE**[1]).

segregation ▶ **noun** [mass noun] the action or state of setting someone or something apart from other people or things or being set apart: *the segregation of pupils with learning difficulties.*

■the enforced separation of different racial groups in a country, community, or establishment: *an official policy of racial segregation.* ■ Genetics the separation of pairs of alleles at meiosis and their independent transmission via separate gametes.

– DERIVATIVES **segregational** adjective, **segregationist** adjective & noun (in the racial sense).

segue /ˈsɛgweɪ/ ▶ **verb** (**segues**, **segued**, **seguing**) [no obj., with adverbial] (in music and film) move without interruption from one song, melody, or scene to another: *allowing one song to segue into the next.*

▶ **noun** an uninterrupted transition from one piece of music or film scene to another.

– ORIGIN Italian, literally 'follows'.

seguidilla /ˌsɛgɪˈdiːljə, -ˈdiːjə/ ▶ **noun** a Spanish dance in triple time.

– ORIGIN mid 18th cent.: Spanish, from *seguida* 'sequence', from *seguir* 'follow'.

Seguridad /sɪˌgʊərɪˈdad, Spanish seˌɣuriˈðað/ ▶ **noun** the Spanish security service.

– ORIGIN Spanish, literally 'Security'.

Sehnsucht /ˈzeɪnzuːxt, German ˈzeːnzʊxt/ ▶ **noun** [mass noun] poetic/literary yearning; wistful longing.

– ORIGIN German.

sei ▶ **noun** another term for **SEI WHALE**.

seicento /seɪˈtʃɛntəʊ/ ▶ **noun** [mass noun] [often as modifier] the style of Italian art and literature of the 17th century: *Florentine seicento painting.*

S

– DERIVATIVES **seicentist** noun.
– ORIGIN Italian, '600', shortened from *mille seicento* '1600', used with reference to the years 1600–99.

seiche /seɪʃ/ ▶ **noun** a temporary disturbance or oscillation in the water level of a lake or partially enclosed body of water, especially one caused by changes in atmospheric pressure.
– ORIGIN mid 19th cent.: from Swiss French, perhaps from German *Seiche* 'sinking (of water)'.

seidel /ˈzʌɪd(ə)l/ ▶ **noun** dated a beer mug or glass.
▪ the contents of such a vessel: *I drank **a seidel of** beer.*
– ORIGIN early 20th cent.: from German *Seidel*, originally denoting a measure between a third and a half of a litre.

Seidlitz powder /ˈsɛdlɪts/ ▶ **noun** a laxative preparation containing tartaric acid, sodium potassium tartrate, and sodium bicarbonate which effervesces when mixed with water.
– ORIGIN late 18th cent.: named with reference to the mineral water of *Seidlitz*, a village in Bohemia.

seif /siːf, seɪf/ (in full **seif dune**) ▶ **noun** a sand dune in the form of a long narrow ridge.
– ORIGIN early 20th cent.: from Arabic *sayf* 'sword' (because of the shape).

seigneur /seɪˈnjəː/ (also **seignior** /ˈseɪnjə/) ▶ **noun** chiefly historical a feudal lord; the lord of a manor.
– DERIVATIVES **seigneurial** adjective.
– ORIGIN late 16th cent.: from Old French, from Latin *senior* 'older, elder'.

seigniorage /ˈseɪnjərɪdʒ/ (also **seignorage**) ▶ **noun** [mass noun] profit made by a government by issuing currency, especially the difference between the face value of coins and their production costs.
▪ historical the Crown's right to a percentage on bullion brought to a mint for coining. ▪ [count noun] historical a thing claimed by a sovereign or feudal superior as a prerogative.
– ORIGIN late Middle English: from Old French *seignorage*, from *seigneur* (see **SEIGNEUR**).

seigniory /ˈseɪnjəri/ (also **seigneury**) ▶ **noun** (pl. **-ies**) a feudal lordship; the position, authority, or domain of a feudal lord.
– ORIGIN Middle English: from Old French *seignorie*, from *seigneur* (see **SEIGNEUR**).

Seikan Tunnel /ˈseɪkan/ the world's longest underwater tunnel, linking the Japanese islands of Hokkaido and Honshu under the Tsugaru Strait. Completed in 1988, the tunnel is 51.7 km (32.3 miles) in length.

Seine /seɪn, French sɛn/ a river of northern France. Rising north of Dijon, it flows north-westwards for 761 km (473 miles), through the cities of Troyes and Paris to the English Channel near Le Havre.

seine /seɪn/ ▶ **noun** (also **seine net**) a fishing net which hangs vertically in the water with floats at the top and weights at the bottom edge, the ends being drawn together to encircle the fish.
▶ **verb** [with obj.] fish (an area) with a seine: *the fishermen then seine the weir.*
▪ catch (fish) with a seine: *they seine whitefish and salmon.*
– DERIVATIVES **seiner** noun.
– ORIGIN Old English *segne*, of West Germanic origin, via Latin from Greek *sagēnē*; reinforced in Middle English by Old French *saine*.

seise ▶ **verb** see **SEIZE** (sense 3).

seisin /ˈsiːzɪn/ (also **seizin**) ▶ **noun** [mass noun] Law possession of land by freehold.
▪ Brit. historical possession, especially of land: *Richard Fitzhugh did not take **seisin of** his lands until 1480.*
– ORIGIN Middle English: from Old French *seisine*, from *saisir* 'seize'.

seismic /ˈsʌɪzmɪk/ ▶ **adjective** of or relating to earthquakes or other vibrations of the earth and its crust.
▪ relating to or denoting geological surveying methods involving vibrations produced artificially by explosions. ▪ figurative of enormous proportions or effect: *there are seismic pressures threatening American society.*
– DERIVATIVES **seismical** adjective, **seismically** adverb.
– ORIGIN mid 19th cent.: from Greek *seismos* 'earthquake' (from *seien* 'to shake') + **-IC**.

seismicity /sʌɪzˈmɪsɪti/ ▶ **noun** [mass noun] Geology the occurrence or frequency of earthquakes in a region: *the high seismicity of the area.*

seismic reflection ▶ **noun** [mass noun] Geology the reflection of elastic waves at boundaries between different rock formations, especially as a technique for prospecting or research.

seismic refraction ▶ **noun** [mass noun] Geology the refraction of elastic waves on passing between formations of rock having different seismic velocities.

seismic velocity ▶ **noun** Geology the velocity of propagation of elastic waves in a particular rock.

seismic wave ▶ **noun** Geology an elastic wave in the earth produced by an earthquake or other means.

seismo- ▶ **combining form** of an earthquake; relating to earthquakes: *seismograph.*
– ORIGIN from Greek *seismos* 'earthquake'.

seismogram /ˈsʌɪzmə(ʊ)gram/ ▶ **noun** a record produced by a seismograph.

seismograph /ˈsʌɪzmə(ʊ)grɑːf/ ▶ **noun** an instrument that measures and records details of earthquakes, such as force and duration.
– DERIVATIVES **seismographic** adjective, **seismographical** adjective.

seismology /sʌɪzˈmɒlədʒi/ ▶ **noun** [mass noun] the branch of science concerned with earthquakes and related phenomena.
– DERIVATIVES **seismological** adjective, **seismologically** adverb, **seismologist** noun.

seismometer /sʌɪzˈmɒmɪtə/ ▶ **noun** another term for **SEISMOGRAPH**.

seismosaurus /ˈsʌɪzmə(ʊ)sɔːrəs/ ▶ **noun** a huge late Jurassic dinosaur known from only a few bones, probably the longest ever animal with a length of up to 35–45 m, and one of the heaviest at up to 100 metric tons.
• Genus *Seismosaurus*, infraorder Sauropoda, order Saurischia.
– ORIGIN modern Latin, from **SEISMO-** 'of an earthquake' + *sauros* 'lizard'.

sei whale /seɪ/ ▶ **noun** a small rorqual with dark steely-grey skin and white grooves on the belly.
• *Balaenoptera borealis*, family Balaenopteridae.
– ORIGIN early 20th cent.: from Norwegian *sejhval*.

seiza /ˈseɪzə/ ▶ **noun** [in sing.] an upright kneeling position which is traditionally used in Japan in meditation and as part of the preparation in martial arts.
– ORIGIN Japanese, from *sei* 'correct' + *za* 'sitting'.

seize ▶ **verb 1** [with obj.] take hold of suddenly and forcibly: *she jumped up and seized his arm | she **seized hold of** the door handle.*
▪ capture (a place) using force: *army rebels seized an air force base.* ▪ assume (power or control) by force: *the current President seized power in a coup.* ▪ (of the police or another authority) take possession of (something) by warrant or legal right; confiscate; impound: *police in Rotterdam have seized 726 lb of cocaine.* ▪ take (an opportunity or initiative) eagerly and decisively: *he seized his chance to attack as Delaney hesitated.* ▪ (of a feeling or pain) affect (someone) suddenly or acutely: *he was seized by the most dreadful fear.* ▪ strongly appeal to or attract (the imagination or attention): *the story of the king's escape seized the public imagination.* ▪ formal understand (something) quickly or clearly: *he always strains to seize the most sombre truths.*
2 [no obj.] (of a machine with moving parts or a moving part in a machine) become stuck or jammed: *the engine **seized up** after only three weeks.*
3 (also **seise**) (**be seized of**) English Law be in legal possession of: *the court is currently seized of custody applications.*
▪ historical have or receive freehold possession of (property): *any person who is seized of land has a protected interest in that land.* ▪ be aware or informed of: *the judge was fully seized of the point.*
4 Nautical, archaic fasten or attach (someone or something) to something by binding with turns of rope.
– PHRASES **seize the day** make the most of the present moment. [ORIGIN: see **CARPE DIEM**.]
– DERIVATIVES **seizable** adjective, **seizer** noun.
– ORIGIN Middle English: from Old French *seizir* 'give seisin', from medieval Latin *sacire*, in the phrase *ad proprium sacire* 'claim as one's own', from a Germanic base meaning 'procedure'.
▶ **seize on/upon** take eager advantage of (something); exploit for one's own purposes: *the government has eagerly seized on the evidence to deny any link between deprivation and crime.*

seizin ▶ **noun** variant spelling of **SEISIN**.

seizing ▶ **noun** Nautical, archaic a length of cord or rope used for fastening or tying.

seizure ▶ **noun 1** [mass noun] the action of capturing someone or something using force: *the seizure of the Assembly building | the Nazi seizure of power.*
▪ the action of confiscating or impounding property by warrant of legal right.
2 a sudden attack of illness, especially a stroke or an epileptic fit: *the patient **had a seizure**.*

sejant /ˈsiːdʒ(ə)nt/ ▶ **adjective** [usu. postpositive] Heraldry (of an animal) sitting upright.
– ORIGIN late 15th cent.: alteration of an Old French variant of *seant* 'sitting', from the verb *seoir*, from Latin *sedere* 'sit'.

Sejm /seɪm/ (also **Seym**) ▶ **noun** the lower house of parliament in Poland.
– ORIGIN Polish.

Sekhmet /ˈsɛkmɛt/ Egyptian Mythology a ferocious lioness-goddess, counterpart of the gentle cat-goddess Bastet and wife of Ptah at Memphis.

Sekt /zɛkt/ ▶ **noun** [mass noun] a German sparkling white wine.
– ORIGIN German.

selachian /sɪˈleɪkɪən/ Zoology ▶ **noun** an elasmobranch fish of a group that comprises the sharks and dogfishes.
• The former group Selachii, subclass Elasmobranchii: now treated as one, two, or three superorders.
▶ **adjective** of or relating to the selachians.
– ORIGIN mid 19th cent.: from modern Latin *Selachii* (from Greek *selakhos* 'shark') + **-AN**.

seladang /səˈlɑːdaŋ/ ▶ **noun** another term for **GAUR**.
– ORIGIN early 19th cent.: from Malay.

selaginella /ˌsɛlədʒɪˈnɛlə, sɪˌladʒɪˈnɛlə/ ▶ **noun** a creeping moss-like plant of a genus which includes the lesser clubmosses.
• Genus *Selaginella*, family Selaginellaceae.
– ORIGIN modern Latin, diminutive of Latin *selago* 'clubmoss'.

selah /ˈsiːlə, -lɑː/ ▶ **exclamation** (in the Bible) occurring frequently at the end of a verse in Psalms and Habakkuk, probably as a musical direction.
– ORIGIN from Hebrew *selāh*.

Selangor /səˈlaŋə/ a state of Malaysia, on the west coast of the Malay Peninsula; capital, Shah Alam.

Selcraig /ˈsɛlkreɪg/ see **SELKIRK**.

seldom ▶ **adverb** not often; rarely: *Islay is seldom visited by tourists | he was seldom absent |* [in combination] *an old seldom-used church.*
▶ **adjective** [attrib.] dated not common; infrequent: *a great but seldom pleasure.*
– ORIGIN Old English *seldan*, of Germanic origin; related to Dutch *zelden* and German *selten*, from a base meaning 'strange, wonderful'.

select ▶ **verb** [with obj.] carefully choose as being the best or most suitable: *children must select their GCSE subjects |* [with obj. and infinitive] *he has been selected to take part |* [no obj.] *you can **select from** a range of quality products.*
▪ [no obj.] (**select for/against**) Biology (in terms of evolution) determine whether (a characteristic or organism) will survive: *a phenotype can be **selected against**.* ▪ use a mouse or keystrokes to mark (something) on a computer screen for a particular operation.
▶ **adjective** (of a group of people or things) carefully chosen from a larger number as being the best or most valuable: *he joined his select team of young Intelligence operatives.*
▪ (of a place or group of people) only used by or consisting of a wealthy or sophisticated elite; exclusive: *the opera was seen by a small and highly select audience.*
– DERIVATIVES **selectable** adjective, **selectness** noun.
– ORIGIN mid 16th cent.: from Latin *select-* 'chosen', from the verb *seligere*, from *se-* 'apart' + *legere* 'choose'.

select committee ▶ **noun** a small parliamentary committee appointed for a special purpose: [in titles] *the Commons Select Committee on the Environment.*

selectee ▶ **noun** a person who is selected.
▪ US a conscript.

selection ▶ **noun** [mass noun] **1** the action or fact of carefully choosing someone or something as being the best or most suitable: *such men decided the selection of candidates | some local Tories objected to his selection.*
▪ [count noun] a number of carefully chosen things: *the publication of a selection of his poems.* ▪ [count noun] a range of things from which a choice may be made: *the restaurant offers a wide selection of hot and cold dishes.*

■ [count noun] a horse or horses tipped as worth bets in a race or meeting.

2 Biology a process in which environmental or genetic influences determine which types of organism thrive better than others, regarded as a factor in evolution. See also **NATURAL SELECTION**.

3 Austral. historical the action of choosing and acquiring plots of land for small farming on terms favourable to the buyer.

■ [count noun] a plot of land acquired in such a way.

– ORIGIN early 17th cent.: from Latin *selectio(n-)*, from *seligere* 'select by separating off' (see **SELECT**).

selectional ▶ adjective Linguistics denoting or relating to the process by which only certain words or structures can occur naturally, normally, or correctly in the context of other words.

– DERIVATIVES **selectionally** adverb.

selection pressure ▶ noun Biology an agent of differential mortality or fertility that tends to make a population change genetically.

selection rule ▶ noun Physics a rule which describes whether particular quantum transitions in an atom or molecule are allowed or forbidden.

selective ▶ adjective relating to or involving the selection of the most suitable or best qualified: *the mini-cow is the result of generations of selective breeding.* ■ (of a person) tending to choose carefully: *he is very selective in his reading.* ■ (of a process or agent) affecting some things and not others: *modern pesticides are more selective in effect.* ■ chiefly Electronics operating at or responding to a particular frequency.

– DERIVATIVES **selectively** adverb.

selective attention ▶ noun [mass noun] Psychology the capacity for or process of reacting to certain stimuli selectively when several occur simultaneously.

selectiveness ▶ noun another term for **SELECTIVITY**.

selective service ▶ noun [mass noun] N. Amer. service in the armed forces under conscription.

selectivity ▶ noun [mass noun] the quality of carefully choosing someone or something as the best or most suitable: *provision is organized on the principle of selectivity.* ■ the property of affecting some things and not others. ■ Electronics the ability of a device to respond to a particular frequency without interference from others.

selectman ▶ noun (pl. **-men**) a member of the local government board of a New England town.

selector ▶ noun a person or thing that selects something, in particular: ■ a person appointed to select a representative team in a sport. ■ a device for selecting a particular gear or other setting of a machine or device.

Selene /sɪˈliːni/ Greek Mythology the goddess of the moon who fell in love with Endymion.

– ORIGIN from Greek *selēnē* 'moon'.

selenic acid ▶ noun [mass noun] Chemistry a crystalline acid analogous to sulphuric acid, made by oxidizing some selenium compounds.

● Chem. formula: H_2SeO_4.

– DERIVATIVES **selenate** noun.

selenite /ˈsɛlɪnʌɪt/ ▶ noun [mass noun] a form of gypsum occurring as transparent crystals or thin plates.

– ORIGIN mid 17th cent.: via Latin from Greek *selēnitēs lithos* 'moonstone', from *selēnē* 'moon' + *lithos* 'stone'.

selenium /sɪˈliːnɪəm/ ▶ noun [mass noun] the chemical element of atomic number 34, a grey crystalline non-metal with semiconducting properties. (Symbol: **Se**)

– DERIVATIVES **selenide** noun.

– ORIGIN early 19th cent.: modern Latin, from Greek *selēnē* 'moon'.

selenium cell ▶ noun a photoelectric device containing a piece of selenium.

seleno- ▶ combining form of, relating to, or shaped like the moon: *selenography.*

– ORIGIN from Greek *selēnē* 'moon'.

selenodont /sɪˈliːnə(ʊ)dɒnt/ ▶ adjective Zoology (of molar teeth) having crescent-shaped ridges on the grinding surfaces, characteristic of the ruminants.

■ (of an ungulate) having such teeth.

– ORIGIN late 19th cent.: from **SELENO-** 'moon-shaped' + Greek *odous, odont-* 'tooth'.

selenography /ˌsɛlɪˈnɒɡrəfi, ˌsiː-/ ▶ noun [mass noun] the scientific mapping of the moon; lunar geography.

– DERIVATIVES **selenographer** noun, **selenographic** adjective, **selenographical** adjective.

selenology /ˌsɛlɪˈnɒlədʒi, ˌsiː-/ ▶ noun [mass noun] the scientific study of the moon.

– DERIVATIVES **selenologist** noun.

Seles /ˈsɛlɛs/, Monica (b.1973), American tennis player, born in Yugoslavia. She became the youngest woman to win a grand slam singles title with her victory in the French Open in 1990. She was stabbed on court by a fan of Steffi Graf in 1993, but she returned to play in 1995 and won the Australian Open in 1996.

Seleucid /sɪˈluːsɪd/ ▶ adjective relating to or denoting a dynasty ruling over Syria and a great part of western Asia from 311 to 65 BC. Its capital was at Antioch.

▶ noun a member of this dynasty.

– ORIGIN from *Seleucus* Nicator (the name of the founder, one of Alexander the Great's generals) + **-ID**[3].

self ▶ noun (pl. **selves**) a person's essential being that distinguishes them from others, especially considered as the object of introspection or reflexive action: *our alienation from our true selves* | [in sing.] *guilt can be turned against the self* | [mass noun] *language is an aspect of a person's sense of self.* ■ [with adj.] a person's particular nature or personality; the qualities that make a person individual or unique: *by the end of the round he was back to his old self* | *Paula seemed to be her usual cheerful self.* ■ [mass noun] one's own interests or pleasure: *to love in an unpossessive way implies the total surrender of self.*

▶ pronoun (pl. **selves**) oneself, in particular: ■ [with adj.] (**one's self**) used ironically to refer in specified glowing terms to oneself or someone else: *an article with a picture of my good self.* ■ used on counterfoils, cheques, and other papers to refer to the holder or person who has signed.

▶ adjective [attrib.] (of a trimming or cover) of the same material and colour as the rest of the item: *a button-through style with self belt.*

▶ verb [with obj.] chiefly Botany self-pollinate; self-fertilize: [as noun **selfing**] *the flowers never open and pollination is normally by selfing.* ■ [usu. as adj. **selfed**] Genetics cause (an animal or plant) to breed with or fertilize one of the same hybrid origin or strain: *progeny were derived from selfed crosses.*

– ORIGIN Old English, of Germanic origin; related to Dutch *zelf* and German *selbe*. Early use was emphatic, expressing the sense '(I) myself', '(he) himself', etc. The verb dates from the early 20th cent.

self- /sɛlf/ ▶ combining form of or directed towards oneself or itself: *self-hatred.* ■ by one's own efforts; by its own action: *self-acting.* ■ on, in, for, or relating to oneself or itself: *self-adhesive.*

self-abandonment (also **self-abandon**) ▶ noun [mass noun] the action of completely surrendering oneself to a desire or impulse.

– DERIVATIVES **self-abandoned** adjective.

self-abasement ▶ noun [mass noun] the belittling or humiliation of oneself.

self-abnegation /ˌabnɪˈɡeɪʃ(ə)n/ ▶ noun [mass noun] the denial or abasement of oneself: *she turned the letter into a grovelling form of self-abnegation.*

self-absorption ▶ noun [mass noun] **1** preoccupation with one's own emotions, interests, or situation.

2 Physics the absorption by a body of radiation which it has itself emitted.

– DERIVATIVES **self-absorbed** adjective.

self-abuse ▶ noun [mass noun] behaviour which causes damage or harm to oneself.

■ used euphemistically to refer to masturbation.

self-accusation ▶ noun [mass noun] the action of accusing oneself, stemming from feelings of guilt.

– DERIVATIVES **self-accusatory** adjective.

self-acting ▶ adjective archaic (of a machine or operation) acting without external influence or control; automatic.

self-actualization (also **-isation**) ▶ noun [mass noun] the realization or fulfilment of one's talents and potentialities, especially considered as a drive or need present in everyone.

self-addressed ▶ adjective (especially of an envelope) bearing one's own address: *enclose a self-addressed envelope.*

self-adhesive ▶ adjective coated with a sticky substance; adhering without requiring moistening.

self-adjusting ▶ adjective (chiefly of machinery) adjusting itself to meet varying requirements.

– DERIVATIVES **self-adjustment** noun.

self-advancement ▶ noun [mass noun] the advancement or promotion of oneself or one's interests: *a positive step in women's self-advancement.*

self-advertisement ▶ noun [mass noun] the active publicization of oneself: *he turned the group into a vehicle for self-advertisement.*

– DERIVATIVES **self-advertiser** noun, **self-advertising** adjective.

self-advocacy ▶ noun [mass noun] the action of representing oneself or one's views or interests.

self-affirmation ▶ noun [mass noun] the recognition and assertion of the existence and value of one's individual self.

self-aggrandizement /əˈɡrandɪzm(ə)nt/ (also **-isement**) ▶ noun [mass noun] the action or process of promoting oneself as being powerful or important.

– DERIVATIVES **self-aggrandizing** adjective.

self-alienation ▶ noun [mass noun] the process of distancing oneself from one's own feelings or activities, such as may occur in mental illness or as a symptom of emotional distress.

self-aligning ▶ adjective (of a bearing or machine part) capable of aligning itself automatically.

self-analysis ▶ noun [mass noun] the analysis of oneself, in particular one's motives and character.

– DERIVATIVES **self-analysing** adjective.

self-annihilation ▶ noun [mass noun] the annihilation or obliteration of self, especially as a process of mystical contemplation.

self-appointed ▶ adjective [attrib.] having assumed a position or role without the endorsement of others: *self-appointed experts.*

self-approbation ▶ noun another term for **SELF-APPROVAL**.

self-approval ▶ noun [mass noun] approval or appreciation of oneself.

– DERIVATIVES **self-approving** adjective, **self-approvingly** adverb.

self-assembly ▶ noun [mass noun] the construction of an object, especially a piece of furniture, from materials sold in kit form: *you can buy it as a flat-pack for self-assembly.* ■ Biology the spontaneous formation of a ribosome, virus, or other body in a medium containing the appropriate components.

– DERIVATIVES **self-assemble** verb.

self-assertion ▶ noun [mass noun] the confident and forceful expression or promotion of oneself, one's views, or one's desires.

– DERIVATIVES **self-asserting** adjective (dated), **self-assertive** adjective, **self-assertiveness** noun.

self-assessment ▶ noun [mass noun] assessment or evaluation of oneself or one's actions and attitudes, in particular, of one's performance at a job or learning task considered in relation to an objective standard.

■ calculation of one's own taxable liability.

self-assurance ▶ noun [mass noun] confidence in one's own abilities or character.

– DERIVATIVES **self-assured** adjective, **self-assuredly** adverb.

self-awareness ▶ noun [mass noun] conscious knowledge of one's own character, feelings, motives, and desires: *the process can be painful but it leads to greater self-awareness.*

– DERIVATIVES **self-aware** adjective.

self-balancing ▶ adjective (of a system) capable of achieving equilibrium or equality of its elements by processes inherent within it: *society is postulated as a self-balancing system based on consensus.* ■ (of an account record) having the debit side equal to the credit side.

▶ noun [mass noun] the process by which a system achieves and maintains a steady state by internal forces.

self-betrayal ▶ noun [mass noun] the intentional or inadvertent revelation of the truth about one's actions or thoughts.

self-build ▶ noun [mass noun] [often as modifier] Brit. the building of homes by their owners: *self-build*

schemes | *self-build is the cheapest way to get a home to your specification.*
– DERIVATIVES **self-builder** noun.

self-cancelling ▶ adjective **1** having elements which contradict or negate one another: *some of the speculation had been self-cancelling, with newspapers predicting that the government would take quite opposite courses.*
2 (of a mechanical device) designed to stop working automatically when no longer required.

self-catering Brit. ▶ adjective (of a holiday, accommodation, or the terms of these) offering facilities for people to cook their own meals: *guests stay in self-catering apartments.*
▶ noun [mass noun] the action of holidaying or staying in accommodation with facilities to cook one's own meals: *self-catering in southern Portugal is easy.*

self-censorship ▶ noun [mass noun] the exercising of control over what one says and does, especially to avoid castigation: *a climate of self-censorship, fear, and hypocrisy.*

self-centred ▶ adjective preoccupied with oneself and one's affairs: *he's far too self-centred to care what you do.*
– DERIVATIVES **self-centredly** adverb, **self-centredness** noun.

self-certification ▶ noun [mass noun] the practice of attesting something about oneself or one's company in a formal statement, rather than being obliged to ask a disinterested party to do so: *the applicability of self-certification to aircraft safety tests.*
▪ the practice, for the purpose of claiming sick pay, by which an employee rather than a doctor declares in writing that an absence was due to illness.
– DERIVATIVES **self-certificate** noun.

self-certify ▶ verb [with obj.] Brit. attest or confirm (one's financial standing) in a formal statement: *if you wish to self-certify your earnings, you will have to supply accounts for the year.*
▪ [as adj. **self-certified**] (of a loan or mortgage) obtained as a result of attesting or confirming one's financial standing in this way.

self-cleaning ▶ adjective (of an object or apparatus) able to clean itself: *a self-cleaning oven.*

self-closing ▶ adjective (especially of a door or valve) closing automatically.

self-cocking ▶ adjective (of a gun) having a hammer that is raised by the trigger, not by hand.

self-colour ▶ noun a single uniform colour: [as modifier] *a self-colour carpet.*
▪ the natural colour of something.
– DERIVATIVES **self-coloured** adjective.

self-compatible ▶ adjective Botany (of a plant or species) able to be fertilized by its own pollen.

self-conceit ▶ noun another term for SELF-CONGRATULATION.
– DERIVATIVES **self-conceited** adjective.

self-concept ▶ noun Psychology an idea of the self constructed from the beliefs one holds about oneself and the responses of others.

self-condemnation ▶ noun [mass noun] the blaming of oneself: *guilt and self-condemnation were riding her hard.*
▪ the inadvertent revelation of one's wrongdoing.
– DERIVATIVES **self-condemned** adjective, **self-condemning** adjective.

self-confessed ▶ adjective [attrib.] having openly admitted to being a person with certain characteristics: *a self-confessed chocoholic.*
– DERIVATIVES **self-confessedly** adverb, **self-confession** noun, **self-confessional** adjective.

self-confidence ▶ noun [mass noun] a feeling of trust in one's abilities, qualities, and judgement.
– DERIVATIVES **self-confident** adjective, **self-confidently** adverb.

self-congratulation ▶ noun [mass noun] undue complacency or pride regarding one's personal achievements or qualities; self-satisfaction: *a hefty dose of self-congratulation about how noble we are.*
– DERIVATIVES **self-congratulatory** adjective.

self-conscious ▶ adjective feeling undue awareness of oneself, one's appearance, or one's actions: *I feel a bit self-conscious parking my scruffy old car | a self-conscious laugh.*
▪ Philosophy & Psychology having knowledge of one's own existence, especially the knowledge of oneself as a conscious being. ▪ (especially of an action or intention) deliberate and with full awareness,

especially affectedly so: *her self-conscious identification with the upper classes.*
– DERIVATIVES **self-consciously** adverb, **self-consciousness** noun.

self-consistent ▶ adjective not having parts or aspects which are in conflict or contradiction with each other; consistent: *the theory is both rigorous and self-consistent.*
– DERIVATIVES **self-consistency** noun.

self-contained ▶ adjective **1** (of a thing) complete, or having all that is needed, in itself.
▪ chiefly Brit. (of accommodation) having its own kitchen and bathroom, and typically its own private entrance: *a group of self-contained flats.*
2 (of a person) quiet and independent; not depending on or influenced by others.
– DERIVATIVES **self-containment** noun (only in sense 2).

self-contempt ▶ noun [mass noun] contempt or loathing for oneself or one's actions: *they expressed self-contempt for having wasted so many hours in front of the idiot box.*
– DERIVATIVES **self-contemptuous** adjective.

self-contradiction ▶ noun [mass noun] inconsistency between aspects or parts of a whole: *deconstruction is interested in exploring language and revealing self-contradiction and instability* | [count noun] *we no longer see a puzzling self-contradiction in masochism.*
– DERIVATIVES **self-contradicting** adjective, **self-contradictory** adjective.

self-control ▶ noun [mass noun] the ability to control oneself, in particular one's emotions and desires or the expression of them in one's behaviour, especially in difficult situations: *Lucy silently struggled for self-control.*
– DERIVATIVES **self-controlled** adjective.

self-correcting ▶ adjective correcting oneself or itself without external help: *the scientific process is self-correcting* | *a self-correcting optical finder.*
– DERIVATIVES **self-correct** verb, **self-correction** noun.

self-created ▶ adjective created by oneself or itself: *his self-created role as the bad boy of the music scene.*
– DERIVATIVES **self-creating** adjective, **self-creation** noun.

self-critical ▶ adjective critical of oneself, one's abilities, or one's actions in a self-aware or unduly disapproving manner: *she felt miserably self-critical for her reluctance to go.*
– DERIVATIVES **self-criticism** noun.

self-deceit ▶ noun another term for SELF-DECEPTION.

self-deceiving ▶ adjective allowing oneself to believe that a false or unvalidated feeling, idea, or situation is true: *I prefer my cynicism to your self-deceiving optimism.*
– DERIVATIVES **self-deceiver** noun.

self-deception ▶ noun [mass noun] the action or practice of allowing oneself to believe that a false or unvalidated feeling, idea, or situation is true: *Jane remarked on men's capacity for self-deception.*
– DERIVATIVES **self-deceptive** adjective.

self-defeating ▶ adjective (of an action or policy) unable to achieve the end it is designed to bring about.

self-defence ▶ noun [mass noun] the defence of one's person or interests, especially through the use of physical force, which is permitted in certain cases as an answer to a charge of violent crime: *he claimed self-defence in the attempted murder charge* | [as modifier] *self-defence classes.*
– DERIVATIVES **self-defensive** adjective.

self-definition ▶ noun [mass noun] definition of one's individuality and one's role in life; such definition of a group by its members: *the struggle for national self-definition.*
▪ definition of something which is arrived at independently: *every attempt is made to avoid leading questions and to promote the respondent's self-definition of the issues to be discussed.*

self-delight ▶ noun [mass noun] delight in oneself or one's existence.

self-delusion ▶ noun [mass noun] the action of deluding oneself; failure to recognize reality: *he retreats into a world of fantasy and self-delusion.*

self-denial ▶ noun [mass noun] the denial of one's own interests and needs; self-sacrifice.
– DERIVATIVES **self-denying** adjective.

self-denying ordinance ▶ noun a resolution (1645) of the Long Parliament depriving members of parliament of civil and military office.

self-dependence ▶ noun [mass noun] reliance on one's own strengths rather than on others; independence.

self-deprecating ▶ adjective modest about or critical of oneself, especially humorously so: *self-deprecating jokes.*
– DERIVATIVES **self-deprecatingly** adverb, **self-deprecation** noun, **self-deprecatory** adjective.

self-depreciatory ▶ adjective another term for SELF-DEPRECATING.
– DERIVATIVES **self-depreciation** noun.

self-despair ▶ noun [mass noun] despair or dismay about oneself or one's actions.

self-destroying ▶ adjective destroying or capable of destroying oneself or itself; self-destructive.

self-destruct ▶ verb [no obj.] (of a thing) destroy itself by exploding or disintegrating automatically, having been preset to do so: *the tape would automatically self-destruct after twenty minutes.*
▪ [as modifier] denoting a device that enables or causes something to destroy itself in such a way: *the self-destruct button.*
– DERIVATIVES **self-destruction** noun, **self-destructive** adjective, **self-destructively** adverb.

self-determination ▶ noun [mass noun] the process by which a country determines its own statehood and forms its own allegiances and government: *the changes cannot be made until the country's right to self-determination is recognized.*
▪ the process by which a person controls their own life.

self-development ▶ noun [mass noun] the process by which a person's character or abilities are gradually developed: *graduates have stressed the value of their courses for self-development.*

self-devotion ▶ noun [mass noun] the devotion of oneself to a person or cause.

self-diffusion ▶ noun [mass noun] Chemistry the migration of constituent atoms or molecules within the bulk of a substance, especially in a crystalline solid.

self-directed ▶ adjective (of an emotion, statement, or activity) directed at one's self: *she grimaces with a bitter self-directed humour.*
▪ (of an activity) under one's own control: *this gives learners guidance in their self-directed learning.* ▪ (of a person) showing initiative and the ability to organize oneself.
– DERIVATIVES **self-direction** noun.

self-discipline ▶ noun [mass noun] the ability to control one's feelings and overcome one's weaknesses; the ability to pursue what one thinks is right despite temptations to abandon it.
– DERIVATIVES **self-disciplined** adjective.

self-discovery ▶ noun [mass noun] the process of acquiring insight into one's own character.

self-disgust ▶ noun [mass noun] profound revulsion at one's own character or actions: *his descent into drunkenness filled him with self-disgust.*

self-doubt ▶ noun [mass noun] lack of confidence in oneself and one's abilities: *his later years were plagued by self-doubt.*

self-dramatization (also **-isation**) ▶ noun [mass noun] dramatization of one's own situation or feelings for effect.

self-drive ▶ adjective **1** Brit. (of a hired vehicle) driven by the person who hires the vehicle, rather than a professional driver: *a self-drive removal van.*
2 (of a holiday) involving use of one's own car rather than transport arranged by the operator.

self-educated ▶ adjective educated largely through one's own efforts, rather than by formal instruction: *he was a self-made and almost self-educated businessman.*
– DERIVATIVES **self-education** noun.

self-effacing ▶ adjective not claiming attention for oneself; retiring and modest: *his demeanour was self-effacing, gracious, and polite.*
– DERIVATIVES **self-effacement** noun, **self-effacingly** adverb.

self-employed ▶ adjective working for oneself as

a freelance or the owner of a business rather than for an employer: *a self-employed builder.*
■relating to or designed for people working for themselves: *the rules for self-employed pension plans have been altered.*
– DERIVATIVES **self-employment** noun.

self-enclosed ▶ adjective (of a person, community, or system) not choosing to or able to communicate with others or with external systems: *the family is a self-enclosed unit.*

self-esteem ▶ noun [mass noun] confidence in one's own worth or abilities; self-respect: *assertiveness training for those with low self-esteem.*

self-evaluation ▶ noun another term for SELF-ASSESSMENT.

self-evident ▶ adjective not needing to be demonstrated or explained; obvious: *self-evident truths* | [with clause] *it is self-evident that childhood experiences must have a profound effect upon our beliefs about ourselves.*
– DERIVATIVES **self-evidence** noun, **self-evidently** adverb.

self-examination ▶ noun [mass noun] the study of one's own behaviour and motivations: *a period of considerable self-doubt and self-examination.*
■the action of examining one's own body for signs of illness.

self-excited ▶ adjective Physics relating to or denoting a dynamo-electric machine or analogous system that generates or excites its own magnetic field.

self-explanatory ▶ adjective easily understood; not needing explanation: *the film's title is fairly self-explanatory.*

self-expression ▶ noun [mass noun] the expression of one's feelings, thoughts, or ideas, especially in writing, art, music, or dance.
– DERIVATIVES **self-expressive** adjective.

self-faced ▶ adjective (of stone) having an undressed surface.

self-feeder ▶ noun **1** a furnace or machine that renews its own fuel or material automatically.
2 a device for supplying food to farm animals automatically.
– DERIVATIVES **self-feeding** adjective.

self-fertile ▶ adjective Botany (of a plant) capable of self-fertilization.
– DERIVATIVES **self-fertility** noun.

self-fertilization (also **-isation**) ▶ noun [mass noun] Biology the fertilization of plants and some invertebrate animals by their own pollen or sperm rather than that of another individual.
– DERIVATIVES **self-fertilized** adjective, **self-fertilizing** adjective.

self-financing ▶ adjective (of an organization or enterprise) having or generating enough income to finance itself.
– DERIVATIVES **self-financed** adjective.

self-flagellation ▶ noun [mass noun] the action of flogging oneself, especially as a form of religious discipline.
■figurative excessive criticism of oneself.

self-flattery ▶ noun [mass noun] the holding of an unjustifiably high opinion of oneself or one's actions.
– DERIVATIVES **self-flattering** adjective.

self-forgetful ▶ adjective forgetful of one's self or one's needs.
– DERIVATIVES **self-forgetfulness** noun.

self-fulfilling ▶ adjective (of an opinion or prediction) bound to be proved correct or to come true as a result of behaviour caused by its being expressed: *expecting something to be bad can turn out to be a self-fulfilling prophecy.*

self-fulfilment (US **-fulfillment**) ▶ noun [mass noun] the fulfilment of one's hopes and ambitions: *it is the striving for self-fulfilment which guides and gives consistency to our lives.*

self-generating ▶ adjective generated by itself, rather than by some external force: *the strident activity of the industrial scene seems to be self-generating.*

self-glorification ▶ noun [mass noun] exaltation of oneself and one's abilities: *they fought not merely for self-glorification but for the common good.*

self-governing ▶ adjective exercising control over one's own affairs, in particular:
■(of a British hospital or school) having opted out of

local authority control. ■(of a former colony or dependency) administering its own affairs.

self-government ▶ noun [mass noun] **1** government of a country by its own people, especially after having been a colony.
2 another term for SELF-CONTROL.
– DERIVATIVES **self-governed** adjective.

self-gravitation ▶ noun [mass noun] Astronomy the gravitational forces acting among the components of a massive body.

self-hatred (also **self-hate**) ▶ noun [mass noun] intense dislike of oneself.

self-heal ▶ noun a purple-flowered Eurasian plant of the mint family, which was formerly widely used for healing wounds.
● *Prunella vulgaris*, family Labiatae.

self-help ▶ noun [mass noun] the use of one's own efforts and resources to achieve things without relying on others: *popular capitalism necessitates a reduction in the role of the state and an increasing reliance on self-help.*
■[as modifier] designed to assist people in achieving things for themselves: *when I suffered from depression I went to a self-help group.*

selfhood ▶ noun [mass noun] the quality that constitutes one's individuality; the state of having an individual identity.

self-identification ▶ noun [mass noun] the attribution of certain characteristics or qualities to oneself: *self-identification by the old person as sick or inadequate.*

self-identity ▶ noun [mass noun] the recognition of one's potential and qualities as an individual, especially in relation to social context: *caring can become the defining characteristic of women's self-identity.*

self-image ▶ noun the idea one has of one's abilities, appearance, and personality: *poverty causes lowered self-respect and self-image.*

self-immolation ▶ noun [mass noun] the offering of oneself as a sacrifice, especially by burning; such suicidal action in the name of a cause or strongly held belief.

self-importance ▶ noun [mass noun] an exaggerated sense of one's own value or importance: *he was a big, blustering, opinionated cop, full of self-importance.*
– DERIVATIVES **self-important** adjective, **self-importantly** adverb.

self-imposed ▶ adjective (of a task or circumstance) imposed on oneself, not by an external force: *he went into self-imposed exile.*

self-improvement ▶ noun [mass noun] the improvement of one's knowledge, status, or character by one's own efforts.

self-incompatible ▶ adjective Botany (of a plant or species) unable to be fertilized by its own pollen.
– DERIVATIVES **self-incompatibility** noun.

self-induced ▶ adjective **1** brought about by oneself: *self-induced vomiting.*
2 produced by electrical self-induction.

self-inductance ▶ noun Physics a measure or coefficient of self-induction in a circuit, usually measured in henries.
■[mass noun] the property of an electric circuit that permits self-induction.

self-induction ▶ noun [mass noun] Physics the induction of an electromotive force in a circuit when the current in that circuit is varied. Compare with MUTUAL INDUCTION.
– DERIVATIVES **self-inductive** adjective.

self-indulgence ▶ noun [mass noun] the quality of being self-indulgent.
■[count noun] something done in a self-indulgent way: *Sunday's simple-minded pleasures and self-indulgences.*

self-indulgent ▶ adjective characterized by doing or tending to do exactly what one wants, especially when this involves pleasure or idleness: *a self-indulgent extra hour of sleep.*
■(of a creative work) lacking economy and control.
– DERIVATIVES **self-indulgently** adverb.

self-inflicted ▶ adjective (of a wound or other harm) inflicted on oneself.

self-insurance ▶ noun [mass noun] insurance of oneself or one's interests by maintaining a fund to cover possible losses rather than by purchasing an insurance policy.

self-interest ▶ noun [mass noun] one's personal interest or advantage, especially when pursued without regard for others.

self-interested ▶ adjective motivated by one's personal interest or advantage, especially without regard for others: *many groups pursue self-interested aims.*

self-involved ▶ adjective wrapped up in oneself or one's own thoughts.
– DERIVATIVES **self-involvement** noun.

selfish ▶ adjective (of a person, action, or motive) lacking consideration for others; concerned chiefly with one's own personal profit or pleasure: *I joined them for selfish reasons.*
– DERIVATIVES **selfishly** adverb, **selfishness** noun.

selfism ▶ noun [mass noun] concentration on one's own interests; self-centredness or self-absorption.
– DERIVATIVES **selfist** noun.

self-justification ▶ noun [mass noun] the justification or excusing of oneself or one's actions.
– DERIVATIVES **self-justificatory** adjective, **self-justifying** adjective.

self-knowledge ▶ noun [mass noun] understanding of oneself or one's own motives or character.
– DERIVATIVES **self-knowing** adjective.

selfless ▶ adjective concerned more with the needs and wishes of others than with one's own; unselfish: *an act of selfless devotion.*
– DERIVATIVES **selflessly** adverb, **selflessness** noun.

self-limiting ▶ adjective relating to or denoting something which limits itself, in particular:
■Medicine (of a condition) ultimately resolving itself without treatment. ■(in psychology) preventing the development or expression of the self.

self-liquidating ▶ adjective denoting an asset that earns back its original cost out of income over a fixed period.
■denoting a loan used to finance a project that will bring a sufficient return to pay back the loan and its interest and leave a profit. ■denoting a sales promotion offer that pays for itself by generating increased sales.

self-loading ▶ adjective (especially of a gun) loading automatically: *a self-loading pistol.*
– DERIVATIVES **self-loader** noun.

self-locking ▶ adjective locking itself shut or in a fixed position: *self-locking screws.*

self-love ▶ noun [mass noun] regard for one's own well-being and happiness (chiefly considered as a desirable rather than narcissistic characteristic).

self-made ▶ adjective having become successful or rich by one's own efforts: *a self-made millionaire.*
■made by oneself: *his self-made fortune* | *a self-made kite.*

self-management ▶ noun [mass noun] management of or by oneself; the taking of responsibility for one's own behaviour and well-being.
■the distribution of political control to individual regions of a state, especially as a form of socialism practised by its own members. ■management of an organization.
– DERIVATIVES **self-managing** adjective.

self-mastery ▶ noun [mass noun] self-control.

selfmate ▶ noun [mass noun] Chess a problem in which the solver's task is to force the opponent to deliver checkmate.

self-mocking ▶ adjective mocking oneself: *a wry, self-mocking smile.*
– DERIVATIVES **self-mockery** noun, **self-mockingly** adverb.

self-mortification ▶ noun [mass noun] the subjugation of appetites or desires by self-denial or self-discipline as an aspect of religious devotion: *voluntary self-mortification such as fasting.*

self-motivated ▶ adjective motivated to do or achieve something because of one's own enthusiasm or interest, without needing pressure from others: *she's a very independent self-motivated individual.*
– DERIVATIVES **self-motivating** adjective, **self-motivation** noun.

self-mutilation ▶ noun [mass noun] the mutilation of oneself, especially as a symptom of mental or emotional disturbance.

self-neglect ▶ noun [mass noun] neglect of oneself, especially one's physical well-being.

selfness ▶ noun [mass noun] a person's essential individuality.
■archaic selfishness; self-regard.

self-opinionated ▶ adjective having an arrogantly high regard for oneself or one's own opinions: *a pompous, self-opinionated bully.*
– DERIVATIVES **self-opinion** noun.

self-parodic ▶ adjective another term for **SELF-PARODYING**.

self-parody ▶ noun [mass noun] the intentional or inadvertent parodying or exaggeration of one's usual behaviour or speech: *they are soft-spoken and clean-cut to the point of self-parody.*

self-parodying ▶ adjective appearing to parody one's usual behaviour or speech, especially inadvertently: *pathetic, self-parodying former beauty queens propped up by surgery and cosmetics.*

self-perpetuating ▶ adjective perpetuating itself or oneself without external agency or intervention: *the self-perpetuating power of the bureaucracy.*
– DERIVATIVES **self-perpetuation** noun.

self-pity ▶ noun [mass noun] excessive, self-absorbed unhappiness over one's own troubles.

self-pitying ▶ adjective characterized by self-pity: *he was in one of his self-pitying moods.*
– DERIVATIVES **self-pityingly** adverb.

self-policing ▶ noun [mass noun] the process of keeping order or maintaining control within a community without accountability or reference to an external authority.
▶ adjective (of a community) independently responsible for keeping and maintaining order: *as long as the Internet community was relatively small, it could be self-policing.*

self-pollination ▶ noun [mass noun] Botany the pollination of a flower by pollen from the same flower or from another flower on the same plant.
– DERIVATIVES **self-pollinated** adjective, **self-pollinating** adjective, **self-pollinator** noun.

self-portrait ▶ noun a portrait that an artist produces of themselves.
– DERIVATIVES **self-portraiture** noun.

self-possessed ▶ adjective calm, confident, and in control of one's feelings; composed.
– DERIVATIVES **self-possession** noun.

self-preservation ▶ noun [mass noun] the protection of oneself from harm or death, especially regarded as a basic instinct in human beings and animals.

self-proclaimed ▶ adjective [attrib.] described as or proclaimed to be such by oneself, without endorsement by others: *exercise books written by self-proclaimed experts.*

self-propagating ▶ adjective (especially of a plant) able to propagate itself.
– DERIVATIVES **self-propagation** noun.

self-propelled ▶ adjective moving or able to move without external propulsion or agency: *a self-propelled weapon.*
– DERIVATIVES **self-propelling** adjective.

self-protection ▶ noun [mass noun] protection of oneself or itself.
– DERIVATIVES **self-protective** adjective.

self-raising flour ▶ noun [mass noun] Brit. flour that has a raising agent already added.

self-rating ▶ noun [mass noun] evaluation of one's own character, feelings, or behaviour, used as a tool in psychology to quantify people's perception of themselves or assess mental health risks.

self-realization (also **-isation**) ▶ noun [mass noun] fulfilment of one's own potential.

self-referential ▶ adjective (especially of a literary or other creative work) making reference to itself, its author or creator, or their other work: *self-referential elements in Donne's poems.*
– DERIVATIVES **self-referentiality** noun, **self-referentially** adverb.

self-reflection ▶ noun [mass noun] meditation or serious thought about one's character, actions, and motives.
– DERIVATIVES **self-reflective** adjective.

self-reflexive ▶ adjective containing a reflection or image of itself; self-referential: *sociology's self-reflexive critique.*

self-regard ▶ noun [mass noun] regard or consideration for oneself; self-respect.
■conceit; vanity.

– DERIVATIVES **self-regarding** adjective.

self-regulating ▶ adjective regulating itself without intervention from external bodies: *advertising is governed by a self-regulating system.*
– DERIVATIVES **self-regulation** noun, **self-regulatory** adjective.

self-reliance ▶ noun [mass noun] reliance on one's own powers and resources rather than those of others.
– DERIVATIVES **self-reliant** adjective, **self-reliantly** adverb..

self-renewal ▶ noun [mass noun] the process of renewing oneself or itself.

self-reproach ▶ noun [mass noun] reproach or blame directed at oneself: *the bitter tears of self-reproach.*
– DERIVATIVES **self-reproachful** adjective.

self-respect ▶ noun [mass noun] pride and confidence in oneself; a feeling that one is behaving with honour and dignity.

self-respecting ▶ adjective having self-respect: *proud, self-respecting mountain villagers.*
■[attrib.] often humorous a person who merits a particular role or name: *no self-respecting editor would run such an article.*

self-restraint ▶ noun [mass noun] restraint imposed by oneself on one's own actions; self-control.
– DERIVATIVES **self-restrained** adjective.

self-revealing ▶ adjective revealing one's character or motives, especially inadvertently: *his most intimate and self-revealing book.*
– DERIVATIVES **self-revelation** noun, **self-revelatory** adjective.

Selfridge /ˈselfrɪdʒ/, Harry Gordon (1858–1947), American-born British businessman. In 1906 he came to England and began to build the department store in Oxford Street, London, that bears his name; it opened in 1909.

self-righteous ▶ adjective having or characterized by a certainty, especially an unfounded one, that one is totally correct or morally superior: *self-righteous indignation and complacency.*
– DERIVATIVES **self-righteously** adverb, **self-righteousness** noun.

self-righting ▶ adjective (of a boat) designed to right itself when capsized.

self-rising flour ▶ noun US term for **SELF-RAISING FLOUR**.

self-rule ▶ noun another term for **SELF-GOVERNMENT** (in sense 1).

self-sacrifice ▶ noun [mass noun] the giving up of one's own interests or wishes in order to help others or advance a cause.
– DERIVATIVES **self-sacrificial** adjective, **self-sacrificing** adjective.

selfsame ▶ adjective [attrib.] (usu. **the selfsame**) exactly the same: *he was standing in the selfsame spot you're filling now.*

self-satisfied ▶ adjective excessively and unwarrantedly satisfied with oneself or one's achievements; smugly complacent: *a pompous, self-satisfied fool | a self-satisfied smirk | a self-satisfied air.*
– DERIVATIVES **self-satisfaction** noun.

self-sealing ▶ adjective sealing itself without the usual process or procedure, in particular: ■(of a pneumatic tyre, fuel tank, etc.) able to seal small punctures automatically. ■(of an envelope) self-adhesive.

self-seed ▶ verb [no obj.] (of a plant) propagate itself by seed: [as adj. **self-seeding**] *the early-blooming, self-seeding drumstick primrose.*
– DERIVATIVES **self-seeder** noun.

self-seeking ▶ adjective having concern for one's own welfare and interests before those of others: *the self-seeking aggrandizement of Party bosses.*
▶ noun [mass noun] concern for oneself before others.
– DERIVATIVES **self-seeker** noun.

self-selection ▶ noun [mass noun] 1 the action of putting oneself forward for something.
2 [often as modifier] the action of selecting something for oneself: *a self-selection buffet.*
– DERIVATIVES **self-selecting** adjective (only in sense 1).

self-service ▶ adjective denoting a shop, restaurant, or other outlet where customers select goods for themselves and pay at a checkout: *a self-service cafeteria.*

■denoting a machine that provides goods after the insertion of coins.
▶ noun [mass noun] the system whereby customers select goods for themselves and pay at a checkout: *providing quick self-service.*

self-serving ▶ adjective & noun another term for **SELF-SEEKING**.

self-shifter ▶ noun a car with an automatic gearbox.

self-similar ▶ adjective Mathematics (of an object or set of objects) similar to itself at a different time, or to a copy of itself on a different scale.
– DERIVATIVES **self-similarity** noun.

self-sow ▶ verb [no obj.] (of a plant) propagate itself by seed: [as adj. **self-sown**] *a batch of self-sown seedlings.*

self-starter ▶ noun 1 a person who is sufficiently motivated or ambitious to start a new career or business or to pursue further education without the help of others: *he was the self-starter who worked his way up from messenger boy to account executive.*
2 dated the starter of a motor-vehicle engine.
– DERIVATIVES **self-starting** adjective.

self-sterile ▶ adjective Biology incapable of self-fertilization.
– DERIVATIVES **self-sterility** noun.

self-stimulation ▶ noun [mass noun] 1 used euphemistically to refer to masturbation.
2 Physiology a phenomenon which occurs in the hypothalamus and other areas of the brain, in which the propagation of electrical stimulation has positive reinforcing properties which act to maintain and perpetuate the impulses.

self-styled ▶ adjective [attrib.] using a description or title that one has given oneself: *self-styled experts | the self-styled President of Bougainville.*

self-subsistent ▶ adjective subsistent without dependence on or support from external agencies: *this colony was virtually self-subsistent, in management methods as in food.*

self-sufficient ▶ adjective needing no outside help in satisfying one's basic needs, especially with regard to the production of food: *I don't think Botswana, due to the climate, could ever be self-sufficient in food.*
■emotionally and intellectually independent: *their son was a little bit of a loner and very self-sufficient.*
– DERIVATIVES **self-sufficiency** noun, **self-sufficiently** adverb.

self-suggestion ▶ noun another term for **AUTO-SUGGESTION**.

self-supporting ▶ adjective 1 having the resources to be able to survive without outside assistance.
2 staying up or upright without being supported by something else: *arches were originally self-supporting structures.*
– DERIVATIVES **self-support** noun.

self-surrender ▶ noun [mass noun] the surrender of oneself or one's will to an external influence, an emotion, or another person.

self-sustaining ▶ adjective able to continue in a healthy state without outside assistance: *the studies throw doubt on whether these businesses are really self-sustaining.*
– DERIVATIVES **self-sustained** adjective.

self-system ▶ noun Psychology the complex of drives and responses relating to the self; the set of potentialities which develop in an individual's character in response to parental and other external influence.

self-tailing ▶ adjective (of a winch) designed to maintain constant tension in the rope round it so that it does not slip.

self-tapping ▶ adjective (of a screw) able to cut a thread in the material into which it is inserted.

self-taught ▶ adjective having acquired knowledge or skill on one's own initiative rather than through formal instruction or training: *a self-taught graphic artist.*

self-timer ▶ noun a mechanism in a camera that introduces a delay between the operation of the shutter release and the opening of the shutter, so that the photographer can be included in the photograph.

self-transcendence ▶ noun [mass noun] the overcoming of the limits of the individual self and its desires in spiritual contemplation and realization.

self-understanding ▶ **noun** [mass noun] awareness of and ability to understand one's own actions and reactions.

self-willed ▶ **adjective** obstinately doing what one wants in spite of the wishes or orders of others: *the child may be very obstinate and self-willed.*
– DERIVATIVES **self-will** noun.

self-winding ▶ **adjective** (chiefly of a watch) wound by some automatic means, such as an electric motor or the movement of the wearer, rather than by hand.

self-worth ▶ **noun** another term for **SELF-ESTEEM**.

Seljuk /ˈsɛldʒuːk/ ▶ **noun** a member of any of the Turkish dynasties which ruled Asia Minor in the 11th to 13th centuries, successfully invading the Byzantine Empire and defending the Holy Land against the Crusaders.
▶ **adjective** of or relating to the Seljuks.
– DERIVATIVES **Seljukian** /-ˈdʒuːkɪən/ adjective & noun.
– ORIGIN from Turkish *seljūq*, the name of the reputed ancestor of the dynasty.

selkie (also **selky** or **silkie**) ▶ **noun** (pl. **-ies**) Scottish a mythical creature that resembles a seal in the water but assumes human form on land.
– ORIGIN from *selch*, variant of **SEAL**, + **-IE**.

Selkirk /ˈsɛlkəːk/, Alexander (1676–1721), Scottish sailor; also called *Alexander Selcraig*. While on a privateering expedition in 1704 Selkirk quarrelled with his captain and was put ashore, at his own request, on one of the uninhabited Juan Fernandez Islands, where he remained until 1709. His experiences formed the basis of Daniel Defoe's novel *Robinson Crusoe* (1719).

Selkirkshire a former county of SE Scotland. It was made a part of Borders region (now Scottish Borders) in 1975.

sell ▶ **verb** (past and past participle **sold**) [with obj.] **1** give or hand over (something) in exchange for money: *they had sold the car | the family business had been **sold off** |* [with two objs] *I was trying to sell him my butterfly collection.*
■ have a stock of (something) available for sale: *the store sells hi-fis, TVs, videos, and other electrical goods.* ■ [no obj.] (of a thing) be purchased: *this magazine of yours won't sell.* ■ (of a publication or recording) attain sales of (a specified number of copies): *the album sold 6 million copies in the United States.* ■ [no obj.] (**sell for/at**) be available for sale at (a specified price): *these antiques of the future sell for about £375.* ■ [no obj.] (**sell out**) sell all of one's stock of something: *they had nearly **sold out of** the initial run of 75,000 copies.* ■ [no obj.] (**sell out**) be all sold: *it was clear that the performances would not sell out.* ■ [no obj.] (**sell through**) (of a product) be purchased by a customer from a retail outlet. ■ [no obj.] (**sell up**) sell all of one's property, possessions, or assets: *Ernest sold up and retired.* ■ (**sell oneself**) have sex in exchange for money: *if she was going to sell herself then it would be as well not to come too cheap.* ■ archaic offer (something) dishonourably for money or other reward; make a matter of corrupt bargaining: *do not your lawyers sell all their practice, as your priests their prayers?* ■ (**sell someone out**) betray someone for one's own financial or material benefit: *the clansmen became tenants and the chiefs sold them out.* ■ [no obj.] (**sell out**) abandon one's principles for reasons of expedience: *the prime minister has come under fire for **selling out to** the United States.*
2 persuade someone of the merits of: *he sold the idea of making a film about Tchaikovsky | he could get work but he just won't sell himself.*
■ be the reason for (something) being bought: *what sells CDs to most people is convenience.* ■ cause (someone) to become enthusiastic about: [as adj. **sold**] *I'm just not **sold on** the idea.*
3 archaic trick or deceive (someone): *what we want is to go out of here quiet, and talk this show up, and sell the rest of the town.*
▶ **noun** informal **1** an act of selling or attempting to sell something: *every other television commercial is a sell for Australian lager.*
2 a disappointment, typically one arising from being deceived as to the merits of something: *actually, Hawaii's a bit of a sell—not a patch on Corfu.*
– PHRASES **sell someone a bill of goods** see **BILL OF GOODS**. **sell someone down the river** see **RIVER**. **sell someone a** (or **the**) **dummy** see **DUMMY**. **sell the pass** see **PASS**[2]. **sell someone a pup** see **PUP**. **sell someone/thing short** fail to recognize or state the true value of: *don't sell yourself short—you've got what it takes.* **sell one's soul** (**to the devil**) do or be willing to do anything, no matter how wrong it is, in order to achieve one's objective: *universities and polytechnics are selling their souls for commercial success.*
– DERIVATIVES **sellable** adjective.
– ORIGIN Old English *sellan* (verb), of Germanic origin; related to Old Norse *selja* 'give up, sell'. Early use included the sense 'give, hand (something) over voluntarily in response to a request'.

sella /ˈsɛlə/ (in full **sella turcica** /ˈtəːkɪkə/) ▶ **noun** (pl. **sellae** /ˈsɛliː/ or **sellae turcicae** /ˈtəːkɪkiː/) Anatomy a depression in the sphenoid bone, containing the pituitary gland.
– ORIGIN late 17th cent.: from Latin, 'saddle', (in full) 'Turkish saddle'.

Sellafield the site of a nuclear power station and reprocessing plant on the coast of Cumbria in NW England. It was the scene in 1957 of a fire which caused a serious escape of radioactive material. Former name (1947–81) **WINDSCALE**.

sell-by date ▶ **noun** chiefly Brit. a date marked on a perishable product indicating the recommended time by which it should be sold: *crisps past their sell-by date.*
■ informal a time after which something or someone is no longer considered desirable or effective: *do broadcasters have a sell-by date?*

seller ▶ **noun** **1** a person who sells something: *street sellers of newspapers, flowers, etc.*
■ (**the seller**) the party in a legal transaction who is selling: *the seller may accept the buyer's offer.*
2 [with adj.] a product that sells in some specified way: *the book became the biggest seller in the history of royal publishing.*
– PHRASES **seller's** (or **sellers'**) **market** an economic situation in which goods or shares are scarce and sellers can keep prices high.

Sellers, Peter (1925–80), English comic actor. He made his name in *The Goon Show*, a radio series of the 1950s, but is best known for the 'Pink Panther' series of films of the 1960s and 1970s, in which he played the French detective Inspector Clouseau.

sell-in ▶ **noun** [mass noun] the sale of goods to retail traders prior to public retailing.

selling point ▶ **noun** a feature of a product for sale that makes it attractive to customers.

selling race ▶ **noun** a horse race after which the winning horse must be auctioned.

sell-off ▶ **noun** a sale of assets, typically at a low price, carried out in order to dispose of them rather than as normal trade.
■ chiefly US a sale of shares, bonds, or commodities, especially one that causes a fall in price.

Sellotape Brit. ▶ **noun** [mass noun] trademark transparent adhesive tape.
▶ **verb** [with obj. and adverbial] fasten or stick with this type of tape: *there was a note Sellotaped to my door.*
– ORIGIN 1940s: from an alteration of **CELLULOSE** + **TAPE**.

sell-out ▶ **noun** **1** the selling of an entire stock of something, especially tickets for an entertainment or sports event.
■ an event for which all tickets are sold: *the game is sure to be a sell-out.*
2 a sale of a business or company.
■ a betrayal of one's principles for reasons of expedience: *the sell-out of socialist economic policy.*

sell-through ▶ **noun** [mass noun] the ratio of the quantity of goods sold by a retail outlet to the quantity distributed to it wholesale: *the sell-through was amazing, 60 per cent.*
■ the retail sale of something, typically a pre-recorded video cassette, as opposed to its rental: [as modifier] *the burgeoning sell-through market.*

Selous /səˈluː/, Frederick Courteney (1851–1917), English explorer, naturalist, and soldier. From 1890 he was involved in the British South Africa Company, negotiating mineral and land rights. The Selous Game Reserve in Tanzania is named after him.

seltzer /ˈsɛltsə/ (also **seltzer water**) ▶ **noun** [mass noun] dated soda water.
■ medicinal mineral water from Niederselters in Germany.
– ORIGIN mid 18th cent.: alteration of German *Selterser*, from (*Nieder*)*selters* (see above).

selva ▶ **noun** a tract of land covered by dense equatorial forest, especially in the Amazon basin.
– ORIGIN mid 19th cent.: from Spanish or Portuguese, from Latin *silva* 'wood'.

selvedge /ˈsɛlvɪdʒ/ (chiefly N. Amer. also **selvage**) ▶ **noun** an edge produced on woven fabric during manufacture that prevents it from unravelling.
■ Geology a zone of altered rock, especially volcanic glass, at the edge of a rock mass.
– ORIGIN late Middle English: from an alteration of **SELF** + **EDGE**, on the pattern of early modern Dutch *selfegghe*. The geological term dates from the 1930s.

selves plural form of **SELF**.

Selye /ˈsɛljeɪ/, Hans Hugo Bruno (1907–82), Austrian-born Canadian physician. He showed that environmental stress and anxiety could result in the release of hormones that, over a long period, could produce biochemical and physiological disorders.

Selznick /ˈsɛlznɪk/, David O. (1902–65), American film producer; full name *David Oliver Selznick*. He produced such films as *King Kong* (1933) for RKO and *Anna Karenina* (1935) for MGM before establishing his own production company in 1936 and producing such screen classics as *Gone with the Wind* (1939) and *Rebecca* (1940).

SEM ▶ **abbreviation for** scanning electron microscope.

semanteme /sɪˈmantiːm/ ▶ **noun** Linguistics a minimal distinctive unit of meaning. Compare with **SEMEME**.
– ORIGIN early 20th cent.: from French *sémantème*, from *sémantique* (see **SEMANTIC**), on the pattern of words such as *morphème* 'morpheme'.

semantic /sɪˈmantɪk/ ▶ **adjective** relating to meaning in language or logic.
– DERIVATIVES **semantically** adverb.
– ORIGIN mid 17th cent.: from French *sémantique*, from Greek *sēmantikos* 'significant', from *sēmainein* 'signify', from *sēma* 'sign'.

semantic field ▶ **noun** Linguistics a lexical set of semantically related items, for example verbs of perception.

semanticity /ˌsɪmanˈtɪsɪti/ ▶ **noun** [mass noun] the quality that a linguistic system has of being able to convey meanings, in particular by reference to the world of physical reality.

semantics ▶ **plural noun** [usu. treated as sing.] the branch of linguistics and logic concerned with meaning. The two main areas are **logical semantics**, concerned with matters such as sense and reference and presupposition and implication, and **lexical semantics**, concerned with the analysis of word meanings and relations between them, such as synonymy and antonymy.
■ the meaning of a word, phrase, sentence, or text: *such quibbling over semantics may seem petty stuff.*
– DERIVATIVES **semantician** noun, **semanticist** noun.

semaphore ▶ **noun** [mass noun] a system of sending messages by holding the arms or two flags or poles in certain positions according to an alphabetic code.
■ [count noun] an apparatus for signalling in this way, consisting of an upright with movable parts. ■ [count noun] a signal sent by semaphore.
▶ **verb** [with obj.] send (a message) by semaphore or by signals resembling semaphore: *Josh stands facing the rear and semaphoring the driver's intentions to frustrated queues of following cars.*
– DERIVATIVES **semaphoric** adjective, **semaphorically** adverb.
– ORIGIN early 19th cent. (denoting a signalling apparatus): from French *sémaphore*, formed irregularly from Greek *sēma* 'sign' + *-phoros*.

Semarang /səˈmɑːraŋ/ a port in Indonesia, on the north coast of Java; pop. 1,249,200 (1990).

semasiology /sɪˌmeɪzɪˈɒlədʒi/ ▶ **noun** [mass noun] the branch of knowledge that deals with concepts and the terms that represent them. Compare with **ONOMASIOLOGY**.
– DERIVATIVES **semasiological** adjective.
– ORIGIN mid 19th cent.: from German *Semasiologie*, from Greek *sēmasia* 'meaning', from *sēmainein* 'signify'.

semblable /ˈsɛmbləb(ə)l/ ▶ **noun** poetic/literary a counterpart or equal to someone: *there was Dodge, her semblable, her conspirator.*
– ORIGIN Middle English (as an adjective meaning 'like, similar'): from Old French, from *sembler* 'seem'.

semblance ▶ **noun** [mass noun] the outward appearance or apparent form of something,

especially when the reality is different: *she tried to force her thoughts back into some semblance of order.*
■archaic resemblance; similarity: *it bears some semblance to the thing I have in mind.*
– ORIGIN Middle English: from Old French, from *sembler* 'seem', from Latin *similare*, *simulare* 'simulate'.

seme /siːm/ ▶ noun another term for SEMANTEME.
– ORIGIN mid 19th cent.: from Greek *sēma* 'sign'.

semé /ˈsɛmi, ˈsɛmeɪ/ (also **semée**) ▶ adjective Heraldry covered with small bearings of indefinite number (e.g. stars, fleurs-de-lis) arranged all over the field.
– ORIGIN late Middle English: French, literally 'sown', past participle of *semer*.

Semei /səˈmeɪ/ (also **Semey**) an industrial city and river port in eastern Kazakhstan, on the Irtysh River close to the border with Russia; pop. 338,800 (1990). Founded in the 18th century, it was known as Semipalatinsk until 1991.

Semele /ˈsɛmɪli/ Greek Mythology the mother, by Zeus, of Dionysus. The fire of Zeus's thunderbolts killed her but made her child immortal.

sememe /ˈsɛmiːm, ˈsiːm-/ ▶ noun Linguistics the unit of meaning carried by a morpheme. Compare with SEMANTEME.
– ORIGIN early 20th cent.: from SEME + -EME.

semen /ˈsiːmən/ ▶ noun [mass noun] the male reproductive fluid, containing spermatozoa in suspension.
– ORIGIN late Middle English: from Latin, literally 'seed', from *serere* 'to sow'.

semester /sɪˈmɛstə/ ▶ noun a half-year term in a school or university, especially in North America, typically lasting for fifteen to eighteen weeks.
– ORIGIN early 19th cent.: from German *Semester*, from Latin *semestris* 'six-monthly', from *sex* 'six' + *mensis* 'month'.

Semey variant spelling of SEMEI.

semi ▶ noun (pl. **semis**) informal **1** Brit. a semi-detached house: *a three-bedroomed semi.*
2 a semi-final: *they defeated them in the semi.*
3 N. Amer. a semi-trailer: *she pulled into the path of a semi.*
– ORIGIN early 20th cent.: abbreviation.

semi- ▶ prefix **1** half: *semicircular.*
■occurring or appearing twice in a specified period: *semi-annual.*
2 partly; in some degree or particular: *semiconscious.*
■almost: *semi-darkness.*
– ORIGIN from Latin; related to Greek *hemi-*.

semi-acoustic ▶ adjective (of a guitar) having both one or more pickups and a hollow body, typically with f-holes.
▶ noun a semi-acoustic guitar.

semi-annual ▶ adjective occurring twice a year: *their semi-annual meetings.*
– DERIVATIVES **semi-annually** adverb.

semiaquatic ▶ adjective (of an animal) living partly on land and partly in water: *semiaquatic crocodiles.*
■(of a plant) growing in very wet or waterlogged ground.

semi-automatic ▶ adjective partially automatic: *a semi-automatic gearbox.*
■(of a firearm) having a mechanism for self-loading but not for continuous firing: *semi-automatic rifles.*
▶ noun a semi-automatic firearm.

semi-autonomous ▶ adjective **1** (of a country, state, or community) having a degree of, but not complete, self-government: *Russia's semi-autonomous republics.*
2 acting independently to some degree: *semi-autonomous working groups.*

semi-basement ▶ noun a storey of a building partly below ground level.

semibold ▶ adjective Printing printed in a typeface with thick strokes but not as thick as bold.

semibreve /ˈsɛmɪbriːv/ ▶ noun Music, chiefly Brit. a note having the time value of two minims or four crotchets, represented by a ring with no stem. It is the longest note now in common use. Also called WHOLE NOTE.

semicircle ▶ noun a half of a circle or of its circumference.
■a set of objects arranged in a semicircle: *chairs were in a semicircle round the hearth.*

– ORIGIN early 16th cent.: from Latin *semicirculus* (see SEMI-, CIRCLE).

semicircular ▶ adjective forming or shaped like a semicircle: *a semicircular driveway.*

semicircular canals ▶ plural noun three fluid-filled bony channels in the inner ear. They are situated at right angles to each other and provide information about orientation to the brain to help maintain balance.

semi-classical ▶ adjective **1** (of music) having elements both of classical music and of other more popular genres.
2 Physics (of a theory or method) intermediate between a classical or Newtonian description and one based on quantum mechanics or relativity.

semicolon /ˈsɛmɪˌkəʊlən, -ˈkəʊlən/ ▶ noun a punctuation mark (;) indicating a pause, typically between two main clauses, that is more pronounced than that indicated by a comma.

semiconducting ▶ adjective (of a material or device) having the properties of a semiconductor.

semiconductor ▶ noun a solid substance that has a conductivity between that of an insulator and that of most metals, either due to the addition of an impurity or because of temperature effects. Devices made of semiconductors, notably silicon, are essential components of most electronic circuits.

semi-conscious ▶ adjective (of a person) only partially conscious: *he dragged out the semi-conscious pilot.*
■(of a feeling or memory) of which the person experiencing it is only vaguely or partially aware: *semi-conscious obsessions.*

semi-conservative ▶ adjective Biochemistry relating to or denoting replication of a nucleic acid in which one complete strand of each double helix is directly derived from the parent molecule.
– DERIVATIVES **semi-conservatively** adverb.

semi-crystalline ▶ adjective Chemistry (of a solid) possessing crystalline character to some degree.

semi-cylinder ▶ noun Geometry half of a cylinder cut longitudinally.
– DERIVATIVES **semi-cylindrical** adjective.

semi-darkness ▶ noun [mass noun] a light level in which it is possible to see, but not clearly.

semidemisemiquaver ▶ noun Music, chiefly Brit. another term for HEMIDEMISEMIQUAVER.

semi-deponent ▶ adjective (of a Latin verb) having active forms in present tenses, and passive forms with active sense in perfect tenses.

semi-derelict ▶ adjective in a partially derelict state: *a semi-derelict farmhouse.*

semi-detached ▶ adjective (of a house) joined to another house on one side only by a common wall.
▶ noun Brit. a semi-detached house.

semidiameter /ˌsɛmɪdʌɪˈamɪtə/ ▶ noun Geometry half of a diameter.
– ORIGIN late Middle English: from late Latin.

semi-documentary ▶ adjective (of a film) having a factual background and a fictitious story.
▶ noun a semi-documentary film.

semi-dome ▶ noun Architecture a half-dome formed by vertical section.

semi-double ▶ adjective (of a flower) intermediate between single and double in having only the outer stamens converted to petals.

semi-elliptical ▶ adjective having the shape of half of an ellipse bisected by one of its diameters, especially the major axis.

semi-final ▶ noun a match or round immediately preceding the final, the winner of which goes on to the final.
– DERIVATIVES **semi-finalist** noun.

semi-finished ▶ adjective prepared for the final stage of manufacture: *crude steel and semi-finished metal products.*

semi-fitted ▶ adjective (of a garment) shaped to the body but not closely fitted: *a single-breasted semi-fitted jacket.*

semi-fluid ▶ adjective having a thick consistency between solid and liquid.
▶ noun a semi-fluid substance.

semi-independent ▶ adjective partially free from outside control; not wholly depending on

another's authority: *detachments are semi-independent units that are armed differently from their regiment.*
■(of a country or region) partially self-governing. ■ (of an institution) not wholly supported by public funds.

semi-infinite ▶ adjective Mathematics (of a line or solid) limited in one direction and stretching to infinity in the other.

semi-invalid ▶ noun a partially disabled or somewhat infirm person.

semilethal ▶ adjective Genetics relating to or denoting an allele or chromosomal abnormality which impairs the viability of most of the individuals homozygous for it.

semi-liquid ▶ adjective & noun another term for SEMI-FLUID.

semi-literate ▶ adjective unable to read or write with ease or fluency; poorly educated: *a high proportion of the population is still relatively poor and semi-literate.*
■(of a text) poorly written: *the semi-literate glossies.*
▶ noun a person who is poorly educated or unable to read or write with ease or fluency.
– DERIVATIVES **semi-literacy** noun.

Sémillon /ˈsɛmɪjõ/ ▶ noun [mass noun] a variety of white wine grape grown in France and elsewhere.
■a white wine made from this grape.
– ORIGIN French dialect, based on Latin *semen* 'seed'.

semilunar ▶ adjective chiefly Anatomy shaped like a half-moon or crescent.
– ORIGIN late Middle English: from medieval Latin *semilunaris* (see SEMI-, LUNAR).

semilunar bone ▶ noun another term for *lunate bone* (see LUNATE).

semilunar cartilage ▶ noun a crescent-shaped cartilage in the knee.

semilunar valve ▶ noun Anatomy each of a pair of valves in the heart, at the bases of the aorta and the pulmonary artery, consisting of three cusps or flaps which prevent the flow of blood back into the heart.

semimajor axis ▶ noun Geometry either of the halves of the major axis of an ellipse.

semimetal ▶ noun Chemistry an element (e.g. arsenic, antimony, or tin) whose properties are intermediate between those of metals and solid non-metals or semiconductors.
– DERIVATIVES **semimetallic** adjective.
– ORIGIN mid 17th cent.: from modern Latin *semimetallum* (see SEMI-, METAL).

semiminor axis ▶ noun Geometry either of the halves of the minor axis of an ellipse.

semi-modal ▶ noun a verb that functions to some extent like a modal verb, typically in the way it forms negative and interrogative constructions. English semi-modals include *need* and *dare.*

semi-monocoque ▶ adjective relating to or denoting aircraft or vehicle structures combining a load-bearing shell with integral frames.

semi-monthly ▶ adjective chiefly N. Amer. occurring or published twice a month: *semi-monthly pay days.*

seminal ▶ adjective **1** (of a work, event, moment, or figure) strongly influencing later developments: *his seminal work on chaos theory.*
2 of, relating to, or denoting semen.
■Botany of, relating to, or derived from the seed of a plant.
– DERIVATIVES **seminally** adverb.
– ORIGIN late Middle English (in sense 2): from Old French *seminal* or Latin *seminalis*, from *semen* 'seed'. Sense 1 dates from the mid 17th cent.

seminal vesicle ▶ noun Anatomy each of a pair of glands which open into the vas deferens near to its junction with the urethra and secrete many of the components of semen.

seminar /ˈsɛmɪnɑː/ ▶ noun a conference or other meeting for discussion or training.
■a class at university in which a topic is discussed by a teacher and a small group of students.
– ORIGIN late 19th cent.: from German *Seminar*, from Latin *seminarium* (see SEMINARY).

seminary /ˈsɛmɪn(ə)ri/ ▶ noun (pl. **-ies**) a training college for priests or rabbis.
■archaic, figurative a place or thing in which something is developed or cultivated: *a glossary would have been a nursery and seminary of blunder.*
– DERIVATIVES **seminarian** /-ˈnɛːrɪən/ noun, **seminarist** noun.
– ORIGIN late Middle English (denoting a seed plot):

from Latin *seminarium* 'seed plot', neuter of *seminarius* 'of seed', from *semen* 'seed'.

seminiferous /ˌsɛmɪˈnɪf(ə)rəs/ ▶ adjective producing or conveying semen.
– ORIGIN late 17th cent.: from Latin *semen, semin-* 'seed' + -FEROUS.

Seminole /ˈsɛmɪnəʊl/ ▶ noun (pl. same or **Seminoles**) **1** a member of an American Indian people of the Creek confederacy, noted for resistance in the 19th century to encroachment on their land in Georgia and Florida. Many were resettled in Oklahoma.
2 [mass noun] the Muskogean language of the Seminoles, now with fewer than 10,000 speakers.
▶ adjective of or relating to the Seminoles or their language.
– ORIGIN via Creek from American Spanish *cimarrón* 'wild, untamed'.

semiochemical /ˌsiːmɪə(ʊ)ˈkɛmɪk(ə)l/ ▶ noun Biochemistry a pheromone or other chemical that conveys a signal from one organism to another so as to modify the behaviour of the recipient organism.

semi-official ▶ adjective having some, but not full, official authority or recognition: *a semi-official visit*.
– DERIVATIVES **semi-officially** adverb.

semiology /ˌsiːmɪˈɒlədʒi, ˌsɛmɪ-/ ▶ noun [mass noun] another term for SEMIOTICS.
– DERIVATIVES **semiological** adjective, **semiologist** noun.
– ORIGIN early 20th cent.: from Greek *sēmeion* 'sign' (from *sēma* 'mark') + -LOGY.

semi-opaque ▶ adjective not fully clear or transparent.

semi-opera ▶ noun a drama or similar entertainment with a substantial proportion of vocal music in addition to instrumental movements.

semiosis /ˌsiːmɪˈəʊsɪs, ˌsɛmɪ-/ ▶ noun [mass noun] Linguistics the process of signification in language or literature.
– ORIGIN early 20th cent.: from Greek *sēmeiosis* '(inference from) a sign'.

semiotics /ˌsiːmɪˈɒtɪks, ˌsɛmɪ-/ ▶ plural noun [treated as sing.] the study of signs and symbols and their use or interpretation.
– DERIVATIVES **semiotic** adjective, **semiotically** adverb, **semiotician** /-ˈtɪʃ(ə)n/ noun.
– ORIGIN late 19th cent.: from Greek *sēmeiotikos* 'of signs', from *sēmeioun* 'interpret as a sign'.

Semipalatinsk /ˌsɛmɪpəˈlɑːtɪnsk/ former name (until 1991) for SEMEI.

semipalmated /ˌsɛmɪpalˈmeɪtɪd/ ▶ adjective used in names of wading birds that have toes webbed for part of their length, e.g. **semipalmated sandpiper**.

semi-Pelagian /ˌsɛmɪpɪˈleɪdʒɪən/ (also **semi-pelagian**) Christian Theology ▶ adjective denoting the doctrine that the first steps towards good can be taken by the human will, though supervening divine grace is needed for salvation. It was (questionably) attributed to John Cassian (d.435), and was generally held to be heretical. See also PELAGIUS.
▶ noun a person who holds this doctrine.
– DERIVATIVES **semi-Pelagianism** noun.

semi-permanent ▶ adjective less than permanent, but with some stability or endurance: *the company employs him on a semi-permanent basis*.
– DERIVATIVES **semi-permanently** adverb.

semipermeable ▶ adjective (of a material or membrane) allowing certain substances to pass through it but not others, especially allowing the passage of a solvent but not of certain solutes.

semi-precious ▶ adjective denoting minerals which can be used as gems but are considered to be less valuable than precious stones.

semi-pro ▶ adjective & noun (pl. -os) informal short for SEMI-PROFESSIONAL.

semi-professional ▶ adjective receiving payment for an activity but not relying entirely on it for a living: *a semi-professional musician*.
■ involving or suitable for people engaged in an activity on such a basis: *training at semi-professional level*.
▶ noun a person who is engaged in an activity on such a basis.

semi-prone position ▶ noun another term for RECOVERY POSITION.

semiquaver /ˈsɛmɪˌkweɪvə/ ▶ noun Music, chiefly Brit. a note having the time value of a sixteenth of a semibreve or half a quaver, represented by a large dot with a two-hooked stem. Also called SIXTEENTH NOTE.

semiquinone /ˌsɛmɪˈkwɪnəʊn/ ▶ noun Chemistry a compound derived from a quinone, in which one of the two oxygen atoms is ionized or bonded to a hydrogen atom.

Semiramis /sɪˈmɪrəmɪs/ Greek Mythology the daughter of an Assyrian goddess who married an Assyrian king. After his death she ruled for many years and became one of the founders of Babylon. She is thought to have been based on the historical queen Sammuramat (*c*.800 BC).

semi-retired ▶ adjective having retired or withdrawn from employment or an occupation but continuing to work part-time or occasionally.
– DERIVATIVES **semi-retirement** noun.

semi-rigid ▶ adjective stiff and solid, but not inflexible: *a semi-rigid polyethylene hose*.
■ (of an airship) having a stiffened keel attached to a flexible gas container. ■ (of an inflatable boat) having a rigid hull and inflatable sponsons.

semi-skilled ▶ adjective (of work or a worker) having or needing some, but not extensive, training: *assembly lines of semi-skilled workers*.

semi-skimmed Brit. ▶ adjective (of milk) having had some of the cream removed.
▶ noun [mass noun] semi-skimmed milk.

semi-solid ▶ adjective highly viscous; slightly thicker than semi-fluid.

semi-submersible ▶ adjective denoting an oil or gas drilling platform or barge with submerged hollow pontoons able to be flooded with water when the vessel is anchored on site in order to provide stability.
▶ noun an oil rig of this type.

semi-sweet ▶ adjective (of food) slightly sweetened, but less so than normal: *semi-sweet chocolates*.
■ (of wine) neither dry nor sweet; slightly sweeter than medium dry.

semi-synthetic ▶ adjective Chemistry (of a substance) made by synthesis from a naturally occurring material.

Semite /ˈsiːmʌɪt, ˈsɛm-/ ▶ noun a member of any of the peoples who speak or spoke a Semitic language, including in particular the Jews and Arabs.
– ORIGIN from modern Latin *Semita*, via late Latin from Greek *Sēm* 'Shem', son of Noah in the Bible, from whom these people were traditionally supposed to be descended.

Semitic /sɪˈmɪtɪk/ ▶ adjective **1** relating to or denoting a family of languages that includes Hebrew, Arabic, and Aramaic and certain ancient languages such as Phoenician and Akkadian, constituting the main subgroup of the Afro-Asiatic family.
2 of or relating to the peoples who speak these languages, especially Hebrew and Arabic.

semitone ▶ noun Music the smallest interval used in classical Western music, equal to a twelfth of an octave or half a tone; a half step.

semi-trailer ▶ noun chiefly N. Amer. a trailer having wheels at the back but supported at the front by a towing vehicle.
■ an articulated lorry.

semi-transparent ▶ adjective partially or imperfectly transparent.

semi-tropics ▶ plural noun another term for SUBTROPICS.
– DERIVATIVES **semi-tropical** adjective.

semivowel ▶ noun a speech sound intermediate between a vowel and a consonant, e.g. *w* or *y*.
– ORIGIN mid 16th cent.: from SEMI- + VOWEL, on the pattern of Latin *semivocalis*.

Semmelweis /ˈzɛm(ə)lvʌɪs/, Ignaz Philipp (1818–65), Hungarian obstetrician; Hungarian name *Ignác Fülöp Semmelweis*. He discovered the infectious character of puerperal fever and advocated rigorous cleanliness and the use of antiseptics by doctors examining patients.

semmit /ˈsɛmɪt/ ▶ noun Scottish an undershirt; a vest.
– ORIGIN late Middle English: of unknown origin.

semolina ▶ noun [mass noun] the hard grains left after the milling of flour, used in puddings and in pasta.
■ a pudding made of this.
– ORIGIN late 18th cent.: from Italian *semolino*, diminutive of *semola* 'bran', from Latin *simila* 'flour'.

semper fidelis /ˌsɛmpə fɪˈdeɪlɪs/ ▶ adjective always faithful (the motto of the US Marine Corps).
– ORIGIN Latin.

sempervivum /ˌsɛmpəˈvʌɪvəm/ ▶ noun a plant of a genus that includes the houseleek.
● Genus *Sempervivum*, family Crassulaceae.
– ORIGIN modern Latin, from Latin *semper* 'always' + *vivus* 'living'.

sempiternal /ˌsɛmpɪˈtəːn(ə)l/ ▶ adjective eternal and unchanging; everlasting: *the sempiternal sadness of the industrial background*.
– DERIVATIVES **sempiternally** adverb, **sempiternity** noun.
– ORIGIN late Middle English: from Old French *sempiternel* or late Latin *sempiternalis*, from Latin *sempiternus*, from *semper* 'always' + *aeternus* 'eternal'.

semplice /ˈsɛmplɪtʃeɪ/ ▶ adverb Music (as a direction) in a simple style of performance.
– ORIGIN Italian, literally 'simple'.

sempre /ˈsɛmpreɪ/ ▶ adverb Music (in directions) throughout; always: *sempre forte*.
– ORIGIN Italian.

sempstress /ˈsɛm(p)strɪs/ ▶ noun another term for SEAMSTRESS.

Semtex ▶ noun [mass noun] a very pliable, odourless plastic explosive.
– ORIGIN 1980s: probably a blend of *Semtin* (the name of a village in the Czech Republic near the place of production) and EXPLOSIVE.

SEN ▶ abbreviation for (in the UK) State Enrolled Nurse.

Sen. ▶ abbreviation for ■ N. Amer. Senate. ■ N. Amer. Senator. ■ Senior.

sen /sɛn/ ▶ noun (pl. same) a monetary unit of Brunei, Cambodia, Indonesia, and Malaysia, equal to one hundredth of a dollar in Brunei, one hundredth of a riel in Cambodia, one hundredth of a rupiah in Indonesia, and one hundredth of a ringgit in Malaysia. [ORIGIN: representing CENT.]
■ a former monetary unit in Japan, equal to one hundredth of a yen. [ORIGIN: Japanese.]

Senanayake /ˌsɛnəˈnʌɪəkə/, Don Stephen (1884–1952), Sinhalese statesman, Prime Minister of Ceylon 1947–52. As Prime Minister he presided over Ceylon's achievement of full dominion status within the Commonwealth.

senarius /sɪˈnɛːrɪəs/ ▶ noun (pl. **senarii** /-ɪiː, -ɪʌɪ/) Prosody a verse of six feet, especially an iambic trimeter.
– ORIGIN mid 16th cent.: from Latin (see SENARY).

senary /ˈsiːnəri, ˈsɛn-/ ▶ adjective rare relating to or based on the number six.
– ORIGIN late 16th cent.: from Latin *senarius* 'containing six', based on *sex* 'six'.

senate ▶ noun any of various legislative or governing bodies, in particular: ■ the smaller upper assembly in the US, US states, France, and other countries. ■ the state council of the ancient Roman republic and empire, which shared legislative power with the popular assemblies, administration with the magistrates, and judicial power with the knights. ■ the governing body of a university or college.
– ORIGIN Middle English: from Old French *senat*, from Latin *senatus*, from *senex* 'old man'.

senator ▶ noun **1** a member of a senate, in particular a member of the US Senate: [as title] *Senator Vandenburg*.
2 Scots Law a Lord of Session.
– DERIVATIVES **senatorial** adjective, **senatorship** noun.
– ORIGIN Middle English (denoting a member of the ancient Roman senate): from Old French *senateur*, from Latin *senator* (see SENATE).

senatus consultum /sɛˌnɑːtuːs kɒnˈsʌltəm/ ▶ noun (pl. **senatus consulta** /kɒnˈsʌltə/) a decree of the ancient Roman senate.
– ORIGIN Latin.

send¹ ▶ verb (past and past participle **sent**) **1** [with obj.] cause to go or be taken to a particular destination; arrange for the delivery of, especially by post: *we*

S

sent a reminder letter but received no reply | [with two objs] *he sent her a nice little note.*
■ order or instruct to go to a particular destination or in a particular direction: *the BBC sent me to Washington to cover the trial.* ■ [no obj., with infinitive] send a message or letter: *he sent to invite her to supper.* ■ [with obj. and adverbial of direction] cause to move sharply or quickly; propel: *the volcano sent clouds of ash up four miles into the air.* ■ (**send someone to**) arrange for someone to go to (an institution) and stay there for a particular purpose: *many parents prefer to send their children to single-sex schools.*
2 [with obj. and complement] cause to be in a specified state: *while driving in London I was sent crazy by roadworks and closed bridges.*
■ [with obj.] informal affect with powerful emotion; put into ecstasy: *it's the spectacle and music that send us, not the words.*
– PHRASES **send someone flying** cause someone to be knocked violently off balance or to the ground. **send someone packing** see **PACK**[1]. **send someone to Coventry** see **COVENTRY**. **send someone to the showers** see **SHOWER**. **send word** send a message: *he sent word that he was busy.*
– DERIVATIVES **sendable** adjective, **sender** noun.
– ORIGIN Old English *sendan*, of Germanic origin; related to Dutch *zenden* and German *senden*.
▶ **send away for** order or request that (something) be sent to one: *you can send away for the recipe.*
send someone down Brit. **1** expel a student from a university. **2** informal sentence someone to imprisonment: *you're going to get sent down for possessing drugs.*
send something down Cricket bowl a ball or an over: *Bainbridge sent down 25 overs and finished with 5 for 44.*
send for order or instruct (someone) to come to one; summon: *if you don't go I shall send for the police.* ■ order by post: *send for our mail order catalogue.*
send something in submit material to be considered for a competition or possible publication: *don't forget to send in your entries for our summer competition.*
send off for another way of saying ***send away for*** above.
send someone off instruct someone to go; arrange for someone's departure: *she sent him off to a lecturing engagement.* ■ (of a referee, especially in soccer or rugby) order a player to leave the field and take no further part in the game: *the goalkeeper was sent off for a professional foul.*
send something off dispatch something by post: *please take a moment or two to send off a cheque to a good cause.*
send something on transmit mail or luggage to a further destination or in advance of one's own arrival: *I've got your catalogue—would you like me to send it on?*
send something out 1 produce or give out something; emit something: *radar signals were sent out in powerful pulses.* **2** dispatch items to a number of people; distribute something widely: *the company sent out written information about the stock.*
send someone up US sentence someone to imprisonment: *he was sent up for arson.*
send someone/thing up informal give an exaggerated imitation of someone or something in order to ridicule them: *we used to send him up something rotten.*

send[2] ▶ noun & verb variant spelling of **SCEND**.

Sendai /sɛnˈdʌɪ/ a city in Japan, situated near the NE coast of the island of Honshu; pop. 918,000 (1990). It is the capital of the region of Tohoku.

Sendai virus /ˈsɛndʌɪ/ ▶ noun [mass noun] Biology a parainfluenza virus which causes disease of the upper respiratory tract in mice and is used in the laboratory to produce cell fusion.

sendal /ˈsɛnd(ə)l/ ▶ noun historical a fine, rich silk material, chiefly used to make ceremonial robes and banners.
– ORIGIN Middle English: from Old French *cendal*, ultimately from Greek *sindōn*.

Sendero Luminoso /senˈðero lumiˈnoso/ Spanish name for **SHINING PATH**.

sending ▶ noun an unpleasant or evil thing or creature supposedly sent by someone with paranormal or magical powers to warn, punish, or take revenge on a person.
– ORIGIN mid 19th cent.: from Old Norse.

send-off ▶ noun a celebratory demonstration of goodwill at a person's departure: *I got an affectionate send-off from my colleagues.*

send-up ▶ noun informal an act of imitating someone or something in order to ridicule them; a parody: *a delicious send-up of a speech given by a trendy academic.*

sene /ˈsɛni/ ▶ noun (pl. same or **senes**) a monetary unit of Samoa, equal to one hundredth of a tala.
– ORIGIN Samoan.

Seneca[1] /ˈsɛnɪkə/, Lucius Annaeus (c.4 BC–AD 65), Roman statesman, philosopher, and dramatist; known as **Seneca the Younger**. Son of Seneca the Elder, he became tutor to Nero in 49 and was appointed consul in 57. His *Epistulae Morales* is a notable Stoic work.

Seneca[2] /ˈsɛnɪkə/, Marcus (or Lucius) Annaeus (c.55 BC–c.39 AD), Roman rhetorician, born in Spain; known as **Seneca the Elder**. Father of Seneca the Younger, he is best known for his works on rhetoric, only parts of which survive.

Seneca[3] /ˈsɛnɪkə/ ▶ noun (pl. same or **Senecas**) **1** a member of an American Indian people that was one of the five nations comprising the original Iroquois confederacy.
2 [mass noun] the Iroquoian language of this people, now with few speakers.
▶ adjective of or relating to this people or their language.
– ORIGIN via Dutch from Algonquian.

senecio /səˈniːsɪəʊ, -ʃɪəʊ/ ▶ noun (pl. **-os**) a plant of a genus that includes the ragworts and groundsels. Many kinds are cultivated as ornamentals and some are poisonous weeds of grassland.
● Genus *Senecio*, family Compositae.
– ORIGIN modern Latin, from Latin, literally 'old man, groundsel', with reference to the hairy white fruits.

Senegal /ˌsɛnɪˈɡɔːl/ a country on the coast of West Africa; pop. 7,632,000 (est. 1991); languages, French (official), Wolof, and other West African languages; capital, Dakar.

Part of the Mali empire in the 14th and 15th centuries, the area was colonized by the French and became part of French West Africa in 1895. Briefly a partner in the Federation of Mali (1959), Senegal withdrew and became a fully independent republic in 1960. The Gambia forms an enclave within Senegal.

– DERIVATIVES **Senegalese** /-ɡəˈliːz/ adjective & noun.

Senegambia /ˌsɛnəˈɡambɪə/ a region of West Africa consisting of the Senegal and Gambia Rivers and the area between them. It lies mostly in Senegal and western Mali.

senesce /sɪˈnɛs/ ▶ verb [no obj.] Biology (of a living organism) deteriorate with age.
– ORIGIN mid 17th cent.: from Latin *senescere*, from *senex* 'old'.

senescence /sɪˈnɛs(ə)ns/ ▶ noun [mass noun] Biology the condition or process of deterioration with age.
■ loss of a cell's power of division and growth.
– DERIVATIVES **senescent** adjective.

seneschal /ˈsɛnɪʃ(ə)l/ ▶ noun **1** historical the steward or major-domo of a medieval great house.
2 chiefly historical a governor or other administrative or judicial officer.
– ORIGIN Middle English: from Old French, from medieval Latin *seniscalus*, from a Germanic compound of words meaning 'old' and 'servant'.

senex /ˈsɛnɛks/ ▶ noun (pl. **senes** /ˈsɛneɪs/) (in literature, especially comedy) an old man as a stock figure.
– ORIGIN late 19th cent.: from Latin, 'old man'.

senhor /sɛnˈjɔː/ ▶ noun (in Portuguese-speaking countries) a man (often used as a title or polite form of address): *Senhor Emilio Sofia Rosa.*
– ORIGIN Portuguese, from Latin *senior* (see **SENIOR**).

senhora /sɛnˈjɔːrə/ ▶ noun (in Portuguese-speaking countries) a woman, especially a married woman (often used as a title or polite form of address): *I look forward to hearing what Senhora Rocha decides.*
– ORIGIN Portuguese, feminine of **SENHOR**.

senhorita /ˌsɛnjəˈriːtə/ ▶ noun (in Portuguese-speaking countries) a young woman, especially an unmarried one (often used as a title or polite form of address).
– ORIGIN Portuguese, diminutive of **SENHORA**.

senile ▶ adjective (of a person) having or showing the weaknesses or diseases of old age, especially a loss of mental faculties: *she couldn't cope with her senile husband.*
■ (of a condition) characteristic of or caused by old age: *senile decay.*
▶ noun a senile person: *you never know where you stand with these so-called seniles.*
– DERIVATIVES **senility** noun.
– ORIGIN mid 17th cent.: from French *sénile* or Latin *senilis*, from *senex* 'old man'.

senile dementia ▶ noun [mass noun] severe mental deterioration in old age, characterized by loss of memory and control of bodily functions.

senile plaque ▶ noun Medicine a microscopic mass of fragmented and decaying nerve terminals around an amyloid core, numbers of which occur in the brains of people with Alzheimer's disease.

senior /ˈsiːnɪə, ˈsiːnjə/ ▶ adjective **1** of a more advanced age: *he is 20 years **senior to** Leonard.*
■ Brit. of, for, or denoting schoolchildren above a certain age, typically eleven. ■ US of the final year at a university or high school. ■ relating to or denoting competitors of above a certain age or of the highest status in a particular sport. ■ (often **Senior**) [postpositive] (in names) denoting the elder of two who have the same name in a family, especially a father as distinct from his son: *Henry James senior.*
2 holding a high and authoritative position: *he is a senior Finance Ministry official.*
■ [predic.] (**senior to**) holding a higher position than: *the people senior to me in my department.*
▶ noun a person who is a specified number of years older than someone else: *she was only two years his senior.*
■ an elderly person, especially an old-age pensioner. ■ a student in one of the higher forms of a senior school. ■ a competitor of above a certain age or of the highest status in a particular sport: *at fourteen you move up to the seniors.*
– DERIVATIVES **seniority** noun.
– ORIGIN late Middle English: from Latin, literally 'older, older man', comparative of *senex*, *sen-* 'old man, old'.

senior aircraftman ▶ noun a male rank in the RAF, above leading aircraftman and below junior technician.

senior aircraftwoman ▶ noun a female rank in the RAF, above leading aircraftwoman and below junior technician.

senior chief petty officer ▶ noun a rank in the US navy, above chief petty officer and below master chief petty officer.

senior citizen ▶ noun an elderly person, especially an old-age pensioner.

senior combination room ▶ noun a term used at Cambridge University for **SENIOR COMMON ROOM**.

senior common room ▶ noun Brit. a room used for social purposes by fellows, lecturers, and other senior members of a college.
■ [treated as sing. or pl.] the senior members of a college regarded collectively.

senior high school ▶ noun N. Amer. a secondary school typically comprising the three highest grades.

senior master sergeant ▶ noun a rank of non-commissioned officer in the US air force, above master sergeant and below chief master sergeant.

senior nursing officer ▶ noun Brit. the person in charge of nursing services in a hospital.

senior registrar ▶ noun Brit. a hospital doctor undergoing specialist training, one grade below that of consultant.

Senior Service ▶ noun Brit. the Royal Navy.

seniti /ˈsɛnɪti/ ▶ noun (pl. same) a monetary unit of Tonga, equal to one hundredth of a pa'anga.
– ORIGIN Tongan.

Senna, Ayrton (1960–94), Brazilian motor-racing driver. He won the Formula One world championship in 1988, 1990, and 1991. He died from injuries sustained in a crash during the Italian Grand Prix in 1994.

senna ▶ noun the cassia tree.
■ [mass noun] a laxative prepared from the dried pods of this tree. ■ used in names of similar plants of the pea family, e.g. **bladder senna**, **scorpion senna**.
– ORIGIN mid 16th cent.: from medieval Latin *sena*, from Arabic *sanā*.

Sennacherib /sɪˈnakərɪb/ (d.681 BC) king of Assyria 705–681, son of Sargon II. In 701 he put down a Jewish rebellion, laying siege to Jerusalem but sparing it from destruction (according to 2 Kings

19:35). He also rebuilt the city of Nineveh and made it his capital.

sennet /ˈsɛnɪt/ ▶**noun** (in the stage directions of Elizabethan plays) a call on a trumpet or cornet to signal the ceremonial entrance or exit of an actor.
– ORIGIN late 16th cent.: perhaps a variant of **SIGNET**.

sennight /ˈsɛnʌɪt/ ▶**noun** archaic a week.
– ORIGIN Old English *seofon nihta* 'seven nights'.

sennit ▶**noun** [mass noun] plaited straw, hemp, or similar fibrous material used in making hats.
■Nautical variant spelling of **SINNET**.

Senoi /sɛˈnɔɪ/ ▶**noun** (pl. same) a member of an aboriginal people of western Malaysia.
▶**adjective** of or relating to this people.
– ORIGIN a local name.

señor /sɛˈnjɔː/ ▶**noun** (pl. **señores** /-reɪz/) a title or form of address used of or to a Spanish-speaking man, corresponding to Mr or sir: *he is certain his information is correct, señor.*
– ORIGIN Spanish, from Latin *senior* (see **SENIOR**).

señora /sɛˈnjɔːrə/ ▶**noun** a title or form of address used of or to a Spanish-speaking woman, corresponding to *Mrs* or *madam*: *Señora Dolores.*
– ORIGIN Spanish, feminine of **SEÑOR**.

señorita /ˌsɛnjəˈriːtə/ ▶**noun** a title or form of address used of or to a Spanish-speaking unmarried woman, corresponding to *Miss*: *a beautiful señorita.*
– ORIGIN Spanish, diminutive of **SEÑORA**.

Senr ▶**abbreviation for** Senior (in names).

sensate /ˈsɛnseɪt, -sət/ ▶**adjective** poetic/literary able to perceive with the senses; sensing: *the infant stretches, sensate, wakening.*
■perceived by the senses: *you are immersed in an illusionary, yet sensate, world.*
– ORIGIN mid 17th cent.: from late Latin *sensatus* 'having senses', from *sensus* (see **SENSE**).

sensation ▶**noun** **1** a physical feeling or perception resulting from something that happens to or comes into contact with the body: *a burning sensation in the middle of the chest.*
■[mass noun] the capacity to have such feelings or perceptions: *they had lost sensation in one or both forearms.* ■an inexplicable awareness or impression: [with clause] *she had the eerie* ***sensation that*** *she was being watched.*
2 a widespread reaction of interest and excitement: *his arrest for poisoning* ***caused a sensation.***
■a person, object, or event that arouses such interest and excitement: *she was a sensation, the talk of the evening.*
– ORIGIN early 17th cent.: from medieval Latin *sensatio(n-)*, from Latin *sensus* (see **SENSE**).

sensational ▶**adjective** (of an event, a person, or a piece of information) causing great public interest and excitement: *a sensational murder trial.*
■(of an account or a publication) presenting information in a way that is intended to provoke public interest and excitement, at the expense of accuracy: *cheap sensational periodicals.* ■informal very good indeed; very impressive or attractive: *you look sensational | a sensational view.*
– DERIVATIVES **sensationally** adverb.

sensationalism ▶**noun** [mass noun] **1** (especially in journalism) the use of exciting or shocking stories or language at the expense of accuracy, in order to provoke public interest or excitement: *media sensationalism.*
2 Philosophy another term for **PHENOMENALISM**.
– DERIVATIVES **sensationalist** noun & adjective, **sensationalistic** adjective.

sensationalize (also **-ise**) ▶**verb** [with obj.] (especially of a newspaper) present information about (something) in a way that provokes public interest and excitement, at the expense of accuracy: *the papers want to sensationalize the tragedy that my family has suffered.*

sense ▶**noun** **1** a faculty by which the body perceives an external stimulus; one of the faculties of sight, smell, hearing, taste, and touch: *the bear has a keen sense of smell which enables it to hunt at dusk.*
2 a feeling that something is the case: *she had the sense of being a political outsider.*
■an awareness or feeling that one is in a specified state: *you can improve your general health and sense of well-being.* ■(**sense of**) a keen intuitive awareness of or sensitivity to the presence or importance of something: *she had a fine sense of comic timing.*
3 [mass noun] a sane and realistic attitude to situations and problems: *he earned respect by the good sense he showed at meetings.*
■a reasonable or comprehensible rationale: *I can't see* ***the sense*** *in leaving all the work to you.*
4 a way in which an expression or a situation can be interpreted; a meaning: *it is not clear which sense of the word 'characters' is intended in this passage.*
5 chiefly Mathematics & Physics a property (e.g. direction of motion) distinguishing a pair of objects, quantities, effects, etc. which differ only in that each is the reverse of the other.
■[as modifier] Genetics relating to or denoting a coding sequence of nucleotides, complementary to an antisense sequence.
▶**verb** [with obj.] perceive by a sense or senses: *with the first frost, they could sense a change in the days.*
■be aware of: *she could sense her father's anger rising.* ■[with clause] be aware that something is the case without being able to define exactly how one knows: *he could sense that he wasn't liked.* ■(of a machine or similar device) detect: *an optical fibre senses a current flowing in a conductor.*
– PHRASES **bring someone to their** (or **come to one's**) **senses** restore someone to (or regain) consciousness. ■cause someone to (or start to) think and behave reasonably after a period of folly or irrationality. **in a** (or **one**) **sense** used to indicate a particular interpretation of a statement or situation: *in a sense, behaviour cannot develop independently of the environment.* **in one's senses** fully aware and in control of one's thoughts and words; sane: *would any man in his senses invent so absurd a story?* **make sense** be intelligible, justifiable, or practicable. **make sense of** find meaning or coherence in: *she must try to make sense of what was going on.* **out of one's senses** in or into a state of madness. **a sense of direction** a person's ability to know without explicit guidance the direction in which they are or should be moving. **take leave of one's senses** (in hyperbolic use) go mad.
– ORIGIN late Middle English (as a noun in the sense 'meaning'): from Latin *sensus* 'faculty of feeling, thought, meaning', from *sentire* 'feel'. The verb dates from the mid 16th cent.

sense datum ▶**noun** Philosophy an immediate object of perception, which is not a material object; a sense impression.

sensei /sɛnˈseɪ/ ▶**noun** (pl. same) (in martial arts) a teacher: [as title] *Sensei Ritchie began work.*
– ORIGIN Japanese, from *sen* 'previous' + *sei* 'birth'.

senseless ▶**adjective** **1** [often as complement] (of a person) unconscious: *the attack left a policeman beaten senseless.*
■incapable of sensation: *she knocked the glass from the girl's senseless fingers.*
2 (especially of violent or wasteful action) without discernible meaning or purpose: *in Vietnam I saw the senseless waste of human beings.*
■lacking common sense; wildly foolish: *it was as senseless as crossing Death Valley on foot.*
– DERIVATIVES **senselessly** adverb, **senselessness** noun.

sense organ ▶**noun** an organ of the body which responds to external stimuli by conveying impulses to the sensory nervous system.

sensibility ▶**noun** (pl. **-ies**) [mass noun] the ability to appreciate and respond to complex emotional or aesthetic influences; sensitivity: *the study of literature leads to a growth of intelligence and sensibility.*
■(**sensibilities**) a person's delicate sensitivity that makes them readily offended or shocked: *the scale of the poverty revealed by the survey shocked people's sensibilities.* ■Zoology, dated sensitivity to sensory stimuli.
– ORIGIN late Middle English (denoting the power of sensation): from late Latin *sensibilitas*, from *sensibilis* 'that can be perceived by the senses' (see **SENSIBLE**).

sensible ▶**adjective** **1** (of a statement or course of action) chosen in accordance with wisdom or prudence; likely to be of benefit: *I cannot believe that it is sensible to spend so much | a sensible diet.*
■(of a person) possessing or displaying prudence: *he was a sensible and capable boy.* ■(of an object) practical and functional rather than decorative: *Mum always made me have sensible shoes.*
2 archaic readily perceived; appreciable: *it will effect a sensible reduction in these figures.*
■[predic.] (**sensible of/to**) able to notice or appreciate; not unaware of: *we are sensible of the difficulties he faces.*
– DERIVATIVES **sensibleness** noun, **sensibly** adverb.
– ORIGIN late Middle English (also in the sense 'perceptible by the senses'): from Old French, or from Latin *sensibilis*, from *sensus* (see **SENSE**).

sensillum /sɛnˈsɪləm/ ▶**noun** (pl. **sensilla** /sɛnˈsɪlə/) Zoology (in arthropods and some other invertebrates) a simple sensory receptor consisting of a modified cell or small group of cells of the cuticle or epidermis, typically hair- or rod-shaped.
– ORIGIN early 20th cent.: modern Latin, diminutive of Latin *sensus* 'sense'.

sensitive ▶**adjective** **1** quick to detect or respond to slight changes, signals, or influences: *the new method of protein detection was more sensitive than earlier ones | spiders are* ***sensitive to*** *vibrations on their web.*
■easily damaged, injured, or distressed by slight changes: *the committee called for improved protection of wildlife in environmentally sensitive areas.* ■(of photographic materials) prepared so as to respond rapidly to the action of light. ■(of a market) unstable and liable to quick changes of price because of outside influences.
2 (of a person or a person's behaviour) having or displaying a quick and delicate appreciation of others' feelings: *I pay tribute to the Minister for his sensitive handling of the bill.*
■easily offended or upset: *I suppose I shouldn't be so sensitive.*
3 kept secret or with restrictions on disclosure to avoid endangering security: *he was suspected of passing sensitive information to other countries.*
▶**noun** a person who is believed to respond to paranormal influences.
– DERIVATIVES **sensitively** adverb, **sensitiveness** noun.
– ORIGIN late Middle English (in the sense 'sensory'): from Old French *sensitif, -ive* or medieval Latin *sensitivus*, formed irregularly from Latin *sentire* 'feel'. The current senses date from the early 19th cent.

sensitive period ▶**noun** Psychology a time or stage in a person's development when they are more responsive to certain stimuli and quicker to learn particular skills.

sensitive plant ▶**noun** **1** a tropical American plant of the pea family, whose leaflets fold together and leaves bend down when touched. A common weed of sugar cane, it has become naturalized throughout the tropics.
• *Mimosa pudica*, family Leguminosae.
2 figurative a delicate or sensitive person.

sensitivity ▶**noun** (pl. **-ies**) [mass noun] the quality or condition of being sensitive: *a total lack of common decency and sensitivity* | [count noun] *he has* ***a sensitivity to*** *cow's milk.*
■(**sensitivities**) a person's feelings which might be easily offended or hurt; sensibilities: *the only rules that matter are practical ones that respect local sensitivities.*

sensitize (also **-ise**) ▶**verb** [with obj.] cause (someone or something) to respond to certain stimuli; make sensitive: *the introductory section aims to* ***sensitize*** *students* ***to*** *the methodology of the course.*
■make (photographic film) sensitive to light: *the kit sensitizes any 35 mm film in hours.* ■(often **be sensitized to**) make (an organism) abnormally sensitive to a foreign substance: *the workers had been immunologically sensitized to the enzyme.*
– DERIVATIVES **sensitization** noun, **sensitizer** noun.

sensitometer /ˌsɛnsɪˈtɒmɪtə/ ▶**noun** Photography a device for measuring the sensitivity of photographic equipment to light.

sensor ▶**noun** a device which detects or measures a physical property and records, indicates, or otherwise responds to it.
– ORIGIN 1950s: from **SENSORY**, on the pattern of *motor.*

sensorimotor /ˌsɛns(ə)rɪˈməʊtə/ ▶**adjective** [attrib.] Physiology (of nerves or their actions) having or involving both sensory and motor functions or pathways.

sensorineural /ˌsɛns(ə)rɪˈnjʊər(ə)l/ ▶**adjective** Medicine (of hearing loss) caused by a lesion or disease of the inner ear or the auditory nerve.

sensorium /sɛnˈsɔːrɪəm/ ▶**noun** (pl. **sensoria** /-rɪə/ or **sensoriums**) the sensory apparatus or faculties considered as a whole: *virtual reality technology directed at recreating the human sensorium.*

– DERIVATIVES **sensorial** adjective, **sensorially** adverb.
– ORIGIN mid 17th cent.: from late Latin, from Latin *sens-* 'perceived', from the verb *sentire*.

sensory ▶ **adjective** of or relating to sensation or the physical senses; transmitted or perceived by the senses: *sensory input*.
– DERIVATIVES **sensorily** adverb.
– ORIGIN mid 18th cent.: from Latin *sens-* 'perceived' (from the verb *sentire*) or from the noun **SENSE** + **-ORY**[2].

sensory deprivation ▶ **noun** [mass noun] a process by which someone is deprived of normal external stimuli such as sight and sound for an extended period of time, especially as an experimental technique in psychology.

sensual /ˈsɛnsjʊəl, -ʃʊəl/ ▶ **adjective** of or arousing gratification of the senses and physical, especially sexual, pleasure: *the production of the ballet is sensual and passionate*.
– DERIVATIVES **sensualism** noun, **sensualist** noun, **sensualize** (also **-ise**) verb, **sensually** adverb.
– ORIGIN late Middle English (in the sense 'sensory'): from late Latin *sensualis*, from *sensus* (see **SENSE**).

USAGE The words **sensual** and **sensuous** are frequently used interchangeably to mean 'gratifying the senses', especially in a sexual sense. Strictly speaking, this goes against a traditional distinction, by which **sensuous** is a more neutral term, meaning 'relating to the senses rather than the intellect', as in *swimming is a beautiful, **sensuous** experience*, while **sensual** relates to gratification of the senses, especially sexually, as in *a **sensual** massage*. In fact the word **sensuous** is thought to have been invented by Milton (1641) in a deliberate attempt to avoid the sexual overtones of **sensual**. In practice, the connotations are such that it is difficult to use **sensuous** in this sense. While traditionalists struggle to maintain a distinction, the evidence from the British National Corpus and elsewhere suggests that the 'neutral' use of **sensuous** is rare in modern English. If a neutral use is intended it is advisable to use alternative wording.

sensuality ▶ **noun** [mass noun] the enjoyment, expression, or pursuit of physical, especially sexual, pleasure: *he ate the grapes with surprising sensuality*.
▪ the condition of being pleasing or fulfilling to the senses: *life can dazzle with its sensuality, its colour*.
– ORIGIN Middle English (denoting the animal side of human nature): from Old French *sensualite*, from late Latin *sensualitas*, from *sensualis* (see **SENSUAL**).

sensu lato /ˌsɛnsuː ˈlɑːtəʊ/ ▶ **adverb** formal in the broad sense.
– ORIGIN Latin.

sensum /ˈsɛnsəm/ ▶ **noun** (pl. **sensa** /-sə/) Philosophy a sense datum.
– ORIGIN mid 19th cent.: modern Latin, 'something sensed', neuter past participle of Latin *sentire* 'feel'.

sensuous /ˈsɛnsjʊəs, ˈsɛnʃʊəs/ ▶ **adjective** **1** relating to or affecting the senses rather than the intellect: *the work showed a deliberate disregard of the more sensuous and immediately appealing aspects of painting*.
2 attractive or gratifying physically, especially sexually: *her voice was rather deep but very sensuous*.
– DERIVATIVES **sensuously** adverb, **sensuousness** noun.
– ORIGIN mid 17th cent.: from Latin *sensus* 'sense' + **-OUS**.

USAGE On the use of the words **sensuous** and **sensual**, see usage at **SENSUAL**.

sensu stricto /ˌsɛnsuː ˈstrɪktəʊ/ ▶ **adverb** formal strictly speaking; in the narrow sense: *the process was one of substitution rather than change sensu stricto*.
– ORIGIN Latin, 'in the restricted sense'.

sent[1] past and past participle of **SEND**[1].

sent[2] /ˈsɛnt/ ▶ **noun** a monetary unit of Estonia, equal to one hundredth of a kroon.
– ORIGIN respelling of **CENT**.

sente /ˈsɛnti/ ▶ **noun** (pl. **lisente** /lɪˈsɛnti/) a monetary unit of Lesotho, equal to one hundredth of a loti.
– ORIGIN Sesotho.

sentence ▶ **noun** **1** a set of words that is complete in itself, typically containing a subject and predicate, conveying a statement, question, exclamation, or command, and consisting of a main clause and sometimes one or more subordinate clauses.
▪ Logic a series of signs or symbols expressing a proposition in an artificial or logical language.
2 the punishment assigned to a defendant found guilty by a court: *her husband is **serving** a three-year **sentence** for fraud*.
▪ the punishment fixed by law for a particular offence: *slander of an official carried an eight-year prison sentence*.
▶ **verb** [with obj.] declare the punishment decided for (an offender): *ten army officers were **sentenced to** death*.
– PHRASES **under sentence of** having been condemned to: *he was under sentence of death*.
– ORIGIN Middle English (in the senses 'way of thinking, opinion', 'court's declaration of punishment', and 'gist (of a piece of writing)'): via Old French from Latin *sententia* 'opinion', from *sentire* 'feel, be of the opinion'.

sentence adverb ▶ **noun** Grammar an adverb or adverbial phrase that expresses a writer's or speaker's attitude to the content of the sentence in which it occurs (such as *frankly, obviously*), or places the sentence in a particular context (such as *technically, politically*).

USAGE The traditional definition of an adverb is that it is a word that modifies the meaning of a verb, an adjective, or another adverb, as in, for example, *he shook his head **sadly***. However, another important function of some adverbs is to comment on a whole sentence, either expressing the speaker's attitude or classifying the discourse. For example, in ***sadly**, he is rather overbearing*, **sadly** does not mean that he is overbearing in a sad manner: it expresses the speaker's attitude to what is being stated. Traditionalists take the view that the use of sentence adverbs is inherently suspect and that they should always be paraphrased, e.g. using such wording as ***it is sad that** he is rather overbearing*. A particular objection is raised to the sentence adverbs **hopefully** and **thankfully**, since they cannot even be paraphrased in the usual way (see **usage** at **HOPEFULLY** and **THANKFULLY**). However, there is overwhelming evidence that such usages are well established and widely accepted in everyday speech and writing.

sentential /sɛnˈtɛnʃ(ə)l/ ▶ **adjective** Grammar & Logic of or relating to a sentence: *sentential meaning*.

sententious /sɛnˈtɛnʃəs/ ▶ **adjective** given to moralizing in a pompous or affected manner: *he tried to encourage his men with sententious rhetoric*.
– DERIVATIVES **sententiously** adverb, **sententiousness** noun.
– ORIGIN late Middle English: from Latin *sententiosus*, from *sententia* 'opinion' (see **SENTENCE**). The original sense was 'full of meaning or wisdom', later becoming depreciatory.

sentient /ˈsɛnʃ(ə)nt/ ▶ **adjective** able to perceive or feel things: *she had been instructed from birth in the equality of all sentient life forms*.
– DERIVATIVES **sentience** noun, **sentiently** adverb.
– ORIGIN early 17th cent.: from Latin *sentient-* 'feeling', from the verb *sentire*.

sentiment ▶ **noun** **1** a view of or attitude towards a situation or event; an opinion: *I agree with your sentiments regarding the road bridge*.
▪ [mass noun] general feeling or opinion: *the council sought steps to control the rise of racist sentiment*. ▪ archaic the expression of a view or desire especially as formulated for a toast.
2 a feeling or emotion: *an intense sentiment of horror*.
▪ [mass noun] exaggerated and self-indulgent feelings of tenderness, sadness, or nostalgia: *many of the appeals rely on treacly sentiment*.
– ORIGIN late Middle English (in the senses 'personal experience' and 'physical feeling, sensation'): from Old French *sentement*, from medieval Latin *sentimentum*, from Latin *sentire* 'feel'.

sentimental ▶ **adjective** of or prompted by feelings of tenderness, sadness, or nostalgia: *she felt a sentimental attachment to the place creep over her*.
▪ (of a work of literature, music, or art) dealing with feelings of tenderness, sadness, or nostalgia in an exaggerated and self-indulgent way: *a sentimental ballad*. ▪ (of a person) excessively prone to feelings of tenderness, sadness, or nostalgia: *I'm a sentimental old fool*.
– PHRASES **sentimental value** the value of something to someone because of personal or emotional associations rather than material worth.
– DERIVATIVES **sentimentally** adverb.

sentimentalism ▶ **noun** [mass noun] the excessive expression of feelings of tenderness, sadness, or nostalgia in behaviour, writing, or speech: *the author blends realism with surrealism, journalism with sentimentalism*.
– DERIVATIVES **sentimentalist** noun.

sentimentality ▶ **noun** (pl. **-ies**) [mass noun] excessive tenderness, sadness, or nostalgia: *there are passages which verge on sentimentality* | [count noun] *sentimentalities of this kind seem reserved, in her, for people she does not know*.

sentimentalize (also **-ise**) ▶ **verb** [with obj.] treat (someone or something) with exaggerated and self-indulgent feelings of tenderness, sadness, or nostalgia: [as adj. **sentimentalized**] *the impossibly sentimentalized and saintly ideal of the Virgin Mother*.
– DERIVATIVES **sentimentalization** noun.

sentinel /ˈsɛntɪn(ə)l/ ▶ **noun** a soldier or guard whose job is to stand and keep watch.
▪ figurative something that appears to be standing guard or keeping watch. ▪ Medicine a thing that acts as an indicator of the presence of disease: [as modifier] *the first national HIV sentinel surveillance programme in the developing world*.
▶ **verb** (**sentinelled**, **sentinelling**; US **sentineled**, **sentineling**) [with obj.] station a soldier or guard by (a place) to keep watch: *a wide course had been roped off and **sentinelled with** police* | figurative *trees sentinelled the trenches*.
– PHRASES **stand sentinel** (of a soldier) keep watch: *soldiers stood sentinel with their muskets* | figurative *a tall round tower standing sentinel over the river*.
– ORIGIN late 16th cent.: from French *sentinelle*, from Italian *sentinella*, of unknown origin.

sentry ▶ **noun** (pl. **-ies**) a soldier stationed to keep guard or to control access to a place.
– PHRASES **stand sentry** keep guard or control access to a place.
– ORIGIN early 17th cent.: perhaps from obsolete *centrinel*, variant of **SENTINEL**.

sentry box ▶ **noun** a structure providing shelter for a standing sentry.

sentry-go ▶ **noun** [mass noun] Military the duty of being a sentry.

Senufo /səˈnuːfəʊ/ ▶ **noun** **1** (pl. same) a member of a West African people inhabiting parts of the Ivory Coast, Mali, and Burkina.
2 [mass noun] the language of this people, which belongs to the Gur group and has many different dialects.
▶ **adjective** of or relating to this people or their language.
– ORIGIN Akan.

Senussi /sɛˈnuːsi/ ▶ **noun** (pl. same or **Senussis**) a member of a North African Muslim religious fraternity founded in 1837 by Sidi Muhammad ibn Ali es-Senussi (d.1859).

Seoul /səʊl/ the capital of South Korea, situated in the north-west of the country on the Han River; pop. 10,627,790 (1990). It was the capital of the Korean Yi dynasty from the late 14th century until 1910, when Korea was annexed by the Japanese. Extensively developed under Japanese rule, it became the capital of South Korea after the partition of 1945.

sepal ▶ **noun** Botany each of the parts of the calyx of a flower, enclosing the petals and typically green and leaf-like.
– ORIGIN early 19th cent.: from French *sépale*, modern Latin *sepalum*, from Greek *skepē* 'covering', influenced by French *pétale* 'petal'.

separable ▶ **adjective** able to be separated or treated separately: *body and soul are not separable*.
▪ Grammar (of a German prefix) separated from the base verb when inflected. ▪ Grammar (of a German verb) consisting of a prefix and a base verb which are separated when inflected, for example *einführen*. ▪ Grammar (of an English phrasal verb) allowing the insertion of the direct object between the base verb and the particle, e.g. *look it over* as opposed to *go over it*.
– DERIVATIVES **separability** noun, **separableness** noun, **separably** adverb.
– ORIGIN late Middle English: from Latin *separabilis*, from *separare* 'disjoin, divide' (see **SEPARATE**).

separate ▶ **adjective** /ˈsɛp(ə)rət/ forming or viewed as a unit apart or by itself: *this raises two separate issues* | *he regards the study of literature as quite **separate from** life*.
▪ not joined or touching physically: *a bathroom and separate WC*. ▪ different; distinct: *melt the white and plain chocolate in separate bowls*.
▶ **verb** /ˈsɛpəreɪt/ **1** [with obj.] cause to move or be apart: *police were trying to separate two rioting mobs* | *they were separated by the war*.

■form a distinction or boundary between (people, places, or things): *only a footpath separated their garden from the shore | six years separated the two brothers.* ■ [no obj.] become detached or disconnected: *the second stage of the rocket failed to separate.* ■ [no obj.] leave another person's company: *they separated at the corner, agreeing to meet within two hours.* ■ [no obj.] stop living together as a couple: *after her parents separated she was brought up by her mother |* [as adj. **separated**] *her parents are separated.* ■ (often **be separated**) US discharge or dismiss (someone) from service or employment: *this year one million veterans will be separated from the service.*

2 divide or cause to divide into constituent or distinct elements: [no obj.] *the processed milk had* ***separated into*** *curds and whey |* [with obj.] *separate the eggs and beat the egg yolks.*

■[with obj.] extract or remove for use or rejection: *the skins are separated from the juice before fermentation |* figurative *we need to separate fact from speculation.* ■ [with obj.] distinguish between; consider individually: *we cannot separate his thinking from his activity.* ■ (of a factor or quality) distinguish (someone or something) from others: *his position separates him from those who might share his interests.* ■ [with obj.] (**separate something off**) make something form, or view something as, a unit apart or by itself: *the organ loft separating off the choir.*

▶**noun** /ˈsɛp(ə)rət/ (**separates**) things forming units by themselves, in particular:

■individual items of clothing, such as skirts, jackets, or trousers, suitable for wearing in different combinations. ■ the self-contained, free-standing components of a sound-reproduction system. ■ portions into which a soil, sediment, etc. can be sorted according to particle size, mineral composition, or other criteria.

– PHRASES **go one's separate ways** leave in a different direction from someone with whom one has just travelled or spent time. ■ end a romantic, professional, or other relationship. **separate but equal** US historical racially segregated but ensuring equal opportunities to all races. **separate the men from the boys** see **MAN**. **separate the sheep from the goats** divide people or things into superior and inferior groups. [ORIGIN: with biblical allusion to Matt. 25:33.] **separate the wheat from the chaff** see **CHAFF**[1].

– DERIVATIVES **separately** adverb, **separateness** noun.

– ORIGIN late Middle English: from Latin *separat-* 'disjoined, divided', from the verb *separare*, from *se-* 'apart' + *parare* 'prepare'.

separate maintenance ▶**noun** see **MAINTENANCE** (sense 2).

separate school ▶**noun** Canadian a school receiving pupils from a particular religious group.

separation ▶**noun** [mass noun] **1** the action or state of moving or being moved apart: *the damage that might arise from the separation of parents and children.*

■the state in which a husband and wife remain married but live apart: *legal grounds for divorce or separation |* [count noun] *she and her husband have agreed to a* ***trial separation***. See also **LEGAL SEPARATION** (sense 1).

2 the division of something into constituent or distinct elements: *prose structured into short sentences with meaningful* ***separation into*** *paragraphs.*

■the process of distinguishing between two or more things: *religion involved the separation of the sacred and the profane |* [count noun] *the constitution imposed a clear* ***separation between*** *church and state.* ■ the process of sorting and then extracting or removing a specified substance for use or rejection. ■ short for **COLOUR SEPARATION**. ■ (also **stereo separation**) distinction or difference between the signals carried by the two channels of a stereophonic system. ■ Physics & Aeronautics the generation of a turbulent boundary layer between the surface of a body and a moving fluid, or between two fluids moving at different speeds.

– PHRASES **separation of powers** an act of vesting the legislative, executive, and judiciary powers of government in separate bodies.

– ORIGIN late Middle English: via Old French from Latin *separatio(n-)*, from *separare* 'disjoin, divide' (see **SEPARATE**).

separation anxiety ▶**noun** [mass noun] Psychiatry anxiety provoked in a young child by separation or the threat of separation from its mother or main carer.

separation order ▶**noun** a court order for the legal separation of a married couple.

separatism ▶**noun** [mass noun] the advocacy or practice of separation of a certain group of people from a larger body on the basis of ethnicity, religion, or gender: *Kurdish separatism.*

separatist ▶**noun** a person who supports the separation of a particular group of people from a larger body on the basis of ethnicity, religion, or gender: *his parents were religious separatists.*

▶**adjective** of or relating to such separation or those supporting it: *a separatist rebellion.*

separative ▶**adjective** technical tending to cause division into constituent or individual elements.

separator ▶**noun** a machine or device that separates something into its constituent or distinct elements: *a magnetic separator.*

■something that keeps two or more things apart: *a separator means you can cook more than one thing at once.*

Sepedi /sɛˈpɛːdi/ ▶**noun** [mass noun] a Bantu language of southern Africa, the main member of the North Sotho group.

Sephadex /ˈsɛfədɛks/ ▶**noun** [mass noun] trademark a preparation of dextran used as a gel in chromatography, electrophoresis, and other separation techniques.

– ORIGIN 1950s: of unknown origin.

Sephardi /sɪˈfɑːdi/ ▶**noun** (pl. **Sephardim** /-dɪm/) a Jew of Spanish or Portuguese descent. They retain their own distinctive dialect of Spanish (Ladino), customs, and rituals, preserving Babylonian Jewish traditions rather than the Palestinian ones of the Ashkenazim. Compare with **ASHKENAZI**.

■any Jew of the Middle East or North Africa.

– DERIVATIVES **Sephardic** adjective.

– ORIGIN modern Hebrew, from *sĕpāraḏ*, a country mentioned in Obad. 20 and taken to be Spain.

Sepharose /ˈsɛfərəʊz/ ▶**noun** [mass noun] trademark a preparation of agarose used as a gel in chromatography, electrophoresis, and other separation techniques.

– ORIGIN 1960s: of unknown origin.

sephira /ˈsɛfɪrɑː/ ▶**noun** (pl. **sephiroth** /ˈsɛfɪrəʊθ/) (in the Kabbalah) each of the ten attributes or emanations surrounding the Infinite and by means of which it relates to the finite. They are represented as spheres on the Tree of Life.

– ORIGIN from Hebrew *sĕpīrāh*.

sepia /ˈsiːpɪə/ ▶**noun** [mass noun] a reddish-brown colour associated particularly with monochrome photographs of the 19th and early 20th centuries.

■a brown pigment prepared from a black fluid secreted by cuttlefish, used in monochrome drawing and in watercolours. ■ [count noun] a drawing done with this pigment. ■ a blackish fluid secreted by a cuttlefish as a defensive screen.

▶**adjective** of a reddish-brown colour: *old sepia photographs.*

– ORIGIN late Middle English (denoting a cuttlefish): via Latin from Greek *sēpia* 'cuttlefish'. The current senses date from the early 19th cent.

sepoy /ˈsiːpɔɪ, sɪˈpɔɪ/ ▶**noun** historical an Indian soldier serving under British or other European orders.

■(in the Indian subcontinent) a police constable.

– ORIGIN from Urdu and Persian *sipāhī* 'soldier', from *sipāh* 'army'.

Sepoy Mutiny another term for **INDIAN MUTINY**.

seppuku /sɛˈpuːkuː/ ▶**noun** another term for **HARA-KIRI**.

– ORIGIN Japanese, from *setsu* 'to cut' + *fuku* 'abdomen'.

seps /sɛps/ ▶**noun** an African lizard with a snake-like body and very short or non-existent legs.

• Genera *Tetradactylus*, family Gerrhosauridae: several species, formerly regarded as skinks.

– ORIGIN mid 16th cent. (denoting a venomous serpent described by classical authors): via Latin from Greek *sēps*, from the base of *sēpein* 'make rotten'.

sepsis /ˈsɛpsɪs/ ▶**noun** [mass noun] Medicine the presence in tissues of harmful bacteria and their toxins, typically through infection of a wound.

– ORIGIN late 19th cent.: modern Latin, from Greek *sēpsis*, from *sēpein* 'make rotten'.

Sept. ▶**abbreviation for** ■ September. ■ Septuagint.

sept ▶**noun** a clan, originally one in Ireland.

– ORIGIN early 16th cent.: probably an alteration of **SECT**.

sept- ▶**combining form** variant spelling of **SEPTI-** (as in *septcentenary*).

septa plural form of **SEPTUM**.

septage /ˈsɛptɪdʒ/ ▶**noun** [mass noun] excrement and other waste material contained in or removed from a septic tank.

– ORIGIN 1970s: from **SEPTIC**, on the pattern of *sewage*.

septal[1] ▶**adjective** relating to or acting as a partition, in particular:

■Anatomy & Biology relating to a septum or septa. ■ Archaeology (of a stone or slab) separating compartments in a burial chamber.

septal[2] ▶**adjective** of or relating to a sept or clan.

septarium /sɛpˈtɛːrɪəm/ ▶**noun** (pl. **septaria** /-rɪə/) Geology a concretionary nodule, typically of ironstone, having radial cracks filled with calcite or another mineral.

– DERIVATIVES **septarian** adjective.

– ORIGIN late 18th cent.: modern Latin, from Latin *septum* 'enclosure'.

septate ▶**adjective** Anatomy & Biology having or partitioned by a septum or septa.

– DERIVATIVES **septation** noun.

septcentenary /ˌsɛp(t)sɛnˈtiːn(ə)ri, -ˈtɛn-/ ▶**noun** (pl. **-ies**) the seven-hundredth anniversary of a significant event.

▶**adjective** of or relating to a seven-hundredth anniversary.

September ▶**noun** the ninth month of the year, in the northern hemisphere usually considered the first month of autumn: *sow the plants in early September | a course commencing this September.*

– ORIGIN late Old English, from Latin, from *septem* 'seven' (being originally the seventh month of the Roman year).

septenarius /ˌsɛptɪˈnɛːrɪəs/ ▶**noun** (pl. **septenarii** /-rɪʌɪ/) Prosody a verse line of seven feet, especially a trochaic or iambic tetrameter catalectic.

– ORIGIN early 19th cent.: from Latin, from *septeni* 'in sevens', from *septem* 'seven'.

septenary /ˈsɛptɪn(ə)ri, -ˈtiːn(ə)ri/ ▶**adjective** of, relating to, or divided into seven.

▶**noun** (pl. **-ies**) a group or set of seven, in particular:

■a period of seven years. ■ Music the seven notes of the diatonic scale. ■ a septenarius.

– ORIGIN late Middle English: from Latin *septenarius* (see **SEPTENARIUS**).

septennial ▶**adjective** recurring every seven years.

■lasting for or relating to a period of seven years.

– ORIGIN mid 17th cent.: from late Latin *septennis* (from Latin *septem* 'seven' + *annus* 'year') + **-AL**.

septennium /sɛpˈtɛnɪəm/ ▶**noun** (pl. **septennia** /-nɪə/ or **septenniums**) rare a specified period of seven years.

– ORIGIN mid 19th cent.: from late Latin, from Latin *septem* 'seven' + *annus* 'year'.

septet /sɛpˈtɛt/ (also **septette**) ▶**noun** a group of seven people playing music or singing together.

■a composition for such a group.

– ORIGIN early 19th cent.: from German *Septett*, from Latin *septem* 'seven'.

septi- (also **sept-**) ▶**combining form** seven; having seven: *septivalent.*

– ORIGIN from Latin *septem* 'seven'.

septic /ˈsɛptɪk/ ▶**adjective 1** (chiefly of a wound or a part of the body) infected with bacteria: *his feet had gone septic.*

2 [attrib.] denoting a drainage system incorporating a septic tank.

▶**noun** N. Amer. a drainage system incorporating a septic tank.

– DERIVATIVES **septically** adverb, **septicity** /-ˈtɪsɪti/ noun.

– ORIGIN early 17th cent.: via Latin from Greek *sēptikos*, from *sēpein* 'make rotten'.

septicaemia /ˌsɛptɪˈsiːmɪə/ (US **septicemia**) ▶**noun** [mass noun] blood poisoning, especially that caused by bacteria or their toxins.

– DERIVATIVES **septicaemic** adjective.

– ORIGIN mid 19th cent.: modern Latin, from Greek *sēptikos* + *haima* 'blood'.

septic tank ▶**noun** a tank, typically underground, in which sewage is collected and allowed to decompose through bacterial activity before draining by means of a soakaway.

septillion /sɛpˈtɪljən/ ▶**cardinal number** (pl. **septillions** or (with numeral) same) a thousand raised to the eighth power (10^{24}).

■ dated, chiefly Brit. a million raised to the seventh power (10^{42}).
– ORIGIN late 17th cent.: from French, from *million*, by substitution of the prefix *septi-* 'seven' (from Latin *septimus* 'seventh') for the initial letters.

septimal /ˈsɛptɪm(ə)l/ ▶ **adjective** of or relating to the number seven.
– ORIGIN mid 19th cent.: from Latin *septimus* 'seventh' (from *septem* 'seven') + **-AL**.

septime /ˈsɛptɪm, -tiːm/ ▶ **noun** Fencing the seventh of the eight parrying positions.
– ORIGIN late 19th cent.: from Latin *septimus* 'seventh'.

septivalent /ˌsɛptɪˈveɪl(ə)nt/ ▶ **adjective** Chemistry another term for **HEPTAVALENT**.

septoria /sɛpˈtɔːrɪə/ ▶ **noun** [mass noun] a fungus of a genus that includes many kinds that cause diseases in plants.
● Genus *Septoria*, subdivision Deuteromycotina.
■ leaf spot disease caused by such a fungus.
– ORIGIN modern Latin, from Latin *septum* (see **SEPTUM**).

septuagenarian /ˌsɛptjʊədʒɪˈnɛːrɪən/ ▶ **noun** a person who is between 70 and 79 years old.
– ORIGIN late 18th cent.: from Latin *septuagenarius* (based on *septuaginta* 'seventy') + **-AN**.

Septuagesima /ˌsɛptjʊəˈdʒɛsɪmə/ (also **Septuagesima Sunday**) the Sunday before Sexagesima.
– ORIGIN late Middle English: from Latin, 'seventieth (day)', probably named by analogy with **QUINQUAGESIMA**.

Septuagint /ˈsɛptjʊədʒɪnt/ ▶ **noun** a Greek version of the Hebrew Bible (or Old Testament), including the Apocrypha, made for Greek-speaking Jews in Egypt in the 3rd and 2nd centuries BC and adopted by the early Christian Churches.
– ORIGIN mid 16th cent. (originally denoting the translators themselves): from Latin *septuaginta* 'seventy', because of the tradition that it was produced, under divine inspiration, by seventy-two translators working independently.

septum /ˈsɛptəm/ ▶ **noun** (pl. **septa** /-tə/) chiefly Anatomy & Biology a partition separating two chambers, such as that between the nostrils or the chambers of the heart.
– ORIGIN mid 17th cent.: from Latin *septum*, from *sepire* 'enclose', from *sepes* 'hedge'.

septuple /ˈsɛptjʊp(ə)l, sɛpˈtjuːp(ə)l/ rare ▶ **adjective** [attrib.] consisting of seven parts or elements.
■ consisting of seven times as much or as many as usual. ■ (of time in music) having seven beats in a bar.
▶ **verb** [with obj.] multiply (something) by seven; increase sevenfold.
– ORIGIN early 17th cent. (as a verb): from late Latin *septuplus*, from Latin *septem* 'seven'.

septuplet /ˈsɛptjʊplɪt, sɛpˈtjuːplɪt/ ▶ **noun 1** (usu. **septuplets**) each of seven children born at one birth.
2 Music a group of seven notes to be performed in the time of four or six.
– ORIGIN late 19th cent.: from Latin *septuplus* (see **SEPTUPLE**), on the pattern of words such as *triplet*.

sepulchral /sɪˈpʌlkr(ə)l/ ▶ **adjective** of or relating to a tomb or interment: *sepulchral monuments.*
■ gloomy; dismal: *a speech delivered in sepulchral tones.*
– DERIVATIVES **sepulchrally** adverb.
– ORIGIN early 17th cent.: from French *sépulchral* or Latin *sepulchralis*, from *sepulcrum* (see **SEPULCHRE**).

sepulchre /ˈsɛp(ə)lkə/ (US **sepulcher**) ▶ **noun** a small room or monument, cut in rock or built of stone, in which a dead person is laid or buried.
▶ **verb** [with obj.] chiefly poetic/literary lay or bury in or as if in a sepulchre: *tomes are soon out of print and sepulchred in the dust of libraries.*
■ serve as a burial place for: *when ocean shrouds and sepulchres our dead.*
– ORIGIN Middle English: via Old French from Latin *sepulcrum* 'burial place', from *sepelire* 'bury'.

sepulture /ˈsɛp(ə)ltʃə/ ▶ **noun** [mass noun] archaic burial; interment: *the rites of sepulture.*
– ORIGIN Middle English: via Old French from Latin *sepultura*, from *sepelire* 'bury'.

seq. (also **seqq.**) ▶ **adverb** short for **ET SEQ.**

sequacious /sɪˈkweɪʃəs/ ▶ **adjective** formal (of a person) lacking independence or originality of thought.
– DERIVATIVES **sequaciously** adverb, **sequacity** /sɪˈkwasɪti/ noun.
– ORIGIN mid 17th cent.: from Latin *sequax*, *sequac-* 'following' (from *sequi* 'follow') + **-IOUS**.

sequel ▶ **noun** a published, broadcast, or recorded work that continues the story or develops the theme of an earlier one.
■ something that takes place after or as a result of an earlier event: *this encouragement to grow potatoes had a disastrous sequel some fifty years later.*
– PHRASES **in the sequel** Brit. formal as things develop.
– ORIGIN late Middle English (in the senses 'body of followers', 'descendants' and 'consequence'): from Old French *sequelle* or Latin *sequella*, from *sequi* 'follow'.

sequela /sɪˈkwiːlə/ ▶ **noun** (pl. **sequelae** /-liː/) (usu. **sequelae**) Medicine a condition which is the consequence of a previous disease or injury: *the long-term sequelae of infection.*
– ORIGIN late 18th cent.: from Latin, from *sequi* 'follow'.

sequence ▶ **noun 1** a particular order in which related events, movements, or things follow each other: *the content of the programme should follow a logical sequence.*
■ Music a repetition of a phrase or melody at a higher or lower pitch. ■ Biochemistry the order in which amino-acid or nucleotide residues are arranged in a protein, DNA, etc.
2 a set of related events, movements, or things that follow each other in a particular order: *a gruelling sequence of exercises | a sonnet sequence.*
■ a set of three or more playing cards of the same suit next to each other in value, for example 10, 9, 8. ■ Mathematics an infinite ordered series of numerical quantities.
3 a part of a film dealing with one particular event or topic: *the famous underwater sequence.*
4 (in the Eucharist) a hymn said or sung after the Gradual or Alleluia that precedes the Gospel.
▶ **verb** [with obj.] arrange in a particular order: *trainee librarians decide how a set of misfiled cards could be sequenced.*
■ Biochemistry ascertain the sequence of amino-acid or nucleotide residues in (a protein, DNA, etc.).
– PHRASES **in sequence** in a given order.
– ORIGIN late Middle English (in sense 4): from late Latin *sequentia*, from Latin *sequent-* 'following', from the verb *sequi* 'follow'.

sequence dancing ▶ **noun** [mass noun] a type of ballroom dancing in which the couples all perform the same steps and movements simultaneously.

sequence of tenses ▶ **noun** [mass noun] Grammar the dependence of the tense of a subordinate verb on the tense of the verb in the main clause (e.g. *I think that you are wrong; I thought that you* were *wrong*).

sequencer ▶ **noun 1** a programmable electronic device for storing sequences of musical notes, chords, or rhythms and transmitting them when required to an electronic musical instrument.
2 Biochemistry an apparatus for determining the sequence of amino acids or other monomers in a biological polymer.

sequent ▶ **adjective** archaic following in a sequence or as a logical conclusion.
– DERIVATIVES **sequently** adverb.
– ORIGIN mid 16th cent.: from Old French, or from Latin *sequent-* 'following' (see **SEQUENCE**).

sequential ▶ **adjective** forming or following in a logical order or sequence: *a series of sequential steps.*
■ chiefly Computing performed or used in sequence: *sequential processing of data files.*
– DERIVATIVES **sequentiality** noun, **sequentially** adverb.
– ORIGIN early 19th cent. (as a medical term in the sense 'following as a secondary condition'): from **SEQUENCE**, on the pattern of *consequential*.

sequential access ▶ **noun** [mass noun] access to a computer data file that requires the user to read through the file from the beginning in the order in which it is stored. Compare with **DIRECT ACCESS**.

sequential circuit ▶ **noun** Electronics a circuit whose output depends on the order or timing of the inputs. Compare with **COMBINATIONAL CIRCUIT**.

sequester /sɪˈkwɛstə/ ▶ **verb** [with obj.] **1** isolate or hide away (someone or something): *she is sequestered in deepest Dorset | the artist* **sequestered himself** *in his studio for two years.*
■ Chemistry form a chelate or other stable compound with (an ion, atom, or molecule) so that it is no longer available for reactions.
2 another term for **SEQUESTRATE**.
– ORIGIN late Middle English: from Old French *sequestrer* or late Latin *sequestrare* 'commit for safe keeping', from Latin *sequester* 'trustee'.

sequestered ▶ **adjective** (of a place) isolated and hidden away: *a wild sequestered spot.*

sequestrate /sɪˈkwɛstreɪt, ˈsiːkwɪs-/ ▶ **verb** [with obj.] take legal possession of (assets) until a debt has been paid or other claims have been met: *the power of courts to sequestrate the assets of unions.*
■ take forcible possession of (something); confiscate: *compensation for Jewish property sequestrated by the Libyan regime.* ■ legally place (the property of a bankrupt) in the hands of a trustee for division among the creditors: [as adj. **sequestrated**] *a trustee in a sequestrated estate.* ■ declare (someone) bankrupt: *two more poll tax rebels were sequestrated.*
– DERIVATIVES **sequestrable** adjective, **sequestrator** /ˈsiːkwɪˌstreɪtə/ noun.
– ORIGIN late Middle English (in the sense 'separate from general access'): from late Latin *sequestrat-* 'given up for safe keeping', from the verb *sequestrare* (see **SEQUESTER**).

sequestration /ˌsiːkwɪˈstreɪʃ(ə)n/ ▶ **noun** [mass noun] the action of taking legal possession of assets until a debt has been paid or other claims have been met: *if such court injunctions are ignored, sequestration of trade union assets will follow.*
■ the action of taking forcible possession of something; confiscation: *he demanded the sequestration of the incriminating correspondence.* ■ [count noun] an act of declaring someone bankrupt. ■ Chemistry the action of sequestering a substance.

sequestrum /sɪˈkwɛstrəm/ ▶ **noun** (pl. **sequestra** /-trə/) Medicine a piece of dead bone tissue formed within a diseased or injured bone, typically in chronic osteomyelitis.
– DERIVATIVES **sequestral** adjective, **sequestrectomy** /ˌsiːkwɪˈstrɒktəmi/ noun (pl. **-ies**).
– ORIGIN mid 19th cent.: modern Latin, neuter of Latin *sequester* 'standing apart'.

sequin ▶ **noun 1** a small, shiny disc sewn as one of many on to clothing for decoration.
2 historical a Venetian gold coin.
– DERIVATIVES **sequinned** (also **sequined**) adjective.
– ORIGIN late 16th cent. (in sense 2): from French, from Italian *zecchino*, from *zecca* 'a mint', from Arabic *sikka* 'a die for coining'. Sense 1 dates from the late 19th cent.

sequoia /sɪˈkwɔɪə/ ▶ **noun** a redwood tree, especially the California redwood.
– ORIGIN from modern Latin *Sequoia* (genus name), from *Sequoya*, the name of the Cherokee Indian who invented the Cherokee syllabary.

Sequoia National Park a national park in the Sierra Nevada of California, east of Fresno. It was established in 1890 to protect groves of giant sequoia trees, of which the largest, the General Sherman Tree, is thought to be between 3,000 and 4,000 years old.

sera plural form of **SERUM**.

serac /ˈsɛrak, sɛˈrak/ ▶ **noun** a pinnacle or ridge of ice on the surface of a glacier.
– ORIGIN mid 19th cent.: from Swiss French *sérac*, originally the name of a compact white cheese.

seraglio /sɛˈrɑːlɪəʊ, sɪ-/ ▶ **noun** (pl. **-os**) **1** the women's apartments (harem) in a Muslim palace.
■ another term for **HAREM** (in sense 2).
2 (**the Seraglio**) historical a Turkish palace, especially the Sultan's court and government offices at Constantinople.
– ORIGIN late 16th cent.: from Italian *serraglio*, via Turkish from Persian *sarāy* 'palace'; compare with **SERAI**.

serai /səˈrʌɪ/ ▶ **noun** another term for **CARAVANSERAI** (in sense 1).

Seraing /səˈraŋ/ an industrial town in Belgium, on the River Meuse just south-west of Liège; pop. 60,840 (1991).

Seram Sea variant spelling of **CERAM SEA**.

serang /səˈraŋ/ ▶ **noun** Indian an Asian head of a Lascar crew.
– ORIGIN from Persian and Urdu *sar-hang* 'commander', from *sar* 'head' + *hang* 'authority'.

serape /sɛˈrɑːpeɪ/ (also **sarape**) ▶ **noun** a shawl or blanket worn as a cloak by people from Latin America.
– ORIGIN Mexican Spanish.

seraph /ˈsɛrəf/ ▶ **noun** (pl. **seraphim** /-fɪm/ or **seraphs**) an angelic being, regarded in traditional

Christian angelology as belonging to the highest order of the ninefold celestial hierarchy, associated with light, ardour, and purity.
– ORIGIN Old English, back-formation from *seraphim* (plural), via late Latin and Greek from Hebrew *śĕrāpīm*. Compare with **CHERUB**.

seraphic /səˈrafɪk/ ▶**adjective** characteristic of or resembling a seraph or seraphim: *a seraphic smile.*
– DERIVATIVES **seraphically** adverb.
– ORIGIN mid 17th cent.: from medieval Latin *seraphicus*, from late Latin *seraphim* (see **SERAPH**).

Seraphic Doctor the nickname of St Bonaventura.

Serapis /ˈsɛrəpɪs, səˈreɪp-/ Egyptian Mythology a god whose cult was developed by Ptolemy I at Memphis as a combination of Apis and Osiris, to unite Greeks and Egyptians in a common worship.

seraskier /ˌsɛrəˈskɪə/ ▶**noun** historical the commander-in-chief and minister of war of the Ottoman Empire.
– ORIGIN Turkish, from Persian *sar'askar* 'head (of the) army'.

Serb ▶**noun** a native or national of Serbia, or a person of Serbian descent.
▶**adjective** of or relating to Serbia, the Serbs, or their language.
– ORIGIN from Serbo-Croat *Srb*.

Serbia /ˈsəːbɪə/ a republic in the Balkans, part of Yugoslavia; pop. 9,660,000 (1986); official language, Serbo-Croat; capital, Belgrade.

Serbia was conquered by the Turks in the 14th century, regaining independence in 1878. Serbian rivalry with the Austro-Hungarian empire contributed to the outbreak of the First World War, after which Serbia was absorbed into the kingdom of Serbs, Croats, and Slovenes (named Yugoslavia from 1929). In 1991–2 four out of the six Yugoslav republics seceded; Serbia became involved in armed conflict with neighbouring Croatia, the civil war in Bosnia, and the suppression of Albanian nationalism in Kosovo. Serbia and Montenegro now comprise Yugoslavia.

Serbian ▶**noun 1** [mass noun] the Southern Slavic language of the Serbs, almost identical to Croatian but written in the Cyrillic alphabet. See **SERBO-CROAT**.
2 another term for **SERB**.
▶**adjective** of or relating to Serbia, the Serbs, or their language.

Serbo- ▶**combining form** Serbian; Serbian and ...: *Serbo-Croat.*
■relating to Serbia.

Serbo-Croat /ˌsəːbəʊˈkrəʊat/ (also **Serbo-Croatian** /-krəʊˈeɪʃ(ə)n/) ▶**noun** [mass noun] the Southern Slavic language spoken in Serbia, Croatia, and elsewhere in the former Yugoslavia. Serbo-Croat is generally classed as one language, but comprises two closely similar forms: Serbian, written in the Cyrillic alphabet, and Croat, written in the Roman alphabet.
▶**adjective** of or relating to this language.

Sercial /ˈsəːsɪəl/ ▶**noun** a variety of wine grape grown chiefly in Madeira.
■a dry light Madeira made from this grape.
– ORIGIN Portuguese.

sere[1] ▶**adjective** variant spelling of **SEAR**.

sere[2] /sɪə/ ▶**noun** Ecology a natural succession of plant (or animal) communities, especially a full series from uncolonized habitat to the appropriate climax vegetation. Compare with **SUCCESSION**.
– ORIGIN early 20th cent.: from Latin *serere* 'join in a series'.

Seremban /səˈrɛmbən/ the capital of the state of Negri Sembilan in Malaysia, situated in the south-west of the Malay Peninsula; pop. 136,252 (1980).

serenade ▶**noun** a piece of music sung or played in the open air, typically by a man at night under the window of his beloved.
■another term for **SERENATA**.
▶**verb** [with obj.] entertain (someone) with a serenade: *a strolling guitarist serenades the diners.*
– DERIVATIVES **serenader** noun.
– ORIGIN mid 17th cent.: from French *sérénade*, from Italian *serenata*, from *sereno* 'serene'.

serenata /ˌsɛrəˈnɑːtə/ ▶**noun** Music a cantata with a pastoral subject.
■a simple form of suite for orchestra or wind band.
– ORIGIN Italian, 'serenade' (see **SERENADE**).

serendipity /ˌsɛr(ə)nˈdɪpɪti/ ▶**noun** [mass noun] the occurrence and development of events by chance in a happy or beneficial way: *a fortunate stroke of serendipity* | [count noun] *a series of small serendipities.*
– DERIVATIVES **serendipitous** adjective, **serendipitously** adverb.
– ORIGIN 1754: coined by Horace Walpole, suggested by *The Three Princes of Serendip*, the title of a fairy tale in which the heroes 'were always making discoveries, by accidents and sagacity, of things they were not in quest of'.

serene ▶**adjective** calm, peaceful, and untroubled; tranquil: *her eyes were closed and she looked very serene* | *serene certainty.*
▶**noun** (usu. **the serene**) archaic an expanse of clear sky or calm sea: *not a cloud obscured the deep serene.*
– DERIVATIVES **serenely** adverb.
– ORIGIN late Middle English (describing the weather or sky as 'clear, fine, and calm'): from Latin *serenus*.

Serengeti /ˌsɛrənˈgɛti/ a vast plain in Tanzania, to the west of the Great Rift Valley. In 1951 the Serengeti National Park was created to protect the area's large numbers of wildebeest, zebra, and Thomson's gazelle.

Serenissima /ˌsɛrəˈnɪsɪmə/ ▶**noun** (**La Serenissima, the Serenissima**) Venice.
– ORIGIN Italian, feminine of *serenissimo* 'most serene'.

serenity ▶**noun** (pl. **-ies**) [mass noun] the state of being calm, peaceful, and untroubled: *an oasis of serenity amidst the bustling city.*
– ORIGIN late Middle English: from Old French *serenite*, from Latin *serenitas*, from *serenus* 'clear, fair' (see **SERENE**).

serf ▶**noun** an agricultural labourer bound by the feudal system who was tied to working on his lord's estate.
– DERIVATIVES **serfage** noun, **serfdom** noun.
– ORIGIN late 15th cent. (in the sense 'slave'): from Old French, from Latin *servus* 'slave'.

serge /səːdʒ/ ▶**noun** [mass noun] a durable twilled woollen or worsted fabric.
– ORIGIN late Middle English: from Old French *sarge*, from a variant of Latin *serica* (*lana*) 'silken (wool)', from *sericus* (see **SILK**).

sergeant ▶**noun** a rank of non-commissioned officer in the army or air force, above corporal and below staff sergeant.
■Brit. a police officer ranking below an inspector. ■US a police officer ranking below a lieutenant.
– DERIVATIVES **sergeancy** noun (pl. **-ies**).
– ORIGIN Middle English: from Old French *sergent*, from Latin *servient-* 'serving', from the verb *servire*. Early use was as a general term meaning 'attendant, servant' and 'common soldier'; the term was later applied to specific official roles.

sergeant-at-arms ▶**noun** chiefly US variant spelling of **SERJEANT-AT-ARMS**.

Sergeant Baker ▶**noun** Austral. a brightly coloured edible marine fish with two elongated dorsal fin rays, occurring in warm Australian coastal waters.
• *Aulopus purpurissatus*, family Aulopidae.
– ORIGIN late 19th cent.: of unknown origin.

sergeant fish ▶**noun** another term for **COBIA**.

sergeant major ▶**noun 1** a warrant officer in the British army whose job is to assist the adjutant of a regiment or battalion (**regimental sergeant major**) or a subunit commander (**company sergeant major**, **battery sergeant major**, etc.).
2 a high rank of non-commissioned officer in the US army, above master sergeant and below warrant officer.
3 a fish with boldly striped sides which lives in warm seas, typically on coral reefs.
• *Abudefduf saxatilis*, family Pomacentridae.

serger /ˈsəːdʒə/ ▶**noun** a sewing machine used for overcasting to prevent material from fraying at the edge.

Sergipe /səːˈʒiːpi/ a state in eastern Brazil, on the Atlantic coast; capital, Aracajú.

Sergius, St /ˈsəːdʒɪəs/ (1314–92), Russian monastic reformer and mystic; Russian name *Svyatoi Sergi Radonezhsky*. He founded forty monasteries, re-establishing the monasticism which had been lost through the Tartar invasion, and inspired the resistance which saved Russia from the Tartars in 1380. Feast day, 25 September.

Sergt ▶**abbreviation for** Sergeant.

serial ▶**adjective 1** consisting of, forming part of, or taking place in a series: *a serial publication.*
■Music using transformations of a fixed series of notes.
■Computing (of a device) involving the transfer of data as a single sequence of bits. See also **SERIAL PORT**.
■Computing (of a processor) running only a single task, as opposed to multitasking. ■Linguistics (of verbs) used in sequence to form a construction, as in *they wanted, needed, longed for peace.*
2 [attrib.] (of a criminal) repeatedly committing the same offence and typically following a characteristic, predictable behaviour pattern: *a suspected serial rapist.*
■(of a person) repeatedly following the same behaviour pattern: *he was a serial adulterer.* ■denoting an action or behaviour pattern that is committed or followed repeatedly: *serial killings* | *serial monogamy.*
▶**noun** a story or play appearing in regular instalments on television or radio or in a magazine or newspaper: *a new three-part drama serial.*
■(usu. **serials**) (in a library) a periodical.
– DERIVATIVES **seriality** noun, **serially** adverb.
– ORIGIN mid 19th cent.: from **SERIES** + **-AL**, perhaps suggested by French *sérial*.

serialism ▶**noun** [mass noun] Music a compositional technique in which a fixed series of notes, especially the twelve notes of the chromatic scale, are used to generate the harmonic and melodic basis of a piece and are subject to change only in specific ways. The first fully serial movements appeared in 1923 in works by Arnold Schoenberg. See also **TWELVE-NOTE**.
– DERIVATIVES **serialist** adjective & noun.

serialize (also **-ise**) ▶**verb** [with obj.] **1** publish or broadcast (a story or play) in regular instalments: *sections of the book were serialized in the Sunday Times.*
2 arrange (something) in a series.
■Music compose according to the techniques of serialism.
– DERIVATIVES **serialization** noun.

serial number ▶**noun** a number showing the position of an item in a series, especially one printed on a banknote or manufactured article for the purposes of identification.

serial port ▶**noun** Computing a connector by which a device that sends data one bit at a time may be connected to a computer.

serial section ▶**noun** Biology each of a series of thin sections through tissue cut in successive parallel planes, especially for mounting on microscope slides.
– DERIVATIVES **serial sectioning** noun.

seriate technical ▶**adjective** /ˈsɪərɪət/ arranged or occurring in one or more series.
▶**verb** /ˈsɪərɪeɪt/ [with obj.] arrange (items) in a sequence according to prescribed criteria.
– DERIVATIVES **seriation** noun.
– ORIGIN mid 19th cent.: back-formation from *seriation*, from **SERIES**.

seriatim /ˌsɪərɪˈeɪtɪm, ˌsɛrɪ-/ ▶**adverb** formal taking one subject after another in regular order; point by point: *it is proposed to deal with these matters seriatim.*
– ORIGIN late 15th cent.: from medieval Latin, from Latin *series*, on the pattern of Latin *gradatim* and *literatim*.

sericite /ˈsɛrɪsʌɪt/ ▶**noun** [mass noun] a fine-grained fibrous variety of muscovite, found chiefly in schist.
– ORIGIN mid 19th cent.: from Latin *sericum* 'silk' + **-ITE**[1].

sericulture /ˈsɛrɪˌkʌltʃə/ ▶**noun** [mass noun] the production of silk and the rearing of silkworms for this purpose.
– DERIVATIVES **sericultural** adjective, **sericulturist** noun.
– ORIGIN mid 19th cent.: abbreviation of French *sériciculture*, from late Latin *sericum* 'silk' + French *culture* 'cultivation'.

seriema /ˌsɛrɪˈiːmə/ (also **cariama**) ▶**noun** a large ground-dwelling South American bird related to the bustards, with a long neck and legs and a crest above the bill.
• Family Cariamidae: two genera and species.
– ORIGIN mid 19th cent.: modern Latin, from Tupi *siriema* 'crested'.

series ▶**noun** (pl. same) a number of things, events, or people of a similar kind or related nature coming one after another: *the explosion was the latest in a* **series of** *accidents* | *he gave a* **series of** *lectures on modern art.*
■[usu. with adj. or noun modifier] a set of related television or radio programmes, especially of a specified kind: *a*

new drama series. ■ a set of books, maps, periodicals, or other documents published in a common format or under a common title. ■ a set of games played between two teams: *the Test series against Australia.* ■ a line of products, especially vehicles or machines, sharing features of design or assembly and marketed with a separate number from other lines: [as modifier] *a series III SWB Land Rover.* ■ a set of stamps, banknotes, or coins issued at a particular time. ■ [as modifier] denoting electrical circuits or components arranged so that the current passes through each successively. The opposite of **PARALLEL**. ■ Geology (in chronostratigraphy) a range of strata corresponding to an epoch in time, being a subdivision of a system and itself subdivided into stages: *the Pliocene series.* ■ Mathematics a set of quantities constituting a progression or having the several values determined by a common relation. ■ Phonetics a group of speech sounds having at least one phonetic feature in common but distinguished in other respects. ■ Music another term for **TONE ROW**.
– PHRASES **in series** (of a set of batteries or electrical components) arranged so that the current passes through each successively.
– ORIGIN early 17th cent.: from Latin, literally 'row, chain', from *serere* 'join, connect'.

serif /ˈsɛrɪf/ ▶ **noun** a slight projection finishing off a stroke of a letter, as in T contrasted with I.
– DERIVATIVES **seriffed** adjective.
– ORIGIN mid 19th cent.: perhaps from Dutch *schreef* 'dash, line', of Germanic origin.

serigraph /ˈsɛrɪɡrɑːf/ ▶ **noun** chiefly N. Amer. a printed design produced by means of a silk screen.
– DERIVATIVES **serigrapher** noun, **serigraphy** noun.
– ORIGIN late 19th cent.: formed irregularly from Latin *sericum* 'silk' + **-GRAPH**.

serin /ˈsɛrɪn/ ▶ **noun** a small Eurasian and North African finch related to the canary, with a short bill and typically streaky plumage.
• Genus *Serinus*, family Fringillidae: several species, in particular the **European serin** (*S. serinus*).
– ORIGIN mid 16th cent. (denoting a canary): from French, 'canary', of unknown ultimate origin.

serine /ˈsɪəriːn, ˈsɛr-/ ▶ **noun** [mass noun] Biochemistry a hydrophilic amino acid which is a constituent of most proteins.
• Chem. formula: $CH_2OHCHNH_2COOH$.
– ORIGIN late 19th cent.: from Latin *sericum* 'silk' + **-INE**[4].

serio-comic /ˌsɪərɪəʊ/ ▶ **adjective** combining the serious and the comic; serious in intention but jocular in manner or vice versa: *a telling serio-comic critique.*
– DERIVATIVES **serio-comically** adverb.

serious ▶ **adjective 1** (of a person) solemn or thoughtful in character or manner: *her face grew serious.*
■ (of a subject, state, or activity) demanding careful consideration or application: *marriage is a serious matter.* ■ (of thought or discussion) careful or profound: *we give serious consideration to safety recommendations.* ■ (of music, literature, or other art forms) requiring deep reflection and inviting a considered response: *he bridges the gap between serious and popular music.*
2 acting or speaking sincerely and in earnest, rather than in a joking or half-hearted manner: *suddenly he wasn't teasing any more—he was deadly serious | actors who are* ***serious about*** *their work.*
3 significant or worrying because of possible danger or risk; not slight or negligible: *she escaped serious injury | Haydn was Mozart's only serious rival.*
4 [attrib.] informal substantial in terms of size, number, or quality: *he suddenly had serious money to spend | a serious chocolate cheesecake.*
– DERIVATIVES **seriousness** noun.
– ORIGIN late Middle English: from Old French *serieux* or late Latin *seriosus*, from Latin *serius* 'earnest, serious'.

seriously ▶ **adverb 1** in a solemn or considered manner: *the doctor looked seriously at him.*
2 with earnest intent; not lightly or superficially: *I seriously considered cancelling my subscription.*
■ really or sincerely (used especially to indicate a response of surprise or shock): *do you seriously believe that I would jeopardize my career by such acts?* ■ [sentence adverb] used to add sincerity to a statement that is to follow, especially after a facetious exchange of remarks: ***seriously though****, short cuts rarely work.* ■ informal used to indicate surprise at what someone has said and to check whether they really meant it: *'I'm dying to know.' 'Seriously?' 'Of course.'*
3 to a degree that is significant or worrying because of possible danger or risk: *the amount of fat you eat can seriously affect your health* | [as submodifier] *three men are seriously ill in hospital.*
4 [as submodifier] informal substantially: *he was seriously rich | I drove to the station in a seriously bad mood.*
– PHRASES **take someone/thing seriously** regard someone or something as important and worthy of attention.

serjeant ▶ **noun** (in official lists) a sergeant in the Foot Guards.
– ORIGIN Middle English: variant (commonly used in legal contexts) of **SERGEANT**.

serjeant-at-arms (also **sergeant-at-arms**) ▶ **noun** (pl. **serjeants-at-arms**) an official of a legislative assembly whose duty includes maintaining order and security.
■ Brit. historical a knight or armed officer in the service of the monarch or a lord.

serjeant-at-law ▶ **noun** (pl. **serjeants-at-law**) Brit. historical a barrister of the highest rank.

serjeanty ▶ **noun** (pl. **-ies**) Brit. historical a form of feudal tenure conditional on rendering some specified personal service to the monarch.

sermon ▶ **noun** a talk on a religious or moral subject, especially one given during a church service and based on a passage from the Bible.
■ a printed transcript of such a talk: *a volume of sermons.* ■ informal a long or tedious piece of admonition or reproof; a lecture.
– DERIVATIVES **sermonic** adjective.
– ORIGIN Middle English (also in the sense 'speech, discourse'): from Old French, from Latin *sermo(n-)* 'discourse, talk'.

sermonize (also **-ise**) ▶ **verb** [no obj.] compose or deliver a sermon.
■ deliver an opinionated and dogmatic talk to someone: *they confidently sermonize on the fixed nature of identity* | [with obj.] *I just don't like being sermonized.*
– DERIVATIVES **sermonizer** noun.

Sermon on the Mount ▶ **noun** the discourse of Christ recorded in Matt. 5–7, including the Beatitudes and the Lord's Prayer.

sero- ▶ **combining form** relating to serum: *serotype.*
■ involving a serous membrane: *serositis.*
– ORIGIN representing **SERUM**.

seroconvert /ˌsɪərəʊkənˈvəːt/ ▶ **verb** [no obj.] Medicine (of a person) undergo a change from a seronegative to a seropositive condition.
– DERIVATIVES **seroconversion** noun.

serodiagnosis ▶ **noun** [mass noun] Medicine diagnosis based on the study of blood sera.
– DERIVATIVES **serodiagnostic** adjective.

serology /sɪəˈrɒlədʒi/ ▶ **noun** [mass noun] the scientific study or diagnostic examination of blood serum, especially with regard to the response of the immune system to pathogens or introduced substances.
– DERIVATIVES **serologic** adjective, **serological** adjective, **serologically** adverb, **serologist** noun.

seronegative ▶ **adjective** Medicine giving a negative result in a test of blood serum, e.g. for the presence of a virus.
– DERIVATIVES **seronegativity** noun.

seropositive ▶ **adjective** Medicine giving a positive result in a test of blood serum, e.g. for the presence of a virus.
– DERIVATIVES **seropositivity** noun.

seroprevalence /ˌsɪərəʊˈprɛvələns/ ▶ **noun** [mass noun] Medicine the level of a pathogen in a population, as measured in blood serum.

serosa /sɪˈrəʊsə/ ▶ **noun** [mass noun] Physiology the tissue of a serous membrane.
– DERIVATIVES **serosal** adjective.
– ORIGIN modern Latin, feminine of medieval Latin *serosus* 'serous'.

serositis /ˌsɪrəˈsʌɪtɪs/ ▶ **noun** [mass noun] Medicine inflammation of a serous membrane.

serotine /ˈsɛrətiːn/ ▶ **noun** a medium-sized insectivorous bat found in Eurasia and Africa:
• a chiefly Eurasian bat (genus *Eptesicus*, family Vespertilionidae, in particular the widespread *E. serotinus*).
• an African bat (genus *Pipistrellus*, family Vespertilionidae).
– ORIGIN late 18th cent.: from French *sérotine*, from Latin *serotinus* 'of the evening, late', from *serus* 'late'.

serotonin /ˌsɛrəˈtəʊnɪn/ ▶ **noun** Biochemistry a compound present in blood platelets and serum, which constricts the blood vessels and acts as a neurotransmitter.
• Alternative name: **5-hydroxytryptamine**; chem. formula: $C_{10}H_{12}N_2O$.
– ORIGIN 1940s: from **SERUM** + **TONIC** + **-IN**[1].

serotype /ˈsɪərə(ʊ)tʌɪp/ Microbiology ▶ **noun** a serologically distinguishable strain of a micro-organism.
▶ **verb** [with obj.] assign (a micro-organism) to a particular serotype.
– DERIVATIVES **serotypic** /ˌsɪərə(ʊ)ˈtɪpɪk/ adjective.

serous /ˈsɪərəs/ ▶ **adjective** Physiology of, resembling, or producing serum.
– DERIVATIVES **serosity** noun.
– ORIGIN late Middle English: from French *séreux* or medieval Latin *serosus*, from *serum* (see **SERUM**).

serous membrane ▶ **noun** a mesothelial tissue which lines certain internal cavities of the body, forming a smooth, transparent, two-layered membrane lubricated by a fluid derived from serum. The peritoneum, pericardium, and pleura are serous membranes.

serow /ˈsɛrəʊ/ ▶ **noun** a goat-antelope with short sharp horns, long coarse hair, and a beard, native to forested mountain slopes of SE Asia, Taiwan, and Japan.
• Genus *Capricornis*, family Bovidae: two species.
– ORIGIN mid 19th cent.: probably from Lepcha *sā-ro*.

Serpens /ˈsəːp(ə)nz/ Astronomy a large constellation (the Serpent) on the celestial equator, said to represent the snake coiled around Ophiuchus. It is divided into two parts by Ophiuchus, **Serpens Caput** (the 'head') and **Serpens Cauda** (the 'tail').
■ [as genitive **Serpentis** /səːˈpɛntɪs/] used with preceding letter or numeral to designate a star in this constellation: *the star Beta Serpentis.*
– ORIGIN Latin.

serpent ▶ **noun 1** chiefly poetic/literary a large snake.
■ (**the Serpent**) a biblical name for Satan (see Gen. 3, Rev. 20). ■ a dragon or other mythical snake-like reptile. ■ figurative a sly or treacherous person, especially one who exploits a position of trust in order to betray it.
2 historical a bass wind instrument made of leather-covered wood in three U-shaped turns, with a cup-shaped mouthpiece and few keys. It was played in military and church bands from the 17th to 19th centuries.
– ORIGIN Middle English: via Old French from Latin *serpent-* 'creeping', from the verb *serpere*.

Serpentes /səːˈpɛntiːz/ Zoology another term for **OPHIDIA**.
– ORIGIN Latin, 'reptiles'.

serpentine /ˈsəːp(ə)ntʌɪn/ ▶ **adjective** of or like a serpent or snake: *serpentine coils.*
■ winding and twisting like a snake: *serpentine country lanes.* ■ complex, cunning, or treacherous: *his charm was too subtle and serpentine for me.*
▶ **noun 1** [mass noun] a dark green mineral consisting of hydrated magnesium silicate, sometimes mottled or spotted like a snake's skin.
2 a thing in the shape of a winding curve or line, in particular:
■ (**the Serpentine**) a winding lake in Hyde Park, London, constructed in 1730. ■ a riding exercise consisting of a series of half-circles made alternately to right and left.
3 historical a kind of cannon, used especially in the 15th and 16th centuries.
▶ **verb** [no obj., with adverbial of direction] move or lie in a winding path or line: *fresh tyre tracks serpentined back towards the hopper.*
– ORIGIN late Middle English: via Old French from late Latin *serpentinus* (see **SERPENT**).

serpentine verse ▶ **noun** Prosody a metrical line beginning and ending with the same word.

serpentinite /ˈsəːp(ə)ntɪˌnʌɪt/ ▶ **noun** [mass noun] Geology a dark, typically greenish metamorphic rock, consisting largely of serpentine or related minerals, formed when mafic igneous rocks are altered by water.
– ORIGIN 1930s: from **SERPENTINE** + **-ITE**[1].

serpentinize /ˈsəːp(ə)ntɪˌnʌɪz/ (also **-ise**) ▶ **verb** [with obj.] Geology convert into serpentine.
– DERIVATIVES **serpentinization** noun.

serpiginous /səːˈpɪdʒɪnəs/ ▶ **adjective** Medicine (of a skin lesion or ulcerated region) having a wavy margin.
– ORIGIN late Middle English: from medieval Latin

serpigo, serpigin- 'ringworm' (from Latin *serpere* 'to creep') + **-ous**.

SERPS /səːps/ ▶ **abbreviation for** (in the UK) state earnings-related pension scheme.

serpulid /ˈsəːpjʊlɪd/ ▶ **noun** Zoology a small marine fan worm which lives in a twisted shell-like tube, typically in colonies, with retractable tentacles for filter-feeding.
● Family Serpulidae, class Polychaeta.
– ORIGIN late 19th cent.: from modern Latin *Serpulidae* (plural), from late Latin *serpula* 'small serpent', from Latin *serpere* 'to creep'.

serranid /səˈranɪd, ˈsɛrə-/ ▶ **noun** Zoology a fish of the sea bass family (Serranidae), whose members are predatory marine fish with a spiny dorsal fin.
– ORIGIN mid 20th cent.: from modern Latin *Serranidae*, from the genus name *Serranus*, from Latin *serra* 'saw'.

serrate /ˈsɛreɪt/ ▶ **adjective** chiefly Botany serrated: *leaves with serrate margins.*
– ORIGIN mid 17th cent.: from late Latin *serratus*, from Latin *serra* 'saw'.

serrated ▶ **adjective** having or denoting a jagged edge; saw-like: *a knife with a serrated edge.*

serration ▶ **noun** (usu. **serrations**) a tooth or point of a serrated edge or surface: *a heavy-duty knife with sawtooth serrations.*

serried ▶ **adjective** [attrib.] (of rows of people or things) standing close together: *serried ranks of soldiers | the serried rows of vines.*
– ORIGIN mid 17th cent.: past participle of *serry* 'press close', probably from French *serré* 'close together', based on Latin *sera* 'lock'.

sertão /ˈsɛːtãʊ/ ▶ **noun** (pl. **-os**) (in Brazil) an arid region of scrub.
– ORIGIN early 19th cent.: Portuguese.

Sertoli cell /sɛːˈtəʊli/ ▶ **noun** Anatomy a type of somatic cell around which spermatids develop in the tubules of the testis.
– ORIGIN late 19th cent.: named after Enrico *Sertoli* (1842–1910), Italian histologist.

serum /ˈsɪərəm/ ▶ **noun** (pl. **sera** /-rə/ or **serums**) [mass noun] an amber-coloured, protein-rich liquid which separates out when blood coagulates.
■ the blood serum of an animal, used especially to provide immunity to a pathogen or toxin by inoculation or as a diagnostic agent.
– ORIGIN late 17th cent.: from Latin, literally 'whey'.

serum hepatitis ▶ **noun** [mass noun] a viral form of hepatitis transmitted through infected blood products, causing fever, debility, and jaundice.

serum sickness ▶ **noun** [mass noun] an allergic reaction to an injection of serum, typically mild and characterized by skin rashes, joint stiffness, and fever.

serval /ˈsəːv(ə)l/ ▶ **noun** a slender African wild cat with long legs, large ears, and a black-spotted orange-brown coat.
● Felis serval, family Felidae.
– ORIGIN late 18th cent.: from French, from Portuguese *cerval* 'deer-like', from *cervo* 'deer', from Latin *cervus*.

servant ▶ **noun** a person who performs duties for others, especially a person employed in a house on domestic duties or as a personal attendant.
■ a person employed in the service of a government: *a government servant.* See also **CIVIL SERVANT, PUBLIC SERVANT.** ■ a devoted and helpful follower or supporter: *he was a great servant of the Labour Party.*
– ORIGIN Middle English: from Old French, literally '(person) serving', present participle (used as a noun) of *servir* 'to serve'.

serve ▶ **verb** [with obj.] **1** perform duties or services for (another person or an organization): *Malcolm has served the church very faithfully.*
■ provide (an area or group of people) with a product or service: *a hospital which serves a large area of Wales.* ■ [no obj.] be employed as a member of the armed forces: *he had hoped to serve with the Medical Corps.* ■ spend (a period) in office, in an apprenticeship, or in prison: *he is serving a ten-year jail sentence.* **2** present (food or drink) to someone: *they serve wine instead of beer* | [with obj. and complement] *serve white wines chilled.*
■ present (someone) with food or drink: *the cafe refused to serve him with the tea* | [with two objs] *Peter served them generous portions of soup.* ■ (of food or drink) be enough for: *the recipe serves four people.* ■ attend to (a customer in a shop): *she turned to serve the impatient*

customer. ■ supply (goods) to a customer. ■ [no obj.] Christian Church act as a server at the celebration of the Eucharist. ■ [with two objs] archaic play (a trick) on (someone): *I remember the trick you served me.* **3** Law deliver (a document such as a summons or writ) in a formal manner to the person to whom it is addressed: *the court then issues the summons and serves it on your debtor.*
■ deliver a document to (someone) in such a way: *they were just about to serve him with a writ.* **4** be of use in achieving or satisfying: *this book will serve a useful purpose* | *the union came into existence to serve the interests of musicians.*
■ [no obj.] be of some specified use: *the square now serves as the town's chief car park* | [with infinitive] *sweat serves to cool down the body.* ■ [with obj. and adverbial] treat (someone) in a specified way: *Cornish houseowners wonder if they are being fairly served.* ■ (of a male breeding animal) copulate with (a female). **5** [no obj.] (in tennis and other racket sports) hit the ball or shuttlecock to begin play for each point of a game: *he tossed the ball up to serve* | [with obj.] *serve the ball on to the front wall.* **6** Nautical bind (a rope) with thin cord to protect or strengthen it. **7** Military operate (a gun): *before long Lodge was the only man in his section able to serve the guns.*
▶ **noun 1** (in tennis and other racket sports) an act of hitting the ball or shuttlecock to start play: *he was let down by an erratic serve.* **2** Austral. informal a reprimand: *he would be willing to give the country a serve in an English newspaper.*
– PHRASES **if my memory serves me** if I remember correctly. **serve at table** act as a waiter. **serve someone right** be someone's deserved punishment or misfortune: *it would serve you right if Jeff walked out on you.* **serve one's time** (chiefly US also **serve out one's time**) hold office for the normal period. ■ (also **serve time**) spend time in office, in an apprenticeship, or in prison. **serve one's/its turn** be useful. ■ (**serve someone's turn**) be useful to someone. **serve two masters** take orders from two superiors or follow two conflicting or opposing principles or policies at the same time. [ORIGIN: with biblical allusion to Matt. 6:24.]
– ORIGIN Middle English: from Old French *servir*, from Latin *servire*, from *servus* 'slave'.
▶ **serve out** Tennis win the final game of a set or match while serving: *Fitzgerald then served out for the set.*

serve-and-volley ▶ **adjective** Tennis [attrib.] denoting a style of play in which the server moves close to the net after serving, ready to play an attacking volley off the service return.
– DERIVATIVES **serve-and-volleyer** noun.

server ▶ **noun** a person or thing that provides a service or commodity, in particular:
■ a computer or computer program which manages access to a centralized resource or service in a network. ■ (in tennis and other racket sports) the player who serves. ■ N. Amer. a waiter or waitress. ■ Christian Church a person assisting the celebrant at the celebration of the Eucharist.

servery ▶ **noun** (pl. **-ies**) Brit. a counter, service hatch, or room from which meals are served.

Servian[1] /ˈsəːvɪən/ ▶ **adjective** of or relating to Servius Tullius, the semi-legendary sixth king of ancient Rome (fl. 6th century BC).

Servian[2] /ˈsəːvɪən/ ▶ **noun** & **adjective** archaic variant of **SERBIAN**.

Servian wall a wall encircling the ancient city of Rome, said to have been built by Servius Tullius, the semi-legendary sixth king of ancient Rome (fl. 6th century BC).

service ▶ **noun 1** [mass noun] the action of helping or doing work for someone: *millions are involved in voluntary service.*
■ [count noun] an act of assistance: *he has done us a great service* | *he volunteered his services as a driver.* ■ assistance or advice given to customers during and after the sale of goods: *they aim to provide better quality of service.* ■ short for **SERVICE INDUSTRY.** ■ the action or process of serving food and drinks to customers: *they complained of poor bar service.* ■ short for **SERVICE CHARGE**: *service is included in the final bill.* ■ a period of employment with a company or organization: *he retired after 40 years' service.* ■ employment as a servant: *the pitifully low wages gained from domestic service.* See also **in service** below. ■ the use which can be made of a machine: *the computer should provide good service for years.* ■ the provision of the necessary maintenance work for a machine: *they phoned for*

service on their air conditioning. ■ [usu. in sing.] a periodic routine inspection and maintenance of a vehicle or other machine: *he took his car in for a service.* ■ (**the services**) the armed forces: [as modifier] (**service**) *service personnel.* ■ (**services**) chiefly Brit. an area with parking beside a major road supplying petrol, refreshments, and other amenities to motorists. **2** a system supplying a public need such as transport, communications, or utilities such as electricity and water: *a regular bus service.*
■ a public department or organization run by the state: *the probation service.* **3** a ceremony of religious worship according to a prescribed form; the prescribed form for such a ceremony: *a funeral service.* **4** [with modifier] a set of matching crockery used for serving a particular meal: *a dinner service.* **5** [mass noun] (in tennis and other racket sports) the action or right of serving to begin play.
■ [count noun] a serve. **6** [mass noun] Law the formal delivery of a document such as a writ or summons.
▶ **verb** [with obj.] **1** (usu. **be serviced**) perform routine maintenance or repair work on (a vehicle or machine): *ensure that gas appliances are serviced regularly.*
■ supply and maintain systems for public utilities and transport and communications in (an area): *the village is small and well serviced.* ■ perform a service or services for (someone): *her life is devoted to servicing others.* ■ pay interest on (a debt): *taxpayers are paying $250 million just to service that debt.* **2** (of a male animal) mate with (a female animal).
■ vulgar slang (of a man) have sexual intercourse with (a woman).
– PHRASES **be at someone's service** be ready to assist someone whenever possible. **be of service** be available to assist someone. **in service 1** in or available for use. **2** dated employed as a servant. **out of service** not available for use. **see service** serve in the armed forces: *he saw service in both world wars.* ■ be used: *the building later saw service as a blacksmith's shop.* **take service** with Brit. dated become a servant to or worker for: *government officials took service with the new rulers.*
– ORIGIN Old English (denoting religious devotion or a form of liturgy), from Old French *servise* or Latin *servitium* 'slavery', from *servus* 'slave'. The early sense of the verb (mid 19th cent.) was 'be of service to, provide with a service'.

serviceable ▶ **adjective** fulfilling its function adequately; usable: *an ageing but still serviceable water supply system.*
■ functional and durable rather than attractive. ■ in working order: *only twelve aircraft were fully serviceable this morning.*
– DERIVATIVES **serviceability** noun, **serviceably** adverb.
– ORIGIN Middle English (in the sense 'willing to be of service'): from Old French *servisable*, from *servise* (see **SERVICE**).

service area ▶ **noun 1** chiefly Brit. a roadside area where services are available to motorists.
2 the area transmitted by a broadcasting station.

serviceberry ▶ **noun 1** the fruit of the service tree.
2 another term for **JUNEBERRY**.

service book ▶ **noun** a book of authorized forms of worship used in a church.

service bureau ▶ **noun** Computing an organization providing services such as scanning, pre-press, and colour printing.

service ceiling ▶ **noun** the maximum height at which an aircraft can sustain a specified rate of climb dependent on engine type.

service charge ▶ **noun** an extra charge made for serving customers in a restaurant.
■ a charge made for maintenance on a property which has been leased.

service club ▶ **noun** N. Amer. an association of business or professional people with the aims of promoting community welfare and goodwill.

service contract ▶ **noun 1** a contract of employment.
2 a business agreement between a contractor and customer covering the maintenance and servicing of equipment over a specified period.

service dress ▶ **noun** [mass noun] Brit. military uniform worn on formal but not ceremonial occasions.

service flat ▶ **noun** Brit. a rented flat in which domestic service and sometimes meals are provided by the management.

service game ▶ **noun** (in tennis and other racket sports) a game in which a particular player serves.

service industry ▶ **noun** a business that does work for a customer, and occasionally provides goods, but is not involved in manufacturing.

service line ▶ **noun** (in tennis, badminton, and other sports) a line on a court marking the limit of the area into which the ball must be served.
■ (especially in handball and paddleball) a line on a court marking the boundary of the area in which the server must be standing when serving.

serviceman ▶ **noun** (pl. **-men**) **1** a man serving in the armed forces.
2 a man providing maintenance on machinery, especially domestic machinery.

service mark ▶ **noun** a legally registered name or designation used in the manner of a trademark to distinguish an organization's services from those of its competitors.

service module ▶ **noun** a detachable compartment of a spacecraft carrying fuel and supplies.

service provider ▶ **noun** Computing a company which allows its subscribers access to the Internet.

service road ▶ **noun** a subsidiary road running parallel to a main road and giving access to houses, shops, or businesses.

service station ▶ **noun** an establishment beside a road selling petrol and oil and typically having the facilities to carry out maintenance.
■ Brit. another term for **SERVICE AREA** (in sense 1).

service tree ▶ **noun** a Eurasian tree of the rose family, closely related to the rowan.
• Genus *Sorbus*, family Rosaceae: the southern European **true service tree** (*S. domestica*), with compound leaves and green-brown fruits that are edible when overripe, and the **wild service tree** (*S. torminalis*), with lobed leaves and brown berries.
– ORIGIN mid 16th cent.: *service* from an alteration of the plural of obsolete *serve*, from Old English *syrfe*, based on Latin *sorbus*.

servicewoman ▶ **noun** (pl. **-women**) a woman serving in the armed forces.

serviette ▶ **noun** Brit. a table napkin.
– ORIGIN late 15th cent.: from Old French, from *servir* 'to serve'.

servile ▶ **adjective 1** having or showing an excessive willingness to serve or please others: *bowing his head in a servile manner.*
2 of or characteristic of a slave or slaves.
– DERIVATIVES **servilely** adverb, **servility** noun.
– ORIGIN late Middle English (in the sense 'suitable for a slave or for the working class'): from Latin *servilis*, from *servus* 'slave'.

serving ▶ **noun** a quantity of food suitable for or served to one person: *a large* **serving of** *spaghetti.*

servingman ▶ **noun** (pl. **-men**) archaic a male servant or attendant.

servingwoman ▶ **noun** (pl. **-women**) archaic a female servant or attendant.

S

Servite /ˈsəːvʌɪt/ ▶ **noun** a friar or nun of the Catholic religious order of the Servants of Blessed Mary, founded in 1233.
▶ **adjective** of or relating to this order.
– ORIGIN from medieval Latin *Servitae* (plural), from Latin, from *Servi Beatae Mariae*, the formal title of the order (see above).

servitor /ˈsəːvɪtə/ ▶ **noun** archaic a person who serves or attends on a social superior.
■ historical an Oxford undergraduate performing menial duties in exchange for assistance from college funds.
– DERIVATIVES **servitorship** noun.
– ORIGIN Middle English: via Old French from late Latin, from *servit-* 'served', from the verb *servire* (see **SERVE**).

servitude /ˈsəːvɪtjuːd/ ▶ **noun** [mass noun] the state of being a slave or completely subject to someone more powerful.
■ Law, archaic the subjection of property to an easement.
– ORIGIN late Middle English: via Old French from Latin *servitudo*, from *servus* 'slave'.

servo ▶ **noun** (pl. **-os**) short for **SERVOMECHANISM** or **SERVOMOTOR**.
■ [as modifier] relating to or involving a servomechanism: *hydraulic and electrical servo systems.*
– ORIGIN late 19th cent.: from Latin *servus* 'slave'.

servomechanism ▶ **noun** a powered mechanism producing motion or forces at a higher level of energy than the input level, e.g. in the brakes and steering of large motor vehicles, especially where feedback is employed to make the control automatic.

servomotor ▶ **noun** the motive element in a servomechanism.

sesame /ˈsɛsəmi/ ▶ **noun** [mass noun] a tall annual herbaceous plant of tropical and subtropical areas of the Old World, cultivated for its oil-rich seeds.
• *Sesamum indicum*, family Pedaliaceae.
■ (**sesame seed**) the edible seeds of this plant, which are used whole or have the oil extracted.
– PHRASES **open sesame** a free or unrestricted means of admission or access: *academic success is not an automatic open sesame to the job market.* [ORIGIN: from the magic formula in the tale of Ali Baba and the Forty Thieves (see **ALI BABA**).]
– ORIGIN late Middle English: via Latin from Greek *sēsamon, sēsamē*; compare with Arabic *simsim*.

sesamoid /ˈsɛsəmɔɪd/ (also **sesamoid bone**) ▶ **noun** a small independent bone or bony nodule developed in a tendon where it passes over an angular structure, typically in the hands and feet. The kneecap is a particularly large sesamoid bone.
– ORIGIN late 17th cent.: from **SESAME** (with reference to the similarity in shape of a sesame seed) + **-OID**.

sesamum /ˈsɛsəməm/ ▶ **noun** another term for **SESAME**.
– ORIGIN mid 16th cent.: via Latin from Greek.

sesh ▶ **noun** informal term for **SESSION**.

Sesotho /sɛˈsuːtuː/ ▶ **noun** [mass noun] the South Sotho language of the Basotho people, an official language in Lesotho and South Africa, with over 5 million speakers.
▶ **adjective** of or relating to this language.
– ORIGIN the name in Sesotho.

sesqui- ▶ **combining form** denoting one and a half: *sesquicentenary.*
■ Chemistry (of a compound) in which a particular element or group is present in a ratio of 3:2 compared with another: *sesquioxide.*
– ORIGIN from Latin *semi-* (see **SEMI-**) + *que* 'and'.

sesquialtera /ˌsɛskwɪˈalt(ə)rə/ ▶ **adjective** [attrib.] Music relating to or denoting a ratio of 3:2, as in an interval of a fifth.
■ denoting a mixture stop in an organ, typically consisting of two ranks of narrow-scaled open flue pipes.
– ORIGIN late Middle English: from Latin, feminine of *sesquialter*, from *sesqui* (see **SESQUI-**) + *alter* 'second'.

sesquicentenary /ˌsɛskwɪsɛnˈtiːn(ə)ri, -ˈtɛn-/ ▶ **noun** (pl. **-ies**) the one-hundred-and-fiftieth anniversary of a significant event.
▶ **adjective** of or relating to such an anniversary.

sesquicentennial /ˌsɛskwɪsɛnˈtɛnɪəl/ ▶ **adjective** of or relating to a sesquicentenary.
▶ **noun** a sesquicentenary.

sesquioxide /ˌsɛskwɪˈɒksʌɪd/ ▶ **noun** Chemistry an oxide in which oxygen is present in the ratio of three atoms to two of another element.

sesquipedalian /ˌsɛskwɪpɪˈdeɪlɪən/ ▶ **adjective** formal (of a word) polysyllabic; long: *sesquipedalian surnames.*
■ characterized by long words; long-winded: *the sesquipedalian prose of scientific journals.*
– ORIGIN mid 17th cent.: from Latin *sesquipedalis* 'a foot and a half long', from *sesqui-* (see **SESQUI-**) + *pes, ped-* 'foot'.

sesquiterpene /ˌsɛskwɪˈtəːpiːn/ ▶ **noun** Chemistry a terpene with the formula $C_{15}H_{24}$, or a simple derivative of such a compound.

sess ▶ **noun** variant spelling of **CESS**[1].

sessile /ˈsɛsʌɪl, ˈsɛsɪl/ ▶ **adjective** Biology (of an organism, e.g. a barnacle) fixed in one place; immobile.
■ Botany & Zoology (of a plant or animal structure) attached directly by its base without a stalk or peduncle: *sporangia may be stalked or sessile.*
– ORIGIN early 18th cent.: from Latin *sessilis*, from *sess-* 'seated', from the verb *sedere*.

sessile oak ▶ **noun** a Eurasian oak tree with stalkless egg-shaped acorns, common in hilly areas with poor soils. Also called **DURMAST OAK**.
• *Quercus petraea*, family Fagaceae.

session ▶ **noun 1** a meeting of a deliberative or judicial body to conduct its business.
■ a period during which such meetings are regularly held: *legislation to curb wildcat strikes will be introduced during the coming parliamentary session.* ■ the governing body of a Presbyterian Church. See also **KIRK SESSION**.
2 [often with modifier] a period devoted to a particular activity: *gym is followed by a training session.*
■ informal a period of heavy or sustained drinking. ■ a period of recording music in a studio, especially by a session musician: *he did the sessions for a Great Country Hits album.* ■ an academic year. ■ the period during which a school has classes.
– PHRASES **in session** assembled for or proceeding with business.
– DERIVATIVES **sessional** adjective.
– ORIGIN late Middle English: from Old French, or from Latin *sessio(n-)*, from *sess-* 'seated' (see **SESSILE**).

session clerk ▶ **noun** a chief lay official in the session of a Presbyterian Church.

session musician ▶ **noun** a freelance musician hired to play on recording sessions.

sesterce /ˈsɛstəːs/ (also **sestertius** /sɛˈstəːʃəs/) ▶ **noun** (pl. **sesterces** /-siːz/ or **sestertii** /-ˈstəːʃiː/) an ancient Roman coin and monetary unit equal to one quarter of a denarius.
– ORIGIN from Latin *sestertius* (*nummus*) '(coin) that is two and a half (asses)'.

sestet /sɛsˈtɛt/ ▶ **noun** Prosody the last six lines of a sonnet.
■ Music, rare a sextet.
– ORIGIN early 19th cent.: from Italian *sestetto*, from *sesto*, from Latin *sextus* 'a sixth'.

sestina /sɛˈstiːnə/ ▶ **noun** Prosody a poem with six stanzas of six lines and a final triplet, all stanzas having the same six words at the line-ends in six different sequences.
– ORIGIN mid 19th cent.: from Italian, from *sesto* (see **SESTET**).

Set /sɛt/ variant spelling of **SETH**.

set[1] ▶ **verb** (**setting**; past and past participle **set**) **1** [with obj. and usu. with adverbial] put, lay, or stand (something) in a specified place or position: *Delaney set the mug of tea down | Catherine set a chair by the bed.*
■ (**be set**) be situated or fixed in a specified place or position: *the village was set among olive groves on a hill.* ■ represent (a story, play, film, or scene) as happening at a specified time or in a specified place: *a private-eye novel set in Berlin.* ■ mount a precious stone in (something, typically a piece of jewellery): *a bracelet set with emeralds.* ■ mount (a precious stone) in something. ■ Printing arrange (type) as required. ■ Printing arrange the type for (a piece of text): *article headings will be set in Times fourteen point.* ■ prepare (a table) for a meal by placing cutlery, crockery, etc. on it in their proper places. ■ (**set something to**) provide (music) so that a written work can be produced in a musical form: *a form of poetry which can be set to music.* ■ Bell-ringing move (a bell) so that it rests in an inverted position ready for ringing. ■ [no obj.] (of a dancer) acknowledge another dancer, typically one's partner, using the steps prescribed: *the gentleman* **sets to** *and turns with the lady on his left hand.* ■ cause (a hen) to sit on eggs. ■ place (eggs) for a hen to sit on. ■ put (a seed or plant) in the ground to grow. ■ give the teeth of (a saw) an alternate outward inclination. ■ Sailing put (a sail) up in position to catch the wind: *a safe distance from shore all sails were set.* See also **set sail** below.
2 [with obj. and usu. with adverbial] put or bring into a specified state: *the Home Secretary set in motion a review of the law* | [with obj. and complement] *the hostages were set free.*
■ [with obj. and present participle] cause (someone or something) to start doing something: *the incident set me thinking.* ■ [with obj. and infinitive] instruct (someone) to do something: *he'll set a man to watch you.* ■ give someone (a task): [with two objs] *the problem we have been set.* ■ devise (a test) and give it to someone to do. ■ establish as (an example) for others to follow, copy, or try to achieve: *the scheme sets a precedent for other companies.* ■ establish (a record): *his time in the 25 m freestyle set a national record.* ■ decide on: *they set a date for a full hearing at the end of February.* ■ fix (a price, value, or limit) on something: *the unions had set a limit on the size of the temporary workforce.*
3 [with obj.] adjust the hands of (a clock or watch), typically to show the right time.
■ adjust (an alarm clock) to sound at the required time. ■ adjust (a device or its controls) so that it performs a particular operation: *you have to be careful*

not to set the volume too high. ■ Electronics cause (a binary device) to enter the state representing the numeral 1.

4 [no obj.] harden into a solid or semi-solid state: *cook for a further thirty-five minutes until the filling has set.* ■ [with obj.] arrange (the hair) while damp so that it dries in the required style: *she had set her hair on small rollers.* ■ [with obj.] put parts of (a broken or dislocated bone or limb) into the correct position for healing. ■ [with obj.] deal with (a fracture or dislocation) in this way. ■ (of a bone) be restored to its normal condition by knitting together again after being broken: *dogs' bones soon set.* ■ (with reference to a person's face) assume or cause to assume a fixed or rigid expression: [no obj.] *her features never set into a civil parade of attention* | [with obj.] *Travis's face was set as he looked up.* ■ (of the eyes) become fixed in position or in the feeling they are expressing: *his bright eyes set in an expression of mocking amusement.* ■ (of a hunting dog) adopt a rigid attitude indicating the presence of game.

5 [no obj.] (of the sun, moon, or another celestial body) appear to move towards and below the earth's horizon as the earth rotates: *the sun was setting and a warm, red glow filled the sky.*

6 [no obj., with adverbial of direction] (of a tide or current) take or have a specified direction or course: *a fair tide can be carried well past Lands End before the stream sets to the north.*

7 [with obj.] chiefly N. Amer. start (a fire).

8 [with obj.] (of blossom or a tree) form into or produce (fruit). ■ [no obj.] (of fruit) develop from blossom. ■ (of a plant) produce (seed): *the herb has flowered and started to set seed.*

9 informal or dialect sit: *a perfect lady—just set in her seat and stared.*

– PHRASES **set one's heart** (or **hopes**) **on** have a strong desire for or to do: *she had her heart set on going to university.* **set out one's stall** display or show off one's abilities, attributes, or experience in order to convince someone of one's suitability for something: *he wanted to set out his stall as someone who would balance the books and create a firm financial situation.* **set sail** hoist the sails of a boat. ■ begin a voyage: *tomorrow we set sail for France.* **set one's teeth** clench one's teeth together. ■ become resolute: *they have set their teeth against a change which would undermine their prospects of forming a government.* **set up shop** see SHOP. **set the wheels in motion** do something to begin a process or put a plan into action.

– ORIGIN Old English *settan*, of Germanic origin; related to Dutch *zetten*, German *setzen*, also to SIT.

▶ **set about 1** start doing something with vigour or determination: *it would be far better to admit the problem openly and set about tackling it.* **2** Brit. informal attack (someone).

set someone against cause someone to be in opposition or conflict with: *he hadn't meant any harm but his few words had set her against him.*

set something against offset something against: *wives' allowances can henceforth be set against investment income.*

set someone apart give someone an air of unusual superiority: *his try-scoring ability and self-effacing modesty have set him apart.*

set something apart separate something and keep it for a special purpose: *there were books and rooms set apart as libraries.*

set something aside 1 save or keep something, typically money or time, for a particular purpose: *the bank expected to set aside about $700 million for restructuring.* ■ remove land from agricultural production. **2** annul a legal decision or process.

set someone/thing back 1 delay or impede the progress of someone or something: *this incident undoubtedly set back research.* **2** informal (of a purchase) cost someone a particular amount of money: *that must have set you back a bit.*

set something by archaic or US save something for future use.

set someone down stop and allow someone to alight from a vehicle.

set something down record something in writing. ■ establish something authoritatively as a rule or principle to be followed: *the Association set down codes of practice for all members to comply with.*

set forth begin a journey or trip.

set something forth state or describe something in writing or speech: *the principles and aims set forth in the Social Charter.*

set forward archaic start on a journey.

set in (of something unpleasant or unwelcome) begin and seem likely to continue: *tables should be treated with preservative before the bad weather sets in.*

set something in insert something, especially a sleeve, into a garment.

set off begin a journey.

set someone off cause someone to start doing something, especially laughing or talking: *anything will set him off laughing.*

set something off 1 detonate a bomb. ■ cause an alarm to go off. ■ cause a series of things to occur: *the fear is that this could set off a chain reaction in other financial markets.* **2** serve as decorative embellishment to: *a pink carnation set off nicely by a red bow tie and cream shirt.*

set something off against another way of saying *set something against* above.

set on (or **upon**) attack (someone) violently.

set someone/thing on (or **upon**) cause or urge a person or animal to attack: *I was asked to leave and threatened with having dogs set upon me.*

set out begin a journey. ■ aim or intend to do something: *she drew up a grandiose statement of what her organization should set out to achieve.*

set something out arrange or display something in a particular order or position. ■ present information or ideas in a well-ordered way in writing or speech: *this chapter sets out the debate surrounding pluralism.*

set to begin doing something vigorously: *she set to with bleach and scouring pads to render the vases spotless.*

set someone up 1 establish someone in a particular capacity or role: *his father set him up in business.* **2** restore or enhance the health of someone: *after my operation the doctor recommended a cruise to set me up again.* **3** informal make an innocent person appear guilty of something: *suppose Lorton had set him up for Newley's murder?*

set something up 1 place or erect something in position: *police set up a roadblock on Lower Thames Street.* **2** establish a business, institution, or other organization. ■ make the arrangements necessary for something: *he asked if I would like him to set up a meeting with the president.* **3** begin making a loud sound.

set oneself up as establish oneself in (a particular occupation): *he set himself up as a druggist in Leamington.* ■ claim to be or act like a specified kind of person (used to indicate scepticism as to someone's right or ability to do so): *he set himself up as a crusader for higher press and broadcasting standards.*

set² ▶ noun **1** a group or collection of things that belong together or resemble one another or are usually found together: *a set of false teeth* | *a new cell with two sets of chromosomes* | *a spare set of clothes.* ■ a collection of implements, containers, or other objects customarily used together for a specific purpose: *an electric fondue set.* ■ a group of people with common interests or occupations or of similar social status: *it was a fashionable haunt of the literary set.* ■ a group of pupils or students of the same average ability in a particular subject who are taught together: *the policy of allocating pupils to mathematics sets.* ■ (in tennis, darts, and other games) a group of games counting as a unit towards a match, only the player or side that wins a defined number or proportion of the games being awarded a point towards the final score: *he took the first set 6–3.* ■ (in jazz or popular music) a sequence of songs or pieces performed together and constituting or forming part of a live show or recording: *a short four-song set.* ■ a group of people making up the required number for a square dance or similar country dance. ■ a fixed number of repetitions of particular bodybuilding exercise. ■ Mathematics & Logic a collection of distinct entities regarded as a unit, being either individually specified or (more usually) satisfying specified conditions: *the set of all positive integers.*

2 [in sing.] the way in which something is set, disposed, or positioned: *the shape and set of the eyes.* ■ the posture or attitude of a part of the body, typically in relation to the impression this gives of a person's feelings or intentions: *the determined set of her upper torso.* ■ short for MINDSET. ■ the action of a current or tide of flowing in a particular direction: *the rudder kept the dinghy straight against the set of the tide.* ■ Austral./NZ informal a grudge: *most of them hear a thing or two and then get a set on you.* ■ an arrangement of the hair when damp so that it dries in the required style: *a shampoo and set.* ■ Bell-ringing the inverted position of a bell when it is ready for ringing. ■ (also **dead set**) a setter's pointing in the presence of game. ■ an alternating outward inclination of the teeth of a saw. ■ a warp or bend in wood, metal, or another material caused by continued strain or pressure.

3 a radio or television receiver: *a TV set.*

4 a collection of scenery, stage furniture, and other articles used for a particular scene in a play or film. ■ the place or area in which filming is taking place or a play is performed: *the magazine has interviews on set with top directors.*

5 a cutting, young plant, or bulb used in the propagation of new plants. ■ a young fruit that has just formed.

6 the last coat of plaster on a wall.

7 Printing the amount of spacing in type controlling the distance between letters. ■ the width of a piece of type.

8 variant spelling of SETT.

9 Snooker another term for PLANT (in sense 4).

– PHRASES **make a dead set at** Brit. make a determined attempt to win the affections of. [ORIGIN: by association with hunting (see *dead set* above.]

– ORIGIN late Middle English: partly from Old French *sette*, from Latin *secta* 'sect', partly from SET¹.

set³ ▶ adjective **1** fixed or arranged in advance: *try to feed the puppy at set times each day.* ■ (of a view or habit) unlikely to change: *I've been on my own a long time and I'm rather set in my ways.* ■ (of a person's expression) held for an unnaturally long time without changing, typically as a reflection of determination. ■ (of a meal or menu in a restaurant) offered at a fixed price with a limited choice of dishes. ■ (of a book) prescribed for study as part of a particular course or for an examination. ■ having a conventional or predetermined wording; formulaic: *witnesses often delivered their testimony according to a set speech.* See also SET PHRASE.

2 [predic.] ready, prepared, or likely to do something: *'All set for tonight?' he asked* | [with infinitive] *water costs look set to increase.* ■ (**set against**) firmly opposed to: *last night you were dead set against the idea.* ■ (**set on**) determined to do (something): *he's set on marrying that girl.*

– ORIGIN late Old English, past participle of SET¹.

seta /ˈsiːtə/ ▶ noun (pl. **setae** /-tiː/) chiefly Zoology a stiff hair-like or bristle-like structure, especially in an invertebrate. ■ Botany (in a moss or liverwort) the stalk supporting the capsule.

– DERIVATIVES **setaceous** /-ˈteɪʃəs/ adjective, **setal** adjective.

– ORIGIN late 18th cent.: from Latin, 'bristle'.

set-aside ▶ noun [mass noun] the policy of taking land out of production to reduce crop surpluses. ■ land taken out of production in this way: *he has fifty acres of set-aside.*

setback ▶ noun **1** a reversal or check in progress: *a serious setback for the peace process.* **2** Architecture a plain, flat offset in a wall. **3** N. Amer. the distance by which a building or part of a building is set back from the property line.

se-tenant /siːˈtɛnənt/ ▶ adjective Philately (of stamps, especially stamps of different designs) joined together side by side as when printed: *a se-tenant block of four stamps.*

– ORIGIN early 20th cent.: from French, literally 'holding together'.

Seth /sɛθ/ (also **Set**) Egyptian Mythology an evil god who murdered his brother Osiris and wounded Osiris's son Horus. Seth is represented as having the head of an animal with a long pointed snout.

seth /seɪt/ ▶ noun Indian a merchant or banker. ■ a rich man. ■ used as a title for a person of high social status: *'Have you come back happy and well, Sethji?'*

– ORIGIN from Hindi *seṭh*, from Sanskrit *śreṣṭha* 'best, chief'.

SETI ▶ abbreviation for search for extraterrestrial intelligence, the designation of a series of projects based mainly on attempts to detect artificial radio transmissions from outer space.

set-in ▶ adjective [attrib.] (of a sleeve) made separately and inset into a garment.

set-net ▶ noun a fishing net fastened in position, into which fish are driven.

– DERIVATIVES **set-netter** noun.

set-off ▶ noun **1** an item or amount that is or may

be set off against another in the settlement of accounts.
■Law a counterbalancing debt pleaded by the defendant in an action to recover money due. ■ dated a counterbalancing or compensating circumstance or condition: *as a set-off against such discussions there had come an improvement in their pecuniary position.*
2 a step or shoulder at which the thickness of part of a building or machine is reduced.
3 [mass noun] Printing the unwanted transference of ink from one printed sheet or page to another before it has set.

seton /ˈsiːt(ə)n/ ▶noun Medicine, historical a skein of cotton or other absorbent material passed below the skin and left with the ends protruding, to promote drainage of fluid or to act as a counterirritant.
– ORIGIN late Middle English: from medieval Latin *seto(n-)*, apparently from Latin *seta* 'bristle'.

setose /ˈsiːtəʊs, -z/ ▶adjective chiefly Zoology bearing bristles or setae; bristly.
– ORIGIN mid 17th cent.: from Latin *seta* 'bristle' + **-OSE**[1].

set phrase ▶noun an unvarying phrase having a specific meaning, such as 'raining cats and dogs', or being the only context in which a word appears, for example 'amends' in 'make amends'.

set piece ▶noun a thing that has been carefully or elaborately planned or composed, in particular:
■a self-contained passage or section of a novel, play, film, or piece of music arranged in an elaborate or conventional pattern for maximum effect: *the film lurches from one comic set piece to another.* ■a formal and carefully structured speech. ■a carefully organized and practised move in a team game by which the ball is returned to play, as at a scrum or a free kick. ■an arrangement of fireworks forming a picture or design.

set point ▶noun (in tennis and other sports) a point which if won by one of the players or sides will also win them a set.

set screw ▶noun a screw for adjusting or clamping parts of a machine.

set scrum ▶noun Rugby another term for **SCRUM**.

set shot ▶noun Basketball a shot at the basket made without jumping.

set square ▶noun a right-angled triangular plate for drawing lines, especially at 90°, 45°, 60°, or 30°.
■a form of T-square with an additional arm turning on a pivot for drawing lines at fixed angles to the head.

Setswana /sɛˈtswɑːnə/ ▶noun [mass noun] the Bantu language of the Tswana people, related to the Sotho languages and spoken by over 3 million people in southern Africa.
▶adjective of or relating to this language.
– ORIGIN the name in Setswana.

sett (also **set**) ▶noun **1** the earth or burrow of a badger.
2 a granite paving block.
3 the particular pattern of stripes in a tartan.
– ORIGIN Middle English: variant of **SET**[2], the spelling with *-tt* prevailing in technical senses.

settee ▶noun a long upholstered seat for more than one person, typically with a back and arms.
– ORIGIN early 18th cent.: perhaps a fanciful variant of **SETTLE**[2].

setter ▶noun **1** a dog of a large long-haired breed trained to stand rigid when scenting game.
2 [usu. in combination] a person or thing that sets something: *the battle between wage-setters and policy-makers.*

set theory ▶noun [mass noun] the branch of mathematics which deals with the formal properties of sets as units (without regard to the nature of their individual constituents) and the expression of other branches of mathematics in terms of sets.
– DERIVATIVES **set-theoretic** adjective, **set-theoretical** adjective.

setting /ˈsɛtɪŋ/ ▶noun **1** the place or type of surroundings where something is positioned or where an event takes place: *a romantic house in a wonderful setting beside the River Wye.*
■the place and time at which a play, novel, or film is represented as happening: *short stories with a contemporary setting.* ■a piece of metal in which a precious stone or gem is fixed to form a piece of jewellery. ■a piece of vocal or choral music composed for particular words: *a setting of Yevtushenko's bleak poem.* ■ short for **PLACE SETTING**.
2 a speed, height, or temperature at which a machine or device can be adjusted to operate: *if you find the room getting too hot, check the thermostat setting.*

setting lotion ▶noun [mass noun] lotion applied to damp hair prior to being set, enabling it to keep its shape longer.

settle[1] ▶verb **1** [with obj.] resolve or reach an agreement about (an argument or problem): *every effort was made to settle the dispute.*
■end (a legal dispute) by mutual agreement: *the matter was settled out of court* | [no obj.] *he sued for libel and then settled out of court.* ■determine; decide on: *exactly what goes into the legislation has not been settled* | [no obj.] *they had not yet **settled on** a date for the wedding.* ■pay (a debt or account): *his bill was settled by charge card* | [no obj.] *I **settle up with** your brother for my board and lodging.* ■(**settle something on**) give money or property to (someone) through a deed of settlement or a will. ■[no obj.] (**settle for**) accept or agree to (something that one considers to be less than satisfactory): *it was too cold for champagne so they settled for a cup of tea.* ■ dated silence (someone considered a nuisance) by some means: *he told me to hold my tongue or he would find a way to settle me.*
2 [no obj.] adopt a more steady or secure style of life, especially in a permanent job and home: *one day I will **settle down** and raise a family.*
■[with adverbial of place] make one's permanent home somewhere: *in 1863 the family settled in London.* ■begin to feel comfortable or established in a new home, situation, or job: *she **settled in** happily with a foster family* | *he had **settled into** his new job.* ■[with obj.] establish a colony in: *European immigrants settled much of Australia.* ■(**settle down to**) turn one's attention to; apply oneself to: *Catherine settled down to her studies.* ■become or make calmer or quieter: [no obj.] *after a few months the controversy settled down* | [with obj.] *try to settle your puppy down before going to bed.*
3 [no obj., with adverbial of place] sit or come to rest in a comfortable position: *he settled into an armchair.*
■[with obj. and adverbial of place] make (someone) comfortable in a particular place or position: *she allowed him to settle her in the taxi.* ■[with obj.] move or adjust (something) so that it rests securely: *she settled her bag on her shoulder.* ■fall or come down on to a surface: *dust from the mill had settled on the roof.* ■[no obj.] (of suspended particles) sink slowly in a liquid to form sediment; (of a liquid) become clear or still through this process: *sediment settles near the bottom of the tank* | *he watched his pint settling.* ■[no obj.] (of an object or objects) gradually sink down under its or their own weight: *they listened to the soft ticking and creaking as the house settled.* ■[no obj.] (of a ship) begin to sink.
– PHRASES **settle one's affairs** (or **estate**) make any necessary arrangements, such as writing a will, before one's death. **settle someone's hash** see **HASH**[1].
– ORIGIN Old English *setlan* 'to seat, place', from **SETTLE**[2].
– DERIVATIVES **settleable** adjective.

settle[2] ▶noun a wooden bench with a high back and arms, typically incorporating a box under the seat.
– ORIGIN Old English *setl* 'a place to sit', of Germanic origin; related to German *Sessel* and Latin *sella* 'seat', also to **SIT**.

settlement ▶noun **1** an official agreement intended to resolve a dispute or conflict: *unions succeeded in reaching a pay settlement* | [mass noun] *the settlement of the Palestinian problem.*
■a formal arrangement made between the parties to a lawsuit in order to resolve it, especially out of court: *the award was made as an out-of-court settlement by the driver's insurance firm.*
2 a place, typically one which has hitherto been uninhabited, where people establish a community: *the little settlement of Buttermere.*
■[mass noun] the process of settling in such a place: *a continent where settlement is at the mercy of geography.* ■[mass noun] the action of allowing or helping people to do this: *Israel's settlement of immigrants in the occupied territories.*
3 Law an arrangement whereby property passes to a succession of people as dictated by the settlor.
■the amount or property given: *Philippa brought him her handsome dower settlement from the Warwick estates.* ■ short for **MARRIAGE SETTLEMENT**.
4 [mass noun] the action or process of settling an account.
5 [mass noun] subsidence of the ground or a structure built on it: *a boundary wall, which has cracked due to settlement, is to be replaced.*

Settlement, Act of a statute of 1701 that vested the British Crown in Sophia of Hanover (granddaughter of James I of England and VI of Scotland) and her Protestant heirs, so excluding Roman Catholics, including the Stuarts, from the succession. Sophia's son became George I.

settlement house ▶noun an institution in an inner-city area, typically sponsored by a church or college, providing educational, recreational, and other social services to the community.

settler ▶noun a person who settles in an area, typically one with no or few previous inhabitants.

settling time ▶noun technical the time taken for a measuring or control instrument to get within a certain distance of a new equilibrium value without subsequently deviating from it by that amount.

settlor /ˈsɛtlə/ ▶noun Law a person who makes a settlement, especially of a property.

set-to ▶noun (pl. **-os**) informal a fight or argument: *we had a little set-to in the pub.*

set-top box ▶noun a device which converts a digital television signal to analogue for viewing on a conventional set.

Setúbal /səˈtuːb(ə)l/ a port and industrial town on the coast of Portugal, south of Lisbon; pop. 83,550 (1991).

set-up ▶noun [usu. in sing.] informal **1** the way in which something, especially an organization or equipment, is organized, planned, or arranged: *would you feel comfortable in a team-teaching set-up?*
■an organization or arrangement: *a set-up called Film Education.* ■a set of equipment needed for a particular activity or purpose: *I have a recording set-up in my house.* ■(in a ball game) a pass or play intended to provide an opportunity for another player to score.
2 a scheme or trick intended to incriminate or deceive someone: *'Listen. He didn't die. It was a set-up'.*
■chiefly N. Amer. a contest with a pre-arranged outcome.

Seurat /ˈsɔːrʌ, French sœra/, Georges Pierre (1859–91), French painter. The founder of neo-Impressionism, he is chiefly associated with pointillism, which he developed during the 1880s. Among his major paintings using this technique is *Sunday Afternoon on the Island of La Grande Jatte* (1884–6).

sev /seɪv/ ▶noun [mass noun] an Indian snack consisting of long, thin strands of gram flour, deep-fried and spiced.
– ORIGIN Hindi.

Sevastopol /Russian sʲivaˈstopəlʲ/ Ukrainian and Russian name for **SEBASTOPOL**.

seven ▶cardinal number equivalent to the sum of three and four; one more than six, or three less than ten; 7: *two sevens are fourteen* | *the remaining seven were sentenced to terms of imprisonment.* (Roman numeral: **vii**, **VII**.)
■a group or unit of seven people or things: *animals were offered for sacrifice in sevens.* ■seven years old: *my mother died when I was seven.* ■seven o'clock: *the meeting doesn't finish until seven.* ■a size of garment or other merchandise denoted by seven. ■a playing card with seven pips. ■(**sevens**) seven-a-side rugby.
– ORIGIN Old English *seofon*, of Germanic origin; related to Dutch *zeven* and German *sieben*, from an Indo-European root shared by Latin *septem* and Greek *hepta*.

seven deadly sins ▶plural noun (**the seven deadly sins**) (in Christian tradition) the sins of pride, covetousness, lust, anger, gluttony, envy, and sloth.

sevenfold ▶adjective seven times as great or as numerous: *profits have recorded a sevenfold increase to £218 million.*
■having seven parts or elements: *the sevenfold purpose of religious education.*
▶adverb by seven times; to seven times the number or amount: *his rent had gone up sevenfold.*

Seven Hills of Rome the seven hills on which the ancient city of Rome was built: Aventine, Caelian, Capitoline, Esquiline, Quirinal, Viminal, and Palatine.

Seven Sages seven wise Greeks of the 6th century BC, to each of whom a moral saying is attributed. The seven, named in a traditional list found in Plato, are Bias, Chilon, Cleobulus, Periander, Pittacus, Solon, and Thales.

seven seas ▶ **plural noun** (**the seven seas**) all the oceans of the world (conventionally listed as the Arctic, Antarctic, North Pacific, South Pacific, North Atlantic, South Atlantic, and Indian Oceans).

Seven Sisters (**the Seven Sisters**) Astronomy the star cluster of the Pleiades.

Seven Sleepers (in early Christian legend) seven noble Christian youths of Ephesus who fell asleep in a cave while fleeing from the Decian persecution and awoke 187 years later.

seventeen ▶ **cardinal number** one more than sixteen, or seven more than ten; 17: *seventeen years later* | *a list of names, seventeen in all.* (Roman numeral **xvii** or **XVII**)
■ seventeen years old: *he joined the Marines at seventeen.* ■ a size of garment or other merchandise denoted by seventeen. ■ a set or team of seventeen individuals.
– DERIVATIVES **seventeenth** adjective & noun.
– ORIGIN Old English *seofontīene*, from the Germanic base of **SEVEN**.

seventh ▶ **ordinal number** constituting number seven in a sequence; 7th: *his seventh goal of the season* | *the seventh of June* | *he was the seventh of eight children.*
■ (**a seventh/one seventh**) each of seven equal parts into which something is or may be divided. ■ the seventh finisher or position in a race or competition: *Jo Richardson came seventh.* ■ seventhly (used to introduce a seventh point or reason). ■ Music an interval spanning seven consecutive notes in a diatonic scale. ■ Music the note which is higher by this interval than the tonic of a diatonic scale or root of a chord. ■ Music a chord in which the seventh note of the scale forms an important component.
– PHRASES **in seventh heaven** see **HEAVEN**.
– DERIVATIVES **seventhly** adverb.

Seventh-Day Adventist ▶ **noun** a member of a strict Protestant sect which preaches the imminent return of Christ to Earth (originally expecting the Second Coming in 1844) and observes Saturday as the sabbath. See also **ADVENTIST**.

seventy ▶ **cardinal number** (pl. **-ies**) **1** the number equivalent to the product of seven and ten; ten less than eighty; 70: *about seventy people attended* | *seventy were arrested.* (Roman numeral: **lxx** or **LXX**)
■ (**seventies**) the numbers from seventy to seventy-nine, especially the years of a century or of a person's life: *Dad was now in his seventies.* ■ seventy years old: *she was nearly seventy.* ■ seventy miles an hour: *doing about seventy.* ■ a size of garment or other merchandise denoted by seventy.
– DERIVATIVES **seventieth** ordinal number, **seventyfold** adjective & adverb.
– ORIGIN Old English *hundseofontig*, from *hund-* (of uncertain origin) + *seofon* 'seven'.

seventy-eight (usu. **78**) ▶ **noun** an old gramophone record designed to be played at 78 rpm.

Seven Wonders of the World the seven most spectacular man-made structures of the ancient world.

> Traditionally they comprise (1) the pyramids of Egypt, especially those at Giza; (2) the Hanging Gardens of Babylon; (3) the Mausoleum of Halicarnassus; (4) the temple of Artemis at Ephesus in Asia Minor; (5) the Colossus of Rhodes; (6) the huge ivory and gold statue of Zeus at Olympia in the Peloponnese, made by Phidias *c.*430 BC; (7) the Pharos of Alexandria (or in some lists, the walls of Babylon).

seven year itch ▶ **noun** [in sing.] a supposed tendency to infidelity after seven years of marriage.

Seven Years War a war (1756–63) which ranged Britain, Prussia, and Hanover against Austria, France, Russia, Saxony, Sweden, and Spain.

> Its main issues were the struggle between Britain and France for supremacy overseas, and that between Prussia and Austria for the domination of Germany. The British made substantial gains over France abroad, capturing French Canada and undermining French influence in India. The war was ended by the Treaties of Paris and Hubertusburg in 1763, leaving Britain the supreme European naval and colonial power and Prussia in an appreciably stronger position than before in central Europe.

sever ▶ **verb** [with obj.] divide by cutting or slicing, especially suddenly and forcibly: *the head was* ***severed from*** *the body* | [as adj. **severed**] *severed limbs.*
■ put an end to (a connection or relationship); break off: *notice is sufficient to sever the joint tenancy.*
– DERIVATIVES **severable** adjective.
– ORIGIN Middle English: from Anglo-Norman French *severer*, from Latin *separare* 'disjoin, divide'.

several ▶ **determiner** & **pronoun** more than two but not many: [as determiner] *the author of several books* | [as pronoun] *the programme is one of several in the UK* | ***several of*** *his friends attended.*
▶ **adjective** separate or respective: *the two levels of government sort out their several responsibilities.*
■ Law applied or regarded separately. Often contrasted with **JOINT**.
– DERIVATIVES **severally** adverb.
– ORIGIN late Middle English: from Anglo-Norman French, from medieval Latin *separalis*, from Latin *separ* 'separate, different'.

severalty ▶ **noun** [mass noun] archaic the condition of being separate.
– ORIGIN late Middle English: from Anglo-Norman French *severalte*, from *several* (see **SEVERAL**).

severance ▶ **noun** [mass noun] the action of ending a connection or relationship: *the severance and disestablishment of the Irish Church* | [count noun] *a complete* ***severance of*** *links with the Republic.*
■ the state of being separated or cut off: *she works on the feeling of severance, of being deprived of her mother.* ■ dismissal or discharge from employment: [as modifier] *employees were offered severance terms.* ■ short for **SEVERANCE PAY**.
– ORIGIN late Middle English: from Anglo-Norman French, based on Latin *separare* (see **SEVER**).

severance pay ▶ **noun** an amount paid to an employee on the early termination of a contract.

severe ▶ **adjective 1** (of something bad or undesirable) very great; intense: *a severe shortage of technicians* | *a severe attack of asthma* | *damage is not too severe.*
■ demanding great ability, skill, or resilience: *a severe test of stamina.*
2 strict or harsh: *the charges would have warranted a severe sentence* | *he is unusually* ***severe on*** *what he regards as tendentious pseudo-learning.*
3 very plain in style or appearance: *she wore another severe suit, grey this time.*
– DERIVATIVES **severely** adverb, **severity** noun.
– ORIGIN mid 16th cent. (in sense 2): from French *sévère* or Latin *severus.*

Severn a river of SW Britain. Rising in central Wales, it flows north-east then south in a broad curve for some 290 km (180 miles) to its mouth on the Bristol Channel. The estuary is spanned by a suspension bridge north of Bristol, opened in 1966, and a second bridge a few miles to the south, opened in 1996.

Severnaya Zemlya /ˌsɛvɛːˌnʌɪə zɪmˈljɑː/ a group of uninhabited islands in the Arctic Ocean off the north coast of Russia, to the north of the Taimyr Peninsula.

Severodvinsk /ˌsɛvərəˈdvɪnsk/ a port in NW Russia, on the White Sea coast west of Archangel; pop. 250,000 (1990).

Severus /sɪˈvɪərəs/, Septimius (146–211), Roman emperor 193–211; full name *Lucius Septimius Severus Pertinax.* He reformed the imperial administration and the army. In 208 he led an army to Britain to suppress a rebellion in the north of the country and later died at York.

severy /ˈsɛvəri/ ▶ **noun** (pl. **-ies**) Architecture a bay or compartment in a vaulted ceiling.
– ORIGIN late Middle English: from Old French *civoire* 'ciborium' (see **CIBORIUM**).

seviche /sɛˈviːtʃeɪ/ ▶ **noun** variant spelling of **CEVICHE**.

Seville /səˈvɪl/ a city in southern Spain, the capital of Andalusia, situated on the Guadalquivir River; pop. 683,490 (1991). A leading cultural centre of Moorish Spain, it was reclaimed by the Spanish in 1248, and rapidly became prominent as a centre of trade with the colonies of the New World. Spanish name **SEVILLA** /seˈβija/.

Seville orange /ˈsɛvɪl/ ▶ **noun** a bitter orange used for marmalade.

Sevin /ˈsɛvɪn/ ▶ **noun** trademark for **CARBARYL**.
– ORIGIN 1950s: of unknown origin.

Sèvres /ˈsɛvr(ə), French sɛvʀ/ ▶ **noun** [mass noun] a type of fine porcelain characterized by elaborate decoration on backgrounds of intense colour, made at Sèvres in the suburbs of Paris.

sevruga /sɛvˈruːɡə/ ▶ **noun** a migratory sturgeon found only in the basins of the Caspian and Black Seas, much fished for its caviar.
• *Acipenser stellatus*, family Acipenseridae.
■ [mass noun] caviar obtained from this fish.
– ORIGIN late 16th cent.: from Russian *sevryuga.*

sew ▶ **verb** (past participle **sewn** or **sewed**) [with obj.] join, fasten, or repair (something) by making stitches with a needle and thread or a sewing machine: *she sewed the seams and hemmed the border* | [no obj.] *I don't even sew very well.*
■ [with obj. and adverbial] attach (something) to something else by sewing: *she could sew the veil on properly in the morning.* ■ make (a garment) by sewing.
– ORIGIN Old English *siwan*, of Germanic origin, from an Indo-European root shared by Latin *suere* and Greek *suein.*
▶ **sew something up** informal bring something to a favourable conclusion: *they had the match sewn up by half-time.* ■ achieve exclusive control over something: *the US courier market has been more or less sewn up by two companies.*

sewage /ˈsuːɪdʒ/ ▶ **noun** [mass noun] waste water and excrement conveyed in sewers.
– ORIGIN mid 19th cent.: from **SEWER**[1], by substitution of the suffix **-AGE**.

sewage farm ▶ **noun** a place where sewage is treated, especially for use as an agricultural fertilizer.

sewage works ▶ **noun** [treated as sing. or pl.] a place where sewage is treated so that the resultant effluent can be returned safely to a river, the sea, etc.

sewellel /sɪˈwɛləl/ ▶ **noun** another term for **MOUNTAIN BEAVER**.
– ORIGIN early 19th cent.: from Chinook Jargon *šwalál* 'robe of mountain-beaver skin'.

sewen ▶ **noun** variant spelling of **SEWIN**.

sewer[1] /ˈsuːə, ˈsjuːə/ ▶ **noun** an underground conduit for carrying off drainage water and waste matter.
– ORIGIN Middle English (denoting a watercourse to drain marshy land): from Old Northern French *seuwiere* 'channel to drain the overflow from a fish pond', based on Latin *ex-* 'out of' + *aqua* 'water'.

sewer[2] /ˈsəʊə/ ▶ **noun** a person that sews.

sewerage ▶ **noun** [mass noun] the provision of drainage by sewers.
■ US term for **SEWAGE**.

sewer rat ▶ **noun** another term for **BROWN RAT**.

sewin /ˈsjuːɪn/ (also **sewen**) ▶ **noun** (in Wales) a sea trout.
– ORIGIN mid 16th cent.: of unknown origin.

sewing ▶ **noun** [mass noun] the action or activity of sewing.
■ work that is to be or is being sewn: *she put down her sewing.*

sewing machine ▶ **noun** a machine with a mechanically driven needle for sewing or stitching cloth.

sewn past participle of **SEW**.

sex ▶ **noun 1** [mass noun] (chiefly with reference to people) sexual activity, including specifically sexual intercourse: *he enjoyed talking about sex* | *she didn't want to* ***have sex with*** *him.*
■ [in sing.] a person's genitals (used in novels to avoid more vulgar or anatomically explicit terms).
2 either of the two main categories (male and female) into which humans and most other living things are divided on the basis of their reproductive functions: *adults of both sexes.*
■ [mass noun] the fact of belonging to one of these categories: *direct discrimination involves treating someone less favourably on the grounds of their sex.* ■ the group of all members of either of these categories: *she was well known for her efforts to improve the social condition of her sex.*
▶ **verb** [with obj.] **1** determine the sex of: *sexing fish.*
2 (**sex someone up**) informal arouse or attempt to arouse someone sexually.
– DERIVATIVES **sexer** noun.
– ORIGIN late Middle English (denoting the two categories, male and female): from Old French *sexe* or Latin *sexus.*

> **USAGE** On the difference in use between the words **sex** (in sense 2 above) and **gender**, see **usage** at **GENDER**.

sex- ▶ **combining form** variant spelling of **SEXI-**, shortened before a vowel (as in *sexennial*), or shortened before a consonant (as in *sexfoil*).

sex act ▶ noun any sexual act.
■ **(the sex act)** the act of sexual intercourse.

sexagenarian /ˌsɛksədʒɪ'nɛːrɪən/ ▶ noun a person who is between 60 and 69 years old.
– ORIGIN mid 18th cent.: from Latin *sexagenarius* (based on *sexaginta* 'sixty') + -AN.

Sexagesima /ˌsɛksə'dʒɛsɪmə/ (also **Sexagesima Sunday**) the Sunday before Quinquagesima.
– ORIGIN late Middle English: from ecclesiastical Latin, literally 'sixtieth (day)', probably named by analogy with QUINQUAGESIMA.

sexagesimal /ˌsɛksə'dʒɛsɪm(ə)l/ ▶ adjective **1** of, relating to, or reckoning by sixtieths.
2 of or relating to the number sixty.
▶ noun (also **sexagesimal fraction**) a fraction based on sixtieths (i.e. with a denominator equal to a power of sixty), as in the divisions of the degree and hour.
– DERIVATIVES **sexagesimally** adverb.
– ORIGIN late 17th cent.: from Latin *sexagesimus* 'sixtieth' + -AL.

sex appeal ▶ noun [mass noun] the quality of being attractive in a sexual way: *she just oozes sex appeal.*

sex bomb ▶ noun informal a woman who is very sexually attractive.

sexcapade ▶ noun informal, chiefly US a sexual escapade; an illicit affair.
– ORIGIN 1960s: blend of SEX and ESCAPADE.

sexcentenary /sɛk(s)sɛn'tiːn(ə)ri, -'tɛn-/ ▶ noun (pl. **-ies**) the six-hundredth anniversary of a significant event.
▶ adjective of or relating to a six-hundredth anniversary.

sex change ▶ noun a change in a person's physical sexual characteristics, typically by surgery and hormone treatment.

sex chromatin ▶ noun [mass noun] Biology material found only in the nuclei of female cells (especially as the Barr body) and believed to represent the inactivated X chromosome.

sex chromosome ▶ noun a chromosome concerned in determining the sex of an organism, typically one of two kinds.

In humans and other mammals females have two similar sex chromosomes (XX) while males have dissimilar ones (XY). In birds and some other animals, females have dissimilar sex chromosomes (ZW) and males similar ones (WW). Some other organisms have a sex chromosome present only in one sex.

sex crime ▶ noun informal a crime involving sexual assault or having a sexual motive.

sex discrimination (also **sexual discrimination**) ▶ noun [mass noun] discrimination in employment and opportunity against a person (typically a woman) on grounds of sex.

sex drive ▶ noun [mass noun] the urge to seek satisfaction of sexual needs.

sexed ▶ adjective **1** [with submodifier] having specified sexual appetites: *highly sexed heterosexual males.*
2 [attrib.] having sexual characteristics: *the effects of family and kinship relations on the construction of sexed individuals.*

sexennial /sɛk'sɛnɪəl/ ▶ adjective recurring every six years.
■ lasting for or relating to a period of six years.
– ORIGIN mid 17th cent.: from SEXENNIUM + -AL.

sexennium /sɛk'sɛnɪəm/ ▶ noun (pl. **sexennia** /-nɪə/ or **sexenniums**) rare a specified period of six years.
– ORIGIN 1950s: from Latin, from *sex* 'six' + *annus* 'year'.

sexfoil ▶ noun (especially in architecture) an ornamental design having six leaves or petals radiating from a common centre.
– ORIGIN late 17th cent.: from SEXI- 'six', on the pattern of words such as *trefoil.*

sex hormone ▶ noun a hormone, such as oestrogen or testosterone, affecting sexual development or reproduction.

sexi- (also **sex-** before a vowel) ▶ combining form six; having six: *sexivalent.*
– ORIGIN from Latin *sex* 'six'.

sex industry ▶ noun (**the sex industry**) used euphemistically to refer to prostitution.

sexism ▶ noun [mass noun] prejudice, stereotyping, or discrimination, typically against women, on the basis of sex.
– DERIVATIVES **sexist** adjective & noun.

sexivalent /ˌsɛksɪ'veɪl(ə)nt/ ▶ adjective Chemistry another term for HEXAVALENT.

sex kitten ▶ noun informal a young woman who asserts or exploits her sexual attractiveness.

sexless ▶ adjective **1** lacking in sexual desire, interest, activity, or attractiveness: *I've no patience with pious, sexless females.*
2 neither male nor female: *the stylized and sexless falsetto.*
– DERIVATIVES **sexlessly** adverb, **sexlessness** noun.

sex life ▶ noun a person's sexual activity and relationships considered as a whole.

sex-linked ▶ adjective chiefly Biology tending to be associated with one sex or the other.
■ (of a gene or heritable characteristic) carried by a sex chromosome.

sex maniac ▶ noun informal a person whose need for sexual gratification is excessive or obsessive.

sex object ▶ noun a person regarded by another only in terms of their sexual attractiveness or availability: *we're now in a period when it is permissible for women to make men into sex objects.*

sex offender ▶ noun a person who commits a crime involving a sexual act.

sexology ▶ noun [mass noun] the study of human sexual life or relationships.
– DERIVATIVES **sexological** adjective, **sexologist** noun.

sexpartite /sɛks'pɑːtʌɪt/ ▶ adjective divided or involving division into six parts: *the sexpartite vault is of 12th-century construction.*
– ORIGIN mid 18th cent.: from SEXI- 'six' + PARTITE, on the pattern of words such as *bipartite.*

sexpert ▶ noun informal an expert in sexual matters.

sexploitation ▶ noun informal the commercial exploitation of sex, sexual attractiveness, or sexually explicit material.
– ORIGIN 1940s: blend of SEX and *exploitation* (see EXPLOIT).

sexpot ▶ noun informal a sexy person.

sex role ▶ noun the role or behaviour learned by a person as appropriate to their sex, determined by the prevailing cultural norms.

sex-starved ▶ adjective lacking and strongly desiring sexual gratification.

sex symbol ▶ noun a person widely noted for their sexual attractiveness.

sext ▶ noun a service forming part of the Divine Office of the Western Christian Church, traditionally said (or chanted) at the sixth hour of the day (i.e. noon).
– ORIGIN late Middle English: from Latin *sexta (hora)* 'sixth (hour)', from *sextus* 'sixth'.

Sextans /'sɛkst(ə)nz/ Astronomy a faint constellation (the Sextant), lying on the celestial equator between Leo and Hydra.
■ [as genitive **Sextantis** /sɛk'stantɪs/] used with preceding letter or numeral to designate a star in this constellation: *the star Alpha Sextantis.*
– ORIGIN Latin.

sextant /'sɛkst(ə)nt/ ▶ noun an instrument with a graduated arc of 60° and a sighting mechanism, used for measuring the angular distances between objects and especially for taking altitudes in navigation and surveying.
– ORIGIN late 16th cent. (denoting the sixth part of a circle): from Latin *sextans, sextant-* 'sixth part', from *sextus* 'sixth'.

sextet (also **sextette**) ▶ noun a group of six people playing music or singing together.
■ a composition for such a group. ■ a set of six people or things: *a sextet of new releases.*
– ORIGIN mid 19th cent.: alteration of SESTET, suggested by Latin *sex* 'six'.

sex therapy ▶ noun [mass noun] counselling or other therapy which addresses a person's psychological or physical sexual problems.
– DERIVATIVES **sex therapist** noun.

sextile /'sɛkstʌɪl, -tɪl/ ▶ noun [mass noun] Astrology an aspect of 60° (one sixth of a circle): *the Jupiter–Saturn cycle is now in sextile to its most difficult period.*
– ORIGIN late Middle English: from Latin *sextilis*, from *sextus* 'sixth'.

sextillion /sɛks'tɪljən/ ▶ cardinal number (pl. **sextillions** or (with numeral) same) a thousand raised to the seventh power (10²¹).

■ dated, chiefly Brit. a million raised to the sixth power (10³⁶).
– DERIVATIVES **sextillionth** ordinal number.
– ORIGIN late 17th cent.: from *million*, by substitution of the prefix *sexti-* 'six' (from Latin *sextus* 'sixth') for the initial letters.

sextodecimo /ˌsɛkstə(ʊ)'dɛsɪməʊ/ (abbrev.: **16mo**) ▶ noun (pl. **-os**) a size of book page that results from folding each printed sheet into sixteen leaves (thirty-two pages).
■ a book of this size.
– ORIGIN late 17th cent.: from Latin *sexto decimo*, ablative of *sextus decimus* 'sixteenth'.

sexton ▶ noun a person who looks after a church and churchyard, typically acting as bell-ringer and gravedigger.
– ORIGIN Middle English: from Anglo-Norman French *segrestein*, from medieval Latin *sacristanus* (see SACRISTAN).

sexton beetle ▶ noun another term for BURYING BEETLE.

sex tourism ▶ noun [mass noun] the organization of holidays with the purpose of taking advantage of the lack of restrictions imposed on sexual activity and prostitution by some foreign countries.

sextuple /'sɛkstjʊp(ə)l, sɛks'tjuːp(ə)l/ ▶ adjective [attrib.] consisting of six parts or things.
■ six times as much or as many.
▶ noun a sixfold number or amount.
▶ verb [with obj.] multiply by six; increase sixfold.
– DERIVATIVES **sextuply** adverb.
– ORIGIN early 17th cent.: from medieval Latin *sextuplus*, formed irregularly from Latin *sex* 'six', on the pattern of late Latin *quintuplus* 'quintuple'.

sextuplet /'sɛkstjʊplɪt, sɛks'tjuːplɪt/ ▶ noun **1** each of six children born at one birth.
2 Music a group of six notes to be performed in the time of four.
– ORIGIN mid 19th cent.: from SEXTUPLE, on the pattern of words such as *triplet.*

sex typing ▶ noun [mass noun] **1** Psychology & Sociology the stereotypical categorization of people, or their appearance or behaviour, according to conventional perceptions of what is typical of each sex.
2 Biology the process of determining the sex of a person or other organism, especially in difficult cases where special tests are necessary.
– DERIVATIVES **sex-typed** adjective.

sexual ▶ adjective **1** relating to the instincts, physiological processes, and activities connected with physical attraction or intimate physical contact between individuals: *she had felt the thrill of a sexual attraction.*
2 of or relating to the two sexes or to gender: *sensitivity about sexual stereotypes.*
■ of or characteristic of one sex or the other: *the hormones which control the secondary sexual characteristics.* ■ Biology being of one sex or the other; capable of sexual reproduction.
– DERIVATIVES **sexually** adverb.
– ORIGIN mid 17th cent.: from late Latin *sexualis*, from Latin *sexus* 'sex'.

sexual dimorphism ▶ noun [mass noun] Zoology distinct difference in size or appearance between the sexes of an animal in addition to the sexual organs themselves.

sexual harassment ▶ noun [mass noun] harassment (typically of a woman) in a workplace, or other professional or social situation, involving the making of unwanted sexual advances or obscene remarks.

sexual intercourse ▶ noun [mass noun] sexual contact between individuals involving penetration, especially the insertion of a man's erect penis into a woman's vagina, typically culminating in orgasm and the ejaculation of semen.

sexual inversion ▶ noun see INVERSION (sense 4).

sexuality ▶ noun (pl. **-ies**) [mass noun] capacity for sexual feelings: *she began to understand the power of her sexuality.*
■ [count noun] a person's sexual orientation or preference: *people with proscribed sexualities.* ■ sexual activity.

sexualize (also **-ise**) ▶ verb [with obj.] make sexual; attribute sex or a sex role to: [as adj. **sexualized**] *sexualized images of women.*
– DERIVATIVES **sexualization** noun.

sexual politics ▶ plural noun [treated as sing.] the

principles determining the relationship of the sexes; relations between the sexes regarded in terms of power.

sexual reproduction ▶ **noun** [mass noun] Biology the production of new living organisms by combining genetic information from two individuals of different types (sexes). In most higher organisms, one sex (male) produces a small motile gamete which travels to fuse with a larger stationary gamete produced by the other (female).

sexual revolution ▶ **noun** the liberalization of established social and moral attitudes to sex, particularly (**the sexual revolution**) that occurring in western countries during the 1960s, as the women's movement and developments in contraception instigated changes in attitudes towards sex and women's sexuality, and sexual equality became an aim of society.

sexual selection ▶ **noun** [mass noun] Biology natural selection arising through preference by one sex for certain characteristics in individuals of the other sex.

sex worker ▶ **noun** used euphemistically to refer to a prostitute.

sexy ▶ **adjective** (**sexier**, **sexiest**) sexually attractive or exciting: *sexy French underwear.*
■ sexually aroused: *neither of them was feeling sexy.* ■ informal exciting; appealing: *I've climbed most of the really sexy west coast mountains.*
– DERIVATIVES **sexily** adverb, **sexiness** noun.

Seychelles /seɪˈʃɛlz, -ˈʃɛl/ (also **the Seychelles**) a country consisting of a group of about ninety islands in the Indian Ocean, about 1,000 km (600 miles) NE of Madagascar; pop. 69,000 (est. 1991); languages, French Creole (official), English, French; capital, Victoria.

> The islands were uninhabited until the mid 18th century, when the French annexed them. The Seychelles were captured by Britain during the Napoleonic Wars and administered from Mauritius before becoming a separate colony in 1903 and an independent republic within the Commonwealth in 1976.

– DERIVATIVES **Seychellois** /ˌseɪʃɛlˈwʌ/ adjective & noun (pl. same).

Seyfert galaxy /ˈsiːfəːt/ ▶ **noun** Astronomy a galaxy of a type characterized by a bright compact core that shows strong infrared emission.
– ORIGIN named after Carl K. *Seyfert* (1911–60), American astronomer.

Seym /seɪm/ ▶ **noun** variant spelling of **SEJM**.

Seymour[1] /ˈsiːmɔː/, Jane (*c.*1509–37), third wife of Henry VIII and mother of Edward VI. She married Henry in 1536 and finally provided the king with the male heir he wanted, although she died twelve days afterwards.

Seymour[2] /ˈsiːmɔː/, Lynn (b.1939), Canadian ballet dancer; born *Lynn Springbett*. From 1957 she danced for the Royal Ballet. Her most acclaimed roles came in Frederick Ashton's *Five Brahms Waltzes in the Manner of Isadora Duncan* and *A Month in the Country* (both 1976).

sez ▶ **verb** non-standard spelling of 'says', used in representing uneducated speech: *'I've got a paper 'ere that sez they can't come in.'*

Sezession /German ˌzetsɛˈsioːn/ (also **Secession** /sɪˈsɛʃ(ə)n/) ▶ **noun** (**the Sezession**) a radical movement involving groups of avant-garde German and Austrian artists who, from 1892, organized exhibitions independently of the traditional academies. The **Vienna Secession** founded by Gustav Klimt in 1897 helped to launch the Jugendstil.
– ORIGIN German, literally 'secession'.

SF ▶ **abbreviation for** ■ Finland (international vehicle registration). [ORIGIN: from Finnish *Suomi* + Swedish *Finland*.] ■ science fiction. ■ Sinn Fein.

sf Music ▶ **abbreviation for** sforzando.

SFA ▶ **abbreviation for** ■ Scottish Football Association. ■ (in the UK) Securities and Futures Authority.

Sfax /sfaks/ (also **Safaqis**) a port on the east coast of Tunisia; pop. 230,900 (1994). It is a centre for the region's phosphate industry.

sforzando /sfɔːˈtsandəʊ/ (also **sforzato** /-ˈtsɑːtəʊ/) Music ▶ **adverb & adjective** (especially as a direction) with sudden emphasis.
▶ **noun** (pl. **sforzandos** or **sforzandi** /-di/) a sudden or marked emphasis.
– ORIGIN Italian, literally 'using force'.

sfumato /sfʊˈmɑːtəʊ/ ▶ **noun** [mass noun] Art the technique of allowing tones and colours to shade gradually into one another, producing softened outlines or hazy forms.
– ORIGIN mid 19th cent.: Italian, literally 'shaded off', past participle of *sfumare*.

SFX ▶ **abbreviation for** special effects.
– ORIGIN *FX* representing a pronunciation of *effects*.

sfz Music ▶ **abbreviation for** sforzando.

SG ▶ **abbreviation for**
■ Law Solicitor General. ■ Physics specific gravity.

Sg ▶ **symbol for** the chemical element seaborgium.

sgd ▶ **abbreviation for** signed.

SGML Computing ▶ **abbreviation for** Standard Generalized Mark-up Language, an international standard for defining methods of encoding electronic texts to describe layout, structure, syntax, etc., which can then be used for analysis or to display the text in any desired format.

SGP ▶ **abbreviation for** Singapore (international vehicle registration).

sgraffito /sgraˈfiːtəʊ/ ▶ **noun** (pl. **sgraffiti** /-ti/) [mass noun] a form of decoration made by scratching through a surface to reveal a lower layer of a contrasting colour, typically done in plaster or stucco on walls, or in slip on ceramics before firing.
– ORIGIN mid 18th cent.: Italian, literally 'scratched away', past participle of *sgraffiare*.

's-Gravenhage /ˌsxraːvənˈhaːxə/ Dutch name for **HAGUE, THE**.

Sgt ▶ **abbreviation for** Sergeant.

sh. Brit. ▶ **abbreviation for** shilling(s).

Shaanxi /ʃɑːnˈʃiː/ (also **Shensi**) a mountainous province of central China; capital, Xian. It is the site of the earliest settlements of the ancient Chinese civilizations.

Shaba /ˈʃɑːbə/ a copper-mining region of SE Zaire (Democratic Republic of Congo); capital, Lubumbashi. Former name (until 1972) **KATANGA**.

Shabaka /ˈʃabəkə/ (d.698 BC), Egyptian pharaoh, founder of the 25th dynasty, reigned 712–698 BC; known as **Sabacon**. He promoted the cult of Amun and revived the custom of pyramid burial in his own death arrangements.

shabash /ˈʃɑːbɑːʃ/ ▶ **exclamation** Indian well done!
– ORIGIN from Urdu and Persian *šābāš*, from *šād* 'joyful' + *bāš!* (imperative) 'be!'.

Shabbat /ʃaˈbat/ ▶ **noun** (among Sephardic Jews and in Israel) the Sabbath. Compare with **SHABBOS**.
– ORIGIN from Hebrew *šabbāṯ*.

Shabbos /ˈʃabəs/ (also **Shabbes**) ▶ **noun** (among Ashkenazic Jews) the Sabbath. Compare with **SHABBAT**.
– ORIGIN Yiddish, from Hebrew *šabbāṯ*.

shabby ▶ **adjective** (**shabbier**, **shabbiest**) in poor condition through long use or lack of care: *a conscript in a shabby uniform saluted the car.*
■ dressed in old or worn clothes. ■ (of behaviour) mean and unfair: *Snooping, was he? That's a shabby trick.*
– DERIVATIVES **shabbily** adverb, **shabbiness** noun.
– ORIGIN mid 17th cent.: from dialect *shab* 'scab' (from a Germanic base meaning 'itch') + **-Y**[1].

shabrack /ˈʃabrak/ ▶ **noun** historical a cavalry saddlecloth used in European armies.
– ORIGIN early 19th cent.: from German *Schabracke*, of east European origin; compare with Russian *shabrak*.

shabti /ˈʃabti/ (also **ushabti**) ▶ **noun** (pl. **shabtis**) each of a set of wooden, stone, or faience figurines, in the form of mummies, placed in an ancient Egyptian tomb to do any work that the dead person might be called upon to do in the afterlife.
– ORIGIN from Egyptian *šbty*, literally 'answerer'.

shabu-shabu /ˌʃabuːˈʃabuː/ ▶ **noun** [mass noun] a Japanese dish of pieces of thinly sliced beef or pork cooked quickly with vegetables in boiling water and then dipped in sauce.
– ORIGIN Japanese.

shack ▶ **noun** a roughly built hut or cabin.
▶ **verb** [no obj.] (**shack up**) informal move in or live with someone as a lover.
– ORIGIN late 19th cent.: perhaps from Mexican *jacal*, Nahuatl *xacatli* 'wooden hut'. The early sense of the verb was 'live in a shack' (originally a US usage).

shackland ▶ **noun** (in South Africa, chiefly KwaZulu/Natal) a hastily erected urban shack settlement, not officially proclaimed as a residential area.

shackle ▶ **noun 1** (**shackles**) a pair of fetters connected together by a chain, used to fasten a prisoner's wrists or ankles together.
■ figurative used in reference to something that restrains or impedes: *society is going to throw off **the shackles of** racism and colonialism.*
2 a metal link, typically U-shaped, closed by a bolt, used to secure a chain or rope to something.
■ a pivoted link connecting a spring in a vehicle's suspension to the body of the vehicle.
▶ **verb** [with obj.] chain with shackles.
■ figurative restrain; limit: *they seek to shackle the oil and gas companies by imposing new controls.*
– ORIGIN Old English *sc(e)acul* 'fetter', of Germanic origin; related to Dutch *schakel* 'link, coupling'.

shackle lock ▶ **noun** another term for **D-LOCK**.

Shackleton, Sir Ernest Henry (1874–1922), British explorer. During one of his Antarctic expeditions (1914–16), Shackleton's ship *Endurance* was crushed in the ice. Shackleton and his crew eventually reached an island, from where he and five others set out in an open boat on a 1,300-km (800-mile) voyage to South Georgia to get help.

shacky ▶ **adjective** N. Amer. informal (of a building) dilapidated or ramshackle.

shad ▶ **noun** (pl. same or **shads**) a herring-like fish that spends much of its life in the sea, typically entering rivers to spawn. It is an important food fish in many regions.
● Genera *Alosa* and *Caspialosa*, family Clupeidae: several species. See **ALLIS SHAD** and **TWAITE SHAD**.
– ORIGIN Old English *sceadd*, of unknown origin.

shadbush (also **shadblow**) ▶ **noun** North American term for **JUNEBERRY**.
– ORIGIN early 19th cent.: so named because it flowers at the same time as shad are found in the rivers.

shadchan /ˈʃadxən, ˈʃɒd-/ (also **shadkhan**) ▶ **noun** (pl. same /ˈʃadxɛn/, **shadchanim** /ˈʃadxənɪm/, or **shadchans**) a Jewish professional matchmaker or marriage broker.
– ORIGIN from Yiddish *shadkhn*, based on Hebrew *šiddēḵ* 'negotiate'.

Shaddai /ˈʃadʌɪ/ ▶ **noun** one of the names given to God in the Hebrew Bible.
– ORIGIN Hebrew, translated as 'Almighty' in English versions of the Bible, but of uncertain meaning.

shaddock /ˈʃadək/ ▶ **noun** another term for **POMELO**.
– ORIGIN late 17th cent.: named after Captain *Shaddock*, who introduced it to the West Indies in the 17th cent.

shaddup /ʃʌˈdʌp/ ▶ **exclamation** informal be quiet!: *'Shaddup! If he wants to confess, let him.'*
– ORIGIN 1950s: representing a pronunciation of *shut up*.

shade ▶ **noun 1** [mass noun] comparative darkness and coolness caused by shelter from direct sunlight: *sitting in the shade | this area will be **in shade** for much of the day.*
■ the darker part of a picture. ■ (usu. **shades**) poetic/literary a shadow or area of darkness: *the shades of evening drew on.* ■ figurative a position of relative inferiority or obscurity: *her elegant pink and black ensemble would **put** most outfits **in the shade**.* ■ historical a portrait in silhouette.
2 a colour, especially with regard to how light or dark it is or as distinguished from one nearly like it: *various shades of blue* | [mass noun] *Maria's eyes darkened **in shade**.*
■ Art a slight degree of difference between colours. ■ a slightly differing variety of something: *politicians of all shades of opinion.* ■ [in sing.] a slight amount of something: *the goal had more than **a shade of** good fortune about it.*
3 a lampshade.
■ (often **shades**) N. Amer. a screen or blind on a window. ■ an eyeshade. ■ (**shades**) informal sunglasses.
4 poetic/literary a ghost.
■ (**the Shades**) the underworld; Hades.
▶ **verb** [with obj.] **1** screen from direct light: *she shaded her eyes against the sun.*
■ cover, moderate, or exclude the light of: *he shaded the torch with his hand.*
2 darken or colour (an illustration or diagram) with parallel pencil lines or a block of colour: *she shaded in the outline of a chimney.*
■ [no obj., with adverbial] (of a colour or something

coloured) gradually change into another colour: *the sky shaded from turquoise to night blue.*
3 informal narrowly win or gain an advantage in (a contest): *the Welsh side shaded a tight, tough first half.*
4 make a slight reduction in the amount, rate, or price of: *banks may shade the margin over base rate they charge customers.*
■[no obj.] decline slightly in price, amount, or rate: [with complement] *their shares shaded 10p to 334p.*
– PHRASES **a shade ——** a little ——: *he was a shade hung-over.* **shades of ——** used to suggest reminiscence of or comparison with someone or something specified: *colleges were conducting campaigns to ban Jewish societies—shades of Nazi Germany.*
– DERIVATIVES **shadeless** adjective, **shader** noun.
– ORIGIN Old English *sc(e)adu*, of Germanic origin. Compare with **SHADOW**.

shading ▶ **noun** [mass noun] **1** the darkening or colouring of an illustration or diagram with parallel lines or a block of colour.
■[count noun] a very slight variation, typically in colour or meaning: *the shadings of opinion even among those who are in broad agreement.*
2 a layer of paint or material used to provide shade, especially for plants: *liquid greenhouse shading.*

shadkhan ▶ **noun** variant spelling of **SHADCHAN**.

shadoof /ʃəˈduːf/ ▶ **noun** a pole with a bucket and counterpoise used especially in Egypt for raising water.
– ORIGIN mid 19th cent.: from Egyptian Arabic *šādūf*.

shadow ▶ **noun 1** a dark area or shape produced by a body coming between rays of light and a surface: *trees cast long shadows.*
■[mass noun] partial or complete darkness, especially as produced in this way: *the north side of the cathedral was deep in shadow* | (**shadows**) *a stranger slowly approached from the shadows.* ■[mass noun] the shaded part of a picture. ■ a dark patch or area on a surface: *there are dark shadows beneath your eyes.* ■ a region of opacity on a radiograph: *shadows on his lungs.* ■ short for **EYESHADOW**.
2 figurative used in reference to proximity, ominous oppressiveness, or sadness and gloom: *the shadow of war fell across Europe* | *only one shadow lay over Sally's life.*
■used in reference to something insubstantial or fleeting: *a freedom that was more shadow than substance.* ■ used in reference to a position of relative inferiority or obscurity: *he* **lived in the shadow of** *his father.* ■ [with negative] the slightest trace of something: *she knew* **without a shadow of a doubt** *that he was lying.* ■ a weak or inferior remnant or version of something: *this fine-looking, commanding man had become* **a shadow of** *his former self.* ■ an expression of perplexity or sadness: *a shadow crossed Maria's face.*
3 an inseparable attendant or companion: *her faithful shadow, a Yorkshire terrier called Heathcliffe.*
■a person secretly following and observing another. ■ a person that accompanies someone in their daily activities at work in order to gain experience at or insight into a job. ■ [usu. as modifier] Brit. the opposition counterpart of a government minister: *the shadow Chancellor.*
▶ **verb** [with obj.] **1** (often **be shadowed**) envelop in shadow; cast a shadow over: *the market is shadowed by St Margaret's church* | *a hood shadowed her face.*
2 follow and observe (someone) closely and typically secretly: *he had been up all night shadowing a team of poachers.*
■Brit. (of an opposition politician) be the counterpart of (a government minister or a ministry). ■ accompany (someone) in their daily activities at work in order to gain experience at or insight into a job.
– PHRASES **be frightened of one's shadow** be very timid or nervous. **wear oneself to a shadow** completely exhaust oneself through overwork.
– DERIVATIVES **shadower** noun, **shadowless** adjective.
– ORIGIN Old English *scead(u)we* (noun), oblique case of *sceadu* (see **SHADE**), *sceadwian* 'screen or shield from attack', of Germanic origin; related to Dutch *schaduw* and German *Schatten* (nouns), from an Indo-European root shared by Greek *skotos* 'darkness'.

shadow-box ▶ **verb** [no obj.] spar with an imaginary opponent as a form of training.

shadowgraph ▶ **noun** an image formed by the shadow of an object on a surface.
■an image formed when light shone through a fluid is refracted differently by regions of different density. ■ a radiograph.

shadowland ▶ **noun** poetic/literary a place in shadow.
■(usu. **shadowlands**) an indeterminate borderland between places or states, typically represented as an abode of ghosts and spirits: *voices laughing in the shadowlands of my recall.*

shadow mask ▶ **noun** a perforated metal screen situated directly behind the phosphor screen in certain types of colour television tube, having a pattern of precisely located holes through which the electron beams pass so as to strike the correct dots on the phosphor screen.

shadow price ▶ **noun** Economics the estimated price of a good or service for which no market price exists.

shadow stitch ▶ **noun** [mass noun] a criss-cross embroidery stitch used on sheer materials for filling in spaces, worked on the reverse side so as to show through in a shadowy way with an outline resembling a backstitch.

shadow theatre ▶ **noun** a display in which the shadows of flat jointed puppets are cast on a screen which is viewed by the audience from the other side. Such shows originated in the Far East, and were popular in London and Paris in the 18th and 19th centuries; they survive in traditional form in Java and Bali.

shadow work ▶ **noun** [mass noun] embroidery done in shadow stitch.

shadowy ▶ **adjective** (**shadowier**, **shadowiest**) full of shadows: *a long, shadowy, cobbled passage.*
■of uncertain identity or nature: *a shadowy figure appeared through the mist* | *the shadowy world of covert operations.* ■ insubstantial; unreal: *they were attacked by a swarm of shadowy, ethereal forms.*
– DERIVATIVES **shadowiness** noun.

shady ▶ **adjective** (**shadier**, **shadiest**) situated in or full of shade: *shady woods.*
■giving shade from sunlight: *they sprawled under a shady carob tree.* ■ informal of doubtful honesty or legality: *he was involved in his grandmother's shady deals.*
– DERIVATIVES **shadily** adverb, **shadiness** noun.

shaft ▶ **noun 1** a long, narrow part or section forming the handle of a tool or club, the body of a spear or arrow, or similar: *the shaft of a golf club* | *the shaft of a feather.*
■an arrow or spear. ■ a column, especially the main part between the base and capital. ■ a long cylindrical rotating rod for the transmission of motive power in a machine. ■ each of the pair of poles between which a horse is harnessed to a vehicle. ■ a ray of light or bolt of lightning: ***a shaft of** sunlight.* ■ a sudden flash of a quality or feeling; *a* ***shaft of** inspiration.* ■ a remark intended to be witty, wounding, or provoking: *he directs his shafts against her.* ■ vulgar slang a man's penis. ■ (**the shaft**) N. Amer. informal harsh or unfair treatment: *the executives continue to raise their pay while the workers* ***get the shaft.***
2 a long, narrow, typically vertical hole that gives access to a mine, accommodates a lift in a building, or provides ventilation.
▶ **verb 1** [no obj., with adverbial of direction] (of light) shine in beams: *brilliant sunshine shafted through the skylight.*
2 [with obj.] vulgar slang (of a man) have sexual intercourse with (a woman).
■informal treat (someone) harshly or unfairly: *I suppose she'll get a lawyer and I'll be shafted.*
– DERIVATIVES **shafted** adjective [in combination] *a long-shafted harpoon.*
– ORIGIN Old English *scæft*, *sceaft* 'handle, pole', of Germanic origin; related to Dutch *schaft*, German *Schaft*, and perhaps also to **SCEPTRE**. Early senses of the verb (late Middle English) were 'fit with a handle' and 'send out shafts of light'.

shaft drive ▶ **noun** a mechanism in which power is transmitted from an engine by means of a driveshaft, especially to the wheels of a vehicle or a boat's propeller.
– DERIVATIVES **shaft-driven** adjective.

Shaftesbury /ˈʃɑːftsb(ə)ri/, Anthony Ashley Cooper, 7th Earl of (1801–85), English philanthropist and social reformer. A dominant figure of the 19th-century social reform movement, he inspired much of the legislation designed to improve conditions for the large working class created as a result of the Industrial Revolution. His reforms included the introduction of the ten-hour working day (1847).

shaft grave ▶ **noun** a type of grave found in late Bronze Age Greece and Crete in which the burial chamber is approached by a vertical shaft sometimes lined with stones and roofed over with beams.

shaft horsepower ▶ **noun** [mass noun] the power delivered to a propeller or turbine shaft.

shafting ▶ **noun 1** [mass noun] a system of connected shafts for transmitting motive power in a machine.
2 vulgar slang an act of sexual intercourse.

shag[1] ▶ **noun 1** [usu. as modifier] a carpet or rug with a long, rough pile: *wall-to-wall shag carpet.*
■[as modifier] (of a pile) long and rough: *a shag pile.* ■ [mass noun] cloth with a velvet nap on one side.
2 a thick, tangled hairstyle or mass of hair: *her hair was cut short in a boyish shag* | [as modifier] *a shag cut.*
3 (also **shag tobacco**) [mass noun] a coarse kind of cut tobacco.
– ORIGIN late Old English *sceacga* 'rough matted hair', of Germanic origin; related to Old Norse *skegg* 'beard' and **SHAW**[2].

shag[2] ▶ **noun** a western European and Mediterranean cormorant with greenish-black plumage and a long curly crest in the breeding season.
• *Phalacrocorax aristotelis*, family Phalacrocoracidae.
■chiefly NZ any cormorant.
– ORIGIN mid 16th cent.: perhaps a use of **SHAG**[1], with reference to the bird's 'shaggy' crest.

shag[3] Brit. vulgar slang ▶ **verb** (**shagged**, **shagging**) [with obj.] have sexual intercourse with (someone).
▶ **noun** an act of sexual intercourse.
■[with adj.] a sexual partner of a specified ability.
– DERIVATIVES **shagger** noun.
– ORIGIN late 18th cent.: of unknown origin.

shag[4] ▶ **noun** a dance originating in the US in the 1930s and 1940s, characterized by vigorous hopping from one foot to the other.
– ORIGIN of obscure derivation; perhaps from obsolete *shag* 'waggle'.

shag[5] ▶ **verb** [with obj.] Baseball chase or catch (fly balls) for practice.
– ORIGIN early 20th cent.: of unknown origin.

shagbark hickory ▶ **noun** see **HICKORY**.

shagged ▶ **adjective** Brit. informal exhausted: *they were too shagged to do any cleaning* | *the* ***shagged-out*** *and work-weary 1990s.*
■damaged, ruined, or useless: *I thought my hearing was shagged because I play the drums.*

shaggy ▶ **adjective** (**shaggier**, **shaggiest**) (of hair or fur) long, thick, and unkempt: *the mountain goat has a long, shaggy coat.*
■having long, thick, unkempt hair or fur: *a huge shaggy Alsatian.* ■ of or having a covering resembling rough, thick hair.
– PHRASES **shaggy-dog story** a long, rambling story or joke, typically one that is amusing only because it is absurdly inconsequential or pointless. [ORIGIN: originally an anecdote of this type, about a shaggy-haired dog (1945).]
– DERIVATIVES **shaggily** adverb, **shagginess** noun.

shaggy ink cap ▶ **noun** a common mushroom which has a tall narrow white cap covered with shaggy scales, occurring worldwide and edible when young.
• *Coprinus comatus*, family Coprinaceae, class Hymenomycetes.

shagreen /ʃaˈgriːn/ ▶ **noun** [mass noun] **1** sharkskin used as a decorative material or, for its natural rough surface of pointed scales, as an abrasive.
2 a kind of untanned leather with a rough granulated surface.
– ORIGIN late 17th cent.: variant of **CHAGRIN** in the literal sense 'rough skin'.

Shah[1] /ʃɑː/, Karim Al-Hussain, see **AGA KHAN**.

Shah[2] /ʃɑː/, Reza, see **PAHLAVI**[1].

shah /ʃɑː/ ▶ **noun** historical a title of the former monarch of Iran.
– DERIVATIVES **shahdom** noun.
– ORIGIN mid 16th cent.: from Persian *šāh*, from Old Persian *ḵšāyaṯiya* 'king'.

shahada /ʃaˈhɑːdə/ (also **shahadah**) ▶ **noun** the Muslim profession of faith ('there is no god but Allah, and Muhammad is the messenger of Allah').
– ORIGIN from Arabic *šahāda* 'testimony, evidence'.

Shah Alam /ˈɑːləm/ the capital of the state of Selangor in Malaysia, near the west coast of the Malay Peninsula; pop. 24,140 (1980).

shahid /ʃəˈhiːd/ (also **shaheed**) ▶ **noun** a Muslim martyr.

– ORIGIN late 19th cent.: from Arabic *šhīd* 'witness, martyr'.

shahtoosh /ʃɑːˈtuːʃ/ ▶ **noun** [mass noun] high-quality wool from the neck hair of the Himalayan ibex.
■ fabric woven from this.

– ORIGIN mid 19th cent.: via Punjabi from Persian *šāh* 'king' + Kashmiri *tośa* 'fine shawl material'.

shaikh ▶ **noun** variant spelling of **SHEIKH**.

Shaitan /ʃeɪˈtɑːn/ ▶ **noun** (in Muslim countries) the Devil, Satan, or an evil spirit.
■ (**shaitan**) an evilly disposed, vicious, or cunning person or animal.

– ORIGIN from Arabic *šayṭān*.

Shaka /ˈʃakə/ (also **Chaka**) (*c.*1787–1828), Zulu chief 1816–28. He reorganized his forces and waged war against the Nguni clans, subjugating them and forming a Zulu empire in SE Africa.

shake ▶ **verb** (past **shook**; past participle **shaken**) **1** [no obj.] (of a structure or area of land) tremble or vibrate: *buildings shook in Sacramento and tremors were felt in Reno.*
■ [with obj.] cause to tremble or vibrate: *a severe earthquake shook the area.* ■ (of a person, part of the body, or the voice) tremble uncontrollably from a strong emotion such as fear or anger: *Luke was* ***shaking with*** *rage | her voice* ***shook with*** *passion.*
2 [with obj.] move (an object) up and down or from side to side with rapid, forceful, jerky movements: *she stood in the hall and shook her umbrella.*
■ [with obj. and adverbial] remove (an object or substance) from something by movements of this kind: *they shook the sand out of their shoes.* ■ informal get rid of or put an end to (something unwanted): *he was unable to* ***shake off*** *the memories of the trenches.* ■ grasp (someone) and move them roughly to and fro, either in anger or to rouse them from sleep: [with obj. and complement] *he gently shook the driver awake and they set off.* ■ brandish in anger or as a warning; make a threatening gesture with: *men shook their fists and shouted.*
3 [with obj.] upset the composure of; shock or astonish: *rumours of a further loss shook the market | the fall* ***shook*** *him* ***up*** *quite badly |* [as adj. **shaken**] *a visibly shaken band were allowed back on stage.*
■ [with obj. and adverbial] cause a change of mood or attitude by shocking or disturbing (someone): *he had to shake himself out of his lethargy.* ■ weaken or impair (confidence, a belief, etc.), especially by shocking or disturbing: *the escalation in costs is certain to shake the confidence of private investors.*

▶ **noun 1** an act of shaking: *with a shake of its magnificent antlers the stag charged down the slope |* [mass noun] *camera shake causes the image to become blurred.*
■ informal an earth tremor. ■ an amount of something that is sprinkled by shaking a container: *add a few* ***shakes*** *of sea salt and black pepper.* ■ short for **MILKSHAKE**. ■ (**the shakes**) informal a fit of trembling or shivering: *I wouldn't go in there, it gives me the shakes.*
2 Music a trill.

– PHRASES **get** (or **give someone**) **a fair shake** informal get (or give someone) just treatment or a fair chance: *I do not believe he gave the industry a fair shake.* **in two shakes** (**of a lamb's tail**) informal very quickly: *I'll be back to you in two shakes.* **more —— than one can shake a stick at** informal used to emphasize the largeness of an amount: *a team with more experience than you can shake a stick at.* **no great shakes** informal not very good or significant: *it is no great shakes as a piece of cinema.* **shake the dust off one's feet** leave indignantly or disdainfully. **shake hands** (**with someone**) (or **shake someone by the hand** or **shake someone's hand**) clasp someone's right hand in one's own at meeting or parting, in reconciliation or congratulation, or as a sign of agreement. **shake one's head** turn one's head from side to side in order to indicate refusal, denial, disapproval, or incredulity: *she shook her head in disbelief.* **shake** (or **quake**) **in one's shoes** (or **boots**) tremble with apprehension. **shake a leg** informal make a start; rouse oneself: *come on, shake a leg.*

– ORIGIN Old English *sc(e)acan* (verb), of Germanic origin.

▶ **shake down** become established in a new place or situation; settle down: *it was disruptive to the industry as it was shaking down after deregulation.*
shake someone down N. Amer. informal extort money from someone.
shake something down cause something to fall or settle by shaking.
shake someone off get away from someone by shaking their grip loose. ■ manage to evade or outmanoeuvre someone who is following or pestering one: *he thought he had shaken off his pursuer.* ■ (in sport, especially a race) outdistance another competitor: *in the final lap she looked as though she had shaken off the Dutch girl.*
shake something off successfully deal with or recover from an illness or injury: *Sheedy has shaken off a calf injury.*
shake on informal confirm (an agreement) by shaking hands: *they shook on the deal.*
shake something out 1 empty something out by shaking a container: *he shook out a handful of painkillers.* ■ figurative get rid of or abandon an attitude or practice: *we are going to shake out the old attitudes.* **2** spread or open something such as a cloth or garment by shaking it: *she shook out the newspaper.* ■ restore something crumpled to its natural shape by shaking: *she undid her helmet and shook out her frizzled hair.* ■ Sailing unwind or untie a reef to increase the area of a sail.
shake someone up rouse someone from lethargy, apathy, or complacency: *he had to do something to shake the team up – we lacked spark.*
shake something up 1 mix ingredients by shaking: *use soap flakes shaken up in the water to make bubbles.* **2** make radical changes to the organization or structure of an institution or system: *he presented plans to shake up the legal profession.*

shakedown ▶ **noun** informal, chiefly N. Amer. **1** a makeshift bed.
2 radical change or restructuring, particularly in a hierarchical organization or group: *a major British monarchy shakedown.*
■ a thorough search of a person or place. ■ a swindle; a piece of extortion. ■ a test of a new product or model, especially a vehicle or ship: *he gave the car its first ever shakedown at Silverstone.*

shake hole ▶ **noun** another term for **SINKHOLE**.

shaken past participle of **SHAKE**.

shake-out ▶ **noun** informal an upheaval or reorganization of a business, market, or organization due to competition and typically involving streamlining and redundancies.

shaker ▶ **noun 1** [with modifier] a container used for mixing ingredients by shaking: *a cocktail shaker.*
■ a container with a pierced top from which a powdered substance such as flour or salt is poured by shaking.
2 (**Shaker**) a member of an American religious sect, the United Society of Believers in Christ's Second Coming, established in England *c.*1750 and living simply in celibate mixed communities. [ORIGIN: so named from the wild, ecstatic movements engaged in during worship.]
■ [as modifier] denoting a style of elegantly functional furniture traditionally produced by Shaker communities.

– DERIVATIVES **Shakerism** noun (in sense 2).

Shakeress ▶ **noun** a female Shaker.

Shakespeare, William (1564–1616), English dramatist.

> His plays are written mostly in blank verse and include comedies, such as *A Midsummer Night's Dream* and *As You Like It*; historical plays, including *Richard III* and *Henry V*; the Greek and Roman plays, which include *Julius Caesar* and *Antony and Cleopatra*; enigmatic comedies such as *All's Well that Ends Well* and *Measure for Measure*; the great tragedies, *Hamlet*, *Othello*, *King Lear*, and *Macbeth*; and the group of tragicomedies with which he ended his career, such as *The Winter's Tale* and *The Tempest*. He also wrote more than 150 sonnets, published in 1609.

– DERIVATIVES **Shakespearean** /ʃeɪkˈspɪərɪən/ (also **Shakespearian**) noun & adjective.

shake-up ▶ **noun** informal a radical reorganization.

Shakhty /ˈʃɑːkti/ a coal-mining city in SW Russia, situated in the Donets Basin north-east of Rostov; pop. 227,000 (1990).

shako /ˈʃeɪkəʊ, ˈʃakəʊ/ ▶ **noun** (pl. **-os**) a cylindrical or conical military hat with a peak and a plume or pompom.

– ORIGIN early 19th cent.: via French from Hungarian *csákó* (*süveg*) 'peaked (cap)', from *csák* 'peak', from German *Zacken* 'spike'.

Shakti /ˈʃʌktiː/ (also **Sakti**) ▶ **noun** [mass noun] Hinduism the female principle of divine energy, especially when personified as the supreme deity. See also **DEVI** and **PARVATI**.

– ORIGIN from Sanskrit *śakti* 'power, divine energy'.

shakudo /ˈʃakuːdəʊ/ ▶ **noun** [mass noun] a Japanese alloy of copper and gold, typically having a blue patina.

– ORIGIN mid 19th cent.: Japanese, from *shaku* 'red' + *dō* 'copper'.

shakuhachi /ˌʃakʊˈhatʃi/ ▶ **noun** (pl. **shakuhachis**) a Japanese bamboo flute, held vertically when played.

– ORIGIN late 19th cent.: Japanese, from *shaku*, a measure of length (approx. 0.33 metre) + *hachi* 'eight (tenths)'.

shaky ▶ **adjective** (**shakier**, **shakiest**) shaking or trembling: *she managed a shaky laugh.*
■ unstable because of poor construction or heavy use: *a cracked, dangerously shaky table.* ■ not safe or reliable; liable to fail or falter: *thoroughly shaky evidence | after a shaky start the Scottish team made superb efforts.*

– DERIVATIVES **shakily** adverb, **shakiness** noun.

shale ▶ **noun** [mass noun] soft finely stratified sedimentary rock that formed from consolidated mud or clay and can be split easily into fragile plates.

– DERIVATIVES **shaly** (also **shaley**) adjective.

– ORIGIN mid 18th cent.: probably from German *Schale*; related to English dialect *shale* 'dish' (see **SCALE**[2]).

shale oil ▶ **noun** [mass noun] oil obtained from bituminous shale.

shall ▶ **modal verb** (3rd sing. present **shall**) **1** (in the first person) expressing the future tense: *this time next week I shall be in Scotland | we shan't be gone long.*
2 expressing a strong assertion or intention: *they shall succeed | you shall not frighten me out of this.*
3 expressing an instruction or command: *you shall not steal.*
4 used in questions indicating offers or suggestions: *shall I send you the book? | shall we go?*

– ORIGIN Old English *sceal*, of Germanic origin; related to Dutch *zal* and German *soll*, from a base meaning 'owe'.

> **USAGE** There is considerable confusion about when to use **shall** and **will**. The traditional rule in standard British English is that **shall** is used with first person pronouns (**I** and **we**) to form the future tense, while **will** is used with second and third persons (**you**, **he**, **she**, **it**, **they**), e.g. *I* ***shall*** *be late*; *she* ***will*** *not be there.* When expressing a strong determination to do something the traditional rule is that **will** is used with the first person, and **shall** with the second and third persons, e.g. *I* ***will*** *not tolerate this*; *you* ***shall*** *go to school.* In practice, however, **shall** and **will** are today used more or less interchangeably in statements (though not in questions). Given that the forms are frequently contracted (**we'll**, **she'll**, etc.) there is often no need to make a choice between **shall** and **will**, another factor no doubt instrumental in weakening the distinction. In modern English the interchangeable use of **shall** and **will** is an acceptable part of standard British and US English.

shallop /ˈʃaləp/ ▶ **noun** chiefly historical a light sailing boat used mainly for coastal fishing or as a tender.
■ a large heavy boat with one or more masts and carrying fore-and-aft or lug sails and sometimes equipped with guns.

– ORIGIN late 16th cent.: from French *chaloupe*, from Dutch *sloep* 'sloop'.

shallot /ʃəˈlɒt/ ▶ **noun 1** a small bulb which resembles an onion and is used for pickling or as a substitute for onion.
2 the plant which produces these bulbs, each mature bulb producing a cluster of smaller bulbs.
• *Allium ascalonicum*, family Liliaceae (or Alliaceae).

– ORIGIN mid 17th cent.: shortening of *eschalot*, from French *eschalotte*, alteration of Old French *eschaloigne* (in Anglo-Norman French *scaloun*: see **SCALLION**).

shallow ▶ **adjective** of little depth: *serve the noodles in a shallow bowl | being fairly shallow, the water was warm.*
■ situated at no great depth: *the shallow bed of the North Sea.* ■ varying only slightly from a specified or understood line or direction, especially the horizontal: *a shallow roof.* ■ not exhibiting, requiring, or capable of serious thought: *a shallow analysis of contemporary society.* ■ (of breathing) taking in little air.

▶ **noun** (**shallows**) an area of the sea, a lake, or a river where the water is not very deep.

▶ **verb** [no obj.] (of the sea, a lake, or a river) become less

deep over time or in a particular place: *the boat ground to a halt where the water shallowed.*
– DERIVATIVES **shallowly** adverb, **shallowness** noun.
– ORIGIN late Middle English: obscurely related to **SHOAL**².

Shalmaneser III /ˌʃalməˈniːzə/ (d.824 BC), king of Assyria 859–824. Most of his reign was devoted to the expansion of his kingdom and the conquest of neighbouring lands. According to Assyrian records he defeated an alliance of Syrian kings and the king of Israel in a battle at Qarqar on the Orontes in 853 BC.
– ORIGIN from *Salmanasar*, the Latin form of the name in the Vulgate (2 Kings 17–19).

shalom /ʃəˈlɒm/ ▸ exclamation used as salutation by Jews at meeting or parting, meaning 'peace'.
– ORIGIN from Hebrew *šālōm*.

shalt archaic second person singular of **SHALL**.

shalwar /ʃʌlˈwɑː/ ▸ noun variant spelling of **SALWAR**.

sham ▸ noun 1 a thing that is not what it is purported to be: *our current free health service is a sham.*
■ [mass noun] pretence. ■ a person who pretends to be someone or something they are not: *he was a sham, totally unqualified for his job as a senior doctor.*
2 N. Amer. short for **PILLOW SHAM**.
▸ adjective bogus; false: *a clergyman who arranged a sham marriage.*
▸ verb (**shammed**, **shamming**) [no obj.] falsely present something as the truth: *was he ill or was he shamming?*
■ [with obj.] pretend to be or to be experiencing: *she shams indifference* | [no obj., with complement] *the opossum escapes danger by shamming dead.*
– DERIVATIVES **shammer** noun.
– ORIGIN late 17th cent.: perhaps a northern English dialect variant of the noun **SHAME**.

shama /ˈʃɑːmə/ ▸ noun a long-tailed South Asian forest thrush, typically having blackish plumage with a rufous belly.
● Genus *Copsychus*, family Turdidae: five species.
– ORIGIN mid 19th cent.: from Hindi *śyāma*, from Sanskrit.

shamal /ʃəˈmɑːl/ ▸ noun a hot, dry north-westerly wind blowing across the Persian Gulf in summer, typically causing sandstorms.
– ORIGIN late 17th cent.: from Arabic *šamāl* 'north (wind)'.

shaman /ˈʃamən, ˈʃeɪm-/ ▸ noun (pl. **shamans**) a person regarded as having access to, and influence in, the world of good and evil spirits, especially among some peoples of northern Asia and North America. Typically such people enter a trance state during a ritual, and practise divination and healing.
– DERIVATIVES **shamanic** /ʃəˈmanɪk/ adjective, **shamanism** noun, **shamanist** noun & adjective, **shamanistic** adjective, **shamanize** (also **-ise**) verb.
– ORIGIN late 17th cent.: from German *Schamane* and Russian *shaman*, from Tungus *šaman*.

shamateur ▸ noun derogatory a sports player who makes money from sporting activities though classified as amateur.
– DERIVATIVES **shamateurism** noun.
– ORIGIN late 19th cent.: blend of **SHAM** and **AMATEUR**.

shamba /ˈʃambə/ ▸ noun (in East Africa) a cultivated plot of ground; a farm or plantation.
– ORIGIN Kiswahili.

shamble ▸ verb [no obj., with adverbial of direction] (of a person) move with a slow, shuffling, awkward gait: *he shambled off down the corridor* | [as adj. **shambling**] *a big, shambling, shy man.*
▸ noun [in sing.] a slow, shuffling, awkward gait.
– ORIGIN late 16th cent.: probably from dialect *shamble* 'ungainly', perhaps from the phrase *shamble legs*, with reference to the legs of trestle tables (such as would be used in a meat market: see **SHAMBLES**).

shambles ▸ plural noun [treated as sing.] 1 informal a state of total disorder: *my career is in a shambles.*
2 a butcher's slaughterhouse (archaic except in place names).
■ a scene of carnage: *the room was a shambles—their throats had been cut and they lay in a waste of blood.*
– ORIGIN late Middle English (in the sense 'meat market'): plural of earlier *shamble* 'stool, stall', of

West Germanic origin, from Latin *scamellum*, diminutive of *scamnum* 'bench'.

shambly ▸ adjective informal (of a building) ramshackle; rickety.
■ (of a person) awkward; ungainly.

shambolic ▸ adjective informal, chiefly Brit. chaotic, disorganized, or mismanaged: *the department's shambolic accounting.*
– ORIGIN 1970s: from **SHAMBLES**, probably on the pattern of *symbolic.*

shame ▸ noun [mass noun] a painful feeling of humiliation or distress caused by the consciousness of wrong or foolish behaviour: *she was hot with shame* | *he felt a pang of shame at telling Alice a lie.*
■ a loss of respect or esteem; dishonour: *the incident had brought shame on his family.* ■ used to reprove someone for something of which they should be ashamed: *shame on you for hitting a woman.* ■ [in sing.] a regrettable or unfortunate situation or action: *it is a shame that they are not better known.* ■ [count noun] a person, action, or situation that brings a loss of respect or honour: *ignorance of Latin would be a disgrace and a shame to any public man.*
▸ verb [with obj.] (of a person, action, or situation) make (someone) feel ashamed: *I tried to shame him into giving some away.*
■ cause (someone) to feel ashamed or inadequate by outdoing or surpassing them: *she shames me with her eighty-year-old energy.*
▸ exclamation 1 used to express sympathy or pity: *people's response when they hear you live in England is 'Oh shame! That terrible climate!'*
2 S. African used to express sentimental pleasure, especially at something small and endearing: *look at the foals—shame, aren't they sweet?*
– PHRASES **put someone to shame** disgrace or embarrass someone by outdoing or surpassing them: *she puts me to shame, she's so capable.*
– ORIGIN Old English *sc(e)amu* (noun), *sc(e)amian* 'feel shame', of Germanic origin; related to Dutch *schamen* (verb) and German *Scham* (noun), *schämen* (verb).

shame culture ▸ noun Anthropology a culture in which conformity of behaviour is maintained through the individual's fear of being shamed.

shamefaced ▸ adjective feeling or expressing shame or embarrassment: *all the boys looked shamefaced.*
– DERIVATIVES **shamefacedly** adverb, **shamefacedness** noun.
– ORIGIN mid 16th cent. (in the sense 'modest, shy'): alteration of archaic *shamefast*, by association with **FACE**.

shameful ▸ adjective worthy of or causing shame or disgrace: *a shameful accusation.*
– DERIVATIVES **shamefully** adverb [as submodifier] *record companies are shamefully slow in fulfilling orders*, **shamefulness** noun.
– ORIGIN Old English *sc(e)amful* 'modest, shamefaced' (see **SHAME, -FUL**).

shameless ▸ adjective (of a person or their conduct) characterized by or showing a lack of shame: *his shameless hypocrisy.*
– DERIVATIVES **shamelessly** adverb, **shamelessness** noun.
– ORIGIN Old English *sc(e)amlēas* (see **SHAME, -LESS**).

shamiana /ˈʃɑːmɪɑːnə/ ▸ noun Indian a marquee.
– ORIGIN via Urdu from Persian *shāmiyāna*.

Shamir /ʃaˈmɪə/, Yitzhak (b.1915), Polish-born Israeli statesman, Prime Minister 1983–4 and 1986–92; Polish name *Yitzhak Jazernicki*. Under his leadership Israel did not retaliate when attacked by Iraqi missiles during the Gulf War, thereby possibly averting an escalation of the conflict.

shamisen ▸ noun variant spelling of **SAMISEN**.

shammy (also **shammy leather**) ▸ noun (pl. **-ies**) informal term for **CHAMOIS** (in sense 2).
– ORIGIN early 18th cent.: a phonetic spelling.

shampoo ▸ noun [mass noun] a liquid preparation containing soap for washing the hair: *he smelt clean, of soap and shampoo* | [count noun] *an anti-dandruff shampoo.*
■ a similar substance for cleaning a carpet, soft furnishings, or a car. ■ [count noun] an act of washing or cleaning something, especially the hair, with shampoo: *a shampoo and set.*
▸ verb (**shampoos**, **shampooed**) [with obj.] wash or clean (something, especially the hair) with shampoo: *Dolly was sitting in the bath shampooing her hair.*

■ (**shampoo something in/out**) wash something in or out of the hair using shampoo: *apply oil to wet hair, otherwise it will be difficult to shampoo it out.*
– ORIGIN mid 18th cent. (in the sense 'massage (as part of a Turkish bath process)'): from Hindi *cāmpo!* 'press!', imperative of *cāmpnā.*

shamrock ▸ noun a low-growing clover-like plant with three-lobed leaves, used as the national emblem of Ireland.
● The shamrock of legend has been identified with a number of different plants in the family Leguminosae, in particular the lesser yellow trefoil (*Trifolium minus*).
■ a spray or leaf of this plant.
– ORIGIN late 16th cent.: from Irish *seamróg* 'trefoil' (diminutive of *seamar* 'clover').

shamus /ˈʃeɪməs/ ▸ noun N. Amer. informal a private detective.
– ORIGIN 1920s: of unknown origin.

Shan /ʃɑːn/ ▸ noun (pl. same or **Shans**) 1 a member of a people living mainly in northern Burma (Myanmar) and adjacent parts of southern China.
2 [mass noun] the language of this people, related to Thai and having about 2.5 million speakers.
▸ adjective of or relating to this people or their language.
– ORIGIN Burmese.

Shandong /ʃanˈdʊŋ/ (also **Shantung**) a coastal province of eastern China; capital, Jinan. It occupies the Shandong Peninsula, separating southern Bo Hai from the Yellow Sea.

shandy ▸ noun (pl. **-ies**) [mass noun] beer mixed with a non-alcoholic drink (typically lemonade).
– ORIGIN late 19th cent.: abbreviation of *shandygaff*, in the same sense, of unknown origin.

Shang /ʃaŋ/ a dynasty which ruled China during part of the 2nd millennium BC, probably the 16th–11th centuries. The period encompassed the invention of Chinese ideographic script and the discovery and development of bronze casting.

Shangaan /ˈʃaŋgɑːn/ ▸ noun (pl. same or **Shangaans**) 1 a member of the Tsonga people of southern Africa.
2 [mass noun] the Bantu language of this people.
▸ adjective of or relating to this people or their language.
– ORIGIN probably named after the founding chief *Soshangane.*

Shanghai /ʃaŋˈhʌɪ/ a city on the east coast of China, a port on the estuary of the Yangtze; pop. 7,780,000 (1990). Opened for trade with the west in 1842, Shanghai contained until the Second World War areas of British, French, and American settlement. It was the site in 1921 of the founding of the Chinese Communist Party. It is now China's most populous city.

shanghai¹ /ʃaŋˈhʌɪ/ ▸ verb (**shanghais**, **shanghaied**, **shanghaiing**) [with obj.] historical force (someone) to join a ship lacking a full crew by drugging them or using other underhand means.
■ informal coerce or trick (someone) into a place or position or into doing something: *Brady shanghaied her into his Jaguar and roared off.*
– ORIGIN late 19th cent.: from **SHANGHAI**.

shanghai² /ʃaŋˈhʌɪ/ Austral./NZ ▸ noun (pl. **shanghais**) a catapult.
▸ verb (**shanghais**, **shanghaied**, **shanghaiing**) [with obj.] shoot with a catapult.
■ [with obj. and adverbial of direction] catapult in a particular direction: *the springy, resilient saplings would shanghai him backwards.*
– ORIGIN mid 19th cent.: probably an alteration of Scots dialect *shangan* 'a stick cleft at one end'.

Shango /ˈʃaŋgəʊ/ ▸ noun [mass noun] a religious cult originating in western Nigeria and now practised chiefly in parts of the Caribbean.
■ (also **Shangor**) [count noun] an African god of thunder significant to this cult. ■ [count noun] a dance associated with this cult.
– ORIGIN 1950s: from Yoruba.

Shangri-La /ˌʃaŋgrɪˈlɑː/ a Tibetan utopia in James Hilton's novel *Lost Horizon* (1933).
■ [as noun **a Shangri-La**] a place regarded as an earthly paradise, especially when involving a retreat from the pressures of modern civilization.
– ORIGIN from *Shangri* (an invented name) + Tibetan *la* 'mountain pass'.

shank ▸ noun 1 (often **shanks**) a person's leg, especially the part from the knee to the ankle: *the old man's thin, bony shanks showed through his trousers.*

▪the lower part of an animal's foreleg. ▪ this part of an animal's leg as a cut of meat.

2 the shaft or stem of a tool or implement, in particular:

▪a long narrow part of a tool connecting the handle to the operational end. ▪ the cylindrical part of a bit by which it is held in a drill. ▪ the long stem of a key, spoon, anchor, etc. ▪ the straight part of a nail or fish-hook.

3 a part or appendage by which something is attached to something else, especially a wire loop attached to the back of a button.

▪the band of a ring rather than the setting or gemstone.

4 the narrow middle of the sole of a shoe.

▶**verb** [with obj.] Golf strike (the ball) with the heel of the club: *I shanked a shot and hit a person on a shoulder.*

– DERIVATIVES **shanked** adjective [usu. in combination] *a long-shanked hook.*

– ORIGIN Old English *sceanca*, of West Germanic origin; related to Dutch *schenk* 'leg bone' and High German *Schenkel* 'thigh'. The use of the verb as a golfing term dates from the 1920s.

Shankar[1] /ˈʃaŋkə/, Ravi (b.1920), Indian sitar player and composer. From the mid 1950s he toured Europe and the US giving sitar recitals, doing much to stimulate contemporary Western interest in Indian music.

Shankar[2] /ˈʃaŋkə/, Uday (1900–77), Indian dancer, brother of Ravi Shankar. He introduced Anna Pavlova to Indian dance and performed with her in his ballet *Krishna and Radha* (1923). He later toured the world with his own company, introducing Indian dance to European audiences.

shanking ▶**noun** [mass noun] **1** Golf the action of striking the ball with the heel of the club.

2 any of a number of plant diseases resulting in the darkening and shrivelling of a plant or fruit from the base of a stem or stalk.

Shankly, Bill (1913–81), Scottish footballer and manager; full name *William Shankly.* He was a renowned manager of Liverpool (1960–74), with whom he had great success in Britain and Europe.

Shanks's pony (also **Shanks's mare**) ▶**noun** used to refer to one's own legs and the action of walking as a means of conveyance.

– ORIGIN late 18th cent.: first recorded as *shanks-nag* in R. Fergusson's *Poems* (1785).

Shannon[1] the longest river of Ireland. It rises in County Leitrim near Lough Allen and flows 390 km (240 miles) south and west to its estuary on the Atlantic.

▪an international airport in the Republic of Ireland, situated on the River Shannon west of Limerick. ▪ a shipping forecast area in the NE Atlantic to the south-west of Ireland.

Shannon[2], Claude Elwood (b.1916), American engineer. He was the pioneer of mathematical communication theory, which has become vital to the design of both communication and electronic equipment. He also investigated digital circuits, and was the first to use the term *bit* to denote a unit of information.

Shannon's theorem (also **Shannon's information theorem**) a theorem defining the maximum capacity of a communication channel to carry information with no more than an arbitrary error rate, given the bandwidth and signal-to-noise ratio.

– ORIGIN mid 20th cent.: named after C. E. Shannon (see **SHANNON**[2]).

shanny ▶**noun** (pl. **-ies**) a small greenish-brown European blenny (fish) of the shoreline and intertidal waters.

• *Blennius pholis*, family Blenniidae.

– ORIGIN mid 19th cent.: of unknown origin; compare with earlier *shan*, in the same sense.

Shansi /ʃanˈsiː/ variant spelling of **SHANXI**.

shan't ▶**contraction of** shall not.

shanti /ˈʃɑːnti/ ▶**noun** [mass noun] Indian peace: [as exclamation] *'Shanti! Shanti! you must not let anger possess you like that.'*

– ORIGIN from Sanskrit *śānti* 'peace, tranquillity'.

Shantou /ʃanˈtaʊ/ a port in the province of Guangdong in SE China, situated on the South China Sea at the mouth of the Han River; pop. 860,000 (1990). It was designated a treaty port in 1869. Former name **SWATOW**.

Shantung /ʃanˈtʊŋ/ variant spelling of **SHANDONG**.

shantung /ʃanˈtʌŋ/ ▶**noun** [mass noun] a dress fabric spun from tussore silk with random irregularities in the surface texture.

– ORIGIN late 19th cent.: from **SHANTUNG**, where it was originally made.

shanty[1] ▶**noun** (pl. **-ies**) a small, crudely built shack.

– ORIGIN early 19th cent. (originally a North American usage): perhaps from Canadian French *chantier* 'lumberjack's cabin, logging camp'.

shanty[2] (also **chanty** or **sea shanty**) ▶**noun** (pl. **-ies**) a song with alternating solo and chorus, of a kind originally sung by sailors while performing physical labour together.

– ORIGIN mid 19th cent.: probably from French *chantez!* 'sing!', imperative plural of *chanter.*

shantyman ▶**noun** (pl. **-men**) N. Amer. a lumberjack.

shanty town ▶**noun** a deprived area on the outskirts of a town consisting of large numbers of shanty dwellings.

Shanxi /ʃanˈʃiː/ (also **Shansi**) a province of north central China, to the south of Inner Mongolia; capital, Taiyuan.

SHAPE ▶**abbreviation for** Supreme Headquarters Allied Powers Europe.

shape ▶**noun 1** the external form or appearance characteristic of someone or something; the outline of an area or figure: *she liked the shape of his nose | house plants come in all shapes and sizes |* [mass noun] *chest freezers are square or rectangular in shape.*

▪a person or thing that is difficult to see and identify clearly: *he saw a shape through the mist.* ▪ [usu. with adj. or noun modifier] a specific form or guise assumed by someone or something: *a fiend in human shape.* ▪ a piece of material, paper, etc., made or cut in a particular form: *stick paper shapes on for the puppet's eyes and nose.*

2 [mass noun] [with adj.] the particular condition or state of someone or something: *he was in no shape to drive | the building was in poor shape.*

▪the distinctive nature or qualities of something: *debates about the future shape of British society.* ▪ definite or orderly arrangement: *check that your structure will give shape to your essay.*

▶**verb** [with obj.] (often **be shaped**) give a particular shape or form to: *most caves are shaped by the flow of water through limestone | shape the dough into two-inch balls.*

▪make (something) fit the form of something else: [with obj. and infinitive] *suits have been shaped to fit so snugly that no curve is undefined.* ▪ determine the nature of; have a great influence on: *his childhood was shaped by a loving relationship with his elder brother.* ▪ [no obj., with adverbial] develop in a particular way; progress: *the yacht was shaping well in trials.* ▪ form or produce (a sound or words). ▪ [no obj.] (of a sports player or athlete) take up a stance or set oneself to perform a particular action: [with infinitive] *I had plenty of time and shaped to kick to the near touchline.*

– PHRASES **get into shape** (or **get someone into shape**) become (or make someone) physically fitter by exercise: *if you're thinking of getting into shape, take it easy and build up slowly.* **in any (way,) shape or form** in any manner or under any circumstances (used for emphasis): *96 per cent of the electorate voted against Europeanization in any shape or form.* **in (good) shape** in good physical condition. **in the shape of** represented or embodied by: *retribution arrived in the shape of my irate father.* ▪ by way of; in the nature of: *there had been little or nothing in the shape of academic planning.* **lick** (or **knock** or **whip**) **someone/thing into shape** act forcefully to bring someone or something into a fitter, more efficient, or better organized state: *the bank were eager to whip the company into shape for eventual sale.* **out of shape 1** (of an object) not having its usual or original shape, especially after being bent or knocked: *check that the pipe end and compression nut are not bent out of shape.* **2** (of a person) in poor physical condition; unfit. **the shape of things to come** the way the future is likely to develop. [ORIGIN: the title of a novel by H. G. Wells (1933).] **shape up or ship out** informal, chiefly N. Amer. used as an ultimatum to someone to improve their performance or behaviour or face being made to leave. **take shape** assume a distinct form; develop into something definite or tangible: *the past few months have seen the state's health insurance legislation begin to take shape.*

– DERIVATIVES **shapable** (also **shapeable**) adjective, **shaped** adjective [usu. in combination] *egg-shaped | X-shaped*, **shaper** noun.

– ORIGIN Old English *gesceap* 'external form', also 'creation', *sceppan* 'create', of Germanic origin.

▶**shape up** develop or happen in a particular way: *it was shaping up to be another bleak year.* ▪ (**shape something up**) informal improve something: *department stores have been forced to shape up their acts.* ▪ become physically fit: *I need to shape up.*

shaped charge ▶**noun** an explosive charge with a cavity which causes the blast to be concentrated into a small area.

shapeless ▶**adjective** (especially of a garment) lacking a distinctive or attractive shape: *she wore a shapeless frock and no make-up.*

– DERIVATIVES **shapelessly** adverb, **shapelessness** noun.

shapely ▶**adjective** (**shapelier**, **shapeliest**) (especially of a woman or part of her body) having an attractive or well-proportioned shape: *however much she ate made no difference to her shapely figure.*

– DERIVATIVES **shapeliness** noun.

shape memory ▶**noun** [mass noun] Metallurgy a property exhibited by certain alloys of recovering their initial shape when they are heated after having been plastically deformed.

shape-shifter ▶**noun** (chiefly in fiction) a person or being with the ability to change their physical form at will.

– DERIVATIVES **shape-shifting** noun & adjective.

shapka /ˈʃapkə/ ▶**noun** a brimless Russian hat of fur or sheepskin.

– ORIGIN 1940s: Russian, literally 'hat'.

Shapley /ˈʃapli/, Harlow (1885–1972), American astronomer. He carried out an extensive survey of galaxies and used his studies on the distribution of globular star clusters to locate the likely centre of the Galaxy and to infer its structure and dimensions. He found that the solar system is located on the Galaxy's edge and not at its centre.

sharara /ʃʌˈrɑːrə/ ▶**noun** a pair of loose pleated trousers worn by women from the Indian subcontinent, typically with a kameez and dupatta.

– ORIGIN from Urdu.

shard ▶**noun** a piece of broken ceramic, metal, glass, or rock, typically having sharp edges: *shards of glass flew in all directions.*

– ORIGIN Old English *sceard* 'gap, notch, potsherd', of Germanic origin: related to Dutch *schaarde* 'notch', also to **SHEAR**.

share[1] ▶**noun** a part or portion of a larger amount which is divided among a number of people, or to which a number of people contribute: *under the proposals, investors would pay a greater share of the annual fees required | we gave them all the chance to have a share in the profits.*

▪one of the equal parts into which a company's capital is divided, entitling the holder to a proportion of the profits: *he's selling his shares in BT.* ▪ part-proprietorship of property held by joint owners: *Jake had a share in a large, seagoing vessel.* ▪ [in sing.] the allotted or due amount of something that a person expects to have or to do, or that is expected to be accepted or done by them: *she's done more than her **fair share of** globetrotting.* ▪ [in sing.] a person's part in or contribution to something: *she can't take a share in childcare – she's a nervous wreck.*

▶**verb** [with obj.] have a portion of (something) with another or others: *he **shared** the pie **with** her | all members of the band equally share the band's profits.*

▪[with obj. and adverbial] give a portion of (something) to another or others: *they shared out the peanuts.* ▪ use, occupy, or enjoy (something) jointly with another or others: *they once shared a flat in Chelsea |* [no obj.] *there weren't enough plates so we had to share |* [as adj. **shared**] *a shared bottle of wine.* ▪ possess (a view or quality) in common with others: *other countries don't share our reluctance to eat goat meat.* ▪ [no obj.] (**share in**) (of a number of people or organizations) have a part in (something, especially an activity): *UK companies would share in the development of three oil platforms.* ▪ tell someone about (something), especially something personal: *she had never **shared** the secret **with** anyone before.*

– PHRASES **share and share alike** have or receive an equal share: *I've no money—we all share and share alike in camp.*

– DERIVATIVES **shareable** (also **sharable**) adjective, **sharer** noun.

– ORIGIN Old English *scearu* 'division, part into which something may be divided', of Germanic origin; related to Dutch *schare* and German *Schar*

S

'troop, multitude', also to **SHEAR**. The verb dates from the late 16th cent.

share[2] ▶ **noun** short for **PLOUGHSHARE**.

share capital ▶ **noun** [mass noun] the part of the capital of a company that comes from the issue of shares.

sharecropper ▶ **noun** chiefly US a tenant farmer who gives a part of each crop as rent.
– DERIVATIVES **sharecrop** verb (**-cropped**, **-cropping**).

shared care ▶ **noun** [mass noun] (in the UK) an arrangement between a welfare agency and the family of a mentally or physically ill person for the provision of respite care or emergency assistance.

shared ownership ▶ **noun** [mass noun] (in Britain) a system by which the occupier of a dwelling buys a proportion of the property, and pays rent on the remainder, typically to a local authority or housing association.

share-farmer ▶ **noun** chiefly Austral./NZ a tenant farmer who receives an agreed share of the profits from the owner.
– DERIVATIVES **share-farming** noun.

shareholder ▶ **noun** an owner of shares in a company.
– DERIVATIVES **shareholding** noun.

share option ▶ **noun** a benefit in the form of an option given by a company to an employee to buy a share in the company at a discount or at a stated fixed price.

share-out ▶ **noun** an act of sharing something out, especially money.

share premium ▶ **noun** Finance the amount by which the amount received by a company for a stock issue exceeds its face value.

shareware ▶ **noun** [mass noun] Computing software that is available free of charge and often distributed informally for evaluation, after which a fee may be requested for continued use.

sharia /ʃəˈriːə/ (also **shariah** or **shariat** /ʃəˈriːət/) ▶ **noun** [mass noun] Islamic canonical law based on the teachings of the Koran and the traditions of the Prophet (Hadith and Sunna), prescribing both religious and secular duties and sometimes retributive penalties for lawbreaking. It has generally been supplemented by legislation adapted to the conditions of the day, though the manner in which it should be applied in modern states is a subject of dispute between Islamic fundamentalists and modernists.
– ORIGIN from Arabic *šarī'a*; the variant *shariat* from Urdu and Persian.

sharif /ʃəˈriːf/ (also **shereef** or **sherif**) ▶ **noun** **1** a descendant of Muhammad through his daughter Fatima, entitled to wear a green turban or veil.
2 a Muslim ruler, magistrate, or religious leader.
– DERIVATIVES **sharifian** adjective.
– ORIGIN from Arabic *šarīf* 'noble', from *šarafa* 'be exalted'.

Sharjah /ˈʃɑːdʒə/ one of the seven member states of the United Arab Emirates; pop. 400,300 (1995). Arabic name **ASH SHARIQAH**.
■ its capital city, situated on the Persian Gulf; pop. 125,000 (1984).

shark[1] ▶ **noun** **1** a long-bodied chiefly marine fish with a cartilaginous skeleton, a prominent dorsal fin, and tooth-like scales. Most sharks are predatory, though the largest kinds feed on plankton, and some can grow to a large size.
• Several orders (or superorders) of the subclass Elasmobranchii: many families.
2 a small SE Asian freshwater fish with a shark-like tail, popular in aquaria.
• Two species in the family Cyprinidae: the small **red-tailed black shark** (*Labeo bicolor*), and the larger **black shark** (*Morulius chrysophekadion*).
3 a light greyish-brown European moth, the male of which has pale silvery hindwings.
• Genus *Cucullia*, family Noctuidae: several species, including **the shark** (*C. umbratica*).
– ORIGIN late Middle English: of unknown origin.

shark[2] ▶ **noun** informal **1** a person who unscrupulously exploits or swindles others: *Coleby was a shark, not the sort of man to pay more when he could pay less* | [with modifier] *property sharks want to develop the site*. See also **LOAN SHARK**.
2 US an expert in a specified field: *a poor shark*.
– ORIGIN late 16th cent.: perhaps from German *Schurke* 'worthless rogue', influenced by **SHARK**[1].

shark bait ▶ **noun** [mass noun] food suspended in the sea to attract sharks for hunting or photography.
■ Austral./NZ informal a lone swimmer well out from shore.

sharkskin ▶ **noun** [mass noun] the rough scaly skin of a shark, sometimes used as shagreen.
■ a stiff, slightly lustrous synthetic fabric.

shark-sucker ▶ **noun** another term for **REMORA**.

Sharma /ˈʃɑːmə/, Shankar Dayal (b.1918), Indian statesman, President 1992–7. A member of the Congress party, Sharma served as Vice-President 1987–92.

Sharon[1] /ˈʃarən/ a fertile coastal plain in Israel, lying between the Mediterranean Sea and the hills of Samaria.

Sharon[2] /ʃəˈrɒn/, Ariel (b.1928), Israeli general and Likud statesman, Prime Minister since 2001.

sharon fruit /ˈʃɛːr(ə)n, ˈʃar(ə)n/ ▶ **noun** a persimmon, especially one of an early fruiting orange variety grown in Israel.
– ORIGIN from **SHARON**[1].

Sharp, Cecil (James) (1859–1924), English collector of folk songs and folk dances. From 1904 onwards he published a number of collections of songs and dances, stimulating a revival of interest in English folk music. Sharp also founded the English Folk Dance Society in 1911.

sharp ▶ **adjective** **1** (of an object) having an edge or point that is able to cut or pierce something: *cut the cake with a very sharp knife* | *keep tools sharp*.
■ producing a sudden, piercing physical sensation or effect: *I suddenly felt a sharp pain in my back*. ■ (of a food, taste, or smell) acidic and intense: *fresh goats' milk cheese has a slightly sharper flavour than fromage frais*. ■ (of a sound) sudden and penetrating: *there was a sharp crack of thunder*. ■ (of words or a speaker) intended or intending to criticize or hurt: *she feared his sharp tongue*. ■ (of an emotion or experience) felt acutely or intensely; painful: *her sharp disappointment was tinged with embarrassment*. ■ (of sand or gravel) composed of angular grains.
2 tapering to a point or edge: *a sharp pencil* | *her face was thin and her nose sharp*.
■ distinct in outline or detail; clearly defined: *the job was a sharp contrast from her past life* | *the scene was as sharp and clear in his mind as a film*. ■ informal (of clothes or their wearer) smart and stylish: *they were greeted by a young man in a sharp suit*.
3 (of an action or change) sudden and marked: *there was a sharp increase in interest rates* | *he heard her sharp intake of breath*.
■ (of a bend, angle, or turn) making a sudden change of direction: *the bus creaked round a sharp hairpin bend*. ■ having or showing speed of perception, comprehension, or response: *her sharp eyes missed nothing* | *his old mind was not so sharp as it once was* | *he had a sharp sense of humour*. ■ quick to take advantage, especially in an unscrupulous or dishonest way: *Paul's a sharp operator*.
4 (of musical sound) above true or normal pitch.
■ [postpositive] (of a note) a semitone higher than a specified note: *F sharp*. ■ (of a key) having a sharp or sharps in the signature.
▶ **adverb** **1** precisely (used after an expression of time): *the meeting starts at 7.30 sharp*.
2 in a sudden or abrupt way: *we had to turn sharp right to get into the kitchen* | *he was brought up sharp by Helen's voice*.
3 above the true or normal pitch of musical sound: *he heard him playing a little sharp on the high notes*.
▶ **noun** **1** a musical note raised a semitone above natural pitch.
■ the sign (♯) indicating this.
2 a long, sharply pointed needle used for general sewing.
■ (usu. **sharps**) a thing with a sharp edge, such as a blade or a fragment of glass: *the safe disposal of sharps and clinical waste*.
3 informal a swindler or cheat. See also **CARD SHARP**.
▶ **verb** [with obj.] **1** [usu. as adj. **sharped**] Music, US raise the pitch of (a note).
2 archaic cheat or swindle (someone), especially at cards: *the fellow is drunk, let's sharp him*. [ORIGIN: late 17th cent.: from **SHARPER**; compare with **SHARK**[2].]
– PHRASES **sharp as a tack** N. Amer. extremely clever or astute. **the sharp end** see **END**.
– DERIVATIVES **sharply** adverb, **sharpness** noun.
– ORIGIN Old English *sc(e)arp*, of Germanic origin; related to Dutch *scherp* and German *scharf*.

Shar Pei /ʃɑː ˈpeɪ/ (also **shar pei**) ▶ **noun** (pl. **Shar Peis**) a compact squarely built dog of a breed of Chinese origin, with a characteristic wrinkly skin and short bristly coat of a fawn, cream, black, or red colour.
– ORIGIN 1970s: from Chinese *shā pí*, literally 'sand skin'.

sharpen ▶ **verb** make or become sharp: [with obj.] *she sharpened her pencil* | [no obj.] *her tone sharpened to exasperation*.
■ improve or cause to improve: [no obj.] *they've got to sharpen up in front of the goal* | [with obj.] *students will sharpen up their reading skills*.
– DERIVATIVES **sharpener** noun.

sharper ▶ **noun** informal a swindler, especially at cards.

Sharpeville massacre the killing of sixty-seven anti-apartheid demonstrators by security forces at Sharpeville, a black township south of Johannesburg, on 21 March 1960. Following the massacre, the South African government banned the African National Congress and the Pan-Africanist Congress.

sharp-featured ▶ **adjective** (of a person) having well-defined facial features.

sharpie ▶ **noun** (pl. **-ies**) **1** a sharp-prowed, flat-bottomed New England sailing boat, with one or two masts each rigged with a triangular sail.
2 informal, chiefly N. Amer. a dishonest and cunning person, especially a cheat.
3 Austral. informal a young person resembling a skinhead, with close-cropped hair and distinctive dress.

sharpish informal ▶ **adjective** fairly sharp.
▶ **adverb** chiefly Brit. quickly; soon: *I'd slip away sharpish if I were you*.

sharp practice ▶ **noun** [mass noun] dishonest or barely honest dealings.

sharp-set ▶ **adjective** dated very hungry.

sharpshooter ▶ **noun** a person who is very skilled in shooting.
– DERIVATIVES **sharpshooting** noun & adjective.

sharp-tongued ▶ **adjective** (of a person) given to using cutting, harsh, or critical language.

sharp-witted ▶ **adjective** (of a person) quick to notice and understand things.
– DERIVATIVES **sharp-wittedly** adverb, **sharp-wittedness** noun.

shashlik /ˈʃaʃlɪk/ ▶ **noun** (pl. same or **shashliks**) (in Asia and eastern Europe) a mutton kebab.
– ORIGIN from Russian *shashlyk*, based on Turkish *şiş* 'spit, skewer'; compare with **SHISH KEBAB**.

Shasta daisy /ˈʃastə/ ▶ **noun** a tall Pyrenean plant which bears a single large white daisy-like flower.
• *Leucanthemum maximum* or its hybrids, family Compositae.
– ORIGIN mid 19th cent.: named after Mount *Shasta* in California.

shastra /ˈʃɑːstrə/ (also **sastra**) ▶ **noun** (in Hinduism and some forms of Buddhism) a work of sacred scripture.
– ORIGIN from Sanskrit *śāstra*.

shat past and past participle of **SHIT**.

Shatt al-Arab /ˌʃat al ˈarəb/ a river of SW Asia, formed by the confluence of the Tigris and Euphrates Rivers and flowing 195 km (120 miles) through SE Iraq to the Persian Gulf. Its lower course forms the border between Iraq and Iran.

shatter ▶ **verb** break or cause to break suddenly and violently into pieces: [no obj.] *bullets riddled the bar top, glasses shattered, bottles exploded* | [with obj.] *the window was shattered by a stone*.
■ [with obj.] damage or destroy (something abstract): *the crisis will shatter their confidence*. ■ [with obj.] upset (someone) greatly: *everyone was shattered by the news* | [as adj. **shattering**] *he found it a shattering experience*. ■ [with obj.] [usu. as adj. **shattered**] informal exhaust (someone): *I usually feel too shattered to do more than crawl into bed*.
– DERIVATIVES **shatterer** noun, **shatteringly** adverb, **shatterproof** adjective.
– ORIGIN Middle English (in the sense 'scatter, disperse'): perhaps imitative; compare with **SCATTER**.

shatter cone ▶ **noun** Geology a fluted conical structure produced in rock by intense mechanical shock, such as that associated with meteoritic impact.

shauri /ˈʃaʊriː/ ▶ **noun** (pl. **shauris** or **shauries**) (in East Africa) a debate, argument, or problematic issue.
– ORIGIN Kiswahili.

shave ▶ **verb** 1 [no obj.] cut the hair off one's face with a razor: *he washed, shaved, and had breakfast.* ■ [with obj.] cut the hair off (a part of the body) with a razor: *she shaved her legs.* ■ [with obj.] cut the hair off the face or another part of the body of (someone) with a razor: *his wife washed and shaved him.* ■ cut (hair) off with a razor: *professional male swimmers* ***shave off*** *their body hair.*
2 [with obj.] cut (a thin slice or slices) from the surface of something: *scrape a large sharp knife across the surface,* ***shaving off*** *rolls of very fine chocolate.* ■ reduce by a small amount: *they shaved profit margins.* ■ remove (a small amount) from something: *she* ***shaved*** *0.5 seconds* ***off*** *the British junior record.*
3 [with obj.] pass or send something close to (something else), missing it narrowly: *Scott shaved the post in the 29th minute.*
▶ **noun** 1 an act of shaving hair from the face or a part of the body: *he couldn't* ***have a shave*** | *the razor will probably last several shaves.*
2 a tool used for shaving very thin slices or layers from wood or other material.
– ORIGIN Old English *sc(e)afan* 'scrape away the surface of (something) by paring', of Germanic origin; related to Dutch *schaven* and German *schaben.*

shavehook ▶ **noun** a tool used to remove paint from moulded areas.

shaveling /ˈʃeɪvlɪŋ/ ▶ **noun** archaic, derogatory a clergyman or priest with a tonsured head.

shaven ▶ **adjective** shaved: *a boy with a shaven head* | [in combination] *shaven-headed monks.*

shaver ▶ **noun** 1 an electric razor.
2 informal a young lad: *little shavers and their older brothers.*

shavetail ▶ **noun** US military slang, often derogatory a newly commissioned officer, especially a second lieutenant. ■ informal an inexperienced person: [as modifier] *the shavetail Assistant District Attorney.*
– ORIGIN figuratively, from the early sense 'untrained pack animal' (identified by a shaven tail).

Shavian /ˈʃeɪvɪən/ ▶ **adjective** of, relating to, or in the manner of G. B. Shaw, his writings, or ideas.
▶ **noun** an admirer of Shaw or his work.
– ORIGIN from *Shavius* (Latinized form of *Shaw*) + **-AN**.

shaving ▶ **noun** 1 a thin strip cut off a surface: *she brushed wood shavings from her knees.*
2 [mass noun] the action of shaving.

Shavuoth /ʃəˈvuːəs, ʃaːvʊˈɒt/ (also **Shavuot**) ▶ **noun** a major Jewish festival held on the 6th (and usually the 7th) of Sivan, fifty days after the second day of Passover. It was originally a harvest festival, but now also commemorates the giving of the Law (the Torah). Also called **PENTECOST**, **FEAST OF WEEKS**.
– ORIGIN from Hebrew *šāḇūʿōṯ* 'weeks', with reference to the weeks between Passover and Pentecost.

Shaw, (George) Bernard (1856–1950), Irish dramatist and writer. His best-known plays combine comedy with a questioning of conventional morality and thought; they include *Man and Superman* (1903), *Pygmalion* (1913), and *St Joan* (1923). A socialist, he became an active member of the Fabian Society. Nobel Prize for Literature (1925).

shaw[1] ▶ **noun** Farming, chiefly Scottish the parts of a potato plant that appear above the ground.
– ORIGIN early 19th cent.: perhaps a variant of the noun **SHOW**.

shaw[2] ▶ **noun** archaic, chiefly Scottish a small group of trees; a thicket.
– ORIGIN Old English *sceaga*, of Germanic origin; related to **SHAG**[1].

shawl ▶ **noun** a piece of fabric worn by women over the shoulders or head or wrapped round a baby.
– DERIVATIVES **shawled** adjective.
– ORIGIN from Urdu and Persian *šāl*, probably from *Shāliāt*, the name of a town in India.

shawl collar ▶ **noun** a rounded turned-down collar, without lapel notches, that extends down the front of a garment.

shawm /ʃɔːm/ ▶ **noun** a medieval and Renaissance wind instrument, forerunner of the oboe, with a double reed enclosed in a wooden mouthpiece, and having a penetrating tone.
– ORIGIN Middle English: from Old French *chalemel*, via Latin from Greek *kalamos* 'reed'.

Shawnee /ʃɔːˈniː/ ▶ **noun** (pl. same or **Shawnees**) 1 a member of an American Indian people living formerly in the eastern US and now chiefly in Oklahoma.
2 [mass noun] the Algonquian language of this people, now with few speakers.
▶ **adjective** of or relating to the Shawnee or their language.
– ORIGIN the name in Delaware.

shay ▶ **noun** informal term for **CHAISE** (in sense 1).
– ORIGIN early 18th cent.: back-formation from **CHAISE**, interpreted as plural.

shaykh ▶ **noun** variant spelling of **SHEIKH**.

shazam /ʃəˈzam/ ▶ **exclamation** used to introduce an extraordinary deed, story, or transformation: *She prayed for his arrival and shazam! There he was.*
– ORIGIN 1940s: an invented word, used by conjurors.

Shcherbakov /ˌʃtʃəːbəˈkɒf/ former name (1946–57) for **RYBINSK**.

shchi /ʃtʃiː/ ▶ **noun** [mass noun] a type of Russian cabbage soup.
– ORIGIN Russian.

she ▶ **pronoun** [third person singular] used to refer to a woman, girl, or female animal previously mentioned or easily identified: *my sister told me that she was not happy.* ■ used to refer to a ship, vehicle, country, or other inanimate thing regarded as female: *I was aboard the St Roch shortly before she sailed for the Northwest Passage.* ■ used to refer to a person or animal of unspecified sex: *only include your child if you know she won't distract you.* ■ Austral./NZ informal it (used to refer to something not usually regarded as female): *reckon some decent weather and* ***she'll be right.*** ■ any female person: *she who rocks the cradle rules the world.*
▶ **noun** [in sing.] a female; a woman: *society would label him a slut if he were a she.* ■ [in combination] female: *a she-bear* | *a she-wolf.*
– PHRASES **who's she—the cat's mother?** Brit. informal used as a mild reproof, especially to a child, for impolite use of the pronoun *she* when a person's name would have been clearer or more well-mannered. ■ expressing the speaker's belief that a woman or girl has a high opinion of herself or is putting on airs.
– ORIGIN Middle English: probably a phonetic development of the Old English feminine personal pronoun *hēo, hīe.*

USAGE 1 For a discussion of whether to say *I am older than* **she** or *I am older than* **her**, see **usage** at **PERSONAL PRONOUN** and **THAN**.
2 The use of the pronoun **he** to refer to a person of unspecified sex, once quite acceptable, has become problematic in recent years and is now usually regarded as old-fashioned or sexist. One of the responses to this has been to use **she** in the way that **he** has been used, as in *only include your* **child** *if you know* **she** *won't distract you.* In some types of writing, for example books on childcare or child psychology, use of **she** has become quite common. In most contexts, however, it is likely to be distracting in the same way that **he** now is, and alternatives such as 'he or she' or 'they' are preferable. See **usage** at **HE** and **THEY**.

s/he ▶ **pronoun** a written representation of 'he or she' used as a neutral alternative to indicate someone of either sex.

shea /ʃiː, ˈʃiːə/ (also **shea tree**) ▶ **noun** a small tropical African tree which bears oily nuts from which shea butter is obtained.
● *Vitellaria paradoxa* (or *Butyrospermum parkii*), family Sapotaceae.
– ORIGIN late 18th cent.: from Mande *sye.*

shea butter ▶ **noun** [mass noun] a fatty substance obtained from the nuts of the shea tree, used in cosmetic skin preparations, food, and lighting.

sheading /ˈʃiːdɪŋ/ ▶ **noun** each of the six administrative divisions of the Isle of Man.
– ORIGIN late 16th cent.: variant of *shedding* (see **SHED**[2]).

sheaf ▶ **noun** (pl. **sheaves**) a bundle of grain stalks laid lengthways and tied together after reaping. ■ a bundle of objects of one kind, especially papers: *he waved* ***a sheaf of*** *papers in the air.*
▶ **verb** [with obj.] bundle into sheaves.
– ORIGIN Old English *scēaf*, of Germanic origin; related to Dutch *schoof* 'sheaf' and German *Schaub* 'wisp of straw', also to the verb **SHOVE**.

shealing ▶ **noun** variant spelling of **SHIELING**.

shear ▶ **verb** (past participle **shorn** or **sheared**) 1 [with obj.] cut the wool off (a sheep or other animal). ■ cut off (something such as hair, wool, or grass), with scissors or shears: *I'll* ***shear off*** *all that fleece.* ■ (**be shorn of**) have something cut off: *they were shorn of their hair* | figurative *the richest man in the US was shorn of nearly $2 billion.*
2 break off or cause to break off, owing to a structural strain: [no obj.] *the derailleur sheared and jammed in the rear wheel* | [with obj.] *the left wing had been almost completely* ***sheared off.***
▶ **noun** [mass noun] a strain produced by pressure in the structure of a substance, when its layers are laterally shifted in relation to each other. See also **WIND SHEAR**.
– DERIVATIVES **shearer** noun.
– ORIGIN Old English *sceran* (originally in the sense 'cut through with a weapon'), of Germanic origin; related to Dutch and German *scheren*, from a base meaning 'divide, shear, shave'.

USAGE The two verbs **shear** and **sheer** are sometimes confused: see **usage** at **SHEER**[2].

Shearer, Moira (b.1926), Scottish ballet dancer and actress; full name *Moira Shearer King*. A ballerina with Sadler's Wells from 1942, she is perhaps best known for her portrayal of a dedicated ballerina in the film *The Red Shoes* (1948).

shearling ▶ **noun** a sheep that has been shorn once: [as modifier] *a group of shearling rams.* ■ [mass noun] wool or fleece from such a sheep. ■ chiefly US a coat made from or lined with such wool.

shears (also **a pair of shears**) ▶ **plural noun** a cutting instrument in which two blades move past each other, like scissors but typically larger: *garden shears.*
– ORIGIN Old English *scēara* (plural) 'scissors, cutting instrument', of Germanic origin; related to Dutch *schaar* and German *Schere*, also to **SHEAR**.

shearwater ▶ **noun** 1 a long-winged seabird related to the petrels, often flying low over the surface of the water far from land.
● Family Procellariidae: three genera, in particular *Puffinus*, and many species.
2 North American term for **SKIMMER** (in sense 2).

sheatfish /ˈʃiːtfɪʃ/ ▶ **noun** (pl. same or **-fishes**) another term for **WELS**.
– ORIGIN late 16th cent.: from an alteration of **SHEATH** + **FISH**[1].

sheath ▶ **noun** (pl. **sheaths** /ʃiːðz, ʃiːθs/) a close-fitting cover for something, especially something that is elongated in shape, in particular: ■ a cover for the blade of a knife or sword. ■ a structure in living tissue which closely envelops another: *the fatty sheath around nerve fibres.* ■ (also **sheath dress**) a woman's close-fitting dress: *a tight sheath of black and gold lurex.* ■ a protective covering around an electric cable. ■ a condom.
– DERIVATIVES **sheathless** adjective.
– ORIGIN Old English *scǣth, scēath* 'scabbard', of Germanic origin; related to Dutch *schede*, German *Scheide*, also to the verb **SHED**[2].

sheathbill ▶ **noun** a mainly white pigeon-like bird with a horny sheath around the base of the bill, breeding on the coasts of sub-Antarctic islands and feeding by scavenging.
● Family Chionididae and genus *Chionis*: two species.

sheathe /ʃiːð/ ▶ **verb** [with obj.] put (a weapon such as a knife or sword) into a sheath. ■ (often **be sheathed in**) encase (something) in a close-fitting or protective covering: *her legs were sheathed in black stockings.*
– ORIGIN late Middle English: from **SHEATH**.

sheathing /ˈʃiːðɪŋ/ ▶ **noun** [mass noun] protective casing or covering.

sheath knife ▶ **noun** a short knife similar to a dagger, carried in a sheath.

sheave[1] ▶ **verb** another term for **SHEAF**.
– ORIGIN late 16th cent.: from **SHEAVES**.

sheave[2] ▶ **noun** a wheel with a groove for a rope to run on, as in a pulley block.
– ORIGIN Middle English: from a Germanic base meaning 'wheel, pulley'.

sheaves plural form of **SHEAF**.

Sheba /ˈʃiːbə/ the biblical name of Saba in SW Arabia. The queen of Sheba visited King Solomon in Jerusalem (1 Kings 10).
– ORIGIN from Hebrew *šəḇāʾ.*

shebang /ʃɪˈbaŋ/ ▶ **noun** 1 [in sing.] informal a matter,

operation, or set of circumstances: *the Mafia boss who's running* **the whole shebang**.
2 N. Amer. archaic a rough hut or shelter.
– ORIGIN mid 19th cent.: of unknown origin.

Shebat /'ʃiːbat/ ▶ **noun** variant spelling of **SEBAT**.

shebeen /ʃɪ'biːn/ ▶ **noun** (especially in Ireland, Scotland, and South Africa) an unlicensed establishment or private house selling alcoholic liquor and typically regarded as slightly disreputable.
■(in South Africa) an informal licensed drinking place in a township.
– ORIGIN late 18th cent.: from Anglo-Irish *síbín*, from *séibe* 'mugful'.

shed[1] ▶ **noun** a simple roofed structure, typically made of wood or metal, used for garden storage, to shelter animals, or as a workshop.
■a larger structure, typically with one or more sides open, for storing or maintaining vehicles or other machinery: *a shed is required for the three shunt engines.* ■ Austral./NZ an open-sided building for shearing sheep or milking cattle.
▶**verb** (**shedded**, **shedding**) [with obj.] (usu. **be shedded**) park (a vehicle) in a depot.
– ORIGIN late 15th cent.: apparently a variant of the noun **SHADE**.

shed[2] ▶ **verb** (**shedding**; past and past participle **shed**) [with obj.] (of a tree or other plant) allow (leaves or fruit) to fall to the ground: *both varieties shed leaves in winter.*
■(of a reptile, insect, etc.) allow (its skin or shell) to come off, to be replaced by another one that has grown underneath. ■ (of a mammal) lose (hair) as a result of moulting, disease, or age. ■ take off (clothes). ■ discard (something undesirable, superfluous, or outdated): *many firms use relocation as an opportunity to shed jobs.* ■ have the property of preventing (something) from being absorbed: *latigo leather has a superior ability to shed water, sweat, and salt.* ■ accidentally allow (something) to fall off or spill: *a lorry shed its load of steel bars.* ■ eliminate part of (an electrical power load) by disconnecting circuits.
– PHRASES **shed (someone's) blood** be injured or killed (or kill or injure someone). **shed light on** see **LIGHT**[1]. **shed tears** weep; cry.
– ORIGIN Old English *sc(e)ādan* 'separate out (one selected group), divide', also 'scatter', of Germanic origin; related to Dutch and German *scheiden*. Compare with **SHEATH**.

she'd ▶ **contraction of** she had; she would.

shedder ▶ **noun** a person or thing that sheds something.
■a female salmon after spawning.

she-devil ▶ **noun** a malicious or spiteful woman.

shedhand ▶ **noun** Austral./NZ a labourer employed to do unskilled work in a shearing shed.

Sheela-na-gig /ˌʃiːlənə'gɪg/ ▶ **noun** a medieval stone figure of a naked female with the legs wide apart and the hands emphasizing the genitals, found in churches in Britain and Ireland.
– ORIGIN from Irish *Síle na gcíoch* 'Julia of the breasts'.

sheen ▶ **noun** [in sing.] a soft lustre on a surface: *black crushed velvet with a slight sheen* | figurative *he seemed to shine with that unmistakable showbiz sheen.*
▶**verb** poetic/literary shine or cause to shine softly: [with obj.] *men entered with rain sheening their steel helms* | [no obj.] *her black hair sheened in the sun.*
– ORIGIN early 17th cent.: from obsolete *sheen* 'beautiful, resplendent'; apparently related to the verb **SHINE**.

sheeny ▶ **adjective** (of an object) having a sheen on its surface; lustrous: *a sheeny gold tie.*
▶**noun** N. Amer. an offensive term for a Jewish person.

sheep ▶ **noun** (pl. same) **1** a domesticated ruminant mammal with a thick woolly coat and (typically only in the male) curving horns. It is kept in flocks for its wool or meat, and is proverbial for its tendency to follow others in the flock.
● *Ovis aries*, family Bovidae, descended from the wild mouflon.
■a wild mammal related to this, such as the argali, bighorn, bharal, and urial.
2 a person who is too easily influenced or led: *party members should not follow their leader like sheep.*
3 a person regarded as a protected follower of God. [ORIGIN: with biblical allusion to Luke 15:6.]
■a member of a minister's congregation.
– PHRASES **count sheep** count imaginary sheep jumping over a fence one by one in an attempt to send oneself to sleep. **make sheep's eyes at someone** look at someone in a foolishly amorous way.
– DERIVATIVES **sheeplike** adjective.
– ORIGIN Old English *scēp*, *scǣp*, *scēap*, of West Germanic origin; related to Dutch *schaap* and German *Schaf*.

sheep bot ▶ **noun** see **NOSTRIL FLY**.

sheep dip ▶ **noun** [mass noun] a liquid preparation for cleansing sheep of parasites or preserving their wool.
■[count noun] a place where sheep are dipped in such a preparation.

sheepdog ▶ **noun** a dog trained to guard and herd sheep.
■a dog of a breed suitable for this.

sheepdog trials ▶ **plural noun** a public competitive display of the skills of sheepdogs.

sheepfold ▶ **noun** a sheep pen.

sheepish ▶ **adjective** (of a person or expression) showing embarrassment from shame or a lack of self-confidence: *a sheepish grin.*
– DERIVATIVES **sheepishly** adverb, **sheepishness** noun.

sheep laurel ▶ **noun** a North American kalmia which is sometimes cultivated as an ornamental.
● *Kalmia angustifolia*, family Ericaceae.

sheep run ▶ **noun** (especially in Australia) an extensive tract of land on which sheep are pastured.

sheep's-bit ▶ **noun** a blue-flowered European plant which resembles a scabious.
● *Jasione montana*, family Campanulaceae.

sheep scab ▶ **noun** [mass noun] an intensely itching skin disease of sheep caused by a parasitic mite.
● The mite is *Psoroptes communis*, family Psoroptidae.

sheep's fescue ▶ **noun** [mass noun] a small wiry pasture grass, common on chalk downland.
● *Festuca ovina*, family Gramineae.

sheepshank ▶ **noun** a kind of knot used to shorten a rope temporarily, made by taking two bights of rope and securing them to the standing rope with two half hitches.

sheepshead ▶ **noun** (pl. same) any of a number of boldly marked edible game fishes which live in warm American waters.
● a black and silver striped porgy of Atlantic coastal and brackish waters (*Archosargus probatocephalus*, family Sparidae). ● (**California sheepshead**) a black and red wrasse of Californian coastal waters (*Semicossyphus pulcher*, family Labridae).

sheepskin ▶ **noun 1** a sheep's skin with the wool on, especially when made into a garment or rug: [as modifier] *a sheepskin coat.*
■[mass noun] leather from a sheep's skin used in bookbinding.
2 (in South Africa) a party with country dancing. [ORIGIN: originally held to celebrate sheep shearing.]

sheep's sorrel (N. Amer. **sheep sorrel**) ▶ **noun** a sorrel which is common on acid soils in north temperate regions.
● *Rumex acetosella*, family Polygonaceae.

sheep tick ▶ **noun** a large tick that infests many mammals, including humans, and frequently transmits diseases. Also called **CASTOR BEAN TICK**.
● *Ixodes ricinus*, family Ixodidae.

sheep walk ▶ **noun** Brit. a tract of land on which sheep are pastured.

sheer[1] ▶ **adjective 1** [attrib.] nothing other than; unmitigated (used for emphasis): *she giggled with sheer delight* | *it's been sheer hard work.*
2 (especially of a cliff or wall) perpendicular or nearly so: *the sheer ice walls.*
3 (of a fabric) very thin; diaphanous: *sheer white silk chiffon.*
▶**adverb 1** perpendicularly: *the ridge fell sheer, in steep crags.*
2 archaic completely; right: *she went sheer forward when the door was open.*
▶**noun** a very fine or diaphanous fabric or article.
– DERIVATIVES **sheerly** adverb, **sheerness** noun.
– ORIGIN Middle English (in the sense 'exempt, cleared'): probably an alteration of dialect *shire* 'pure, clear', from the Germanic base of the verb **SHINE**. In the mid 16th cent. the word was used to describe clear, pure water, and also in sense 3.

sheer[2] ▶ **verb** [no obj., with adverbial] (typically of a boat) swerve or change course quickly: *the boat sheered off to beach further up the coast.*
■figurative avoid or move away from an unpleasant topic: *her mind* **sheered away** *from images she didn't want to dwell on.*
▶**noun** a sudden deviation from a course, especially by a boat.
– ORIGIN early 17th cent.: perhaps from Middle Low German *scheren* 'to shear'.

USAGE The two verbs **sheer** and **shear** have a similar origin but do not have identical meanings. **Sheer**, the less common verb, means 'swerve or change course quickly', as in *the boat* **sheers off** *the bank.* **Shear**, on the other hand, usually means 'cut the wool off (a sheep)' and can also mean 'break off (usually as a result of structural strain)', as in *the pins broke and the wing part* **sheared off**.

sheer[3] ▶ **noun** [mass noun] the upward slope of a ship's lines towards the bow and stern.
– ORIGIN late 17th cent.: probably from the noun **SHEAR**.

sheer legs ▶ **plural noun** [treated as sing.] a hoisting apparatus made from poles joined at or near the top and separated at the bottom, used for masting ships, installing engines, and hauling heavy objects.

sheet[1] ▶ **noun 1** a large rectangular piece of cotton or other fabric, used on a bed to cover the mattress and as a layer beneath blankets when these are used.
■used in comparisons to describe the pallor of a person who is ill or has had a shock: *Are you OK? You're* **as white as a sheet**. ■ a broad flat piece of material such as metal or glass: *the small pipe has been formed from a flat sheet of bronze.*
2 a rectangular piece of paper, especially one of a standard size produced commercially and used for writing and printing on: ***a sheet of*** *unmarked paper.*
■a quantity of text or other information contained on such a piece of paper: *he produced yet another* **sheet of** *figures.* ■ a flat piece of paper as opposed to a reel of continuous paper, the bound pages of a book, or a folded map. ■ all the postage stamps printed on one piece of paper: *a sheet of 1p stamps.* ■ a map, especially one part of a series covering a larger area.
3 an extensive unbroken surface area of something: *Loch Affric is* **a** *lovely* **sheet of** *water among trees* | [as modifier] *sheet ice.*
■a broad moving mass of flames or water: *the rain was still falling in sheets.*
▶**verb 1** [with obj.] cover with or wrap in a sheet of cloth: *lorry drivers don't sheet their loads.*
2 [no obj., with adverbial of direction] (of rain) fall in large quantities: *rain sheeted down.*
– ORIGIN Old English *scēte*, *scīete*, of Germanic origin; related to the verb **SHOOT** in its primary sense 'to project'.

sheet[2] Nautical ▶ **noun 1** a rope attached to the lower corner of a sail for securing or extending the sail or for altering its direction.
2 (**sheets**) the space at the bow or stern of an open boat.
▶**verb** [with obj.] (**sheet something in/out**) make a sail more or less taut.
■(**sheet something home**) extend a sail by tightening the sheets so that the sail is set as flat as possible.
– PHRASES **two** (or **three**) **sheets to the wind** informal drunk.
– ORIGIN Old English *scēata* 'lower corner of a sail', of Germanic origin; related to Old Norse *skauti* 'kerchief' (see also **SHEET**[1]).

sheet anchor ▶ **noun** figurative a person or thing that is very dependable and relied upon in the last resort.
– ORIGIN late 15th cent. (denoting an additional anchor for use in emergencies): perhaps related to obsolete *shot*, denoting two cables spliced together, later influenced by **SHEET**[2].

sheet bend ▶ **noun** a method of temporarily fastening one rope through the loop of another.

sheeted ▶ **adjective 1** covered with or enveloped in a sheet of cloth: *the sheeted body.*
2 Geology (of rock) fissured or divided into layers, especially by faulting.

sheet feeder ▶ **noun** Computing a device for feeding paper into a printer a sheet at a time.

sheeting ▶ **noun** [mass noun] material formed into or used as a sheet: *a window covered with plastic sheeting.*

sheetlet ▶ **noun** a small unseparated sheet of postage stamps.

S

sheet lightning ▶ **noun** [mass noun] lightning with its brightness diffused by reflection within clouds.

sheet metal ▶ **noun** [mass noun] metal formed into thin sheets, typically by rolling or hammering.

sheet music ▶ **noun** [mass noun] printed music, as opposed to performed or recorded music.
■ music published in single or interleaved sheets, not bound.

Sheetrock ▶ **noun** [mass noun] trademark, chiefly US a plasterboard made of gypsum layered between sheets of heavy paper.

Sheffield an industrial city in northern England, a unitary council formerly in Yorkshire; pop. 500,500 (1991). Sheffield is famous for the manufacture of cutlery and silverware and for the production of steel.

Sheffield plate ▶ **noun** [mass noun] copper plated with silver by rolling and edging with silver film and ribbon, especially as produced in Sheffield between 1760 and 1840.

sheikh /ʃeɪk, ʃiːk/ (also **shaikh**, **shaykh**, or **sheik**) ▶ **noun** **1** an Arab leader, in particular the chief or head of an Arab tribe, family, or village.
2 a leader in a Muslim community or organization.
– DERIVATIVES **sheikhdom** noun.
– ORIGIN late 16th cent.: based on Arabic *šayḵ* 'old man, sheikh', from *šāḵa* 'be or grow old'.

sheila ▶ **noun** Austral./NZ informal a girl or young woman.
– ORIGIN mid 19th cent. (originally as *shaler*): of unknown origin, later assimilated to the given name *Sheila*.

sheitel /ˈʃeɪt(ə)l/ ▶ **noun** (among orthodox Ashkenazic Jews) a wig worn by a married woman.
– ORIGIN late 19th cent.: from Yiddish *sheytl*, from a Germanic base meaning 'crown of the head'.

shekel /ˈʃɛk(ə)l/ ▶ **noun** the basic monetary unit of modern Israel, equal to 100 agora.
■ historical a silver coin and unit of weight used in ancient Israel and the Middle East. ■ (**shekels**) informal money; wealth.
– ORIGIN from Hebrew *šeqel*, from *šāqal* 'weigh'.

Shekinah /ʃɪˈkʌɪnə/ (also **Shekhinah**) ▶ **noun** [mass noun] Jewish & Christian Theology the glory of the divine presence, conventionally represented as light or interpreted symbolically (in Kabbalism as a divine feminine aspect).
– ORIGIN mid 17th cent.: from late Hebrew, from *šākan* 'dwell, rest'.

shelduck /ˈʃɛldʌk/ ▶ **noun** (pl. same or **shelducks**) a large goose-like Old World duck with brightly coloured plumage, typically showing black and white wings in flight.
● Genus *Tadorna*, family Anatidae: several species, in particular *T. tadorna* of Eurasian coasts, with white, greenish-black, and chestnut plumage.
– ORIGIN early 18th cent.: probably from dialect *sheld* 'pied' (related to Middle Dutch *schillede* 'variegated') + **DUCK**[1]. The term *sheldrake* dates from Middle English.

shelf[1] ▶ **noun** (pl. **shelves**) a flat length of wood or rigid material, attached to a wall or forming part of a piece of furniture, that provides a surface for the storage or display of objects.
■ a ledge of rock or protruding strip of land. ■ a submarine bank, or a part of the continental shelf.
– PHRASES **off the shelf** not designed or made to order but taken from existing stock or supplies: *off-the-shelf software packages.* **on the shelf** (of people or things) no longer useful or desirable: *an injury which has kept him on the shelf.* ■ (especially of a woman) past an age when one might expect to have the opportunity to marry. ■ (of a music recording or a film) awaiting release on the market after being recorded.
– DERIVATIVES **shelf-ful** noun (pl. **-fuls**), **shelf-like** adjective.
– ORIGIN Middle English: from Middle Low German *schelf*; related to Old English *scylfe* 'partition', *scylf* 'crag'.

shelf[2] Austral. informal ▶ **noun** (pl. **shelfs**) an informer.
▶ **verb** [with obj.] inform upon (someone).
– ORIGIN early 20th cent. (as a noun): probably from the phrase *on the shelf* 'out of the way'.

shelf life ▶ **noun** the length of time for which an item remains usable, fit for consumption, or saleable.

shelf mark ▶ **noun** a notation on a book showing its place in a library.

shelf room ▶ **noun** [mass noun] the amount of available space on a shelf.

shell ▶ **noun** **1** the hard protective outer case of a mollusc or crustacean: *cowrie shells* | [mass noun] *the technique of carving shell.*
■ the thin outer covering of an animal's egg, which is hard and fragile in that of a bird but leathery in that of a reptile. ■ the outer case of a nut kernel or seed. ■ the carapace of a tortoise, turtle, or terrapin. ■ the wing cases of a beetle. ■ the integument of an insect pupa or chrysalis. ■ (**one's shell**) figurative used with reference to a state of shyness or introversion: *she'll soon come out of her shell with the right encouragement.*
2 something resembling or likened to a shell because of its shape or its function as an outer case: *pasta shells* | *baked pastry shells filled with cheese.*
■ the walls of an unfinished or gutted building or other structure: *the hotel was a shell, the roof having collapsed completely.* ■ figurative an outer form without substance: *he was a shell of the man he had been previously.* ■ a light racing boat. ■ the metal framework of a vehicle body. ■ an inner or roughly made coffin. ■ the handguard of a sword. ■ Physics each of a set of orbitals around the nucleus of an atom, occupied or able to be occupied by electrons of similar energies.
3 an explosive artillery projectile or bomb: *the sound of the shell passing over, followed by the explosion* | [as modifier] *shell holes.*
■ a hollow metal or paper case used as a container for fireworks, explosives, or cartridges. ■ N. Amer. a cartridge.
4 Computing short for **SHELL PROGRAM**.
▶ **verb** [with obj.] **1** bombard with shells: *the guns started shelling their positions.*
■ (usu. **be shelled**) Baseball score heavily against (an opposing pitcher or team).
2 remove the shell or pod from (a nut or seed): *they were shelling peas* | [as adj. **shelled**] *shelled Brazil nuts.*
– DERIVATIVES **shelled** adjective [in combination] *a soft-shelled clam*, **shell-less** adjective, **shelly** adjective.
– ORIGIN Old English *scell* (noun), of Germanic origin; related to Dutch *schel* 'scale, shell', also to **SCALE**[1]. The verb dates from the mid 16th cent. in sense 2.
▶ **shell something out** (or **shell out**) informal pay a specified amount of money, especially an amount that is resented as being excessive: *he has had to shell out £500 a week hiring a bodyguard.*

she'll ▶ **contraction of** she shall; she will.

shellac /ʃəˈlak/ ▶ **noun** [mass noun] lac resin melted into thin flakes, used for making varnish.
▶ **verb** (**shellacked**, **shellacking**) [with obj.] **1** [often as adj. **shellacked**] varnish (something) with shellac.
2 (usu. **be shellacked**) N. Amer. informal defeat or beat (someone) decisively: *they were shellacked in the 1982 election.*
– ORIGIN mid 17th cent.: from **SHELL** + **LAC**[1], translating French *laque en écailles* 'lac in thin plates'.

shellback ▶ **noun** N. Amer. informal an old or experienced sailor, especially one who has crossed the equator.

shell bit ▶ **noun** a gouge-shaped boring bit.

shell company ▶ **noun** a non-trading company used as a vehicle for various financial manoeuvres or kept dormant for future use in some other capacity.

shell egg ▶ **noun** an egg bought or sold in its natural state in the shell.

Shelley[1], Mary (Wollstonecraft) (1797–1851), English writer, daughter of William Godwin and Mary Wollstonecraft. She eloped with Percy Bysshe Shelley in 1814 and married him in 1816. She is chiefly remembered as the author of the Gothic novel *Frankenstein, or the Modern Prometheus* (1818).

Shelley[2], Percy Bysshe (1792–1822), English poet. He was a leading figure of the romantic movement with radical political views. Notable works include *Queen Mab* (political poems, 1813), *Prometheus Unbound* (lyrical drama, 1820), *The Defence of Poetry* (essay, 1821), and *Adonais* (1821), an elegy on the death of Keats.

shellfire ▶ **noun** [mass noun] bombardment by shells.

shellfish ▶ **noun** (pl. same) an aquatic shelled mollusc (e.g. an oyster or cockle) or a crustacean (e.g. a crab or shrimp), especially one that is edible.
■ [mass noun] such molluscs or crustaceans as food.

shell game ▶ **noun** N. Amer. another term for **THIMBLERIG**.
■ a deceptive and evasive action or ploy, especially a political one: *he played a shell game, misleading the tax department about his real worth.*

shell heap ▶ **noun** Archaeology a mound of domestic waste consisting mainly of shells, common at prehistoric sites.

shell jacket ▶ **noun** an army officer's tight-fitting undress jacket reaching to the waist.
■ the jacket of a shell suit.

shell-like ▶ **adjective** resembling a shell in shape or appearance: *a creature with a shell-like carapace.*
▶ **noun** Brit. informal a person's ear: *Prentice had a word in somebody's shell-like.*

shell lime ▶ **noun** [mass noun] fine-quality lime produced by roasting seashells.

shell money ▶ **noun** [mass noun] chiefly historical shells used as a medium of exchange, especially wampum.

shell mound ▶ **noun** another term for **SHELL HEAP**.

shell pink ▶ **noun** [mass noun] a delicate pale pink.

shell program ▶ **noun** Computing a program which provides an interface between the user and the operating system.

shell shock ▶ **noun** [mass noun] psychological disturbance caused by prolonged exposure to active warfare, especially being under bombardment. Also called **COMBAT FATIGUE**.
– DERIVATIVES **shell-shocked** adjective.
– ORIGIN First World War: with reference to exposure to shellfire.

shell suit ▶ **noun** a casual outfit consisting of a loose jacket and trousers with elasticated waist or cut all-in-one, with a soft lining and a shiny polyester outer shell.

shell top ▶ **noun** a short sleeveless top, typically having button fastenings down the back and a simple shape with a high neckline.

shell-work ▶ **noun** [mass noun] ornamentation consisting of shells cemented on to a surface.

Shelta /ˈʃɛltə/ ▶ **noun** [mass noun] an ancient secret language used by Irish and Welsh tinkers and gypsies, and based largely on altered Irish or Gaelic words.
– ORIGIN late 19th cent.: of unknown origin.

shelter ▶ **noun** a place giving temporary protection from bad weather or danger.
■ a place providing food and accommodation for the homeless. ■ an animal sanctuary. ■ [mass noun] a shielded or safe condition; protection: *he hung back in the shelter of a rock* | *you're welcome to take shelter from the storm.*
▶ **verb** [with obj.] protect or shield from something harmful, especially bad weather: *the hut sheltered him from the cold wind* | [as adj. **sheltered**] *the plants need a shady, sheltered spot in the garden.*
■ [no obj., with adverbial of place] find refuge or take cover from bad weather or danger: *people were sheltering under store canopies and trees.* ■ prevent (someone) from having to do or face something difficult or unpleasant: [as adj. **sheltered**] *I was a mathematics don at Cambridge living a rather sheltered life.* ■ protect (income) from taxation: *only your rental income can be sheltered.*
– DERIVATIVES **shelterer** noun, **shelterless** adjective.
– ORIGIN late 16th cent.: perhaps an alteration of obsolete *sheltron* 'phalanx', from Old English *scieldtruma*, literally 'shield troop'.

shelter belt ▶ **noun** a line of trees or shrubs planted to protect an area, especially a field of crops, from fierce weather.

sheltered housing (also **sheltered accommodation**) ▶ **noun** [mass noun] Brit. accommodation for the elderly or handicapped consisting of private independent units with some shared facilities and a warden.

shelterwood ▶ **noun** [mass noun] mature trees left standing to provide shelter in which saplings can grow.

sheltie (also **shelty**) ▶ **noun** (pl. **-ies**) a Shetland pony or sheepdog.
– ORIGIN early 17th cent.: probably representing an Orkney pronunciation of Old Norse *Hjalti* 'Shetlander'.

shelve[1] ▶ **verb** [with obj.] **1** place or arrange (items, especially books) on a shelf.
■ figurative decide not to proceed with (a project or plan),

S

either temporarily or permanently: *plans to reopen the school have been shelved.*
2 fit with shelves: *one whole long wall was shelved.*
– DERIVATIVES **shelver** noun.
– ORIGIN late 16th cent. (in the sense 'project like a shelf' (Shakespearean usage)): from *shelves*, plural of **SHELF**[1].

shelve[2] ▶ verb [no obj., with adverbial] (of ground) slope downwards in a specified manner or direction: *the ground shelved gently down to the water.*
– ORIGIN late Middle English: origin uncertain; perhaps from **SHELF**[1].

shelves plural form of **SHELF**[1].

shelving ▶ noun [mass noun] shelves collectively: *a lack of shelving and cupboards.*
■ the action of shelving something.

Shem /ʃɛm/ (in the Bible) a son of Noah (Gen. 10:21), traditional ancestor of the Semites.

Shema /ʃɛˈmɑː/ a Hebrew text consisting of three passages from the Pentateuch (Deuteronomy 6:4, 11:13–21; Numbers 15:37–41) and beginning 'Hear O Israel, the Lord our God is one Lord'. It forms an important part of Jewish evening and morning prayer and is used as a Jewish confession of faith.
– ORIGIN Hebrew, literally 'hear', the first word of Deut. 6:4.

she-male ▶ noun informal a transvestite.
■ a passive male homosexual.

shemozzle /ʃɪˈmɒz(ə)l/ (also **schemozzle**) ▶ noun informal a state of chaos and confusion; a muddle.
– ORIGIN late 19th cent.: Yiddish, suggested by late Hebrew *šel-lō'-mazzāl* 'of no luck'.

shen /ʃɛn/ ▶ noun (pl. same) (in Chinese thought) the spiritual element of a person's psyche.
– ORIGIN from Chinese *shén*.

Shenandoah /ˌʃɛnənˈdəʊə/ a river of Virginia. Rising in two headstreams, one on each side of the Blue Ridge Mountains, it flows some 240 km (150 miles) northwards to join the Potomac at Harpers Ferry.

Shenandoah National Park a national park in the Blue Ridge Mountains of northern Virginia, situated to the south-east of the Shenandoah River. It was established in 1935.

shenanigans /ʃɪˈnanɪɡ(ə)nz/ ▶ plural noun informal secret or dishonest activity or manoeuvring: *bookies try to depress the favourite's official starting price by last-minute shenanigans.*
■ silly or high-spirited behaviour; mischief.
– ORIGIN mid 19th cent.: of unknown origin.

sheng /ʃʌŋ/ ▶ noun (pl. same) a Chinese form of mouth organ with about seventeen reed pipes of bamboo set in a rounded windchest.
– ORIGIN late 18th cent.: from Chinese *shēng*.

Shensi /ʃɛnˈsiː/ variant of **SHAANXI**.

Shenyang /ʃɛnˈjaŋ/ a city in NE China; pop. 4,500,000 (1990). An important Manchurian city between the 17th and early 20th centuries, it is now the capital of the province of Liaoning. Former name **MUKDEN**.

Shenzhen /ʃɛnˈʒɛn/ an industrial city in southern China, just north of Hong Kong; pop. 875,100 (1990).

she-oak ▶ noun another term for **CASUARINA**.

Sheol /ˈʃiːəʊl, ˈʃiːɒl/ the Hebrew underworld, abode of the dead.
– ORIGIN Hebrew.

shepherd ▶ noun a person who tends and rears sheep.
■ figurative a member of the clergy who provides spiritual care and guidance for a congregation.
▶ verb [with obj.] [usu. as noun **shepherding**] tend (sheep) as a shepherd.
■ [with obj. and adverbial of direction] guide or direct in a particular direction: *we were shepherded around with great ceremony.* ■ give guidance to (someone), especially on spiritual matters: *she had to submit the control of her career and money to a group who shepherded her.*
– ORIGIN Old English *scēaphierde*, from **SHEEP** + obsolete *herd* 'herdsman'.

shepherd dog ▶ noun a sheepdog.

shepherdess /ˈʃɛpədɪs, ˌʃɛpəˈdɛs/ ▶ noun a female shepherd.
■ an idealized or romanticized rustic maiden in pastoral literature.

shepherd satellite (also **shepherd moon**) ▶ noun Astronomy a small moon orbiting close to a planetary ring, especially of Saturn, and whose gravitational field confines the ring within a narrow band.

shepherd's crook ▶ noun a staff with a hook at one end used by shepherds.

shepherd's needle ▶ noun a white-flowered Eurasian plant of the parsley family, with long needle-shaped fruit.
● *Scandix pecten-veneris*, family Umbelliferae.

shepherd's pie ▶ noun a dish of minced meat under a layer of mashed potato.

shepherd's plaid ▶ noun a small black-and-white check pattern.
■ [mass noun] woollen cloth with this pattern.

shepherd's purse ▶ noun a widely distributed white-flowered weed of the cabbage family, with triangular or heart-shaped seed pods.
● *Capsella bursa-pastoris*, family Cruciferae.

sherardize /ˈʃɛrədʌɪz/ (also **-ise**) ▶ verb [with obj.] coat (iron or steel) with zinc by heating it in contact with zinc dust.
– ORIGIN early 20th cent.: from the name of *Sherard Cowper-Coles* (1867–1936), English inventor, + **-IZE**.

Sheraton /ˈʃɛrət(ə)n/ ▶ adjective [attrib.] (of furniture) designed, made by, or in the simple, delicate, and graceful style of the English furniture-maker Thomas Sheraton (1751–1806).

sherbet ▶ noun [mass noun] Brit. a flavoured sweet effervescent powder eaten alone or made into a drink.
■ (especially in Arab countries) a cooling drink of sweet diluted fruit juices. ■ N. Amer. water ice; sorbet. ■ Austral. humorous beer.
– ORIGIN early 17th cent.: from Turkish *şerbet*, Persian *šerbet*, from Arabic *šarba* 'drink', from *šariba* 'to drink'. Compare with **SYRUP**.

sherd /ʃəːd/ ▶ noun another term for **POTSHERD**.

shereef (also **sherif**) ▶ noun variant spelling of **SHARIF**.

Sheridan /ˈʃɛrɪd(ə)n/, Richard Brinsley (1751–1816), Irish dramatist and Whig politician. His plays are comedies of manners; they include *The Rivals* (1775) and *The School for Scandal* (1777). In 1780 he entered Parliament, becoming a celebrated orator and holding senior government posts.

sheriff ▶ noun (also **high sheriff**) (in England and Wales) the chief executive officer of the Crown in a county, having various administrative and judicial functions.
■ an honorary officer elected annually in some English towns. ■ (in Scotland) a judge. ■ US an elected officer in a county, responsible for keeping the peace.
– DERIVATIVES **sheriffdom** noun, **sheriffhood** noun, **sheriffship** noun.
– ORIGIN Old English *scīrgerēfa* (see **SHIRE**, **REEVE**[1]).

sheriff clerk ▶ noun (in Scotland) the clerk of a sheriff's court.

sheriff court ▶ noun (in Scotland) a judicial court for civil cases, equivalent to a county court.

sheriff-depute ▶ noun (pl. **sheriff-deputes**) historical (in Scotland) the chief judge of a county or district.

sheriff principal ▶ noun (pl. **sheriffs principal**) (in Scotland) each of six chief judges.

Sherlock ▶ noun informal a person who investigates mysteries or shows great perceptiveness: *it doesn't take a Sherlock to figure out that she's lying to me.*
– ORIGIN early 20th cent.: from *Sherlock* Holmes (see **HOLMES**[3]).

Sherman, William Tecumseh (1820–91), American general. In 1864 in the American Civil War he became chief Union commander in the west. He set out with 60,000 men on a march through Georgia, during which he crushed Confederate forces and broke civilian morale by his policy of deliberate destruction of the territory he passed through.

Sherpa /ˈʃəːpə/ ▶ noun (pl. same or **Sherpas**) a member of a Himalayan people living on the borders of Nepal and Tibet, renowned for their skill in mountaineering.
■ a civil servant or diplomat who undertakes preparatory political work prior to a summit conference.
– ORIGIN from Tibetan *sharpa* 'inhabitant of an eastern country'.

Sherrington, Sir Charles Scott (1857–1952), English physiologist. He contributed greatly to the understanding of the nervous system and introduced the concept of reflex actions and the reflex arc. Nobel Prize for Physiology or Medicine (1932).

sherry ▶ noun (pl. **-ies**) [mass noun] a fortified wine originally and mainly from southern Spain, often drunk as an aperitif.
– ORIGIN late 16th cent.: alteration of archaic *sherris*, interpreted as plural, from Spanish (*vino de*) *Xeres* 'Xeres (wine)' (Xeres being the former name of **JEREZ**).

's-Hertogenbosch /ˌs(h)ɛːrˈtəʊxən'bɒs/ a city in the southern Netherlands, the capital of North Brabant; pop. 92,060 (1991).

sherwani /ʃəːˈwɑːniː/ ▶ noun (pl. **sherwanis**) a knee-length coat buttoning to the neck, worn by men from the Indian subcontinent.
– ORIGIN from Urdu and Persian *širwānī* 'from Shirvan' (referring to a town in NE Persia).

she's ▶ contraction of she is; she has.

Shetland Islands /ˈʃɛtlənd/ (also **Shetland** or **the Shetlands**) a group of about 100 islands off the north coast of Scotland, north-east of the Orkneys, constituting the administrative region of Shetland; pop. 22,020 (1991); chief town, Lerwick. Together with the Orkney Islands the Shetland Islands became a part of Scotland in 1472, having previously been ruled by Norway and Denmark.
– DERIVATIVES **Shetlander** noun.

Shetland lace ▶ noun [mass noun] a black or white bobbin lace made from Shetland wool.
■ knitwear made using openwork stitches to give a lacey effect.

Shetland pony ▶ noun a pony of a small hardy rough-coated breed.

Shetland sheep ▶ noun a sheep of a hardy short-tailed breed native to Shetland and bred especially for its fine wool.

Shetland sheepdog ▶ noun a small dog of a collie-like breed.

Shetland wool ▶ noun [mass noun] a type of fine loosely twisted wool from Shetland sheep.

Shevardnadze /ˌʃɛvaːdˈnɑːdzɪ/, Eduard (Amvrosievich) (b.1928), Soviet statesman and head of state of Georgia since 1992. He was Minister of Foreign Affairs 1985–90 under President Gorbachev before becoming head of state of his native Georgia.

Shevat /ˈʃiːvat/ ▶ noun variant spelling of **SEBAT**.

shew ▶ verb old-fashioned variant spelling of **SHOW**.

shewbread /ˈʃəʊbrɛd/ ▶ noun [mass noun] twelve loaves placed every Sabbath in the Jewish Temple and eaten by the priests at the end of the week.
– ORIGIN mid 16th cent.: suggested by German *Schaubrot*, representing Hebrew *leḥem pānīm*, literally 'bread of the face (of God)'.

shh (also **sh**) ▶ exclamation used to call for silence: *'Shh! Keep your voice down!'*
– ORIGIN mid 19th cent.: variant of **HUSH**.

Shia /ˈʃiːə/ (also **Shi'a**) ▶ noun (pl. same or **Shias**) [mass noun] one of the two main branches of Islam, followed especially in Iran, that rejects the first three Sunni caliphs and regards Ali, the fourth caliph, as Muhammad's first true successor. Compare with **SUNNI**.
■ [count noun] a Muslim who adheres to this branch of Islam.
– ORIGIN from Arabic *šī'a* 'party (of Ali)'.

shiatsu /ʃɪˈatsuː/ ▶ noun [mass noun] a form of therapy of Japanese origin based on the same principles as acupuncture, in which pressure is applied to certain points on the body using the hands.
– ORIGIN 1960s: Japanese, literally 'finger pressure'.

shibboleth /ˈʃɪbəlɛθ/ ▶ noun a custom, principle, or belief distinguishing a particular class or group of people, especially a long-standing one regarded as outmoded or no longer important: *Labour's socialist shibboleths.*
– ORIGIN mid 17th cent.: from Hebrew *šibbōlet* 'ear of corn', used as a test of nationality by its difficult pronunciation (Judg. 12:6).

shicer /ˈʃʌɪsə/ ▶ noun Austral. informal a worthless thing or person, especially a swindler.
■ Mining an unproductive claim or mine.
– ORIGIN mid 19th cent.: from German *Scheisser* 'contemptible person'.

shicker /ˈʃɪkə/ (also **shikker**) US & Austral./NZ informal

▶ adjective (also **shickered**, **shikkered**) [predic.] drunk: *they got shickered, talked cars and deals.*
▶ noun a drunk.
– ORIGIN late 19th cent.: from Yiddish *shiker*, from Hebrew *šikkōr*, from *šākar* 'be drunk'.

shidduch /ˈʃɪdəx/ ▶ noun (pl. **shidduchim**) a Jewish arranged marriage.
– ORIGIN late 19th cent.: Yiddish, from Hebrew *šiddūḵ* 'negotiation (of a marriage)'.

shied past and past participle of **SHY**[2].

shield ▶ noun **1** a broad piece of metal or another suitable material, held by straps or a handle attached on one side, used as a protection against blows or missiles.
2 something shaped like a shield, in particular:
■ a sporting trophy consisting of an engraved metal plate mounted on a piece of wood. ■ a US police officer's badge. ■ Heraldry a stylized representation of a shield used for displaying a coat of arms. ■ Geology a large rigid area of the earth's crust, typically of Precambrian rock, which has been unaffected by later orogenic episodes, e.g. the Canadian Shield.
3 a person or thing providing protection: *a protective coating of grease provides a shield against abrasive dirt.*
■ a protective plate or screen on machinery or equipment. ■ a device or material that prevents or reduces the emission of light or other radiation. ■ a hard flat or convex part of an animal, especially a shell.
▶ verb [with obj.] protect (someone or something) from a danger, risk, or unpleasant experience: *he pulled the cap lower to shield his eyes from the glare | these people have been completely shielded from economic forces.*
■ prevent from being seen: *the rocks she sat behind shielded her from the lodge.* ■ enclose or screen (a piece of machinery) to protect the user. ■ prevent or reduce the escape of sound, light, or other radiation from (something): *uranium shutters shield the cobalt radioactive source.*
– DERIVATIVES **shieldless** adjective.
– ORIGIN Old English *scild* (noun), *scildan* (verb), of Germanic origin; related to Dutch *schild* and German *Schild*, from a base meaning 'divide, separate'.

shield bug ▶ noun a broad shield-shaped bug which is typically brightly coloured or boldly marked. It emits a foul smell when handled or molested. Also called **STINK BUG**.
● Pentatomidae and other families, suborder Heteroptera.

shield fern ▶ noun any of a number of ferns that have circular shield-like scales protecting the spore cases:
● a European fern of damp woodland (genus *Polystichum*, family Dryopteridaceae). ● N. Amer. an evergreen fern (genus *Thelypteris*, family Thelypteridaceae). ● Austral. a fern of forested country (family Aspidiaceae).

shieldtail snake (also **shield-tailed snake**) ▶ noun a burrowing snake which has a flat disc formed from an enlarged scale on the upper surface of the tail, native to the rainforests of southern India and Sri Lanka.
● *Rhinophis*, *Uropeltis*, and other genera, family Uropeltidae: numerous species.

shield volcano ▶ noun Geology a broad domed volcano with gently sloping sides, characteristic of the eruption of fluid, basaltic lava.

shieling /ˈʃiːlɪŋ/ (also **shealing**) ▶ noun Scottish a roughly constructed hut used while pasturing animals.
■ an area of pasture.
– ORIGIN mid 16th cent.: from Scots *shiel* 'hut' (of unknown origin) + **-ING**[1].

shift /ʃɪft/ ▶ verb move or cause to move from one place to another, especially over a small distance: [with obj.] *a team from the power company came to shift the cables away from the house* | [no obj.] *the roof cracked and shifted.*
■ [no obj.] change the position of one's body, especially because one is nervous or uncomfortable: *he shifted a little in his chair.* ■ [with obj.] change the emphasis, direction, or focus of: *she's shifting the blame on to me.* ■ [no obj.] change in emphasis, direction, or focus: *the wind had shifted to the east | the balance of power shifted abruptly.* ■ [no obj.] Brit. informal move quickly: *you'll have time for a bite if you shift.* ■ (**shift oneself**) [in imperative] Brit. informal used to tell someone to move from a place or rouse themselves from a state of inactivity: *shift yourself, Ruby, do something useful and get the plates.* ■ [with obj.] Computing move (data) to the right or left in a register: *the partial remainder is shifted left.* ■ [with obj.] Brit. remove (a stain). ■ [with obj.] informal sell (something): *a lot of high-priced product you simply don't know how to shift.* ■ [with obj.] Brit. informal eat or drink (something) hastily or in large amounts. ■ [no obj.] chiefly N. Amer. change gear in a vehicle: *she shifted down to fourth.* ■ [no obj.] archaic be evasive or indirect: *they know not how to shift and rob as the old ones do.*
▶ noun **1** a slight change in position, direction, or tendency: *a shift of wind took us by surprise | a* **shift in** *public opinion.*
■ [mass noun] Astronomy the displacement of spectral lines. See also **RED SHIFT**. ■ (also **shift key**) a key on a typewriter or computer keyboard used to switch between two sets of characters or functions, principally between lower- and upper-case letters. ■ short for **SOUND SHIFT**. ■ N. Amer. the gear lever or gear-changing mechanism in a motor vehicle. ■ [mass noun] Building the positioning of successive rows of bricks so that their ends do not coincide. ■ Computing a movement of the digits of a word in a register one or more places to left or right, equivalent to multiplying or dividing the corresponding number by a power of whatever number is the base. ■ American Football a change of position by two or more players before the ball is put into play.
2 one of two or more recurring periods in which different groups of workers do the same jobs in relay: *the night shift.*
■ a group of workers who work in this way.
3 (also **shift dress**) a woman's straight unwaisted dress.
■ historical a long, loose-fitting undergarment.
4 archaic an ingenious or devious device or stratagem: *the thousand shifts and devices of which Hannibal was a master.*
– PHRASES **make shift** do what one wants to do in spite of not having ideal conditions. **shift for oneself** manage as best one can without help. **shift one's ground** say or write something that contradicts something one has previously written or said. **shifting sands** something that is constantly changing, especially unpredictably: *whether something is accepted depends upon* **the shifting sands of** *taste.*
– DERIVATIVES **shiftable** adjective.
– ORIGIN Old English *sciftan* 'arrange, divide, apportion', of Germanic origin; related to German *schichten* 'to layer, stratify'. A common Middle English sense 'change, replace' gave rise to the noun sense 3 (via the notion of changing one's clothes) and sense 2 (via the concept of relays of workers).

shifter ▶ noun [usu. in combination] a person or thing that shifts something: *each morning the rock-shifters travel by donkey cart to start work.*
■ N. Amer. a gearbox of a motor vehicle or a set of gear levers on a bicycle: *a new, improved five-speed shifter.*

shifting cultivation (also **shifting agriculture**) ▶ noun [mass noun] a form of agriculture, used especially in tropical Africa, in which an area of ground is cleared of vegetation and cultivated for a few years and then abandoned for a new area until its fertility has been naturally restored.

shiftless ▶ adjective (of a person or action) characterized by laziness, indolence, and a lack of ambition: *a shiftless lot of good-for-nothings.*
– DERIVATIVES **shiftlessly** adverb, **shiftlessness** noun.

shift lever ▶ noun chiefly N. Amer. another term for **GEAR LEVER**.

shift register ▶ noun Computing a register that is designed to allow the bits of its contents to be moved to left or right.

shift work ▶ noun [mass noun] work comprising recurring periods in which different groups of workers do the same jobs in relay.

shifty ▶ adjective (**shiftier**, **shiftiest**) informal **1** (of a person or their manner) appearing deceitful or evasive: *he had a shifty look about him.*
2 constantly changing; shifting: *it was a close race in a shifty wind on smooth water.*
– DERIVATIVES **shiftily** adverb, **shiftiness** noun.

shigella /ʃɪˈgɛlə/ ▶ noun a bacterium that is an intestinal pathogen of humans and other primates, some kinds of which cause dysentery.
● Genus *Shigella*; Gram-negative rods.
– ORIGIN modern Latin, from the name of Kiyoshi *Shiga* (1870–1957), Japanese bacteriologist, + the diminutive suffix *-ella*.

shih-tzu /ʃiːˈtsuː/ ▶ noun a dog of a breed with long silky erect hair and short legs.
– ORIGIN 1920s: from Chinese *shizi* 'lion'.

shiitake /ʃɪˈtɑːkeɪ, ʃiː-/ (also **shitake**, **shiitake mushroom**) ▶ noun an edible mushroom which grows on fallen timber, cultivated in Japan and China.
● *Lentinus edodes*, family Pleurotaceae, class Hymenomycetes.
– ORIGIN late 19th cent.: from Japanese, from *shii*, denoting a kind of oak, + *take* 'mushroom'.

Shiite /ˈʃiːʌɪt/ (also **Shi'ite**) ▶ noun an adherent of the Shia branch of Islam.
▶ adjective of or relating to Shia.
– DERIVATIVES **Shiism** /ˈʃiːɪz(ə)m/ (also **Shi'ism**) noun.

Shijiazhuang /ˌʃiːdʒɪəˈʒwaŋ/ a city in NE central China, capital of Hebei province; pop. 1,320,000 (1990).

shikar /ʃɪˈkɑː/ ▶ noun [mass noun] Indian hunting as a sport.
– ORIGIN from Urdu and Persian *šikār*.

shikara /ʃɪˈkɑːrə/ ▶ noun Indian **1** (in Kashmir) a houseboat.
■ variant spelling of **SHIKARI** (in sense 2).
2 a spire on a Hindu temple.
– ORIGIN via Kashmiri from Persian *šikārī* 'of hunting'.

shikari /ʃɪˈkɑːriː/ ▶ noun (pl. **shikaris**) Indian **1** a hunter.
■ a guide on hunting expeditions.
2 (also **shikara**) (in Kashmir) a light, flat-bottomed boat.
– ORIGIN via Urdu from Persian *šikārī* 'of hunting'.

shikker ▶ adjective & noun variant spelling of **SHICKER**.

Shikoku /ʃɪˈkəʊkuː/ the smallest of the four main islands of Japan, constituting an administrative region; pop. 4,195,000 (1990); capital, Matsuyama. It is divided from Kyushu to the west and southern Honshu to the north by the Inland Sea.

shikra /ˈʃɪkrə/ ▶ noun a small stocky sparrowhawk found in Africa and Central and South Asia.
● Genus *Accipiter*, family Accipitridae: two species, in particular the widespread *A. badius*.
– ORIGIN mid 19th cent.: from Persian and Urdu *šikara*.

shiksa /ˈʃɪksə/ ▶ noun often derogatory (used especially by Jews) a gentile girl or woman.
– ORIGIN late 19th cent.: from Yiddish *shikse*, from Hebrew *šiqṣāh* (from *šeqeṣ* 'detested thing' + the feminine suffix *-āh*).

shill N. Amer. informal ▶ noun an accomplice of a hawker, gambler, or swindler who acts as an enthusiastic customer to entice or encourage others.
▶ verb [no obj.] act or work as such a person.
– ORIGIN early 20th cent.: probably from earlier *shillaber*, of unknown origin.

shillelagh /ʃɪˈleɪlə, -li/ ▶ noun a thick stick of blackthorn or oak used in Ireland, typically as a weapon.
– ORIGIN late 18th cent.: from the name of the town *Shillelagh*, in Co. Wicklow, Ireland.

shilling ▶ noun **1** a former British coin and monetary unit equal to one twentieth of a pound or twelve pence.
2 the basic monetary unit in Kenya, Tanzania, and Uganda, equal to 100 cents.
– PHRASES **not the full shilling** Brit. informal not intelligent or quick thinking. **take the King's** (or **Queen's**) **shilling** Brit. enlist as a soldier. [ORIGIN: with reference to the former practice of paying a shilling to a soldier who enlisted.]
– ORIGIN Old English *scilling*, of Germanic origin; related to Dutch *schelling* and German *Schilling*.

Shillong /ʃɪˈlɒŋ/ a city in the far north-east of India, capital of the state of Meghalaya; pop. 130,690 (1991).

Shilluk /ʃɪˈluːk/ ▶ noun (pl. same or **Shilluks**) **1** a member of a Sudanese people living mainly on the west bank of the Nile.
2 [mass noun] the Nilotic language of this people.
▶ adjective of or relating to this people or their language.
– ORIGIN the name in Shilluk.

shilly-shally ▶ verb (**-ies**, **-ied**) [no obj.] fail to act resolutely or decisively: *the government shilly-shallied about the matter.*
▶ noun [mass noun] indecisive behaviour.
– DERIVATIVES **shilly-shallyer** (also **-shallier**) noun.
– ORIGIN mid 18th cent.: originally as *shill I, shall I*, reduplication of *shall I?*

Shilton, Peter (b.1949), English footballer. He played

S

in goal for a number of clubs, including Nottingham Forest, and made a record 1,000th league appearance in 1996. For England he won a record 125 caps (1970–90).

shim ▶ noun a washer or thin strip of material used to align parts, make them fit, or reduce wear.
▶ verb (**shimmed**, **shimming**) [with obj.] wedge (something) or fill up (a space) with a shim.
– ORIGIN early 18th cent.: of unknown origin.

shimiyana /ˌʃɪmɪˈjɑːnə/ ▶ noun [mass noun] S. African a home-brewed liquor of sugar or treacle and water, fermented in the sun.
– ORIGIN from Zulu *isishimeyana*.

shimmer ▶ verb [no obj.] shine with a soft tremulous light: *the sea shimmered in the sunlight.*
▶ noun [in sing.] a light with such qualities: *a pale shimmer of moonlight.*
– DERIVATIVES **shimmeringly** adverb, **shimmery** adjective.
– ORIGIN late Old English *scymrian*, of Germanic origin; related to German *schimmern*, also to **SHINE**. The noun dates from the early 19th cent.

shimmy ▶ noun (pl. **-ies**) **1** a kind of ragtime dance in which the whole body shakes or sways.
■ [mass noun] shaking, especially abnormal vibration of the wheels of a motor vehicle: *steering stabilizers reduce shimmy even from oversized tyres.*
2 archaic informal term for **CHEMISE**.
▶ verb (**-ies**, **-ied**) [no obj.] dance the shimmy.
■ shake or vibrate abnormally: *he braked hard and felt the car shimmy dangerously.* ■ move with a graceful swaying motion: *her hair swung in waves as she shimmied down the catwalk.* ■ [with adverbial of direction] move swiftly and effortlessly: *he shimmied right to the top of one of the chimneys.*
– ORIGIN early 20th cent.: of unknown origin.

shin ▶ noun the front of the leg below the knee.
■ a cut of beef from the lower part of a cow's leg.
▶ verb (**shinned**, **shinning**) [no obj.] (**shin up/down**) climb quickly up or down by gripping with one's arms and legs: *he shinned up a tree.*
– ORIGIN Old English *scinu*, probably from a Germanic base meaning 'narrow or thin piece'; related to German *Schiene* 'thin plate' and Dutch *scheen*. The verb was originally in nautical use (early 19th cent.).

Shin Bet /ʃɪn ˈbɛt/ (also **Shin Beth**) the principal security service of Israel, concerned primarily with counter-espionage.
– ORIGIN modern Hebrew, the initial letters of the first two words of *šērûṯ biṭṭāḥōn kĕlālī* '(general) security service'.

shin bone ▶ noun the tibia.

shindig ▶ noun informal a large, lively party, especially one celebrating something.
■ a noisy disturbance or quarrel.
– ORIGIN mid 19th cent.: probably from the nouns **SHIN** and **DIG**, influenced later by **SHINDY**.

shindy ▶ noun (pl. **-ies**) informal a noisy disturbance or quarrel: *there were plenty of gulls **kicking up a shindy**.*
■ a large, lively party.
– ORIGIN early 19th cent.: perhaps an alteration of **SHINTY**.

shine ▶ verb (past and past participle **shone** or **shined**) **1** [no obj.] (of the sun or another source of light) give out a bright light: *the sun shone through the window.*
■ glow or be bright with reflected light: *I could see his eyes shining in the light of the fire.* ■ [with obj. and adverbial of direction] direct (a torch or other light) somewhere in order to see something in the dark: *he shone the torch around the room before entering.* ■ (of something with a smooth surface) reflect light because clean or polished: *my shoes were polished until they shone like glass.* ■ (of a person's eyes) be bright with the expression of a particular emotion: *his eyes **shone with** excitement.* ■ [often as adj. **shining**] figurative be brilliant or excellent at something: *he has set a **shining example** with his model behaviour* | *a boy who **shone at** nothing.* ■ (**shine through**) figurative (of a quality or skill) be clearly evident: *at Murrayfield his talent shone through.*
2 (past and past participle **shined**) [with obj.] make (an object made of leather, metal, or wood) bright by rubbing it; polish: *his shoes were shined to perfection.*
▶ noun [in sing.] a quality of brightness, especially through reflecting light: *a shine of saliva on his chin.*
■ a high polish or sheen; a lustre: *use boot polish to try and get a shine* | *my hair has lost its shine.* ■ an act of rubbing something to give it a shiny surface: *Archie's shoes got a quick shine from a boy with a buffing cloth.*
– PHRASES **take the shine off** spoil the brilliance or excitement of: *these concerns are taking the shine off Britain's economic recovery.* **take a shine to** informal develop a liking for.
– ORIGIN Old English *scīnan*, of Germanic origin; related to Dutch *schijnen* and German *scheinen*.
– DERIVATIVES **shiningly** adverb.

shiner ▶ noun **1** a thing that shines or reflects light: *moonlight blanked the weakest shiners, but the powerful stars were gleaming.*
■ [in combination] a person or thing that polishes something: *shoeshiners.*
2 informal a black eye.
3 a small silvery North American freshwater fish which typically has colourful markings.
• *Notropis* and other genera, family Cyprinidae: several species.

shingle[1] ▶ noun [mass noun] a mass of small rounded pebbles, especially on a seashore.
– DERIVATIVES **shingly** adjective.
– ORIGIN late Middle English: of unknown origin.

shingle[2] ▶ noun **1** a rectangular wooden tile used on walls or roofs.
2 dated a woman's short haircut in which the hair tapers from the back of the head to the nape of the neck. [ORIGIN: so named because of the layering.]
3 N. Amer. a small signboard, especially one found outside a doctor's or lawyer's office.
▶ verb [with obj.] **1** roof or clad with shingles: [as adj. **shingled**] *a tower surmounted by a shingled spire.*
2 dated cut (a woman's hair) in a shingle.
– PHRASES **hang out one's shingle** N. Amer. begin to practise a profession.
– ORIGIN Middle English (as a noun): apparently from Latin *scindula*, earlier *scandula* 'a split piece of wood'.

shingleback (also **shingleback lizard**) ▶ noun a slow-moving heavily built lizard with scales resembling those of pine cones, occurring in arid regions of Australia.
• *Trachydosaurus rugosus*, family Scincidae.

shingles ▶ plural noun [treated as sing.] Medicine an acute painful inflammation of the nerve ganglia, with a skin eruption often forming a girdle around the middle of the body. It is caused by the same virus as chickenpox. Also called **HERPES ZOSTER**.
– ORIGIN late Middle English: representing medieval Latin *cingulus*, variant of Latin *cingulum* 'girdle', from *cingere* 'gird'.

shin guard ▶ noun another term for **SHIN PAD**.

Shining Path a Peruvian Maoist revolutionary movement and terrorist organization, founded in 1970 and led by Abimael Guzmán (b.1934) until his capture and imprisonment in 1992. At first the movement operated in rural areas, but in the 1980s it began to launch terrorist attacks in Peruvian towns and cities.
– ORIGIN translating Spanish **SENDERO LUMINOSO**.

Shinkansen /ˈʃiːnkɑːnˌsɛn/ ▶ noun (pl. same) (in Japan) a railway system carrying high-speed passenger trains.
■ a train operating on such a system.
– ORIGIN Japanese, from *shin* 'new' + *kansen* 'main line'.

shinny[1] ▶ verb (**-ies**, **-ied**) North American term for **SHIN**: *he loved to shinny up that tree.*
– ORIGIN late 19th cent.: from the noun **SHIN** + **-Y**[2].

shinny[2] (also **shinny hockey**) ▶ noun [mass noun] N. Amer. an informal form of ice hockey played especially by children, on the street or on ice, often with a ball or other object in place of a puck.
– ORIGIN variant of **SHINTY**.

Shinola /ʃʌɪˈnəʊlə/ ▶ noun [mass noun] US trademark a brand of boot polish.
■ informal used as a euphemism for 'shit': *there'll be the same old Shinola on television.*
– PHRASES **neither shit nor Shinola** vulgar slang neither one thing nor the other. **not know shit from Shinola** vulgar slang used to indicate that someone is ignorant or innocent.
– ORIGIN early 20th cent.: from **SHINE** + *-ola* (suffix chiefly in US usage).

shin pad ▶ noun a pad worn to protect the shins when playing soccer, hockey, and other sports.

shinplaster ▶ noun historical, informal **1** US & Austral. a banknote or promissory note regarded as having little or no value.
2 Canadian a twenty-five cent bill.
– ORIGIN so named because of the resemblance to a square piece of paper soaked in vinegar and used to bandage the shin.

shin splints ▶ plural noun [treated as sing. or pl.] acute pain in the shin and lower leg caused by prolonged running, typically on hard surfaces.

Shinto /ˈʃɪntəʊ/ ▶ noun [mass noun] a Japanese religion dating from the early 8th century and incorporating the worship of ancestors and nature spirits and a belief in sacred power (**kami**) in both animate and inanimate things. It was the state religion of Japan until 1945. See also **AMATERASU**.
– DERIVATIVES **Shintoism** noun, **Shintoist** noun.
– ORIGIN Japanese, from Chinese *shen dao* 'way of the gods'.

shinty ▶ noun (pl. **-ies**) [mass noun] a Scottish twelve-a-side game resembling hockey, played with curved sticks and taller goalposts and derived from the Irish game of hurling.
– ORIGIN mid 18th cent. (earlier as *shinny*): apparently from the cry *shin ye, shin you, shin t' ye*, used in the game, of unknown origin; compare with **SHINNY**[2].

shiny ▶ adjective (**shinier**, **shiniest**) (of a smooth surface) reflecting light, typically because very clean or polished: *shiny hair* | *shiny black shoes.*
– DERIVATIVES **shinily** adverb, **shininess** noun.

ship ▶ noun a large boat for transporting people or goods by sea.
■ a sailing vessel with a bowsprit and three or more square-rigged masts. ■ informal any boat, especially a racing boat. ■ a spaceship. ■ N. Amer. an aircraft.
▶ verb (**shipped**, **shipping**) **1** [with obj. and adverbial of direction] (often **be shipped**) transport (goods or people) on a ship: *the wounded soldiers were shipped home.*
■ transport by some other means: *he was captured and **shipped off** to a labour camp.* ■ [with obj.] Electronics make (a product) available for purchase. ■ [no obj.] dated embark on a ship: *people wishing to get from London to New York ship at Liverpool.* ■ (of a sailor) take service on a ship: *Jack, you shipped with the Admiral once, didn't you?*
2 [with obj.] (of a boat) take in (water) over the side.
3 [with obj.] take (oars) from the rowlocks and lay them inside a boat.
■ fix (something such as a rudder or mast) in its place on a ship.
– PHRASES **a sinking ship** used in various phrases to describe an organization or endeavour that is failing, usually in the context of criticizing someone for leaving it: *they have fled like rats from a sinking ship.* **ship a sea** Brit. (of a boat) be flooded by a wave. **take ship** set off on a voyage by ship; embark: *they were due to take ship for Rhodes.* **when someone's ship comes in** (or **home**) when someone's fortune is made.
– DERIVATIVES **shipless** adjective, **shippable** adjective.
– ORIGIN Old English *scip* (noun), late Old English *scipian* (verb), of Germanic origin; related to Dutch *schip* and German *Schiff*.

-ship ▶ suffix forming nouns: **1** denoting a quality or condition: *companionship* | *friendship.*
2 denoting status, office, or honour: *ambassadorship* | *citizenship.*
■ denoting a tenure of office: *chairmanship.*
3 denoting a skill in a certain capacity: *workmanship.*
4 denoting the collective individuals of a group: *membership.*
– ORIGIN Old English *-scipe*, *scype*, of Germanic origin.

shipboard ▶ noun [as modifier] used or occurring on board a ship: *shipboard life.*
– PHRASES **on shipboard** on board a ship.

ship-breaker ▶ noun a contractor who breaks up old ships for scrap.

shipbroker ▶ noun a broker who specializes in arranging charters, cargo space, and passenger bookings on ships.

shipbuilder ▶ noun a person or company whose job or business is the design and construction of ships.
– DERIVATIVES **shipbuilding** noun.

ship burial ▶ noun Archaeology a burial in a wooden ship under a mound. The custom was reserved for those who were particularly honoured in Scandinavia and parts of the British Isles in the pagan Anglo-Saxon and Viking periods (6th–11th centuries AD).

ship canal ▶ noun a canal wide and deep enough for ships to travel along it.

ship chandler ▶ noun see **CHANDLER**.

shiplap ▶ verb [with obj.] fit (boards) together by

halving so that each overlaps the one below: [as adj. **shiplapped**] *shiplapped pine used as facing for the first floor.*

▶ **noun** [mass noun] boards which have been fitted together in this way, typically used for cladding.
■ [count noun] [usu. as modifier] a joint between boards made by halving: *a shiplap joint.*

Shipley, Jenny (b.1952), New Zealand National Party stateswoman, Prime Minister 1997–9; full name *Jennifer Mary Shipley.*

shipload ▶ **noun** as much cargo or as many people as a ship can carry.

shipmaster ▶ **noun** a ship's captain.

shipmate ▶ **noun** a fellow member of a ship's crew.

shipment ▶ **noun** [mass noun] the action of shipping goods: *logs waiting for shipment* | [count noun] *shipments begin this month.*
■ [count noun] a quantity of goods shipped; a consignment.

ship money ▶ **noun** [mass noun] historical a tax raised in England in medieval times to provide ships for the navy.

ship of the desert ▶ **noun** poetic/literary a camel.

ship of the line ▶ **noun** historical a sailing warship of the largest size, used in the line of battle.

shipowner ▶ **noun** a person owning a ship or shares in a ship.

shippen /ˈʃɪp(ə)n/ ▶ **noun** variant spelling of **SHIPPON**.

shipper ▶ **noun** a person or company that transports or receives goods by sea, land, or air.
– ORIGIN late Old English *scipere* 'sailor'. Current senses date from the mid 18th cent.

shipping ▶ **noun** [mass noun] ships considered collectively, especially those in a particular area or belonging to a particular country: *the volume of shipping using these ports.*
■ the transport of goods by sea or some other means.

shipping agent ▶ **noun** a licensed agent in a port who transacts a ship's business, such as insurance or documentation, for the owner.

shipping bill ▶ **noun** (in the UK) a form used by Customs and Excise before goods can be exported from the country or removed from a bonded warehouse.

shipping master ▶ **noun** Brit. an official presiding over the signing-on and discharging of seamen.

shipping office ▶ **noun** the office of a shipping agent or shipping master.

shippon /ˈʃɪp(ə)n/ (also **shippen**) ▶ **noun** dialect a cattle shed.
– ORIGIN Old English *scypen*, of Germanic origin.

ship rat ▶ **noun** another term for **BLACK RAT**.

ship-rigged ▶ **adjective** (of a sailing ship) square-rigged.

ship's biscuit ▶ **noun** [mass noun] a very hard, coarse kind of biscuit formerly taken on sea voyages.

ship's boat ▶ **noun** a small boat carried on board a ship.

ship's company ▶ **noun** the crew of a ship.

ship's corporal ▶ **noun** see **CORPORAL**[1] (sense 2).

shipshape ▶ **adjective** in good order; trim and neat: *he checked that everything was shipshape and Bristol fashion.*

ship's husband ▶ **noun** an agent who is responsible for providing maintenance and supplies for a ship in port.
– DERIVATIVES **ship's husbandry** noun.

ship-to-shore ▶ **adjective** from a ship to land: *ship-to-shore phone calls.*
▶ **noun** a radio-telephone connecting a ship to land, or connecting a train or other vehicle to a control centre.

shipway ▶ **noun** a slope on which a ship is built and down which it slides to be launched.

shipworm ▶ **noun** another term for **TEREDO**.

shipwreck ▶ **noun** the destruction of a ship at sea by sinking or breaking up, for example in a storm or after striking a rock.
■ a ship so destroyed: *the detritus of a forgotten shipwreck in an Arctic sea.*
▶ **verb** (**be shipwrecked**) (of a person or ship) suffer a shipwreck.

shipwright ▶ **noun** a shipbuilder.

shipyard ▶ **noun** an enclosed area of land where ships are built and repaired.

shiralee /ˈʃɪrəli:/ ▶ **noun** Austral. informal a bundle of personal belongings or blankets carried by a tramp.
– ORIGIN late 19th cent.: of unknown origin.

Shiraz[1] /ˈʃɪəraz, ʃɪˈraz/ a city in SW central Iran; pop. 965,000 (1991). The city is noted for the school of miniature painting based there between the 14th and 16th centuries, and for the manufacture of carpets.

Shiraz[2] /ˈʃɪəraz, ʃɪˈraz/ ▶ **noun** [mass noun] a variety of black wine grape.
■ a red wine made from this grape.
– ORIGIN from **SHIRAZ**[1], apparently an alteration of French *syrah*, influenced by the belief that the vine was brought from Iran by the Crusades.

shire /ˈʃaɪə/ ▶ **noun 1** Brit. a county, especially in England.
■ (**the Shires**) used in reference to parts of England regarded as strongholds of traditional rural culture, especially the rural Midlands. ■ historical an administrative district in medieval times ruled jointly by an alderman and a sheriff.
2 Austral. a rural area with its own elected council.
– ORIGIN Old English *scīr* 'care, official charge, county', of Germanic origin.

-shire /ʃɪə, ʃə/ ▶ **combining form** forming the names of counties: *Oxfordshire* | *South Yorkshire.*

shire county ▶ **noun** (in the UK) a non-metropolitan county (in existence since 1974).

shire horse ▶ **noun** a heavy powerful horse of a draught breed, originally from the English Midlands.

shirk ▶ **verb** [with obj.] avoid or neglect (a duty or responsibility): *I do not shirk any responsibility in this matter.*
▶ **noun** archaic a person who shirks.
– DERIVATIVES **shirker** noun.
– ORIGIN mid 17th cent. (in the sense 'practise fraud or trickery'): from obsolete *shirk* 'sponger', perhaps from German *Schurke* 'scoundrel'.

shirr /ʃə:/ ▶ **verb** [with obj.] **1** gather (an area of fabric or part of a garment) by means of drawn or elasticized threads in parallel rows: [as adj. **shirred**] *a swimsuit with a shirred front* | [as noun **shirring**] *shirring is flattering to all figure types* | [as noun modifier] *shirring elastic.*
2 US bake (an egg without its shell).
– ORIGIN mid 19th cent.: of unknown origin.

shirt ▶ **noun** a garment for the upper body made of cotton or a similar fabric, with a collar and sleeves, and with buttons down the front.
■ [usu. with modifier] a similar garment of stretchable material without full fastenings, worn as casual wear or for sports: *a rugby shirt.* ■ [with modifier] Brit. used to refer to membership of a particular sports team: *Smith increased his chances of a Great Britain shirt with a penalty shot save.*
– PHRASES **keep your shirt on** informal don't lose your temper; stay calm. **lose one's shirt** informal lose all one's possessions. **put one's shirt on** Brit. informal bet all one has on; be sure of: *they'll confirm it's him, I'll put my shirt on it.* **the shirt off one's back** informal one's last remaining possessions.
– DERIVATIVES **shirted** adjective [often in combination] *white-shirted bouncers,* **shirtless** adjective.
– ORIGIN Old English *scyrte*, of Germanic origin; related to Old Norse *skyrta* (compare with **SKIRT**), Dutch *schort*, German *Schürze* 'apron', also to **SHORT**; probably from a base meaning 'short garment'.

shirt dress ▶ **noun** a dress with a collar and button fastening in the style of a shirt, typically cut without a seam at the waist.

shirt front ▶ **noun** the breast of a shirt, in particular that of a stiffened evening shirt.

shirting ▶ **noun** [mass noun] a material for making shirts, especially a fine cotton in plain colours or incorporating a traditional woven stripe.

shirtlifter ▶ **noun** Brit. informal, derogatory a homosexual.

shirtsleeve ▶ **noun** (usu. **shirtsleeves**) the sleeve of a shirt: *he rolled up his shirtsleeves.*
– PHRASES **in (one's) shirtsleeves** wearing a shirt with nothing over it.
– DERIVATIVES **shirtsleeved** adjective.

shirt tail ▶ **noun** the lower, typically curved, part of a shirt which comes below the waist.

shirtwaist ▶ **noun** N. Amer. a woman's blouse resembling a shirt.
■ (also **shirtwaist dress**) another term for **SHIRTWAISTER**.

shirtwaister ▶ **noun** a woman's dress with a seam at the waist, its bodice incorporating a collar and button fastening in the style of a shirt.

shirty ▶ **adjective** (**shirtier**, **shirtiest**) Brit. informal ill-tempered; querulous: *she got quite shirty.*
– DERIVATIVES **shirtily** adverb, **shirtiness** noun.

shisham /ˈʃɪʃəm/ (also **shisham tree**) ▶ **noun** an Indian tree of the pea family, which produces useful timber.
● *Dalbergia sissoo*, family Leguminosae.
– ORIGIN mid 19th cent.: from Persian and Urdu *šīšam.*

shish kebab /ˌʃɪʃ kɪˈbab/ ▶ **noun** a dish of pieces of marinated meat and vegetables cooked and served on skewers.
– ORIGIN from Turkish *şiş kebap*, from *şiş* 'skewer' + *kebap* 'roast meat'.

shit vulgar slang ▶ **verb** (**shitting**; past and past participle **shitted** or **shit** or **shat**) [no obj.] expel faeces from the body.
■ (**shit oneself**) soil one's clothes as a result of expelling faeces accidentally. ■ (**shit oneself**) figurative be very frightened.
▶ **noun** [mass noun] faeces.
■ [in sing.] an act of defecating. ■ [count noun] a contemptible or worthless person. ■ something worthless; rubbish; nonsense. ■ unpleasant experiences or treatment. ■ personal belongings; stuff. ■ an intoxicating drug, especially cannabis.
▶ **exclamation** an exclamation of disgust, anger, or annoyance.
– PHRASES **be shitting bricks** be extremely nervous or frightened. **get one's shit together** organize oneself so as to be able to deal with or achieve something. **in the shit** in trouble; in a difficult situation. **no shit** used as a way of confirming or seeking confirmation of the truth of a statement. **not give a shit** not care at all. **not know shit** not know anything. **shit for brains** chiefly N. Amer. a stupid person. **be up shit creek** (also **be up shit creek without a paddle**) be in an awkward predicament. **when the shit hits the fan** when the disastrous consequences of something become public.
– ORIGIN Old English *scitte* 'diarrhoea', of Germanic origin; related to Dutch *schijten*, German *scheissen* (verb). The term was originally neutral and used without vulgar connotation.

shitake ▶ **noun** variant spelling of **SHIITAKE**.

shitbag ▶ **noun** vulgar slang a contemptible or worthless person.

shite ▶ **noun** & **exclamation** vulgar slang another term for **SHIT**.

shit-eating ▶ **adjective** vulgar slang, chiefly US smug; self-satisfied.

shitepoke ▶ **noun** N. Amer. informal any of a number of birds of the heron family.
● Several species in the family Ardeidae, in particular the green-backed *Butorides striatus.*
– ORIGIN late 18th cent.: from **SHITE** (because of the bird's habit of defecating when disturbed) + the noun **POKE**[1].

shitface ▶ **noun** vulgar slang an obnoxious person.

shit-faced ▶ **adjective** [predic.] vulgar slang drunk or under the influence of drugs.

shithole ▶ **noun** vulgar slang an extremely dirty, shabby, or otherwise unpleasant place.

shit-hot ▶ **adjective** vulgar slang excellent, typically with regard to a particular skill or sphere.

shithouse ▶ **noun** vulgar slang a toilet.
■ figurative an extremely unpleasant place.
– PHRASES **be built like a brick shithouse** (of a person) having a very solid physique.

shitkicker ▶ **noun** N. Amer. vulgar slang **1** an unsophisticated or oafish person, especially one from a rural area.
2 (**shitkickers**) substantially made boots with thick soles and typically with reinforced toes.

shitless ▶ **adjective** (in phrase **be scared** (or **bored**) **shitless**) vulgar slang be extremely frightened (or bored).

shitlist ▶ **noun** N. Amer. vulgar slang a list of those who one dislikes or plans to harm.

shit-scared ▶ **adjective** vulgar slang terrified.

shit stirrer ▶ noun vulgar slang a person who takes pleasure in causing trouble or discord.
– DERIVATIVES **shit stirring** noun.

shitty ▶ adjective (**shittier, shittiest**) vulgar slang **1** (of a person or action) contemptible; worthless. ■(of an experience or situation) unpleasant; awful. **2** covered with excrement.

shitwork ▶ noun [mass noun] vulgar slang work considered to be menial or routine.

shiur /ˈʃiːʊə/ ▶ noun (pl. **shiurim** /-rɪm/) Judaism a Talmudic study session, usually led by a rabbi.
– ORIGIN from Hebrew šīˈūr 'measure, portion'.

shiv /ʃɪv/ ▶ noun N. Amer. informal a knife or razor used as a weapon.
– ORIGIN probably from Romany *chiv* 'blade'.

Shiva /ˈʃiːvə, ˈʃɪvə/ (also **Siva**) (in Indian religion) a god associated with the powers of reproduction and dissolution.

> Shiva is regarded by some as the supreme being and by others as forming a triad with Brahma and Vishnu. He is worshipped in many aspects: as destroyer, ascetic, lord of the cosmic dance, and lord of beasts, and through the symbolic lingam. His wife is Parvati.

– ORIGIN from Sanskrit *Śiva*, literally 'the auspicious one'.

shiva /ˈʃɪvə/ (also **shivah**) ▶ noun [mass noun] Judaism a period of seven days' formal mourning for the dead, beginning immediately after the funeral.
– ORIGIN from Hebrew *šiḇˈāh* 'seven'.

Shivaji /ʃɪˈvɑːdʒi/ (also **Sivaji**) (1627–80), Indian raja of the Marathas 1674–80. He raised a successful Hindu revolt against Muslim rule in 1659 and expanded Maratha territory. After being crowned raja he blocked Mogul expansionism by forming an alliance with the sultans in the south.

shivaree /ˌʃɪvəˈriː/ ▶ noun chiefly US variant spelling of **CHARIVARI**.

shive /ʃʌɪv/ ▶ noun a broad bung hammered into a hole in the top of a cask when the cask has been filled.
– ORIGIN Middle English: related to **SHEAVE**². The original sense was 'slice (of bread)', later 'piece of split wood'; the current sense dates from the mid 19th cent.

shiver¹ ▶ verb [no obj.] (of a person or animal) shake slightly and uncontrollably as a result of being cold, frightened, or excited: *they shivered in the damp foggy cold.*
▶ noun a momentary trembling movement: *she gave a little shiver as the wind flicked at her bare arms* | *the way he looked at her sent shivers down her spine.*
■(**the shivers**) a spell or an attack of trembling, typically as a result of fear or horror: *a look that gave him the shivers.*
– DERIVATIVES **shiverer** noun, **shiveringly** adverb, **shivery** adjective.
– ORIGIN Middle English *chivere*, perhaps an alteration of dialect *chavele* 'to chatter', from Old English *ceafl* 'jaw'.

shiver² ▶ noun (usu. **shivers**) each of the small fragments into which something such as glass is shattered when broken: a splinter.
▶ verb [no obj.] rare break into such splinters or fragments: *the world seemed to shiver into a million splinters of prismatic colour.*
– PHRASES **shiver my timbers** a mock oath attributed to sailors.
– ORIGIN Middle English: from a Germanic base meaning 'to split'; related to German *Schiefer* 'slate'.

shivoo /ʃɪˈvuː/ ▶ noun Austral./NZ informal, dated a party or celebration; a revel.
– ORIGIN late 19th cent.: from obsolete *shiveau*, of unknown origin.

Shiv Sena /ʃɪv ˈseɪnə/ ▶ noun a Hindu nationalist organization centred in Maharashtra.
– ORIGIN from Sanskrit *śiva* 'auspicious' + *sena* 'army'.

Shizuoka /ˌʃɪzuˈəʊkə/ a port on the south coast of the island of Honshu in Japan; pop. 472,200 (1990).

Shkodër /ˈʃkɔːdə/ a city in NW Albania, near the border with Montenegro; pop. 81,900 (1990). Italian name **SCUTARI**.

shlub /ʃlʌb/ ▶ noun variant spelling of **SCHLUB**.

shm ▶ abbreviation for simple harmonic motion.

shmatte /ˈʃmatə/ ▶ noun variant spelling of **SCHMATTE**.

shmear /ʃmiːə/ ▶ noun & verb variant spelling of **SCHMEAR**.

shmeer /ʃmiːə/ ▶ noun & verb variant spelling of **SCHMEAR**.

shmo ▶ noun (pl. **-oes**) variant spelling of **SCHMO**.

sho ▶ adverb non-standard spelling of **SURE**, representing its pronunciation in the southern US: *ah sho is glad tuh have yuh.*

Shoah /ˈʃəʊə/ ▶ noun (**the Shoah**) another term for the Holocaust (see **HOLOCAUST** sense 1).
– ORIGIN modern Hebrew, literally 'catastrophe'.

shoal¹ ▶ noun a large number of fish swimming together: *a shoal of bream.* Compare with **SCHOOL**².
■informal, chiefly Brit. a large number of people: *Liverpool are again without a shoal of injured defenders.*
▶ verb [no obj.] (of fish) form shoals.
– ORIGIN late 16th cent.: probably from Middle Dutch *schōle* 'troop'. Compare with **SCHOOL**².

shoal² ▶ noun an area of shallow water.
■a submerged sandbank visible at low water. ■(usu. **shoals**) figurative a hidden danger or difficulty: *he alone could safely guide them through Hollywood's treacherous shoals.*
▶ verb [no obj.] (of water) become shallower.
▶ adjective dialect or N. Amer. (of water) shallow.
– DERIVATIVES **shoaly** adjective.
– ORIGIN Old English *sceald* (adjective), of Germanic origin; related to **SHALLOW**.

shoat /ʃəʊt/ (also **shote**) ▶ noun US a young pig, especially one which is newly weaned.
– ORIGIN late Middle English: of unknown origin; compare with West Flemish *schote*.

shochet /ˈʃɒkɛt, -x-/ ▶ noun (pl. **shochetim** /-ɪm/) a person officially certified as competent to kill cattle and poultry in the manner prescribed by Jewish law.
– ORIGIN late 19th cent.: from Hebrew *šōḥēt* 'slaughtering'.

shochu /ˈʃəʊtʃuː/ ▶ noun [mass noun] a rough Japanese spirit distilled from any of various ingredients, including sake dregs.
– ORIGIN from Japanese *shōchū*.

shock¹ ▶ noun **1** a sudden upsetting or surprising event or experience: *it was a shock to face such hostile attitudes when I arrived.*
■a feeling of disturbed surprise resulting from such an event: *her death gave us all a terrible shock* | [mass noun] *her eyes opened wide in shock.* ■[mass noun] an acute medical condition associated with a fall in blood pressure, caused by such events as loss of blood, severe burns, bacterial infection, allergic reaction, or sudden emotional stress, and marked by cold, pallid skin, irregular breathing, rapid pulse, and dilated pupils: *he died of shock due to massive abdominal haemorrhage.* ■a disturbance causing instability in an economy: *trading imbalances caused by the two oil shocks.* ■ short for **ELECTRIC SHOCK**.
2 a violent shaking movement caused by an impact, explosion, or tremor: *earthquake shocks* | [mass noun] *rackets today don't bend or absorb shock the way wooden rackets do.*
■chiefly N. Amer. short for **SHOCK ABSORBER**.
▶ verb **1** [with obj.] (often **be shocked**) cause (someone) to feel surprised and upset: *she was shocked at the state of his injuries.*
■offend the moral feelings of; outrage: *the revelations shocked the nation.* ■ [no obj.] experience such feelings: *he shocked so easily.* ■(usu. **be shocked**) affect with physiological shock, or with an electric shock.
2 [no obj.] archaic collide violently: *carriage after carriage shocked fiercely against the engine.*
– PHRASES **short, sharp shock** Brit. a brief but harsh custodial sentence handed down to an offender in an attempt to discourage them from committing further offences. ■ a severe measure taken in order to effect quick results.
– DERIVATIVES **shockability** noun, **shockable** adjective.
– ORIGIN mid 16th cent.: from French *choc* (noun), *choquer* (verb), of unknown origin. The original senses were 'throw (troops) into confusion by charging at them' and 'an encounter between charging forces', giving rise to the notion of 'sudden violent blow or impact'.

shock² ▶ noun a group of twelve sheaves of grain placed upright and supporting each other to allow the grain to dry and ripen.
▶ verb [with obj.] arrange (sheaves of grain) in such a group.
– ORIGIN Middle English: perhaps from Middle Dutch, Middle Low German *schok*, of unknown origin.

shock³ ▶ noun an unkempt or thick mass of hair: *a man with a shock of hair.*
– ORIGIN mid 17th cent.: origin uncertain; compare with obsolete *shough*, denoting a breed of lapdog. The word originally denoted a dog with long shaggy hair, and was then used as an adjective meaning 'unkempt, shaggy'. The current sense dates from the early 19th cent.

shock absorber ▶ noun a device for absorbing jolts and vibrations, especially on a vehicle.

shock brigade ▶ noun (in the former USSR) a body of workers who exceeded production quotas and were assigned to an especially urgent or arduous task.

shock cord ▶ noun [mass noun] heavy elasticated cord; bungee cord.

shocker ▶ noun informal **1** something that shocks, especially through being unacceptable or sensational: *the play's penultimate sequence is a shocker.*
■a person who behaves badly or acts in a sensational manner: *I was a shocker when I was younger.*
2 Brit. a shock absorber.

shock-headed ▶ adjective having thick, shaggy, and unkempt hair.

shock-horror ▶ adjective [attrib.] informal causing great public outrage: *a shock-horror TV advertising campaign.*

shocking ▶ adjective causing indignation or disgust; offensive: *shocking behaviour.*
■causing a feeling of surprise and dismay: *she brought shocking news.* ■ Brit. informal very bad: *I've got a shocking cold.*
– DERIVATIVES **shockingly** adverb, **shockingness** noun.

shocking pink ▶ noun [mass noun] a vibrant shade of pink.

shock jock ▶ noun a disc jockey on a talk-radio show who expresses opinions in a deliberately offensive or provocative way.

Shockley, William (Bradford) (1910–89), American physicist. Shockley and his researchers at Bell Laboratories developed the transistor in 1948 and in 1958 he shared with them the Nobel Prize for Physics. He later became a controversial figure because of his views on a supposed connection between race and intelligence.

shockproof ▶ adjective **1** designed to resist damage when dropped or knocked: *a shockproof watch.*
2 not easily shocked: *fifth-form grammar-school boys consider themselves a rather shockproof lot.*

shock stall ▶ noun [mass noun] a marked increase in drag and a loss of lift and control on an aircraft approaching the speed of sound.

shock tactics ▶ plural noun a strategy using sudden violent or extreme action to shock someone into doing something.

shock therapy (also **shock treatment**) ▶ noun [mass noun] treatment of chronic mental conditions by electroconvulsive therapy or by inducing physiological shock.
■figurative sudden and drastic measures taken to solve an intractable problem.

shock troops ▶ plural noun a group of people likened to troops trained specially for carrying out a sudden assault.

shock wave ▶ noun a sharp change of pressure in a narrow region travelling through a medium, especially air, caused by explosion or by a body moving faster than sound: *charting the shock waves of the explosion* | figurative *the oil embargo sent shock waves through the American economy.*

shock worker ▶ noun (in the former USSR) a member of a shock brigade.

shod past and past participle of **SHOE**.

shoddy ▶ adjective (**shoddier, shoddiest**) badly made or done: *we're not paying good money for shoddy goods.*
■figurative lacking moral principle; sordid: *a shoddy misuse of the honours system.*
▶ noun [mass noun] an inferior quality yarn or fabric made from the shredded fibre of waste woollen cloth or clippings.
– DERIVATIVES **shoddily** adverb, **shoddiness** noun.
– ORIGIN mid 19th cent.: of unknown origin.

shoe ▶ noun **1** a covering for the foot, typically made of leather, with a sturdy sole and not reaching above the ankle.

■a horseshoe.
2 something resembling a shoe in shape or use, in particular:
■a drag for a wheel. ■short for **BRAKE SHOE**. ■a socket, especially on a camera, for fitting a flash unit or other accessory. ■a metal rim or ferrule, especially on the runner of a sledge. ■a step for a mast. ■a box from which cards are dealt in casinos at baccarat or some other card games.
▶**verb** (**shoes, shoeing**; past and past participle **shod**) [with obj.] (often **be shod**) fit (a horse) with a shoe or shoes.
■(**be shod**) [with adverbial] (of a person) be wearing shoes of a specified kind: *his large feet were shod in trainers* ■protect (the end of an object such as a pole) with a metal shoe: *the four wooden baulks were each shod with heavy iron heads.* ■fit a tyre to (a wheel).
– PHRASES **be** (or **put oneself**) **in another person's shoes** be (or put oneself) in another person's situation or predicament: *if I'd been in your shoes I'd have walked out on him.* **dead men's shoes** property or a position coveted by a prospective successor but available only on a person's death. **if the shoe fits, wear it** N. Amer. see ***if the cap fits, wear it*** (at **CAP**). **shoe leather** informal used in reference to the wear on shoes through walking: *you can save on shoe leather by giving us your instructions over the telephone.* **wait for the other shoe to drop** N. Amer. informal be prepared for a further or consequential event or complication to occur.
– DERIVATIVES **shoeless** adjective.
– ORIGIN Old English *scōh* (noun), *scōg(e)an* (verb), of Germanic origin; related to Dutch *schoen* and German *Schuh*.

shoebill (also **shoe-billed stork**) ▶**noun** another term for **WHALE-HEADED STORK**.

shoeblack ▶**noun** dated, chiefly Brit. a person who cleans the shoes of passers-by for payment.

shoebox ▶**noun** a box in which a pair of shoes is delivered or sold.
■used in references to very small or uniform rooms or spaces: *a shoebox of a room.*

shoehorn ▶**noun** a curved instrument used for easing one's heel into a shoe.
▶**verb** [with obj. and adverbial] force into an inadequate space: *people were shoehorned into cramped corners.*

shoelace ▶**noun** a cord or leather strip passed through eyelets or hooks on opposite sides of a shoe and pulled tight and fastened.

shoemaker ▶**noun** a person who makes shoes and other footwear as a profession.
– DERIVATIVES **shoemaking** noun.

Shoemaker–Levy 9 /'liːvi/ a comet discovered in March 1993, when it had just broken up as a result of passing very close to Jupiter. In July 1994 more than twenty separate fragments impacted successively on Jupiter, causing large explosions in its atmosphere.
– ORIGIN named after Carolyn (born 1929) and Eugene *Shoemaker* (1928–97), American astronomers, and David *Levy* (born 1948), Canadian astronomer, discoverers of the comet.

shoepack ▶**noun** N. Amer. a commercially manufactured oiled leather boot, typically having a rubber sole.
– ORIGIN mid 18th cent.: from Delaware (Unami) *sippack* 'shoes', from *čipahkpo* 'moccasins', later assimilated to **SHOE** and **PACK**[1].

shoeshine ▶**noun** chiefly N. Amer. an act of polishing someone's shoes, especially for payment: [as modifier] *a shoeshine boy.*
– DERIVATIVES **shoeshiner** noun.

shoestring ▶**noun** **1** informal a small or inadequate budget: *they proved capable of producing high-quality material **on a shoestring*** | [as modifier] *a shoestring budget.*
2 N. Amer. a shoelace.
▶**adjective** [attrib.] N. Amer. (of a save or tackle in sport) near or around the ankles or feet, or just above the ground.

shoestring potatoes ▶**plural noun** N. Amer. potatoes cut into long thin strips and deep-fried.

shoe tree ▶**noun** a shaped block inserted into a shoe when it is not being worn to keep the shoe in shape.

shofar /'ʃəʊfə/ ▶**noun** (pl. **shofars** or **shofroth** /'ʃəʊfrəʊt/) a ram's-horn trumpet used by Jews in religious ceremonies and as an ancient battle signal.
– ORIGIN from Hebrew *šōpār*, (plural) *šōpārōṯ*.

shogun /'ʃəʊɡʊn/ ▶**noun** a hereditary commander-in-chief in feudal Japan. Because of the military power concentrated in his hands and the consequent weakness of the nominal head of state (the mikado or emperor), the shogun was generally the real ruler of the country until feudalism was abolished in 1867.
– DERIVATIVES **shogunate** /-nət/ noun.
– ORIGIN Japanese, from Chinese *jiāng jūn* 'general'.

shoji /'ʃəʊdʒi/ (also **shoji screen**) ▶**noun** (pl. same or **shojis**) (in Japan) a sliding outer or inner door made of a latticed screen covered with white paper.
– ORIGIN from Japanese *shōji*.

Sholapur /'ʃəʊləpʊə/ a city in western India, on the Deccan plateau in the state of Maharashtra; pop. 604,000 (1991).

Shona /'ʃəʊnə/ ▶**noun** (pl. same or **Shonas**) **1** a member of a group of peoples inhabiting parts of southern Africa. The Shona comprise over three quarters of the population of Zimbabwe, and smaller groups live in South Africa, Zambia, and Mozambique. See also **MASHONA**.
2 [mass noun] any of the closely related Bantu languages spoken by these peoples, with over 5 million speakers altogether.
▶**adjective** of or relating to the Shona or their languages.
– ORIGIN a local name.

shone past and past participle of **SHINE**.

shonky Austral./NZ informal ▶**adjective** (**shonkier, shonkiest**) dishonest, unreliable, or illegal, especially in a devious way: *shonky political goings on.*
▶**noun** (also **shonk**) a person engaged in suspect business activities.
– ORIGIN 1970s: perhaps from English dialect *shonk* 'smart'.

shoo ▶**exclamation** a word said to frighten or drive away a person or animal.
▶**verb** (**shoos, shooed**) [with obj. and adverbial of direction] make (a person or animal) go away by waving one's arms at them, saying 'shoo', or otherwise acting in a discouraging manner: *I went to comfort her but she shooed me away.*
– ORIGIN a natural exclamation: first recorded in late Middle English. The verb use dates from the early 17th cent.

shoo-fly pie ▶**noun** N. Amer. a rich tart made of treacle baked in a pastry case with a crumble topping.
– ORIGIN from the US interjection *shoo-fly* (referring to the need to wave flies away from the sweet treacle).

shoo-in ▶**noun** chiefly N. Amer. a person or thing that is certain to succeed, especially someone who is certain to win a competition: *he was **a shoo-in for** re-election.*
– ORIGIN 1930s: from the earlier use of the term denoting the winner of a rigged horse race.

shook[1] past of **SHAKE**. ▶**adjective** [predic.] informal **1** (**shook up**) emotionally or physically disturbed; upset: *she looks pretty shook up from the letter.*
2 (**shook on**) Austral./NZ keen on; enthusiastic about: *those stories you read about where two blokes get shook on the same sheila.*

shook[2] ▶**noun** N. Amer. a set of components ready for assembly into a box or cask.
– ORIGIN late 18th cent.: of unknown origin.

shoot ▶**verb** (past and past participle **shot**) **1** [with obj.] kill or wound (a person or animal) with a bullet or arrow: *he was shot in the leg during an armed robbery* | [with obj. and complement] *troops **shot dead** 29 people.*
■[no obj.] fire a bullet from a gun or discharge an arrow from a bow: *he shot at me twice* | *the troops were ordered to **shoot to kill*** | [with obj.] *they shot a volley of arrows into the village.* ■[no obj., with adverbial] use a firearm with a specified degree of skill: *we shot well against Spain.* ■cause (a gun) to fire. ■[with obj. and adverbial] damage or remove (something) with a bullet or missile: *Guy, shoot their hats off.* ■[no obj.] hunt game with a gun: *we go to Scotland to shoot every autumn.* ■[no obj.] (**shoot over**) shoot game over (an estate or other area of countryside). ■shoot game in or on (an estate, cover, etc.).
2 [no obj., with adverbial of direction] move suddenly and rapidly in a particular direction: *the car shot forward* | *Ward's hand shot out, grabbing his arm.*
■[with obj. and adverbial of direction] cause to move suddenly and rapidly in a particular direction: *he would have fallen if Marc hadn't shot out a hand to stop him* | *Beauchamp shot United into the lead.* ■[with obj.] direct (a glance, question, or remark) at someone: [with two objs] *Luke shot her a quick glance* | [with direct speech] *'I can't believe what I'm hearing,' she **shot back**.* ■[no obj., in imperative] used to invite a comment or question: *'May I just ask you one more question?' 'Shoot'.* ■(of a pain) move with a sharp stabbing sensation: *Claudia felt a shaft of pain shoot through her chest* | figurative *a pang of regret shot through her.* ■[with obj.] (of a boat) sweep swiftly down or under (rapids, a waterfall, or a bridge). ■[with obj.] informal (of a motor vehicle) pass (a traffic light at red). ■Cricket (of a ball) dart along the ground after pitching. ■extend sharply in a particular direction: *a road that seemed to just shoot upwards at a terrifying angle.* ■[with obj.] move (a door bolt) to fasten or unfasten a door.
3 [no obj.] (in football, hockey, basketball, etc.) kick, hit, or throw the ball or puck in an attempt to score a goal: *Williams twice shot wide* | [with obj.] *after school, we'd go straight out in the alley to shoot baskets.*
■[with obj.] informal make (a specified score) for a round of golf: *in the second round he shot a 65.* ■[with obj.] N. Amer. informal play a game of (pool, dice, or cards).
4 [with obj.] film or photograph (a scene, film, etc.): *she has just been commissioned to shoot a video* | [no obj.] *point the camera and just shoot—nothing could be easier.*
5 [no obj.] (of a plant or seed) send out buds or shoots; germinate.
■(of a bud or shoot) appear; sprout.
6 [with obj.] informal inject oneself or another person with (a narcotic drug): *he shot dope into his arm.*
7 [with obj.] plane (the edge of a board) accurately.
▶**noun** **1** a young branch or sucker springing from the main stock of a tree or other plant: *he nipped off the new shoots that grew where the leaves joined the stems.*
2 an occasion when a group of people hunt and shoot game for sport: *a grouse shoot.*
■Brit. land used for shooting game. ■a shooting match or contest: *activities include a weekly rifle shoot.*
3 an occasion when a professional photographer takes photographs or when a film or video is being made: *a photo shoot* | *a fashion shoot.*
4 variant spelling of **CHUTE**[1].
5 a rapid in a stream: *follow the portages that skirt all nine shoots of whitewater.*
▶**exclamation** N. Amer. informal used as a euphemism for 'shit': *shoot, it was a great day to be alive.*
– PHRASES **have shot one's bolt** see **BOLT**[1]. **shoot the breeze** (or **the bull**) N. Amer. informal have a casual conversation. **shoot one's cuffs** pull one's shirt cuffs out to project beyond the cuffs of one's jacket or coat. **shoot from the hip** informal react suddenly or without careful consideration of one's words or actions. **shoot oneself in the foot** informal inadvertently make a situation worse for oneself. **shoot it out** informal engage in a decisive confrontation, typically a gun battle. **shoot a line** Brit. informal describe something in an exaggerated, untruthful, or boastful way: *he never shot a line about his escapades.* **shoot one's mouth off** informal talk boastfully or indiscreetly.
– DERIVATIVES **shootable** adjective.
– ORIGIN Old English *scēotan*, of Germanic origin; related to Dutch *scieten* and German *sciessen*, also to **SHEET**[1], **SHOT**[1], and **SHUT**.
▶**shoot someone/thing down** kill or wound someone by shooting them, especially in a ruthless way: *troops shot down 28 demonstrators.* ■bring down an aircraft, missile, or pilot by shooting at it. ■figurative crush someone or their opinions by forceful criticism or argument: *she tried to argue and got **shot down in flames** for her trouble.*
shoot through Austral./NZ informal leave, typically to escape from or avoid someone or something: *me wife's shot through and I can't pay the rent.* [ORIGIN: 1940s: from *shoot through like a Bondi tram* (Bondi being the name of Sydney suburb).]
shoot up **1** (especially of a child) grow taller rapidly: *when she hit thirteen she shot up to a startling 5 foot 9.* ■(of a price or amount) rise suddenly. **2** see ***shoot someone/thing up*** (sense 2) below.
shoot someone/thing up **1** cause great damage to something by shooting; kill or wound someone by shooting: *the police shot up our building.* **2** (also **shoot up**) informal inject a narcotic drug; inject someone with a narcotic drug: *she went home and shot up alone in her room* | *I was shooting up cocaine.* | *shoot people up with the new chemical and see what happens.*

shoot-'em-up ▶**noun** informal a fast-moving story or film, of which gunfire is a dominant feature.
■a simple, strategyless computer game in which the

sole objective is to kill as many enemies as possible to achieve a high score.

shooter ▶ noun **1** a person who uses a gun either regularly or on a particular occasion.
■ informal a gun.
2 a member of a team in games such as netball and basketball whose role is to attempt to score goals.
■ a person who throws a dice.
3 Cricket a bowled ball that moves rapidly along the ground after pitching.
4 informal, chiefly N. Amer. a small alcoholic drink, especially of spirits: *geez, he could use a shooter of whiskey.*

shooting ▶ noun [mass noun] the action or practice of shooting: *the unprovoked shooting of civilians by soldiers* | [count noun] *20,000 fatal shootings a year.*
■ the sport or pastime of shooting with a gun. ■ the right of shooting game over an area of land. ■ [count noun] an estate or other area rented to shoot over.
▶ adjective moving or growing quickly: *shooting beams of light played over the sea.*
■ (of a pain) sudden and piercing.
– PHRASES **the whole shooting match** informal everything: *the whole shooting match is being computerized.*

shooting board ▶ noun a board with a step-shaped profile used to guide the motion of a plane relative to a workpiece to ensure accurate planing.

shooting box ▶ noun Brit. a lodge used by hunters in the shooting season.

shooting brake ▶ noun Brit. dated an estate car.

shooting coat ▶ noun a padded waterproof coat with large pockets, worn when shooting game.
■ archaic term for **MORNING COAT**.

shooting gallery ▶ noun a room or fairground booth used for recreational shooting at targets with guns or air guns.
■ N. Amer. informal a place used for taking drugs, especially injecting heroin.

shooting iron ▶ noun informal, chiefly US a firearm.

shooting jacket ▶ noun another term for **SAFARI JACKET**.

shooting range ▶ noun an area provided with targets for the controlled practice of shooting.

shooting star[1] ▶ noun a small, rapidly moving meteor burning up on entering the earth's atmosphere.

shooting star[2] ▶ noun a North American plant with white, pink, or purple hanging flowers with backward curving petals. The flowers are carried above the leaves on slender stems and turn to face up following fertilization.
• Genus *Dodecatheon*, family Primulaceae.

shooting stick ▶ noun a walking stick with a handle that unfolds to form a seat and a sharpened end which can be stuck firmly in the ground.

shooting war ▶ noun a war in which there is armed conflict, as opposed to a cold war or war of nerves, for example.

shoot-out ▶ noun informal a decisive gun battle.
■ (also **penalty shoot-out**) Soccer a tiebreaker decided by each side taking a specified number of penalty shots.

shop ▶ noun **1** a building or part of a building where goods or services are sold: *a video shop* | *a barber's shop.*
■ [in sing.] informal an act of going shopping: *she slogged her way round the supermarket doing the weekly shop.*
2 [usu. with modifier] a place where things are manufactured or repaired; a workshop: *an auto repair shop.*
■ a room or department in a factory where a particular stage of production is carried out: *the machine shop.* ■ informal the place where one works: *she pointed to the classroom ceiling—'I live here, over the shop.'*
▶ verb (**shopped**, **shopping**) **1** [no obj.] go to a shop or shops to buy goods: *she* ***shopped for*** *groceries twice a week.*
■ (**shop around**) look for the best available price or rate for something: *they shopped around for cheaper food.* ■ N. Amer. short for **WINDOW-SHOP**.
2 [with obj.] informal, chiefly Brit. inform on (someone): *she shopped her husband to bosses for taking tools home.*
– PHRASES **all over the shop** see **ALL**. **set up shop** establish oneself in a business: *he set up shop as a hairdresser in Soho.* **talk shop** discuss matters concerning one's work, especially at a social occasion when this is inappropriate.
– ORIGIN Middle English: shortening of Old French *eschoppe* 'lean-to booth', of West Germanic origin; related to German *Schopf* 'porch' and English dialect *shippon* 'cattle shed'. The verb is first recorded (mid 16th cent.) in the sense 'imprison' (from an obsolete slang use of the noun for 'prison'), hence sense 2.

shopaholic ▶ noun informal a compulsive shopper.
– ORIGIN 1980s: blend of **SHOP** and **ALCOHOLIC**.

shop assistant ▶ noun Brit. a person who serves customers in a shop.

shop boy ▶ noun dated, a male shop assistant.

shop class ▶ noun N. Amer. a class in which practical skills such as carpentry or engineering are taught: *back in high school I made a wooden dummy in shop class.*

shopfitter ▶ noun a person whose job it is to fit the counters, shelves, etc. with which a shop is equipped.
– DERIVATIVES **shopfitting** noun.

shop floor ▶ noun [in sing.] Brit. the part of a workshop or factory where production as distinct from administrative work is carried out: *working conditions on the shop floor.*

shopfront ▶ noun the facade of a shop.

shop girl ▶ noun dated a female shop assistant.

shophouse ▶ noun (in SE Asia) a shop opening on to the pavement and also used as the owner's residence.

shopkeeper ▶ noun the owner and manager of a shop.
– DERIVATIVES **shopkeeping** noun.

shoplifting ▶ noun [mass noun] the action of stealing goods from a shop while pretending to be a customer.
– DERIVATIVES **shoplift** verb, **shoplifter** noun.

shopman ▶ noun (pl. **-men**) Brit. dated a male shop assistant or shopkeeper.

shoppe /ʃɒp, 'ʃɒpi/ ▶ noun a shop with spurious old-fashioned charm or quaintness: *the mishmash of the usual Tourist Gift Shoppe.*

shopper ▶ noun a person who is shopping.
■ Brit. a bag for holding shopping, that is attached to wheels and pushed or pulled along: *a four-wheeled tartan shopper.* ■ a small-wheeled bicycle with a basket, designed for use while shopping.

shopping ▶ noun [mass noun] [often as modifier] the purchasing of goods from shops: *a busy shopping area.*
■ goods bought from shops, especially food and household goods: *a bag of shopping.*

shopping cart ▶ noun North American term for **SHOPPING TROLLEY**.

shopping centre ▶ noun an area or complex of shops.

shopping list ▶ noun a list of purchases to be made.
■ a list of items to be considered or acted on: *a lengthy shopping list of detailed proposals.*

shopping mall ▶ noun see **MALL** (sense 1).

shopping trolley ▶ noun Brit. a bag or basket on wheels for carrying shopping, in particular a large wire basket on wheels provided for the use of supermarket customers.

shop-soiled ▶ adjective Brit. (of an article) made dirty or imperfect by being displayed or handled in a shop.

shop steward ▶ noun a person elected by workers, for example in a factory, to represent them in dealings with management.

shop talk ▶ noun [mass noun] conversation about one's occupation or business at an informal or social occasion.

shopwalker ▶ noun Brit. dated a senior employee in a large shop who supervises assistants, directs customers, and answers queries.

shop window ▶ noun a window of a shop, in which goods are displayed: *looking in a shop window.*
■ (**the shop window**) figurative a position that allows a person or organization to demonstrate their strengths: *he is keen to put himself in the shop window.*

shopworn ▶ adjective chiefly US another term for **SHOP-SOILED**.

shore[1] ▶ noun the land along the edge of a sea, lake, or other large body of water: *I took the tiller and made for the shore.*
■ Law the land between ordinary high- and low-water marks. ■ (usu. **shores**) a country or other geographic area bounded by a coast: *record companies have been anxious to import the music to American shores.*
– PHRASES **in shore** on the water near land or nearer to land. **on shore** ashore; on land: *are any of the crew left on shore?*
– DERIVATIVES **shoreless** adjective, **shoreward** adjective & adverb, **shorewards** adverb.
– ORIGIN Middle English: from Middle Dutch, Middle Low German *schōre*; perhaps related to the verb **SHEAR**.

shore[2] ▶ noun a prop or beam set obliquely against something weak or unstable as a support.
▶ verb [with obj.] support or hold up (something) with such props or beams: *rescue workers had to* ***shore up*** *the building, which was in danger of collapse* | figurative *tax relief to help* ***shore up*** *the ailing airline industry.*
– ORIGIN Middle English: from Middle Dutch, Middle Low German *schore* 'prop', of unknown origin.

shore[3] archaic past of **SHEAR**.

shore-based ▶ adjective operating from or based on a shore: *shore-based guns.*

shorebird ▶ noun a bird that frequents the shore.
■ chiefly N. Amer. a wader of the order Charadriiformes, such as a sandpiper.

shore crab ▶ noun a crab which inhabits the seashore and shallow waters.
• Several species, in particular the dark green **common shore crab** (*Carcinus maenas*, family Carcinidae) of Europe.

shorelark ▶ noun a widespread lark of open country, especially the Arctic and mountains, the male having a black and white head pattern and two small black horn-like crests.
• Genus *Eremophila*, family Alaudidae: two species, in particular *E. alpestris*. North American name: **horned lark**.

shore leave ▶ noun [mass noun] leisure time spent ashore by a sailor: *the hall was full of sailors* ***on shore leave.***

shoreline ▶ noun the line along which a large body of water meets the land: *he walked along the shoreline.*

shoreside ▶ noun the edge of a shore: [as modifier] *a shoreside restaurant.*
■ the side of something nearest the shore: *men on the shoreside of each boat were poling it upriver.*

shoreweed ▶ noun [mass noun] a small European plant with grass-like leaves, growing in mud and shallow water at the edge of ponds.
• *Littorella uniflora*, family Plantaginaceae.

shoring ▶ noun [mass noun] shores or props used to support or hold up something weak or unstable.

shorn past participle of **SHEAR**.

short ▶ adjective **1** measuring a small distance from end to end: *short, dark hair* | *a short flight of steps* | *the bed was too short for him.*
■ (of a journey) covering a small distance: *the hotel is a short walk from the sea.* ■ (of a garment or sleeves on a garment) only covering the top part of a person's arms or legs: *a short skirt.* ■ (of a person) small in height: *he is short and tubby.* ■ (of a ball in cricket, a shot in tennis, etc.) travelling only a small distance before bouncing: *he uses his opportunities to attack every short ball.* ■ Cricket (of a ball) pitching relatively near the bowler. ■ Cricket denoting fielding positions relatively close to the batsman: *short midwicket.*
2 lasting or taking a small amount of time: *visiting London for a short break* | *a short conversation.*
■ [attrib.] seeming to last less time than is the case; passing quickly: *in 10 short years all this changed.* ■ (of a person's memory) retaining things for only a small amount of time: *he has a short memory for past misdeeds.* ■ Stock Exchange (of stocks or other securities or commodities) sold in advance of being acquired, with reliance on the price falling so that a profit can be made. ■ Stock Exchange (of a broker, position in the market, etc.) buying or based on such stocks or other securities or commodities. ■ denoting or having a relatively early date for the maturing of a bill of exchange.
3 relatively small in extent: *a short speech* | *he wrote a short book.*
■ [predic.] (**short of/on**) not having enough of (something); lacking or deficient in: *they were short of provisions* | *I know you're short on cash.* ■ [predic.] in insufficient supply: *food is short.* ■ [predic.] (of a person) terse; uncivil: *he was often sharp and rather* ***short with*** *her.*
4 Phonetics (of a vowel) categorized as short with regard to quality and length (e.g. in standard British English the vowel /ʊ/ in *good* is short as distinct from the long vowel /uː/ in *food*).

S

■Prosody (of a vowel or syllable) having the lesser of the two recognized durations.
5 (of odds or a chance) reflecting or representing a high level of probability: *they have been backed at short odds to win thousands of pounds.*
6 (of pastry) containing a high proportion of fat to flour and therefore crumbly.
■(of clay) having poor plasticity.
▶**adverb** (chiefly in sport) at, to, or over a relatively small distance: *you go deep and you go short.*
■not as far as the point aimed at; not far enough: *all too often you pitch the ball short.*
▶**noun 1** Brit. informal a strong alcoholic drink, especially spirits, served in small measures.
2 a short film as opposed to a feature film.
■a short sound such as a short signal in Morse code or a short vowel or syllable: *her call was two longs and a short.* ■ a short circuit.
3 Stock Exchange a person who sells short.
■(**shorts**) Stock Exchange short-dated stocks.
4 (**shorts**) a mixture of bran and coarse flour.
▶**verb** short-circuit or cause to short-circuit: [no obj.] *the electrical circuit had* **shorted out** | [with obj.] *if the contact terminals are shorted, the battery quickly overheats.* [ORIGIN: early 20th cent.: abbreviation.]
– PHRASES **be caught** (or Brit. **taken**) **short** be put at a disadvantage: *the troubled company has been caught short by price competition in a recession-stricken market.* ■ Brit. informal urgently need to urinate or defecate. **a brick short of a load, two sandwiches short of a picnic,** etc. informal (of a person) stupid; crazy: *she's two bricks short of a load.* **bring** (or **pull**) **someone up short** make someone check or pause abruptly: *he was entering the office when he was brought up short by the sight of John.* **come short** fail to reach a goal or standard: *we're so close to getting the job done, but we keep* **coming up** *short.* ■ S. African get into trouble: *if you try to trick him you'll come short.* **for short** as an abbreviation or nickname: *the File Transfer Protocol, or ftp for short.* **get** (or **have**) **someone by the short and curlies** (or **short hairs**) informal have complete control of a person. [ORIGIN: from military slang, referring to pubic hair.] **go short** not have enough of something, especially food: *you won't go short when I die.* **in short** to sum up; briefly: *he was a faithful, orthodox party member; a Stalinist in short.* **in short order** chiefly US immediately; rapidly: *after the killing the camp had been shut down in short order.* **in the short run** in the near future. **in short supply** scarce. **in the short term** in the near future. **little** (or **nothing**) **short of** almost (or equal to); little (or nothing) less than: *he regarded the cost of living as little short of scandalous.* **make short work of** accomplish, consume, or destroy quickly: *we made short work of our huge portions.* **short and sweet** brief and pleasant: *his comments were short and sweet.* **the short end of the stick** an outcome in which one has less advantage than others. **short for** an abbreviation or nickname for: *I'm Robbie—short for Roberta.* **short of** less than: *he died at sixty-one, four years short of his pensionable age.* ■ not reaching as far as: *a rocket failure left a satellite tumbling in an orbit far short of its proper position.* ■ without going so far as (some extreme action): *short of putting out an all-persons alert, there's little else we can do.* **short of breath** panting; short-winded. **short, sharp shock** see **SHOCK**[1]. **stop short** stop suddenly or abruptly. **stop short of** not go as far as (some extreme action): *the measures stopped short of establishing direct trade links.*
– DERIVATIVES **shortish** adjective, **shortness** noun.
– ORIGIN Old English *sceort,* of Germanic origin; related to **SHIRT** and **SKIRT**.

short-acting ▶**adjective** (chiefly of a drug) having effects that only last for a short time.

shortage ▶**noun** a state or situation in which something needed cannot be obtained in sufficient amounts: *a* **shortage of** *hard cash | food shortages |* [mass noun] *the problems of land shortage in the countryside.*

short-arm ▶**adjective** denoting a blow or throw executed with the arm not fully extended or with motion from the elbow only.

short-arse ▶**noun** informal, derogatory a person of small stature.

short back and sides ▶**noun** Brit. a haircut in which the hair is cut short at the back and the sides.

shortbread ▶**noun** [mass noun] a crisp, rich, crumbly type of biscuit made with butter, flour, and sugar.

shortcake ▶**noun** [mass noun] **1** another term for **SHORTBREAD**.
2 N. Amer. a rich dessert made from short pastry and topped with fruit and whipped cream.

short change ▶**noun** [mass noun] insufficient money given as change.
▶**verb** (**short-change**) [with obj.] cheat by giving short change: *I'm sure I was short-changed at the bar.*
■treat unfairly by withholding something of value: [as adj. **short-changed**] *I felt short-changed when United left five of their stars at home.*

short circuit ▶**noun** an electrical circuit in a device of lower resistance than that of a normal circuit, typically resulting from the unintended contact of components and consequent accidental diversion of the current.
▶**verb** (**short-circuit**) (with reference to an electrical device) malfunction or fail or cause to do this as a result of a short circuit across it: [no obj.] *the birds caused the electricity supply to short-circuit |* [with obj.] *water had leaked into the washing machine's motor, short-circuiting it.*
■[with obj.] figurative shorten (a process or activity) by using a more direct (but often improper) method: *the normal processes of a democracy should not be short-circuited.*

shortcoming ▶**noun** (usu. **shortcomings**) a fault or failure to meet a certain standard, typically in a person's character, a plan, or a system: *he discussed the* **shortcomings of** *his wife.*

short commons ▶**plural noun** see **COMMONS**.

short corner ▶**noun** (in field hockey) a penalty hit or kick taken from a spot on the goal line relatively close to the goalposts (but not within ten yards).

short covering ▶**noun** [mass noun] the buying in of stocks or other securities or commodities that have been sold short, typically to avoid loss when prices move upwards.

shortcrust (also **shortcrust pastry**) ▶**noun** [mass noun] Brit. crumbly pastry made with flour, fat, and a little water, and typically used for pies, flans, and tarts.

short cut ▶**noun** an alternative route that is shorter than the one usually taken.
■figurative an accelerated way of doing or achieving something: *teaching no longer offered a short cut to secure employment.*

short-dated ▶**adjective** (of a stock or bond) due for early payment or redemption.

short-day ▶**adjective** [attrib.] (of a plant) needing a daily period of darkness of more than a certain length to initiate flowering which therefore happens naturally as the days shorten in the autumn.

short division ▶**noun** [mass noun] arithmetical division in which the quotient is written directly without a succession of intermediate workings.

short-eared owl ▶**noun** a migratory day-flying owl that frequents open country, found in northern Eurasia and North and South America.
• *Asio flammeus*, family Strigidae.

shorten ▶**verb** make or become shorter: [with obj.] *he shortened his stride | patients whose waiting time had been shortened |* [no obj.] *as skirts shortened, so heels rose | around mid September, days shorten and temperatures dip.*
■[with obj.] Sailing reduce the amount of (sail spread). ■ (with reference to gambling odds) make or become shorter; decrease: [with obj.] *Ladbrokes shortened Nashwan's odds from 2–1 to 7–4 |* [no obj.] *the odds had shortened to 14–1.* ■ [with obj.] Prosody & Phonetics make (a vowel or syllable) short.

short end ▶**noun** (**the short end**) the part of a stock market which deals in short-term stocks or other securities or commodities.

shortening ▶**noun** [mass noun] fat used for making pastry.

shortfall ▶**noun** a deficit of something required or expected: *they are facing an expected $10 billion* **shortfall in** *revenue.*

short field ▶**noun** Baseball the part of the outfield nearest the infield: *he hit the next hard into short field.*

short-fused ▶**adjective** informal quick-tempered.

shorthair ▶**noun** a cat of a short-haired breed.

shorthand ▶**noun** [mass noun] a method of rapid writing by means of abbreviations and symbols, used especially for taking dictation. The major systems of shorthand currently in use are those devised in 1837 by Sir Isaac Pitman and (in the US) in 1888 by **John R. Gregg** (1867–1948).
■[in sing.] a short and simple way of expressing or referring to something: *poetry for him is simply a* **shorthand for** *literature that has aesthetic value.*

short-handed ▶**adjective** not having enough or the usual number of staff or crew: *the kitchen was a bit short-handed.*

shorthand typist ▶**noun** Brit. a typist qualified to take and transcribe shorthand.

short haul ▶**noun** a relatively short distance in terms of travel or the transport of goods: *it is only a short haul over the mountains to Los Angeles |* [as modifier] *short-haul routes.*

short head Horse Racing, Brit. ▶**noun** a length less than that of a horse's head (used in referring to the distance by which a horse wins or loses): *he lost* **by a short head.**
▶**verb** (**short-head**) [with obj.] narrowly beat.

shorthold ▶**adjective** English Law relating to or denoting a tenancy whereby the tenant agrees to rent a property for a stated term, at the end of which the landlord may recover it.

shorthorn ▶**noun** an animal of a breed of cattle with short horns.

short hundredweight ▶**noun** see **HUNDREDWEIGHT**.

shortie ▶**noun** variant spelling of **SHORTY**.

short leet ▶**noun** & **verb** Scottish term for **SHORTLIST**.

shortlist ▶**noun** a list of selected candidates from which a final choice is made: *a shortlist of four companies.*
▶**verb** [with obj.] put (someone or something) on a shortlist: *the novel was* **shortlisted for** *the Booker Prize.*

short-lived ▶**adjective** lasting only a short time: *a short-lived romance | these benefits are likely to be short-lived.*

shortly ▶**adverb 1** in a short time; soon: *the new database will shortly be available for consultation | the flight was hijacked* **shortly after** *takeoff.*
2 in a few words; briefly: *they received a letter shortly outlining the proposals.*
■abruptly, sharply, or curtly: *'Do you like cricket?' 'I do not,' she said shortly.*
– ORIGIN Old English *scortlīce* (see **SHORT**, **-LY**[2]).

short mark ▶**noun** another term for **BREVE** (in sense 2).

short measure ▶**noun** an amount, especially of alcohol, less than that which is declared or paid for.

short metre (abbrev.: **SM**) ▶**noun** a metrical pattern for hymns in which the stanzas have four lines with 6, 6, 8, and 6 syllables.

short order ▶**noun** N. Amer. an order or dish of food which can be quickly prepared and served: *a short order of souvlaki |* [as modifier] *I'm a short-order cook.*
– PHRASES **in short order** see **SHORT**.

Short Parliament the first of two parliaments summoned by Charles I in 1640 (the other being the Long Parliament). Due to its insistence on seeking a general redress of grievances against him before granting the money he required, Charles dismissed it after only three weeks.

short-pitched ▶**adjective** Cricket (of a delivery) bowled so that the ball bounces relatively near the bowler: *fast, short-pitched bowling.*

short-range ▶**adjective** [attrib.] **1** (especially of a vehicle or missile) only able to be used or be effective over short distances: *short-range nuclear weapons.*
2 of or over a short period of future time: *short-range schemes | short-range forecasting.*

short rib ▶**noun 1** Brit. another term for **FLOATING RIB**.
2 (**short ribs**) N. Amer. a narrow cut of beef containing the ends of the ribs near to the breastbone.

short-run ▶**adjective** taken or considered on a short timescale; short-term: *periods of often violent short-run price volatility.*
■Printing produced in or relating to a print run of relatively few copies.

shorts ▶**plural noun** short trousers that reach only to the knees or thighs: *cycling shorts.*
■N. Amer. men's underpants.

short score ▶ **noun** Music a score in which the parts are condensed on to a small number of staves.

short shrift ▶ **noun** [mass noun] rapid and unsympathetic dismissal; curt treatment: *the judge gave **short shrift to** an argument based on the right to free speech.*
■archaic little time between condemnation and execution or punishment.

short sight ▶ **noun** [mass noun] the inability to see things clearly unless they are relatively close to the eyes, owing to the focusing of rays of light by the eye at a point in front of the retina. Also called **MYOPIA**.

short-sighted ▶ **adjective** having short sight.
■figurative lacking imagination or foresight: *a short-sighted government.*
– DERIVATIVES **short-sightedly** adverb, **short-sightedness** noun.

short-sleeved ▶ **adjective** having sleeves that do not reach below the elbow: *a short-sleeved silk top.*

short-staffed ▶ **adjective** [predic.] having too few or fewer than the usual number of staff.

short-stay ▶ **adjective** [attrib.] denoting a place in which someone or something stays or remains for only a short period: *short-stay accommodation.*
■denoting a person staying somewhere for only a short period of time: *short-stay patients.*

shortstop /ˈʃɔːtstɒp/ ▶ **noun** Baseball a fielder positioned between second and third base.

short story ▶ **noun** a story with a fully developed theme but significantly shorter and less elaborate than a novel.

short subject ▶ **noun** chiefly US a short film, typically one shown before the screening of a feature film.

short suit ▶ **noun** (in bridge or whist) a holding of only one or two cards of one suit in a hand.

short-tailed vole ▶ **noun** another term for **FIELD VOLE**.

short temper ▶ **noun** a tendency to lose one's temper quickly.
– DERIVATIVES **short-tempered** adjective.

short tennis ▶ **noun** [mass noun] tennis played on a small court with a small racket and a soft ball, used especially as an introduction to the game for children.

short-term ▶ **adjective** occurring in or relating to a relatively short period of future time: *it might be a wise short-term investment.*

short-termism ▶ **noun** [mass noun] concentration on short-term projects or objectives for immediate profit at the expense of long-term security.

short time ▶ **noun** [mass noun] the condition of working fewer than the regular hours per day or days per week: *staff have agreed to work on short time.*

short-timer ▶ **noun** US military slang a person nearing the end of their period of military service.

short title ▶ **noun** an abbreviated form of a title of a book or document.

short ton ▶ **noun** see **TON**[1].

short trousers ▶ **plural noun** trousers reaching only to the knee, as worn typically by young boys.

short view ▶ **noun** (**the short view**) consideration of the present and immediate future only: *You will say I was taking the short view.*

short waist ▶ **noun** archaic a woman's dress with a high waist.

short wave ▶ **noun** a radio wave of a wavelength between about 10 and 100 m (and a frequency of about 3 to 30 MHz): [as modifier] *a short-wave transmitter.*
■[mass noun] broadcasting using radio waves of this wavelength: [as modifier] *short-wave radio.*

short weight ▶ **noun** [mass noun] weight that is less than that declared: *unscrupulous retailers give short weight by including an excessive amount of packaging.*

short-winded ▶ **adjective** (of a person) out of breath or quickly becoming so.

shortwing ▶ **noun** a small South Asian songbird of the thrush family, with long legs, short wings and tail, and dark brown or blue plumage.
• Family Turdidae: two genera, in particular *Brachypteryx*, and several species.

shorty (also **shortie**) ▶ **noun** (pl. **-ies**) informal a person who is shorter than average (often used as a nickname).
■[often as modifier] a short garment, especially a short dress, nightdress, or raincoat: *she pulled on a shorty nightshirt.*

Shoshone /ʃə'ʃəʊni/ ▶ **noun** (pl. same or **Shoshones**)
1 a member of an American Indian people living chiefly in Wyoming, Idaho, and Nevada.
2 [mass noun] the Uto-Aztecan language of this people.
▶ **adjective** of or relating to the Shoshone or their language.
– ORIGIN of unknown origin.

Shoshonean ▶ **noun** [mass noun] a branch of the Uto-Aztecan language family that includes Comanche and Shoshone.
▶ **adjective** of, relating to, or denoting this group of languages.

Shostakovich /ˌʃɒstəˈkəʊvɪtʃ/, Dmitri (Dmitrievich) (1906–75), Russian composer. He developed a highly personal style and, although he experimented with atonality and twelve-note techniques, his music always returned to a basic tonality. He is best known for his fifteen symphonies.

shot[1] ▶ **noun** **1** the firing of a gun or cannon: *he brought down a caribou with a single shot to the neck* | figurative *the opening shots have been fired in a legal battle over repairs.*
■an attempt to hit a target by shooting: *he asked me if I would like to **have a shot** at a pheasant.* ■ figurative a critical or aggressive remark: *Paul tried one last shot—'You realize what you want will cost more money?'* ■ [with adj.] a person with a specified level of ability in shooting: *he was an excellent shot at short and long distances.*
2 a hit, stroke, or kick of the ball in sports such as football, tennis, or golf: *his partner pulled off a winning backhand shot.*
■an attempt to drive the ball into goal; an attempt to score: *he **took a shot** that the goalie stopped.* ■ informal an attempt to do something: *several of the competitors will **have a shot** at the all-round title.*
3 (pl. same) a ball of stone or metal used as a missile shot from a large gun or cannon.
■(also **lead shot**) [mass noun] tiny lead pellets used in quantity in a single charge or cartridge in a shotgun.
■ a heavy ball thrown by a shot-putter.
4 a photograph: *she **took a shot** of me holding a lamp near my face.*
■a film sequence photographed continuously by one camera: *the movie's opening shot is of a character walking across a featureless landscape.* ■ [mass noun] the range of a camera's view: *a prop man was standing just **out of shot**.*
5 informal a small alcoholic drink, especially of spirits: *he took a shot of whisky.*
■an injection of a drug or vaccine: *he took a shot of impure heroin.*
6 [usu. with modifier] the launch of a space rocket: *a moon shot.*
– PHRASES **give it one's best shot** informal do the best that one can. **like a shot** informal without hesitation; willingly: *'Would you go back?' 'Like a shot.'* **not a shot in one's locker** Brit. no money or chances left. **a shot across the bows** see **BOW**[3]. **a shot in the arm** informal an encouraging stimulus: *the movie was a real shot in the arm for our crew.* **a shot in the dark** see **DARK**.
– ORIGIN Old English *sc(e)ot, gesc(e)ot* of Germanic origin; related to German *Geschoss*, from the base of the verb **SHOOT**.

shot[2] past and past participle of **SHOOT**. ▶ **adjective**
1 (of coloured cloth) woven with a warp and weft of different colours, giving a contrasting effect when looked at from different angles: *a dress of shot silk.*
■interspersed with a different colour: *dark hair **shot with** silver.*
2 informal ruined or worn out: *a completely shot engine will put you out of the race* | *my nerves are shot.*
■[predic.] US & Austral./NZ drunk.
– PHRASES **get** (or **be**) **shot of** Brit. informal get (or be) rid of. **shot through with** suffused with (a particular feature or quality): *the mist was shot through with orange spokes of light.* **shot to pieces** (or **to hell**) informal ruined.

shot[3] ▶ **noun** [in sing.] Brit. informal, dated a bill or one's share of it, especially in a pub: *he had paid her shot.*
– ORIGIN late Middle English: from **SHOT**[1]; compare with Old English *scēotan* 'shoot, pay, contribute' and **SCOT**.

shot-blast ▶ **verb** [with obj.] clean or strip (a metal or other surface) by directing a high-speed stream of steel particles at it.

shotcrete ▶ **noun** another term for **GUNITE**.
– ORIGIN 1950s: from **SHOT**[2] + **CONCRETE**.

shote ▶ **noun** variant spelling of **SHOAT**.

shot-firer ▶ **noun** a person who fires a blasting charge, for example in mining.

shot glass ▶ **noun** N. Amer. a small glass used for serving spirits.

shotgun ▶ **noun** a smooth-bore gun for firing small shot at short range.

shotgun marriage (also **shotgun wedding**) ▶ **noun** informal an enforced or hurried wedding, especially because the bride is pregnant.

shotgun microphone ▶ **noun** another term for **GUN MICROPHONE**.

shot hole ▶ **noun** **1** a hole made by the passage of a shot.
2 a hole bored in rock for the insertion of a blasting charge.
3 a small round hole made in a leaf by a fungus or bacterium, especially in a fruit tree following an attack of leaf spot: [as modifier] *shot hole disease.*
■a small hole made in wood by a boring beetle: [as modifier] *shot-hole borer.*

shotmaking ▶ **noun** [mass noun] the playing of aggressive or decisive strokes in tennis, golf, and other games.
– DERIVATIVES **shotmaker** noun.

Shotokan /ʃə(ʊ)ˈtəʊkan/ ▶ **noun** [usu. as modifier] the style of karate which is now the most widespread in the UK and a number of other countries.
– ORIGIN Japanese, from *shō* 'right, true' + *to* 'way' + *kan* 'kan'.

shot-peen ▶ **verb** shape (sheet metal) by bombarding it with a stream of metal shot.

shot-put (also **shot-putting**) ▶ **noun** an athletic contest in which a very heavy round ball is thrown as far as possible.
– DERIVATIVES **shot-putter** noun.

shotted ▶ **adjective** filled or weighted with shot.

shotten herring /ˈʃɒt(ə)n/ ▶ **noun** a herring that has spawned.
■archaic a weakened or dispirited person.
– ORIGIN Middle English: *shotten*, archaic past participle of **SHOOT**, in the specialized sense 'discharge (spawn)'.

shottist ▶ **noun** S. African a person who is skilled in shooting and takes part in shooting competitions.

shot tower ▶ **noun** historical a tower in which shot was made from molten lead poured through sieves at the top and falling into water at the bottom.

should ▶ **modal verb** (3rd sing. **should**) **1** used to indicate obligation, duty, or correctness, typically when criticizing someone's actions: *he should have been careful* | *I think we should trust our people more* | *you shouldn't have gone.*
■indicating a desirable or expected state: *by now pupils should be able to read with a large degree of independence.*
■ used to give or ask advice or suggestions: *you should go back to bed* | *what should I wear?* ■ (**I should**) used to give advice: *I should hold out if I were you.*
2 used to indicate what is probable: *£348 m should be enough to buy him out* | *the bus should arrive in a few minutes.*
3 formal expressing the conditional mood:
■(in the first person) indicating the consequence of an imagined event: *if I were to obey my first impulse, I should spend my days writing letters.* ■ referring to a possible event or situation: *if you should change your mind, I'll be at the hotel* | *should anyone arrive late, admission is likely to be refused.*
4 used in a clause with 'that' after a main clause describing feelings: *it is astonishing that we should find violence here.*
5 used in a clause with 'that' expressing purpose: *in order that training should be effective it must be planned systematically.*
6 (in the first person) expressing a polite request or acceptance: *I should like some more, if I may* | *we should be grateful for your advice.*
7 (in the first person) expressing a conjecture or hope: *he'll have a sore head, I should imagine* | *'It won't happen again.' 'I should hope not.'*
8 used to emphasize to a listener how striking an event is or was: *you should have seen Marge's face.*
■(**who/what should —— but**) emphasizing how surprising an event was: *I was in this shop when who should I see across the street but Tobias.*
– ORIGIN Old English *sceolde*: past of **SHALL**.

USAGE As with **shall** and **will**, there is confusion about when to use **should** and **would**. The traditional rule is that **should** is used with first person pronouns (**I** and **we**), as in *I said I* ***should*** *be late*, and **would** is used with second and third persons (**you**, **he**, **she**, **it**, **they**), as in *you didn't say you* ***would*** *be late*. In practice, **would** is normally used instead of **should** in reported speech and conditional clauses: *I said I* ***would*** *be late; if we had known we* ***would*** *have invited her.* In spoken and informal contexts the issue rarely arises, since the distinction is obscured by the use of the contracted forms **I'd**, **we'd**, etc.
In modern English, uses of **should** are dominated by the senses relating to obligation (for which **would** cannot be substituted), as in *you* ***should*** *go out more often*, and for related emphatic uses, as in *you* ***should*** *have seen her face!*

shoulder ▶**noun 1** the upper joint of each of a person's arms and the part of the body between this and the neck.
■(in quadrupeds) the joint of the upper forelimb and the adjacent part of the back. ■ the part of a bird or insect at which the wing is attached. ■a joint of meat from the upper foreleg and shoulder blade of an animal: *a shoulder of lamb.* ■ a part of a garment covering the shoulder: *a jacket with padded shoulders.* ■ (**shoulders**) the upper part of the back and arms: *a tall youth with broad shoulders.* ■ (**shoulders**) figurative this part of the body regarded as bearing responsibility or hardship or providing strength: *all accounts place the blame squarely on his shoulders.*
2 a part of something resembling a shoulder in shape, position, or function: *the shoulder of a pulley.*
■a point at which a steep slope descends from a plateau or highland area: *the shoulder of the hill sloped down* | *a resort sheltered by the shoulder of Ben Nevis.*
3 another term for **HARD SHOULDER**.
▶**verb 1** [with obj.] put (something heavy) over one's shoulder or shoulders to carry: *we shouldered our crippling backpacks and set off slowly up the hill.*
■figurative take on (a burden or responsibility): *the day-to-day work will be shouldered by an action group.*
2 [with obj. and adverbial of direction] push (someone or something) out of one's way with one's shoulder: *she shouldered him brusquely aside.*
■[no obj., with adverbial of direction] move in this way: *he shouldered past a woman with a baby* | *he* ***shouldered his way*** *through the seething mass of children.*
– PHRASES **be looking over one's shoulders** be anxious or insecure about a possible danger: *takeovers are the thing that keeps suppliers looking over their shoulders.* **put one's shoulder to the wheel** set to work vigorously. **shoulder arms** hold a rifle against the right side of the body, barrel upwards. **a shoulder to cry on** someone who listens sympathetically to someone's problems. **shoulder to shoulder** side by side: *everyone is bunched together shoulder to shoulder.* ■ acting together towards a common aim: with united effort: *we fought shoulder to shoulder with the rest of the country.*
– DERIVATIVES **shouldered** adjective [in combination] *broad-shouldered.*
– ORIGIN Old English *sculdor*, of West Germanic origin; related to Dutch *schouder* and German *Schulter.*

shoulder bag ▶**noun** a bag with a long strap that is hung over the shoulder.

shoulder belt ▶**noun** a bandolier or other strap passing over one shoulder and under the opposite arm.

shoulder blade ▶**noun** either of the large, flat, triangular bones which lie against the ribs in the upper back and provide attachments for the bone and muscles of the upper arm. Also called **SCAPULA**.

shoulder-charge ▶**verb** [with obj.] charge at (a person or obstacle) with the shoulder first.
▶**noun** a charge made leading with the shoulder.

shoulder-high ▶**adjective** & **adverb** up to or at the height of the shoulders: [as adj.] *a glade of shoulder-high grass* | [as adv.] *he was lifted shoulder-high.*

shoulder holster ▶**noun** a gun holster worn under the armpit.

shoulder-in ▶**noun** (in dressage) a movement in which the horse moves parallel to the side of the arena, with its hindquarters carried closer to the wall than its shoulders and its body curved towards the centre.

shoulder joint ▶**noun** the joint connecting an upper limb or forelimb to the body. It is a ball-and-socket joint in which the head of the humerus fits into the socket of the scapula.

shoulder knot ▶**noun** a knot of ribbon, metal, or lace worn as part of a ceremonial dress.

shoulder pad ▶**noun** a spongy, shaped pad sewn into the shoulder of a garment to provide bulk and shape.
■a hard, protective pad for the shoulders used in certain sports, such as ice hockey and American football.

shoulder season (also **shoulder period**) ▶**noun** a travel period between peak and off-peak seasons.

shoulder stand ▶**noun** a gymnastic movement in which, starting from a supine position, the torso and legs are raised vertically over the head and supported on the shoulders and arms.

shoulder strap ▶**noun** a narrow strip of material going over the shoulder from front to back of a garment.
■a long strap attached to a bag for carrying it over the shoulder. ■ a strip of cloth from shoulder to collar on a military uniform bearing a symbol of rank. ■ a similar strip on a raincoat.

shouldn't ▶**contraction of** should not.

shout ▶**verb 1** [no obj.] (of a person) utter a loud call or cry, typically as an expression of a strong emotion: *she shouted for joy.*
■[reporting verb] say something very loudly; call out: [with obj.] *he leant out of his window and shouted abuse at them* | *I* ***shouted out*** *a warning* | [with direct speech] *'Come back!' she shouted.* ■ (**shout at**) speak loudly and angrily to; insult or scold loudly: *he apologized because he had shouted at her in front of them all.* ■ [with obj.] (**shout someone down**) prevent someone from speaking or being heard by shouting: *he was shouted down as he tried to explain the decision.* ■ [with obj.] figurative indicate or express (a particular quality or characteristic) unequivocally or powerfully: *from crocodile handbag to gold-trimmed shoes she shouted money.*
2 [with two objs] Austral./NZ informal treat (someone) to (something, especially a drink): *I'll shout you a beer.*
■[no obj.] buy a round of drinks: *anyone shooting a hole in one must shout for all players present on the course.*
▶**noun 1** a loud cry expressing a strong emotion or calling attention: *his words were interrupted by warning shouts.*
■informal an emergency call-out for the fire brigade or the police.
2 (**one's shout**) Brit. informal one's turn to buy a round of drinks: *'Do you want another drink? My shout.'*
– PHRASES **all over bar the shouting** informal (of a contest) almost finished and therefore virtually decided. **give someone a shout** informal call for someone's attention. ■ call on or get in touch with someone. **in with a shout** informal having a good chance: *they were definitely in with a shout of bringing off a victory.* **shout something from the rooftops** talk about something openly and jubilantly, especially something that is personal or has previously been kept secret. **shout the odds** talk loudly and opinionatedly.
– DERIVATIVES **shouter** noun, **shouty** adjective (informal).
– ORIGIN late Middle English: perhaps related to **SHOOT**; compare with Old Norse *skúta* 'a taunt', also with the verb **SCOUT**[2].

shouting match ▶**noun** a loud quarrel.

shove ▶**verb** [with obj.] push (someone or something) roughly: *police started* ***pushing and shoving*** *people down the street* | [no obj.] *kids pushed, kicked, and shoved.*
■[no obj., with adverbial of direction] make one's way by pushing someone or something: *Woolley shoved past him.* ■ [with obj. and adverbial of place] put (something) somewhere carelessly or roughly: *she shoved the books into her briefcase.* ■ (**shove it**) informal used to express angry dismissal of something: *I should have told the selectors to shove it.*
▶**noun** [usu. in sing.] a strong push: *she gave him a hefty shove and he nearly fell.*
– ORIGIN Old English *scūfan* (verb), of Germanic origin; related to Dutch *schuiven* and German *schieben*, also to **SHUFFLE**.
▶**shove off 1** [usu. in imperative] informal go away: *shove off—you're bothering the customers.* **2** push away from the shore in a boat.
shove up move oneself to make room for someone.

shove-halfpenny ▶**noun** [mass noun] a game in which coins are struck so that they slide across a marked board on a table.

shovel ▶**noun** a tool resembling a spade with a broad blade and typically upturned sides, used for moving coal, earth, snow, or other material.
■a machine or part of a machine having a similar shape or function. ■an amount of something carried or moved with a shovel: *a few* ***shovels of*** *earth.*
▶**verb** (**shovelled**, **shovelling**; US **shoveled**, **shoveling**) [with obj. and adverbial] move (coal, earth, snow, or similar) with a shovel: *she shovelled coal on the fire.*
■informal put or push (something, typically food) somewhere quickly and in large quantities: *Dave was shovelling pasta into his mouth.*
– DERIVATIVES **shovelful** noun (pl. **-fuls**).
– ORIGIN Old English *scofl*, of Germanic origin; related to Dutch *schoffel*, German *Schaufel*, also to the verb **SHOVE**.

shovelboard ▶**noun** [mass noun] Brit. a game played by pushing discs with the hand or with a long-handled shovel over a marked surface.
– ORIGIN mid 16th cent.: alteration of obsolete *shoveboard*, from **SHOVE** + **BOARD**.

shoveler (also **shoveller**) ▶**noun** a dabbling duck with a long broad bill.
• Genus *Anas*, family Anatidae: four species, in particular *A. clypeata* of Eurasia and North America.
– ORIGIN late Middle English (denoting a spoonbill): alteration of earlier *shovelard*, from **SHOVEL**, perhaps influenced by *mallard*.

shovel hat ▶**noun** a black felt hat with a low round crown and a broad brim turned up at the sides, formerly worn especially by clergymen.

shovelhead (also **shovelhead shark**) ▶**noun** another term for **BONNETHEAD**.

shoveller (US **shoveler**) ▶**noun** a person or thing that shovels something: *a snow shoveller.*

shovel pass ▶**noun** American Football an underarm pass made with a shovelling movement of the arms.

show ▶**verb** (past participle **shown** or **showed**) **1** be or allow or cause to be visible: [no obj.] *wrinkles were starting to show on her face* | [no obj., with complement] *the muscles of her jaws showed white through the skin* | [with obj.] *a white blouse will show the blood.*
■[with obj.] offer, exhibit, or produce (something) for scrutiny or inspection: *an alarm salesperson should show an ID card* | [with two objs] *he wants to show you all his woodwork stuff.* ■ [with obj.] put on display in an exhibition or competition: *he ceased rather early in his career to show his work* | [no obj.] *other artists who showed there included Robert Motherwell.* ■ [with obj.] present (a film or television programme) on a screen for public viewing. ■ [no obj.] (of a film) be presented in this way: *a movie showing at the Venice Film Festival.* ■ [with obj.] indicate (a particular time, measurement, etc.): *a travel clock showing the time in different cities.* ■ [with obj.] represent or depict in art: *a postcard showing the Wicklow Mountains.* ■ (**show oneself**) allow oneself to be seen; appear in public: *he was amazed that she would have the gall to show herself.* ■ [no obj.] informal arrive or turn up for an appointment or at a gathering: *her date failed to show.* ■ [no obj.] N. Amer. finish third or in the first three in a race. ■ [no obj.] informal (of a woman) be visibly pregnant: *Shirl was four months gone and just starting to show.*
2 [with obj.] display or allow to be perceived (a quality, emotion, or characteristic): *it was Frank's turn to show his frustration* | *his sangfroid showed signs of cracking.*
■accord or treat someone with (a specified quality): *he urged his soldiers fight them and show no mercy* | [with two objs] *he has learned to show women some respect.* ■ [no obj.] (of an emotion) be noticeable: *he tried not to let his relief show.*
3 [with obj.] demonstrate or prove: *experts say this shows the benefit of regular inspections* | [with clause] *the figures show that the underlying rate of inflation continues to fall.*
■(**show oneself**) prove or demonstrate oneself to be: [with infinitive] *she showed herself to be a harsh critic* | [with complement] *the youth soon showed himself a canny batsman.* ■ cause to understand or be capable of doing something by explanation or demonstration: *he showed the boy how to operate the machine.* ■ [with obj. and adverbial of direction] conduct or lead: *show them in, please.*
▶**noun 1** a spectacle or display of something, typically an impressive one: *spectacular shows of bluebells.*
2 a public entertainment, in particular:
■a play or other stage performance, especially a musical. ■ a light entertainment programme on television or radio. ■ [usu. with adj. or noun modifier] an event or competition involving the public display or

S

exhibition of animals, plants, or products: *the annual agricultural show*. ■ informal an undertaking, project, or organization: *I man a desk in a little office. I don't run the show*. ■ US & Austral./NZ informal an opportunity for doing something; a chance: *I didn't have a show*.
3 an outward appearance or display of a quality or feeling: *Joanie was frightened of any show of affection*. ■ an outward display intended to give a particular, false impression: *Drew made a show of looking around for firewood* | [mass noun] *they are all show and no go*.
4 Medicine a discharge of blood and mucus from the vagina at the onset of labour or menstruation.
– PHRASES **all over the show** another way of saying *all over the place* (see ALL). **for show** for the sake of appearance rather than for use. **get** (or **keep**) **the show on the road** informal begin (or succeed in continuing with) an undertaking or enterprise: *'Let's get this show on the road—we're late already'*. **give the** (**whole**) **show away** demonstrate the inadequacies or reveal the truth of something. **good** (or **bad** or **poor**) **show!** informal, dated used to express approval (or disapproval or dissatisfaction). **have something** (or **nothing**) **to show for** have a (or no) visible result of (one's work or experience): *a year later, he had nothing to show for his efforts*. **on show** being exhibited. **show one's cards** another way of saying *show one's hand* below. **show cause** Law produce satisfactory grounds for application of (or exemption from) a procedure or penalty. **show (someone) a clean pair of heels** informal run away extremely fast. **show someone the door** dismiss or eject someone from a place. **show one's face** appear in public: *she had been up in court and was so ashamed she could hardly show her face*. **show the flag** see FLAG¹. **show one's hand** (in a card game) reveal one's cards. ■ figurative disclose one's plans: *he needed hard evidence, and to get it he would have to show his hand*. **show of force** a demonstration of the forces at one's command and of one's readiness to use them. **show of hands** the raising of hands among a group of people to indicate a vote for or against something, with numbers typically being estimated rather than counted. **show one's teeth** Brit. use one's power or authority in an aggressive or intimidating way: *the council showed its teeth for the first time by imposing an economic embargo*. **show the way** indicate the direction to be followed to a particular place. ■ indicate what can or should be done by doing it first: *Morgan showed the way by becoming Deputy Governor of Jamaica*. **show willing** display a willingness to help or to do something.
– ORIGIN Old English *scēawian* 'look at, inspect', from a West Germanic base meaning 'look'; related to Dutch *schouwen* and German *schauen*.
▶ **show something forth** archaic exhibit: *the heavens show forth the glory of God*.
show off informal make a deliberate or pretentious display of one's abilities or accomplishments.
show someone/thing off display or cause others to take notice of someone or something that is a source of pride: *his jeans were tight-fitting, showing off his compact figure*.
show out Bridge reveal that one has no cards of a particular suit.
show someone round (or chiefly N. Amer. **around**) act as a guide for someone to points of interest in a place or building.
show through (of one's real feelings) be revealed inadvertently.
show up 1 be conspicuous or clearly visible. **2** informal arrive or turn up for an appointment or gathering.
show someone/thing up make someone or something conspicuous or clearly visible: *a rising moon showed up the wild seascape*. ■ expose someone or something as being bad or faulty in some way: *it's a pity they haven't showed up the authorities for what they are*. ■ (**show someone up**) informal embarrass or humiliate someone: *she says I showed her up in front of her friends*.

Showa /ˈʃəʊwə/ ▶ noun [usu. as modifier] the period when Japan was ruled by the emperor Hirohito.
– ORIGIN Japanese, from *shō* 'bright, clear' + *wa* 'harmony'.

show-and-tell ▶ noun [mass noun] chiefly N. Amer. a teaching method, used especially in teaching young children, in which pupils are encouraged to bring items they have selected to class and describe them to their classmates.

show bag ▶ noun Austral. a bag of goods, especially

trade samples or publicity material, available at events such as annual shows.

showband ▶ noun a band which plays cover versions of popular songs.
■ a band, especially a jazz band, which performs with theatrical extravagance.

showbiz ▶ noun informal term for SHOW BUSINESS.
– DERIVATIVES **showbizzy** adjective.

showboat ▶ noun (in the US) a river steamer on which theatrical performances are given.
■ informal, chiefly US a show-off; an exhibitionist.
▶ verb [no obj.] informal, chiefly US show off: [as adj. **showboating**] *a lot of showboating politicians*.
– DERIVATIVES **showboater** noun.

show business ▶ noun [mass noun] the theatre, films, television, and pop music as a profession or industry.

showcard ▶ noun a large card bearing a conspicuous design, used especially in advertising, market research, and teaching.

showcase ▶ noun a glass case used for displaying articles in a shop or museum.
■ a place or occasion for presenting something favourably to general attention: *the gallery will provide a showcase for Scotland's young photographers*.
▶ verb [with obj.] exhibit; display: *the albums showcase his production skills*.

showdown ▶ noun a final test or confrontation intended to settle a dispute.
■ (in poker or brag) the requirement at the end of a round that the players who remain in should show their cards to determine which is the strongest hand.

shower /ˈʃaʊə/ ▶ noun **1** a brief and usually light fall of rain, hail, sleet, or snow.
■ a mass of small things falling or moving at the same time: *a shower of dust sprinkled his face*. ■ figurative a large number of things happening or given to someone at the same time: *he was pleased by the shower of awards*. ■ a group of particles produced by a cosmic-ray particle in the earth's atmosphere.
2 a cubicle or bath in which a person stands under a spray of water to wash.
■ the apparatus that produces such a spray of water. ■ (US also **shower bath**) an act of washing oneself in a shower.
3 [often with modifier] N. Amer. a party at which presents are given to someone, typically a woman who is about to get married or have a baby: *she loved going to baby showers*.
4 [in sing.] Brit. informal a group of people perceived as incompetent, stupid, or worthless: *look at this lot—what a shower!*
▶ verb **1** [no obj., with adverbial of direction] (of a mass of small things) fall or be thrown in a shower: *bits of broken glass showered over me*.
■ [with obj. and adverbial of direction] cause (a mass of small things) to fall in a shower: *his hooves showered sparks across the concrete floor*. ■ [with obj.] (**shower someone with**) throw (a number of small things) all at once towards someone: *hooligans showered him with rotten eggs*. ■ [with obj.] (**shower someone with**) give someone a great number of (things): *he showered her with kisses*. ■ [with obj.] (**shower something on/upon**) give a great number of things to (someone): *senior officers showered praise on their young policewomen*.
2 [no obj.] wash oneself in a shower.
– PHRASES **send someone to the showers** N. Amer. informal fail early on in a race or contest.
– ORIGIN Old English *scūr* 'light fall of rain, hail, etc.', of Germanic origin; related to Dutch *schoer* and German *Schauer*.

showerproof ▶ adjective (of a garment) resistant to light rain.
▶ verb [with obj.] make showerproof.

showery ▶ adjective (of weather or a period of time) characterized by frequent showers of rain.

showgirl ▶ noun an actress who sings and dances in musicals, variety acts, and similar shows.

showground ▶ noun an area of land on which a show takes place.

show house (also **show home**) ▶ noun Brit. a house on a newly built estate which is furnished and decorated to be shown to prospective buyers.

showing ▶ noun [mass noun] the action of showing something or the fact of being shown: *alsatian dog, championship quality, excellent results in showing*. ■ [count noun] a presentation of a cinema film or television programme: *another showing of the three-part series*. ■ [count noun] [with adj.] a performance of a specified quality: *despite poor opinion poll showings, the*

party selected him as its candidate. ■ the way in which something is argued or represented: *on her own showing she would make a more suitable wife for him than her twin*.
– ORIGIN Old English *scēawung*.

showjumping ▶ noun [mass noun] the competitive sport of riding horses over a course of fences and other obstacles in an arena, with penalty points for errors.
– DERIVATIVES **showjump** verb, **showjumper** noun.

showman ▶ noun (pl. **-men**) a person who produces or presents shows as a profession, especially the proprietor, manager, or MC of a circus, fair, or other variety show.
■ a person skilled in dramatic or entertaining presentation, performance, or publicity.
– DERIVATIVES **showmanship** noun.

Show Me State informal name for MISSOURI.

shown past participle of SHOW.

show-off ▶ noun informal a person who acts pretentiously or who publicly parades themselves, their possessions, or their accomplishments.

showpiece ▶ noun something which attracts attention or admiration as an outstanding example of its type: *the factory has expanded and become a showpiece of British industry*.
■ something which offers a particular opportunity for a display of skill: *the serenade was a showpiece for the wind section*. ■ an item of work presented for exhibition or display.

showplace ▶ noun a place of beauty or interest attracting many visitors.

showreel ▶ noun a short videotape containing examples of an actor's or director's work for showing to potential employers.

showroom ▶ noun a room used to display goods for sale, such as appliances, cars, or furniture.

show-stopper ▶ noun informal a performance or item receiving prolonged applause.
■ something that is striking or has great popular appeal: *the brilliant orange flowers against the bronze-green foliage were a show-stopper* | *a show-stopper of a smile*.
– DERIVATIVES **show-stopping** adjective.

show trial ▶ noun a judicial trial held in public with the intention of influencing or satisfying public opinion, rather than of ensuring justice.

show window ▶ noun a shop window looking on to a street, used for exhibiting goods.

showy ▶ adjective (**showier**, **showiest**) having a striking appearance or style, typically by being excessively bright, colourful, or ostentatious: *showy flowers* | *she wore a great deal of showy costume jewellery*.
– DERIVATIVES **showily** adverb, **showiness** noun.

shoyu /ˈʃəʊjuː/ ▶ noun [mass noun] a type of Japanese soy sauce.
– ORIGIN from Japanese *shōyu*.

s.h.p. ▶ abbreviation for shaft horsepower.

shrank past of SHRINK.

shrapnel /ˈʃrapn(ə)l/ ▶ noun [mass noun] fragments of a bomb, shell, or other object thrown out by an explosion.
– ORIGIN early 19th cent.: named after General Henry *Shrapnel* (1761–1842), the British soldier who invented the shell.

shred ▶ noun (usu. **shreds**) a strip of some material, such as paper, cloth, or food, that has been torn, cut, or scraped from something larger: *her beautiful dress was torn to shreds* | figurative *my reputation will be in shreds*.
■ [often with negative] a very small amount: *we have not a shred of evidence to go on*.
▶ verb (**shredded**, **shredding**) [with obj.] tear or cut into shreds: [as adj. **shredded**] *shredded cabbage*.
– ORIGIN late Old English *scrēad* 'piece cut off', *scrēadian* 'trim, prune', of West Germanic origin; related to SHROUD.

shredder ▶ noun **1** a machine or other device for shredding something, especially documents. **2** informal a snowboarder.

Shreveport /ˈʃriːvpɔːt/ an industrial city in NW Louisiana, on the Red River near the border with Texas; pop. 198,525 (1990).

shrew ▶ noun a small mouse-like insectivorous mammal with a long pointed snout and tiny eyes.
● Family Soricidae: many genera, in particular *Sorex* and *Crocidura*, and numerous species.

▪a bad-tempered or aggressively assertive woman.
– DERIVATIVES **shrewish** adjective, **shrewishly** adverb, **shrewishness** noun.
– ORIGIN Old English *scrēawa*, *scrǣwa* of Germanic origin; related words in Germanic languages have senses such as 'dwarf', 'devil', or 'fox'.

shrewd ▶ **adjective 1** having or showing sharp powers of judgement; astute: *she was shrewd enough to guess the motive behind his gesture | a shrewd career move.*
2 archaic (especially of weather) piercingly cold: *a shrewd east wind.*
▪(of a blow) severe; *a bayonet's shrewd thrust.* ▪ mischievous; malicious.
– DERIVATIVES **shrewdly** adverb, **shrewdness** noun.
– ORIGIN Middle English (in the sense 'evil in nature or character'): from SHREW in the sense 'evil person or thing', or as the past participle of obsolete *shrew* 'to curse'. The word developed the sense 'cunning', and gradually gained a favourable connotation during the 17th cent.

shrew-mole ▶ **noun** a small shrew-like mole with a long tail, native to Asia and North America.
● *Neurotrichus* and other genera, family Talpidae: five species, including *N. gibbsii* of the western US.

Shrewsbury /ˈʃrəʊzb(ə)ri, ˈʃruːz-/ a town in western England, the county town of Shropshire, situated on the River Severn near the border with Wales; pop. 59,170 (1981).

Shri /ʃriː/ ▶ **noun** Indian variant spelling of SRI.

shriek ▶ **verb** [no obj.] utter a high-pitched piercing sound or words, especially as an expression of terror, pain, or excitement: *the audience **shrieked with laughter** |* [with direct speech] *'There it is!' she shrieked |* [with obj.] *she was shrieking abuse at a taxi.*
▪(of something inanimate) make a high-pitched screeching sound: *the wheels shrieked as the car sped away.* ▪ figurative be very obvious or strikingly discordant: *the answer **shrieked at** her all too clearly | the patterned carpets shrieked at Blanche from the shabby store.*
▶ **noun 1** a high-pitched piercing cry or sound; a scream: *shrieks of laughter.*
2 informal an exclamation mark.
– DERIVATIVES **shrieker** noun.
– ORIGIN late 15th cent. (as a verb): imitative; compare with dialect *screak*, Old Norse *skrækja*, also with SCREECH.

shrieval /ˈʃriːv(ə)l/ ▶ **adjective** chiefly historical of or relating to a sheriff.
– ORIGIN late 17th cent.: from *shrieve*, obsolete variant of SHERIFF.

shrievalty ▶ **noun** (pl. **-ies**) chiefly historical the office, jurisdiction, or tenure of a sheriff.

shrift ▶ **noun** [mass noun] archaic confession, especially to a priest: *go to shrift.* See also SHORT SHRIFT.
▪absolution by a priest.
– ORIGIN Old English *scrift* 'penance imposed after confession', from SHRIVE.

shrike ▶ **noun** a songbird with a strong sharply hooked bill, often impaling its prey of small birds, lizards, and insects on thorns. Also called BUTCHER-BIRD.
● Family Laniidae: several genera and numerous species, especially in Africa, e.g. the **great grey shrike** (*Lanius excubitor*), of both Eurasia and North America.
▪used in names of similar birds of other families, e.g. **cuckoo-shrike**, **pepper-shrike**.
– ORIGIN mid 16th cent.: perhaps related to Old English *scrīc* 'thrush' and Middle Low German *schrīk* 'corncrake', of imitative origin.

shrill ▶ **adjective** (of a voice or sound) high-pitched and piercing: *a shrill laugh.*
▪derogatory (especially of a complaint or demand) loud and forceful: *a concession to their shrill demands.*
▶ **verb** [no obj.] make a shrill noise: *a piercing whistle shrilled through the night air.*
▪speak or cry with a shrill voice: [with direct speech] *'For God's sake!' shrilled Jan.*
▶ **noun** [in sing.] a shrill sound or cry: *the rising shrill of women's voices.*
– DERIVATIVES **shrillness** noun, **shrilly** adverb.
– ORIGIN late Middle English: of Germanic origin; related to Low German *schrell* 'sharp in tone or taste'.

shrimp ▶ **noun** (pl. same or **shrimps**) a small free-swimming crustacean with an elongated body, typically marine and frequently of commercial importance as food.
● *Pandalus*, *Crangon*, and other genera, order Decapoda.
▪informal, derogatory a small, physically weak person.
▶ **verb** [no obj.] fish for shrimps: [as modifier] (**shrimping**) *a shrimping net.*
– ORIGIN Middle English: probably related to Middle Low German *schrempen* 'to wrinkle', Middle High German *schrimpfen* 'to contract', also to SCRIMP.

shrimper ▶ **noun 1** a boat designed or used for catching shrimps.
2 a person who fishes for shrimps.

shrimp plant ▶ **noun** an evergreen Mexican shrub with clusters of small flowers in pinkish-brown bracts that are said to resemble shrimps, widely grown as a house plant.
● *Justicia brandegeana*, family Acanthaceae.

shrine ▶ **noun** a place regarded as holy because of its associations with a divinity or a sacred person or relic, typically marked by a building or other construction.
▪a place associated with or containing memorabilia of a particular revered person or thing: *her grave has become a shrine for fans from all over the world.* ▪ a casket containing sacred relics; a reliquary. ▪ a niche or enclosure containing a religious statue or other object.
▶ **verb** [with obj.] poetic/literary enshrine.
– ORIGIN Old English *scrīn* 'cabinet, chest, reliquary', of Germanic origin; related to Dutch *schrijn* and German *Schrein*, from Latin *scrinium* 'chest for books'.

Shriner /ˈʃrʌɪnə/ ▶ **noun** a member of the Order of Nobles of the Mystic Shrine, a charitable society founded in the US in 1872.

shrink ▶ **verb** (past **shrank**; past participle **shrunk** or (especially as adj.) **shrunken**) **1** become or make smaller in size or amount; contract or cause to contract: [no obj.] *the workforce has shrunk to less than a thousand |* [with obj.] *the summer sun had shrunk and dried the wood.*
▪[no obj.] (of clothes or material) become smaller as a result of being immersed in water. ▪ [as adj. **shrunken**] (especially of a person's face or other part of the body) withered, wrinkled, or shrivelled through old age or illness: *a tiny shrunken face and enormous eyes.* ▪ [no obj.] (**shrink into oneself**) become withdrawn. ▪ [with obj.] (**shrink something on**) slip a metal tyre or other fitting on to (something) while it is expanded with heat and allow it to tighten in place.
2 [no obj., with adverbial of direction] move back or away, especially because of fear or disgust: *she shrank away from him, covering her face | he shrank back against the wall.*
▪[often with negative] (**shrink from**) be averse to or unwilling to do (something difficult or unappealing): *I don't shrink from my responsibilities.*
▶ **noun** informal a psychiatrist: *you should see a shrink.* [ORIGIN: from *headshrinker.*]
– DERIVATIVES **shrinkable** adjective, **shrinker** noun, **shrinkingly** adverb.
– ORIGIN Old English *scrincan*, of Germanic origin; related to Swedish *skrynka* 'to wrinkle'.

shrinkage ▶ **noun** [mass noun] the process, fact, or amount of shrinking: *give long curtains good hems to allow for shrinkage.*
▪an allowance made for reduction in the takings of a business due to wastage or theft.

shrinkfit ▶ **adjective** denoting clothing, especially denim jeans, designed to shrink to the desired size after initial washing.

shrinking violet ▶ **noun** [often with negative] informal an exaggeratedly shy person: *Dorothy is no shrinking violet when it comes to expressing her views.*

shrink-resistant ▶ **adjective** (of textiles or garments) resistant to shrinkage.

shrink-wrap ▶ **verb** [with obj.] package (an article) by enclosing it in clinging transparent plastic film that shrinks tightly on to it: [as adj. **shrink-wrapped**] *shrink-wrapped blocks of cheese.*
▪[as adj. **shrink-wrapped**] Computing (of a product) sold commercially as a ready-made software package.
▶ **noun** [mass noun] clinging transparent plastic film used to enclose an article as packaging.

shrive /ʃrʌɪv/ ▶ **verb** (past **shrove**; past participle **shriven**) [with obj.] archaic (of a priest) hear the confession of, assign penance to, and absolve.
▪(**shrive oneself**) present oneself to a priest for confession, penance, and absolution.
– ORIGIN Old English *scrīfan* 'impose as a penance', of Germanic origin; related to Dutch *schrijven* and German *schreiben* 'write', from Latin *scribere* 'write'.

shrivel ▶ **verb** (**shrivelled**, **shrivelling**; US **shriveled**, **shriveling**) wrinkle and contract or cause to wrinkle and contract, especially due to loss of moisture: [no obj.] *the flowers simply **shrivelled up** |* [with obj.] *a heatwave so intense that it shrivelled the grapes in every vineyard.*
▪[no obj.] figurative lose momentum, will, or desire; become insignificant or ineffectual: *as American interest shrivelled, so did the government's.* ▪ [with obj.] figurative cause to feel worthless or insignificant: *she shrivelled him with one glance.*
– ORIGIN mid 16th cent.: perhaps of Scandinavian origin; compare with Swedish dialect *skryvla* 'to wrinkle'.

shriven past participle of SHRIVE.

Shropshire a county of England, situated on the border with Wales; county town, Shrewsbury.

shroud ▶ **noun 1** a length of cloth or an enveloping garment in which a dead person is wrapped for burial: *he was buried in a linen shroud.*
▪figurative a thing that envelops or obscures something: *a **shroud of** mist | they operate behind a **shroud of** secrecy.*
▪ technical a protective casing or cover.
2 (**shrouds**) a set of ropes forming part of the standing rigging of a sailing boat and supporting the mast or topmast.
▪(also **shroud line**) each of the lines joining the canopy of a parachute to the harness.
▶ **verb** [with obj.] wrap or dress (a body) in a shroud for burial.
▪figurative cover or envelop so as to conceal from view: *mountains shrouded by cloud | the mystery which shrouds the origins of the universe.*
– ORIGIN late Old English *scrūd* 'garment, clothing', of Germanic origin, from a base meaning 'cut'; related to SHRED. An early sense of the verb (Middle English) was 'cover so as to protect'.

shroud-laid ▶ **adjective** (of rope) made of four strands laid right-handed on a core.

shrove past of SHRIVE.

Shrovetide ▶ **noun** Shrove Tuesday and the two days preceding it, when it was formerly customary to attend confession.
– ORIGIN late Middle English: of obscure origin; the first element related to SHRIVE.

Shrove Tuesday ▶ **noun** the day before Ash Wednesday. Though named for its former religious significance, it is chiefly marked by feasting and celebration, which traditionally preceded the observance of the Lenten fast. Also called PANCAKE DAY. Compare with MARDI GRAS.

shrub[1] ▶ **noun** a woody plant which is smaller than a tree and has several main stems arising at or near the ground.
– DERIVATIVES **shrubby** adjective.
– ORIGIN Old English *scrubb*, *scrybb* 'shrubbery'; compare with West Flemish *schrobbe* 'vetch', Norwegian *skrubba* 'dwarf cornel', also with SCRUB[2].

shrub[2] ▶ **noun** [mass noun] **1** a drink made of sweetened fruit juice and spirits, typically rum or brandy.
2 N. Amer. a slightly acid cordial made from fruit juice and water .
– ORIGIN early 18th cent.: from Arabic *šurb*, *šarāb*, from *šariba* 'to drink'; compare with SHERBET and SYRUP.

S

shrubbery ▶ **noun** (pl. **-ies**) an area in a garden planted with shrubs.

shrug ▶ **verb** (**shrugged**, **shrugging**) [with obj.] raise (one's shoulders) slightly and momentarily to express doubt, ignorance, or indifference: *Jimmy looked enquiringly at Pete who shrugged his shoulders |* [no obj.] *he just shrugged and didn't look interested.*
▪(**shrug something off**) dismiss something as unimportant: *the managing director shrugged off the criticism.*
▶ **noun** an act or instance of shrugging one's shoulders: *she lifted her shoulders in a dismissive shrug.*
– ORIGIN late Middle English (in the sense 'fidget'): of unknown origin.

shrunk (also **shrunken**) past participle of SHRINK.

shtetl /ˈʃtɛt(ə)l/ ▶ **noun** (pl. **shtetlach** /ˈʃtɛtlaːx/ or **shtetls**) historical a small Jewish town or village in eastern Europe.
– ORIGIN 1940s: Yiddish, 'little town'.

shtick /ʃtɪk/ ▶ **noun** informal an attention-getting or theatrical routine, gimmick, or talent.
– ORIGIN 1960s: Yiddish, from German *Stück* 'piece'.

shtook /ʃtʊk/ (also **schtuck**) ▶ **noun** [mass noun] informal trouble: *I'm **in shtook** with my boss.*

– ORIGIN 1930s: of unknown origin.

shtum /ʃtʊm/ (also **schtum**) informal ▶ **adjective** silent; non-communicative: *he kept shtum about the fact that he was sent down for fraud.*
▶ **verb** (**shtummed**, **shtumming**) [no obj.] be or become quiet and non-communicative: *you start to say something and then just when it's getting interesting you shtum up.*
– ORIGIN 1950s: Yiddish, from German *stumm*.

shtup /ʃtʊp/ (also **schtup**) vulgar slang ▶ **verb** (**shtupped**, **shtupping**) [with obj.] have sexual intercourse with (someone).
▶ **noun** an act of sexual intercourse.
– ORIGIN 1960s: Yiddish.

shubunkin /ʃʊˈbʌŋkɪn/ ▶ **noun** a goldfish of an ornamental variety, having black spots, red patches, and long fins and tail.
– ORIGIN early 20th cent.: from Japanese.

shuck /ʃʌk/ chiefly N. Amer. ▶ **noun 1** an outer covering such as a husk or pod, especially the husk of an ear of maize.
■ the shell of an oyster or clam. ■ the integument of certain insect pupae or larvae.
2 informal a person or thing regarded as worthless or contemptible: *William didn't dig the idea at all and said it was a shuck.*
▶ **exclamation** (**shucks**) informal used to express surprise, regret, irritation, or, in response to praise, self-deprecation: *'Thank you for getting it.' 'Oh, shucks, it was nothing.'* See also **AW-SHUCKS**.
▶ **verb** [with obj.] **1** remove the shucks from maize or shellfish: *shuck and drain the oysters.*
■ informal take off (a garment): *she shucked off her nightdress and started dressing.* ■ informal abandon; get rid of: *the regime's ability to **shuck off** its totalitarian characteristics.*
2 informal cause (someone) to believe something that is not true; fool or tease.
– DERIVATIVES **shucker** noun.
– ORIGIN late 17th cent.: of unknown origin.

shudder ▶ **verb** [no obj.] (of a person) tremble convulsively, typically as a result of fear or repugnance: *he shuddered with revulsion* | [with infinitive] figurative *I **shudder to think** of retirement.*
■ (especially of a vehicle, machine, or building) shake or vibrate deeply: *the train shuddered and edged forward.* ■ [usu. as adj. **shuddering**] (of a person's breathing) be unsteady, especially as a result of emotional disturbance: *he drew a deep, shuddering breath.*
▶ **noun** an act of shuddering: *the elevator rose with a shudder* | figurative *the pound's devaluation **sent shudders through** the market.*
– PHRASES **give someone the shudders** informal cause someone to feel repugnance or fear.
– DERIVATIVES **shudderingly** adverb, **shuddery** adjective.
– ORIGIN Middle English (as a verb): from Middle Dutch *schüderen*, from a Germanic base meaning 'shake'.

shuffle /ˈʃʌf(ə)l/ ▶ **verb 1** [no obj., with adverbial] walk by dragging one's feet along or without lifting them fully from the ground: *I stepped into my skis and shuffled to the edge of the steep slope* | [as adj. **shuffling**] *she heard Gran's shuffling steps.*
■ shift one's position while sitting or move one's feet while standing, typically because of boredom, nervousness, or embarrassment: *Christine shuffled uneasily in her chair* | [with obj.] *Ben shuffled his feet in the awkward silence.*
2 [with obj.] rearrange (a pack of cards) by sliding them over each other quickly.
■ move (people or things) around so as to occupy different positions or to be in a different order. ■ [no obj.] (**shuffle through**) sort or look through (a number of things) hurriedly: *he shuffled through the papers on his desk.*
3 [with obj.] (**shuffle something into**) put part of one's body into (an item of clothing), typically in a clumsy way: *shuffling her feet into a pair of shoes, she tiptoed out of the room.*
■ (**shuffle something off**) get out of or avoid a responsibility or obligation: *some hospitals can shuffle off their responsibilities by claiming to have no suitable facilities.* ■ [no obj.] archaic behave in a shifty or evasive manner: *Mr Milles did not frankly own it, but seem'd to shuffle about it.* ■ [no obj.] (**shuffle out of**) archaic get out of (a difficult situation) in an underhand or evasive manner: *he shuffles out of the consequences by vague charges of undue influence.*
▶ **noun 1** [in sing.] a shuffling movement, walk, or sound: *there was a shuffle of approaching feet.*
■ a quick dragging or scraping movement of the feet in dancing. ■ a dance performed with such steps. ■ a piece of music for or in the style of such a dance. ■ a rhythmic motif based on such a dance step and typical of early jazz, consisting of alternating crotchets and quavers in a triplet pattern.
2 an act of shuffling a pack of cards.
■ a change of order or relative positions; a reshuffle: *the Prime Minister may have to consider a cabinet shuffle in the spring.* ■ a facility on a CD player for playing tracks in an arbitrary order: [as modifier] *a shuffle facility.*
3 archaic a piece of equivocation or subterfuge.
– PHRASES **be** (or **get**) **lost in the shuffle** N. Amer. informal be overlooked or missed in a confused or crowded situation. **shuffle off this mortal coil** see **COIL**[2].
– DERIVATIVES **shuffler** noun.
– ORIGIN mid 16th cent.: perhaps from Low German *schuffeln* 'walk clumsily', also 'deal dishonestly, shuffle (cards)', of Germanic origin; related to **SHOVE** and **SCUFFLE**.

shuffleboard ▶ **noun** North American term for **SHOVELBOARD**.

shufti /ˈʃʊfti/ ▶ **noun** (pl. **shuftis**) Brit. informal a look or reconnoitre, especially a quick one: *I'll take a shufti round the wood while I'm about it.*
– ORIGIN 1940s (originally military slang): from Arabic *šāfa* 'try to see'.

shul /ʃuːl/ ▶ **noun** a synagogue.
– ORIGIN late 19th cent.: Yiddish, from German *Schule* 'school'.

Shumen /ˈʃuːmən/ an industrial city in NE Bulgaria; pop. 126,350 (1990).

shun ▶ **verb** (**shunned**, **shunning**) [with obj.] persistently avoid, ignore, or reject (someone or something) through antipathy or caution: *he shunned fashionable society* | [as adj. **shunned**] *the shunned wife's quiet divorce.*
– ORIGIN Old English *scunian* 'abhor, shrink back with fear, seek safety from an enemy', of unknown origin.

shunt ▶ **verb 1** [with obj. and adverbial of direction] push or pull (a train or part of a train) from the main line to a siding or from one line of rails to another: *their train had been shunted into a siding.*
■ (usu. **be shunted**) push or shove (someone or something): *chairs were being shunted to and fro.* ■ direct or divert (someone or something) to a less important place or position: *amateurs were gradually being shunted to filing jobs.*
2 [with obj.] provide (an electrical current) with a conductor joining two points of a circuit, through which more or less of the current may be diverted.
▶ **noun 1** an act of pushing or shoving something.
■ Brit. informal a motor accident, especially a collision of vehicles travelling one close behind the other.
2 an electrical conductor joining two points of a circuit, through which more or less of a current may be diverted.
■ Surgery an alternative path for the passage of the blood or other body fluid: [as modifier] *shunt surgery.*
– ORIGIN Middle English (in the sense 'move suddenly aside'): perhaps from **SHUN**.

shunter ▶ **noun** a small locomotive used for shunting.
■ a railway worker engaged in such work, especially to couple and uncouple wagons.

shura /ˈʃʊərə/ ▶ **noun** [mass noun] Islam the principle of consultation, in particular as applied to government.
■ [count noun] a consultative council.
– ORIGIN from Arabic *šūrā* 'consultation'.

shuriken /ˈʃʊərɪkɛn/ ▶ **noun** a weapon in the form of a star with projecting blades or points, used as a missile in some martial arts.
– ORIGIN Japanese, literally 'dagger in the hand'.

shush /ʃʊʃ, ʃʌʃ/ ▶ **exclamation** be quiet: *'Shush! Do you want to wake everyone?'*
▶ **noun 1** an utterance of 'shush': *the thumps were followed by shushes from the aunts.*
■ [mass noun] informal silence: *could we have a little shush please?*
2 a soft swishing or rustling sound.
▶ **verb 1** [with obj.] tell or signal (someone) to be silent: *she shushed him with a wave.*
■ [no obj.] become or remain silent: *Beth told her to shush.*
2 [no obj., usu. with adverbial of direction] move with or make a soft swishing or rustling sound: *I stood to watch a big liner shushing slowly past* | [as noun **shushing**] *she could hear the gentle shushing of the waves.*
– ORIGIN 1920s: imitative.

shu-shu /ˈʃuːʃuː/ W. Indian ▶ **noun** [mass noun] rumour; gossip: *the shu-shu is that he is being paid his full salary ever since he was ordered back to work.*
▶ **verb** [no obj.] speak at close range in a low tone, typically to exchange gossip.
– ORIGIN from French *chuchoter* 'to whisper'.

shut ▶ **verb** (**shutting**; past and past participle **shut**) [with obj.] move (something) into position so that it blocks an opening: *shut the window, please* | *she shut her lips tight* | [as adj. **shut**] *she slammed the door shut.*
■ [no obj.] (of something that can block an opening) be moved or be able to be moved into position: *the door shut behind him.* ■ block an opening into (something) by moving something into position: *he shut the box and locked it.* ■ (**shut it**) [in imperative] informal stop talking; be quiet. ■ [with obj. and adverbial] keep (someone or something) in a place by closing something such as a door: *it was his own dog which he had accidentally shut outside.* ■ fold or bring together the sides of (something) so as to close it: *he shut his book.* ■ prevent access to or along: *they ought to shut the path up to that terrible cliff.* ■ chiefly Brit. make or become unavailable for business or service, either permanently or until it is next due to be open: [with obj.] *we shut the shop for lunch* | [no obj.] *the accident and emergency departments will shut.*
– PHRASES **be** (or **get**) **shut of** informal be (or get) rid of: *I'd be glad to be shut of him.* **shut the door on** (or **to**) see **DOOR**. **shut one's eyes to** see **EYE**. **shut one's mind to** see **MIND**. **shut the stable door after the horse has bolted** see **STABLE DOOR**. **shut up shop** cease trading, either temporarily or permanently. ■ informal stop some activity: *flowers that come in one great burst, then shut up shop for the rest of the year.* **shut your face** (or **mouth** or **trap**)**!** informal used as a rude or angry way of telling someone to be quiet .
– ORIGIN Old English *scyttan* 'put (a bolt) in position to hold fast', of West Germanic origin; related to Dutch *schutten* 'shut up, obstruct', also to **SHOOT**.
▶ **shut down** (or **shut something down**) cease (or cause something to cease) business or operation: *the plant's operators decided to shut down the reactor.*
shut someone/thing in keep someone or something inside a place by closing something such as a door: *her parents shut her in an upstairs room.* ■ enclose or surround a place: *the village is shut in by the mountains on either side.* ■ trap something by shutting a door or drawer on it: *you shut your finger in the door.*
shut off (or **shut something off**) (used especially in relation to water, electricity, or gas) stop (or cause something to stop) flowing: *he was about to shut off the power.* ■ stop (or cause something to stop) working: *the engines shut off automatically.* ■ (**shut something off**) block the entrances and exits of something: *the six compartments were being shut off from each other.*
shut oneself off isolate oneself from other people.
shut someone/thing out keep someone or something out of a place or situation: *the door swung to behind them, shutting out some of the noise* ■ prevent an opponent from scoring in a game. ■ screen someone or something from view: *clouds shut out the stars.* ■ prevent something from occurring: *there was a high-mindedness which shut out any consideration of alternatives.* ■ block something such as a painful memory from the mind: *anything he didn't like he shut out.*
shut up (or **shut someone up**) [often in imperative] informal stop (or cause someone to stop) talking: *just shut up and listen.*
shut something up close all doors and windows of a building or room, typically because it will be unoccupied for some time.

shutdown ▶ **noun** a closure of a factory or system, typically a temporary closure due to a fault or for maintenance.
■ a turning off of a computer or computer system.

Shute, Nevil (1899–1960), English novelist; pseudonym of *Nevil Shute Norway*. After the Second World War he settled in Australia, which provides the setting for his later novels. Notable works: *A Town Like Alice* (1950) and *On the Beach* (1957).

shut-eye ▶ **noun** [mass noun] informal sleep: *we'd better get some shut-eye.*

shut-in ▶ **noun 1** a person confined indoors,

especially as a result of either physical or mental disability.

2 a state or period in which an oil or gas well has available but unused capacity.

shut-off ▶ **noun** [usu. as modifier] a device used for stopping a supply or operation: *a shut-off valve.*
■ [mass noun] the cessation of flow, supply, or activity.

shutout ▶ **noun** N. Amer. a play, game, or inning in which the opposition is prevented from scoring.

shut-out bid ▶ **noun** Bridge a high bid intended to end the auction; a pre-emptive bid.

shutter ▶ **noun 1** each of a pair of hinged panels fixed inside or outside a window that can be closed for security or privacy or to keep out the light.
2 Photography a device that opens and closes to expose the film in a camera.
3 Music the blind enclosing the swell box in an organ, used for controlling the volume of sound.
▶ **verb** [with obj.] close the shutters of (a window or building): *the windows were shuttered against the afternoon heat* | [as adj. **shuttered**] *barred and shuttered shops.*
– PHRASES **put up the shutters** (of a business) cease trading for the day or permanently.
– DERIVATIVES **shutterless** adjective.

shutterbug ▶ **noun** informal, chiefly N. Amer. an enthusiastic photographer.

shuttering ▶ **noun** [mass noun] wood in planks or strips used as a temporary structure for fencing to contain setting concrete, to support the sides of earth trenches, or similar.
■ [count noun] a temporary structure of this kind.

shutter priority ▶ **noun** [mass noun] Photography a system used in some automatic cameras in which the shutter speed is selected by the user and the appropriate aperture is then set by the camera. Compare with **APERTURE PRIORITY**.

shutter release ▶ **noun** the button on a camera that is pressed to make the shutter open.

shutter speed ▶ **noun** Photography the nominal time for which a shutter is open at a given setting.

shuttle ▶ **noun 1** a form of transport that travels regularly between two places: *the nine o'clock shuttle from Edinburgh* | [as modifier] *a shuttle bus service from the city centre.*
■ short for **SPACE SHUTTLE**.
2 a bobbin with two pointed ends used for carrying the weft thread across between the warp threads in weaving.
■ a bobbin carrying the lower thread in a sewing machine.
3 short for **SHUTTLECOCK**.
▶ **verb** [no obj., with adverbial of direction] travel regularly between two or more places: *the Secretary of State shuttled to and fro seeking compromise.*
■ [with obj. and adverbial of direction] transport in a shuttle: *the river taxi shuttled employees between the newspaper's offices and the capital.*
– ORIGIN Old English *scytel* 'dart, missile', of Germanic origin; compare with Old Norse *skutill* 'harpoon'; related to **SHOOT**. Sense 1 and the verb are from the movement of the bobbin from one side of the loom to the other and back.

shuttlecock ▶ **noun** a cork to which feathers are attached to form a cone shape, or a similar object of plastic, struck with rackets in the games of badminton and battledore.

shuttle diplomacy ▶ **noun** [mass noun] negotiations conducted by a mediator who travels between two or more parties that are reluctant to hold direct discussions.

shy[1] ▶ **adjective** (**shyer**, **shyest**) **1** having or showing nervousness or timidity in the company of other people: *I was pretty shy at school* | *a shy smile.*
■ [predic.] (**shy of/about**) slow or reluctant to do (something): *the wealthy have become less shy of displaying their privilege.* ■ [in combination] having a dislike of or aversion to a specified thing: *they were a little camera-shy.* ■ (of a wild mammal or bird) reluctant to remain in sight of humans.
2 [predic.] (**shy of**) informal less than; short of: *the shares are 29p shy of their flotation price.*
■ before: *he left school just shy of his fourteenth birthday.*
3 (of a plant) not bearing flowers or fruit well or prolifically.
▶ **verb** (**-ies**, **-ied**) [no obj.] (especially of a horse) start suddenly aside in fright at an object, noise, or movement.
■ (**shy from**) avoid doing or becoming involved in (something) due to nervousness or a lack of confidence: *don't shy away from saying what you think.*
▶ **noun** a sudden startled movement, especially of a frightened horse.
– DERIVATIVES **shyer** noun, **shyly** adverb, **shyness** noun.
– ORIGIN Old English *scēoh* '(of a horse) easily frightened', of Germanic origin; related to German *scheuen* 'shun', *scheuchen* 'scare'; compare with **ESCHEW**. The verb dates from the mid 17th cent.

shy[2] dated ▶ **verb** (**-ies**, **-ied**) [with obj.] fling or throw (something) at a target: *he tore the spectacles off and shied them at her.*
▶ **noun** (pl. **-ies**) an act of flinging or throwing something at a target.
– PHRASES **have a shy at** try to hit something, especially with a ball or stone. ■ archaic attempt to do or obtain something. ■ archaic jeer at: *you are always having a shy at Lady Ann and her relations.*
– ORIGIN late 18th cent.: of unknown origin.

Shylock a Jewish moneylender in Shakespeare's *Merchant of Venice*, who lends money to Antonio but demands in return a pound of Antonio's own flesh should the debt not be repaid on time.
■ [as noun **a Shylock**] a moneylender who charges extremely high rates of interest.

shyster ▶ **noun** informal a person, especially a lawyer, who uses unscrupulous, fraudulent, or deceptive methods in business.
– ORIGIN mid 19th cent.: said to be from *Scheuster*, the name of a lawyer whose behaviour provoked accusations of 'scheuster' practices, perhaps reinforced by German *Scheisser* 'worthless person'.

SI ▶ **abbreviation for** ■ the international system of units of measurement. [ORIGIN: from French *Système International*.] ■ Law statutory instrument.

Si ▶ **symbol for** the chemical element silicon.

si /siː/ ▶ **noun** Music another term for **TE**.
– ORIGIN early 18th cent.: from the initial letters of *Sancte Iohannes*, the closing words of a Latin hymn (see **SOLMIZATION**).

Siachen Glacier /sɪˈɑːtʃən/ a glacier in the Karakoram mountains in NW India, situated at an altitude of some 5,500 m (17,800 ft). Extending over 70 km (44 miles), it is one of the world's longest glaciers.

sial /ˈsʌɪəl/ ▶ **noun** [mass noun] Geology the material of the upper or continental part of the earth's crust, characterized as relatively light and rich in silica and alumina. Contrasted with **SIMA**.
– ORIGIN 1920s: from the initial letters of **SILICA** and **ALUMINA**.

sialagogue /ˈsʌɪələgɒg/ ▶ **noun** Medicine a drug that promotes the secretion of saliva.
– ORIGIN late 18th cent.: from French, from Greek *sialon* 'saliva' + *agōgos* 'leading'.

sialic acid /sʌɪˈalɪk/ ▶ **noun** [mass noun] Biochemistry a substance present in saliva which consists of acyl derivatives of neuraminic acid.
– ORIGIN 1950s: *sialic* from Greek *sialon* 'saliva' + **-IC**.

sialidase /sʌɪˈalɪdeɪz/ ▶ **noun** another term for **NEURAMINIDASE**.
– ORIGIN 1950s: from Greek *sialon* 'saliva' + **-IDE** + **-ASE**.

Sialkot /sɪˈɑːlkɒt/ an industrial city in the province of Punjab, in Pakistan; pop. 296,000 (1981).

Siam /sʌɪˈam/ former name (until 1939) for **THAILAND**.

Siam, Gulf of former name for the Gulf of Thailand (see **THAILAND, GULF OF**).

siamang /ˈsʌɪəmaŋ, ˈsiːə-/ ▶ **noun** a large black gibbon native to Sumatra and Malaya.
• *Hylobates syndactylus*, family Hylobatidae.
– ORIGIN early 19th cent.: from Malay.

Siamese ▶ **noun** (pl. same) **1** dated a native of Siam (now Thailand) in SE Asia.
2 old-fashioned term for **THAI** (the language).
3 (also **Siamese cat**) a cat of a lightly built short-haired breed characterized by slanting blue eyes and typically pale fur with darker points.
▶ **adjective** dated of or concerning Siam, its people, or language.

Siamese fighting fish ▶ **noun** see **FIGHTING FISH**.

Siamese twins ▶ **plural noun** twins that are physically joined at birth, sometimes sharing organs, and sometimes separable by surgery (depending on the degree of fusion).
– ORIGIN with reference to the *Siamese* men Chang and Eng (1811–74), who, despite being joined at the waist, led an active life.

Sian variant of **XIAN**.

SIB ▶ **abbreviation for** Securities and Investment Board, a regulatory body that oversees London's financial markets.

sib ▶ **noun 1** chiefly Zoology a brother or sister; a sibling.
2 Anthropology a group of people recognized by an individual as his or her kindred.
– ORIGIN Old English 'related by birth or descent', of unknown origin. Sense 1 dates from the early 20th cent.

Sibelius /sɪˈbeɪlɪəs/, Jean (1865–1957), Finnish composer; born *Johan Julius Christian Sibelius*. His affinity for his country's landscape and legends, especially the epic *Kalevala*, is expressed in a series of symphonic poems including *The Swan of Tuonela* (1893), *Finlandia* (1899), and *Tapiola* (1925).

Šibenik /ˈʃɪbɛnɪk/ an industrial city and port in Croatia, on the Adriatic coast; pop. 41,000 (1991).

Siberia /sʌɪˈbɪərɪə/ a vast region of Russia, extending from the Urals to the Pacific and from the Arctic coast to the northern borders of Kazakhstan, Mongolia, and China. Noted for the severity of its winters, it was traditionally used as a place of exile; it is now a major source of minerals and hydroelectric power.
– DERIVATIVES **Siberian** adjective & noun.

Siberian tiger ▶ **noun** a tiger of a large and threatened race with a long thick coat, found in SE Siberia and NE China.

sibia /ˈsɪbɪə/ ▶ **noun** a South Asian songbird of the babbler family, typically having a blackish or greyish head and a long tail.
• Genus *Heterophasia* (and *Crocias*), family Timaliidae: several species.
– ORIGIN from Nepalese *sibya*.

sibilant ▶ **adjective** Phonetics (of a speech sound) sounded with a hissing effect, for example *s*, *sh*.
■ making or characterized by a hissing sound: *his sibilant whisper.*
▶ **noun** Phonetics a sibilant speech sound.
– DERIVATIVES **sibilance** noun.
– ORIGIN mid 17th cent.: from Latin *sibilant-* 'hissing', from the verb *sibilare*.

Sibiu /siːˈbjuː/ an industrial city in central Romania; pop. 188,000 (1990).

siblicide /ˈsɪblɪsʌɪd/ ▶ **noun** [mass noun] Zoology the killing of a sibling or siblings, as a behaviour pattern typical in various animal groups.

sibling ▶ **noun** each of two or more children or offspring having one or both parents in common; a brother or sister.
– ORIGIN Old English in the sense 'relative' (see **SIB**, **-LING**). The current sense dates from the early 20th cent.

sibship ▶ **noun** chiefly Zoology a group of offspring having the same two parents.
■ [mass noun] Anthropology the state of belonging to a sib or the same sib.

sibyl ▶ **noun** a woman in ancient times supposed to utter the oracles and prophecies of a god.
■ poetic/literary a woman able to foretell the future.
– ORIGIN from Old French *Sibile* or medieval Latin *Sibilla*, via Latin from Greek *Sibulla*.

sibylline /ˈsɪbɪlʌɪn/ ▶ **adjective** chiefly poetic/literary of, relating to, or characteristic of a sibyl; prophetic and mysterious.
– ORIGIN late 16th cent.: from Latin *Sibillinus*, from *Sibylla* (see **SIBYL**).

Sibylline books ▶ **plural noun** a collection of oracles belonging to the ancient Roman state and used for guidance by magistrates and others.

sic /sɪk/ ▶ **adverb** used in brackets after a copied or quoted word that appears odd or erroneous to show that the word is quoted exactly as it stands in the original, as in *a story must hold a child's interest and 'enrich his* (sic) *life'.*
– ORIGIN Latin, literally 'so, thus'.

siccative /ˈsɪkətɪv/ ▶ **noun** a drying agent used as a component of paint.
– ORIGIN late Middle English: from late Latin *siccativus*, from *siccare* 'to dry'.

sice[1] /sʌɪs/ ▶ **noun** (especially in gambling) the six on a dice.
– ORIGIN late Middle English: from Old French *sis*, from Latin *sex* 'six'.

sice² ▶ **noun** variant spelling of **SYCE**.

Sichuan /sɪˈtʃwɑːn/ (also **Szechuan** or **Szechwan**) a province of west central China; capital, Chengdu.

Sicilia /siˈtʃilja/ Italian name for **SICILY**.

siciliano /sɪˌtʃɪlɪˈɑːnəʊ, -ˌsɪlɪ-/ (also **siciliana**) ▶ **noun** (pl. **-os**) a dance, song, or instrumental piece in 6/8 or 12/8 time, typically in a minor key, and evoking a pastoral mood.
– ORIGIN Italian, literally 'Sicilian'.

Sicilian Vespers a massacre of French inhabitants of Sicily, which began near Palermo at the time of vespers on Easter Monday in 1282. The ensuing war resulted in the replacement of the unpopular French Angevin dynasty by the Spanish House of Aragon.

Sicily a large Italian island in the Mediterranean, off the south-western tip of Italy; capital, Palermo. It is separated from the Italian mainland by the Strait of Messina and its highest point is the volcano Mount Etna. Italian name **SICILIA**.
– DERIVATIVES **Sicilian** /sɪˈsɪlɪən/ adjective & noun.

sick¹ ▶ **adjective** **1** affected by physical or mental illness: *nursing very sick children* | *half my staff were off sick* | [as plural noun **the sick**] *visiting the sick and the elderly.*
■of or relating to those who are ill: *the company organized a sick fund for its workers.* ■ figurative (of an organization, system, or society) suffering from serious problems, especially of a financial nature: *the British economy remains sick.* ■ archaic pining or longing for someone or something: *he was* **sick for** *a sight of her.*
2 [predic.] feeling nauseous and wanting to vomit: *he was starting to feel sick* | *Mark felt sick with fear.*
■[attrib.] (of an emotion) so intense as to cause one to feel unwell or nauseous: *he had a sick fear of returning.* ■ informal disappointed, mortified, or miserable: *he looked pretty sick at that, but he eventually agreed.*
3 [predic.] (**sick of**) intensely annoyed with or bored by (someone or something) as a result of having had too much of them: *I'm absolutely sick of your moods.*
4 informal (especially of humour) having something unpleasant such as death, illness, or misfortune as its subject and dealing with it in an offensive way: *this was someone's idea of a sick joke.*
■(of a person) having abnormal or unnatural tendencies; perverted: *he is a deeply sick man from whom society needs to be protected.*
▶ **noun** [mass noun] Brit. informal vomit.
▶ **verb** [with obj.] (**sick something up**) Brit. informal bring something up by vomiting.
– PHRASES **be sick 1** be ill. **2** Brit. vomit. **get sick 1** be ill. **2** US vomit. **make someone sick** cause someone to vomit or feel nauseous or unwell. ■ cause someone to feel intense annoyance or disgust: *you're so damned self-righteous you make me sick!* **—— oneself sick** do something to such an extent that one feels nauseous or unwell (often used for emphasis): *she was* **worrying herself sick** *about Mike.* **on the sick** Brit. informal receiving sickness benefit. **sick and tired of** informal annoyed about or bored with (something) and unwilling to put up with it any longer: *I am sick and tired of all the criticism.* **(as) sick as a dog** informal extremely ill. **(as) sick as a parrot** informal extremely disappointed. **the sick man of ——** a country that is politically or economically unsound, especially in comparison with its neighbours in the region specified: *the country had been the sick man of Europe for too long.* [ORIGIN: from a use of *sick man*, frequently applied in the late 19th cent. to the Sultan of Turkey, later extended to Turkey and other countries.] **sick to death of** informal another way of saying ***sick and tired of*** above. **sick to one's stomach** nauseous. ■ disgusted.
– DERIVATIVES **sickish** adjective.
– ORIGIN Old English *sēoc* 'affected by illness', of Germanic origin; related to Dutch *ziek* and German *siech.*

sick² ▶ **verb** [with obj.] (**sick something on**) set a dog on (someone or something): *the plan was to surprise the heck out of the grizzly by sicking the dog on him.*
■(**sick someone on**) informal set someone to pursue, keep watch on, or accompany (another).
– ORIGIN mid 19th cent.: dialect variant of **SEEK**.

sick bag ▶ **noun** a paper bag provided in an aircraft or ship as a receptacle for vomit.

sickbay ▶ **noun** a room or building set aside for the treatment or accommodation of the sick, especially within a military base, ship, or school.

sickbed ▶ **noun** an invalid's bed (often used to refer to the state or condition of being an invalid): *he had climbed from his sickbed to help the club.*

sick benefit ▶ **noun** informal short for **SICKNESS BENEFIT**.

sick building syndrome ▶ **noun** [mass noun] a condition affecting office workers, typically marked by headaches and respiratory problems, attributed to unhealthy or stressful factors in the working environment such as poor ventilation.

sick call ▶ **noun 1** a visit to a sick person, typically one made by a doctor or priest.
2 Military a summons for those reporting sick to attend for treatment.

sicken ▶ **verb 1** [with obj.] (often **be sickened**) make (someone) feel disgusted or appalled: *she was sickened by the bomb attack.*
■[no obj.] archaic feel disgust or horror: *he* **sickened at** *the thought.*
2 [no obj.] become ill: *Dawson sickened unexpectedly and died in 1916.*
■(**sicken for**) begin to show symptoms of (a particular illness): *I hope I'm not sickening for a cold.*

sickener ▶ **noun 1** informal something which causes disgust or severe disappointment.
2 (**the sickener**) a poisonous toadstool with a red cap and a white or cream-coloured stem and gills, found commonly in both Eurasia and North America.
● Genus *Russula*, family Russulaceae, class Hymenomycetes, in particular *R. emetica*.

sickening ▶ **adjective** causing or liable to cause a feeling of nausea or disgust: *a sickening stench of blood* | *she hit the ground with a sickening thud.*
■informal causing irritation or annoyance.
– DERIVATIVES **sickeningly** adverb.

Sickert /ˈsɪkət/, Walter Richard (1860–1942), British painter, of Danish and Anglo-Irish descent. His subjects are mainly urban scenes and figure compositions, particularly pictures of the theatre and music hall, and drab domestic interiors.

sick headache ▶ **noun** a headache accompanied by nausea, particularly a migraine.

sickie ▶ **noun** informal **1** chiefly Brit. a period of sick leave, typically one taken when one is not actually ill.
2 another word for **SICKO**.

sickle ▶ **noun** a short-handled farming tool with a semicircular blade, used for cutting corn, lopping, or trimming.
– ORIGIN Old English *sicol, sicel*, of Germanic origin; related to Dutch *sikkel* and German *Sichel*, based on Latin *secula*, from *secare* 'to cut'.

sick leave ▶ **noun** [mass noun] leave of absence granted because of illness.

sicklebill ▶ **noun** any of a number of birds with a long narrow downcurved bill:
● a tropical American hummingbird (genus *Eutoxeres*, family Trochilidae: two species). ● a New Guinea bird of paradise (two genera in the family Paradisaeidae).

sickle-cell anaemia (also **sickle-cell disease**) ▶ **noun** [mass noun] a severe hereditary form of anaemia in which a mutated form of haemoglobin distorts the red blood cells into a crescent shape at low oxygen levels. It is commonest among those of African descent.

sickle-cell trait ▶ **noun** [mass noun] a relatively mild condition caused by the presence of a single gene for sickle-cell anaemia, producing a smaller amount of abnormal haemoglobin and conferring some resistance to malaria.

sickle feather ▶ **noun** each of the long middle feathers of a cock's tail.

sick list ▶ **noun** a list, especially in the army or navy, of people who are ill and unable to work.

sickly ▶ **adjective** (**sicklier, sickliest**) **1** often ill; in poor health: *she was a thin, sickly child.*
■(of a person's complexion or expression) indicative of poor health: *his usual sickly pallor.* ■ poetic/literary (of a place, climate, or time) causing or characterized by unhealthiness: *a deep sickly vaporous swamp.*
2 (of a flavour, smell, colour, or light) unpleasant as to induce discomfort or nausea: *the walls were painted a sickly green* | *she liked her coffee sweet and sickly.*
■excessively sentimental or mawkish: *a sickly fable of delicate young lovers.*
– DERIVATIVES **sickliness** noun.
– ORIGIN late Middle English: probably suggested by Old Norse *sjúkligr.*

sick-making ▶ **adjective** informal nauseatingly unpleasant or shocking: *a sick-making stench.*
■overly sentimental, coy, or trite.

sickness ▶ **noun** [mass noun] **1** the state of being ill: *she was absent through sickness* | [as modifier] *a sickness allowance.*
■[often with adj. or noun modifier] a particular type of illness or disease: *botulism causes fodder sickness of horses* | [count noun] *a woman suffering an incurable sickness.*
2 the feeling or fact of being affected with nausea or vomiting: *she felt a wave of sickness wash over her* | *travel sickness.*
– ORIGIN Old English *sēocnesse* (see **SICK¹**, **-NESS**).

sickness benefit ▶ **noun** [mass noun] (in the UK) benefit paid weekly by the state to an individual for sickness which interrupts paid employment.

sick note ▶ **noun** a note to be given to an employer, teacher, or person in authority confirming that an absence was due to sickness.

sick nurse ▶ **noun** dated a nurse who looks after the sick and infirm (as distinct from a children's nurse).

sicko ▶ **noun** (pl. **-os**) informal a mentally ill or perverted person, especially one who is sadistic.

sick-out ▶ **noun** informal, chiefly N. Amer. a period of unwarranted sick leave taken as a form of group industrial action.

sickroom ▶ **noun** a room in a school or place of work occupied by or set apart for people who are unwell.

sida /ˈsʌɪdə/ ▶ **noun** a plant of the mallow family, native to tropical and warm regions.
● Genus *Sida*, family Malvaceae.
– ORIGIN modern Latin, from Greek *sidē* 'pomegranate tree', also 'water lily'.

sidalcea /sɪˈdalsɪə/ ▶ **noun** a herbaceous North American plant of the mallow family, several kinds of which are cultivated as ornamentals.
● Genus *Sidalcea*, family Malvaceae.
– ORIGIN modern Latin, from *Sida* + *Alcea*, names of related genera.

siddha /ˈsɪdʌ/ ▶ **noun** Hinduism an ascetic who has achieved enlightenment.
– ORIGIN Sanskrit.

Siddhartha Gautama /sɪˌdɑːtə ˈgaʊtəmə/ see **BUDDHA**.

siddhi /ˈsɪdi/ ▶ **noun** Hinduism **1** [mass noun] complete understanding; enlightenment.
2 (pl. **siddhis**) a paranormal power possessed by a siddha.
– ORIGIN Sanskrit.

Siddons /ˈsɪd(ə)nz/, Mrs Sarah (1755–1831), English actress, sister of John Kemble; born *Sarah Kemble*. She was an acclaimed tragic actress, noted particularly for her role as Lady Macbeth.

side ▶ **noun 1** a position to the left or right of an object, place, or central point: *a town on the other side of the river* | *on either side of the entrance was a garden* | *Rona tilted her head to one side.*
■either of the two halves of an object, surface, or place regarded as divided by an imaginary central line: *she lay on her side of the bed* | *the left side of the brain.* ■ the right or the left part of a person's or animal's body, especially of the human torso: *he has been paralysed down his right side since birth.* ■ [in sing.] a place or position closely adjacent to someone: *his wife stood* **at his side**. ■ either of the lateral halves of the body of a butchered animal, or an animal or fish prepared for eating: *a side of beef.*
2 an upright or sloping surface of a structure or object that is not the top or bottom and generally not the front or back: *a car crashed into the side of the house* | *line the sides of the cake tin* | [as modifier] *a side entrance.*
■each of the flat surfaces of a solid object. ■ either of the two surfaces of something flat and thin, such as paper or cloth. ■ the amount of writing needed to fill one side of a sheet of paper: *she told us not to write more than three sides.* ■ either of the two faces of a record or of the two separate tracks on a length of recording tape. ■ Brit. informal a television channel considered as one of two or more that are available: *What's on the other side?* ■ W. Indian either of a pair of things: *a pair of shoes, one side winged by a bullet.*
3 a part or region near the edge and away from the

S

middle of something: *a minibus was parked at the side of the road | cottages on the south side of the green.*

■[as modifier] subsidiary to or less important than something: *a side dish of fresh vegetables.* ■ chiefly N. Amer. a dish served as subsidiary to the main one: *sides of German potato salad and red cabbage.* ■ each of the lines forming the boundary of a plane rectilinear figure: *the farm buildings formed three sides of a square.*

4 a person or group opposing another or others in a dispute, contest, or debate: *the two sides agreed to resume border trade | whose side are you on?*

■a sports team. ■ the position, interests, or attitude of one person or group, especially when regarded as being in opposition to another or others: *Mrs Burt hasn't kept her side of the bargain | the conservationists are on the city's side of the case.* ■ a particular aspect of something, especially a situation or a person's character: *her ability to put up with his disagreeable side.* ■ a person's kinship or line of descent as traced through either their father or mother: *Richard was of French descent on his mother's side.*

5 (also **side spin**) [mass noun] horizontal spinning motion given to a ball.

■chiefly Brit. spin given to the cue ball in snooker and billiards by hitting it on one side, not centrally.

6 [mass noun] [usu. with negative] Brit. informal boastfulness or pretentiousness of manner or attitude: *there was absolutely no side to him.*

▶**verb 1** [no obj.] (**side with/against**) support or oppose in a conflict, dispute, or debate: *he felt that Max had betrayed him by siding with Beatrice.*

2 [with obj.] provide with a side or sides; form the side of: *the hills that side a long valley.*

– PHRASES **by** (or **at**) **someone's side** close to someone, especially so as to give them comfort or moral support: *a stepson who stayed by your side when your own son deserted you.* **by the side of** close to: *a house by the side of the road.* **from side to side 1** alternately left and right from a central point: *I shook my head frantically from side to side.* **2** across the entire width; right across: *the fleet stretched four miles from side to side.* **have something on one's side** (or **something is on one's side**) something is operating to one's advantage: *now he had time on his side, Thomas relaxed a little.* **let the side down** Brit. fail to meet the expectations of one's colleagues or friends, especially by mismanaging something or otherwise causing them embarrassment. **on/from every side** (or **on/from all sides**) in or from all directions; everywhere: *there were shouts now from all sides.* **on** (or **to**) **one side** out of one's way; aside. ■ to be dealt with or considered later, especially because tending to distract one from something more important: *before the kick-off a player has to set his disappointments and frustrations to one side.* **on the —— side** tending towards being ——; rather —— (used to qualify an adjective): *these boots are a bit on the tight side.* **on the side 1** in addition to one's regular job or as a subsidiary source of income: *no one lived in the property, but the caretaker made a little on the side by letting rooms out.* **2** secretly, especially with regard to a relationship in addition to one's legal or regular partner: *Brian had a mistress on the side.* **3** N. Amer. served separately from the main dish: *a club sandwich with french fries on the side.* **side by side** (of two or more people or things) close together and facing the same way: *on we jogged, side by side, for a mile.* ■ together: *we have been using both systems, side by side, for two years.* ■ (of people or groups) supporting each other; in cooperation: *the two institutions worked side by side in complete harmony.* **side of the fence** see **FENCE**. **take sides** support one person or cause against another or others in a dispute, conflict, or contest: *I do not want to take sides in this matter.* **take** (or **draw**) **someone to/on one side** speak to someone in private, especially so as to advise or warn them about something. **this side of 1** before (a particular time, date, or event): *this side of midnight.* ■ yet to reach (a particular age): *I'm this side of forty-five.* **2** informal used in superlative expressions to denote that something is comparable with a paragon or model of its kind: *the finest coffee this side of Brazil.* (**on**) **this side of the grave** in life.

– DERIVATIVES **sideless** adjective.

– ORIGIN Old English *sīde* 'left or right part of the body', of Germanic origin; related to Dutch *zijde* and German *Seite*, probably from a base meaning 'extending lengthways'.

sidearm /ˈsʌɪdɑːm/ ▶**adjective** [attrib.] (of a throw, pitch, or cast) performed or delivered with a sweeping motion of the arm from the side of the body at or below shoulder level.

■(of a person, typically a baseball pitcher) using such a sweeping motion of the arm.

▶**adverb** in a sidearm manner: *I could throw sidearm.*

▶**verb** [with obj.] chiefly Baseball throw or pitch a ball to (someone) with such a sweeping motion of the arm.

■throw or pitch (a ball or other object) in this way.

– DERIVATIVES **sidearmer** noun.

side arms ▶**plural noun** weapons worn at a person's side such as pistols or other small firearms (or, formerly, swords or bayonets).

sideband ▶**noun** Telecommunications one of two frequency bands either side of the carrier wave, which contain the modulated signal.

sidebar ▶**noun** chiefly N. Amer. a short article in a newspaper or magazine, typically boxed, placed alongside a main article and containing additional or explanatory material.

■a secondary, additional, or incidental thing; a side issue. ■ (also **sidebar conference**) (in a court of law) a discussion between the lawyers and the judge held out of earshot of the jury.

side bet ▶**noun** a bet over and above the main bet, especially on a subsidiary issue.

sideboard ▶**noun 1** a flat-topped piece of furniture with cupboards and drawers, used for storing crockery, glasses, and table linen.

2 (usu. **sideboards**) Brit. a sideburn.

3 a board forming the side, or a part of the side, of a structure, especially a removable board at the side of a cart or lorry.

sideburn ▶**noun** (usu. **sideburns**) a strip of hair grown by a man down each side of the face in front of his ears.

– ORIGIN late 19th cent.: originally *burnside*, from the name of General *Burnside* (1824–81), who affected this style.

sidecar ▶**noun 1** a small, low vehicle attached to the side of a motorcycle for carrying passengers.

2 a cocktail of brandy and lemon juice with orange liqueur.

3 another term for **JAUNTING CAR**.

side chain ▶**noun** Chemistry a group of atoms attached to the main part of a molecule with a ring or chain structure.

side chair ▶**noun** an upright wooden chair without arms.

side chapel ▶**noun** a subsidiary chapel opening off the side aisle in a large church.

sidecut ▶**noun** a curve in the side of a ski or snowboard which allows it to turn more smoothly.

sided ▶**adjective** [in combination] having sides of a specified number or type: *narrow, steep-sided canyons.*

– DERIVATIVES **sidedly** adverb [in combination], **sidedness** noun.

side door ▶**noun** a door in or at the side of a building.

■figurative an indirect means of access.

side drum ▶**noun** a small drum in the form of a short cylinder with a membrane at each end, the upper one being struck with hard sticks and the lower one often fitted with rattling cords or wires (snares).

– ORIGIN late 18th cent.: so named because it was originally played, suspended from the drummer's side.

side effect ▶**noun** a secondary, typically undesirable effect of a drug or medical treatment: *many anti-cancer drugs now in use have toxic side effects.*

side-foot ▶**verb** [with obj.] kick (a ball) with the inside of the foot, especially in soccer.

side glance ▶**noun** a sideways or brief glance.

sidehill ▶**noun** N. Amer. a hillside.

side issue ▶**noun** a point or topic connected to or raised by some other issue, but not as important, especially one that distracts attention from that which is important.

sidekick ▶**noun** informal a person's assistant or close associate, especially one who has less authority than that person.

sidelight ▶**noun 1** a light placed at the side of something.

■Brit. a small light on either side of the front of a motor vehicle, used in poor light when full headlights are not required, to warn of the vehicle's presence. ■ (**sidelights**) a ship's navigation lights. ■ figurative a piece of incidental information that helps to clarify or enliven a subject. ■ [mass noun] natural light coming from the side.

2 a narrow window or pane of glass set alongside a door or larger window.

sideline ▶**noun 1** an activity done in addition to one's main job, especially to earn extra income: [as modifier] *a sideline career as a stand-up comic.*

■an auxiliary line of goods or trade: *electronic handbooks are a lucrative sideline for the firm.*

2 (usu. **sidelines**) either of the two lines bounding the longer sides of a football field, basketball court, or similar.

■the area immediately outside such lines as a place for non-players, substitutes, or spectators.

▶**verb** [with obj.] (often **be sidelined**) cause (a player) to be unable to play in a team or game: *an ankle injury has sidelined him for two weeks.*

■figurative remove from the centre of activity or attention; place in a less influential position: *back-bench MPs have been sidelined and excluded from decision-making.*

– PHRASES **on** (or **from**) **the sidelines** in (or from) a position where one is observing a situation but is unable or unwilling to be directly involved in it.

sidelong ▶**adjective** & **adverb** directed to or from one side; sideways: [as adj.] *Steve gave her a sidelong glance* | [as adv.] *he looked sidelong at her with a quick smile.*

– ORIGIN late Middle English: alteration of earlier *sideling*, from **SIDE** + the adverbial suffix *-ling*.

sideman ▶**noun** (pl. **-men**) a supporting musician in a jazz band or rock group.

sidemeat ▶**noun** [mass noun] N. Amer. salt pork or bacon, typically cut from the side of the pig.

side-necked turtle ▶**noun** a freshwater turtle with a relatively long head and neck that is retracted sideways into the shell for defence.

• Suborder Pleurodira: families Chelidae (South America and Australasia) and Pelomedusidae (South America and southern Africa), and several genera.

side note ▶**noun** a marginal note in a text.

side-on ▶**adverb** with the side of someone or something towards something else: *the ship was wallowing side-on to the swell.*

▶**adjective** directed from or towards a side: *a shot of the crowd from the side-on camera.*

■(of a collision) involving the side of a vehicle.

side plate ▶**noun** a plate smaller than a dinner plate, typically about 15–20 cm in diameter, used for bread or other accompaniments to a meal.

side pond ▶**noun** a pond positioned beside a canal lock in such a way that water can flow into or out of it when the lock is operated.

sidereal /sʌɪˈdɪərɪəl/ ▶**adjective** of or with respect to the distant stars (i.e. the constellations or fixed stars, not the sun or planets).

– ORIGIN mid 17th cent.: from Latin *sidereus* (from *sidus, sider-* 'star') + **-AL**.

sidereal clock ▶**noun** Astronomy a clock measuring sidereal time in terms of 24 equal divisions of a sidereal day.

sidereal day ▶**noun** Astronomy the time between two consecutive transits of the First Point of Aries. It represents the time taken by the earth to rotate on its axis relative to the stars, and is almost four minutes shorter than the solar day because of the earth's orbital motion.

sidereal month ▶**noun** Astronomy the time it takes the moon to orbit once around the earth with respect to the stars (approximately 27¼ days).

sidereal period ▶**noun** Astronomy the period of revolution of one body about another with respect to the distant stars.

sidereal time ▶**noun** [mass noun] Astronomy time reckoned from the motion of the earth (or a planet) relative to the distant stars (rather than with respect to the sun).

sidereal year ▶**noun** Astronomy the orbital period of the earth around the sun, taking the stars as a reference frame. It is 20 minutes longer than the tropical year because of precession.

siderite /ˈsʌɪdərʌɪt, ˈsɪd-/ ▶**noun 1** [mass noun] a brown mineral consisting of ferrous carbonate, occurring as the main component of some kinds of ironstone or as rhombohedral crystals in mineral veins.

2 a meteorite consisting mainly of nickel and iron.

– DERIVATIVES **sideritic** adjective.

– ORIGIN late 16th cent. (denoting lodestone): from Greek *sidēros* 'iron' + **-ITE**[1].

sidero-[1] ▶ **combining form** of or relating to the stars: *siderostat*.
– ORIGIN from Latin *sidus*, *sider-* 'star'.

sidero-[2] ▶ **combining form** of or relating to iron: *siderophore*.
– ORIGIN from Greek *sidēros* 'iron'.

side road ▶ noun a minor or subsidiary road, especially one joining or diverging from a main road.

siderophore /ˈsɪdərə(ʊ)ˌfɔː, ˈsʌɪ-/ ▶ noun Biochemistry a molecule which binds and transports iron in micro-organisms.

siderostat /ˈsɪd(ə)rə(ʊ)stat, ˈsʌɪ-/ ▶ noun Astronomy an instrument used for keeping the image of a celestial object in a fixed position.

side-saddle ▶ noun a saddle in which the rider has both feet on the same side of the horse. It is typically used by a woman rider wearing a skirt.
▶ adverb sitting in this position on a horse.

side salad ▶ noun a salad served as a side dish.

side shoot ▶ noun a shoot growing from the side of a plant's stem.

sideshow ▶ noun a small show or stall at an exhibition, fair, or circus.
■ figurative a minor or diverting incident or issue, especially one which distracts attention from something more important.

side-slip ▶ noun a sideways skid or slip.
■ Aeronautics a sideways movement of an aircraft, especially downwards towards the inside of a turn. ■ (in skiing and surfing) an act of travelling down a slope or wave in a direction not in line with one's skis or board.
▶ verb [no obj.] skid or slip sideways: *the weight counteracts the tyre's tendency to side-slip.*
■ Aeronautics move in a side-slip. ■ (in skiing and surfing) travel sideways or in any direction not in line with one's skis or board.

sidesman ▶ noun (pl. **-men**) Brit. a churchwarden's assistant, who performs such duties as showing worshippers to their seats and taking the collection during a church service.

side spin ▶ noun see **SIDE** (sense 5).

side split ▶ noun Canadian a split-level house with fewer storeys on one side than the other.

side-splitting ▶ adjective informal extremely amusing: *side-splitting anecdotes.*

sidestep ▶ verb (**-stepped**, **-stepping**) [with obj.] avoid (someone or something) by stepping sideways: *he sidestepped a defender and crossed the ball.*
■ figurative avoid dealing with or discussing (something problematic or disagreeable): *he neatly sidestepped the questions about riots.* ■ [no obj.] Skiing climb or descend by lifting alternate skis while facing sideways on the slope.
▶ noun a step taken sideways, typically to avoid someone or something.
– DERIVATIVES **sidestepper** noun.

side stream ▶ noun a tributary stream.

sidestream smoke ▶ noun [mass noun] smoke that passes from a cigarette into the surrounding air, rather than into the smoker's lungs.

side street ▶ noun a minor or subsidiary street.

sidestroke ▶ noun [in sing.] a swimming stroke similar to the breaststroke in which the swimmer lies on their side.

side suit ▶ noun Bridge a suit other than the trump suit.

sideswipe ▶ noun **1** a passing critical remark about someone or something.
2 chiefly N. Amer. a glancing blow from or on the side of something, especially a motor vehicle.
▶ verb [with obj.] chiefly N. Amer. strike (someone or something) with or as if with a glancing blow: *Curtis jerked the wheel hard over and sideswiped the other car.*

side table ▶ noun a table placed at the side of a room or apart from the main table.

side tone ▶ noun [mass noun] feedback in a telephone receiver, in particular the reproduction of the user's own voice.

sidetrack ▶ verb [with obj.] (usu. **be/get sidetracked**)
1 cause (someone) to be distracted from an immediate or important issue: *he does not let himself get sidetracked by fads and trends.*

■ divert (a project or debate) away from a central issue or previously determined plan: *the effort at reform has been sidetracked for years.*
2 chiefly US direct (a train) into a branch line or siding.
■ divert (a well or borehole) to reach a productive deposit or to avoid an obstruction.
▶ noun a minor path or track.
■ chiefly US a railway branch line or siding. ■ a well or borehole which runs partly to one side of the original line of drilling.

side trip ▶ noun a minor excursion during a voyage or trip.

side valve ▶ noun a valve in an internal-combustion engine mounted alongside the cylinder.

side view ▶ noun a view from the side.

sidewalk ▶ noun N. Amer. a pavement.

side wall ▶ noun a wall forming the side of a structure or room.
■ the side of a tyre, typically untreaded and marked or coloured distinctively.

sideward ▶ adjective another term for **SIDEWAYS**.
▶ adverb (also **sidewards**) another term for **SIDEWAYS**.

sideways ▶ adverb & adjective to, towards, or from the side: [as adv.] *she tilted her body sideways* | [as adj.] *he hurried towards his office without a sideways glance.*
■ [as adv.] with one side facing forward: *the lorry slid sideways across the road.* ■ so as to occupy a job or position at the same level as one previously held rather than be promoted or demoted: [as adj.] *after the reshuffle there were sideways moves for ministers.* ■ by an indirect way: [as adv.] *he came into politics sideways, as campaign manager for Ronald Reagan.* ■ [as adj.] from an unconventional or unorthodox viewpoint: *take a sideways look at daily life.*
– PHRASES **knock someone sideways** see **KNOCK**. **sideways on** from the side; side-on.

side-wheeler ▶ noun N. Amer. a steamer with paddle wheels on either side.

side whiskers ▶ plural noun whiskers or sideburns on a man's cheeks.

sidewind /ˈsʌɪdwʌɪnd/ ▶ verb [no obj.] [often as noun **sidewinding**] (of a sidewinder or other snake) move sideways in a series of S-shaped curves.

side wind ▶ noun a wind blowing predominantly from one side.
■ figurative an indirect agency or influence.

sidewinder[1] /ˈsʌɪdˌwʌɪndə/ ▶ noun a pale-coloured, nocturnal, burrowing rattlesnake that moves sideways over sand by throwing its body into S-shaped curves. It is found in the deserts of North America.
● *Crotalus cerastes*, family Viperidae.

sidewinder[2] /ˈsʌɪdˌwɪndə/ ▶ noun US a heavy blow with the fist delivered from or on the side.

sidewise ▶ adverb & adjective another term for **SIDEWAYS**.

Sidhe /ʃiː/ ▶ plural noun the fairy people of Irish folklore, said to live beneath the hills and often identified as the remnant of the ancient Tuatha Dé Danann.
– ORIGIN from Irish *aos sidhe* 'people of the fairy mound'.

Sidi bel Abbès /ˌsɪdɪ bɛl əˈbɛs/ a town in northern Algeria, situated to the south of Oran; pop. 186,000 (1989).

siding ▶ noun **1** a short track at the side of and opening on to a railway line, used chiefly for shunting or stabling trains.
■ N. Amer. a loop line. ■ S. African a scheduled stop for goods and passenger trains, often in open country, for farming produce to be loaded and passengers taken on board.
2 [mass noun] N. Amer. cladding material for the outside of a building.

sidle ▶ verb [no obj., with adverbial of direction] walk in a furtive, unobtrusive, or timid manner, especially sideways or obliquely: *I sidled up to her.*
▶ noun [in sing.] an instance of walking in this way.
– ORIGIN late 17th cent.: back-formation from *sideling* (see **SIDELONG**).

Sidney, Sir Philip (1554–86), English poet, courtier, and soldier. His best-known work is *Arcadia* (published posthumously in 1590), a pastoral prose romance including poems in a wide variety of verse forms.

Sidon /ˈsʌɪd(ə)n/ a city in Lebanon, on the

Mediterranean coast south of Beirut; pop. 38,000 (1988). Founded in the 3rd millennium BC, it was a Phoenician seaport and city state. Arabic name **SAIDA**.

Sidra, Gulf of /ˈsɪdrə/ (also **Gulf of Sirte**) a broad inlet of the Mediterranean on the coast of Libya, between the towns of Benghazi and Misratah.

SIDS ▶ abbreviation for sudden infant death syndrome, a technical term for **COT DEATH**.

Siebengebirge /ˈziːb(ə)nɡəˌbɪəɡə, German ˈziːbŋɡəˌbɪrɡə/ a range of hills in western Germany, on the right bank of the Rhine south-east of Bonn.

siege ▶ noun a military operation in which enemy forces surround a town or building, cutting off essential supplies, with the aim of compelling the surrender of those inside: *Verdun had withstood a siege of ten weeks* | [as modifier] *siege warfare.*
■ a similar operation by a police or other force to compel the surrender of an armed person.
– PHRASES **lay siege to** conduct a siege of (a place): *government forces laid siege to the building* | figurative *the press laid siege to her flat.* **under siege** (of a place) undergoing a siege.
– ORIGIN Middle English: from Old French *sege*, from *asegier* 'besiege'.

siege economy ▶ noun an economy in which import controls are imposed and the export of capital is curtailed.

siege gun ▶ noun a heavy gun used in attacking a place under siege.

siege mentality ▶ noun a defensive or paranoid attitude based on the belief that others are hostile towards one.

siege train ▶ noun a set of artillery and other equipment for a siege, together with troops and transport vehicles.

Siegfried /ˈsiːɡfriːd/ the hero of the first part of the Nibelungenlied. A prince of the Netherlands, Siegfried obtains a hoard of treasure by killing the dragon Fafner. He marries Kriemhild, and helps Gunther to win Brunhild before being killed by Hagen.

Siegfried Line the line of defence constructed by the Germans along the western frontier of Germany before the Second World War.
■ another term for **HINDENBURG LINE**.

Sieg Heil /ziːk ˈhʌɪl/ ▶ exclamation a victory salute used originally by Nazis at political rallies.
– DERIVATIVES **Sieg-Heiling** adjective.
– ORIGIN German, literally 'hail victory!'.

Siemens /ˈsiːmənz/ a German family of scientific entrepreneurs and engineers. **Ernst Werner von Siemens** (1816–92) was an electrical engineer who developed the process of electroplating, devised an electric generator which used an electromagnet, and pioneered electrical traction. His brother **Karl Wilhelm** (1823–83) (also known as *Sir Charles William Siemens*) moved to England, where he developed the open-hearth steel furnace and designed the cable-laying steamship *Faraday*. Their brother **Friedrich** (1826–1904) applied the principles of the open-hearth furnace to glass-making.

siemens /ˈsiːmənz/ (abbrev.: **S**) ▶ noun Physics the SI unit of conductance, equal to one reciprocal ohm.
– ORIGIN 1930s: named after K. W. von **SIEMENS**.

Siena /sɪˈɛnə/ a city in west central Italy, in Tuscany; pop. 57,745 (1990). In the 13th and 14th centuries it was the centre of a flourishing school of art. Its central square is the venue for the noted Palio horse race.
– DERIVATIVES **Sienese** /sɪəˈniːz/ adjective & noun.

sienna ▶ noun [mass noun] a kind of ferruginous earth used as a pigment in painting, normally yellowish-brown in colour (**raw sienna**) or deep reddish-brown when roasted (**burnt sienna**).
■ the colour of this pigment.
– ORIGIN late 18th cent.: from Italian (*terra di*) *Sienna* 'earth of) Siena'.

Sierpinski triangle /ʃɪəˈpɪnski/ (also **Sierpinski gasket**) ▶ noun Mathematics a fractal based on a triangle with four equal triangles inscribed in it. The central triangle is removed and each of the other three treated as the original was, and so on, creating an infinite regression in a finite space.
– ORIGIN 1970s: named after Waclaw *Sierpiński* (1882–1969), Polish mathematician.

sierra /sɪˈɛrə, sɪˈɛːrə/ ▶ noun **1** (especially in Spanish-

speaking countries or the western US) a long jagged mountain chain.
2 a code word representing the letter S, used in radio communication.
– ORIGIN mid 16th cent.: Spanish, from Latin *serra* 'saw'.

Sierra Club a North American environmental group, founded in 1892. The pioneering naturalist John Muir was its first president.

Sierra Leone /lɪˈəʊn/ a country on the coast of West Africa; pop. 4,239,000 (est. 1991); languages, English (official), English Creole, Temne, and other West African languages; capital, Freetown.

> An area of British influence from the late 18th century, the district around Freetown on the coast became a colony in 1807, serving as a centre for operations against slave traders. The large inland territory was not declared a protectorate until 1896. Sierra Leone achieved independence within the Commonwealth in 1961 but was suspended from the organization in 1997 following military coups in 1992 and 1997.

– DERIVATIVES **Sierra Leonean** adjective & noun.

Sierra Madre /ˈmɑːdreɪ/ a mountain system in Mexico, extending from the border with the US in the north to the southern border with Guatemala.

Sierra Nevada /nəˈvɑːdə/ **1** a mountain range in southern Spain, in Andalusia, south-east of Granada.
2 a mountain range in eastern California. Rising sharply from the Great Basin in the east, it descends more gently to California's Central Valley in the west.

siesta /sɪˈɛstə/ ▶**noun** an afternoon rest or nap, especially one taken during the hottest hours of the day in a hot climate.
– ORIGIN mid 17th cent.: Spanish, from Latin *sexta (hora)* 'sixth hour'.

sieve /sɪv/ ▶**noun** a utensil consisting of a wire or plastic mesh held in a frame, used for straining solids from liquids, for separating coarser from finer particles, or for reducing soft solids to a pulp.
■used figuratively with reference to the fact that a sieve does not hold all its contents: *she's forgotten all the details already, she's got **a mind like a sieve**.*
▶**verb** [with obj.] put (a food substance or other material) through a sieve.
■[no obj.] (**sieve through**) figurative examine in detail: *lawyers had sieved through her contract.*
– DERIVATIVES **sieve-like** adjective.
– ORIGIN Old English *sife* (noun), of West Germanic origin; related to Dutch *zeef* and German *Sieb*.

sieve cell ▶**noun** Botany a sieve element of a primitive type present in ferns and gymnosperms, with narrow pores and no sieve plate.

sieve element ▶**noun** Botany an elongated cell in the phloem of a vascular plant, in which the primary wall is perforated by pores through which water is conducted.

sieve plate ▶**noun** Botany an area of relatively large pores present in the common end walls of sieve tube elements.
■Zoology a perforated plate in the integument of an invertebrate, especially the madreporite of an echinoderm.

sievert /ˈsiːvət/ (abbrev.: **Sv**) ▶**noun** Physics the SI unit of dose equivalent (the biological effect of ionizing radiation), defined as that which delivers a joule of energy per kilogram of recipient mass.
– ORIGIN 1940s: named after Rolf M. *Sievert* (1896–1966), Swedish radiologist.

sieve tube ▶**noun** Botany a series of sieve tube elements placed end to end to form a continuous tube.

sieve tube element (also **sieve tube member**) ▶**noun** Botany a sieve element of a type present in angiosperms, a series of which are joined end to end to form sieve tubes, with sieve plates between the elements.

sifaka /sɪˈfakə/ ▶**noun** a large gregarious lemur which leaps from tree to tree in an upright position.
• Genus *Propithecus*, family Indriidae: two species.
– ORIGIN mid 19th cent.: from Malagasy.

sift ▶**verb** [with obj.] put (a fine, loose, or powdery substance) through a sieve so as to remove lumps or large particles: *sift the flour into a large bowl.*
■figurative examine (something) thoroughly so as to isolate that which is most important or useful: *until we sift the evidence ourselves, we can't comment objectively* | [no obj.] *the fourth stage involves **sifting through** the data and evaluating it.* ■(**sift something out**) separate something, especially something to be discarded, from something else: *he asked for streamlined procedures to sift out frivolous applications.* ■cause to flow or pass as through a sieve: *Miranda sifted the warm sand through her fingers.* ■[no obj., with adverbial of direction] (of snow, ash, light, or similar) descend or float down lightly or sparsely as if sprinkled from a sieve: *ash began to sift down round them.*
▶**noun** [usu. in sing.] an act of sifting something, especially so as to isolate that which is most important or useful: *a careful archaeological sift must be made through the debris.*
■an amount of sifted material: *the floor was dusted with a fine sift of flour.*
– DERIVATIVES **sifter** noun.
– ORIGIN Old English *siftan*, of West Germanic origin; related to Dutch *ziften*, also to **SIEVE**.

SIG Computing ▶**abbreviation for** special interest group, a type of newsgroup.

Sig. ▶**abbreviation for** Signor.

sig ▶**noun** Computing, informal a short personalized message at the end of an e-mail message.
– ORIGIN 1990s: abbreviation of **SIGNATURE**.

Sigatoka /ˌsɪgəˈtəʊkə/ ▶**noun** [mass noun] a fungal disease of banana plants characterized by elongated spots on the leaves, which then rot completely.
• The fungus is *Mycosphaerella musicola*, subdivision Ascomycotina.
– ORIGIN 1920s: named after a district in Fiji.

sigh ▶**verb** [no obj.] emit a long, deep, audible breath expressing sadness, relief, tiredness, or similar: *Harry sank into a chair and sighed with relief.*
■figurative (of the wind or something through which the wind blows) make a sound resembling this: *a breeze made the treetops sigh.* ■(**sigh for**) poetic/literary feel a deep yearning for (someone or something lost, unattainable, or distant): *he sighed for days gone by.*
▶**noun** a long, deep, audible exhalation expressing sadness, relief, tiredness, or similar: *she let out a long sigh of despair* | figurative *the councils **heaved a sigh of relief** when they saved over £6 m between them.*
■figurative a gentle sound resembling this, especially one made by the wind.
– ORIGIN Middle English (as a verb): probably a back-formation from *sighte*, past tense of *siche*, *sike*, from Old English *sīcan*.

sight ▶**noun 1** [mass noun] the faculty or power of seeing: *Joseph lost his sight as a baby* | [as modifier] *a sight test.*
■the action or fact of seeing someone or something: *I've always been scared of the sight of blood.* ■the area or distance within which someone can see or something can be seen: *he now refused to let Rose out of his sight.* ■dated a person's view or consideration: *we are all equal **in the sight of God**.*
2 a thing that one sees or that can be seen: *John was a familiar sight in the bar for many years* | *he was getting used to seeing unpleasant sights.*
■(**sights**) places of interest to tourists and visitors in a city, town, or other place: *she offered to show me the sights.* ■(**a sight**) informal a person or thing having a ridiculous, repulsive, or dishevelled appearance: *'I must look a frightful sight,' she said.*
3 (usu. **sights**) a device on a gun or optical instrument used for assisting a person's precise aim or observation.
▶**verb 1** [with obj.] manage to see or observe (someone or something); catch an initial glimpse of: *tell me when you sight London Bridge* | [as noun **sighting**] *the unseasonal sighting of a cuckoo.*
2 [no obj., with adverbial of direction] take aim by looking through the sights of a gun: *she sighted down the barrel.*
■take a detailed visual measurement of something with or as with a sight. ■[with obj.] adjust the sight of (a firearm or optical instrument).
– PHRASES **at first sight** on first seeing or meeting someone: *it was love at first sight.* ■after an initial impression (which is then found to be different from what is actually the case): *the debate is more complex than it seems at first sight.* **catch** (or **get**) **a sight of** glimpse for a moment; suddenly notice: *when she caught sight of him she smiled.* **in sight** visible: *no other vehicle was in sight.* ■near at hand; close to being achieved or realized: *the minister insisted that agreement was in sight.* **in** (or **within**) **sight of** so as to see or be seen from: *I climbed the hill and came in sight of the house.* ■within reach of; close to attaining: *he was safe for the moment and in sight of victory.* **in** (or **within**) **one's sights** visible, especially through the sights of one's gun. ■within the scope of one's ambitions or expectations: *he had the prize firmly in his sights.* **lose sight of** be no longer able to see. ■fail to consider, be aware of, or remember: *we should not lose sight of the fact that the issues involved are moral ones.* **not a pretty sight** informal not a pleasant spectacle or situation. **on** (or **at**) **sight** as soon as someone or something has been seen: *in Africa, paramilitary game wardens shoot poachers on sight.* **out of sight 1** not visible: *she saw them off, waving until the car was out of sight.* **2** (also **outasight**) [often as exclamation] informal extremely good; excellent. **out of sight, out of mind** proverb you soon forget people or things that are no longer visible or present. (**get**) **out of my sight!** go away at once! **raise** (or **lower**) **one's sights** become more (or less) ambitious; increase (or lower) one's expectations. **set one's sights on** have as an ambition; hope strongly to achieve or reach: *Katherine set her sights on university.* **a sight ——** informal used to indicate that something is so described to a considerable extent: *the old lady is a sight cleverer than Sarah* | *he's a sight too full of himself.* **a sight for sore eyes** informal a person or thing that one is extremely pleased or relieved to see. **a sight to behold** a person or thing that is particularly impressive or worth seeing.
– DERIVATIVES **sighter** noun.
– ORIGIN Old English *(ge)sihth* 'something seen', of West Germanic origin; related to Dutch *zicht* and German *Gesicht* 'sight, face, appearance'. The verb dates from the mid 16th cent. (in sense 2).

sight deposit ▶**noun** a bank deposit that can be withdrawn immediately without notice or penalty.

sighted ▶**adjective** (of a person) having the ability to see; not blind: *a sighted guide is needed* | [as plural noun **the sighted**] *the blind leading the sighted, I thought.*
■[in combination] having a specified kind of sight: *the keen-sighted watcher may catch a glimpse.*

sight gag ▶**noun** informal a visual joke.

sight glass ▶**noun** a transparent tube or window through which the level of liquid in a reservoir or supply line can be checked visually.

sighting shot ▶**noun** an experimental shot to guide shooters in adjusting their sights.

sightless ▶**adjective** unable to see; blind: *blank, sightless eyes.*
■poetic/literary invisible.
– DERIVATIVES **sightlessly** adverb, **sightlessness** noun.

sight line ▶**noun** a hypothetical line from someone's eye to what is seen (used especially with reference to good or bad visibility): *the authorities require good sight lines at road junctions.*

sightly ▶**adjective** pleasing to the eye: *metal guards can also be used but are less sightly.*
– DERIVATIVES **sightliness** noun.

sight-read ▶**verb** [with obj.] read and perform (music) at sight, without preparation.
– DERIVATIVES **sight-reader** noun.

sight screen ▶**noun** Cricket a large white screen placed near the boundary in line with the wicket to help the batsman see the ball.

sightseeing ▶**noun** [mass noun] the activity of visiting places of interest in a particular location: [as modifier] *a sightseeing tour.*
– DERIVATIVES **sightsee** verb, **sightseer** noun.

sight-sing ▶**verb** [with obj.] sing (music) at sight, without preparation.

sight unseen ▶**adverb** without the opportunity to look at the object in question beforehand: *they bought their computers sight unseen through the mail.*
■without being seen: *what other treasures remain sight unseen?*

sightworthy ▶**adjective** rare worth seeing or visiting.

sigil /ˈsɪdʒɪl/ ▶**noun** an inscribed or painted symbol considered to have magical power.
■archaic a seal: *the supply wains bore the High King's sigil.* ■poetic/literary a sign or symbol.
– ORIGIN late Middle English: from late Latin *sigillum* 'sign'.

SIGINT /ˈsɪgɪnt/ ▶**abbreviation for** signals intelligence.

siglum /ˈsɪgləm/ ▶**noun** (pl. **sigla** /-lə/) a letter or symbol which stands for a word or name, especially

S

to denote a particular manuscript or edition of a text.

– ORIGIN early 18th cent.: from late Latin *sigla* (plural), perhaps from *singula*, neuter plural of *singulus* 'single'.

sigma /ˈsɪgmə/ ▶ **noun** the eighteenth letter of the Greek alphabet (Σ, σ), transliterated as 's'.

• The form ς is used instead of σ at the end of a word. The uncial form, resembling the letter c, is also sometimes used.

■ (**Sigma**) [followed by Latin genitive] Astronomy the eighteenth star in a constellation: *Sigma Octantis*. ■ Chemistry & Physics relating to or denoting an electron or orbital with zero angular momentum about an internuclear axis.

▶ **symbol for** ■ (Σ) mathematical sum. ■ (σ) standard deviation.

– ORIGIN Greek.

sigmate /ˈsɪgmət/ ▶ **adjective** having the shape of a Σ or a letter S.

sigmoid /ˈsɪgmɔɪd/ ▶ **adjective 1** curved like the uncial sigma; crescent-shaped.

2 S-shaped.

▶ **noun** Anatomy short for **SIGMOID COLON**.

– DERIVATIVES **sigmoidal** adjective.

– ORIGIN late 17th cent.: from Greek *sigmoeidēs*, from *sigma* (see **SIGMA**).

sigmoid colon ▶ **noun** Anatomy the S-shaped last part of the large intestine, leading into the rectum.

sigmoidoscopy /ˌsɪgmɔɪˈdɒskəpi/ ▶ **noun** [mass noun] examination of the sigmoid colon by means of a flexible tube inserted through the anus.

– DERIVATIVES **sigmoidoscope** noun, **sigmoidoscopic** adjective.

sign ▶ **noun 1** an object, quality, or event whose presence or occurrence indicates the probable presence or occurrence of something else: *flowers are often given as a sign of affection* | [with clause] *the shops are full, which is a sign that the recession is past its worst*.

■ something regarded as an indication or evidence of what is happening or going to happen: *the signs are that counterfeiting is growing at an alarming rate*. ■ [with negative] used to indicate that someone or something is not present where they should be or are expected to be: *there was still no sign of her*. ■ Medicine an indication of a disease detectable by a medical practitioner even if not apparent to the patient. Compare with **SYMPTOM**. ■ a miracle regarded as evidence of supernatural power (chiefly in biblical and literary use). ■ [mass noun] N. Amer. the trail of a wild animal: *wolverine sign*.

2 a gesture or action used to convey information or instructions: *she gave him the thumbs-up sign*.

■ a notice that is publicly displayed giving information or instructions in a written or symbolic form: *I didn't see the 'Stop' sign*. ■ an action or reaction that conveys something about someone's state or experiences: *she gave no sign of having seen him*. ■ a gesture used in a system of sign language. ■ [mass noun] short for **SIGN LANGUAGE**. ■ a symbol or word used to represent an operation, instruction, concept, or object in algebra, music, or other subjects. ■ a word or gesture given according to prior arrangement as a means of identification; a password.

3 (also **zodiacal sign**) Astrology each of the twelve equal sections into which the zodiac is divided, named from the constellations formerly situated in each, and associated with successive periods of the year according to the position of the sun on the ecliptic: *a person born under the sign of Virgo*.

4 Mathematics the positiveness or negativeness of a quantity.

▶ **verb 1** [with obj.] write one's name on (a letter, card, or similar item) to identify oneself as the writer or sender: *the card was signed by the whole class*.

■ indicate agreement with or authorization of the contents of (a document or other written or printed material) by attaching a signature: *the two countries signed a non-aggression treaty*. ■ write (one's name) for purposes of identification or authorization: *she signed her name in the book* | [with obj. and complement] *she signed herself Imogen* | [no obj.] *he signed on the dotted line*. ■ engage (someone, typically a sports player or a musician) to work for one by signing a contract with them: *the manager plans to sign a new goalkeeper*. ■ [no obj.] sign a contract committing oneself to work for a particular person or organization: *a new striker has signed for Blackburn*.

2 [no obj.] use gestures to convey information or instructions: [with infinitive] *she signed to her husband to leave the room*.

■ communicate in sign language: *she was learning to sign*. ■ [with obj.] express or perform (something) in sign language: [as adj. **signed**] *the theatre routinely puts on signed performances*. ■ [with obj.] (usu. **be signed**) indicate with signposts or other markers: *the footpath is signed by the gate*. ■ archaic [with obj.] mark or consecrate with the sign of the cross.

– PHRASES **sign of the cross** a Christian sign made in blessing or prayer by tracing a cross from the forehead to the chest and to each shoulder, or in the air. **sign of the times** something judged to exemplify or indicate the nature or quality of a particular period, typically something unwelcome or unpleasant: *the theft was a sign of the times*. **signed, sealed, and delivered** (or **signed and sealed**) formally and officially agreed and in effect.

– DERIVATIVES **signer** noun.

– ORIGIN Middle English: from Old French *signe* (noun), *signer* (verb), from Latin *signum* 'mark, token'.

▶ **sign something away/over** officially relinquish rights or property by signing a deed: *I have no intention of signing away my inheritance*.

sign for sign a receipt to confirm that one has received (something delivered or handed over).

sign in sign a register on arrival, typically in a hotel.

sign someone in record someone's arrival in a register.

sign off 1 conclude a letter, broadcast, or other message: *he signed off with a few words of advice*. ■ conclude an activity: *he signed off from school athletics with a double in the shot*. ■ sign to record that one is leaving work for the day. ■ Bridge indicate by a conventional bid that one is seeking to end the bidding. **2** Brit. register to stop receiving unemployment benefit after finding work.

sign someone off record that someone is entitled to miss work, typically because of illness.

sign off on US informal assent or give one's approval to: *it was hard to get celebrities to sign off on those issues*.

sign on 1 commit oneself to employment, membership of a society, or some other undertaking: *I'll sign on with a nursing agency*. **2** Brit. register as unemployed.

sign someone on take someone into one's employment.

sign out sign a register to record one's departure, typically from a hotel.

sign someone out authorize someone's release or record their departure by signing a register.

sign something out sign to indicate that one has borrowed or hired something: *I signed out the keys*.

sign up commit oneself to a period of employment or education or to some other undertaking: *he signed up for a ten-week course*. ■ enlist in the armed forces. ■ (also **sign something up**) conclude a business deal: *the company has already signed up a few orders*.

sign someone up formally engage someone in employment.

Signac /ˈsiːnjak/, Paul (1863–1935), French neo-Impressionist painter. A pointillist painter, he had a technique that was freer than Seurat's and was characterized by the use of small dashes and patches of pure colour rather than dots.

signage ▶ **noun** [mass noun] chiefly N. Amer. signs collectively, especially commercial or public display signs.

signal[1] ▶ **noun 1** a gesture, action, or sound that is used to convey information or instructions, typically by pre-arrangement between the parties concerned: *the firing of the gun was the signal for a chain of beacons to be lit* | [with infinitive] *the policeman raised his hand as a signal to stop*.

■ an indication of a state of affairs: *the markets are waiting for a clear signal about the direction of policy*. ■ an event or statement that provides the impulse or occasion for something specified to happen: *the champion's announcement that he was retiring was the signal for scores of journalists to gather at his last match*. ■ an apparatus on a railway, typically a coloured light or a semaphore, giving indications to train drivers of whether or not the line is clear. ■ Bridge a pre-arranged convention of bidding or play intended to convey information to one's partner.

2 an electrical impulse or radio wave transmitted or received: *equipment for receiving TV signals*.

▶ **verb** (**signalled**, **signalling**; US **signaled**, **signaling**) [no obj.] transmit information or instructions by means of a gesture, action, or sound: *hold your fire until I signal*.

■ [with obj. and infinitive] instruct (someone) to do something by means of gestures or signs rather than explicit orders: *she signalled Charlotte to be silent*. ■ (of a cyclist, motorist, or vehicle) indicate an intention to turn in a specified direction using an extended arm or flashing indicator: [with complement] *Stone signalled right* | [with infinitive] *the truck signalled to turn left*. ■ [with obj.] indicate the existence or occurrence of (something) by actions or sounds: *the Community could signal displeasure by refusing to cooperate*. ■ [with clause] give an indication of a state of affairs: *she gave a glance which signalled that her father was being secretive*.

– DERIVATIVES **signaller** noun.

– ORIGIN late Middle English: from Old French, from medieval Latin *signale*, neuter of late Latin *signalis*, from Latin *signum* 'mark, token' (see **SIGN**). The verb dates from the early 19th cent.

signal[2] ▶ **adjective** [attrib.] striking in extent, seriousness, or importance; outstanding: *he attacked the government for their signal failure of leadership*.

– DERIVATIVES **signally** adverb.

– ORIGIN early 17th cent.: from French *signalé*, from the Italian past participle *segnalato* 'distinguished, made illustrious', from *segnale* 'a signal'.

signal box (chiefly US also **signal tower**) ▶ **noun** Brit. a building beside a railway track from which signals, points, and other equipment are controlled.

signal-caller ▶ **noun** American Football a player who signals the next play or formation to other team members.

signalize (also **-ise**) ▶ **verb** [with obj.] **1** mark or indicate (something), especially in a striking or conspicuous manner: *people seek to change their name to signalize a change in status that has taken place*.

■ archaic make (something) noteworthy or remarkable: *a little flower with not much to signalize it*.

2 US & Austral. provide (an intersection) with traffic signals.

signalman ▶ **noun** (pl. **-men**) a railway worker responsible for operating signals and points.

■ a person responsible for sending and receiving naval or military signals.

signals intelligence ▶ **noun** [mass noun] the branch of military intelligence concerned with the monitoring, interception, and interpretation of radio and radar signals, and telemetry.

signal-to-noise ratio ▶ **noun** the ratio of the strength of an electrical or other signal carrying information to that of unwanted interference, generally expressed in decibels.

■ informal a measure of how much useful information there is in a system, such as the Internet, as a proportion of the entire contents.

signatory /ˈsɪgnət(ə)ri/ ▶ **noun** (pl. **-ies**) a party that has signed an agreement, especially a state that has signed a treaty: *Britain is a signatory to the convention* | [as modifier] *the signatory states*.

– ORIGIN late 19th cent.: from Latin *signatorius* 'of sealing', from *signat-* 'marked (with a cross)', from the verb *signare*.

signature ▶ **noun 1** a person's name written in a distinctive way as a form of identification in authorizing a cheque or document or concluding a letter.

■ [mass noun] the action of signing a document: *the licence was sent to the customer for signature*. ■ a distinctive pattern, product, or characteristic by which someone or something can be identified: *the chef produced the pâté that was his signature* | [as modifier] *his signature dish*.

2 Music short for **KEY SIGNATURE** or **TIME SIGNATURE**.

3 Printing a letter or figure printed at the foot of one or more pages of each sheet of a book as a guide in binding.

■ a printed sheet after being folded to form a group of pages.

4 N. Amer. the part of a medical prescription that gives instructions about the use of the medicine or drug prescribed.

– ORIGIN mid 16th cent. (as a Scots legal term, denoting a document presented by a writer to the Signet): from medieval Latin *signatura* 'sign manual' (in late Latin denoting a marking on sheep), from Latin *signare* 'to sign, mark'.

signature tune ▶ **noun** chiefly Brit. a distinctive piece of music associated with a particular programme or performer on television or radio.

signboard ▶ **noun** a board displaying the name or logo of a business or product.

■ chiefly N. Amer. a board displaying a sign to direct traffic or travellers.

S

signed-rank test ▶ noun Statistics a non-parametric test for comparing two sets of values by calculating the distribution of positive or negative differences in ranking of corresponding pairs.

signee ▶ noun a person who has signed a contract or other official document.

signet ▶ noun historical a small seal, especially one set in a ring, used instead of or with a signature to give authentication to an official document.
■ (usu. **the Signet**) the royal seal formerly used for special purposes in England and Scotland, and in Scotland later as the seal of the Court of Session.
– ORIGIN late Middle English: from Old French, or from medieval Latin *signetum*, diminutive of *signum* 'token, seal'.

signet ring ▶ noun a ring with letters or a design carved on it.

signifiant /ˌsiːnjiˈfjɔ̃/ ▶ noun another term for SIGNIFIER.

significance ▶ noun [mass noun] **1** the quality of being worthy of attention; importance: *adolescent education was felt to be a social issue of some significance.*
2 the meaning to be found in words or events: *the significance of what was happening was clearer to me than to her.*
3 (also **statistical significance**) the extent to which a result deviates from that expected to arise simply from random variation or errors in sampling.
– ORIGIN late Middle English (denoting unstated meaning): from Old French, or from Latin *significantia*, from *significare* 'indicate, portend'.

significant ▶ adjective **1** sufficiently great or important to be worthy of attention; noteworthy: *a significant increase in sales.*
2 having a particular meaning; indicative of something: *in times of stress her dreams seemed to her especially significant.*
■ suggesting a meaning or message that is not explicitly stated: *she gave him a significant look.*
3 Statistics of, relating to, or having significance.
– DERIVATIVES **significantly** adverb.
– ORIGIN late 16th cent. (in sense 2): from Latin *significant-* 'indicating', from the verb *significare* (see SIGNIFY).

significant figure ▶ noun Mathematics each of the digits of a number that are used to express it to the required degree of accuracy, starting from the first non-zero digit.

significant other ▶ noun a person with whom someone has an established romantic or sexual relationship.

signification ▶ noun [mass noun] the representation or conveying of meaning.
■ [count noun] an exact meaning or sense.
– ORIGIN Middle English: via Old French from Latin *significatio(n-)*, from *significare* 'indicate' (see SIGNIFY).

significative /sɪɡˈnɪfɪkətɪv/ ▶ adjective rare being a symbol or sign of something; having a meaning.

significator ▶ noun Astrology (in a horary chart) the planet which signifies the inquirer, or the subject of the question.
■ a card chosen to represent the inquirer in a tarot reading.

signifié /ˌsiːnjiˈfjeɪ/ ▶ noun another term for SIGNIFIED.

signified ▶ noun Linguistics the meaning or idea expressed by a sign, as distinct from the physical form in which it is expressed. Compare with SIGNIFIER.

signifier ▶ noun Linguistics a sign's physical form (such as a sound, printed word, or image) as distinct from its meaning. Compare with SIGNIFIED.

signify ▶ verb (**-ies**, **-ied**) **1** [with obj.] be an indication of: *this decision signified a fundamental change in their priorities.*
■ be a symbol of; have as meaning: *the church used this image to signify the Holy Trinity.* ■ (of a person) indicate or declare (a feeling or intention): *signify your agreement by signing the letter below.* ■ [no obj.] [with negative] be of importance: *the locked door doesn't necessarily signify.*
2 [no obj.] US informal (among black Americans) exchange boasts or insults as a game or ritual.
– ORIGIN Middle English: from Old French *signifier*,

signing ▶ noun [mass noun] **1** the action of writing one's signature on an official document: *the signing of the Anglo-French agreement to build Concorde.*
■ the action of recruiting someone, especially to a professional sports team or record company: *the signing of overseas players.* ■ [count noun] Brit. a person who has recently been recruited, especially to join a professional sports team or record company: *Manchester United's latest signing.* ■ [count noun] an event in a bookshop or other place at which an author signs a number of books to gain publicity and sales.
2 sign language.
3 the provision of signs in a street or other place.

sign language ▶ noun [mass noun] a system of communication using visual gestures and signs, as used by deaf people.

sign-off ▶ noun Bridge a bid indicating that the bidder wishes to end bidding.

signor /ˈsiːnjɔː, siːˈnjɔː/ (also **signore**) ▶ noun (pl. **signori** /-ˈnjɔːriː/) a title or form of address used or to an Italian-speaking man, corresponding to *Mr* or *sir*: *Signor Ugolotti* | *I am a man of honour, Signor.*
– ORIGIN Italian, from Latin *senior* (see SENIOR).

signora /siːˈnjɔːrə/ ▶ noun a title or form of address used of or to an Italian-speaking married woman, corresponding to *Mrs* or *madam*: *good night, Signora.*
– ORIGIN Italian, feminine of *signor* (see SIGNOR).

signorina /ˌsiːnjəˈriːnə/ ▶ noun a title or form of address used of or to an Italian-speaking unmarried woman, corresponding to *Miss*: *Signorina Rosalba.*
– ORIGIN Italian, diminutive of *signora* (see SIGNORA).

signory /ˈsiːnjəri/ ▶ noun (pl. **-ies**) **1** another term for SEIGNIORY.
2 historical the governing body of a medieval Italian republic. [ORIGIN: influenced by Italian *signoria*.]

signpost ▶ noun a sign giving information such as the direction and distance to a nearby town, typically found at a road junction.
▶ verb [with obj.] provide (an area) with a signpost or signposts: *most of the walks were well signposted.*
■ chiefly Brit. indicate (a place or feature) with a signpost: *Battle is clearly signposted off all the main roads.*

sign-up ▶ noun [mass noun] [usu. as modifier] the action of enrolling for something or of enrolling or employing someone: *a sign-up fee of £29.95.*

signwriter (also **sign painter**) ▶ noun a person who paints commercial signs and advertisements.
– DERIVATIVES **signwriting** noun.

sigri /ˈsiːɡri/ ▶ noun (pl. **sigris**) (in the Indian subcontinent) a type of brazier.
– ORIGIN from Punjabi *sagrī*.

Sigurd /ˈsɪɡʊəd/ (in Norse legend) the Norse equivalent of Siegfried, husband of Gudrun.

Sihanouk /ˈsiːənʊk/, Norodom (b.1922), Cambodian king 1941–55 and since 1993, Prime Minister 1955–60, and head of state 1960–70 and 1975–6. After Cambodian independence in 1953, Sihanouk abdicated in favour of his father in order to become Prime Minister. On his father's death Sihanouk proclaimed himself head of state. He was ousted in a US-backed coup and was briefly reinstated by the Khmer Rouge. Sihanouk was crowned for the second time in 1993.

sika /ˈsiːkə/ (also **sika deer**) ▶ noun a forest-dwelling deer with a greyish winter coat that turns yellowish-brown with white spots in summer. It is native to Japan and SE Asia and naturalized in Britain and elsewhere.
● *Cervus nippon*, family Cervidae.
– ORIGIN late 19th cent.: from Japanese *shika*.

sike /sʌɪk/ ▶ noun Scottish & N. English a small stream or rill, typically one that flows through marshy ground and is often dry in summer.
– ORIGIN Old English *sic.*

Sikh /siːk/ ▶ noun an adherent of Sikhism.
▶ adjective of or relating to Sikhs or Sikhism.
– ORIGIN from Punjabi 'disciple', from Sanskrit *śiṣya*.

Sikhism /ˈsiːkɪz(ə)m, ˈsɪk-/ ▶ noun [mass noun] a monotheistic religion founded in Punjab in the 15th century by Guru Nanak.

Sikh teaching centres on spiritual liberation and social justice and harmony, though the community took on a militant aspect during early conflicts. The last guru, Gobind Singh (1666–1708), passed his authority to the scripture, the Adi Granth, and to the Khalsa, the body of initiated Sikhs.

Sikh Wars a series of wars between the Sikhs and the British in 1845 and 1848–9, culminating in the British annexation of Punjab.

Siking /ʃiːˈkɪŋ/ former name for XIAN.

Sikkim /ˈsɪkɪm/ a state of NE India, in the eastern Himalayas between Bhutan and Nepal, on the border with Tibet; capital, Gangtok. After British rule it became an Indian protectorate, becoming a state of India in 1975.
– DERIVATIVES **Sikkimese** adjective & noun.

Sikorsky /sɪˈkɔːski/, Igor (Ivanovich) (1889–1972), Russian-born American aircraft designer. He built the first large four-engined aircraft, the Grand (1913), in his native country and went on to establish the Sikorsky company in the US. In 1939 he developed the first mass-produced helicopter.

Siksika /ˈsɪksɪkə/ ▶ plural noun the northernmost of the three peoples forming the Blackfoot confederacy.
– ORIGIN from Blackfoot *siksi-* 'black' + *ka-* 'foot'.

silage /ˈsʌɪlɪdʒ/ ▶ noun [mass noun] grass or other green fodder compacted and stored in airtight conditions, typically in a silo, without first being dried, and used as animal feed in the winter.
▶ verb [no obj.] [often as noun **silaging**] make silage.
■ [with obj.] preserve (grass and other green fodder) as silage.
– ORIGIN late 19th cent.: alteration of ENSILAGE, influenced by SILO.

silane /ˈsʌɪleɪn/ ▶ noun [mass noun] Chemistry a colourless gaseous compound of silicon and hydrogen which has strong reducing properties and is spontaneously flammable in air.
● Chem. formula: SiH_4.
■ [count noun] any of the large class of hydrides of silicon analogous to the alkanes.
– ORIGIN early 20th cent.: from SILICON + -ANE[2].

silastic /sɪˈlastɪk/ ▶ noun [mass noun] trademark silicone rubber.
– ORIGIN 1940s: blend of SILICON and ELASTIC.

Silat /sɪˈlat/ ▶ noun [mass noun] the Malay art of self-defence, practised as a martial art or accompanied by drums as a ceremonial display or dance.
– ORIGIN Malay.

Silbury Hill /ˈsɪlb(ə)ri/ a Neolithic monument near Avebury in Wiltshire, a flat-topped conical mound more than 40 m (130 ft) high, which is the largest man-made prehistoric mound in Europe.

Silchester /ˈsɪltʃɪstə/ a village in Hampshire, situated to the south-west of Reading. It is the site of an important town of pre-Roman and Roman Britain, known to the Romans as Calleva Atrebatum.

sild ▶ noun (pl. same) a small immature herring, especially one caught in northern European seas.
– ORIGIN 1920s: from Danish and Norwegian.

silence ▶ noun [mass noun] complete absence of sound: *sirens pierce the silence of the night* | [count noun] *an eerie silence descended over the house.*
■ the fact or state of abstaining from speech: *Karen had withdrawn into sullen silence* | *she was reduced to silence for a moment.* ■ the avoidance of mentioning or discussing something: *politicians keep their silence on the big questions.* ■ [count noun] a short appointed period of time during which people stand still and do not speak as a sign of respect for a dead person or group of people: *the game was preceded by a two-minute silence in his memory.*
▶ verb [with obj.] (often **be silenced**) cause to become silent; prohibit or prevent from speaking: *she was silenced by the Inspector's stern look* | *the team's performance silenced their critics* | *freedom of the press cannot be silenced by tanks.*
■ [usu. as adj. **silenced**] fit (a gun or an exhaust system) with a silencer: *a silenced .22 rifle.*
– PHRASES **in silence** without speech or other sound: *we finished our meal in silence.* **silence is golden** proverb it's often wise to say nothing.
– ORIGIN Middle English: from Old French, from Latin *silentium*, from *silere* 'be silent'.

silencer ▶ noun a device for reducing the noise emitted by a mechanism, especially a gun or exhaust system.

silent ▶ adjective not making or accompanied by any sound: *the wood was still and silent.*
■(of a person) not speaking: *she fell silent for a moment.* ■ not expressed aloud: *a silent prayer.* ■ (of a letter) written but not pronounced, e.g. *b* in *doubt*. ■ (of a film) without an accompanying soundtrack. ■ saying or recording nothing on a particular subject: *the poems are silent on the question of marriage.* ■ (of a person) not prone to speak much; taciturn: *I'm the strong, silent type.*
– PHRASES **(as) silent as the grave** see **GRAVE**[1]. **the silent majority** the majority of people, regarded as holding moderate opinions but rarely expressing them. **the silent treatment** a stubborn refusal to talk to someone, especially after a recent argument or disagreement.
– DERIVATIVES **silently** adverb.
– ORIGIN late 15th cent. (in the sense 'not speaking'): from Latin *silent-* 'being silent', from the verb *silere*.

silent partner ▶ noun North American term for **SLEEPING PARTNER**.

Silenus /sʌɪˈliːnəs/ Greek Mythology an aged woodland deity, one of the sileni, who was entrusted with the education of Dionysus. He is depicted either as dignified and musical, or as an old drunkard.
■[as noun **a silenus**] (pl. **sileni** /-nʌɪ/) a woodland spirit, usually depicted in art as old and having ears like those of a horse.

Silesia /sʌɪˈliːzɪə, -ˈliːʒə/ a region of central Europe, centred on the upper Oder valley, now largely in SW Poland. It was partitioned at various times between the states of Prussia, Austria–Hungary, Poland, and Czechoslovakia.
– DERIVATIVES **Silesian** adjective & noun.

silex /ˈsʌɪlɛks/ ▶ noun [mass noun] silica, especially quartz or flint.
– ORIGIN late 16th cent.: from Latin, 'flint'.

silhouette /ˌsɪlʊˈɛt/ ▶ noun the dark shape and outline of someone or something visible against a lighter background, especially in dim light.
■a representation of someone or something showing the shape and outline only, typically coloured in solid black.
▶ verb [with obj.] (usu. **be silhouetted**) cast or show (someone or something) as a dark shape and outline against a lighter background: *the castle was silhouetted against the sky.*
– PHRASES **in silhouette** seen or placed as a silhouette.
– ORIGIN late 18th cent.: named (although the reason remains obscure) after Étienne de *Silhouette* (1709–67), French author and politician.

silica /ˈsɪlɪkə/ ▶ noun [mass noun] a hard, unreactive, colourless compound which occurs as the mineral quartz and as a principal constituent of sandstone and other rocks.
● Alternative name: **silicon dioxide**; chem. formula: SiO_2.
– DERIVATIVES **siliceous** /-ˈlɪʃəs/ (also **silicious**) adjective.
– ORIGIN early 19th cent.: from Latin *silex*, *silic-* 'flint', on the pattern of words such as *alumina*.

silica gel ▶ noun [mass noun] hydrated silica in a hard granular hygroscopic form used as a desiccant.

silicate /ˈsɪlɪkeɪt, -kət/ ▶ noun Chemistry a salt in which the anion contains both silicon and oxygen, especially one of the anion SiO_4^{2-}.
■any of the many minerals consisting of silica combined with metal oxides, forming a major component of the rocks of the earth's crust.

silicic /sɪˈlɪsɪk/ ▶ adjective Geology (of rocks) rich in silica.

silicic acid ▶ noun [mass noun] Chemistry a weakly acidic colloidal hydrated form of silica made by acidifying solutions of alkali metal silicates.

siliciclastic /sɪˌlɪsɪˈklastɪk/ ▶ adjective Geology relating to or denoting clastic rocks consisting largely of silica or silicates.

silicide /ˈsɪlɪsʌɪd/ ▶ noun Chemistry a binary compound of silicon with another element or group.

silicify /sɪˈlɪsɪfʌɪ/ ▶ verb (**-ies**, **-ied**) [with obj.] (usu. **be silicified**) convert into or impregnate with silica.
– DERIVATIVES **silicification** noun.

silicon /ˈsɪlɪk(ə)n/ ▶ noun [mass noun] the chemical element of atomic number 14, a non-metal with semiconducting properties, used in making electronic circuits. Pure silicon exists in a shiny dark grey crystalline form and as an amorphous powder. (Symbol: **Si**)
– ORIGIN early 19th cent.: alteration of earlier *silicium*, from Latin *silex*, *silic-* 'flint', on the pattern of *carbon* and *boron*.

silicon carbide ▶ noun [mass noun] a hard refractory crystalline compound of silicon and carbon; carborundum.
● Chem. formula: SiC.

silicon chip ▶ noun a microchip.

silicone /ˈsɪlɪkəʊn/ ▶ noun any of a class of synthetic materials which are polymers with a chemical structure based on chains of alternate silicon and oxygen atoms, with organic groups attached to the silicon atoms. Such compounds are typically resistant to chemical attack and insensitive to temperature changes and are used to make rubber and plastics and in polishes and lubricants.
▶ verb [with obj.] (usu. **be siliconed**) join or otherwise treat (something) with a silicone.

siliconize /ˈsɪlɪk(ə)nʌɪz/ (also **-ise**) ▶ verb [with obj.] [often as adj. **siliconized**] coat or otherwise treat (something) with silicone.

Silicon Valley a name given to an area between San Jose and Palo Alto in Santa Clara County, California, USA, noted for its computing and electronics industries.

silicosis /ˌsɪlɪˈkəʊsɪs/ ▶ noun [mass noun] Medicine lung fibrosis caused by the inhalation of dust containing silica.
– DERIVATIVES **silicotic** adjective.

siliqua /ˈsɪlɪkwə/ (also **silique** /sɪˈliːk/) ▶ noun (pl. **siliquae** /-kwiː/ or **siliques** /sɪˈliːks/) **1** Botany the long, narrow seed pod of many plants of the cabbage family, splitting open when mature.
2 a Roman silver coin of the 4th and 5th centuries AD, worth 1⁄24 solidus.
– DERIVATIVES **siliquose** /-kwəʊs/ adjective.
– ORIGIN Latin, literally 'pod'.

silk ▶ noun [mass noun] a fine, strong, soft lustrous fibre produced by silkworms in making cocoons and collected to make thread and fabric.
■a similar fibre spun by some other insect larvae and by most spiders. ■ [often as modifier] thread or fabric made from the fibre produced by the silkworm: *a silk shirt.* ■ (**silks**) garments made from such fabric, especially as worn by a jockey in the colours of a particular horse owner. ■ [count noun] Riding a cover worn over a riding hat made from a silk-like fabric. ■ [count noun] Brit. informal a Queen's (or King's) Counsel. [ORIGIN: so named because of the right accorded to wear a gown made of this cloth.] ■ (**silks**) the silky styles of the female maize flower.
– PHRASES **take silk** Brit. become a Queen's (or King's) Counsel.
– DERIVATIVES **silk-like** adjective.
– ORIGIN Old English *sioloc*, *seolec*, from late Latin *sericum*, neuter of Latin *sericus*, based on Greek *Sēres*, the name given to the inhabitants of the Far Eastern countries from which silk first came overland to Europe.

silk cotton ▶ noun another term for **KAPOK**.

silk-cotton tree ▶ noun a tree which produces silk cotton.
● Two species in the family Bombacaceae: the **Indian silk-cotton tree** (*Bombax ceiba*) and the ceiba.

silk dupion ▶ noun see **DUPION**.

silken ▶ adjective made of silk: *a silken ribbon.*
■soft or lustrous like silk: *silken hair.*
– ORIGIN Old English *seolcen* (see **SILK**, **-EN**[2]).

silk gland ▶ noun a gland in a silkworm, spider, or other arthropod that secretes the substance which hardens as threads of silk or web.

silk hat ▶ noun a man's tall, cylindrical hat covered with black silk plush.

silkie ▶ noun (pl. **-ies**) **1** a small chicken of a breed characterized by long soft plumage.
2 variant spelling of **SELKIE**.

silk moth ▶ noun a large moth with a caterpillar that spins a protective silken cocoon:
● (**the silk moth**) a domesticated Asian moth whose larva is the chief commercial silkworm (*Bombyx mori*, family Bombycidae). ● (also **giant silk moth**) a saturniid moth.

Silk Road (also **Silk Route**) an ancient caravan route linking Xian in central China with the eastern Mediterranean. It was established during the period of Roman rule in Europe, and took its name from the silk which was brought to the west from China.

silk screen ▶ noun a screen of fine mesh used in screen printing.
■a print made by screen printing.
▶ verb (**silk-screen**) [with obj.] print, decorate, or reproduce using a silk screen.

silk-stocking ▶ adjective N. Amer. wealthy; aristocratic: *a silk-stocking district* | *a silk-stocking crowd.*

silkworm ▶ noun the commercially bred caterpillar of the domesticated silk moth (*Bombyx mori*), which spins a silk cocoon that is processed to yield silk fibre.
■[with modifier] a commercial silk-yielding caterpillar of a saturniid moth. See **TUSSORE**.
– ORIGIN Old English *seolcwyrm* (see **SILK**, **WORM**).

silky ▶ adjective (**silkier**, **silkiest**) of or resembling silk, especially in being soft, fine, and lustrous: *the fur felt silky and soft.*
■(of a person or their speech or manner) suave and smooth, especially in a way intended to be persuasive: *a silky, seductive voice.*
– DERIVATIVES **silkily** adverb, **silkiness** noun.

silky oak ▶ noun a tall Australian tree which yields silky-textured timber similar to oak.
● Several species in the family Proteaceae, in particular *Cardwellia sublimis* and the frequently cultivated *Grevillea robusta*.

sill (also chiefly Building **cill**) ▶ noun a shelf or slab of stone, wood, or metal at the foot of a window or doorway.
■a strong horizontal member at the base of any structure, e.g. in the frame of a motor or rail vehicle. ■ Geology a tabular sheet of igneous rock intruded between and parallel with the existing strata. Compare with **DYKE**[1]. ■ an underwater ridge or rock ledge extending across the bed of a body of water.
– ORIGIN Old English *syll*, *sylle* 'horizontal beam forming a foundation', of Germanic origin; related to German *Schwelle* 'threshold'.

sillabub ▶ noun archaic spelling of **SYLLABUB**.

sillimanite /ˈsɪlɪmənʌɪt/ ▶ noun [mass noun] an aluminosilicate mineral typically occurring as fibrous masses, commonly in schist or gneiss.
– ORIGIN mid 19th cent.: from the name of Benjamin *Silliman* (1779–1864), American chemist + **-ITE**[1].

Sillitoe /ˈsɪlɪtəʊ/, Alan (b.1928), English writer, noted for his novels about working-class provincial life. Notable works: *The Loneliness of the Long-Distance Runner* (1959) and *Saturday Night and Sunday Morning* (1958).

silly ▶ adjective (**sillier**, **silliest**) **1** having or showing a lack of common sense or judgement; absurd and foolish: *another of his silly jokes* | *'Don't be silly!' she said.*
■ridiculously trivial or frivolous: *he would brood about silly things.* ■ [as complement] used to convey that an activity or process has been engaged in to such a degree that someone is no longer capable of thinking or acting sensibly: *he often drank himself silly* | *his mother worried herself silly over him.* ■ archaic (especially of a woman, child, or animal) helpless; defenceless.
2 [attrib.] Cricket denoting fielding positions very close to the batsman: *silly mid-on.*
▶ noun (pl. **-ies**) informal a foolish person (often used as a form of address): *Come on, silly.*
– PHRASES **the silly season** chiefly Brit. high summer regarded as the season when newspapers often publish trivial material because of a lack of important news.
– DERIVATIVES **sillily** adverb, **silliness** noun.
– ORIGIN late Middle English (in the sense 'deserving of pity or sympathy'): alteration of dialect *seely* 'happy', later 'innocent, feeble', from a West Germanic base meaning 'luck, happiness'. The sense 'foolish' developed via the stages 'feeble' and 'unsophisticated, ignorant'.

silly billy ▶ noun informal, chiefly Brit. a stupid or foolish person.

silo /ˈsʌɪləʊ/ ▶ noun (pl. **-os**) **1** a tall tower or pit on a farm used to store grain.
■a pit or other airtight structure in which green crops are compressed and stored as silage.
2 an underground chamber in which a guided missile is kept ready for firing.
– ORIGIN mid 19th cent.: from Spanish, via Latin from Greek *siros* 'corn-pit'.

Siloam /sʌɪˈləʊəm/ (in the New Testament) a spring and pool of water near Jerusalem, where a man born blind was told by Jesus to wash, thereby gaining sight (John 9:7).

siloxane /sɪˈlɒkseɪn/ ▶ noun Chemistry a compound

having a molecular structure based on a chain of alternate silicon and oxygen atoms, especially (as in silicone) with organic groups attached to the silicon atoms.
– ORIGIN early 20th cent.: blend of **SILICON** and **OXYGEN** + -**ANE**².

silt ▶ noun [mass noun] fine sand, clay, or other material carried by running water and deposited as a sediment, especially in a channel or harbour. ■[count noun] a bed or layer of such material. ■ technical sediment whose particles are between clay and sand in size (typically 0.002–0.06 mm).
▶ verb [no obj.] become filled or blocked with silt: *the river's mouth had silted up* | [as noun silting] *the silting of the river estuary.* ■[with obj.] fill or block with silt.
– DERIVATIVES **siltation** noun, **silty** adjective.
– ORIGIN late Middle English: probably originally denoting a salty deposit and of Scandinavian origin, related to Danish and Norwegian *sylt* 'salt marsh', also to **SALT**.

siltstone ▶ noun [mass noun] fine-grained sedimentary rock consisting of consolidated silt.

Silurian /sʌɪˈljʊərɪən, sɪ-/ ▶ adjective Geology of, relating to, or denoting the third period of the Palaeozoic era, between the Ordovician and Devonian periods. ■[as noun **the Silurian**] the Silurian period or the system of rocks deposited during it.

The Silurian lasted from about 439 to 409 million years ago. The first true fish and land plants appeared, and the end of the period is marked by the climax of the Caledonian orogeny.

– ORIGIN early 18th cent.: from Latin *Silures* (denoting a people of ancient SE Wales) + -**IAN**.

siluroid /sɪˈljʊərɔɪd/ Zoology ▶ noun a fish of an order (Siluriformes) that comprises the catfishes.
▶ adjective of or relating to fish of this order.
– ORIGIN mid 19th cent.: from *Silurus* (genus name) + -**OID**.

silvan ▶ adjective variant spelling of **SYLVAN**.

Silvanus /sɪlˈveɪnəs, sɪlˈvɑːnəs/ Roman Mythology an Italian woodland deity identified with Pan.

silver ▶ noun [mass noun] 1 a precious shiny greyish-white metal, the chemical element of atomic number 47. (Symbol: **Ag**)

A transition metal, silver is found in nature in the uncombined state as well as in ores. It is valued for use in jewellery and other ornaments and formerly in coins, and the decomposition of silver salts by the action of light (depositing metallic silver) is the basis of photography.

2 a shiny grey-white colour or appearance like that of silver: *the dark hair was now highlighted with silver.* 3 silver dishes, containers, or cutlery: *thieves stole £5,000 worth of silver* | *the family silver.* ■household cutlery of any material. 4 coins made from silver or from a metal that resembles silver. ■chiefly Scottish money. 5 [count noun] short for **SILVER MEDAL**.
▶ verb [with obj.] [often as adj. **silvered**] coat or plate with silver: *large silvered candlesticks.* ■provide (mirror glass) with a backing of a silver-coloured material in order to make it reflective. ■ poetic/literary (especially of the moon) give a silvery appearance to: *the brilliant moon silvered the turf.* ■ turn (a person's hair) grey or white. ■ [no obj.] (of a person's hair) turn grey or white.
– PHRASES **be born with a silver spoon in one's mouth** be born into a wealthy family of high social standing. **every cloud has a silver lining** proverb every difficult or sad situation has a comforting or more hopeful aspect, even though this may not be immediately apparent. **the silver screen** the cinema industry; cinema films collectively: *stars of the silver screen.*
– ORIGIN Old English *seolfor*, of Germanic origin; related to Dutch *zilver* and German *Silber*.

silver age ▶ noun a period regarded as notable but inferior to a golden age, such as that of so-called silver Latin literature.

silverback ▶ noun a mature male mountain gorilla, which is distinguished by an area of white or silvery hair across the back and is the dominant member of its social group.

silver band ▶ noun Brit. a brass band playing silver-plated instruments.

silverberry ▶ noun (pl. -ies) a North American shrub related to the oleaster, with red-brown stems and silvery leaves, flowers, and berries.
● *Elaeagnus commutata*, family Elaeagnaceae.

silverbill ▶ noun a small African and Asian waxbill related to the mannikins, with a conical pale blue-grey bill.
● Genus *Lonchura*, family Estrildidae: three species.

silver birch ▶ noun a Eurasian birch with silver-grey bark, common on poorer soils to the northern limit of tree growth.
● *Betula pendula*, family Betulaceae.
■N. Amer. another term for **PAPER BIRCH**.

silver disc ▶ noun a framed silver-coloured disc awarded to a recording artist or group for sales of a recording exceeding a specified figure (lower than those required for a gold disc).

silver drummer ▶ noun see **DRUMMER** (sense 3).

silver-eared mesia ▶ noun see **MESIA**.

silvereye ▶ noun an Australasian songbird of the white-eye family, with mainly greenish plumage and a white ring round the eye.
● Genus *Zosterops*, family Zosteropidae: two or three species.

silver fern ▶ noun 1 another term for **PONGA**. 2 a stylized fern leaf in silver, as an emblem of New Zealand.

silver fir ▶ noun a fir tree with foliage that appears silvery or bluish because of whitish lines on the undersides of the needles.
● Genus *Abies*, family Pinaceae: several species, in particular *A. alba*.

silverfish ▶ noun (pl. same or -fishes) 1 a silvery bristletail that lives in houses and other buildings, chiefly nocturnal and feeding on starchy materials.
● *Lepisma saccharina*, family Lepismatidae. 2 a silver-coloured fish, especially a goldfish of an unpigmented variety.

silver fox ▶ noun a red fox of a North American variety which has black fur with white tips. ■[mass noun] the fur of this animal.

silver gilt ▶ noun [mass noun] gilded silver. ■an imitation gilding of yellow lacquer over silver leaf.

silvering ▶ noun [mass noun] silver-coloured material used to coat glass in order to make it reflective.

silver jubilee ▶ noun the twenty-fifth anniversary of a significant event.

silver Latin ▶ noun [mass noun] literary Latin from the death of Augustus (AD 14) to the mid second century.

silver leaf ▶ noun 1 a fungal disease of ornamental and fruit trees, especially plum trees, resulting in silvery discoloration of the leaves.
● The fungus is *Chondrostereum purpureum*, family Stereaceae, class Hymenomycetes. 2 silver that has been beaten into a very thin sheet, suitable for applying to surfaces as a decoration.

silver-line ▶ noun [with modifier] either of two European moths with two or three whitish lines on the forewing:
● (**brown silver-line**) a light brown moth whose larvae feed on bracken (*Petrophora chlorosata*, family Geometridae).
● (**silver-lines**) a moth with mainly green forewings (genera *Pseudoips* and *Bena*, family Noctuidae).

silver medal ▶ noun a medal made of or coloured silver, customarily awarded for second place in a race or competition.

silvern /ˈsɪlv(ə)n/ ▶ adjective archaic term for **SILVER**.
– ORIGIN Old English *seolfren, silfren* (see **SILVER**, -**N**¹).

silver paper ▶ noun [mass noun] 1 chiefly Brit. foil made of aluminium or other silver-coloured metal. 2 archaic fine white tissue paper.

silver plate ▶ noun [mass noun] a thin layer of silver electroplated or otherwise applied as a coating to another metal. ■objects coated with silver. ■ plates, dishes, etc. made of silver.
▶ verb (**silver-plate**) [with obj.] cover (something) with a thin layer of silver.

silverpoint ▶ noun [mass noun] the art of drawing with a silver-pointed instrument on paper prepared with a coating of powdered bone or zinc white, creating a fine indelible line composed of metal fragments.

silver salmon ▶ noun another term for **COHO**.

silver sand ▶ noun Brit. a fine, white sand used in gardening.

silver service ▶ noun [mass noun] a style of serving food at formal meals in which the server uses a silver spoon and fork in one hand to serve the food item by item on to the diner's plate.

silverside ▶ noun 1 [mass noun] Brit. the upper side of a round of beef from the outside of the leg. 2 (also **silversides**) a small, slender, chiefly marine fish with a bright silver line along its sides.
● Family Atherinidae: several genera and species.

silversmith ▶ noun a person who makes silver articles.
– DERIVATIVES **silversmithing** noun.

silver solder ▶ noun [mass noun] a brazing alloy consisting largely of copper and silver.

silver standard ▶ noun historical a system by which the value of a currency is defined in terms of silver, for which the currency may be exchanged.

Silver State informal name for **NEVADA**.

Silverstone a motor-racing circuit near Towcester in Northamptonshire.

silversword ▶ noun a Hawaiian plant of the daisy family, which has long narrow leaves with silvery hairs and clusters of purplish flowers.
● Genus *Argyroxiphium*, family Compositae.

silver thaw ▶ noun a glassy coating of ice formed on the ground or an exposed surface by freezing rain or the refreezing of thawed ice.

silver tongue ▶ noun a tendency to be eloquent and persuasive in speaking.
– DERIVATIVES **silver-tongued** adjective.

silver tree ▶ noun a South African tree which has light silvery-green leaves covered with very fine down.
● *Leucadendron argenteum*, family Proteaceae.

silverware ▶ noun [mass noun] dishes, containers, or cutlery made of or coated with silver, or made of a material resembling silver.

silver wedding ▶ noun the twenty-fifth anniversary of a wedding.

silverweed ▶ noun [mass noun] a yellow-flowered herbaceous potentilla with silvery compound leaves, a common grassland weed of north temperate regions.
● *Potentilla anserina*, family Rosaceae.

silvery ▶ adjective like silver in colour or appearance; shiny and grey-white: *shoals of silvery fish.* ■(of a person's hair) grey-white and lustrous. ■(of a sound) gentle, clear, and melodious: *a little silvery laugh.*
– DERIVATIVES **silveriness** noun.

silver Y ▶ noun a greyish-brown European moth that has purple-tinged wings with a white Y-shaped mark on the forewings.
● *Autographa gamma*, family Noctuidae.

silviculture /ˈsɪlvɪˌkʌltʃə/ ▶ noun [mass noun] the growing and cultivation of trees.
– DERIVATIVES **silvicultural** adjective, **silviculturist** noun.
– ORIGIN late 19th cent.: from French *sylviculture*, from Latin *silva* 'wood' + French *culture* 'cultivation'.

sim ▶ noun informal a video game that simulates an activity such as flying an aircraft or playing a sport.
– ORIGIN late 20th cent.: abbreviation of *simulation* (see **SIMULATE**).

sima /ˈsʌɪmə/ ▶ noun [mass noun] Geology the material of the lower part of the earth's crust, underlying both the ocean and the continents, characterized as relatively heavy and rich in silica and magnesia. Contrasted with **SIAL**.
– ORIGIN early 20th cent.: blend of **SILICA** + **MAGNESIUM**.

simazine /ˈsɪməziːn, ˈsʌɪ-/ ▶ noun [mass noun] a synthetic compound derived from triazine and used as a herbicide, especially to kill broad-leaved weeds and grasses before they emerge.
– ORIGIN 1950s: blend of **SYMMETRICAL** and **TRIAZINE**.

Simbirsk /sɪmˈbɪəsk/ a city in European Russia, a port on the River Volga south-east of Nizhni Novgorod; pop. 638,000 (1990). Between 1924 and 1992 it was called Ulyanovsk, in honour of Lenin (Vladimir Ilich Ulyanov), who was born there in 1870.

simcha /ˈsɪmtʃə, -xə/ ▶ noun a Jewish private party or celebration.
– ORIGIN from Hebrew *śimḥāh* 'rejoicing'.

Simenon /ˈsiːmənɒ̃/, Georges (Joseph Christian) (1903–89), Belgian-born French novelist. He is best known for his series of detective novels featuring Commissaire Maigret.

Simeon /ˈsɪmɪən/ (in the Bible) a Hebrew patriarch, son of Jacob and Leah (Gen. 29:33).
■the tribe of Israel traditionally descended from him.

Simeon Stylites, St /stʌɪˈlʌɪtiːz/ (c.390–459), Syrian monk. After living in a monastic community he became the first to practise an extreme form of asceticism which involved living on top of a pillar.

Simferopol /ˌsɪmfəˈrɒp(ə)l/ a city in the Crimea; pop. 348,900 (1990). It was settled by the Tartars in the 16th century, when it was known as Ak-Mechet, and was seized in 1736 by the Russians.

simian /ˈsɪmɪən/ ▶ **adjective** relating to, resembling, or affecting apes or monkeys: *simian immunodeficiency virus*. Compare with **PROSIMIAN**.
▶ **noun** an ape or monkey.
– ORIGIN early 17th cent.: from Latin *simia* 'ape', perhaps via Latin from Greek *simos* 'flat-nosed'.

Simien jackal /ˈsɪmɪən/ (also **Simien fox** or **Simian**) ▶ **noun** an endangered jackal with a bright reddish coat and white underparts, native to the mountain grasslands of Ethiopia.
● *Canis simensis*, family Canidae.
– ORIGIN named after the *Simien* Mountains of Ethiopia.

similar ▶ **adjective** having a resemblance in appearance, character, or quantity, without being identical: *a soft cheese* **similar to** *brie* | *northern India and similar areas*.
■Geometry (of geometrical figures) having the same shape, with the same angles and proportions, though of different sizes.
▶ **noun** chiefly archaic a person or thing similar to another.
■(usu. **similars**) a substance that produces effects resembling the symptoms of particular diseases (the basis of homeopathic treatment): *the principle of treatment by similars*.
– ORIGIN late 16th cent. (also as a term in anatomy meaning 'homogeneous'): from French *similaire* or medieval Latin *similaris*, from Latin *similis* 'like'.

USAGE The standard construction for **similar** is with **to**, as in *I've had problems* ***similar to*** *yours*. However, in British English, the construction **similar as** is sometimes used instead, as in *I've had* ***similar*** *problems* ***as*** *yourself*. This is not accepted as correct in standard English.

similarity ▶ **noun** (pl. **-ies**) the state or fact of being similar: *the similarity of symptoms makes them hard to diagnose*.
■(usu. **similarities**) a similar feature or aspect: *the similarities between people of different nationalities*.

similarly ▶ **adverb** [usu. as submodifier] in a similar way: *a similarly priced property*.
■[sentence adverb] used to indicate a similarity between two facts or events: *The diaries of politicians tend to be self-justificatory. Similarly, autobiographies may be idealized*.

simile /ˈsɪmɪli/ ▶ **noun** a figure of speech involving the comparison of one thing with another thing of a different kind, used to make a description more emphatic or vivid (e.g. *as brave as a lion*).
■[mass noun] the use of such a method of comparison.
– ORIGIN late Middle English: from Latin, neuter of *similis* 'like'.

S

similitude /sɪˈmɪlɪtjuːd/ ▶ **noun** [mass noun] the quality or state of being similar to something.
■[count noun] archaic a comparison between two things. ■[count noun] archaic a person or thing resembling someone or something else.
– ORIGIN late Middle English: from Old French, from Latin *similitudo*, from *similis* 'like'.

Simla /ˈsɪmlə/ a city in NE India, capital of the state of Himachal Pradesh; pop. 109,860 (1991).

SIMM Computing ▶ **abbreviation** for single in-line memory module, containing RAM chips.

Simmental /ˈsɪm(ə)ntɑːl/ ▶ **noun** an animal of a red and white breed of cattle farmed for both meat and milk.
– ORIGIN 1950s: named after a valley in central Switzerland.

simmer ▶ **verb** [no obj.] (of water or food that is being heated) stay just below boiling point while bubbling gently: *the goulash was simmering slowly in the oven* | figurative *the disagreement simmered for years and eventually boiled over*.
■[with obj.] keep (something) at such a point when cooking or heating it: *simmer the sauce gently until thickened*. ■be in a state of suppressed anger or excitement: *she was simmering with resentment*.
■(**simmer down**) become calmer and quieter.
▶ **noun** [in sing.] a state or temperature just below boiling point: *bring the water to a simmer*.
– ORIGIN mid 17th cent.: alteration of dialect *simper* (in the same sense), perhaps imitative.

Simnel /ˈsɪmn(ə)l/, Lambert (c.1475–1525), English pretender and rebel. He was trained by Yorkists to impersonate firstly one of the Princes in the Tower and subsequently the Earl of Warwick in an attempt to overthrow Henry VII.

simnel cake /ˈsɪmn(ə)l/ ▶ **noun** chiefly Brit. a rich fruit cake, typically with a marzipan covering and decoration, eaten especially at Easter or during Lent.
– ORIGIN mid 17th cent.: *simnel* from Old French *simenel*, based on Latin *simila* or Greek *semidalis* 'fine flour'.

simoleon /sɪˈməʊlɪən/ ▶ **noun** US informal a dollar.
– ORIGIN late 19th cent.: perhaps on the pattern of *napoleon*.

Simon[1], (Marvin) Neil (b.1927), American dramatist. Most of his plays are wry comedies portraying aspects of middle-class life; they include *Barefoot in the Park* (1963) and *The Odd Couple* (1965).

Simon[2], Paul (b.1942), American singer and songwriter. He achieved fame with **Art Garfunkel** (b.1941) for the albums *Sounds of Silence* (1966) and *Bridge Over Troubled Water* (1970). The duo split up in 1970 and Simon went on to pursue a successful solo career, recording albums such as *Graceland* (1986).

Simon, St an Apostle; known as **Simon the Zealot**. According to one tradition he preached and was martyred in Persia along with St Jude. Feast day (with St Jude), 28 October.

Simonides /sʌɪˈmɒnɪdiːz/ (c.556–468 BC), Greek lyric poet. Much of his poetry, which includes elegies, odes, and epigrams, celebrates the heroes of the Persian Wars.

simonize /ˈsʌɪmənʌɪz/ ▶ **verb** [with obj.] US polish (a motor vehicle).
– ORIGIN 1930s: from the proprietary name *Simoniz* + **-IZE**.

simon-pure ▶ **adjective** completely genuine, authentic, or honest.
– ORIGIN late 18th cent.: from (*the real*) *Simon Pure*, a character in Centlivre's *Bold Stroke for a Wife* (1717), who for part of the play is impersonated by another character.

Simon Says ▶ **noun** [mass noun] a children's game in which players must obey the leader's instructions if (and only if) they are prefaced with the words 'Simon says'.

simony /ˈsʌɪməni, ˈsɪm-/ ▶ **noun** [mass noun] chiefly historical the buying or selling of ecclesiastical privileges, for example pardons or benefices.
– DERIVATIVES **simoniac** /-ˈməʊnɪak/ adjective & noun, **simoniacal** /-ˈnʌɪək(ə)l/ adjective.
– ORIGIN Middle English: from Old French *simonie*, from late Latin *simonia*, from Simon Magus (Acts 8:18).

simoom /sɪˈmuːm/ (also **simoon** /-muːn/) ▶ **noun** a hot, dry, dust-laden wind blowing in the desert, especially in Arabia.
– ORIGIN late 18th cent.: from Arabic *samūm*, from *samma* 'to poison'.

simp ▶ **noun** N. Amer. informal a silly or foolish person.
– ORIGIN early 20th cent.: abbreviation of **SIMPLETON**.

simpatico /sɪmˈpatɪkəʊ/ ▶ **adjective** (of a person) likeable and easy to get on with.
■having or characterized by shared attributes or interests; compatible: *a simpatico relationship*.
– ORIGIN Italian and Spanish.

simper ▶ **verb** [no obj.] smile or gesture in an affectedly coquettish, coy, or ingratiating manner: *she simpered, looking pleased with herself*.
▶ **noun** [usu. in sing.] an affectedly coquettish, coy, or ingratiating smile or gesture: *an exaggerated simper*.
– DERIVATIVES **simperingly** adverb.
– ORIGIN mid 16th cent.: of unknown origin; compare with German *zimpfer* 'elegant, delicate'.

simple ▶ **adjective** (**simpler**, **simplest**) **1** easily understood or done; presenting no difficulty: *a simple solution* | *camcorders are now so simple to operate*.
■plain, basic, or uncomplicated in form, nature, or design; without much decoration or ornamentation: *a simple white blouse* | *the house is furnished in a simple country style*. ■[attrib.] used to emphasize the fundamental and straightforward nature of something: *the simple truth*.
2 composed of a single element; not compound.
■Mathematics denoting a group that has no proper normal subgroup. ■Botany (of a leaf or stem) not divided or branched. ■(of a lens, microscope, etc.) consisting of a single lens or component. ■(in English grammar) denoting a tense formed without an auxiliary, for example *sang* as opposed to *was singing*. ■(of interest) payable on the sum loaned only. Compare with **COMPOUND**[1].
3 of or characteristic of low rank or status; humble and unpretentious: *a simple Buddhist monk*.
4 of low or abnormally low intelligence.
▶ **noun** chiefly historical a medicinal herb, or a medicine made from one: *the gatherers of simples*.
– DERIVATIVES **simpleness** noun.
– ORIGIN Middle English: from Old French, from Latin *simplus*. The noun sense (mid 16th cent.) originally referred to a medicine made from one constituent, especially from one plant.

simple eye ▶ **noun** a small eye of an insect or other arthropod which has only one lens, typically present in one or more pairs. Also called **OCELLUS**. Contrasted with **COMPOUND EYE**.

simple fracture ▶ **noun** a fracture of the bone only, without damage to the surrounding tissues or breaking of the skin.

simple harmonic motion ▶ **noun** [mass noun] Physics oscillatory motion under a retarding force proportional to the amount of displacement from an equilibrium position.

simple interval ▶ **noun** Music an interval of one octave or less.

simple machine ▶ **noun** Mechanics any of the basic mechanical devices for applying a force, such as an inclined plane, wedge, or lever.

simple majority ▶ **noun** a majority in which the highest number of votes cast for any one candidate, issue, or item exceeds the second-highest number, while not constituting an absolute majority.

simple-minded ▶ **adjective** having or showing very little intelligence or judgement.
– DERIVATIVES **simple-mindedly** adverb, **simple-mindedness** noun.

simple sentence ▶ **noun** a sentence consisting of only one clause, with a single subject and predicate.

Simple Simon ▶ **noun** a foolish or gullible person.
– ORIGIN probably from the name of a character who features in various nursery rhymes.

simple time ▶ **noun** [mass noun] musical rhythm or metre in which each beat in a bar may be subdivided simply into halves or quarters. Compare with **COMPOUND TIME**.

simpleton ▶ **noun** a foolish or gullible person.
– ORIGIN mid 17th cent.: from **SIMPLE**, on the pattern of surnames derived from place names ending in *-ton*.

simplex ▶ **adjective** technical composed of or characterized by a single part or structure.
■(of a communication system, computer circuit, etc.) only allowing transmission of signals in one direction at a time.
▶ **noun** a simple or uncompounded word.
– ORIGIN late 16th cent.: from Latin, literally 'single', variant of *simplus* 'simple'.

simplex method ▶ **noun** Mathematics a standard method of maximizing a linear function of several variables under several constraints on other linear functions.

simpliciter /sɪmˈplɪsɪtə/ ▶ **adverb** chiefly Law simply; unconditionally: *restraint is imposed in order to prevent competition simpliciter*.
– ORIGIN Latin, literally 'simply'.

simplicity ▶ **noun** [mass noun] the quality or condition of being easy to understand or do: *for the sake of simplicity, this chapter will concentrate upon one theory*.
■the quality or condition of being plain or natural: *the grandeur and simplicity of Roman architecture*. ■[count noun] a thing that is plain, natural, or easy to understand: *the simplicities of pastoral living*.
– PHRASES **be simplicity itself** be extremely easy.
– ORIGIN late Middle English: from Old French *simplicite* or Latin *simplicitas*, from *simplex* (see **SIMPLEX**).

simplify ▶ **verb** (**-ies**, **-ied**) [with obj.] make (something) simpler or easier to do or understand: *an overhaul of court procedure to simplify litigation.*
– DERIVATIVES **simplification** noun.
– ORIGIN mid 17th cent.: from French *simplifier*, from medieval Latin *simplificare*, from Latin *simplus* (see **SIMPLE**).

simplism /ˈsɪmplɪz(ə)m/ ▶ **noun** [mass noun] rare the oversimplification of an issue.

simplistic ▶ **adjective** treating complex issues and problems as if they were much simpler than they really are: *simplistic solutions.*
– DERIVATIVES **simplistically** adverb.

Simplon /ˈsɪmplɒn/ a pass in the Alps in southern Switzerland, consisting of a road built by Napoleon in 1801–5 at an altitude of 2,028 m (6,591 ft) and a railway tunnel (built in 1922) which links Switzerland and Italy.

simply ▶ **adverb 1** in a straightforward or plain manner: *speaking simply and from the heart.*
2 merely; just: *simply complete the application form.*
■[as submodifier] absolutely; completely (used for emphasis): *it makes Trevor simply furious.* ■ [sentence adverb] used to introduce a short summary of a situation: *quite simply, some things have to be taught.*

Simpson[1], Sir James Young (1811–71), Scottish surgeon and obstetrician. He discovered the usefulness of chloroform as an anaesthetic shortly after the first use of ether.

Simpson[2], O. J. (b.1947), American football player, actor, and celebrity; full name *Orenthal James Simpson*. He was arrested in 1994, accused of murdering his wife and her male companion, but was acquitted after a lengthy, high-profile trial.

Simpson[3], Wallis (1896–1986), American wife of Edward, Duke of Windsor (Edward VIII); born *Wallis Warfield*. Her relationship with the king caused a scandal in view of her impending second divorce and forced the king's abdication in 1936.

Simpson Desert a desert in central Australia, situated between Alice Springs and the Channel Country to the east.
– ORIGIN named in 1929 after A. A. *Simpson*, president of the Royal Geographical Society of Australia at that time.

Simpson's rule Mathematics an arithmetical rule for estimating the area under a curve where the values of an odd number of ordinates, including those at each end, are known.
– ORIGIN late 19th cent.: named after Thomas *Simpson* (1710–61), English mathematician.

simul /ˈsɪm(ə)l/ ▶ **noun** Chess a display in which a player plays a number of games simultaneously against different opponents.
– ORIGIN 1960s: abbreviation of **SIMULTANEOUS**.

simulacrum /ˌsɪmjʊˈleɪkrəm/ ▶ **noun** (pl. **simulacra** /-krə/ or **simulacrums**) an image or representation of someone or something.
■an unsatisfactory imitation or substitute.
– ORIGIN late 16th cent.: from Latin, from *simulare* (see **SIMULATE**).

simulant ▶ **noun** a thing which simulates or resembles something else: *jade simulants.*
– ORIGIN mid 18th cent.: from Latin *simulant-* 'copying, representing', from the verb *simulare.*

simulate /ˈsɪmjʊleɪt/ ▶ **verb** [with obj.] imitate the appearance or character of: *red ochre intended to simulate blood* | [as adj. **simulated**] *a simulated leather handbag.*
■pretend to have or feel (an emotion): *it was impossible to force a smile, to simulate pleasure.* ■ produce a computer model of: *future population changes were simulated by computer.*
– DERIVATIVES **simulation** noun, **simulative** adjective.
– ORIGIN mid 17th cent.: from Latin *simulat-* 'copied, represented', from the verb *simulare*, from *similis* 'like'.

simulator ▶ **noun** a machine designed to provide a realistic imitation of the controls and operation of a vehicle, aircraft, or other complex system, used for training purposes.
■(also **simulator program**) a program enabling a computer to execute programs written for a different computer.

simulcast /ˈsɪm(ə)lkɑːst/ ▶ **noun** a simultaneous transmission of the same programme on radio and television, or on two or more channels.
■N. Amer. a live transmission of a public celebration or sports event: *simulcasts of live races.*
▶ **verb** [with obj.] broadcast (a programme) in such a way: *it will be simulcast live to 201 countries.*
– ORIGIN 1940s: blend of **SIMULTANEOUS** and **BROADCAST**.

simultaneous /ˌsɪm(ə)lˈteɪnɪəs/ ▶ **adjective** occurring, operating, or done at the same time: *a simultaneous withdrawal of troops* | *simultaneous translation.*
– DERIVATIVES **simultaneity** /-təˈniːɪti, -təˈneɪɪti/ noun, **simultaneously** adverb, **simultaneousness** noun.
– ORIGIN mid 17th cent.: based on Latin *simul* 'at the same time', probably influenced by late Latin *momentaneus.*

simultaneous equations ▶ **plural noun** equations involving two or more unknowns that are to have the same values in each equation.

simurg /sɪˈməːg/ ▶ **noun** (in Persian mythology) a large mythical bird of great age, believed to have the power of reasoning and speech.
– ORIGIN from Persian *sīmurǵ*, from Pahlavi *sēn* 'eagle' + *murǵ* 'bird'.

sin[1] /sɪn/ ▶ **noun** an immoral act considered to be a transgression against divine law: *a sin in the eyes of God* | [mass noun] *the human capacity for sin.*
■an act regarded as a serious or regrettable fault, offence, or omission: *he committed the unforgivable sin of refusing to give interviews.*
▶ **verb** (**sinned**, **sinning**) [no obj.] commit a sin: *I sinned and brought shame down on us.*
■(**sin against**) offend against (God, a person, or a principle): *Lord, we have sinned against you.*
– PHRASES (**as**) —— **as sin** informal having a particular undesirable quality to a high degree: *as ugly as sin* | *miserable as sin.* **for one's sins** humorous, chiefly Brit. used to suggest that a task or duty is so onerous or unpleasant that it must be a punishment. **live in sin** informal, dated live together as though married. **sin of commission** a sinful action. **sin of omission** a sinful failure to perform an action.
– DERIVATIVES **sinless** adjective, **sinlessly** adverb, **sinlessness** noun.
– ORIGIN Old English *synn* (noun), *syngian* (verb); probably related to Latin *sons, sont-* 'guilty'.

sin[2] /sʌɪn/ ▶ **abbreviation for** sine.

Sinai /ˈsʌɪnʌɪ, -nɪʌɪ/ an arid mountainous peninsula in NE Egypt, extending into the Red Sea between the Gulf of Suez and the Gulf of Aqaba. It was occupied by Israel between 1967 and 1982. In the south is Mount Sinai, where, according to the Bible, Moses received the Ten Commandments (Exod. 19–34).

Sinaitic /ˌsʌɪneɪˈɪtɪk/ ▶ **adjective** of or relating to Mount Sinai or the Sinai peninsula.

Sinaloa /ˌsiːnəˈləʊə/ a state on the Pacific coast of Mexico; capital, Culiacán Rosales.

Sinanthropus /sɪˈnanθrəpəs/ ▶ **noun** a former genus name applied to some fossil hominids found in China in 1926. See **PEKING MAN**.
– ORIGIN modern Latin, from **SINO-** 'Chinese' (because remains were found near Beijing) + Greek *anthrōpos* 'man'.

Sinatra /sɪˈnɑːtrə/, Frank (1915–98), American singer and actor; full name *Francis Albert Sinatra*. His many hits include 'Night and Day' and 'My Way'. Notable films: *From Here to Eternity* (1953), for which he won an Oscar.

Sinbad the Sailor (also **Sindbad**) the hero of one of the tales in the *Arabian Nights*, who relates the fantastic adventures he meets with in his voyages.

sin bin informal ▶ **noun** (in sport) a box or bench to which offending players can be sent for a period as a penalty during a game, especially in ice hockey.
■Brit. a place where offenders are sent for detention, punishment, or rehabilitation.
▶ **verb** (**sin-bin**) [with obj.] send (a player) to a sin bin as a penalty.

since ▶ **preposition**, **conjunction**, & **adverb 1** in the intervening period between (the time mentioned) and the time under consideration, typically the present: [as prep.] *she has suffered from cystic fibrosis since 1984* | *the worst property slump since the war* | [as conjunction] *I've felt better since I've been here* | [as adv.] *she ran away on Friday and we haven't seen her since.*
2 [conjunction] for the reason that: because: *delegates were delighted, since better protection of rhino reserves will help protect other rare species.*
3 [adverb] ago: *the settlement had vanished long since.*
– ORIGIN late Middle English: contraction of obsolete *sithence*, or from dialect *sin* (both from dialect *sithen* 'thereupon, afterwards, ever since').

sincere ▶ **adjective** (**sincerer**, **sincerest**) free from pretence or deceit; proceeding from genuine feelings: *they offer their sincere thanks to Paul.*
■(of a person) saying what they genuinely feel or believe; not dishonest or hypocritical.
– DERIVATIVES **sincereness** noun, **sincerity** noun.
– ORIGIN mid 16th cent. (also in the sense 'not falsified, unadulterated'): from Latin *sincerus* 'clean, pure'.

sincerely ▶ **adverb** in a sincere or genuine way: *I sincerely hope that we shall have a change of government* | [as submodifier] *sincerely held differences of belief.*
– PHRASES **yours sincerely** (US also **sincerely yours**) a formula used to end a letter, typically a formal one in which the recipient is addressed by name.

sinciput /ˈsɪnsɪpʌt/ ▶ **noun** Anatomy the front of the skull from the forehead to the crown.
– DERIVATIVES **sincipital** /-ˈsɪpɪt(ə)l/ adjective.
– ORIGIN late 16th cent.: from Latin, from *semi-* 'half' + *caput* 'head'.

Sinclair[1] /ˈsɪŋkleː/, Sir Clive (Marles) (b.1940), English electronics engineer and entrepreneur. He founded a research and development company and launched a range of innovative products including pocket calculators and personal computers. A three-wheeled electric car, the C5, failed to achieve commercial success.

Sinclair[2] /ˈsɪŋkleː/, Upton (Beall) (1878–1968), American novelist and social reformer. He agitated for social justice in seventy-nine books, including *The Jungle* (1906) and the eleven-volume 'Lanny Budd' series (1940–53).

Sind /sɪnd/ a province of SE Pakistan, traversed by the lower reaches of the Indus; capital, Karachi.

Sindebele /sɪnˈdeɪbəli, ˌsɪndɛˈbeɪli/ ▶ **noun** another term for **NDEBELE** (the language).

Sindhi /ˈsɪndi/ ▶ **noun** (pl. **Sindhis**) **1** a native or inhabitant of Sind.
2 [mass noun] the Indic language of Sind, used also in western India and having about 14 million speakers.
▶ **adjective** of or relating to the province of Sind or its people, or the Sindhi language.
– ORIGIN from Persian and Urdu *sindī*, from Sanskrit *sindhu* 'river' (specifically the Indus).

sine /sʌɪn/ ▶ **noun** Mathematics the trigonometric function that is equal to the ratio of the side opposite a given angle (in a right-angled triangle) to the hypotenuse.
– ORIGIN late 16th cent.: from Latin *sinus* 'curve', used in medieval Latin as a translation of Arabic *jayb* 'pocket, sine'.

sinecure /ˈsʌɪnɪkjʊə, ˈsɪn-/ ▶ **noun** a position requiring little or no work but giving the holder status or financial benefit.
– DERIVATIVES **sinecurism** noun, **sinecurist** noun.
– ORIGIN mid 17th cent.: from Latin *sine cura* 'without care'.

sine curve (also **sine wave**) ▶ **noun** a curve representing periodic oscillations of constant amplitude as given by a sine function. Also called **SINUSOID**.

sine die /ˌsiːneɪ ˈdiːeɪ, ˌsʌɪni ˈdʌɪiː/ ▶ **adverb** (with reference to business or proceedings that have been adjourned) with no appointed date for resumption: *the case was adjourned sine die.*
– ORIGIN Latin, literally 'without a day'.

sine qua non /kweɪ ˈnɒn, kwɑː ˈnəʊn/ ▶ **noun** an essential condition; a thing that is absolutely necessary: *grammar and usage are the sine qua non of language teaching and learning.*
– ORIGIN Latin, literally '(cause) without which not'.

sinew ▶ **noun** a piece of tough fibrous tissue uniting muscle to bone; a tendon or ligament.
■(usu. **sinews**) figurative the parts of a structure, system, or thing that give it strength or bind it together: *the sinews of government.*
▶ **verb** [with obj.] [usu. as adj. **sinewed**] poetic/literary strengthen with or as if with sinews: *the sinewed shape of his back.*
– DERIVATIVES **sinewless** adjective, **sinewy** adjective.
– ORIGIN Old English *sin(e)we* 'tendon', of Germanic origin; related to Dutch *zeen* and German *Sehne.*

sinfonia /sɪnˈfəʊnɪə, ˌsɪnfəˈniːə/ ▶ **noun** Music a symphony.
■(in baroque music) an orchestral piece used as an introduction to an opera, cantata, or suite. ■ a small symphony orchestra.

– ORIGIN Italian.

sinfonia concertante ▶ **noun** a piece of music for orchestra with one or (usually) more soloists, typically from the 18th century.
– ORIGIN Italian, literally 'harmonizing symphony'.

sinfonietta /ˌsɪnfəʊnɪˈɛtə/ ▶ **noun** Music a short or simple symphony.
■ a small symphony orchestra.
– ORIGIN Italian, diminutive of *sinfonia* (see **SINFONIA**).

sinful ▶ **adjective** wicked and immoral; committing or characterized by the committing of sins: *sinful men* | *a sinful way of life.*
■ highly reprehensible: *a sinful waste.*
– DERIVATIVES **sinfully** adverb, **sinfulness** noun.
– ORIGIN Old English *synfull* (see **SIN**[1], **-FUL**).

sing ▶ **verb** (past **sang**; past participle **sung**) [no obj.] make musical sounds with the voice, especially words with a set tune: *Bella sang to the baby.*
■ [with obj.] perform (a song, words, or tune) in this way: *someone started singing 'God Save the Queen'* | [as noun **singing**] *the singing of hymns in Latin.* ■ (**sing along**) sing in accompaniment to a song or piece of music. ■ (**sing something out**) call something out loudly; shout: *he sang out a greeting.* ■ (of a bird) make characteristic melodious whistling and twittering sounds: *the birds were singing in the chestnut trees.* ■ make a high-pitched whistling or buzzing sound: *the kettle was beginning to sing.* ■ (of a person's ear) be affected with a continuous buzzing sound, especially as the after-effect of a blow or loud noise: *a stinging slap that made my ear sing.* ■ informal act as an informer to the police: *a leading terrorist was* **singing like a canary.** ■ [with obj.] recount or celebrate in a work of literature, especially poetry: *poetry should sing the strangeness and variety of the human race* | [no obj.] *these poets* **sing of** *the North American experience.* ■ archaic compose poetry.
▶ **noun** [in sing.] informal an act or spell of singing.
■ [count noun] US a meeting for amateur singing.
– PHRASES **all-singing, all-dancing** Brit. informal having a large number and variety of impressive features. **sing a different tune** (or **song**) change one's opinion about or attitude towards someone or something. **sing for one's supper** see **SUPPER**. **sing from the same hymn** (or **song**) **sheet** Brit. informal present a united front in public by not disagreeing with one another. **sing in** (or **out**) **the new** (or **old**) **year** celebrate the new year (or the end of the previous year) with singing. **sing the praises of** see **PRAISE**. **sing someone to sleep** cause someone to fall asleep by singing gently to them.
– DERIVATIVES **singable** adjective, **singingly** adverb.
– ORIGIN Old English *singan* (verb), of Germanic origin; related to Dutch *zingen* and German *singen*.

sing. ▶ **abbreviation for** singular.

singalong ▶ **noun** an informal occasion when people sing together in a group.
■ [usu. as modifier] a light popular song or tune to which one can easily sing along in accompaniment: *an album featuring simple, singalong tunes.*

Singapore /ˌsɪŋəˈpɔː/ a country in SE Asia consisting of the island of Singapore (linked by a causeway to the southern tip of the Malay Peninsula) and some fifty-four smaller islands; pop. 3,045,000 (est. 1991); official languages, Malay, Chinese, Tamil, and English; capital, Singapore City.

> Established as a trading post under the East India Company in 1819, Singapore came under British colonial rule in 1867 as part of the Straits Settlements with Penang and Malacca. Singapore rapidly grew to become the most important commercial centre and naval base in SE Asia. After the Second World War it became first a British Crown Colony in 1946 and then a self-governing state within the Commonwealth in 1959. Federated with Malaysia in 1963, it declared full independence two years later.

– DERIVATIVES **Singaporean** /-ˈpɔːrɪən/ adjective & noun.

Singapore sling ▶ **noun** a cocktail made from gin and cherry brandy.

singe ▶ **verb** (**singeing**) [with obj.] burn (something) superficially or lightly: *the fire had singed his eyebrows* | [as adj. **singed**] *a smell of singed feathers.*
■ [no obj.] be burnt in this way: *the heat was so intense I could feel the hairs on my hands singe.* ■ burn the bristles or down off (the carcass of a pig or fowl) to prepare it for cooking.
▶ **noun** a superficial burn.
– ORIGIN Old English *sencgan*, of West Germanic origin; related to Dutch *zengen*.

Singer[1], Isaac Bashevis (1904–91), Polish-born American novelist and short-story writer. His work blends realistic detail and elements of fantasy, mysticism, and magic to portray the lives of Polish Jews from many periods. Nobel Prize for Literature (1978).

Singer[2], Isaac Merrit (1811–75), American inventor. In 1851 he designed and built the first commercially successful sewing machine.

singer ▶ **noun** a person who sings, especially professionally: *a pop singer.*

singer-songwriter ▶ **noun** a person who sings and writes popular songs, especially professionally.

Singh /sɪŋ/ ▶ **noun** a title or surname adopted by certain warrior castes of northern India, especially by male members of the Sikh Khalsa.
– ORIGIN from Punjabi *siṅgh* 'lion', from Sanskrit *siṃha* 'lion'.

Singhalese /ˌsɪŋɡəˈliːz/ ▶ **noun** & **adjective** variant spelling of **SINHALESE**.

singing hinny ▶ **noun** a kind of currant cake baked on a griddle, originating in northern England.

singing saw ▶ **noun** another term for **MUSICAL SAW**.

single ▶ **adjective 1** [attrib.] only one; not one of several: *a single red rose* | *the kingdom was ruled over by a single family.*
■ regarded separately or as distinct from each other or others in a group: *she wrote down every single word* | *alcohol is the single most important cause of violence.* ■ [with negative] even one (used for emphasis): *they didn't receive a single reply.* ■ designed or suitable for one person: *a single bed.* ■ archaic not accompanied or supported by others; alone.
2 unmarried or not involved in a stable sexual relationship: *a single mother.*
3 [attrib.] consisting of one part: *the studio was a single large room.*
■ Brit. (of a ticket) valid for an outward journey only, not for the return. ■ (of a flower) having only one whorl of petals. ■ denoting an alcoholic drink that consists of one measure of spirits: *a single whisky.*
4 archaic free from duplicity or deceit; ingenuous: *a pure and single heart.*
▶ **noun 1** an individual person or thing rather than part of a pair or a group.
■ a short record with one song on each side. ■ (**singles**) people who are unmarried or not involved in a stable sexual relationship: [as modifier] *a singles bar.* ■ Brit. a ticket that is valid only for an outward journey. ■ a bedroom, especially in a hotel, that is suitable for one person. ■ a single measure of spirits. ■ US informal a one-dollar note.
2 a play that scores one point, in particular:
■ Cricket a hit for one run. ■ Baseball a hit which allows the batter to proceed safely to first base.
3 (**singles**) (especially in tennis and badminton) a game or competition for individual players, not pairs or teams.
4 (usu. **singles**) Bell-ringing a system of change-ringing in which one pair of bells change places at each round.
▶ **verb** [with obj.] **1** (**single someone/thing out**) choose someone or something from a group for special treatment: *one newspaper was* **singled out for** *criticism.*
2 thin out (seedlings or saplings).
3 reduce (a railway track) to a single line.
4 [no obj.] Baseball hit a single.
■ [with obj.] cause (a run) to be scored by hitting a single. ■ [with obj.] advance (a runner) by hitting a single.
– DERIVATIVES **singleness** noun, **singly** adverb.
– ORIGIN Middle English: via Old French from Latin *singulus*, related to *simplus* 'simple'.

single acrostic ▶ **noun** an acrostic using the first letter only of each line.

single-acting ▶ **adjective** (of an engine) having pressure applied only to one side of the piston.

single-action ▶ **adjective** (of a gun) needing to be cocked by hand before it can be fired.

single-blind ▶ **adjective** [attrib.] denoting a test or experiment in which information that may bias the results is concealed from either tester or subject.

single bond ▶ **noun** a chemical bond in which one pair of electrons is shared between two atoms.

single-breasted ▶ **adjective** (of a jacket or coat) showing only one row of buttons at the front when fastened.

single carriageway ▶ **noun** a road with only one lane in each direction.

single-cell protein ▶ **noun** [mass noun] protein derived from a culture of single-celled organisms, used especially as a food supplement.

single combat ▶ **noun** [mass noun] fighting between two people: *he defeated the enemy champion* **in single combat.**

single-copy ▶ **adjective** Genetics (of a gene or genetic sequence) present in a genome in only one copy.

single cream ▶ **noun** [mass noun] Brit. thin cream with a relatively low fat content.

single-cut ▶ **adjective** (of a file) having grooves cut in one direction only, not crossing each other.

single-decker ▶ **noun** chiefly Brit. a bus having only one floor or level.

single digging ▶ **noun** [mass noun] (in gardening) digging in which only the topsoil is turned over, to the depth of one spit.

single end ▶ **noun** Scottish a single room.

single-ended ▶ **adjective** (of an electronic device) designed for use with unbalanced signals and therefore having one input and one output terminal connected to earth.

single-entry ▶ **adjective** denoting a system of bookkeeping in which each transaction is entered in one account only.

Single European Act (abbrev.: **SEA**) a decree providing for the establishment of a single European market from 1 January 1993, and giving greater powers to the European Parliament. It came into force on 1 July 1987.

single file ▶ **noun** [in sing.] a line of people or things arranged one behind another: *we trooped along* **in single file** | [as modifier] *a single-file column.*
▶ **adverb** one behind another: *we walked single file.*

single-foot ▶ **verb** [no obj.] N. Amer. (of a horse) walk by moving both legs on each side in alternation, each foot falling separately.

single-handed ▶ **adverb** & **adjective 1** done without help from anyone else: [as adv.] *sailing single-handed round the world* | [as adj.] *a single-handed crusade.*
2 done or designed to be used with one hand: [as adv.] *the tool is easy to use single-handed* | [as adj.] *a single-handed axe.*
– DERIVATIVES **single-handedly** adverb.

single-hander ▶ **noun** a boat or other craft that can be sailed single-handed.
■ a person who sails a boat or yacht single-handed.

single-lens reflex ▶ **adjective** denoting a reflex camera in which the lens that forms the image on the film also provides the image in the viewfinder.

single malt (also **single malt whisky**) ▶ **noun** [mass noun] whisky unblended with any other malt.

single market ▶ **noun** an association of countries trading with each other without restrictions or tariffs. The European single market came into effect on 1 January 1993.

single-minded ▶ **adjective** having or concentrating on only one aim or purpose: *the single-minded pursuit of profit.*
– DERIVATIVES **single-mindedly** adverb, **single-mindedness** noun.

single parent ▶ **noun** a person bringing up a child or children without a partner.

single seater ▶ **noun** a vehicle or aircraft for one person: [as modifier] *a single-seater glider.*

single-source ▶ **verb** [with obj.] give a franchise to a single supplier for (a particular product).

single stick ▶ **noun** Fencing a stick of about a sword's length.
■ [mass noun] fencing with such a stick.

singlet ▶ **noun 1** chiefly Brit. a sleeveless garment worn under or instead of a shirt; a vest.
2 Physics a single unresolvable line in a spectrum, not part of a multiplet.
■ a state or energy level with zero spin, giving a single value for a particular quantum number. ■ Chemistry an atomic or molecular state in which all electron spins are paired.
– ORIGIN mid 18th cent. (originally denoting a man's short jacket): from **SINGLE** (because the garment was unlined) + **-ET**[1], on the pattern of *doublet*.

singleton ▶ **noun** a single person or thing of the

kind under consideration: *splitting the clumps of plants into singletons.*
■[often as modifier] a child or animal born singly, rather than one of a multiple birth: *singleton boys.* ■ a person who is not married or in a long-term relationship. ■ (in card games, especially bridge) a card that is the only one of its suit in a hand. ■ Mathematics & Logic a set which contains exactly one element.
– ORIGIN late 19th cent.: from **SINGLE**, on the pattern of *simpleton*.

single transferable vote ▶ noun an electoral system of proportional representation in which a person's vote can be transferred to a second or further competing candidate (according to the voter's stated order of preference) if the candidate of first choice is eliminated during a succession of counts or has more votes than are needed for election.

singletree ▶ noun North American term for **SWINGLETREE**.

single-vision ▶ adjective denoting glasses of which each lens is a single optical element; not bifocal.

Sing Sing a New York State prison, built in 1825–8 at Ossining village on the Hudson River and formerly notorious for its severe discipline. Official name **OSSINING CORRECTIONAL FACILITY**.

sing-song ▶ adjective (of a person's voice) having a repeated rising and falling rhythm: *the sing-song voices of children reciting tables.*
▶ noun **1** Brit. informal an informal gathering for singing.
2 [in sing.] a sing-song way of speaking.
▶ verb (past and past participle **sing-songed**) [no obj.] speak or recite something in a sing-song manner.

singsong girl ▶ noun (in China) a female entertainer.
■informal a prostitute.

Singspiel /ˈzɪŋʃpiːl/ ▶ noun (pl. **Singspiele**) /-ə/ a form of German light opera, typically with spoken dialogue, popular especially in the late 18th century.
– ORIGIN from German *singen* 'sing' + *Spiel* 'play'.

singular ▶ adjective **1** exceptionally good or great; remarkable: *he had the singular good fortune not to die in the trenches.*
■dated strange or eccentric in some respect: *no explanation accompanied this rather singular statement.* ■ Mathematics possessing unique properties. ■ Mathematics (of a square matrix) having a zero determinant. ■ Mathematics denoting a point that is a singularity.
2 Grammar (of a word or form) denoting or referring to just one person or thing.
3 single; unique: *she always thought of herself as singular, as his only daughter.*
▶ noun (usu. **the singular**) Grammar the singular form of a word: *the first person singular.*
– ORIGIN Middle English (in the sense 'solitary, single', also 'beyond the average'): from Old French *singuler*, from Latin *singularis*, from *singulus* (see **SINGLE**).

singularity ▶ noun (pl. **-ies**) **1** [mass noun] the state, fact, quality or condition of being singular: *he believed in the singularity of all cultures.*
■[count noun] a peculiarity or odd trait.
2 Physics & Mathematics a point at which a function takes an infinite value, especially in space-time when matter is infinitely dense, such as at the centre of a black hole.
– ORIGIN Middle English: from Old French *singularite*, from late Latin *singularitas*, from *singularis* 'alone (of its kind)' (see **SINGULAR**).

singularize (also **-ise**) ▶ verb [with obj.] rare **1** make distinct or conspicuous.
2 give a singular form to (a word).
– DERIVATIVES **singularization** noun.

singularly ▶ adverb in a remarkable or noticeable way: *you have singularly failed to live up to your promises* | [as submodifier] *six houses built from a singularly unattractive deep red brick.*
■dated in a strange or eccentric way: *Charlotte thought her very singularly dressed.*

sinh /ʃʌɪn, sɪntʃ, sʌɪˈneɪtʃ/ Mathematics ▶ abbreviation for hyperbolic sine.
– ORIGIN late 19th cent.: from *sin(e)* + *h(yperbolic)*.

Sinhalese /ˌsɪnhəˈliːz, ˌsɪnə-/ (also **Singhalese**, **Sinhala** /sɪnˈhɑːlə/) ▶ noun (pl. same) **1** a member of a people originally from northern India, now forming the majority of the population of Sri Lanka.
2 [mass noun] an Indic language spoken by this people, descended from Sanskrit. It has about 13 million speakers.
▶ adjective of or relating to this people or language.
– ORIGIN from Sanskrit *Siṅhala* 'Sri Lanka' + **-ESE**.

Sining variant of **XINING**.

sinister ▶ adjective **1** giving the impression that something harmful or evil is happening or will happen: *there was something sinister about that murmuring voice.*
2 [attrib.] archaic & Heraldry of, on, or towards the left-hand side (in a coat of arms, from the bearer's point of view, i.e. the right as it is depicted). The opposite of **DEXTER**[1].
– DERIVATIVES **sinisterly** adverb, **sinisterness** noun.
– ORIGIN late Middle English (in the sense 'malicious, underhand'): from Old French *sinistre* or Latin *sinister* 'left'.

sinistral /ˈsɪnɪstr(ə)l/ ▶ adjective of or on the left side or the left hand (the opposite of **DEXTRAL**), in particular:
■left-handed. ■ Geology relating to or denoting a strike-slip fault in which the motion of the block on the further side of the fault from an observer is towards the left. ■ Zoology (of a spiral mollusc shell) with whorls rising to the left and coiling in a clockwise direction.
▶ noun a left-handed person.
– DERIVATIVES **sinistrality** noun, **sinistrally** adverb.

Sinitic /sɪˈnɪtɪk/ ▶ adjective of, relating to, or denoting the division of the Sino-Tibetan language family that includes the many forms of Chinese.

sink[1] ▶ verb (past **sank**; past participle **sunk**) **1** [no obj.] go down below the surface of something, especially of a liquid; become submerged: *he saw the coffin sink below the surface of the waves.*
■(of a ship) go to the bottom of the sea or some other body of water because of damage or a collision: *the trawler sank with the loss of all six crew.* ■ figurative disappear and not be seen or heard of again: *the film* ***sank*** *virtually* ***without trace.*** ■ [with obj.] cause (a ship) to go to the bottom of the sea or other body of water: *a freak wave sank their boat near the shore.* ■ [with obj.] figurative cause to fail: *this pledge could sink the government.* ■ [with obj.] figurative conceal, keep in the background, or ignore: *they agreed to sink their differences.*
2 [no obj.] descend from a higher to a lower position; drop downwards: *Sam felt the ground sinking beneath his feet* | *you can relax on the veranda as the sun sinks low.*
■(of a person) lower oneself or drop down gently: *she sank back on to her pillow.* ■ [with adverbial of direction] gradually penetrate into the surface of something: *her feet sank into the thick pile of the carpet.* ■ (**sink in**) figurative (of words or facts) be fully understood or realized: *Peter read the letter twice before its meaning sank in.* ■ [with obj.] (**sink something into**) cause something sharp to penetrate (a surface): *the dog sank its teeth into her arm.*
3 [no obj.] gradually decrease or decline in value, amount, quality, or intensity: *their output sank to a third of the pre-war figure* | *the reputation of the Council sank to a very low level.*
■lapse or fall into a particular state or condition, typically one that is unwelcome or unpleasant: *he* ***sank into*** *a coma after suffering a brain haemorrhage.* ■ be overwhelmed by a darker mood; become depressed: *her heart sank as she thought of Craig.* ■ approach death: *the doctor concluded that the lad was sinking fast.*
4 [with obj.] insert beneath a surface by digging or hollowing out: *rails fixed in place with screws sunk below the surface of the wood.*
■excavate (a well) or bore (a shaft) vertically downwards: *they planned to sink a gold mine in Oklahoma.* ■ pocket (a ball) in snooker or billiards. ■ Golf hit the ball into the hole with (a putt or other shot). ■ informal drink (alcohol), especially rapidly: *English players sinking a few post-match lagers.* ■ [with obj. and adverbial] insert into something: *Kelly stood watching, her hands sunk deep into her pockets.*
5 [with obj.] (**sink something in/into**) put money or energy into (something); invest something in: *many investors sank their life savings into the company.*
– PHRASES **a** (or **that**) **sinking feeling** an unpleasant feeling caused by the realization that something unpleasant or undesirable has happened or is about to happen. **sink or swim** fail or succeed entirely by one's own efforts.
– DERIVATIVES **sinkable** adjective, **sinkage** noun.
– ORIGIN Old English *sincan*, of Germanic origin; related to Dutch *zinken* and German *sinken*.

> **USAGE** Historically, the past tense of **sink** has been both **sank** and **sunk** (*the boat* ***sank***; *the boat* ***sunk***), and the past participle has been both **sunk** and **sunken** (*the boat had already* ***sunk***; *the boat had already* ***sunken***). In modern English, however, the past is generally **sank** (occasionally **sunk**) and the past participle is always **sunk**. The form **sunken** now only survives as an adjective, as in ***sunken*** *garden*; ***sunken*** *cheeks*.

sink[2] ▶ noun a fixed basin with a water supply and outflow pipe.
■short for **SINKHOLE**. ■ a pool or marsh in which a river's water disappears by evaporation or percolation. ■ technical a body or process which acts to absorb or remove energy or a particular component from a system: *a heat sink* | *the oceans can act as a* ***sink for*** CO_2. The opposite of **SOURCE**. ■ [usu. as modifier] figurative a school or estate situated in a socially deprived area: *the local sink school.* ■ figurative a place of vice or corruption: ***a sink of*** *unnatural vice, pride, and luxury.*
– ORIGIN Middle English: from **SINK**[1].

sinker ▶ noun **1** a weight used to sink a fishing line or sounding line.
2 (also **sinker ball**) Baseball a pitch which drops markedly as it nears home plate.
3 a type of windsurfing board of insufficient buoyancy to support its crew unless moving fast.
4 US a doughnut.

sinkhole ▶ noun a cavity in the ground, especially in a limestone formation, caused by water erosion and providing a route for surface water to disappear underground.

Sinkiang /sɪnˈkjaŋ/ variant of **XINJIANG**.

sinking fund ▶ noun a fund formed by periodically setting aside money for the gradual repayment of a debt or replacement of a wasting asset.

sinner ▶ noun a person who transgresses against divine law by committing an immoral act or acts.

sinnet /ˈsɪnɪt/ (also **sennit**) ▶ noun [mass noun] Nautical braided cordage in flat, round, or square form, made from three to nine cords.
– ORIGIN early 17th cent.: of unknown origin.

Sinn Fein /ʃɪn ˈfeɪn, Irish ˌʃʲiːnʲ ˈfʲeːnʲ/ a political movement and party seeking a united republican Ireland.

> Founded in 1905, Sinn Fein became increasingly committed to Republicanism after the failure of the Home Rule movement. Having won a majority of Irish seats in the 1918 general election, its members refused to go to Westminster and set up their own parliament in Ireland in 1919. After a split in the 1920s, when many of its members joined Fianna Fáil, the party began to function as the political wing of the IRA.

– DERIVATIVES **Sinn Feiner** noun.
– ORIGIN from Irish *sinn féin* 'we ourselves'.

Sino- /ˈsʌɪnəʊ/ ▶ combining form Chinese; Chinese and ...: *Sino-American.*
■relating to China.

sino-atrial /ˌsʌɪnəʊˈeɪtrɪəl/ ▶ adjective Anatomy of, relating to, or denoting a small body of specialized muscle tissue (the **sino-atrial node**) in the wall of the right atrium of the heart that acts as a pacemaker by producing a contractile signal at regular intervals.
– ORIGIN early 20th cent.: from **SINUS** + *atrial* (see **ATRIUM**).

sin-offering ▶ noun (in traditional or ancient Judaism) an offering made as an atonement for sin.

Sino-Japanese Wars two wars (1894–5, 1937–45) fought between China and Japan.

> The first war, caused by rivalry over Korea, was ended by a treaty in Japan's favour and led to the eventual overthrow of the Manchus in 1912. In the second war Japanese expansionism led to trouble in Manchuria in 1931 and to the establishment of a Japanese puppet state (Manchukuo) a year later.

sinology /sʌɪˈnɒlədʒi, sɪ-/ ▶ noun [mass noun] the study of Chinese language, history, customs, and politics.
– DERIVATIVES **sinological** adjective, **sinologist** noun.

Sino-Tibetan ▶ adjective of, relating to, or denoting a large language family of eastern Asia which includes Chinese, Burmese, Tibetan, and (in some classifications) Thai. They are tonal languages, but the exact relationships between them are far from clear.
▶ noun [mass noun] this language family.

sinsemilla /ˌsɪnsəˈmɪlə/ ▶ noun [mass noun] cannabis

S

of a variety which has a particularly high concentration of narcotic agents.
– ORIGIN 1970s: from American Spanish, literally 'without seed'.

sin tax ▶ noun informal a tax on items considered undesirable, such as alcohol or tobacco.

sinter /'sɪntə/ ▶ noun [mass noun] **1** Geology a hard siliceous or calcareous deposit precipitated from mineral springs.
2 solid material which has been sintered, especially a mixture of iron ore and other materials prepared for smelting.
▶ verb [with obj.] make (a powdered material) coalesce into a solid or porous mass by heating it (and usually also compressing it) without liquefaction.
■[no obj.] coalesce in this way.
– ORIGIN late 18th cent. (as a noun): from German *Sinter*; compare with CINDER.

Sint Maarten /sɪnt 'maːrtə(n)/ Dutch name for ST MARTIN.

Sint-Niklaas /sɪnt 'nɪklaːs/ an industrial town in northern Belgium, south-west of Antwerp; pop. 68,200 (1991). French name ST NICOLAS.

Sintra /'siːntrə/ (also **Cintra**) a small town in western Portugal, situated in a mountainous area to the north-west of Lisbon; pop. 20,000 (1981).

Sintu /'sɪntuː/ ▶ adjective & noun South African term for BANTU (the language family), used to avoid the offensive connotations of 'Bantu'.
– ORIGIN 1970s: from the Bantu elements (i)si- denoting language or culture, and -ntu '(African) person'.

sinuate /'sɪnjʊət/ ▶ adjective Botany & Zoology having a wavy or sinuous margin; with alternate rounded notches and lobes.
– ORIGIN late 17th cent.: from Latin *sinuatus*, past participle of *sinuare* 'to bend'.

Sinuiju /'ʃɪnədʒuː/ a city and port in North Korea, situated on the Yalu River near its mouth on the Yellow Sea; pop. 500,000 (1984).

sinuosity /ˌsɪnjʊ'ɒsɪti/ ▶ noun (pl. **-ies**) [mass noun] the ability to curve or bend easily and flexibly.
■[count noun] a bend, especially in a stream or road.
– ORIGIN late 16th cent.: from French *sinuosité* or medieval Latin *sinuositas*, from *sinuosus* (see SINUOUS).

sinuous /'sɪnjʊəs/ ▶ adjective having many curves and turns: *the river follows a sinuous trail through the dale*.
■lithe and supple: *the sinuous grace of a cat*.
– DERIVATIVES **sinuously** adverb, **sinuousness** noun.
– ORIGIN late 16th cent.: from French *sinueux* or Latin *sinuosus*, from *sinus* 'a bend'.

sinus /'saɪnəs/ ▶ noun **1** (often **sinuses**) Anatomy & Zoology a cavity within a bone or other tissue, especially one in the bones of the face or skull connecting with the nasal cavities.
■an irregular venous or lymphatic cavity, reservoir, or dilated vessel. ■ Medicine an infected tract leading from a deep-seated infection and discharging pus to the surface. ■ Botany a rounded notch between two lobes on the margin of a leaf or petal.
2 [as modifier] Physiology relating to or denoting the sino-atrial node of the heart or its function as a pacemaker: *sinus rhythm | sinus tachycardia*.
– ORIGIN late Middle English (in the medical sense): from Latin, literally 'a recess, bend'.

sinusitis /ˌsaɪnə'saɪtɪs/ ▶ noun [mass noun] Medicine inflammation of a nasal sinus.

sinusoid /'saɪnəsɔɪd/ ▶ noun **1** a curve having the form of a sine wave.
2 Anatomy a small irregularly shaped blood vessel found in certain organs, especially the liver.
– DERIVATIVES **sinusoidal** adjective, **sinusoidally** adverb.
– ORIGIN early 19th cent.: from French *sinusoïde*, from Latin *sinus* (see SINUS).

sinus venosus /viː'nəʊsəs/ ▶ noun Zoology the first chamber of the heart in fish, amphibians, and reptiles, emptying into the right atrium.
– ORIGIN early 19th cent.: modern Latin, literally 'venous cavity'.

Sion /'saɪən/ ▶ noun variant spelling of ZION.

-sion ▶ suffix forming nouns such as *mansion*, *persuasion*.
– ORIGIN from Latin participial stems ending in -s + -ION.

Siouan /'suːən/ ▶ noun [mass noun] a family of North

American Indian languages spoken by the Sioux and related people, including Dakota, Hidatsa, and Crow.
▶ adjective of, relating to, or denoting this language family.

Sioux /suː/ ▶ noun (pl. same) another term for the Dakota people of North America or their language. See DAKOTA².
▶ adjective of or relating to this people or their language.
– ORIGIN North American French, from *Nadouessioux* from Ojibwa (Ottawa dialect) *nātowēssiwak*, by substitution of the French plural ending -x for the Ojibwa plural -ak.

sip ▶ verb (**sipped**, **sipping**) [with obj.] drink (something) by taking small mouthfuls: *I sat sipping coffee* | [no obj.] *she sipped at her tea*.
▶ noun a small mouthful of liquid: *she took a sip of the red wine*.
– DERIVATIVES **sipper** noun.
– ORIGIN late Middle English: perhaps a modification of SUP¹, as symbolic of a less vigorous action.

sipe /saɪp/ ▶ noun a groove or channel in the tread of a tyre to improve its grip.
– ORIGIN 1950s: from dialect *sipe* 'oozing, trickling', of unknown origin.

siphon /'saɪf(ə)n/ (also **syphon**) ▶ noun a tube used to convey liquid upwards from a container and then down to a lower level by gravity. Once the liquid has been forced into the tube, typically by suction, atmospheric pressure on the remainder in the container maintains the flow.
■Zoology a tubular organ in an aquatic animal, especially a mollusc, through which water is drawn in or expelled. ■ see SODA SIPHON.
▶ verb [with obj.] draw off or convey (liquid) by means of a siphon.
■figurative draw off or transfer over a period of time, especially illegally or unfairly: *he's been siphoning money off the firm*.
– DERIVATIVES **siphonage** noun, **siphonal** adjective (Zoology), **siphonic** /-'fɒnɪk/ adjective.
– ORIGIN late Middle English: from French, or via Latin from Greek *siphōn* 'pipe'. The verb dates from the mid 19th cent.

Siphonaptera /ˌsaɪfə'napt(ə)rə/ Entomology an order of insects that comprises the fleas.
– DERIVATIVES **siphonapteran** noun & adjective.
– ORIGIN modern Latin (plural), from Greek *siphōn* 'tube' + *apteros* 'wingless'.

Siphonophora /ˌsaɪfə'nɒf(ə)rə/ Zoology an order of colonial marine coelenterates that includes the Portuguese man-of-war, having a float or swimming bell for drifting or swimming on the open sea.
– DERIVATIVES **siphonophore** /saɪ'fɒnəfɔː/ noun.
– ORIGIN modern Latin (plural), from Greek *siphōn* 'tube' + *pherein* 'to bear'.

siphuncle /'saɪfʌŋk(ə)l/ ▶ noun Zoology (in shelled cephalopods such as nautiloids and ammonoids) a calcareous tube containing living tissue running through all the shell chambers, serving to pump fluid out of vacant chambers in order to adjust buoyancy.
– ORIGIN mid 18th cent.: from Latin *siphunculus* 'small tube'.

Siphunculata /saɪˌfʌŋkjʊ'laːtə/ Entomology another term for ANOPLURA.
– ORIGIN modern Latin (plural), from Latin *siphunculus* 'little pipe'.

sippet ▶ noun a small piece of bread or toast, used to dip into soup or sauce or as a garnish.
– ORIGIN mid 16th cent.: apparently a diminutive of SOP.

Sipuncula /saɪ'pʌŋkjʊlə/ Zoology a small phylum that comprises the peanut worms. Also called SIPUNCULIDA.
– DERIVATIVES **sipunculan** noun & adjective, **sipunculid** noun & adjective.
– ORIGIN modern Latin (plural), from *Sipunculus* (genus name), based on a variant of Latin *siphunculus* 'small tube'.

Sir. ▶ abbreviation for (in biblical references) Sirach (Apocrypha).

sir (also **Sir**) ▶ noun used as a polite or respectful way of addressing a man, especially one in a position of authority: *excuse me, sir*.
■used to address a man at the beginning of a formal

or business letter: *Dear Sir*. ■ used as a title before the forename of a knight or baronet. ■ another expression for SIREE.
– ORIGIN Middle English: reduced form of SIRE.

Siracusa /ˌsɪra'kuːza/ Italian name for SYRACUSE 1.

sirdar ▶ noun variant spelling of SARDAR.

Sirdaryo /ˌsɪrdɑ:'jəʊ/ a river of central Asia. Rising in two headstreams in the Tien Shan mountains in eastern Uzbekistan, it flows for some 2,220 km (1,380 miles) west and north-west through southern Kazakhstan to the Aral Sea. Russian name SYR-DARYA.

sire /saɪə/ ▶ noun **1** the male parent of an animal, especially a stallion or bull kept for breeding.
2 archaic a respectful form of address for someone of high social status, especially a king.
■a father or other male forebear.
▶ verb [with obj.] be the male parent of (an animal).
■poetic/literary (of a person) be the father of.
– ORIGIN Middle English (in sense 2): from Old French, from an alteration of Latin *senior* (see SENIOR). Sense 1 dates from the early 16th cent.

siree /sɪ'riː/ (also **sirree**) ▶ exclamation N. Amer. informal used for emphasis, especially after *yes* and *no*: *he's not the type to treat young employees like mud, no siree*.
– ORIGIN early 19th cent.: from SIR + the emphatic suffix -ee.

siren ▶ noun **1** a device that makes a loud prolonged signal or warning sound: *ambulance sirens*.
2 Greek Mythology each of a number of women or winged creatures whose singing lured unwary sailors on to rocks.
■a woman who is considered to be alluring or fascinating but also dangerous in some way.
3 an eel-like American amphibian with tiny forelimbs, no hindlimbs, small eyes, and external gills, typically living in muddy pools.
● Family Sirenidae: genera *Siren* and *Pseudobranchus*, and three species, including the **greater siren** (*S. lacertina*).
– PHRASES **siren song** (or **call**) used in reference to the appeal of something that is alluring but also potentially harmful or dangerous: *a mountaineer who hears the siren song of K2*.
– ORIGIN Middle English (denoting an imaginary type of snake): from Old French *sirene*, from late Latin *Sirena*, feminine of Latin *Siren*, from Greek *Seirēn*.

Sirenia /saɪ'riːnɪə/ Zoology an order of large aquatic plant-eating mammals which includes the manatees and dugong. They live chiefly in tropical coastal waters and are distinguished by paddle-like forelimbs and a tail flipper replacing hindlimbs.
● Order Sirenia: two families and four living species.
– DERIVATIVES **sirenian** noun & adjective.
– ORIGIN modern Latin (see SIREN).

siren suit ▶ noun a one-piece garment for the whole body which is easily put on or taken off, originally designed for use in air-raid shelters.

Sir Galahad ▶ noun see GALAHAD.

Sirius /'sɪrɪəs/ Astronomy the brightest star in the sky, south of the celestial equator in the constellation Canis Major. It is a binary star with a dim companion, which is a white dwarf. Also called DOG STAR.
– ORIGIN Latin, from Greek *seirios astēr* 'scorching star'.

sirloin ▶ noun [mass noun] the choicer part of a loin of beef: [as modifier] *fresh sirloin steaks*.
– ORIGIN late Middle English: from Old French (see SUR-¹, LOIN).

sirocco /sɪ'rɒkəʊ/ (also **scirocco**) ▶ noun (pl. **-os**) a hot wind, often dusty or rainy, blowing from North Africa across the Mediterranean to southern Europe.
– ORIGIN early 17th cent.: via French from Italian *scirocco*, based on Spanish Arabic *šalūk* 'east wind'.

sirrah /'sɪrə/ ▶ noun archaic used as a term of address for a man or boy, especially one younger or of lower status than the speaker.
– ORIGIN early 16th cent.: probably from SIRE, when still two syllables in Middle English, with the second syllable assimilated to AH.

sirtaki /sɜː'taːki/ ▶ noun variant spelling of SYRTAKI.

Sirte, Gulf of /'sɜːti/ another name for SIDRA, GULF OF.

sirup ▶ noun US spelling of SYRUP.

sirupy ▶ adjective US spelling of SYRUPY.

SIS ▶ **abbreviation for** (in the UK) Secret Intelligence Service. See **MI6**.

sis¹ /sɪs/ ▶ **noun** informal a person's sister (often used as a form of address): *where are you going, sis?*
– ORIGIN mid 17th cent.: abbreviation.

sis² /sɪs, səs/ ▶ **exclamation** S. African informal used to express disappointment, disgust, or contempt.
– ORIGIN from Afrikaans *sies*.

sisal /ˈsʌɪs(ə)l/ ▶ **noun** [mass noun] a Mexican agave with large fleshy leaves, cultivated for fibre production.
• *Agave sisalana*, family Agavaceae.
■ the fibre made from this plant, used especially for ropes or matting.
– ORIGIN mid 19th cent.: from *Sisal*, the name of a port in Yucatán, Mexico.

siskin ▶ **noun** a small songbird related to the goldfinch, with yellow and black in the plumage.
• Genus *Carduelis* (and *Serinus*), family Fringillidae: the North Eurasian (**spruce**) **siskin** (*C. spinus*), with dark-streaked greenish-yellow plumage, and several species in the New World.
– ORIGIN mid 16th cent.: from Middle Dutch *siseken*, a diminutive related to German *Zeisig*, of Slavic origin.

Sisley /ˈsɪsli, ˈsɪzli/, Alfred (1839–99), French Impressionist painter, of English descent. He is chiefly remembered for his paintings of the countryside around Paris in the 1870s, with their concentration on reflecting surfaces and fluid brushwork.

sissy (also **cissy**) informal ▶ **noun** (pl. **-ies**) a person regarded as effeminate or cowardly.
▶ **adjective** (**sissier**, **sissiest**) feeble and cowardly.
– DERIVATIVES **sissified** adjective, **sissiness** noun, **sissyish** adjective.
– ORIGIN mid 19th cent. (in the sense 'sister'): from **SIS¹** + **-Y²**.

sister ▶ **noun 1** a woman or girl in relation to other daughters and sons of her parents.
■ a close female friend or associate, especially a female fellow member of a trade union or other organization. ■ (often **Sister**) a member of a religious order of women. ■ a fellow woman seen in relation to feminist issues. ■ informal, chiefly N. Amer. a black woman (chiefly used as a term of address by other black people). ■ [usu. as modifier] a thing, especially an organization, which bears a relationship to another of common origin or allegiance or mutual association: *Securicor and its sister company Securicor Services | a sister ship.*
2 (often **Sister**) Brit. a senior female nurse, typically in charge of a ward.
– DERIVATIVES **sisterliness** noun, **sisterly** adjective.
– ORIGIN Old English, of Germanic origin; related to Dutch *zuster* and German *Schwester*, from an Indo-European root shared by Latin *soror*.

sister city ▶ **noun** a city that is twinned with another.

sister-german ▶ **noun** (pl. **sisters-german**) archaic a sister sharing both parents with another.

sisterhood ▶ **noun 1** [mass noun] the relationship between sisters.
■ the feeling of kinship with and closeness to a group of women or all women.
2 (often **Sisterhood**) an association, society, or community of women linked by a common interest, religion, or trade.

sister-in-law ▶ **noun** (pl. **sisters-in-law**) the sister of one's wife or husband.
■ the wife of one's brother or brother-in-law.

Sister of Mercy ▶ **noun** a member of an order of women founded for educational or charitable purposes, especially that founded in Dublin in 1827.

Sistine /ˈsɪstiːn, -tʌɪn/ ▶ **adjective** of or relating to any of the popes called Sixtus, especially Sixtus IV.
– ORIGIN from Italian *Sistino*, from *Sisto* 'Sixtus'.

Sistine Chapel a chapel in the Vatican, built in the late 15th century by Pope Sixtus IV, containing a painted ceiling and fresco of the Last Judgement by Michelangelo and also frescoes by Botticelli.

sistrum /ˈsɪstrəm/ ▶ **noun** (pl. **sistra** /-trə/) a musical instrument of ancient Egypt consisting of a metal frame with transverse metal rods which rattled when the instrument was shaken.
– ORIGIN late Middle English: via Latin from Greek *seistron*, from *seiein* 'to shake'.

Siswati /sɪˈswɑːti/ ▶ **noun** another term for **SWAZI** (the language).

Sisyphean /ˌsɪsɪˈfiːən/ ▶ **adjective** (of a task) such that it can never be completed.
– ORIGIN late 16th cent.: from Latin *Sisypheius* (based on Greek *Sisuphos*: see **SISYPHUS**) + **-AN**.

Sisyphus /ˈsɪsɪfəs/ Greek Mythology the son of Aeolus, punished in Hades for his misdeeds in life by being condemned to the eternal task of rolling a large stone to the top of a hill, from which it always rolled down again.

sit ▶ **verb** (**sitting**; past and past participle **sat** /sat/) **1** [no obj.] adopt or be in a position in which one's weight is supported by one's buttocks rather than one's feet and one's back is upright: *you'd better **sit down** | I sat next to him at dinner.*
■ [with obj.] cause to adopt or be in such a position: *sit yourself down and I'll bring you some tea.* ■ (of an animal) rest with the hind legs bent and the body close to the ground: *it is important for a dog to sit when instructed.* ■ (of a bird) rest on a branch; perch. ■ (of a bird) remain on its nest to incubate its egg: [as adj. **sitting**] *a sitting hen.* ■ [with obj.] ride or keep one's seat on (a horse). ■ [with obj.] N. Amer. not use (a player) in a game: *the manager must decide who to sit in the World Series.* ■ [with obj.] (of a table, room, or building) be large enough for (a specified number of seated people): *the chapel sat about 3,000 people.* ■ (**sit for**) pose, typically in a seated position, for (an artist or photographer): *Walter Deverell asked her to sit for him.* ■ [no obj., with adverbial of place] be or remain in a particular position or state: *the fridge was sitting in a pool of water.* ■ [with adverbial] (of an item of clothing) fit a person well or badly as specified: *the blue uniform sat well on his big frame.* ■ (**sit with**) be harmonious with: *his shyness doesn't sit easily with Hollywood tradition.*
2 [no obj.] (of a parliament, committee, court of law, etc.) be engaged in its business: *Parliament continued sitting until March 16.*
■ serve as a member of a council, jury, or other official body: *they were determined that women jurists should sit on the tribunal.* ■ (**sit for**) Brit. be the Member of Parliament for (a particular constituency).
3 [with obj.] Brit. take (an examination): *pupils are required to sit nine subjects at GCSE* | [no obj.] *he was about to **sit for** his Cambridge entrance exam.*
4 [no obj., in combination] live in someone's house while they are away and look after their pet or pets: *Fenella had been cat-sitting for me.* See also **BABYSIT**.
▶ **noun** [in sing.] **1** a period of sitting: *a sit in the shade.*
2 archaic the way in which an item of clothing fits someone: *the sit of her frock.*
– PHRASES **sit at someone's feet** be someone's pupil or follower. **sit in judgement** see **JUDGEMENT**. **sit on the fence** see **FENCE**. **sit on one's arse** vulgar slang do nothing; fail to take action. **sit on one's hands** take no action. **sit (heavy) on the stomach** (of food) take a long time to be digested. **sit on someone's tail** drive extremely close behind another vehicle, typically while waiting for a chance to overtake. **sit tight** informal remain firmly in one's place. ■ refrain from taking action or changing one's mind: *we're advising our clients to sit tight and neither to buy nor sell.* **sit up (and take notice)** informal suddenly start paying attention or have one's interest aroused.
– ORIGIN Old English *sittan*, of Germanic origin; related to Dutch *zitten*, German *sitzen*, from an Indo-European root shared by Latin *sedere* and Greek *hezesthai*.

USAGE In sentences such as *we were **sat** there for hours* the use of the past participle **sat** with the verb 'to be' is informal and not part of standard English. Originally only in dialect, it is now common in British (though not US) English. Standard English uses the present participle **sitting** in similar contexts, as in *we were **sitting** there for hours.*

▶ **sit back** relax: *sit back and enjoy the music.* ■ take no action; choose not to become involved: *I can't just sit back and let Liz get on with it.*
sit by take no action in order to prevent something undesirable from occurring: *I'm not going to sit by and let an innocent man go to jail.*
sit down 1 archaic encamp outside a city in order to besiege it: *with a large force he **sat down before** Ravenna.* **2** Brit. accept or put up with an unwelcome situation or development: *if they think I'm going to **sit down under** it, they can think again.*
sit in 1 (of a group of people) occupy a place as a form of protest. **2** attend a meeting or discussion without taking an active part in it: *I sat in on a training session for therapists.*
sit in for temporarily carry out the duties of (another person).
sit on informal **1** fail to deal with: *she sat on the article until a deadline galvanized her into putting words to paper.* **2** subdue (someone), typically by saying something intended to discomfit or embarrass them. ■ suppress (something): *I want this story sat on.*
sit something out not take part in a particular event or activity: *he had to sit out Sheffield Wednesday's UEFA Cup game.* ■ wait without moving or taking action until a particular unwelcome situation or process is over: *most of the workers seem to be sitting the crisis out, waiting to see what will happen.*
sit through stay until the end of (a tedious or lengthy meeting or performance).
sit up (or **sit someone up**) **1** move (or cause someone to move) from a lying or slouching to a sitting position: *Amy sat up and rubbed her eyes | I'll sit you up on the pillows.* **2** refrain from going to bed until a later time than usual: *we sat up late to watch a horror film.*

Sita /ˈsiːtɑː/ (in the Ramayana) the wife of Rama. She is the Hindu model of the ideal woman, an incarnation of Lakshmi.
– ORIGIN from Sanskrit *Sītā*, literally 'furrow'.

sitar /ˈsɪtɑː, sɪˈtɑː/ ▶ **noun** a large, long-necked Indian lute with movable frets, played with a wire pick.
– DERIVATIVES **sitarist** /sɪˈtɑːrɪst/ noun.
– ORIGIN via Urdu from Persian *sitār*, from *sih* 'three' + *tār* 'string'.

sitatunga /ˌsɪtəˈtʌŋɡə/ ▶ **noun** a brown or greyish antelope with splayed hoofs and, in the male, spiral horns, inhabiting swampy areas in central and East Africa.
• *Tragelaphus spekii*, family Bovidae.
– ORIGIN late 19th cent.: from Kiswahili.

sitcom ▶ **noun** informal a situation comedy.
– ORIGIN 1960s: abbreviation.

sit-down ▶ **adjective** [attrib.] (of a meal) eaten sitting at a table.
■ (of a protest) in which demonstrators occupy their workplace or sit down on the ground in a public place, refusing to leave until their demands are met.
▶ **noun** a period of sitting down; a short rest.
■ a sit-down protest.

site ▶ **noun** an area of ground on which a town, building, or monument is constructed: *the proposed site of a hydroelectric dam.*
■ a place where a particular event or activity is occurring or has occurred: *the site of the battle of Flodden | materials for repairs are always **on site**.* ■ short for **BUILDING SITE**. ■ short for **CAMPSITE** or **CARAVAN SITE**.
▶ **verb** [with obj. and adverbial of place] (usu. **be sited**) fix or build (something) in a particular place: *the rectory is sited behind the church* | [as noun **siting**] *decisions concerning the siting of nuclear power plants.*
– ORIGIN late Middle English (as a noun): from Anglo-Norman French, or from Latin *situs* 'local position'. The verb dates from the late 16th cent.

sitella ▶ **noun** variant spelling of **SITTELLA**.

sit-in ▶ **noun** a form of protest in which demonstrators occupy a place, refusing to leave until their demands are met.

Sitka /ˈsɪtkə/ (also **Sitka spruce**) ▶ **noun** a fast-growing North American spruce tree, widely cultivated for its strong lightweight timber.
• *Picea sitchensis*, family Pinaceae.
– ORIGIN late 19th cent.: named after *Sitka*, a town in Alaska.

sitkamer /ˈsɪtkamər/ ▶ **noun** South African term for **SITTING ROOM**.
– ORIGIN Afrikaans.

sitrep ▶ **noun** informal a report on the current military situation in a particular area.
– ORIGIN 1940s: from *sit(uation) rep(ort)*.

sits vac ▶ **plural noun** Brit. informal situations vacant (see **SITUATION**).
– ORIGIN 1960s: abbreviation.

Sittang /ˈsɪtaŋ/ a river of southern Burma (Myanmar). Rising in the Pegu mountains, it flows some 560 km (350 miles) south into the Bay of Bengal at the Gulf of Martaban.

sittella /sɪˈtɛlə/ (also **sitella**) ▶ **noun** a small Australasian songbird of the nuthatch family, typically having a black cap or head.
• Genus *Neositta*, family Sittidae: two species, in particular the **varied sittella** (*N. chrysoptera*) of Australia.
– ORIGIN mid 19th cent.: from modern Latin *Sittella* (former genus name), from Greek *sittē* 'nuthatch'.

S

sitter ▶ noun **1** a person who sits, especially for a portrait or examination.
■ a sitting hen.
2 [usu. in combination] a person who looks after children, pets, or a house while the parents or owners are away: *a house-sitter.*
■ a person who provides care and companionship for people who are ill.
3 informal (in sport) an easy catch or shot.

sitting ▶ noun a continuous period of being seated, especially when engaged in a particular activity: *the joint was eaten at one sitting.*
■ a period of time spent as a model for an artist or photographer. ■ a scheduled period of time when a group of people are served a meal, especially in a restaurant: *there will be two sittings for Christmas lunch.* ■ a period of time during which a committee or parliament is engaged in its normal business. ■ Law, Brit. a period of time when a law court holds sessions: *a special sitting of Basildon magistrates.*
▶ adjective [attrib.] **1** denoting a person who has sat down or the position of such a person: *a sitting position.*
■ (of an animal or bird) not running or flying.
2 (of an MP or other elected representative) current; present: *the resignation of the sitting member.*
3 (of a hen or other bird) settled on eggs for the purpose of incubating them.

Sitting Bull (*c.*1831–90), Sioux chief; Sioux name *Tatanka Iyotake.* As the main chief of the Sioux peoples from about 1867, Sitting Bull led the Sioux in the fight to retain their lands; this resulted in the massacre of General Custer and his men at Little Bighorn.

sitting duck (also **sitting target**) ▶ noun informal a person or thing with no protection against an attack or other source of danger.

sitting room ▶ noun chiefly Brit. a room in a house in which people can sit down and relax.

sitting tenant ▶ noun Brit. a tenant already in occupation of premises, especially when there is a change of owner.

situate ▶ verb /ˈsɪtʃʊeɪt, -tjʊ-/ [with obj. and adverbial of place] (usu. **be situated**) fix or build (something) in a certain place or position: *the pilot light is usually situated at the front of the boiler* | [as adj., with submodifier] (**situated**) *a conveniently situated hotel.*
■ put in context; describe the circumstances surrounding (something): *it is necessary to situate these ideas in the wider context of the class structure.* ■ (**be situated**) [with adverbial] be in a specified financial or marital position: *Amy is now comfortably situated.*
▶ adjective /ˈsɪtʃʊət, -tjʊət/ Law or archaic situated.
– ORIGIN late Middle English: from medieval Latin *situat-* 'placed', from the verb *situare*, from Latin *situs* 'site'.

situation ▶ noun **1** a set of circumstances in which one finds oneself; a state of affairs: *the situation between her and Jake had come to a head* | *the political situation in Russia.*
2 the location and surroundings of a place: *the situation of the town is pleasant.*
3 formal a position of employment; a job.
– PHRASES **situations vacant** (or **wanted**) chiefly Brit. lists of jobs offered (or sought), especially in a newspaper.
– DERIVATIVES **situational** adjective, **situationally** adverb.
– ORIGIN late Middle English (in sense 2): from French, or from medieval Latin *situatio(n-)*, from *situare* 'to place' (see **SITUATE**). Sense 1 dates from the early 18th cent.

situation comedy ▶ noun a television or radio series in which the same set of characters are involved in various amusing situations.

situation ethics ▶ plural noun [treated as sing.] Philosophy the doctrine of flexibility in the application of moral laws according to circumstances.

situationism ▶ noun [mass noun] the theory that human behaviour is determined by surrounding circumstances rather than by personal qualities.
– DERIVATIVES **situationist** noun & adjective.

sit-up ▶ noun a physical exercise designed to strengthen the abdominal muscles, in which a person sits up from a supine position without using the arms for leverage.

sit-upon ▶ noun informal, humorous a person's buttocks.

situs /ˈsʌɪtəs/ ▶ noun Law, chiefly US the place to which for purposes of legal jurisdiction or taxation a property belongs.

situs inversus /ˌsʌɪtəs ɪnˈvəːsəs, ˌsiːtəs/ ▶ noun [mass noun] Medicine an uncommon condition in which the heart and other organs of the body are transposed through the sagittal plane to lie on the opposite (left or right) side from the usual.
– ORIGIN late 19th cent.: from Latin *situs inversus viscerum* 'inverted placing of the internal organs'.

Sitwell, Dame Edith (Louisa) (1887–1964), English poet and critic. Her early verse, with that of her brothers **Osbert** (1892–1969) and **Sacheverell** (1897–1988), marked a revolt against the prevailing Georgian style of the day. In 1923 she attracted attention with *Façade*, a group of poems in notated rhythm recited to music by William Walton.

sitz-bath /ˈsɪts/ ▶ noun a bath in which only the buttocks and hips are immersed in water.
– ORIGIN mid 19th cent.: partial translation of German *Sitzbad*, from *sitzen* 'sit' + *Bad* 'bath'.

sitzfleisch /ˈzɪtsflʌɪʃ/ ▶ noun [mass noun] informal, chiefly US a person's buttocks.
■ power to endure or to persevere in an activity; staying power.
– ORIGIN from German, from *sitzen* 'sit' + *Fleisch* 'flesh'.

sitzkrieg /ˈzɪtskriːg/ ▶ noun a war, or a phase of a war, in which there is little or no active warfare.
– ORIGIN 1940s: suggested by **BLITZKRIEG**, from German *sitzen* 'sit'.

Siva /ˈsiːvə, ˈʃiːvə/ variant spelling of **SHIVA**.
– DERIVATIVES **Sivaism** noun, **Sivaite** noun & adjective.

Sivaji variant spelling of **SHIVAJI**.

Sivan /ˈsiːvɑːn/ ▶ noun (in the Jewish calendar) the ninth month of the civil and third of the religious year, usually coinciding with parts of May and June.
– ORIGIN from Hebrew *sīwān*.

Siwalik Hills /sɪˈwɑːlɪk/ a range of foothills in the southern Himalayas, extending from NE India across Nepal to Sikkim.

Siwash /ˈsʌɪwɒʃ/ ▶ noun derogatory **1** an American Indian of the northern Pacific coast.
2 another term for **CHINOOK JARGON**.
▶ adjective derogatory of or relating to American Indians of the northern Pacific coast.
▶ verb [no obj.] camp without a tent.
– ORIGIN Chinook Jargon, from Canadian French *sauvage* 'wild'.

Siwash sweater ▶ noun Canadian a thick sweater made by Siwash Indians and decorated with symbols from their mythology.

six ▶ cardinal number equivalent to the product of two and three; one more than five, or four less than ten; 6: *she's lived here six months* | *six of the people arrested have been charged* | *a six-week tour.* (Roman numeral: **vi** or **VI**.)
■ a group or unit of six people or things. ■ six years old: *a child of six.* ■ six o'clock: *it's half past six.* ■ Cricket a hit that reaches the boundary without first striking the ground, scoring six runs. Compare with **FOUR**. ■ a size of garment or other merchandise denoted by six. ■ a playing card or domino with six pips. ■ a group of six Brownies or Cubs. ■ (**the Six**) another name for **LES SIX**.
– PHRASES **at sixes and sevens** in a state of total confusion or disarray. **knock** (or **hit**) **someone for six** Brit. informal utterly surprise or overcome someone. **six feet under** informal dead and buried. **six of one and half a dozen of the other** used to convey that there is little real difference between two alternatives.
– ORIGIN Old English *siex, six, syx*, of Germanic origin; related to Dutch *zes* and German *sechs*, from an Indo-European root shared by Latin *sex* and Greek *hex*.

Six, Les see **LES SIX**.

sixain /ˈsɪkseɪn/ ▶ noun a six-line stanza.
– ORIGIN late 16th cent.: from French, from *six* 'six'.

Six Counties the counties of Northern Ireland.

Six Day War a war, 5–10 June 1967, in which Israel occupied Sinai, the Old City of Jerusalem, the West Bank, and the Golan Heights and defeated an Egyptian, Jordanian, and Syrian alliance. Arab name **JUNE WAR**.

sixer ▶ noun **1** the leader of a group of six Brownies or Cubs.
2 Cricket, chiefly Indian a hit for six runs.
3 US a six-pack.

sixfold ▶ adjective six times as great or as numerous: *a sixfold increase in their overheads.*
■ having six parts or elements: *a sixfold plan of action.*
▶ adverb by six times; to six times the number or amount: *coal prices have risen sixfold.*

six-gun ▶ noun another term for **SIX-SHOOTER**.

Six Nations ▶ plural noun (**the Six Nations**) the peoples of the Iroquois confederacy.

six-pack ▶ noun **1** a pack of six cans of beer held together with a plastic fastener.
2 informal a set of well-developed abdominal muscles.

sixpence ▶ noun Brit. a coin worth six old pence (2½ p), withdrawn in 1980.
■ the sum of six pence, especially before decimalization (1971).
– PHRASES **on a sixpence** Brit. informal used to refer to a manoeuvre that can be performed by a moving vehicle or person within a small area or short distance: *the car stops on a sixpence.*

sixpenny ▶ adjective [attrib.] Brit. costing or worth six pence, especially before decimalization (1971).

six-pounder ▶ noun a gun discharging a shot that weighs six pounds.

six-shooter ▶ noun a revolver with six chambers.

sixte /sɪkst/ ▶ noun Fencing the sixth of the eight parrying positions.
– ORIGIN late 19th cent.: French, from Latin *sextus* 'sixth'.

sixteen ▶ cardinal number equivalent to the product of four and four; one more than fifteen, or six more than ten; 16: *sixteen miles east of Dublin* | *sixteen of our eighteen patients.* (Roman numeral: **xvi** or **XVI**.)
■ a size of garment or other merchandise denoted by sixteen. ■ sixteen years old: *a daughter of sixteen.*
– DERIVATIVES **sixteenth** ordinal number.
– ORIGIN Old English *siextīene* (see **SIX**, **-TEEN**).

sixteenmo ▶ noun (pl. **-os**) another term for **SEXTODECIMO**.

sixteenth note ▶ noun Music, chiefly N. Amer. a semiquaver.

sixth ▶ ordinal number constituting number six in a sequence; 6th: *her sixth novel* | *the sixth of the month* | *to the original five categories we add a sixth.*
■ (**a sixth/one sixth**) each of six equal parts into which something is or may be divided: *a sixth of the total population.* ■ the sixth finisher or position in a race or competition: *he could only finish sixth.* ■ chiefly Brit. the sixth form of a school or college. ■ sixthly (used to introduce a sixth point or reason): *sixth, given all the facts there is no logical reason why we can't make a decision.* ■ Music an interval spanning six consecutive notes in a diatonic major or minor scale, e.g. C to A (**major sixth**) or A to F (**minor sixth**). ■ Music the note which is higher by this interval than the tonic of a scale or root of a chord.
– DERIVATIVES **sixthly** adverb.

sixth-form college ▶ noun Brit. a college for pupils in their final years of secondary education, starting at the age of 16.

sixth sense ▶ noun [in sing.] a supposed intuitive faculty giving awareness not explicable in terms of normal perception: *some sixth sense told him he was not alone.*

sixty ▶ cardinal number (pl. **-ies**) the number equivalent to the product of six and ten; ten more than fifty; 60: *a crew of sixty* | *sixty bedrooms* | *sixty per cent of the children.* (Roman numeral: **lx** or **LX**.)
■ (**sixties**) the numbers from sixty to sixty-nine, especially the years of a century or of a person's life: *Morris was in his early sixties* | *the flower children of the sixties.* ■ sixty miles an hour: *they were doing sixty.* ■ sixty years old: *he retired at sixty.* ■ a size of garment or other merchandise denoted by sixty.
– DERIVATIVES **sixtieth** ordinal number, **sixtyfold** adjective & adverb.
– ORIGIN Old English *siextig* (see **SIX**, **-TY**[2]).

sixty-fourmo ▶ noun (pl. **-os**) a size of book in which each leaf is one sixty-fourth the size of a printing sheet.
■ a book of this size.

sixty-fourth note ▶ noun Music, chiefly N. Amer. a hemidemisemiquaver.

sixty-four thousand dollar question ▶ noun informal something that is not known and on which a great deal depends.
– ORIGIN 1940s: originally *sixty-four dollar question,*

b but | d dog | f few | g get | h he | j yes | k cat | l leg | m man | n no | p pen | r red | s sit | t top | v voice | w we | z zoo | ʃ she | ʒ decision | θ thin | ð this | ŋ ring | x loch | tʃ chip | dʒ jar

from a question posed for the top prize in a broadcast quiz show.

sixty-nine ▶ noun another term for SOIXANTE-NEUF.

sizable ▶ adjective variant spelling of SIZEABLE.

sizar /ˈsaɪzə/ ▶ noun an undergraduate at Cambridge University or at Trinity College, Dublin, receiving financial help from the college and formerly having certain menial duties.
– DERIVATIVES **sizarship** noun.
– ORIGIN late 16th cent.: from obsolete *size* 'ration of bread, beer, etc.' + -AR³.

size¹ ▶ noun **1** [mass noun] the relative extent of something; a thing's overall dimensions or magnitude; how big something is: *the schools varied in size* | *a forest the size of Wales* | [count noun] *firms of all sizes*.
■ extensive dimensions or magnitude: *she seemed slightly awed by the size of the building.*
2 each of the classes, typically numbered, into which garments or other articles are divided according to how large they are: *I can never find anything in my size.*
■ a person or garment corresponding to such a numbered class: *she's a size 10.*
▶ verb [with obj.] alter or sort in terms of size or according to size: *twist drills are sized in millimetres.*
■ (**size something up**) estimate or measure something's dimensions: *she was trying to size up a room with a tape measure.* ■ (**size someone/thing up**) informal form an estimate or rough judgement of someone or something: *the two men sized each other up.*
▶ adjective [in combination] having a specified size; sized: *marble-size chunks of hail.*
– PHRASES **of a size** (of two or more people or things) having the same dimensions. **of some size** fairly large. **that's about the size of it** informal said to confirm someone's assessment of a situation, especially of one regarded as bad. **to size** to the dimensions wanted: *the PVC sheet is easily cut to size.*
– DERIVATIVES **sizer** noun.
– ORIGIN Middle English (also in the sense 'assize, ordinance fixing a rate of payment'): from Old French *sise*, from *assise* 'ordinance', or a shortening of ASSIZE.

size² ▶ noun [mass noun] a gelatinous solution used in glazing paper, stiffening textiles, and preparing plastered walls for decoration.
▶ verb [with obj.] treat with size to glaze or stiffen.
– ORIGIN Middle English: perhaps the same word as SIZE¹.

sizeable (also **sizable**) ▶ adjective fairly large: *a sizeable proportion of the population* | *a sizeable apartment.*
– DERIVATIVES **sizeably** adverb.

sized ▶ adjective [in combination or with submodifier] having a specified size: *comfortably sized rooms.*

Sizewell a village on the Suffolk coast, the site of two nuclear power stations including a pressurized-water reactor.

sizzle ▶ verb [no obj.] (of food) make a hissing sound when frying or cooking: *the bacon began to sizzle in the pan.*
■ [often as adj. **sizzling**] informal be very hot: *the sizzling summer temperatures.* ■ [often as adj. **sizzling**] informal be very exciting or passionate, especially sexually: *that was the start of a sizzling affair.*
▶ noun [in sing.] a hissing sound, as of food frying or cooking: *the sizzle of hot dogs.*
■ [mass noun] informal a state or quality of great excitement or passion: *it would be a waste not to cast him in roles requiring some sexual sizzle.*
– DERIVATIVES **sizzler** noun.
– ORIGIN early 17th cent.: imitative.

SJ ▶ abbreviation for Society of Jesus.

Sjælland /ˈsjɛlan/ Danish name for ZEALAND.

sjambok /ˈʃambɒk/ ▶ noun (in South Africa) a long, stiff whip, originally made of rhinoceros hide.
▶ verb [with obj.] flog with a sjambok.
– ORIGIN from South African Dutch *tjambok*, via Malay from Urdu *chābuk*.

SJC ▶ abbreviation for (in the US) Supreme Judicial Court.

Sjögren's syndrome /ˈʃɔːɡrən/ (also **Sjögren's disease**) ▶ noun [mass noun] Medicine a chronic autoimmune condition characterized by degeneration of the salivary and lachrymal glands, causing dryness of the mouth and eyes.

– ORIGIN 1930s: named after Henrik S. C. *Sjögren* (1899–1986), Swedish physician.

SK ▶ abbreviation for Saskatchewan (in official postal use).

ska /skɑː/ ▶ noun [mass noun] a style of fast popular music having a strong offbeat and originating in Jamaica in the 1960s, a forerunner of reggae.
– ORIGIN 1960s: of unknown origin.

skaapsteker /ˈskɑːpˌsteɪkə/ ▶ noun S. African a greyish-brown snake of southern Africa, which is venomous but rarely dangerous.
● Genus *Psammophylax*, family Colubridae: two species.
– ORIGIN early 19th cent.: via Afrikaans from Dutch *schaap* 'sheep' + *steker* 'stinger'.

skag (also **scag**) ▶ noun [mass noun] informal, chiefly US heroin.
– ORIGIN early 20th cent.: of unknown origin.

Skagerrak /ˈskaɡərak/ (**the Skagerrak**) a strait separating southern Norway from the NW coast of Denmark.

skald /skɔːld, skald/ (also **scald**) ▶ noun historical (in ancient Scandinavia) a composer and reciter of poems honouring heroes and their deeds.
– DERIVATIVES **skaldic** adjective.
– ORIGIN from Old Norse *skáld*, of unknown origin.

Skanda /ˈskandə/ Hinduism the Hindu war god, first son of Shiva and Parvati and brother of Ganesha. He is depicted as a boy or youth, sometimes with six heads and often with his mount, a peacock.

skank /skaŋk/ ▶ noun **1** a steady-paced dance performed to reggae music, characterized by rhythmically bending forward, raising the knees, and extending the hands palms-downwards.
■ [mass noun] reggae music suitable for such dancing.
2 informal, chiefly N. Amer. a person perceived to be extremely sleazy or unpleasant.
▶ verb [no obj.] [often as adj. **skanking**] play reggae music or dance in this style.
■ informal walk or move in a sexually suggestive way.
– ORIGIN 1970s: of unknown origin.

skanky ▶ adjective informal, chiefly N. Amer. very unpleasant; revolting.

Skara Brae /ˌskɑːrə ˈbreɪ, ˌskarə/ a late Neolithic (3rd millennium BC) settlement on Mainland in the Orkney Islands.

skarn /skɑːn/ ▶ noun [mass noun] Geology lime-bearing siliceous rock produced by the metamorphic alteration of limestone or dolomite.
– ORIGIN early 20th cent.: from Swedish, literally 'dung, filth'.

skat ▶ noun [mass noun] a three-handed trick-taking card game with bidding, played chiefly in Germany.
– ORIGIN mid 19th cent.: from German, from Italian *scarto* 'a discard', from *scartare* 'discard'.

skate¹ ▶ noun an ice skate or roller skate.
■ short for SKATEBOARD. ■ a device, typically with wheels on the underside, used to move a heavy or unwieldy object.
▶ verb [no obj.] move on ice skates or roller skates in a gliding fashion: *the boys were skating on the ice.*
■ [with obj.] perform a (specified figure) on skates: *double-eight figures skated entirely on one foot.* ■ ride on a skateboard. ■ (**skate over/round/around**) figurative pass over or refer only fleetingly to (a subject or problem): *she seemed to skate over the next part of her story.*
■ (**skate through**) figurative make quick and easy progress through: *he admits he had expected to skate through the system.*
– PHRASES **get one's skates on** Brit. informal make haste; hurry up.
– DERIVATIVES **skater** noun.
– ORIGIN mid 17th cent. (originally as the plural *scates*): from Dutch *schaats* (singular but interpreted as plural), from Old French *eschasse* 'stilt'.

skate² ▶ noun (pl. same or **skates**) a typically large marine fish of the ray family with a cartilaginous skeleton and a flattened diamond-shaped body.
● Family Rajidae: numerous species, in particular the commercially valuable *Raja batis.*
■ [mass noun] the flesh of a skate or thornback used as food.
– ORIGIN Middle English: from Old Norse *skata.*

skate³ ▶ noun S. African informal an uncouth and disreputable white man.
– ORIGIN 1970s: of unknown origin.

skateboard ▶ noun a short narrow board with two small wheels fixed to the bottom of either end, on which (as a recreation or sport) a person can ride in a standing or crouching position, propelling

themselves by occasionally pushing one foot against the ground.
▶ verb [no obj.] [often as noun **skateboarding**] ride on a skateboard.
– DERIVATIVES **skateboarder** noun.

skatepark ▶ noun an area designated and equipped for skateboarding.

skating ▶ noun [mass noun] the action or activity of skating on ice skates, roller skates, or a skateboard as a sport or pastime.

skating rink ▶ noun an expanse of ice artificially made for skating, or a floor used for roller skating.

skean /skiːn, ˈskiːən/ ▶ noun a dagger formerly used in Ireland and Scotland.
– ORIGIN late Middle English: from Irish and Scottish Gaelic *sgian* 'knife'.

skean-dhu /ˈduː/ ▶ noun a dagger worn in the stocking as part of Highland dress.
– ORIGIN early 19th cent.: from SKEAN + Scottish Gaelic *dubh* 'black'.

skebenga /skəˈbɛŋɡə/ ▶ noun S. African a gangster; a bandit.
– ORIGIN from Zulu *isigebengu* 'bandit, plunderer'.

sked informal, chiefly N. Amer. ▶ noun short for SCHEDULE.
▶ verb (**skedded**, **skedding**) short for SCHEDULE.

skedaddle /skɪˈdad(ə)l/ ▶ verb [no obj.] informal depart quickly or hurriedly; run away.
– ORIGIN mid 19th cent.: of unknown origin.

skedonk /skəˈdɒŋk/ ▶ noun S. African informal an old, battered car.
– ORIGIN of unknown origin.

skeet (also **skeet shooting**) ▶ noun [mass noun] a shooting sport in which a clay target is thrown from a trap to simulate the flight of a bird.
– ORIGIN 1920s: apparently a pseudo-archaic alteration of the verb SHOOT.

skeeter¹ ▶ noun informal, chiefly N. Amer. & Austral. a mosquito.
– ORIGIN mid 19th cent.: shortened form, representing a casual pronunciation.

skeeter² ▶ verb variant spelling of SKITTER.

skeg ▶ noun a tapering or projecting after section of a vessel's keel.
■ a fin underneath the rear of a surfboard.
– ORIGIN early 17th cent.: from Old Norse *skegg* 'beard', perhaps from Dutch *scheg.*

skein /skeɪn/ ▶ noun a length of thread or yarn, loosely coiled and knotted.
■ a tangled or complicated arrangement, state, or situation: *the skeins of her long hair* | figurative *a skein of lies.* ■ a flock of wild geese or swans in flight, typically in a V-shaped formation.
– ORIGIN Middle English: shortening of Old French *escaigne*, of unknown origin.

skeletal /ˈskɛlɪt(ə)l, skəˈliːt(ə)l/ ▶ adjective of, relating to, or functioning as a skeleton: *the skeletal remains of aquatic organisms.*
■ very thin; emaciated: *a small, skeletal boy clothed in rags.* ■ existing only in outline or as a framework of something: *a skeletal plot for a novel* | *the skeletal leaves of long-faded roses.*
– DERIVATIVES **skeletally** adverb.

skeletal muscle ▶ noun a muscle which is connected to the skeleton to form part of the mechanical system which moves the limbs and other parts of the body.
■ another term for STRIATED MUSCLE.

skeleton ▶ noun an internal or external framework of bone, cartilage, or other rigid material supporting or containing the body of an animal or plant.
■ used in exaggerated reference to a very thin or emaciated person or animal: *she was no more than a skeleton at the end.* ■ the remaining part of something after its life or usefulness is gone: *the chapel was stripped to a skeleton of its former self.* ■ the supporting framework, basic structure, or essential part of something: *the concrete skeleton of an unfinished building* | *the skeleton of a report.* ■ [as modifier] denoting the essential or minimum number of people, things, or parts necessary for something: *there was only a skeleton staff on duty.*
– PHRASES **skeleton in the cupboard** (US **skeleton in the closet**) a discreditable or embarrassing fact that someone wishes to keep secret.
– DERIVATIVES **skeletonize** (also **-ise**) verb.
– ORIGIN late 16th cent.: modern Latin, from Greek, neuter of *skeletos* 'dried up', from *skellein* 'dry up'.

Skeleton Coast an arid coastal area in Namibia.

Comprising the northern part of the Namib desert, it extends from Walvis Bay in the south to the border with Angola.

skeleton key ▶ noun a key designed to fit many locks by having the interior of the bit hollowed.

skelf /skɛlf/ ▶ noun Scottish **1** a splinter; a sliver.
2 informal a person who is a nuisance.
– ORIGIN late Middle English (in the sense 'shelf'): probably from Middle Low German *schelf*; compare with **SHELF**[1]. Sense 1 dates from the early 17th cent.

skelly[1] /ˈskɛli/ ▶ adjective Scottish cross-eyed.
– ORIGIN late 18th cent.: based on Old Norse *skjálgr* 'wry, oblique'.

skelly[2] ▶ noun variant spelling of **SCHELLY**.

skelm /ˈskɛl(ə)m/ S. African ▶ noun a scoundrel.
– ORIGIN early 17th cent.: from Dutch *schelm*, from German.

skelp /skɛlp/ ▶ verb [with obj.] Scottish & N. English strike, slap, or smack.
– ORIGIN late Middle English: probably imitative.

Skelton, John (*c.*1460–1529), English poet. Court poet to Henry VIII, he wrote verse consisting of short irregular rhyming lines with rhythms based on colloquial speech.

skene /ˈskiːniː/ ▶ noun (in ancient Greek theatre) a three-dimensional structure which formed part of the stage or set.
– ORIGIN from Greek *skēnē* 'hut, tent'.

skep (also **skip**) ▶ noun a straw or wicker beehive.
▪ archaic a wooden or wicker basket.
– ORIGIN late Old English *sceppe* 'basket', from Old Norse *skeppa* 'basket, bushel'.

skeptic ▶ noun US spelling of **SCEPTIC**.

skeptical ▶ adjective US spelling of **SCEPTICAL**.

skerm /skɛr(ə)m/ ▶ noun (in southern Africa) a temporary dwelling for nomads or travellers.
▪ a screen or hide for hunters or game watchers.
– ORIGIN Afrikaans.

skerrick /ˈskɛrɪk/ ▶ noun [usu. with negative] informal Austral./NZ the smallest bit: *there's not a skerrick of food in the house.*
– ORIGIN early 19th cent.: of unknown origin. The word is also recorded as an English slang term meaning 'halfpenny'.

skerry /ˈskɛri/ ▶ noun (pl. **-ies**) Scottish a reef or rocky island.
– ORIGIN early 17th cent.: Orkney dialect, from Old Norse *sker*.

sketch ▶ noun **1** a rough or unfinished drawing or painting, often made to assist in making a more finished picture: *a charcoal sketch.*
▪ a brief written or spoken account or description of someone or something, giving only basic details: *a biographical sketch of Ernest Hemingway.* ▪ a rough or unfinished version of any creative work.
2 a short humorous play or performance, consisting typically of one scene in a revue or comedy programme.
3 informal, dated a comical or amusing person or thing.
▶ verb [with obj.] make a rough drawing of: *as they talked, Modigliani began to sketch her* | [no obj.] *Jeanne sketched and painted whenever she had the time.*
▪ give a brief account or general outline of: *they sketched out the prosecution case.* ▪ perform (a gesture) with one's hands or body: *he sketched a graceful bow in her direction.*
– DERIVATIVES **sketcher** noun.
– ORIGIN mid 17th cent.: from Dutch *schets* or German *Skizze*, from Italian *schizzo*, from *schizzare* 'make a sketch', based on Greek *skhedios* 'done extempore'.

sketchbook (also **sketch pad**) ▶ noun a pad of drawing paper for sketching on.

sketch map ▶ noun a roughly drawn map that shows only basic details.

sketchy ▶ adjective (**sketchier**, **sketchiest**) not thorough or detailed: *the information they had was sketchy.*
▪ (of a picture) resembling a sketch; consisting of outline without much detail.
– DERIVATIVES **sketchily** adverb, **sketchiness** noun.

skeuomorph /ˈskjuːə(ʊ)mɔːf/ ▶ noun an object or feature which imitates the design of a similar artefact in another material.
– DERIVATIVES **skeuomorphic** adjective.
– ORIGIN late 19th cent.: from Greek *skeuos* 'container, implement' + *morphē* 'form'.

skew ▶ adjective **1** neither parallel nor at right angles to a specified or implied line; askew; crooked: *his hat looked slightly skew* | *a skew angle.*
▪ Statistics (of a statistical distribution) not symmetrical.
2 Mathematics (of a pair of lines) neither parallel nor intersecting.
▪ (of a curve) not lying in a plane.
▶ noun an oblique angle; a slant.
▪ a bias towards one particular group or subject: *the paper had a working-class skew.* ▪ [mass noun] Statistics the state of not being symmetrical.
▶ verb [no obj., with adverbial] suddenly change direction or position: *the car had skewed across the track.*
▪ twist or turn or cause to do this: *he skewed around in his saddle* | [with obj.] *his leg was skewed in and pushed against the other one.* ▪ [with obj.] make biased or distorted in a way that is regarded as inaccurate, unfair, or misleading: *the curriculum is skewed towards the practical subjects.* ▪ [with obj.] Statistics cause (a distribution) to be asymmetrical.
– PHRASES **on the skew** neither parallel nor at right angles to a specified or implied line; askew.
– DERIVATIVES **skewness** noun.
– ORIGIN late Middle English (as a verb in the sense 'move obliquely'): shortening of Old Northern French *eskiuwer*, variant of Old French *eschiver* 'eschew'. The adjective and noun (early 17th cent.) are from the verb.

skew arch (also **skew bridge**) ▶ noun an arch (or bridge) with the line of the arch not at right angles to the abutment.

skewback ▶ noun the sloping face of the abutment on which an extremity of an arch rests.

skewbald ▶ adjective (of an animal) with irregular patches of white and another colour (properly not black). Compare with **PIEBALD**.
▶ noun a skewbald animal, especially a horse.
– ORIGIN mid 17th cent.: from obsolete *skewed* 'skewbald' (of uncertain origin), on the pattern of *piebald*.

skewer ▶ noun a long piece of wood or metal used for holding pieces of food, typically meat, together during cooking.
▶ verb [with obj.] fasten together or pierce with a pin or skewer: [as adj. **skewered**] *skewered meat and fish.*
▪ informal criticize (someone) sharply.
– ORIGIN late Middle English: of unknown origin.

skew gear ▶ noun a gear consisting of two cogwheels having non-parallel, non-intersecting axes.

skew-symmetric ▶ adjective (of a matrix) having all the elements of the principal diagonal equal to zero, and each of the remaining elements equal to the negative of the element in the corresponding position on the other side of the diagonal.

skew-whiff ▶ adverb & adjective informal, chiefly Brit. not straight; askew: [as adv.] *he knocked my wig skew-whiff.*

ski ▶ noun (pl. **skis**) each of a pair of long narrow pieces of hard flexible material, typically pointed and turned up at the front, fastened under the feet for travelling over snow.
▪ a similar device attached beneath a vehicle or aircraft. ▪ [as modifier] of, relating to, or used for skiing: *a ski instructor* | *ski boots.* ▪ another term for **WATERSKI**.
▶ verb (**skis**, **skied**, **skiing** or **ski-ing**) [no obj.] travel over snow on skis; take part in the sport or recreation of skiing: *they skied down the mountain.*
▪ [with obj.] ski on (a particular ski run or type of snow): *off-piste spring snow is easy to ski.*
– DERIVATIVES **skiable** adjective.
– ORIGIN mid 18th cent.: from Norwegian, from Old Norse *skíth* 'billet, snowshoe'.

skiagraphy /skʌɪ-/ ▶ noun variant spelling of **SCIAGRAPHY**.

Skiathos /skiːˈaθɒs/ a Greek island in the Aegean Sea, the most westerly of the Northern Sporades group. Greek name **Skíathos** /ˈskiaθɔs/.

ski binding ▶ noun see **BINDING** (sense 2).

ski boat ▶ noun a small powerboat used for towing waterskiers.
▪ S. African a broad flat-bottomed boat with two watertight holds and two outboard motors, designed for offshore angling.

ski-bob ▶ noun a device resembling a bicycle with skis instead of wheels, used for sliding down snow-covered slopes.
▶ verb [no obj.] ride a ski-bob.
– DERIVATIVES **ski-bobber** noun.

skid ▶ verb (**skidded**, **skidding**) **1** [no obj.] (of a vehicle) slide, typically sideways or obliquely, on slippery ground or as a result of stopping or turning too quickly: *the taxi cab skidded to a halt.*
▪ slip; slide: *Barbara's foot skidded and she fell to the floor.* ▪ [with obj.] cause to skid: *he skidded his car.* ▪ [with obj.] N. Amer. move a heavy object on skids: *they skidded the logs down the hill to the waterfront.* ▪ figurative decline; deteriorate: *its shares have skidded 29% since March.*
2 [with obj.] fasten a skid to (a wheel) as a brake.
▶ noun **1** an act of skidding or sliding: *the Volvo went into a skid.*
2 a runner attached to the underside of an aircraft for use when landing on snow or grass.
▪ N. Amer. each of a set of wooden rollers used for moving a log or other heavy object.
3 a braking device consisting of a wooden or metal shoe preventing a wheel from revolving.
4 a beam or plank of wood used to support a ship under construction or repair.
– PHRASES **hit the skids** informal begin a rapid decline or deterioration. **on the skids** informal (of a person or their career) in a bad state; failing. **put the skids under** informal hasten the decline or failure of.
– ORIGIN late 17th cent. (as a noun in the sense 'supporting beam'): perhaps related to Old Norse *skíth* (see **SKI**).

skid lid ▶ noun Brit. informal a crash helmet.

Skidoo /skɪˈduː/ (also **skidoo**) trademark, chiefly N. Amer.
▶ noun a motorized toboggan.
▶ verb (**skidoos**, **skidooed**) [no obj.] [usu. as noun **skidooing**] ride on a Skidoo.
– ORIGIN mid 20th cent.: an arbitrary formation from **SKI**.

skidoo /skɪˈduː/ (also **skiddoo**) ▶ verb (**skidoos**, **skidooed**) [no obj.] N. Amer. informal, dated leave somewhere quickly.
– PHRASES **twenty-three skidoo** a hasty departure.
– ORIGIN early 20th cent.: perhaps from **SKEDADDLE**. The term is said to have been used originally in reference to male onlookers chased by police from the Flatiron Building, 23rd Street, New York, where the skirts of female passers-by were raised by winds intensified by the building's design.

skidpan (N. Amer. **skidpad**) ▶ noun a slippery road surface prepared for drivers to practise control of skidding.

skid road ▶ noun N. Amer. a road formed of skids along which logs were hauled.
▪ historical a part of a town frequented by loggers.
▪ another term for **SKID ROW**.

skid row ▶ noun informal, chiefly N. Amer. a run-down part of a town frequented by vagrants and alcoholics.
▪ figurative a desperately unfortunate or difficult situation: *with no money to spend, the club are* **on skid row**.
– ORIGIN 1930s: alteration of **SKID ROAD**.

skidsteer loader ▶ noun a farm vehicle with a large bucket or fork at the front end.

skier[1] ▶ noun a person who skis.

skier[2] ▶ noun variant spelling of **SKYER**.

skiff ▶ noun a light rowing boat or sculling boat, typically for one person.
– ORIGIN late 15th cent.: from French *esquif*, from Italian *schifo*, of Germanic origin; related to **SHIP**.

skiffle ▶ noun [mass noun] **1** Brit. a kind of folk music with a blues or jazz flavour that was popular in the 1950s, played by a small group and often incorporating improvised instruments such as washboards.
2 US a style of 1920s and 1930s jazz deriving from blues, ragtime, and folk music, using both improvised and conventional instruments.
– ORIGIN 1920s: perhaps imitative.

ski-flying ▶ noun [mass noun] a form of ski jumping from a higher slope so that the skier jumps further.

skiing ▶ noun [mass noun] the action of travelling over snow on skis, especially as a sport or recreation. Competitive skiing falls into two categories: **Nordic** (cross-country racing and jumping) and **Alpine** (downhill or straight racing, and slalom racing round a series of markers).

skijoring /ˈskiːdʒɔːrɪŋ, -ˈdʒɔː-/ ▶ noun [mass noun] the action of being pulled over snow or ice on skis by a horse or dog, as a sport or recreation activity.
– DERIVATIVES **skijorer** noun.
– ORIGIN 1920s: from Norwegian *skikjøring*, from *ski* 'ski' + *kjøre* 'drive'.

ski jump ▶ noun a steep slope levelling off before a

sharp drop to allow a skier to leap through the air. ▪a leap made from such a slope.
– DERIVATIVES **ski jumper** noun, **ski jumping** noun.

skilfish ▶noun (pl. same or **-fishes**) a large fish of the North Pacific which is an important food fish in Japan.
• *Erilepis zonifer*, family Anoplopomatidae.
– ORIGIN late 19th cent.: from Haida *sqil*.

skilful (also chiefly N. Amer. **skillful**) ▶adjective having or showing skill: *a skilful midfielder.*
– DERIVATIVES **skilfully** adverb, **skilfulness** noun.

ski lift ▶noun a system used to transport skiers up a slope to the top of a run, typically consisting of moving seats attached to an overhead cable.

skill ▶noun [mass noun] the ability to do something well; expertise: *difficult work, taking great skill.*
▪[count noun] a particular ability: *the basic skills of cookery.*
▶verb [with obj.] [usu. as noun **skilling**] train (a worker) to do a particular task.
– DERIVATIVES **skilless** adjective (archaic).
– ORIGIN late Old English *scele* 'knowledge', from Old Norse *skil* 'discernment, knowledge'.

skilled ▶adjective having or showing the knowledge, ability, or training to perform a certain activity or task well: *a lab technician **skilled** in electronics | skilled draughtsmen.*
▪based on such training or experience; showing expertise: *skilled legal advice.* ▪(of work) requiring special abilities or training: *a highly skilled job.*

skillet ▶noun Brit. historical a small metal cooking pot with a long handle, typically having legs.
▪a frying pan.
– ORIGIN Middle English: perhaps from Old French *escuelete*, diminutive of *escuele* 'platter', from late Latin *scutella*.

skillful ▶adjective chiefly N. Amer. variant spelling of **SKILFUL**.

skilly ▶noun [mass noun] Brit., chiefly historical thin broth, typically made from oatmeal and water and flavoured with meat.
– ORIGIN mid 19th cent.: abbreviation of archaic *skilligalee*, a fanciful formation.

skim ▶verb (**skimmed**, **skimming**) **1** [with obj.] remove (a substance) from the surface of a liquid: *as the scum rises, **skim** it **off**.*
▪remove a substance from the surface of (a liquid): *bring to the boil, then skim it to remove any foam.* ▪informal steal or embezzle (money), especially in small amounts over a period of time: *she was skimming money from the household kitty.*
2 [no obj., with adverbial of direction] go or move quickly and lightly over or on a surface or through the air: *he let his fingers skim across her shoulders.*
▪[with obj.] pass over (a surface), nearly or lightly touching it in the process: *we stood on the bridge, watching swallows skimming the water.* ▪[with obj.] throw (a flat stone) low over an expanse of water so that it bounces on the surface several times. ▪[with obj.] read (something) quickly or cursorily so as to note only the important points: *he sat down and skimmed the report* | [no obj.] *she **skimmed through** the newspaper.* ▪(**skim over**) deal with or treat (a subject) briefly or superficially.
▶noun **1** a thin layer of a substance on the surface of a liquid: ***a skim of** ice.*
2 an act of reading something quickly or superficially: *a quick skim through the pamphlet.*
– ORIGIN Middle English (in the sense 'remove scum from (a liquid)'): back-formation from **SKIMMER**, or from Old French *escumer*, from *escume* 'scum, foam'.

ski mask ▶noun a protective covering for the head and face, with holes for the eyes, nose, and mouth.

skimboard ▶noun a type of surfboard, typically round or short, used for riding shallow water.

skimmed milk (N. Amer. also **skim milk**) ▶noun [mass noun] milk from which the cream has been removed.

skimmer ▶noun **1** a person or thing that skims, in particular:
▪a utensil or device for removing a substance from the surface of a liquid. ▪a device or craft designed to collect oil spilled on water. ▪a hydroplane, hydrofoil, hovercraft, or other vessel that has little or no displacement at speed.
2 a long-winged seabird related to the terns, feeding by flying low over the water surface with its knife-like extended lower mandible immersed.
• Genus *Rynchops*, family Rynchopidae (or Laridae): three species, one each in Africa, Asia, and America.
3 chiefly US a flat, broad-brimmed straw hat.
▪informal a close-fitting dress.
4 North American term for **DARTER** (in sense 3).
– ORIGIN Middle English: from Old French *escumoir*, from *escumer* 'skim', from *escume* 'scum'.

skimmia /ˈskɪmɪə/ ▶noun an evergreen East Asian shrub with creamy-white flowers and red berries.
• Genus *Skimmia*, family Rutaceae.
– ORIGIN modern Latin, from Japanese.

skimmington ▶noun historical a procession made through a village intended to bring ridicule on and make an example of a nagging wife or an unfaithful husband.
– PHRASES **ride skimmington** hold such a procession.
– ORIGIN early 17th cent.: perhaps from *skimming-ladle*, used as a thrashing instrument during the procession.

skimobile /ˈskiːməbiːl/ ▶noun N. Amer. a motor vehicle for travelling over snow, with caterpillar tracks at the back and steerable skis in front.

skimp ▶verb [no obj.] expend or use less time, money, or material on something than is necessary in an attempt to economize: *don't **skimp on** insurance when you book your holidays.*
▶noun informal a fashionably short or revealing garment: *she wore a yellow skimp.*
– ORIGIN late 18th cent.: of unknown origin; compare with **SCAMP**[2] and **SCRIMP**.

skimpy ▶adjective (**skimpier**, **skimpiest**) (of clothes) short and revealing: *a skimpy dress.*
▪providing or consisting of less than is needed; meagre: *my knowledge of music is extremely skimpy.*
– DERIVATIVES **skimpily** adverb, **skimpiness** noun.

skin ▶noun **1** the thin layer of tissue forming the natural outer covering of the body of a person or animal: *I use body lotion to keep my skin supple* | [mass noun] *a flap of skin.*
▪the skin of a dead animal with or without the fur, used as material for clothing or other items: [mass noun] *is this real crocodile skin?* ▪a container made from the skin of an animal such as a goat, used for holding liquids.
2 an outer layer or covering, in particular:
▪the peel or outer layer of certain fruits or vegetables. ▪the thin outer covering of a sausage. ▪a thin layer forming on the surface of certain hot liquids, such as milk, as they cool. ▪informal a cigarette paper. ▪the outermost layer of a structure such as a building or aircraft. ▪(usu. **skins**) a strip of sealskin or other material attached to the underside of a ski to prevent a skier slipping backwards during climbing.
2 Brit. informal a skinhead.
3 (usu. **skins**) informal (especially in jazz) a drum or drum head.
4 [as modifier] informal relating to or denoting pornographic literature or films: *the skin trade.*
5 [mass noun] US a card game in which each player has one card which they bet will not be the first to be matched by a card dealt from the pack.
▶verb (**skinned**, **skinning**) **1** [with obj.] remove the skin from (an animal or a fruit or vegetable).
▪(in hyperbolic use) punish severely: *Dad would **skin** me alive if I forgot it.* ▪graze (a part of one's body): *he scrambled down from the tree with such haste that he skinned his knees.* ▪informal take money from or swindle (someone). ▪Soccer, informal (of a player) take the ball past (a defender) with ease.
2 [with obj.] archaic cover with skin: *the wound was skinned, but the strength of his thigh was not restored.*
▪[no obj.] (of a wound) form new skin: *the hole in his skull **skinned over**.*
– PHRASES **be skin and bone** (of a person or animal) be very thin. **by the skin of one's teeth** by a very narrow margin; only just: *I only got away by the skin of my teeth.* [ORIGIN: from a misquotation of Job 19:20: 'I am escaped with the skin of my teeth' (i.e. and nothing else). Current use reflects a different sense.] **get under someone's skin** informal **1** annoy or irritate someone intensely: *it was the sheer effrontery of them which got under my skin.* **2** fill someone's mind in a compelling and persistent way. **3** reach or display a deep understanding of someone: *movies that get under the skin of the British national character.* **give someone (some) skin** US black slang shake or slap hands together as a gesture or friendship or solidarity. **have a thick** (or **thin**) **skin** be insensitive (or oversensitive) to criticism or insults. **it's no skin off my nose** (or US **off my back**) informal used to indicate that one is not offended or adversely affected by something: *'I've not much appetite, I'm afraid.' 'No skin off my nose.'* **keep** (or **sleep in**) **a whole skin** archaic escape being wounded or injured. **skin and blister** Brit. rhyming slang a person's sister. **skin one's teeth** W. Indian laugh, especially inappropriately or unexpectedly. **there's more than one way to skin a cat** proverb there's more than one way of achieving one's aim. **under the skin** in reality, as opposed to superficial appearances: *he still believes that all women are goddesses under the skin.*
– DERIVATIVES **skinless** adjective, **skin-like** adjective.
– ORIGIN late Old English *scinn*, from Old Norse *skinn*; related to Dutch *schinden* 'flay, peel' and German *schinden*.
▶**skin up** Brit. informal make a cannabis cigarette.

skin beetle ▶noun chiefly N. Amer. a beetle that feeds on carrion, hide, or similar material, and is sometimes a serious pest of stored goods.
• Several species in the families Dermestidae and Trogidae.

skincare ▶noun [mass noun] the use of cosmetics to care for the skin: [as modifier] *skincare products.*

skin-deep ▶adjective not deep or lasting; superficial: *their left-wing attitudes were only skin-deep.*

skinder /ˈskənə, ˈskɪnə/ S. African informal ▶noun [mass noun] gossip: *we can catch up on the skinder.*
▶verb [no obj.] engage in gossip.
– ORIGIN from Afrikaans *skinder* 'to slander, gossip'.

skin diving ▶noun [mass noun] the action or sport of swimming under water without a diving suit, typically in deep water using an aqualung and flippers.
– DERIVATIVES **skin-dive** verb, **skin-diver** noun.

skin effect ▶noun [mass noun] Physics the tendency of a high-frequency alternating current to flow through only the outer layer of a conductor.

skinflint ▶noun informal a person who spends as little money as possible; a miser.

skinfold ▶noun a fold of skin and underlying fat formed by pinching, the thickness of which is a measure of nutritional status.

skin friction ▶noun [mass noun] Physics friction at the surface of a solid and a fluid in relative motion.

skinful ▶noun [in sing.] Brit. informal enough alcoholic drink to make one drunk: *he had a skinful on New Year's eve.*

skin game ▶noun N. Amer. informal a rigged gambling game; a swindle.

skin graft ▶noun a surgical operation in which a piece of healthy skin is transplanted to a new site or to a different individual.
▪a piece of skin transferred in this way.

skinhead ▶noun a young person of a subculture characterized by close-cropped hair and heavy boots, often perceived as aggressive, violent, and racist.

skink ▶noun a smooth-bodied lizard with short or absent limbs, typically burrowing in sandy ground, and occurring throughout tropical and temperate regions.
• Family Scincidae: numerous genera and species.
– ORIGIN late 16th cent.: from French *scinc* or Latin *scincus*, from Greek *skinkos*.

skinned ▶adjective [in combination] having a skin of a specified type: *a fair-skinned woman.*
– PHRASES **be thin-skinned** (or **thick-skinned**) be sensitive (or insensitive) to criticism or insults.

Skinner, Burrhus Frederic (1904–90), American behaviourist psychologist. He promoted the view that the proper aim of psychology should be to predict behaviour, and hence be able to control it.

skinner ▶noun **1** a person who skins animals or prepares skins.
▪a person who deals in animal skins; a furrier.
2 Horse Racing, Austral. informal a result that is very profitable to bookmakers.

Skinner box ▶noun Psychology an apparatus for studying instrumental conditioning in animals (typically rats or pigeons) in which the animal is isolated and provided with a lever or switch which it learns to use to obtain a reward, such as a food pellet, or to avoid a punishment, such as an electric shock.

skinny informal ▶adjective (**skinnier**, **skinniest**) (of a person or part of their body) unattractively thin: *his skinny arms.*
▪(of an article of clothing) tight-fitting: *a skinny black jumper.*
▶noun (**the skinny**) US confidential information on a

S

particular person or topic: *the inside skinny is that he didn't know the deal was in the works.*
– DERIVATIVES **skinniness** noun.

skinny-dip ▶ **verb** [no obj.] informal swim naked.
▶ **noun** a naked swim.

skinnymalinks /ˈskɪnɪməlɪŋks/ (also **skinny-malink**) ▶ **noun** Scottish a very thin person.
– ORIGIN late 19th cent.: origin uncertain; a Scottish children's song related the adventures of a thin man known as 'Skinamalinky Long Leg'.

skinny-rib ▶ **noun** a tightly fitting sweater or cardigan, originally fashionable in the 1960s.

skin-pop informal, chiefly N. Amer. ▶ **verb** [with obj.] inject (a drug, typically a narcotic) subcutaneously.
▶ **noun** a subcutaneous injection of a drug, typically a narcotic.
– DERIVATIVES **skin-popper** noun.

skint ▶ **adjective** Brit. informal (of a person) having little or no money available: *I'm a bit skint just now.*
– ORIGIN 1920s: variant of colloquial *skinned*, in the same sense, past participle of **SKIN**.

skin test ▶ **noun** a test to determine whether an immune reaction is elicited when a substance is applied to or injected into the skin.
▶ **verb** (**skin-test**) [with obj.] [usu. as noun **skin-testing**] perform such a test on (someone).

skintight ▶ **adjective** (of a garment) very close-fitting.

skin tonic ▶ **noun** a cosmetic astringent used to refresh and tighten facial skin.

skip[1] ▶ **verb** (**skipped**, **skipping**) [no obj., with adverbial of direction] move along lightly, stepping from one foot to the other with a hop or bounce: *she began to skip down the path.*
■ [no obj.] jump over a rope which is held at both ends by oneself or two other people and turned repeatedly over the head and under the feet, as a game or for exercise. ■ [with obj.] N. Amer. jump over (a rope) in such a way. ■ [with obj.] jump lightly over: *the children used to skip the puddles.* ■ [with obj.] omit (part of a book that one is reading, or a stage in a sequence that one is following): *the video manual allows the viewer to skip sections he's not interested in* | [no obj.] *she disliked him so much that she* **skipped over** *any articles which mentioned him.* ■ [with obj.] fail to attend or deal with as appropriate; miss: *I wanted to skip my English lesson to visit my mother* | *try not to skip breakfast.* ■ [no obj.] move quickly and in an unmethodical way from one point or subject to another: *Marian skipped half-heartedly through the book.* ■ [with obj.] informal depart quickly and secretly from: *she skipped her home amid rumours of a romance.* ■ [no obj.] informal run away; disappear: *I'm not giving them a chance to* **skip off** *again.* ■ (**skip it**) informal abandon an undertaking, conversation, or activity: *after several wrong turns in our journey, we almost decided to skip it.* ■ [with obj.] throw (a stone) so that it ricochets off the surface of water.
▶ **noun** a light, bouncing step; a skipping movement: *he moved with a strange, dancing skip.*
■ Computing an act of passing over part of a sequence of data or instructions. ■ N. Amer. informal a person who defaults or absconds.
– ORIGIN Middle English: probably of Scandinavian origin.

skip[2] ▶ **noun 1** Brit. a large transportable open-topped container for building and other refuse.
2 a cage or bucket in which men or materials are lowered and raised in mines and quarries.
■ variant spelling of **SKEP**.

skip[3] ▶ **noun** the captain or director of a side at bowls or curling.
▶ **verb** (**skipped**, **skipping**) [with obj.] act as skip of (a side).
– ORIGIN early 19th cent. (originally Scots): abbreviation of **SKIPPER**[1].

ski pants ▶ **plural noun** trousers worn for skiing.
■ women's trousers imitating a style of these, made of stretchy fabric with tapering legs and an elastic stirrup under each foot.

skipjack ▶ **noun 1** (also **skipjack tuna**) a small tuna with dark horizontal stripes, widely distributed throughout tropical and temperate seas. Also called **BONITO** or **OCEANIC BONITO**.
● *Katsuwonus* (or *Euthynnus*) *pelamis*, family Scombridae.
2 another term for **CLICK BEETLE**.
3 a sloop-rigged sailing boat of a kind used off the east coast of the US.
– ORIGIN early 18th cent.: from the verb **SKIP**[1] + **JACK**[1]. Sense 1 is from the fish's habit of jumping out of the water; senses 2 and 3 arose in the 19th cent.

ski-plane ▶ **noun** an aeroplane having its undercarriage fitted with skis for landing on snow or ice.

ski pole ▶ **noun** either of two light metal poles held by a skier to assist in balance or propulsion.

skipper[1] informal ▶ **noun** the captain of a ship or boat, especially a small trading or fishing vessel.
■ the captain of a side in a game or sport. ■ the captain of an aircraft.
▶ **verb** [with obj.] act as captain of.
– ORIGIN late Middle English: from Middle Dutch, Middle Low German *schipper*, from *schip* 'ship'.

skipper[2] ▶ **noun 1** a person or thing that skips.
■ used in the names of small insects and crustaceans that skip or hop, e.g. **cheese-skipper**.
2 a small brownish moth-like butterfly with rapid darting flight.
● Family Hesperiidae: numerous genera.
3 the Atlantic saury (see **SAURY**).

skipper[3] ▶ **noun** S. African a long-sleeved sweatshirt or T-shirt.
– ORIGIN of unknown origin.

skippet ▶ **noun** chiefly historical a small round wooden box used to preserve documents and seals.
– ORIGIN late Middle English: of unknown origin.

skipping rope ▶ **noun** Brit. a length of rope used for skipping, typically with a handle at each end.

skirl /skəːl/ ▶ **noun** a shrill sound, especially that of bagpipes.
▶ **verb** [no obj.] (of bagpipes) make such a sound.
– ORIGIN late Middle English (as a verb): probably of Scandinavian origin; ultimately imitative.

skirmish ▶ **noun** an episode of irregular or unpremeditated fighting, especially between small or outlying parts of armies or fleets.
■ a short argument: *there was a skirmish over the budget.*
▶ **verb** [no obj.] [often as noun **skirmishing**] engage in a skirmish: *reports of skirmishing along the border.*
– DERIVATIVES **skirmisher** noun.
– ORIGIN Middle English (as a verb): from Old French *eskirmiss-*, lengthened stem of *eskirmir*, from a Germanic verb meaning 'defend'.

skirr /skəː/ ▶ **verb** [no obj., with adverbial of direction] rare move rapidly, especially with a whirring sound: *five dark birds rose skirring away.*
– ORIGIN mid 16th cent.: perhaps related to **SCOUR**[1] or **SCOUR**[2].

skirret /ˈskɪrɪt/ ▶ **noun** an East Asian plant of the parsley family, formerly cultivated in Europe for its edible carrot-like root.
● *Sium sisarum*, Umbelliferae.
– ORIGIN Middle English *skirwhit(e)*, perhaps from Scots *skire* 'bright, clear' + **WHITE**.

skirt ▶ **noun 1** a woman's outer garment fastened around the waist and hanging down around the legs.
■ the part of a coat or dress that hangs below the waist. ■ [mass noun] informal women regarded as objects of sexual desire: *so, Sandro, off to chase some skirt?* ■ the curtain that hangs round the base of a hovercraft to contain the air cushion. ■ a surface that conceals or protects the wheels or underside of a vehicle or aircraft. ■ a small flap on a saddle, covering the bar from which the stirrup leather hangs. ■ archaic an edge, border, or extreme part.
2 [mass noun] an animal's diaphragm and other membranes as food: *bits of beef skirt.*
■ [count noun] Brit. a cut of meat from the lower flank.
▶ **verb** [with obj.] go round or past the edge of: *he did not go through the city but skirted it.*
■ be situated along or around the edge of: *the fields that skirted the highway were full of cattle.* ■ [no obj.] (**skirt along/around**) go along or around (something) rather than directly through or across it: *the river valley skirts along the northern slopes of the hills.* ■ attempt to ignore; avoid dealing with: *there was a subject she was always skirting* | [no obj.] *the treaty* **skirted around** *the question of political cooperation.*
– DERIVATIVES **skirted** adjective [in combination] *a full-skirted dress.*
– ORIGIN Middle English: from Old Norse *skyrta* 'shirt'; compare with synonymous Old English *scyrte*, also with **SHORT**. The verb dates from the early 17th cent.

skirt-chaser ▶ **noun** informal a man who pursues women amorously and is fickle in his affections.

skirting (also **skirting board**) ▶ **noun** Brit. a wooden board running along the base of an interior wall.

ski stick ▶ **noun** old-fashioned term for **SKI POLE**.

skit ▶ **noun** a short comedy sketch or piece of humorous writing, especially a parody: *a skit on daytime magazine programmes.*
– ORIGIN early 18th cent. (in the sense 'satirical comment or attack'): related to the rare verb *skit* 'move lightly and rapidly', perhaps from Old Norse (compare with *skjóta* 'shoot').

skite /skʌɪt/ informal ▶ **verb** [no obj.] **1** Austral./NZ boast: *she had a silk dress and used to skite about it.*
2 [with adverbial of direction] move quickly and forcefully, especially when glancing off a surface: *rain skited off her coat.*
▶ **noun 1** Austral./NZ a boaster. [ORIGIN: mid 19th cent.: from Scots and northern English dialect, denoting a person regarded with contempt; compare with **BLATHERSKITE**.]
■ [mass noun] boasting; boastfulness.
2 Scottish a drinking bout; a spree: *he only drank brandy when he was* **on a skite**.
– ORIGIN early 18th cent. (in sense 2 of the verb): perhaps of Old Norse origin; compare with **SKIT**.

ski touring ▶ **noun** [mass noun] a form of skiing in which people travel across mountainous terrain, both skiing downhill and climbing using skins.
– DERIVATIVES **ski tour** noun, **ski tourer** noun.

ski tow ▶ **noun 1** a type of ski lift, with a moving rope or bars suspended from a moving overhead cable.
2 a tow rope for waterskiers.

skitter (also **skeeter**) ▶ **verb** [no obj.] **1** [no obj., with adverbial of direction] move lightly and quickly or hurriedly: *the girls skittered up the stairs* | figurative *her mind skittered back to that day at the office.*
2 [with obj.] draw (bait) jerkily across the surface of the water as a technique in fishing.
– ORIGIN mid 19th cent.: apparently a frequentative of **SKITE**.

skittery ▶ **adjective** restless; skittish: *a skittery horse.*

skittish ▶ **adjective** lively and unpredictable; playful: *my skittish and immature mother.*
■ (especially of a horse) nervous; inclined to shy.
– DERIVATIVES **skittishly** adverb, **skittishness** noun.
– ORIGIN late Middle English: perhaps from the rare verb *skit* 'move lightly and rapidly'.

skittle ▶ **noun 1** (**skittles**) [treated as sing.] a game played with wooden pins, typically nine in number, set up at the end of an alley to be bowled down with a wooden ball or disc.
■ (in full **table skittles**) a game played with similar pins set up on a board to be knocked down by swinging a suspended ball. ■ Brit. informal chess that is not played seriously.
2 a pin used in the game of skittles.
▶ **verb** [with obj.] knock over as if in a game of skittles: *she put her hand out and skittled a row of bottles.*
■ (often **be skittled**) Cricket get (batsmen) out in rapid succession: *Pakistan were* **skittled out** *for 93.*
– ORIGIN mid 17th cent.: of unknown origin. The word *skyttel* exists in Danish and Swedish in the sense 'shuttle, child's marble', but there is no evidence to connect this with the game of skittles.

skive[1] /skʌɪv/ Brit. informal ▶ **verb** [no obj.] avoid work or a duty by staying away or leaving early; shirk: *I* **skived off** *school* | [with obj.] *she used to skive lessons.*
▶ **noun** [in sing.] an instance of avoiding work or a duty in this way.
■ an easy option.
– DERIVATIVES **skiver** noun.
– ORIGIN early 20th cent.: perhaps from French *esquiver* 'slink away'.

skive[2] /skʌɪv/ ▶ **verb** [with obj.] technical pare (the edge of a piece of leather or other material) so as to reduce its thickness.
– ORIGIN early 19th cent.: from Old Norse *skífa*; related to **SHIVE**.

skivvy ▶ **noun** (pl. **-ies**) **1** Brit. informal a low-ranking female domestic servant.
■ a person doing work that is poorly paid and considered menial.
2 (also **skivvy shirt**) US a lightweight high-necked long-sleeved garment.
■ a T-shirt or short-sleeved vest.
3 (**skivvies**) N. Amer. trademark underwear of vest and underpants. [ORIGIN: originally a US navy term.]
▶ **verb** (**-ies**, **-ied**) [no obj.] informal do menial household tasks; work as a skivvy.
– ORIGIN early 20th cent.: of unknown origin.

skokiaan /ˈskɒkɪɑːn/ ▶ **noun** [mass noun] S. African an illicit home-brewed liquor made of yeast, sugar, and water.

– ORIGIN perhaps from Zulu *isikokeyana* 'small enclosure', referring to the practice of hiding illicit liquor in holes in the ground.

skol /skɒl, skəʊl/ (also **skoal**) ▶ exclamation used to express friendly feelings towards one's companions before drinking.

– ORIGIN early 17th cent. (a Scots use): from Danish and Norwegian *skaal*, Swedish *skål*, from Old Norse *skál* 'bowl'; perhaps introduced through the visit of James VI to Denmark in 1589.

skolly /'skɒli/ ▶ noun (pl. **-ies**) S. African informal a petty criminal of mixed ethnic origin; a hooligan.

– ORIGIN Afrikaans, probably from Dutch *schoelje* 'rogue'.

skookum /'sku:kəm/ N. Amer. ▶ adjective informal (of a person or animal) strong, vigorous, or impressive.

▶ noun archaic a street party or trade fair.

– ORIGIN mid 19th cent.: from Chinook Jargon.

skookum house ▶ noun N. Amer. informal a jail.

Skopje /'skɒpjeɪ/ the capital of the republic of Macedonia, situated in the north on the Vardar River; pop. 440,500 (1994). Founded by the Romans, it became the capital of Macedonia in 1945.

skosh /skəʊʃ/ ▶ noun US informal a small amount; a little.

– PHRASES **a skosh** somewhat; slightly: *it's a skosh more formal than one might like.*

– ORIGIN 1950s: from Japanese *sukoshi*.

Skraeling /'skreɪlɪŋ/ ▶ noun an Inuit or other indigenous inhabitant of Greenland or Vinland (on the NE coast of North America) at the time of early Norse settlement.

– ORIGIN from Old Norse *Skræling(j)ar* (plural).

Skryabin variant spelling of SCRIABIN.

skua /'skju:ə/ ▶ noun a large brownish predatory seabird related to the gulls, pursuing other birds to make them disgorge fish they have caught.

● Family Stercorariidae: genera *Catharacta* (four larger species) and *Stercorarius* (three smaller species, North American name: **jaeger**).

– ORIGIN late 17th cent.: modern Latin, from Faroese *skúvur*, from Old Norse *skufr* (apparently imitative).

skulduggery /skʌl'dʌg(ə)ri/ (also **skullduggery**) ▶ noun [mass noun] underhand or unscrupulous behaviour; trickery: *a firm that investigates commercial skulduggery.*

– ORIGIN mid 19th cent.: alteration of Scots *sculduddery*, of unknown origin.

skulk ▶ verb [no obj.] keep out of sight, typically with a sinister or cowardly motive: *don't skulk outside the door like a spy!*

■ [with adverbial of direction] move stealthily or furtively: *he spent most of his time skulking about the corridors.* ■ shirk duty.

▶ noun a group of foxes.

– DERIVATIVES **skulker** noun.

– ORIGIN Middle English: of Scandinavian origin; compare with Norwegian *skulka* 'lurk', and Danish *skulke*, Swedish *skolka* 'shirk'.

skull ▶ noun a bone framework enclosing the brain of a vertebrate; the skeleton of a person's or animal's head.

■ informal a person's head or brain: *a skull crammed with too many thoughts.*

▶ verb [with obj.] hit (someone) on the head.

– PHRASES **out of one's skull** informal **1** out of one's mind; crazy. **2** very drunk. **skull and crossbones** a representation of a skull with two thigh bones crossed below it as an emblem of piracy or death.

– DERIVATIVES **skulled** adjective [in combination] *long-skulled.*

– ORIGIN Middle English *scolle*; of unknown origin; compare with Old Norse *skoltr.*

skullcap ▶ noun **1** a small close-fitting peakless cap.

■ a protective helmet, in particular one worn by jockeys or horse riders. **2** the top part of the skull. **3** a widely distributed plant of the mint family, whose tubular flowers have a helmet-shaped cup at the base.

● Genus *Scutellaria*, family Labiatae.

skull session ▶ noun US informal a discussion or conference, especially to discuss policies, tactics, and manoeuvres.

skunk ▶ noun **1** a cat-sized American mammal of the weasel family, with distinctive black-and-white striped fur. When threatened it squirts a fine spray of foul-smelling irritant liquid from its anal glands towards its attacker.

● *Mephitis* and other genera, family Mustelidae: several species, in particular the **striped skunk** (*M. mephitis*).

■ [mass noun] the fur of the skunk. ■ informal short for SKUNKWEED. ■ informal a contemptible person.

▶ verb [with obj.] N. Amer. informal **1** (often **be skunked**) defeat (someone) overwhelmingly in a game or contest, especially by preventing them from scoring at all. **2** dated fail to pay (a bill or creditor).

– ORIGIN mid 17th cent.: from Abnaki *segankw*; variants occur in many other American Indian dialects.

skunk cabbage ▶ noun a North American plant of the arum family, the flower of which has a distinctive unpleasant smell.

● Two species in the family Araceae: the western *Lysichiton americanum*, with a stalked yellow flower, and the eastern *Symplocarpus foetidus*, with a greenish purple flower.

skunkweed ▶ noun [mass noun] cannabis of a variety which has a high concentration of narcotic agents.

skunkworks ▶ plural noun [usu. treated as sing.] US informal an experimental laboratory or department of a company or institution, typically smaller than and independent of its main research division.

skutterudite /'skʊt(ə)rə,daɪt/ ▶ noun [mass noun] a grey metallic mineral, typically forming cubic or octahedral crystals, consisting chiefly of an arsenide of cobalt and nickel.

– ORIGIN mid 19th cent.: from *Skutterud* (now Skotterud), a village in SE Norway, + -ITE[1].

sky ▶ noun (pl. **-ies**) (often **the sky**) the region of the atmosphere and outer space seen from the earth: *hundreds of stars shining in the sky* | [mass noun] *Dorcas had never seen so much sky.*

■ poetic/literary heaven; heavenly power: *the just vengeance of incensed skies.*

▶ verb (**-ies, -ied**) [with obj.] informal hit (a ball) high into the air: *he skied his tee shot.*

■ hang (a picture) very high on a wall, especially in an exhibition.

– PHRASES **out of a clear blue sky** see BLUE[1]. **the sky is the limit** informal there is practically no limit (to something such as a price that can be charged or the opportunities afforded to someone). **to the skies** very highly; enthusiastically: *he wrote to his sister praising Lizzie to the skies.* **under the open sky** out of doors.

– DERIVATIVES **skyey** adjective, **skyless** adjective.

– ORIGIN Middle English (also in the plural denoting clouds), from Old Norse *ský* 'cloud'. The verb dates from the early 19th cent.

sky blue ▶ noun [mass noun] a bright clear blue.

sky-blue pink ▶ noun [mass noun] humorous a non-existent colour.

skybox ▶ noun N. Amer. a luxurious enclosed seating area high up in a sports arena.

sky burial ▶ noun a Tibetan funeral ritual involving the exposure of a dismembered corpse to sacred vultures.

skycap ▶ noun N. Amer. a porter at an airport.

sky-clad ▶ adjective naked (used especially in connection with modern pagan ritual).

– ORIGIN early 20th cent.: probably a translation of Sanskrit *Digāmbara*, denoting a Jain sect.

sky cloth ▶ noun a backdrop painted or coloured to represent the sky.

skydiving ▶ noun [mass noun] the sport of jumping from an aircraft and performing acrobatic manoeuvres in the air under free fall before landing by parachute.

– DERIVATIVES **skydive** verb, **skydiver** noun.

Skye a mountainous island of the Inner Hebrides, recently linked to the west coast of Scotland by a bridge; chief town, Portree. It is the largest and most northerly island of the group.

skyer (also **skier**) ▶ noun Cricket a hit which goes very high.

Skye terrier ▶ noun a small long-haired terrier of a slate-coloured or fawn-coloured Scottish breed.

skyflower ▶ noun a shrub of the verbena family, with clusters of lilac flowers and yellow berries, native to Central and South America.

● *Duranta erecta*, family Verbenaceae.

skyglow ▶ noun [mass noun] brightness of the night sky in a built-up area as a result of light pollution.

sky-high ▶ adverb & adjective as if reaching the sky; very high: [as adv.] *they saved a president from being blown sky-high.*

■ at or to a very high level; very great: [as adj.] *sky-high premiums.*

skyhook ▶ noun **1** dated an imaginary or fanciful device by which something could be suspended in the air.

2 Climbing a small flattened hook, with an eye for attaching a rope, fixed temporarily into a rock face. **3** Basketball a very high-arcing hook shot.

skyjack ▶ verb [with obj.] hijack (an aircraft).

▶ noun an act of skyjacking.

– DERIVATIVES **skyjacker** noun.

– ORIGIN 1960s: blend of SKY and HIJACK.

Skylab an American orbiting space laboratory launched in 1973, used for experiments in zero gravity and for astrophysical studies until 1974.

skylark ▶ noun a common Eurasian and North African lark of farmland and open country, noted for its prolonged song given in hovering flight.

● Genus *Alauda*, family Alaudidae: two species, in particular the widespread *A. arvensis*.

▶ verb [no obj.] pass time by playing tricks or practical jokes; indulge in horseplay: *he was skylarking with a friend when he fell into a pile of boxes.* [ORIGIN: late 17th cent. (originally in nautical use): by association with the verb LARK[2].]

skylight ▶ noun a window set in a roof or ceiling at the same angle.

skylight filter ▶ noun Photography a very slightly pink filter that reduces haze and excessive blueness of the sky in photographs by absorbing ultraviolet light.

skyline ▶ noun an outline of land and buildings defined against the sky: *the skyline of the city.*

skylit (also **skylighted**) ▶ adjective fitted with or lit by a skylight or skylights.

sky pilot ▶ noun informal a clergyman.

skyr /skɪə/ ▶ noun [mass noun] an Icelandic dish consisting of curdled milk.

– ORIGIN Icelandic.

skyrocket ▶ noun a rocket designed to explode high in the air as a signal or firework.

▶ verb (**-rocketed, -rocketing**) [no obj.] informal (of a price, rate, or amount) increase very steeply or rapidly: *the cost of the welfare system has skyrocketed.*

skysail /'skaɪseɪl, -s(ə)l/ ▶ noun a light sail above the royal in a square-rigged ship.

skyscape ▶ noun a view of an expanse of sky.

■ a picture of such a view.

skyscraper ▶ noun a very tall building of many storeys.

sky surfing ▶ noun [mass noun] the sport of jumping from an aircraft and surfing through the air on a board before landing by parachute.

skywalk ▶ noun another term for SKYWAY (in sense 2).

skyward ▶ adverb (also **skywards**) towards the sky: *flames were now shooting skyward.*

▶ adjective moving or directed towards the sky: *the city was heavily guarded by skyward laser batteries.*

skywatch ▶ verb [no obj.] informal observe or monitor the sky, especially for heavenly bodies or aircraft.

– DERIVATIVES **skywatcher** noun.

sky wave ▶ noun a radio wave reflected from the ionosphere.

skyway ▶ noun chiefly N. Amer. **1** a recognized route followed by aircraft.

2 a covered overhead walkway between buildings. **3** a raised motorway.

skywriting ▶ noun [mass noun] words in the form of smoke trails made by an aeroplane, especially for advertising.

slab ▶ noun a large, thick, flat piece of stone or concrete, typically square or rectangular in shape: *paving slabs* | *she settled on a slab of rock.*

■ a flat, heavy table top or counter, used during the preparation of food: *a fishmonger's slab.* ■ a large, thick slice or piece of cake, bread, chocolate, etc.: *a slab of bread and cheese.* ■ Climbing a large, smooth body of rock lying at a sharp angle to the horizontal. ■ an outer piece of timber sawn from a log. ■ Brit. a table used for laying a body on in a mortuary.

▶ verb (**slabbed, slabbing**) [with obj.] [often as noun **slabbing**] remove slabs from (a log or tree) to prepare it for sawing into planks.

– DERIVATIVES **slabby** adjective.

– ORIGIN Middle English: of unknown origin.

slab avalanche ▶ **noun** an avalanche formed by a sheet of snow breaking along a fracture line.

slabbed ▶ **adjective** covered with slabs: *a slabbed patio area.*

slabber chiefly Scottish & Irish ▶ **verb** [no obj.] dribble at the mouth; slaver: *he was slabbering like a child.*
■ [with obj.] splatter or splash (something): *his trouser legs were slabbered with mud.* ■ chatter, especially about matters of little importance: [as noun **slabbering**] *all the slabbering you do gets Bobby into some trouble.*
▶ **noun** a dribble of saliva.
– ORIGIN mid 16th cent. (in the sense 'dribble on'): related to dialect *slab* 'muddy place, puddle'.

slack[1] ▶ **adjective 1** not taut or held tightly in position; loose: *a slack rope | her mouth went slack.*
2 (of business or trade) characterized by a lack of work or activity; quiet: *business was rather slack.*
■ slow or sluggish: *they were working at a slack pace.* ■ having or showing laziness or negligence: *slack accounting procedures.*
3 W. Indian lewd: *the veteran king of slack chat.*
■ W. Indian (of a person, typically a woman) promiscuous.
4 (of a tide) neither ebbing nor flowing: *soon the water will become slack, and the tide will turn.*
▶ **noun 1** [mass noun] the part of a rope or line which is not held taut; the loose or unused part: *I picked up the rod and wound in the slack.*
2 (**slacks**) casual trousers.
3 informal a spell of inactivity or laziness: *he slept deeply, refreshed by a little slack in the daily routine.*
▶ **verb** [with obj.] **1** loosen (something, especially a rope).
■ reduce the intensity or speed of (something); slacken: *the horse slacked his pace.* ■ [no obj.] (**slack off**) decrease in quantity or intensity: *the flow of blood slacked off.* ■ [no obj.] Brit. informal work slowly or lazily: *she ticked off her girls if they were slacking.* ■ [no obj.] (**slack up**) slow down: *the animal doesn't slack up until he reaches the trees.*
2 slake (lime).
▶ **adverb** loosely: *their heads were hanging slack in attitudes of despair.*
– PHRASES **cut someone some slack** N. Amer. informal allow someone some leeway in their conduct. **take** (or **pick**) **up the slack 1** use up a surplus or improve the use of resources to avoid an undesirable lull in business: *as domestic demand starts to flag, foreign demand will help pick up the slack.* **2** pull on the loose end or part of a rope in order to make it taut.
– DERIVATIVES **slackly** adverb, **slackness** noun.
– ORIGIN Old English *slæc* 'inclined to be lazy, unhurried', of Germanic origin; related to Latin *laxus* 'loose'.

slack[2] ▶ **noun** [mass noun] coal dust or small pieces of coal.
– ORIGIN late Middle English: probably from Low German or Dutch.

slacken ▶ **verb** make or become slack: [with obj.] *he slackened his grip | the joints can be tightened and slackened off again |* [no obj.] *the pace never slackens.*

slacker ▶ **noun** informal a person who avoids work or effort.
■ US a person who evades military service. ■ chiefly US a young person (especially in the 1990s) of a subculture characterized by apathy and aimlessness.

slack water ▶ **noun** the state of the tide when it is turning, especially at low tide.

slag ▶ **noun 1** [mass noun] stony waste matter separated from metals during the smelting or refining of ore.
■ similar material produced by a volcano; scoria.
2 Brit. informal, derogatory a promiscuous woman.
■ a contemptible or insignificant person.
▶ **verb** (**slagged**, **slagging**) **1** [no obj.] [usu. as noun **slagging**] produce deposits of slag.
2 [with obj.] Brit. informal criticize (someone) in an abusive and insulting manner: *we used to hate each other and slag each other off.*
– DERIVATIVES **slaggy** adjective (**slaggier**, **slaggiest**).
– ORIGIN mid 16th cent.: from Middle Low German *slagge*, perhaps from *slagen* 'strike', with reference to fragments formed by hammering. The verb sense 'criticize' dates from the 1970s.

slag heap ▶ **noun** a hill or area of refuse from a mine or industrial site.

slag wool ▶ **noun** [mass noun] mineral wool made from blast-furnace slag.

slain past participle of **SLAY**[1].

slainte /ˈslɑːntʃə/ ▶ **exclamation** used to express friendly feelings towards one's companions before drinking.
– ORIGIN from Scottish Gaelic *slàinte*, literally 'health'.

slake ▶ **verb** [with obj.] **1** quench or satisfy (one's thirst): *slake your thirst with citron pressé.*
■ figurative satisfy (desires): *restaurants worked to slake the Italian obsession with food.*
2 combine (quicklime) with water to produce calcium hydroxide.
– ORIGIN Old English *slacian* 'become less eager', also 'slacken', from the adjective *slæc* 'slack'; compare with Dutch *slaken* 'diminish, relax'.

slaked lime ▶ **noun** see **LIME**[1].

slalom /ˈslɑːləm/ ▶ **noun** a ski race down a winding course marked out by poles.
■ a sporting event on water with a winding course marked out by obstacles, typically a canoe or sailing race.
▶ **verb** [no obj., with adverbial of direction] move or race in a winding path, avoiding obstacles: *she drove with reckless speed, slaloming in and out of the stalled cars.*
– DERIVATIVES **slalomer** noun.
– ORIGIN 1920s: from Norwegian, literally 'sloping track'.

slam[1] ▶ **verb** (**slammed**, **slamming**) [with obj.] shut (a door, window, or lid) forcefully and loudly: *he slams the door behind him as he leaves.*
■ [no obj.] be closed forcefully and loudly: *she heard a car door slam.* ■ [with obj. and adverbial] push or put somewhere with great force: *Charlie slammed down the phone.* ■ [no obj.] (**slam into**) crash into; collide heavily with: *the car mounted the pavement, slamming into a lamp post.* ■ [with obj. and adverbial of direction] informal hit (something) with great force in a particular direction: *he slammed a shot into the net.* ■ put (something) into action suddenly or forcefully: *I slammed on the brakes.* ■ [no obj., with adverbial of direction] move violently or loudly: *he slammed out of the room.* ■ [with obj.] (usu. **be slammed**) informal criticize severely: *a new TV soap was slammed as being cynical and irresponsible.* ■ [with obj.] informal, chiefly US score points against or gain a victory over (someone) easily.
▶ **noun 1** [usu. in sing.] a loud bang caused by the forceful shutting of something such as a door: *the back door closed with a slam.*
2 (usu. **the slam**) N. Amer. informal prison. [ORIGIN: abbreviation of **SLAMMER**.]
3 chiefly US a poetry contest in which competitors recite their entries and are judged by members of the audience, the winner being elected after several elimination rounds. [ORIGIN: of unknown origin.]
– ORIGIN late 17th cent.: probably of Scandinavian origin; compare with Old Norse *slam(b)ra.*

slam[2] ▶ **noun** Bridge a grand slam (all thirteen tricks) or small slam (twelve tricks), for which bonus points are scored if bid and made.
– ORIGIN early 17th cent. (originally the name of a card game): perhaps from obsolete *slampant* 'trickery'.

slam-bang informal, chiefly N. Amer. ▶ **adjective** exciting and energetic: *a slam-bang action cartoon.*
■ with no niceties, subtleties, or restraints; direct and forceful: *the slam-bang world of daily journalism.*
▶ **adverb** suddenly and forcefully or violently: *I walked slam-bang into this character.*

slam-dancing ▶ **noun** [mass noun] chiefly N. Amer. a form of dancing to rock music in which the dancers deliberately collide with one another.
– DERIVATIVES **slam-dance** verb, **slam dancer** noun.

slam dunk ▶ **noun** Basketball a shot in which a player thrusts the ball down through the basket.
■ [usu. as modifier] US informal something reliable or unfailing; a foregone conclusion or certainty: *the film season's one slam-dunk hit.*
▶ **verb** (**slam-dunk**) [with obj.] thrust (the ball) down through the basket.
■ US informal defeat or dismiss decisively: *they continue to slam-dunk every proposal we make.*

slammer ▶ **noun 1** (usu. **the slammer**) informal prison.
2 chiefly N. Amer. a person who deliberately collides with others when slam-dancing.
3 (also **tequila slammer**) a cocktail made with tequila and champagne or another fizzy drink, which is covered, slammed on the table, and then drunk in one.

slander ▶ **noun** [mass noun] Law the action or crime of making a false spoken statement damaging to a person's reputation: *he is suing the TV company for slander.* Compare with **LIBEL**.
■ [count noun] a false and malicious spoken statement: *I've had just about all I can stomach of your slanders.*
▶ **verb** [with obj.] make false and damaging statements about (someone): *they were accused of slandering the head of state.*
– DERIVATIVES **slanderer** noun, **slanderous** adjective, **slanderously** adverb.
– ORIGIN Middle English: from Old French *esclandre*, alteration of *escandle*, from late Latin *scandalum* (see **SCANDAL**).

slang ▶ **noun** [mass noun] a type of language that consists of words and phrases that are regarded as very informal, are more common in speech than writing, and are typically restricted to a particular context or group of people: *grass is slang for marijuana | army slang.*
▶ **verb** [with obj.] informal attack (someone) using abusive language: *he watched ideological groups slanging one another.*
– ORIGIN mid 18th cent.: of unknown origin.

slanging match ▶ **noun** chiefly Brit. a prolonged exchange of insults.

slangy ▶ **adjective** (**slangier**, **slangiest**) using or denoting slang: *the style is so slangy as to be incomprehensible | a slangy, stand-up comedian.*
■ (of a person or their manner) flashy or pretentious, especially in a vulgar way.
– DERIVATIVES **slangily** adverb, **slanginess** noun.

slant ▶ **verb** [no obj., with adverbial of direction] slope or lean in a particular direction; diverge from a vertical or horizontal line: *a ploughed field slanted up to the skyline |* [as adj. **slanting**] *the slanting beams of the roof.*
■ (especially of light or shadow) fall in an oblique direction: *the early sun slanted across the mountains.* ■ [with obj.] cause (something) to lean or slope in such a way: *slant your skis as you turn to send up a curtain of water.* ■ [with obj.] [often as adj. **slanted**] present or view (information) from a particular angle, especially in a biased or unfair way: *slanted news coverage.*
▶ **noun 1** [in sing.] a sloping position: *the hedge grew* **at a slant** *| cut flower stems* **on the slant**.
2 a particular point of view from which something is seen or presented: *a new* **slant on** *science.*
▶ **adjective** [attrib.] sloping: *slant pockets.*
– ORIGIN late Middle English: variant of dialect *slent*, of Scandinavian origin, probably influenced by **ASLANT**.

slant-eyed ▶ **adjective** (of a person) having slanting eyes (often used as an insult towards people of oriental origin).

slant height ▶ **noun** the height of a cone from the vertex to the periphery, rather than the centre, of the base.

slantwise ▶ **adjective** & **adverb** at an angle or in a sloping direction: [as adj.] *a slantwise glance |* [as adv.] *the bird veers and drops slantwise toward the wood.*

slap[1] ▶ **verb** (**slapped**, **slapping**) [with obj.] hit (someone or something) with the palm of one's hand or a flat object: *my sister slapped my face.*
■ [no obj., with adverbial] hit against or into something with the sound of such an action: *water* **slapped against** *the boat.* ■ (**slap someone down**) informal reprimand someone forcefully. ■ [with obj. and adverbial] put or apply (something) somewhere quickly, carelessly, or forcefully: *slap on a bit of make-up.* ■ (**slap something on**) informal impose a fine or other penalty on: *the government had slapped an embargo on imports.*
▶ **noun 1** a blow with the palm of the hand or a flat object: *he gave her a slap across her cheek.*
■ a sound made or as if made by such an action: *she heard the slap of water against the harbour wall.*
2 [mass noun] informal make-up, especially when applied thickly or carelessly.
▶ **adverb** informal suddenly and directly, especially with great force: *storming out of her room, she went slap into Luke.*
■ exactly; right: *we passed slap through the middle of an enemy armoured unit.*
– PHRASES **slap in the face** an unexpected rejection or affront. **slap on the back** congratulations or commendations: *they deserve a hearty slap on the back for their efforts.* **slap someone on the back** congratulate someone. **slap on the wrist** a mild reprimand or punishment.
– ORIGIN late Middle English (as a verb): probably imitative. The noun dates from the mid 17th cent.

slap[2] ▶ **adjective** S. African lacking strength, energy, or discipline; ineffectual: *the book took her three years to write because she was very slap.*

▪(of food) soft or runny: *the chips were crisp outside and slap inside.*

– ORIGIN Afrikaans, literally 'dangling, flabby'.

slap and tickle ▶ **noun** [mass noun] Brit. informal physical amorous play.

slap bang ▶ **adverb** informal **1** exactly; right: *your property happens to be slap bang in the middle of our site.*

2 in a sudden and violent way: *you came slap bang against the rock.*

slap bass ▶ **noun** [mass noun] a style of playing double bass or bass guitar by pulling and releasing the strings sharply against the fingerboard, used for effect in jazz or popular music.

slapdash ▶ **adjective** done too hurriedly and carelessly: *he gave a slapdash performance.*

▶ **adverb** dated hurriedly and carelessly.

slap-happy ▶ **adjective** informal **1** casual or flippant in a cheerful and often irresponsible way: *he possessed sauntering slap-happy courage.*

▪(of an action or operation) unmethodical; poorly thought out: *slap-happy surveying methods.*

2 dazed or stupefied from happiness or relief: *she's a bit slap-happy after such a narrow escape.*

slaphead ▶ **noun** derogatory a bald or balding man.

slapjack ▶ **noun** N. Amer. a kind of pancake cooked on a griddle.

slapper ▶ **noun 1** Brit. informal, derogatory a promiscuous or vulgar woman.

2 informal term for **SLAP SHOT**.

slap shot ▶ **noun** Ice Hockey a hard shot made by raising the stick just above or below the waist before striking the puck with a sharp slapping motion.

slapstick ▶ **noun** [mass noun] comedy based on deliberately clumsy actions and humorously embarrassing events: [as modifier] *slapstick humour.*

▪[count noun] a device consisting of two flexible pieces of wood joined together at one end, used by clowns and in pantomime to produce a loud slapping noise.

slap-up ▶ **adjective** [attrib.] informal, chiefly Brit. (of a meal or celebration) large and sumptuous: *a slap-up dinner.*

slash ▶ **verb** [with obj.] cut (something) with a violent sweeping movement, typically using a knife or sword: *a tyre was slashed on my car | they cut and **slashed their way** to the river |* [no obj.] *the man **slashed at** him with a sword.*

▪informal reduce (a price, quantity, etc.) greatly: *the workforce has been slashed by 2,000.* ▪archaic lash, whip, or thrash severely. ▪archaic crack (a whip). ▪archaic criticize (someone or something) severely.

▶ **noun 1** a cut made with a wide, sweeping stroke: *the man took a mighty slash at his head with a large sword.*

▪a wound or gash made by such an action: *he staggered over with a crimson slash across his temple.* ▪figurative a bright patch or flash of colour or light: *the foliage is handsome—yellow and gold with the odd **slash of** red.*

2 an oblique stroke (/) in print or writing, used between alternatives (e.g. *and/or*), in fractions (e.g. *3/4*), in ratios (e.g. *miles/day*), or between separate elements of a text.

▪[as modifier] denoting or belonging to a genre of fiction, chiefly published in fanzines, in which any of various male pairings from the popular media is portrayed as having a homosexual relationship. [ORIGIN: 1980s: from *slash* denoting an oblique printed stroke, linking adjoining names or initials (as in *Kirk/Spock* and *K/S*: the latter is also used as an alternative name for the genre, taken from the names of characters in *Star Trek*, a US science-fiction television programme).]

3 [in sing.] Brit. informal an act of urinating.

4 [mass noun] N. Amer. debris resulting from the felling or destruction of trees.

– ORIGIN late Middle English: perhaps imitative, or from Old French *esclachier* 'break in pieces'. The noun dates from the late 16th cent.

slash-and-burn ▶ **adjective** [attrib.] of, relating to, or denoting a method of agriculture in which existing vegetation is cut down and burned off before new seeds are sown, typically used as a method for clearing forest land for farming.

▪figurative aggressive and merciless: *her slash-and-burn campaigning style.*

slashed ▶ **adjective** (of a garment) having slits to show the lining material or skin beneath: *she wore slashed jeans.*

slasher ▶ **noun** informal **1** a person or thing that slashes, in particular:

▪any of various tools for cutting wood. ▪US a sporting competitor who is quick, agile, and skilled at cutting through the opposition.

2 (also **slasher film**) a horror film, especially one in which victims (typically women or teenagers) are slashed with knives and razors.

slashing ▶ **adjective** [attrib.] informal vigorously incisive or effective: *a slashing magazine attack on her.*

slash pine ▶ **noun** a pine growing in a low-lying coastal region (slash) of the south-eastern US, Central America, and the Caribbean.

• Genus *Pinus*, family Pinaceae: several species, in particular *P. caribaea.*

slash pocket ▶ **noun** a pocket set in a garment with a slit for the opening.

slasto /ˈslastəʊ/ ▶ **noun** [mass noun] S. African trademark a slate-like shale used for flooring and tiling.

– ORIGIN blend of **SLATE** and **STONE**.

slat ▶ **noun** a thin, narrow piece of wood, plastic, or metal, especially one of a series which overlap or fit into each other, as in a fence or a Venetian blind.

– ORIGIN late Middle English (in the sense 'roofing slate'): shortening of Old French *esclat* 'splinter', from *esclater* 'to split'. The current sense dates from the mid 18th cent.

slate ▶ **noun 1** [mass noun] a fine-grained grey, green, or bluish-purple metamorphic rock easily split into smooth, flat plates.

▪[count noun] a flat plate of such rock used as roofing material.

2 a flat plate of slate used for writing on, typically framed in wood, formerly used in schools.

▪a list of candidates for election to a post or office, typically a group sharing a set of political views: *candidates on the left's slate won 74 per cent of constituency votes.* ▪chiefly N. Amer. a range of something on offer: *the company has revealed details of a $60 m slate of film productions.* ▪a board showing the identifying details of a take of a film, which is held in front of the camera at its beginning and end.

3 [mass noun] [usu. as modifier] a bluish-grey colour: *suits of slate grey.*

▶ **verb** [with obj.] **1** cover (something, especially a roof) with slates.

2 Brit. informal criticize severely: *his work was slated by the critics.*

3 (usu. **be slated**) chiefly N. Amer. schedule; plan: *London shows are slated for late June |* [with obj. and infinitive] *the former brickyard is slated to be renovated.*

▪(usu. **be slated**) chiefly N. Amer. nominate (someone) as a candidate for an office or post: *I understand that I am being slated for promotion.*

4 identify (a take) using a slate.

– PHRASES **on the** (or **one's**) **slate** Brit. to be paid for later; on credit: *'Five quid,' said the barman. 'Put it on my slate,' I suggested.* **wipe the slate clean** see **WIPE**.

– DERIVATIVES **slaty** adjective.

– ORIGIN Middle English *sclate*, *sklate*, shortening of Old French *esclate*, feminine synonymous with *esclat* 'piece broken off' (see **SLAT**). Sense 3 of the verb arose from the practice of noting a name on a writing slate.

slate-coloured ▶ **adjective** of a dark bluish or greenish grey.

slate pencil ▶ **noun** chiefly historical a pencil made of soft slate used for writing on slate.

slater ▶ **noun 1** a person who slates roofs for a living.

2 a woodlouse or similar isopod crustacean.

• Several species in the order Isopoda. See also **SEA SLATER**.

slather /ˈslaðə/ ▶ **noun** (often **slathers**) N. Amer. informal a large amount.

▶ **verb** [with obj.] informal spread or smear (a substance) thickly or liberally: ***slather on** some tanning lotion.*

▪spread or smear a substance thickly or liberally on: *scones **slathered with** clotted cream.*

– PHRASES **open slather** Austral./NZ informal freedom to act without restriction; free rein: *you've got an open slather here, lad—do what you like.*

– ORIGIN early 19th cent.: of unknown origin.

slatted ▶ **adjective** having slats: *a slatted bench.*

slattern /ˈslat(ə)n/ ▶ **noun** dated a dirty, untidy woman.

– DERIVATIVES **slatternliness** noun, **slatternly** adjective.

– ORIGIN mid 17th cent.: related to *slattering* 'slovenly', from dialect *slatter* 'to spill, slop', frequentative of *slat* 'strike', of unknown origin.

slaughter /ˈslɔːtə/ ▶ **noun** [mass noun] the killing of animals for food.

▪the killing of a large number of people or animals in a cruel or violent way; massacre: *the slaughter of 20 peaceful demonstrators.* ▪[count noun] informal a thorough defeat: *a magnificent 5–0 slaughter of Coventry.*

▶ **verb** [with obj.] (usu. **be slaughtered**) kill (animals) for food.

▪kill (people or animals) in a cruel or violent way, typically in large numbers: *innocent civilians are being slaughtered.* ▪informal defeat (an opponent) thoroughly: *the first team were slaughtered.*

– DERIVATIVES **slaughterer** noun, **slaughterous** adjective.

– ORIGIN Middle English (as a noun): from Old Norse *slátr* 'butcher's meat'; related to **SLAY**[1]. The verb dates from the mid 16th cent.

slaughterhouse ▶ **noun** a place where animals are slaughtered for food.

Slav /slɑːv/ ▶ **noun** a member of a group of peoples in central and eastern Europe speaking Slavic languages.

▶ **adjective** another term for **SLAVIC**.

– ORIGIN from medieval Latin *Sclavus*, late Greek *Sklabos*, later also from medieval Latin *Slavus*.

slave ▶ **noun** chiefly historical a person who is the legal property of another and is forced to obey them.

▪a person who works very hard without proper remuneration or appreciation: *by the time I was ten, I had become her slave, doing all the housework.* ▪a person who is excessively dependent upon or controlled by something: *the poorest people of the world are **slaves to** the banks | she was no **slave to** fashion.* ▪a device, or part of one, directly controlled by another: [as modifier] *a slave cassette deck.* Compare with **MASTER**[1].

▶ **verb** [no obj.] work excessively hard: *after **slaving away** for fourteen years all he gets is two thousand.*

▪[with obj.] subject (a device) to control by another: *should the need arise, the two channels can be slaved together.*

– ORIGIN Middle English: shortening of Old French *esclave*, equivalent of medieval Latin *sclava* (feminine) 'Slavonic (captive)': the Slavonic peoples had been reduced to a servile state by conquest in the 9th cent.

slave bangle (also **slave bracelet**) ▶ **noun** a bangle or bracelet worn above the elbow.

slave bell ▶ **noun** (in South Africa) a large bell hung between two whitewashed pillars, formerly used to summon slaves and mark the beginning and end of work periods.

Slave Coast a part of the west coast of Africa, between the Volta River and Mount Cameroon, from which slaves were exported in the 16th–19th centuries.

slave-driver ▶ **noun** a person who oversees and urges on slaves at work.

▪informal a person who works others very hard.

– DERIVATIVES **slave-drive** verb.

slave labour ▶ **noun** [mass noun] labour which is coerced and inadequately rewarded, or people that do it: *most of production is carried out by slave labour.*

slave-making ant (also **slave-maker ant**) ▶ **noun** an ant that raids the nests of other ant species and steals the pupae, which later become workers in the new colony.

• Several species in the family Formicidae, in particular the European *Formica sanguinea*. See also **AMAZON ANT**.

slaver[1] /ˈsleɪvə/ ▶ **noun** chiefly historical a person dealing in or owning slaves.

▪a ship used for transporting slaves.

slaver[2] /ˈslavə, ˈsleɪvə/ ▶ **noun** [mass noun] saliva running from the mouth.

▪archaic, figurative excessive or obsequious flattery.

▶ **verb** [no obj.] let saliva run from the mouth: *the Labrador was slavering at the mouth.*

▪show excessive desire: *suburbanites **slavering over** drop-dead models.*

– ORIGIN Middle English: probably from Low German; compare with **SLOBBER**.

slavery ▶ **noun** [mass noun] the state of being a slave: *thousands had been sold into slavery.*

▪the practice or system of owning slaves. ▪a condition compared to that of a slave in respect of exhausting labour or restricted freedom: *female domestic slavery.* ▪excessive dependence on or devotion to something: ***slavery to** tradition.*

Slave State (also **slave state**) ▶ **noun** historical any of the Southern states of the US in which slavery was legal before the Civil War.

slave trade ▶ **noun** [mass noun] chiefly historical the procuring, transporting, and selling of human

S

beings as slaves, in particular the former trade in African blacks as slaves by European countries and North America.
– DERIVATIVES **slave trader** noun.

Slavey /ˈsleɪvi/ ▶ **noun** **1** a member of a Dene people of NW Canada.
2 [mass noun] either of the two languages (**North** and **South Slavey**) spoken by this people.
▶ **adjective** of or relating to this people or their languages.

slavey ▶ **noun** (pl. **-eys**) Brit. informal, dated a maidservant, especially a hard-worked one.

Slavic /ˈslɑːvɪk, ˈslavɪk/ ▶ **adjective** of, relating to, or denoting the branch of the Indo-European language family that includes Russian, Ukrainian, and Belorussian (**Eastern Slavic**), Polish, Czech, Slovak, and Sorbian (**Western Slavic**), and Bulgarian, Serbo-Croat, Macedonian, and Slovene (**Southern Slavic**).
■ of, relating to, or denoting the peoples of central and eastern Europe who speak any of these languages.
▶ **noun** the Slavic languages collectively. See also **SLAVONIC**.

slaving ▶ **noun** [mass noun] [usu. as modifier] chiefly historical the action or process of enslaving people: *a slaving expedition.*

slavish ▶ **adjective** relating to or characteristic of a slave, typically by behaving in a servile or submissive way: *he noted the slavish, feudal respect they had for her.*
■ showing no attempt at originality, constructive interpretation, or development: *a slavish adherence to protocol.*
– DERIVATIVES **slavishly** adverb, **slavishness** noun.

Slavonian grebe /sləˈvəʊnɪən/ ▶ **noun** a North Eurasian and North American grebe with reddish underparts and a black and gold crest.
● *Podiceps auritus*, family Podicipedidae. North American name: **horned grebe**.

Slavonic /sləˈvɒnɪk/ ▶ **adjective** & **noun** another term for **SLAVIC**. See also **CHURCH SLAVONIC**.
– ORIGIN from medieval Latin *S(c)lavonicus*, from *S(c)lavonia* 'country of the Slavs', from *Sclavus* (see **SLAV**).

slaw ▶ **noun** [mass noun] N. Amer. coleslaw.
– ORIGIN late 18th cent.: from Dutch *sla*, shortened from *salade* 'salad'.

slay[1] ▶ **verb** (past **slew**; past participle **slain**) [with obj.] archaic or poetic/literary kill (a person or animal) in a violent way: *St George slew the dragon.*
■ (usu. **be slain**) N. Amer. murder (someone) (used chiefly in journalism): *a man was slain with a shotgun* | [as noun **slaying**] *a gangland slaying.* ■ informal greatly impress or amuse (someone): *you slay me, you really do.*
– DERIVATIVES **slayer** noun.
– ORIGIN Old English *slēan* 'strike, kill', of Germanic origin; related to Dutch *slaan* and German *schlagen*.

slay[2] ▶ **noun** variant spelling of **SLEY**.

SLBM ▶ **abbreviation** for submarine-launched ballistic missile.

SLD ▶ **abbreviation** for Social and Liberal Democrats.

SLE ▶ **abbreviation** for systemic lupus erythematosus.

sleaze ▶ **noun** [mass noun] immoral, sordid, and corrupt behaviour or material, especially in business or politics: *political campaigns that are long on sleaze and short on substance.*
■ [count noun] informal, chiefly US a sordid, corrupt, or immoral person.
▶ **verb** [no obj., with adverbial] informal behave in an immoral, corrupt, or sordid way: *you're the last person who has to sleaze around bars.*
– ORIGIN 1960s: back-formation from **SLEAZY**.

sleazeball (also **sleazebag**) ▶ **noun** informal, chiefly N. Amer. a disreputable, disgusting, or despicable person (also used as a general term of abuse).

sleazoid (also **sleazo**) (pl. **-os**)) informal, chiefly US ▶ **adjective** sleazy, sordid, or despicable: *a sleazoid lawyer.*
▶ **noun** a sleazy, sordid, or despicable person.

sleazy ▶ **adjective** (**sleazier**, **sleaziest**) **1** (of a person or situation) sordid, corrupt, or immoral.
■ (of a place) squalid and seedy: *a sleazy all-night cafe.*
2 dated (of textiles and clothing) flimsy.
– DERIVATIVES **sleazily** adverb, **sleaziness** noun.
– ORIGIN mid 17th cent.: of unknown origin.

sled ▶ **noun** & **verb** (**sledded**, **sledding**) North American term for **SLEDGE[1]**.
– ORIGIN Middle English: from Middle Low German *sleddde*; related to the verb **SLIDE**.

sledge[1] ▶ **noun** a vehicle on runners for conveying loads or passengers over snow or ice, either pushed, pulled, drawn by horses or dogs, or allowed to slide downhill.
■ Brit. a toboggan.
▶ **verb** [no obj., with adverbial of direction] ride on a sledge: *they sledged down the slopes in the frozen snow* | [as noun **sledging**] *I love sledging.*
■ [with obj. and adverbial of direction] carry (passengers or a load) on a sledge: *the task of sledging 10-metre lifeboats across tundra.*
– ORIGIN late 16th cent. (as a noun): from Middle Dutch *sleedse*; related to **SLED**. The verb dates from the early 18th cent.

sledge[2] ▶ **noun** a sledgehammer.
▶ **verb** [with obj.] [usu. as noun **sledging**] Cricket (of a fielder) make offensive remarks to (an opposing batsman) in order to break their concentration.
– ORIGIN Old English *slecg* (noun), from a Germanic base meaning 'to strike', related to **SLAY[1]**. The current sense of the verb dates from the late 20th cent.

sledgehammer ▶ **noun** a large, heavy hammer used for such jobs as breaking rocks and driving in fence posts.
■ [as modifier] powerful; forceful: *sledgehammer blows.* ■ [as modifier] figurative ruthless, insensitive, or using unnecessary force: *under his sledgehammer direction, anything of subtlety is swamped.*
▶ **verb** [with obj.] hit with a sledgehammer.

sleek ▶ **adjective** (of hair, fur, or skin) smooth and glossy: *he was tall, with sleek, dark hair.*
■ (of a person or animal) having smooth, glossy skin, hair, or fur, often taken as a sign of physical fitness: *a sleek black cat.* ■ (of a person) having a wealthy and well-groomed appearance: *a sleek and ambitious junior Minister.* ■ (of an object) having an elegant, streamlined shape or design: *his sleek black car slid through the traffic.* ■ ingratiating; unctuous: *she gave Guy a sleek smile to underline her words.*
▶ **verb** [with obj. and adverbial of direction] make (the hair) smooth and glossy, typically by applying pressure or moisture to it: *her black hair was sleeked down.*
▶ **adverb** poetic/literary in a smooth manner: *the hiss of water sliding sleek against the hull.*
– DERIVATIVES **sleekly** adverb, **sleekness** noun, **sleeky** adjective.
– ORIGIN late Middle English: a later variant of **SLICK** (adjective and verb).

sleep ▶ **noun** [mass noun] a condition of body and mind such as that which typically recurs for several hours every night, in which the nervous system is inactive, the eyes closed, the postural muscles relaxed, and consciousness practically suspended: *I was on the verge of sleep* | [in sing.] *a good night's sleep.*
■ chiefly poetic/literary a state compared to or resembling this, such as death or complete silence or stillness: *a photograph of the poet in his last sleep.* ■ a gummy secretion found in the corners of the eyes after sleep: *she sat up, rubbing the sleep from her eyes.*
▶ **verb** (past and past participle **slept** /slɛpt/) [no obj.] rest in such a condition; be asleep: *she slept for half an hour* | [as adj. **sleeping**] *he looked at the sleeping child.*
■ (**sleep through**) fail to be woken by: *he was so tired he slept through the alarm.* ■ [with adverbial] have sexual intercourse or be involved in a sexual relationship: *I won't sleep with a man who doesn't respect me.* ■ [with obj.] (**sleep something off/away**) dispel the effects of or recover from something by going to sleep: *she thought it wise to let him sleep off his hangover.* ■ [with obj.] provide (a specified number of people) with beds, rooms, or places to stay the night: *studios sleeping two people cost £70 a night.* ■ figurative be inactive or dormant: *Copenhagen likes to be known as the city that never sleeps.* ■ poetic/literary be at peace in death; lie buried: *he sleeps in Holywell cemetery.*
– PHRASES **one could do something in one's sleep** informal one regards something as so easy that it will require no effort or conscious thought to accomplish: *she knew the music perfectly, could sing it in her sleep.* **get to sleep** manage to fall asleep. **go to sleep** fall asleep. ■ (of a limb) become numb as a result of prolonged pressure. **let sleeping dogs lie** proverb avoid interfering in a situation that is currently causing no problems but may well do so as a result of such interference. **lose sleep** see **LOSE**. **put someone to sleep** make someone unconscious by using drugs, alcohol, or an anaesthetic. ■ (also **send someone to sleep**) bore someone greatly. **put something to sleep** kill an animal, especially an old or badly injured one, painlessly (used euphemistically). ■ Computing put a computer on standby while it is not being used. **sleep easy** see **EASY**. **sleep like a log** (or **top**) sleep very soundly. **sleep on it** informal delay making a decision on something until the following day so as to have more time to consider it. **the sleep of the just** a deep, untroubled sleep. **sleep rough** see **ROUGH**. **sleep tight** [usu. in imperative] sleep well (said to someone when parting from them at night). **sleep with one eye open** sleep very lightly, aware of what is happening around one.
– ORIGIN Old English *slēp*, *slǣp* (noun), *slēpan*, *slǣpan* (verb), of Germanic origin; related to Dutch *slapen* and German *schlafen*.
▶ **sleep around** informal have many casual sexual partners.
sleep in remain asleep or in bed later than usual in the morning. ◂ sleep by night at one's place of work.
sleep out sleep outdoors.
sleep over N. Amer. spend the night at a place other than one's own home: *Katie was asked to sleep over with Jenny.*

sleeper ▶ **noun** **1** a person or animal who is asleep.
■ [with adj.] a person with a specified sleep pattern: *he was a light sleeper, for long periods an insomniac.*
2 a thing used for or connected with sleeping, in particular:
■ a train carrying sleeping cars. ■ a sleeping car. ■ a berth in a sleeping car. ■ informal a sleeping pill. ■ (usu. **sleepers**) chiefly N. Amer. a sleepsuit for a baby or small child. ■ N. Amer. a sofa or chair that converts into a bed.
3 a film, book, play, etc. that achieves sudden unexpected success after initially attracting very little attention, typically one that proves popular without much promotion or expenditure.
■ an antique whose true value goes unrecognized for some time. ■ (also **sleeper agent**) a secret agent who remains inactive for a long period while establishing a secure position.
4 Brit. a ring or post worn in a pierced ear to keep the hole from closing.
5 chiefly Brit. a wooden or concrete beam laid transversely under railway track to support it.
6 a stocky fish with mottled coloration which occurs widely in warm seas and fresh water.
● *Dormitator* and other genera, family Gobiidae (or Eleotridae): many species. See also **COCKABULLY**.

sleep-in ▶ **noun** **1** a period of sleeping on the premises where one works, as part of one's duties.
■ [as modifier] denoting a person who sleeps on the premises where they work: *a sleep-in housekeeper.*
2 a form of protest in which the participants sleep overnight in premises which they have occupied: *a student sleep-in began last night.*

sleeping bag ▶ **noun** a warm lined padded bag to sleep in, especially when camping.

sleeping car (Brit. also **sleeping carriage**) ▶ **noun** a railway carriage provided with beds or berths.

sleeping draught ▶ **noun** Brit. dated a drink or drug intended to induce sleep.

sleeping partner ▶ **noun** Brit. a partner not sharing in the actual work of a firm.

sleeping pill ▶ **noun** a tablet of a drug which helps to induce sleep, such as chloral hydrate or a barbiturate sedative.

sleeping policeman ▶ **noun** Brit. a hump in the road intended to cause traffic to reduce speed.

sleeping sickness ▶ **noun** [mass noun] **1** a tropical disease caused by a parasitic protozoan (trypanosome) which is transmitted by the bite of the tsetse fly. It causes fever, chills, pain in the limbs, and anaemia, and eventually affects the nervous system causing extreme lethargy and death. Also called **TRYPANOSOMIASIS**.
2 US term for **SLEEPY SICKNESS**.

sleep-learning ▶ **noun** [mass noun] learning by hearing while asleep, typically by playing a tape recording of what is to be learned.

sleepless ▶ **adjective** characterized by or experiencing lack of sleep: *another sleepless night* | *Lisa lay sleepless.*
■ chiefly poetic/literary continually active or moving: *the sleepless river.*
– DERIVATIVES **sleeplessly** adverb, **sleeplessness** noun.

sleep mode ▶ **noun** Electronics a power-saving mode of operation in which devices or parts of devices are switched off until needed.

sleep-out ▶ **noun** an occasion of sleeping outdoors.

■Austral./NZ a veranda, porch, or outbuilding providing sleeping accommodation.

sleepover ▶**noun** chiefly N. Amer. an occasion of spending the night away from home.

sleepsuit ▶**noun** Brit. a young child's one-piece garment, typically worn as nightwear.

sleepwalk ▶**verb** [no obj.] walk around and sometimes perform other actions while asleep.
▶**noun** an instance of such activity.
– DERIVATIVES **sleepwalker** noun.

sleepy ▶**adjective** (**sleepier**, **sleepiest**) needing or ready for sleep: *the wine had made her sleepy.*
■showing the effects of sleep: *she rubbed her sleepy eyes.* ■ inducing sleep; soporific: *the sleepy heat of the afternoon.* ■ (of a place) without much activity: *he turned off the road into a sleepy little town.* ■ (of a business, organization, or industry) lacking the ability or will to respond to change; not dynamic: *the one-time sleepy world of pensions.*
– DERIVATIVES **sleepily** adverb, **sleepiness** noun.

sleepyhead ▶**noun** a sleepy or inattentive person (usually as a form of address): *come on, sleepyhead, time to get up.*

sleepy sickness ▶**noun** [mass noun] Brit. encephalitis lethargica, a brain infection causing drowsiness and sometimes coma. See also **SLEEPING SICKNESS**.

sleet ▶**noun** [mass noun] rain containing some ice, as when snow melts as it falls.
■US a thin coating of ice formed by sleet or rain freezing on coming into contact with a cold surface.
▶**verb** [no obj.] (**it sleets**, **it is sleeting**, etc.) sleet falls: *it was sleeting so hard we could barely see.*
– DERIVATIVES **sleety** adjective.
– ORIGIN Middle English: of Germanic origin; probably related to Middle Low German *slōten* (plural) 'hail' and German *Schlosse* 'hailstone'.

sleeve ▶**noun 1** the part of a garment that wholly or partly covers a person's arm: *a shirt with the sleeves rolled up.*
■(also **record sleeve** or **album sleeve**) a protective paper or cardboard cover for a record. ■ a protective or connecting tube fitting over or enclosing a rod, spindle, or smaller tube.
2 a windsock.
■a drogue towed by an aircraft.
– PHRASES **up one's sleeve** (of a strategy, idea, or resource) kept secret and in reserve for use when needed: *he was new to the game but had a few tricks up his sleeve.* **wear one's heart on one's sleeve** see **HEART**.
– DERIVATIVES **sleeved** adjective [often in combination] *a cap-sleeved shirt*, **sleeveless** adjective.
– ORIGIN Old English *slēfe*, *slīef(e)*, *slȳf*; related to Middle Dutch *sloove* 'covering'.

sleeve board ▶**noun** a small ironing board over which a sleeve is pulled for pressing.

sleeveen /ˈsliːviːn, sliːˈviːn/ ▶**noun** Irish informal an untrustworthy or cunning person.
– ORIGIN mid 19th cent.: from Irish *slíbhín* 'trickster'.

sleeve link ▶**noun** Brit. dated a cufflink.

sleeve note ▶**noun** Brit. an article printed on a record sleeve giving information about the music or musician.

sleeve nut ▶**noun** a long nut with right-hand and left-hand screw threads for drawing together conversely threaded pipes or shafts.

sleeve valve ▶**noun** a valve in the form of a cylinder which slides to cover and uncover an inlet or outlet.

sleeving ▶**noun** [mass noun] Brit. tubular covering for electrical or other cables.

sleigh ▶**noun** a sledge drawn by horses or reindeer, especially one used for passengers.
▶**verb** [no obj.] [usu. as noun **sleighing**] ride on a sleigh.
– ORIGIN early 17th cent. (originally a North American usage): from Dutch *slee*; related to **SLED**.

sleigh bed ▶**noun** chiefly N. Amer. a bed resembling a sleigh, with outward curving head- and footboards.

sleigh bell ▶**noun** a tinkling bell attached to the harness of a sleigh horse.

sleight /slʌɪt/ ▶**noun** [mass noun] poetic/literary the use of dexterity or cunning, especially so as to deceive: *except by sleight of logic, the two positions cannot be harmonized.*
– PHRASES **sleight of hand** manual dexterity, typically in performing conjuring tricks: *a nifty bit of sleight of hand got the ashtray into the correct position.*
■ skilful deception: *this is financial sleight of hand of the worst sort.*
– ORIGIN Middle English *sleghth* 'cunning, skill', from Old Norse *slœgth*, from *slœgr* 'sly'.

slender ▶**adjective** (**slenderer**, **slenderest**) **1** (of a person or part of the body) gracefully thin: *her slender neck.*
■(especially of a rod or stem) of small girth or breadth: *slender iron railings.*
2 (of something abstract) barely sufficient in amount or basis: *people of slender means | a slender majority of four.*
– DERIVATIVES **slenderly** adverb, **slenderness** noun.
– ORIGIN late Middle English: of unknown origin.

slenderize (also **-ise**) ▶**verb** [with obj.] [usu. as adj. **slenderizing**] chiefly N. Amer. make (a person or a part of their body) appear more slender: *my mother has always held that dark colours are slenderizing.*
■[no obj.] (of a person) lose weight; become slim. ■ figurative reduce the size of (something): *a campaign promise that he would slenderize the executive branch.*

slender loris ▶**noun** see **LORIS**.

slept past and past participle of **SLEEP**.

sleuth /sluːθ/ informal ▶**noun** a detective.
▶**verb** [no obj.] [often as noun **sleuthing**] carry out a search or investigation in the manner of a detective: *scientists began their genetic sleuthing for honey mushrooms four years ago.*
■[with obj.] dated investigate (someone or something).
– ORIGIN Middle English (originally in the sense 'track', in **SLEUTH-HOUND**): from Old Norse *slóth*; compare with **SLOT**[2]. Current senses date from the late 19th cent.

sleuth-hound ▶**noun** dated a bloodhound.
■informal an eager investigator; a detective.

S level ▶**noun** (in the UK except Scotland) an examination, or a pass of one, typically taken together with an A level in the same subject, but having a more advanced syllabus.
– ORIGIN abbreviation of *Special level* or (formerly) *Scholarship level*.

slew[1] (also **slue**) ▶**verb 1** [no obj., with adverbial of direction] (of a vehicle or person) turn or slide violently or uncontrollably in a particular direction: *the Renault slewed from side to side in the snow.*
■[with obj.] turn or slide (something, especially a vehicle) in such a way: *he managed to slew the aircraft round before it settled on the runway.*
2 [no obj.] (of an electronic device) undergo slewing.
▶**noun** [in sing.] a violent or uncontrollable sliding movement: *I was assaulted by the thump and slew of the van.*
– ORIGIN mid 18th cent. (originally in nautical use): of unknown origin.

slew[2] past of **SLAY**[1].

slew[3] ▶**noun** informal, chiefly N. Amer. a large number or quantity of something: *he asked me a slew of questions.*
– ORIGIN mid 19th cent.: from Irish *sluagh*.

slewing ▶**noun** [mass noun] Electronics the response of an electronic device to a sudden large increase in input, especially one that causes the device to respond at its maximum rate.

slew rate ▶**noun** Electronics the maximum rate at which an amplifier can respond to an abrupt change of input level.

sley /sleɪ/ (also **slay**) ▶**noun** a tool used in weaving to force the weft into place.
– ORIGIN Old English *slege*; related to **SLAY**[1].

slice ▶**noun 1** a thin, broad piece of food, such as bread, meat, or cake, cut from a larger portion: *four slices of bread | potato slices.*
■a portion or share of something: *local authorities control a huge slice of public spending.*
2 Golf a stroke which makes the ball curve away to the right (for a left-handed player, the left), typically inadvertently.
■(in other sports) a shot or stroke made with glancing contact so that the ball travels forward spinning.
3 a utensil with a broad, flat blade for lifting foods such as cake and fish.
▶**verb** [with obj.] **1** cut (something, especially food) into slices: *slice the onion into rings | [as adj.* **sliced**] *a sliced loaf.*
■(**slice something off/from**) cut something or a piece of something off or from (something larger), typically with one clean cut: *he sliced a corner from a fried egg |* figurative *he sliced 70 seconds off the record.* ■ cut with or as if with a sharp implement: *the bomber's wings were slicing the air with some efficiency |* [no obj.] *the blade sliced into his palm.* ■ [no obj., with adverbial of direction] move easily and quickly: *Grimsby sliced through Swindon's defence.*
2 Golf strike (the ball) or play (a stroke) so that the ball curves away to the right (for a left-handed player, the left), typically inadvertently.
■(in other sports) propel (the ball) with a glancing contact so that it travels forward spinning: *Evans went and sliced a corner into his own net.*
– PHRASES **a slice of the action** see *a piece of the action* at **PIECE**. **slice of life** a realistic representation of everyday experience in a film, play, or book.
– DERIVATIVES **sliceable** adjective, **slicer** noun [often in combination] *a bacon-slicer.*
– ORIGIN Middle English (in the sense 'fragment, splinter'): shortening of Old French *esclice* 'splinter', from the verb *esclicier*, of Germanic origin; related to German *schleissen* 'to slice', also to **SLIT**.

slick ▶**adjective 1** (of an action or thing) done or operating in an impressively smooth, efficient, and apparently effortless way: *Rangers have been entertaining crowds with a slick passing game.*
■(of a thing) superficially impressive or efficient in presentation: *the brands are backed by slick advertising.* ■ (of a person or their behaviour) smart, adroit, or clever; glibly assured: *a salesperson may be viewed as a slick confidence trickster.*
2 (of skin or hair) smooth and glossy: *a dandy-looking dude with a slick black ponytail.*
■(of a surface) smooth, wet, and slippery: *she tumbled back against the slick, damp wall.*
▶**noun 1** an oil slick.
■a small smear or patch of a glossy or wet substance, especially a cosmetic: *a slick of lip balm.*
2 (usu. **slicks**) a racing-car or bicycle tyre without a tread, for use in dry weather conditions.
3 N. Amer. informal a glossy magazine.
4 N. Amer. informal a smart, clever, or glibly assured person.
▶**verb 1** [with obj. and adverbial] make (one's hair) flat, smooth, and glossy by applying water, oil, or cream to it: *his damp hair was slicked back | [as adj., in combination* **slicked**] *his slicked-down hair.*
■cover with a film of liquid; make wet or slippery: *she woke to find her body slicked with sweat | [as adj., in combination* **-slicked**] *a rain-slicked road.*
2 (**slick someone/thing up**) N. Amer. make someone or something smart, tidy, or stylish.
– DERIVATIVES **slickly** adverb, **slickness** noun.
– ORIGIN Middle English (in the senses 'glossy' and 'make smooth or glossy'): probably from Old English and related to Old Norse *slíkr* 'smooth'; compare with **SLEEK**.

slickenside ▶**noun** (usu. **slickensides**) Geology a polished and striated rock surface that results from friction along a fault or bedding plane.
– ORIGIN mid 18th cent.: from a dialect variant of the adjective **SLICK** + **SIDE**.

slicker chiefly N. Amer. ▶**noun 1** informal a convincing rogue.
■short for **CITY SLICKER**.
2 a raincoat made of smooth material.

slide ▶**verb** (past and past participle **slid**) [no obj., with adverbial of direction] move along a smooth surface while maintaining continuous contact with it: *she slid down the bank into the water | [as adj.* **sliding**] *the tank should have a sliding glass cover.*
■[with obj. and adverbial of direction] move (something) along a surface in such a way: *she slid the keys over the table.* ■ move smoothly, quickly, or unobtrusively: *I quickly slid into a seat at the back of the hall.* ■ [with obj. and adverbial of direction] move (something) in such a way: *she slid the bottle into her pocket.* ■ change gradually to a worse condition or lower level: *the country faces the prospect of sliding from recession into slump.*
▶**noun 1** a structure with a smooth sloping surface for children to slide down.
■a smooth stretch or slope of ice or packed snow for sliding or tobogganing on. ■ an act of moving along a smooth surface while maintaining continuous contact with it: *use an ice axe to halt a slide on ice and snow.* ■ Baseball a sliding approach made to a base along the ground. ■ a decline in value or quality: *the current slide in house prices.*
2 a part of a machine or instrument that slides.
■the place on a machine or instrument where a sliding part operates. ■ [mass noun] slide guitar: *I'd been playing slide for years.*
3 (also **microscope slide**) a rectangular piece of

S

glass on which an object is mounted or placed for examination under a microscope.
■ a mounted transparency, especially one placed in a projector for viewing on a screen: [as modifier] *a slide show.*
4 Brit. a hairslide.
– PHRASES **let something slide** negligently allow something to deteriorate: *Papa had let the business slide after Mama's death.*
– DERIVATIVES **slidable** adjective, **slidably** adverb.
– ORIGIN Old English *slīdan* (verb); related to **SLED** and **SLEDGE**[1]. The noun, first in the sense 'act of sliding', is recorded from the late 16th cent.

slide duplicator (also **slide copier**) ▶ **noun** Photography an optical device attached to the front of camera lens for rephotographing a transparency.

slide fastener ▶ **noun** N. Amer. a zip fastener or similar fastening device.

slide guitar ▶ **noun** [mass noun] a style of guitar playing in which a glissando effect is produced by moving a bottleneck or similar device over the strings, used especially in blues.

slide projector ▶ **noun** a piece of equipment used for displaying photographic slides on a screen.

slider ▶ **noun 1** a North American freshwater turtle with a red or yellow patch on the side of the head.
• Genus *Trachemys* (or *Pseudemys*), family Emydidae: several species, in particular the **pond slider** (*T. scripta*).
2 Electronics a knob or lever which is moved horizontally or vertically to control a variable, such as the volume of a radio.
■ Computing an icon mimicking such a knob or lever.
3 Baseball a pitch that moves laterally as it nears home plate.

slide rule ▶ **noun** a ruler with a sliding central strip, marked with logarithmic scales and used for making rapid calculations, especially multiplication and division.

slide valve ▶ **noun** a piece that opens and closes an aperture by sliding across it.

sliding door ▶ **noun** a door drawn across an aperture on a groove or suspended from a track, rather than turning on hinges.

sliding scale ▶ **noun** a scale of fees, taxes, wages, etc., that varies in accordance with variation of some standard.

sliding seat ▶ **noun** a seat able to slide to and fro on runners, especially one in a racing rowing boat used to adjust the length of a stroke.

slight ▶ **adjective 1** small in degree; inconsiderable: *a slight increase | a slight ankle injury | the chance of success is very slight.*
■ (especially of a creative work) not profound or substantial; rather trivial or superficial: *a slight plot.*
2 (of a person or their build) not sturdy and strongly built: *she was slight and delicate-looking.*
▶ **verb** [with obj.] **1** insult (someone) by treating or speaking of them without proper respect or attention: *he was desperate not to slight a guest* | [as adj. **slighting**] *slighting references to Roman Catholics.*
2 archaic raze or destroy (a fortification).
▶ **noun** an insult caused by a failure to show someone proper respect or attention: *an unintended slight can create grudges | he was seething at the* **slight to** *his authority.*
– PHRASES **not in the slightest** not at all: *he didn't mind in the slightest.* **the slightest ——** [usu. with negative] any —— whatsoever: *I don't have the slightest idea.*
– DERIVATIVES **slightingly** adverb, **slightish** adjective, **slightness** noun.
– ORIGIN Middle English; the adjective from Old Norse *sléttr* 'smooth' (an early sense in English), of Germanic origin; related to Dutch *slechts* 'merely' and German *schlicht* 'simple', *schlecht* 'bad'; the verb (originally in the sense 'make smooth or level'), from Old Norse *slétta*. The sense 'treat with disrespect' dates from the late 16th cent.

slightly ▶ **adverb 1** to a small degree; inconsiderably: *he lowered his voice slightly* | [as submodifier] *they are all slightly different.*
2 (with reference to a person's build) in a slender way: *a slightly built girl.*

Sligo /ˈslʌɪɡəʊ/ a county of the Republic of Ireland, in the west in the province of Connacht.
■ its county town, a seaport on Sligo Bay, an inlet of the Atlantic; pop. 17,300 (1991).

slily ▶ **adverb** variant spelling of *slyly* (see **SLY**).

slim ▶ **adjective** (**slimmer**, **slimmest**) **1** (of a person or their build) gracefully thin; slenderly built (used approvingly): *her slim figure | the girls were tall and slim.*
■ (of a thing) small in width and typically long and narrow in shape: *a slim gold band encircled her wrist.* ■ (of a garment) cut on slender lines; designed to make the wearer appear slim: *a pair of slim, immaculately cut trousers.* ■ (of a business or other organization) reduced to a smaller size in the hope that it will become more efficient.
2 (of something abstract, especially a chance or margin) very small: *there was just a slim chance of success | the evidence is slim.*
3 S. African crafty; sly; unscrupulous. [ORIGIN: Dutch.]
▶ **verb** (**slimmed**, **slimming**) [no obj.] make oneself thinner by dieting and sometimes exercising: *I must slim down a bit* | [as noun **slimming**] *an aid to slimming.*
■ [with obj.] make (a person or a bodily part) thinner in such a way: *how can I* **slim down** *my hips?* ■ [with obj.] reduce (a business or other organization) to a smaller size in the hope of making it more efficient: *restructuring and slimming down the organization.*
▶ **noun 1** [in sing.] a course or period of slimming: *a sponsored slim.*
2 (also **slim disease**) African term for **AIDS**.
– DERIVATIVES **slimly** adverb, **slimness** noun.
– ORIGIN mid 17th cent.: from Low German or Dutch (from a base meaning 'slanting, cross, bad'), of Germanic origin. The pejorative sense found in Dutch and German existed originally in the English noun *slim* 'lazy or worthless person'; compare with the South African usage 'crafty, sly' (sense 3).

slime ▶ **noun** [mass noun] a moist, soft, and slippery substance, typically regarded as repulsive: *the cold stone was wet with slime.*
▶ **verb** [with obj.] cover with slime: *what grass remained was slimed over with pale brown mud.*
– ORIGIN Old English *slīm*, of Germanic origin; related to Dutch *slijm* and German *Schleim* 'mucus, slime', Latin *limus* 'mud', and Greek *limnē* 'marsh'.

slimeball ▶ **noun** informal a repulsive or despicable person.

slime mould ▶ **noun** a simple organism that consists of an acellular mass of creeping jelly-like protoplasm containing nuclei, or a mass of amoeboid cells. When it reaches a certain size it forms a large number of spore cases.
• Division Myxomycota, kingdom Fungi, in particular the class Myxomycetes; also treated as protozoan (phylum Gymnomyxa, kingdom Protista).

slim jim ▶ **noun** informal a very slim person or thing, in particular:
■ (**slim jims**) a pair of long narrow trousers. ■ US a long thin variety of smoked sausage. ■ (trademark in the US) a long flexible metal strip with a hooked end, used by car thieves and others for accessing a locked vehicle.

slimline ▶ **adjective** (of a person or article) slender in design or build.
■ figurative stripped of unnecessary elements; economical: *a slimline orchestra.* ■ (of food or drink) low in calories: *slimline tonic.*

slimmer ▶ **noun** a person who is trying to make themselves thinner by dieting and sometimes exercising.

slim volume ▶ **noun** a book, typically of verse, by a little-known author.

slimy ▶ **adjective** (**slimier**, **slimiest**) covered by or having the feel or consistency of slime: *the thick, slimy mud | the walls were slimy with lichen.*
■ informal disgustingly immoral, dishonest, or obsequious: *he was a slimy people-pleaser.*
– DERIVATIVES **slimily** adverb, **sliminess** noun.

sling[1] ▶ **noun 1** a flexible strap or belt used in the form of a loop to support or raise a hanging weight: *the horse had to be supported by a sling fixed to the roof.*
■ a bandage or soft strap looped round the neck to support an injured arm: *she had her arm in a sling.* ■ a pouch or frame for carrying a baby, supported by a strap round the neck or shoulders. ■ a short length of rope used to provide additional support for the body in abseiling or climbing.
2 a simple weapon in the form of a strap or loop, used to hurl stones or other small missiles.
3 Austral. informal a bribe or gratuity.
▶ **verb** (past and past participle **slung**) **1** [with obj. and adverbial of place] suspend or arrange (something), especially with a strap or straps, so that it hangs loosely in a particular position: *a hammock was slung between two trees.*
■ carry (something, especially a garment) loosely and casually about one's person: *he had his jacket slung over one shoulder.*
2 [with obj. and adverbial of direction] informal throw; fling (often used to express the speaker's casual attitude): *sling a few things into your knapsack.*
■ hurl (a stone or other missile) from a sling or similar weapon. ■ hoist or transfer (something) with a sling: *horse after horse was slung up from the barges.* ■ [no obj.] Austral. informal pay a bribe or gratuity.
– PHRASES **put someone's** (or **have one's**) **ass in a sling** N. Amer. vulgar slang cause someone to be (or be) in trouble. **sling beer** N. Amer. informal work as a bartender. **sling hash** (or **plates**) N. Amer. informal serve food in a cafe or diner. **sling one's hook** see **HOOK**. **slings and arrows** used with reference to adverse factors or circumstances: *the slings and arrows of outrageous critics.* [ORIGIN: with reference to Shakespeare's *Hamlet* III. i. 58.]
– DERIVATIVES **slinger** noun.
– ORIGIN Middle English: probably from Low German, of symbolic origin; compare with German *Schlinge* 'noose, snare'. Sense 2 of the verb is from Old Norse *slyngva*.
▶ **sling off** Austral./NZ informal mock; make fun: *I wasn't slinging off at your religion.*

sling[2] ▶ **noun** a sweetened drink of spirits, especially gin, and water. See also **SINGAPORE SLING**.
– ORIGIN mid 18th cent.: of unknown origin.

slingback ▶ **noun** a shoe held in place by a strap around the ankle above the heel: [as modifier] *high-heeled slingback shoes.*

sling-bag ▶ **noun** Brit. an informal bag, typically made of fabric, with a long strap for hanging it from the shoulder.

slingshot ▶ **noun** a hand-held catapult.
■ a shot from a hand-held catapult. ■ [often as modifier] the effect of the gravitational pull of a celestial body in accelerating and changing the course of another body or a spacecraft.
▶ **verb** (**-shotting**; past and past participle **-shot** or **-shotted**) forcefully accelerate or cause to accelerate through use of gravity: [no obj.] *the car would hit the first dip, then slingshot off the second rise* | [with obj.] *Jupiter's gravity slingshots the fragments toward Earth.*

slink ▶ **verb** (past and past participle **slunk**) [no obj., with adverbial of direction] move smoothly and quietly with gliding steps, in a stealthy or sensuous manner: *the fox came slinking through the bracken.*
■ come or go unobtrusively or furtively: *all the staff have slunk off home.*
▶ **noun** [in sing.] an act of moving in this way: *she moved with a sensuous slink.*
– ORIGIN Old English *slincan* 'crawl, creep'; compare with Middle Dutch and Middle Low German *slinken* 'subside, sink'.

slinky ▶ **adjective** (**slinkier**, **slinkiest**) informal graceful and sinuous in movement, line, or figure: *a slinky black evening dress.*
– DERIVATIVES **slinkily** adverb, **slinkiness** noun.

slip[1] ▶ **verb** (**slipped**, **slipping**) **1** [no obj.] (of a person or animal) slide unintentionally for a short distance, typically losing one's balance or footing: *I slipped over on the ice | he kept slipping in the mud.*
■ [with adverbial of direction] (of a thing) accidentally slide or move out of position or from someone's grasp: *the envelope slipped through Luke's fingers | a wisp of hair had slipped down over her face.* ■ fail to grip or make proper contact with a surface: *the front wheels began to slip* | [as adj. **slipping**] *a badly slipping clutch.* ■ [with adverbial of direction] go or move quietly or quickly, without attracting notice: *we slipped out by a back door.* ■ pass or change to a lower, worse, or different condition, typically in a gradual or imperceptible way: *many people feel standards have slipped* | [with complement] *the bank's shares slipped 1.5p to 227p.* ■ (**be slipping**) informal be behaving in a way that is not up to one's usual level of performance: *you're slipping, Doyle—you need a holiday.* ■ (**slip away/by**) (of time) elapse: *the night was slipping away.* ■ [with obj. and adverbial of direction] put (something) in a particular place or position quietly, quickly, or stealthily: *she slipped the map into her pocket* | [with two objs] *I slipped him a tenner to keep quiet.* ■ (**slip into/out of**) put on or take off (a garment) quickly and easily. ■ (**slip something in**) insert a remark smoothly or adroitly into a conversation.
2 [with obj.] escape or get loose from (a means of restraint): *the giant balloon slipped its moorings.*
■ [no obj.] (**slip out**) (of a remark) be uttered inadvertently. ■ (of a thought or fact) fail to be remembered by (one's mind or memory); elude (one's notice): *a beautiful woman's address was never likely to slip his mind.* ■ release (an animal, typically a

hunting dog) from restraint. ■ Knitting move (a stitch) to the other needle without knitting it. ■ release (the clutch of a motor vehicle) slightly or for a moment. ■ (of an animal) produce (dead young) prematurely; abort.

▶ noun **1** an act of sliding unintentionally for a short distance: *a single slip could send them plummeting down the mountainside.*
■ a fall to a lower level or standard: *a continued slip in house prices.* ■ [mass noun] relative movement of an object or surface and a solid surface in contact with it. ■ a reduction in the movement of a pulley or other mechanism due to slipping of the belt, rope, etc. ■ a sideways movement of an aircraft in flight, typically downwards towards the centre of curvature of a turn. ■ [mass noun] Geology the extent of relative horizontal displacement of corresponding points on either side of a fault plane.
2 a minor or careless mistake: *the judge made a slip in his summing up.*
3 a loose-fitting garment, typically a short petticoat: *a silk slip* | [as modifier] *a slip dress.*
4 Cricket a fielding position (often one of two or more in an arc) close behind the batsman on the off side, for catching balls edged by the batsman: *he was caught in the slips for 32* | *King is at first slip.*
■ a fielder at this position.
5 short for SLIPWAY.
6 (usu. **slips**) a leash which enables a dog to be released quickly.
7 Knitting short for SLIP STITCH: *one colour at a time should be knitted in striped slip.*
– PHRASES **give someone the slip** informal evade or escape from someone. **let something slip 1** reveal something inadvertently in the course of a conversation: [with clause] *Clive had let slip he was married.* **2** archaic release a hound from the leash so as to begin the chase: *let slip the dogs of war.* **let something slip through one's fingers** (or **grasp**) lose hold or possession of something. **slip of the pen** (or **the tongue**) a minor mistake in writing (or speech). **slip through the net** see NET[1]. **there's many a slip 'twixt cup and lip** proverb many things can go wrong between the start of a project and its completion; nothing is certain until it has happened.
– ORIGIN Middle English (in the sense 'move quickly and softly'): probably from Middle Low German *slippen* (verb); compare with SLIPPERY.

▶ **slip away** die peacefully (used euphemistically): *he lay there and quietly slipped away.*
slip something over on informal, dated take advantage of (someone) by trickery.
slip up informal make a careless error: *they often slipped up when it came to spelling.*

slip² ▶ noun **1** a small piece of paper, typically a form for writing on or one giving printed information: *his monthly salary slip* | *complete the tear-off slip below.*
■ Printing a printer's proof on a long piece of paper; a galley proof. ■ a long, narrow strip of a thin material such as wood.
2 a cutting taken from a plant for grafting or planting; a scion.
– PHRASES **a slip of a —** used to denote a small, slim person: *you are little more than a slip of a girl.*
– ORIGIN late Middle English: probably from Middle Dutch, Middle Low German *slippe* 'cut, strip'.

slip³ ▶ noun [mass noun] a creamy mixture of clay, water, and typically a pigment of some kind, used especially for decorating earthenware.
– ORIGIN mid 17th cent.: of obscure origin; compare with Norwegian *slip(a)* 'slime'.

slip-carriage (also **slip-coach**) ▶ noun Brit. historical a railway carriage on an express which could be detached so as to come to rest at a station where the rest of the train did not stop.

slip case ▶ noun a close-fitting case open at one side or end for an object such as a book.

slip casting ▶ noun [mass noun] the manufacture of ceramic ware by allowing slip to solidify in a mould.
– DERIVATIVES **slip-cast** adjective.

slip cover ▶ noun a loose cover, in particular a detachable cover for a chair or sofa.
■ a jacket or slip case for a book.

slip form ▶ noun a mould in which a concrete structure of uniform cross section is cast by filling the mould with liquid concrete and then continuously moving and refilling it at a

sufficiently slow rate for the emerging part to have partially set.

slip knot ▶ noun **1** a knot that can be undone by a pull.
2 a running knot.

slip-on ▶ adjective (especially of shoes or clothes) having no (or few) fastenings and therefore able to be put on and taken off quickly.
▶ noun a shoe or garment that can be easily slipped on and off.

slipover ▶ noun a pullover, typically one without sleeves.
▶ adjective (**slip-over**) [attrib.] (of a garment) designed to be put on over the head: *a slip-over sweater.*

slippage ▶ noun [mass noun] the action or process of something slipping or subsiding; the amount or extent of this: *£16 million has been spent on cracks and slippage.*
■ failure to meet a standard or deadline: the extent of this: *slippage on any job will entail slippage on the overall project.*

slipped ▶ adjective Heraldry (of a flower or leaf) depicted with a stalk.

slipped disc ▶ noun a cartilaginous disc between vertebrae in the spine that is displaced or partly protruding, pressing on nearby nerves and causing back pain or sciatica.

slipper ▶ noun a comfortable slip-on shoe that is worn indoors.
■ a light slip-on shoe, especially one used for dancing.
▶ verb [with obj.] beat (someone) with a slipper.
– DERIVATIVES **slippered** adjective.

slipper bath ▶ noun Brit., chiefly historical a bath with one high end to lean against and the other end covered in.

slipperette ▶ noun (trademark in the US) a soft slipper or similar foot covering, especially a disposable slipper of a kind distributed to airline passengers.

slipper flower ▶ noun another term for CALCEOLARIA.

slipper limpet ▶ noun a mollusc which has an oval shell with an internal ledge, giving the empty shell a slipper-like appearance. Also called **BOAT SHELL** in North America.
● Genus *Crepidula*, family Crepidulidae, class Gastropoda: many species, especially the North American *C. fornicata*, which has become a serious pest of oyster beds in Europe.

slipper orchid ▶ noun another term for LADY'S SLIPPER.

slipper satin ▶ noun [mass noun] a fine-quality semi-glossy satin, used in dressmaking and for dancing slippers.

slipper sock ▶ noun a thick sock, typically with a leather sole, for use as a slipper.

slippery ▶ adjective (of a surface or object) difficult to hold firmly or stand on because it is smooth, wet, or slimy: *slippery ice* | *her hand was slippery with sweat.*
■ (of a person) evasive and unpredictable; not to be relied on: *Martin's a slippery customer.* ■ (of a word or concept) elusive in meaning because changing according to one's point of view: *the word 'intended' is a decidedly slippery one.*
– PHRASES **slippery slope** an idea or course of action which will lead to something unacceptable, wrong, or disastrous: *he is on the slippery slope towards a life of crime.*
– DERIVATIVES **slipperily** adverb, **slipperiness** noun.
– ORIGIN late 15th cent.: from dialect *slipper* 'slippery', probably suggested by Luther's *schlipfferig*.

slippery elm ▶ noun a North American elm with coarsely textured leaves and rough outer bark.
● *Ulmus fulva*, family Ulmaceae.
■ [mass noun] the mucilaginous inner bark of this tree used medicinally.

slippery hitch ▶ noun a kind of knot made fast by catching part of the rope beneath the loop, released by pulling on the free end.

slippy ▶ adjective (**slippier**, **slippiest**) informal slippery: *the towpath was slippy with mud* | *slippy tyres.*
– PHRASES **look** (or **be**) **slippy** Brit. dated be quick.
– DERIVATIVES **slippiness** noun.

slip ring ▶ noun a ring in a dynamo or electric motor which is attached to and rotates with the shaft, passing an electric current to a circuit via a fixed brush pressing against it.

slip road ▶ noun Brit. a road entering or leaving a motorway or dual carriageway.

slip-rope ▶ noun a mooring rope with both ends on board ship, enabling the crew to cast off without disembarking.

slip sheet ▶ noun Printing a sheet of paper placed between newly printed sheets to prevent set-off or smudging.

slipshod ▶ adjective (typically of a person or method of work) characterized by a lack of care, thought, or organization: *he'd caused many problems with his slipshod management.*
■ archaic (of shoes) worn down at the heel.
– ORIGIN late 16th cent. (originally in the sense 'wearing slippers or loose shoes'): from the verb SLIP[1] + SHOD.

slip-slop ▶ noun South African term for FLIP-FLOP.

slip stitch ▶ noun **1** (in sewing) a loose stitch joining layers of fabric and not visible externally.
2 [mass noun] [often as modifier] Knitting a type of stitch in which the stitches are moved from one needle to the other without being knitted: *a slip stitch pattern.*
▶ verb (**slip-stitch**) [with obj.] sew or knit with stitches of such kinds.

slipstone ▶ noun a shaped oilstone used to sharpen gouges.

slipstream ▶ noun a current of air or water driven back by a revolving propeller or jet engine.
■ the partial vacuum created in the wake of a moving vehicle, often used by other vehicles in a race to assist in overtaking. ■ figurative an assisting force regarded as drawing something along behind something else: *when the US economy booms, the rest of the world is pulled along in the slipstream.*
▶ verb [no obj.] (especially in motor racing) follow closely behind another vehicle, travelling in its slipstream and awaiting an opportunity to overtake.
■ [with obj.] travel in the slipstream of (someone), especially in order to overtake them.

slip-up ▶ noun informal a mistake or blunder.

slipware ▶ noun [mass noun] pottery decorated with slip (see SLIP[3]).

slipway ▶ noun a slope built leading into water, used for launching and landing boats and ships or for building and repairing them.

slit ▶ noun a long, narrow cut or opening: *make a slit in the stem under a bud* | *arrow slits.*
▶ verb (**slitting**; past and past participle **slit**) [with obj.] make a long, narrow cut in (something): *give me the truth or I will slit your throat* | [with obj. and complement] *he slit open the envelope.*
■ cut (something) into strips: *a wide recording head magnetizes the tape before it is slit to domestic size.* ■ (past and past participle **slitted**) form (one's eyes) into slits; squint.
– DERIVATIVES **slitter** noun.
– ORIGIN late Old English *slite* (noun); related to Old English *slītan* 'split, rend' (of Germanic origin).

slit-eyed ▶ adjective (of a person or expression) having long narrow eyes or narrowing the eyes by squinting.

slither ▶ verb [no obj., with adverbial of direction] move smoothly over a surface with a twisting or oscillating motion: *I spied a baby adder slithering away.*
■ slide or slip unsteadily on a loose or slippery surface: *we slithered down a snowy mountain track.*
▶ noun **1** [in sing.] a movement in such a manner: *a snake-like slither across the grass.*
2 a sliver: *a slither of bacon.*
– DERIVATIVES **slithery** adjective.
– ORIGIN Middle English: alteration of the dialect verb *slidder*, frequentative from the base of SLIDE.

slit lamp ▶ noun Medicine a lamp which emits a narrow but intense beam of light, used for examining the interior of the eye.

slit limpet ▶ noun a limpet-like marine mollusc which has a characteristic slit in the margin of the shell.
● Genus *Emarginula*, family Fissurellidae, class Gastropoda.

slit pocket ▶ noun a side pocket with a vertical opening.

slit trench ▶ noun a narrow trench for a soldier or a small group of soldiers and their equipment.

slitty ▶ adjective (**slittier**, **slittiest**) chiefly derogatory (of the eyes) long and narrow.

Sliven /'sliːv(ə)n/ a commercial city in east central

Bulgaria, in the foothills of the Balkan Mountains; pop. 150,210 (1990).

sliver /ˈslɪvə, ˈslʌɪ-/ ▶ **noun** a small, thin, narrow piece of something cut or split off a larger piece: *a sliver of cheese* | figurative *there was a sliver of light under his door.*
■ a strip of loose untwisted textile fibres produced by carding.
▶ **verb** [with obj.] [usu. as adj. **slivered**] cut or break (something) into small, thin, narrow pieces: *slivered almonds.*
■ convert (textile fibres) into slivers.
– ORIGIN late Middle English: from dialect *slive* 'cleave'.

slivovitz /ˈslɪvəvɪts/ ▶ **noun** [mass noun] a type of plum brandy made chiefly in the former Yugoslavia and in Romania.
– ORIGIN from Serbo-Croat *šljivovica*, from *šljiva* 'plum'.

Sloane[1], Sir Hans (1660–1753), Irish physician and naturalist. He endowed the Chelsea Physic Garden, and his books and specimens formed the basis of the British Museum Library and the Natural History Museum in London.

Sloane[2] (also **Sloane Ranger**) ▶ **noun** Brit. informal a fashionable upper-class young person (typically a woman) of independent means, especially one living in London.
– DERIVATIVES **Sloaney** adjective.
– ORIGIN 1970s: from *Sloane* Square, London (+ Lone *Ranger*, the name of a fictitious cowboy hero).

slob ▶ **noun 1** informal a lazy and slovenly person.
2 [mass noun] Irish muddy land.
▶ **verb** [no obj.] informal behave in a lazy and slovenly manner: *when your body is your fortune, you can't afford to slob out.*
– DERIVATIVES **slobbish** adjective, **slobby** adjective.
– ORIGIN late 18th cent.: from Irish *slab* 'mud', from Anglo-Irish *slab* 'ooze, sludge', probably of Scandinavian origin.

slobber ▶ **verb** [no obj.] have saliva dripping copiously from the mouth: *Fido tended to slobber* | [as adj. **slobbering**] *big slobbering kisses.*
■ (**slobber over**) figurative show excessive enthusiasm for: *news executives slobbered over him for autographs.*
▶ **noun** [mass noun] saliva dripping copiously from the mouth.
– DERIVATIVES **slobbery** adjective.
– ORIGIN late Middle English: probably from Middle Dutch *slobberen* 'walk through mud', also 'feed noisily', of imitative origin.

sloe ▶ **noun** another term for **BLACKTHORN.**
■ the small bluish-black fruit of the blackthorn, with a sharp sour taste.
– ORIGIN Old English *slā(h)*, of Germanic origin; related to Dutch *slee* and German *Schlehe*, from an Indo-European root probably shared by Latin *livere* 'be blue' and Serbo-Croat *šljiva* 'plum'.

sloe-eyed ▶ **adjective** having attractive dark, typically almond-shaped eyes.

sloe gin ▶ **noun** [mass noun] a liqueur made by steeping sloes in gin.

slog ▶ **verb** (**slogged**, **slogging**) **1** [no obj.] work hard over a period of time: *they were slogging away to meet a deadline.*
■ [with adverbial of direction] walk or move with difficulty or effort: *I slogged through the heather in the heat.*
2 [with obj.] hit forcefully and typically wildly, especially in boxing or cricket: *batsmen careering down the pitch to slog the ball up in the air* | [no obj.] *the fighters were slogging away.*
■ (**slog it out**) fight or compete fiercely: *they'll be slogging it out in the first round of the cup next Sunday.*
▶ **noun 1** [usu. in sing.] a spell of difficult, tiring work or travelling: *it would be a hard slog back to the camp* | [mass noun] *it wasn't all slog during those years.*
2 a forceful and uncontrolled hit, especially in cricket: *a slog hit the fielder on the helmet.*
– DERIVATIVES **slogger** noun.
– ORIGIN early 19th cent.: of unknown origin; compare with **SLUG**[2].

slogan ▶ **noun** a short and striking or memorable phrase used in advertising.
■ a motto associated with a political party or movement or other group. ■ historical a Scottish Highland war cry.
– ORIGIN early 16th cent.: from Scottish Gaelic *sluagh-ghairm*, from *sluagh* 'army' + *gairm* 'shout'.

sloganeer chiefly US ▶ **verb** [no obj.] [usu. as noun

sloganeering] employ or invent slogans, especially in a political context.
▶ **noun** a person who does this.

sloka /ˈʃləʊkə/ ▶ **noun** a couplet of Sanskrit verse, especially one in which each line contains sixteen syllables.
– ORIGIN from Sanskrit *śloka* 'noise, praise'.

slo-mo ▶ **noun** informal short for **SLOW MOTION.**

sloop ▶ **noun** a one-masted sailing boat with a mainsail and jib rigged fore and aft.
■ (also **sloop of war**) historical a small square-rigged sailing warship with two or three masts. ■ historical a small anti-submarine warship used for convoy escort in the Second World War.
– ORIGIN early 17th cent.: from Dutch *sloep(e)*, of unknown origin.

sloosh Brit. informal ▶ **noun** a rushing of water; an energetic rinsing: *a sloosh with this mouthwash helps loosen plaque.*
■ [mass noun] the heavy splashing or rushing noise made in this way: *the sloosh of water in the culverts.*
▶ **verb** [no obj., with adverbial] (of liquid) flow or pour with a rush: *she gazed at the torrent of water slooshing downstream.*
■ [with obj.] rinse (something) with a rush of water: *sloosh down the changing-room floor.*
– ORIGIN early 20th cent.: imitative.

sloot /sluːt/ (also **sluit**) ▶ **noun** S. African a deep gully eroded by rainfall.
■ historical a narrow water channel constructed for irrigation.
– ORIGIN Afrikaans, from Dutch *sloot* 'ditch'.

slop[1] ▶ **verb** (**slopped**, **slopping**) **1** [no obj., with adverbial of direction] (of a liquid) spill or flow over the edge of a container, typically as a result of careless handling: *water slopped over the edge of the sink.*
■ [with obj.] cause (a liquid) to spill or overflow in such a way: *in spite of his care he slopped some water.* ■ [with obj. and adverbial] apply or put (something) somewhere in a casual or careless manner: *they spent their weekend slopping on paint.* ■ (**slop through**) wade through (a wet or muddy area): *they were slopping through paddy fields.*
2 [with obj.] feed slops to (an animal).
3 [no obj.] chiefly N. Amer. speak or write in a sentimentally effusive manner; gush: *she slopped over her dog.*
▶ **noun 1** (**slops**) waste water from a kitchen, bathroom, or chamber pot that has to be emptied by hand: *sink slops.*
■ semi-liquid kitchen refuse, often used as animal food. ■ unappetizing weak, semi-liquid food.
2 [mass noun] chiefly N. Amer. sentimental language or material: *country music is not all commercial slop.*
3 Nautical a choppy sea.
– ORIGIN mid 16th cent. (in the sense 'to spill, splash'): probably related to **SLIP**[3]. Early use of the noun denoted 'slushy mud', the first of the current senses ('unappetizing food') dating from the mid 17th cent.

slop about/around chiefly Brit. (of a person) dress in an untidy or casual manner: *at weekends he would slop about in his oldest clothes.*
slop out (especially in prison) empty the contents of a chamber pot: [as noun **slopping out**] *the indignity of slopping out.*

slop[2] ▶ **noun** archaic **1** a workman's loose outer garment.
2 (**slops**) wide, baggy trousers common in the 16th and early 17th centuries, especially as worn by sailors.
■ clothes and bedding supplied to sailors by the navy. ■ chiefly Brit. ready-made or cheap clothing.
– ORIGIN late Middle English (in sense 1): from the second element of Old English *oferslop* 'surplice', of Germanic origin.

slop basin (also N. Amer. **slop bowl**) ▶ **noun** Brit. a bowl for the dregs of cups of tea or coffee.

slop bucket ▶ **noun** a bucket for removing waste from a kitchen or chamber pot.

slope ▶ **noun 1** a surface of which one end or side is at a higher level than another; a rising or falling surface: *he slithered helplessly down the slope.*
■ a difference in level or sideways position between the two ends or sides of a thing: *the roof should have a slope sufficient for proper drainage* | [mass noun] *the backward slope of the chair.* ■ (often **slopes**) a part of the side of a hill or mountain, especially as a place for skiing: *a ten-minute cable car ride delivers you to the slopes.* ■ the gradient of a graph at any point. ■ Electronics the mutual conductance of a valve,

numerically equal to the gradient of one of the characteristic curves of the valve.
2 US informal, offensive an oriental person, especially a Vietnamese.
▶ **verb** [no obj.] **1** (of a surface or line) be inclined from a horizontal or vertical line; slant up or down: *the garden sloped down to a stream* | *the ceiling sloped* | [as adj. **sloping**] *a sloping floor.*
■ [with obj.] place or arrange in such a position or inclination: *Poole sloped his shoulders* | [as adj. **sloped**] *a sloped leather writing surface.*
2 [no obj., with adverbial of direction] informal move in an idle or aimless manner: *I had seen Don sloping about the beach.*
– PHRASES **at the slope** Military (of a rifle) held with the barrel on the left shoulder and the butt in the left hand. **slope arms** Military hold a rifle at the slope.
– ORIGIN late 16th cent. (as a verb): from the obsolete adverb *slope*, a shortening of **ASLOPE**. The use of the verb with reference to aimless or unobtrusive movement may be related to **LOPE**.

slope off informal leave unobtrusively, typically in order to evade work or duty: *the men sloped off looking ashamed of themselves.*

sloppy ▶ **adjective** (**sloppier**, **sloppiest**) **1** (of semi-fluid matter) containing too much liquid; watery and disagreeable or unsatisfactory: *do not make the concrete too sloppy.*
2 careless and unsystematic; excessively casual: *your speech has always been sloppy.*
■ (of a garment) casual and loose-fitting: *wearing a sloppy sweater and jeans.*
3 (of literature or behaviour) weakly or foolishly sentimental: *lovers of sloppy romance.*
– DERIVATIVES **sloppily** adverb, **sloppiness** noun.

sloppy joe ▶ **noun** informal **1** a long, loose-fitting sweater.
2 N. Amer. a hamburger in which the minced-beef filling is made into a kind of meat sauce, typically with tomatoes and spices.

slosh ▶ **verb 1** [no obj., with adverbial of direction] (of liquid in a container) move irregularly with a splashing sound: *water in the boat sloshed about under our feet* | figurative *there is so much money now sloshing around in professional tennis.*
■ (of a person) move through liquid with a splashing sound: *they sloshed up the tracks in the dank woods.* ■ [with obj. and adverbial of direction] pour (liquid) clumsily: *she sloshed coffee into a cracked cup.*
2 [with obj.] Brit. informal hit (someone) hard.
▶ **noun 1** an act or sound of splashing: *the distant slosh of the washing machine in the basement.*
■ a quantity of liquid that is poured out: *I gave Michael and myself another slosh of rye.*
2 Brit. informal a heavy blow.
– ORIGIN early 19th cent.: variant of the noun **SLUSH**.

sloshed ▶ **adjective** informal drunk: *I drank a lot of wine and got sloshed.*

sloshy ▶ **adjective** (**sloshier**, **sloshiest**) **1** wet and sticky; slushy: *the hoofprints are sloshy depressions.*
2 excessively sentimental; sloppy: *the programme is a sloshy and patronizing affair.*

slot[1] ▶ **noun 1** a long, narrow aperture or slit in a machine for something to be inserted: *he slid a coin into the slot of the jukebox.*
■ a groove or channel into which something fits or in which something works, such as one in the head of a screw.
2 an allotted place in an arrangement or scheme such as a broadcasting schedule: *a late-night television slot* | *landing slots at Heathrow airport.*
▶ **verb** (**slotted**, **slotting**) [with obj. and adverbial of direction] place (something) into a long, narrow aperture: *he slotted a cassette into the tape machine* | *the plates come in sections that can be slotted together.*
■ [no obj.] be placed or able to be placed into such an aperture: *the processors will slot into a personal computer.* ■ Brit. informal (of a soccer player) score (a goal) with a precise shot: *he slotted in the opening goal.* ■ [no obj.] (**slot in/into**) (of a person) fit easily into (a new role or situation): *employers look for someone who will slot into the office culture.*
– DERIVATIVES **slotted** adjective.
– ORIGIN late Middle English (in the sense 'slight depression running down the middle of the chest', surviving as a Scots term): from Old French *esclot*, of obscure origin.

slot[2] ▶ **noun** (usu. **slots**) the track of a deer, visible as slotted footprints in soft ground.

– ORIGIN late 16th cent.: from Old French *esclot* 'hoofprint of a horse', probably from Old Norse *slóth* 'trail'; compare with **SLEUTH**.

slotback ▶ noun American Football a back between the tackle and the split end.

slot car ▶ noun N. Amer. an electrically driven miniature racing car which travels in a slot in a track.

sloth /slәʊθ/ ▶ noun **1** [mass noun] reluctance to work or make an effort; laziness: *he should overcome his natural sloth and complacency.*
2 a slow-moving tropical American mammal that hangs upside down from the branches of trees using its long limbs and hooked claws.
• Families Bradypodidae (three species of **three-toed sloth** in genus *Bradypus*) and Megalonychidae (two species of **two-toed sloth** in genus *Choloepus*), order Xenarthra (or Edentata).
– ORIGIN Old English: from **SLOW** + **-TH**[2].

sloth bear ▶ noun a shaggy-coated nocturnal Indian bear which uses its long curved claws for hanging upside down like a sloth and for opening termite mounds to feed on the insects.
• *Melursus ursinus*, family Ursidae.

slothful ▶ adjective lazy: *fatigue made him slothful.*
– DERIVATIVES **slothfully** adverb, **slothfulness** noun.

slot machine ▶ noun a machine worked by the insertion of a coin, in particular:
■ Brit. a vending machine selling small items. ■ a fruit machine.

slotted spoon ▶ noun a large spoon with slots for straining food.

slouch ▶ verb **1** [no obj., with adverbial] stand, move, or sit in a lazy, drooping way: *he slouched against the wall* | (**be slouched**) *he was slouched in his chair.*
2 [with obj.] dated bend one side of the brim of (a hat) downwards.
▶ noun [in sing.] **1** a lazy, drooping posture or movement: *his stance was a round-shouldered slouch.*
2 [usu. with negative] informal an incompetent person: *my brother was no slouch at making a buck.*
3 a downward bend of a hat brim.
– DERIVATIVES **slouchy** adjective.
– ORIGIN early 16th cent. (in the sense 'lazy, slovenly person'): of unknown origin. *Slouching* was used to mean 'hanging down, drooping' (specifically describing a hat with a brim hanging over the face), and 'having an awkward posture' from the 17th cent.

slouch hat ▶ noun a hat with a wide flexible brim.

Slough /slaʊ/ a town to the west of London; pop. 97,400 (1981).

slough[1] /slaʊ/ ▶ noun a swamp.
■ figurative a situation characterized by lack of progress or activity: *the economic slough of the interwar years.* ■ N. Amer. a muddy side channel or inlet.
– DERIVATIVES **sloughy** adjective.
– ORIGIN Old English *slōh, slō(g)*, of unknown origin.

slough[2] /slʌf/ ▶ verb [with obj.] (of an animal, especially a snake, or a person) cast off or shed (an old skin or dead skin): *a snake **sloughs off** its old skin* | figurative *he is concerned to **slough off** the country's bad environmental image.*
■ [no obj.] (**slough off**) (of dead skin) drop off; be shed. ■ [no obj.] (**slough away/down**) (of soil or rock) collapse or slide into a hole or depression.
▶ noun [mass noun] the dropping off of dead tissue from living flesh: *the drugs can cause blistering and slough.*
– DERIVATIVES **sloughy** adjective.
– ORIGIN Middle English (as a noun denoting a skin, especially the outer skin shed by a snake): perhaps related to Low German *slu(we)* 'husk, peel'. The verb dates from the early 18th cent.

Slough of Despond /slaʊ/ a deep boggy place in John Bunyan's *The Pilgrim's Progress* between the City of Destruction and the gate at the beginning of Christian's journey.
■ [as noun] a state of hopeless depression: *while everyone is having a blast I am sinking into the Slough of Despond.*

Slovak /'slәʊvak/ ▶ noun **1** a native or national of Slovakia, or a person of Slovak descent.
2 [mass noun] the Western Slavic language of Slovakia, with about 5 million speakers.
▶ adjective of or relating to this people or their language.
– ORIGIN the name in Slovak, from a Slavic root shared with **SLOVENE** and perhaps related to *slovo* 'word'.

Slovakia /slә'vakɪә, -'vɑːkɪә/ a country in central Europe; pop. 5,268,935 (1991); official language, Slovak; capital, Bratislava.

> Slovakia was dominated by Hungary until it declared independence in 1918 and united with the Czech-speaking areas of Bohemia and Moravia to form Czechoslovakia. The eastern of the two constituent republics of Czechoslovakia, Slovakia became independent on the partition of that country on 1 January 1993.

– DERIVATIVES **Slovakian** adjective & noun.

sloven /'slʌv(ә)n/ ▶ noun dated a person who is habitually untidy or careless.
– ORIGIN late 15th cent. (in the sense 'person with base manners'): perhaps from Flemish *sloef* 'dirty' or Dutch *slof* 'careless, negligent'.

Slovene /'slәʊviːn, slәʊ'viːn/ ▶ noun **1** a native or national of Slovenia, or a person of Slovene descent.
2 [mass noun] the Southern Slavic language of this people, with about 2 million speakers.
▶ adjective of or relating to Slovenia, its people, or their language.
– ORIGIN from Slovene *Slovenec*, from a Slavic root shared with **SLOVAK** and perhaps related to *slovo* 'word'.

Slovenia /slә'viːnɪә/ a country in SE Europe, formerly a constituent republic of Yugoslavia; pop. 1,962,000 (est. 1991); official language, Slovene; capital, Ljubljana.

> Slovenia formed part of the Austrian empire and in 1919 was ceded to the kingdom of Serbs, Croats, and Slovenes (named Yugoslavia from 1929) of which it remained a constituent republic until it declared its independence in 1991.

Slovenian ▶ noun & adjective another term for **SLOVENE**.

slovenly ▶ adjective (especially of a person or their appearance) untidy and dirty: *he was upbraided for his slovenly appearance.*
■ (especially of a person or action) careless; excessively casual: *slovenly speech.*
– DERIVATIVES **slovenliness** noun.

slow ▶ adjective **1** moving or operating, or designed to do so, only at a low speed; not quick or fast: *until recently, diesel cars were slow and noisy* | *a slow dot-matrix printer.*
■ taking a long time to perform a specified action: *she was rather a slow reader* | [with infinitive] *large organizations can be slow to change.* ■ lasting or taking a long time: *a slow process* | *the journey home was slow.* ■ [attrib.] not allowing or intended for fast travel: *the slow lane.* ■ (of a sports field or ground) likely to make the ball bounce or run slowly or to prevent competitors from travelling fast.
2 [predic. or as complement] (of a clock or watch) showing a time earlier than the correct time: *the clock was five minutes slow.*
3 not prompt to understand, think, or learn: *he's so slow, so unimaginative.*
4 uneventful and rather dull: *a slow and mostly aimless narrative.*
■ (of business) with little activity; slack: *sales were slow.*
5 Photography (of a film) needing long exposure.
■ (of a lens) having a small aperture.
6 (of a fire or oven) burning or giving off heat gently: *bake the dish in a preheated slow oven.*
▶ adverb at a slow pace; slowly: *the train went slower and slower* | [in combination] *a slow-moving river.*
▶ verb [no obj.] reduce one's speed or the speed of a vehicle or process: *the train slowed to a halt* | *investment has **slowed down*** | [with obj.] *he slowed the car.*
■ (**slow down/up**) live or work less actively or intensely: *I wasn't feeling well and had to slow down.*
– PHRASES **slow but** (or **and**) **sure** not quick but achieving the required result eventually: *I am making good progress—slow but sure.*
– DERIVATIVES **slowish** adjective, **slowness** noun.
– ORIGIN Old English *slāw* 'slow-witted, sluggish', of Germanic origin.

> **USAGE** The word **slow** is normally used as an adjective (*a **slow** learner*; *the journey was **slow***). It is also used as an adverb in certain specific contexts, including compounds such as **slow-acting** and **slow-moving** and in the expression **go slow**. Other adverbial use is informal and usually regarded as non-standard, as for example in *he drives too **slow*** and *go as **slow** as you can*. In such contexts standard English uses **slowly** instead. The use of **slow** and **slowly** in this respect contrasts with the use of **fast**, which is completely standard in use as both an adjective and an adverb; there is no word 'fastly'.

slowcoach ▶ noun Brit. informal a person who acts or moves slowly: *'Come on, slowcoach,' urged George.*

slow cooker ▶ noun a large electric pot used for cooking food, especially stews, very slowly.

slowdown ▶ noun an act of slowing down: *a traffic slowdown in the passing lane.*
■ a decline in economic activity.

slow drag ▶ noun a slow blues rhythm or piece of music.
▶ verb (**slow-drag**) [no obj.] dance to such a rhythm.

slow handclap ▶ noun [in sing.] an instance of slow, rhythmic clapping by an audience as a sign of displeasure or impatience.

slow loris ▶ noun see **LORIS**.

slowly ▶ adverb at a slow speed; not quickly: *they moved forward slowly.*
– PHRASES **slowly but surely** achieving the desired results gradually and reliably rather than quickly and spectacularly: *the new church began, slowly but surely, to grow.*

slow march ▶ noun [in sing.] a military marching pace approximately half the speed of the quick march.

slow match ▶ noun [mass noun] historical a slow-burning wick or cord for lighting explosives.

slow motion ▶ noun [mass noun] the action of showing film or playing back video more slowly than it was made or recorded, so that the action appears much slower than in real life: *the scene was shown **in slow motion*** | [as modifier] *a slow-motion sequence.*

slow neutron ▶ noun a neutron with low kinetic energy especially after moderation.

slowpoke ▶ noun informal North American term for **SLOWCOACH**.

slow puncture ▶ noun chiefly Brit. a puncture causing only gradual deflation of a tyre.

slow reactor ▶ noun Physics a nuclear reactor using mainly slow neutrons.

slow-scan ▶ adjective [attrib.] Telecommunications scanning at a much slower rate than usual, so that the resulting signal has a much smaller bandwidth: *a slow-scan transmission.*

slow-twitch ▶ adjective [attrib.] Physiology (of a muscle fibre) contracting slowly, providing endurance rather than strength.

slow virus ▶ noun a virus or virus-like organism that multiplies slowly in the host organism and has a long incubation period.

slow-worm ▶ noun a small snake-like Eurasian legless lizard that is typically brownish or copper-coloured and which gives birth to live young. Also called **BLINDWORM**.
• *Anguis fragilis*, family Anguidae.
– ORIGIN Old English *slāwyrm*, from *slā-* (of uncertain origin) + *wyrm* 'snake'.

SLR ▶ abbreviation for ■ self-loading rifle. ■ single-lens reflex.

slub[1] ▶ noun a lump or thick place in yarn or thread.
■ [mass noun] fabric woven from yarn with such a texture.
▶ adjective [attrib.] (of fabric) having an irregular appearance caused by uneven thickness of the warp.
– DERIVATIVES **slubbed** adjective.
– ORIGIN early 19th cent.: of unknown origin.

slub[2] ▶ noun [mass noun] wool that has been slightly twisted in preparation for spinning.
▶ verb (**slubbed**, **slubbing**) [with obj.] twist (wool) in this way.
– ORIGIN mid 19th cent.: of unknown origin.

sludge ▶ noun [mass noun] thick, soft, wet mud or a similar viscous mixture of liquid and solid components, especially the product of an industrial or refining process.
■ dirty oil, especially in the sump of an internal-combustion engine. ■ [usu. as modifier] a dark, muddy shade of brown or green: *a trendy sludge green.* ■ sea ice newly formed in small pieces.
– DERIVATIVES **sludgy** adjective.
– ORIGIN early 17th cent.: of uncertain origin; compare with **SLUSH**.

slue ▶ verb & noun variant spelling of **SLEW**[1].

slug[1] ▶ noun **1** a tough-skinned terrestrial mollusc which typically lacks a shell and secretes a film of mucus for protection. It can be a serious plant pest. See also **SEA SLUG**.

S

• Order Stylommatophora, class Gastropoda.
2 an amount of an alcoholic drink, typically liquor, that is gulped or poured: *he took **a slug of** whisky.* [ORIGIN: mid 18th cent.: figuratively from sense 3.]
3 an elongated, typically rounded piece of metal: *the reactor uses embedded **slugs of** uranium.*
■ a bullet, especially one of lead. ■ a missile for an air gun. ■ a distinct mass of any substance: *removing spent **slugs of** gum from under the bench.* ■ a line of type in Linotype printing.
▶ **verb** (**slugged**, **slugging**) [with obj.] drink (something, typically alcohol) in a large draught; swig: *she picked up her drink and slugged it straight back.*
– ORIGIN late Middle English (in the sense 'sluggard'): probably of Scandinavian origin; compare with Norwegian dialect *slugg* 'large heavy body'. Sense 1 dates from the early 18th cent.

slug[2] informal, chiefly N. Amer. ▶ **verb** (**slugged**, **slugging**) [with obj.] strike (someone) with a hard blow: *he was the one who'd get slugged.*
■ (**slug it out**) settle a dispute or contest by fighting or competing fiercely: *they went outside to slug it out.*
▶ **noun** a hard blow.
– DERIVATIVES **slugger** noun.
– ORIGIN mid 19th cent.: of unknown origin; compare with the verb **SLOG**.

slugabed ▶ **noun** a lazy person who stays in bed late.
– ORIGIN late 16th cent.: from the rare verb *slug* 'be lazy or slow' + **ABED**.

slugfest ▶ **noun** N. Amer. informal a tough and challenging contest, especially in sports such as boxing and baseball.
– ORIGIN early 20th cent.: from **SLUG**[2] + **-FEST**.

sluggard ▶ **noun** a lazy, sluggish person.
– DERIVATIVES **sluggardliness** noun, **sluggardly** adjective.
– ORIGIN Middle English: from the rare verb *slug* 'be lazy or slow' + **-ARD**.

sluggish ▶ **adjective** slow-moving or inactive: *a sluggish stream.*
■ lacking energy or alertness: *Alex woke late feeling tired and sluggish.* ■ slow to respond or make progress: *the car had been sluggish all morning.*
– DERIVATIVES **sluggishly** adverb, **sluggishness** noun.
– ORIGIN late Middle English: from the noun **SLUG**[1] or the verb *slug* (see **SLUGGARD**) + **-ISH**[1].

slug pellet ▶ **noun** a pellet containing a substance poisonous to slugs, placed among growing plants to prevent them being damaged.

sluice /sluːs/ ▶ **noun** **1** (also **sluice gate**) a sliding gate or other device for controlling the flow of water, especially one in a lock gate.
■ (also **sluiceway**) an artificial water channel for carrying off overflow or surplus water. ■ (in gold mining) a channel or trough constructed with grooves into which a current of water is directed in order to separate gold from the ore containing it.
2 an act of rinsing or showering with water: *a sluice with cold water.*
▶ **verb** [with obj.] wash or rinse freely with a stream or shower of water: *she sluiced her face in cold water | crews **sluiced down** the decks of their ship.*
■ [no obj., with adverbial of direction] (of water) pour, flow, or shower freely: *the waves sluiced over them.*
– ORIGIN Middle English (as a noun): from Old French *escluse* 'sluice gate', based on Latin *excludere* 'exclude'. The verb dates from the late 16th cent.

sluit /sluːt, ˈsluːɪt/ ▶ **noun** variant spelling of **SLOOT**.

slum ▶ **noun** a squalid and overcrowded urban street or district inhabited by very poor people.
■ a house or building unfit for human habitation.
▶ **verb** (**slummed**, **slumming**) [no obj.] informal spend time at a lower social level than one's own through curiosity or for charitable purposes: *day trippers slumming among the quaintly dangerous natives.*
■ (**slum it**) put up with conditions that are less comfortable or of a lower quality than one is used to: *businessmen are having to slum it in aircraft economy class seats.*
– DERIVATIVES **slummer** noun, **slumminess** noun, **slummy** adjective.
– ORIGIN early 19th cent. (originally slang, in the sense 'room'): of unknown origin.

slumber poetic/literary ▶ **verb** [no obj.] sleep: *Sleeping Beauty slumbered in her forest castle |* figurative *the village street slumbered under the afternoon sun.*
▶ **noun** (often **slumbers**) a sleep: *scaring folk from their slumbers.*
– DERIVATIVES **slumberer** noun, **slumberous** (also **slumbrous**) adjective.
– ORIGIN Middle English: alteration of Scots and northern English *sloom*, in the same sense. The *-b-* was added for ease of pronunciation.

slumberland ▶ **noun** [mass noun] poetic/literary or humorous the state of being asleep.

slumber party ▶ **noun** N. Amer. a party for teenagers, typically girls, in which all the guests stay the night at the house where the party is held.

slumgullion /slʌmˈɡʌljən/ ▶ **noun** [mass noun] N. Amer. informal cheap or insubstantial stew.

slumlord ▶ **noun** N. Amer. informal a landlord of slum property, especially one who profiteers.

slummock Brit. informal ▶ **noun** a dirty, untidy, or slovenly person.
▶ **verb** [no obj.] behave in a lazy, indolent, or clumsy way: *you've slummocked in bed for weeks.*
– ORIGIN mid 19th cent.: of unknown origin.

slump ▶ **verb** [no obj.] **1** [with adverbial] sit, lean, or fall heavily and limply: *she slumped against the cushions |* (**be slumped**) *Denis was slumped in his seat.*
2 undergo a sudden severe or prolonged fall in price, value, or amount: *land prices slumped.*
■ fail or decline substantially: *United **slumped to** another one-nil defeat.*
▶ **noun** a sudden severe or prolonged fall in the price, value, or amount of something: *a slump in annual profits.*
■ a prolonged period of abnormally low economic activity, typically bringing widespread unemployment. ■ a period of substantial failure or decline: *Arsenal's recent slump.*
– DERIVATIVES **slumpy** adjective.
– ORIGIN late 17th cent. (in the sense 'fall into a bog'): probably imitative and related to Norwegian *slumpe* 'to fall'.

slung past and past participle of **SLING**[1].

slung shot ▶ **noun** a hard object, such as a metal ball, attached by a strap or thong to the wrist and used as a weapon.

slunk past and past participle of **SLINK**.

slur ▶ **verb** (**slurred**, **slurring**) [with obj.] **1** speak (words or speech) indistinctly so that the sounds run into one another: *he was slurring his words like a drunk.*
■ [no obj.] (of words or speech) be spoken in this way: *his speech was beginning to slur.* ■ pass over (a fact or aspect) so as to conceal or minimize it: *essential attributes are being **slurred over** or ignored.*
2 Music perform (a group of two or more notes) legato: [as adj. **slurred**] *a group of slurred notes.*
■ mark (notes) with a slur.
3 chiefly US make damaging or insulting insinuations or allegations about: *try and slur the integrity of the police to secure an acquittal.*
▶ **noun** **1** an insinuation or allegation about someone that is likely to insult them or damage their reputation: *the comments were a **slur on** staff at the hospital.*
2 an act of speaking indistinctly so that sounds or words run into one another or a tendency to speak in such a way: *there was a mean slur in his voice.*
3 Music a curved line used to show that a group of two or more notes are to be sung to one syllable or played or sung legato.
– ORIGIN early 17th cent.: of unknown origin. The Middle English noun *slur* 'thin, fluid mud' gave rise to the early verb senses 'smear, smirch' and 'disparage (a person)', later 'gloss over (a fault)', whence current usage.

slurp ▶ **verb** [with obj.] eat or drink (something) with a loud sucking noise: *she slurped her coffee |* [no obj.] *he slurped noisily from a wine cup.*
▶ **noun** a loud sucking sound made while eating or drinking: *she drank it down with a loud slurp.*
– DERIVATIVES **slurpy** adjective.
– ORIGIN mid 17th cent.: from Dutch *slurpen*.

slurry ▶ **noun** (pl. **-ies**) [mass noun] a semi-liquid mixture, typically of fine particles of manure, cement, or coal and water.
– ORIGIN late Middle English: related to dialect *slur* 'thin mud', of unknown origin.

slush ▶ **noun** [mass noun] **1** partially melted snow or ice: *the snow was turning into brown slush in the gutters.*
■ watery mud.
2 informal excessive sentiment: *the slush of Hollywood's romantic fifties films.*
▶ **verb** [no obj.] make a squelching or splashing sound: *there was water slushing around in the galley.*
– ORIGIN mid 17th cent.: probably imitative; compare with **SLOSH**.

slush fund ▶ **noun** a reserve of money used for illicit purposes, especially political bribery.
– ORIGIN mid 19th cent.: originally nautical slang denoting money collected to buy luxuries, from the sale of watery food known as *slush*.

slushy ▶ **adjective** (**slushier**, **slushiest**)
1 resembling, consisting of, or covered with slush: *slushy snow.*
2 informal excessively sentimental: *slushy novels.*
– DERIVATIVES **slushiness** noun.

slut ▶ **noun** a slovenly or promiscuous woman.
– DERIVATIVES **sluttish** adjective, **sluttishness** noun.
– ORIGIN Middle English: of unknown origin.

sly ▶ **adjective** (**slyer**, **slyest**) having or showing a cunning and deceitful nature: *she had a sly personality.*
■ (of a remark, glance, or facial expression) showing in an insinuating way that one has some secret knowledge that may be harmful or embarrassing: *he gave a sly grin.* ■ (of an action) surreptitious: *a sly sip of water.*
– PHRASES **on the sly** in a secretive fashion: *she was drinking on the sly.*
– DERIVATIVES **slyly** (also **slily**) adverb, **slyness** noun.
– ORIGIN Middle English (also in the sense 'dexterous'): from Old Norse *slœgr* 'cunning', originally 'able to strike' from the verb *slá*; compare with **SLEIGHT**.

slyboots ▶ **noun** informal a sly person.

sly grog ▶ **noun** [mass noun] Austral./NZ informal liquor sold illicitly.

slype /slʌɪp/ ▶ **noun** a covered way or passage between a cathedral transept and the chapter house or deanery.
– ORIGIN mid 19th cent.: perhaps a variant of dialect *slipe* 'long narrow piece of ground'.

SM ▶ **abbreviation for** ■ sadomasochism. ■ Sergeant Major. ■ short metre.

Sm ▶ **symbol for** the chemical element samarium.

smack[1] ▶ **noun** a sharp slap or blow, typically one given with the palm of the hand: *she gave Mark a smack across the face.*
■ a loud, sharp sound made by such a blow or a similar action: *she closed the ledger with a smack.* ■ a loud kiss: *I was saluted with two hearty smacks on my cheeks.*
▶ **verb** [with obj.] strike (someone or something), typically with the palm of the hand and as a punishment: *Jessica smacked his face, quite hard.*
■ [with obj. and adverbial of place] smash, drive, or put forcefully into or on to something: *he smacked a fist into the palm of a black-gloved hand.* ■ part (one's lips) noisily in eager anticipation or enjoyment of food, drink, or other pleasures. ■ archaic crack (a whip).
▶ **adverb** (also **smack bang**) informal **1** in a sudden and violent way: *I ran smack into the back of a parked truck.*
2 exactly; precisely: *our mother's house was smack in the middle of the city.*
– PHRASES **a smack in the face** (or **eye**) informal a strong rebuff.
– ORIGIN mid 16th cent. (in the sense 'part (one's lips) noisily'): from Middle Dutch *smacken*, of imitative origin; compare with German *schmatzen* 'eat or kiss noisily'.

smack[2] ▶ **verb** [no obj.] (**smack of**) have a flavour of; taste of: *the tea smacked strongly of tannin.*
■ suggest the presence or effects of (something wrong or unpleasant): *the whole thing smacks of a cover-up.*
▶ **noun** (**a smack of**) a flavour or taste of: *anything with even a modest smack of hops dries the palate.*
■ a trace or suggestion of: *I hear the smack of collusion between them.*
– ORIGIN Old English *smæc* 'flavour, smell', of Germanic origin; related to Dutch *smaak* and German *Geschmack*.

smack[3] ▶ **noun** a single-masted sailing boat used for coasting or fishing.
– ORIGIN early 17th cent.: from Dutch *smak*, of unknown ultimate origin.

smack[4] ▶ **noun** [mass noun] informal heroin.
– ORIGIN 1940s: probably an alteration of Yiddish *shmek* 'a sniff'.

smack dab ▶ **adverb** N. Amer. informal exactly; precisely: *here I am in Bolivia, smack dab in the heart of South America.*

smacker (also **smackeroo**) ▶ noun informal **1** a loud kiss.
2 Brit. one pound sterling: *300,000 smackers.*
■ N. Amer. one dollar.

small ▶ adjective of a size that is less than normal or usual: *the room was small and quiet | the small hill that sheltered the house.*
■ not great in amount, number, strength, or power: *a rather small amount of money.* ■ not fully grown or developed; young: *as a small boy, he spent his days either reading or watching cricket.* ■ used of the first letter of a word that has both a general and a specific use to show that in this case the general use is intended: *they are diehard conservatives, with a small c.* ■ insignificant; unimportant: *these are small points.* ■ archaic low or inferior in rank or position; socially undistinguished: *at dinner, some of the smaller neighbours were invited.* ■ [attrib.] little; hardly any: *the captain had been paying small attention.* ■ [attrib.] (of a business or its owner) operating on a modest scale: *a small farmer.* ■ (of a voice) lacking strength and confidence: *'I'm scared,' she said in a small voice.*
▶ noun (**smalls**) Brit. informal small items of clothing, especially underwear.
▶ adverb into small pieces: *the okra cut up small.*
■ in a small size: *you shouldn't write so small.*
– PHRASES **feel** (or **look**) **small** feel (or look) contemptibly weak or insignificant. **in a small way** on a small scale: *in a small way his life has been improved.* **it is** (or **what**) **a small world** used to express surprise at meeting an acquaintance or discovering a personal connection in a distant place or an unexpected context. **no small ——** a good deal of ——: *a matter of no small consequence.* **small is beautiful** used, especially in environmentalism, to express the belief that something small-scale is better than a large-scale equivalent. [ORIGIN: the title of a book by E. F. Schumacher (1973).] **the small of the back** the part of a person's back where the spine curves in at the level of the waist. **small potatoes** informal something insignificant or unimportant: *her business was small potatoes.* **small profits and quick returns** the policy of a cheap shop which relies on low prices and a large turnover. **small wonder** not very surprising: *it's small wonder that her emotions had see-sawed.*
– DERIVATIVES **smallish** adjective, **smallness** noun.
– ORIGIN Old English *smæl*, of Germanic origin; related to Dutch *smal* and German *schmal*.

small ad ▶ noun a small advertisement in a newspaper, typically one inserted by a private individual in a classified section.

small arms ▶ plural noun portable firearms, especially rifles, pistols, and light machine guns.

small beer ▶ noun [mass noun] **1** chiefly Brit. a thing that is considered unimportant: *even with £10,000 to invest, you are still small beer for most stockbrokers.*
2 archaic weak beer.

small-bore ▶ adjective denoting a firearm with a narrow bore, in international and Olympic shooting generally .22 inch calibre (5.6 millimetre bore).
■ N. Amer. informal trivial; unimportant: *small-bore economic issues.*

small bower ▶ noun see BOWER[2].

small calorie ▶ noun see CALORIE.

small-cap ▶ adjective [attrib.] Finance denoting or relating to the stock of a company with a small capitalization.

small capital ▶ noun a capital letter which is of the same height as a lower-case x in the same typeface, as THIS.

small change ▶ noun [mass noun] coins of low value.
■ figurative a thing that is considered trivial: *his wrongdoings were small change compared to a lot of happenings in the city.*

small circle ▶ noun a circle on the surface of a sphere whose plane does not pass through the sphere's centre.

small claims court ▶ noun a local court in which claims for small sums of money can be heard and decided quickly and cheaply, without legal representation.

small clause ▶ noun Linguistics a clause which contains neither a finite verb nor the infinitive marker 'to', for example *him groan* in *I heard him groan.*

small coal ▶ noun another term for SLACK[2].

small end ▶ noun (in a piston engine) the end of the connecting rod connected to the piston.

small forward ▶ noun Basketball a versatile forward who is effective outside the key as well as near the net.

small fry ▶ plural noun young fish, animals, or children.
■ insignificant people or things: *high-ranking officials escaped prosecution while numerous small fry were imprisoned.*

smallgoods ▶ plural noun Austral. cooked meats and meat products.

smallholding ▶ noun Brit. an agricultural holding smaller than a farm.
■ [mass noun] the practice of farming such a piece of land: *cooperation with neighbours is the key to successful smallholding.*
– DERIVATIVES **smallholder** noun.

small hours ▶ plural noun (**the small hours**) the early hours of the morning after midnight: *she returned in the small hours.*

small intestine ▶ noun the part of the intestine that runs between the stomach and the large intestine; the duodenum, jejunum, and ileum collectively.

small letter ▶ noun a lower-case letter, as distinct from a capital letter.

small-minded ▶ adjective having or showing rigid opinions or a narrow outlook; petty: *my family are small-minded provincials.*
– DERIVATIVES **small-mindedly** adverb, **small-mindedness** noun.

smallmouth ▶ noun N. Amer. the smallmouth bass. See BLACK BASS.

smallpox ▶ noun [mass noun] an acute contagious viral disease, with fever and pustules usually leaving permanent scars. It was effectively eradicated through vaccination by 1979. Also called VARIOLA.

small print ▶ noun [mass noun] printed matter in small type.
■ inconspicuous details or conditions printed in an agreement or contract, especially ones that may prove unfavourable: *check the small print and make sure you know your rights.*

small-reed ▶ noun a reed-like grass which grows in damp woods and marshes in temperate regions.
● Genus *Calamagrostis*, family Gramineae.

small-scale ▶ adjective of limited size or extent: *a small-scale research project | small-scale manufacturing.*

small screen ▶ noun (**the small screen**) television as a medium: *transplanting the timeless values of good literature to the small screen.*

small slam ▶ noun Bridge the bidding and winning of twelve of the thirteen tricks.

small stores ▶ plural noun small items for personal use on a sea voyage.

small-sword ▶ noun chiefly historical a light tapering thrusting-sword used for duelling.

small talk ▶ noun [mass noun] polite conversation about unimportant or uncontroversial matters, especially as engaged in on social occasions: *propriety required that he face these people and make small talk.*

small-time ▶ adjective informal unimportant; minor: *a small-time gangster.*
– DERIVATIVES **small-timer** noun.

small-town ▶ adjective of, relating to, or characteristic of a small town, especially as considered to be unsophisticated or petty: *small-town gossip.*

smalt /smɔːlt, smɒlt/ ▶ noun [mass noun] chiefly historical glass coloured blue with cobalt oxide.
■ a pigment made by pulverizing such glass.
– ORIGIN mid 16th cent.: from French, from Italian *smalto*, of Germanic origin; related to SMELT[1].

smaltite /ˈsmɔːltʌɪt, ˈsmɒl-/ ▶ noun [mass noun] a grey metallic mineral consisting chiefly of cobalt arsenide, typically occurring as cubic or octahedral crystals.
– ORIGIN mid 19th cent.: from *smaltine* (a rare word with the same sense) + -ITE[1].

smarm informal ▶ verb **1** [no obj.] chiefly Brit. behave in an ingratiating way in order to gain favour: *I smarmed my way into the air force.*
2 [with obj.] smooth down (one's hair), especially with water, oil, or gel: *he had smarmed his hair down.*

▶ noun [mass noun] ingratiating behaviour: *it takes a combination of smarm and confidence to persuade them.*
– ORIGIN mid 19th cent. (originally dialect in the sense 'smear, bedaub'): of unknown origin.

smarmy ▶ adjective (**smarmier**, **smarmiest**) informal ingratiating and wheedling in a way that is perceived as insincere or excessive: *a smarmy, unctuous reply.*
– DERIVATIVES **smarmily** adverb, **smarminess** noun.

smart ▶ adjective **1** (of a person) clean, tidy, and well-dressed: *you look very smart.*
■ (of clothes) attractively neat and stylish: *a smart blue skirt.* ■ (of a thing) bright and fresh in appearance: *a smart green van.* ■ (of a person or place) fashionable and upmarket: *a smart restaurant.*
2 informal having or showing a quick-witted intelligence: *if he was that smart he would never have been tricked.*
■ (of a device) capable of independent and seemingly intelligent action: *hi-tech smart weapons.* ■ chiefly N. Amer. showing impertinence by making clever or sarcastic remarks: *don't get smart or I'll whack you one.*
3 quick; brisk: *I gave him a smart salute.*
■ painfully severe: *a dog that snaps is given a smart blow.*
▶ verb [no obj.] (of a wound or part of the body) cause a sharp, stinging pain: *the wound was smarting* | [as adj. **smarting**] *Susan rubbed her smarting eyes.*
■ (of a person) feel upset and annoyed: *defence chiefs are still smarting from the government's cuts.*
▶ noun **1** (**smarts**) N. Amer. informal intelligence; acumen: *I don't think I have the smarts for it.*
2 [mass noun] sharp stinging pain: *the smart of the recent blood-raw cuts.*
■ archaic mental pain or suffering: *sorrow is the effect of smart, and smart the effect of faith.*
▶ adverb archaic in a quick or brisk manner: *it is better for tenants to be compelled to pay up smart.*
– PHRASES **look smart** chiefly Brit. be quick: *come up here, and look smart about it!*
– DERIVATIVES **smartingly** adverb, **smartly** adverb, **smartness** noun.
– ORIGIN Old English *smeortan* (verb), of West Germanic origin; related to German *schmerzen*; the adjective is related to the verb, the original sense (late Old English) being 'causing sharp pain'; from this arose 'keen, brisk', whence the current senses of 'mentally sharp' and 'neat in a brisk, sharp style'.

smart alec (also **smart aleck**) informal ▶ noun a person considered irritating because they know a great deal or always have a clever answer to a question.
▶ adjective having or showing an irritating, know-all attitude: *a smart-alec answer.*
– DERIVATIVES **smart-alecky** adjective.
– ORIGIN mid 19th cent.: from SMART + *Alec*, diminutive of the given name *Alexander.*

smart-arse (US **smart-ass**) ▶ noun informal another term for SMART ALEC.

smart card ▶ noun a plastic card with a built-in microprocessor, used typically to perform financial transactions.

smarten ▶ verb [with obj.] make (something) smarter in appearance: *he spent part of the proceeds on smartening up his flat.*
■ [no obj.] (**smarten up**) make one's appearance smarter: *if there was water to spare I would smarten up and shave.*

smartish ▶ adverb informal, chiefly Brit. quickly; briskly: *get over here smartish!*

smart money ▶ noun [mass noun] money bet or invested by people with expert knowledge: *the smart money in entertainment is invested in copyright.*
■ knowledgeable people collectively: *the smart money in music programming is abandoning pop.*

smart mouth N. Amer. informal ▶ noun an ability or tendency to make cheeky retorts; impudence: *why do you hide behind that smart mouth all the time?*
▶ verb (**smart-mouth**) [no obj.] make impudent remarks.
■ [with obj.] make impudent remarks to.
– DERIVATIVES **smart-mouthed** adjective.

smart quotes ▶ plural noun Computing quotation marks which, although all keyed the same, are automatically interpreted and set as opening or closing marks (inverted or raised commas) rather than vertical lines.

smart set ▶ noun (**the smart set**) fashionable people considered as a group.

smartweed ▶ noun [mass noun] chiefly N. Amer. a plant

of the dock family, typically having slender leaves and a short spike of tiny compact flowers.
● Genus *Polygonum*, family Polygonaceae: several species.

smarty ▶ noun (pl. **-ies**) informal **1** a know-all. **2** dated a smartly dressed person; a member of a smart set.

smarty-pants (Brit. also **smarty-boots**) ▶ noun another term for **SMARTY** (in sense 1).

smash ▶ verb **1** [with obj.] violently break (something) into pieces: *the thief smashed a window to get into the car* | *gone are the days when he smashed up hotels.*
■ [no obj.] be violently broken into pieces; shatter: *the glass ball smashed instantly on the pavement.* ■ violently knock down or crush inwards: *soldiers smashed down doors.* ■ crash and severely damage (a vehicle): *my Land Rover's been smashed up.* ■ hit or attack (someone) very violently: *Donald smashed him over the head.* ■ easily or comprehensively beat (a record): *he smashed the course record.* ■ completely defeat, destroy, or foil (something regarded as hostile or dangerous): *a deliberate attempt to smash the trade union movement.* ■ [no obj.] informal, dated (of a business) go bankrupt; fail financially.
2 [no obj., with adverbial of direction] move so as to hit or collide with something with great force and impact: *their plane smashed into a mountainside.*
■ [with obj. and adverbial of direction] (in sport) strike (the ball) or score (a goal, run, etc.) with great force: *he smashed home the Tranmere winner.* ■ [with obj.] (in tennis, badminton, and similar sports) strike (the ball or shuttlecock) downwards with a hard overarm stroke.
▶ noun **1** an act or sound of something smashing: *he heard the smash of glass.*
■ a violent collision or impact between vehicles: *a car smash.* ■ a violent blow: *a forearm smash.* ■ a stroke in tennis, badminton, and similar sports in which the ball is hit downwards with a hard overarm volley. ■ informal, dated a bankruptcy or financial failure.
2 (also **smash hit**) informal a very successful song, film, show, or performer: *a box office smash.*
3 a mixture of spirits (typically brandy) with flavoured water and ice.
▶ adverb with a sudden, violent shattering: *they were together for an instant, and then smash it was all gone.*
– PHRASES **go to smash** informal, dated be ruined or destroyed: *he sees the community going to smash.*
– ORIGIN early 18th cent. (as a noun): probably imitative, representing a blend of words such as *smack*, *smite* with *bash*, *mash*, etc.

smash-and-grab ▶ adjective [attrib.] denoting a robbery in which the thief smashes a shop window and seizes goods: *a smash-and-grab raid on a jeweller.*
▶ noun a robbery of this type.

smashed ▶ adjective **1** violently or badly broken or shattered: *a smashed collar bone.*
2 [predic.] informal very drunk: *when they go back to the barracks, the single men get smashed.*

smasher ▶ noun **1** Brit. informal a very attractive or impressive person or thing: *the night nurse was a smasher.*
2 [usu. in combination] a person or device that breaks something up: *riot police had clashed with window-smashers.*

smashing ▶ adjective informal, chiefly Brit. excellent; wonderful: *you look smashing!*
– DERIVATIVES **smashingly** adverb.

smash-up ▶ noun informal a violent collision, especially of cars.

smatterer ▶ noun dated a person who studies a subject in a superficial way or has only a slight knowledge of it.

smattering (also **smatter**) ▶ noun a slight superficial knowledge of a language or subject: *Edward had only a smattering of Welsh.*
■ a small amount of something: *a smattering of snow.*
– ORIGIN mid 16th cent.: from *smatter* 'talk ignorantly, prate' (surviving in Scots), of unknown origin.

smaze ▶ noun [mass noun] a mixture of smoke and haze.

SME ▶ abbreviation for Suriname (international vehicle registration).

smear ▶ verb [with obj.] coat or mark (something) messily or carelessly with a greasy or sticky substance: *his face was smeared with dirt.*
■ [with obj. and adverbial] spread (a greasy or sticky substance) over something: *she smeared sunblock on her skin.* ■ figurative damage the reputation of (someone) by false accusations; slander: *someone was trying to smear her by faking letters.* ■ messily blur the outline of

(something such as writing or paint); smudge: *her lipstick was smeared.*
▶ noun **1** a mark or streak of a greasy or sticky substance: *there was an oil smear on his jacket.*
■ figurative a false accusation intended to damage someone's reputation: *the popular press were indulging in unwarranted smears.* ■ a sample of material spread thinly on a microscope slide for examination, typically for medical diagnosis: *the smears were stained for cryptosporidium.* ■ short for **SMEAR TEST**.
2 Climbing an insecure foothold.
– DERIVATIVES **smeary** adjective, **smearer** noun.
– ORIGIN Old English *smierwan* (verb), *smeoru* 'ointment, grease', of Germanic origin; related to German *schmieren* (verb), *Schmer* (noun).

smear campaign ▶ noun a plan to discredit a public figure by making false accusations.

smear test ▶ noun a test to detect signs of cervical cancer. See **CERVICAL SMEAR**.

smectic /ˈsmɛktɪk/ ▶ adjective denoting or involving a state of a liquid crystal in which the molecules are oriented in parallel and arranged in well-defined planes. Compare with **NEMATIC**.
▶ noun a substance of this type.
– ORIGIN late 17th cent.: via Latin from Greek *smēktikos* 'cleansing' (because of the soap-like consistency).

smectite /ˈsmɛktʌɪt/ ▶ noun [mass noun] a clay mineral (e.g. bentonite) which undergoes reversible expansion on absorbing water.
– ORIGIN early 19th cent.: from Greek *smēktis* 'fuller's earth' + **-ITE**[1].

smegma /ˈsmɛɡmə/ ▶ noun [mass noun] a sebaceous secretion in the folds of the skin, especially under a man's foreskin.
– ORIGIN early 19th cent.: via Latin from Greek *smēgma* 'soap', from *smēkhein* 'cleanse'.

smell ▶ noun [mass noun] the faculty or power of perceiving odours or scents by means of the organs in the nose: *a highly developed sense of smell* | *dogs locate the bait by smell.*
■ [count noun] a quality in something that is perceived by this faculty; an odour or scent: *lingering kitchen smells* | *a smell of coffee.* ■ an unpleasant odour: *twenty-seven cats lived there—you can imagine the smell!* ■ [in sing.] an act of inhaling in order to ascertain an odour or scent: *have a smell of this.*
▶ verb (past and past participle **smelt** or **smelled**) **1** [with obj.] perceive or detect the odour or scent of (something): *I think I can smell something burning.*
■ sniff at (something) in order to perceive or detect its odour or scent: *the dogs smell each other.* ■ [no obj.] have or use a sense of smell: *becoming deaf or blind or unable to smell.* ■ (**smell something out**) detect or discover something by the faculty of smell: *his nose can smell out an animal from ten miles away.* ■ detect or suspect (something) by means of instinct or intuition: *he can smell trouble long before it gets serious* | *he can smell out weakness in others.*
2 [no obj.] emit an odour or scent of a specified kind: *the place smelled of damp* | [with complement] *the food smelt and tasted good* | [as adj., in combination **-smelling**] *pungent-smelling food.*
■ have a strong or unpleasant odour: *if I don't get a bath soon I'll start to smell* | *it smells in here.* ■ appear in a certain way; be suggestive of something: *it smells like a hoax to me.*
– PHRASES **smell blood** discern weakness or vulnerability in an opponent. **smell a rat** informal begin to suspect trickery or deception. **smell the roses** N. Amer. informal enjoy or appreciate what is often ignored.
– DERIVATIVES **smellable** adjective, **smeller** noun.
– ORIGIN Middle English: of unknown origin.

smelling bottle ▶ noun chiefly historical a small bottle containing smelling salts or perfume.

smelling salts ▶ plural noun chiefly historical a pungent substance sniffed as a restorative in cases of faintness or headache, typically consisting of ammonium carbonate mixed with perfume.

smelly ▶ adjective (**smellier**, **smelliest**) having a strong or unpleasant smell: *smelly feet.*
– DERIVATIVES **smelliness** noun.

smelt[1] ▶ verb [with obj.] [often as noun **smelting**] extract (metal) from its ore by a process involving heating and melting: *tin smelting.*
■ extract a metal from (ore) in this way.
– ORIGIN mid 16th cent.: from Middle Dutch, Middle Low German *smelten*; related to the verb **MELT**.

smelt[2] past and past participle of **SMELL**.

smelt[3] ▶ noun (pl. same or **smelts**) a small silvery

fish which lives in both marine and fresh water and is sometimes fished commercially, in particular:
● a fish of the northern hemisphere (family Osmeridae: *Osmerus* and other genera). ● a fish of Australasian waters (family Retropinnidae: several genera).
– ORIGIN Old English; obscurely related to various European names of fish; compare with **SMOLT**.

smelter ▶ noun an installation or factory for smelting a metal from its ore.
■ a person engaged in the business of smelting.

Smersh /smɜːʃ/ the popular name for the Russian counter-espionage organization responsible for maintaining security within the Soviet armed and intelligence services.
– ORIGIN abbreviation of Russian *Smert' shpionam*, literally 'death to spies'.

Smetana /ˈsmɛtənə/, Bedřich (1824–84), Czech composer. Regarded as the founder of Czech music, he was dedicated to the cause of Czech nationalism, as is apparent in his operas, such as *The Bartered Bride* (1866) and in the cycle of symphonic poems *Ma Vlast* ('My Country' 1874–9).

smetana /ˈsmɛtənə/ ▶ noun [mass noun] sour cream.
– ORIGIN Russian, from *smetat* 'sweep off'.

smew /smjuː/ ▶ noun a small migratory merganser of northern Eurasia, the male of which has white plumage with a crest and fine black markings.
● *Mergus albellus*, family Anatidae.
– ORIGIN late 17th cent.: obscurely related to Dutch *smient* 'wigeon' and German *Schmeiente* 'small wild duck'.

smidge ▶ noun informal another term for **SMIDGEN**: *a smidge over five foot two.*

smidgen (also **smidgeon** or **smidgin**) ▶ noun informal a small amount of something: *add a smidgen of cayenne.*
– ORIGIN mid 19th cent.: perhaps from Scots *smitch* in the same sense.

smilax /ˈsmʌɪlaks/ ▶ noun **1** a widely distributed climbing shrub with hooks and tendrils. Several South American species yield sarsaparilla from their roots, and some are cultivated as ornamentals.
● Genus *Smilax*, family Liliaceae.
2 a climbing asparagus, the decorative foliage of which is used by florists.
● *Asparagus* (or *Myrsiphyllum*) *asparagoides*, family Liliaceae.
– ORIGIN late 16th cent.: via Latin from Greek, literally 'bindweed'.

smile ▶ verb [no obj.] form one's features into a pleased, kind, or amused expression, typically with the corners of the mouth turned up and the front teeth exposed: *she was smiling* | *he smiled at Shelley* | [as adj. **smiling**] *smiling faces.*
■ [with obj.] express (a feeling) with such an expression: *he smiled his admiration of the great stone circle.* ■ [with obj.] give (a smile) of a specified kind: *Guy smiled a grim smile.* ■ (**smile at/on/upon**) regard favourably or indulgently: *at first fortune smiled on him.* ■ [often as adj. **smiling**] poetic/literary (especially of landscape) have a bright or pleasing aspect: *smiling groves and terraces.*
▶ noun a pleased, kind, or amused facial expression, typically with the corners of the mouth turned up and the front teeth exposed: *he flashed his most winning smile* | *she greeting us all with a smile.*
– PHRASES **be all smiles** informal (of a person) look very cheerful and pleased, especially in contrast to a previous mood. **come up smiling** informal recover from adversity and cheerfully face what is to come.
– DERIVATIVES **smiler** noun, **smilingly** adverb.
– ORIGIN Middle English: perhaps of Scandinavian origin; related to **SMIRK**.

smiley (also **smilie**) ▶ adjective informal smiling; cheerful: *he drew a smiley face.*
▶ noun (pl. **-eys** or **-ies**) a symbol which, when viewed sideways, represents a smiling face, formed by the characters :-) and used in electronic communications to indicate that the writer is pleased or joking.

smirch /smɜːtʃ/ ▶ verb [with obj.] make (something) dirty; soil: *the window was smirched by heat and smoke.*
■ figurative discredit (a person or their reputation); taint: *I am not accustomed to having my honour smirched.*
▶ noun a dirty mark or stain.
■ figurative a blot on someone's character; a flaw.
– ORIGIN late 15th cent.: probably symbolic.

smirk ▶ verb [no obj.] smile in an irritatingly smug, conceited, or silly way: *Dr Ali smirked in triumph.*
▶ noun a smug, conceited, or silly smile: *Gloria pursed her mouth in a self-satisfied smirk.*

– DERIVATIVES **smirker** noun, **smirkily** adverb, **smirkingly** adverb, **smirky** adjective.
– ORIGIN Old English *sme(a)rcian*, from a base shared by **SMILE**. The early sense was 'to smile'; it later gained a notion of smugness or silliness.

smit /smɪt/ archaic past participle of **SMITE**.

smite ▶ verb (past **smote**; past participle **smitten**) [with obj.] poetic/literary strike with a firm blow: *he smites the water with his sword.*
■ archaic defeat or conquer (a people or land): *he may smite our enemies.* ■ (usu. **be smitten**) figurative (especially of disease) attack or affect severely: *various people had been smitten with untimely summer flu.* ■ (**be smitten**) be strongly attracted to someone or something: *she was so smitten with the boy.*
▶ noun archaic a heavy blow or stroke with a weapon or the hand: *the kirk rang with slaps and smites.*
– DERIVATIVES **smiter** noun.
– ORIGIN Old English *smītan* 'to smear, blemish', of Germanic origin; related to Dutch *smijten* and German *schmeissen* 'to fling'.

Smith[1], Adam (1723–90), Scottish economist and philosopher. Often regarded as the founder of modern economics, he advocated minimal state interference in economic matters and discredited mercantilism. Notable works: *Inquiry into the Nature and Causes of the Wealth of Nations* (1776).

Smith[2], Bessie (1894–1937), American blues singer. She made over 150 recordings, including some with Benny Goodman and Louis Armstrong.

Smith[3], David (Roland) (1906–65), American sculptor. His early work is marked by recurring motifs of human violence and greed. These later give way to a calmer, more monumental style, as in the *Cubi* series.

Smith[4], Ian (Douglas) (b.1919), Rhodesian statesman, Prime Minister 1964–79. In 1965 he issued a unilateral declaration of independence from Britain (UDI) because he would not agree to black majority rule. He eventually resigned in 1979.

Smith[5], Joseph (1805–44), American religious leader and founder of the Church of Jesus Christ of Latter-Day Saints (the Mormons).

Smith[6], Stevie (1902–71), English poet and novelist; pseudonym of *Florence Margaret Smith*. She is mainly remembered for her witty, caustic, and enigmatic verse; collections include *A Good Time was Had By All* (1937) and *Not Waving But Drowning* (1957).

Smith[7], Sydney (1771–1845), English Anglican churchman, essayist, and wit. He is notable for his *Letters of Peter Plymley* (1807), which defended Catholic Emancipation.

Smith[8], William (1769–1839), English land surveyor and geologist, known as the father of English geology. He produced the first geological map of England and Wales, based on the different types of strata, distinguished by characteristic assemblages of fossils, found in different places.

smith ▶ noun a worker in metal.
■ short for **BLACKSMITH**.
▶ verb [with obj.] treat (metal) by heating, hammering, and forging it: *tin-bronze was cast into ingots before being smithed into bracelets.*
– ORIGIN Old English, of Germanic origin; related to Dutch *smid* and German *Schmied*.

-smith ▶ combining form denoting a person skilled in creating something with a specified material: *goldsmith* | *wordsmith*.

smithereens /ˌsmɪðəˈriːnz/ (also **smithers** /ˈsmɪðəz/) ▶ plural noun informal small pieces: *a grenade blew him to smithereens.*
– ORIGIN early 19th cent.: probably from Irish *smidirín*.

smithery ▶ noun [mass noun] the work of or goods made by a smith.

Smithfield a part of London containing the city's principal meat market.

Smithsonian Institution /smɪθˈsəʊnɪən/ a US foundation for education and scientific research in Washington DC, opened in 1846 and now responsible for administering many museums, art galleries, and other establishments. It originated in a £100,000 bequest in the will of the English chemist and mineralogist James Smithson (1765–1829).

smithsonite /ˈsmɪθs(ə)nʌɪt/ ▶ noun [mass noun] a yellow, grey, or green mineral consisting of zinc carbonate typically occurring as crusts or rounded masses.
– ORIGIN mid 19th cent.: from the name *Smithson* (see **SMITHSONIAN INSTITUTION**) + **-ITE**[1].

smithy /ˈsmɪði/ ▶ noun (pl. **-ies**) a blacksmith's workshop; a forge.
– ORIGIN Middle English, from Old Norse *smithja*.

smitten past participle of **SMITE**.

smock ▶ noun a loose dress or blouse for a woman or child, with the upper part closely gathered in smocking.
■ a loose overall worn to protect one's clothes: *an artist's smock.* ■ (also **smock-frock**) historical a smocked linen overgarment worn by an agricultural worker.
▶ verb [with obj.] [usu. as adj. **smocked**] decorate (something) with smocking: *smocked dresses.*
– ORIGIN Old English *smoc* 'woman's loose-fitting undergarment'; probably related to Old English *smūgan* 'to creep' and Old Norse *smjúga* 'put on a garment, creep into'. The use of the verb as a needlework term dates from the late 19th cent.

smocking ▶ noun [mass noun] decoration on a garment created by gathering a section of the material into tight pleats and holding them together with parallel stitches in an ornamental pattern.

smog ▶ noun [mass noun] fog or haze intensified by smoke or other atmospheric pollutants.
– DERIVATIVES **smoggy** adjective.
– ORIGIN early 20th cent.: blend of **SMOKE** and **FOG**[1].

smoke ▶ noun **1** [mass noun] a visible suspension of carbon or other particles in air, typically one emitted from a burning substance: *bonfire smoke.*
■ [count noun] an act of smoking tobacco: *I'm dying for a smoke.* ■ [count noun] informal a cigarette or cigar.
2 (**the Smoke**) Brit. dated a big city, especially London: *she was offered a job in the Smoke.*
▶ verb **1** [no obj.] emit smoke or visible vapour: *heat the oil until it just smokes* | [as adj. **smoking**] *they huddled round his smoking fire in the winter damp.*
■ inhale and exhale the smoke of tobacco or a drug: *Janine was sitting at the kitchen table smoking* | [as noun **smoking**] *the effect of smoking on health* | [with obj.] *he smoked forty cigarettes a day.*
2 [with obj.] [often as adj. **smoked**] cure or preserve (meat or fish) by exposure to smoke: *smoked salmon.*
■ treat (glass) so as to darken it: *the smoked glass of his lenses.* ■ fumigate, cleanse, or purify by exposure to smoke. ■ subdue (insects, especially bees) by exposing them to smoke. ■ (**smoke someone/thing out**) drive someone or something out of a place by using smoke: *we will fire the roof and smoke him out.* ■ (**smoke someone out**) figurative force someone to make something known: *as the press smokes him out on other human rights issues, he will be revealed as a social conservative.*
3 [with obj.] N. Amer. informal kill (someone) by shooting.
■ defeat overwhelmingly in a fight or contest.
4 [with obj.] archaic make fun of (someone): *we baited her and smoked her.*
– PHRASES **go up in smoke** informal be destroyed by fire. ■ figurative (of a plan) come to nothing: *more than one dream is about to go up in smoke.* **no smoke without fire** (or **where there's smoke there's fire**) proverb there's always some reason for a rumour. **smoke and mirrors** N. Amer. the obscuring or embellishing of the truth of a situation with misleading or irrelevant information: *the budget process is an exercise in smoke and mirrors.* [ORIGIN: with reference to illusion created by conjuring tricks.] **smoke like a chimney** smoke tobacco incessantly.
– DERIVATIVES **smokable** (also **smokeable**) adjective.
– ORIGIN Old English *smoca* (noun), *smocian* (verb), from the Germanic base of *smēocan* 'emit smoke'; related to Dutch *smook* and German *Schmauch*.

smoke alarm ▶ noun a fire-protection device that automatically detects and gives a warning of the presence of smoke.

smoke ball ▶ noun a projectile filled with material which emits dense smoke on ignition, used to conceal military operations.

smoke bomb ▶ noun a bomb that emits dense smoke as it explodes.

smokebox ▶ noun a device for catching or producing and containing smoke, in particular:
■ an oven for smoking food. ■ the chamber in a steam engine or boiler between the flues and the funnel or chimney stack. ■ another term for **SMOKER** (in sense 4).

smoke bush ▶ noun another term for **SMOKE TREE**.

smoke-dry ▶ verb [with obj.] cure (meat or fish) by exposing it to smoke.

smoke-free ▶ adjective without smoke: *a smoke-free environment.*
■ where smoking is not permitted: *a smoke-free train.*

smoke-ho ▶ noun variant of **SMOKO**.

smokehouse ▶ noun chiefly N. Amer. a shed or room for curing food by exposure to smoke.

smokejumper ▶ noun N. Amer. a firefighter who arrives by parachute to extinguish a forest fire.

smokeless ▶ adjective producing or emitting little or no smoke: *smokeless fuel.*

smokeless zone ▶ noun Brit. a district in which it is illegal to create smoke and where only smokeless fuel may be used.

smoker ▶ noun **1** a person who smokes tobacco regularly.
■ a train compartment in which smoking is allowed.
2 a person or device that smokes fish or meat.
3 chiefly N. Amer. an informal social gathering for men.
4 a device which emits smoke for subduing bees in a hive.

smoke ring ▶ noun a ring-shaped puff of smoke exhaled by a smoker.

smoke room ▶ noun Brit. another term for **SMOKING ROOM**.

smoker's cough ▶ noun a persistent cough caused by excessive smoking.

smokescreen ▶ noun a cloud of smoke created to conceal military operations.
■ figurative a ruse designed to disguise someone's real intentions or activities: *he tried to create a smokescreen by quibbling about the statistics.*

smoke shop ▶ noun N. Amer. a shop selling tobacco products and smoking equipment.

smoke signal ▶ noun a column of smoke used as a way of conveying a message to a distant person.
■ figurative an indication of someone's intentions or views: *a series of political smoke signals has aroused hopes for a fresh initiative on Northern Ireland.*

smokestack ▶ noun a chimney or funnel for discharging smoke from a locomotive, ship, factory, etc.

smokestone ▶ noun another term for **SMOKY QUARTZ**.

smoke tree ▶ noun a Eurasian shrub or small tree which bears feathery plumes of purple or reddish flowers and fruit, giving it a smoky appearance.
• *Cotinus coggygria* (formerly *Rhus cotinus*), family Anacardiaceae.

smoke tunnel ▶ noun a form of wind tunnel using thin jets of smoke to show the motion of air.

smokie ▶ noun Scottish a smoked haddock.

smoking divan ▶ noun see **DIVAN** (sense 3).

smoking gun (also **smoking pistol**) ▶ noun figurative a piece of incontrovertible incriminating evidence.

smoking jacket ▶ noun a man's comfortable jacket, typically made of velvet, formerly worn while smoking after dinner.

smoking room ▶ noun a room set aside for smoking in a hotel or other public building.

smoko /ˈsməʊkəʊ/ (also **smoke-ho**) ▶ noun (pl. **-os**) Austral./NZ informal a rest from work for a smoke; a tea break.

smoky ▶ adjective (**smokier**, **smokiest**) **1** filled with or smelling of smoke: *a smoky office.*
■ producing or obscured by a great deal of smoke: *smoky factory chimneys.* ■ having the taste or aroma of smoked food: *smoky bacon.* ■ like smoke in colour or appearance: *smoky eyes.*
– DERIVATIVES **smokily** adverb, **smokiness** noun.

smoky quartz ▶ noun [mass noun] a semi-precious variety of quartz ranging in colour from light greyish-brown to nearly black.

smolder ▶ verb US spelling of **SMOULDER**.

Smolensk /sməˈljɛnsk/ a city in western European Russia, on the River Dnieper close to the border with Belarus; pop. 346,000 (1990).

Smollett /ˈsmɒlɪt/, Tobias (George) (1721–71), Scottish novelist. His humorous and fast-moving picaresque novels include *The Adventures of Roderick Random* (1748) and *The Adventures of Peregrine Pickle* (1751).

smolt /sməʊlt/ ▶ noun a young salmon (or trout) after the parr stage, when it becomes silvery and migrates to the sea for the first time.
– ORIGIN late Middle English (originally Scots and northern English): of unknown origin; compare with **SMELT**³.

smooch informal ▶ verb [no obj.] kiss and cuddle amorously: *the young lovers smooched in their car.* ■ Brit. dance slowly in a close embrace.
▶ noun a kiss or a spell of amorous kissing and cuddling: *a slurpy smooch on the ear.* ■ Brit. a period of slow dancing in a close embrace: *they suggest a dance but it turns into a smooch.*
– DERIVATIVES **smoocher** noun, **smoochy** adjective (**smoochier, smoochiest**).
– ORIGIN 1930s: from dialect *smouch*, of imitative origin.

smoodge (also **smooge**) Austral./NZ informal ▶ verb [no obj.] behave in an ingratiating manner: *he used to hang around here smoodging to mum.*
▶ noun [mass noun] affectionate flattery: *what's wrong with a bit of smoodge between friends?*
– DERIVATIVES **smoodger** noun.
– ORIGIN early 20th cent.: probably an alteration of dialect *smouch* 'kiss, sidle up to'.

smoor /smʊə/ S. African ▶ noun [mass noun] a type of stew.
▶ verb [with obj.] braise or stew (meat or fish).
– ORIGIN Afrikaans.

smooth ▶ adjective 1 having an even and regular surface; free from perceptible projections, lumps, or indentations: *smooth flat rocks.* ■ (of a person's face or skin) not wrinkled, pitted, or hairy: *a smooth skin tans more easily.* ■ (of a liquid) with an even consistency; without lumps: *cook gently until the sauce is smooth.* ■ (of the sea or another body of water) without heavy waves; calm: *the smooth summer sea.* ■ (of movement) without jerks: *the trucks gave a smooth ride | graphics are excellent, with fast, smooth scrolling.* ■ (of an action, event, or process) without problems or difficulties: *the group's expansion into the US market was not quite so smooth.* ■ denoting the face of a tennis or squash racket without the projecting loops from the stringing process (used as a call when the racket is spun to decide the right to serve first or to choose ends).
2 (of food or drink) without harshness or bitterness: *a lovely, smooth, very fruity wine.* ■ (of a person or their manner, actions, or words) suavely charming in a way considered to be unctuous: *his voice was infuriatingly smooth.*
▶ verb (also **smoothe**) [with obj.] give (something) a flat, regular surface or appearance by running one's hand over it: *she smoothed out the newspaper.* ■ rub off the rough edges of (something): *you can use glasspaper to smooth the joint.* ■ deal successfully with (a problem, difficulty, or perceived fault): *these doctrinal disputes were smoothed over.* ■ free (a course of action) from difficulties or problems: *a conference would be held to smooth the way for the establishment of the provisional government.* ■ modify (a graph, curve, etc.) so as to lessen irregularities: *values are collected over a long period of time so that fluctuations are smoothed out.*
▶ adverb archaic in a way that is without difficulties: *the course of true love never did run smooth.*
– PHRASES **smooth someone's ruffled feathers** see **RUFFLE**.
– DERIVATIVES **smoothable** adjective, **smoother** noun, **smoothish** adjective, **smoothly** adverb, **smoothness** noun.
– ORIGIN Old English *smōth*, probably of Germanic origin, though no cognates are known. The verb dates from Middle English.

smooth-bore ▶ noun [often as modifier] a gun with an unrifled barrel: *smooth-bore muskets.*

smooth breathing ▶ noun see **BREATHING** (sense 2).

smooth-faced ▶ adjective 1 concealing one's true feelings by a show of friendliness.
2 clean-shaven.

smooth hound ▶ noun a small European shark which typically lives close to the bottom in shallow waters.
● Genus *Mustelus*, family Triakidae: two species.

smoothie ▶ noun 1 informal a man with a smooth, suave manner: *a smoothie with an eye for a pretty girl.*
2 chiefly US a thick, smooth drink of fresh fruit puréed with milk, yogurt, or ice cream.

smoothing iron ▶ noun historical a flat iron.

smoothing plane ▶ noun a small plane for finishing the surface of wood.

smooth muscle ▶ noun [mass noun] Physiology muscle tissue in which the contractile fibrils are not highly ordered, occurring in the gut and other internal organs and not under voluntary control. Often contrasted with **STRIATED MUSCLE**.

smooth newt ▶ noun a small yellowish-brown smooth-skinned newt that is widely distributed throughout Europe and western Asia.
● *Triturus vulgaris*, family Salamandridae.

smooth snake ▶ noun a harmless Eurasian snake which is grey to reddish in colour, typically living in heathy country where it feeds on lizards.
● *Coronella austriaca*, family Colubridae.

smooth talk ▶ noun [mass noun] charming or flattering language, especially when used to persuade someone to do something.
▶ verb (**smooth-talk**) [with obj.] use such language to (someone), especially to persuade them to do something: *don't try to smooth-talk me | [as adj. **smooth-talking**] a smooth-talking salesman.*
– DERIVATIVES **smooth-talker** noun.

smooth tongue ▶ noun [in sing.] the ability or tendency to use insincere flattery or persuasion: *your smooth tongue could even turn your mistakes to your advantage.*
– DERIVATIVES **smooth-tongued** adjective.

smorgasbord /ˈsmɔːɡəsbɔːd/ ▶ noun a range of open sandwiches and delicacies served as hors d'oeuvres or a buffet.
■ figurative a wide range of something; a variety: *the album is a smorgasbord of different musical styles.*
– ORIGIN Swedish, from *smörgås* '(slice of) bread and butter' (from *smör* 'butter' + *gås* 'goose, lump of butter') + *bord* 'table'.

smorzando /smɔːˈtsandəʊ/ Music ▶ adverb & adjective (especially as a direction) dying away.
– ORIGIN Italian, literally 'extinguishing'.

smote past of **SMITE**.

smother ▶ verb [with obj.] kill (someone) by covering their nose and mouth so that they suffocate. ■ extinguish (a fire) by covering it. ■ (**smother someone/thing in/with**) cover someone or something entirely with: *rich orange sorbets smothered in fluffy whipped cream.* ■ make (someone) feel trapped and oppressed by acting in an overly protective manner towards them. ■ suppress (a feeling or action): *she smothered a sigh.* ■ (in sport) stop the motion of (the ball or a shot): *the goalkeeper was able to smother the ball.* ■ cook in a covered container: [as adj. **smothered**] *smothered fried chicken.*
▶ noun a mass of something that stifles or obscures: *all this vanished in a smother of foam.*
– ORIGIN Middle English (as a noun in the sense 'stifling smoke'): from the base of Old English *smorian* 'suffocate'.

smothered mate ▶ noun [mass noun] Chess checkmate in which the king has no vacant square to move to and is checkmated by a knight.

smoulder (US also **smolder**) ▶ verb [no obj.] burn slowly with smoke but no flame: *the bonfire still smouldered, the smoke drifting over the paddock.* ■ show or feel barely suppressed anger, hatred, or another powerful emotion: *Anna smouldered with indignation | [as adj. **smouldering**] he met her smouldering eyes.* ■ exist in a suppressed or concealed state: *the controversy smouldered on for several years | [as adj. **smouldering**] smouldering rage.*
▶ noun [mass noun] smoke coming from a fire that is burning slowly without a flame: *the last acrid smoulder of his cigarette.*
– DERIVATIVES **smoulderingly** adverb.
– ORIGIN late Middle English: related to Dutch *smeulen*.

SMPTE ▶ abbreviation for Society of Television and Motion Picture Engineers (used to denote a time coding system for synchronizing video and audio tapes).

smriti /ˈsmrɪti/ ▶ noun (pl. **smritis**) a Hindu religious text containing traditional teachings on religion, such as the Mahabharata.
– ORIGIN from Sanskrit *smṛti* 'remembrance'.

SMSgt ▶ abbreviation for Senior Master Sergeant.

smudge¹ ▶ noun a blurred or smeared mark on the surface of something: *a smudge of blood on the floor.* ■ an indistinct or blurred view or image: *the low smudge of hills on the horizon.*
▶ verb [with obj.] cause (something) to become messily

smeared by rubbing it: *she dabbed her eyes, careful not to smudge her make-up.*
■ [no obj.] become smeared when rubbed: *mascaras that smudge or flake around the eyes.* ■ make blurred or indistinct: *the photograph had been smudged by the photocopier and was by no means as clear as the original.*
– DERIVATIVES **smudgeless** adjective.
– ORIGIN late Middle English (as a verb in the sense 'soil, stain'): of unknown origin. The noun dates from the late 18th cent.

smudge² ▶ noun N. Amer. a smoky outdoor fire that is lit to keep off insects or protect plants against frost.
– ORIGIN mid 18th cent. (in the sense 'suffocating smoke'), of unknown origin related to obsolete *smudge* 'cure (herring) by smoking', of obscure origin.

smudge pot ▶ noun N. Amer. a container for a smudge (see **SMUDGE**²).

smudgy ▶ adjective (**smudgier, smudgiest**) smeared or blurred from being smudged: *a smudgy photograph.*
– DERIVATIVES **smudgily** adverb, **smudginess** noun.

smug ▶ adjective (**smugger, smuggest**) having or showing an excessive pride in oneself or one's achievements: *he was feeling smug after his win.*
– DERIVATIVES **smugly** adverb, **smugness** noun.
– ORIGIN mid 16th cent. (originally in the sense 'neat, spruce'): from Low German *smuk* 'pretty'.

smuggle ▶ verb [with obj.] move (goods) illegally into or out of a country: *he's been smuggling cigarettes from Gibraltar into Spain | [as noun **smuggling**] cocaine smuggling has increased alarmingly.* ■ [with obj. and adverbial of direction] convey (someone or something) somewhere secretly and illicitly: *he smuggled out a message.*
– DERIVATIVES **smuggler** noun.
– ORIGIN late 17th cent.: from Low German *smuggelen*, of unknown ultimate origin.

smush /smʌʃ/ ▶ verb [with obj.] N. Amer. informal crush; smash: *they smushed marshmallows in their mouths.*
– ORIGIN early 19th cent.: alteration of **MUSH**¹.

smut ▶ noun 1 a small flake of soot or other dirt: *all those black smuts from the engine.* ■ a mark or smudge made by such a flake: *the curtains were grey with city smuts.*
2 [mass noun] a fungal disease of cereals in which parts of the ear change to black powder.
● The fungi belong to *Ustilago* and other genera, order Ustilaginales, class Teliomycetes.
3 [mass noun] obscene or lascivious talk, writing, or pictures: *porn, in this view, is far from being harmless smut.*
▶ verb (**smutted, smutting**) [with obj.] [often as adj. **smutted**] mark with flakes or soot or other dirt: *the smutted sky.* ■ infect (a plant) with smut: *smutted wheat.*
– DERIVATIVES **smuttily** adverb, **smuttiness** noun, **smutty** adjective (**smuttier, smuttiest**).
– ORIGIN late Middle English (in the sense 'defile, corrupt, make obscene'): related to German *schmutzen*; compare with **SMUDGE**¹. The noun dates from the mid 17th cent.

smut ball ▶ noun a grain of wheat or another cereal affected by smut.

smut mill ▶ noun a machine for removing smut from cereal grain.

Smuts /smʌts/, Jan (Christiaan) (1870–1950), South African statesman and soldier, Prime Minister 1919–24 and 1939–48. He led Boer forces during the Second Boer War, but afterwards supported the policy of Anglo-Boer cooperation. He commanded Allied troops against German East Africa (1916) and later helped to found the League of Nations.

Smyrna /ˈsmɜːnə/ an ancient city on the west coast of Asia Minor, on the site of modern Izmir in Turkey.

SN ▶ abbreviation for Senegal (international vehicle registration).

Sn ▶ symbol for the chemical element tin.
– ORIGIN from late Latin *stannum* 'tin'.

snack ▶ noun a small amount of food eaten between meals.
■ a light meal that is eaten in a hurry or in a casual manner. ■ Austral. informal a thing that is easy to accomplish: *it'll be a snack.*
▶ verb [no obj.] eat a snack: *she likes to snack on yogurt.*
– ORIGIN Middle English (originally in the sense 'snap, bite'): from Middle Dutch *snac(k)*, from

snacken 'to bite', variant of *snappen*. Senses relating to food date from the late 17th cent.

snack bar ▶ noun a place where snacks are sold.

snackette ▶ noun W. Indian a small shop selling snacks, cigarettes, and minor groceries.

snaffle ▶ noun (also **snaffle bit**) (on a bridle) a simple bit, typically a jointed one, used with a single set of reins.
  ■ (also **snaffle bridle**) a bridle with such a bit.
▶ verb [with obj.] informal take (something) for oneself, typically quickly or without permission: *shall we snaffle some of Bernard's sherry?*
– ORIGIN mid 16th cent. (denoting a bridle bit): probably from Low German or Dutch; compare with Middle Low German, Middle Dutch *snavel* 'beak, mouth'. The verb (mid 19th cent.) is perhaps a different word.

snafu /snaˈfuː, ˈsnafuː/ informal, chiefly N. Amer. ▶ noun a confused or chaotic state; a mess: *an enormous amount of my time was devoted to untangling snafus.*
▶ adjective in utter confusion or chaos: *our refrigeration plant is snafu.*
▶ verb [with obj.] throw (a situation) into chaos: *you ignored his orders and snafued everything.*
– ORIGIN 1940s: acronym from *situation normal: all fouled (or fucked) up.*

snag[1] ▶ noun **1** an unexpected or hidden obstacle or drawback: *there's one small snag.*
  2 a sharp, angular, or jagged projection: *keep an emery board handy in case of nail snags.*
  ■ a rent or tear in fabric caused by such a projection.
  3 N. Amer. a dead tree.
▶ verb (**snagged**, **snagging**) [with obj.] catch or tear (something) on a projection: *thorns snagged his sweater.*
  ■ [no obj.] become caught on a projection: *radio aerials snagged on bushes and branches.* ■ N. Amer. informal catch or obtain (someone or something): *it's the first time they've snagged the star for a photo.*
– DERIVATIVES **snaggy** adjective (only in sense 2).
– ORIGIN late 16th cent. (in sense 2): probably of Scandinavian origin. The early sense 'stump sticking out from a tree trunk' gave rise to a US sense 'submerged piece of timber obstructing navigation', of which sense 1 is originally a figurative use. Current verb senses arose in the 19th cent.

snag[2] ▶ noun Austral. informal a sausage.
– ORIGIN 1940s: of unknown origin.

snaggle ▶ noun a tangled or knotted mass.
▶ verb [no obj.] become knotted or tangled: *the column of smoke snaggled for a moment.*
– ORIGIN early 20th cent.: from the noun **SNAG**[1] + **-LE**[2].

snaggle-tooth ▶ noun **1** (pl. **snaggle-teeth**) an irregular or projecting tooth.
  2 (pl. **snaggle-tooths**) a small deep-sea fish with large fangs at the front of the jaws and a number of light organs on the body.
  ● Family Astronesthidae: several genera and species.
– DERIVATIVES **snaggle-toothed** adjective.

snail ▶ noun a mollusc with a single spiral shell into which the whole body can be withdrawn.
  ● Most orders in the class Gastropoda.
– DERIVATIVES **snail-like** adjective.
– ORIGIN Old English *snæg(e)l*, of Germanic origin; related to German *Schnecke.*

snailfish ▶ noun (pl. same or **-fishes**) a small fish of cool or cold seas, with loose jelly-like skin and typically a ventral sucker. Also called **SEA SNAIL**.
  ● *Liparis* and other genera, family Cyclopteridae: several species, including *L. liparis* of the North Atlantic.

snail mail ▶ noun [mass noun] informal the ordinary postal system as opposed to electronic mail.
  ■ correspondence sent using the postal system.

snail's pace ▶ noun [in sing.] an extremely slow speed: *he drove at a snail's pace.*
– DERIVATIVES **snail-paced** adjective.

snake ▶ noun **1** a long limbless reptile which has no eyelids, a short tail, and jaws that are capable of considerable extension. Some snakes have a venomous bite.
  ● Suborder Ophidia (or Serpentes), order Squamata: many families.
  ■ (in general use) a limbless lizard or amphibian.
  2 (also **snake in the grass**) a treacherous or deceitful person: *that man is a cold-blooded snake.*
  3 (**the snake**) a former system of interconnected exchange rates for the currencies of EC countries.

4 (in full **plumber's snake**) a long flexible wire for clearing obstacles in piping.
▶ verb [no obj., with adverbial of direction] move or extend with the twisting motion of a snake: *a rope snaked down.*
– DERIVATIVES **snake-like** adjective.
– ORIGIN Old English *snaca*, of Germanic origin.

snakebark maple ▶ noun a maple tree with longitudinal pale stripes on the bark.
  ● Genus *Acer*, family Aceraceae: several species, in particular *A. davidii* (of eastern Asia) and the moosewood.

snakebird ▶ noun another term for **DARTER** (in sense 1).

snakebite ▶ noun Brit. a drink consisting of draught cider and lager in equal proportions.

snakebitten ▶ adjective N. Amer. informal doomed to misfortune; unlucky: *the snakebitten space shuttle chalked up a fourth launch delay.*

snake charmer ▶ noun an entertainer who appears to make snakes move by playing music.

snake dance ▶ noun a dance in which the performers handle live snakes, imitate the motions of snakes, or form a line which moves in a zigzag fashion, in particular a ritual dance of the North American Hopi Indians involving the handling of live rattlesnakes.
▶ verb (**snake-dance**) [no obj.] dance in any of these ways.

snake eyes ▶ plural noun [treated as sing.] a throw of two ones with a pair of dice.
  ■ figurative the worst possible result; a complete lack of success: *his elegant, amusing book sadly came up snake eyes.*

snake fence (also **snake-rail fence**) ▶ noun N. Amer. a fence made of roughly split rails or poles joined in a zigzag pattern with their ends crossing.

snakefish ▶ noun (pl. same or **-fishes**) see **CUTLASSFISH, LIZARDFISH**.

snake fly ▶ noun a slender woodland insect with transparent wings and a long 'neck' which allows the head to be raised above the body.
  ● Family Raphidiidae, order Neuroptera: *Raphidia* and other genera.

snakehead ▶ noun a freshwater fish with a broad, heavily scaled head and a long cylindrical body, native to tropical Africa and Asia.
  ● Family Channidae: several genera and species.

snake lizard ▶ noun a nocturnal legless lizard native to Australia and New Guinea.
  ● *Delma, Lialis*, and other genera, family Pygopodidae: many species, in particular *D. nasuta* and *L. burtonis.*

snakelocks anemone ▶ noun a sea anemone of cool seas, with long snake-like tentacles. It has symbiotic algae living in its cells and giving it a green colour.
  ● *Anemonia viridis*, order Actiniaria.

snake mackerel ▶ noun another term for **ESCOLAR**.

snake oil ▶ noun [mass noun] informal, chiefly N. Amer. a substance with no real medicinal value sold as a remedy for all diseases: *some kelp products are snake oil, but the good ones promote plant growth* | figurative *the president's foreign policy is snake oil.*

snakepit ▶ noun a pit containing poisonous snakes.
  ■ figurative a scene of vicious behaviour or ruthless competition: *the literary snakepits of New York.*

snake-rail fence ▶ noun another term for **SNAKE FENCE**.

Snake River a river of the north-western US. Rising in Yellowstone National Park in Wyoming, it flows for 1,670 km (1,038 miles) through Idaho into the state of Washington, where it joins the Columbia River.

snakeroot ▶ noun **1** any of a number of North American plants reputed to contain an antidote to snake poison, in particular:
  ● (**Virginian snakeroot**) a birthwort with long heart-shaped leaves and curved tubular flowers (*Aristolochia serpentaria*, family Aristolochiaceae). ● (**white snakeroot**) a poisonous plant which causes milk-sickness in livestock (*Eupatorium rugosum*, family Compositae).
  2 any of a number of plants thought to resemble a snake in shape, in particular **Indian snakeroot** (see **RAUWOLFIA**).

snakes and ladders ▶ plural noun [treated as sing.] a children's game in which players move counters along a board, gaining an advantage by moving up pictures of ladders or a disadvantage by moving down pictures of snakes.

snake's head ▶ noun a Eurasian fritillary with flowers chequered in red and purple, typically growing in damp hay meadows and water meadows.
  ● *Fritillaria meleagris*, family Liliaceae.

snakeskin ▶ noun [mass noun] [often as modifier] the skin of a snake: *snakeskin boots.*

snakeweed ▶ noun [mass noun] old-fashioned term for **BISTORT**.

snakewood ▶ noun **1** a tree or shrub which has timber from which a snakebite antidote or other medicinal extract is obtained.
  ● Several species, in particular the tree *Strychnos minor* (or *colubrina*) (family Loganiaceae), of the Indian subcontinent.
  2 a tropical American tree which has timber with a snakeskin pattern, used for decorative work.
  ● *Brosimum rubescens*, family Moraceae.

snaky ▶ adjective (**-ier**, **-iest**) like a snake in appearance; long and sinuous: *a long snaky whip.*
  ■ of the supposed nature of a snake in showing coldness, venom, or cunning: *a snaky friend.*
  ■ Austral./NZ informal angry; irritable: *what are you snaky about?*
– DERIVATIVES **snakily** adverb, **snakiness** noun.

snap ▶ verb (**snapped**, **snapping**) **1** break or cause to break suddenly and completely, typically with a sharp cracking sound: [no obj.] *guitar strings kept snapping* | [with obj.] *dead twigs can be snapped off.*
  ■ [no obj.] emit a sudden, sharp cracking sound: *banners snapping in the breeze.* ■ [no obj.] (of an animal) make a sudden audible bite: *a dog was snapping at his heels.*
  ■ [with obj. and complement or adverbial] cause to move or alter in a specified way with a brisk movement and typically a sharp sound: *Rosa snapped her bag shut.*
  ■ [no obj., with complement or adverbial] move or alter in this way: *his mouth snapped into a tight, straight line.* ■ [no obj.] figurative suddenly lose one's self-control: *she claims she snapped after years of violence.* ■ [reporting verb] say something quickly and irritably to someone: [no obj.] *McIllvanney snapped at her* | [with direct speech] *'I really don't much care,' she snapped.*
  2 [with obj.] take a snapshot of: *he planned to spend the time snapping rare wildlife* | [no obj.] *photographers were snapping away at her.*
  3 [with obj.] American Football put (the ball) into play by a quick backward movement.
▶ noun **1** a sudden, sharp cracking sound or movement: *she closed her purse with a snap.*
  ■ [in sing.] a hurried, irritable tone or manner: *'I'm still waiting,' he said with a snap.* ■ [mass noun] vigour or liveliness of style or action; zest: *the snap of the dialogue.*
  2 a snapshot: *holiday snaps.*
  3 [mass noun] Brit. a card game in which cards from two piles are turned over simultaneously and players call 'snap' as quickly as possible when two similar cards are exposed.
  ■ [as exclamation] said when one notices that one has or does the identical thing to someone else: *'Snap!' They looked at each other's ties with a smile.*
  4 [mass noun] N. English food, especially food taken to work to be eaten during a break.
  5 [in sing.] N. Amer. informal an easy task: *a control panel that makes operation a snap.*
  6 (usu. **snaps**) N. Amer. a press stud.
▶ adjective [attrib.] done or taken on the spur of the moment, unexpectedly, or without notice: *a snap judgement* | *he could call a snap election.*
– PHRASES **in a snap** informal, chiefly N. Amer. in a moment; almost immediately: *gourmet-quality meals are ready in a snap.* **snap one's fingers** see **FINGER**. **snap someone's head off** see **HEAD**.
– DERIVATIVES **snappingly** adverb.
– ORIGIN late 15th cent. (in the senses 'make a sudden audible bite' and 'quick sharp biting sound'): probably from Middle Dutch or Middle Low German *snappen* 'seize'; partly imitative.
▶ **snap out of** [often in imperative] informal get out of (a bad or unhappy mood) by a sudden effort: *come on, Fran—snap out of it!*
snap something up quickly and eagerly buy or secure something that is in short supply or being sold cheaply: *all the tickets have been snapped up.*

snap-action ▶ adjective [attrib.] **1** denoting a switch or relay that makes and breaks contact rapidly, whatever the speed of the activating mechanism.
  2 denoting a gun whose hinged barrel is secured by a spring catch.
▶ noun (**snap action**) the operation of such a switch, relay, or gun.

snap bean ▶ **noun** N. Amer. a bean of a variety grown for its edible pods.
– ORIGIN late 18th cent.: so named because the pods are broken into pieces to be eaten.

snap-brim ▶ **adjective** (of a hat) with a brim that can be turned up and down at opposite sides.

snapdragon ▶ **noun** a plant bearing spikes of brightly coloured two-lobed flowers which gape like a mouth when a bee lands on the curved lip.
• *Antirrhinum majus*, family Scrophulariaceae.

snap fastener ▶ **noun** another term for **PRESS STUD**.

snap-hook (also **snap-link**) ▶ **noun** a hook with a spring allowing the entrance but preventing the escape of a cord, link, etc.

snap-lock ▶ **adjective** denoting a device or component which is fastened automatically when pushed into position: *the top is secured by snap-lock buckles.*

snap-on (also **snap-in**) ▶ **adjective** [attrib.] denoting a cover or attachment that is attached or secured with a snap.

snap pea ▶ **noun** another term for **SUGAR SNAP**.

snapper ▶ **noun 1** a marine fish that is typically reddish and is valued as food:
• a fish of a widespread tropical family (Lutjanidae, the **snapper family**), which snaps its toothed jaws. See also **RED SNAPPER**. • a fish of Australasian coastal waters (*Chrysophrys auratus*, family Sparidae).
2 another term for **SNAPPING TURTLE**.
3 informal a photographer.
4 N. Amer. a paper cracker, or the part of a cracker that makes a bang.
5 American Football a centre player.

snapping turtle ▶ **noun** a large American freshwater turtle with a long neck and strong hooked jaws.
• Family Chelydridae: *Chelydra serpentina* and the alligator snapper.

snappish ▶ **adjective** (of a dog) irritable and inclined to bite.
■ irritable and curt: *she was often snappish with the children.*
– DERIVATIVES **snappishly** adverb, **snappishness** noun.

snappy ▶ **adjective** (**snappier**, **snappiest**) informal **1** irritable and inclined to speak sharply; snappish: *anything unusual made her snappy and nervous.*
2 cleverly concise; neat: *snappy catchphrases.*
■ neat and elegant: *a snappy dresser.*
– PHRASES **make it snappy** be quick about it: *into bed and make it snappy!*
– DERIVATIVES **snappily** adverb, **snappiness** noun.

snap roll ▶ **noun** a manoeuvre in which an aircraft makes a single quick revolution about its longitudinal axis while flying horizontally.

snapshot ▶ **noun 1** an informal photograph taken quickly, typically with a small hand-held camera.
■ a brief look or summary: *this excellent book can only be a snapshot of a complex industry.* ■ Computing a record of the contents of a storage location or data file at a given time.
2 (**snap shot**) a shot in soccer or hockey taken quickly with little backlift.

snare ▶ **noun 1** a trap for catching birds or mammals, typically one having a noose of wire or cord.
■ figurative a thing likely to lure or tempt someone into harm or error: *seducers laid their snares for innocent provincials.* ■ Surgery a wire loop for severing polyps or other growths.
2 a length of wire, gut, or hide stretched across a drumhead to produce a rattling sound.
■ (also **snare drum**) another term for **SIDE DRUM**. [ORIGIN: probably from Middle Low German, Middle Dutch *snare* 'harp string'.]
▶ **verb** [with obj.] catch (a bird or mammal) in a snare.
■ figurative catch or trap (someone): *five blackmailers were snared in a police sting.*
– DERIVATIVES **snarer** noun.
– ORIGIN late Old English *sneare*, from Old Norse *snara*.

snarf ▶ **verb** [with obj.] informal, chiefly US eat or drink quickly or greedily: *they* **snarfed up** *frozen yogurt.*
– ORIGIN 1950s: perhaps imitative.

snark ▶ **noun** an imaginary animal (used to refer to someone or something that is difficult to track down).
– ORIGIN 1876: nonsense word coined by Lewis Carroll in *The Hunting of the Snark.*

snarky ▶ **adjective** (**-ier**, **-iest**) N. Amer. informal (of a person, words, or a mood) sharply critical; cutting: *the kid who makes snarky remarks in class.*

snarl[1] ▶ **verb** [no obj.] (of an animal such as a dog) make an aggressive growl with bared teeth: [as adj. **snarling**] *snarling alsatians.*
■ [reporting verb] (of a person) say something in an angry, bad-tempered voice: *I used to* **snarl at** *anyone I disliked* | [with direct speech] *'Shut your mouth!' he snarled* | [with obj.] *he snarled a few choice remarks at them.*
▶ **noun** an act or sound of snarling: *the cat drew its mouth back in a snarl.*
– DERIVATIVES **snarler** noun, **snarlingly** adverb, **snarly** adjective.
– ORIGIN late 16th cent.: extension of obsolete *snar*, of Germanic origin; related to German *schnarren* 'rattle, snarl', probably imitative.

snarl[2] ▶ **verb** [with obj.] **1** (**snarl something up**) entangle or impede something: *the trailing lead got snarled up in a bramble bush.*
■ [no obj.] (**snarl up**) become entangled or impeded: *the promising opening soon snarls up in a mess of motives.*
2 decorate (metalwork) with raised shapes by hammering the underside.
▶ **noun** a knot or tangle: *snarls of wild raspberry plants.*
– ORIGIN late Middle English (in the senses 'snare, noose' and 'catch in a snare'): from **SNARE**.

snarling iron ▶ **noun** a tool struck with a hammer to create decorative raised work on metal.

snarl-up ▶ **noun** informal a traffic jam.
■ a muddle or mistake: *there's a snarl-up in editing.*

snash ▶ **noun** [mass noun] Scottish insolence; abuse: *he did not have to take this snash.*
– ORIGIN late 18th cent.: probably imitative.

snatch ▶ **verb** [with obj.] quickly seize (something) in a rude or eager way: *she snatched a biscuit from the plate* | figurative *a victory snatched from the jaws of defeat.*
■ informal steal (something) or kidnap (someone), typically by seizing or grabbing suddenly: *a mission to snatch Winston Churchill.* ■ [no obj.] (**snatch at**) hastily or ineffectually attempt to seize (something): *she snatched at the handle.* ■ quickly secure or obtain (something) when a chance presents itself: *snatching a few hours' sleep.* ■ [no obj.] (**snatch at**) eagerly take or accept (an offer or opportunity): *I snatched at the chance.*
▶ **noun 1** an act of snatching or quickly seizing something: *a quick snatch of breath.*
■ a short spell of doing something: *brief snatches of sleep.* ■ a fragment of song or talk: *picking up snatches of conversation.* ■ informal a kidnapping or theft.
2 Weightlifting the rapid raising of a weight from the floor to above the head in one movement.
3 vulgar slang a woman's genitals.
– DERIVATIVES **snatcher** noun [in combination] *a bag-snatcher*, **snatchy** adjective.
– ORIGIN Middle English *sna(c)che* (verb) 'suddenly snap at', (noun) 'a snare'; perhaps related to **SNACK**.

snatch squad ▶ **noun** a group of police officers or soldiers detailed to seize troublemakers in a crowd.

snavel /ˈsnav(ə)l/ (also **snavle** or **snavvle**) ▶ **verb** [with obj.] Austral. informal steal; grab: *they'll snavel all the land.*
– ORIGIN late 18th cent. (originally English slang): perhaps a variant of **SNAFFLE**.

snazzy ▶ **adjective** (**snazzier**, **snazziest**) informal stylish and attractive: *snazzy little silk dresses.*
– DERIVATIVES **snazzily** adverb, **snazziness** noun.
– ORIGIN 1960s: of unknown origin.

sneak ▶ **verb** (past and past participle **sneaked** or informal, chiefly N. Amer. **snuck**) **1** [no obj., with adverbial of direction] move or go in a furtive or stealthy manner: *I sneaked out by the back exit.*
■ [with obj. and adverbial of direction] convey (someone or something) in such a way: *someone sneaked a camera inside.* ■ [with obj.] do or obtain (something) in a stealthy or furtive way: *she sneaked a glance at her watch.* ■ (**sneak up on**) creep up on (someone) without being detected: *he sneaks up on us slyly.*
2 [no obj.] Brit. informal (especially in children's use) inform an adult or person in authority of a companion's misdeeds; tell tales: *she* **sneaked on** *us.*
▶ **noun** informal **1** Brit. (especially in children's use) someone who informs an adult or person in authority of a companion's misdeeds; a telltale.
■ a furtive and contemptible person: *he was branded a prying sneak for eavesdropping on intimate conversation.*
2 (usu. **sneaks**) N. Amer. short for **SNEAKER**.
▶ **adjective** [attrib.] acting or done surreptitiously, unofficially, or without warning: *a sneak thief* | *a sneak preview.*
– ORIGIN late 16th cent.: probably dialect; perhaps related to obsolete *snike* 'to creep'.

USAGE The traditional standard past form of **sneak** is **sneaked** (*she* **sneaked** *round the corner*). An alternative past form, **snuck** (*she* **snuck** *past me*), arose in the US in the 19th century. Until very recently **snuck** was confined to US dialect use and was regarded as non-standard. However, in the last few decades its use has spread, particularly in the US, where it is now generally regarded as a standard alternative to **sneaked**. In the Oxford Reading Programme, there are equal numbers of US citations for **snuck** and **sneaked**.

sneakbox ▶ **noun** US a small, flat boat masked with brush or weeds, used in wildfowl shooting.

sneaker ▶ **noun** chiefly N. Amer. a soft shoe worn for sports or casual occasions.

sneaking ▶ **adjective** [attrib.] **1** (of a feeling) persistent in one's mind but reluctantly held or not fully recognized; nagging: *I've a sneaking suspicion they'll do well.*
2 informal furtive and contemptible: *an unpleasant, sneaking habit.*
– DERIVATIVES **sneakingly** adverb.

sneaky ▶ **adjective** (**sneakier**, **sneakiest**) furtive; sly: *sneaky, underhand tactics.*
■ (of a feeling) secret; reluctant: *I developed a sneaky fondness for the old lady.*
– DERIVATIVES **sneakily** adverb, **sneakiness** noun.

sneck Scottish & N. English ▶ **noun** a latch on a door or window.
▶ **verb** [with obj.] close or fasten (a door or window) with a latch.
– ORIGIN Middle English: obscurely related to **SNATCH**.

sneer ▶ **noun** a contemptuous or mocking smile, remark, or tone: *he acknowledged their presence with a condescending sneer.*
▶ **verb** [no obj.] smile or speak in a contemptuous or mocking manner: *she had* **sneered at** *their bad taste* | [with direct speech] *'I see you're conservative in your ways,' David sneered.*
– DERIVATIVES **sneerer** noun, **sneeringly** adverb.
– ORIGIN late Middle English: probably of imitative origin.

sneeze ▶ **verb** [no obj.] make a sudden involuntary expulsion of air from the nose and mouth due to irritation of one's nostrils: *the smoke made her sneeze.*
▶ **noun** an act or the sound of expelling air from the nose in such a way: *he stopped a sudden sneeze.*
– PHRASES **not to be sneezed at** informal not to be rejected without careful consideration; worth having or taking into account: *a saving of £550 was not to be sneezed at.*
– DERIVATIVES **sneezer** noun, **sneezy** adjective.
– ORIGIN Middle English: apparently an alteration of Middle English *fnese* due to misreading or misprinting (after initial *fn-* had become unfamiliar), later adopted because it sounded appropriate.

sneeze machine ▶ **noun** S. African a cannon-like device used for spraying tear gas.

sneezeweed ▶ **noun** [mass noun] a yellow-flowered North American plant of the daisy family. Some kinds are toxic to grazing animals and some are used by American Indians in the treatment of colds.
• Genus *Helenium*, family Compositae.

sneezewort ▶ **noun** a Eurasian plant related to the yarrow, whose dried leaves induce sneezing.
• *Achillea ptarmica*, family Compositae.

snell N. Amer. ▶ **noun** a short line of gut or horsehair by which a fish-hook is attached to a longer line.
▶ **verb** [with obj.] tie or fasten (a hook) to a line: [as adj. **snelled**] *a snelled or long-shanked hook.*
– ORIGIN mid 19th cent.: of unknown origin.

Snellen test /ˈsnɛl(ə)n/ ▶ **noun** an eyesight test using rows of letters printed in successively decreasing sizes (the **Snellen scale**) of which patients are asked to read as many as they can.
– ORIGIN mid 19th cent.: named after Hermann *Snellen* (1834–1908), Dutch ophthalmologist.

Snell's law Physics a law stating that the ratio of the sines of the angles of incidence and refraction of a wave are constant when it passes between two given media.

– ORIGIN late 19th cent.: named after Willebrord Van Roijen *Snell* (1591–1626), Dutch mathematician.

snib chiefly Scottish & Irish ▶**noun** a lock, latch, or fastening for a door or window.
▪the small catch on a Yale lock which holds the bolt in or out.
▶**verb** (**snibbed**, **snibbing**) [with obj.] bolt, fasten, or lock (a door).
– ORIGIN early 19th cent.: perhaps from Low German *snibbe* 'beak-like point'.

snick ▶**verb** [with obj.] **1** cut a small notch or incision in (something): *the stem can be carefully snicked to allow the bud to swell.*
▪Cricket deflect (the ball) slightly with the edge of the bat; deflect a ball delivered by (a bowler) in this way.
2 cause (something) to make a sharp clicking sound: [with obj. and complement] *he placed the pen in the briefcase and snicked it shut.*
▪[no obj.] make such a sound: *the bolt snicked into place.*
▶**noun 1** a small notch or cut: *he had several shaving snicks.*
▪Cricket a slight deflection of the ball by the bat.
2 a sharp click: *he heard the snick of the latch.*
– ORIGIN late 17th cent.: probably from obsolete *snick or snee* 'fight with knives'.

snicker ▶**verb** [no obj.] give a smothered or half-suppressed laugh; snigger.
▪(of a horse) whinny.
▶**noun** a smothered laugh; a snigger.
▪a whinny.
– DERIVATIVES **snickeringly** adverb.
– ORIGIN late 17th cent.: imitative.

snicket ▶**noun** chiefly N. English a narrow passage between houses; an alleyway.
– ORIGIN late 19th cent.: of unknown origin.

snide ▶**adjective 1** derogatory or mocking in an indirect way: *snide remarks about my mother.*
▪chiefly US (of a person) devious and underhand: *a snide divorce lawyer.*
2 counterfeit; inferior: *snide Rolex watches.*
▶**noun** an unpleasant or underhand person or remark.
– DERIVATIVES **snidely** adverb, **snideness** noun, **snidey** adjective.
– ORIGIN mid 19th cent. (originally slang in sense 2): of unknown origin.

sniff ▶**verb** [no obj.] draw up air audibly through the nose to detect a smell, to stop it running, or to express contempt: *his dog* **sniffed at** *my trousers* | [with direct speech] *'You're behaving in an unladylike fashion,' sniffed Mother.*
▪[with obj.] draw in (a scent, substance, or air) through the nose. ▪ [usu. with negative] (**sniff at**) show contempt or dislike for: *the price is not to be sniffed at.* ▪ (**sniff around/round**) informal investigate covertly, especially in an attempt to find out confidential or incriminating information about someone. ▪ [with obj.] (**sniff something out**) informal discover something by investigation: *he made millions sniffing out tax loopholes for companies.*
▶**noun** an act or sound of drawing air through the nose: *he gave a sniff of disapproval.*
▪an amount of air or other substance taken up in such a way: *his drug use was confined to a* **sniff of** *amyl nitrite.* ▪ [in sing.] informal a hint or sign: *they're off at the first* **sniff of** *trouble.* ▪ [in sing.] informal a small chance: *the Olympic hosts will at least* **get a sniff at** *a medal.*
– ORIGIN Middle English: imitative.

sniffer ▶**noun 1** a person who sniffs, especially one who sniffs a drug or toxic substance: *he gave a sniff which suggested that the sniffer had eaten better food.*
▪informal a device for detecting an invisible and dangerous substance, such as gas or radiation: *electronic sniffers are used to detect the presence of a nuclear mass.*
2 informal a person's nose.
3 (also **sniffer program**) a computer program that detects and records a variety of restricted information, especially the secret passwords needed to gain access to files or networks.

sniffer dog ▶**noun** informal a dog trained to find drugs or explosives by smell.

sniffle ▶**verb** [no obj.] sniff slightly or repeatedly, typically because of a cold or fit of crying.
▶**noun** an act of sniffing in such a way: *he was restraining his sniffles rather well.*
▪a head cold causing a running nose and sniffing: *she had a slight cough and a sniffle.*
– DERIVATIVES **sniffler** noun, **sniffly** adjective.
– ORIGIN mid 17th cent.: imitative; compare with **SNIVEL**.

sniffy ▶**adjective** (**sniffier**, **sniffiest**) informal scornful; contemptuous: *some people are sniffy about tea bags.*
– DERIVATIVES **sniffily** adverb, **sniffiness** noun.

snifter ▶**noun** informal a small quantity of an alcoholic drink: *care to join me for a snifter?*
▪chiefly N. Amer. a balloon glass for brandy.
– ORIGIN mid 19th cent.: imitative; compare with dialect *snift* 'to snort'.

snifter valve (also **snifting valve**) ▶**noun** a valve on a steam engine that allows air in or out.

snig ▶**verb** (**snigged**, **snigging**) [with obj.] Austral./NZ drag (a heavy load, especially timber) using ropes or chains: *bullock teams would snig the logs to the winder.*
– ORIGIN late 18th cent.: of unknown origin.

snigger ▶**noun** a smothered or half-suppressed laugh.
▶**verb** [no obj.] give such a laugh: *the boys at school were sure to snigger at him behind his back* | [with direct speech] *'Doesn't he look a fool?' they sniggered.*
– DERIVATIVES **sniggerer** noun, **sniggeringly** adverb.
– ORIGIN early 18th cent.: later variant of **SNICKER**.

sniggery ▶**adjective** informal characterized by or liable to cause sniggering: *sniggery jokes.*

snigging chain ▶**noun** Austral./NZ a chain used to move logs.

sniggle ▶**verb** [no obj.] fish for eels by pushing a baited hook into holes in which they are hiding.
– ORIGIN mid 17th cent.: frequentative, based on earlier *snig* 'small eel', of unknown origin.

snip ▶**verb** (**snipped**, **snipping**) [with obj.] cut (something) with scissors or shears, typically with small quick strokes: *she was snipping a few dead heads off the roses* | [no obj.] *she inspected the embroidery,* **snipping at** *loose threads.*
▶**noun 1** an act of cutting something in such a way: *he took a snip at a dandelion on the grass.*
▪a small piece of something that has been cut off: *the collage consists of snips of wallpaper.*
2 [in sing.] Brit. informal a surprisingly cheap item; a bargain: *the wine is a snip at £2.65.*
▪dated a thing that is easily achieved.
3 (**snips**) hand shears, especially for cutting metal: *use tin snips.*
4 N. Amer. informal a small or insignificant person: *imagine that little snip telling me I was wrong!*
– ORIGIN mid 16th cent. (in the sense 'a shred'): from Low German *snip* 'small piece', of imitative origin.

snipe /snʌɪp/ ▶**noun** (pl. same or **snipes**) a wading bird of marshes and wet meadows, with brown camouflaged plumage, a long straight bill, and typically a drumming display flight. See also **PAINTED SNIPE**, **SEED-SNIPE**.
● *Gallinago* and other genera, family Scolopacidae: several species, e.g. the **common snipe** (*G. gallinago*).
▶**verb** [no obj.] shoot at someone from a hiding place, especially accurately and at long range: *the soldiers in the trench* **sniped at** *us.*
▪make a sly or petty verbal attack: *the state governor constantly* **sniped at** *the president* | [as noun **sniping**] *there has been some sniping about inept leadership.*
– DERIVATIVES **sniper** noun.
– ORIGIN Middle English: probably of Scandinavian origin; compare with Icelandic *mýrisnípa*; obscurely related to Dutch *snip* and German *Schnepfe*.

snipe eel ▶**noun** a slender marine eel with a long, thin beak-like snout, typically occurring in deep water.
● Family Nemichthyidae: several genera and species.

snipefish ▶**noun** (pl. same or **-fishes**) a marine fish that has a long, slender snout with the mouth at the tip.
● Family Macrorhamphosidae: several genera and species.

snipe fly ▶**noun** a slender, long-legged predatory fly which catches insect prey on the wing.
● Family Rhagionidae: many genera and species.

snippet ▶**noun** a small piece or brief extract: *snippets of information about the war.*
– DERIVATIVES **snippety** adjective.

snippy ▶**adjective** (**snippier**, **snippiest**) informal curt or sharp, especially in a condescending way: *a snippy note from our landlord.*
– DERIVATIVES **snippily** adverb, **snippiness** noun.

snit ▶**noun** N. Amer. informal a fit of irritation; a sulk: *the ambassador and delegation had withdrawn in a snit.*
– ORIGIN 1930s: of unknown origin.

snitch informal ▶**verb 1** [with obj.] steal.
2 [no obj.] inform on someone: *she wouldn't tell who* **snitched on** *me.*
▶**noun** an informer.
– ORIGIN late 17th cent.: of unknown origin.

snivel ▶**verb** (**snivelled**, **snivelling**; US **sniveled**, **sniveling**) [no obj.] cry and sniffle: *Kate started to snivel, looking sad and stunned.*
▪complain in a whining or tearful way: *he shouldn't snivel about his punishment* | [as adj. **snivelling**] *you snivelling little brat!*
▶**noun** a slight sniff indicating suppressed emotion or crying: *Lucy's torrent of howls weakened to a snivel.*
– DERIVATIVES **sniveller** noun, **snivellingly** adverb.
– ORIGIN late Old English (recorded only in the verbal noun *snyflung* 'mucus'), from *snofl*, in the same sense; compare with **SNUFFLE**.

snob ▶**noun** a person with an exaggerated respect for high social position or wealth who seeks to associate with social superiors and dislikes people or activities regarded as lower-class.
▪[with adj. or noun modifier] a person who believes that their tastes in a particular area are superior to those of other people: *a musical snob.*
– DERIVATIVES **snobbery** noun (pl. **-ies**), **snobbism** noun, **snobby** adjective (**snobbier**, **snobbiest**).
– ORIGIN late 18th cent. (originally dialect in the sense 'cobbler'): of unknown origin; early senses conveyed a notion of 'lower status or rank', later denoting a person seeking to imitate those of superior social standing or wealth. Folk etymology connects the word with Latin *sine nobilitate* 'without nobility' but the first recorded sense has no connection with this.

snobbish ▶**adjective** of, characteristic of, or like a snob: *the writer takes a rather snobbish tone.*
– DERIVATIVES **snobbishly** adverb, **snobbishness** noun.

SNOBOL /ˈsnəʊbɒl/ ▶**noun** [mass noun] a high-level computer programming language used especially in manipulating textual data.
– ORIGIN 1960s: formed from letters taken from *string-oriented symbolic language*, on the pattern of *COBOL*.

snob value ▶**noun** [mass noun] value attached to something for its power to indicate supposed social superiority; cachet: *the 'Lancashire' coffin was more expensive and carried snob value.*

sno-cone ▶**noun** variant spelling of **SNOW CONE**.

snoek /snuːk/ ▶**noun** South African term for **BARRACOUTA**.
– ORIGIN Afrikaans from Dutch, 'pike'; compare with **SNOOK**[2].

snog Brit. informal ▶**verb** (**snogged**, **snogging**) [with obj.] kiss and caress amorously: *he snogged my girl at a party* | [no obj.] *the pair were snogging on the sofa.*
▶**noun** an act or spell of amorous kissing and caressing: *he gave her a proper snog, not just a peck.*
– DERIVATIVES **snogger** noun.
– ORIGIN 1940s: of unknown origin.

snood /snuːd/ ▶**noun 1** an ornamental hairnet or fabric bag worn over the hair at the back of a woman's head.
▪historical a ribbon or band worn by unmarried women in Scotland to confine their hair.
2 a wide ring of knitted material worn as a hood or scarf.
3 a short line attaching a hook to a main line in sea fishing.
– ORIGIN Old English *snōd*, of unknown origin.

snook[1] /snuːk/ ▶**noun** (in phrase **cock a snook**) informal, chiefly Brit. place one's hand so that the thumb touches one's nose and the fingers are spread out, in order to express contempt.
▪ figurative openly show contempt or a lack of respect for someone or something: *he spent a lifetime cocking a snook at the art world.*
– ORIGIN late 18th cent.: of unknown origin.

snook[2] /snuːk/ ▶**noun** a large edible game fish of the Caribbean which is sometimes found in brackish water.
● *Centropomus undecimalis*, family Centropomidae.
– ORIGIN late 17th cent.: from Dutch *snoek* (see **SNOEK**).

snooker ▶**noun** [mass noun] a game played with cues on a billiard table in which the players use a cue ball (white) to pocket the other balls (fifteen red and six coloured) in a set order.
▪[count noun] a position in a game of snooker or pool in which a player cannot make a direct shot at any permitted ball: *he needed a snooker to have a chance of winning the frame.*

▶ **verb** [with obj.] subject (oneself or one's opponent) to a snooker.
■ figurative leave (someone) in a difficult position; thwart: *I managed to lose my flat keys—that was me snookered.* ■ figurative US trick, entice, or trap: *they were **snookered** into buying books at prices that were too high.*
– ORIGIN late 19th cent.: of unknown origin.

snoop informal ▶ **verb** [no obj.] investigate or look around furtively in an attempt to find out something, especially information about someone's private affairs: *your sister might find the ring if she goes **snooping about*** | [as adj. **snooping**] *snooping neighbours.*
▶ **noun** [in sing.] an act of looking around in such a way: *I could go back to her cottage and have another snoop.*
■ a person who investigates in such a way; a detective.
– DERIVATIVES **snooper** noun, **snoopy** adjective.
– ORIGIN mid 19th cent.: from Dutch *snoepen* 'eat on the sly'.

snooperscope ▶ **noun** a device which converts infrared radiation into a visible image, used for seeing in the dark.

snoot ▶ **noun 1** informal a person's nose.
2 informal a person who shows contempt for those considered to be of a lower social class: *the snoots complain that the paper has lowered its standards.*
3 a tubular or conical attachment used to produce a narrow beam from a spotlight.
▶ **adjective** informal stylish and sophisticated: *a snoot silk shirt.*
– ORIGIN mid 19th cent.: variant of **SNOUT**.

snootful ▶ **noun** as much as one can take of something, especially alcoholic drink: *for a hundred kopecks, you get a snootful of vodka.*

snooty ▶ **adjective** (**snootier**, **snootiest**) informal showing disapproval or contempt towards others, especially those considered to belong to a lower social class: *snooty neighbours.*
– DERIVATIVES **snootily** adverb, **snootiness** noun.
– ORIGIN early 20th cent.: from **SNOOT** + **-Y**[1]; compare with **SNOTTY**.

snooze informal ▶ **noun** a short, light sleep, especially during the day: *he settled in the grass for a snooze.*
▶ **verb** [no obj.] have a short, light sleep: *the children play beach games while the adults snooze in the sun.*
– DERIVATIVES **snoozer** noun, **snoozy** adjective (**snoozier**, **snooziest**).
– ORIGIN late 18th cent.: of unknown origin.

snooze button ▶ **noun** a control on a clock which sets an alarm to repeat after a short interval, allowing time for a little more sleep.

snore ▶ **noun** a snorting or grunting sound in a person's breathing while they are asleep: *she lay on the mattress listening to Sally's snores.*
■ informal a thing that is extremely boring: *she sings a version of 'Passionate Kisses' that's a certified snore.*
▶ **verb** [no obj.] make such a sound while asleep: *he was snoring loudly* | [as noun **snoring**] *you keep me awake all night with your snoring.*
– DERIVATIVES **snorer** noun.
– ORIGIN Middle English (in the sense 'a snort, snorting'): probably imitative; compare with **SNORT**.

snorkel /ˈsnɔːk(ə)l/ ▶ **noun 1** a tube for a swimmer to breathe through while under water.
2 (**Snorkel**) trademark a type of hydraulically elevated platform for firefighting.
▶ **verb** (**snorkelled**, **snorkelling**; US **snorkeled**, **snorkeling**) [no obj.] [often as noun **snorkelling**] swim using a snorkel: *the sea is incredibly clear—ideal for snorkelling* | *snorkel around the unspoilt coral reefs.*
– DERIVATIVES **snorkeller** noun.
– ORIGIN 1940s: from German *Schnorchel*.

Snorri Sturluson /ˌsnɔːrɪ ˈstəːləs(ə)n/ (1178–1241), Icelandic historian and poet. A leading figure of medieval Icelandic literature, he wrote the *Younger Edda* or *Prose Edda* and the *Heimskringla*, a history of the kings of Norway from mythical times to the year 1177.

snort ▶ **noun 1** an explosive sound made by the sudden forcing of breath through a person's nose, used to express indignation, derision, or incredulity: *he gave a snort of disgust.*
■ a similar sound made by an animal, typically when excited or frightened. ■ informal an inhaled dose of an illegal powdered drug, especially cocaine: *they were high on a few snorts.* ■ informal a measure of an alcoholic drink: *a bottle of rum was opened and they took a good long snort.*
▶ **verb** [no obj.] make a sudden sound through one's nose, especially to express indignation or derision: *she snorted with laughter* | [with direct speech] *'How perfectly ridiculous!' he snorted.*
■ (of an animal) make such a sound, especially when excited or frightened. ■ [with obj.] informal inhale (an illegal drug).
– ORIGIN late Middle English (as a verb, also in the sense 'snore'): probably imitative; compare with **SNORE**. The noun dates from the early 19th cent.

snorter ▶ **noun** informal **1** a person or thing that snorts, especially someone who inhales cocaine.
2 Brit. dated a thing that is an extreme or remarkable example of its kind, especially for its strength or severity: *the opening batsman fended off a snorter.*

snot ▶ **noun** [mass noun] informal nasal mucus.
■ [count noun] a contemptible or worthless person.
– ORIGIN late Middle English: probably from Middle Dutch, Middle Low German; related to **SNOUT**.

snot-nosed ▶ **adjective** informal childish and inexperienced (used as a general term of abuse): *a boy at thirteen is a **snot-nosed kid**.*
■ (of a person) considering oneself superior; conceited: *a snot-nosed snob.*

snot rag ▶ **noun** informal a handkerchief.

snotter[1] ▶ **noun** (usu. **snotters**) informal, chiefly Scottish a piece or drop of nasal mucus.

snotter[2] ▶ **noun** Nautical a fitting which holds the heel of a sprit close to the mast.
■ a length of rope with an eye spliced in each end.
– ORIGIN mid 18th cent.: of unknown origin.

snotty ▶ **adjective** (**snottier**, **snottiest**) informal **1** full of or covered with nasal mucus: *a snotty nose.*
2 having or showing a superior or conceited attitude: *a snotty letter.*
– DERIVATIVES **snottily** adverb, **snottiness** noun.

snotty-nosed ▶ **adjective** informal another term for **SNOT-NOSED**.

snout ▶ **noun 1** the projecting nose and mouth of an animal, especially a mammal.
■ derogatory a person's nose. ■ the projecting front or end of something such as a pistol.
2 Brit. informal a cigarette.
■ [mass noun] tobacco. [ORIGIN: late 19th cent.: of unknown origin.]
3 Brit. informal a police informer.
4 (also **snout moth**) a European moth with long palps that extend in front of the head like a snout.
• *Hypsena* and other genera, family Noctuidae, in particular **the snout** (*H. proboscidalis*).
– DERIVATIVES **snouted** adjective [often in combination] *long-snouted baboons*, **snouty** adjective.
– ORIGIN Middle English: from Middle Dutch, Middle Low German *snūt*; related to **SNOT**.

snout beetle ▶ **noun** North American term for **WEEVIL**.

snout butterfly ▶ **noun** a butterfly with long palps that extend in front of the head like a snout.
• Subfamily Libytheinae, family Nymphalidae: several species, including the nettle-tree butterfly.

Snow, C. P., 1st Baron Snow of Leicester (1905–80), English novelist and scientist; full name *Charles Percy Snow*. He is best known for his sequence of eleven novels *Strangers and Brothers*, which deals with moral dilemmas in the academic world, and for his lecture *Two Cultures* (1959).

snow ▶ **noun** [mass noun] **1** atmospheric water vapour frozen into ice crystals and falling in light white flakes or lying on the ground as a white layer: *we were trudging through deep snow* | (**snows**) *the first snows of winter.*
2 something that resembles snow in colour or texture, in particular:
■ a mass of flickering white spots on a television or radar screen, caused by interference or a poor signal. ■ informal cocaine. ■ a dessert or other dish resembling snow: *vanilla snow.* ■ [with modifier] a frozen gas resembling snow: *carbon dioxide snow.*
▶ **verb 1** [no obj.] (**it snows**, **it is snowing**, etc.) snow falls: *it's not snowing so heavily now.*
■ (**be snowed in/up**) be confined or blocked by a large quantity of snow: *I was snowed in for a week.* ■ [with obj.] figurative used to describe the arrival of an overwhelming quantity of something: *in the last week it had snowed letters and business.* ■ [with obj.] sprinkle or scatter (something), causing it to fall like snow: *the ceiling is snowing green flakes of paint on to the seats.*
2 [with obj.] informal, chiefly N. Amer. mislead or charm (someone) with elaborate and insincere words: *they would snow the public into believing that all was well.*
– DERIVATIVES **snowless** adjective, **snowlike** adjective.
– ORIGIN Old English *snāw*, of Germanic origin; related to Dutch *sneeuw* and German *Schnee*, from an Indo-European root shared by Latin *nix*, *niv-* and Greek *nipha*.
▶ **snow someone under** (usu. **be snowed under**) overwhelm someone with a large quantity of something, especially work: *he's been snowed under with urgent cases.*

snowball ▶ **noun 1** a ball of packed snow, especially one made for throwing at other people for fun.
■ figurative a thing that grows rapidly in intensity or importance: [as modifier] *the bustle has a snowball effect on the day's turnover.* ■ a dessert resembling a ball of snow, especially one containing or covered in ice cream.
2 a cocktail containing advocaat and lemonade.
▶ **verb 1** [with obj.] throw snowballs at: *I made sure the other kids stopped snowballing Celia.*
2 [no obj.] increase rapidly in size, intensity, or importance: *the campaign was snowballing.*
– PHRASES **a snowball's chance** (**in hell**) informal no chance at all: *the scheme has a snowball's chance in hell of being accepted.*

snowball tree (also **snowball bush**) ▶ **noun** a guelder rose of a sterile variety which produces large globular white flower heads.

snowbell ▶ **noun** an Asian tree related to the storax, bearing clusters of fragrant white hanging flowers at midsummer.
• *Styrax japonica*, family Styracaceae.

snowberry ▶ **noun** a North American shrub of the honeysuckle family, bearing white berries and often cultivated as an ornamental or for hedging.
• *Symphoricarpos albus*, family Caprifoliaceae.

snowbird ▶ **noun 1** N. Amer. informal a northerner who moves to a warmer Southern state in the winter.
2 a widespread and variable junco with grey or brown upper parts and a white belly.
• *Junco hyemalis*, family Emberizidae (subfamily Emberizinae). Alternative name: **dark-eyed junco**.
■ the snow bunting.

snow-blind ▶ **adjective** temporarily blinded by the glare of light reflected by a large expanse of snow.
– DERIVATIVES **snow blindness** noun.

snowblink ▶ **noun** a white reflection in the sky of snow or ice on the ground.

snowblower ▶ **noun** a machine that clears fallen snow by blowing it out to the side of the road.

snowboard ▶ **noun** a board resembling a short, broad ski, used for sliding downhill on snow.
▶ **verb** [no obj.] slide downhill on such a board: [as noun **snowboarding**] *the thrills of snowboarding.*
– DERIVATIVES **snowboarder** noun.

snow boot ▶ **noun** a warm waterproof boot worn in the snow.

snowbound ▶ **adjective** prevented from travelling or going out by snow or snowy weather: *he was snowbound in the nearby mountains.*
■ covered in snow or inaccessible because of it: *a snowbound Alpine village.*

snow bunting ▶ **noun** a northern bunting that breeds mainly in the Arctic, the male having white plumage with a black back in the breeding season.
• *Plectrophenax nivalis*, family Emberizidae (subfamily Emberizinae).

snow cannon ▶ **noun** a machine which makes artificial snow and blows it on to ski slopes.

snowcap ▶ **noun 1** a covering of snow on the top of a mountain.
2 a small Central American hummingbird with mainly purple plumage and a white crown.
• *Microchera albocoronata*, family Trochilidae.
– DERIVATIVES **snow-capped** adjective (in sense 1).

snowcat ▶ **noun** a tracked vehicle for travelling over snow.
– ORIGIN 1940s: from **SNOW** + **CATERPILLAR**.

snow chains ▶ **plural noun** a pair or set of meshes of metal chain, fitted around a vehicle's tyres to give extra grip in snow.

snowcock ▶ **noun** a large partridge found in the high mountains of Central and East Asia, with predominantly grey and white plumage.
• Genus *Tetraogallus*, family Phasianidae: five species.

snow cone (also **sno-cone**) ▶ **noun** N. Amer. & W. Indian a paper cup of crushed ice flavoured with fruit syrup.

snow crab ▶ **noun** an edible spider crab found off the eastern seaboard of Canada.

• *Chionoecetes opilio*, section Oxyrhyncha.

Snowdon a mountain in NW Wales. Rising to 1,085 m (3,560 ft), it is the highest mountain in Wales. Welsh name **YR WYDDFA**.

Snowdonia /snəʊˈdəʊnɪə/ a massif region in NW Wales, forming the heart of the Snowdonia National Park. Its highest peak is Snowdon.

snowdrift ▶ **noun** a bank of deep snow heaped up by the wind.

snowdrop ▶ **noun** a bulbous European plant which bears drooping white flowers during the late winter.
• *Galanthus nivalis*, family Liliaceae (or Amaryllidaceae).

snowfall ▶ **noun** a fall of snow: *heavy snowfalls made travel absolutely impossible* | [mass noun] *he was forced back by high winds and snowfall*.
■ [mass noun] the quantity of snow falling within a given area in a given time: *the average snowfall is 7.5 m a year*.

snowfield ▶ **noun** a permanent wide expanse of snow in mountainous or polar regions.

snowflake ▶ **noun 1** a flake of snow, especially a feathery ice crystal, typically displaying delicate sixfold symmetry.
2 a white-flowered Eurasian plant related to and resembling the snowdrop, typically blooming in the summer or autumn.
• Genus *Leucojum*, family Liliaceae (or Amaryllidaceae).

snow flea ▶ **noun** either of two small insects that appear on or near snow in northern regions or on mountains:
• a small flightless scorpion fly which feeds on mosses (family Boreidae, including the Eurasian *Boreus hyemalis*); North American name: **snow scorpion fly**. • a springtail that often swarms on snow, making it appear black (family Isotomidae, including the Alpine *Isotoma saltans* and the North American *Hypogastrura nivicola*).

snow goose ▶ **noun** a gregarious goose that breeds in Arctic Canada and Greenland, typically having white plumage with black wing tips.
• *Anser caerulescens*, family Anatidae.

snow gun ▶ **noun** another term for **SNOW CANNON**.

snow hole ▶ **noun** a hole in snow used as a temporary shelter, typically one made for the purpose.

snow-in-summer ▶ **noun** [mass noun] either of two white-flowered plants with silvery-green leaves:
• a low-growing southern European plant of the pink family (*Cerastium tomentosum*, family Caryophyllaceae). • an evergreen Australian shrub of the daisy family (*Helichrysum rosmarinifolium*, family Compositae).

snow job ▶ **noun** informal a deception or concealment of one's real motive in an attempt to flatter or persuade: *we shall need to* **do a snow job on** *him*.

snow leopard ▶ **noun** a rare large cat which has pale grey fur patterned with dark blotches and rings, living in the Altai mountains, Hindu Kush, and Himalayas. Also called **OUNCE**².
• *Panthera uncia*, family Felidae.

snowline ▶ **noun** (usu. **the snowline**) the altitude above which some snow remains on the ground in a particular place throughout the year.
■ the altitude above which there is snow on the ground in a particular place at a given time.

snow machine ▶ **noun** N. Amer. another term for **SNOWMOBILE**.

snowman ▶ **noun** (pl. **-men**) a representation of a human figure created with compressed snow.

snowmelt ▶ **noun** [mass noun] chiefly N. Amer. the melting of fallen snow: *heavy rains combine with rapid snowmelt*.
■ water that results from this: *the day was spring-like and the snowmelt shone in blue and gold*.

snowmobile /ˈsnəʊməbiːl/ ▶ **noun** a motor vehicle, especially one with runners or caterpillar tracks, for travelling over snow.

snowpack ▶ **noun** a mass of lying snow that is compressed and hardened by its own weight.

snow partridge ▶ **noun** a Himalayan partridge with fine black and white bars on the upper parts and a red bill and legs.
• *Lerwa lerwa*, family Phasianidae.

snow pea ▶ **noun** chiefly N. Amer. another term for **MANGETOUT**.

snowplough (US **snowplow**) ▶ **noun 1** an implement or vehicle for clearing roads of thick snow by pushing it aside.
2 Skiing an act of turning the points of one's skis inwards in order to slow down or turn.
▶ **verb** [no obj.] ski with the tips of one's skis pointing inwards in order to slow down or turn.

snowscape ▶ **noun** a landscape covered in snow.
■ a picture of such a landscape.

snowshoe ▶ **noun** a flat device resembling a racket, which is attached to the sole of a boot and used for walking on snow.
▶ **verb** [no obj., with adverbial of direction] travel wearing snowshoes: *we snowshoed down into the next valley*.
– DERIVATIVES **snowshoer** noun.

snowshoe hare (N. Amer. also **snowshoe rabbit**) ▶ **noun** a North American hare with large hairy hind feet, fairly small ears, and a white winter coat.
• *Lepus americanus*, family Leporidae.

snowstorm ▶ **noun** a heavy fall of snow, especially with a high wind.
■ figurative a shower or large quantity of something: *it swam away in a flurry of wings and flippers, raising a snowstorm of foam*. ■ a toy or ornament consisting of a model of a scene in a liquid containing white particles which, when shaken, mimics a snowstorm.

snowsure ▶ **adjective** (of a ski resort or slope) likely to have enough snow to ski on during the season.

snow vole ▶ **noun** a vole with a pale coat and long tail, occurring in mountainous country from SW Europe to Iran.
• *Microtus nivalis*, family Muridae.

snow-white ▶ **adjective** of a pure white colour: *perfect spotless utensils on a snow-white tablecloth*.

snowy ▶ **adjective** (**snowier**, **snowiest**) covered with snow: *snowy mountains*.
■ (of weather or a period of time) characterized by snowfall: *a snowy January day*. ■ of or like snow, especially in being pure white: *snowy hair*.
– DERIVATIVES **snowily** adverb, **snowiness** noun.

snowy mespilus ▶ **noun** a white-flowered shrub or small tree of the rose family which is often grown as an ornamental.
• Genus *Amelanchier*, family Rosaceae: several species.
– ORIGIN modern Latin *Mespilus* (genus name), from Latin *mespilus* 'medlar tree'.

snowy owl ▶ **noun** a large northern owl that breeds mainly in the Arctic tundra, the male being entirely white and the female having darker markings.
• *Nyctea scandiaca*, family Strigidae.

SNP ▶ **abbreviation for** Scottish National Party.

Snr ▶ **abbreviation for** Senior: *John Hammond Snr*.

snub ▶ **verb** (**snubbed**, **snubbing**) [with obj.] **1** rebuff, ignore, or spurn disdainfully: *he snubbed faculty members and students alike* | *he snubbed her request to wind up the debate*.
2 check the movement of (a horse or boat), especially by a rope wound round a post: *a horse snubbed to a tree*.
▶ **noun** an act of showing disdain or a lack of cordiality by rebuffing or ignoring someone or something: *the move was a* **snub to** *the government*.
▶ **adjective** (of a person's nose) short and turned up at the end: [in combination] *snub-nosed*.
– ORIGIN Middle English (as a verb, originally in the sense 'rebuke with sharp words'): from Old Norse *snubba* 'chide, check the growth of'. The adjective dates from the early 18th cent.

snubber ▶ **noun 1** a simple kind of shock absorber.
2 an electric circuit intended to suppress voltage spikes.

snuck informal, chiefly N. Amer. past and past participle of **SNEAK**.

snuff¹ ▶ **verb** [with obj.] extinguish (a candle): *a breeze* **snuffed out** *the candle*.
■ informal put an end to (something) in a brutal manner: *his life was snuffed out by a sniper's bullet*. ■ (**snuff it**) Brit. informal die. ■ dated trim the charred wick from (a candle).
▶ **noun** the charred part of a candle wick.
– ORIGIN late Middle English: of unknown origin.

snuff² ▶ **noun** [mass noun] powdered tobacco that is sniffed up the nostril rather than smoked: *a pinch of snuff*.
▶ **verb** [with obj.] inhale or sniff at (something): *they stood* **snuffing up** *the keen cold air*.
■ [no obj.] archaic sniff up powdered tobacco.
– PHRASES **up to snuff** informal **1** up to the required standard: *they need a million dollars to get their facilities up to snuff*. ■ in good health: *he hadn't felt up to snuff all summer*. **2** Brit. archaic not easily deceived; knowing: *an up-to-snuff old vagabond*.
– ORIGIN late Middle English (as a verb): from Middle Dutch *snuffen* 'to snuffle'. The noun dates from the late 17th cent. and is probably an abbreviation of Dutch *snuftabak*.

snuff-coloured ▶ **adjective** (chiefly of clothing) of a dark yellowish-brown colour.

snuffer ▶ **noun** a small hollow metal cone on the end of a handle, used to extinguish a candle by smothering the flame.
■ (**snuffers**) an implement resembling scissors with an inverted metal cup attached to one blade, used to extinguish a candle or trim its wick.

snuffle ▶ **verb** [no obj.] breathe noisily through the nose due to a cold or crying: *Alice was weeping quietly, snuffling a little*.
■ (especially of an animal) make repeated sniffing sounds as though smelling at something: *the collie snuffled around his boots* | [as noun **snuffling**] *she heard a strange, persistent snuffling*.
▶ **noun** a sniff or sniffing sound: *a silence broken only by the faint snuffles of the dogs*.
■ (usu. **the snuffles**) informal a cold or other infection that causes sniffing: *he went down with the snuffles*.
– DERIVATIVES **snuffler** noun, **snuffly** adjective.
– ORIGIN late 16th cent.: probably from Low German and Dutch *snuffelen*; compare with **SNUFF**² and **SNIVEL**.

snuff movie ▶ **noun** informal a pornographic film or video recording of an actual murder.

snuffy¹ ▶ **adjective** (**snuffier**, **snuffiest**) archaic supercilious or contemptuous: *some snuffy old stockbroker*.
■ easily offended; annoyed.

snuffy² ▶ **adjective** archaic resembling powdered tobacco in colour or substance.

snug ▶ **adjective** (**snugger**, **snuggest**) **1** comfortable, warm, and cosy; well protected from the weather or cold: *she was safe and snug in Ruth's arms* | *a snug cottage*.
■ archaic (of an income or employment) allowing one to live in comfort and comparative ease.
2 (especially of clothing) very tight or close-fitting: *a well-shaped hood for a snug fit*.
▶ **noun** Brit. a small, comfortable public room in a pub or inn.
▶ **verb** [with obj. and adverbial of direction] chiefly N. Amer. place (something) safely or cosily: *she tucks him in, snugging the blanket up to his chin*.
■ [no obj., with adverbial of direction] settle comfortably and cosily: *the passengers snugged down amongst the cargo*.
– PHRASES **snug as a bug (in a rug)** humorous in an extremely comfortable position or situation.
– DERIVATIVES **snugly** adverb, **snugness** noun.
– ORIGIN late 16th cent. (originally in nautical use in the sense 'shipshape, compact, prepared for bad weather'): probably of Low German or Dutch origin.

snuggery ▶ **noun** (pl. **-ies**) a cosy or comfortable place, especially someone's private room or den.
■ Brit. archaic another term for **SNUG**.

snuggle ▶ **verb** settle or move into a warm, comfortable position: [no obj., with adverbial] *I* **snuggled down** *in my sleeping bag* | [with obj. and adverbial] *she snuggled her head into his shoulder*.
– ORIGIN late 17th cent.: frequentative of the verb **SNUG**.

So. ▶ **abbreviation for** South.

so¹ ▶ **adverb 1** [as submodifier] to such a great extent: *the words tumbled out* **so** *fast* **that** *I could barely hear them* | *don't look so worried* | *I'm not* **so** *foolish* **as to** *say that*.
■ extremely; very much (used for emphasis): *she looked so pretty* | *I do love it so*. ■ informal used with a gesture to indicate size: *the bird was about so long*.
2 [as submodifier] [with negative] to the same extent (used in comparisons): *he isn't* **so** *bad* **as** *you'd think* | *help without which he would not have done so well*.
3 referring back to something previously mentioned:
■ that is the case: *'Has somebody called an ambulance?' 'I believe so.'* | *if she notices, she never says so*. ■ the truth: *I hear that you're a writer—is that so?* ■ similarly; and also: *times have changed and so have I*. ■ expressing agreement: *'There's another one.' 'So there is.'* ■ Irish used for emphasis in a formula added at the end of a statement: *your old man was the salt of the earth, so he was*. ■ informal used to emphatically contradict a negative statement: *it is so!*
4 in the way described or demonstrated; thus: *hold your arms so* | **so it was that** *he was still a bachelor*.
▶ **conjunction 1** and for this reason; therefore: *it was still painful so I went to see a specialist* | *you know I'm telling the truth, so don't interrupt*.

■(**so that**) with the result that: *it was overgrown with brambles, so that I had difficulty making any progress.*
2 (**so that**) with the aim that; in order that: *they whisper to each other so that no one else can hear.*
3 and then; as the next step: *and so to the final.*
4 introducing a question: *so, what did you do today?* ■introducing a question following on from what was said previously: *so what did he do about it?* ■ (also **so what?**) informal why should that be considered significant?: *'He came into the shop this morning.' 'So?' | so what if he failed?*
5 introducing a statement which is followed by a defensive comment: *so I'm a policeman—what's wrong with that?*
6 introducing a concluding statement: *so that's that.*
7 in the same way; correspondingly: ***just as** bad money drives out good, **so** does bad art drive out the good.*
– PHRASES **and so on** (or **forth**) and similar things; et cetera: *these savouries include cheeses, cold meats, and so on.* **just so much** chiefly derogatory emphasizing a large amount of something: *it's just so much ideological cant.* **not so much —— as ——** not —— but rather ——: *the novel was not so much unfinished as unfinishable.* **only so much** a limited amount: *there is only so much you can do to protect yourself.* **or so** see **OR**[1]. **so as to do something** in order to do something: *she had put her hair up so as to look older.* **so be it** an expression of acceptance or resignation. **so far** see **FAR**. **so far so good** see **FAR**. **so long!** informal goodbye till we meet again. **so long as** see **LONG**[1]. **so many** (or **much**) indicating a particular but unspecified quantity: *so many hours at such-and-such a speed.* **so much as** [with negative] even: *he sat down without so much as a word to anyone.* **so much for 1** indicating that one has finished talking about something: *So much for the melodic line. We now turn our attention to the accompaniment.* **2** suggesting that something has not been successful or useful: *so much for that idea!* **so much so that** to such an extent that: *I was fascinated by the company, so much so that I wrote a book about it.* **so to speak** (or **say**) used to highlight the fact that one is describing something in an unusual or metaphorical way: *delving into the body's secrets, I looked death in the face, so to speak.*
– ORIGIN Old English *swā*, of Germanic origin; related to Dutch *zo* and German *so*.

so[2] ▶**noun** variant spelling of **SOH**.

-so ▶**combining form** equivalent to **-SOEVER**.

soak ▶**verb** [with obj.] **1** make or allow (something) to become thoroughly wet by immersing it in liquid: *soak the beans overnight in water.* ■[no obj.] be immersed in water or another liquid: *she spent some time soaking in a hot bath.* ■ (of a liquid) cause (something or someone) to become extremely wet: *the rain poured down, soaking their hair.* ■ [no obj., with adverbial of direction] (of a liquid) penetrate or permeate completely: *cold water was soaking into my shoes.* ■ (**soak something off/out**) remove something by immersing it in water for a period of time: *don't disturb the wound—soak the dressing off if necessary.* ■ (**soak oneself in**) immerse oneself in (a particular experience, activity, or interest): *he soaked himself in the music of Mozart.*
2 informal impose heavy charges or taxation on: *VAT would not soak the rich—it would soak the everyday guy struggling to stay afloat.*
3 [no obj.] archaic, informal drink heavily: *you keep soaking in taverns.*
▶**noun 1** [in sing.] an act of immersing someone or something in liquid for a period of time: *I'm looking forward to a long soak in the bath.*
2 informal a heavy drinker: *his daughter stayed up to put the **old soak** to bed.*
3 Austral./NZ a hollow where rainwater collects; a waterhole.
– DERIVATIVES **soakage** noun.
– ORIGIN Old English *socian* 'become saturated with a liquid by immersion'; related to *sūcan* 'to suck'.
▶**soak something up** absorb a liquid: *use clean tissues to soak up any droplets of water.* ■ figurative expose oneself to or experience (something beneficial or enjoyable): *lie back and soak up the Mediterranean sun | he spends his time painting and soaking up the culture.* ■ informal cost or use up money: *the project had soaked up over £1 billion.*

soakaway ▶**noun** Brit. a pit, typically filled with hard core, into which waste water is piped so that it drains slowly out into the surrounding soil.

soaked ▶**adjective** extremely wet; saturated: *my shirt is soaked through | she was soaked to the skin |* [in combination] figurative *a sun-soaked beach.*

soaker ▶**noun 1** a sheet of metal used in roofing to keep out rain.
2 a liquid containing detergent in which dirty clothing is soaked before washing.

soaking ▶**adjective** extremely wet; wet through: *his jacket was soaking.*
▶**noun** an act of wetting something thoroughly: *in spring, give the soil a good soaking.*

so-and-so ▶**noun** (pl. **-os**) a person or thing whose name the speaker does not need to specify or does not know or remember.
■informal a person who is disliked or is considered to have a particular characteristic, typically an unfavourable one: *nosy old so-and-so!*

Soane, Sir John (1753–1837), English architect. His later work avoided unnecessary ornament and adopted structural necessity as the basis of design. His designs included the Bank of England (1788–1833, since rebuilt) and his house in London, now a museum.

soap ▶**noun 1** [mass noun] a substance used with water for washing and cleaning, made of a compound of natural oils or fats with sodium hydroxide or another strong alkali, and typically having perfume and colouring added: *a bar of soap.*
2 informal a soap opera: *the soaps are top of the ratings.*
▶**verb** [with obj.] wash with soap: *she soaped her face.*
– PHRASES **no soap** N. Amer. informal used to convey that there is no chance of something happening or occurring: *They needed a writer with some enthusiasm. No soap.*
– DERIVATIVES **soapless** adjective.
– ORIGIN Old English *sāpe*, of West Germanic origin; related to Dutch *zeep* and German *Seife*. The verb dates from the mid 16th cent.

soapberry ▶**noun** a tree or shrub with berries that produce a soapy froth when crushed, in particular:
● a plant with saponin-rich berries that are used as a soap substitute (genus *Sapindus*, family Sapindaceae). ● a North American shrub with edible berries (*Shepherdia canadensis*, family Elaeagnaceae).
■the berry of any of these plants.

soapbox ▶**noun** a box or crate used as a makeshift stand by a public speaker: [as modifier] *a soapbox orator.* ■figurative a thing that provides an opportunity for someone to air their views publicly: *fanzines are soapboxes for critical sporting fans.* ■ chiefly historical a box or crate in which soap is packed and transported.

soap bubble ▶**noun** an iridescent bubble consisting of air in a thin film of soapy water.

soapfish ▶**noun** (pl. same or **-fishes**) a stout-bodied fish of tropical seas which produces large amounts of toxic mucus from the skin, making it a soapy feel when handled.
● Family Grammistidae, several genera and species.

soap flakes ▶**plural noun** soap in the form of thin flakes used for washing clothes.

soap opera ▶**noun** a television or radio drama serial dealing typically with daily events in the lives of the same group of characters.
– ORIGIN 1930s: so named because such serials were originally sponsored in the US by soap manufacturers.

soap powder ▶**noun** [mass noun] detergent in the form of a powder, used for washing clothes.

soapstone ▶**noun** [mass noun] a soft rock consisting largely of talc. Compare with **STEATITE**.

soapsuds ▶**plural noun** another term for **SUDS**.

soapwort ▶**noun** a European plant of the pink family, with fragrant pink or white flowers and leaves that were formerly used to make soap.
● *Saponaria officinalis*, family Caryophyllaceae.

soapy ▶**adjective** (**soapier**, **soapiest**) **1** containing or covered with soap: *hot soapy water.*
■of or like soap: *his hands smelled soapy.* ■ (of a person or behaviour) unpleasantly flattering and ingratiating: *a soapy, worshipful look.*
2 informal characteristic of a soap opera: *soapy little turns of plot.*
– DERIVATIVES **soapily** adverb, **soapiness** noun.

soar ▶**verb** [no obj.] fly or rise high in the air: *the bird spread its wings and soared into the air |* figurative *when she heard his voice, her spirits soared.*
■maintain height in the air without flapping wings or using engine power: *the gulls soared on the summery winds.* ■ increase rapidly above the usual level: *the cost of living continued to soar |* [as adj. **soaring**] *the soaring crime rate.*
– DERIVATIVES **soarer** noun, **soaringly** adverb.
– ORIGIN late Middle English: shortening of Old French *essorer*, based on Latin *ex-* 'out of' + *aura* 'breeze'.

soaraway ▶**adjective** [attrib.] making or characterized by rapid or impressive progress: *a soaraway success.*

Soave /ˈswɑːveɪ, səʊˈɑːveɪ/ ▶**noun** [mass noun] a dry white wine produced in the region of northern Italy around Soave.

Soay sheep /ˈsəʊeɪ/ ▶**noun** a small domesticated sheep of a primitive breed with brown fleece and horns in both sexes, formerly confined to the island of Soay in the St Kilda group.

sob ▶**verb** (**sobbed**, **sobbing**) [no obj.] cry noisily, making loud, convulsive gasps: *he broke down and sobbed like a child | he sobbed himself to sleep.*
■[with obj.] say while crying noisily: *she **sobbed out** her troubles to him |* [with direct speech] *'I thought they'd killed you,' he sobbed weakly.*
▶**noun** an act or sound of sobbing: *with a sob of despair she threw herself on to the bed.*
– DERIVATIVES **sobbingly** adverb.
– ORIGIN Middle English: perhaps of Dutch or Low German origin; compare with Dutch dialect *sabben* 'to suck'.

soba /ˈsəʊbə/ ▶**noun** [mass noun] Japanese noodles made from buckwheat flour.
– ORIGIN Japanese.

sober ▶**adjective** (**soberer**, **soberest**) not affected by alcohol; not drunk.
■serious, sensible, and solemn: *a sober view of life | his expression became sober.* ■ muted in colour: *a sober grey suit.*
▶**verb** make or become sober after drinking alcohol: [with obj.] *that coffee **sobered** him **up** |* [no obj.] *I ought to **sober up** a bit.*
■make or become more serious, sensible, and solemn: [no obj.] *his expression sobered her |* [as adj. **sobering**] *a sobering thought.*
– PHRASES (**as**) **sober as a judge** completely sober.
– DERIVATIVES **soberingly** adverb, **soberly** adverb.
– ORIGIN Middle English: from Old French *sobre*, from Latin *sobrius*.

Sobers, Gary (b.1936), West Indian cricketer; full name *Sir Garfield St Aubrun Sobers*. During his test career he scored more than 8,000 runs and took 235 wickets.

sobersides ▶**noun** informal, chiefly N. Amer. a sedate and serious person.
– DERIVATIVES **sobersided** adjective.

Sobieski /səˈbjɛski/, John, see **JOHN III**.

sobriety /səˈbrʌɪəti/ ▶**noun** [mass noun] the state of being sober: *the price of beer compelled me to maintain a certain level of sobriety.*
■the quality of being staid or solemn.
– ORIGIN late Middle English: from Old French *sobriete* or Latin *sobrietas*, from *sobrius* (see **SOBER**).

sobriquet /ˈsəʊbrɪkeɪ/ (also **soubriquet**) ▶**noun** a person's nickname.
– ORIGIN mid 17th cent.: French, originally in the sense 'tap under the chin', of unknown origin.

sob sister ▶**noun** informal **1** a female journalist who writes articles with sentimental appeal or answers readers' problems.
2 an actress who plays sentimental roles.

sob story ▶**noun** informal a story or explanation intended to make someone feel sympathy for the person relating it.

sob stuff ▶**noun** [mass noun] informal, sentimental speech or writing: *cut the sob stuff and tell me what happened that night.*

Soc. ▶**abbreviation for** ■ Socialist. ■ Society.

soc /sɒʃ/ ▶**noun** N. Amer. informal (in an academic context) sociology: [as modifier] *she's a soc major.*

soca /ˈsəʊkə/ ▶**noun** [mass noun] calypso music with elements of soul, originally from Trinidad.
– ORIGIN 1970s: blend of **SOUL** and **CALYPSO**.

socage /ˈsɒkɪdʒ/ (also **soccage**) ▶**noun** [mass noun] historical a feudal tenure of land involving payment of rent or other non-military service to a superior.
– ORIGIN Middle English: from Anglo-Norman French, from *soc*, variant of **SOKE**.

so-called ▶**adjective** [attrib.] used to show that something or someone is commonly designated by

the name or term specified: *Western Countries belonging to the so-called Paris club.*
■used to express one's view that such a name or term is inappropriate: *she could trust him more than any of her so-called friends.*

soccer ▶ **noun** [mass noun] a form of football played by two teams of eleven players with a round ball which may not be handled during play except by the goalkeepers. The object of the game is to score goals by kicking or heading the ball into the opponents' goal. Also called **FOOTBALL** (in the UK) and **ASSOCIATION FOOTBALL**.
– ORIGIN late 19th cent.: shortening of **Assoc.** + **-ER**[3].

Sochi /ˈsɒtʃi/ a port and holiday and health resort in SW Russia, situated in the western foothills of the Caucasus, on the Black Sea coast close to the border with Georgia; pop. 339,000 (1990).

sociable ▶ **adjective** willing to talk and engage in activities with other people; friendly: *being a sociable person, Eva loved entertaining.*
■(of a place, occasion, or activity) marked by friendliness: *a very sociable little village.*
▶ **noun 1** historical an open carriage with facing side seats.
2 historical a tricycle with two seats side by side.
3 chiefly Brit. an S-shaped couch for two people who sit partially facing each other.
4 US dated an informal social gathering: *a church sociable.*
– DERIVATIVES **sociability** noun, **sociableness** noun, **sociably** adverb.
– ORIGIN mid 16th cent.: from French, or from Latin *sociabilis*, from *sociare* 'unite', from *socius* 'companion'.

social ▶ **adjective 1** [attrib.] of or relating to society or its organization: *alcoholism is recognized as a major social problem | the social structure of Europe had become more fluid.*
■of or relating to rank and status in society: *a recent analysis of social class in Britain | her mother is a lady of the highest social standing.* ■ needing companionship and therefore best suited to living in communities: *we are social beings as well as individuals.* ■ relating to or designed for activities in which people meet each other for pleasure: *Guy led a full social life | staff facilities included a social club and leisure complex.*
2 Zoology (of a bird) gregarious; breeding or nesting in colonies.
■(of an insect) living together in organized communities, typically with different castes, as ants, bees, wasps, and termites do. ■ (of a mammal) living together in groups, typically in a hierarchical system with complex communication.
▶ **noun** an informal social gathering, especially one organized by the members of a particular club or group: *a church social.*
– DERIVATIVES **sociality** noun, **socially** adverb *the provision and support to families who are socially disadvantaged.*
– ORIGIN late Middle English: from Old French, or from Latin *socialis* 'allied', from *socius* 'friend'.

Social and Liberal Democrats (abbrev.: **SLD**) (in the UK) a political party formed in 1988 from a majority of the membership of the Liberal Party and the Social Democratic Party. It was officially renamed in 1989 as the Liberal Democrats.

social anthropology ▶ **noun** see **ANTHROPOLOGY**.

social assistance ▶ **noun** Canadian term for **SOCIAL SECURITY**.

social climber ▶ **noun** derogatory a person who is anxious to gain a higher social status.
– DERIVATIVES **social climbing** noun.

social conscience ▶ **noun** a sense of responsibility or concern for the problems and injustices of society.

social contract (also **social compact**) ▶ **noun** an implicit agreement among the members of a society to cooperate for social benefits, for example by sacrificing some individual freedom for state protection. Theories of a social contract became popular in the 16th, 17th, and 18th centuries among theorists such as Thomas Hobbes, John Locke, and Jean-Jacques Rousseau, as a means of explaining the origin of government and the obligations of subjects.

social credit ▶ **noun** [mass noun] the economic theory that consumer purchasing power should be increased either by subsidizing producers so that they can lower prices or by distributing the profits of industry to consumers.

social Darwinism ▶ **noun** [mass noun] the theory that individuals, groups, and peoples are subject to the same Darwinian laws of natural selection as plants and animals. Now largely discredited, social Darwinism was advocated by Herbert Spencer and others in the late 19th and early 20th centuries and was used to justify political conservatism, imperialism, and racism and to discourage intervention and reform.

social democracy ▶ **noun** [mass noun] a socialist system of government achieved by democratic means.
– DERIVATIVES **social democrat** noun.

Social Democratic and Labour Party (abbrev.: **SDLP**) a left-of-centre political party in Northern Ireland, formed in 1970 and supported largely by Catholics. It calls for the establishment of a united Ireland by constitutional means, and rejects the violent tactics of the IRA.

Social Democratic Party (abbrev.: **SDP**) a UK political party with moderate socialist aims, founded in 1981 by a group of former Labour MPs and disbanded in 1990 after political regroupings.

social disease ▶ **noun** informal a venereal disease.

social distance ▶ **noun** [mass noun] the perceived or desired degree of remoteness between a member of one social group and the members of another, as evidenced in the level of intimacy tolerated between them.

social engineering ▶ **noun** [mass noun] the application of sociological principles to specific social problems.

social fact ▶ **noun** a thing originating in the institutions or culture of a society which affects the behaviour or attitudes of an individual member of that society.

social fund ▶ **noun** (in the UK) a social security fund from which loans or grants are made to people in need.

social geography ▶ **noun** [mass noun] the study of people and their environment with particular emphasis on social factors.

social gospel ▶ **noun** Christian faith practised as a call not just to personal conversion but to social reform.
– DERIVATIVES **social gospeller** noun.

social inquiry report ▶ **noun** (in the UK) a report made by a probation officer or social worker on a person's character and circumstances, which may be required by a court before sentencing.

social insurance ▶ **noun** [mass noun] a system of compulsory contribution to provide state assistance in sickness, unemployment, etc.

socialism ▶ **noun** [mass noun] a political and economic theory of social organization which advocates that the means of production, distribution, and exchange should be owned or regulated by the community as a whole.
■policy or practice based on this theory. ■ (in Marxist theory) a transitional social state between the overthrow of capitalism and the realization of Communism.

The term 'socialism' has been used to describe positions as far apart as anarchism, Soviet state Communism, and social democracy; however, it necessarily implies an opposition to the untrammelled workings of the economic market. The socialist parties that have arisen in most European countries from the late 19th century have generally tended towards social democracy.

– DERIVATIVES **socialist** noun & adjective, **socialistic** adjective, **socialistically** adverb.
– ORIGIN early 19th cent.: from French *socialisme*, from *social* (see **SOCIAL**).

socialist realism ▶ **noun** [mass noun] the theory of art, literature, and music officially sanctioned by the state in some Communist countries (especially in the Soviet Union under Stalin), by which artistic work was supposed to reflect and promote the ideals of a socialist society.

socialite ▶ **noun** a person who is well known in fashionable society and is fond of social activities and entertainment.

socialize (also **-ise**) ▶ **verb 1** [no obj.] mix socially with others: *he didn't mind* ***socializing with*** *his staff.*
2 [with obj.] make (someone) behave in a way that is acceptable to their society: *newcomers are* ***socialized into*** *orthodox ways* | [as adj. **socializing**] *a socializing effect.*
3 [with obj.] organize according to the principles of socialism: [as adj. **socialized**] *socialized economies.*
– DERIVATIVES **socialization** noun (in senses 2 and 3).

socialized medicine ▶ **noun** [mass noun] US the provision of medical and hospital care for all by means of public funds.

social ladder ▶ **noun** another term for **SOCIAL SCALE**.

social market economy (also **social market**) ▶ **noun** an economic system based on a free market operated in conjunction with state provision for those unable to sell their labour, such as the elderly or unemployed.

social partner ▶ **noun** an individual or organization, such as an employer, trade union, or employee, participating in a cooperative relationship for the mutual benefit of all concerned.

social process ▶ **noun** the pattern of growth and change in a society over the years.

social psychology ▶ **noun** [mass noun] the branch of psychology that deals with social interactions, including their origins and their effects on the individual.
– DERIVATIVES **social psychologist** noun.

social realism ▶ **noun** [mass noun] the realistic depiction in art of contemporary life, as a means of social or political comment.

social scale (also **social ladder**) ▶ **noun** (usu. **the social scale**) the hierarchical structure of society or of a society: *two men at opposite ends of the social scale.*

social science ▶ **noun** [mass noun] the scientific study of human society and social relationships.
■[count noun] a subject within this field, such as economics or politics.
– DERIVATIVES **social scientist** noun.

social secretary ▶ **noun** a person who arranges the social activities of a person or organization.

social security ▶ **noun** [mass noun] (in the UK) monetary assistance from the state for people with an inadequate or no income.
■(**Social Security**) (in the US) a federal insurance scheme providing benefits for pensioners, the unemployed, and the disabled.

social service ▶ **noun** (**social services**) government services provided for the benefit of the community, such as education, medical care, and housing.
■[mass noun] activity aiming to promote the welfare of others.

social studies ▶ **plural noun** [treated as sing.] various aspects or branches of the study of human society, considered as an educational discipline.

social unit ▶ **noun** an individual, or a group or community, considered as a discrete constituent of a society or larger group.

social wage ▶ **noun** the amenities provided within a society from public funds.

social work ▶ **noun** [mass noun] work carried out by trained personnel with the aim of alleviating the conditions of those people in a community suffering from social deprivation.
– DERIVATIVES **social worker** noun.

societal /səˈsʌɪt(ə)l/ ▶ **adjective** of or relating to society or social relations: *societal change.*
– DERIVATIVES **societally** adverb.

society ▶ **noun** (pl. **-ies**) **1** [mass noun] the aggregate of people living together in a more or less ordered community: *drugs, crime, and other dangers to society.*
■the community of people living in a particular country or region and having shared customs, laws, and organizations: *the ethnic diversity of British society* | [count noun] *modern industrial societies.* ■ [with adj.] a specified section of such a community: *no one in polite society uttered the word.* ■ (also **high society**) the aggregate of people who are fashionable, wealthy, and influential, regarded as forming a distinct group in a community: [as modifier] *a society wedding.* ■ [count noun] a plant or animal community.
2 an organization or club formed for a particular purpose or activity: [in names] *the Royal Society for the Protection of Birds.*
3 [mass noun] the situation of being in the company of other people: *she shunned the society of others.*

S

– ORIGIN mid 16th cent. (in the sense 'companionship, friendly association with others'): from French *société*, from Latin *societas*, from *socius* 'companion'.

Society Islands a group of islands in the South Pacific, forming part of French Polynesia.
– ORIGIN named in honour of the *Royal Society* by Captain Cook, who visited the islands in 1769.

Society of Jesus official name for the Jesuits (see JESUIT).

socio- /ˈsəʊsɪəʊ, ˈsəʊʃɪəʊ/ ▶ combining form **1** relating to society; society and ...: *socio-economic*.
2 relating to sociology; sociology and ...: *sociolinguistics*.
– ORIGIN from Latin *socius* 'companion'.

sociobiology ▶ noun [mass noun] the scientific study of the biological (especially ecological and evolutionary) aspects of social behaviour in animals and humans.
– DERIVATIVES **sociobiological** adjective, **sociobiologically** adverb, **sociobiologist** noun.

sociocultural ▶ adjective combining social and cultural factors.
– DERIVATIVES **socioculturally** adverb.

socioecology ▶ noun [mass noun] the branch of science that deals with the interactions among the members of a species, and between them and the environment.
– DERIVATIVES **socioecological** adjective, **socioecologist** noun.

socio-economic ▶ adjective relating to or concerned with the interaction of social and economic factors.
– DERIVATIVES **socio-economically** adverb.

sociolect /ˈsəʊsɪə(ʊ)lɛkt, ˈsəʊʃɪə(ʊ)-/ ▶ noun the dialect of a particular social class.
– ORIGIN 1970s: from SOCIO- + -*lect* as in DIALECT.

socio-legal ▶ adjective **1** relating to the relationship between law and society.
2 combining social and legal factors.

sociolinguistics ▶ plural noun [treated as sing.] the study of language in relation to social factors, including differences of regional, class, and occupational dialect, gender differences, and bilingualism.
– DERIVATIVES **sociolinguist** noun, **sociolinguistic** adjective, **sociolinguistically** adverb.

sociology ▶ noun [mass noun] the study of the development, structure, and functioning of human society.
■ the study of social problems.
– DERIVATIVES **sociological** adjective, **sociologically** adverb, **sociologist** noun.
– ORIGIN mid 19th cent.: from French *sociologie* (see SOCIO-, -LOGY).

sociometry /ˌsəʊsɪˈɒmɪtri, ˌsəʊʃɪ-/ ▶ noun [mass noun] the study of relationships within a group of people.
– DERIVATIVES **sociometric** adjective, **sociometrically** adverb, **sociometrist** noun.

sociopath /ˈsəʊsɪə(ʊ)paθ, ˈsəʊʃɪə(ʊ)-/ ▶ noun a person with a personality disorder manifesting itself in extreme antisocial attitudes and behaviour.
– DERIVATIVES **sociopathic** adjective, **sociopathy** noun.

socio-political ▶ adjective combining social and political factors.

sock ▶ noun **1** a garment for the foot and lower part of the leg, typically knitted from wool, cotton, or nylon.
■ a removable inner sole placed inside a shoe or boot for added warmth or to improve the fit. ■ a white marking on the lower part of a horse's leg, not extending as far as the knee or hock. Compare with STOCKING.
2 informal a hard blow: *a sock on the jaw*.
■ [mass noun] US force or emphasis: *we have enough speed and sock in our line-up to score runs*.
▶ verb informal [with obj.] hit forcefully: *Jess socked his father across the face*.
■ (often **be socked with**) affect disadvantageously: *consumers have been socked with huge price increases*.
– PHRASES **knock** (or **blow**) **someone's socks off** informal amaze or impress someone. **knock the socks off** informal surpass or beat: —— **one's socks off** informal do something with great energy and enthusiasm: *she acted her socks off*. **pull one's socks up** informal make an effort to improve one's work,

performance, or behaviour. **put a sock in it** [usu. in imperative] Brit. informal stop talking. **sock and buskin** archaic the theatrical profession; drama. **sock it to someone** informal attack or make a forceful impression on someone.
– ORIGIN Old English *socc* 'light shoe', of Germanic origin, from Latin *soccus* 'comic actor's shoe, light low-heeled slipper', from Greek *sukkhos*.

▶ **sock something away** N. Amer. put money aside as savings: *you'll need to sock away about $900 a month.*
sock something in (or **sock in**) N. Amer. (of weather) envelop: *the beach was socked in with fog*.

socket ▶ noun **1** a natural or artificial hollow into which something fits or in which something revolves: *the eye socket*.
■ the part of the head of a golf club into which the shaft is fitted.
2 an electrical device receiving a plug or light bulb to make a connection.
▶ verb (**socketed, socketing**) [with obj.] **1** place in or fit with a socket.
2 Golf old-fashioned term for SHANK.
– ORIGIN Middle English (in the sense 'head of a spear, resembling a ploughshare'): from an Anglo-Norman French diminutive of Old French *soc* 'ploughshare', probably of Celtic origin.

socket outlet ▶ noun a socket for an electric plug that is fixed to a wall and connected to an electricity supply.

socket set ▶ noun a number of detachable sockets of different sizes for use with a socket wrench.

socket wrench (also **socket spanner**) ▶ noun a ratchet tool with a series of detachable sockets for tightening and untightening nuts of different sizes.

sockeye (also **sockeye salmon**) ▶ noun a commercially valuable salmon of the North Pacific and rivers draining into it. Also called RED SALMON.
● *Oncorhynchus nerka*, family Salmonidae. See also KOKANEE.
– ORIGIN late 19th cent.: from Salish *sukai*, literally 'fish of fishes'.

socking ▶ adverb [as submodifier] Brit. informal used for emphasis: *a brooch with a socking great diamond in the middle*.

socko ▶ adjective informal, chiefly US stunningly effective or successful: *a sell-out, socko performance*.
– ORIGIN 1920s: from SOCK in the sense 'forceful blow' + -O.

socle /ˈsəʊk(ə)l, ˈsɒk-/ ▶ noun Architecture a plain low block or plinth serving as a support for a column, urn, statue, etc. or as the foundation of a wall.
– ORIGIN early 18th cent.: from French, from Italian *zoccolo*, literally 'wooden shoe', from Latin *socculus*, from *soccus* (see SOCK).

Socotra /səˈkəʊtrə/ an island in the Arabian Sea near the mouth of the Gulf of Aden; capital, Tamridah. It is administered by Yemen.

Socrates /ˈsɒkrətiːz/ (469–399 BC), ancient Athenian philosopher. As represented in the writings of his disciple Plato, he engaged in dialogue with others in an attempt to reach understanding and ethical concepts by exposing and dispelling error (the **Socratic method**). Charged with introducing strange gods and corrupting the young, Socrates was sentenced to death and died by drinking hemlock.

Socratic /səˈkratɪk/ ▶ adjective of or relating to Socrates or his philosophy.
▶ noun a follower of Socrates.
– DERIVATIVES **Socratically** adverb.

Socratic elenchus ▶ noun see ELENCHUS.

Socratic irony ▶ noun [mass noun] a pose of ignorance assumed in order to entice others into making statements that can then be challenged.

Socred /ˈsəʊkrɛd/ ▶ noun Canadian a political party or an individual advocating social credit.
– ORIGIN 1950s: contraction of *social credit*.

sod¹ ▶ noun (**the sod**) the surface of the ground, with the grass growing on it.
■ a piece of this.
▶ verb (**sodded, sodding**) [with obj.] rare cover with sods or pieces of turf.
– PHRASES **under the sod** dead and buried in a grave.
– ORIGIN late Middle English: from Middle Dutch, Middle Low German *sode*, of unknown ultimate origin.

sod² vulgar slang, chiefly Brit. ▶ noun an unpleasant or obnoxious person.

■ [with adj.] a person of a specified kind. ■ something that is difficult or causes problems.
▶ verb (**sodded, sodding**) [with obj., usu. in imperative] used to express one's anger or annoyance at someone or something.
■ [no obj.] (**sod off**) [in imperative] go away. ■ [as adj. **sodding**] used as a general term of contempt.
– PHRASES **sod all** absolutely nothing.
– ORIGIN early 19th cent.: abbreviation of SODOMITE.

soda ▶ noun [mass noun] **1** (also **soda water**) carbonated water (originally made with sodium bicarbonate) drunk alone or with spirits or wine: *a whisky and soda*.
■ chiefly N. Amer. a sweet carbonated drink: *a can of soda*.
2 sodium carbonate, especially as a natural mineral or as an industrial chemical.
■ sodium in chemical combination: *nitrate of soda*.
– ORIGIN late Middle English (in sense 2): from medieval Latin, from Arabic *suwwad* 'saltwort'.

soda ash ▶ noun [mass noun] commercially manufactured anhydrous sodium carbonate.

soda bread ▶ noun [mass noun] bread leavened with baking soda.

soda cracker ▶ noun N. Amer. a thin, crisp biscuit leavened with baking soda.

soda fountain ▶ noun chiefly US a device that dispenses soda water or soft drinks.
■ a shop or counter selling drinks from such a device.

soda jerk (also **soda jerker**) ▶ noun N. Amer. informal, dated a person who serves and sells soft drinks, ice cream, and confectionery at a soda fountain.

soda lake ▶ noun a salt lake with a high content of sodium salts.

soda lime ▶ noun [mass noun] a mixture of calcium oxide and sodium hydroxide.

sodalite /ˈsəʊdəlʌɪt/ ▶ noun [mass noun] a blue mineral consisting chiefly of an aluminosilicate and chloride of sodium, occurring chiefly in alkaline igneous rocks.
– ORIGIN early 19th cent.: from SODA + -LITE.

sodality /səʊˈdalɪti/ ▶ noun (pl. -**ies**) a confraternity or association, especially a Roman Catholic religious guild or brotherhood.
– ORIGIN early 17th cent.: from French *sodalité* or Latin *sodalitas*, from *sodalis* 'comrade'.

soda pop ▶ noun [mass noun] US informal a sweet carbonated drink.

soda siphon ▶ noun a bottle from which carbonated water is dispensed by allowing the gas pressure to force it out.

soda water ▶ noun see SODA (sense 1).

sodbuster ▶ noun N. Amer. informal a farmer or farm worker who ploughs the land.

sodden ▶ adjective saturated with liquid, especially water; soaked through: *his clothes were sodden*.
■ [in combination] having drunk an excessive amount of a particular alcoholic drink: *a whisky-sodden criminal*.
▶ verb [with obj.] archaic saturate (something) with water.
– DERIVATIVES **soddenly** adverb, **soddenness** noun.
– ORIGIN Middle English (in the sense 'boiled, cooked by boiling'): archaic past participle of SEETHE.

Soddy, Frederick (1877–1956), English physicist. He assisted William Ramsay in the discovery of helium and formulated a theory of isotopes, the word *isotope* being coined by him in 1913, after work on radioactive decay. Nobel Prize for Chemistry (1921).

sodger /ˈsɒdʒə/ ▶ noun non-standard spelling of SOLDIER, used to represent regional pronunciation.

sodium ▶ noun [mass noun] the chemical element of atomic number 11, a soft silver-white reactive metal of the alkali-metal group. (Symbol: **Na**)
– DERIVATIVES **sodic** adjective (Mineralogy).
– ORIGIN early 19th cent.: from SODA + -IUM.

sodium amytal ▶ noun see AMYTAL.

sodium bicarbonate ▶ noun [mass noun] a soluble white powder used in fire extinguishers and effervescent drinks and as a raising agent in baking. Also called BAKING SODA.
● Chem. formula: $NaHCO_3$.

sodium carbonate ▶ noun [mass noun] a white alkaline compound with many commercial applications including the manufacture of soap and glass. Also called WASHING SODA.
● Chem. formula: Na_2CO_3.

sodium chloride ▶ noun [mass noun] a colourless

crystalline compound occurring naturally in seawater and halite; common salt.
● Chem. formula: NaCl.

sodium cromoglycate ▶ noun see **CROMOGLYCATE**.

sodium hydroxide ▶ noun [mass noun] a strongly alkaline white deliquescent compound used in many industrial processes, e.g. the manufacture of soap and paper. Also called **CAUSTIC SODA**.
● Chem. formula: NaOH.

sodium thiosulphate ▶ noun [mass noun] a white soluble compound used in photography as a fixer to dissolve unchanged silver halides. Also called **HYPO**[1].
● Chem. formula: $Na_2S_2O_3$.

sodium-vapour lamp (also **sodium lamp**) ▶ noun a lamp in which an electrical discharge in sodium vapour gives a yellow light, typically used in street lighting.

Sodom /ˈsɒdəm/ a town in ancient Palestine, probably south of the Dead Sea. According to Gen. 19:24 it was destroyed by fire from heaven, together with Gomorrah, for the wickedness of its inhabitants.
■ [as noun **a Sodom**] a wicked or depraved place.

sodomite /ˈsɒdəmʌɪt/ ▶ noun a person who engages in anal intercourse.
– DERIVATIVES **sodomitic** adjective, **sodomitical** adjective.
– ORIGIN Middle English (in the sense 'sodomy'): via Old French from late Latin *Sodomita*, from Greek *Sodomitēs* 'inhabitant of Sodom'.

sodomy ▶ noun [mass noun] anal intercourse.
– DERIVATIVES **sodomize** (also **-ise**) verb.
– ORIGIN Middle English: from medieval Latin *sodomia*, from late Latin *peccatum Sodomiticum* 'sin of Sodom' (after Gen. 19:5, which implies that the men of Sodom practised homosexual rape) (see **SODOM**).

Sodor /ˈsəʊdə/ a medieval diocese comprising the Hebrides and the Isle of Man. **Sodor and Man** has been the official name for the Anglican diocese of the Isle of Man since 1684.
– ORIGIN from Norse *Sudhr-eyjar* 'southern isles'; the islands belonged formerly to Norway.

Sod's Law another name for **MURPHY'S LAW**.

SOE ▶ abbreviation for Special Operations Executive.

soever ▶ adverb archaic or poetic/literary of any kind; to any extent: *how great soever the assurance is.*

-soever ▶ combining form of any kind; to any extent: *whatsoever | whosoever.*
– ORIGIN Middle English: originally as the phrase *so ever.*

sofa ▶ noun a long upholstered seat with a back and arms, for two or more people.
– ORIGIN early 17th cent.: from French, based on Arabic *ṣuffa*.

sofa bed ▶ noun a sofa that can be converted into a bed, typically for occasional use.

Sofar /ˈsəʊfɑː/ (also **SOFAR**) ▶ noun [mass noun] a system in which the sound waves from an underwater explosion are detected and located by three or more listening stations, useful in determining the position at sea of survivors of a disaster.
– ORIGIN 1940s: from *So(und) f(ixing) a(nd) r(anging)*.

soffit /ˈsɒfɪt/ ▶ noun the underside of an architectural structure, such as an arch, a balcony, or overhanging eaves.
– ORIGIN early 17th cent.: from French *soffite* or Italian *soffitto*, based on Latin *suffixus* 'fastened below'.

Sofia /ˈsəʊfɪə, səˈfiːə/ the capital of Bulgaria; pop. 1,220,900 (1990). An ancient Thracian settlement, it became a province of Rome in the first century AD. It was held by the Turks between the late 14th and late 19th centuries and became the capital of Bulgaria in 1879.

S. of S. ▶ abbreviation for Song of Songs (in biblical references).

soft ▶ adjective **1** easy to mould, cut, compress, or fold; not hard or firm to the touch: *soft margarine | the ground was soft beneath their feet.*
■ having a smooth surface or texture that is pleasant to touch; not rough or coarse: *soft crushed velvet | her hair felt very soft.* ■ rounded; not angular: *the soft edges of their adobe home.*
2 having a pleasing quality involving a subtle effect

or contrast rather than sharp definition: *the soft glow of the lamps | the moon's pale light cast soft shadows.*
■ (of a voice or sound) quiet and gentle: *they spoke in soft whispers.* ■ (of rain, wind, or other natural force) not strong or violent: *a soft breeze rustled the trees.* ■ dialect (of the weather) rainy, moist, or thawing. ■ (of a consonant) pronounced as a fricative (as *c* in *ice*). ■ (of a market, currency, or commodity) falling or likely to fall in value.
3 sympathetic, lenient, or compassionate, especially to a degree perceived as excessive; not strict or sufficiently strict: *the government is not becoming soft on crime | Julia's soft heart was touched by his grief.*
■ (of words or language) not harsh or angry; conciliatory; soothing: *he was no good with soft words, gentle phrases.* ■ willing to compromise in political matters: *candidates ranging from far right to soft left.* ■ informal (of a job or way of life) requiring little effort. ■ informal foolish; silly: *he must be going soft in the head.* ■ [predic.] (**soft on**) informal infatuated with: *was Brendan soft on her?*
4 (of a drink) not alcoholic.
■ (of a drug) not likely to cause addiction. ■ (of water) free from mineral salts that make lathering difficult. ■ (of radiation) having little penetrating power. ■ (of a detergent) biodegradable. ■ (also **soft-core**) (of pornography) suggestive or erotic but not explicit.
▶ adverb softly: *I can just speak soft and she'll hear me.*
■ in a weak or foolish way: *don't talk soft.*
– PHRASES **have a soft spot for** be fond of or affectionate towards. **soft option** an easier alternative: *probation should in no sense be seen as a soft option by the judiciary.* **soft touch** (also **easy touch**) informal a person who readily gives or does something if asked.
– DERIVATIVES **softish** adjective, **softness** noun.
– ORIGIN Old English *sōfte* 'agreeable, calm, gentle', of West Germanic origin; related to Dutch *zacht* and German *sanft*.

softa /ˈsɒftə/ ▶ noun a Muslim student of sacred law and theology.
– ORIGIN Turkish, from Persian *sūkta* 'burnt, on fire'.

softback ▶ adjective & noun another term for **PAPERBACK**.

softball ▶ noun [mass noun] a modified form of baseball played on a smaller field with a larger, softer ball, seven rather than nine innings, and underarm pitching. The game evolved in the US during the late 19th century from a form of indoor baseball.
■ [count noun] a ball used in this game.

soft-boiled ▶ adjective (of an egg) boiled for a short time, leaving the yolk soft or liquid.

soft box ▶ noun Photography a frame with a cloth covering used to diffuse the light from a flash or floodlight.

soft-centred ▶ adjective (of a sweet) having a soft filling.
■ (of a person) having a compassionate or sentimental nature.

soft clam ▶ noun another term for **SOFTSHELL CLAM**.

soft coal ▶ noun [mass noun] bituminous coal.

soft copy ▶ noun Computing a legible version of a piece of information not printed on a physical medium, especially as stored or displayed on a computer.

soft coral ▶ noun see **CORAL** (sense 2).

soft-core ▶ adjective another term for **SOFT** (in sense 4).

softcover ▶ adjective & noun another term for **PAPERBACK**.

soft crab ▶ noun another term for **SOFTSHELL CRAB**.

soften ▶ verb make or become less hard: [with obj.] *plant extracts to soften and moisturize the skin* | [no obj.] *let the vegetables soften over a low heat.*
■ make or become less severe: [no obj.] *her expression softened at the sight of Diane's white face.* ■ [with obj.] undermine the resistance of (someone): *the blockade appears a better weapon with which to soften them up for eventual surrender.* ■ [with obj.] remove mineral salts from (water).

softener ▶ noun a substance or device that softens something, especially a fabric conditioner.

softening of the brain ▶ noun [mass noun] informal or archaic mental deterioration, especially senile

dementia, supposedly resulting from degeneration of the brain tissue.

soft focus ▶ noun [mass noun] deliberate slight blurring or lack of definition in a photograph or film.
▶ adjective (**soft-focus**) characterized by or producing such a lack of definition.

soft fruit ▶ noun Brit. a small stoneless fruit, such as a strawberry or a blackcurrant.

soft furnishings ▶ plural noun Brit. items made of cloth, such as curtains, chair coverings, etc., used to decorate a room.

soft goods ▶ plural noun Brit. textiles.

soft-headed ▶ adjective lacking wisdom or intelligence.
– DERIVATIVES **soft-headedness** noun.

soft-hearted ▶ adjective kind and compassionate.
– DERIVATIVES **soft-heartedness** noun.

soft hyphen ▶ noun a hyphen inserted into a word in word processing, to be displayed or typeset only if it falls at the end of a line of text.

softie (also **softy**) ▶ noun (pl. **-ies**) informal a soft-hearted, weak, or sentimental person.

soft iron ▶ noun [mass noun] iron that has a low carbon content and is easily magnetized and demagnetized, used to make the cores of solenoids and other electrical equipment.

soft landing ▶ noun a controlled landing of a spacecraft during which no serious damage is incurred.
– DERIVATIVES **soft-land** verb.

soft loan ▶ noun a loan, typically one to a developing country, made on terms very favourable to the borrower.

softly ▶ adverb in a quiet voice or manner: *'Can't you sleep?' she asked softly | the door opened softly.*
■ with a gentle or slow movement: *he touched her cheek softly.* ■ in a pleasantly subdued manner: *the room was softly lit by a lamp.*

softly-softly ▶ adjective [attrib.] cautious and patient: *he urged the president to use a softly-softly approach to the crisis.*

soft-nosed ▶ adjective (of a bullet) expanding on impact.

soft palate ▶ noun the fleshy, flexible part towards the back of the roof of the mouth.

soft-paste ▶ adjective denoting artificial porcelain, typically made with white clay and ground glass and fired at a comparatively low temperature.

soft pedal ▶ noun a pedal on a piano that can be pressed to make the tone softer. See also **UNA CORDA**.
▶ verb (**soft-pedal**) [with obj.] Music play with the soft pedal down.
■ refrain from emphasizing the more unpleasant aspects of; play down: *the administration's decision to soft-pedal the missile program.*

soft roe ▶ noun see **ROE**[1].

soft rot ▶ noun [mass noun] any of a number of bacterial and fungal diseases of fruit and vegetables in which the tissue becomes soft and slimy.
■ any of a number of fungal conditions affecting timber, which becomes soft and friable.

soft sell ▶ noun [in sing.] subtly persuasive selling.
▶ verb (**soft-sell**) [with obj.] sell (something) by using such a method.

softshell (also **softshell turtle**) ▶ noun a freshwater turtle with a flattened leathery shell, native to Asia, Africa, and North America.
● Family Trionychidae: several genera and many species, including the **spiny softshell** (*Apalone* (or *Trionyx*) *spinifera*) of North America.

softshell clam ▶ noun a marine bivalve mollusc with a thin shell and a long siphon, valued as food on the east coast of North America. Also called **SOFT CLAM**, **STEAMER CLAM**.
● Genus *Mya*, family Myidae, especially *M. arenaria*.

softshell crab ▶ noun chiefly N. Amer. a crab, especially a blue crab, that has recently moulted and has a new shell that is still soft and edible. Also called **SOFT CRAB**.

soft-shoe ▶ noun a kind of tap dance performed in soft-soled shoes.
▶ verb [no obj.] perform a dance of this kind.
■ [no obj., with adverbial of direction] move quietly and carefully so as not to draw attention to oneself: *I soft-shoed after*

him | figurative *he soft-shoed into a safer topic of conversation.*

soft shoulder ▶ noun chiefly N. Amer. an unmetalled strip of land at the side of a road.

soft soap ▶ noun [mass noun] **1** a semi-fluid soap, especially one made with potassium rather than sodium salts.
2 informal persuasive flattery.
▶ verb (**soft-soap**) [with obj.] informal use flattery in order to persuade or cajole (someone) to do something.

soft sore ▶ noun another term for **CHANCROID**.

soft-spoken ▶ adjective speaking or said with a gentle, quiet voice.

soft sugar ▶ noun [mass noun] Brit. granulated or powdered sugar.

soft tack ▶ noun [mass noun] archaic bread or other nourishing food, especially as eaten by sailors or soldiers.

soft target ▶ noun a person or thing that is relatively unprotected or vulnerable, especially to military or terrorist attack.

soft-top ▶ noun a motor vehicle having a roof that can be folded back.
■ (**soft top**) a roof of this type.

soft toy ▶ noun a children's toy, typically a toy animal, made of fabric stuffed with a soft filling.

software ▶ noun [mass noun] the programs and other operating information used by a computer. Compare with **HARDWARE**.

soft wheat ▶ noun [mass noun] wheat of a variety having a soft grain rich in starch.

softwood ▶ noun [mass noun] **1** the wood from a conifer (such as pine, fir, or spruce) as distinguished from that of broadleaved trees.
■ [count noun] a tree producing such wood.
2 (in gardening) young pliable growth on shrubs and other plants from which cuttings can be taken.

softy ▶ noun variant spelling of **SOFTIE**.

soggy ▶ adjective (**soggier**, **soggiest**) extremely wet and soft: *the pastry is a bit soggy.*
– DERIVATIVES **soggily** adverb, **sogginess** noun.
– ORIGIN early 18th cent. (in the sense 'boggy'): from dialect *sog* 'a swamp' + **-Y**[1].

Sogne Fjord /ˈsɒŋ/ a fjord on the west coast of Norway. The longest and deepest fjord in the country, it extends inland for some 200 km (125 miles), with a maximum depth of 1,308 m (4,291 ft). Norwegian name **SOGNAFJORDEN** /ˈsɒŋnə-ˌfjuːrən/.

sogo shosha /ˌsəʊɡəʊ ˈʃəʊʃə/ ▶ noun (pl. same) a very large Japanese company that trades internationally in a wide range of goods and services.
– ORIGIN Japanese, from *sōgō* 'comprehensive' + *shōsha* 'mercantile society'.

soh /səʊ/ (also **so** or **sol**) ▶ noun Music (in tonic sol-fa) the fifth note of a major scale.
■ the note G in the fixed-doh system.
– ORIGIN Middle English *sol*: representing (as an arbitrary name for the note) the first syllable of *solve*, taken from a Latin hymn (see **SOLMIZATION**).

SOHO ▶ adjective relating to a market for cheap consumer electronics used by individuals and small companies.
– ORIGIN 1990s: acronym from *small office home office*.

soi-disant /ˌswɑːdiːˈzɒ̃/ ▶ adjective self-styled; so-called: *a soi-disant novelist.*
– ORIGIN French, from *soi* 'oneself' + *disant* 'saying'.

soigné /ˈswɑːnjeɪ/ ▶ adjective (fem. **soignée** pronunc. same) dressed very elegantly; well groomed: *she was dark, petite, and soignée.*
– ORIGIN past participle of French *soigner* 'take care of', from *soin* 'care'.

soigneur /swʌnˈjɜː/ ▶ noun Cycling a person who gives training, massage, and other assistance to a team, especially during a race.
– ORIGIN French, from *soigner* 'take care of'.

soil[1] /sɔɪl/ ▶ noun [mass noun] the upper layer of earth in which plants grow, a black or dark brown material typically consisting of a mixture of organic remains, clay, and rock particles.
■ the territory of a particular nation: *the stationing of US troops on Japanese soil.*
– DERIVATIVES **soil-less** adjective.
– ORIGIN late Middle English: from Anglo-Norman French, perhaps representing Latin *solium* 'seat', by association with *solum* 'ground'.

soil[2] ▶ verb [with obj.] make dirty: *he might soil his expensive suit* | [as adj. **soiled**] *a soiled T-shirt.*
■ (especially of a child, patient, or pet) make dirty by defecating in or on. ■ figurative bring discredit to; tarnish: *what good is there in soiling your daughter's reputation?*
▶ noun [mass noun] waste matter, especially sewage containing excrement. See also **NIGHT SOIL**.
■ [count noun] archaic a stain or discolouring mark.
– ORIGIN Middle English (as a verb): from Old French *soiller*, based on Latin *sucula*, diminutive of *sus* 'pig'. The earliest use of the noun (late Middle English) was 'muddy wallow for wild boar'; current noun senses date from the early 16th cent.

soil[3] ▶ verb [with obj.] rare feed (cattle) on fresh-cut green fodder (originally for the purpose of purging them).
– ORIGIN early 17th cent.: perhaps from **SOIL**[2].

soil mechanics ▶ plural noun [usu. treated as sing.] the branch of science concerned with the properties and behaviour of soil as they affect its use in civil engineering.

soil pipe ▶ noun a sewage or waste water pipe.

soil science ▶ noun [mass noun] the branch of science concerned with the formation, nature, ecology, and classification of soil.

soil stack ▶ noun the pipe which takes all the waste water from the upstairs plumbing system of a building.

soirée /ˈswɑːreɪ/ ▶ noun an evening party or gathering, typically in a private house, for conversation or music.
– ORIGIN French, from *soir* 'evening'.

soixante-neuf /ˌswasɒntˈnɜːf/ ▶ noun [mass noun] informal sexual activity between two people involving mutual oral stimulation of their genitals.
– ORIGIN French, literally 'sixty-nine', from the position of the couple.

sojourn /ˈsɒdʒ(ə)n, -dʒɜːn/ formal ▶ noun a temporary stay: *her sojourn in Rome.*
▶ verb [no obj., with adverbial of place] stay somewhere temporarily: *she had sojourned once in Egypt.*
– DERIVATIVES **sojourner** noun.
– ORIGIN Middle English: from Old French *sojourner*, based on Latin *sub-* 'under' + late Latin *diurnum* 'day'.

Soka Gakkai /ˌsəʊkə ˈɡakʌɪ/ a political and lay religious organization founded in Japan in 1930, based on the teachings of the Nichiren Buddhist sect.
– ORIGIN Japanese, from *sō* 'create' + *ka* 'value' + *gakkai* '(learned) society'.

sokaiya /ˈsəʊkʌɪjə/ ▶ noun (pl. same) a holder of shares in a Japanese company who tries to extort money from it by threatening to cause trouble for executives at a general meeting of the shareholders.
– ORIGIN Japanese, from *sōkai* 'general meeting' + *-ya* 'dealer'.

soke ▶ noun Brit. historical a right of local jurisdiction.
■ a district under a particular jurisdiction; a minor administrative district.
– ORIGIN late Old English, back-formation from obsolete *soken* 'habitual visiting of a place'.

Sokol /ˈsɒkɒl/ ▶ noun a Slav gymnastic society aiming to promote a communal spirit and physical fitness, originating in Prague in 1862.
– ORIGIN Czech, literally 'falcon' (the emblem of the society).

Sol /sɒl/ Roman Mythology the sun, especially when personified as a god.
– ORIGIN Latin.

sol[1] /sɒl/ ▶ noun variant of **SOH**.

sol[2] /sɒl/ ▶ noun Chemistry a fluid suspension of a colloidal solid in a liquid.
– ORIGIN late 19th cent.: abbreviation of **SOLUTION**.

sol[3] /sɒl/ (also **nuevo sol**) ▶ noun (pl. **soles** /ˈsɒlɛz, ˈsəʊlɛz/) the basic monetary unit of Peru, equal to 100 cents. It replaced the inti in 1991.
– ORIGIN Spanish, literally 'sun'.

-sol ▶ combining form in nouns denoting different kinds and states of soil: *histosol* | *vertisol.*
– ORIGIN from Latin *solum* 'soil'.

sola[1] /ˈsəʊlə/ ▶ noun an Indian swamp plant of the pea family, with stems that yield the pith that is used to make sola topis.
● *Aeschynomene indica*, family Leguminosae.

– ORIGIN mid 19th cent.: from Bengali *solā*, Hindi *solā*.

sola[2] ▶ noun feminine form of **SOLUS**.

solace /ˈsɒlɪs/ ▶ noun [mass noun] comfort or consolation in a time of great distress or sadness: *she sought solace in her religion.*
▶ verb [with obj.] give solace to.
– ORIGIN Middle English: from Old French *solas* (noun), *solacier* (verb), based on Latin *solari* 'to console'.

solan /ˈsəʊlən/ (also **solan goose**) ▶ noun the northern gannet. See **GANNET** (sense 1).
– ORIGIN late Middle English: probably from Old Norse *súla* 'gannet' + *and-* 'duck'.

solanaceous /ˌsɒləˈneɪʃəs/ ▶ adjective Botany of, relating to, or denoting plants of the nightshade family (Solanaceae).
– ORIGIN early 19th cent.: from modern Latin *Solanaceae* (plural), based on Latin *solanum* 'nightshade', + **-OUS**.

solander /səˈlandə/ (also **solander box**) ▶ noun a protective box made in the form of a book, for holding such items as botanical specimens, maps, and colour plates.
– ORIGIN late 18th cent.: named after Daniel C. Solander (1736–82), Swedish botanist.

solanine /ˈsɒlənɪn/ ▶ noun [mass noun] Chemistry a poisonous compound which is present in green potatoes and in related plants. It is a steroid glycoside of the saponin group.
– ORIGIN mid 19th cent.: from French, from the genus name *Solanum* + **-INE**[4].

solanum /səˈleɪnəm/ ▶ noun a plant of a genus that includes the potato and woody nightshade.
● Genus *Solanum*, family Solanaceae.
– ORIGIN Latin.

solar[1] /ˈsəʊlə/ ▶ adjective of, relating to, or determined by the sun: *solar radiation.*
■ relating to or denoting energy derived from the sun's rays: *solar heating.*
▶ noun Brit. an upper chamber in a medieval house.
– ORIGIN late Middle English: from Latin *solaris*, from *sol* 'sun'.

solar[2] /ˈsɒlə, ˈsəʊlə/ ▶ noun Brit. an upper chamber in a medieval house.
– ORIGIN Middle English: from Anglo-Norman French *soler*, from Latin *solarium* 'gallery. terrace'.

solar battery (also **solar cell**) ▶ noun a device converting solar radiation into electricity.

solar constant ▶ noun Physics the rate at which energy reaches the earth's surface from the sun, usually taken to be 1,388 watts per square metre.

solar day ▶ noun the time between successive meridian transits of the sun at a particular place.

solar eclipse ▶ noun an eclipse in which the sun is obscured by the moon.

solar energy ▶ noun [mass noun] radiant energy emitted by the sun.
■ another term for **SOLAR POWER**.

solar flare ▶ noun Astronomy a brief eruption of intense high-energy radiation from the sun's surface, associated with sunspots and causing radio and magnetic disturbances on the earth.

solarium /səˈlɛːrɪəm/ ▶ noun (pl. **solariums** or **solaria** /-rɪə/) a room equipped with sunlamps or sunbeds which can be used to acquire an artificial suntan.
■ a room fitted with extensive areas of glass to admit sunlight.
– ORIGIN mid 19th cent.: from Latin, literally 'sundial, place for sunning oneself', from *sol* 'sun'.

solarize (also **-ise**) ▶ verb [with obj.] Photography change the relative darkness of (a part of an image) by overexposure to light.
– DERIVATIVES **solarization** noun.

solar mass ▶ noun Astronomy the mass of the sun used as a unit of mass, equal to 1.989×10^{30} kg.

solar myth ▶ noun a myth ascribing the sun's course or attributes to a particular god or hero.

solar panel ▶ noun a panel designed to absorb the sun's rays as a source of energy for generating electricity or heating.

solar plexus ▶ noun a complex of ganglia and radiating nerves of the sympathetic system at the pit of the stomach.

solar pond ▶ noun a pool of very salty water in

which convection is inhibited, allowing accumulation of energy from solar radiation in the lower layers.

solar power ▶ noun [mass noun] power obtained by harnessing the energy of the sun's rays.

solar system ▶ noun Astronomy the collection of nine planets and their moons in orbit round the sun, together with smaller bodies in the form of asteroids, meteoroids, and comets.

solar wind ▶ noun the continuous flow of charged particles from the sun which permeates the solar system.

solar year ▶ noun see YEAR (sense 1).

SOLAS /ˈsəʊlas/ ▶ noun [mass noun] [usu. as modifier] the provisions made during a series of international conventions governing maritime safety.
– ORIGIN 1960s: acronym from *safety of life at sea*.

solatium /səˈleɪʃɪəm/ ▶ noun (pl. **solatia** /-ʃɪə/) informal a thing given to someone as a compensation or consolation: *a suitable solatium in the form of an apology was offered to him.*
– ORIGIN early 19th cent.: from Latin, literally 'solace'.

sola topi ▶ noun an Indian sun hat made from the pith of the stems of sola plants.

sold past and past participle of SELL.

soldanella /ˌsɒldəˈnɛlə/ ▶ noun a dwarf European alpine plant with bell-shaped flowers that have fringed petals and often appear in snow.
● Genus *Soldanella*, family Primulaceae.
– ORIGIN modern Latin, from Italian, of unknown ultimate origin.

solder /ˈsəʊldə, ˈsɒldə/ ▶ noun [mass noun] a low-melting alloy, especially one based on lead and tin or (for higher temperatures) on brass or silver, used for joining less fusible metals.
▶ verb [with obj.] join with solder.
– DERIVATIVES **solderable** adjective, **solderer** noun.
– ORIGIN Middle English: from Old French *soudure*, from the verb *souder*, from Latin *solidare* 'fasten together', from *solidus* 'solid'.

soldering iron ▶ noun an electrical tool used for melting solder and applying it to metals that are to be joined.

soldi plural form of SOLDO.

soldier ▶ noun 1 a person who serves in an army.
■(also **common soldier** or **private soldier**) a private in an army.
2 Entomology a wingless caste of ant or termite with a large specially modified head and jaws, involved chiefly in defence.
3 Brit. informal a strip of bread or toast, used for dipping into a soft-boiled egg.
■[usu. as modifier] an upright brick, timber, or other building element.
▶ verb [no obj.] serve as a soldier: [as noun **soldiering**] *soldiering was what the Colonel understood.*
■(**soldier on**) informal carry on doggedly; persevere: *Graham wasn't enjoying this, but he soldiered on.*
– DERIVATIVES **soldierly** adjective, **soldiership** noun (archaic).
– ORIGIN Middle English: from Old French *soldier*, from *soulde* '(soldier's) pay', from Latin *solidus* (see SOLIDUS). The verb dates from the early 17th cent.

soldier arch ▶ noun a flat or gently curved arch made from upright bricks.

soldier beetle ▶ noun an elongated flying beetle with soft downy wing cases, typically found on flowers where it hunts other insects.
● Family Cantharidae: several genera.

soldierfish ▶ noun (pl. same or **-fishes**) a squirrelfish that is typically bright red in colour.
● Several genera and species in the family Holocentridae.

soldier fly ▶ noun a bright metallic fly with a flattened body, which frequently basks in the sun with its wings folded flat over the body.
● Family Stratiomyidae: many genera.

soldier of Christ ▶ noun an active or proselytizing Christian.

soldier of fortune ▶ noun a person who works as a soldier for any country or group that will pay them; a mercenary.

soldiery ▶ noun (pl. **-ies**) soldiers collectively: *the town was filled with disbanded soldiery.*
■[mass noun] military training or knowledge: *the arts of soldiery.*

soldo /ˈsɒldəʊ/ ▶ noun (pl. **soldi** /ˈsɒldi/) a former

Italian coin and monetary unit worth the twentieth part of a lira.
– ORIGIN Italian, from Latin *solidus* (see SOLIDUS).

Sole a shipping forecast area in the NE Atlantic, covering the western approaches to the English Channel.

sole[1] ▶ noun the undersurface of a person's foot: *the soles of their feet were nearly black with dirt.*
■the section forming the underside of a piece of footwear (typically excluding the heel when this forms a distinct part). ■ the part of the undersurface of a person's foot between the toes and the instep. ■ the undersurface of a tool or implement such as a plane or the head of a golf club. ■ the floor of a ship's cabin or cockpit.
▶ verb [with obj.] (usu. **be soled**) put a new sole on to (a shoe).
– DERIVATIVES **soled** adjective [in combination] *rubber-soled shoes.*
– ORIGIN Middle English: from Old French, from Latin *solea* 'sandal, sill', from *solum* 'bottom, pavement, sole'; compare with Dutch *zool* and German *Sohle*.

sole[2] ▶ noun a marine flatfish of almost worldwide distribution, important as a food fish.
● Several species in the families Soleidae, Pleuronectidae, and Bothidae. See DOVER SOLE, LEMON SOLE.
– ORIGIN Middle English: from Old French, from Provençal *sola*, from Latin *solea* (see SOLE[1]), named from its shape.

sole[3] ▶ adjective [attrib.] one and only: *my sole aim was to contribute to the national team.*
■belonging or restricted to one person or group of people: *loans can be in sole or joint names | the health club is for the sole use of our guests.* ■ archaic (especially of a woman) unmarried. ■ archaic alone, unaccompanied.
– ORIGIN late Middle English (also in the senses 'secluded' and 'unrivalled'): from Old French *soule*, from Latin *sola*, feminine of *solus* 'alone'.

solebar ▶ noun a longitudinal structural piece forming part of the underframe of a railway vehicle.

solecism /ˈsɒlɪsɪz(ə)m/ ▶ noun a grammatical mistake in speech or writing.
■a breach of good manners; a piece of incorrect behaviour.
– DERIVATIVES **solecistic** /-ˈsɪstɪk/ adjective.
– ORIGIN mid 16th cent.: from French *solécisme*, or via Latin from Greek *soloikismos*, from *soloikos* 'speaking incorrectly'.

solely /ˈsəʊlli/ ▶ adverb not involving anyone or anything else; only: *he is solely responsible for any debts the company may incur | people are appointed solely on the basis of merit.*

solemn ▶ adjective formal and dignified: *a solemn procession.*
■not cheerful or smiling; serious: *Tim looked very solemn.* ■ characterized by deep sincerity: *he swore a solemn oath to keep faith.*
– DERIVATIVES **solemnly** adverb, **solemnness** noun.
– ORIGIN Middle English (in the sense 'associated with religious rites'): from Old French *solemne*, from Latin *sollemnis* 'customary, celebrated at a fixed date', from *sollus* 'entire'.

solemnity /səˈlɛmnɪti/ ▶ noun (pl. **-ies**) [mass noun] the state or quality of being serious and dignified: *his ashes were laid to rest with great solemnity.*
■[count noun] (usu. **solemnities**) a formal, dignified rite or ceremony: *the ritual of the church was observed in all its solemnities.*
– ORIGIN Middle English (in the sense 'observance of formality and ceremony', frequently in the phrases *in solemnity*, *with solemnity*): from Old French *solemnite*, from Latin *sollemnitas*, from *sollemnis* (see SOLEMN).

solemnize /ˈsɒləmnaɪz/ (also **-ise**) ▶ verb [with obj.] duly perform (a ceremony, especially that of marriage).
■mark with a formal ceremony.
– DERIVATIVES **solemnization** noun.
– ORIGIN late Middle English: from Old French *solemniser*, from medieval Latin *solemnizare*, from Latin *sollemnis* (see SOLEMN).

Solemn League and Covenant an agreement made in 1643 between the English Parliament and the Scottish Covenanters during the English Civil War, by which the Scots would provide military aid in return for the establishment of a Presbyterian system in England,

Scotland, and Ireland. Although the Scottish support proved crucial in the Parliamentary victory, the principal Presbyterian leaders were expelled from Parliament in 1647 and the covenant was never honoured.

Solemn Mass ▶ noun another term for HIGH MASS.

solenodon /səˈlɛnədɒn/ ▶ noun a forest-dwelling mammal with a long flexible snout and a stiff muscular tail, occurring only in Cuba and Hispaniola.
● Family Solenodontidae and genus *Solenodon*: two species.
– ORIGIN modern Latin, from Greek *sōlēn* 'channel, pipe' + *odō* (variant of *odous*, *odont-*) 'tooth'.

solenoid /ˈsɒlɪnɔɪd, ˈsəʊl-/ ▶ noun a cylindrical coil of wire acting as a magnet when carrying electric current.
– DERIVATIVES **solenoidal** adjective.
– ORIGIN early 19th cent.: from French *solénoïde*, from Greek *sōlēn* 'channel, pipe'.

Solent /ˈsəʊlənt/ (**the Solent**) a channel between the NW coast of the Isle of Wight and the mainland of southern England.

soleplate ▶ noun 1 a metal plate forming the base of an electric iron, machine saw, or other machine.
2 a horizontal timber at the base of a wall frame.

solera /səˈlɛːrə/ ▶ noun (also **solera system**) [mass noun] a Spanish method of producing wine, especially sherry and Madeira, whereby small amounts of younger wines stored in an upper tier of casks are systematically blended with the more mature wine in the casks below.
■(also **solera wine**) [count noun] a blend of sherry or Malaga wine produced by the solera system. ■ [count noun] a wine cask, typically one with a capacity of four hogsheads, on the bottom tier of the solera system and containing the oldest wine.
– ORIGIN Spanish, literally 'cross-beam, stone base'.

Soleure /sɒˈlɛːr/ French name for SOLOTHURN.

soleus /ˈsəʊ(ʊ)lɪəs/ (also **soleus muscle**) ▶ noun Anatomy a broad muscle in the lower calf, below the gastrocnemius, which flexes the foot to point the toes downwards.
– ORIGIN late 17th cent.: modern Latin, from Latin *solea* 'sole'.

sol-fa /ˈsɒlfɑː/ ▶ noun short for TONIC SOL-FA.
▶ verb (**sol-fas**, **sol-faed**, **sol-faing**) [with obj.] sing using the sol-fa syllables.

solfatara /ˌsɒlfəˈtɑːrə/ ▶ noun Geology a volcanic crater emitting only sulphurous and other gases.
– ORIGIN late 18th cent.: from the name of a volcano near Naples, from Italian *solfo* 'sulphur'.

solfège /ˈsɒlfɛʒ/ ▶ noun another term for SOLFEGGIO.
– ORIGIN French.

solfeggio /sɒlˈfɛdʒɪəʊ/ ▶ noun (pl. **solfeggi** /-dʒi/) Music an exercise in singing using sol-fa syllables.
■[mass noun] solmization.
– ORIGIN Italian.

soli plural form of SOLO.

solicit ▶ verb (**solicited**, **soliciting**) [with obj.] ask for or try to obtain (something) from someone: *he called a meeting to solicit their views* | [no obj.] *don't solicit for money.*
■ask (someone) for something: *historians and critics are solicited for opinions by the auction houses.* ■ [no obj.] accost someone and offer one's or someone else's services as a prostitute: [as noun **soliciting**] *although prostitution was not itself an offence, soliciting was.*
– DERIVATIVES **solicitation** noun.
– ORIGIN late Middle English: from Old French *solliciter*, from Latin *sollicitare* 'agitate', from *sollicitus* 'anxious', from *sollus* 'entire' + *citus* (past participle of *ciere* 'set in motion').

solicitor ▶ noun 1 Brit. a member of the legal profession qualified to deal with conveyancing, the drawing up of wills, and other legal matters. A solicitor may also advise clients, instruct barristers, and represent clients in some courts. Compare with BARRISTER, ATTORNEY.
■N. Amer. the chief law officer of a city, town, or government department.
2 N. Amer. a person who tries to obtain business orders, advertising, etc.; a canvasser.
– ORIGIN late Middle English (denoting an agent or deputy): from Old French *solliciteur*, from *solliciter* (see SOLICIT).

Solicitor General ▶ noun (pl. **Solicitors General**) (in the UK) the Crown law officer below the

Attorney General or (in Scotland) below the Lord Advocate.
■(in the US) the law officer below the Attorney General.

solicitous ▶ **adjective** characterized by or showing interest or concern: *she was always solicitous about the welfare of her students* | *a solicitous enquiry.*
■archaic eager or anxious to do something: *he was solicitous to cultivate her mamma's good opinion.*
– DERIVATIVES **solicitously** adverb, **solicitousness** noun.
– ORIGIN mid 16th cent.: from Latin *sollicitus* (see **SOLICIT**) + **-OUS**.

solicitude ▶ **noun** [mass noun] care or concern for someone or something: *I was touched by his solicitude.*
– ORIGIN late Middle English: from Old French *sollicitude*, from Latin *sollicitudo*, from *sollicitus* (see **SOLICITOUS**).

solid ▶ **adjective** (**solider, solidest**) **1** firm and stable in shape; not liquid or fluid: *the stream was frozen solid* | *solid fuels.*
■strongly built or made of strong materials; not flimsy or slender: *a solid door with good, secure locks.* ■ having three dimensions: *a solid figure with six plane faces.* ■ [attrib.] concerned with objects having three dimensions: *solid geometry.*
2 not hollow or containing spaces or gaps: *a sculpture made out of solid rock* | *a solid mass of flowers* | *the shops were packed solid.*
■consisting of the same substance throughout: *solid silver cutlery.* ■ (of typesetting) without extra space between the lines of characters. ■ (of a line or surface) without spaces; unbroken: *the solid outline encloses the area within which we measured.* ■ (of time) uninterrupted; continuous: *a solid day of meetings* | [postpositive] *it poured for two hours solid.*
3 dependable; reliable: *the defence is solid* | *there is solid evidence of lower inflation.*
■sound but without any special qualities or flair: *the rest of the acting is solid.* ■ unanimous or undivided: *they received solid support from their teammates.* ■ [predic.] (**solid with**) US informal on good terms with: *he thought he could put himself* ***in solid with*** *you by criticizing her.*
4 Austral./NZ informal severe; unfair: *they'll be* ***solid on*** *him for that mistake.*
▶ **noun** a substance or object that is solid rather than liquid or fluid.
■(**solids**) food that is not liquid: *she drinks only milk and rarely eats solids.* ■ Geometry a body or geometric figure having three dimensions.
– DERIVATIVES **solidly** adverb, **solidness** noun.
– ORIGIN late Middle English: from Latin *solidus*; related to *salvus* 'safe' and *sollus* 'entire'.

solidago /ˌsɒlɪˈdeɪɡəʊ/ ▶ **noun** (pl. **-os**) a plant of the genus *Solidago* in the daisy family, especially (in gardening) goldenrod.
– ORIGIN modern Latin, from a medieval Latin alteration of late Latin *consolida* 'comfrey'.

solid angle ▶ **noun** a three-dimensional analogue of an angle, such as that subtended by a cone or formed by planes meeting at a point. It is measured in steradians.

solidarity ▶ **noun 1** [mass noun] unity or agreement of feeling or action, especially among individuals with a common interest; mutual support within a group: *factory workers voiced solidarity with the striking students.*
2 (**Solidarity**) an independent trade union movement in Poland which developed into a mass campaign for political change and inspired popular opposition to Communist regimes across eastern Europe. Formed in 1980 under the leadership of Lech Wałęsa, it was banned in 1981 following the imposition of martial law. Legalized again in 1989, it won a majority in the elections of that year. [ORIGIN: translating Polish *Solidarność*.]
– ORIGIN mid 19th cent.: from French *solidarité*, from *solidaire* 'solidary'.

solidary ▶ **adjective** (of a group or community) characterized by solidarity or coincidence of interests.
– ORIGIN early 19th cent.: from French *solidaire*, from *solide* 'solid'.

solid-body ▶ **adjective** denoting or relating to an electric guitar without a soundbox, the strings being mounted on a solid shaped block forming the guitar body.

solid-drawn ▶ **adjective** (of a tube) pressed or drawn out from a solid bar of metal.

solidi plural form of **SOLIDUS**.

solidify ▶ **verb** (**-ies, -ied**) make or become hard or solid: [no obj.] *the magma slowly solidifies and forms crystals.*
■[with obj.] figurative make stronger; reinforce: *social and political pressures helped to solidify national identities.*
– DERIVATIVES **solidification** noun, **solidifier** noun.

solidity ▶ **noun** [mass noun] the quality or state of being firm or strong in structure: *the sheer strength and solidity of Romanesque architecture.*
■the quality of being substantial or reliable in character: *he exuded an aura of reassuring solidity.*

solid solution ▶ **noun** Chemistry a solid mixture containing a minor component uniformly distributed within the crystal lattice of the major component.

solid South ▶ **noun** (**the solid South**) chiefly historical the politically united Southern states of America, traditionally regarded as giving unwavering electoral support to the Democratic Party.

solid state ▶ **noun** [mass noun] the state of matter in which materials are not fluid but retain their boundaries without support, the atoms or molecules occupying fixed positions with respect to each other and unable move freely.
▶ **adjective** (**solid-state**) (of a device) making use of the electronic properties of solid semiconductors (as opposed to valves).

solidus /ˈsɒlɪdəs/ ▶ **noun** (pl. **solidi** /-dʌɪ/) **1** chiefly Brit. another term for **SLASH** (in sense 2).
2 (also **solidus curve**) Chemistry a curve in a graph of the temperature and composition of a mixture, below which the substance is entirely solid.
3 historical a gold coin of the later Roman Empire. [ORIGIN: from Latin *solidus* (*nummus*).]
– ORIGIN Latin, literally 'solid'.

solifluction /ˌsɒlɪˈflʌkʃ(ə)n, ˌsəʊlɪ-/ ▶ **noun** [mass noun] Geology the gradual movement of wet soil or other material down a slope, especially where frozen subsoil acts as a barrier to the percolation of water.
– ORIGIN early 20th cent.: from Latin *solum* 'soil' + *fluctio(n-)* 'flowing', from the verb *fluere*.

solifuge /ˈsɒlɪfjuːdʒ/ (also **solifugid** /sɒˈlɪfjʊdʒɪd/) ▶ **noun** Zoology a sun spider.
– ORIGIN mid 17th cent.: from Latin *solifuga*.

Solihull /ˈsɒlɪhʌl, ˌsəʊlɪˈhʌl/ a town in the Midlands, forming part of the conurbation of Birmingham; pop. 94,600 (1981).

soliloquy /səˈlɪləkwi/ ▶ **noun** (pl. **-ies**) an act of speaking one's thoughts aloud when by oneself or regardless of any hearers, especially by a character in a play.
■a part of a play involving such an act.
– DERIVATIVES **soliloquist** noun, **soliloquize** (also **-ise**) verb.
– ORIGIN Middle English: from late Latin *soliloquium*, from Latin *solus* 'alone' + *loqui* 'speak'.

Soliman /ˈsɒlɪmən/ variant spelling of **SULEIMAN I**.

solipsism /ˈsɒlɪpsɪz(ə)m/ ▶ **noun** [mass noun] the view or theory that the self is all that can be known to exist.
– DERIVATIVES **solipsist** noun, **solipsistic** adjective, **solipsistically** adverb.
– ORIGIN late 19th cent.: from Latin *solus* 'alone' + *ipse* 'self' + **-ISM**.

solitaire /ˈsɒlɪtɛː, ˌsɒlɪˈtɛː/ ▶ **noun 1** [mass noun] a game for one player played by removing pegs one at a time from a board by jumping others over them from adjacent holes, the object being to be left with only one peg.
■the card game patience.
2 a diamond or other gem set in a piece of jewellery by itself.
■a ring set with such a gem.
3 either of two large extinct flightless birds related to the dodo, found on two of the Mascarene Islands until they were exterminated in the 18th century.
• Family Raphidae: the **Rodriguez solitaire** (*Pezophaps solitaria*), and the poorly known **Réunion solitaire** (*Ornithaptera solitaria*).
4 a large American thrush with mainly grey plumage and a short bill.
• Genus *Myadestes*, family Turdidae: several species.
– ORIGIN early 18th cent.: from French, from Latin *solitarius* (see **SOLITARY**).

solitary ▶ **adjective** done or existing alone: *I live a pretty solitary life* | *tigers are essentially solitary.*
■(of a place) secluded or isolated: *solitary farmsteads.* ■ [attrib.] [often with negative] single; only: *we have not a solitary shred of evidence to go on.* ■ (of a bird, mammal, or insect) living alone or in pairs, especially in contrast to related social forms: *a solitary wasp.* ■ (of a flower or other part) borne singly.
▶ **noun** (pl. **-ies**) **1** a recluse or hermit.
2 informal short for **SOLITARY CONFINEMENT**.
– DERIVATIVES **solitarily** adverb, **solitariness** noun.
– ORIGIN Middle English: from Latin *solitarius*, from *solus* 'alone'.

solitary confinement ▶ **noun** the isolation of a prisoner in a separate cell as a punishment.

solitary wave ▶ **noun** another term for **SOLITON**.

soliton /ˈsɒlɪtɒn/ ▶ **noun** Physics a quantum or quasiparticle propagated as a travelling non-dissipative wave which is neither preceded nor followed by another such disturbance.
– ORIGIN 1960s: from **SOLITARY** + **-ON**.

solitude ▶ **noun** [mass noun] the state or situation of being alone: *she savoured her few hours of freedom and solitude.*
■[count noun] a lonely or uninhabited place.
– ORIGIN Middle English: from Old French, or from Latin *solitudo*, from *solus* 'alone'.

solmization /ˌsɒlmɪˈzeɪʃ(ə)n/ (also **-isation**) ▶ **noun** [mass noun] Music a system of associating each note of a scale with a particular syllable, especially to teach singing.

The commonest European system, still in use, originally named the notes *ut, re, mi, fa, sol, la* in groups of six (hexachords) beginning on G, C, or F, using syllables from a Latin hymn for St John the Baptist's Day in which each phrase begins on the next note in the scale: '*Ut* queant laxis *re*sonare fibris *Mi*ra gestorum *fa*muli tuorum, *Sol*ve polluti *la*bili reatum, Sancte Iohannes'. A seventh note *si* was added later (from the initials of Sancte Iohannes). Modern systems typically use the sequence as arbitrarily adapted in the 19th century: *doh, ray, me, fah, soh, la, te*, with doh being C in the fixed-doh system and the keynote in the movable-doh or tonic sol-fa system.

– DERIVATIVES **solmizate** verb.
– ORIGIN mid 18th cent.: from French *solmisation*, based on *sol* 'soh' + *mi* (see **ME**[2]).

Solnhofen /ˈzəʊlnˌhəʊf(ə)n, German ˈzoːlnˌhoːfn/ a village in Bavaria, Germany, near which there are extensive, thinly stratified beds of lithographic limestone dating from the Upper Jurassic period. These beds are noted as the chief source of archaeopteryx fossils.

solo ▶ **noun** (pl. **-os**) **1** a thing done by one person unaccompanied, in particular:
■(pl. **solos** or **soli**) a piece of vocal or instrumental music or a dance, or a part or passage in one, for one performer. ■ an unaccompanied flight by a pilot in an aircraft.
2 (also **solo whist**) [mass noun] a card game resembling whist in which the players make bids and the highest bidder plays against the others in an attempt to win a specified number of tricks.
■a bid by which a player undertakes to win five tricks in this game.
3 a motorbike without a sidecar.
▶ **adjective** & **adverb** for or done by one person alone; unaccompanied: [as adj.] *a solo album* | [as adv.] *she'd spent most of her life flying solo.*
■(of a motorbike) without a sidecar: *a solo machine.*
▶ **verb** (**-oes, -oed**) [no obj.] perform something unaccompanied, in particular:
■perform an unaccompanied piece of music or a part or passage in one. ■ fly an aircraft unaccompanied. ■ undertake solo climbing.
– ORIGIN late 17th cent. (as a musical term): from Italian, from Latin *solus* 'alone'.

solo climbing ▶ **noun** [mass noun] the sport of climbing unaided by ropes and other equipment, and without the assistance of other people.
– DERIVATIVES **solo climber** noun.

soloist ▶ **noun** a musician or singer who performs a solo.

Solomon /ˈsɒləmən/, son of David, king of ancient Israel *c.*970–*c.*930 BC. In the Bible Solomon is traditionally associated with the Song of Solomon, Ecclesiastes, and Proverbs, while his wisdom is illustrated by the Judgement of Solomon. Discontent with his rule, however, led to the secession of the northern tribes in the reign of his son Rehoboam.
■[as noun] (usu. **a Solomon**) a very wise person.
– DERIVATIVES **Solomonic** /sɒləˈmɒnɪk/ adjective.

Solomon Gundy ▶ **noun** West Indian and Canadian term for **SALMAGUNDI**.
– ORIGIN alteration.

Solomon Islands (also **the Solomons**) a country

consisting of a group of islands in the SW Pacific, to the east of New Guinea; pop. 326,000 (est. 1991); languages, English (official), Pidgin, local Austronesian languages; capital, Honiara.

The islands were divided between Britain and Germany in the late 19th century; the southern islands became a British protectorate in 1893 while the north remained German until mandated to Australia in 1920. With the exception of the northern part of the chain (now part of Papua New Guinea), the Solomons became self-governing in 1976 and fully independent within the Commonwealth two years later.

– DERIVATIVES **Solomon Islander** noun.

Solomon's seal ▶ noun **1** a figure like the Star of David.
2 a widely distributed plant of the lily family, having arching stems that bear a double row of broad leaves with drooping green and white flowers in their axils.
• Genus *Polygonatum*, family Liliaceae: many species.

Solon /ˈsəʊlɒn/ (*c.*630–*c.*560 BC), Athenian statesman and lawgiver. One of the Seven Sages, he revised the code of laws established by Draco, making it less severe. His division of the citizens into four classes based on wealth rather than birth laid the foundations of Athenian democracy.

solo stop ▶ noun an organ stop especially suitable for imitating a solo performance on another instrument.

Solothurn /ˈzəʊləʊˌtʊən, German ˈzoːloˌtʊrn/ a canton in NW Switzerland, in the Jura mountains. French name **SOLEURE**.
■ its capital, a town on the River Aare; pop. 15,430 (1990).

solo whist ▶ noun see **SOLO** (sense 2).

solstice /ˈsɒlstɪs/ ▶ noun either of the two times in the year, the **summer solstice** and the **winter solstice**, when the sun reaches its highest or lowest point in the sky at noon, marked by the longest and shortest days.
– DERIVATIVES **solstitial** adjective.
– ORIGIN Middle English: from Old French, from Latin *solstitium*, from *sol* 'sun' + *stit-* 'stopped, stationary' (from the verb *sistere*).

Solti /ˈʃɒlti/, Sir Georg (1912–97), Hungarian-born British conductor. He revivified Covent Garden as musical director (1961–71) and was conductor of the Chicago Symphony Orchestra (1969–91) and the London Philharmonic Orchestra (1979–83).

solubilize /ˈsɒljʊbɪlʌɪz/ (also **-ise**) ▶ verb [with obj.] technical make (a substance) soluble or more soluble.
– DERIVATIVES **solubilization** noun.

soluble ▶ adjective **1** (of a substance) able to be dissolved, especially in water: *the poison is soluble in alcohol.*
2 (of a problem) able to be solved.
– DERIVATIVES **solubility** noun.
– ORIGIN late Middle English: from Old French, from late Latin *solubilis*, from *solvere* (see **SOLVE**).

soluble glass ▶ noun another term for **WATER GLASS** (in sense 1).

solunar /sɒˈluːnə/ ▶ adjective of or relating to the combined influence or conjunction of the sun and moon.
– ORIGIN late 18th cent.: blend of **SOL** and **LUNAR**.

solus /ˈsəʊləs/ ▶ adjective (fem. **sola** /-lə/) alone or unaccompanied (used especially as a stage direction).
– ORIGIN Latin.

solute /ˈsɒljuːt, sɒˈljuːt/ ▶ noun the minor component in a solution, dissolved in the solvent.
– ORIGIN late 19th cent.: from Latin *solutum*, neuter of *solutus* 'loosened', past participle of the verb *solvere*.

solution ▶ noun **1** a means of solving a problem or dealing with a difficult situation: *there are no easy solutions to financial and marital problems.*
■ the correct answer to a puzzle: *the solution to this month's crossword.*
2 a liquid mixture in which the minor component (the solute) is uniformly distributed within the major component (the solvent).
■ [mass noun] the process or state of being dissolved in a solvent.
3 [mass noun] archaic the action of separating or breaking down; dissolution: *the solution of British supremacy in South Africa.*
– ORIGIN late Middle English: from Old French, from Latin *solutio(n-)*, from *solvere* 'loosen' (see **SOLVE**).

solution set ▶ noun Mathematics the set of all the solutions of an equation or condition.

Solutrean /səˈluːtrɪən/ ▶ adjective Archaeology of, relating to, or denoting an Upper Palaeolithic culture of central and SW France and parts of Iberia. It is dated to about 21,000–18,000 years ago, following the Aurignacian and preceding the Magdalenian.
■ [as noun **the Solutrean**] the Solutrean culture or period.
– ORIGIN late 19th cent.: from *Solutré*, the site of a cave in eastern France, where objects from this culture were found, + **-AN**.

solvate Chemistry ▶ verb /sɒlˈveɪt/ [with obj.] (of a solvent) enter into reversible chemical combination with (a dissolved molecule, ion, etc.).
▶ noun /ˈsɒlveɪt/ a more or less loosely bonded complex formed between a solvent and a dissolved species.
– DERIVATIVES **solvation** noun.
– ORIGIN early 20th cent.: formed irregularly from **SOLVE** + **-ATE**[1].

Solvay process /ˈsɒlveɪ/ ▶ noun [mass noun] Chemistry an industrial process for obtaining sodium carbonate from limestone, ammonia, and brine.
– ORIGIN late 19th cent.: named after Ernest Solvay (1838–1922), Belgian chemist.

solve ▶ verb [with obj.] find an answer to, explanation for, or means of effectively dealing with (a problem or mystery): *the policy could solve the town's housing crisis | a murder investigation that has never been solved.*
– DERIVATIVES **solvable** adjective, **solver** noun.
– ORIGIN late Middle English (in the sense 'loosen, dissolve, untie'): from Latin *solvere* 'loosen, unfasten'.

solvent ▶ adjective **1** having assets in excess of liabilities; able to pay one's debts: *interest rate rises have very severe effects on normally solvent companies.*
2 [attrib.] able to dissolve other substances: *osmotic, chemical, or solvent action.*
▶ noun the liquid in which a solute is dissolved to form a solution.
■ a liquid, typically one other than water, used for dissolving other substances. ■ figurative something that acts to weaken or dispel a particular attitude or situation: *an unrivalled* **solvent of** *social prejudices.*
– DERIVATIVES **solvency** noun (in sense 1 of the adjective).
– ORIGIN mid 17th cent.: from Latin *solvent-* 'loosening, unfastening, paying', from the verb *solvere*.

solvent abuse ▶ noun [mass noun] the use of certain volatile organic solvents as intoxicants by inhalation, e.g. glue-sniffing.

solvent extraction ▶ noun [mass noun] Chemistry the partial removal of a substance from a solution or mixture by dissolving it in another, immiscible solvent in which it is more soluble.

Solway Firth an inlet of the Irish Sea, separating Cumbria (in England) from Dumfries and Galloway (in Scotland).

Solyman variant spelling of **SULEIMAN I**.

Solzhenitsyn /ˌsɒlʒəˈniːtsɪn/, Alexander (b.1918), Russian novelist; Russian name *Aleksandr Isaevich Solzhenitsyn*. He spent eight years in a labour camp for criticizing Stalin and began writing on his release. From 1963 his books were banned in the Soviet Union, and he was exiled in 1974, eventually returning to Russia in 1994. Notable works: *One Day in the Life of Ivan Denisovich* (1962) and *The Gulag Archipelago* (1973). Nobel Prize for Literature (1970).

Som. ▶ abbreviation for Somerset.

som /səʊm/ ▶ noun (pl. same) the basic monetary unit of Kyrgyzstan, equal to 100 tiyin.

soma[1] /ˈsəʊmə/ ▶ noun [usu. in sing.] Biology the parts of an organism other than the reproductive cells.
■ the body as distinct from the soul, mind, or psyche.
– ORIGIN late 19th cent.: from Greek *sōma* 'body'.

soma[2] /ˈsəʊmə/ ▶ noun [mass noun] Hinduism an intoxicating drink prepared from a plant and used in Vedic ritual, believed to be the drink of the gods.
– ORIGIN from Sanskrit *sōma*.

somaesthetic /ˌsəʊmiːsˈθɛtɪk/ (US **somesthetic**) ▶ adjective another term for **SOMATOSENSORY**.
– ORIGIN late 19th cent.: from Greek *sōma* 'body' + **AESTHETIC**.

Somali /səˈmɑːli/ ▶ noun (pl. same or **Somalis**) a member of a mainly Muslim people of Somalia.
■ [mass noun] the Cushitic language of this people, the official language of Somalia, also spoken in Djibouti and parts of Kenya and Ethiopia, and having over 6 million speakers. ■ a native or national of Somalia.
▶ adjective of or relating to Somalia, the Somalis, or their language.
– DERIVATIVES **Somalian** adjective & noun.
– ORIGIN the name in Somali.

Somalia /səˈmɑːlɪə/ a country in the Horn of Africa; pop. 8,041,000 (est. 1991); official languages, Somali and Arabic; capital, Mogadishu.

The area of the Horn of Africa was divided between British and Italian spheres of influence in the late 19th century, and the modern republic of Somalia became independent in 1960 following the unification of the former British Somaliland and Italian Somalia. Civil war broke out in Somalia in 1988 and led to the overthrow of the government in 1991; the US intervened militarily 1992–4. In 1991 northern Somalia declared itself independent as the Somaliland Republic.

Somali Peninsula another name for **HORN OF AFRICA**.

soman /ˈsəʊmən/ ▶ noun [mass noun] a lethal organophosphorus nerve gas, developed in Germany during the Second World War.
– ORIGIN 1950s: from German, of unknown origin.

somatic /səˈmatɪk/ ▶ adjective of or relating to the body, especially as distinct from the mind.
– DERIVATIVES **somatically** adverb.
– ORIGIN late 18th cent.: from Greek *sōmatikos*, from *sōma* 'body'.

somatic cell ▶ noun Biology any cell of a living organism other than the reproductive cells.

somatization /ˌsəʊmətʌɪˈzeɪʃ(ə)n/ ▶ noun [mass noun] Psychiatry the production of recurrent and multiple medical symptoms with no discernible organic cause: [as modifier] *somatization disorder.*

somato- ▶ combining form of or relating to the human or animal body: *somatotype.*
– ORIGIN from Greek *sōma, sōmat-* 'body'.

somatomedin /ˌsəʊmətə(ʊ)ˈmiːdɪn/ ▶ noun [mass noun] Biochemistry a hormone which acts as an intermediate in the stimulation of tissue growth by growth hormone.
– ORIGIN 1970s: from **SOMATO-** 'of the body' + *(inter)med(iary)* + **-IN**[1].

somatopleure /ˌsəʊmətə(ʊ)ˈplʊə/ ▶ noun Embryology a layer of tissue in a vertebrate embryo comprising the ectoderm and the outer layer of mesoderm, and giving rise to the amnion, chorion, and part of the body wall. Often contrasted with **SPLANCHNOPLEURE**.
– ORIGIN late 19th cent.: from **SOMATO-** 'of the body' + Greek *pleura* 'side'.

somatosensory ▶ adjective Physiology relating to or denoting a sensation (such as pressure, pain, or warmth) which can occur anywhere in the body, in contrast to one localized at a sense organ (such as sight, balance, or taste). Also called **SOMAESTHETIC**.

somatostatin /ˌsəʊmətə(ʊ)ˈstatɪn/ ▶ noun [mass noun] Biochemistry a hormone secreted in the pancreas and pituitary gland which inhibits gastric secretion and somatotrophin release.

somatotrophin /ˌsəʊmətə(ʊ)ˈtrəʊfɪn/ ▶ noun [mass noun] Biochemistry a growth hormone secreted by the anterior pituitary gland.

somatotype ▶ noun a category to which people are assigned according to the extent to which their bodily physique conforms to a basic type (usually endomorphic, mesomorphic, or ectomorphic).
– DERIVATIVES **somatotyping** noun.
– ORIGIN 1940s: coined by W. H. Sheldon in *Varieties of Human Physique*.

sombre (US also **somber**) ▶ adjective dark or dull in colour or tone; gloomy: *the night skies were sombre and starless.*
■ oppressively solemn or sober in mood; grave: *he looked at her with a sombre expression.*
– DERIVATIVES **sombrely** adverb, **sombreness** noun.
– ORIGIN mid 18th cent.: from French, based on Latin *sub* 'under' + *umbra* 'shade'.

sombrero /sɒmˈbrɛːrəʊ/ ▶ noun (pl. **-os**) a broad-brimmed felt or straw hat, typically worn in Mexico and the south-western US.
– ORIGIN Spanish, from *sombra* 'shade' (see **SOMBRE**).

some ▶ determiner **1** an unspecified amount or number of: *I made some money running errands | he played some records for me.*
2 used to refer to someone or something that is unknown or unspecified: *she married some newspaper*

S

magnate twice her age | there must be some mistake | he's in ***some kind of*** *trouble.*
3 (used with a number) approximately: *some thirty different languages are spoken.*
4 (pronounced stressing 'some') a considerable amount or number of: *he went to some trouble | I've known you for some years now.*
5 (pronounced stressing 'some') at least a small amount or number of: *he liked some music but generally wasn't musical.*
6 (pronounced stressing 'some') expressing admiration of something notable: *that was some goal.*
■used ironically to express disapproval or disbelief: *Mr Power gave his stock reply. Some help. | not that Jennifer would ever be on the dole. Some chance of that.*
▶**pronoun 1** an unspecified number or amount of people or things: *here are* ***some of*** *our suggestions | if you want whisky I'll give you some.*
2 (pronounced stressing 'some') at least a small amount or number of people or things: *surely some have noticed.*
▶**adverb** informal, chiefly N. Amer. to some extent; quite a lot: *he needs feeding up some.*
– PHRASES **and then some** informal and plenty more than that: *we got our money's worth and then some.* **some few** see **FEW**. **some little** a considerable amount of: *we are going to be working together for some little time yet.*
– ORIGIN Old English *sum*, of Germanic origin, from an Indo-European root shared by Greek *hamōs* 'somehow' and Sanskrit *sama* 'any, every'.

-some[1] ▶**suffix** forming adjectives meaning:
1 productive of: *loathsome.*
2 characterized by being: *wholesome.*
■apt to: *tiresome.*
– ORIGIN Old English *-sum*.

-some[2] ▶**suffix** (forming nouns) denoting a group of a specified number: *foursome.*
– ORIGIN Old English *sum* 'some'.

-some[3] ▶**combining form** denoting a portion of a body, especially a particle of a cell: *chromosome.*
– ORIGIN from Greek *sōma* 'body'.

somebody ▶**pronoun 1** some person; someone.
2 a person of importance or authority: *I'd like to be somebody* | [as noun] *nobodies who want to become somebodies.*

some day (also **someday**) ▶**adverb** at some time in the future: *some day I'll live in the countryside.*

somehow ▶**adverb** in some way; by some means: *somehow I managed to get the job done.*
■for a reason that is not known or specified: *he looked different somehow.*

someone ▶**pronoun 1** an unknown or unspecified person; some person: *there's someone at the door | someone from the audience shouted out.*
2 a person of importance or authority: *a small-time lawyer keen to be someone.*

someplace ▶**adverb** & **pronoun** informal, chiefly N. Amer. another term for **SOMEWHERE**.

somersault /ˈsʌməsɒlt, -sɔːlt/ ▶**noun** an acrobatic movement in which a person turns head over heels in the air or on the ground and lands or finishes on their feet.
■figurative a dramatic upset or reversal of policy or opinion: *Paula's stomach* ***turned a somersault.***
▶**verb** [no obj.] perform such an acrobatic feat, or make a similar movement accidentally: *his car somersaulted into a ditch.*
– ORIGIN mid 16th cent. (as a noun): from Old French *sombresault*, from Provençal *sobresaut*, from *sobre* 'above' + *saut* 'leap'.

Somerset /ˈsʌməsɛt/ a county of SW England, on the Bristol Channel; county town, Taunton.

somesthetic ▶**adjective** US spelling of **SOMAESTHETIC**.

something ▶**pronoun 1** a thing that is unspecified or unknown: *we stopped for something to eat | I knew something terrible had happened | something about her frightened me.*
2 used in various expressions indicating that a description or amount being stated is not exact: *a wry look,* ***something between*** *amusement and regret | grassland totalling* ***something over*** *three hundred acres | there were* ***something like*** *fifty applications.*
▶**adverb** [as submodifier] **1** informal used for emphasis with a following adjective functioning as an adverb: *my back hurts something terrible | he used to take the mickey out of me something awful.*
2 archaic or dialect to some extent; somewhat: *the people were something scared.*
– PHRASES **or something** informal added as a reference to an unspecified alternative similar to the thing mentioned: *you look like you just climbed a mountain or something.* **quite** (or **really**) **something** informal something considered impressive or notable. **something else** informal an exceptional person or thing: *the reaction from the crowd was something else.* **something of** to some degree: *Richard was something of an expert at the game.* **something or other** see **OTHER**. **there is something in —— ——** is worth considering; there is some truth in ——: *people think I'm stupid because I think there's something in this alien business.* **thirty-something** (**forty-something**, etc.) informal an unspecified age between thirty and forty (forty and fifty, etc.).
– ORIGIN Old English *sum thing* (see **SOME**, **THING**).

sometime ▶**adverb** at some unspecified or unknown time: *you must come and have supper sometime | sometime after six everybody left.*
■archaic at one time; formerly: *the Emperor Constantine used this speech sometime unto his bishops.*
▶**adjective 1** former: *the sometime editor of the paper.*
2 N. Amer. occasional: *a sometime contributor.*

sometimes ▶**adverb** occasionally, rather than all of the time: *sometimes I want to do things on my own.*

someway ▶**adverb** (often **someways**) informal, chiefly N. Amer. in some way or manner; by some means: *we've got to make money someway.*

somewhat ▶**adverb** to a moderate extent or by a moderate amount; rather: *matters have improved somewhat since then* | [as submodifier] *a somewhat thicker book.*
– PHRASES **somewhat of** something of: *it was* ***somewhat of a*** *disappointment.*

somewhen ▶**adverb** informal at some time: *somewhen between 1918 and 1930.*

somewhere ▶**adverb** in or to some place: *I've seen you somewhere before | can we go somewhere warm?*
■used to indicate an approximate amount: *it cost* ***somewhere around*** *two thousand dollars.*
▶**pronoun** some unspecified place: *in search of somewhere to live.*
– PHRASES **get somewhere** informal make progress; achieve success.

somite /ˈsəʊmʌɪt/ ▶**noun** Zoology each of a number of body segments containing the same internal structures, clearly visible in invertebrates such as earthworms but also present in the embryonic stages of vertebrates. Also called **METAMERE**.
– ORIGIN mid 19th cent.: from Greek *sōma* 'body' + **-ITE**[1].

Somme /sɒm/ a river of northern France. Rising east of Saint-Quentin, it flows through Amiens to the English Channel north-east of Dieppe. The upper valley of the Somme was the scene of heavy fighting in the First World War.

Somme, Battle of the a major battle of the First World War between the British and the Germans, on the Western Front in northern France July–November 1916. More than a million men on both sides were killed or wounded.

sommelier /ˈsɒm(ə)ljeɪ, səˈmɛljeɪ/ ▶**noun** a wine waiter.
– ORIGIN early 19th cent.: French, literally 'butler'.

sommer /ˈsɒmə/ ▶**adverb** S. African informal just; simply: *I used to just sommer sit there.*
– ORIGIN Afrikaans.

somnambulism /sɒmˈnambjʊlɪz(ə)m/ ▶**noun** [mass noun] sleepwalking.
– DERIVATIVES **somnambulant** adjective, **somnambulantly** adverb, **somnambulist** noun, **somnambulistic** adjective, **somnambulistically** adverb.
– ORIGIN late 18th cent.: from French *somnambulisme*, from Latin *somnus* 'sleep' + *ambulare* 'to walk'.

somniferous /sɒmˈnɪf(ə)rəs/ ▶**adjective** tending to induce sleep; soporific.
– ORIGIN early 17th cent.: from Latin *somnifer* (from *somnium* 'dream') + **-OUS**.

somnolent /ˈsɒmnəl(ə)nt/ ▶**adjective** sleepy; drowsy.
■causing or suggestive of drowsiness: *a somnolent summer day.* ■ Medicine abnormally drowsy.
– DERIVATIVES **somnolence** noun, **somnolency** noun, **somnolently** adverb.
– ORIGIN late Middle English (in the sense 'causing sleepiness'): from Old French *sompnolent* or Latin *somnolentus*, from *somnus* 'sleep'.

Somoza /səˈməʊzə/ the name of a family of Nicaraguan statesmen:
■**Anastasio** (1896–1956), President 1937–47 and 1951–6; full name *Anastasio Somoza García*. He took presidential office following a military coup in 1936. Somoza ruled Nicaragua as a virtual dictator and was assassinated.
■**Luis** (1922–67), President 1957–63, son of Anastasio; full name *Luis Somoza Debayle*.
■**Anastasio** (1925–80), President 1967–79, younger brother of Luis; full name *Anastasio Somoza Debayle*. His dictatorial regime was overthrown by the Sandinistas and he was assassinated while in exile in Paraguay.

son ▶**noun** a boy or man in relation to either or both of his parents.
■a male offspring of an animal. ■a male descendant: *the sons of Adam.* ■ (**the Son**) (in Christian belief) the second person of the Trinity; Christ. ■a man considered in relation to his native country or area: *one of Norfolk's most famous sons.* ■ a man regarded as the product of a particular person, influence, or environment: *sons of the church.* ■ (also **my son**) used by an elder person as a form of address for a boy or young man: *'You're on private land, son'.*
– PHRASES **son of a bitch** (pl. **sons of bitches**) used as a general term of contempt or abuse. **son of a gun** (pl. **sons of guns**) informal a jocular or affectionate way of addressing or referring to someone. [ORIGIN: with reference to the guns carried aboard ships: the epithet is said to have been applied originally to babies born at sea to women allowed to accompany their husbands.]
– DERIVATIVES **sonship** noun.
– ORIGIN Old English *sunu*, of Germanic origin; related to Dutch *zoon* and German *Sohn*, from an Indo-European root shared by Greek *huios*.

sonar /ˈsəʊnɑː/ ▶**noun** [mass noun] a system for the detection of objects under water by emitting sound pulses and detecting or measuring their return after being reflected.
■[count noun] an apparatus used in this system. ■ the method of echolocation used in air or water by animals such as whales and bats.
– ORIGIN 1940s: from *so(und) na(vigation and) r(anging)*, on the pattern of *radar*.

sonata /səˈnɑːtə/ ▶**noun** a classical composition for an instrumental soloist, often with a piano accompaniment. It is typically in several movements with one (especially the first) or more in sonata form.
– ORIGIN late 17th cent.: Italian, literally 'sounded' (originally as distinct from 'sung'), feminine past participle of *sonare*.

sonata form ▶**noun** [mass noun] a type of composition in three sections (exposition, development, and recapitulation) in which two themes or subjects are explored according to set key relationships. It forms the basis for much classical music, including the sonata, symphony, and concerto.

sonatina /ˌsɒnəˈtiːnə/ ▶**noun** a simple or short sonata.
– ORIGIN mid 18th cent.: Italian, diminutive of **SONATA**.

sonde /sɒnd/ ▶**noun** an instrument probe that automatically transmits information about its surroundings underground, under water, in the atmosphere, etc.
– ORIGIN early 20th cent.: from French, literally 'sounding (line)'.

Sondheim /ˈsɒndhʌɪm/, Stephen (Joshua) (b.1930), American composer and lyricist. He became famous with his lyrics for Leonard Bernstein's *West Side Story* (1957). He has since written a number of musicals, including *A Little Night Music* (1973) and *Sweeney Todd* (1979).

sone /səʊn/ ▶**noun** a unit of subjective loudness, equal to 40 phons.
– ORIGIN 1930s: from Latin *sonus* 'a sound'.

son et lumière /ˌsɒn eɪ ˈluːmjɛː, French sɔ̃ e lymjɛʀ/ ▶**noun** an entertainment held by night at a historic monument or building, telling its history by the use of lighting effects and recorded sound.
– ORIGIN French, literally 'sound and light'.

Song /sɒŋ/ variant spelling of **SUNG**.

song ▶**noun** a short poem or other set of words set to music or meant to be sung: *a pop song.*
■[mass noun] singing or vocal music: *the pilgrims* ***broke into song.*** ■a musical composition suggestive of a

song. ■ [mass noun] the musical phrases uttered by some birds, whales, and insects, typically forming a recognizable and repeated sequence and used chiefly for territorial defence or for attracting mates. ■ a poem, especially one in rhymed stanzas: *The Song of Hiawatha.* ■ [mass noun] archaic poetry.
– PHRASES **for a song** informal very cheaply: *the place was going for a song.* **on song** Brit. informal performing well: *will Swindon be on song for the new season?* **a song and dance** informal a fuss or commotion: *she would be sure to make a song and dance about her aching feet.* ■ N. Amer. a long explanation that is pointless or deliberately evasive.
– ORIGIN Old English *sang,* of Germanic origin; related to Dutch *zang* and German *Sang,* also to **SING**.

songbird ▶ noun **1** a bird with a musical song.
2 Ornithology a perching bird of an advanced group distinguished by having the muscles of the syrinx attached to the bronchial semi-rings; an oscine passerine.
● Suborder Oscines, order Passeriformes; in Europe 'songbird' is effectively synonymous with 'passerine' or 'perching bird'.

songbook ▶ noun a book containing a collection of songs with music.

song cycle ▶ noun a set of related songs, often on a romantic theme, intended to form a single musical entity.

song flight ▶ noun [mass noun] territorial display flight that involves song, as in the skylark.

song form ▶ noun a form used in the composition of a song, in particular a simple melody and accompaniment or a three-part work in which the third part is a repetition of the first.

Songhai /ˈsɒŋˈɡʌɪ/ ▶ noun (pl. same or **Songhais**) **1** a member of a people of West Africa living mainly in Niger and Mali.
2 [mass noun] the Nilo-Saharan language of this people, with about 2 million speakers.
▶ adjective of or relating to this people or their language.
– ORIGIN the name in Songhai.

Song Hong /sɒŋ ˈhɒŋ/ Vietnamese name for **RED RIVER** (in sense 1).

Song of Songs a book of the Bible containing an anthology of Hebrew love poems traditionally ascribed to Solomon but in fact dating from a much later period. Jewish and Christian writers have interpreted the book allegorically as representing God's relationship with his people, or with the soul. Also called **Song of Solomon, Canticles.**

Song of the Three Holy Children a book of the Apocrypha, telling of three Hebrew exiles thrown into a furnace by Nebuchadnezzar.

songololo /ˌsɒŋɡɒˈlɒlɒ/ ▶ noun (pl. **-os**) S. African a millipede which curls up into a pinwheel-shaped coil when disturbed.
● *Julus terrestris,* class Diplopoda.
– ORIGIN early 20th cent.: from Xhosa *i-songololo,* Zulu *i-shongololo* (from *ukus(h)onga* 'roll up').

songsmith ▶ noun informal a person who writes popular songs.

song sparrow ▶ noun a sparrow-like North American bird related to the buntings, noted for its constant and characteristic song.
● *Melospiza melodia,* family Emberizidae (subfamily Emberizinae).

songster ▶ noun a person who sings, especially fluently and skilfully.
■ a person who writes songs or verse. ■ a songbird.
– ORIGIN Old English *sangestre* (see **SONG, -STER**).

songstress ▶ noun a female songster.

song thrush ▶ noun a common European and central Asian thrush with a buff spotted breast, having a loud song in which each phrase is repeated two or three times.
● *Turdus philomelos,* family Turdidae.

songwriter ▶ noun a person who writes popular songs or the music for them.
– DERIVATIVES **songwriting** noun.

sonic ▶ adjective relating to or using sound waves.
■ denoting or having a speed equal to that of sound.
– DERIVATIVES **sonically** adverb.
– ORIGIN 1920s: from Latin *sonus* 'sound' + **-IC**.

sonicate /ˈsɒnɪkeɪt/ Biochemistry ▶ verb [with obj.] (usu. **be sonicated**) subject (a biological sample) to

ultrasonic vibration so as to fragment the cells, macromolecules, and membranes.
▶ noun a biological sample which has been subjected to such treatment.
– ORIGIN 1950s: from **SONIC** + **-ATE**[2].

sonic barrier ▶ noun another term for **SOUND BARRIER**.

sonic boom ▶ noun a loud explosive noise caused by the shock wave from an aircraft or other object travelling faster than the speed of sound.

sonics ▶ plural noun musical sounds artificially produced or reproduced.

Soninke /sɒˈniːŋkeɪ/ ▶ noun (pl. same or **Soninkes**)
1 a member of a West African people living in Mali and Senegal.
2 [mass noun] the language of this people, which belongs to the Mande group and has about 1 million speakers.
▶ adjective of or relating to this people or their language.
– ORIGIN the name in Soninke.

son-in-law ▶ noun (pl. **sons-in-law**) the husband of one's daughter.

sonnet ▶ noun a poem of fourteen lines using any of a number of formal rhyme schemes, in English typically having ten syllables per line.
▶ verb (**sonneted, sonneting**) [no obj.] archaic compose sonnets.
■ [with obj.] celebrate in a sonnet.
– ORIGIN mid 16th cent.: from French, or from Italian *sonetto,* diminutive of *suono* 'a sound'.

sonneteer /ˌsɒnɪˈtɪə/ ▶ noun a writer of sonnets.

sonny ▶ noun informal used by an older person as a familiar form of address to a young boy.
■ (also **Sonny Jim**) used as a humorous or patronizing way of addressing a man: *look, sonny, that's all I can tell you.*

sono- /ˈsəʊnəʊ, ˈsɒnəʊ/ ▶ combining form of or relating to sound: *sonometer.*
– ORIGIN from Latin *sonus* 'sound'.

sonobuoy ▶ noun a buoy equipped to detect underwater sounds and transmit them by radio.

sonogram ▶ noun **1** a graph representing a sound, showing the distribution of energy at different frequencies.
2 a visual image produced from an ultrasound examination.
– DERIVATIVES **sonograph** noun.

sonography /səˈnɒɡrəfi/ ▶ noun [mass noun] **1** the analysis of sound using an instrument which produces a graphical representation of its component frequencies.
2 another term for **ULTRASONOGRAPHY**.
– DERIVATIVES **sonograph** noun, **sonographic** adjective.

sonoluminescence ▶ noun [mass noun] Physics luminescence excited in a substance by the passage of sound waves through it.
– DERIVATIVES **sonoluminescent** adjective.

sonometer /səˈnɒmɪtə/ ▶ noun another term for **MONOCHORD**.

Sonora /səˈnɔːrə/ a state of NW Mexico, on the Gulf of California; capital, Hermosillo.

Sonora Desert an arid region of North America, comprising SE California and SW Arizona in the US and, in Mexico, much of Baja California and the western part of Sonora.

Sonoran /səˈnɔːrən/ ▶ adjective relating to, denoting, or characteristic of a biogeographical region including desert areas of the south-western US and central Mexico.
– ORIGIN late 19th cent.: from **SONORA** + **-AN**.

sonorant /ˈsɒn(ə)r(ə)nt, səˈnɔːr(ə)nt/ ▶ noun Phonetics a sound produced with the vocal cords so positioned that spontaneous voicing is possible; a vowel, a glide, or a liquid or nasal consonant.
– ORIGIN 1930s: from **SONOROUS** + **-ANT**.

sonority /səˈnɒrɪti/ ▶ noun [mass noun] the quality or fact of being sonorous.
■ Phonetics the relative loudness of a speech sound.

sonorous /ˈsɒn(ə)rəs, səˈnɔːrəs/ ▶ adjective (of a person's voice or other sound) imposingly deep and full.
■ capable of producing a deep or ringing sound: *the alloy is sonorous and useful in making bells.* ■ (of a speech or style) using imposing language: *he relished the sonorous words of condemnation.*

– DERIVATIVES **sonorously** adverb, **sonorousness** noun.
– ORIGIN early 17th cent.: from Latin *sonorus* (from *sonor* 'sound') + **-OUS**.

sonsy /ˈsɒnsi/ (also **sonsie**) ▶ adjective (**sonsier, sonsiest**) Scottish poetic/literary having an attractive and healthy appearance.
– ORIGIN mid 16th cent. (also in the sense 'lucky'): from Irish and Scottish Gaelic *sonas* 'good fortune' (from *sona* 'fortunate') + **-Y**[1].

Sontag /ˈsɒntag/, Susan (b.1933), American writer and critic. She established her reputation as a radical intellectual with *Against Interpretation* (essays, 1966). Other notable works: *On Photography* (1976); *Illness as Metaphor* (1979).

Soochow /suːˈtʃaʊ/ variant of **SUZHOU**.

sook /suːk, sʊk/ ▶ noun informal, chiefly Austral./NZ & Canadian
1 a person lacking spirit or self-confidence; a coward.
2 a hand-reared calf.
– ORIGIN mid 19th cent.: dialect variant of the noun **SUCK**.

sool /suːl/ ▶ verb [with obj.] chiefly Austral./NZ (of a dog) attack or worry (an animal).
■ urge or goad (someone) into doing something.
– DERIVATIVES **sooler** noun.
– ORIGIN late 19th cent.: variant of dialect *sowl* 'seize by the ears', of unknown origin.

soon ▶ adverb **1** in or after a short time: *everyone will soon know the truth | he'll be home soon | they arrived soon after 7.30.*
■ early: *how soon can you get here? | it's a pity you have to leave so soon | I wish you'd told me sooner | it was too soon to know.*
2 used to indicate one's preference in a particular matter: *I'd just as soon Tim did it | I would sooner resign than transfer to Toronto.*
– PHRASES **no sooner —— than** used to convey that the second event mentioned happens immediately after the first: *she had no sooner spoken than the telephone rang.* **sooner or later** at some future time; eventually: *you'll have to tell him sooner or later.* **sooner rather than later** before much time has gone by: *I would be grateful if you would come to your senses sooner rather than later.*
– DERIVATIVES **soonish** adverb.
– ORIGIN Old English *sōna* 'immediately', of West Germanic origin.

USAGE In standard English, the phrase **no sooner** is followed by **than**, as in *we had no sooner arrived than we had to leave.* This is because **sooner** is a comparative, and comparatives are followed by **than** (*earlier than; better than,* and so on). It is incorrect to follow **no sooner** with **when** rather than **than**, as in *we had no sooner arrived when we had to leave.*

Sooner State informal name for **OKLAHOMA**.
– ORIGIN *Sooner* in the sense 'one who acts prematurely', i.e. a person who tried to get into the frontier territory of Oklahoma before the US government opened it to settlers in 1889.

soot ▶ noun [mass noun] a deep black powdery or flaky substance consisting largely of amorphous carbon, produced by the incomplete burning of organic matter.
▶ verb [with obj.] cover or clog (something) with soot.
– PHRASES **(as) black as soot** intensely black.
– ORIGIN Old English *sōt,* of Germanic origin; related to German dialect *Sott,* from an Indo-European root shared by the verb **SIT**.

sooth /suːθ/ ▶ noun [mass noun] archaic truth.
– PHRASES **in sooth** in truth; really.
– ORIGIN Old English *sōth* (originally as an adjective in the sense 'genuine, true'), of Germanic origin.

soothe ▶ verb [with obj.] gently calm (a person or their feelings): *a shot of brandy might soothe his nerves |* [as adj.] **soothing** *she put on some soothing music.*
■ reduce pain or discomfort in (a part of the body): *to soothe the skin try chamomile or thyme.* ■ relieve or ease (pain): *it contains a mild anaesthetic to soothe the pain.*
– DERIVATIVES **soother** noun, **soothingly** adverb.
– ORIGIN Old English *sōthian* 'verify, show to be true', from *sōth* 'true' (see **SOOTH**). In the 16th cent. the verb passed through the senses 'corroborate (a statement)', 'humour (a person)' by expressing assent and 'flatter by one's assent', whence 'mollify, appease' (late 17th cent.).

soothsayer ▶ noun a person supposed to be able to foresee the future.
– DERIVATIVES **soothsaying** noun.

– ORIGIN Middle English (in the sense 'person who speaks the truth'): see **SOOTH**.

sooty ▶ **adjective** (**sootier**, **sootiest**) covered with or coloured like soot: *his olive skin and sooty eyes.*
■ used in names of birds and other animals that are mainly blackish or brownish black, e.g. **sooty tern**.
– DERIVATIVES **sootily** adverb, **sootiness** noun.

sooty mould ▶ **noun** [mass noun] a black velvety mould that grows on the surfaces of leaves and stems affected by honeydew.
● Family Capnodiaceae, subdivision Ascomycotina.

sop ▶ **noun 1** a thing given or done as a concession of no great value to appease someone whose main concerns or demands are not being met: *my agent telephones as a sop but never finds me work.*
2 a piece of bread dipped in gravy, soup, or sauce.
▶ **verb** (**sopped**, **sopping**) [with obj.] (**sop something up**) soak up liquid using an absorbent substance: *he used some bread to sop up the sauce.*
■ archaic wet thoroughly; soak.
– ORIGIN Old English *soppian* 'dip (bread) in liquid', *sopp* (noun), probably from the base of Old English *sūpan* 'sup'. Sense 1 (mid 17th cent.) alludes to the sop used by Aeneas on his visit to Hades to appease Cerberus.

sopaipilla /ˌsɒpʌɪˈpiːljə, -ˈpiːjə/ ▶ **noun** (especially in New Mexico) a deep-fried pastry, typically square, eaten with honey or sugar or as a bread.
– ORIGIN American Spanish.

sophism /ˈsɒfɪz(ə)m/ ▶ **noun** a fallacious argument, especially one used deliberately to deceive.
– ORIGIN late Middle English: from Old French *sophime*, via Latin from Greek *sophisma* 'clever device', from *sophizesthai* 'become wise' (see **SOPHIST**).

sophist /ˈsɒfɪst/ ▶ **noun** a paid teacher of philosophy and rhetoric in Greece in the Classical and Hellenistic periods, associated in popular thought with moral scepticism and specious reasoning.
■ a person who reasons with clever but fallacious arguments.
– DERIVATIVES **sophistic** /-ˈfɪstɪk/ adjective, **sophistical** /səˈfɪstɪk(ə)l/ adjective, **sophistically** adverb.
– ORIGIN mid 16th cent.: via Latin from Greek *sophistēs*, from *sophizesthai* 'devise, become wise', from *sophos* 'wise'.

sophisticate ▶ **verb** [with obj.] cause (a person or their thoughts, attitudes, and expectations) to become less simple or straightforward through education or experience: *readers who have been sophisticated by modern literary practice.*
■ develop (something such as a piece of equipment or a technique) into a more complex form: *a function that many other software applications have sophisticated.* ■ [no obj.] archaic talk or reason in an impressively complex and educated manner. ■ archaic mislead or corrupt (a person, an argument, the mind, etc.) by sophistry: *books of casuistry, which sophisticate the understanding and defile the heart.*
▶ **adjective** archaic sophisticated.
▶ **noun** a person with much worldly experience and knowledge of fashion and culture: *he is still the butt of jokes made by New York sophisticates.*
– DERIVATIVES **sophistication** noun.
– ORIGIN late Middle English (as an adjective in the sense 'adulterated', and as a verb in the sense 'mix with a foreign substance'): from medieval Latin *sophisticatus* 'tampered with', past participle of the verb *sophisticare*, from *sophisticus* 'sophistic'. The shift of sense probably occurred first in the adjective *unsophisticated*, from 'uncorrupted' via 'innocent' to 'inexperienced, uncultured'. The noun dates from the early 20th cent.

sophisticated ▶ **adjective** (of a machine, system, or technique) developed to a high degree of complexity: *highly sophisticated computer systems.*
■ (of a person or their thoughts, reactions, and understanding) aware of and able to interpret complex issues; subtle: *discussion and reflection are necessary for a sophisticated response to a text.* ■ having, revealing, or proceeding from a great deal of worldly experience and knowledge of fashion and culture: *a chic, sophisticated woman | a young man with sophisticated tastes.* ■ appealing to people with such knowledge of experience: *a sophisticated restaurant.*
– DERIVATIVES **sophisticatedly** adverb.

sophistry /ˈsɒfɪstri/ ▶ **noun** (pl. **-ies**) [mass noun] the use of fallacious arguments, especially with the intention of deceiving.
■ [count noun] a fallacious argument.

Sophocles /ˈsɒfəkliːz/ (c.496–406 BC), Greek dramatist. His seven surviving plays are notable for their complexity of plot and depth of characterization, and for their examination of the relationship between mortals and the divine order. Notable plays: *Antigone* and *Oedipus Rex* (also called *Oedipus Tyrannus*).

sophomore /ˈsɒfəmɔː/ ▶ **noun** N. Amer. a second-year university or high-school student.
– DERIVATIVES **sophomoric** adjective.
– ORIGIN mid 17th cent.: perhaps from earlier *sophumer*, from *sophum*, *sophom* (obsolete variants of **SOPHISM**) + **-ER**[1].

sophomoric /ˌsɒfəˈmɒrɪk/ ▶ **adjective** of, relating to, or characteristic of a sophomore: *my sophomoric years.*
■ pretentious or juvenile: *sophomoric double entendres.*

Sophy /ˈsəʊfi/ ▶ **noun** (pl. **-ies**) historical a former title for the ruler of Persia associated especially with the Safavid dynasty.
– ORIGIN from Arabic *Ṣafī-al-dīn* 'pure of religion'.

soporific /ˌsɒpəˈrɪfɪk/ ▶ **adjective** tending to induce drowsiness or sleep: *the motion of the train had a somewhat soporific effect.*
■ sleepy or drowsy: *some medicine made her soporific.*
■ tediously boring or monotonous: *a libel trial is in large parts intensely soporific.*
▶ **noun** drug or other agent of this kind.
– DERIVATIVES **soporifically** adverb.
– ORIGIN mid 17th cent.: from Latin *sopor* 'sleep' + **-IFIC**.

sopping ▶ **adjective** saturated with liquid; wet through: *get those sopping clothes off* | [as submodifier] *the handkerchief was sopping wet.*
– ORIGIN mid 19th cent.: present participle of **SOP**.

soppy ▶ **adjective** (**soppier**, **soppiest**) Brit. informal self-indulgently sentimental: *I look at babies with a soppy smile on my face.*
■ lacking spirit and common sense; feeble: *my little sisters were too soppy for our adventurous games.*
– DERIVATIVES **soppily** adverb, **soppiness** noun.
– ORIGIN early 19th cent. (in the sense 'soaked with water'): from **SOP** + **-Y**[1].

sopranino /ˌsɒprəˈniːnəʊ/ ▶ **noun** Music (pl. **-os**) an instrument, especially a recorder or saxophone, higher than soprano.
– ORIGIN early 20th cent.: Italian, diminutive of **SOPRANO**.

soprano /səˈprɑːnəʊ/ ▶ **noun** (pl. **-os**) the highest singing voice.
■ a female or boy singer with such a voice. ■ a part written for such a voice. ■ [usu. as modifier] an instrument of a high or the highest pitch in its family: *a soprano saxophone.*
– ORIGIN mid 18th cent.: Italian, from *sopra* 'above', from Latin *supra*.

soprano clef ▶ **noun** Music an obsolete clef placing middle C on the lowest line of the stave.

soprano recorder ▶ **noun** North American term for **DESCANT RECORDER**.

Sopwith /ˈsɒpwɪθ/, Sir Thomas (Octave Murdoch) (1888–1989), English aircraft designer. During the First World War he designed the fighter biplane the Sopwith Camel, while in the Second World War, as chairman of the Hawker Siddeley company, he was responsible for the production of aircraft such as the Hurricane fighter.

sora /ˈsɔːrə, ˈsəʊrə/ (also **sora crake** or **rail**) ▶ **noun** a common small brown and grey American crake, frequenting marshes.
● *Porzana carolina*, family Rallidae.
– ORIGIN early 18th cent.: probably from an American Indian language.

Sorb /sɔːb/ ▶ **noun** a member of a Slavic people living in parts of SE Brandenburg and eastern Saxony. Also called **WEND**.
– ORIGIN from German *Sorbe*.

sorb /sɔːb/ ▶ **noun** the fruit of the true service tree.
– ORIGIN early 16th cent.: from French *sorbe* or Latin *sorbus* 'service tree', *sorbum* 'serviceberry'.

sorbent /ˈsɔːb(ə)nt/ ▶ **noun** Chemistry a substance which has the property of collecting molecules of another substance by sorption.
– ORIGIN early 20th cent.: from *sorb* 'take up by sorption', on the pattern of *absorbent*.

sorbet /ˈsɔːbeɪ, -bɪt/ ▶ **noun** a water ice.
■ archaic an Arabian sherbet.
– ORIGIN late 16th cent.: from French, from Italian *sorbetto*, from Turkish *şerbet*, based on Arabic *šariba* 'to drink'; compare with **SHERBET**.

Sorbian /ˈsɔːbɪən/ ▶ **adjective** of or relating to the Sorbs or their language.
▶ **noun** the traditional language of the Sorbs, a Slavic language related to Polish and Czech. It has been revived from near extinction and has around 70,000 speakers. Also called **WENDISH** or **LUSATIAN**.

sorbitan /ˈsɔːbɪtan/ ▶ **noun** [usu. as modifier] Chemistry any of a group of compounds which are cyclic ethers derived from sorbitol or its derivatives.
– ORIGIN 1930s: blend of **SORBITOL** and **ANHYDRIDE**.

sorbitol /ˈsɔːbɪtɒl/ ▶ **noun** [mass noun] Chemistry a sweet-tasting crystalline compound found in some fruit.
● A hexahydric alcohol; chem. formula: $CH_2OH(CHOH)_4CH_2OH$.
– ORIGIN late 19th cent.: from **SORB** + **-ITE**[1] + **-OL**.

Sorbonne /sɔːˈbɒn, French sɔʀbɔn/ the seat of the faculties of science and literature of the University of Paris.
– ORIGIN originally a theological college founded by Robert de Sorbon, chaplain to Louis IX, c.1257.

sorbus /ˈsɔːbəs/ ▶ **noun** a tree or shrub of a genus which includes the rowan, service tree, and whitebeam.
● Genus *Sorbus*, family Rosaceae: many species.
– ORIGIN modern Latin, from Latin *sorbus* 'service tree'.

sorcerer ▶ **noun** a person who claims or is believed to have magic powers; a wizard.
– ORIGIN late Middle English: from *sorser* (from Old French *sorcier*, based on Latin *sors*, *sort-* 'lot') + **-ER**[1].

sorceress ▶ **noun** a female sorcerer; a witch.

sorcery ▶ **noun** [mass noun] the use of magic, especially black magic.
– DERIVATIVES **sorcerous** adjective.

sordid ▶ **adjective** involving ignoble actions and motives; arousing moral distaste and contempt: *the story paints a sordid picture of bribes and scams.*
■ dirty or squalid: *the overcrowded housing conditions were sordid and degrading.*
– DERIVATIVES **sordidly** adverb, **sordidness** noun.
– ORIGIN late Middle English (as a medical term in the sense 'purulent'): from French *sordide* or Latin *sordidus*, from *sordere* 'be dirty'. The current senses date from the early 17th cent.

sordino /sɔːˈdiːnəʊ/ ▶ **noun** (pl. **sordini** /-ni/) Music a mute for a musical instrument.
■ (**sordini**) (on a piano) the dampers.
– ORIGIN late 16th cent.: from Italian, from *sordo* 'mute', from Latin *surdus*.

sordor /ˈsɔːdə/ ▶ **noun** [mass noun] chiefly poetic/literary physical or moral sordidness.
– ORIGIN early 19th cent.: from **SORDID**, on the pattern of the pair *squalid*, *squalor*.

sore ▶ **adjective** (of a part of one's body) painful or aching: *my feet were sore and my head ached.*
■ [predic.] suffering pain from a part of one's body: *he was sore from the long ride.* ■ [predic.] informal, chiefly US upset and angry: *I didn't even know they were sore at us.*
■ [attrib.] severe; urgent: *we're in sore need of him.*
▶ **noun** a raw or painful place on the body: *all of us had sores and infections on our hands.*
■ a cause or source of distress or annoyance: *there's no point raking over the past and opening old sores.*
▶ **adverb** archaic extremely; severely: *they were sore afraid.*
– PHRASES **sore point** a subject or issue about which someone feels distressed or annoyed and which it is therefore advisable to avoid in conversation with them. **stand** (or **stick**) **out like a sore thumb** be very obviously different from the surrounding people or things.
– DERIVATIVES **soreness** noun.
– ORIGIN Old English *sār* (noun and adjective), *sāre* (adverb), of Germanic origin; related to Dutch *zeer* 'sore' and German *sehr* 'very'. The original sense was 'causing intense pain, grievous', whence the adverbial use.

sorehead ▶ **noun** N. Amer. informal a person who is in a bad temper or easily irritated.

sorel /ˈsɒr(ə)l/ ▶ **noun** Brit. a male fallow deer in its third year.
– ORIGIN late 15th cent.: variant of **SORREL**[2].

sorely ▶ **adverb** to a very high degree or level of intensity (especially of an unwelcome or unpleasant state or emotion): *she would sorely miss his company | help was sorely needed.*
– ORIGIN Old English *sārlīce* (see **SORE**, **-LY**[2]).

sorghum /ˈsɔːgəm/ ▶ **noun** [mass noun] a cereal which

is native to warm regions of the Old World and is a major source of grain and stockfeed.
• Genus *Sorghum*, family Gramineae: many species, in particular *S. bicolor* and its cultivars.
– ORIGIN late 16th cent.: modern Latin, from Italian *sorgo*, perhaps based on a variant of Latin *syricum* 'Syrian'.

sori plural form of **SORUS**.

Soroptimist /səˈrɒptɪmɪst/ ▶ **noun** a member of an international association of clubs for professional and business women founded in California in 1921.
– ORIGIN 1920s: from Latin *soror* 'sister' + *optimist* (see **OPTIMISM**).

sororal /səˈrɔːr(ə)l/ ▶ **adjective** formal of or like a sister or sisters.
– ORIGIN mid 17th cent.: from Latin *soror* 'sister' + **-AL**.

sorority /səˈrɒrɪti/ ▶ **noun** (pl. **-ies**) N. Amer. a society for female students in a university or college.
– ORIGIN mid 16th cent.: from medieval Latin *sororitas*, or from Latin *soror* 'sister' (on the pattern of *fraternity*).

sorosis /səˈrəʊsɪs/ ▶ **noun** (pl. **soroses** /-siːz/) Botany a fleshy multiple fruit, e.g. a pineapple or mulberry, derived from the ovaries of several flowers.
– ORIGIN mid 19th cent.: modern Latin, from Greek *sōros* 'heap'.

sorption /ˈsɔːpʃ(ə)n/ ▶ **noun** [mass noun] Chemistry absorption and adsorption considered as a single process.
– ORIGIN early 20th cent.: back-formation from **ABSORPTION** and **ADSORPTION**.

sorrel[1] /ˈsɒr(ə)l/ ▶ **noun 1** a European plant of the dock family, with arrow-shaped leaves that are used in salads and cookery for their acidic flavour. See also **WOOD SORREL**.
• Genus *Rumex*, family Polygonaceae: several species, including the **English sorrel** (*R. acetosa*) and the more slender-leaved **French sorrel** (*R. scutatus*).
2 (also **red sorrel**) a tall annual Caribbean hibiscus with red flowers and stems.
• *Hibiscus sabdariffa*, family Malvaceae.
■ [mass noun] a sweet red drink made from the sepals of these flowers.
– ORIGIN late Middle English: from Old French *sorele*, of Germanic origin; related to **SOUR**.

sorrel[2] /ˈsɒr(ə)l/ ▶ **noun** a horse with a light reddish-brown coat.
■ [mass noun] [usu. as modifier] a light reddish-brown colour: *a sorrel mare with four white socks.*
– ORIGIN Middle English: from Old French *sorel*, from *sor* 'yellowish', from a Germanic adjective meaning 'dry'.

sorrel tree ▶ **noun** another term for **SOURWOOD**.

Sorrento /səˈrɛntəʊ/ a town on the west coast of central Italy, situated on a peninsula separating the Bay of Naples, which it faces, from the Gulf of Salerno; pop. 17,500 (1990).

sorrow ▶ **noun** [mass noun] a feeling of deep distress caused by loss, disappointment, or other misfortune suffered by oneself or others: *a bereaved person needs time to work through their sorrow.*
■ [count noun] an event or circumstance that causes such a feeling: *it was a great sorrow to her when they separated.* ■ the outward expression of grief; lamentation.
▶ **verb** [no obj.] feel or display deep distress: [as adj. **sorrowing**] *the sorrowing widower found it hard to relate to his sons.*
– ORIGIN Old English *sorh, sorg* (noun), *sorgian* (verb), of Germanic origin; related to Dutch *zorg* and German *Sorge*.

sorrowful ▶ **adjective** feeling or showing grief: *she looked at him with sorrowful eyes.*
■ causing grief: *the sorrowful news of his father's death.*
– DERIVATIVES **sorrowfully** adverb, **sorrowfulness** noun.
– ORIGIN Old English *sorhful* (see **SORROW**, **-FUL**).

sorry ▶ **adjective** (**sorrier**, **sorriest**) **1** [predic.] feeling distress, especially through sympathy with someone else's misfortune: *I was sorry to hear about what happened to your family.*
■ (**sorry for**) filled with compassion for: *he couldn't help feeling sorry for her when he heard how she'd been treated.* ■ feeling regret or penitence: *he said he was sorry he had upset me | I'm sorry if I was a bit brusque.* ■ used as an expression of apology: *sorry—I was trying not to make a noise.* ■ used as a polite request that someone should repeat something that one has failed to hear or understand: *I'm sorry—you were saying?*
2 [attrib.] in a poor or pitiful state or condition: *he looks a sorry sight with his broken jaw.*
■ unpleasant and regrettable, especially on account of incompetence or misbehaviour: *we feel so ashamed that we keep quiet about the whole sorry business.*
– PHRASES **sorry for oneself** sad and self-pitying.
– DERIVATIVES **sorrily** adverb, **sorriness** noun.
– ORIGIN Old English *sārig* 'pained, distressed', of West Germanic origin, from the base of the noun **SORE**. The shortening of the root vowel has given the word an apparent connection with the unrelated **SORROW**.

sort ▶ **noun 1** a category of things or people having some common feature; a type: *if only we knew the sort of people she was mixing with | a radical change poses **all sorts of** questions.*
■ [with adj.] informal a person of a specified character or nature: *Frank was a genuinely friendly sort.* ■ archaic a manner or way: *in law also the Judge is **in a sort** superior to his King.*
2 [mass noun] Computing the arrangement of data in a prescribed sequence.
▶ **verb** [with obj.] **1** arrange systematically in groups; separate according to type, class, etc.: *she **sorted out** the clothes, some to be kept, some to be thrown away.*
■ (**sort through**) look at (a group of things) one after another in order to classify them or make a selection: *she sat down and sorted through her mail.*
2 resolve (a problem or difficulty): *the teacher helps the children to **sort out** their problems.*
■ resolve the problems or difficulties of (someone): *I need time to **sort** myself **out**.*
– PHRASES **after a sort** dated after a fashion. **in some sort** to a certain extent: *I am in some sort indebted to you.* **it takes all sorts to make a world** proverb people vary greatly in character, tastes, and abilities (often used as a comment on what the speaker feels to be strange behaviour): *he was wearing make-up—well, it takes all sorts.* **nothing of the sort** used as an emphatic way of denying permission or refuting an earlier statement or assumption: *'I'll pay.' 'You'll do nothing of the sort.'* **of a sort** (or **of sorts**) informal of a somewhat unusual and typically inferior kind: *the training camp actually became a tourist attraction of sorts.* **out of sorts** slightly unwell: *feeling nauseous and generally out of sorts.* ■ in low spirits; irritable: *the trying events of the day had put him out of sorts.* **sort of** informal to some extent; in some way or other (used to convey inexactness or vagueness): *'Do you see what I mean?' 'Sort of,' answered Jean cautiously.* **sort out the men from the boys** show or prove who is the best at a particular activity. **the —— sort** the kind of person likely to do or be involved with the thing specified: *she'd never imagined Steve to be the marrying sort.*
– DERIVATIVES **sortable** adjective, **sorter** noun.
– ORIGIN late Middle English: from Old French *sorte*, from an alteration of Latin *sors, sort-* 'lot, condition'.

USAGE The construction **these sort of**, as in *I don't want to answer **these sort of** questions*, is technically ungrammatical. This is because **these** is plural and needs to agree with a plural noun (in this case **sorts** rather than **sort**). However, the construction is undoubtedly common and has in fact been used for hundreds of years. There are some grammarians who analyse the construction differently, seeing the words 'these sort of' as a single invariable unit. For more details, see **usage** at **KIND**[1].

▶ **sort someone out** informal deal with someone who is causing trouble, typically by restraining, reprimanding, or punishing them: *if he can't pay you, I'll sort him out.*
sort something out 1 separate something from a mixed group: *she started **sorting out** the lettuce **from** the spinach.* **2** arrange; prepare: *they are anxious to sort out travelling arrangements.*

sortal /ˈsɔːt(ə)l/ Linguistics & Philosophy ▶ **adjective** denoting or relating to a term representing a semantic feature that applies to an entity as long as it exists, classifying it as being of a particular kind.
▶ **noun** a term of this kind, for example *human* as opposed to *engineer*.

sorted ▶ **adjective** Brit. informal organized; arranged; fixed up: *'And your social commitments?' 'They're well sorted' | he's working on that old car he's been trying to get sorted.*
■ (of a person) having obtained illegal drugs. ■ (of a person) confident, organized, and emotionally well balanced: *after a while, you realize they're not as sorted as they seem | a pretty sorted kind of bloke.*

sortes /ˈsɔːtiːz, ˈsɔːteɪz/ (also **sortes Biblicae** /ˈbɪblɪkiː/) ▶ **plural noun** [treated as sing.] divination, or the seeking of guidance, by chance selection of a passage in the Bible or another text regarded as authoritative.
– ORIGIN Latin, 'chance selections (of the Bible)'.

sortie ▶ **noun** an attack made by troops coming out from a position of defence.
■ an operational flight by a single military aircraft. ■ a short trip or journey: *I went on a shopping sortie.*
▶ **verb** (**sorties**, **sortied**, **sortieing**) [no obj.] come out from a defensive position to make an attack.
– ORIGIN late 18th cent.: from French, feminine past participle of *sortir* 'go out'.

sortilege /ˈsɔːtɪlɪdʒ/ ▶ **noun** [mass noun] chiefly historical the practice of foretelling the future from a card or other item drawn at random from a collection.
– ORIGIN late Middle English: via Old French from medieval Latin *sortilegium* 'sorcery', from Latin *sortilegus* 'sorcerer', from Latin *sors, sort-* 'lot, chance' + *legere* 'choose'.

sorting office ▶ **noun** an office in which mail is sorted according to its destination.

sortition ▶ **noun** [mass noun] the action of selecting or determining something by the casting or drawing of lots.
– ORIGIN late 16th cent.: from Latin *sortitio(n-)*, from *sortire* 'divide or obtain by lot'.

sort-out ▶ **noun** an act of tidying or organizing things by separating them into categories: *start your kitchen reorganization with a sort-out.*

sorus /ˈsɔːrəs/ ▶ **noun** (pl. **sori** /-rʌɪ/) Botany a cluster of spore-producing receptacles on the underside of a fern frond.
■ a gamete-producing or fruiting body in certain algae and fungi.
– ORIGIN mid 19th cent.: modern Latin, from Greek *sōros* 'heap'.

SOS ▶ **noun** (pl. **SOSs**) an international code signal of extreme distress, used especially by ships at sea.
■ an urgent appeal for help. ■ Brit. a message broadcast to an untraceable person in an emergency.
– ORIGIN early 20th cent.: letters chosen as being easily transmitted and recognized in Morse code; by folk etymology an abbreviation of *save our souls*.

sosatie /səˈsɑːti/ ▶ **noun** (pl. **-ies**) a South African dish of cubes of curried or spiced meat grilled on a skewer.
– ORIGIN Afrikaans; compare with **SATAY**.

Sosnowiec /sɒsˈnɒvjɛts/ an industrial mining town in SW Poland, west of Cracow; pop. 259,350 (1990).

so-so ▶ **adjective** neither very good nor very bad: *a happy ending to a so-so season | 'How are you?' 'So-so.'*

sostenuto /ˌsɒstəˈnuːtəʊ/ Music ▶ **adjective** (of a passage of music) to be played in a sustained or prolonged manner.
▶ **noun** (pl. **-os**) a passage to be played in a sustained and prolonged manner.
■ [mass noun] performance in this manner.
– ORIGIN Italian, 'sustained'.

sot ▶ **noun** a habitual drunkard.
▶ **verb** (**sotted**, **sotting**) [no obj.] archaic drink habitually.
– DERIVATIVES **sottish** adjective.
– ORIGIN late Old English *sott* 'foolish person', from medieval Latin *sottus*, reinforced by Old French *sot* 'foolish'. The current sense of the noun dates from the late 16th cent.

soteriology /sə(ʊ),tɪərɪˈɒlədʒi, sɒ-/ ▶ **noun** [mass noun] Theology the doctrine of salvation.
– DERIVATIVES **soteriological** adjective.
– ORIGIN mid 19th cent.: from Greek *sōtēria* 'salvation' + **-LOGY**.

Sothic /ˈsəʊθɪk, ˈsɒθ-/ ▶ **adjective** of or relating to Sirius (the Dog Star), especially with reference to the ancient Egyptian year fixed by its heliacal rising.
– ORIGIN early 19th cent.: from Greek *Sōthis* (from an Egyptian name of the Dog Star) + **-IC**.

Sotho /ˈsuːtuː/ ▶ **noun** (pl. same or **-os**) **1** a member of a group of peoples living chiefly in Botswana, Lesotho, and northern South Africa.
2 [mass noun] the group of Bantu languages spoken by these peoples, of which the most important are Sepedi (also called **North Sotho**) and Sesotho (also called **South Sotho**). The term **Western Sotho** is sometimes used of the related language Setswana.

S

▶**adjective** of or relating to this people or their languages.
– ORIGIN the stem of **BASOTHO** and **SESOTHO**.

sotol /ˈsəʊtəʊl/ ▶**noun** [mass noun] a North American desert plant of the agave family, with spiny-edged leaves and small white flowers.
• Genus *Dasylirion*, family Agavaceae: several species.
■an alcoholic drink made from the sap of this plant.
– ORIGIN late 19th cent.: via American Spanish from Nahuatl *tzotolli*.

sotto voce /ˌsɒtəʊ ˈvəʊtʃeɪ/ ▶**adverb** & **adjective** (of singing or a spoken remark) in a quiet voice: [as adv.] *'It won't be cheap,' he added sotto voce* | [as adj.] *a sotto voce remark.*
– ORIGIN from Italian *sotto* 'under' + *voce* 'voice'.

sou /suː/ ▶**noun** historical a former French coin of low value.
■[usu. with negative] informal a very small amount of money: *he didn't have a sou.*
– ORIGIN French, originally as *sous* (plural), from Old French *sout* from Latin *solidus* (see **SOLIDUS**).

soubise /suːˈbiːz/ ▶**noun** [mass noun] a thick white sauce made with onion purée and often served with fish or eggs.
– ORIGIN named after Charles de Rohan *Soubise* (1715–87), French general and courtier.

soubresaut /ˈsuːbrəsəʊ/ ▶**noun** (pl. pronounced same) Ballet a straight-legged jump from both feet with the toes pointed and feet together, one behind the other.
– ORIGIN French.

soubrette /suːˈbrɛt/ ▶**noun** a minor female role in a comedy, typically that of a pert maidservant.
– ORIGIN mid 18th cent.: French, from Provençal *soubreto*, feminine of *soubret* 'coy', from *sobrar*, from Latin *superare* 'be above'.

soubriquet /ˈsuːbrɪkeɪ/ ▶**noun** variant spelling of **SOBRIQUET**.

souchong /ˈsuːʃɒŋ/ ▶**noun** [mass noun] a fine black variety of China tea.
– ORIGIN mid 18th cent.: from Chinese *siú* 'small' + *chúng* 'sort'.

soucouyant /ˌsuːkuːˈjɒ̃/ ▶**noun** (in eastern Caribbean folklore) a malignant witch believed to shed her skin by night and suck the blood of her victims.
– ORIGIN West Indian creole.

souffle /ˈsuːf(ə)l/ ▶**noun** Medicine a low murmuring or blowing sound heard through a stethoscope.
– ORIGIN late 19th cent.: from French, from *souffler* 'to blow', from Latin *sufflare*.

soufflé ▶**noun** a light, spongy baked dish made typically by adding flavoured egg yolks to stiffly beaten egg whites.
■any of various light sweet or savoury dishes made with beaten egg whites.
– ORIGIN French, literally 'blown', past participle of *souffler* (see **SOUFFLE**).

Soufrière /ˌsuːfrɪˈɛː/ **1** a dormant volcano on the French island of Guadeloupe in the Caribbean. Rising to 1,468 m (4,813 ft), it is the highest peak in the Lesser Antilles.
2 an active volcanic peak on the island of St Vincent in the Caribbean. It rises to a height of 1,234 m (4,006 ft).
– ORIGIN French, from *soufre* 'sulphur'.

sough /saʊ, sʌf/ ▶**verb** [no obj.] (of the wind in trees, the sea, etc.) make a moaning, whistling, or rushing sound.
▶**noun** [in sing.] a sound of this type.
– ORIGIN Old English *swōgan*, of Germanic origin.

sought past and past participle of **SEEK**.

sought after ▶**adjective** much in demand; generally desired: *the most expensive and sought-after perfume.*

souk /suːk/ (also **suk**, **sukh**, or **suq**) ▶**noun** an Arab market or marketplace; a bazaar.
– ORIGIN from Arabic *sūḳ*.

soukous /ˈsuːkuːs/ ▶**noun** [mass noun] a style of African popular music characterized by syncopated rhythms and intricate contrasting guitar melodies, originating in Zaire (Democratic Republic of Congo).
– ORIGIN perhaps from French *secouer* 'to shake'.

soul ▶**noun 1** the spiritual or immaterial part of a human being or animal, regarded as immortal.
■a person's moral or emotional nature or sense of identity: *in the depths of her soul, she knew he would betray her.* ■[mass noun] emotional or intellectual energy or intensity, especially as revealed in a work of art or an artistic performance: *their interpretation lacked soul.* ■short for **SOUL MUSIC**.
2 a person regarded as the embodiment of a specified quality: *he was **the soul of** discretion.*
■an individual person: *I'll never tell a soul.* ■a person regarded with affection or pity: *she's a nice old soul.*
– PHRASES **bare one's soul** see **BARE**. **the life and soul of the party** see **LIFE**. **lost soul** a soul that is damned. ■chiefly humorous a person who seems unable to cope with everyday life. **sell one's soul (to the devil)** see **SELL**. **upon my soul** dated an exclamation of surprise.
– DERIVATIVES **souled** adjective [in combination] *she was a great-souled character.*
– ORIGIN Old English *sāwol*, *sāw(e)l*, of Germanic origin; related to Dutch *ziel* and German *Seele*.

soul case ▶**noun** N. Amer. & W. Indian informal the body.

soul catcher ▶**noun** (among various North American Indian peoples) a hollowed bone tube used by a medicine man to contain the soul of a sick person.

soul-destroying ▶**adjective** (of an activity) unbearably monotonous.

soul food ▶**noun** [mass noun] food traditionally associated with black people of the southern US.

soulful ▶**adjective** expressing or appearing to express deep and often sorrowful feeling: *she gave him a soulful glance.*
– DERIVATIVES **soulfully** adverb, **soulfulness** noun.

soul kiss ▶**noun** another term for **FRENCH KISS**.

soulless ▶**adjective** (of a building, room, or other place) lacking character and individuality: *she found the apartment beautiful but soulless.*
■(of an activity) tedious and uninspiring: *soulless, non-productive work.* ■lacking or suggesting the lack of human feelings and qualities: *two soulless black eyes were watching her.*
– DERIVATIVES **soullessly** adverb, **soullessness** noun.

soulmate ▶**noun** a person ideally suited to another as a close friend or romantic partner.

soul music ▶**noun** [mass noun] a kind of music incorporating elements of rhythm and blues and gospel music, popularized by American blacks. Characterized by an emphasis on vocals and an impassioned improvisatory delivery, it is associated with performers such as Marvin Gaye, Aretha Franklin, James Brown, and Otis Redding.

soul-searching ▶**noun** [mass noun] deep and anxious consideration of one's emotions and motives or of the correctness of a course of action.
▶**adjective** involving or expressing such consideration: *long, soul-searching conversations about religion.*

soulster ▶**noun** informal a singer of soul music.

Soumak /ˈsuːmak/ ▶**noun** a rug or carpet made in the neighbourhood of Shemakha in Azerbaijan, distinguished by a flat, napless surface and loose threads at the back.
– ORIGIN early 20th cent.: perhaps an alteration of *Shemakha* (see above).

sound[1] ▶**noun** [mass noun] vibrations that travel through the air or another medium and can be heard when they reach a person's or animal's ear: *light travels faster than sound.*
■[count noun] a group of vibrations of this kind; a thing that can be heard: *she heard the sound of voices in the hall* | *don't make a sound.* ■the area or distance within which something can be heard: *we were always **within sound of** the train whistles.* ■short for **SPEECH SOUND**. ■the ideas or impressions conveyed by words: *you've had a hard day, **by the sound of it**.* ■(also **musical sound**) sound produced by continuous and regular vibrations, as opposed to noise. ■music, speech, and sound effects when recorded, used to accompany a film or video production, or broadcast: [as modifier] *a sound studio.* ■broadcasting by radio as distinct from television. ■the distinctive quality of the music of a particular composer or performer or of the sound produced by a particular musical instrument: *the sound of the Beatles.* ■(**sounds**) informal music, especially popular music: *sounds of the Sixties.*
▶**verb** [no obj.] emit sound: *a loud buzzer sounded.*
■[with obj.] cause (something) to emit sound: *she sounded the horn.* ■[with obj.] give an audible signal to warn of or indicate (something): *a different bell begins to sound midnight.* ■[with obj.] say (something); utter: *a Labour back-bencher sounded a warning.* ■convey a specified impression when heard: [with complement] *he sounded worried.* ■(of something or someone that has been described to one) convey a specified impression: *it sounds as though you really do believe that* | [with complement] *the house sounds lovely.* ■[with obj.] test (the lungs or another body cavity) by noting the sound they produce: *the doctor sounded her chest.*
– DERIVATIVES **soundless** adjective, **soundlessly** adverb, **soundlessness** noun.
– ORIGIN Middle English *soun*, from Anglo-Norman French *soun* (noun), *suner* (verb), from Latin *sonus*. The form with *-d* was established in the 16th cent.
▶**sound off** express one's opinions in a loud or forceful manner.

sound[2] ▶**adjective 1** in good condition; not damaged, injured, or diseased: *they returned **safe and sound*** | *he was not of sound mind.*
■based on reason, sense, or judgement: *sound advice for healthy living* | *the scientific content is sound.* ■competent, reliable, or holding acceptable views: *he's a bit stuffy, but he's very **sound on** his law.* ■financially secure: *she could get her business on a sound footing for the first time.* ■Brit. informal excellent: *He ate his lasagne with relish. 'It's sound, this.'*
2 (of sleep) deep and undisturbed.
■(of a person) tending to sleep deeply.
3 severe: *such people should be given a sound thrashing.*
▶**adverb** soundly: *he was sound asleep.*
– PHRASES (**as**) **sound as a bell** in perfect condition.
– DERIVATIVES **soundly** adverb, **soundness** noun.
– ORIGIN Middle English: from Old English *gesund*, of West Germanic origin; related to Dutch *gezond* and German *gesund*.

sound[3] ▶**verb 1** [with obj.] ascertain (the depth of water in the sea, a lake, or a river), typically by means of a line or pole or using sound echoes.
■find the depth of water in (a ship's hold). ■Medicine examine (a person's bladder or other internal cavity) with a long surgical probe.
2 [with obj.] question (someone), typically in a cautious or discreet way, as to their opinions or feelings on a subject: *we'll **sound out** parliament first.*
■inquire into (someone's opinions of feelings) in this way: *officials arrived to **sound out** public opinion at meetings in factories.*
3 [no obj.] (especially of a whale) dive down steeply to a great depth.
▶**noun** a long surgical probe, typically with a curved, blunt end.
– DERIVATIVES **sounder** noun.
– ORIGIN late Middle English: from Old French *sonder*, based on Latin *sub-* 'below' + *unda* 'wave'.

sound[4] ▶**noun** a narrow stretch of water forming an inlet or connecting two wider areas of water such as two seas or a sea and a lake.
■(**the Sound**) another name for **{*COBAR*}**RESUND.
– ORIGIN Middle English: from Old Norse *sund* 'swimming, strait'; related to **SWIM**.

soundalike ▶**noun** a person or thing that closely resembles another in sound, especially someone whose voice or style of speaking or singing is very similar to that of a famous person.

sound barrier ▶**noun** (**the sound barrier**) the increased drag, reduced controllability, and other effects which occur when an aircraft approaches the speed of sound, formerly regarded as an obstacle to supersonic flight.

sound bite ▶**noun** a short extract from a recorded interview, chosen for its pungency or aptness.

soundboard (also **sounding board**) ▶**noun** a thin sheet of wood over which the strings of a piano or similar instrument are positioned to increase the sound produced.

soundbox ▶**noun** the hollow chamber forming the body of a stringed musical instrument and providing resonance.

sound card ▶**noun** a device which can be slotted into a computer to allow the use of audio components for multimedia applications.

soundcheck ▶**noun** a test of sound equipment before a musical performance or recording to check that the desired sound is being produced.

sound conditioner ▶**noun** a device designed to mask or block out undesirable sounds by generating white noise or some other continuous, unobtrusive sound.

sound effect ▶**noun** a sound other than speech or music made artificially for use in a play, film, or other broadcast production.

sound engineer ▶**noun** a technician dealing with acoustics for a broadcast or musical performance.

Soundex ▶**noun** [mass noun] Computing a phonetic

coding system intended to suppress spelling variations, used especially to encode surnames for the linkage of medical and other records: [as modifier] *Soundex searches.*
– ORIGIN 1950s: from **SOUND**[1] + the arbitrary ending *-ex.*

soundhole ▶ **noun** an aperture in the belly of a stringed instrument.

sounding[1] ▶ **noun** [mass noun] the action or process of measuring the depth of the sea or other body of water.
■ a measurement taken by sounding. ■ the determination of any physical property at a depth in the sea or at a height in the atmosphere. ■ (**soundings**) figurative information or evidence ascertained as a preliminary step before deciding on a course of action: *he's been* **taking soundings** *about the possibility of moving his offices.* ■ (**soundings**) archaic the area of sea close to the shore which is shallow enough for the bottom to be reached by means of a sounding line.

sounding[2] ▶ **adjective** [attrib.] archaic giving forth sound, especially loud or resonant sound: *he went in with a sounding plunge.*
■ having an imposing sound but little substance: *the orator has been apt to deal in sounding commonplaces.*

sounding board ▶ **noun** 1 a board or screen placed over or behind a pulpit or stage to reflect a speaker's voice forward.
■ another term for **SOUNDBOARD**.
2 a person or group whose reactions to suggested ideas are used as a test of their validity or likely success before they are made public.
■ a channel through which ideas are disseminated.

sounding line ▶ **noun** a weighted line with distances marked off at regular intervals, used to measure the depth of water under a boat.

sounding rod ▶ **noun** a rod used to measure the depth of water under a boat or in a ship's hold or other container.

sound post ▶ **noun** a small wooden rod wedged between the front and back surfaces of a violin or similar instrument and modifying its vibrations.

sound pressure ▶ **noun** [mass noun] Physics the difference between the instantaneous pressure at a point in the presence of a sound wave and the static pressure of the medium.

soundproof ▶ **adjective** preventing, or constructed of material that prevents, the passage of sound.
▶ **verb** [with obj.] make (a room or building) resistant to the passage of sound.

soundscape ▶ **noun** a piece of music considered in terms of its component sounds: *his lush keyboard soundscapes.*

sound shift ▶ **noun** Linguistics a systematic change in the pronunciation of a set of speech sounds as a language evolves.

sound spectrograph ▶ **noun** an instrument for analysing sound into its frequency components.

sound stage ▶ **noun** an area of a film studio with acoustic properties suitable for the recording of sound, typically used to record dialogue.

sound symbolism ▶ **noun** [mass noun] the partial representation of the sense of a word by its sound, as in *bang, fizz,* and *slide.* See also **ONOMATOPOEIA**.

sound system ▶ **noun** a set of equipment for the reproduction and amplification of sound.

soundtrack ▶ **noun** a recording of the musical accompaniment of a film.
■ a strip on the edge of a film on which the sound component is recorded.
▶ **verb** [with obj.] provide (a film) with a soundtrack: *it is soundtracked by the great Ennio Morricone.*

sound wave ▶ **noun** Physics a wave of compression and rarefaction, by which sound is propagated in an elastic medium such as air.

soup ▶ **noun** [mass noun] 1 a liquid dish, typically savoury and made by boiling meat, fish, or vegetables etc. in stock or water: *a bowl of tomato soup.*
■ figurative a substance or mixture perceived to resemble soup in appearance or consistency: *the waves and the water beyond have become a thick brown soup.*
2 US informal nitroglycerine or gelignite, especially as used for safe-breaking.
3 informal the chemicals in which film is developed.
– PHRASES **from soup to nuts** N. Amer. informal from beginning to end; completely: *I know all about that game from soup to nuts.* **in the soup** informal in trouble.
– ORIGIN Middle English: from Old French *soupe* 'sop, broth (poured on slices of bread)', from late Latin *suppa*, of Germanic origin.
▶ **soup something up** informal increase the power and efficiency of an engine or other machine. ■ make something more elaborate or impressive: *we had to soup up the show for the new venue.* [ORIGIN: 1930s, perhaps influenced by **SUPER-**.]

soup and fish ▶ **noun** Brit. informal, dated men's evening dress.
– ORIGIN so named from the traditional first two courses of a formal dinner.

soupçon /'su:psɒn, -sɔ̃/ ▶ **noun** [in sing.] a very small quantity of something: *a soupçon of mustard.*
– ORIGIN mid 18th cent.: French, from Old French *souspeçon*, from medieval Latin *suspectio* (see **SUSPICION**).

soup kitchen ▶ **noun** a place where free food is served to those who are homeless or destitute.

soup plate ▶ **noun** a deep, wide-rimmed plate in which soup is served.

soup spoon ▶ **noun** a large spoon with a round bowl, used for eating soup.

soupy ▶ **adjective** (**soupier, soupiest**) having the appearance or consistency of soup: *a soupy stew.*
■ (of the air or climate) humid. ■ informal mawkishly sentimental: *soupy nostalgia.*
– DERIVATIVES **soupily** adverb, **soupiness** noun.

sour ▶ **adjective** having an acid taste like lemon or vinegar: *she sampled the wine and found it was sour.*
■ (of food, especially milk or bread) having gone bad because of fermentation. ■ having a rancid smell: *her breath was always sour.* ■ figurative feeling or expressing resentment, disappointment, or anger: *she was a different woman from the sour, bored creature I had known.* ■ (of soil) deficient in lime and usually dank. ■ (of petroleum or natural gas) containing a relatively high proportion of sulphur.
▶ **noun** [with modifier] a drink made by mixing an alcoholic drink with lemon juice or lime juice: *a rum sour.*
▶ **verb** make or become sour: [with obj.] *water soured with tamarind* | [as adj. **soured**] *soured cream* | [no obj.] *a bowl of milk was souring in the sun.*
■ make or become unpleasant, acrimonious, or difficult: [with obj.] *a dispute soured relations between the two countries for over a year* | [no obj.] *many friendships have soured over borrowed money.*
– PHRASES **go** (or **turn**) **sour** become less pleasant or attractive; turn out badly: *the vision of bedsit freedom soon turned sour.* **sour grapes** used to refer to an attitude in which someone disparages or affects to despise something because they cannot have it themselves. [ORIGIN: with allusion to Aesop's fable *The Fox and the Grapes.*]
– DERIVATIVES **sourish** adjective, **sourly** adverb, **sourness** noun.
– ORIGIN Old English *sūr*, of Germanic origin; related to Dutch *zuur* and German *sauer.*

source ▶ **noun** a place, person, or thing from which something comes or can be obtained: *mackerel is a good source of fish oil.*
■ a spring or fountain head from which a river or stream issues: *the source of the Nile.* ■ a person who provides information: *military sources announced a reduction in strategic nuclear weapons.* ■ a book or document used to provide evidence in research. ■ technical a body or process by which energy or a particular component enters a system. The opposite of **SINK**[2]. ■ Electronics a part of a field-effect transistor from which carriers flow into the interelectrode channel.
▶ **verb** [with obj.] (often **be sourced**) obtain from a particular source: *each type of coffee is sourced from one country.*
■ find out where (something) can be obtained: *she was called upon to source a supply of carpet.*
– PHRASES **at source** at the point of origin or issue: *reduction of pollution at source.* ■ used to show that a sum is deducted from earnings or other payments before they are made: *your pension contribution will be deducted at source.*
– ORIGIN late Middle English: from Old French *sours(e)*, past participle of *sourdre* 'to rise', from Latin *surgere.*

sourcebook ▶ **noun** a collection of writings and articles on a particular subject, especially one used as a basic introduction to that subject.

source code ▶ **noun** [mass noun] Computing a text listing of commands to be compiled or assembled into an executable computer program.

source criticism ▶ **noun** [mass noun] the analysis and study of the sources used by biblical authors.

source program ▶ **noun** Computing a program written in a language other than machine code, typically a high-level language.

source rock ▶ **noun** Geology a rock formation from which later sediments are derived or in which a particular mineral originates.
■ a sediment containing sufficient organic matter to be a future source of hydrocarbons.

sour cream ▶ **noun** [mass noun] cream which has been deliberately fermented by the addition of certain bacteria.

sourdough ▶ **noun** 1 [mass noun] leaven for making bread, consisting of fermenting dough, originally that left over from a previous baking.
■ bread made using such leaven.
2 N. Amer. an experienced prospector in the western US or Canada; an old timer.

sour grass ▶ **noun** [mass noun] grass which is coarse, unpalatable, or of very low nutritional value.
● Species in several genera of the family Gramineae, in particular *Elionurus* (in South Africa), and *Andropogon* and *Valota* (in the Caribbean).

sour mash ▶ **noun** [mass noun] US a mash used in distilling certain malt whiskeys.
■ whiskey distilled from this.

sourpuss ▶ **noun** informal a bad-tempered or habitually sullen person.
– ORIGIN 1930s (originally US): from **SOUR** + **PUSS**[2].

soursop ▶ **noun** 1 a large acidic custard apple with white fibrous flesh.
2 the evergreen tropical American tree which bears this fruit.
● *Annona muricata*, family Annonaceae.

sourveld /'saʊəvɛlt/ ▶ **noun** [mass noun] S. African land covered with coarse vegetation, or the vegetation itself.
– ORIGIN partial translation of South African Dutch *zuurveld.*

sourwood ▶ **noun** a North American tree of the heather family, which has acid-tasting leaves. Also called **SORREL TREE**.
● *Oxydendrum arboreum*, family Ericaceae.

sous- /su:(z)/ ▶ **prefix** (in words adopted from French) subordinate: *sous-chef.*
– ORIGIN from French *sous* 'under'.

Sousa /'su:zə/, John Philip (1854–1932), American composer and conductor. His works include more than a hundred marches, for example *The Stars and Stripes.*

sousaphone /'su:zəfəʊn/ ▶ **noun** an American form of tuba with a wide bell pointing forward above the player's head, used in marching bands.
– DERIVATIVES **sousaphonist** /-'zɒf(ə)nɪst/ noun.
– ORIGIN 1920s: named after J. P. **SOUSA**, on the pattern of *saxophone.*

souse /saʊs/ ▶ **verb** [with obj.] soak in or drench with liquid: *the chips were well soused with vinegar.*
■ [often as adj. **soused**] put (gherkins, fish, etc.) in pickle or a marinade: *soused herring.* ■ [as adj. **soused**] informal drunk: *I was soused to the eyeballs.*
▶ **noun** 1 [mass noun] liquid, typically salted, used for pickling.
■ N. Amer. & W. Indian food, especially a pig's head, in pickle.
2 informal a drunkard.
■ dated a drinking bout.
– ORIGIN late Middle English (as a noun denoting pickled meat): from Old French *sous* 'pickle', of Germanic origin; related to **SALT**.

souslik /'su:slɪk/ (also **suslik**) ▶ **noun** a short-tailed ground squirrel native to Eurasia and the Arctic.
● Genus *Spermophilus*, family Sciuridae: several species, in particular the **European souslik** (*S. citellus*).
– ORIGIN late 18th cent.: from Russian.

sou-sou /'su:su:/ ▶ **noun** W. Indian a cooperative savings system in which each person contributes the same fixed amount each week, and the whole amount is taken by a different member each time.
– ORIGIN from Yoruba.

Sousse /su:s/ (also **Susah, Susa**) a port and resort on the east coast of Tunisia; pop. 125,000 (1994).

sous vide /su: 'vi:d/ ▶ **noun** [mass noun] a method of treating food by partial cooking followed by vacuum-sealing and chilling.

▶ **adjective** & **adverb** (of food or cooking) involving such preparation: [as adj.] *a convection oven can be used in sous vide operations* | [as adv.] *cooking cuisine sous vide.*
– ORIGIN French, literally 'under vacuum'.

soutache /suːˈtaʃ/ ▶ **noun** a narrow, flat ornamental braid used to trim garments.
– ORIGIN mid 19th cent.: from French, from Hungarian *sujtás*.

soutane /suːˈtɑːn/ ▶ **noun** a type of cassock worn by Roman Catholic priests.
– ORIGIN mid 19th cent.: from French, from Italian *sottana*, from *sotto* 'under', from Latin *subtus*.

souteneur /ˌsuːtəˈnəː/ ▶ **noun** a pimp.
– ORIGIN French, literally 'protector'.

souter /ˈsuːtə/ (also **soutar**) ▶ **noun** Scottish & N. English a shoemaker.
– ORIGIN Old English *sūtere*, from Latin *sutor*, from *suere* 'sew'.

souterrain /ˈsuːtəreɪn/ ▶ **noun** chiefly Archaeology an underground chamber or passage.
– ORIGIN mid 18th cent.: from French, from *sous* 'under' + *terre* 'earth'.

south ▶ **noun** (usu. **the south**) **1** the direction towards the point of the horizon 90° clockwise from east, or the point on the horizon itself: *the breeze came from the south* | *they trade with the countries to the south.*
▪ the compass point corresponding to this.
2 the southern part of the world or of a specified country, region, or town: *he was staying in the south of France.*
▪ (usu. **the South**) the southern part of England. ▪ (usu. **the South**) the Southern states of the United States. ▪ (usu. **the South**) the less industrialized and economically advanced nations of the world.
3 [as name] (**South**) Bridge the player sitting opposite and partnering North.
▶ **adjective** [attrib.] **1** lying towards, near, or facing the south: *the south coast.*
▪ (of a wind) blowing from the south.
2 of or denoting the southern part of a specified area, city, or country or its inhabitants: *South America.*
▶ **adverb** to or towards the south: *they journeyed south along the valley* | *the village is a few miles* ***south of*** *Cambridge.*
▶ **verb** [no obj.] move towards the south: *the wind southed a point or two.*
▪ (of a celestial body) cross the meridian.
– PHRASES **down south** informal to or in the south of a country. **south by east** (or **west**) between south and south-south-east (or south-south-west).
– ORIGIN Old English *sūth*, of Germanic origin; related to Low German *sud*.

South Africa a country occupying the southernmost part of the continent of Africa; pop. 36,762,000 (est. 1991); languages: official languages, English, Afrikaans, Zulu, Xhosa, and other languages; administrative capital, Pretoria; seat of legislature, Cape Town.

> Settled by the Dutch in the 17th century, the area of the Cape came under British administration in 1806. There followed inland expansion and British dominance of local populations, culminating in victory in the Zulu and Boer Wars at the end of the 19th century. The colonies of Natal, the Cape, Transvaal, and Orange Free State joined to form the self-governing Union of South Africa in 1910. In 1961 South Africa became a republic and left the Commonwealth. From 1948 it pursued a policy of white minority rule (apartheid), which led to international diplomatic isolation. A gradual dismantling of apartheid began in 1990 following the release of the African National Congress leader Nelson Mandela. Majority rule was achieved after the country's first democratic elections in April 1994, won by the ANC. South Africa rejoined the Commonwealth in 1994.

– DERIVATIVES **South African** adjective & noun.

South African Dutch ▶ **noun** [mass noun] the Afrikaans language from the 17th to the 19th centuries, during its development from Dutch.
▶ **adjective** dated or derogatory of or relating to Afrikaans-speaking South Africans.

South America a continent comprising the southern half of the American land mass, connected to North America by the Isthmus of Panama. It includes the Falkland Islands, the Galapagos Islands, and Tierra del Fuego. (See also **AMERICA**.)
– DERIVATIVES **South American** adjective & noun.

Southampton /saʊθˈ(h)am(p)tə(ʊ)n, saʊˈθam(p)t(ə)n/ an industrial city and seaport on the south coast of England, a unitary council formerly in Hampshire; pop. 194,400 (1991). It lies at the end of Southampton Water, an inlet of the English Channel opposite the Isle of Wight.

South Atlantic Ocean see **ATLANTIC OCEAN**.

South Australia a state comprising the central southern part of Australia; capital, Adelaide. Constituted as a semi-independent colony in 1836, it became a Crown Colony in 1841 and was federated with the other states of Australia in 1901.

South Bank the area adjacent to the southern bank of the River Thames, especially the cultural complex located between Westminster and Blackfriars Bridges in London.

southbound ▶ **adjective** travelling or leading towards the south: *southbound traffic* | *the southbound carriageway of the A1.*

South Carolina a state of the US on the Atlantic coast; pop. 3,486,700 (1990); capital, Columbia. The region was permanently settled by the English from 1663. Separated from North Carolina in 1729, South Carolina became one of the original thirteen states of the Union (1788). In 1860 it was the first state to secede from the Union, precipitating the American Civil War.
– DERIVATIVES **South Carolinian** noun & adjective.

South China Sea see **CHINA SEA**.

South Dakota a state in the north central US; pop. 696,000 (1990); capital, Pierre. Acquired partly by the Louisiana Purchase in 1803, it became a part of the former Dakota Territory in 1861. It separated from North Dakota in 1889, becoming the 40th state of the US.
– DERIVATIVES **South Dakotan** noun & adjective.

South Devon ▶ **noun** an animal of a breed of large light red or fawn cattle.

Southdown ▶ **noun** a sheep of a breed raised especially for mutton, originally on the South Downs of Hampshire and Sussex.

south-east ▶ **noun 1** (usu. **the south-east**) the direction towards the point of the horizon midway between south and east, or the point on the horizon itself: *a ship was coming in from the south-east.*
▪ the compass point corresponding to this.
2 the south-eastern part of a country, region, or town.
▶ **adjective** [attrib.] **1** lying towards, near, or facing the south-east: *a table stood in the south-east corner.*
▪ (of a wind) blowing from the south-east.
2 of or denoting the south-eastern part of a specified country, region, or town or its inhabitants: *South-East Asia.*
▶ **adverb** to or towards the south-east: *turn south-east to return to your starting point.*
– DERIVATIVES **south-eastern** adjective.

South-East Asia Treaty Organization (abbrev.: **SEATO**) a defence alliance which existed between 1954 and 1977 for countries of SE Asia and part of the SW Pacific, to further a US policy of containing Communism. Its members were Australia, Britain, France, New Zealand, Pakistan, the Philippines, Thailand, and the US.

southeaster ▶ **noun** a wind blowing from the south-east.

south-easterly ▶ **adjective** & **adverb** another term for **SOUTH-EAST**.
▶ **noun** another term for **SOUTHEASTER**.

South-East Iceland a shipping forecast area covering part of the NE Atlantic between Iceland and the Faroes.

south-eastward ▶ **adverb** (also **south-eastwards**) towards the south-east: *he walked south-eastwards from the river.*
▶ **adjective** situated in, directed toward, or facing the south-east.

Southend-on-Sea a resort town on the Thames estuary east of London; pop. 153,700 (1991).

South Equatorial Current an ocean current that flows westwards across the Pacific Ocean just south of the equator.

southerly ▶ **adjective** & **adverb** in a southward position or direction: [as adj.] *the most southerly of the Greek islands* | [as adv.] *they made off southerly.*
▪ (of a wind) blowing from the south: [as adj.] *a southerly gale* | [as adv.] *the wind had backed southerly.*
▶ **noun** (often **southerlies**) a wind blowing from the south.

southern ▶ **adjective 1** [attrib.] situated in the south or directed towards or facing the south: *the southern hemisphere.*
▪ (of a wind) blowing from the south.
2 living in or originating from the south: *the southern rural poor.*
▪ of, relating to, or characteristic of the south or its inhabitants: *a faintly southern accent.*
– DERIVATIVES **southernmost** adjective.
– ORIGIN Old English *sūtherne* (see **SOUTH**, **-ERN**).

Southern Alps a mountain range in South Island, New Zealand. Running roughly parallel to the west coast, it extends for almost the entire length of the island. At Mount Cook, its highest peak, it rises to 3,764 m (12,349 ft).

Southern Baptist ▶ **noun** a member of a large convention of Baptist churches established in the US in 1845, typically having a fundamentalist and evangelistic approach to Christianity.

Southern blot ▶ **noun** Biology a procedure for identifying specific sequences of DNA, in which fragments separated on a gel are transferred directly to a second medium on which assay by hybridization may be carried out.
– ORIGIN late 20th cent.: named after Edwin M. *Southern* (born 1938), British biochemist.

Southern Comfort ▶ **noun** [mass noun] trademark a whisky-based alcoholic drink of US origin.

Southern Cone ▶ **noun** the region of South America comprising the countries of Brazil, Paraguay, Uruguay, Argentina, and Chile.

Southern Cross Astronomy the constellation Crux.

southerner ▶ **noun** a native or inhabitant of the south, especially of the southern United States or southern England.

southern-fried ▶ **adjective** chiefly US (of food, especially chicken) coated in flour, egg, and breadcrumbs and then deep-fried.

southern hemisphere the half of the earth that is south of the equator.

Southern Lights another name for the aurora australis. See **AURORA**.

Southern Ocean the expanse of ocean surrounding Antarctica.

Southern Paiute ▶ **noun** & **adjective** see **PAIUTE**.

Southern Rhodesia see **ZIMBABWE**.

southernwood ▶ **noun** a bushy artemisia of southern Europe. Also called **LAD'S LOVE**.
• *Artemisia abrotanum*, family Compositae.

Southey /ˈsʌði, ˈsaʊði/, Robert (1774–1843), English poet. Associated with the Lake Poets, he is best known for his shorter poems, such as the 'Battle of Blenheim' (1798). He was made Poet Laureate in 1813.

South Georgia a barren island in the South Atlantic, situated 1,120 km (700 miles) east of the Falkland Islands, of which it is a dependency. It was first explored in 1775 by Captain James Cook, who named the island after George III.

South Glamorgan a former county of South Wales, on the Bristol Channel, dissolved in 1996.

southing ▶ **noun** [mass noun] distance travelled or measured southward, especially at sea.
▪ [count noun] a figure or line representing southward distance on a map. ▪ Astronomy the transit of a celestial object, especially the sun, across the meridian due south of the observer. ▪ [count noun] Astronomy the angular distance of a star or other object south of the celestial equator.

South Island the more southerly and larger of the two main islands of New Zealand, separated from North Island by Cook Strait.

South Korea a country in the Far East, occupying the southern part of the peninsula of Korea; pop. 42,793,000 (est. 1990); official language, Korean; capital, Seoul. Official name **REPUBLIC OF KOREA**.

> South Korea was formed in 1948, when Korea was partitioned along the 38th parallel; the Korean War (1950–3) has been followed by decades of hostility between North and South Korea. An emerging industrial power, South Korea has had one of the world's fastest-growing economies since the 1960s.

– DERIVATIVES **South Korean** adjective & noun.

South Orkney Islands a group of uninhabited islands in the South Atlantic, lying to the north-east of the Antarctic Peninsula. Discovered in 1821, the islands are administered as part of the British Antarctic Territory.

South Ossetia an autonomous region of Georgia, situated in the Caucasus on the border with Russia; capital, Tskhinvali. (See also **OSSETIA**.)

South Pacific Commission an agency established in 1947 to promote the economic and social stability of the islands in the South Pacific, having twenty-seven member governments and administrations.

southpaw ▶ noun a left-handed boxer who leads with the right hand.
■ Baseball a left-handed pitcher. ■ informal, chiefly US left-hander in any sphere.
– ORIGIN mid 19th cent. (denoting the left hand or a punch with the left hand): the usage in baseball is from the orientation of the diamond to the same points of the compass, causing the pitcher to have his left hand on the south side of his body.

South Pole ▶ noun see POLE².

Southport a resort town in NW England, on the Irish Sea coast north of Liverpool; pop. 90,960 (1981).

South Sandwich Islands a group of uninhabited volcanic islands in the South Atlantic, lying 480 km (300 miles) south-east of South Georgia. They are administered from the Falkland Islands.

South Sea (also **South Seas**) archaic the southern Pacific Ocean.

South Sea Bubble a speculative boom in the shares of the South Sea Company in 1720 which ended with the failure of the company and a general financial collapse.

South Shetland Islands a group of uninhabited islands in the South Atlantic, lying north of the Antarctic Peninsula. Discovered in 1819, the islands are administered as part of the British Antarctic Territory.

South Shields a port on the coast of NE England, at the mouth of the Tyne opposite North Shields; pop. 87,125 (1981).

south-south-east ▶ noun the compass point or direction midway between south and south-east.

south-south-west ▶ noun the compass point or direction midway between south and south-west.

South Uist see UIST.

South Utsire see UTSIRE.

southward /ˈsaʊθwəd/ Nautical /ˈsʌðəd/ ▶ adjective in a southerly direction: employment and people began a southward drift.
▶ adverb (also **southwards**) towards the south: the village stretches southwards across the plain.
▶ noun (**the southward**) the direction or region to the south: cool air from the ocean to the southward.
– DERIVATIVES **southwardly** adverb.

south-west ▶ noun 1 (usu. **the south-west**) the direction towards the point of the horizon midway between south and west, or the point of the horizon itself: clouds uncoiled from the south-west.
■ the compass point corresponding to this.
2 the south-western part of a country, region, or town.
▶ adjective [attrib.] 1 lying towards, near, or facing the south-west: the south-west tower collapsed in a storm.
■ (of a wind) blowing from the south-west.
2 of or denoting the south-western part of a specified country, region, or town or its inhabitants: south-west London.
▶ adverb to or towards the south-west: they drove directly south-west.
– DERIVATIVES **south-western** adjective.

South West Africa former name for NAMIBIA.

South West Africa People's Organization (abbrev.: SWAPO) a nationalist organization formed in Namibia in 1964–6 to oppose the illegitimate South African rule over the region. It waged a guerrilla campaign, operating largely from Angola; it eventually gained UN recognition, and won elections in 1989.

southwester ▶ noun a wind blowing from the south-west.

south-westerly ▶ adjective & adverb another term for SOUTH-WEST.
▶ noun another term for SOUTHWESTER.

south-westward ▶ adverb (also **south-westwards**) towards the south-west: the governor sent two companies of foot soldiers south-westwards.

▶ adjective situated in, directed toward, or facing the south-west: the south-westward extension of the valley.

South Yorkshire a metropolitan county of northern England.

Soutine /suːˈtiːn/, Chaim (1893–1943), French painter, born in Lithuania. A major exponent of expressionism, he produced pictures of grotesque figures during the 1920s, while from 1925 he increasingly painted still lifes.

souvenir /ˌsuːvəˈnɪə/ ▶ noun a thing that is kept as a reminder of a person, place, or event.
▶ verb [with obj.] informal take as a memento: many parts of the aircraft have been souvenired.
– ORIGIN late 18th cent.: from French, from souvenir 'remember', from Latin subvenire 'occur to the mind'.

souvlaki /suːˈvlɑːki/ ▶ noun (pl. **souvlakia** /-kɪə/ or **souvlakis**) [mass noun] a Greek dish of pieces of meat grilled on a skewer: a generous plate of souvlaki | [count noun] souvlakia in pitta.
– ORIGIN modern Greek.

sou'wester /saʊˈwɛstə/ ▶ noun a waterproof hat with a broad flap covering the neck.

SOV ▶ noun Brit. informal a pound sterling.
– ORIGIN early 19th cent.: abbreviation of SOVEREIGN.

sovereign ▶ noun 1 a supreme ruler, especially a monarch.
2 a former British gold coin worth one pound sterling, now only minted for commemorative purposes.
▶ adjective possessing supreme or ultimate power: the Assembly was sovereign over the Council.
■ [attrib.] (of a nation or state) fully independent and determining its own affairs: a sovereign, democratic republic. ■ [attrib.] (of affairs) subject to a specified state's control without outside interference: criticism was seen as interference in China's sovereign affairs.
■ [attrib.] archaic or poetic/literary possessing royal power and status: our most sovereign lord the King. ■ [attrib.] dated very good or effective: a sovereign remedy for all ills.
– DERIVATIVES **sovereignly** adverb.
– ORIGIN Middle English: from Old French soverain, based on Latin super 'above'. The change in the ending was due to association with REIGN.

sovereign good ▶ noun (**the sovereign good**) the greatest good, especially that of a state or its people.

sovereign pontiff ▶ noun see PONTIFF.

sovereignty ▶ noun (pl. **-ies**) [mass noun] supreme power or authority: the sovereignty of Parliament.
■ the authority of a state to govern itself or another state: national sovereignty. ■ [count noun] a self-governing state.
– ORIGIN late Middle English: from Old French sovereinete, from soverain (see SOVEREIGN).

soviet /ˈsəʊvɪət, ˈsɒv-/ ▶ noun 1 an elected local, district, or national council in the former USSR.
■ a revolutionary council of workers or peasants in Russia before 1917.
2 (**Soviet**) a citizen of the former USSR.
▶ adjective (**Soviet**) of or concerning the former Soviet Union: the Soviet leader.
– DERIVATIVES **Sovietization** noun, **Sovietize** (also **-ise**) verb.
– ORIGIN early 20th cent.: from Russian sovet 'council'.

Sovietologist /ˌsəʊvɪəˈtɒlədʒɪst, ˌsɒv-/ ▶ noun a person who studies the former Soviet Union.
– DERIVATIVES **Sovietological** adjective, **Sovietology** noun.

Soviet Union a former federation of Communist republics occupying the northern half of Asia and part of eastern Europe; capital, Moscow. Full name UNION OF SOVIET SOCIALIST REPUBLICS.

Created from the Russian empire in the aftermath of the 1917 Russian Revolution, the Soviet Union was the largest country in the world. It comprised fifteen republics: Russia, Belarus, Ukraine, Georgia, Armenia, Moldova, Azerbaijan, Kazakhstan, Kyrgyzstan, Turkmenistan, Tajikistan, Uzbekistan, and the three Baltic states (annexed in 1940). After the Second World War, the Soviet Union emerged as a superpower in rivalry with the US, leading to the cold war. Decades of repression and economic failure eventually led to attempts at liberalization and economic reform under President Mikhail Gorbachev during the 1980s. The USSR was formally dissolved in 1991, some of its constituents joining a looser confederation, the Commonwealth of Independent States.

sovkhoz /ˈsɒvkɒz, sʌvˈkɔːz/ ▶ noun (pl. same, **sovkhozes** /ˈsɒvkɒzɪz, sʌvˈkɔːzɪz/, or **sovkhozy**

/ˈsɒvkɒzi, sʌvˈkɔːzi/) a state-owned farm in the former USSR.
– ORIGIN Russian, from sov(etskoe) khoz(yaĭstvo) 'Soviet farm'.

sow¹ /səʊ/ ▶ verb (past **sowed** /səʊd/; past participle **sown** /səʊn/ or **sowed**) [with obj.] plant (seed) by scattering it on or in the earth: fill a pot with compost and sow a thin layer of seeds on top.
■ plant the seeds of (a plant or crop): catch crops should be sown after minimal cultivation. ■ plant (a piece of land) with seed: the field used to be sown with oats. ■ (be sown with) be thickly covered with: we walked through a valley sown with boulders. ■ lay or plant (an explosive mine) or cover (territory) with mines: the field had both British and German mines sown in it. ■ cause to appear or spread: the new policy has sown confusion and doubt.
– PHRASES **sow the seed** (or **seeds**) **of** do something which will eventually bring about (a particular result, especially a disastrous one): the seeds of dissension had been sown.
– DERIVATIVES **sower** noun.
– ORIGIN Old English sāwan, of Germanic origin; related to Dutch zaaien and German säen.

sow² /saʊ/ ▶ noun 1 an adult female pig, especially one which has farrowed.
■ the female of certain other mammals, e.g. the guinea pig.
2 a large block of metal (larger than a 'pig') made by smelting.
– PHRASES **you can't make a silk purse out of a sow's ear** proverb you can't create a fine product from inferior materials.
– ORIGIN Old English sugu; related to Dutch zeug, German Sau, from an Indo-European root shared by Latin sus and Greek hus 'pig'.

sowback /ˈsaʊbak/ ▶ noun a low ridge of sand.

sowbread /ˈsaʊbrɛd/ ▶ noun a cyclamen with pale pink or white flowers and leaves that do not appear until late summer after flowering, native to southern Eurasia.
● Cyclamen hederifolium, family Primulaceae.
– ORIGIN mid 16th cent.: so named because the roots are reputedly eaten by wild boars in Sicily.

sow bug /saʊ/ ▶ noun chiefly N. Amer. another term for WOODLOUSE.

sowel /ˈsaʊəl/ ▶ noun non-standard spelling of SOUL, used to represent Scottish or Irish dialectal speech.

Soweto /səˈwɛtəʊ, -ˈweɪtəʊ/ a large urban area, consisting of several townships, in South Africa south-west of Johannesburg. In 1976 demonstrations against the compulsory use of Afrikaans in schools resulted in violent police activity and the deaths of hundreds of people.
– DERIVATIVES **Sowetan** noun & adjective.
– ORIGIN from So(uth) We(stern) To(wnships).

sown past participle of SOW¹.

sowthistle /ˈsaʊθɪs(ə)l/ ▶ noun a Eurasian plant with yellow flowers, thistle-like leaves, and milky sap. Also called MILK THISTLE.
● Genus Sonchus, family Compositae.

sox ▶ noun chiefly N. Amer. non-standard plural spelling of SOCK (in sense 1 of the noun).

Soxhlet /ˈsɒkslət/ ▶ noun [as modifier] Chemistry denoting a form of condensing apparatus used for the continuous solvent extraction of a solid.
– ORIGIN late 19th cent.: named after Franz Soxhlet (1848–1926), Belgian chemist.

soy ▶ noun 1 (also **soy sauce**) [mass noun] a sauce made with fermented soya beans, used in Chinese and Japanese cooking.
2 another term for SOYA.
– ORIGIN from Japanese shō-yu, from Chinese shi-yu, from shi 'salted beans' + yu 'oil'.

soya ▶ noun [mass noun] 1 protein derived from the beans of an Asian plant, used as a replacement for animal protein in certain foods.
■ (also **soya sauce**) chiefly Brit. see SOY (sense 1).
2 the widely cultivated plant of the pea family which produces these beans.
● Glycine max, family Leguminosae.
– ORIGIN late 17th cent.: from Dutch soja, from Malay soi (see SOY).

soya meal ▶ noun [mass noun] the residue of soya bean seeds after the extraction of their oil, used as animal feed.

soya milk ▶ noun [mass noun] the liquid obtained by suspending soya bean flour in water, used as a fat-free substitute for milk, particularly by vegans.

soybean (also **soya bean**) ▶ noun a bean of the soya plant.

Soyinka /ʃɔɪˈɪŋkə/, Wole (b.1934), Nigerian dramatist, novelist, and critic. In 1986 he became the first African to receive the Nobel Prize for Literature. Notable works: *The Lion and the Jewel* (play, 1959) and *The Interpreters* (novel, 1965).

Soyuz /sɔɪˈjuːz, ˈsɔɪjɒz/ a series of manned Soviet orbiting spacecraft, used to investigate the operation of orbiting space stations.

sozzled ▶ adjective informal very drunk: *Uncle Brian's sozzled!*
– ORIGIN late 19th cent.: past participle of dialect *sozzle* 'mix sloppily', probably of imitative origin.

SP ▶ abbreviation for starting price.

sp. ▶ abbreviation for species (usually singular).

Spa /spɑː/ a small town in eastern Belgium, south-east of Liège; pop. 10,140 (1991). It has been celebrated since medieval times for the curative properties of its mineral springs.

spa ▶ noun a mineral spring considered to have health-giving properties.
■ a place or resort with such a spring. ■ a commercial establishment offering health and beauty treatment through such means as steam baths, exercise equipment, and massage. ■ (also **spa bath** or **pool**) a bath containing hot aerated water.
– ORIGIN early 17th cent.: from **Spa**.

space ▶ noun [mass noun] **1** a continuous area or expanse which is free, available, or unoccupied: *a table took up much of the space* | [count noun] *we shall all be living together in a small space* | *he reversed out of the parking space.*
■ [count noun] an area of land which is not occupied by buildings: *she had a love of open spaces.* ■ [count noun] a blank between printed, typed, or written words, characters, numbers, etc. ■ [count noun] Music each of the four gaps between the five lines of a stave. ■ an interval of time (often used to suggest that the time is short considering what has happened or been achieved in it): *both their cars were stolen in the space of three days.* ■ pages in a newspaper, or time between television or radio programmes, available for advertising. ■ (also **commercial space**) an area rented or sold as business premises. ■ the amount of paper used or needed to write about a subject: *there is no space to give further details.* ■ the freedom and scope to live, think, and develop in a way that suits one: *a teenager needing her own space.* ■ Telecommunications one of two possible states of a signal in certain systems. The opposite of **MARK**[1].
2 the dimensions of height, depth, and width within which all things exist and move: *the work gives the sense of a journey in space and time.*
■ (also **outer space**) the physical universe beyond the earth's atmosphere. ■ the near-vacuum extending between the planets and stars, containing small amounts of gas and dust. ■ Mathematics a mathematical concept generally regarded as a set of points having some specified structure.
▶ verb **1** [with obj.] (usu. **be spaced**) position (two or more items) at a distance from one another: *the houses are spaced out.*
■ (in printing or writing) put blanks between (words, letters, or lines): [as noun **spacing**] *the default setting is single line spacing.*
2 (**be spaced out** or chiefly US **space out**) informal be or become euphoric or disorientated, especially from taking drugs; cease to be aware of one's surroundings: *I was so tired that I began to feel totally spaced out* | *I kind of space out for a few minutes.*
– PHRASES **watch this space** informal further developments are expected and more information will be given later.
– DERIVATIVES **spacer** noun.
– ORIGIN Middle English: shortening of Old French *espace*, from Latin *spatium*. Current verb senses date from the late 17th cent.

space age ▶ noun (**the space age**) the era starting when the exploration of space became possible.
▶ adjective (**space-age**) very modern; technologically advanced: *a space-age control room.*

space bar ▶ noun a long key on a typewriter or computer keyboard for making a space between words.

space blanket ▶ noun a light metal-coated sheet designed to retain heat.

space cadet ▶ noun a trainee astronaut.
■ an enthusiast for space travel, typically a young person. ■ informal a person perceived as out of touch with reality.

space capsule ▶ noun a small spacecraft or the part of a larger one that contains the instruments or crew.

space charge ▶ noun Physics a collection of particles with a net electric charge occupying a region, either in free space or in a device.

spacecraft ▶ noun (pl. same or **spacecrafts**) a vehicle used for travelling in space.

space density ▶ noun Astronomy the frequency of occurrence of stars, particles, or other heavenly bodies, per specified volume of space.

spacefaring ▶ noun [mass noun] the action or activity of travelling in space.
– DERIVATIVES **spacefarer** noun.

space flight ▶ noun a journey through space.
■ [mass noun] space travel.

space frame ▶ noun a three-dimensional structural framework which is designed to behave as an integral unit and to withstand loads applied at any point.

space group ▶ noun Crystallography any of 230 symmetry groups used to classify crystal structures.

space heater ▶ noun a self-contained appliance for heating an enclosed space within a building.
– DERIVATIVES **space-heated** adjective, **space heating** noun.

space lattice ▶ noun Crystallography a regular, indefinitely repeated array of points in three dimensions in which the points lie at the intersections of three sets of parallel equidistant planes.

spaceman ▶ noun (pl. **-men**) a male astronaut.

space opera ▶ noun informal, chiefly US a novel, film, or television programme set in outer space, typically of a simplistic and melodramatic nature.

spaceplane ▶ noun an aircraft that takes off and lands conventionally but is capable of entry into orbit or travel through space.

spaceport ▶ noun a base from which spacecraft are launched.

space probe ▶ noun see **PROBE**.

space race ▶ noun (**the space race**) the competition between nations regarding achievements in the field of space exploration.

space rocket ▶ noun a rocket designed to travel through space or to launch a spacecraft.

spaceship ▶ noun a spacecraft, especially one controlled by a crew.

spaceship earth ▶ noun [in sing.] the world considered as possessing finite resources common to all humankind.

space shot ▶ noun the launch of a spacecraft and its subsequent progress in space.

space shuttle ▶ noun a rocket-launched spacecraft able to land like an unpowered aircraft, used to make repeated journeys between the earth and earth orbit.

space station ▶ noun a large artificial satellite used as a long-term base for manned operations in space.

spacesuit ▶ noun a garment designed to allow an astronaut to survive in space.

space telescope ▶ noun an astronomical telescope that operates in space by remote control, to avoid interference by the earth's atmosphere.

space–time ▶ noun [mass noun] Physics the concepts of time and three-dimensional space regarded as fused in a four-dimensional continuum.

space travel ▶ noun [mass noun] travel through outer space.
– DERIVATIVES **space traveller** noun.

space vehicle ▶ noun a spacecraft.

space walk ▶ noun a period of physical activity engaged in by an astronaut in space outside a spacecraft.

space warp ▶ noun an imaginary or hypothetical distortion of space–time that enables space travellers to travel faster than light or otherwise make journeys contrary to the laws of physics.

spacewoman ▶ noun (pl. **-women**) a female astronaut.

spacey (also **spacy**) ▶ adjective (**spacier**, **spaciest**) informal out of touch with reality: *I remember babbling, high and spacey.*
■ (of popular, especially electronic music) drifting and ethereal.

spacial ▶ adjective variant spelling of **SPATIAL**.

spacious ▶ adjective (especially of a room or building) having ample space.
– DERIVATIVES **spaciously** adverb, **spaciousness** noun.
– ORIGIN late Middle English: from Old French *spacios* or Latin *spatiosus*, from *spatium* (see **SPACE**).

spackle /ˈspak(ə)l/ ▶ noun [mass noun] N. Amer. trademark a compound used to fill cracks in plaster and produce a smooth surface before decoration.
▶ verb [with obj.] repair (a surface) or fill (a hole or crack) with spackle.
– ORIGIN 1920s: perhaps a blend of **SPARKLE** and German *Spachtel* 'putty knife, mastic'.

spade[1] ▶ noun a tool with a sharp-edged, typically rectangular, metal blade and a long handle, used for digging or cutting earth, sand, turf, etc.
■ a tool of a similar shape for another purpose, especially one for removing the blubber from a whale.
▶ verb [with obj.] dig over (ground) with a spade: *while spading the soil, I think of the flowers.*
■ [with obj. and adverbial of direction] move (soil) with a spade: *earth is spaded into the grave.*
– PHRASES **call a spade a spade** speak plainly without avoiding unpleasant or embarrassing issues.
– DERIVATIVES **spadeful** noun (pl. **-fuls**).
– ORIGIN Old English *spadu*, *spada*, of Germanic origin; related to Dutch *spade*, German *Spaten*, also to Greek *spathē* 'blade, paddle'.

spade[2] ▶ noun **1** (**spades**) one of the four suits in a conventional pack of playing cards, denoted by a black inverted heart-shaped figure with a small stalk.
■ (**a spade**) a card of this suit.
2 informal, offensive a black person.
– PHRASES **in spades** informal to a very high degree: *he got his revenge now in spades.*
– ORIGIN late 16th cent.: from Italian *spade*, plural of *spada* 'sword', via Latin from Greek *spathē*; compare with **SPADE**[1].

spade beard ▶ noun an oblong-shaped beard.

spadefish ▶ noun (pl. same or **-fishes**) a marine fish with an almost disc-shaped body. It lives in tropical inshore waters, where it often forms schools.
● *Chaetodipterus* and other genera, family Ephippidae: several species, including the western Atlantic *C. faber*.

spadefoot (also **spadefoot toad**) ▶ noun (pl. **spadefoots**) a plump, short-legged burrowing toad with a prominent sharp-edged tubercle on the hind feet, native to North America and Europe.
● Family Pelobatidae: several genera, including *Scaphiophus* (of America) and *Pelobates* (of Europe), and several species, in particular *P. fuscus*.

spade foot ▶ noun a square enlargement at the end of a chair leg.

spade guinea ▶ noun a guinea of George III's reign with a spade-shaped shield on the reverse.

spadework ▶ noun [mass noun] hard or routine preparatory work.

spadille /spəˈdɪl/ ▶ noun (in the card games ombre and quadrille) the ace of spades.
– ORIGIN late 17th cent.: from French, from Spanish *espadilla*, diminutive of *espada* 'sword' (see **SPADE**[2]).

spadix /ˈspeɪdɪks/ ▶ noun (pl. **spadices** /-siːz/) **1** Botany a spike of minute flowers closely arranged round a fleshy axis and typically enclosed in a spathe, characteristic of the arums.
2 Zoology (in certain invertebrates) a part or organ which is more or less conical in shape, e.g. a group of connected tentacles in a nautiloid.
– ORIGIN mid 18th cent.: via Latin from Greek, literally 'palm branch'.

spae /speɪ/ ▶ verb [with obj.] Scottish predict: [with clause] *some Finns had spaed that he should settle in Iceland.*
– ORIGIN Middle English: from Old Norse *spá*, of unknown origin.

spaetzle /ˈʃpɛtslə, ˈʃpɛts(ə)l/ (also **spätzle**) ▶ plural noun [treated as sing. or pl.] small dumplings of a type made in southern Germany and Alsace, consisting of seasoned dough poached in boiling water.
– ORIGIN from German dialect *Spätzle*, literally 'little sparrows'.

spaewife ▶ noun Scottish a woman who is believed to be able to predict the future.

spag bol informal ▶ **abbreviation for** spaghetti Bolognese.

spaghetti /spəˈgɛti/ ▶ **plural noun** pasta made in solid strings, between macaroni and vermicelli in thickness.
– ORIGIN Italian, plural of the diminutive of *spago* 'string'.

spaghetti Bolognese /ˌbɒləˈneɪz/ ▶ **noun** [mass noun] spaghetti served with a sauce of minced beef, tomato, onion, and herbs.
– ORIGIN Italian, literally 'spaghetti of Bologna'.

spaghettification /ˌspagɛˈti:ni/ ▶ **noun** [mass noun] Physics the process by which (in some theories) an object would be stretched and ripped apart by gravitational forces on falling into a black hole.

spaghettini /ˌspagɛˈti:ni/ ▶ **plural noun** pasta in the form of strings of thin spaghetti.
– ORIGIN Italian, diminutive of *spaghetti* 'little strings' (see **SPAGHETTI**).

spaghetti strap ▶ **noun** a thin shoulder strap on an item of women's clothing.

spaghetti western ▶ **noun** informal a western film made cheaply in Europe by an Italian director.

spahi /ˈspɑːhiː/ ▶ **noun** historical **1** a member of the Turkish irregular cavalry.
2 a member of the Algerian cavalry in French service.
– ORIGIN mid 16th cent.: from Turkish *sipahi*, from Persian *sipāhī* (see **SEPOY**).

Spain a country in SW Europe, occupying the greater part of the Iberian peninsula; pop. 39,045,000 (est. 1991); languages, Spanish (official), Catalan; capital, Madrid. Spanish name **España**.

> Spain was dominated by the Moors from about 718 until the rise of independent Christian kingdoms, notably Aragon and Castile, in the medieval period; the last Moorish stronghold, Granada, was won back in the late 15th century. Under the Habsburg kings, 16th-century Spain became the dominant European power, building up a huge empire in America and elsewhere; most of this was lost in the early 19th century. The Spanish Civil War (1936–9) was followed by the establishment of a Fascist dictatorship under General Franco; after his death in 1975 a constitutional monarchy was re-established. Spain became a member of the EC in 1986.

spake archaic or poetic/literary past of **SPEAK**.

spall /spɔːl/ ▶ **verb** [with obj.] break (ore, rock, or stone) into smaller pieces, especially in preparation for sorting.
■ [no obj.] (of ore, rock, or stone) break off in fragments: *cracks below the surface cause slabs of material to spall off.*
▶ **noun** a splinter or chip, especially of rock.
– ORIGIN late Middle English (as a noun): of unknown origin. The verb dates from the mid 18th cent.

Spallanzani /ˌspalanˈzɑːni/, Lazzaro (1729–99), Italian physiologist and biologist. He is known today for his experiments in subjects such as the circulation of the blood and the digestive system of animals. He also disproved the theory of spontaneous generation.

spallation /spɔːˈleɪʃ(ə)n/ ▶ **noun** [mass noun] **1** Physics the break-up of a bombarded nucleus into several parts.
2 Geology separation of fragments from the surface of a rock, especially by interaction with a compression wave.

spalpeen /spalˈpiːn/ ▶ **noun** Irish a rascal.
– ORIGIN late 18th cent. (denoting a migratory farm worker): from Irish *spailpín*, of unknown origin.

spalted /ˈspɔːltɪd/ ▶ **adjective** (of wood) containing blackish irregular lines as a result of fungal decay, and sometimes used to produce a decorative surface.
– ORIGIN 1970s: from dialect *spalt* 'to split, splinter' + **-ED**[1].

spam ▶ **noun** [mass noun] **1** trademark a tinned meat product made mainly from ham.
2 irrelevant or inappropriate messages sent on the Internet to a large number of newsgroups or users.
▶ **verb** [with obj.] send the same message indiscriminately to (large numbers of newsgroups or users) on the Internet.
– DERIVATIVES **spammer** noun.
– ORIGIN 1930s: apparently from *sp(iced h)am*. The Internet sense apparently derives from a sketch by the British 'Monty Python' comedy group, set in a café in which every item on the menu includes spam.

span[1] ▶ **noun** the full extent of something from end to end; the amount of space that something covers: *a warehouse with a clear span of 28 feet.*
■ the length of time for which something lasts: *a short concentration span.* ■ the wingspan of an aircraft or a bird. ■ an arch or part of a bridge between piers or supports. ■ the maximum distance between the tips of the thumb and little finger, taken as the basis of a measurement equal to 9 inches. ■ archaic a short distance or time.
▶ **verb** (**spanned**, **spanning**) [with obj.] (of a bridge, arch, etc.) extend from side to side of: *the stream was spanned by a narrow bridge.*
■ extend across (a period of time or a range of subjects): *their interests span almost all the conventional disciplines.* ■ cover or enclose with the length of one's hand: *her waist was slender enough for him to span with his hands.*
– ORIGIN Old English, 'distance between the tips of the thumb and little finger', of Germanic origin; reinforced in Middle English by Old French *espan*.

span[2] ▶ **noun 1** Nautical a rope with its ends fastened at different points to a spar or other object in order to provide a purchase.
2 a team of people or animals, in particular:
■ N. Amer. a matched pair of horses, mules, or oxen. ■ S. African a team of two or more pairs of oxen. ■ S. African a gang, especially a work gang of prisoners.
3 (**a span**) S. African informal a lot: *thanks a span.*
▶ **verb** [with obj.] S. African yoke (an animal): *he spanned his donkeys to the cart.*
– ORIGIN mid 16th cent. (as a verb): from Dutch or Low German *spannen*. The noun (originally in nautical use) dates from the mid 18th cent.

span[3] ▶ **adjective** see **SPICK AND SPAN**.

span[4] chiefly archaic past of **SPIN**.

spanakopita /ˌspanəˈkɒpɪtə/ ▶ **noun** (in Greek cooking) a filo pastry stuffed with spinach and feta cheese.
– ORIGIN modern Greek, literally 'spinach pie'.

spandex ▶ **noun** [mass noun] trademark a type of stretchy polyurethane fabric.
– ORIGIN 1950s: an arbitrary formation from **EXPAND**.

spandrel /ˈspandrɪl/ ▶ **noun** Architecture the almost triangular space between one side of the outer curve of an arch, a wall, and the ceiling or framework.
■ the space between the shoulders of adjoining arches and the ceiling or moulding above.
– ORIGIN late Middle English: perhaps from Anglo-Norman French *spaund(e)re*, or from *espaundre* 'expand'.

spandrel wall ▶ **noun** a wall built on the curve of an arch, filling in the spandrel.

spang ▶ **adverb** US informal directly; completely: *looking the General right spang in the eye.*
– ORIGIN mid 19th cent.: of unknown origin.

spangle ▶ **noun** a small thin piece of glittering material, typically used in quantity to ornament a dress; a sequin.
■ a spot of bright colour or light.
▶ **verb** [with obj.] [usu. as adj. **spangled**] cover with spangles or other small sparkling objects: *a spangled Christmas doll.*
– DERIVATIVES **spangly** adjective.
– ORIGIN late Middle English: diminutive from obsolete *spang* 'glittering ornament', from Middle Dutch *spange* 'buckle'.

spangle gall ▶ **noun** a reddish disc-shaped gall that forms on the undersides of oak leaves in response to the developing larva of a gall wasp. It results from eggs laid in the summer and alternates with the currant gall.
• The wasp is *Neuroterus quercusbaccarum*, family Cynipidae.

Spanglish /ˈspaŋglɪʃ/ ▶ **noun** [mass noun] hybrid language combining words and idioms from both Spanish and English.

Spaniard /ˈspanjəd/ ▶ **noun 1** a native or national of Spain, or a person of Spanish descent.
2 a spiny rock plant of the parsley family, native to New Zealand.
• Genus *Aciphylla*, family Umbelliferae.
– ORIGIN Middle English: shortening of Old French *Espaignart*, from *Espaigne* 'Spain'.

spaniel ▶ **noun** a dog of a breed with a long silky coat and drooping ears.
■ used in similes and metaphors as a symbol of devotion or obsequiousness: *I followed my uncles around as faithfully as any spaniel.*
– ORIGIN Middle English: from Old French *espaigneul* 'Spanish (dog)', from Latin *Hispaniolus* 'Spanish'.

Spanish ▶ **adjective** of or relating to Spain, its people, or its language.
▶ **noun 1** [as plural noun **the Spanish**] the people of Spain.
2 [mass noun] the main language of Spain and of much of Central and South America (except Brazil) and several other countries. It is a Romance language with over 300 million speakers worldwide.
– DERIVATIVES **Spanishness** noun.
– ORIGIN Middle English: from **SPAIN** + **-ISH**[1], with later shortening of the first vowel.

Spanish America the parts of America once colonized by Spaniards and in which Spanish is still generally spoken, including most of Central and South America (except Brazil) and part of the Caribbean.

Spanish-American War a war between Spain and the United States in the Caribbean and the Philippines in 1898. American public opinion having been aroused by Spanish atrocities in Cuba and the destruction of the warship *Maine* in Santiago harbour, the US declared war and successfully invaded Cuba, Puerto Rico, and the Philippines, all of which Spain gave up by the Treaty of Paris (1898).

Spanish Armada see **ARMADA**.

Spanish bayonet ▶ **noun** a yucca with long stiff sword-shaped leaves and tall slender spikes of white flowers, found from the southern US to the Caribbean.
• *Yucca aloifolia*, family Agavaceae.

Spanish broom ▶ **noun** a Mediterranean broom with fragrant yellow flowers and almost leafless stems which were formerly used in basketry.
• *Spartium junceum*, family Leguminosae.

Spanish chestnut ▶ **noun** see **CHESTNUT** (sense 2).

Spanish Civil War the conflict (1936–9) between Nationalist forces (including monarchists and members of the Falange Party) and Republicans (including socialists and Communists and Catalan and Basque separatists) in Spain.

> It began with a military uprising against the leftist, Republican Popular Front government in July 1936. In bitter fighting the Nationalists, led by General Franco, gradually gained control of the countryside but failed to capture the capital, Madrid. After periods of prolonged stalemate, Franco finally succeeded in capturing Barcelona and Madrid in early 1939. He established a Fascist dictatorship that lasted until his death in 1975.

Spanish-Colonial ▶ **adjective** denoting a style of architecture characteristic of Spanish America.

Spanish flu (also **Spanish influenza**) ▶ **noun** [mass noun] influenza caused by an influenza virus of type A, in particular that of the pandemic which began in 1918.

Spanish fly ▶ **noun** a bright green European blister beetle with a mousy smell.
• *Lytta vesicatoria*, family Meloidae.
■ [mass noun] a toxic preparation of the dried bodies of these beetles, formerly used in medicine as a counterirritant and sometimes taken as an aphrodisiac. Also called **CANTHARIDES**.

Spanish guitar ▶ **noun** the standard six-stringed acoustic guitar, used especially for classical and folk music.

Spanish ibex (also **Spanish goat**) ▶ **noun** see **IBEX**.

Spanish Inquisition an ecclesiastical court established in 1478 and directed originally against converts from Judaism and Islam but later also against Protestants. It operated with great severity and was not suppressed until the early 19th century.

Spanish mackerel ▶ **noun** a large edible game fish related to the mackerel.
• Genus *Scomberomorus*, family Scombridae: several species, in particular *S. maculatus* of the tropical Atlantic, and *S. commerson* of the Indo-Pacific.

Spanish Main the former name for the NW coast of South America between the Orinoco River and Panama, and adjoining parts of the Caribbean Sea.

Spanish Mission ▶ **noun** [as modifier] denoting a style of architecture characteristic of the Catholic missions in Spanish America.

Spanish moss ▶ **noun** [mass noun] a tropical American plant which grows as silvery-green

S

festoons on trees, obtaining water and nutrients directly through its surface.
● *Tillandsia usneoides*, family Bromeliaceae. See also **AIR PLANT**.

Spanish needles ▸ noun an American bur-marigold with prickly fruit.
● *Bidens bipinnata*, family Compositae.

Spanish omelette ▸ noun an omelette containing chopped vegetables, especially potatoes, often served open rather than folded.

Spanish onion ▸ noun a large onion with a mild flavour.

Spanish practice ▸ noun another term for **OLD SPANISH CUSTOM**.

Spanish rice ▸ noun [mass noun] a dish of rice with onions, peppers, tomatoes, and other vegetables, often coloured and flavoured with saffron.

Spanish Sahara former name (1958–75) for **WESTERN SAHARA**.

Spanish Succession, War of the a European war (1701–14), provoked by the death of the Spanish king Charles II without issue. The Grand Alliance of Britain, the Netherlands, and the Holy Roman emperor threw back a French invasion of the Low Countries, and, although the Peace of Utrecht confirmed the accession of a Bourbon king in Spain, prevented Spain and France from being united under one crown.

Spanish Town a town in Jamaica, west of Kingston, the second largest town and a former capital of Jamaica; pop. 110,380 (1991).

Spanish windlass ▸ noun a device for tightening a rope or cable by twisting it using a stick as a lever.

spank ▸ verb [with obj.] slap with one's open hand or a flat object, especially on the buttocks as a punishment: *she was spanked for spilling ink on the carpet.*
▸ noun a slap of this type.
– ORIGIN early 18th cent.: perhaps imitative.

spanker ▸ noun 1 a fore-and-aft sail set on the after side of a ship's mast, especially the mizzenmast.
2 informal, dated a very fine person or thing.

spanking ▸ adjective 1 (especially of a horse or its gait) lively; brisk: *a spanking trot.*
2 informal very good: *we had a spanking time.*
■fine and impressive: *a spanking white Rolls Royce* | [as submodifier] *a spanking new conference centre.*
▸ noun [in sing.] an act of slapping, especially on the buttocks as a punishment for children.

spanner ▸ noun chiefly Brit. a tool with a shaped opening or jaws for gripping and turning a nut or bolt.
– PHRASES **spanner in the works** see **WORK**.
– ORIGIN late 18th cent.: from German *spannen* 'draw tight' + **-ER**[1].

span of control ▸ noun the area of activity, number of functions, people, or things for which an individual or organization is responsible.

spanspek /'spanspɛk/ ▸ noun South African term for **CANTALOUPE**.
– ORIGIN Afrikaans.

spansule /'spansjuːl/ ▸ noun trademark a capsule which when swallowed releases one or more medicinal drugs over a set period.
– ORIGIN mid 20th cent.: blend of the noun **SPAN**[1] and **CAPSULE**.

span-worm ▸ noun North American term for **LOOPER**.

spar[1] ▸ noun a thick, strong pole such as is used for a mast or yard on a ship.
■the main longitudinal beam of an aeroplane wing.
– ORIGIN Middle English: shortening of Old French *esparre*, or from Old Norse *sperra*; related to Dutch *spar* and German *Sparren*.

spar[2] ▸ verb (**sparred**, **sparring**) [no obj.] make the motions of boxing without landing heavy blows, as a form of training: *one contestant broke his nose while sparring.*
■engage in argument, typically of a kind that is prolonged or repeated but not violent: *mother and daughter spar regularly over drink, drugs, and career.* ■ (of a gamecock) fight with the feet or spurs.
▸ noun 1 a period or bout of sparring.
2 informal a close friend.
– ORIGIN Old English *sperran*, *spyrran* 'strike out', of unknown origin; compare with Old Norse *sperrask* 'kick out'.

spar[3] ▸ noun [usu. in combination or with modifier] a

crystalline, easily cleavable, translucent or transparent mineral.
– DERIVATIVES **sparry** adjective.
– ORIGIN late 16th cent.: from Middle Low German; related to Old English *spærstān* 'gypsum'.

sparable /'sparəb(ə)l/ ▸ noun a headless nail used for the soles and heels of shoes.
– ORIGIN early 17th cent.: contraction of *sparrow-bill*, in the same sense.

sparagmos /spə'ragməs/ ▸ noun [mass noun] the dismemberment of a victim, forming a part of some ancient rituals and represented in Greek myths and tragedies.
– ORIGIN Greek, literally 'tearing'.

sparaxis /spə'raksɪs/ ▸ noun a South African plant of the iris family, with slender sword-shaped leaves and showy multicoloured flowers.
● Genus *Sparaxis*, family Iridaceae.
– ORIGIN modern Latin, from Greek, literally 'laceration', from *sparassein* 'to tear'.

spar buoy ▸ noun a buoy made of a spar with one end moored so that the other stands up.

spar deck ▸ noun the light upper deck of a vessel.

spare ▸ adjective 1 additional to what is required for ordinary use: *few people had spare cash for inessentials.*
■not currently in use or occupied: *a spare seat.*
2 with no excess fat; thin: *a spare, bearded figure.*
■elegantly simple: *her clothes are smart and spare in style.*
▸ noun 1 an item kept in case another item of the same type is lost, broken, or worn out.
2 (in tenpin bowling) an act of knocking down all the pins with two balls.
▸ verb 1 [with two objs] give (something of which one has enough) to (someone); afford to give to: *she asked if I could spare her a bob or two.*
■make free or available: *I'm sure you can spare me a moment.* ■ [no obj.] archaic be frugal: *but some will spend, and some will spare.*
2 [with obj.] refrain from killing, injuring, or distressing: *there was no way the men would spare her.*
■[with two objs] refrain from inflicting (something) on (someone): *the country had until now been spared the violence occurring elsewhere.* ■ (**spare oneself**) [with negative] try to ensure or satisfy one's own comfort or needs: *in her concern to help others, she has never spared herself.*
– PHRASES **go spare** Brit. informal 1 become extremely angry or distraught. 2 be unwanted or not needed and therefore available for use: *I didn't have much money going spare.* **spare someone's blushes** see **BLUSH**. **spare no expense** (or **no expense spared**) be prepared to pay any amount (used to indicate the importance of achieving something). **spare the rod and spoil the child** see **ROD**. **spare a thought for** remember: *spare a thought for our volunteer group at Christmas.* **to spare** left over: *that turkey will feed ten people with some to spare.*
– DERIVATIVES **sparely** adverb, **spareness** noun, **sparer** noun (rare).
– ORIGIN Old English *spær* 'not plentiful, meagre', *sparian* 'refrain from injuring', 'refrain from using', of Germanic origin; related to Dutch and German *sparen* 'to spare'.

spare-part surgery ▸ noun [mass noun] informal the treatment of organ failure by surgical transplantation or the insertion of artificial replacements.

spare rib ▸ noun (usu. **spare ribs**) a closely trimmed rib of pork.
– ORIGIN late 16th cent.: probably from Middle Low German *ribbesper* (by transposition of the syllables), and associated with the adjective **SPARE**.

spare time ▸ noun [mass noun] time which is not taken up by one's usual activities; leisure time.

spare tyre ▸ noun an extra tyre carried in a motor vehicle for emergencies.
■informal a roll of fat round a person's waist.

sparge /spɑːdʒ/ chiefly technical ▸ verb [with obj.] moisten by sprinkling with water, especially in brewing.
▸ noun [mass noun] the action of sprinkling or splashing.
■[count noun] a spray of hot water, especially water sprinkled over malt when brewing.
– DERIVATIVES **sparger** noun.
– ORIGIN late 16th cent. (as a verb in the sense 'sprinkle (water) about'): apparently from Latin *spargere* 'to sprinkle'. The current senses date from the early 19th cent.

sparid /'sparɪd, 'spεɪrɪd/ ▸ noun Zoology a fish of the

sea bream family (Sparidae), whose members are marine and have deep bodies with long spiny dorsal fins.
– ORIGIN 1960s: from modern Latin *Sparidae* (plural), via Latin from Greek *sparos* 'sea bream'.

sparing ▸ adjective moderate; economical: *physicians advised sparing use of the ointment.*
– DERIVATIVES **sparingly** adverb, **sparingness** noun.

Spark, Dame Muriel (b.1918), Scottish novelist. Notable works: *The Prime of Miss Jean Brodie* (1961) and *The Mandelbaum Gate* (1965).

spark[1] ▸ noun 1 a small fiery particle thrown off from a fire, alight in ashes, or produced by striking together two hard surfaces such as stone or metal.
■a light produced by a sudden disruptive electrical discharge through the air. ■ a discharge such as this serving to ignite the explosive mixture in an internal-combustion engine. ■ a small bright object or point: *there was a spark of light.* ■ a trace of a specified quality or intense feeling: *a tiny spark of anger flared within her.* ■ a sense of liveliness and excitement: *there was a spark between them at their first meeting.* ■ (also **Spark** or **Sparks**) informal used in the armed forces as a nickname for a radio operator or an electrician.
▸ verb 1 [no obj.] emit sparks of fire or electricity: *the ignition sparks as soon as the gas is turned on.*
■produce sparks at the point where an electric circuit is interrupted.
2 [with obj.] ignite: *the explosion sparked a fire.*
■figurative provide the stimulus for (a dramatic event or process): *the severity of the plan sparked off street protests.*
– PHRASES **spark out** Brit. informal completely unconscious: *I think he would knock Bowe spark out.* **sparks fly** an encounter becomes heated or lively. **strike sparks off each other** (or **one another**) (of two or more people) creatively inspire each other while working on something.
– DERIVATIVES **sparkless** adjective, **sparky** adjective.
– ORIGIN Old English *spærca*, *spearca*, of unknown origin.

spark[2] archaic ▸ noun a lively young fellow.
▸ verb [no obj.] engage in courtship.
– DERIVATIVES **sparkish** adjective.
– ORIGIN early 16th cent.: probably a figurative use of **SPARK**[1].

spark chamber ▸ noun Physics an apparatus designed to show ionizing particles.

spark gap ▸ noun a space between electrical terminals across which a transient discharge passes.

sparking plug ▸ noun Brit. another term for **SPARK PLUG**.

sparkle ▸ verb [no obj.] shine brightly with flashes of light: *her earrings sparkled as she turned her head* | [as adj. **sparkling**] *her sparkling blue eyes.*
■be vivacious and witty: *after a glass of wine, she began to sparkle.* ■ [as adj. **sparkling**] (of wine and similar drinks) effervescent.
▸ noun a glittering flash of light: *there was a sparkle in his eyes.*
■[mass noun] vivacity and wit: *she's got a kind of sparkle.*
– DERIVATIVES **sparklingly** adverb, **sparkly** adjective.
– ORIGIN Middle English: frequentative (verb) or diminutive (noun) of **SPARK**[1].

sparkler ▸ noun 1 a thing that sparkles, in particular:
■a hand-held firework that emits sparks. ■ informal a gemstone, especially a diamond. ■ informal a sparkling wine.
2 a nozzle attached to the spout on a beer pump to give the beer a frothy head.

spark plug ▸ noun a device for firing the explosive mixture in an internal-combustion engine.

sparling ▸ noun an edible European smelt (fish) which migrates into fresh water to spawn.
● *Osmerus eperlanus*, family Osmeridae.
– ORIGIN Middle English: shortening of Old French *esperlinge*, of Germanic origin.

sparring partner ▸ noun a boxer employed to engage in sparring with another as training.
■a person with whom one continually argues or contends.

sparrow ▸ noun 1 a small finch-like Old World bird related to the weaver birds, typically with brown and grey plumage.
● Family Passeridae (or Ploceidae): four genera, in particular *Passer*, and many species, e.g. the cosmopolitan **house sparrow** (*P. domesticus*).

2 [usu. with modifier] any of a number of birds that resemble true sparrows in size or colour:
• an American bunting (many genera in the subfamily Emberizinae, family Emberizidae). • a waxbill, in particular the Java sparrow. • see **HEDGE SPARROW**.
– ORIGIN Old English *spearwa*, of Germanic origin.

sparrow fart ▶ **noun** (in phrase **at sparrow fart**) informal very early in the morning.

sparrow grass ▶ **noun** dialect term for **ASPARAGUS**.
– ORIGIN mid 17th cent.: corruption (by folk etymology) of obsolete *sparagus* 'asparagus'.

sparrowhawk ▶ **noun** a small Old World woodland hawk that preys on small birds.
• Genus *Accipiter*, family Accipitridae: many species, in particular the widespread **northern sparrowhawk** (*A. nisus*).
■ N. Amer. the American kestrel (see **KESTREL**).

sparse ▶ **adjective** thinly dispersed or scattered: *areas of sparse population*.
■ austere; meagre: *an elegantly sparse chamber*.
– DERIVATIVES **sparsely** adverb, **sparseness** noun, **sparsity** noun.
– ORIGIN early 18th cent. (used to descrbe writing in the sense 'widely spaced'): from Latin *sparsus*, past participle of *spargere* 'scatter'.

Sparta /ˈspɑːtə/ a city in the southern Peloponnese in Greece, capital of the department of Laconia; pop. 13,000 (1991). It was a powerful city state in the 5th century BC, defeating its rival Athens in the Peloponnesian War to become the leading city of Greece.

Spartacist /ˈspɑːtəsɪst, -təkɪst/ ▶ **noun** a member of the Spartacus League.

Spartacus /ˈspɑːtəkəs/ (died *c.*71 BC), Thracian slave and gladiator. He led a revolt against Rome in 73, but was eventually defeated by Crassus in 71 and killed in battle.

Spartacus League a German revolutionary socialist group founded in 1916 by Rosa Luxemburg and Karl Liebknecht (1871–1919). At the end of 1918 the group became the German Communist Party, which in 1919 organized an uprising in Berlin that was brutally crushed.
– ORIGIN *Spartacus* was adopted as a pseudonym by Karl Liebknecht.

Spartan[1] ▶ **adjective** of or relating to Sparta in ancient Greece.
■ showing the indifference to comfort or luxury traditionally associated with ancient Sparta: *spartan but adequate rooms*.
▶ **noun** a citizen of Sparta.

Spartan[2] ▶ **noun** a Canadian dessert apple of a variety with crisp white flesh and maroon-flushed yellow skin.

spartina /spɑːˈtʌɪnə, -ˈtiːnə/ (also **spartina grass**) ▶ **noun** a plant of a genus that comprises the cordgrasses.
• Genus *Spartina*, family Gramineae.
– ORIGIN modern Latin, from Greek *spartinē* 'rope'.

spar tree ▶ **noun** Forestry a tree or other tall structure to which cables are attached for hauling logs.

spasm ▶ **noun** a sudden involuntary muscular contraction or convulsive movement.
■ a sudden and brief spell of an activity or sensation: *a spasm of coughing woke him*. ■ [mass noun] prolonged involuntary muscle contraction: *the airways in the lungs go into spasm*.
– ORIGIN late Middle English: from Old French *spasme*, or via Latin from Greek *spasmos*, *spasma*, from *span* 'pull'.

spasmodic ▶ **adjective** occurring or done in brief, irregular bursts: *spasmodic fighting continued*.
■ caused by, subject to, or in the nature of a spasm or spasms: *a spasmodic cough*.
– DERIVATIVES **spasmodically** adverb.
– ORIGIN late 17th cent.: from modern Latin *spasmodicus*, from Greek *spasmōdēs*, from *spasma* (see **SPASM**).

spasmolytic /ˌspazmə(ʊ)ˈlɪtɪk/ Medicine ▶ **adjective** (of a drug or treatment) able to relieve spasm of smooth muscle.
▶ **noun** a drug of this kind.

spasmophilia /ˌspazmə(ʊ)ˈfɪlɪə/ ▶ **noun** [mass noun] Medicine undue tendency of the muscles to contract, caused by ionic imbalance in the blood, or associated with anxiety disorders.
– DERIVATIVES **spasmophile** noun.

Spassky /ˈspaski/, Boris (Vasilevich) (b.1937), Russian chess player, world champion 1969–72. He lived in Paris from 1975 and played for France in the 1984 Olympics.

spastic ▶ **adjective** relating to or affected by muscle spasm.
■ relating to or denoting a form of muscular weakness (**spastic paralysis**) typical of cerebral palsy, caused by damage to the brain or spinal cord and involving reflex resistance to passive movement of the limbs and difficulty in initiating and controlling muscular movement. ■ (of a person) suffering from cerebral palsy. ■ informal, offensive incompetent or uncoordinated.
▶ **noun** a person suffering from cerebral palsy.
■ informal, offensive an incompetent or uncoordinated person.
– DERIVATIVES **spastically** adverb, **spasticity** noun.
– ORIGIN mid 18th cent.: via Latin from Greek *spastikos* 'pulling', from *span* 'pull'.

USAGE The word **spastic** has been used in medical senses since the 18th century. In the 1970s and 1980s it became a term of abuse, used mainly by schoolchildren, directed towards any person regarded as incompetent or physically uncoordinated. Nowadays, the use of the word **spastic**, whether as a noun or as an adjective, is likely to cause offence, and it is preferable to use phrasing such as *people suffering from* ***cerebral palsy*** instead.

spat[1] past and past participle of **SPIT**[1].

spat[2] ▶ **noun 1** (usu. **spats**) historical a short cloth gaiter covering the instep and ankle.
2 a cover for the upper part of an aircraft wheel.
– ORIGIN early 19th cent.: abbreviation of **SPATTERDASH**.

spat[3] informal ▶ **noun** a petty quarrel.
▶ **verb** (**spatted**, **spatting**) [no obj.] quarrel pettily.
– ORIGIN early 19th cent. (originally a US colloquial usage): probably imitative.

spat[4] ▶ **noun** [mass noun] the spawn or larvae of shellfish, especially oysters.
– ORIGIN mid 17th cent.: from Anglo-Norman French, of unknown ultimate origin.

spatchcock ▶ **noun** a chicken or game bird split open and grilled.
▶ **verb** [with obj.] split open (a poultry or game bird) ready for grilling.
■ informal, chiefly Brit. add (a phrase, sentence, clause, etc.) in a context where it is inappropriate: *a new clause has been spatchcocked into the Bill*.
– ORIGIN late 18th cent. (originally an Irish usage): perhaps related to the noun **DISPATCH** + **COCK**[1], but compare with **SPITCHCOCK**.

spate ▶ **noun 1** [usu. in sing.] a large number of similar things or events appearing or occurring in quick succession: *a spate of attacks on holidaymakers*.
2 chiefly Brit. a sudden flood in a river, especially one caused by heavy rains or melting snow.
– PHRASES **in (full) spate** (of a river) overflowing due to a sudden flood. ■ figurative (of a person or action) at the height of activity: *work was in full spate*.
– ORIGIN late Middle English (originally Scots and northern English in the sense 'flood, inundation'): of unknown origin.

spathe /speɪð/ ▶ **noun** Botany a large sheathing bract enclosing the flower cluster of certain plants, especially the spadix of arums and palms.
– ORIGIN late 18th cent.: via Latin from Greek *spathē* 'broad blade'.

spathic iron ore /ˈspaθɪk/ ▶ **noun** another term for **SIDERITE** (in sense 1).
– ORIGIN mid 19th cent.: *spathic* from *spath*, a rare variant of **SPAR**[3], + **-IC**.

spathulate /ˈspatjʊlət/ ▶ **adjective** Botany & Zoology variant spelling of **SPATULATE**.

spatial /ˈspeɪʃ(ə)l/ (also **spacial**) ▶ **adjective** of or relating to space: *the spatial distribution of population*.
– DERIVATIVES **spatiality** noun, **spatialization** (also **-isation**) noun, **spatialize** (also **-ise**) verb, **spatially** adverb.
– ORIGIN mid 19th cent.: from Latin *spatium* 'space' + **-AL**.

spatio-temporal /ˌspeɪʃɪəʊˈtɛmp(ə)r(ə)l/ ▶ **adjective** Physics & Philosophy belonging to both space and time or to space-time.
– DERIVATIVES **spatio-temporally** adverb.

Spätlese /ˈʃpɛtˌleɪzə/ ▶ **noun** (pl. **Spätleses** or **Spätlesen**, /-ˌleɪz(ə)n/) [mass noun] a white wine of German origin or style made from grapes harvested late in the season.
– ORIGIN from German, from *spät* 'late' + *Lese* 'picking, vintage'.

spatter ▶ **verb** [with obj.] cover with drops or spots of something: *passing vehicles* ***spattered*** *his shoes and trousers* ***with*** *mud*.
■ scatter or splash (liquid, mud, etc.) over a surface: *he spatters grease all over the cooker*. ■ [no obj.] fall so as to be scattered over an area: *she watched the raindrops spatter down*.
▶ **noun** a spray or splash of something.
■ a sprinkling: *there was a spatter of freckles over her nose*. ■ a short outburst of sound: *the sharp spatter of shots*.
– ORIGIN mid 16th cent. (in the sense 'splutter while speaking'): frequentative, from a base shared by Dutch, Low German *spatten* 'burst, spout'.

spatterdash ▶ **noun** (usu. **spatterdashes**) historical a long gaiter or legging worn to keep stockings or trousers clean, especially when riding.

spatterdock ▶ **noun** N. Amer. a yellow-flowered water lily.
• Genus *Nuphar*, family Nymphaeaceae: several species, in particular *N. advena*.

spatterware ▶ **noun** [mass noun] pottery decorated by sponging with colour; sponged ware.

spatula ▶ **noun** an implement with a broad, flat, blunt blade, used for mixing and spreading things, especially in cooking and painting.
■ a thin, flat wooden or metal instrument used in medical examinations e.g. for holding down the tongue or taking cell samples.
– ORIGIN early 16th cent.: from Latin, variant of *spathula*, diminutive of *spatha* (see **SPATHE**).

spatulate /ˈspatjʊlət/ ▶ **adjective** having a broad, rounded end: *his thick, spatulate fingers*.
■ (also **spathulate**) Botany & Zoology broad at the apex and tapered to the base: *large spatulate leaves*.

spätzle ▶ **plural noun** variant spelling of **SPAETZLE**.

spavin /ˈspavɪn/ ▶ **noun** a disorder of a horse's hock. See **BOG SPAVIN**, **BONE SPAVIN**.
– DERIVATIVES **spavined** adjective.
– ORIGIN late Middle English: shortening of Old French *espavin*, variant of *esparvain*, of Germanic origin.

spawn ▶ **verb** [no obj.] (of a fish, frog, mollusc, crustacean, etc.) release or deposit eggs: *the fish spawn among fine-leaved plants* | [with obj.] *a large brood is spawned*.
■ (**be spawned**) (of a fish, frog, etc.) be laid as eggs. ■ [with obj.] (of a person) produce (offspring, typically offspring regarded as undesirable): *why had she married a man who could spawn a boy like that?* ■ [with obj.] produce or generate, especially in large numbers: *the decade spawned a bewildering variety of books on the forces*.
▶ **noun** [mass noun] the eggs of fish, frogs, etc.: *the fish covers its spawn with gravel*.
■ the process of producing such eggs. ■ the product or offspring of a person or place (used to express distaste or disgust): *the spawn of chaos: demons and sorcerers*. ■ the mycelium of a fungus, especially a cultivated mushroom.
– DERIVATIVES **spawner** noun.
– ORIGIN late Middle English: shortening of Anglo-Norman French *espaundre* 'to shed roe', variant of Old French *espandre* 'pour out', from Latin *expandere* 'expand'.

spay ▶ **verb** [with obj.] (usu. **be spayed**) sterilize (a female animal) by removing the ovaries.
– ORIGIN late Middle English: shortening of Old French *espeer* 'cut with a sword', from *espee* 'sword', from Latin *spatha* (see **SPATHE**).

spaz (also **spazz**) informal, chiefly US ▶ **noun** (pl. **spazzes**) offensive short for **SPASTIC**.
▶ **verb** [no obj.] (**spaz out**) lose physical or emotional control: *if I didn't have it, I'd spaz out*.
– ORIGIN 1960s: abbreviation of **SPASTIC**.

spaza /ˈspɑːzə/ ▶ **noun** (in South Africa) a small unofficial store in a township, often based in a private house.
– ORIGIN township slang, literally 'camouflaged', of unknown origin.

SPCK ▶ **abbreviation** for Society for Promoting Christian Knowledge.

speak ▶ **verb** (past **spoke**; past participle **spoken**) [no obj.] **1** say something in order to convey information, an opinion, or a feeling: *in his agitation he was unable to speak* | *she refused to speak about the incident*.
■ have a conversation: *I wish to* ***speak*** *privately* ***with*** *you* | *I'll* ***speak to*** *him if he rings up*. ■ [with obj.] utter (a word, message, speech, etc.): *patients copy words spoken by the*

S

therapist. ■ [with obj.] communicate in or be able to communicate in (a specified language): *my mother spoke Russian.* ■ make a speech before an audience or a contribution to a debate: *twenty thousand people attended to hear him speak.* ■ (**speak for**) express the views or position of (another person or group): *he claimed to speak for the majority of local people.* ■ convey one's views or position indirectly: *speaking through his solicitor, he refused to join the debate.* ■ (**speak of**) mention or discuss in speech or writing: *the books speak of betrayal.* ■ (of behaviour, a quality, an event, etc.) serve as evidence for something: *her harping on him spoke strongly of a crush* | [with obj.] *his frame spoke tiredness.* ■ [with obj. and infinitive or adverbial] archaic show or manifest (someone or something) to be in a particular state or to possess a certain quality: *she had seen nothing that spoke him of immoral habits.* ■ (of an object that typically makes a sound when it functions) make a characteristic sound: *the gun spoke again.* ■ (of an organ pipe or other musical instrument) make a sound: *insufficient air circulates for the pipes to speak.* ■ (of a hound) bark. ■ [with obj.] Nautical, archaic hail and hold communication with (a ship) at sea.

2 (**speak to**) talk to in order to reprove or advise: *she tried to speak to Seb about his drinking.*

■ talk to in order to give or extract information: *he had spoken to the police.* ■ discuss or comment on formally: *the Church wants to speak to real issues.* ■ appeal or relate to: *the story spoke to him directly.*

– PHRASES **not to speak of** used in introducing a further factor to be considered: *the rent had to be paid, not to speak of school fees.* **nothing** (or **no** —— or **none**) **to speak of** used to indicate that there is some but very little of something: *I've no capital—well, none to speak of.* **something speaks for itself** something's implications are so clear that it needs no supporting evidence or comments: *the figures speak for themselves.* **speak for oneself** give one's own opinions. ■ [in imperative] used to tell someone that what they have said may apply to them but does not apply to others: *'This is such a boring place.' 'Speak for yourself—I like it.'* **speak in tongues** speak in an unknown language during religious worship. **speaking of** used to introduce a statement or question about a topic recently alluded to: *speaking of cost, can I afford to buy it?* **speak one's mind** express one's feelings or opinions frankly. **speak volumes** (of a gesture, circumstance, or object) convey a great deal: *a look that spoke volumes.* ■ be good evidence for: *his record speaks volumes for his determination.* **speak well** (or **ill**) **of** praise (or criticize).

– DERIVATIVES **speakable** adjective.

– ORIGIN Old English *sprecan*, later *specan*, of West Germanic origin; related to Dutch *spreken* and German *sprechen*.

▶ **speak out** (or **up**) express one's feelings or opinions frankly and publicly: *the government will be forthright in speaking out against human rights abuses.*

speak up 1 speak more loudly: *We can't hear you. Speak up!* **2** see **SPEAK OUT**.

speak up for speak in defence or support of: *there was no independent body to speak up for press freedoms.*

-speak ▶ **combining form** forming nouns denoting a manner of speaking, characteristic of a specified field or group: *technospeak.*

– ORIGIN on the pattern of (*New*)*speak*.

speakeasy ▶ **noun** (pl. **-ies**) informal (in the US during Prohibition) an illicit liquor shop or drinking club.

speaker ▶ **noun 1** a person who speaks.

■ a person who delivers a speech or lecture. ■ [usu. with modifier or in combination] a person who speaks a specified language: *he is a fluent English and French speaker.*

2 (**Speaker**) the presiding officer in a legislative assembly, especially the House of Commons.

3 short for **LOUDSPEAKER**.

– DERIVATIVES **speakership** noun (in sense 2).

speakerphone ▶ **noun** chiefly N. Amer. a telephone with a loudspeaker and microphone, which does not need to be held in the hand.

speaking ▶ **noun** [mass noun] the action of conveying information or expressing one's thoughts and feelings in spoken language.

■ the activity of delivering speeches or lectures: *public speaking.*

▶ **adjective** [attrib.] used for or engaged in speech: *you have a clear speaking voice.*

■ conveying meaning as though in words: *she gave him a speaking look.* ■ (of a portrait) so like the subject as to seem to be alive and capable of speech: *a speaking likeness.* ■ [in combination] able to communicate in a specified language: *an English-speaking guide.*

– PHRASES **on speaking terms 1** slightly acquainted. **2** sufficiently friendly to talk to each other: *she parted from her mother barely on speaking terms.* —— **speaking** used to indicate the degree of accuracy intended in a statement or the point of view from which it is made: *broadly speaking, there are three major models for local-central relations.* **speaking in tongues** another term for **GLOSSOLALIA**.

speaking clock ▶ **noun** (**the speaking clock**) Brit. a telephone service giving the correct time in recorded speech.

speaking trumpet ▶ **noun** historical an instrument for making the voice carry, especially at sea.

speaking tube ▶ **noun** a pipe for conveying a person's voice from one room or building to another.

spear ▶ **noun** a weapon with a pointed tip, typically of steel, and a long shaft, used for thrusting or throwing.

■ a similar barbed instrument used for catching fish. ■ archaic a spearman. ■ a plant shoot, especially a pointed stem of asparagus or broccoli.

▶ **verb** [with obj.] pierce or strike with a spear or other pointed object: *she speared her last chip with her fork.*

– ORIGIN Old English *spere*, of Germanic origin; compare with Dutch *speer* and German *Speer*.

spear-carrier ▶ **noun** an actor with a walk-on part.

■ an unimportant participant in something.

spearfish ▶ **noun** (pl. same or **-fishes**) a billfish that resembles the marlin.

• Genus *Tetrapturus*, family Istiophoridae: several species.

speargrass ▶ **noun** [mass noun] **1** any of a number of grasses with hard pointed seed heads, some of which are sharp enough to harm livestock.

• *Heteropogon*, *Stipa*, and other genera, family Gramineae.

2 chiefly NZ any of a number of spiny or prickly plants, in particular the piripiri and the Spaniard.

speargun ▶ **noun** a gun used to propel a spear in underwater fishing.

spearhead ▶ **noun** the point of a spear.

■ an individual or group chosen to lead an attack or movement: *she became the spearhead of a health education programme.*

▶ **verb** [with obj.] lead (an attack or movement): *he's spearheading a campaign to reduce the number of accidents at work.*

spearman ▶ **noun** (pl. **-men**) chiefly historical a man, especially a soldier, who uses a spear.

Spearman's rank correlation ▶ **noun** a product-moment correlation coefficient devised as a measure of the degree of agreement between two rankings. (Symbol: ρ)

– ORIGIN early 20th cent.: named after Charles E. Spearman (1863–1945), English psychologist.

spearmint ▶ **noun** [mass noun] the common garden mint, which is used as a culinary herb and to flavour chewing gum.

• *Mentha spicata*, family Labiatae.

spear side ▶ **noun** the male side or members of a family. The opposite of **DISTAFF SIDE**.

spearwort ▶ **noun** a European buttercup of marshes and ditches, with thick hollow stems and long narrow spear-shaped leaves.

• Genus *Ranunculus*, family Ranunculaceae: the **lesser spearwort** (*R. flammula*) and the less common **greater spearwort** (*R. lingua*).

spec[1] ▶ **noun** (in phrase **on spec**) informal in the hope of success but without any specific plan or instructions: *he built the factory on spec and hoped someone would buy it.*

– ORIGIN late 18th cent.: abbreviation of **SPECULATION**.

spec[2] ▶ **noun** informal a detailed working description.

– ORIGIN 1950s: abbreviation of **SPECIFICATION**.

speccy ▶ **adjective** variant spelling of **SPECKY**.

special ▶ **adjective** better, greater, or otherwise different from what is usual: *they always made a special effort at Christmas.*

■ exceptionally good or precious: *she's a very special person.* ■ belonging specifically to a particular person or place: *we want to preserve our town's special character.* ■ designed or organized for a particular person, purpose, or occasion: *we will return by special coaches.* ■ (of a subject) studied in particular depth. ■ used to denote education for children with particular needs, especially those with learning difficulties. ■ Mathematics denoting a group consisting of matrices of unit determinant.

▶ **noun** a thing, such as an event, product, or broadcast, that is designed or organized for a particular occasion or purpose: *television's election night specials.*

■ a dish not on the regular menu at a restaurant but served on a particular day. ■ a person assigned to a special duty; a special constable or special correspondent. ■ informal a product or service offered at a temporarily reduced price.

– PHRASES **on special** short for ***on special offer*** (see **OFFER**).

– DERIVATIVES **specialness** noun.

– ORIGIN Middle English: shortening of Old French *especial* 'especial' or Latin *specialis*, from *species* 'appearance' (see **SPECIES**).

Special Air Service (abbrev.: **SAS**) (in the UK) a specialist army regiment trained in commando techniques of warfare, formed during the Second World War and used in clandestine operations, frequently against terrorists.

Special Boat Service (abbrev.: **SBS**) (also **Special Boat Section**) (in the UK) a nautical counterpart of the SAS, provided by the Royal Marines.

Special Branch (in the UK) the police department dealing with political security.

special case ▶ **noun 1** a situation or person that has unusual qualities or needs.

2 Law a written statement of fact presented by litigants to a court.

special constable ▶ **noun** (in the UK) a person who is trained to act as a police officer on particular occasions, especially in times of emergency.

special correspondent ▶ **noun** a journalist writing for a newspaper on special events or a special area of interest.

special delivery ▶ **noun** [mass noun] (in the UK) guaranteed delivery of a letter within the UK the day after posting.

■ (in the US) delivery of mail outside normal hours on payment of an additional fee. ■ [count noun] a letter or parcel sent by a special-delivery service.

special development area (also **special area**) ▶ **noun** (in the UK) a district for which special economic provision is made in legislation.

special drawing rights (abbrev.: **SDR**) ▶ **plural noun** a form of international money, created by the International Monetary Fund, and defined as a weighted average of various convertible currencies.

special edition ▶ **noun** an edition of a newspaper, magazine, television programme, etc. which differs from the usual format, especially in concentrating on one particularly important story.

special effects ▶ **plural noun** illusions created for films and television by props, camerawork, computer graphics, etc.

special intention ▶ **noun** (in the Roman Catholic Church) a special aim or purpose for which a mass is celebrated or prayers are said.

special interest (also **special interest group**) ▶ **noun** N. Amer. a group of people or an organization seeking or receiving special advantages, typically through political lobbying.

specialist ▶ **noun** a person who concentrates primarily on a particular subject or activity; a person highly skilled in a specific and restricted field.

■ a person highly trained in a particular branch of medicine.

▶ **adjective** possessing or involving detailed knowledge or study of a restricted topic: *the project may involve people with specialist knowledge.*

■ [attrib.] concentrating on a restricted field, market, or area of activity: *a specialist electrical shop.*

– DERIVATIVES **specialism** noun.

speciality /ˌspɛʃɪˈalɪti/ (chiefly N. Amer. & Medicine also **specialty**) ▶ **noun** (pl. **-ies**) a pursuit, area of study, or skill to which someone has devoted much time and effort and in which they are expert: *his speciality was watercolours.*

■ a product, especially a type of food, which a person or region is famous for making well. ■ [as modifier] meeting particular tastes or needs: *speciality potatoes for salads.* ■ (often **specialty**) a branch of medicine or surgery.

– ORIGIN late Middle English (denoting the quality of being special or distinctive): from Old French *especialite* or late Latin *specialitas*, from Latin *specialis* (see **SPECIAL**).

specialize (also **-ise**) ▶ **verb** [no obj.] concentrate on and become expert in a particular subject or skill: *he could **specialize in** tropical medicine.*
■ confine oneself to providing a particular product or service: *the firm **specialized in** commercial brochures.* ■ make a habit of engaging in a particular activity: *a group of writers have **specialized in** attacking the society they live in.* ■ [with obj.] (often **be specialized**) Biology adapt or set apart (an organ or part) to serve a special function or to suit a particular way of life: *zooids specialized for different functions.*
– DERIVATIVES **specialization** noun.
– ORIGIN early 17th cent.: from French *spécialiser*, from *spécial* 'special'.

specialized (also **-ised**) ▶ **adjective** requiring or involving detailed and specific knowledge or training: *skilled treatment for these patients is very specialized.*
■ concentrating on a small area of a subject: *periodicals have become more and more specialized.* ■ designed for a particular purpose: *specialized software.*

special jury ▶ **noun** Brit. historical a jury with members of a particular social standing. Compare with **COMMON JURY**.

special licence ▶ **noun** Brit. a licence allowing a marriage to take place at a time or place not normally permitted.

specially ▶ **adverb** for a special purpose: *a new coat and hat, bought specially* | [as submodifier] *a specially commissioned report.*

USAGE On the differences between **specially** and **especially**, see usage at **ESPECIALLY**.

special needs ▶ **plural noun** (in the context of children at school) particular educational requirements resulting from learning difficulties, physical disability, or emotional and behavioural difficulties.

Special Operations Executive (abbrev.: **SOE**) a secret British military service during the Second World War, set up in 1940 to carry out clandestine operations and coordinate with resistance movements in Europe and later the Far East.

special pleading ▶ **noun** [mass noun] argument in which the speaker deliberately ignores aspects that are unfavourable to their point of view.
■ appeals to give a particular interest group special treatment.

special school ▶ **noun** (in the UK) a school catering for children with special needs.

special sort ▶ **noun** Printing a character, such as an accented letter or a symbol, that is not normally included in any font.

special team ▶ **noun** American Football a squad that is used for kick-offs, punts, and other special plays.

specialty /ˈspɛʃ(ə)lti/ ▶ **noun** (pl. **-ies**) **1** chiefly N. Amer. & Medicine another term for **SPECIALITY**.
2 Law a contract under seal.
– ORIGIN Middle English (denoting special affection or attachment): shortening of Old French *especialte*, from *especial* (see **SPECIAL**).

special verdict ▶ **noun** Law a verdict that requires an answer to a specific detailed question.
■ a verdict that an accused is not guilty by reason of insanity.

speciation /ˌspiːʃɪˈeɪʃ(ə)n, ˌspiːs-/ ▶ **noun** [mass noun] Biology the formation of new and distinct species in the course of evolution.
– DERIVATIVES **speciate** verb.

specie /ˈspiːʃiː, ˈspiːʃi/ ▶ **noun** [mass noun] money in the form of coins rather than notes.
– PHRASES **in specie 1** in coin. **2** Law in the real, precise, or actual form specified: *the plaintiff could not be sure of recovering his goods in specie.*
– ORIGIN mid 16th cent. (in sense 2): from Latin, ablative of *species* 'form, kind', in the phrase *in specie* 'in the actual form'.

species /ˈspiːʃiːz, -ʃɪz, ˈspiːs-/ ▶ **noun** (pl. same) **1** (abbrev.: **sp.**, **spp.**) Biology a group of living organisms consisting of similar individuals capable of exchanging genes or interbreeding. The species is the principal natural taxonomic unit, ranking below a genus and denoted by a Latin binomial, e.g. *Homo sapiens*.
■ Logic a group subordinate to a genus and containing individuals agreeing in some common attributes and called by a common name. ■ a kind or sort: *a species of invective at once tough and suave.* ■ used humorously to refer to people who share a characteristic or occupation: *a political species that is becoming more common, the environmental statesman.* ■ Chemistry & Physics a particular kind of atom, molecule, ion, or particle: *a new molecular species.*
2 Christian Church the visible form of each of the elements of consecrated bread and wine in the Eucharist.
– ORIGIN late Middle English: from Latin, literally 'appearance, form, beauty', from *specere* 'to look'.

speciesism /ˈspiːʃiːˌzɪz(ə)m, ˈspiːs-/ ▶ **noun** [mass noun] the assumption of human superiority leading to the exploitation of animals.
– DERIVATIVES **speciesist** adjective & noun.

species rose ▶ **noun** a rose belonging to a distinct species and not to one of the many varieties produced by hybridization.

specific /spəˈsɪfɪk/ ▶ **adjective 1** clearly defined or identified: *savings were made by increasing the electricity supply only until it met specific development needs.*
■ precise and clear in making statements or issuing instructions: *when ordering goods be specific.* ■ belonging or relating uniquely to a particular subject: *information needs are often very **specific to** companies and individuals.*
2 Biology of, relating to, or connected with species or a species.
3 (of a duty or a tax) levied at a fixed rate per physical unit of the thing taxed, regardless of its price.
4 Physics of or denoting a number equal to the ratio of the value of some property of a given substance to the value of the same property of some other substance used as a reference, such as water, or of a vacuum, under equivalent conditions.
■ of or denoting a physical quantity expressed in terms of a unit mass, volume, or other measure, in order to give a value independent of the properties or scale of the particular system studied.
▶ **noun 1** chiefly dated a medicine or remedy effective in treating a particular disease or part of the body.
2 (usu. **specifics**) a precise detail.
– DERIVATIVES **specifically** adverb, **specificity** /ˌspɛsɪˈfɪsɪti/ noun, **specificness** noun.
– ORIGIN mid 17th cent. (originally in the sense 'having a special determining quality'): from late Latin *specificus*, from Latin *species* (see **SPECIES**).

specific activity ▶ **noun** Physics the activity of a given radioisotope per unit mass.

specification /ˌspɛsɪfɪˈkeɪʃ(ə)n/ ▶ **noun** an act of describing or identifying something precisely or of stating a precise requirement: *give a full specification of the job advertised* | [mass noun] *there was no clear specification of objectives.*
■ (usu. **specifications**) a detailed description of the design and materials used to make something. ■ a standard of workmanship, materials, required to be met in a piece of work: *everything was built to a higher specification.* ■ a description of an invention accompanying an application for a patent.
– ORIGIN late 16th cent.: from medieval Latin *specificatio(n-)*, from late Latin *specificare* (see **SPECIFY**).

specific charge ▶ **noun** Physics the ratio of the charge of an ion or subatomic particle to its mass.

specific disease ▶ **noun** a disease caused by a particular and characteristic organism.

specific epithet ▶ **noun** chiefly Botany & Microbiology the second element in the Latin binomial name of a species, which follows the generic name and distinguishes the species from others in the same genus. Compare with **SPECIFIC NAME**, **TRIVIAL NAME**.

specific gravity ▶ **noun** another term for **RELATIVE DENSITY**.

specific heat capacity ▶ **noun** Physics the heat required to raise the temperature of the unit mass of a given substance by a given amount (usually one degree).

specific name ▶ **noun** chiefly Botany & Microbiology the Latin binomial name of a species, consisting of the generic name followed by the specific epithet.
■ chiefly Zoology another term for **SPECIFIC EPITHET**.

specific performance ▶ **noun** [mass noun] Law the performance of a contractual duty, as ordered in cases where damages would not be adequate remedy.

specify ▶ **verb** (**-ies**, **-ied**) [with obj.] identify clearly and definitely: *the coup leader promised an election but did not specify a date.*
■ [with clause] state a fact or requirement clearly and precisely: *the agency failed to **specify that** the workers were not their employees.* ■ include in an architect's or engineer's specifications: *naval architects specified circular portholes.*
– DERIVATIVES **specifiable** adjective, **specifier** noun.
– ORIGIN Middle English: from Old French *specifier* or late Latin *specificare* (see **SPECIFIC**).

specimen /ˈspɛsɪmɪn/ ▶ **noun** an individual animal, plant, piece of a mineral, etc. used as an example of its species or type for scientific study or display.
■ an example of something such as a product or piece of work, regarded as typical of its class or group. ■ a sample for medical testing, especially of urine. ■ informal used to refer humorously to a person or animal: *in her he found himself confronted by a sorrier specimen than himself.*
– ORIGIN early 17th cent. (in the sense 'pattern, model'): from Latin, from *specere* 'to look'.

specimen plant (also **specimen tree**) ▶ **noun** an unusual or impressive plant or tree grown as a focus of interest in a garden.

specious /ˈspiːʃəs/ ▶ **adjective** superficially plausible, but actually wrong: *a specious argument.*
■ misleading in appearance, especially misleadingly attractive: *the music trade gives Golden Oldies a specious appearance of novelty.*
– DERIVATIVES **speciously** adverb, **speciousness** noun.
– ORIGIN late Middle English (in the sense 'beautiful'): from Latin *speciosus* 'fair', from *species* (see **SPECIES**).

speck ▶ **noun** a tiny spot: *the figure in the distance had become a mere speck.*
■ a small particle of a substance: *specks of dust.* ■ a rotten spot in fruit.
▶ **verb** [with obj.] (usu. **be specked**) mark with small spots: *their skin was specked with goose pimples.*
– DERIVATIVES **speckless** adjective.
– ORIGIN Old English *specca*; compare with the noun **SPECKLE**.

speckle ▶ **noun** (usu. **speckles**) a small spot or patch of colour.
▶ **verb** [with obj.] [often as adj. **speckled**] mark with a large number of small spots or patches of colour: *a large speckled brown egg.*
– ORIGIN late Middle English (as a noun): from Middle Dutch *spekkel*; the verb (late 16th cent.) from the noun or a back-formation from **SPECKLED**.

speckled trout ▶ **noun** N. Amer. the brook charr. See **CHARR**.

speckled wood ▶ **noun** a brown Eurasian butterfly with cream or orange markings, favouring light woodland habitats.
• *Pararge aegeria*, subfamily Satyrinae, family Nymphalidae.

specky (also **speccy**) ▶ **adjective** informal (of a person) wearing spectacles.

specs ▶ **plural noun** informal a pair of spectacles.
– ORIGIN early 19th cent.: abbreviation.

spect ▶ **verb** non-standard form of **EXPECT** representing childish pronunciation: *I spect they've been to a party.*

spectacle ▶ **noun** a visually striking performance or display: *the acrobatic feats make a good spectacle* | [mass noun] *the show is pure spectacle.*
■ an event or scene regarded in terms of its visual impact: *the spectacle of a city's mass grief.*
– PHRASES **make a spectacle of oneself** draw attention to oneself by behaving in a ridiculous way in public.
– ORIGIN Middle English: via Old French from Latin *spectaculum* 'public show', from *spectare*, frequentative of *specere* 'to look'.

spectacled ▶ **adjective** wearing spectacles.
■ used in names of animals with markings on the face or elsewhere that resemble spectacles.

spectacled bear ▶ **noun** a South American bear with a black or dark brown coat and white markings around the eyes.
• *Tremarctos ornatus*, family Ursidae.

spectacled caiman ▶ **noun** a small South American caiman with a bony ridge between the eyes which gives the appearance of spectacles.
• *Caiman sclerops*, family Alligatoridae.

spectacled cobra ▶ **noun** an Asian cobra with a

S

marking on the hood that resembles spectacles. Also called **INDIAN COBRA**.

● *Naja naja*, family Elapidae.

spectacles ▸ plural noun Brit. a pair of glasses.

spectacular ▸ adjective beautiful in a dramatic and eye-catching way: *spectacular mountain scenery.* ■ strikingly large or obvious: *the party suffered a spectacular loss in the election.* ▸ noun an event such as a pageant or musical, produced on a large scale and with striking effects.
– DERIVATIVES **spectacularly** adverb.
– ORIGIN late 17th cent.: from **SPECTACLE**, on the pattern of words such as *oracular*.

spectate ▸ verb [no obj.] be a spectator, especially at a sporting event: *the two of us spectated at the first race.*
– ORIGIN early 18th cent.: back-formation from **SPECTATOR**.

spectator ▸ noun a person who watches at a show, game, or other event.
– DERIVATIVES **spectatorial** adjective (rare).
– ORIGIN late 16th cent.: from French *spectateur* or Latin *spectator*, from *spectare* 'gaze at, observe' (see **SPECTACLE**).

spectator sport ▸ noun a sport that many people find entertaining to watch.

specter ▸ noun US spelling of **SPECTRE**.

spectinomycin /ˌspɛktɪnə(ʊ)ˈmʌɪsɪn/ ▸ noun [mass noun] Medicine a bacterial antibiotic used as an alternative to penicillin.
● The drug is obtained from the bacterium *Streptomyces spectabilis*.
– ORIGIN 1960s: from the specific epithet *spectabilis* (see above), literally 'visible, remarkable' + **-MYCIN**.

Spector /ˈspɛktə/, Phil (b.1940), American record producer and songwriter. He pioneered a 'wall of sound' style, using echo and tape loops, and had a succession of hit recordings in the 1960s with groups such as the Ronettes and the Crystals.

spectra plural form of **SPECTRUM**.

spectral ▸ adjective **1** of or like a ghost. [ORIGIN: early 18th cent.: from **SPECTRE** + **-AL**.]
2 of or concerning spectra or the spectrum. [ORIGIN: mid 19th cent.: from **SPECTRUM** + **-AL**.]
– DERIVATIVES **spectrally** adverb.

spectral index ▸ noun an exponential factor relating the flux density of a radio source to its frequency.

spectral tarsier ▸ noun a tarsier which has a tail with a long bushy tuft and a scaly base, native to Sulawesi.
● *Tarsius spectrum*, family Tarsiidae.

spectral type (also **spectral class**) ▸ noun Astronomy the group in which a star is classified according to its spectrum, especially using the Harvard classification.

spectre (US **specter**) ▸ noun a ghost. ■ something widely feared as a possible unpleasant or dangerous occurrence: *the spectre of nuclear holocaust.*
– ORIGIN early 17th cent.: from French *spectre* or Latin *spectrum* (see **SPECTRUM**).

spectro- ▸ combining form representing **SPECTRUM**.

spectrogram ▸ noun a photographic or other visual or electronic representation of a spectrum.

spectrograph ▸ noun an apparatus for photographing or otherwise recording spectra.
– DERIVATIVES **spectrographic** adjective, **spectrographically** adverb, **spectrography** noun.

spectroheliograph /ˌspɛktrə(ʊ)ˈhiːlɪəɡrɑːf/ ▸ noun an instrument for taking photographs of the sun in light of one wavelength only.

spectrohelioscope /ˌspɛktrə(ʊ)ˈhiːlɪəskəʊp/ ▸ noun a device similar to a spectroheliograph which produces a directly observable monochromatic image of the sun.

spectrometer /spɛkˈtrɒmɪtə/ ▸ noun an apparatus used for recording and measuring spectra, especially as a method of analysis.
– DERIVATIVES **spectrometric** adjective, **spectrometry** noun.

spectrophotometer /ˌspɛktrə(ʊ)fəʊˈtɒmɪtə/ ▸ noun an apparatus for measuring the intensity of light in a part of the spectrum, especially as transmitted or emitted by particular substances.
– DERIVATIVES **spectrophotometric** /-təˈmɛtrɪk/ adjective, **spectrophotometrically** adverb, **spectrophotometry** noun.

spectroscope ▸ noun an apparatus for producing and recording spectra for examination.

spectroscopy ▸ noun [mass noun] the branch of science concerned with the investigation and measurement of spectra produced when matter interacts with or emits electromagnetic radiation.
– DERIVATIVES **spectroscopic** adjective, **spectroscopically** adverb, **spectroscopist** noun.

spectrum ▸ noun (pl. **spectra** /-trə/) **1** a band of colours, as seen in a rainbow, produced by separation of the components of light by their different degrees of refraction according to wavelength. ■ (**the spectrum**) the entire range of wavelengths of electromagnetic radiation. ■ an image or distribution of components of any electromagnetic radiation arranged in a progressive series according to wavelength. ■ a similar image or distribution of components of sound, particles, etc., arranged according to such characteristics as frequency, charge, and energy.
2 used to classify something, or suggest that it can be classified, in terms of its position on a scale between two extreme or opposite points: *the left or the right of the political spectrum.* ■ a wide range: *self-help books are covering a broader and broader spectrum.*
– ORIGIN early 17th cent. (in the sense 'spectre'): from Latin, literally 'image, apparition', from *specere* 'to look'.

spectrum analyser ▸ noun a device for analysing a system of oscillations, especially sound, into its separate components.

specula plural form of **SPECULUM**.

specular /ˈspɛkjʊlə/ ▸ adjective of, relating to, or having the properties of a mirror.
– ORIGIN late 16th cent. (in *specular stone*, a substance formerly used as glass): from Latin *specularis*, from *speculum* (see **SPECULUM**).

speculate /ˈspɛkjʊleɪt/ ▸ verb [no obj.] **1** form a theory or conjecture about a subject without firm evidence: *my colleagues speculate about my private life* | [with clause] *observers speculated that the authorities wished to improve their image.*
2 invest in stocks, property, or other ventures in the hope of gain but with the risk of loss: *he didn't look as though he had the money to speculate in shares.*
– DERIVATIVES **speculation** noun, **speculator** noun.
– ORIGIN late 16th cent.: from Latin *speculat-* 'observed from a vantage point', from the verb *speculari*, from *specula* 'watchtower', from *specere* 'to look'.

speculative ▸ adjective **1** engaged in, expressing, or based on conjecture rather than knowledge: *he gave her a speculative glance.*
2 (of an investment) involving a high risk of loss. ■ (of a business venture) undertaken on the chance of success, without a pre-existing contract.
– DERIVATIVES **speculatively** adverb, **speculativeness** noun.

speculative builder ▸ noun a person who has houses erected without securing buyers in advance.

speculum /ˈspɛkjʊləm/ ▸ noun (pl. **specula** /-lə/) **1** Medicine a metal instrument that is used to dilate an orifice or canal in the body to allow inspection. **2** Ornithology a bright patch of plumage on the wings of certain birds, especially a strip of metallic sheen on the secondary flight feathers of many ducks. **3** a mirror or reflector of glass or metal, especially (formerly) a metallic mirror in a reflecting telescope. ■ short for **SPECULUM METAL**.
– ORIGIN late Middle English: from Latin, literally 'mirror', from *specere* 'to look'.

speculum metal ▸ noun [mass noun] an alloy of copper and tin used to make mirrors, especially formerly for telescopes.

sped past and past participle of **SPEED**.

speech ▸ noun **1** [mass noun] the expression of or the ability to express thoughts and feelings by articulate sounds: *he was born deaf and without the power of speech.* ■ a person's style or speaking: *she wouldn't accept his correction of her speech.*
2 a formal address or discourse delivered to an audience: *the headmistress made a speech about how much they would miss her.* ■ a sequence of lines written for one character in a play.

– ORIGIN Old English *sprǣc, sprēc*, later *spēc*, of West Germanic origin: related to Dutch *spraak*, German *Sprache*, also to **SPEAK**.

speech act ▸ noun Linguistics & Philosophy an utterance considered as an action, particularly with regard to its intention, purpose, or effect.

speech centre (also **speech area**) ▸ noun a region of the brain involved in the comprehension or production of speech.

speech community ▸ noun a group of people sharing a common language or dialect.

speech day ▸ noun Brit. an annual celebration held at some schools, especially public schools, at which speeches are made and prizes are presented.

speechify ▸ verb (**-ies**, **-ied**) [no obj.] [often as noun **speechifying**] deliver a speech, especially in a tedious or pompous way: *the after-dinner speechifying begins.*
– DERIVATIVES **speechification** noun, **speechifier** noun.

speechless ▸ adjective unable to speak, especially as the temporary result of shock or some strong emotion: *he was speechless with rage.*
– DERIVATIVES **speechlessly** adverb, **speechlessness** noun.
– ORIGIN Old English *spǣclēas* (see **SPEECH**, **-LESS**).

speech pathology ▸ noun another term for **SPEECH THERAPY**.
– DERIVATIVES **speech pathologist** noun.

speech-reading ▸ noun [mass noun] lip-reading.

speech sound ▸ noun a phonetically distinct unit of speech.

speech synthesis ▸ noun [mass noun] the process of generating spoken language by machine on the basis of written input.

speech therapy ▸ noun [mass noun] training to help people with speech and language problems to speak more clearly.
– DERIVATIVES **speech therapist** noun.

speech-writer ▸ noun a person employed to write speeches for others to deliver.

speed ▸ noun **1** the rate at which someone or something moves or operates or is able to move or operate: *the car has a top speed of 147 mph.* ■ [mass noun] rapidity of movement or action: *the accident was due to excessive speed* | figurative *they were bemused by the speed of events.* ■ each of the possible gear ratios of a bicycle. ■ chiefly US or dated each of the possible gear ratios of a motor vehicle. ■ the sensitivity of photographic film to light. ■ the light-gathering power or f-number of a camera lens. ■ the duration of a photographic exposure.
2 [mass noun] informal an amphetamine drug, especially methamphetamine.
3 [mass noun] archaic success; prosperity: *wish me good speed.*
▸ verb (past and past participle **sped**) **1** [no obj., with adverbial of direction] move quickly: *I got into the car and home we sped.* ■ (past and past participle **speeded**) [no obj.] (of a motorist) travel at a speed that is greater than the legal limit: *the car that crashed was speeding.* ■ (past and past participle **speeded**) (**speed up**) move or work more quickly: *you force yourself to speed up because you don't want to keep others waiting.* ■ (past and past participle **speeded**) [with obj.] cause to move, act, or happen more quickly: *recent initiatives have sought to speed up decision-making.*
2 [no obj.] archaic make prosperous or successful: *may God speed you.*
3 [no obj.] informal take or be under the influence of an amphetamine drug: *more kids than ever are speeding, tripping, and getting stoned.*
– PHRASES **at speed** quickly: *a car flashed past them at speed.* **up to speed** operating at full speed. ■ (of a person or company) performing at an anticipated rate or level. ■ (of a person) fully informed or up to date: *that reminds me to bring you up to speed on the soap opera.*
– DERIVATIVES **speeder** noun.
– ORIGIN Old English *spēd* (noun), *spēdan* (verb), from the Germanic base of Old English *spōwan* 'prosper, succeed', a sense reflected in early usage.

speed bag ▸ noun N. Amer. a small punchbag used by boxers for practising quick punches.

speedball ▸ noun **1** informal a mixture of cocaine with heroin.
2 a small punchball used by boxers for practising quick punches.

3 [mass noun] US a ball game resembling soccer but in which the ball may be handled.

speedboat ▶ **noun** a motor boat designed for high speed.

speed bump (Brit. also **speed hump**) ▶ **noun** a ridge set at intervals in a road surface to control the speed of vehicles.

speed camera ▶ **noun** a roadside camera triggered by speeding vehicles, taking either video footage or a photograph of the vehicle with a record of its speed.

speed limit ▶ **noun** the maximum speed at which a vehicle may legally travel on a particular stretch of road.

speed limiter ▶ **noun** see **LIMITER**.

speed merchant ▶ **noun** informal **1** a motorist who enjoys driving fast.
2 Cricket & Baseball a fast bowler or pitcher.

speedo ▶ **noun** (pl. **-os**) **1** informal short for **SPEEDOMETER**.
2 trademark, chiefly US a swimming costume.

speedometer /spiːˈdɒmɪtə/ ▶ **noun** an instrument on a vehicle's dashboard indicating its speed.

speed-read ▶ **verb** [with obj.] read rapidly by assimilating several phrases or sentences at once.
– DERIVATIVES **speed-reader** noun.

speedster ▶ **noun** informal a person or thing that operates well at high speed, for example a fast runner or car.

speed trap ▶ **noun** a radar trap.

speed-up ▶ **noun** an increase in speed, especially in a person's or machine's rate of working.

speedway ▶ **noun** [mass noun] a form of motorcycle racing in which the riders race several laps around an oval dirt track, typically in a stadium.
■ [count noun] a stadium or track used for this sport. ■ N. Amer. a road or track used for motor-car racing. ■ N. Amer. a highway for fast motor traffic.

speedwell ▶ **noun** a small creeping herbaceous plant of north temperate regions, with small blue or pink flowers.
• Genus *Veronica*, family Scrophulariaceae: several species, including the **germander speedwell**.

speedwriting ▶ **noun** [mass noun] trademark a form of shorthand using the letters of the alphabet.
– DERIVATIVES **speedwriter** noun.

speedy ▶ **adjective** (**speedier**, **speediest**) **1** done or occurring quickly: *a speedy recovery.*
2 moving quickly: *a speedy winger.*
– DERIVATIVES **speedily** adverb, **speediness** noun.

speedy trial ▶ **noun** chiefly US Law a criminal trial held after minimal delay, as considered to be a citizen's constitutional right.

Speenhamland system /ˈspiːnəmland/ ▶ **noun** historical a system of poor relief first adopted in the late 18th century and established throughout rural England in succeeding years.
– ORIGIN first adopted in *Speenhamland*, an English village near Newbury, Berks.

Speer /spɪə, German ʃpeːɐ/, Albert (1905–81), German architect and Nazi government official, designer of the Nuremberg stadium for the 1934 Nazi Party congress. He was also Minister for Armaments and Munitions. Following the Nuremberg trials, he served twenty years in Spandau prison.

speiss /spʌɪs/ ▶ **noun** [mass noun] a mixture of impure arsenides and antimonides of nickel, cobalt, iron, and other metals, produced in the smelting of cobalt and other ores.
– ORIGIN late 18th cent.: from German *Speise* 'food, amalgam'.

spekboom /ˈspɛkbʊəm/ ▶ **noun** S. African a South African shrub with succulent leaves, which is used for fodder during times of drought.
• *Portulacaria afra*, family Portulacaceae.
– ORIGIN mid 19th cent.: from Afrikaans, from *spek* 'bacon' + *boom* 'tree'.

Speke /spiːk/, John Hanning (1827–64), English explorer. With Sir Richard Burton, he became the first European to discover Lake Tanganyika (1858). He also discovered Lake Victoria, naming it in honour of the queen.

speleology /ˌspiːlɪˈɒlədʒi, ˌspɛl-/ ▶ **noun** [mass noun] the study or exploration of caves.
– DERIVATIVES **speleological** adjective, **speleologist** noun.
– ORIGIN late 19th cent.: from French *spéléologie*, via Latin from Greek *spēlaion* 'cave'.

speleothem /ˈspiːlɪə(ʊ)θɛm/ ▶ **noun** Geology a structure formed in a cave by the deposition of minerals from water, e.g. a stalactite or stalagmite.
– ORIGIN 1950s: from Greek *spēlaion* 'cave' + *thema* 'deposit'.

spell[1] ▶ **verb** (past and past participle **spelled** or chiefly Brit. **spelt**) [with obj.] write or name the letters that form (a word) in correct sequence: *Dolly spelled her name* | [no obj.] *journals have a house style about how to spell.*
■ (of letters) make up or form (a word): *the letters spell the word 'how'.* ■ be recognizable as a sign or characteristic of: *she had the chic, efficient look that spells Milan.* ■ lead to: *the plans would spell disaster for the economy.*
– ORIGIN Middle English: shortening of Old French *espeller*, from the Germanic base of **SPELL**[2].
▶ **spell something out** speak the letters that form a word in sequence. ■ explain something in detail: *I'll spell out the problem again.*

spell[2] ▶ **noun** a form of words used as a magical charm or incantation.
■ a state of enchantment caused by such a form of words: *the magician may **cast a spell on** himself.* ■ an ability to control or influence people as though one had magical power over them: *she is afraid that you are waking from her spell.*
– PHRASES **under a spell** not fully in control of one's thoughts and actions, as though in a state of enchantment. **under someone's spell** so devoted to someone that they seem to have magic power over one.
– ORIGIN Old English *spel(l)* 'narration', of Germanic origin.

spell[3] ▶ **noun** a short period: *I want to get away from racing for a spell.*
■ a period spent in an activity: *a spell of greenhouse work.* ■ Austral. a period of rest from work. ■ Cricket a series of overs during a session of play in which a particular bowler bowls.
▶ **verb** [with obj.] chiefly N. Amer. allow (someone) to rest briefly by taking their place in some activity: *I got sleepy and needed her to spell me for a while at the wheel.*
■ [no obj.] Austral. take a brief rest: *I'll spell for a bit.*
– ORIGIN late 16th cent.: variant of dialect *spele* 'take the place of', of unknown origin. The early sense of the noun was 'shift of relief workers'.

spell[4] ▶ **noun** a splinter of wood.
– ORIGIN late Middle English: perhaps a variant of obsolete *speld* 'chip, splinter'.

spellbind ▶ **verb** (past and past participle **spellbound**) [with obj.] hold the complete attention of (someone) as though by magic; fascinate: *the singer **held** the audience **spellbound**.*
– DERIVATIVES **spellbinder** noun, **spellbindingly** adverb.

spell check Computing ▶ **noun** [often as modifier] a check of the spelling in a file of text using a spellchecker.
■ a spellchecker.
▶ **verb** [with obj.] check the spelling in (a text) using a spellchecker.

spellchecker ▶ **noun** a computer program which checks the spelling of words in files of text, typically by comparison with a stored list of words.

speller ▶ **noun** [with adj.] a person who spells with a specified ability: *a very weak speller.*
■ chiefly N. Amer. a book for teaching spelling. ■ another term for **SPELLCHECKER**.

spelling ▶ **noun** [mass noun] the process or activity of writing or naming the letters of a word.
■ [count noun] the way a word is spelled: *the spelling of his name was influenced by French.* ■ a person's ability to spell words: *her spelling was deplorable.*

spelling bee ▶ **noun** a spelling competition.

spelling checker ▶ **noun** another term for **SPELLCHECKER**.

spelt[1] past and past participle of **SPELL**[1].

spelt[2] ▶ **noun** [mass noun] an old kind of wheat with bearded ears and spikelets that each contain two narrow grains, not widely grown but favoured as a health food. Compare with **EINKORN**, **EMMER**.
• *Triticum spelta*, family Gramineae.
– ORIGIN late Old English, from Old Saxon *spelta*. The word was rare until the 16th cent., when it was readopted from Middle Dutch.

spelter /ˈspɛltə/ ▶ **noun** [mass noun] commercial crude smelted zinc.
■ a solder or other alloy in which zinc is the main constituent.
– ORIGIN mid 17th cent.: compare with Old French *espeautre*, Middle Dutch *speauter*; related to **PEWTER**.

spelunking /spɪˈlʌŋkɪŋ/ ▶ **noun** [mass noun] N. Amer. the exploration of caves, especially as a hobby.
– DERIVATIVES **spelunker** noun.
– ORIGIN 1940s: from obsolete *spelunk* 'cave' (from Latin *spelunca*) + **-ING**[1].

Spence, Sir Basil (Urwin) (1907–76), British architect, born in India. He designed the new Coventry cathedral (1962).

spence ▶ **noun** archaic a larder.
– ORIGIN late Middle English: shortening of Old French *despense*, from Latin *dispensa*, feminine past participle of *dispendere* (see **DISPENSE**).

Spencer[1], Herbert (1820–1903), English philosopher and sociologist. He sought to apply the theory of natural selection to human societies, developing social Darwinism and coining the phrase the 'survival of the fittest' (1864).

Spencer[2], Sir Stanley (1891–1959), English painter. He is best known for his religious and visionary works in the modern setting of his native village of Cookham in Berkshire, such as *Resurrection: Cookham* (1926).

spencer[1] ▶ **noun** a short, close-fitting jacket, worn by women and children in the early 19th century.
■ a thin woollen vest, worn by women for extra warmth in winter.
– ORIGIN probably named after the second Earl *Spencer* (1758–1834), English politician.

spencer[2] ▶ **noun** Sailing a trysail.
– ORIGIN mid 19th cent.: of unknown origin.

Spencerian /spɛnˈsɪərɪən/ ▶ **adjective** of or relating to a style of sloping handwriting widely taught in American schools from around 1850.

spend ▶ **verb** (past and past participle **spent**) [with obj.] pay out (money) in buying or hiring goods or services: *the firm has **spent** £100,000 **on** hardware and software.*
■ pay out (money) for a particular person's benefit or for the improvement of something: *the college **spent** £140 **on** each of its students.* ■ used to show the activity in which someone is engaged or the place where they are living over a period of time: *she spent a lot of time travelling.* ■ use or give out the whole of; exhaust: *she couldn't buy any more because she had already spent her money* | *the initial surge of interest had **spent itself**.*
▶ **noun** informal an amount of money paid for a particular purpose or over a particular period of time: *the average spend at the cafe is about £10 a head.*
– PHRASES **spend a penny** Brit. informal urinate (used euphemistically). [ORIGIN: with reference to the coin-operated locks of public toilets.]
– DERIVATIVES **spendable** adjective, **spender** noun.
– ORIGIN Old English *spendan*, from Latin *expendere* 'pay out'; partly also a shortening of obsolete *dispend*, from Latin *dispendere* 'pay out'.

Spender, Sir Stephen (1909–95), English poet and critic. In his critical work *The Destructive Element* (1935) Spender defended the importance of political subject matter in literature.

spending money ▶ **noun** [mass noun] money available to be spent on pleasures and entertainment.

spendthrift ▶ **noun** a person who spends money in an extravagant, irresponsible way.

Spengler /ˈspɛŋglə, German ˈʃpɛŋlɐ/, Oswald (1880–1936), German philosopher. In his book *The Decline of the West* (1918–22) he argues that civilizations undergo a seasonal cycle of a thousand years and are subject to growth and decay analogous to biological species.

Spenser, Edmund (*c.*1552–99), English poet. He is best known for his allegorical romance the *Faerie Queene* (1590; 1596), celebrating Queen Elizabeth I and written in the Spenserian stanza.
– DERIVATIVES **Spenserian** adjective.

Spenserian stanza /spɛnˈsɪərɪən/ ▶ **noun** the stanza used by Spenser in the *Faerie Queene*, consisting of eight iambic pentameters and an alexandrine, with the rhyming scheme *ababbcbcc*.

spent past and past participle of **SPEND**. ▶ **adjective** having been used and unable to be used again: *a spent matchstick.*
■ having no power or energy left: *the movement has become a spent force.*

spent tan ▶ **noun** see **TAN**[1] (sense 2).

a **cat** | ɑː **arm** | ɛ **bed** | ɛː **hair** | ə **ago** | əː **her** | ɪ **sit** | i **cosy** | iː **see** | ɒ **hot** | ɔː **saw** | ʌ **run** | ʊ **put** | uː **too** | ʌɪ **my** | aʊ **how** | eɪ **day** | əʊ **no** | ɪə **near** | ɔɪ **boy** | ʊə **poor** | ʌɪə **fire** | aʊə **sour**

sperm ▶ noun (pl. same or **sperms**) **1** short for SPERMATOZOON.
 ■ [mass noun] informal semen. [ORIGIN: late Middle English: via late Latin from Greek *sperma* 'seed', from *speirein* 'to sow'.]
2 short for SPERM WHALE.
 ■ [mass noun] short for SPERMACETI or SPERM OIL.

spermaceti /ˌspəːməˈsiːti, -ˈsɛti/ ▶ noun [mass noun] a white waxy substance produced by the sperm whale, formerly used in candles and ointments. It is present in a rounded organ in the head, where it focuses acoustic signals and aids in the control of buoyancy.
 – ORIGIN late 15th cent.: from medieval Latin, from late Latin *sperma* 'sperm' + *ceti* 'of a whale' (genitive of *cetus*, from Greek *kētos* 'whale'), from the belief that it was whale spawn.

spermatheca /ˌspəːməˈθiːkə/ ▶ noun (pl. **spermathecae** /-ˈθiːkiː/) Zoology (in a female or hermaphrodite invertebrate) a receptacle in which sperm is stored after mating.
 – ORIGIN early 19th cent.: from late Latin *sperma* 'sperm' + THECA.

spermatic ▶ adjective of or relating to sperm or semen.
 – DERIVATIVES **spermatically** adverb.
 – ORIGIN late Middle English: via late Latin from Greek *spermatikos*, from *sperma* (see SPERM).

spermatic cord ▶ noun a bundle of nerves, ducts, and blood vessels connecting the testicles to the abdominal cavity.

spermatid /ˈspəːmətɪd/ ▶ noun Biology an immature male sex cell formed from a spermatocyte, which may develop into a spermatozoon without further division.
 – DERIVATIVES **spermatidal** /ˌspəːməˈtʌɪd(ə)l/ adjective.

spermato- ▶ combining form Biology relating to sperm or seeds: *spermatophore* | *spermatozoid*.
 – ORIGIN from Greek *sperma*, *spermat-* 'sperm'.

spermatocyte /ˈspəːmət(ə)sʌɪt, spəˈmat-/ ▶ noun Biology a cell produced at the second stage in the formation of spermatozoa, formed from a spermatogonium and dividing by meiosis into spermatids.

spermatogenesis /ˌspəːmətə(ʊ)-, spəˌmatə(ʊ)ˈdʒɛnɪsɪs, / ▶ noun [mass noun] Biology the production or development of mature spermatozoa.

spermatogonium /ˌspəːmətə(ʊ)-, spəˌmatə(ʊ)ˈɡəʊnɪəm, / ▶ noun (pl. **spermatogonia** /-nɪə/) Biology a cell produced at an early stage in the formation of spermatozoa, formed in the wall of a seminiferous tubule and giving rise by mitosis to spermatocytes.
 – DERIVATIVES **spermatogonial** adjective.
 – ORIGIN late 19th cent.: from SPERM + modern Latin *gonium* (from Greek *gonos* 'offspring, seed').

spermatophore /ˈspəːmətə(ʊ)fɔː, spəˈmat-/ ▶ noun Zoology a protein capsule containing a mass of spermatozoa, transferred during mating in various insects, arthropods, cephalopod molluscs, etc.

spermatophyte /ˈspəːmətə(ʊ)fʌɪt, spəˈmat-/ ▶ noun Botany a plant of a large division that comprises those that bear seeds, including the gymnosperms and angiosperms.
 ● Division Spermatophyta.

spermatozoid /ˌspəːmətə(ʊ)ˈzəʊɪd, spəˌmat-/ ▶ noun Botany a motile male gamete produced by a lower plant or a gymnosperm. Also called ANTHEROZOID.

spermatozoon /ˌspəːmətə(ʊ)ˈzəʊɒn, spəˌmat-/ ▶ noun (pl. **spermatozoa** /-ˈzəʊə/) Biology the mature motile male sex cell of an animal, by which the ovum is fertilized, typically having a compact head and one or more long flagella for swimming.
 – DERIVATIVES **spermatozoal** adjective, **spermatozoan** adjective.
 – ORIGIN mid 19th cent.: from Greek *sperma*, *spermat-* 'seed' + *zōion* 'animal'.

sperm bank ▶ noun a place where semen is kept in cold storage for use in artificial insemination.

sperm count ▶ noun a measure of the number of spermatozoa per ejaculation or per measured amount of semen, used as an indication of a man's fertility.

spermicide ▶ noun a substance that kills spermatozoa, used as a contraceptive.
 – DERIVATIVES **spermicidal** adjective.

spermidine /ˈspəːmɪdiːn/ ▶ noun [mass noun] Biochemistry a colourless compound with a similar distribution and effect to spermine.
 ● A polyamine; chem. formula: $H_2N(CH_2)_3NH(CH_2)_4NH_2$.
 – ORIGIN 1920s: from SPERM + -IDE + -INE⁴.

spermine /ˈspəːmiːn/ ▶ noun [mass noun] Biochemistry a deliquescent compound which acts to stabilize various components of living cells and is widely distributed in living and decaying tissues.
 ● A polyamine; chem. formula: $(H_2N(CH_2)_3NH(CH_2)_2)_2$.

spermo- ▶ combining form equivalent to SPERMATO-.

sperm oil ▶ noun [mass noun] an oil found with spermaceti in the head of the sperm whale, used formerly as a lubricant.

sperm whale ▶ noun a toothed whale with a massive head, typically feeding at great depths on squid, formerly valued for the spermaceti and sperm oil in its head and the ambergris in its intestines.
 ● Family Physeteridae: two genera and three species, in particular the very large *Physeter macrocephalus* (also called CACHALOT).
 – ORIGIN mid 19th cent.: *sperm*, abbreviation of SPERMACETI.

spessartine /ˈspɛsətiːn/ ▶ noun [mass noun] a form of garnet containing manganese and aluminium, occurring as orange-red to dark brown crystals.
 – ORIGIN mid 19th cent.: from French, from *Spessart*, the name of a district in NW Bavaria, + -INE⁴.

spew ▶ verb [with obj.] expel large quantities of (something) rapidly and forcibly: *buses were spewing out black clouds of exhaust.*
 ■ [no obj., with adverbial of direction] be poured or forced out in large quantities: *great screeds of paper spewed out of the computer.* ■ [no obj.] informal vomit.
 – DERIVATIVES **spewer** noun.
 – ORIGIN Old English *spīwan*, *spēowan*, of Germanic origin; related to German *speien*.

Spey /speɪ/ a river of east central Scotland. Rising in the Grampian Mountains east of the Great Glen, it flows 171 km (108 miles) north-eastwards to the North Sea.

SPF ▶ abbreviation for sun protection factor (indicating the effectiveness of protective skin preparations).

sphagnum /ˈsfaɡnəm/ ▶ noun [mass noun] a plant of a genus that comprises the peat mosses.
 ● Genus *Sphagnum*, family Sphagnaceae.
 – ORIGIN mid 18th cent.: modern Latin, from Greek *sphagnos*, denoting a kind of moss.

sphalerite /ˈsfalərʌɪt/ ▶ noun [mass noun] a shiny mineral, yellow to dark brown or black in colour, consisting of zinc sulphide.
 – ORIGIN mid 19th cent.: from Greek *sphaleros* 'deceptive' + -ITE¹. Compare with BLENDE.

sphene /sfiːn/ ▶ noun [mass noun] a greenish-yellow or brown mineral consisting of a silicate of calcium and titanium, occurring in granitic and metamorphic rocks in wedge-shaped crystals.
 – ORIGIN early 19th cent.: from French *sphène*, from Greek *sphēn* 'wedge'.

sphenoid /ˈsfiːnɔɪd/ Anatomy ▶ noun (also **sphenoid bone**) a compound bone which forms the base of the cranium, behind the eye and below the front part of the brain. It has two pairs of broad lateral 'wings' and a number of other projections, and contains two air-filled sinuses.
 ▶ adjective of or relating to this bone.
 – DERIVATIVES **sphenoidal** adjective.
 – ORIGIN mid 18th cent.: from modern Latin *sphenoides*, from Greek *sphēnoeidēs*, from *sphēn* 'wedge'.

Sphenopsida /sfɛˈnɒpsɪdə/ Botany a class of pteridophyte plants that comprises the horsetails and their extinct relatives.
 – DERIVATIVES **sphenopsid** noun & adjective.
 – ORIGIN modern Latin (plural), from Greek *sphēn* 'wedge' + *opsis* 'appearance'.

sphere ▶ noun **1** a round solid figure, or its surface, with every point on its surface equidistant from its centre.
 ■ an object having this shape; a ball or globe. ■ a globe representing the earth. ■ chiefly poetic/literary a celestial body. ■ poetic/literary the sky perceived as a vault upon or in which celestial bodies are represented as lying. ■ each of a series of revolving concentrically arranged spherical shells in which celestial bodies were formerly thought to be set in a fixed relationship.
 2 an area of activity, interest, or expertise; a section of society or an aspect of life distinguished and unified by a particular characteristic: *political reforms to match those in the economic sphere.*
 ▶ verb [with obj.] archaic enclose in or as if in a sphere.
 ■ form into a rounded or perfect whole.
 – PHRASES **music (or harmony) of the spheres** the natural harmonic tones supposedly produced by the movement of the celestial bodies or the bodies fixed in them. **sphere of influence (or interest)** a country or area in which another country has power to affect developments though it has no formal authority. ■ a field or area in which an individual or organization has power to affect events and developments.
 – DERIVATIVES **spheral** adjective (archaic).
 – ORIGIN Middle English: from Old French *espere*, from late Latin *sphera*, earlier *sphaera*, from Greek *sphaira* 'ball'.

-sphere ▶ combining form **1** denoting a structure or region of spherical form, especially a region round the earth: *ionosphere*.
 – ORIGIN from SPHERE, on the pattern of (atmo)sphere.

spheric /ˈsfɛrɪk/ ▶ adjective spherical.
 – DERIVATIVES **sphericity** noun.

spherical ▶ adjective shaped like a sphere.
 ■ of or relating to the properties of spheres. ■ formed inside or on the surface of a sphere.
 – DERIVATIVES **spherically** adverb.
 – ORIGIN late 15th cent.: via late Latin from Greek *sphairikos*, from *sphaira* (see SPHERE).

spherical aberration ▶ noun a loss of definition in the image arising from the surface geometry of a spherical mirror or lens.

spherical angle ▶ noun an angle formed by the intersection of two great circles of a sphere.

spherical coordinates (also **spherical polar coordinates**) ▶ plural noun three coordinates that define the location of a point in three-dimensional space. They are the length of its radius vector r, the angle θ between the vertical plane containing this vector and the x-axis, and the angle φ between this vector and the horizontal x–y plane.
 ● Usually written (r, θ, φ).

spherical triangle ▶ noun a triangle formed by three arcs of great circles on a sphere.

spherical trigonometry ▶ noun [mass noun] the branch of trigonometry concerned with the measurement of the angles and sides of spherical triangles.

spheroid /ˈsfɪərɔɪd/ ▶ noun a sphere-like but not perfectly spherical body.
 ■ a solid generated by a half-revolution of an ellipse about its major axis (**prolate spheroid**) or minor axis (**oblate spheroid**).
 – DERIVATIVES **spheroidal** adjective, **spheroidicity** noun.

spheroplast /ˈsfɪərəplast, -plaːst/ ▶ noun Biology a bacterium or plant cell bound by its plasma membrane, the cell wall being deficient or lacking and the whole having a spherical form.

spherule /ˈsfɛrjuːl/ ▶ noun a small sphere.
 – DERIVATIVES **spherular** adjective.
 – ORIGIN mid 17th cent.: from late Latin *sphaerula*, diminutive of Latin *sphaera* (see SPHERE).

spherulite /ˈsfɛrjʊlʌɪt/ ▶ noun chiefly Geology a small spheroidal mass of crystals (especially of a mineral) grouped radially around a point.
 – DERIVATIVES **spherulitic** adjective.
 – ORIGIN early 19th cent.: from SPHERULE + -ITE¹.

sphincter /ˈsfɪŋktə/ ▶ noun Anatomy a ring of muscle surrounding and serving to guard or close an opening or tube, such as the anus or the openings of the stomach.
 – DERIVATIVES **sphincteral** adjective, **sphincteric** adjective.
 – ORIGIN late 16th cent.: via Latin from Greek *sphinktēr*, from *sphingein* 'bind tight'.

sphingid /ˈsfɪndʒɪd/ ▶ noun Entomology a moth of the hawkmoth family (Sphingidae).
 – ORIGIN early 20th cent.: from modern Latin *Sphingidae* (plural), from Greek *Sphinx* (see SPHINX).

sphingo- ▶ combining form used in the names of various related compounds isolated from the brain and nervous tissue: *sphingomyelin*.
 – ORIGIN from Greek *Sphinx*, *Sphing-* 'Sphinx', originally in *sphingosine*, with reference to the enigmatic nature of the compound.

sphingolipid /ˌsfɪŋɡə(ʊ)ˈlɪpɪd/ ▶ noun Biochemistry any of a class of compounds which are fatty acid derivatives of sphingosine and occur chiefly in the cell membranes of the brain and nervous tissue.

sphingomyelin /ˌsfɪŋɡə(ʊ)ˈmʌɪəlɪn/ ▶ **noun** [mass noun] Biochemistry a substance which occurs widely in brain and nervous tissue, consisting of complex phosphoryl derivatives of sphingosine and choline.

sphingosine /ˈsfɪŋɡə(ʊ)sʌɪn/ ▶ **noun** [mass noun] Biochemistry a basic compound which is a constituent of a number of substances important in the metabolism of nerve cells, especially sphingomyelins.
• A crystalline alcohol; chem. formula: $C_{18}H_{37}NO_2$.

sphinx ▶ **noun 1** (**Sphinx**) Greek Mythology a winged monster of Thebes, having a woman's head and a lion's body. It propounded a riddle about the three ages of man, killing those who failed to solve it, until Oedipus was successful, whereupon the Sphinx committed suicide.
■ an ancient Egyptian stone figure having a lion's body and a human or animal head, especially the huge statue near the Pyramids at Giza. ■ an enigmatic or inscrutable person.
2 North American term for **HAWKMOTH**.
– ORIGIN late Middle English: via Latin from Greek *Sphinx*, apparently from *sphingein* 'draw tight'.

sphygmo- /ˈsfɪɡməʊ/ ▶ **combining form** Physiology of or relating to the pulse or pulsation: *sphygmograph*.
– ORIGIN from Greek *sphugmos* 'pulse'.

sphygmograph ▶ **noun** an instrument which produces a line recording the strength and rate of a person's pulse.

sphygmomanometer /ˌsfɪɡməʊməˈnɒmɪtə/ ▶ **noun** an instrument for measuring blood pressure, typically consisting of an inflatable rubber cuff which is applied to the arm and connected to a column of mercury next to a graduated scale, enabling the determination of systolic and diastolic blood pressure by increasing and gradually releasing the pressure in the cuff.
– DERIVATIVES **sphygmomanometry** noun.

Sphynx /sfɪŋks/ ▶ **noun** a cat of a hairless breed, originally from North America.

spic ▶ **noun** US informal, offensive a Spanish-speaking person from Central or South America or the Caribbean, especially a Mexican.
– ORIGIN early 20th cent.: abbreviation of US slang *spiggoty*, in the same sense, of uncertain origin: perhaps an alteration of *speak the* in 'no speak the English'.

Spica /ˈspiːkə/ Astronomy the brightest star in the constellation Virgo.
– ORIGIN Latin, literally 'ear of wheat (in the hand of the goddess)'.

spica /ˈspʌɪkə/ ▶ **noun** Medicine a bandage folded into a spiral arrangement resembling an ear of wheat or barley.
– ORIGIN late 17th cent.: from Latin, literally 'spike, ear of corn'; related to *spina* 'spine'. The current sense is influenced by Greek *stakhus* 'ear of wheat'.

spic and span ▶ **adjective** variant spelling of **SPICK AND SPAN**.

spiccato /spɪˈkɑːtəʊ/ Music ▶ **noun** [mass noun] a style of staccato playing on stringed instruments involving bouncing the bow on the strings.
▶ **adjective** & **adverb** performed or to be performed in this style.
– ORIGIN Italian, literally 'detailed, distinct'.

spice ▶ **noun 1** an aromatic or pungent vegetable substance used to flavour food, e.g. cloves, pepper, or mace: *the cake is packed with spices* | [mass noun] *sift together flour, baking powder, and mixed spice*.
■ [mass noun] an element providing interest and excitement: *healthy rivalry adds spice to the game*. ■ [mass noun] N. English sweets; confectionery.
2 [mass noun] a russet colour.
▶ **verb** [with obj.] [often as adj. **spiced**] flavour with spice: *turbot with a spiced sauce*.
■ add an interesting or piquant quality to; make more exciting: *she was probably adding details to spice up the story*.
– ORIGIN Middle English: shortening of Old French *espice*, from Latin *species* 'sort, kind', in late Latin 'wares'.

spicebush ▶ **noun** a North American shrub with aromatic leaves, bark, and fruit. The leaves were formerly used for a tea and the fruit as an allspice substitute.
• *Lindera benzoin*, family Lauraceae.

Spice Islands former name for **MOLUCCA ISLANDS**.

spick and span (also **spic and span**) ▶ **adjective** neat, clean, and well looked after: *my little house is spick and span*.
– ORIGIN late 16th cent. (in the sense 'brand new'): from *spick and span new*, emphatic extension of dialect *span new*, from Old Norse *spán-nýr*, from *spánn* 'chip' + *nýr* 'new'; *spick* influenced by Dutch *spiksplinternieuw*, literally 'splinter new'.

spicule /ˈspɪkjuːl/ ▶ **noun 1** technical a minute sharp-pointed object or structure that is typically present in large numbers, such as a fine particle of ice.
■ Zoology each of the small needle-like or sharp-pointed structures of calcite or silica which make up the skeleton of a sponge.
2 Astronomy a short-lived, relatively small radial jet of gas in the chromosphere or lower corona of the sun.
– DERIVATIVES **spicular** adjective, **spiculate** /-lət/ adjective, **spiculation** noun.
– ORIGIN late 18th cent.: from modern Latin *spicula*, *spiculum*, diminutives of *spica* 'ear of grain'.

spicy (also **spicey**) ▶ **adjective** (**spicier**, **spiciest**) flavoured with or fragrant with spice: *pasta in a spicy tomato sauce*.
■ exciting or entertaining, especially through being mildly indecent: *spicy jokes and suggestive songs*.
– DERIVATIVES **spicily** adverb, **spiciness** noun.

spider ▶ **noun** an eight-legged predatory arachnid with an unsegmented body consisting of a fused head and thorax and a rounded abdomen. Spiders have fangs which inject poison into their prey, and most kinds spin webs in which to capture insects.
• Order Araneae, class Arachnida.
■ used in names of similar or related arachnids, e.g. **sea spider**, **sun spider**. ■ any object resembling a spider, especially one having numerous or prominent legs or radiating spokes. ■ Brit. a set of radiating elastic ties used to hold a load in place on a vehicle.
▶ **verb** [no obj., with adverbial of direction] move in a scuttling manner suggestive of a spider: *a treecreeper spidered head first down the tree trunk*.
■ form a pattern suggestive of a spider or its web.
– DERIVATIVES **spiderish** adjective.
– ORIGIN late Old English *spīthra*, from *spinnan* (see **SPIN**).

spider beetle ▶ **noun** a small long-legged scavenging beetle, the female of which has a rounded body that gives it a spider-like appearance.
• Family Ptinidae: *Ptinus* and other genera.

spider crab ▶ **noun** a crab with long thin legs and a compact pear-shaped body, which is camouflaged in some kinds by attached sponges and seaweed.
• Majidae and other families, order Decapoda: *Macropodia* and other genera.

spider flower ▶ **noun** a plant with clusters of flowers which have long protruding stamens or styles, giving the flower head a spider-like appearance.
• a South American plant (genus *Cleome*, family Capparidaceae, in particular *C. hassleriana*). • an Australian grevillea.

spider-hunting wasp ▶ **noun** a fast-moving digger wasp that provisions its nest burrow with spiders that it has caught and paralysed.
• Family Pompilidae: many genera.

spider lily ▶ **noun** a lily that typically has long slender petals or elongated petal-like parts around the flower.
• *Hymenocallis* and other genera, family Liliaceae (or Amaryllidaceae).

spiderman ▶ **noun** (pl. **-men**) Brit. informal a person who works at great heights in building work.

spider mite ▶ **noun** an active plant-feeding mite which resembles a minute spider and is frequently a serious garden and greenhouse pest.
• Family Tetranychidae: many species, in particular the **red spider mite** (*Tetranychus urticae*).

spider monkey ▶ **noun** a South American monkey with very long limbs and a long prehensile tail.
• Genus *Brachyteles*, family Cebidae: four species.

spider naevus ▶ **noun** a cluster of minute red blood vessels visible under the skin, occurring typically during pregnancy or as a symptom of certain diseases (e.g. cirrhosis or acne rosacea).

spider orchid ▶ **noun** an orchid with a flower that is said to resemble a spider.
• Several genera in the family Orchidaceae, in particular *Ophrys* of Europe, related to the bee orchid, *Caladenia* of Australia, with long narrow petals and sepals, and the epiphytic **tree spider orchids** (*Dendrobium*) of Australia.

spider plant ▶ **noun** a plant of the lily family which has long narrow leaves with a central yellow stripe, native to southern Africa and popular as a house plant.
• *Chlorophytum comosum*, family Liliaceae.

spider vein ▶ **noun** another term for **THREAD VEIN**.

spiderweb ▶ **noun** a web made by a spider.
■ a thing resembling such a web: *the spiderweb of overhead transmission lines*. ■ a type of turquoise criss-crossed with fine dark lines.
▶ **verb** (**-webbed**, **-webbing**) [with obj.] cover with a pattern resembling a spiderweb: *a glass block spiderwebbed with cracks*.

spiderwort ▶ **noun** an American plant whose flowers bear long hairy stamens.
• Genus *Tradescantia*, family Commelinaceae: several species, including the blue-flowered North American *T. virginiana*, from which many cultivars have been derived.

spidery ▶ **adjective** resembling a spider, especially having long, thin, angular lines like a spider's legs: *the letters were written in a spidery hand*.

spiegeleisen /ˈspiːɡ(ə)lˌʌɪz(ə)n/ ▶ **noun** [mass noun] an alloy of iron and manganese, used in steel-making.
– ORIGIN mid 19th cent.: from German, from *Spiegel* 'mirror' + *Eisen* 'iron'.

spiel /ʃpiːl, spiːl/ informal ▶ **noun** a long or fast speech or story, typically one intended as a means of persuasion or as an excuse but regarded with scepticism or contempt by those who hear it.
▶ **verb** [with obj.] reel off; recite: *he solemnly spieled all he knew*.
■ [no obj.] speak glibly or at length.
– ORIGIN late 19th cent.: from German *Spiel* 'a game'.

Spielberg /ˈspiːlbəːɡ/, Steven (b.1947), American film director and producer. His science-fiction and adventure films such as *ET* (1982) and *Jurassic Park* (1993) broke box office records, while *Schindler's List* (1993) won seven Oscars.

spieler /ˈʃpiːlə, ˈspiːlə/ informal ▶ **noun 1** a glib or voluble speaker.
2 Austral./NZ a gambler or swindler.
3 a gambling club.
– ORIGIN mid 19th cent.: from German *Spieler* 'player' (see **SPIEL**).

spiff ▶ **verb** [with obj.] (**spiff someone/thing up**) informal make someone or something attractive, smart, or stylish: *he arrived all spiffed up in a dinner jacket*.
– ORIGIN late 19th cent.: perhaps from dialect *spiff* 'well-dressed'.

spiffing ▶ **adjective** Brit. informal, dated excellent; splendid: *it's a frightfully spiffing idea*.
– ORIGIN late 19th cent.: of unknown origin.

spifflicate /ˈspɪflɪkeɪt/ (also **spiflicate**) ▶ **verb** [with obj.] informal, humorous treat roughly or severely; destroy: *the mosquito was spifflicated*.
– DERIVATIVES **spifflication** noun.
– ORIGIN mid 18th cent.: a fanciful formation.

spiffy ▶ **adjective** (**spiffier**, **spiffiest**) N. Amer. informal smart in appearance: *a spiffy new outfit*.
– DERIVATIVES **spiffily** adverb.
– ORIGIN mid 19th cent.: of unknown origin.

spignel /ˈspɪɡn(ə)l/ ▶ **noun** an aromatic white-flowered plant of the parsley family, found on mountains in Europe.
• *Meum athamanticum*, family Umbelliferae.
– ORIGIN early 16th cent.: perhaps from Anglo-Norman French *spigurnelle*, the name of an unidentified plant.

spigot /ˈspɪɡət/ ▶ **noun 1** a small peg or plug, especially for insertion into the vent of a cask.
2 US a tap.
■ a device for controlling the flow of liquid in a tap.
3 the plain end of a section of a pipe fitting into the socket of the next one.
– ORIGIN Middle English: perhaps an alteration of Provençal *espigou(n)*, from Latin *spiculum*, diminutive of *spicum*, variant of *spica* (see **SPICA**).

spike[1] ▶ **noun 1** a thin, pointed piece of metal, wood, or another rigid material.
■ a large stout nail, especially one used to fasten a rail to a railway sleeper. ■ each of several metal points set into the sole of a running shoe to prevent slipping. ■ (**spikes**) a pair of running shoes with such metal points. ■ chiefly Brit. a pointed metal rod standing on a base and used for filing paper items such as bills, or journalistic material considered for

S

publication and rejected. ■ informal a hypodermic needle.

2 a sharp increase in the magnitude or concentration of something: *the oil price spike.*

■ Electronics a pulse of very short duration in which a rapid increase in voltage is followed by a rapid decrease.

3 Brit. informal the casual ward of a hostel offering temporary accommodation for the homeless.

▶ **verb** [with obj.] **1** impale on or pierce with a sharp point: *she spiked another oyster.*

■ Baseball injure (a player) with the spikes on one's shoes. ■ (of a newspaper editor) reject (a story) by or as if by filing it on a spike: *the editors deemed the article in bad taste and spiked it.* ■ stop the progress of (a plan or undertaking); put an end to: *he doubted they would spike the entire effort over this one negotiation.* ■ historical render (a gun) useless by plugging up the vent with a spike.

2 form into or cover with sharp points: *his hair was matted and spiked with blood.*

■ [no obj.] take on a sharp, pointed shape: *lightning spiked across the sky.* ■ [no obj.] increase and then decrease sharply; reach a peak: *oil prices would spike and fall again.*

3 informal add alcohol or a drug to contaminate (drink or food) surreptitiously: *she bought me an orange juice and spiked it with vodka.* [ORIGIN: late 19th cent.: originally US slang.]

■ add sharp or pungent flavouring to (food or drink): *spike the liquid with lime or lemon juice.* ■ enrich (a nuclear reactor or its fuel) with a particular isotope.

4 (in volleyball) hit (the ball) forcefully from a position near the net so that it moves downward into the opposite court.

■ American Football fling (the ball) forcefully to the ground, typically in celebration of a touchdown or victory.

– PHRASES **spike someone's guns** thwart someone's plans.

– ORIGIN Middle English: perhaps from Middle Low German, Middle Dutch *spiker*, related to **SPOKE**[1]. The verb dates from the early 17th cent.

spike[2] ▶ **noun** Botany a flower cluster formed of many flower heads attached directly to a long stem. Compare with **CYME**, **RACEME**.

– ORIGIN late Middle English (denoting an ear of corn): from Latin *spica* (see **SPICA**).

spike heel ▶ **noun** a high tapering heel on a woman's shoe.

spikelet ▶ **noun** Botany the basic unit of a grass flower, consisting of two glumes or outer bracts at the base and one or more florets above.

spikemoss ▶ **noun** a chiefly tropical creeping clubmoss which has branching stems with hair-like spines on the leaf margins, small spore-bearing cones, and typically a mat-like growth.

● Genus *Selaginella* and family Selaginellaceae, class Lycopsida.

spikenard /ˈspʌɪknɑːd/ ▶ **noun** **1** [mass noun] historical a costly perfumed ointment much valued in ancient times.

2 the Himalayan plant of the valerian family that produces the rhizome from which this ointment was prepared. See also **PLOUGHMAN'S SPIKENARD**.

● *Nardostachys grandiflora*, family Valerianaceae.

– ORIGIN Middle English: from medieval Latin *spica nardi* (see **SPIKE**[2], **NARD**), translating Greek *nardostakhus*.

spiky ▶ **adjective** (**spikier**, **spikiest**) like a spike or spikes or having many spikes: *he has short spiky hair.*

■ informal easily offended or annoyed.

– DERIVATIVES **spikily** adverb, **spikiness** noun.

spile /spʌɪl/ ▶ **noun** **1** a small wooden peg or spigot for stopping a cask.

■ N. Amer. a small wooden or metal spout for tapping the sap from a sugar maple.

2 a large, heavy timber driven into the ground to support a superstructure.

▶ **verb** [with obj.] chiefly US or dialect broach (a cask) with a peg in order to draw off liquid.

– ORIGIN early 16th cent.: from Middle Dutch, Middle Low German, 'wooden peg'; in sense 2 apparently an alteration of **PILE**[2].

spilite /ˈspʌɪlʌɪt, ˈspɪl-/ ▶ **noun** [mass noun] Geology an altered form of basalt, rich in albite and commonly amygdaloidal in texture, typical of basaltic lava solidified under water.

– DERIVATIVES **spilitic** /spʌɪˈlɪtɪk/ adjective.

– ORIGIN mid 19th cent.: from French *spillite*, from Greek *spilos* 'spot, stain'.

spill[1] ▶ **verb** (past and past participle **spilt** or **spilled**) [with obj.] cause or allow (liquid) to flow over the edge of its container, especially unintentionally: *you'll spill that tea if you're not careful* | figurative *azaleas spilled cascades of flowers over the pathways.*

■ [no obj.] (of liquid) flow over the edge of its container: *some of the wine spilled on to the floor* | figurative *years of frustration spilled over into violence.* ■ [no obj.] (of the contents of something) be emptied out on to a surface: *passengers' baggage had* **spilled out** *of the hold.* ■ cause or allow (the contents of something) to be emptied out on to a surface: *the bag fell to the floor,* **spilling out** *its contents.* ■ [no obj., with adverbial of direction] (of a number of people) move out of somewhere quickly: *students began to spill out of the building.* ■ (in the context of ball games) drop (the ball). ■ informal reveal (confidential information) to someone: *he was reluctant to spill her address.* ■ cause (someone) to fall off a horse or bicycle: *the horse was wrenched off course, spilling his rider.* ■ Sailing let (wind) out of a sail, typically by slackening the sheets.

▶ **noun** **1** a quantity of liquid that has spilled or been spilt: *a 25-tonne oil spill* | *wipe up spills immediately.*

■ an instance of a liquid spilling or being spilt: *he was absolved from any blame for the oil spill.*

2 a fall from a horse or bicycle.

3 Austral. a vacating of all or several posts in a cabinet or parliamentary party to allow reorganization after one important change of office.

– PHRASES **spill the beans** informal reveal secret information unintentionally or indiscreetly. **spill (someone's) blood** kill or wound people. **spill one's guts** informal reveal copious information to someone in an uninhibited way.

– ORIGIN Old English *spillan* 'kill, destroy, waste, shed (blood)'; of unknown origin.

– DERIVATIVES **spiller** noun.

spill[2] ▶ **noun** a thin strip of wood or paper used for lighting a fire, candle, pipe, etc.

– ORIGIN Middle English (in the sense 'sharp fragment of wood'): obscurely related to **SPILE**. The current sense dates from the early 19th cent.

spillage ▶ **noun** [mass noun] the action of causing or allowing a liquid to spill, or liquid spilled in this way: *accidents involving chemical spillage* | [count noun] *oil spillages at sea.*

Spillane /spɪˈleɪn/, Mickey (b.1918), American writer; pseudonym of *Frank Morrison Spillane*. His popular detective novels include *My Gun Is Quick* (1950) and *The Big Kill* (1951).

spillikin /ˈspɪlɪkɪn/ ▶ **noun** **1** (**spillikins**) a game played with a heap of small rods of wood, bone, or plastic, in which players try to remove one at a time without disturbing the others.

2 a splinter or fragment.

– ORIGIN mid 18th cent.: from **SPILL**[2] + **-KIN**.

spillover ▶ **noun** an instance of overflowing or spreading into another area: *there has been a spillover into state schools of the ethos of independent schools.*

■ a thing that spreads or has spread into another area: *the village was a spillover from a neighbouring, larger village.* ■ [usu. as modifier] an unexpected consequence, repercussion, or by-product: *the spillover effect of the quarrel.*

spillway ▶ **noun** a passage for surplus water from a dam.

■ a natural drainage channel cut by water formed by melting of glaciers or ice fields.

spilt past and past participle of **SPILL**[1].

spilth ▶ **noun** [mass noun] archaic the action of spilling; material that is spilt.

spin ▶ **verb** (**spinning**; past and past participle **spun**) **1** turn or cause to turn or whirl round quickly: [no obj.] *the girl* **spun round** *in alarm* | *the rear wheels spun violently* | [with obj.] *he fiddled with the radio, spinning the dial.*

■ [no obj.] (of a person's head) give a sensation of dizziness: *the figures were enough to make her head spin.* ■ [with obj.] toss (a coin). ■ [with obj.] chiefly Cricket impart a revolving motion to (a ball) when bowling. ■ [no obj.] chiefly Cricket (of a ball) move through the air with such a revolving motion. ■ [with obj.] give (a news story) a favourable emphasis or slant. ■ [with obj.] spin-dry (clothes). ■ [with obj.] play (a record). ■ [with obj.] shape (sheet metal) by pressure applied during rotation on a lathe: [as adj. **spun**] *spun metal components.*

2 [with obj.] draw out (wool, cotton, or other material) and convert it into threads, either by hand or with machinery: *they* **spin** *wool* **into** *the yarn for weaving* | [as adj. **spun**] *spun glass.*

■ make (threads) in this way: *this method is used to spin filaments from syrups.* ■ (of a spider or a silkworm or other insect) produce (gossamer or silk) or construct (a web or cocoon) by extruding a fine viscous thread from a special gland.

3 [no obj.] fish with a spinner: *they were spinning for salmon in the lake.*

▶ **noun** **1** a rapid turning or whirling motion: *he concluded the dance with a double spin.*

■ [mass noun] revolving motion imparted to a ball in a game, especially cricket, tennis, or snooker: *this racket enables the player to impart more spin to the ball* | [as modifier] *a spin bowler.* ■ [in sing.] a favourable bias or slant in a news story: *he tried to put a positive spin on the president's campaign.* ■ [usu. in sing.] a fast revolving motion of an aircraft as it descends rapidly: *he tried to stop the plane from* **going into a spin**. ■ Physics the intrinsic angular momentum of a subatomic particle.

2 [in sing.] informal a brief trip in a vehicle for pleasure: *a spin around town.*

3 [with adj.] [in sing.] Austral./NZ informal a piece of good or bad luck: *Kevin had had a rough spin.*

– PHRASES **spin one's wheels** N. Amer. informal waste one's time or efforts. **spin a yarn** tell a long, far-fetched story.

– ORIGIN Old English *spinnan* 'draw out and twist (fibre)'; related to German *spinnen*. The noun dates from the mid 19th cent.

▶ **spin something off** (of a parent company) turn a subsidiary into a new and separate company.

spin out N. Amer. (of a driver or car) lose control, especially in a skid.

spin something out **1** make something last as long as possible: *they seem keen to spin out the debate through their speeches and interventions.* ■ spend or occupy time aimlessly or without profit: *Shane and Mary played games to spin out the afternoon.* **2** (**spin someone/thing out**) Cricket dismiss a batsman or side by spin bowling.

spina bifida /ˌspʌɪnə ˈbɪfɪdə/ ▶ **noun** [mass noun] a congenital defect of the spine in which part of the spinal cord and its meninges are exposed through a gap in the backbone. It often causes paralysis of the lower limbs, and sometimes mental handicap.

– ORIGIN early 18th cent.: modern Latin (see **SPINE**, **BIFID**).

spinach /ˈspɪnɪdʒ, -ɪtʃ/ ▶ **noun** an edible Asian plant of the goosefoot family, with large, dark green leaves which are widely eaten as a vegetable.

● *Spinacia oleracea*, family Chenopodiaceae.

– DERIVATIVES **spinachy** adjective.

– ORIGIN Middle English: probably from Old French *espinache*, via Arabic from Persian *aspānāk*.

spinach beet ▶ **noun** beet of a variety which is cultivated for its leaves, which resemble spinach in taste and appearance.

● *Beta vulgaris* subsp. (or var.) *cicla*, family Chenopodiaceae.

spinal ▶ **adjective** of or relating to the spine: *spinal injuries.*

■ relating to or forming the central axis or backbone of something: *the building of a new spinal road.*

– DERIVATIVES **spinally** adverb.

– ORIGIN late 16th cent.: from late Latin *spinalis*, from Latin *spina* (see **SPINE**).

spinal canal ▶ **noun** a cavity which runs successively through each of the vertebrae and encloses the spinal cord.

spinal column ▶ **noun** the spine; the backbone.

spinal cord ▶ **noun** the cylindrical bundle of nerve fibres and associated tissue which is enclosed in the spine and connects nearly all parts of the body to the brain, with which it forms the central nervous system.

spinal tap ▶ **noun** North American term for **LUMBAR PUNCTURE**.

spindle ▶ **noun** **1** a slender rounded rod with tapered ends used in hand spinning to twist and wind thread from a mass of wool or flax held on a distaff.

■ a pin or rod used on a spinning wheel to twist and wind the thread. ■ a pin bearing the bobbin of a spinning machine. ■ a measure of length for yarn, equal to 15,120 yards (13,826 metres) for cotton or 14,400 yards (13,167 metres) for linen. ■ N. Amer. a pointed metal rod on a base, used for filing paper items. ■ a turned piece of wood used as a banister or chair leg.

2 a rod or pin serving as an axis that revolves or on which something revolves.

■ the vertical rod at the centre of a record turntable which keeps the record in place during play.

3 Biology a slender mass of microtubules formed

S

when a cell divides. At metaphase the chromosomes become attached to it by their centromeres before being pulled towards its ends.
4 (also **spindle tree** or **bush**) a Eurasian shrub or small tree with slender toothed leaves and pink capsules containing bright orange seeds. The hard timber was formerly used for making spindles.
• Genus *Euonymus*, family Celastraceae: several species, in particular *E. europaea*.
– ORIGIN Old English *spinel*, from the base of the verb **SPIN**.

spindle-back ▶ adjective (of a chair) with a back consisting of framed cylindrical bars.

spindle cell ▶ noun a narrow, elongated cell, in particular:
■ Medicine a cell of this shape indicating the presence of a type of sarcoma. ■ Zoology a cell of this shape present in the blood of most non-mammalian vertebrates, functioning as a platelet.

spindle-shanks ▶ plural noun dated long thin legs.
■ [treated as sing.] a person with long thin legs.
– DERIVATIVES **spindle-shanked** adjective.

spindle-shaped ▶ adjective having a circular cross section and tapering towards each end.

spindle shell ▶ noun a predatory marine mollusc which has a shell that forms a long slender spiral with a narrow canal extending downwards from the aperture.
• *Neptunea antiqua* (family Buccinidae) of northern seas, and *Fusinus* and other genera (family Fasciolariidae) of tropical and temperate seas, class Gastropoda.

spindle whorl ▶ noun chiefly Archaeology a whorl or small pulley used to weight a spindle.

spindly ▶ adjective (of a person or limb) long or tall and thin: *spindly arms and legs.*
■ (of a thing) thin and weak or insubstantial in construction: *spindly chairs.*

spin doctor ▶ noun informal a spokesperson employed to give a favourable interpretation of events to the media, especially on behalf of a political party.

spin-down ▶ noun [mass noun] a decrease in the speed of rotation of a spinning object, in particular a heavenly body or a computer disc.

spindrift ▶ noun [mass noun] spray blown from the crests of waves by the wind.
■ driving snow or sand.
– ORIGIN early 17th cent. (originally Scots): variant of *spoondrift*, from archaic *spoon* 'run before wind or sea' + the noun **DRIFT**.

spin dryer ▶ noun a machine for drying wet clothes by spinning them in a revolving perforated drum.
– DERIVATIVES **spin-dry** verb.

spine ▶ noun **1** a series of vertebrae extending from the skull to the small of the back, enclosing the spinal cord and providing support for the thorax and abdomen; the backbone.
■ figurative a thing's central feature or main source of strength: *players who will form the spine of our side | Puerto Rico's mountainous spine.* ■ [mass noun] figurative resolution or strength of character. ■ the part of a book's jacket or cover that encloses the inner edges of the pages, facing outwards when the book is on a shelf and typically bearing the title and the author's name. ■ (also **pay spine**) a linear pay scale operated by some large organizations that allows flexibility for local and specific conditions.
2 Zoology & Botany any hard pointed defensive projection or structure, such as a prickle of a hedgehog, a spike-like projection on a sea urchin, a sharp ray in a fish's fin, or a spike on the stem of a plant.
■ Geology a tall mass of viscous lava extruded from a volcano.
– DERIVATIVES **spined** adjective [in combination] *broken-spined paperbacks.*
– ORIGIN late Middle English: shortening of Old French *espine*, or from Latin *spina* 'thorn, prickle, backbone'.

spine-chiller ▶ noun a story or film that inspires terror and excitement.

spine-chilling ▶ adjective inspiring terror or terrified excitement: *a spine-chilling silence.*

spinel /spɪˈnɛl, ˈspɪn(ə)l/ ▶ noun [mass noun] a hard glassy mineral occurring as octahedral crystals of variable colour and consisting chiefly of magnesium and aluminium oxides.
■ [count noun] Chemistry any of a class of oxides including this, containing aluminium and another metal and having the general formula MAl_2O_4.
– ORIGIN early 16th cent.: from French *spinelle*, from Italian *spinella*, diminutive of *spina* 'thorn'.

spineless ▶ adjective **1** having no spine or backbone; invertebrate.
■ figurative (of a person) lacking energy or resolution; weak and purposeless: *a spineless coward.*
2 (of an animal or plant) lacking spines: *spineless forms of prickly pear have been selected.*
– DERIVATIVES **spinelessly** adverb, **spinelessness** noun.

spinel ruby ▶ noun [mass noun] a deep red variety of spinel, often of gem quality.

spinet /spɪˈnɛt, ˈspɪnɪt/ ▶ noun **1** historical a small harpsichord with the strings set obliquely to the keyboard, popular in the 18th century.
2 US a type of small upright piano.
– ORIGIN mid 17th cent.: shortening of obsolete French *espinette*, from Italian *spinetta* 'virginal, spinet', diminutive of *spina* 'thorn' (see **SPINE**), the strings being plucked by quills.

spinetail ▶ noun any of a number of birds with pointed feather tips projecting beyond the tail:
• (also **spine-tailed swift**) a mainly African and Asian swift (several genera in the family Apodidae). • a small tropical American ovenbird (*Synallaxis* and other genera, family Furnariidae). • Austral. another term for **LOGRUNNER**.

spine-tingling ▶ adjective informal thrilling or pleasurably frightening: *a spine-tingling adventure.*

spinifex /ˈspɪnɪfɛks/ ▶ noun a grass with coarse spiny leaves and spiny flower heads which break off and are blown about like tumbleweed, occurring from East Asia to Australia.
• Genus *Spinifex*, family Gramineae.
– ORIGIN early 19th cent.: modern Latin, from Latin *spina* 'thorn' + *-fex* from *facere* 'make'.

spinifexbird ▶ noun a secretive warbler that frequents thickets of spinifex in central Australia.
• *Eremiornis carteri*, family Sylviidae.

spinnaker /ˈspɪnəkə/ ▶ noun a large three-cornered sail, typically bulging when full, set forward of the mainsail of a racing yacht when running before the wind.
– ORIGIN mid 19th cent.: apparently a fanciful formation from *Sphinx*, the name of the yacht first using it, perhaps influenced by **SPANKER**.

spinner ▶ noun **1** a person occupied in making thread by spinning.
2 Cricket a bowler who is expert in spinning the ball.
■ a spun ball.
3 (also **spinnerbait**) Fishing a lure designed to revolve when pulled through the water.
■ a type of fishing fly, used chiefly for trout.
4 a metal fairing that is attached to and revolves with the propeller boss of an aircraft in order to streamline it.

spinner dolphin ▶ noun a dolphin of warm seas which has a long slender beak, noted for rotating several times while leaping into the air.
• Genus *Stenella*, family Delphinidae: two species, in particular *S. longirostris*.

spinneret /ˈspɪnərɛt/ ▶ noun Zoology any of a number of different organs through which the silk, gossamer, or thread of spiders, silkworms, and certain other insects is produced.
■ (in the production of man-made fibres) a cap or plate with a number of small holes through which a fibre-forming solution is forced.

spinney ▶ noun (pl. **-eys**) Brit. a small area of trees and bushes.
– ORIGIN late 16th cent.: shortening of Old French *espinei*, from an alteration of Latin *spinetum* 'thicket', from *spina* 'thorn'.

spinning ▶ noun [mass noun] the action or process of spinning; the conversion of fibres into thread or yarn.

spinning jenny ▶ noun historical a machine for spinning with more than one spindle at a time, patented by James Hargreaves in 1770.

spinning mule ▶ noun see **MULE**[1] (sense 3).

spinning top ▶ noun see **TOP**[2] (sense 1).

spinning wheel ▶ noun a household machine for spinning yarn or thread with a spindle driven by a wheel attached to a crank or treadle.

spin-off ▶ noun a by-product or incidental result of a larger project: *the commercial spin-off from defence research.*
■ a product marketed by its association with a popular television programme, film, personality, etc.: [as modifier] *spin-off merchandising.* ■ a business or organization developed out of or by members of another organization, in particular a subsidiary of a parent company that has been sold off, creating a new company.

Spinone /spɪˈnəʊni/ ▶ noun (pl. **Spinoni**) a wire-haired gun dog of an Italian breed, typically white with brown markings, drooping ears, and a docked tail.
– ORIGIN 1940s: Italian.

spinose /ˈspʌɪnəʊs, spʌɪˈnəʊs/ (also **spinous** /ˈspʌɪnəs/) ▶ adjective chiefly Botany & Zoology having spines; spiny: *spinose forms will need care in collecting.*

spin-out ▶ noun N. Amer. informal **1** another term for **SPIN-OFF**.
2 a skidding spin by a vehicle out of control.

Spinoza /spɪˈnəʊzə/, Baruch (or Benedict) de (1632–77), Dutch philosopher, of Portuguese-Jewish descent. Spinoza espoused a pantheistic system, seeing 'God or nature' as a single infinite substance, with mind and matter being two incommensurable ways of conceiving the one reality.
– DERIVATIVES **Spinozism** noun, **Spinozist** noun & adjective, **Spinozistic** adjective.

spin-stabilized (also **-ised**) ▶ adjective (of a satellite or spacecraft) stabilized in a desired orientation by being made to rotate about an axis.
– DERIVATIVES **spin-stabilization** noun.

spinster ▶ noun an unmarried woman, typically an older woman beyond the usual age for marriage.
– DERIVATIVES **spinsterhood** noun, **spinsterish** adjective.
– ORIGIN late Middle English (in the sense 'woman who spins'): from the verb **SPIN** + **-STER**; in early use the term was appended to names of women to denote their occupation. The current sense dates from the early 18th cent.

USAGE The development of the word **spinster** is a good example of the way in which a word acquires strong connotations to the extent that it can no longer be used in a neutral sense. From the 17th century the word was appended to names as the official legal description of an unmarried woman: *Elizabeth Harris of London, Spinster*; this type of use survives today in some legal and religious contexts. In modern everyday English, however, **spinster** cannot be used to mean simply 'unmarried woman'; it is now always a derogatory term, referring or alluding to a stereotype of an older woman who is unmarried, childless, prissy, and repressed.

spinthariscope /spɪnˈθarɪskəʊp/ ▶ noun Physics an instrument that shows the incidence of alpha particles by flashes on a fluorescent screen.
– ORIGIN early 20th cent.: formed irregularly from Greek *spintharis* 'spark' + **-SCOPE**.

spinto /ˈspɪntəʊ/ ▶ noun (pl. **-os**) a lyric soprano or tenor voice of powerful dramatic quality.
■ a singer with such a voice.
– ORIGIN 1950s: Italian, literally 'pushed', past participle of *spingere* 'push'.

spinulose /ˈspɪnjʊləʊs/ ▶ adjective Botany & Zoology having small spines.
– ORIGIN early 19th cent.: from modern Latin *spinulosus*, from *spinula*, diminutive of *spina* 'thorn, spine'.

spiny ▶ adjective (**spinier**, **spiniest**) full of or covered with prickles: *a spiny cactus.*
■ informal difficult to understand or handle: *a spiny problem.*
– DERIVATIVES **spininess** noun.

spiny anteater ▶ noun another term for **ECHIDNA**.

spiny dogfish ▶ noun another term for **SPUR-DOG**.

spiny-headed worm ▶ noun another term for **THORNY-HEADED WORM**.

spiny lobster ▶ noun a large edible crustacean with a spiny shell and long heavy antennae, but lacking the large claws of true lobsters.
• Family Palinuridae: several genera and species, in particular *Palinurus vulgaris* of European waters, and the American genus *Panulirus*.

spiny mouse ▶ noun a mouse that has spines mixed with the hair on its back, native to Africa and SW Asia.
• Genus *Acomys*, family Muridae: several species.

spiracle /ˈspʌɪrək(ə)l/ ▶ noun Zoology an external respiratory opening, especially each of a number of pores on the body of an insect, or each of a pair of

vestigial gill slits behind the eye of a cartilaginous fish.
– DERIVATIVES **spiracular** adjective.
– ORIGIN late 18th cent.: from Latin *spiraculum*, from *spirare* 'breathe'.

spiraea /spʌɪˈriːə/ (chiefly US also **spirea**) ▶**noun** a shrub of the rose family, with clusters of small white or pink flowers. Found throughout the northern hemisphere, it is widely cultivated as a garden ornamental.
• Genus *Spiraea*, family Rosaceae.
– ORIGIN modern Latin, from Greek *speiraia*, from *speira* 'a coil'.

spiral ▶**adjective** winding in a continuous and gradually widening (or tightening) curve, either around a central point on a flat plane or about an axis so as to form a cone: *a spiral pattern*.
■winding in a continuous curve of constant diameter about a central axis, as though along a cylinder; helical. ■(of a stairway) constantly turning in one direction as it rises, around a solid or open centre. ■Medicine (of a fracture) curving round a long bone lengthwise. ■short for **SPIRAL-BOUND**: *a spiral notebook*.
▶**noun 1** a spiral curve, shape, or pattern: *he spotted a spiral of smoke*.
■a spiral spring. ■Astronomy short for **SPIRAL GALAXY**.
2 (also **vicious spiral**) a progressive rise or fall of prices, wages, etc., each responding to an upward or downward stimulus provided by a previous one: *an inflationary spiral*.
■a process of deterioration through the continuous increase or decrease of a specified feature: *this spiral of deprivation and environmental degradation*.
▶**verb** (**spiralled**, **spiralling**; US **spiraled**, **spiraling**) **1** [no obj., with adverbial of direction] move in a spiral course: *a wisp of smoke spiralled up from the trees*.
■[with obj. and adverbial] cause to have a spiral shape or follow a spiral course: *spiral the bandage round the injured limb*.
2 [no obj.] show a continuous and dramatic increase: *inflation continued to spiral* | [as adj. **spiralling**] *he needed to relax after the spiralling tensions of the day*.
■(**spiral down/downward**) decrease or deteriorate continuously: *he expects the figures to spiral down further*.
– DERIVATIVES **spirally** adverb.
– ORIGIN mid 16th cent. (as an adjective): from medieval Latin *spiralis*, from Latin *spira* 'coil' (see **SPIRE**[2]).

spiral-bound ▶**adjective** (of a book or notepad) bound with a wire or plastic spiral threaded through a row of holes along one edge.

spiral galaxy ▶**noun** a galaxy in which the stars and gas clouds are concentrated mainly in one or more spiral arms.

spirant /ˈspʌɪr(ə)nt/ ▶**adjective** Phonetics (of a consonant) uttered with a continuous expulsion of breath.
▶**noun** such a consonant; a fricative.
– DERIVATIVES **spirantization** noun, **spirantize** (also **-ise**) verb.
– ORIGIN mid 19th cent.: from Latin *spirant-* 'breathing', from the verb *spirare*.

S

spire[1] ▶**noun** a tapering conical or pyramidal structure on the top of a building, typically a church tower.
■the continuation of a tree trunk above the point where branching begins, especially in a tree of a tapering form. ■a long tapering object: *spires of delphiniums*.
– DERIVATIVES **spired** adjective, **spiry** adjective.
– ORIGIN Old English *spīr* 'tall slender stem of a plant'; related to German *Spier* 'tip of a blade of grass'.

spire[2] ▶**noun** Zoology the upper tapering part of the spiral shell of a gastropod mollusc, comprising all but the whorl containing the body.
– ORIGIN mid 16th cent. (in the general sense 'a spiral'): from French, or via Latin from Greek *speira* 'a coil'.

spirea ▶**noun** US variant spelling of **SPIRAEA**.

spire shell ▶**noun** a marine or freshwater mollusc with a long conical spiral shell.
• Hydrobiidae and related families, class Gastropoda.

spirillum /spʌɪˈrɪləm/ ▶**noun** (pl. **spirilla** /-lə/) a bacterium with a rigid spiral structure, found in stagnant water and sometimes causing disease.
• Genus *Spirillum*; Gram-negative.
– ORIGIN modern Latin, irregular diminutive of Latin *spira* 'a coil'.

spirit ▶**noun 1** the non-physical part of a person which is the seat of emotions and character; the soul: *we seek a harmony between body and spirit*.
■such a part regarded as a person's true self and as capable of surviving physical death or separation: *a year after he left, his spirit is still present*. ■such a part manifested as an apparition after their death; a ghost. ■a supernatural being: *shrines to nature spirits*. ■(**Spirit**) short for **HOLY SPIRIT**. ■archaic a highly refined substance or fluid thought to govern vital phenomena.
2 [in sing.] those qualities regarded as forming the definitive or typical elements in the character of a person, nation, or group or in the thought and attitudes of a particular period: *the university is a symbol of the nation's egalitarian spirit*.
■[with adj.] a person identified with their most prominent mental or moral characteristics or with their role in a group or movement: *he was a leading spirit in the conference*. ■a specified emotion or mood, especially one prevailing at a particular time: *I hope the team will build on this* ***spirit of*** *confidence*. ■(**spirits**) a person's mood: *the warm weather lifted everyone's spirits after the winter*. ■[mass noun] the quality of courage, energy, and determination or assertiveness: *his visitors admired his spirit and good temper*. ■the attitude or intentions with which someone undertakes or regards something: *he confessed in a spirit of self-respect, not defiance*. ■the real meaning or the intention behind something as opposed to its strict verbal interpretation: *the rule had been broken in spirit if not in letter*.
3 (usu. **spirits**) chiefly Brit. strong distilled liquor such as brandy, whisky, gin, or rum.
■[mass noun] [with modifier] a volatile liquid, especially a fuel, prepared by distillation: *aviation spirit*. ■archaic a solution of volatile components extracted from something, typically by distillation or by solution in alcohol: ***spirits of*** *turpentine*.
▶**verb** (**spirited**, **spiriting**) [with obj. and adverbial of direction] convey rapidly and secretly: *stolen cows were* ***spirited away*** *some distance to prevent detection*.
– PHRASES **enter into the spirit** join wholeheartedly in an event, especially one of celebration and festivity: *he* ***entered into the spirit of*** *the occasion by dressing as a pierrot*. **in** (or **in the**) **spirit** in thought or intention though not physically: *he couldn't be here in person, but he is with us in spirit*. **the spirit is willing but the flesh is weak** proverb someone has good intentions but fails to live up to them. [ORIGIN: with biblical allusion to Matt. 26:41.] **when the spirit moves someone** when someone feels inclined to do something: *he can be quite candid when the spirit moves him*. [ORIGIN: a phrase originally in Quaker use, with reference to the Holy Spirit.] **the spirit world** (in animistic and occult belief) the non-physical realm in which disembodied spirits have their existence.
▶**spirit someone up** archaic stimulate, animate, or cheer up someone.
– ORIGIN Middle English: from Anglo-Norman French, from Latin *spiritus* 'breath, spirit', from *spirare* 'breathe'.

spirited ▶**adjective 1** full of energy, enthusiasm, and determination: *a spirited campaigner for women's rights*.
2 [in combination] having a specified character, outlook on life, or mood: *he was a warm-hearted, generous-spirited man*.
– DERIVATIVES **spiritedly** adverb, **spiritedness** noun.

spirit gum ▶**noun** [mass noun] a quick-drying solution of gum, chiefly used by actors to attach false hair to their faces.

spiritism ▶**noun** another term for **SPIRITUALISM** (in sense 1).
– DERIVATIVES **spiritist** adjective & noun, **spiritistic** adjective.

spirit lamp ▶**noun** a lamp burning volatile spirits, especially methylated spirits, instead of oil.

spiritless ▶**adjective** lacking courage, vigour, or vivacity: *Ruth and I played a spiritless game of Scrabble*.
– DERIVATIVES **spiritlessly** adverb, **spiritlessness** noun.

spirit level ▶**noun** a device consisting of a sealed glass tube partially filled with alcohol or other liquid, containing an air bubble whose position reveals whether a surface is perfectly level.

spirit of hartshorn ▶**noun** see **HARTSHORN**.

spirit of wine (also **spirits of wine**) ▶**noun** [mass noun] archaic purified alcohol.

spiritous ▶**adjective** another term for **SPIRITUOUS**.

spirits of salt ▶**noun** archaic term for **HYDROCHLORIC ACID**.

spiritual /ˈspɪrɪtʃʊəl, -tjʊəl/ ▶**adjective 1** of, relating to, or affecting the human spirit or soul as opposed to material or physical things: *I'm responsible for his spiritual welfare* | *the spiritual values of life*.
■(of a person) not concerned with material values or pursuits.
2 of or relating to religion or religious belief: *Iran's spiritual leader*.
▶**noun** (also **negro spiritual**) a religious song of a kind associated with black Christians of the southern US, and thought to derive from the combination of European hymns and African musical elements by black slaves.
– PHRASES **one's spiritual home** a place in which one feels a profound sense of belonging: *I had always thought of Italy as my spiritual home*.
– DERIVATIVES **spirituality** noun, **spiritually** adverb.
– ORIGIN Middle English: from Old French *spirituel*, from Latin *spiritualis*, from *spiritus* (see **SPIRIT**).

spiritualism ▶**noun** [mass noun] **1** a system of belief or religious practice based on supposed communication with the spirits of the dead, especially through mediums.
2 Philosophy the doctrine that the spirit exists as distinct from matter, or that spirit is the only reality.
– DERIVATIVES **spiritualist** noun, **spiritualistic** adjective.

spiritualize (also **-ise**) ▶**verb** [with obj.] elevate to a spiritual level.
– DERIVATIVES **spiritualization** noun.

spirituous /ˈspɪrɪtjʊəs/ ▶**adjective** formal or archaic containing much alcohol; distilled: *spirituous beverages*.
– ORIGIN late 16th cent. (in the sense 'spirited, lively'): from Latin *spiritus* 'spirit' + **-OUS**, or from French *spiritueux*.

spiritus /ˈspɪrɪtʊs/ ▶**noun** Latin term for **BREATH**, often used figuratively to mean spirit.

spiritus rector /ˈrɛktɔː/ ▶**noun** [mass noun] a ruling or directing spirit.
– ORIGIN Latin.

spiro-[1] ▶**combining form 1** spiral; in a spiral: *spirochaete*.
2 Chemistry denoting a molecule with two rings with one atom common to both: *spironolactone*.
– ORIGIN from Latin *spira*, Greek *speira* 'a coil'.

spiro-[2] ▶**combining form** relating to breathing: *spirometer*.
– ORIGIN formed irregularly from Latin *spirare* 'breathe'.

spirochaete /ˈspʌɪrə(ʊ)kiːt/ (US **spirochete**) ▶**noun** a flexible spirally twisted bacterium, especially one that causes syphilis.
• *Treponema* and other genera, order Spirochaetales; Gram-negative.
– ORIGIN late 19th cent.: from **SPIRO-**[1] 'in a spiral' + Greek *khaitē* 'long hair'.

spirograph ▶**noun 1** an instrument for recording breathing movements.
2 (**Spirograph**) trademark a toy which is used to draw intricate curved patterns using interlocking plastic cogs and toothed rings of different sizes.
– DERIVATIVES **spirographic** adjective (only in sense 1).

spirogyra /ˌspʌɪrə(ʊ)ˈdʒʌɪrə/ ▶**noun** Botany a filamentous green alga of a genus that includes blanket weed.
• Genus *Spirogyra*, division Chlorophyta.
– ORIGIN modern Latin, from **SPIRO-**[1] 'spiral' + Greek *guros*, *gura* 'round'.

spirometer /spʌɪˈrɒmɪtə/ ▶**noun** an instrument for measuring the air capacity of the lungs.
– DERIVATIVES **spirometry** noun.

spironolactone /ˌspʌɪrənə(ʊ)ˈlaktəʊn/ ▶**noun** [mass noun] Medicine a steroid drug which promotes sodium excretion and is used in the treatment of certain types of oedema and hypertension.
– ORIGIN 1960s: from **SPIRO-**[1] (in sense 2) + **LACTONE**, with the insertion of **-ONE**.

spirt ▶**verb** & **noun** old-fashioned spelling of **SPURT**.

spirulina /ˌspɪrʊˈlʌɪnə, ˌspʌɪrʊ-/ ▶**noun** [mass noun] filamentous cyanobacteria which form tangled masses in warm alkaline lakes in Africa and Central and South America.
• Genus *Spirulina*, division Cyanobacteria.

■(usu. **Spirulina**) the substance of such growths dried and prepared as a food or food additive, which is a rich source of many vitamins and minerals.
– ORIGIN modern Latin, from *spirula* 'small spiral (shell)'.

spit[1] ▶**verb** (**spitting**; past and past participle **spat** or **spit**) [no obj.] **1** eject saliva forcibly from one's mouth, sometimes as a gesture of contempt or anger: *Todd spat in Hugh's face.*
■[with obj.] forcibly eject (food or liquid) from one's mouth: *the baby* **spat out** *its porridge.* ■ (**spit up**) N. Amer. (especially of a baby) vomit or regurgitate food. ■ [with obj.] utter in a hostile or aggressive way: *she spat abuse at the jury* | [with direct speech] *'Go to hell!' she spat.* ■ be extremely angry or frustrated: *he was spitting with sudden fury.* ■ (of a fire or something being cooked) emit small bursts of sparks or hot fat with a series of short, explosive noises. ■ (of a cat) make a hissing noise as a sign of anger or hostility.
2 (**it spits**, **it is spitting**, etc.) Brit. light rain falls: *it began to spit.*
▶**noun 1** [mass noun] saliva, typically that which has been ejected from a person's mouth.
■short for **CUCKOO SPIT**.
2 an act of spitting.
– PHRASES **be the spit** (or **the dead spit**) **of** informal look exactly like: *Felix is the spit of Rosa's brother.* **spit blood** (or Austral. **chips**) feel or express vehement anger: *it was enough to make anyone spit blood!* **spit** (**out**) **the dummy** Austral. informal behave in a bad-tempered or petulant way. **spit in the eye** (or **face**) **of** show contempt or scorn for. **spit in** (or **into**) **the wind** used to suggest that it is futile or pointless to do something. **spit it out** informal used to urge someone to say or confess something quickly: *spit it out, man, I haven't got all day.* **spit-and-sawdust** Brit. informal used to describe a bar that appears dirty or run-down: *the old-fashioned spit-and-sawdust pub.*
– ORIGIN Old English *spittan*, of imitative origin.

spit[2] ▶**noun 1** a long, thin metal rod pushed through meat in order to hold and turn it while it is roasted over an open fire: *chicken cooked on a spit.*
2 a narrow point of land projecting into the sea: *a narrow spit of land shelters the bay.*
▶**verb** (**spitted**, **spitting**) [with obj.] put a spit through (meat) in order to roast it over an open fire: *he spitted the rabbit and cooked it.*
– DERIVATIVES **spitty** adjective.
– ORIGIN Old English *spitu*, of West Germanic origin; related to Dutch *spit* and German *Spiess*.

spit[3] ▶**noun** (pl. same or **spits**) a layer of earth whose depth is equal to the length of the blade of a spade: *break up the top spit with a fork.*
– ORIGIN early 16th cent.: from Middle Dutch and Middle Low German; probably related to **SPIT**[2].

spit and polish ▶**noun** [mass noun] thorough or exaggerated cleaning and polishing, especially by a soldier: *they gave the dining room some extra spit and polish.*

spitball ▶**noun 1** a piece of paper that has been chewed and shaped into a ball for use as a missile.
2 Baseball an illegal pitch made with a ball moistened with saliva or sweat to make it move erratically.
▶**verb** [with obj.] US informal throw out (a suggestion) for discussion: *I'm just spitballing a few ideas.*
– DERIVATIVES **spitballer** noun.

spitchcock ▶**noun** an eel that has been split and grilled or fried.
▶**verb** [no obj.] prepare (an eel or other fish) in this way.
– ORIGIN late 15th cent.: of unknown origin; compare with **SPATCHCOCK**.

spit curl ▶**noun** North American term for **KISS-CURL**.

spit dog ▶**noun** a firedog with a hook on its upright for supporting a spit.

spite ▶**noun** [mass noun] a desire to hurt, annoy, or offend someone: *he'd think I was saying it out of spite.*
■[count noun] archaic an instance of such a desire; a grudge: *it seemed as if the wind* **had a spite at** *her.*
▶**verb** [with obj.] deliberately hurt, annoy, or offend (someone): *he put the house up for sale to spite his family.*
– PHRASES **in spite of** without being affected by the particular factor mentioned: *he was suddenly cold in spite of the sun.* **in spite of oneself** although one did not want or expect to do so: *Oliver smiled in spite of himself.*
– ORIGIN Middle English: shortening of Old French *despit* 'contempt', *despiter* 'show contempt for'.

spiteful ▶**adjective** showing or caused by malice: *the teachers made spiteful little jokes about me.*
– DERIVATIVES **spitefully** adverb, **spitefulness** noun.

spitfire ▶**noun** a person with a fierce temper.

Spithead /spɪtˈhɛd/ a channel between the NE coast of the Isle of Wight and the mainland of southern England. It offers sheltered access to Southampton Water and deep anchorage.

spit-roast ▶**verb** [with obj.] [usu. as adj. **spit-roasted**] cook (a piece of meat) on a spit: *spit-roasted lamb.*

Spitsbergen /ˈspɪtsˌbəːg(ə)n/ a Norwegian island in the Svalbard archipelago, in the Arctic Ocean north of Norway; principal settlement, Longyearbyen.

spitter ▶**noun 1** a person who spits.
2 another term for **SPITBALL** (in sense 2).

spitting cobra ▶**noun** an African cobra that defends itself by spitting venom from the fangs, typically at the aggressor's eyes.
• Genera *Naja* and *Hemachatus*, family Elapidae: three species, in particular the **black-necked spitting cobra** (*N. nigricollis*).

spitting image ▶**noun** (**the spitting image of**) informal the exact double of (another person or thing): *she's the spitting image of her mum.*

spittle ▶**noun** [mass noun] saliva, especially as ejected from the mouth.
– DERIVATIVES **spittly** adjective.
– ORIGIN late 15th cent.: alteration of dialect *spattle*, by association with **SPIT**[1].

spittlebug ▶**noun** another term for **FROGHOPPER**.

spittoon /spɪˈtuːn/ ▶**noun** a metal or earthenware pot typically having a funnel-shaped top, used for spitting into.

Spitz, Mark (Andrew) (b.1950), American swimmer. He won seven gold medals in the 1972 Olympic Games at Munich and set twenty-seven world records for free style and butterfly (1967–72).

spitz ▶**noun** a dog of a small breed with a pointed muzzle, especially a Pomeranian.
– ORIGIN mid 19th cent.: from German *Spitz(hund)*, from *spitz* 'pointed' + *Hund* 'dog'.

spiv ▶**noun** Brit. informal a man, typically characterized by flashy dress, who makes a living by disreputable dealings.
– DERIVATIVES **spivvish** adjective, **spivvy** adjective.
– ORIGIN 1930s: perhaps related to **SPIFFY**.

splake /spleɪk/ ▶**noun** a hybrid trout of North American lakes.
• Produced by crossing the speckled trout (*S. fontinalis*) with the lake trout (*Salvelinus namaycush*).
– ORIGIN 1950s: blend of *speckled* and **LAKE**[1].

splanchnic /ˈsplaŋknɪk/ ▶**adjective** of or relating to the viscera or internal organs, especially those of the abdomen.
– ORIGIN late 17th cent.: from modern Latin *splanchnicus*, from Greek *splankhnikos*, from *splankhna* 'entrails'.

splanchnopleure /ˌsplaŋknə(ʊ)ˈplʊə/ ▶**noun** Embryology a layer of tissue in a vertebrate embryo comprising the endoderm and the inner layer of mesoderm, and giving rise to the gut, lungs, and yolk sac. Often contrasted with **SOMATOPLEURE**.
– ORIGIN late 19th cent.: from Greek *splankhna* 'entrails' + *pleura* 'side'.

splash ▶**noun** a sound made by something striking or falling into liquid: *we hit the water with a mighty splash.*
■a spell of moving about in water energetically: *the girls joined them for a final splash in the pool.* ■ a small quantity of liquid that has fallen or been dashed against a surface: *a* **splash of** *gravy.* ■ a small quantity of liquid added to a drink: *a* **splash of** *lemonade.* ■ a bright patch of colour: *add a red scarf to give* **a splash of** *colour.* ■ informal a prominent or sensational news feature or story: *a front-page splash.* ■ informal a striking, ostentatious, or exciting effect or event: *there's going to be a big splash when Mike returns to the ring.*
▶**verb** [with obj. and adverbial of direction] cause (liquid) to strike or fall on something in irregular drops: *she splashed cold water on to her face.*
■[with obj.] make wet by doing this: *they splashed each other with water.* ■ [no obj., with adverbial of direction] (of a liquid) fall or be scattered in irregular drops: *a tear fell and splashed on to the pillow.* ■ [no obj., with adverbial] strike or move around in a liquid, causing it to fly about noisily: *a stone splashed into the water* | *she splashed up the path.* ■ (**be splashed with**) be decorated with scattered patches of: *a field splashed with purple clover.* ■ [with obj.] print (a story or photograph, especially a sensational one) in a prominent place in a newspaper or magazine: *the story was* **splashed across** *the front pages.*
– PHRASES **make a splash** informal attract a great deal of attention.
– ORIGIN early 18th cent. (as a verb): alteration of **PLASH**[1].
▶**splash down** (of a spacecraft) land on water.
splash out (or **splash money out**) Brit. informal spend money freely: *she* **splashed out on** *a Mercedes.*

splashback ▶**noun** Brit. a panel behind a sink or cooker that protects the wall from splashes.

splashboard ▶**noun** a screen designed to protect the passengers of a vehicle or boat from splashes.

splashdown ▶**noun** the alighting of a returning spacecraft on the sea, with the assistance of parachutes.

splashy ▶**adjective** (**splashier**, **splashiest**) **1** characterized by water flying about noisily in irregular drops: *a splashy waterfall.*
■characterized by irregular patches of bright colour: *splashy floral silks.*
2 informal attracting a great deal of attention; elaborately or ostentatiously impressive: *I don't care for splashy Hollywood parties.*

splat[1] ▶**noun** a piece of thin wood in the centre of a chair back.
– ORIGIN mid 19th cent.: from obsolete *splat* 'split up'; related to **SPLIT**.

splat[2] informal ▶**noun** a sound of something soft and wet or heavy striking a surface: *the goblin makes a huge splat as he hits the ground.*
▶**adverb** with a sound of this type: *he lands splat on his right elbow.*
▶**verb** (**splatted**, **splatting**) [with obj.] crush or squash (something) with a sound of this type: *he was splatting a bug.*
■[no obj.] land or be squashed with a sound of this type.
– ORIGIN late 19th cent.: abbreviation of **SPLATTER**.

splatter ▶**verb** [with obj.] splash with a sticky or viscous liquid: *a passing cart rolled by, splattering him with mud.*
■splash (such a liquid) over a surface or object. ■ [no obj., with adverbial] (of such a liquid) splash: *heavy droplets of rain splatter on to the windscreen.* ■ informal prominently or sensationally publish (a story) in a newspaper: *the story is* **splattered over** *pages two and three.*
▶**noun 1** a spot or trail of a sticky or viscous liquid splashed over a surface or object: *each puddle we crossed threw* **a splatter of** *mud on the windshield.*
2 [as modifier] informal denoting or referring to films featuring many violent and gruesome deaths: *a splatter movie.*
– ORIGIN late 18th cent.: imitative.

splatterpunk ▶**noun** [mass noun] informal a literary genre characterized by the explicit description of horrific, violent, or pornographic scenes.

splay ▶**verb** [with obj.] thrust or spread (things, especially limbs or fingers) out and apart: *her hands were splayed across his broad shoulders* | *he stood with his legs and arms* **splayed out**.
■[no obj.] (especially of limbs or fingers) be thrust or spread out and apart: *his legs* **splayed out** *in front of him.* ■ [no obj.] (of a thing) diverge in shape or position; become wider or more separated: *the river* **splayed out**, *deepening to become an estuary.* ■ [usu. as adj. **splayed**] construct (a window, doorway, or aperture) so that it diverges or is wider at one side of the wall than the other: *the walls are pierced by splayed window openings.*
▶**noun 1** a widening or outward tapering of something, in particular:
■a tapered widening of a road at an intersection to increase visibility. ■ a splayed window aperture or other opening.
2 a surface making an oblique angle with another, such as the splayed side of a window or embrasure.
■[mass noun] the degree of bevel or slant of a surface.
▶**adjective** [usu. in combination] turned outward or widened: *the girls were sitting splay-legged.*
– ORIGIN Middle English (in the sense 'unfold to view, display'): shortening of the verb **DISPLAY**.

splay-foot ▶**noun** a broad flat foot turned outward.
– DERIVATIVES **splay-footed** adjective.

spleen ▶**noun 1** Anatomy an abdominal organ involved in the production and removal of blood cells in most vertebrates and forming part of the immune system.
2 [mass noun] bad temper; spite: *he could* **vent his spleen**

on the institutions which had duped him. [ORIGIN: from the earlier belief that the spleen was the seat of such emotions.]
– DERIVATIVES **spleenful** adjective.
– ORIGIN Middle English: shortening of Old French *esplen*, via Latin from Greek *splēn*.

spleenwort ▶ noun a small fern which grows in rosettes on rocks and walls, typically with rounded or triangular lobes on a slender stem. Spleenworts were formerly used to treat disorders of the spleen.
• Genus *Asplenium*, family Aspleniaceae.

splen- ▶ combining form Anatomy of or relating to the spleen: *splenectomy.*
– ORIGIN from Greek *splēn* 'spleen'.

splendent ▶ adjective archaic shining brightly.
■ illustrious; great.
– ORIGIN late 15th cent.: from Latin *splendent-* 'shining', from the verb *splendere*.

splendid ▶ adjective magnificent; very impressive: *a splendid view of Windsor Castle | his robes were splendid.*
■ informal excellent; very good: *a splendid fellow* | [as exclamation] *'Is your family well? Splendid!'*
– PHRASES **splendid isolation** used to emphasize the isolation of a person or thing: *the stone stands* **in** *splendid isolation near the moorland road.* [ORIGIN: 1896: first applied to the period from 1890 to 1907 when Britain pursued a policy of diplomatic and commercial non-involvement.]
– DERIVATIVES **splendidly** adverb [as submodifier] *a splendidly ornate style*, **splendidness** noun.
– ORIGIN early 17th cent.: from French *splendide* or Latin *splendidus*, from *splendere* 'shine, be bright'.

splendiferous /splɛnˈdɪf(ə)rəs/ ▶ adjective informal, humorous splendid: *a splendiferous Sunday dinner.*
– DERIVATIVES **splendiferously** adverb, **splendiferousness** noun.
– ORIGIN mid 19th cent.: formed irregularly from **SPLENDOUR**.

splendour (US **splendor**) ▶ noun [mass noun] magnificent and splendid appearance; grandeur: *the barren splendour of the Lake District.*
■ (**splendours**) magnificent features or qualities: *the splendours of the imperial court.*
– ORIGIN late Middle English: from Anglo-Norman French *splendur* or Latin *splendor*, from *splendere* 'shine, be bright'.

splenectomy /splɪˈnɛktəmi/ ▶ noun (pl. **-ies**) a surgical operation involving removal of the spleen.

splenetic /splɪˈnɛtɪk/ ▶ adjective **1** bad-tempered; spiteful: *a splenetic rant.*
2 archaic term for **SPLENIC**.
– DERIVATIVES **splenetically** adverb (only in sense 1).
– ORIGIN late Middle English (as a noun denoting a person with a diseased spleen): from late Latin *spleneticus*, from Greek *splēn* (see **SPLEEN**).

splenic /ˈsplɛnɪk, ˈspliːnɪk/ ▶ adjective of or relating to the spleen: *the splenic artery.*
– ORIGIN early 17th cent.: from French *splénique*, or via Latin from Greek *splēnikos*, from *splēn* (see **SPLEEN**).

splenitis /splɪˈnʌɪtɪs/ ▶ noun [mass noun] Medicine inflammation of the spleen.

splenium /ˈspliːnɪəm/ ▶ noun Anatomy the thick posterior part of the corpus callosum of the brain.
– DERIVATIVES **splenial** adjective.
– ORIGIN mid 19th cent.: from Latin.

splenius /ˈspliːnɪəs/ (also **splenius muscle**) ▶ noun (pl. **splenii** /-nɪʌɪ/) Anatomy any of two pairs of muscles attached to the vertebrae in the neck and upper back which draw back the head.
– ORIGIN mid 18th cent.: modern Latin, from Greek *splēnion* 'bandage'.

splenomegaly /ˌspliːnə(ʊ)ˈmɛg(ə)li/ ▶ noun [mass noun] abnormal enlargement of the spleen.
– ORIGIN early 20th cent.: from **SPLEN-** 'spleen' + Greek *megas*, *megal-* 'great'.

splice ▶ verb [with obj.] join or connect (a rope or ropes) by interweaving the strands at the ends: *we learned how to weave and splice ropes | a cord was* **spliced on** | figurative *the work splices detail and generalization.*
■ join (pieces of timber, film, or tape) at the ends: *commercials can be* **spliced in** *later | I was* **splicing together** *a video from the footage on opium-growing.*
■ Genetics join or insert (a gene or gene fragment).
▶ noun a join consisting of two ropes, pieces of timber, or similar joined together at the ends.
■ the wedge-shaped tang of a cricket-bat handle, forming a joint with the blade.
– PHRASES **get** (or **be**) **spliced** informal get married. **splice the main brace** Brit. historical (in the navy) serve out an extra tot of rum.
– DERIVATIVES **splicer** noun.
– ORIGIN early 16th cent.: probably from Middle Dutch *splissen*, of unknown origin.

spliff ▶ noun informal a cannabis cigarette.
– ORIGIN 1930s: of unknown origin.

spline /splʌɪn/ ▶ noun **1** a rectangular key fitting into grooves in the hub and shaft of a wheel, especially one formed integrally with the shaft which allows movement of the wheel on the shaft.
■ a corresponding groove in a hub along which the key may slide.
2 a slat.
■ a flexible wood or rubber strip used especially in drawing large curves.
3 (also **spline curve**) Mathematics a continuous curve constructed so as to pass through a given set of points and have a certain number of continuous derivatives.
▶ verb [with obj.] secure (a part) by means of a spline.
■ [usu. as adj. **splined**] fit with a spline: *splined freewheels.*
– ORIGIN mid 18th cent. (originally East Anglian dialect): perhaps related to **SPLINTER**.

splint ▶ noun **1** a strip of rigid material used for supporting and immobilizing a broken bone when it has been set: *she had to wear splints on her legs.*
2 a long, thin strip of wood used to light a fire.
■ a rigid or flexible strip, especially of wood, used in basketwork.
3 a bony enlargement on the inside of a horse's leg, on the splint bone.
4 S. African a fragment of diamond.
▶ verb [with obj.] secure (a broken limb) with a splint or splints: *his leg was splinted.*
– ORIGIN Middle English (in sense 2; also denoting a section of armour): from Middle Dutch, Middle Low German *splinte* 'metal plate or pin'; related to **SPLINTER**.

splint bone ▶ noun either of two small bones in the foreleg of horse or other large quadruped, lying behind and close to the cannon bone.

splinter ▶ noun a small, thin, sharp piece of wood, glass, or similar material broken off from a larger piece: *a splinter of ice.*
▶ verb break or cause to break into small sharp fragments: [no obj.] *the soap box splintered* | figurative *the party had begun to splinter into factions* | [with obj.] *he crashed into a fence, splintering the wooden barricade.*
– DERIVATIVES **splintery** adjective.
– ORIGIN Middle English: from Middle Dutch *splinter*, *splenter*; related to **SPLINT**.

splinter bar ▶ noun Brit. another term for **SWINGLETREE**.

splinter group (also **splinter party**) ▶ noun a small organization, typically a political party, that has broken away from a larger one.

splinter-proof ▶ adjective **1** capable of withstanding splinters from bursting shells or bombs: *splinter-proof shutters.*
2 not producing splinters when broken: *splinter-proof glass.*

Split /splɪt/ a seaport on the coast of southern Croatia; pop. 189,300 (1991). Founded as a Roman colony in 78 BC, it contains the ruins of the palace of the emperor Diocletian, built in about AD 300.

split ▶ verb (**splitting**; past and past participle **split**) **1** break or cause to break forcibly into parts, especially into halves or along the grain: [no obj.] *the ice cracked and heaved and split* | [with obj.] *split and toast the muffins.*
■ remove or be removed by breaking, separating, or dividing: [with obj.] *the point was pressed against the edge of the flint to* **split off** *flakes* | [no obj.] *an incentive for regions to* **split away** *from countries.* ■ divide or cause to divide into parts or elements: [no obj.] *the river had* **split into** *a number of channels* | [with obj.] **splitting** *water* **into** *oxygen and hydrogen.* ■ [with obj.] divide and share (something, especially resources or responsibilities): *they met up and split the booty.* ■ [with obj.] cause the fission of (an atom).
2 (with reference to a group of people) divide into two or more groups: [no obj.] *let's* **split up** *and find the other two* | [with obj.] *once again the family was split up.*
■ [no obj.] end a marriage or an emotional or working relationship: *after the band* **split up** *Tex became a railway clerk.* ■ [with obj.] (often **be split**) (of an issue) cause (a group) to be divided because of opposing views: *the party was deeply* **split over** *its future direction.*
3 [no obj.] informal (of one's head) suffer great pain from a headache: *my head is splitting* | [as adj. **splitting**] *a splitting headache.*
4 [no obj.] Brit. informal betray the secrets of or inform on someone: *I told him I wouldn't* **split on** *him.*
5 [no obj.] informal leave a place, especially suddenly: *'Let's split,' Harvey said.*
▶ noun **1** a tear, crack, or fissure in something, especially down the middle or along the grain: *light squeezed through a small split in the curtain.*
■ an instance or act of splitting or being split; a division: *the split between the rich and the poor.* ■ a separation into parties or within a party; a schism: *the accusations caused a split in the party.* ■ an ending of a marriage or an emotional or working relationship: *a much-publicized split with his wife.*
2 (**the splits**) Brit. (in gymnastics and dance) an act of leaping in the air or sitting down with the legs straight and at right angles to the body, one in front and the other behind, or one at each side: *I could never* **do the splits** *before.*
3 a thing that is divided or split, in particular:
■ a bun, roll, or cake that is split or cut in half. ■ a split osier used in basketwork. ■ each strip of steel or cane that makes up the reed in a loom. ■ half a bottle or glass of champagne or other liquor. ■ a single thickness of split hide. ■ (in tenpin bowling) a formation of standing pins after the first ball in which there is a gap between two pins or groups of pins, making a spare unlikely. ■ N. Amer. a drawn match or series. ■ US a split-level house.
4 the time taken to complete a recognized part of a race, or the point in the race where such a time is measured.
– PHRASES **split the difference** take the average of two proposed amounts. **split hairs** see **HAIR**. **split one's sides** (N. Amer. also **split a gut**) informal be convulsed with laughter: *the dynamic comedy duo will have you splitting your sides with laughter.* **split the ticket** (or **one's vote**) US vote for candidates of more than one party. **split the vote** (of a candidate or minority party) attract votes from another candidate or party with the result that both are defeated by a third.
– ORIGIN late 16th cent. (originally in the sense 'break up (a ship)', describing the force of a storm or rock): from Middle Dutch *splitten*, of unknown ultimate origin.

split-brain ▶ adjective [attrib.] Psychiatry (of a person or animal) having the corpus callosum severed or absent, so as to eliminate the main connection between the two hemispheres of the brain.

split decision ▶ noun a decision based on a majority verdict rather than on a unanimous one, especially as to the winner on points of a boxing match.

split end ▶ noun **1** (usu. **split ends**) a tip of a person's hair which has split from dryness or ill-treatment.
2 American Football an offensive end positioned on the line of scrimmage but some distance away from the other linemen.

split-half ▶ adjective [attrib.] Statistics relating to or denoting a technique of splitting a body of supposedly homogeneous data into two halves and calculating the results separately for each to assess their reliability.

split image ▶ noun an image in a rangefinder or camera focusing system that has been bisected by optical means, the halves being aligned only when the system is in focus.

split infinitive ▶ noun a construction consisting of an infinitive with an adverb or other word inserted between *to* and the verb, e.g. *she seems to really like it.*

USAGE *You have* **to really watch** *him;* **to boldly go** *where no man has gone before.* It is still widely held that splitting infinitives—separating the infinitive marker **to** from the verb, as in the above examples—is wrong. The dislike of split infinitives is long-standing but is not well founded, being based on an analogy with Latin. In Latin, infinitives consist of only one word (e.g. *crescere* 'to grow'; *amare* 'to love'), which makes them impossible to split: therefore, so the argument goes, they should not be split in English either. But English is not the same as Latin. In particular, the placing of an adverb in English is extremely important in giving the appropriate emphasis: *you really have* **to watch** *him* and **to go** *boldly where no man has gone before*, examples where the infinitive is not split, convey a different emphasis or sound awkward. In the modern context, some traditionalists may continue to hold up the split infinitive as an error in

English. However, in standard English the principle of allowing split infinitives is broadly accepted as both normal and useful.

split-level ▶ adjective **1** (of a building) having a room or rooms higher than others by less than a whole storey: *a large split-level house.*
■(of a room) having its floor on two levels.
2 (of a cooker) having the oven and hob in separately installed units.
▶ noun a split-level building.

split pea ▶ noun a pea dried and split in half for cooking.

split personality ▶ noun less common term for **MULTIPLE PERSONALITY**.
■archaic term for **SCHIZOPHRENIA**.

split-phase ▶ adjective denoting or relating to an induction motor or other device utilizing two or more voltages at different phases produced from a single-phase supply.

split pin ▶ noun a metal cotter pin with two arms passed through a hole, held in place by the springing apart of the arms.

split-rail ▶ adjective denoting a fence or enclosure made from pieces of wood split lengthwise from logs.

split ring ▶ noun a small steel ring with two spiral turns, such as a key ring.

split run ▶ noun a print run of a newspaper during which some articles or advertisements are changed so as to produce different editions.

split screen ▶ noun a cinema, television, or computer screen on which two or more separate images are displayed.

split second ▶ noun a very brief moment of time: *for a split second, I hesitated.*
▶ adjective very rapid or accurate: *split-second timing is crucial.*

split shift ▶ noun a working shift comprising two or more separate periods of duty in a day.

split shot ▶ noun **1** [mass noun] small pellets used to weight a fishing line.
2 Croquet a stroke driving two touching balls in different directions.

splitter ▶ noun **1** a person or thing occupied in or designed for splitting something: *a log splitter.*
■a person, especially a taxonomist, who attaches more importance to differences than to similarities in classification. Contrasted with **LUMPER**.
2 informal a severe headache.

splittism ▶ noun [mass noun] (among communists, or in communist countries) the pursuance of factional interests in opposition to official Communist Party policy.
– DERIVATIVES **splittist** noun.

splodge ▶ noun & verb Brit. another term for **SPLOTCH**.
– DERIVATIVES **splodgy** adjective.

splosh informal ▶ verb [no obj., with adverbial of direction] make a soft splashing sound as one moves: *he sploshed across the road.*
▶ noun **1** a soft splashing sound: *a quiet splosh.*
■a splash of liquid: *sploshes of wine.*
2 [mass noun] dated money.
– ORIGIN mid 19th cent.: imitative.

splotch informal ▶ noun a daub, blot, or smear of something, typically a liquid: *a splotch of red in a larger area of yellow.*
▶ verb [with obj.] (usu. **be splotched**) make such a daub, blot, or smear on: *a rag splotched with grease.*
– DERIVATIVES **splotchy** adjective.
– ORIGIN early 17th cent.: perhaps a blend of **SPOT** and obsolete *plotch* 'blotch'.

splurge informal ▶ noun an act of spending money freely or extravagantly: *the annual pre-Christmas splurge.*
■a large or excessive amount of something: *there has recently been a splurge of teach-yourself books.*
▶ verb [with obj.] spend (money) freely or extravagantly: *I'd splurged about £2,500 on clothes* | [no obj.] *we splurged on T-bone steaks.*
– ORIGIN early 19th cent. (originally US): probably imitative.

splurt informal ▶ noun a sudden gush, especially of saliva.
■a sudden brief outburst of something: *I let out a splurt of laughter.*

▶ verb [with obj.] push out with force; spit out: *the rear wheels splurted gravel.*
– ORIGIN late 18th cent.: imitative.

splutter ▶ verb [no obj.] make a series of short explosive spitting or choking sounds: *she coughed and spluttered, tears coursing down her face.*
■[reporting verb] say something rapidly, indistinctly, and with a spitting sound, as a result of anger, embarrassment, or another strong emotion: [with obj.] *he began to splutter excuses* | [with direct speech] *'How dare you?' she spluttered.* ■ [with obj.] spit (something) out from one's mouth noisily and in small splashes: *spluttering brackish water, he struggled to regain his feet.*
▶ noun a short explosive spitting or choking noise.
– DERIVATIVES **splutterer** noun, **splutteringly** adverb.
– ORIGIN late 17th cent.: imitative; compare with **SPUTTER**.

Spock, Benjamin McLane (1903–98), American paediatrician and writer; known as **Dr Spock**. His influential manual *The Common Sense Book of Baby and Child Care* (1946) challenged traditional ideas in child-rearing in favour of a psychological approach.

spod ▶ noun Brit. informal a dull or socially inept person, especially someone who is excessively studious.
– DERIVATIVES **spoddy** adjective.

Spode /spəʊd/ ▶ noun [mass noun] trademark fine pottery or porcelain made at the factories of the English potter Josiah Spode (1755–1827) or his successors, characteristically consisting of ornately decorated and gilded services and large vases.

spodic /'spɒdɪk/ ▶ adjective Soil Science denoting a soil horizon rich in aluminium oxide and organic matter and typically also containing iron oxide, produced by percolating water.
– ORIGIN 1960s: from Greek *spodos* 'ashes, embers' + -IC.

spodosol /'spɒdə(ʊ)sɒl/ ▶ noun Soil Science a soil of an order characterized by a spodic horizon and including most podzols.
– ORIGIN 1960s: from Greek *spodos* 'ashes, embers' + -SOL + Latin *solum* 'soil'.

spodumene /'spɒdjʊmiːn/ ▶ noun [mass noun] a translucent, typically greyish-white aluminosilicate mineral which is an important source of lithium.
– ORIGIN early 19th cent.: from French *spodumène*, from Greek *spodoumenos* 'burning to ashes', present participle of *spodousthai*, from *spodos* 'ashes'.

spoil ▶ verb (past and past participle **spoilt** (chiefly Brit.) or **spoiled**) [with obj.] **1** diminish or destroy the value or quality of: *I wouldn't want to spoil your fun* | *a series of political blunders spoilt their chances of being re-elected.*
■prevent someone from enjoying (an occasion or event): *she was afraid of spoiling Christmas for the rest of the family.* ■ mark (a ballot paper) incorrectly so as to make one's vote invalid, especially as a gesture of protest. ■ [no obj.] (of food) become unfit for eating: *I've got some ham that'll spoil if we don't eat it tonight.*
2 harm the character of (a child) by being too lenient or indulgent: *the last thing I want to do is spoil Thomas* | [as adj. **spoilt** or **spoiled**] *a spoilt child.*
■treat with great or excessive kindness, consideration, or generosity: *breakfast in bed—you're spoiling me!*
3 [no obj.] (**be spoiling for**) be extremely or aggressively eager for: *Cooper was spoiling for a fight.*
4 archaic rob (a place or a person) of goods or possessions by force or violence.
▶ noun **1** (usu. **spoils**) goods stolen or taken forcibly from a person or place: *the looters carried their spoils away.*
2 [mass noun] waste brought up during the course of an excavation or a dredging or mining operation: *colliery spoil.*
– PHRASES **be spoilt for choice** Brit. have so many possibilities to choose from that it is difficult to do so.
– ORIGIN Middle English (in the sense 'to plunder'): shortening of Old French *espoille* (noun), *espoillier* (verb), from Latin *spoliare*, from *spolium* 'plunder, skin stripped from an animal', or a shortening of **DESPOIL**.

spoilage ▶ noun [mass noun] **1** the action of spoiling, especially the deterioration of food and perishable goods.
2 waste produced by material being spoilt, especially paper that is spoilt in printing.

spoiler ▶ noun **1** a person or thing that spoils.
■(especially in a political context) a person who obstructs or prevents an opponent's success while having no chance of winning a contest themselves.

■a news story published with the intention of reducing the impact of a related item published elsewhere by diverting attention from it. ■an electronic device for preventing unauthorized copying of sound recordings by means of a disruptive signal inaudible on the original.
2 a flap on an aircraft or glider which can be projected from the surface of a wing in order to create drag and so reduce speed.
■a similar device on a motor vehicle intended to prevent it being lifted off the road when travelling at very high speeds.

spoiling tactics ▶ plural noun a strategy designed to obstruct or prevent the success of a project or an opponent.

spoilsman ▶ noun (pl. **-men**) US a person who seeks to profit by the spoils system; a person who supports this system.

spoilsport ▶ noun a person who behaves in a way that spoils others' pleasure, especially by not joining in an activity.

spoils system ▶ noun chiefly US the practice of a successful political party giving public office to its supporters.

spoilt chiefly Brit. past and past participle of **SPOIL**.

Spokane /spə(ʊ)ˈkæn/ a city in eastern Washington, situated on the falls of the Spokane River, near the border with Idaho; pop. 177,200 (1990).

spoke[1] ▶ noun each of the bars or wire rods connecting the centre of a wheel to its outer edge.
■each of a set of radial handles projecting from a ship's wheel. ■ each of the metal rods in an umbrella to which the material is attached.
– PHRASES **put a spoke in someone's wheel** Brit. prevent someone from carrying out a plan.
– DERIVATIVES **spoked** adjective [in combination] *a wire-spoked wheel.*
– ORIGIN Old English *spāca*, of West Germanic origin; related to Dutch *speek*, German *Speiche*, from the base of **SPIKE**[1].

spoke[2] past of **SPEAK**.

spoken past participle of **SPEAK**. ▶ adjective [in combination] speaking in a specified way: *a blunt-spoken man.*
– PHRASES **be spoken for** be already claimed, owned, or reserved. ■(of a person) already have a romantic commitment: *he knows Claudine is spoken for.*

spokeshave /'spəʊkʃeɪv/ ▶ noun a small plane with a handle on each side of its blade, used for shaping curved surfaces (originally wheel spokes).
▶ verb [with obj.] shape with a plane of this type.

spokesman ▶ noun (pl. **-men**) a person, especially a man, who makes statements on behalf of a group: *a spokesman for Greenpeace.*
– ORIGIN early 16th cent.: formed irregularly from **SPOKE**[2], on the pattern of words such as *craftsman*.

spokesperson ▶ noun (pl. **-persons** or **-people**) a spokesman or spokeswoman (used as a neutral alternative).

spokeswoman ▶ noun (pl. **-women**) a woman who makes statements on behalf of a group.

Spoleto /spəˈleɪtəʊ/ a town in Umbria, in central Italy; pop. 38,030 (1990). It was one of Italy's principal cities from the 6th to the 8th century AD.

spoliation /ˌspəʊlɪˈeɪʃ(ə)n/ ▶ noun [mass noun] **1** the action of ruining or destroying something: *the spoliation of the countryside.*
2 the action of taking goods or property from somewhere by violent means: *the spoliation of the Church.*
– DERIVATIVES **spoliator** noun.
– ORIGIN late Middle English (denoting pillaging): from Latin *spoliatio(n-)*, from the verb *spoliare* 'strip, deprive' (see **SPOIL**).

spondaic /spɒnˈdeɪɪk/ ▶ adjective Prosody of or concerning spondees.
■(of a hexameter) having a spondee as its fifth foot.
– ORIGIN late 16th cent.: via French or late Latin from Greek *spondeiakos*, from *spondeios* (see **SPONDEE**).

spondee /'spɒndiː/ ▶ noun Prosody a foot consisting of two long (or stressed) syllables.
– ORIGIN late Middle English: from Old French, or via Latin from Greek *spondeios (pous)* '(foot) of a libation', from *spondē* 'libation' (being characteristic of music accompanying libations).

spondulicks /spɒnˈd(j)uːlɪks/ (also **spondulix**) ▶ **plural noun** Brit. informal money.
– ORIGIN mid 19th cent.: of unknown origin.

spondylitis /ˌspɒndɪˈlʌɪtɪs/ ▶ **noun** [mass noun] Medicine inflammation of the joints of the backbone. See also **ANKYLOSING SPONDYLITIS**.
– ORIGIN mid 19th cent.: from Latin *spondylus* 'vertebra' (from Greek *spondulos*) + **-ITIS**.

spondylosis /ˌspɒndɪˈləʊsɪs/ ▶ **noun** [mass noun] Medicine a painful condition of the spine resulting from the degeneration of the intervertebral discs.
– ORIGIN early 20th cent.: from Greek *spondulos* 'vertebra' + **-OSIS**.

sponge ▶ **noun 1** a primitive sedentary aquatic invertebrate with a soft porous body that is typically supported by a framework of fibres or calcareous or glassy spicules. Sponges draw in a current of water to extract nutrients and oxygen.
• Phylum Porifera: several classes.
2 a piece of a soft, light, porous substance originally consisting of the fibrous skeleton of such an invertebrate but now usually made of synthetic material. Sponges absorb liquid and are used for washing and cleaning.
■ [in sing.] an act of wiping or cleaning with a sponge: *they gave him a quick* ***sponge down***. ■ [mass noun] such a substance used as padding or insulating material: *the headguard is padded with sponge*. ■ a piece of such a substance impregnated with spermicide and inserted into a woman's vagina as a form of barrier contraceptive. ■ informal a heavy drinker. ■ [mass noun] [with modifier] metal in a porous form, typically prepared by reduction without fusion or by electrolysis: *platinum sponge*.
3 (also **sponge cake**) a very light cake made with eggs, sugar, and flour but little or no fat: *a chocolate sponge* | [mass noun] *the gateau is made with moist sponge*.
■ short for **SPONGE PUDDING**.
4 informal a person who lives at someone else's expense.
▶ **verb** (**sponging** or **spongeing**) **1** [with obj.] wipe, rub, or clean with a wet sponge or cloth: *she* ***sponged*** *him* ***down*** *in an attempt to cool his fever*.
■ remove or wipe away (liquid or a mark) in such a way: *I'll go and* ***sponge*** *this orange juice* ***off*** *my dress*. ■ give a decorative mottled or textured effect to (a painted wall or surface) by applying a different shade of paint with a sponge.
2 [no obj.] informal obtain or accept money or food from other people without doing or intending to do anything in return: *they found they could earn a perfectly good living by* ***sponging off*** *others*.
■ [with obj.] obtain (something) in such a way: *he edged closer, clearly intending to sponge money from her*.
– DERIVATIVES **spongeable** adjective, **sponge-like** adjective.
– ORIGIN Old English (in sense 2 of the noun), via Latin from Greek *spongia*, later form of *spongos*, reinforced in Middle English by Old French *esponge*.

sponge bag ▶ **noun** Brit. a toilet bag.

sponge bath ▶ **noun** North American term for **BLANKET BATH**.

sponge cloth ▶ **noun 1** [mass noun] soft, lightly woven cloth with a slightly wrinkled surface.
2 a cloth made from a thin spongy material, used for cleaning.

sponge pudding ▶ **noun** Brit. a steamed or baked pudding of fat, flour, and eggs.

sponger ▶ **noun 1** informal a person who lives at others' expense.
2 a person who applies paint to pottery using a sponge.

sponge rubber ▶ **noun** [mass noun] rubber latex processed into a sponge-like substance.

sponge tree ▶ **noun** another term for **OPOPANAX** (in sense 1).

spongiform /ˈspʌndʒɪfɔːm/ ▶ **adjective** chiefly Veterinary Medicine having, relating to, or denoting a porous structure or consistency resembling that of a sponge.

spongin /ˈspʌn(d)ʒɪn/ ▶ **noun** [mass noun] Biochemistry the horny or fibrous substance found in the skeleton of many sponges.

spongy /ˈspʌn(d)ʒi/ ▶ **adjective** (**spongier**, **spongiest**) like a sponge, especially in being porous, compressible, elastic, or absorbent: *a soft, spongy blanket of moss*.
■ (of metal) having an open, porous structure: *spongy platinum*. ■ (chiefly of a motor vehicle's braking system) lacking firmness.
– DERIVATIVES **spongily** adverb, **sponginess** noun.

sponson /ˈspɒns(ə)n/ ▶ **noun** a projection on the side of a boat, ship, or seaplane, in particular:
■ a gun platform standing out from a warship's side. ■ a short subsidiary wing that serves to stabilize a seaplane. ■ a buoyancy chamber fitted to a boat's hull, especially on a canoe. ■ a triangular platform supporting the wheel on a paddle steamer.
– ORIGIN mid 19th cent.: of unknown origin.

sponsor ▶ **noun 1** a person or organization that provides funds for a project or activity carried out by another, in particular:
■ an individual or organization that pays some or all of the costs involved in staging a sporting or artistic event in return for advertising. ■ a person who pledges to donate a certain amount of money to another person after they have participated in a fund-raising event organized on behalf of a charity. ■ chiefly US a business or organization that pays for or contributes to the costs of a radio or television programme in return for advertising.
2 a person who introduces and supports a proposal for legislation: *a leading sponsor of the bill*.
■ a person taking official responsibility for the actions of another: *they act as informants, sponsors, and contacts for new immigrants*. ■ a godparent at a child's baptism. ■ (especially in the Roman Catholic Church) a person presenting a candidate for confirmation.
▶ **verb** [with obj.] **1** provide funds for (a project or activity or the person carrying it out): *Joe is being sponsored by a government training scheme*.
■ pay some or all of the costs involved in staging (a sporting or artistic event) in return for advertising. ■ pledge to donate a certain sum of money to (someone) after they have participated in a fund-raising event organized on behalf of a charity. ■ [often as adj. **sponsored**] pledge to donate money because someone is taking part in (such an event): *they raised £70 by a sponsored walk*.
2 introduce and support (a proposal) in a legislative assembly: *a Labour MP sponsored the bill*.
■ propose and organize (negotiations or talks) between other people or groups: *the USA sponsored negotiations between the two sides*.
– DERIVATIVES **sponsorship** noun.
– ORIGIN mid 17th cent. (as a noun): from Latin, from *spondere* 'promise solemnly' (see **SPONSION**). The verb dates from the late 19th cent.

spontaneous /spɒnˈteɪnɪəs/ ▶ **adjective** performed or occurring as a result of a sudden inner impulse or inclination and without premeditation or external stimulus: *the audience broke into spontaneous applause* | *a spontaneous display of affection*.
■ (of a person) having an open, natural, and uninhibited manner. ■ (of a process or event) occurring without apparent external cause: *spontaneous miscarriages*. ■ archaic (of a plant) growing naturally and without being tended or cultivated. ■ Biology (of movement or activity in an organism) instinctive or involuntary: *the spontaneous mechanical activity of circular smooth muscle*.
– DERIVATIVES **spontaneity** noun, **spontaneously** adverb.
– ORIGIN mid 17th cent.: from late Latin *spontaneus* (from *(sua) sponte* 'of (one's) own accord') + **-OUS**.

spontaneous combustion ▶ **noun** [mass noun] the ignition of organic matter (e.g. hay or coal) without apparent cause, typically through heat generated internally by rapid oxidation.

spontaneous generation ▶ **noun** [mass noun] historical the supposed production of living organisms from non-living matter, as inferred from the apparent appearance of life in some infusions.

spoof informal ▶ **noun 1** a humorous imitation of something, typically a film or a particular genre of film, in which its characteristic features are exaggerated for comic effect: *a Robin Hood spoof*.
2 a trick played on someone as a joke.
▶ **verb** [with obj.] **1** imitate (something) while exaggerating its characteristic features for comic effect: *it is a movie that spoofs other movies*.
2 hoax or trick (someone): *they proceeded to spoof Western intelligence with false information*.
■ interfere with (radio or radar signals) so as to make them useless.
– DERIVATIVES **spoofer** noun, **spoofery** noun.
– ORIGIN late 19th cent.: coined by Arthur Roberts (1852–1933), English comedian.

spook informal ▶ **noun 1** a ghost.
■ S. African a thing that people are frightened of, especially without justification (used in political contexts): *the far-right spook will stay a spook for a long time yet*.
2 chiefly N. Amer. a spy: *a CIA spook*.
3 S. African an armoured vehicle used to detect mines.
4 offensive, dated, chiefly US a black person.
▶ **verb** [with obj.] **1** frighten; unnerve: *they spooked a couple of grizzly bears*.
■ [no obj.] (especially of an animal) take fright suddenly: *he'll spook if we make any noise*.
2 S. African clear (an area) of mines: *a road that hasn't been spooked*.
– ORIGIN early 19th cent.: from Dutch, of unknown origin.

spooky ▶ **adjective** (**spookier**, **spookiest**) informal **1** sinister or ghostly in a way that causes fear and unease: *I bet this place is really spooky late at night*.
2 chiefly N. Amer. (of a person or animal) easily frightened; nervous.
– DERIVATIVES **spookily** adverb, **spookiness** noun.

spool ▶ **noun** a cylindrical device on which film, magnetic tape, thread, or other flexible materials can be wound; a reel: *spools of electrical cable*.
■ a cylindrical device attached to a fishing rod and used for winding and unwinding the line as required. ■ [as modifier] denoting furniture of a style popular in England in the 17th century and North America in the 19th century, typically ornamented with a series of small knobs resembling spools: *a narrow spool bed*.
▶ **verb 1** [with obj. and adverbial] wind (magnetic tape or thread) on to a spool: *he was trying to spool his tapes back into the cassettes with a pencil eraser*.
■ [no obj., with adverbial] be wound on or off a spool: *the plastic reel allows the line to run free as it spools out*.
2 [with obj.] Computing send (data that is intended for printing or processing on a peripheral device) to an intermediate store: *users can set which folder they wish to spool files to*. [ORIGIN: acronym from *simultaneous peripheral operation online*.]
3 [no obj.] (of an engine) increase its speed of rotation, typically to that required for operation: *a jet engine can take up to six seconds to* ***spool up***.
– ORIGIN Middle English (denoting a cylinder on to which spun thread is wound): shortening of Old French *espole* or from Middle Low German *spōle*, of West Germanic origin; related to Dutch *spoel* and German *Spule*. The verb dates from the early 17th cent.

spoon ▶ **noun 1** an implement consisting of a small, shallow oval or round bowl on a long handle, used for eating, stirring, and serving food.
■ the contents of such an implement: *three* ***spoons of*** *sugar*. ■ (**spoons**) a pair of spoons held in the hand and beaten together rhythmically as a percussion instrument.
2 a thing resembling a spoon in shape, in particular:
■ (also **spoon bait**) a fishing lure designed to wobble when pulled through the water. ■ an oar with a broad curved blade. ■ Golf, dated a club with a slightly concave wooden head.
▶ **verb 1** [with obj. and adverbial of direction] convey (food) somewhere by using a spoon: *Rosie spooned sugar into her mug*.
■ hit (a ball) up into the air with a soft or weak stroke: *he spooned his shot high over the bar*.
2 [no obj.] informal, dated (of two people) behave in an amorous way; kiss and cuddle: *I saw them spooning on the beach*.
– DERIVATIVES **spooner** noun, **spoonful** noun (pl. **-fuls**).
– ORIGIN Old English *spōn* 'chip of wood', of Germanic origin; related to German *Span* 'shaving'. Sense 1 is of Scandinavian origin. The verb dates from the early 18th cent.

spoonbill ▶ **noun** a tall mainly white or pinkish wading bird related to ibises, having a long bill with a very broad flat tip.
• Genera *Platalea* and *Ajaia*, family Threskiornithidae: several species.

spoon bread ▶ **noun** [mass noun] US soft maize bread.

spoonerism ▶ **noun** a verbal error in which a speaker accidentally transposes the initial sounds or letters of two or more words, often to humorous effect, as in the sentence *you have hissed the mystery lectures*.
– ORIGIN early 20th cent.: named after the Revd W. A. *Spooner* (1844–1930), an English scholar who reputedly made such errors in speaking.

spoon-feed ▶ **verb** [with obj.] feed (someone) by using a spoon.
■figurative provide (someone) with so much help or information that they do not need to think for themselves.

spoonworm ▶ **noun** an unsegmented worm-like marine invertebrate that lives in burrows, crevices, or discarded shells. They typically have a sausage-shaped body with a long proboscis that can be extended over the seabed.
• Phylum Echiura.

spoony informal ▶ **adjective** (**spoonier**, **spooniest**) dated sentimentally or foolishly amorous: *I was spoony over Miss Talmadge to the point of idolatry.*
■archaic foolish; silly.
▶ **noun** (pl. **-ies**) archaic a simple, silly, or foolish person.
– DERIVATIVES **spoonily** adverb, **spooniness** noun.

spoor /spʊə, spɔː/ ▶ **noun** the track or scent of an animal: *they searched around the hut for a spoor* | [mass noun] *the trail is marked by wolf spoor.*
■S. African the track of a wagon or motor vehicle.
▶ **verb** [with obj.] follow the track or scent of (an animal or person): *taking the spear, he set off to spoor the man.*
– DERIVATIVES **spoorer** noun.
– ORIGIN early 19th cent.: from Afrikaans, from Middle Dutch *spor*, of Germanic origin.

Sporades /ˈspɒrədiːz/ two groups of Greek islands in the Aegean Sea. The **Northern Sporades**, which lie close to the east coast of mainland Greece, include the islands of Euboea, Skiros, Skiathos, and Skopelos. The **Southern Sporades**, situated off the west coast of Turkey, include Rhodes and the other islands of the Dodecanese.

sporadic /spəˈradɪk/ ▶ **adjective** occurring at irregular intervals or only in a few places; scattered or isolated: *sporadic fighting broke out.*
– DERIVATIVES **sporadically** adverb.
– ORIGIN late 17th cent.: via medieval Latin from Greek *sporadikos*, from *sporas*, *sporad-* 'scattered'; related to *speirein* 'to sow'.

sporangiophore /spəˈran(d)ʒɪə(ʊ),fɔː/ ▶ **noun** Botany (in a fungus) a specialized hypha bearing sporangia.

sporangium /spəˈran(d)ʒɪəm/ ▶ **noun** (pl. **sporangia** /-dʒɪə/) Botany (in ferns and lower plants) a receptacle in which asexual spores are formed.
– DERIVATIVES **sporangial** adjective.
– ORIGIN early 19th cent.: modern Latin, from Greek *spora* 'spore' + *angeion* 'vessel'.

spore ▶ **noun** Biology a minute, typically one-celled, reproductive unit capable of giving rise to a new individual without sexual fusion, characteristic of lower plants, fungi, and protozoans.
■Botany (in a plant exhibiting alternation of generations) a haploid reproductive cell which gives rise to a gametophyte. ■Microbiology (in bacteria) a rounded resistant form adopted by a bacterial cell in adverse conditions.
– ORIGIN mid 19th cent.: from modern Latin *spora*, from Greek *spora* 'sowing, seed', from *speirein* 'to sow'.

sporo- ▶ **combining form** Biology of or relating to spores: *sporogenesis.*
– ORIGIN from Greek *spora* 'spore'.

sporocyst ▶ **noun** Zoology a parasitic fluke in the initial stage of infection in a snail host, developed from a miracidium.
■(in parasitic sporozoans) an encysted zygote in an invertebrate host.

sporogenesis /ˌspɒrə(ʊ)ˈdʒɛnɪsɪs, ˌspɔːrə(ʊ)-/ ▶ **noun** [mass noun] chiefly Botany the process of spore formation.

sporogenous /spəˈrɒdʒɪnəs/ ▶ **adjective** chiefly Botany (of an organism or tissue) producing spores.

sporogony /spəˈrɒgəni/ ▶ **noun** [mass noun] Zoology the asexual process of spore formation in parasitic sporozoans.

sporophore /ˈspɒrəfɔː, ˈspɔː-/ ▶ **noun** Botany the spore-bearing structure of a fungus.

sporophyte /ˈspɒrəfʌɪt, ˈspɔː-/ ▶ **noun** Botany (in the life cycle of plants with alternating generations) the asexual and usually diploid phase, producing spores from which the gametophyte arises. It is the dominant form in vascular plants, e.g. the frond of a fern.
– DERIVATIVES **sporophytic** adjective.

Sporozoa /ˌspɒrəˈzəʊə/ Zoology & Medicine a phylum of mainly parasitic spore-forming protozoans that have a complex life cycle with sexual and asexual generations. They include the organisms that cause malaria, babesiosis, coccidiosis, and toxoplasmosis. Also called **APICOMPLEXA**.
– DERIVATIVES **sporozoan** noun & adjective.
– ORIGIN modern Latin (plural), from **SPORE** + Greek *zōia* 'animals'.

sporozoite /ˌspɒrə(ʊ)ˈzəʊʌɪt, ˌspɔː-/ ▶ **noun** Zoology & Medicine a motile spore-like stage in the life cycle of some parasitic sporozoans (e.g. the malaria organism), which is typically the infective agent introduced into a host.
– ORIGIN late 19th cent.: from **SPORO-** 'relating to spores' + Greek *zōion* 'animal' + **-ITE**[1].

sporran /ˈspɒr(ə)n/ ▶ **noun** a small pouch worn around the waist so as to hang in front of the kilt as part of men's Scottish Highland dress.
– ORIGIN mid 18th cent.: from Scottish Gaelic *sporan*.

sport ▶ **noun 1** an activity involving physical exertion and skill in which an individual or team competes against another or others for entertainment: *team sports such as soccer and rugby* | [mass noun] *I used to play a lot of sport* | [as modifier] (**sports**) *a sports centre.*
■(**sports**) Brit. an occasion on which people compete in various athletic activities: *I won the 200 metres in the school sports.* ■[mass noun] [usu. with adj.] success or pleasure derived from an activity such as hunting or fishing: *I have heard there is good sport to be had in Buttermere.* ■[mass noun] dated entertainment; fun: *it was considered great sport to catch him out.* ■archaic a source of amusement or entertainment: *I do not wish to show myself the sport of a man like Wildeve.*
2 informal a person who behaves in a good or specified way in response to teasing, defeat, or a similarly trying situation: *go on, be a sport!* | *Angela's a bad sport.*
■chiefly Austral./NZ used as a friendly form of address, especially between men who do not know each other: *hold on, sport!*
3 Biology an animal or plant showing abnormal or striking variation from the parent type, especially in form or colour, as a result of spontaneous mutation.
▶ **verb 1** [with obj.] wear or display (a distinctive or noticeable item): *he was sporting a huge handlebar moustache.*
2 [no obj.] amuse oneself or play in a lively, energetic way: *the children sported in the water.*
– PHRASES **in sport** for fun: *I have assumed the name was given more or less in sport.* **make sport of** dated make fun of. **the sport of kings** horse racing.
– DERIVATIVES **sporter** noun.
– ORIGIN late Middle English (in the sense 'pastime, entertainment'): shortening of **DISPORT**.

sportif /spɔːˈtiːf/ ▶ **adjective** (of a person) active or interested in athletic sports: *he was sportif and ready for action.*
■(of an action or event) intended in fun or as a joke. ■(of a garment or style of dress) suitable for sport or informal wear; casual.
▶ **noun** a person who is active or interested in sport.
– ORIGIN French.

sporting ▶ **adjective 1** [attrib.] connected with or interested in sport: *a major sporting event.*
2 fair and generous in one's behaviour or treatment of others, especially in a game or contest: *it was jolly sporting of you to let me have first go.*
– DERIVATIVES **sportingly** adverb (only in sense 2).

sporting chance ▶ **noun** [in sing.] a reasonable chance of winning or succeeding: *I'll give you a sporting chance.*

sportive ▶ **adjective** playful; light-hearted.
■archaic amorous or lustful.
– DERIVATIVES **sportively** adverb, **sportiveness** noun.

sports bar ▶ **noun** a bar where televised sport is shown continuously.

sports car ▶ **noun** a low-built car designed for performance at high speeds, often having a roof that can be folded back.

sportscast ▶ **noun** chiefly N. Amer. a broadcast of sports news or a sports event.
– DERIVATIVES **sportscaster** noun.

sports day ▶ **noun** Brit. an occasion on which the pupils of a school compete in various races and athletic events.

sports finder ▶ **noun** Photography a direct-vision viewfinder typically consisting of a simple frame which allows action outside the field of view of the camera to be seen. This is often fitted to twin-lens reflex cameras.

sports jacket (US also **sport jacket** or **sports coat**) ▶ **noun** a man's jacket resembling a suit jacket, for informal wear.

sportsman ▶ **noun** (pl. **-men**) a man who takes part in a sport, especially as a professional.
■a person who behaves sportingly. ■dated a man who hunts or shoots wild animals as a pastime.
– DERIVATIVES **sportsmanlike** adjective, **sportsmanship** noun.

sportsperson ▶ **noun** (pl. **-persons** or **-people**) a sportsman or sportswoman (used as a neutral alternative).

sportster ▶ **noun** a sports car.

sportswear ▶ **noun** [mass noun] clothes worn for sport or for casual outdoor use.

sportswoman ▶ **noun** (pl. **-women**) a woman who takes part in sport, especially professionally.
– DERIVATIVES **sportswomanship** noun.

sport utility (also **sport utility vehicle**) ▶ **noun** a high-performance four-wheel-drive vehicle.

sporty ▶ **adjective** (**sportier**, **sportiest**) informal fond of or good at sport: *tracksuits don't necessarily mean you're sporty.*
■(of clothing) casual yet attractively stylish: *a sporty outfit.* ■(of a car) compact and with fast acceleration: *the sporty 1.5 litre coupe.*
– DERIVATIVES **sportily** adverb, **sportiness** noun.

sporulate /ˈspɒrjʊleɪt/ ▶ **verb** [no obj.] Biology produce or form a spore or spores.
– DERIVATIVES **sporulation** noun.

s'pose ▶ **verb** non-standard spelling of **SUPPOSE**, representing informal speech.

spot ▶ **noun 1** a small round or roundish mark, differing in colour or texture from the surface around it: *ladybirds have black spots on their red wing covers.*
■a small mark or stain: *a spot of mildew on the wall.* ■a pimple. ■archaic a moral blemish or stain. ■short for **PENALTY SPOT**. ■chiefly N. Amer. a pip on a domino, playing card, or dice. ■[in combination] informal, chiefly N. Amer. a banknote of a specified value: *a ten-spot.*
2 a particular place or point: *a nice secluded spot* | *an ideal picnic spot.*
■[with adj. or noun modifier] a small feature or part of something with a particular quality: *his bald spot* | *there was one bright spot in a night of dismal failure.* ■a position within a listing; a ranking: *the runner-up spot.* ■a place for an individual item within a show: *she couldn't do her usual singing spot in the club.*
3 informal, chiefly Brit. a small amount of something: *a spot of rain* | *a spot of bother flared up.*
■dated a small alcoholic drink: *may I offer you a spot?*
4 [as modifier] denoting a system of trading in which commodities or currencies are delivered and paid for immediately after a sale: *trading in the spot markets* | *the current spot price.*
5 short for **SPOTLIGHT**.
6 (also **spot board**) a board for working plaster before application.
▶ **verb** (**spotted**, **spotting**) **1** [with obj.] see, notice, or recognize (someone or something) that is difficult to detect or that one is searching for: *Andrew spotted the advert in the paper* | *the men were spotted by police.*
■(usu. **be spotted**) recognize that (someone) has a particular talent, especially for sport or show business: *we were spotted by a talent scout.* ■[no obj.] Military locate an enemy's position, typically from the air: *they were spotting for enemy aircraft.*
2 [with obj.] (usu. **be spotted**) mark with spots: *the velvet was spotted with stains.*
■[no obj.] become marked with spots: *a damp atmosphere causes the flowers to spot.* ■cover (a surface or area) thinly: *thorn trees spotted the land.* ■archaic stain or sully the moral character or qualities of. ■[no obj.] (**it spots**, **it is spotting**, etc.) rain slightly: *it was still spotting with rain.*
3 [with obj.] place (a ball) on its designated starting point on a billiard table.
4 [with two objs] N. Amer. informal give or lend (money) to (someone): *I'll spot you $300.*
■allow (an advantage) to (someone) in a game or sport: *the higher-rated team spots the lower-rated team the difference in their handicaps.*
– PHRASES **hit the spot** informal be exactly what is required: *the cup of coffee hit the spot.* **in a spot** informal in a difficult situation. **on the spot 1** without any delay; immediately: *he offered me the job on the spot.* **2** at the scene of an action or event: *journalists on the spot reported no progress.* **3** chiefly Brit. (with reference to an action) performed without moving from one's original position: *running on the spot.* **put**

S

someone on the spot informal force someone into a situation in which they must make a difficult decision or answer a difficult question.
– ORIGIN Middle English: perhaps from Middle Dutch *spotte*. The sense 'notice, recognize' arose from the early 19th-cent. slang use 'note as a suspect or criminal'.

spot advertising ▶ **noun** [mass noun] television advertising occupying a short break during or between programmes.

spot ball ▶ **noun** Billiards one of two white cue balls, distinguished from the other by two black spots.

spot check ▶ **noun** a test made without warning on a randomly selected subject.
▶ **verb** (**spot-check**) [with obj.] subject (someone or something) to such a test.

spot height ▶ **noun** the altitude of a point, especially as shown on a map.

spot kick ▶ **noun** another term for **PENALTY KICK**.

spotlamp ▶ **noun** another term for **SPOTLIGHT**.

spotless ▶ **adjective** absolutely clean or pure; immaculate: *a spotless white apron*.
– DERIVATIVES **spotlessly** adverb, **spotlessness** noun.

spotlight ▶ **noun** a lamp projecting a narrow, intense beam of light directly on to a place or person, especially a performer on stage.
■ a beam of light from a lamp of this kind: *the knife flashed in the spotlight*. ■ (**the spotlight**) figurative intense scrutiny or public attention: *she was constantly in the media spotlight*.
▶ **verb** (past and past participle **-lighted** or **-lit**) [with obj.] illuminate with a spotlight: *the dancers are spotlighted from time to time throughout the evening*.
■ figurative direct attention to (a particular problem or situation): *the protest spotlighted the overcrowding in British prisons*.

spot meter ▶ **noun** Photography a photometer that measures the intensity of light received within a cone of small angle, usually 2° or less.

spot on ▶ **adjective** & **adverb** Brit. informal completely accurate or accurately: [as adj.] *your reviews are spot on*.

spotted ▶ **adjective** marked or decorated with spots.
– DERIVATIVES **spottedness** noun.

spotted deer ▶ **noun** another term for **CHITAL**.

spotted dick ▶ **noun** [mass noun] Brit. a suet pudding containing currants.

spotted dog ▶ **noun 1** a Dalmatian dog.
2 Brit. another term for **SPOTTED DICK**.

spotted fever ▶ **noun** [mass noun] any of a number of diseases characterized by fever and skin spots:
■ cerebrospinal meningitis. ■ typhus. ■ (also **Rocky Mountain spotted fever**) a rickettsial disease transmitted by ticks.

spotted flycatcher ▶ **noun** a common migratory Old World flycatcher with grey-brown plumage.
• *Muscicapa striata*, family Muscicapidae.

spotted hyena ▶ **noun** a southern African hyena which has a greyish-yellow to reddish coat with irregular dark spots, and a loud laughing call.
• *Crocuta crocuta*, family Hyaenidae.

spotted orchid ▶ **noun** a common Eurasian orchid with spotted leaves and flowers varying from purple to white, with darker markings on the lip.
• Genus *Dactylorhiza*, family Orchidaceae: several species, in particular the **common spotted orchid** (*D. fuchsii*), which grows chiefly on calcareous soils, and the **heath spotted orchid** (*D. maculata*), of damp acid soils.

spotter ▶ **noun** [often in combination] a person that looks for or observes a particular thing as a hobby or job: *bus-spotters*.
■ an aviator or aircraft employed in locating or observing enemy positions: [as modifier] *spotter planes*. ■ US informal a person employed by a company or business to keep watch on employees or customers.

spotty ▶ **adjective** (**spottier**, **spottiest**) marked with spots: *a spotty purple flower*.
■ Brit. (of a person) having pimples: *a spotty youth*. ■ chiefly N. Amer. of uneven quality; patchy: *his spotty record on the environment*.
– DERIVATIVES **spottily** adverb, **spottiness** noun.

spot-weld ▶ **verb** [with obj.] join by welding at a number of separate points: *the wire was spot-welded in place*.
▶ **noun** (**spot weld**) each of the welds so made.
– DERIVATIVES **spot-welder** noun.

spousal /ˈspaʊz(ə)l/ ▶ **adjective** [attrib.] Law, chiefly N. Amer. of or relating to marriage or to a husband or wife: *the spousal benefits of married couples*.

spouse /spaʊz, -s/ ▶ **noun** a husband or wife, considered in relation to their partner.
– ORIGIN Middle English: from Old French *spous(e)*, variant of *espous(e)*, from Latin *sponsus* (masculine), *sponsa* (feminine), past participles of *spondere* 'betroth'.

spout ▶ **noun 1** a tube or lip projecting from a container, through which liquid can be poured: *a teapot with a chipped spout*.
■ a pipe or trough through which water may be carried away or from which it can flow out. ■ a sloping trough for conveying something to a lower level; a chute. ■ historical a lift in a pawnshop used to convey pawned items up for storage.
2 a stream of liquid issuing from somewhere with great force: *the tall spouts of geysers*.
■ the plume of water vapour ejected from the blowhole of a whale: *the spout of an occasional whale*.
▶ **verb** [with obj.] **1** send out (liquid) forcibly in a stream: *volcanoes spouted ash and lava*.
■ [no obj., with adverbial] (of a liquid) flow out of somewhere in such a way: *blood was spouting from the cuts on my hand*. ■ (of a whale or dolphin) eject (water vapour and air) through its blowhole.
2 express (one's views or ideas) in a lengthy, declamatory, and unreflecting way: *he was spouting platitudes about our furry friends*.
– PHRASES **put something up the spout** Brit. informal, dated pawn something. **up the spout** Brit. informal **1** no longer working or likely to be useful or successful. **2** (of a woman) pregnant. **3** (of a bullet or cartridge) in the barrel of a gun and ready to be fired.
– DERIVATIVES **spouted** adjective, **spouter** noun, **spoutless** adjective.
– ORIGIN Middle English (as a verb): from Middle Dutch *spouten*, from an imitative base shared by Old Norse *spýta* 'to spit'.

spp. ▶ **abbreviation for** species (plural).

SPQR ▶ **abbreviation for** ■ historical the Senate and people of Rome. [ORIGIN: from Latin *Senatus Populusque Romanus*.] ■ humorous small profits and quick returns.

Spr ▶ **abbreviation for** (in the UK) Sapper.

Sprachgefühl /ˈʃprɑːxɡəˌfuːl, German ˈʃpraːxɡəˌfyːl/ ▶ **noun** [mass noun] intuitive feeling for the natural idiom of a language.
■ the essential character of a language.
– ORIGIN German, from *Sprache* 'speech, a language' + *Gefühl* 'feeling'.

spraddle ▶ **verb** [with obj.] [usu. as adj. **spraddled**] chiefly W. Indian & N. Amer. spread (one's legs) far apart: *the cat's spraddled hind legs*.
– ORIGIN mid 17th cent. (in the sense 'sprawl'): probably from *sprad*, dialect past participle of **SPREAD**.

sprag ▶ **noun 1** a simple brake on a vehicle, especially a stout stick or bar inserted between the spokes of a wheel to check its motion.
2 a prop in a coal mine.
– ORIGIN mid 19th cent: of unknown origin.

sprain ▶ **verb** [with obj.] wrench or twist the ligaments of (an ankle, wrist, or other joint) violently so as to cause pain and swelling but not dislocation: *he left in a wheelchair after spraining an ankle*.
▶ **noun** the result of such a wrench or twist of a joint.
– ORIGIN early 17th cent.: of unknown origin.

spraing /spreɪŋ/ ▶ **noun** [mass noun] a viral disease of potatoes characterized by curved lesions inside the tubers and rings or lesions on the leaves.
– ORIGIN early 16th cent. (originally Scots, denoting a brightly coloured stripe): apparently of Scandinavian origin; compare with Norwegian *sprang* 'lace, fringe'.

spraint /spreɪnt/ (also **spraints**) ▶ **noun** [mass noun] the droppings of an otter.
– ORIGIN late Middle English: from Old French *espreintes*, from *espraindre* 'squeeze out', based on Latin *exprimere* 'to express'.

sprang past of **SPRING**.

sprat ▶ **noun** a small marine fish of the herring family, widely caught for food and fish products.
• *Sprattus* and other genera, family Clupeidae: several species, in particular *S. sprattus* of European inshore waters.
■ any of a number of small fishes that resemble the true sprats, e.g. the sand eel.
▶ **verb** (**spratted**, **spratting**) [no obj.] fish for sprats.
– PHRASES **a sprat to catch a mackerel** Brit. a small expenditure made, or a small risk taken, in the hope of a large or significant gain.
– ORIGIN late 16th cent.: variant of Old English *sprot*, of unknown origin.

Spratly Islands /ˈspratli/ a group of small islands and coral reefs in the South China Sea, between Vietnam and Borneo. Dispersed over a distance of some 965 km (600 miles), the islands are variously claimed by China, Taiwan, Vietnam, the Philippines, and Malaysia.

sprauncy /ˈsprɔːnsi/ ▶ **adjective** (**sprauncier**, **spraunciest**) Brit. informal smart or showy in appearance.
– ORIGIN 1950s: perhaps related to dialect *sprouncey* 'cheerful'.

sprawl ▶ **verb** [no obj., with adverbial] sit, lie, or fall with one's arms and legs spread out in an ungainly way: *the door shot open, sending him sprawling across the pavement* | *she lay sprawled on the bed*.
■ spread out over a large area in an untidy or irregular way: *the town sprawled along several miles of cliff top* | [as adj. **sprawling**] *the sprawling suburbs*.
▶ **noun** [usu. in sing.] an ungainly or carelessly relaxed position in which one's arms and legs are spread out: *she fell into a sort of luxurious sprawl*.
■ a group or mass of something that has spread out in an untidy or irregular way: *a sprawl of buildings*. ■ [mass noun] the expansion of an urban or industrial area into the adjoining countryside in a way perceived to be disorganized and unattractive: *the growth of urban sprawl*.
– DERIVATIVES **sprawlingly** adverb.
– ORIGIN Old English *spreawlian* 'move the limbs convulsively'; related to Danish *sprælle* 'kick or splash about'. The noun dates from the early 18th cent.

spray[1] ▶ **noun** [mass noun] liquid that is blown or driven through the air in the form of tiny drops: *a torrent of white foam and spray* | [count noun] *a fine spray of mud*.
■ a liquid preparation which can be forced out of a can or other container in such a form: *a can of insect spray*. ■ [count noun] a can or container holding such a preparation. ■ [count noun] an act of applying such a preparation: *refresh your flowers with a quick spray*.
▶ **verb** [with obj. and adverbial of direction] apply (liquid) to someone or something in the form of a shower of tiny drops: *the product can be sprayed on to wet or dry hair*.
■ [with obj.] sprinkle or cover (someone or something) with a shower of tiny drops of liquid: *she sprayed herself with perfume*. ■ [no obj., with adverbial of direction] (of liquid) be driven through the air or forced out of something in such a form: *water sprayed into the air*. ■ [with obj.] treat (a plant) with insecticide or herbicide in such a way: *avoid spraying your plants with pesticides*. ■ scatter (something) somewhere with great force: *the truck shuddered to a halt, spraying gravel from under its wheels*. ■ [with obj.] fire a rapid succession of bullets at: *enemy gunners sprayed the decks of the warships*. ■ [with obj.] (of a male cat) direct a stream of urine over (an object or area) to mark a territory. ■ [with obj.] (in a sporting context) kick, hit, or throw (the ball) in an unpredictable or inaccurate direction: *he began his round by spraying his fairway shots*.
– DERIVATIVES **sprayable** adjective.
– ORIGIN early 17th cent. (earlier as *spry*): related to Middle Dutch *spra(e)yen* 'sprinkle'.

spray[2] ▶ **noun** a stem or small branch of a tree or plant, bearing flowers and foliage: *a spray of honeysuckle*.
■ a bunch of cut flowers arranged in an attractive way. ■ a brooch in the form of a bouquet of flowers.
– ORIGIN Middle English: representing late Old English *(e)sprei*, recorded in personal and place names, of unknown origin.

spraydeck ▶ **noun** a flexible cover which is fitted to the opening in the top of a kayak to form a waterproof seal around the canoeist's body.

spray-dry ▶ **verb** [with obj.] dry (a foodstuff or a ceramic material) by spraying particles of it into a current of hot air, the water in the particles being rapidly evaporated.
– DERIVATIVES **spray-dryer** noun.

sprayer ▶ **noun** a piece of equipment used for spraying liquid, typically one that diffuses insecticide or herbicide over crops, plants, and trees.
■ a person who sprays something as part of their occupation: *a paint-sprayer*.

spray gun ▶ **noun** a device resembling a gun which

is used to spray a liquid such as paint or pesticide under pressure.

spray-paint ▶ verb [with obj.] (often **be spray-painted**) paint (an image or message) on to a surface with a spray.
■ paint (a surface) with a spray: *they were spray-painting sidewalks and buildings.*

sprayskirt ▶ noun another term for SPRAYDECK.

spread ▶ verb (past and past participle **spread**) **1** [with obj.] open out (something) so as to extend its surface area, width, or length: *I spread a towel on the sand and sat down | she helped Colin to* ***spread out*** *the map.*
■ stretch out (arms, legs, hands, fingers, or wings) so that they are far apart: *the swan spread its wings.*
2 [no obj., with adverbial] extend over a large or increasing area: *rain over north-west Scotland will spread south-east during the day.*
■ (**spread out**) (of a group of people) move apart so as to cover a wider area: *the Marines spread out across the docks.* ■ [with obj. and adverbial] distribute or disperse (something) over a certain area: *volcanic eruptions spread dust high into the stratosphere.* ■ gradually reach or cause to reach a larger and larger area or more and more people: [no obj.] *the violence spread from the city centre to the suburbs* | [with obj.] *she's always spreading rumours about other people.* ■ (of people, animals, or plants) become distributed over a large or larger area: *the owls have spread as far north as Kuala Lumpur.* ■ [with obj. and adverbial] distribute (something) in a specified way: *you can* ***spread*** *the payments* ***over*** *as long a period as you like.*
3 [with obj. and adverbial] apply (a substance) to an object or surface in an even layer: *he sighed, spreading jam on a croissant.*
■ cover (a surface) with a substance in such a way: *spread each slice thinly with mayonnaise.* ■ [no obj., with adverbial] be able to be applied in such a way: *a tub of unsalted butter that spreads so well.*
4 [with obj.] archaic lay (a table) for a meal.
▶ noun **1** [mass noun] the fact or process of spreading over an area: *the spread of Aids | the spread of the urban population into rural areas.*
2 the extent, width, or area covered by something: *the male's antlers can attain a spread of six feet.*
■ the wingspan of a bird. ■ an expanse or amount of something: *the green spread of the park.* ■ N. Amer. a large farm or ranch.
3 the range or variety of something: *a wide spread of ages.*
■ the difference between two rates or prices: *the very narrow spread between borrowing and deposit rates.* ■ short for POINT SPREAD.
4 a soft paste that can be applied in a layer to bread or other food.
5 an article or advertisement covering several columns or pages of a newspaper or magazine, especially one on two facing pages: *a double-page spread.*
■ N. Amer. a bedspread.
6 informal a large and impressively elaborate meal.
– PHRASES **spread like wildfire** see WILDFIRE. **spread oneself too thin** be involved in so many different activities or projects that one's time and energy are not used to good effect. **spread one's wings** see WING.
– DERIVATIVES **spreadable** adjective.
– ORIGIN Old English *-sprǣdan* (used in combinations), of West Germanic origin; related to Dutch *spreiden* and German *spreiten.*

spread betting ▶ noun [mass noun] a form of gambling in which the amount of money won or lost depends upon the degree to which a score or result in a sporting fixture or other event exceeds or falls short of a level specified by the gambler.

spreadeagle ▶ verb [with obj.] (usu. **be spreadeagled**) stretch (someone) out with their arms and legs extended: *he lay spreadeagled in the road.*
■ informal utterly defeat (an opponent in a sporting contest). ■ [no obj.] Skating perform a spread eagle.
▶ noun (**spread eagle**) an emblematic representation of an eagle with its legs and wings extended.
■ Skating a straight glide made with the feet in a line, with the heels touching, and the arms stretched out to either side.
▶ adjective US **1** stretched out with one's arms and legs extended: *prisoners are chained to their beds, spreadeagle, for days at a time.*
2 dated loudly or aggressively patriotic about the United States: *spreadeagle oratory.*

spreader ▶ noun a device used for spreading or scattering a substance over a wide area.
■ a person who spreads or disseminates something: *they were spreaders of terror.* ■ a plant that grows over a wide area. ■ a bar attached to the mast of a yacht in order to spread the angle of the upper shrouds.

spreadsheet ▶ noun a computer program used chiefly for accounting, in which figures arranged in the rows and columns of a grid can be manipulated and used in calculations.
▶ verb [no obj.] [usu. as noun **spreadsheeting**] use such a computer program.

Sprechgesang /ˈʃprɛxɡəˌzaŋ, German ˈʃprɛçɡəˌzaŋ/ ▶ noun [mass noun] Music a style of dramatic vocalization intermediate between speech and song.
– ORIGIN German, literally 'speech song'.

Sprechstimme /ˈʃprɛxˌʃtɪmə, German ˈʃprɛçˌʃtɪmə/ ▶ noun [mass noun] Music another term for SPRECHGESANG.
■ the kind of voice used in Sprechgesang.
– ORIGIN German, literally 'speech voice'.

spree ▶ noun a spell or sustained period of unrestrained activity of a particular kind: *he went on a six-month crime spree | a shopping spree.*
■ a spell of unrestrained drinking.
▶ verb (**sprees, spreed, spreeing**) [no obj.] dated take part in a spree.
■ [with obj.] spend (money) recklessly: *it was his custom to spree his money in a single night.*
– PHRASES **on the spree** dated engaged in a spell of unrestrained drinking.
– ORIGIN late 18th cent.: of unknown origin.

spreite /ˈʃprʌɪtə/ ▶ noun (pl. **spreiten** or **spreites**) Palaeontology a banded pattern of uncertain origin found in the infill of the burrows of certain fossil invertebrates.
– ORIGIN 1960s: from German *Spreite* 'layer, lamina'.

sprew /spruː/ (also **spreeu** /ˈspriːuː/) ▶ noun (pl. **sprews** or **spreeus**) S. African a southern African starling with variegated or iridescent plumage, especially a glossy starling.
● *Lamprotornis* and other genera, family Sturnidae.
– ORIGIN late 18th cent.: from Dutch *spreeuw* 'starling'.

sprezzatura /ˌsprɛtsəˈt(j)ʊərə/ ▶ noun [mass noun] studied carelessness, especially as a characteristic quality or style of art or literature.
– ORIGIN Italian.

sprig[1] ▶ noun a small stem bearing leaves or flowers, taken from a bush or plant: *a sprig of holly.*
■ a descendant or younger member of a family or social class: *a sprig of the French nobility.* ■ archaic, chiefly derogatory a young man. ■ a small moulded decoration applied to a piece of pottery before firing.
▶ verb decorate (pottery) with small, separately moulded designs.
– DERIVATIVES **spriggy** adjective.
– ORIGIN Middle English: from or related to Low German *sprick.*

sprig[2] ▶ noun a small tapering tack with no head, used chiefly to hold glass in a window frame until the putty dries.
– ORIGIN Middle English: of unknown origin.

sprigged ▶ adjective (chiefly of fabric or paper) decorated with a design of sprigs of leaves or flowers.
■ (of china) decorated with small, separately moulded designs.

sprightly (also **spritely**) ▶ adjective (**sprightlier, sprightliest**) (especially of an old person) lively; full of energy: *she was quite sprightly for her age.*
– DERIVATIVES **sprightliness** noun.
– ORIGIN late 16th cent.: from *spright* (rare variant of SPRITE) + -LY[1].

spring ▶ verb (past **sprang** or chiefly N. Amer. **sprung**; past participle **sprung**) **1** [no obj., with adverbial of direction] move or jump suddenly or rapidly upwards or forwards: *I sprang out of bed* | figurative *they sprang to her defence.*
■ [no obj., with complement or adverbial] move rapidly or suddenly from a constrained position by or as if by the action of a spring: *the drawer sprang open.* ■ [with obj.] operate or cause to operate by means of a mechanism: [with obj.] *he prepared to spring his trap* | [no obj.] *the engine sprang into life.* ■ [with obj.] cause (a game bird) to rise from cover. ■ [with obj.] informal bring about the escape or release of (a prisoner): *the president sought to spring the hostages.*
2 [no obj.] (**spring from**) originate or arise from: *madness and creativity could spring from the same source.*
■ appear suddenly or unexpectedly from: *tears sprang from his eyes.* ■ (**spring up**) suddenly develop or appear: *a terrible storm sprang up.* ■ [with obj.] (**spring something on**) present or propose something suddenly or unexpectedly to (someone): *we decided to spring a surprise on them.*
3 [with obj.] [usu. as adj. **sprung**] cushion or fit (a vehicle or item of furniture) with springs: *a fully sprung bed.*
4 [no obj.] (especially of wood) become warped or split.
■ [with obj.] (of a boat) suffer splitting of (a mast or other part).
5 [no obj.] (**spring for**) N. Amer. & Austral. informal pay for, especially as a treat for someone else: *don't spring for the album until you've heard it.*
■ [with obj.] archaic spend (money): *he might spring a few shillings more.*
▶ noun **1** the season after winter and before summer, in which vegetation begins to appear, in the northern hemisphere from March to May and in the southern hemisphere from September to November: *in spring the garden is a feast of blossom* | [as modifier] *spring rain* | figurative *he was in the spring of his years.*
■ Astronomy the period from the vernal equinox to the summer solstice. ■ short for SPRING TIDE.
2 an elastic device, typically a helical metal coil, that can be pressed or pulled but returns to its former shape when released, used chiefly to exert constant tension or absorb movement.
■ [mass noun] the ability to spring back strongly; elasticity: *the mattress has lost its spring.*
3 [in sing.] a sudden jump upwards or forwards: *with a sudden spring, he leapt on to the table.*
■ informal, dated an escape or release from prison.
4 a place where water or oil wells up from an underground source, or the basin or flow formed in such a way: [as modifier] *spring water.*
■ figurative the origin or a source of something: *the place was a spring of musical talent.*
5 an upward curvature of a ship's deck planking from the horizontal.
■ a split in a wooden plank or spar under strain.
6 Nautical a hawser laid out diagonally aft from a ship's bow or forward from a ship's stern and secured to a fixed point in order to prevent movement or assist manoeuvring.
– PHRASES **spring a leak** (of a boat or container) develop a leak. [ORIGIN: originally a phrase in nautical use, referring to timbers springing out of position.]
– DERIVATIVES **springless** adjective, **springlet** noun (poetic/literary), **springlike** adjective.
– ORIGIN Old English *spring* (noun), *springan* (verb), of Germanic origin; related to Dutch and German *springen.* Early use in the senses 'head of a well' and 'rush out in a stream' gave rise to the figurative use 'originate'.

USAGE In British English the standard past tense is **sprang** (*she* ***sprang*** *forward*), while in US English the past can be either **sprang** or **sprung** (*I* ***sprung*** *out of bed*).

spring balance ▶ noun a balance that measures weight by the tension of a spring.

spring beauty ▶ noun a spring-flowering succulent plant.
● Genera *Claytonia* and *Montia*, family Portulacaceae: several species, in particular the American *M. perfoliata*, naturalized in Britain, and *C. virginica*, sometimes cultivated as an ornamental.

springboard ▶ noun **1** a strong, flexible board from which someone may jump in order to gain added impetus when performing a dive or a gymnastic movement.
■ figurative a thing that lends impetus or assistance to a particular action, enterprise, or development: *an economic plan that may be the springboard for recovery.*
2 Canadian & Austral. a platform fixed to the side of a tree and used by a lumberjack when working at some height from the ground.

springbok /ˈsprɪŋbɒk/ ▶ noun **1** (S. African also **springbuck**) a gazelle with a characteristic habit of leaping (pronking) when disturbed, forming large herds on arid plains in southern Africa.
● *Antidorcas marsupialis*, family Bovidae.
2 (**Springbok**) a member of a sports team selected to represent South Africa, especially in rugby union.
– ORIGIN late 18th cent.: from Afrikaans, from Dutch *springen* 'to spring' + *bok* 'antelope'.

S

spring break ▶ noun N. Amer. a week's holiday for school and college students at Easter.
– DERIVATIVES **spring breaker** noun.

spring chicken ▶ noun **1** [usu. with negative] informal a young person: *you're no spring chicken yourself any more*.
2 a young chicken for eating (originally available only in spring).

spring clean ▶ noun Brit. a thorough cleaning of a house or room, typically undertaken in spring.
▶ verb (**spring-clean**) [with obj.] clean (a home or room) thoroughly: *it was Veronica who spring-cleaned the flat*.

springe /sprɪn(d)ʒ/ ▶ noun a noose or snare for catching small game.
– ORIGIN Middle English: from the base of **SPRING**.

spring equinox ▶ noun the equinox in spring, on about 20 March in the northern hemisphere and 22 September in the southern hemisphere.
■ Astronomy the equinox in March. Also called **VERNAL EQUINOX**.

springer ▶ noun **1** (also **springer spaniel**) a small spaniel of a breed originally used to spring game. There are two main breeds, the **English springer**, typically black and white or brown and white, and the less common red and white **Welsh springer**.
2 Architecture the lowest stone in an arch, where the curve begins.
3 a cow or heifer near to calving.
4 S. African any of a number of marine fish noted for leaping out of the water, in particular:
■ the tenpounder. ■ the skipjack tuna.

spring fever ▶ noun [mass noun] a feeling of restlessness and excitement felt at the beginning of spring.

Springfield 1 the state capital of Illinois; pop. 105,230 (1990). It was the home and burial place of Abraham Lincoln.
2 a city in SW Massachusetts, on the Connecticut River; pop. 156,980 (1990). It was first settled in 1636.
3 a city in SW Missouri, on the northern edge of the Ozark Mountains; pop. 140,490 (1990).

spring greens ▶ plural noun the leaves of young cabbage plants of a variety that does not develop a heart.

springhare /ˈsprɪŋhɛː/ (also **springhaas** /ˈsprɪŋhɑːs/) ▶ noun (pl. **springhares** or **springhaas**) a large nocturnal burrowing rodent resembling a miniature kangaroo, with a rabbit-like head, a long bushy tail, and long hindlimbs, native to southern Africa.
● *Pedetes capensis*, the only member of the family Pedetidae.

spring-loaded ▶ adjective containing a compressed or stretched spring pressing one part against another: *a spring-loaded clothes peg*.

spring lock ▶ noun a type of lock with a spring-loaded bolt which requires a key only to open it, as distinct from a deadlock.

spring mattress ▶ noun a mattress containing springs in a frame.

spring onion ▶ noun chiefly Brit. an onion taken from the ground before the bulb has formed, typically eaten raw in salad.

spring peeper ▶ noun see **PEEPER**[2].

spring roll ▶ noun a Chinese snack consisting of a pancake filled with vegetables and sometimes meat, rolled into a cylinder and fried.

Springsteen, Bruce (b.1949), American rock singer, songwriter, and guitarist, noted for his songs about working-class life in the US. Notable albums: *Born to Run* (1975) and *Born in the USA* (1984).

springtail ▶ noun a minute primitive wingless insect which has a spring-like organ under the abdomen that enables it to leap when disturbed. Springtails are abundant in the soil and leaf litter.
● Order Collembola: many families.

springtide ▶ noun poetic/literary term for **SPRINGTIME**.

spring tide ▶ noun a tide just after a new or full moon, when there is the greatest difference between high and low water.

springtime ▶ noun the season of spring.

springy ▶ adjective (**springier**, **springiest**) springing back quickly when squeezed or stretched; elastic: *the springy turf*.
■ (of movements) light and confident: *he left the room with a springy step*.

– DERIVATIVES **springily** adverb, **springiness** noun.

sprinkle ▶ verb **1** [with obj. and adverbial] scatter or pour small drops or particles of a substance over (an object or surface): *I sprinkled the floor with water*.
■ scatter or pour (small drops or particles of a substance) over an object or surface: *sprinkle sesame seeds over the top*. ■ figurative distribute or disperse something randomly or irregularly throughout (something): *he sprinkled his conversation with quotations*. ■ figurative place or attach (a number of things) at irregularly spaced intervals: *a dress with little daisies sprinkled all over it*.
2 [no obj.] (**it sprinkles**, **it is sprinkling**, etc.) N. Amer. rain very lightly: *it began to sprinkle*.
▶ noun **1** a small quantity or amount of something scattered over an object or surface: *a generous sprinkle of pepper* | figurative *fiction with a sprinkle of fact*.
2 [in sing.] N. Amer. a light rain.
3 (**sprinkles**) chiefly N. Amer. tiny sugar shapes, typically strands and balls, used for decorating cakes and desserts.
– ORIGIN late Middle English: perhaps from Middle Dutch *sprenkelen*.

sprinkler ▶ noun a device that sprays water.
■ a device used for watering lawns. ■ an automatic fire extinguisher installed in the ceilings of a building.

sprinkling ▶ noun a small thinly distributed amount of something: *a sprinkling of grey in his hair*.

sprint ▶ verb [no obj., with adverbial of direction] run at full speed over a short distance: *I saw Charlie sprinting through the traffic towards me*.
▶ noun an act or short spell of running at full speed.
■ a short, fast race in which the competitors run a distance of 400 metres or less: *the 100 metres sprint*. ■ a short, fast race in cycling, swimming, horse racing, etc.
– DERIVATIVES **sprinter** noun.
– ORIGIN late 18th cent. (as a dialect term meaning 'a bound or spring'): related to Swedish *spritta*.

sprinting ▶ noun [mass noun] the competitive athletic sport of running distances of 400 metres or less.

sprit ▶ noun Sailing a small spar reaching diagonally from a mast to the upper outer corner of a sail.
– ORIGIN Old English *sprēot* '(punting) pole'; related to **SPROUT**.

sprite ▶ noun **1** an elf or fairy.
2 a computer graphic which may be moved on-screen and otherwise manipulated as a single entity.
3 a faint flash, typically red, sometimes emitted in the upper atmosphere over a thunderstorm owing to the collision of high-energy electrons with air molecules.
– ORIGIN Middle English: alteration of *sprit*, a contraction of **SPIRIT**.

spritely ▶ adjective variant spelling of **SPRIGHTLY**.

spritsail /ˈsprɪts(ə)l, -seɪl/ ▶ noun a sail extended by a sprit.
■ a sail extended by a yard set under a ship's bowsprit.

spritz chiefly N. Amer. ▶ verb [with obj.] squirt or spray something at or on to (something) in quick short bursts: *she spritzed her neck with cologne*.
▶ noun an act or an instance of squirting or spraying in quick short bursts.
■ a container of something that is sprayed, especially hairspray: *a spritz of your favourite perfume*.
– ORIGIN early 20th cent.: from German *spritzen* 'to squirt'.

spritzer ▶ noun a mixture of wine and soda water.
– ORIGIN 1960s: from German *Spritzer* 'a splash'.

sprocket ▶ noun each of several projections on the rim of a wheel that engage with the links of a chain or with holes in film, tape, or paper.
■ (also **sprocket wheel**) a wheel with projections of this kind.
– ORIGIN mid 16th cent. (denoting a triangular piece of timber used in a roof): of unknown origin.

sprog Brit. informal, chiefly derogatory ▶ noun a child.
■ a military recruit or trainee.
▶ verb (**sprogged**, **sprogging**) [no obj.] have a baby.
– ORIGIN 1940s (originally services' slang in the sense 'new recruit'): perhaps from obsolete *sprag* 'lively young man', of unknown origin.

sprosser /ˈsprɒsə/ ▶ noun another term for **THRUSH NIGHTINGALE**.
– ORIGIN late 19th cent.: from German.

sprout ▶ verb [no obj.] (of a plant) put forth shoots: *the weeds begin to sprout*.

■ [with obj.] grow (plant shoots or hair): *many black cats sprout a few white hairs*. ■ [no obj.] (of a plant, flower, or hair) start to grow; spring up: *crocuses sprouted up from the grass* | figurative *forms of nationalism sprouted as the system collapsed*.
▶ noun **1** a shoot of a plant.
2 short for **BRUSSELS SPROUT**.
– ORIGIN Middle English: of West Germanic origin; related to Dutch *spruiten* and German *spriessen*.

spruce[1] ▶ adjective neat in dress and appearance: *he looked as spruce as if he were heading for a meeting with his bank manager*.
▶ verb [with obj.] (**spruce someone/thing up**) make a person or place smarter or tidier: *the fund will be used to spruce up historic buildings*.
– DERIVATIVES **sprucely** adverb, **spruceness** noun.
– ORIGIN late 16th cent.: perhaps from **SPRUCE**[2] in the obsolete sense 'Prussian', in the phrase *spruce (leather) jerkin*.

spruce[2] ▶ noun a widespread coniferous tree which has a distinctive conical shape and hanging cones, widely grown for timber, pulp, and Christmas trees.
● Genus *Picea*, family Pinaceae: many species.
– ORIGIN late Middle English (denoting Prussia or something originating in Prussia): alteration of obsolete *Pruce* 'Prussia'. The application to the tree dates from the early 17th cent.

spruce[3] ▶ verb [no obj.] Brit. informal, dated engage in pretence or deception, especially by feigning illness: *he's no fool; he'd have known if she was sprucing*.
■ [with obj.] deceive: *they spruced you proper*.
– DERIVATIVES **sprucer** noun.
– ORIGIN early 20th cent.: of unknown origin.

spruce beer ▶ noun [mass noun] a fermented drink using spruce twigs and needles as flavouring.

spruce budworm ▶ noun the brown caterpillar of a small North American moth which is a serious pest of spruce and other conifers.
● *Choristoneura fumiferana*, family Tortricidae.

sprue[1] /spruː/ ▶ noun a channel through which metal or plastic is poured into a mould.
■ a piece of metal or plastic which has solidified in a sprue, especially one joining a number of small moulded plastic items.
– ORIGIN early 19th cent.: of unknown origin.

sprue[2] /spruː/ ▶ noun [mass noun] disease of the small intestine causing malabsorption of food, in particular:
■ (also **tropical sprue**) a disease characterized by ulceration of the mouth and chronic enteritis, suffered by visitors to tropical regions from temperate countries. ■ (also **non-tropical sprue**) another term for **COELIAC DISEASE**.
– ORIGIN late 19th cent.: from Dutch *spruw* 'thrush'; perhaps related to Flemish *spruwen* 'sprinkle'.

spruik /spruːk/ ▶ verb [no obj.] Austral./NZ informal speak in public, especially to advertise a show: *men who spruik outside striptease joints*.
– DERIVATIVES **spruiker** noun.
– ORIGIN early 20th cent.: of unknown origin.

spruit /spreɪt/ ▶ noun S. African a small watercourse, typically dry except during the rainy season.
– ORIGIN Dutch; related to **SPROUT**.

sprung past participle and (especially in North America) past of **SPRING**.

sprung rhythm ▶ noun [mass noun] a poetic metre approximating to speech, each foot having one stressed syllable followed by a varying number of unstressed ones.
– ORIGIN late 19th cent.: coined by G. M. Hopkins, who used the metre.

spry ▶ adjective (**spryer**, **spryest**) (especially of an old person) active; lively: *he continued to look spry and active well into his eighties*.
– DERIVATIVES **spryly** adverb, **spryness** noun.
– ORIGIN mid 18th cent.: of unknown origin.

spud ▶ noun **1** informal a potato.
■ chiefly US a foolish or incompetent person.
2 a small, narrow spade for cutting the roots of plants, especially weeds.
3 [often as modifier] a short length of pipe that is used to connect two components or that takes the form of a projection from a fitting to which a pipe may be screwed: *a spud washer*.
4 a type of ice chisel.
▶ verb (**spudded**, **spudding**) [with obj.] **1** dig up or cut (plants, especially weeds) with a spud.
2 make the initial drilling for (an oil well).
– ORIGIN late Middle English (denoting a short

knife): of unknown origin. The sense 'potato' (dating from the mid 19th cent.) was originally slang and dialect.

spud-bashing ▶ **noun** [mass noun] Brit. informal the action of peeling potatoes, especially for a prolonged period.

spud wrench ▶ **noun** a long bar with a socket on the end for tightening bolts.

spue ▶ **verb** archaic spelling of **SPEW**.

spumante /spuːˈmanteɪ, -ˈmanti/ ▶ **noun** [mass noun] an Italian sparkling white wine.
– ORIGIN Italian, literally 'sparkling'.

spume /spjuːm/ poetic/literary ▶ **noun** [mass noun] froth or foam, especially that found on waves.
▶ **verb** [no obj.] form or produce a mass of froth or foam: *water was spuming under the mill.*
– DERIVATIVES **spumous** adjective, **spumy** adjective.
– ORIGIN late Middle English: from Old French *(e)spume* or Latin *spuma*.

spumoni /spuːˈməʊni/ (also **spumone**) ▶ **noun** [mass noun] N. Amer. a kind of ice-cream dessert with different colours and flavours in layers.
– ORIGIN from Italian *spumone*, from *spuma* 'foam'.

spun past and past participle of **SPIN**.

spunk ▶ **noun** [mass noun] **1** informal courage and determination.
2 Brit. vulgar slang semen.
3 [count noun] Austral. informal a sexually attractive person.
– ORIGIN mid 16th cent. (in the sense 'a spark, vestige'): of unknown origin; perhaps a blend of **SPARK**[1] and obsolete *funk* 'spark'.

spunky ▶ **adjective** (**spunkier**, **spunkiest**) informal **1** courageous and determined: *a spunky performance.*
2 chiefly Austral. sexually attractive: *a top chick with a spunky boyfriend.*
– DERIVATIVES **spunkily** adverb.

spun silk ▶ **noun** [mass noun] a cheap material made of short-fibred and waste silk.

spun sugar ▶ **noun** [mass noun] hardened sugar syrup drawn out into long filaments and used to make candyfloss or as a decoration for sweet dishes.

spun yarn ▶ **noun** [mass noun] Nautical cord made by twisting loose strands of rope together.

spur ▶ **noun 1** a device with a small spike or a spiked wheel that is worn on a rider's heel and used for urging a horse forward.
■ figurative a thing that prompts or encourages someone; an incentive: *profit was both the spur and the reward of enterprise.* ■ a hard spike on the back of the leg of a cock or male game bird, used in fighting. ■ a steel point fastened to the leg of a gamecock. ■ a climbing iron.
2 a thing that projects or branches off from a main body, in particular:
■ a projection from a mountain or mountain range. ■ a short branch road or railway line. ■ Botany a slender tubular projection from the base of a flower, e.g. a honeysuckle or orchid, typically containing nectar. ■ a short fruit-bearing side shoot.
3 a small, single-pointed support for ceramic ware in a kiln.
▶ **verb** (**spurred**, **spurring**) [with obj.] **1** urge (a horse) forward by digging one's spurs into its sides: *she spurred her horse towards the hedge.*
■ give an incentive or encouragement to (someone): *her sons' passion for computer games **spurred** her **on** to set up a software shop.* ■ cause or promote the development of; stimulate: *governments cut interest rates to spur demand.*
2 prune in (a side shoot of a plant) so as to form a spur close to the stem: ***spur back** the lateral shoots.*
– PHRASES **on the spur of the moment** on a momentary impulse; without premeditation. **put** (or **set**) **spurs to** use one's spurs to urge on (a horse).
– DERIVATIVES **spurless** adjective, **spurred** adjective.
– ORIGIN Old English *spora, spura*, of Germanic origin; related to Dutch *spoor* and German *Sporn*, also to **SPURN**.

spur-dog ▶ **noun** a large white-spotted grey dogfish with venomous spines in front of the dorsal fins. It occurs in the North Atlantic and the Mediterranean, often in large shoals.
• *Squalus acanthias*, family Squalidae.

spurfowl ▶ **noun** an Asian and African game bird related to the partridges, with spurs on the legs.
• Genus *Galloperdix* of Asia (three species), and the **red-necked spurfowl** or francolin (*Francolinus afer*) of Africa, family Phasianidae.

spurge /spəːdʒ/ ▶ **noun** a herbaceous plant or shrub with milky latex and very small typically greenish flowers. Many kinds are cultivated as ornamentals and some are of commercial importance.
• Genus *Euphorbia*, family Euphorbiaceae: numerous species.
– ORIGIN late Middle English: shortening of Old French *espurge*, from *espurgier*, from Latin *expurgare* 'cleanse' (because of the purgative properties of the milky latex).

spur gear ▶ **noun** another term for **SPUR WHEEL**.

spurge laurel ▶ **noun** a low-growing evergreen Eurasian shrub with leathery leaves, small green flowers, and black poisonous berries.
• *Daphne laureola*, family Thymelaeaceae.

spurious /ˈspjʊərɪəs/ ▶ **adjective** not being what it purports to be; false or fake: *separating authentic and spurious claims.*
■ (of a line of reasoning) apparently but not actually valid: *this spurious reasoning results in nonsense.* ■ archaic (of offspring) illegitimate.
– DERIVATIVES **spuriously** adverb, **spuriousness** noun.
– ORIGIN late 16th cent. (in the sense 'born out of wedlock'): from Latin *spurius* 'false' + **-OUS**.

spurn ▶ **verb** [with obj.] reject with disdain or contempt: *he spoke gruffly, as if afraid that his invitation would be spurned.*
■ archaic strike, tread, or push away with the foot: *with one touch of my feet, I spurn the solid Earth.*
▶ **noun** archaic an act of spurning.
– DERIVATIVES **spurner** noun.
– ORIGIN Old English *spurnan, spornan*; related to Latin *spernere* 'to scorn'; compare with **SPUR**.

spurrey /ˈspʌri/ (also **spurry**) ▶ **noun** (pl. **-eys** or **-ies**) a small widely distributed plant of the pink family, with pink or white flowers.
• Genera *Spergula* and *Spergularia*, family Caryophyllaceae: several species, in particular **corn spurrey** (*Spergula arvensis*), a spindly weed of cornfields, and **sand spurrey** (*Spergularia rubra*), of sandy and gravelly soils.
– ORIGIN late 16th cent.: from Dutch *spurrie*; probably related to medieval Latin *spergula*.

spurrier /ˈspʌrɪə, ˈspəː-/ ▶ **noun** rare a person who makes spurs.

spur royal ▶ **noun** historical a gold coin worth fifteen shillings, made chiefly in the reign of James I and bearing a representation of a sun with rays.

spurt ▶ **verb** [no obj., with adverbial of direction] gush out in a sudden and forceful stream: *he cut his finger, and blood spurted over the sliced potatoes.*
■ [with obj. and adverbial of direction] cause to gush out suddenly: *the kettle boiled and spurted scalding water everywhere.* ■ move with a sudden burst of speed: *the other car had spurted to the top of the ramp* | figurative *the shares spurted to 375p.*
▶ **noun** a sudden gushing stream: *a sudden spurt of blood gushed into her eyes.*
■ a sudden marked burst or increase of activity or speed: *late in the race he **put on a spurt** and reached second place* | *a growth spurt.*
– ORIGIN mid 16th cent.: of unknown origin.

spur wheel ▶ **noun** a gearwheel with teeth projecting parallel to the wheel's axis.

sputnik /ˈspʊtnɪk, ˈspʌt-/ ▶ **noun** each of a series of Soviet artificial satellites, the first of which (launched on 4 October 1957) was the first satellite to be placed in orbit.
– ORIGIN Russian, literally 'fellow-traveller'.

sputter ▶ **verb 1** [no obj.] make a series of soft explosive sounds, typically when being heated or as a symptom of a fault: *the engine sputtered and stopped.*
■ [reporting verb] speak in a series of incoherent bursts as a result of indignation or some other strong emotion: [with direct speech] *'But … but …' she sputtered.* ■ [with obj.] emit with a spitting sound: *the goose is in the oven, sputtering fat.* ■ [with adverbial] figurative proceed or develop in a spasmodic and feeble way: *strikes in the public services sputtered on.*
2 [with obj.] Physics deposit (metal) on a surface by using fast ions to eject particles of it from a target.
■ cover (a surface) with metal by this method.
▶ **noun** a series of soft explosive sounds, typically produced by an engine or by something heating or burning: *the sputter of the motor died away.*
– DERIVATIVES **sputterer** noun.
– ORIGIN late 16th cent. (as a verb): from Dutch *sputteren*, of imitative origin.

sputum /ˈspjuːtəm/ ▶ **noun** [mass noun] a mixture of saliva and mucus coughed up from the respiratory tract, typically as a result of infection or other disease and often examined microscopically to aid medical diagnosis.
– ORIGIN late 17th cent.: from Latin, neuter past participle of *spuere* 'to spit'.

spy ▶ **noun** (pl. **-ies**) a person who secretly collects and reports information on the activities, movements, and plans of an enemy or competitor.
■ a person who keeps watch on others secretly: [as modifier] *a spy camera.*
▶ **verb** (**-ies**, **-ied**) [no obj.] work for a government or other organization by secretly collecting information about enemies or competitors: *he agreed to spy for the West.*
■ (**spy on**) observe (someone) furtively: *the couple were spied on by reporters.* ■ [with obj.] discern or make out, especially by careful observation: *he could spy a figure in the distance.* ■ [with obj.] (**spy something out**) collect information about something to use in deciding how to act: *he would go and spy out the land.*
– ORIGIN Middle English: shortening of Old French *espie* 'espying', *espier* 'espy', of Germanic origin, from an Indo-European root shared by Latin *specere* 'behold, look'.

spyglass ▶ **noun** a small telescope.

spyhole ▶ **noun** Brit. a peephole, especially one in a door for observing callers before opening.

spymaster ▶ **noun** the head of an organization of spies.

sq ▶ **abbreviation for** square: *51,100 sq km.*

SQL Computing ▶ **abbreviation for** Structured Query Language, an international standard for database manipulation.

Sqn Ldr ▶ **abbreviation for** Squadron Leader.

squab /skwɒb/ ▶ **noun 1** a young unfledged pigeon.
2 Brit. the padded back or side of a vehicle seat.
■ a thick stuffed cushion, especially one covering the seat of a chair or sofa.
▶ **adjective** archaic (of a person) short and fat.
– ORIGIN mid 17th cent. (in the sense 'inexperienced person'): of unknown origin; compare with obsolete *quab* 'shapeless thing' and Swedish dialect *skvabba* 'fat woman'.

squabble ▶ **noun** a noisy quarrel about something petty or trivial: *family squabbles.*
▶ **verb** [no obj.] quarrel noisily over a trivial matter: *the boys were squabbling over a ball.*
– DERIVATIVES **squabbler** noun.
– ORIGIN early 17th cent.: probably imitative; compare with Swedish dialect *skvabbel* 'a dispute'.

squab pie ▶ **noun** Brit. **1** pigeon pie.
2 archaic a pie with a thick crust containing mutton, pork, onions, and apples. [ORIGIN: early 18th cent.: regional use, chiefly current in western and south-western counties.]

squacco heron /ˈskwakəʊ/ ▶ **noun** a small crested buff and white heron found in southern Europe, the Middle East, and Africa.
• *Ardeola ralloides*, family Ardeidae.
– ORIGIN mid 18th cent.: *squacco* from Italian dialect *sguacco*.

squad ▶ **noun** [treated as sing. or pl.] a small group of people having a particular task: *an assassination squad.*
■ a small number of soldiers assembled for drill or assigned to some special task. ■ a group of sports players or competitors from which a team is chosen: *Ireland's World Cup squad.* ■ a division of a police force dealing with a particular crime or type of crime: *the regional crime squad.*
– ORIGIN mid 17th cent.: shortening of French *escouade*, variant of *escadre*, from Italian *squadra* 'square'.

squad car ▶ **noun** a police patrol car.

squaddie (also **squaddy**) ▶ **noun** (pl. **-ies**) Brit. informal a private soldier.

squadron ▶ **noun** an operational unit in an air force consisting of two or more flights of aircraft and the personnel required to fly them.
■ a principal division of an armoured or cavalry regiment, consisting of two or more troops. ■ a group of warships detached on a particular duty or under the command of a flag officer. ■ informal a large group of people or things: *he immediately commissioned a squadron of architects.*
– ORIGIN mid 16th cent. (originally denoting a group of soldiers in square formation): from Italian *squadrone*, from *squadra* 'square'.

squadron leader ▶ **noun** a rank of officer in the

S

RAF, above flight lieutenant and below wing commander.

squalamine /ˈskweɪləmiːn/ ▶ **noun** [mass noun] Biochemistry a compound of the steroid type found in sharks, which has antibiotic properties.
– ORIGIN late 20th cent.: from Latin *squalus* (denoting a kind of marine fish and used as a rare term in English for 'shark') + **AMINE**.

squalene /ˈskweɪliːn/ ▶ **noun** [mass noun] Biochemistry an oily liquid hydrocarbon which occurs in shark liver oil and human sebum, and is a metabolic precursor of sterols.
• A triterpenoid; chem. formula: $C_{30}H_{50}$.
– ORIGIN early 20th cent.: from Latin *squalus* (see **SQUALAMINE**) + **-ENE**.

squalid ▶ **adjective** (of a place) extremely dirty and unpleasant, especially as a result of poverty or neglect: *the squalid, overcrowded prison.*
■ showing or involving a contemptible lack of moral standards: *a squalid attempt to save themselves from electoral embarrassment.*
– DERIVATIVES **squalidly** adverb, **squalidness** noun.
– ORIGIN late 16th cent.: from Latin *squalidus*, from *squalere* 'be rough or dirty'.

squall /skwɔːl/ ▶ **noun** a sudden violent gust of wind or localized storm, especially one bringing rain, snow, or sleet: *low clouds and squalls of driving rain.*
■ a loud cry: *he emitted a short mournful squall.*
▶ **verb** [no obj.] (of a baby or small child) cry noisily and continuously: *Sarah was squalling in her crib.*
– DERIVATIVES **squally** adjective.
– ORIGIN mid 17th cent.: probably an alteration of **SQUEAL**, influenced by **BAWL**.

squall line ▶ **noun** Meteorology a narrow band of high winds and storms associated with a cold front.

squalor /ˈskwɒlə/ ▶ **noun** [mass noun] a state of being extremely dirty and unpleasant, especially as a result of poverty or neglect: *they lived in squalor and disease.*
– ORIGIN early 17th cent.: from Latin, from *squalere* 'be dirty'.

Squamata /skwəˈmɑːtə/ Zoology a large order of reptiles which comprises the snakes, lizards, and worm lizards.
– DERIVATIVES **squamate** adjective & noun.
– ORIGIN modern Latin (plural), from Latin *squama* 'scale'.

squamocolumnar /ˌskweɪmə(ʊ)kəˈlʌmnə/ ▶ **adjective** Anatomy relating to or denoting a junction between layers of stratified squamous cells and columnar cells in epithelial tissue.

squamosal /skwəˈməʊs(ə)l/ ▶ **noun** Zoology the squamous portion of the temporal bone, especially when this forms a separate bone which, in mammals, articulates with the lower jaw.
– ORIGIN mid 19th cent.: from Latin *squamosus* (from *squama* 'scale') + **-AL**.

squamous /ˈskweɪməs/ ▶ **adjective** covered with or characterized by scales: *a squamous black hide.*
■ Anatomy relating to, consisting of, or denoting a layer of epithelium that consists of very thin flattened cells: *squamous cell carcinoma.* ■ [attrib.] Anatomy denoting the flat portion of the temporal bone which forms part of the side of the skull.
– ORIGIN late Middle English: from Latin *squamosus*, from *squama* 'scale'.

squamule /ˈskweɪmjuːl/ ▶ **noun** Botany & Zoology a small scale.
– DERIVATIVES **squamulose** adjective.
– ORIGIN mid 18th cent.: from Latin *squamula*, diminutive of *squama* 'scale'.

squander ▶ **verb** [with obj.] waste (something, especially money or time) in a reckless and foolish manner: *entrepreneurs squander their profits on expensive cars.*
■ allow (an opportunity) to pass or be lost: *the team squandered several good scoring chances.*
– DERIVATIVES **squanderer** noun.
– ORIGIN late 16th cent.: of unknown origin.

square ▶ **noun 1** a plane figure with four equal straight sides and four right angles.
■ a thing having such a shape or approximately such a shape: *she tore a bit of cloth into a four-inch square.* ■ a thing having the shape or approximate shape of a cube: *a small square of chocolate.* ■ an open (typically four-sided) area surrounded by buildings in a village, town, or city: *a market square* | [in place names] *Leicester Square.* ■ an open area at the meeting of streets. ■ a small square area on the board used in a game. ■ Cricket a closer-cut area at the centre of a ground, any strip of which may be prepared as a wicket. ■ an area within a military barracks or camp used for drill. ■ US a block of buildings bounded by four streets. ■ historical a body of infantry drawn up in rectangular form. ■ a unit of 100 square ft used as a measure of flooring, roofing, etc. ■ a square scarf. ■ Brit. a mortar board. ■ the portion of the cover of a bound book which projects beyond the pages.
2 the product of a number multiplied by itself: *a circle's area is proportional to the square of its radius.*
3 an L-shaped or T-shaped instrument used for obtaining or testing right angles: *a carpenter's square.*
■ [mass noun] Astrology an aspect of 90° (one quarter of a circle): *Venus **in square to** Jupiter.*
4 informal a person considered to be old-fashioned or boringly conventional in attitude or behaviour.
■ N. Amer. a cigarette containing tobacco rather than cannabis.
5 N. Amer. informal a square meal: *three squares a day.*
▶ **adjective 1** having the shape or approximate shape of a square: *a square table.*
■ having the shape or approximate shape of a cube: *a square block of flats.* ■ having or in the form of two right angles: *a suitable length of wood with square ends.* ■ having an outline resembling two corners of a square: *his square jaw.* ■ broad and solid in shape: *he was short and square.*
2 denoting a unit of measurement equal to the area of a square whose side is of the unit specified: *30,000 square feet of new gallery space.*
■ [postpositive] denoting the length of each side of a square shape or object: *the office was fifteen feet square.*
3 at right angles; perpendicular: *these lines must be **square to** the top and bottom marked edges.*
■ Cricket & Soccer in a direction transversely across the field or pitch. ■ Astrology having or denoting an aspect of 90°: *Jupiter is square to the Sun.*
4 level or parallel: *place two pieces of wood one on top of the other, ensuring that they are exactly square.*
■ properly arranged; in good order: *we should get everything square before we leave.* ■ compatible or in agreement: *he wanted to make sure we were **square with** the court's decision and not subject to a lawsuit.* ■ fair and honest: *she'd been as square with him as anybody could be.*
5 (of two people) owing nothing to each other: *an acknowledgement that we are square.*
■ with both players or sides having equal scores in a game: *the goal brought the match **all square** once again.*
6 informal old-fashioned or boringly conventional: *Elvis was anything but square.*
7 (of rhythm) simple and straightforward.
▶ **adverb 1** directly; straight: *it hit me square in the forehead.*
■ informal fairly; honestly: *I'd acted square and on the level with him.*
2 Cricket & Soccer in a direction transversely across the field or pitch: *the ball bounced almost square to the left.*
▶ **verb** [with obj.] **1** make square or rectangular; give a square or rectangular cross section to: *you can **square off** the other edge.*
■ [usu. as adj. **squared**] mark out in squares: *a sheet of squared paper.*
2 multiply (a number) by itself: *5 squared equals 25.*
■ [usu. as postpositive adj.] (**squared**) convert (a linear unit of measurement) to a unit of area equal to a square whose side is of the unit specified: *there were only three people per kilometre squared.*
3 make compatible; reconcile: *I'm able to **square** my profession **with** my religious beliefs.*
■ [no obj.] be compatible: *do those announcements really **square with** the facts?*
4 balance (an account): *institutions are anxious to square their books before the election.*
■ settle or pay (a bill or debt): *would you **square up** the bill?* ■ make the score of (a match or game) even: [with obj. and complement] *his goal squared the match 1–1.* ■ informal secure the help, acquiescence, or silence of (someone), especially by offering an inducement: *trying to square the press.*
5 bring (one's shoulders) into a position in which they appear square and broad, typically to prepare oneself for a difficult task or event: *chin up, shoulders squared, she stepped into the room.*
■ (**square oneself**) adopt a posture of defence.
6 pass (a ball) across the field, especially towards the centre.
7 Sailing set (a yard or other part of a ship) at right angles to the keel or other point of reference.
8 Astrology (of a planet) have a square aspect with (another planet or position): *Saturn squares the Sun on the 17th.*
– PHRASES **back to** (or **at**) **square one** informal back to where one started, with no progress having been made. **on the square 1** informal honest; straightforward. **2** having membership of the Freemasons. **out of square** not at right angles. **square accounts with** see **ACCOUNT**. **square the circle** construct a square equal in area to a given circle (a problem incapable of a purely geometrical solution). ■ do something that is considered to be impossible. **a square deal** see **DEAL**[1]. **a square peg in a round hole** see **PEG**.
– DERIVATIVES **squareness** noun, **squarer** noun, **squarish** adjective.
– ORIGIN Middle English: shortening of Old French *esquare* (noun), *esquarre* (past participle, used as an adjective), *esquarrer* (verb), based on Latin *quadra* 'square'.
▶ **square something away** N. Amer. arrange or deal with in a satisfactory way: *don't you worry, we'll get things squared away.*
square off 1 N. Amer. another way of saying ***square up*** below. **2** Austral. settle a difference; set matters right.
square someone off Austral. conciliate or placate someone.
square up assume the attitude of a person about to fight: *he has been known to **square up to** people who have enraged him.* ■ (**square up to**) face and tackle (a difficulty or problem) resolutely: *the Party squared up to the necessity of facing fascism with military sanctions.*

square-bashing ▶ **noun** [mass noun] Brit. informal military drill performed repeatedly on a barrack square.

square brackets ▶ **plural noun** brackets of the form [ ].

square-built ▶ **adjective** having a comparatively broad or square shape.

square cut ▶ **noun** Cricket a cut hit square on the offside.
▶ **verb** (**square-cut**) [with obj.] hit (the ball) with such a stroke; hit a ball delivered by (a bowler) with such a stroke.

square dance ▶ **noun** a country dance, originating in the US, that starts with four couples facing one another in a square, with the steps and movements shouted out by a caller.
▶ **verb** (**square-dance**) [no obj.] [often as noun **square-dancing**] participate in a square dance.
– DERIVATIVES **square dancer** noun.

square eyes ▶ **plural noun** Brit. humorous used in reference to eyes supposedly affected by excessive television viewing: *he watched so much TV he'd got square eyes.*
■ [treated as sing.] used as a nickname or taunt for a person who watches too much television.
– DERIVATIVES **square-eyed** adjective.

square go ▶ **noun** Scottish an unarmed brawl.

squarehead ▶ **noun** N. Amer. informal **1** a stupid or inept person.
2 offensive a person of Germanic or Scandinavian origin.

square knot ▶ **noun** another term for **REEF KNOT**.

square law ▶ **noun** Physics a law relating two variables one of which varies (directly or inversely) as the square of the other. See also **INVERSE SQUARE LAW**.

square leg ▶ **noun** Cricket a fielding position level with the batsman, approximately halfway towards the boundary on the leg side.
■ a fielder at this position.

squarely ▶ **adverb** directly, without deviating to one side: *Ashley looked at him squarely.*
■ in a direct and uncompromising manner; without equivocation: *they placed the blame squarely on the president.*

square meal ▶ **noun** a substantial, satisfying, and balanced meal: *three square meals a day.*
– ORIGIN said to derive from nautical use, with reference to the square platters on which meals were served on board ship.

square measure ▶ **noun** a unit of measurement relating to area.

Square Mile an informal name for the City of London.

square number ▶ **noun** the product of a number multiplied by itself, e.g. 1, 4, 9, 16.

square perch ▶ **noun** see **PERCH**[3] (sense 2).

S

square piano ▶ noun an early type of piano, small and oblong in shape.

square pole ▶ noun another term for **PERCH**[3] (in sense 2).

square-rigged ▶ adjective (of a sailing ship) having the principal sails at right angles to the length of the ship, supported by horizontal yards attached to the mast or masts.

square-rigger ▶ noun a square-rigged sailing ship.

square rod ▶ noun another term for **PERCH**[3] (in sense 2).

square root ▶ noun a number which produces a specified quantity when multiplied by itself.

square sail ▶ noun a four-cornered sail supported by a yard attached to a mast.

square-shouldered ▶ adjective (of a person) having broad shoulders that do not slope.

square-tail ▶ noun a fish of warm seas which has a slender cylindrical body and long tail, the base of which is square in cross section.
• Family Tetragonuridae and genus *Tetragonurus*: several species.

square-toed ▶ adjective (of shoes or boots) having broad, square toes.
■ archaic old-fashioned or formal.

square wave ▶ noun Electronics a periodic wave that varies abruptly in amplitude between two fixed values, spending equal times at each.

squark /skwɑːk/ ▶ noun Physics the supersymmetric counterpart of a quark, with spin 0 instead of ½.
– ORIGIN 1980s: from *s(uper)* + **QUARK**[1].

squash[1] ▶ verb [with obj.] crush or squeeze (something) with force so that it becomes flat, soft, or out of shape: *wash and squash the cans before depositing them* | [as adj. **squashed**] *a squashed packet of cigarettes.*
■ [with obj. and adverbial] squeeze or force (someone or something) into a small or restricted space: *she squashed some of her clothes inside the bag.* ■ [no obj., with adverbial of direction] make one's way into a small or restricted space: *I squashed into the middle of the crowd.* ■ suppress, stifle, or subdue (a feeling, conjecture, or action): *the mournful sound did nothing to squash her high spirits.* ■ firmly reject (an idea or suggestion): *the proposal was immediately squashed by the Heritage Department.* ■ silence or discomfit (someone), typically by making a remark intended to embarrass or humiliate them: *she needled him with such venom that Seb was visibly squashed.*
▶ noun **1** [in sing.] a state of being squeezed or forced into a small or restricted space: *it was a bit of a squash but he didn't seem to mind.*
■ [count noun] dated a social gathering or informal meeting: *a poetry squash in London.*
2 [mass noun] Brit. a concentrated liquid made from fruit juice and sugar, which is diluted to make a drink: *orange squash.*
3 (also **squash rackets**) [mass noun] a game in which two players use rackets to hit a small, soft rubber ball against the walls of a closed court.
4 Biology a preparation of softened tissue that has been made thin for microscopic examination by gently compressing or tapping it.
– ORIGIN mid 16th cent. (as a verb): alteration of **QUASH**.

squash[2] ▶ noun (pl. same or **squashes**) **1** an edible gourd, the flesh of which may be cooked and eaten as a vegetable.
2 the trailing plant of the gourd family which produces this fruit.
• Genus *Cucurbita*, family Cucurbitaceae: many species and varieties, including the **winter squashes** and **summer squashes**.
– ORIGIN mid 17th cent.: abbreviation of Narragansett *asquutasquash*.

squashberry ▶ noun (pl. **-ies**) a North American viburnum which bears edible berries.
• *Viburnum edule*, family Caprifoliaceae.

squash blossom ▶ noun [as modifier] denoting a type of silver jewellery made by Navajos characterized by designs resembling the flower of the squash plant.

squash bug ▶ noun a bug which resembles a shield bug, several American kinds being serious pests of squashes and similar fruit.
• Family Coreidae, suborder Heteroptera: many species, in particular the North American *Anasasa tristis*.

squashy ▶ adjective easily crushed or squeezed into a different shape; having a soft consistency: *a big, squashy leather chair.*
– DERIVATIVES **squashily** adverb, **squashiness** noun.

squat ▶ verb (**squatted**, **squatting**) **1** [no obj.] crouch or sit with one's knees bent and one's heels close to or touching one's buttocks or the back of one's thighs: *I **squatted down** in front of him.*
■ [with obj.] Weightlifting crouch down in such a way and rise again while holding (a specified weight) behind one's neck: *he can squat 850 pounds.*
2 [no obj.] unlawfully occupy an uninhabited building or settle on a piece of land: *eight families are squatting in the house.*
■ [with obj.] occupy (an uninhabited building) in such a way.
▶ adjective (**squatter**, **squattest**) short and thickset; disproportionately broad or wide: *he was muscular and squat* | *a squat grey house.*
▶ noun **1** [in sing.] a position in which one's knees are bent and one's heels are close to or touching one's buttocks or the back of one's thighs.
■ Weightlifting an exercise in which a person squats down and rises again while holding a barbell at shoulder level. ■ (in gymnastics) an exercise involving a squatting movement or action.
2 a building occupied by people living in it without the legal right to do so.
■ an unlawful occupation of an uninhabited building.
3 N. Amer. informal short for **DIDDLY-SQUAT**.
– DERIVATIVES **squatly** adverb, **squatness** noun.
– ORIGIN Middle English (in the sense 'thrust down with force'): from Old French *esquatir* 'flatten', based on Latin *coactus*, past participle of *cogere* 'compel' (see **COGENT**). The current sense of the adjective dates from the mid 17th cent.

squatt ▶ noun the larva of the common housefly, used by anglers as bait.
– ORIGIN 1930s: perhaps from the adjective **SQUAT**.

squatter ▶ noun **1** a person who unlawfully occupies an uninhabited building or unused land.
■ N. Amer. & Austral. historical a settler with no legal title to the land occupied, typically one on land not yet allocated by a government.
2 Austral. a large-scale sheep or cattle farmer.
■ Austral./NZ historical a person occupying a tract of pastoral land as a tenant of the Crown.

squat thrust ▶ noun an exercise in which the legs are thrust backwards to their full extent from a squatting position with the hands on the floor.

squaw /skwɔː/ ▶ noun offensive an American Indian woman or wife.
■ N. Amer., offensive a woman or wife.
– ORIGIN mid 17th cent.: from Narragansett *squaws* 'woman', with related forms in many Algonquin dialects.

USAGE Until relatively recently, the word **squaw** was used neutrally in anthropological and other contexts to mean 'an American Indian woman or wife'. With changes in the political climate in the second half of the 20th century, however, the derogatory attitudes of the past towards American Indian women have meant that, in modern North American English, the word cannot be used in any sense without being offensive. In British English, the word has not acquired offensive connotations to the same extent, but it is nevertheless uncommon here too and now regarded as old-fashioned.

squawfish ▶ noun (pl. same or **-fishes**) a large predatory freshwater fish of the carp family, with a slender body and large mouth, found in western North America.
• Genus *Ptychocheilus*, family Cyprinidae: several species, in particular the **northern squawfish** (*P. oregonensis*).
– ORIGIN late 19th cent.: the word derives from the former importance to American Indians of such fish, as food.

squawk ▶ verb [no obj.] (of a bird) make a loud, harsh, noise: *the geese flew upriver, squawking.*
■ [with direct speech] (of a person) say something in a loud, discordant tone: *'What are you doing?' she squawked.* ■ complain or protest about something.
▶ noun a loud harsh or discordant noise made by a bird or a person.
■ a complaint or protest: *her plan provoked a loud squawk from her friends.*
– DERIVATIVES **squawker** noun.
– ORIGIN early 19th cent.: imitative.

squawk box ▶ noun informal, chiefly US a loudspeaker, in particular one that is part of an intercom system.

squaw man ▶ noun N. Amer. offensive a white or black man married to an American Indian woman.

squawroot ▶ noun either of two North American plants:
• a yellow-brown parasitic plant related to the broomrape (*Conopholis americana*, family Orobanchaceae). • the blue cohosh. See **COHOSH**.

squeak ▶ noun a short, high-pitched sound or cry: *the door opened with a slight squeak.*
■ [with negative] a single remark, statement, or communication: *I didn't hear a squeak from him for months.*
▶ verb [no obj.] **1** make a high-pitched sound or cry: *he oiled the hinges to stop them squeaking.*
■ [with direct speech] say something in a nervous or excited high-pitched tone: *'You're scaring me,' she squeaked.* ■ informal inform on someone.
2 [with adverbial] informal succeed in achieving something by a very narrow margin: *the bill squeaked through with just six votes to spare.*
– ORIGIN late Middle English (as a verb): imitative; compare with Swedish *skväka* 'croak', also with **SQUEAL** and **SHRIEK**. The noun dates from the early 17th cent.

squeaker ▶ noun a person or thing that squeaks: *children blowing party squeakers.*
■ informal, chiefly N. Amer. a competition or election won or likely to be won by a narrow margin. ■ chiefly Brit. a young pigeon.

squeaky ▶ adjective (**squeakier**, **squeakiest**) having or making a high-pitched sound or cry: *a high, squeaky voice.*
– DERIVATIVES **squeakily** adverb, **squeakiness** noun.

squeaky clean ▶ adjective informal completely clean: *plates licked squeaky clean.*
■ beyond reproach; without vice: *politicians who are less than squeaky clean.*

squeal ▶ noun a long, high-pitched cry or noise: *we heard a splash and a squeal* | *they drew up with a squeal of brakes.*
▶ verb [no obj.] **1** make a such a cry or noise: *the girls squealed with delight.*
■ [with direct speech] say something in a high-pitched, excited tone: *'Don't you dare!' she squealed.* ■ complain or protest about something: *the bookies only squealed because we beat them.*
2 informal inform on someone to the police or a person in authority: *she feared they would victimize her for **squealing on** their pals.*
– DERIVATIVES **squealer** noun (especially in sense 2).
– ORIGIN Middle English (as a verb): imitative. The noun dates from the mid 18th cent.

squeamish ▶ adjective (of a person) easily made to feel sick, faint, or disgusted, especially by unpleasant images, such as the sight of blood: *he was a bit squeamish at the sight of the giant needles.*
■ (of a person) having strong moral views; scrupulous: *she was not squeamish about using her social influence in support of her son.*
– DERIVATIVES **squeamishly** adverb, **squeamishness** noun.
– ORIGIN late Middle English: alteration of dialect *squeamous*, from Anglo-Norman French *escoymos*, of unknown origin.

squeegee /ˈskwiːdʒiː/ ▶ noun a scraping implement with a rubber-edged blade set on a handle, typically used for cleaning windows.
■ a similar small instrument or roller used especially in photography for squeezing water out of prints.
■ [usu. as modifier] informal a person who cleans the windscreen of a car stopped in traffic and then demands payment from the driver: *squeegee merchants at every road junction.*
▶ verb (**squeegees**, **squeegeed**, **squeegeeing**) [with obj.] clean or scrape (something) with a squeegee: *squeegee the shower doors while the surfaces are still wet.*
– ORIGIN mid 19th cent.: from archaic *squeege* 'to press', strengthened form of **SQUEEZE**.

squeeze ▶ verb **1** [with obj.] firmly press (something soft or yielding), typically with one's fingers: *Kate squeezed his hand affectionately* | [no obj.] *he squeezed with all his strength.*
■ [with obj. and adverbial] extract (liquid or a soft substance) from something by compressing or twisting it firmly: ***squeeze out** as much juice as you can* | [as adj., with submodifier] (**squeezed**) *freshly squeezed orange juice.* ■ [with obj. and adverbial] obtain (something) from someone with difficulty: *councils will want to **squeeze** as much money **out of** taxpayers as they can.* ■ informal pressurize (someone) in order to obtain something from them: *she used the opportunity to squeeze him for information.* ■ (especially in a financial or commercial

S

context) have a damaging or restricting effect on: *the economy is being squeezed by foreign debt repayments.* ■ (**squeeze something off**) informal shoot a round or shot from a gun: *squeeze off a few well-aimed shots.* ■ (**squeeze something off**) informal take a photograph: *he squeezed off a half-dozen Polaroids.* ■ Bridge force (an opponent) to discard a guarding or potentially winning card.
2 [no obj., with adverbial of direction] manage to get into or through a narrow or restricted space: *Sarah squeezed in beside her | he found a hole in the hedge and* ***squeezed his way*** *through.*
■ [with obj. and adverbial of direction] manage to force into or through such a space: *she squeezed herself into her tightest pair of jeans.* ■ [no obj.] (**squeeze up**) move closer to someone or something so that one is pressed tightly against them or it: *he guided her towards a seat, motioning for everyone to squeeze up and make room.* ■ [with obj.] (**squeeze someone/thing in**) manage to find time for someone or something: *she may be able to squeeze you in, if you play your cards right.* ■ [with obj.] (**squeeze someone/thing out**) force someone or something out of a domain or activity: *workers have been squeezed out of their jobs.*
▶**noun 1** an act of pressing something with one's fingers: *a gentle squeeze of the trigger.*
■ a hug. ■ a state of forcing oneself or being forced into a small or restricted space: *it was* ***a tight squeeze*** *in the tiny hall.* ■ dated a crowded social gathering. ■ a small amount of liquid extracted from something by pressing it firmly with one's fingers: *a* ***squeeze of*** *lemon juice.* ■ a strong financial demand or pressure, typically a restriction on borrowing, spending, or investment in a financial crisis: *industry faced higher costs and a* ***squeeze on*** *profits.* ■ a moulding or cast of an object, or an impression or copy of a design, obtained by pressing a pliable substance round or over it. ■ [mass noun] informal money illegally extorted or exacted from someone: *he was out to extract some squeeze from her.* ■ Bridge a tactic that forces an opponent to discard an important card. ■ (also **squeeze play**) Baseball an act of hitting a ball short to the infield to enable a runner on third base to start for home as soon as the ball is pitched.
2 N. Amer. informal a person's girlfriend or boyfriend: *the poor guy just lost his* ***main squeeze.***
– PHRASES **put the squeeze on** informal coerce or pressurize (someone). **squeeze one's eyes shut** close one's eyes tightly.
– DERIVATIVES **squeezable** adjective, **squeezer** noun.
– ORIGIN mid 16th cent.: from earlier *squise*, from obsolete *queise*, of unknown origin.

squeeze bottle ▶**noun** a container made of flexible plastic which is squeezed to extract the contents.

squeeze box ▶**noun** informal an accordion or concertina.

squeezy ▶**adjective 1** (especially of a container) flexible and able to be squeezed to force out the contents.
2 archaic having a restricted or confined character: *a squeezy little room.*

squelch ▶**verb** [no obj.] make a soft sucking sound such as that made by treading heavily through mud: *bedraggled guests squelched across the lawns to seek shelter.*
■ informal forcefully silence or suppress: *property developers tried to squelch public protest.*
▶**noun 1** a soft sucking sound made when pressure is applied to liquid or mud: *the squelch of their feet.*
2 (also **squelch circuit**) Electronics a circuit that suppresses the output of a radio receiver if the signal strength falls below a certain level.
– DERIVATIVES **squelcher** noun, **squelchy** adjective.
– ORIGIN early 17th cent. (originally denoting a heavy crushing fall on to something soft): imitative.

squib ▶**noun 1** a small firework that burns with a hissing sound before exploding.
■ a short piece of satirical writing. ■ N. Amer. a short news item or filler in a newspaper.
2 informal a small, slight, or weak person, especially a child.
3 American Football a short kick on a kick-off.
▶**verb** (**squibbed**, **squibbing**) **1** [with obj.] American Football kick (the ball) a comparatively short distance on a kick-off; execute (a kick) in this way.
2 [no obj.] archaic utter, write, or publish a satirical or sarcastic attack.
■ [with obj.] lampoon: *the mendicant parson, whom I am so fond of squibbing.*
– ORIGIN early 16th cent. (in sense 1): of unknown origin; perhaps imitative of a small explosion. The verb was first recorded in sense 2 (late 16th cent.).

SQUID ▶**noun** Physics a device used in particular in sensitive magnetometers, which consists of a superconducting ring containing one or more Josephson junctions. A change by one flux quantum in the ring's magnetic flux linkage produces a sharp change in its impedance.
– ORIGIN 1960s: acronym from *superconducting quantum interference device.*

squid ▶**noun** (pl. same or **squids**) an elongated, fast-swimming cephalopod mollusc with eight arms and two long tentacles, typically able to change colour.
● Order Teuthoidea and Vampyromorpha, class Cephalopoda, in particular the common genus *Loligo*. See also **GIANT SQUID**.
■ [mass noun] this mollusc used as food. ■ an artificial bait for fish imitating a squid in form.
▶**verb** (**squidded**, **squidding**) [no obj.] fish using squid as bait.
– ORIGIN late 16th cent.: of unknown origin.

squidge ▶**verb** informal [with obj.] squash or crush.
■ [no obj.] make a noise like soft mud yielding to pressure; squelch: *squidging mud between our toes.*
– ORIGIN late 19th cent.: perhaps imitative.

squidgy ▶**adjective** (**squidgier**, **squidgiest**) informal, chiefly Brit. soft, spongy, and moist: *a squidgy cream cake.*

squiffed ▶**adjective** N. Amer. informal slightly drunk.
– ORIGIN late 19th cent.: variant of **SQUIFFY**.

squiffy ▶**adjective** (**squiffier**, **squiffiest**) informal
1 chiefly Brit. slightly drunk: *I feel quite squiffy.*
2 askew; awry: *the graphics make your eyes go squiffy.*
– ORIGIN mid 19th cent.: of unknown origin.

squiggle ▶**noun** a short line that curls and loops in an irregular way: *some prescriptions are a series of meaningless squiggles.*
▶**verb** chiefly US [no obj.] wriggle; squirm: *a thin worm that squiggled in his palm.*
■ [with obj.] squeeze (something) from a tube so as to make irregular, curly lines on a surface.
– DERIVATIVES **squiggly** adjective.
– ORIGIN early 19th cent.: perhaps a blend of **SQUIRM** and **WIGGLE** or **WRIGGLE**.

squill ▶**noun 1** (also **sea squill**) a coastal Mediterranean plant of the lily family, with broad leaves, white flowers, and a very large bulb.
● *Drimia* (or *Urginea*) *maritima*, family Liliaceae.
■ (also **squills**) [mass noun] an extract of the bulb of this plant, which is poisonous and has medicinal and other uses.
2 [usu. with modifier] a small plant of the lily family, which resembles a hyacinth and has slender strap-like leaves and small clusters of violet-blue or blue-striped flowers.
● Several species in the family Liliaceae: genus *Scilla*, including the **spring squill** (*S. verna*), and the **striped squill** (*Puschkinia scilloides*).
– ORIGIN late Middle English: via Latin from Greek *skilla.*

squillion /ˈskwɪljən/ ▶**cardinal number** (pl. **squillions** or (with numeral) same) informal an indefinite very large number: ***squillions of*** *pounds.*
– ORIGIN 1940s: fanciful formation on the pattern of *billion* and *trillion.*

squinancywort /ˈskwɪnənsɪˌwəːt/ ▶**noun** a small Eurasian plant of delicate appearance, with fine narrow leaves and scented white or lilac flowers. It was formerly used in the treatment of quinsy.
● *Asperula cynanchica*, family Rubiaceae.
– ORIGIN early 18th cent.: from medieval Latin *squinantia* (apparently formed by confusion of Greek *sunankhē* with *kunankhē* 'cynanche', both denoting throat diseases) + **WORT**.

squinch[1] ▶**noun** a straight or arched structure across an interior angle of a square tower to carry a superstructure such as a dome.
– ORIGIN late 15th cent.: alteration of obsolete *scunch*, abbreviation of **SCUNCHEON**.

squinch[2] ▶**verb** [with obj.] chiefly US tense up the muscles of (one's eyes or face): *Gina* ***squinched*** *her face* ***up.***
■ [no obj.] (of a person's eyes) narrow so as to be almost closed, typically in reaction to strong light: *he flicked on the inside light, which made my eyes* ***squinch up.*** ■ [no obj.] crouch down in order to make oneself seem smaller or to occupy less space: *I squinched down under the sheet.*
– ORIGIN early 19th cent.: perhaps a blend of the verbs **SQUEEZE** and **PINCH**.

squint ▶**verb 1** [no obj.] look at someone or something with one or both eyes partly closed in an attempt to see more clearly or as a reaction to strong light: *the bright sun made them squint.*
■ [with obj.] partly close (one's eyes) for such reasons.
2 [no obj.] have eyes that look in different directions: *Melanie did not squint.*
■ (of a person's eye) have a deviation in the direction of its gaze: *her left eye squinted slightly.*
▶**noun 1** [in sing.] a permanent deviation in the direction of the gaze of one eye: *I had a bad squint.*
2 [in sing.] informal a quick or casual look: *let me have a squint.*
3 an oblique opening through a wall in a church permitting a view of the altar from an aisle or side chapel.
▶**adjective** chiefly Scottish not straight or level.
– DERIVATIVES **squinter** noun, **squinty** adjective [often in combination] *squinty-eyed.*
– ORIGIN mid 16th cent. (in the sense 'squinting', as in **SQUINT-EYED**): shortening of **ASQUINT**.

squint-eyed ▶**adjective** derogatory **1** (of a person) having a squint.
2 archaic spiteful.

squire ▶**noun 1** a man of high social standing who owns and lives on an estate in a rural area, especially the chief landowner in such an area: *the squire of Radbourne Hall |* [as title] *Squire Trelawny.*
■ Brit. informal used by a man as a friendly or humorous form of address to another man. ■ US archaic a title given to a magistrate, lawyer, or judge in some rural districts.
2 historical a young nobleman acting as an attendant to a knight before becoming a knight himself.
3 Austral. a subadult snapper fish (*Chrysophrys auratus*).
▶**verb** [with obj.] (of a man) accompany or escort (a woman): *she was squired around Rome by a reporter.*
■ dated (of a man) have a romantic relationship with (a woman).
– DERIVATIVES **squiredom** noun, **squireship** noun.
– ORIGIN Middle English (in sense 2): shortening of Old French *esquier* 'esquire'.

squirearch /ˈskwʌɪəˌrɑːk/ ▶**noun** a member of the squirearchy.
– DERIVATIVES **squirearchical** adjective.
– ORIGIN mid 19th cent.: back-formation from **SQUIREARCHY**, on the pattern of words such as *monarch.*

squirearchy /ˈskwʌɪəˌrɑːki/ ▶**noun** (pl. **-ies**) landowners collectively, especially when considered as a class having political or social influence.
– ORIGIN late 18th cent.: from **SQUIRE**, on the pattern of words such as *hierarchy.*

squireen /ˌskwʌɪəˈriːn/ ▶**noun** Brit. a small landowner, especially one in Ireland.
– ORIGIN early 19th cent.: from **SQUIRE** + *-een* (representing the Irish diminutive suffix *-ín*).

squirl ▶**noun** informal an ornamental flourish or curve, especially in handwriting.
– ORIGIN mid 19th cent.: perhaps a blend of **SQUIGGLE** and **TWIRL** or **WHIRL**.

squirm ▶**verb** [no obj.] wriggle or twist the body from side to side, especially as a result of nervousness or discomfort: *all my efforts to squirm out of his grasp were useless.*
■ show or feel embarrassment or shame.
▶**noun** [in sing.] a wriggling movement.
– DERIVATIVES **squirmer** noun, **squirmy** adjective.
– ORIGIN late 17th cent.: symbolic of writhing movement; probably associated with **WORM**.

squirrel ▶**noun 1** an agile tree-dwelling rodent with a bushy tail, typically feeding on nuts and seeds.
● Family Sciuridae: several genera, in particular *Sciurus*, and numerous species.
■ a related rodent of this family (see **GROUND SQUIRREL**, **FLYING SQUIRREL**). ■ [mass noun] the fur of the squirrel.
▶**verb** (**squirrelled**, **squirrelling**; US also **squirreled**, **squirreling**) **1** [with obj.] (**squirrel something away**) hide money or something of value in a safe place: *the money was squirrelled away in foreign bank accounts.*
2 [no obj., with adverbial of direction] move in an inquisitive and restless manner: *they were squirrelling around in the woods in search of something.*
– ORIGIN Middle English: shortening of Old French *esquireul*, from a diminutive of Latin *sciurus*, from Greek *skiouros*, from *skia* 'shade' + *oura* 'tail'. Current verb senses date from the early 20th cent.

squirrel cage ▶ **noun** a rotating cylindrical cage in which a small captive animal can exercise as on a treadmill.
■ a monotonous or repetitive activity or way of life: *running madly about in a squirrel cage of activity.* ■ a form of rotor used in small electric motors, resembling a cylindrical cage.

squirrelfish ▶ **noun** (pl. same or **-fishes**) a chiefly nocturnal large-eyed marine fish that is typically brightly coloured and lives around rocks or coral reefs in warm seas.
● Family Holocentridae: several genera and species.

squirrelly ▶ **adjective 1** relating to or resembling a squirrel: *the chipmunks were little squirrelly things.*
2 informal, chiefly N. Amer. restless, nervous, or unpredictable.
■ eccentric or mad.

squirrel monkey ▶ **noun** a small South American monkey with a non-prehensile tail, typically moving through trees by leaping.
● Genus *Saimiri*, family Cebidae: five species, in particular *S. sciureus*.

squirrel-tail grass ▶ **noun** [mass noun] a kind of barley with bushy spikelets, sometimes cultivated as an ornamental grass.
● *Hordeum jubatum*, family Gramineae.

squirt ▶ **verb** [with obj. and adverbial of direction] cause (a liquid) to be ejected from a small opening in something in a thin, fast stream or jet: *she squirted soda into a glass.*
■ cause (a container of liquid) to eject its contents in this way: *some youngsters squirted a water pistol in her face.* ■ [with obj.] wet (someone or something) with a jet or stream of liquid in this way: *she squirted me with scent.* ■ [no obj., with adverbial of direction] (of a liquid) be ejected from something in this way. ■ [no obj., with adverbial of direction] (of an object) move suddenly and unpredictably: *he got his glove on the ball but it squirted away.* ■ transmit (information) in highly compressed or speeded-up form.
▶ **noun 1** a thin stream or small quantity of liquid ejected from something: *a quick squirt of perfume.*
■ a small device from which a liquid may be ejected in a thin, fast stream. ■ a compressed radio signal transmitted at high speed.
2 informal a person perceived to be insignificant, impudent, or presumptuous: *what did he see in this patronizing little squirt?*
– DERIVATIVES **squirter** noun.
– ORIGIN Middle English (first recorded as a verb): imitative.

squirt boat ▶ **noun** a small, highly manoeuvrable kayak.

squirt gun ▶ **noun** N. Amer. a water pistol.

squirting cucumber ▶ **noun** a Mediterranean plant of the gourd family, bearing a small cucumber-like fruit which falls readily when ripe and forcibly expels an irritant pulp containing its seeds.
● *Ecballium elaterium*, family Cucurbitaceae.

squish ▶ **verb** [no obj.] make a soft squelching sound when walked on or in: *the mud squished under my shoes.*
■ yield easily to pressure when squeezed or squashed: *strawberries so ripe that they squished if picked too firmly.* ■ [with obj.] informal squash (something): *Naomi was furiously squishing her ice cream in her bowl.* ■ [with adverbial of direction] squeeze oneself into somewhere: *she squished in among them on the couch.*
▶ **noun** [in sing.] a soft squelching sound.
– DERIVATIVES **squishy** adjective (**squishier**, **squishiest**).
– ORIGIN mid 17th cent.: imitative.

squit informal Brit. ▶ **noun 1** a small or insignificant person.
2 (**the squits**) diarrhoea.
– ORIGIN early 19th cent.: perhaps related to dialect *squit* 'to squirt.'

squitters ▶ **plural noun** informal diarrhoea.
– ORIGIN mid 17th cent.: perhaps from dialect *squit* 'to squirt'.

squiz Austral./NZ informal ▶ **noun** a look or glance.
▶ **verb** [with obj.] look or glance at.
– ORIGIN early 20th cent.: probably a blend of **QUIZ**[2] and **SQUINT**.

Sr ▶ **abbreviation for** ■ senior (in names): *E. T. Krebs Sr.* ■ Señor. ■ Signor. ■ Sister (in a religious order): [as a title] *Sr Agatha.*
▶ **symbol for** the chemical element strontium.

sr ▶ **abbreviation for** steradian(s).

SRAM ▶ **noun** Electronics a type of memory chip which is faster and requires less power than dynamic memory.
– ORIGIN abbreviation of *static random-access memory.*

Sranan /ˈsrɑːnən/ ▶ **noun** another term for **TAKI-TAKI**.
– ORIGIN from Taki-Taki *Sranan tongo*, literally 'Surinam tongue'.

Sri /sri/ (also **Shri**) ▶ **noun** Indian a title of respect used before the name of a man, a god, or a sacred book: *Sri Chaudhuri.*
– ORIGIN from Sanskrit *Śrī* 'beauty, fortune', used as an honorific title.

Sri Lanka /srɪ ˈlaŋkə, ʃrɪ/ an island country off the SE coast of India; pop. 17,194,000 (est. 1991); languages, Sinhalese (official), Tamil; capital, Colombo. Former name (until 1972) **CEYLON**.

The island was ruled by a strong native dynasty from the 12th century but was successively dominated by the Portuguese, Dutch, and British from the 16th century and finally annexed by the British in 1815. A Commonwealth state from 1948, the country became an independent republic in 1972. Since 1981 there has been fighting between government forces and Tamil separatist guerrillas.

– DERIVATIVES **Sri Lankan** adjective & noun.

Srinagar /srɪˈnʌɡə/ a city in NW India, the summer capital of the state of Jammu and Kashmir, situated on the Jhelum River in the foothills of the Himalayas; pop. 595,000 (1991).

SRN ▶ **abbreviation for** State Registered Nurse.

SRO ▶ **abbreviation for** ■ (in the UK) self-regulatory organization, a body that regulates the activities of investment businesses. ■ N. Amer. single room occupancy. ■ standing room only.

SS[1] ▶ **abbreviation for** ■ Saints: *the Church of SS Peter and Paul.* ■ Baseball shortstop. ■ social security. ■ steamship: *the SS Canberra.*

SS[2] the Nazi special police force. Founded in 1925 by Hitler as a personal bodyguard, the SS provided security forces (including the Gestapo) and administered the concentration camps.
– ORIGIN abbreviation of German *Schutzstaffel* 'defence squadron'.

SSAFA ▶ **abbreviation for** (in the UK) Soldiers', Sailors', and Airmen's Families Association.

SSB ▶ **abbreviation for** single sideband transmission, a type of amplitude modulation in which the carrier wave and one sideband are suppressed in order to occupy less bandwidth.

SSC ▶ **abbreviation for** (in Scotland) Solicitor in the Supreme Court. ■ Physics superconducting super collider.

SSE ▶ **abbreviation for** south-south-east.

SSP ▶ **abbreviation for** (in the UK) statutory sick pay.

ssp. ▶ **abbreviation for** subspecies (usually singular).

sspp. ▶ **abbreviation for** subspecies (plural).

SSR historical ▶ **abbreviation for** Soviet Socialist Republic.

SSRC ▶ **abbreviation for** (in the UK) Social Science Research Council.

SSSI ▶ **abbreviation for** (in the UK) Site of Special Scientific Interest.

SST ▶ **abbreviation for** supersonic transport.

SSW ▶ **abbreviation for** south-south-west.

ST ▶ **abbreviation for** stokes.

St ▶ **abbreviation for** ■ Saint: *St George.* ■ Physics stokes.

st ▶ **abbreviation for** ■ stone (in weight). ■ Cricket (on scorecards) stumped by.

-st ▶ **suffix** variant spelling of **-EST**[2].

Sta. ▶ **abbreviation for** railway station.

stab ▶ **verb** (**stabbed**, **stabbing**) [with obj.] (of a person) thrust a knife or other pointed weapon into (someone) so as to wound or kill: *he stabbed him in the stomach* | [as noun **stabbing**] *the fatal stabbings of four women.*
■ [no obj.] make a thrusting gesture or movement at something with a pointed object: *she stabbed at the earth with the fork* | [with obj.] *she stabbed the air with her forefinger* ■ [no obj.] (**stab into/through**) (of a sharp or pointed object) violently pierce: *a sharp end of wicker stabbed into his sole.* ■ [no obj.] (**stab at**) (of a pain or painful thing) cause a sudden sharp sensation: [as adj. **stabbing**] *I felt a stabbing pain in my chest.*
▶ **noun 1** a thrust with a knife or other pointed weapon: [as modifier] *multiple stab wounds.*
■ a wound made in such a way: *she had a deep stab in the back.* ■ a thrusting movement with a finger or other pointed object: *impatient stabs of his finger.* ■ a sudden sharp feeling or pain: *she felt a stab of jealousy.*
2 (**stab at**) informal an attempt to do (something): *Meredith made a feeble stab at joining in.*
– PHRASES **a stab in the back** a treacherous act or statement. **stab someone in the back** betray someone. **a stab in the dark** see **DARK**.
– DERIVATIVES **stabber** noun.
– ORIGIN late Middle English: of unknown origin.

Stabat Mater /ˌstɑːbat ˈmɑːtə, ˈmeɪtə/ ▶ **noun** a medieval Latin hymn on the suffering of the Virgin Mary at the Crucifixion.
– ORIGIN from the opening words *Stabat mater dolorosa* 'Stood the mother, full of grief'.

stabilator /ˈsteɪbɪleɪtə/ ▶ **noun** a combined stabilizer and elevator at the tail of an aircraft.

stabile /ˈsteɪbʌɪl/ ▶ **noun** Art a free-standing abstract sculpture or structure, typically of wire or sheet metal, in the style of a mobile but rigid and stationary.
– ORIGIN 1940s: from Latin *stabilis* 'stable', influenced by **MOBILE**.

stability ▶ **noun** [mass noun] the state of being stable: *there are fears for the political stability of the area.*
– ORIGIN Middle English: from Old French *stablete*, from Latin *stabilitas*, from *stabilis* 'stable'.

stabilize (also **-ise**) ▶ **verb** [with obj.] make or become stable: [no obj.] *his condition appears to have stabilized* | [with obj.] *an emergency programme designed to stabilize the economy.*
■ [with obj.] cause (an object or structure) to be unlikely to overturn: *the craft was stabilized by throwing out the remaining ballast.*
– DERIVATIVES **stabilization** noun.

stabilizer (also **-iser**) ▶ **noun** a thing used to keep something steady or stable, in particular:
■ the horizontal tailplane of an aircraft. ■ a gyroscopic device used to reduce the rolling of a ship. ■ (**stabilizers**) Brit. a pair of small supporting wheels fitted on either side of the rear wheel of a child's bicycle. ■ a substance which prevents the breakdown of emulsions, especially in foods and paints. ■ a financial mechanism that prevents unsettling fluctuation in an economic system.

stable[1] ▶ **adjective** (**stabler**, **stablest**) (of an object or structure) not likely to give way or overturn; firmly fixed: *specially designed dinghies that are very stable.*
■ (of a patient or their medical condition) not deteriorating in health after an injury or operation: *he is now in a stable condition in hospital.* ■ (of a person) sane and sensible; not easily upset or disturbed: *the officer concerned is mentally and emotionally stable.* ■ not likely to change or fail; firmly established: *a stable relationship* | *prices have remained relatively stable.* ■ not liable to undergo chemical decomposition, radioactive decay, or other physical change.
– DERIVATIVES **stably** adverb.
– ORIGIN Middle English: from Anglo-Norman French, from Latin *stabilis*, from the base of *stare* 'to stand'.

stable[2] ▶ **noun** a building set apart and adapted for keeping horses.
■ an establishment where racehorses are kept and trained. ■ the racehorses of a particular training establishment. ■ an organization or establishment providing the same background or training for its members: *the player comes from the same stable as Agassi.*
▶ **verb** [with obj.] put or keep (a horse) in a specially adapted building.
■ put or base (a train) in a depot.
– DERIVATIVES **stableful** noun (pl. **-fuls**).
– ORIGIN Middle English: shortening of Old French *estable* 'stable, pigsty', from Latin *stabulum*, from the base of *stare* 'to stand'.

stable boy ▶ **noun** a boy or man employed in a stable.

stable companion ▶ **noun** another term for **STABLEMATE**.

stable door ▶ **noun** the door of a stable, divided into two parts horizontally allowing one half to be shut and the other left open.
– PHRASES **shut** (or **bolt**) **the stable door after the horse has bolted** try to avoid or prevent something bad or unwelcome when it is already too late to do so.

stable equilibrium ▶ **noun** a state in which a body tends to return to its original position after being disturbed.

S

stable fly ▶ **noun** a bloodsucking fly related to the housefly, that bites large mammals including humans.
• *Stomoxis calcitrans*, family Muscidae.

Stableford /ˈsteɪb(ə)lfəd/ ▶ **noun** [mass noun] [usu. as modifier] a form of stroke-play golf in which points are awarded according to the number of strokes taken to complete each hole: *a Stableford competition.*
– ORIGIN named after Frank B. *Stableford* (*c.* 1870–1959), the American doctor who devised it.

stable girl ▶ **noun** a girl or woman employed in a stable.

stable lad ▶ **noun** Brit. a person employed in a stable.

stableman ▶ **noun** (pl. **-men**) chiefly US a person employed in a stable.

stablemate ▶ **noun** a horse, especially a racehorse, from the same establishment as another.
▪ a person or product from the same organization or background as another: *the Daily Mirror and its Scottish stablemate the Daily Record.*

stable vice ▶ **noun** see **VICE**[1].

stabling ▶ **noun** [mass noun] accommodation for horses.

stablish ▶ **verb** archaic form of **ESTABLISH**.

staccato /stəˈkɑːtəʊ/ chiefly Music ▶ **adverb** & **adjective** with each sound or note sharply detached or separated from the others: [as adj.] *a staccato rhythm.* Compare with **LEGATO**, **MARCATO**.
▶ **noun** (pl. **-os**) [mass noun] performance in this manner.
▪ a noise or speech resembling a series of short, detached musical notes: *her heels made a rapid staccato on the polished boards.*
– ORIGIN Italian, literally 'detached'.

staccato mark ▶ **noun** a dot or stroke above or below a note indicating that it is to be played staccato.

stack ▶ **noun 1** a pile of objects, typically one that is neatly arranged: *a stack of boxes.*
▪ (**a stack of/stacks of**) informal a large quantity of something: *there's stacks of work for me now.* ▪ a rectangular or cylindrical pile of hay or straw or of grain in sheaf. ▪ a vertical arrangement of hi-fi or guitar amplification equipment. ▪ a number of aircraft flying in circles at different altitudes around the same point while waiting for permission to land at an airport. ▪ a pyramidal group of rifles. ▪ (**the stacks**) units of shelving in part of a library normally closed to the public, used to store books compactly. ▪ Computing a set of storage locations which store data in such a way that the most recently stored item is the first to be retrieved.
2 a chimney, especially one on a factory, or a vertical exhaust pipe on a vehicle.
▪ (also **sea stack**) Brit. a column of rock standing in the sea, remaining after erosion of cliffs.
3 Brit. a measure for a pile of wood of 108 cu. ft (3.06 cubic metres).
▶ **verb** [with obj.] **1** arrange (a number of things) in a pile, typically a neat one: *the books had been stacked up in neat piles | she stood up, beginning to stack the plates.*
▪ fill or cover (a place or surface) with piles of things, typically neat ones: *he spent most of the time stacking shelves.* ▪ cause (an aircraft) to fly in circles while waiting for permission to land at an airport: *I hope we aren't stacked for hours over Kennedy.*
2 shuffle or arrange (a pack of cards) dishonestly so as to gain an unfair advantage.
▪ (**be stacked against/in favour of**) used to refer to a situation which is such that an unfavourable or a favourable outcome is overwhelmingly likely: *the odds were stacked against Fiji in the World Cup | conditions were heavily stacked in favour of the Americas.*
3 [no obj.] (in snowboarding) fall over.
– PHRASES **stack arms** see ***pile arms*** at **PILE**[1].
– DERIVATIVES **stackable** adjective, **stacker** noun.
– ORIGIN Middle English: from Old Norse *stakkr* 'haystack', of Germanic origin.
▶ **stack up** (or **stack something up**) **1** form or cause to form a large quantity; build up: *cars stack up behind every bus, while passengers queue to pay fares.*
2 N. Amer. informal measure up; compare: *our rural schools stack up well against their urban counterparts.* ▪ [usu. with negative] make sense; correspond to reality: *to blame the debacle on the antics of a rogue trader is not credible—it doesn't stack up.*

stacked ▶ **adjective 1** (of a number of things) put or arranged in a stack or stacks: *the stacked chairs.*
▪ (of a place or surface) filled or covered with goods: *the stacked shelves.* ▪ (of a machine) having sections that are arranged vertically: *full-sized washer/dryers are replacing stacked units.* ▪ (of a heel) made from thin layers of wood, plastic, or another material glued one on top of the other.
2 (of a pack of cards) shuffled or arranged dishonestly so as to gain an unfair advantage.
3 informal (of a woman) having large breasts.
4 Computing (of a task) placed in a queue for subsequent processing.
▪ (of a stream of data) stored in such a way that the most recently stored item is the first to be retrieved.

stackyard ▶ **noun** a farmyard or enclosure where stacks of hay, straw, or grain in sheaf are stored.

staddle ▶ **noun** a platform or framework supporting a stack or rick.
▪ (also **staddle stone**) a stone, especially one resembling a mushroom in shape, supporting a framework or rick.
– ORIGIN Old English *stathol* 'base, support', of Germanic origin; related to the verb **STAND**.

stadium ▶ **noun** (pl. **stadiums** or **stadia** /ˈsteɪdɪə/)
1 an athletic or sports ground with tiers of seats for spectators.
▪ (in ancient Rome or Greece) a track for a foot race or chariot race.
2 (pl. **stadia**) an ancient Roman or Greek measure of length, about 185 metres. [ORIGIN: originally denoting the length of a stadium.]
– ORIGIN late Middle English (in sense 2): via Latin from Greek *stadion*. Sense 1 dates from the mid 19th cent.

stadtholder /ˈstadˌhəʊldə, ˈstat-/ (also **stadholder**) ▶ **noun** (from the 15th century to the late 18th century) the chief magistrate of the United Provinces of the Netherlands.
– DERIVATIVES **stadtholdership** noun.
– ORIGIN mid 16th cent.: from Dutch *stadhouder* 'deputy', from *stad* 'place' + *houder* 'holder', translating medieval Latin *locum tenens*.

Staël, Mme de, see **DE STAËL**.

staff[1] ▶ **noun 1** [treated as sing. or pl.] all the people employed by a particular organization: *a staff of 600 | hospital staff were not to blame.*
▪ the teachers in a school or college: [as modifier] *a staff meeting.*
2 [treated as sing. or pl.] a group of officers assisting an officer in command of an army formation or administration headquarters.
▪ (usu. **Staff**) short for **STAFF SERGEANT**.
3 a long stick used as a support when walking or climbing or as a weapon.
▪ a rod or sceptre held as a sign of office or authority. ▪ short for **FLAGSTAFF**. ▪ Surveying a rod for measuring distances or heights. ▪ Brit. a spindle in a watch. ▪ Brit. a token in the form of a rod given to a train driver as authority to proceed over a single-track line.
4 Music another term for **STAVE** (in sense 2).
▶ **verb** [with obj.] (usu. **be staffed**) provide (an organization, business, etc.) with staff: *legal advice centres are staffed by volunteer lawyers |* [as adj., with submodifier] (**staffed**) *all units are fully staffed.*
– PHRASES **the staff of life** a staple food, especially bread.
– ORIGIN Old English *stæf* (in sense 3), of Germanic origin; related to Dutch *staf* and German *Stab*.

staff[2] ▶ **noun** [mass noun] a mixture of plaster of Paris, cement, or a similar material, used for temporary building work.
– ORIGIN late 19th cent.: of unknown origin.

Staffa /ˈstafə/ a small uninhabited island of the Inner Hebrides, west of Mull. It is the site of Fingal's Cave and is noted for its basalt columns.

staffage /stəˈfɑːʒ/ ▶ **noun** [mass noun] accessory items in a painting, especially figures or animals in a landscape picture.
– ORIGIN late 19th cent.: from German, from *staffieren* 'decorate', perhaps from Old French *estoffer*, from *estoffe* 'stuff'.

staff association ▶ **noun** an association of employees performing some of the functions of a trade union, such as representing its members in discussions with management.

staff college ▶ **noun** a college at which military officers are trained for staff duties.

staffer ▶ **noun** chiefly US a member of the staff of an organization, especially of a newspaper.

staff notation ▶ **noun** [mass noun] Music notation by means of a stave, especially as distinct from the tonic sol-fa.

staff nurse ▶ **noun** Brit. an experienced nurse less senior than a sister or charge nurse.

staff officer ▶ **noun** a military officer serving on the staff of a military headquarters or government department.

Stafford /ˈstafəd/ an industrial town in central England, to the south of Stoke-on-Trent; pop. 62,240 (1981).

Staffordshire a county of central England; county town, Stafford.

Staffordshire bull terrier ▶ **noun** a dog of a small stocky breed of terrier, with a short, broad head and dropped ears.

staffroom ▶ **noun** chiefly Brit. a common room for teachers in a school or college.

Staffs. ▶ **abbreviation for** Staffordshire.

staff sergeant ▶ **noun** a rank of non-commissioned officer in the army, above sergeant and below warrant officer.
▪ a rank of non-commissioned officer in the US air force, above airman and below technical sergeant.

stag ▶ **noun 1** a male deer, especially a male red deer after its fifth year.
▪ a turkeycock over one year old. ▪ [usu. as modifier] a social gathering attended by men only: *a stag event.* ▪ chiefly N. Amer. a person who attends a social gathering unaccompanied by a partner.
2 Stock Exchange, Brit. a person who applies for shares in a new issue with a view to selling at once for a profit.
▶ **adverb** chiefly N. Amer. without a partner at a social gathering: *a lot of boys went stag.*
▶ **verb** (**stagged**, **stagging**) [with obj.] **1** Stock Exchange, Brit. buy (shares in a new issue) and sell them at once for a profit.
2 N. Amer. informal roughly cut (a garment, especially a pair of trousers) to make it shorter: [as adj. **stagged**] *stagged jeans.* [ORIGIN: early 20th cent.: used originally of loggers' trousers.]
– ORIGIN Middle English (as a noun): related to Old Norse *steggr* 'male bird', Icelandic *steggi* 'tomcat'.

stag beetle ▶ **noun** a large dark beetle, the male of which has large branched jaws that resemble a stag's antlers.
• Family Lucanidae: several species, including the European *Lucanus cervus*.

stage ▶ **noun 1** a point, period, or step in a process or development: *there is no need at this stage to give explicit details | I was in the early stages of pregnancy.*
▪ a section of a journey or race: *the final stage of the journey is made by coach.* ▪ Brit. short for **FARE STAGE**. ▪ each of two or more a sections of a rocket or spacecraft that have their own engines and are jettisoned in turn when their propellant is exhausted. ▪ [with modifier] Electronics a specified part of a circuit, typically one consisting of a single amplifying transistor or valve with the associated equipment.
2 a raised floor or platform, typically in a theatre, on which actors, entertainers, or speakers perform: *there are only two characters on stage.*
▪ (**the stage**) the acting or theatrical profession: *I've always wanted to go on the stage.* ▪ [in sing.] a scene of action or forum of debate, especially in a particular political context: *Britain is playing a leading role on the international stage.*
3 a floor or level of a building or structure: *the upper stage was added in the 17th century.*
▪ (on a microscope) a raised and usually movable plate on which a slide or object is placed for examination.
4 Geology (in chronostratigraphy) a range of strata corresponding to an age in time, forming a subdivision of a series.
▪ (in palaeoclimatology) a period of time marked by a characteristic climate: *the Boreal stage.*
5 archaic term for **STAGECOACH**.
▶ **verb** [with obj.] **1** present a performance of (a play or other show): *the show is being staged at the Grand Opera House in Belfast.*
▪ (of a person or group) organize and participate in (a public event): *UDF supporters staged a demonstration in Sofia.* ▪ cause (something dramatic or unexpected) to happen: *the President's attempt to stage a comeback | the dollar staged a partial recovery.*
2 Medicine diagnose or classify (a disease or patient) as having reached a particular stage in the expected progression of the disease.
– PHRASES **hold the stage** dominate a scene of action or forum of debate. **set the stage for** prepare the conditions for (the occurrence or beginning of something): *these churchmen helped to*

set the stage for popular reform. **stage left** (or **right**) on the left (or right) side of a stage from the point of view of a performer facing the audience.
– DERIVATIVES **stageability** noun, **stageable** adjective.
– ORIGIN Middle English (denoting a floor of a building, a platform, or a stopping-place): shortening of Old French *estage* 'dwelling', based on Latin *stare* 'to stand'. Current senses of the verb date from the early 17th cent.

stagecoach ▶ noun a large closed horse-drawn vehicle formerly used to carry passengers and often mail along a regular route between two places.

stagecraft ▶ noun [mass noun] skill or experience in writing or staging plays.

stage direction ▶ noun an instruction in the text of a play, especially one indicating the movement, position, or tone of an actor, or the sound effects and lighting.

stage door ▶ noun an actors' and workmen's entrance from the street to the area of a theatre behind the stage.

stage fright ▶ noun [mass noun] nervousness before or during an appearance before an audience.

stagehand ▶ noun a person who moves scenery or props before or during the performance of a play.

stage-manage ▶ verb [with obj.] be responsible for the lighting and other technical arrangements for (a stage play).
■ arrange and control (something) carefully in order to create a certain effect: *he stage-managed his image with astounding success.*
– DERIVATIVES **stage management** noun.

stage manager ▶ noun the person responsible for the lighting and other technical arrangements for a stage play.

stage name ▶ noun a name assumed for professional purposes by an actor or other performer.

stage play (also **stage production**) ▶ noun a play performed on stage rather than broadcast or made into a film.

stage presence ▶ noun [mass noun] the ability to command the attention of a theatre audience by the impressiveness of one's manner or appearance.

stager ▶ noun archaic an actor.

stage-struck ▶ adjective having a passionate desire to become an actor.

stage whisper ▶ noun a loud whisper uttered by an actor on stage, intended to be heard by the audience but supposedly unheard by other characters in the play.
■ any loud whisper intended to be overheard.

stagey ▶ adjective variant spelling of STAGY.

stagflation ▶ noun [mass noun] Economics persistent high inflation combined with high unemployment and stagnant demand in a country's economy.
– ORIGIN 1960s: blend of *stagnation* (see STAGNATE) and INFLATION.

stagger ▶ verb **1** [no obj.] walk or move unsteadily, as if about to fall: *he staggered to his feet, swaying a little.*
■ [with obj. and adverbial of direction] figurative continue in existence or operation uncertainly or precariously: *the treasury staggered from one crisis to the next.* ■ archaic waver in purpose; hesitate. ■ archaic (of a blow) cause (someone) to walk or move unsteadily, as if about to fall: *the collision staggered her and she fell.*
2 [with obj.] astonish or deeply shock: *I was staggered to find it was six o'clock* | [as adj. **staggering**] *the staggering bills for maintenance and repair.*
3 [with obj.] arrange (events, payments, hours, etc.) so that they do not occur at the same time; spread over a period of time: *meetings are staggered throughout the day.*
■ arrange (objects or parts of an object) in a zigzag order or so that they are not in line: *stagger the screws at each joint.*
▶ noun [in sing.] **1** an unsteady walk or movement: *the pub is within an easy stagger of his office.*
2 an arrangement of things in a zigzag order or so that they are not in line, in particular: ■ (**the stagger**) the arrangement of the runners in lanes on a running track at the start of a race, so that the runner in the inside lane is positioned behind those in the next lane and so on until the outside lane. ■ [mass noun] an arrangement of the wings of a biplane so that their front edges are not in line.

– DERIVATIVES **staggerer** noun, **staggeringly** adverb [as submodifier] *a staggeringly unjust society.*
– ORIGIN late Middle English (as a verb): alteration of dialect *stacker*, from Old Norse *stakra*, frequentative of *staka* 'push, stagger'. The noun dates from the late 16th cent.

staggering bob ▶ noun [mass noun] Austral. informal a very young calf.
■ [mass noun] veal from such a calf.

staggers ▶ plural noun [usu. treated as sing.] any of several parasitic or acute deficiency diseases of farm animals characterized by staggering or loss of balance.
■ the inability to stand or walk steadily, especially as a result of giddiness.

staghorn (also **stag's horn**) ▶ noun **1** [mass noun] the antler of a stag, used to make handles for knives and walking sticks.
2 short for STAGHORN CORAL, STAGHORN FERN, or STAG'S-HORN FUNGUS.

staghorn coral ▶ noun a large stony coral with antler-like branches.
● Genus *Acropora*, order Scleractinia, in particular *A. cervicornis.*

staghorn fern (also **stag's-horn fern**) ▶ noun a fern which has fronds that resemble antlers, occurring in tropical rainforests where it typically grows as an epiphyte.
● Genus *Platycerium*, family Polypodiaceae.

staghound ▶ noun a large dog of a breed used for hunting deer by sight or scent.

staging ▶ noun **1** an instance or method of presenting a play or other dramatic performance: *one of the better stagings of* Hamlet | [mass noun] *the quality of staging and design.*
■ an instance of organizing a public event or protest: *the fourteenth staging of the championships.*
2 a stage or set of stages or temporary platforms arranged as a support for performers or between different levels of scaffolding.
■ Brit. a shelving unit for plants in a greenhouse.
3 [mass noun] Medicine diagnosis or classification of the particular stage reached by a progressive disease.
4 [mass noun] the arrangement of stages in a rocket or spacecraft.
■ the separation and jettisoning of a stage from the remainder of a rocket when its propellant is spent.

staging area (also **staging point**) ▶ noun a stopping place or assembly point en route to a destination.

staging post ▶ noun a place at which people, vehicles, or aircraft regularly stop when making a particular journey.

stagnant /ˈstagnənt/ ▶ adjective (of a body of water or the atmosphere of a confined space) having no current or flow and often having an unpleasant smell as a consequence: *a stagnant ditch.*
■ figurative showing no activity; dull and sluggish: *a stagnant economy.*
– DERIVATIVES **stagnancy** noun, **stagnantly** adverb.
– ORIGIN mid 17th cent.: from Latin *stagnant-* 'forming a pool of standing water', from the verb *stagnare*, from *stagnum* 'pool'.

stagnate /stagˈneɪt, ˈstagneɪt/ ▶ verb [no obj.] (of water or air) cease to flow or move; become stagnant.
■ figurative cease developing; become inactive or dull: *teaching can easily stagnate into a set of routines* | [as adj. **stagnating**] *stagnating consumer confidence.*
– DERIVATIVES **stagnation** noun.
– ORIGIN mid 17th cent.: from Latin *stagnat-* 'settled as a still pool', from the verb *stagnare*, from *stagnum* 'pool'.

stag night (also **stag party**) ▶ noun chiefly Brit. a celebration held for a man shortly before his wedding, attended by his male friends only.
■ N. Amer. any party attended by men only.

stag's horn ▶ noun variant form of STAGHORN.

stag's-horn fungus (also **staghorn fungus**) ▶ noun a small fungus of dead wood, which forms black velvety antler-shaped fruiting bodies with white tips, common in both Eurasia and North America.
● *Xylaria hypoxylon*, family Xylariaceae, subdivision Ascomycotina.

stagy /ˈsteɪdʒi/ (also **stagey**) ▶ adjective (**stagier**, **stagiest**) excessively theatrical; exaggerated: *a stagy melodramatic voice.*
– DERIVATIVES **stagily** adverb, **staginess** noun.

staid ▶ adjective sedate, respectable, and unadventurous: *staid law firms.*
– DERIVATIVES **staidly** adverb, **staidness** noun.
– ORIGIN mid 16th cent.: archaic past participle of STAY[1].

stain ▶ verb [with obj.] **1** mark (something) with coloured patches or dirty marks that are not easily removed: *her clothing was stained with blood* | [as adj. **stained**] *a stained beer mat* | [no obj.] *red powder paint can stain.*
■ [no obj.] be marked or be liable to be marked with such patches. ■ figurative damage or bring disgrace to (the reputation or image of someone or something): *the awful events would unfairly stain the city's reputation.* ■ suffuse (something) with brighter or darker colour: *the flush stained her cheeks again.*
2 colour (a material or object) by applying a penetrative dye or chemical: *wood can always be stained to a darker shade.*
▶ noun **1** a coloured patch or dirty mark that is difficult to remove: *there were mud stains on my shoes.*
■ a thing that damages or brings disgrace to someone or something's reputation: *he regarded his time in gaol as a stain on his character.* ■ a patch of brighter or deeper colour that suffuses something: *the sun left a red stain behind as it retreated.*
2 a penetrative dye or chemical used in colouring a material or object.
■ Biology a special dye used to colour organic tissue so as to make the structure visible for microscopic examination. ■ Heraldry any of the minor colours used in blazoning and liveries, especially tenné and sanguine.
– DERIVATIVES **stainable** adjective, **stainer** noun.
– ORIGIN late Middle English (as a verb): shortening of archaic *distain*, from Old French *desteindre* 'tinge with a colour different from the natural one'. The noun was first recorded (mid 16th cent.) in the sense 'defilement, disgrace'.

stained glass ▶ noun [mass noun] coloured glass used to form decorative or pictorial designs, notably for church windows, both by painting and especially by setting contrasting pieces in a lead framework like a mosaic.

Stainer, Sir John (1840–1901), English composer. He is remembered for his church music, including hymns, cantatas, and the oratorio *Crucifixion* (1887).

stainless ▶ adjective unmarked by or resistant to stains or discoloration.
■ figurative (of a person or their reputation) free from wrongdoing or disgrace: *her supposedly stainless past.*

stainless steel ▶ noun [mass noun] a form of steel containing chromium, resistant to tarnishing and rust.

stair ▶ noun (usu. **stairs**) a set of steps leading from one floor of a building to another, typically inside the building: *he came up the stairs.*
■ single step in such a set: *the bottom stair.*
– ORIGIN Old English *stæger*, of Germanic origin; related to Dutch *steiger* 'scaffolding', from a base meaning 'climb'.

staircase ▶ noun a set of stairs and its surrounding walls or structure.
■ Brit. a set of stairs and the rooms leading off it in a large building, especially a school or college.

staircase shell ▶ noun another term for WENTLETRAP.

stairhead ▶ noun chiefly Brit. a landing at the top of a set of stairs.

stairlift ▶ noun a lift in the form of a chair that can be raised or lowered at the edge of a domestic staircase, used for carrying a person who is unable to go up or down the stairs.

stair rod ▶ noun a rod for securing a carpet in the angle between two steps.
– PHRASES **rain** (or **come down in**) **stair rods** Brit. informal rain very heavily.

stairway ▶ noun a set of steps or stairs and its surrounding walls or structure.

stairwell ▶ noun a shaft in a building in which a staircase is built.

staithe /steɪð/ ▶ noun (in the north and east of England) a landing stage for loading or unloading cargo boats.
– ORIGIN Middle English: from Old Norse *stǫth* 'landing stage'.

stake[1] ▶ noun **1** a strong wooden or metal post with a point at one end, driven into the ground to

support a tree, form part of a fence, act as a boundary mark, etc.
▪a long vertical rod used in basket-making. ▪a metalworker's small anvil, typically with a projection for fitting into a socket on a bench.
2 (**the stake**) historical a wooden post to which a person was tied before being burned alive as a punishment.
3 a territorial division of the Mormon Church under the jurisdiction of a president.
▶**verb** [with obj.] **1** support (a tree or plant) with a stake or stakes.
2 (**stake something out**) mark an area with stakes so as to claim ownership of it: *the boundary between the two manors was properly staked out* | figurative *the local dog staked out his territory.*
▪be assertive in defining and defending a position or policy: *Elena was staking out a role for herself as a formidable political force.*
– PHRASES **go to the stake for** used to emphasize that one would do anything to defend a particular belief, opinion, or person. **pull up stakes** N. Amer. move or go to live elsewhere. **stake a claim** assert one's right to something.
– ORIGIN Old English *staca*, of West Germanic origin; related to Dutch *staak*, also to **STICK**[2].
▶**stake someone/thing out** informal continuously watch a place or person in secret: *they'd staked out Culley's flat for half a day.*

stake[2] ▶**noun** (usu. **stakes**) a sum of money or something else of value gambled on the outcome of a risky game or venture: *playing dice for high stakes* | figurative *the opposition* ***raised the stakes*** *in the battle for power.*
▪a share or interest in a business, situation, or system: *GM acquired a 50 per cent stake in Saab.* ▪ (**stakes**) prize money, especially in horse racing. ▪ [in names] (**stakes**) a horse race in which all the owners of the racehorses running contribute to the prize money: *the horse is to run in the Craven Stakes.* ▪ [with modifier] (**stakes**) a situation involving competition in a specified area: *we will keep you one step ahead in the fashion stakes.*
▶**verb** [with obj.] **1** gamble (money or something else of value) on the outcome of a game or race: *one gambler staked everything he'd got and lost* | figurative *it was risky to* ***stake*** *his reputation* ***on*** *on one big success.*
2 US informal give financial or other support to: *he* ***staked*** *him* ***to*** *an education at the École des Beaux-Arts.*
– PHRASES **at stake 1** to be won or lost; at risk: *people's lives could be at stake.* **2** at issue or in question: *the logical response is to give up, but there's more at stake than logic.*
– ORIGIN late Middle English: perhaps a specialized usage of **STAKE**[1], from the notion of an object being placed as a wager on a post or stake.

stake boat ▶**noun** an anchored boat used to mark the course for a boat race.

stake body ▶**noun** US a body for a lorry having a flat open platform with removable posts along the sides.

stakebuilding ▶**noun** [mass noun] Finance the building up of a holding of shares in a company.

stakeholder ▶**noun 1** (in gambling) an independent party with whom each of those who make a wager deposits the money or counters wagered.
2 a person with an interest or concern in something, especially a business.
▪[as modifier] denoting a type of organization or system in which all the members or participants are seen as having an interest in its success: *a stakeholder economy.*

stake net ▶**noun** a fishing net hung on stakes.

stake-out ▶**noun** informal a period of secret surveillance of a building or an area by police in order to observe someone's activities.

staker ▶**noun 1** a person who gambles money on the outcome of a game or race.
2 Canadian a person who makes a mining claim.

Stakhanovite /stəˈkɑːnəvʌɪt, -ˈkanə-/ ▶**noun** a worker in the former USSR who was exceptionally hard-working and productive.
▪an exceptionally hard-working or zealous person.
– DERIVATIVES **Stakhanovism** noun, **Stakhanovist** noun & adjective.
– ORIGIN 1930s: from the name of Aleksei Grigorevich *Stakhanov* (1906–1977), Russian coal miner.

stalactite /ˈstaləktʌɪt/ ▶**noun** a tapering structure hanging like an icicle from the roof of a cave, formed of calcium salts deposited by dripping water.
– DERIVATIVES **stalactitic** adjective.
– ORIGIN late 17th cent.: from modern Latin *stalactites*, from Greek *stalaktos* 'dripping', based on *stalassein* 'to drip'.

Stalag /ˈstalag, ˈʃtalag/ ▶**noun** (in the Second World War) a German prison camp, especially for non-commissioned officers and privates.
– ORIGIN German, contraction of *Stammlager*, from *Stamm* 'base, main stock' + *Lager* 'camp'.

stalagmite /ˈstaləgmʌɪt/ ▶**noun** a mound or tapering column rising from the floor of a cave, formed of calcium salts deposited by dripping water and often uniting with a stalactite.
– DERIVATIVES **stalagmitic** adjective.
– ORIGIN late 17th cent.: from modern Latin *stalagmites*, from Greek *stalagma* 'a drop', based on *stalassein* (see **STALACTITE**).

stale[1] ▶**adjective** (**staler**, **stalest**) (of food) no longer fresh and pleasant to eat; hard, musty, or dry: *stale bread.*
▪no longer new and interesting or exciting: *their marriage had gone stale.* ▪ [predic.] (of a person) no longer able to perform well or creatively because of having done something for too long: *a top executive tends to get stale.* ▪ (of a cheque or legal claim) invalid because out of date.
▶**verb** make or become stale: [no obj.] *she would cut up yesterday's leftover bread, staling now.*
– DERIVATIVES **stalely** adverb, **staleness** noun.
– ORIGIN Middle English (describing beer in the sense 'clear from long standing, strong'): probably from Anglo-Norman French and Old French, from *estaler* 'to halt'; compare with the verb **STALL**.

stale[2] ▶**verb** [no obj.] (of an animal, especially a horse) urinate.
– ORIGIN late Middle English: perhaps from Old French *estaler* 'come to a stand, halt' (compare with **STALE**[1]).

stalemate ▶**noun** [mass noun] Chess a position counting as a draw, in which a player is not in check but cannot move except into check.
▪a situation in which further action or progress by opposing or competing parties seems impossible: *the war had again reached stalemate.*
▶**verb** [with obj.] bring to or cause to reach stalemate: [as adj. **stalemated**] *the currently stalemated peace talks.*
– ORIGIN mid 18th cent.: from obsolete *stale* (from Anglo-Norman French *estale* 'position', from *estaler* 'be placed') + **MATE**[2].

Stalin[1] /ˈstɑːlɪn/ (also **Stalino**) former name (1924–61) for **DONETSK**.

Stalin[2] /ˈstɑːlɪn/, Joseph (1879–1953), Soviet statesman, General Secretary of the Communist Party of the USSR 1922–53; born *Iosif Vissarionovich Dzhugashvili.*

His adoptive name Stalin means 'man of steel'. Having isolated his political rival Trotsky, by 1927 Stalin was the uncontested leader of the Communist Party. In 1928 he launched a succession of five-year plans for rapid industrialization and the enforced collectivization of agriculture; as a result of this process some 10 million peasants are thought to have died. His large-scale purges of the intelligentsia in the 1930s were equally ruthless. After the victory over Hitler in 1945 he maintained a firm grip on neighbouring Communist states.

Stalinabad /ˈstɑːlɪnəbad/ former name (1929–61) for **DUSHANBE**.

Stalingrad /ˈstɑːlɪngrad/ former name (1925–61) for **VOLGOGRAD**.

Stalingrad, Battle of a long and bitterly fought battle of the Second World War, in which the German advance into the Soviet Union was turned back at Stalingrad in 1942–3. The Germans surrendered after suffering more than 300,000 casualties.

Stalinism ▶**noun** [mass noun] the ideology and policies adopted by Stalin, based on centralization, totalitarianism, and the pursuit of communism.
▪any rigid centralized authoritarian form of communism.
– DERIVATIVES **Stalinist** noun & adjective.

Stalino /ˈstɑːlɪnəʊ/ see **STALIN**[1].

Stalin Peak former name (1933–1962) for **COMMUNISM PEAK**.

stalk[1] ▶**noun** the main stem of a herbaceous plant: *he chewed a stalk of grass.*
▪the slender attachment or support of a leaf, flower, or fruit: *the acorns grow on stalks.* ▪a similar support for a sessile animal, or for an organ in an animal. ▪a slender support or stem of something: *drinking glasses with long stalks.* ▪ (in a vehicle) a lever on the steering column controlling the indicators, lights, etc.
– DERIVATIVES **stalked** adjective [in combination] *rough-stalked meadow grass*, **stalkless** adjective, **stalk-like** adjective, **stalky** adjective.
– ORIGIN Middle English: probably a diminutive of dialect *stale* 'rung of a ladder, long handle'.

stalk[2] ▶**verb 1** [with obj.] pursue or approach stealthily: *a cat stalking a bird.*
▪harass or persecute (someone) with unwanted and obsessive attention: *for five years she was stalked by a man who would taunt and threaten her.* ▪chiefly poetic/literary move silently or threateningly through (a place): *the tiger stalks the jungle* | figurative *fear stalked the camp.*
2 [no obj., with adverbial of direction] stride somewhere in a proud, stiff, or angry manner: *without another word she turned and stalked out.*
▶**noun 1** a stealthy pursuit of someone or something.
2 a stiff, striding gait.
– ORIGIN late Old English *-stealcian* (in *bistealcian* 'walk cautiously or stealthily'), of Germanic origin; related to **STEAL**.

stalker ▶**noun** a person who stealthily hunts or pursues an animal or another person.
▪a person who harasses or persecutes someone with unwanted and obsessive attention.

stalk-eyed ▶**adjective** (of a crustacean) having eyes mounted on stalks.

stalking horse ▶**noun** a screen traditionally made in the shape of a horse behind which a hunter may stay concealed when stalking prey.
▪a false pretext concealing someone's real intentions. ▪a candidate in an election for the leadership of a political party who stands only in order to provoke the election and thus allow a stronger candidate to come forward.
– ORIGIN early 16th cent.: from the former practice of using a horse trained to allow a fowler to hide behind it, or under its coverings, until within easy range of prey.

stall ▶**noun 1** a stand, booth, or compartment for the sale of goods in a market or large covered area: *fruit and vegetable stalls.*
2 an individual compartment for an animal in a stable or cowshed, enclosed on three sides.
▪a stable or cowshed. ▪N. Amer. a marked-out parking space for a vehicle. ▪ (also **starting stall**) a cage-like compartment in which a horse is held immediately prior to the start of a race. ▪a compartment for one person in a shower room, toilet, or similar.
3 a fixed seat in the choir or chancel of a church, more or less enclosed at the back and sides and often canopied, typically reserved for a particular member of the clergy.
4 (**stalls**) Brit. the seats on the ground floor in a theatre.
5 an instance of an engine, vehicle, aircraft, or boat stalling: *speed must be maintained to avoid a stall and loss of control.*
▶**verb 1** [no obj.] (of a motor vehicle or its engine) stop running, typically because of an overload on the engine: *her car stalled at the crossroads.*
▪(of an aircraft or its pilot) stop flying and begin to fall because the speed is too low or the angle of attack too large to maintain adequate lift. ▪Sailing have insufficient wind power in the sails to give controlled motion. ▪ [with obj.] cause (an engine, vehicle, aircraft, or boat) to stall.
2 [no obj.] (of a situation or process) stop making progress: *his career had stalled, hers taken off.*
▪[with obj.] delay, obstruct, or block the progress of (something): *the government has stalled the much-needed project.* ▪speak or act in a deliberately vague way in order to gain more time to deal with a question or issue; prevaricate: *she was* ***stalling for time.*** ▪ [with obj.] delay or divert (someone) by acting in such a way: *stall him until I've had time to take a look.*
3 [with obj.] put or keep (an animal) in a stall, especially in order to fatten it.
– PHRASES **set out one's stall** Brit. make one's position on an issue very clear.
– ORIGIN Old English *steall* 'stable or cattle shed', of Germanic origin; related to Dutch *stal*, also to **STAND**. Early senses of the verb included 'reside, dwell' and 'bring to a halt'.

stallage /ˈstɔːlɪdʒ/ ▶**noun** [mass noun] Brit., chiefly historical rental, taxation, or fees charged for the holding of a stall in a market.

b **but** | d **dog** | f **few** | g **get** | h **he** | j **yes** | k **cat** | l **leg** | m **man** | n **no** | p **pen** | r **red** | s **sit** | t **top** | v **voice** | w **we** | z **zoo** | ʃ **she** | ʒ decision | θ **thin** | ð **this** | ŋ **ring** | x **loch** | tʃ **chip** | dʒ **jar**

■the right to hold a stall in a market.
– ORIGIN Middle English: shortening of Old French *estalage*, from *estal* 'stall'.

stall-feed ▶ **verb** [with obj.] feed and keep (an animal) in a stall, especially in order to fatten it.

stallholder ▶ **noun** Brit. a person owning or running a stall at a market.

stallion ▶ **noun** an uncastrated adult male horse.
– ORIGIN Middle English: from an Anglo-Norman French variant of Old French *estalon*, from a derivative of a Germanic base shared by **STALL**.

stall turn ▶ **noun** an aerobatic manoeuvre in which the aircraft climbs vertically before being stalled, when it turns on one wing into a dive.

stalwart /'stɔːlwət, 'stal-/ ▶ **adjective** loyal, reliable, and hard-working: *he remained a stalwart supporter of the cause.*
■dated strongly built and sturdy: *he was of stalwart build.*
▶ **noun** a loyal, reliable, and hard-working supporter or participant in an organization or team: *the stalwarts of the Labour Party.*
– DERIVATIVES **stalwartly** adverb, **stalwartness** noun.
– ORIGIN late Middle English: Scots variant of obsolete *stalworth*, from Old English *stǣl* 'place' + *weorth* 'worth'.

Stamboul /stam'buːl/ archaic name for **ISTANBUL**.

stamen /'steɪmən/ ▶ **noun** Botany the male fertilizing organ of a flower, typically consisting of a pollen-containing anther and a filament.
– ORIGIN mid 17th cent.: from Latin, literally 'warp in an upright loom, thread'.

stamina ▶ **noun** [mass noun] the ability to sustain prolonged physical or mental effort: *their secret is stamina rather than speed.*
– ORIGIN late 17th cent. (in the sense 'rudiments, essential elements of something'): from Latin, plural of **STAMEN** in the sense 'threads spun by the Fates'.

staminate /'stamɪnət/ ▶ **adjective** Botany (of a plant or flower) having stamens but no pistils. Compare with **PISTILLATE**.

staminode /'stamɪnəʊd/ ▶ **noun** Botany a sterile or abortive stamen, frequently resembling a stamen without its anther.

stammer ▶ **verb** [no obj.] speak with sudden involuntary pauses and a tendency to repeat the initial letters of words.
■[with obj.] utter (words) in such a way: *I* **stammered out** *my history* | [with direct speech] *'I ... I can't,' Isabel stammered.*
▶ **noun** [in sing.] a tendency to stammer: *as a young man, he had a dreadful stammer.*
– DERIVATIVES **stammerer** noun, **stammeringly** adverb.
– ORIGIN late Old English *stamerian*, of West Germanic origin; related to **STUMBLE**. The noun dates from the late 18th cent.

stamp ▶ **verb** [with obj.] **1** bring down (one's foot) heavily on the ground or on something on the ground: *he stamped his foot in frustration* | [no obj.] *he threw his cigarette down and stamped on it* | figurative *Robertson stamped on all these suggestions.*
■[with obj. and adverbial] crush, flatten, or remove with a heavy blow from one's foot: *he stamped out the flames before they could grow.* ■ (**stamp something out**) suppress or put an end to something by taking decisive action: *urgent action is required to stamp out corruption.* ■ [no obj., with adverbial of direction] walk with heavy, forceful steps: *John stamped off, muttering.*
2 impress a pattern or mark, especially an official one, on (a surface, object, or document) using an engraved or inked block or die or other instrument: *the woman stamped my passport.*
■impress (a pattern or mark) on something in such a way: *a key with a number* **stamped on** *the shaft* | figurative *he must be able to* **stamp** *his authority* **on** *his team.* ■ make (something) by cutting it out with a die or mould: *the knives are* **stamped out from** *a flat strip of steel.* ■ figurative reveal or mark out as having a particular character, quality, or ability: *his style* **stamps** *him* **as** *a player to watch.*
3 fix a postage stamp or stamps on to (a letter): *Annie stamped the envelope for her.*
4 crush or pulverize (ore).
▶ **noun 1** an instrument for stamping a pattern or mark, in particular an engraved or inked block or die.
■a mark or pattern made by such an instrument, especially one indicating official validation or certification: *passports with visa stamps* | figurative *the emperor gave them his stamp of approval.* ■ figurative a characteristic or distinctive impression or quality: *the whole project has the stamp of authority.* ■ a particular class or type of person or thing: *empiricism of this stamp has been especially influential in British philosophy.*
2 a small adhesive piece of paper stuck to something to show that an amount of money has been paid, in particular a postage stamp: *a first-class stamp* | *TV licence stamps.*
3 an act or sound of stamping with the foot: *the stamp of boots on the bare floor.*
4 a block for crushing ore in a stamp mill.
– DERIVATIVES **stamper** noun.
– ORIGIN Middle English (in the sense 'crush to a powder'): of Germanic origin; related to German *stampfen* 'stamp with the foot'; reinforced by Old French *estamper* 'to stamp'. Compare with **STOMP**.

Stamp Act ▶ **noun** an act regulating stamp duty.

stamp collecting ▶ **noun** [mass noun] the collection and study of postage stamps as objects of interest or value; philately.
– DERIVATIVES **stamp collector** noun.

stamp duty ▶ **noun** a duty levied on the legal recognition of certain documents.

stamped addressed envelope ▶ **noun** a self-addressed envelope with a stamp affixed, typically enclosed with a letter for an expected reply.

stampede ▶ **noun** a sudden panicked rush of a number of horses, cattle, or other animals.
■a sudden rapid movement or reaction of a mass of people in response to a particular circumstance or stimulus: *a stampede of bargain hunters.* ■ [often in names] (in North America) a rodeo: *the Calgary Stampede.*
▶ **verb** [no obj.] (of horses, cattle, or other animals) rush wildly in a sudden mass panic: *the nearby sheep stampeded as if they sensed impending danger.*
■[no obj., with adverbial of direction] (of people) move rapidly in a mass: *the children stampeded through the kitchen, playing tag or hide-and-seek.* ■ [with obj.] cause (people or animals) to move in such a way: *the raiders stampeded 200 mules* | figurative *don't let them* **stampede** *us* **into** *anything.*
– DERIVATIVES **stampeder** noun.
– ORIGIN early 19th cent.: Mexican Spanish use of Spanish *estampida* 'crash, uproar', of Germanic origin; related to the verb **STAMP**.

stamp hinge ▶ **noun** a small piece of gummed transparent paper used for fixing postage stamps in an album.

stamping ground (N. Amer. also **stomping ground**) ▶ **noun** a place where someone regularly spends time; a favourite haunt.

stamp mill ▶ **noun** a mill for crushing ore.

stamp office ▶ **noun** Brit. an office for the issue of government stamps and the receipt of stamp duty.

stamp paper ▶ **noun** [mass noun] the gummed marginal paper at the edge of a sheet of postage stamps.

stance /stɑːns, stans/ ▶ **noun 1** the way in which someone stands, especially when deliberately adopted (as in cricket, golf, and other sports); a person's posture: *she altered her stance, resting all her weight on one leg.*
■the attitude of a person or organization towards something; a standpoint: *the party is changing its* **stance on** *Europe.*
2 Scottish a site on a street for a market, street vendor's stall, or taxi rank.
3 Climbing a ledge or foothold on which a belay can be secured.
– ORIGIN Middle English (denoting a standing place): from French, from Italian *stanza*.

stanch[1] /stɔːn(t)ʃ, stɑːn(t)ʃ/ ▶ **verb** chiefly US variant spelling of **STAUNCH**[2].

stanch[2] /stɔːn(t)ʃ/ ▶ **adjective** variant spelling of **STAUNCH**[1] (in sense 2).

stanchion /'stanʃ(ə)n/ ▶ **noun** an upright bar, post, or frame forming a support or barrier.
– DERIVATIVES **stanchioned** adjective.
– ORIGIN Middle English: from Anglo-Norman French *stanchon*, from Old French *estanchon*, from *estance* 'a support', probably based on Latin *stant-* 'standing', from the verb *stare*.

stand ▶ **verb** (past and past participle **stood**) **1** [no obj., usu. with adverbial of place] have or maintain an upright position, supported by one's feet: *Lionel stood in the doorway* | *she stood still, heart hammering.*
■rise to one's feet: *the two men* **stood up** *and shook hands.* ■ [no obj., with adverbial of direction] move to and remain in a specified position: *she stood aside to let them enter.* ■ [with obj. and adverbial of place] place or set in an upright or specified position: *don't stand the plant in direct sunlight.*
2 [no obj., with adverbial of place] (of an object, building, or settlement) be situated in a particular place or position: *the town stood on a hill* | *the hotel stands in three acres of gardens.*
■(of a building or other vertical structure) remain upright and entire rather than fall into ruin or be destroyed: *after the storms only one house was left standing.* ■ remain valid or unaltered: *my decision stands* | *he won 31 caps–a record which stood for 42 years.* ■ (especially of a vehicle) remain stationary: *the train now standing at platform 3.* ■ (of a liquid) collect and remain motionless: *soil where water stands in winter.* ■ (of food, a mixture, or liquid) rest without disturbance, typically so as to infuse or marinate: *pour boiling water over the fruit and leave it to stand for 5 minutes.* ■ [no obj., with adverbial of direction] (of a ship) remain on a specified course: *the ship was standing north.*
3 [no obj., with complement] be in a specified state or condition: *since mother's death the house had stood empty* | *sorry, darling–I stand corrected.*
■adopt a particular attitude towards a matter or issue: *students should consider where they stand on this issue.* ■ be of a specified height: *Sampson was a small man, standing 5 ft 4 in tall.* ■ (**stand at**) be at (a particular level or value): *the budget stood at £2,000 million per annum.* ■ [no obj., with infinitive] be in a situation where one is likely to do something: *investors stood to lose heavily.* ■ act in a specified capacity: *he stood security for the government's borrowings.* ■ (also **stand at stud**) [no obj.] (of a stallion) be available for breeding.
4 [with obj. and often modal] withstand (an experience or test) without being damaged: *small, stable boats that could stand the punishment of heavy seas* | *will your cooker stand the strain of the festive season?*
■[usu. with negative] informal be able to endure or tolerate: *I can't stand the way Mum talks to him.* ■ [with modal and negative] informal strongly dislike: *I can't stand brandy.*
5 [no obj.] Brit. be a candidate in an election: *he* **stood for** *parliament in 1968.*
6 [no obj.] act as umpire in a cricket match.
7 [usu. with two objs] provide (food or drink) for someone at one's own expense: *somebody in the bar would stand him a coffee.*
▶ **noun 1** [usu. in sing.] an attitude towards a particular issue; a position taken in an argument: *the party's tough stand on immigration* | *his traditionalist stand.*
■a determined effort to resist or fight for something: *this was not the moment to* **make a stand for** *independence* | *we have to* **take a stand against** *racism.* ■ an act of holding one's ground against or halting to resist an opposing force: *Custer's legendary last stand.* ■ Cricket another term for **PARTNERSHIP**: *they shared a second-wicket stand of 135.*
2 a place where or object on which someone or something stands, sits, or rests, in particular:
■a large raised tiered structure for spectators, typically at a sporting venue: *United's manager watched from the stands.* ■ a rack, base, or piece of furniture for holding, supporting, or displaying something: *a microphone stand.* ■ a small stall or booth in a street, market, or public building from which goods are sold: *a hot-dog stand.* ■ chiefly Brit. an upright structure on which an organization displays promotional material at an exhibition. ■ a raised platform for a band, orchestra, or speaker. ■ (**the stand**) (also **witness stand**) a witness box: *Sergeant Harris took the stand.* ■ the place where someone typically stands or sits: *she took her stand in front of the desks.* ■ a place where vehicles, typically taxis, wait for passengers.
3 [usu. in sing.] a cessation from motion or progress: *the train drew to a stand by the signal box.*
■the mean sea level at a particular period in the past. ■ the state of the tide at high or low water when there is little change in water level. ■ each halt made on a touring theatrical production to give one or more performances.
4 a group of growing plants of a specified kind, especially trees: *a stand of poplars.*
5 S. African a plot of land. [ORIGIN: perhaps from Afrikaans *standplaas* 'standing place'.]
– PHRASES **as it stands** in its present condition: *there are no merits in the Bill as it stands.* ■ (also **as things stand**) in the present circumstances: *the country would struggle, as it stands, to host the next World Cup.* **be at a stand** archaic be perplexed and unable to take action. **it stands to reason** see **REASON**. **stand and deliver!** historical a highwayman's order to hand over money and valuables. **stand a chance** see **CHANCE**. **stand easy!** see **EASY**. **stand one's**

ground maintain one's position, typically in the face of opposition: *she stood her ground, refusing to let him intimidate her.* **stand someone in good stead** see **STEAD**. **stand on me** informal, dated rely on me; believe me. **stand on one's own (two) feet** be or become self-reliant or independent. **stand out a mile** see **MILE**. **stand out like a sore thumb** see **SORE**. **stand pat** see **PAT**[2]. **stand treat** dated bear the expense of treating someone to something. **stand trial** be tried in a court of law. **stand up and be counted** state publicly one's support for someone or something. **will the real —— please stand up** informal used rhetorically to indicate that the specified person should clarify their position or reveal their true character: *he was so different from the unhappy man of a week ago—would the real Jack Lawrence please stand up?*

– DERIVATIVES **stander** noun.

– ORIGIN Old English *standan* (verb), *stand* (noun), of Germanic origin, from an Indo-European root shared by Latin *stare* and Greek *histanai*, also by the noun **STEAD**.

USAGE The use of the past participle **stood** with the verb 'to be', as in *we were* **stood** *in a line for hours*, is not acceptable in standard English, where the present participle **standing** should be used instead. See also usage at **SIT**.

▶**stand alone** be unequalled: *when it came to fun Fergus stood alone.*

stand aside take no action to prevent, or not involve oneself in, something that is happening: *the army had stood aside as the monarchy fell.* ■ another way of saying ***stand down*** (in sense 1) below.

stand back withdraw from a situation emotionally in order to view it more objectively. ■ another way of saying ***stand aside*** above.

stand by 1 be present while something bad is happening but fail to take any action to stop it: *he was beaten to the ground as onlookers stood by.* **2** support or remain loyal to (someone), typically in a time of need: *she had stood by him during his years in prison.* ■ adhere to or abide by (something promised, stated, or decided): *the government must stand by its pledges.* **3** be ready to deal or assist with something: *two battalions were on their way, and a third was standing by.*

stand down 1 withdraw or resign from a position or office: *he stood down as leader of the party.* **2** (**stand down** or **stand someone down**) relax or cause to relax after a state of readiness: *if something doesn't happen soon, I reckon they'll stand us down.* **3** (of a witness) leave the witness box after giving evidence.

stand for 1 be an abbreviation of or symbol for: *BBC stands for British Broadcasting Corporation.* **2** [with negative] informal refuse to endure or tolerate: *I won't stand for any nonsense.* **3** support (a cause or principle): *we stand for animal welfare.*

stand in 1 deputize: *Brown* **stood in for** *the injured Simpson.* **2** Nautical sail closer to the shore.

stand in with dated be in league or partnership with.

stand off move or keep away: *the women stood off at a slight distance.* ■ Nautical sail further away from the shore.

stand someone off 1 keep someone away: repel someone. **2** Brit. another way of saying ***lay someone off*** (see **LAY**[1]).

stand on 1 be scrupulous in the observance of: *call me Alexander—don't let's stand on formality.* **2** Nautical continue on the same course.

stand out 1 project from a surface: *the veins in his neck stood out.* ■ be easily noticeable: *he was one of those men who stood out in a crowd.* ■ be clearly better or more significant than someone or something: *four issues stand out as being of crucial importance.* **2** persist in opposition or support of something: *she* **stood out against** *public opinion | the company* **stood out for** *the product it wanted.*

stand over 1 stand close to (someone) so as to watch, supervise, or intimidate them. **2** (**stand over** or **stand something over**) be postponed or postpone to be dealt with at a later date: *a number of points were stood over to a further meeting.*

stand to [often in imperative] Military stand ready for an attack, especially one before dawn or after dark.

stand up (of an argument, claim, evidence, etc.) remain valid after close scrutiny or analysis.

stand someone up informal fail to keep an appointment with a boyfriend or girlfriend.

stand up for speak or act in support of: *she learned to* **stand up for** *herself.*

stand up to 1 make a spirited defence against: *giving workers the confidence to stand up to their employers.* **2** be resistant to the harmful effects of (prolonged wear or use).

stand-alone ▶ **adjective** (of computer hardware or software) able to operate independently of other hardware or software.

standard ▶ **noun 1** a level of quality or attainment: *their restaurant offers a high standard of service | the government's ambition to raise standards in schools.* ■ a required or agreed level of quality or attainment: *half of the beaches fail to comply with European standards |* [mass noun] *their tap water was not* **up to standard**. ■ Brit. historical (in elementary schools) a grade of proficiency tested by examination or the form or class preparing pupils for such a grade. ■ S. African (often with a specifying number) a class or year in a high school: *his education ended at standard six.*

2 an idea or thing used as a measure, norm, or model in comparative evaluations: *the wages are low by today's standards | the system had become an industry standard.* ■ (**standards**) principles of conduct informed by notions of honour and decency: *a decline in moral standards.* ■ a form of language that is widely accepted as the usual form. ■ the prescribed weight of fine metal in gold or silver coins: *the sterling standard for silver.* ■ a system by which the value of a currency is defined in terms of gold or silver or both. ■ a measure for timber, equivalent to 165 cu. ft (4.67 cubic metres).

3 an object that is supported in an upright position, in particular: ■ a military or ceremonial flag carried on a pole or hoisted on a rope. ■ used in names of newspapers: *a report in the Evening Standard.* ■ a tree or shrub that grows on an erect stem of full height. ■ a shrub grafted on an erect stem and trained in tree form. ■ Botany the large, frequently erect uppermost petal of a papilionaceous flower. Also called **VEXILLUM**. ■ Botany one of the inner petals of an iris flower, frequently erect. ■ an upright water or gas pipe.

4 (especially with reference to jazz or blues) a tune or song of established popularity.

▶ **adjective 1** used or accepted as normal or average: *the standard rate of income tax | it is standard practice in museums to register objects as they are acquired.* ■ (of a size, measure, design, etc.) such as is regularly used or produced; not special or exceptional: *all these doors come in a range of standard sizes.* ■ (of a work, repertoire, or writer) viewed as authoritative or of permanent value and so widely read or performed: *his essays on the interpretation of reality became a standard text.* ■ denoting or relating to the form of a language widely accepted as the usual correct form: *speakers of standard English.*

2 [attrib.] (of a tree or shrub) growing on an erect stem of full height. ■ (of a shrub) grafted on an erect stem and trained in tree form: *standard roses.*

– PHRASES **raise one's** (or **the**) **standard** chiefly figurative take up arms: *he is the only one who has dared raise his standard against her.*

– DERIVATIVES **standardly** adverb.

– ORIGIN Middle English (denoting a flag raised on a pole as a rallying point, the authorized exemplar of a unit of measurement, or an upright timber): shortening of Old French *estendart*, from *estendre* 'extend'; in sense 3, influenced by the verb **STAND**.

standard assessment task (abbrev.: **SAT**) ▶ **noun** (in the UK) a standard test given to schoolchildren to assess their progress in a core subject of the national curriculum.

standard-bearer ▶ **noun** a soldier who is responsible for carrying the distinctive flag of a unit, regiment, or army. ■ a leading figure in a cause or movement: *the announcement made her a standard-bearer for gay rights.*

Standardbred ▶ **noun** N. Amer. a horse of a breed able to attain a specified speed, developed especially for trotting.

standard cost ▶ **noun** the estimated cost of a process, resource, or item used in a manufacturing enterprise, entered in an account and compared with the actual cost so that anomalies are readily detectable.

– DERIVATIVES **standard costing** noun.

standard deviation ▶ **noun** Statistics a quantity calculated to indicate the extent of deviation for a group as a whole.

standard error ▶ **noun** Statistics a measure of the statistical accuracy of an estimate, equal to the standard deviation of the theoretical distribution of a large population of such estimates.

standard gauge ▶ **noun** a railway gauge of 4 ft 8½ inches (1.435 m), standard in Britain and many other parts of the world.

Standard Grade ▶ **noun** (in Scotland) an examination equivalent to the GCSE.

standardize (also **-ise**) ▶ **verb** [with obj.] cause (something) to conform to a standard: *Jones's effort to standardize oriental spelling.* ■ [no obj.] (**standardize on**) adopt (something) as one's standard: *we could standardize on US equipment.* ■ determine the properties of by comparison with a standard.

– DERIVATIVES **standardizable** adjective, **standardization** noun, **standardizer** noun.

standard lamp ▶ **noun** chiefly Brit. a lamp with a tall stem whose base stands on the floor.

standard lens ▶ **noun** a camera lens with a focal length approximately equal to the diagonal of the negative (taken as 50 mm for a 35 mm camera), giving a field of view similar to that of the naked eye.

standard model ▶ **noun** (**the standard model**) Physics a mathematical description of the elementary particles of matter and the electromagnetic, weak, and strong forces by which they interact.

standard of living ▶ **noun** the degree of wealth and material comfort available to a person or community.

standard time ▶ **noun** [mass noun] a uniform time for places in approximately the same longitude, established in a country or region by law or custom.

standard wire gauge ▶ **noun** see **WIRE GAUGE**.

standby ▶ **noun** (pl. **standbys**) [mass noun] readiness for duty or immediate deployment: *buses were placed* **on standby** *for the journey to London.* ■ the state of waiting to secure an unreserved place for a journey or performance, allocated on the basis of earliest availability: *passengers were obliged to go* **on standby**. ■ [count noun] a person waiting to secure such a place. ■ [count noun] a person or thing ready to be deployed immediately, especially if needed as backup in an emergency: *a generator was kept as a standby in case of power failure |* [as modifier] *a standby rescue vessel.* ■ [as modifier] denoting or relating to an economic or financial measure prepared for implementation in specified circumstances: *a standby credit facility.*

stand-down ▶ **noun** chiefly Military a period of relaxation after a state of alert. ■ an off-duty period.

standee /stanˈdiː/ ▶ **noun** chiefly US a person who stands, especially in a passenger vehicle when all the seats are occupied or at a performance or sporting event.

stand-in ▶ **noun** a person who stands in for another, especially in a match or performance; a substitute: [as modifier] *a stand-in goalkeeper.*

standing ▶ **noun 1** [mass noun] position, status, or reputation: *their standing in the community | a man of high social standing.* ■ (**standings**) the table of scores indicating the relative positions of competitors in a sporting contest: *she heads the world championship standings.*

2 [mass noun] used to specify the length of time that something has lasted or that someone has fulfilled a particular role: *an inter-departmental squabble* **of long standing**.

3 a stall for cattle and horses.

▶ **adjective** [attrib.] **1** (of a jump or a start in a running race) performed from rest or an upright position, without a run-up or the use of starting blocks.

2 remaining in force or use; permanent: *he has a standing invitation to visit them | a standing army.*

3 (of water) stagnant or still.

4 (of corn) not yet reaped and so still erect.

5 Printing (of metal type) kept set up after use.

– PHRASES **all standing** Sailing (chiefly with reference to a boat's stopping) without time to lower the sails. **in good standing** in favour or on good terms with someone: *the companies wanted to stay* **in good standing with** *the government.* **leave someone/thing standing** informal be much better or make much faster progress than someone or something else: *in the personal fitness stakes he left her standing.*

standing committee ▶ noun a permanent committee that meets regularly.

standing count (also **standing eight count**) ▶ noun Boxing a count of eight taken on a boxer who has not been knocked down but who appears temporarily unfit to continue fighting.

standing crop ▶ noun a growing crop, especially of a cereal.
■ [mass noun] Ecology the total biomass of an ecosystem or any of its components at a given time.

standing joke ▶ noun something that regularly causes amusement or provokes ridicule.

standing order ▶ noun **1** Brit. an instruction to a bank by the holder of an account to make regular fixed payments to a particular person or organization. **2** Brit. an order for a commodity placed on a regular basis with a retailer such as a newsagent. **3** an order or ruling governing the procedures of a parliament or other society or council. **4** a military order or ruling that is retained irrespective of changing conditions.

standing ovation ▶ noun a period of prolonged applause during which the crowd or audience rise to their feet.

standing part ▶ noun the end of a rope or sheet in a ship's rigging which is made fast, as distinct from the end to be hauled on.

standing rigging ▶ noun see RIGGING¹ (sense 1).

standing room ▶ noun [mass noun] space available for people to stand rather than sit in a vehicle, building, or stadium.

standing stone ▶ noun another term for MENHIR.

standing wave ▶ noun Physics a vibration of a system in which some particular points remain fixed while others between them vibrate with the maximum amplitude. Compare with TRAVELLING WAVE.

standish ▶ noun chiefly historical a stand for holding pens, ink, and other writing equipment.
– ORIGIN Middle English: commonly held to be from the verb STAND + DISH, but evidence of such a use of *dish* is lacking.

stand of arms ▶ noun Brit. archaic a complete set of weapons for one man.

stand of colours ▶ noun Brit. a battalion's flags.

stand-off ▶ noun **1** chiefly US a stalemate or deadlock between two equally matched opponents in a dispute or conflict: *the 16-day-old stand-off was no closer to being resolved.* **2** Rugby short for STAND-OFF HALF.

stand-off half ▶ noun Rugby a halfback who forms a link between the scrum half and the three-quarters.

stand-offish ▶ adjective informal distant and cold in manner; unfriendly.
– DERIVATIVES **stand-offishly** adverb, **stand-offishness** noun.

stand oil ▶ noun [mass noun] linseed oil or another drying oil thickened by heating, used in paints, varnishes, and printing inks.

standout informal ▶ noun chiefly N. Amer. a person or thing of exceptional ability or high quality: *standouts include the home-made ravioli and the pizzas.*
▶ adjective [attrib.] exceptionally good: *he became a standout quarterback in the NFL.*

standpipe ▶ noun a vertical pipe extending from a water supply, especially one connecting a temporary tap to the mains.

standpoint ▶ noun an attitude to or outlook on issues, typically arising from one's circumstances or beliefs: *she writes on religion from the standpoint of a believer.*
■ the position from which someone is able to view a scene or an object.

standstill /ˈstan(d)stɪl/ ▶ noun [in sing.] a situation or condition in which there is no movement or activity at all: *the traffic came to a standstill.*

standstill agreement ▶ noun Finance an agreement between two countries in which a debt owed by one to the other is held in abeyance for a specified period.
■ an agreement between a company and a bidder for the company in which the bidder agrees to buy no more shares for a specified period.

stand-to ▶ noun [mass noun] Military the state of readiness for action or attack.

■ the formal start to a day of military operations.

stand-up ▶ adjective [attrib.] **1** involving, done by, or engaged in by people standing up: *a stand-up party.*
■ such that people have to stand rather than sit: *a stand-up bar.* ■ (of a comedian) performing by standing in front of an audience and telling jokes. ■ (of comedy) performed in such a way: *his stand-up routine depends on improvised observations.*
2 (of a fight or argument) involving direct, loud, and often violent confrontation: *she had a stand-up row with her husband.*
■ US informal courageous and loyal in a combative way.
3 designed to stay upright or erect.
▶ noun **1** a comedian who performs by standing in front of an audience and telling jokes.
■ [mass noun] comedy performed in such a way: *he began doing stand-up when he was fifteen.* ■ a brief monologue by a television news reporter.
2 a fight or argument involving direct, loud, and often violent confrontation.

Stanford /ˈstanfəd/, Sir Charles (Villiers) (1852–1924), British composer, born in Ireland. He is noted especially for his Anglican church music and numerous choral works.

Stanhope /ˈstanəp/, Lady Hester Lucy (1776–1839), English traveller. Granted a pension on the death of her uncle, Pitt the Younger, she settled in a ruined convent in the Lebanon Mountains in 1814 and participated in Middle Eastern politics for several years.

stanhope /ˈstanəp, -həʊp/ ▶ noun historical a light open horse-drawn carriage for one person, with two or four wheels.
– ORIGIN early 19th cent.: named after Fitzroy *Stanhope* (1787–1864), an English clergyman for whom the first one was made.

Stanier /ˈstanɪə/, Sir William (Arthur) (1876–1965), English railway engineer. He is chiefly remembered for his standard locomotive designs for the London Midland and Scottish Railway.

Stanislaus, St /ˈstanɪslɔːs/ (1030–79), patron saint of Poland; Polish name *Stanisław* /staˈniswaf/; known as St Stanislaus of Cracow. As bishop of Cracow (1072–79) he excommunicated King Boleslaus II. According to tradition Stanislaus was murdered by Boleslaus while taking Mass. Feast day, 11 April (formerly 7 May).

Stanislavsky /ˌstanɪsˈlafski/, Konstantin (Sergeevich) (1863–1938), Russian theatre director and actor; born *Konstantin Sergeevich Alekseev*. Stanislavsky trained his actors to take a psychological approach and use latent powers of self-expression when taking on roles; his theory and technique were later developed into method acting.

stank past of STINK.

Stanley¹ (also **Port Stanley**) the chief port and town of the Falkland Islands, situated on the island of East Falkland; pop. 1,557 (1991).

Stanley², Sir Henry Morton (1841–1904), Welsh explorer; born *John Rowlands*. As a newspaper correspondent he was sent in 1869 to central Africa to find David Livingstone; two years later he found him at Lake Tanganyika. After Livingstone's death in 1873 Stanley continued his explorations in Africa, charting Lake Victoria, tracing the course of the Congo, and mapping Lake Albert.

Stanley, Mount a mountain in the Ruwenzori range in central Africa, on the border between Zaire (Democratic Republic of Congo) and Uganda. Its highest peak, Margherita Peak, which rises to 5,110 m (16,765 ft), is the third-highest peak in Africa. African name MOUNT NGALIEMA.
– ORIGIN named after Sir Henry M. *Stanley*, the first European to reach it (1889).

Stanley crane ▶ noun another term for BLUE CRANE.

Stanley Cup a trophy awarded annually to the North American ice-hockey team that wins the championship in the National Hockey League.
– ORIGIN named after Lord *Stanley* of Preston (1841–1908), the Governor General of Canada who donated the trophy in 1893.

Stanley knife ▶ noun Brit. trademark a utility knife with a short, strong replaceable blade.

Stanleyville /ˈstanlɪvɪl/ former name (1882–1966) for KISANGANI.

stannary /ˈstan(ə)ri/ ▶ noun (pl. **-ies**) (usu. **the stannaries**) Brit., chiefly historical a tin-mining district in Cornwall or Devon.
– ORIGIN late Middle English: from medieval Latin *stannaria* (plural), from late Latin *stannum* 'tin'.

stannary court ▶ noun Brit. historical a legal body for the regulation of tin miners in the stannaries.

stannic /ˈstanɪk/ ▶ adjective Chemistry of tin with a valency of four; of tin(IV). Compare with STANNOUS.
– ORIGIN late 18th cent.: from late Latin *stannum* 'tin' + -IC.

stannous /ˈstanəs/ ▶ adjective Chemistry of tin with a valency of two; of tin(II). Compare with STANNIC.
– ORIGIN mid 19th cent.: from late Latin *stannum* 'tin' + -OUS.

Stansted /ˈstanstɪd/ an international airport in Essex, north-east of London.

stanza /ˈstanzə/ ▶ noun a group of lines forming the basic recurring metrical unit in a poem; a verse.
■ a group of four lines in some Greek and Latin metres.
– DERIVATIVES **stanza'd** (also **stanzaed**) adjective, **stanzaic** /-ˈzeɪk/ adjective.
– ORIGIN late 16th cent.: from Italian, literally 'standing place', also 'stanza'.

stapedial /stəˈpiːdɪəl/ ▶ adjective [attrib.] Anatomy & Zoology of or relating to the stapes.
– ORIGIN late 19th cent.: from modern Latin *stapedius* (denoting the muscle attached to the neck of the stapes) + -AL.

stapelia /stəˈpiːlɪə/ ▶ noun a succulent African plant with large star-shaped fleshy flowers that have bold markings and a foetid carrion-like smell which attracts pollinating flies. Also called CARRION FLOWER.
● Genus *Stapelia*, family Asclepiadaceae.
– ORIGIN modern Latin, named after Jan Bode von *Stapel* (died 1636), Dutch botanist.

stapes /ˈsteɪpiːz/ ▶ noun (pl. same) Anatomy a small stirrup-shaped bone in the middle ear, transmitting vibrations from the incus to the inner ear. Also called STIRRUP.
– ORIGIN mid 17th cent.: modern Latin, from medieval Latin *stapes* 'stirrup'.

staph /staf/ ▶ noun informal **1** Medicine short for STAPHYLOCOCCUS. **2** Entomology short for STAPHYLINID.

staphylinid /ˌstafɪˈlɪnɪd, -ˈlʌɪn-/ ▶ noun Entomology a beetle of a family (Staphylinidae) that comprises the rove beetles.
– ORIGIN late 19th cent.: from modern Latin *Staphylinidae* (plural), from the genus name *Staphylinus*, from Greek *staphulinos*, denoting a kind of insect.

staphylococcus /ˌstafɪlə(ʊ)ˈkɒkəs/ ▶ noun (pl. **staphylococci** /-ˈkɒk(s)ʌɪ, -ˈkɒk(s)iː/) a bacterium of a genus that includes many pathogenic kinds that cause pus formation, especially in the skin and mucous membranes.
● Genus *Staphylococcus*; Gram-positive cocci in clusters.
– DERIVATIVES **staphylococcal** adjective.
– ORIGIN modern Latin, from Greek *staphulē* 'bunch of grapes' + *kokkos* 'berry'.

staple¹ ▶ noun a piece of bent metal or wire pushed through something or clipped over it as a fastening, in particular:
■ a piece of thin wire with a long centre portion and two short end pieces which are driven by a stapler through sheets of paper to fasten them together. ■ a small U-shaped metal bar with pointed ends for driving into wood to hold attachments such as electric wires, battens, or sheets of cloth in place.
▶ verb [with obj. and adverbial of place] attach or secure with a staple or staples: *Merrill stapled a batch of papers together.*
– ORIGIN Old English *stapol*, of Germanic origin; related to Dutch *stapel* 'pillar' (a sense reflected in English in early use).

staple² ▶ noun **1** a main or important element of something, especially of a diet: *bread, milk, and other staples | Greek legend was the staple of classical tragedy.*
■ a main item of trade or production: *rubber became the staple of the Malayan economy.*
2 the fibre of cotton or wool considered with regard to its length and degree of fineness.
3 [often with modifier] historical a centre of trade, especially in a specified commodity: *proposals were made for a wool staple at Pisa.*
▶ adjective [attrib.] main or important, especially in

terms of consumption: *the staple foods of the poor* | figurative *violence is the staple diet of the video generation.*
■ most important in terms of trade or production: *rice was the staple crop grown in most villages.*
– ORIGIN Middle English (in sense 3): from Old French *estaple* 'market', from Middle Low German, Middle Dutch *stapel* 'pillar, emporium'; related to **STAPLE**[1].

staple gun ▶ **noun** a hand-held mechanical tool for driving staples into a hard surface.

stapler ▶ **noun** a device for fastening together sheets of paper with a staple or staples.

star ▶ **noun 1** a fixed luminous point in the night sky which is a large, remote incandescent body like the sun.

> True stars were formerly known as the **fixed stars**, to distinguish them from the planets or **wandering stars**. They are gaseous spheres consisting primarily of hydrogen and helium, there being an equilibrium between the compressional force of gravity and the outward pressure of radiation resulting from internal thermonuclear fusion reactions. Some six thousand stars are visible to the naked eye, but there are actually more than a hundred thousand million in our own Galaxy, while billions of other galaxies are known.

2 a conventional or stylized representation of a star, typically one having five or more points: *the walls were painted with silver moons and stars.*
■ a symbol of this shape used to indicate a category of excellence: *the hotel has three stars* | [as modifier] *MPs suggested giving ferries star ratings.* ■ an asterisk. ■ used in names of starfishes and similar echinoderms with five or more radiating arms, e.g. **cushion star**, **brittlestar**. ■ a white patch on the forehead of a horse or other animal. ■ (also **star connection**) [usu. as modifier] a Y-shaped arrangement of three-phase electrical windings. ■ (also **star network**) [usu. as modifier] a data or communication network in which all nodes are independently connected to one central unit.
3 a famous or exceptionally talented performer in the world of entertainment or sport: *a pop star* | [as modifier] *singers of **star quality**.*
■ an outstandingly good or successful person or thing in a group: *a **rising star** in the party* | [as modifier] *Elinor was a star pupil.*
4 Astrology a planet, constellation, or configuration regarded as influencing someone's fortunes or personality: *his golf destiny was written in the stars.*
■ (**stars**) a horoscope published in a newspaper or magazine: *what do my stars say?*
▶ **verb** (**starred**, **starring**) [with obj.] **1** (of a film, play, or other show) have (someone) as a principal performer: *a film starring Liza Minnelli.*
■ [no obj.] (of a performer) have a principal role in a film, play, or other show: *McQueen had **starred in** such epics as* The Magnificent Seven | [as adj. **starring**] *his first starring role.* ■ [no obj.] (of a person) perform brilliantly or prominently in a game or other event: *Bernie Slaven **starred** in the win over Leeds.*
2 decorate or cover with star-shaped marks or objects: *thick grass **starred with** flowers.*
■ mark (something) for special notice or recommendation with an asterisk or other star-shaped symbol: *the activities listed below are starred according to their fitness ratings* | [as adj., in combination **-starred**] *Michelin-starred restaurants.* ■ make a radiating crack in (glass, ice, etc.): *the third bullet starred the windshield.*
– PHRASES **my stars!** informal, dated an expression of astonishment. **reach for the stars** have high or ambitious aims. **see stars** see flashes of light, especially as a result of being hit on the head. **someone's star is rising** see **RISE**. **stars in one's eyes** used to describe someone who is idealistically hopeful or enthusiastic about their future: *a singer selected from hundreds of applicants with stars in their eyes.*
– DERIVATIVES **starless** adjective, **starlike** adjective.
– ORIGIN Old English *steorra*, of Germanic origin; related to Dutch *ster*, German *Stern*, from an Indo-European root shared by Latin *stella* and Greek *astēr*.

star anise ▶ **noun** [mass noun] **1** a small star-shaped fruit with one seed in each arm. It has an aniseed flavour and is used unripe in Asian cookery.
2 the small Chinese evergreen tree from which this spice is obtained.
• *Illicium verum*, family Illiciaceae.

star-apple ▶ **noun** an edible purple fruit with a star-shaped cross section.
• This is produced by the evergreen tropical American tree *Chrysophyllum cainito* (family Sapotaceae).

Stara Zagora /ˌstɑːrə zəˈɡɔːrə/ a city in east central Bulgaria; pop. 188,230 (1990). It was held by the Turks from 1370 until 1877, when it was destroyed by them during the Russo-Turkish War. It has since been rebuilt as a modern planned city.

starboard /ˈstɑːbɔːd, -bəd/ ▶ **noun** the side of a ship or aircraft that is on the right when one is facing forward. The opposite of **PORT**[3].
▶ **verb** [with obj.] turn (a ship or its helm) to starboard.
– ORIGIN Old English *stēorbord* 'rudder side' (see **STEER**[1], **BOARD**), because early Teutonic sailing vessels were steered with a paddle over the right side.

starboard watch ▶ **noun** see **WATCH** (in sense 2).

starburst ▶ **noun** a pattern of lines or rays radiating from a central object or source of light: [as modifier] *a starburst pattern.*
■ an explosion producing such an effect. ■ a camera lens attachment that produces a pattern of rays around the image of a source of light. ■ a period of intense activity in a galaxy involving the formation of stars.

starch ▶ **noun** [mass noun] an odourless, tasteless white substance occurring widely in plant tissue and obtained chiefly from cereals and potatoes. It is a polysaccharide which functions as a carbohydrate store and is an important constituent of the human diet.
■ food containing this substance. ■ powder or spray made from this substance and used before ironing to stiffen fabric or clothing. ■ figurative stiffness of manner or character: *the starch in her voice.*
▶ **verb** [with obj.] stiffen (fabric or clothing) with starch: [as adj. **starched**] *his immaculately starched shirt.*
■ N. Amer. informal (of a boxer) defeat (an opponent) by a knockout.
– PHRASES **take the starch out of someone** US deflate or humiliate someone.
– DERIVATIVES **starcher** noun.
– ORIGIN Old English (recorded only in the past participle *sterced* 'stiffened'), of Germanic origin; related to Dutch *sterken*, German *stärken* 'strengthen', also to **STARK**.

Star Chamber an English court of civil and criminal jurisdiction that developed in the late 15th century, trying especially those cases affecting the interests of the Crown. It was noted for its arbitrary and oppressive judgements and was abolished in 1641.

starch-reduced ▶ **adjective** (of food) containing less than the normal proportion of starch.

starchy ▶ **adjective** (**starchier**, **starchiest**) **1** (of food or diet) containing a lot of starch.
2 (of clothing) stiff with starch.
■ informal very stiff, formal, or prim in manner or character: *the manager is usually a bit starchy.*
– DERIVATIVES **starchily** adverb, **starchiness** noun.

star cloud ▶ **noun** a region where stars appear to be especially numerous and close together.

star connection ▶ **noun** see **STAR** (sense 2).

star-crossed ▶ **adjective** poetic/literary (of a person or a plan) thwarted by bad luck.

stardom ▶ **noun** [mass noun] the state or status of being a famous or exceptionally talented performer in the world of entertainment or sport.

stardust ▶ **noun** [mass noun] (especially in the context of success in the world of entertainment or sport) a magical or charismatic quality or feeling: *he slipped past four defenders as though stardust had been sprinkled in his boots.*

stare ▶ **verb** [no obj.] look fixedly or vacantly at someone or something with one's eyes wide open: *he stared at her in amazement* | *Robyn sat staring into space, her mind numb.*
■ (of a person's eyes) be wide open, with a fixed or vacant expression: *her grey eyes stared back at him.* ■ [no obj., with adverbial of direction] (of a thing) be unpleasantly prominent or striking: *the obituaries stared out at us.* ■ [with obj.] (**stare someone into**) reduce someone to (a specified condition) by looking fixedly at them: *Sandra stared him into silence.*
▶ **noun** a long fixed or vacant look: *she gave him a cold stare.*
– PHRASES **be staring something in the face** be on the verge of defeat, death, or another unpleasant fate: *Everton were staring defeat in the face.* **stare someone in the eye** (or **face**) look fixedly or boldly at someone. **stare someone in the face** be glaringly apparent or obvious: *the answer had been staring him in the face.*
– DERIVATIVES **starer** noun.
– ORIGIN Old English *starian*, of Germanic origin, from a base meaning 'be rigid'.
▶ **stare someone out** (or **down**) look fixedly at someone until they feel forced to lower their eyes or turn away.

stare decisis /ˌstɛːrɪ dɪˈsʌɪzɪs, ˌstɑːreɪ dɪˈsiːsɪs/ ▶ **noun** [mass noun] Law the legal principle of determining points in litigation according to precedent.
– ORIGIN Latin, literally 'stand by things decided'.

starfish ▶ **noun** (pl. same or **-fishes**) a marine echinoderm with five or more radiating arms. The undersides of the arms bear tube feet for locomotion and, in predatory species, for opening the shells of molluscs.
• Class Asteroidea.

starflower ▶ **noun** a plant with starlike flowers, in particular:
• a small North American woodland plant (*Trientalis borealis*, family Primulaceae). • a star of Bethlehem.

starfruit ▶ **noun 1** another term for **CARAMBOLA**.
2 a small European plant with tiny white flowers and six-pointed star-shaped fruit, living in or close to shallow fresh water.
• *Damasonium alisma*, family Alismataceae.

stargazer ▶ **noun 1** informal an astronomer or astrologer.
2 Austral. informal a horse that turns its head when galloping.
3 a fish of warm seas that normally lies buried in the sand with only its eyes, which are on top of the head, protruding:
• a widely distributed fish that has electric organs (family Uranoscopidae: several genera). • (**sand stargazer**) a western Atlantic fish (family Dactyloscopidae: several genera).
– DERIVATIVES **stargaze** verb.

stargazy pie /ˈstɑːɡeɪzi/ ▶ **noun** [mass noun] a kind of fish pie traditionally made in Cornwall, with the heads of the fish appearing through the crust.

stark ▶ **adjective 1** severe or bare in appearance or outline: *the ridge formed a stark silhouette against the sky.*
■ unpleasantly or sharply clear; impossible to avoid: *his position is **in stark contrast to** that of Curran* | *the **stark reality** of life for deprived minorities.*
2 [attrib.] complete; sheer: *he came running back in stark terror.*
■ rare completely naked.
3 archaic or poetic/literary stiff, rigid, or incapable of movement: *a human body lying stiff and stark by the stream.*
■ physically strong or powerful: *the dragoons were stark fellows.*
– PHRASES **stark naked** completely naked. **stark raving** (or **staring**) **mad** informal completely crazy.
– DERIVATIVES **starkly** adverb [as submodifier] *the reality is starkly different*, **starkness** noun.
– ORIGIN Old English *stearc* 'unyielding, severe', of Germanic origin; related to Dutch *sterk* and German *stark* 'strong'.

Stark effect ▶ **noun** [mass noun] Physics the splitting of a spectrum line into several components by the application of an electric field.
– ORIGIN early 20th cent.: named after Johannes Stark (1874–1957), German physicist.

starkers ▶ **adjective** [predic.] informal, chiefly Brit. completely naked.

starlet ▶ **noun 1** informal a young actress with aspirations to become a star: *a Hollywood starlet.*
■ a promising young sports player.
2 another term for **CUSHION STAR**.

starlight ▶ **noun** [mass noun] the light that comes from the stars.

Starling, Ernest Henry (1866–1927), English physiologist and founder of the science of endocrinology. He demonstrated the existence of peristalsis, and coined the term *hormone* for the substance secreted by the pancreas which stimulates the secretion of digestive juices.

starling[1] ▶ **noun** a gregarious Old World songbird with a straight bill, typically with dark lustrous or iridescent plumage but sometimes brightly coloured.
• Family Sturnidae (the **starling family**): many genera and numerous species, in particular the speckled **common** (or **European**) **starling** (*Sturnus vulgaris*), widely introduced elsewhere. The starling family also includes the mynahs, grackles, and (usually) the oxpeckers.
– ORIGIN Old English *stærlinc*, from *stær* 'starling' (of Germanic origin) + **-LING**.

S

starling[2] ▶ **noun** a wooden pile erected with others around or just upstream of a bridge or pier to protect it from the current or floating objects.
– ORIGIN late 17th cent.: perhaps a corruption of dialect *staddling* 'staddle'.

starlit ▶ **adjective** lit or made brighter by stars: *a clear starlit night.*

star network ▶ **noun** see **STAR** (in sense 2).

star-nosed mole ▶ **noun** a mole with a number of fleshy radiating tentacles around its nostrils, native to north-eastern North America.
● *Condylura cristata*, family Talpidae.

star of Bethlehem ▶ **noun** a plant of the lily family with star-shaped flowers which typically have green stripes on the outer surface, found in temperate regions of the Old World.
● Genera *Ornithogalum* and *Gagea*, family Liliaceae: several species, including the white-flowered *O. umbellatum* and the yellow-flowered *G. luteum*.

Star of David ▶ **noun** a six-pointed figure consisting of two interlaced equilateral triangles, used as a Jewish and Israeli symbol.

Starr, Ringo (b.1940), English rock and pop drummer; born *Richard Starkey*. He replaced Pete Best in the Beatles in 1962.

star route ▶ **noun** US a postal delivery route served by a private contractor.

star ruby ▶ **noun** a cabochon ruby reflecting an opalescent starlike image owing to its regular internal structure.

starry ▶ **adjective** (**starrier**, **starriest**) **1** full of or lit by stars: *a starry sky.*
■resembling a star in brightness or shape: *tiny white starry flowers.*
2 informal of, relating to, or characteristic of stars in the world of entertainment: *the series had the benefit of a starry cast.*
– DERIVATIVES **starrily** adverb, **starriness** noun.

starry-eyed ▶ **adjective** naively enthusiastic or idealistic; failing to recognize the practical realities of a situation.

Stars and Bars ▶ **plural noun** [treated as sing.] historical the flag of the Confederate States.

Stars and Stripes ▶ **plural noun** [treated as sing.] the national flag of the US.

star sapphire ▶ **noun** a cabochon sapphire that reflects a starlike image resulting from its regular internal structure.

star shell ▶ **noun** an explosive projectile designed to burst in the air and light up an enemy's position.

starship ▶ **noun** (in science fiction) a large manned spaceship used for interstellar travel.

star sign ▶ **noun** a sign of the zodiac.

star-spangled ▶ **adjective** poetic/literary covered, glittering, or decorated with stars: *the star-spangled horizon.*
■figurative glitteringly successful: *a star-spangled career.* ■ used humorously with reference to the American national flag and a perceived American identity: *star-spangled decency.*

Star-spangled Banner a song written in 1814 with words composed by Francis Scott Key (1779–1843) and a tune adapted from that of a popular English drinking song, *To Anacreon in Heaven*. It was officially adopted as the US national anthem in 1931.

star stream ▶ **noun** Astronomy a systematic drift of stars in the same general direction within a galaxy.

star-struck ▶ **adjective** fascinated or greatly impressed by famous people, especially those connected with the cinema or the theatre: *I was a star-struck cinema-goer.*

star-studded ▶ **adjective** **1** (of the night sky) filled with stars.
2 informal featuring a number of famous people, especially actors or sports players: *a star-studded cast.*

START ▶ **abbreviation for** Strategic Arms Reduction Talks.

start ▶ **verb** **1** [no obj.] come into being; begin or be reckoned from a particular point in time or space: *the season starts in September | we ate before the film started | below Roaring Springs the real desert starts.*
■[with infinitive or present participle] embark on a continuing action or a new venture: *I started to chat to him | we plan to start building in the autumn.* ■ use a particular point, action, or circumstance as an opening for a course of action: *the teacher can* **start by** *capitalizing on children's curiosity | I shall* **start with** *the case you mention first.* ■ [no obj., with adverbial of direction] begin to move or travel: *we started out into the snow | he started for the door.* ■ [with obj.] begin to attend (an educational establishment) or engage in (an occupation, especially a profession): *she will start school today | he started work at a travel agent.* ■ begin one's working life: *he started as a mess orderly | he* **started off** *as doctor in the house.* ■ [with obj.] begin to live through (a period distinguished by a specified characteristic): *they started their married life.* ■ cost at least a specified amount: *fees* **start at** *around £300.*
2 [with obj.] cause (an event or process) to happen: *two men started the blaze which caused the explosion | those women started all the trouble.*
■bring (a project or an institution) into being; cause to take effect or begin to work or operate: *I'm starting a campaign to get the law changed.* ■ cause (a machine) to begin to work: *we had trouble starting the car | he* **starts up** *his van.* ■ [no obj.] (of a machine or device) begin operating or being used: *the noise of a lorry* **starting up** *| there was a moment of silence before the organ started.* ■ cause or enable (someone or something) to begin doing or pursuing something: *his father* **started** *him* **off** *in business |* [with obj. and present participle] *what he said started me thinking.* ■ give a signal to (competitors) to start in a race.
3 [no obj.] give a small jump or make a sudden jerking movement from surprise or alarm: *'Oh my!' she said, starting.*
■[no obj., with adverbial of direction] poetic/literary move or appear suddenly: *she had seen Meg start suddenly from a thicket.* ■ (of eyes) bulge so as to appear to burst out of their sockets: *his eyes* **started out of** *his head like a hare's.* ■ be displaced or displace by pressure or shrinkage: [no obj.] *the mortar in the joints had started.* ■ [with obj.] rouse (game) from its lair.
▶**noun** [usu. in sing.] **1** the point in time or space at which something has its origin; the beginning of something: *he takes over as chief executive at the start of next year | the event was a shambles from start to finish | his bicycle was found close to the start of a forest trail.*
■the point or moment at which a race begins. ■ an act of beginning to do or deal with something: *I can* **make a start on** *cleaning up | an early start enabled us to avoid the traffic.* ■ used to indicate that a useful initial contribution has been made but that more remains to be done: *if he would tell her who had put him up to it, it would be a start.* ■a person's position or circumstances at the beginning of their life, especially a position of advantage: *she's anxious to give her baby the best* **start in life**. ■ an advantage consisting in having set out in a race or on journey earlier than one's rivals or opponents: *he would have a ninety-minute* **start on** *them.*
2 a sudden movement of surprise or alarm: *she awoke* **with a start** *| the woman* **gave** *a nervous* **start**.
■dated a surprising occurrence: *you hear of some rum starts there.*
– PHRASES **don't start** (or **don't you start**) informal used to tell someone not to grumble or criticize: *don't start—I do my fair share.* **for a start** informal used to introduce or emphasize the first or most important of a number of considerations: *this side are at an advantage—for a start, there are more of them.* **get the start of** dated gain an advantage over. **start a family** conceive one's first child. **start a hare** see **HARE**. **start something** informal cause trouble. **to start with** at the beginning of a series of events or period of time: *she wasn't very keen on the idea to start with.* ■ as the first thing to be taken into account: *to start with, I was feeling down.*
– ORIGIN Old English *styrtan* 'to caper, leap', of Germanic origin; related to Dutch *storten* 'push' and German *stürzen* 'fall headlong, fling'. From the sense 'sudden movement' arose the sense 'initiation of movement, setting out on a journey' and hence 'beginning (of a process, etc.)'.
▶**start in** informal begin doing something, especially talking: *people groan when she starts in about her acting ambitions.* ■ (**start in on**) N. Amer. begin to do or deal with: *she started in on her face.* ■ (**start in on**) N. Amer. attack verbally; begin to criticize.
start off (or **start someone/thing off**) begin (or cause someone or something to begin) working, operating, or dealing with something: *treatment should start off with attention to diet | what started you off on this search?* ■ (**start off**) begin a meal: *she* **started off with** *porridge.*
start on 1 begin to work on or deal with: *I'm starting on a new book.* **2** informal begin to talk to someone, especially in a critical or hostile way: *she started on about my not having proper furniture.*
start over N. Amer. make a new beginning: *could you face going back to school and starting over?*
start out (or **up**) embark on a venture or undertaking, especially a commercial one: *the company will start out with a hundred employees.*

starter ▶ **noun** a person or thing that starts an event, activity, or process, in particular:
■chiefly Brit. the first course of a meal, especially one with three or more courses. ■ an automatic device for starting a machine, especially the engine of a vehicle. ■ a person who gives the signal for the start of a race. ■ [with adj.] a horse, competitor, or player taking part in a race or game at the start: *the trainer has confirmed Cool Ground as a definite starter.* ■ Baseball the pitcher who starts the game. ■ [with adj.] a person or thing that starts in a specified way, especially with reference to time or speed: *he was a* **late starter** *in photography | I'm just a* **slow starter**. ■ a topic, question, or other item with which to start a group discussion or course of study: *material to act as a* **starter for** *discussion.* ■ (**a starter**) informal a plan or idea that has a chance of succeeding and is therefore worthy of consideration: *she began to think that she must move away, yet she knew that it was not even a starter.* ■ (also **starter culture**) a bacterial culture used to initiate souring in making yogurt, cheese, or butter. ■ a preparation of chemicals to initiate the breakdown of vegetable matter in making compost. ■ a railway signal controlling the starting of trains from a station or other location.
– PHRASES **for starters** informal first of all; to start with. **under starter's orders** (of horses, runners, or other competitors) ready to start a race and just waiting for the signal.

starter home ▶ **noun** a compact house or flat specifically designed and built to meet the requirements of young people buying their first home.

starting block ▶ **noun** (usu. **starting blocks**) a shaped rigid block for bracing the feet of a runner at the start of a race.

starting gate ▶ **noun** (usu. **the starting gate**) a restraining structure incorporating a barrier that is raised at the start of a race, especially in horse racing and skiing, to ensure a simultaneous start.

starting handle ▶ **noun** chiefly historical a crank for starting the engine of a car.

starting pistol ▶ **noun** a pistol used to give the signal for the start of a race.

starting point ▶ **noun** a place that marks the beginning of a journey.
■a basis for or introduction to study, discussion, or further development.

starting post ▶ **noun** a post or other marker indicating the place at which a race is to start.

starting price ▶ **noun** the final odds at the start of a horse race.

starting stall ▶ **noun** see **STALL** (sense 2).

startle ▶ **verb** [with obj.] cause (a person or animal) to feel sudden shock or alarm: *a sudden sound in the doorway startled her |* [with infinitive] *he was startled to see a column of smoke.*
– DERIVATIVES **startler** noun.
– ORIGIN Old English *steartlian* 'kick, struggle', from the base of **START**. The early sense gave rise to 'move quickly, caper' (typically said of cattle), whence '(cause to) react with fear' (late 16th cent.).

startling ▶ **adjective** very surprising, astonishing, or remarkable: *he bore a startling likeness to their father | she had startling blue eyes.*
– DERIVATIVES **startlingly** adverb [as submodifier] *a startlingly good memory.*

Start Point a headland on the south coast of Devon, to the south-west of Torquay.

start-up ▶ **noun** [mass noun] the action or process of setting something in motion: *the start-up of marketing in Europe |* [as modifier] *start-up costs.*
■[count noun] a newly established business: *problems facing start-ups and small firms in rural areas.*

star turn ▶ **noun** the person or act that gives the most heralded or impressive performance in a programme.

starve ▶ **verb** [no obj.] **1** (of a person or animal) suffer severely or die from hunger: *she left her animals to starve | seven million* **starved to death** *|* [as adj. **starving**] *the world's starving children.*
■[with obj.] cause (a person or animal) to suffer severely or die from hunger: *for a while she had considered starving herself.* ■ (**be starving** or **starved**) informal feel very hungry: *I don't know about you, but I'm starving.*

S

■ (**starve someone out** or **into**) force someone out of a place or into a specified state by stopping supplies of food: *the Royalists were starved out after eleven days | German U-boats hoping to starve Britain into submission.* ■ [with obj.] (usu. **be starved of** or US **for**) deprive of something necessary: *the arts are being starved of funds.*

2 archaic be freezing cold: *pull down that window for we are perfectly starving here.*

– DERIVATIVES **starvation** noun.

– ORIGIN Old English *steorfan* 'to die', of Germanic origin, probably from a base meaning 'be rigid' (compare with **STARE**); related to Dutch *sterven* and German *sterben*.

starveling /ˈstɑːvlɪŋ/ archaic ▶**noun** an under-nourished or emaciated person or animal.
▶**adjective** (of a person or animal) lacking enough food; emaciated: *a starveling child.*

Star Wars popular name for **STRATEGIC DEFENSE INITIATIVE**.

starwort ▶**noun** any of a number of plants with starlike flowers or leaves.
• *Stellaria* (family Caryophyllaceae), *Callitriche* (family Callitrichaceae), and other genera: several species, including the greater stitchwort.

stash[1] informal ▶**verb** [with obj. and adverbial of place] store (something) safely and secretly in a specified place: *their wealth had been* **stashed away** *in Swiss banks.*
▶**noun 1** a secret store of something: *the man grudgingly handed over* **a stash of** *notes.*
■ a quantity of an illegal drug, especially one kept for personal use: *one prisoner tried to swallow his stash.*
2 dated a hiding place or hideout.
– ORIGIN late 18th cent.: of unknown origin.

stash[2] ▶**noun** US informal a moustache.
– ORIGIN 1940s: shortened form.

Stasi /ˈstɑːzi, ˈʃtɑː-/ the internal security force of the former German Democratic Republic, abolished in 1989.
– ORIGIN German, from *Sta(ats)si(cherheitsdienst)* 'state security service'.

stasis /ˈsteɪsɪs, ˈsta-/ ▶**noun** [mass noun] formal or technical a period or state of inactivity or equilibrium.
■ Medicine a stoppage of flow of a body fluid.
– ORIGIN mid 18th cent.: modern Latin, from Greek, literally 'standing, stoppage', from *sta-* base of *histanai* 'to stand'.

-stasis ▶**combining form** (pl. **-stases**) Physiology slowing down; stopping: *haemostasis.*
– DERIVATIVES **-static** combining form in corresponding adjectives.
– ORIGIN from Greek *stasis* 'standing, stoppage'.

stat[1] /stat/ informal ▶**abbreviation for** ■ photostat. ■ statistic. ■ statistics: [as modifier] *a stat sheet.* ■ thermostat.

stat[2] /stat/ ▶**adverb** (in a medical direction or prescription) immediately.
– ORIGIN late 19th cent.: abbreviation of Latin *statim.*

-stat ▶**combining form** denoting instruments, substances, etc. maintaining a controlled state: *thermostat | haemostat.*
– ORIGIN partly from *(helio)stat*, partly a back-formation from **STATIC**.

statant /ˈsteɪtənt/ ▶**adjective** [usu. postpositive] Heraldry (of an animal) standing with all four paws on the ground.
– ORIGIN late 15th cent.: formed irregularly from Latin *stat-* 'fixed, stationary' (from the verb *stare* 'to stand')' + **-ANT**.

state ▶**noun 1** the particular condition that someone or something is in at a specific time: *the state of the company's finances | we're worried about her* **state of mind**.
■ a physical condition as regards internal or molecular form or structure: *water in a liquid state.* ■ [in sing.] (**a state**) informal an agitated or anxious condition: *don't* **get into a state**. ■ [in sing.] informal a dirty or untidy condition: *look at the state of you—what a mess!* ■ Physics short for **QUANTUM STATE**.
2 a nation or territory considered as an organized political community under one government: *the state of Israel.*
■ an organized political community or area forming part of a federal republic: *the German state of Bavaria.* ■ (**the States**) informal term for **UNITED STATES**.
3 the civil government of a country: *services provided by the state* | [in combination] *state-owned companies* | [mass noun] *a minister engaged in* **matters of state**.
■ (**the States**) the legislative body in Jersey, Guernsey, and Alderney.
4 [mass noun] pomp and ceremony associated with monarchy or high levels of government: *he was buried* **in state**.
5 [usu. with adj.] an impression taken from an etched or engraved plate at a particular stage.
■ a particular printed version of the first edition of a book, distinguished from others by pre-publication changes.
▶**adjective** [attrib.] **1** of, provided by, or concerned with the civil government of a country: *the future of state education | a state secret.*
2 used or done on ceremonial occasions; involving the ceremony associated with a head of state: *the Queen pays a state visit to Malaysia on Saturday.*
▶**verb 1** [reporting verb] express something definitely or clearly in speech or writing: [with clause] *the report stated that more than 51 per cent of voters failed to participate* | [with direct speech] *'Money hasn't changed me,' she stated firmly* | [with obj.] *people will be invited to state their views.*
■ [with obj.] chiefly Law specify the facts of (a case) for consideration: *judges must give both sides an equal opportunity to state their case.*
2 [with obj.] Music present or introduce (a theme or melody) in a composition.
– PHRASES **state of affairs** (or **things**) a situation or set of circumstances: *the survey revealed a sorry state of affairs in schools.* **state of the art** the most recent stage in the development of a product, incorporating the newest ideas and the most up-to-date features. ■ [as modifier] incorporating the newest ideas and the most up-to-date features: *a new state-of-the-art hospital.* **state of emergency** a situation of national danger or disaster in which a government suspends normal constitutional procedures in order to regain control: *the government has declared a state of emergency.* **state of grace** a condition of being free from sin. **state of life** (in religious contexts) a person's occupation, calling, or status. **the state of play** Brit. the current situation in an ongoing process, especially one involving opposing or competing parties. ■ the score at a particular time in a cricket or football match. **state of war** a situation when war has been declared or is in progress.
– DERIVATIVES **statable** adjective.
– ORIGIN Middle English (as a noun): partly a shortening of **ESTATE**, partly from Latin *status* 'manner of standing, condition' (see **STATUS**). The current verb senses date from the mid 17th cent.

state capitalism ▶**noun** [mass noun] a political system in which the state has control of production and the use of capital.

statecraft ▶**noun** [mass noun] the skilful management of state affairs; statesmanship: *issues of statecraft require great deliberation.*

State Department (in the US) the department in the government dealing with foreign affairs.

State Enrolled Nurse (abbrev.: **SEN**) ▶**noun** (in the UK) a nurse enrolled on a state register and having a qualification lower than that of a State Registered Nurse.

state function ▶**noun** Physics a quantity in thermodynamics, such as entropy or enthalpy, that has a unique value for each given state of a system.

statehood ▶**noun** [mass noun] the status of being a recognized independent nation: *the Jewish struggle for statehood.*

state house ▶**noun 1** (in the US) the building where the legislature of a state meets.
2 NZ a private house that is owned and let by the government.

stateless ▶**adjective** (of a person) not recognized as a citizen of any country.
– DERIVATIVES **statelessness** noun.

statelet ▶**noun** a small state, especially one that is closely affiliated to or has emerged from the break-up of a larger state.

stately ▶**adjective** (**statelier**, **stateliest**) having a dignified, unhurried, and rather grand manner; majestic in manner and appearance: *a stately procession | his tall and stately wife.*
– DERIVATIVES **stateliness** noun.

stately home ▶**noun** Brit. a large and fine house that is occupied or was formerly occupied by an aristocratic family.

state machine ▶**noun** Electronics a device which can be in one of a set number of stable conditions depending on its previous condition and on the present values of its inputs.

statement ▶**noun** a definite or clear expression of something in speech or writing: *do you agree with this statement? | this is correct as a* **statement of fact** | [mass noun] *Minton's love of clear statement.*
■ an official account of facts, views, or plans, especially one for release to the media: *the ministers issued a joint statement calling for negotiations.* ■ a formal account of events given by a witness, defendant, or other party to the police or in a court of law: *she* **made a statement** *to the police.* ■ a document setting out items of debit and credit between a bank or other organization and a customer. ■ (in the UK) an official assessment made by a local education authority concerning a child's special educational needs.
▶**verb** [with obj.] officially assess (a child) as having special educational needs.

statement of claim ▶**noun** English Law a pleading served by the plaintiff in a High Court action containing the allegations made against the defendant and the relief sought by the plaintiff. See also **CLAIM** (sense 1).

Staten Island /ˈstat(ə)n/ an island borough of New York City, in the south-west of the city; pop. 378,980 (1990).
– ORIGIN named by early Dutch settlers after the *Staten* or States General of the Netherlands.

State of the Union message (also **State of the Union address**) ▶**noun** a yearly address delivered in January by the President of the US to Congress, giving the administration's view of the state of the nation and plans for legislation.

state pension ▶**noun** see **PENSION**[1].

state prisoner ▶**noun** another term for **PRISONER OF STATE**.

stater /ˈsteɪtə/ ▶**noun** historical an ancient Greek gold or silver coin.
– ORIGIN via late Latin from Greek *statēr*, from a base meaning 'weigh'.

State Registered Nurse (abbrev.: **SRN**) ▶**noun** (in the UK) a nurse enrolled on a state register and more highly qualified than a State Enrolled Nurse.

stateroom /ˈsteɪtruːm, -rʊm/ ▶**noun** a large room in a palace or public building, for use on formal occasions.
■ a captain's or superior officer's room on a ship. ■ a private compartment on a ship. ■ US a private compartment on a train.

state's attorney ▶**noun** US a lawyer representing a state in court.

state school ▶**noun** Brit. a school that is funded and controlled by the state and for which no fees are charged.

state's evidence ▶**noun** [mass noun] US Law evidence for the prosecution given by a participant in or accomplice to the crime being tried.

States General (also **Estates General**) ▶**noun** historical the legislative body in the Netherlands from the 15th to 18th centuries, and in France until 1789, representing the three estates of the realm (i.e. the clergy, the nobility, and the commons).

stateside /ˈsteɪtsʌɪd/ ▶**adjective** & **adverb** informal, chiefly US of, in, or towards the US (used in reference to the US from elsewhere or from the geographically separate states of Alaska and Hawaii): [as adj.] *stateside police departments* | [as adv.] *they were headed stateside.*

statesman /ˈsteɪtsmən/ ▶**noun** (pl. **-men**) a skilled, experienced, and respected political leader or figure.
– DERIVATIVES **statesmanlike** adjective, **statesmanship** noun.
– ORIGIN late 16th cent.: from *state's man*, translating French *homme d'état.*

state socialism ▶**noun** [mass noun] a political system in which the state has control of industries and services.

states' rights ▶**plural noun** (in the US) the rights and powers held by individual states rather than by the federal government.

stateswoman ▶**noun** (pl. **-women**) a skilled, experienced, and respected female political leader.

state trial ▶**noun** a trial in which prosecution is made by the state.

state university ▶**noun** (in the US) a university managed by the public authorities of a particular state.

S

state vector ▶ **noun** Physics a vector in a space whose dimensions correspond to all the independent wave functions of a system, the instantaneous value of the vector conveying all possible information about the state of the system at that instant.

statewide ▶ **adjective** & **adverb** extending throughout a particular state in the US: [as adj.] *a statewide health system.*

static /ˈstatɪk/ ▶ **adjective 1** lacking in movement, action, or change, especially in a way viewed as undesirable or uninteresting: *demand has grown in what was a fairly static market | the whole ballet appeared too static.*
■ Computing (of a process or variable) not able to be changed during a set period, for example while a program is running.
2 Physics concerned with bodies at rest or forces in equilibrium. Often contrasted with **DYNAMIC**.
■ (of an electric charge) having gathered on or in an object that cannot conduct a current. ■ acting as weight but not moving. ■ of statics.
3 Computing (of a memory or store) not needing to be periodically refreshed by an applied voltage.
▶ **noun** [mass noun] crackling or hissing noises on a telephone, radio, or other telecommunication system.
■ short for **STATIC ELECTRICITY**. ■ informal, chiefly US angry or critical talk or behaviour: *the reception was going sour, breaking up into static.*
– DERIVATIVES **statically** adverb.
– ORIGIN late 16th cent. (denoting the science of weight and its effects): via modern Latin from Greek *statikē (tekhnē)* 'science of weighing'; the adjective from modern Latin *staticus*, from Greek *statikos* 'causing to stand', from the verb *histanai*. Sense 1 of the adjective dates from the mid 19th cent.

static cling ▶ **noun** [mass noun] chiefly N. Amer. the adhering of a garment to the wearer's body or to another garment, caused by a build-up of static electricity.

statice /ˈstatɪsi/ ▶ **noun** another term for **SEA LAVENDER**.
– ORIGIN mid 18th cent.: from modern Latin *statice* (former genus name), based on Greek, feminine of *statikos* 'causing to stand still' (with reference to medicinal use of the plant to staunch blood).

static electricity ▶ **noun** [mass noun] a stationary electric charge, typically produced by friction, which causes sparks or crackling or the attraction of dust or hair.

static line ▶ **noun** a length of cord used instead of a rip cord for opening a parachute, attached at one end to the aircraft and temporarily snapped to the parachute at the other.

static pressure ▶ **noun** [mass noun] Physics the pressure of a fluid on a body when the latter is at rest relative to it.

statics ▶ **plural noun 1** [usu. treated as sing.] the branch of mechanics concerned with bodies at rest and forces in equilibrium. Compare with **DYNAMICS** (sense 1).
2 another term for **STATIC**.

station ▶ **noun 1** a place where passenger trains stop on a railway line, typically with platforms and buildings: *a railway station* | [in names] *Paddington Station.*
2 [usu. with modifier] a place or building where a specified activity or service is based: *a research station in the rainforest | coastal radar stations.*
■ a small military base, especially of a specified kind: *a naval station.* ■ N. Amer. a subsidiary post office. ■ Austral./NZ a large sheep or cattle farm.
3 [with modifier] a company involved in broadcasting of a specified kind: *a radio station.*
4 the place where someone or something stands or is placed on military or other duty: *the lookout resumed his station in the bow.*
■ [count noun] dated one's social rank or position: *Karen was getting ideas* **above her station**.
5 Botany a particular site at which an interesting or rare plant grows.
6 short for **STATION OF THE CROSS**.
▶ **verb** [with obj. and adverbial of place] put in or assign to a specified place for a particular purpose, especially a military one: *troops* **were stationed in** *the town | a young girl had* **stationed herself** *by the door.*
– ORIGIN Middle English (as a noun): via Old French from Latin *statio(n-)*, from *stare* 'to stand'. Early use referred generally to 'position', especially 'position in life, status', and specifically, in ecclesiastical use, to 'a holy place of pilgrimage (visited as one of a succession)'. The verb dates from the late 16th cent.

stationary ▶ **adjective** not moving or not intended to be moved: *a car collided with a stationary vehicle.*
■ Astronomy (of a planet) having no apparent motion in longitude. ■ not changing in quantity or condition: *a stationary population.*
– ORIGIN late Middle English: from Latin *stationarius* (originally in the sense 'belonging to a military station'), from *statio(n-)* 'standing' (see **STATION**).

stationary bicycle (also **stationary bike**) ▶ **noun** an exercise bike.

stationary engine ▶ **noun** an engine that remains in a fixed position, especially one that drives generators or other machinery in a building.

stationary point ▶ **noun** Mathematics a point on a curve where the gradient is zero.

stationary state ▶ **noun** an unvarying condition in a physical process.

stationary wave ▶ **noun** Physics another term for **STANDING WAVE**.

station bill ▶ **noun** a list showing the prescribed stations of a ship's crew.

station break ▶ **noun** N. Amer. a pause between broadcast programmes for an announcement of the identity of the station transmitting them.

stationer ▶ **noun** a person or shop selling paper, pens, and other writing and office materials.
– ORIGIN Middle English (in the sense 'bookseller'): from medieval Latin *stationarius* 'tradesman (at a fixed location, i.e. not itinerant)'. Compare with **STATIONARY**.

stationery ▶ **noun** [mass noun] writing and other office materials.

Stationery Office ▶ **noun** (in the UK) a government department that publishes governmental publications and provides stationery for government offices.

station hand ▶ **noun** Austral. a worker on a large sheep or cattle farm.

station house ▶ **noun** US a police or fire station.

station-keeping ▶ **noun** [mass noun] the maintenance of a ship's proper position relative to others in a fleet.

stationmaster ▶ **noun** an official in charge of a railway station.

Station of the Cross ▶ **noun** (usu. **Stations of the Cross**) one of a series of fourteen pictures or carvings representing successive incidents during Jesus' progress from Pilate's house to his crucifixion at Calvary, before which devotions are performed in some Churches.

station pointer ▶ **noun** a navigational instrument that fixes a ship's position on a chart by determining its place relative to two landmarks or conspicuous objects at sea.

station sergeant ▶ **noun** Brit. a sergeant in charge of a police station.

station-sow ▶ **verb** [with obj.] plant (seeds) singly or in groups at set intervals along a row or drill.

station wagon ▶ **noun** chiefly US an estate car.

statism /ˈsteɪtɪz(ə)m/ ▶ **noun** [mass noun] a political system in which the state has substantial centralized control over social and economic affairs: *the rise of authoritarian statism.*
– DERIVATIVES **statist** noun & adjective.

statistic ▶ **noun** a fact or piece of data obtained from a study of a large quantity of numerical data: *the statistics show that the crime rate has increased.*
■ an event or person regarded as no more than such a piece of data (used to suggest an inappropriately impersonal approach): *he was just another statistic.*
▶ **adjective** another term for **STATISTICAL**.
– ORIGIN late 18th cent.: from German *statistisch* (adjective), *Statistik* (noun).

statistical ▶ **adjective** of or relating to the use of statistics: *a statistical comparison.*
– DERIVATIVES **statistically** adverb [sentence adverb] *these differences were not statistically significant.*

statistical inference ▶ **noun** [mass noun] the theory, methods, and practice of forming judgements about the parameters of a population and the reliability of statistical relationships, typically on the basis of random sampling.

statistical linguistics ▶ **plural noun** [treated as sing.] the application of statistical techniques to language analysis, typically using a large machine-readable corpus, in order to discover general principles of linguistic behaviour, genre difference, etc.

statistical mechanics ▶ **plural noun** [treated as sing.] the description of physical phenomena in terms of a statistical treatment of the behaviour of large numbers of atoms or molecules, especially as regards the distribution of energy among them.

statistical physics ▶ **plural noun** [treated as sing.] a branch of physics concerned with large numbers of particles to which statistics can be applied.

statistical significance ▶ **noun** see **SIGNIFICANCE**.

statistical tables ▶ **plural noun** the values of the cumulative distribution functions, probability functions, or probability density functions of certain common distributions presented as reference tables for different values of their parameters.

statistician ▶ **noun** an expert in the preparation and analysis of statistics.

statistics ▶ **plural noun** [treated as sing.] the practice or science of collecting and analysing numerical data in large quantities, especially for the purpose of inferring proportions in a whole from those in a representative sample.

Statius /ˈsteɪʃəs/, Publius Papinius (*c.*45–96 AD), Roman poet. He is best known for the *Silvae*, a miscellany of poems addressed to friends, and the *Thebais*, an epic concerning the bloody quarrel between the sons of Oedipus.

stative /ˈsteɪtɪv/ Linguistics ▶ **adjective** (of a verb) expressing a state or condition rather than an activity or event, such as *be* or *know*, as opposed to *run* or *grow*. Contrasted with **DYNAMIC**.
▶ **noun** a stative verb.
– ORIGIN mid 17th cent.: from Latin *stativus*, from *stat-* 'stopped, standing', from the verb *stare*.

stato- ▶ **combining form** relating to statics: *statocyst.*
– ORIGIN from Greek *statos* 'standing'.

statoblast /ˈstatə(ʊ)blast/ ▶ **noun** Zoology (in bryozoans) a resistant reproductive body produced asexually.

statocyst ▶ **noun** Zoology a small organ of balance and orientation in some aquatic invertebrates, consisting of a sensory vesicle or cell containing statoliths. Also called **OTOCYST**.

statolith ▶ **noun** Zoology a calcareous particle in the statocysts of invertebrates, which stimulates sensory receptors in response to gravity, so enabling balance and orientation.
■ another term for **OTOLITH**.

stator /ˈsteɪtə/ ▶ **noun** the stationary portion of an electric generator or motor, especially of an induction motor.
■ a row of small stationary aerofoils fixed to the casing of an axial-flow turbine, positioned between the rotors.
– ORIGIN late 19th cent.: from **STATIONARY**, on the pattern of *rotor*.

statoscope ▶ **noun** a form of aneroid barometer for measuring minute variations of pressure, used especially to indicate the altitude of an aircraft.
– ORIGIN early 20th cent.: from Greek *statos* 'standing' + **-SCOPE**.

stats ▶ **plural noun** informal short for **STATISTICS**.

statuary /ˈstatjʊəri, -tʃʊə-/ ▶ **noun** [mass noun] sculpture consisting of statues; statues regarded collectively: *fragments of broken statuary | classical statuary.*
■ archaic the art or practice of making statues. ■ [count noun] archaic a sculptor.
– ORIGIN mid 16th cent.: from Latin *statuarius*, from *statua* (see **STATUE**).

statuary marble ▶ **noun** [mass noun] fine-grained white marble suitable for making statues.

statue /ˈstatjuː, -tʃuː/ ▶ **noun** a carved or cast figure of a person or animal, especially one that is life-size or larger.
– DERIVATIVES **statued** adjective.
– ORIGIN Middle English: from Old French, from Latin *statua*, from *stare* 'to stand'.

Statue of Liberty see **LIBERTY, STATUE OF**.

statuesque /ˌstatjʊˈɛsk, -tʃʊ-/ ▶ **adjective** (especially

of a woman) attractively tall and dignified: *her statuesque beauty.*
– DERIVATIVES **statuesquely** adverb, **statuesqueness** noun.
– ORIGIN late 18th cent.: from **STATUE**, on the pattern of *picturesque*.

statuette ▶ noun a small statue or figurine, especially one that is smaller than life-size.
– ORIGIN mid 19th cent.: from French, diminutive of *statue.*

stature ▶ noun [mass noun] a person's natural height: *a man of short stature* | *she was small in stature.*
■ importance or reputation gained by ability or achievement: *an architect of international stature.*
– DERIVATIVES **statured** adjective [in combination] *a short-statured fourteen-year-old.*
– ORIGIN Middle English: via Old French from Latin *statura*, from *stare* 'to stand'. The sense 'importance' dates from the mid 19th cent.

status ▶ noun **1** the relative social, professional, or other standing of someone or something: *an improvement in the status of women.*
■ [mass noun] high rank or social standing: *those who enjoy wealth and status.* ■ the official classification given to a person, country, or organization, determining their rights or responsibilities: *the duchy had been elevated to the status of a principality.*
2 the position of affairs at a particular time, especially in political or commercial contexts: *an update on the status of the bill.*
– ORIGIN late 18th cent. (as a legal term meaning 'legal standing'): from Latin, literally 'standing', from *stare* 'to stand'.

status asthmaticus /ˌsteɪtəs asˈmatɪkəs/ ▶ noun [mass noun] Medicine a severe condition in which asthma attacks follow one another without pause.
– ORIGIN modern Latin.

status bar ▶ noun Computing a horizontal bar, usually at the bottom of the screen or window, showing information about a document being edited or a program running.

status epilepticus /ˌɛpɪˈlɛptɪkəs/ ▶ noun [mass noun] Medicine a dangerous condition in which epileptic fits follow one another without recovery of consciousness between them.
– ORIGIN modern Latin.

status quo /ˈkwəʊ/ ▶ noun (usu. **the status quo**) the existing state of affairs, especially regarding social or political issues: *they have a vested interest in maintaining the status quo.*
– ORIGIN Latin, literally 'the state in which'.

status quo ante /kwəʊ ˈanti/ ▶ noun (usu. **the status quo ante**) the previously existing state of affairs.
– ORIGIN Latin, literally 'the state in which before'.

status symbol ▶ noun a possession that is taken to indicate a person's wealth or high social or professional status.

statute /ˈstatjuːt, -tʃuːt/ ▶ noun a written law passed by a legislative body: *the Act consolidated statutes dealing with non-fatal offences* | [mass noun] *immunities granted to trade unions* by statute.
■ a rule of an organization or institution: *the appointment will be subject to the statutes of the university.* ■ archaic (in biblical use) a law or decree made by a sovereign, or by God.
– ORIGIN Middle English: from Old French *statut*, from late Latin *statutum*, neuter past participle of Latin *statuere* 'set up' from *status* 'standing' (see **STATUS**).

statute-barred ▶ adjective English Law (especially of a debt claim) no longer legally enforceable owing to a prescribed period of limitation having lapsed.

statute book ▶ noun a book in which laws are written.
■ (**the statute book**) a nation's laws regarded collectively: *the bill failed to reach the statute book.*

statute law ▶ noun [mass noun] the body of principles and rules of law laid down in statutes. Compare with **COMMON LAW**, **CASE LAW**.

statute mile ▶ noun see **MILE**.

statute of limitations ▶ noun Law a statute prescribing a period of limitation for the bringing of actions of certain kinds.

statutes at large ▶ plural noun chiefly US a country's statutes in their original version, regardless of later modifications.

statutory /ˈstatjʊt(ə)ri, -tʃʊ-/ ▶ adjective required,

permitted, or enacted by statute: *statutory controls over prices.*
■ having come to be required or expected through being done or made regularly: *the statutory Christmas phone call to his mother.*
– DERIVATIVES **statutorily** adverb.

statutory declaration ▶ noun Law a prescribed declaration made under statutory authority before a justice of the peace, commissioner of oaths, or notary public.

statutory instrument ▶ noun Law a government or executive order of subordinate legislation.

statutory order ▶ noun Law former term for **STATUTORY INSTRUMENT**.

statutory rape ▶ noun [mass noun] US Law sexual intercourse with a minor.

statutory tenant ▶ noun Law a person who is legally entitled to remain in a property although their original tenancy has expired.

staunch¹ /stɔːn(t)ʃ/ ▶ adjective **1** very loyal and committed in attitude: *a staunch supporter of the anti-nuclear lobby* | *a staunch Catholic.*
2 (of a wall) of strong or firm construction.
■ (also **stanch**) archaic (of a ship) watertight.
– DERIVATIVES **staunchly** adverb [as submodifier] *a staunchly Royalist county*, **staunchness** noun.
– ORIGIN late Middle English (in the sense 'watertight'): from Old French *estanche*, feminine of *estanc*, from a Romance base meaning 'dried up, weary'. Sense 1 dates from the early 17th cent.

staunch² /stɔːn(t)ʃ, stɑːn(t)ʃ/ (chiefly US also **stanch**) ▶ verb [with obj.] stop or restrict (a flow of blood) from a wound: *he staunched the blood with whatever came to hand* | figurative *the company did nothing to stanch the tide of rumours.*
■ stop the flow of blood from (a wound).
– ORIGIN Middle English: from Old French *estanchier*, from the base of **STAUNCH¹**.

staurolite /ˈstɔːrəlʌɪt/ ▶ noun [mass noun] a brown glassy mineral that occurs as hexagonal prisms often twinned in the shape of a cross. It consists of a silicate of aluminium and iron.
– ORIGIN early 19th cent.: from Greek *stauros* 'cross' + **-LITE**.

Stavanger /stəˈvaŋə/ a seaport in SW Norway; pop. 98,180 (1991). It is an important centre servicing offshore oilfields in the North Sea.

stave ▶ noun **1** a vertical wooden post or plank in a building or other structure.
■ any of the lengths of wood fixed side by side to make a barrel, bucket, or other container. ■ a strong wooden stick or iron pole used as a weapon.
2 (also **staff**) Music a set of five parallel lines on any one or between any adjacent two of which a note is written to indicate its pitch.
3 a verse or stanza of a poem.
▶ verb [with obj.] **1** (past and past participle **staved** or **stove**) (**stave something in**) break something by forcing it inwards or piercing it roughly with a hole: *the door was staved in.*
2 (past and past participle **staved**) (**stave something off**) avert or delay something bad or dangerous: *a reassuring presence can stave off a panic attack.*
– ORIGIN Middle English: back-formation from **STAVES**. Current senses of the verb date from the early 17th cent.

stave church ▶ noun a church of a type built in Norway from the 11th to the 13th century, the walls of which were constructed of upright planks or staves.

stave rhyme ▶ noun [mass noun] alliteration, especially in old Germanic poetry.

stavesacre /ˈsteɪvˌzeɪkə/ ▶ noun a southern European larkspur whose seeds were formerly used as an insecticide.
● *Delphinium staphisagria*, family Ranunculaceae.
– ORIGIN late Middle English: via Latin from Greek *staphis agria* 'wild raisin'.

Stavropol /ˈstavrəpɒl, stavˈrɒp(ə)l/ **1** a krai (administrative territory) in southern Russia, in the northern Caucasus.
■ its capital city; pop. 324,000 (1990).
2 former name (until 1964) for **TOGLIATTI**.

stay¹ ▶ verb **1** [no obj., usu. with adverbial] remain in the same place: *you stay here and I'll be back soon* | *Jenny decide to stay at home with their young child* | *he stayed with the firm as a consultant.*
■ (**stay for/to**) delay leaving so as to join in (an activity): *why not stay to lunch?* ■ (**stay down**) (of food)

remain in the stomach, rather than be thrown up as vomit. ■ (**stay with**) remain in the mind or memory of (someone): *Gary's words stayed with her all evening.*
2 [no obj., with complement or adverbial] remain in a specified state or position: *her ability to stay calm* | *tactics used to stay in power* | *I managed to stay out of trouble.*
■ (**stay with**) continue or persevere with (an activity or task): *the incentive needed to stay with a healthy diet.* ■ (**stay with**) (of a competitor or player) keep up with (another) during a race or match. ■ short for *stay the course* below: *the boat made a good race for half the course but could not stay.*
3 [no obj.] (of a person) live somewhere temporarily as a visitor or guest: *the girls had gone to stay with friends* | *Minton invited him to stay the night.*
■ Scottish & S. African live permanently: *where do you stay?*
4 [with obj.] stop, delay, or prevent (something), in particular suspend or postpone (judicial proceedings) or refrain from pressing (charges).
■ assuage (hunger) for a short time: *I grabbed something to stay the pangs of hunger.* ■ poetic/literary curb; check: *he tries to stay the destructive course of barbarism.* ■ [no obj., in imperative] archaic wait a moment in order to allow someone time to think or speak: *stay, stand apart, I know not which is which.*
5 [with obj.] (usu. **be stayed**) poetic/literary support or prop up.
▶ noun **1** a period of staying somewhere, in particular of living somewhere temporarily as a visitor or guest: *an overnight stay at a luxury hotel.*
2 poetic/literary a curb or check: *there is likely to be a good public library as a stay against boredom.*
■ Law a suspension or postponement of judicial proceedings: *a stay of prosecution.*
3 a device used as a brace or support.
■ (**stays**) historical a corset made of two pieces laced together and stiffened by strips of whalebone.
4 [mass noun] archaic power of endurance.
– PHRASES **be here** (or **have come**) **to stay** informal be permanent or widely accepted: *the private sector is here to stay and likely to expand.* **stay the course** (or **distance**) keep going strongly to the end of a race or contest. ■ pursue a difficult task or activity to the end. **a stay of execution** a delay in carrying out a court order. **stay put** (of a person or object) remain somewhere without moving or being moved. **stay well** S. African used on departing as an expression of good wishes from the person leaving to the one staying.
– ORIGIN late Middle English (as a verb): from Anglo-Norman French *estai-*, stem of Old French *ester*, from Latin *stare* 'to stand'; in the sense 'support' (senses 5 of the verb and 3 of the noun), partly from Old French *estaye* (noun), *estayer* (verb), of Germanic origin.
▶ **stay on** continue to study, work, or be somewhere after others have left: *75 per cent of sixteen-year-olds stay on in full-time education.*
stay over (of a guest or visitor) sleep somewhere, especially at someone's home, for the night.
stay up not go to bed: *they stayed up all night.*

stay² ▶ noun a large rope, wire, or rod used to support a ship's mast, leading from the masthead to another mast or spar or down to another part of the ship.
■ a guy or rope supporting a flagstaff or other upright pole. ■ a supporting wire or cable on an aircraft.
▶ verb [with obj.] secure or steady (a mast) by means of stays.
– PHRASES **be in stays** (of a sailing ship) be head to the wind while tacking. **miss stays** (of a sailing ship) fail in an attempt to go about from one tack to another.
– ORIGIN Old English *stæg*, of Germanic origin; related to Dutch *stag*, from a base meaning 'be firm'.

stay-at-home informal ▶ adjective [attrib.] preferring to be at home rather than to travel, socialize, or go out to work.
▶ noun a person who lives in such a way.

stay bar ▶ noun a support used in building or in machinery.

stayer ▶ noun **1** a tenacious person or thing, especially a horse able to hold out to the end of a race.
2 a person who lives somewhere temporarily as a visitor or guest.

staying power ▶ noun [mass noun] informal the ability to maintain an activity or commitment despite fatigue or difficulty; stamina: *do you have the staying power to study alone at home?*

stay-in strike ▶ **noun** Brit. a sit-down strike.

Stayman /ˈsteɪmən/ (also **Stayman Winesap**) ▶ **noun** an apple of a deep red variety with a mildly tart flavour which is used for cooking and as a dessert apple, originating in the US.

stay rod ▶ **noun** another term for **STAY BAR**.

staysail /ˈsteɪseɪl, -s(ə)l/ ▶ **noun** a triangular fore-and-aft sail extended on a stay.

stay stitching ▶ **noun** [mass noun] stitching placed along a bias or curved seam to prevent the fabric of a garment from stretching while the garment is being made.

stay-up ▶ **adjective** denoting stockings that have elasticated tops and stay in position without a need for suspenders.
▶ **noun** (usu. **stay-ups**) a stocking of this type.

STD ▶ **abbreviation for** ■ Doctor of Sacred Theology. [ORIGIN: from Latin *Sanctae Theologiae Doctor*.] ■ sexually transmitted disease. ■ Brit. subscriber trunk dialling.

stead ▶ **noun** the place or role that someone or something should have or fill (used in referring to a substitute): *you wish to have him superseded and to be appointed **in his stead**.*
– PHRASES **stand someone in good stead** be advantageous or useful to someone over time or in the future: *his early training stood him in good stead.*
– ORIGIN Old English *stede* 'place', of Germanic origin; related to Dutch *stad* 'town', German *Statt* 'place', *Stadt* 'town', from an Indo-European root shared by the verb **STAND**.

steadfast /ˈstɛdfɑːst, -fəst/ ▶ **adjective** resolutely or dutifully firm and unwavering: *steadfast loyalty.*
– DERIVATIVES **steadfastly** adverb, **steadfastness** noun.
– ORIGIN Old English *stedefæst* 'standing firm' (see **STEAD, FAST**[1]).

Steadicam ▶ **noun** trademark a lightweight mounting for a film camera which keeps it steady for filming when hand-held or moving.

steading ▶ **noun** Scottish & N. English a farm and its buildings; a farmstead.

steady ▶ **adjective** (**steadier**, **steadiest**) **1** firmly fixed, supported, or balanced; not shaking or moving: *the lighter the camera, the harder it is to hold steady* | *he refilled her glass with a steady hand.*
■ not faltering or wavering; controlled: *a steady gaze* | *she tried to keep her voice steady.* ■ (of a person) sensible, reliable, and self-restrained: *a solid, steady young man.*
2 regular, even, and continuous in development, frequency, or intensity: *a steady decline in the national birth rate* | *sales remain steady.*
■ not changing; regular and established: *I thought I'd better get a steady job* | *a steady boyfriend.*
▶ **verb** (**-ies**, **-ied**) make or become steady: [with obj.] *I took a deep breath to steady my nerves* | [as adj. **steadying**] *she's the one steadying influence in his life* | [no obj.] *by the beginning of May prices had steadied.*
▶ **exclamation** used as a warning to someone to keep calm or take care: *Steady now! We don't want you hurting yourself.*
▶ **noun** (pl. **-ies**) **1** informal a person's regular boyfriend or girlfriend: *his steady chucked him two weeks ago.*
2 a strut for stabilizing a caravan or other vehicle when stationary.
– PHRASES **go steady** informal have a regular romantic or sexual relationship with a particular person. **steady on!** Brit. used as a way of exhorting someone to calm down or be more reasonable in what they are saying or doing.
– DERIVATIVES **steadier** noun, **steadily** adverb, **steadiness** noun.
– ORIGIN Middle English (in the sense 'unwavering, without deviation'): from **STEAD** + **-Y**[1]. The verb dates from the mid 16th cent.

steady-going ▶ **adjective** (of a person) moderate and sensible in behaviour; level-headed.

steady state ▶ **noun** an unvarying condition in a physical process, especially as in the theory that the universe is eternal and maintained by constant creation of matter.

The steady state theory postulates that the universe maintains a constant average density, with more matter continuously created to fill the void left by galaxies that are receding from one another. The theory has now largely been abandoned in favour of the big bang theory and an evolving universe.

steak ▶ **noun** [mass noun] high-quality beef taken from the hindquarters of the animal, typically cut into thick slices that are cooked at speed by grilling or frying.
■ [count noun] a thick slice of such beef or other high-quality meat or fish: *a fillet steak* | *a salmon steak.* ■ poorer-quality beef that is cubed or minced and cooked more slowly by braising or stewing: *braising steak* | [as modifier] *steak and kidney pie.*
– ORIGIN Middle English: from Old Norse *steik*; related to *steikja* 'roast on a spit' and *stikna* 'be roasted'.

steak au poivre /əʊ ˈpwɑːvr(ə)/ ▶ **noun** [mass noun] steak coated liberally with crushed peppercorns before cooking.
– ORIGIN French, literally 'steak with pepper'.

steak Diane ▶ **noun** [mass noun] a dish consisting of thin slices of steak fried with seasonings, especially Worcestershire sauce.

steakhouse ▶ **noun** a restaurant that specializes in serving steaks.

steak knife ▶ **noun** a knife with a serrated blade for use when eating steak.

steak tartare ▶ **noun** [mass noun] a dish consisting of raw minced steak mixed with raw egg, onion, and seasonings and shaped into small cakes or patties.

steal ▶ **verb** (past **stole**; past participle **stolen**) **1** [with obj.] take (another person's property) without permission or legal right and without intending to return it: *thieves stole her bicycle* | [no obj.] *she was found guilty of stealing from her employers* | [as adj. **stolen**] *stolen goods.*
■ dishonestly pass off (another person's ideas) as one's own: *accusations that one group had stolen ideas from the other were soon flying.* ■ take the opportunity to give or share (a kiss) when it is not expected or when people are not watching: *he stole kisses in shop doorways.* ■ (in various sports) gain (an advantage, a run, or possession of the ball) unexpectedly or by exploiting the temporary distraction of an opponent. ■ Baseball run to (a base) while the pitcher is in the act of delivery.
2 [no obj., with adverbial of direction] move somewhere quietly or surreptitiously: *he stole down to the kitchen* | figurative *a delicious languor was stealing over her.*
■ [with obj. and adverbial of direction] direct (a look) quickly and unobtrusively: *he stole a furtive glance at her.*
▶ **noun** [in sing.] **1** informal a bargain: *at £59.95 it's an absolute steal.*
2 chiefly N. Amer. an act of stealing something: *New York's biggest art steal.*
■ an idea taken from another work: *the chorus is a steal from The Smiths' 'London'.* ■ Baseball an act of stealing a base.
– PHRASES **steal someone blind** informal rob or cheat someone in a comprehensive or merciless way. **steal a march on** gain an advantage over (someone), typically by acting before they do: *stores that open on Sunday are stealing on march on their competitors.* **steal someone's heart** win someone's love. **steal the show** attract the most attention and praise. **steal someone's thunder** win praise for oneself by pre-empting someone else's attempt to impress.
– DERIVATIVES **stealer** noun [in combination] *a sheep-stealer.*
– ORIGIN Old English *stelan* (verb), of Germanic origin; related to Dutch *stelen* and German *stehlen*.

stealth ▶ **noun** **1** [mass noun] cautious and surreptitious action or movement: *the silence and stealth of a hungry cat* | *privatization **by stealth**.*
2 [as modifier] (chiefly of aircraft) designed in accordance with technology which makes detection by radar or sonar difficult: *a stealth bomber.*
– ORIGIN Middle English (in the sense 'theft'): probably representing an Old English word related to **STEAL**, + **-TH**[2].

stealthy ▶ **adjective** (**stealthier**, **stealthiest**) behaving, done, or made in a cautious and surreptitious manner, so as not to be seen or heard: *stealthy footsteps.*
– DERIVATIVES **stealthily** adverb, **stealthiness** noun.

steam ▶ **noun** [mass noun] the vapour into which water is converted when heated, forming a white mist of minute water droplets in the air.
■ the invisible gaseous form of water, formed by boiling, from which this vapour condenses. ■ the expansive force of this vapour used as a source of power for machines: *the equipment was originally powered by steam* | [as modifier] *a steam train.* ■ locomotives and railway systems powered in this way: *we were trainspotters in the last years of steam.* ■ figurative energy and momentum or impetus: *the anti-corruption drive **gathered steam**.*
▶ **verb** **1** [no obj.] give off or produce steam: *a mug of coffee was steaming at her elbow.*
■ (**steam up** or **steam something up**) become or cause to become covered or misted over with steam: [no obj.] *the glass keeps steaming up* | [with obj.] *the warm air had begun to steam up the windows.* ■ (often **be/get steamed up**) informal be or become extremely agitated or angry: *you got all steamed up over nothing!* | *after steaming behind the closed door in his office, he came out and screamed at her.*
2 [with obj.] cook (food) by heating it in steam from boiling water: *steam the vegetables until just tender.*
■ [no obj.] (of food) cook in this way: *add the mussels and leave them to steam.* ■ clean or otherwise treat with steam: *he steamed his shirts in the bathroom to remove the odour.* ■ [with obj. and complement or adverbial] apply steam to (something fixed with adhesive) so as to open or loosen it: *he'd steamed the letter open and then resealed it.* ■ generate steam in and operate (a steam locomotive).
3 [no obj., with adverbial of direction] (of a ship or train) travel somewhere under steam power: *the 11.54 steamed into the station.*
■ informal come, go, or move somewhere rapidly or in a forceful way: *Jeremy steamed in ten minutes late* | figurative *the company has steamed ahead with its investment programme.* ■ [no obj.] (**steam in**) Brit. informal start or join a fight. ■ [no obj.] [often as noun **steaming**] informal (of a gang of thieves) move rapidly through a public place, stealing things or robbing people on the way.
– PHRASES **get up** (or **pick up**) **steam** **1** generate enough pressure to drive a steam engine. **2** (of a project in its early stages) gradually gain more impetus and driving force: *his campaign steadily picked up steam.* **have steam coming out of one's ears** informal be extremely angry or irritated. **in steam** (of a steam locomotive) ready for work, with steam in the boiler. **let** (or **blow**) **off steam** informal (of a person) get rid of pent-up energy or strong emotion. **run out of** (or **lose**) **steam** informal lose impetus or enthusiasm: *a rebellion that had run out of steam.* **under one's own steam** (with reference to travel) without assistance from others: *we're going to have to get there under our own steam.* **under steam** (of a machine) being operated by steam.
– ORIGIN Old English *stēam* 'vapour', *stēman* 'emit a scent, be exhaled', of Germanic origin; related to Dutch *stoom* 'steam'.

steam age ▶ **noun** the time when trains were drawn by steam locomotives.

steam bath ▶ **noun** a room that is filled with hot steam for the purpose of cleaning and refreshing the body and for relaxation.
■ a session in such a bath.

steam beer ▶ **noun** [mass noun] US trademark an effervescent beer brewed chiefly in the western US.

steamboat ▶ **noun** a boat that is propelled by a steam engine, especially (in the US) a paddle-wheel craft of a type used widely on rivers in the 19th century.

steam distillation ▶ **noun** [mass noun] Chemistry distillation of a liquid in a current of steam, used especially to purify liquids that are not very volatile and are immiscible with water.

steamed ▶ **adjective** [predic.] Brit. informal extremely drunk: *we went out and got steamed.*

steam engine ▶ **noun** an engine that uses the expansion or rapid condensation of steam to generate power.
■ a steam locomotive.

steamer ▶ **noun** **1** a ship or boat powered by steam.
■ informal a steam locomotive.
2 a type of saucepan in which food can be steamed.
■ a device used to direct a jet of hot steam on to a garment in order to remove creases.
3 informal a wetsuit.

steamer clam ▶ **noun** another term for **SOFTSHELL CLAM**.

steamer duck ▶ **noun** a sturdily built greyish duck which churns the water with its wings when fleeing danger, typically flightless and native to southern South America.
● Genus *Tachyeres*, family Anatidae: several species, including the flightless *T. brachypterus* of the Falkland Islands.

steamer rug ▶ **noun** US a rug of a kind formerly

S

used on board a passenger ship for keeping warm on deck.

steamer trunk ▶ **noun** a sturdy trunk designed or intended for use on board a steamship.

steam gauge ▶ **noun** a pressure gauge attached to a steam boiler.

steam hammer ▶ **noun** a large steam-powered hammer used in forging.

steam heat ▶ **noun** [mass noun] heat produced by steam, especially by a central heating system in a building or on a train or ship that uses steam.
▶ **verb** (**steam-heat**) [with obj.] heat (something) by passing hot steam through it, especially at high pressure.

steamie ▶ **noun** (pl. **-ies**) Scottish, informal a communal wash house.

steaming ▶ **adjective** **1** giving off steam: *a basin of steaming water.*
2 Brit. informal extremely drunk.
3 Brit. informal very angry.
▶ **adverb** [as submodifier] (**steaming hot**) extremely hot.

steam iron ▶ **noun** an electric iron that emits steam from holes in its flat surface, as an aid to ironing articles that are completely dry.

steam jacket ▶ **noun** a steam-filled casing that is fitted around a cylinder in order to heat its contents.

steam organ ▶ **noun** a fairground pipe organ that is driven by a steam engine and played by means of a keyboard or a system of punched cards.

steamroll ▶ **verb** chiefly N. Amer. another term for **STEAMROLLER**.

steamroller ▶ **noun** a heavy, slow-moving vehicle with a roller, used to flatten the surfaces of roads during construction.
■ figurative an oppressive and relentless power or force: *victims of an ideological steamroller.*
▶ **verb** [with obj.] (of a government or other authority) forcibly pass (a measure) by restricting debate or otherwise overriding opposition: *the government's trying to* **steamroller** *a law* **through**.
■ force (someone) into doing or accepting something: *an attempt to* **steamroller** *the country* **into** *political reforms.*

steam shovel ▶ **noun** an excavator that is powered by steam.

steam table ▶ **noun** N. Amer. (in a cafeteria or restaurant) a table with slots to hold food containers which are kept hot by steam circulating beneath them.

steam-tight ▶ **adjective** not allowing steam to pass through: *steam-tight joints.*

steam turbine ▶ **noun** a turbine in which a high-velocity jet of steam rotates a bladed disc or drum.

steamy ▶ **adjective** (**steamier**, **steamiest**) producing, filled with, or clouded with steam: *a small steamy kitchen.*
■ (of a place or its atmosphere) hot and humid: *the hot, steamy jungle.* ■ informal depicting or involving erotic sexual activity: *steamy sex scenes | a steamy affair.*
– DERIVATIVES **steamily** adverb, **steaminess** noun.

stearic acid /ˈstɪərɪk, stɪˈarɪk/ ▶ **noun** Chemistry a solid saturated fatty acid obtained from animal or vegetable fats.
● Chem. formula: $CH_3(CH_2)_{16}COOH$.
– DERIVATIVES **stearate** /ˈstɪəreɪt/ noun.
– ORIGIN mid 19th cent.: *stearic* from French *stéarique*, from Greek *stear* 'tallow'.

stearin /ˈstɪərɪn/ ▶ **noun** [mass noun] a white crystalline substance which is the main constituent of tallow and suet. It is a glyceryl ester of stearic acid.
■ a mixture of fatty acids used in candle-making.
– ORIGIN early 19th cent.: from French *stéarine*, from Greek *stear* 'tallow'.

steatite /ˈstɪətʌɪt/ ▶ **noun** [mass noun] the mineral talc occurring in consolidated form, especially as soapstone.
– DERIVATIVES **steatitic** adjective.
– ORIGIN mid 18th cent.: via Latin from Greek *steatitēs*, from *stear, steat-* 'tallow'.

steato- ▶ **combining form** relating to fatty matter or tissue: *steatosis.*
– ORIGIN from Greek *stear, steat-* 'tallow, fat'.

steatopygia /ˌstɪətə(ʊ)ˈpɪdʒɪə/ ▶ **noun** [mass noun] accumulation of large amounts of fat on the buttocks, especially as a normal condition in the Khoikhoi and other peoples of arid parts of southern Africa.
– DERIVATIVES **steatopygous** /ˌstɪətə(ʊ)ˈpʌɪɡəs, ˌstɪəˈtɒpɪɡəs/ adjective.
– ORIGIN early 19th cent.: modern Latin, from Greek *stear, steat-* 'tallow' + *pugē* 'rump'.

steatorrhoea /ˌstɪətə(ʊ)ˈriːə/ ▶ **noun** [mass noun] Medicine the excretion of abnormal quantities of fat with the faeces owing to reduced absorption of fat by the intestine.

steatosis /ˌstɪəˈtəʊsɪs/ ▶ **noun** [mass noun] Medicine infiltration of liver cells with fat, associated with disturbance of the metabolism by, for example, alcoholism, malnutrition, pregnancy, or drug therapy.

Stedman /ˈstɛdmən/ ▶ **adjective** [attrib.] Bell-ringing relating to or denoting a method of change-ringing: *Stedman triples.*
– ORIGIN mid 18th cent.: named after Fabian *Stedman*, the English printer (*fl.* 1670) who devised it.

steed ▶ **noun** archaic or poetic/literary a horse being ridden or available for riding.
– ORIGIN Old English *stēda* 'stallion'; related to **STUD**[2].

steel ▶ **noun** [mass noun] a hard, strong grey or bluish-grey alloy of iron with carbon and usually other elements, used extensively as a structural and fabricating material.
■ used as a symbol or embodiment of strength and firmness: *nerves of steel* | [as modifier] *a steel will.* ■ [count noun] a rod of roughened steel on which knives are sharpened.
▶ **verb** [with obj.] mentally prepare (oneself) to do or face something difficult: *his team were* **steeling themselves for** *disappointment* | [with infinitive] *she steeled herself to remain calm.*
– ORIGIN Old English *stȳle, stēli*, of Germanic origin; related to Dutch *staal*, German *Stahl*, also to **STAY**[2]. The verb dates from the late 16th cent.

steel band ▶ **noun** a band that plays music on steel drums.

steel blue ▶ **noun** [mass noun] a dark bluish-grey colour.

steel drum ▶ **noun** a percussion instrument originating in Trinidad, made out of an oil drum with one end beaten down and divided by grooves into sections to give different notes. Also called **PAN**[1] (especially by players).

Steele, Sir Richard (1672–1729), Irish essayist and dramatist. He founded and wrote for the periodicals the *Tatler* (1709–11) and the *Spectator* (1711–12), the latter in collaboration with Joseph Addison.

steel engraving ▶ **noun** [mass noun] the process or action of engraving a design into a steel plate.
■ [count noun] a print made from an engraved steel plate.

steel grey ▶ **noun** [mass noun] a dark purplish-grey colour: [as modifier] *the steel-grey November sky.*

steelhead (also **steelhead trout**) ▶ **noun** a rainbow trout of a large migratory race.

steel pan ▶ **noun** another term for **STEEL DRUM**.

steel wool ▶ **noun** [mass noun] fine strands of steel matted together into a mass, used as an abrasive.

steelwork ▶ **noun** [mass noun] articles of steel.

steelworks ▶ **plural noun** [usu. treated as sing.] a factory where steel is manufactured.
– DERIVATIVES **steelworker** noun.

steely ▶ **adjective** (**steelier**, **steeliest**) resembling steel in colour, brightness, or strength: *a steely blue.*
■ figurative coldly determined; hard: *there was a steely edge to his questions.*
– DERIVATIVES **steeliness** noun.

steelyard /ˈstiːljɑːd, ˈstɪljəd/ ▶ **noun** an apparatus for weighing that has a short arm taking the item to be weighed and a long graduated arm along which a weight is moved until it balances.

steen /stɪən, stiːn/ (also **stein**) ▶ **noun** [mass noun] a variety of white grape grown in South Africa.
■ the wine made from this grape. ■ (**stein**) a blended semi-sweet white wine, typically containing steen grapes.
– ORIGIN South African Dutch, elliptically from *steendruiven*, literally 'stone grapes'.

steenbok /ˈstiːnbɒk, ˈsteɪn-/ (also **steinbok** or **steenbuck**) ▶ **noun** a small African antelope with large ears, a small tail, and smooth upright horns.
● *Raphiceros campestris*, family Bovidae.
– ORIGIN late 18th cent.: from Dutch, from *steen* 'stone' + *bok* 'buck'.

steenbras /ˈstiːnbras, -brɑːs/ ▶ **noun** (pl. same) S. African an edible South African sea bream of shallow waters.
● *Sparodon* and other genera, family Sparidae.
– ORIGIN early 17th cent.: from Afrikaans, from Dutch *steen* 'stone' + *brasen* 'bream'.

steep[1] ▶ **adjective** **1** (of a slope, flight of stairs, or angle) rising or falling sharply; almost perpendicular: *she pushed the bike up the steep hill.*
■ (of a rise or fall in an amount) very large or rapid: *the steep rise in unemployment.*
2 informal (of a price or demand) not reasonable; excessive: *a steep membership fee.*
■ dated (of a claim or account) exaggerated or incredible: *this is a rather steep statement.*
▶ **noun** chiefly Skiing or poetic/literary a steep mountain slope: *hair-raising steeps.*
– DERIVATIVES **steepish** adjective, **steeply** adverb, **steepness** noun.
– ORIGIN Old English *stēap* 'extending to a great height', of West Germanic origin; related to **STEEPLE** and **STOOP**[1].

steep[2] ▶ **verb** [with obj.] soak (food or tea) in water or other liquid so as to extract its flavour or to soften it: *the chillies are steeped in olive oil* | [no obj.] *the noodles should be left to steep for 3–4 minutes.*
■ soak or saturate (cloth) in water or other liquid. ■ figurative (usu. **be steeped in**) surround or fill with a quality or influence: *a city steeped in history.*
– ORIGIN Middle English: of Germanic origin; related to **STOUP**.

steepen ▶ **verb** become or cause to become steeper: [no obj.] *the snow improved as the slope steepened.*

steeple ▶ **noun** a church tower and spire.
■ a spire on the top of a church tower or roof. ■ archaic a tall tower of a church or other building.
– DERIVATIVES **steepled** adjective.
– ORIGIN Old English *stēpel*, of Germanic origin; related to **STEEP**[1].

steeplechase ▶ **noun** a horse race run on a racecourse having ditches and hedges as jumps.
■ a running race in which runners must clear hurdles and water jumps.
– DERIVATIVES **steeplechaser** noun, **steeplechasing** noun.
– ORIGIN late 18th cent.: from **STEEPLE** (because originally a steeple marked the finishing point across country) + **CHASE**[1].

steeple-crowned ▶ **adjective** (of a hat) having a tall, pointed crown.

steeplejack ▶ **noun** a person who climbs tall structures such as chimneys and steeples in order to carry out repairs.

steer[1] ▶ **verb** [with obj.] (of a person) guide or control the movement of (a vehicle, vessel, or aircraft), for example by turning a wheel or operating a rudder: *he steered the boat slowly towards the busy quay* | [no obj.] *he let Lily steer.*
■ [no obj., with adverbial of direction] (of a vehicle, vessel, or aircraft) be guided in a specified direction in such a way: *the ship* **steered into** *port.* ■ [with obj. and adverbial of direction] follow (a course) in a specified direction: *the fishermen were steering a direct course for Koepang* | [no obj.] figurative *try to steer away from foods based on sugar.* ■ [with obj. and adverbial of direction] guide the movement or course of (someone or something): *he had steered her to a chair* | figurative *he made an attempt to steer the conversation back to Heather.*
▶ **noun** **1** [mass noun] the type of steering of a vehicle: *some cars boast four-wheel steer.*
2 informal a piece of advice or information concerning the development of a situation: *the need for the NHS to be given a clear steer as to its future direction.*
– PHRASES **steer clear of** take care to avoid or keep away from: *his programme steers clear of prickly local issues.* **steer a middle course** see **MIDDLE**.
– DERIVATIVES **steerable** adjective.
– ORIGIN Old English *stīeran*, of Germanic origin; related to Dutch *sturen* and German *steuern*.

steer[2] ▶ **noun** another term for **BULLOCK**.
– ORIGIN Old English *stēor*, of Germanic origin; related to Dutch *stier* and German *Stier*.

steerage ▶ **noun** [mass noun] **1** historical the part of a ship providing accommodation for passengers with the cheapest tickets: *poor emigrants in steerage.*
2 archaic or poetic/literary the action of steering a boat.

steerage way ▶ **noun** [mass noun] the rate of headway required if a ship is to be controlled by the helm.

steer-by-wire ▶ noun [mass noun] [often as modifier] a semi-automatic and typically computer-regulated system for controlling the engine, handling, suspension, and other functions of a motor vehicle.

steerer ▶ noun a person or mechanism that steers a vehicle or vessel.
■ US informal a person who takes or entices someone to meet a racketeer or swindler.

steering ▶ noun [mass noun] the action of steering a vehicle, vessel, or aircraft.
■ the mechanism in a vehicle, vessel, or aircraft which makes it possible to steer it in different directions.

steering column ▶ noun a shaft that connects the steering wheel of a vehicle to the rest of the steering mechanism.

steering committee (also **steering group**) ▶ noun a committee that decides on the priorities or order of business of an organization and manages the general course of its operations.

steering wheel ▶ noun a wheel that a driver rotates in order to steer a vehicle.

steersman ▶ noun (pl. **-men**) a person who is steering a boat or ship.

steeve[1] ▶ noun (in a sailing ship) the angle of the bowsprit in relation to the horizontal.
▶ verb [with obj.] (usu. **be steeved**) give (the bowsprit) a specified inclination.
– ORIGIN mid 17th cent.: of unknown origin.

steeve[2] ▶ noun a derrick consisting of a long pole with a block at the end.
– ORIGIN late 15th cent. (as a verb): from Old French *estiver* or Spanish *estibar*, from Latin *stipare* 'pack tight'. The noun is first recorded as a 19th-cent. US term.

Stefan–Boltzmann law /ˌstɛfan'bɔʊltsmən/ Physics a law stating that the total radiation emitted by a black body is proportional to the fourth power of its absolute temperature.
– ORIGIN late 19th cent.: named after Josef *Stefan* (1835–93), Austrian physicist, and L. **BOLTZMANN**.

stegosaur /'stɛgəsɔː/ (also **stegosaurus** /ˌstɛgə'sɔːrəs/) ▶ noun a small-headed quadrupedal herbivorous dinosaur of the Jurassic and early Cretaceous periods, with a double row of large bony plates or spines along the back.
● Infraorder Stegosauria, order Ornithischia: several genera, including *Stegosaurus*.
– ORIGIN modern Latin, from Greek *stegē* 'covering' + *sauros* 'lizard'.

Steiermark /'ʃtaɪəˌmark/ German name for **STYRIA**.

Stein /staɪn/, Gertrude (1874–1946), American writer. Stein developed an esoteric stream-of-consciousness style, notably in *The Autobiography of Alice B. Toklas* (1933). Her home in Paris became a focus for the avant-garde during the 1920s and 1930s.

stein[1] /staɪn/ ▶ noun a large earthenware beer mug.
– ORIGIN mid 19th cent.: from German *Stein*, literally 'stone'.

stein[2] ▶ noun variant spelling of **STEEN**.

Steinbeck /'staɪnbɛk/, John (Ernst) (1902–68), American novelist. His work, for example *Of Mice and Men* (1937) and *The Grapes of Wrath* (1939), is noted for its sympathetic and realistic portrayal of the migrant agricultural workers of California. Nobel Prize for Literature (1962).

steinbock /'staɪnbɒk/ ▶ noun (pl. same or **-bocks**) an ibex, especially one living in the Alps.
– ORIGIN late 17th cent.: from German, from *Stein* 'stone' + *Bock* 'buck'.

steinbok /'staɪnbɒk/ ▶ noun variant spelling of **STEENBOK**.

Steiner /'ʃtaɪnə, 'st-/, Rudolf (1861–1925), Austrian philosopher, founder of anthroposophy. He founded the Anthroposophical Society in 1912, aiming to integrate the practical and psychological in education. The society has contributed to child-centred education, especially with its Steiner schools.

Steinway /'staɪnweɪ/, Henry (Engelhard) (1797–1871), German piano-builder, resident in the US from 1849; born *Heinrich Engelhard Steinweg*. He founded his famous piano-making firm in New York in 1853.

stela /'stiːlə/ ▶ noun (pl. **stelae** /-liː/) Archaeology an upright stone slab or column typically bearing a commemorative inscription or relief design, often serving as a gravestone.
– ORIGIN late 18th cent.: via Latin from Greek (see **STELE**).

Stelazine /'stɛləziːn/ ▶ noun trademark for **TRIFLUOPERAZINE**.
– ORIGIN 1950s: of unknown origin.

stele /stiːl, 'stiːli/ ▶ noun **1** Botany the central core of the stem and root of a vascular plant, consisting of the vascular tissue (xylem and phloem) and associated supporting tissue. Also called **VASCULAR CYLINDER**.
2 Archaeology another term for **STELA**.
– DERIVATIVES **stelar** adjective (in sense 1).
– ORIGIN early 19th cent.: from Greek *stēlē* 'standing block'.

Stella /'stɛlə/, Frank (Philip) (b.1936), American painter, an important figure in minimalism known for his series of all-black paintings.

Stella Maris /ˌstɛlə 'mɑːrɪs/ ▶ noun chiefly poetic/literary a female protector or guiding spirit at sea (a title sometimes given to the Virgin Mary).
– ORIGIN Latin, literally 'star of the sea'.

stellar /'stɛlə/ ▶ adjective of or relating to a star or stars: *stellar structure and evolution*.
■ informal, chiefly N. Amer. featuring or having the quality of a star performer or performers: *a stellar cast had been assembled*.
– DERIVATIVES **stelliform** adjective.
– ORIGIN mid 17th cent.: from late Latin *stellaris*, from Latin *stella* 'star'.

stellarator /'stɛləreɪtə/ ▶ noun Physics a toroidal apparatus for producing controlled fusion reactions in hot plasma, where all the controlling magnetic fields inside it are produced by external windings.
– ORIGIN 1950s: from **STELLAR** (with reference to the fusion processes in stars), on the pattern of *generator*.

stellar wind ▶ noun Astronomy a continuous flow of charged particles from a star.

stellate /'stɛleɪt, -lət/ ▶ adjective technical arranged in a radiating pattern like that of a star.
– DERIVATIVES **stellated** adjective.
– ORIGIN mid 17th cent.: from Latin *stellatus*, from *stella* 'star'.

Stellenbosch /'stɛlənbɒs/ a university town in SW South Africa, just east of Cape Town; pop. 43,000 (1985).

Steller /'stɛlə/, Georg Wilhelm (1709–46), German naturalist and geographer. Steller was a research member of Vitus Bering's second expedition to Kamchatka and Alaska and described many new birds and mammals, several of which now bear his name.

Steller's sea cow ▶ noun a very large relative of the dugong that was formerly found in the area of the Bering Sea and Kamchatka Peninsula, discovered and exterminated in the 18th century.
● *Hydrodamalis gigas*, family Dugongidae.

stellium /'stɛliəm/ ▶ noun Astrology another term for **SATELLITIUM**.

stem[1] ▶ noun **1** the main body or stalk of a plant or shrub, typically rising above ground but occasionally subterranean.
■ the stalk supporting a fruit, flower, or leaf, and attaching it to a larger branch, twig, or stalk.
2 a long, thin supportive or main section of something: *the main stem of the wing feathers*.
■ the slender part of a wine glass between the base and the bowl. ■ the tube of a tobacco pipe. ■ a rod or cylinder in a mechanism, for example the sliding shaft of a bolt or the winding pin of a watch. ■ a vertical stroke in a letter or musical note.
3 Grammar the root or main part of a noun, adjective, or other word, to which inflections or formative elements are added.
■ archaic or poetic/literary the main line of descent of a family or nation: *the Hellenic tribes were derived from the Aryan stem*.
4 the main upright timber or metal piece at the bow of a ship, to which the ship's sides are joined at the front end.
5 US informal a pipe used for smoking crack or opium.
▶ verb (**stemmed**, **stemming**) **1** [no obj.] (**stem from**) originate in or be caused by: *many of the universities' problems stem from rapid expansion.*

2 [with obj.] remove the stems from (fruit or tobacco leaves).
3 [with obj.] (of a boat) make headway against (the tide or current).
– PHRASES **from stem to stern** from the front to the back, especially of a ship: *surges of water rocked their boats from stem to stern.*
– DERIVATIVES **stemless** adjective, **stem-like** adjective.
– ORIGIN Old English *stemn, stefn*, of Germanic origin; related to Dutch *stam* and German *Stamm*. Sense 4 is related to Dutch *steven*, German *Steven*.

stem[2] ▶ verb (**stemmed**, **stemming**) **1** [with obj.] stop or restrict (the flow of something): *a nurse did her best to stem the bleeding* | figurative *an attempt to stem the rising tide of unemployment.*
2 [no obj.] Skiing slide the tail of one ski or both skis outwards in order to turn or slow down.
– ORIGIN Middle English (in the sense 'to stop, delay': from Old Norse *stemma*, of Germanic origin. The skiing term (early 20th cent.) is from the German verb *stemmen*.

stem cell ▶ noun Biology an undifferentiated cell of a multicellular organism which is capable of giving rise to indefinitely more cells of the same type, and from which certain other kinds of cell arise by differentiation.

stem ginger ▶ noun [mass noun] a superior grade of crystallized or preserved ginger.

stemma /'stɛmə/ ▶ noun (pl. **stemmata** /-mətə/) a recorded genealogy of a family; a family tree.
■ a diagram showing the relationship between a text and its various manuscript versions.
– ORIGIN mid 17th cent.: via Latin from Greek *stemma* 'wreath', from *stephein* 'wreathe, crown'.

stemmatics /stɛ'matɪks/ ▶ plural noun [treated as sing.] the branch of study concerned with analysing the relationship of surviving variant versions of a text to each other, especially so as to reconstruct a lost original.

stemmed ▶ adjective [attrib.] **1** [in combination] having a stem of a specified length or kind: *red-stemmed alder bushes.*
2 (of fruit or leaves) having had the stems removed.

stemple ▶ noun archaic each of a number of crossbars in a mineshaft, serving as supports or steps.
– ORIGIN mid 17th cent.: perhaps related to German *Stempel*.

stem stitch ▶ noun [mass noun] an embroidery stitch forming a continuous line of long, overlapped stitches, typically used to represent narrow stems.

stem turn ▶ noun Skiing a turn made by stemming with the upper ski and lifting the lower one parallel to it towards the end.

stemware ▶ noun [mass noun] N. Amer. goblets and stemmed glasses regarded collectively.

stem-winder ▶ noun US **1** informal an entertaining and rousing speech: *a stem-winder of a speech.*
2 dated a watch wound by turning a knob on the end of a stem.
– ORIGIN sense 1 from the notion of 'winding up' or causing a lively reaction from those listening.

stench ▶ noun a strong and very unpleasant smell: *the stench of rotting fish.*
– ORIGIN Old English *stenc* 'smell', of Germanic origin; related to Dutch *stank*, German *Gestank*, also to the verb **STINK**.

stencil ▶ noun a thin sheet of card, plastic, or metal with a pattern or letters cut out of it, used to produce the cut design on the surface below by the application of ink or paint through the holes.
■ a design produced by such a sheet: *a floral stencil around the top of the room.*
▶ verb (**stencilled**, **stencilling**; US **stenciled**, **stenciling**) [with obj.] decorate (a surface) with such a design: *the walls had been stencilled with designs* | [as noun **stencilling**] *the art of stencilling.*
■ produce (a design) with a stencil: *stencil a border around the door* | [as adj. **stencilled**] *the stencilled letters.*
– ORIGIN early 18th cent.: from earlier *stansel* 'ornament with various colours' (based on Latin *scintilla* 'spark').

Stendhal /'stɒdaːl, French stɛdal/ (1783–1842), French novelist; pseudonym of *Marie Henri Beyle*. His two best-known novels are *Le Rouge et le noir* (1830), relating the rise and fall of a young man from the provinces, and *La Chartreuse de Parme* (1839).

Sten gun ▶ noun a type of lightweight British submachine gun.

– ORIGIN 1940s: from the initials of the inventors' surnames, Shepherd and Turpin, suggested by **BREN**.

Steno /ˈstiːnəʊ/, Nicolaus (1638–86), Danish anatomist and geologist; Danish name *Niels Steensen*. His ideas on the geological history of the earth are now regarded as fundamental—that fossils are the petrified remains of living organisms, that many rocks arise from consolidation of sediments, and that such rocks occur in layers in the order in which they were laid down.

steno /ˈstɛnəʊ/ ▶ **noun** (pl. **-os**) N. Amer. informal a shorthand typist: *it was written by the little steno herself.*
■ [as modifier] short for **STENOGRAPHY**.

stenography /stɪˈnɒɡrəfi/ ▶ **noun** [mass noun] N. Amer. the action or process of writing in shorthand and transcribing the shorthand on a typewriter.
– DERIVATIVES **stenographer** noun, **stenographic** adjective.
– ORIGIN early 17th cent.: from Greek *stenos* 'narrow' + **-GRAPHY**.

stenohaline /ˌstɛnəʊˈheɪlʌɪn, -liːn/ ▶ **adjective** Ecology (of an aquatic organism) able to tolerate only a narrow range of salinity. Often contrasted with **EURYHALINE**.
– ORIGIN 1930s: from Greek *stenos* 'narrow' + *halinos* 'of salt'.

stenosis /stɪˈnəʊsɪs/ ▶ **noun** (pl. **stenoses**) [mass noun] Medicine the abnormal narrowing of a passage in the body.
– DERIVATIVES **stenosed** adjective, **stenosing** adjective, **stenotic** adjective.
– ORIGIN late 19th cent.: modern Latin, from Greek *stenōsis* 'narrowing', from *stenoun* 'make narrow', from *stenos* 'narrow'.

stenothermal /ˌstɛnə(ʊ)ˈθəːm(ə)l/ ▶ **adjective** Ecology (of an organism) able to tolerate only a small range of temperature. Often contrasted with **EURYTHERMAL**.
– ORIGIN late 19th cent.: from Greek *stenos* 'narrow' + **THERMAL**.

stenotopic /ˌstɛnə(ʊ)ˈtɒpɪk/ ▶ **adjective** Ecology (of an organism) able to tolerate only a restricted range of habitats or ecological conditions. Often contrasted with **EURYTOPIC**.
– ORIGIN 1940s: from Greek *stenos* 'narrow' + *topos* 'place' + **-IC**.

stenotype ▶ **noun** a machine resembling a typewriter that is used for recording speech in syllables or phonemes.
– DERIVATIVES **stenotypist** noun.
– ORIGIN late 19th cent.: from **STENOGRAPHY** + **TYPE**.

stent[1] ▶ **noun** **1** Medicine a splint placed temporarily inside a duct, canal, or blood vessel to aid healing or relieve an obstruction.
■ an impression or cast of a part or body cavity, used to maintain pressure so as to promote healing, especially of a skin graft.
2 [mass noun] (also **Stents**) trademark a substance used in dentistry for taking impressions of the teeth.
– ORIGIN late 19th cent.: from the name of Charles T. *Stent* (1807–85), English dentist. The sense 'splint' dates from the 1960s.

stent[2] historical, chiefly Scottish ▶ **noun** an assessment of property made for purposes of taxation.
■ the amount or value assessed; a tax.
▶ **verb** [with obj.] assess and charge (a person or a community) for purposes of taxation.
– ORIGIN Middle English: from Old French *estente* 'valuation', related to Anglo-Norman French *extente* (see **EXTENT**).

stenter ▶ **noun** another term for **TENTER**[1].
– ORIGIN from Scots *stent* 'set up (a tent)' (perhaps a shortening of **EXTEND**) + **-ER**[1].

stentor /ˈstɛntə/ ▶ **noun** **1** poetic/literary a person with a powerful voice.
2 Zoology a sedentary trumpet-shaped single-celled animal that is widespread in fresh water.
• Genus *Stentor*, phylum Ciliophora, kingdom Protista.
– ORIGIN early 17th cent.: from Greek *Stentōr*, the name of a herald in the Trojan War.

stentorian /stɛnˈtɔːrɪən/ ▶ **adjective** (of a person's voice) loud and powerful: *a stentorian roar.*

step ▶ **noun** **1** an act or movement of putting one leg in front of the other in walking or running: *Ron took a step back | she turned and retraced her steps.*
■ the distance covered by such a movement: *Richard came a couple of steps nearer.* ■ [usu. in sing.] a person's particular way of walking: *she left the room with a springy step.* ■ one of the sequences of movement of the feet which make up a dance. ■ a short or easily walked distance: *the market is only a short step from the end of the lake.*
2 a flat surface, especially one in a series, on which to place one's foot when moving from one level to another: *the bottom step of the staircase | a flight of marble steps.*
■ a doorstep: *there was a pint of milk on the step.* ■ a rung of a ladder. ■ **(steps)** (or **a pair of steps**) Brit. a stepladder. ■ Climbing a foothold cut in a slope of ice. ■ a block fixed to a boat's keel in order to take the base of a mast or other fitting. ■ Physics an abrupt change in the value of a quantity, especially voltage.
3 a measure or action, especially one of a series taken in order to deal with or achieve a particular thing: *the government must* ***take steps*** *to discourage age discrimination | a major step forward in the fight against terrorism.*
■ a stage in a gradual process: *sales are up, which is a step in the right direction.* ■ a particular position or grade on an ascending or hierarchical scale: *the first step on the managerial ladder.*
4 Music, chiefly US an interval in a scale; a tone (whole step) or semitone (half step).
5 [mass noun] step aerobics: [as modifier] *a step class.*
▶ **verb** (**stepped**, **stepping**) **1** [no obj., with adverbial] lift and set down one's foot or one foot after the other in order to walk somewhere or move to a new position: *Claudia tried to step back | I accidentally stepped on his foot.*
■ [as imperative] used as a polite or deferential way of asking someone to walk a short distance for a particular purpose: *please step this way.* ■ **(step it)** dated perform a dance: *they stepped it down the room between the lines of dancers.* ■ take a particular course of action: *he stepped out of retirement to answer an SOS call from his old club.*
2 [with obj.] Nautical set up (a mast) in its step.
– PHRASES **break step** stop walking or marching in step with others. **fall into step** change the way one is walking so that one is walking in step with another person. **in** (or **out of**) **step** putting (or not putting) one's feet forward alternately in the same rhythm as the people one is walking, marching, or dancing with. ■ figurative conforming (or not conforming) to what others are doing or thinking: *the party is clearly* ***out of step with*** *voters.* ■ Physics (of two or more oscillations or other cyclic phenomena) having (or not having) the same frequency and always in the same phase. **follow** (or **tread**) **in someone's steps** do as someone else did, especially in making a journey or following a career. **keep step** remain walking, marching, or dancing in step. **mind** (or **watch**) **one's step** used as a warning to someone to walk or act carefully. **one step ahead** managing to avoid competition or danger from someone or something: *I try to keep one step ahead of the rest of the staff.* **step by step** so as to progress gradually and carefully from one stage to the next: *I'll explain it to you step by step |* [as modifier] *a step-by-step guide.* **step into the breach** see **BREACH**. **step into someone's shoes** take control of a task or job from another person. **step on it** (or **step on the gas**) informal go faster, typically in a motor vehicle. **step on someone's toes** see ***tread on someone's toes*** at **TREAD**. **step out of line** behave inappropriately or disobediently.
– DERIVATIVES **step-like** adjective.
– ORIGIN Old English *stæpe*, *stepe* (noun), *stæppan*, *steppan* (verb), of Germanic origin; related to Dutch *steppen* and German *stapfen*.
▶ **step aside** another way of saying ***step down*** below.
step back mentally withdraw from a situation in order to consider it objectively.
step down withdraw or resign from an important position or office: *Mr Krenz stepped down as party leader a week ago.*
step something down decrease voltage by using a transformer.
step forward offer one's help or services: *a company has stepped forward to sponsor the team.*
step in become involved in a difficult or problematic situation, especially in order to help or prevent something from happening. ■ act as a substitute for someone: *Lucy stepped in at very short notice to take Joan's place.*
step out 1 leave a room or building, typically for a short time. **2** N. Amer. informal go out with: *he was* ***stepping out with*** *a redheaded waitress.* **3** walk with long or vigorous steps: *she enjoyed the outing, stepping out manfully.*
step something up increase the amount, speed, or intensity of something: *police decided to step up security plans for the match.* ■ increase voltage using a transformer.

step- ▶ **combining form** denoting a relationship resulting from a remarriage: *stepmother.*
– ORIGIN Old English *stēop-*, from a Germanic base meaning 'bereaved, orphaned'.

step aerobics ▶ **plural noun** [mass noun] a type of aerobics that involves stepping up on to and down from a portable block.

Stepanakert /stʲipanəˈkʲɛrt/ Russian name for **XANKÄNDI**.

stepbrother ▶ **noun** a son of one's step-parent, by a marriage other than that with one's own father or mother.

stepchild ▶ **noun** (pl. **-children**) a child of one's husband or wife by a previous marriage.

step-cut ▶ **adjective** (of a gem) cut in straight facets round the centre.

stepdad ▶ **noun** informal term for **STEPFATHER**.

stepdaughter ▶ **noun** a daughter of one's husband or wife by a previous marriage.

stepfamily ▶ **noun** (pl. **-ies**) a family that is formed on the remarriage of a divorced or widowed person and that includes a child or children.

stepfather ▶ **noun** a man who is married to one's mother after the divorce of one's parents or the death of one's father.

step function ▶ **noun** Mathematics & Electronics a function that increases or decreases abruptly from one constant value to another.

stephanotis /ˌstɛfəˈnəʊtɪs/ ▶ **noun** a Madagascan climbing plant which is cultivated for its fragrant waxy white flowers.
• Genus *Stephanotis*, family Asclepiadaceae.
– ORIGIN modern Latin, from Greek, literally 'fit for a wreath', from *stephanos* 'wreath'.

Stephen (*c.*1097–1154), grandson of William the Conqueror, king of England 1135–54. Stephen seized the throne from Matilda a few months after the death of Henry I. Civil war followed until Matilda was defeated and forced to leave England in 1148.

Stephen, St[1] (died *c.*35), Christian martyr. One of the original seven deacons in Jerusalem appointed by the Apostles, he was charged with blasphemy and stoned, thus becoming the first Christian martyr. Feast day (in the Western Church) 26 December; (in the Eastern Church) 27 December.

Stephen, St[2] (*c.*977–1038), king and patron saint of Hungary, reigned 1000–38. The first king of Hungary, he took steps to Christianize the country. Feast day, 2 September or (in Hungary) 20 August.

Stephenson, George (1781–1848), British engineer, a pioneer of steam locomotives and railways. He built his first locomotive in 1814 and by 1825 had designed and driven an engine for the Stockton and Darlington Railway. With his son Robert (1803–59) he built the famous *Rocket* (1829), the prototype for all future steam locomotives. Robert is also famous as a bridge designer.

step-in ▶ **adjective** [attrib.] denoting a garment or pair of shoes that is put on by being stepped into and has no need for fastenings.
▶ **noun** (**step-ins**) **1** a pair of such shoes; slip-ons.
2 dated, chiefly N. Amer. a pair of women's briefs.

stepladder ▶ **noun** a short folding ladder with flat steps and a small platform.

stepmother ▶ **noun** a woman who is married to one's father after the divorce of one's parents or the death of one's mother.

stepmum ▶ **noun** informal term for **STEPMOTHER**.

step-parent ▶ **noun** a stepfather or stepmother.

steppe /stɛp/ ▶ **noun** (often **steppes**) a large area of flat unforested grassland in SE Europe or Siberia.
– ORIGIN late 17th cent.: from Russian *step'*.

stepped ▶ **adjective** having or formed into a step or series of steps: *a building with stepped access.*
■ carried out or occurring in stages or with pauses rather than continuously: *a stepped scale of discounts.*

steppe lemming ▶ **noun** a burrowing vole-like central Asian rodent with a black dorsal stripe, sometimes a serious pest of crops and pasture.

S

● *Lagurus lagurus*, family Muridae.

stepper ▶ noun **1** an electric motor or other device which moves or rotates in a series of small discrete steps.
2 a portable block used in step aerobics.

stepping stone ▶ noun a raised stone used singly or in a series as a place on which to step when crossing a stream or muddy area.
■ figurative an undertaking or event that helps one to make progress towards a specified goal: *the school championships are a stepping stone to international competition.*

step response ▶ noun Electronics the output of a device in response to an abrupt change in voltage.

stepsister ▶ noun a daughter of one's step-parent by a marriage other than with one's own father or mother.

stepson ▶ noun a son of one's husband or wife by a previous marriage.
– ORIGIN Old English *stēopsunu* (see STEP-, SON).

step wedge ▶ noun Photography a series of contiguous uniformly shaded rectangles, growing progressively darker from white (or light grey) at one end to black (or dark grey) at the other.

stepwise ▶ adverb & adjective in a series of distinct stages; not continuously: [as adv.] *concentrations of the acid tend to decrease stepwise.*

-ster ▶ suffix **1** denoting a person engaged in or associated with a particular activity or thing: *maltster* | *songster.*
2 denoting a person having a particular quality: *youngster.*
– ORIGIN Old English *-estre, -istre*, etc., of Germanic origin.

steradian /stəˈreɪdɪən/ (abbrev.: **sr**) ▶ noun the SI unit of solid angle, equal to the angle at the centre of a sphere subtended by a part of the surface equal in area to the square of the radius.
– ORIGIN late 19th cent.: from Greek *stereos* 'solid' + RADIAN.

sterane /ˈstɪəreɪn, ˈstɛreɪn/ ▶ noun Chemistry any of a class of saturated polycyclic hydrocarbons which are found in crude oils and are derived from the sterols of ancient organisms.
– ORIGIN 1950s: from STEROID + -ANE².

stercoraceous /ˌstəːkəˈreɪʃəs/ ▶ adjective technical consisting of or resembling dung or faeces.
– ORIGIN mid 18th cent.: from Latin *stercus, stercor-* 'dung' + -ACEOUS.

stere /stɪə/ ▶ noun a unit of volume equal to one cubic metre.
– ORIGIN late 18th cent.: from French *stère*, from Greek *stereos* 'solid'.

stereo /ˈstɛrɪəʊ, ˈstɪərɪəʊ/ ▶ noun (pl. **-os**) **1** [mass noun] sound that is directed through two or more speakers so that it seems to surround the listener and to come from more than one source; stereophonic sound.
■ [count noun] a CD, cassette, or record player that has two or more speakers and produces stereo sound.
2 Photography another term for stereoscope.
3 Printing short for STEREOTYPE.
▶ adjective **1** short for STEREOPHONIC: *stereo equipment* | *stereo sound.*
2 Photography short for *stereoscopic* (see STEREOSCOPE).

stereo- ▶ combining form relating to solid forms having three dimensions: *stereography.*
■ relating to a three-dimensional effect, arrangement, etc.: *stereochemistry* | *stereophonic* | *stereoscope.*
– ORIGIN from Greek *stereos* 'solid'.

stereobate /ˈstɛrɪə(ʊ)beɪt, ˈstɪə-/ ▶ noun Architecture a solid mass of masonry serving as a foundation for a wall or row of columns.
– ORIGIN mid 19th cent.: from French *stéréobate*, via Latin from Greek *stereobatēs*, from Greek *stereos* 'solid' + *batēs* 'base' (from *bainein* 'to walk').

stereocamera ▶ noun Photography a camera for simultaneously taking two photographs of the same thing from adjacent viewpoints, so that they will form a stereoscopic pair.

stereochemistry ▶ noun [mass noun] the branch of chemistry concerned with the three-dimensional arrangement of atoms and molecules and the effect of this on chemical reactions.
– DERIVATIVES **stereochemical** adjective, **stereochemically** adverb.

stereognosis /ˌstɛrɪə(ʊ)ˈnəʊsɪs, ˌstɪə-/ ▶ noun [mass noun] Psychology the mental perception of depth or three-dimensionality by the senses, usually in reference to the ability to perceive the form of solid objects by touch.
– DERIVATIVES **stereognostic** adjective.
– ORIGIN early 20th cent.: from Greek *stereos* 'solid' + *gnōsis* 'knowledge'.

stereogram ▶ noun **1** a diagram or computer-generated image giving a three-dimensional representation of a solid object or surface.
2 a stereo radiogram.

stereography ▶ noun [mass noun] the depiction or representation of three-dimensional things by projection on to a two-dimensional surface, e.g. in cartography.
– DERIVATIVES **stereograph** noun, **stereographic** adjective.

stereoisomer /ˌstɛrɪəʊˈʌɪsəmə, ˌstɪə-/ ▶ noun Chemistry each of two or more compounds differing only in the spatial arrangement of their atoms.
– DERIVATIVES **stereoisomeric** adjective, **stereoisomerism** noun.

stereolithography ▶ noun [mass noun] a technique or process for creating three-dimensional objects, in which a computer-controlled moving laser beam is used to build up the required structure, layer by layer, from a liquid polymer that hardens on contact with laser light.
– DERIVATIVES **stereolithographic** adjective.

stereometry ▶ noun [mass noun] Geometry the measurement of solid bodies.

stereomicroscope ▶ noun a binocular microscope that gives a relatively low-power stereoscopic view of the subject.

stereophonic /ˌstɛrɪə(ʊ)ˈfɒnɪk, ˌstɪərɪə(ʊ)-/ ▶ adjective (of sound recording and reproduction) using two or more channels of transmission and reproduction so that the reproduced sound seems to surround the listener and to come from more than one source.
– DERIVATIVES **stereophonically** adverb, **stereophony** /-ˈɒf(ə)ni/ noun.

stereopsis /ˌstɛrɪˈɒpsɪs, ˌstɪərɪ-/ ▶ noun [mass noun] the perception of depth produced by the reception in the brain of visual stimuli from both eyes in combination; binocular vision.
– DERIVATIVES **stereoptic** adjective.
– ORIGIN early 20th cent.: from STEREO- 'three-dimensional' + Greek *opsis* 'sight'.

stereopticon /ˌstɛrɪˈɒptɪk(ə)n, ˌstɪərɪ-/ ▶ noun a slide projector that combines two images to create a three-dimensional effect, or makes one image dissolve into another.
– ORIGIN mid 19th cent.: from STEREO- 'three-dimensional' + Greek *optikon*, neuter of *optikos* 'relating to vision'.

stereoscope /ˈstɛrɪə(ʊ)skəʊp, ˈstɪə-/ ▶ noun a device by which two photographs of the same object taken at slightly different angles are viewed together, creating an impression of depth and solidity.
– DERIVATIVES **stereoscopic** adjective, **stereoscopically** adverb, **stereoscopy** noun.

stereoselective /ˌstɛrɪəʊsɪˈlɛktɪv, ˌstɪə-/ ▶ adjective Chemistry (of a reaction) preferentially producing a particular stereoisomeric form of the product, irrespective of the configuration of the reactant.
– DERIVATIVES **stereoselectivity** noun.

stereo separation ▶ noun see SEPARATION (sense 2).

stereospecific ▶ adjective Chemistry another term for STEREOSELECTIVE.
– DERIVATIVES **stereospecifically** adverb, **stereospecificity** noun.

stereospondyl /ˌstɛrɪə(ʊ)ˈspɒndɪl, ˌstɪə-/ ▶ noun a fossil amphibian with a broad flat head, occurring in the Permian and Triassic periods.
● Suborder Stereospondyli, order Temnospondyli: several families.
– ORIGIN early 20th cent.: from modern Latin *Stereospondyli* (plural), from Greek *stereos* 'solid' + *spondulos* 'vertebra'.

stereotactic /ˌstɛrɪə(ʊ)ˈtaktɪk, ˌstɪərɪə(ʊ)-/ (also **stereotaxic** /-ˈtaksɪk/) ▶ adjective relating to or denoting techniques for surgical treatment or scientific investigation that permit the accurate positioning of probes inside the brain or other parts of the body.
– DERIVATIVES **stereotactically** adverb.

stereotaxis /ˌstɛrɪə(ʊ)ˈtaksɪs, ˌstɪərɪə(ʊ)-/ (also **stereotaxy** /-ˈtaksi/) ▶ noun [mass noun] the use of stereotactic instruments or devices in surgery or research.
– ORIGIN late 19th cent.: from STEREO- three-dimensional + Greek *taxis* 'orientation'.

stereotype ▶ noun **1** a widely held but fixed and oversimplified image or idea of a particular type of person or thing: *the stereotype of the woman as the carer* | *sexual and racial stereotypes.*
■ a person or thing that conforms to such an image: *don't treat anyone as a stereotype.*
2 a relief printing plate cast in a mould made from composed type or an original plate.
▶ verb view or represent as a stereotype: *the city is too easily stereotyped as an industrial wasteland* | [as adj. **stereotyped**] *the film is weakened by its stereotyped characters.*
– DERIVATIVES **stereotypic** adjective, **stereotypical** adjective, **stereotypically** adverb.
– ORIGIN late 18th cent.: from French *stéréotype* (adjective).

stereotypy /ˈstɛrɪə(ʊ)ˌtʌɪpi, ˈstɪə-/ ▶ noun [mass noun] the persistent repetition of an act, especially by an animal, for no obvious purpose.

steric /ˈstɛrɪk, ˈstɪərɪk/ ▶ adjective Chemistry of or relating to the spatial arrangement of atoms in a molecule, especially as it affects chemical reactions.
– DERIVATIVES **sterically** adverb.
– ORIGIN late 19th cent.: formed irregularly from Greek *stereos* 'solid' + -IC.

sterigma /stəˈrɪgmə/ ▶ noun (pl. **sterigmata** /stəˈrɪgmətə/) Botany (in some fungi) a spore-bearing projection from a cell.
– ORIGIN mid 19th cent.: modern Latin, from Greek *stērigma* 'a support', from *stērizein* 'to support'.

sterilant /ˈstɛrɪl(ə)nt/ ▶ noun an agent used to destroy micro-organisms; a disinfectant.
■ a chemical agent used to destroy pests and diseases in the soil, especially fungi and nematodes.

sterile ▶ adjective **1** not able to produce children or young: *the disease had made him sterile.*
■ (of a plant) not able to produce fruit or seeds. ■ (of land or soil) too poor in quality to produce crops. ■ lacking in imagination, creativity, or excitement; uninspiring or unproductive: *he found the fraternity's teachings sterile.*
2 free from bacteria or other living micro-organisms; totally clean: *a sterile needle and syringes.*
– DERIVATIVES **sterilely** adverb, **sterility** noun.
– ORIGIN late Middle English: from Old French, or from Latin *sterilis*; related to Greek *steira* 'barren cow'. Sense 2 dates from the late 19th cent.

sterilize (also **-ise**) ▶ verb [with obj.] **1** make (something) free from bacteria or other living micro-organisms: *babies' feeding equipment can be cleaned and sterilized* | [as adj. **sterilized**] *sterilized jars.*
2 (usu. **be sterilized**) deprive (a person or animal) of the ability to produce offspring, typically by removing or blocking the sex organs.
■ make (land or water) unable to produce crops or support life.
– DERIVATIVES **sterilizable** adjective, **sterilization** noun, **sterilizer** noun.

sterlet /ˈstəːlɪt/ ▶ noun a small sturgeon of the Danube basin and Caspian Sea area, farmed and commercially fished for its flesh and caviar.
● *Acipenser ruthenus*, family Acipenseridae.
– ORIGIN late 16th cent.: from Russian *sterlyad'*.

sterling ▶ noun [mass noun] British money: *prices in sterling are shown* | [as modifier] *issues of sterling bonds.*
■ short for STERLING SILVER: [as modifier] *a sterling spoon.*
▶ adjective chiefly Brit. (of a person or their work, efforts, or qualities) excellent or valuable: *this organization does sterling work for youngsters.*
– ORIGIN Middle English: probably from *steorra* 'star' + -LING (because some early Norman pennies bore a small star). Until recently one popular theory was that the coin was originally made by *Easterling* moneyers (from the 'eastern' Hanse towns), but the stressed first syllable would not have been dropped.

sterling area a group of countries, most belonging to the British Commonwealth, that formerly pegged their exchange rates to sterling or kept their reserves in sterling rather than gold or dollars.

sterling silver ▶ noun [mass noun] silver of 92¼ per cent purity.

S

Sterlitamak /ˌstɛːlɪtəˈmɑːk/ an industrial city in southern Russia, situated on the Belaya River to the north of Orenburg; pop. 250,000 (1990).

stern[1] ▶ adjective (of a person or their manner) serious and unrelenting, especially in the assertion of authority and exercise of discipline: *a smile transformed his stern face* | *Mama looked stern.*
■ (of an act or statement) strict and severe; using extreme measures or terms: *stern measures to restrict vehicle growth.* ■ (of competition or opposition) putting someone or something under extreme pressure: *the past year has been a stern test of the ability of British industry.*
– PHRASES **be made of sterner stuff** have a stronger character and be more able to overcome problems than others: *whereas James was deeply wounded by the failure, George was made of sterner stuff.* [ORIGIN: from Shakespeare's *Julius Caesar* (III. 2. 93).] **the sterner sex** archaic men regarded collectively and in contrast to women.
– DERIVATIVES **sternly** adverb, **sternness** noun.
– ORIGIN Old English *styrne*, probably from the West Germanic base of the verb **STARE**.

stern[2] ▶ noun the rearmost part of a ship or boat: *he stood at the stern of the yacht.*
■ humorous a person's bottom: *my stern can't take too much sun.*
– DERIVATIVES **sterned** adjective [in combination] *a square-sterned vessel*, **sternmost** adjective, **sternwards** adverb.
– ORIGIN Middle English: probably from Old Norse *stjórn* 'steering', from *stýra* 'to steer'.

sternal ▶ adjective of or relating to the sternum: *the sternal area* | *sternal muscles.*

sternal rib ▶ noun another term for **TRUE RIB**.

sterndrive ▶ noun an inboard engine connected to an outboard drive unit at the rear of a powerboat.

Sterne /stəːn/, Laurence (1713–68), Irish novelist. He is best known for his nine-volume work *The Life and Opinions of Tristram Shandy* (1759–67), which parodied the developing conventions of the novel form.

Stern Gang the British name for a militant Zionist group that campaigned in Palestine during the 1940s for the creation of a Jewish state. Founded by Avraham Stern (1907–42) as an offshoot of Irgun, the group assassinated the British Minister for the Middle East, Lord Moyne, and Count Bernadotte, the UN mediator for Palestine.

sternite ▶ noun Entomology (in an insect) a sclerotized plate forming the sternum of a segment. Compare with **TERGITE**.

Sterno /ˈstəːnəʊ/ ▶ noun [mass noun] US trademark flammable hydrocarbon jelly supplied in cans for use as fuel for cooking stoves.
– ORIGIN early 20th cent.: from the name of *Sternau* and Co., New York, + **-O**.

sternocleidomastoid /ˌstəːnə(ʊ)ˌklʌɪdə(ʊ)ˈmastɔɪd/ (also **sternocleidomastoid muscle**) ▶ noun Anatomy each of a pair of long muscles which connect the sternum, clavicle, and mastoid process of the temporal bone and serve to turn and nod the neck.

sternomastoid /ˌstəːnə(ʊ)ˈmastɔɪd/ ▶ noun another term for **STERNOCLEIDOMASTOID**.

sternpost ▶ noun the central upright support at the stern of a boat, traditionally bearing the rudder.

sternsheets ▶ plural noun the flooring planks in a boat's after section, or the seating in this section of an open boat.

sternum /ˈstəːnəm/ ▶ noun (pl. **sternums** or **sterna** /-nə/) the breastbone.
■ Zoology a thickened ventral plate on each segment of the body of an arthropod.
– ORIGIN mid 17th cent.: modern Latin from Greek *sternon* 'chest'.

sternutation /ˌstəːnjʊˈteɪʃ(ə)n/ ▶ noun [mass noun] formal the action of sneezing.
– ORIGIN late Middle English: from Latin *sternutatio(n-)*, from the verb *sternutare*, frequentative of *sternuere* 'to sneeze'.

sternutator /ˈstəːnjʊˌteɪtə/ ▶ noun technical an agent that causes sneezing.
■ an agent used in chemical warfare that causes irritation to the nose and eyes, pain in the chest, and nausea.
– DERIVATIVES **sternutatory** /-ˈnjuːtət(ə)ri/ adjective & noun (pl. **-ies**).

sternway ▶ noun [mass noun] backward movement of a ship: *we begin making sternway towards the shoal.*

sternwheeler ▶ noun a steamer propelled by a paddle wheel positioned at the stern.

steroid /ˈstɪərɔɪd, ˈstɛrɔɪd/ ▶ noun Biochemistry any of a large class of organic compounds with a characteristic molecular structure containing four rings of carbon atoms (three six-membered and one five). They include many hormones, alkaloids, and vitamins.
■ short for **ANABOLIC STEROID**.
– DERIVATIVES **steroidal** adjective.
– ORIGIN 1930s: from **STEROL** + **-OID**.

sterol /ˈstɪərɒl, ˈstɛrɒl/ ▶ noun Biochemistry any of a group of naturally occurring unsaturated steroid alcohols, typically waxy solids.
– ORIGIN early 20th cent.: independent usage of the ending of words such as **CHOLESTEROL** and **ERGOSTEROL**.

stertorous /ˈstəːt(ə)rəs/ ▶ adjective (of breathing) noisy and laboured.
– DERIVATIVES **stertorously** adverb.
– ORIGIN early 19th cent.: from modern Latin *stertor* 'snoring sound' (from Latin *stertere* 'to snore') + **-OUS**.

stet ▶ verb (**stetted**, **stetting**) [no obj., in imperative] let it stand (used as an instruction on a printed proof to indicate that a correction or alteration should be ignored).
■ [with obj.] write such an instruction against (something corrected or deleted).
▶ noun such an instruction made on a printed proof.
– ORIGIN Latin, 'let it stand', from *stare* 'to stand'.

stethoscope /ˈstɛθəskəʊp/ ▶ noun a medical instrument for listening to the action of someone's heart or breathing, typically having a small disc-shaped resonator that is placed against the chest, and two tubes connected to earpieces.
– DERIVATIVES **stethoscopic** adjective
– ORIGIN early 19th cent.: from French *stéthoscope*, from Greek *stēthos* 'breast' + *skopein* 'look at'.

Stetson /ˈstɛts(ə)n/ ▶ noun (trademark in the US) a hat with a high crown and a very wide brim, traditionally worn by cowboys and ranchers in the US.
– ORIGIN late 19th cent.: named after John B. *Stetson* (1830–1906), American hat manufacturer.

Stettin /ʃtɛˈtiːn/ German name for **SZCZECIN**.

steups /stʃuːps/ ▶ verb [no obj.] make a noise by sucking air and saliva through the teeth, typically to express annoyance or derision.
▶ noun an expression of annoyance or derision made in such a way.
– ORIGIN imitative.

stevedore /ˈstiːvədɔː/ ▶ noun a person employed at a dock to load and unload goods from ships.
– ORIGIN late 18th cent.: from Spanish *estivador*, from *estivar* 'stow a cargo', from Latin *stipare* (see **STEEVE**[2]).

Stevenage /ˈstiːvənɪdʒ/ a town in Hertfordshire; pop. 74,520 (1981). It was designated a planned urban centre in 1946 and was developed as a new town.

Stevengraph /ˈstiːv(ə)ngrɑːf/ ▶ noun a type of small picture made from brightly coloured woven silk, produced during the late 19th century.
– ORIGIN named after Thomas *Stevens* (1828–88), English weaver, whose firm made them.

Stevens, Wallace (1879–1955), American poet. He wrote poetry privately and mostly in isolation from the literary community, developing an original and colourful style. His *Collected Poems* (1954) won a Pulitzer Prize.

Stevenson, Robert Louis (Balfour) (1850–94), Scottish novelist, poet, and travel writer. Stevenson made his name with the adventure story *Treasure Island* (1883). Other notable works: *The Strange Case of Dr Jekyll and Mr Hyde* and *Kidnapped* (both 1886).

stevioside /ˈstiːvɪ(ə)sʌɪd/ ▶ noun [mass noun] a sweet compound of the glycoside class obtained from the leaves of a Paraguayan shrub and used as a food sweetener.
● The shrub is *Stevia rebaudiana* (family Compositae).
– ORIGIN 1930s: from the genus name *Stevia* (from the name of P. J. *Esteve* (died 1566), Spanish botanist) + **-OSE**[2] + **-IDE**.

stew[1] ▶ noun 1 [mass noun] a dish of meat and vegetables cooked slowly in liquid in a closed dish or pan: *lamb stew* | [count noun] *add to casseroles, stews, and sauces.*
2 [in sing.] informal a state of great anxiety or agitation: *she's in a right old stew.*
3 archaic a heated public room used for hot steam baths.
■ a brothel.
▶ verb [with obj.] cook (meat, fruit, or other food) slowly in liquid in a closed dish or pan: *a new way to stew rhubarb* | [no obj.] *add the beef and stew gently.*
■ [no obj.] (of meat, fruit, or other food) be cooked in such a way. ■ [no obj.] Brit. (of tea) become strong and bitter with prolonged brewing. ■ [no obj.] informal remain in a heated or stifling atmosphere: *sweaty clothes left to stew in a plastic bag.* ■ [no obj.] informal worry about something, especially on one's own: *James will be expecting us, so we will let him stew a bit.* ■ (be **stewed in**) poetic/literary be steeped in or imbued with: *politics there are stewed in sexual prejudice and privilege.*
– PHRASES **stew in one's own juice** informal suffer anxiety or the unpleasant consequences of one's own actions without the consoling intervention of others.
– ORIGIN Middle English (in the sense 'cauldron'): from Old French *estuve* (related to *estuver* 'heat in steam'), probably based on Greek *tuphos* 'smoke, steam'. Sense 1 (mid 18th cent.) is directly from the verb (dating from late Middle English).

stew[2] ▶ noun Brit. a pond or large tank for keeping fish for eating.
■ an artificial oyster bed.
– ORIGIN Middle English: from Old French *estui*, from *estoier* 'confine'.

stew[3] ▶ noun N. Amer. informal an air steward or stewardess.
– ORIGIN 1970s: abbreviation.

steward ▶ noun 1 a person who looks after the passengers on a ship, aircraft, or train and brings them meals.
■ a person responsible for supplies of food to a college, club, or other institution.
2 an official appointed to supervise arrangements or keep order at a large public event, for example a race, match, or demonstration.
■ short for **SHOP STEWARD**.
3 a person employed to manage another's property, especially a large house or estate.
■ Brit., chiefly historical an officer of the royal household, especially an administrator of Crown estates: [in titles] *Chief Steward of the Duchy of Lancaster.* ■ a person whose responsibility it is to take care of something: *farmers pride themselves on being stewards of the countryside.*
▶ verb [with obj.] 1 (of an official) supervise arrangements or keep order at (a large public event): *the event was organized and stewarded properly.*
2 manage or look after (another's property).
– DERIVATIVES **stewardship** noun.
– ORIGIN Old English *stīweard*, from *stig* (probably in the sense 'house, hall') + *weard* 'ward'. The verb dates from the early 17th cent.

stewardess /ˈstjuːədɪs, ˌstjuːəˈdɛs/ ▶ noun a woman who is employed to look after the passengers on a ship or aircraft.

Stewart[1] ▶ adjective & noun variant spelling of **STUART**[5].

Stewart[2], Jackie (b.1939), British motor-racing driver; born *John Young Stewart*. He was three times world champion (1969; 1971; 1973).

Stewart[3], James (Maitland) (1908–97), American actor, famous for roles in which he was seen as embodying the all-American hero. His films include *The Philadelphia Story* (1940), which earned him an Oscar, Frank Capra's *It's a Wonderful Life* (1946), Alfred Hitchcock's *Vertigo* (1958), and westerns such as *The Man from Laramie* (1955).

Stewart Island an island of New Zealand, situated off the south coast of South Island, from which it is separated by the Foveaux Strait; chief settlement, Oban.
– ORIGIN named after Captain William *Stewart*, a whaler and sealer who made a survey of the island in 1809.

stewartry (also **stewardry**) ▶ noun (pl. **-ies**) a former territorial division of Scotland (abolished in 1747) under the jurisdiction of a steward.
■ (**The Stewartry**) the Kirkcudbright district of Galloway.

stewbum ▶ noun US informal an alcoholic, especially one who has become vagrant.

stewed ▶ **adjective** (of food) cooked slowly in liquid in a closed dish or pan: *stewed apple.*
■ Brit. (of tea) tasting strong and bitter because of prolonged brewing. ■ [predic.] informal drunk: *we got stewed at their party.*

stewing ▶ **adjective** [attrib.] (of meat or other food) suitable for stewing: *a pound of stewing steak.*

stewpot ▶ **noun** a large pot in which stews are cooked.

stg ▶ **abbreviation for** sterling.

Sth ▶ **abbreviation for** south.

sthenic /ˈsθɛnɪk/ ▶ **adjective** Medicine, dated of or having a high or excessive level of strength and energy.
– ORIGIN late 18th cent.: from Greek *sthenos* 'strength', on the pattern of *asthenic*.

stibnite /ˈstɪbnʌɪt/ ▶ **noun** [mass noun] a lead-grey mineral, typically occurring as striated prismatic crystals, which consists of antimony sulphide and is the chief ore of antimony.
– ORIGIN mid 19th cent.: from Latin *stibium* 'black antimony' + **-INE**[4] + **-ITE**[1].

stichomythia /ˌstɪkə(ʊ)ˈmɪθɪə/ ▶ **noun** [mass noun] dialogue in which two characters speak alternate lines of verse, used as a stylistic device in ancient Greek drama.
– ORIGIN mid 19th cent.: modern Latin, from Greek *stikhomuthia*, from *stikhos* 'row, line of verse' + *muthos* 'speech, talk'.

stick[1] ▶ **noun** **1** a thin piece of wood that has fallen or been cut off a tree.
2 a piece of such wood trimmed for a particular purpose, in particular:
■ a long, thin piece of wood used for support in walking or as a weapon with which to hit someone or something. ■ (in hockey, polo, and other games) a long, thin implement, typically made of wood, with a curved head or angled blade that is used to hit or direct the ball or puck. ■ [usu. with modifier] a short, thin piece of wood used to impale food: *lolly sticks.* ■ (**the sticks**) informal goalposts or cricket stumps. ■ (**sticks**) (in field hockey) the foul play of raising the stick above the shoulder. ■ Nautical, archaic a mast or spar. ■ figurative a piece of basic furniture: *every* ***stick of furniture*** *just vanished.*
3 something resembling or likened to a stick, in particular:
■ a long, thin piece of something: ***a stick of*** *dynamite | cinnamon sticks.* ■ US a quarter-pound pack of butter or margarine. ■ a conductor's baton. ■ a gear or control lever. ■ (in extended and metaphorical use) referring to a very thin person or limb: *the girl was a stick | her arms were* ***like sticks.*** ■ a number of bombs or paratroopers dropped rapidly from an aircraft. ■ a small group of soldiers assigned to a particular duty: ***a stick of*** *heavily armed guards.*
4 a threat of punishment or unwelcome measures (often contrasted with the offer of reward as a means of persuasion): *training that relies more on the carrot than on the stick.*
■ [mass noun] Brit. informal severe criticism or treatment: *I* ***took a lot of stick*** *from the press.*
5 (**the sticks**) informal, derogatory rural areas far from cities or civilization: *he felt hard done by living* ***out in the sticks.***
6 [with adj.] informal, dated a person of a specified kind: *Janet's not such a bad* ***old stick*** *sometimes.*
7 Stock Exchange a large quantity of unsold stock, especially the proportion of shares which must be taken up by underwriters after an unsuccessful issue.
– PHRASES **up the stick** Brit. informal pregnant. **up sticks** Brit. informal go to live elsewhere. [ORIGIN: from nautical slang *to up sticks* 'set up a boat's mast' (ready for departure).]
– DERIVATIVES **sticklike** adjective.
– ORIGIN Old English *sticca* 'peg, stick, spoon', of West Germanic origin; related to Dutch *stek* 'cutting from a plant' and German *Stecken* 'staff, stick'.

stick[2] ▶ **verb** (past and past participle **stuck**) **1** [with obj.] (**stick something in/into/through**) push a sharp or pointed object into or through (something): *he stuck his fork into the sausage | the candle was stuck in a straw-covered bottle.*
■ (**stick something on**) fix something on (a point or pointed object): *stick the balls of wool on knitting needles.* ■ [no obj.] (**stick in/into/through**) (of a pointed object) be or remain fixed with its point embedded in (something): *there was a slim rod sticking into the ground beside me.* ■ [with obj. and adverbial] insert, thrust, or push: *a youth with a cigarette stuck behind one ear | she stuck out her tongue at him.* ■ [no obj., with adverbial of direction] protrude or extend in a certain direction: *his front teeth* ***stick out*** *| Sue's hair was* ***sticking up*** *at all angles.* ■ [with obj. and adverbial of place] put somewhere, typically in a quick or careless way: *just stick that sandwich on my desk.* ■ informal used to express angry dismissal of a particular thing: *he told them they could stick the job—he didn't want it anyway.* ■ informal cause to incur an expense or loss: *she stuck me for all of last month's rent.* ■ stab or pierce with a sharp object: [as adj. **stuck**] *he screamed like a stuck pig.*
2 [no obj.] adhere or cling to a substance or surface: *the plastic seats* ***stuck to*** *my skin.*
■ [with obj. and adverbial of place] fasten or cause to adhere to an object or surface: *she stuck the stamp on the envelope.* ■ be or become fixed or jammed in one place as a result of an obstruction: *he drove into a bog, where his wheels stuck fast.* ■ remain in a static condition; fail to progress: *he lost a lot of weight but had stuck at 15 stone.* ■ (of a feeling or thought) remain persistently in one's mind: *one particular incident sticks in my mind.* ■ informal be or become convincing, established, or regarded as valid: *the authorities couldn't make the charges stick | the name stuck and Anastasia she remained.* ■ (in pontoon and similar card games) decline to add to one's hand.
3 (**be stuck**) be fixed in a particular position or unable to move or be moved: *Sara tried to open the window but it was stuck | we got stuck in a traffic jam | the cat's stuck up a tree.*
■ be unable to progress with a task or find the answer or solution to something: *I'm doing the crossword and I've got stuck.* ■ [with adverbial of place] informal be or remain in a specified place or situation, typically one perceived as tedious or unpleasant: *I don't want to be stuck in an office all my life.* ■ (**be stuck for**) be at a loss for or in need of: *I'm not usually stuck for words.* ■ (**be stuck with**) informal be unable to get rid of or escape from: *like it or not, she and Grant were stuck with each other.* ■ (**be stuck on**) informal be infatuated with: *he's too good for Jenny, even though she's so stuck on him.*
4 [often with negative] Brit. informal accept or tolerate (an unpleasant or unwelcome person or situation): *I can't stick Geoffrey—he's a real old misery.*
■ (**stick it out**) informal put up with or persevere with something difficult or disagreeable.
– PHRASES **get stuck in** (or **into**) Brit. informal start doing (something) enthusiastically or with determination: *we got stuck into the decorating.* **stick at nothing** allow nothing to deter one from achieving one's aim, however wrong or dishonest: *he would stick at nothing to preserve his privileges.* **stick 'em up!** informal hands up! (spoken typically by a person threatening someone else with a gun). **stick in one's throat** (or **craw**) be difficult or impossible to accept; be a source of continuing annoyance. ■ (of words) be difficult or impossible to say: *she couldn't say 'Thank you'—the words stuck in her throat.* **stick it to** informal, chiefly US treat (someone) harshly or severely. **stick one** (or **it**) **on** Brit. informal hit (someone). **stick one's neck out** informal risk incurring criticism or anger by acting or speaking boldly. **stick out a mile** see **MILE**. **stick out like a sore thumb** see **SORE**. **stick to one's guns** see **GUN**. **stick to one's ribs** (of food) be filling and nourishing: *a bowl of soup that will stick to your ribs.*
– ORIGIN Old English *stician*, of Germanic origin; related to German *sticken* 'embroider', from an Indo-European root shared by Greek *stizein* 'to prick', *stigma* 'a mark' and Latin *instigare* 'spur on'. Early senses included 'pierce' and 'remain fixed (by its embedded pointed end)'.
▶ **stick around** informal remain in or near a place: *I'd like to stick around and watch the game.*
stick at informal persevere with (a task or endeavour) in a steady and determined way.
stick by 1 continue to support or be loyal to (someone), typically during difficult times: *I love him and whatever happens I'll stick by him.* **2** another way of saying ***stick to*** in sense 2 below.
stick something on informal place the blame for a mistake or wrongdoing on (someone).
stick out be extremely noticeable: *many important things had happened to him, but one stuck out.*
stick out for refuse to accept less than (what one has asked for); persist in demanding (something): *they offered him a Rover but Vic stuck out for a Jaguar.*
stick to 1 continue or confine oneself to doing or using (a particular thing): *I'll stick to bitter lemon, thanks.* ■ not move or digress from (a path or a subject). **2** adhere to (a commitment, belief, or rule): *the government stuck to their election pledges.*
stick together informal remain united or mutually loyal: *we Europeans must stick together.*
stick someone/thing up informal, chiefly US rob someone at gunpoint.
stick up for support or defend (a person or cause).
stick with informal **1** persevere or continue with: *I'm happy to stick with the present team.* **2** another way of saying ***stick by*** above.

stickability ▶ **noun** [mass noun] informal a person's ability to persevere with something; staying power: *the secret of success is stickability.*

stickball ▶ **noun** [mass noun] N. Amer. an informal game played with a stick and a ball, derived from the rules of baseball or lacrosse.

sticker ▶ **noun 1** an adhesive label or notice, generally printed or illustrated.
2 informal a determined or persistent person.

sticker price ▶ **noun** N. Amer. the advertised retail price of an article.

sticker shock ▶ **noun** [mass noun] US informal shock or dismay experienced by the potential buyers of a particular product on discovering its high or increased price.

stick-handle ▶ **verb** [no obj.] [usu. as noun **stick-handling**] Ice Hockey control the puck with one's stick.

sticking plaster ▶ **noun** chiefly Brit. a piece of flexible material with an adhesive backing for covering cuts or small wounds, available in a roll or as individual patches.

sticking point ▶ **noun** a point at which an obstacle arises in progress towards an agreement or goal.

stick insect ▶ **noun** a long, slender, slow-moving insect that resembles a twig. Many species appear to lack males and the females lay fertile eggs without mating.
● Family Phasmatidae, order Phasmida: many genera.

stick-in-the-mud ▶ **noun** informal a person who is dull and unadventurous and who resists change.

stickleback ▶ **noun** a small fish with sharp spines along its back, able to live in both salt and fresh water and found in both Eurasia and North America.
● Family Gasterosteidae: several genera and species, including the common and widespread **three-spined stickleback** (*Gasterosteus aculeatus*).
– ORIGIN late Middle English: from Old English *sticel* 'thorn, sting' + *bæc* 'back'.

stickler ▶ **noun** a person who insists on a certain quality or type of behaviour: ***a stickler for*** *accuracy | a stickler when it comes to timekeeping.*
– ORIGIN mid 16th cent. (in the sense 'umpire'): from obsolete *stickle* 'be umpire', alteration of obsolete *stightle* 'to control', frequentative of Old English *stiht(i)an* 'set in order'.

stick-nest rat ▶ **noun** a fluffy-haired gregarious Australian rat which builds nests of interwoven sticks.
● Genus *Leporillus*, family Muridae: two species, in particular *L. conditor.*

stickpin ▶ **noun** N. Amer. a straight pin with an ornamental head, worn to keep a tie in place or as a brooch.

stickseed ▶ **noun** a plant of the borage family which bears small barbed seeds.
● Genera *Hackelia* and *Lappula*, family Boraginaceae: several species, in particular *H. floribunda*, which resembles a forget-me-not.

stick shift ▶ **noun** N. Amer. a gear lever or manual transmission.

stick-to-it-iveness ▶ **noun** [mass noun] N. Amer. informal perseverance; persistence.

stickum /ˈstɪkəm/ ▶ **noun** [mass noun] informal, chiefly N. Amer. a sticky or adhesive substance; gum or paste.
– ORIGIN early 20th cent.: from the verb **STICK**[2] + *-um* (representing the pronoun *them*).

stick-up ▶ **noun** informal, chiefly US an armed robbery in which a gun is used to threaten people.

stickweed ▶ **noun** [mass noun] US any of a number of North American plants with hooked or barbed seeds, e.g. ragweed.

sticky ▶ **adjective** (**stickier**, **stickiest**) **1** tending or designed to stick to things on contact or covered with something that sticks: *sticky cakes and pastries | sticky tape.*
■ (of a substance) glutinous; viscous: *the dough should be moist but not sticky.* ■ (of prices, interest rates, or wages) slow to change or react to change.

2 (of the weather) hot and damp; muggy: *it was an unusually hot and sticky summer.*
■damp with sweat: *she felt hot and sticky and changed her clothes.*
3 informal involving problems; difficult or awkward: *the relationship is going through a sticky patch.*
– PHRASES **come to a sticky end** see **END**. **sticky fingers** informal a propensity to steal.
– DERIVATIVES **stickily** adverb, **stickiness** noun.

stickybeak Austral./NZ informal ▶**noun** an inquisitive and prying person.
▶**verb** [no obj.] pry into other people's affairs: *I don't mean to stickybeak, but when is he going to leave?*

sticky end ▶**noun** Biochemistry an end of a DNA double helix at which a few unpaired nucleotides of one strand extend beyond the other.

sticky-fingered ▶**adjective** informal given to stealing: *a sticky-fingered con artist.*

stiction /ˈstɪkʃ(ə)n/ ▶**noun** [mass noun] Physics the friction which tends to prevent stationary surfaces from being set in motion.

Stieglitz /ˈstiːɡlɪts/, Alfred (1864–1946), American photographer, husband of Georgia O'Keefe. He was important for his pioneering work to establish photography as a fine art in the US.

stifado /stɪˈfɑːdəʊ/ ▶**noun** [mass noun] a Greek dish of meat stewed with onions and sometimes tomatoes.
– ORIGIN from modern Greek *stiphado*.

stiff ▶**adjective** **1** not easily bent or changed in shape; rigid: *a stiff black collar | stiff cardboard.*
■not moving as freely as is usual or desirable; difficult to turn or operate: *a stiff drawer | the shower tap is a little stiff.* ■(of a person or part of the body) unable to move easily and without pain: *he was stiff from sitting on the desk | a stiff back.* ■(of a person or their manner) not relaxed or friendly; constrained: *she greeted him with stiff politeness.*
2 severe or strong: *they face stiff fines and a possible jail sentence | a stiff increase in taxes.*
■(of a wind) blowing strongly: *a stiff breeze stirring the lake.* ■requiring strength or effort; difficult: *a long stiff climb up the bare hillside.* ■(of an alcoholic drink) strong: *a stiff measure of brandy.*
3 [predic.] (**stiff with**) informal full of: *the place is stiff with alarm systems.*
4 (—— **stiff**) informal having a specified unpleasant feeling to an extreme extent: *she was scared stiff | I was bored stiff with my project.*
▶**noun** informal **1** a dead body.
2 chiefly N. Amer. a boring, conventional person: *ordinary working stiffs in respectable offices.*
3 (**the stiffs**) Brit. a sports club's reserve team.
▶**verb** [with obj.] informal **1** (often **be stiffed**) N. Amer. cheat (someone) out of something, especially money.
■fail to leave (someone) a tip.
2 N. Amer. ignore deliberately; snub.
3 kill: *I want to get those pigs who stiffed your doctor.*
■[no obj.] be unsuccessful: *as soon as he began singing about the wife and kids, his albums stiffed.*
– PHRASES **stiff as a board** informal (of a person or part of the body) extremely stiff. **a stiff upper lip** a quality of uncomplaining stoicism: *senior managers had to keep a stiff upper lip and remain optimistic.*
– DERIVATIVES **stiffish** adjective, **stiffly** adverb, **stiffness** noun.
– ORIGIN Old English *stīf*, of Germanic origin; related to Dutch *stijf*.

stiff-arm ▶**verb** [with obj.] tackle or fend off (a person) by extending an arm rigidly (illegal in rugby).

stiffen ▶**verb** make or become stiff or rigid: [with obj.] *he stiffened his knees in an effort to prevent them trembling* | [no obj.] *my back stiffens up and I can't bend.*
■[with obj.] support or strengthen (a garment or fabric), typically by adding tape or an adhesive layer. ■figurative make or become stronger or more steadfast: [with obj.] *outrage over the murders stiffened the government's resolve to confront the Mafia* | [no obj.] *the regime's resistance stiffened.*
– DERIVATIVES **stiffener** noun.

stiffening ▶**noun** [mass noun] material used to stiffen a garment, fabric, or other object.

stiff-necked ▶**adjective** (of a person or their behaviour) haughty and stubborn.

stifftail (also **stiff-tailed duck**) ▶**noun** a diving duck with a stiff tail of pointed feathers, often held up at an angle.
● Family Anatidae: four genera, in particular *Oxyura*, and several species, e.g. the ruddy duck.

stiffy (also **stiffie**) ▶**noun** (pl. **-ies**) vulgar slang an erection of a man's penis.

stifle[1] ▶**verb** [with obj.] **1** make (someone) unable to breathe properly; suffocate: *those in the streets were stifled by the fumes* | [as adj. **stifling**] *stifling heat.*
2 restrain (a reaction) or stop oneself acting on (an emotion): *she stifled a giggle | she stifled a desire to turn and flee* | [as adj. **stifled**] *she gave a stifled cry of disappointment.*
■prevent or constrain (an activity or idea): *high taxes were stifling private enterprise.*
– DERIVATIVES **stifler** noun, **stiflingly** adverb [as submodifier] *a stiflingly hot day.*
– ORIGIN late Middle English: perhaps from a frequentative of Old French *estouffer* 'smother, stifle'.

stifle[2] (also **stifle joint**) ▶**noun** a joint in the legs of horses, dogs, and other animals, equivalent to the knee in humans.
– ORIGIN Middle English: of unknown origin.

stifle bone ▶**noun** the bone in front of a stifle.

stigma /ˈstɪɡmə/ ▶**noun** (pl. **stigmas** or especially in sense 2 **stigmata** /-mətə, -ˈmɑːtə/) **1** a mark of disgrace associated with a particular circumstance, quality, or person: *the stigma of mental disorder | to be a non-reader carries a social stigma.*
2 (**stigmata**) (in Christian tradition) marks corresponding to those left on Christ's body by the Crucifixion, said to have been impressed by divine favour on the bodies of St Francis of Assisi and others.
3 Medicine a visible sign or characteristic of a disease.
■a mark or spot on the skin.
4 Botany (in a flower) the part of a pistil that receives the pollen during pollination.
– ORIGIN late 16th cent. (denoting a mark made by pricking or branding): via Latin from Greek *stigma* 'a mark made by a pointed instrument, a dot'; related to **STICK**[1].

stigmaria /stɪɡˈmɛːrɪə/ ▶**noun** (pl. **stigmariae** /-ˈmɛːrɪiː/) Palaeontology a fossilized root of a giant lycopod, common in Carboniferous coal measures.
● Class Lycopsida, in particular the genera *Lepidodendron* and *Sigillaria*.
– DERIVATIVES **stigmarian** adjective.
– ORIGIN mid 19th cent.: modern Latin, from Greek *stigma*, with reference to the scars where rootlets were attached, covering the fossils.

stigmatic ▶**adjective** **1** of or relating to a stigma or stigmas, in particular constituting or conveying a mark of disgrace.
2 another term for **ANASTIGMATIC**.
▶**noun** a person bearing stigmata.
– DERIVATIVES **stigmatically** adverb.
– ORIGIN late 16th cent. (in the sense '(person) marked with a blemish or deformity'): from Latin *stigma, stigmat-* + **-IC**.

stigmatist ▶**noun** another term for **STIGMATIC**.

stigmatize (also **-ise**) ▶**verb** [with obj.] **1** (usu. **be stigmatized**) describe or regard as worthy of disgrace or great disapproval: *the institution was stigmatized as a last resort for the destitute.*
2 mark with stigmata.
– DERIVATIVES **stigmatization** noun.
– ORIGIN late 16th cent. (in the sense 'mark with a brand'): from French *stigmatiser* or medieval Latin *stigmatizare*, from Greek *stigmatizein*, from *stigma* (see **STIGMA**).

Stijl see **DE STIJL**.

stilb ▶**noun** a unit of luminance equal to one candela per square centimetre.
– ORIGIN 1940s: from French, from Greek *stilbein* 'to glitter'.

stilbene /ˈstɪlbiːn/ ▶**noun** [mass noun] Chemistry a synthetic aromatic hydrocarbon which forms phosphorescent crystals and is used in dye manufacture.
● Alternative name: *trans*-**1,2-diphenylethene**; chem. formula: $C_6H_5CH{=}CHC_6H_5$.
– ORIGIN mid 19th cent.: from Greek *stilbein* 'to glitter' + **-ENE**.

stilboestrol /stɪlˈbiːstrɒl/ (US **stilbestrol**) ▶**noun** [mass noun] Biochemistry a powerful synthetic oestrogen used in hormone therapy, as a post-coital contraceptive, and as a growth-promoting agent for livestock.
– ORIGIN 1930s: from **STILBENE** + **OESTRUS** + **-OL**.

stile[1] ▶**noun** an arrangement of steps that allows people but not animals to climb over a fence or wall.
– ORIGIN Old English *stigel*, from a Germanic root meaning 'to climb'.

stile[2] ▶**noun** a vertical piece in the frame of a panelled door or sash window. Compare with **RAIL**[1] (sense 3).
– ORIGIN late 17th cent.: probably from Dutch *stijl* 'pillar, doorpost'.

stiletto ▶**noun** (pl. **-os**) **1** chiefly Brit. a woman's shoe with a thin, high tapering heel.
■(also **stiletto heel**) a heel on such a shoe.
2 a short dagger with a tapering blade.
■a sharp-pointed tool for making eyelet holes.
– ORIGIN early 17th cent.: from Italian, diminutive of *stilo* 'dagger'.

still[1] ▶**adjective** not moving or making a sound: *she sat very still, her eyes closed.*
■(of air or water) undisturbed by wind, sound, or current; calm and tranquil: *her voice carried on the still air | a still autumn day.* ■(of a drink) not effervescent.
▶**noun** **1** [mass noun] deep silence and calm; stillness: *the still of the night.*
2 an ordinary static photograph as opposed to a motion picture, especially a single shot from a cinema film: *film stills* | [as modifier] *stills photography.*
▶**adverb** **1** up to and including the present or the time mentioned; even now (or then) as formerly: *he still lives with his mother | it was still raining.*
■referring to something that will or may happen in the future: *we could still win.*
2 nevertheless; all the same: *I'm afraid he's crazy. Still, he's harmless.*
3 even (used with comparatives for emphasis): *write, or better still, type, captions for the pictures | Hank, already sweltering, began to sweat still more profusely.*
▶**verb** make or become still; quieten: [with obj.] *she raised her hand, stilling Erica's protests* | [no obj.] *the din in the hall stilled.*
– PHRASES **still and all** informal nevertheless; even so. **still small voice** the voice of one's conscience (with reference to 1 Kings 19:12). **still waters run deep** proverb a quiet or placid manner may conceal a passionate nature.
– DERIVATIVES **stillness** noun.
– ORIGIN Old English *stille* (adjective and adverb), *stillan* (verb), of West Germanic origin, from a base meaning 'be fixed, stand'.

still[2] ▶**noun** an apparatus for distilling alcoholic drinks such as whisky.
– ORIGIN mid 16th cent.: from the rare verb *still* 'extract by distillation', shortening of **DISTIL**.

stillage ▶**noun** a wooden rack or pallet for holding stored goods off the floor or separating goods in transit.
– ORIGIN late 16th cent. (originally denoting a stand for casks): apparently from Dutch *stellagie* 'scaffold', from *stellen* 'to place'.

stillbirth ▶**noun** the birth of an infant that has died in the womb (strictly, after having survived through at least the first 28 weeks of pregnancy, earlier instances being regarded as abortion or miscarriage).

stillborn ▶**adjective** (of an infant) born dead.
■figurative (of a proposal or plan) having failed to develop or succeed; unrealized: *the proposed wealth tax was stillborn.*

still-hunt chiefly N. Amer. ▶**verb** [no obj.] [often as noun **still-hunting**] hunt game stealthily; stalk.
▶**noun** a stealthy hunt for game.

still life ▶**noun** (pl. **still lifes**) a painting or drawing of an arrangement of objects, typically including fruit and flowers and objects contrasting with these in texture, such as bowls and glassware.
■[mass noun] this type or genre of painting or drawing.

still room ▶**noun** Brit. historical a room in a large house used by the housekeeper for the storage of preserves, cakes, and liqueurs and the preparation of tea and coffee.
– ORIGIN early 18th cent.: a term used earlier for a room in a house where a still was kept for the distillation of perfumes and cordials.

Stillson /ˈstɪls(ə)n/ (also **Stillson wrench**) ▶**noun** a large wrench with jaws that tighten as pressure is increased.
– ORIGIN early 20th cent.: named after Daniel C. *Stillson* (1830–99), its American inventor.

stilly poetic/literary ▶**adverb** quietly and with little movement: *the birds rested stilly.*

▶ **adjective** still and quiet: *the stilly night.*

stilt ▶ **noun 1** either of a pair of upright poles with supports for the feet enabling the user to walk at a distance above the ground.
■ each of a set of posts or piles supporting a building. ■ a small, flat, three-pointed support for ceramic ware in a kiln.
2 a long-billed wading bird with predominantly black and white plumage and very long slender reddish legs.
● Family Recurvirostridae: two genera, in particular *Himantopus*, and several species.
– PHRASES **on stilts 1** supported by stilts. **2** (of language) bombastic or stilted: *he is talking nonsense on stilts, and he knows it.*
– ORIGIN Middle English: of Germanic origin; related to Dutch *stelt* and German *Stelze*. Sense 2 dates from the late 18th cent.

stilt bug ▶ **noun** a plant bug with very long slender legs.
● Family Berytidae, suborder Heteroptera: many genera.

stilted ▶ **adjective 1** (of a manner of talking or writing) stiff and self-conscious or unnatural: *we made stilted conversation.*
2 standing on stilts: *villages of stilted houses.*
■ Architecture (of an arch) with pieces of upright masonry between the imposts and the springers.
– DERIVATIVES **stiltedly** adverb, **stiltedness** noun.

Stilton ▶ **noun** [mass noun] trademark a kind of strong rich cheese, often with blue veins, originally made at various places in Leicestershire.
– ORIGIN so named because it was formerly sold to travellers at a coaching inn in Stilton (now in Cambridgeshire).

stimulant ▶ **noun** a substance that raises levels of physiological or nervous activity in the body.
■ something that increases activity, interest, or enthusiasm in a specified field: *population growth is a major stimulant to industrial development.*
▶ **adjective** raising levels of physiological or nervous activity in the body: *caffeine has stimulant effects on the heart.*
– ORIGIN early 18th cent.: from Latin *stimulant-* 'urging, goading', from the verb *stimulare*.

stimulate ▶ **verb** [with obj.] raise levels of physiological or nervous activity in (the body or any biological system): *the women are given fertility drugs to stimulate their ovaries.*
■ encourage interest or activity in (a person or animal): *the reader could not fail to be stimulated by the ideas presented* | [as adj. **stimulating**] *a rich and stimulating working environment.* ■ encourage development of or increased activity in (a state or process): *the courses stimulate a passion for learning* | *tax changes designed to stimulate economic growth.*
– DERIVATIVES **stimulatingly** adverb, **stimulation** noun, **stimulative** adjective, **stimulator** noun, **stimulatory** adjective.
– ORIGIN mid 16th cent. (in the sense 'sting, afflict'): from Latin *stimulat-* 'urged, goaded', from the verb *stimulare*.

stimulus /ˈstɪmjʊləs/ ▶ **noun** (pl. **stimuli** /-lʌɪ, -liː/) a thing or event that evokes a specific functional reaction in an organ or tissue: *areas of the brain which respond to auditory stimuli.*
■ a thing that rouses activity or energy in someone or something; a spur or incentive: *if the tax were abolished, it would act as a stimulus to exports.* ■ an interesting and exciting quality: *she loved the stimulus of the job.*
– ORIGIN late 17th cent.: from Latin, 'goad, spur, incentive'.

sting ▶ **noun 1** a small sharp-pointed organ at the end of the abdomen of bees, wasps, ants, and scorpions, capable of inflicting a painful or dangerous wound by injecting poison.
■ any of a number of minute hairs or other organs of plants, jellyfishes, etc., which inject a poisonous or irritating fluid when touched. ■ a wound from such an animal or plant organ: *a wasp or bee sting.* ■ a sharp tingling or burning pain or sensation: *I felt the sting of the cold, bitter air.* ■ [in sing.] figurative a hurtful quality or effect: *I recalled the sting of his betrayal* | *she smiled to take the sting out of her words.*
2 informal a carefully planned operation, typically one involving deception: *five blackmailers were jailed last week after they were snared in a police sting.*
▶ **verb** (past and past participle **stung**) **1** [with obj.] wound or pierce with a sting: *he was stung by a jellyfish* | [no obj.] *a nettle stings if you brush it lightly.*
2 feel or cause to feel a sharp tingling or burning pain or sensation: [no obj.] *her eyes stung as if she might cry again* | [with obj.] *the brandy stung his throat* | [as adj. **stinging**] *a stinging pain.*
■ [with obj.] figurative (typically of something said) hurt or upset (someone): *stung by her mockery, Frank hung his head.* ■ (**sting someone into**) provoke someone to do (something) by causing annoyance or offence: *he was stung into action by an article in the paper.*
3 [with obj.] informal swindle or exorbitantly overcharge (someone): *there were fears that as President he would sting them with stiffer tax bills.*
– PHRASES **sting in the tail** an unexpected, typically unpleasant or problematic end to something: *the Budget comes with a sting in the tail—future tax increases.*
– DERIVATIVES **stingingly** adverb, **stingless** adjective.
– ORIGIN Old English *sting* (noun), *stingan* (verb), of Germanic origin.

stingaree /ˌstɪŋgəˈriː, ˈstɪŋgəriː/ ▶ **noun** a cinnamon-brown stingray occurring on sand flats in shallow Australian waters.
● *Urolophus testaceus*, family Urolophidae.
■ US & Austral. informal any stingray.
– ORIGIN mid 19th cent.: alteration of **STINGRAY**.

stinge ▶ **noun** informal a mean or ungenerous person.
– ORIGIN early 20th cent.: back-formation from **STINGY**.

stinger ▶ **noun 1** an insect or animal that stings, such as a bee or jellyfish.
■ the part of an insect or animal that holds a sting. ■ informal a painful blow: *he suffered a stinger on his right shoulder.*
2 (**Stinger**) (trademark in the US) a device consisting of a spiked metal ribbon that is placed across a road to stop vehicles by puncturing their tyres.

stinging nettle ▶ **noun** a Eurasian nettle covered in minute hairs that inject irritants when they are touched. These include histamine, which causes itching, and acetylcholine, which causes a burning sensation.
● Genus *Urtica*, family Urticaceae: several species, in particular *U. dioica*.

stingray ▶ **noun** a bottom-dwelling marine ray with a flattened diamond-shaped body and a long poisonous serrated spine at the base of the tail.
● Families Dasyatidae (the **long-tailed stingrays**) and Urolophidae (the **short-tailed stingrays**): several species.

stingy /ˈstɪn(d)ʒi/ ▶ **adjective** (**stingier**, **stingiest**) informal mean; ungenerous: *his employer is stingy and idle.*
– DERIVATIVES **stingily** adverb, **stinginess** noun.
– ORIGIN mid 17th cent.: perhaps a dialect variant of the noun **STING** + **-Y**[1].

stink ▶ **verb** (past **stank** or **stunk**; past participle **stunk**) [no obj.] **1** have a strong unpleasant smell: *the place stank like a sewer* | *his breath* **stank of** *drink.*
■ [with obj.] (**stink a place out/up**) fill a place with such a smell: *her perfume stank the place out.*
2 informal be very unpleasant, contemptible, or scandalous: *he thinks the values of the society in which he lives stink.*
■ (**stink of**) be highly suggestive of (something regarded with disapproval): *the whole affair stinks of a set-up.* ■ (**stink of**) have or appear to have a scandalously large amount of (something, especially money): *the whole place was luxurious and stank of money.*
▶ **noun** [in sing.] **1** a strong unpleasant smell; a stench: *the stink of the place hit me as I went in.*
2 informal a row or fuss: *a silly move now would* **kick up a stink** *we couldn't handle.*
▶ **adjective** W. Indian **1** having a strong unpleasant smell: *'What you doing with that stink dog?'*
2 contemptible; corrupt: *the whole episode is so stink that the principal asked for an immediate transfer of the teacher.*
– PHRASES **like stink** informal extremely hard or intensely: *she's working like stink to get everything ready.*
– ORIGIN Old English *stincan*, of West Germanic origin; related to Dutch and German *stinken*, also to **STENCH**.

stinkard /ˈstɪŋkəd/ ▶ **noun 1** archaic a smelly or despicable person.
2 a member of a lower social order in some American Indian communities.

stink badger ▶ **noun** a SE Asian badger with a long mobile snout, short stout limbs, and anal glands that contain a foul-smelling liquid which can be squirted at an attacker.
● Genus *Mydaus*, family Mustelidae: two species, including the teledu.

stink bomb ▶ **noun** a small glass container holding a sulphurous compound that is released when the container is thrown to the ground and broken, emitting a strong and very unpleasant smell.

stink bug ▶ **noun** another term for **SHIELD BUG**.

stinker ▶ **noun** informal a person or thing that smells very bad.
■ a very bad or unpleasant person or thing: *have those little stinkers been bullying you?* ■ a difficult task: *Tackled the crossword yet? It's a stinker.*

stinkhorn ▶ **noun** a widely distributed fungus which has a tall whitish stem with a rounded greenish-brown gelatinous head that turns into a foul-smelling slime containing the spores.
● Family Phallaceae, class Gasteromycetes: many species, including the common European *Phallus impudicus*.

stinking ▶ **adjective** foul-smelling: *he was locked in a stinking cell.*
■ informal very bad or unpleasant: *a stinking cold.*
▶ **adverb** [as submodifier] informal extremely: *she is obviously stinking rich* | *I want to get stinking drunk and forget.*
– DERIVATIVES **stinkingly** adverb.

stinking cedar ▶ **noun** a tree of the yew family found only in Florida, with fetid leaves, branches, and timber.
● *Torreya taxifolia*, family Taxaceae. Alternative name: **Florida torreya**.

stinking dungworm ▶ **noun** another term for **BRANDLING**.

stinking hellebore ▶ **noun** a European hellebore with greenish purple-tipped flowers.
● *Helleborus foetidus*, family Ranunculaceae.

stinking iris ▶ **noun** another term for **GLADDON**.

stinking smut ▶ **noun** another term for **BUNT**[2].

stinko ▶ **adjective** informal extremely drunk.

stinkpot ▶ **noun 1** informal, chiefly US a vehicle that emits foul-smelling exhaust fumes.
■ an unpleasant person (used as a term of abuse).
2 (also **stinkpot turtle**) an American musk turtle with a domed shell, typically living in muddy-bottomed waters and producing a strong unpleasant smell when disturbed.
● *Kinosternon odoratum* (or *Sternotherus odoratus*), family Kinosternidae.

stinkweed ▶ **noun** [mass noun] any of a number of plants with a strong or foetid smell, e.g. (N. Amer.) jimson weed.

stinkwood ▶ **noun** any of a number of trees that yield timber with an unpleasant odour, in particular:
● (**black stinkwood**) a South African tree (*Ocotea bullata*, family Lauraceae). ● a New Zealand tree (*Coprosoma foetidissima*, family Rubiaceae).

stinky ▶ **adjective** (**stinkier**, **stinkiest**) informal having a strong or unpleasant smell: *stinky cigarette smoke.*
■ very disagreeable and unpleasant: *a stinky job.*

stint[1] ▶ **verb** [with obj.] [often with negative] supply a very ungenerous or inadequate amount of (something): *stowage room hasn't been stinted.*
■ restrict (someone) in the amount of something (especially money) given or permitted: *to avoid having to stint yourself, budget in advance.* ■ [no obj.] be very economical or mean about spending or providing something: *he doesn't* **stint on** *wining and dining.*
▶ **noun 1** a person's fixed or allotted period of work: *his varied career included a stint as a magician.*
2 [mass noun] limitation of supply or effort: *a collector with an eye for quality and the means to indulge it* **without stint**.
– ORIGIN Old English *styntan* 'make blunt', of Germanic origin; related to **STUNT**[1].

stint[2] ▶ **noun** a small short-legged sandpiper of northern Eurasia and Alaska, with a brownish back and white underparts.
● Genus *Calidris*, family Scolopacidae: four species.
– ORIGIN Middle English: of unknown origin.

stipe /stʌɪp/ ▶ **noun** Botany a stalk or stem, especially the stem of a seaweed or fungus or the stalk of a fern frond.
– ORIGIN late 18th cent.: from French, from Latin *stipes* (see **STIPES**).

stipend /ˈstʌɪpɛnd/ ▶ **noun** a fixed regular sum paid as a salary or as expenses to a clergyman, teacher, or public official.
– ORIGIN late Middle English: from Old French *stipendie* or Latin *stipendium*, from *stips* 'wages' + *pendere* 'to pay'.

S

stipendiary /stʌɪˈpɛndɪəri, stɪ-/ ▶ **adjective** receiving a stipend; working for payment rather than on a voluntary, unpaid basis: *stipendiary clergy* | *a stipendiary magistrate.*
▪of, relating to, or of the nature of a stipend: *stipendiary obligations.*
▶ **noun** (pl. **-ies**) a person receiving a stipend.
– ORIGIN late Middle English (as a noun): from Latin *stipendiarius*, from *stipendium* (see **STIPEND**).

stipes /ˈstʌɪpiːz/ ▶ **noun** (pl. **stipites** /ˈstɪpɪtiːz/) Zoology a part or organ resembling a stalk, especially the second joint of the maxilla of an insect.
▪Botany more technical term for **STIPE**.
– ORIGIN mid 18th cent.: from Latin, literally 'log, tree trunk'.

stipitate ▶ **adjective** chiefly Botany (especially of a fungus) having a stipe or a stipes.

stipple ▶ **verb** [with obj.] (in drawing, painting, and engraving) mark (a surface) with numerous small dots or specks: [as noun **stippling**] *the miniaturist's use of stippling.*
▪produce a decorative effect on (paint or other material) by roughening its surface when it is wet.
▶ **noun** [mass noun] the process or technique of stippling a surface, or the effect so created.
– DERIVATIVES **stippler** noun.
– ORIGIN mid 17th cent.: from Dutch *stippelen*, frequentative of *stippen* 'to prick', from *stip* 'a point'.

stipulate[1] /ˈstɪpjʊleɪt/ ▶ **verb** [with obj.] demand or specify (a requirement), typically as part of a bargain or agreement: *he stipulated certain conditions before their marriage* | [as adj. **stipulated**] *the stipulated time has elapsed.*
– DERIVATIVES **stipulation** noun, **stipulator** noun.
– ORIGIN early 17th cent.: from Latin *stipulat-* 'demanded as a formal promise', from the verb *stipulari*.

stipulate[2] /ˈstɪpjʊlət/ ▶ **adjective** Botany (of a leaf or plant) having stipules.
– ORIGIN late 18th cent.: from Latin *stipula* (see **STIPULE**) + **-ATE**[2].

stipule /ˈstɪpjuːl/ ▶ **noun** Botany a small leaf-like appendage to a leaf, typically borne in pairs at the base of the leaf stalk.
– DERIVATIVES **stipular** adjective.
– ORIGIN late 18th cent.: from French *stipule* or Latin *stipula* 'straw'.

stir[1] ▶ **verb** (**stirred, stirring**) **1** [with obj.] move a spoon or other implement round and round in (a liquid or other substance) in order to mix it thoroughly: *Desmond stirred his tea and ate a biscuit* | [no obj.] *pour in the cream and stir well.*
▪(**stir something in/into**) add an ingredient to (a liquid or other substance) in such a way: *stir in the flour and cook gently for two minutes.*
2 [no obj.] move or begin to move slightly: *nothing stirred except the wind.*
▪[with obj.] cause to move or be disturbed slightly: *a gentle breeze stirred the leaves* | *cloudiness is caused by the fish* ***stirring up*** *mud.* ▪(of a person or animal) rise or wake from sleep: *no one else had stirred yet.* ▪(**stir from/out of**) (of a person) leave or go out of (a place): *as he grew older, he seldom stirred from his club.* ▪begin or cause to begin to be active or to develop: [no obj.] *the 1960s, when the civil rights movement stirred* | [with obj.] *a voice* ***stirred*** *her* ***from*** *her reverie* | *he even* ***stirred himself*** *to play an encore.*
3 [with obj.] arouse strong feeling in (someone); move or excite: *they will be* ***stirred to action*** *by what is written* | *he* ***stirred up*** *the sweating crowd.*
▪arouse or prompt (a feeling or memory) or inspire (the imagination): *the story stirred many memories of my childhood* | *the rumours had* ***stirred up*** *his anger.*
4 [no obj.] Brit. informal deliberately cause trouble between others by spreading rumours or gossip: *Francis was always stirring, trying to score off people.*
▶ **noun** [in sing.] **1** a slight physical movement: *I stood, straining eyes and ears for the faintest stir.*
▪a commotion: *the event caused quite a stir.* ▪an initial sign of a specified feeling: *Caroline felt a stir of anger deep within her breast.*
2 an act of mixing food or drink with a spoon or other implement: *he gives his Ovaltine a stir.*
– PHRASES **stir the blood** make someone excited or enthusiastic. **stir one's stumps** [often in imperative] Brit. informal, dated (of a person) begin to move or act.
– ORIGIN Old English *styrian*, of Germanic origin; related to German *stören* 'disturb'.
▶**stir something up** cause or provoke trouble or bad feeling: *he accused me of trying to stir up trouble.*

stir[2] ▶ **noun** informal prison: *I've spent twenty-eight years in stir.*
– ORIGIN mid 19th cent.: perhaps from Romany *sturbin* 'jail'.

stirabout ▶ **noun** [mass noun] chiefly Irish porridge made by stirring oatmeal in boiling water or milk.

stir-crazy ▶ **adjective** informal, chiefly US psychologically disturbed, especially as a result of being confined or imprisoned.

stir-fry ▶ **verb** [with obj.] fry (meat, fish, or vegetables) rapidly over a high heat while stirring briskly: [as adj. **stir-fried**] *stir-fried beef.*
▶ **noun** a dish cooked by such a method.

stirk /stəːk/ ▶ **noun** dialect a yearling bullock or heifer.
– ORIGIN Old English *stirc*, perhaps from *stēor* 'steer' + *-oc* (see **-OCK**).

Stirling[1] a town in central Scotland, on the River Forth, administrative centre of Stirling region; pop. 27,900 (1991).

Stirling[2], James (1692–1770), Scottish mathematician. His main work, *Methodus Differentialis* (1730), was concerned with summation and interpolation. A formula named after him, giving the approximate value of the factorial of large numbers, was actually first worked out by the French-born mathematician **Abraham De Moivre** (1667–1754).

Stirling[3], Sir James Fraser (1926–92), Scottish architect. Working at first in a brutalist style, he became known for his use of geometric shapes and coloured decoration in public buildings such as the Neuestaatsgalerie in Stuttgart (1977).

Stirling[4], Robert (1790–1878), Scottish engineer and Presbyterian minister. In 1816 he was co-inventor (with his brother) of a type of external-combustion engine using heated air.

Stirling engine ▶ **noun** a machine used to provide power or refrigeration, operating on a closed cycle in which a working fluid is cyclically compressed and expanded at different temperatures.

stirrer ▶ **noun** an object or mechanical device used for stirring something.
▪informal a person who deliberately causes trouble between others by spreading rumours or gossip.

stirring ▶ **adjective 1** causing great excitement or strong emotion; rousing: *stirring songs.*
2 archaic moving briskly; active.
▶ **noun** an initial sign of activity, movement, or emotion: *the first stirrings of anger.*
– DERIVATIVES **stirringly** adverb.

stirrup ▶ **noun 1** each of a pair of devices attached to each side of a horse's saddle, in the form of a loop with a flat base to support the rider's foot.
2 (**stirrups** or **lithotomy stirrups**) a pair of metal supports in which a woman's ankles may be placed during gynaecological examinations and childbirth, to hold her legs in a position which will facilitate medical examination or intervention.
3 (also **stirrup bone**) another term for **STAPES**.
4 (**stirrups**) short for **STIRRUP PANTS**.
– ORIGIN Old English *stigrāp*, from the Germanic base of obsolete *sty* 'climb' + **ROPE**.

stirrup cup ▶ **noun** a cup of wine or other alcoholic drink offered to a person on horseback who is about to depart on a journey.

stirrup iron ▶ **noun** the metal loop of a stirrup, in which the rider's foot rests.

stirrup leather ▶ **noun** the strap attaching a stirrup iron to a saddle.

stirrup pants ▶ **plural noun** a pair of women's or girls' stretch trousers having a band of elastic at the bottom of each leg which passes under the arch of the foot.

stirrup pump ▶ **noun** chiefly historical a portable hand-operated water pump with a footrest resembling a stirrup, used to extinguish small fires.

stishovite /ˈstɪʃəvʌɪt/ ▶ **noun** [mass noun] a mineral that is a dense polymorph of silica and is formed at very high pressures, especially in meteorite craters.
– ORIGIN 1960s: from the name of Sergei M. *Stishov*, 20th-cent. Russian chemist, + **-ITE**[1].

stitch ▶ **noun 1** a loop of thread or yarn resulting from a single pass or movement of the needle in sewing, knitting, or crocheting.
▪a loop of thread used to join the edges of a wound or surgical incision: *he had to have sixteen stitches to his head.* ▪[usu. with modifier] a method of sewing, knitting, or crocheting producing a particular pattern or design: *basic embroidery stitches.* ▪[in sing., usu. with negative] informal the smallest item of clothing: *nymphs with come-hither looks and not a stitch on.*
2 a sudden sharp pain in the side of the body, caused by strenuous exercise: *he was panting and had a stitch.*
▶ **verb** [with obj.] make, mend, or join (something) with stitches: *stitch a plain seam with right sides together* | *they stitched the cut on her face* | [as adj., in combination] (**-stitched**) *English dresses.*
– PHRASES **in stitches** informal laughing uncontrollably: *his unique brand of droll self-mockery* ***had*** *his audiences* ***in stitches.*** **a stitch in time saves nine** proverb if you sort out a problem immediately it may save a lot of extra work later.
– DERIVATIVES **stitcher** noun, **stitchery** noun.
– ORIGIN Old English *stice* 'a puncture, stabbing pain', of Germanic origin; related to German *Stich* 'a sting, prick', also to **STICK**[2]. The sense 'loop' (in sewing etc.) arose in Middle English.
▶**stitch someone up** Brit. informal manipulate a situation so that someone is placed in a disadvantageous position or wrongly blamed for something: *he was stitched up by outsiders and ousted as chairman.*
stitch something up (or **together**) Brit. informal arrange or secure a deal or agreement to one's advantage: *the company has stitched up major deals all over the world to boost sales.*

stitchbird ▶ **noun** a rare New Zealand honeyeater with mainly dark brown or blackish plumage and a sharp call that resembles the word 'stitch'.
● *Notiomystis cincta*, family Meliphagidae.

stitching ▶ **noun** [mass noun] a row of stitches sewn on to cloth: *the gloves were white with black stitching.*
▪the action or work of stitching or sewing: *one of the mares cut her leg and it required stitching.*

stitch-up ▶ **noun** Brit. informal an act of placing someone in a position in which they will be wrongly blamed for something, or of manipulating a situation to one's advantage.

stitchwort ▶ **noun** a straggling European plant of the pink family with a slender stem and white starry flowers. It was formerly thought to cure a stitch in the side.
● Genus *Stellaria*, family Caryophyllaceae: several species, in particular **greater stitchwort** (*S. holostea*).

stiver /ˈstʌɪvə/ ▶ **noun** a small coin formerly used in the Netherlands, equal to one twentieth of a guilder.
▪archaic any coin of low value. ▪[with negative] archaic a very small or insignificant amount: *they didn't care a stiver.*
– ORIGIN from Dutch *stuiver*, denoting a small coin; probably related to the noun **STUB**.

STM ▶ **abbreviation for** scanning tunnelling microscope.

stoa /ˈstəʊə/ ▶ **noun** a classical portico or roofed colonnade.
▪(**the Stoa**) the great hall in Athens in which the ancient Greek philosopher Zeno gave the founding lectures of the Stoic school of philosophy.
– ORIGIN Greek.

stoat ▶ **noun** a small carnivorous mammal of the weasel family which has chestnut fur with white underparts and a black-tipped tail. It is native to both Eurasia and North America and in northern areas the coat turns white in winter. Compare with **ERMINE, WEASEL**.
● *Mustela erminea*, family Mustelidae. North American name: **short-tailed weasel**.
– ORIGIN late Middle English: of unknown origin.

stob /stɒb/ ▶ **noun** dialect, chiefly Scottish & US a broken branch or a stump.
▪a stake used for fencing.
– ORIGIN Middle English: variant of **STUB**.

stochastic /stəˈkastɪk/ ▶ **adjective** randomly determined; having a random probability distribution or pattern that may be analysed statistically but may not be predicted precisely.
– DERIVATIVES **stochastically** adverb.
– ORIGIN mid 17th cent.: from Greek *stokhastikos*, from *stokhazesthai* 'aim at, guess', from *stokhos* 'aim'.

stock ▶ **noun 1** [mass noun] the goods or merchandise kept on the premises of a shop or warehouse and available for sale or distribution: *the store has a very low turnover of stock* | [count noun] *buy now, while stocks last!* | [as modifier] *stock shortages.*
▪a supply or quantity of something accumulated or available for future use: *I need to replenish my* ***stock of***

S

wine | [count noun] *fish stocks are being dangerously depleted.* ■ farm animals such as cattle, pigs, and sheep, bred and kept for their meat or milk; livestock. ■ short for **ROLLING STOCK**. ■ (also **film stock**) photographic film that has not been exposed or processed. ■ the undealt cards of the pack, left on the table to be drawn from in some card games.

2 [mass noun] the capital raised by a business or corporation through the issue and subscription of shares: *between 1982 and 1986 the value of the company's stock rose by 86%.*
■ (usu. **stocks**) a portion of this as held by an individual or group as an investment: *she owned £3000 worth of stocks and shares.* ■ (usu. **stocks**) the shares of a particular company, type of company, or industry: *blue-chip stocks.* ■ securities issued by the government in fixed units with a fixed rate of interest: *government gilt-edged stock.* ■ figurative a person's reputation or popularity: *I felt I was right, but my stock was low with this establishment.*

3 [mass noun] liquid made by cooking bones, meat, fish, or vegetables slowly in water, used as a basis for the preparation of soup, gravy, or sauces: *a pint of chicken stock.*
■ [with modifier] the raw material from which a specified commodity can be manufactured: *the fat can be used as soap stock.*

4 [mass noun] [usu. with adj. or noun modifier] a person's ancestry or line of descent: *her mother was of French stock* | *both of them came from peasant stock.*
■ a breed, variety, or population of an animal or plant.

5 the trunk or woody stem of a living tree or shrub, especially one into which a graft (scion) is inserted.
■ the perennial part of a herbaceous plant, especially a rhizome.

6 a herbaceous European plant that is widely cultivated for its fragrant flowers, which are typically lilac, pink, or white. [ORIGIN: mid 17th cent.: from *stock-gillyflower*.]
● Genus *Matthiola*, family Cruciferae: several species, in particular the **Brompton stock** (*M. incana*) and the **night-scented stock** (*M. bicornis*).

7 (**the stocks**) [treated as sing. or pl.] historical an instrument of punishment consisting of an adjustable wooden structure with holes for securing a person's feet and hands, in which criminals were locked and exposed to public ridicule or assault.

8 the part of a rifle or other firearm to which the barrel and firing mechanism are attached, held against one's shoulder when firing the gun.
■ the crossbar of an anchor. ■ the handle of something such as a whip or fishing rod. ■ short for **HEADSTOCK** (in sense 1). ■ short for **TAILSTOCK**.

9 a band of white material tied like a cravat and worn as a part of formal horse-riding dress.
■ a piece of black material worn under a clerical collar.

10 (**stocks**) a frame used to support a ship or boat out of water, especially when under construction.

11 short for **STOCK BRICK**.

▶ **adjective** [attrib.] **1** (of a product or type of product) usually kept in stock and thus regularly available for sale: *25 per cent off stock items.*
2 (of a phrase or expression) so regularly used as to be automatic or hackneyed: *their stock response to the refugee crisis was 'We can't take everyone'.*
■ denoting a conventional character type or situation that recurs in a particular genre of literature, theatre, or film: *the stock characters in every cowboy film.* ■ denoting or relating to cinematic footage that can be regularly used in different productions, typically that of outdoor scenes used to add realism to a production shot in an indoor set.

▶ **verb** [with obj.] **1** have or keep a supply of (a particular product or type or product) available for sale: *most supermarkets now stock a range of organic produce.*
■ provide or fill with goods, items, or a supply of something: *I must* **stock up** *the fridge* | [as adj., with submodifier or in combination] (**stocked**) *a well-stocked shop.* ■ [no obj.] (**stock up**) amass supplies of something, typically for a particular occasion or purpose: *I'm stocking up for Christmas* | *you'd better* **stock up** *with fuel.*
2 fit (a rifle or other firearm) with a stock.

– PHRASES **in** (or **out of**) **stock** (of goods) available (or unavailable) for immediate sale in a shop. **on the stocks** in construction or preparation: *also on the stocks is a bill to bring about tax relief for these businesses.* **put stock in** [often with negative] have a specified amount of belief or faith in: *I don't put much stock in modern medicine.* **stock and station** Austral./NZ denoting a firm or agent dealing in farm products and supplies. **take stock** review or make an overall assessment of a particular situation, typically as a prelude to making a decision: *he needed a period of peace and quiet in order to* **take stock** *of his life.*

– DERIVATIVES **stockless** adjective.

– ORIGIN Old English *stoc(c)* 'trunk, block of wood, post', of Germanic origin; related to Dutch *stok* and German *Stock* 'stick'. The notion 'store, fund' (senses 1 and 2) arose in late Middle English and is of obscure origin, perhaps expressing 'growth from a central stem' or 'firm foundation'.

stockade ▶ **noun** a barrier formed from upright wooden posts or stakes, especially as a defence against attack or as a means of confining animals.
■ an enclosure bound by such a barrier: *we got ashore and into the stockade.* ■ chiefly N. Amer. a military prison.
▶ **verb** [with obj.] [usu. as adj. **stockaded**] enclose (an area) by erecting such a barrier.
– ORIGIN early 17th cent.: shortening of obsolete French *estocade*, alteration of *estacade*, from Spanish *estacada*, from the Germanic base of the noun **STAKE**[1].

stock book ▶ **noun** a book used by a business to keep records of quantities of goods acquired, held in stock, and disposed of.

stockbreeder ▶ **noun** a farmer who breeds livestock.
– DERIVATIVES **stockbreeding** noun.

stock brick ▶ **noun** a hard solid brick pressed in a mould.

stockbroker ▶ **noun** a broker who buys and sells securities on a stock exchange on behalf of clients.
– DERIVATIVES **stockbrokerage** noun, **stockbroking** noun.

stockbroker belt ▶ **noun** Brit. an affluent residential area outside a large city.

stock car ▶ **noun 1** an ordinary car that has been strengthened for use in a type of race in which competing cars collide with each other.
2 N. Amer. a railway wagon for transporting livestock.

stock company ▶ **noun** US a repertory company that is largely based in one theatre.

stock control ▶ **noun** [mass noun] the regulation of the acquisition of stocks of goods needed by a business for the purposes of its trade.

stock cube ▶ **noun** a cube of concentrated dehydrated meat, vegetable, or fish stock for use in cooking.

stock dove ▶ **noun** a grey Eurasian and North African pigeon, resembling a small wood pigeon, and nesting in holes in trees.
● *Columba oenas*, family Columbidae.

stocker ▶ **noun 1** N. Amer. a farm animal, typically a young steer or heifer, destined for slaughter but kept until matured or fattened.
2 a person whose job is to fill the shelves of a shop or supermarket with merchandise.
3 N. Amer. informal a stock car.

stock exchange ▶ **noun** a market in which securities are bought and sold: *the company was floated on the Stock Exchange.*
■ (**the Stock Exchange**) the level of prices in such a market: *a plunge in the Stock Exchange during the election campaign.*

stockfeed ▶ **noun** [mass noun] food for livestock.

stockfish ▶ **noun** (pl. same or **-fishes**) **1** a commercially valuable hake of coastal waters of southern Africa.
● *Merluccius capensis*, family Merlucciidae.
2 [mass noun] cod or a similar fish split and dried in the open air without salt.
– ORIGIN Middle English (in sense 2): from Middle Low German, Middle Dutch *stokvisch*, of unknown origin; sense 1 (early 19th cent.) from South African Dutch.

Stockhausen /ˈstɒkˌhaʊz(ə)n, ˈʃtɒk-/, Karlheinz (b.1928), German composer. An important avant-garde composer and exponent of serialism, he co-founded an electronic music studio for West German radio, and in 1980 embarked on his *Licht* cycle of musical ceremonies.

stockholder ▶ **noun 1** chiefly N. Amer. a shareholder.
2 a holder of supplies for manufacturers.
– DERIVATIVES **stockholding** noun.

Stockholm /ˈstɒkhəʊm/ the capital of Sweden, a seaport on the east coast, situated on the mainland and on numerous adjacent islands; pop. 674,450 (1990).

Stockholm syndrome ▶ **noun** [mass noun] feelings of trust or affection felt by some victims of kidnapping or hostage-taking towards their captor.
– ORIGIN 1970s: with reference to a bank robbery in Stockholm.

Stockholm tar ▶ **noun** [mass noun] a kind of tar prepared from resinous pinewood and used in particular in shipbuilding and as an ingredient of ointments.

stockhorse ▶ **noun** Austral./NZ a stockman's horse.

stockinet (also **stockinette**) ▶ **noun** [mass noun] a soft, loosely knitted stretch fabric, formerly used for making underwear and now used for cleaning, wrapping, or bandaging.
– ORIGIN late 18th cent.: probably an alteration of *stocking-net*.

stocking ▶ **noun** a women's garment, typically made of translucent nylon or silk, that fits closely over the foot and is held up by suspenders or an elasticated strip at the upper thigh.
■ short for **CHRISTMAS STOCKING**. ■ US or archaic a long sock worn by men. ■ [usu. with modifier] a cylindrical bandage or other medical covering for the leg resembling a stocking, especially an elasticated support used in the treatment of disorders of the veins. ■ a white marking of the lower part of a horse's leg, extending as far as, or just beyond, the knee or hock.
– PHRASES **in** (**one's**) **stockinged feet** without shoes: *she stood five feet ten in her stockinged feet.*
– DERIVATIVES **stockinged** adjective [in combination] *her black-stockinged legs*, **stockingless** adjective.
– ORIGIN late 16th cent.: from **STOCK** in the dialect sense 'stocking' + **-ING**[1].

stocking cap ▶ **noun** a knitted conical hat with a long tapered end, often bearing a tassle, that hangs down.

stocking filler (N. Amer. **stocking stuffer**) ▶ **noun** Brit. a small present suitable for putting in a Christmas stocking.

stocking mask ▶ **noun** a nylon stocking pulled over the face to disguise the features, used by criminals.

stocking stitch ▶ **noun** [mass noun] a knitting stitch consisting of alternate rows of plain and purl stitch.

stock-in-trade ▶ **noun** [mass noun] the typical subject or commodity a person, company, or profession uses or deals in: *information is our stock-in-trade.*
■ qualities, ideas, or behaviour characteristic of a person or their work: *flippancy is his stock-in-trade.* ■ the goods kept in hand by a business for the purposes of its trade.

stockist ▶ **noun** Brit. a retailer that stocks goods of a particular type for sale: *one of the country's largest stockists of Italian designer labels.*

stockjobber ▶ **noun 1** Brit. another term for **JOBBER** (in sense 1).
2 US derogatory a stockbroker.
– DERIVATIVES **stockjobbing** noun.

stocklist ▶ **noun** Brit. a publication listing a retailer's stock of goods with current prices.

stockman ▶ **noun** (pl. **-men**) **1** Austral./NZ a person who looks after livestock.
■ US an owner of livestock.
2 US a person who looks after a stockroom or warehouse.

stock market ▶ **noun** (usu. **the stock market**) a stock exchange.

stock option ▶ **noun** another term for **SHARE OPTION**.

stock-out ▶ **noun** a situation in which an item is out of stock.

stockpile ▶ **noun** a large accumulated stock of goods or materials, especially one held in reserve for use at a time of shortage or other emergency.
▶ **verb** [with obj.] accumulate a large stock of (goods or materials): *he claimed that the weapons were being stockpiled.*
– DERIVATIVES **stockpiler** noun.

Stockport an industrial town in NW England, near Manchester; pop. 130,000 (est. 1991).

stockpot ▶ **noun** a pot in which stock for soup is prepared by long, slow cooking.

stock-proof ▶ **adjective** (of a fence or other barrier) effective in preventing livestock from straying.

S

stockroom ▶ noun a room in which quantities of goods are stored.

stock split ▶ noun N. Amer. an issue of new shares in a company to existing shareholders in proportion to their current holdings.

stock-still ▶ adverb without any movement; completely still: *he stood stock-still.*

stocktaking ▶ noun [mass noun] the action or process of recording the amount of stock held by a business: *the shop is closed for stocktaking.*
■ the action of reviewing and assessing one's situation and options.
– DERIVATIVES **stocktake** noun, **stocktaker** noun.

Stockton-on-Tees an industrial town in NE England, a port on the River Tees near its mouth on the North Sea; pop. 170,200 (1991). The town developed after the opening in 1825 of the Stockton and Darlington Railway, the first passenger rail service in the world.

stock whip ▶ noun a whip used for driving cattle.

stocky ▶ adjective (**stockier**, **stockiest**) (of a person) broad and sturdily built.
– DERIVATIVES **stockily** adverb, **stockiness** noun.

stockyard ▶ noun N. Amer. a large yard containing pens and sheds in which livestock is kept and sorted.

stodge ▶ noun [mass noun] informal, chiefly Brit. food that is heavy, filling, and high in carbohydrates: *she ate her way through a plateful of stodge.*
■ figurative dull and uninspired material or work.
– ORIGIN late 17th cent. (as a verb in the sense 'stuff to stretching point'): symbolic, suggested by **STUFF** and **PODGE**.

stodgy ▶ adjective (**stodgier**, **stodgiest**) 1 Brit. (of food) heavy, filling, and high in carbohydrates.
■ chiefly US bulky or heavy in appearance: *this stodgy three-storey building.*
2 dull and uninspired: *some of the material is rather stodgy and top-heavy with facts.*
– DERIVATIVES **stodginess** noun, **stodgily** adverb.

stoep /stuːp/ ▶ noun S. African a terraced veranda in front of a house.
– ORIGIN Afrikaans, from Dutch; related to **STEP**.

stog ▶ verb (**be stogged**) dialect be stuck or bogged down: *people are stogged in their misery.*
– ORIGIN early 19th cent.: perhaps symbolic and suggested by **STICK**[2] and **BOG**.

stogy /ˈstəʊɡi/ (also **stogie**) ▶ noun (pl. **-ies**) N. Amer. a long, thin, cheap cigar.
– ORIGIN mid 19th cent. (originally as *stoga*): short for *Conestoga* in Pennsylvania.

stoic /ˈstəʊɪk/ ▶ noun 1 a person who can endure pain or hardship without showing their feelings or complaining.
2 (**Stoic**) a member of the ancient philosophical school of Stoicism.
▶ adjective 1 another term for **STOICAL**.
2 (**Stoic**) of or belonging to the Stoics or their school of philosophy.
– ORIGIN late Middle English: via Latin from Greek *stōïkos*, from **STOA** (with reference to Zeno's teaching in the *Stoa Poikilē* or Painted Porch, at Athens).

stoical /ˈstəʊɪk(ə)l/ ▶ adjective enduring pain and hardship without showing one's feelings or complaining: *he taught a stoical acceptance of suffering.*
– DERIVATIVES **stoically** adverb.

stoichiometric /ˌstɔɪkɪə(ʊ)ˈmɛtrɪk/ ▶ adjective Chemistry of or relating to stoichiometry.
■ relating to or denoting quantities of reactants in simple integral ratios, as prescribed by an equation or formula.
– DERIVATIVES **stoichiometrically** adverb.

stoichiometry /ˌstɔɪkɪˈɒmɪtri/ ▶ noun [mass noun] Chemistry the relationship between the relative quantities of substances taking part in a reaction or forming a compound, typically a ratio of whole integers.
– ORIGIN early 19th cent.: from Greek *stoikheion* 'element' + **-METRY**.

stoicism /ˈstəʊɪsɪz(ə)m/ ▶ noun [mass noun] 1 the endurance of pain or hardship without the display of feelings and without complaint.
2 (**Stoicism**) an ancient Greek school of philosophy founded at Athens by Zeno of Citium. The school taught that virtue, the highest good, is based on knowledge; the wise live in harmony with the

divine Reason (also identified with Fate and Providence) that governs nature, and are indifferent to the vicissitudes of fortune and to pleasure and pain.

stoke ▶ verb [with obj.] add coal or other solid fuel to (a fire, furnace, or boiler).
■ encourage or incite (a strong emotion or tendency): *his composure had the effect of stoking her anger | the Chancellor was stoking up a consumer boom.* ■ [often as adj. **stoked**] informal excite or thrill: *when they told me I was on the team, I was stoked.* ■ [no obj.] informal consume a large quantity of food or drink to give one energy: *Carol was at the coffee machine, stoking up for the day.*
– ORIGIN mid 17th cent.: back-formation from **STOKER**.

stokehold ▶ noun a compartment in a steamship in which the boilers and furnace are housed.

stokehole ▶ noun a space in front of a furnace in which a stoker works.

Stoke-on-Trent a city on the River Trent, a unitary council formerly in Staffordshire; pop. 244,800 (1991). It has long been the centre of the Staffordshire pottery industries.

Stoker, Bram (1847–1912), Irish novelist and theatre manager; full name *Abraham Stoker*. He was secretary and touring manager to the actor Henry Irving but is chiefly remembered as the author of the vampire story *Dracula* (1897).

stoker ▶ noun a person who tends the furnace on a steamship or steam train.
■ a mechanical device for supplying fuel to a firebox or furnace, especially on a steam locomotive.
– ORIGIN mid 17th cent.: from Dutch, from *stoken* 'stoke (a furnace)', from Middle Dutch *stoken* 'push, poke'; related to **STICK**[1].

stokes (abbrev.: **ST**) ▶ noun (pl. same) Physics the cgs unit of kinematic viscosity, corresponding to a dynamic viscosity of 1 poise and a density of 1 gram per cubic centimetre, equivalent to 10^{-4} square metres per second.
– ORIGIN mid 20th cent.: from the name of Sir G. *Stokes* (see **STOKES' LAW**).

Stokes' law Physics 1 a law stating that in fluorescence the wavelength of the emitted radiation is longer than that of the radiation causing it. This is not true in all cases.
2 an expression describing the resisting force on a particle moving through a viscous fluid and showing that a maximum velocity is reached in such cases, e.g. for an object falling under gravity through a fluid.
– ORIGIN late 19th cent.: named after Sir George *Stokes* (1819–1903), British physicist.

Stokes' theorem Mathematics a theorem proposing that the surface integral of the curl of a function over any surface bounded by a closed path is equal to the line integral of a particular vector function round that path.
– ORIGIN late 19th cent.: named after Sir G. *Stokes* (see **STOKES' LAW**).

Stokowski /stəˈkɒfski/, Leopold (1882–1977), British-born American conductor, of Polish descent. He is best known for arranging and conducting the music for Walt Disney's film *Fantasia* (1940), which sought to bring classical music to cinema audiences by means of cartoons.

stokvel /ˈstɒkfɛl/ ▶ noun (in South Africa) a savings or investment society to which members regularly contribute an agreed amount and from which they receive a lump sum payment.
■ (in South Africa) a society formed to hold regular parties that are funded by the members and generate profits for the hosts. ■ a party held by such a society.
– ORIGIN from an Africanized pronunciation of *stock-fair*, denoting a periodical gathering of buyers and sellers of livestock.

STOL Aeronautics ▶ abbreviation for short take-off and landing.

stole[1] ▶ noun a woman's long scarf or shawl, especially of fur or similar material, worn loosely over the shoulders.
■ a priest's silk vestment worn over the shoulders and hanging down to the knee or below.
– ORIGIN Old English (in the senses 'long robe' and 'priest's vestment'), via Latin from Greek *stolē* 'clothing', from *stellein* 'array'.

stole[2] past of **STEAL**.

stolen past participle of **STEAL**.

stolid ▶ adjective (of a person) calm, dependable, and showing little emotion or animation.
– DERIVATIVES **stolidity** noun, **stolidly** adverb, **stolidness** noun.
– ORIGIN late 16th cent.: from obsolete French *stolide* or Latin *stolidus* (perhaps related to *stultus* 'foolish').

stollen /ˈstɒlən, ˈʃtɒ-/ ▶ noun a rich German fruit and nut loaf.
– ORIGIN from German *Stollen*.

stolon /ˈstəʊlɒn/ ▶ noun 1 Botany a creeping horizontal plant stem or runner that takes root at points along its length to form new plants.
■ an arching stem of a plant that roots at the tip to form a new plant, as in the bramble.
2 Zoology the branched stem-like structure of some colonial hydroid coelenterates, attaching the colony to the substrate.
– DERIVATIVES **stolonate** adjective, **stoloniferous** adjective.
– ORIGIN early 17th cent.: from Latin *stolo, stolon-* 'shoot, scion'.

stoma /ˈstəʊmə/ ▶ noun (pl. **stomas** or **stomata** /-mətə/) Botany any of the minute pores in the epidermis of the leaf or stem of a plant, forming a slit of variable width which allows movement of gases in and out of the intercellular spaces. Also called **STOMATE**.
■ Zoology a small mouth-like opening in some lower animals. ■ Medicine an artificial opening made into a hollow organ, especially one on the surface of the body leading to the gut or trachea.
– DERIVATIVES **stomal** adjective (Medicine).
– ORIGIN late 17th cent.: modern Latin, from Greek *stoma* 'mouth'.

stomach ▶ noun 1 the internal organ in which the first part of digestion occurs, being (in humans and many mammals) a pear-shaped enlargement of the alimentary canal linking the oesophagus to the small intestine.
■ each of four such organs in a ruminant (the rumen, reticulum, omasum, and abomasum). ■ any of a number of analogous organs in lower animals. ■ the front part of the body between the chest and thighs; the belly: *Blake hit him in the stomach.* ■ [in sing.] the stomach viewed as the seat of hunger, nausea, anxiety, or other unsettling feelings: *Virginia had a sick feeling in her stomach.*
2 [in sing.] [usu. with negative] an appetite for food or drink: *she doesn't have the stomach to eat anything.*
■ a desire or inclination for something involving conflict, difficulty, or unpleasantness: *the teams proved to have no stomach for a fight | [with infinitive] frankly, I don't have the stomach to find out.*
▶ verb [with obj.] (usu. **cannot stomach**) consume (food or drink) without feeling or being sick: *if you cannot stomach orange juice, try apple juice.*
■ endure or accept (an obnoxious thing or person): *I can't stomach the self-righteous attitude of some managers.*
– PHRASES **an army marches on its stomach** a group of soldiers or workers can only fight or function effectively if they have been well fed. [ORIGIN translating French *c'est la soupe qui fait le soldat*, a maxim of Napoleon.] **on a full** (or **an empty**) **stomach** after having eaten (or having not eaten): *I think better on a full stomach.* **a strong stomach** an ability to see or do unpleasant things without feeling sick or squeamish.
– DERIVATIVES **stomachful** noun (pl. **-fuls**).
– ORIGIN Middle English: from Old French *estomac, stomaque*, via Latin from Greek *stomakhos* 'gullet', from *stoma* 'mouth'. The early sense of the verb was 'be offended at, resent' (early 16th cent.).

stomacher ▶ noun historical a V-shaped piece of decorative cloth, worn over the chest and stomach by men and women in the 16th century, later only by women.
– ORIGIN late Middle English: probably a shortening of Old French *estomachier*, from *estomac* (see **STOMACH**).

stomachic /stəˈmakɪk/ dated ▶ adjective promoting the appetite or assisting digestion.
▶ noun a medicine or tonic of this kind.

stomach muscles ▶ plural noun the muscles constituting the front wall of the abdomen.

stomach pump ▶ noun a syringe attached to a long tube, used for extracting the contents of a person's stomach (for example, if they have taken poison).

stomach tube ▶ noun a tube passed into the

stomach via the gullet for cleansing or emptying it or for introducing food.

stomata plural form of **STOMA**.

stomatal /ˈstəʊmət(ə)l, ˈstɒ-/ ▶ **adjective** chiefly Botany of or relating to a stoma or stomata.

stomate /ˈstəʊmeɪt/ ▶ **noun** Botany another term for **STOMA**.
– ORIGIN mid 19th cent.: apparently an English singular of **STOMATA**.

stomatitis /ˌstəʊməˈtʌɪtɪs, ˌstɒ-/ ▶ **noun** [mass noun] Medicine inflammation of the mucous membrane of the mouth.
– ORIGIN mid 19th cent.: modern Latin, from *stoma, stomat-* 'mouth' + **-ITIS**.

stomatogastric /ˌstəʊmətə(ʊ)ˈgastrɪk, ˌstɒmətə(ʊ)-, bstəˌmatə(ʊ)-/ ▶ **adjective** chiefly Zoology relating to or connected with the mouth and stomach, particularly denoting a system of visceral nerves in invertebrates.
– ORIGIN mid 19th cent.: from Greek *stoma, stomat-* 'mouth' + **GASTRIC**.

stomp ▶ **verb** [no obj., with adverbial of direction] tread heavily and noisily, typically in order to show anger: *Martin stomped off to the spare room.*
■ [no obj.] (**stomp on**) tread heavily or stamp on: *I stomped on the accelerator.* ■ [with obj.] chiefly US deliberately trample or tread heavily on: *Cobb proceeded to kick and stomp him viciously.* ■ [with obj.] stamp (one's feet). ■ [no obj.] dance with heavy stamping steps.
▶ **noun** (in jazz or popular music) a tune or song with a fast tempo and a heavy beat.
■ a lively dance performed to such music, involving heavy stamping.
– DERIVATIVES **stomper** noun, **stompy** adjective.
– ORIGIN early 19th cent. (originally US dialect): variant of the verb **STAMP**.

stompie /ˈstɒmpi/ ▶ **noun** (pl. **-ies**) S. African informal a half-smoked cigarette kept for later use.
– PHRASES **pick up stompies** break into a conversation of which one has heard only the end.
– ORIGIN Afrikaans, diminutive of *stomp* 'stump'.

stomping ▶ **adjective** (of music) having a lively stamping rhythm.

stomping ground ▶ **noun** N. Amer. another term for **STAMPING GROUND**.

Stone, Oliver (b.1946), American film director, screenwriter, and producer. He has won Oscars for his adaptation of the novel *Midnight Express* (1978) and his direction of *Platoon* (1986) and *Born on the Fourth of July* (1989), both of which indict American involvement in the Vietnam War.

stone ▶ **noun 1** [mass noun] hard solid non-metallic mineral matter of which rock is made, especially as a building material.
■ [count noun] a small piece of rock found on the ground. ■ in extended use with reference to weight or lack of feeling, expression, or movement: *Isabel stood as if* ***turned to stone*** | *her face became* ***as hard as stone*** | *the elevator* ***dropped like a stone***. ■ [count noun] Astronomy a meteorite made of rock, as opposed to metal. ■ [count noun] Medicine a calculus; a gallstone or kidney stone.
2 a piece of stone shaped for a purpose, especially one of commemoration, ceremony, or demarcation: *a memorial stone* | *boundary stones.*
■ a gem or jewel. ■ short for **CURLING STONE**. ■ a round piece or counter, originally made of stone, used in various board games, especially the Japanese game of go. ■ a large flat table or sheet, originally made of stone and now usually of metal, on which pages of type are made up.
3 a hard seed in a cherry, plum, peach, and some other fruits.
4 (pl. same) Brit. a unit of weight equal to 14 lb (6.35 kg): *I weighed 10 stone.*
5 [mass noun] a natural shade of whitish or brownish-grey: [as modifier] *stone stretch trousers.*
▶ **verb** [with obj.] **1** throw stones at: *policemen were stoned by the crowd.*
■ chiefly historical execute (someone) by throwing stones at them: *Stephen* ***was stoned to death*** *in Jerusalem.*
2 remove the stone from (a fruit): [as adj. **stoned**] *add 50 g of stoned black olives.*
3 build, face, or pave with stone.
– PHRASES **be written** (or **engraved** or **set**) **in stone** used to emphasize that something is fixed and unchangeable: *anything can change—nothing is written in stone.* **cast** (or **throw**) **the first stone** be the first to make an accusation (used to emphasize that a potential critic is not wholly blameless). [ORIGIN: with biblical allusion to John 8:7.] **leave no stone unturned** try every possible course of action in order to achieve something. **stone me!** (or **stone the crows!**) Brit. informal an exclamation of surprise or shock. **a stone's throw** a short distance: *the Sea Life Centre is* ***just a stone's throw from*** *the sea itself.*
– DERIVATIVES **stoneless** adjective.
– ORIGIN Old English *stān* (noun), of Germanic origin; related to Dutch *steen* and German *Stein*. The verb dates from Middle English (first recorded in sense 1).

Stone Age a prehistoric period when weapons and tools were made of stone or of organic materials such as bone, wood, or horn.

> The Stone Age covers a period of about 2.5 million years, from the first use of tools by the ancestors of man (*Australopithecus*) to the introduction of agriculture and the first towns. It is subdivided into the Palaeolithic, Mesolithic, and Neolithic periods, and is succeeded in Europe by the Bronze Age (or, sometimes, the Copper Age) about 5,000–4,000 years ago.

stone boat ▶ **noun** N. Amer. a flat-bottomed sled used for transporting stones and other heavy objects.

stone broke ▶ **adjective** North American term for **STONY BROKE**.

stonechat ▶ **noun** a small Old World songbird of the thrush family, having bold markings and a call like two stones being knocked together.
● Genus *Saxicola*, family Turdidae: three or four species, in particular the widespread *S. torquata*, the male of which has a black head and orange breast.

stone china ▶ **noun** [mass noun] a kind of very hard earthenware resembling porcelain.

stone circle ▶ **noun** a megalithic monument of a type found mainly in western Europe, consisting of stones, typically standing stones, arranged more or less in a circle.

> The earliest stone circles date from the Neolithic period. In the early Bronze Age many hundreds of small circles were constructed in western Britain, often from quite small stones. Circles often appear to be aligned astronomically, especially with particular sunrise or sunset positions, and it is generally agreed that they had a ritual function.

stone cold ▶ **adjective** completely cold.
▶ **adverb** (**stone-cold**) [as submodifier] completely: *stone-cold sober.*

stone crab ▶ **noun** a large, heavy edible crab of the Gulf of Mexico and Caribbean area.
● *Menippe mercenaria*, family Xanthidae.

stonecrop ▶ **noun** a small fleshy-leaved plant which typically has star-shaped yellow or white flowers and grows among rocks or on walls.
● Genus *Sedum*, family Crassulaceae: many species, including **yellow** (or **biting**) **stonecrop** (*S. acre*), whose tiny leaves have a bitter, peppery taste.

stone curlew ▶ **noun** a large-eyed plover-like bird with mottled brownish plumage, inhabiting open stony or sandy country. Also called **THICK-KNEE**.
● Family Burhinidae: two genera and several species, in particular *Burhinus oedicnemus* of Eurasia and Africa.

stoned ▶ **adjective** informal under the influence of drugs, especially cannabis.
■ very drunk: *they're in the local pubs* ***getting stoned***.

stone dead ▶ **adjective** [predic.] completely dead.

stone deaf ▶ **adjective** completely deaf.

stone face ▶ **noun** informal a face which reveals no emotions.
– DERIVATIVES **stone-faced** adjective.

stonefish ▶ **noun** (pl. same or **-fishes**) a chiefly marine fish of bizarre appearance which lives in the tropical Indo-Pacific. It rests motionless in the sand with its venomous dorsal spines projecting and is a frequent cause of injury to swimmers.
● Family Synanceiidae: several genera and species, including *Synanceia verrucosa* (also called **DEVILFISH**.)

stonefly ▶ **noun** (pl. **-flies**) a slender insect with transparent membranous wings, the larvae of which live in clean running water. The adults are used as bait by fly fishermen.
● Order Plecoptera: many families.

stone fruit ▶ **noun** a fruit with flesh or pulp enclosing a stone, such as a peach, plum, or cherry.

stoneground ▶ **adjective** (of flour) ground with millstones.

stonehatch ▶ **noun** dialect the ringed plover, which lines its nest with tiny pebbles.

Stonehenge a megalithic monument on Salisbury Plain in Wiltshire. Completed in several constructional phases from *c.*2950 BC, it is composed of a circle of sarsen stones surrounded by a bank and ditch and enclosing a circle of smaller bluestones. Within this inner circle is a horseshoe arrangement of five trilithons with the axis aligned on the midsummer sunrise, an orientation that was probably for ritual purposes.
– ORIGIN from Old English *stān* 'stone' + an element related to *hengan* 'to hang'.

stone-lily ▶ **noun** (pl. **-ies**) dated a fossilized sea lily.

stone marten ▶ **noun** a Eurasian marten that has chocolate-brown fur with a white throat. Also called **BEECH MARTEN**.
● *Martes foina*, family Mustelidae.

stonemason ▶ **noun** a person who cuts, prepares, and builds with stone.
– DERIVATIVES **stonemasonry** noun.

Stone of Scone /skuːn/ the stone on which medieval Scottish kings were crowned. It was brought to England by Edward I and preserved in the coronation chair in Westminster Abbey, and returned to Scotland in 1996. Also called **CORONATION STONE**, **STONE OF DESTINY**.

stone pine ▶ **noun** an umbrella-shaped southern European pine tree with large needles, very large glossy brown cones, and seeds that are eaten as 'pine nuts'. Also called **UMBRELLA PINE**.
● *Pinus pinea*, family Pinaceae. See also **AROLLA**.

stoner ▶ **noun 1** informal a person who regularly takes drugs, especially cannabis.
2 [in combination] Brit. a person or thing that weighs a specified number of stone: *a couple of 16-stoners.*

stonewall ▶ **verb** [with obj.] delay or block (a request, process, or person) by refusing to answer questions or by giving evasive replies, especially in politics: [as noun **stonewalling**] *the art of stonewalling and political intimidation.*
■ [no obj.] Cricket bat extremely defensively.
– DERIVATIVES **stonewaller** noun.

stoneware ▶ **noun** [mass noun] a type of pottery which is impermeable and partly vitrified but opaque.

stonewashed (also **stonewash**) ▶ **adjective** (of a garment or fabric, especially denim) washed with abrasives to produce a worn or faded appearance.

stonework ▶ **noun** [mass noun] the parts of a building that are made of stone.
■ the work of a mason: *a masterpiece of clever stonework.*
– DERIVATIVES **stoneworker** noun.

stonewort ▶ **noun** a freshwater plant with whorls of slender leaves, related to green algae. Many kinds become encrusted with chalky deposits, giving them a stony feel.
● *Chara* and other genera in the class Charophyceae, division Chlorophyta; sometimes placed in its own division (Charophyta).

stonk military slang ▶ **noun** a concentrated artillery bombardment.
▶ **verb** [with obj.] bombard with concentrated artillery fire.
– ORIGIN 1940s: said to be formed from elements of the artillery term *Standard Regimental Concentration*.

stonker ▶ **noun** Brit. informal something which is very large or impressive of its kind: *it's a real stonker of a plan.*

stonkered ▶ **adjective** [predic.] Austral./NZ informal utterly exhausted or defeated.
■ drunk.
– ORIGIN 1920s: from Scots and northern English *stonk* 'game of marbles', perhaps of imitative origin.

stonking ▶ **adjective** Brit. informal used to emphasize something remarkable or exciting: *a stonking 207 mph maximum speed* | [as submodifier] *a stonking good model.*
– ORIGIN 1980s: from the verb **STONK**.

stony ▶ **adjective** (**stonier**, **stoniest**) covered with or full of small pieces of rock: *rough stony paths.*
■ made of or resembling stone: *stony steps.* ■ not having or showing feeling or sympathy: *Lucenzo's hard, stony eyes* | [in combination] *he walked away, stony-faced.* ■ Astronomy (of a meteorite) consisting mostly of rock, as opposed to metal.
– PHRASES **fall on stony ground** (of words or a suggestion) be ignored or badly received. [ORIGIN: with biblical reference to the parable of the sower (Matt. 13:5).]
– DERIVATIVES **stonily** adverb, **stoniness** noun.
– ORIGIN Old English *stānig* (see **STONE**, **-Y**[1]).

S

stony broke (N. Amer. **stone broke**) ▶ adjective Brit. informal entirely without money.

stony coral ▶ noun see CORAL (sense 2).

stony-hearted ▶ adjective very cruel or unfeeling.

stony-iron Astronomy ▶ adjective (of a meteorite) containing appreciable quantities of both rock and iron.
▶ noun a stony-iron meteorite.

stood past and past participle of STAND.

stooge ▶ noun 1 derogatory a person who serves merely to support or assist others, particularly in doing unpleasant work: *party stooges put there to do a job on behalf of central office.*
  ■ a person who is employed to assume a particular role while keeping their true identity hidden: *a police stooge.*
  2 a performer whose act involves being the butt of a comedian's jokes.
▶ verb [no obj.] 1 move about aimlessly; drift or cruise: *she stooged around in the bathroom for a while.*
  2 perform a role that involves being the butt of a comedian's jokes.
− ORIGIN early 20th cent.: of unknown origin.

stook /stʊk, stuːk/ ▶ noun Brit. a group of sheaves of grain stood on end in a field.
▶ verb [with obj.] arrange in stooks.
− ORIGIN Middle English (as a noun): from or related to Middle Low German *stūke.*

stool ▶ noun 1 a seat without a back or arms, typically resting on three or four legs or on a single pedestal.
  2 a piece of faeces.
  3 a root or stump of a tree or plant from which shoots spring.
  4 US a decoy bird in hunting.
▶ verb [no obj.] (of a plant) throw up shoots from the root.
  ■ [with obj.] cut back (a plant) to or near ground level in order to induce new growth.
− PHRASES **at stool** Medicine when defecating. **fall between two stools** Brit. fail to be or take one of two satisfactory alternatives.
− ORIGIN Old English, of Germanic origin; related to Dutch *stoel,* German *Stuhl,* also to STAND. Current senses of the verb date from the late 18th cent.

stoolball ▶ noun [mass noun] a team game played in the UK, chiefly by women and girls, with a bat and ball and pairs of batters scoring runs between bases.
− ORIGIN said to be so named from the use of a *stool* as a wicket when forms of this game were played in Elizabethan times.

stoolie ▶ noun N. Amer. informal short for STOOL PIGEON.

stool pigeon ▶ noun a police informer.
  ■ a person acting as a decoy.
− ORIGIN late 19th cent.: so named from the original use of a pigeon fixed to a stool as a decoy.

stoop¹ ▶ verb [no obj.] 1 bend one's head or body forwards and downwards: *he stooped down and reached towards the coin | Linda stooped to pick up the bottles |* [with obj.] *the man stoops his head.*
  ■ have the head and shoulders habitually bent forwards: *he tends to stoop when he walks |* [as adj. **stooping**] *a thin, stooping figure.* ■ (of a bird of prey) swoop down on a quarry.
  2 lower one's moral standards so far as to do something reprehensible: *Craig wouldn't stoop to thieving | she was unwilling to believe that anyone could stoop so low as to steal from a dead woman.*
  ■ [with infinitive] archaic condescend to do something: *the princes now and then stooped to pay a nominal homage.*
▶ noun 1 [in sing.] a posture in which the head and shoulders are habitually bent forwards: *a tall, thin man with a stoop.*
  2 the downward swoop of a bird of prey.
− ORIGIN Old English *stūpian* (verb), of Germanic origin; related to the adjective STEEP¹. Both senses of the noun date from the late 16th cent.

stoop² ▶ noun N. Amer. a porch with steps in front of a house or other building.
− ORIGIN mid 18th cent.: from Dutch *stoep* (see STOEP).

stoop ball ▶ noun [mass noun] N. Amer. a ball game resembling baseball in which the ball is thrown against a building rather than to a batter.

stooped ▶ adjective (of a person) having the head and shoulders habitually bent forwards: *a thin, stooped figure.*

stoop labour ▶ noun [mass noun] N. Amer. agricultural labour performed in a stooping or squatting position.

stoor ▶ noun variant of STOUR.

stop ▶ verb (**stopped**, **stopping**) 1 [no obj.] (of an event, action, or process) come to an end; cease to happen: *his laughter stopped as quickly as it had begun | the rain had stopped and the clouds had cleared.*
  ■ [with present participle] cease to perform a specified action or have a specified experience: *she stopped giggling |* [with obj.] *he stopped work for tea.* ■ [with present participle] abandon a specified practice or habit: *I've stopped eating meat.* ■ stop moving or operating: *he stopped to look at the view | my watch has stopped.* ■ (of a bus or train) call at a designated place to pick up or set down passengers: *main-line trains stop at platform 7.* ■ Brit. informal stay somewhere for a short time: *you'll have to stop the night.*
  2 [with obj.] cause (an action, process, or event) to come to an end: *this harassment has got to be stopped.*
  ■ prevent (an action or event) from happening: *a security guard was killed trying to stop a raid.* ■ prevent or dissuade (someone) from continuing in an activity or achieving an aim: *a campaign is under way to stop the bombers.* ■ [with obj. and present participle] prevent (someone or something) from performing a specified action or undergoing a specified experience: *several attempts were made to stop him giving evidence | you can't stop me from getting what I want.* ■ cause or order to cease moving or operating: *he stopped his car by the house | police were given powers to stop and search suspects.* ■ informal be hit by (a bullet). ■ instruct a bank to withhold payment on (a cheque). ■ refuse to supply as usual; withhold or deduct: *they would stop money off you if you were late.* ■ Boxing defeat (an opponent) by a knockout: *he was stopped in the sixth by Tyson.* ■ pinch back (a plant).
  3 [with obj.] block or close up (a hole or leak): *he tried to stop the hole with the heel of his boot | the stile has been stopped up.*
  ■ Brit. dated put a filling in (a tooth). ■ block the mouth of (a fox's earth) prior to a hunt. ■ plug the upper end of (an organ pipe), giving a note an octave lower. ■ obtain the required pitch from (the string of a violin or similar instrument) by pressing at the appropriate point with the finger. ■ make (a rope) fast with a stopper.
  4 [no obj.] W. Indian be or behave in a particular way: *'Why was she so?' 'I don't know, you know how dem old people stop.'*
  ■ [with complement] remain in a particular state or condition: *he said I mustn't stop barefooted, so I had to buy a pair of new shoes.*
▶ noun 1 a cessation of movement or operation: *all business came to a stop | there were constant stops and changes of pace.*
  ■ a break or halt during a journey: *allow an hour or so for driving and as long as you like for stops | the flight landed for a refuelling stop.* ■ a place designated for a bus or train to halt and pick up or set down passengers: *the bus was pulling up at her stop.* ■ an object or part of a mechanism which is used to prevent something from moving: *the shelves have special stops to prevent them from being pulled out too far.* ■ Brit. dated a punctuation mark, especially a full stop. ■ used in telegrams to indicate a full stop: *MEET YOU AT THE AIRPORT STOP.* ■ Phonetics a consonant produced with complete closure of the vocal tract. ■ Bridge a high card that prevents the opponents from establishing a particular suit; a control. ■ Nautical a short length of rope used to secure something; a stopper.
  2 a set of organ pipes of a particular tone and range of pitch.
  ■ (also **stop knob**) a knob, lever, or similar device in an organ or harpsichord which brings into play a set of pipes or strings of a particular tone and range of pitch.
  3 Photography the effective diameter of a lens.
  ■ a device for reducing this. ■ a unit of change of relative aperture or exposure (with a reduction of one stop equivalent to halving it).
− PHRASES **pull out all the stops** make a very great effort to achieve something: *the director pulled out all the stops to meet the impossible deadline.* ■ do something very elaborately or on a grand scale: *they gave a Christmas party and pulled out all the stops.* [ORIGIN: with reference to the stops of an organ.] **put a stop to** cause (an activity) to end: *she would have to put a stop to all this nonsense.* **stop at nothing** be utterly ruthless or determined in one's attempt to achieve something: *he would stop at nothing to retain his position of power.* **stop dead** (or **short**) suddenly cease moving, speaking, or acting. **stop**

one's ears put one's fingers in one's ears to avoid hearing something. **stop someone's mouth** induce someone to keep silent about something. **stop payment** instruct a bank to withhold payment on a cheque. **stop the show** (of a performer) provoke prolonged applause or laughter, causing an interruption.
− DERIVATIVES **stoppable** adjective.
− ORIGIN Old English (for)*stoppian* 'block up (an aperture)', of West Germanic origin; related to German *stopfen,* from late Latin *stuppare* 'to stuff'.
▶ **stop by/in** call briefly and informally as a visitor. **stop something down** Photography reduce the aperture of a lens with a diaphragm. **stop off** (or **over**) pay a short visit en route to one's ultimate destination when travelling: *I stopped off to visit him and his wife | he decided to stop over in Paris.* **stop out** Brit. informal stay out, especially longer or later than might be expected. **stop something out** cover an area that is not to be printed or etched when making a print or etching. **stop up** Brit. informal refrain from going to bed; stay up.

stopband ▶ noun Electronics a band of frequencies which are attenuated by a filter.

stopbank ▶ noun Austral./NZ an embankment built to prevent a river flooding.

stop bath ▶ noun Photography a bath for stopping the action of a preceding bath by neutralizing any of its chemical still present.

stop bead ▶ noun a bead or narrow moulding to stop movement, e.g. to prevent a sash window swinging back into the room.

stop bit ▶ noun Telecommunications (in asynchronous data transfers) one of a pattern of bits which indicate the end of a character or of the whole transmission.

stopcock ▶ noun an externally operated valve regulating the flow of a liquid or gas through a pipe, in particular one on the water main supplying a house.

stope /stəʊp/ ▶ noun (usu. **stopes**) a step-like working in a mine.
▶ verb [no obj.] [usu. as noun **stoping**] (in mining) excavate a series of steps or layers in (the ground or rock).
  ■ [as noun **stoping**] Geology the process by which country rock is broken up and removed by the upward movement of magma.
− ORIGIN mid 18th cent.: apparently related to the noun STEP.

Stopes /stəʊps/, Marie (Charlotte Carmichael) (1880–1958), Scottish birth-control campaigner. Her book *Married Love* (1918) was a frank treatment of sexuality within marriage. In 1921 she founded the pioneering Mothers' Clinic for Birth Control in London.

stopgap ▶ noun a temporary way of dealing with a problem or satisfying a need: *transplants are only a stopgap until more sophisticated alternatives can work.*

stop-go ▶ noun [mass noun] [usu. as modifier] alternate stopping and restarting of progress: *stop-go driving.*
  ■ Brit. the alternate restriction and stimulation of economic demand by a government: *stop-go policies.*

stop knob ▶ noun the knob controlling a stop on an organ or harpsichord.

stop light ▶ noun 1 Brit. a red traffic light.
  ■ N. Amer. a set of traffic lights.
  2 (also Brit. **stop lamp**) another term for BRAKE LIGHT.

stop list ▶ noun 1 a list of people or groups deprived of particular rights, privileges, or services, in particular a list of people with whom members of an association are forbidden to do business.
  2 a list of words automatically omitted from a computer-generated concordance or index, typically the most frequent words, which would slow down processing unacceptably.

stop-loss ▶ adjective Finance denoting or relating to an order to sell a security or commodity at a specified price in order to limit a loss.

stop-motion ▶ noun [mass noun] [usu. as modifier] a cinematographic technique whereby the camera is repeatedly stopped and started, for example to give animated figures the impression of movement.

stop-off ▶ noun another term for STOPOVER.

stop-out ▶ noun Brit. informal a person who stays out late at night.

stopover ▶ **noun** a break in a journey: *a brief stopover at Shannon Airport.*
■ a place where a journey is broken.

stoppage ▶ **noun** an instance of movement, activity, or supply stopping or being stopped: *a power stoppage.*
■ a blockage in a narrow passage, such as the barrel of a gun. ■ a cessation of work by employees in protest at the terms set by their employers. ■ (**stoppages**) Brit. deductions from one's wages by an employer for the payment of tax, National Insurance, and other costs: *£3.40 an hour before stoppages.* ■ Boxing a knockout.

stoppage time ▶ **noun** another term for **INJURY TIME**.

Stoppard /ˈstɒpɑːd/, Sir Tom (b.1937), British dramatist, born in Czechoslovakia; born *Thomas Straussler.* His best-known plays are comedies, often dealing with metaphysical and ethical questions, for example *Rosencrantz and Guildenstern are Dead* (1966), which is based on the characters in *Hamlet.*

stopper ▶ **noun** **1** a plug for sealing a hole, especially in the neck of a bottle or other container.
2 [in combination] a person or thing that halts or obstructs a specified thing: *a crime-stopper.*
■ (in soccer or American football) a player whose function is to block attacks on goal from the middle of the field. ■ Baseball a starting pitcher depended on to win a game or reverse a losing streak, or a relief pitcher who prevents the opposing team from scoring highly. ■ (in sailing or climbing) a rope or clamp for preventing a rope or cable from being run out. ■ Bridge another term for **CONTROL**.
▶ **verb** [usu. as adj. **stoppered**] use a stopper to seal (a bottle or other container): *a small stoppered jar.*
– PHRASES **put a** (or **the**) **stopper on** informal prevent from happening or continuing.

stopping ▶ **noun** Brit. dated a filling for a tooth.

stopping place ▶ **noun** a point or establishment at which to stop during a journey.

stopping train ▶ **noun** a train which stops at most or all intermediate stations on a particular line.

stopple US ▶ **noun** a stopper or plug.
▶ **verb** [with obj.] seal with a stopper.
– ORIGIN Middle English: partly a shortening of Old French *estouppail* 'bung', reinforced by the verb **STOP**.

stop press ▶ **noun** [mass noun] Brit. late news inserted in a newspaper or periodical either at the last moment before printing or after printing has begun (especially as a heading): [as modifier] *stop-press news.*

stop-start (also **stop-and-start**) ▶ **adjective** informal alternately stopping and starting; progressing interruptedly: *stop-start journeys.*

stopstreet ▶ **noun** S. African an intersection at which there is a sign immediately before the point of entry, instructing motor vehicles to stop before proceeding across.

stop time ▶ **noun** [mass noun] (in jazz) a rhythmic device whereby a chord or accent is played only on the first beat of every bar or every other bar, typically accompanying a solo.

stop valve ▶ **noun** a valve used to stop the flow of liquid in a pipe.

stop volley ▶ **noun** Tennis a volley played close to the net whereby the player allows the racket to be knocked backwards by the ball and sends it only just back over the net.

stopwatch ▶ **noun** a special watch with buttons that start, stop, and then zero the hands, used to time races.

storage ▶ **noun** [mass noun] the action or method of storing something for future use: *the chair can be folded flat for easy storage* | [as modifier] *the room lacked storage space.*
■ the retention of retrievable data on a computer or other electronic system. ■ space available for storing something, in particular allocated space in a warehouse: *Cooper had put much of the furniture into storage.* ■ the cost of storing something in a warehouse.

storage battery (also **storage cell**) ▶ **noun** a battery (or cell) used for storing electrical energy.

storage device ▶ **noun** a piece of computer equipment on which information can be stored.

storage heater ▶ **noun** Brit. an electric heater that accumulates heat in water or bricks during the night (when electricity is cheaper) and releases it during the day.

storage ring ▶ **noun** Physics an approximately circular accelerator in which particles can be effectively stored by being made to circulate continuously at high energy.

storax /ˈstɔːraks/ (also **styrax**) ▶ **noun** **1** [mass noun] a rare fragrant gum resin obtained from an East Mediterranean tree, sometimes used in medicine, perfumery, and incense.
■ (**Levant** or **liquid storax**) a liquid balsam obtained from the Asian liquidambar tree.
2 a tropical or subtropical tree or shrub with showy white flowers in drooping clusters.
• Genus *Styrax*, family Styracaceae: several species, in particular *S. officinalis*, from which storax resin is obtained.
– ORIGIN late Middle English: from Latin, from a variant of Greek *sturax.*

store ▶ **noun** **1** a quantity or supply of something kept for use as needed: *the squirrel has* **a store of** *food* | figurative *her vast* **store of** *knowledge.*
■ a place where things are kept for future use or sale: *a grain store.* ■ (**stores**) supplies of equipment and food kept for use by members of an army, navy, or other institution, or the place where they are kept. ■ Brit. a computer memory.
2 chiefly N. Amer. a shop of any size or kind: *a health-food store.*
■ Brit. a large shop selling different types of goods. ■ Brit. (also **stores**) a shop selling basic necessities: *a well-stocked village store.*
3 a sheep, steer, cow, or pig acquired or kept for fattening.
▶ **verb** [with obj.] keep or accumulate (something) for future use: *a small room used for storing furniture* | figurative *the scheme could* **store up** *serious future problems.*
■ retain or enter (information) for future electronic retrieval: *the data is* **stored on** *disk.* ■ (**be stored with**) have a supply of (something useful): *a mind well stored with esoteric knowledge.*
– PHRASES **in store** **1** in a safe place while not being used or displayed: *items* **held in store**. **2** coming in the future; about to happen: *he did not yet know what* **lay in store for** *him.* **set** (or **lay** or **put**) **store by** (or **on**) consider (something) to be of a particular degree of importance or value: *many people set much store by privacy.*
– DERIVATIVES **storable** adjective, **storer** noun.
– ORIGIN Middle English: shortening of Old French *estore* (noun), *estorer* (verb), from Latin *instaurare* 'renew'; compare with **RESTORE**.

store-and-forward ▶ **adjective** [attrib.] Telecommunications relating to or denoting a data network in which messages are routed to one or more intermediate stations where they may be stored before being forwarded to their destinations.

store-bought ▶ **adjective** N. Amer. informal, dated bought ready-made from a shop; not home-made.

store card ▶ **noun** a credit card that can be used only in one store or chain of stores.

storefront ▶ **noun** chiefly N. Amer. **1** another term for **SHOPFRONT**.
2 a room or set of rooms facing the street on the ground floor of a commercial building, typically used as a shop: [as modifier] *a bright storefront eatery.*

storehouse ▶ **noun** a building used for storing goods.
■ a large supply of something: *an enormous storehouse of facts.*

storekeeper ▶ **noun** **1** a person responsible for stored goods.
2 N. Amer. a shopkeeper.

storeman ▶ **noun** (pl. **-men**) Brit. a man responsible for stored goods.

storeroom ▶ **noun** a room in which items are stored.

storey (N. Amer. also **story**) ▶ **noun** (pl. **-eys** or **-ies**) a part of a building comprising all the rooms that are on the same level: [in combination] *a three-storey building.*
– DERIVATIVES **storeyed** (N. Amer. also **storied**) adjective [in combination] *four-storeyed houses.*
– ORIGIN late Middle English: shortening of Latin *historia* 'history, story', a special use in Anglo-Latin, perhaps originally denoting a tier of painted windows or sculptures on the front of a building (representing a historical subject).

storiated /ˈstɔːrɪeɪtɪd/ ▶ **adjective** rare decorated with historical, legendary, or emblematic designs.
– DERIVATIVES **storiation** noun.
– ORIGIN late 19th cent.: compare with **HISTORIATED**.

storied ▶ **adjective** [attrib.] poetic/literary celebrated in or associated with stories or legends: *the island's storied past.*

stork ▶ **noun** a very tall long-legged wading bird with a long heavy bill and typically with white and black plumage.
• Family Ciconiidae: several genera and species, in particular the **white stork** (*Ciconia ciconia*), with black wing tips and a reddish bill and legs, often nesting on tall buildings in Europe.
■ the white stork as the pretended bringer of babies.
– ORIGIN Old English *storc*, of Germanic origin; probably related to **STARK** (because of its rigid stance).

storksbill ▶ **noun** a European plant related to the cranesbill, with small pink flowers and fruits that have long twisted beaks.
• Genus *Erodium*, family Geraniaceae.

storm ▶ **noun** **1** a violent disturbance of the atmosphere with strong winds and usually rain, thunder, lightning, or snow.
■ (also **storm system**) an intense low-pressure weather system; a cyclone. ■ a wind of force 10 on the Beaufort scale (48–55 knots or 88–102 kph). ■ a heavy discharge of missiles or blows: *two men were taken by* **a storm of** *bullets.*
2 [usu. in sing.] a tumultuous reaction; an uproar or controversy: *the book caused a storm in America* | *she has been at the centre of a storm concerning payments.*
■ a violent or noisy outburst of a specified feeling or reaction: *the disclosure raised* **a storm of** *protest.*
3 (**storms**) N. Amer. storm windows.
4 a direct assault by troops on a fortified place.
▶ **verb** **1** [no obj., with adverbial of direction] move angrily or forcefully in a specified direction: *she burst into tears and stormed off* | *he stormed out of the house.*
■ [with direct speech] shout (something) angrily; rage: *'Don't patronize me!' she stormed.* ■ move forcefully and decisively to a specified position in a game or contest: *Chester stormed back with two goals in five minutes.*
2 [with obj.] (of troops) suddenly attack and capture (a building or other place) by means of force: *Indian commandos stormed a hijacked plane early today* | [as noun **storming**] *the storming of the Bastille.*
3 [no obj.] (**it storms**, **it is storming**, etc.) (of the weather) be violent, with strong winds and usually rain, thunder, lightning, or snow.
– PHRASES **go down a storm** be enthusiastically received by an audience. **the lull** (or **calm**) **before the storm** a period of unusual tranquillity or stability that seems likely to presage difficult times. **storm and stress** another term for **STURM UND DRANG**. **a storm in a teacup** Brit. great anger or excitement about a trivial matter. **take something by storm** (of troops) capture a place by a sudden and violent attack. ■ have great and rapid success in a particular place or with a particular group of people: *his first collection took the fashion world by storm.* —— **up a storm** chiefly N. Amer. perform the specified action with great enthusiasm and energy: *the band could really* **play up a storm**.
– DERIVATIVES **stormproof** adjective.
– ORIGIN Old English, of Germanic origin; related to Dutch *storm* and German *Sturm*, probably also to the verb **STIR**[1]. The verb dates from late Middle English in sense 3.

storm beach ▶ **noun** an expanse of sand or gravel thrown up on the coast by storms.

stormbound ▶ **adjective** prevented by storms from starting or continuing a journey.

storm centre ▶ **noun** the central point around which controversy or trouble happens: *Lusignan seems to have been the storm centre of the revolt.*

storm cloud ▶ **noun** a heavy, dark rain cloud.
■ (**storm clouds**) used in reference to a threatening or ominous state of affairs: *the beginning of the decade saw* **storm clouds gathering** *over Europe.*

stormcock ▶ **noun** dialect the mistle thrush.

storm collar ▶ **noun** a high coat collar that can be turned up and fastened.

storm cone ▶ **noun** (in the UK) a black conical object hoisted by coastguards as a gale warning, the number and arrangement of cones giving information about wind direction and strength.

storm cuff ▶ **noun** a tight-fitting inner cuff,

S

typically an elasticated one, which prevents rain or wind from getting inside a coat.

storm door ▶ **noun** chiefly N. Amer. an additional outer door for protection in bad weather or winter.

storm drain (US **storm sewer**) ▶ **noun** a drain built to carry away excess water in times of heavy rain.

stormer ▶ **noun** [usu. in sing.] Brit. informal something particularly impressive or good of its kind: *a stormer of an album | the engine is a real stormer.*

storm flap ▶ **noun** a piece of material designed to protect an opening or fastening on a tent or coat from the effects of rain.

storm glass ▶ **noun** a sealed tube containing a solution of which the clarity is thought to change when storms approach.

storming ▶ **adjective** [attrib.] Brit. informal (of a performance, especially in sport or music) outstandingly vigorous or impressive: *his storming finish carried him into third place.*

storm jib ▶ **noun** Sailing a small heavy jib for use in a high wind.

storm lantern ▶ **noun** chiefly Brit. a hurricane lamp.

Stormont Castle /ˈstɔːmɒnt/ a castle in Belfast which was, until 1972, the seat of the Parliament of Northern Ireland and is now the headquarters of the Northern Ireland Assembly.

storm petrel ▶ **noun** a small seabird of the open ocean, typically having blackish plumage and a white rump, and formerly believed to be a harbinger of bad weather.
• Family Hydrobatidae: several genera and many species, e.g. *Hydrobates pelagicus* of the NE Atlantic and Mediterranean.

storm sail ▶ **noun** a sail of smaller size and stronger material than the corresponding one used in ordinary weather.

storm sewer ▶ **noun** US variant of **STORM DRAIN**.

storm signal ▶ **noun** a lamp, flag, or other device used to give a visible warning of an approaching storm.

storm surge ▶ **noun** a rising of the sea as a result of wind and atmospheric pressure changes associated with a storm.

storm troops ▶ **plural noun** another term for **SHOCK TROOPS**.
■ (**Storm Troops**) historical the Nazi political militia; the Brownshirts.
– DERIVATIVES **storm trooper** noun.

storm water ▶ **noun** [mass noun] surface water in abnormal quantity resulting from heavy falls of rain or snow.

storm window ▶ **noun** chiefly N. Amer. a window fixed on outside a normal window for protection and insulation in bad weather or winter.

stormy ▶ **adjective** (**stormier**, **stormiest**) (of weather) characterized by strong winds and usually rain, thunder, lightning, or snow: *a dark and stormy night.*
■ (of the sea or sky) having large waves or dark clouds because of windy or rainy conditions: *grey and stormy skies.* ■ full of angry or violent outbursts of feeling: *a long and stormy debate | a stormy relationship.*
– DERIVATIVES **stormily** adverb, **storminess** noun.

S

stormy petrel ▶ **noun** dated term for **STORM PETREL**.
■ figurative a person who delights in conflict or attracts controversy.

Stornoway /ˈstɔːnəweɪ/ a port on the east coast of Lewis, in the Outer Hebrides; pop. 5,925 (1991). The administrative centre of the Western Isles, it is noted for the manufacture of Harris tweed.

Storting /ˈstɔːtɪŋ/ the Norwegian parliament.
– ORIGIN Norwegian, from *stor* 'great' + *ting* 'assembly'.

story¹ ▶ **noun** (pl. **-ies**) **1** an account of imaginary or real people and events told for entertainment: *an adventure story | I'm going to tell you a story.*
■ a plot or storyline: *the novel has a good story.* ■ a report of an item of news in a newspaper, magazine, or news broadcast: *stories in the local papers.* ■ a piece of gossip; a rumour: *there have been lots of stories going around, as you can imagine.* ■ informal a false statement or explanation; a lie: *Ellie never* **told stories***—she had always believed in the truth.*
2 an account of past events in someone's life or in the evolution of something: *the story of modern farming | the film is based on a true story.*
■ a particular person's representation of the facts of a matter, especially as given in self-defence: *during police interviews, Harper changed his story.* ■ [in sing.] a situation viewed in terms of the information known about it or its similarity to another: *having such information is useful, but it is not the whole story | many children with leukaemia now survive—twenty years ago it was a very different story.*
– PHRASES **but that's another story** informal used after raising a matter to indicate that one does not want to expand on it for now. **end of story** informal used to emphasize that there is nothing to add on a matter just mentioned: *Men don't cry in public. End of story.* **it's a long story** informal used to indicate that, for now, one does not want to talk about something that is too painful and involved. **it's** (or **that's**) **the story of one's life** informal used to lament the fact that a particular misfortune has happened too often in one's experience. **the same old story** used to indicate that a particular bad situation is tediously familiar: *United kept on trying but it was the same old story—no luck.* **the story goes** it is said or rumoured: ***the story goes that*** *he's fallen out with his friends.* **to cut** (or N. Amer. **make**) **a long story short** used to end an account of events quickly: *to cut a long story short, I married Stephen.*
– ORIGIN Middle English (denoting a historical account or representation): shortening of Anglo-Norman French *estorie*, from Latin *historia* (see **HISTORY**).

story² ▶ **noun** N. Amer. variant spelling of **STOREY**.

storyboard ▶ **noun** a sequence of drawings, typically with some directions and dialogue, representing the shots planned for a film or television production.

storybook ▶ **noun** a book containing a story or collection of stories intended for children.
■ [as modifier] denoting something that is as idyllically perfect as things typically are in storybooks: *it was a storybook finish to an illustrious career.*

story editor ▶ **noun** an editor who advises on the content and form of film or television scripts.

storyline ▶ **noun** the plot of a novel, play, film, or other narrative form.

storyteller ▶ **noun** a person who tells stories.
– DERIVATIVES **storytelling** noun & adjective.

stot ▶ **verb** (**stotted**, **stotting**) **1** /stəʊt, stɒt/ Scottish bounce or cause to bounce against a surface: [with obj.] *I stotted the ball off the back wall.*
■ [no obj.] move unsteadily; stagger or lurch: *he's been up there stotting aboot the mountain.*
2 /stɒt/ [no obj.] another term for **PRONK**.
– ORIGIN early 16th cent.: of unknown origin.

stotin /stɒˈtiːn/ ▶ **noun** a monetary unit of Slovenia, equal to one hundredth of a tolar.
– ORIGIN Slovene.

stotinka /stɒˈtɪŋkə/ ▶ **noun** (pl. **stotinki** /stɒˈtɪŋki/) a monetary unit of Bulgaria, equal to one hundredth of a lev.
– ORIGIN Bulgarian, literally 'one hundredth'.

stotty /ˈstɒti/ (also **stotty cake**) ▶ **noun** (pl. **-ies**) [mass noun] N. English a kind of coarse bread made from spare scraps of white dough.
■ [count noun] a soft roll made from this.
– ORIGIN of unknown origin.

stoup /stuːp/ ▶ **noun** a basin for holy water, especially on the wall near the door of a Roman Catholic church for worshippers to dip their fingers in before crossing themselves.
■ archaic or historical a flagon or beaker for drink.
– ORIGIN Middle English (in the sense 'pail, small cask'): from Old Norse *staup*, of Germanic origin; related to the verb **STEEP²**.

Stour /ˈstaʊə/ **1** a river of southern England which rises in west Wiltshire and flows south-east to meet the English Channel east of Bournemouth.
2 (also /stʊə/) a river of eastern England which rises south-east of Cambridge and flows south-eastwards to the North Sea.
3 a river of central England which rises west of Wolverhampton and flows south-westwards through Stourbridge and Kidderminster to meet the Severn at Stourport-on-Severn.

stour /stʊə/ (also **stoor**) ▶ **noun** [mass noun] Scottish & N. English dust forming a cloud or deposited in a mass.
– DERIVATIVES **stoury** adjective.
– ORIGIN late Middle English: of uncertain origin.

stoush /staʊʃ/ Austral./NZ informal ▶ **verb** [with obj.] hit; fight with: *get out of that car while I stoush you.*
▶ **noun** a brawl or other fight.
– ORIGIN late 19th cent.: of unknown origin.

stout ▶ **adjective** **1** (of a person) rather fat or of heavy build: *stout middle-aged men.*
■ (of an object) strong and thick: *Billy had armed himself with a stout stick | stout walking boots.*
2 (of an act, quality, or person) brave and determined: *he put up a stout defence in court.*
▶ **noun** [mass noun] a kind of strong, dark beer brewed with roasted malt or barley.
– DERIVATIVES **stoutish** adjective, **stoutly** adverb, **stoutness** noun.
– ORIGIN Middle English: from Anglo-Norman French and Old French dialect, of West Germanic origin; perhaps related to **STILT**. The noun (late 17th cent.) originally denoted any strong beer and is probably elliptical for *stout ale*.

stout-hearted ▶ **adjective** courageous or determined.
– DERIVATIVES **stout-heartedly** adverb, **stout-heartedness** noun.

stove¹ ▶ **noun** an apparatus for cooking or heating that operates by burning fuel or using electricity.
■ Brit. a hothouse for plants.
▶ **verb** [with obj.] **1** fumigate or disinfect (a house) with sulphur or other fumes.
2 treat (an object) by heating it in a stove in order to apply a desired surface coating.
3 Brit. force or raise (plants) in a hothouse.
– ORIGIN Middle English (in the sense 'sweating-room'): from Middle Dutch or Middle Low German *stove*; perhaps related to the noun **STEW¹**. Current verb senses date from the early 17th cent.

stove² past and past participle of **STAVE**.

stoved ▶ **adjective** [attrib.] Brit. (of vegetables or meat) stewed.

stove-enamel Brit. ▶ **noun** [mass noun] a heatproof enamel produced by heat treatment in a stove, or a paint imitating it.
▶ **verb** [with obj.] [usu. as adj. **stove-enamelled**] give (something) a finish of this kind.

stovepipe ▶ **noun** the pipe taking the smoke and gases from a stove up through a roof or to a chimney.

stovepipe hat ▶ **noun** a silk hat resembling a top hat but much taller.

stovies /ˈstəʊvɪz/ ▶ **plural noun** Scottish a dish of potatoes stewed in a pot.
– ORIGIN late 19th cent.: from Scots *stove* 'stew (meat or vegetables)', perhaps partly from Dutch *stoven*.

stow ▶ **verb** [with obj. and adverbial] pack or store (an object) carefully and neatly in a particular place: *Barney began stowing her luggage into the boot | she* **stowed** *the map* **away** *in the glove compartment.*
– PHRASES **stow it!** informal used as a way of urging someone to be quiet or to stop doing something.
– ORIGIN late Middle English: shortening of **BESTOW**.
▶ **stow away** conceal oneself on a ship, aircraft, or other passenger vehicle in order to travel secretly or without paying the fare: *he stowed away on a ship bound for South Africa.*

stowage ▶ **noun** [mass noun] the action of stowing something.
■ space for stowing something in: *there is plenty of stowage beneath the berth.*

stowaway ▶ **noun** a person who stows away.

Stowe, Harriet (Elizabeth) Beecher (1811–96), American novelist. She won fame with her anti-slavery novel *Uncle Tom's Cabin* (1852), which strengthened the contemporary abolitionist cause with its descriptions of the sufferings caused by slavery.

STP ▶ **abbreviation for** ■ Physiology short-term potentiation. ■ Chemistry standard temperature and pressure. ■ Professor of Sacred Theology. [ORIGIN: from Latin *Sanctae Theologiae Professor*.]

str. ▶ **abbreviation for** ■ strait. ■ Rowing stroke.

strabismus /strəˈbɪzməs/ ▶ **noun** [mass noun] abnormal alignment of the eyes; the condition of having a squint.
– DERIVATIVES **strabismic** adjective.
– ORIGIN late 17th cent.: modern Latin, from Greek *strabismos*, from *strabizein* 'to squint', from *strabos* 'squinting'.

Strabo /ˈstreɪbəʊ/ (*c.*63 BC–*c.*23 AD), historian and geographer of Greek descent. His only extant work, *Geographica*, in seventeen volumes, provides a detailed physical and historical geography of the ancient world during the reign of Augustus.

stracciatella /ˌstratʃəˈtɛlə/ ▶ **noun** [mass noun] an Italian soup containing eggs and cheese.
– ORIGIN Italian.

Strachey /ˈstreɪtʃi/, (Giles) Lytton (1880–1932), English biographer. A prominent member of the Bloomsbury Group, he achieved recognition with *Eminent Victorians* (1918), which attacked the literary Establishment through its satirical biographies of Florence Nightingale, General Gordon, and others.

Strad ▶ **noun** informal a Stradivarius.
– ORIGIN late 19th cent.: abbreviation.

straddle ▶ **verb** [with obj.] sit or stand with one leg on either side of: *he turned the chair round and straddled it.*
■ place (one's legs) wide apart: *he shifted his legs, straddling them to keep his balance.* ■ [no obj.] archaic stand, walk, or sit with one's legs wide apart. ■ extend across or be situated on both sides of: *a mountain range straddling the Franco-Swiss border.* ■ N. Amer. take up or maintain an equivocal position with regard to (a political issue): *a man who had straddled the issue of taxes.* ■ fire at (a target) with shots or bombs so that they fall short of and beyond it.
▶ **noun 1** an act of sitting or standing with one's legs wide apart.
2 Stock Exchange a simultaneous purchase of options to buy and to sell a security or commodity at a fixed price, allowing the purchaser to make a profit whether the price of the security or commodity goes up or down.
– DERIVATIVES **straddler** noun.
– ORIGIN mid 16th cent.: alteration of dialect *striddle*, back-formation from dialect *striddling* 'astride', from **STRIDE** + the adverbial suffix *-ling*.

Stradivari /ˌstradɪˈvɑːri/, Antonio (*c.*1644–1737), Italian violin-maker. He devised the proportions of the modern violin, giving a more powerful and rounded sound than earlier instruments possessed. About 650 of his celebrated violins, violas, and violoncellos are still in existence.

Stradivarius /ˌstradɪˈvɛːrɪəs/ ▶ **noun** a violin or other stringed instrument made by Antonio Stradivari or his followers.
– ORIGIN mid 19th cent.: Latinized form of **STRADIVARI**.

strafe /strɑːf, streɪf/ ▶ **verb** [with obj.] attack repeatedly with bombs or machine-gun fire from low-flying aircraft: *military aircraft strafed the village.*
▶ **noun** an attack from low-flying aircraft.
– ORIGIN early 20th cent.: humorous adaptation of the German First World War catchphrase *Gott strafe England* 'may God punish England'.

straggle ▶ **verb** [no obj., usu. with adverbial of direction] move along slowly, typically in a small irregular group, so as to remain some distance behind the person or people in front: *half the men were already straggling back into the building* | [as adj. **straggling**] *the straggling crowd of refugees.*
■ grow, spread, or be laid out in an irregular, untidy way: *her hair was straggling over her eyes.*
▶ **noun** an untidy or irregularly arranged mass or group of something: *a straggle of cottages.*
– DERIVATIVES **straggler** noun, **straggly** adjective.
– ORIGIN late Middle English: perhaps from dialect *strake* 'go'.

straight ▶ **adjective 1** extending or moving uniformly in one direction only; without a curve or bend: *a long, straight road.*
■ Geometry (of a line) lying on the shortest path between any two of its points. ■ (of an aim, blow, or course) going direct to the intended target: *a straight punch to the face.* ■ (of hair) not curly or wavy. ■ (of a garment) not flared or fitted closely to the body: *a straight skirt.* ■ (of an arch) flat-topped.
2 properly positioned so as to be level, upright, or symmetrical: *he made sure his tie was straight.*
■ [predic.] in proper order or condition: *it'll take a long time to get the place straight.*
3 not evasive; honest: *a straight answer* | *thank you for being straight with me.*
■ simple; straightforward: *a straight choice between nuclear power and penury.* ■ (of a look) bold and steady: *he gave her a straight, no-nonsense look.* ■ (of thinking) clear, logical, and unemotional.
4 [attrib.] in continuous succession: *he scored his fourth straight win.*
5 (of an alcoholic drink) undiluted; neat: *straight brandy.*
6 (especially of drama) serious as opposed to comic or musical; employing the conventional techniques of its art form: *a straight play.*
■ informal (of a person) conventional or respectable: *she looked pretty straight in her school clothes.* ■ informal heterosexual.
▶ **adverb 1** in a straight line; directly: *he was gazing straight at her* | *keep* **straight on**.
■ with no delay or diversion; directly or immediately: *after dinner we went straight back to our hotel* | *I fell into bed and went straight to sleep.* ■ archaic at once; immediately: *I'll fetch up the bath to you straight.*
2 in or into a level, even, or upright position: *he pulled his clothes straight* | *sit up straight!*
3 correctly; clearly: *I'm so tired I can hardly think straight.*
■ honestly and directly; in a straightforward manner: *I told her straight—the kid's right.*
4 without a break; continuously: *he remembered working sixteen hours straight.*
▶ **noun 1** a part of something that is not curved or bent, especially the concluding stretch of a racecourse: *he pulled away in the straight to win by half a second.*
■ archaic a form or position that is not curved or bent: *the rod flew back to the straight.*
2 Poker a continuous sequence of five cards.
3 informal a conventional person.
■ a heterosexual.
4 S. African informal (in township slang) a 750 ml bottle of liquor. [ORIGIN: perhaps a transferred sense of US slang *straight* 'unadulterated whisky'.]
– PHRASES **get something straight** make a situation clear, especially by reaching an understanding. **go straight** live an honest life after being a criminal. **a straight face** a blank or serious facial expression, especially when trying not to laugh: *my father* **kept a straight face** *when he joked.* **the straight and narrow** the honest and morally acceptable way of living: *he's making a real effort to get back on the straight and narrow.* **straight away** immediately. **a straight fight** Brit. a contest between just two opponents, especially in an election. **straight from the shoulder 1** dated (of a blow) swift and well delivered. **2** (of words) frank or direct: *sometimes he spoke straight from the shoulder and sometimes in puzzles.* **straight off** (or **out**) informal without hesitation or deliberation: *Wendy drank half the bottle straight off.* **straight up** informal **1** Brit. truthfully; honestly: *come on, Bert, I won't hurt you—straight up.* **2** chiefly N. Amer. unmixed; unadulterated: *a dry Martini served straight up.*
– DERIVATIVES **straightish** adjective, **straightly** adverb, **straightness** noun.
– ORIGIN Middle English (as an adjective and adverb): archaic past participle of **STRETCH**.

straight-ahead ▶ **adjective** (especially of popular music) straightforward, simple, or unadorned.

straight angle ▶ **noun** Mathematics an angle of 180°.

straight-arm ▶ **verb** [with obj.] US informal ward off (an opponent) or remove (an obstacle) with the arm unflexed: *I straight-armed the woman leaning in on her.*

straight arrow ▶ **noun** N. Amer. informal an honest, morally upright person.

straightaway ▶ **adverb** variant spelling of ***straight away*** at **STRAIGHT**.
▶ **adjective** N. Amer. extending or moving in a straight line.
▶ **noun** N. Amer. a straight section of a road or racetrack.

straight chain ▶ **noun** Chemistry a chain of atoms in a molecule, usually carbon atoms, that is neither branched nor formed into a ring.

straight chair ▶ **noun** a straight-backed side chair.

straight-cut ▶ **adjective** (of tobacco) cut lengthwise into long silky fibres.

straight edge ▶ **noun** a bar with one accurately straight edge, used for testing whether something else is straight.

straight-eight ▶ **noun** an internal-combustion engine with eight cylinders in line.
■ a vehicle with an engine of this type.

straighten ▶ **verb** make or become straight: [with obj.] *she helped him straighten his tie* | [no obj.] *where the river straightened he took his chance to check the barometer.*
■ [with obj.] make tidy or put in order again: *he sat down at his desk, straightening his things that Lee had moved* | *they are asking for help in* **straightening out** *their lives.* ■ [no obj.] stand or sit erect after bending: *he* **straightened up**, *using the bedside table for support.* ■ (**straighten up**) (of a vehicle, ship, or aircraft) stop turning and move in a straight line.
– DERIVATIVES **straightener** noun.

straight-faced ▶ **adjective** with a blank or serious facial expression.

straight flush ▶ **noun** (in poker or brag) a hand of cards all of one suit and in a continuous sequence (for example, the seven, eight, nine, ten, and jack of spades).

straightforward ▶ **adjective** uncomplicated and easy to do or understand: *in a straightforward case no fees will be charged.*
■ (of a person) honest and frank: *a straightforward young man.*
– DERIVATIVES **straightforwardly** adverb, **straightforwardness** noun.

straightjacket ▶ **noun** & **verb** variant spelling of **STRAITJACKET**.

straight-laced ▶ **adjective** variant spelling of **STRAIT-LACED**.

straight-line ▶ **adjective** containing, characterized by, or relating to straight lines or motion in a straight line: *a straight-line graph* | *the Porsche's straight-line stability.*
■ Finance of or relating to a method of depreciation allocating a given percentage of the cost of an asset each year for a fixed period.

straight man ▶ **noun** the person in a comedy duo who speaks lines which give a comedian the opportunity to make jokes.

straight razor ▶ **noun** North American term for **CUT-THROAT RAZOR**.

straight shooter ▶ **noun** informal, chiefly N. Amer. an honest and forthright person.
– DERIVATIVES **straight-shooting** adjective.

straight-six ▶ **noun** an internal-combustion engine with six cylinders in line.
■ a vehicle with an engine of this type.

straight stitch ▶ **noun** a single short separate embroidery stitch.

straight time ▶ **noun** [mass noun] chiefly US normal working hours, paid at a regular rate.

straight-up ▶ **adjective** N. Amer. informal honest; trustworthy: *you sounded like a straight-up guy.*

straightway ▶ **adverb** archaic form of ***straight away*** (see **STRAIGHT**).

strain[1] ▶ **verb 1** [with obj.] force (a part of one's body or oneself) to make a strenuous or unusually great effort: *I stopped and listened, straining my ears for any sound.*
■ injure (a limb, muscle, or organ) by overexerting it or twisting it awkwardly: *on cold days you are more likely to strain a muscle* | *glare from the screen can strain your eyes.* ■ [no obj.] make a strenuous and continuous effort: *his voice was so quiet that I had to strain to hear it.* ■ make severe or excessive demands on: *he strained her tolerance to the limit.* ■ [no obj.] pull or push forcibly at something: *the bear* **strained at** *the chain around its neck* | *his stomach was swollen,* **straining against** *the thin shirt.* ■ stretch (something) tightly: *the barbed wire fence was strained to posts six feet high.* ■ archaic embrace (someone) tightly: *she strained the infant to her bosom again.*
2 [with obj.] pour (a mainly liquid substance) through a porous or perforated device or material in order to separate out any solid matter: *strain the custard into a bowl.*
■ cause liquid to drain off (food which has been boiled, soaked, or canned) by using such a device. ■ drain off (liquid) in this way: ***strain off*** *the surplus fat.*
▶ **noun 1** a force tending to pull or stretch something to an extreme or damaging degree: *the usual type of chair puts an enormous strain on the spine* | [mass noun] *aluminium may bend under strain.*
■ Physics the magnitude of a deformation, equal to the change in the dimension of a deformed object divided by its original dimension. ■ an injury to a part of the body caused by overexertion or twisting a muscle awkwardly: *he has a slight groin strain.*
2 a severe or excessive demand on the strength, resources, or abilities of someone or something: *the accusations* **put a strain on** *relations between the two countries* | [mass noun] *she's obviously* **under** *considerable* **strain**.
■ [mass noun] a state of tension or exhaustion resulting from this: *the telltale signs of nervous strain.*
3 (usu. **strains**) the sound of piece of music as it is played or performed: *from within the flat could be heard the strains of country and western music.*
– PHRASES **at (full) strain** archaic using the utmost

S

effort. **strain every nerve** see **NERVE**. **strain at the leash** see **LEASH**.
– DERIVATIVES **strainable** adjective.
– ORIGIN Middle English (as a verb): from Old French *estreindre*, from Latin *stringere* 'draw tight'. Current senses of the noun arose in the mid 16th cent.

strain² ▶ **noun 1** a breed, stock, or variety of an animal or plant developed by breeding.
■a natural or cultured variety of a micro-organism with a distinct form, biochemistry, or virulence.
2 a particular tendency as part of a person's character: *there was a powerful strain of insanity on her mother's side of the family.*
■a variety of a particular abstract thing: *a strain of feminist thought.*
– ORIGIN Old English *strīon* 'acquisition, gain', of Germanic origin; related to Latin *struere* 'to build up'.

strained ▶ **adjective 1** (of an atmosphere, situation, or relationship) not relaxed or comfortable; tense or uneasy: *there was a strained silence | relations between the two countries were strained.*
■(of a person) showing signs of tiredness or nervous tension: *Jean's pale, strained face.* ■ (of an appearance or performance) produced by deliberate effort rather than natural impulse; artificial or forced: *I put on my strained smile for the next customer.* ■ (of a statement or representation) laboured or far-fetched: *my example may seem a little strained and artificial.*
2 (of a limb or muscle) injured by overexertion or twisting.
3 (of a mainly liquid substance) having been strained to separate out any solid matter.

strain energy ▶ **noun** [mass noun] Mechanics energy stored in an elastic body under loading.

strainer ▶ **noun** a device having holes punched in it or made of crossed wires for separating solid matter from a liquid: *a tea strainer.*

strain gauge ▶ **noun** a device for indicating the strain of a material or structure at the point of attachment.

strait ▶ **noun 1** (also **straits**) a narrow passage of water connecting two seas or two large areas of water: [in place names] *the Straits of Gibraltar.*
2 (**straits**) used in reference to a situation characterized by a specified degree of trouble or difficulty: *the economy is* **in dire straits** *| redundancy left him in severe financial straits.*
▶ **adjective** archaic (of a place) of limited spatial capacity; narrow or cramped: *the road was so strait that a handful of men might have defended it.*
■close, strict, or rigorous: *my captivity was strait as ever.*
– DERIVATIVES **straitly** adverb, **straitness** noun.
– ORIGIN Middle English: shortening of Old French *estreit* 'tight, narrow', from Latin *strictus* 'drawn tight' (see **STRICT**).

straiten ▶ **verb** archaic make or become narrow: [with obj.] *the passage was straitened by tables.*

straitened ▶ **adjective 1** characterized by poverty: *they lived in straitened circumstances.*
2 restricted in range or scope: *their straitened horizons.*

straitjacket (also **straightjacket**) ▶ **noun** a strong garment with long sleeves which can be tied together to confine the arms of a violent prisoner or mental patient.
■used in reference to something which restricts freedom of action, development, or expression: *the government is operating in an economic straitjacket.*
▶ **verb** (**-jacketed**, **-jacketing**) [with obj.] restrain with a straitjacket.
■impose severely restrictive measures on (a person or activity): *the treaty should not be used as a tool to straitjacket international trade.*

strait-laced (also **straight-laced**) ▶ **adjective** having or showing very strict moral attitudes.

Straits Settlements a former British Crown Colony in SE Asia. Established in 1867, it comprised Singapore, Penang, and Malacca, and later included Labuan, Christmas Island, and the Cocos Islands. It was disbanded in 1946.

strake ▶ **noun 1** a continuous line of planking or plates from the stem to the stern of a ship or boat.
2 a protruding ridge fitted to an aircraft or other structure to improve aerodynamic stability.
– ORIGIN Middle English: from Anglo-Latin *stracus*, *straca*; probably from the Germanic base of the verb **STRETCH**.

Stralsund /ˈstrɑːlzʊnt/ a town and fishing port in northern Germany, on the Baltic coast opposite the island of Rügen; pop. 71,620 (1991).

stramash /strəˈmaʃ/ ▶ **noun** Scottish & N. English an uproar; a row.
– ORIGIN late 18th cent.: apparently imitative.

stramonium /strəˈməʊnɪəm/ ▶ **noun** [mass noun] a preparation of the dried leaves or poisonous seeds of the thorn apple, with medical and other uses.
– ORIGIN mid 17th cent.: modern Latin (part of the plant's binomial), perhaps an alteration of Tartar *turman* 'horse medicine'.

strand¹ ▶ **verb** [with obj.] drive or leave (a boat, sailor, or sea creature) aground on a shore: *the ships were stranded in shallow water |* [as adj. **stranded**] *a stranded whale.*
■leave (someone) without the means to move from somewhere: *two of the firm's lorries are stranded in France.*
▶ **noun** poetic/literary the shore of a sea, lake, or large river: *a heron glided to rest on a pebbly strand.*
– ORIGIN Old English (as a noun), of unknown origin. The verb dates from the early 17th cent.

strand² ▶ **noun** a single thin length of something such as thread, fibre, or wire, especially as twisted together with others: *a strand of cotton | strands of grass.*
■a string of beads or pearls. ■ an element that forms part of a complex whole: *Marxist theories evolved from different strands of social analysis.*
– ORIGIN late 15th cent.: of unknown origin.

stranded ▶ **adjective** [attrib.] (of thread, rope, or similar) arranged in single thin lengths twisted together: *stranded cotton |* [in combination] figurative *the many-stranded passions of the country.*

strandloper /ˈstrantˌlʊəpə/ (also **strandlooper**) ▶ **noun** chiefly S. African a person who collects items on the shore; a beachcomber.
■(**Strandloper**) a member of a Khoisan people who lived on the southern shores of southern Africa from prehistoric times until the present millennium.
– ORIGIN Afrikaans, from *strand* 'seashore' + *loper* 'runner'.

strandwolf /ˈstrantvɒlf, ˈstrandwʊlf/ ▶ **noun** S. African the brown hyena, which often frequents the shore, where it scavenges dead fish and birds.
• *Hyaena brunnea*, family Hyaenidae.
– ORIGIN late 18th cent.: from South African Dutch, from *strand* 'beach' + *wolf* 'wolf'.

strange ▶ **adjective 1** unusual or surprising in a way that is unsettling or hard to understand: *children have some strange ideas | he's a very strange man |* [with clause] ***it is strange how*** *things change.*
2 not previously visited, seen, or encountered; unfamiliar or alien: *she found herself in bed in a strange place | a harsh accent that was* **strange to** *his ears.*
■[predic.] (**strange to/at/in**) archaic unaccustomed to or unfamiliar with: *I am strange to the work.*
– PHRASES **feel strange** (of a person or part of the body) feel unwell; have unpleasant sensations: *her head still felt strange.* ■ be uncomfortable or ill at ease in a situation: *the family had expected to feel strange in Stephen's company.* **strange to say** (or poetic/literary **tell**) it is surprising or unusual that: *strange to say, I didn't really like carol singers.*
– DERIVATIVES **strangely** adverb [as submodifier] *the house was strangely quiet |* [sentence adverb] ***strangely enough****, people were able to perform this task without difficulty.*
– ORIGIN Middle English: shortening of Old French *estrange*, from Latin *extraneus* 'external, strange'.

strange attractor ▶ **noun** Mathematics an equation or fractal set representing a complex pattern of behaviour in a chaotic system.

strangeness ▶ **noun** [mass noun] **1** the state or fact of being strange.
2 Physics one of six flavours of quark.

strange particle ▶ **noun** Physics a subatomic particle classified as having a non-zero value for strangeness.

stranger ▶ **noun** a person whom one does not know or with whom one is not familiar: *don't talk to strangers | she remained* ***a stranger to*** *him.*
■a person who does not know, or is not known in, a particular place or community: *I'm* ***a stranger in*** *these parts | he must have been* ***a stranger to*** *the village.* ■ (**stranger to**) a person entirely unaccustomed to (a feeling, experience, or situation): *he* ***is no stranger to*** *controversy.* ■ a person who is not a member or official of the House of Commons.
– PHRASES **hello, stranger!** humorous used to greet someone whom one has not seen for some time.
– ORIGIN late Middle English: shortening of Old French *estrangier*, from Latin *extraneus* (see **STRANGE**).

strangle ▶ **verb** [with obj.] squeeze or constrict the neck of (a person or animal), especially so as to cause death: *the victim was strangled with a scarf.*
■[as adj. **strangled**] sounding as though the speaker's throat is constricted: *a series of strangled gasps.* ■ suppress (an impulse, action, or sound): *she strangled a sob.* ■ hamper or hinder the development or activity of: *they allowed bureaucracy to strangle initiative.*
– DERIVATIVES **strangler** noun.
– ORIGIN Middle English: shortening of Old French *estrangler*, from Latin *strangulare*, from Greek *strangalan*, from *strangalē* 'halter', related to *strangos* 'twisted'.

stranglehold ▶ **noun** [in sing.] a grip around the neck of another person that can kill by asphyxiation if held for long enough.
■complete or overwhelming control: *in France, supermarkets have less of a* ***stranglehold on*** *food supplies.*

strangles ▶ **plural noun** [usu. treated as sing.] a bacterial infection of the upper respiratory tract of horses, causing enlargement of the lymph nodes in the throat, which may impair breathing.
• This disease is caused by the bacterium *Streptococcus equi.*
– ORIGIN early 17th cent.: plural of obsolete *strangle* 'strangulation', from **STRANGLE**.

strangulate /ˈstraŋgjʊleɪt/ ▶ **verb** [with obj.] [often as adj. **strangulated**] **1** Medicine prevent circulation of the blood supply through (a part of the body, especially a hernia) by constriction: *a strangulated hernia.*
2 informal strangle; throttle: *the poor woman died strangulated.*
■[as adj. **strangulated**] sounding as though the speaker's throat is constricted: *a strangulated cry.*
– ORIGIN mid 17th cent. (in the sense 'suffocate'): from Latin *strangulat-* 'choked', from the verb *strangulare* (see **STRANGLE**).

strangulation ▶ **noun** [mass noun] **1** the action or state of strangling or being strangled: *death due to strangulation.*
■the process or state of severely restricting the activities or supplies of an area or community or of undergoing such restrictions: *economic strangulation.*
2 Medicine the condition in which circulation of blood to a part of the body (especially a hernia) is cut off by constriction.

strangury /ˈstraŋgjʊri/ ▶ **noun** [mass noun] a condition caused by blockage or irritation at the base of the bladder, resulting in severe pain and a strong desire to urinate.
– DERIVATIVES **strangurious** /-ˈgjʊərɪəs/ adjective.
– ORIGIN late Middle English: via Latin from Greek *strangouria*, from *stranx*, *strang-* 'drop squeezed out' + *ouron* 'urine'.

Stranraer /stranˈrɑː/ a port and market town in SW Scotland, in Dumfries and Galloway; pop. 10,170 (1984). It is the terminus of a ferry service from Northern Ireland.

strap ▶ **noun** a strip of leather, cloth, or other flexible material, often with a buckle, used to fasten, secure, or carry something or to hold on to something: *her bra strap | the strap of his shoulder bag.*
■a strip of metal, often hinged, used to fasten or secure something. ■ (**the strap**) punishment by beating with a strip of leather.
▶ **verb** (**strapped**, **strapping**) **1** [with obj. and adverbial of place] fasten or secure in a specified place or position with a strap or seat belt: *I had to strap the bag to my bicycle | the children were strapped into their car seats.*
■[with obj.] Brit. bind (an injured part of the body) with adhesive plaster: *the goalkeeper's knee was* ***strapped up****.*
2 [with obj.] beat (someone) with a strip of leather: *I expected when my dad walked in that he'd strap him.*
– ORIGIN late 16th cent. (denoting a trap for birds, also a piece of timber fastening two objects together): dialect form of **STROP¹**.

straphanger ▶ **noun** informal a standing passenger in a bus or train.
■chiefly US a person who commutes to work by public transport.
– DERIVATIVES **strap-hang** verb.

strap hinge ▶ **noun** a hinge with long leaves or flaps for screwing on to the surface of a door or gate.

strapless ▶ **adjective** (especially of a dress or bra) without shoulder straps.

strapline ▶ **noun** a subsidiary heading or caption in a newspaper or magazine.

strap-on ▶ **adjective** able to be attached by a strap or straps.

strappado /strəˈpɑːdəʊ, -eɪdəʊ/ ▶ **noun** (pl. **-os**) (usu. **the strappado**) historical a form of punishment or torture in which the victim was secured to a rope and made to fall from a height almost to the ground before being stopped with an abrupt jerk.
▪the instrument used for inflicting this punishment or torture.
– ORIGIN mid 16th cent.: from French *(e)strapade*, from Italian *strappata*, from *strappare* 'to snatch'.

strapped ▶ **adjective** informal short of money: *I'm constantly strapped for cash.*

strapper ▶ **noun** chiefly Austral. a person who grooms racehorses.

strapping[1] ▶ **adjective** (especially of a young person) big and strong: *they had three strapping sons.*

strapping[2] ▶ **noun** [mass noun] adhesive plaster for binding injured parts of the body.
▪strips of leather or pliable metal used to hold, strengthen, or fasten something.

strappy ▶ **adjective** (of shoes or clothes) having eye-catching straps: *white strappy sandals.*

strapwork ▶ **noun** [mass noun] ornamentation imitating pierced and interlaced straps.

Strasberg /ˈstrazbəːg/, Lee (1901–82), American actor, director, and drama teacher, born in Austria; born *Israel Strassberg*. As artistic director of the Actors' Studio in New York City (1948–82) he was the leading figure in the development of method acting in the US.

Strasbourg /ˈstrazbəːg, French stʀasbuʀ/ a city in NE France, in Alsace, close to the border with Germany; pop. 255,940 (1990). Annexed by Germany in 1870, it was returned to France after the First World War. It is the headquarters of the Council of Europe and of the European Parliament.

strata plural form of **STRATUM**.

stratagem /ˈstratədʒəm/ ▶ **noun** a plan or scheme, especially one used to outwit an opponent or achieve an end: *a series of devious stratagems.*
▪[mass noun] archaic skill in devising such plans or schemes; cunning.
– ORIGIN late 15th cent. (originally denoting a military ploy): from French *stratagème*, via Latin from Greek *stratēgēma*, from *stratēgein* 'be a general', from *stratēgos*, from *stratos* 'army' + *agein* 'to lead'.

stratal ▶ **adjective** relating or belonging to strata or a stratum.

strategic /strəˈtiːdʒɪk/ ▶ **adjective** relating to the identification of long-term or overall aims and interests and the means of achieving them: *strategic planning for the organization is the responsibility of top management.*
▪carefully designed or planned to serve a particular purpose or advantage: *alarms are positioned at strategic points around the prison.* ▪relating to the gaining of overall or long-term military advantage: *Newark Castle was of strategic importance | a hazard to British strategic and commercial interests.* ▪(of human or material resources) essential in fighting a war: *the strategic forces on Russian territory.* ▪(of bombing or weapons) done or for use against industrial areas and communication centres of enemy territory as a long-term military objective: *strategic nuclear missiles.* Often contrasted with **TACTICAL**.
– DERIVATIVES **strategical** adjective, **strategically** adverb [as submodifier] *a strategically placed mirror.*
– ORIGIN early 19th cent.: from French *stratégique*, from Greek *stratēgikos*, from *stratēgos* (see **STRATAGEM**).

Strategic Arms Limitation Talks (abbrev. **SALT**) a series of negotiations between the US and the Soviet Union aimed at the limitation or reduction of nuclear armaments, which produced the Strategic Arms Limitation Treaty. The talks were organized from 1968 onwards and held in stages until superseded by the START negotiations in 1983.

Strategic Arms Reduction Talks (abbrev. **START**) a series of arms-reduction negotiations between the US and the Soviet Union begun in 1983. The Intermediate Nuclear Forces (INF) treaty was signed in 1987 and the Strategic Arms Reduction Treaty in 1991.

Strategic Defense Initiative (abbrev.: **SDI**) a projected US system of defence against nuclear weapons, using satellites armed with lasers to intercept and destroy intercontinental ballistic missiles. The project was renamed the **BALLISTIC MISSILE DEFENSE ORGANIZATION** in 1993. Popularly known as **STAR WARS**.

strategist ▶ **noun** a person skilled in planning action or policy, especially in war or politics.

strategize (also **-ise**) ▶ **verb** [no obj.] N. Amer. devise a strategy or strategies.

strategy /ˈstratɪdʒi/ ▶ **noun** (pl. **-ies**) a plan of action or policy designed to achieve a major or overall aim: *time to develop a coherent economic strategy* | [mass noun] *shifts in marketing strategy.*
▪[mass noun] the art of planning and directing overall military operations and movements in a war or battle. Often contrasted with ***tactics*** (see **TACTIC**). ▪a plan for such military operations and movements: *non-provocative defence strategies.*
– ORIGIN early 19th cent.: from French *stratégie*, from Greek *stratēgia* 'generalship', from *stratēgos* (see **STRATAGEM**).

Stratford-upon-Avon a town in Warwickshire, on the River Avon; pop. 20,100 (1981). Famous as the birth and burial place of William Shakespeare, it is the site of the Royal Shakespeare Theatre.
– DERIVATIVES **Stratfordian** noun.

strath /straθ/ ▶ **noun** Scottish a broad mountain valley.
– ORIGIN mid 16th cent.: from Scottish Gaelic *srath*.

Strathclyde /straθˈklʌɪd/ a former local government region in west central Scotland, dissolved in 1996.

strathspey /straθˈspeɪ/ ▶ **noun** a slow Scottish dance.
▪a piece of music for such a dance, typically in four-four time.
– ORIGIN mid 18th cent.: from *Strathspey*, the name of the valley of the River Spey.

stratified sample ▶ **noun** Statistics a sample that is drawn from a number of separate strata of the population, rather than at random from the whole population, in order that it should be representative.

stratiform /ˈstratɪfɔːm/ ▶ **adjective** technical arranged in layers: *stratiform clouds.*
▪Geology (of a mineral deposit) formed parallel to the bedding planes of the surrounding rock.

stratify /ˈstratɪfʌɪ/ ▶ **verb** (**-ies**, **-ied**) [with obj.] [usu. as adj. **stratified**] form or arrange into strata: *socially stratified cities* | [no obj.] *the residues have begun to stratify.*
▪arrange or classify: *stratifying patients into well-defined risk groups.* ▪place (seeds) close together in layers in moist sand or peat to preserve them or to help them germinate. ▪[no obj.] (of seeds) be germinated by this method.
– DERIVATIVES **stratification** noun.

stratigraphy /strəˈtɪgrəfi/ ▶ **noun** [mass noun] the branch of geology concerned with the order and relative position of strata and their relationship to the geological timescale.
▪the analysis of the order and position of layers of archaeological remains. ▪the structure of a particular set of strata.
– DERIVATIVES **stratigrapher** noun, **stratigraphic** adjective, **stratigraphical** adjective.
– ORIGIN mid 19th cent.: from **STRATUM** + **-GRAPHY**.

stratocracy /strəˈtɒkrəsi/ ▶ **noun** (pl. **-ies**) [mass noun] rare government by military forces.
▪[count noun] a military government.

stratocumulus /ˌstratə(ʊ)ˈkjuːmjʊləs, ˌstreɪ-, ˌstrɑː-/ ▶ **noun** [mass noun] cloud forming a low layer of clumped or broken grey masses.

stratopause /ˈstratə(ʊ)pɔːz, ˌstreɪ-, ˌstrɑː-/ ▶ **noun** the interface between the stratosphere and the ionosphere.
– ORIGIN 1950s: from **STRATOSPHERE**, suggested by **TROPOPAUSE**.

stratosphere /ˈstratəˌsfɪə/ ▶ **noun** the layer of the earth's atmosphere above the troposphere, extending to about 50 km above the earth's surface (the lower boundary of the mesosphere).
▪figurative the very highest levels of a profession or other sphere, or of prices or other quantities: *her next big campaign launched her into the fashion stratosphere.*
– DERIVATIVES **stratospheric** /-ˈsfɛrɪk/ adjective, **stratospherically** adverb.

stratovolcano /ˌstratəʊvɒlˈkeɪnəʊ/ ▶ **noun** (pl. **-oes**) a volcano built up of alternate layers of lava and ash.

stratum /ˈstrɑːtəm, ˈstreɪtəm/ ▶ **noun** (pl. **strata** /-tə/) **1** a layer or a series of layers of rock in the ground: *a stratum of flint.*
▪a thin layer within any structure: *thin strata of air.*
2 a level or class to which people are assigned according to their social status, education, or income: *members of other social strata.*
▪Statistics a group into which members of a population are divided in stratified sampling.
– ORIGIN late 16th cent. (in the sense 'layer or coat of a substance'): modern Latin, from Latin, literally 'something spread or laid down', neuter past participle of *sternere* 'strew'.

> **USAGE** In Latin, the word **stratum** is singular and its plural form is **strata**. In English, this distinction is maintained. It is therefore incorrect to use **strata** as a singular or to create the form **stratas** as the plural: *a series of overlying **strata** not a series of overlying **stratas**, and a new **stratum** was uncovered not a new **strata** was uncovered.*

stratum corneum /ˌstrɑːtəm ˈkɔːnɪəm/ ▶ **noun** Anatomy the horny outer layer of the skin.
– ORIGIN Latin, literally 'horny layer'.

stratus /ˈstrɑːtəs, ˈstreɪtəs/ ▶ **noun** [mass noun] cloud forming a continuous horizontal grey sheet, often with rain or snow.
– ORIGIN early 19th cent.: modern Latin, from Latin, literally 'strewn', past participle of *sternere*.

Strauss[1] /straʊs, ʃt-/ the name of two Austrian composers:
▪**Johann** (1804–49), a leading composer of waltzes; known as **Strauss the Elder**. His best-known work is the *Radetzky March* (1838).
▪**Johann** (1825–99), son of Strauss the Elder; known as **Strauss the Younger**. He became known as 'the waltz king', composing many famous waltzes, such as *The Blue Danube* (1867). He is also noted for the operetta *Die Fledermaus* (1874).

Strauss[2] /straʊs, ʃt-/, Richard (1864–1949), German composer. With the librettist Hugo von Hofmannsthal he produced operas such as *Der Rosenkavalier* (1911). Often regarded as the last of the 19th-century romantic composers, Strauss is also well known for the symphonic poem *Also Sprach Zarathustra* (1896).

stravaig /strəˈveɪg/ (also **stravage**) ▶ **verb** [no obj., with adverbial of direction] chiefly Scottish & Irish wander about aimlessly: *stravaiging about the roads.*
– ORIGIN late 18th cent.: probably a shortening of obsolete *extravage* 'digress, ramble'.

Stravinsky /strəˈvɪnski/, Igor (Fyodorovich) (1882–1971), Russian-born composer, resident in the US from 1939. He made his name with the ballets *The Firebird* (1910) and *The Rite of Spring* (1913); both shocked Paris audiences with their irregular rhythms and frequent dissonances. Stravinsky later developed a neoclassical style typified by *The Rake's Progress* (opera, 1948–51) and experimented with serialism in *Threni*.

straw ▶ **noun** **1** [mass noun] dried stalks of grain, used especially as fodder or as material for thatching, packing, or weaving: [as modifier] *a straw hat.*
▪a pale yellow colour like that of straw: [as modifier] *a dull straw colour.* ▪used in reference to something insubstantial or worthless: *it seemed as if the words were merely straw.* ▪[count noun] [with negative] anything or at all (used to emphasize how little something is valued): *if he finds you here, my life **won't be worth a straw**.*
2 a single dried stalk of grain: *the tramp sat chewing a straw.*
▪a stalk of grain or something similar used in drawing lots: *we had to **draw straws** for the food we had.*
3 a thin hollow tube of paper or plastic for sucking drink from a glass or bottle.
– PHRASES **clutch** (or **grasp** or **catch**) **at straws** be in such a desperate situation as to resort to even the most unlikely means of salvation. [ORIGIN: from the proverb *a drowning man will clutch at a straw.*] **draw the short straw** be the unluckiest of a group of people, especially in being chosen to perform an unpleasant task. **the last** (or **final**) **straw** a further difficulty or annoyance, typically minor in itself but coming on top of a whole series of difficulties, that makes a situation unbearable:

S

his affair was the last straw. [ORIGIN: from the proverb *the last straw breaks the (laden) camel's back.*] **a straw in the wind** a slight hint of future developments.
– DERIVATIVES **strawy** adjective.
– ORIGIN Old English *strēaw*, of Germanic origin; related to Dutch *stroo* and German *Stroh*, also to **STREW**.

strawberry ▶ noun **1** a sweet soft red fruit with a seed-studded surface.
2 the low-growing plant which produces this fruit, having white flowers, lobed leaves, and runners, and found throughout north temperate regions.
• Genus *Fragaria*, family Rosaceae; the commercial strawberry is usually *F.* × *ananassa*.
3 [mass noun] a deep pinkish-red colour.
– ORIGIN Old English *strēa(w)berige*, *strēowberige* (see **STRAW**, **BERRY**).

strawberry blonde (also **strawberry blond**) ▶ adjective (of hair) of a light reddish-blonde colour.
■ (of a person) having hair of such a colour.
▶ noun [mass noun] a light reddish-blonde hair colour.
■ [count noun] a person who has hair of such a colour.

strawberry mark ▶ noun a soft red birthmark.

strawberry roan ▶ adjective denoting an animal's coat which is chestnut mixed with white or grey.
▶ noun a strawberry roan animal.

strawberry tree ▶ noun a small evergreen European tree which bears clusters of whitish flowers late in the year, often at the same time as the strawberry-like fruit from the previous season's flowers.
• *Arbutus unedo*, family Ericaceae.

strawboard ▶ noun [mass noun] board made of straw pulp, used in building (faced with paper) and in book covers.

straw boss ▶ noun N. Amer. informal a junior supervisor, especially a worker who has some responsibility but little authority.

strawflower ▶ noun an everlasting flower of the daisy family.
• Several species in the family Compositae, in particular the Australian *Helichrysum bracteatum* and plants of the genus *Helipterum*.

straw man ▶ noun another term for ***man of straw*** at **MAN**.

straw poll (N. Amer. also **straw vote**) ▶ noun an unofficial ballot conducted as a test of opinion: *I **took a straw poll** among my immediate colleagues.*

stray ▶ verb [no obj.] move without a specific purpose or by mistake, especially so as to get lost or arrive somewhere where one should not be: *I strayed a few blocks in the wrong direction | the military arrested anyone who **strayed into** the exclusion zone.*
■ move so as to escape from control or leave the place where one should be: *dog owners are urged not to allow their dogs to stray* | figurative *I appear to have strayed a long way from our original topic.* ■ [no obj., with adverbial of direction] (of the eyes or a hand) move idly or casually in a specified direction: *her eyes strayed to the telephone.* ■ (of a person who is married or in a long-term relationship) be unfaithful: *men who stray are seen as more exciting and desirable.* ■ [no obj., with adverbial of direction] poetic/literary wander or roam in a specified direction: *over these mounds the Kurdish shepherd strays.*
▶ adjective [attrib.] **1** not in the right place; not where it should be or where other items of the same kind are: *he pushed a few stray hairs from her face.*
■ appearing somewhere by chance or accident; not part of a general pattern or plan: *she was killed by a stray bullet.* ■ (of a domestic animal) having no home or having wandered away from home: *stray dogs.*
2 Physics (of a physical quantity) arising as a consequence of the laws of physics, not by deliberate design, and usually having a detrimental effect on the operation or efficiency of equipment: *stray capacitance.*
▶ noun **1** a stray person or thing, especially a domestic animal.
2 (**strays**) electrical phenomena interfering with radio reception.
– DERIVATIVES **strayer** noun.
– ORIGIN Middle English: shortening of Anglo-Norman French and Old French *estrayer* (verb), Anglo-Norman French *strey* (noun), partly from **ASTRAY**.

streak ▶ noun **1** a long, thin line or mark of a different substance or colour from its surroundings: *a streak of oil.*
■ Microbiology a narrow line of bacteria smeared on the surface of a solid culture medium.
2 an element of a specified kind in someone's character: *there's a streak of insanity in the family | Lucy had a ruthless streak.*
■ [usu. with adj.] a continuous period of specified success or luck: *the theatre is **on a winning streak** | Hull ended their four-game **losing streak**.*
3 informal an act of running naked in a public place so as to shock or amuse others: *a streak for charity.*
▶ verb **1** [with obj.] cover (a surface) with streaks: *tears streaking her face, Cynthia looked up | his beard was **streaked with** grey.*
■ dye (hair) with long, thin lines of a different, typically lighter colour than one's natural hair colour: [with obj. and complement] *hair that was streaked blonde.* ■ Microbiology smear (a needle, swab, etc.) over the surface of a solid culture medium to initiate a culture.
2 [no obj., with adverbial of direction] move very fast in a specified direction: *the cat leaped free and streaked across the street.*
3 [no obj.] informal run naked in a public place so as to shock or amuse others.
– PHRASES **like a streak** informal very fast: *he is off like a streak.* **streak of lightning** a flash of lightning.
– DERIVATIVES **streaker** noun (only in sense 3 of the verb).
– ORIGIN Old English *strica*, of Germanic origin; related to Dutch *streek* and German *Strich*, also to **STRIKE**. The sense 'run naked' was originally US slang.

streaking ▶ noun [mass noun] long, thin lines of a different colour from their surroundings, especially on dyed hair.

streaky ▶ adjective (**streakier**, **streakiest**) having streaks of different colours or textures: *streaky blond hair.*
■ Brit. (of bacon) from the belly, thus having alternate strips of fat and lean. ■ informal, chiefly N. Amer. variable in quality; not predictable or reliable: *King has always been a famously streaky hitter.*
– DERIVATIVES **streakily** adverb, **streakiness** noun.

stream ▶ noun **1** a small, narrow river.
2 a continuous flow of liquid, air, or gas: *Frank blew out **a stream of** smoke | the blood gushed out in scarlet streams.*
■ a mass of people or things moving continuously in the same direction: *there is **a** steady **stream of** visitors.* ■ a large number of things that happen or come one after the other: *a woman screamed **a stream of** abuse.* ■ Computing a continuous flow of data or instructions, typically one having a constant or predictable rate.
3 Brit. a group in which schoolchildren of the same age and ability are taught: *children in the top streams.*
▶ verb **1** [no obj., with adverbial of direction] (of liquid) run or flow in a continuous current in a specified direction: *she sat with tears **streaming down** her face* | figurative *sunlight **streamed through** the windows.*
■ (of a mass of people or things) move in a continuous flow in a specified direction: *he was watching the taxis **streaming past**.*
2 [no obj.] (usu. **be streaming**) (of a person or part of the body) produce a continuous flow of liquid; run with liquid: *my eyes were streaming | I woke up in the night, **streaming with** sweat* | [with obj.] *his mouth was streaming blood.*
3 [no obj.] (of hair, clothing, etc.) float or wave at full extent in the wind: *her black cloak **streamed behind** her.*
4 Brit. put (schoolchildren) in groups of the same age and ability to be taught together: [as noun **streaming**] *streaming within comprehensive schools is common practice.*
– PHRASES **against** (or **with**) **the stream** against (or with) the prevailing view or tendency: *a world in which the demand for quality does not run against the stream.* **on stream** in or into operation or existence; available: *more jobs are **coming on stream**.*
– DERIVATIVES **streamlet** noun.
– ORIGIN Old English *strēam* (noun), of Germanic origin; related to Dutch *stroom*, German *Strom*, from an Indo-European root shared by Greek *rhein* 'to flow'.

streamer ▶ noun **1** a long, narrow strip of material used as a decoration or symbol: *plastic party streamers* | figurative *a streamer of smoke.*
■ [usu. as modifier] a banner headline in a newspaper: *a streamer head in the student paper.* ■ [usu. as modifier] Fishing a fly with feathers attached: *a streamer fly.* ■ Astronomy an elongated mass of luminous matter, e.g. in aurorae or the sun's corona.
2 Computing short for **TAPE STREAMER**.

streamer weed ▶ noun [mass noun] a freshwater plant with long fronds that stream and wave in the current, especially water crowfoot.

streamflow ▶ noun the flow of water in a stream or river.

streaming ▶ adjective [attrib.] **1** (of a cold) accompanied by copious running of the nose and eyes.
2 Computing relating to or making use of a form of tape transport, used mainly to provide back-up storage, in which data may be transferred in bulk while the tape is in motion.

streamline ▶ verb [with obj.] [usu. as adj. **streamlined**] design or provide with a form that presents very little resistance to a flow of air or water, increasing speed and ease of movement: *streamlined passenger trains.*
■ figurative make (an organization or system) more efficient and effective by employing faster or simpler working methods: *the company streamlined its operations by removing whole layers of management.*
▶ noun a line along which the flow of a moving fluid is least turbulent.
▶ adjective **1** (of fluid flow) free from turbulence.
2 dated having a streamlined shape: *a streamline aeroplane.*

stream of consciousness ▶ noun Psychology a person's thoughts and conscious reactions to events, perceived as a continuous flow. The term was introduced by William James in his *Principles of Psychology* (1890).
■ a literary style in which a character's thoughts, feelings, and reactions are depicted in a continuous flow uninterrupted by objective description or conventional dialogue. James Joyce, Virginia Woolf, and Marcel Proust are among its notable early exponents.

streel /striːl/ Irish ▶ noun a disreputable, untidy person, especially a woman.
▶ verb [no obj., with adverbial of direction] (of a person) wander aimlessly: *youngsters streeling through the house.*
■ [with obj.] trail or drag: *streeling bits of coloured cloth.*
– DERIVATIVES **streelish** adjective.
– ORIGIN early 19th cent.: from Irish *s(t)raoill(e)* 'untidy or awkward person'.

Streep, Meryl (b.1949), American actress; born *Mary Louise Streep*. She won Oscars for her parts in *Kramer vs Kramer* (1980) and *Sophie's Choice* (1982).

street ▶ noun a public road in a city, town, or village, typically with houses and buildings on one or both sides: *the narrow, winding streets of Edinburgh* | [in place names] *45 Lake Street.*
■ US used to refer to the financial markets and activities on Wall Street. ■ (**the street/streets**) the roads or public areas of a city or town: *every week, fans stop me in the street.* ■ [as modifier] of or relating to the outlook, values, or lifestyle of those young people who are perceived as composing a fashionable urban subculture: *London street style.* ■ [as modifier] denoting someone who is homeless: *the street kids of the city.*
– PHRASES **not in the same street** Brit. informal far inferior in terms of ability. **on the streets 1** homeless. **2** working as a prostitute. **streets ahead** Brit. informal greatly superior: *the restaurant is streets ahead of its local rivals.* **up** (or **right up**) **one's street** (or N. Amer. **alley**) informal well suited to one's tastes, interests, or abilities: *this job would be right up your street.*
– DERIVATIVES **streeted** adjective [in combination] *a many-streeted tangle of low, brick buildings,* **streetward** adjective & adverb.
– ORIGIN Old English *strǣt*, of West Germanic origin, from late Latin *strāta (via)* 'paved (way)', feminine past participle of *sternere* 'lay down'.

street Arab ▶ noun archaic a raggedly dressed homeless child wandering the streets.

streetcar ▶ noun N. Amer. a tram.

street credibility (also informal **street cred**) ▶ noun [mass noun] acceptability among young fashionable urban people.

street cries ▶ plural noun the cries used by street traders to advertise their wares.

street door ▶ noun the main door of a house opening on the street.

street entertainer ▶ noun a person who entertains the public in the street, especially with music, acting, or juggling.
– DERIVATIVES **street entertainment** noun.

street furniture ▶ **noun** [mass noun] objects placed or fixed in the street for public use, such as postboxes, road signs, and benches.

street jewellery ▶ **noun** [mass noun] Brit. enamel advertising plates as collectors' items.

street-legal ▶ **adjective** (of a vehicle) meeting all legal requirements for use on ordinary roads.

street light (also **street lamp**) ▶ **noun** a light illuminating a road, typically mounted on a tall post.
– DERIVATIVES **street lighting** noun.

street name ▶ **noun** N. Amer. the name of a stockbroking firm, bank, or dealer in which stock is held on behalf of a purchaser.

street-smart ▶ **adjective** chiefly N. Amer. another term for **STREETWISE**.

street theatre ▶ **noun** [mass noun] drama performed on the streets, typically in an informal or improvised manner.

street trader ▶ **noun** a person who sells something in the street, either from a stall or van or with their goods laid out on the pavement.
– DERIVATIVES **street trading** noun.

street value ▶ **noun** the price a commodity, especially an amount of drugs, would fetch if sold illicitly: *detectives seized drugs with a street value of £300,000.*

streetwalker ▶ **noun** a prostitute who seeks clients in the street.
– DERIVATIVES **streetwalking** noun & adjective.

streetwise ▶ **adjective** informal having the skills and knowledge necessary for dealing with modern urban life, especially the difficult or criminal aspects of it: *I wasn't streetwise enough to figure out what he had in mind.*
■ reflective of modern urban life, especially that of urban youth: *streetwise fashion.*

Strega /ˈstreɪɡə/ ▶ **noun** [mass noun] trademark a kind of orange-flavoured Italian liqueur.
– ORIGIN Italian, literally 'witch'.

Streisand /ˈstrʌɪs(ə)nd, -sand/, Barbra (Joan) (b.1942), American singer, actress, and film director. She won an Oscar for her performance in *Funny Girl* (1968). She later played the lead in *A Star is Born* (1976); the film's song 'Evergreen', composed by Streisand, won an Oscar.

strelitzia /strəˈlɪtsɪə/ ▶ **noun** a southern African plant of the genus *Strelitzia* (family Strelitziaceae), especially (in gardening) a bird of paradise flower.
– ORIGIN named after Charlotte of Mecklenburg-Strelitz (1744–1818), queen of George III.

strength /strɛŋθ, strɛŋkθ/ ▶ **noun** **1** [mass noun] the quality or state of being strong, in particular:
■ physical power and energy: *cycling can help you build up your strength.* ■ the emotional or mental qualities necessary in dealing with situations or events that are distressing or difficult: *many people find strength in religion* | *it takes strength of character to admit one needs help.* ■ the capacity of an object or substance to withstand great force or pressure: *they were taking no chances with the strength of the retaining wall.* ■ the influence or power possessed by a person, organization, or country: *the political and military strength of European governments.* ■ the degree of intensity of a feeling or belief: *street protests demonstrated the strength of feeling against the president.* ■ the cogency of an argument or case: *the strength of the argument for property taxation.* ■ the potency, intensity, or speed of a force or natural agency: *the wind had markedly increased in strength.* ■ the potency or degree of concentration of a drug, chemical, or drink: *it's double the strength of your average beer* | [count noun] *the solution comes in two strengths.* ■ Bridge the potential of a hand to win tricks, arising from the number and type of high cards it contains.
2 a good or beneficial quality or attribute of a person or thing: *the strengths and weaknesses of their sales and marketing operation* | *his strength was his obsessive single-mindedness.*
■ poetic/literary a person or thing perceived as a source of mental or emotional support: *he was my closest friend, my strength and shield.*
3 [mass noun] the number of people comprising a group, typically a team or army: *the peacetime strength of the army was 415,000.*
■ a number of people required to make such a group complete: *we are now more than 100 officers* ***below strength*** | *some units will be maintained* ***at full strength*** *while others will rely on reserves* | [in combination] *an under-strength side.*
– PHRASES **from strength** from a secure or advantageous position: *it makes sense to negotiate from strength.* **give me strength!** used as an expression of exasperation or annoyance. **go from strength to strength** develop or progress with increasing success. **in strength** in large numbers: *security forces were out in strength.* **on the strength of** on the basis or with the justification of: *I joined the bank on the strength of an MA in English.* **the strength of** chiefly Austral./NZ the point or meaning of; the truth about: *you've about got the strength of it, Mick.* **tower** (or **pillar**) **of strength** a person who can be relied upon to give a great deal of support and comfort to others.
– DERIVATIVES **strengthless** adjective.
– ORIGIN Old English *strengthu*, from the Germanic base of **STRONG**.

strengthen /ˈstrɛŋθ(ə)n, -ŋkθ(ə)n/ ▶ **verb** make or become stronger: [with obj.] *he advises an application of fluoride to strengthen the teeth* | [no obj.] *the wind won't strengthen until after dark.*
– PHRASES **strengthen someone's hand** (or **hands**) enable or encourage a person to act more vigorously or effectively.
– DERIVATIVES **strengthener** noun.

strenuous /ˈstrɛnjʊəs/ ▶ **adjective** requiring or using great exertion: *the government made strenuous efforts to upgrade the quality of the teaching profession.*
– DERIVATIVES **strenuously** adverb, **strenuousness** noun.
– ORIGIN early 17th cent.: from Latin *strenuus* 'brisk' + **-OUS**.

strep ▶ **noun** Medicine, informal short for **STREPTOCOCCUS**.

Strepsiptera /strɛpˈsɪptərə/ Entomology an order of minute parasitic insects which comprises the stylops.
– DERIVATIVES **strepsipteran** noun & adjective.
– ORIGIN modern Latin (plural), from Greek *strepsi-* (combining form of *strephein* 'to turn') + *pteron* 'wing'.

strepto- ▶ **combining form** twisted; in the form of a twisted chain: *streptomycete.*
■ associated with streptococci or streptomycetes: *streptokinase.*
– ORIGIN from Greek *streptos* 'twisted', from *strephein* 'to turn'.

streptocarpus /ˌstrɛptə(ʊ)ˈkɑːpəs/ ▶ **noun** an African plant with funnel-shaped flowers which are typically pink, white, or violet, some kinds of which have only one large leaf. They are widely cultivated as indoor or greenhouse plants. Also called **CAPE PRIMROSE**.
• Genus *Streptocarpus*, family Gesneriaceae.
– ORIGIN modern Latin, from **STREPTO-** 'twisted' + Greek *karpos* 'fruit'.

streptococcus /ˌstrɛptə(ʊ)ˈkɒkəs/ ▶ **noun** (pl. **streptococci** /-ˈkɒk(s)ʌɪ, -ˈkɒk(s)iː/) a bacterium of a genus that includes the agents of souring of milk and dental decay, and haemolytic pathogens causing various infections such as scarlet fever and pneumonia.
• Genus *Streptococcus*; Gram-positive cocci in pairs and chains.
– DERIVATIVES **streptococcal** adjective.

streptokinase /ˌstrɛptə(ʊ)ˈkʌɪneɪz/ ▶ **noun** [mass noun] Biochemistry an enzyme produced by some streptococci which is involved in breaking down red blood cells. It is used to treat inflammation and blood clots.

streptomycete /ˌstrɛptə(ʊ)ˈmʌɪsiːt/ ▶ **noun** (pl. **streptomycetes** /-ˈmʌɪsiːts, -mʌɪˈsiːtiːz/) a bacterium which occurs chiefly in soil as aerobic saprophytes resembling moulds, several of which are important sources of antibiotics.
• *Streptomyces* and related genera, order Actinomycetales; Gram-positive filaments forming chains of spores.
– ORIGIN 1950s: Anglicized singular of modern Latin *Streptomyces*, from **STREPTO-** 'twisted' + Greek *mukēs, mukēt-* 'fungus'.

streptomycin /ˌstrɛptə(ʊ)ˈmʌɪsɪn/ ▶ **noun** [mass noun] Medicine an antibiotic that was the first drug to be successful against tuberculosis but is now chiefly used with other drugs because of its toxic side effects.
• This antibiotic is produced by the bacterium *Streptomyces griseus*.

stress ▶ **noun** [mass noun] **1** pressure or tension exerted on a material object: *the distribution of stress is uniform across the bar.*
■ the degree of this measured in units of force per unit area.
2 a state of mental or emotional strain or tension resulting from adverse or very demanding circumstances: *he's obviously* ***under*** *a lot of* ***stress*** | [in combination] *stress-related illnesses.*
■ [count noun] something that causes such a state: *the stresses and strains of public life.*
3 particular emphasis or importance: *he has started to* ***lay*** *greater* ***stress on*** *the government's role in industry.*
■ emphasis given to a particular syllable or word in speech, typically through a combination of relatively greater loudness, higher pitch, and longer duration: *normally, the stress falls on the first syllable.*
▶ **verb** **1** [reporting verb] give particular emphasis or importance to (a point, statement, or idea) made in speech or writing: [with obj.] *they stressed the need for reform* | [with clause] *she was anxious to stress that her daughter's safety was her only concern* | [with direct speech] *'I want it done very, very neatly,' she stressed.*
■ [with obj.] give emphasis to (a syllable or word) when pronouncing it.
2 subject to pressure or tension: *this type of workout does stress the shoulder and knee joints.*
3 [with obj.] cause mental or emotional strain or tension in: *I avoid many of the things that used to stress me before* | [as adj. **stressed**] *she should see a doctor if she is feeling particularly* ***stressed out.***
■ [no obj.] informal become tense or anxious; worry: *don't stress—there's plenty of time to get a grip on the situation.*
– DERIVATIVES **stressless** adjective, **stressor** noun (only in sense 3 of the verb).
– ORIGIN Middle English (denoting hardship or force exerted on a person for the purpose of compulsion): shortening of **DISTRESS**, or partly from Old French *estresse* 'narrowness, oppression', based on Latin *strictus* 'drawn tight' (see **STRICT**).

stress fracture ▶ **noun** a fracture of a bone caused by repeated (rather than sudden) mechanical stress.

stressful ▶ **adjective** causing mental or emotional stress: *corporate finance work can be stressful.*
– DERIVATIVES **stressfully** adverb, **stressfulness** noun.

stress incontinence ▶ **noun** [mass noun] a condition (found chiefly in women) in which there is involuntary emission of urine when pressure within the abdomen increases suddenly, as in coughing or jumping.

stress-timed ▶ **adjective** (of a language) characterized by a rhythm in which primary stresses occur at roughly equal intervals, irrespective of the number of unstressed syllables in between. English is a stress-timed language. Contrasted with **SYLLABLE-TIMED**.

stretch ▶ **verb** [no obj.] **1** (of something soft or elastic) be made or be capable of being made longer or wider without tearing or breaking: *my jumper stretched in the wash* | *rubber will stretch easily when pulled.*
■ [with obj.] cause to do this: *stretch the elastic.* ■ [with obj. and adverbial] pull (something) tightly from one point to another or across a space: *small squares of canvas were stretched over the bamboo frame.* ■ last or cause to last longer than expected: [no obj.] *her nap had stretched to two hours* | [with obj.] *stretch your weekend into a mini summer vacation.* ■ [no obj.] (of finances or resources) be sufficient or adequate for a certain purpose: *my budget won't* ***stretch to*** *a weekend at a health farm.* ■ [with obj.] make great demands on the capacity or resources of: *the cost of the court case has* ***stretched*** *their finances* ***to the limit.*** ■ [with obj.] cause (someone) to make maximum use of their talents or abilities: *it's too easy—it doesn't stretch me.* ■ [with obj.] adapt or extend the scope of (something) in a way that exceeds a reasonable or acceptable limit: *to describe her as sweet would be stretching it a bit.*
2 straighten or extend one's body or a part of one's body to its full length, typically so as to tighten one's muscles or in order to reach something: *the cat yawned and stretched* | [with obj.] *stretching my cramped legs* | *we lay* ***stretched out*** *on the sand.*
3 [no obj., with adverbial] extend or spread over an area or period of time: *the beach stretches for over four miles* | *the long hours of night stretched ahead of her.*
▶ **noun** **1** an act of stretching one's limbs or body: *I got up and had a stretch.*
■ [mass noun] the fact or condition of a muscle being stretched: *she could feel the stretch and pull of the muscles in her legs.* ■ [mass noun] [usu. as modifier] the capacity of a material or garment to stretch or be stretched; elasticity: *stretch jeans.* ■ a difficult or demanding

S

task: *it was a stretch for me sometimes to come up with the rent.*
2 a continuous area or expanse of land or water: *a treacherous stretch of road.*
■a continuous period of time: *long stretches of time.* ■ informal a period of time spent in prison: *a four-year stretch for tax fraud.* ■ chiefly N. Amer. a straight part of a racetrack, typically the home straight: *he made a promising start, but faded down the stretch.* ■ Sailing the distance covered on one tack.
3 [usu. as modifier] informal a motor vehicle or aircraft modified so as to have extended seating or storage capacity: *a black stretch limo.*
– PHRASES **at full stretch** with a part of one's body fully extended. ■ using the maximum amount of one's resources or energy: *increased export business kept our production plants at full stretch.* **at a stretch 1** in one continuous period: *I often had to work for over twenty hours at a stretch.* **2** used to indicate that something is just possible but only with difficulty or in extreme circumstances: *it is aimed at one age group, adults, or, at a stretch, business studies students.* **by no** (or **not by any**) **stretch of the imagination** used to emphasize that something is definitely not the case: *by no stretch of the imagination could Carl ever be called good-looking.* **stretch one's legs** go for a short walk, typically after sitting in one place for some time. **stretch a point** allow or do something not usually acceptable, typically as a result of the particular circumstances: *since your daughter is one of my regular patients, I'm stretching a point.* **stretch one's wings** see **WING**.
– DERIVATIVES **stretchability** noun, **stretchable** adjective.
– ORIGIN Old English *streccan*, of West Germanic origin; related to Dutch *strekken* and German *strecken*. The noun dates from the late 16th cent.

stretcher ▶ **noun 1** a framework of two poles with a long piece of canvas slung between them, used for carrying sick, injured, or dead people.
2 a thing that stretches something, in particular:
■a wooden frame over which a canvas is spread and tautened ready for painting. ■ [with modifier] a rod or frame used for expanding or tautening a specified thing: *sail stretchers.* ■ archaic, informal an exaggeration or lie.
3 a rod or bar joining and supporting chair legs.
■a board in a boat against which a rower presses the feet for support.
4 a brick or stone laid with its long side along the face of a wall. Compare with **HEADER** (sense 3).
▶ **verb** [with obj.] (usu. **be stretchered**) carry (a sick or injured person) somewhere on a stretcher: *their striker had to be stretchered off following a tackle.*

stretcher-bearer ▶ **noun** a person who helps to carry the sick or injured on stretchers, especially in time of war or at the scene of an accident.

stretcher party ▶ **noun** a group of stretcher-bearers.

stretch marks ▶ **plural noun** streaks or stripes on the skin, especially on the abdomen, caused by distention of the skin from obesity or during pregnancy.

stretch receptor ▶ **noun** Physiology a sensory receptor that responds to the stretching of surrounding muscle tissue and so contributes to the coordination of muscle activity.

stretchy ▶ **adjective** (**-ier, -iest**) (especially of material or a garment) able to stretch or be stretched easily: *stretchy miniskirts.*
– DERIVATIVES **stretchiness** noun.

stretto /ˈstrɛtəʊ/ Music ▶ **noun** (pl. **stretti**) a passage, especially at the end of an aria or movement, to be performed in quicker time.
■a section at the end of a fugue in which successive introductions of the theme follow at shorter intervals than before, increasing the sense of excitement.
▶ **adverb** (as a direction) in quicker time.
– ORIGIN Italian, literally 'narrow'.

streusel /ˈstrɔɪz(ə)l, ˈstruːz(ə)l/ ▶ **noun** a crumbly topping or filling made from fat, flour, sugar, and often cinnamon.
■a cake or pastry with such a topping.
– ORIGIN from German *Streusel*, from *streuen* 'sprinkle'.

strew ▶ **verb** (past participle **strewn** or **strewed**) [with obj.] (usu. **be strewn**) scatter or spread (things) untidily over a surface or area: *a small room with newspapers strewn all over the floor.*
■(usu. **be strewn with**) cover (a surface or area) with untidily scattered things: *the table was strewn with books and papers* | [as adj., in combination **strewn**] *boulder-strewn slopes.* ■ be scattered or spread untidily over (a surface or area): *leaves strewed the path.*
– DERIVATIVES **strewer** noun.
– ORIGIN Old English *stre(o)wian*, of Germanic origin; related to Dutch *strooien*, German *streuen*, from an Indo-European root shared by Latin *sternere* 'lay flat'.

strewn field ▶ **noun** Geology a region of the earth's surface over which tektites of a similar age and presumed origin are found.

strewth (also **struth**) ▶ **exclamation** informal used to express surprise or dismay.
– ORIGIN late 19th cent.: contraction of *God's truth*.

stria /ˈstrʌɪə/ ▶ **noun** (pl. **striae** /-iː/) technical a linear mark, slight ridge, or groove on a surface, often one of a number of similar parallel features.
■Anatomy any of a number of longitudinal collections of nerve fibres in the brain.
– ORIGIN late 17th cent. (as a scientific term): from Latin, literally 'furrow'.

striate technical ▶ **adjective** /ˈstrʌɪət, ˈstrʌɪeɪt/ marked with striae: *the striate cortex.*
▶ **verb** /strʌɪˈeɪt/ [with obj.] [usu. as adj. **striated**] mark with striae: *striated bark.*
– DERIVATIVES **striation** noun.

striated muscle ▶ **noun** [mass noun] Physiology muscle tissue in which the contractile fibrils in the cells are aligned in parallel bundles, so that their different regions form stripes visible in a microscope. Muscles of this type are attached to the skeleton by tendons and are under voluntary control. Also called **SKELETAL MUSCLE**. Often contrasted with **SMOOTH MUSCLE**.

striatum /strʌɪˈeɪtəm/ ▶ **noun** (pl. **striata** /strʌɪˈeɪtə/) Anatomy short for **CORPUS STRIATUM**.
– DERIVATIVES **striatal** adjective.

stricken North American or archaic past participle of **STRIKE**. ▶ **adjective** seriously affected by an undesirable condition or unpleasant feeling: *the pilot landed the stricken aircraft* | *Raymond was stricken with grief* | [in combination] *the farms were drought-stricken.*
■(of a face or look) showing great distress: *she looked at Anne's stricken face, contorted with worry.*
– PHRASES **stricken in years** dated used euphemistically to describe someone old and feeble.

strickle ▶ **noun 1** a rod used to level off a heaped measure.
2 a whetting tool.
– ORIGIN Old English *stricel* (in sense 1); related to **STRIKE**. Sense 2 dates from the mid 17th cent.

strict ▶ **adjective** demanding that rules concerning behaviour are obeyed and observed: *my father was very strict* | *a strict upbringing.*
■(of a rule or discipline) demanding total obedience or observance; rigidly enforced: *civil servants are bound by strict rules on secrecy.* ■ (of a person) following rules or beliefs exactly: *a strict vegetarian.* ■ exact in correspondence or adherence to something; not allowing or admitting deviation or relaxation: *a strict interpretation of the law.*
– DERIVATIVES **strictness** noun.
– ORIGIN late Middle English (in the sense 'restricted in space or extent'): from Latin *strictus*, past participle of *stringere* 'tighten, draw tight'.

strict construction ▶ **noun** Law a literal interpretation of a statute or document by a court.

strict liability ▶ **noun** [mass noun] Law liability which does not depend on actual negligence or intent to harm.

strictly ▶ **adverb 1** in a way that involves rigid enforcement or that demands obedience: *he's been brought up strictly.*
2 used to indicate that one is applying words or rules exactly or rigidly: [sentence adverb] *strictly speaking, ham is a cured, cooked leg of pork* | [as submodifier] *to be strictly accurate, there are two Wolvertons.*
■with no exceptions; completely or absolutely: *these foods are strictly forbidden.* ■ no more than; purely: *that visit was strictly business* | *his attitude and manner were strictly professional.*

stricture /ˈstrɪktʃə/ ▶ **noun 1** a restriction on a person or activity: *the strictures imposed by the British Board of Film Censors.*
2 a sternly critical or censorious remark or instruction: *his strictures on their lack of civic virtue.*
3 Medicine abnormal narrowing of a canal or duct in the body: *a colonic stricture* | [mass noun] *jaundice caused by bile duct stricture.*
– DERIVATIVES **strictured** adjective.
– ORIGIN late Middle English (in sense 3): from Latin *strictura*, from *stringere* 'draw tight' (see **STRICT**). Another sense of the Latin verb, 'touch lightly', gave rise to sense 2 via an earlier meaning 'incidental remark'.

stride ▶ **verb** (past **strode**; past participle **stridden**) **1** [no obj., with adverbial of direction] walk with long, decisive steps in a specified direction: *he strode across the road* | figurative *striding confidently towards the future.*
■[with obj.] walk about or along (a street or other place) in this way: *a woman striding the cobbled streets.*
2 [no obj.] (**stride across/over**) cross (an obstacle) with one long step: *by giving a little leap she could stride across like a grown-up.*
■[with obj.] poetic/literary bestride: *new wealth enabled Britain to stride the world once more.*
▶ **noun 1** a long, decisive step: *he crossed the room in a couple of strides.*
■[in sing.] the length of a step or manner of taking steps in walking or running: *the horse shortened its stride* | *he followed her with an easy stride.*
2 (usu. **strides**) a step or stage in progress towards an aim: *great strides have been made towards equality.*
■(**one's stride**) a good or regular rate of progress, especially after a slow or hesitant start: *the speaker was getting into his stride.*
3 (**strides**) Brit. informal trousers.
4 [as modifier] denoting or relating to a rhythmic style of jazz piano playing in which the left hand alternately plays single bass notes on the downbeat and chords an octave higher on the upbeat: *a stride pianist.*
– PHRASES **break (one's) stride** slow or interrupt the pace at which one walks or moves. **match someone stride for stride** manage to keep up with a competitor. **take something in one's stride** deal with something difficult or unpleasant in a calm and accepting way: *I told her what had happened and she took it all in her stride.*
– DERIVATIVES **strider** noun.
– ORIGIN Old English *stride* (noun) 'single long step', *stridan* (verb) 'stand or walk with the legs wide apart', probably from a Germanic base meaning 'strive, quarrel'; related to Dutch *strijden* 'fight' and German *streiten* 'quarrel'.

strident ▶ **adjective** loud and harsh; grating: *his voice had become increasingly sharp, almost strident.*
■presenting a point of view, especially a controversial one, in an excessively and unpleasantly forceful way: *public pronouncements on the crisis became less strident.* ■ Phonetics another term for **SIBILANT**.
– DERIVATIVES **stridency** noun, **stridently** adverb.
– ORIGIN mid 17th cent.: from Latin *strident-* 'creaking', from the verb *stridere*.

stridor /ˈstrʌɪdə/ ▶ **noun** [mass noun] a harsh or grating sound: *the engines' stridor increased.*
■Medicine a harsh vibrating noise when breathing, caused by obstruction of the windpipe or larynx.
– ORIGIN mid 17th cent.: from Latin, from *stridere* 'to creak'.

stridulate /ˈstrɪdjʊleɪt/ ▶ **verb** [no obj.] (of an insect, especially a male cricket or grasshopper) make a shrill sound by rubbing the legs, wings, or other parts of the body together.
– DERIVATIVES **stridulant** adjective, **stridulation** noun, **stridulatory** adjective.
– ORIGIN mid 19th cent.: from French *striduler*, from Latin *stridulus* 'creaking', from the verb *stridere*.

strife ▶ **noun** [mass noun] angry or bitter disagreement over fundamental issues; conflict: *strife within the community* | *ethnic and civil strife.*
■Austral. trouble, disgrace, or difficulty of any kind.
– ORIGIN Middle English: shortening of Old French *estrif* (related to Old French *estriver* 'strive').

strigil /ˈstrɪdʒɪl/ ▶ **noun** an instrument with a curved blade used, especially by ancient Greeks and Romans, to scrape sweat and dirt from the skin in a hot-air bath or after exercise; a scraper.
■Entomology a comb-like structure on the forelegs of some insects, used chiefly for grooming.
– ORIGIN from Latin *strigilis*, from *stringere* 'touch lightly'. The term in entomology dates from the late 19th cent.

strigose /ˈstrʌɪgəʊs/ ▶ **adjective** Botany covered with short stiff adpressed hairs.

S

▪Entomology finely grooved or furrowed.
– ORIGIN late 18th cent.: from Latin *striga* 'swath, furrow' + **-OSE**[1].

strike ▶verb (past and past participle **struck** /strʌk/) **1** [with obj.] hit forcibly and deliberately with one's hand or a weapon or other implement: *he raised his hand, as if to strike me* | *one man was struck on the head with a stick* | [no obj.] *Ewan* ***struck out at*** *her.* ▪inflict (a blow): [with two objs] *he struck her two blows on the leg.* ▪accidentally hit (a part of one's body) against something: *she fell, striking her head against the side of the boat.* ▪come into forcible contact or collision with: *he was struck by a car in Whitepark Road.* ▪(of a beam or ray of light or heat) fall on (an object or surface): *the light struck her ring, reflecting off the diamond.* ▪(in sporting contexts) hit or kick (a ball) so as to score a run, point, or goal: *he struck the ball into the back of the net.* ▪[no obj.] (of a clock) indicate the time by sounding a chime or stroke: [with complement] *the church clock struck twelve.* ▪[no obj.] (of time) be indicated in this way: *eight o'clock struck.* ▪ignite (a match) by rubbing it briskly against an abrasive surface. ▪produce (fire or a spark) as a result of friction: *his iron stick struck sparks from the pavement.* ▪bring (an electric arc) into being. ▪produce (a musical note) by pressing or hitting a key.
2 [with obj.] (of a disaster, disease, or other unwelcome phenomenon) occur suddenly and have harmful or damaging effects on: *an earthquake struck the island* | [no obj.] *tragedy struck when Nick was killed in a car crash* | [as adj., in combination **struck**] *storm-struck areas.* ▪[no obj.] carry out an aggressive or violent action, typically without warning: *it was eight months before the murderer struck again.* ▪(usu. **be struck down**) kill or seriously incapacitate (someone): *he was struck down by a mystery virus.* ▪(**strike something into**) cause or create a particular strong emotion in (someone): *drugs—a subject guaranteed to strike fear into parents' hearts.* ▪[with obj. and complement] cause (someone) to be in a specified state: *he was struck dumb.*
3 [with obj.] (of a thought or idea) come into the mind of (someone) suddenly or unexpectedly: *a disturbing thought struck Melissa.* ▪cause (someone) to have a particular impression: [with clause] *it struck him that Marjorie was unusually silent* | *the idea* ***struck*** *her* ***as*** *odd.* ▪(**be struck by/with**) find particularly interesting, noticeable, or impressive: *Lucy was struck by the ethereal beauty of the scene.* ▪(**be struck on**) informal be deeply fond of or infatuated with: *she was rather struck on Angus, wasn't she?*
4 [no obj.] (of employees) refuse to work as a form of organized protest, typically in an attempt to obtain a particular concession or concessions from their employer: *workers may strike over threatened job losses.* ▪[with obj.] N. Amer. undertake such action against (an employer).
5 [with obj.] cancel, remove, or cross out with or as if with a pen: ***strike*** *his name* ***from*** *the list* | *the Court of Appeal* ***struck out*** *the claim for exemplary damages* | ***striking*** *words* ***through*** *with a pen.* ▪(**strike someone off**) officially remove someone from membership of a professional group: *he was struck off by the Law Society and will never practise as a solicitor again.* ▪(**strike something down**) N. Amer. abolish a law or regulation: *the law was struck down by the Supreme Court.*
6 [with obj.] make (a coin or medal) by stamping metal. ▪(in cinematography) make (another print) of a film. ▪reach, achieve, or agree to (something involving agreement, balance, or compromise): *the team has* ***struck a deal*** *with a sports marketing agency* | *you have to* ***strike a happy medium.*** ▪(in financial contexts) reach (a figure) by balancing an account: *last year's loss was struck after allowing for depreciation of £67 million.* ▪Canadian form (a committee): *the government struck a committee to settle the issue.*
7 [with obj.] discover (gold, minerals, or oil) by drilling or mining. ▪[no obj.] (**strike on/upon**) discover or think of, especially unexpectedly or by chance: *pondering, she struck upon a brilliant idea.* ▪come to or reach: *several days out of the village, we struck the Gilgit Road.*
8 [no obj., with adverbial of direction] move or proceed vigorously or purposefully: *she* ***struck out*** *into the lake with a practised crawl* | *he struck off down the track.* ▪(**strike out**) start out on a new or independent course or endeavour: *after two years he was able to strike out on his own* | *he's struck out as a private eye.*
9 [with obj.] take down (a tent or the tents of an encampment): *it took ages to strike camp.* ▪dismantle (theatrical scenery): *the minute we finish this evening, they'll start striking the set.* ▪lower or take down (a flag or sail), especially as a salute or to signify surrender: *the ship struck her German colours.*
10 [with obj.] insert (a cutting of a plant) in soil to take root. ▪[no obj.] (of a plant or cutting) develop roots: *small conifers will strike from cuttings.* ▪[no obj.] (of a young oyster) attach itself to a bed.
11 [no obj.] Fishing secure a hook in the mouth of a fish by jerking or tightening the line after it has taken the bait or fly.
▶noun **1** a refusal to work organized by a body of employees as a form of protest, typically in an attempt to gain a concession or concessions from their employer: *dockers voted for an all-out strike* | [mass noun] *local government workers* ***went on strike*** | [as modifier] *strike action.* ▪[with modifier] a refusal to do something expected or required, typically by a body of people, with a similar aim: *a rent strike.*
2 a sudden attack, typically a military one: *the threat of nuclear strikes.* ▪(in sporting contexts) an act of hitting or kicking a ball, typically so as to score a point or goal: *his 32nd-minute strike helped the team to end a run of three defeats.* ▪(in tenpin bowling) an act of knocking down all the pins with one's first ball. ▪Fishing an act or instance of jerking or tightening the line to secure a fish that has already taken the bait or fly.
3 a discovery of gold, minerals, or oil by drilling or mining: *the Lena goldfields strike of 1912.*
4 Baseball a batter's unsuccessful attempt to hit a pitched ball. ▪a pitch that passes through the strike zone. ▪US something to one's discredit: *when they returned from Vietnam they had* ***two strikes against*** *them.*
5 the horizontal or compass direction of a stratum, fault, or other geological feature.
6 short for **FLY STRIKE**.
– PHRASES **strike an attitude** (or **pose**) hold one's body in a particular position to create an impression: *striking a dramatic pose, Antonia announced that she was leaving.* **strike a balance** see **BALANCE**. **strike a blow for** (or **at/against**) do something to help (or hinder) a cause, belief, or principle: *just by finishing the race, she hopes to strike a blow for womankind.* **strike a chord** see **CHORD**[2]. **strike at the root** (or **roots**) **of** see **ROOT**[1]. **strike hands** archaic (of two people) clasp hands to seal a deal or agreement. **strike home** see **HOME**. **strike (it) lucky** Brit. informal have good luck in a particular matter. **strike it rich** informal acquire a great deal of money, typically in a sudden or unexpected way. **strike a light** Brit. informal, dated used as an expression of surprise, dismay, or alarm. **strike me pink** Brit. informal, dated used to express astonishment or indignation. **strike while the iron is hot** make use of an opportunity immediately. [ORIGIN: with reference to smithing.]
– ORIGIN Old English *strīcan* 'go, flow' and 'rub lightly', of West Germanic origin; related to German *streichen* 'to stroke', also to **STROKE**. The sense 'deliver a blow' dates from Middle English.
▶**strike back 1** retaliate: *he* ***struck back at*** *critics who claim he is too negative.* **2** (of a gas burner) burn from an internal point before the gas has become mixed with air.
strike in archaic intervene in a conversation or discussion.
strike someone out (or **strike out**) Baseball dismiss someone (or be dismissed) by means of three strikes. ▪(**strike out**) N. Amer. informal fail or be unsuccessful: *the company struck out the first time it tried to manufacture personal computers.*
strike up (or **strike something up**) (of a band or orchestra) begin to play a piece of music: *they struck up the 'Star-Spangled Banner'.* ▪(**strike something up**) begin a friendship or conversation with someone, typically in a casual way.

strike-breaker ▶noun a person who works or is employed in place of others who are on strike, thereby making the strike ineffectual.
– DERIVATIVES **strike-break** verb.

strike force ▶noun [treated as sing. or pl.] a military force equipped and organized for sudden attack. ▪informal the forwards in a soccer team.

strikeout ▶noun Baseball an out called when a batter has made three strikes.
▶adjective Computing (of text) having a horizontal line through the middle; crossed out.

strike pay ▶noun [mass noun] money paid to strikers by their trade union.

strike price ▶noun Finance **1** the price fixed by the seller of a security after receiving bids in a tender offer, typically for a sale of gilt-edged securities or a new stock market issue.
2 the price at which a put or call option can be exercised.

striker ▶noun **1** an employee on strike.
2 the player who is to strike the ball in a game; a player considered in terms of ability to strike the ball: *a gifted striker of the ball.* ▪(chiefly in soccer) a forward or attacker.
3 Brit. a device striking the primer in a gun.

strike rate ▶noun the success rate of a sports team, typically in scoring goals or runs.

striker plate ▶noun a metal plate attached to a door jamb or lidded container, against which the end of a spring-lock bolt strikes when the door or lid is closed.

strike-slip fault ▶noun Geology a fault in which rock strata are displaced mainly in a horizontal direction, parallel to the line of the fault.

strike zone ▶noun Baseball an imaginary area over home plate extending from the armpits to the knees of a batter in the batting position.

striking ▶adjective **1** attracting attention by reason of being unusual, extreme, or prominent: *the murder bore a striking similarity to an earlier shooting* | [with clause] *it is* ***striking that*** *no research into the problem is occurring.* ▪dramatically good-looking or beautiful: *she is naturally striking* | *a striking landscape.*
2 [attrib.] (of an employee) on strike: *striking mineworkers.*
▶noun [mass noun] the action of striking: *substantial damage was caused by the striking of a submerged object.*
– PHRASES **within striking distance** see **DISTANCE**.
– DERIVATIVES **strikingly** adverb [as submodifier] *a strikingly beautiful girl.*

striking circle ▶noun an elongated semicircle on a hockey field in front of the goal, from within which the ball must be hit in order to score.

striking plate ▶noun another term for **STRIKER PLATE**.

striking price ▶noun another term for **STRIKE PRICE**.

strimmer ▶noun trademark an electrically powered grass trimmer with a nylon cutting cord which rotates rapidly on a spindle.
– ORIGIN 1970s: probably a blend of **STRING** and **TRIMMER**.

Strindberg /ˈstrɪndbəːg/, (Johan) August (1849–1912), Swedish dramatist and novelist. His satire *The Red Room* (1879) is regarded as Sweden's first modern novel. His later plays are typically tense, psychic dramas, such as *A Dream Play* (1902).

Strine /strʌɪn/ (also **strine**) informal ▶noun [mass noun] the English language as spoken by Australians; the Australian accent, especially when considered pronounced or uneducated. ▪[count noun] an Australian.
▶adjective of or relating to Australians or Australian English: *he spoke with a broad Strine accent.*
– ORIGIN 1960s: representing *Australian* in Strine.

string ▶noun **1** [mass noun] material consisting of threads of cotton, hemp, or other material twisted together to form a thin length. ▪[count noun] a piece of such material used to tie round or attach to something. ▪[count noun] a piece of catgut or similar material interwoven with others to form the head of a sports racket. ▪[count noun] a length of catgut or wire on a musical instrument, producing a note by vibration. ▪(**strings**) the stringed instruments in an orchestra. ▪[as modifier] of, relating to, or consisting of stringed instruments: *a string quartet.*
2 a set of things tied or threaded together on a thin cord: *she wore* ***a string of*** *agates round her throat.* ▪a sequence of similar items or events: ***a string of*** *burglaries.* ▪Computing a linear sequence of characters, words, or other data. ▪a group of racehorses trained at one stable. ▪a reserve team or player holding a specified position in an order of preference: *the village team held Rangers' second string to a 0–0 draw.* ▪a player assigned a specified rank in a team in an individual sport such as squash: *Taylor lost in straight games to third string Baines.*
3 a tough piece of fibre in vegetables, meat, or other food, such as a tough elongated piece connecting the two halves of a bean pod.

S

a cat | ɑː arm | ɛ bed | ɛː hair | ə ago | əː her | ɪ sit | i cosy | iː see | ɒ hot | ɔː saw | ʌ run | ʊ put | uː too | ʌɪ my | aʊ how | eɪ day | əʊ no | ɪə near | ɔɪ boy | ʊə poor | ʌɪə fire | aʊə sour

4 short for STRINGBOARD.
5 Physics a hypothetical one-dimensional subatomic particle having the dynamical properties of a flexible loop.
■(also **cosmic string**) a hypothetical thread-like concentration of energy within the structure of space-time.
▶verb (past and past participle **strung**) **1** [with obj. and adverbial] hang (something) so that it stretches in a long line: *lights were strung across the promenade.*
■thread (a series of small objects) on a string: *he collected stones with holes in them and strung them on a strong cord.* ■ (**be strung**) be arranged in a long line: *the houses were strung along the road.* ■ (**string something together**) add items to one another to form a series or coherent whole: *he can't string two sentences together.*
2 [with obj.] fit a string or strings to (a musical instrument, a racket, or a bow): *the harp had been newly strung.*
3 [with obj.] remove the strings from (a bean).
4 [with obj.] informal, chiefly N. Amer. hoax: *I'm not stringing you—I'll eat my shirt if it's not true.*
5 [no obj.] work as a stringer in journalism: *he strings for almost every French radio service.*
6 [no obj.] Billiards determine the order of play by striking the cue ball from baulk to rebound off the top cushion, first stroke going to the player whose ball comes to rest nearer the bottom cushion.
– PHRASES **have many strings to one's bow** see BOW[1]. **how long is a piece of string?** used to indicate that something cannot be given a finite measurement. **no strings attached** informal used to show that an offer or opportunity carries no special conditions or restrictions. **on a string** under one's control or influence: *I keep all three men on a string and never make a choice.*
– DERIVATIVES **stringless** adjective, **string-like** adjective.
– ORIGIN Old English *streng* (noun), of Germanic origin; related to German *Strang*, also to STRONG. The verb (dating from late Middle English) is first recorded in the senses 'arrange in a row' and 'fit with a string'.
▶**string along** informal stay with or accompany a person or group casually or as long as it is convenient.
string someone along informal mislead someone deliberately over a length of time, especially about one's intentions: *she had no plans to marry him—she was just stringing him along.*
string something out cause something to stretch out; prolong something. ■ (**string out**) stretch out into a long line: *the runners string out in a line across the road.* ■ (**be strung out**) be nervous or tense: *I often felt strung out by daily stresses.* ■ (**be strung out**) N. Amer. be under the influence of alcohol or drugs: *he died, strung out on booze and cocaine.*
string someone/thing up **1** hang something up on strings. ■ kill someone by hanging. **2** (**be strung up**) Brit. be tense or nervous.

string bass ▶noun (especially among jazz musicians) a double bass.

string bean ▶noun **1** any of various beans eaten in their fibrous pods, especially runner beans or French beans.
2 informal a tall thin person.

string bed ▶noun (in India) a charpoy.

stringboard ▶noun a supporting timber or skirting in which the ends of the steps in a staircase are set. Also called STRINGER.

string course ▶noun a raised horizontal band or course of bricks on a building.

stringed ▶adjective [attrib.] (of a musical instrument) having strings: [in combination] *a three-stringed fiddle.*

stringendo /strɪnˈdʒɛndəʊ/ Music ▶adverb & adjective (especially as a direction) with increasing speed.
▶noun (pl. **stringendos** or **stringendi**) a passage performed or marked to be performed in this way.
– ORIGIN Italian, literally 'squeezing, binding together'.

stringent /ˈstrɪn(d)ʒ(ə)nt/ ▶adjective (of regulations, requirements, or conditions) strict, precise, and exacting: *California's air pollution guidelines are stringent.*
– DERIVATIVES **stringency** noun, **stringently** adverb.
– ORIGIN mid 17th cent. (in the sense 'compelling, convincing'): from Latin *stringent-* 'drawing tight', from the verb *stringere*.

stringer ▶noun **1** a longitudinal structural piece in a framework, especially that of a ship or aircraft.
2 informal a newspaper correspondent not on the regular staff of a newspaper, especially one retained on a part-time basis to report on events in a particular place.
3 a stringboard.

stringhalt /ˈstrɪŋhɔːlt/ ▶noun a condition affecting one or both of a horse's hind legs, causing exaggerated bending of the hock.

string line ▶noun Billiards another term for BAULK LINE.

string orchestra ▶noun an orchestra consisting only of bowed string instruments of the violin family.

stringpiece ▶noun a long piece supporting and connecting the parts of a wooden framework.

string quartet ▶noun a chamber music ensemble consisting of first and second violins, viola, and cello.
■a piece of music for such an ensemble.

string theory ▶noun [mass noun] a cosmological theory based on the existence of cosmic strings. See also STRING (sense 5).

string tie ▶noun a very narrow necktie.

string vest ▶noun a vest made of a meshed fabric, typically worn by men as underwear.

stringy ▶adjective (**stringier**, **stringiest**) (especially of hair) resembling string; long, thin, and lustreless.
■(of a person) tall, wiry, and thin. ■ (of food) containing tough fibres and so hard to eat. ■ (of a liquid) viscous; forming strings.
– DERIVATIVES **stringily** adverb, **stringiness** noun.

stringy-bark ▶noun Austral. an Australian eucalyptus with tough fibrous bark.
• Several species in the genus *Eucalyptus*, family Myrtaceae.

strip[1] ▶verb (**stripped**, **stripping**) [with obj.] **1** remove all coverings from: *they stripped the bed.*
■remove the clothes from (someone): [with obj. and complement] *the man had been stripped naked.* ■ [no obj.] take off one's clothes: *I was tempted to **strip off** for a swim | she **stripped down** to her underwear.* ■ pull or tear off (a garment or covering): *she **stripped off** her shirt |* figurative *strip away the hype and you'll find original thought.* ■ remove bark and branches from (a tree). ■ remove paint from (a surface) with solvent. ■ remove (paint) in this way: *strip off the existing paint.* ■ remove the stems from (tobacco). ■ milk (a cow) to the last drop.
2 leave bare of accessories or fittings: *thieves stripped the room of luggage.*
■remove the accessory fittings of or take apart (a machine, motor vehicle, etc.) to inspect or adjust it: *the tank was **stripped down** piece by piece.*
3 (**strip someone of**) deprive someone of (rank, power, or property): *the lieutenant was stripped of his rank.*
4 sell off (the assets of a company) for profit.
■Finance divest (a bond) of its interest coupons so that it and they may be sold separately.
5 tear the thread or teeth from (a screw, gearwheel, etc.).
■[no obj.] (of a screw, gearwheel, etc.) lose its thread or teeth.
6 [no obj.] (of a bullet) be fired from a rifled gun without spin owing to a loss of surface.
▶noun **1** an act of undressing, especially in a striptease: *she got drunk and did a strip on top of the piano.*
■[as modifier] used for or involving the performance of stripteases: *a campaigner against strip joints.*
2 Brit. the identifying outfit worn by the members of a sports team while playing. [ORIGIN: late 20th cent.: possibly from the notion of clothing to which a player with a striptease 'strips' down.]
– ORIGIN Middle English (as a verb): of Germanic origin; related to Dutch *stropen*.

strip[2] ▶noun **1** a long, narrow piece of cloth, paper, plastic, or some other material: *a **strip of** linen.*
■a long, narrow area of land. ■ chiefly N. Amer. a main road in or leading out of a town, lined with shops, restaurants, and other facilities. ■ [mass noun] steel or other metal in the form of narrow flat bars.
2 a comic strip.
■Brit. a programme broadcast regularly at the same time: *he hosts a weekly two-hour advice strip.*
– ORIGIN late Middle English: from or related to Middle Low German *strippe* 'strap, thong', probably also to STRIPE.

strip cropping ▶noun [mass noun] US cultivation in which different crops are sown in alternate strips to prevent soil erosion.

stripe ▶noun **1** a long narrow band or strip, typically of the same width throughout its length, differing in colour or texture from the surface on either side of it: *a pair of blue shorts with pink stripes.*
■archaic a blow with a scourge or lash.
2 a chevron sewn on to a uniform to denote military rank.
■chiefly N. Amer. a type or category: *entrepreneurs **of** all **stripes** are joining in the offensive.*
▶verb [with obj.] (usu. **be striped**) mark with stripes: *her body was striped with bands of sunlight.*
– ORIGIN late Middle English: perhaps a back-formation from STRIPED, of Dutch or Low German origin; compare with Middle Dutch and Middle Low German *strīpe*.

striped ▶adjective marked with or having stripes: [in combination] *a green-striped coat.*

striped bass ▶noun a large bass of North American coastal waters, with dark horizontal stripes along the upper sides, migrating up streams to breed.
• *Morone* (or *Roccus*) *saxatilis*, family Perchichthyidae.

striped hyena ▶noun a hyena with numerous black stripes on the body and legs, living in steppe and desert areas from NE Africa to India.
• *Hyaena hyaena*, family Hyaenidae.

striped muscle ▶noun another term for STRIATED MUSCLE.

striped polecat ▶noun another term for ZORILLA.

stripey ▶adjective variant spelling of STRIPY.

strip light ▶noun Brit. a tubular fluorescent lamp.

stripling ▶noun archaic or humorous a young man.
– ORIGIN Middle English: probably from STRIP[2] (from the notion of 'narrowness', i.e. slimness) + -LING.

strip mall ▶noun N. Amer. a shopping mall located on a busy main road.

strip mill ▶noun a mill in which steel slabs are rolled into strips.

strip-mine chiefly US ▶verb [with obj.] obtain (ore or coal) by opencast mining: *lignite coal is strip-mined at depths of 15 to 35 metres |* [as noun **strip-mining**] *protected lands opened up to strip-mining for coal.*
■subject (an area of land) to opencast mining.
▶noun (**strip mine**) a mine worked by this method.

stripped-down ▶adjective [attrib.] reduced to essentials: *a pretty, stripped-down ballad.*
■(of a machine, motor vehicle, etc.) having had all fittings removed; dismantled.

stripper ▶noun **1** a device used for stripping something: *a wire stripper removes insulation from flex.*
■[mass noun] solvent for removing paint.
2 a striptease performer.

strippergram ▶noun a novelty greetings message delivered by a man or woman who accompanies it with a striptease act.

strip poker ▶noun [mass noun] a form of poker in which a player with a losing hand takes off an item of clothing as a forfeit.

strip-search ▶verb [with obj.] search (someone) for concealed items, typically drugs or weapons, in a way that involves the removal of all their clothes.
▶noun an act of searching someone in such a way.

striptease ▶noun a form of entertainment in which a performer gradually undresses to music in a way intended to be sexually exciting.
– DERIVATIVES **stripteaser** noun.

stripy (also **stripey**) ▶adjective striped: *a stripy T-shirt.*

strive ▶verb (past **strove** or **strived**; past participle **striven** or **strived**) [no obj.] make great efforts to achieve or obtain something: *national movements were **striving for** independence |* [with infinitive] *we must strive to secure steady growth.*
■struggle or fight vigorously: *scholars must **strive against** bias.*
– DERIVATIVES **striver** noun.
– ORIGIN Middle English: shortening of Old French *estriver*; related to *estrif* 'strife'.

strobe informal ▶noun **1** a stroboscope.
■a stroboscopic lamp: [as modifier] *strobe lights dazzled her.*
2 US an electronic flash for a camera.

S

▶**verb** [no obj.] **1** flash intermittently: *the light of the fireworks strobed around the room.*
■[with obj.] light as if with a stroboscope: *a neon sign strobed the room.*
2 exhibit or give rise to strobing: *he explained that the stripes I was wearing would strobe.*
– ORIGIN 1940s: abbreviation of *stroboscopic* (see **STROBOSCOPE**).

strobilus /ˈstrəʊbɪləs/ ▶**noun** (pl. **strobili** /-lʌɪ, -liː/) Botany the cone of a pine, fir, or other conifer.
■a cone-like structure, such as the flower of the hop.
– ORIGIN mid 18th cent.: from late Latin, from Greek *strobilos*, from *strephein* 'to twist'.

strobing /ˈstrəʊbɪŋ/ ▶**noun** [mass noun] **1** irregular movement and loss of continuity sometimes seen in lines and stripes in a television picture.
2 jerkiness in what should be a smooth movement of an image on a screen.

stroboscope /ˈstrəʊbəskəʊp/ ▶**noun** Physics an instrument for studying periodic motion or determining speeds of rotation by shining a bright light at intervals so that a moving or rotating object appears stationary.
■a lamp made to flash intermittently, especially for this purpose.
– DERIVATIVES **stroboscopic** adjective, **stroboscopically** adverb.
– ORIGIN mid 19th cent.: from Greek *strobos* 'whirling' + **-SCOPE**.

strode past of **STRIDE**.

stroganoff /ˈstrɒgənɒf/ ▶**noun** [mass noun] a dish in which the central ingredient, typically strips of beef, is cooked in a sauce containing sour cream.
– ORIGIN named after Count Pavel *Stroganov* (1772–1817), Russian diplomat.

stroke ▶**noun 1** an act of hitting or striking someone or something; a blow: *he received three strokes of the cane.*
■a method of striking the ball in sports or games. ■ Golf an act of hitting the ball with a club, as a unit of scoring: *he won by two strokes.* ■ the sound made by a striking clock.
2 an act of moving one's hand or an object across a surface, applying gentle pressure: *massage the cream into your skin using light upward strokes.*
■a mark made by drawing a pen, pencil, or paintbrush in one direction across paper or canvas: *the paint had been applied in careful, regular strokes.* ■ a line forming part of a written or printed character. ■ a short printed or written diagonal line typically separating characters or figures.
3 a movement, especially one of a series, in which something moves out of its position and back into it; a beat: *the ray swam with effortless strokes of its huge wings.*
■the whole motion of a piston in either direction. ■ the rhythm to which a series of repeated movements is performed: *the rowers sing to keep their stroke.* ■ a movement of the arms and legs forming one of a series in swimming. ■ style of moving the arms and legs in swimming: *front crawl is a popular stroke.* ■ (in rowing) the mode or action of moving the oar. ■ (also **stroke oar**) the oar or oarsman nearest the stern of a boat, setting the timing for the other rowers.
4 a sudden disabling attack or loss of consciousness caused by an interruption in the flow of blood to the brain, especially through thrombosis.
▶**verb** [with obj.] **1** move one's hand with gentle pressure over (a surface, especially hair, fur, or skin), typically repeatedly; caress: *he put his hand on her hair and stroked it.*
■[with obj. and adverbial of place] apply (something) to a surface using a gentle movement: *she strokes blue eyeshadow on her eyelids.* ■ N. Amer. informal reassure or flatter (someone), especially in order to gain their cooperation: *production executives were expert at stroking stars and brokering talent.*
2 act as the stroke of (a boat or crew): *he stroked the coxed four to victory.*
3 hit or kick (a ball) smoothly and deliberately: *Markwick stroked the ball home.*
■score (a run or point) in such a manner: *the senior stroked a two-run single.*
– PHRASES **at a** (or **one**) **stroke** by a single action having immediate effect: *attitudes cannot be changed at one stroke.* **not** (or **never**) **do a stroke of work** do no work at all. **on the stroke of ——** precisely at the specified time: *he arrived on the stroke of two.* **put someone off their stroke** disconcert someone so that they do not work or perform as well as they might; break the pattern or rhythm of someone's work. **stroke of business** a profitable transaction. **stroke of genius** an outstandingly brilliant and original idea. **stroke of luck** (or **good luck**) a fortunate occurrence that could not have been predicted or expected.
– ORIGIN Old English *strācian* 'caress lightly', of Germanic origin; related to Dutch *streek* 'a stroke', German *streichen* 'to stroke', also to **STRIKE**. The earliest noun sense 'blow' is first recorded in Middle English.

stroke play ▶**noun** [mass noun] play in golf in which the score is reckoned by counting the number of strokes taken overall, as opposed to the number of holes won.

stroll ▶**verb** [no obj., with adverbial of direction] walk in a leisurely way: *I strolled around the city.*
■figurative achieve a sporting victory easily, without effort: *the horse strolled home by 12 lengths.*
▶**noun** a short leisurely walk.
■figurative a victory or objective that is easily achieved.
– ORIGIN early 17th cent. (in the sense 'roam as a vagrant'): probably from German *strollen, strolchen*, from *Strolch* 'vagabond', of unknown ultimate origin.

stroller ▶**noun 1** a person taking a leisurely walk: *shady gardens where strollers could relax.*
2 N. Amer. a pushchair.
3 S. African a young urban vagrant; a street child.

strolling players ▶**plural noun** historical a troupe of itinerant actors.

stroma /ˈstrəʊmə/ ▶**noun** (pl. **stromata** /-mətə/)
1 [mass noun] Anatomy & Biology the supportive tissue of an epithelial organ, tumour, gonad, etc., consisting of connective tissues and blood vessels.
■the spongy framework of protein fibres in a red blood cell or platelet. ■ Botany the matrix of a chloroplast, in which the grana are embedded.
2 Botany a cushion-like mass of fungal tissue, having spore-bearing structures either embedded in it or on its surface.
– DERIVATIVES **stromal** adjective (chiefly Anatomy), **stromatic** adjective (chiefly Botany).
– ORIGIN mid 19th cent.: modern Latin, via late Latin from Greek *strōma* 'coverlet'.

stromatolite /strə(ʊ)ˈmatəlʌɪt/ ▶**noun** a calcareous mound built up of layers of lime-secreting cyanobacteria and trapped sediment, found in Precambrian rocks as the earliest known fossils, and still being formed in lagoons in Australasia.
– ORIGIN 1930s: from modern Latin *stroma, stromat-* 'layer, covering' + **-LITE**.

stromatoporoid /ˌstrəʊməˈtɒpərɔɪd/ ▶**noun** an extinct sessile coral-like marine organism of uncertain relationship which built up calcareous masses composed of laminae and pillars, occurring from the Cambrian to the Cretaceous.
– ORIGIN late 19th cent.: from modern Latin *Stromatopora* (genus name), from *stroma, stromat-* 'layer, covering' + *-pora* (on the pattern of *madrepora*).

Stromboli /ˈstrɒmbəli, strɒmˈbəʊli/ a volcanic island in the Mediterranean, the most north-easterly of the Lipari Islands.

Strombolian /strɒmˈbəʊlɪən/ ▶**adjective** Geology denoting volcanic activity of the kind typified by Stromboli, with continual mild eruptions in which lava fragments are ejected.

strong ▶**adjective** (**stronger, strongest**) **1** having the power to move heavy weights or perform other physically demanding tasks: *she cut through the water with her strong arms.*
■[attrib.] able to perform a specified action well and powerfully: *he was not a strong swimmer.* ■ exerting great force: *a strong current.* ■ (of an argument or case) likely to succeed because of sound reasoning or convincing evidence: *there is a strong argument for decentralization.* ■ possessing skills and qualities that create a likelihood of success: *the competition was too strong.* ■ powerfully affecting the mind, senses, or emotions: *his imagery made a strong impression on the critics.* ■ used after a number to indicate the size of a group: *a hostile crowd several thousands strong.*
2 able to withstand great force or pressure: *cotton is strong, hard-wearing, and easy to handle.*
■(of a person's constitution) not easily affected by disease or hardship. ■ (of a person's nervous or emotional state) not easily disturbed or upset: *driving on these motorways requires strong nerves.* ■ (of a person's character) showing determination, self-control, and good judgement: *only a strong will enabled him to survive.* ■ in a secure financial position: *the company's chip business remains strong.* ■ (of a market) having steadily high or rising prices. ■ offering security and advantage: *the company was in a strong position to negotiate a deal.* ■ (of a belief or feeling) intense and firmly held. ■ (of a relationship) lasting and remaining warm despite difficulties.
3 very intense: *a strong smell.*
■(of something seen or heard) not soft or muted; clear or prominent: *she should wear strong colours.* ■ (of food or its flavour) distinctive and pungent: *strong cheese.* ■ (of a solution or drink) containing a large proportion of a particular substance; concentrated: *a cup of strong coffee.* ■ (of language or actions) forceful and extreme, especially excessively or unacceptably so: *the government were urged to take strong measures against the perpetrators of violence.* ■ Chemistry (of an acid or base) fully ionized into cations and anions in solution; having (respectively) a very low or a very high pH.
4 Grammar denoting a class of verbs in Germanic languages that form the past tense and past participle by a change of vowel within the stem rather than by addition of a suffix (e.g. *swim, swam, swum*).
5 Physics of, relating to, or denoting the strongest of the known kinds of force between particles, which acts between nucleons and other hadrons when closer than about 10^{-13} cm (so binding protons in a nucleus despite the repulsion due to their charge), and which conserves strangeness, parity, and isospin.
– PHRASES **come on strong** informal **1** behave aggressively or assertively, especially in making sexual advances to someone. **2** improve one's position considerably: *he came on strong towards the end of the round.* **going strong** informal continuing to be healthy, vigorous, or successful: *the programme is still going strong after twelve series.* **strong on** good at: *he is strong on comedy.* ■ possessing large quantities of: *our pizza wasn't strong on pine nuts.* **strong meat** Brit. ideas or language likely to be found unacceptably forceful or extreme. **one's strong point** something at which one excels: *arithmetic had never been my strong point.*
– DERIVATIVES **strongish** adjective, **strongly** adverb.
– ORIGIN Old English, of Germanic origin; related to Dutch and German *streng*, also to **STRING**.

strong-arm ▶**adjective** [attrib.] using or characterized by force or violence: *they were furious at what they said were government strong-arm tactics.*
▶**verb** [with obj.] use force or violence against: *the culprit shouted before being strong-armed out of the door.*

strongbox ▶**noun** a small lockable box, typically made of metal, in which valuables may be kept.

strong breeze ▶**noun** a wind of force 6 on the Beaufort scale (22–27 knots or 40–50 kph).

strong drink ▶**noun** [mass noun] alcohol, especially spirits.

strong gale ▶**noun** a wind of force 9 on the Beaufort scale (41–47 knots or 75–87 kph).

stronghold ▶**noun** a place that has been fortified so as to protect it against attack.
■a place where a particular cause or belief is strongly defended or upheld: *a Labour stronghold.*

strong interaction ▶**noun** Physics interaction at short distances between certain subatomic particles mediated by the strong force.

strongman ▶**noun** (pl. **-men**) a man of great physical strength, especially one who performs feats of strength as a form of entertainment.
■a leader who rules by the exercise of threats, force, or violence.

strong-minded ▶**adjective** not easily influenced by others; resolute and determined.
– DERIVATIVES **strong-mindedness** noun.

strongpoint ▶**noun** a specially fortified defensive position.

strongroom ▶**noun** a room, typically one in a bank, designed to protect valuable items against fire and theft.

strong safety ▶**noun** American Football a defensive back positioned opposite the strong side who usually covers the tight end.

strong suit ▶**noun** (in bridge or whist) a holding of a number of high cards of one suit in a hand.
■a desirable quality that is particularly prominent in someone's character or an activity at which they excel: *compassion is not Jack's strong suit.*

S

strongyle /ˈstrɒndʒɪl/ ▶ **noun** a nematode worm of a group that includes several common disease-causing parasites of mammals and birds.
• Genus *Strongylus* or family Strongylidae, class Phasmida. See also **REDWORM** (sense 2).
– ORIGIN mid 19th cent.: from modern Latin *Strongylus*, from Greek *strongulos* 'round'.

strongyloidiasis /ˌstrɒndʒɪlɔɪˈdʌɪəsɪs/ ▶ **noun** [mass noun] infestation with threadworms of a type found in tropical and subtropical regions, chiefly affecting the small intestine and causing ulceration and diarrhoea.
• The worms belong to the genus *Strongyloides*, class Phasmida, in particular *S. stercoralis*.

strontia /ˈstrɒnʃ(ɪ)ə/ ▶ **noun** [mass noun] Chemistry strontium oxide, a white solid resembling quicklime.
• Chem. formula: SrO.
– ORIGIN early 19th cent.: from earlier *strontian*, denoting native strontium carbonate from *Strontian*, a parish in the Highland region of Scotland, where it was discovered.

strontianite /ˈstrɒnʃ(ə)nʌɪt/ ▶ **noun** [mass noun] a rare pale greenish-yellow or white mineral consisting of strontium carbonate.
– ORIGIN late 18th cent.: from *strontian* (see **STRONTIA**) + **-ITE**[1].

strontium /ˈstrɒntɪəm, ˈstrɒnʃ(ɪ)əm/ ▶ **noun** [mass noun] the chemical element of atomic number 38, a soft silver-white metal of the alkaline earth series. Its salts are used in fireworks and flares because they give a brilliant red light. (Symbol: **Sr**)
– ORIGIN early 19th cent.: from **STRONTIA** + **-IUM**.

strop[1] ▶ **noun** a device, typically a strip of leather, for sharpening razors.
▪ S. African a leather strap, especially the strap on a yoke that is fastened under the throat of a draught animal. [ORIGIN: Afrikaans, from Dutch *strop* 'noose'.] ▪ Nautical a collar of leather or spliced rope or iron used for handling cargo.
▶ **verb** (**stropped**, **stropping**) [with obj.] sharpen on or with a strop: *he stropped a knife razor-sharp on his belt.*
– ORIGIN late Middle English (in the sense 'thong', also as a nautical term): probably a West Germanic adoption of Latin *stroppus* 'thong'.

strop[2] ▶ **noun** [usu. in sing.] Brit. informal a bad mood; a temper: *Nathalie gets in a strop and makes to leave.*
– ORIGIN late 20th cent.: probably a back-formation from **STROPPY**.

strophanthin /strə(ʊ)ˈfanθɪn/ ▶ **noun** [mass noun] Medicine a poisonous substance of the glycoside class, obtained from certain African trees and used as a heart stimulant.
• This substance is obtained from trees of the genera *Strophanthus* and *Acokanthera* (family Apocynaceae).
– ORIGIN late 19th cent.: from modern Latin *strophanthus* (from Greek *strophos* 'twisted cord' + *anthos* 'flower', referring to the long segments of the corolla) + **-IN**[1].

strophe /ˈstrəʊfi/ ▶ **noun** the first section of an ancient Greek choral ode or of one division of it.
▪ a group of lines forming a section of a lyric poem.
– DERIVATIVES **strophic** adjective.
– ORIGIN early 17th cent.: from Greek *strophē*, literally 'turning', from *strephein* 'to turn': the term originally denoted a movement from right to left made by a Greek chorus, or lines of choral song recited during this.

stroppy ▶ **adjective** (**stroppier**, **stroppiest**) Brit. informal bad-tempered and argumentative.
– DERIVATIVES **stroppily** adverb, **stroppiness** noun.
– ORIGIN 1950s: perhaps an abbreviation of **OBSTREPEROUS**.

stroud /straʊd/ ▶ **noun** [mass noun] coarse woollen fabric, formerly used in the manufacture of blankets.

strove past of **STRIVE**.

strow /strəʊ/ ▶ **verb** (past participle **strown** /strəʊn/ or **strowed**) archaic variant of **STREW**.

struck past and past participle of **STRIKE**.

struck joint ▶ **noun** a masonry joint in which the mortar between two courses of bricks is sloped inwards so as to be flush with the surface of one but below that of the other.

structural ▶ **adjective** of, relating to, or forming part of the structure of a building or other item: *the blast left ten buildings with major structural damage.*
▪ of or relating to the arrangement of and relations between the parts or elements of a complex whole: *there have been structural changes in the industry.*
– DERIVATIVES **structurally** adverb.

structural engineering ▶ **noun** [mass noun] the branch of civil engineering that deals with large modern buildings and similar structures.
– DERIVATIVES **structural engineer** noun.

structural formula ▶ **noun** Chemistry a formula which shows the arrangement of atoms in the molecule of a compound.

structuralism ▶ **noun** [mass noun] a method of interpretation and analysis of aspects of human cognition, behaviour, culture, and experience, which focuses on relationships of contrast between elements in a conceptual system that reflect patterns underlying a superficial diversity.
▪ the doctrine that structure is more important than function.

Originating in the structural linguistics of Ferdinand de Saussure, and extended into anthropology by Claude Lévi-Strauss, structuralism was adapted to a wide range of social and cultural studies, especially in the 1960s, by writers such as Roland Barthes, Louis Althusser, and Jacques Lacan.

– DERIVATIVES **structuralist** noun & adjective.

structural linguistics ▶ **plural noun** [treated as sing.] the branch of linguistics that deals with language as a system of interrelated structures, in particular the theories and methods of Leonard Bloomfield, emphasizing the accurate identification of syntactic and lexical form as opposed to meaning and historical development.

structural steel ▶ **noun** [mass noun] strong mild steel in shapes suited to construction work.

structural unemployment ▶ **noun** [mass noun] unemployment resulting from industrial reorganization, typically due to technological change, rather than fluctuations in supply or demand.

structuration ▶ **noun** [mass noun] the state or process of organization in a structured form.

structure ▶ **noun** the arrangement of and relations between the parts or elements of something complex: *the two sentences have equivalent syntactic structures.*
▪ the organization of a society or other group and the relations between its members, determining its working. ▪ a building or other object constructed from several parts. ▪ [mass noun] the quality of being organized: *we shall use three headings to give some structure to the discussion.*
▶ **verb** [with obj.] (often **be structured**) construct or arrange according to a plan; give a pattern or organization to: *services must be structured so as to avoid pitfalls.*
– DERIVATIVES **structureless** adjective.
– ORIGIN late Middle English (denoting the process of building): from Old French, or from Latin *structura*, from *struere* 'to build'. The verb is rarely found before the 20th cent.

structure plan ▶ **noun** a plan drawn up by a local planning authority for the use of a prescribed area of land.

strudel /ˈstruːd(ə)l, ˈʃtruː-/ ▶ **noun** a confection of thin pastry rolled up round a fruit filling and baked.
– ORIGIN from German *Strudel*, literally 'whirlpool'.

struggle ▶ **verb** [no obj.] make forceful or violent efforts to get free of restraint or constriction: *before she could struggle, he lifted her up* | [with infinitive] *he struggled to break free.*
▪ strive to achieve or attain something in the face of difficulty or resistance: [with infinitive] *many families on income support have to struggle to make ends meet.* ▪ (**struggle with**) have difficulty handling or coping with: *passengers struggle with bags and briefcases.* ▪ engage in conflict: *politicians continued to struggle over familiar issues.* ▪ [no obj., with adverbial of direction] make one's way with difficulty: *it took us all day to struggle back to our bivouac.* ▪ have difficulty in gaining recognition or a living: *new authors are struggling in the present climate.*
▶ **noun** a forceful or violent effort to get free of restraint or resist attack.
▪ a conflict or contest: *a power struggle for the leadership.* ▪ a great physical effort: *with a struggle, she pulled the pram up the slope.* ▪ a determined effort under difficulties: *the centre is the result of the scientists' struggle to realize their dream.* ▪ a very difficult task: *it was a struggle to make herself understood.*
– PHRASES **the struggle for existence** (or **life**) the competition between organisms, especially as an element in natural selection, or between people seeking a livelihood.
– DERIVATIVES **struggler** noun.
– ORIGIN late Middle English: frequentative, perhaps of imitative origin. The noun dates from the late 17th cent.

strum ▶ **verb** (**strummed**, **strumming**) [with obj.] play (a guitar or similar instrument) by sweeping the thumb or a plectrum up or down the strings.
▪ play (a tune) in such a way: *he strummed a few chords.* ▪ [no obj.] play casually or unskilfully on a stringed or keyboard instrument.
▶ **noun** [in sing.] the sound made by strumming: *the brittle strum of acoustic guitars.*
▪ an instance or spell of strumming.
– DERIVATIVES **strummer** noun.
– ORIGIN late 18th cent.: imitative; compare with **THRUM**[1].

struma /ˈstruːmə/ ▶ **noun** (pl. **strumae** /-miː/) Medicine a swelling of the thyroid gland; a goitre.
– ORIGIN mid 16th cent. (in the Latin sense): modern Latin, from Latin, 'scrofulous tumour'.

strumous /ˈstruːməs/ ▶ **adjective** archaic scrofulous.
– ORIGIN late 16th cent.: from Latin *strumosus*, from *struma* (see **STRUMA**).

strumpet ▶ **noun** archaic a female prostitute or a promiscuous woman.
– ORIGIN Middle English: of unknown origin.

strung past and past participle of **STRING**.

strut ▶ **noun 1** a rod or bar forming part of a framework and designed to resist compression.
2 [in sing.] a stiff, erect, and apparently arrogant or conceited gait: *that old confident strut and swagger has returned.*
▶ **verb** (**strutted**, **strutting**) **1** [no obj., with adverbial] walk with a stiff, erect, and apparently arrogant or conceited gait: *peacocks strut through the grounds.*
2 [with obj.] brace (something) with a strut or struts: *the holes were close-boarded and strutted.*
– PHRASES **strut one's stuff** informal dance or behave in a confident and expressive way.
– DERIVATIVES **strutter** noun, **struttingly** adverb.
– ORIGIN Old English *strūtian* 'protrude stiffly', of Germanic origin. Current senses date from the late 16th cent.

struth ▶ **exclamation** variant spelling of **STREWTH**.

Struve /ˈstruːvə/, Otto (1897–1963), Russian-born American astronomer. He was mainly interested in spectroscopic investigations into the composition, evolution, and rotation of stars, but his most important contribution was his discovery of the presence of ionized hydrogen in interstellar space (1938).

strychnine /ˈstrɪkniːn, -ɪn/ ▶ **noun** [mass noun] a bitter and highly poisonous compound obtained from nux vomica and related plants. An alkaloid, it has occasionally been used as a stimulant.
– ORIGIN early 19th cent.: from French, via Latin from Greek *strukhnos*, denoting a kind of nightshade.

Sts ▶ **abbreviation for** Saints.

Stuart[1], Charles Edward (1720–88), son of James Stuart, pretender to the British throne; known as **the Young Pretender** or **Bonnie Prince Charlie**. He led the Jacobite uprising of 1745–6. However, he was driven back to Scotland and defeated at the Battle of Culloden (1746).

Stuart[2], James (Francis Edward) (1688–1766), son of James II (James VII of Scotland), pretender to the British throne; known as **the Old Pretender**. He arrived in Scotland too late to alter the outcome of the 1715 Jacobite uprising and left the leadership of the 1745–6 uprising to his son Charles Edward Stuart.

Stuart[3], John McDouall (1815–66), Scottish explorer. He was a member of Charles Sturt's third expedition to Australia (1844–6) and subsequently crossed Australia from south to north and back again, at his sixth attempt (1860–2).

Stuart[4], Mary, see **MARY, QUEEN OF SCOTS**.

Stuart[5] (also **Stewart**) ▶ **adjective** of or relating to the royal family ruling Scotland 1371–1714 and Britain 1603–1649 and 1660–1714.
▶ **noun** a member of this family.

stub ▶ **noun 1** the truncated remnant of a pencil, cigarette, or similar-shaped object after use.
▪ a truncated or unusually short thing: *he wagged his little stub of tail.* ▪ [as modifier] denoting a projection or

hole that goes only part of the way through a surface: *a stub tenon.*
2 the counterfoil of a cheque, receipt, ticket, or other document.
▶**verb** (**stubbed**, **stubbing**) [with obj.] **1** accidentally strike (one's toe) against something: *I stubbed my toe, swore, and tripped.*
2 extinguish (a lighted cigarette) by pressing the lighted end against something: *she* ***stubbed out*** *her cigarette in the overflowing ashtray.*
3 grub up (a plant) by the roots: *he was found to have* ***stubbed up*** *a hedge.*
– ORIGIN Old English *stub(b)* 'stump of a tree', of Germanic origin. The verb is first recorded (late Middle English) in sense 3; sense 1 of the verb (mid 19th cent.) was originally a US usage.

stub axle ▶**noun** an axle supporting only one wheel of a pair on opposite sides of a vehicle.

stubble ▶**noun** [mass noun] the cut stalks of cereal plants left sticking out of the ground after the grain is harvested.
■short, stiff hairs growing on a man's face when he has not shaved for a while.
– DERIVATIVES **stubbled** adjective, **stubbly** adjective.
– ORIGIN Middle English: from Anglo-Norman French *stuble*, from Latin *stupla*, *stupula*, variants of *stipula* 'straw'.

stubborn ▶**adjective** having or showing dogged determination not to change one's attitude or position on something, especially in spite of good arguments or reasons to do so: *you're a silly, stubborn old woman.*
■difficult to move, remove, or cure: *the removal of stubborn screws.*
– DERIVATIVES **stubbornly** adverb, **stubbornness** noun.
– ORIGIN Middle English (originally in the sense 'untameable, implacable'): of unknown origin.

Stubbs[1], George (1724–1806), English painter and engraver. He is particularly noted for his sporting scenes and paintings of horses and lions, such as the *Mares and Foals in a Landscape* series (*c.*1760–70).

Stubbs[2], William (1825–1901), English historian and ecclesiastic. He wrote the influential *Constitutional History of England* (three volumes 1874–8). He was also bishop of Chester (1884–8) and of Oxford (1888–1901).

stubby ▶**adjective** (**stubbier**, **stubbiest**) short and thick: *Blufton pointed with a stubby finger.*
▶**noun** (pl. **-ies**) Austral./NZ informal a squat bottle of beer holding normally 375 cl.
– DERIVATIVES **stubbily** adverb, **stubbiness** noun.

stucco ▶**noun** [mass noun] fine plaster used for coating wall surfaces or moulding into architectural decorations.
▶**verb** (**-oes**, **-oed**) [with obj.] [usu. as adj. **stuccoed**] coat or decorate with such plaster: *a stuccoed house.*
– ORIGIN late 16th cent. (as a noun): from Italian, of Germanic origin.

stuck past participle of **STICK**[2].

stuck-up ▶**adjective** informal staying aloof from others because one thinks one is superior.

stud[1] ▶**noun** **1** a large-headed piece of metal that pierces and projects from a surface, especially for decoration.
■a small, simple piece of jewellery for wearing in pierced ears or nostrils. ■a fastener consisting of two buttons joined with a bar, used in formal wear to fasten a shirt front or to fasten a collar to a shirt. ■(usu. **studs**) a small projection fixed to the base of footwear, especially sports boots, to allow the wearer to grip the ground. ■(usu. **studs**) a small metal piece set into the tyre of a motor vehicle to improve roadholding in slippery conditions. ■a small object projecting slightly from a road surface as a marker.
2 an upright timber in the wall of a building to which laths and plasterboard are nailed.
■US the height of a room as indicated by the length of this.
3 a rivet or crosspiece in each link of a chain cable.
▶**verb** (**studded**, **studding**) [with obj.] (usu. **be studded**) decorate or augment (something) with many studs or similar small objects: *a dagger* ***studded with*** *precious diamonds.*
■strew or cover (something) with a scattering of small objects or features: *the sky was clear and* ***studded with*** *stars.*
– ORIGIN Old English *studu*, *stuthu* 'post, upright prop'; related to German *stützen* 'to prop'. The sense 'ornamental metal knob' arose in late Middle English.

stud[2] ▶**noun** **1** an establishment where horses or other domesticated animals are kept for breeding: [as modifier] *a stud farm* | [mass noun] *the horse was retired* ***to stud.***
■a collection of horses or other domesticated animals belonging to one person. ■(also **stud horse**) a stallion. ■informal a young man thought to be very active sexually or regarded as a good sexual partner.
2 (also **stud poker**) [mass noun] a form of poker in which the first card of a player's hand is dealt face down and the others face up, with betting after each round of the deal.
– ORIGIN Old English *stōd*, of Germanic origin; related to German *Stute* 'mare', also to **STAND**.

stud book ▶**noun** a book containing the pedigrees of horses.

studding ▶**noun** [mass noun] studs collectively. See **STUD**[1] (sense 2).

studdingsail /ˈstʌns(ə)l/ ▶**noun** (on a square-rigged sailing ship) an additional sail set at the end of a yard in light winds.
– ORIGIN mid 16th cent.: *studding* perhaps from Middle Low German, Middle Dutch *stōtinge* 'a thrusting'.

student ▶**noun** a person who is studying at a university or other place of higher education.
■chiefly N. Amer. a school pupil. ■[as modifier] denoting someone who is studying in order to enter a particular profession: *a group of student nurses.* ■a person who takes an interest in a particular subject: *a* ***student of*** *the free market.*
– DERIVATIVES **studentship** noun Brit., **studenty** adjective Brit. (informal).
– ORIGIN late Middle English: from Latin *student-* 'applying oneself to', from the verb *studere*, related to *studium* 'painstaking application'.

student-at-law ▶**noun** Canadian an articling law student.

Student's t-test ▶**noun** a test for statistical significance that uses tables of a statistical distribution called **Student's *t*-distribution**, which is that of a fraction (*t*) whose numerator is drawn from a normal distribution with a mean of zero, and whose denominator is the root mean square of *k* terms drawn from the same normal distribution (where *k* is the number of degrees of freedom).
– ORIGIN early 20th cent.: *Student*, the pseudonym of William Sealy Gosset (1876–1937), English brewery employee.

stud horse ▶**noun** see **STUD**[2].

studied ▶**adjective** (of a quality or result) achieved or maintained by careful and deliberate effort: *he treated them with studied politeness.*
– DERIVATIVES **studiedly** adverb, **studiedness** noun.

studio ▶**noun** (pl. **-os**) **1** a room where an artist, photographer, sculptor, etc. works.
■a place where performers, especially dancers, practise and exercise. ■a room where musical or sound recordings can be made. ■a room from which television programmes are broadcast, or in which they are recorded. ■a place where cinema films are made or produced.
2 a film or television production company.
3 a studio flat.
– ORIGIN early 19th cent.: from Italian, from Latin *studium* (see **STUDY**).

studio couch ▶**noun** chiefly N. Amer. a sofa bed.

studio flat ▶**noun** (also N. Amer. **studio apartment**) Brit. a flat containing one main room.

studio portrait ▶**noun** a large photograph for which the sitter is posed, typically taken in the photographer's studio.

studio theatre ▶**noun** a small theatre where experimental and innovative productions are staged.

studious ▶**adjective** spending a lot of time studying or reading: *he was quiet and studious.*
■done deliberately or with a purpose in mind: *his studious absence from public view.* ■showing great care or attention: *a studious inspection.*
– DERIVATIVES **studiously** adverb, **studiousness** noun.
– ORIGIN Middle English: from Latin *studiosus*, from *studium* 'painstaking application'.

studmuffin ▶**noun** N. Amer. informal a man perceived as sexually attractive, typically one with well-developed muscles.

stud poker ▶**noun** see **STUD**[2] (sense 2).

study ▶**noun** (pl. **-ies**) **1** [mass noun] the devotion of time and attention to acquiring knowledge on an academic subject, especially by means of books: *the study of English* | *an application to continue full-time study.*
■(**studies**) activity of this type as pursued by one person: *some students may not be able to resume their studies.* ■[count noun] an academic book or article on a particular topic: *a study of Jane Austen's novels.* ■(**studies**) used in the title of an academic subject: *an undergraduate course in transport studies.*
2 a detailed investigation and analysis of a subject or situation: *a study of a sample of 5,000 children* | [mass noun] *the study of global problems.*
■a portrayal in literature or another art form of an aspect of behaviour or character: *a complex study of a gay teenager.* ■archaic a thing that is or deserves to be investigated; the subject of an individual's study: *I have made it my study to examine the nature and character of the Indians.* ■archaic the object or aim of someone's endeavours: *the acquisition of a fortune is the study of all.* ■[with adj.] theatrical slang a person who memorizes a role at a specified speed: *I'm a quick study.*
3 a room used or designed for reading, writing, or academic work.
4 a piece of work, especially a drawing, done for practice or as an experiment.
■a musical composition designed to develop a player's technical skill.
5 (**a study in**) a thing or person that is an embodiment or good example of something: *he perched on the edge of the bed, a study in confusion and misery.*
■informal an amusing or remarkable thing or person: *Ira's face was a study as he approached the car.*
▶**verb** (**-ies**, **-ied**) [with obj.] **1** devote time and attention to acquiring knowledge on (an academic subject), especially by means of books: *students studying A-level drama.*
■investigate and analyse (a subject or situation) in detail: *he has been studying mink for many years.* ■[no obj.] apply oneself to study: *he spent his time listening to the radio rather than studying.* ■[no obj.] acquire academic knowledge at an educational establishment: *he studied at the Kensington School of Art.* ■[no obj.] (**study up**) US learn intensively about something, especially in preparation for a test of knowledge: *schoolchildren* ***studying up on*** *their forebears' games and chores.* ■(of an actor) try to learn (the words of one's role). ■W. Indian give serious thought or consideration to: *the people here don't make so much noise, so the government don't have us to study.*
2 look at closely in order to observe or read: *she bent her head to study the plans.*
3 archaic make an effort to achieve (a result) or take into account (a person or their wishes): *with no husband to study, housekeeping is mere play.*
– PHRASES **in a brown study** absorbed in one's thoughts. [ORIGIN: apparently originally from *brown* in the sense 'gloomy'.]
– ORIGIN Middle English: shortening of Old French *estudie* (noun), *estudier* (verb), both based on Latin *studium* 'zeal, painstaking application'.

study bedroom ▶**noun** Brit. a room used both as a bedroom and as a study, typically by a student who is resident at a university.

study group ▶**noun** a group of people who meet to study a particular subject and then report their findings or recommendations.

study hall ▶**noun** [mass noun] N. Amer. the period of time in a school curriculum set aside for the preparation of school work.
■a schoolroom used for such work.

stuff ▶**noun** [mass noun] **1** matter, material, articles, or activities of a specified or indeterminate kind that are being referred to, indicated, or implied: *a lorry picked the stuff up* | *a girl who's good at the technical stuff.*
■a person's belongings, equipment, or baggage: *he took his stuff and went.* ■Brit. informal, dated worthless or foolish ideas, speech, or writing; rubbish: [as exclamation] ***stuff and nonsense!*** ■informal drink or drugs. ■(**the stuff**) informal money. ■(**one's stuff**) things in which one is knowledgeable and experienced; one's area of expertise: *he* ***knows his stuff*** *and can really write.*
2 the basic constituents or characteristics of something or someone: *Healey was made of sterner stuff* | *such a trip was the stuff of his dreams.*
3 Brit. dated woollen fabric, especially as distinct from silk, cotton, and linen: [as modifier] *her dark stuff gown.*

S

4 N. Amer. (in sport) spin given to a ball to make it vary its course.
■ a player's ability to produce such spin or control the speed of delivery of a ball.
▶ **verb** [with obj.] **1** fill (a receptacle or space) tightly with something: *an old teapot **stuffed full of** cash* | figurative *his head has been **stuffed with** myths and taboos.*
■ informal force or cram (something) tightly into a receptacle or space: *he stuffed a thick wad of notes into his jacket pocket.* ■ informal hastily or clumsily push (something) into a space: *Sadie took the coin and stuffed it in her coat pocket.* ■ fill (the cavity of an item of food) with a savoury or sweet mixture, especially before cooking: *chicken stuffed with mushrooms and breadcrumbs.* ■ (**be stuffed up**) (of a person) have one's nose blocked up with catarrh as a result of a cold. ■ informal fill (oneself) with large amounts of food: *he **stuffed himself with** Parisian chocolates.* ■ [no obj.] informal eat greedily: *I find myself stuffing wildly, mostly when I'm babysitting.* ■ fill out the skin of (a dead animal or bird) with material to restore the original shape and appearance: *he took the bird to a taxidermist to be stuffed* | [as adj. **stuffed**] *a stuffed parrot.* ■ informal fill (envelopes) with identical copies of printed matter: *they spent the whole time in a back room stuffing envelopes.* ■ US place bogus votes in (a ballot box).
2 [usu. in imperative] Brit. informal used to express indifference towards or rejection of (something): *stuff the diet!*
3 Brit. informal defeat heavily in sport: *Town got stuffed every week.*
4 Brit. vulgar slang (of a man) have sexual intercourse with (a woman).
– PHRASES **and stuff** informal said in vague reference to additional things of a similar nature to those specified: *all that running and swimming and stuff.* **bit of stuff** see **BIT**[1]. **get stuffed** [usu. in imperative] Brit. informal said in anger to tell someone to go away or as an expression of contempt. **not give a stuff** Brit. informal said to express indifference or contempt: *I couldn't give a stuff what they think.* **stuff it** Brit. informal said to express indifference, resignation, or rejection: *Stuff it, I'm 61, what do I care?* **that's the stuff** Brit. informal said in approval of what has just been done or said.
– DERIVATIVES **stuffer** noun [in combination] *a sausage-stuffer.*
– ORIGIN Middle English (denoting material for making clothes): shortening of Old French *estoffe* 'material, furniture', *estoffer* 'equip, furnish', from Greek *stuphein* 'draw together'.

stuffed shirt ▶ **noun** informal a conservative, pompous person.

stuff gown ▶ **noun** Brit. a gown worn by a barrister who is not a Queen's (or King's) Counsel.

stuffing ▶ **noun** [mass noun] **1** a mixture used to stuff poultry or meat before cooking.
2 padding used to stuff cushions, furniture, or soft toys.
– PHRASES **knock** (or **take**) **the stuffing out of** informal severely impair the confidence or strength of (someone).

stuffing box ▶ **noun** a casing in which material such as greased wool is compressed around a shaft or axle to form a seal against gas or liquid, used for instance where the propeller shaft of a boat passes through the hull.

stuff sack ▶ **noun** a bag into which a sleeping bag, clothing, and other items can be stuffed or packed for ease of carrying or when not in use.

stuffy ▶ **adjective** (**stuffier**, **stuffiest**) (of a place) lacking fresh air or ventilation: *a stuffy, overcrowded office.*
■ (of a person's nose) blocked up and making breathing difficult, typically as a result of illness. ■ (of a person) not receptive to new or unusual ideas and behaviour; conventional and narrow-minded: *he was steady and rather stuffy.*
– DERIVATIVES **stuffily** adverb, **stuffiness** noun.

Stuka /ˈstuːkə, ˈʃt-/ ▶ **noun** a type of German military aircraft (the Junkers Ju 87) designed for dive-bombing, much used in the Second World War.
– ORIGIN contraction of German *Sturzkampfflugzeug* 'dive-bomber'.

stultify /ˈstʌltɪfʌɪ/ ▶ **verb** (**-ies**, **-ied**) [with obj.] **1** [usu. as adj. **stultifying**] cause to lose enthusiasm and initiative, especially as a result of a tedious or restrictive routine: *the mentally stultifying effects of a disadvantaged home.*
2 cause (someone) to appear foolish or absurd: *Counsel is not expected to **stultify himself** in an attempt to advance his client's interests.*
– DERIVATIVES **stultification** noun, **stultifier** noun.
– ORIGIN mid 18th cent.: from late Latin *stultificare*, from Latin *stultus* 'foolish'.

stum /stʌm/ ▶ **noun** [mass noun] unfermented grape juice.
▶ **verb** (**stummed**, **stumming**) [with obj.] **1** prevent or stop the fermentation of (wine) by fumigating a cask with burning sulphur.
2 renew the fermentation of (wine) by adding stum.
– ORIGIN mid 17th cent.: from Dutch *stom* (noun), *stommen* (verb), from *stom* 'dumb'.

stumble ▶ **verb** [no obj.] trip or momentarily lose one's balance; almost fall: *her foot caught a shoe and she stumbled.*
■ [with adverbial of direction] trip repeatedly as one walks: *his legs still weak, he stumbled after them.* ■ make a mistake or repeated mistakes in speaking: *she **stumbled over** the words.* ■ (**stumble across/on/upon**) find or encounter by chance: *a policeman had stumbled across a gang of youths.*
▶ **noun** an act of stumbling.
■ a stumbling walk: *he parodied my groping stumble across the stage.*
– DERIVATIVES **stumbler** noun, **stumblingly** adverb.
– ORIGIN Middle English (as a verb): from Old Norse, from the Germanic base of **STAMMER**.

stumblebum ▶ **noun** informal, chiefly US a clumsy or inept person.

stumbling block ▶ **noun** a circumstance that causes difficulty or hesitation: *a major stumbling block to the acceptance of homeopathy.*

stumer /ˈstjuːmə/ ▶ **noun** Brit. informal **1** a worthless cheque or a counterfeit coin or note.
2 a failure: *his piece was a stumer, a complete flop.*
– ORIGIN late 19th cent.: of unknown origin.

stump ▶ **noun** **1** the bottom part of a tree left projecting from the ground after most of the trunk has fallen or been cut down.
■ the small projecting remnant of something that has been cut or broken off or worn away: *the stump of an amputated arm.*
2 Cricket each of the three upright pieces of wood which form a wicket.
■ (**stumps**) close of play in a cricket match.
3 Art a cylinder with conical ends made of rolled paper or other soft material, used for softening or blending marks made with a crayon or pencil.
4 [as modifier] engaged in or involving political campaigning: *he is an inspiring stump speaker.* [ORIGIN: referring to the use of a tree stump, from which an orator would speak.]
▶ **verb** [with obj.] **1** (usu. **be stumped**) (of a question or problem) be too hard for; baffle: *education chiefs were stumped by some of the exam questions.*
■ (**be stumped**) be at a loss; be unable to work out what to do or say: *detectives are **stumped for** a reason for the attack.*
2 Cricket (of a wicketkeeper) dismiss (a batsman) by dislodging the bails with the ball while the batsman is out of the crease but not running.
3 [no obj., with adverbial of direction] walk stiffly and noisily: *he stumped away on short thick legs.*
4 chiefly US travel around (a district) making political speeches: *there is no chance that he will be well enough to stump the country* | [no obj.] *the two men had come to the city to stump for the presidential candidate.*
5 use a stump on (a drawing, line, etc.).
– PHRASES **on the stump** informal engaged in political campaigning. **up a stump** US informal in a situation too difficult for one to manage.
– ORIGIN Middle English (denoting a part of a limb remaining after an amputation): from Middle Low German *stump(e)* or Middle Dutch *stomp*. The early sense of the verb was 'stumble'.
▶ **stump something up** Brit. informal pay a sum of money: *a buyer would have to stump up at least £8.5 million for the site.*

stumper ▶ **noun** informal **1** a puzzling question.
2 Cricket a wicketkeeper.

stumpnose ▶ **noun** (pl. same) chiefly S. African a southern African sea bream, popular with anglers.
• *Rhabdosargus* and other genera, family Sparidae: several species, in particular the **white stumpnose** (*R. globiceps*), which is of commercial importance.

stump work ▶ **noun** [mass noun] a type of raised embroidery popular between the 15th and 17th centuries and characterized by elaborate designs padded with wool or hair.

stumpy ▶ **adjective** (**stumpier**, **stumpiest**) short and thick; squat: *weak stumpy legs.*
– DERIVATIVES **stumpily** adverb, **stumpiness** noun.

stun ▶ **verb** (**stunned**, **stunning**) [with obj.] knock unconscious or into a dazed or semi-conscious state: *the man was strangled after being stunned by a blow to the head.*
■ (usu. **be stunned**) astonish or shock (someone) so that they are temporarily unable to react: *the community was stunned by the tragedy.* ■ (of a sound) deafen temporarily: *anyone inside the room that was bombed would be temporarily blinded and stunned.*
– ORIGIN Middle English: shortening of Old French *estoner* 'astonish'.

stung past and past participle of **STING**.

stun grenade ▶ **noun** a grenade that stuns people with its sound and flash, without causing serious injury.

stun gun ▶ **noun** a device used to immobilize an attacker without causing serious injury, typically by administering an electric shock.

stunk past and past participle of **STINK**.

stunner ▶ **noun** informal a strikingly beautiful or impressive person or thing: *the girl was a stunner.*
■ an amazing turn of events.

stunning ▶ **adjective** extremely impressive or attractive: *she looked stunning.*
– DERIVATIVES **stunningly** adverb.

stunsail /ˈstʌns(ə)l/ (also **stuns'l**) ▶ **noun** another term for **STUDDINGSAIL**.
– ORIGIN mid 18th cent.: contraction.

stunt[1] ▶ **verb** [with obj.] [often as adj. **stunted**] retard the growth or development of: *trees damaged by acid rain had stunted branches.*
■ frustrate and spoil: *she was concerned at the stunted lives of those around her.*
– DERIVATIVES **stuntedness** noun.
– ORIGIN late 16th cent. (in the sense 'bring to an abrupt halt'): from dialect *stunt* 'foolish, stubborn', of Germanic origin; perhaps related to **STUMP**.

stunt[2] ▶ **noun** an action displaying spectacular skill and daring.
■ something unusual done to attract attention: *the story was spread as a publicity stunt to help sell books.*
▶ **verb** [no obj.] perform stunts, especially aerobatics: *agile terns are stunting over the water.*
– ORIGIN late 19th cent. (originally US college slang): of unknown origin.

stuntman ▶ **noun** (pl. **-men**) a man employed to take an actor's place in performing dangerous stunts.

stuntwoman ▶ **noun** (pl. **-women**) a woman employed to take an actor's place in performing dangerous stunts.

stupa /ˈstuːpə/ ▶ **noun** a dome-shaped building erected as a Buddhist shrine.
– ORIGIN from Sanskrit *stūpa*.

stupe[1] /stjuːp/ archaic ▶ **noun** a piece of soft cloth or cotton wool dipped in hot water and used to make a poultice.
▶ **verb** [with obj.] treat with such a poultice.
– ORIGIN late Middle English (as a noun): via Latin from Greek *stupē*.

stupe[2] /stjuːp/ ▶ **noun** informal a stupid person.
– ORIGIN mid 18th cent.: abbreviation of **STUPID**.

stupefacient /ˌstjuːpɪˈfeɪʃ(ə)nt/ Medicine ▶ **adjective** (chiefly of a drug) causing semi-consciousness.
▶ **noun** a drug of this type.
– ORIGIN mid 17th cent.: from Latin *stupefacient-* 'stupefying', from the verb *stupefacere*.

stupefy /ˈstjuːpɪfʌɪ/ ▶ **verb** (**-ies**, **-ied**) [with obj.] make (someone) unable to think or feel properly: *the offence of administering drugs to a woman with intent to stupefy her.*
■ astonish and shock: *the amount they spend on clothes would appal their parents and stupefy their grandparents.*
– DERIVATIVES **stupefaction** noun, **stupefier** noun, **stupefyingly** adverb [as submodifier] *a stupefyingly tedious task.*
– ORIGIN late Middle English: from French *stupéfier*, from Latin *stupefacere*, from *stupere* 'be struck senseless'.

stupendous /stjuːˈpɛndəs/ ▶ **adjective** informal extremely impressive: *I have the most stupendous views.*
– DERIVATIVES **stupendously** adverb, **stupendousness** noun.

– ORIGIN mid 16th cent.: from Latin *stupendus* 'to be wondered at' (gerundive of *stupere*) + **-OUS**.

stupid ▶ adjective (**stupider**, **stupidest**) lacking intelligence or common sense: *I was stupid enough to think she was perfect.*
▪dazed and unable to think clearly: *apprehension was numbing her brain and making her stupid.* ▪ informal used to express exasperation or boredom: *she told him to stop messing about with his stupid painting.*
▶ noun informal a stupid person (often used as a term of address): *you're not a coward, stupid!*
– DERIVATIVES **stupidity** noun, **stupidly** adverb.
– ORIGIN mid 16th cent.: from French *stupide* or Latin *stupidus*, from *stupere* 'be amazed or stunned'.

stupidness ▶ noun [mass noun] chiefly W. Indian foolish or nonsensical talk or behaviour: *girl, what stupidness are you talking?*

stupor /ˈstjuːpə/ ▶ noun [in sing.] a state of near-unconsciousness or insensibility: *a drunken stupor.*
– DERIVATIVES **stuporous** adjective.
– ORIGIN late Middle English: from Latin, from *stupere* 'be amazed or stunned'.

sturdy ▶ adjective (**sturdier**, **sturdiest**) (of a person or their body) strongly and solidly built: *he had a sturdy, muscular physique.*
▪strong enough to withstand rough work or treatment: *the bike is sturdy enough to cope with bumpy tracks.* ▪ showing confidence and determination: *the townspeople have a sturdy independence.*
▶ noun [mass noun] vertigo in sheep caused by a tapeworm larva encysted in the brain.
– DERIVATIVES **sturdied** adjective (from the noun), **sturdily** adverb, **sturdiness** noun.
– ORIGIN Middle English (in the senses 'reckless, violent' and 'intractable, obstinate'): shortening of Old French *esturdi* 'stunned, dazed'. The derivation remains obscure; thought by some to be based on Latin *turdus* 'a thrush' (compare with the French phrase *soûl comme une grive* 'drunk as a thrush').

sturgeon /ˈstəːdʒ(ə)n/ ▶ noun a very large primitive fish with bony plates on the body. It occurs in temperate seas and rivers of the northern hemisphere, especially central Eurasia, and is of commercial importance for its caviar and flesh.
• Family Acipenseridae: several genera and species.
– ORIGIN Middle English: from Anglo-Norman French, of Germanic origin; related to Dutch *steur* and German *Stör*.

Sturmabteilung /ˈʃtʊəmabˌtʌɪlʊŋ, German ˈʃtʊrmapˌtaɪlʊŋ/ (abbrev.: **SA**) see **BROWNSHIRT**.
– ORIGIN German, literally 'storm division'.

Sturmer /ˈstəːmə/ (also **Sturmer pippin**) ▶ noun an eating apple of a late-ripening variety with a mainly yellowish-green skin and firm yellowish flesh.
– ORIGIN mid 19th cent.: named after the village of *Sturmer*, on the Essex–Suffolk border, where it was first grown.

Sturm und Drang /ˌʃtʊəm ʊnt ˈdraŋ, German ˌʃtʊrm ʊnt ˈdraŋ/ ▶ noun [mass noun] a literary and artistic movement in Germany in the late 18th century, influenced by Jean-Jacques Rousseau and characterized by the expression of emotional unrest and a rejection of neoclassical literary norms.
– ORIGIN German, literally 'storm and stress'.

Sturt /stəːt/, Charles (1795–1869), English explorer. He led three expeditions into the Australian interior, becoming the first European to discover the Darling River (1828) and the source of the Murray (1830).

Sturt's desert rose ▶ noun see **DESERT ROSE** (sense 3).

stutter ▶ verb [no obj.] talk with continued involuntary repetition of sounds, especially initial consonants: *the child was stuttering in fright.*
▪[with obj.] utter in such a way: *he shyly **stuttered out** an invitation to the cinema* | [with direct speech] *'W-what's happened?' she stuttered.* ▪(of a machine or gun) produce a series of short, sharp sounds: *she flinched as a machine gun stuttered nearby.*
▶ noun a tendency to stutter while speaking.
▪a series of short, sharp sounds produced by a machine or gun.
– DERIVATIVES **stutterer** noun, **stutteringly** adverb.
– ORIGIN late 16th cent. (as a verb): frequentative of dialect *stut*, of Germanic origin; related to German *stossen* 'strike against'.

Stuttgart /ˈʃtʊtgɑːt, German ˈʃtʊtgart/ an industrial city in western Germany, the capital of Baden-Württemberg, on the Neckar River; pop. 591,950 (1991).

sty[1] ▶ noun (pl. **-ies**) a pigsty.
▶ verb (**-ies**, **-ied**) [with obj.] archaic keep (a pig) in a sty: *the most beggarly place that ever pigs were stied in.*
– ORIGIN Old English *stī-* (in *stīfearh* 'sty pig'), probably identical with *stig* 'hall' (see **STEWARD**), of Germanic origin.

sty[2] (also **stye**) ▶ noun (pl. **sties** or **styes**) an inflamed swelling on the edge of an eyelid, caused by bacterial infection of the gland at the base of an eyelash.
– ORIGIN early 17th cent.: from dialect *styany*, from *styan* (from Old English *stīgend* 'riser') + **EYE**.

Stygian /ˈstɪdʒɪən/ ▶ adjective of or relating to the River Styx.
▪poetic/literary very dark: *the Stygian crypt.*

stylar /ˈstʌɪlə/ ▶ adjective Botany of or relating to the style or styles of a flower.

style ▶ noun **1** a manner of doing something: *different styles of management.*
▪a way of painting, writing, composing, building, etc., characteristic of a particular period, place, person, or movement. ▪ a way of using language: *he never wrote in a journalistic style* | [mass noun] *students should pay attention to style and idiom.* ▪ [usu. with negative] a way of behaving or approaching a situation that is characteristic of or favoured by a particular person: *backing out isn't my style.* ▪ an official or legal title: *the partnership traded **under the style of** Storr and Mortimer.*
2 a distinctive appearance, typically determined by the principles according to which something is designed: *the pillars are no exception to the general style.*
▪a particular design of clothing. ▪ a way of arranging the hair.
3 [mass noun] elegance and sophistication: *a sophisticated nightspot with style and taste.*
4 a rod-like object or part, in particular:
▪archaic term for **STYLUS** (in sense 2). ▪ Botany (in a flower) a narrow, typically elongated extension of the ovary, bearing the stigma. ▪ Zoology (in an invertebrate) a small, slender pointed appendage; a stylet.
▶ verb [with obj.] **1** design or make in a particular form: *the yacht is well proportioned and conservatively styled.*
▪arrange (hair) in a particular way: *he styled her hair by twisting it up to give it body.*
2 [with obj. and complement] designate with a particular name, description, or title: *the official is styled principal and vice-chancellor of the university.*
– PHRASES **in style** (or **in grand style**) in an impressive, grand, or luxurious way.
– DERIVATIVES **styleless** adjective, **stylelessness** noun, **styler** noun.
– ORIGIN Middle English (denoting a stylus, also a literary composition, an official title, or a characteristic manner of literary expression): from Old French *stile*, from Latin *stilus*. The verb dates (first in sense 2) from the early 16th cent.

-style ▶ suffix (forming adjectives and adverbs) in a manner characteristic of: *family-style* | *church-style.*
– ORIGIN from **STYLE**.

style sheet ▶ noun Computing a type of template file consisting of font and layout settings to give a standardized look to certain documents.

stylet /ˈstʌɪlɪt/ ▶ noun **1** Medicine a slender probe.
▪a wire or piece of plastic run through a catheter or cannula in order to stiffen it or to clear it.
2 Zoology (in an invertebrate) a small style, especially a piercing mouthpart of an insect.
– ORIGIN late 17th cent.: from French *stilet*, from Italian *stiletto* (see **STILETTO**).

styli plural form of **STYLUS**.

stylish ▶ adjective having or displaying a good sense of style: *these are elegant and stylish performances.*
▪fashionably elegant: *a stylish and innovative range of jewellery.*
– DERIVATIVES **stylishly** adverb, **stylishness** noun.

stylist ▶ noun **1** a person who works creatively in the fashion and beauty industry, in particular:
▪a designer of fashionable styles of clothing. ▪ a hairdresser.
2 a person noted for elegant work or performance, in particular:
▪a writer noted for taking great pains over the style in which he or she writes. ▪ (in sport or music) a person who performs with style.

stylistic ▶ adjective of or concerning style, especially literary style: *the stylistic conventions of magazine stories.*
– DERIVATIVES **stylistically** adverb.
– ORIGIN mid 19th cent.: from **STYLIST**, suggested by German *stilistisch*.

stylistics ▶ plural noun [treated as sing.] the study of the distinctive styles found in particular literary genres and in the works of individual writers.

stylite /ˈstʌɪlʌɪt/ ▶ noun historical an ascetic living on top of a pillar, especially in ancient or medieval Syria, Turkey, and Greece in the 5th century AD.
– ORIGIN mid 17th cent.: from ecclesiastical Greek *stulitēs*, from *stulos* 'pillar'.

stylize (also **-ise**) ▶ verb [with obj.] [usu. as adj. **stylized**] depict or treat in a mannered and non-realistic style: *gracefully shaped vases decorated with stylized but recognizable white lilies.*
– DERIVATIVES **stylization** noun.
– ORIGIN late 19th cent.: from **STYLE**, suggested by German *stilisiren*.

stylo /ˈstʌɪləʊ/ ▶ noun (pl. **-os**) informal short for **STYLOGRAPH**.

stylobate /ˈstʌɪlə(ʊ)beɪt/ ▶ noun a continuous base supporting a row of columns in classical Greek architecture.
– ORIGIN late 17th cent.: via Latin from Greek *stulobatēs*, from *stulos* 'pillar' + *batēs* 'base' (from *bainein* 'to walk').

stylograph ▶ noun a kind of fountain pen having a fine perforated tube instead of a split nib.
– DERIVATIVES **stylographic** adjective.
– ORIGIN mid 19th cent.: from **STYLUS** + **-GRAPH**.

styloid ▶ adjective technical resembling a stylus or pen.
▶ noun short for **STYLOID PROCESS**.

styloid process ▶ noun Anatomy a slender projection of bone, such as that from the lower surface of the temporal bone of the skull, or those at the lower ends of the ulna and radius.

stylolite /ˈstʌɪlə(ʊ)lʌɪt/ ▶ noun Geology an irregular surface or seam within a limestone or other sedimentary rock, characterized by irregular interlocking pegs and sockets around 1 cm in depth and a concentration of insoluble minerals.
▪a grooved peg forming part of such a seam.
– ORIGIN mid 19th cent.: from Greek *stulos* 'column' + **-LITE**.

stylometry /stʌɪˈlɒmɪtri/ ▶ noun [mass noun] the statistical analysis of variations in literary style between one writer or genre and another.
– DERIVATIVES **stylometric** /ˌstʌɪləˈmɛtrɪk/ adjective.

stylophone ▶ noun a miniature electronic musical instrument producing a distinctive buzzing sound when a stylus is drawn along its metal keyboard.

stylopized /ˈstʌɪləpʌɪzd/ (also **-ised**) ▶ adjective Entomology (of a bee or other insect) parasitized by a stylops.

stylops /ˈstʌɪlɒps/ ▶ noun (pl. same) a minute insect that spends part or all of its life as an internal parasite of other insects, especially bees or wasps. The males are winged and the females typically retain a grub-like form and remain parasitic.
• Order Strepsiptera, in particular genus *Stylops*, family Stylopidae.
– DERIVATIVES **stylopid** /stʌɪˈlɒpɪd/ noun & adjective.
– ORIGIN late 19th cent.: modern Latin, from Greek *stulos* 'column' + *ōps* 'eye, face'.

stylus /ˈstʌɪləs/ ▶ noun (pl. **styli** /-lʌɪ, -liː/ or **styluses**) **1** a hard point, typically of diamond or sapphire, following a groove in a gramophone record and transmitting the recorded sound for reproduction.
▪a similar point producing such a groove when recording sound.
2 an ancient writing implement, consisting of a small rod with a pointed end for scratching letters on wax-covered tablets, and a blunt end for obliterating them.
▪an implement of similar shape used especially for engraving and tracing. ▪ Computing a pen-like device used to input handwritten text or drawings directly into a computer.
– ORIGIN early 18th cent. (as a modern Latin term in botany: see **STYLE**): erroneous spelling of Latin *stilus*.

stymie /ˈstʌɪmi/ ▶ verb (**stymies**, **stymied**, **stymying** or **stymieing**) [with obj.] informal prevent or hinder the progress of: *the changes must not be allowed to stymie new medical treatments.*
– ORIGIN mid 19th cent. (originally a golfing term,

S

denoting a situation on the green where a ball obstructs the shot of another player): of unknown origin.

styptic /ˈstɪptɪk/ Medicine ▶ adjective (of a substance) capable of causing bleeding to stop when it is applied to a wound.
▶ noun a substance of this kind.
− ORIGIN late Middle English: via Latin from Greek *stuptikos*, from *stuphein* 'to contract'.

styptic pencil ▶ noun a stick of a styptic substance, used to treat small cuts.

styrax /ˈstʌɪraks/ ▶ noun variant of **STORAX**.

styrene /ˈstʌɪriːn/ ▶ noun [mass noun] Chemistry an unsaturated liquid hydrocarbon obtained as a petroleum by-product. It is easily polymerized and is used to make plastics and resins.
● Chem. formula: $C_6H_5CH{=}CH_2$.
− ORIGIN late 19th cent.: from **STYRAX** + **-ENE**.

Styria /ˈstɪrɪə/ a mountainous state of SE Austria; capital, Graz. German name **STEIERMARK**.

styrofoam ▶ noun [mass noun] (trademark in the US) a kind of expanded polystyrene.
− ORIGIN 1950s: from **POLYSTYRENE** + **FOAM**.

Styx /stɪks/ Greek Mythology one of the nine rivers in the underworld, over which Charon ferried the souls of the dead.
− ORIGIN from Greek *Stux*, from *stugnos* 'hateful, gloomy'.

suasion /ˈsweɪʒ(ə)n/ ▶ noun [mass noun] formal persuasion as opposed to force or compulsion.
− ORIGIN late Middle English: from Old French, or from Latin *suasio(n-)*, from *suadere* 'to urge'.

suasive /ˈsweɪsɪv/ ▶ adjective serving to persuade.
■ Grammar denoting a class of English verbs, for example *insist*, whose meaning includes the notion of persuading and which take a subordinate clause whose verb may either be in the subjunctive or take a modal.

suave /swɑːv/ ▶ adjective (**suaver**, **suavest**) (especially of a man) charming, confident, and elegant: *all the waiters were suave and deferential*.
− DERIVATIVES **suavely** adverb, **suaveness** noun, **suavity** /-vɪti/ noun (pl. **-ies**).
− ORIGIN late Middle English (in the sense 'gracious, agreeable'): from Old French, or from Latin *suavis* 'agreeable'. The current sense dates from the mid 19th cent.

sub informal ▶ noun **1** a submarine.
■ N. Amer. short for **SUBMARINE SANDWICH**.
2 a subscription.
3 a substitute, especially in a sporting team.
4 a subeditor.
5 Brit. an advance or loan against expected income.
▶ verb (**subbed**, **subbing**) **1** [no obj.] act as a substitute for someone: *he often subbed for Walker at the goal line.*
2 [with obj.] Brit. lend or advance a sum to (someone) against expected income: *who'll sub me till Thursday?*
3 [with obj.] subedit: *reporters submit copy which is mercilessly subbed and rewritten.*

sub- ▶ prefix **1** at, to, or from a lower level or position: *subalpine.*
■ lower in rank: *subaltern | subdeacon.* ■ of a smaller size; of a subordinate nature: *subculture.*
2 somewhat; nearly; more or less: *subantarctic.*
3 denoting subsequent or secondary action of the same kind: *sublet | subdivision.*
4 denoting support: *subvention.*
5 Chemistry in names of compounds containing a relatively small proportion of a component: *suboxide.*
− ORIGIN from Latin *sub* 'under, close to'.

> **USAGE** Sub- is also found assimilated in the following forms: **suc-** before **c**; **suf-** before **f**; **sug-** before **g**; **sup-** before **p**; **sur-** before **r**; **sus-** before **c, p, t**.

subacid ▶ adjective (of a fruit) moderately sharp to the taste.
− ORIGIN mid 17th cent.: from Latin *subacidus* (see **SUB-**, **ACID**).

subacute ▶ adjective **1** Medicine (of a condition) between acute and chronic.
2 moderately acute in shape or angle.

subadult ▶ noun Zoology an animal that is not fully adult.

subaerial ▶ adjective Geology existing, occurring, or formed in the open air or on the earth's surface, not under water or underground.
− DERIVATIVES **subaerially** adverb.

subagency ▶ noun (pl. **-ies**) a subordinate commercial, political, or other agency.
− DERIVATIVES **subagent** noun.

subalpine ▶ adjective of or situated on the higher slopes of mountains just below the treeline.

subaltern /ˈsʌb(ə)lt(ə)n/ ▶ noun an officer in the British army below the rank of captain, especially a second lieutenant.
▶ adjective **1** of lower status: *the private tutor was a recognized subaltern part of the bourgeois family.*
2 Logic, dated (of a proposition) implied by another proposition (e.g. as a particular affirmative is by a universal one), but not implying it in return.
− ORIGIN late 16th cent. (as an adjective): from late Latin *subalternus*, from Latin *sub-* 'next below' + *alternus* 'every other'.

subantarctic ▶ adjective of or relating to the region immediately north of the Antarctic Circle.

sub-aqua ▶ adjective of or relating to swimming or exploring under water, especially with an aqualung: *sub-aqua equipment.*
▶ noun [mass noun] underwater swimming or exploration with an aqualung.
− ORIGIN 1950s: from **SUB-** 'under' + Latin *aqua* 'water'.

sub-aquatic ▶ adjective underwater: *a narrow sub-aquatic microclimate.*

subaqueous ▶ adjective existing, formed, or taking place under water.
■ figurative lacking in substance or strength: *the light that filtered through the leaves was pale, subaqueous.*

subarachnoid ▶ adjective Anatomy denoting or occurring in the fluid-filled space around the brain between the arachnoid membrane and the pia mater, through which major blood vessels pass.

subarctic ▶ adjective of or relating to the region immediately south of the Arctic Circle.

sub-assembly ▶ noun (pl. **-ies**) a unit assembled separately but designed to be incorporated with other units into a larger manufactured product.

Sub-Atlantic ▶ adjective Geology of, relating to, or denoting the fifth climatic stage of the postglacial period in northern Europe, following the Sub-Boreal stage (from about 2,800 years ago to the present day). The climate has been cooler and wetter than in the earlier postglacial periods.
■ [as noun **the Sub-Atlantic**] the Sub-Atlantic climatic stage.

subatomic ▶ adjective smaller than or occurring within an atom.

subatomic particle ▶ noun see **PARTICLE** (sense 1).

subaudition ▶ noun a thing that is not stated, only implied or inferred.
− ORIGIN late 18th cent.: from late Latin *subauditio(n-)*, from *subaudire* 'understand'.

sub-basement ▶ noun a storey below a basement.

Sub-Boreal /ˈbɔːrɪəl/ ▶ adjective Geology of, relating to, or denoting the fourth climatic stage of the postglacial period in northern Europe, between the Atlantic and Sub-Atlantic stages (about 5,000 to 2,800 years ago). The stage corresponds to the Neolithic period and Bronze Age, and the climate was cooler and drier than previously but still warmer than today.
■ [as noun **the Sub-Boreal**] the Sub-Boreal climatic stage.

sub-breed ▶ noun a minor variant of a breed; a secondary breed.

Subbuteo /sʌˈbjuːtɪəʊ/ ▶ noun trademark a table-top version of soccer in which players use their fingers to flick miniature figures of their footballers at the ball in order to strike it towards the goal.
− ORIGIN 1940s: punningly from Latin *Falco subbuteo* 'hobby falcon', represented on Subbuteo products.

subcarrier ▶ noun Telecommunications a carrier wave modulated by a signal wave and then used with other subcarriers to modulate the main carrier wave.

subcategory ▶ noun (pl. **-ies**) a secondary or subordinate category.
− DERIVATIVES **subcategorization** noun, **subcategorize** (also **-ise**) verb.

subclass ▶ noun a secondary or subordinate class.
■ Biology a taxonomic category that ranks below class and above order.

sub-clause ▶ noun **1** chiefly Law a subsidiary section of a clause of a bill, contract, or treaty.
2 Grammar a subordinate clause.

subclavian /sʌbˈkleɪvɪən/ ▶ adjective Anatomy relating to or denoting an artery or vein which serves the neck and arm on the left or right side of the body.
− ORIGIN mid 17th cent.: from modern Latin *subclavius*, from *sub* 'under' + *clavis* 'key' (see **CLAVICLE**), + **-IAN**.

subclinical ▶ adjective Medicine relating to or denoting a disease which is not severe enough to present definite or readily observable symptoms.

subcommittee ▶ noun a committee composed of some members of a larger committee, board, or other body and reporting to it.

subcompact ▶ noun N. Amer. a motor vehicle which is smaller than a compact.

subconical ▶ adjective approximately conical.

subconscious ▶ adjective of or concerning the part of the mind of which one is not fully aware but which influences one's actions and feelings: *my subconscious fear.*
▶ noun (**one's/the subconscious**) this part of the mind (not in technical use in psychoanalysis, where *unconscious* is preferred).
− DERIVATIVES **subconsciously** adverb, **subconsciousness** noun.

subcontinent ▶ noun a large distinguishable part of a continent, such as North America or southern Africa. See also **INDIAN SUBCONTINENT**.
− DERIVATIVES **subcontinental** adjective.

subcontract ▶ verb /sʌbkən'trakt/ [with obj.] employ a firm or person outside one's company to do (work) as part of a larger project: *we would subcontract the translation work out.*
■ [no obj.] (of a firm or person) carry out work for a company as part of a larger project.
▶ noun /sʌbˈkɒntrakt/ a contract for a company or person to do work for another company as part of a larger project.

subcontractor ▶ noun a firm or person that carries out work for a company as part of a larger project.

subcontrary /sʌbˈkɒntrəri/ Logic, dated ▶ adjective denoting propositions which can both be true, but cannot both be false (e.g. *some X are Y* and *some X are not Y*).
▶ noun (pl. **-ies**) a proposition of this kind.
− ORIGIN late 16th cent.: from late Latin *subcontrarius*, translation of Greek *hupenantios*.

subcortical ▶ adjective below the cortex.
■ Anatomy relating to or denoting the region of the brain below the cortex.

subcostal ▶ adjective Anatomy beneath a rib; below the ribs.

subcritical ▶ adjective Physics below a critical threshold, in particular:
■ (in nuclear physics) containing or involving less than the critical mass. ■ (of a flow of fluid) slower than the speed at which waves travel in the fluid.

subculture ▶ noun a cultural group within a larger culture, often having beliefs or interests at variance with those of the larger culture.
− DERIVATIVES **subcultural** adjective.

subcutaneous ▶ adjective Anatomy & Medicine situated or applied under the skin: *subcutaneous fat.*
− DERIVATIVES **subcutaneously** adverb.

subdeacon ▶ noun (in some Christian Churches) a minister of an order ranking below deacon. Now largely obsolete in the Western Church, the liturgical role being taken by other ministers.
− DERIVATIVES **subdiaconate** noun.

subdirectory ▶ noun (pl. **-ies**) Computing a directory below another directory in a hierarchy.

subdivide ▶ verb [with obj.] divide (something that has already been divided or that is a separate unit): *the heading was subdivided into eight separate sections.*
− ORIGIN late Middle English: from Latin *subdividere* (see **SUB-**, **DIVIDE**).

subdivision ▶ noun [mass noun] the action of subdividing or being subdivided.
■ [count noun] a secondary or subordinate division. ■ [count noun] US & Austral. an area of land divided into plots for sale; an area of housing. ■ Biology any taxonomic subcategory, especially (in botany) one that ranks below division and above class.

subdominant ▶ noun Music the fourth note of the diatonic scale of any key.

subduction /səbˈdʌkʃ(ə)n/ ▶ **noun** [mass noun] Geology the sideways and downward movement of the edge of a plate of the earth's crust into the mantle beneath another plate.
– DERIVATIVES **subduct** verb.
– ORIGIN 1970s: via French from Latin *subductio(n-)*, from *subduct-* 'drawn from below', from the verb *subducere*.

subdue ▶ **verb** (**subdues**, **subdued**, **subduing**) [with obj.] overcome, quieten, or bring under control (a feeling or person): *she managed to subdue an instinct to applaud.*
■ bring (a country or people) under control by force: *Charles went on a campaign to subdue the Saxons.*
– DERIVATIVES **subduable** adjective.
– ORIGIN late Middle English: from Anglo-Norman French *suduire*, from Latin *subducere*, literally 'draw from below'.

subdued ▶ **adjective 1** (of a person or their manner) quiet and rather reflective or depressed: *I felt strangely subdued as I drove home.*
2 (of colour or lighting) soft and restrained: *a subdued plaid shirt.*

subdural /sʌbˈdjʊər(ə)l/ ▶ **adjective** Anatomy situated or occurring between the dura mater and the arachnoid membrane of the brain and spinal cord.

subedit ▶ **verb** (**subedited**, **subediting**) [with obj.] chiefly Brit. check, correct, and adjust the extent of (the text of a newspaper or magazine before printing), typically also writing headlines and captions: *he wrote articles on sport while subediting the* Oxford Magazine.
– DERIVATIVES **subeditor** noun.

suberin /ˈsjuːb(ə)rɪn/ ▶ **noun** [mass noun] Botany an inert impermeable waxy substance present in the cell walls of corky tissues.
– ORIGIN mid 19th cent.: from Latin *suber* 'cork' + **-IN**[1].

suberize /ˈsjuːb(ə)rʌɪz/ (also **-ise**) ▶ **verb** [with obj.] [usu. as adj. **suberized**] Botany impregnate (the wall of a plant cell) with suberin: *suberized cell walls.*
– DERIVATIVES **suberization** noun.

subfamily ▶ **noun** (pl. **-ies**) a subdivision of a group.
■ Biology a taxonomic category that ranks below family and above tribe or genus, usually ending in *-inae* (in zoology) or *-oideae* (in botany).

subfloor ▶ **noun** the foundation for a floor in a building.

subform ▶ **noun** a subordinate or secondary form.

subframe ▶ **noun** a supporting frame, especially one into which a window or door is set, or one to which the engine or suspension of a car without a true chassis is attached.

subfusc /ˈsʌbfʌsk, sʌbˈfʌsk/ ▶ **adjective** poetic/literary dull; gloomy: *the light was subfusc and aqueous.*
▶ **noun** [mass noun] Brit. the formal clothing worn for examinations and formal occasions at some universities.
– ORIGIN early 18th cent.: from Latin *subfuscus*, from *sub-* 'somewhat' + *fuscus* 'dark brown'.

subgenus ▶ **noun** (pl. **subgenera**) Biology a taxonomic category that ranks below genus and above species.
– DERIVATIVES **subgeneric** adjective.

subglacial ▶ **adjective** Geology situated or occurring underneath a glacier or ice sheet.

subgroup ▶ **noun** a subdivision of a group.
■ Mathematics a group whose members are all members of another group, both being subject to the same operations.

subharmonic ▶ **noun** an oscillation with a frequency equal to an integral submultiple of another frequency.
▶ **adjective** denoting or involving a subharmonic.

sub-heading (also **sub-head**) ▶ **noun** a heading given to a subsection of a piece of writing.

subhuman ▶ **adjective** of a lower order of being than the human.
■ Zoology (of a primate) closely related to humans. ■ derogatory (of people or their behaviour) not worthy of a human being; debased or depraved: *he regards all PR people as subhuman.*
▶ **noun** a subhuman creature or person.

subjacent /səbˈdʒeɪs(ə)nt/ ▶ **adjective** technical situated below something else.
– DERIVATIVES **subjacency** noun.
– ORIGIN late 16th cent.: from Latin *subjacent-* 'lying underneath', from *sub-* 'under' + *jacere* 'to lie'.

subject ▶ **noun** /ˈsʌbdʒɪkt/ **1** a person or thing that is being discussed, described, or dealt with: *I've said all there is to be said on the subject | he's the subject of a major new biography.*
■ a person or circumstance giving rise to a specified feeling, response, or action: *the incident was the* **subject** *of international condemnation.* ■ Grammar a noun phrase functioning as one of the main components of a clause, being the element about which the rest of the clause is predicated. ■ Logic the part of a proposition about which a statement is made. ■ Music a theme of a fugue or of a piece in sonata form; a leading phrase or motif. ■ a person who is the focus of scientific or medical attention or experiment.
2 a branch of knowledge studied or taught in a school, college, or university.
3 a citizen or member of a state other than its supreme ruler.
4 Philosophy a thinking or feeling entity; the conscious mind; the ego, especially as opposed to anything external to the mind.
■ the central substance or core of a thing as opposed to its attributes.
▶ **adjective** /ˈsʌbdʒɪkt/ [predic.] (**subject to**) **1** likely or prone to be affected by (a particular condition or occurrence, typically an unwelcome or unpleasant one): *he was subject to bouts of manic depression.*
2 dependent or conditional upon: *the proposed merger is subject to the approval of the shareholders.*
3 under the authority of: *ministers are subject to the laws of the land.*
■ [attrib.] under the control or domination of (another ruler, country, or government): *the Greeks were the first subject people to break free from Ottoman rule.*
▶ **adverb** /ˈsʌbdʒɪkt/ (**subject to**) conditionally upon: *subject to the EC's agreement, we intend to set up an enterprise zone in the area.*
▶ **verb** /səbˈdʒɛkt/ [with obj.] **1** (**subject someone/thing to**) cause or force to undergo (a particular experience of form of treatment): *he'd subjected her to a terrifying ordeal.*
2 bring (a person or country) under one's control or jurisdiction, typically by using force: *the city had been* **subjected to** *Macedonian rule.*
– DERIVATIVES **subjection** noun, **subjectless** adjective.
– ORIGIN Middle English (in the sense '(person) owing obedience'): from Old French *suget*, from Latin *subjectus* 'brought under', past participle of *subicere*, from *sub-* 'under' + *jacere* 'throw'. Senses relating to philosophy, logic, and grammar are derived ultimately from Aristotle's use of *to hupokeimenon* meaning 'material from which things are made' and 'subject of attributes and predicates'.

subject catalogue ▶ **noun** a catalogue, especially in a library, that is arranged according to the subjects treated.

subjective ▶ **adjective 1** based on or influenced by personal feelings, tastes, or opinions: *his views are highly subjective | there is always the danger of making a subjective judgement.* Contrasted with **OBJECTIVE**.
■ dependent on the mind or on an individual's perception for its existence.
2 Grammar of, relating to, or denoting a case of nouns and pronouns used for the subject of a sentence.
▶ **noun** (**the subjective**) Grammar the subjective case.
– DERIVATIVES **subjectively** adverb, **subjectiveness** noun, **subjectivity** noun.
– ORIGIN late Middle English (originally in the sense 'characteristic of a political subject, submissive'): from Latin *subjectivus*, from *subject-* 'brought under' (see **SUBJECT**).

subjective case ▶ **noun** Grammar the nominative.

subjectivism ▶ **noun** [mass noun] Philosophy the doctrine that knowledge is merely subjective and that there is no external or objective truth.
– DERIVATIVES **subjectivist** noun & adjective.

subject matter ▶ **noun** [mass noun] the topic dealt with or the subject represented in a debate, exposition, or work of art.

subjoin ▶ **verb** [with obj.] formal add (comments or supplementary information) at the end of a speech or text.
– ORIGIN late 16th cent.: from obsolete French *subjoindre*, from Latin *subjungere*, from *sub-* 'in addition' + *jungere* 'to join'.

sub judice /sʌb ˈdʒuːdɪsi, sʊb ˈjuːdɪkeɪ/ ▶ **adjective** Law under judicial consideration and therefore prohibited from public discussion elsewhere: *the cases were still sub judice.*
– ORIGIN Latin, literally 'under a judge'.

subjugate /ˈsʌbdʒʊgeɪt/ ▶ **verb** [with obj.] bring under domination or control, especially by conquest: *the invaders had soon subjugated most of the native population.*
■ (**subjugate someone/thing to**) make someone or something subordinate to: *the new ruler firmly subjugated the Church to the state.*
– DERIVATIVES **subjugation** noun, **subjugator** noun.
– ORIGIN late Middle English: from late Latin *subjugat-* 'brought under a yoke', from the verb *subjugare*, based on *jugum* 'yoke'.

subjunct /ˈsʌbjʌŋ(k)t/ ▶ **noun** Grammar an adverb or prepositional phrase used in a role that does not form part of the basic clause structure, for example *kindly* in *he kindly offered to help.*
– ORIGIN early 20th cent.: from Latin *subjunctus*, past participle of *subjungere* (see **SUBJOIN**).

subjunctive /səbˈdʒʌŋ(k)tɪv/ Grammar ▶ **adjective** relating to or denoting a mood of verbs expressing what is imagined or wished or possible. Compare with **INDICATIVE**.
▶ **noun** a verb in the subjunctive mood.
■ (**the subjunctive**) the subjunctive mood.
– DERIVATIVES **subjunctively** adverb.
– ORIGIN mid 16th cent.: from French *subjonctif, -ive* or late Latin *subjunctivus*, from *subjungere* (see **SUBJOIN**), rendering Greek *hupotaktikos* 'subjoined'.

USAGE … *if I* **were** *you; the report recommends that he* **face** *the tribunal; it is important that they* **be** *aware of the provisions of the act.* These sentences all contain a verb in the **subjunctive mood**. The subjunctive is used to express situations which are hypothetical or not yet realized, and is typically used for what is imagined, hoped for, demanded, or expected. In English the subjunctive mood is fairly uncommon (especially in comparison with other languages such as French and Spanish), mainly because most of the functions of the subjunctive are covered by modal verbs such as **might**, **could**, and **should**. In fact, in English the subjunctive is often indistinguishable from the ordinary **indicative mood**, since its form in most contexts is identical. It is distinctive only in the third person singular, where the normal indicative **-s** ending is absent (*he* **face** rather than *he* **faces** in the example above), and in the verb 'to be' (*I* **were** rather than *I* **was** and *they* **be** rather than *they* **are** in the examples above). In modern English the subjunctive mood still exists but is regarded in many contexts as optional. Use of the subjunctive tends to convey a more formal tone but there are few people who would regard its absence as actually wrong. Today it survives mostly in fixed expressions, as in **be** *that as it may; God* **help** *you;* **perish** *the thought;* and **come** *what may.*

subkingdom ▶ **noun** Biology a taxonomic category that ranks below kingdom and above phylum or division.

sublanguage ▶ **noun** a specialized language or jargon associated with a specific group or context.

sublate /səˈbleɪt/ ▶ **verb** [with obj.] Philosophy assimilate (a smaller entity) into a larger one: *fragmented aspects of the self the subject is unable to sublate.*
– DERIVATIVES **sublation** noun.
– ORIGIN mid 19th cent.: from Latin *sublat-* 'taken away', from *sub-* 'from below' + *lat-* (from the stem of *tollere* 'take away').

sublateral ▶ **noun** a side shoot developing from a lateral shoot or branch of a plant.

sublease ▶ **noun** a lease of a property by a tenant to a subtenant.
▶ **verb** another term for **SUBLET**.

sub-lessee ▶ **noun** a person who holds a sublease.

sub-lessor ▶ **noun** a person who grants a sublease.

sublet ▶ **verb** /sʌbˈlɛt/ (**subletting**; past and past participle **sublet**) [with obj.] lease (a property) to a subtenant: *I quit my job and sublet my apartment.*
▶ **noun** /ˈsʌblɛt/ another term for **SUBLEASE**.
■ informal a property that has been subleased.

sublethal ▶ **adjective** having an effect less than lethal.

sub lieutenant ▶ **noun** a rank of officer in the Royal Navy, above midshipman and below lieutenant.

sublimate /ˈsʌblɪmeɪt/ ▶ **verb 1** [with obj.] (in psychoanalytic theory) divert or modify (an instinctual impulse) into a culturally higher or socially more acceptable activity: *people who will*

S

*sublimate sexuality **into** activities which help to build up and preserve civilization.*
■transform (something) into a purer or idealized form: *attractive rhythms are **sublimated** and integrated **into** a much larger context.*
2 Chemistry another term for **SUBLIME**.
▶**noun** /also 'sʌblɪmət/ Chemistry a solid deposit of a substance which has sublimed.
– DERIVATIVES **sublimation** noun.
– ORIGIN late Middle English (in the sense 'raise to a higher status'): from Latin *sublimat-* 'raised up', from the verb *sublimare*.

sublime ▶**adjective** (**sublimer**, **sublimest**) of such excellence, grandeur, or beauty as to inspire great admiration or awe: *Mozart's sublime piano concertos* | [as noun **the sublime**] *experiences that ranged **from the sublime to the ridiculous**.*
■used to denote the extreme or unparalleled nature of a person's attitude or behaviour: *he had the sublime confidence of youth.*
▶**verb 1** [no obj.] Chemistry (of a solid substance) change directly into vapour when heated, typically forming a solid deposit again on cooling.
■[with obj.] cause (a substance) to do this: *these crystals could be sublimed under a vacuum.*
2 [with obj.] archaic elevate to a high degree of moral or spiritual purity or excellence.
– DERIVATIVES **sublimely** adverb, **sublimity** noun.
– ORIGIN late 16th cent. (in the sense 'dignified, aloof'): from Latin *sublimis*, from *sub-* 'up to' + a second element perhaps related to *limen* 'threshold', *limus* 'oblique'.

Sublime Porte ▶**noun** see **PORTE**.

subliminal /sə'blɪmɪn(ə)l/ ▶**adjective** Psychology (of a stimulus or mental process) below the threshold of sensation or consciousness; perceived by or affecting someone's mind without their being aware of it.
– DERIVATIVES **subliminally** adverb.
– ORIGIN late 19th cent.: from **SUB-** 'below' + Latin *limen*, *limin-* 'threshold' + **-AL**.

subliminal advertising ▶**noun** [mass noun] the use by advertisers of images and sounds to influence consumers' responses without their being conscious of it.

sublingual ▶**adjective** Anatomy & Medicine situated or applied under the tongue.
■denoting a pair of small salivary glands beneath the tongue.
– DERIVATIVES **sublingually** adverb.

sublittoral /sʌb'lɪt(ə)r(ə)l/ chiefly Ecology ▶**adjective** (of a marine animal, plant, or deposit) living, growing, or accumulating near to or just below the shore.
■relating to or denoting a biogeographic zone extending (in the sea) from the average line of low tide to the edge of the continental shelf or (in a large lake) beyond the littoral zone but still well lit.
▶**noun** (**the sublittoral**) the sublittoral zone.

Sub-Lt. ▶**abbreviation for** Sub Lieutenant.

sublunar ▶**adjective** Astronomy within the moon's orbit and subject to its influence.

sublunary /sʌb'lu:n(ə)ri/ ▶**adjective** poetic/literary belonging to this world as contrasted with a better or more spiritual one: *the concept was irrational to sublunary minds.*
– ORIGIN late 16th cent. (in the sense 'terrestrial'): from modern Latin *sublunaris*.

subluxation /ˌsʌblʌk'seɪʃ(ə)n/ ▶**noun** Medicine a partial dislocation.
■a slight misalignment of the vertebrae, regarded in chiropractic theory as the cause of many health problems.
– ORIGIN late 17th cent.: from modern Latin *subluxatio(n-)* (see **SUB-**, **LUXATE**).

sub-machine gun ▶**noun** a hand-held lightweight machine gun.

submandibular /ˌsʌbman'dɪbjʊlə/ ▶**adjective** Anatomy situated beneath the jaw or mandible.
■relating to or affecting a submandibular gland.

submandibular gland ▶**noun** Anatomy either of a pair of salivary glands situated below the parotid glands. Also called **SUBMAXILLARY GLAND**.

submarginal ▶**adjective** (of land) not allowing profitable farming or cultivation.

submarine ▶**noun** a warship with a streamlined hull designed to operate completely submerged in the sea for long periods, equipped with an internal store of air and a periscope and typically armed with torpedoes and/or missiles.
■a submersible craft of any kind. ■N. Amer. a submarine sandwich.
▶**adjective** existing, occurring, done, or used under the surface of the sea: *submarine volcanic activity.*
– DERIVATIVES **submariner** noun.

submarine sandwich ▶**noun** N. Amer. another term for **HOAGIE**.

submaxillary gland /ˌsʌbmak'sɪləri/ ▶**noun** another term for **SUBMANDIBULAR GLAND**.

submediant ▶**noun** Music the sixth note of the diatonic scale of any key.

submenu ▶**noun** Computing a menu accessed from a more general menu.

submerge ▶**verb** [with obj.] (usu. **be submerged**) cause to be under water: *houses had been flooded and cars submerged.*
■[no obj.] descend below the surface of an area of water: *the U-boat had had time to submerge.* ■completely cover or obscure: *the tensions submerged earlier in the campaign now came to the fore.*
– DERIVATIVES **submergence** noun, **submergible** adjective.
– ORIGIN early 17th cent.: from Latin *submergere*, from *sub-* 'under' + *mergere* 'to dip'.

submerse /səb'mə:s/ ▶**verb** [with obj.] submerge: *pellets were then submersed in agar.*
▶**adjective** Botany denoting or characteristic of a plant growing entirely under water. Contrasted with **EMERSE**.
– DERIVATIVES **submersion** noun.
– ORIGIN late Middle English: from Latin *submers-* 'plunged below', from the verb *submergere* (see **SUBMERGE**).

submersible ▶**adjective** designed to be completely submerged and/or to operate while submerged.
▶**noun** a small boat or other craft of this kind, especially one designed for research and exploration.

submicroscopic ▶**adjective** too small to be seen by an ordinary light microscope.

subminiature ▶**adjective** of greatly reduced size.
■(of a camera) very small and using 16-mm film.

submission ▶**noun** [mass noun] **1** the action or fact of accepting or yielding to a superior force or to the will or authority of another person: *they were forced into submission.*
■[count noun] Wrestling an act of surrendering to a hold by one's opponent. ■archaic humility; meekness: *servile flattery and submission.*
2 the action of presenting a proposal, application, or other document for consideration or judgement: *reports should be prepared for submission at partners' meetings.*
■[count noun] a proposal, application, or other document presented in this way. ■[count noun] Law a proposition or argument presented by counsel to a judge or jury.
– ORIGIN late Middle English: from Old French, or from Latin *submissio(n-)*, from the verb *submittere* (see **SUBMIT**).

submissive ▶**adjective** ready to conform to the authority or will of others; meekly obedient or passive.
– DERIVATIVES **submissively** adverb, **submissiveness** noun.
– ORIGIN late 16th cent.: from **SUBMISSION**, on the pattern of pairs such as *remission*, *remissive*.

submit ▶**verb** (**submitted**, **submitting**) **1** [no obj.] accept or yield to a superior force or to the authority or will of another person: *the original settlers were forced to **submit to** Bulgarian rule.*
■(**submit oneself**) consent to undergo a certain treatment: *he **submitted himself to** a body search.* ■[with obj.] subject to a particular process, treatment, or condition: *samples **submitted to** low pressure while being airfreighted.* ■agree to refer a matter to a third party for decision or adjudication: *the United States refused to **submit to** arbitration.*
2 [with obj.] present (a proposal, application, or other document) to a person or body for consideration or judgement: *the panel's report was **submitted to** a parliamentary committee.*
■[with clause] (especially in judicial contexts) suggest; argue: *he submitted that such measures were justified.*
– DERIVATIVES **submitter** noun.
– ORIGIN late Middle English: from Latin *submittere*, from *sub-* 'under' + *mittere* 'send, put'. Sense 2 'present for judgement' dates from the mid 16th cent.

submodifier ▶**noun** Grammar an adverb used in front of an adjective or another adverb to modify its meaning, for example *very* in *very cold* or *unusually* in *an unusually large house.*
– DERIVATIVES **submodification** noun, **submodify** verb.

submontane /ˌsʌb'mɒnteɪn/ ▶**adjective** passing under or through mountains.
■situated in the foothills or lower slopes of a mountain range.

submucosa /ˌsʌbmjʊ:'kəʊsə/ ▶**noun** (pl. **submucosae**) Physiology the layer of areolar connective tissue lying beneath a mucous membrane.
– DERIVATIVES **submucosal** adjective.
– ORIGIN late 19th cent.: from modern Latin *submucosa (membrana)*, feminine of *submucosus* 'submucous'.

submultiple ▶**noun** a number that can be divided exactly into a specified number.
▶**adjective** being such a number.

submunition /ˌsʌbmju:'nɪʃ(ə)n/ ▶**noun** a small weapon or device that is part of a larger warhead and separates from it prior to impact.

subnetwork (also **subnet**) ▶**noun** Computing a part of a larger network such as the Internet.

subnormal ▶**adjective** not meeting standards or reaching a level regarded as usual, especially with respect to intelligence or development.
– DERIVATIVES **subnormality** noun.

sub-nuclear ▶**adjective** Physics occurring in or smaller than an atomic nucleus.

suboptimal ▶**adjective** technical of less than the highest standard or quality.

sub-orbital ▶**adjective 1** situated below or behind the orbit of the eye.
2 of, relating to, or denoting a trajectory that does not complete a full orbit of the earth or other celestial body.

suborder ▶**noun** Biology a taxonomic category that ranks below order and above family.

subordinary ▶**noun** (pl. **-ies**) Heraldry a simple device or bearing that is less common than the ordinaries (e.g. roundel, orle, lozenge).

subordinate ▶**adjective** /sə'bɔ:dɪnət/ lower in rank or position: *his subordinate officers.*
■of less or secondary importance: *in adventure stories, character must be **subordinate to** action.*
▶**noun** /sə'bɔ:dɪnət/ a person under the authority or control of another within an organization.
▶**verb** /sə'bɔ:dɪneɪt/ [with obj.] treat or regard as of lesser importance than something else: *practical considerations were **subordinated to** political expediency.*
■make subservient to or dependent on something else.
– DERIVATIVES **subordinately** adverb, **subordination** noun, **subordinative** adjective.
– ORIGIN late Middle English: from medieval Latin *subordinatus* 'placed in an inferior rank', from Latin *sub-* 'below' + *ordinare* 'ordain'.

subordinate clause ▶**noun** a clause, typically introduced by a conjunction, that forms part of and is dependent on a main clause (e.g. 'when it rang' in 'she answered the phone when it rang').

subordinated debt ▶**noun** Finance a debt owed to an unsecured creditor that can only be paid, in the event of a liquidation, after the claims of secured creditors have been met.

subordinate legislation ▶**noun** [mass noun] Law law which is enacted under delegated powers, such as statutory instruments.

subordinating conjunction ▶**noun** a conjunction that introduces a subordinating clause, e.g. *although*, *because*. Contrasted with **COORDINATING CONJUNCTION**.

suborn /sə'bɔ:n/ ▶**verb** [with obj.] bribe or otherwise induce (someone) to commit an unlawful act such as perjury: *he was accused of conspiring to suborn witnesses.*
– DERIVATIVES **subornation** noun, **suborner** noun.
– ORIGIN mid 16th cent.: from Latin *subornare* 'incite secretly', from *sub-* 'secretly' + *ornare* 'equip'.

suboscine /sʌb'ɒsʌɪn, -sɪn/ ▶**adjective** Ornithology of, relating to, or denoting passerine birds of a division that includes those other than songbirds, found chiefly in America. Compare with **OSCINE**.
• Suborder Deutero-Oscines, order Passeriformes.

suboxide ▶**noun** Chemistry an oxide containing the lowest or an unusually small proportion of oxygen.

subparallel ▶**adjective** chiefly Geology almost parallel.

subphylum ▶ noun (pl. **subphyla**) Zoology a taxonomic category that ranks below phylum and above class.

sub-plot ▶ noun a subordinate plot in a play, novel, or similar work.

subpoena /sə'piːnə/ Law ▶ noun (in full **subpoena ad testificandum**) a writ ordering a person to attend a court: *a subpoena may be issued to compel their attendance* | [mass noun] *they were all* ***under subpoena*** *to appear.*
▶ verb (**subpoenas**, **subpoenaed** or **subpoena'd**, **subpoenaing**) [with obj.] summon (someone) with a subpoena: *the Queen is above the law and cannot be subpoenaed.*
■ require (a document or other evidence) to be submitted to a court of law: *the decision to subpoena government records.*
– ORIGIN late Middle English (as a noun): from Latin *sub poena* 'under penalty' (the first words of the writ). Use as a verb dates from the mid 17th cent.

subpoena duces tecum /ˌdjuːsiːz 'tiːkəm/ ▶ noun Law a writ ordering a person to attend a court and bring relevant documents.
– ORIGIN Latin, literally 'under penalty you shall bring with you'.

sub-postmaster ▶ noun chiefly Brit. a man in charge of a sub-post office.

sub-postmistress ▶ noun chiefly Brit. a woman in charge of a sub-post office.

sub-post office ▶ noun (in the UK) a small local post office offering fewer services than a main post office.

subprogram ▶ noun Computing another term for **SUBROUTINE**.

subregion ▶ noun a division of a region.
– DERIVATIVES **subregional** adjective.

subrogation /ˌsʌbrə'geɪʃ(ə)n/ ▶ noun [mass noun] Law the substitution of one person or group by another in respect of a debt or insurance claim, accompanied by the transfer of any associated rights and duties.
– DERIVATIVES **subrogate** /'sʌbrəgeɪt/ verb.
– ORIGIN late Middle English (in the general sense 'substitution'): from late Latin *subrogatio(n-)*, from *subrogare* 'choose as substitute', from *sub-* 'in place of another' + *rogare* 'ask'.

sub rosa /sʌb 'rəʊzə/ ▶ adjective & adverb formal happening or done in secret: [as adv.] *the committee operates sub rosa* | [as adj.] *sub rosa inspections.*
– ORIGIN Latin, literally 'under the rose', as an emblem of secrecy.

subroutine ▶ noun Computing a set of instructions designed to perform a frequently used operation within a program.

sub-Saharan ▶ adjective [attrib.] from or forming part of the African regions south of the Sahara desert.

subsample ▶ noun a sample drawn from a larger sample.
▶ verb [with obj.] take such a sample from.

subscribe ▶ verb **1** [no obj.] arrange to receive something, typically a publication, regularly by paying in advance: ***subscribe to*** *the magazine for twelve months and receive a free limited-edition T-shirt.*
■ contribute or undertake to contribute a certain sum of money to a particular fund, project, or charitable cause, typically on a regular basis: *he is one of the millions who* ***subscribe to*** *the NSPCC* | [with obj.] *he* ***subscribed*** *£400* ***to*** *the campaign.* ■ (**subscribe to**) figurative express or feel agreement with (an idea or proposal): *we prefer to subscribe to an alternative explanation.* ■ [with obj.] apply to participate in: *the course has been fully subscribed.* ■ apply for or undertake to pay for an issue of shares: *they* ***subscribed to*** *the July rights issue at 300p a share* | [with obj.] *the issue was fully subscribed.* ■ [with obj.] pay or guarantee (money) for an issue of shares: *10 million 50p units will be distributed to savers in proportion to the funds they subscribe.* ■ [with obj.] (of a bookseller) agree before publication to take (a certain number of copies of a book): *most of the first print run of 15,000 copies has been subscribed.*
2 [with obj.] formal sign (a will, contract, or other document): *he subscribed the will as a witness.*
■ sign (one's name) on such a document. ■ (**subscribe oneself**) [with complement] archaic sign oneself as: *he ventured still to subscribe himself her most obedient servant.*
– DERIVATIVES **subscriber** noun.
– ORIGIN late Middle English (in the sense 'sign at the bottom of a document'): from Latin *subscribere*, from *sub-* 'under' + *scribere* 'write'.

subscriber trunk dialling ▶ noun [mass noun] Brit. the automatic connection of trunk calls by dialling without the assistance of an operator.

subscript ▶ adjective (of a letter, figure, or symbol) written or printed below the line.
▶ noun a subscript letter, figure, or symbol.
■ Computing a symbol (notionally written as a subscript but in practice usually not) used in a program, alone or with others, to specify one of the elements of an array.
– ORIGIN early 18th cent.: from Latin *subscript-* 'written below', from the verb *subscribere* (see **SUBSCRIBE**).

subscription ▶ noun **1** [mass noun] the action of making or agreeing to make an advance payment in order to receive or participate in something or as a donation: *the newsletter is available only on subscription* | [count noun] *take out a one-year subscription.*
■ [count noun] a payment of such a type: *membership of the club is available at an annual subscription of £300.* ■ a system in which the production of a book is wholly or partly financed by advance orders.
2 formal a signature or short piece of writing at the end of a document: *he signed the letter and added a subscription.*
■ archaic a signed declaration or agreement.
– ORIGIN late Middle English (in sense 2): from Latin *subscriptio(n-)*, from *subscribere* 'write below' (see **SUBSCRIBE**).

subscription concert ▶ noun one of a series of concerts for which tickets are sold mainly in advance.

subsea ▶ adjective (especially of processes or equipment used in the oil industry) situated or occurring beneath the surface of the sea.

subsection ▶ noun a division of a section.

subsellium /səb'sɛlɪəm/ ▶ noun (pl. **subsellia** /-lɪə/) another term for **MISERICORD** (in sense 1).
– ORIGIN Latin, from *sub-* 'secondary' + *sella* 'seat'.

subsequence[1] /'sʌbsɪkw(ə)ns/ ▶ noun [mass noun] formal the state of following something, especially as a result or effect: *an affair which appeared in due subsequence in the newspapers.*

subsequence[2] /'sʌbˌsiːkw(ə)ns/ ▶ noun a sequence contained in or forming part of another sequence.
■ Mathematics a sequence derived from another by the omission of a number of terms.

subsequent ▶ adjective coming after something in time; following: *the theory was developed* ***subsequent to*** *the earthquake of 1906.*
■ Geology (of a stream or valley) having a direction or character determined by the resistance to erosion of the underlying rock, and typically following the strike of the strata.
– DERIVATIVES **subsequently** adverb.
– ORIGIN late Middle English: from Old French, or from Latin *subsequent-* 'following after' (from the verb *subsequi*).

subserve ▶ verb [with obj.] help to further or promote: *they extended the uses of writing to subserve their political interest.*
– ORIGIN mid 17th cent.: from Latin *subservire* (see **SUB-**, **SERVE**).

subservient ▶ adjective prepared to obey others unquestioningly: *she was* ***subservient to*** *her parents.*
■ less important; subordinate: *Marxism makes freedom* ***subservient to*** *control.* ■ serving as a means to an end: *the whole narration is* ***subservient to*** *the moral plan of exemplifying twelve virtues in twelve knights.*
– DERIVATIVES **subservience** noun, **subserviency** noun, **subserviently** adverb.
– ORIGIN mid 17th cent.: from Latin *subservient-* 'subjecting to, complying with', from the verb *subservire* (see **SUBSERVE**).

subset ▶ noun a part of a larger group of related things.
■ Mathematics a set of which all the elements are contained in another set.

subshrub ▶ noun Botany a dwarf shrub, especially one that is woody only at the base.
– DERIVATIVES **subshrubby** adjective.

subside ▶ verb [no obj.] **1** become less intense, violent, or severe: *I'll wait a few minutes until the storm subsides.*
■ lapse into silence or inactivity: *Fergus opened his mouth to protest again, then subsided.* ■ (**subside in/into**) give way to (an overwhelming feeling, especially laughter): *Anthony and Mark subsided into mirth.*
2 (of water) go down to a lower or the normal level: *the floods subside almost as quickly as they arise.*
■ (of the ground) cave in; sink: *the island is subsiding.* ■ (of a building or other structure) sink lower into the ground: *a ditch which caused the tower to subside slightly.* ■ (of a swelling) reduce until gone: *it took seven days for the swelling to subside completely.* ■ [no obj., with adverbial] sink into a sitting, kneeling, or lying position: *Patrick subsided into his seat.*
– ORIGIN late 17th cent.: from Latin *subsidere*, from *sub-* 'below' + *sidere* 'settle' (related to *sedere* 'sit').

subsidence /səb'sʌɪd(ə)ns, 'sʌbsɪd(ə)ns/ ▶ noun [mass noun] the gradual caving in or sinking of an area of land.
– ORIGIN mid 17th cent.: from Latin *subsidentia* 'sediment', from the verb *subsidere* (see **SUBSIDE**).

subsidiarity /səbˌsɪdɪ'arɪti/ ▶ noun [mass noun] (in politics) the principle that a central authority should have a subsidiary function, performing only those tasks which cannot be performed at a more local level.

subsidiary ▶ adjective less important than but related or supplementary to: *a subsidiary flue of the main chimney.*
■ [attrib.] (of a company) controlled by a holding or parent company.
▶ noun (pl. **-ies**) a company controlled by a holding company.
■ rare a thing that is of lesser importance than but related to something else.
– DERIVATIVES **subsidiarily** adverb (rare).
– ORIGIN mid 16th cent. (in the sense 'serving to help or supplement'): from Latin *subsidiarius*, from *subsidium* 'support, assistance' (see **SUBSIDY**).

subsidize (also **-ise**) ▶ verb [with obj.] support (an organization or activity) financially: *the mining industry continues to be subsidized.*
■ pay part of the cost of producing (something) to reduce prices for the buyer: *the government subsidizes basic goods including sugar, petroleum, and wheat.*
– DERIVATIVES **subsidization** noun, **subsidizer** noun.

subsidy ▶ noun (pl. **-ies**) **1** a sum of money granted by the state or a public body to assist an industry or business so that the price of a commodity or service may remain low or competitive: *a farm subsidy* | [mass noun] *the rail service now operates without subsidy.*
■ a sum of money granted to support an arts organization or other undertaking held to be in the public interest. ■ a sum of money paid by one state to another for the preservation of neutrality, the promotion of war, or to repay military aid. ■ a grant or contribution of money.
2 historical a parliamentary grant to the sovereign for state needs.
■ a tax levied on a particular occasion.
– ORIGIN late Middle English: from Anglo-Norman French *subsidie*, from Latin *subsidium* 'assistance'.

subsist ▶ verb [no obj.] **1** maintain or support oneself, especially at a minimal level: *he* ***subsisted on*** *welfare and casual labour.*
■ [with obj.] archaic provide sustenance for: *the problem of subsisting the poor in a period of high bread prices.*
2 chiefly Law remain in being, force, or effect.
■ (**subsist in**) be attributable to: *the effect of genetic maldevelopment may subsist in chromosomal mutation.*
– DERIVATIVES **subsistent** adjective.
– ORIGIN mid 16th cent. (in the sense 'continue to exist'): from Latin *subsistere* 'stand firm', from *sub-* 'from below' + *sistere* 'set, stand'.

subsistence ▶ noun [mass noun] **1** the action or fact of maintaining or supporting oneself at a minimum level: *the minimum income needed for subsistence.*
■ the means of doing this: *the garden provided not only subsistence but a little cash crop* | [count noun] *the agricultural working class were deprived of a subsistence.* ■ [as modifier] denoting or relating to production at a level sufficient only for one's own use or consumption, without any surplus for trade: *subsistence agriculture.*
2 chiefly Law the state of remaining in force or effect: *rights of occupation normally only continue during the subsistence of the marriage.*

subsistence allowance (also **subsistence money**) ▶ noun chiefly Brit. an allowance or advance on someone's pay, typically granted as travelling expenses.

subsistence level (also **subsistence wage**)

▶ **noun** a standard of living (or wage) that provides only the bare necessities of life.

subsoil ▶ **noun** [mass noun] the soil lying immediately under the surface soil.
▶ **verb** [with obj.] [usu. as noun **subsoiling**] plough (land) so as to cut into the subsoil.

subsoiler ▶ **noun** a kind of plough with no mouldboard, used to loosen the soil at some depth below the surface without turning it over.

subsong ▶ **noun** [mass noun] Ornithology birdsong that is softer and less well defined than the usual territorial song, sometimes heard only at close quarters as a quiet warbling.

subsonic ▶ **adjective** relating to or flying at a speed or speeds less than that of sound.
– DERIVATIVES **subsonically** adverb.

subspace ▶ **noun 1** Mathematics a space that is wholly contained in another space, or whose points or elements are all in another space.
2 [mass noun] (in science fiction) a hypothetical space-time continuum used for communication at a speed faster than that of light.

sub specie aeternitatis /sʌb ˈspiːʃiː ɪˌtəːnɪˈtɑːtɪs/ ▶ **adverb** viewed in relation to the eternal; in a universal perspective: *sub specie aeternitatis the authors have got it about right.*
– ORIGIN Latin, literally 'under the aspect of eternity'.

subspecies (abbrev.: **subsp.** or **ssp.**) ▶ **noun** (pl. same) Biology a taxonomic category that ranks below species, usually a fairly permanent geographically isolated race. Subspecies are designated by a Latin trinomial, e.g. (in zoology) *Ursus arctos horribilis* or (in botany) *Beta vulgaris* subsp. *crassa*. Compare with **FORM** (in sense 3) and **VARIETY** (in sense 2).
– DERIVATIVES **subspecific** adjective.

substage ▶ **noun** [usu. as modifier] an apparatus fixed beneath the ordinary stage of a compound microscope to support mirrors and other accessories.

substance ▶ **noun 1** a particular kind of matter with uniform properties: *a steel tube coated with a waxy substance.*
■ an intoxicating, stimulating, or narcotic chemical or drug, especially an illegal one.
2 [mass noun] the real physical matter of which a person or thing consists and which has a tangible, solid presence: *proteins compose much of the actual substance of the body.*
■ the quality of having a solid basis in reality or fact: *the claim has no substance.* ■ the quality of being dependable or stable: *some were inclined to knock her for her lack of substance.*
3 [mass noun] the quality of being important, valid, or significant: *he had yet to accomplish anything of substance.*
■ the most important or essential part of something; the real or essential meaning: *the substance of the Maastricht Treaty.* ■ the subject matter of a text, speech, or work of art, especially as contrasted with the form or style in which it is presented. ■ wealth and possessions: *a woman of substance.* ■ Philosophy the essential nature underlying phenomena, which is subject to changes and accidents.
– PHRASES **in substance** essentially: *basic rights are equivalent in substance to human rights.*
– ORIGIN Middle English (denoting the essential nature of something): from Old French, from Latin *substantia* 'being, essence', from *substant-* 'standing firm', from the verb *substare*.

substance P ▶ **noun** [mass noun] Biochemistry a compound thought to be involved in the synaptic transmission of pain and other nerve impulses. It is a polypeptide with eleven amino-acid residues.

sub-standard ▶ **adjective 1** below the usual or required standard: *sub-standard housing.*
2 another term for **NON-STANDARD**.

substantial ▶ **adjective 1** of considerable importance, size, or worth: *a substantial amount of cash.*
■ strongly built or made: *a row of substantial Victorian villas.* ■ (of a meal) large and filling. ■ important in material or social terms; wealthy: *a substantial Devon family.*
2 concerning the essentials of something: *there was substantial agreement on changing policies.*
3 real and tangible rather than imaginary: *spirits are shadowy, human beings substantial.*
– DERIVATIVES **substantiality** noun.
– ORIGIN Middle English: from Old French *substantiel* or Christian Latin *substantialis*, from *substantia* 'being, essence' (see **SUBSTANCE**).

substantialism ▶ **noun** [mass noun] Philosophy the doctrine that behind phenomena there are substantial realities.
– DERIVATIVES **substantialist** noun & adjective.

substantialize (also **-ise**) ▶ **verb** [with obj.] give (something) substance or actual existence: *the universe is a series of abstract truths, substantialized by their reference to God.*

substantially ▶ **adverb 1** to a great or significant extent: *profits grew substantially* | [as submodifier] *substantially higher pension costs.*
2 for the most part; essentially: *things will remain substantially the same over the next ten years.*

substantiate /səbˈstanʃɪeɪt/ ▶ **verb** [with obj.] provide evidence to support or prove the truth of: *they had found nothing to substantiate the allegations.*
– DERIVATIVES **substantiation** noun.
– ORIGIN mid 17th cent.: from medieval Latin *substantiat-* 'given substance', from the verb *substantiare*.

substantive /ˈsʌbst(ə)ntɪv/ ▶ **adjective** /also səbˈstantɪv/ **1** having a firm basis in reality and so important, meaningful, or considerable: *there is no substantive evidence for the efficacy of these drugs.*
2 having a separate and independent existence.
■ (of a rank or appointment) not acting or temporary; permanent. ■ (of a dye) not needing a mordant. ■ (of an enactment, motion, or resolution) made in due form as such; not amended.
3 (of law) defining rights and duties as opposed to giving the rules by which such things are established.
▶ **noun** Grammar, dated a noun.
– DERIVATIVES **substantival** /-ˈtʌɪv(ə)l/ adjective, **substantively** adverb.
– ORIGIN late Middle English (in the sense 'having an independent existence'): from Old French *substantif, -ive* or late Latin *substantivus*, from *substantia* 'essence' (see **SUBSTANCE**).

substation ▶ **noun 1** a set of equipment reducing the high voltage of electrical power transmission to that suitable for supply to consumers.
2 a subordinate station for the police or fire service.
■ N. Amer. a small post office, for example one situated within a larger shop.

substellar ▶ **adjective** Astronomy relating to or denoting a body much smaller than a typical star whose mass is not great enough to support main sequence hydrogen burning.

substituent /səbˈstɪtjʊənt/ ▶ **noun** Chemistry an atom or group of atoms taking the place of another atom or group or occupying a specified position in a molecule.
– ORIGIN late 19th cent.: from Latin *substituent-* 'standing in place of', from the verb *substituere* (see **SUBSTITUTE**).

substitute ▶ **noun** a person or thing acting or serving in place of another: *soya milk is used as a* ***substitute for*** *dairy milk.*
■ a sports player nominated as eligible to replace another after a match has begun. ■ a person or thing that becomes the object of love or another emotion which is deprived of its natural outlet: *a father substitute.* ■ Scots Law a deputy: *a sheriff substitute.*
▶ **verb** [with obj.] use or add in place of: *dried rosemary can be* ***substituted for*** *the fresh herb.*
■ [no obj.] act or serve as a substitute: *I found someone to* ***substitute for*** *me.* ■ replace (someone or something) with another: *customs officers* ***substituted*** *the drugs* ***with*** *another substance* | *this was substituted by a new clause.* ■ replace (a sports player) with a substitute during a match: *he was substituted eleven minutes from time.* ■ Chemistry replace (an atom or group in a molecule, especially a hydrogen atom) with another. ■ [as adj. **substituted**] Chemistry (of a compound) in which one or more hydrogen atoms have been replaced by other atoms or groups: *a substituted terpenoid.*
– DERIVATIVES **substitutability** noun, **substitutable** adjective, **substitutive** adjective.
– ORIGIN late Middle English (denoting a deputy or delegate): from Latin *substitutus* 'put in place of', past participle of *substituere*, based on *statuere* 'set up'.

USAGE Traditionally, the verb **substitute** is followed by **for** and means 'put (someone or something) in place of another', as in *she* ***substituted*** *the fake vase* ***for*** *the real one.* From the late 17th century **substitute** has also been used with **with** or **by** to mean 'replace (something) with something else', as in *she* ***substituted*** *the real vase* ***with*** *the fake one.* This can be confusing, since the two sentences shown above mean the same thing, yet the object of the verb and the object of the preposition have swapped positions. Despite the potential confusion, the second, newer use is well established, especially in some scientific contexts, and, though still disapproved of by traditionalists, is now generally regarded as part of normal standard English.

substitution ▶ **noun** [mass noun] the action of replacing someone or something with another person or thing: ***substitution of*** *rail services* ***with*** *buses* | [count noun] *a tactical substitution.*
– DERIVATIVES **substitutional** adjective, **substitutionary** adjective.

substorm ▶ **noun** a localized disturbance of the earth's magnetic field in high latitudes, typically manifested as an aurora.

substrate /ˈsʌbstreɪt/ ▶ **noun** a substance or layer which underlies something, or on which some process occurs, in particular:
■ the surface or material on or from which an organism lives, grows, or obtains its nourishment. ■ the substance on which an enzyme acts. ■ a material which provides the surface on which something is deposited or inscribed, for example the silicon wafer used to manufacture integrated circuits.
– ORIGIN early 19th cent.: Anglicized form of **SUBSTRATUM**.

substratum /sʌbˈstrɑːtəm, -ˈstreɪtəm/ ▶ **noun** (pl. **substrata**) an underlying layer or substance, in particular a layer of rock or soil beneath the surface of the ground.
■ a foundation or basis of something: *there is a broad* ***substratum of*** *truth in it.*
– ORIGIN mid 17th cent.: modern Latin, neuter past participle (used as a noun) of Latin *substernere*, from *sub-* 'below' + *sternere* 'strew'. Compare with **STRATUM**.

substructure ▶ **noun** an underlying or supporting structure.
– DERIVATIVES **substructural** adjective.

subsume /səbˈsjuːm/ ▶ **verb** [with obj.] (often **be subsumed**) include or absorb (something) in something else: *most of these phenomena can be* ***subsumed under*** *two broad categories.*
– DERIVATIVES **subsumable** adjective, **subsumption** noun.
– ORIGIN mid 16th cent. (in the sense 'subjoin, add'): from medieval Latin *subsumere*, from *sub-* 'from below' + *sumere* 'take'. The current sense dates from the early 19th cent.

subsurface ▶ **noun** the stratum or strata below the earth's surface.

subsystem ▶ **noun** a self-contained system within a larger system.

subtenant ▶ **noun** a person who leases property from a tenant.
– DERIVATIVES **subtenancy** noun.

subtend /sʌbˈtɛnd/ ▶ **verb** [with obj.] **1** (of a line, arc, or figure) form (an angle) at a particular point when straight lines from its extremities are joined at that point.
■ (of an angle or chord) have bounding lines or points that meet or coincide with those of (a line or arc).
2 Botany (of a bract) extend under (a flower) so as to support or enfold it.
– ORIGIN late 16th cent. (in sense 1): from Latin *subtendere*, from *sub-* 'under' + *tendere* 'stretch'. Sense 2 dates from the late 19th cent.

subtense ▶ **noun** Geometry a subtending line, especially the chord of an arc.
■ the angle subtended by a line at a point.
– ORIGIN early 17th cent.: from modern Latin *subtensa* (*linea*), feminine past participle of *subtendere* (see **SUBTEND**).

subterfuge /ˈsʌbtəfjuːdʒ/ ▶ **noun** [mass noun] deceit used in order to achieve one's goal.
■ [count noun] a statement or action resorted to in order to deceive.
– ORIGIN late 16th cent.: from French, or from late Latin *subterfugium*, from Latin *subterfugere* 'escape secretly', from *subter-* 'beneath' + *fugere* 'flee'.

subterminal ▶ **adjective** technical near the end of a chain or other structure.

subterranean /ˌsʌbtəˈreɪnɪən/ ▶ **adjective** existing, occurring, or done under the earth's surface.
■ secret; concealed: *the subterranean world of the behind-the-scenes television power brokers.*
– DERIVATIVES **subterraneously** adverb.
– ORIGIN early 17th cent.: from Latin *subterraneus* (from *sub-* 'below' + *terra* 'earth') + **-AN**.

subterranean clover ▶ **noun** a European clover, naturalized as a weed of pastures in Australia, whose fruiting heads bury themselves in the ground.
• *Trifolium subterraneum*, family Leguminosae.

subtext ▶ **noun** an underlying and often distinct theme in a piece of writing or conversation.

subtilize /ˈsʌtɪlʌɪz/ (also **-ise**) ▶ **verb** [with obj.] archaic make more subtle; refine.
– DERIVATIVES **subtilization** noun.

subtitle ▶ **noun 1** (**subtitles**) captions displayed at the bottom of a cinema or television screen that translate or transcribe the dialogue or narrative.
2 a subordinate title of a published work or article giving additional information about its content.
▶ **verb** [with obj.] (usu. **be subtitled**) **1** provide (a film or programme) with subtitles: *much of the film is subtitled.*
2 provide (a published work or article) with a subtitle: *the novel was aptly subtitled.*

subtle ▶ **adjective** (**subtler**, **subtlest**) (especially of a change or distinction) so delicate or precise as to be difficult to analyse or describe: *his language expresses rich and subtle meanings.*
■ (of a mixture or effect) delicately complex and understated: *subtle lighting.* ■ making use of clever and indirect methods to achieve something: *he tried a more subtle approach.* ■ capable of making fine distinctions: *a subtle mind.* ■ arranged in an ingenious and elaborate way. ■ archaic crafty; cunning.
– DERIVATIVES **subtleness** noun, **subtly** adverb.
– ORIGIN Middle English (also in the sense 'not easily understood'): from Old French *sotil*, from Latin *subtilis*.

subtlety ▶ **noun** (pl. **-ies**) [mass noun] the quality or state of being subtle: *the textural subtlety of Degas.*
■ [count noun] a subtle distinction, feature, or argument: *the subtleties of English grammar.*
– ORIGIN Middle English: from Old French *soutilte*, from Latin *subtilitas*, from *subtilis* 'fine, delicate' (see **SUBTLE**).

subtonic ▶ **noun** Music the note below the tonic, the seventh note of the diatonic scale of any key.

subtopia ▶ **noun** [mass noun] Brit. unsightly, sprawling suburban development.
– DERIVATIVES **subtopian** adjective.
– ORIGIN 1950s: blend of **SUBURB** and **UTOPIA**.

subtotal ▶ **noun** the total of one set of a larger group of figures to be added.
▶ **verb** (**subtotalled**, **subtotalling**; US **subtotaled**, **subtotaling**) [with obj.] add (numbers) so as to obtain a subtotal.
▶ **adjective** Medicine (of an injury or a surgical operation) partial; not total.

subtract ▶ **verb** [with obj.] take away (a number or amount) from another to calculate the difference: *subtract 43 from 60.*
■ take away (something) from something else so as to decrease the size, number, or amount: *programs were added and subtracted as called for.*
– DERIVATIVES **subtracter** noun, **subtractive** adjective.
– ORIGIN mid 16th cent.: from Latin *subtract-* 'drawn away', from *sub-* 'from below' + *trahere* 'to draw'.

subtraction ▶ **noun** [mass noun] the process or skill of taking one number or amount away from another: *subtraction of this figure from the total.*
■ Mathematics the process of taking a matrix, vector, or other quantity away from another under specific rules to obtain the difference.

subtrahend /ˈsʌbtrəˌhɛnd/ ▶ **noun** Mathematics a quantity or number to be subtracted from another.
– ORIGIN late 17th cent.: from Latin *subtrahendus* 'to be taken away', gerundive of *subtrahere* (see **SUBTRACT**).

subtropics ▶ **plural noun** (**the subtropics**) the regions adjacent to or bordering on the tropics.
– DERIVATIVES **subtropical** adjective.

Subud /sʊˈbuːd/ a movement, founded in 1947 and led by the Javanese mystic Pak Muhammad Subuh, based on a system of exercises by which the individual seeks to approach a state of perfection through divine power.
– ORIGIN contraction of Javanese *susila budhi dharma*, from Sanskrit *suśīla* 'good disposition' + *buddhi* 'understanding' + *dharma* 'religious duty'.

subulate /ˈsjuːbjʊlət, -leɪt/ ▶ **adjective** Botany & Zoology (of a part) slender and tapering to a point; awl-shaped.
– ORIGIN mid 18th cent.: from Latin *subula* 'awl' + **-ATE**².

subumbrella ▶ **noun** Zoology the concave inner surface of the umbrella of a jellyfish or other medusa.
– DERIVATIVES **subumbrellar** adjective.

sub-underwrite ▶ **verb** [with obj.] Finance underwrite (part of a liability underwritten by another).
– DERIVATIVES **sub-underwriter** noun.

subungulate /sʌbˈʌŋgjʊlət, -leɪt/ ▶ **noun** Zoology a mammal of a diverse group that probably evolved from primitive ungulates, comprising the elephants, hyraxes, sirenians, and perhaps the aardvark.

subunit ▶ **noun** a distinct component of something: *chemical subunits of human DNA.*

suburb ▶ **noun** an outlying district of a city, especially a residential one.
– ORIGIN Middle English: from Old French *suburbe* or Latin *suburbium*, from *sub-* 'near to' + *urbs, urb-* 'city'.

suburban ▶ **adjective** of or characteristic of a suburb: *suburban life.*
■ contemptibly dull and ordinary: *Elizabeth despised Ann's house-proudness as deeply suburban.*
– DERIVATIVES **suburbanite** noun, **suburbanization** noun, **suburbanize** (also **-ise**) verb.

suburbia ▶ **noun** [mass noun] the suburbs or their inhabitants viewed collectively.

subvent ▶ **verb** [with obj.] formal support or assist by the payment of a subvention.
– ORIGIN early 20th cent.: from Latin *subvent-* 'assisted', from the verb *subvenire* (see **SUBVENTION**).

subvention ▶ **noun** a grant of money, especially from a government.
– ORIGIN late Middle English (in the sense 'provision of help'): from Old French, from late Latin *subventio(n-)*, from Latin *subvenire* 'assist', from *sub-* 'from below' + *venire* 'come'.

subversive ▶ **adjective** seeking or intended to subvert an established system or institution: *subversive literature.*
▶ **noun** a person with such aims.
– DERIVATIVES **subversively** adverb, **subversiveness** noun.
– ORIGIN mid 17th cent.: from medieval Latin *subversivus*, from the verb *subvertere* (see **SUBVERT**).

subvert ▶ **verb** [with obj.] undermine the power and authority of (an established system or institution): *an attempt to subvert democratic government.*
– DERIVATIVES **subversion** noun, **subverter** noun.
– ORIGIN late Middle English: from Old French *subvertir* or Latin *subvertere*, from *sub-* 'from below' + *vertere* 'to turn'.

subvocal ▶ **adjective** (of a word or sound) barely audible: *a subvocal sigh.*
■ Psychology & Philosophy relating to or denoting an unarticulated level of speech comparable to thought: *almost all of what is called 'thinking' is subvocal talk.*

subvocalize (also **-ise**) ▶ **verb** [with obj.] utter (words or sounds) with the lips silently or with barely audible sound, especially when talking to oneself, memorizing something, or reading.
– DERIVATIVES **subvocalization** noun.

subway ▶ **noun 1** Brit. a tunnel under a road for use by pedestrians.
2 chiefly N. Amer. an underground railway.

subway series ▶ **noun** (in the US) a series of baseball games played between two teams in the same city, especially New York.

subwoofer ▶ **noun** a loudspeaker component designed to reproduce very low bass frequencies.

sub-zero ▶ **adjective** (of temperature) lower than zero; below freezing.

suc- ▶ **prefix** variant spelling of **SUB-** assimilated before *c* (as in *succeed*, *succussion*).

succah /ˈsʊkə/ (also **sukkah**) ▶ **noun** a booth in which a practising Jew spends part of the Feast of Tabernacles.
– ORIGIN late 19th cent.: from Hebrew *sukkāh* 'hut'.

succedaneum /ˌsʌksɪˈdeɪnɪəm/ ▶ **noun** (pl. **succedanea** /-nɪə/) dated or poetic/literary a substitute, especially for a medicine or drug.
– DERIVATIVES **succedaneous** adjective.
– ORIGIN early 17th cent.: modern Latin, neuter of Latin *succedaneus* 'following after', from *succedere* 'come close after' (see **SUCCEED**).

succeed ▶ **verb 1** [no obj.] achieve what one aims or wants to: *he* **succeeded in** *winning a pardon.*
■ (of a plan, request, or undertaking) lead to the desired result: *a mission which could not possibly succeed.*
2 [with obj.] take over a throne, inheritance, office, or other position from: *he would succeed Hawke as Prime Minister.*
■ [no obj.] become the new rightful holder of an inheritance, office, title, or property: *he* **succeeded to** *his father's kingdom.* ■ come after and take the place of: *her embarrassment was succeeded by fear.*
– PHRASES **nothing succeeds like success** proverb success leads to opportunities for further and greater successes.
– DERIVATIVES **succeeder** noun (archaic).
– ORIGIN late Middle English: from Old French *succeder* or Latin *succedere* 'come close after', from *sub-* 'close to' + *cedere* 'go'.

succentor /səkˈsɛntə/ ▶ **noun** a precentor's deputy in some cathedrals.
– ORIGIN early 17th cent.: from late Latin, from Latin *succinere* 'sing to, chime in', from *sub-* 'subordinately' + *canere* 'sing'.

succès de scandale /sʊkˌseɪ də skɒnˈdɑːl, French syksɛ də skɑ̃dal/ ▶ **noun** a success due to notoriety or a thing's scandalous nature.
– ORIGIN French, literally 'success of scandal'.

succès d'estime /sʊkˌseɪ dɛˈstiːm, French syksɛ dɛstim/ ▶ **noun** (pl. same) a success through critical appreciation, as opposed to popularity or commercial gain.
– ORIGIN French, literally 'success of opinion'.

success ▶ **noun** [mass noun] the accomplishment of an aim or purpose: *the president had some* **success in** *restoring confidence.*
■ the attainment of popularity or profit: *the success of his play.* ■ [count noun] a person or thing that achieves desired aims or attains prosperity: *I must make a success of my business.* ■ archaic the outcome of an undertaking, specified as achieving or failing to achieve its aims: *the good or ill success of their maritime enterprises.*
– ORIGIN mid 16th cent.: from Latin *successus*, from the verb *succedere* 'come close after' (see **SUCCEED**).

successful ▶ **adjective** accomplishing an aim or purpose: *a successful attack on the town.*
■ having achieved popularity, profit, or distinction: *a successful actor.*
– DERIVATIVES **successfully** adverb, **successfulness** noun.

succession ▶ **noun 1** a number of people or things sharing a specified characteristic and following one after the other: *she had been secretary to a succession of board directors.*
■ Geology a group of strata representing a single chronological sequence.
2 [mass noun] the action or process of inheriting a title, office, property, etc.: *the new king was already elderly at the time of his succession.*
■ the right or sequence of inheriting a position, title, etc.: *the* **succession to** *the Crown was disputed.* ■ Ecology the process by which a plant or animal community successively gives way to another until a stable climax is reached. Compare with **SERE**².
– PHRASES **in quick** (or **rapid**) **succession** following one another at short intervals. **in succession** following one after the other without interruption: *she won the race for the second year in succession.* **in succession to** inheriting or elected to the place of: *he was elevated to the Lords in succession to his father.* **settle the succession** determine who shall succeed someone.
– DERIVATIVES **successional** adjective.
– ORIGIN Middle English (denoting legal transmission of an estate or the throne to another, also in the sense 'successors, heirs'): from Old French, or from Latin *successio(n-)*, from the verb *succedere* (see **SUCCEED**). The term in ecology dates from the mid 19th cent.

S

Succession, Act of (in English history) each of three Acts of Parliament passed during the reign of Henry VIII regarding the succession of his children.

The first (1534) declared Henry's marriage to Catherine of Aragon to be invalid, fixing the succession on any child born to Henry's new wife Anne Boleyn. The second (1536) cancelled this, asserting the rights of Jane Seymour and her issue, while the third (1544) determined the order of succession of Henry's three children, the future Edward VI, Mary I, and Elizabeth I.

succession state ▶ **noun** a country resulting from the partition of another one.

successive ▶ **adjective** [attrib.] following one another or following others: *they were looking for their fifth successive win.*
– DERIVATIVES **successively** adverb, **successiveness** noun.
– ORIGIN late Middle English: from medieval Latin *successivus*, from *success-* 'followed closely', from the verb *succedere* (see **SUCCEED**).

successor ▶ **noun** a person or thing that succeeds another: *Schoenberg saw himself as a natural* ***successor to*** *the German romantic school.*

success story ▶ **noun** informal a successful person or thing.

succinct /sək'sɪŋ(k)t/ ▶ **adjective** (especially of something written or spoken) briefly and clearly expressed: *use short, succinct sentences.*
– DERIVATIVES **succinctly** adverb, **succinctness** noun.
– ORIGIN late Middle English (in the sense 'encircled'): from Latin *succinctus* 'tucked up', past participle of *succingere*, from *sub-* 'from below' + *cingere* 'gird'.

succinic acid /sʌk'sɪnɪk/ ▶ **noun** [mass noun] Biochemistry a crystalline organic acid which occurs in living tissue as an intermediate in glucose metabolism.
• Chem. formula: $HOOC(CH_2)_2COOH$.
– DERIVATIVES **succinate** /'sʌksɪneɪt/ noun.
– ORIGIN late 18th cent.: *succinic* from French *succinique*, from Latin *succinum* 'amber' (from which it was first derived).

succinylcholine /ˌsʌksɪnʌɪl'kəʊliːn/ ▶ **noun** [mass noun] Medicine a synthetic compound used as a short-acting muscle relaxant and local anaesthetic. It is an ester of choline with succinic acid.

succor ▶ **noun** & **verb** US spelling of **SUCCOUR**.

succory /'sʌk(ə)ri/ ▶ **noun** another term for **CHICORY** (in sense 1).
– ORIGIN mid 16th cent.: alteration of obsolete French *cicorée*.

succotash /'sʌkətaʃ/ ▶ **noun** [mass noun] US a dish of maize and lima beans boiled together.
– ORIGIN mid 18th cent.: from Narragansett *msiquatash* (plural).

Succoth /sʊ'kəʊt, 'sʌkəθ/ ▶ **noun** a major Jewish festival held in the autumn (beginning on the 15th day of Tishri) to commemorate the sheltering of the Israelites in the wilderness. It is marked by the erection of small booths covered in natural materials. Also called **FEAST OF TABERNACLES**.
– ORIGIN from Hebrew *sukkōṯ*, plural of *sukkāh* 'thicket, hut'.

succour /'sʌkə/ (US **succor**) ▶ **noun** [mass noun] assistance and support in times of hardship and distress.
■ (**succours**) archaic reinforcements of troops.
▶ **verb** [with obj.] give assistance or aid to: *prisoners of war were liberated and succoured.*
– DERIVATIVES **succourless** adjective.
– ORIGIN Middle English: via Old French from medieval Latin *succursus*, from Latin *succurrere* 'run to the help of', from *sub-* 'from below' + *currere* 'run'.

succubous /'sʌkjʊbəs/ ▶ **adjective** Botany (of a liverwort) having leaves obliquely inserted on the stem so that their upper edges are overlapped by the lower edges of the leaves above. Often contrasted with **INCUBOUS**.
– ORIGIN mid 19th cent.: from late Latin *succubare* 'lie under' + **-OUS**.

succubus /'sʌkjʊbəs/ ▶ **noun** (pl. **succubi** /-bʌɪ/) a female demon believed to have sexual intercourse with sleeping men.
– ORIGIN late Middle English: from medieval Latin *succubus* 'prostitute', from *succubare*, from *sub-* 'under' + *cubare* 'to lie'.

succulent ▶ **adjective** (of food) tender, juicy, and tasty.
■ Botany (of a plant, especially a xerophyte) having thick fleshy leaves or stems adapted to storing water.
▶ **noun** Botany a succulent plant.
– DERIVATIVES **succulence** noun, **succulently** adverb.
– ORIGIN early 17th cent.: from Latin *succulentus*, from *succus* 'juice'.

succumb ▶ **verb** [no obj.] fail to resist (pressure, temptation, or some other negative force): *he has become the latest to* ***succumb to*** *the strain of football management.*
■ die from the effect of a disease or injury.
– ORIGIN late 15th cent. (in the sense 'bring low, overwhelm'): from Old French *succomber* or Latin *succumbere*, from *sub-* 'under' + a verb related to *cubare* 'to lie'.

succursal /sə'kɔːs(ə)l/ ▶ **adjective** (of a religious establishment such as a monastery) subsidiary to a principal establishment.
– ORIGIN mid 19th cent.: from French *succursale*, from medieval Latin *succursus*, from the verb *succurrere* (see **SUCCOUR**).

succuss /sə'kʌs/ ▶ **verb** [with obj.] (in preparing homeopathic remedies) shake (a solution) vigorously.
– DERIVATIVES **succussion** noun.
– ORIGIN mid 19th cent.: from Latin *succuss-* 'shaken', from the verb *succutere*, from *sub-* 'away' + *quatere* 'to shake'.

such ▶ **determiner**, **predeterminer**, & **pronoun 1** of the type previously mentioned: [as determiner] *I have been involved in many such courses* | [as predeterminer] *I longed to find a kindred spirit, and in him I thought I had found such a person* | [as pronoun] *we were second-class citizens and they treated us* ***as such.***
2 (**such —— as/that**) of the type about to be mentioned: [as determiner] *there is no such thing as a free lunch* | [as predeterminer] *the farm is organized in such a way that it can be run by two adults* | [as pronoun] *the wound was such that I had to have stitches.*
3 to so high a degree; so great (often used to emphasize a quality): [as determiner] *this material is of* ***such*** *importance* ***that*** *it has a powerful bearing on the case* | [as predeterminer] *autumn's such a beautiful season* | [as pronoun] ***such is*** *the elegance of his typeface* ***that*** *it is still a favourite of designers.*
– PHRASES **and such** and similar things: *he had activities like the scouts and Sunday school and such.* **as such** [often with negative] in the exact sense of the word: *it is possible to stay overnight here although there is no guest house as such.* **such-and-such** used to refer vaguely to a person or thing that does not need to be specified: *so many enterprises to be sold by such-and-such a date.* **such as 1** for example: *wild flowers such as mountain pansy and wild thyme.* **2** of a kind that; like: *an event such as we've shared.* **3** archaic those who: *such as alter in a moment, win not credit in a month.* **such as it is** (or **they are**) what little there is; for what it's worth: *the plot, such as it is, takes road movie form.* **such a one** such a person or thing: *what was the reward for* ***such a one as*** *Fox?* **such that** to the extent that: *the linking of sentences such that they constitute a narrative.*
– ORIGIN Old English *swilc, swylc*; related to Dutch *zulk*, German *solch*, from the Germanic bases of **SO**[1] and **ALIKE**.

suchlike ▶ **pronoun** things of the type mentioned: *carpets, old chairs, tables, and suchlike.*
▶ **determiner** of the type mentioned: *food, drink, clothing, and suchlike provisions.*

Suchou variant of **SUZHOU**.

Suchow /suː'tʃaʊ/ variant of **XUZHOU**.

suck ▶ **verb 1** [with obj.] draw into the mouth by contracting the muscles of the lip and mouth to make a partial vacuum: *they suck mint juleps through straws.*
■ hold (something) in the mouth and draw at it by contracting the lip and cheek muscles: *she sucked a mint* | [no obj.] *the child* ***sucked on*** *her thumb.* ■ draw milk, juice, or other fluid from (something) into the mouth or by suction: *she sucked each segment of the orange carefully.* ■ [with obj. and adverbial of direction] draw in a specified direction by creating a vacuum: *he was sucked under the surface of the river.* ■ figurative involve (someone) in something without their choosing: *I didn't want to be* ***sucked into*** *the role of dutiful daughter.* ■ [no obj.] (of a pump) make a gurgling sound as a result of drawing air instead of water.
2 [no obj.] N. Amer. informal be very bad, disagreeable, or disgusting: *I love your country but your weather sucks.* [ORIGIN: by association with vulgar slang **SUCKHOLE**.]
▶ **noun** an act of sucking something.
■ the sound made by water retreating and drawing at something: *the soft suck of the sea against the sand.*
▶ **exclamation** (**sucks**) Brit. informal used to express derision and defiance: ***sucks to*** *them!*
– PHRASES **give suck** archaic give milk from the breast or teat; suckle. **suck someone dry** exhaust someone's physical, material, or emotional resources. **suck it and see** Brit. informal used to suggest that the only way to know if something will work or be suitable is to try it. **suck it up** US informal accept a hardship.
– ORIGIN Old English *sūcan* (verb), from an Indo-European imitative root; related to **SOAK**.
▶ **suck up** informal behave obsequiously, especially for one's own advantage: *he has risen to where he is mainly by* ***sucking up to*** *the president.*

sucker ▶ **noun 1** a person or thing that sucks, in particular:
■ a rubber cup that adheres to a surface by suction. ■ a flat or concave organ enabling an animal to cling to a surface by suction. ■ the piston of a suction pump. ■ a pipe through which liquid is drawn by suction.
2 informal a gullible or easily deceived person.
■ (**a sucker for**) a person especially susceptible to or fond of a specified thing: *I always was a sucker for a good fairy tale.*
3 informal, chiefly US a thing or person not specified by name: *he's one strong sucker.*
4 Botany a shoot springing from the base of a tree or other plant, especially one arising from the root below ground level at some distance from the main stem or trunk.
■ a side shoot from an axillary bud, as in tomato plants or maize.
5 a freshwater fish with thick lips that are used to suck up food from the bottom, native to North America and Asia.
• Family Catostomidae: many genera and species.
6 N. Amer. informal a lollipop.
▶ **verb 1** [no obj.] Botany (of a plant) produce suckers: *it spread rapidly after being left undisturbed to sucker.*
2 [with obj.] informal, chiefly US fool or trick (someone): *they got suckered into accepting responsibility.*

suckerfish ▶ **noun** (pl. same or **-fishes**) another term for **REMORA**.

sucker punch ▶ **noun** an unexpected punch or blow.
▶ **verb** (**sucker-punch**) [with obj.] hit (someone) with such a punch or blow: *his father sucker-punched him and knocked him out.*

sucket spoon /'sʌkɪt/ (also **sucket fork**) ▶ **noun** a utensil for eating fruit, having a two-pronged fork at one end and a spoon at the other.
– ORIGIN late 15th cent.: *sucket*, alteration of obsolete *succate*, variant of *succade* 'sweetmeats', of unknown origin.

suckhole ▶ **noun 1** US informal a whirlpool.
2 Canadian & Austral. vulgar slang a sycophant.
▶ **verb** [no obj.] Canadian & Austral. vulgar slang behave in a sycophantic way towards someone.

sucking ▶ **adjective** (of a child or animal) not yet weaned.

sucking disc ▶ **noun** Zoology an animal's sucker, especially one on the end of each tube foot of an echinoderm.

suckle ▶ **verb** [with obj.] feed (a baby or young animal) from the breast or teat: *a mother pig suckling a huge litter.*
■ [no obj.] (of a baby or young animal) feed by sucking the breast or teat: *the infant's biological need to suckle.*
– ORIGIN late Middle English: probably a back-formation from **SUCKLING**.

suckler ▶ **noun** an unweaned animal, especially a calf.
■ a cow used to breed and suckle calves for beef.

Suckling, Sir John (1609–42), English poet, dramatist, and Royalist leader. His poems include 'Ballad upon a Wedding', published in the collection *Fragmenta Aurea* (1646).

suckling ▶ **noun** an unweaned child or animal: [as modifier] *roast suckling pig.*
– ORIGIN Middle English: from the verb **SUCK** + **-LING**.

S

suck-up ▶ **noun** N. Amer. informal a person who behaves obsequiously, especially for their own advantage.

sucky ▶ **adjective** informal **1** ingratiating and obsequious: *Tommy immediately put on his sucky expression.*
2 disagreeable; unpleasant: *her sucky state job.*

sucralfate /ˈs(j)uːkr(ə)lˌfeɪt/ ▶ **noun** [mass noun] Medicine a drug used in the treatment of gastric and duodenal ulcers. It is a complex of aluminium hydroxide and a sulphate derivative of sucrose.
– ORIGIN 1960s: blend of **SUCROSE**, **ALUMINIUM**, and *sulfate* (see **SULPHATE**).

sucrase /ˈs(j)uːkreɪz/ ▶ **noun** another term for **INVERTASE**.

Sucre[1] /ˈsuːkreɪ/ the judicial capital and seat of the judiciary of Bolivia; pop. 130,950 (1992). It is situated in the Andes, at an altitude of 2,700 m (8,860 ft). Named Chuquisaca by the Spanish in 1539, the city was renamed in 1825 in honour of Antonio José de Sucre.

Sucre[2] /ˈsuːkreɪ/, Antonio José de (1795–1830), Venezuelan revolutionary and statesman, President of Bolivia 1826–8. He served as Simón Bolívar's Chief of Staff, liberating Ecuador, Peru, and Bolivia from the Spanish, and was the first President of Bolivia.

sucre /ˈsuːkreɪ/ ▶ **noun** the basic monetary unit of Ecuador, equal to 100 centavos.
– ORIGIN named after A. J. de *Sucre* (see **SUCRE**[2]).

sucrier /ˈsuːkrɪeɪ/ ▶ **noun** a sugar bowl, typically made of porcelain and with a cover.
– ORIGIN mid 19th cent.: French, from *sucre* 'sugar'.

sucrose /ˈs(j)uːkrəʊz, -əʊs/ ▶ **noun** [mass noun] Chemistry a compound which is the chief component of cane or beet sugar.
• A disaccharide containing glucose and fructose units; chem. formula: $C_{12}H_{22}O_{11}$.
– ORIGIN mid 19th cent.: from French *sucre* 'sugar' + **-OSE**[2].

suction ▶ **noun** [mass noun] the production of a partial vacuum by the removal of air in order to force fluid into a vacant space or procure adhesion.
▶ **verb** [with obj. and adverbial of direction] remove (something) using suction: *physicians used a tube to suction out the gallstones.*
– ORIGIN early 17th cent.: from late Latin *suctio(n-)*, from Latin *sugere* 'suck'.

suction pump ▶ **noun** a pump for drawing liquid through a pipe into a chamber emptied by a piston.

suctorial /sʌkˈtɔːrɪəl/ ▶ **adjective** chiefly Zoology adapted for sucking (used for example of the mouthparts of some insects).
■ (of an animal) having a sucker for feeding or adhering to something.
– DERIVATIVES **suctorially** adverb.
– ORIGIN mid 19th cent.: from modern Latin *suctorius* (from Latin *sugere* 'suck') + **-AL**.

Sudan /suːˈdɑːn, -ˈdan/ (also **the Sudan**) **1** a country in NE Africa south of Egypt, with a coastline on the Red Sea; pop. 25,855,000 (est. 1991); languages, Arabic (official), Dinka, Hausa, and other languages; capital, Khartoum.

> Under Arab rule from the 13th century, the country was conquered by Egypt in 1820–2. Sudan was separated from its northern neighbour by the Mahdist revolt of 1881–98 and administered after the reconquest of 1898 as an Anglo-Egyptian condominium. It became an independent republic in 1956, but has suffered severely as a result of protracted civil war between the Islamic government in the north and separatist forces in the south.

2 a vast region of North Africa, extending across the width of the continent from the southern edge of the Sahara to the tropical equatorial zone in the south.
– DERIVATIVES **Sudanese** /ˌsuːdəˈniːz/ adjective & noun.
– ORIGIN from Arabic *sūdān*, literally 'country of the blacks'.

sudan grass ▶ **noun** [mass noun] a Sudanese sorghum cultivated for fodder in dry regions of the US.
• *Sorghum sudanense*, family Gramineae.

sudarium /s(j)uːˈdɛːrɪəm/ ▶ **noun** (pl. **sudaria** /-rɪə/) (in the Roman Catholic Church) another term for **VERONICA** (in sense 2).
– ORIGIN early 17th cent.: from Latin, literally 'napkin', from *sudor* 'sweat'.

sudatorium /ˌs(j)uːdəˈtɔːrɪəm/ ▶ **noun** (pl. **sudatoria** /-rɪə/) a room, especially in ancient Roman times, used for hot-air or steam baths.
– ORIGIN Latin, neuter of *sudatorius*, from *sudare* 'to sweat'.

Sudbury /ˈsʌdb(ə)ri/ a city in SW central Ontario; pop. 110,670 (1991). It lies at the centre of Canada's largest mining region.

sudd /sʌd/ ▶ **noun** (**the sudd**) an area of floating vegetation in a stretch of the White Nile, thick enough to impede navigation.
– ORIGIN Arabic, literally 'obstruction'.

sudden ▶ **adjective** occurring or done quickly and unexpectedly or without warning: *a sudden bright flash.*
▶ **adverb** poetic/literary or informal suddenly: *sudden there swooped an eagle downward.*
– PHRASES **(all) of a sudden** suddenly: *I feel really tired all of a sudden.* **on a sudden** archaic way of saying ***all of a sudden***.
– DERIVATIVES **suddenness** noun.
– ORIGIN Middle English: from Anglo-Norman French *sudein*, from an alteration of Latin *subitaneus*, from *subitus* 'sudden'.

sudden death ▶ **noun** [mass noun] informal a means of deciding the winner in a tied match, in which play continues and the winner is the first side or player to score: [as modifier] *a sudden-death play-off.*

sudden infant death syndrome ▶ **noun** technical term for **COT DEATH**.

suddenly ▶ **adverb** quickly and unexpectedly: *George II died suddenly* | [sentence adverb] *suddenly I heard a loud scream.*

Sudetenland /suːˈdeɪt(ə)nˌland/ an area in the north-west part of the Czech Republic, on the border with Germany. Allocated to Czechoslovakia after the First World War, it became an object of Nazi expansionist policies and was ceded to Germany as a result of the Munich Agreement of September 1938. In 1945 the area was returned to Czechoslovakia. Czech name **SUDETY** /ˈsuːdɛtiː/.

sudoriferous /ˌs(j)uːdəˈrɪf(ə)rəs/ ▶ **adjective** (of a gland) secreting sweat.
– ORIGIN late 16th cent. (in the sense 'sudorific'): from late Latin *sudorifer* (from Latin *sudor* 'sweat') + **-OUS**.

sudorific /ˌs(j)uːdəˈrɪfɪk/ Medicine ▶ **adjective** relating to or causing sweating.
▶ **noun** a drug that induces sweating.
– ORIGIN early 17th cent.: from modern Latin *sudorificus*, from Latin *sudor* 'sweat'.

Sudra /ˈsuːdrə, ˈʃuːdrə/ ▶ **noun** a member of the worker caste, lowest of the four Hindu castes.
– ORIGIN from Sanskrit *śūdra*.

suds ▶ **plural noun** froth made from soap and water.
■ N. Amer. informal beer.
▶ **verb** [with obj.] chiefly N. Amer. lather, cover, or wash in soapy water: *Martha sudsed my back.*
■ [no obj.] form suds: *soft baby soap that sudsed.*
– DERIVATIVES **sudsy** adjective.
– ORIGIN mid 19th cent.: of uncertain sense development but perhaps originally denoting the flood water of the fens; compare with Middle Low German *sudde*, Middle Dutch *sudse* 'marsh, bog'; probably related to **SEETHE**.

sudser /ˈsʌdzə/ ▶ **noun** N. Amer. informal a soap opera.

sue ▶ **verb** (**sues**, **sued**, **suing**) **1** [with obj.] institute legal proceedings against (a person or institution), typically for redress: *she is to sue the baby's father* | [no obj.] *I* ***sued for*** *breach of contract.*
2 [no obj.] formal appeal formally to a person for something: *the rebels were forced to* ***sue for*** *peace.*
– DERIVATIVES **suer** noun.
– ORIGIN Middle English: from Anglo-Norman French *suer*, based on Latin *sequi* 'follow'. Early senses were very similar to those of the verb *follow.*

suede ▶ **noun** [mass noun] leather, especially kidskin, with the flesh side rubbed to make a velvety nap.
– ORIGIN mid 17th cent.: from French (*gants de*) *Suède* '(gloves of) Sweden'.

suedehead ▶ **noun** a young person of a subculture characterized by an appearance similar to that of skinheads but generally with slightly longer hair and smarter clothes.

suerte /ˈswɛːteɪ/ ▶ **noun** an action or pass performed by a bullfighter.
■ each of the three stages of a bullfight.
– ORIGIN Spanish, literally 'chance, fate'.

suet /ˈs(j)uːɪt/ ▶ **noun** [mass noun] the hard white fat on the kidneys and loins of cattle, sheep, and other animals, used to make foods including puddings, pastry, and mincemeat.
– DERIVATIVES **suety** adjective.
– ORIGIN Middle English: from Anglo-Norman French, from the synonymous word *su*, from Latin *sebum* 'tallow'.

Suetonius /swiːˈtəʊnɪəs/ (*c.*69–*c.*150 AD), Roman biographer and historian; full name *Gaius Suetonius Tranquillus*. His surviving works include *Lives of the Caesars*.

suet pudding ▶ **noun** a pudding of suet and flour, typically boiled or steamed.

Suez, Isthmus of /ˈsuːɪz/ an isthmus between the Mediterranean and the Red Sea, connecting Egypt and Africa to the Sinai peninsula and Asia. The port of Suez lies in the south. The isthmus is traversed by the Suez Canal.

Suez Canal a shipping canal connecting the Mediterranean at Port Said with the Red Sea. It was constructed between 1859 and 1869 by Ferdinand de Lesseps. In 1875 it came under British control; its nationalization by Egypt in 1956 prompted the Suez crisis.

Suez crisis a short conflict following the nationalization of the Suez Canal by President Nasser of Egypt in 1956. Britain and France made a military alliance with Israel to regain control of the canal, but international criticism forced the withdrawal of forces.

suf- ▶ **prefix** variant spelling of **SUB-** assimilated before *f* (as in *suffocate*, *suffuse*).

suffer ▶ **verb** [with obj.] **1** experience or be subjected to (something bad or unpleasant): *he'd suffered intense pain* | [no obj.] *he'd suffered a great deal since his arrest* | [as noun **suffering**] *weapons that cause unnecessary suffering.*
■ [no obj.] (**suffer from**) be affected by or subject to (an illness or ailment): *his daughter suffered from agoraphobia.* ■ [no obj.] become or appear worse in quality: *his relationship with Anne did suffer.* ■ [no obj.] archaic undergo martyrdom or execution.
2 archaic tolerate: *France will no longer suffer the existing government.*
■ [with obj. and infinitive] allow (someone) to do something: *my conscience would not suffer me to accept any more.*
– PHRASES **not suffer fools gladly** be impatient or intolerant towards people one regards as foolish or unintelligent. [ORIGIN: with biblical allusion to 2 Cor. 11–19.]
– DERIVATIVES **sufferable** adjective, **sufferer** noun (only in sense 1).
– ORIGIN Middle English: from Anglo-Norman French *suffrir*, from Latin *sufferre*, from *sub-* 'from below' + *ferre* 'to bear'.

sufferance ▶ **noun** [mass noun] **1** absence of objection rather than genuine approval; toleration: *Charles was only here* ***on sufferance****.*
■ Law the condition of the holder of an estate who continues to hold it after the title has ceased, without the express permission of the owner: *an estate at sufferance.* ■ archaic patient endurance.
2 archaic the suffering or undergoing of something bad or unpleasant.
– ORIGIN Middle English (in sense 2): from Anglo-Norman French *suffraunce*, from late Latin *sufferentia*, from *sufferre* (see **SUFFER**).

suffice /səˈfʌɪs/ ▶ **verb** [no obj.] be enough or adequate: *a quick look should suffice* | [with infinitive] *two examples should suffice to prove the contention.*
■ [with obj.] meet the needs of: *simple mediocrity cannot suffice them.*
– PHRASES **suffice (it) to say** used to indicate that one is saying enough to make one's meaning clear while withholding something for reasons of discretion or brevity: *suffice it to say that they were not considered suitable for this project.*
– ORIGIN Middle English: from Old French *suffis-*, stem of *suffire*, from Latin *sufficere* 'put under, meet the need of', from *sub-* 'under' + *facere* 'make'.

sufficiency ▶ **noun** (pl. **-ies**) [mass noun] the condition or quality of being adequate or sufficient.
■ [in sing.] an adequate amount of something, especially of something essential: *a* ***sufficiency*** *of good food.* ■ archaic self-sufficiency or independence of character, especially of an arrogant or imperious sort.
– ORIGIN late 15th cent. (denoting sufficient means or wealth): from late Latin *sufficientia*, from the verb *sufficere* (see **SUFFICE**).

sufficient ▶ **adjective** & **determiner** enough; adequate: [as adj.] *he had a small private income which was*

sufficient for her needs | [as determiner] *they had sufficient resources to survive.*
– DERIVATIVES **sufficiently** adverb.
– ORIGIN Middle English (in the sense 'legally satisfactory'): from Old French, or from Latin *sufficient-* 'meeting the need of' (see **SUFFICE**).

sufficient reason ▶ noun [mass noun] Philosophy the principle (associated particularly with G.W. Leibniz) that all events must ultimately be explicable in terms of the reasons a divine being would have had to choose one alternative rather than another.

suffix /ˈsʌfɪks/ ▶ noun **1** a morpheme added at the end of a word to form a derivative (e.g. *-ation, -fy, -ing, -itis*).
2 Mathematics another term for **SUBSCRIPT**.
▶ verb /also səˈfɪks/ [with obj.] append, especially as a suffix.
– DERIVATIVES **suffixation** noun.
– ORIGIN late 18th cent. (as a noun): from modern Latin *suffixum*, neuter past participle (used as a noun) of Latin *suffigere*, from *sub-* 'subordinately' + *figere* 'fasten'.

suffocate ▶ verb die or cause to die from lack of air or inability to breathe: [no obj.] *ten detainees suffocated in an airless police cell* | [with obj.] *she was suffocated by fumes from the boiler.*
■ have or cause to have difficulty in breathing: [no obj.] *he was suffocating, his head jammed up against the back of the sofa* | [with obj.] *you're suffocating me—I can scarcely breathe* | [as adj. **suffocating**] *the suffocating heat.* ■ figurative feel or cause to feel trapped and oppressed: [as adj. **suffocated**] *I felt suffocated by London.*
– DERIVATIVES **suffocatingly** adverb, **suffocation** noun.
– ORIGIN late 15th cent.: from Latin *suffocat-* 'stifled', from the verb *suffocare*, from *sub-* 'below' + *fauces* 'throat'.

Suffolk[1] /ˈsʌfək/ a county of eastern England, on the coast of East Anglia; county town, Ipswich.

Suffolk[2] /ˈsʌfək/ (also **Suffolk sheep**) ▶ noun a sheep of a large black-faced breed with a short fleece.

Suffolk punch ▶ noun see **PUNCH**[4] (sense 2).

suffragan /ˈsʌfrəg(ə)n/ (also **suffragan bishop** or **bishop suffragan**) ▶ noun a bishop appointed to help a diocesan bishop.
■ a bishop in relation to his archbishop or metropolitan.
– ORIGIN late Middle English: from Anglo-Norman French and Old French, representing medieval Latin *suffraganeus* 'assistant (bishop)', from Latin *suffragium* (see **SUFFRAGE**).

suffrage /ˈsʌfrɪdʒ/ ▶ noun **1** [mass noun] the right to vote in political elections.
■ [count noun] archaic a vote given in assent to a proposal or in favour of the election of a particular person.
2 (usu. **suffrages**) (in the Book of Common Prayer) the intercessory petitions pronounced by a priest in the Litany.
■ a series of petitions pronounced by the priest with the responses of the congregation. ■ archaic intercessory prayers, especially those for the dead.
– ORIGIN late Middle English (in the sense 'intercessory prayers', also 'assistance'): from Latin *suffragium*, reinforced by French *suffrage*. The modern sense of 'right to vote' was originally US (dating from the late 18th cent.).

suffragette /ˌsʌfrəˈdʒɛt/ ▶ noun historical a woman seeking the right to vote through organized protest.

> In the UK in the early 20th century the suffragettes initiated a campaign of demonstrations and militant action, under the leadership of the Pankhursts, after the repeated defeat of women's suffrage bills in Parliament. In 1918 they won the vote for women over the age of 30, and ten years later were given full equality with men in voting rights.

suffragi /sʊˈfrɑːgi/ ▶ noun (pl. **suffragis**) (in Arabic-speaking countries) a waiter or butler.
– ORIGIN via Egyptian from Turkish *sofracı*, based on Arabic *ṣufra* 'food'.

suffragist ▶ noun chiefly historical a person advocating the extension of suffrage, especially to women.
– DERIVATIVES **suffragism** noun.

suffuse /səˈfjuːz/ ▶ verb [with obj.] gradually spread through or over: *her cheeks were suffused with colour* | *the first half of the poem is suffused with idealism.*
– DERIVATIVES **suffusion** noun.
– ORIGIN late 16th cent.: from Latin *suffus-* 'poured into', from *sub-* 'below, from below' + *fundere* 'pour'.

Sufi /ˈsuːfi/ ▶ noun (pl. **Sufis**) a Muslim ascetic and mystic.
– DERIVATIVES **Sufic** adjective.
– ORIGIN mid 17th cent.: from Arabic *ṣūfī*, perhaps from *ṣūf* 'wool' (referring to the woollen garment worn).

Sufism ▶ noun [mass noun] the mystical system of the Sufis.

> Sufism is the esoteric dimension of the Islamic faith, the spiritual path to mystical union with God. It is influenced by other faiths, such as Buddhism, and reached its peak in the 13th century. There are many Sufi orders, the best-known being the dervishes.

sug /sʌg/ ▶ verb (**sugged, sugging**) [no obj.] informal sell or attempt to sell a product under the guise of conducting market research: *a market researcher claims the firm is sugging.*
– ORIGIN 1980s: acronym from *sell under the guise*.

sug- ▶ prefix variant spelling of **SUB-** assimilated before g (as in *suggest*).

sugan /ˈsuːg(ə)n/ ▶ noun Irish a straw rope.
■ (also **sugan chair**) a chair with a seat made from woven straw ropes.
– ORIGIN late 17th cent.: from Irish *súgán*.

sugar ▶ noun **1** [mass noun] a sweet crystalline substance obtained from various plants, especially sugar cane and sugar beet, consisting essentially of sucrose, and used as a sweetener in food and drink.
■ [count noun] a lump or teaspoonful of this, used to sweeten tea or coffee. ■ informal, chiefly US used as a term of endearment or an affectionate form of address: *what's wrong, sugar?* ■ [as exclamation] informal used as a euphemism for 'shit'. ■ informal a narcotic drug, especially heroin or LSD.
2 Biochemistry any of the class of soluble, crystalline, typically sweet-tasting carbohydrates found in living tissues and exemplified by glucose and sucrose.
▶ verb [with obj.] sweeten, sprinkle, or coat with sugar: *Mother absent-mindedly sugared her tea* | [as adj. **sugared**] *sugared almonds.*
■ figurative make more agreeable or palatable: *the novel was preachy but sugared heavily with jokes.* ■ [no obj.] [usu. as noun **sugaring**] Entomology spread a mixture of sugar, treacle, beer, etc., on a tree trunk in order to catch moths.
– PHRASES **sugar the pill** see **PILL**[1].
– DERIVATIVES **sugarless** adjective.
– ORIGIN Middle English: from Old French *sukere*, from Italian *zucchero*, probably via medieval Latin from Arabic *sukkar*.

sugar apple ▶ noun another term for **SWEETSOP**.

sugar bean ▶ noun a French bean of a reddish mottled variety widely eaten in South Africa.

sugar beet ▶ noun [mass noun] beet of a variety from which sugar is extracted. It provides an important alternative sugar source to cane, and the pulp which remains after processing is used as stockfeed.

sugarbird ▶ noun **1** a southern African songbird with a long fine bill and very long tail, feeding on nectar and insects.
• Genus *Promerops*, family Promeropidae (or Meliphagidae): two species.
2 W. Indian another term for **BANANAQUIT**.

sugar bush ▶ noun **1** a plantation of sugar maples.
2 South African term for **PROTEA**.

sugar candy ▶ noun another term for **CANDY**.

sugar cane ▶ noun [mass noun] a perennial tropical grass with tall stout jointed stems from which sugar is extracted. The fibrous residue can be used as fuel, in fibreboard, and for a number of other purposes.
• Genus *Saccharum*, family Gramineae: several species, in particular *S. officinarum* and its hybrids.

sugar-coat ▶ verb [with obj.] coat (an item of food) with sugar: [as adj. **sugar-coated**] *sugar-coated almonds.*
■ make superficially attractive or acceptable: *you won't see him sugar-coat the truth.* ■ make excessively sentimental: *the film-makers' proficiency is overpowered by their tendency to sugar-coat the material.*

sugarcraft ▶ noun [mass noun] the art of creating confectionery or cake decorations from sugar paste.

sugar cube ▶ noun a sugar lump.

sugar daddy ▶ noun informal a rich older man who lavishes gifts on a young woman in return for her company or sexual favours.

sugar glider ▶ noun a flying phalanger that feeds on wattle gum and eucalyptus sap, native to Australia, New Guinea, and Tasmania.
• *Petaurus breviceps*, family Petauridae.

sugar gum ▶ noun an Australian eucalyptus with sweet foliage which is attractive to cattle and sheep.
• Genus *Eucalyptus*, family Myrtaceae: several species, in particular *E. cladocalyx*.

sugaring ▶ noun [mass noun] **1** (also **sugaring off**) N. Amer. the boiling down of maple sap until it thickens into syrup or crystallizes into sugar.
2 a method of removing unwanted hair by applying a mixture of lemon juice, sugar, and water to the skin and then peeling it off together with the hair.

sugar kelp ▶ noun [mass noun] a large brown seaweed with a long crinkly blade-like frond that grows up to 3 m in length and young stems that are edible.
• *Lactaria saccharina*, class Phaeophyceae.

sugarloaf ▶ noun a conical moulded mass of sugar (used chiefly in similies and metaphors to describe the shape of other objects): [as modifier] *a sugarloaf hat.*

Sugar Loaf Mountain a rocky peak situated to the north-east of Copacabana Beach, in Rio de Janeiro, Brazil. It rises to a height of 390 m (1,296 ft).

sugar lump ▶ noun a small cube of compacted sugar used for sweetening hot drinks.

sugar maple ▶ noun a North American maple, from the sap of which maple sugar and maple syrup are made. Also called **ROCK MAPLE** in North America.
• *Acer saccharum*, family Aceraceae.

sugar of lead ▶ noun [mass noun] Chemistry, dated lead acetate, a soluble white crystalline salt.
• Chem. formula: $Pb(CH_3CO_2)_2$.
– ORIGIN mid 17th cent.: so named because of its sweet taste.

sugarplum ▶ noun chiefly archaic a crystallized plum.
■ a small round sweet of flavoured boiled sugar.

sugar snap (also **sugar snap pea, sugar pea**) ▶ noun mangetout, especially of a variety with thicker and more rounded pods.

sugar soap ▶ noun [mass noun] Brit. an alkaline preparation containing washing soda and soap, used for cleaning or removing paint.

sugary ▶ adjective containing much sugar: *energy-restoring, sugary drinks.*
■ resembling or coated in sugar: *a sugary texture.* ■ excessively sentimental: *sugary romance.*
– DERIVATIVES **sugariness** noun.

suggest ▶ verb [reporting verb] put forward for consideration: [with clause] *I suggest that we wait a day or two* | [with direct speech] *'Maybe you ought to get an expert,' she suggested* | [with obj.] *Ruth suggested a holiday.*
■ [with obj.] cause one to think that (something) exists or is the case: *finds of lead coffins suggested a cemetery north of the river* | [with clause] *the temperature wasn't as tropical as the bright sunlight may have suggested* ■ state or express indirectly: [with clause] *are you suggesting that I should ignore her?* | [with obj.] *the seduction scenes suggest his guilt and her loneliness.* ■ [with obj.] evoke: *the theatrical interpretation of weather and water almost suggests El Greco.* ■ (**suggest itself**) (of an idea) come into one's mind.
– DERIVATIVES **suggester** noun.
– ORIGIN early 16th cent.: from Latin *suggest-* 'suggested, prompted', from the verb *suggerere*, from *sub-* 'from below' + *gerere* 'bring'.

suggestible ▶ adjective open to suggestion; easily swayed: *a suggestible client would comply.*
– DERIVATIVES **suggestibility** noun.

suggestion ▶ noun an idea or plan put forward for consideration.
■ [mass noun] the action of doing this: ***at my suggestion**, the museum held an exhibition of his work.* ■ something that implies or indicates a certain fact or situation: *there is no suggestion that he was involved in any wrongdoing.* ■ a slight trace or indication of something: *there was a suggestion of a smile on his lips.* ■ [mass noun] the action or process of calling up an idea or thought in someone's mind by associating it with other things: *the power of suggestion.* ■ [mass noun] Psychology the influencing of a person to accept an idea, belief, or impulse uncritically, especially as a technique in hypnosis or other therapies. ■ Psychology a belief or impulse of this type.
– ORIGIN Middle English (in the sense 'an incitement to evil'): via Old French from Latin *suggestio(n-)*, from the verb *suggerere* (see **SUGGEST**).

suggestive ▶ **adjective** tending to suggest an idea: *there were various suggestive pieces of evidence.* ■ indicative or evocative: *flavours* ***suggestive of*** *coffee and blackberry.* ■ making someone think of sex and sexual relationships: *a suggestive remark.*
– DERIVATIVES **suggestively** adverb, **suggestiveness** noun.

suh /sʌ/ ▶ **noun** non-standard spelling of **SIR**, used in representing British dialect or southern US or black speech.

Sui /sweɪ/ a dynasty which ruled in China AD 581–618 and reunified the country.

suicidal ▶ **adjective** deeply unhappy or depressed and likely to commit suicide: *far from being suicidal, he was clearly enjoying life.* ■ relating to or likely to lead to suicide: *I began to take her suicidal tendencies seriously.* ■ likely to have a disastrously damaging effect on oneself or one's interests: *a suicidal career move.*
– DERIVATIVES **suicidally** adverb.

suicide /ˈs(j)uːɪsʌɪd/ ▶ **noun** [mass noun] the action of killing oneself intentionally: *he* ***committed suicide*** *at the age of forty* | [count noun] *gun control laws may reduce suicides.* ■ [count noun] a person who does this. ■ a course of action which is disastrously damaging to oneself or one's own interests: *it would be political suicide to restrict criteria for unemployment benefit.* ■ [as modifier] relating to or denoting a military operation carried out by people who do not expect to survive it: *a suicide bomber.*
▶ **verb** [no obj.] intentionally kill oneself: *she suicided in a very ugly manner.*
– ORIGIN mid 17th cent.: from modern Latin *suicida* 'act of suicide', *suicidium* 'person who commits suicide', from Latin *sui* 'of oneself' + *caedere* 'kill'.

suicide pact ▶ **noun** an agreement between two or more people to commit suicide together.

suicide squeeze ▶ **noun** Baseball an act of running for home by a runner on third base as the ball is pitched.

sui generis /ˌsuːʌɪ ˈdʒɛn(ə)rɪs, suːiː, sjuː-, ˈgɛn-/ ▶ **adjective** unique: *the sui generis nature of animals.*
– ORIGIN Latin, literally 'of its own kind'.

sui juris /ˈdʒʊərɪs, ˈjʊə-/ ▶ **adjective** Law of age; independent: *the beneficiaries are all sui juris.*
– ORIGIN Latin, literally 'of one's own right'.

suint /swɪnt/ ▶ **noun** [mass noun] the natural grease in sheep's wool, from which lanolin is obtained.
– ORIGIN late 18th cent.: from French, from *suer* 'sweat'.

Suisse /sɥis/ French name for **SWITZERLAND**.

suit ▶ **noun 1** a set of outer clothes made of the same fabric and designed to be worn together, typically consisting of a jacket and trousers or a jacket and skirt. ■ a set of clothes to be worn on a particular occasion or for a particular activity: *a jogging suit.* ■ a complete set of pieces of armour for covering the whole body. ■ a complete set of sails required for a ship or for a set of spars. ■ (usu. **suits**) informal a high-ranking executive in a business or organization, typically one regarded as exercising influence in an impersonal way: *maybe now the suits in Washington will listen.*
2 any of the sets distinguished by their pictorial symbols into which a pack of playing cards is divided, in conventional packs comprising spades, hearts, diamonds, and clubs.
3 short for **LAWSUIT**. ■ the process of trying to win a woman's affection, typically with a view to marriage: *he could not compete with John's charms in Marian's eyes and his suit came to nothing.* ■ poetic/literary a petition or entreaty made to a person in authority.
▶ **verb 1** [with obj.] be convenient for or acceptable to: *he lied whenever it suited him* | [no obj.] *the flat has two bedrooms—if it suits, you can have one of them.* ■ (**suit oneself**) [often in imperative] act entirely according to one's own wishes (often used to express the speaker's annoyance): *'I'm not going to help you.' 'Suit yourself.'* ■ go well with or enhance the features, figure, or character of (someone): *the dress didn't suit her.* ■ (**suit something to**) archaic adapt or make appropriate for (something): *they took care to suit their answers to the questions put to them.*
2 [no obj.] N. Amer. put on clothes, especially for a particular activity: *I* ***suited up*** *and entered the water.*
– PHRASES **suit the action to the word** carry out one's stated intentions. **suit someone's book** Brit. informal be convenient or acceptable to someone. **suit someone down to the ground** Brit. be extremely convenient or appropriate for someone.
– ORIGIN Middle English: from Anglo-Norman French *siwte*, from a feminine past participle of a Romance verb based on Latin *sequi* 'follow'. Early senses included 'attendance at a court' and 'legal process'; senses 1 and 2 derive from an earlier meaning 'set of things to be used together'. The verb sense 'make appropriate' dates from the late 16th cent.

suitable ▶ **adjective** right or appropriate for a particular person, purpose, or situation: *these toys are not* ***suitable for*** *children under five.*
– DERIVATIVES **suitability** noun, **suitableness** noun, **suitably** adverb.
– ORIGIN late 16th cent.: from the verb **SUIT**, on the pattern of *agreeable.*

suitcase ▶ **noun** a case with a handle and a hinged lid, used for carrying clothes and other personal possessions.
– DERIVATIVES **suitcaseful** noun (pl. **-fuls**).

suite /swiːt/ ▶ **noun 1** a set of things belonging together, in particular: ■ a set of rooms designated for one person's or family's use or for a particular purpose. ■ a set of furniture of the same design. ■ Music a set of instrumental compositions, originally in dance style, to be played in succession. ■ Music a set of selected pieces from an opera or musical, arranged to be played as one instrumental work. ■ Computing a set of programs with a uniform design and the ability to share data. ■ Geology a group of minerals, rocks, or fossils occurring together and characteristic of a location or period.
2 a group of people in attendance on a monarch or other person of high rank.
– ORIGIN late 17th cent.: from French, from Anglo-Norman French *siwte* (see **SUIT**).

suited ▶ **adjective 1** [predic.] right or appropriate for a particular person, purpose, or situation: *the task is ideally* ***suited to*** *a computer.*
2 [in combination] wearing a suit of clothes of a specified type, fabric, or colour: *a dark-suited man* | *sober-suited lawyers.*

suiting ▶ **noun** [mass noun] fabric of a suitable quality for making suits, trousers, jackets, and skirts. ■ suits collectively.

suitor /ˈs(j)uːtə/ ▶ **noun 1** a man who pursues a relationship with a particular woman, with a view to marriage.
2 a prospective buyer of a business or corporation.
– ORIGIN late Middle English (in the sense 'member of a retinue', also in sense 2): from Anglo-Norman French *seutor*, from Latin *secutor*, from *sequi* 'follow'.

suji /ˈsuːʒi/ ▶ **noun** Indian term for **SEMOLINA**.

suk (also **sukh**) ▶ **noun** variant spelling of **SOUK**.

Sukarno /suːˈkɑːnəʊ/, Achmad (1901–70), Indonesian statesman, President 1945–67. He led the struggle for independence, which was formally granted in 1949, but lost power in the 1960s after having been implicated in the abortive communist coup of 1965.

Sukhotai /ˌsʊkəˈtʌɪ/ (also **Sukhothai**) a town in NW central Thailand; pop. 22,600 (1990). It was formerly the capital of an independent state of the same name, which flourished from the mid 13th to the mid 14th centuries.

sukiyaki /ˌsʊkɪˈjaki, -ˈjɑːki/ ▶ **noun** [mass noun] a Japanese dish of sliced meat, especially beef, fried rapidly with vegetables and sauce.
– ORIGIN Japanese.

sukkah ▶ **noun** variant spelling of **SUCCAH**.

Sukkur /ˈsʌkə/ a city in SE Pakistan, on the Indus River; pop. 350,000 (est. 1991). Nearby is the Sukkur Barrage, a dam constructed across the Indus which directs water through irrigation channels to a large area of the Indus valley.

Sukuma /sʊˈkuːmə, sʊˈkjuːmə/ ▶ **noun** (pl. same or **Sukumas**) **1** a member of a people inhabiting west central Tanzania.
2 [mass noun] the Bantu language of this people, related to Nyamwezi and having around 4 million speakers.
▶ **adjective** of or relating to this people or their language.
– ORIGIN a local name.

Sulawesi /ˌsʊləˈweɪsi/ a mountainous island in the Greater Sunda group in Indonesia, situated to the east of Borneo; chief town, Ujung Pandang. It is noted as the habitat of numerous endemic species. Former name **CELEBES**.

Sulaymaniyah /ˌsʊlɪməˈniːə/ a town in NE Iraq, in the mountainous region of southern Kurdistan; pop. 279,400 (est. 1985). It is the capital of a Kurdish governorate of the same name. Full name **AS SULAYMANIYAH**.

sulcate /ˈsʌlkeɪt/ ▶ **adjective** Botany & Zoology marked with parallel grooves.
– ORIGIN mid 18th cent.: from Latin *sulcatus* 'furrowed', past participle of *sulcare.*

sulcus /ˈsʌlkəs/ ▶ **noun** (pl. **sulci** /-sʌɪ/) Anatomy a groove or furrow, especially one on the surface of the brain.
– ORIGIN mid 17th cent.: from Latin, 'furrow, wrinkle'.

Suleiman I /ˈsuːlɪmən, ˌsuːleɪˈmɑːn/ (also **Soliman** or **Solyman**) (*c.*1494–1566), sultan of the Ottoman Empire 1520–66; also known as **Suleiman the Magnificent** or **Suleiman the Lawgiver**. The Ottoman Empire reached its fullest extent under his rule.

sulfa- ▶ **combining form** US spelling of **SULPHA-**.

sulfur etc. ▶ **noun** US spelling of **SULPHUR** etc.

sulk ▶ **verb** [no obj.] be silent, morose, and bad-tempered out of annoyance or disappointment: *he was sulking over the break-up of his band.*
▶ **noun** a period of gloomy and bad-tempered silence stemming from annoyance and resentment: *she was* ***in a fit of the sulks.***
– DERIVATIVES **sulker** noun.
– ORIGIN late 18th cent.: perhaps a back-formation from **SULKY**.

sulky ▶ **adjective** (**sulkier**, **sulkiest**) morose, bad-tempered, and resentful; refusing to be cooperative or cheerful: *disappointment was making her sulky.* ■ expressing or suggesting gloom and bad temper: *she had a sultry, sulky mouth.* ■ figurative not quick to work or respond: *a sulky fire.*
▶ **noun** (pl. **-ies**) a light two-wheeled horse-drawn vehicle for one person, used chiefly in trotting races.
– DERIVATIVES **sulkily** adverb, **sulkiness** noun.
– ORIGIN mid 18th cent.: perhaps from obsolete *sulke* 'hard to dispose of', of unknown origin.

sull /sʌl/ ▶ **verb** [no obj.] US informal, dialect (of an animal) refuse to advance. ■ (of a person) become sullen; sulk: *don't* ***sull up*** *on me, let's get it aired.*
– ORIGIN mid 19th cent.: back-formation from **SULLEN**.

Sulla /ˈsʌlə/ (138–78 BC), Roman general and politician; full name *Lucius Cornelius Sulla Felix*. After a victorious campaign against Mithridates VI, Sulla invaded Italy in 83. He was elected dictator in 82 and implemented constitutional reforms in favour of the Senate.

sullage /ˈsʌlɪdʒ/ ▶ **noun** [mass noun] waste from household sinks, showers, and baths, but not toilets. ■ archaic refuse, especially sewage.
– ORIGIN mid 16th cent.: perhaps from Anglo-Norman French *suillage*, from *suiller* 'to soil'.

sullen ▶ **adjective** bad-tempered and sulky: *a sullen pout* | figurative *a sullen sunless sky.* ■ (especially of water) slow-moving: *rivers in sullen, perpetual flood.*
▶ **noun** (**the sullens**) archaic a sulky or depressed mood.
– DERIVATIVES **sullenly** adverb, **sullenness** noun.
– ORIGIN Middle English (in the senses 'solitary, averse to company', and 'unusual'): from Anglo-Norman French *sulein*, from *sol* 'sole'.

Sullivan, Sir Arthur (Seymour) (1842–1900), English composer. His fame rests on the fourteen light operas which he wrote in collaboration with the librettist W. S. Gilbert.

sully /ˈsʌli/ ▶ **verb** (**-ies**, **-ied**) [with obj.] poetic/literary or ironic damage the purity or integrity of; defile: *they were outraged that anyone should sully their good name.*
– ORIGIN late 16th cent.: perhaps from French *souiller* 'to soil'.

sulpha /ˈsʌlfə/ (US **sulfa**) ▶ **noun** [mass noun] [usu. as modifier] the sulphonamide family of drugs: *a succession of life-saving sulpha drugs.*
– ORIGIN 1940s: abbreviation (see **SULPHA-**).

sulpha- (US **sulfa-**) ▶ **combining form** in names of drugs derived from sulphanilamide.
– ORIGIN abbreviation of **SULPHANILAMIDE**.

S

sulphadiazine /ˌsʌlfəˈdʌɪəziːn/ (US **sulfadiazine**) ▶noun [mass noun] Medicine a sulphonamide antibiotic used to treat meningococcal meningitis.

sulphadimidine /ˌsʌlfəˈdɪmɪdiːn/ (US **sulfadimidine**) ▶noun [mass noun] Medicine a sulphonamide antibiotic used chiefly to treat human urinary infections and to control respiratory disease in pigs.
– ORIGIN mid 20th cent.: from SULPHA- + DI-¹ + PYRIMIDINE.

sulphamethoxazole /ˌsʌlfəmɪˈtɒksəzəʊl/ (US **sulfamethoxazole**) ▶noun [mass noun] Medicine a sulphonamide antibiotic used to treat respiratory and urinary tract infections, and as a component of the preparation co-trimoxazole.

sulphamic acid /sʌlˈfamɪk/ (US **sulfamic acid**) ▶noun [mass noun] Chemistry a strongly acid crystalline compound used in cleaning agents and to make weedkiller.
● Chem. formula: HOSO₂NH₂.
– DERIVATIVES **sulphamate** /ˈsʌlfəmeɪt/ noun.
– ORIGIN mid 19th cent.: *sulphamic* from SULPHUR + AMIDE + -IC.

sulphanilamide /ˌsʌlfəˈnɪləmʌɪd/ (US **sulfanilamide**) ▶noun Medicine a synthetic compound with antibacterial properties which is the basis of the sulphonamide drugs.
● Alternative name: *p*-**aminobenzenesulphonamide**; chem. formula: (H₂N)C₆H₄(SO₂NH₂).
– ORIGIN 1930s: from *sulphanilic* (from SULPHUR + ANILINE + -IC) + AMIDE.

sulphapyridine /ˌsʌlfəˈpɪrɪdiːn/ (US **sulfapyridine**) ▶noun [mass noun] Medicine a sulphonamide antibiotic used to treat some forms of dermatitis.

sulphasalazine /ˌsʌlfəˈsaləziːn/ (US **sulfasalazine**) ▶noun [mass noun] Medicine a sulphonamide antibiotic used to treat ulcerative colitis and Crohn's disease.
– ORIGIN mid 20th cent.: from SULPHA- + *sal(icylic acid)* + AZINE.

sulphate /ˈsʌlfeɪt/ (US **sulfate**) ▶noun Chemistry a salt or ester of sulphuric acid, containing the anion SO₄²⁻ or the divalent group —OSO₂O—.
– ORIGIN late 18th cent.: from French *sulfate*, from Latin *sulphur* (see SULPHUR).

sulphide /ˈsʌlfʌɪd/ (US **sulfide**) ▶noun Chemistry a binary compound of sulphur with another element or group.

sulphite /ˈsʌlfʌɪt/ (US **sulfite**) ▶noun Chemistry a salt of sulphurous acid, containing the anion SO₃²⁻.
– ORIGIN late 18th cent.: from French *sulfite*, alteration of *sulfate* (see SULPHATE).

sulphonamide /sʌlˈfɒnəmʌɪd/ (US **sulfonamide**) ▶noun Medicine any of a class of synthetic drugs, derived from sulphanilamide, which are able to prevent the multiplication of some pathogenic bacteria.
– ORIGIN late 19th cent.: from SULPHONE + AMIDE.

sulphonate /ˈsʌlfəneɪt/ (US **sulfonate**) Chemistry ▶noun a salt or ester of a sulphonic acid.
▶verb [with obj.] convert (a compound) into a sulphonate, typically by reaction with sulphuric acid.
– DERIVATIVES **sulphonation** noun.

sulphone /ˈsʌlfəʊn/ (US **sulfone**) ▶noun Chemistry an organic compound containing a sulphonyl group linking two organic groups.
– ORIGIN late 19th cent.: from German *Sulfon*, from *Sulfur* (see SULPHUR).

sulphonic acid (US **sulfonic**) ▶noun Chemistry an organic acid containing the group —SO₂OH.

sulphonyl /ˈsʌlfənʌɪl, -nɪl/ (US **sulfonyl**) ▶noun [as modifier] Chemistry of or denoting a divalent radical, —SO₂—, derived from a sulphonic acid group.

sulphur (US & Chemistry **sulfur**) ▶noun 1 [mass noun] the chemical element of atomic number 16, a yellow combustible non-metal. (Symbol: **S**)
■ the material of which hellfire and lightning were formerly believed to consist. ■ a pale greenish-yellow colour: [as modifier] *the bird's sulphur-yellow throat.*

Sulphur occurs uncombined in volcanic and sedimentary deposits, as well as being a constituent of many minerals and petroleum. It is normally a bright yellow crystalline solid, but several other allotropic forms can be made. Sulphur is an ingredient of gunpowder, and is used in making matches and as an antiseptic and fungicide.

2 an American butterfly with predominantly yellow wings that may bear darker patches.
● *Colias, Phoebis,* and other genera, family Pieridae.

▶verb [with obj.] disinfect or fumigate with sulphur.
– DERIVATIVES **sulphury** adjective.
– ORIGIN Middle English: from Anglo-Norman French *sulfre,* from Latin *sulfur, sulphur.*

USAGE In general use the standard British spelling is **sulphur** and the standard US spelling is **sulfur**. In chemistry, however, the **-f-** spelling is now the standard form in all related words in the field in both British and US contexts.

sulphur candle ▶noun a candle containing sulphur, burnt to produce sulphur dioxide for fumigation.

sulphur dioxide ▶noun [mass noun] Chemistry a colourless pungent toxic gas formed by burning sulphur in air.
● Chem. formula: SO₂.

sulphureous /sʌlˈfjʊərɪəs/ (US **sulfureous**) ▶adjective of, like, or containing sulphur.
– ORIGIN early 16th cent.: from Latin *sulphureus* (from SULPHUR) + -OUS.

sulphuretted hydrogen /ˈsʌlfjʊˈrɛtɪd/ (US **sulfureted**) ▶noun Chemistry archaic term for HYDROGEN SULPHIDE.

sulphuric /sʌlˈfjʊərɪk/ (US **sulfuric**) ▶adjective containing sulphur or sulphuric acid: *the sulphuric by-products of wood fires.*
– ORIGIN late 18th cent.: from French *sulfurique,* from Latin (as SULPHUR).

sulphuric acid ▶noun [mass noun] a strong acid made by oxidizing solutions of sulphur dioxide and used in large quantities as an industrial and laboratory reagent. The concentrated form is an oily, dense, corrosive liquid.
● Chem. formula: H₂SO₄.

sulphurous /ˈsʌlf(ə)rəs/ (US **sulfurous**) ▶adjective (chiefly of vapour or smoke) containing or derived from sulphur: *wafts of sulphurous fumes.*
■ like sulphur in colour; pale yellow. ■ marked by bad temper, anger, or profanity: *a sulphurous glance.*
– ORIGIN late Middle English: from Latin *sulphurosus,* from *sulphur* (see SULPHUR).

sulphurous acid ▶noun [mass noun] Chemistry an unstable weak acid formed when sulphur dioxide dissolves in water. It is used as a reducing and bleaching agent.
● Chem. formula: H₂SO₃.

sulphur spring ▶noun a spring of which the water contains sulphur or its compounds.

sulphur tuft ▶noun a common European toadstool with a sulphur-yellow cap and yellowish gills and stem, growing throughout the year in clumps on tree stumps.
● *Hypholoma fasciculare,* family Strophariaceae, class Hymenomycetes.

Sulpician /sʌlˈpɪʃɪən, sʌlˈpɪʃ(ə)n/ ▶noun a member of a congregation of secular Roman Catholic priests founded in 1642 by a priest of St Sulpice, Paris, mainly to train candidates for holy orders.
▶adjective relating to or denoting this congregation.

sultan ▶noun 1 a Muslim sovereign.
■ (the Sultan) historical the sultan of Turkey.
2 a bird of a breed of white domestic chicken from Turkey.
– DERIVATIVES **sultanate** noun.
– ORIGIN mid 16th cent.: from French, or from medieval Latin *sultanus,* from Arabic *sultān* 'power, ruler'.

sultana ▶noun 1 a small light brown seedless raisin used in foods such as puddings and cakes.
2 a wife or concubine of a sultan.
■ any other woman in a sultan's family.
– ORIGIN late 16th cent. (in sense 2): from Italian, feminine of *sultano* (see SULTAN). Sense 1 dates from the mid 19th cent.

sultry /ˈsʌltri/ ▶adjective (**sultrier, sultriest**) 1 (of the air or weather) hot and humid.
2 (of a person, especially a woman) attractive in a way that suggests a passionate nature.
– DERIVATIVES **sultrily** adverb, **sultriness** noun.
– ORIGIN late 16th cent.: from obsolete *sulter* 'swelter'.

sulu /ˈsuːluː/ ▶noun (pl. **sulus**) a length of cotton or other light fabric wrapped about the body as a sarong, worn from the waist by men and full-length by women from the Melanesian Islands.
– ORIGIN Fijian.

Sulu Sea /ˈsuːluː/ a sea in the Malay Archipelago, encircled by the NE coast of Borneo and the western islands of the Philippines.

sum ▶noun 1 a particular amount of money: *they could not afford such a sum.*
2 (**the sum of**) the total amount resulting from the addition of two or more numbers, amounts, or items: *the sum of two prime numbers.*
■ the total amount of something that exists: *the sum of his own knowledge.*
3 an arithmetical problem, especially at an elementary level.
▶verb (**summed, summing**) [with obj.] technical find the sum of (two or more amounts): *if we sum these equations we obtain X.*
■ [no obj.] (**sum to**) (of two or more amounts) add up to a specified total: *these probabilities must sum to 1.*
– PHRASES **in sum** to sum up: *this interpretation does little, in sum, to add to our understanding.*
– ORIGIN Middle English: via Old French from Latin *summa* 'main part, sum total', feminine of *summus* 'highest'.
▶**sum up** give a brief summary of something: *Gerard will open the debate and I will sum up.* ■ Law (of a judge) review the evidence at the end of a case, and direct the jury regarding points of law.
sum someone/thing up express a concise idea of the nature or character of a person or thing: *selfish—that summed her up.*

sumac /ˈs(j)uːmak, ˈʃuː-/ (also **sumach**) ▶noun a shrub or small tree with compound leaves, reddish hairy fruits in persistent conical clusters, and bright autumn colours.
● Genera *Rhus* and *Cotinus,* family Anacardiaceae: several species, including the Mediterranean *R. coriaria* and the North American **staghorn sumac** (*R. typhina*), often grown as an ornamental.
– ORIGIN Middle English (denoting the dried and ground leaves of *R. coriaria* used in tanning and dyeing): from Old French *sumac* or medieval Latin *sumac(h),* from Arabic *summāk.*

Sumatra /suːˈmɑːtrə/ a large island of Indonesia, situated to the south-west of the Malay Peninsula, from which it is separated by the Strait of Malacca; chief city, Medan.
– DERIVATIVES **Sumatran** adjective & noun.

Sumatran rhinoceros ▶noun a rare hairy two-horned rhinoceros found in montane rainforests from Malaysia to Borneo.
● *Dicerorhinus sumatrensis,* family Rhinocerotidae.

Sumba /ˈsʊmbə/ an island of the Lesser Sunda group in Indonesia, lying to the south of the islands of Flores and Sumbawa; chief town, Waingapu. Also called **SANDALWOOD ISLAND**.

Sumbawa /sʊmˈbɑːwə/ an island in the Lesser Sunda group in Indonesia, situated between Lombok and Flores.

Sumer /ˈsuːmə/ an ancient region of SW Asia in present-day Iraq, comprising the southern part of Mesopotamia. From the 4th millennium BC it was the site of city states which became part of ancient Babylonia.

Sumerian /suːˈmɪərɪən, sjuː-/ ▶adjective of or relating to Sumer, its ancient language, or the early and non-Semitic element it contributed to Babylonian civilization.
▶noun 1 a member of the indigenous non-Semitic people of ancient Babylonia.
2 [mass noun] the Sumerian language.

The Sumerians had the oldest known written language, whose relationship to any other language is unclear. Theirs is the first historically attested civilization and they invented cuneiform writing, the sexagesimal system of mathematics, and the socio-political institution of the city state. Their art, literature, and theology had a profound influence long after their demise *c.*2000 BC.

– ORIGIN late 19th cent.: from French *sumérien,* from SUMER.

Sumgait /sʊmɡaˈjit/ Russian name for **SUMQAYIT**.

sumi /ˈsuːmi/ ▶noun [mass noun] a type of black Japanese ink prepared in solid sticks and used for painting and writing.
– ORIGIN early 20th cent.: Japanese, literally 'ink, blacking'.

sumi-e /ˈsuːmɪeɪ/ ▶noun [mass noun] Japanese ink painting using sumi.
– ORIGIN early 20th cent.: from SUMI + Japanese *e* 'painting'.

summa /ˈsʊmə, ˈsʌmə/ ▶noun (pl. **summae** /-miː/) chiefly archaic a summary of a subject.

– ORIGIN early 18th cent.: from Latin, literally 'sum total' (a sense reflected in Middle English).

summa cum laude /ˌsʌmə kʌm ˈlɔːdeɪ, ˌsʊmə kʊm ˈlaʊdeɪ/ ▶ adverb & adjective chiefly N. Amer. with the highest distinction: [as adv.] *he graduated summa cum laude* | [as adj.] *three scientific degrees, all summa cum laude.*
– ORIGIN Latin, literally 'with highest praise'.

summand /ˈsʌmand/ ▶ noun Mathematics a quantity to be added to another.
– ORIGIN mid 19th cent.: from Latin *summandus* 'to be added', gerundive of *summare*.

summarize (also **-ise**) ▶ verb [with obj.] give a brief statement of the main points of (something): *these results can be summarized in the following table* | [no obj.] *to summarize, there are three main categories.*
– DERIVATIVES **summarization** noun, **summarizer** noun.

summary ▶ noun (pl. **-ies**) a brief statement or account of the main points of something: *a summary of Chapter Three.*
▶ adjective **1** dispensing with needless details or formalities; brief: *summary financial statements.*
2 Law (of a judicial process) conducted without the customary legal formalities: *summary arrest.*
■ (of a conviction) made by a judge or magistrate without a jury.
– PHRASES **in summary** in short: *in summary, there is no clear case for one tax system compared to another.*
– DERIVATIVES **summarily** adverb, **summariness** noun.
– ORIGIN late Middle English (as an adjective): from Latin *summarius*, from *summa* 'sum total' (see **SUM**).

summary jurisdiction ▶ noun [mass noun] Law the authority of a court to use summary proceedings and arrive at a judgement.

summary offence ▶ noun Law an offence within the scope of a summary court.

summat /ˈsʌmət/ ▶ pronoun N. English non-standard spelling of **SOMETHING**.

summation /sʌˈmeɪʃ(ə)n/ ▶ noun [mass noun] **1** the process of adding things together: *the summation of numbers of small pieces of evidence.*
■ [count noun] a sum total of things added together.
2 the process of summing something up: *these will need summation in a single document.*
■ [count noun] a summary.
– DERIVATIVES **summational** adjective, **summative** adjective.

summer[1] ▶ noun the warmest season of the year, in the northern hemisphere from June to August and in the southern hemisphere from December to February: *the plant flowers in late summer* | *a long hot summer* | [as modifier] *summer holidays* | figurative *the golden summer of her life.*
■ Astronomy the period from the summer solstice to the autumnal equinox. ■ (**summers**) poetic/literary years, especially of a person's age: *a girl of sixteen or seventeen summers.*
▶ verb [no obj., with adverbial of place] spend the summer in a particular place: *well over 100 birds summered there in 1976.*
■ [with obj.] pasture (cattle) for the summer.
– DERIVATIVES **summery** adjective.
– ORIGIN Old English *sumor*, of Germanic origin; related to Dutch *zomer*, German *Sommer*, also to Sanskrit *samā* 'year'.

summer[2] (also **summer tree**) ▶ noun a horizontal bearing beam, especially one supporting joists or rafters.
– ORIGIN Middle English: from Old French *somier* 'packhorse', from late Latin *sagmarius*, from Greek *sagma* 'packsaddle'.

summer camp ▶ noun (especially in North America) a camp providing recreational and sporting facilities for children during the summer holiday period.

summer cypress ▶ noun another term for **KOCHIA**.

summer house ▶ noun a small building in a garden, used for sitting in during fine weather.

summer lightning ▶ noun [mass noun] distant sheet lightning without audible thunder, typically occurring on a summer night.

Summer Palace a palace (now in ruins) of the former Chinese emperors near Beijing.

summer pudding ▶ noun [mass noun] Brit. a pudding of soft summer fruit encased in bread or sponge.

summersault ▶ noun & verb archaic spelling of **SOMERSAULT**.

summer sausage ▶ noun [mass noun] N. Amer. a type of hard dried and smoked sausage which is similar to salami in preparation and can be made in winter to keep until summer.

summer school ▶ noun a course of lectures held during school and university summer vacations, taken as part of an academic course or as an independent course of study for professional or personal purposes.

summer season ▶ noun the summer period when most people take holidays.

summer solstice ▶ noun the solstice at midsummer, at the time of the longest day, about 21 June in the northern hemisphere and 22 December in the southern hemisphere.
■ Astronomy the solstice in June.

summer squash ▶ noun a squash which is eaten before the seeds and rind have hardened and which does not keep.
● Cultivars of *Cucurbita pepo* var. *melopepo*, family Cucurbitaceae.

summer stock ▶ noun [mass noun] chiefly N. Amer. theatrical productions by a repertory company organized for the summer season, especially at holiday resorts.

summertime ▶ noun the season or period of summer: *in summertime trains run every ten minutes.*

summer time ▶ noun [mass noun] Brit. time as adjusted to achieve longer evening daylight in summer by setting clocks an hour ahead of the standard time. Compare with **DAYLIGHT SAVING TIME**.

summer tree ▶ noun see **SUMMER**[2].

summer-weight ▶ adjective (of clothes) made of light fabric and therefore cool to wear.

summing-up ▶ noun a restatement of the main points of an argument, case, etc.
■ Law a judge's review of evidence at the end of a case, with a direction to the jury regarding points of law.

summit ▶ noun **1** the highest point of a hill or mountain.
■ figurative the highest attainable level of achievement: *the dramas are considered to form one of the summits of world literature.*
2 a meeting between heads of government.
– ORIGIN late Middle English (in the general sense 'top part'): from Old French *somete*, from *som* 'top', from Latin *summum*, neuter of *summus* 'highest'.

summiteer ▶ noun **1** a participant in a meeting between heads of government.
2 a climber who has reached the summit of a mountain.

summon ▶ verb [with obj.] authoritatively or urgently call on (someone) to be present, especially as a defendant or witness in a law court: *the pope summoned Anselm to Rome.*
■ urgently demand (help): *she summoned medical assistance.* ■ call people to attend (a meeting): *he summoned a meeting of head delegates.* ■ bring to the surface (a particular quality or reaction) from within oneself: *she managed to summon up a smile.*
■ (**summon something up**) call an image to mind: *names that summon up images of far-off places.*
– DERIVATIVES **summonable** adjective, **summoner** noun.
– ORIGIN Middle English: from Old French *somondre*, from Latin *summonere* 'give a hint', later 'call, summon', from *sub-* 'secretly' + *monere* 'warn'.

summons ▶ noun (pl. **summonses**) an order to appear before a judge or magistrate, or the writ containing it: *a summons for non-payment of a parking ticket.*
■ an authoritative or urgent call to someone to be present or to do something: [with infinitive] *they might receive a summons to fly to France next day.*
▶ verb [with obj.] chiefly Law serve (someone) with a summons: [with obj. and infinitive] *he has been summonsed to appear in court next month.*
– ORIGIN Middle English: from Old French *sumunse*, from an alteration of Latin *summonita*, feminine past participle of *summonere* (see **SUMMON**).

summum bonum /ˌsʊməm ˈbɒnəm, ˌsʌməm ˈbəʊnəm/ ▶ noun the highest good, especially as the ultimate goal according to which values and priorities are established in an ethical system.
– ORIGIN Latin.

sumo /ˈsuːməʊ/ ▶ noun (pl. **-os**) [mass noun] a Japanese form of heavyweight wrestling, in which a wrestler wins a bout by forcing his opponent outside a marked circle or by making him touch the ground with any part of his body except the soles of his feet.
■ [count noun] a sumo wrestler.
– ORIGIN from Japanese *sūmo*.

sump ▶ noun a pit or hollow in which liquid collects, in particular:
■ the base of an internal-combustion engine, which serves as a reservoir of oil for the lubrication system. ■ a depression in the floor of a mine or cave in which water collects. ■ a cesspool.
– ORIGIN Middle English (in the sense 'marsh'): from Middle Dutch or Low German *sump*, or (in the mining sense) from German *Sumpf*; related to **SWAMP**.

sumph /sʌmf/ ▶ noun Scottish a stupid or clumsy person.
– ORIGIN early 18th cent.: of unknown origin.

sumpter /ˈsʌm(p)tə/ ▶ noun archaic a pack animal.
– ORIGIN Middle English: from Old French *sommetier*, via late Latin from Greek *sagma, sagmat-* 'packsaddle'; compare with **SUMMER**[2].

sumptuary /ˈsʌm(p)tjʊəri/ ▶ adjective [attrib.] chiefly historical relating to or denoting laws that limit private expenditure on food and personal items.
– ORIGIN early 17th cent.: from Latin *sumptuarius*, from *sumptus* 'cost, expenditure', from *sumere* 'take'.

sumptuous ▶ adjective splendid and expensive-looking: *the banquet was a sumptuous, luxurious meal.*
– DERIVATIVES **sumptuosity** noun, **sumptuously** adverb, **sumptuousness** noun.
– ORIGIN late Middle English (in the sense 'made or produced at great cost'): from Old French *somptueux*, from Latin *sumptuosus*, from *sumptus* 'expenditure' (see **SUMPTUARY**).

Sumqayit /ˌsʊmkɑːˈjiːt/ an industrial city in eastern Azerbaijan, on the Caspian Sea; pop. 234,600 (1990). Russian name **SUMGAIT**.

sum total ▶ noun another term for **SUM** (in sense 2).

Sumy /ˈsuːmi/ an industrial city in NE Ukraine, near the border with Russia; pop. 296,000 (1990).

Sun. ▶ abbreviation for Sunday.

sun ▶ noun **1** (also **Sun**) the star round which the earth orbits.
■ any similar star in the universe, with or without planets.

> The sun is the central body of the solar system. It provides the light and energy that sustains life on earth, and its changing position relative to the earth's axis determines the terrestrial seasons. The sun is a star of a type known as a G2 dwarf, a sphere of hydrogen and helium 1.4 million km in diameter which obtains its energy from nuclear fusion reactions deep within its interior, where the temperature is about 15 million degrees. The surface is a little under 6,000°C.

2 [mass noun] (usu. **the sun**) the light or warmth received from the earth's sun: *we sat outside in the sun.*
■ poetic/literary a person or thing regarded as a source of glory or inspiration or understanding: *the rhetoric faded before the sun of reality.* ■ poetic/literary used with reference to someone's success or prosperity: *the sun of the Plantagenets went down in clouds.*
3 poetic/literary a day or a year: *after going so many suns without food, I was sleeping.*
▶ verb (**sunned, sunning**) (**sun oneself**) sit or lie in the sun: *Buzz could see Clare sunning herself on the terrace below.*
■ [with obj.] expose (something) to the sun, especially to warm or dry it: *the birds are sunning their wings.*
– PHRASES **against the sun** Nautical against the direction of the sun's apparent movement (in the northern hemisphere); from right to left or anticlockwise. **catch the sun** see **CATCH**. **make hay while the sun shines** see **HAY**[1]. **on which the sun never sets** (of an empire) worldwide. [ORIGIN: applied in the 17th cent. to the Spanish dominions, later to the British Empire.] **shoot the sun** Nautical ascertain the altitude of the sun with a sextant in order to determine one's latitude. **under the sun** on earth; in existence (used in expressions emphasizing the large number of something): *they exchanged views on every subject under the sun.* **with the sun** Nautical in the direction of the sun's apparent movement (in the northern hemisphere); from left to right or clockwise.
– DERIVATIVES **sunless** adjective, **sunlessness** noun,

sunlike adjective, **sunward** adjective & adverb, **sunwards** adverb.

– ORIGIN Old English *sunne*, of Germanic origin; related to Dutch *zon* and German *Sonne*, from an Indo-European root shared by Greek *hēlios* and Latin *sol*.

sun-and-planet gear ▶ noun a system of gearwheels consisting of a central wheel (a **sun gear** or **sun wheel**) around which one or more outer wheels (**planet gears** or **planet wheels**) travel.

sun-baked ▶ adjective (especially of the ground) exposed to the heat of the sun and therefore dry and hard.

sunbath ▶ noun a period of sunbathing: *an upstairs deck on which you could take a sunbath.*

sunbathe ▶ verb [no obj.] sit or lie in the sun, especially to tan the skin: [as noun **sunbathing**] *it was too hot for sunbathing.*
– DERIVATIVES **sunbather** noun.

sunbeam ▶ noun a ray of sunlight.

sun bear (also **Malayan sun bear**) ▶ noun a small mainly nocturnal bear which has a brownish-black coat with a light-coloured mark on the chest, native to SE Asia.
● *Helarctos malayanus*, family Ursidae.

sunbed ▶ noun Brit. a lounger used for sunbathing on.
■ an apparatus used for acquiring a tan, consisting of two banks of sunlamps between which one lies or stands.

sunbelt ▶ noun a strip of territory receiving a high amount of sunshine, especially the southern US from California to Florida.

sunbird ▶ noun a small, brightly coloured Old World songbird with a long downcurved bill, feeding on nectar and resembling a hummingbird (but not able to hover).
● Family Nectariniidae: four genera, in particular *Nectarinia*, and numerous species.

sunbittern ▶ noun a tropical American wading bird with a long bill, neck, and legs, having mainly greyish plumage but showing chestnut and orange on the wings when they are spread in display.
● *Eurypyga helias*, the only member of the family Eurypygidae.
– ORIGIN late 19th cent.: so named because of the pattern on the spread wings, that resembles a sunset.

sunblind ▶ noun Brit. an awning erected over a window in sunny weather.

sunblock ▶ noun [mass noun] a cream or lotion for protecting the skin from the sun and preventing sunburn.

sun bonnet ▶ noun a child's close-fitting peaked cotton hat that protects the head and neck from the sun.

sunburn ▶ noun [mass noun] reddening, inflammation, and, in severe cases, blistering and peeling of the skin caused by overexposure to the ultraviolet rays of the sun.
▶ verb (past and past participle **sunburned** or **sunburnt**) (**be sunburned**) (of a person or bodily part) suffer from sunburn: *most of us managed to get sunburnt.*
■ [usu. as adj. **sunburned** or **sunburnt**] tanned; brown from exposure to the sun: *a handsome sunburned face.* ■ [no obj.] suffer from sunburn: *a complexion that sunburnt easily.*

sunburst ▶ noun a sudden brief appearance of the full sun from behind clouds.
■ a decoration or ornament resembling the sun and its rays: [as modifier] *a pair of sunburst diamond earrings.* ■ a pattern of irregular concentric bands of colour with the brightest at the centre.

suncream ▶ noun [mass noun] a creamy preparation spread over a person's skin to protect it from sunburn and often to promote a suntan.

sundae ▶ noun a dish of ice cream with added ingredients such as fruit, nuts, and syrup.
– ORIGIN late 19th cent. (originally US): perhaps an alteration of **SUNDAY**, either because the dish was made with ice cream left over from Sunday and sold cheaply on the Monday, or because it was sold only on Sundays, a practice devised (according to some accounts) to circumvent Sunday legislation.

Sunda Islands /ˈsʌndə/ a chain of islands in the south-western part of the Malay Archipelago, consisting of two groups: the **Greater Sunda Islands**, which include Sumatra, Java, Borneo, and Sulawesi, and the **Lesser Sunda Islands**, which lie to the east of Java and include Bali, Sumbawa, Flores, Sumba, and Timor.

sun dance ▶ noun a dance performed by North American Indians in honour of the sun.

Sundanese /ˌsʌndəˈniːz/ ▶ noun (pl. same) **1** a member of a mainly Muslim people of western Java.
2 [mass noun] the Indonesian language of this people, with around 25 million speakers.
▶ adjective of or relating to the Sundanese or their language.
– ORIGIN from Sundanese *Sunda*, the western part of Java, + **-ESE**.

Sundarbans /ˈsʊndəbʌnz/ a region of swampland in the Ganges delta, extending from the mouth of the River Hooghly in West Bengal to that of the Tetulia in Bangladesh.

Sunday ▶ noun the day of the week before Monday and following Saturday, observed by Christians as a day of rest and religious worship and (together with Saturday) forming part of the weekend: *they left town on Sunday* | *many people work on Sundays* | [as modifier] *Sunday evening.*
■ informal (**the Sundays**) the newspapers published each Sunday.
▶ adverb chiefly N. Amer. on Sunday: *the concert will be held Sunday.*
■ (**Sundays**) on Sundays; each Sunday: *the programme is repeated Sundays at 9 p.m.*
– ORIGIN Old English *Sunnandæg* 'day of the sun', translation of Latin *dies solis*; compare with Dutch *zondag* and German *Sonntag.*

Sunday best ▶ noun (**one's Sunday best**) a person's best clothes, worn on Sundays or special occasions.

Sunday driver ▶ noun a person perceived as driving in an amateurish and unskilful way.

Sunday observance ▶ noun [mass noun] the Christian principle of keeping Sunday as a day of rest and worship.

Sunday painter ▶ noun an amateur painter, especially one with little training.

Sunday punch ▶ noun informal, chiefly US a powerful or devastating punch or other attacking action.

Sunday school ▶ noun a class held on Sundays to teach children about Christianity.

sun deck ▶ noun **1** the deck, or part of a deck, of a yacht or cruise ship that is open to the sky.
2 N. Amer. a terrace or balcony positioned to catch the sun.

sunder ▶ verb [with obj.] poetic/literary split apart: *the crunch of bone when it is sundered.*
– PHRASES **in sunder** apart or into pieces: *hew their bones in sunder!*
– ORIGIN late Old English *sundrian*; related to German *sondern.*

Sunderland an industrial city in NE England, a port at the mouth of the River Wear; pop. 286,800 (1991).

sundew ▶ noun a small carnivorous plant of boggy places, with rosettes of leaves that bear sticky glandular hairs. These trap insects, which are then digested.
● Genus *Drosera*, family Droseraceae: many species, including the common European *D. rotundifolia.*

sundial ▶ noun **1** an instrument showing the time by the shadow of a pointer cast by the sun on to a plate marked with the hours of the day.
2 (also **sundial shell**) a mollusc with a flattened spiral shell that is typically patterned in shades of brown, living in tropical and subtropical seas.
● Family Architectonicidae, class Gastropoda.

sun disc ▶ noun (especially in ancient Egypt) a winged disc representing a sun god.

sun dog ▶ noun another term for **PARHELION**.

sundown ▶ noun [in sing.] chiefly N. Amer. the time in the evening when the sun disappears or daylight fades.

sundowner ▶ noun **1** Brit. informal an alcoholic drink taken at sunset.
2 Austral. a tramp arriving at a sheep station in the evening under the pretence of seeking work, so as to obtain food and shelter.

sundress ▶ noun a light, loose, sleeveless dress, typically having a wide neckline and thin shoulder straps.

sundrops ▶ noun a day-flowering North American plant with yellow flowers, related to the evening primrose.
● Genera *Oenothera* and *Calylophus*, family Onagraceae.

sundry ▶ adjective [attrib.] of various kinds; several: *prawn and garlic vol-au-vents and sundry other delicacies.*
▶ noun (pl. **-ies**) **1** (**sundries**) various items not important enough to be mentioned individually: *a drugstore selling magazines, newspapers, and sundries.*
2 Cricket Australian term for **EXTRA**.
– ORIGIN Old English *syndrig* 'distinct, separate'; related to **SUNDER**.

sun-dry ▶ verb [with obj.] [usu. as adj. **sun-dried**] dry (something, especially food) in the sun, as opposed to using artificial heat: *sun-dried tomatoes.*

sunfast ▶ adjective US (of a dye or fabric) not prone to fade in sunlight.

sun filter ▶ noun another term for **SUNSCREEN**.

sunfish ▶ noun (pl. same or **-fishes**) **1** a large deep-bodied marine fish of warm seas, with tall dorsal and anal fins near the rear of the body and a very short tail. Also called **MOLA**.
● Family Molidae: three genera and several species, in particular the very large **ocean sunfish** (*Mola mola*).
2 a nest-building freshwater fish that is native to North America and popular in aquaria, e.g. the pumpkinseed.
● Several genera and species in the family Centrarchidae (the **sunfish family**). This family also includes sporting fish such as the black basses, rock bass, bluegill, and crappies.

sunflower ▶ noun a tall North American plant of the daisy family, with very large golden-rayed flowers. Sunflowers are cultivated for their edible seeds which are an important source of oil for cooking and margarine.
● *Helianthus annuus*, family Compositae.

Sunflower State informal name for **KANSAS**.

Sung /sʊŋ/ (also **Song**) a dynasty that ruled in China AD 960–1279. The period was marked by the first use of paper money and by advances in printing, firearms, shipbuilding, clockmaking, and medicine.

sung past participle of **SING**.

sungazer ▶ noun a burrowing colonial girdled lizard native to Africa, noted for apparently staring at the sun while basking. Also called **GIANT ZONURE**.
● *Cordylus giganteus*, family Cordylidae.

sun gear ▶ noun see **SUN-AND-PLANET GEAR**.

sunglasses ▶ plural noun glasses tinted to protect the eyes from sunlight or glare.

sun-grazing ▶ adjective Astronomy (of a comet) having an orbit which passes close to the sun.

sungrebe ▶ noun a grebe-like tropical American waterbird of the finfoot family, with a striped head and black-spotted yellow feet.
● *Heliornis fulica*, family Heliornithidae. Alternative name: **American finfoot**.

sun hat ▶ noun a broad-brimmed hat that protects the head and neck from the sun.

sun helmet ▶ noun chiefly historical a rigid hat made of cork or a similar material, worn in tropical climates.

suni /ˈsuːni/ ▶ noun a dark brown dwarf antelope native to southern Africa.
● *Neotragus moschatus*, family Bovidae.
– ORIGIN late 19th cent.: a local word.

sun in splendour ▶ noun Heraldry the sun as heraldically blazoned, depicted with rays and often a human face.

sunk past and past participle of **SINK**[1].

sunken ▶ adjective **1** [attrib.] having sunk or been submerged in water: *the wreck of a sunken ship.*
2 having sunk below the usual or expected level: *she produced a sunken fruit cake from a tin.*
■ [attrib.] at a lower level than the surrounding area: *a sunken garden.* ■ (of a person's eyes or cheeks) deeply recessed, especially as a result of illness, hunger, or stress: *her face was white, with sunken cheeks.*
– ORIGIN late Middle English: past participle of **SINK**[1].

sunk fence ▶ noun a ditch with one side formed by a wall or with a fence running along the bottom.

Sun King the nickname of Louis XIV of France (see **LOUIS**[1]).

sun-kissed ▶ adjective made warm or brown by

the sun: *the sun-kissed resort of Acapulco* | *her sun-kissed shoulders.*

sunlamp ▶ noun **1** a lamp emitting ultraviolet rays used as a substitute for sunlight, typically to produce an artificial suntan or in therapy. **2** a large lamp with a parabolic reflector used in film-making.

sunlight ▶ noun [mass noun] light from the sun: *a shaft of sunlight.*

sunlit ▶ adjective illuminated by direct light from the sun: *clear sunlit waters.*

sun lounge ▶ noun Brit. a room with large windows and sometimes a glass roof, designed to allow in a lot of sunlight.

sunlounger ▶ noun Brit. a lounger used for sunbathing.

Sunna /ˈsʊnə, ˈsʌnə/ ▶ noun the traditional portion of Muslim law based on Muhammad's words or acts, accepted (together with the Koran) as authoritative by Muslims and followed particularly by Sunni Muslims.
– ORIGIN Arabic, literally 'form, way, course, rule'.

Sunni /ˈsʊni, ˈsʌni/ ▶ noun (pl. same or **Sunnis**) [mass noun] one of the two main branches of Islam, commonly described as orthodox, and differing from Shia in its understanding of the Sunna and in its acceptance of the first three caliphs. Compare with **SHIA**.
■ [count noun] a Muslim who adheres to this branch of Islam.
– DERIVATIVES **Sunnite** adjective & noun.
– ORIGIN Arabic, literally 'custom, normative rule'.

sunnies ▶ plural noun Austral. informal sunglasses.

sunny ▶ adjective (**sunnier, sunniest**) bright with sunlight: *a sunny day.*
■ (of a place) receiving much sunlight: *Seefeld is set high on a sunny plateau.* ■ (of a person or their temperament) cheery and bright: *he had a sunny disposition.*
– DERIVATIVES **sunnily** adverb, **sunniness** noun.

sunny side ▶ noun the side of something that receives the sun for longest: *a well-known hotel on the sunny side of Söll.*
■ the more cheerful or pleasant aspect of a state of affairs: *he was fond of the sunny side of life.*
– PHRASES **sunny side up** N. Amer. (of an egg) fried on one side only.

sunray ▶ noun a ray of sunlight.
■ a radiating line or broadening stripe resembling a ray of the sun.

sunray pleats ▶ plural noun widening pleats radiating out from a skirt's waistband.
– DERIVATIVES **sunray-pleated** adjective.

sunrise ▶ noun the time in the morning when the sun appears or full daylight arrives: *an hour before sunrise.*
■ the colours and light visible in the sky on an occasion of the sun's first appearance in the morning, considered as a view or spectacle: *a spectacular sunrise over the summit of the mountain.*

sunrise industry ▶ noun a new and growing industry, especially in electronics or tele-communications.

sunroof ▶ noun a panel in the roof of a car that can be opened for extra ventilation.

sunroom ▶ noun chiefly N. Amer. another term for **SUN LOUNGE**.

sun rose ▶ noun another term for **ROCK ROSE**.

sun scald ▶ noun [mass noun] damage to plant tissue, especially bark or fruit, caused by exposure to excessive sunlight.

sunscreen ▶ noun [mass noun] a cream or lotion rubbed on to the skin to protect it from the sun.
■ [count noun] an active ingredient of creams and lotions of this kind and other preparations for the skin.

sunset ▶ noun [in sing.] the time in the evening when the sun disappears or daylight fades: *sunset was still a couple of hours away.*
■ [count noun] the colours and light visible in the sky on an occasion of the sun's disappearance in the evening, considered as a view or spectacle: *a blue and gold sunset.* ■ figurative a period of decline, especially the last years of a person's life: *the sunset of his life.*

sunset industry ▶ noun an old and declining industry.

sunset provision ▶ noun N. Amer. a stipulation that an agency or programme be disbanded or

terminated at the end of a fixed period unless it is formally renewed.

sunset shell ▶ noun a burrowing bivalve mollusc with a long oval shell which (in some kinds) is pinkish with ray-like markings.
● Genus *Gari*, family Psammobiidae (or Sanguinolariidae).

sunshade ▶ noun a parasol, awning, or other device giving protection from the sun.

sunshine ▶ noun [mass noun] **1** direct sunlight unbroken by cloud, especially over a comparatively large area: *we walked in the warm sunshine.*
■ figurative cheerfulness; happiness: *their colourful music can bring a ray of sunshine.*
2 Brit. informal used as a friendly or sometimes threatening form of address: *hand it over, sunshine.*
– DERIVATIVES **sunshiny** adjective.

sunshine law ▶ noun US a law requiring certain proceedings of government agencies to be open or available to the public.

sunshine roof ▶ noun Brit. old-fashioned term for **SUNROOF**.

Sunshine State ▶ noun any of the states of New Mexico, South Dakota, California, and Florida.

sun sign ▶ noun Astrology another term for **BIRTH SIGN**.

sunspace ▶ noun N. Amer. a room or area in a building having a glass roof and walls and intended to maximize the power of the sun's rays.

sun spider ▶ noun a fast-moving predatory arachnid with a pair of massive vertical pincers (chelicerae). Sun spiders live chiefly in warm deserts; many are active by day, and some grow to a large size.
● Order Solifugae (or Solpugida).

sunspot ▶ noun Astronomy a spot or patch appearing from time to time on the sun's surface, appearing dark by contrast with its surroundings.

> Sunspots are regions of lower surface temperature and are believed to form where loops in the sun's magnetic field intersect the surface; an individual spot may persist for several weeks. The number of sunspots on the solar surface fluctuates according to a regular cycle, with times of maximum sunspot activity recurring every eleven years.

sun squirrel ▶ noun an African tree squirrel that typically has a dark ringed tail, noted for basking in the sun, which often causes bleaching of the fur.
● Genus *Heliosciurus*, family Sciuridae: five species.

sunstar ▶ noun a widely distributed starfish with a large number of arms.
● Genus *Solaster*, class Asteroidea.

sunstone ▶ noun a chatoyant gem consisting of feldspar, with a red or gold lustre.

sunstroke ▶ noun [mass noun] heatstroke brought about by excessive exposure to the sun.

sunsuit ▶ noun a child's suit of clothes, typically consisting of shorts and top, worn in hot sunny weather.

suntan ▶ noun a browning of the skin caused by exposure to the sun: *he had acquired quite a suntan.*
▶ verb [with obj.] [usu. as adj. **suntanned**] expose to the sun in order to achieve such a brown colour: *a suntanned face.*

suntrap ▶ noun Brit. a place sheltered from the wind and positioned to receive much sunshine.

sunup ▶ noun [in sing.] chiefly N. Amer. the time in the morning when the sun appears or full daylight arrives: *they worked from sunup to sundown.*

sun visor ▶ noun a small screen above a vehicle's windscreen, attached by a hinge so that it can be lowered to protect the occupants' eyes from bright sunlight.

sun wheel ▶ noun see **SUN-AND-PLANET GEAR**.

sunyata /ˈʃuːnjətɑː, ˈsuː-/ ▶ noun [mass noun] Buddhism the doctrine that phenomena are devoid of an immutable or determinate intrinsic nature. It is often regarded as a means of gaining an intuition of ultimate reality. Compare with **TATHATA**.
– ORIGIN from Sanskrit *śūnyatā* 'emptiness'.

Sun Yat-sen /ˌsʊn jatˈsɛn/ (also **Sun Yixian** /ˌsʊn jiːˈʃiːˈan/) (1866–1925), Chinese Kuomintang statesman, provisional President of the Republic of China 1911–12 and President of the Southern Chinese Republic 1923–5. He organized the Kuomintang force and played a vital part in the revolution of 1911 which overthrew the Manchu dynasty. Following opposition, however, he

resigned as President to establish a secessionist government at Guangzhou.

Suomi /ˈsuɒmi/ Finnish name for **FINLAND**.

sup[1] ▶ verb (**supped, supping**) [with obj.] dated or N. English take (drink or liquid food) by sips or spoonfuls: *she supped up her soup delightedly* | [no obj.] *he was supping straight from the bottle.*
▶ noun a sip of liquid: *he took another sup of wine.*
■ [mass noun] N. English & Irish alcoholic drink.
– ORIGIN Old English *sūpan* (verb), *sūpa* (noun), of Germanic origin; related to Dutch *zuipen*, German *saufen* 'to drink'.

sup[2] ▶ verb (**supped, supping**) [no obj.] dated eat supper: *you'll sup on seafood delicacies.*
– PHRASES **he who sups with the devil should have a long spoon** proverb a person who has dealings with a dangerous or wily person should be cautious.
– ORIGIN Middle English: from Old French *super*, of Germanic origin; related to **SUP**[1].

sup- ▶ prefix variant spelling of **SUB-** assimilated before p (as in *suppurate*).

Supadriv /ˈsuːpədraɪv/ ▶ noun trademark a type of cross-head screwdriver with extra ridges between the arms of the cross.

super ▶ adjective **1** informal very good or pleasant; excellent: *Julie was a super girl* | [as exclamation] *You're both coming in? Super!*
2 (of a manufactured product) of extra fine quality: *a super quality binder.*
3 Building, chiefly Brit. short for **SUPERFICIAL** (used in expressing quantities of material).
▶ adverb [as submodifier] informal especially; particularly: *he's been super understanding.*
▶ noun informal **1** a superintendent.
2 archaic an extra, unwanted, or unimportant person; a supernumerary.
■ theatrical slang, dated or N. Amer. an extra.
3 [mass noun] superphosphate.
4 [mass noun] superfine fabric or manufacture.
– ORIGIN mid 19th cent.: abbreviation.

super- ▶ combining form above; over; beyond: *superlunary* | *superstructure.*
■ to a great or extreme degree: *superabundant* | *supercool.* ■ extra large of its kind: *supercontinent.* ■ having greater influence, capacity, etc. than another of its kind: *superbike* | *superpower.* ■ of a higher kind (especially in names of classificatory divisions): *superfamily.*
– ORIGIN from Latin *super-*, from *super* 'above, beyond'.

superabound ▶ verb [no obj.] archaic be very or too abundant: *the capitalists do not need to combine when labour superabounds.*
– ORIGIN late Middle English (in the sense 'be more abundant'): from late Latin *superabundare* (see **SUPER-**, **ABOUND**).

superabundant ▶ adjective more formal or literary term for **OVER-ABUNDANT**.
– DERIVATIVES **superabundance** noun, **superabundantly** adverb.
– ORIGIN late Middle English (in the sense 'very plentiful'): from late Latin *superabundant-* 'abounding to excess', from the verb *superabundare.*

superacid ▶ noun Chemistry a solution of a strong acid in a very acidic (usually non-aqueous) solvent, functioning as a powerful protonating agent.
– DERIVATIVES **superacidity** noun.

superadd ▶ verb [with obj.] rare add (something) to what has already been added: [as adj. **superadded**] *the presence of superadded infection by bacteria.*
– DERIVATIVES **superaddition** noun.
– ORIGIN late Middle English: from Latin *superaddere* (see **SUPER-**, **ADD**).

superadiabatic /ˌsjuːpəreɪdɪəˈbatɪk, -adɪə-/ ▶ adjective chiefly Meteorology relating to or denoting a temperature gradient which is steeper than that occurring in adiabatic conditions.

superalloy ▶ noun an alloy capable of withstanding high temperatures, high stresses, and often highly oxidizing atmospheres.

superaltar ▶ noun a portable slab of stone consecrated for use where there is no consecrated altar.
– ORIGIN Middle English: from medieval Latin *superaltare*, from *super-* 'over' + late Latin *altar(e)* 'altar'.

superannuate /ˌsjuːpərˈanjʊeɪt/ ▶ verb [with obj.] (usu. **be superannuated**) retire (someone) with a

pension: *his pilot's licence was withdrawn and he was superannuated.*
■[as adj. **superannuated**] (of a post or employee) belonging to a superannuation scheme: *she is not superannuated and has no paid holiday.* ■ [usu. as adj. **superannuated**] cause to become obsolete through age or new technological or intellectual developments: *superannuated computing equipment.*
– DERIVATIVES **superannuable** adjective.
– ORIGIN mid 17th cent.: back-formation from *superannuated*, from medieval Latin *superannuatus*, from Latin *super-* 'over' + *annus* 'year'.

superannuation ▶ noun [mass noun] [usu. as modifier] regular payment made into a fund by an employee towards a future pension: *a superannuation fund.*
■a pension of this type paid to a retired person. ■ the process of superannuating an employee.

superb ▶ adjective **1** excellent: *a superb performance.*
2 impressively splendid: *a superb mausoleum.*
■used in names of birds with attractive or colourful plumage, e.g. **superb lyrebird**.
– DERIVATIVES **superbly** adverb, **superbness** noun.
– ORIGIN mid 16th cent. (in sense 2): from Latin *superbus* 'proud, magnificent'.

superbike ▶ noun a high-performance motorcycle.

Super Bowl ▶ noun (in the US) the National Football League championship game played annually between the champions of the National and the American Football Conferences.

superbug ▶ noun **1** a bacterium that is useful in biotechnology, typically one that has been genetically engineered to enhance its usefulness for a particular purpose.
2 a strain of bacteria that has become resistant to antibiotic drugs.
■an insect that is difficult to control or eradicate, especially because it has become immune to insecticides.

supercalender ▶ verb [with obj.] give a highly glazed finish to (paper) by calendering it more than calendered paper.

supercar ▶ noun a high-performance sports car.

supercargo ▶ noun (pl. **-oes** or **-os**) a representative of the ship's owner on board a merchant ship, responsible for overseeing the cargo and its sale.
– ORIGIN late 17th cent.: alteration of earlier *supracargo*, from Spanish *sobrecargo*, from *sobre* 'over' + *cargo* 'cargo'.

supercede ▶ verb variant spelling of **SUPERSEDE**.

USAGE The spelling **supercede** is generally regarded as an error: see usage at **SUPERSEDE**.

supercharge ▶ verb [with obj.] fit or design (an internal-combustion engine) with a supercharger: [as adj. **supercharged**] *a supercharged 3.8-litre V6.*
■[usu. as adj. **supercharged**] supply with extra energy or power: *a supercharged computer.* ■ [as adj. **supercharged**] having powerful emotional overtones or associations: *appeasement is one of those supercharged words, like terrorism and fascism.*

supercharger ▶ noun a device that increases the pressure of the fuel-air mixture in an internal-combustion engine, fitted in order to achieve greater efficiency.

superciliary /ˌs(j)uːpəˈsɪlɪəri/ ▶ adjective [attrib.] Anatomy of or relating to the eyebrow or the region over the eye.
– ORIGIN mid 18th cent.: from Latin *supercilium* 'eyebrow' (from *super-* 'above' + *cilium* 'eyelid') + **-ARY**[1].

supercilious ▶ adjective behaving or looking as though one thinks one is superior to others: *a supercilious lady's maid.*
– DERIVATIVES **superciliously** adverb, **superciliousness** noun.
– ORIGIN early 16th cent.: from Latin *superciliosus* 'haughty', from *supercilium* 'eyebrow'.

superclass ▶ noun Biology a taxonomic category that ranks above class and below phylum.

supercluster ▶ noun Astronomy a cluster of galaxies which themselves occur as clusters.

supercoil Biochemistry ▶ noun another term for **SUPERHELIX**.
▶ verb [with obj.] form (a substance) into a superhelix: [as adj. **supercoiled**] *a supercoiled circular DNA molecule.*

supercollider ▶ noun Physics a collider in which superconducting magnets are used to accelerate particles to energies of millions of megavolts.

supercomputer ▶ noun a particularly powerful mainframe computer.
– DERIVATIVES **supercomputing** noun.

superconductivity ▶ noun [mass noun] Physics the property of zero electrical resistance in some substances at very low absolute temperatures.
– DERIVATIVES **superconduct** verb, **superconducting** adjective, **superconductive** adjective.

superconductor ▶ noun Physics a substance capable of becoming superconducting at sufficiently low temperatures.
■a substance in the superconducting state.

superconscious ▶ adjective transcending human or normal consciousness.
– DERIVATIVES **superconsciously** adverb, **superconsciousness** noun.

supercontinent ▶ noun each of several large land masses (notably Pangaea, Gondwana, and Laurasia) thought to have divided to form the present continents in the geological past.

supercool ▶ verb [with obj.] Chemistry cool (a liquid) below its freezing point without solidification or crystallization.
■[no obj.] Biology (of a living organism) survive body temperatures below the freezing point of water.
▶ adjective informal extremely attractive, impressive, or calm: *the supercool tracks in this collection.*

supercritical ▶ adjective Physics above a critical threshold, in particular:
■(in nuclear physics) containing or involving more than the critical mass. ■ (of a flow of fluid) faster than the speed at which waves travel in the fluid. ■ denoting an aerofoil or aircraft wing designed to tolerate shock-wave formation at transonic speeds. ■ of, relating to, or denoting a fluid at a temperature and pressure greater than its critical temperature and pressure.

super-duper ▶ adjective humorous super; marvellous.

superego ▶ noun (pl. **-os**) Psychoanalysis the part of a person's mind that acts as a self-critical conscience, reflecting social standards learned from parents and teachers. Compare with **EGO** and **ID**.

superelevation ▶ noun [mass noun] the amount by which the outer edge of a curve on a road or railway is banked above the inner edge.

supereminent ▶ adjective old-fashioned term for **PRE-EMINENT**.
– DERIVATIVES **supereminence** noun, **supereminently** adverb.
– ORIGIN mid 16th cent.: from Latin *supereminent-* 'rising above', from the verb *supereminere* 'rise above' (see **SUPER-**, **EMINENT**).

supererogation /ˌs(j)uːpərɛrəˈɡeɪʃ(ə)n/ ▶ noun [mass noun] the performance of more work than duty requires.
– PHRASES **works of supererogation** (in the Roman Catholic Church) actions believed to form a reserve fund of merit that can be drawn on by prayer in favour of sinners.
– DERIVATIVES **supererogatory** /-ɪˈrɒɡət(ə)ri/ adjective.
– ORIGIN early 16th cent.: from late Latin *supererogatio(n-)*, from *supererogare* 'pay in addition', from *super-* 'over' + *erogare* 'pay out'.

superette ▶ noun US a small supermarket.
– ORIGIN 1930s: from **SUPERMARKET** + **-ETTE**.

superfamily ▶ noun (pl. **-ies**) Biology a taxonomic category that ranks above family and below order.

superfatted ▶ adjective (of soap) containing excess fats compared with its alkali content.

superfecundation /ˌs(j)uːpəfɛk(ə)nˈdeɪʃ(ə)n, -fiːk-/ ▶ noun Medicine & Zoology fertilization of a second ovum during the same oestrus cycle as a result of a second mating, leading to fetuses of the same age but different parentage.

superfetation /ˌs(j)uːpəfiːˈteɪʃ(ə)n/ ▶ noun [mass noun] Medicine & Zoology fertilization of a second ovum after the start of pregnancy, leading to fetuses of different ages.
■figurative the accretion of one thing on another: *the superfetation of ideas.*
– ORIGIN early 17th cent.: from French *superfétation* or modern Latin *superfetatio(n-)*, from Latin *superfetare*, from *super-* 'above' + *fetus* 'foetus'.

superficial ▶ adjective existing or occurring at or on the surface: *the building suffered only superficial damage.*
■situated or occurring on the skin or immediately beneath it: *the superficial muscle groups.* ■ appearing to be true or real only until examined more closely: *the resemblance between the breeds is superficial.* ■ not thorough, deep, or complete; cursory: *he had only the most superficial knowledge of foreign countries.* ■ not having or showing any depth of character or understanding: *perhaps I was a superficial person.* ■ Building, chiefly Brit. denoting a quantity of a material expressed in terms of area covered rather than linear dimension or volume.
– DERIVATIVES **superficiality** /-ʃɪˈalɪti/ noun (pl. **-ies**), **superficially** adverb, **superficialness** noun.
– ORIGIN late Middle English: from late Latin *superficialis*, from Latin *superficies* (see **SUPERFICIES**).

superficies /ˌs(j)uːpəˈfɪʃiːz/ ▶ noun (pl. same) archaic a surface: *the superficies of a sphere.*
■an outward part or appearance: *the superficies of life.*
– ORIGIN mid 16th cent.: from Latin, from *super-* 'above' + *facies* 'face'.

superfine ▶ adjective **1** of especially high quality: *superfine cotton shirtings.*
2 (of fibres or an instrument) very thin: *superfine tweezers.*
■consisting of especially small particles: *superfine face powder.*
– ORIGIN late 16th cent. (in the sense 'excessively elegant'): from **SUPER-** 'to a high degree' + **FINE**[1].

superfluidity ▶ noun [mass noun] Physics the property of flowing without friction or viscosity, as in liquid helium below about 2.18 kelvins.
– DERIVATIVES **superfluid** noun & adjective.

superfluity /ˌs(j)uːpəˈfluːɪti/ ▶ noun (pl. **-ies**) [in sing.] an unnecessarily or excessively large amount or number of something: *a* ***superfluity of*** *unoccupied time.*
■an unnecessary thing: *they thought the garrison a superfluity.* ■ [mass noun] the state of being superfluous: *footservants who had nothing to do but to display their own superfluity.*
– ORIGIN late Middle English: from Old French *superfluite*, from late Latin *superfluitas*, from Latin *superfluus* 'running over' (see **SUPERFLUOUS**).

superfluous ▶ adjective unnecessary, especially through being more than enough: *the purchaser should avoid asking for superfluous information.*
– DERIVATIVES **superfluously** adverb, **superfluousness** noun.
– ORIGIN late Middle English: from Latin *superfluus*, from *super-* 'over' + *fluere* 'to flow'.

superfly informal, chiefly US ▶ adjective (of clothing or a person's appearance) bright and ostentatious.
▶ noun (pl. **-flies**) an ostentatious, self-confident person.
– ORIGIN 1970s: the adjective from **SUPER-** + **FLY**[3]; the noun from the name of a character in the blaxploitation film *Superfly* (1972).

superfusion ▶ noun [mass noun] Physiology the technique of running a stream of liquid over the surface of a piece of suspended tissue, keeping it viable and allowing observation of the interchange of substances.

supergalaxy ▶ noun (pl. **-ies**) another term for **SUPERCLUSTER**.

supergene[1] ▶ adjective [attrib.] Geology relating to or denoting the deposition or enrichment of mineral deposits by solutions moving downward through the rocks.

supergene[2] ▶ noun Genetics a group of closely linked genes, typically having related functions.

supergiant ▶ noun Astronomy a very large star that is even brighter than a giant, often despite being relatively cool.

superglue ▶ noun a very strong quick-setting adhesive, based on cyanoacrylates or similar polymers.
▶ verb (**-glues**, **-glued**, **-gluing** or **-glueing**) [with obj.] stick with superglue: *he superglued his hands together.*

supergrass ▶ noun Brit. informal a police informer who implicates a large number of people.

supergravity ▶ noun [mass noun] Physics gravity as described or predicted by a supersymmetric quantum field theory.

supergroup ▶ noun an exceptionally successful rock group, in particular one formed by musicians already famous from playing in other groups.

superheat Physics ▶ verb [with obj.] heat (a liquid) under pressure above its boiling point without vaporization.

S

■heat (a vapour) above its temperature of saturation. ■ heat to a very high temperature. ▶ **noun** [mass noun] the excess of temperature of a vapour above its temperature of saturation.

– DERIVATIVES **superheater** noun.

superheavy ▶ **adjective** Physics relating to or denoting an element with an atomic mass or atomic number greater than those of the naturally occurring elements, especially one belonging to a group above atomic number 110 having proton/neutron ratios which in theory confer relatively long half-lives.

superheavyweight ▶ **noun** [mass noun] a weight above heavyweight in boxing and other sports. In the amateur boxing scale it begins at 91 kg. ■[count noun] a boxer or other competitor of this weight.

superhelix ▶ **noun** (pl. **superhelices**) Biochemistry a helical structure formed from a number of protein or nucleic acid chains which are individually helical.

– DERIVATIVES **superhelical** adjective.

superhero ▶ **noun** (pl. **-oes**) a benevolent fictional character with superhuman powers, such as Superman.

superhet ▶ **noun** informal short for SUPERHETERODYNE.

superheterodyne /ˌs(j)uːpəˈhɛt(ə)rə(ʊ)dʌɪn/ ▶ **adjective** denoting or using a system of radio and television reception in which the receiver produces a tunable signal which is combined with the incoming signal to produce a predetermined intermediate frequency, on which most of the amplification is formed. ▶ **noun** a superheterodyne receiver.

– ORIGIN 1920s: from SUPERSONIC + HETERODYNE.

superhighway ▶ **noun** 1 N. Amer. a dual carriageway with controlled access. 2 (also **information superhighway**) an extensive electronic network such as the Internet, used for the rapid transfer of information such as sound, video, and graphics in digital form.

superhuman ▶ **adjective** having or showing exceptional ability or powers: *the pilot made one last superhuman effort not to come down right on our heads.*

– DERIVATIVES **superhumanly** adverb.
– ORIGIN mid 17th cent.: from late Latin *superhumanus* (see SUPER-, HUMAN).

superimpose ▶ **verb** [with obj.] place or lay (one thing) over another, typically so that both are still evident: *the number will appear on the screen, superimposed on a flashing button* | [as adj. **superimposed**] *different stone tools were found in superimposed layers.*

– DERIVATIVES **superimposable** adjective, **superimposition** noun.

superincumbent /ˌs(j)uːp(ə)rɪnˈkʌmb(ə)nt/ ▶ **adjective** poetic/literary lying on something else: *the crushing effect of the superincumbent masonry.*

superinduce ▶ **verb** [with obj.] introduce or induce in addition: *both genes are known to be superinduced in fibroblasts by inhibition of protein synthesis.*

– ORIGIN mid 16th cent.: from Latin *superinducere* 'cover over, bring from outside' (see SUPER-, INDUCE).

superinfection ▶ **noun** [mass noun] Medicine infection occurring after or on top of an earlier infection, especially following treatment with broad-spectrum antibiotics.

superintend ▶ **verb** [with obj.] be responsible for the management or arrangement of (an activity or organization); oversee: *he superintended a land reclamation scheme.*

– DERIVATIVES **superintendence** noun, **superintendency** noun.
– ORIGIN early 17th cent.: from ecclesiastical Latin *superintendere*, translating Greek *episkopein*.

superintendent ▶ **noun** a person who manages or superintends an organization or activity. ■(in the UK) a police officer ranking above chief inspector. ■(in the US) a high-ranking official, especially the chief of a police department. ■ N. Amer. the caretaker of a building.

– ORIGIN mid 16th cent.: from ecclesiastical Latin *superintendent-* 'overseeing', from the verb *superintendere* (see SUPERINTEND).

superior ▶ **adjective** 1 higher in rank, status, or quality: *a superior officer* | *it is **superior to** every other car on the road.* ■of high standard or quality: *superior malt whiskies.*

■ greater in size or power: *deploying superior force.* ■ [predic.] (**superior to**) above yielding to or being influenced by: *I felt superior to any accusation of anti-Semitism.* ■ having or showing an overly high opinion of oneself; supercilious: *that girl was frightfully superior.* 2 chiefly Anatomy further above or out; higher in position. ■(of a letter, figure, or symbol) written or printed above the line. ■ Astronomy (of a planet) having an orbit further from the sun than the earth's. ■ Botany (of the ovary of a flower) situated above the sepals and petals. ▶ **noun** 1 a person or thing superior to another in rank, status, or quality, especially a colleague in a higher position: *obeying their superiors' orders.* ■the head of a monastery or other religious institution. 2 Printing a superior letter, figure, or symbol.

– DERIVATIVES **superiorly** adverb (usu. in sense 2 of the adjective).
– ORIGIN late Middle English: from Old French *superiour*, from Latin *superior*, comparative of *superus* 'that is above', from *super* 'above'.

Superior, Lake the largest of the five Great Lakes of North America, on the border between Canada and the US. With an area of 82,350 sq. km (31,800 sq. miles), it is the largest freshwater lake in the world.

superior conjunction ▶ **noun** Astronomy a conjunction of Mercury or Venus with the sun, when the planet and the earth are on opposite sides of the sun.

superior court ▶ **noun** Law 1 (in England) a higher court whose decisions have weight as precedents and which is not subject to control by any other court except by way of appeal. 2 (in some states of the US) a court of appeals or a court of general jurisdiction.

superiority ▶ **noun** [mass noun] the state of being superior: *an attempt to establish **superiority over** others* | *the allies have achieved air superiority.* ■a supercilious manner or attitude: *he attacked the media's smug superiority.*

superiority complex ▶ **noun** an attitude of superiority which conceals actual feelings of inferiority and failure.

superius /s(j)uːˈpɪərɪəs/ ▶ **noun** [mass noun] the highest voice part in early choral music; the cantus.

– ORIGIN late 18th cent.: from Latin, neuter (used as a noun) of *superior* (see SUPERIOR).

superjacent /ˌs(j)uːpəˈdʒeɪs(ə)nt/ ▶ **adjective** technical lying over or above something else; overlying.

– ORIGIN late 16th cent.: from Latin *superjacent-*, from *super-* 'over' + *jacere* 'to lie'.

superlative /s(j)uːˈpəːlətɪv/ ▶ **adjective** 1 of the highest quality or degree: *a superlative piece of skill.* 2 Grammar (of an adjective or adverb) expressing the highest or a very high degree of a quality (e.g. *bravest, most fiercely*). Contrasted with POSITIVE and COMPARATIVE. ▶ **noun** 1 Grammar a superlative adjective or adverb. ■(the superlative) the highest degree of comparison. 2 (usu. **superlatives**) an exaggerated or hyperbolical expression of praise: *the critics ran out of superlatives to describe him.*

– DERIVATIVES **superlatively** adverb [as submodifier] *he was superlatively fit,* **superlativeness** noun.
– ORIGIN late Middle English: from Old French *superlatif, -ive*, from late Latin *superlativus*, from Latin *superlatus* 'carried beyond', past participle of *superferre*.

superlattice ▶ **noun** Metallurgy & Physics an ordered arrangement of certain atoms in a solid solution which is superimposed on the solvent crystal lattice.

superluminal /ˌs(j)uːpəˈluːmɪn(ə)l/ ▶ **adjective** Physics denoting or having a speed greater than that of light.

– ORIGIN 1950s: from SUPER- 'above' + Latin *lumen, lumin-* 'a light' + -AL.

superlunary /ˌs(j)uːpəˈluːnəri/ ▶ **adjective** belonging to a higher world; celestial.

– ORIGIN early 17th cent.: from medieval Latin *superlunaris* (see SUPER-, LUNAR).

supermajority ▶ **noun** (pl. **-ies**) a number that is much more than half of a total, especially in a vote.

superman ▶ **noun** (pl. **-men**) 1 chiefly Philosophy the ideal superior man of the future. See ÜBERMENSCH.

2 (**Superman**) a US cartoon character having great strength, the ability to fly, and other extraordinary powers. ■(a superman) informal a man with exceptional physical or mental ability.

– ORIGIN early 20th cent.: from SUPER- 'exceptional' + MAN, coined by G. B. Shaw in imitation of German *Übermensch* (used by Nietzsche).

supermarket ▶ **noun** a large self-service shop selling foods and household goods.

supermassive ▶ **adjective** Astronomy having a mass many times (typically between 10^6 and 10^9 times) that of the sun: *a supermassive star.*

supermini ▶ **noun** (pl. **superminis**) a motor car of the smallest type that is widely produced.

supermodel ▶ **noun** a successful fashion model who has reached the status of a celebrity.

supermundane /ˌs(j)uːpəˈmʌndeɪn/ ▶ **adjective** rare above or superior to the earth or worldly affairs.

supernal /s(j)uːˈpəːn(ə)l/ ▶ **adjective** chiefly poetic/literary of or relating to the sky or the heavens; celestial. ■of exceptional quality or extent: *he is the supernal poet of our age* | *supernal erudition.*

– DERIVATIVES **supernally** adverb.
– ORIGIN late Middle English: from Old French, or from medieval Latin *supernalis*, from Latin *supernus*, from *super* 'above'.

supernatant /ˌs(j)uːpəˈneɪt(ə)nt/ technical ▶ **adjective** denoting the liquid lying above a solid residue after crystallization, precipitation, centrifugation, or other process. ▶ **noun** a volume of supernatant liquid.

supernatural ▶ **adjective** (of a manifestation or event) attributed to some force beyond scientific understanding or the laws of nature: *a supernatural being.* ■unnaturally or extraordinarily great: *a woman of supernatural beauty.* ▶ **noun** (the supernatural) manifestations or events considered to be of supernatural origin, such as ghosts.

– DERIVATIVES **supernaturalism** noun, **supernaturalist** noun, **supernaturally** adverb [as submodifier] *the monster was supernaturally strong.*

supernormal ▶ **adjective** exceeding or beyond the normal; exceptional: *a supernormal human.*

– DERIVATIVES **supernormality** noun.

supernova /ˌs(j)uːpəˈnəʊvə/ ▶ **noun** (pl. **supernovae** /-viː/ or **supernovas**) Astronomy a star that suddenly increases greatly in brightness because of a catastrophic explosion that ejects most of its mass.

supernumerary /ˌs(j)uːpəˈnjuːm(ə)r(ə)ri/ ▶ **adjective** present in excess of the normal or requisite number, in particular: ■(of a person) not belonging to a regular staff but engaged for extra work. ■ not wanted or needed; redundant: *books were obviously supernumerary, and he began jettisoning them.* ■ Botany & Zoology denoting a structure or organ occurring in addition to the normal ones: *a pair of supernumerary teats.* ■(of an actor) appearing on stage but not speaking. ▶ **noun** (pl. **-ies**) a supernumerary person or thing.

– ORIGIN early 17th cent.: from late Latin *supernumerarius* '(soldier) added to a legion after it is complete', from Latin *super numerum* 'beyond the number'.

superorder ▶ **noun** Biology a taxonomic category that ranks above order and below class.

superordinate /ˌs(j)uːpərˈɔːdɪnət/ ▶ **noun** a thing that represents a superior order or category within a system of classification: *a pair of compatibles must have a common superordinate.* ■a person who has authority over or control of another within an organization. ■ Linguistics a word whose meaning includes the meaning of one or more other words: *'bird' is the superordinate of 'canary'.* ▶ **adjective** superior in status: *senior staff's superordinate position.*

– ORIGIN early 17th cent.: from SUPER- 'above', on the pattern of *subordinate.*

superoxide ▶ **noun** Chemistry an oxide containing the anion O_2^-.

superphosphate ▶ **noun** [mass noun] a fertilizer made by treating phosphate rock with sulphuric or phosphoric acid.

superplastic Metallurgy ▶ **adjective** (of a metal or alloy) capable of extreme plastic extension under load. ▶ **noun** a metal or alloy having this property.

– DERIVATIVES **superplasticity** noun.

superpose ▶ **verb** [with obj.] place (something) on or above something else, especially so that they coincide: [as adj. **superposed**] *a border of superposed triangles.*
– DERIVATIVES **superposition** noun.
– ORIGIN early 19th cent.: from French *superposer*, from *super-* 'above' + *poser* 'to place'.

superpower ▶ **noun** a very powerful and influential nation (used especially with reference to the US and the former USSR when these were perceived as the two most powerful nations in the world).

supersaturate ▶ **verb** [with obj.] Chemistry increase the concentration of (a solution) beyond saturation point.
– DERIVATIVES **supersaturation** noun.

superscalar ▶ **adjective** denoting a computer architecture where several instructions are loaded at once and, as far as possible, are executed simultaneously, shortening the time taken to run the whole program.

superscribe ▶ **verb** [with obj.] write or print (an inscription) at the top of or on the outside of a document.
■ write or print an inscription at the top of or on the outside of (a document). ■ write or print (a letter, word, symbol, or line of writing or printing) above an existing letter, word, or line.
– DERIVATIVES **superscription** noun.
– ORIGIN late 15th cent.: from Latin *superscribere*, from *super-* 'over' + *scribere* 'write'.

superscript ▶ **adjective** (of a letter, figure, or symbol) written or printed above the line.
▶ **noun** a superscript letter, figure, or symbol.
– ORIGIN late 19th cent. (as an adjective): from Latin *superscriptus* 'written above', past participle of *superscribere*.

supersede /ˌs(j)uːpəˈsiːd/ ▶ **verb** [with obj.] take the place of (a person or thing previously in authority or use); supplant: *the older models have now been superseded.*
– DERIVATIVES **supersession** noun.
– ORIGIN late 15th cent. (in the sense 'postpone, defer'): from Old French *superseder*, from Latin *supersedere* 'be superior to', from *super-* 'above' + *sedere* 'sit'. The current sense dates from the mid 17th cent.

USAGE The standard spelling is **supersede** rather than **supercede**. The word is derived from the Latin verb *supersedere* but has been influenced by the presence of other words in English spelled with a **c**, such as **intercede** and **accede**. The **c** spelling is recorded as early as the 16th century; although still often regarded as incorrect, it is now being entered without comment in some modern dictionaries.

superset ▶ **noun** Mathematics a set which includes another set or sets.

supersonic ▶ **adjective** involving or denoting a speed greater than that of sound.
– DERIVATIVES **supersonically** adverb.

supersonics ▶ **plural noun** [treated as sing.] another term for **ULTRASONICS**.

superspace ▶ **noun** [mass noun] Physics a concept of space-time in which points are defined by more than four coordinates.
■ a space of infinitely many dimensions postulated to contain actual space-time and all possible spaces.

superspecies ▶ **noun** (pl. same) Biology a group of largely allopatric species which are descended from a common evolutionary ancestor and are closely related but too distinct to be regarded as subspecies of one species.

superstar ▶ **noun** a high-profile and extremely successful performer or sports player.
– DERIVATIVES **superstardom** noun.

superstate ▶ **noun** a large and powerful state formed from a federation or union of nations: *we are not advocates of a European superstate.*

superstition ▶ **noun** [mass noun] excessively credulous belief in and reverence for supernatural beings: *he dismissed the ghost stories as mere superstition.*
■ [count noun] a widely held but unjustified belief in supernatural causation leading to certain consequences of an action or event, or a practice based on such a belief: *she touched her locket for luck, a superstition she had had since childhood.*
– DERIVATIVES **superstitious** adjective, **superstitiously** adverb, **superstitiousness** noun.
– ORIGIN Middle English: from Old French, or from Latin *superstitio(n-)*, from *super-* 'over' + *stare* 'to stand' (perhaps from the notion of 'standing over' something in awe).

superstore ▶ **noun** a very large out-of-town supermarket.

superstratum /s(j)uːpəˈstrɑːtəm, -ˈstreɪtəm/ ▶ **noun** (pl. **superstrata** /-tə/) an overlying stratum.

superstring ▶ **noun** Physics a subatomic particle in a version of string theory that incorporates supersymmetry.

superstructure ▶ **noun** a structure built on top of something else.
■ the parts of a ship, other than masts and rigging, built above its hull and main deck. ■ the part of a building above its foundations. ■ a concept or idea based on others. ■ (in Marxist theory) the institutions and culture considered to result from or reflect the economic system underlying a society.
– DERIVATIVES **superstructural** adjective.

supersymmetry ▶ **noun** [mass noun] Physics a very general type of mathematical symmetry which relates fermions and bosons.
– DERIVATIVES **supersymmetric** adjective.

supertanker ▶ **noun** a very large oil tanker.

supertax ▶ **noun** [mass noun] an additional tax on something already taxed.

supertonic ▶ **noun** Music the second note of the diatonic scale of any key; the note above the tonic.

Super Tuesday ▶ **noun** US, informal a day on which several states hold primary elections.

superunleaded ▶ **adjective** denoting unleaded petrol with a higher octane rating than that of regular unleaded petrol, achieved by the addition of aromatic hydrocarbons.
▶ **noun** [mass noun] petrol of this type.

supervene /ˌs(j)uːpəˈviːn/ ▶ **verb** [no obj.] occur later than a specified or implied event or action, typically in such a way as to change the situation: [as adj. **supervening**] *any plan that is made is liable to be disrupted by supervening events.*
■ Philosophy (of a fact or property) be entailed by or consequent on the existence or establishment of another: *the view that mental events supervene upon physical ones.*
– DERIVATIVES **supervenient** adjective, **supervention** noun.
– ORIGIN mid 17th cent.: from Latin *supervenire*, from *super-* 'in addition' + *venire* 'come'.

supervise ▶ **verb** [with obj.] observe and direct the execution of (a task, project, or activity): *the sergeant left to supervise the loading of the lorries.*
■ observe and direct the work of (someone): *nurses were supervised by a consultant psychiatrist.* ■ keep watch over (someone) in the interest of their or others' security: *the prisoners were supervised by two officers.*
– DERIVATIVES **supervision** noun, **supervisor** noun, **supervisory** adjective.
– ORIGIN late 15th cent. (in the sense 'survey, peruse'): from medieval Latin *supervis-* 'surveyed, supervised', from *supervidere*, from *super-* 'over' + *videre* 'to see'.

supervision order ▶ **noun** English Law a court order placing a child or young person under the supervision of a local authority or a probation officer in a case of delinquency or where care proceedings are appropriate.

supervoltage ▶ **noun** [usu. as modifier] Medicine a voltage in excess of 200 kV used in X-ray radiotherapy: *supervoltage therapy.*

superwoman ▶ **noun** (pl. **-women**) informal a woman with exceptional physical or mental ability, especially one who successfully manages a home, brings up children, and has a full-time job.

supinate /ˈs(j)uːpɪneɪt/ ▶ **verb** [with obj.] technical put or hold (a hand, foot, or limb) with the palm or sole turned upwards: [as adj. **supinated**] *a supinated foot.* Compare with **PRONATE**.
– DERIVATIVES **supination** noun.
– ORIGIN mid 19th cent.: back-formation from *supination*, from Latin *supinatio(n-)*, from *supinare* 'lay backwards', from *supinus* (see **SUPINE**).

supinator ▶ **noun** Anatomy a muscle whose contraction produces or assists in the supination of a limb or part of a limb.
■ any of several specific muscles in the forearm.

supine /ˈs(j)uːpʌɪn/ ▶ **adjective 1** (of a person) lying face upwards.
■ technical having the front or ventral part upwards. ■ (of the hand) with the palm upwards.
2 failing to act or protest as a result of moral weakness or indolence: *the government was supine in the face of racial injustice.*
▶ **noun** a Latin verbal noun used only in the accusative and ablative cases, especially to denote purpose (e.g. *mirabile dictu* 'wonderful to relate').
– DERIVATIVES **supinely** adverb, **supineness** noun.
– ORIGIN late Middle English: the adjective from Latin *supinus* 'bent backwards' (related to *super* 'above'); the noun from late Latin *supinum*, neuter of *supinus*.

supper ▶ **noun** an evening meal, typically a light or informal one: *we had a delicious cold supper* | [mass noun] *I was sent to bed without any supper.*
■ [with modifier] Scottish a meal consisting of the specified food with chips: *a fish supper.*
– PHRASES **sing for one's supper** earn a favour or benefit by providing a service in return: *the cruise lecturers are academics singing for their supper.*
– DERIVATIVES **supperless** adjective.
– ORIGIN Middle English: from Old French *super* 'to sup' (used as a noun) (see **SUP**[2]).

supper club ▶ **noun** a restaurant or nightclub serving suppers and usually providing entertainment.

supplant ▶ **verb** [with obj.] supersede and replace: *the socialist society which Marx believed would eventually supplant capitalism.*
– DERIVATIVES **supplanter** noun.
– ORIGIN Middle English: from Old French *supplanter* or Latin *supplantare* 'trip up', from *sub-* 'from below' + *planta* 'sole'.

supple ▶ **adjective** (**suppler**, **supplest**) bending and moving easily and gracefully; flexible: *her supple fingers* | figurative *my mind is becoming more supple.*
■ not stiff or hard; easily manipulated: *this body oil leaves your skin feeling deliciously supple.*
▶ **verb** [with obj.] make more flexible.
– DERIVATIVES **supplely** (also **supply**) adverb, **suppleness** noun.
– ORIGIN Middle English: from Old French *souple*, from Latin *supplex*, *supplic-* 'submissive', from *sub-* 'under' + *placere* 'propitiate'.

supplejack ▶ **noun** either of two New World twining plants:
• a tall North American climber (*Berchemia scandens*, family Rhamnaceae). • a plant of the Caribbean and tropical America (*Paullinia plumieri*, family Sapindaceae).

supplement ▶ **noun 1** something which completes or enhances something else when added to it: *the handout is a* ***supplement to*** *the official manual.*
■ a substance taken to remedy the deficiencies in a person's diet: *multivitamin supplements.* ■ a separate section, especially a colour magazine, added to a newspaper or periodical. ■ an additional charge payable for an extra service or facility: *the single room supplement is £2 per night.*
2 Geometry the amount by which an angle is less than 180°.
▶ **verb** [with obj.] add an extra element or amount to: *she took the job to supplement her husband's income.*
– DERIVATIVES **supplemental** adjective, **supplementally** adverb, **supplementation** noun.
– ORIGIN late Middle English: from Latin *supplementum*, from *supplere* 'fill up, complete' (see **SUPPLY**[1]).

supplementary ▶ **adjective** completing or enhancing something: *the centre's work was to be seen as* ***supplementary to*** *orthodox treatment and not a substitute for it.*
▶ **noun** a supplementary person or thing.
■ Brit. a question asked in parliament following the answer to a tabled one.
– DERIVATIVES **supplementarily** adverb.

supplementary angle ▶ **noun** Mathematics either of two angles whose sum is 180°.

supplementary benefit ▶ **noun** [mass noun] (in the UK) a weekly allowance formerly paid by the state to those with an income below a certain level, now replaced by **INCOME SUPPORT**.

suppletion /səˈpliːʃ(ə)n/ ▶ **noun** Linguistics the occurrence of an unrelated form to fill a gap in a conjugation (e.g. *went* as the past tense of *go*).
– DERIVATIVES **suppletive** adjective.
– ORIGIN Middle English: from Old French, from

medieval Latin *suppletio(n-)*, from *supplere* 'fill up, make full' (see **SUPPLY**[1]).

Supplex /ˈsʌplɛks/ ▶ **noun** [mass noun] trademark a synthetic stretchable fabric which is permeable to air and water vapour, used in sports and outdoor clothing.

suppliant /ˈsʌplɪənt/ ▶ **noun** a person making a humble plea to someone in power or authority.
▶ **adjective** making or expressing a plea, especially to someone in power or authority: *their faces were suppliant.*
– DERIVATIVES **suppliantly** adverb.
– ORIGIN late Middle English (as a noun): from French, 'beseeching', present participle of *supplier*, from Latin *supplicare* (see **SUPPLICATE**).

supplicate /ˈsʌplɪkeɪt/ ▶ **verb** [no obj.] ask or beg for something earnestly or humbly: [with infinitive] *the plutocracy supplicated to be made peers.*
– DERIVATIVES **supplicant** adjective & noun, **supplication** noun, **supplicatory** adjective.
– ORIGIN late Middle English: from Latin *supplicat-* 'implored', from the verb *supplicare*, from *sub-* 'from below' + *placere* 'propitiate'.

supply[1] /səˈplʌɪ/ ▶ **verb** (**-ies**, **-ied**) [with obj.] make (something needed or wanted) available to someone; provide: *the farm supplies apples to cider makers.*
■ provide (someone) with something needed or wanted: *they struggled to **supply** the besieged island **with** aircraft.* ■ be a source of (something needed): *eat foods which supply a significant amount of dietary fibre.* ■ be adequate to satisfy (a requirement or demand): *the two reservoirs supply about 1% of the city's needs.* ■ archaic take over (a place or role left by someone else): *when she died, no one could supply her place.*
▶ **noun** (pl. **-ies**) a stock of a resource from which a person or place can be provided with the necessary amount of that resource: *there were fears that the drought would limit the exhibition's water supply.*
■ [mass noun] the action of providing what is needed or wanted: *the deal involved the supply of forty fighter aircraft.* ■ [mass noun] Economics the amount of a good or service offered for sale. ■ (**supplies**) the provisions and equipment necessary for an army or for people engaged in a particular project or expedition. ■ (**supplies**) Brit. a grant of money by Parliament for the costs of government. ■ [usu. as modifier] a person, especially a schoolteacher, acting as a temporary substitute for another. ■ [as modifier] providing necessary goods and equipment: *a supply ship.*
– PHRASES **in short supply** not easily obtainable; scarce: *he meant to go, but time and petrol were in short supply.* **on supply** (of a schoolteacher) acting as a temporary substitute for another. **supply and demand** the amount of a good or service available and the desire of buyers for it, considered as factors regulating its price: *by the law of supply and demand the cost of health care will plummet.*
– DERIVATIVES **supplier** noun.
– ORIGIN late Middle English: from Old French *soupleer*, from Latin *supplere* 'fill up', from *sub-* 'from below' + *plere* 'fill'. The early sense of the noun was 'assistance, relief' (chiefly a Scots use).

supply[2] /ˈsʌpli/ ▶ **adverb** variant spelling of ***supplely*** (see **SUPPLE**).

supply chain ▶ **noun** the sequence of processes involved in the production and distribution of a commodity.

supply-side ▶ **adjective** [attrib.] Economics denoting or relating to a policy designed to increase output and employment by changing the conditions under which goods and services are supplied, especially by measures which reduce government involvement in the economy and allow the free market to operate.
– DERIVATIVES **supply-sider** noun.

support ▶ **verb** [with obj.] **1** bear all or part of the weight of; hold up: *the dome was supported by a hundred white columns.*
■ produce enough food and water for; be capable of sustaining: *the land had lost its capacity to support life.* ■ be capable of fulfilling (a role) adequately: *tutors gain practical experience which helps them support their tutoring role.* ■ endure; tolerate: *at work during the day I could support the grief.*
2 give assistance to, especially financially; enable to function or act: *the government gives £2,500 million a year to support the activities of the voluntary sector.*
■ provide with a home and the necessities of life: *my main concern was to support my family.* ■ give comfort and emotional help to: *I like to visit her to support her.* ■ approve of and encourage: *the proposal was supported by many delegates.* ■ suggest the truth of; corroborate: *the studies support our findings.* ■ be actively interested in and concerned for the success of (a particular sports team). ■ [as adj. **supporting**] (of an actor or a role) important in a play or film but subordinate to the leading parts. ■ (of a pop or rock group or performer) function as a secondary act to (another) at a concert.
3 Computing (of a computer or operating system) allow the use or operation of (a program, language, or device): *the new versions do not support the graphical user interface standard.*
▶ **noun 1** a thing that bears the weight of something or keeps it upright: *the best support for a camera is a tripod.*
■ [mass noun] the action or state of bearing the weight of something or someone or of being so supported: *she clutched the sideboard for support.*
2 [mass noun] material assistance: *he urged that military support be sent to protect humanitarian convoys* | [as modifier] *support staff.*
■ comfort and emotional help offered to someone in distress: *she's been through a bad time and needs our support.* ■ approval and encouragement: *the policies of reform enjoy widespread support.* ■ a secondary act at a pop or rock concert. ■ technical help given to the user of a computer or other product.
– PHRASES **in support of** giving assistance to: *air operations in support of the British Commonwealth forces.* ■ showing approval of: *the paper printed many letters in support of the government.* ■ attempting to promote or obtain: *a strike in support of an 8.5% pay rise.*
– DERIVATIVES **supportability** noun, **supportable** adjective.
– ORIGIN Middle English (originally in the sense 'tolerate, put up with'): from Old French *supporter*, from Latin *supportare*, from *sub-* 'from below' + *portare* 'carry'.

supporter ▶ **noun 1** a person who approves of and encourages someone or something (typically a public figure, a movement or party, or a policy): *Labour supporters.*
■ a person who is actively interested in and wishes success for a particular sports team.
2 Heraldry a representation of an animal or other figure, typically one of a pair, holding up or standing beside an escutcheon.

supportive ▶ **adjective** providing encouragement or emotional help: *the staff are extremely **supportive of** each other.*
– DERIVATIVES **supportively** adverb, **supportiveness** noun.

supportive therapy ▶ **noun** [mass noun] treatment designed to improve, reinforce, or sustain a patient's physiological well-being or psychological self-esteem and self-reliance.

support price ▶ **noun** a minimum price guaranteed to a farmer for agricultural produce and maintained by subsidy or the buying in of surplus stock.

suppose ▶ **verb 1** [with clause] assume that something is the case on the basis of evidence or probability but without proof or certain knowledge: *I suppose I got there about half past eleven.*
■ used to make a reluctant or hesitant admission: *I'm quite a good actress, I suppose.* ■ used to introduce a hypothesis and trace or ask about what follows from it: *suppose he had been murdered—what then?* ■ [in imperative] used to introduce a suggestion: *suppose we leave this to the police.* ■ (of a theory or argument) assume or require that something is the case as a precondition: *the procedure supposes that a will has already been proved* | [with obj.] *the theory supposes a predisposition to interpret utterances.* ■ [with obj.] believe to exist or to possess a specified characteristic: *he **supposed** the girl **to be** about twelve* | [as adj. **supposed**] *people admire their supposed industriousness.*
2 (**be supposed to do something**) be required to do something because of the position one is in or an agreement one has made: *I'm supposed to be meeting someone at the airport.*
■ [with negative] be forbidden to do something: *I shouldn't have been in the study—I'm not supposed to go in there.*
– PHRASES **I suppose so** used to express hesitant or reluctant agreement.
– DERIVATIVES **supposable** adjective.
– ORIGIN Middle English: from Old French *supposer*, from Latin *supponere* (from *sub-* 'from below' + *ponere* 'to place'), but influenced by Latin *suppositus* 'set under' and Old French *poser* 'to place'.

supposedly ▶ **adverb** [sentence adverb] according to what is generally assumed or believed (often used to indicate that the speaker doubts the truth of the statement): *the adverts are aimed at women, supposedly because they do the shopping.*

supposition ▶ **noun** an uncertain belief: *they were working on the supposition that his death was murder* | [mass noun] *their outrage was based on supposition and hearsay.*
– DERIVATIVES **suppositional** adjective.
– ORIGIN late Middle English (as a term in scholastic logic): from Old French, or from late Latin *suppositio(n-)* (translating Greek *hupothesis* 'hypothesis'), from the verb *supponere* (see **SUPPOSE**).

suppositious ▶ **adjective** based on assumption rather than fact: *most of the evidence is purely suppositious.*
– DERIVATIVES **suppositiously** adverb., **suppositiousness** noun.
– ORIGIN early 17th cent. (in the sense 'supposititious'): partly a contraction of **SUPPOSITITIOUS**, reinforced by **SUPPOSITION**.

supposititious /səˌpɒzɪˈtɪʃəs/ ▶ **adjective** substituted for the real thing; not genuine: *the supposititious heir to the throne.*
– DERIVATIVES **supposititiously** adverb, **supposititiousness** noun.
– ORIGIN early 17th cent.: from Latin *supposititius* (from *supponere* 'to substitute') + **-OUS**.

suppository ▶ **noun** (pl. **-ies**) a solid medical preparation in a roughly conical or cylindrical shape, designed to be inserted into the rectum or vagina to dissolve.
– ORIGIN late Middle English: from medieval Latin *suppositorium*, neuter (used as a noun) of late Latin *suppositorius* 'placed underneath'.

suppress ▶ **verb** [with obj.] forcibly put an end to: *the rising was savagely suppressed.*
■ prevent the development, action, or expression of (a feeling, impulse, idea, etc.); restrain: *she could not suppress a rising panic.* ■ prevent the dissemination of (information): *the report had been suppressed.* ■ prevent or inhibit (a process or reaction): *use of the drug suppressed the immune response.* ■ partly or wholly eliminate (electrical interference). ■ Psychoanalysis consciously inhibit (an unpleasant idea or memory) to avoid considering it.
– DERIVATIVES **suppressible** adjective, **suppressive** adjective, **suppressor** noun.
– ORIGIN late Middle English: from Latin *suppress-* 'pressed down', from the verb *supprimere*, from *sub-* 'down' + *premere* 'to press'.

suppressant ▶ **noun** a drug or other substance which acts to suppress or restrain something: *an appetite suppressant.*

suppression ▶ **noun** [mass noun] the action of suppressing something such as an activity or publication: *the Communist Party's forcible suppression of the opposition in 1948.*
■ Medicine stoppage or reduction of a discharge or secretion. ■ Biology the absence or non-development of a part or organ that is normally present. ■ Genetics the cancelling of the effect of one mutation by a second mutation. ■ Psychology the restraint or repression of an idea, activity, or reaction by something more powerful. ■ Psychoanalysis the conscious inhibition of unacceptable memories, impulses, or desires. ■ prevention of electrical interference.

suppressor cell (also **suppressor T cell**) ▶ **noun** Physiology a lymphocyte which can suppress antibody production by other lymphoid cells.

suppurate /ˈsʌpjʊreɪt/ ▶ **verb** [no obj.] undergo the formation of pus; fester.
– DERIVATIVES **suppuration** noun, **suppurative** /-rətɪv/ adjective.
– ORIGIN late Middle English (in the sense 'cause to form pus'): based on Latin *sub-* 'below' + *pus, pur-* 'pus'.

supra /ˈs(j)uːprə/ ▶ **adverb** formal used in academic or legal texts to refer to someone or something mentioned above or earlier: *the recent work by McAuslan and others (supra).*
– ORIGIN Latin.

supra- /ˈs(j)uːprə/ ▶ **prefix 1** above: *suprarenal.*
2 beyond; transcending: *supranational.*
– ORIGIN from Latin *supra* 'above, beyond, before in time'.

suprachiasmatic nucleus /ˌs(j)uːprəˌkʌɪəz-

S

ˈmatɪk/ ▶ **noun** Anatomy each of a pair of small nuclei in the hypothalamus of the brain, above the optic chiasma, thought to be concerned with the regulation of physiological circadian rhythms.

supramolecular ▶ **adjective** Biochemistry relating to or denoting structures composed of several or many molecules.

supramundane /s(j)uːprəˈmʌndeɪn/ ▶ **adjective** transcending or superior to the physical world.

supranational ▶ **adjective** having power or influence that transcends national boundaries or governments: *supranational law.*
– DERIVATIVES **supranationalism** noun, **supranationality** noun.

supranuclear ▶ **adjective** Anatomy situated, occurring, or originating above a nucleus of the central nervous system.

supraoptic ▶ **adjective** Anatomy situated above the optic chiasma.

supraorbital ▶ **adjective** Anatomy situated above the orbit of the eye.

suprarenal ▶ **adjective** Anatomy another term for **ADRENAL**.

suprasegmental Linguistics ▶ **adjective** denoting a feature of an utterance other than the consonantal and vocalic components, for example (in English) stress and intonation.
▶ **noun** such a feature.

supremacist ▶ **noun** an advocate of the supremacy of a particular group, especially one determined by race or sex: *a white supremacist.*
▶ **adjective** relating to or advocating such supremacy.
– DERIVATIVES **supremacism** noun.

supremacy /s(j)uːˈprɛməsi/ ▶ **noun** [mass noun] the state or condition of being superior to all others in authority, power, or status: *the supremacy of the king.*

Supremacy, Act of (in English history) either of two Acts of Parliament of 1534 and 1559 (particularly the former), which established Henry VIII and Elizabeth I as supreme heads of the Church of England and excluded the authority of the Pope.

suprematism ▶ **noun** [mass noun] the Russian abstract art movement developed by Kazimir Malevich *c.*1915, characterized by simple geometrical shapes and associated with ideas of spiritual purity.
– DERIVATIVES **suprematist** noun.

supreme ▶ **adjective** (of authority or an office, or someone holding it) superior to all others: *a unified force with a supreme commander.*
■ strongest, most important, or most powerful: *on the race track he* **reigned supreme**. ■ very great or intense; extreme: *he was nerving himself for a supreme effort.* ■ (of a penalty or sacrifice) involving death: *our comrades who made the supreme sacrifice.* ■ [postpositive] used to indicate that someone or something is very good at or well known for a specified activity: *people expected the marathon runner supreme to win.*
▶ **noun** (also **suprême**) [mass noun] a rich cream sauce.
■ a dish served in such a sauce: *chicken supreme.* [ORIGIN: from French *suprême*.]
– PHRASES **the Supreme Being** a name for God.
– DERIVATIVES **supremely** adverb.
– ORIGIN late 15th cent. (in the sense 'highest'): from Latin *supremus*, superlative of *superus* 'that is above', from *super* 'above'.

supreme court ▶ **noun** the highest judicial court in a country or state.
■ (in full **Supreme Court of Judicature**) (in England and Wales) the highest court below the House of Lords, divided into the High Court, the Court of Appeal, and the Crown Court.

supreme pontiff ▶ **noun** see **PONTIFF**.

Supreme Soviet ▶ **noun** the governing council of the former USSR or one of its constituent republics. That of the USSR was its highest legislative authority and was composed of two equal chambers: the Soviet of Union and the Soviet of Nationalities.

supremo /s(j)uːˈpriːməʊ, -ˈpreɪməʊ/ ▶ **noun** (pl. **-os**) Brit. informal a person in overall charge of an organization or activity: *the Channel Four supremo.*
■ a person with great authority or skill in a certain area: *an interior by design supremo Kelly.*
– ORIGIN Spanish, literally 'supreme'.

supremum /s(j)uːˈpriːməm/ ▶ **noun** Mathematics the smallest quantity that is greater than or equal to each of a given set or subset of quantities. The opposite of **INFIMUM**.
– ORIGIN 1940s: from Latin *suppremum* 'highest part'.

Supt ▶ **abbreviation for** Superintendent.

suq ▶ **noun** variant spelling of **SOUK**.

sur-[1] ▶ **prefix** equivalent to **SUPER-**.
– ORIGIN from French.

sur-[2] ▶ **prefix** variant spelling of **SUB-** assimilated before *r* (as in *surrogate*).

sura /ˈsʊərə/ (also **surah**) ▶ **noun** a chapter or section of the Koran.
– ORIGIN from Arabic *sūra*.

Surabaya /ˌsʊərəˈbʌɪə/ a seaport in Indonesia, on the north coast of Java; pop. 2,473,200 (1990). It is Indonesia's principal naval base and its second largest city.

surah /ˈsʊərə, ˈsjʊərə/ ▶ **noun** [mass noun] a soft twilled silk fabric used in dressmaking.
– ORIGIN late 19th cent.: representing the French pronunciation of **SURAT**, where it was originally made.

surahi /sʊˈrɑːhi/ ▶ **noun** (pl. **surahis**) an Indian clay pot with a long neck, used for storing water.
– ORIGIN via Urdu from Arabic *ṣurāḥiya* 'pure wine'.

sural /ˈs(j)ʊər(ə)l/ ▶ **adjective** Anatomy of or relating to the calf of the leg.
– ORIGIN early 17th cent.: from modern Latin *suralis*, from Latin *sura* 'calf'.

suramin /ˈsʊərəmɪn/ ▶ **noun** [mass noun] Medicine a synthetic compound derived from urea, used to treat trypanosomiasis, onchocerciasis, and filariasis.
– ORIGIN 1940s: of unknown origin.

Surat /ˈsʊərət, sʊˈrat/ a city in the state of Gujarat in western India, a port on the Tapti River near its mouth on the Gulf of Cambay; pop. 1,497,000 (1991). It was the site of the first trading post of the East India Company, established in 1612.

surcease ▶ **noun** [mass noun] archaic or US cessation: *he teased us without surcease.*
■ relief or consolation: *drugs are taken to provide surcease from intolerable psychic pain.*
▶ **verb** [no obj.] archaic cease.
– ORIGIN late Middle English (as a verb): from Old French *sursis*, past participle of Old French *surseoir* 'refrain, delay', from Latin *supersedere* (see **SUPERSEDE**). The change in the ending was due to association with **CEASE**; the noun dates from the late 16th cent.

surcharge ▶ **noun 1** an additional charge or payment: *we guarantee that no surcharges will be added to the cost of your holiday.*
■ a charge made by assessors as a penalty for false returns of taxable property. ■ Brit. an amount in an official account not passed by the auditor and having to be refunded by the person responsible. ■ the showing of an omission in an account for which credit should have been given.
2 a mark printed on a postage stamp changing its value.
▶ **verb** [with obj.] **1** exact an additional charge or payment from: *retailers will be able to surcharge credit-card users.*
2 mark (a postage stamp) with a surcharge.
– ORIGIN late Middle English (as a verb): from Old French *surcharger* (see **SUR-**[1], **CHARGE**). The early sense of the noun (late 15th cent.) was 'excessive load'.

surcingle /ˈsəːsɪŋg(ə)l/ ▶ **noun** a wide strap which runs over the back and under the belly of a horse, used to keep a rug or other equipment in place.
– ORIGIN Middle English: from Old French *surcengle*, based on *cengle* 'girth', from Latin *cingula*, from *cingere* 'gird'.

surcoat /ˈsəːkəʊt/ ▶ **noun** historical a loose robe worn over armour.
■ a similar sleeveless garment worn as part of the insignia of an order of knighthood. ■ an outer coat of rich material.
– ORIGIN Middle English: from Old French *surcot*, from *sur* 'over' + *cot* 'coat'.

surd /səːd/ ▶ **adjective 1** Mathematics (of a number) irrational.
2 Phonetics (of a speech sound) uttered with the breath and not the voice (e.g. *f, k, p, s, t*).
▶ **noun 1** Mathematics a surd number, especially the irrational root of an integer.
2 Phonetics a surd consonant.
– ORIGIN mid 16th cent.: from Latin *surdus* 'deaf, mute'; as a mathematical term, translating Greek (Euclid) *alogos* 'irrational, speechless', apparently via Arabic *jiḏr aṣamm*, literally 'deaf root'. Sense 2 dates from the mid 18th cent.

sure /ʃʊə, ʃɔː/ ▶ **adjective 1** [predic.] [often with clause] confident in what one thinks or knows; having no doubt that one is right: *I'm sure I've seen that dress before | she had to check her diary to be* **sure of** *the day of the week.*
■ (**sure of**) having a certain prospect or confident anticipation of: *the Gunners are sure of a UEFA Cup place.* ■ [with infinitive] certain to do something: *it's sure to rain before morning.* ■ true beyond any doubt: *what is sure is that learning is a complex business.* ■ [attrib.] able to be relied on or trusted: *her neck was red—a sure sign of agitation.* ■ confident; assured: *the drawings impress by their sure sense of rhythm.*
▶ **adverb** informal certainly (used for emphasis): *Texas sure was a great place to grow up.*
■ [as an exclamation] used to show assent: *'Are you serious?' 'Sure.'*
– PHRASES **be sure** [usu. in imperative] do not fail (used to emphasize an invitation or instruction): [with infinitive] *be sure to pop in* | [with clause] *be sure that you know what is required.* **for sure** informal without doubt: *I can't say for sure what Giles really wanted.* **make sure** [usu. with clause] establish that something is definitely so; confirm: *go and make sure she's all right.* ■ ensure that something is done or happens: *he made sure that his sons were well educated.* **(as) sure as eggs is eggs** (also **as sure as fate**) without any doubt. **sure enough** informal used to introduce a statement that confirms something previously predicted: *when X-rays were taken, sure enough, there was the needle.* **sure of oneself** very confident of one's own abilities or views: *he's very sure of himself.* **sure thing** informal a certainty. ■ [as exclamation] chiefly N. Amer. certainly; of course: *'Can I watch?' 'Sure thing.'* **to be sure** used to concede the truth of something that conflicts with another point that one wishes to make: *the ski runs are very limited, to be sure, but excellent for beginners.* ■ used for emphasis: *what an extraordinary woman she was, to be sure.*
– DERIVATIVES **sureness** noun.
– ORIGIN Middle English: from Old French *sur*, from Latin *securus* 'free from care'.

sure-fire ▶ **adjective** [attrib.] informal certain to succeed: *bad behaviour is a sure-fire way of getting attention.*

sure-footed ▶ **adjective** unlikely to stumble or slip: *tough, sure-footed hill ponies.*
■ confident and competent: *the challenges of the 1990s demand a responsible and sure-footed government.*
– DERIVATIVES **sure-footedly** adverb, **sure-footedness** noun.

surely ▶ **adverb 1** [sentence adverb] used to emphasize the speaker's firm belief that what they are saying is true and often their surprise that there is any doubt of this: *if there is no will, then surely the house goes automatically to you.*
■ without doubt; certainly: *if he did not heed the warning, he would surely die.* ■ [as exclamation] informal, chiefly N. Amer. of course; yes: *'You'll wait for me?' 'Surely.'*
2 with assurance or confidence: *no one knows how to move the economy quickly and surely in that direction.*

Sûreté /ˈsjʊəteɪ, French syʀte/ (also **Sûreté nationale** /ˌnasjəˈnɑːl, French nasjɔnal/) the French police department of criminal investigation.
– ORIGIN French, literally '(National) Security'.

surety /ˈʃʊərɪti, ˈʃʊəti/ ▶ **noun** (pl. **-ies**) a person who takes responsibility for another's performance of an undertaking, for example their appearing in court or the payment of a debt.
■ money given to support an undertaking that someone will perform a duty, pay their debts, etc.; a guarantee: *the magistrate granted bail with a surety of £500.* ■ [mass noun] the state of being sure or certain of something: *I was enmeshed in the surety of my impending fatherhood.*
– PHRASES **of** (or **for**) **a surety** archaic for certain: *who can tell that for a surety?* **stand surety** become a surety; stand bail: *Alfonso agreed to* **stand surety for** *his friend's behaviour.*
– DERIVATIVES **suretyship** noun.
– ORIGIN Middle English (in the sense 'something given to support an undertaking that someone will fulfil an obligation'): from Old French *surte*, from Latin *securitas* (see **SECURITY**).

surf ▶ **noun** [mass noun] the mass or line of foam formed by waves breaking on a seashore or reef: *the roar of the surf.*
■ [in sing.] a spell of surfing: *he went for an early surf.*

▶**verb** [no obj.] ride on the crest of a wave, typically towards the shore while riding on a surfboard: *learning to surf.*
■[with obj.] ride (a wave) towards the shore in such a way: *he has built a career out of surfing big waves.* ■ informal ride on the roof or outside of a fast-moving vehicle, typically a train, for excitement: *he fell to his death while surfing on a 70 mph train.* ■ [with obj.] move from site to site on (the Internet).
– DERIVATIVES **surfer** noun, **surfy** adjective.
– ORIGIN late 17th cent.: apparently from obsolete *suff,* of unknown origin, perhaps influenced by the spelling of *surge.*

surface ▶**noun 1** the outside part or uppermost layer of something (often used when describing its texture, form, or extent): *the earth's surface | poor road surfaces.*
■the level top of something: *roll out the dough on a floured surface.* ■ (also **surface area**) the area of such an outer part or uppermost layer: *the surface area of a cube.* ■ [in sing.] the upper limit of a body of liquid: *fish floating on the surface of the water.* ■ [in sing.] what is apparent on a casual view or consideration of someone or something, especially as distinct from feelings or qualities which are not immediately obvious: *Tom was a womanizer, but on the surface he remained respectable* | [as modifier] *we need to go beyond surface appearances.*
2 Geometry a set of points that has length and breadth but no thickness.
▶**adjective** [attrib.] of, relating to, or occurring on the upper or outer part of something: *surface workers at Cornish copper mines.*
■denoting ships which travel on the surface of the water as distinct from submarines: *the surface fleet.* ■ carried by or denoting transportation by sea or overland as contrasted with by air: *surface mail.*
▶**verb 1** [no obj.] rise or come up to the surface of the water or the ground: *he surfaced from his dive.*
■come to people's attention; become apparent: *the row first surfaced two years ago.* ■ informal (of a person) appear after having been asleep: *it was almost 11.30 before Anthony surfaced.*
2 [with obj.] (usu. **be surfaced**) provide (something, especially a road) with a particular upper or outer layer: *a small path surfaced with terracotta tiles.*
– DERIVATIVES **surfaced** adjective [often in combination] *a smooth-surfaced cylinder,* **surfacer** noun.
– ORIGIN early 17th cent.: from French (see **SUR-**[1], **FACE**), suggested by Latin *superficies.*

surface-active ▶**adjective** (of a substance, such as a detergent) tending to reduce the surface tension of a liquid in which it is dissolved.

surface chemistry ▶**noun** [mass noun] the branch of chemistry concerned with the processes occurring at interfaces between phases, especially that between liquid and gas.

surface effect ▶**noun** an effect associated with or only encountered near a surface, in particular that associated with an air-cushion vehicle (hovercraft) in which the cushion is sealed by rigid side walls and flexible seals fore and aft.

surface-mount ▶**adjective** (of an electronic component) having leads that are designed to be soldered on the side of a circuit board that the body of the component is mounted on. Often contrasted with **THROUGH-HOLE**.

surface noise ▶**noun** [mass noun] extraneous noise in playing a gramophone record, caused by imperfections in the grooves or in the pickup system.

surface structure ▶**noun** [mass noun] (in transformational grammar) the structure of a well-formed phrase or sentence in a language, as opposed to its underlying logical form. Contrasted with **DEEP STRUCTURE**.

surface tension ▶**noun** [mass noun] the tension of the surface film of a liquid caused by the attraction of the particles in the surface layer by the bulk of the liquid, which tends to minimize surface area.

surface-to-air ▶**adjective** [attrib.] (of a missile) designed to be fired from the ground or a vessel at an aircraft.

surface-to-surface ▶**adjective** [attrib.] (of a missile) designed to be fired from one point on the ground or a vessel at another such point or vessel.

surface water ▶**noun** [mass noun] **1** water that collects on the surface of the ground.
2 (also **surface waters**) the top layer of a body of water: *the surface water of a pond or lake.*

surfactant /sə'fakt(ə)nt/ ▶**noun** a substance which tends to reduce the surface tension of a liquid in which it is dissolved.
– ORIGIN 1950s: from *surf(ace)-act(ive)* + **-ANT**.

surfbird ▶**noun** a small migratory wader of the sandpiper family, with mainly dark grey plumage and a short bill and legs, breeding in Alaska.
• *Aphriza virgata,* family Scolopacidae.

surfboard ▶**noun** a long, narrow shaped board used in surfing.

surfcasting ▶**noun** [mass noun] fishing by casting a line into the sea from the shore.
– DERIVATIVES **surfcaster** noun.

surfeit ▶**noun** [usu. in sing.] an excessive amount of something: *a surfeit of food and drink.*
■archaic an illness caused or regarded as being caused by excessive eating or drinking: *he died of a surfeit.*
▶**verb** (**surfeited**, **surfeiting**) [with obj.] (usu. **be surfeited with**) cause (someone) to desire no more of something as a result of having consumed or done it to excess: *I am surfeited with shopping.*
■[no obj.] archaic consume too much of something: *he never surfeited on rich wine.*
– ORIGIN Middle English: from Old French *surfeit,* based on Latin *super-* 'above, in excess' + *facere* 'do'.

surficial /sə'fɪʃ(ə)l/ ▶**adjective** Geology of or relating to the earth's surface: *surficial deposits.*
– DERIVATIVES **surficially** adverb.
– ORIGIN late 19th cent.: from **SURFACE**, on the pattern of *superficial.*

surfie ▶**noun** informal, chiefly Austral. a surfing enthusiast, especially a young man.

surfing ▶**noun** [mass noun] the sport or pastime of being carried to the shore on the crest of large waves while standing or lying on a surfboard.

surf lifesaver ▶**noun** see **LIFESAVER** (sense 2).

surf music ▶**noun** [mass noun] a style of popular music originating in the US in the early 1960s, characterized by high harmony vocals and typically having lyrics relating to surfing.

surf 'n' turf (also **surf and turf**) ▶**noun** [mass noun] chiefly N. Amer. a dish containing both seafood and meat, typically shellfish and steak.

surfperch ▶**noun** (pl. same or **-perches**) a deep-bodied live-bearing fish of the North Pacific, living chiefly in coastal waters. Also called **SEA PERCH**.
• Family Embiotocidae: several genera and species.

surf-riding ▶**noun** another term for **SURFING**.

surge ▶**noun** a sudden powerful forward or upward movement, especially by a crowd or by a natural force such as the waves or tide: *flooding caused by tidal surges.*
■a sudden large increase, typically a brief one which happens during an otherwise stable or quiescent period: *the firm predicted a 20% surge in sales.* ■ a powerful rush of an emotion or feeling: *Sophie felt a surge of anger.* ■ a sudden marked increase in voltage or current in an electric circuit.
▶**verb** [no obj., usu. with adverbial] (of a crowd or a natural force) move suddenly and powerfully forward or upward: *the journalists surged forward.*
■increase suddenly and powerfully, typically during an otherwise stable or quiescent period: *shares surged to a record high.* ■ (of an emotion or feeling) affect someone powerfully and suddenly: *indignation surged up within her.* ■ (of an electric voltage or current) increase suddenly. ■ Nautical (of a rope, chain, or windlass) slip back with a jerk.
– ORIGIN late 15th cent. (in the sense 'fountain, stream'): the noun (in early use) from Old French *sourgeon*; the verb partly from the Old French stem *sourge-,* based on Latin *surgere* 'to rise'. Early senses of the verb included 'rise and fall on the waves' and 'swell with great force'.

surge chamber ▶**noun** another term for **SURGE TANK**.

surgeon ▶**noun** a medical practitioner qualified to practise surgery.
■a doctor in the navy.
– ORIGIN Middle English: from Anglo-Norman French *surgien,* contraction of Old French *serurgien,* based on Latin *chirurgia,* from Greek *kheirourgia* 'handiwork, surgery', from *kheir* 'hand' + *ergon* 'work'.

surgeonfish ▶**noun** (pl. same or **-fishes**) a deep-bodied and typically brightly coloured tropical marine fish with a scalpel-like spine on each side of the tail.
• Family Acanthuridae: several genera and many species. See also **TANG**[3], **UNICORN FISH**.

surgeon general ▶**noun** (pl. **surgeons general**) (chiefly in the US) the head of a public health service or of the medical service of an army, navy, or air force.

surgeon's knot ▶**noun** a reef knot with one or more extra turns in the first half knot.
– ORIGIN from the use of such a knot to tie a ligature in surgery.

surgery ▶**noun** (pl. **-ies**) **1** [mass noun] the branch of medicine concerned with treatment of injuries or disorders of the body by incision or manipulation, especially with instruments: *cardiac surgery.*
2 Brit. a place where a doctor, dentist, or other medical practitioner treats or advises patients.
■[in sing.] an occasion on which such treatment or consultation occurs: *Doctor Bailey had finished his evening surgery.* ■ an occasion on which an MP, lawyer, or other professional person gives advice.
– ORIGIN Middle English: from Old French *surgerie,* contraction of *serurgerie,* from *serurgien* (see **SURGEON**).

surge tank ▶**noun** a tank connected to a pipe carrying a liquid and intended to neutralize sudden changes of pressure in the flow by filling when the pressure increases and emptying when it drops.

surgical ▶**adjective** of, relating to, or used in surgery: *a surgical dressing | a surgical ward.*
■(of a special garment or appliance) worn to correct or relieve an injury, illness, or deformity: *surgical stockings.* ■ figurative denoting something done with great precision, especially a swift and highly accurate military attack from the air: *surgical bombing.*
– DERIVATIVES **surgically** adverb.
– ORIGIN late 18th cent. (earlier as *chirurgical*): from French *cirurgical,* from Old French *sirurgie* (see **SURGERY**).

surgical spirit ▶**noun** [mass noun] Brit. methylated spirit (often with other ingredients such as oil of wintergreen) used in medical practice, especially for cleansing the skin before injections or surgery.

suricate /'s(j)ʊərɪkeɪt/ ▶**noun** a gregarious burrowing meerkat with dark bands on the back and a black-tipped tail, native to southern Africa.
• *Suricata suricatta,* family Herpestidae.
– ORIGIN late 18th cent.: via French from a local African word.

Suriname /ˌsʊərɪ'nam, -'nɑːmə/ (also **Surinam** /-'nam/) a country on the NE coast of South America; pop. 402,900 (est. 1994); languages, Dutch (official), Creoles, Hindi; capital, Paramaribo. Former name (until 1948) **DUTCH GUIANA**.

Colonized by the Dutch and the English from the 17th century, Suriname became fully independent in 1975. The population is descended largely from African slaves and Asian workers brought in to work on sugar plantations; there is also a small American Indian population.

– DERIVATIVES **Surinamer** noun, **Surinamese** /-nə'miːz/ adjective & noun.

Suriname toad ▶**noun** an aquatic South American toad with a flat body and long webbed feet, the female of which carries the eggs and tadpoles in pockets on her back.
• *Pipa pipa,* family Pipidae.

surjection /səː'dʒɛkʃ(ə)n/ ▶**noun** Mathematics an onto mapping.
– DERIVATIVES **surjective** adjective.

surly ▶**adjective** (**surlier**, **surliest**) bad-tempered and unfriendly: *the porter left with a surly expression.*
– DERIVATIVES **surlily** adverb, **surliness** noun.
– ORIGIN mid 16th cent. (in the sense 'lordly, haughty, arrogant'): alteration of obsolete *sirly* (see **SIR**, **-LY**[1]).

surmise /sə'mʌɪz/ ▶**verb** [no obj.] [usu. with clause] suppose that something is true without having evidence to confirm it: *he surmised that something must be wrong* | [with direct speech] *'I don't think they're locals,' she surmised.*
▶**noun** a supposition that something may be true, even though there is no evidence to confirm it: *Charles was glad to have his surmise confirmed* | [mass noun] *all these observations remain surmise.*
– ORIGIN late Middle English (in the senses 'formal allegation' and 'allege formally'): from Anglo-Norman French and Old French *surmise,* feminine past participle of *surmettre* 'accuse', from late Latin *supermittere* 'put in afterwards', from *super-* 'over' + *mittere* 'send'.

surmount ▶ **verb** [with obj.] **1** overcome (a difficulty or obstacle): *all manner of cultural differences were surmounted.*
2 (usu. **be surmounted**) stand or be placed on top of: *the tomb was surmounted by a sculptured angel.*
– DERIVATIVES **surmountable** adjective.
– ORIGIN late Middle English (also in the sense 'surpass, be superior to'): from Old French *surmonter* (see **SUR-**[1], **MOUNT**[1]).

surmullet ▶ **noun** a red mullet that is widely distributed in the tropical Indo-Pacific.
• *Pseudupeneus fraterculus*, family Mullidae.
– ORIGIN late 17th cent.: from French *surmulet*, from Old French *sor* 'red' + *mulet* 'mullet'.

surname ▶ **noun** a hereditary name common to all members of a family, as distinct from a Christian or other given name.
■ archaic a name, title, or epithet added to a person's name, especially one indicating their birthplace or a particular quality or achievement: *Simeon of the pillar, by surname Stylites.*
▶ **verb** [with obj.] (usu. **be surnamed**) give a surname to: *Eddie Penham, so aptly surnamed, had produced a hand-painted sign for us.*
– ORIGIN Middle English: partial translation of Anglo-Norman French *surnoun*, suggested by medieval Latin *supernomen*.

surpass ▶ **verb** [with obj.] exceed; be greater than: *pre-war levels of production were surpassed in 1929.*
■ be better than: *he continued to surpass me at all games.* ■ (**surpass oneself**) do or be better than ever before: *the organist was surpassing himself.* ■ [as adj. **surpassing**] dated or poetic/literary incomparable or outstanding: *a picture of surpassing beauty.*
– DERIVATIVES **surpassable** adjective, **surpassingly** adverb.
– ORIGIN mid 16th cent.: from French *surpasser*, from *sur-* 'above' + *passer* 'to pass'.

surplice /ˈsəːplɪs/ ▶ **noun** a loose white linen vestment varying from hip-length to calf-length, worn over a cassock by clergy and choristers at Christian church services.
– DERIVATIVES **surpliced** adjective.
– ORIGIN Middle English: from Old French *sourpelis*, from medieval Latin *superpellicium*, from *super-* 'above' + *pellicia* 'fur garment'.

surplus ▶ **noun** an amount of something left over when requirements have been met; an excess of production or supply over demand: *exports of food surpluses.*
■ an excess of income or assets over expenditure or liabilities in a given period, typically a financial year: *a trade surplus of $1,395 million.* ■ the excess value of a company's assets over the face value of its stock.
▶ **adjective** more than what is needed or used; excess: *make the most of your surplus cash | the firm told 284 employees that they were* ***surplus to requirements****.*
■ denoting a shop selling excess or out-of-date military equipment or clothing: *she had picked up her boots in an army surplus store.*
– ORIGIN late Middle English: from Old French *sourplus*, from medieval Latin *superplus*, from *super-* 'in addition' + *plus* 'more'.

surplus value ▶ **noun** [mass noun] Economics (in Marxist theory) the excess of value produced by the labour of workers over the wages they are paid.

surprise ▶ **noun** **1** an unexpected or astonishing event, fact, or thing: *the announcement was a complete surprise.*
■ [mass noun] a feeling of mild astonishment or shock caused by something unexpected: *much to her surprise, she'd missed him.* ■ [as modifier] denoting something made, done, or happening unexpectedly: *a surprise attack.*
2 [as modifier] Bell-ringing denoting a complex method of change-ringing: *surprise major.*
▶ **verb** [with obj.] (often **be surprised**) (of something unexpected) cause (someone) to feel mild astonishment or shock: *I* ***was surprised at*** *his statement | [with obj. and clause] Joe was surprised that he enjoyed the journey | [with infinitive] she was surprised to learn that he was forty | [as adj.* ***surprising****] a surprising sequence of events.*
■ capture, attack, or discover suddenly and unexpectedly; catch unawares: *he surprised a gang stealing scrap metal.*
– PHRASES **surprise, surprise** informal said when giving someone a surprise. ■ said ironically when one believes that something was entirely predictable: *we entrust you with Jason's care and, surprise surprise, you make a mess of it.* **take someone/thing by surprise** attack or capture someone or something unexpectedly. ■ (**take someone by surprise**) happen when someone is not prepared or is expecting something different: *the question took David by surprise.*
– DERIVATIVES **surprisedly** adverb, **surprisingly** adverb [as submodifier] *the profit margin in advertising is surprisingly low* | [sentence adverb] *not surprisingly, his enthusiasm knew no bounds,* **surprisingness** noun.
– ORIGIN late Middle English (in the sense 'unexpected seizure of a place, or attack on troops'): from Old French, feminine past participle of *surprendre*, from medieval Latin *superprehendere* 'seize'.

surra /ˈsʊərə, ˈsʌrə/ ▶ **noun** [mass noun] a parasitic disease of camels and other mammals caused by trypanosomes, transmitted by biting flies and occurring chiefly in North Africa and Asia.
– ORIGIN late 19th cent.: from Marathi *sūra* 'air breathed through the nostrils'.

surreal ▶ **adjective** having the qualities of surrealism; bizarre: *a surreal mix of fact and fantasy.*
– DERIVATIVES **surreality** noun, **surreally** adverb.
– ORIGIN 1930s: back-formation from **SURREALISM**.

surrealism ▶ **noun** [mass noun] a 20th-century avant-garde movement in art and literature which sought to release the creative potential of the unconscious mind, for example by the irrational juxtaposition of images.

> Launched in 1924 by a manifesto of André Breton and having a strong political content, the movement grew out of symbolism and Dada and was strongly influenced by Sigmund Freud. In the visual arts its most notable exponents were André Masson, Jean Arp, Joan Miró, René Magritte, Salvador Dali, Max Ernst, Man Ray, and Luis Buñuel.

– DERIVATIVES **surrealist** noun & adjective, **surrealistic** adjective, **surrealistically** adverb.
– ORIGIN early 20th cent.: from French *surréalisme* (see **SUR-**[1], **REALISM**).

surrebuttal /ˌsʌrɪˈbʌtəl/ ▶ **noun** another term for **SURREBUTTER**.

surrebutter /ˌsʌrɪˈbʌtə/ ▶ **noun** Law, archaic a plaintiff's reply to the defendant's rebutter.
– ORIGIN late 16th cent.: from **SUR-**[1] 'in addition' + **REBUTTER**, on the pattern of *surrejoinder*.

surrejoinder /ˌsʌrɪˈdʒɔɪndə/ ▶ **noun** Law, archaic a plaintiff's reply to the defendant's rejoinder.
– ORIGIN mid 16th cent.: from **SUR-**[1] 'in addition' + **REJOINDER**.

surrender ▶ **verb** [no obj.] cease resistance to an enemy or opponent and submit to their authority: *over 140 rebels surrendered to the authorities.*
■ [with obj.] give up or hand over (a person, right, or possession), typically on compulsion or demand: *in 1815 Denmark* ***surrendered*** *Norway* ***to*** *Sweden | the UK is opposed to surrendering its monetary sovereignty.* ■ [with obj.] (in a sporting context) lose (a point, game, or advantage): *she surrendered only twenty games in her five qualifying matches.* ■ (**surrender to**) abandon oneself entirely to (a powerful emotion or influence); give in to: *he was surprised that Miriam should surrender to this sort of jealousy | he* ***surrendered himself*** *to the mood of the hills.* ■ [with obj.] (of a person assured) cancel (a life insurance policy) and receive back a proportion of the premiums paid. ■ [with obj.] give up (a lease) before its expiry.
▶ **noun** [mass noun] the action of surrendering: *the final surrender of Germany on 8 May 1945 | [count noun] the colonel was anxious to negotiate a surrender.*
■ the giving up of a lease before its expiry. ■ the action of surrendering a life insurance policy.
– PHRASES **surrender to bail** Law duly appear in court after release on bail.
– ORIGIN late Middle English (chiefly in legal use): from Anglo-Norman French (see **SUR-**[1], **RENDER**).

surrender value ▶ **noun** the amount payable to a person who surrenders a life insurance policy.

surreptitious /ˌsʌrəpˈtɪʃəs/ ▶ **adjective** kept secret, especially because it would not be approved of: *low wages were supplemented by surreptitious payments from tradesmen.*
– DERIVATIVES **surreptitiously** adverb, **surreptitiousness** noun.
– ORIGIN late Middle English (in the sense 'obtained by suppression of the truth'): from Latin *surreptitius* (from the verb *surripere*, from *sub-* 'secretly' + *rapere* 'seize') + **-OUS**.

Surrey a county of SE England; county town, Kingston-upon-Thames.

surrey ▶ **noun** (pl. **-eys**) historical (in the US) a light four-wheeled carriage with two seats facing forwards.
– ORIGIN late 19th cent.: originally denoting a *Surrey cart*, first made in **SURREY**, from which the carriage was later adapted.

surrogacy /ˈsʌrəgəsi/ ▶ **noun** [mass noun] the action or state of being a surrogate.
■ the process of giving birth as a surrogate mother or of arranging such a birth.

surrogate /ˈsʌrəgət/ ▶ **noun** a substitute, especially a person deputizing for another in a specific role or office: *wives of MPs are looked on as* ***surrogates for*** *their husbands while the latter are at Westminster.*
■ (in the Christian Church) a bishop's deputy who grants marriage licences. ■ (in the US) a judge in charge of probate, inheritance, and guardianship.
– ORIGIN early 17th cent.: from Latin *surrogatus*, past participle of *surrogare* 'elect as a substitute', from *super-* 'over' + *rogare* 'ask'.

surrogate mother ▶ **noun** **1** a person, animal, or thing which takes on all or part of the role of mother to another person or animal.
2 a woman who bears a child on behalf of another woman, either from her own egg fertilized by the other woman's partner, or from the implantation in her womb of a fertilized egg from the other woman.

surround ▶ **verb** [with obj.] (usu. **be surrounded**) be all round (someone or something): *the hotel is surrounded by its own gardens* | figurative *he loves to* ***surround himself with*** *family and friends* | [as adj. **surrounding**] *the surrounding countryside.*
■ (of troops, police, etc.) encircle (someone or something) so as to cut off communication or escape: *troops surrounded the parliament building.* ■ be associated with: *the killings were surrounded by controversy.*
▶ **noun** a thing that forms a border or edging around an object: *an oak fireplace surround.*
■ (usu. **surrounds**) the area encircling something; surroundings: *the beautiful surrounds of Connemara.*
– ORIGIN late Middle English (in the sense 'overflow'): from Old French *souronder*, from late Latin *superundare*, from *super-* 'over' + *undare* 'to flow' (from *unda* 'a wave'); later associated with **ROUND**. Current senses of the noun date from the late 19th cent.

surroundings ▶ **plural noun** the things and conditions around a person or thing: *I took up the time admiring my surroundings.*

surround sound ▶ **noun** [mass noun] a system of stereophony involving three or more speakers surrounding the listener so as to give a more realistic effect.

surtax ▶ **noun** [mass noun] an additional tax on something already taxed, especially a higher rate of tax on incomes above a certain level.
– ORIGIN late 19th cent.: from French *surtaxe* (see **SUR-**[1], **TAX**).

Surtees /ˈsəːtiːz/, Robert Smith (1805–64), English journalist and novelist. He is best remembered for his comic sketches of Mr Jorrocks, the sporting Cockney grocer, collected in *Jorrocks's Jaunts and Jollities* (1838).

surtitle ▶ **noun** (usu. **surtitles**) a caption projected on a screen above the stage in an opera, translating the text being sung.
▶ **verb** [with obj.] provide (an opera production) with surtitles.

surtout /ˈsəːtuː, səːˈtuː(t)/ ▶ **noun** historical a man's greatcoat of a similar style to a frock coat.
– ORIGIN late 17th cent.: from French, from *sur* 'over' + *tout* 'everything'.

Surtsey /ˈsəːtsi/ a small island to the south of Iceland, formed by a volcanic eruption in 1963.

surveillance /səˈveɪl(ə)ns, -ˈveɪəns/ ▶ **noun** [mass noun] close observation, especially of a suspected spy or criminal: *he found himself put* ***under surveillance*** *by British military intelligence.*
– ORIGIN early 19th cent.: from French, from *sur-* 'over' + *veiller* 'watch' (from Latin *vigilare* 'keep watch').

survey ▶ **verb** /səˈveɪ/ [with obj.] **1** (of a person or their eyes) look carefully and thoroughly at (someone or something), especially so as to appraise them: *her green eyes surveyed him coolly | I surveyed the options.*
■ investigate the opinions or experience of (a group of people) by asking them questions: *95% of patients surveyed were satisfied with the health service.*

■ investigate (behaviour or opinions) by questioning a group of people: *the investigator surveyed the attitudes and beliefs held by residents.*
2 examine and record the area and features of (an area of land) so as to construct a map, plan, or description: *he surveyed the coasts of New Zealand.*
■ Brit. examine and report on the condition of (a building), especially for a prospective buyer: *the cottage didn't look unsafe, but he had it surveyed.*
▶ **noun** /'sɜːveɪ/ **1** a general view, examination, or description of someone or something: *the author provides a survey of the relevant literature.*
■ an investigation of the opinions or experience of a group of people, based on a series of questions.
2 Brit. an act of surveying a building: *the building society will insist that you have a survey done.*
■ a written report detailing the findings of this.
3 an act of surveying an area of land: *the flight involved a detailed aerial survey of military bases.*
■ a map, plan, or detailed description obtained in such a way. ■ a department carrying out the surveying of land: *the British Geological Survey.*
– ORIGIN late Middle English (in the sense 'examine and ascertain the condition of'): from Anglo-Norman French *surveier*, from medieval Latin *supervidere*, from *super-* 'over' + *videre* 'to see'. The early sense of the noun (late 15th cent.) was 'supervision'.

Surveyor a series of unmanned American spacecraft sent to the moon between 1966 and 1968, five of which successfully made soft landings.

surveyor ▶ **noun** a person who examines the condition of land and buildings professionally.
■ Brit. an official inspector of something, especially for measurement and valuation purposes. ■ a person who investigates or examines something, especially boats for seaworthiness.
– DERIVATIVES **surveyorship** noun.
– ORIGIN late Middle English (denoting a supervisor): from Anglo-Norman French *surveiour*, from the verb *surveier* (see **SURVEY**).

surveyor general ▶ **noun** (pl. **surveyors general** or **surveyor generals**) historical a chief supervisor in certain departments of the British government.

survivable ▶ **adjective** (of an accident or ordeal) able to be survived; not fatal: *air crashes are becoming more survivable.*

survival ▶ **noun** [mass noun] the state or fact of continuing to live or exist, typically in spite of an accident, ordeal, or difficult circumstances: *the animal's chances of survival were pretty low* | figurative *he was fighting for his political survival.*
■ [count noun] an object or practice that has continued to exist from an earlier time: *his shorts were a survival from his army days.*
– PHRASES **survival of the fittest** Biology the continued existence of organisms which are best adapted to their environment, with the extinction of others, as a concept in the Darwinian theory of evolution. Compare with **NATURAL SELECTION**.

survival bag ▶ **noun** a large bag made of plastic or metal foil, used in an emergency by climbers and others as a protection against exposure.

survival curve ▶ **noun** a graph showing the proportion of a population living after a given age, or at a given time after contracting a serious disease or receiving a radiation dose.

survivalism ▶ **noun** [mass noun] **1** the policy of trying to ensure one's own survival or that of one's social or national group.
2 the practising of outdoor survival skills as a sport or hobby.
– DERIVATIVES **survivalist** noun & adjective.

survival kit ▶ **noun** a pack of emergency equipment, including food, medical supplies, and tools, especially as carried by members of the armed forces.
■ a collection of items to help someone in a particular situation: *a supply-teacher survival kit.*

survival value ▶ **noun** [mass noun] the property of an ability, faculty, or characteristic that makes individuals possessing it more likely to survive, thrive, and reproduce: *everyone knows that a bad smell is of survival value to the skunk.*

survive ▶ **verb** [no obj.] continue to live or exist, especially in spite of danger or hardship: *against all odds the child survived.*
■ [with obj.] continue to live or exist in spite of (an accident or ordeal): *he has survived several assassination attempts.* ■ [with obj.] remain alive after the death of (a particular person): *he was survived by his wife and six children* | [as adj. **surviving**] *there were no surviving relatives.* ■ [no obj.] manage to keep going in difficult circumstances: *she had to work day and night and survive on two hours sleep.*
– ORIGIN late Middle English: from Old French *sourvivre*, from Latin *supervivere*, from *super-* 'in addition' + *vivere* 'live'.

survivor ▶ **noun** a person who survives, especially a person remaining alive after an event in which others have died: *the sole survivor of the massacre.*
■ the remainder of a group of people or things: *a survivor from last year's team.* ■ a person who copes well with difficulties in their life: *she is a born survivor.* ■ Law a joint tenant who has the right to the whole estate on the other's death.

survivorship ▶ **noun** [mass noun] the state or condition of being a survivor; survival.
■ chiefly Zoology the proportion of a population surviving to a given age.

survivorship curve ▶ **noun** chiefly Zoology a survival curve.

Surya /'suːrɪə/ Hinduism the sun god of later Hindu mythology, originally one of several solar deities in the Vedic religion.
– ORIGIN from Sanskrit *sūrya* 'sun'.

Sus. ▶ **abbreviation for** (in biblical references) Susanna (Apocrypha).

sus /sʌs/ Brit. informal ▶ **noun** [mass noun] suspicion of having committed a crime: *he was picked up* **on sus**.
■ [as modifier] historical of, relating to, or denoting a law under which a person could be arrested on suspicion of having committed an offence: *the sus law.* ■ variant spelling of **suss** (in sense 1).
▶ **adjective** variant spelling of **SUSS**.

sus- ▶ **prefix** variant spelling of **SUB-** before *c, p, t* (as in *susceptible, suspend, sustain*).

Susa /'suːsə/ **1** an ancient city of SW Asia, one of the chief cities of the kingdom of Elam and later capital of the Persian Achaemenid dynasty.
2 another name for **SOUSSE**.

Susah /'suːsə/ another name for **SOUSSE**.

Susanna (in the Apocrypha) a woman of Babylon falsely accused of adultery by two elders but saved by the sagacity of Daniel.
■ the book of the Apocrypha telling the story of Susanna.

susceptibility ▶ **noun** (pl. **-ies**) **1** [mass noun] the state or fact of being likely or liable to be influenced or harmed by a particular thing: *lack of exercise increases* **susceptibility to** *disease.*
■ (**susceptibilities**) a person's feelings, typically considered as being easily hurt: *I was so careful not to offend their susceptibilities.*
2 Physics the ratio of magnetization to a magnetizing force.

susceptible /sə'sɛptɪb(ə)l/ ▶ **adjective 1** likely or liable to be influenced or harmed by a particular thing: *patients with liver disease may be* **susceptible to** *infection.*
■ (of a person) easily influenced by feelings or emotions; sensitive: *they only do it to tease him—he's too susceptible.*
2 [predic.] (**susceptible of**) capable or admitting of: *the problem is not susceptible of a simple solution.*
– DERIVATIVES **susceptibly** adverb.
– ORIGIN early 17th cent.: from late Latin *susceptibilis*, from Latin *suscipere* 'take up, sustain', from *sub-* 'from below' + *capere* 'take'.

susceptive ▶ **adjective** archaic receptive or sensitive to something; susceptible.
– ORIGIN late Middle English: from late Latin *susceptivus*, from *suscept-* 'taken up', from the verb *suscipere* (see **SUSCEPTIBLE**).

sushi /'suːʃi, 'sʊʃi/ ▶ **noun** [mass noun] a Japanese dish consisting of small balls or rolls of vinegar-flavoured cold rice served with a garnish of vegetables, egg, or raw seafood.
– ORIGIN Japanese.

suslik /'sʌslɪk/ ▶ **noun** variant spelling of **SOUSLIK**.

suspect ▶ **verb** /sə'spɛkt/ [with obj.] **1** have an idea or impression of the existence, presence, or truth of (something) without certain proof: *if you suspect a gas leak, do not turn on an electric light* | [with clause] *she suspected that he might be bluffing* | [as adj. **suspected**] *a suspected heart condition.*
■ believe or feel that (someone) is guilty of an illegal, dishonest, or unpleasant act, without certain proof: *parents* **suspected of** *child abuse.*
2 doubt the genuineness or truth of: *a broker whose honesty he had no reason to suspect.*
▶ **noun** /'sʌspɛkt/ a person thought to be guilty of a crime or offence: *the police have arrested a suspect.*
▶ **adjective** /'sʌspɛkt/ not to be relied on or trusted; possibly dangerous or false: *a suspect package was found on the platform.*
– ORIGIN Middle English (originally as an adjective): from Latin *suspectus* 'mistrusted', past participle of *suspicere*, from *sub-* 'from below' + *specere* 'to look'.

suspend ▶ **verb** [with obj.] (usu. **be suspended**) **1** temporarily prevent from continuing or being in force or effect: *work on the dam was suspended.*
■ officially prohibit (someone) from holding their usual post or carrying out their usual role for a particular length of time: *two officers were* **suspended from** *duty pending the outcome of the investigation.* ■ defer or delay (an action, event, or judgement): *the judge suspended judgement until January 15.* ■ Law (of a judge or court) cause (an imposed sentence) to be unenforced as long as no further offence is committed within a specified period: *the sentence was suspended for six months* | [as adj. **suspended**] *a suspended jail sentence.*
2 hang (something) from somewhere: *the light was* **suspended from** *the ceiling.*
3 (**be suspended**) (of solid particles) be dispersed throughout the bulk of a fluid: *the paste contains collagen suspended in a salt solution.*
– PHRASES **suspend disbelief** temporarily allow oneself to believe something that isn't true, especially in order to enjoy a work of fiction. **suspend payment** (of a company) cease to meet its financial obligations as a result of insolvency or insufficient funds.
– ORIGIN Middle English: from Old French *suspendre* or Latin *suspendere*, from *sub-* 'from below' + *pendere* 'hang'.

suspended animation ▶ **noun** [mass noun] the temporary cessation of most vital functions without death, as in a dormant seed or a hibernating animal.

suspended ceiling ▶ **noun** a ceiling with a space between it and the floor above from which it hangs.

suspender ▶ **noun 1** (usu. **suspenders**) Brit. an elastic strap attached to a belt or garter, fastened to the top of a stocking to hold it up.
2 (**suspenders**) N. Amer. a pair of braces for holding up trousers.

suspender belt ▶ **noun** Brit. a woman's undergarment consisting of a decorative belt and elastic suspenders to which the tops of stockings are fastened.

suspense ▶ **noun** [mass noun] **1** a state or feeling of excited or anxious uncertainty about what may happen: *come on, Fran, don't keep me in suspense!*
■ a quality in a work of fiction that arouses excited expectation or uncertainty about what may happen: *a tale of mystery and suspense* | [as modifier] *a suspense novel.*
2 chiefly Law the temporary cessation or suspension of something.
– DERIVATIVES **suspenseful** adjective.
– ORIGIN late Middle English: from Old French *suspens* 'abeyance', based on Latin *suspensus* 'suspended, hovering, doubtful', past participle of *suspendere* (see **SUSPEND**).

suspense account ▶ **noun** an account in the books of an organization in which items are entered temporarily before allocation to the correct or final account.

suspension ▶ **noun 1** [mass noun] the action of suspending someone or something or the condition of being suspended, in particular:
■ the temporary prevention of something from continuing or being in force or effect: *the suspension of military action.* ■ the official prohibition of someone from holding their usual post or carrying out their usual role for a particular length of time: *the investigation led to the suspension of several officers* | [count noun] *a four-match suspension.* ■ [count noun] Music a discord made by prolonging a note of a chord into the following chord.
2 [mass noun] the system of springs and shock absorbers by which a vehicle is supported on its wheels: *the rear suspension deforms slightly on corners.*
3 a mixture in which particles are dispersed throughout the bulk of a fluid: *a suspension of maize starch in arachis oil.*
■ [mass noun] the state of being dispersed in such a way: *the agitator in the vat keeps the slurry* **in suspension**.

S

– ORIGIN late Middle English: from French, or from Latin *suspensio(n-)*, from the verb *suspendere* (see **SUSPEND**).

suspension bridge ▶ noun a bridge in which the weight of the deck is supported by vertical cables suspended from further cables that run between towers and are anchored in abutments at each end.

suspension feeder ▶ noun Zoology an aquatic animal which feeds on particles of organic matter suspended in the water, especially a bottom-dwelling filter feeder.

suspensive ▶ adjective **1** of or relating to the deferral or suspension of an event, action, or legal obligation.
2 causing suspense.
– DERIVATIVES **suspensively** adverb, **suspensiveness** noun.

suspensory ▶ adjective **1** holding and supporting an organ or part: *a suspensory ligament.*
2 of or relating to the deferral or suspension of an event, action, or legal obligation: *a suspensory requirement.*
– ORIGIN late Middle English: from medieval Latin *suspensorius* 'used for hanging something up', from Latin *suspendere* (see **SUSPEND**).

suspicion ▶ noun **1** a feeling or thought that something is possible, likely, or true: *she had a sneaking **suspicion that** he was laughing at her.*
■ a feeling or belief that someone is guilty of an illegal, dishonest, or unpleasant action: *police would not say what aroused their suspicions* | [mass noun] *he was arrested **on suspicion of** murder.* ■ [mass noun] cautious distrust: *her activities were regarded with suspicion by the headmistress.*
2 a very slight trace of something: ***a suspicion of** a smile.*
– PHRASES **above suspicion** too obviously good or honest to be thought capable of wrongdoing. **under suspicion** thought to be guilty of wrongdoing.
– ORIGIN Middle English: from Anglo-Norman French *suspeciun*, from medieval Latin *suspectio(n-)*, from *suspicere* 'mistrust'. The change in the second syllable was due to association with Old French *suspicion* (from Latin *suspicio(n-)* 'suspicion').

suspicious ▶ adjective having or showing a cautious distrust of someone or something: *he was **suspicious of** her motives* | *she gave him a suspicious look.*
■ causing one to have the idea or impression that something or someone is of questionable, dishonest, or dangerous character or condition: *they are not treating the fire as suspicious.* ■ having the belief or impression that someone is involved in an illegal or dishonest activity: *police were called when staff became suspicious.*
– DERIVATIVES **suspiciously** adverb [as submodifier] *it's suspiciously cheap*, **suspiciousness** noun.
– ORIGIN Middle English: from Old French *suspicious*, from Latin *suspiciosus*, from *suspicio(n-)* (see **SUSPICION**).

suspire /sə'spʌɪə/ ▶ verb [no obj.] poetic/literary breathe.
– DERIVATIVES **suspiration** noun.
– ORIGIN late Middle English (in the sense 'yearn after'): from Latin *suspirare*, from *sub-* 'from below' + *spirare* 'breathe'.

Susquehanna /ˌsʌskwə'hanə/ a river of the north-eastern US. It has two headstreams, one rising in New York State and one in Pennsylvania, which meet in central Pennsylvania. The river then flows 240 km (150 miles) south to Chesapeake Bay.

suss Brit. informal ▶ verb (**sussed**, **sussing**) [with obj.] realize; grasp: *he's sussed it* | [with clause] *she **sussed out** right away that there was something fishy going on.*
■ discover the true character or nature of: *I reckon I've **got** him **sussed**.*
▶ noun **1** (also **sus**) a police suspect: *he's the number one suss.*
2 [mass noun] [with adj. or noun modifier] knowledge or awareness of a specified kind: *his lack of business suss.*
▶ adjective (also **sus**) shrewd and wary: *he is too suss a character to fall into that trap.*
– ORIGIN 1930s: abbreviation of **SUSPECT**, **SUSPICION**.

sussed ▶ adjective Brit. informal (of a person) clever and well informed: *the band were sussed and streetwise.*

Sussex[1] a former county of southern England. It was divided in 1974 into the counties of East Sussex and West Sussex.

Sussex[2] ▶ noun a speckled or red bird of a domestic English breed of chicken.

sustain ▶ verb [with obj.] **1** strengthen or support physically or mentally: *this thought had sustained him throughout the years* | [as adj. **sustaining**] *a sustaining breakfast of bacon and eggs.*
■ cause to continue or be prolonged for an extended period or without interruption: *he cannot sustain a normal conversation* | [as adj. **sustained**] *several years of sustained economic growth.* ■ (of a performer) represent (a part or character) convincingly: *he sustained the role of Creon with burly resilience.* ■ bear (the weight of an object) without breaking or falling: *he sagged against her so that she could barely sustain his weight* | figurative *his health will no longer enable him to sustain the heavy burdens of office.*
2 undergo or suffer (something unpleasant, especially an injury): *he died after sustaining severe head injuries.*
3 uphold, affirm, or confirm the justice or validity of: *the allegations of discrimination were sustained.*
▶ noun [mass noun] Music an effect or facility on a keyboard or electronic instrument whereby a note can be sustained after the key is released.
– DERIVATIVES **sustainedly** adverb, **sustainer** noun, **sustainment** noun.
– ORIGIN Middle English: from Old French *soustenir*, from Latin *sustinere*, from *sub-* 'from below' + *tenere* 'hold'.

sustainable ▶ adjective able to be maintained at a certain rate or level: *sustainable fusion reactions.*
■ Ecology (especially of development, exploitation, or agriculture) conserving an ecological balance by avoiding depletion of natural resources. ■ able to be upheld or defended: *sustainable definitions of good educational practice.*
– DERIVATIVES **sustainability** noun (Ecology), **sustainably** adverb (Ecology).

sustained-release ▶ adjective [attrib.] Medicine denoting a drug preparation in a capsule containing numerous tiny pellets with different coatings that release their contents steadily over a long period.

sustained yield ▶ noun [mass noun] a level of exploitation or crop production which is maintained by restricting the quantity harvested to avoid long-term depletion.

sustenance ▶ noun [mass noun] food and drink regarded as a source of strength; nourishment: *poor rural economies turned to potatoes for sustenance.*
■ the maintaining of someone or something in life or existence: *he kept two or three cows for the sustenance of his family* | *the sustenance of parliamentary democracy.*
– ORIGIN Middle English: from Old French *soustenance*, from the verb *soustenir* (see **SUSTAIN**).

sustentation /ˌsʌst(ə)n'teɪʃ(ə)n/ ▶ noun [mass noun] formal the support or maintenance of someone or something, especially through the provision of money: *provision is made for the sustentation of preachers.*
– ORIGIN late Middle English: from Old French, or from Latin *sustentatio(n-)*, from *sustentare* 'uphold, sustain', frequentative of *sustinere* (see **SUSTAIN**).

Susu /'suːsuː/ ▶ noun (pl. same) **1** a member of a West African people of NW Sierra Leone and the southern coast of Guinea.
2 the language of this people, which belongs to the Mande group and has about 700,000 speakers.
▶ adjective of or relating to this people or their language.
– ORIGIN the name in Susu.

susurration /ˌs(j)uːsʌ'reɪʃ(ə)n/ (also **susurrus** /s(j)uː'sʌrəs/) ▶ noun [mass noun] poetic/literary whispering or rustling.
– ORIGIN late Middle English: from late Latin *susurratio(n-)*, from Latin *susurrare* 'to murmur, hum'.

Sutherland[1] /'sʌðələnd/ a former county of Scotland, since 1975 a district of Highland region.

Sutherland[2] /'sʌðələnd/, Graham (Vivian) (1903–80), English painter. During the Second World War he was an official war artist. His post-war work included the tapestry *Christ in Majesty* (1962) in Coventry cathedral.

Sutherland[3] /'sʌðələnd/, Dame Joan (b.1926), Australian operatic soprano, noted for her dramatic coloratura roles, particularly the title role in Donizetti's *Lucia di Lammermoor.*

Sutlej /'sʌtlɪdʒ/ a river of northern India and Pakistan which rises in the Himalayas in SW Tibet, and flows for 1,450 km (900 miles) westwards through India into Punjab province in Pakistan, where it joins the Chenab River to form the Panjnad and eventually join the Indus. It is one of the five rivers that gave Punjab its name.

sutler /'sʌtlə/ ▶ noun historical a person who followed an army and sold provisions to the soldiers.
– ORIGIN late 16th cent.: from obsolete Dutch *soeteler*, from *soetelen* 'perform mean duties'.

sutra /'suːtrə/ ▶ noun a rule or aphorism in Sanskrit literature, or a set of these on grammar or Hindu law or philosophy. See also **KAMA SUTRA**.
■ a Buddhist or Jainist scripture.
– ORIGIN from Sanskrit *sūtra* 'thread, rule', from *siv* 'sew'.

suttee /sʌ'tiː, 'sʌti/ (also **sati**) ▶ noun (pl. **suttees** or **satis**) [mass noun] the former Hindu practice of a widow immolating herself on her husband's funeral pyre.
■ [count noun] a widow who committed such an act.
– ORIGIN Hindi, from Sanskrit *satī* 'faithful wife', from *sat* 'good'.

Sutton Coldfield a town in the west Midlands of England, just north of Birmingham; pop. 86,494 (1981).

Sutton Hoo the site in Suffolk of a Saxon ship burial of the 7th century AD, containing magnificent grave goods including jewellery and gold coins.

suture /'suːtʃə/ ▶ noun **1** a stitch or row of stitches holding together the edges of a wound or surgical incision.
■ a thread or wire used for this. ■ [mass noun] the action of stitching together the edges of a wound or incision.
2 a seam-like immovable junction between two bones, such as those of the skull.
■ Zoology a similar junction, such as between the sclerites of an insect's body. ■ Geology a line of junction formed by two crustal plates which have collided.
▶ verb [with obj.] stitch up (a wound or incision) with a suture: *the small incision was sutured.*
– DERIVATIVES **sutural** adjective.
– ORIGIN late Middle English: from French, or from Latin *sutura*, from *suere* 'sew'.

SUV ▶ abbreviation for sport utility vehicle.

Suva /'suːvə/ the capital of Fiji, situated on the SE coast of the island of Viti Levu; pop. 71,600 (1986).

Suwannee /sʊ'wɒni/ (also **Swanee**) a river of the south-eastern US. Rising in SE Georgia, it flows for some 400 km (250 miles) south-west through northern Florida to the Gulf of Mexico.

suxamethonium /ˌsʌksəmɪ'θəʊnɪəm/ ▶ noun another term for **SUCCINYLCHOLINE**.
– ORIGIN 1950s: from *sux-* (representing the pronunciation of *succ-* in **SUCCINIC ACID**) + *methonium*, a complex cation.

suzerain /'suːzəreɪn/ ▶ noun a sovereign or state having some control over another state that is internally autonomous.
■ historical a feudal overlord.
– DERIVATIVES **suzerainty** noun.
– ORIGIN early 19th cent.: from French, apparently from *sus* 'above' (from Latin *su(r)sum* 'upward'), suggested by *souverain* 'sovereign'.

Suzhou /suː'dʒəʊ/ (also **Suchou** or **Soochow**) a city in eastern China, in the province of Jiangsu, situated west of Shanghai on the Grand Canal; pop. 840,000 (1990). Founded in the 6th century BC, it was the capital of the ancient Wu kingdom.

Suzman /'sʊzmən/, Helen (b.1917), South African politician, of Lithuanian-Jewish descent. From 1961 to 1974 she was the sole MP opposed to apartheid.

Suzuki /sʊ'zuːki/ ▶ adjective relating to or denoting a method of teaching the violin, typically to very young children in large groups, developed by Shin'ichi Suzuki (1898–1998), Japanese educationalist and violin teacher.

Sv ▶ abbreviation for sievert(s).

s.v. ▶ abbreviation used in textual references before a word or heading to indicate that a specified item can be found under it: *the dictionary lists 'rural policeman' (s.v. 'rural').*
– ORIGIN from Latin *sub voce* or *sub verbo*, literally 'under the word or voice'.

Svalbard /'svɑːlbɑː/ a group of islands in the Arctic Ocean about 640 km (400 miles) north of Norway;

pop. 3,700 (1995). They came under Norwegian sovereignty in 1925. The chief settlement (on Spitsbergen) is Longyearbyen.

Svedberg /ˈsvɛdbəːɡ/ (also **Svedberg unit**) (abbrev.: **S**) ▶ **noun** Biochemistry a unit of time equal to 10^{-13} seconds, used in expressing sedimentation coefficients.

svelte ▶ **adjective** (of a person) slender and elegant.
– ORIGIN early 19th cent.: from French, from Italian *svelto*.

Sven /svɛn/ variant spelling of **SWEYN I**.

Svengali /svɛnˈɡɑːli/ a musician in George du Maurier's novel *Trilby* (1894) who trains Trilby's voice and controls her stage singing hypnotically.
■ [as noun **a Svengali**] a person who exercises a controlling or mesmeric influence on another, especially for a sinister purpose.

Sverdlovsk /svɛːdˈlɒfsk/ former name (1924–91) for **EKATERINBURG**.

Sverige /ˈsvarjə/ Swedish name for **SWEDEN**.

Svetambara /swɛˈtɑːmbərə/ ▶ **noun** a member of one of the two principal sects of Jainism, which was formed as a result of doctrinal schism *c.*80 AD and survives today in parts of India. The sect's adherents practise asceticism and wear white clothing. See also **DIGAMBARA**.
– ORIGIN from Sanskrit *śvetāmbara*, literally 'white-clad'.

Sveti Konstantin /ˌsvɛtɪ ˌkɒnstanˈtiːn/ another name for **DROUZHBA**.

SVGA ▶ **abbreviation for** super video graphics array, a high-resolution standard for monitors and screens.

S-VHS ▶ **abbreviation for** super video home system, an improved version of VHS using the same tape cassettes as the standard version.

Svizzera /ˈzvittsera/ Italian name for **SWITZERLAND**.

SW ▶ **abbreviation for** ■ south-west. ■ south-western.

SWA ▶ **abbreviation for** Namibia (international vehicle registration).
– ORIGIN from *South West Africa*.

swab ▶ **noun 1** an absorbent pad or piece of material used in surgery and medicine for cleaning wounds, applying medication, or taking specimens.
■ a specimen of a secretion taken with a swab for examination: *he had taken throat swabs.*
2 a mop or other absorbent device for cleaning or mopping up a floor or other surface.
3 archaic a term of abuse or contempt for a person.
■ US another term for **SWABBIE**.
▶ **verb** (**swabbed**, **swabbing**) [with obj.] clean (a wound or surface) with a swab: ***swabbing down** the decks | swab a patch of skin with alcohol.*
■ [with adverbial] absorb or clear (moisture) with a swab: *the blood was swabbed away.*
– ORIGIN mid 17th cent. (in the sense 'mop for cleaning the decks'): back-formation from *swabber* 'sailor detailed to swab decks', from early modern Dutch *zwabber*, from a Germanic base meaning 'splash' or 'sway'.

swabbie ▶ **noun** (pl. **-ies**) US Nautical slang a member of the navy, typically one who is of low rank.

Swabia /ˈsweɪbɪə/ a former duchy of medieval Germany. The region is now divided between SW Germany, Switzerland, and France. German name **SCHWABEN**.
– DERIVATIVES **Swabian** adjective & noun.

swacked ▶ **adjective** N. Amer. informal drunk.
– ORIGIN 1930s: past participle of Scots *swack* 'fling, strike heavily'.

swaddle ▶ **verb** [with obj.] wrap (someone, especially a baby) in garments or cloth: *she swaddled the baby tightly | figurative they have grown up swaddled in consumer technology.*
– ORIGIN Middle English: frequentative of **SWATHE**[2].

swaddling clothes ▶ **plural noun** narrow bands of cloth formerly wrapped round a newborn child to restrain its movements and quieten it.

swadeshi /swaˈdɛʃi/ ▶ **adjective** Indian (of manufactured goods) made in India from Indian-produced materials.
– ORIGIN via Hindi from Sanskrit *svadeśīya* 'of one's own country', from *sva* 'own' + *deśa* 'country'.

swag ▶ **noun 1** an ornamental festoon of flowers, fruit, and greenery: *ribbon-tied swags of flowers.*
■ a carved or painted representation of such a festoon: *fine plaster swags.* ■ a curtain or piece of fabric fastened so as to hang in a drooping curve.
2 [mass noun] informal money or goods taken by a thief or burglar: *garden machinery is the most popular swag.*
3 Austral./NZ a traveller's or miner's bundle of personal belongings.
▶ **verb** (**swagged**, **swagging**) [with obj.] **1** arrange in or decorate with a swag or swags of fabric: *swag the fabric gracefully over the curtain tie-backs* | [as adj. **swagged**] *the swagged contours of nomads' tents.*
2 Austral./NZ travel with one's personal belongings in a bundle: ***swagging it** in Queensland | **swagging my way** up to the Northern Territory.*
3 [no obj.] chiefly poetic/literary hang heavily: *the crinkly old hide swags here and there.*
■ sway from side to side: *the stout chief sat swagging from one side to the other of the carriage.*
– ORIGIN Middle English (in the sense 'bulging bag'): probably of Scandinavian origin. The original sense of the verb (early 16th cent.) was 'cause to sway or sag'.

swage /sweɪdʒ/ ▶ **noun 1** a shaped tool or die for giving a desired form to metal by hammering or pressure.
2 a groove, ridge, or other moulding on an object.
▶ **verb** [with obj.] shape (metal) using a swage, especially in order to reduce its cross section.
■ [with adverbial] join (metal pieces) together by this process.
– ORIGIN late Middle English (in sense 2): from Old French *souage* 'decorative groove', of unknown origin.

swage block ▶ **noun** a grooved or perforated block for shaping metal.

swagger ▶ **verb** [no obj., with adverbial of direction] walk or behave in a very confident and typically arrogant or aggressive way: *he swaggered along the corridor* | [as adj. **swaggering**] *a swaggering gait.*
▶ **noun** [in sing.] a very confident and typically arrogant or aggressive gait or manner: *they strolled around the camp with an exaggerated swagger.*
▶ **adjective 1** [attrib.] denoting a coat or jacket cut with a loose flare from the shoulders.
2 Brit. informal, dated smart or fashionable: *I'll take you somewhere swagger.*
– DERIVATIVES **swaggerer** noun, **swaggeringly** adverb.
– ORIGIN early 16th cent.: apparently a frequentative of the verb **SWAG**.

swagger stick ▶ **noun** a short cane carried by a military officer.

swagman ▶ **noun** (pl. **-men**) Austral./NZ a person carrying a swag.

Swahili /swəˈhiːli, swɑː-/ ▶ **noun** (pl. same) **1** [mass noun] a Bantu language widely used as a lingua franca in East Africa and having official status in several countries. There are probably fewer than 2 million native speakers, but it is in everyday use by over 20 million. Also called **KISWAHILI**.
2 a member of a people of Zanzibar and nearby coastal regions, descendants of the original speakers of Swahili.
▶ **adjective** of or relating to this language or to the people who are its native speakers.
– ORIGIN from Arabic *sawāḥil*, plural of *sāḥil* 'coast'.

swain ▶ **noun** archaic a country youth.
■ poetic/literary a young lover or suitor.
– ORIGIN late Old English (denoting a young man attendant on a knight), from Old Norse *sveinn* 'lad'.

swale ▶ **noun** chiefly US & dialect a low or hollow place, especially a marshy depression between ridges.
– ORIGIN early 16th cent.: of unknown origin; probably taken to America from the eastern counties, where it is still in use.

Swaledale ▶ **noun** a sheep of a small hardy breed with long coarse wool.
– ORIGIN early 20th cent.: from the name of a region in North Yorkshire.

swallow[1] ▶ **verb** [with obj.] cause or allow (something, especially food or drink) to pass down the throat: *she swallowed a mouthful slowly.*
■ [no obj.] perform the muscular movement of the oesophagus required to do this, especially through fear or nervousness: *she swallowed hard, sniffing back her tears.* ■ put up with or meekly accept (something insulting or unwelcome): *he seemed ready to swallow any insult.* ■ believe unquestioningly (a lie or unlikely assertion): *she had swallowed his story hook, line, and sinker.* ■ resist expressing (a feeling) or uttering (words): *he swallowed his pride.* ■ take in and cause to disappear; engulf: *the dark mist **swallowed** her **up**.* ■ completely use up (money or resources): *debts **swallowed up** most of the money he had got for the house.*
▶ **noun** an act of swallowing something, especially food or drink: *he downed his drink in one swallow.*
■ an amount of something swallowed in one action: *he said he'd like just **a swallow of** pie.*
– DERIVATIVES **swallowable** adjective.
– ORIGIN Old English *swelgan*, of Germanic origin; related to Dutch *zwelgen* and German *schwelgen*.

swallow[2] ▶ **noun** a migratory swift-flying songbird with a forked tail and long pointed wings, feeding on insects in flight. Compare with **WOODSWALLOW**.
● Family Hirundinidae: several genera, in particular *Hirundo*, and numerous species, e.g. the widespread *H. rustica* (North American name: **barn swallow**).
– PHRASES **one swallow does not make a summer** proverb a single fortunate event doesn't mean that what follows will also be good.
– ORIGIN Old English *swealwe*, of Germanic origin; related to Dutch *zwaluw* and German *Schwalbe*.

swallow dive ▶ **noun** Brit. a dive performed with one's arms outspread until close to the water.

swallower ▶ **noun 1** [usu. in combination] a person or thing that swallows something: *pill-swallowers.*
2 a slender deep-sea fish with very large jaws and a distensible stomach, enabling it to swallow very large prey.
● Family Chiasmodontidae: *Chiasmodon* and other genera.

swallow hole ▶ **noun** another term for **SINKHOLE**.

swallowtail ▶ **noun 1** (also **swallowtail butterfly**) a large brightly coloured butterfly with tail-like projections on the hindwings.
● Family Papilionidae: many species, including the European *Papilio machaon*, of fenland country.
2 [usu. as modifier] a deeply forked tail; a thing resembling such a tail in shape: *swallowtail suits.*
– DERIVATIVES **swallow-tailed** adjective.

swallow-tailed moth ▶ **noun** a pale yellowish European moth with short tail-like projections on the hindwings.
● *Ourapteryx sambucaria*, family Geometridae.

swallow-wort ▶ **noun 1** a plant of the milkweed family, the follicles of which suggest a swallow with outstretched wings, often becoming a weed.
● Several species in the family Asclepiadaceae, in particular the European **black swallow-wort** (*Cynanchum* (or *Vincetoxicum*) *nigrum*), and the American *Asclepias curassavica*.
2 Brit. the greater celandine, formerly believed to be used by swallows to restore their sight.

swam past of **SWIM**.

swami /ˈswɑːmi/ ▶ **noun** (pl. **swamis**) a Hindu male religious teacher: [as title] *Swami Satchidananda.*
– ORIGIN from Hindi *swāmī* 'master, prince', from Sanskrit *svāmin*.

Swammerdam /ˈswamədam/, Jan (1637–80), Dutch naturalist and microscopist. He classified insects into four groups and was the first to observe red blood cells.

swamp ▶ **noun** an area of low-lying, uncultivated ground where water collects; a bog or marsh.
■ used to emphasize the degree to which a piece of ground is waterlogged: *the ceaseless deluge had turned the lawn into a swamp.*
▶ **verb** [with obj.] overwhelm or flood with water: *a huge wave swamped the canoes.*
■ figurative overwhelm with an excessive amount of something; inundate: *feelings of guilt suddenly swamped her | the country **was swamped with** goods from abroad.* ■ [no obj.] (of a boat) become overwhelmed with water and sink.
– DERIVATIVES **swampy** adjective.
– ORIGIN early 17th cent.: probably ultimately from a Germanic base meaning 'sponge' or 'fungus'.

swamp cabbage ▶ **noun** the skunk cabbage of western North America (*Lysichiton americanum*), the leaves of which are sometimes used in cooking.

swamp cypress ▶ **noun** a deciduous North American conifer with exposed root buttresses, typically growing in swamps and on water margins. Also called **BALD CYPRESS**.
● *Taxodium distichum*, family Taxodiaceae.

swamp deer ▶ **noun** a deer that inhabits swamps and grassy plains in India and Nepal. Also called **BARASINGHA**.
● *Cervus duvaucelli*, family Cervidae.

swamper ▶ **noun** informal, dated **1** N. Amer. an assistant to the captain of a riverboat or to a lorry driver.

S

2 N. Amer. a worker who trims felled trees and clears a road for lumberers in a forest.
3 US a native or inhabitant of a swampy region.

swamp fever ▶**noun** [mass noun] **1** a contagious viral disease of horses that causes anaemia and emaciation and is usually fatal.
2 dated malaria.

swamphen /ˈswɒmphɛn/ (also **purple swamphen**) ▶**noun** a marshbird of the rail family, with a purplish-blue head and breast and a large red bill, found throughout the Old World.
• *Porphyrio porphyrio*, family Rallidae.

swampland ▶**noun** [mass noun] (also **swamplands**) land consisting of swamps.

swamp mahogany ▶**noun** an Australian eucalyptus with long leaves and dark fibrous bark, grown elsewhere as an ornamental and as a shelter-belt tree.
• *Eucalyptus robusta*, family Myrtaceae.

swamp rat ▶**noun** an African rodent that frequents dense vegetation on swampy ground.
• Three genera in the family Muridae, in particular the vole-like *Otomys* (also called **VLEI RAT**) and the slender *Malacomys*: several species.

swamp snake ▶**noun** an olive-coloured venomous snake living in marshy and wet country on the east coast of Australia.
• *Hemiaspis signata*, family Elapidae.

swamp wallaby ▶**noun** a large wallaby living in forests and damp thickets in eastern Australia.
• *Wallabia bicolor*, family Macropodidae.

Swan, Sir Joseph Wilson (1828–1914), English physicist and chemist. He devised an electric light bulb in 1860 and in 1883 he formed a partnership with Thomas Edison to manufacture it.

swan ▶**noun** a large waterbird with a long flexible neck, short legs, webbed feet, a broad bill, and typically all-white plumage.
• Genus *Cygnus* (and *Coscoroba*): several species.
▶**verb** (**swanned**, **swanning**) [no obj., with adverbial of direction] Brit. informal move about or go somewhere in a casual, relaxed way, typically perceived as irresponsible or ostentatious by others: *swanning around Europe nowadays are we?*
– DERIVATIVES **swanlike** adjective.
– ORIGIN Old English, of Germanic origin; related to Dutch *zwaan* and German *Schwan*. The current sense of the verb originated as military slang, referring to the free movement of armoured vehicles.

swan dive ▶**noun** N. Amer. a swallow dive.
▶**verb** [no obj.] (**swan-dive**) perform a swan drive.

Swanee /ˈswɒni/ variant spelling of **SUWANNEE**.

Swanee whistle ▶**noun** a musical instrument (often a toy) in the form of a pipe with a plunger instead of finger holes, so that the player slides from note to note.

swank informal ▶**verb** [no obj.] display one's wealth, knowledge, or achievements in a way that is intended to impress others: ***swanking about**, playing the dashing young master spy.*
▶**noun** [mass noun] behaviour, talk, or display intended to impress others: *a little money will buy you a good deal of swank.*
▶**adjective** North American term for **SWANKY**.
– ORIGIN early 19th cent.: of unknown origin.

swankpot ▶**noun** Brit. informal, dated a person attempting to impress others.

swanky ▶**adjective** (**swankier**, **swankiest**) informal stylishly luxurious and expensive: *directors with swanky company cars.*
▪ using one's wealth, knowledge, or achievements to try to impress others.
– DERIVATIVES **swankily** adverb, **swankiness** noun.

swan mussel ▶**noun** a large European freshwater mussel of still or slow-moving water, the larvae of which parasitize fish.
• *Anodonta cygnea*, family Unionidae.

swan neck ▶**noun** a curved structure shaped like a swan's neck: [as modifier] *a small swan-neck dispenser.*
– DERIVATIVES **swan-necked** adjective.

swannery ▶**noun** (pl. **-ies**) Brit. a place set aside for swans to breed.

Swan River a river of Western Australia. Rising as the Avon to the south-east of Perth, it flows north and west through Perth to the Indian ocean at Fremantle. It was the site of the first free European settlement in Western Australia.

swansdown ▶**noun** [mass noun] **1** the fine down of a swan, used for trimmings and powder puffs.
2 a thick cotton fabric with a soft nap on one side.
▪ a soft, thick fabric made from wool mixed with a little silk or cotton.

Swansea /ˈswɒnzi/ a city in South Wales, on the Bristol Channel; pop. 182,100 (1991). Welsh name **ABERTAWE**.

Swanson, Gloria (1899–1983), American actress; born *Gloria May Josephine Svensson*. She was a major star of silent films such as *Sadie Thompson* (1928) but is now chiefly known for her performance as the fading movie star in *Sunset Boulevard* (1950).

swansong ▶**noun** a person's final public performance or professional activity before retirement: *he has decided to make this tour his swansong.*
– ORIGIN early 19th cent.: suggested by German *Schwanengesang*, a song like that fabled to be sung by a dying swan.

swan-upping ▶**noun** Brit. the annual practice of catching the swans on the River Thames and marking them to indicate their ownership.

swap (also **swop**) ▶**verb** (**swapped**, **swapping**) [with obj.] take part in an exchange of: *we swapped phone numbers | I'd **swap** places **with** you any day* | [no obj.] *I was wondering if you'd like to **swap with** me.*
▪ give (one thing) and receive something else in exchange: ***swap** one of your sandwiches **for** a cheese and pickle?* ▪ substitute (one thing) for another: *I swapped my busy life in London **for** a peaceful village retreat.*
▶**noun** an act of exchanging one thing for another: *let's **do a swap**.*
▪ a thing that has been or may be given in exchange for something else: *I've got one already, but I'll keep this as a swap.* ▪ Finance an exchange of liabilities between two borrowers, either so that each acquires access to funds in a currency they need or so that a fixed interest rate is exchanged for a floating rate.
– DERIVATIVES **swappable** adjective, **swapper** noun.
– ORIGIN Middle English (originally in the sense 'throw forcibly'): probably imitative of a resounding blow. Current senses have arisen from an early use meaning 'strike hands as a token of agreement'.

swapfile ▶**noun** Computing a file on a hard disk used to provide space for programs which have been transferred from the processor's memory.

swap meet ▶**noun** chiefly N. Amer. a gathering at which enthusiasts or collectors trade or exchange items of common interest: *a computer swap meet.*
▪ a flea market.

SWAPO /ˈswɑːpəʊ/ (also **Swapo**) ▶**abbreviation for** South West Africa People's Organization.

swap shop ▶**noun** informal an agency which provides a communication channel for people with articles to exchange or trade.
▪ an event to which people are invited to bring articles for exchange or trade.

swaption ▶**noun** Finance an option giving the right but not the obligation to engage in a swap.
– ORIGIN 1980s: blend of **SWAP** and **OPTION**.

Swaraj /swəˈrɑːdʒ/ ▶**noun** [mass noun] historical self-government or independence for India.
– DERIVATIVES **Swarajist** noun.
– ORIGIN from Sanskrit *svarājya*, from *sva* 'own' + *rājya* 'rule'; compare with **RAJ**.

sward /swɔːd/ ▶**noun** an expanse of short grass.
▪ Farming the upper layer of soil, especially when covered with grass.
– DERIVATIVES **swarded** adjective.
– ORIGIN Old English *sweard* 'skin'. The sense 'upper layer of soil' developed in late Middle English (at first in phrases such as *sward of the earth*) .

sware archaic past of **SWEAR**.

swarf /swɑːf/ ▶**noun** [mass noun] fine chips or filings of stone, metal, or other material produced by a machining operation.
– ORIGIN mid 16th cent.: either from Old English *geswearf* 'filings' or from Old Norse *svarf* 'file dust'.

swarm ▶**noun** a large or dense group of insects, especially flying ones.
▪ a large number of honeybees that leave a hive en masse with a newly fertilized queen in order to establish a new colony. ▪ (**a swarm/swarms of**) a large number of people or things: *a swarm of journalists.* ▪ a series of similar-sized earthquakes occurring together, typically near a volcano. ▪ Astronomy a large number of minor celestial objects occurring together in space, especially a dense shower of meteors.
▶**verb 1** [no obj.] (of insects) move in or form a swarm: [as adj. **swarming**] *swarming locusts.*
▪ (of honeybees, ants, or termites) issue from the nest in large numbers in order to mate and found new colonies: *the bees had swarmed and left the hive.*
2 [no obj., with adverbial] move somewhere in large numbers: *protesters were swarming into the building.*
▪ (**swarm with**) (of a place) be crowded or overrun with (moving people or things): *the place was swarming with police.*
– ORIGIN Old English *swearm* (noun), of Germanic origin; related to German *Schwarm*, probably also to the base of Sanskrit *svarati* 'it sounds'.
▶**swarm up** climb (something) rapidly by gripping it with one's hands and feet, alternately hauling and pushing oneself upwards: *I swarmed up the mast.* [ORIGIN: mid 16th cent.: of unknown origin.]

swarmer (also **swarmer cell**) ▶**noun** Biology another term for **ZOOSPORE**.

swart /swɔːt/ ▶**adjective** archaic or poetic/literary swarthy.
– ORIGIN Old English *sweart*, of Germanic origin; related to Dutch *zwart* and German *schwarz*.

swart gevaar /ˌswart xəˈfɑː/ ▶**noun** (in South Africa) a threat perceived as being posed by black people to whites.
– ORIGIN Afrikaans, literally 'black danger'.

swarthy ▶**adjective** (**swarthier**, **swarthiest**) dark-skinned: *swarthy Spaniards with gleaming teeth.*
– DERIVATIVES **swarthily** adverb, **swarthiness** noun.
– ORIGIN late 16th cent.: alteration of obsolete *swarty* (see **SWART**).

swash[1] ▶**verb** [no obj.] **1** (of water or an object in water) move with a splashing sound: *the water swashed and rippled around the car wheels.*
2 archaic (of a person) flamboyantly swagger about or wield a sword: *he swashed about self-confidently.*
▶**noun** the rush of seawater up the beach after the breaking of a wave.
▪ archaic the motion or sound of water dashing or washing against something.
– ORIGIN mid 16th cent. (in the sense 'make a noise like swords clashing or beating on shields'): imitative.

swash[2] ▶**adjective** Printing denoting an ornamental written or printed character, typically a capital letter.
– ORIGIN late 17th cent.: of unknown origin.

swashbuckle ▶**verb** [no obj.] [usu. as adj. **swashbuckling**] engage in daring and romantic adventures with ostentatious bravado or flamboyance: *a crew of swashbuckling buccaneers.*
– ORIGIN late 19th cent.: back-formation from **SWASHBUCKLER**.

swashbuckler ▶**noun** a swashbuckling person.
▪ a film or book portraying such a person.
– ORIGIN mid 16th cent.: from **SWASH**[1] + **BUCKLER**.

swash plate ▶**noun** an inclined disc revolving on an axle and giving reciprocating motion to a part in contact with it.

swastika /ˈswɒstɪkə/ ▶**noun** an ancient symbol in the form of an equal-armed cross with each arm continued at a right angle, used (in clockwise form) as the emblem of the German Nazi party.
– ORIGIN late 19th cent.: from Sanskrit *svastika*, from *svasti* 'well-being', from *su* 'good' + *asti* 'being'.

swat ▶**verb** (**swatted**, **swatting**) [with obj.] hit or crush (something, especially an insect) with a sharp blow from a flat object: *I swatted a mosquito that had landed on my wrist* | [no obj.] ***swatting at** a fly.*
▪ hit (someone) with a sharp blow: *she swatted him over the head with a rolled-up magazine.*
▶**noun** such a sharp blow: *the dog gave the hedgehog a sideways swat.*
– ORIGIN early 17th cent. (in the sense 'sit down'): northern English dialect and US variant of **SQUAT**.

swatch ▶**noun** a sample, especially of fabric.
▪ a collection of such samples, especially in the form of a book. ▪ a patch or area of a material or surface: *the sunset had filled the sky with swatches of deep orange.*
– ORIGIN early 16th cent. (originally Scots and northern English, denoting the counterfoil of a tally, and later a tally fixed to a piece of cloth before dyeing): of unknown origin.

swathe[1] /swɔːθ, swɒθ/ (chiefly N. Amer. also **swath** /sweɪð/) ▶**noun** (pl. **swathes** or **swaths** /swɔːθs, swɔːðs, swɒθs/) **1** a row or line of grass, corn, or other crop as it falls or lies when mown or reaped.

■ a strip left clear by the passage of a mowing machine or scythe: *the combine had cut a deep swathe around the border of the fields.*
2 a broad strip or area of something: *vast swathes of countryside* | figurative *a significant swathe of popular opinion.*
– PHRASES **cut a swathe through** pass through (something) causing great damage, destruction, or change: *Aids has cut a swathe through battalions of ordinary people.* **cut a wide swath** US attract a great deal of attention by trying to impress others.
– ORIGIN Old English *swæth*, *swathu* 'track, trace', of West Germanic origin; related to Dutch *zwad(e)* and German *Schwade*. In Middle English the term denoted a measure of the width of grassland, probably reckoned by a sweep of the mower's scythe.

swathe² /sweɪð/ ▶ **verb** [with obj.] (usu. **be swathed in**) wrap in several layers of fabric: *his hands were swathed in bandages.*
▶ **noun** a piece or strip of material in which something is wrapped.
– ORIGIN late Old English *swath-* (noun), *swathian* (verb); compare with **SWADDLE**.

swather /ˈswɔːθə, ˈswɒθə/ ▶ **noun** a device on a mowing machine for raising uncut fallen grain and marking the line between cut and uncut grain.

Swatow /swɒˈtaʊ/ former name for **SHANTOU**.

sway ▶ **verb** move or cause to move slowly or rhythmically backwards and forwards or from side to side: [no obj.] *he swayed slightly on his feet* | [as adj. **swaying**] *swaying palm trees* | [with obj.] *wind rattled and swayed the trees.*
■ [with obj.] control or influence (a person or course of action): *he's easily swayed by other people.* ■ poetic/literary rule; govern: *now let the Lord forever reign and sway us as he will.*
▶ **noun** [mass noun] **1** a rhythmical movement from side to side: *the easy sway of her hips.*
2 rule; control: *the part of the continent* **under** *Russia's sway.*
– PHRASES **hold sway** have great power or influence over a particular person, place, or domain.
– ORIGIN Middle English: corresponding in sense to Low German *swājen* 'be blown to and fro' and Dutch *zwaaien* 'swing, walk totteringly'.

swayback ▶ **noun** an abnormally hollowed back, especially in a horse; lordosis.
– DERIVATIVES **sway-backed** adjective.

sway bar ▶ **noun** N. Amer. another term for **ANTI-ROLL BAR**.

Swazi /ˈswɑːzi/ ▶ **noun** (pl. same or **Swazis**) **1** a member of a people inhabiting Swaziland and parts of eastern Transvaal.
■ a native or national of Swaziland.
2 [mass noun] the Nguni language of this people, an official language in Swaziland and South Africa with about 1.6 million speakers. Also called **SISWATI**.
▶ **adjective** of or relating to Swaziland, the Swazis, or their language.
– ORIGIN from the name of *Mswati*, a 19th-century king of the Swazis.

Swaziland a small landlocked kingdom in southern Africa, bounded by South Africa and Mozambique; pop. 825,000 (est. 1991); official languages, Swazi and English; capital, Mbabane.

Swaziland was a South African protectorate from 1894 and came under British rule in 1902 after the Second Boer War. In 1968 it became a fully independent Commonwealth state.

SWB ▶ **abbreviation for** short wheelbase.

swear ▶ **verb** (past **swore**; past participle **sworn**) **1** [reporting verb] make a solemn statement or promise undertaking to do something or affirming that something is the case: [with clause] *Maria made me swear I would never tell anyone* | *I* **swear by** *all I hold dear that I had nothing to do with it* | [with infinitive] *he swore to obey the rules* | [with direct speech] *'Never again,' she swore, 'will I be short of money'* | [with obj.] *they were reluctant to swear allegiance.*
■ [with obj.] take (an oath): *he forced them to swear an oath of loyalty to him.* ■ [with obj.] take a solemn oath as to the truth of (a statement): *I asked him if he would swear a statement to this effect.* ■ [with obj.] (**swear someone in**) admit someone to a particular office or position by directing them to take a formal oath: *he was sworn in as president on 10 July.* ■ [with obj.] make (someone) promise to observe a certain course of action: *I've been* **sworn to** *secrecy.* ■ [no obj., usu. with negative] (**swear to**) express one's assurance that something is the case: *I couldn't swear to it, but I'm pretty sure it's his writing.* ■ [no obj.] (**swear off**) informal promise to abstain from: *I'd sworn off alcohol.* ■ [no obj.] (**swear by**) informal have or express great confidence in the use, value, or effectiveness of: *Iris swears by her yoga.*
2 [no obj.] use offensive language, especially as an expression of anger: *Peter swore under his breath.*
– PHRASES **swear blind** (or N. Amer. **swear up and down**) Brit. informal affirm something emphatically: *his informant swore blind that the weapons were still there.*
– DERIVATIVES **swearer** noun.
– ORIGIN Old English *swerian* of Germanic origin; related to Dutch *zweren*, German *schwören*, also to **ANSWER**.
▶ **swear something out** US Law obtain the issue of (a warrant for arrest) by making a charge on oath.

swear word ▶ **noun** an offensive word, used especially as an expression of anger.

sweat ▶ **noun 1** [mass noun] moisture exuded through the pores of the skin, typically in profuse quantities as a reaction to heat, physical exertion, fever, or fear.
■ [count noun] an instance of exuding moisture in this way over a period of time: *even thinking about him made me* **break out in a sweat** | *we'd all* **worked up a sweat** *in spite of the cold.* ■ [count noun] informal a state of flustered anxiety or distress: *I don't believe he'd* **get into** *such* **a sweat** *about a girl.* ■ informal hard work; effort: *computer graphics take a lot of the sweat out of animation.* ■ [in sing.] informal a laborious task or undertaking: *helping to run the meeting was a bit of a sweat.*
2 (**sweats**) chiefly N. Amer. informal term for **SWEATSUIT** or **SWEATPANTS**.
■ [as modifier] denoting loose casual garments made of thick, fleecy cotton: *sweat tops and bottoms.*
▶ **verb** (past and past participle **sweated** or US **sweat**) **1** [no obj.] exude sweat: *he was sweating profusely.*
■ [with obj.] (**sweat something out/off**) get rid of (something) from the body by exuding sweat: *a well-hydrated body sweats out waste products more efficiently.* ■ [with obj.] cause (a person or animal) to exude sweat by exercise or exertion: *cold as it was, the climb had sweated him.* ■ (of food or an object) ooze or exude beads of moisture on to its surface: *cheese stored at room temperature will quickly begin to sweat.* ■ (of a person) exert a great deal of strenuous effort: *I've* **sweated over** *this for six months.* ■ (of a person) be or remain in a state of extreme anxiety, typically for a prolonged period: *I let her sweat for a while, then I asked her out again.* ■ [with obj.] US informal worry about (something): *he's not going to have a lot of time to sweat the details.*
2 [with obj.] heat (chopped vegetables) slowly in a pan with a small amount of fat, so that they cook in their own juices: *sweat the celery and onions with olive oil and seasoning.*
■ [no obj.] (of chopped vegetables) be cooked in this way: *let the chopped onion sweat gently for five minutes.*
3 [with obj. and adverbial] subject (metal) to surface melting, especially to fasten or join by solder without a soldering iron: *the tyre is sweated on to the wooden parts.*
– PHRASES **break sweat** (or US **break a sweat**) informal exert oneself physically. **by the sweat of one's brow** by one's own hard work, typically manual labour. **don't sweat it** US informal used to urge someone not to worry. **no sweat** informal used to convey that one perceives no difficulty or problem with something: *'We haven't any decaf, I'm afraid.' 'No sweat.'* **sweat blood** informal make an extraordinarily strenuous effort to do something: *she's sweated blood to support her family.* ■ be extremely anxious: *we've been sweating blood over the question of what is right.* **sweat buckets** informal sweat profusely. **sweat bullets** N. Amer. informal be extremely anxious or nervous. **sweat it out** informal endure an unpleasant experience, typically one involving physical exertion in great heat: *about 1,500 runners are expected to sweat it out in this year's run.* ■ wait in a state of extreme anxiety for something to happen or be resolved: *he sweated it out until the lab report was back.* **sweat the small stuff** US informal worry about trivial things.
– ORIGIN Old English *swāt* (noun), *swǣtan* (verb), of Germanic origin; related to Dutch *zweet* and German *Schweiss*, from an Indo-European root shared by Latin *sudor*.

sweatband ▶ **noun** a band of absorbent material worn around the head or wrist to soak up sweat, especially by participants in sport.
■ a band of absorbent material lining a hat.

sweated ▶ **adjective** relating to or denoting manual workers employed at very low wages for long hours and under poor conditions: *the use of sweated labour by unscrupulous employers.*

sweat equity ▶ **noun** [mass noun] N. Amer. informal an interest in a property earned by a tenant in return for labour towards upkeep or restoration.

sweater ▶ **noun 1** a knitted garment worn on the upper body, typically with long sleeves, put on over the head.
2 dated an employer who works employees hard in poor conditions for low pay.

sweat gland ▶ **noun** a small gland that secretes sweat, situated in the dermis of the skin. Such glands are found over most of the body, and have a simple coiled tubular structure.

sweating sickness ▶ **noun** any of various fevers with intense sweating, epidemic in England in the 15th–16th centuries.

sweat lodge ▶ **noun** a hut, typically dome-shaped and made with natural materials, used by North American Indians for ritual steam baths as a means of purification.

sweatpants ▶ **plural noun** loose, warm trousers with an elasticated or drawstring waist, worn when exercising or as leisurewear.

sweatshirt ▶ **noun** a loose, warm sweater, typically made of cotton, worn when exercising or as leisurewear.

sweatshop ▶ **noun** a factory or workshop, especially in the clothing industry, where manual workers are employed at very low wages for long hours and under poor conditions.

sweat sock ▶ **noun** N. Amer. a thick, absorbent calf-length sock, often worn with trainers.

sweatsuit ▶ **noun** a suit consisting of a sweatshirt and sweatpants, worn when exercising or as leisurewear.

sweaty ▶ **adjective** (**sweatier**, **sweatiest**) exuding, soaked in, or inducing sweat: *my feet got so hot and sweaty.*
– DERIVATIVES **sweatily** adverb, **sweatiness** noun.

Swede ▶ **noun** a native or national of Sweden, or a person of Swedish descent.
– ORIGIN from Middle Low German and Middle Dutch *Swēde*, probably from Old Norse *Svíthjóth*, from *Svíar* 'Swedes' + *thjóth* 'people'.

swede ▶ **noun 1** Brit. a large, round yellow-fleshed root which is eaten as a vegetable. Also called **RUTABAGA** in North America.
2 the European plant of the cabbage family which produces this root.
• *Brassica napus*, family Cruciferae: 'napobrassica' group.
– ORIGIN early 19th cent.: from **SWEDE**, being first introduced into Scotland from Sweden in 1781–2.

Sweden a country occupying the eastern part of the Scandinavian peninsula; pop. 8,590,630 (1990); official language, Swedish; capital, Stockholm. Swedish name **SVERIGE**.

Originally united in the 12th century, Sweden formed part of the Union of Kalmar with Denmark and Norway from 1397 until its re-emergence as an independent kingdom in 1523. Between 1814 and 1905 it was united with Norway. A constitutional monarchy, Sweden has pursued a policy of non-alignment, and it remained neutral in the two world wars. Sweden joined the European Union in 1995.

Swedenborg /ˈswiːd(ə)nbɔːɡ/, Emanuel (1688–1772), Swedish scientist, philosopher, and mystic. The spiritual beliefs which he expounded after a series of mystical experiences blended Christianity with pantheism and theosophy.
– DERIVATIVES **Swedenborgian** /ˌswiːd(ə)nˈbɔːɡɪən/ adjective & noun.

Swede saw ▶ **noun** chiefly Canadian a type of saw with a bow-like tubular frame and many cutting teeth.
– ORIGIN *Swede* in the sense 'Swedish'.

swedge /swɛdʒ/ Scottish informal ▶ **noun** a fight or brawl.
▶ **verb** [no obj.] fight or brawl.
– ORIGIN perhaps related to dialect *swag* 'sway heavily'.

Swedish ▶ **adjective** of or relating to Sweden, its people, or their language.
▶ **noun** [mass noun] the Scandinavian language of Sweden, also spoken in parts of Finland. It has over 8 million speakers.

Swedish massage ▶ **noun** [mass noun] a popular

S

general purpose system of massage, devised in Sweden.

Sweeney ▶ **noun** (**the Sweeney**) Brit. informal the members of a police flying squad.
– ORIGIN 1930s: from rhyming slang *Sweeney* Todd, a barber who murdered his customers.

sweep ▶ **verb** (past and past participle **swept**) **1** [with obj.] clean (an area) by brushing away dirt or litter: *I've swept the floor | Greg* ***swept out*** *the kitchen.*
■[with obj. and adverbial of direction] move or remove (dirt or litter) in such a way: *she swept the tea leaves into a dustpan.* ■ [with obj. and adverbial of direction] move or push (someone or something) with great force: *I was swept along by the crowd.* ■ [with obj. and adverbial of direction] brush (hair) back from one's face or upwards: *long hair swept up into a high chignon.* ■ search (an area) for something: *the detective swept the room for hair and fingerprints.* ■ examine (a place or thing) for electronic listening devices: *the line is swept every fifteen minutes.* ■ cover (an entire area) with a gun: *they were trying to get the Lewis gun up behind some trees from where they would sweep the trench.* ■ Cricket hit (the ball) on the leg side by bringing the bat across the body from a half-kneeling position; hit a ball delivered by (a bowler) with such a stroke.
2 [no obj., with adverbial of direction] move swiftly and smoothly: *a large black car swept past the open windows* | figurative *a wave of sympathy swept over him.*
■[with obj. and adverbial of direction] cause to move swiftly and smoothly: *he swept his hand round the room.* ■ (of a person) move in a confident and stately manner: *she swept magnificently from the hall.* ■ (of a geographical or natural feature) extend continuously in a particular direction, especially in a curve: *green forests swept down the hillsides.* ■ [with obj.] look swiftly over: *her eyes swept the room.* ■ affect (an area or place) swiftly and widely: *violence swept the country* | [no obj.] *the rebellion had swept through all four of the country's provinces.* ■ [with obj.] N. Amer. win all the games in (a series); take each of the winning or main places in (a contest or event): *we knew we had to sweep these three home games.*
▶ **noun 1** an act of sweeping something with a brush: *I was giving the floor a quick sweep.*
■short for **CHIMNEY SWEEP**.
2 a long, swift, curving movement: *a grandiose sweep of his hand.*
■a comprehensive search or survey of a place or area: *the police finished their sweep through the woods.* ■ Electronics the movement of a beam across the screen of a cathode ray tube. ■ (often **sweeps**) N. Amer. a survey of the ratings of television stations, carried out at regular intervals to determine advertising rates. ■ Cricket an attacking stroke in which the bat is brought across the body from a half-kneeling position to hit the ball to leg.
3 a long, typically curved stretch of road, river, country, etc.: *we could see a wide sweep of country perhaps a hundred miles across.*
■a curved part of a drive in front of a building: *one fork of the drive continued on to the gravel sweep.* ■ figurative the range or scope of something: *the whole sweep of the history of the USSR.*
4 informal a sweepstake.
5 N. Amer. an instance of winning every event, award, or place in a contest: *a World Series sweep.*
6 a long heavy oar used to row a barge or other vessel: [as modifier] *a big, heavy sweep oar.*
7 a sail of a windmill.
8 a long pole mounted as a lever for raising buckets from a well.
– PHRASES **make a clean sweep** see **CLEAN**. **sweep the board** win every event or prize in a contest. **sweep someone off their feet** see **FOOT**. **sweep something under the carpet** see **CARPET**.
– ORIGIN Old English *swāpan* (verb), of Germanic origin; related to German *schweifen* 'sweep in a curve'.
▶**sweep something away** (or **aside**) remove, dispel, or abolish something in a swift and sudden way: *Nahum's smile swept away the air of apprehensive gloom.*

sweepback ▶ **noun** [mass noun] the angle at which an aircraft's wing is set back from a right angle to the body.

sweeper ▶ **noun 1** a person or device that cleans a floor or road by sweeping.
2 Soccer a player stationed behind the other defenders, free to defend at any point across the field and sometimes initiate and support attacks.
3 a small nocturnal shoaling fish of reefs and coastal waters, occurring chiefly in the tropical Indo-Pacific.
● Family Pempheridae: several genera and species, including the western Atlantic **glassy sweeper** (*Pempheris schomburgki*), with transparent young.

sweeping ▶ **adjective** wide in range or effect: *we cannot recommend any sweeping alterations.*
■extending or performed in a long, continuous curve: *sweeping, desolate moorlands | a smooth sweeping motion.* ■ (of a statement) taking no account of particular cases or exceptions; too general: *a sweeping assertion.*
▶ **noun** (**sweepings**) dirt or refuse collected by sweeping: *the sweepings from the house.*
– DERIVATIVES **sweepingly** adverb, **sweepingness** noun.

sweep second hand ▶ **noun** a second hand on a clock or watch, moving on the same dial as the other hands.

sweepstake ▶ **noun** (also **sweepstakes**) a form of gambling, especially on horse races, in which all the stakes are divided among the winners: [as modifier] *a sweepstake ticket.*
■a race on which money is bet in this way. ■ a prize or prizes won in a sweepstake.

sweet ▶ **adjective 1** having the pleasant taste characteristic of sugar or honey; not salt, sour, or bitter: *a cup of hot sweet tea* | figurative *a sweet taste of success.*
■(of air, water, or food) fresh, pure, and untainted: *lungfuls of the clean, sweet air.* ■ [often in combination] smelling pleasant like flowers or perfume; fragrant: *sweet-smelling flowers.*
2 pleasing in general; delightful: *it was the sweet life he had always craved.*
■highly satisfying or gratifying: *some sweet, short-lived revenge.* ■ [often as exclamation] informal used in expressions of assent or approval: *Yeah, I'd like to come to the party. Sweet, mate.* ■ working, moving, or done smoothly or easily: *the sweet handling of this motorcycle.* ■ (of sound) melodious or harmonious: *the sweet notes of the flute.* ■ chiefly US denoting music, especially jazz, played at a steady tempo without improvisation.
3 (of a person or action) pleasant and kind or thoughtful: *a very sweet nurse came along.*
■(especially of a person or animal) charming and endearing: *a sweet little cat.* ■ [predic.] (**sweet on**) informal, dated infatuated or in love with: *she seemed quite sweet on him.* ■ dear; beloved: *my sweet love.* ■ archaic used as a respectful form of address: *go to thy rest, sweet sir.*
4 used for emphasis in various phrases and exclamations: *What had happened? Sweet nothing.*
■(**one's own sweet ——**) used to emphasize the unpredictable individuality of someone's actions: *I'd rather carry on in my own sweet way.*
▶ **noun 1** Brit. a small shaped piece of confectionery made with sugar: *a bag of sweets.*
2 Brit. a sweet dish forming a course of a meal; a pudding or dessert.
3 used as an affectionate form of address to a person one is very fond of: *hello, my sweet.*
4 (**the sweet**) archaic or poetic/literary the sweet part or element of something: *you have had the bitter, now comes the sweet.*
■(**sweets**) the pleasures or delights found in something: *the sweets of office.*
– PHRASES **keep someone sweet** informal keep someone well disposed towards oneself, especially by favours or bribery. **she's sweet** Austral. informal all is well. **sweet dreams** used to express good wishes to a person going to bed. **sweet sixteen** used to refer to the age of sixteen as characterized by prettiness and innocence in a girl.
– DERIVATIVES **sweetish** adjective, **sweetly** adverb.
– ORIGIN Old English *swēte*, of Germanic origin; related to Dutch *zoet*, German *süss*, from an Indo-European root shared by Latin *suavis* and Greek *hēdus*.

sweet alyssum ▶ **noun** see **ALYSSUM**.

sweet-and-sour ▶ **adjective** [attrib.] (especially of Chinese-style food) cooked in a sauce containing sugar and either vinegar or lemon.

sweet balm ▶ **noun** see **BALM** (sense 3).

sweet basil ▶ **noun** see **BASIL**.

sweet bay ▶ **noun** see **BAY**[2].

sweetbread ▶ **noun** the thymus gland (or, rarely, the pancreas) of an animal, especially as used for food.

sweetbriar ▶ **noun 1** a Eurasian wild rose with fragrant leaves and flowers.
● *Rosa rubiginosa*, family Rosaceae.
2 W. Indian a spiny acacia with fragrant yellow flowers.
● Genus *Acacia*, family Leguminosae: *A. farnesiana*, an Old World tree which is grown throughout the tropics and yields an essential oil used in perfumery, and the tropical American *A. tortuosa*.

sweet butter ▶ **noun** [mass noun] a type of unsalted butter made from fresh pasteurized cream.

sweet chestnut ▶ **noun** see **CHESTNUT**.

sweet cicely ▶ **noun** a white-flowered European plant of the parsley family, with large fern-like leaves and a scent which resembles aniseed.
● *Myrrhis odorata*, family Umbelliferae.

sweetcorn ▶ **noun** [mass noun] maize of a variety with kernels that have a high sugar content. It is grown for human consumption and is harvested while slightly immature.
■the kernels of this plant eaten as a vegetable.

sweeten ▶ **verb** make or become sweet or sweeter, especially in taste: [with obj.] *a cup of coffee sweetened with saccharin* | [no obj.] *her smile sweetened.*
■[with obj.] make more agreeable or acceptable: *there is no way to sweeten the statement.* ■ [with obj.] informal induce (someone) to be well disposed or helpful to oneself: *I am in the process of* ***sweetening*** *him* ***up.***
– PHRASES **sweeten the pill** see **PILL**[1].

sweetener ▶ **noun** a substance used to sweeten food or drink, especially one other than sugar.
■informal, chiefly Brit. an inducement, typically in the form of money or a concession: *a sweetener may persuade them to sell.*

sweet Fanny Adams ▶ **noun** see **FANNY ADAMS** (sense 1).

sweet fennel ▶ **noun** see **FENNEL**.

sweet flag ▶ **noun** an Old World waterside plant of the arum family, with leaves that resemble those of the iris. It is used medicinally and as a flavouring. Also called **CALAMUS**.
● *Acorus calamus*, family Araceae.

sweet gale ▶ **noun** another term for **BOG MYRTLE**.
– ORIGIN mid 17th cent.: *gale* from Old English *gagel, gagelle*, of Germanic origin; related to Dutch *gagel*, German *Gagel*.

sweet galingale ▶ **noun** another term for **GALINGALE** (in sense 1).

sweetgrass ▶ **noun** [mass noun] any of a number of grasses which possess a sweet flavour, making them attractive to livestock, or a sweet smell, resulting in their former use as herbs for strewing or burning.
● *Glyceria, Hierochloe*, and other genera, family Gramineae.

sweet gum ▶ **noun** the North American liquidambar, which yields a balsam and decorative heartwood which is marketed as satin walnut.
● *Liquidambar styraciflua*, family Hamamelidaceae.

sweetheart ▶ **noun** used as a term of endearment or affectionate form of address: *don't worry, sweetheart, I've got it all worked out.*
■a person that one is in love with: *the pair were childhood sweethearts.* ■ a particularly lovable or pleasing person or thing: *he is an absolute sweetheart.* ■ [as modifier] informal denoting an arrangement reached privately by two sides, especially an employer and a trade union, in their own interests: *a sweetheart agreement.*

sweetheart neckline ▶ **noun** a neckline on a dress or blouse that is low at the front and shaped like the top of a heart.

sweetheart rose ▶ **noun** N. Amer. a rose with small pink, white, or yellow flowers that are particularly attractive as buds.

sweetie informal ▶ **noun 1** Brit. a sweet.
2 (also **sweetie-pie**) used as a term of endearment (especially as a form of address).
3 a green-skinned grapefruit of a variety noted for its sweet taste.

sweeting ▶ **noun 1** an apple of a sweet-flavoured variety.
2 archaic darling.

sweetlips (also **sweetlip**) ▶ **noun** (pl. same) a patterned grunt (fish) that changes its colour and markings with age, occurring in the Indo-Pacific.
● *Plectorhynchus* and other genera, family Pomadasyidae: several species, including the **oriental sweetlips** (*P. orientalis*).

sweetmeal ▶ **noun** [mass noun] [usu. as modifier] Brit. sweetened wholemeal: *a sweetmeal biscuit.*

sweetmeat ▶ **noun** archaic an item of confectionery or sweet food.

sweet milk ▶ **noun** [mass noun] fresh whole milk, as opposed to buttermilk.

sweetness ▶ **noun** [mass noun] the quality of being sweet.

▪used as an affectionate form of address, though often ironically: *I've just got to go, sweetness.*

– PHRASES **sweetness and light** social or political harmony: *Khrushchev's next visit to the West was one of sweetness and light.* ▪a reasonable and peaceable person: *when he's around she's all sweetness and light.* [ORIGIN: taken from Swift and used with aesthetic or moral reference, first by Arnold in *Culture and Anarchy* (1869).]

sweet pea ▶ **noun** a climbing plant of the pea family, widely cultivated for its colourful fragrant flowers.

● Genus *Lathyrus*, family Leguminosae: several species, in particular *L. odoratus*, which originated in southern Italy and Sicily.

sweet pepper ▶ **noun** a large green, yellow, orange, or red variety of capsicum which has a mild or sweet flavour and is often eaten raw. Also called **BELL PEPPER** in North America.

● *Capsicum annuum* var. *annuum*, '*grossum*' group (or var. *grossum*).

sweet potato ▶ **noun 1** an edible tropical tuber with white slightly sweet flesh.

2 the Central American climbing plant which yields this tuber, widely cultivated in warm countries.

● *Ipomoea batatas*, family Convolvulaceae.

sweet rocket ▶ **noun** a herbaceous plant of the cabbage family, cultivated for its long spikes of mauve or white flowers which are fragrant in the evening.

● *Hesperis matronalis*, family Cruciferae.

sweetsop ▶ **noun 1** a round or heart-shaped custard apple which has a green scaly rind and a sweet pulp. Also called **SUGAR APPLE**.

2 the tropical American evergreen shrub which yields this fruit.

● *Annona squamosa*, family Annonaceae.

sweet spot ▶ **noun** informal the point or area on a bat, club, or racket at which it makes most effective contact with the ball.

sweet sultan ▶ **noun** a Near Eastern plant of the daisy family, with sweet-scented flowers, slender stems, and narrow grey-green leaves.

● *Centaurea moschata*, family Compositae.

sweet talk informal ▶ **verb** (**sweet-talk**) [with obj.] insincerely praise (someone) in order to persuade them to do something: *detectives* ***sweet-talked*** *them* ***into*** *confessing.*

▶ **noun** [mass noun] insincere praise used to persuade someone to do something.

sweet tooth ▶ **noun** [usu. in sing.] (pl. **sweet tooths**) a great liking for sweet-tasting foods.

– DERIVATIVES **sweet-toothed** adjective.

sweetveld /ˈswiːtfɛlt/ ▶ **noun** [mass noun] S. African land on which plants providing nutritious grazing grow.

▪nutritious vegetation.

– ORIGIN probably partly translating Dutch *zoeteveld*; compare with **SOURVELD**.

sweet vernal grass ▶ **noun** see **VERNAL GRASS**.

sweet violet ▶ **noun** a sweet-scented Old World violet with heart-shaped leaves, used in perfumery and as a flavouring.

● *Viola odorata*, family Violaceae.

sweet william ▶ **noun** a fragrant European garden pink with flattened clusters of vivid red, pink, or white flowers.

● *Dianthus barbatus*, family Caryophyllaceae.

sweet woodruff ▶ **noun** see **WOODRUFF**.

swell ▶ **verb** (past participle **swollen** or **swelled**) [no obj.] (especially of a part of the body) become larger or rounder in size, typically as a result of an accumulation of fluid: *her bruised knee was already* ***swelling up*** | figurative *the sky was black and swollen with rain* | [as adj. **swollen**] *swollen glands.*

▪become or make greater in intensity, number, amount, or volume: [no obj.] *the murmur swelled to a roar* | [as adj. **swelling**] *the swelling ranks of Irish singer-songwriters* | [with obj.] *the population was swollen by refugees.* ▪be intensely affected or filled with a particular emotion: *she felt herself* ***swell with*** *pride.*

▶ **noun 1** [in sing.] a full or gently rounded shape or form: *the soft swell of her breast.*

▪a gradual increase in sound, amount, or intensity: *a huge swell in the popularity of one-day cricket.* ▪a welling up of a feeling: *a swell of pride swept over George.*

2 [usu. in sing.] a slow, regular movement of the sea in rolling waves that do not break: *there was a heavy swell.*

3 a mechanism for producing a crescendo or diminuendo in an organ or harmonium.

4 informal, dated a person of wealth or high social position, typically one perceived as fashionable or stylish: *a crowd of city swells.*

▶ **adjective** N. Amer. informal, dated excellent; very good: *you're looking swell.*

▪archaic smart; fashionable: *a swell boulevard.*

▶ **adverb** N. Amer. informal, dated excellently; very well: *everything was just going swell.*

– PHRASES **someone's head swells** someone becomes conceited: *I am not saying this to make your head swell* | *if I say this, you'll get* ***swollen-headed.***

– ORIGIN Old English *swellan* (verb), of Germanic origin; related to German *schwellen*. Current senses of the noun date from the early 16th cent.; the informal adjectival use derives from noun sense 4 (late 18th cent.).

swell box ▶ **noun** a part of a large organ in which some of the pipes are enclosed, with a movable shutter for controlling the sound level.

swelling ▶ **noun** an abnormal enlargement of a part of the body, typically as a result of an accumulation of fluid.

▪a natural rounded protuberance: *the lobes are prominent swellings on the base of the brain.*

swell organ ▶ **noun** a section of a large organ consisting of pipes enclosed in a swell box, usually played with an upper keyboard.

swelter ▶ **verb** [no obj.] (of a person or the atmosphere at a particular time or place) be uncomfortably hot: *Barney sweltered in his doorman's uniform* | [as adj. **sweltering**] *a sweltering English summer.*

▶ **noun** [in sing.] an uncomfortably hot atmosphere: *the swelter of the afternoon had cooled.*

– DERIVATIVES **swelteringly** adverb.

– ORIGIN Middle English: from the base of dialect *swelt* 'perish', of Germanic origin.

swept past and past participle of **SWEEP**.

swept-back ▶ **adjective** [attrib.] (of an aircraft wing) positioned to point somewhat backwards.

swept-up ▶ **adjective** another term for **UPSWEPT**.

swept volume ▶ **noun** the volume through which a piston or plunger moves as it makes a stroke.

swept-wing ▶ **adjective** [attrib.] (of an aircraft) having swept-back wings.

swerve ▶ **verb** change or cause to change direction abruptly: [no obj.] *a lorry swerved across her path* | [with obj.] *O'Hara swerved the motorcycle round the corner.*

▶ **noun** an abrupt change of direction: *do not make sudden swerves, particularly around parked vehicles.*

▪[mass noun] divergence from a straight course imparted to a ball or other object, especially in soccer, cricket, or snooker.

– DERIVATIVES **swerver** noun.

– ORIGIN Old English *sweorfan* 'depart, leave, turn aside', of Germanic origin; related to Middle Dutch *swerven* 'to stray'.

Sweyn I /sweɪn/ (also **Sven**) (d.1014), king of Denmark *c.*985–1014; known as **Sweyn Forkbeard**. From 1003 he launched a series of attacks on England, finally driving Ethelred the Unready to flee to Normandy at the end of 1013. Sweyn then became king of England but died five weeks later.

SWG ▶ **abbreviation for** (in the UK) standard wire gauge, denoting a series of standard sizes in which wire is made.

swidden /ˈswɪd(ə)n/ ▶ **noun** an area of land cleared for cultivation by slashing and burning vegetation.

▪[mass noun] the method of clearing land in this way: *the practice of swidden.*

▶ **verb** [with obj.] clear (land) by slashing and burning vegetation.

– ORIGIN late 18th cent. (as a verb, originally dialect): variant of dialect *swithen* 'to burn'.

Swift, Jonathan (1667–1745), Irish satirist, poet, and Anglican cleric; known as **Dean Swift**. He is best known for *Gulliver's Travels* (1726), a satire on human society in the form of a fantastic tale of travels in imaginary lands.

swift ▶ **adjective** happening quickly or promptly: *a remarkably swift recovery.*

▪moving or capable of moving at high speed: *the water was very swift* | *the swiftest horse in his stable.*

▶ **adverb** poetic/literary except in combination swiftly: *streams which ran swift and very clear* | *a swift-acting poison.*

▶ **noun 1** a swift-flying insectivorous bird with long slender wings and a superficial resemblance to a swallow, spending most of its life on the wing.

● Family Apodidae: several genera and numerous species, in particular the common **Eurasian swift** (*Apus apus*).

2 (also **swift moth**) a moth, typically yellow-brown in colour, with fast darting flight. The eggs are scattered in flight and the larvae live underground feeding on roots, where they can be a serious pest.

● Family Hepialidae: *Hepialus* and other genera.

3 a light, adjustable reel for holding a skein of silk or wool.

– DERIVATIVES **swiftly** adverb, **swiftness** noun.

– ORIGIN Old English (as an adjective), from the Germanic base of Old English *swifan* 'move in a course, sweep'. The bird name dates from the mid 17th cent.

swift fox ▶ **noun** a small fox with a yellowish-buff coat and a black-tipped tail, living on the plains of North America.

● *Vulpes velox*, family Canidae.

swiftlet ▶ **noun** a small swift found in South Asia and Australasia.

● Genera *Aerodramus* and *Collocalia*, family Apodidae: many species.

swifty (also **swiftie**) ▶ **noun** (pl. **-ies**) informal, chiefly Austral. **1** a deceptive trick: *they had hoped to* ***pull a swifty.***

2 a person who acts or thinks quickly: *boy, are you a swifty.*

swig ▶ **verb** (**swigged**, **swigging**) [with obj.] drink in large draughts: *Dave swigged the wine in five gulps* | [no obj.] *Ratagan* ***swigged at*** *his beer.*

▶ **noun** a large draught of drink: *he took a swig of tea.*

– DERIVATIVES **swigger** noun.

– ORIGIN mid 16th cent. (as a noun in the obsolete sense 'liquor'): of unknown origin.

swill ▶ **verb 1** [with obj.] Brit. wash or rinse out (an area or container) by pouring large amounts of water or other liquid over or into it: *I* ***swilled out*** *the mug.*

▪cause (liquid) to swirl round in a container or cavity: *she gently* ***swilled*** *her brandy* ***round*** *her glass.* ▪[no obj., with adverbial] (of a liquid) move or splash about over a surface: *the icy water swilled round us.*

2 [with obj.] drink (something) greedily or in large quantities: *they whiled away their evening swilling pints of bitter* | [as adj. **swilling**] *his beer-swilling pals.*

▪accompany (food) with large quantities of drink: *a feast swilled down with pints of cider.*

▶ **noun 1** [mass noun] kitchen refuse and scraps of waste food mixed with water for feeding to pigs.

▪alcohol of inferior quality: *the beer was just warm swill.*

2 a large mouthful of a drink: *a swill of ale.*

– DERIVATIVES **swiller** noun [usu. in combination] *beer-swillers.*

– ORIGIN Old English *swillan*, *swilian* (verb), of unknown origin. The noun dates from the mid 16th cent.

swim ▶ **verb** (**swimming**; past **swam**; past participle **swum**) **1** [no obj.] propel the body through water by using the limbs, or (in the case of a fish or other aquatic animal) by using fins, tail, or other bodily movement: *they swam ashore* | *Adrian taught her to swim breaststroke.*

▪[with obj.] cross (a particular stretch of water) in this way: *she swam the Channel.* ▪float on or at the surface of a liquid: *bubbles swam on the surface.* ▪[with obj.] cause to float or move across water: *the Russians were able to swim their infantry carriers across.*

2 [no obj.] be immersed in or covered with liquid: *mashed potatoes* ***swimming in*** *gravy.*

3 [no obj.] appear to reel or whirl before one's eyes: *Emily rubbed her eyes as the figures swam before her eyes.*

▪experience a dizzily confusing sensation in one's head: *the drink made his head swim.*

▶ **noun 1** an act or period of swimming: *we went for a swim in the river.*

2 a pool in a river which is a particularly good spot for fishing: *he landed two 5 lb chub from the same swim.*

– PHRASES **in the swim** involved in or aware of current affairs or events. **swim with** (or **against**) **the tide** act in accordance with (or against) the prevailing opinion or tendency.

– DERIVATIVES **swimmable** adjective, **swimmer** noun.

– ORIGIN Old English *swimman* (verb), of Germanic origin; related to Dutch *zwemmen* and German *schwimmen*.

USAGE In standard English, the past tense of **swim** is **swam** (*she* **swam** *to the shore*) and the past participle is **swum** (*she had never* **swum** *there before*). In the 17th and 18th centuries **swam** and **swum** were used interchangeably for the past participle, but this is not acceptable in standard modern English.

swim bladder ▶ **noun** Zoology a gas-filled sac present in the body of many bony fishes, used to maintain and control buoyancy.

swimfeeder ▶ **noun** Fishing a small perforated container for bait which is cast into the water or attached to a lure to attract fish.

swimmeret /ˈswɪmərɛt/ ▶ **noun** another term for **PLEOPOD**.

swimming ▶ **noun** [mass noun] the sport or activity of propelling oneself through water using the limbs.

swimming bath ▶ **noun** (also **swimming baths**) Brit. a swimming pool, especially a public indoor one.

swimming costume ▶ **noun** Brit. a garment worn for swimming, especially a woman's one-piece swimsuit.

swimming crab ▶ **noun** a coastal crab which has paddle-like rear legs for swimming.
• Family Portunidae: many species, including the **velvet swimming crab** (*Macropipus puber*).

swimming hole ▶ **noun** chiefly N. Amer. a bathing place in a stream or river.

swimmingly ▶ **adverb** smoothly and satisfactorily: *things are going swimmingly.*

swimming pool ▶ **noun** an artificial pool for swimming in.

swimming trunks (also **swim trunks**) ▶ **plural noun** shorts worn by men for swimming.

swimsuit ▶ **noun** a woman's one-piece swimming costume.
– DERIVATIVES **swimsuited** adjective.

swimwear ▶ **noun** [mass noun] clothing worn for swimming.

Swinburne, Algernon Charles (1837–1909), English poet and critic. Associated as a poet with the Pre-Raphaelites, he also contributed to the revival of interest in Elizabethan and Jacobean drama and produced influential studies of William Blake and the Brontës.

swindle ▶ **verb** [with obj.] use deception to deprive (someone) of money or possessions: *a businessman swindled investors* **out of** *millions of pounds.*
■ obtain (money) fraudulently: *he was said to have swindled £62.5 million from the state-owned cement industry.*
▶ **noun** a fraudulent scheme or action: *he is mixed up in a £10 million insurance swindle.*
– DERIVATIVES **swindler** noun.
– ORIGIN late 18th cent.: back-formation from *swindler*, from German *Schwindler* 'extravagant maker of schemes, swindler', from *schwindeln* 'be giddy', also 'tell lies'.

Swindon an industrial town in central England, a unitary council formerly in Wiltshire; pop. 100,000 (est. 1991). An old market town, it developed rapidly after railway engineering works were established there in 1841 and again in the 1950s as an overspill town for London.

S

swine ▶ **noun** (pl. same) **1** formal or US a pig.
2 (pl. same or **swines**) informal a person regarded by the speaker with contempt and disgust: *what an arrogant, unfeeling swine!*
■ a thing that is very difficult or unpleasant to deal with: *mist is a swine in unfamiliar country.*
– DERIVATIVES **swinish** adjective, **swinishly** adverb, **swinishness** noun.
– ORIGIN Old English *swīn*, of Germanic origin; related to Dutch *zwijn* and German *Schwein*, also to **SOW**[2].

swine fever ▶ **noun** [mass noun] an intestinal viral disease of pigs.

swineherd ▶ **noun** chiefly historical a person who tends pigs.
– ORIGIN Old English, from **SWINE** + obsolete *herd* 'herdsman'.

swine vesicular disease ▶ **noun** [mass noun] an infectious viral disease of pigs causing mild fever and blisters around the mouth and feet.

swing ▶ **verb** (past and past participle **swung**) **1** move or cause to move back and forth or from side to side while or as if suspended: [no obj.] *her long black skirt swung about her legs* | [with obj.] *a priest began swinging a censer* | [as adj. **swinging**] *local girls with their castanets and their swinging hips.*
■ [often with adverbial or complement] move or cause to move in alternate directions or in either direction on an axis: [no obj.] *a wooden gate swinging crazily on its hinges* | [with obj.] *he swung the heavy iron door to.* ■ [with obj.] turn (a ship or aircraft) to all compass points in succession, in order to test compass error. ■ informal be executed by hanging: *now he was going to swing for it.*
2 [no obj., with adverbial of direction] move by grasping a support from below and leaping: *we swung across like two trapeze artists* | (**swing oneself**) *the Irishman swung himself into the saddle.*
■ move quickly round to the opposite direction: *Ronni had swung round to face him.* ■ move with a rhythmic swaying gait: *the riflemen swung along smartly.*
3 [with adverbial of direction] move or cause to move in a smooth, curving line: [with obj.] *he swung her bag up on to the rack* | [no obj.] *the cab swung into the car park.*
■ [with obj.] bring down (something held) with a curving movement, typically in order to hit an object: *I swung the club and missed the ball.* ■ [no obj.] (**swing at**) attempt to hit or punch, typically with a wide curving movement of the arm: *he swung at me with the tyre wrench.* ■ throw (a punch) with such a movement: *she swung a punch at him.* ■ [with obj.] Cricket (of a bowler) make a delivery of (a ball) deviate (typically sideways) from a regular course in the air. ■ [no obj.] Cricket (of a ball) deviate in such a way.
4 shift or cause to shift from one opinion, mood, or state of affairs to another: [no obj.] *opinion swung in the Chancellor's favour* | [with obj.] *the failure to seek a peace could swing sentiment the other way.*
■ [with obj.] have a decisive influence on (something, especially a vote or election): *an attempt to swing the vote in their favour.* ■ [with obj.] informal succeed in bringing about: *with us backing you we might be able to swing something.*
5 [no obj.] play music with an easy flowing but vigorous rhythm: *the band swung on.*
■ (of music) be played with such a rhythm.
6 [no obj.] informal (of an event, place, or way of life) be lively, exciting, or fashionable.
7 [no obj.] informal be promiscuous, especially by engaging in group sex or swapping sexual partners.
▶ **noun 1** a seat suspended by ropes or chains, on which someone may sit and swing back and forth.
■ a spell of swinging on such an apparatus.
2 an act of swinging: *with the swing of her arm, the knife flashed through the air.*
■ the manner in which a golf club or a bat is swung: *improve your golf swing.* ■ [mass noun] the motion of swinging: *this short cut gave her hair new movement and swing.* ■ [in sing.] a smooth flowing rhythm or action: *they came with a steady swing up the last reach.* ■ [mass noun] Cricket sideways deviation of the ball from a regular path: [as modifier] *a swing bowler.*
3 a discernible change in opinion, especially the amount by which votes or points scored change from one side to another: *a five per cent swing to Labour.*
4 [mass noun] a style of jazz or dance music with an easy flowing but vigorous rhythm.
■ the rhythmic feeling or drive of such music.
5 N. Amer. a swift tour involving a number of stops, especially one undertaken as part of a political campaign.
– PHRASES **get (back) into the swing of things** informal get used to (or return to) being easy and relaxed about an activity or routine one is engaged in. **go with a swing** informal (of a party or other event) be lively and enjoyable. **in full swing** at the height of activity: *by nine-thirty the dance was in full swing.* **swing the lead** Brit. informal malinger; shirk one's duty. [ORIGIN: with nautical allusion to the lump of lead suspended by a string, slowly lowered to ascertain the depth of water.] **swings and roundabouts** Brit. a situation in which different actions or options result in no eventual gain or loss: *the advantages of a small company over a large one is a matter of swings and roundabouts.* [ORIGIN: from the colloquial phrase *to gain on the swings and lose on the roundabouts.*] **swing into action** quickly begin acting or operating.
– DERIVATIVES **swinger** noun.
– ORIGIN Old English *swingan* 'to beat, whip', also 'rush', *geswing* 'a stroke with a weapon', of Germanic origin; related to German *schwingen* 'brandish'.

swingback ▶ **adjective** (of a coat) cut to swing as the wearer moves.

swingbin ▶ **noun** Brit. a rubbish bin with a lid that swings shut after being pushed open.

swingboat ▶ **noun** chiefly Brit. a boat-shaped swing with seats for several people at fairs.

swing bridge ▶ **noun** a bridge over water that can be rotated horizontally to allow ships through.

swingby /ˈswɪŋbʌɪ/ ▶ **noun** a change in the flight path of a spacecraft using the gravitational pull of a celestial body. Compare with **SLINGSHOT**.

swing coat ▶ **noun** a coat cut so as to swing when the wearer moves.

swing door (N. Amer. also **swinging door**) ▶ **noun** a door that can be opened in either direction and is closed by a spring device when released.

swinge ▶ **verb** (**swingeing**) [with obj.] poetic/literary strike hard; beat.
– ORIGIN Old English *swengan* 'shake, shatter, move violently', of Germanic origin.

swingeing ▶ **adjective** chiefly Brit. severe or otherwise extreme: *swingeing cuts in public expenditure.*
– DERIVATIVES **swingeingly** adverb.

swinging ▶ **adjective** informal (of a person, place, or way of life) lively, exciting, and fashionable: *a swinging resort* | *the Swinging Sixties.*
■ sexually liberated or promiscuous.
– DERIVATIVES **swingingly** adverb.

swingle ▶ **noun 1** a wooden tool for beating flax and removing the woody parts from it.
2 the swinging part of a flail.
▶ **verb** [with obj.] beat (flax) with such a tool.
– ORIGIN Middle English: from Middle Dutch *swinghel*, from the base of the verb **SWING**.

swingletree /ˈswɪŋ(ə)ltriː/ ▶ **noun** chiefly Brit. a crossbar pivoted in the middle, to which the traces are attached in a horse-drawn cart or plough.

swingometer /swɪŋˈɒmɪtə/ ▶ **noun** informal a device or computerized display used to demonstrate the effect of a political swing on an election.

swing set ▶ **noun** N. Amer. a frame for children to play on, typically including one or more swings and a slide.

swing shift ▶ **noun** US a work shift from afternoon to late evening.

swing ticket ▶ **noun** an information tag attached by a string to an article for sale.

swing vote ▶ **noun** chiefly US a vote that has a decisive influence on the result of a poll.
– DERIVATIVES **swing voter** noun.

swing-wing ▶ **noun** [usu. as modifier] an aircraft wing that can move from a right-angled to a swept-back position: *swing-wing fighter bombers.*
■ an aircraft with wings of this design.

swingy ▶ **adjective** (**swingier**, **swingiest**) **1** (of music) characterized by swing (see **SWING** (sense 4 of the noun)).
2 (of a skirt, coat, or other garment) cut so as to swing as the wearer moves.

swipe informal ▶ **verb** [with obj.] **1** hit or try to hit with a swinging blow: *she swiped me right across the nose* | [no obj.] *she lifted her hand to* **swipe at** *a cat.*
2 steal: *someone swiped one of his sausages.*
3 pass (a swipe card) through the electronic device that reads it.
▶ **noun** a sweeping blow: *he missed the ball with his first swipe.*
■ an attack or criticism: *he* **took a swipe at** *his critics.*
– DERIVATIVES **swiper** noun.
– ORIGIN mid 18th cent.: perhaps a variant of **SWEEP**.

swipe card ▶ **noun** a plastic card such as a credit card or ID card bearing magnetically encoded information which is read when the edge of the card is slid through an electronic device.

swipple ▶ **noun** dialect the swinging part of a flail.
– ORIGIN late Middle English: probably based on the verb **SWEEP**.

swirl ▶ **verb** [no obj.] move in a twisting or spiralling pattern: *the smoke was swirling around him* | [as adj. **swirling**] figurative *a flood of swirling emotions.*
■ [with obj.] cause to move in such a pattern: *swirl a little cream into the soup.*
▶ **noun** a quantity of something moving in such a pattern: *swirls of dust swept across the floor.*
■ a twisting or spiralling movement or pattern: *she emerged with a swirl of skirts* | *swirls of colour.*
– DERIVATIVES **swirly** adjective.
– ORIGIN late Middle English (originally Scots in the sense 'whirlpool'): perhaps of Low German or

Dutch origin; compare with Dutch *zwirrelen* 'to whirl'.

swish ▶ **verb** [no obj., with adverbial of direction] move with a hissing or rushing sound: *a car swished by.*
■ [with obj.] cause to move with such a sound: *a girl came in, swishing her long skirts.* ■ aim a swinging blow at something: *he* **swished at** *a bramble with a piece of stick.* ■ [with obj.] Basketball sink (a shot) without the ball touching the backboard or rim.
▶ **noun 1** a hissing or rustling sound: *he could hear the swish of a distant car.*
■ a rapid swinging movement: *the cow gave a swish of its tail.* ■ Basketball, informal a shot that goes through the basket without touching the backboard or rim.
2 US informal, offensive an effeminate male homosexual.
▶ **adjective** Brit. informal impressively smart and fashionable: *dinner at a swish hotel.*
– ORIGIN mid 18th cent.: imitative.

swishy ▶ **adjective 1** making a swishing sound or movement.
2 informal effeminate.

Swiss ▶ **adjective** of or relating to Switzerland or its people.
■ [as plural noun **the Swiss**] the people of Switzerland.
▶ **noun** (pl. same) a native or national of Switzerland, or a person of Swiss descent.
– ORIGIN early 16th cent.: from French *Suisse*, from Middle High German *Swīz* 'Switzerland'.

Swiss army knife (also **Swiss army penknife**) ▶ **noun** a penknife incorporating several blades and other tools such as scissors and screwdrivers.

Swiss chard ▶ **noun** see **CHARD**.

Swiss cheese ▶ **noun** [mass noun] cheese from Switzerland, typically containing large holes.
■ used figuratively to refer something that is full of holes, gaps, or defects: *the team has Swiss cheese for a defence.*

Swiss cheese plant ▶ **noun** a large monstera with perforated leaves (supposedly resembling the holes in a Swiss cheese), popularly grown as a house plant while young, and with creamy arum-like spathes followed by pineapple-flavoured fruit when mature.
• *Monstera deliciosa*, family Araceae.

Swiss Confederation the confederation of cantons forming Switzerland.

Swiss darning ▶ **noun** [mass noun] a technique in which coloured stitches are sewn on to knitted garments to make patterns or motifs that seem to have been knitted.

Swiss guard ▶ **noun** [often treated as pl.] Swiss mercenaries employed as a special guard, formerly by sovereigns of France, now only at the Vatican.

Swiss roll ▶ **noun** Brit. a cylindrical cake with a spiral cross section, made from a flat sponge cake spread with a filling such as jam and rolled up.

switch ▶ **noun 1** a device for making and breaking the connection in an electric circuit: *the guard hit a switch and the gate swung open.*
■ Computing a program variable which activates or deactivates a certain function of a program.
2 an act of adopting one policy or way of life, or choosing one type of item, in place of another; a change, especially a radical one: *his friends were surprised at his switch from newspaper owner to farmer.*
3 a slender flexible shoot cut from a tree.
4 N. Amer. a set of points on a railway track.
5 a tress of false or detached hair tied at one end, used in hairdressing to supplement natural hair.
▶ **verb** [with obj.] **1** change the position, direction, or focus of: *the company switched the boats to other routes.*
■ adopt (something different) in place of something else; change: *she's managed to switch careers.* ■ [no obj.] adopt a new policy, position, way of life, etc.: *she worked as a librarian and then switched to journalism.* ■ substitute (two items) for each other; exchange: *after ten minutes, listener and speaker switch roles.*
2 archaic beat or flick with or as if with a switch.
– DERIVATIVES **switchable** adjective.
– ORIGIN late 16th cent. (denoting a thin tapering riding whip): probably from Low German.
▶ **switch something off** turn off an electrical device.
■ (**switch off**) informal cease to pay attention: *as he waffles on, I switch off.*
switch something on turn on an electrical device.

switchback ▶ **noun 1** Brit. a road, path, or railway with alternate sharp ascents and descents.
■ a roller coaster.
2 N. Amer. a 180° bend in a road or path, especially one leading up the side of a mountain.

switchblade ▶ **noun** chiefly N. Amer. another term for **FLICK KNIFE**.

switchboard ▶ **noun** an installation for the manual control of telephone connections in an office, hotel, or other large building.
■ another term for **HELPLINE**. ■ an apparatus for varying connections between electric circuits in other applications.

switched-on Brit. informal ▶ **adjective** aware of what is going on or what is up to date; alert: *your shortcomings will be apparent to a switched-on youngster.*

switcher ▶ **noun 1** US a shunting engine.
2 a piece of electronic equipment used to select or combine different video and audio signals.

switcheroo /ˌswɪtʃəˈruː/ ▶ **noun** N. Amer. informal a change, reversal, or exchange, especially a surprising or deceptive one.
– ORIGIN late 20th cent.: from the noun **SWITCH** + *-eroo* in the sense 'unexpected'.

switchgear ▶ **noun** [mass noun] **1** switching equipment used in the transmission of electricity.
2 the switches or electrical controls in a motor vehicle.

switchgrass ▶ **noun** [mass noun] a tall North American panic grass which forms large clumps.
• *Panicum virgatum*, family Gramineae.

switch-hitter ▶ **noun** Baseball an ambidextrous batter.
■ N. Amer. informal a bisexual.
– DERIVATIVES **switch-hitting** adjective.

switch-over ▶ **noun** an instance of adopting a new policy, position, way of life, etc.: *a switch-over by the bulk of the Labour vote would give the Lib Dems victory.*

switch selling ▶ **noun** [mass noun] a sales technique whereby cheap or non-existent goods are placed on offer on favourable terms to entice the consumer into buying similar but more expensive items.

switchyard ▶ **noun** chiefly N. Amer. **1** the part of a railway yard taken up by points, in which trains are made up.
2 an enclosed area of a power system containing the switchgear.

swither Scottish ▶ **verb** [no obj.] be uncertain as to which course of action to choose: *Leonard swithered as to whether he should enter the arts or commerce.*
▶ **noun** [in sing.] a state of uncertainty.
– ORIGIN early 16th cent.: of unknown origin.

Swithin, St (also **Swithun**) (d.862), English ecclesiastic. He was bishop of Winchester from 852. The tradition that if it rains on St Swithin's Day it will do so for the next forty days may have its origin in the heavy rain said to have occurred when his relics were to be transferred to a shrine in Winchester cathedral. Feast day, 15 July.

Switzerland a mountainous, landlocked country in central Europe; pop. 6,673,850 (1990); official languages, French, German, Italian, and Romansh; capital, Berne. French name **SUISSE**, German name **SCHWEIZ**, Italian name **SVIZZERA**; also called by its Latin name **HELVETIA**.

> Switzerland emerged as an independent country in the 14th and 15th centuries, when the states or cantons formed a confederation to defeat first their Habsburg overlords and then their Burgundian neighbours. After a period of French domination (1798–1815) the Swiss Confederation's neutrality was guaranteed by the other European powers. Neutral in both world wars, Switzerland has emerged as an international financial centre and as the headquarters of several international organizations such as the Red Cross.

swive /swʌɪv/ ▶ **verb** [with obj.] archaic or humorous have sexual intercourse with.
– ORIGIN Middle English: apparently from the Old English verb *swīfan* 'move (along a course), sweep'.

swivel ▶ **noun** a coupling between two parts enabling one to revolve without turning the other.
▶ **verb** (**swivelled**, **swivelling**; US **swiveled**, **swiveling**) [often with adverbial] turn around a point or axis or on a swivel: [no obj.] *he swivelled in the chair* | [with obj.] *she swivelled her eyes round.*
– ORIGIN Middle English, from the base of Old English *swīfan* 'to move (along a course), sweep'.

swivel chair ▶ **noun** a chair with a seat able to be turned on its base to face in any direction.

swivet /ˈswɪvɪt/ ▶ **noun** [in sing.] chiefly US a fluster or panic: *the incomprehensible did not throw him into a swivet.*
– ORIGIN late 19th cent.: of unknown origin.

swizz (also **swiz**) ▶ **noun** [usu. in sing.] Brit. informal a thing that is disappointing or represents a mild swindle: *what a swizz!*
– ORIGIN early 20th cent.: abbreviation of **SWIZZLE**[2].

swizzle[1] ▶ **noun** a mixed alcoholic drink, especially a frothy one of rum or gin and bitters.
▶ **verb** [with obj.] stir (a drink) with a swizzle stick.
– ORIGIN early 19th cent.: of unknown origin.

swizzle[2] ▶ **noun** Brit. informal another term for **SWIZZ**.
– ORIGIN early 20th cent.: probably an alteration of **SWINDLE**.

swizzle stick ▶ **noun** a stick used for frothing up still drinks or taking the fizz out of sparkling ones.

swollen past participle of **SWELL**.

swoon ▶ **verb** [no obj.] faint from extreme emotion: *I don't want a nurse who swoons at the sight of blood.*
■ be emotionally affected by someone or something that one admires; become ecstatic: *the administration is so busy* **swooning over** *celebs that it has lost its senses.*
▶ **noun** an occurrence of fainting: *her strength ebbed away and she fell into a swoon.*
– ORIGIN Middle English: the verb from obsolete *swown* 'fainting', the noun from *aswoon* 'in a faint', both from Old English *geswōgen* 'overcome'.

swoop ▶ **verb 1** [no obj., with adverbial of direction] (especially of a bird) move rapidly downwards through the air: *the barn owl can* **swoop down on** *a mouse in total darkness* | *the aircraft swooped in to land.*
■ carry out a sudden attack, especially in order to make a capture or arrest: *armed police* **swooped on** *a flat after a tip-off.*
2 [with obj.] informal seize with a sweeping motion: *she* **swooped up** *the hen in her arms.*
▶ **noun** a swooping or snatching movement or action: *four members were arrested following a swoop by detectives on their homes.*
– PHRASES **at** (or **in**) **one fell swoop** see **FELL**[4].
– ORIGIN mid 16th cent. (in the sense 'sweep along in a stately manner'): perhaps a dialect variant of Old English *swāpan* (see **SWEEP**). The early sense of the noun was 'a blow, stroke'.

swoosh /swuːʃ, swʊʃ/ ▶ **noun** the sound produced by a sudden rush of air or liquid: *the swoosh of surf.*
▶ **verb** [no obj., with adverbial of direction] move with such a sound: *swooshing down beautiful ski slopes.*
– ORIGIN mid 19th cent.: imitative.

swop ▶ **verb** & **noun** variant spelling of **SWAP**.

sword ▶ **noun** a weapon with a long metal blade and a hilt with a handguard, used for thrusting or striking and now typically worn as part of ceremonial dress.
■ (**the sword**) poetic/literary military power, violence, or destruction: *not many perished by the sword.* ■ (**swords**) one of the suits in a tarot pack.
– PHRASES **beat** (or **turn**) **swords into ploughshares** devote resources to peaceful rather than warlike ends. [ORIGIN: with biblical allusion to Is. 2:4 and Mic. 4:3.] **he who lives by the sword dies by the sword** proverb those who commit violent acts must expect to suffer violence themselves. **put to the sword** kill, especially in war. **the sword of justice** judicial authority.
– DERIVATIVES **sword-like** adjective.
– ORIGIN Old English *sw(e)ord*, of Germanic origin; related to Dutch *zwaard* and German *Schwert*.

sword-and-sorcery ▶ **noun** [mass noun] a genre of fiction characterized by heroic adventures and elements of fantasy.

sword-bearer ▶ **noun** an official who carries a sword for a sovereign or other dignitary on formal occasions.

swordbill (also **sword-billed hummingbird**) ▶ **noun** a mainly green hummingbird with a very long bill, found in northern South America.
• *Ensifera ensifera*, family Trochilidae.

sword dance ▶ **noun** a dance in which the performers brandish swords or step around swords laid on the ground, originally as a tribal preparation for war or as a victory celebration.

sword fern ▶ **noun** a fern with long slender fronds.
• Genera *Polystichum* and *Nephrolepis*, family Dryopteridaceae: several species, including the North American *P. munitum* and the tropical *N. exaltata*.

swordfish ▶ **noun** (pl. same or **-fishes**) a large edible marine fish with a streamlined body and a long

flattened sword-like snout, related to the billfishes and popular as a game fish.
• *Xiphias gladius*, the only member of the family Xiphiidae.

sword knot ▶ **noun** a ribbon or tassel attached to a sword hilt, originally for securing it to the wrist.

sword lily ▶ **noun** a gladiolus.

sword of Damocles /ˈdaməkliːz/ ▶ **noun** see **DAMOCLES**.

sword of state ▶ **noun** the sword carried in front of a sovereign on state occasions.

swordplay ▶ **noun** [mass noun] the activity or skill of fencing with swords or foils.
■ figurative repartee; skilful debate: *this intellectual swordplay went on for several minutes.*

swordsman ▶ **noun** (pl. **-men**) a man who fights with a sword (typically with his level of skill specified): *an expert swordsman.*
– DERIVATIVES **swordsmanship** noun.

swordstick ▶ **noun** a hollow walking stick containing a blade that can be used as a sword.

sword-swallower ▶ **noun** a person who passes (or pretends to pass) a sword blade down their throat and gullet as entertainment.

swordtail ▶ **noun** a live-bearing freshwater fish of Central America, popular in aquaria. The lower edge of the tail is elongated and brightly marked in the male.
• *Xiphophorus helleri*, family Poeciliidae.

swore past of **SWEAR**.

sworn past participle of **SWEAR**. ▶ **adjective** [attrib.] **1** (of testimony or evidence) given under oath: *he made a sworn statement.*
2 determined to remain in the role or condition specified: *they were sworn enemies.*

swot Brit. informal ▶ **verb** (**swotted**, **swotting**) [no obj.] study assiduously: *kids swotting for GCSEs.*
▶ **noun** a person who studies hard, especially one regarded as spending too much time studying: *at school I wasn't a swot, but I wasn't a layabout either.*
– DERIVATIVES **swotty** adjective.
– ORIGIN mid 19th cent.: dialect variant of **SWEAT**.
▶ **swot up on** study (a subject) intensively, especially in preparation for something: *teachers spend their evenings swotting up on jargon* | (**swot something up**) *I've always been interested in old furniture and I've swotted it up a bit.*

SWOT analysis ▶ **noun** a study undertaken by an organization to identify its internal strengths and weaknesses, as well as its external opportunities and threats.
– ORIGIN late 20th cent.: *SWOT*, acronym from *strengths, weaknesses, opportunities, threats.*

swum past participle of **SWIM**.

swung past and past participle of **SWING**.

swung dash ▶ **noun** a dash (~) in the form of a reverse *s* on its side.

swy /swʌɪ/ ▶ **noun** Austral. another term for the game of **TWO-UP**.
– ORIGIN 1940s: from German *zwei* 'two'.

SY ▶ **abbreviation for** steam yacht: *the SY Morning.*

-sy ▶ **suffix** forming diminutive nouns and adjectives such as *folksy, mopsy*, also pet names such as *Patsy.*
– ORIGIN variant of **-Y**[2].

sybarite /ˈsɪbərʌɪt/ ▶ **noun** a person who is self-indulgent in their fondness for sensuous luxury.
– DERIVATIVES **sybaritism** noun.
– ORIGIN mid 16th cent. (originally denoting an inhabitant of Sybaris, an ancient Greek city in southern Italy, noted for luxury): via Latin from Greek *Subaritēs.*

sybaritic /ˌsɪbəˈrɪtɪk/ ▶ **adjective** fond of sensuous luxury or pleasure; self-indulgent: *their opulent and sybaritic lifestyle.*

sycamine /ˈsɪkəmɪn, -ʌɪn/ ▶ **noun** (in biblical use) the black mulberry tree (see Luke 17:6; in modern versions translated as 'mulberry tree').
– ORIGIN early 16th cent.: via Latin from Greek *sukaminos* 'mulberry tree', from Hebrew *šiqmāh* 'sycamore', assimilated to Greek *sukon* 'fig'.

sycamore ▶ **noun 1** a large Eurasian maple with winged fruits, native to central and southern Europe. It is planted as a fast-growing ornamental but tends to displace native trees.
• *Acer pseudoplatanus*, family Aceraceae.
2 N. Amer. the buttonwood tree.
3 (also **sycomore** or **sycomore fig**) (in biblical use) a fig tree that grows in the Middle East.
• *Ficus sycomorus*, family Moraceae.
– ORIGIN Middle English: from Old French *sic(h)amor*, via Latin from Greek *sukomoros*, from *sukon* 'fig' + *moron* 'mulberry'.

syce /sʌɪs/ (also **sice**) ▶ **noun** (especially in India) a groom (taking care of horses).
– ORIGIN from Persian and Urdu *sā'is*, from Arabic.

sycon /ˈsʌɪkɒn/ ▶ **noun** Zoology a sponge of a grade of structure showing some folding of the body wall, with choanocytes only lining radial canals. Compare with **ASCON** and **LEUCON**.
– DERIVATIVES **syconoid** adjective.
– ORIGIN late 19th cent.: adopted as a genus name from Greek *sukon* 'fig'.

syconium /sʌɪˈkəʊnɪəm/ ▶ **noun** (pl. **syconia** /-nɪə/) Botany a fleshy hollow receptacle that develops into a multiple fruit, as in the fig.
– ORIGIN mid 19th cent.: modern Latin, from Greek *sukon* 'fig'.

sycophant /ˈsɪkəfant/ ▶ **noun** a person who acts obsequiously towards someone in order to gain advantage; a servile flatterer.
– DERIVATIVES **sycophancy** noun, **sycophantic** adjective, **sycophantically** adverb.
– ORIGIN mid 16th cent. (denoting an informer): from French *sycophante*, or via Latin from Greek *sukophantēs* 'informer', from *sukon* 'fig' + *phainein* 'to show'; the association with informing against the illegal exportation of figs from ancient Athens (recorded by Plutarch) is not substantiated.

sycosis /sʌɪˈkəʊsɪs/ ▶ **noun** [mass noun] inflammation of the hair follicles in the bearded part of the face, caused by bacterial infection.
– ORIGIN late 16th cent. (originally denoting any fig-shaped skin ulcer): modern Latin, from Greek *sukōsis*, from *sukon* 'fig'.

Sydenham /ˈsɪd(ə)nəm/, Thomas (*c.*1624–89), English physician, known as 'the English Hippocrates'. He emphasized the healing power of nature, made a study of epidemics, and explained the nature of the type of chorea that is named after him.

Sydenham's chorea ▶ **noun** a form of chorea chiefly affecting children, associated with rheumatic fever. Formerly called **ST VITUS'S DANCE**.

Sydney the capital of New South Wales in SE Australia; pop. 3,097,950 (1991). It was the first British settlement in Australia and is the country's largest city and chief port. It has a fine natural harbour, crossed by the Sydney Harbour Bridge (opened 1932), and a striking opera house (opened 1973).

syenite /ˈsʌɪənʌɪt/ ▶ **noun** [mass noun] Geology a coarse-grained grey igneous rock composed mainly of alkali feldspar and ferromagnesian minerals such as hornblende.
– DERIVATIVES **syenitic** adjective.
– ORIGIN late 18th cent.: from French *syénite*, from Latin *Syenites* (*lapis*) '(stone) of *Syene*' (from Greek *Suēnē* 'Aswan', a town in Egypt).

Syktyvkar /ˌsɪktɪfˈkɑː/ a city in NW Russia, capital of the autonomous republic of Komi; pop. 235,000 (1990).

syl- ▶ **prefix** variant spelling of **SYN-** assimilated before *l* (as in *syllogism*).

syllabary /ˈsɪləb(ə)ri/ ▶ **noun** (pl. **-ies**) a set of written characters representing syllables and (in some languages or stages of writing) serving the purpose of an alphabet.
– ORIGIN mid 19th cent.: from modern Latin *syllabarium*, from Latin *syllaba* (see **SYLLABLE**).

syllabi plural form of **SYLLABUS**.

syllabic /sɪˈlabɪk/ ▶ **adjective 1** of, relating to, or based on syllables: *a system of syllabic symbols.*
■ Prosody based on the number of syllables: *the recreation of classical syllabic metres.* ■ (of a consonant, especially a nasal or other continuant) constituting a whole syllable, such as the *m* in *Mbabane* or the *l* in *bottle.* ■ articulated in syllables: *syllabic singing.*
– DERIVATIVES **syllabically** adverb, **syllabicity** noun.
– ORIGIN early 18th cent.: from French *syllabique* or late Latin *syllabicus*, from Greek *sullabikos*, from *sullabē* 'syllable'.

syllabification /sɪˌlabɪfɪˈkeɪʃ(ə)n/ (also **syllabication**) ▶ **noun** [mass noun] the division of words into syllables, either in speech or in writing.
– DERIVATIVES **syllabify** verb (**-ies**, **-ied**).

syllabize (also **-ise**) ▶ **verb** [with obj.] divide into or articulate by syllables.
– ORIGIN late 16th cent.: via medieval Latin from Greek *sullabizein*, from *sullabē* 'syllable'.

syllable /ˈsɪləb(ə)l/ ▶ **noun** a unit of pronunciation having one vowel sound, with or without surrounding consonants, forming the whole or a part of a word; for example, there are two syllables in *water* and three in *inferno*.
■ a character or characters representing a syllable. ■ [usu. with negative] the least amount of speech or writing; the least mention of something: *I'd never have breathed a syllable if he'd kept quiet.*
▶ **verb** [with obj.] pronounce (a word or phrase) clearly, syllable by syllable.
– PHRASES **in words of one syllable** using very simple language; expressed plainly.
– DERIVATIVES **syllabled** adjective [usu. in combination] *poems of few-syllabled lines.*
– ORIGIN late Middle English: from an Anglo-Norman French alteration of Old French *sillabe*, via Latin from Greek *sullabē*, from *sun-* 'together' + *lambanein* 'take'.

syllable-timed ▶ **adjective** (of a language) characterized by a rhythm in which syllables occur at roughly equivalent time intervals, irrespective of the stress placed on them. French is a syllable-timed language. Contrasted with **STRESS-TIMED**.

syllabub /ˈsɪləbʌb/ ▶ **noun** a whipped cream dessert, typically flavoured with white wine or sherry.
– ORIGIN of unknown origin.

syllabus /ˈsɪləbəs/ ▶ **noun** (pl. **syllabuses** or **syllabi** /-bʌɪ/) **1** the subjects in a course of study or teaching: *there isn't time to cover the syllabus* | *the history syllabus.*
2 (in the Roman Catholic Church) a summary of points decided by papal decree regarding heretical doctrines or practices.
– ORIGIN mid 17th cent. (in the sense 'concise table of headings of a discourse'): modern Latin, originally a misreading of Latin *sittybas*, accusative plural of *sittyba*, from Greek *sittuba* 'title slip, label'.

syllepsis /sɪˈlɛpsɪs/ ▶ **noun** (pl. **syllepses** /-siːz/) a figure of speech in which a word is applied to two others in different senses (e.g. *caught the train and a bad cold*) or to two others of which it grammatically suits only one (e.g. *neither they nor it is working*). Compare with **ZEUGMA**.
– DERIVATIVES **sylleptic** adjective.
– ORIGIN late Middle English: via late Latin from Greek *sullēpsis* 'taking together'.

syllogism /ˈsɪləˌdʒɪz(ə)m/ ▶ **noun** an instance of a form of reasoning in which a conclusion is drawn (whether validly or not) from two given or assumed propositions (premises) that each share a term with the conclusion, and that share a common or middle term not present in the conclusion (e.g. *all dogs are animals; all animals have four legs; therefore all dogs have four legs*).
■ [mass noun] deductive reasoning as distinct from induction: *logic is rules or syllogism.*
– DERIVATIVES **syllogistic** adjective, **syllogistically** adverb.
– ORIGIN late Middle English: via Old French or Latin from Greek *sullogismos*, from *sullogizesthai*, from *sun-* 'with' + *logizesthai* 'to reason' (from *logos* 'reasoning').

syllogize /ˈsɪlədʒʌɪz/ (also **-ise**) ▶ **verb** [no obj.] use syllogisms.
■ [with obj.] put (facts or an argument) in the form of syllogism.
– ORIGIN late Middle English: via Old French or late Latin from Greek *sullogizesthai* (see **SYLLOGISM**).

sylph /sɪlf/ ▶ **noun 1** an imaginary spirit of the air.
■ a slender woman or girl.
2 a mainly dark green and blue hummingbird, the male of which has a long forked tail.
• Genus *Aglaiocercus* (and *Neolesbia*), family Trochilidae: three species.
– ORIGIN mid 17th cent.: from modern Latin *sylphes*, *sylphi* and the German plural *Sylphen*, perhaps based on Latin *sylvestris* 'of the woods' + *nympha* 'nymph'.

sylphlike ▶ **adjective** (of a woman or girl) slender and graceful.

sylvan (also **silvan**) ▶ **adjective** chiefly poetic/literary consisting of or associated with woods; wooded: *trees and contours all add to a sylvan setting.*
■ pleasantly rural or pastoral: *vistas of sylvan charm.*
– ORIGIN mid 16th cent. (as a noun denoting an

inhabitant of the woods): from French *sylvain* or Latin *Silvanus* 'woodland deity', from *silva* 'a wood'.

Sylvaner /sɪlˈvɑːnə/ ▶ noun [mass noun] a variety of wine grape first developed in German-speaking districts, the dominant form being a white grape.
■ a white wine made from this grape.
– ORIGIN German.

sylvatic /sɪlˈvatɪk/ ▶ adjective Veterinary Medicine relating to or denoting certain diseases when contracted by wild animals, and the pathogens causing them: *an epidemic of sylvatic plague among prairie dogs.*
– ORIGIN 1930s: from Latin *silvaticus*, from *silva* 'wood'.

Sylvian fissure /ˈsɪlvɪən/ (also **fissure of Sylvius**) ▶ noun Anatomy a large diagonal fissure on the lateral surface of the brain which separates off the temporal lobe.
– ORIGIN mid 19th cent.: named after François de la Boë *Sylvius* (1614–72), Flemish anatomist.

sylvine /ˈsɪlviːn/ ▶ noun another term for **SYLVITE**.

sylvinite /ˈsɪlvɪnʌɪt/ ▶ noun [mass noun] a mixture of the minerals sylvite and halite, mined as a source of potash.
– ORIGIN late 19th cent.: from **SYLVINE** + **-ITE**[1].

sylvite /ˈsɪlvʌɪt/ ▶ noun [mass noun] a colourless or white mineral consisting of potassium chloride, occurring typically as cubic crystals.
– ORIGIN mid 19th cent.: from modern Latin (*sal digestivus*) *Sylvii*, the old name of this salt, + **-ITE**[1].

sym- ▶ prefix variant spelling of **SYN-** assimilated before *b*, *m*, *p* (as in *symbiosis*, *symmetry*, *symphysis*).

symbiont /ˈsɪmbɪɒnt, -bʌɪ-/ ▶ noun Biology either of two organisms that live in symbiosis with one another.
– ORIGIN late 19th cent.: formed irregularly from Greek *sumbiōn* 'living together', present participle of *sumbioun* (see **SYMBIOSIS**).

symbiosis /ˌsɪmbɪˈəʊsɪs, -bʌɪ-/ ▶ noun (pl. **symbioses** /-siːz/) [mass noun] Biology interaction between two different organisms living in close physical association, typically to the advantage of both. Compare with **ANTIBIOSIS**.
■ [count noun] a mutually beneficial relationship between different people or groups: *a perfect mother and daughter symbiosis.*
– DERIVATIVES **symbiotic** /-ˈɒtɪk/ adjective, **symbiotically** adverb.
– ORIGIN late 19th cent.: modern Latin, from Greek *sumbiōsis* 'a living together', from *sumbioun* 'live together', from *sumbios* 'companion'.

symbol ▶ noun a thing that represents or stands for something else, especially a material object representing something abstract: *the limousine was another symbol of his wealth and authority.*
■ a mark or character used as a conventional representation of an object, function, or process, e.g. the letter or letters standing for a chemical element or a character in musical notation. ■ a shape or sign used to represent something such as an organization, e.g. a red cross or a Star of David.
▶ verb (**symbolled**, **symbolling**; US **symboled**, **symboling**) [with obj.] archaic symbolize.
– ORIGIN late Middle English (denoting the Apostles' Creed): from Latin *symbolum* 'symbol, Creed (as the mark of a Christian)', from Greek *sumbolon* 'mark, token', from *sun-* 'with' + *ballein* 'to throw'.

symbolic ▶ adjective 1 serving as a symbol: *a repeating design symbolic of eternity.*
■ significant purely in terms of what is being represented or implied: *the release of the dissident was an important symbolic gesture.*
2 involving the use of symbols or symbolism: *the symbolic meaning of motifs and designs.*
– DERIVATIVES **symbolical** adjective, **symbolically** adverb.
– ORIGIN mid 17th cent.: from French *symbolique* or late Latin *symbolicus*, from Greek *sumbolikos*. The adjective *symbolical* dates from the early 17th cent.

symbolic interactionism ▶ noun [mass noun] Sociology the view of social behaviour that emphasizes linguistic or gestural communication and its subjective understanding, especially the role of language in the formation of the child as a social being.

symbolic logic ▶ noun [mass noun] the use of symbols to denote propositions, terms, and relations in order to assist reasoning.

symbolism ▶ noun [mass noun] 1 the use of symbols to represent ideas or qualities: *in China, symbolism in gardens achieved great subtlety.*
■ symbolic meaning attributed to natural objects or facts: *the old-fashioned symbolism of flowers.*
2 (also **Symbolism**) an artistic and poetic movement or style using symbolic images and indirect suggestion to express mystical ideas, emotions, and states of mind. It originated in late 19th century France and Belgium, with important figures including Mallarmé, Maeterlinck, Verlaine, Rimbaud, and Redon.
– DERIVATIVES **symbolist** noun & adjective.

symbolize (also **-ise**) ▶ verb [with obj.] be a symbol of: *the ceremonial dagger symbolizes justice.*
■ represent by means of symbols: *a tendency to symbolize the father as the sun.*
– DERIVATIVES **symbolization** noun.

symbology ▶ noun [mass noun] the study or use of symbols.
■ symbols collectively: *the use of religious symbology.*

symmetrical ▶ adjective made up of exactly similar parts facing each other or around an axis; showing symmetry.
– DERIVATIVES **symmetric** adjective, **symmetrically** adverb.

symmetry /ˈsɪmɪtri/ ▶ noun (pl. **-ies**) [mass noun] the quality of being made up of exactly similar parts facing each other or around an axis: *this series has a line of symmetry through its centre* | *a crystal structure with hexagonal symmetry.*
■ correct or pleasing proportion of the parts of a thing: *an overall symmetry making the poem pleasant to the ear.* ■ similarity or exact correspondence between different things: *families where there is symmetry between husband and wife on the paid job dimension* | [count noun] *history sometimes exhibits weird symmetries between events.* ■ [count noun] Physics & Mathematics a law or operation where a physical property or process has an equivalence in two or more directions.
– DERIVATIVES **symmetrize** (also **-ise**) verb.
– ORIGIN mid 16th cent. (denoting proportion): from French *symétrie* or Latin *symmetria*, from Greek, from *sun-* 'with' + *metron* 'measure'.

symmetry breaking ▶ noun [mass noun] Physics the absence or reduction of manifest symmetry in a situation despite its presence in the laws of nature underlying it.

Symons /ˈsʌɪmənz/, Julian (Gustave) (b.1912), English writer of detective fiction. His psychological crime fiction includes the novels *The Colour of Murder* (1957) and *The Progress of a Crime* (1960).

sympathectomy /ˌsɪmpəˈθɛktəmi/ ▶ noun [mass noun] the surgical cutting of a sympathetic nerve or removal of a ganglion to relieve a condition affected by its stimulation.

sympathetic ▶ adjective 1 feeling, showing, or expressing sympathy: *he was sympathetic towards staff with family problems* | *he spoke in a sympathetic tone.*
■ [predic.] showing approval of or favour towards an idea or action: *he was sympathetic to evolutionary ideas.*
2 pleasant or agreeable, in particular:
■ (of a person) attracting the liking of others: *Audrey develops as a sympathetic character.* ■ (of a structure) designed in a sensitive or fitting way: *buildings that were sympathetic to their surroundings.*
3 relating to or denoting the part of the autonomic nervous system consisting of nerves arising from ganglia near the middle part of the spinal cord, supplying the internal organs, blood vessels, and glands, and balancing the action of the parasympathetic nerves.
4 relating to, producing, or denoting an effect which arises in response to a similar action elsewhere.
– DERIVATIVES **sympathetically** adverb.
– ORIGIN mid 17th cent. (in the sense 'relating to an affinity or paranormal influence', as in **SYMPATHETIC MAGIC**): from **SYMPATHY**, on the pattern of *pathetic*.

sympathetic magic ▶ noun [mass noun] primitive or magical ritual using objects or actions resembling or symbolically associated with the event or person over which influence is sought.

sympathetic string ▶ noun each of a group of additional wire strings fitted to certain stringed instruments to give extra resonance.

sympathique /ˌsãpaˈtiːk/ ▶ adjective (of a person) agreeably in tune with another's personality or mood: *he is sympathique to women.*

■ (of a place) pleasantly and comfortably appropriate to one's tastes or inclinations: *the most important quality of a restaurant is a sympathique atmosphere.*
– ORIGIN French.

sympathize (also **-ise**) ▶ verb [no obj.] 1 feel or express sympathy: *it is easy to understand and sympathize with his predicament.*
2 agree with a sentiment or opinion: *they sympathize with critiques of traditional theory.*
– DERIVATIVES **sympathizer** noun.
– ORIGIN late 16th cent. (in the sense 'suffer with another person'): from French *sympathiser*, from *sympathie* 'sympathy, friendly understanding' (see **SYMPATHY**).

sympatholytic /ˌsɪmpəθə(ʊ)ˈlɪtɪk/ Medicine ▶ adjective (of a drug) antagonistic to or inhibiting the transmission of nerve impulses in the sympathetic nervous system.
▶ noun a drug having this effect, often used in the treatment of high blood pressure.

sympathomimetic /ˌsɪmpəθə(ʊ)mɪˈmɛtɪk, -mʌɪ-/ Medicine ▶ adjective (of a drug) producing physiological effects characteristic of the sympathetic nervous system by promoting the stimulation of sympathetic nerves.
▶ noun a drug having this effect, often used in nasal decongestants.

sympathy ▶ noun (pl. **-ies**) 1 [mass noun] feelings of pity and sorrow for someone else's misfortune: *they had great sympathy for the flood victims.*
■ (one's **sympathies**) formal expression of such feelings; condolences: *all Tony's friends joined in sending their sympathies to his widow Jean.*
2 [mass noun] understanding between people; common feeling: *the special sympathy between the two boys was obvious to all.*
■ (**sympathies**) support in the form of shared feelings or opinions: *his sympathies lay with his constituents.* ■ agreement with or approval of an opinion or aim; a favourable attitude: *I have some sympathy for this view.* ■ (in **sympathy**) relating harmoniously to something else; in keeping: *repairs had to be in sympathy with the original structure.* ■ the state or fact of responding in a way similar or corresponding to an action elsewhere: *the magnetic field oscillates in sympathy.*
– ORIGIN late 16th cent. (in sense 2): via Latin from Greek *sumpatheia*, from *sumpathēs*, from *sun-* 'with' + *pathos* 'feeling'.

sympatric /sɪmˈpatrɪk/ ▶ adjective Biology (of animals or plants, especially of related species or populations) occurring within the same geographical area; overlapping in distribution. Compare with **ALLOPATRIC**.
■ (of speciation) taking place without geographical separation.
– DERIVATIVES **sympatry** noun.
– ORIGIN early 20th cent.: from **SYM-** 'with, together' + Greek *patra* 'fatherland' + **-IC**.

sympetalous /sɪmˈpɛt(ə)ləs/ ▶ adjective Botany (of a flower or corolla) having the petals united along their margins to form a tubular shape.
– DERIVATIVES **sympetaly** noun.

symphonic ▶ adjective (of music) relating to or having the form or character of a symphony: *Franck's Symphonic Variations.*
■ relating to or written for a symphony orchestra: *symphonic and chamber music.*
– DERIVATIVES **symphonically** adverb.

symphonic poem ▶ noun another term for **TONE POEM**.

symphonist ▶ noun a composer of symphonies.

symphony ▶ noun (pl. **-ies**) an elaborate musical composition for full orchestra, typically in four movements, at least one of which is traditionally in sonata form.
■ chiefly historical an orchestral interlude in a large-scale vocal work. ■ something regarded, typically favourably, as a composition of different elements: *autumn is a symphony of texture and pattern.* ■ chiefly N. Amer. (especially in names of orchestras) short for **SYMPHONY ORCHESTRA**: *the Boston Symphony.*
– ORIGIN Middle English (denoting any of various instruments such as the dulcimer or the virginal): from Old French *symphonie*, via Latin from Greek *sumphōnia*, from *sumphōnos* 'harmonious', from *sun-* 'together' + *phōnē* 'sound'.

symphony orchestra ▶ noun a large classical orchestra, including string, wind, brass, and percussion instruments.

Symphyla /sɪm'fʌɪlə/ Zoology a small class of myriapod invertebrates which resemble the centipedes. They are small eyeless animals with one pair of legs per segment, typically living in soil and leaf mould.
– DERIVATIVES **symphylan** noun & adjective.
– ORIGIN modern Latin (plural), from **SYM-** 'together' + Greek *phulē, phulon* 'tribe'.

symphysis /'sɪmfɪsɪs/ ▶ **noun** (pl. **symphyses** /-siːz/)
1 [mass noun] the process of growing together.
2 a place where two bones are closely joined, either forming an immovable joint (as between the pubic bones in the centre of the pelvis) or completely fused (as at the midline of the lower jaw).
– DERIVATIVES **symphyseal** /-'fɪzɪəl/ adjective, **symphysial** /-'fɪzɪəl/ adjective.
– ORIGIN late 16th cent. (in sense 2): modern Latin, from Greek *sumphusis*, from *sun-* 'together' + *phusis* 'growth'.

symplasm /'sɪmplaz(ə)m/ ▶ **noun** Botany a symplast, especially the cytoplasm of which it is composed.
– DERIVATIVES **symplasmic** adjective.

symplast /'sɪmplast, -plɑːst/ ▶ **noun** Botany a continuous network of interconnected plant cell protoplasts.
– DERIVATIVES **symplastic** adjective.
– ORIGIN 1930s: from German *Symplast*.

sympodium /sɪm'pəʊdɪəm/ ▶ **noun** (pl. **sympodia** /-dɪə/) Botany the apparent main axis or stem of a plant, made up of successive secondary axes due to the death of each season's terminal bud, as in the vine.
– DERIVATIVES **sympodial** adjective.
– ORIGIN mid 19th cent.: modern Latin, from Greek *syn-* 'together' + *pous, pod-* 'foot'.

symposiast /sɪm'pəʊzɪast/ ▶ **noun** a participant in a symposium.

symposium /sɪm'pəʊzɪəm/ ▶ **noun** (pl. **symposia** /-zɪə/ or **symposiums**) a conference or meeting to discuss a particular subject.
■ a collection of essays or papers on a particular subject by a number of contributors. ■ a drinking party or convivial discussion, especially as held in ancient Greece after a banquet (and notable as the title of a work by Plato).
– ORIGIN late 16th cent. (denoting a drinking party): via Latin from Greek *sumposion*, from *sumpotēs* 'fellow drinker', from *sun-* 'together' + *potēs* 'drinker'.

symptom ▶ **noun** Medicine a physical or mental feature which is regarded as indicating a condition of disease, particularly such a feature that is apparent to the patient: *dental problems may be a symptom of other illness*. Compare with **SIGN** (in sense 1).
■ a sign of the existence of something, especially of an undesirable situation: *the government was plagued by leaks—a symptom of divisions and poor morale*.
– DERIVATIVES **symptomless** adjective.
– ORIGIN late Middle English *synthoma*, from medieval Latin, based on Greek *sumptōma* 'chance, symptom', from *sumpiptein* 'happen'; later influenced by French *symptome*.

symptomatic ▶ **adjective** serving as a symptom or sign, especially of something undesirable: *these difficulties are symptomatic of fundamental problems*.
■ exhibiting or involving symptoms: *patients with symptomatic coeliac disease | symptomatic patients*.
– DERIVATIVES **symptomatically** adverb.

symptomatology /ˌsɪm(p)tə(ʊ)mə'tɒlədʒi/ ▶ **noun** [mass noun] the set of symptoms characteristic of a medical condition or exhibited by a patient.

sympto-thermal method /ˌsɪmptə(ʊ)'θəːm(ə)l/ ▶ **noun** a contraceptive method based on the monitoring of a woman's body temperature and of physical symptoms related to ovulation, enabling awareness of the time of the month at which sexual intercourse is most likely to lead to pregnancy.

syn- ▶ **prefix** united; acting or considered together: *synchrony | syncarpous*.
– ORIGIN from Greek *sun* 'with'.

synaesthesia /ˌsɪnɪs'θiːzɪə/ (US **synesthesia**) ▶ **noun** [mass noun] Physiology & Psychology the production of a sense impression relating to one sense or part of the body by stimulation of another sense or part of the body.
– DERIVATIVES **synaesthete** /sɪn'iːsθiːt, -'ɛs-/ noun, **synaesthetic** adjective.
– ORIGIN late 19th cent.: modern Latin, from **SYN-** 'with', on the pattern of *anaesthesia*.

synagogue /'sɪnəgɒg/ ▶ **noun** the building where a Jewish assembly or congregation meets for religious observance and instruction.
■ such a Jewish assembly or congregation.
– DERIVATIVES **synagogal** adjective, **synagogical** adjective.
– ORIGIN Middle English: via Old French and late Latin from Greek *sunagōgē* 'meeting', from *sun-* 'together' + *agein* 'bring'.

synapomorphy /sɪ'napə(ʊ)ˌmɔːfi/ ▶ **noun** (pl. **-ies**) [mass noun] Biology the possession by two organisms of a characteristic (not necessarily the same in each) that is derived from one characteristic in an organism from which they both evolved.
■ [count noun] a characteristic derived in this way.
– ORIGIN 1960s: from **SYN-** 'together' + **APO-** 'away from' + Greek *morphē* 'form'.

synapse /'sʌɪnaps, 'sɪn-/ ▶ **noun** a junction between two nerve cells, consisting of a minute gap across which impulses pass by diffusion of a neurotransmitter.
– ORIGIN late 19th cent.: from Greek *sunapsis*, from *sun-* 'together' + *hapsis* 'joining', from *haptein* 'to join'.

synapsid /sʌɪ'napsɪd, sɪ-/ ▶ **noun** a fossil reptile of a Permian and Triassic group, the members of which show increasingly mammalian characteristics and include the ancestors of mammals. Also called **MAMMAL-LIKE REPTILE**.
● Subclass Synapsida; includes the pelycosaurs and the therapsids.
– ORIGIN early 20th cent.: from modern Latin *Synapsida*, from Greek *sun-* 'together' + *apsis, apsid-* 'arch'.

synapsis /sɪ'napsɪs/ ▶ **noun** [mass noun] Biology the fusion of chromosome pairs at the start of meiosis.
– ORIGIN late 19th cent.: modern Latin, from Greek *sunapsis* 'connection, junction'.

synaptic /sɪ'naptɪk, sʌɪ-/ ▶ **adjective** Anatomy of or relating to a synapse or synapses between nerve cells: *the synaptic membrane*.
– DERIVATIVES **synaptically** adverb.

synaptonemal complex /sɪˌnaptə(ʊ)'niːm(ə)l, sʌɪ-/ ▶ **noun** Biology a ladder-like series of parallel threads visible in electron microscopy adjacent to and coaxial with pairing chromosomes in meiosis.
– ORIGIN 1950s: from *synapto-* (combining form of **SYNAPSIS**) + Greek *nēma* 'thread' + **-AL**.

synarchy /'sɪnɑːki/ ▶ **noun** [mass noun] joint rule or government by two or more individuals or parties.
– DERIVATIVES **synarchic** adjective, **synarchist** noun.
– ORIGIN mid 18th cent.: from Greek *sunarkhia*, from *sunarkhein* 'rule jointly'.

synarthrosis /ˌsɪnɑː'θrəʊsɪs/ ▶ **noun** (pl. **synarthroses** /-siːz/) Anatomy an immovably fixed joint between bones connected by fibrous tissue (for example, the sutures of the skull).
– ORIGIN late 16th cent.: from modern Latin, from Greek *sunarthrōsis*, from *sun-* 'together' + *arthrōsis* 'jointing' (from *arthron* 'joint').

synastry /sɪ'nastri/ ▶ **noun** [mass noun] Astrology comparison between the horoscopes of two or more people in order to determine their likely compatibility and relationship.
– ORIGIN mid 17th cent.: via late Latin from Greek *sunastria*, from *sun-* 'together' + *astēr, astr-* 'star'.

sync (also **synch**) informal ▶ **noun** [mass noun] synchronization: *images flash on to your screen* **in sync with** *the music*.
▶ **verb** [with obj.] synchronize: *the flash needs to be synced to your camera*.
– PHRASES **in** (or **out of**) **sync** working well (or badly) together; in (or out of) agreement: *her eyes and her brain seemed to be seriously out of sync*.
– ORIGIN 1920s: abbreviation.

syncarpous /sɪn'kɑːpəs/ ▶ **adjective** Botany (of a flower, fruit, or ovary) having the carpels united. Often contrasted with **APOCARPOUS**.
– ORIGIN mid 19th cent.: from **SYN-** 'together' + Greek *karpos* 'fruit' + **-OUS**.

synchondrosis /ˌsɪŋkɒn'drəʊsɪs/ ▶ **noun** (pl. **synchondroses** /-siːz/) Anatomy an almost immovable joint between bones bound by a layer of cartilage, as in the spinal vertebrae.
– ORIGIN late 16th cent.: from modern Latin, from Greek *sunkhondrōsis*, from *sun-* 'together' + *khondros* 'cartilage'.

synchro /'sɪŋkrəʊ/ ▶ **noun 1** short for **SYNCHROMESH**.
2 synchronized or synchronization: *tape editing with synchro start*.
3 short for **SYNCHRONIZED SWIMMING**.

synchro- ▶ **combining form** synchronous: *synchrotron*.

synchrocyclotron /ˌsɪŋkrə(ʊ)'sʌɪklə(ʊ)trɒn/ ▶ **noun** Physics a cyclotron able to achieve higher energies by decreasing the frequency of the accelerating electric field as the particles increase in energy and mass.

synchromesh ▶ **noun** [mass noun] a system of gear changing, especially in motor vehicles, in which the driving and driven gearwheels are made to revolve at the same speed during engagement by means of a set of friction clutches, thereby easing the change.
– ORIGIN 1920s: contraction of *synchronized mesh*.

synchronic /sɪŋ'krɒnɪk/ ▶ **adjective** concerned with something, especially a language, as it exists at one point in time: *synchronic linguistics*. Often contrasted with **DIACHRONIC**.
– DERIVATIVES **synchronically** adverb.
– ORIGIN 1920s: from late Latin *synchronus* (see **SYNCHRONOUS**) + **-IC**.

synchronicity /ˌsɪŋkrə'nɪsɪti/ ▶ **noun** [mass noun]
1 the simultaneous occurrence of events which appear significantly related but have no discernible causal connection: *such synchronicity is quite staggering*.
2 another term for **SYNCHRONY** (in sense 1).

synchronism /'sɪŋkrənɪz(ə)m/ ▶ **noun** another term for **SYNCHRONY**.
– DERIVATIVES **synchronistic** adjective, **synchronistically** adverb.
– ORIGIN late 16th cent.: from Greek *sunkhronismos*, from *sunkhronos* (see **SYNCHRONOUS**).

synchronize /'sɪŋkrənʌɪz/ (also **-ise**) ▶ **verb** [with obj.] cause to occur or operate at the same time or rate: *soldiers used watches to synchronize movements | synchronize your hand gestures with your main points*.
■ [no obj.] occur at the same time or rate: *sometimes converging swells will synchronize to produce a peak*. ■ adjust (a clock or watch) to show the same time as another: *It is now 05.48. Synchronize watches*. ■ [no obj.] tally; agree: *their version failed to synchronize with the police view*. ■ coordinate; combine: *both media* **synchronize** *national interests* **with** *multinational scope*.
– DERIVATIVES **synchronization** noun, **synchronizer** noun.

synchronized swimming ▶ **noun** [mass noun] a sport in which members of a team of swimmers perform coordinated or identical movements in time to music.
– DERIVATIVES **synchronized swimmer** noun.

synchronous /'sɪŋkrənəs/ ▶ **adjective 1** existing or occurring at the same time: *glaciations were approximately synchronous in both hemispheres*.
2 (of a satellite or its orbit) making or denoting an orbit around the earth or another celestial body in which one revolution is completed in the period taken for the body to rotate about its axis.
– DERIVATIVES **synchronously** adverb.
– ORIGIN mid 17th cent.: from late Latin *synchronus* (from Greek *sunkhronos*, from *sun-* 'together' + *khronos* 'time') + **-OUS**.

synchronous motor ▶ **noun** an electric motor having a speed exactly proportional to the current frequency.

synchrony /'sɪŋkrəni/ ▶ **noun** [mass noun] **1** simultaneous action, development, or occurrence.
■ the state of operating or developing according to the same time scale as something else: *some individuals do not remain* **in synchrony with** *the twenty-four-hour day*.
2 synchronic treatment or study: *the structuralist distinction between synchrony and diachrony*.
– ORIGIN mid 19th cent.: from Greek *sunkhronos* (see **SYNCHRONOUS**).

synchrotron /'sɪŋkrə(ʊ)trɒn/ ▶ **noun** Physics a cyclotron in which the magnetic field strength increases with the energy of the particles to keep their orbital radius constant.

synchrotron radiation ▶ **noun** [mass noun] Physics polarized radiation emitted by a charged particle spinning in a magnetic field.

syncline /'sɪŋklʌɪn/ ▶ **noun** Geology a trough or fold of stratified rock in which the strata slope upwards from the axis. Compare with **ANTICLINE**.
– DERIVATIVES **synclinal** adjective.

S

– ORIGIN late 19th cent.: from **SYN-** 'together' + Greek *klinein* 'to lean', on the pattern of *incline*.

syncopate /ˈsɪŋkəpeɪt/ ▶ **verb** [with obj.] **1** [usu. as adj. **syncopated**] displace the beats or accents in (music or a rhythm) so that strong beats become weak and vice versa: *syncopated dance music.*
2 shorten (a word) by dropping sounds or letters in the middle, as in *symbology* for *symbolology*, or *Gloster* for *Gloucester*.
– DERIVATIVES **syncopation** noun, **syncopator** noun.
– ORIGIN early 17th cent.: from late Latin *syncopat-* 'affected with syncope', from the verb *syncopare* 'to swoon' (see **SYNCOPE**).

syncope /ˈsɪŋkəpi/ ▶ **noun** [mass noun] **1** Medicine temporary loss of consciousness caused by a fall in blood pressure.
2 Grammar the omission of sounds or letters from within a word, for example when *library* is pronounced /ˈlʌɪbri/.
– DERIVATIVES **syncopal** adjective.
– ORIGIN late Middle English: via late Latin from Greek *sunkopē*, from *sun-* 'together' + *koptein* 'strike, cut off'.

syncretism /ˈsɪŋkrɪtɪz(ə)m/ ▶ **noun** [mass noun] **1** the amalgamation or attempted amalgamation of different religions, cultures, or schools of thought.
2 Linguistics the merging of different inflectional varieties of a word during the development of a language.
– DERIVATIVES **syncretic** adjective, **syncretist** noun & adjective, **syncretistic** adjective.
– ORIGIN early 17th cent.: from modern Latin *syncretismus*, from Greek *sunkrētismos*, from *sunkrētizein* 'unite against a third party', from *sun-* 'together' + *krēs* 'Cretan' (originally with reference to ancient Cretan communities).

syncretize (also **-ise**) ▶ **verb** [with obj.] attempt to amalgamate or reconcile (differing things, especially religious beliefs, cultural elements, or schools of thought).
– DERIVATIVES **syncretization** noun.

syncytium /sɪnˈsɪtɪəm/ ▶ **noun** (pl. **syncytia** /-tɪə/) Biology a single cell or cytoplasmic mass containing several nuclei, formed by fusion of cells or by division of nuclei.
■ Embryology material of this kind forming the outermost layer of the trophoblast.
– DERIVATIVES **syncytial** adjective.
– ORIGIN late 19th cent.: from **SYN-** 'together' + **-CYTE** 'cell' + **-IUM**.

syndactyly /sɪnˈdaktɪli/ ▶ **noun** [mass noun] Medicine & Zoology the condition of having some or all of the fingers or toes wholly or partly united, either naturally (as in web-footed animals) or as a malformation.
– ORIGIN mid 19th cent.: from **SYN-** 'united' + Greek *daktulos* 'finger' + **-Y**[3].

syndesmosis /ˌsɪndɛzˈməʊsɪs/ ▶ **noun** (pl. **syndesmoses** /-siːz/) Anatomy an immovable joint in which bones are joined by connective tissue (e.g. between the fibula and tibia at the ankle).
– ORIGIN late 16th cent.: modern Latin, from Greek *sundesmos* 'binding, fastening'.

syndetic /sɪnˈdɛtɪk/ ▶ **adjective** Grammar of or using conjunctions.
– ORIGIN early 17th cent.: from Greek *sundetikos*, from *sundein* 'bind together'.

syndic ▶ **noun** **1** a government official in various countries.
2 (in the UK) a business agent of certain universities and corporations, especially a member of a senate committee at Cambridge University.
– DERIVATIVES **syndical** adjective.
– ORIGIN early 17th cent.: from French, via late Latin from Greek *sundikos*, from *sun-* 'together' + *dikē* 'justice'.

syndicalism ▶ **noun** [mass noun] historical a movement for transferring the ownership and control of the means of production and distribution to workers' unions. Influenced by Proudhon and by the French social philosopher Georges Sorel (1847–1922), syndicalism developed in French trade unions during the late 19th century and was at its most vigorous between 1900 and 1914, particularly in France, Italy, Spain, and the US.
– DERIVATIVES **syndicalist** noun & adjective.
– ORIGIN early 20th cent.: from French *syndicalisme*, from *syndical*, from *syndic* 'a delegate' (see **SYNDIC**).

syndicate ▶ **noun** /ˈsɪndɪkət/ a group of individuals or organizations combined to promote some common interest: *large-scale buyouts involving a syndicate of financial institutions | a crime syndicate.*
■ an association or agency supplying material simultaneously to a number of newspapers or periodicals. ■ a committee of syndics.
▶ **verb** /ˈsɪndɪkeɪt/ [with obj.] (usu. **be syndicated**) control or manage by a syndicate: *the loans are syndicated to a group of banks.*
■ publish or broadcast (material) simultaneously in a number of newspapers, television stations, etc.: *her cartoon strip is syndicated in 1,400 newspapers worldwide.* ■ sell (a horse) to a syndicate: *the stallion was syndicated for a record $5.4 million.*
– DERIVATIVES **syndication** noun.
– ORIGIN early 17th cent. (denoting a committee of syndics): from French *syndicat*, from medieval Latin *syndicatus*, from late Latin *syndicus* 'delegate of a corporation' (see **SYNDIC**). Current verb senses date from the late 19th cent.

syndiotactic /ˌsɪndʌɪə(ʊ)ˈtaktɪk/ ▶ **adjective** Chemistry (of a polymer or polymeric structure) in which the repeating units have alternating stereochemical configurations.
– ORIGIN 1950s: from Greek *sunduo* 'two together' + *taktos* 'arranged' + **-IC**.

syndrome ▶ **noun** a group of symptoms which consistently occur together or a condition characterized by a set of associated symptoms: *a rare syndrome in which the production of white blood cells is damaged.*
■ a characteristic combination of opinions, emotions, or behaviour: *the 'Not In My Back Yard' syndrome.*
– DERIVATIVES **syndromic** adjective.
– ORIGIN mid 16th cent.: modern Latin, from Greek *sundromē*, from *sun-* 'together' + *dramein* 'to run'.

syne /sʌɪn/ ▶ **adverb** Scottish ago. See also **AULD LANG SYNE**, **LANG SYNE**.
– ORIGIN Middle English: contraction of dialect *sithen* 'ever since'.

synecdoche /sɪˈnɛkdəki/ ▶ **noun** a figure of speech in which a part is made to represent the whole or vice versa, as in *England lost by six wickets* (meaning 'the English cricket team').
– DERIVATIVES **synecdochic** adjective, **synecdochical** adjective, **synecdochically** adverb.
– ORIGIN late Middle English: via Latin from Greek *sunekdokhē*, from *sun-* 'together' + *ekdekhesthai* 'take up'.

synecology /ˌsɪnɪˈkɒlədʒi/ ▶ **noun** [mass noun] the ecological study of whole plant or animal communities. Contrasted with **AUTECOLOGY**.
– DERIVATIVES **synecological** /-ˌiːkəˈlɒdʒɪk(ə)l, -ˌɛk-/ adjective, **synecologist** noun.
– ORIGIN early 20th cent.: from **SYN-** 'together' + **ECOLOGY**.

synectics /sɪˈnɛktɪks/ ▶ **plural noun** [treated as sing.] trademark (in the US) a problem-solving technique which seeks to promote creative thinking, typically among small groups of people of diverse experience and expertise.
– ORIGIN 1960s: from late Latin *synecticus* (based on Greek *sunekhein* 'hold together'), on the pattern of *dialectics*.

syneresis /sɪˈnɪərɪsɪs/ ▶ **noun** (pl. **synereses** /-siːz/) [mass noun] **1** the contraction of two vowels into a diphthong or single vowel.
2 Chemistry the contraction of a gel accompanied by the separating out of liquid.
– ORIGIN late 16th cent.: via late Latin from Greek *sunairesis*, based on *sun-* 'together' + *hairein* 'take'.

synergist ▶ **noun** a substance, organ, or other agent that participates in an effect of synergy.
– DERIVATIVES **synergistic** adjective, **synergistically** adverb.

synergy /ˈsɪnədʒi/ (also **synergism**) ▶ **noun** [mass noun] the interaction or cooperation of two or more organizations, substances, or other agents to produce a combined effect greater than the sum of their separate effects: *the synergy between artist and record company.*
– DERIVATIVES **synergetic** adjective, **synergic** adjective.
– ORIGIN mid 19th cent.: from Greek *sunergos* 'working together', from *sun-* 'together' + *ergon* 'work'.

synesthesia ▶ **noun** US spelling of **SYNAESTHESIA**.

synfuel /ˈsɪnfjʊəl, sɪnˈfjuːəl/ ▶ **noun** [mass noun] fuel made from coal, oil shale, etc., as a substitute for a petroleum product.

syngamy /ˈsɪŋgəmi/ ▶ **noun** [mass noun] Biology the fusion of two cells, or of their nuclei, in reproduction.
– ORIGIN early 20th cent.: from **SYN-** 'with' + Greek *gamos* 'marriage'.

syngas ▶ **noun** short for **SYNTHESIS GAS**.

Synge /sɪŋ/, J. M. (1871–1909), Irish dramatist; full name *Edmund John Millington Synge*. *The Playboy of the Western World* (1907) caused riots at the Abbey Theatre, Dublin, because of its explicit language and its implication that Irish peasants would condone a brutal murder.

syngeneic /ˌsɪndʒɪˈniːɪk, ˌsɪndʒɪˈneɪɪk/ ▶ **adjective** Medicine & Biology (of organisms or cells) genetically similar or identical and hence immunologically compatible, especially so closely related that transplantation does not provoke an immune response.
– ORIGIN 1960s: from **SYN-** 'together' + Greek *genea* 'race, stock' + **-IC**.

syngenetic /ˌsɪndʒɪˈnɛtɪk/ ▶ **adjective** Geology relating to or denoting a mineral deposit or formation produced at the same time as the enclosing or surrounding rock.

synod /ˈsɪnəd, -ɒd/ ▶ **noun** **1** an assembly of the clergy and sometimes also the laity in a diocese or other division of a particular Church.
2 a Presbyterian ecclesiastical court above the presbyteries and subject to the General Assembly.
– ORIGIN late Middle English: via late Latin from Greek *sunodos* 'meeting', from *sun-* 'together' + *hodos* 'way'.

synodic /sɪˈnɒdɪk/ ▶ **adjective** Astronomy relating to or involving the conjunction of stars, planets, or other celestial objects.
– ORIGIN mid 17th cent.: via late Latin from Greek *sunodikos*, from *sunodos* (see **SYNOD**).

synodical ▶ **adjective** **1** Christian Church of, relating to, or constituted as a synod: *synodical government.*
2 Astronomy another term for **SYNODIC**.
– DERIVATIVES **synodal** adjective (only in sense 1).

synodic month ▶ **noun** Astronomy another term for **LUNAR MONTH**.

synodic period ▶ **noun** Astronomy the time between successive conjunctions of a planet with the sun.

synonym /ˈsɪnənɪm/ ▶ **noun** a word or phrase that means exactly or nearly the same as another word or phrase in the same language, for example *shut* is a synonym of *close*.
■ a person or thing so closely associated with a particular quality or idea that the mention of their name calls it to mind: *the Victorian age is a synonym for sexual puritanism.* ■ Biology a taxonomic name which has the same application as another, especially one which has been superseded and is no longer valid.
– DERIVATIVES **synonymic** adjective, **synonymity** noun.
– ORIGIN late Middle English: via Latin from Greek *sunōnumon*, neuter (used as a noun) of the adjective *sunōnumos*, from *sun-* 'with' + *onoma* 'name'.

synonymous /sɪˈnɒnɪməs/ ▶ **adjective** (of a word or phrase) having the same meaning as another word or phrase in the same language: *aggression is often taken as synonymous with violence.*
■ closely associated with or suggestive of something: *his deeds had made his name synonymous with victory.*
– DERIVATIVES **synonymously** adverb, **synonymousness** noun.

synonymy /sɪˈnɒnɪmi/ ▶ **noun** [mass noun] the state of being synonymous.
– ORIGIN mid 16th cent.: via late Latin from Greek *sunōnumia*, from *sunōnumos* (see **SYNONYM**).

synopsis /sɪˈnɒpsɪs/ ▶ **noun** (pl. **synopses** /-siːz/) a brief summary or general survey of something: *a synopsis of the insurance cover provided is set out below.*
■ an outline of the plot of a play, film, or book.
– DERIVATIVES **synopsize** (also **-ise**) verb.
– ORIGIN early 17th cent.: via late Latin from Greek, from *sun-* 'together' + *opsis* 'seeing'.

synoptic ▶ **adjective** **1** of or forming a general summary or synopsis: *a synoptic outline of the contents.*
■ taking or involving a comprehensive mental view: *a synoptic model of higher education.*
2 of or relating to the Synoptic Gospels.
▶ **noun** (**Synoptics**) the Synoptic Gospels.
– DERIVATIVES **synoptical** adjective, **synoptically** adverb.

– ORIGIN early 17th cent.: from Greek *sunoptikos*, from *sunopsis* (see **SYNOPSIS**).

Synoptic Gospels ▶ **plural noun** the Gospels of Matthew, Mark, and Luke, which describe events from a similar point of view, as contrasted with that of John.

synoptist ▶ **noun** the writer of a Synoptic Gospel.

synostosis /ˌsɪnɒˈstəʊsɪs/ ▶ **noun** (pl. **synostoses** /-siːz/) [mass noun] Physiology & Medicine the union or fusion of adjacent bones by the growth of bony substance, either as a normal process during growth or as the result of ankylosis.
– ORIGIN mid 19th cent.: from **SYN-** 'together' + Greek *osteon* 'bone' + **-OSIS**.

synovial /sʌɪˈnəʊvɪəl, sɪ-/ ▶ **adjective** relating to or denoting a type of joint which is surrounded by a thick flexible membrane forming a sac into which is secreted a viscous fluid that lubricates the joint.
– ORIGIN mid 18th cent.: from modern Latin *synovia*, probably formed arbitrarily by Paracelsus.

synovitis /ˌsʌɪnə(ʊ)ˈvʌɪtɪs, ˌsɪn-/ ▶ **noun** [mass noun] Medicine inflammation of a synovial membrane.

synsacrum /sɪnˈseɪkrəm, sɪnˈsakrəm/ ▶ **noun** (pl. **synsacra** /-krə/ or **synsacrums**) Zoology an elongated composite sacrum containing a number of fused vertebrae, present in birds and some extinct reptiles.

syntactic /sɪnˈtaktɪk/ ▶ **adjective** of or according to syntax: *syntactic analysis*.
– DERIVATIVES **syntactical** adjective, **syntactically** adverb.
– ORIGIN early 19th cent.: from Greek *suntaktikos*, from *suntassein* 'arrange together' (see **SYNTAX**).

syntagm /ˈsɪntam/ (also **syntagma** /sɪnˈtagmə/) ▶ **noun** (pl. **syntagms** or **syntagmas** or **syntagmata** /-mətə/) a linguistic unit consisting of a set of linguistic forms (phonemes, words, or phrases) that are in a sequential relationship to one another. Often contrasted with **PARADIGM**.
▪ the relationship between any two such forms.
– ORIGIN mid 17th cent.: via late Latin from Greek *suntagma*, from *suntassein* 'arrange together'.

syntagmatic /ˌsɪntagˈmatɪk/ ▶ **adjective** of or denoting the relationship between two or more linguistic units used sequentially to make well-formed structures. Contrasted with **PARADIGMATIC**.
– DERIVATIVES **syntagmatically** adverb, **syntagmatics** noun.

syntax /ˈsɪntaks/ ▶ **noun** [mass noun] the arrangement of words and phrases to create well-formed sentences in a language: *the syntax of English*.
▪ a set of rules for or an analysis of this: *generative syntax*. ▪ the branch of linguistics that deals with this.
– ORIGIN late 16th cent.: from French *syntaxe*, or via late Latin from Greek *suntaxis*, from *sun-* 'together' + *tassein* 'arrange'.

syntenic /sɪnˈtɛnɪk/ ▶ **adjective** Genetics (of genes) occurring on the same chromosome: *syntenic sequences*.
– DERIVATIVES **synteny** noun.
– ORIGIN 1970s: from **SYN-** 'together' + Greek *tainia* 'band, ribbon' + **-IC**.

synth ▶ **noun** informal short for **SYNTHESIZER**.
– DERIVATIVES **synthy** adjective.

synthase /ˈsɪnθeɪz/ ▶ **noun** [often with modifier] Biochemistry an enzyme which catalyses the linking together of two molecules, especially without the direct involvement of ATP: *nitric oxide synthases*. Compare with **LIGASE**.

synthesis /ˈsɪnθɪsɪs/ ▶ **noun** (pl. **syntheses** /-siːz/) [mass noun] combination or composition, in particular:
▪ the combination of ideas to form a theory or system: *the synthesis of intellect and emotion in his work* | [count noun] *the ideology represented a synthesis of certain ideas*. Often contrasted with **ANALYSIS**. ▪ the production of chemical compounds by reaction from simpler materials: *the synthesis of methanol from carbon monoxide and hydrogen*. ▪ (in Hegelian philosophy) the final stage in the process of dialectical reasoning, in which a new idea resolves the conflict between thesis and antithesis. ▪ Grammar the process of making compound and derivative words. ▪ Linguistics the tendency in a language to use inflected forms rather than word order to express grammatical structure.
– DERIVATIVES **synthesist** noun.
– ORIGIN early 17th cent.: via Latin from Greek *sunthesis*, from *suntithenai* 'place together'.

synthesis gas ▶ **noun** [mass noun] a mixture of carbon monoxide and hydrogen produced industrially, especially from coal, and used as a feedstock in making synthetic chemicals.

synthesize /ˈsɪnθɪsʌɪz/ (also **synthetize**, **-ise**) ▶ **verb** [with obj.] make (something) by synthesis, especially chemically: *man synthesizes new chemical poisons and sprays the countryside wholesale*.
▪ combine (a number of things) into a coherent whole: *pupils should synthesize the data they have gathered* | *Darwinian theory has been synthesized with modern genetics*. ▪ produce (sound) electronically: *trigger chips that synthesize speech* | [as adj. **synthesized**] *synthesized chords*.

synthesizer ▶ **noun** an electronic musical instrument, typically operated by a keyboard, producing a wide variety of sounds by generating and combining signals of different frequencies.

synthetic /sɪnˈθɛtɪk/ ▶ **adjective** (of a substance) made by chemical synthesis, especially to imitate a natural product: *synthetic rubber*.
▪ (of an emotion or action) not genuine; insincere: *their tears are a bit synthetic*. ▪ Logic (of a proposition) having truth or falsity determinable by recourse to experience. Compare with **ANALYTIC**. ▪ Linguistics (of a language) characterized by the use of inflections rather than word order to express grammatical structure. Contrasted with **ANALYTIC** and **AGGLUTINATIVE**.
▶ **noun** (usu. **synthetics**) a synthetic material or chemical, especially a textile fibre.
– DERIVATIVES **synthetical** adjective, **synthetically** adverb.
– ORIGIN late 17th cent.: from French *synthétique* or modern Latin *syntheticus*, from Greek *sunthetikos*, based on *suntithenai* 'place together'.

synthetic resin ▶ **noun** see **RESIN**.

synthon /ˈsɪnθɒn/ ▶ **noun** Chemistry a constituent part of a molecule to be synthesized which is regarded as the basis of a synthetic procedure.
– ORIGIN 1960s: from **SYNTHESIS** + **-ON**.

syntonic /sɪnˈtɒnɪk/ ▶ **adjective** Psychology (of a person) responsive to and in harmony with their environment so that affect is appropriate to the given situation: *culturally syntonic*.
▪ [in combination] (of a psychiatric condition or psychological process) consistent with other aspects of an individual's personality and belief system: *this phobia was ego-syntonic*. ▪ historical relating to or denoting the lively and responsive type of temperament which was considered liable to manic-depressive psychosis. See also **CYCLOTHYMIA**.
– DERIVATIVES **syntone** noun.
– ORIGIN late 19th cent.: from German *Syntonie* 'state of being syntonic' + **-IC**.

syntype ▶ **noun** Botany & Zoology each of a set of type specimens of equal status, upon which the description and name of a new species is based. Compare with **HOLOTYPE**.

syphilis ▶ **noun** [mass noun] a chronic bacterial disease that is contracted chiefly by infection during sexual intercourse, but also congenitally by infection of a developing fetus.
● This is caused by the spirochaete *Treponema pallidum*. The infection progresses in four successive stages: **primary syphilis**, characterized by a chancre in the part infected; **secondary syphilis**, affecting chiefly the skin, lymph nodes, and mucous membranes; **tertiary syphilis**, involving the spread of tumour-like lesions (gummas) throughout the body, frequently damaging the cardiovascular and central nervous systems; **quaternary syphilis** neurosyphilis.
– DERIVATIVES **syphilitic** adjective & noun.
– ORIGIN early 18th cent.: modern Latin, from *Syphilis, sive Morbus Gallicus*, the title of a Latin poem (1530), from the name of the character *Syphilus*, the supposed first sufferer of the disease.

syphon ▶ **noun** & **verb** variant spelling of **SIPHON**.

SYR ▶ **abbreviation for** Syria (international vehicle registration).

Syracuse 1 /ˈsʌɪrəˌkjuːz/ a port on the east coast of Sicily; pop. 125,440 (1990). It became a flourishing centre of Greek culture, especially in the 5th and 4th centuries BC under the rule of Dionysius I and II. It was taken by the Romans at the end of the 3rd century BC. Italian name **SIRACUSA**.
2 /ˈsɪrəˌkjuːz/ a city in New York State, to the south-east of Lake Ontario; pop. 163,860 (1990). The site of salt springs, it was an important centre of salt production during the 19th century.

Syrah /ˈsiːrə/ ▶ **noun** another term for **SHIRAZ**[2].

Syr-Darya /ˌsɪrdarʲˈja/ Russian name for **SIRDARYO**.

syrette /sɪˈrɛt/ ▶ **noun** Medicine trademark a disposable injection unit comprising a collapsible tube with an attached hypodermic needle and a single dose of a drug, commonly morphine.
– ORIGIN 1940s: from **SYRINGE** + **-ETTE**.

Syria /ˈsɪrɪə/ a country in the Middle East with a coastline on the eastern Mediterranean Sea; pop. 12,824,000 (est. 1991); official language, Arabic; capital, Damascus.

Syria was the site of various early civilizations, notably that of the Phoenicians. Falling successively within the empires of Persia, Macedon, and Rome, it became a centre of Islamic power and civilization from the 7th century and a province of the Ottoman Empire in 1516. After the Turkish defeat in the First World War Syria was mandated to France, becoming independent with the ejection of Vichy troops by the Allies in 1941. From 1958 to 1961 Syria was united with Egypt as the United Arab Republic.

– DERIVATIVES **Syrian** adjective & noun.

Syriac /ˈsɪrɪak/ ▶ **noun** [mass noun] the language of ancient Syria, a western dialect of Aramaic in which many important early Christian texts are preserved, and which is still used by Syrian Christians as a liturgical language.
▶ **adjective** of or relating to this language.

syringa /sɪˈrɪŋgə/ ▶ **noun 1** a plant of the genus *Syringa* (family Oleaceae), especially (in gardening) the lilac.
2 informal a mock orange.
– ORIGIN modern Latin, from Greek *surinx*, *suring-* 'tube' (with reference to the use of its stems as pipe-stems).

syringe /sɪˈrɪn(d)ʒ, ˈsɪ-/ ▶ **noun** Medicine a tube with a nozzle and piston or bulb for sucking in and ejecting liquid in a thin stream, used for cleaning wounds or body cavities, or fitted with a hollow needle for injecting or withdrawing fluids.
▪ any similar device used in gardening or cooking.
▶ **verb** (**syringing**) [with obj.] spray liquid into (the ear or a wound) with a syringe: *I had my ears syringed*.
▪ spray liquid over (plants) with a syringe: *syringe the leaves frequently during warm weather*.
– ORIGIN late Middle English: from medieval Latin *syringa*, from *syrinx* (see **SYRINX**).

syringomyelia /sɪˌrɪŋgə(ʊ)mʌɪˈiːlɪə/ ▶ **noun** [mass noun] Medicine a chronic progressive disease in which longitudinal cavities form in the cervical region of the spinal cord. This characteristically results in wasting of the muscles in the hands and a loss of sensation.
– ORIGIN late 19th cent.: modern Latin, from Greek *surinx*, *suring-* 'tube, channel' + *muelos* 'marrow'.

syrinx /ˈsɪrɪŋks/ ▶ **noun** (pl. **syrinxes**) **1** a set of pan pipes.
2 Ornithology the lower larynx or voice organ in birds, situated at or near the junction of the trachea and bronchi and well-developed in songbirds.
– ORIGIN early 17th cent.: via Latin from Greek *surinx* 'pipe, channel'.

Syro- /ˈsʌɪrəʊ/ ▶ **combining form** Syrian; Syrian and ...: *Syro-Palestinian*.
▪ relating to Syria.

syrphid /ˈsəːfɪd/ ▶ **noun** Entomology a fly of the hoverfly family (Syrphidae).
– ORIGIN late 19th cent.: from modern Latin *Syrphidae* (plural), from the genus name *Syrphus*, from Greek *surphos* 'gnat'.

syrtaki /səːˈtaki/ (also **sirtaki**) ▶ **noun** (pl. **syrtakis**) a Greek folk dance in which dancers form a line or chain.
– ORIGIN modern Greek, from Greek *surtos* 'drawn, led' + the diminutive suffix *-aki*.

syrup (US also **sirup**) ▶ **noun** [mass noun] a thick sweet liquid made by dissolving sugar in boiling water, often used for preserving fruit.
▪ a thick sweet liquid containing medicine or used as a drink: *cough syrup*. ▪ a thick, sticky liquid obtained from sugar cane as part of the processing of sugar. ▪ figurative excessive sweetness or sentimentality of style or manner: *Mr Gurney's poems are almost all of them syrup*.
– ORIGIN late Middle English: from Old French *sirop* or medieval Latin *siropus*, from Arabic *šarāb* 'beverage'; compare with **SHERBET** and **SHRUB**[2].

syrup of figs ▶ **noun** [mass noun] a laxative syrup made from dried figs, typically with senna and carminatives.

syrupy (US also **sirupy**) ▶ **adjective** having the consistency or sweetness of syrup: *syrupy puddings*.

■figurative excessively sentimental: *a particularly syrupy moment from a corny film.*

sysop /ˈsɪsɒp/ ▶ **noun** Computing a system operator.
– ORIGIN 1980s: abbreviation.

system ▶ **noun 1** a set of connected things or parts forming a complex whole, in particular:
■ a set of things working together as parts of a mechanism or an interconnecting network: *the state railway system | fluid is pushed through a system of pipes or channels.* ■ Physiology a set of organs in the body with a common structure or function: *the digestive system.* ■ the human or animal body as a whole: *you need to get the cholesterol out of your system.* ■ Computing a group of related hardware units or programs or both, especially when dedicated to a single application. ■ Geology (in chronostratigraphy) a major range of strata that corresponds to a period in time, subdivided into series. ■ Astronomy a group of celestial objects connected by their mutual attractive forces, especially moving in orbits about a centre: *the system of bright stars known as the Gould Belt.* ■ short for **CRYSTAL SYSTEM**.
2 a set of principles or procedures according to which something is done; an organized scheme or method: *a multiparty system of government | the public-school system.*
■ [mass noun] orderliness; method: *there was no system at all in the company.* ■ a method of choosing one's procedure in gambling. ■ a set of rules used in measurement or classification: *the metric system.* ■ **(the system)** the prevailing political or social order, especially when regarded as oppressive and intransigent: *don't try bucking the system.*
3 Music a set of staves in a musical score joined by a brace.
– PHRASES **get something out of one's system** informal get rid of a preoccupation or anxiety: *yelling is an ace way of getting stress out of your system.*
– DERIVATIVES **systemless** adjective.
– ORIGIN early 17th cent.: from French *système* or late Latin *systema*, from Greek *sustēma*, from *sun-* 'with' + *histanai* 'set up'.

systematic ▶ **adjective** done or acting according to a fixed plan or system; methodical: *a systematic search of the whole city.*
– DERIVATIVES **systematically** adverb, **systematist** /ˈsɪstəmətɪst/ noun.
– ORIGIN early 18th cent.: from French *systématique*, via late Latin from late Greek *sustēmatikos*, from *sustēma* (see **SYSTEM**).

systematic desensitization (also **-isation**)

▶ **noun** [mass noun] Psychiatry a treatment for phobias in which the patient is exposed to progressively more anxiety-provoking stimuli and taught relaxation techniques.

systematic error ▶ **noun** Statistics an error having a non-zero mean, so that its effect is not reduced when observations are averaged.

systematics ▶ **plural noun** [treated as sing.] the branch of biology that deals with classification and nomenclature; taxonomy.

systematic theology ▶ **noun** [mass noun] a form of theology in which the aim is to arrange religious truths in a self-consistent whole.
– DERIVATIVES **systematic theologian** noun.

systematize /ˈsɪstəməˌtʌɪz/ (also **-ise**) ▶ **verb** [with obj.] arrange according to an organized system; make systematic: *Galen set about systematizing medical thought* | [as adj. **systematized**] *systematized reading schemes.*
– DERIVATIVES **systematization** noun, **systematizer** noun.

system building ▶ **noun** [mass noun] **1** systematic thought; the process of building an intellectual system.
2 a method of construction using standardized prefabricated components.

systemic /sɪˈstɛmɪk, -ˈstiːm-/ ▶ **adjective 1** of or relating to a system, especially as opposed to a particular part: *the disease is localized rather than systemic.*
■ (of an insecticide, fungicide, or similar substance) entering the plant via the roots or shoots and passing through the tissues.
2 Physiology denoting the part of the circulatory system concerned with the transport of oxygen to and carbon dioxide from the body in general, especially as distinct from the pulmonary part concerned with the transport of oxygen from and carbon dioxide to the lungs.
– DERIVATIVES **systemically** adverb.
– ORIGIN early 19th cent.: formed irregularly from **SYSTEM** + **-IC**.

systemic grammar (also **systemic linguistics**) ▶ **noun** [mass noun] Linguistics a method of analysis based on the conception of language as a network of systems determining the options from which speakers choose in accordance with their communicative goals.

system integrator (also **systems integrator**) ▶ **noun** see **INTEGRATOR**.

systemize (also **-ise**) ▶ **verb** another term for **SYSTEMATIZE**.
– DERIVATIVES **systemization** noun, **systemizer** noun.

system operator (also **systems operator**) ▶ **noun** Computing a person who manages the operation of a computer system, especially an electronic bulletin board.

systems analyst ▶ **noun** a person who analyses a complex process or operation in order to improve its efficiency, especially by applying a computer system.
– DERIVATIVES **systems analysis** noun.

systole /ˈsɪst(ə)li/ ▶ **noun** Physiology the phase of the heartbeat when the heart muscle contracts and pumps blood from the chambers into the arteries. Often contrasted with **DIASTOLE**.
– DERIVATIVES **systolic** /-ˈstɒlɪk/ adjective.
– ORIGIN late 16th cent.: via late Latin from Greek *sustolē*, from *sustellein* 'to contract'.

syzygy /ˈsɪzɪdʒi/ ▶ **noun** (pl. **-ies**) Astronomy a conjunction or opposition, especially of the moon with the sun: *the planets were aligned in syzygy.*
■ a pair of connected or corresponding things.
– ORIGIN early 17th cent.: via late Latin from Greek *suzugia*, from *suzugos* 'yoked, paired', from *sun-* 'with, together' + the stem of *zeugnunai* 'to yoke'.

Szczecin /ˈʃtʃɛtʃɪn/ a city in NW Poland, a port on the Oder River near the border with Germany; pop. 413,437 (1990). German name **STETTIN**.

Szechuan /sɛˈtʃwɑːn/ (also **Szechwan**) variant of **SICHUAN**.

Szeged /ˈsɛgɛd/ a city in southern Hungary, a port on the River Tisza near the border with Serbia; pop. 178,500 (1993).

Szent-Györgyi /sɛntˈdʒɜːdʒi/, Albert von (1893–1986), American biochemist, born in Hungary. He discovered ascorbic acid, later identified with vitamin C.

Szilard /ˈsɪlɑːd/, Leo (1898–1964), Hungarian-born American physicist and molecular biologist. He fled from Nazi Germany to the US, where he became a central figure in the Manhattan Project to develop the atom bomb.

Tt

T¹ (also **t**) ▶ **noun** (pl. **Ts** or **T's**) **1** the twentieth letter of the alphabet.
■ denoting the next after S in a set of items, categories, etc.
2 (**T**) (also **tee**) a shape like that of a capital T: [in combination] *make a T-shaped wound in the rootstock and insert the cut´ bud.* See also **T-JUNCTION**, **T-SQUARE**, etc.
− PHRASES **cross the T** historical (of a naval force) cross in front of an enemy force approximately at right angles, securing a tactical advantage for gunnery. **to a T** informal exactly; to perfection: *I baked it to a T, and of course it was delicious.*

T² ▶ **abbreviation for** ■ [in combination] (in units of measurement) tera- (10¹²): *12 Tbytes of data storage.* ■ tesla. ■ Thailand (international vehicle registration). ■ (in names of sports clubs) Town: *Mansfield T.*
▶ **symbol for** ■ temperature. ■ Chemistry the hydrogen isotope tritium.

t ▶ **abbreviation for** imperial or metric ton(s).
▶ **symbol for** (*t*) Statistics a number characterizing the distribution of a sample taken from a population with a normal distribution (see **STUDENT'S T-TEST**).

't ▶ **contraction of** the word 'it', attached to the end of a verb, especially in the transcription of regional spoken use: *I'll never do't again.*

-t¹ ▶ **suffix** equivalent to -ED² (as in *crept, sent, spoilt*).

-t² ▶ **suffix** equivalent to -EST² (as in *shalt*).

TA ▶ **abbreviation for** (in the UK) Territorial Army.

Ta ▶ **symbol for** the chemical element tantalum.

ta ▶ **exclamation** Brit. informal thank you.
− ORIGIN late 18th cent.: a child's word.

TAB ▶ **abbreviation for** ■ Austral./NZ Totalizator Agency Board. ■ typhoid–paratyphoid A and B vaccine.

tab¹ ▶ **noun 1** a small flap or strip of material attached to or projecting from something, used to hold or manipulate it, or for identification and information.
■ a similar piece of material forming part of a garment: [as modifier] *shirts with tab collars.* ■ Military, Brit. a marking on the collar distinguishing an officer of high rank or (formerly) a staff officer. ■ chiefly N. Amer. a strip or ring of metal attached to the top of a canned drink and pulled to open the can.
2 informal, chiefly N. Amer. a restaurant bill.
3 (**tabs**) short for **TABLEAU CURTAINS**.
4 Aeronautics a part of a control surface, typically hinged, that modifies the action or response of the surface.
▶ **verb** (**tabbed**, **tabbing**) [with obj.] mark or identify with a projecting piece of material: *he opened the book at a page tabbed by a cloth bookmark.*
■ figurative, chiefly US identify as being of a specified type or suitable for a specified position: *he was tabbed by the President as the next Republican National Committee chairman.*
− PHRASES **keep tabs** (or **a tab**) **on** informal monitor the activities or development of; keep under observation. **pick up the tab** informal, chiefly N. Amer. pay for something: *my company will pick up the tab for all moving expenses.*
− DERIVATIVES **tabbed** adjective.
− ORIGIN late Middle English: perhaps related to **TAG**¹.

tab² ▶ **noun** short for **TABULATOR**.

▶ **verb** (**tabbed**, **tabbing**) short for **TABULATE**.

tab³ ▶ **noun** informal a tablet, especially one containing an illicit drug.
− ORIGIN 1960s: abbreviation.

tab⁴ ▶ **noun** N. Amer. informal a tabloid newspaper.

tabac /ta'bak, French taba/ ▶ **noun** (pl. pronounced same) (in French-speaking countries) a tobacconist's shop.
− ORIGIN French, literally *tobacco*.

tabanca /ta'baŋka/ ▶ **noun** [mass noun] W. Indian a painful feeling of unrequited love, typically for a former lover and causing unbalanced or violent behaviour.
− ORIGIN probably from Kikongo *tabaka* 'buy up or sell out completely'.

tabard /'tabəd, -aːd/ ▶ **noun** a sleeveless jerkin consisting only of front and back pieces with a hole for the head.
■ historical a coarse garment of this kind as the outer dress of medieval peasants and clerics, or worn as a surcoat over armour. ■ a herald's official coat emblazoned with the arms of the sovereign.
− ORIGIN Middle English: from Old French *tabart*, of unknown origin.

tabaret /'tabərɪt/ ▶ **noun** [mass noun] an upholstery fabric of alternate satin and watered silk stripes.
− ORIGIN late 18th cent.: probably from **TABBY**.

Tabasco¹ /tə'baskəʊ/ a state of SE Mexico, on the Gulf of Mexico; capital, Villahermosa.

Tabasco² /tə'baskəʊ/ (also **Tabasco sauce**) ▶ **noun** [mass noun] trademark a pungent sauce made from the fruit of a capsicum pepper.
● The plant is *Capsicum frutescens* (or *C. annuum*), family Solanaceae.
− ORIGIN late 19th cent.: named after the state of *Tabasco* (see **TABASCO**¹).

tabbouleh /tə'buːleɪ, 'tabuːleɪ/ ▶ **noun** [mass noun] an Arab salad of cracked wheat mixed with finely chopped ingredients such as tomatoes, onions, and parsley.
− ORIGIN from Arabic *tabbūla*.

tabby ▶ **noun** (pl. **-ies**) **1** (also **tabby cat**) a grey or brownish cat mottled or streaked with dark stripes. [ORIGIN: late 17th cent. (as *tabby cat*): said to be so named from its striped colouring.]
2 [mass noun] a fabric with a watered pattern, typically silk.
3 [mass noun] a plain weave.
4 [mass noun] a type of concrete made of lime, shells, gravel, and stones, which dries very hard. [ORIGIN: early 19th cent. (originally *tabby work*): perhaps a different word, or from a resemblance in colour to that of a tabby cat.]
5 a small moth with dark wavy markings on the forewings.
● Genus *Aglossa* (family Pyralidae), often found in barns and warehouses, and genus *Epizeuxis* (family Noctuidae).
▶ **adjective** (of a cat) grey or brownish in colour and streaked with dark stripes.
− ORIGIN late 16th cent. (denoting a kind of silk taffeta, originally striped, later with a watered finish: see sense 2): from French *tabis*, based on Arabic *al-'Attābiyya*, the name of the quarter of Baghdad where tabby was manufactured.

tabernacle /'tabə,nak(ə)l/ ▶ **noun 1** (in biblical use) a fixed or movable habitation, typically of light construction.
■ a tent used as a sanctuary for the Ark of the Covenant by the Israelites during the Exodus and until the building of the Temple.
2 a meeting place for worship used by Nonconformists or Mormons.
3 an ornamented receptacle or cabinet in which a pyx containing the reserved sacrament may be placed in Catholic churches, usually on or above an altar.
■ archaic a canopied niche or recess in the wall of a church.
4 a partly open socket or double post on a sailing boat's deck into which a mast is fixed, with a pivot near the top so that the mast can be lowered to pass under bridges.
− DERIVATIVES **tabernacled** adjective.
− ORIGIN Middle English: via French from Latin *tabernaculum* 'tent', diminutive of *taberna* 'hut, tavern'.

tabernacle clock ▶ **noun** a small clock having a metal case in the form of a tower.

tabes /'teɪbiːz/ ▶ **noun** [mass noun] Medicine emaciation. See also **TABES DORSALIS**.
− DERIVATIVES **tabetic** /tə'bɛtɪk/ adjective.
− ORIGIN late 16th cent.: from Latin, literally 'wasting away'.

tabescent /tə'bɛs(ə)nt/ ▶ **adjective** wasting away.
− ORIGIN late 19th cent.: from Latin *tabescent-* 'beginning to waste away', from the verb *tabescere*, from *tabere* 'waste away'.

tabes dorsalis /dɔː'seɪlɪs/ ▶ **noun** another term for **LOCOMOTOR ATAXIA**.
− ORIGIN modern Latin, literally 'wasting of the back'.

tabi /'taːbi/ ▶ **noun** (pl. same) a thick-soled Japanese ankle sock with a separate section for the big toe.
− ORIGIN Japanese.

tabla /'tablə, 'tʌblə/ ▶ **noun** a pair of small hand drums fixed together, used in Indian music; one is slightly larger than the other and is played using pressure from the heel of the hand to vary the pitch.
− ORIGIN from Persian and Urdu *tablah*, Hindi *tablā*, from Arabic *tabl* 'drum'.

tablature /'tablətʃə/ ▶ **noun** [mass noun] chiefly historical a form of musical notation indicating fingering rather than the pitch of notes, written on lines corresponding to, for example, the strings of a lute or the holes on a flute.
− ORIGIN late 16th cent.: from French, probably from Italian *tavolatura*, from *tavolare* 'set to music'.

table ▶ **noun 1** a piece of furniture with a flat top and one or more legs, providing a level surface on which objects may be placed, and which can be used for such purposes as eating, writing, working, or playing games.
■ [in sing.] food provided in a restaurant or household: *he was reputed to have the finest French table of the time.* ■ a group seated at table for a meal: *the whole table was in gales of laughter.* ■ (**the table**) a meeting place for formal discussions held to settle an issue or dispute: *the negotiating table.* ■ [in sing.] Bridge the dummy hand (which is exposed on the table).

2 a set of facts or figures systematically displayed, especially in columns.
■ a list of rivals or competitors showing their positions relative to one another; a league table. ■ **(tables)** multiplication tables: *children at the school have spelling tests and learn their tables.* ■ Computing a collection of data stored in memory as a series of records, each defined by a unique key stored with it.
3 a flat surface, in particular:
■ Architecture a flat, typically rectangular, vertical surface. ■ a horizontal moulding, especially a cornice. ■ a slab of wood or stone bearing an inscription. ■ a flat surface of a gem. ■ a cut gem with two flat faces. ■ each half or quarter of a folding board for backgammon.
▶ **verb** [with obj.] **1** Brit. present formally for discussion or consideration at a meeting: *an MP tabled an amendment to the bill.*
2 chiefly US postpone consideration of: *I'd like the issue to be tabled for the next few months.*
3 Sailing strengthen (a sail) by making a hem at the edge.
– PHRASES **lay something on the table 1** make something known so that it can be freely and sensibly discussed. **2** chiefly US postpone something indefinitely. **on the table** offered for discussion: *our offer remains on the table.* **turn the tables** reverse one's position relative to someone else, especially by turning a position of disadvantage into one of advantage. **under the table 1** informal used to show that someone is very drunk: *by 3.30 everybody was under the table.* **2** another term for **under the counter** (see **COUNTER**[1]).
– DERIVATIVES **tableful** noun (pl. **-fuls**).
– ORIGIN Old English *tabule* 'flat slab, inscribed tablet', from Latin *tabula* 'plank, tablet, list'. reinforced in Middle English by Old French *table*.

tableau /'tablǝʊ/ ▶ **noun** (pl. **tableaux** /-lǝʊz/) a group of models or motionless figures representing a scene from a story or from history; a tableau vivant.
– ORIGIN late 17th cent. (in the sense 'picture', figuratively 'picturesque description'): from French, literally 'picture', diminutive of *table* (see **TABLE**).

tableau curtains ▶ **plural noun** (in the theatre) a pair of curtains drawn open by diagonal cords fixed to the lower inner corners.

tableau vivant /ˌtablǝʊ 'viːvɒ̃, French tablo vivɑ̃/ ▶ **noun** (pl. **tableaux vivants** pronunc. same) chiefly historical a silent and motionless group of people arranged to represent a scene or incident.
– ORIGIN French, literally 'living picture'.

tablecloth ▶ **noun** a cloth spread over a table, especially during meals.
■ figurative (in South Africa) the layer of cloud which often covers the top of Table Mountain.

table d'hôte /ˌtɑːbl(ǝ) 'dǝʊt, French tabl dot/ ▶ **noun** a restaurant meal offered at a fixed price and with few if any choices.
– ORIGIN early 17th cent.: French, literally 'host's table'. The term originally denoted a table in a hotel or restaurant where all guests ate together, hence a meal served there at a stated time and for a fixed price.

table knife ▶ **noun** a knife used at meals, especially for eating the main course.

table lamp ▶ **noun** a small lamp designed to stand on a table.

tableland ▶ **noun** a broad, high, level region; a plateau.

table licence ▶ **noun** Brit. a licence permitting a restaurateur or hotelier to serve alcoholic drinks only with meals.

table linen ▶ **noun** [mass noun] fabric items used at mealtimes, such as tablecloths and napkins, collectively.

table manners ▶ **plural noun** a pattern of behaviour that is conventionally required of someone while eating at table.

table mat ▶ **noun** a small mat used for protecting the surface of a table from hot dishes.

Table Mountain a flat-topped mountain near the south-west tip of South Africa, overlooking Cape Town and Table Bay, rising to a height of 1,087 m (3,563 ft).

table napkin ▶ **noun** another term for **NAPKIN** (in sense 1).

table salt ▶ **noun** [mass noun] salt suitable for sprinkling on food at meals.

table skittles ▶ **noun** see **SKITTLE** (sense 1).

tablespoon ▶ **noun** a large spoon for serving food.
■ (abbrev.: **tbsp** or **tbs**) the amount held by such a spoon, in the UK considered to be 15 millilitres when used as a measurement in cookery.
– DERIVATIVES **tablespoonful** noun (pl. **-fuls**).

tablet ▶ **noun** a flat slab of stone, clay, or wood, used especially for an inscription.
■ a small disc or cylinder of a compressed solid substance, typically a measured amount of a medicine or drug; a pill. ■ Brit. a small flat piece of soap. ■ Architecture another term for **TABLE** (in sense 3). ■ N. Amer. a writing pad. ■ a kind of token giving authority for a train to proceed over a single-track line.
– ORIGIN Middle English: from Old French *tablete*, from a diminutive of Latin *tabula* (see **TABLE**).

table talk ▶ **noun** [mass noun] informal conversation carried on at meals.

table tennis ▶ **noun** [mass noun] an indoor game based on tennis, played with small bats and a ball bounced on a table divided by a net.

table top ▶ **noun** the horizontal top part of a table.
■ [as modifier] small or portable enough to be placed or used on a table: *are you interested in a plumbed-in water filter or would a table-top model suit you better?*

table-top sale ▶ **noun** Brit. an occasion when participants sell unwanted possessions from tables, especially one where at least some of the proceeds go to charity.

table-turning ▶ **noun** [mass noun] a process or phenomenon in which a table is turned or moved supposedly by spiritual agency acting through a group of people who have placed their hands on its surface.

tableware ▶ **noun** [mass noun] crockery, cutlery, and glassware used for serving and eating meals at a table.

table wine ▶ **noun** [mass noun] wine of moderate quality considered suitable for drinking with a meal.

tablier /'tablɪeɪ/ ▶ **noun** historical a part of a woman's dress resembling an apron.
– ORIGIN mid 19th cent.: from French, based on Latin *tabula* (see **TABLE**).

tabloid ▶ **noun** a newspaper having pages half the size of those of the average broadsheet, typically popular in style and dominated by headlines, photographs, and sensational stories.
– ORIGIN late 19th cent.: from **TABLET** + **-OID**. Originally the proprietary name of a medicine sold in tablets, the term came to denote any small medicinal tablet; the current sense reflects the notion of 'concentrated, easily assimilable'.

taboo (also **tabu**) ▶ **noun** (pl. **taboos** or **tabus**) a social or religious custom prohibiting or restricting a particular practice or forbidding association with a particular person, place, or thing.
▶ **adjective** prohibited or restricted by social custom: *sex was a taboo subject.*
■ designated as sacred and prohibited: *the burial ground was seen as a taboo place.*
▶ **verb** (**taboos**, **tabooed** or **tabus**, **tabued**) [with obj.] place under such prohibition: *traditional societies taboo female handling of food during this period.*
– ORIGIN late 18th cent.: from Tongan *tabu* 'set apart, forbidden'; introduced into English by Captain Cook.

tabor /'teɪbǝ/ ▶ **noun** historical a small drum, especially one used simultaneously by the player of a simple pipe.
– ORIGIN Middle English: from Old French *tabour* 'drum'; perhaps related to Persian *tabīra* 'drum'. Compare with **TAMBOUR**.

tabouret /'tabǝrɛt, -reɪ/ (US also **taboret**) ▶ **noun** a low stool or small table.
– ORIGIN mid 17th cent.: from French, 'stool', diminutive of *tabour* 'drum' (see **TABOR**).

Tabriz /tǝ'briːz/ a city in NW Iran; pop. 1,089,000 (1991). It lies at about 1,367 m (4,485 ft) above sea level at the centre of a volcanic region and has been subject to frequent destructive earthquakes.

Tabriz rug ▶ **noun** a rug made in Tabriz, the older styles of which typically have a rich decorative medallion pattern.

tabular /'tabjʊlǝ/ ▶ **adjective 1** (of data) consisting of or presented in columns or tables: *a tabular presentation of running costs.*
2 broad and flat like the top of a table: *a huge tabular iceberg.*

■ (of a crystal) relatively broad and thin, with two well-developed parallel faces.
– DERIVATIVES **tabularly** adverb.
– ORIGIN mid 17th cent. (in sense 2): from Latin *tabularis*, from *tabula* (see **TABLE**).

tabula rasa /ˌtabjʊlǝ 'rɑːzǝ/ ▶ **noun** (pl. **tabulae rasae** /ˌtabjʊliː 'rɑːziː/) an absence of preconceived ideas or predetermined goals; a clean slate: *the team did not have complete freedom and a tabula rasa from which to work.*
■ the human mind, especially at birth, viewed as having no innate ideas.
– ORIGIN Latin, literally 'scraped tablet', denoting a tablet with the writing erased.

tabulate /'tabjʊleɪt/ ▶ **verb** [with obj.] arrange (data) in tabular form: [as adj. **tabulated**] *tabulated results.*
– DERIVATIVES **tabulation** noun.
– ORIGIN early 17th cent. (originally Scots in the sense 'enter on a roll'): in modern use from **TABLE** + **-ATE**[3].

tabulator ▶ **noun** a person or thing that arranges data in tabular form.
■ a facility in a word-processing program, or a device on a typewriter, used for advancing to a sequence of set positions in tabular work.

tabun /'tɑːbʊn/ ▶ **noun** [mass noun] an organophosphorus nerve gas, developed in Germany during the Second World War.
– ORIGIN German, of unknown origin.

tacamahac /'takǝmǝˌhak/ ▶ **noun** another term for **BALSAM POPLAR**.
– ORIGIN late 16th cent. (originally denoting the aromatic resin of *Bursera simaruba*: see **ELEMI**): from obsolete Spanish *tacamahaca*, from Aztec *tecomahiyac*.

tacan /'takǝn/ ▶ **noun** [mass noun] an electronic ultra-high-frequency navigational aid system for aircraft, which measures bearing and distance from a ground beacon.
– ORIGIN 1950s: from *ta(ctical) a(ir) n(avigation)*.

tac-au-tac /'takǝʊˌtak/ ▶ **noun** Fencing a parry combined with a riposte.
– ORIGIN early 20th cent.: French, literally 'clash for clash', from imitative *tac*.

tacet /'tasɪt, 'teɪ-/ ▶ **verb** [no obj.] Music (as a direction) indicating that a voice or instrument is silent.
– ORIGIN Latin, literally 'is silent', from *tacere* 'be silent'.

tach /tak/ ▶ **noun** N. Amer. informal short for **TACHOMETER**.

tache ▶ **noun** variant spelling of **TASH**.

tachi /'tatʃi/ ▶ **noun** historical a long, single-edged samurai sword with a slightly curved blade, worn slung from the belt.
– ORIGIN Japanese.

Taching /tɑːˈtʃɪŋ/ variant of **DAQING**.

tachism /'taʃɪz(ǝ)m/ (also **tachisme**) ▶ **noun** [mass noun] a style of painting adopted by some French artists from the 1940s, involving the use of dabs or splotches of colour, similar in aims to abstract expressionism.
– ORIGIN 1950s: from French *tachisme*, from *tache* 'a stain'.

tachistoscope /tǝ'kɪstǝˌskǝʊp/ ▶ **noun** an instrument used for exposing objects to the eye for a very brief measured period of time.
– DERIVATIVES **tachistoscopic** adjective, **tachistoscopically** adverb.
– ORIGIN late 19th cent.: from Greek *takhistos* 'swiftest' + **-SCOPE**.

tacho /'takǝʊ/ ▶ **noun** (pl. **-os**) Brit. informal short for **TACHOGRAPH** or **TACHOMETER**.

tacho- ▶ **combining form** relating to speed: *tachograph.*
– ORIGIN from Greek *takhos* 'speed'.

tachograph ▶ **noun** a tachometer providing a record of engine speed over a period, especially in a commercial road vehicle.

tachometer /ta'kɒmɪtǝ/ ▶ **noun** an instrument which measures the working speed of an engine (especially in a road vehicle), typically in revolutions per minute.

tachy- ▶ **combining form** rapid: *tachycardia.*
– ORIGIN from Greek *takhus* 'swift'.

tachycardia /ˌtakɪˈkɑːdɪǝ/ ▶ **noun** [mass noun] an abnormally rapid heart rate.

– ORIGIN late 19th cent.: from **TACHY-** 'swift' + Greek *kardia* 'heart'.

tachygraphy /ta'kɪɡrəfi/ ▶ **noun** [mass noun] stenography or shorthand, especially that of ancient or medieval scribes.
– DERIVATIVES **tachygraphic** adjective.

tachykinin /ˌtakɪ'kʌɪnɪn/ ▶ **noun** Biochemistry any of a class of substances formed in bodily tissue in response to injury and having a rapid stimulant effect on smooth muscle.

tachymeter /ta'kɪmɪtə/ ▶ **noun 1** a theodolite for the rapid measurement of distances in surveying. **2** a facility on a watch for measuring speed.
– DERIVATIVES **tachymetric** adjective.

tachyon /'takɪɒn/ ▶ **noun** Physics a hypothetical particle that travels faster than light.
– ORIGIN 1960s: from **TACHY-** 'swift' + **-ON**.

tachyphylaxis /ˌtakɪfɪ'laksɪs/ ▶ **noun** [mass noun] Medicine rapidly diminishing response to successive doses of a drug, rendering it less effective. The effect is common with drugs acting on the nervous system.

tachypnoea /ˌtakɪp'niːə/ (US **tachypnea**) ▶ **noun** [mass noun] Medicine abnormally rapid breathing.
– ORIGIN late 19th cent.: from **TACHY-** 'swift' + Greek *pnoē* 'breathing'.

tacit /'tasɪt/ ▶ **adjective** understood or implied without being stated: *your silence may be taken to mean tacit agreement.*
– DERIVATIVES **tacitly** adverb.
– ORIGIN early 17th cent. (in the sense 'wordless, noiseless'): from Latin *tacitus*, past participle of *tacere* 'be silent'.

taciturn /'tasɪtəːn/ ▶ **adjective** (of a person) reserved or uncommunicative in speech; saying little.
– DERIVATIVES **taciturnity** noun, **taciturnly** adverb.
– ORIGIN late 18th cent.: from Latin *taciturnus*, from *tacitus* (see **TACIT**).

Tacitus /'tasɪtəs/ (*c.*56–*c.*120 AD), Roman historian; full name *Publius*, or *Gaius*, *Cornelius Tacitus*. His *Annals* (covering the years 14–68) and *Histories* (69–96) are major works on the history of the Roman Empire.

tack¹ ▶ **noun 1** a small, sharp, broad-headed nail. ■N. Amer. a drawing pin.
2 a long stitch used to fasten fabrics together temporarily, prior to permanent sewing.
3 Sailing an act of changing course by turning a boat's head into and through the wind, so as to bring the wind on the opposite side. ■a boat's course relative to the direction of the wind: *the brig bowled past* **on the opposite tack**. ■ a distance sailed between such changes of course. ■ figurative a method of dealing with a situation or problem; a course of action or policy: *as she could not stop him going she tried another tack and insisted on going with him.*
4 Sailing a rope for securing the corner of certain sails. ■the corner to which such a rope is fastened.
5 [mass noun] the quality of being sticky: *cooking the sugar to caramel gives tack to the texture.*
▶**verb 1** [with obj. and adverbial] fasten or fix in place with tacks: *he used the tool to* **tack down** *sheets of fibreboard.* ■fasten (pieces of cloth) together temporarily with long stitches. ■ (**tack something on**) add or append something to something already existing.
2 [no obj.] Sailing change course by turning a boat's head into and through the wind. Compare with **WEAR²**. [ORIGIN: from the practice of shifting ropes (see sense 4) to change direction.] ■[with obj.] alter the course of (a boat) in such a way. ■ [with adverbial of direction] make a series of such changes of course while sailing: *she spent the entire night tacking back and forth.* ■ figurative make a change in one's conduct, policy, or direction of attention.
– PHRASES **on the port** (or **starboard**) **tack** Sailing with the wind coming from the port (or starboard) side of the boat.
– DERIVATIVES **tacker** noun.
– ORIGIN Middle English (in the general sense 'something that fastens one thing to another'): probably related to Old French *tache* 'clasp, large nail'.

tack² ▶ **noun** [mass noun] equipment used in horse riding, including the saddle and bridle.
– ORIGIN late 18th cent. (originally dialect in the general sense 'apparatus, equipment'): contraction of **TACKLE**. The current sense dates from the 1920s.

tack³ ▶ **noun** [mass noun] informal cheap, shoddy, or tasteless material.
– ORIGIN 1980s: back-formation from **TACKY²**.

tack coat ▶ **noun** (in road-making) a thin coating of tar or asphalt applied before a road is laid to form an adhesive bond.

tackie /'taki/ ▶ **noun** (pl. **-ies**) S. African informal a rubber-soled canvas shoe; a sports shoe. ■a tyre.
– PHRASES **a piece of old tackie** an easy task. **tread tackie** drive; accelerate.
– ORIGIN perhaps from **TACKY¹**, with reference to the adhesion of the rubber.

tackle ▶ **noun 1** [mass noun] the equipment required for a task or sport: *fishing tackle.* ■(also **wedding tackle**) Brit. vulgar slang a man's genitals.
2 a mechanism consisting of ropes, pulley blocks, hooks, or other things for lifting heavy objects. ■the running rigging and pulleys used to work a boat's sails.
3 Soccer & Hockey an act of playing the ball, or attempting to do so, when it is in the possession of an opponent. ■American Football & Rugby an act of seizing and attempting to stop a player in possession of the ball.
4 American Football a player who lines up next to the end along the line of scrimmage.
▶**verb** [with obj.] make determined efforts to deal with (a problem or difficult task): *police have launched an initiative to tackle rising crime.* ■initiate discussion with (someone) about a disputed or sensitive issue: *a young man tackled him over why the council had spent money on a swimming pool.* ■ chiefly Soccer & Hockey try to take the ball from (an opponent) by intercepting them. ■ American Football & Rugby try to stop the forward progress of (the ball-carrier) by seizing them and knocking them to the ground.
– DERIVATIVES **tackler** noun.
– ORIGIN Middle English (denoting equipment for a specific task): probably from Middle Low German *takel*, from *taken* 'lay hold of'. Early senses of the verb (late Middle English) described the provision and handling of a ship's equipment.

tackle block ▶ **noun** a pulley over which a rope runs.

tackle fall ▶ **noun** a rope for applying force to the blocks of a tackle. See **TACKLE** (sense 2).

tack room ▶ **noun** a room in a stable building where saddles, bridles, and other equipment are kept.

tacky¹ ▶ **adjective** (**tackier**, **tackiest**) (of glue, paint, or other substances) retaining a slightly sticky feel; not fully dry: *the paint was still tacky.*
– DERIVATIVES **tackiness** noun.

tacky² ▶ **adjective** (**tackier**, **tackiest**) informal showing poor taste and quality: *even in her faintly tacky costumes, she won our hearts.*
– DERIVATIVES **tackily** adverb, **tackiness** noun.
– ORIGIN early 19th cent.: of unknown origin. Early use was as a noun denoting a horse of little value, later applied to a poor white in some Southern states of the US, hence 'shabby, cheap, in bad taste' (mid 19th cent.).

taco /'takəʊ, 'tɑːkəʊ/ ▶ **noun** (pl. **-os**) a Mexican dish consisting of a folded or rolled tortilla filled with various mixtures, such as seasoned mince, chicken, or beans.
– ORIGIN Mexican Spanish, from Spanish, literally 'plug, wad'.

taco chip ▶ **noun** a fried fragment of a taco, flavoured with chilli and spices and eaten as a snack.

taconite /'takənʌɪt/ ▶ **noun** [mass noun] a low-grade iron ore consisting largely of chert, occurring chiefly around Lake Superior in North America.
– ORIGIN early 20th cent.: from the name of the *Taconic* Range of mountains, US, + **-ITE¹**.

tacrine /'takriːn/ ▶ **noun** [mass noun] Medicine a synthetic drug used in Alzheimer's disease to inhibit the breakdown of acetylcholine by cholinesterase and thereby enhance neurological function.
• An acridine derivative; chem formula: $C_{13}H_{15}N_2Cl$.
– ORIGIN 1960s: from *t(etra-)* + *acr(id)ine*.

tact ▶ **noun** [mass noun] adroitness and sensitivity in dealing with others or with difficult issues: *the inspector broke the news to me with tact and consideration.*
– ORIGIN mid 17th cent. (denoting the sense of touch): via French from Latin *tactus* 'touch, sense of touch', from *tangere* 'to touch'.

tactful ▶ **adjective** having or showing adroitness and sensitivity in dealing with others or with difficult issues: *they need a tactful word of advice.*
– DERIVATIVES **tactfully** adverb, **tactfulness** noun.

tactic ▶ **noun** an action or strategy carefully planned to achieve a specific end. ■(**tactics**) [also treated as sing.] the art of disposing armed forces in order of battle and of organizing operations, especially during contact with an enemy. Often contrasted with **STRATEGY**.
– DERIVATIVES **tactician** noun.
– ORIGIN mid 18th cent.: from modern Latin *tactica*, from Greek *taktikē* (*tekhnē*) '(art) of tactics', feminine of *taktikos*, from *taktos* 'ordered, arranged', from the base of *tassein* 'arrange'.

tactical ▶ **adjective** of, relating to, or constituting actions carefully planned to gain a specific military end: *as a tactical officer in the field he had no equal.* ■(of bombing or weapons) done or for use in immediate support of military or naval operations. Often contrasted with **STRATEGIC**. ■ (of a person or their actions) showing adroit planning; aiming at an end beyond the immediate action: *in a tactical retreat, she moved into a hotel with her daughters.* ■ (of voting) aimed at preventing the strongest candidate from winning by supporting the next strongest, without regard to one's true political allegiance.
– DERIVATIVES **tactically** adverb.
– ORIGIN late 16th cent. (in the sense 'relating to military or naval tactics'): from Greek *taktikos* (see **TACTIC**) + **-AL**.

tacticity ▶ **noun** [mass noun] Chemistry the stereochemical arrangement of the units in the main chain of a polymer.

tactile ▶ **adjective** of or connected with the sense of touch: *vocal and visual signals become less important as tactile signals intensify.* ■perceptible by touch or apparently so; tangible. ■ designed to be perceived by touch: *tactile exhibitions help blind people enjoy the magic of sculpture.* ■ (of a person) given to touching others, especially as an unselfconscious expression of sympathy or affection.
– DERIVATIVES **tactility** noun.
– ORIGIN early 17th cent. (in the sense 'perceptible by touch, tangible'): from Latin *tactilis*, from *tangere* 'to touch'.

tactless ▶ **adjective** having or showing a lack of adroitness and sensitivity in dealing with others or with difficult issues: *a tactless remark.*
– DERIVATIVES **tactlessly** adverb, **tactlessness** noun.

tactual ▶ **adjective** another term for **TACTILE**.

tactus /'taktəs/ ▶ **noun** Music a principal accent or rhythmic unit, especially in 15th- and 16th-century music.
– ORIGIN Latin.

tad informal ▶ **adverb** (**a tad**) to a small extent; somewhat: *Mark looked a tad embarrassed.*
▶ **noun** [in sing.] a small amount of something: *crumpets sweetened with* **a tad of** *honey.*
– ORIGIN late 19th cent. (denoting a small child): origin uncertain, perhaps from **TADPOLE**. The current usage dates from the 1940s.

ta-da /tə'dɑː/ (also **ta-dah**) ▶ **exclamation** an imitation of a fanfare (typically used to indicate an impressive entrance or a dramatic announcement).
– ORIGIN late 20th cent.: imitative.

tadger ▶ **noun** variant spelling of **TODGER**.

Tadjik ▶ **noun** & **adjective** variant spelling of **TAJIK**.

Tadmur /'tadmʊə/ (also **Tadmor** /-mɔː/) another name for **PALMYRA**.

tadpole ▶ **noun** the tailed aquatic larva of an amphibian (frog, toad, newt, or salamander), breathing through gills and lacking legs until its later stages of development.
– ORIGIN late 15th cent.: from Old English *tāda* 'toad' + **POLL** (probably because the tadpole seems to consist of a large head and a tail in its early development stage).

Tadzhik ▶ **noun** & **adjective** variant spelling of **TAJIK**.

Tadzhikistan variant spelling of **TAJIKISTAN**.

taedium vitae /ˌtiːdɪəm 'viːtʌɪ, 'vʌɪtiː/ ▶ **noun** [mass noun] a state of extreme ennui; weariness of life.
– ORIGIN Latin.

Taegu /ta'ɡuː/ a city in SE South Korea; pop. 2,228,830 (1990). Nearby is the Haeinsa temple, established in AD 802, which contains 80,000

Buddhist printing blocks dating from the 13th century.

Taejon /taˈdʒɒn/ a city in central South Korea; pop. 1,062,080 (1990).

tae kwon do /ˌtʌɪ kwɒn ˈdəʊ/ ▶ noun [mass noun] a modern Korean martial art similar to karate.
– ORIGIN Korean, literally 'art of hand and foot fighting', from *tae* 'kick' + *kwon* 'fist' + *do* 'art, method'.

tael /teɪl/ ▶ noun a weight used in China and the Far East, originally of varying amount but later fixed at about 38 grams (1⅓ oz.).
■ a former Chinese monetary unit based on the value of this weight of standard silver.
– ORIGIN from Malay *tahil* 'weight'.

taenia /ˈtiːnɪə/ (US **tenia**) ▶ noun (pl. **taeniae** /-niːiː/ or **taenias**) 1 Anatomy a flat ribbon-like structure in the body.
■ (**taeniae coli** /ˈkəʊlʌɪ/) the smooth longitudinal muscles of the colon.
2 Architecture a fillet between a Doric architrave and frieze.
3 (in ancient Greece) a band or ribbon worn round a person's head.
– DERIVATIVES **taenioid** adjective.
– ORIGIN mid 16th cent. (in sense 2): via Latin from Greek *tainia* 'band, ribbon'.

taeniodont /ˈtiːnɪə(ʊ)dɒnt/ ▶ noun a primitive fossil herbivorous mammal from the Palaeocene and Eocene of North America, with deep powerful jaws and short stout limbs.
● Suborder Taeniodonta, order Cimolesta.
– ORIGIN 1930s: from modern Latin *Taeniodontia* (order name), from Greek *tainia* 'band, ribbon' + *odous, odont-* 'tooth'.

taffeta /ˈtafɪtə/ ▶ noun [mass noun] a fine lustrous silk or similar synthetic fabric with a crisp texture.
– ORIGIN late Middle English (originally denoting a plain-weave silk): from Old French *taffetas* or medieval Latin *taffata*, based on Persian *tāftan* 'to shine'.

taffrail ▶ noun a rail round a ship's stern.
– ORIGIN early 19th cent.: alteration (by association with **RAIL**[1]), of obsolete *tafferel* 'panel', used to denote the flat part of a ship's stern above the transom, from Dutch *tafereel*.

Taffy (also **Taff**) ▶ noun Brit. informal, often offensive (pl. **-ies**) a Welshman.
– ORIGIN mid 17th cent.: representing a supposed Welsh pronunciation of the given name *Davy* or *David* (Welsh *Dafydd*).

taffy ▶ noun (pl. **-ies**) [mass noun] 1 N. Amer. a sweet similar to toffee, made from brown sugar or treacle, boiled with butter and pulled until glossy.
2 US informal insincere flattery.
– ORIGIN early 19th cent.: earlier form of **TOFFEE**.

tafia /ˈtafɪə/ ▶ noun [mass noun] W. Indian a drink similar to rum, distilled from molasses or waste from the production of brown sugar.
– ORIGIN via French from West Indian creole, alteration of **RATAFIA**.

Taft /taft/, William Howard (1857–1930), American Republican statesman, 27th President of the US 1909–13. His presidency is remembered for its dollar diplomacy and tariff laws.

tag[1] ▶ noun 1 a label attached to someone or something for the purpose of identification or to give other information.
■ an electronic device that can be attached to someone or something for monitoring purposes, e.g. to track offenders under house arrest or to deter shoplifters. ■ a nickname or description popularly given to someone or something. ■ US a licence plate of a motor vehicle. ■ Computing a character or set of characters appended to an item of data in order to identify it.
2 a small piece or part that is attached to a main body.
■ a ragged lock of wool on a sheep. ■ the tip of an animal's tail when it is distinctively coloured. ■ a loose or spare end of something; a leftover. ■ a metal or plastic point at the end of a shoelace that stiffens it, making it easier to insert through an eyelet.
3 a frequently repeated quotation or stock phrase.
■ Theatre a closing speech addressed to the audience. ■ the refrain of a song. ■ a musical phrase added to the end of a piece. ■ Grammar a short phrase or clause added to an already complete sentence, as in *I like it, I do*. See also **TAG QUESTION**.
▶ verb (**tagged**, **tagging**) [with obj.] 1 attach a label to:

mothers suspected that their babies had been wrongly tagged during an alarm at the hospital.
■ [with obj. and adverbial or complement] give a specified name or description to: *he left because he didn't want to be tagged as a soap star*. ■ attach an electronic tag to: [as noun **tagging**] *the tagging of remand prisoners*. ■ Computing add a character or set of characters to (an item of data) in order to identify it for later retrieval. ■ Biology & Chemistry label (something) with a radioactive isotope, fluorescent dye, or other marker: *pieces of DNA tagged with radioactive particles*.
2 [with obj. and adverbial] add to something, especially as an afterthought or with no real connection: *she meant to **tag** her question **on** at the end of her remarks*.
■ [no obj., with adverbial] follow or accompany someone, especially without invitation: *that'll teach you not to tag along where you're not wanted*. ■ [with obj.] Brit. informal follow closely: *we were tagged—that car was following us*.
3 shear away ragged locks of wool from (sheep).
– ORIGIN late Middle English (denoting a narrow hanging section of a decoratively slashed garment): of unknown origin; compare with **DAG**. The verb dates from the early 17th cent.

tag[2] ▶ noun [mass noun] a children's game in which one chases the rest, and anyone who is caught then becomes the pursuer.
■ [as modifier] denoting a form of wrestling involving tag teams. See **TAG TEAM**. ■ Baseball the action of tagging a runner.
▶ verb (**tagged**, **tagging**) [with obj.] touch (someone being chased) in a game of tag.
■ Baseball put (a runner) out by touching with the ball or with the hand holding the ball.
– ORIGIN mid 18th cent.: perhaps a variant of **TIG**.

Tagalog /təˈɡɑːlɒɡ/ ▶ noun 1 a member of a people originally of central Luzon in the Philippine Islands.
2 [mass noun] the Austronesian language of this people, with over 17 million speakers. Its vocabulary has been much influenced by Spanish and English, and to some extent by Chinese and Arabic, and it is the basis of a standardized national language of the Philippines (Filipino).
▶ adjective of or relating to this people or their language.
– ORIGIN the name in Tagalog, from *tagá* 'native' + *ilog* 'river'.

Tagamet /ˈtaɡəmɛt/ ▶ noun trademark for **CIMETIDINE**.
– ORIGIN 1970s: an arbitrary formation.

Taganrog /ˌtaɡənˈrɒɡ/ an industrial port in SW Russia, on the Gulf of Taganrog, an inlet of the Sea of Azov; pop. 293,000 (1990). It was founded in 1698 by Peter the Great as a fortress and naval base.

tagati /təˈɡɑːti/ ▶ noun (pl. same or **abatagati**) (among some South African peoples) an evil witch or wizard.
■ [mass noun] witchcraft.
▶ verb [no obj.] (among some South African peoples) practise witchcraft.
■ [with obj.] bewitch (someone).
– ORIGIN from Xhosa and Zulu *umthakathi* 'wizard'.

tag day ▶ noun North American term for **FLAG DAY**.

tag end ▶ noun chiefly US the last remaining part of something: *the tag end of the season*.

tagetes /təˈdʒiːtiːz/ ▶ noun a plant of the genus *Tagetes* in the daisy family, especially (in gardening) an African or French marigold.
– ORIGIN modern Latin, from Latin *Tages*, the name of an Etruscan god.

tagliatelle /ˌtaljəˈtɛleɪ, -li/ ▶ plural noun pasta in narrow ribbons.
– ORIGIN Italian, from *tagliare* 'to cut'.

tag line ▶ noun informal, chiefly N. Amer. a catchphrase or slogan, especially as used in advertising, or the punchline of a joke.

tagma /ˈtaɡmə/ ▶ noun (pl. **tagmata** /-mətə/) Zoology (in the bodies of arthropods and some other segmented animals) a morphologically distinct region, typically comprising several adjoining segments, such as the head, thorax, and abdomen of insects.
– DERIVATIVES **tagmatize** verb (also **-ise**).
– ORIGIN early 20th cent.: from Greek, literally 'something arranged', from *tassein* 'set in order'.

tagmeme /ˈtaɡmiːm/ ▶ noun Linguistics (in tagmemics) a slot in a syntactic frame which may be filled by any member of a set of appropriate linguistic items.

– ORIGIN 1930s: from Greek *tagma* 'arrangement' + **-EME**.

tagmemics /taɡˈmiːmɪks/ ▶ plural noun [treated as sing.] Linguistics a mode of linguistic analysis based on identifying the function of each grammatical position in the sentence or phrase and the class of words by which it can be filled.
– DERIVATIVES **tagmemic** adjective.

Tagore /təˈɡɔː/, Rabindranath (1861–1941), Indian writer and philosopher. His poetry pioneered the use of colloquial Bengali, and his own translations established his reputation in the West. Nobel Prize for Literature (1913).

tag question ▶ noun Grammar a question converted from a statement by an appended interrogative formula, e.g. *it's nice out, isn't it?*

tag sale ▶ noun US a sale of miscellaneous second-hand items.

tag team ▶ noun a pair of wrestlers who fight as a team, taking the ring alternately. One team member cannot enter the ring until the other tags or touches hands with him or her on leaving.
■ informal, chiefly N. Amer. a pair of people working together.

tagua nut /ˈtaɡwə/ ▶ noun another term for **IVORY NUT**.
– ORIGIN mid 19th cent.: *tagua*, via Spanish from Quechua *tawa*.

Tagus /ˈteɪɡəs/ a river in SW Europe, the longest river of the Iberian peninsula, which rises in the mountains of eastern Spain and flows over 1,000 km (625 miles) generally westwards into Portugal, where it turns south-westwards, emptying into the Atlantic near Lisbon. Spanish name **TAJO**, Portuguese name **TEJO**.

tahini /tɑːˈhiːni/ (also **tahina** /tɑːˈhiːnə/) ▶ noun [mass noun] a Middle Eastern paste or spread made from ground sesame seeds.
– ORIGIN from modern Greek *takhini*, based on Arabic *taḥana* 'to crush'.

Tahiti /təˈhiːti/ an island in the central South Pacific, one of the Society Islands, forming part of French Polynesia; pop. 115,820 (1988); capital, Papeete. One of the largest islands in the South Pacific, it was claimed for France in 1768 and declared a French colony in 1880.

Tahitian /tɑːˈhiːʃ(ə)n, -ˈhiːtɪən/ ▶ noun 1 a native or national of Tahiti, or a person of Tahitian descent.
2 [mass noun] the language of Tahiti, a Polynesian language with about 125,000 speakers.
▶ adjective of or relating to Tahiti, its people, or their language.

tahr /tɑː/ (also **thar**) ▶ noun a goat-like mammal inhabiting cliffs and mountain slopes in Oman, southern India, and the Himalayas.
● Genus *Hemitragus*, family Bovidae: three species.
– ORIGIN mid 19th cent.: a local word in Nepal.

tahsil /tɑːˈsiːl/ ▶ noun variant of **TEHSIL**.

Tai /tʌɪ/ ▶ adjective of, relating to, or denoting a family of tonal SE Asian languages, including Thai and Lao, of uncertain affinity to other language groups (sometimes being linked with the Sino-Tibetan family).

tai /tʌɪ/ ▶ noun (pl. same) a deep red-brown Pacific sea bream, eaten as a delicacy in Japan.
● *Pagrus major*, family Sparidae.
– ORIGIN early 17th cent.: from Japanese.

Tai'an /tʌɪˈɑːn/ a city in NE China, in Shandong province; pop. 1,370,000 (1986).

t'ai chi ch'uan /ˌtʌɪ tʃiː ˈtʃwɑːn/ (also **t'ai chi** /ˌtʌɪ ˈtʃiː/) ▶ noun [mass noun] 1 a Chinese martial art and system of callisthenics, consisting of sequences of very slow controlled movements.
2 (in Chinese philosophy) the ultimate source and limit of reality, from which spring yin and yang and all of creation.
– ORIGIN Chinese, literally 'great ultimate boxing', from *tái* 'extreme' + *ji* 'limit' + *quán* 'fist, boxing'.

Taichung /tʌɪˈtʃʊŋ/ a city in west central Taiwan; pop. 774,000 (1991).

Ta'if /ˈtɑːɪf/ a city in western Saudi Arabia, situated to the south-east of Mecca in the Asir Mountains; pop. 204,850 (est. 1986). It is the unofficial seat of government of Saudi Arabia during the summer.

Taig /teɪɡ/ ▶ noun informal, offensive (in Northern Ireland) a Protestant name for a Catholic.
– ORIGIN 1970s: variant of *Teague*, Anglicized spelling

of the Irish name *Tadhg*, used since the mid 17th cent. as a nickname for an Irishman.

taiga /ˈtʌɪɡə/ ▶ **noun** [mass noun] (often **the taiga**) the swampy coniferous forest of high northern latitudes, especially that between the tundra and steppes of Siberia.
– ORIGIN late 19th cent.: from Russian *taĭga*, from Mongolian.

taiko /ˈtʌɪkəʊ/ ▶ **noun** (pl. same or **-os**) a Japanese barrel-shaped drum.
– ORIGIN late 19th cent.: Japanese.

tail[1] ▶ **noun 1** the hindmost part of an animal, especially when prolonged beyond the rest of the body, such as the flexible extension of the backbone in a vertebrate, the feathers at the hind end of a bird, or a terminal appendage in an insect. ■a thing resembling an animal's tail in its shape or position, typically something extending downwards or outwards at the end of something: *the trailed tail of a capital Q* | *the cars were head to tail.* ■ the rear part of an aeroplane, with the tailplane and rudder. ■ the lower or hanging part of a garment, especially the back of a shirt or coat. ■ (**tails**) informal a tailcoat; a man's formal evening suit with such a coat: *the men looked debonair in white tie and tails.* ■ the luminous trail of particles following a comet. ■ the lower end of a pool or stream. ■ the exposed end of a slate or tile in a roof. ■ a slender backward prolongation of each hindwing in some butterflies. ■ Mathematics an extremity of a curve approaching the horizontal axis of a graph, especially that of a frequency distribution.
2 the end of a long train or line of people or vehicles: *a catering truck at the tail of the convoy.*
■[in sing.] the final, more distant, or weaker part of something: *the forecast says we're in for the tail of a hurricane.* ■ Cricket the end of the batting order, with the weakest batsmen. ■ informal a person secretly following another to observe their movements.
3 informal, chiefly N. Amer. a person's buttocks.
■vulgar slang a woman's genitals. ■ [mass noun] informal women collectively regarded as a means of sexual gratification: *my wife thinks going out with you guys will keep me from chasing tail.*
4 (**tails**) the side of a coin without the image of a head on it (used when tossing a coin to determine a winner).
▶**verb** [with obj.] **1** informal follow and observe (someone) closely, especially in secret: *was it Special Branch who were tailing Mills just before the murder?*
■[no obj., with adverbial of direction] follow: *they went to their favourite cafe—Owen and Sally tailed along.*
2 [no obj., with adverbial of direction] N. Amer. (of an object in flight) drift or curve in a particular direction: *the next pitch tailed in on me at the last second.*
3 rare provide with a tail: *her calligraphy was topped by banners of black ink and tailed like the haunches of fabulous beasts.*
4 archaic join (one thing) to another: *each new row of houses tailed on its drains to those of its neighbours.*
5 pull on the end of (a rope) after it has been wrapped round the drum of a winch a few times, in order to prevent slipping when the winch rotates.
– PHRASES **chase one's (own) tail** informal rush around ineffectually. **on someone's tail** following someone closely: *a police car stayed on his tail for half a mile.* **a piece of tail** see **PIECE**. **the tail of one's eye** dated the outer corner of one's eye. **the tail wags the dog** the less important or subsidiary factor, person, or thing dominates a situation; the usual roles are reversed: *the financing system is becoming the tail that wags the dog.* **with one's tail between one's legs** informal in a state of dejection or humiliation. **with one's tail up** informal in a confident or cheerful mood.
– DERIVATIVES **tailed** adjective [in combination] *a white-tailed deer*, **tailless** adjective.
– ORIGIN Old English *tæg(e)l*, from a Germanic base meaning 'hair, hairy tail'; related to Middle Low German *tagel* 'twisted whip, rope's end'. The early sense of the verb (early 16th cent.) was 'fasten to the back of something'.
▶**tail back** Brit. (of traffic) become congested and form a tailback.
tail something in (or **into**) insert the end of a beam, stone, or brick, into (a wall).
tail off (or **away**) gradually diminish in amount, strength, or intensity: *the economic boom was beginning to tail off.*

tail[2] ▶ **noun** [mass noun] Law, chiefly historical limitation of ownership, especially of an estate or title limited to a person and their heirs: *the land was held* **in tail** *general.* See also **FEE TAIL**.
– ORIGIN Middle English (denoting a tallage): from Old French *taille* 'notch, tax', from *taillier* 'to cut', based on Latin *talea* 'twig, cutting'.

tailback ▶ **noun 1** Brit. a long queue of stationary or slow-moving traffic extending back from a busy junction or similar obstruction on the road.
2 American Football the offensive back stationed furthest from the line of scrimmage.

tailboard ▶ **noun** Brit. a tailgate.

tail bone ▶ **noun** less technical term for **COCCYX**.

tail boom ▶ **noun** a main spar of several making up the longitudinal framework carrying the tail of an aeroplane when not supported by the fuselage.

tailcoat ▶ **noun** Brit. a man's formal morning or evening coat, with a long skirt divided at the back into tails and cut away in front.

tail comb ▶ **noun** a comb with a tapering tail or handle used in styling to lift, divide, or curl the hair.

tail covert ▶ **noun** (in a bird's tail) each of the smaller feathers covering the bases of the main feathers.

taildragger ▶ **noun** an aeroplane that lands and taxies on a tail wheel or tail skid, its nose off the ground.

tail end ▶ **noun** [in sing.] the last or hindmost part of something: *we joined the tail end of a queue.*
■Cricket another term for **TAIL**[1].
– DERIVATIVES **tail-ender** noun (Cricket).

tail-end Charlie ▶ **noun** informal a person or thing that brings up the rear in a group or formation.
■a member of the crew of a military aircraft who operates a gun from a compartment at the rear.

tail fin ▶ **noun** Zoology a fin at the posterior extremity of a fish's body, typically continuous with the tail. Also called **CAUDAL FIN**.
■Aeronautics a projecting vertical surface on the tail of an aircraft, providing stability and typically housing the rudder. ■ an upswept projection on each rear corner of a motor car, popular in the 1950s.

tail gas ▶ **noun** [mass noun] gas produced in a refinery and not required for further processing.

tailgate ▶ **noun** a hinged flap at the back of a lorry or truck which may be lowered or removed when loading or unloading the vehicle.
■the door at the back of an estate or hatchback car. ■ [as modifier] N. Amer. relating to or denoting an informal meal served from the back of a parked vehicle: *a tailgate picnic.* ■ [as modifier] denoting a style of jazz trombone playing characterized by improvisation in the manner of the early New Orleans musicians.
▶**verb** informal, chiefly US drive too closely behind another vehicle: [with obj.] *he started tailgating the motorist in front* | [no obj.] *drivers who will tailgate at 90 mph.*
– DERIVATIVES **tailgater** noun.

tailing ▶ **noun 1** (**tailings**) the residue of something, especially ore.
■[mass noun] grain or flour of inferior quality.
2 [mass noun] the action of cutting the stalks or ends off fruit or vegetables, in preparation for cooking: *the green beans only needed topping and tailing.*
3 the part of a beam or projecting brick or stone embedded in a wall.

taille /tɑːj, French taj/ ▶ **noun** (pl. pronounced same) **1** (in France before 1789) a tax levied on the common people by the king or an overlord. [ORIGIN: compare with **TAIL**[2].]
2 Music, historical the register of a tenor or similar voice, or an instrument of this register.
3 [mass noun] the juice produced from a second pressing of the grapes during winemaking, generally considered inferior because it contains less sugar, more tannin, and has lower acidity than the first pressing.
■low-quality wine made from this residue.
– ORIGIN French.

Tailleferre /tʌɪˈfɛː, French tajfɛʀ/, Germaine (1892–1983), French composer and pianist. A member of Les Six, she composed concertos for unusual combinations of instruments.

tailleur /tɑːˈjəː/ ▶ **noun** (pl. pronounced same) dated or formal a woman's tailor-made suit.
– ORIGIN French.

tail light (also **tail lamp**) ▶ **noun** a red light at the rear of a motor vehicle, train, or bicycle.

tail male ▶ **noun** [mass noun] Law, historical the limitation of the succession of property or title to male descendants.

tail-off ▶ **noun** [in sing.] a decline or gradual reduction in something: *a tail-off in customers.*

tailor ▶ **noun 1** a person whose occupation is making fitted clothes such as suits, trousers, and jackets to fit individual customers.
2 (also **tailorfish**) another term for **BLUEFISH**.
▶**verb** [with obj.] (usu. **be tailored**) (of a tailor) make (clothes) to fit individual customers: *he was wearing a sports coat which had obviously been tailored in London.*
■make or adapt for a particular purpose or person: *arrangements can be* **tailored** *to meet individual requirements.*
– ORIGIN Middle English: from Anglo-Norman French *taillour*, literally 'cutter', based on late Latin *taliare* 'to cut'. The verb dates from the mid 17th cent.

tailorbird ▶ **noun** a small South Asian warbler that makes a row of holes in one or two large leaves and stitches them together with cottony fibres or silk to form a container for the nest.
● Genus *Orthotomus*, family Sylviidae: several species.

tailored ▶ **adjective 1** (of clothes) smart, fitted, and well cut: *a tailored charcoal-grey suit.*
■[with submodifier] (of clothes) cut in a particular way: *her clothes were well tailored and expensive.*
2 made or adapted for a particular purpose or person: *specially tailored courses can be run on request.*

tailoring ▶ **noun** [mass noun] the activity or trade of a tailor.
■the style or cut of a garment or garments.

tailor-made ▶ **adjective** (of clothes) made by a tailor for a particular customer: *tailor-made suits.*
■made, adapted, or suited for a particular purpose or person: *he was* **tailor-made for** *the job.*
▶**noun** a garment that has been specially made for a particular customer: *a lady in a red tailor-made.*
■a cigarette made in a factory, rather than being hand-rolled.

tailor's chalk ▶ **noun** [mass noun] hard chalk or soapstone used in tailoring and dressmaking for marking fabric.

tailor's twist ▶ **noun** [mass noun] strong silk thread used by tailors.

tailpiece ▶ **noun** a final or end part of something, in particular:
■a part added to the end of a story or piece of writing. ■ a small decorative design at the foot of a page or the end of a chapter or book. ■ the piece at the base of a violin or other stringed instrument to which the strings are attached.

tailpipe ▶ **noun** the rear section of the exhaust pipe of a motor vehicle.

tailplane ▶ **noun** Brit. a horizontal aerofoil at the tail of an aircraft.

tail race ▶ **noun** a fast-flowing stretch of a river or stream below a dam or watermill.

tail rhyme ▶ **noun** Prosody a rhyme involving couplets, triplets, or stanzas, each with a tag or additional short line.

tail rotor ▶ **noun** Aeronautics an auxiliary rotor at the tail of a helicopter designed to counterbalance the torque of the main rotor.

tail skid ▶ **noun** a support for the tail of an aircraft when on the ground.

tail slide ▶ **noun** a backward movement of an aircraft from a vertical stalled position.

tailspin ▶ **noun** a spin by an aircraft.
■a state or situation characterized by chaos, panic, or loss of control: *the rise in interest rates sent the stock market into a tailspin.*
▶**verb** (**-spinning**; past and past participle **-spun**) [no obj.] become out of control: *an economy tailspinning into chaos.*

tailstock ▶ **noun** the adjustable part of a lathe holding the fixed spindle.

tail-walk ▶ **verb** [no obj., usu. with adverbial of direction] (of a fish) move over the surface of water by propulsion with the tail.
– DERIVATIVES **tail-walking** noun.

tailwater ▶ **noun** [mass noun] the water in a mill race below the wheel, or in a canal below a lock.

tailwheel ▶ **noun** a wheel supporting the tail of an aircraft, designed to ease handling while on the ground.

tailwind ▶ noun a wind blowing in the direction of travel of a vehicle or aircraft; a wind blowing from behind.

taimen /ˈtʌɪmən/ ▶ noun (pl. same) a food fish that is closely related to the huchen, widespread in Siberia and East Asia.
• *Hucho taimen*, family Salmonidae.
– ORIGIN 1970s: from Russian.

Taimyr Peninsula /tʌɪˈmɪə/ (also **Taymyr**) a vast, almost uninhabited peninsula on the north coast of central Russia, extending into the Arctic Ocean and separating the Kara Sea from the Laptev Sea. Its northern tip is the northernmost point of Asia.

Tainan /tʌɪˈnɑːn/ a city on the SW coast of Taiwan; pop. 690,000 (1991). Settled from mainland China in 1590, it is one of the oldest cities on the island and was its capital from 1684 until 1885, when it was replaced by Taipei. Its original name was Taiwan, the name later given to the whole island.

Taino /ˈtʌɪnəʊ/ ▶ noun [mass noun] an extinct Caribbean language of the Arawakan group.
– ORIGIN from Taino *taino* 'noble, lord'.

taint ▶ noun a trace of a bad or undesirable quality or substance: *the taint of corruption which adhered to the government.*
▪ a thing whose influence or effect is perceived as contaminating or undesirable: *the taint that threatens to stain most of the company's other partners.* ▪ an unpleasant smell: *the lingering taint of creosote.*
▶ verb [with obj.] (often **be tainted**) contaminate or pollute (something): *the air was tainted by fumes from the cars.*
▪ affect with a bad or undesirable quality: *his administration was tainted by scandal.* ▪ [no obj.] archaic (of food or water) become contaminated or polluted.
– DERIVATIVES **taintless** adjective (poetic/literary).
– ORIGIN Middle English (as a verb in the sense 'convict, prove guilty'): partly from Old French *teint* 'tinged', based on Latin *tingere* 'to dye, tinge'; partly a shortening of **ATTAINT**.

taipan[1] /ˈtʌɪpan/ ▶ noun a foreigner who is head of a business in China or Hong Kong.
– ORIGIN mid 19th cent.: from Chinese (Cantonese dialect) *daaihbāan*.

taipan[2] /ˈtʌɪpan/ ▶ noun a large, brown, highly venomous Australian snake.
• Genus *Oxyuranus*, family Elapidae: two species, in particular *O. scutellatus*.
– ORIGIN 1930s: from Wik Munkan (an extinct Aboriginal language of North Queensland) *dhayban*.

Taipei /tʌɪˈpeɪ/ the capital of Taiwan; pop. 2,718,000 (1991). It developed as an industrial city in the 19th century, and became the capital in 1885.

Taiping Rebellion /tʌɪˈpɪŋ/ a sustained uprising against the Qing dynasty in China 1850–64.

The rebellion was led by Hong Xiuquan (1814–64), who had founded a religious group inspired by elements of Christian theology and proposing egalitarian social policies. His large army captured Nanjing in 1853 but was eventually defeated at Shanghai at the hands of an army trained by the British general Charles Gordon.

– ORIGIN *Taiping* from Chinese *T'ai-p'ing-wang* 'Prince of great peace', a title given to Hong Xiuquan.

Taiwan /tʌɪˈwɑːn/ an island country off the SE coast of China; pop. 20,400,000 (1991); official language, Mandarin Chinese; capital, Taipei. Official name **REPUBLIC OF CHINA**. Former name **FORMOSA**.

In 1949, towards the end of the war with the Communist regime of mainland China, Chiang Kai-shek withdrew there with 500,000 nationalist Kuomintang troops. Taiwan became the headquarters of the Kuomintang, which has held power continuously since then. Since the 1950s Taiwan has undergone steady economic growth. In 1971 it lost its seat in the United Nations to the People's Republic of China, which regards Taiwan as one of its provinces.

– DERIVATIVES **Taiwanese** /ˌtʌɪwəˈniːz/ adjective & noun.

Taiyuan /ˌtʌɪjʊˈɑːn/ a city in northern China, capital of Shanxi province; pop. 1,900,000 (1990).

Tai Yue Shan /ˌtʌɪ jʊeɪ ˈʃan/ Chinese name for **LANTAU**.

Ta'iz /taˈɪz/ a city in SW Yemen; pop. 290,100 (est. 1993). It was the administrative capital of Yemen from 1948 to 1962.

taj /tɑːdʒ/ ▶ noun a tall conical cap worn by a dervish.
▪ historical a crown worn by an Indian prince of high rank.
– ORIGIN mid 19th cent.: from Persian *tāj* 'crown'.

Tajik /tɑːˈdʒiːk/ (also **Tadjik** or **Tadzhik**) ▶ noun **1** a member of a mainly Muslim people inhabiting Tajikistan and parts of neighbouring countries.
▪ a native or national of the republic of Tajikistan.
2 [mass noun] (also **Tajiki** /tɑːˈdʒiːki/) the language of the Tajiks, a member of the Iranian branch of the Indo-European family.
▶ adjective of or relating to Tajikistan, the Tajiks, or their language.
– ORIGIN from Persian *tājik* 'a Persian, someone who is neither an Arab nor a Turk'.

Tajikistan /təˌdʒiːkɪˈstɑːn, -ˈstan/ (also **Tadzhikistan**) a mountainous republic in central Asia, north of Afghanistan; pop. 5,412,000 (est. 1991); languages, Tajik (official), Russian; capital, Dushanbe.

The region was conquered by the Mongols in the 13th century and absorbed into the Russian empire during the 1880s and 1890s. From 1929 Tajikistan formed a constituent republic of the USSR; it became an independent republic within the Commonwealth of Independent States in 1991.

Taj Mahal /ˌtɑːʒ məˈhɑːl, ˌtɑːdʒ/ a mausoleum at Agra built by the Mogul emperor Shah Jahan (1592–1666) in memory of his favourite wife, completed *c.*1649. Set in formal gardens, the domed building in white marble is reflected in a pool flanked by cypresses.
– ORIGIN perhaps a corruption of Persian *Mumtaz Mahal*, from *mumtāz* 'chosen one' (the title of the wife of Shah Jahan) and *mahal* 'abode'.

Tajo /ˈtaxo/ Spanish name for **TAGUS**.

taka /ˈtɑːkɑː/ ▶ noun (pl. same) the basic monetary unit of Bangladesh, equal to 100 poisha.
– ORIGIN from Bengali *ṭākā*.

takahe /ˈtɑːkəhi/ ▶ noun a large, rare flightless rail with bluish-black and olive-green plumage and a large red bill, found in mountain grassland in New Zealand.
• *Porphyrio mantelli*, family Rallidae.
– ORIGIN mid 19th cent.: from Maori.

take ▶ verb (past **took**; past participle **taken**) [with obj.] **1** lay hold of (something) with one's hands; reach for and hold: *he leaned forward to take her hand.*
▪ [with obj. and adverbial of direction] remove (someone or something) from a particular place: *he took an envelope from his inside pocket | the police took him away.* ▪ consume as food, drink, medicine, or drugs: *take an aspirin and lie down.* ▪ capture or gain possession of by force or military means: *twenty of their ships were sunk or taken | the French took Ghent.* ▪ (in bridge, whist, and similar card games) win (a trick). ▪ Chess capture (an opposing piece or pawn). ▪ Cricket dismiss a batsman from (his wicket). ▪ dispossess someone of (something); steal or illicitly remove: *someone must have sneaked in here and taken it.* ▪ subtract: *take two from ten | add the numbers together and take away five.* ▪ occupy (a place or position): *we found that all the seats were taken.* ▪ buy or rent (a house). ▪ agree to buy (an item): *I'll take the one on the end.* ▪ (**be taken**) humorous (of a person) already be married or in a romantic relationship. ▪ [in imperative] use or have ready to use: *take half the marzipan and roll out.* ▪ [usu. in imperative] use as an instance or example in support of an argument: *let's take Napoleon, for instance.* ▪ Brit. regularly buy or subscribe to (a particular newspaper or periodical). ▪ ascertain by measurement or observation: *the nurse takes my blood pressure.* ▪ write down: *he was taking notes.* ▪ make (a photograph) with a camera. ▪ (usu. **be taken**) (especially of illness) suddenly strike or afflict (someone): *mum's been taken bad.* ▪ have sexual intercourse with.
2 [with obj. and usu. with adverbial] carry or bring with one; convey: *he took along a portfolio of his drawings | the drive takes you through some wonderful scenery | [with two objs] I took him a letter.*
▪ accompany or guide (someone) to a specified place: *I'll take you to your room | he called to take her out for a meal.* ▪ bring into a specified state: *the invasion took Europe to the brink of war.* ▪ use as a route or a means of transport: *take the A43 towards Bicester | we took the night train to Scotland.*
3 accept or receive (someone or something): *she was advised to take any job offered | they don't take children.*
▪ understand or accept as valid: *I take your point.* ▪ acquire or assume (a position, state, or form): *teaching methods will take various forms | he took office in September.* ▪ receive (a specified amount of money) as payment or earnings: *on its first day of trading the shop took 1.6 million roubles.* ▪ achieve or attain (a victory or result): *John Martin took the men's title.* ▪ act on (an opportunity): *he took his chance to get out while the house was quiet.* ▪ experience or be affected by: *the lad took a savage beating.* ▪ [with obj. and adverbial] react to or regard (news or an event) in a specified way: *she took the news well | everything you say, he takes it the wrong way.* ▪ [with obj. and adverbial] deal with (a physical obstacle or course) in a specified way: *he takes the corners with no concern for his own safety.* ▪ regard or view in a specified way: *he somehow took it as a personal insult | [with obj. and infinitive] I fell over what I took to be a heavy branch.* ▪ (**be taken by/with**) be attracted or charmed by: *Billie was very taken with him.* ▪ submit to, tolerate, or endure: *they refused to take it any more | some people found her hard to take.* ▪ (**take it**) [with clause] assume: *I take it that someone is coming to meet you.*
4 make, undertake, or perform (an action or task): *Lucy took a deep breath | the key decisions are still to be taken.*
▪ conduct (a ceremony or gathering). ▪ be taught or examined in (a subject): *some degrees require a student to take a secondary subject.* ▪ Brit. obtain (an academic degree) after fulfilling the required conditions: *she took a degree in business studies.*
5 require or use up (a specified amount of time): *the jury took an hour and a half to find McPherson guilty | [with two objs] it takes me about a quarter of an hour to walk to work.*
▪ (of a task or situation) need or call for (a particular person or thing): *it will take an electronics expert to dismantle it.* ▪ hold; accommodate: *an exclusive island hideaway that takes just twenty guests.* ▪ wear or require (a particular size of garment or type of complementary article): *he only takes size 5 boots.*
6 [no obj.] (of a plant or seed) take root or begin to grow; germinate: *the fuchsia cuttings had taken and were looking good.*
▪ (of an added substance) become successfully established.
7 Grammar have or require as part of the appropriate construction: *verbs which take both the infinitive and the finite clause as their object.*
▶ noun **1** a scene or sequence of sound or vision photographed or recorded continuously at one time: *he completed a particularly difficult scene in two takes.*
▪ a particular version of or approach to something: *his own whimsical take on life.*
2 an amount of something gained or acquired from one source or in one session: *the take from commodity taxation.*
▪ chiefly US the money received at a cinema or theatre for seats.
3 Printing an amount of copy set up at one time or by one compositor.
– PHRASES **be on the take** informal take bribes. **be taken ill** become ill suddenly. **have what it takes** informal have the necessary qualities for success. **take a chair** sit down. **take advantage of** (or **take advice** etc.) see **ADVANTAGE**, **ADVICE**, etc. **take something as read** Brit. accept something without considering or discussing it; assume something. **take the biscuit** (or **cake**) informal (of a person or incident) be the most remarkable or foolish of their kind. **take a lot of** (or **some**) —— be difficult to do or effect in the specified way: *he might take some convincing.* **take someone in hand** undertake to control or reform someone. **take something in hand** start doing or dealing with a task. **take ill** (US **sick**) informal become ill, especially suddenly. **take something ill** archaic resent something done or said. **take it from me** I can assure you: *take it from me, kid—I've been there, done it, seen it all.* **take it on one** (or **oneself**) **to do something** decide to do something without asking for permission or advice. **take it or leave it** [usu. in imperative] said to express that the offer one has made is not negotiable and that one is indifferent to another's reaction to it: *that's the deal—take it or leave it.* **take it out of 1** exhaust the strength of (someone): *parties and tours can take it out of you, especially if you are over 65.* **2** Brit. take reprisals against. **take someone out of themselves** make a person forget their worries. **take that!** exclaimed when hitting someone or taking decisive action against them. **take one's time** not hurry.
– DERIVATIVES **takable** (also **takeable**) adjective.
– ORIGIN late Old English *tacan* 'get (especially by force), capture', from Old Norse *taka* 'grasp, lay hold of', of unknown ultimate origin.
▶ **take after** resemble (a parent or ancestor): *the rest of us take after our mother.*
take against Brit. begin to dislike (someone), often for no strong or obvious reason: *from the moment he arrived, they took against this talented loudmouth.*
take something apart dismantle something.
▪ (**take someone/thing apart**) informal attack, criticize, or defeat someone or something in a vigorous or forceful way.

t

take something away Brit. buy food at a cafe or restaurant for eating elsewhere: *he ordered a lamb madras to take away.*
take away from detract from: *that shouldn't take away from the achievement of the French.*
take someone back strongly remind someone of a past time: *if 'Disco Inferno' doesn't take you back, the bell-bottom pants will.*
take something back 1 retract a statement: *I take back nothing of what I said.* **2** return unsatisfactory goods to a shop. ■ (of a shop) accept such goods. **3** Printing transfer text to the previous line.
take something down 1 write down spoken words: *I took down the address.* **2** dismantle and remove a structure: *the old Norman church was taken down in 1819.*
take from another way of saying ***take away from***.
take someone in 1 accommodate someone as a lodger or because they are homeless or in difficulties. **2** cheat, fool, or deceive someone: *she tried to pass this off as an amusing story, but nobody was taken in.*
take something in 1 undertake work at home. **2** make a garment tighter by altering its seams. ■ Sailing furl a sail. **3** include or encompass something: *the sweep of his arm took in most of Main Street.* ■ fully understand or absorb something heard or seen: *she took in the scene at a glance.* **4** visit or attend a place or event in a casual way or on the way to another: *he'd maybe take in a movie, or just relax.*
take off 1 (of an aircraft or bird) become airborne. ■ (of an enterprise) become successful or popular: *the newly launched electronic newspaper has really taken off.* **2** (also **take oneself off**) depart hastily: *the officer took off after his men.*
take someone off informal, chiefly Brit. mimic someone humorously.
take something off 1 remove clothing from one's or another's body: *she took off her cardigan.* **2** deduct part of an amount. **3** choose to have a period away from work: *I took the next day off.*
take on Brit. informal become very upset, especially needlessly: *don't take on so—no need to upset yourself.*
take someone on 1 engage an employee. **2** be willing or ready to meet an adversary or opponent, especially a stronger one: *a group of villagers has taken on the planners.*
take something on 1 undertake a task or responsibility, especially a difficult one: *whoever takes on the trout farm will have their work cut out.* **2** acquire a particular meaning or quality: *the subject has taken on a new significance in the past year.*
take someone out Bridge respond to a bid or double by one's partner by bidding a different suit.
take someone/thing out informal kill, destroy, or disable someone or something.
take something out 1 obtain an official document or service: *you can take out a loan for a specific purchase.* ■ get a licence or summons issued. **2** chiefly US another way of saying ***take something away***.
take something out on relieve frustration or anger by attacking or mistreating (a person or thing not responsible for such feelings).
take something over 1 (also **take over**) assume control of something: *British troops had taken over the German trenches.* ■ (of a company) buy out another. ■ become responsible for a task in succession to another: *he will take over as chief executive in April.* **2** Printing transfer text to the next line.
take to 1 begin or fall into the habit of: *he took to hiding some secret supplies in his desk.* **2** form a liking for: *Mrs Brady never took to Moran.* ■ develop an ability for (something), especially quickly or easily: *I took to pole-vaulting right away.* **3** go to (a place) to escape danger or an enemy: *they took to the hills.*
take someone up adopt someone as a protégé.
take something up 1 become interested or engaged in a pursuit: *she took up tennis at the age of 11.* ■ begin to hold or fulfil a position or post: *he left to take up an appointment as a missionary.* ■ accept an offer or challenge. **2** occupy time, space, or attention: *I don't want to take up any more of your time.* **3** pursue a matter later or further: *he'll have to take it up with the bishop.* ■ (also **take up**) resume speaking after an interruption: *I took up where I had left off.* **4** shorten a garment by turning up the hem.
take someone up on 1 challenge or question a speaker on (a particular point): *the interviewer did not take him up on his quotation.* **2** accept (an offer or challenge) from someone: *I'd like to take you up on that offer.*
take up with begin to associate with (someone), especially in a way disapproved of by the speaker: *he's taken up with a divorced woman, I understand.*

takeaway ▶ **noun 1** Brit. a restaurant or shop selling cooked food to be eaten elsewhere: *the menu from a Chinese takeaway* | [as modifier] *a takeaway pizza.*
■ a meal or dish of such food.
2 Golf another term for **BACKSWING**.

takedown chiefly N. Amer. ▶ **noun 1** a wrestling manoeuvre in which an opponent is swiftly brought to the mat from a standing position.
2 informal a police raid or arrest.
3 [as modifier] denoting a firearm with the capacity to have the barrel and magazine detached from the stock.

take-home pay ▶ **noun** [mass noun] the pay received by an employee after the deduction of tax and insurance.

take-off ▶ **noun 1** [mass noun] the action of becoming airborne: *the plane accelerated down the runway for take-off* | [count noun] *a perfect take-off.*
2 an act of mimicking someone or something: *the film is a take-off of Star Wars.*

takeout ▶ **noun 1** chiefly N. Amer. a takeaway.
2 Bridge a bid (in a different suit) made in response to a bid or double by one's partner.

take-out double ▶ **noun** Bridge a double which, by convention, requires one's partner to bid, used to convey information rather than to score penalty points. Often contrasted with **BUSINESS DOUBLE**.

takeover ▶ **noun** an act of assuming control of something, especially the buying-out of one company by another.

taker ▶ **noun 1** [in combination] a person who takes a specified thing: *a drug-taker* | *a risk-taker.*
2 a person who takes a bet or accepts an offer or challenge: *there were plenty of takers when I offered a small wager.*

take-up ▶ **noun** [mass noun] **1** the acceptance of something offered: *education is aiding the take-up of birth control.*
2 Stock Exchange the action of paying in full for securities originally bought on margin.

takht /tɑːkt/ ▶ **noun** (in Eastern countries) a sofa or long bench, or a bed.
– ORIGIN from Persian *takt*.

takin /ˈtɑːkɪn/ ▶ **noun** a large heavily built goat-antelope found in steep, dense woodlands of the eastern Himalayas.
• *Budorcas taxicolor*, family Bovidae.
– ORIGIN mid 19th cent.: a local word.

taking ▶ **noun 1** [mass noun] the action or process of taking something: *the taking of life.*
2 (**takings**) the amount of money earned by a business from the sale of goods or services: *the big test for the shop's new look is whether it'll boost takings.*
▶ **adjective** dated (of a person) captivating in manner; charming: *he was not a very taking person, she felt.*
– PHRASES **for the taking** ready or available for someone to take advantage of: *the fourth game was Wright's for the taking.*
– DERIVATIVES **takingly** adverb.

Taki-Taki /ˈtɑːkɪˌtɑːki/ ▶ **noun** [mass noun] an English-based creole language of Suriname. Also called **SRANAN**.
– ORIGIN an alteration of **TALKEE-TALKEE**.

Taklimakan Desert /ˌtakləməˈkɑːn/ (also **Takla Makan**) a desert in the Xinjiang autonomous region of NW China, lying between the Kunlun Shan and Tien Shan mountains and forming the greater part of the Tarim Basin.

Takoradi /ˌtɑːkəˈrɑːdi/ a seaport in western Ghana, on the Gulf of Guinea; pop. 615,000 (1984). It is part of the joint urban area of Sekondi-Takoradi and is one of the major seaports of West Africa.

tala[1] /ˈtɑːlə/ ▶ **noun** a traditional rhythmic pattern in classical Indian music.
– ORIGIN from Sanskrit *tāla* 'handclapping, musical time'.

tala[2] /ˈtɑːlə/ ▶ **noun** (pl. same or **talas**) the basic monetary unit of Samoa, equal to 100 sene.
– ORIGIN from Samoan *tālā*.

Talaing /təˈlʌɪŋ/ ▶ **noun** (pl. same or **Talaings**) & **adjective** another term for **MON**.
– ORIGIN the name in Burmese.

talapoin /ˈtaləpɔɪn/ ▶ **noun 1** a Buddhist monk or priest.
2 a small West African monkey that lives in large groups near watercourses and in swamp forest.
• *Miopithecus talapoin*, family Cercopithecidae.
– ORIGIN late 16th cent.: from Portuguese *talapão*, from Mon *tala pói*, literally 'lord of merit', used as a respectful title for a Buddhist monk.

talaq /taˈlɑːk/ ▶ **noun** [mass noun] (in Islamic law) divorce effected by the husband's threefold repetition of the word 'talaq', this constituting a formal repudiation of his wife.
– ORIGIN from Arabic *ṭalāq*, from *ṭalaqa* 'repudiate'.

talaria /təˈlɛːrɪə/ ▶ **plural noun** (in Roman mythology) winged sandals as worn by certain gods and goddesses, especially Mercury.
– ORIGIN Latin, neuter plural of *talaris*, from *talus* 'ankle'.

Talbot /ˈtɔːlbət, ˈtɒl-/, (William Henry) Fox (1800–77), English pioneer of photography. He produced the first photograph on paper in 1835. Five years later he discovered a process for producing a negative from which multiple positive prints could be made, though the independently developed daguerreotype proved to be superior.

talbot /ˈtɔːlbət, ˈtɒl-/ ▶ **noun** a dog of an extinct light-coloured breed of hound with large ears and heavy jaws.
– ORIGIN late Middle English: probably from the family name *Talbot*; the term was also used to denote the representation of such a dog in the badge and supporters of the Talbot family, earls of Shrewsbury.

talc ▶ **noun** [mass noun] talcum powder.
■ a white, grey, or pale green soft mineral with a greasy feel, occurring as translucent masses or laminae and consisting of hydrated magnesium silicate.
▶ **verb** (**talced**, **talcing**) [with obj.] powder or treat (something) with talc.
– DERIVATIVES **talcose** adjective (Geology), **talcy** adjective.
– ORIGIN late 16th cent. (denoting the mineral): from medieval Latin *talcum* (see **TALCUM**).

talcum (also **talcum powder**) ▶ **noun** [mass noun] a cosmetic or toilet preparation consisting of the mineral talc in powdered form, typically perfumed.
▶ **verb** (**talcumed**, **talcuming**) [with obj.] powder (something) with this substance.
– ORIGIN mid 16th cent.: from medieval Latin, from Arabic *ṭalḳ*, from Persian.

tale ▶ **noun 1** a fictitious or true narrative or story, especially one that is imaginatively recounted.
■ a lie.
2 archaic a number or total: *an exact tale of the dead bodies.*
– PHRASES **a tale of a tub** archaic an apocryphal story. **tell tales** see **TELL**[1].
– ORIGIN Old English *talu* 'telling, something told', of Germanic origin; related to Dutch *taal* 'speech' and German *Zahl* 'number', also to **TELL**[1]. Sense 2 is probably from Old Norse.

talebearer ▶ **noun** dated a person who maliciously gossips or reveals secrets.
– DERIVATIVES **talebearing** noun & adjective.

taleggio /taˈlɛdʒɪəʊ/ ▶ **noun** [mass noun] a type of soft Italian cheese made from cows' milk.
– ORIGIN named after the *Taleggio* valley in Lombardy.

talent ▶ **noun 1** [mass noun] natural aptitude or skill: *he possesses more talent than any other player* | [count noun] *she displayed **a talent for** garden design.*
■ people possessing such aptitude or skill: *I signed all the talent in Rome* | [count noun] *Simon is a talent to watch.* ■ informal people regarded as sexually attractive or as prospective sexual partners: *most Saturday nights I have this urge to go on the hunt for new talent.*
2 a former weight and unit of currency, used especially by the ancient Romans and Greeks.
– DERIVATIVES **talentless** adjective.
– ORIGIN Old English *talente*, *talentan* (as a unit of weight), from Latin *talenta*, plural of *talentum* 'weight, sum of money', from Greek *talanton*. Sense 1 is a figurative use with biblical allusion to the parable of the talents (Matt. 25:14–30).

talented ▶ **adjective** having a natural aptitude or skill for something: *a talented young musician.*

talent scout ▶ **noun** a person whose job is to

search for talented performers who can be employed or promoted, especially in sport and entertainment.

talent spotter ▶ **noun** Brit. a talent scout.
– DERIVATIVES **talent-spot** verb.

tales /ˈteɪliːz/ ▶ **noun** Law a writ for summoning substitute jurors when the original jury has become deficient in number.
– ORIGIN from Latin *tales (de circumstantibus)* 'such (of the bystanders)', the first words of the writ.

talesman /ˈteɪliːzmən, ˈteɪlz-/ ▶ **noun** (pl. **-men**) Law a person summoned by a tales.

taleteller ▶ **noun** a person who tells stories.
■ a person who spreads gossip or reveals secrets.
– DERIVATIVES **tale-telling** noun.

tali plural form of **TALUS**[1].

Taliban /ˈtalɪban/ a fundamentalist Muslim movement whose militia took control of much of Afghanistan from early 1995, and in 1996 took Kabul and set up an Islamic state. The Taliban were overthrown by US-led forces and Afghan groups in 2001 following the terrorist attacks on the World Trade Center and the Pentagon.
– ORIGIN from Pashto or Dari, from Persian, literally 'students, seekers of knowledge'.

talik /ˈtalɪk/ ▶ **noun** Geology an area of unfrozen ground surrounded by permafrost.
– ORIGIN 1940s: from Russian, from *tayat'* 'melt'.

talipes /ˈtalɪpiːz/ ▶ **noun** Medicine technical term for **CLUB FOOT**.
– ORIGIN mid 19th cent.: modern Latin, from Latin *talus* 'ankle' + *pes* 'foot'.

talipot /ˈtalɪpɒt/ ▶ **noun** a tall Indian palm with very large fan-shaped leaves and a flower that can reach 8 m tall. The leaves are used as sunshades and for thatching, and to make the material upon which Buddhist sacred books are written.
• *Corypha umbraculifera*, family Palmae.
– ORIGIN late 17th cent.: from Malayalam *tālipat*, from Sanskrit *tālīpatra*, from *tālī* 'palm' + *patra* 'leaf'.

talisman /ˈtalɪzmən/ ▶ **noun** (pl. **talismans**) an object, typically an inscribed ring or stone, that is thought to have magic powers and to bring good luck.
– DERIVATIVES **talismanic** /-ˈmanɪk/ adjective.
– ORIGIN mid 17th cent.: based on Arabic *ṭilsam*, apparently from an alteration of late Greek *telesma* 'completion, religious rite', from *telein* 'complete, perform a rite', from *telos* 'result, end'.

talk ▶ **verb** [no obj.] speak in order to give information or express ideas or feelings; converse or communicate by spoken words: *the two men talked* | *we'd sit and* **talk about** *jazz* | *it was no use* **talking to** *Anthony* | [with obj.] *you're talking rubbish.*
■ have the power of speech: *he can talk as well as you or I can.* ■ discuss personal or intimate feelings: *we need to talk, Maggie.* ■ have formal dealings or discussions; negotiate: *they won't* **talk to** *the regime that killed their families.* ■ (**talk something over/through**) discuss something thoroughly. ■ (**talk at**) address (someone) in a hectoring or self-important way without listening to their replies: *he never talked at you.* ■ (**talk to**) reprimand or scold (someone): *someone will have to talk to Lily.* ■ [with obj.] (**be talking**) informal used to emphasize the seriousness, importance, or extent of the thing one is mentioning or in the process of discussing: *we're talking big money.* ■ [with obj.] use (a particular language) in speech: *we were talking German.* ■ [with obj. and adverbial] persuade or cause (someone) to do something by talking: *don't try to talk me into acting as a go-between.* ■ reveal secret or confidential information; betray secrets. ■ gossip: *you'll have the whole school talking.*
▶ **noun** [mass noun] conversation; discussion: *there was a slight but noticeable lull in the talk.*
■ [count noun] a period of conversation or discussion, especially a relatively serious one: *my mother had a talk with Louis.* ■ [count noun] an informal address or lecture. ■ rumour, gossip, or speculation: *there is* **talk** *of an armistice.* ■ empty promises or boasting: *he's all talk.* ■ (**the talk of**) a current subject of widespread gossip or speculation in (a particular place): *within days I was* **the talk of the town**. ■ (**talks**) formal discussions or negotiations over a period: *peace talks.*
– PHRASES **you can't** (or **can**) (US **shouldn't** or **should**) **talk** informal used to convey that a criticism made applies equally well to the person who has made it: *'He'd chase anything in a skirt!' 'You can't talk!'* **don't talk to me about ——** informal said in protest when someone introduces a subject of which the speaker has had bitter personal experience. **know what one is talking about** be expert or authoritative on a specified subject. **look** (or **hark**) **who's talking** another way of saying *you can't talk*. **now you're talking** see **NOW**. **talk a blue streak** see **BLUE**[1]. **talk about ——!** informal used to emphasize that something is an extreme or striking example of a particular situation, state, or experience: *Talk about hangovers! But aching head or not we were getting ready.* **talk big** informal talk boastfully or overconfidently. **talk dirty** see **DIRTY**. **talk the hind leg off a donkey** Brit. informal talk incessantly. **talk nineteen to the dozen** see **DOZEN**. **talk of the devil** see **DEVIL**. **talk sense into** persuade (someone) to behave more sensibly. **talk shop** see **SHOP**. **talk through one's hat** (or Brit. **arse** or **backside** or US **ass**) informal talk foolishly, wildly, or ignorantly. **talk turkey** see **TURKEY**.
– DERIVATIVES **talker** noun.
– ORIGIN Middle English: frequentative verb from the Germanic base of **TALE** or **TELL**[1].
▶ **talk back** reply defiantly or insolently.
talk down to speak patronizingly or condescendingly to.
talk something out Brit. (in Parliament) block the course of a bill by prolonging discussion to the time of adjournment.
talk someone round (or US **around**) bring someone to a particular point of view by talking.
talk someone through enable someone to perform (a task) by giving them continuous instruction.
talk someone/thing up (or **down**) discuss someone or something in a way that makes them seem more (or less) interesting or attractive.

talkathon ▶ **noun** informal a prolonged discussion or debate.
– ORIGIN 1930s (originally US, denoting a debate artificially prolonged to prevent the progress of a bill): blend of **TALK** and **MARATHON**.

talkative ▶ **adjective** fond of or given to talking: *the talkative driver hadn't stopped chatting.*
– DERIVATIVES **talkatively** adverb, **talkativeness** noun.

talkback ▶ **noun** **1** a system of two-way communication by loudspeaker.
2 another term for **PHONE-IN**.

talkee-talkee /ˈtɔːkɪˌtɔːki/ ▶ **noun** [mass noun] dated an English-based creole or pidgin language, particularly in the Caribbean region. See also **TAKI-TAKI**.
– ORIGIN from **TALK**.

talkfest ▶ **noun** informal, chiefly N. Amer. a session of lengthy discussion or conversation, especially a television chat show or debate.

talkie ▶ **noun** informal a film with a soundtrack, as distinct from a silent film.
– ORIGIN early 20th cent. (originally US in the phrase *the talkies*): from **TALK**, on the pattern of *movie*.

talking ▶ **adjective** [attrib.] engaging in speech.
■ (of an animal or object) able to make sounds similar to those of speech: *the world's greatest talking bird.* ■ silently expressive: *he did have talking eyes.*
▶ **noun** [mass noun] the action of talking; speech or discussion: *I'll do the talking—you just back me up.*
– PHRASES **talking of ——** chiefly Brit. while we are on the subject of ——: *talking of cards, you'd better take a couple of my business cards.*

talking blues ▶ **plural noun** [mass noun] a style of blues music in which the lyrics are more or less spoken rather than sung.

talking book ▶ **noun** a recorded reading of a book, originally designed for use by the blind.

talking drum ▶ **noun** one of a set of West African drums, each having a different pitch, which are beaten to transmit a tonal language.

talking film (also **talking picture**) ▶ **noun** a film with a soundtrack, as distinct from a silent film.

talking head ▶ **noun** informal a presenter or reporter on television who addresses the camera and is viewed in close-up.

talking point ▶ **noun** a topic that invites discussion or argument.

talking shop (also **talk shop**) ▶ **noun** Brit. a place or group regarded as a centre for unproductive talk rather than action.

talking-to ▶ **noun** [in sing.] informal a sharp reprimand.

talk radio ▶ **noun** [mass noun] chiefly N. Amer. a type of radio broadcast in which the presenter talks about topical issues and encourages listeners to ring in to air their opinions.

talk show ▶ **noun** a chat show, especially one in which listeners, viewers, or the studio audience are invited to participate in the discussion.

talktime ▶ **noun** [mass noun] the time during which a mobile telephone is in use to handle calls, especially as a measure of the duration of the telephone's battery.

tall ▶ **adjective** **1** of great or more than average height, especially (with reference to an object) relative to width: *a tall, broad-shouldered man* | *a tall glass of iced tea.*
■ (after a measurement and in questions) measuring a specified distance from top to bottom: *he was over six feet tall* | *how tall are you?* ■ [as adv.] used in reference to proud and confident movement or behaviour: *stop wishing that you were somehow different—start to* **walk tall**!
2 [attrib.] informal (of an account) fanciful and difficult to believe; unlikely: *a tall story.*
– PHRASES **a tall order** an unreasonable or difficult demand.
– DERIVATIVES **tallish** adjective, **tallness** noun.
– ORIGIN late Middle English: probably from Old English *getæl* 'swift, prompt'. Early senses also included 'fine, handsome' and 'bold, strong, good at fighting'.

tallage /ˈtalɪdʒ/ ▶ **noun** historical a form of arbitrary taxation levied by kings on the towns and lands of the Crown, abolished in the 14th century.
■ a tax levied on feudal dependants by their superiors.
– ORIGIN Middle English: from Old French *taillage*, from *tailler* 'to cut' (see **TAIL**[2]).

Tallahassee /ˌtaləˈhasi/ the state capital of Florida; pop. 124,770 (1990).

tallboy ▶ **noun** Brit. a tall chest of drawers, typically one mounted on legs and in two sections, one standing on the other. Compare with **HIGHBOY**.

Talleyrand /ˈtalɪrand, French talɛʀɑ̃/, Charles Maurice de (1754–1838), French statesman; full surname *Talleyrand-Périgord*. Involved in the coup that brought Napoleon to power, he became head of the new government after the fall of Napoleon (1814) and was later instrumental in the overthrow of Charles X and the accession of Louis Philippe (1830).

tall hat ▶ **noun** another term for **TOP HAT**.

Tallinn /ˈtalɪn/ the capital of Estonia, a port on the Gulf of Finland; pop. 505,000 (est. 1989).

Tallis /ˈtalɪs/, Thomas (*c.*1505–85), English composer. Organist of the Chapel Royal jointly with William Byrd, he served under Henry VIII, Edward VI, Mary, and Elizabeth I. His works include the forty-part motet *Spem in Alium*.

tallith /ˈtalɪθ/ ▶ **noun** a fringed shawl traditionally worn by Jewish men at prayer.
– ORIGIN from Rabbinical Hebrew *ṭallīt*, from biblical Hebrew *ṭillēl* 'to cover'.

tallow ▶ **noun** [mass noun] a hard fatty substance made from rendered animal fat, used in making candles and soap.
▶ **verb** [with obj.] archaic smear (something, especially the bottom of a boat) with such a substance.
– DERIVATIVES **tallowy** adjective.
– ORIGIN Middle English: perhaps from Middle Low German; related to Dutch *talk* and German *Talg*.

tallow tree ▶ **noun** a tree with fatty seeds from which vegetable tallow or other oils are extracted.
• Several species and families, in particular the **Chinese** (or **vegetable**) **tallow tree** (*Sapium sebiferum*, family Euphorbiaceae), native to East Asia.

tallow-wood ▶ **noun** a large Australian eucalyptus which yields very hard, greasy timber.
• *Eucalyptus microcorys*, family Myrtaceae.

tall poppy syndrome ▶ **noun** [mass noun] informal, chiefly Austral. a perceived tendency to discredit or disparage those who have achieved notable wealth or prominence in public life.

tall ship ▶ **noun** a sailing ship with a high mast or masts.

tall timber ▶ **noun** [mass noun] N. Amer. dense and uninhabited forest.
■ [count noun] (usu. **tall timbers**) informal a remote or unknown place.

tally ▶ **noun** (pl. **-ies**) **1** a current score or amount: *that takes his tally to 10 goals in 10 games.*

t

■ a record of a score or amount: *I **kept a running tally** of David's debt on a note above my desk.* ■ a particular number taken as a group or unit to facilitate counting. ■ a mark registering such a number. ■ (also **tally stick**) historical a piece of wood scored across with notches for the items of an account and then split into halves, each party keeping one. ■ an account kept in such a way. ■ archaic a counterpart or duplicate of something.
2 a label attached to a plant or tree, or stuck in the ground beside it, that gives information about it, such as its name and class.
▶**verb** (**-ies, -ied**) **1** [no obj.] agree or correspond: *their signatures should **tally with** their names on the register.* **2** [with obj.] calculate the total number of: *the votes were being tallied with abacuses.*
– DERIVATIVES **tallier** noun.
– ORIGIN late Middle English (denoting a notched tally stick): from Anglo-Norman French *tallie*, from Latin *talea* 'twig, cutting'. Compare with **TAIL**².

tally-ho ▶**exclamation** a huntsman's cry to the hounds on sighting a fox.
▶**noun** (pl. **-os**) **1** an utterance of this.
2 historical a fast horse-drawn coach.
▶**verb** (**-oes, -oed**) [no obj.] utter a cry of 'tally-ho'.
– ORIGIN late 18th cent.: apparently an alteration of French *taïaut*, of unknown origin.

tallyman ▶**noun** (pl. **-men**) **1** Brit. a person who sells goods on credit, especially from door to door.
2 a person who keeps a score or record of something.

tally system ▶**noun** Brit. a system of selling goods on short-term credit or an instalment plan.

Talmud /ˈtalmʊd, -məd/ ▶**noun** (**the Talmud**) the body of Jewish civil and ceremonial law and legend comprising the Mishnah and the Gemara. There are two versions of the Talmud: the Babylonian Talmud (which dates from the 5th century AD but includes earlier material) and the earlier Palestinian or Jerusalem Talmud.
– DERIVATIVES **Talmudic** adjective, **Talmudical** adjective, **Talmudist** noun.
– ORIGIN from late Hebrew *talmūḏ* 'instruction', from Hebrew *lāmaḏ* 'learn'.

Talmud Torah ▶**noun** [mass noun] Judaism the field of study that deals with the Jewish law.
■ [count noun] a communal school where children are instructed in Judaism.

talon ▶**noun** **1** a claw, especially one belonging to a bird of prey.
2 the shoulder of a bolt against which the key presses to slide it in a lock.
3 (in various card games) the cards remaining undealt.
4 a printed form attached to a bearer bond that enables the holder to apply for a new sheet of coupons when the existing coupons have been used up.
5 an ogee moulding.
– DERIVATIVES **taloned** adjective.
– ORIGIN late Middle English (denoting any heel-like part or object): from Old French, literally 'heel', from Latin *talus* 'ankle bone, heel'.

taluk /ˈtɑːlʊk/ (also **taluka** /ˈtɑːlʊkɑː/ or **taluq**) ▶**noun** (in the Indian subcontinent) an administrative district for taxation purposes, typically comprising a number of villages.
– ORIGIN via Persian and Urdu from Arabic *ta'allaḳa* 'be connected'.

talus¹ /ˈteɪləs/ ▶**noun** (pl. **tali** /-lʌɪ/) Anatomy the large bone in the ankle, which articulates with the tibia of the leg and the calcaneum and navicular bone of the foot. Also called **ASTRAGALUS**.
– ORIGIN late 16th cent.: from Latin, literally 'ankle, heel'.

talus² /ˈteɪləs/ ▶**noun** (pl. **taluses**) [mass noun] a sloping mass of rock fragments at the foot of a cliff.
■ [count noun] the sloping side of an earthwork, or of a wall that tapers to the top.
– ORIGIN mid 17th cent.: from French, of unknown origin.

TAM ▶**abbreviation for** television audience measurement.

tam ▶**noun** a tam-o'-shanter.
– ORIGIN late 19th cent.: abbreviation.

tamagotchi /ˌtaməˈgɒtʃi/ ▶**noun** trademark an electronic toy displaying a digital image of a creature, which has to be looked after and responded to by the 'owner' as if it were a pet.
– ORIGIN Japanese.

tamale /təˈmɑːleɪ, -ˈmɑːli/ ▶**noun** a Mexican dish of seasoned meat and maize flour steamed or baked in maize husks.
– ORIGIN from Mexican Spanish *tamal*, plural *tamales*, from Nahuatl *tamalli*.

tamandua /təˈmand(j)ʊə, ˌtam(ə)nˈduːə/ ▶**noun** a small nocturnal arboreal anteater with a naked prehensile tail, native to tropical America.
● Genus *Tamandua*, family Myrmecophagidae: two species.
– ORIGIN early 17th cent.: via Portuguese from Tupi *tamanduá*, from *taly* 'ant' + *monduar* 'hunter'.

Tamang /taˈmaŋ/ ▶**noun** (pl. same or **Tamangs**) **1** a member of a Buddhist people inhabiting mountainous parts of Nepal and Sikkim.
2 [mass noun] the Tibeto-Burman language of this people.
▶**adjective** of or relating to this people or their language.
– ORIGIN Nepali, from *rtamaṅ* 'owner of many horses'.

Tamar /ˈteɪmɑː/ a river in SW England which rises in NW Devon and flows 98 km (60 miles) generally southwards, forming the boundary between Devon and Cornwall and emptying into the English Channel through Plymouth Sound.

tamarack /ˈtamərak/ ▶**noun** a slender North American larch.
● *Larix laricina*, family Pinaceae.
– ORIGIN early 19th cent.: from Canadian French *tamarac*, probably of Algonquian origin.

tamarau /ˈtamərau/ ▶**noun** a small brownish-black buffalo similar to the anoa, found only on Mindoro in the Philippines.
● *Bubalus mindorensis*, family Bovidae.
– ORIGIN late 19th cent.: from Tagalog.

tamari /təˈmɑːri/ (also **tamari sauce**) ▶**noun** [mass noun] a variety of rich, naturally fermented soy sauce.
– ORIGIN Japanese.

tamarillo /ˌtaməˈrɪləʊ/ ▶**noun** (pl. **-os**) chiefly Austral./NZ a tropical South American plant of the nightshade family, which bears edible egg-shaped red fruits. Also called **TREE TOMATO**.
● *Cyphomandra betaceae*, family Solanaceae.
■ the fruit of this plant.
– ORIGIN 1960s (originally NZ): an invented name, perhaps suggested by Spanish *tomatillo*, diminutive of *tomate* 'tomato'.

tamarin /ˈtam(ə)rɪn/ ▶**noun** a small forest-dwelling South American monkey of the marmoset family, typically brightly coloured and with tufts and crests of hair around the face and neck.
● Genera *Saguinus* and *Leontopithecus*, family Callitrichidae (or Callithricidae): several species.
– ORIGIN late 18th cent.: from French, from Galibi.

tamarind /ˈtam(ə)rɪnd/ ▶**noun** **1** [mass noun] sticky brown acidic pulp from the pod of a tree of the pea family, widely used as a flavouring in Asian cookery.
■ [count noun] the pod from which this pulp is extracted.
2 the tropical African tree which yields these pods, cultivated throughout the tropics and also grown as an ornamental and shade tree.
● *Tamarindus indica*, family Leguminosae.
– ORIGIN late Middle English: from medieval Latin *tamarindus*, from Arabic *tamr hindī* 'Indian date'.

tamarisk /ˈtam(ə)rɪsk/ ▶**noun** an Old World shrub or small tree with tiny scale-like leaves borne on slender branches, giving it a feathery appearance.
● Genus *Tamarix*, family Tamaricaceae: many species, including the **French tamarisk** (*T. gallica*), a common coastal shrub of SW Europe.
– ORIGIN late Middle English: from late Latin *tamariscus*, variant of Latin *tamarix*, of unknown origin.

tamasha /təˈmɑːʃə/ ▶**noun** Indian a grand show, performance, or celebration, especially one involving dance.
– ORIGIN via Persian and Urdu from Arabic *tamāšā* 'walk about together'.

Tamashek /ˈtaməʃɛk/ ▶**noun** [mass noun] the dialect of Berber spoken by the Tuareg, sometimes regarded as a separate language.
– ORIGIN the name in Berber.

Tamaulipas /ˌtamaʊˈliːpas/ a state of NE Mexico with a coastline on the Gulf of Mexico; capital, Ciudad Victoria.

tambala /tamˈbɑːlə/ ▶**noun** (pl. same or **tambalas**) a monetary unit of Malawi, equal to one hundredth of a kwacha.
– ORIGIN from Nyanja, literally 'cockerel'.

Tambo /ˈtambəʊ/, Oliver (1917–93), South African politician. He joined the African National Congress in 1944, became its acting president in 1967, and was president from 1977 until 1991, when he resigned in favour of the recently released Nelson Mandela.

tambotie /tamˈbʊti, -ˈbuːti, -ˈbəʊti/ ▶**noun** S. African an African tree of the spurge family, with scented timber and caustic sap.
● *Spirostachys africana*, family Euphorbiaceae.
– ORIGIN mid 19th cent.: from Xhosa *um-Thombothi*, literally 'poison tree'.

tambour /ˈtambʊə/ ▶**noun** **1** historical a small drum.
2 something resembling a drum in shape or construction, in particular:
■ a circular frame for holding fabric taut while it is being embroidered. ■ Architecture a wall of circular plan, such as one supporting a dome or surrounded by a colonnade. ■ Architecture each of a sequence of cylindrical stones forming the shaft of a column. ■ Architecture a lobby enclosed by a ceiling and folding doors to prevent draughts, typically within a church porch. ■ a sloping buttress or projection in a real tennis or fives court. ■ [usu. as modifier] a sliding flexible shutter or door on a piece of furniture, made of strips of wood attached to a backing of canvas: *a tambour door.*
▶**verb** [with obj.] [often as adj. **tamboured**] decorate or embroider on a tambour: *a tamboured waistcoat.*
– ORIGIN late 15th cent.: from French *tambour* 'drum'; perhaps related to Persian *tabīra* 'drum'. Compare with **TABOR**.

tamboura /tamˈbʊərə/ (also **tambura**) ▶**noun** **1** a large four-stringed lute used in Indian music as a drone accompaniment. Also called **TANPURA**.
2 a long-necked lute or mandolin of Balkan countries.
– ORIGIN late 16th cent. (denoting a type of long-necked lute): from Arabic *ṭanbūr* or Persian *tunbūra*, both from Persian *dunbara*, literally 'lamb's tail'.

tambourin /ˈtambərɪn/ ▶**noun** a long narrow drum used in Provence.
■ a dance accompanied by such a drum.
– ORIGIN French, diminutive of *tambour* (see **TAMBOUR**).

tambourine /ˌtambəˈriːn/ ▶**noun** a percussion instrument resembling a shallow drum with metal discs in slots around the edge, played by being shaken or hit with the hand.
– DERIVATIVES **tambourinist** noun.
– ORIGIN late 16th cent.: from French *tambourin* (see **TAMBOURIN**).

Tambov /tamˈbɒf/ an industrial city in SW Russia; pop. 307,000 (1990).

tambura ▶**noun** variant spelling of **TAMBOURA**.

tamburitza /tamˈbʊrɪtsə/ ▶**noun** a kind of long-necked mandolin played in Croatia and neighbouring countries.
– ORIGIN Serbo-Croat, diminutive of *tambura* **TAMBOURA**.

tame ▶**adjective** **1** (of an animal) not dangerous or frightened of people; domesticated: *the fish are so tame you have to push them away from your face mask.*
■ not exciting, adventurous, or controversial. ■ informal (of a person) willing to cooperate.
2 US (of a plant) produced by cultivation.
■ (of land) cultivated.
▶**verb** [with obj.] (often **be tamed**) domesticate (an animal).
■ make less powerful and easier to control: *the battle to tame inflation.*
– DERIVATIVES **tameable** (also **tamable**) adjective, **tamely** adverb, **tameness** noun, **tamer** noun [in combination] *a lion-tamer.*
– ORIGIN Old English *tam* (adjective), *temmian* (verb), of Germanic origin; related to Dutch *tam* and German *zahm*, from an Indo-European root shared by Latin *domare* and Greek *daman* 'tame, subdue'.

Tamerlane /ˈtaməleɪn/ (also **Tamburlaine** /ˈtambə-/) (1336–1405), Mongol ruler of Samarkand 1369–1405; Tartar name *Timur Lenk* ('lame Timur'). Leading a force of Mongols and Turks, he conquered Persia, northern India, and Syria and established his capital at Samarkand. He was the ancestor of the Mogul dynasty in India.

Tamil /ˈtamɪl/ ▶**noun** **1** a member of a people inhabiting parts of South India and Sri Lanka.

b **b**ut | d **d**og | f **f**ew | g **g**et | h **h**e | j **y**es | k **c**at | l **l**eg | m **m**an | n **n**o | p **p**en | r **r**ed | s **s**it | t **t**op | v **v**oice | w **w**e | z **z**oo | ʃ **sh**e | ʒ de**c**ision | θ **th**in | ð **th**is | ŋ ri**ng** | x lo**ch** | tʃ **ch**ip | dʒ **j**ar

2 [mass noun] the Dravidian language of the Tamils, spoken by about 50 million people.
▶ **adjective** of or relating to this people or their language.
– DERIVATIVES **Tamilian** adjective & noun.
– ORIGIN the name in Tamil.

Tamil Nadu /ˈnɑːduː/ a state in the extreme south-east of the Indian peninsula, on the Coromandel Coast, with a largely Tamil-speaking, Hindu population; capital, Madras. Tamil Nadu was formerly an ancient kingdom comprising a much larger area, stretching northwards to Orissa and including the Lakshadweep Islands and part of the Malabar Coast. Former name (until 1968) **MADRAS**.

Tamil Tigers a Sri Lankan guerrilla organization founded in 1972 that seeks the establishment of an independent state (Eelam) in the north-east of the country for the Tamil community. Also called **LIBERATION TIGERS OF TAMIL EELAM**.

Tamla Motown /ˈtamlə/ ▶ **noun** trade name for **MOTOWN** (in sense 1).

Tammany /ˈtaməni/ (also **Tammany Hall**) (in the US) a powerful organization within the Democratic Party that was widely associated with corruption. Founded as a fraternal and benevolent society in 1789, it came to dominate political life in New York City in the 19th and early 20th centuries, before being reduced in power by Franklin D. Roosevelt in the early 1930s.
■ [as noun **a Tammany**] a corrupt political organization or group.
– DERIVATIVES **Tammanyite** noun.
– ORIGIN named after an American Indian chief of the late 17th cent., said to have welcomed William Penn, and regarded as 'patron saint' of Pennsylvania and other northern colonies.

tammar wallaby /ˈtamə/ ▶ **noun** a small greyish-brown wallaby found in SW Australia.
● *Macropus eugenii*, family Macropodidae.
– ORIGIN mid 19th cent.: from Gaurna (an Aboriginal language) *tamma*.

Tammerfors /ˌtamərˈfɔrs/ Swedish name for **TAMPERE**.

Tammuz[1] /ˈtamuːz/ Near Eastern Mythology a Mesopotamian god, lover of Ishtar and similar in some respects to the Greek Adonis. He became the personification of the seasonal death and rebirth of crops.
– ORIGIN from Ezek. 8:14, from Akkadian *Dumuzi*.

Tammuz[2] variant spelling of **THAMMUZ**.

tam-o'-shanter /ˌtaməˈʃantə/ ▶ **noun** a round woollen or cloth cap of Scottish origin, with a bobble in the centre.
– ORIGIN mid 19th cent.: named after the hero of Burns's poem *Tam o' Shanter* (1790).

tamoxifen /taˈmɒksɪfɛn/ ▶ **noun** Medicine a synthetic drug used to treat breast cancer and infertility in women. It acts as an oestrogen antagonist.
– ORIGIN 1970s: an arbitrary formation based on **TRANS-**, **AMINE**, **OXY-**[2], **PHENOL**, elements of the drug's chemical name.

tamp ▶ **verb** [with obj.] pack (a blast hole) full of clay or sand to concentrate the force of the explosion: *when the hole was tamped to the top, gunpowder was inserted.*
■ [with obj. and adverbial of direction] ram or pack (a substance) down or into something firmly: *he tamped down the tobacco with his thumb.*
– ORIGIN early 19th cent.: probably a back-formation from *tampin* (interpreted as 'tamping'), variant of **TAMPION**.

Tampa /ˈtampə/ a port and resort on the west coast of Florida; pop. 280,015 (1990).

Tampax (also **tampax**) ▶ **noun** (pl. same) trademark a sanitary tampon.
– ORIGIN 1930s: an arbitrary formation from **TAMPON**.

tamper ▶ **verb** [no obj.] (**tamper with**) interfere with (something) in order to cause damage or make unauthorized alterations: *someone tampered with the brakes of my car.*
▶ **noun** a person or thing that tamps something down, especially a machine or tool for tamping down earth or ballast.
– DERIVATIVES **tamperer** noun.
– ORIGIN mid 16th cent. (in the sense 'busy oneself to a particular end, machinate'): alteration of the verb **TEMPER**.

Tampere /ˈtampəreɪ/ a city in SW Finland; pop. 172,560 (1990). Swedish name **TAMMERFORS**.

tamper-evident ▶ **adjective** (of packaging) designed to reveal any interference with the contents.

tamper-proof ▶ **adjective** made so that it cannot be interfered with or changed.

Tampico /tamˈpiːkəʊ/ one of Mexico's principal seaports, on the Gulf of Mexico; pop. 271,640 (1990).

tampion /ˈtampɪən/ (also **tompion**) ▶ **noun** a wooden stopper for the muzzle of a gun.
■ a plug for the top of an organ pipe.
– ORIGIN late Middle English: from French *tampon* 'tampon'.

tampon ▶ **noun** a plug of soft material inserted into the vagina to absorb menstrual blood.
■ Medicine a plug of material used to stop a wound or block an opening in the body and absorb blood or secretions.
▶ **verb** (**tamponed**, **tamponing**) plug with a tampon.
– ORIGIN mid 19th cent.: from French, nasalized variant of *tapon* 'plug, stopper', ultimately of Germanic origin and related to **TAP**[1].

tamponade /ˌtampəˈneɪd/ ▶ **noun** [mass noun] Medicine
1 (in full **cardiac tamponade**) compression of the heart by an accumulation of fluid in the pericardial sac.
2 the surgical use of a plug of absorbent material.

tam-tam ▶ **noun** a large metal gong.
– ORIGIN mid 19th cent.: perhaps from Hindi *ṭam-ṭam* (see **TOM-TOM**).

Tamworth[1] /ˈtamwəθ, -wəθ/ a town in central England, in Staffordshire; pop. 64,550 (1981).

Tamworth[2] /ˈtamwəθ/ ▶ **noun** a pig of a long-bodied, typically red or brown breed.

Tamworth Manifesto (in English history) an election speech by Sir Robert Peel in 1834 in his Tamworth constituency, in which he accepted the changes instituted by the Reform Act and expressed his belief in moderate political reform. The manifesto is widely held to signal the emergence of the Conservative Party from the old loose grouping of Tory interests.

tan[1] ▶ **noun 1** [mass noun] a yellowish-brown colour: [as modifier] *she dressed quickly in tan cords and a cream woollen top.*
■ [count noun] a golden-brown shade of skin developed by pale-skinned people after exposure to the sun.
2 (also **tanbark**) [mass noun] bark of oak or other trees, bruised and used as a source of tannin for converting hides into leather.
■ (also **spent tan**) such bark from which the tannin has been extracted, used for covering the ground for walking, riding, children's play, etc., and in gardening.
▶ **verb** (**tanned**, **tanning**) **1** [no obj.] (of a pale-skinned person or their skin) become brown or browner after exposure to the sun: *you'll tan very quickly in the pure air.*
■ [with obj.] [usu. as adj. **tanned**] (of the sun) cause (a pale-skinned person or their skin) to become brown or browner: *he looked tanned and fit.*
2 [with obj.] convert (animal skin) into leather by soaking in a liquid containing tannic acid, or by the use of other chemicals.
3 [with obj.] informal, dated beat (someone) repeatedly, especially as a punishment.
▶ **adjective** US (of a pale-skinned person) having golden-brown skin after exposure to the sun: *she looks tall, tan, and healthy.*
– DERIVATIVES **tannable** adjective, **tannish** adjective.
– ORIGIN late Old English *tannian* 'convert into leather', probably from medieval Latin *tannare*, perhaps of Celtic origin; reinforced in Middle English by Old French *tanner*. Early use of the noun (late Middle English) was in sense 2.

tan[2] ▶ **abbreviation** for tangent.

Tana, Lake /ˈtɑːnə/ a lake in northern Ethiopia, the source of the Blue Nile.

tanager /ˈtanədʒə/ ▶ **noun** a small American songbird of the bunting family, the male of which typically has brightly coloured plumage.
● Family Emberizidae (subfamily Thraupinae): many genera, in particular *Tangara*, and numerous species.
– ORIGIN early 17th cent. (originally as *tangara*): from Tupi *tangará*, later refashioned on the pattern of the modern Latin genus name *Tanagra*.

Tanagra /ˈtanəgrə/ an ancient Greek city in Boeotia, site of a battle in 457 BC during the Peloponnesian War. It has given its name to a type of terracotta figurine, often of a young woman, made there and elsewhere mainly in the 4th and 3rd centuries BC.

Tánaiste /ˈtɔːnɪʃtə, Irish ˈtɑːnəʃtʲə/ ▶ **noun** the deputy Prime Minister of the Republic of Ireland.
– ORIGIN from Irish *tánaiste*, literally 'second in excellence'.

Tananarive /ˌtananəˈriːv/ former name (until 1975) for **ANTANANARIVO**.

tanbark /ˈtanbɑːk/ ▶ **noun** see **TAN**[1] (sense 2).

tandem ▶ **noun** a bicycle with seats and pedals for two riders, one behind the other.
■ a carriage driven by two animals harnessed one in front of the other. ■ a group of two people or machines working together.
▶ **adverb** with two or more horses harnessed one behind another: *I rode tandem to Paris.*
■ alongside each other; together.
– PHRASES **in tandem** alongside each other. ■ one behind another.
– ORIGIN late 18th cent.: humorously from Latin, literally 'at length'.

tandoor /ˈtanduə, tanˈduə/ ▶ **noun** a clay oven of a type used originally in northern India and Pakistan.
– ORIGIN from Urdu *tandūr*, from Persian *tanūr*, based on Arabic *tannūr* 'oven'.

tandoori /tanˈduəri/ ▶ **adjective** denoting or relating to a style of Indian cooking based on the use of a tandoor: *tandoori chicken.*
▶ **noun** [mass noun] food or cooking of this type.
■ [count noun] a restaurant serving such food.
– ORIGIN from Urdu and Persian *tandūri*, from *tandūr* (see **TANDOOR**).

Tang /taŋ/ a dynasty ruling China 618–c.906, a period noted for territorial conquest and great wealth and regarded as the golden age of Chinese poetry and art.

tang[1] ▶ **noun 1** [in sing.] a strong taste, flavour, or smell: *the clean salty tang of the sea.*
■ a characteristic quality: *his words came out with a distinct tang of broad Lancashire.*
2 the projection on the blade of a tool such as a knife, by which the blade is held firmly in the handle.
– ORIGIN Middle English (denoting a snake's tongue, formerly believed to be a stinging organ; also denoting the sting of an insect): from Old Norse *tangi* 'point, tang of a knife'.

tang[2] ▶ **verb** [no obj.] make a loud ringing or clanging sound: *the bronze bell tangs.*
– ORIGIN mid 16th cent.: imitative.

tang[3] ▶ **noun** a surgeonfish which occurs around reefs and rocky areas, where it browses on algae.
● Genus *Acanthurus*, family Acanthuridae: several species, in particular the **blue tang** (*A. coeruleus*) of the western Atlantic, and the **convict tang** (*A. triostegus*) of the Indo-Pacific.
– ORIGIN mid 18th cent.: from **TANG**[1].

Tanga /ˈtaŋgə/ one of the principal ports of Tanzania, situated in the north-east of the country on the Indian Ocean; pop. 187,630 (1988).

tanga /ˈtaŋgə/ (also **tanga briefs**) ▶ **noun** Brit. a pair of briefs consisting of small panels connected by strings at the sides.
– ORIGIN early 20th cent. (denoting a loincloth worn by indigenous peoples in tropical America): from Portuguese, ultimately of Bantu origin. The current sense dates from the 1970s.

Tanganyika /ˌtaŋgəˈniːkə, -ˈnjiːkə/ see **TANZANIA**.

Tanganyika, Lake a lake in East Africa, in the Great Rift Valley. The deepest lake in Africa and the longest freshwater lake in the world, it forms most of the border of Zaire (Democratic Republic of Congo) with Tanzania and Burundi.

tangata /ˈtaŋʌtə/ ▶ **noun** (pl. same) [usu. with modifier] (in Maori speech) a person; a human being: *I pray you come back a he tangata, a man.*
– ORIGIN Maori.

tangata whenua /ˌtaŋʌtə ˈfɛnuːə/ ▶ **plural noun** used to describe the Maori people of a particular locality, or as a whole as the original inhabitants of New Zealand.
– ORIGIN Maori, literally 'people of the land'.

Tange /ˈtaŋgeɪ/, Kenzo (b.1913), Japanese architect. His work, for example the Peace Centre at Hiroshima (1955), is characterized by the use of modern materials while retaining a feeling for traditional Japanese architecture.

tangelo /'tan(d)ʒələʊ/ ▶ noun (pl. **-os**) a hybrid of the tangerine and grapefruit.
– ORIGIN early 20th cent.: blend of **TANGERINE** and **POMELO**.

tangent /'tan(d)ʒ(ə)nt/ ▶ noun **1** a straight line or plane that touches a curve or curved surface at a point, but if extended does not cross it at that point.
■figurative a completely different line of thought or action: *Loretta's mind went off at a tangent.* **2** Mathematics the trigonometric function that is equal to the ratio of the sides (other than the hypotenuse) opposite and adjacent to an angle in a right-angled triangle.
▶ adjective (of a line or plane) touching, but not intersecting, a curve or curved surface.
– DERIVATIVES **tangency** noun.
– ORIGIN late 16th cent. (in sense 2 and as an adjective): from Latin *tangent-* 'touching', from the verb *tangere*.

tangential /tan'dʒɛnʃ(ə)l/ ▶ adjective of, relating to, or along a tangent: *a tangential line.*
■diverging from a previous course or line; erratic: *tangential thoughts.* ■hardly touching a matter; peripheral: *the reforms were tangential to efforts to maintain a basic standard of life.*
– DERIVATIVES **tangentially** adverb.

tangerine ▶ noun **1** a small citrus fruit with a loose skin, especially one of a variety with deep orange-red skin.
■[mass noun] a deep orange-red colour. **2** the citrus tree which bears this fruit.
● *Citrus reticulata,* family Rutaceae.
– ORIGIN mid 19th cent.: from *Tanger* (former name of **TANGIER**) + **-INE**[1]. The fruit, exported from Tangier, was originally called the *tangerine orange.*

tangi /'taŋi/ ▶ noun (pl. **tangis**) a ceremonial Maori funeral or wake.
– ORIGIN Maori.

tangible /'tan(d)ʒɪb(ə)l/ ▶ adjective perceptible by touch: *the atmosphere of neglect and abandonment was almost tangible.*
■clear and definite; real: *the emphasis is now on tangible results.*
▶ noun (usu. **tangibles**) a thing that is perceptible by touch.
– DERIVATIVES **tangibility** noun, **tangibleness** noun, **tangibly** adverb.
– ORIGIN late 16th cent.: from French, or from late Latin *tangibilis,* from *tangere* 'to touch'.

Tangier /tan'dʒɪə/ a seaport on the northern coast of Morocco, on the Strait of Gibraltar commanding the western entrance to the Mediterranean; pop. 307,000 (1993). Portuguese from the end of the 15th century, Tangier was ruled by the sultan of Morocco 1684–1904, when it came under international control; it passed to the newly independent monarchy of Morocco in 1956.

tangle[1] ▶ verb [with obj.] (usu. **be tangled**) twist together into a confused mass: *the broom somehow got tangled up in my long skirt.*
■[no obj.] (**tangle with**) informal become involved in a conflict or fight with: *they usually come a cropper when they tangle with the heavy mobs.*
▶ noun a confused mass of something twisted together: *a tangle of golden hair.*
■a confused or complicated state; a muddle. ■ informal a fight, argument, or disagreement.
– PHRASES **a tangled web** a complex, difficult, and confusing situation or thing. [ORIGIN: from 'O what a tangled web we weave, When first we practise to deceive' (Scott's *Marmion*).]
– DERIVATIVES **tangly** adjective.
– ORIGIN Middle English (in the sense 'entangle, catch in a tangle'): probably of Scandinavian origin and related to Swedish dialect *taggla* 'disarrange'.

tangle[2] ▶ noun [mass noun] any of a number of brown seaweeds, especially oarweed.
– ORIGIN mid 16th cent.: probably from Norwegian *tongul.*

tanglefoot ▶ noun [mass noun] N. Amer. material applied to a tree trunk as a grease band, especially to prevent infestation by insects.

tango[1] ▶ noun (pl. **-os**) **1** a ballroom dance originating in Buenos Aires, characterized by marked rhythms and postures and abrupt pauses.
■a piece of music written for or in the style of this dance, typically in a slow, dotted duple rhythm.

2 a code word representing the letter T, used in radio communication.
▶ verb (**-oes, -oed**) [no obj.] dance the tango.
– PHRASES **it takes two to tango** informal both parties involved in a situation or argument are equally responsible for it.
– ORIGIN late 19th cent.: from Latin American Spanish, perhaps of African origin.

tango[2] ▶ noun [mass noun] Brit. informal, dated an orange-yellow colour.
– ORIGIN early 20th cent.: abbreviation of **TANGERINE**, influenced by **TANGO**[1].

tangram /'taŋgram/ ▶ noun a Chinese geometrical puzzle consisting of a square cut into seven pieces which can be arranged to make various other shapes.
– ORIGIN mid 19th cent.: of unknown origin.

Tangshan /taŋ'ʃan/ an industrial city in Hebei province, NE China; pop. 1,500,000 (1990). The city had to be rebuilt after a devastating earthquake in 1976.

Tangut /'taŋguːt/ ▶ noun (pl. same or **Tanguts**) **1** a member of a Tibetan people who established a kingdom in NW China and western Inner Mongolia from the late 10th to the mid 13th centuries. **2** [mass noun] the extinct language of this people.
▶ adjective of or relating to this people or their language.
– ORIGIN apparently from Mongolian, from Chinese *Dǎng Xiàng.*

tangy ▶ adjective (**tangier, tangiest**) having a strong, piquant flavour or smell: *a tangy salad.*
– DERIVATIVES **tanginess** noun.

tanh /tan'eɪtʃ, tanʃ, θan/ Mathematics ▶ abbreviation for hyperbolic tangent.

tania noun variant spelling of **TANNIA**.

tanist /'tanɪst/ ▶ noun the heir apparent to a Celtic chief, typically the most vigorous adult of his kin, elected during the chief's lifetime.
– DERIVATIVES **tanistry** noun.
– ORIGIN mid 16th cent.: from Irish, Scottish Gaelic *tánaiste,* literally 'second in excellence'.

taniwha /'tanɪwɑː, 'tanɪfə/ ▶ noun (pl. same or **taniwhas**) a water monster of Maori legend.
– ORIGIN Maori.

Tanjungkarang /ˌtandʒʊŋkə'raŋ/ see **BANDAR LAMPUNG**.

tank ▶ noun **1** a large receptacle or storage chamber, especially for liquid or gas.
■the container holding the fuel supply in a motor vehicle. ■ a receptacle with transparent sides in which to keep fish; an aquarium. ■ short for **TANK ENGINE**. ■ Indian & Austral./NZ a reservoir. **2** a heavy armoured fighting vehicle carrying guns and moving on a continuous articulated metal track. [ORIGIN: from the use of *tank* as a secret code word during manufacture in 1915.] **3** US informal a cell in a police station or jail.
▶ verb **1** [no obj.] fill the tank of a vehicle with fuel: *the cars stopped to tank up.*
■(**be/get tanked up**) informal drink heavily; become drunk: *they get tanked up before the game.* **2** [no obj.] US informal fail completely, especially at great financial cost.
■[with obj.] N. Amer. informal (in sport) deliberately lose or fail to finish (a match).
– DERIVATIVES **tankful** noun (pl. **-fuls**), **tankless** adjective.
– ORIGIN early 17th cent.: perhaps from Gujarati *tānkū* or Marathi *tānkē* 'underground cistern', from Sanskrit *tadāga* 'pond', probably influenced by Portuguese *tangue* 'pond', from Latin *stagnum.*

tanka[1] /'taŋkə/ ▶ noun (pl. same or **tankas**) a Japanese poem in five lines and thirty-one syllables, giving a complete picture of an event or mood.
– ORIGIN Japanese, from *tan* 'short' + *ka* 'song'.

tanka[2] /'tɑːŋkə/ ▶ noun (pl. **tankas**) a Tibetan religious painting on a scroll, hung as a banner in temples and carried in processions.
– ORIGIN from Tibetan *t'án-ka* 'image, painting'.

tankage ▶ noun [mass noun] **1** the storage capacity of a tank.
■the storage of something in a tank; a charge made for such storage. **2** a fertilizer or animal feed obtained from the residue from tanks in which animal carcasses have been rendered.

tankard ▶ noun a tall beer mug, typically made of

silver or pewter, with a handle and sometimes a hinged lid.
■the contents of or an amount held by such a mug: *I've downed a tankard of ale.*
– ORIGIN Middle English (denoting a large tub for carrying liquid): perhaps related to Dutch *tanckaert.*

tank engine ▶ noun a steam locomotive carrying fuel and water receptacles in its own frame, not in a tender.

tanker ▶ noun a ship, road vehicle, or aircraft for carrying liquids, especially mineral oils, in bulk.
▶ verb [with obj.] (usu. **be tankered**) transport (a liquid) in such a vehicle.

tank farm ▶ noun an area of oil or gas storage tanks.

tank-farming ▶ noun [mass noun] the practice of growing plants in tanks of water without soil.

tank killer ▶ noun an aircraft, vehicle, or missile effective against tanks.

tank top ▶ noun a close-fitting sleeveless top, typically made of wool and worn over a shirt or blouse.

tank town ▶ noun N. Amer. a small unimportant town (used originally of a town at which trains stopped to take on water).

tanner[1] ▶ noun **1** a person who is employed to tan animal hides.
2 a lotion or cream designed to promote the development of a suntan or produce a similar skin colour artificially.

tanner[2] ▶ noun Brit. informal a sixpence.
– ORIGIN early 19th cent.: of unknown origin.

tannery ▶ noun (pl. **-ies**) a place where animal hides are tanned; the workshop of a tanner.

Tannhäuser /'tanˌhɔɪzə, German 'tanˌhɔyzɐ/ (c.1200–c.1270), German poet. In reality a Minnesinger whose works included lyrics and love poetry, he became a legendary figure as a knight who visited Venus's grotto and spent seven years in debauchery, then repented and sought absolution from the Pope.

tannia /'tanɪə/ (also **tania**) ▶ noun a tall Caribbean plant of the arum family, cultivated in the tropics for its edible pear-shaped tubers and large arrow-shaped leaves. Also called **MALANGA**.
● *Xanthosoma sagittifolium,* family Araceae.
■a tuber of this plant. ■ [mass noun] the leaves or tubers of this plant eaten as food.
– ORIGIN mid 18th cent.: from Carib *taya,* Tupi *taña.*

tannic ▶ adjective of or related to tannin: *a dry wine with a slightly tannic aftertaste.*
– ORIGIN late 18th cent.: from French *tannique,* from *tanin* (see **TANNIN**).

tannic acid ▶ noun another term for **TANNIN**.
– DERIVATIVES **tannate** noun.

tannie /'tani/ ▶ noun (pl. **-ies**) S. African a woman who is older than the speaker (often used as a respectful and affectionate title or form of address).
– ORIGIN Afrikaans, literally 'auntie', familiar form of *tante* (see **TANTE**).

tannin ▶ noun [mass noun] a yellowish or brownish bitter-tasting organic substance present in some galls, barks, and other plant tissues, consisting of derivatives of gallic acid.
– ORIGIN early 19th cent.: from French *tanin,* from *tan* 'tanbark' (ultimately related to **TAN**[1]) + **-IN**[1].

tannoy Brit. ▶ noun trademark a type of public address system.
▶ verb [with obj.] transmit or announce over such a system: *the news was tannoyed one afternoon.*
■call for (someone) using a tannoy system.
– ORIGIN 1920s: contraction of *tantalum alloy,* which is used as a rectifier in the system.

Tannu-Tuva /ˌtanuːˈtuːvə/ former name for **TUVA**.

Tanoan /tə'nəʊən/ ▶ noun [mass noun] a small language family comprising a number of Pueblo Indian languages.
▶ adjective of or relating to this language family.
– ORIGIN from Spanish *Tano* + **-AN**.

tanpura /tʌn'puːrə/ ▶ noun another term for **TAMBOURA** (of India).
– ORIGIN mid 19th cent.: variant of **TAMBURA**.

Tansen /'tansɛn/ (c.1500–89), Indian musician and singer. A leading exponent of northern Indian classical music, he became an honoured member of the court of Akbar the Great.

tansu /ˈtansuː/ ▶ **noun** (pl. same) a Japanese chest of drawers or cabinet.
– ORIGIN Japanese.

tansy /ˈtanzi/ ▶ **noun** a plant of the daisy family with yellow flat-topped button-like flower heads and aromatic leaves, formerly used in cookery and medicine.
• Genus *Tanacetum*, family Compositae: several species, in particular the common Eurasian *T. vulgare*.
– ORIGIN Middle English: from Old French *tanesie*, probably from medieval Latin *athanasia* 'immortality', from Greek.

tantalite /ˈtantəlʌɪt/ ▶ **noun** [mass noun] a rare, dense black mineral consisting of a mixed oxide of iron and tantalum, of which it is the principal source.
– ORIGIN early 19th cent.: from **TANTALUM** + **-ITE**[1].

tantalize (also **-ise**) ▶ **verb** [with obj.] torment or tease (someone) with the sight or promise of something that is unobtainable: *such ambitious questions have long tantalized the world's best thinkers.*
■ excite the senses or desires of (someone): *she still tantalized him* | [as adj. **tantalizing**] *the tantalizing fragrance of fried bacon.*
– DERIVATIVES **tantalization** noun, **tantalizer** noun, **tantalizingly** adverb.
– ORIGIN late 16th cent.: from **TANTALUS** + **-IZE**.

tantalum /ˈtantələm/ ▶ **noun** [mass noun] the chemical element of atomic number 73, a hard silver-grey metal of the transition series. (Symbol: **Ta**)
– DERIVATIVES **tantalic** adjective.
– ORIGIN early 19th cent.: from **TANTALUS**, with reference to its frustrating insolubility in acids.

Tantalus /ˈtantələs/ Greek Mythology a Lydian king, son of Zeus and father of Pelops. For his crimes (which included killing Pelops) he was punished by being provided with fruit and water which receded when he reached for them. His name is the origin of the word *tantalize*.

tantalus ▶ **noun** Brit. a stand in which spirit decanters may be locked up though still visible.

tantamount ▶ **adjective** [predic.] (**tantamount to**) equivalent in seriousness to; virtually the same as: *the resignations were tantamount to an admission of guilt.*
– ORIGIN mid 17th cent.: from the earlier verb *tantamount* 'amount to as much', from Italian *tanto montare*.

tante /tɑ̃ːt, tɑːnt, ˈtantə/ ▶ **noun** (especially among those of French, German, or Afrikaans origin) a mature or elderly woman who is related or well known to the speaker (often used as a respectful form of address).
– ORIGIN French, Dutch *tante*, German *Tante* 'aunt'.

tantivy /tanˈtɪvi/ archaic ▶ **noun** (pl. **-ies**) a rapid gallop or ride.
▶ **exclamation** used as a hunting cry.
▶ **adjective** moving or riding swiftly.
– ORIGIN mid 17th cent.: probably imitative of the sound of galloping.

tant mieux /tɒ̃ ˈmjəː, French tɑ̃ mjø/ ▶ **exclamation** so much the better.
– ORIGIN French.

tanto[1] /ˈtantəʊ/ ▶ **noun** (pl. **-os**) a Japanese short sword or dagger.
– ORIGIN Japanese.

tanto[2] /ˈtantəʊ/ ▶ **adverb** [usu. with negative] Music (as a direction) too much: [postpositive as submodifier] *allegro non tanto.*
– ORIGIN Italian.

tant pis /tɒ̃ ˈpiː, French tɑ̃ pi/ ▶ **exclamation** so much the worse; the situation is regrettable but now beyond retrieval.
– ORIGIN French.

tantra /ˈtantrə, ˈtʌntrə/ ▶ **noun** a Hindu or Buddhist mystical or magical text, dating from the 7th century or earlier.
■ [mass noun] adherence to the doctrines or principles of the tantras, involving mantras, meditation, yoga, and ritual.
– DERIVATIVES **tantric** adjective, **tantrism** noun, **tantrist** noun.
– ORIGIN Sanskrit, literally 'loom, groundwork, doctrine', from *tan* 'stretch'.

tantrum ▶ **noun** an uncontrolled outburst of anger and frustration, typically in a young child.
– ORIGIN early 18th cent.: of unknown origin.

Tanzania /ˌtanzəˈnɪə/ a country in East Africa with a coastline on the Indian Ocean; pop. 27,270,000 (est. 1991); official languages, Swahili and English; capital, Dodoma.

Tanzania consists of a mainland area (the former Tanganyika) and the island of Zanzibar. A German colony (German East Africa) from the late 19th century, Tanganyika became a British mandate after the First World War and a trust territory, administered by Britain, after the Second, before becoming independent within the Commonwealth in 1961. It was named Tanzania after its union with Zanzibar in 1964.

– DERIVATIVES **Tanzanian** adjective & noun.

tanzanite /ˈtanzənʌɪt/ ▶ **noun** [mass noun] a blue or violet gem variety of zoisite, containing vanadium.
– ORIGIN 1960s: from **TANZANIA** + **-ITE**[1].

Tao /taʊ, ˈtɑːəʊ/ ▶ **noun** (in Chinese philosophy) the absolute principle underlying the universe, combining within itself the principles of yin and yang and signifying the way, or code of behaviour, that is in harmony with the natural order. The interpretation of Tao in the Tao-te-Ching developed into the philosophical religion of Taoism.
– ORIGIN Chinese, literally '(right) way'.

Taoiseach /ˈtiːʃəx, Irish ˈtiːsʲəx/ ▶ **noun** the Prime Minister of the Irish Republic.
– ORIGIN Irish, literally 'chief, leader'.

Taoism /ˈtaʊɪz(ə)m, ˈtɑːəʊ-/ ▶ **noun** [mass noun] a Chinese philosophy based on the writings of Lao-tzu, advocating humility and religious piety.

The central concept and goal is the Tao, and its most important text is the Tao-te-Ching. Taoism has both a philosophical and a religious aspect. Philosophical Taoism emphasizes inner contemplation and mystical union with nature; wisdom, learning, and purposive action should be abandoned in favour of simplicity and **wu-wei** (non-action, or letting things take their natural course). The religious aspect of Taoism developed later, c.3rd century AD, incorporating certain Buddhist features and developing a monastic system.

– DERIVATIVES **Taoist** /-ɪst/ noun & adjective, **Taoistic** /-ˈɪstɪk/ adjective.

taonga /tɑːˈɒŋɡə/ ▶ **noun** (pl. same) (in Maori culture) an object or natural resource which is highly prized.
– ORIGIN Maori.

Taormina /ˌtɑːɔːˈmiːnə/ a resort town on the east coast of Sicily; pop. 10,905 (1990). It was founded by Greek colonists in the 4th century BC.

Tao-te-Ching /ˌtaʊtiːˈtʃɪŋ/ ▶ **noun** the central Taoist text, ascribed to Lao-tzu, the traditional founder of Taoism. Apparently written as a guide for rulers, it defined the Tao, or way, and established the philosophical basis of Taoism.
– ORIGIN Chinese, literally 'the Book of the Way and its Power'.

tap[1] ▶ **noun 1** a device by which a flow of liquid or gas from a pipe or container can be controlled.
■ a device connected to a telephone used for listening secretly to someone's conversations. ■ an act of listening secretly to someone's telephone conversation. ■ (also **tapping**) Brit. an electrical connection made to some point between the end terminals of a transformer coil or other component.
2 an instrument for cutting a threaded hole in a material.
3 Brit. a taproom.
▶ **verb** (**tapped**, **tapping**) [with obj.] **1** draw liquid through the tap or spout of (a cask, barrel, or other container).
■ draw (liquid) from a cask, barrel, or other container. ■ (often **be tapped**) connect a device to (a telephone) so that conversation can be listened to secretly: *the telephones were tapped by the state security police.* ■ informal obtain money or information from (someone): *he considered whom he could tap for information.* ■ exploit or draw a supply from (a resource): *clients from industry seeking to tap Edinburgh's resources of expertise* | [no obj.] *these magazines have tapped into a target market of consumers.* ■ draw sap from (a tree) by cutting into it.
2 cut a thread in (something) to accept a screw.
– PHRASES **on tap** ready to be poured from a tap. ■ informal freely available whenever needed. ■ N. Amer. informal on schedule to occur.
– DERIVATIVES **tappable** adjective.
– ORIGIN Old English *tæppa* 'peg for the vent-hole of a cask', *tæppian* 'provide (a cask) with a stopper', of Germanic origin; related to Dutch *tap* and German *Zapfen* (nouns).

tap[2] ▶ **verb** (**tapped**, **tapping**) [with obj.] **1** strike (someone or something) with a quick light blow or blows: *one of my staff tapped me on the shoulder.*
■ strike (something) against something else with a quick light blow or blows: *Gloria was tapping her feet in time to the music.* ■ (**tap something out**) produce (a rhythm) with a series of quick light blows on a surface. ■ write or enter (something) using a keyboard or keypad.
2 (usu. **be tapped**) US informal designate or select (someone) for a task or honour, especially membership of an organization or committee.
▶ **noun 1** a quick light blow or the sound of such a blow.
2 [mass noun] tap dancing.
■ [count noun] a piece of metal attached to the toe and heel of a tap dancer's shoe to make a tapping sound.
3 (**taps**) [treated as sing. or pl.] US a bugle call for lights to be put out in army quarters. [ORIGIN: so named because the signal was originally sounded on a drum.]
■ a similar call sounded at a military funeral. ■ Brit. (in the Guide movement) a closing song sung at an evening camp fire or at the end of a meeting.
– DERIVATIVES **tapper** noun.
– ORIGIN Middle English: from Old French *taper*, or of imitative origin; compare with **CLAP**[1] and **RAP**[1].

tapa /ˈtɑːpə/ ▶ **noun** [mass noun] the bark of the paper mulberry tree.
■ (also **tapa cloth**) cloth made from such bark, used in the Pacific islands.
– ORIGIN early 19th cent.: of Polynesian origin.

tapas /ˈtapəs/ ▶ **plural noun** small Spanish savoury dishes, typically served with drinks at a bar.
– ORIGIN Spanish, literally 'cover, lid' (because the dishes were given free with the drink, served on a dish balanced on, therefore 'covering', the glass).

tap changer ▶ **noun** an apparatus for changing the connection to an electrical transformer from one tap to another, so as to vary the turns ratio and hence control the output voltage under a varying load.

tap dance ▶ **noun** a dance performed wearing shoes fitted with metal taps, characterized by rhythmical tapping of the toes and heels.
▶ **verb** [no obj.] (**tap-dance**) perform such a dance.
– DERIVATIVES **tap dancer** noun, **tap-dancing** noun.

tape ▶ **noun** [mass noun] a narrow strip of material, typically used to hold or fasten something: *a reel of tape* | [count noun] *a dirty apron fastened with thin tapes.*
■ [often with modifier] long narrow flexible material with magnetic properties, used for recording sound, pictures, or computer data. ■ [count noun] a cassette or reel containing such material. ■ [count noun] a recording on such a cassette or reel. ■ (also **adhesive tape**) a strip of paper or plastic coated with adhesive, used to stick things together. ■ [count noun] a strip of material stretched across the finishing line of a race, to be broken by the winner. ■ a strip of material used to mark off an area or form a notional barrier. ■ [count noun] a tape measure.
▶ **verb** [with obj.] **1** record (sound or pictures) on audio or video tape: *it is not known who taped the conversation.*
2 fasten or attach (something) with adhesive tape.
3 (**tape something off**) seal or mark off an area or thing with tape.
– PHRASES **have** (or **get**) **someone/thing taped** Brit. informal understand a person or thing fully. **on tape** recorded on magnetic tape.
– ORIGIN Old English *tæppa*, *tæppe*; perhaps related to Middle Low German *teppen* 'pluck, tear'.

tape deck ▶ **noun** a piece of equipment for playing audio tapes, especially as part of a stereo system.

tape echo ▶ **noun** a facility which allows the repeat of a sound to be delayed by adjusting the time lapse between the recording and playback heads of a tape recorder.

tape-grass ▶ **noun** [mass noun] a submerged aquatic plant of the frogbit family, with narrow grass-like leaves. Also called **RIBBON-GRASS** and (in North America) **EELGRASS**.
• Genus *Vallisneria*, family Hydrocharitaceae: several species.

tape hiss ▶ **noun** [mass noun] extraneous high-frequency background noise during the playing of a tape recording.

tape machine ▶ **noun 1** a tape recorder.
2 a machine for receiving and recording telegraph messages on paper tape.

tape measure ▶ **noun** a length of tape or thin flexible metal, marked at graded intervals for measuring.

tapenade /ˈtapənɑːd/ ▶ **noun** [mass noun] a Provençal savoury paste or dip, made from black olives, capers, and anchovies.

a cat | ɑː arm | ɛ bed | ɛː hair | ə ago | əː her | ɪ sit | i cosy | iː see | ɒ hot | ɔː saw | ʌ run | ʊ put | uː too | ʌɪ my | aʊ how | eɪ day | əʊ no | ɪə near | ɔɪ boy | ʊə poor | ʌɪə fire | aʊə sour

– ORIGIN French, from Provençal.

taper ▶ noun a slender candle.
■ a wick coated with wax, used for conveying a flame.
▶ verb diminish or reduce or cause to diminish or reduce in thickness towards one end: [no obj.] *the tail tapers to a rounded tip* | [with obj.] *David asked my dressmaker to taper his trousers.*
■ gradually lessen: *the impact of the dollar's depreciation started to taper off.*
– ORIGIN Old English (denoting any wax candle), dissimilated form (by alteration of p- to t-) of Latin *papyrus* (see **PAPYRUS**), the pith of which was used for candle wicks.

tape recorder ▶ noun an apparatus for recording sounds on magnetic tape and afterwards reproducing them.
– DERIVATIVES **tape-record** verb, **tape recording** noun.

taperer ▶ noun a person carrying a taper in a religious ceremony.

taper pin ▶ noun a short round metal rod having a small degree of taper which enables it to act as a stop or wedge when driven into a hole.

tape streamer ▶ noun Computing a device for writing data very quickly on to magnetic tape, used typically for making back-ups of large amounts of data.

tapestry ▶ noun (pl. **-ies**) a piece of thick textile fabric with pictures or designs formed by weaving coloured weft threads or by embroidering on canvas, used as a wall hanging or soft furnishing.
■ figurative used in reference to an intricate or complex sequence of events: *the loopiness of the Commons adds to life's rich tapestry.*
– DERIVATIVES **tapestried** adjective.
– ORIGIN late Middle English: from Old French *tapisserie*, from *tapissier* 'tapestry worker' or *tapisser* 'to carpet', from *tapis* 'carpet, tapis'.

tapestry moth ▶ noun a drab moth related to the clothes moth, the larvae of which feed on coarse textiles and animal hair.
● *Trichophaga tapetzella*, family Tineidae.

tapetum /təˈpiːtəm/ ▶ noun Zoology a reflective layer of the choroid in the eyes of many animals, causing them to shine in the dark.
– ORIGIN early 18th cent.: from late Latin, from Latin *tapete* 'carpet'.

tapeworm ▶ noun a parasitic flatworm, the adult of which lives in the intestines. It has a long ribbon-like body with many segments that can become independent, and a small head bearing hooks and suckers.
● Class Cestoda, phylum Platyhelminthes.

taphonomy /taˈfɒnəmi/ ▶ noun [mass noun] the branch of palaeontology that deals with the processes of fossilization.
– DERIVATIVES **taphonomic** adjective, **taphonomist** noun.
– ORIGIN 1940s: from Greek *taphos* 'grave' + -NOMY.

tap-in ▶ noun chiefly Soccer & Basketball a relatively gentle, close-range kick or tap scoring a goal.

tapioca /ˌtapɪˈəʊkə/ ▶ noun [mass noun] a starchy substance in the form of hard white grains, obtained from cassava and used in cookery for puddings and other dishes.
– ORIGIN early 18th cent.: from Tupi-Guarani *tipioca*, from *tipi* 'dregs' + *og, ok* 'squeeze out'.

tapir /ˈteɪpə, -ɪə/ ▶ noun a nocturnal hoofed mammal with a stout body, sturdy limbs, and a short flexible proboscis, native to the forests of tropical America and Malaysia.
● Family Tapiridae and genus *Tapirus*: four species, including the black and white **Malayan tapir** (*T. indicus*).
– ORIGIN late 18th cent.: via Spanish and Portuguese from Tupi *tapyra*.

tapis /ˈtapiː/ ▶ noun (pl. same) archaic a tapestry or richly decorated cloth, used as a hanging or a covering for something.
– ORIGIN French, from Old French *tapiz*, via late Latin from Greek *tapētion*, diminutive of *tapēs* 'tapestry'.

tapotement /təˈpəʊtm(ə)nt/ ▶ noun [mass noun] rapid and repeated striking of the body as a technique in massage.
– ORIGIN late 19th cent.: French, from *tapoter* 'to tap'.

tap pants ▶ plural noun US a pair of brief lingerie shorts, usually worn with a camisole top.

tap penalty ▶ noun Rugby a penalty taken by kicking the ball lightly to a teammate.

tappet /ˈtapɪt/ ▶ noun a lever or projecting part on a machine which intermittently makes contact with a cam or other part so as to give or receive motion.
– ORIGIN mid 18th cent.: apparently an irregular diminutive of **TAP**[2].

tapping ▶ noun another term for **TAP**[1] (in sense 1).

taproom ▶ noun a room in which alcoholic drinks, especially beer, are available on tap; a bar in a pub or hotel.

taproot ▶ noun a straight tapering root growing vertically downwards and forming the centre from which subsidiary rootlets spring.

tap shoe ▶ noun a shoe with a specially hardened sole or attached metal plates at toe and heel to make a tapping sound in tap dancing.

tapster ▶ noun archaic a person who draws and serves alcoholic drinks at a bar.
– ORIGIN Old English *tæppestre*, denoting a woman serving ale (see **TAP**[1], **-STER**).

tapu /ˈtɑːpuː/ ▶ adjective NZ forbidden; taboo.
– ORIGIN Maori.

taqueria /ˌtɑːkəˈriːə/ ▶ noun chiefly US a Mexican restaurant specializing in tacos.
– ORIGIN Mexican Spanish.

tar[1] ▶ noun [mass noun] a dark, thick flammable liquid distilled from wood or coal, consisting of a mixture of hydrocarbons, resins, alcohols, and other compounds. It is used in road-making and for coating and preserving timber.
■ a similar substance formed by burning tobacco or other material: [in combination] *low-tar cigarettes.*
▶ verb (**tarred**, **tarring**) [with obj.] [usu. as adj. **tarred**] cover (something) with tar: *a newly tarred road.*
– PHRASES **beat** (or **whale**) **the tar out of** N. Amer. informal beat or thrash severely. **tar and feather** smear with tar and then cover with feathers as a punishment. **tar people with the same brush** consider specified people to have the same faults.
– ORIGIN Old English *teru, teoru*, of Germanic origin; related to Dutch *teer*, German *Teer*, and perhaps ultimately to **TREE**.

tar[2] ▶ noun informal, dated a sailor.
– ORIGIN mid 17th cent.: perhaps an abbreviation of **TARPAULIN**, also used as a nickname for a sailor at this time.

Tara /ˈtɑːrə/ a hill in County Meath in the Republic of Ireland, site in early times of the residence of the high kings of Ireland and still marked by ancient earthworks.

ta-ra ▶ exclamation informal, chiefly N. English goodbye.
– ORIGIN 1950s: variant of **TA-TA**.

Tarabulus Al-Gharb /təˌrɑːbələs alˈɡɑːb/ Arabic name for **TRIPOLI** (in sense 1).

Tarabulus Ash-Sham /aʃˈʃam/ Arabic name for **TRIPOLI** (in sense 2).

taradiddle /ˈtarəˌdɪd(ə)l/ (also **tarradiddle**) ▶ noun informal, chiefly Brit. a petty lie.
■ [mass noun] pretentious nonsense.
– ORIGIN late 18th cent.: perhaps related to **DIDDLE**.

tarakihi /ˌtarəˈkiːhi, ˌtarəˈkiːiː/ ▶ noun a silver marine fish with a black band behind the head, related to the morwong and caught for food off New Zealand coasts.
● *Cheilodactylus macropterus*, family Cheilodactylidae.
– ORIGIN late 19th cent.: from Maori.

taramasalata /ˌtarəməsəˈlɑːtə/ (also **tarama** /ˈtarəmə/) ▶ noun [mass noun] a pinkish paste or dip made from the roe of certain fish, mixed with olive oil and seasoning.
– ORIGIN from modern Greek *taramas* 'roe' (from Turkish *tarama*, denoting a preparation of soft roe or red caviar) + *salata* 'salad'.

Taranaki /ˌtarəˈnɑːki/ Maori name for Mount Egmont (see **EGMONT, MOUNT**).

tarantass /ˌtar(ə)nˈtas/ ▶ noun a four-wheeled, horse-drawn Russian carriage without springs, mounted on a long flexible wooden chassis.
– ORIGIN from Russian *tarantas*.

tarantella /ˌtar(ə)nˈtɛlə/ (also **tarantelle** /-ˈtɛl/) ▶ noun a rapid whirling dance originating in southern Italy.
■ a piece of music written in fast 6/8 time in the style of this dance.
– ORIGIN late 18th cent.: Italian, from the name of the seaport **TARANTO**; so named because it was

thought to be a cure for tarantism, the victim dancing the tarantella until exhausted. See also **TARANTULA**.

Tarantino /ˌtarənˈtiːnəʊ/, Quentin (Jerome) (b.1963), American film director, screenwriter, and actor. He came to sudden prominence with *Reservoir Dogs* (1992), followed in 1994 by *Pulp Fiction*. Both aroused controversy for their amorality and violence but also won admiration for their wit and style.

tarantism /ˈtar(ə)nˌtɪz(ə)m/ ▶ noun [mass noun] a psychological illness characterized by an extreme impulse to dance, prevalent in southern Italy from the 15th to the 17th century, and widely believed at the time to have been caused by the bite of a tarantula.
– ORIGIN mid 17th cent.: from Italian *tarantismo*, from the name of the seaport **TARANTO**, after which the tarantula is also named. Compare with **TARANTELLA**.

Taranto /təˈrantəʊ/ a seaport and naval base in Apulia, SE Italy; pop. 244,030 (1990). Founded by the Greeks in the 8th century BC, it came under Roman rule in 272 BC.

tarantula /təˈrantjʊlə/ ▶ noun **1** a very large hairy spider found chiefly in tropical and subtropical America, some kinds of which are able to catch small lizards, frogs, and birds. Also called **BIRD-EATING SPIDER**.
● Family Theraphosidae, suborder Mygalomorphae.
2 a large black wolf spider of southern Europe, whose bite was formerly believed to cause tarantism.
● *Lycosa tarentula*, family Lycosidae.
– ORIGIN mid 16th cent.: from medieval Latin, from Old Italian *tarantola* 'tarantula', from the name of the seaport **TARANTO**. Compare with **TARANTELLA** and **TARANTISM**.

tarantula hawk ▶ noun a large spider-hunting wasp of the south-west US.
● Genus *Pepsis*, family Pompilidae.

tarata /təˈrɑːtə/ ▶ noun New Zealand term for **LEMONWOOD**.
– ORIGIN Maori.

Tarawa /ˈtarəwə, təˈrɑːwə/ an atoll in the South Pacific, one of the Gilbert Islands; pop. 28,800 (1990). It is the location of Bairiki, the capital of Kiribati.

tar baby ▶ noun informal a difficult problem which is only aggravated by attempts to solve it.
– ORIGIN with allusion to the doll smeared with tar as a trap for Brer Rabbit, in J. C. Harris's *Uncle Remus*.

tarboosh /tɑːˈbuːʃ/ ▶ noun a man's cap similar to a fez, typically of red felt with a tassel at the top.
– ORIGIN early 18th cent.: from Egyptian Arabic *ṭarbūš*, based on Persian *sarpūš*, from *sar* 'head' + *pūš* 'cover'.

tarbrush ▶ noun (**the tarbrush**) offensive black or Indian ancestry.

Tardenoisian /ˌtɑːdɪˈnɔɪzɪən/ ▶ adjective of or relating to a late Mesolithic culture of west and central Europe, especially France, dated to about 8,000–6,000 years ago.
■ [as noun **the Tardenoisian**] the Tardenoisian culture or period.
– ORIGIN 1920s: from French *Tardenoisien*, from the name of *Fère-en-Tardenois* in NE France, where objects from this culture were found.

Tardigrada /ˌtɑːdɪˈɡreɪdə/ Zoology a small phylum that comprises the water bears.
– DERIVATIVES **tardigrade** /ˈtɑːdɪɡreɪd/ noun.
– ORIGIN modern Latin (plural), from Latin *tardigradus*, from *tardus* 'slow' + *gradi* 'to walk'.

tardive dyskinesia /ˌtɑːdɪv ˌdɪskɪˈniːzɪə/ ▶ noun [mass noun] Medicine a neurological disorder characterized by involuntary movements of the face and jaw.
– ORIGIN 1960s: *tardive* from French *tardif, tardive* (see **TARDY**).

tardy ▶ adjective (**tardier**, **tardiest**) delaying or delayed beyond the right or expected time; late: *please forgive this tardy reply.*
■ slow in action or response; sluggish.
– DERIVATIVES **tardily** adverb, **tardiness** noun.
– ORIGIN mid 16th cent.: from French *tardif, -ive*, from Latin *tardus* 'slow'.

tare[1] /tɛː/ ▶ **noun** **1** a vetch, especially the common vetch.
2 (**tares**) (in biblical use) an injurious weed resembling corn when young (Matt. 13:24–30).
– ORIGIN Middle English: of unknown origin.

tare[2] /tɛː/ ▶ **noun** an allowance made for the weight of the packaging in order to determine the net weight of goods.
■ the weight of a motor vehicle, railway carriage, or aircraft without its fuel or load.
– ORIGIN late Middle English: from French, literally 'deficiency, tare', from medieval Latin *tara*, based on Arabic *ṭaraḥa* 'reject, deduct'.

tare and tret ▶ **noun** [mass noun] historical the arithmetical rule used for calculating the net weight of goods by subtracting the tare and the tret from the gross weight.

targa /ˈtɑːɡə/ ▶ **noun** [usu. as modifier] a type of convertible sports car with hood or panel that can be removed, especially leaving a central roll bar for passenger safety: *a targa roof.*
– ORIGIN Italian, literally 'shield', given as a name to a model of Porsche with a detachable hood (1965), probably suggested by the *Targa Florio* ('Florio Shield'), a motor time-trial held annually in Sicily.

targe /tɑːdʒ/ ▶ **noun** archaic term for **TARGET** (in sense 2).
– ORIGIN Old English *targa, targe*, of Germanic origin; reinforced in Middle English by Old French *targe*.

target ▶ **noun** **1** a person, object, or place selected as the aim of an attack.
■ a mark or point at which someone fires or aims, especially a round or rectangular board marked with concentric circles used in archery or shooting. ■ an objective or result towards which efforts are directed: *the car met its sales target in record time.* ■ Phonetics an idealization of the articulation of a speech sound, with reference to which actual utterances can be described. ■ a person or thing against whom criticism or abuse is or may be directed.
2 historical a small, round shield or buckler.
▶ **verb** (**targeted**, **targeting**) [with obj.] (usu. **be targeted**) select as an object of attention or attack: *two men were targeted by the attackers.*
■ aim or direct (something): *a significant nuclear capability targeted on the US.*
– PHRASES **on target** accurately hitting the thing aimed at. ■ proceeding or improving at a good enough rate to achieve an objective.
– DERIVATIVES **targetable** adjective.
– ORIGIN late Middle English (in sense 2): diminutive of **TARGE**. The noun came to denote various round objects. The verb dates from the early 17th cent.

target cell ▶ **noun** **1** Physiology a cell which bears receptors for a hormone, drug, or other signalling molecule, or is the focus of contact by a virus, phagocyte, nerve fibre, etc.
2 Medicine an abnormal form of red blood cell which appears as a dark ring surrounding a dark central spot, typical of certain kinds of anaemia.

target language ▶ **noun** the language into which a text, document, or speech is translated.
■ a foreign language which a person intends to learn.

target man ▶ **noun** Soccer & Hockey a forward used in a central position to whom other players direct long passes.

target organ ▶ **noun** Physiology & Medicine a specific organ on which a hormone, drug, or other substance acts.

Targum /ˈtɑːɡəm/ ▶ **noun** an ancient Aramaic paraphrase or interpretation of the Hebrew Bible, of a type made from about the 1st century AD when Hebrew was ceasing to be a spoken language.
– ORIGIN from Aramaic *targūm* 'interpretation'.

Tar Heel State informal name for **NORTH CAROLINA**.

tariff ▶ **noun** a tax or duty to be paid on a particular class of imports or exports.
■ a list of these taxes. ■ a table of the fixed charges made by a business, especially in a hotel or restaurant. ■ Law a scale of sentences and damages for crimes and injuries of different severities.
▶ **verb** [with obj.] fix the price of (something) according to a tariff: *these services are tariffed by volume.*
– ORIGIN late 16th cent. (also denoting an arithmetical table): via French from Italian *tariffa*, based on Arabic *ʿarrafa* 'notify'.

Tarim /tɑːˈriːm/ a river of NW China, in Xinjiang autonomous region. It rises as the Yarkand in the Kunlun Shan mountains and flows for over 2,000 km (1,250 miles) generally eastwards through the dry Tarim Basin, petering out in the Lop Nor depression. For much of its course the river is unformed, following no clearly defined bed and subject to much evaporation.

tariqa /taˈriːkə/ (also **tariqat** /taˈriːkət/) ▶ **noun** [mass noun] the Sufi doctrine or path of spiritual learning.
■ [count noun] a Sufi missionary.
– ORIGIN from Arabic *ṭarīqa* 'manner, way, creed'.

Tarkovsky /tɑːˈkɒfski/, Andrei (Arsenevich) (1932–86), Russian film director. Featuring a poetic and impressionistic style, his films include *Ivan's Childhood* (1962), *Solaris* (1972), and *The Sacrifice* (1986), which won the special grand prize at Cannes.

tarlatan /ˈtɑːlətən/ ▶ **noun** [mass noun] a thin, open-weave muslin fabric, used for stiffening ball dresses.
– ORIGIN early 18th cent.: from French *tarlatane*, probably of Indian origin.

tarmac ▶ **noun** [mass noun] (trademark in the UK) material used for surfacing roads or other outdoor areas, consisting of broken stone mixed with tar.
■ (**the tarmac**) a runway or other area surfaced with such material.
▶ **verb** (**tarmacked**, **tarmacking**) [with obj.] surface (a road or other outdoor area) with such material: [as adj. **tarmacked**] *there are no tarmacked roads.*
– ORIGIN early 20th cent.: abbreviation of **TARMACADAM**.

tarmacadam /ˌtɑːməˈkadəm/ ▶ **noun** another term for **TARMAC**.
– DERIVATIVES **tarmacadamed** adjective.
– ORIGIN late 19th cent.: from **TAR**[1] + **MACADAM**.

Tarn /tɑːn, French taʀn/ a river of southern France, which rises in the Cévennes and flows 380 km (235 miles) generally south-westwards through deep gorges before meeting the Garonne north-west of Toulouse.

tarn ▶ **noun** a small mountain lake.
– ORIGIN Middle English (originally northern English dialect): from Old Norse *tjǫrn*.

tarnation ▶ **noun** & **exclamation** chiefly N. Amer. used as a euphemism for 'damnation'.
– ORIGIN late 18th cent.: alteration.

tarnish ▶ **verb** lose or cause to lose lustre, especially as a result of exposure to air or moisture: [no obj.] *silver tarnishes too easily* | [with obj.] *lemon juice would tarnish the gilded metal.*
■ figurative make or become less valuable or respected: [with obj.] *his regime had not been tarnished by human rights abuses.*
▶ **noun** [mass noun] dullness of colour; loss of brightness.
■ a film or stain formed on an exposed surface of a mineral or metal. ■ figurative damage or harm done to something.
– DERIVATIVES **tarnishable** adjective.
– ORIGIN late Middle English (as a verb): from French *terniss-*, lengthened stem of *ternir*, from *terne* 'dark, dull'.

Tarnów /ˈtɑːnʊf/ an industrial city in southern Poland; pop. 73,740 (1990).

taro /ˈtɑːrəʊ, ˈtarəʊ/ ▶ **noun** [mass noun] a tropical Asian plant of the arum family which has edible starchy corms and edible fleshy leaves, especially a variety with a large central corm grown as a staple in the Pacific. Also called **DASHEEN**, **COCOYAM**. Compare with **EDDO**.
• *Colocasia esculenta* var. *esculenta*, family Araceae.
■ the corm of this plant.
– ORIGIN mid 18th cent.: of Polynesian origin.

tar oil ▶ **noun** [mass noun] a volatile oil obtained by distilling tar, used by gardeners as an insecticide.

tarot /ˈtarəʊ/ ▶ **noun** [mass noun] (**the Tarot**) playing cards, traditionally a pack of 78 with five suits, used for fortune telling and (especially in Europe) in certain games. The suits are typically swords, cups, coins (or pentacles), batons (or wands), and a permanent suit of trumps.
■ a card game played with such a pack. ■ [count noun] a card from such a pack.
– ORIGIN late 16th cent.: from French, from Italian *tarocchi*, of unknown origin.

tarp ▶ **noun** informal, chiefly N. Amer. a tarpaulin sheet or cover.
– ORIGIN early 20th cent.: abbreviation.

tarpan /ˈtɑːpan/ ▶ **noun** a greyish wild horse that was formerly common in eastern Europe and western Asia, exterminated in 1919.
• *Equus caballus gomelini*, family Equidae.
– ORIGIN Kyrgyz.

tarpaulin /tɑːˈpɔːlɪn/ ▶ **noun** **1** [mass noun] heavy-duty waterproof cloth, originally of tarred canvas.
■ [count noun] a sheet or covering of this.
2 historical a sailor's tarred or oilskin hat.
■ archaic a sailor.
– ORIGIN early 17th cent.: probably from **TAR**[1] + **PALL**[1] + **-ING**[1].

Tarpeia /tɑːˈpiːə/ one of the Vestal Virgins, the daughter of a commander of the Capitol in ancient Rome. According to legend she betrayed the citadel to the Sabines in return for whatever they wore on their arms, hoping to receive their golden bracelets; however, the Sabines killed her by throwing their shields on to her.

Tarpeian Rock /tɑːˈpiːən/ a cliff in ancient Rome, at the south-western corner of the Capitoline Hill, over which murderers and traitors were hurled.

tar pit ▶ **noun** a hollow in which natural tar accumulates by seepage.
■ figurative a complicated or difficult situation or problem.

tarpon /ˈtɑːpɒn/ ▶ **noun** a large tropical marine fish of herring-like appearance.
• Two species in the family Megalopidae: *Tarpon atlanticus*, a prized Atlantic game fish, and *Megalops cyprinoides* of the Indo-Pacific.
– ORIGIN late 17th cent.: probably from Dutch *tarpoen*, perhaps from a Central American language.

Tarquinius /tɑːˈkwɪnɪəs/ the name of two semi-legendary Etruscan kings of ancient Rome; anglicized name *Tarquin*:
■ **Tarquinius Priscus**, reigned *c.*616–*c.*578 BC; full name *Lucius Tarquinius Priscus*. According to tradition he was murdered by the sons of the previous king.
■ **Tarquinius Superbus**, reigned *c.*534–*c.*510 BC; full name *Lucius Tarquinius Superbus*; known as **Tarquin the Proud**. According to tradition he was the son or grandson of Tarquinius Priscus. Noted for his cruelty, he was expelled from the city and the Republic was founded. He repeatedly, but unsuccessfully, attacked Rome, assisted by Lars Porsenna.

tarradiddle ▶ **noun** variant spelling of **TARADIDDLE**.

tarragon /ˈtarəɡ(ə)n/ ▶ **noun** [mass noun] a perennial plant of the daisy family, with narrow aromatic leaves that are used as a culinary herb.
• *Artemisia dracunculus*, family Compositae.
– ORIGIN mid 16th cent.: representing medieval Latin *tragonia* and *tarchon*, perhaps from an Arabic alteration of Greek *drakōn* 'dragon' (by association with *drakontion* 'dragon arum').

Tarragona wine /ˌtarəˈɡəʊnə/ ▶ **noun** [mass noun] a sweet fortified red or white wine produced in the Tarragona region of Spain.

Tarrasa /təˈrasə, Spanish taˈrasa/ (also **Terrassa**) an industrial city in Catalonia, NE Spain; pop. 153,520 (1991).

tarry[1] /ˈtɑːri/ ▶ **adjective** (**tarrier**, **tarriest**) of, like, or covered with tar: *a length of tarry rope.*
– DERIVATIVES **tarriness** noun.

tarry[2] /ˈtari/ ▶ **verb** (**-ies**, **-ied**) [no obj.] dated stay longer than intended; delay leaving a place: *she could tarry a bit and not get home until four.*
– DERIVATIVES **tarrier** noun (rare).
– ORIGIN Middle English: of unknown origin.

tarsal /ˈtɑːs(ə)l/ Anatomy & Zoology ▶ **adjective** of or relating to the tarsus: *the tarsal claws of beetles.*
▶ **noun** a bone of the tarsus.
– ORIGIN early 19th cent.: from **TARSUS** + **-AL**.

tar sand ▶ **noun** (often **tar sands**) Geology a deposit of sand impregnated with bitumen.

tarsi plural form of **TARSUS**.

tarsier /ˈtɑːsɪə/ ▶ **noun** a small insectivorous, tree-dwelling, nocturnal primate with very large eyes, a long tufted tail, and very long hindlimbs, native to the islands of SE Asia.
• Family Tarsiidae and genus *Tarsius*, suborder Prosimii: four species.
– ORIGIN late 18th cent.: from French, from *tarse* 'tarsus', with reference to the animal's long tarsal bones.

tarsometatarsus /ˌtɑːsəʊmɛtəˈtɑːsəs/ ▶ **noun** (pl. **tarsometatarsi** /-sʌɪ, -siː/) Zoology a long bone in the

lower leg of birds and some reptiles, formed by fusion of tarsal and metatarsal structures.
– DERIVATIVES **tarsometatarsal** adjective.

Tarsus /ˈtɑːsəs/ an ancient city in southern Turkey, the capital of Cilicia and the birthplace of St Paul. It is now a market town.

tarsus /ˈtɑːsəs/ ▶ noun (pl. **tarsi** /-sʌɪ, -siː/) **1** Anatomy a group of small bones between the main part of the hindlimb and the metatarsus in terrestrial vertebrates. The seven bones of the human tarsus form the ankle and upper part of the foot. They are the talus, calcaneus, navicular, and cuboid, and the three cuneiform bones.
■Zoology the shank or tarsometatarsus of the leg of a bird or reptile. ■ Zoology the foot or fifth joint of the leg of an insect or other arthropod, typically consisting of several small segments and ending in a claw.
2 Anatomy a thin sheet of fibrous connective tissue which supports the edge of each eyelid.
– ORIGIN late Middle English: modern Latin, from Greek *tarsos* 'flat of the foot, the eyelid'.

tart[1] ▶ noun an open pastry case containing a sweet or savoury filling.
– DERIVATIVES **tartlet** noun.
– ORIGIN late Middle English (denoting a savoury pie): from Old French *tarte* or medieval Latin *tarta*, of unknown origin.

tart[2] ▶ noun informal, derogatory a prostitute or a promiscuous woman.
▶ verb [with obj.] (**tart oneself up**) informal, chiefly Brit. dress or make oneself up in order to look attractive or eye-catching.
■(**tart something up**) decorate or improve the appearance of something: *the page layouts have been tarted up with cartoons.*
– ORIGIN mid 19th cent.: probably an abbreviation of **SWEETHEART**.

tart[3] ▶ adjective sharp or acid in taste: *a tart apple.*
■(of a remark or tone of voice) cutting, bitter, or sarcastic: *I bit back a tart reply.*
– DERIVATIVES **tartly** adverb, **tartness** noun.
– ORIGIN Old English *teart* 'harsh, severe', of unknown origin.

tartan[1] ▶ noun a woollen cloth woven in one of several patterns of coloured checks and intersecting lines, especially of a design associated with a particular Scottish clan.
▶ adjective used allusively in reference to Scotland or the Scots: *the financing proposals for the Scottish parliament amounted to a tartan tax.*
– ORIGIN late 15th cent. (originally Scots): perhaps from Old French *tertaine*, denoting a kind of cloth; compare with *tartarin*, a rich fabric formerly imported from the east through Tartary.

tartan[2] ▶ noun historical a lateen-rigged, single-masted ship used in the Mediterranean.
– ORIGIN early 17th cent.: from French *tartane*, from Italian *tartana*, perhaps from Arabic *ṭarīda*.

Tartar /ˈtɑːtə/ ▶ noun historical a member of the combined forces of central Asian peoples, including Mongols and Turks, who under the leadership of Genghis Khan conquered much of Asia and eastern Europe in the early 13th century, and under Tamerlane (14th century) established an empire with its capital at Samarkand. See also **TATAR**.
■(**tartar**) a harsh, fierce, or intractable person.
– DERIVATIVES **Tartarian** /-ˈtɛːrɪən/ adjective.
– ORIGIN from Old French *Tartare* or medieval Latin *Tartarus*, alteration (influenced by **TARTARUS**) of **TATAR**.

tartar /ˈtɑːtə/ ▶ noun [mass noun] a hard calcified deposit that forms on the teeth and contributes to their decay.
■a deposit of impure potassium hydrogen tartrate formed during the fermentation of wine.
– ORIGIN late Middle English: via medieval Latin from medieval Greek *tartaron*, of unknown origin.

tartare /tɑːˈtɑː/ ▶ adjective [postpositive] (of fish) served raw, typically seasoned and shaped into small cakes. See also **STEAK TARTARE**.
– ORIGIN French, literally 'Tartar'.

tartar emetic ▶ noun [mass noun] a toxic compound used in treating protozoal disease in animals, as a mordant in dyeing, and formerly as an emetic.
● Alternative name: **potassium antimony tartrate**; chem. formula: $K(SbO)C_4H_4O_6$.

tartare sauce (also **tartar sauce**) ▶ noun [mass

noun] a cold sauce, typically eaten with fish, consisting of mayonnaise mixed with chopped onions, gherkins, and capers.

tartaric acid ▶ noun [mass noun] Chemistry a crystalline organic acid which is present especially in unripe grapes and is used in baking powders and as a food additive.
● A dibasic acid; chem. formula: $COOH(CHOH)_2COOH$.
– ORIGIN late 18th cent.: *tartaric* from obsolete French *tartarique*, from medieval Latin *tartarum* (see **TARTAR**).

Tartarus /ˈtɑːt(ə)rəs/ Greek Mythology **1** a primeval god, offspring of Chaos.
2 a part of the underworld where the wicked suffered punishment for their misdeeds, especially those such as Ixion and Tantalus who had committed some outrage against the gods.
– DERIVATIVES **Tartarean** /-ˈtɛːrɪən/ adjective.

Tartary /ˈtɑːtəri/ a historical region of Asia and eastern Europe, especially the high plateau of central Asia and its NW slopes, which formed part of the Tartar empire in the Middle Ages.

tarte Tatin /ˌtɑːt taˈtã/ ▶ noun a type of upside-down apple tart consisting of pastry baked over slices of fruit arranged in caramelized sugar, served fruit side up after cooking.
– ORIGIN French, from *tarte* 'tart' + *Tatin*, the surname of the sisters said to have created the dish.

tartrate /ˈtɑːtreɪt/ ▶ noun Chemistry a salt or ester of tartaric acid.
– ORIGIN late 18th cent.: from French, from *tartre* 'tartar' + **-ATE**[1].

tartrazine /ˈtɑːtrəziːn/ ▶ noun [mass noun] Chemistry a brilliant yellow synthetic dye derived from tartaric acid and used to colour food, drugs, and cosmetics.
– ORIGIN late 19th cent.: from French *tartre* 'tartar' + **AZO-** + **-INE**[4].

Tartuffe /tɑːˈtuːf/ ▶ noun **1** poetic/literary or humorous a religious hypocrite, or a hypocritical pretender to excellence of any kind. [ORIGIN: from the name of the principal character (a religious hypocrite) in Molière's *Tartuffe* (1664).]
2 (**tartuffe**) a sweet truffle. [ORIGIN: from Italian *tartufo*.]
– DERIVATIVES **Tartufferie** (also **Tartuffery**) noun.

tartufo /tɑːˈtuːfəʊ/ ▶ noun **1** an edible fungus, especially the white truffle.
2 an Italian dessert, containing chocolate, of a creamy mousse-like consistency.
– ORIGIN Italian, literally 'truffle'.

tarty ▶ adjective (**tartier**, **tartiest**) informal (of a woman) dressed in a sexually provocative manner that is considered to be in bad taste.
■(of clothes) contributing to a sexually provocative appearance.
– DERIVATIVES **tartily** adverb, **tartiness** noun.

tarweed ▶ noun [mass noun] any of a number of American plants of the daisy family with sticky leaves and heavy scent.
● *Madia*, *Grindelia*, *Hemizonia*, and related genera, family Compositae.

tarwhine /ˈtɑːwʌɪn/ ▶ noun (pl. same) a yellowish sea bream of warm shallow inshore waters, which is an important food and game fish in the Indo-Pacific.
● *Rhabdosargus globiceps*, family Sparidae.
– ORIGIN late 19th cent.: from Dharuk *darawayn* 'a fish'.

Tarzan a fictitious character created by Edgar Rice Burroughs. Tarzan (Lord Greystoke by birth) is orphaned in West Africa in his infancy and reared by apes in the jungle.
■[as noun **a Tarzan**] a man of great agility and powerful physique.

Tas. chiefly Austral. ▶ abbreviation for Tasmania.

tasca /ˈtaska/ ▶ noun (in Spain and Portugal) a tavern or bar, especially one serving food.
– ORIGIN Spanish and Portuguese.

taser /ˈteɪzə/ ▶ noun US trademark a weapon firing barbs attached by wires to batteries, causing temporary paralysis.
– ORIGIN 1970s: from the initial letters of *Tom Swift's electric rifle* (a fictitious weapon), on the pattern of *laser*.

tash (also **tache**) ▶ noun informal a moustache.
– ORIGIN late 19th cent.: shortened form.

Tashi Lama /ˈtaʃi ˌlɑːmə/ ▶ noun another name for **PANCHEN LAMA**.

Tashkent /taʃˈkɛnt/ the capital of Uzbekistan, in

the far north-east of the country in the western foothills of the Tien Shan mountains: pop. 2,094,000 (1990). One of the oldest cities in central Asia, Tashkent was an important centre on the trade route between Europe and the Orient. It became part of the Mongol empire in the 13th century, was captured by the Russians in 1865, and replaced Samarkand as capital of Uzbekistan in 1930.

task ▶ noun a piece of work to be done or undertaken.
▶ verb [with obj.] (usu. **be tasked**) assign such a piece of work to: *NATO troops are tasked with separating the warring parties.*
■make great demands on (someone's resources or abilities): *it tasked his diplomatic skill to effect his departure in safety.*
– PHRASES **take someone to task** reprimand or criticize someone severely for a fault or mistake.
– ORIGIN Middle English: from an Old Northern French variant of Old French *tasche*, from medieval Latin *tasca*, alteration of *taxa*, from Latin *taxare* 'censure, charge' (see **TAX**). An early sense of the verb was 'impose a tax on'.

task force (also **task group**) ▶ noun an armed force organized for a special operation.
■a unit specially organized for a task: *the government has set up a task force to survey mental health services.*

taskmaster ▶ noun a person who imposes a harsh or onerous workload on someone.

Tasman /ˈtazmən/, Abel (Janszoon) (1603–c.1659), Dutch navigator. Sent in 1642 by the Governor General of the Dutch East Indies, Anthony van Diemen (1593–1645), to explore Australian waters, he reached Tasmania (which he named Van Diemen's Land) and New Zealand, and in 1643 arrived at Tonga and Fiji.

Tasmania /tazˈmeɪnɪə/ a state of Australia consisting of the mountainous island of Tasmania itself and several smaller islands; pop. 457,500 (1990); capital, Hobart. It was known as Van Diemen's Land until 1855.
– DERIVATIVES **Tasmanian** adjective & noun.

Tasmanian devil ▶ noun a heavily built marsupial with a large head, powerful jaws, and mainly black fur, found only in Tasmania. It is slow-moving and aggressive, feeding mainly on carrion.
● *Sarcophilus harrisii*, family Dasyuridae.

Tasmanian wolf (also **Tasmanian tiger**) ▶ noun another term for **THYLACINE**.

Tasman Sea an arm of the South Pacific lying between Australia and New Zealand.

Tass /tas/ the official news agency of the former Soviet Union, renamed ITAR-Tass in 1992.
– ORIGIN Russian acronym, from *Telegrafnoe agentstvo Sovetskogo Soyuza* 'Telegraphic Agency of the Soviet Union'.

tass ▶ noun Scottish archaic a cup or small goblet.
■a small draught of an alcoholic drink.
– ORIGIN late 15th cent.: from Old French *tasse* 'cup', via Arabic from Persian *ṭašt* 'bowl'.

tassa drum /ˈtasə/ ▶ noun W. Indian a large one-sided Indian goatskin drum, typically hung from the neck and played with two sticks, and used especially at weddings and religious celebrations.
– ORIGIN *tassa* from Hindi.

tassel[1] ▶ noun a tuft of loosely hanging threads, cords, or other material knotted at one end and attached for decoration to soft furnishings, clothing, or other items.
■the tufted head of some plants, especially a flower head with prominent stamens at the top of a maize stalk.
▶ verb (**tasselled**, **tasselling**; US **tasseled**, **tasseling**) **1** [with obj.] [usu. as adj. **tasselled**] provide with a tassel or tassels: *tasselled curtains.*
2 N. Amer. [no obj.] (of maize or other plants) form tassels.
– ORIGIN Middle English (also denoting a clasp for a cloak): from Old French *tassel* 'clasp', of unknown origin.

tassel[2] (also **torsel**) ▶ noun a small piece of stone or wood supporting the end of a beam or joist.
– ORIGIN mid 17th cent.: from obsolete French, from Latin *taxillus* 'small die'.

tassie ▶ noun Scottish archaic a small cup.

Tasso /ˈtasəʊ/, Torquato (1544–95), Italian poet,

known for his epic poem *Gerusalemme liberata* (1581).

taste ▶ **noun 1** the sensation of flavour perceived in the mouth and throat on contact with a substance: *the wine had a fruity taste.*
■[mass noun] the faculty of perceiving this quality: *birds do not have a highly developed sense of taste.* ■ a small portion of food or drink taken as a sample: *try a taste of gorgonzola.* ■ a brief experience of something, conveying its basic character: *it was his first taste of serious action.*
2 a person's liking for particular flavours: *this pudding is too sweet for my taste.*
■a person's tendency to like and dislike certain things: *he found the aggressive competitiveness of the profession was not* **to his taste**. ■ **(taste for)** a liking for or interest in (something): *have you lost your taste for fancy restaurants?* ■ [mass noun] the ability to discern what is of good quality or of a high aesthetic standard: *she has frightful taste in literature.* ■ [mass noun] conformity or failure to conform with generally held views concerning what is offensive or acceptable: *that's a joke* **in** *very bad* **taste**.
▶**verb** [with obj.] perceive or experience the flavour of: *she had never tasted ice cream before.*
■[no obj.] have a specified flavour: [with complement] *the spinach tastes delicious.* ■ sample or test the flavour of (food or drink) by taking it into the mouth: *the waiter poured some wine for him to taste.* ■ eat or drink a small portion of. ■ have experience of: *the team has not yet tasted victory at home.*
– PHRASES **a bad** (or **bitter** or **nasty**) **taste in the** (or US **someone's**) **mouth** informal a strong feeling of distress or disgust following an experience. **taste blood** see **BLOOD**. **to taste** in the amount needed to give a flavour pleasing to someone eating a dish: *add salt and pepper to taste.*
– ORIGIN Middle English (also in the sense 'touch'): from Old French *tast* (noun), *taster* (verb) 'touch, try, taste', perhaps based on a blend of Latin *tangere* 'to touch' and *gustare* 'to taste'.

taste bud ▶ **noun** (usu. **taste buds**) any of the clusters of bulbous nerve endings on the tongue and in the lining of the mouth which provide the sense of taste.

tasteful ▶ **adjective** showing good aesthetic judgement or appropriate behaviour: *a tasteful lounge bar.*
– DERIVATIVES **tastefully** adverb, **tastefulness** noun.

tasteless ▶ **adjective 1** lacking flavour.
2 considered to be lacking in aesthetic judgement or to offend against what is regarded as appropriate behaviour: *a tasteless joke.*
– DERIVATIVES **tastelessly** adverb, **tastelessness** noun.

tastemaker ▶ **noun** a person who decides or influences what is or will become fashionable.

taster ▶ **noun 1** a person employed to test food or drink for quality by tasting it: *a tea taster.*
■a small cup used by a person tasting wine in such a way. ■ an instrument for extracting a small sample from within a cheese.
2 a small quantity or brief experience of something, intended as a sample: *the song is a taster for the band's new LP.*
– ORIGIN late Middle English: in early use from Anglo-Norman French *tastour*, from Old French *taster* 'to taste'; later from **TASTE** + **-ER**[1].

tastevin /ˈtastəvã, ˌtastəˈvã, French tastəvɛ̃/ ▶ **noun** (pl. pronounced same) a small, shallow silver cup for tasting wines, of a type used in France.
– ORIGIN French, literally 'wine taster'.

tasting ▶ **noun** a gathering at which people sample, compare, and evaluate different wines, or other drinks or food.

tasty ▶ **adjective** (**tastier**, **tastiest**) (of food) having a pleasant, distinct flavour: *a tasty snack.*
■informal, chiefly Brit. attractive; very appealing: *a tasty deal at the building society.* ■ Brit. informal very good; impressive: *he's a bit tasty with a football.*
– DERIVATIVES **tastily** adverb, **tastiness** noun.

tat[1] ▶ **noun** [mass noun] Brit. informal tasteless or shoddy clothes, jewellery, or ornaments.
– ORIGIN mid 19th cent. (in the senses 'rag' and 'person in rags'): probably a back-formation from **TATTY**.

tat[2] ▶ **verb** (**tatted**, **tatting**) [with obj.] make (a decorative mat or edging) by tying knots in thread and using a small shuttle to form lace.
– ORIGIN late 19th cent.: back-formation from **TATTING**.

tat[3] ▶ **noun** see **TIT**[3].

ta-ta ▶ **exclamation** informal, chiefly Brit. goodbye.
– ORIGIN early 19th cent.: of unknown origin; compare with earlier *da-da*.

tatami /təˈtɑːmi/ (also **tatami mat**) ▶ **noun** (pl. same or **tatamis**) a rush-covered straw mat forming a traditional Japanese floor covering.
– ORIGIN Japanese.

Tatar /ˈtɑːtə/ ▶ **noun 1** a member of a Turkic people living in Tatarstan and various other parts of Russia and Ukraine. They are the descendants of the Tartars who ruled central Asia in the 14th century.
2 [mass noun] the Turkic language of this people, with about 6 million speakers.
▶**adjective** of or relating to this people or their language.
– ORIGIN the Turkic name of a Tartar tribe.

Tatarstan /ˌtɑːtəˈstɑːn, -ˈstan/ an autonomous republic in European Russia, in the valley of the River Volga; pop. 3,658,000 (1990); capital, Kazan.

Tate, Nahum (1652–1715), Irish dramatist and poet, resident in London from the 1670s. He was appointed Poet Laureate in 1692.

Tate Gallery a national museum of art at Millbank, London, founded in 1897 by the sugar manufacturer Sir Henry Tate (1819–99) to house his collection of modern British paintings, as a nucleus for a permanent national collection of modern art. It was renamed the Tate Britain in 2000, when the new Tate Modern gallery opened.

tater /ˈteɪtə/ (Brit. also **tatie** /-ti/) ▶ **noun** informal a potato.
– ORIGIN mid 18th cent.: alteration.

Tathagata /təˈtɑːgətə, təˈθɑːgətə/ ▶ **noun** an honorific title of a Buddha, especially the Buddha Gautama, or a person who has attained perfection by following Buddhist principles.
– ORIGIN from Pali *Tathāgata*, from *tathā* 'in that manner' + *gata* 'gone'.

tathata /ˌtatəˈtɑː, ˌtaθəˈtɑː/ ▶ **noun** [mass noun] Buddhism the ultimate nature of all things, as expressed in phenomena but inexpressible in language. Compare with **SUNYATA**.
– ORIGIN Pali, literally 'true state of things'.

Tati /ˈtati/, Jacques (1908–82), French film director and actor; born *Jacques Tatischeff*. He introduced the comically inept character Monsieur Hulot in *Monsieur Hulot's Holiday* (1953), seen again in films including the Oscar-winning *Mon oncle* (1958).

Tatra Mountains /ˈtɑːtrə, ˈtatrə/ (also **the Tatras**) a range of mountains in eastern Europe on the Polish–Slovak border, the highest range in the Carpathians, rising to 2,655 m (8,710 ft) at Mount Gerlachovsky.

tattered ▶ **adjective** torn, old, and in generally poor condition; in tatters: *an old woman in tattered clothes.*
– ORIGIN Middle English (in the sense 'dressed in decoratively slashed or jagged clothing'): apparently originally from the noun *tatter* 'scrap of cloth' + **-ED**[1]; later treated as a past participle.

tatters ▶ **plural noun** irregularly torn pieces of cloth, paper, or other material.
– PHRASES **in tatters** informal torn in many places; in shreds: *wallpaper hung in tatters.* ■ figurative destroyed; ruined: *the ceasefire was in tatters within hours.*
– ORIGIN late Middle English (also in the singular meaning 'scrap of cloth'): from Old Norse *tǫtrar* 'rags'.

tattersall /ˈtatəs(ə)l, -sɔːl/ (also **tattersall check**) ▶ **noun** a woollen fabric with a pattern of coloured checks and intersecting lines, resembling a tartan.
– ORIGIN late 19th cent.: named after **TATTERSALLS**, by association with the traditional design of horse blankets.

Tattersalls /ˈtatəsɔːlz/ an English firm of horse auctioneers founded in 1776 by the horseman Richard Tattersall (1724–95).

tattie ▶ **noun** informal, chiefly Scottish a potato.
– ORIGIN late 18th cent.: alteration.

tatting ▶ **noun** [mass noun] a kind of knotted lace made by hand with a small shuttle, used chiefly for trimming.
■the process of making such lace.
– ORIGIN mid 19th cent.: of unknown origin.

tattle ▶ **noun** [mass noun] gossip; idle talk.
▶**verb** [no obj.] gossip idly.
■report another's wrongdoing; tell tales.
– ORIGIN late 15th cent. (in the sense 'falter, stammer', also 'make meaningless sounds', referring to a small child): from Middle Flemish *tatelen*, *tateren*, of imitative origin.

tattler ▶ **noun 1** a person who engages in gossip or who tells tales.
2 a migratory sandpiper with mainly grey plumage, breeding in NW Canada or eastern Siberia.
• Genus *Heteroscelus*, family Scolopacidae: two species, in particular the **wandering tattler** (*H. incanus*) of Canada.

tattletale US ▶ **noun** a person, especially a child, who reveals secrets or informs on others; a telltale.
▶**verb** [no obj.] reveal someone's secrets; tell tales.

tattoo[1] ▶ **noun** (pl. **tattoos**) an evening drum or bugle signal recalling soldiers to their quarters.
■an entertainment consisting of music, marching, and the performance of displays and exercises by military personnel. ■ a rhythmic tapping or drumming.
– ORIGIN mid 17th cent. (originally as *tap-too*) from Dutch *taptoe!*, literally 'close the tap (of the cask)!'.

tattoo[2] ▶ **verb** (**tattoos**, **tattooed**) [with obj.] mark (a person or a part of the body) with an indelible design by inserting pigment into punctures in the skin: *his cheek was tattooed with a winged fist.*
■make (a design) in such way: *he has a heart tattooed on his left hand.*
▶**noun** (pl. **tattoos**) a design made in such a way.
– DERIVATIVES **tattooer** noun, **tattooist** noun.
– ORIGIN mid 18th cent.: from Tahitian, Tongan, and Samoan *ta-tau* or Marquesan *ta-tu*.

tatty ▶ **adjective** (**tattier**, **tattiest**) informal worn and shabby; in poor condition: *the room was furnished in slightly tatty upholstered furniture.*
■of poor quality: *the high, but generally tatty, output of the current Celtic revival.*
– DERIVATIVES **tattily** adverb, **tattiness** noun.
– ORIGIN early 16th cent. (originally Scots, in the sense 'tangled, matted, shaggy'): apparently ultimately related to Old English *tættec* 'rag', of Germanic origin; compare with **TATTERED**.

Tatum /ˈteɪtəm/, Art (1910–56), American jazz pianist; full name *Arthur Tatum*. Born with cataracts in both eyes, he was almost completely blind. He became famous in the 1930s for his solo and trio work.

tau /tɔː, taʊ/ ▶ **noun** the nineteenth letter of the Greek alphabet (**Τ, τ**), transliterated as 't'.
■**(Tau)** [followed by Latin genitive] Astronomy the nineteenth star on a constellation: *Tau Ceti.* ■ (in full **tau particle** or **tau lepton**) Physics an unstable subatomic particle of the lepton class, with a charge of −1 and a mass roughly 3500 times that of the electron.
– ORIGIN Greek.

tau cross ▶ **noun** a T-shaped cross.

taught past and past participle of **TEACH**.

tau neutrino ▶ **noun** Physics a neutrino of the type associated with the tau particle.

taunt ▶ **noun** a remark made in order to anger, wound, or provoke someone.
▶**verb** [with obj.] provoke or challenge (someone) with insulting remarks: *pupils began taunting her about her weight.*
■reproach (someone) with something in a contemptuous way: *she had* **taunted** *him* **with** *going to another man.*
– DERIVATIVES **taunter** noun, **tauntingly** adverb.
– ORIGIN early 16th cent.: from French *tant pour tant* 'like for like, tit for tat', from *tant* 'so much', from Latin *tantum*, neuter of *tantus*. An early use of the verb was 'exchange banter'.

Taunton /ˈtɔːntən/ the county town of Somerset, in SW England; pop. 48,860 (1981).

tau particle ▶ **noun** see **TAU**.

taupe /təʊp/ ▶ **noun** [mass noun] grey with a tinge of brown: [as modifier] *a taupe overcoat.*
– ORIGIN early 20th cent.: from French, literally 'mole, moleskin', from Latin *talpa*.

Taupo, Lake /ˈtaʊpəʊ/ the largest lake of New Zealand, in the centre of North Island. The town of Taupo is situated on its northern shore. Maori name **TAUPOMOANA**.

Tauranga /taʊˈraŋə/ a port on the Bay of Plenty, North Island, New Zealand; pop. 64,000 (1990).

taurine[1] /ˈtɔːriːn/ ▶ **noun** [mass noun] Biochemistry a sulphur-containing amino acid important in the metabolism of fats.
• Chem. formula: $NH_2CH_2CH_2SO_3H$.

– ORIGIN mid 19th cent.: from Greek *tauros* 'bull' (because it was originally obtained from ox-bile) + **-INE**⁴.

taurine² /ˈtɔːraɪn/ ▶ adjective of or like a bull.
■ of or relating to bullfighting: *taurine skill*.
– ORIGIN early 17th cent.: from Latin *taurinus*, from *taurus* 'bull'.

taurocholic acid /ˌtɔːrə(ʊ)ˈkɒlɪk/ ▶ noun [mass noun] Biochemistry an acid formed by the combination of taurine with cholic acid, occurring in bile.
– DERIVATIVES **taurocholate** noun.
– ORIGIN mid 19th cent.: from Greek *tauros* 'bull' + *kholē* 'bile' + **-IC**.

tauromachy /tɔːˈrɒməki/ ▶ noun (pl. **-ies**) [mass noun] rare bullfighting.
■ [count noun] a bullfight.
– DERIVATIVES **tauromachian** adjective, **tauromachic** adjective.
– ORIGIN mid 19th cent.: from Greek *tauromakhia*, from *tauros* 'bull' + *makhē* 'battle'.

Taurus /ˈtɔːrəs/ **1** Astronomy a constellation (the Bull), said to represent a bull with brazen feet that was tamed by Jason. Its many bright stars include Aldebaran (the bull's eye), and it contains the star clusters of the Hyades and the Pleiades, and the Crab Nebula.
■ [as genitive **Tauri** /ˈtɔːriː/] used with preceding letter or numeral to designate a star in this constellation: *the star Beta Tauri*.
2 Astrology the second sign of the zodiac, which the sun enters on about 21 April.
■ (**a Taurus**) (pl. same) a person born when the sun is in this sign.
– DERIVATIVES **Taurean** /ˈtɔːrɪən, tɔːˈriːən/ noun & adjective (only in sense 2).
– ORIGIN Latin.

Taurus Mountains a range of mountains in southern Turkey, parallel to the Mediterranean coast. Rising to 3,734 m (12,250 ft) at Mount Aladaë, the range forms the southern edge of the Anatolian plateau.

taut ▶ adjective stretched or pulled tight; not slack: *the fabric stays taut without adhesive*.
■ (especially of muscles or nerves) tense; not relaxed. ■ figurative (of writing, music, etc.) concise and controlled: *a taut text of only a hundred and twenty pages*. ■ (of a ship) having a disciplined and efficient crew.
– DERIVATIVES **tauten** verb, **tautly** adverb, **tautness** noun.
– ORIGIN Middle English *tought* 'distended', perhaps originally a variant of **TOUGH**.

tauto- /ˈtɔːtəʊ/ ▶ combining form same: *tautology*.
– ORIGIN from Greek *tauto*, contraction of *to auto* 'the same'.

tautog /tɔːˈtɒg/ ▶ noun a greyish-olive edible wrasse which occurs off the Atlantic coast of North America.
● *Tautoga onitis*, family Labridae.
– ORIGIN mid 17th cent.: from Narragansett *tautauog*, plural of *taut*.

tautology /tɔːˈtɒlədʒi/ ▶ noun (pl. **-ies**) [mass noun] the saying of the same thing twice over in different words, generally considered to be a fault of style (e.g. *they arrived one after the other in succession*).
■ [count noun] a phrase or expression in which the same thing is said twice in different words. ■ Logic a statement that is true by necessity or by virtue of its logical form.
– DERIVATIVES **tautological** adjective, **tautologically** adverb, **tautologist** noun, **tautologize** (also **-ise**) verb, **tautologous** adjective.
– ORIGIN mid 16th cent.: via late Latin from Greek, from *tautologos* 'repeating what has been said', from *tauto-* 'same' + *-logos* (see **-LOGY**).

tautomer /ˈtɔːtəmə/ ▶ noun Chemistry each of two or more isomers of a compound which exist together in equilibrium, and are readily interchanged by migration of an atom or group within the molecule.
– DERIVATIVES **tautomeric** /-ˈmɛrɪk/ adjective, **tautomerism** /-ˈtɒmərɪz(ə)m/ noun.
– ORIGIN early 20th cent.: blend of **TAUTO-** 'same' and **ISOMER**.

tautonym /ˈtɔːtə(ʊ)nɪm/ ▶ noun Botany & Zoology a scientific name in which the same word is used for both genus and species, for example *Vulpes vulpes* (the red fox).
– DERIVATIVES **tautonymy** noun.

Tavel /taˈvɛl/ ▶ noun [mass noun] a fine rosé wine produced at Tavel in the south of France.

Tavener, Sir John (Kenneth) (b.1944), English composer. His music is primarily religious and has been influenced by his conversion to the Russian Orthodox Church.

tavern ▶ noun chiefly archaic or N. Amer. an inn or public house.
– ORIGIN Middle English: from Old French *taverne*, from Latin *taberna* 'hut, tavern'. Compare with **TABERNACLE**.

taverna /taˈvɔːnə/ ▶ noun a small Greek restaurant or cafe.
– ORIGIN modern Greek, from Latin *taberna* (see **TAVERN**).

Taverner, John (c.1490–1545), English composer, an influential writer of early polyphonic church music.

taw¹ /tɔː/ ▶ verb [with obj.] make (hide) into leather without the use of tannin, especially by soaking it in a solution of alum and salt.
– DERIVATIVES **tawer** noun.
– ORIGIN Old English *tawian* 'prepare raw material for use or further processing', of Germanic origin; related to **TOOL**.

taw² /tɔː/ ▶ noun a large marble.
■ [mass noun] a game of marbles. ■ a line from which players throw marbles.
– ORIGIN early 18th cent.: of unknown origin.

tawa¹ /ˈtɑːwə, ˈtaʊə/ ▶ noun a tall New Zealand forest tree of the laurel family, which bears damson-like fruit.
● *Beilschmiedia tawa*, family Lauraceae.
– ORIGIN mid 19th cent.: from Maori.

tawa² /tɑːˈwɑː/ ▶ noun a circular griddle used in the Indian subcontinent, especially for cooking chapattis.
– ORIGIN from Hindi and Punjabi *tavā*.

tawdry ▶ adjective (**tawdrier**, **tawdriest**) showy but cheap and of poor quality: *tawdry jewellery*.
■ sordid or unpleasant: *the tawdry business of politics*.
▶ noun [mass noun] archaic cheap and gaudy finery.
– DERIVATIVES **tawdrily** adverb, **tawdriness** noun.
– ORIGIN early 17th cent.: short for *tawdry lace*, a fine silk lace or ribbon worn as a necklace in the 16th–17th cents, contraction of *St Audrey's lace*: *Audrey* was a later form of *Etheldrida* (died 679), patron saint of Ely where tawdry laces, along with cheap imitations and other cheap finery, were traditionally sold at a fair.

tawny ▶ adjective (**tawnier**, **tawniest**) of an orange-brown or yellowish-brown colour: *tawny eyes*.
▶ noun [mass noun] an orange-brown or yellowish-brown colour: *pine needles turning from tawny to amber*.
– DERIVATIVES **tawniness** noun.
– ORIGIN Middle English: from Old French *tane*, from *tan* 'tanbark'; related to **TAN**¹.

tawny eagle ▶ noun a uniformly brown eagle found in Asia and Africa.
● *Aquila rapax*, family Accipitridae.

tawny grisette ▶ noun a widely distributed edible mushroom with an orange-brown cap, a slender stem, and white gills, growing chiefly in birchwoods.
● *Amanita fulva*, family Amanitaceae, class Hymenomycetes.

tawny owl ▶ noun **1** a common Eurasian owl with either reddish-brown or grey plumage, and a familiar quavering hoot.
● *Strix aluco*, family Strigidae.
2 (**Tawny Owl**) informal (in the UK) the assistant adult leader of a pack of Brownie Guides, officially termed *Assistant Brownie Guider* since 1968.

tawny port ▶ noun [mass noun] a port wine made from a blend of several vintages matured in wood.

tawse /tɔːz/ (also **taws**) ▶ noun Scottish a thong with a slit end, formerly used in schools for punishing children.
– ORIGIN early 16th cent. (denoting a whip for driving a spinning top): apparently the plural of obsolete *taw* 'tawed leather', from **TAW**¹.

tax ▶ noun a compulsory contribution to state revenue, levied by the government on workers' income and business profits, or added to the cost of some goods, services, and transactions.
■ [in sing.] figurative a strain or heavy demand: *a heavy tax on the reader's attention*.
▶ verb [with obj.] **1** impose a tax on (someone or something): *the income will be taxed at the top rate*.

■ pay tax on (something, especially a vehicle). ■ figurative make heavy demands on (someone's powers or resources): *she knew that the ordeal to come must tax all her strength*.
2 confront (someone) with a fault or wrongdoing: *why are you taxing me with these preposterous allegations?*
3 Law examine and assess (the costs of a case).
– DERIVATIVES **taxable** adjective, **taxer** noun.
– ORIGIN Middle English (also in the sense 'estimate or determine the amount of a penalty or damages', surviving in sense 3): from Old French *taxer*, from Latin *taxare* 'to censure, charge, compute', perhaps from Greek *tassein* 'fix'.

taxa plural form of **TAXON**.

taxation ▶ noun [mass noun] the levying of tax.
■ money paid as tax.
– ORIGIN Middle English (in the sense 'the assessment of a penalty or damages'; compare with **TAX**): via Old French from Latin *taxatio(n-)*, from *taxare* 'to censure, charge'.

tax avoidance ▶ noun [mass noun] Brit. the arrangement of one's financial affairs to minimize tax liability within the law. Compare with **TAX EVASION**.

tax break ▶ noun informal a tax concession or advantage allowed by government.

tax code ▶ noun a code number representing the tax-free part of an employee's income, assigned by tax authorities for use by employers in calculating the tax to be deducted under the PAYE system.

tax credit ▶ noun a sum that can be offset against a tax liability.

tax-deductible ▶ adjective able to be deducted from taxable income or the amount of tax to be paid.

tax-disc ▶ noun Brit. a circular label displayed on the windscreen of a motor vehicle, certifying payment of road tax.

tax evasion ▶ noun [mass noun] the illegal non-payment or underpayment of tax. Compare with **TAX AVOIDANCE**.

tax exile ▶ noun a person with a high income or considerable wealth who chooses to live in a country or area with low rates of tax.

tax-free ▶ adjective & adverb (of goods, income, etc.) exempt from tax: [as adj.] *a tax-free lump sum* | [as adv.] *your return is paid to you tax-free*.

tax haven ▶ noun a country or independent area where taxes are levied at a low rate.

taxi ▶ noun (pl. **taxis**) a motor vehicle licensed to transport passengers in return for payment of a fare and typically fitted with a taximeter.
■ a boat or other means of transportation similarly used. ■ (in South Africa) a light vehicle, especially a minibus, transporting passengers along a fixed route for a set fare but not operating to a timetable.
▶ verb (**taxies**, **taxied**, **taxiing** or **taxying**) [no obj., with adverbial of direction] **1** (of an aircraft) move slowly along the ground before take-off or after landing: *the plane taxies up to a waiting limousine*.
■ [with obj.] (of a pilot) cause (an aircraft) to move in such a way.
2 take a taxi as a means of transport: *I would taxi home and sleep till eight*.
– ORIGIN early 20th cent.: abbreviation of *taxi-cab* or *taximeter cab* (see **TAXIMETER**).

taxicab ▶ noun a taxi.

taxi dancer ▶ noun chiefly N. Amer. a professional dance partner.

taxidermist /ˌtaksɪˈdəːmɪst/ ▶ noun a person who practises taxidermy.

taxidermy /ˈtaksɪˌdəːmi/ ▶ noun [mass noun] the art of preparing, stuffing, and mounting the skins of animals with lifelike effect.
– DERIVATIVES **taxidermal** adjective, **taxidermic** adjective, **taxidermically** adverb.
– ORIGIN early 19th cent.: from Greek *taxis* 'arrangement' + *derma* 'skin'.

taximeter ▶ noun a device used in taxis that automatically records the distance travelled and the fare payable.
– ORIGIN late 19th cent.: from French *taximètre*, from *taxe* 'tariff', from the verb *taxer* 'to tax' + *-mètre* '(instrument) measuring'.

taxing ▶ adjective physically or mentally demanding: *they find the work too taxing*.

tax inspector ▶**noun** another term for **INSPECTOR OF TAXES**.

taxi rank (US **taxi stand**) ▶**noun** a place where taxis park while waiting to be hired.

taxis /ˈtaksɪs/ ▶**noun** (pl. **taxes** /ˈtaksiːz/) **1** [mass noun] Surgery the restoration of displaced bones or organs by manual pressure alone.
2 [count noun] Biology a motion or orientation of a cell, organism, or part in response to an external stimulus. Compare with **KINESIS**.
3 [mass noun] Linguistics the systematic arrangement of linguistic units (phonemes, morphemes, words, phrases, or clauses) in linear sequence.
– ORIGIN mid 18th cent. (in sense 1): from Greek, literally 'arrangement', from *tassein* 'arrange'. Sense 2 dates from the late 19th cent.

taxi squad ▶**noun** American Football a group of players taking part in practices and available as reserves for the team.

taxiway ▶**noun** a route along which an aircraft can taxi when moving to or from a runway.

tax loss ▶**noun** Economics a loss that can be offset against taxable profit earned elsewhere or in a different period.

taxman ▶**noun** (pl. **-men**) informal an inspector or collector of taxes.
■(**the taxman**) the government department that collects tax: *he denies conspiracy to cheat the taxman.*

taxol /ˈtaksɒl/ ▶**noun** [mass noun] Medicine, trademark a compound, originally obtained from the bark of the Pacific yew tree, which has been found to inhibit the growth of certain cancers.
– ORIGIN 1970s: from Latin *taxus* 'yew' + **-OL**.

taxon /ˈtaksɒn/ ▶**noun** (pl. **taxa** /ˈtaksə/) Biology a taxonomic group of any rank, such as a species, family, or class.
– ORIGIN 1920s: back-formation from **TAXONOMY**.

taxonomy /takˈsɒnəmi/ ▶**noun** [mass noun] chiefly Biology the branch of science concerned with classification, especially of organisms; systematics.
■the classification of something, especially organisms: *the taxonomy of these fossils.* ■ [count noun] a scheme of classification: *a taxonomy of smells.*
– DERIVATIVES **taxonomic** adjective, **taxonomical** adjective, **taxonomically** adverb, **taxonomist** noun.
– ORIGIN early 19th cent.: coined in French from Greek *taxis* 'arrangement' + *-nomia* 'distribution'.

taxpayer ▶**noun** a person who pays taxes.

tax point ▶**noun** the date on which value added tax becomes chargeable on a transaction.

tax return ▶**noun** a form on which a taxpayer makes an annual statement of income and personal circumstances, used by the tax authorities to assess liability for tax.

tax shelter ▶**noun** a financial arrangement made to avoid or minimize taxes.

tax year ▶**noun** a year as reckoned for taxation (in Britain reckoned from 6 April).

Tay the longest river in Scotland, flowing 192 km (120 miles) eastwards through Loch Tay, entering the North Sea through the Firth of Tay.

Tay, Firth of the estuary of the River Tay, on the North Sea coast of Scotland. It is spanned by the longest railway bridge in Britain, a structure opened in 1888 that has 85 spans and a total length of 3,553 m (11,653 feet); its predecessor collapsed in a gale in 1879 while a passenger train was crossing it.

tayberry ▶**noun** (pl. **-ies**) a dark red soft fruit produced by crossing a blackberry and a raspberry.
– ORIGIN named after the River **TAY** in Scotland, near where it was introduced in 1977.

Taylor[1], Dame Elizabeth (b.1932), American actress, born in England. Notable films include *National Velvet* (made when she was still a child in 1944), *Cleopatra* (1963), and *Who's Afraid of Virginia Woolf?* (1966), for which she won an Oscar. She has been married eight times, including twice to the actor Richard Burton.

Taylor[2], Jeremy (1613–67), English Anglican churchman and writer. Chaplain to Charles I during the English Civil War, he is now remembered chiefly for his devotional writings.

Taylor[3], Zachary (1784–1850), American Whig statesman, 12th President of the US 1849–50. He became a national hero after his victories in the war with Mexico (1846–8).

Taylorism ▶**noun** [mass noun] the principles or practice of scientific management.
– DERIVATIVES **Taylorist** noun & adjective.
– ORIGIN mid 19th cent.: from the name of Frederick W. *Taylor* (1856–1915), the American engineer who expounded the system, + **-ISM**.

Taylor's series ▶**noun** Mathematics an infinite sum giving the value of a function *f*(*z*) in the neighbourhood of a point *a* in terms of the derivatives of the function evaluated at *a*.
– ORIGIN early 19th cent.: named after Brook *Taylor* (1685–1731), English mathematician.

Taymyr Peninsula variant spelling of **TAIMYR PENINSULA**.

tayra /ˈtʌɪrə/ ▶**noun** a large, agile tree-dwelling animal of the weasel family, with a short dark coat, native to Central and South America.
● *Eira barbara*, family Mustelidae.
– ORIGIN mid 19th cent.: from Tupi *taira*.

Tay–Sachs disease /teɪˈsaks/ ▶**noun** [mass noun] an inherited metabolic disorder in which certain lipids accumulate in the brain, causing spasticity and death in childhood.
– ORIGIN early 20th cent.: from the names of Warren *Tay* (1843–27), English ophthalmologist, and Bernard *Sachs* (1858–1944), American neurologist, who described it in 1881 and 1887 respectively.

Tayside a former local government region in eastern Scotland, dissolved in 1996.

tazza /ˈtɑːtsə/ ▶**noun** a saucer-shaped cup mounted on a foot.
– ORIGIN early 19th cent.: from Italian, from Arabic *ṭasa* 'bowl' (see **TASS**).

TB ▶**abbreviation for** ■ terabyte(s). ■ tubercle bacillus; tuberculosis.

Tb ▶**abbreviation for** terabyte(s).
▶**symbol for** the chemical element terbium.

t.b.a. ▶**abbreviation for** to be announced (in notices about events): *7p.m. party with live band t.b.a.*

T-back ▶**noun** a high-cut undergarment or swimming costume having only a thin strip of material passing between the buttocks.
■a style of back on a bra or bikini top in which the shoulder straps meet a supporting lateral strap below the shoulder blades.

T-bar ▶**noun 1** a beam or bar shaped like the letter T.
■(also **T-bar lift**) a type of ski lift in the form of a series of inverted T-shaped bars for towing two skiers at a time uphill. ■ [often as modifier] a T-shaped fastening on a shoe or sandal: *a pair of T-bar sandals.*
2 the horizontal line of the letter *T*.

Tbilisi /ˌtəbɪˈliːsi/ the capital of Georgia; pop. 1,267,500 (1991). From 1845 until 1936 its name was Tiflis.

T-bill ▶**noun** informal short for **TREASURY BILL**.

T-bone (also **T-bone steak**) ▶**noun** a large choice piece of loin steak containing a T-shaped bone.

tbsp (also **tbs**) (pl. same or **tbsps**) ▶**abbreviation for** tablespoonful.

Tc ▶**symbol for** the chemical element technetium.

TCCB ▶**abbreviation for** (in the UK) Test and County Cricket Board.

TCD ▶**abbreviation for** Trinity College, Dublin.

TCDD ▶**abbreviation for** tetrachlorodibenzo-paradioxin (see **DIOXIN**).

T-cell ▶**noun** another term for **T-LYMPHOCYTE**.

tch /tʃ/ ▶**exclamation** used to express irritation, annoyance, or impatience.

tchagra /ˈtʃagrə/ ▶**noun** an African shrike that feeds mainly on the ground, typically having a brown back and black eyestripe.
● Genus *Tchagra*, family Laniidae: several species.
– ORIGIN modern Latin, perhaps imitative.

Tchaikovsky /ˌtʃʌɪˈkɒfski/, Pyotr (Ilich) (1840–93), Russian composer. Notable works include the ballets *Swan Lake* (1877) and *The Nutcracker* (1892), the First Piano Concerto (1875), the opera *Eugene Onegin* (1879), the overture *1812* (1880), and his sixth symphony, the 'Pathétique' (1893).

tchotchke /ˈtʃɒtʃkə/ (also **tsatske**) ▶**noun** US informal **1** a small object that is decorative rather than strictly functional; a trinket.
2 a pretty girl or woman.
– ORIGIN 1960s: Yiddish.

TCP ▶**noun** [mass noun] Brit. trademark a disinfectant and germicidal solution containing various phenols and sodium salicylate.
– ORIGIN 1930s: abbreviation of *trichlorophenyl*, part of the chemical name of one of the ingredients.

TCP/IP Computing, trademark ▶**abbreviation for** transmission control protocol/Internet protocol, used to govern the connection of computer systems to the Internet.

TD ▶**abbreviation for** ■ (in the Republic of Ireland) Teachta Dála, Member of the Dáil: *Tom Meaney TD.* ■ technical drawing. ■ (in the UK) Territorial (Officer's) Decoration. ■ American Football touchdown.

Te ▶**symbol for** the chemical element tellurium.

te (N. Amer. **ti**) ▶**noun** (in tonic sol-fa) the seventh note of a major scale.
■the note B in the fixed-doh system.
– ORIGIN mid 19th cent.: alteration of **SI**, adopted to avoid having two notes (*soh* and *si*) beginning with the same letter (see **SOLMIZATION**).

tea ▶**noun** [mass noun] **1** a hot drink made by infusing the dried, crushed leaves of the tea plant in boiling water, and usually adding a small amount of milk.
■the dried leaves used to make such a drink. ■ [usu. with modifier] a similar drink made from the infused leaves, fruits, or flowers of other plants: *herbal tea* | [count noun] *fruit teas.* ■ W. Indian any hot drink, for example, coffee or cocoa.
2 (also **tea plant**) the evergreen shrub or small tree which produces these leaves, native to South and East Asia and grown as a major cash crop.
● *Camellia sinensis*, family Theaceae.
3 chiefly Brit. a light afternoon meal consisting typically of tea to drink, sandwiches, and cakes.
■Brit. a cooked evening meal. See also **HIGH TEA**. ■ W. Indian breakfast, typically consisting of a hot drink and bread.
▶**verb** (**teaed** or **tea'd**) [no obj., with adverbial] archaic drink tea or take afternoon tea: *I teaed with Professor Herron.*
■[with obj.] give tea to (someone): *I breakfast, tea, and sup my lodgers.*
– PHRASES **not for all the tea in China** informal there is nothing at all that could induce one to do something. **tea and sympathy** informal kind and attentive behaviour towards someone who is upset or in trouble.
– ORIGIN mid 17th cent.: probably via Malay from Chinese (Min dialect) *te*; related to Mandarin *chá*. Compare with **CHAR**[3].

tea bag ▶**noun** a small porous sachet containing tea leaves or powdered tea, on to which boiling water is poured in order to make a drink of tea.

tea ball ▶**noun** a hollow ball of perforated metal to hold tea leaves, over which boiling water is poured in order to make a drink of tea.

tea bread ▶**noun** [mass noun] a type of cake, baked in the shape of a loaf, containing dried fruit that has been soaked in tea before baking.

tea break ▶**noun** Brit. a short rest period during the working day, in which people typically drink a cup of tea or coffee.

tea caddy ▶**noun** a small tin in which tea is kept for daily use.

teacake ▶**noun** Brit. a light yeast-based sweet bun with dried fruit, typically served toasted and buttered.

tea ceremony ▶**noun** an elaborate Japanese ritual of serving and drinking tea, as an expression of Zen Buddhist philosophy.

teach ▶**verb** (past and past participle **taught**) [with obj. and infinitive or clause] show or explain to (someone) how to do something: *she taught him to read* | *he taught me how to ride a bike.*
■[with obj.] give information about or instruction in (a subject or skill): *he came one day each week to teach painting* | [with two objs] *she teaches me French.* ■ [no obj.] give such instruction professionally: *she teaches at the local high school.* ■ [with obj.] encourage someone to accept (something) as a fact or principle: *the philosophy teaches self-control.* ■ [with obj. and clause] cause (someone) to learn or understand something: *she'd been taught that it paid to be passive.* ■ induce (someone) by example or punishment to do or not to do something: *my upbringing taught me never to be disrespectful to elders.* ■ informal make (someone) less inclined to do something: *'I'll teach you to forget my tea,' he said, and gave me six with his cane.*
▶**noun** informal a teacher.
– PHRASES **teach someone a lesson** see **LESSON**. **teach school** US be a schoolteacher.

t

– ORIGIN Old English *tǣcan* 'show, present, point out', of Germanic origin; related to **TOKEN**, from an Indo-European root shared by Greek *deiknunai* 'show', *deigma* 'sample'.

USAGE The verbs **teach** and **learn** do not have the same meaning and should not be used interchangeably: see **usage** at **LEARN**.

teachable ▶ **adjective** **1** (of a person) able to learn by being taught.
2 (of a subject) able to be taught.
– DERIVATIVES **teachability** noun, **teachableness** noun.

teacher ▶ **noun** a person who teaches, especially in a school.
– DERIVATIVES **teacherly** adjective.

teacherage /ˈtiːtʃərɪdʒ/ ▶ **noun** N. Amer. a house or lodgings provided for a teacher by a school.

tea chest ▶ **noun** a light metal-lined wooden box in which tea is transported.

teach-in ▶ **noun** informal an informal lecture and discussion or series of lectures on a subject of public interest.

teaching ▶ **noun** **1** [mass noun] the occupation, profession, or work of a teacher.
2 (**teachings**) ideas or principles taught by an authority: *the teachings of the Koran.*

teaching fellow ▶ **noun** a postgraduate student who carries out teaching or laboratory duties in return for accommodation, tuition, or expenses.

teaching hospital ▶ **noun** a hospital that is affiliated to a medical school, in which medical students receive practical training.

teaching machine ▶ **noun** a machine or computer that gives instruction to a pupil according to a program, reacting to their responses.

Teachta Dála /ˌtjɒxtə ˈdɔːlə, Irish ˌtʲaxtə ˈdɑːlə/ (abbrev.: **TD**) ▶ **noun** (pl. **Teachti** /-ti/) (in the Republic of Ireland) a member of the Dáil or lower House of Parliament.
– ORIGIN Irish.

tea cloth ▶ **noun** a tea towel.

tea cosy ▶ **noun** a thick or padded cover placed over a teapot to keep the tea hot.

teacup ▶ **noun** a cup from which tea is drunk.
■ an amount held by this, about 150 ml.
– DERIVATIVES **teacupful** noun (pl. **-fuls**).

tea dance ▶ **noun** an afternoon tea with dancing, originating in 19th-century society.

tea garden ▶ **noun** **1** a garden in which tea and other refreshments are served to the public.
2 a tea plantation.

tea gown ▶ **noun** dated a long, loose-fitting dress, typically made of fine fabric and lace-trimmed, worn at afternoon tea and popular in the late 19th and early 20th centuries.

teahead ▶ **noun** informal, dated chiefly US a habitual user of cannabis.

teak ▶ **noun** **1** [mass noun] hard durable timber used in shipbuilding and for making furniture.
2 the large deciduous tree native to India and SE Asia which yields this timber.
● *Tectona grandis*, family Verbenaceae.
– ORIGIN late 17th cent.: from Portuguese *teca*, from Tamil and Malayalam *tēkku*.

teal ▶ **noun** (pl. same or **teals**) a small freshwater duck, typically with a greenish band on the wing that is most prominent in flight.
● Genus *Anas*, family Anatidae: several species, in particular the common Eurasian and Canadian (**green-winged**) **teal** (*A. crecca*).
■ (also **teal blue**) [mass noun] a dark greenish-blue colour.
– ORIGIN Middle English: of unknown origin; related to Dutch *teling*.

tea lady ▶ **noun** Brit. a woman employed to make and serve tea in a workplace.

tea leaf ▶ **noun** **1** (**tea leaves**) dried leaves of tea, especially after infusion in tea-making or as dregs.
2 Brit. rhyming slang a thief.

team ▶ **noun** [treated as sing. or pl.] a group of players forming one side in a competitive game or sport.
■ two or more people working together: *a team of researchers.* ■ two or more animals, especially horses, in harness together to pull a vehicle.
▶ **verb** **1** [no obj.] (**team up**) come together as a team to achieve a common goal: *he* **teamed up with** *the band to produce the disc.*
2 [with obj.] (usu. **team something with**) match or coordinate a garment with (another): *a pinstripe suit teamed with a crisp white shirt.*
3 [with obj.] harness (animals, especially horses) together to pull a vehicle: *the horses are teamed in pairs.*
– ORIGIN Old English *tēam* 'team of draught animals', of Germanic origin; related to German *Zaum* 'bridle', also to **TEEM**[1] and **TOW**[1], from an Indo-European root shared by Latin *ducere* 'to lead'.

teammate ▶ **noun** a fellow member of a team.

team ministry ▶ **noun** a group of clergy of incumbent status who minister jointly to several parishes under the leadership of a rector or vicar.

team player ▶ **noun** a person who plays or works well as a member of a team.

team spirit ▶ **noun** [mass noun] feelings of camaraderie among the members of a group, enabling them to cooperate and work well together.

teamster ▶ **noun** **1** US a lorry driver.
■ a member of the Teamsters Union, including lorry drivers, chauffeurs, and warehouse workers.
2 a driver of a team of animals.

team-teaching ▶ **noun** [mass noun] coordinated teaching by a team of teachers working together.

teamwork ▶ **noun** [mass noun] the combined action of a group, especially when effective and efficient.

tea oil ▶ **noun** [mass noun] an oil resembling olive oil obtained from the seeds of the sasanqua and related plants, used chiefly in China and Japan.

tea party ▶ **noun** a social gathering in the afternoon at which tea, cakes, and other light refreshments are served.

tea plant ▶ **noun** another term for **TEA** (in sense 2).

tea planter ▶ **noun** a proprietor or cultivator of a tea plantation.

teapot ▶ **noun** a pot with a handle, spout, and lid, in which tea is brewed and from which it is poured.

teapoy /ˈtiːpɔɪ/ ▶ **noun** a small three-legged table or stand, especially one that holds a tea caddy.
– ORIGIN early 19th cent.: from Hindi *tī-* 'three' + Urdu and Persian *pāī* 'foot', the sense and spelling influenced by **TEA**.

tear[1] /tɛː/ ▶ **verb** (past **tore**; past participle **torn**) **1** [with obj. and adverbial] pull or rip (something) apart or to pieces with force: *I* **tore up** *the letter.*
■ remove by pulling or ripping forcefully: *he tore up the floorboards.* ■ (**be torn between**) figurative have great difficulty in choosing between: *he was torn between his duty and his better instincts.* ■ [with obj.] make a hole or split in (something) by ripping or pulling at it: *she was always tearing her clothes.* ■ make (a hole or split) in something by force: *the blast tore a hole in the wall of a bridge.* ■ [no obj.] come apart; rip: *the material wouldn't tear.* ■ [with obj.] damage (a muscle or ligament) by overstretching it: *he tore a ligament playing squash.*
2 [no obj., with adverbial of direction] informal move very quickly, typically in a reckless or excited manner: *she tore along the footpath on her bike.*
▶ **noun** a hole or split in something caused by it having been pulled apart forcefully.
– PHRASES **tear one's hair out** informal act with or show extreme desperation. **tear someone off a strip** (or **tear a strip off someone**) Brit. informal rebuke someone angrily. **tear someone/thing to shreds** (or **pieces**) informal criticize someone or something forcefully or aggressively. **that's torn it** Brit. informal used to express dismay when something unfortunate has happened to disrupt someone's plans.
– DERIVATIVES **tearable** adjective, **tearer** noun.
– ORIGIN Old English *teran*, of Germanic origin; related to Dutch *teren* and German *zehren*, from an Indo-European root shared by Greek *derein* 'flay'. The noun dates from the early 17th cent.
▶ **tear someone/thing apart** **1** destroy something, especially good relations between people: *a bloody civil war had torn the country apart.* **2** upset someone greatly: *stop crying—it's tearing me apart.* **3** search a place thoroughly: *I'll help you find it; I'll tear your house apart if I have to.* **4** criticize someone or something harshly.
tear oneself away [often with negative] leave despite a strong desire to stay: *she couldn't tear herself away from the view.*
tear someone/thing down **1** demolish something, especially a building. **2** US informal criticize or punish someone severely.
tear into **1** attack verbally: *she tore into him: 'Don't you realize what you've done to me?'* **2** make an energetic or enthusiastic start on: *a jazz trio are tearing into the tune with gusto.*

tear[2] /tɪə/ ▶ **noun** a drop of clear salty liquid secreted from glands in a person's eye when they cry or when the eye is irritated.
– PHRASES **in tears** crying: *he was so hurt by her attitude he was nearly in tears.* **without tears** (of a subject) presented so as to be learned or achieved easily: *tennis without tears.* [ORIGIN: first used in the titles of books by F. L. Mortimer, such as *Reading without Tears* (1857) and *Latin without Tears* (1877).]
– DERIVATIVES **tear-like** adjective.
– ORIGIN Old English *tēar*, of Germanic origin; related to German *Zähre*, from an Indo-European root shared by Old Latin *dacruma* (Latin *lacrima*) and Greek *dakru*.

tearaway ▶ **noun** Brit. a person who behaves in a wild or reckless manner.

teardrop ▶ **noun** a single tear.
■ [as modifier] shaped like a single tear: *a wardrobe with brass teardrop handles.*

tear duct ▶ **noun** a passage through which tears pass from the lachrymal glands to the eye or from the eye to the nose.

tearful ▶ **adjective** crying or inclined to cry: *a tearful infant | Stephen felt tearful.*
■ causing tears; sad or emotional: *a tearful farewell.*
– DERIVATIVES **tearfully** adverb, **tearfulness** noun.

tear gas ▶ **noun** [mass noun] gas that causes severe irritation to the eyes, chiefly used in riot control to force crowds to disperse.
▶ **verb** (**tear-gas**) [with obj.] (usu. **be tear-gassed**) attack with tear gas.

tearing ▶ **adjective** [attrib.] violent; extreme: *he did seem to be in a tearing hurry | the tearing wind.*

tear jerker ▶ **noun** informal a sentimental story, film, or song, calculated to evoke sadness or sympathy.
– DERIVATIVES **tear-jerking** noun & adjective.

tearless ▶ **adjective** not crying: *Mary watched in tearless silence as the coffin was lowered.*
– DERIVATIVES **tearlessly** adverb, **tearlessness** noun.

tear-off ▶ **adjective** denoting something that is removed by being torn off, typically along a perforated line: *please complete the tear-off slip.*

tea room ▶ **noun** **1** a small restaurant or cafe where tea and other light refreshments are served.
2 S. African a shop selling sweets, cigarettes, newspapers, and perishable goods.
3 N. Amer. informal a public toilet used as a meeting place by homosexuals.

tea rose ▶ **noun** a garden rose with flowers that are typically pale yellow with a pink tinge and have a delicate scent said to resemble that of tea.
● Cultivars of the Chinese hybrid *Rosa* × *odorata.*

tear sheet ▶ **noun** a page that can be or has been removed from a newspaper, magazine, or book for use separately.

tear-stained ▶ **adjective** wet with tears: *I looked at the man's tear-stained face.*

tease ▶ **verb** [with obj.] **1** make fun of or attempt to provoke (a person or animal) in a playful way: *I used to tease her about being so house-proud* | [no obj.] *she was just teasing* | [with direct speech] *'Think you're clever, don't you?' she teased.*
■ tempt (someone) sexually with no intention of satisfying the desire aroused.
2 [with obj. and adverbial of direction] gently pull or comb (something tangled, especially wool or hair) into separate strands: *she was teasing out the curls into her usual hairstyle.*
■ (**tease something out**) figurative find something out from a mass of irrelevant information: *a historian who tries to tease out the truth.* ■ chiefly N. Amer. backcomb (hair) in order to make it appear fuller. ■ archaic comb (the surface of woven cloth) to raise a nap.
▶ **noun** informal a person who makes fun of someone playfully or unkindly.
■ a person who tempts someone sexually with no intention of satisfying the desire aroused. ■ [in sing.] an act of making fun of or tempting someone: *she couldn't resist a gentle tease.*
– DERIVATIVES **teasingly** adverb.
– ORIGIN Old English *tǣsan* (in sense 2), of West Germanic origin; related to Dutch *teezen* and German dialect *zeisen*, also to **TEASEL**. Sense 1 is a development of the earlier and more serious

'irritate by annoying actions' (early 17th cent.), a figurative use of the word's original sense.

teasel (also **teazle** or **teazel**) ▶ noun a tall prickly Eurasian plant with spiny purple flower heads.
● Genus *Dipsacus*, family Dipsacaceae: several species, including **fuller's teasel**.
■ a large, dried, spiny head from such a plant, or a device serving as a substitute for one of these, used in the textile industry to raise a nap on woven cloth.
▶ verb [with obj.] [often as noun **teaseling**] chiefly archaic raise a nap on (cloth) with or as if with teasels.
– ORIGIN Old English *tǣsl*, *tǣsel*, of West Germanic origin; related to **TEASE**.

teaser ▶ noun **1** informal a difficult or tricky question or task.
2 a person who makes fun of or provokes others in a playful or unkind way.
■ a person who tempts someone sexually with no intention of satisfying the desire aroused. ■ a short introductory advertisement for a product, especially one that does not mention the name of the thing being advertised. ■ Fishing a lure or bait trailed behind a boat to attract fish. ■ an inferior stallion or ram used to excite mares or ewes before they are served by the stud animal.

tea set /'tiːsɛt/ ▶ noun a set of crockery for serving tea.

tea shop ▶ noun another term for **TEA ROOM** (in sense 1).

Teasmade ▶ noun trademark an automatic tea-maker.

teaspoon ▶ noun a small spoon used typically for adding sugar to and stirring hot drinks or for eating some foods.
■ (abbrev.: **tsp**) the amount held by such a spoon, in the UK considered to be 5 millilitres when used as a measurement in cookery.
– DERIVATIVES **teaspoonful** noun (pl. **-fuls**).

tea-strainer ▶ noun a small device incorporating a fine mesh for straining tea.

teat ▶ noun a nipple of the mammary gland of a female mammal, from which the milk is sucked by the young.
■ Brit. a thing resembling this, especially a perforated plastic bulb by which an infant or young animal can suck milk from a bottle.
– ORIGIN Middle English (superseding earlier **TIT**²): from Old French *tete*, probably of Germanic origin.

teatime ▶ noun chiefly Brit. the time in the afternoon when tea is traditionally served.

tea towel ▶ noun chiefly Brit. a cloth for drying washed crockery, cutlery, and glasses.

tea tray ▶ noun a tray from which tea is served.

tea tree ▶ noun **1** (also **ti tree**) an Australasian flowering shrub or small tree with leaves that are sometimes used for tea.
● Genus *Leptospermum*, family Myrtaceae: several species, in particular the manuka.
2 (also **Duke of Argyll's tea tree**) an ornamental boxthorn native to the Mediterranean.
● *Lycium barbarum*, family Solanaceae.

teazle (also **teazel**) ▶ noun variant spelling of **TEASEL**.

Tebet /'tɛbɛt/ (also **Tevet**) ▶ noun (in the Jewish calendar) the fourth month of the civil and tenth of the religious year, usually coinciding with parts of December and January.
– ORIGIN from Hebrew *ṭēḇēṯ*.

TEC ▶ abbreviation for (in the UK) Training and Enterprise Council.

tec ▶ noun informal, dated a detective.
– ORIGIN late 19th cent.: abbreviation.

tech (also **tec**) ▶ noun informal **1** Brit. a technical college.
2 [mass noun] technology. See also **HIGH TECH**, **LOW TECH**.
■ [count noun] a technician. ■ [count noun] a technical.
– ORIGIN early 20th cent. (originally US): abbreviation.

techie /'tɛki/ (also **techy**) ▶ noun (pl. **-ies**) informal a person who is expert in or enthusiastic about technology, especially computing.
– ORIGIN 1960s: from **TECH** + **-IE**. First recorded as a US slang term for a technical college student, the word was later used as British service slang, denoting a technician. The current sense dates from the 1980s.

technetium /tɛk'niːʃɪəm/ ▶ noun [mass noun] the chemical element of atomic number 43, a radioactive metal. Technetium was the first

element to be created artificially, in 1937, by bombarding molybdenum with deuterons. (Symbol: **Tc**)
– ORIGIN 1940s: modern Latin, from Greek *tekhnētos* 'artificial', from *tekhnasthai* 'make by art', from *tekhnē* 'art'.

technic ▶ noun **1** chiefly US technique.
2 (**technics**) [treated as sing. or pl.] technical terms, details, and methods; technology.
– DERIVATIVES **technicist** noun.
– ORIGIN early 17th cent. (as an adjective in the sense 'to do with art or an art'): from Latin *technicus*, from Greek *tekhnikos*, from *tekhnē* 'art'. The noun dates from the 19th cent.

technical ▶ adjective **1** of or relating to a particular subject, art, or craft, or its techniques: *technical terms*.
■ (especially of a book or article) requiring special knowledge to be understood: *a technical report*.
2 of, involving, or concerned with applied and industrial sciences: *an important technical achievement*.
3 resulting from mechanical failure: *a technical fault*.
4 according to a strict application or interpretation of the law or rules: *the arrest was a technical violation of the treaty*.
▶ noun chiefly N. Amer. a small truck with a machine gun mounted on the back.
■ a gunman who rides in such a truck.

technical college ▶ noun a college of further education providing courses in a range of practical subjects, such as information technology, applied sciences, engineering, agriculture, and secretarial skills.

technical drawing ▶ noun [mass noun] the practice or skill of delineating objects in a precise way using certain techniques of draughtsmanship, as employed in architecture or engineering.
■ [count noun] a drawing produced in such a way.

technical foul ▶ noun Basketball a foul which does not involve contact between opponents.

technicality ▶ noun (pl. **-ies**) a point of law or a small detail of a set of rules: *their convictions were overturned on a technicality*.
■ (**technicalities**) the specific details or terms belonging to a particular field: *he has great expertise in the technicalities of the game*. ■ [mass noun] the state of being technical; the use of technical terms or methods: *the extreme technicality of the proposed constitution*.

technical knockout ▶ noun Boxing the ending of a fight by the referee on the grounds of a contestant's inability to continue, the opponent being declared the winner.

technically ▶ adverb **1** [usu. sentence adverb] according to the facts or exact meaning of something; strictly: *technically, a nut is a single-seeded fruit*.
2 with reference to the technique displayed: *a technically brilliant boxing contest*.
3 involving or regarding the technology available: *technically advanced tools*.

technical sergeant ▶ noun a rank of non-commissioned officer in the US air force, above staff sergeant and below master sergeant.

technical support ▶ noun [mass noun] Computing a service provided by a hardware or software company which provides registered users with help and advice about their products.

technician ▶ noun a person employed to look after technical equipment or do practical work in a laboratory.
■ an expert in the practical application of a science. ■ a person skilled in the technique of an art or craft.

Technicolor ▶ noun [mass noun] trademark a process of colour cinematography using synchronized monochrome films, each of a different colour, to produce a colour print.
■ (**technicolor**) (Brit. also **technicolour**) informal vivid colour: [as modifier] *a technicolor bruise*.
– DERIVATIVES **technicolored** adjective.
– ORIGIN early 20th cent.: blend of **TECHNICAL** and **COLOR**.

technicolor yawn ▶ noun informal, humorous an act of vomiting.

technikon /'tɛknɪkɒn/ ▶ noun (in South Africa) an institution offering technical and vocational education at tertiary level.

– ORIGIN Greek, noun use of the neuter of *tekhnikos* 'relating to skills'.

technique ▶ noun a way of carrying out a particular task, especially the execution or performance of an artistic work or a scientific procedure.
■ [mass noun] skill or ability in a particular field: *he has excellent technique* | [in sing.] *an established athlete with a very good technique*. ■ a skilful or efficient way of doing or achieving something: *tape recording is a good technique for evaluating our own communications*.
– ORIGIN early 19th cent.: from French, from Latin *technicus* (see **TECHNIC**).

techno ▶ noun [mass noun] a style of fast, heavy electronic dance music, typically with few or no vocals.
– ORIGIN 1980s: abbreviation of **TECHNOLOGICAL**.

techno- ▶ combining form relating to technology or its use: *technophobe*.
– ORIGIN from Greek *tekhnē* 'art, craft'.

technobabble ▶ noun [mass noun] informal incomprehensible technical jargon.

technocracy /tɛk'nɒkrəsi/ ▶ noun (pl. **-ies**) [mass noun] the government or control of society or industry by an elite of technical experts.
■ [count noun] an instance or application of this. ■ [count noun] an elite of technical experts.
– ORIGIN early 20th cent.: from Greek *tekhnē* 'art, craft' + **-CRACY**.

technocrat ▶ noun an exponent or advocate of technocracy.
■ a member of a technically skilled elite.
– DERIVATIVES **technocratic** adjective, **technocratically** adverb.

technofear ▶ noun [mass noun] informal fear of using technological equipment, especially computers.

technological ▶ adjective of, relating to, or using technology: *the quickening pace of technological change*.
– DERIVATIVES **technologically** adverb.

technology ▶ noun (pl. **-ies**) [mass noun] the application of scientific knowledge for practical purposes, especially in industry: *advances in computer technology* | [count noun] *recycling technologies*.
■ machinery and equipment developed from such scientific knowledge. ■ the branch of knowledge dealing with engineering or applied sciences.
– DERIVATIVES **technologist** noun.
– ORIGIN early 17th cent.: from Greek *tekhnologia* 'systematic treatment', from *tekhnē* 'art, craft' + *-logia* (see **-LOGY**).

technology park ▶ noun a science park.

technology transfer ▶ noun [mass noun] the transfer of new technology from the originator to a secondary user, especially from developed to underdeveloped countries in an attempt to boost their economies.

technophile ▶ noun a person who is enthusiastic about new technology.
– DERIVATIVES **technophilia** noun, **technophilic** adjective.

technophobe ▶ noun a person who fears, dislikes, or avoids new technology.
– DERIVATIVES **technophobia** noun, **technophobic** adjective.

technospeak ▶ noun another term for **TECHNOBABBLE**.

technostress ▶ noun [mass noun] informal stress or psychosomatic illness caused by working with computer technology on a daily basis.

technostructure ▶ noun [treated as sing. or pl.] a group of technologists or technical experts having considerable control over the workings of industry or government.
– ORIGIN 1960s: coined by J. K. Galbraith.

techy ▶ noun variant spelling of **TECHIE**.

tectonic /tɛk'tɒnɪk/ ▶ adjective **1** Geology of or relating to the structure of the earth's crust and the large-scale processes which take place within it.
2 of or relating to building or construction.
– DERIVATIVES **tectonically** adverb.
– ORIGIN mid 17th cent. (in sense 2): via late Latin from Greek *tektonikos*, from *tektōn* 'carpenter, builder'.

tectonics ▶ plural noun [treated as sing. or pl.] Geology large-scale processes affecting the structure of the earth's crust.

tectonophysics /tɛkˌtɒnə(ʊ)'fɪzɪks/ ▶ **plural noun** [treated as sing.] the branch of geophysics that deals with the forces that cause movement and deformation in the earth's crust.
– ORIGIN 1950s: from **TECTONICS** + **PHYSICS**.

tectonostratigraphic /tɛkˌtɒnə(ʊ)ˌstratɪ'grafɪk/ ▶ **adjective** Geology of or relating to the correlation of rock formations with each other in terms of their connection with a tectonic event.
– ORIGIN 1970s: from **TECTONICS** + stratigraphic (see **STRATIGRAPHY**).

tectorial /tɛk'tɔːrɪəl/ ▶ **adjective** Anatomy forming a covering.
■denoting the membrane covering the organ of Corti in the inner ear.
– ORIGIN late 19th cent.: from Latin *tectorium* 'covering, a cover' (from *tegere* 'to cover') + **-AL**.

tectrices /'tɛktrɪsiːz, tɛk'trʌɪsiːz/ ▶ **plural noun** (sing. **tectrix** /-trɪks/) Ornithology the coverts of a bird.
– ORIGIN late 19th cent.: modern Latin, from Latin *tect-* 'covered', from the verb *tegere*.

tectum /'tɛktəm/ ▶ **noun** Anatomy the uppermost part of the midbrain, lying to the rear of the cerebral aqueduct.
■(in full **optic tectum**) a rounded swelling (colliculus) forming part of this and containing cells involved in the visual system.
– ORIGIN early 20th cent.: from Latin, literally 'roof'.

Ted ▶ **noun** Brit. informal a Teddy boy.
– ORIGIN 1950s: abbreviation.

ted ▶ **verb** (**tedded**, **tedding**) [with obj.] [often as noun **tedding**] turn over and spread out (grass, hay, or straw) to dry or for bedding.
– DERIVATIVES **tedder** noun.
– ORIGIN Middle English: from Old Norse *tethja* 'spread manure' (past tense *tadda*), related to *tad* 'dung'.

teddy ▶ **noun** (pl. **-ies**) **1** (also **teddy bear**) a soft toy bear.
2 a woman's all-in-one undergarment.
– ORIGIN early 20th cent.: from *Teddy*, pet form of the given name *Theodore*: in sense 1 alluding to *Theodore* **ROOSEVELT**[3], an enthusiastic bear-hunter.

Teddy boy ▶ **noun** Brit. (in the 1950s) a young man of a subculture characterized by a style of dress based on Edwardian fashion (typically with drainpipe trousers, bootlace tie, and hair slicked up in a quiff) and a liking for rock and roll music.
– ORIGIN from *Teddy*, pet form of the given name *Edward* (with reference to Edward VII's reign).

Te Deum /ˌtiː 'diːəm, teɪ 'deɪəm/ ▶ **noun** a hymn beginning *Te Deum laudamus*, 'We praise Thee, O God', sung at matins or on special occasions such as a thanksgiving.
■an expression of thanksgiving or exultation.
– ORIGIN Latin.

tedious ▶ **adjective** too long, slow, or dull: tiresome or monotonous: *a tedious journey*.
– DERIVATIVES **tediously** adverb, **tediousness** noun.
– ORIGIN late Middle English: from Old French *tedieus* or late Latin *taediosus*, from Latin *taedium* (see **TEDIUM**).

tedium ▶ **noun** [mass noun] the state of being tedious: *the tedium of car journeys*.
– ORIGIN mid 17th cent.: from Latin *taedium*, from *taedere* 'be weary of'.

tee[1] ▶ **noun** see **T**[1] (sense 2).

tee[2] ▶ **noun 1** a cleared space on a golf course, from which the ball is struck at the beginning of play for each hole.
■a small peg with a concave head which can be placed in the ground to support a golf ball before it is struck from such an area. [ORIGIN: late 17th cent. (originally Scots, as *teaz*): of unknown origin.]
2 a mark aimed at in bowls, quoits, curling, and other similar games. [ORIGIN: late 18th cent. (originally Scots): perhaps the same word as **TEE**[1].]
▶ **verb** (**tees**, **teed**, **teeing**) [no obj.] (usu. **tee up**) Golf place the ball on a tee ready to make the first stroke of the round or hole.
■[with obj.] place (something) in position, especially to be struck: *a wary man tees up the rest of the coconuts*.
▶ **tee off** Golf play the ball from a tee; begin a round or hole of golf. ■ make a start on something. **tee someone off** (usu. **be teed off**) N. Amer. informal make someone angry or annoyed: *Tommy was really teed off at Ernie*.

tee[3] ▶ **noun** informal, chiefly N. Amer. a T-shirt.

tee-hee ▶ **noun** a giggle or titter, especially a derisive one: [as exclamation] *They won't mind what I get up to. Tee-hee!*
▶ **verb** (**tee-hees, tee-heed, tee-heeing**) [no obj.] titter or giggle in such a way.
– ORIGIN Middle English (as a verb): imitative.

teem[1] ▶ **verb** [no obj.] (**teem with**) be full of or swarming with: *every garden is teeming with wildlife* | [as adj. **teeming**] *she walked briskly through the teeming streets*.
– ORIGIN Old English *tēman, tīeman*, of Germanic origin; related to **TEAM**. The original senses included 'give birth to', also 'be or become pregnant', giving rise to 'be full of' in the late 16th cent.

teem[2] ▶ **verb** [no obj.] (of water, especially rain) pour down; fall heavily: *with the rain teeming down at the manor, Italy seemed a long way off*.
– ORIGIN Middle English: from Old Norse *tœma* 'to empty', from *tómr* 'empty'. The original sense was 'to empty', specifically 'to drain liquid from, pour liquid out'; the current sense (originally dialect) dates from the early 19th cent.

teen informal ▶ **adjective** [attrib.] of or relating to teenagers: *a teen idol*.
▶ **noun** a teenager.
– ORIGIN early 19th cent. (as a noun): abbreviation. The adjective dates from the 1940s.

-teen ▶ **suffix** forming the names of numerals from 13 to 19: *fourteen* | *eighteen*.
– ORIGIN Old English, inflected form of **TEN**.

teenage ▶ **adjective** [attrib.] denoting a person between 13 and 19 years old: *a teenage girl*.
■relating to or characteristic of people of this age: *teenage magazines*.
– DERIVATIVES **teenaged** adjective.

teenager ▶ **noun** a person aged between 13 and 19 years.

teens ▶ **plural noun** the years of a person's age from 13 to 19: *they were both in their late teens*.
– ORIGIN late 17th cent.: plural of *teen*, independent usage of **-TEEN**.

teensy /'tiːnzi, -si/ ▶ **adjective** (**teensier, teensiest**) informal tiny: *a teensy bit of custard powder*.
– ORIGIN late 19th cent. (originally US dialect): probably an extension of **TEENY**.

teeny ▶ **adjective** (**teenier, teeniest**) informal tiny: *a teeny bit of criticism*.
– ORIGIN early 19th cent.: variant of **TINY**.

teeny-bopper ▶ **noun** informal a young teenager, especially a girl, who keenly follows the latest fashions in clothes and pop music.
– DERIVATIVES **teeny-bop** adjective.

teeny-weeny (also **teensy-weensy**) ▶ **adjective** informal very tiny: *doesn't he have a teeny-weeny twinge of conscience?*

teepee ▶ **noun** variant spelling of **TEPEE**.

Tees /tiːz/ a river of NE England which rises in Cumbria and flows 128 km (80 miles) generally south-eastwards to the North Sea at Middlesbrough.

tee shirt ▶ **noun** variant spelling of **T-SHIRT**.

Teesside an industrial region in NE England around the lower Tees valley, including Middlesbrough.

Teeswater ▶ **noun** a sheep of a long-woolled breed, first developed in the Tees valley.

teeter ▶ **verb** [no obj., usu. with adverbial] move or balance unsteadily; sway back and forth: *she teetered after him in her high-heeled sandals*.
■(often **teeter between**) figurative be unable to decide between different courses; waver: *she teetered between tears and anger*.
– PHRASES **teeter on the brink** (or **edge**) be very close to a difficult or dangerous situation.
– ORIGIN mid 19th cent.: variant of dialect *titter*, from Old Norse *titra* 'shake, shiver'.

teeter-totter N. Amer. or dialect ▶ **noun** a see-saw.
▶ **verb** [no obj.] teeter; waver.
– ORIGIN late 19th cent.: reduplication of **TEETER** or **TOTTER**.

teeth plural form of **TOOTH**.

teethe ▶ **verb** [no obj.] grow or cut teeth, especially milk teeth.
– ORIGIN late Middle English: from **TEETH**.

teething ▶ **noun** [mass noun] the process of growing one's teeth, especially milk teeth.

teething ring ▶ **noun** a small ring for an infant to bite on while teething.

teething troubles (also **teething problems**) ▶ **plural noun** short-term problems that occur in the early stages of a new project.

teetotal ▶ **adjective** choosing or characterized by abstinence from alcohol: *a teetotal lifestyle*.
– DERIVATIVES **teetotalism** noun.
– ORIGIN mid 19th cent.: emphatic extension of **TOTAL**, apparently first used by Richard Turner, a worker from Preston, in a speech (1833) urging total abstinence from all alcohol, rather than mere abstinence from spirits, advocated by some early temperance reformers.

teetotaller (US **teetotaler**) ▶ **noun** a person who never drinks alcohol.

teetotum /tiː'təʊtəm/ ▶ **noun** a small spinning top spun with the fingers, especially one with four sides lettered to determine whether the spinner has won or lost.
– ORIGIN early 18th cent. (as *T totum*): from *T* (representing *totum*, inscribed on the side of the toy) + Latin *totum* 'the whole' (stake). The letters on the sides (representing Latin words) were *T* (= *totum*), *A* (= *auferre* 'take away'), *D* (= *deponere* 'put down'), and *N* (= *nihil* 'nothing').

teevee ▶ **noun** non-standard spelling of **TV**.

teff /tɛf/ ▶ **noun** [mass noun] an African cereal which is cultivated almost exclusively in Ethiopia, used mainly to make flour.
●*Eragrostis tef*, family Gramineae.
– ORIGIN late 18th cent.: from Amharic *tēf*.

tefillin /tiː'fɪliːn/ ▶ **plural noun** collective term for Jewish phylacteries.
– ORIGIN from Aramaic *tĕpillín* 'prayers'.

TEFL /'tɛf(ə)l/ ▶ **abbreviation for** teaching of English as a foreign language.

Teflon /'tɛflɒn/ ▶ **noun** trademark for **POLYTETRAFLUOROETHYLENE**.
– ORIGIN 1940s: from **TETRA-** 'four' + **FLUORO-** + *-on* on the pattern of words such as *nylon* and *rayon*.

teg ▶ **noun** a sheep in its second year.
– ORIGIN early 16th cent. (as a contemptuous term for a woman; later applied specifically to a ewe in her second year): perhaps related to Swedish *tacka* 'ewe'.

tegmen /'tɛgmɛn/ ▶ **noun** (pl. **tegmina**) Biology a covering structure or roof of an organ, in particular:
■Entomology a sclerotized forewing serving to cover the hindwing in grasshoppers and related insects.
■Botany the delicate inner protective layer of a seed.
■(also **tegmen tympani**) Anatomy a plate of thin bone forming the roof of the middle ear, a part of the temporal bone.
– ORIGIN early 19th cent.: from Latin, 'covering' from *tegere* 'to cover'.

tegmentum /tɛg'mɛntəm/ ▶ **noun** (pl. **tegmenta** /-ə/) Anatomy a region of grey matter on either side of the cerebral aqueduct in the midbrain.
– DERIVATIVES **tegmental** adjective.
– ORIGIN mid 19th cent.: from Latin, variant of *tegumentum* 'tegument'.

tegu /'tɛguː/ ▶ **noun** (pl. same or **tegus**) a large stocky lizard that has dark skin with pale cross-bands of small spots, native to the tropical forests of South America.
●Genus *Tupinambis*, family Teiidae: several species, in particular the **common tegu** (*T. teguixin*).
– ORIGIN 1950s: abbreviation of *teguexin*, from Aztec *tecoixin* 'lizard'.

Tegucigalpa /tɛˌguːsɪ'galpə/ capital of Honduras; pop. 670,100 (est. 1991).

tegula /'tɛgjʊlə/ ▶ **noun** (pl. **tegulae** /-liː/) Entomology a small scale-like sclerite covering the base of the forewing in many insects.
– ORIGIN early 19th cent.: from Latin, literally 'tile', from *tegere* 'to cover'.

tegument /'tɛgjʊm(ə)nt/ ▶ **noun** chiefly Zoology the integument of an organism, especially a parasitic flatworm.
– DERIVATIVES **tegumental** adjective, **tegumentary** adjective.
– ORIGIN late Middle English (in the general sense 'a covering or coating'): from Latin *tegumentum*, from *tegere* 'to cover'.

Tehran /tɛ'rɑːn/ (also **Teheran**) the capital of Iran, situated in the foothills of the Elburz Mountains;

pop. 6,750,000 (1994). It replaced Isfahan as capital of Persia in 1788.

tehsil /tʌˈsiːl/ (also **tahsil**) ▶ noun an administrative area in parts of India.
– ORIGIN from Persian and Urdu *taḥsīl*, from Arabic, 'collection, levying of taxes'.

teichoic acid /tʌɪˈkəʊɪk/ ▶ noun [mass noun] Biochemistry a compound present in the walls of Gram-positive bacteria. It is a polymer of ribitol or glycerol phosphate.
– DERIVATIVES **teichoate** noun.
– ORIGIN 1950s: *teichoic* from Greek *teikhos* 'wall' + **-IC**.

Teilhard de Chardin /ˌteɪɑː də ʃɑːˈdã, French tɛjar də ʃardɛ̃/, Pierre (1881–1955), French Jesuit philosopher and palaeontologist. He is best known for his theory, blending science and Christianity, that man is evolving mentally and socially towards a perfect spiritual state. The Roman Catholic Church declared his views were unorthodox and his major works (e.g. *The Phenomenon of Man*, 1955) were published posthumously.

tein /ˈteɪn/ ▶ noun (pl. same or **teins**) a monetary unit of Kazakhstan, equal to one hundredth of a tenge.

tej /tɛdʒ/ ▶ noun [mass noun] a kind of honey wine or mead, the national drink of Ethiopia.
– ORIGIN probably Amharic.

Tejano /tɛˈhɑːnəʊ/ ▶ noun (pl. **-os**) a Mexican-American inhabitant of southern Texas: [as modifier] *the Tejano upper classes.*
■ [mass noun] a style of folk or popular music originating among such people, with elements from Mexican-Spanish vocal traditions and Czech and German dance tunes and rhythms, traditionally played by small groups featuring accordion and guitar.
– ORIGIN American Spanish, alteration of *Texano* 'Texan'.

Tejo /ˈtəʒu/ Portuguese name for **TAGUS**.

Te Kanawa /teɪ ˈkanəwə, tə, ˈkɑːnəwə/, Dame Kiri (Janette) (b.1944), New Zealand operatic soprano, resident in Britain since 1966. She made her debut in London in 1970 and since then has sung in the world's leading opera houses.

tekke /ˈtɛkeɪ/ ▶ noun (pl. **tekkes**) a monastery of dervishes, especially in Ottoman Turkey.
– ORIGIN Turkish.

tektite /ˈtɛktʌɪt/ ▶ noun Geology a small black glassy object found in numbers over certain areas of the earth's surface, believed to have been formed as molten debris in meteorite impacts and scattered widely through the air.
– ORIGIN early 20th cent.: coined in German from Greek *tēktos* 'molten' (from *tēkein* 'melt') + **-ITE**[1].

tel. (also **Tel.**) ▶ abbreviation for telephone.

telamon /ˈtɛləmən, -mɒn/ ▶ noun (pl. **telamones** /-ˈməʊniːz/) Architecture a male figure used as a pillar to support an entablature or other structure.
– ORIGIN early 17th cent.: via Latin from Greek *telamōnes*, plural of *Telamōn*, the name of a mythical hero.

telangiectasia /tɛˌlandʒɪɛkˈteɪzɪə/ (also **telangiectasis** /tɛˌlandʒɪˈɛktəsɪs/) ▶ noun [mass noun] Medicine a condition characterized by dilatation of the capillaries causing them to appear as small red or purple clusters, often spidery in appearance, on the skin or the surface of an organ.
– DERIVATIVES **telangiectatic** adjective.
– ORIGIN mid 19th cent.: modern Latin, from Greek *telos* 'end' + *angeion* 'vessel' + *ektasis* 'dilatation'.

Tel Aviv /ˌtɛl əˈviːv/ (also **Tel Aviv-Jaffa**) a city on the Mediterranean coast of Israel; pop. 355,200 (1994) (with Jaffa). It was founded as a suburb of Jaffa by Russian Jewish immigrants in 1909 and named Tel Aviv a year later.

telco ▶ noun (pl. **-os**) US a telecommunications company.
– ORIGIN late 20th cent.: abbreviation.

tele ▶ noun non-standard spelling of **TELLY**.

tele- /ˈtɛli/ ▶ combining form **1** to or at a distance: *telekinesis.*
■ used in names of instruments for operating over long distances: *telemeter*. [ORIGIN: from Greek *tēle-* 'far off'.]
2 relating to television: *telecine*. [ORIGIN: abbreviation.]
3 done by means of the telephone: *telemarketing*. [ORIGIN: abbreviation.]

tele-ad ▶ noun an advertisement placed in a newspaper or magazine by telephone.

telebanking ▶ noun another term for **TELEPHONE BANKING**.

telecast ▶ noun a television broadcast.
▶ verb [with obj.] (usu. **be telecast**) transmit by television: *the programme will be telecast simultaneously to nearly 150 cities.*
– DERIVATIVES **telecaster** noun.

telecentre ▶ noun another term for **TELECOTTAGE**.

telecine /ˈtɛlɪˌsɪni/ ▶ noun [mass noun] the broadcasting of cinema film on television.
■ equipment used in such broadcasting.

telecommunication ▶ noun [mass noun] communication over a distance by cable, telegraph, telephone, or broadcasting.
■ (**telecommunications**) [treated as sing.] the branch of technology concerned with such communication.
■ [count noun] formal a message sent by such means.
– ORIGIN 1930s: from French *télécommunication*, from *télé-* 'at a distance' + *communication* 'communication'.

telecommute ▶ verb [no obj.] [usu. as noun **telecommuting**] work from home, communicating with the workplace using equipment such as telephones, fax machines, and modems.
– DERIVATIVES **telecommuter** noun.

telecomputer ▶ noun a device which combines the capabilities of a computer with those of a television and a telephone, particularly for multimedia applications.
– DERIVATIVES **telecomputing** noun.

telecoms (also **telecomms**) ▶ plural noun [treated as sing.] telecommunications.
– ORIGIN 1960s: abbreviation.

teleconference ▶ noun a conference with participants in different locations linked by telecommunication devices.
– DERIVATIVES **teleconferencing** noun.

teleconnection ▶ noun a causal connection or correlation between meteorological or other environmental phenomena which occur a long distance apart.

teleconverter ▶ noun Photography a camera lens designed to be fitted in front of a standard lens to increase its effective focal length.

Telecopier ▶ noun US trademark a device which transmits and reproduces facsimile copies over a telephone line.

telecottage ▶ noun a room or building, especially in a rural area, filled with computer equipment for the shared use of people living in the area.

teledu /ˈtɛlɪduː/ ▶ noun a stink badger that has brownish-black fur with a white stripe along the top of the head and back, native to Sumatra, Java, and Borneo.
● *Mydaus javanensis*, family Mustelidae.
– ORIGIN early 19th cent.: from Javanese.

tele-evangelist ▶ noun variant of **TELEVANGELIST**.

telefacsimile ▶ noun another term for **FAX**[1].

telefax trademark ▶ noun [mass noun] the transmission of documents by fax.
■ [count noun] a document sent in such a way. ■ [count noun] a fax machine.
▶ verb [with obj.] [usu. as adj. **telefaxed**] send (a message) by fax: *telefaxed bills of lading.*
– ORIGIN 1940s: abbreviation of **TELEFACSIMILE**.

teleferic /ˈtɛlɪˈfɛrɪk/ ▶ noun variant spelling of **TÉLÉPHÉRIQUE**.

telefilm ▶ noun a film made for or broadcast on television.

telegenic /ˌtɛlɪˈdʒɛnɪk/ ▶ adjective having an appearance or manner that is appealing on television: *his telegenic charm appears to be his major asset.*
– ORIGIN 1930s (originally US): from **TELE-** 'television' + **-GENIC** 'well suited to', on the pattern of *photogenic*.

telegram ▶ noun a message sent by telegraph and then delivered in written or printed form, used in the UK only for international messages since 1981.
– ORIGIN mid 19th cent.: from **TELE-** 'at a distance' + **-GRAM**[1], on the pattern of *telegraph*.

telegraph ▶ noun **1** [mass noun] a system for transmitting messages from a distance along a wire, especially one creating signals by making and breaking an electrical connection: *news came from the outside world by telegraph.*
■ [count noun] a device for transmitting messages in such a way.
2 (also **telegraph board**) a board displaying scores or other information at a sports match or race meeting.
▶ verb [with obj.] send (someone) a message by telegraph: *I must go and telegraph Mama.*
■ send (a message) by telegraph: *she would rush off to telegraph news to her magazine.* ■ convey (an intentional or unconscious message), especially with facial expression or body language.
– DERIVATIVES **telegrapher** /ˈtɛlɪˌɡrɑːfə, tɪˈlɛɡrəfə/ noun.
– ORIGIN early 18th cent.: from French *télégraphe*, from *télé-* 'at a distance' + *-graphe* (see **-GRAPH**).

telegraphese ▶ noun [mass noun] informal the terse, abbreviated style of language used in telegrams.

telegraphic ▶ adjective **1** of or by telegraphs or telegrams: *the telegraphic transfer of the funds.*
2 (especially of speech) omitting inessential words; concise.
– DERIVATIVES **telegraphically** adverb.

telegraphic address ▶ noun chiefly historical an abbreviated or other registered address for use in telegrams.

telegraphist ▶ noun a person skilled or employed in telegraphy.

telegraph key ▶ noun a button which is pressed to produce a signal when transmitting Morse code.

telegraph plant ▶ noun a tropical Asian plant of the pea family, whose leaves have a spontaneous jerking motion. It is sometimes grown as a curiosity under glass.
● *Codariocalyx motorius* (formerly *Desmodium gyrans*), family Leguminosae.

telegraph pole ▶ noun a tall pole used to carry telegraph or telephone wires above the ground.

telegraphy ▶ noun [mass noun] the science or practice of using or constructing communication systems for the transmission or reproduction of information.

Telegu /ˈtɛlɪɡuː/ ▶ noun variant spelling of **TELUGU**.

telekinesis /ˌtɛlɪkʌɪˈniːsɪs, -kɪˈniːsɪs/ ▶ noun [mass noun] the supposed ability to move objects at a distance by mental power or other non-physical means.
– DERIVATIVES **telekinetic** adjective.
– ORIGIN late 19th cent.: from **TELE-** 'at a distance' + Greek *kinēsis* 'motion' (from *kinein* 'to move').

Telemachus /tɪˈlɛməkəs/ Greek Mythology the son of Odysseus and Penelope.

Telemann /ˈteɪləman, German ˈteːləman/, Georg Philipp (1681–1767), German composer and organist. His prolific output includes six hundred overtures, forty-four Passions, and forty operas.

telemark Skiing ▶ noun (also **telemark turn**) a turn, performed on skis to which only the toe of each boot is fixed, with the outer ski advanced and the knee bent: [as modifier] *telemark skiing.*
▶ verb [no obj., with adverbial] perform such a turn while skiing: *they went telemarking silently through the trees.*
– ORIGIN early 20th cent.: named after *Telemark*, a district in Norway, where it originated.

telemarketing ▶ noun [mass noun] the marketing of goods or services by means of telephone calls, typically unsolicited, to potential customers.
– DERIVATIVES **telemarketer** noun.

telematics ▶ plural noun [treated as sing.] the branch of information technology which deals with the long-distance transmission of computerized information.
– DERIVATIVES **telematic** adjective.
– ORIGIN 1970s: blend of **TELECOMMUNICATION** and **INFORMATICS**.

telemedicine ▶ noun [mass noun] the remote diagnosis and treatment of patients by means of telecommunications technology.

telemessage ▶ noun a message sent by telephone or telex and delivered in written form, which replaced the telegram for inland messages in the UK in 1981.

telemeter /ˈtɛlɪmiːtə, tɪˈlɛmɪtə/ ▶ noun an apparatus for recording the readings of an instrument and transmitting them by radio.
▶ verb [with obj.] transmit (readings) to a distant receiving set or station.

– DERIVATIVES **telemetric** adjective, **telemetry** noun.

telencephalon /ˌtɛlɛnˈsɛf(ə)lɒn, -ˈkɛf-, ˌtiːlɛnˈsɛf(ə)lɒn, -ˈkɛf-/ ▶ noun Anatomy the most highly developed and anterior part of the forebrain, consisting chiefly of the cerebral hemispheres. Compare with **DIENCEPHALON**.
– ORIGIN late 19th cent.: from **TELE-** 'far' + **ENCEPHALON**.

telenovela /ˈtɛlnəʊˌbɛlə/ ▶ noun (in Latin America) a television soap opera.
– ORIGIN Spanish.

teleological argument ▶ noun Philosophy the argument for the existence of God from the evidence of order, and hence design, in nature. Compare with **COSMOLOGICAL ARGUMENT** and **ONTOLOGICAL ARGUMENT**.

teleology /ˌtɛliˈɒlədʒi, ˌtiːl-/ ▶ noun (pl. **-ies**) [mass noun] Philosophy the explanation of phenomena by the purpose they serve rather than by postulated causes.
■ Theology the doctrine of design and purpose in the material world.
– DERIVATIVES **teleologic** adjective, **teleological** adjective, **teleologically** adverb, **teleologism** noun, **teleologist** noun.
– ORIGIN mid 18th cent. (denoting the branch of philosophy that deals with ends or final causes): from modern Latin *teleologia*, from Greek *telos* 'end' + *-logia* (see **-LOGY**).

teleoperation ▶ noun [mass noun] the electronic remote control of machines.
– DERIVATIVES **teleoperate** verb.

teleoperator ▶ noun a machine operated by remote control so as to imitate the movements of its operator.

teleost /ˈtɛliɒst, ˈtiːl-/ ▶ noun Zoology a fish of a large group that comprises all ray-finned fishes apart from the primitive bichirs, sturgeons, paddlefishes, freshwater garfishes, and bowfins.
● Division (or infraclass) Teleostei, subclass Actinopterygii: many orders.
– ORIGIN mid 19th cent.: from Greek *teleos* 'complete' + *osteon* 'bone'.

telepath /ˈtɛlɪpaθ/ ▶ noun a person with the ability to use telepathy.
– ORIGIN late 19th cent. (as a verb, meaning 'to use telepathy'): back-formation from **TELEPATHY**.

telepathy ▶ noun [mass noun] the supposed communication of thoughts or ideas by means other than the known senses.
– DERIVATIVES **telepathic** adjective, **telepathically** adverb, **telepathist** noun, **telepathize** (also **-ise**) verb.

téléphérique /ˌtɛlɪfeˈriːk, French teleferik/ (also **teleferic**) ▶ noun (pl. same) a cableway.
■ a mountain cable car.
– ORIGIN French.

telephone ▶ noun 1 [mass noun] a system for transmitting sound, typically voices, over a distance using wire or radio, by converting acoustic vibrations to electrical signals.
■ [count noun] an instrument used as part of such a system, typically a single unit including a handset with a transmitting microphone and a set of numbered buttons by which a connection can be made to another such instrument.
▶ verb [with obj.] ring or speak to (someone) using the telephone: *he had just finished telephoning his wife.*
■ [no obj.] make a telephone call: *she telephoned for help.* ■ send (a message) by telephone: *Barbara had telephoned the news.*
– PHRASES **on the telephone 1** using the telephone. **2** Brit. connected to a telephone system.
– DERIVATIVES **telephoner** noun, **telephonic** adjective, **telephonically** adverb.

telephone banking ▶ noun [mass noun] a method of banking in which the customer conducts transactions by telephone, typically by means of a computerized system using touch-tone dialling or voice-recognition technology.

telephone book ▶ noun a telephone directory.

telephone box ▶ noun chiefly Brit. a public booth or enclosure housing a payphone.

telephone call ▶ noun a communication or conversation by telephone.

telephone directory ▶ noun a book listing the names, addresses, and telephone numbers of the people in a particular area.

telephone exchange ▶ noun a set of equipment that connects telephone lines during a call.

telephone kiosk ▶ noun see **KIOSK**.

telephone number ▶ noun a number assigned to a particular telephone and used in making connections to it.
■ (usu. **telephone numbers**) informal a number with many digits (used especially to represent a large sum of money): *we're talking telephone numbers in terms of sales.*

telephone operator ▶ noun chiefly US a person who works at the switchboard of a telephone exchange.

telephone tag ▶ noun [mass noun] informal the action of continually trying to reach a person by telephone and failing because they are not there.

telephonist ▶ noun Brit. an operator of a switchboard.

telephony /tɪˈlɛf(ə)ni/ ▶ noun [mass noun] the working or use of telephones.

telephoto (also **telephoto lens**) ▶ noun (pl. **-os**) a lens with a longer focal length than standard, giving a narrow field of view and a magnified image.

teleport ▶ verb (especially in science fiction) transport or be transported across space and distance instantly.
▶ noun 1 a centre providing interconnections between different forms of telecommunications, especially one which links satellites to ground-based communications. [ORIGIN: 1980s: originally the name of such a centre in New York.]
2 an act of teleporting.
– DERIVATIVES **teleportation** noun.
– ORIGIN 1950s: back-formation from *teleportation* (1930s), from **TELE-** 'at a distance' + a shortened form of **TRANSPORTATION**.

telepresence ▶ noun [mass noun] the use of virtual reality technology, especially for remote control of machinery or for apparent participation in distant events.
■ a sensation of being elsewhere, created in such a way.

teleprinter ▶ noun Brit. a device for transmitting telegraph messages as they are keyed, and for printing messages received.

teleprompter ▶ noun North American term for **AUTOCUE**.

telerecord ▶ verb [with obj.] record (a television programme) during transmission.

telerecording ▶ noun a recording of a television programme made while it is being transmitted.

telesales ▶ plural noun the selling of goods or services over the telephone.

telescope ▶ noun an optical instrument designed to make distant objects appear nearer, containing an arrangement of lenses, or of curved mirrors and lenses, by which rays of light are collected and focused and the resulting image magnified.
■ short for **RADIO TELESCOPE**.
▶ verb [with obj.] cause (an object made of concentric tubular parts) to slide into itself, so that it becomes smaller.
■ [no obj.] be capable of sliding together in this way: *five steel sections that telescope into one another.* ■ crush (a vehicle) by the force of an impact. ■ figurative condense or conflate so as to occupy less space or time: *a way of telescoping many events into a relatively brief period.*
– ORIGIN mid 17th cent.: from Italian *telescopio* or modern Latin *telescopium*, from *tele-* 'at a distance' + *-scopium* (see **-SCOPE**).

telescopic ▶ adjective 1 of, relating to, or made with a telescope.
■ capable of viewing and magnifying distant objects. ■ Astronomy visible through a telescope.
2 having or consisting of concentric tubular sections designed to slide into one another: *a telescopic umbrella.*
– DERIVATIVES **telescopically** adverb.

telescopic sight ▶ noun a small telescope used for sighting, typically mounted on a rifle.

Telescopium /ˌtɛlɪˈskəʊpɪəm/ Astronomy an inconspicuous southern constellation (the Telescope), south of Sagittarius.
■ [as genitive **Telescopii** /ˌtɛlɪˈskəʊpiːʌɪ/] used with preceding letter or numeral to designate a star in this constellation: *the star Zeta Telescopii.*
– ORIGIN modern Latin.

teleshopping ▶ noun [mass noun] the ordering of

goods by customers using a telephone or direct computer link.

telesoftware ▶ noun [mass noun] Brit. software transmitted or broadcast via a network or television system.

teletex ▶ noun [mass noun] trademark an enhanced version of telex.
– ORIGIN 1970s: probably a blend of **TELEX** and **TEXT**.

teletext ▶ noun [mass noun] a news and information service in the form of text and graphics, transmitted using the spare capacity of existing television channels to televisions with appropriate receivers.

telethon ▶ noun a very long television programme, typically one broadcast to raise money for a charity.
– ORIGIN 1940s (originally US): from **TELE-** 'at a distance' + *-thon* on the pattern of *marathon*.

teletype ▶ noun trademark a kind of teleprinter.
■ a message received and printed by a teleprinter.
▶ verb [with obj. and usu. with adverbial of direction] send (a message) by means of a teleprinter.

teletypewriter ▶ noun chiefly US a teleprinter.

televangelist (also **tele-evangelist**) ▶ noun chiefly US an evangelical preacher who appears regularly on television to promote beliefs and appeal for funds.
– DERIVATIVES **televangelical** adjective, **televangelism** noun.

televiewer ▶ noun a person who watches television.
– DERIVATIVES **televiewing** noun & adjective.

televise ▶ verb [with obj.] [usu. as adj. **televised**] transmit by television: *a live televised debate between the party leaders.*
– DERIVATIVES **televisable** adjective.
– ORIGIN 1920s: back-formation from **TELEVISION**.

television ▶ noun 1 [mass noun] a system for transmitting visual images and sound which are reproduced on screens, chiefly used to broadcast programmes for entertainment, information, and education.
■ the activity, profession, or medium of broadcasting on television: *neither of my children showed the merest inclination to follow me into television* | [as modifier] *television news.* ■ television programmes: *Dan was sitting on the settee watching television.*
2 (also **television set**) a box-shaped device with a screen for receiving television signals.
– PHRASES **on (the) television** being broadcast by television; appearing in a television programme: *Norman was on television yesterday.*
– ORIGIN early 20th cent.: from **TELE-** 'at a distance' + **VISION**.

televisionary ▶ noun (pl. **-ies**) informal, often humorous an enthusiast for television.
▶ adjective of, relating to, or induced by television: *televisionary indoctrination.*

television station ▶ noun an organization transmitting television programmes.

television tube ▶ noun another term for **PICTURE TUBE**.

televisual ▶ adjective relating to or suitable for television: *the world of televisual images.*
– DERIVATIVES **televisually** adverb.

telework ▶ verb another term for **TELECOMMUTE**.
– DERIVATIVES **teleworker** noun.

telex ▶ noun [mass noun] an international system of telegraphy with printed messages transmitted and received by teleprinters using the public telecommunications network.
■ [count noun] a device used for this. ■ [count noun] a message sent by this system.
▶ verb [with obj.] communicate with (someone) by telex.
■ send (a message) by telex.
– ORIGIN 1930s: blend of **TELEPRINTER** and **EXCHANGE**.

Telford[1] a town in west central England; pop. 115,000 (est. 1991). Named after Thomas Telford, it was designated a new town in 1963.

Telford[2], Thomas (1757–1834), Scottish civil engineer. He built hundreds of miles of roads, more than a thousand bridges (including the Menai suspension bridge 1819–26), and a number of canals, including the Caledonian Canal across Scotland (opened 1822).

telic /ˈtɛlɪk/ ▶ adjective (of an action or attitude) directed or tending to a definite end.

▪ Linguistics (of a verb, conjunction, or clause) expressing purpose.
– DERIVATIVES **telicity** noun.
– ORIGIN mid 19th cent.: from Greek *telikos* 'final', from *telos* 'end'.

Tell, William, a legendary hero of the liberation of Switzerland from Austrian oppression. He was required to hit with an arrow an apple placed on the head of his son, which he did successfully. The events are placed in the 14th century, but there is no evidence for a historical person of this name, and similar legends are of widespread occurrence.

tell[1] ▶ **verb** (past and past participle **told**) **1** [reporting verb] communicate information, facts, or news to someone in spoken or written words: [with obj. and clause] *I told her you were coming* | [with obj. and direct speech] *'We have nothing in common,' she told him* | [with obj.] *he's telling the truth* | [with two objs] *we must be told the facts.*
▪ [with obj. and infinitive] order, instruct, or advise someone to do something: *tell him to go away.* ▪ [with obj.] narrate or relate (a tale or story). ▪ [with obj.] reveal information to (someone) in a non-verbal way: *the figures tell a different story* | [with two objs] *the smile on her face told him everything.* ▪ [no obj.] divulge confidential or private information: *promise you won't tell.* ▪ [no obj.] (**tell on**) informal inform someone of the misdemeanours of: *friends don't tell on each other.*
2 [with clause] decide or determine correctly or with certainty: *you* ***can tell*** *they're in love.*
▪ [with obj. and adverbial] distinguish one person or thing from another; perceive the difference between one person or thing and another: *I* ***can't tell the difference between*** *margarine and butter.*
3 [no obj.] (of an experience or period of time) have a noticeable, typically harmful, effect on someone: *the strain of supporting the family was beginning to* ***tell on*** *him.*
▪ (of a particular factor) play a part in the success or otherwise of someone or something: *lack of fitness* ***told against*** *him on his first run of the season.*
4 [with obj.] archaic count (the members of a series or group): *the shepherd had told all his sheep.*
– PHRASES **as far as one can tell** judging from the available information. **I tell you** (or **I can tell you**) used to emphasize a statement: *that took me by surprise, I can tell you!* **I** (or **I'll**) **tell you what** used to introduce a suggestion: *I tell you what, why don't we meet for lunch tomorrow?* **I told you** (**so**) used as a way of pointing out that one's warnings, although ignored, have been proved to be well founded. **tell one's beads** see **BEAD**. **tell someone's fortune** see **FORTUNE**. **tell it like it is** informal describe the true facts of a situation no matter how unpleasant they may be. **tell its own tale** (or **story**) be significant or revealing, without any further explanation or comment being necessary: *the worried expression on Helen's face told its own tale.* **tell me about it** informal used as an ironic acknowledgement of one's familiarity with a difficult or unpleasant situation or experience described by someone else. **tell me another** informal used as an expression of disbelief or incredulity. **tell something a mile off** see **MILE**. **tell tales** make known or gossip about another person's secrets, wrongdoings, or faults. **tell that to the marines** see **MARINE**. **tell the time** (or US **tell time**) be able to ascertain the time from reading the face of a clock or watch. **tell someone where to get off** (or **where they get off**) informal angrily dismiss or rebuke someone. **tell someone where to put** (or **what to do with**) **something** informal angrily or emphatically reject something: *I told him what he could do with his diamond.* **that would be telling** informal used to convey that one is not prepared to divulge secret or confidential information. **there is no telling** used to convey the impossibility of knowing what has happened or will happen: *there's no telling how she will react.* **to tell** (**you**) **the truth** used as a preface to a confession or admission of something. **you're telling me** informal used to emphasize that one is already well aware of something or in complete agreement with a statement.
– DERIVATIVES **tellable** adjective.
– ORIGIN Old English *tellan* 'relate, count, estimate', of Germanic origin; related to German *zählen* 'reckon, count', *erzählen* 'recount, relate', also to **TALE**.
▶ **tell someone off 1** informal reprimand or scold someone: *my parents told me off for coming home late.* **2** assign a member of a group to a particular task: *there used to be a chap told off every day to fetch us beer.*

tell[2] ▶ **noun** Archaeology (in the Middle East) an artificial mound formed by the accumulated remains of ancient settlements.
– ORIGIN mid 19th cent.: from Arabic *tall* 'hillock'.

Tell el-Amarna see **AMARNA, TELL EL-**.

Teller /ˈtɛlə/, Edward (b.1908), Hungarian-born American physicist. After moving to the US he worked on the first atomic reactor and the first atom bombs. Work under his guidance led to the detonation of the first hydrogen bomb in 1952.

teller ▶ **noun 1** a person employed to deal with customers' transactions in a bank.
▪ historical (in the UK) each of the four officers of the Exchequer responsible for the receipt and payment of moneys. ▪ chiefly N. Amer. a cashpoint machine. [ORIGIN: from *automated teller machine* (see ATM).]
2 a person who tells something: *a foul-mouthed teller of lies.*
3 a person appointed to count votes, especially in a parliament.
– DERIVATIVES **tellership** noun (chiefly historical) (only in sense 1).

tellin /ˈtɛlɪn/ ▶ **noun** a marine bivalve mollusc which lives buried in the sand siphoning detritus from the surface around its burrow.
• Family Tellinidae: *Tellina* and other genera.
– ORIGIN early 18th cent.: from Greek *tellinē*, denoting a kind of shellfish.

telling ▶ **adjective** having a striking or revealing effect; significant: *a telling argument against this theory.*
– DERIVATIVES **tellingly** adverb.

telling-off ▶ **noun** (pl. **tellings-off**) informal, chiefly Brit. a reprimand.

telltale ▶ **adjective** [attrib.] revealing, indicating, or betraying something: *the telltale bulge of a concealed weapon.*
▶ **noun 1** a person, especially a child, who reports others' wrongdoings or reveals their secrets.
2 a device or object that automatically gives a visual indication of the state or presence of something.

tellurian /tɛˈljʊərɪən/ formal or poetic/literary ▶ **adjective** of or inhabiting the earth.
▶ **noun** an inhabitant of the earth.
– ORIGIN mid 19th cent.: from Latin *tellus, tellur-* 'earth' + **-IAN**.

telluric /tɛˈljʊərɪk/ ▶ **adjective** of the earth as a planet.
▪ of the soil.
– ORIGIN mid 19th cent.: from Latin *tellus, tellur-* 'earth' + **-IC**.

telluric acid ▶ **noun** [mass noun] Chemistry a crystalline acid made by oxidizing tellurium dioxide.
• Chem. formula: $Te(OH)_6$.
– DERIVATIVES **tellurate** noun.

tellurite /ˈtɛljʊrʌɪt/ ▶ **noun** Chemistry a salt of the anion TeO_3^{2-}.

tellurium /tɛˈljʊərɪəm/ ▶ **noun** [mass noun] the chemical element of atomic number 52, a brittle, shiny, silvery-white semimetal resembling selenium and occurring mainly in small amounts in metallic sulphide ores. (Symbol: **Te**)
– DERIVATIVES **telluride** /ˈtɛljʊrʌɪd/ noun.
– ORIGIN early 19th cent.: modern Latin, from Latin *tellus, tellur-* 'earth', probably named in contrast to **URANIUM**.

telly ▶ **noun** (pl. **-ies**) Brit. informal term for **TELEVISION**.

telnet Computing ▶ **noun** [mass noun] a network protocol that allows a user on one computer to log in to another computer that is part of the same network.
▪ [count noun] a program that establishes a connection from one computer to another by means of such a protocol. ▪ [count noun] a link established in such a way.
▶ **verb** (**telnetted, telnetting**) [no obj.] informal log into a remote computer using a telnet program.
– DERIVATIVES **telnettable** adjective.
– ORIGIN 1970s: blend of **TELECOMMUNICATION** and **NETWORK**.

telogen /ˈtɛlə(ʊ)dʒ(ə)n, ˈtiːl-/ ▶ **noun** [mass noun] Physiology the resting phase of a hair follicle. Often contrasted with **ANAGEN**.
– ORIGIN 1920s: from Greek *telos* 'end' + **-GEN**.

telolecithal /ˌtiːlə(ʊ)ˈlɛsɪθ(ə)l, ˌtɛl-/ ▶ **adjective** Zoology (of an egg or egg cell) having a large yolk situated at or near one end.
– ORIGIN late 19th cent.: from Greek *telos* 'end' + *lekithos* 'egg yolk' + **-AL**.

telomere /ˈtiːlə(ʊ)mɪə, ˈtɛl-/ ▶ **noun** Genetics a compound structure at the end of a chromosome.
– DERIVATIVES **telomeric** adjective.
– ORIGIN 1940s: from Greek *telos* 'end' + *meros* 'part'.

telophase /ˈtiːlə(ʊ)feɪz, ˈtɛl-/ ▶ **noun** [mass noun] Biology the final phase of cell division, between anaphase and interphase, in which the chromatids or chromosomes move to opposite ends of the cell and two nuclei are formed.
– ORIGIN late 19th cent.: from Greek *telos* 'end' + **PHASE**.

telos /ˈtɛlɒs/ ▶ **noun** (pl. **teloi** /-lɔɪ/) chiefly Philosophy or poetic/literary an ultimate object or aim.
– ORIGIN Greek, literally 'end'.

telson /ˈtɛls(ə)n/ ▶ **noun** Zoology the last segment in the abdomen, or a terminal appendage to it, in crustaceans, chelicerates, and embryonic insects.
– ORIGIN mid 19th cent.: from Greek, literally 'limit'.

Telstar the first of the active communications satellites (i.e. both receiving and retransmitting signals, not merely reflecting signals from the earth). It was launched by the US in 1962 and used in the transmission of television broadcasting and telephone communication.

Telugu /ˈtɛləguː/ (also **Telegu**) ▶ **noun** (pl. same or **Telugus**) **1** a member of a people of SE India.
2 [mass noun] the Dravidian language of this people, with about 54 million speakers, mainly in Andhra Pradesh.
▶ **adjective** of or relating to this people or their language.
– ORIGIN from the name in Telugu, *teluṅgu*.

temazepam /təˈmeɪzɪpam, -ˈmazɪ-/ ▶ **noun** [mass noun] Medicine a compound of the benzodiazepine class used as a tranquillizer and short-acting hypnotic.
• A tricyclic compound; chem. formula: $C_{16}H_{13}ClN_2O_2$.
– ORIGIN 1970s: from *tem-* (of unknown origin), on the pattern of *oxazepam*.

temblor /tɛmˈblɔː/ ▶ **noun** US an earthquake.
– ORIGIN late 19th cent.: from American Spanish.

Tembu /ˈtɛmbuː/ ▶ **noun** (pl. same or **Tembus**) a member of a Xhosa-speaking people originating in present-day KwaZulu/Natal and now living in the Transkei.
▶ **adjective** of or relating to this people.
– ORIGIN from Xhosa *umtembu*.

temenos /ˈtɛmənɒs/ ▶ **noun** (pl. **temenoi** /-nɔɪ/) Archaeology a piece of ground surrounding or adjacent to a temple; a sacred enclosure or precinct.
– ORIGIN early 19th cent.: from Greek, from the stem of *temnein* 'cut off'.

temerarious /ˌtɛməˈrɛːrɪəs/ ▶ **adjective** poetic/literary reckless; rash.
– ORIGIN mid 16th cent.: from Latin *temerarius* (from *temere* 'rashly') + **-OUS**.

temerity /tɪˈmɛrɪti/ ▶ **noun** [mass noun] excessive confidence or boldness; audacity: *no one had the temerity to question his conclusions.*
– ORIGIN late Middle English: from Latin *temeritas*, from *temere* 'rashly'.

Temesvár /ˈtɛmɛʃˌvɑːr/ Hungarian name for **TIMIŞOARA**.

Temne /ˈtɛmni/ ▶ **noun** (pl. same or **Temnes**) **1** a member of a people of Sierra Leone.
2 [mass noun] the Niger–Congo language of this people, the main language of Sierra Leone, with about 1 million speakers.
▶ **adjective** of or relating to this people or their language.
– ORIGIN the name in Temne.

temnospondyl /ˌtɛmnə(ʊ)ˈspɒndɪl/ ▶ **noun** a fossil amphibian of a large group that was dominant from the Carboniferous to the Triassic.
• Order (or grade) Temnospondyli: many families.
– ORIGIN early 20th cent.: from modern Latin *Temnospondyli* (plural), from Greek *temnein* 'to cut' + *spondulos* 'vertebra'.

temp[1] informal ▶ **noun** a temporary employee, typically an office worker who finds employment through an agency.
▶ **verb** [no obj.] work as a temporary employee.
– ORIGIN 1930s (originally US): abbreviation.

temp[2] ▶ **abbreviation** for temperature.

temp. ▶ **abbreviation** in or from the time of: *a Roman aqueduct temp. Augustus.*

– ORIGIN from Latin *tempore*, ablative of *tempus* 'time'.

tempeh /ˈtɛmpeɪ/ ▶ **noun** [mass noun] an Indonesian dish made by deep-frying fermented soya beans.
– ORIGIN from Indonesian *tempe*.

temper ▶ **noun 1** [in sing.] a person's state of mind seen in terms of their being angry or calm: *he rushed out in a very bad temper.*
■a tendency to become angry easily: *I know my temper gets the better of me at times.* ■ an angry state of mind: *Drew had walked out* ***in a temper*** | [mass noun] *I only said it in* ***a fit of temper.***
2 [mass noun] the degree of hardness and elasticity in steel or other metal: *the blade rapidly heats up and the metal loses its temper.*
▶**verb** [with obj.] **1** improve the hardness and elasticity of (steel or other metal) by reheating and then cooling it.
■improve the consistency or resiliency of (a substance) by heating it or adding particular substances to it.
2 (often **be tempered with**) serve as a neutralizing or counterbalancing force to (something): *their idealism is tempered with realism.*
3 tune (a piano or other instrument) so as to adjust the note intervals correctly.
– PHRASES **keep** (or **lose**) **one's temper** refrain (or fail to refrain) from becoming angry. **out of temper** in an irritable mood.
– DERIVATIVES **temperer** noun.
– ORIGIN Old English *temprian* 'bring something into the required condition by mixing it with something else', from Latin *temperare* 'mingle, restrain oneself'. Sense development was probably influenced by Old French *temprer* 'to temper, moderate'. The noun originally denoted a proportionate mixture of elements or qualities, also the combination of the four bodily humours, believed in medieval times to be the basis of temperament, hence sense 1 (late Middle English). Compare with **TEMPERAMENT**.

tempera /ˈtɛmp(ə)rə/ ▶ **noun** [mass noun] a method of painting with pigments dispersed in an emulsion miscible with water, typically egg yolk. The method was used in Europe for fine painting, mainly on wood panels, from the 12th or early 13th century until the 15th, when it began to give way to oils.
■emulsion used in this method of painting.
– ORIGIN mid 19th cent.: from Italian, in the phrase *pingere a tempera* 'paint in distemper'.

temperament ▶ **noun 1** a person's or animal's nature, especially as it permanently affects their behaviour: *she had an artistic temperament.*
■[mass noun] the tendency to behave angrily or emotionally: *he had begun to show signs of temperament.*
2 [mass noun] the adjustment of intervals in tuning a piano or other musical instrument so as to fit the scale for use in different keys; in **equal temperament**, the octave consists of twelve equal semitones.
– ORIGIN late Middle English: from Latin *temperamentum* 'correct mixture', from *temperare* 'mingle'. In early use the word was synonymous with the noun **TEMPER**.

temperamental ▶ **adjective 1** (of a person) liable to unreasonable changes of mood.
2 of or relating to a person's temperament: *they were firm friends in spite of temperamental differences.*
– DERIVATIVES **temperamentally** adverb.

temperance ▶ **noun** [mass noun] abstinence from alcoholic drink: [as modifier] *the temperance movement.*
– ORIGIN Middle English: from Anglo-Norman French *temperaunce*, from Latin *temperantia* 'moderation', from *temperare* 'restrain'.

temperate ▶ **adjective 1** of, relating to, or denoting a region or climate characterized by mild temperatures.
2 showing moderation or self-restraint: *Charles was temperate in his consumption of both food and drink.*
– DERIVATIVES **temperately** adverb, **temperateness** noun.
– ORIGIN late Middle English (in the sense 'not affected by passion or emotion'): from Latin *temperatus* 'mingled, restrained', from the verb *temperare*.

temperate zone ▶ **noun** each of the two belts of latitude between the torrid zone and the northern and southern frigid zones.

temperature ▶ **noun** the degree or intensity of heat present in a substance or object, especially as expressed according to a comparative scale and shown by a thermometer or perceived by touch.
■Medicine the degree of internal heat of a person's body: *I'll* ***take her temperature.*** ■ informal a body temperature above the normal: *he* ***was running a temperature.*** ■ the degree of excitement or tension in a discussion or confrontation: *the temperature of the debate was lower than before.*
– ORIGIN late Middle English: from French *température* or Latin *temperatura*, from *temperare* 'restrain'. The word originally denoted the state of being tempered or mixed, later becoming synonymous with **TEMPERAMENT**. The modern sense dates from the late 17th cent.

temperature coefficient ▶ **noun** Physics a coefficient expressing the relation between a change in a physical property and the change in temperature that causes it.

temperature–humidity index ▶ **noun** a quantity expressing the discomfort felt as a result of the combined effects of the temperature and humidity of the air.

temperature inversion ▶ **noun** see **INVERSION** (sense 2).

-tempered ▶ **combining form** having a specified temper or disposition: *ill-tempered.*
– DERIVATIVES **-temperedly** combining form in corresponding adverbs, **-temperedness** combining form in corresponding nouns.

tempest ▶ **noun** a violent windy storm.
– PHRASES **a tempest in a teapot** North American term for ***a storm in a teacup*** (see **STORM**).
– ORIGIN Middle English: from Old French *tempeste*, from Latin *tempestas* 'season, weather, storm', from *tempus* 'time, season'.

tempestuous /tɛmˈpɛstjʊəs/ ▶ **adjective 1** characterized by strong and turbulent or conflicting emotion: *he had a reckless and tempestuous streak.*
2 very stormy: *a tempestuous wind.*
– DERIVATIVES **tempestuously** adverb, **tempestuousness** noun.
– ORIGIN late Middle English: from late Latin *tempestuosus*, from Latin *tempestas* (see **TEMPEST**).

tempi plural form of **TEMPO**[1].

Templar /ˈtɛmplə/ ▶ **noun** historical a member of the Knights Templars.
– ORIGIN Middle English: from Old French *templier*, from medieval Latin *templarius*, from Latin *templum* (see **TEMPLE**[1]).

template /ˈtɛmplɪt, -pleɪt/ (also **templet**) ▶ **noun 1** a shaped piece of metal, wood, card, plastic, or other material used as a pattern for processes such as cutting out, shaping, or drilling.
■figurative something that serves as a model for others to copy: *the plant was to serve as the template for change throughout the company.* ■ Biochemistry a nucleic acid molecule that acts as a pattern for the sequence of assembly of a protein, nucleic acid, or other large molecule.
2 a timber or plate used to distribute the weight in a wall or under a support.
– ORIGIN late 17th cent. (as *templet*): probably from **TEMPLE**[3] + **-ET**[1]. The change in the ending in the 19th cent. was due to association with **PLATE**.

Temple, Shirley (b.1928), American child star; latterly *Shirley Temple Black*. In the 1930s she appeared in a succession of films, such as *Rebecca of Sunnybrook Farm* (1938). She later became active in Republican politics and represented the US at the United Nations and as an ambassador.

temple[1] ▶ **noun** a building devoted to the worship, or regarded as the dwelling place, of a god or gods or other objects of religious reverence.
■(**the Temple**) either of two successive religious buildings of the Jews in Jerusalem. The first (957–586 BC) was built by Solomon and destroyed by Nebuchadnezzar; it contained the Ark of the Covenant. The second (515 BC–AD 70) was enlarged by Herod the Great from 20 BC and destroyed by the Romans during a Jewish revolt; all that remains is the Wailing Wall. ■(**the Temple**) a group of buildings in Fleet Street, which stand on land formerly occupied by the headquarters of the Knights Templars. Located there are the Inner and Outer Temple, two of the Inns of Court. ■ N. Amer. a synagogue. ■ a place of Christian public worship, especially a Protestant church in France.
– ORIGIN Old English *templ*, *tempel*, reinforced in Middle English by Old French *temple*, both from Latin *templum* 'open or consecrated space'.

temple[2] ▶ **noun** the flat part of either side of the head between the forehead and the ear.
– ORIGIN Middle English: from Old French, from an alteration of Latin *tempora*, plural of *tempus* 'temple of the head'.

temple[3] ▶ **noun** a device in a loom for keeping the cloth stretched.
– ORIGIN late Middle English: from Old French, perhaps ultimately the same word as **TEMPLE**[2].

temple block ▶ **noun** a percussion instrument consisting of a hollow block of wood which is struck with a stick.

templet ▶ **noun** variant spelling of **TEMPLATE**.

tempo[1] ▶ **noun** (pl. **tempos** or **tempi** /-piː/) **1** Music the speed at which a passage of music is or should be played.
2 the rate or speed of motion or activity; pace: *the tempo of life dictated by a heavy workload.*
– ORIGIN mid 17th cent. (as a fencing term denoting the timing of an attack): from Italian, from Latin *tempus* 'time'.

tempo[2] ▶ **noun** (pl. **-os**) (in the Indian subcontinent) a light three-wheeled delivery van.

temporal[1] /ˈtɛmp(ə)r(ə)l/ ▶ **adjective 1** relating to worldly as opposed to spiritual affairs; secular.
2 of or relating to time.
■Grammar relating to or denoting time or tense.
– DERIVATIVES **temporally** adverb.
– ORIGIN Middle English: from Old French *temporel* or Latin *temporalis*, from *tempus*, *tempor-* 'time'.

temporal[2] /ˈtɛmpər(ə)l/ ▶ **adjective** Anatomy of or situated in the temples of the head.
– ORIGIN late Middle English: from late Latin *temporalis*, from *tempora* 'the temples' (see **TEMPLE**[2]).

temporal bone ▶ **noun** Anatomy either of a pair of bones which form part of the side of the skull on each side and enclose the middle and inner ear.

temporalis /ˌtɛmpəˈreɪlɪs/ ▶ **noun** Anatomy a fan-shaped muscle which runs from the side of the skull to the back of the lower jaw and is involved in closing the mouth and chewing.
– ORIGIN late 17th cent.: from late Latin.

temporality ▶ **noun** (pl. **-ies**) **1** [mass noun] the state of existing within or having some relationship with time.
2 (usu. **temporalities**) a secular possession, especially the properties and revenues of a religious body or a member of the clergy.
– ORIGIN late Middle English (denoting temporal matters or secular authority): from late Latin *temporalitas*, from *temporalis* (see **TEMPORAL**[1]).

temporal lobe ▶ **noun** each of the paired lobes of the brain lying beneath the temples, including areas concerned with the understanding of speech.

temporal power ▶ **noun** [mass noun] the power of a bishop or cleric, especially the Pope, in secular matters.

temporary ▶ **adjective** lasting for only a limited period of time; not permanent: *a temporary job.*
▶**noun** (pl. **-ies**) a person employed on a temporary basis, typically an office worker who finds employment through an agency. See also **TEMP**[1].
– DERIVATIVES **temporarily** adverb, **temporariness** noun.
– ORIGIN mid 16th cent.: from Latin *temporarius*, from *tempus*, *tempor-* 'time'.

temporary hardness ▶ **noun** [mass noun] the presence in water of mineral salts (chiefly calcium bicarbonate) that are removed by boiling.

temporize (also **-ise**) ▶ **verb** [no obj.] avoid making a decision or committing oneself in order to gain time: *the opportunity was missed because the queen still temporized.*
– DERIVATIVES **temporization** noun, **temporizer** noun.
– ORIGIN late 16th cent.: from French *temporiser* 'bide one's time', from medieval Latin *temporizare* 'to delay', from Latin *tempus*, *tempor-* 'time'.

temporomandibular joint /ˌtɛmpərəʊmanˈdɪbjʊlə/ ▶ **noun** Anatomy the hinge joint between the temporal bone and the lower jaw.

tempo rubato ▶ **noun** fuller term for **RUBATO**.

Tempranillo /ˌtɛmprəˈniːjəʊ, -ˈniːljəʊ/ ▶ **noun** [mass noun] a variety of wine grape grown in Spain, used to make Rioja wine.

b **b**ut | d **d**og | f **f**ew | g **g**et | h **h**e | j **y**es | k **c**at | l **l**eg | m **m**an | n **n**o | p **p**en | r **r**ed | s **s**it | t **t**op | v **v**oice | w **w**e | z **z**oo | ʃ **sh**e | ʒ deci**s**ion | θ **th**in | ð **th**is | ŋ ri**ng** | x lo**ch** | tʃ **ch**ip | dʒ **j**ar

■a red wine made from this grape.
– ORIGIN named after a village in northern Spain.

temps levé /ˌtã ləˈveɪ/ ▶ **noun** (pl. same) Ballet a movement like a small hop in which there is no transfer of weight from one foot to the other.
– ORIGIN French, literally 'raised time'.

tempt ▶ **verb** [with obj.] entice or attempt to entice (someone) to do or acquire something that they find attractive but know to be wrong or not beneficial: *don't allow impatience to* **tempt** *you* **into** *overexposure and sunburn | there'll always be someone tempted by the rich pickings of poaching |* [with obj. and infinitive] *jobs which involve entertaining may tempt you to drink more than you intend.*
■(**be tempted to do something**) have an urge or inclination to do something: *I was tempted to look at my watch, but didn't dare.* ■ attract; allure: *he was tempted out of retirement to save the team from relegation.* ■ archaic risk provoking (a deity or abstract force), usually with undesirable consequences.
– PHRASES **tempt fate** (or **providence**) do something that is risky or dangerous.
– DERIVATIVES **temptability** noun (rare), **temptable** adjective (rare).
– ORIGIN Middle English: from Old French *tempter* 'to test', from Latin *temptare* 'handle, test, try'.

temptation ▶ **noun** a desire to do something, especially something wrong or unwise: *he resisted the temptation to call Celia at the office |* [mass noun] *we almost gave in to temptation.*
■a thing or course of action that attracts or tempts someone: *the temptations of life in London.* ■ (**the Temptation**) the tempting of Jesus by the Devil (see Matt. 4).
– ORIGIN Middle English: from Old French *temptacion*, from Latin *temptatio(n-)*, from *temptare* 'handle, test, try'.

tempter ▶ **noun** a person or thing that tempts.
■(**the Tempter**) the Devil.
– ORIGIN late Middle English: from Old French *tempteur*, from ecclesiastical Latin *temptator*, from Latin *temptare* 'to handle, test, try'.

tempting ▶ **adjective** appealing to or attracting someone, even if wrong or inadvisable: *a tempting financial offer |* [with infinitive] *it is often tempting to bring about change rapidly.*
– DERIVATIVES **temptingly** adverb.

temptress ▶ **noun** a woman who tempts someone to do something, typically a sexually attractive woman who sets out to allure or seduce someone.

tempura /ˈtɛmpʊrə/ ▶ **noun** [mass noun] a Japanese dish of fish, shellfish, or vegetables, fried in batter.
– ORIGIN Japanese, probably from Portuguese *tempêro* 'seasoning'.

ten ▶ **cardinal number** equivalent to the product of five and two; one more than nine; 10: *the last ten years | the house comfortably sleeps ten | a ten-foot shrub.* (Roman numeral: **x**, **X**)
■a group or unit of ten people or things: *count in tens.* ■ ten years old: *the boy was no more than ten.* ■ ten o'clock: *at about ten at night I got a call.* ■ a size of garment or other merchandise denoted by ten. ■ a ten-pound note or ten-dollar bill: *he took the money in tens.* ■ a playing card with ten pips.
– PHRASES **be ten a penny** see **PENNY**. **ten out of ten** a perfect mark. ■ used to congratulate someone or indicate that they have done something well: *you have to give her ten out of ten for persistence.* **ten to one** very probably: *ten to one you'll never find out who did this.*
– ORIGIN Old English *tēn, tīen*, of Germanic origin; related to Dutch *tien* and German *zehn*, from an Indo-European root shared by Sanskrit *daśa*, Greek *deka*, and Latin *decem*.

ten. Music ▶ **abbreviation for** tenuto.

tenable ▶ **adjective** 1 able to be maintained or defended against attack or objection: *such a simplistic approach is no longer tenable.*
2 (of an office, position, scholarship, etc.) able to be held or used: *a scholarship of £200 per annum tenable for three years.*
– DERIVATIVES **tenability** noun.
– ORIGIN late 16th cent.: from French, from *tenir* 'to hold', from Latin *tenere*.

tenace /ˈtɛnəs/ ▶ **noun** (in bridge, whist, and similar card games) a pair of cards in one hand which rank immediately above and below a card held by an opponent, e.g. the ace and queen in a suit of which an opponent holds the king.

– ORIGIN mid 17th cent.: from French, from Spanish *tenaza*, literally 'pincers'.

tenacious /tɪˈneɪʃəs/ ▶ **adjective** not readily letting go of, giving up, or separated from an object that one holds, a position, or a principle: *a tenacious grip | he was the most tenacious politician in South Korea.*
■not easily dispelled or discouraged; persisting in existence or in a course of action: *a tenacious local legend | you're tenacious and you get at the truth.*
– DERIVATIVES **tenaciously** adverb, **tenaciousness** noun, **tenacity** /tɪˈnasɪti/ noun.
– ORIGIN early 17th cent.: from Latin *tenax, tenac-* (from *tenere* 'to hold') + **-IOUS**.

tenaculum /tɪˈnakjʊləm/ ▶ **noun** (pl. **tenacula** /-lə/) a sharp hook used by a surgeon for picking up small pieces of tissue such as the ends of arteries.
– ORIGIN late 17th cent.: from Latin, literally 'holder, holding instrument', from *tenere* 'to hold'.

tenancy ▶ **noun** (pl. **-ies**) [mass noun] possession of land or property as a tenant: *Holding took over the tenancy of the farm.*

tenancy in common ▶ **noun** Law a shared tenancy in which each holder has a distinct, separately transferable interest.

tenant ▶ **noun** a person who occupies land or property rented from a landlord.
■Law a person holding real property by private ownership.
▶ **verb** [with obj.] (usu. **be tenanted**) occupy (property) as a tenant.
– DERIVATIVES **tenantable** adjective (formal), **tenantless** adjective.
– ORIGIN Middle English: from Old French, literally 'holding', present participle of *tenir*, from Latin *tenere*.

tenant at will ▶ **noun** (pl. **tenants at will**) Law a tenant that can be evicted without notice.

tenant farmer ▶ **noun** a person who farms rented land.

tenantry ▶ **noun** 1 [treated as sing. or pl.] the tenants of an estate.
2 [mass noun] tenancy.

Tencel /ˈtɛnsɛl/ ▶ **noun** [mass noun] trademark a cellulosic fibre obtained from wood pulp using recyclable solvents; a fabric made from this.
– ORIGIN 1960s (proprietary name of various yarns and fabrics): an invented word.

tench ▶ **noun** (pl. same) a European freshwater fish of the carp family, popular with anglers and widely introduced elsewhere.
• *Tinca tinca*, family Cyprinidae.
– ORIGIN Middle English: from Old French *tenche*, from late Latin *tinca*.

Ten Commandments (in the Bible) the divine rules of conduct given by God to Moses on Mount Sinai, according to Exod. 20:1–17.

The commandments are generally enumerated as: have no other gods; do not make or worship idols; do not take the name of the Lord in vain; keep the sabbath holy; honour one's father and mother; do not kill; do not commit adultery; do not steal; do not give false evidence; do not covet another's property or wife.

tend[1] ▶ **verb** [no obj., with infinitive] regularly or frequently behave in a particular way or have a certain characteristic: *written language tends to be formal | her hair tended to come loose.*
■[no obj.] (**tend to/towards**) be liable to possess or display (a particular characteristic): *Walter tended towards corpulence.* ■ [no obj., with adverbial] go or move in a particular direction: *the rate of change of money wages tends to infinity.*
– ORIGIN Middle English (in the sense 'move or be inclined to move in a certain direction'): from Old French *tendre* 'stretch, tend', from Latin *tendere*.

tend[2] ▶ **verb** [with obj.] care for or look after; give one's attention to: *Varela tended plants on the roof |* [no obj.] *for two or three months he* **tended to** *business.*
■US direct or manage; work in: *I've been tending bar at the airport lounge.* ■ archaic wait on as an attendant or servant.
– DERIVATIVES **tendance** noun (archaic).
– ORIGIN Middle English: shortening of **ATTEND**.

tendency ▶ **noun** (pl. **-ies**) an inclination towards a particular characteristic or type of behaviour: *for students, there is a* **tendency to** *socialize in the evenings | criminal tendencies.*
■a group within a larger political party or movement: *the dominant tendency in the party remained right-wing.*

– ORIGIN early 17th cent.: from medieval Latin *tendentia*, from *tendere* 'to stretch' (see **TEND**[1]).

tendentious /tɛnˈdɛnʃəs/ ▶ **adjective** expressing or intending to promote a particular cause or point of view, especially a controversial one: *a tendentious reading of history.*
– DERIVATIVES **tendentiously** adverb, **tendentiousness** noun.
– ORIGIN early 20th cent.: suggested by German *tendenziös*.

tender[1] ▶ **adjective** (**tenderer**, **tenderest**) 1 showing gentleness and concern or sympathy: *he was being so kind and tender.*
■[predic.] (**tender of**) archaic solicitous of; concerned for: *be tender of a lady's reputation.*
2 (of food) easy to cut or chew; not tough: *tender green beans.*
■(of a plant) easily injured by severe weather and therefore needing protection. ■ (of a part of the body) sensitive to pain: *the pale, tender skin of her forearm.* ■ young, immature, and vulnerable: *at the* **tender age of** *five.* ■ requiring tact or careful handling: *the issue of conscription was a particularly tender one.* ■ Nautical (of a ship) leaning or readily inclined to roll in response to the wind.
– PHRASES **tender mercies** used ironically to imply that someone cannot be trusted to look after or treat someone else kindly or well: *they have abandoned their children to the tender mercies of the social services.*
– DERIVATIVES **tenderly** adverb, **tenderness** noun.
– ORIGIN Middle English: from Old French *tendre*, from Latin *tener* 'tender, delicate'.

tender[2] ▶ **verb** [with obj.] offer or present (something) formally: *he tendered his resignation as leader.*
■offer (money) as payment: *she tendered her fare.* ■ [no obj.] make a formal written offer to carry out work, supply goods, or buy land, shares, or another asset for a stated fixed price: *firms of interior decorators have been* **tendering for** *the work.* ■ make such an offer giving (a stated fixed price): *what price should we tender for a contract?* ■ (**tender something out**) seek offers to carry out work at a stated fixed price.
▶ **noun** an offer to carry out work, supply goods, or buy land, shares, or another asset at a stated fixed price.
– PHRASES **put something out to tender** seek offers to carry out work or supply goods at a stated fixed price.
– DERIVATIVES **tenderer** noun.
– ORIGIN mid 16th cent. (as a legal term meaning 'formally offer a plea or evidence, or money to discharge a debt', also as a noun denoting such an offer): from Old French *tendre*, from Latin *tendere* 'to stretch, hold forth' (see **TEND**[1]).

tender[3] ▶ **noun** 1 [with modifier] a vehicle used by a fire service for carrying specified supplies or equipment or fulfilling a specified role.
■a vehicle used in mobile operations by another public service or the armed forces.
2 a dinghy or other boat used to ferry people and supplies to and from a ship.
3 a trailing vehicle closely coupled to a steam locomotive to carry fuel and water.
4 [usu. in combination or with modifier] a person who looks after someone else or a machine or place: *Alexei signalled to one of the engine tenders.*
– ORIGIN late Middle English (in the sense 'attendant, nurse'): from **TEND**[2] or shortening of *attender* (see **ATTEND**).

tender-eyed ▶ **adjective** 1 having gentle eyes.
2 having sore or weak eyes.

tenderfoot ▶ **noun** (pl. **tenderfoots** or **tenderfeet**) 1 chiefly N. Amer. a newcomer or novice, especially a person unaccustomed to the hardships of pioneer life.
2 dated a new member of the Scout or Guide movement who has passed the enrolment tests.

tender-hearted ▶ **adjective** having a kind, gentle, or sentimental nature.
– DERIVATIVES **tender-heartedness** noun.

tenderize (also **-ise**) ▶ **verb** make (meat) more tender by beating or slow cooking.

tenderizer (also **-iser**) ▶ **noun** a thing used to make meat tender, in particular:
■a substance such as papain which is rubbed on to meat or used as a marinade to soften the fibres. ■ a small hammer with teeth on the head, used to beat meat.

tenderloin ▶ **noun** 1 [mass noun] the tenderest part of

t

a loin of beef, pork, etc., taken from under the short ribs in the hindquarters.
■US the undercut of a sirloin.
2 N. Amer. informal a district of a city where vice and corruption are prominent. |ORIGIN: late 19th cent.: originally a term applied to a district of New York, seen as a 'choice' assignment by police because of the bribes offered to them to turn a blind eye.]

tender-minded ▶ adjective easily affected emotionally by other people's distress or by criticism.
– DERIVATIVES **tender-mindedness** noun.

tendinitis /ˌtɛndɪˈnʌɪtəs/ (also **tendonitis** /ˌtɛndə-/) ▶ noun [mass noun] inflammation of a tendon, most commonly from overuse but also from infection or rheumatic disease.

tendon /ˈtɛndən/ ▶ noun a flexible but inelastic cord of strong fibrous collagen tissue attaching a muscle to a bone.
■the hamstring of a quadruped.
– DERIVATIVES **tendinous** adjective.
– ORIGIN late Middle English: from French or medieval Latin tendo(n-), translating Greek tenōn 'sinew', from teinein 'to stretch'.

tendon organ ▶ noun Anatomy a sensory receptor within a tendon that responds to tension and relays impulses to the central nervous system.

tendresse /tɒ̃ˈdrɛs/ (also **tendre** /ˈtɒ̃dr(ə)/) ▶ noun [in sing.] a feeling of fondness or love (used to give an impression of coyness or allusiveness on the part of the speaker): *the local grande dame for whom George had a tendresse.*
– ORIGIN French.

tendril ▶ noun a slender thread-like appendage of a climbing plant, often growing in a spiral form, which stretches out and twines round any suitable support.
■something resembling a plant tendril, especially a slender curl or ringlet of hair.
– ORIGIN mid 16th cent.: probably a diminutive of Old French tendron 'young shoot', from Latin tener 'tender'.

tendu /tɒ̃ˈd(j)uː/ ▶ adjective [postpositive] Ballet (of a position) stretched out or held tautly: *battement tendu.*
– ORIGIN French.

tendu leaf /tɛnˈduː/ ▶ noun [mass noun] the leaves of an Asian ebony tree, gathered in India as a cheap tobacco substitute.
● *Diospyros melanoxylon,* family Ebenaceae.
– ORIGIN Hindi tendu.

Tenebrae /ˈtɛnɪbriː, -breɪ/ ▶ plural noun historical (in the Roman Catholic Church) matins and lauds for the last three days of Holy Week, at which candles were successively extinguished. Several composers have set parts of the office to music.
– ORIGIN Latin, literally 'darkness'.

tenebrionid /tɪˌnɛbrɪˈɒnɪd/ ▶ noun Entomology a beetle of a family (Tenebrionidae) that comprises the darkling beetles.
– ORIGIN 1920s: from modern Latin Tenebrionidae (plural), from tenebrio 'night spirit'.

tenebrism /ˈtɛnəbrɪz(ə)m/ (also **Tenebrism**) ▶ noun [mass noun] a style of painting developed by Caravaggio and other 17th-century Spanish and Italian artists, characterized by predominantly dark tones and shadows with dramatically contrasting effects of light.
– DERIVATIVES **tenebrist** noun.
– ORIGIN from Italian tenebroso 'dark' + -ISM.

tenebrous /ˈtɛnɪbrəs/ ▶ adjective poetic/literary dark; shadowy or obscure.
– ORIGIN late Middle English: via Old French from Latin tenebrosus, from tenebrae 'darkness'.

tenement /ˈtɛnəm(ə)nt/ ▶ noun **1** (especially in Scotland or the US) a room or a set of rooms forming a separate residence within a house or block of flats.
■(also **tenement house**) a house divided into and let in such separate residences.
2 a piece of land held by an owner.
■Law any kind of permanent property, e.g. lands or rents, held from a superior.
– ORIGIN Middle English (in the sense 'tenure, property held by tenure'): via Old French from medieval Latin tenementum, from tenere 'to hold'.

Tenerife /ˌtɛnəˈriːf, Spanish teneˈrife/ a volcanic island in the Atlantic, the largest of the Canary Islands; pop. 771,000 (1990); capital, Santa Cruz.

tenesmus /tɪˈnɛzməs/ ▶ noun [mass noun] Medicine a continual or recurrent inclination to evacuate the bowels, caused by disorder of the rectum or other illness.
– ORIGIN early 16th cent.: via medieval Latin from Greek teinesmos 'straining', from teinein 'stretch, strain'.

tenet /ˈtɛnɪt, ˈtiːnɛt/ ▶ noun a principle or belief, especially one of the main principles of a religion or philosophy: *the tenets of classical liberalism.*
– ORIGIN late 16th cent. (superseding earlier tenent): from Latin, literally 'he holds', from the verb tenere.

tenfold ▶ adjective ten times as great or as numerous: *a tenfold increase in the use of insecticides.*
■having ten parts or elements.
▶ adverb by ten times; to ten times the number or amount: *production increased tenfold.*

ten-gallon hat ▶ noun a large, broad-brimmed hat, traditionally worn by cowboys.

tenge /ˈtɛŋɡeɪ/ ▶ noun (pl. same or **tenges**) **1** the basic monetary unit of Kazakhstan, equal to 100 teins.
2 a monetary unit of Turkmenistan, equal to one hundredth of a manat.

Teng Hsiao-p'ing /ˌtɛŋ ʃaʊˈpɪŋ/ variant of **DENG XIAOPING**.

tenia ▶ noun US spelling of **TAENIA**.

Teniers /ˈtɛnɪəz/, David (1610–90), Flemish painter; known as **David Teniers the Younger**. From 1651 he was court painter to successive regents of the Netherlands.

Ten Lost Tribes of Israel see **LOST TRIBES**.

ten-minute rule ▶ noun a rule of the House of Commons allowing brief discussion of a motion to introduce a bill, each speech being limited to ten minutes.

Tenn. ▶ abbreviation for Tennessee.

Tennant Creek /ˈtɛnənt/ a mining town between Alice Springs and Darwin in Northern Territory, Australia; pop. 3,300 (1986).

tennantite /ˈtɛnəntʌɪt/ ▶ noun [mass noun] a grey-black mineral consisting of a sulphide of copper, iron, and arsenic. It is an important ore of copper.
– ORIGIN mid 19th cent.: from the name of Smithson Tennant (1761–1815), English chemist, + -ITE[1].

tenné /ˈtɛnɪ/ Heraldry ▶ noun [mass noun] orange-brown, as a stain used in blazoning.
▶ adjective [usu. postpositive] of this colour.
– ORIGIN mid 16th cent.: obsolete French, variant of Old French tane (see **TAWNY**).

tenner ▶ noun Brit. informal a ten-pound note.

Tennessee /ˌtɛnəˈsiː/ **1** a river in the south-eastern US, flowing some 1,400 km (875 miles) in a great loop, generally westwards through Tennessee and Alabama, then northwards to re-enter Tennessee, joining the Ohio River in western Kentucky.
2 a state in the central south-eastern US; pop. 4,877,185 (1990); capital, Nashville. Ceded by Britain to the US in 1783, it became the 16th state in 1796.
– DERIVATIVES **Tennessean** noun & adjective.

Tennessee Valley Authority (abbrev.: **TVA**) an independent federal government agency in the US, created in 1933 as part of the New Deal proposals. Responsible for the development of the whole Tennessee river basin, it provides one of the world's greatest irrigation and hydroelectric power systems.

Tennessee Walking Horse ▶ noun a powerful riding horse of a breed with a characteristic fast walking pace.

Tenniel /ˈtɛnɪəl/, Sir John (1820–1914), English illustrator and cartoonist. He illustrated Lewis Carroll's *Alice's Adventures in Wonderland* (1865) and *Through the Looking Glass* (1871).

tennies ▶ plural noun N. Amer. informal tennis shoes.

tennis ▶ noun [mass noun] a game in which two or four players strike a ball with rackets over a net stretched across a court. The usual form (originally called **lawn tennis**) is played with a felt-covered hollow rubber ball on a grass, clay, or artificial surface. See also **REAL TENNIS**.
– ORIGIN late Middle English tenetz, tenes 'real tennis', apparently from Old French tenez 'take, receive' (called by the server to an opponent), imperative of tenir.

tennis elbow ▶ noun [mass noun] inflammation of the tendons of the elbow (epicondylitis) caused by overuse of the muscles of the forearm.

tennis shoe ▶ noun a light canvas or leather soft-soled shoe suitable for tennis or casual wear.

Tenno /ˈtɛnəʊ/ ▶ noun (pl. **-os**) the Emperor of Japan.
– ORIGIN Japanese.

Tennyson /ˈtɛnɪs(ə)n/, Alfred, 1st Baron Tennyson of Aldworth and Freshwater (1809–92), English poet, Poet Laureate from 1850. His reputation was established by *In Memoriam* (1850), a long poem concerned with immortality, change, and evolution. Other notable works: 'The Charge of the Light Brigade' (1854) and *Idylls of the King* (1859).

Tennysonian /ˌtɛnɪˈsəʊnɪən/ ▶ adjective relating to or in the style of Tennyson.
▶ noun an admirer or student of Tennyson or his work.

Tenochtitlán /tɛˌnɒtʃtɪˈtlɑːn/ the ancient capital of the Aztec empire, founded c.1320. In 1521 the Spanish conquistador Cortés destroyed it and established Mexico City on its site.

tenon ▶ noun a projecting piece of wood made for insertion into a mortise in another piece.
▶ verb [with obj.] (usu. **be tenoned**) join by means of a tenon.
■cut as a tenon.
– DERIVATIVES **tenoner** noun.
– ORIGIN late Middle English: from French, from tenir 'to hold', from Latin tenere.

tenon saw ▶ noun a small saw with a strong brass or steel back for precise work.

tenor[1] ▶ noun a singing voice between baritone and alto or counter-tenor, the highest of the ordinary adult male range.
■a singer with such a voice. ■ a part written for such a voice. ■ [usu. as modifier] an instrument, especially a saxophone, trombone, tuba, or viol, of the second or third lowest pitch in its family: *a tenor sax.* ■ (in full **tenor bell**) the largest and deepest bell of a ring or set.
– ORIGIN late Middle English: via Old French from medieval Latin, based on tenere 'to hold'; so named because the tenor part was allotted (and therefore 'held') the melody.

tenor[2] ▶ noun **1** [in sing.] (usu. **the tenor of**) the general meaning, sense, or content of something: *the general tenor of the debate.*
2 [in sing.] (usu. **the tenor of**) a settled or prevailing character or direction, especially the course of a person's life or habits: *the even tenor of life in the kitchen was disrupted the following day.*
3 Law the actual wording of a document.
4 Finance the time that must elapse before a bill of exchange or promissory note becomes due for payment.
– ORIGIN Middle English: from Old French tenour, from Latin tenor 'course, substance, import of a law', from tenere 'to hold'.

tenor clef ▶ noun Music a clef placing middle C on the second-highest line of the stave, used chiefly for cello and bassoon music.

tenorino /ˌtɛnəˈriːnəʊ/ ▶ noun (pl. **tenorini** /-ˈriːni/) a high tenor.
– ORIGIN Italian, diminutive of tenore 'tenor'.

tenorist ▶ noun a person who plays a tenor instrument, especially the tenor saxophone.

tenosynovitis /ˌtɛnəʊˌsʌɪnə(ʊ)ˈvʌɪtɪs/ ▶ noun [mass noun] Medicine inflammation and swelling of a tendon, typically in the wrist, often caused by repetitive movements such as typing.
– ORIGIN late 19th cent.: from Greek tenōn 'tendon' + **SYNOVITIS**.

tenotomy /təˈnɒtəmi/ ▶ noun [mass noun] the surgical cutting of a tendon, especially as a remedy for club foot.
– ORIGIN mid 19th cent.: coined in French from Greek tenōn 'tendon' + -tomia (see **-TOMY**).

tenpin ▶ noun a skittle used in tenpin bowling.
■(**tenpins**) [treated as sing.] US tenpin bowling.

tenpin bowling ▶ noun [mass noun] a game in which ten skittles are set up at the end of a track (typically one of several in a large, automated alley) and bowled down with hard rubber or plastic balls.

tenpounder ▶ noun a large silvery-blue herring-like fish of tropical seas, which is popular as a game fish. Also called **LADYFISH**.
● *Elops saurus* (or *machnata*), family Elopidae.

tenrec /ˈtɛnrɛk/ ▶ noun a small insectivorous

mammal native to Madagascar, different kinds of which resemble hedgehogs, shrews, or small otters.
• Several genera in the family Tenrecidae: many species, including the **common** (or **tailless**) **tenrec** (*Tenrec ecaudatus*), also found in the Comoro islands.
– ORIGIN late 18th cent.: from French *tanrec*, from Malagasy *tàndraka*.

TENS ▶ **abbreviation for** transcutaneous electrical nerve stimulation, a technique intended to provide pain relief by applying electrodes to the skin to block impulses in underlying nerves.

tense[1] ▶ **adjective** (especially of a muscle or someone's body) stretched tight or rigid: *she tried to relax her tense muscles.*
■ (of a person) unable to relax because of nervousness, anxiety, or stimulation: *he was tense with excitement.* ■ (of a situation, event, etc.) causing or showing anxiety and nervousness: *relations between the two neighbouring states had been tense in recent years.* ■ Phonetics (of a speech sound, especially a vowel) pronounced with the vocal muscles stretched tight. The opposite of **LAX**.
▶ **verb** [no obj.] become tense, typically through anxiety or nervousness: *her body **tensed up**.*
■ [with obj.] make (a muscle or one's body) tight or rigid: *carefully stretch and then tense your muscles.*
– DERIVATIVES **tensely** adverb, **tenseness** noun, **tensity** noun (dated).
– ORIGIN late 17th cent.: from Latin *tensus* 'stretched', from the verb *tendere*.

tense[2] ▶ **noun** Grammar a set of forms taken by a verb to indicate the time (and sometimes also the continuance or completeness) of the action in relation to the time of the utterance: *the past tense.*
– DERIVATIVES **tenseless** adjective.
– ORIGIN Middle English (in the general sense 'time'): from Old French *tens*, from Latin *tempus* 'time'.

tensegrity /tɛnˈsɛɡrɪti/ ▶ **noun** [mass noun] Architecture the characteristic property of a stable three-dimensional structure consisting of members under tension that are contiguous and members under compression that are not.
– ORIGIN 1950s: from *tensional integrity*.

tensile /ˈtɛnsʌɪl/ ▶ **adjective** **1** of or relating to tension.
2 capable of being drawn out or stretched.
– DERIVATIVES **tensility** noun.
– ORIGIN early 17th cent. (in sense 2): from medieval Latin *tensilis*, from Latin *tendere* 'to stretch'.

tensile strength ▶ **noun** the resistance of a material to breaking under tension. Compare with **COMPRESSIVE STRENGTH**.

tension ▶ **noun** [mass noun] **1** the state of being stretched tight: *the parachute keeps the cable under tension as it drops.*
■ the state of having the muscles stretched tight, especially as causing strain or discomfort: *the elimination of neck tension can relieve headaches.* ■ a strained state or condition resulting from forces acting in opposition to each other. ■ the degree of tightness of stitches in knitting and machine sewing. ■ electromotive force.
2 mental or emotional strain: *a mind which is affected by stress or tension cannot think as clearly.*
■ a strained political or social state or relationship: *the coup followed months of tension between the military and the government* | [count noun] *racial tensions.* ■ a relationship between ideas or qualities with conflicting demands or implications: *the basic **tension between** freedom and control.*
▶ **verb** [with obj.] apply a force to (something) which tends to stretch it.
– DERIVATIVES **tensional** adjective, **tensionally** adverb, **tensioner** noun, **tensionless** adjective.
– ORIGIN mid 16th cent. (as a medical term denoting a condition or feeling of being physically stretched or strained): from French, or from Latin *tensio(n-)*, from *tendere* 'stretch'.

tensive ▶ **adjective** causing or expressing tension.
■ (of a pain) giving a sensation of tension or tightness.

tenson /ˈtɛns(ə)n/ (also **tenzon**) ▶ **noun** historical a contest in verse-making between troubadours.
■ a piece of verse composed for such a contest.
– ORIGIN mid 19th cent.: from French *tenson* (related to Provençal *tenso*), based on Latin *tendere* 'to stretch'.

tensor /ˈtɛnsə, -sɔː/ ▶ **noun** **1** Mathematics a mathematical object analogous to but more general than a vector, represented by an array of components that are functions of the coordinates of a space.
2 Anatomy a muscle that tightens or stretches a part of the body.
– DERIVATIVES **tensorial** adjective.
– ORIGIN early 18th cent.: modern Latin, from Latin *tendere* 'to stretch'.

tent[1] ▶ **noun** a portable shelter made of cloth, supported by one or more poles and stretched tight by cords or loops attached to pegs driven into the ground.
■ Medicine short for **OXYGEN TENT**.
▶ **verb** **1** [with obj.] cover with or as if with a tent: *the garden had been completely tented over for supper.*
■ arrange in a shape that looks like a tent: *Tim tented his fingers.* ■ [as adj. **tented**] composed of or provided with tents: *they were living in large tented camps.*
2 [no obj.] (especially of travelling circus people) live in a tent.
– ORIGIN Middle English: from Old French *tente*, based on Latin *tent-* 'stretched', from the verb *tendere*. The verb dates from the mid 16th cent.

tent[2] ▶ **noun** [mass noun] a deep red sweet wine chiefly from Spain, used especially as sacramental wine.
– ORIGIN late Middle English: from Spanish *tinto* 'deep-coloured', from Latin *tinctus* 'dyed, stained', from the verb *tingere*.

tent[3] ▶ **noun** Surgery a piece of absorbent material inserted into an opening to keep it open, or especially to widen it gradually as the material absorbs moisture.
– ORIGIN late Middle English (also denoting a surgical probe): from Old French *tente*, from *tenter* 'to probe', from Latin *temptare* 'handle, test, try'.

tentacle ▶ **noun** a slender flexible limb or appendage in an animal, especially around the mouth of an invertebrate, used for grasping, moving about, or bearing sense organs.
■ (in a plant) a tendril or a sensitive glandular hair. ■ something resembling a tentacle in shape or flexibility: *trailing tentacles of vapour.* ■ (usu. **tentacles**) figurative an insidious spread of influence and control: *the Party's tentacles reached into every nook and cranny of people's lives.*
– DERIVATIVES **tentacled** adjective [also in combination], **tentacular** adjective, **tentaculate** adjective.
– ORIGIN mid 18th cent.: Anglicized from modern Latin *tentaculum*, from Latin *tentare*, *temptare* 'to feel, try'.

tentage ▶ **noun** [mass noun] tents collectively.

tentative ▶ **adjective** not certain or fixed; provisional: *a tentative conclusion.*
■ done without confidence; hesitant: *he eventually tried a few tentative steps round his hospital room.*
– DERIVATIVES **tentatively** adverb, **tentativeness** noun.
– ORIGIN late 16th cent.: from medieval Latin *tentativus*, from *tentare*, variant of *temptare* 'handle, try'.

tent caterpillar ▶ **noun** a chiefly American moth caterpillar that lives in groups inside communal silken webs in a tree, which it often defoliates.
• Several species in the family Lasiocampidae, especially *Malacosoma americana*, related to the lackey.

tent dress ▶ **noun** a full, loose-fitting dress that is narrow at the shoulders and very wide at the hem, having no waistline or darts.

tenter[1] ▶ **noun** a framework on which fabric can be held taut for drying or other treatment during manufacture.
– ORIGIN Middle English: from medieval Latin *tentorium*, from *tent-* 'stretched', from the verb *tendere*.

tenter[2] ▶ **noun** Brit. archaic a person in charge of something, especially of machinery in a factory.
– ORIGIN early 19th cent.: from Scots and northern English dialect *tent* 'pay attention', apparently from Middle English *attent* 'heed'.

tenterhook ▶ **noun** historical a hook used to fasten cloth on a drying frame or tenter.
– PHRASES **on tenterhooks** in a state of suspense or agitation because of uncertainty about a future event.

tenth ▶ **ordinal number** constituting number ten in a sequence; 10th: *the tenth century* | *the tenth of September* | *the tenth-floor locker room.*
■ (**a tenth/one tenth**) each of ten equal parts into which something is or may be divided: *a tenth of a litre.* ■ Music an interval or chord spanning an octave and a third in the diatonic scale, or a note separated from another by this interval.
– DERIVATIVES **tenthly** adverb.

tenth-rate ▶ **adjective** informal of extremely poor quality.

tentorium /tɛnˈtɔːrɪəm/ ▶ **noun** (pl. **tentoria** /-rɪə/) **1** Anatomy a fold of the dura mater forming a partition between the cerebrum and cerebellum.
2 Entomology an internal skeletal framework in the head of an insect.
– ORIGIN early 19th cent.: from Latin, literally 'tent'.

tent peg ▶ **noun** see **PEG** (sense 1).

tent stitch ▶ **noun** [mass noun] a series of parallel diagonal stitches.

tenuity /tɪˈnjuːɪti/ ▶ **noun** [mass noun] lack of solidity or substance; thinness.
– ORIGIN late Middle English: from Latin *tenuitas*, from *tenuis* 'thin'.

tenuous ▶ **adjective** very weak or slight: *the tenuous link between interest rates and investment.*
■ very slender or fine; insubstantial: *a tenuous cloud.*
– DERIVATIVES **tenuously** adverb, **tenuousness** noun.
– ORIGIN late 16th cent.: formed irregularly from Latin *tenuis* 'thin' + **-OUS**.

tenure /ˈtɛnjə/ ▶ **noun** [mass noun] **1** the conditions under which land or buildings are held or occupied.
2 the holding of an office: *his tenure of the premiership would be threatened.*
■ [count noun] a period for which an office is held.
3 (also **security of tenure**) guaranteed permanent employment, especially as a teacher or lecturer, after a probationary period.
▶ **verb** [with obj.] give (someone) a permanent post, especially as a teacher or lecturer: *I had recently been tenured and then promoted to full professor.*
■ [as adj. **tenured**] having or denoting such a post: *a tenured faculty member.*
– PHRASES **security of tenure** **1** the right of a tenant of property to occupy it after the lease expires (unless a court should order otherwise). **2** see sense 3 above.
– ORIGIN late Middle English: from Old French, from *tenir* 'to hold', from Latin *tenere*.

tenure track ▶ **noun** [mass noun] [usu. as modifier] chiefly N. Amer. an employment structure whereby the holder of a post, typically an academic one, is guaranteed consideration for eventual tenure: *a tenure-track position.*

tenurial ▶ **adjective** relating to the tenure of land.
– DERIVATIVES **tenurially** adverb.
– ORIGIN late 19th cent.: from medieval Latin *tenura* 'tenure' + **-AL**.

tenuto /təˈnuːtəʊ/ Music ▶ **adverb** & **adjective** (of a note) held for its full time value or slightly more.
▶ **noun** (pl. **-os** or **tenuti**) a note or chord performed in this way.
– ORIGIN Italian, literally 'held', past participle of *tenere*.

ten-week stock ▶ **noun** a stock of a fast-maturing variety which can be made to bloom ten weeks after sowing, widely grown as a bedding plant.
• *Matthiola incana* var. 'Annua', family Cruciferae.

Tenzing Norgay /ˌtɛnsɪŋ ˈnɔːɡeɪ/ (1914–86), Sherpa mountaineer. In 1953, as members of the British expedition, he and Sir Edmund Hillary were the first to reach the summit of Mount Everest.

tenzon /ˈtiːnz(ə)n/ ▶ **noun** variant spelling of **TENSON**.

teocalli /ˌtiːəˈkali/ ▶ **noun** (pl. **teocallis**) a temple of the Aztecs or other Mexican peoples, typically standing on a truncated pyramid.
– ORIGIN American Spanish, from Nahuatl *teo:kalli*, from *teo:tl* 'god' + *kalli* 'house'.

teosinte /ˌtiːəʊˈsɪnteɪ/ ▶ **noun** [mass noun] a Mexican grass which is grown as fodder and is considered to be one of the parent plants of modern maize.
• *Zea mays* subsp. *mexicana*, family Gramineae.
– ORIGIN late 19th cent.: from French *téosinté*, from Nahuatl *teocintli*, apparently from *teo:tl* 'god' + *cintli* 'dried ear of maize'.

Teotihuacán /teɪˌəʊtɪwəˈkɑːn/ the largest city of pre-Columbian America, situated about 40 km (25 miles) north-east of Mexico City. Built *c.*300 BC, it reached its zenith *c.*300–600 AD, when it was the centre of an influential culture which spread throughout Meso-America. It was sacked by the invading Toltecs c.900.

tepache /tɛˈpatʃeɪ/ ▶ **noun** [mass noun] a Mexican drink, typically made with pineapple, water, and brown sugar and partially fermented.
– ORIGIN Mexican Spanish.

tepal /ˈtɛp(ə)l, ˈtiːp(ə)l/ ▶ **noun** Botany a segment of the outer whorl in a flower that has no differentiation between petals and sepals.
– ORIGIN mid 19th cent.: from French *tépale*, blend of *pétale* 'petal' and *sépal* 'sepal'.

tepary bean /ˈtɛpəri/ ▶ **noun** a bean plant native to the south-western US, cultivated in Mexico and Arizona for its drought-resistant qualities.
● *Phaseolus acutifolius*, family Leguminosae.
– ORIGIN early 20th cent.: of unknown origin.

tepee /ˈtiːpiː/ (also **teepee** or **tipi**) ▶ **noun** a conical tent made of skins, cloth, or canvas on a frame of poles, used by American Indians of the Plains and Great Lakes regions.
– ORIGIN mid 18th cent.: from Sioux *tīpī* 'dwelling'.

tephra /ˈtɛfrə/ ▶ **noun** [mass noun] Geology rock fragments and particles ejected by a volcanic eruption.
– ORIGIN 1940s: from Greek, literally 'ash, ashes'.

tephrochronology /ˌtɛfrə(ʊ)krəˈnɒlədʒi/ ▶ **noun** [mass noun] Geology the dating of volcanic eruptions and other events by studying layers of tephra.
– DERIVATIVES **tephrochronological** adjective.

Tepic /tɛˈpiːk/ a city in western Mexico, capital of the state of Nayarit; pop. 238,100 (1990).

tepid ▶ **adjective** (especially of a liquid) only slightly warm; lukewarm.
■ figurative showing little enthusiasm: *the applause was tepid*.
– DERIVATIVES **tepidity** noun, **tepidly** adverb, **tepidness** noun.
– ORIGIN late Middle English: from Latin *tepidus*, from *tepere* 'be warm'.

tepidarium /ˌtɛpɪˈdɛːrɪəm/ ▶ **noun** (pl. **tepidaria** /-rɪə/) a warm room in an ancient Roman bath.
– ORIGIN Latin.

teppan-yaki /ˌtɛpanˈjɑːki/ ▶ **noun** [mass noun] a Japanese dish of meat, fish, or both, fried with vegetables on a hot steel plate forming the centre of the dining table.
– ORIGIN Japanese, from *teppan* 'steel plate' + *yaki* 'to fry'.

tequila /tɛˈkiːlə/ ▶ **noun** [mass noun] a Mexican liquor made from an agave.
– ORIGIN Mexican Spanish, named after the town of *Tequila* in Mexico, where the drink was first produced.

tequila slammer ▶ **noun** see **SLAMMER** (sense 3).

tequila sunrise ▶ **noun** a cocktail containing tequila, orange juice, and grenadine.

ter- ▶ **combining form** three; having three: *tercentenary*.
– ORIGIN from Latin *ter* 'thrice'.

USAGE **Ter-** is commonly replaced by **tri-**, as in **tricentenary**.

tera- /ˈtɛrə/ ▶ **combining form** used in units of measurement: **1** denoting a factor of 10^{12}: *terawatt*. **2** Computing denoting a factor of 2^{40}.
– ORIGIN from Greek *teras* 'monster'.

terabyte (abbrev.: **Tb** or **TB**) ▶ **noun** Computing a unit of information equal to one million million (10^{12}) or strictly, 2^{40} bytes.

teraflop ▶ **noun** Computing a unit of computing speed equal to one million million floating-point operations per second.

terai /təˈrʌɪ/ (also **terai hat**) ▶ **noun** a wide-brimmed felt hat, typically with a double crown, worn chiefly by travellers in subtropical regions.
– ORIGIN late 19th cent.: from *Terai*, the name of a belt of marshy jungle between the Himalayan foothills and plains, from Hindi *tarāī* 'marshy lowlands'.

teraphim /ˈtɛrəfɪm/ ▶ **plural noun** [also treated as sing.] small images or cult objects used as domestic deities or oracles by ancient Semitic peoples.
– ORIGIN late Middle English: via late Latin from Greek *theraphin*, from Hebrew *tĕrāpîm*.

terato- ▶ **combining form** relating to monsters or abnormal forms: *teratology*.
– ORIGIN from Greek *teras*, *terat-* 'monster'.

teratocarcinoma /ˌtɛratəʊkɑːsɪˈnəʊmə/ ▶ **noun** (pl.

teratocarcinomata or **teratocarcinomas**) Medicine a form of malignant teratoma occurring especially in the testis.

teratogen /tɛˈratədʒ(ə)n, ˈtɛrətədʒ(ə)n/ ▶ **noun** an agent or factor which causes malformation of an embryo.
– DERIVATIVES **teratogenic** adjective, **teratogenicity** noun.

teratogenesis /ˌtɛrətə(ʊ)ˈdʒɛnɪsɪs/ ▶ **noun** [mass noun] the process by which congenital malformations are produced in an embryo or fetus.

teratology /ˌtɛrəˈtɒlədʒi/ ▶ **noun** [mass noun] **1** Medicine & Biology the scientific study of congenital abnormalities and abnormal formations. **2** mythology relating to fantastic creatures and monsters.
– DERIVATIVES **teratological** /-təˈlɒdʒɪk(ə)l/ adjective, **teratologist** noun.

teratoma /ˌtɛrəˈtəʊmə/ ▶ **noun** (pl. **teratomas** or **teratomata** /-mətə/) Medicine a tumour composed of tissues not normally present at the site (the site being typically in the gonads).

terawatt /ˈtɛrəwɒt/ ▶ **noun** a unit of power equal to 10^{12} watts or a million megawatts.

terbium /ˈtəːbɪəm/ ▶ **noun** [mass noun] the chemical element of atomic number 65, a silvery-white metal of the lanthanide series. (Symbol **Tb**)
– ORIGIN mid 19th cent.: modern Latin, from *Ytterby*, the name of a village in Sweden where it was discovered. Compare with **ERBIUM** and **YTTERBIUM**.

terbutaline /təːˈbjuːtəliːn/ ▶ **noun** [mass noun] Medicine a synthetic compound with bronchodilator properties, used especially in the treatment of asthma.
● Chem. formula: $C_{12}H_{19}NO_3$.
– ORIGIN 1960s: from **TER-** + **BUTYL** (elements of the systematic name), on the pattern of words such as *isoprenaline*.

terce /təːs/ ▶ **noun** a service forming part of the Divine Office of the Western Christian Church, traditionally said (or chanted) at the third hour of the day (i.e. 9 a.m.).
– ORIGIN late Middle English: from Old French, from Latin *tertia*, feminine of *tertius* 'third'. Compare with **TIERCE**.

tercel /ˈtəːs(ə)l/ (also **tiercel**) ▶ **noun** Falconry the male of a hawk, especially a peregrine or a goshawk. Compare with **FALCON**.
– ORIGIN Middle English: from Old French, based on Latin *tertius* 'third', perhaps from the belief that the third egg of a clutch produced a male.

tercentenary ▶ **noun** (pl. **-ies**) the three-hundredth anniversary of a significant event.
▶ **adjective** of or relating to a three-hundredth anniversary: *his tercentenary year*.

tercentennial ▶ **adjective** & **noun** another term for **TERCENTENARY**.

tercet /ˈtəːsɪt/ ▶ **noun** Prosody a set or group of three lines of verse rhyming together or connected by rhyme with an adjacent triplet.
– ORIGIN late 16th cent.: from French, from Italian *terzetto*, diminutive of *terzo* 'third', from Latin *tertius*.

terebinth /ˈtɛrəbɪnθ/ ▶ **noun** a small southern European tree which was formerly a source of turpentine and galls for tanning.
● *Pistacia terebinthus*, family Anacardiaceae.
– ORIGIN late Middle English: from Old French *therebinte*, or via Latin from Greek *terebinthos*.

terebratulid /ˌtɛrɪˈbratjʊlɪd/ ▶ **noun** Zoology a brachiopod of a mainly fossil order that originated in the Devonian, having a short pedicle and a calcareous loop supporting the tentacles.
● Order Terebratulida, class Articulata: many families.
– ORIGIN 1970s: from modern Latin *Terebratulida*, based on Latin *terebrare* 'to bore'.

teredo /təˈriːdəʊ/ ▶ **noun** Zoology (pl. **-os**) a worm-like bivalve mollusc with reduced shells which it uses to drill into wood. It can cause substantial damage to wooden structures and (formerly) ships. Also called **SHIPWORM**.
● Genus *Teredo*, family Teredinidae: several species, in particular *T. navalis*.
– ORIGIN late Middle English: via Latin from Greek *terēdōn*; related to *teirein* 'rub hard, wear away'.

Terence (c.190–159 BC), Roman comic dramatist; Latin name *Publius Terentius Afer*. His six surviving comedies are based on the Greek New Comedy;

they are marked by more realism and a greater consistency of plot than the works of Plautus.

Terengganu /ˌtɛrɛŋˈɡɑːnuː/ variant of **TRENGGANU**.

terephthalic acid /ˌtɛrɛfˈθalɪk/ ▶ **noun** [mass noun] Chemistry a crystalline organic acid used in making polyester resins and other polymers.
● The *para*-isomer of phthalic acid; chem. formula: $C_6H_4(COOH)_2$.
– DERIVATIVES **terephthalate** noun.
– ORIGIN mid 19th cent.: blend of *terebic* 'of or from turpentine' (from **TEREBINTH**) and **PHTHALIC ACID**.

teres /ˈtɛriːz/ ▶ **noun** Anatomy either of two muscles passing below the shoulder joint from the scapula to the upper part of the humerus, one (**teres major**) drawing the arm towards the body and rotating it inwards, the other (**teres minor**) rotating it outwards.
– ORIGIN early 18th cent.: modern Latin, from Latin, literally 'rounded'.

Teresa, Mother /təˈreɪzə, -ˈriːzə/ (also **Theresa**) (1910–97), Roman Catholic nun and missionary; born *Agnes Gonxha Bojaxhiu* in what is now Macedonia of Albanian parentage. She became an Indian citizen in 1948. She founded the Order of Missionaries of Charity, which became noted for its work among the poor in Calcutta and now operates in many parts of the world. Nobel Peace Prize (1979).

Teresa of Ávila, St /ˈavɪlə/ (1515–82), Spanish Carmelite nun and mystic. She instituted the 'discalced' reform movement with St John of the Cross. Her writings include *The Way of Perfection* (1583) and *The Interior Castle* (1588). Feast day, 15 October.

Teresa of Lisieux, St /liːˈzjəː/ (also **Thérèse**) (1873–97), French Carmelite nun; born *Marie-Françoise Thérèse Martin*. In her autobiography *L'Histoire d'une âme* (1898) she taught that sanctity can be attained through continual renunciation in small matters, and not only through extreme self-mortification. Feast day, 3 October.

Tereshkova /ˌtɛrɪʃˈkəʊvə/, Valentina (Vladimirovna) (b.1937), Russian cosmonaut. In June 1963 she became the first woman in space.

Teresina /ˌtɛrɛˈziːnə/ a river port in NE Brazil, on the Parnaíba river, capital of the state of Piauí; pop. 591,160 (1990).

terete /təˈriːt/ ▶ **adjective** chiefly Botany cylindrical or slightly tapering, and without substantial furrows or ridges.
– ORIGIN early 17th cent.: from Latin *teres*, *teret-* 'rounded off'.

tergal /ˈtəːɡ(ə)l/ ▶ **adjective** Zoology of or relating to a tergum of an arthropod.
– ORIGIN mid 19th cent.: from Latin *tergum* 'back' + **-AL**.

tergite /ˈtəːɡʌɪt/ ▶ **noun** Entomology (in an insect) a sclerotized plate forming the tergum of a segment. Compare with **STERNITE**.
– ORIGIN late 19th cent.: from **TERGUM** + **-ITE**[1].

tergiversate /ˈtəːdʒɪvəˌseɪt, -ˈvəːseɪt/ ▶ **verb** [no obj.] **1** make conflicting or evasive statements; equivocate: *the more she tergiversated, the greater grew the ardency of the reporters for an interview*. **2** change one's loyalties; be apostate.
– DERIVATIVES **tergiversation** noun, **tergiversator** noun.
– ORIGIN mid 17th cent.: from Latin *tergiversat-* 'with one's back turned', from the verb *tergiversari*, from *tergum* 'back' + *vertere* 'to turn'.

tergum /ˈtəːɡəm/ ▶ **noun** (pl. **terga**) Zoology a thickened dorsal plate on each segment of the body of an arthropod.
– ORIGIN early 19th cent.: from Latin, literally 'back'.

-teria ▶ **suffix** denoting self-service establishments: *washeteria*.
– ORIGIN on the pattern of (*cafe*)*teria*.

teriyaki /ˌtɛrɪˈjɑːki/ ▶ **noun** [mass noun] a Japanese dish consisting of fish or meat marinated in soy sauce and grilled.
■ (also **teriyaki sauce**) a mixture of soy sauce, sake, ginger, and other flavourings, used in Japanese cookery as a marinade or glaze for such dishes.
– ORIGIN Japanese.

term ▶ **noun** **1** a word or phrase used to describe a thing or to express a concept, especially in a

particular kind of language or branch of study: *the musical term 'leitmotiv' | a term of abuse.*
■ (**terms**) language used on a particular occasion; a way of expressing oneself: *a protest in the strongest possible terms.* ■ Logic a word or words that may be the subject or predicate of a proposition.
2 a fixed or limited period for which something, for example office, imprisonment, or investment, lasts or is intended to last: *the President is elected for a single four-year term.*
■ archaic the duration of a person's life. ■ (also **term day**) (especially in Scotland) a fixed day of the year appointed for the making of payments, the start or end of tenancies, etc. ■ (also **full term**) [mass noun] the completion of a normal length of pregnancy: *the pregnancy **went to full term** | low birthweight **at term**.* ■ (Brit. also **term of years** or US **term for years**) Law a tenancy of a fixed period. ■ archaic a boundary or limit, especially of time.
3 each of the periods in the year, alternating with holiday or vacation, during which instruction is given in a school, college, or university, or during which a law court holds sessions: *the summer term | term starts tomorrow.*
■ informal the season during which a sport is played: *Wright already has six goals this term.*
4 (**terms**) conditions under which an action may be undertaken or agreement reached; stipulated or agreed requirements: *their solicitors had agreed terms | he could only be dealt with **on his own terms**.*
■ conditions with regard to payment for something; stated charges: *loans on favourable terms.* ■ agreed conditions under which a war or other dispute is brought to an end: *a deal in Bosnia that could force the Serbs to **come to terms**.*
5 Mathematics each of the quantities in a ratio, series, or mathematical expression.
6 Architecture another term for **TERMINUS**.
▶ **verb** [with obj. and usu. with complement] give a descriptive name to; call by a specified term: *he has been termed the father of modern theology.*
– PHRASES **come to terms with** come to accept (a new and painful or difficult event or situation); reconcile oneself to: *she had come to terms with the tragedies in her life.* **in terms of** (or **in —— terms**) with regard to the particular aspect or subject specified: *replacing the printers is difficult to justify in terms of cost | sales are down by nearly 7 per cent in **real terms**.* **the long/short/medium term** used to refer to a time that is a specified way into the future. **on terms** in a state of friendship or equality. ■ (in sport) level in score or on points. **on —— terms** in a specified relation or on a specified footing: *we are all on friendly terms.* **terms of reference** Brit. the range or scope established for an inquiry or discussion.
– ORIGIN Middle English (denoting a limit in space or time, or (in the plural) limiting conditions): from Old French *terme*, from Latin *terminus* 'end, boundary, limit'.

termagant /ˈtəːməg(ə)nt/ ▶ **noun 1** a harsh-tempered or overbearing woman.
2 (**Termagant**) historical an imaginary deity of violent and turbulent character, often appearing in morality plays.
– ORIGIN Middle English (in sense 2): via Old French from Italian *Trivigante*, taken to be from Latin *tri-* 'three' + *vagant-* 'wandering', and to refer to the moon 'wandering' between heaven, earth, and hell under the three names *Selene, Artemis*, and *Persephone*.

term for years ▶ **noun** see **TERM** (sense 2).

terminable ▶ **adjective 1** able to be terminated.
2 coming to an end after a certain time.

terminal ▶ **adjective 1** [attrib.] of, forming, or situated at the end or extremity of something: *a terminal date | the terminal tip of the probe.*
■ of or forming a transport terminal: *terminal platforms.* ■ Zoology situated at, forming, or denoting the end of a part or series of parts furthest from the centre of the body. ■ Botany (of a flower, inflorescence, etc.) borne at the end of a stem or branch. Often contrasted with **AXILLARY**.
2 (of a disease) predicted to lead to death, especially slowly; incurable: *terminal cancer.*
■ [attrib.] suffering from or relating to such a disease: *a hospice for terminal cases.* ■ [attrib.] (of a condition) forming the last stage of such a disease. ■ informal extreme and usually beyond cure or alteration (used to emphasize the extent of something regarded as bad or unfortunate): *you're making a terminal ass of yourself.*
3 done or occurring each school, college, university, or law term: *terminal examinations.*
▶ **noun 1** an end or extremity of something, in particular:
■ the end of a railway or other transport route, or a station at such a point. ■ a departure and arrival building for air passengers at an airport. ■ an installation where oil or gas is stored at the end of a pipeline or at a port.
2 a point of connection for closing an electric circuit.
3 a device at which a user enters data or commands for a computer system and which displays the received output.
4 (also **terminal figure**) another term for **TERMINUS** (in sense 3).
5 Brit. a patient suffering from a terminal illness.
– DERIVATIVES **terminally** adverb [as submodifier] *a terminally ill woman.*
– ORIGIN early 19th cent.: from Latin *terminalis*, from *terminus* 'end, boundary'.

terminal moraine ▶ **noun** Geology a moraine deposited at the point of furthest advance of a glacier or ice sheet.

terminal velocity ▶ **noun** Physics the constant speed that a freely falling object eventually reaches when the resistance of the medium through which it is falling prevents further acceleration.

terminate ▶ **verb** [with obj.] bring to an end: *he was advised to terminate the contract.*
■ [no obj.] (**terminate in**) (of a thing) have its end at (a specified place) or of (a specified form): *the chain terminated in an iron ball covered with spikes.* ■ [no obj.] (of a train, bus, or boat service) end its journey: *the train will terminate at Stratford.* ■ end (a pregnancy) before term by artificial means. ■ chiefly N. Amer. end the employment of (someone); dismiss: *Adamson's putting pressure on me to terminate you.* ■ chiefly N. Amer. assassinate (someone, especially an intelligence agent): *he was terminated by persons unknown.* ■ archaic form the physical end or extremity of (an area).
– PHRASES **terminate someone with extreme prejudice** chiefly US murder or assassinate someone (used as a euphemism).
– ORIGIN late 16th cent. (in the sense 'direct an action towards a specified end'): from Latin *terminat-* 'limited, ended', from the verb *terminare*, from *terminus* 'end, boundary'.

termination ▶ **noun 1** [mass noun] the action of bringing something or coming to an end: *the termination of a contract.*
■ [count noun] chiefly N. Amer. an act of dismissing someone from employment. ■ [count noun] an induced abortion. ■ [count noun] chiefly N. Amer. an assassination, especially of an intelligence agent.
2 an ending or final point of something, in particular:
■ a word's final syllable or letters or letter, especially when constituting an element in inflection or derivation. ■ [with adj.] archaic an ending or result of a specified kind: *a good result and a happy termination.*
– DERIVATIVES **terminational** adjective.
– ORIGIN late Middle English (in the sense 'determination, decision'): from Old French, or from Latin *terminatio(n-)*, from *terminare* 'to limit, end'.

terminator ▶ **noun 1** a person or thing that terminates something.
■ Astronomy the dividing line between the light and dark part of a planetary body. ■ Biochemistry a sequence of polynucleotides that causes transcription to end and the newly synthesized nucleic acid to be released from the template molecule.

terminer ▶ **noun** see **OYER AND TERMINER**.

termini plural form of **TERMINUS**.

terminological inexactitude ▶ **noun** a lie (used as a humorous euphemism).
– ORIGIN first used by Winston Churchill in a Commons speech in 1906.

terminology ▶ **noun** (pl. **-ies**) [mass noun] the body of terms used with a particular technical application in a subject of study, theory, profession, etc.: *the terminology of semiotics* | [count noun] *specialized terminologies for higher education.*
– DERIVATIVES **terminological** adjective, **terminologically** adverb, **terminologist** noun.
– ORIGIN early 19th cent.: from German *Terminologie*, from medieval Latin *terminus* 'term'.

terminus ▶ **noun** (pl. **termini** or **terminuses**) **1** chiefly Brit. the end of a railway or other transport route, or a station at such a point; a terminal.
■ an oil or gas terminal.
2 a final point in space or time; an end or extremity: *the exhibition's terminus is 1962.*
■ Biochemistry the end of a polypeptide or polynucleotide chain or similar long molecule.
3 Architecture a figure of a human bust or an animal ending in a square pillar from which it appears to spring, originally used as a boundary marker in ancient Rome.
– ORIGIN mid 16th cent. (in the sense 'final point in space or time'): from Latin, 'end, limit, boundary'.

terminus ad quem /ˌtəːmɪnəs ad ˈkwɛm/ ▶ **noun** the point at which something ends or finishes.
■ an aim or goal.
– ORIGIN Latin, literally 'end to which'.

terminus ante quem /ˌantɪ ˈkwɛm/ ▶ **noun** the latest possible date for something.
– ORIGIN Latin, literally 'end before which'.

terminus a quo /ɑː ˈkwəʊ/ ▶ **noun** the earliest possible date for something.
■ a starting point or initial impulse.
– ORIGIN Latin, literally 'end from which'.

terminus post quem /pəʊst ˈkwɛm/ ▶ **noun** the earliest possible date for something.
– ORIGIN Latin, literally 'end after which'.

termitarium /ˌtəːmʌɪˈtɛːrɪəm/ ▶ **noun** (pl. **termitaria**) a colony of termites, typically within a mound of cemented earth.
■ a man-made structure or environment that resembles such a colony in some way, such as a tower block.
– ORIGIN mid 19th cent.: modern Latin, from Latin *termes, termit-* 'termite'.

termitary /ˈtəːmɪtəri/ ▶ **noun** (pl. **-ies**) another term for **TERMITARIUM**.

termite /ˈtəːmʌɪt/ ▶ **noun** a small, pale soft-bodied insect that lives in large colonies with several different castes, typically within a mound of cemented earth. Many kinds feed on wood and can be highly destructive to trees and timber. Also called **WHITE ANT**.
● Order Isoptera: several families.
– ORIGIN late 18th cent.: from late Latin *termes, termit-* 'woodworm', alteration of Latin *tarmes*, perhaps by association with *terere* 'to rub'.

termly ▶ **adjective** & **adverb** happening or done once in each school, college, university, or law term: [as adj.] *termly examinations* | [as adv.] *the committee meets termly.*

term of years ▶ **noun** see **TERM** (sense 2).

term paper ▶ **noun** N. Amer. a student's lengthy essay on a subject drawn from the work done during a school or college term.

terms of trade ▶ **plural noun** Economics the ratio of an index of a country's export prices to an index of its import prices.

tern[1] /təːn/ ▶ **noun** a seabird related to the gulls, typically smaller and more slender, with long pointed wings and a forked tail.
● Family Sternidae (or Laridae): several genera, in particular *Sterna*, and many species.
– ORIGIN late 17th cent.: of Scandinavian origin; related to Danish *terne* and Swedish *tärna*, both from Old Norse *therna*.

tern[2] /təːn/ ▶ **noun** rare a set of three, especially three lottery numbers that when drawn together win a large prize.
– ORIGIN late Middle English: apparently from French *terne*, from Latin *terni* 'three at once, three each', from *ter* 'thrice'.

ternary /ˈtəːnəri/ ▶ **adjective** composed of three parts.
■ Mathematics using three as a base.
– ORIGIN late Middle English: from Latin *ternarius*, from *terni* 'three at once'.

ternary form ▶ **noun** [mass noun] Music the form of a movement in which the first subject is repeated after an interposed second subject in a related key.

terne /təːn/ ▶ **noun** [mass noun] (also **terne metal**) a lead alloy containing about 20 per cent tin and often some antimony.
■ (also **terne plate**) thin sheet iron or steel coated with this.
– ORIGIN mid 19th cent. (denoting terne plate): probably from French *terne* 'dull, tarnished'.

ternlet ▶ **noun** Austral., NZ, & Indian a small tern.
● Family Sternidae (or Laridae): several species, in particular the **grey ternlet** (*Procelsterna cerulea*) (alternative name: **blue-grey noddy**).

t

terotechnology /ˌterə(ʊ)tekˈnɒlədʒi, ˌtɪərə(ʊ)-/ ▶ noun [mass noun] Brit. the branch of technology and engineering concerned with the installation and maintenance of equipment.
– DERIVATIVES **terotechnological** adjective, **terotechnologist** noun.
– ORIGIN 1970s: from Greek *tērein* 'take care of' + **TECHNOLOGY**.

terpene /ˈtəːpiːn/ ▶ noun Chemistry any of a large group of volatile unsaturated hydrocarbons found in the essential oils of plants, especially conifers and citrus trees. They are based on a cyclic molecule having the formula $C_{10}H_{16}$.
– ORIGIN late 19th cent.: from German *Terpentin* 'turpentine' + **-ENE**.

terpenoid /ˈtəːpɪnɔɪd/ Chemistry ▶ noun any of a large class of organic compounds including terpenes, diterpenes, and sesquiterpenes. They have unsaturated molecules composed of linked isoprene units, generally having the formula $(C_5H_8)_n$.
▶ adjective denoting such a compound.

terpolymer /təːˈpɒlɪmə/ ▶ noun Chemistry a polymer synthesized from three different monomers.

Terpsichore /təːpˈsɪkəri/ Greek & Roman Mythology the Muse of lyric poetry and dance.
– ORIGIN Greek, literally 'delighting in dancing'.

terpsichorean /ˌtəːpsɪkəˈriːən/ formal or humorous ▶ adjective of or relating to dancing.
▶ noun a dancer.
– ORIGIN early 19th cent.: from *Terpsichore* (used in the 18th cent. to denote a female dancer or the art of dance) + **-AN**.

terra /ˈterə/ ▶ noun [mass noun] [usu. with modifier] land or territory.
– ORIGIN Latin, literally 'earth'.

terra alba /ˈalbə/ ▶ noun [mass noun] pulverized gypsum, especially as an ingredient of medicines.
– ORIGIN Latin, literally 'white earth'.

terrace ▶ noun 1 a level paved area next to a building; a patio.
■ each of a series of flat areas made on a slope, used for cultivation. ■ (usu. **terraces**) Brit. a flight of wide, shallow steps providing standing room for spectators in a stadium, especially a soccer ground. ■ Geology a natural horizontal shelf-like formation, such as a raised beach.
2 chiefly Brit. a row of houses built in one block in a uniform style.
■ a terraced house.
▶ verb [with obj.] make or form (sloping land) into a number of level flat areas resembling a series of steps.
– ORIGIN early 16th cent. (denoting an open gallery, later a platform or balcony in a theatre): from Old French, literally 'rubble, platform', based on Latin *terra* 'earth'.

terraced ▶ adjective 1 (of a house) forming part of a row of houses built in a block in a uniform style.
2 (of land) having been formed into a number of level areas resembling a series of steps.

terraced roof ▶ noun a flat roof, especially the roof of an Indian or Eastern house that is used as a cool resting area.

terracing ▶ noun [mass noun] 1 the action of making a series of flat areas on a slope for cultivation.
■ terraced ground.
2 wide, shallow steps used to provide standing room for spectators in a stadium.

terracotta /ˌterəˈkɒtə/ ▶ noun [mass noun] unglazed, typically brownish-red earthenware, used chiefly as an ornamental building material and in modelling.
■ [count noun] a statuette or other object made of such earthenware. ■ a strong brownish-red or brownish-orange colour.
– ORIGIN early 18th cent.: from Italian *terra cotta* 'baked earth', from Latin *terra cocta*.

terra firma /ˈfəːmə/ ▶ noun [mass noun] dry land; the ground as distinct from the sea or air.
– ORIGIN early 17th cent. (denoting the territories on the Italian mainland which were subject to the state of Venice): from Latin, literally 'firm land'.

terraform ▶ verb [with obj.] (especially in science fiction) transform (a planet) so as to resemble the earth, especially so that it can support human life.
– DERIVATIVES **terraformer** noun.
– ORIGIN 1940s: from Latin *terra* 'earth' + the verb **FORM**.

terrain /tɛˈreɪn/ ▶ noun [mass noun] a stretch of land,

especially with regard to its physical features: *they were delayed by rough terrain*.
– ORIGIN early 18th cent. (denoting part of the training ground in a riding school): from French, from a popular Latin variant of Latin *terrenum*, neuter of *terrenus* (see **TERRENE**).

terra incognita /ɪnˈkɒɡnɪtə, ˌɪnkɒɡˈniːtə/ ▶ noun [mass noun] unknown or unexplored territory.
– ORIGIN Latin, 'unknown land'.

terramare /ˌterəˈmɑːri, -ˈmɛːri/ ▶ noun [mass noun] an ammoniacal earthy deposit found in mounds in prehistoric lake dwellings or settlements, especially in Italy.
■ a dwelling or settlement of this type.
– ORIGIN mid 19th cent.: from French, from Italian dialect *terramara*, from Italian *terra* 'earth' + *marna* 'marl'.

Terramycin /ˌterəˈmʌɪsɪn/ ▶ noun trademark for **OXYTETRACYCLINE**.
– ORIGIN 1950s: from Latin *terra* 'earth' + **-MYCIN**.

terrane /tɛˈreɪn/ ▶ noun Geology a fault-bounded area or region with a distinctive stratigraphy, structure, and geological history.
– ORIGIN early 19th cent: from popular Latin *terranum*. Compare with **TERRAIN**.

terrapin ▶ noun 1 a freshwater turtle, especially one of the smaller kinds of the Old World. Called **TURTLE** in North America.
● Emydidae and other families, order Chelonia: several genera and species, in particular the **European pond terrapin**.
2 (also **diamondback terrapin**) US a small edible turtle with lozenge-shaped markings on its shell, found in coastal marshes of the eastern US.
● *Malaclemys terrapin*, family Emydidae.
3 (**Terrapin**) Brit. trademark a type of prefabricated one-storey building for temporary use.
– ORIGIN early 17th cent. (denoting the diamondback terrapin): of Algonquian origin.

terraqueous /tɛˈreɪkwɪəs/ ▶ adjective consisting of, or formed of, land and water.
– ORIGIN mid 17th cent.: from Latin *terra* 'land' + **AQUEOUS**.

terrarium /tɛˈrɛːrɪəm/ ▶ noun (pl. **terrariums** or **terraria** /-rɪə/) a vivarium for smaller land animals, especially reptiles, amphibians, or terrestrial invertebrates, typically in the form of a glass-fronted case.
■ a sealed transparent globe or similar container in which plants are grown.
– ORIGIN late 19th cent.: modern Latin, from Latin *terra* 'earth', on the pattern of *aquarium*.

terra rossa /ˈrɒsə/ ▶ noun [mass noun] a reddish soil occurring on limestone in Mediterranean climates.
– ORIGIN late 19th cent.: Italian, literally 'red earth'.

terra sigillata /ˌsɪdʒɪˈleɪtə/ ▶ noun [mass noun]
1 astringent clay from Lemnos or Samos, formerly used as a medicine.
2 another term for **SAMIAN WARE**.
– ORIGIN late Middle English: from medieval Latin, literally 'sealed earth'.

Terrassa variant spelling of **TARRASA**.

terrasse /tɛras/ ▶ noun (pl. pronounced same) (in France) a flat, paved area outside a cafe where people sit to take refreshments.
– ORIGIN French, literally 'terrace'.

terrazzo /tɛˈratsəʊ/ ▶ noun [mass noun] flooring material consisting of chips of marble or granite set in concrete and polished to give a smooth surface.
– ORIGIN early 20th cent.: Italian, literally 'terrace', based on Latin *terra* 'earth'.

Terre Haute /ˌterə ˈhəʊt/ a city in western Indiana, on the Wabash River, near the border with Illinois; pop. 57,480 (1990).

terrene /tɛˈriːn/ ▶ adjective archaic of or like earth; earthy.
■ occurring on or inhabiting dry land. ■ of the world; secular rather than spiritual.
– ORIGIN Middle English: from Anglo-Norman French, from Latin *terrenus*, from *terra* 'earth'.

terreplein /ˈtɛːpleɪn/ ▶ noun chiefly historical a level space where a battery of guns is mounted.
– ORIGIN late 16th cent. (denoting a sloping bank behind a rampart): from French *terre-plein*, from Italian *terrapieno*, from *terrapienare* 'fill with earth'.

terrestrial /təˈrɛstrɪəl/ ▶ adjective 1 of, on, or relating to the earth: *increased ultraviolet radiation may disrupt terrestrial ecosystems*.

■ denoting television broadcast using equipment situated on the ground rather than by satellite: *a fifth terrestrial channel*. ■ of or on dry land: *a submarine eruption will be much more explosive than its terrestrial counterpart*. ■ (of an animal) living on or in the ground; not aquatic, arboreal, or aerial. ■ (of a plant) growing on land or in the soil; not aquatic or epiphytic. ■ Astronomy (of a planet) similar in size or composition to the earth, especially being one of the four inner planets. ■ archaic of or relating to the earth as opposed to heaven.
▶ noun an inhabitant of the earth.
– DERIVATIVES **terrestrially** adverb.
– ORIGIN late Middle English (in the sense 'temporal, worldly, mundane'): from Latin *terrestris* (from *terra* 'earth') + **-AL**.

terrestrial globe ▶ noun a spherical representation of the earth with a map on the surface.

terrestrial magnetism ▶ noun [mass noun] the magnetic properties of the earth as a whole.

terrestrial telescope ▶ noun a telescope used for observing terrestrial objects, which gives an uninverted image.

terret /ˈtɛrɪt/ ▶ noun each of the loops or rings on a horse's harness pad for the driving reins to pass through.
– ORIGIN late 15th cent. (denoting either of two rings by which a leash is attached to a hawk's jesses): from Old French *touret*, diminutive of *tour* 'a turn'.

terre verte /tɛː ˈvɛːt/ ▶ noun [mass noun] a greyish-green pigment made from a kind of clay (glauconite) and used especially for watercolours and tempera. Also called **GREEN EARTH**.
– ORIGIN mid 17th cent.: French, literally 'green earth'.

terribilità /ˌtɛrɪbɪlɪˈtaː/ ▶ noun [mass noun] awesomeness or emotional intensity of conception and execution in an artist or work of art, originally as a quality attributed to Michelangelo by his contemporaries.
– ORIGIN Italian.

terrible ▶ adjective extremely and shockingly or distressingly bad or serious: *a terrible crime | terrible pain*.
■ causing or likely to cause terror; sinister: *the stranger gave a terrible smile*. ■ of extremely poor quality: *the terrible conditions in which the ordinary people lived*. ■ [attrib.] informal used to emphasize the extent of something unpleasant or bad: *what a terrible mess*. ■ extremely incompetent or unskilful: *she is terrible at managing her money*. ■ [as complement] feeling or looking extremely unwell: *I was sick all night and felt terrible for two days*. ■ [as complement] (of a person or their feelings) troubled or guilty: *Maria felt terrible because she had forgotten the woman's name*.
– DERIVATIVES **terribleness** noun.
– ORIGIN late Middle English (in the sense 'causing terror'): via French from Latin *terribilis*, from *terrere* 'frighten'.

terribly ▶ adverb 1 [usu. as submodifier] very; extremely: *I'm terribly sorry | it was all terribly frustrating*.
2 very badly or unpleasantly: *they beat me terribly*.
■ very greatly (used to emphasize something bad, distressing, or unpleasant): *your father misses you terribly*.

terricolous /tɛˈrɪkələs/ ▶ adjective Zoology (of an animal such as an earthworm) living on the ground or in the soil.
■ Botany (of a plant, especially a lichen) growing on soil or on the ground.
– ORIGIN mid 19th cent.: from Latin *terricola* 'earth-dweller' (from *terra* 'earth' + *colere* 'inhabit') + **-OUS**.

terrier[1] /ˈtɛrɪə/ ▶ noun 1 a small dog of a breed originally used for turning out foxes and other burrowing animals from their earths.
■ used in similes to emphasize tenacity or eagerness: *she would fight like a terrier for every penny*.
2 (**Terrier**) Brit. informal a member of the Territorial Army.
– ORIGIN late Middle English: from Old French (*chien*) *terrier* 'earth (dog)', from medieval Latin *terrarius*, from Latin *terra* 'earth'.

terrier[2] /ˈtɛrɪə/ ▶ noun historical a register of the lands belonging to a landowner, originally including a list of tenants, their holdings, and the rents paid, later consisting of a description of the acreage and boundaries of the property.
■ an inventory of property or goods.
– ORIGIN late 15th cent.: from Old French *terrier*,

from medieval Latin *terrarius (liber)* '(book) of land', from Latin *terra* 'earth'.

terrific ▶ **adjective 1** of great size, amount, or intensity: *there was a terrific bang.*
■ informal extremely good; excellent: *it's been such a terrific day | you look terrific.*
2 archaic causing terror.
– DERIVATIVES **terrifically** adverb [as submodifier] *she's been terrifically busy lately.*
– ORIGIN mid 17th cent. (in sense 2): from Latin *terrificus*, from *terrere* 'frighten'.

terrify ▶ **verb** (**-ies**, **-ied**) [with obj.] cause to feel extreme fear: *he is* ***terrified of*** *spiders* | [with obj. and clause] *she was terrified he would drop her* | [as adj. **terrifying**] *the terrifying events of the past few weeks.*
– DERIVATIVES **terrifier** noun, **terrifyingly** adverb [as submodifier] *the bombs are terrifyingly accurate.*
– ORIGIN late 16th cent.: from Latin *terrificare*, from *terrificus* 'frightening' (see **TERRIFIC**).

terrigenous /tɛˈrɪdʒɪnəs/ ▶ **adjective** Geology (of a marine deposit) made of material eroded from the land.
– ORIGIN late 17th cent. (in the sense 'produced from the earth, earth-born'): from Latin *terrigenus* (from *terra* 'earth' + *-genus* 'born') + **-OUS**.

terrine /təˈriːn/ ▶ **noun** a meat, fish, or vegetable mixture that has been cooked or otherwise prepared in advance and allowed to cool or set in its container, typically served in slices.
■ a container used for such a dish, typically of an oblong shape and made of earthenware.
– ORIGIN early 18th cent. (denoting a tureen): from French, literally 'large earthenware pot', from *terrin* 'earthen'. Compare with **TUREEN**.

territorial ▶ **adjective 1** of or relating to the ownership of an area of land or sea: *territorial disputes.*
■ Zoology (of an animal or species) defending a territory: *these sharks are aggressively territorial.* ■ of or relating to an animal's territory: *territorial growls.*
2 of or relating to a particular territory, district, or locality: *a bizarre territorial rite.*
■ (usu. **Territorial**) of or relating to a Territory, especially in the US or Canada.
▶ **noun** (**Territorial**) (in the UK) a member of the Territorial Army.
– DERIVATIVES **territoriality** noun, **territorially** adverb.
– ORIGIN early 17th cent.: from late Latin *territorialis*, from Latin *territorium* (see **TERRITORY**).

Territorial Army (in the UK) a volunteer force locally organized to provide a reserve of trained and disciplined manpower for use in an emergency.

territorial imperative ▶ **noun** [usu. in sing.] Zoology & Psychology the need to claim and defend a territory.

territorial waters ▶ **plural noun** the waters under the jurisdiction of a state, especially the part of the sea within a stated distance of the shore (traditionally three miles from low-water mark).

territory ▶ **noun** (pl. **-ies**) **1** an area of land under the jurisdiction of a ruler or state: *the government was prepared to give up the nuclear weapons on its territory* | [mass noun] *sorties into enemy territory.*
■ Zoology an area defended by an animal or group of animals against others of the same sex or species. Compare with **HOME RANGE**. ■ an area defended by a team or player in a game or sport. ■ an area in which one has certain rights or for which one has responsibility with regard to a particular type of activity: *don't go committing murders on my territory.* ■ [mass noun] figurative an area of knowledge, activity, or experience: *the contentious territory of clinical standards* | *the way she felt now—she was in unknown territory.* ■ [mass noun] [with adj. or noun modifier] land with a specified characteristic: *woodland territory.*
2 (**Territory**) (especially in the US, Canada, or Australia) an organized division of a country that is not yet admitted to the full rights of a state.
– PHRASES **go** (or **come**) **with the territory** be an unavoidable result of a particular situation.
– ORIGIN late Middle English: from Latin *territorium*, from *terra* 'land'. The word originally denoted the district surrounding and under the jurisdiction of a town or city, specifically a Roman or provincial city.

terror ▶ **noun 1** [mass noun] extreme fear: *people fled in* ***terror*** | [in sing.] *a terror of darkness.*
■ the use of such fear to intimidate people, especially for political reasons: *weapons of terror.* ■ [in sing.] a person or thing that causes extreme fear: *his delivery is* ***the terror of*** *even world-class batsmen.* ■ (**the Terror**) the period of the French Revolution between mid 1793 and July 1794 when the ruling Jacobin faction, dominated by Robespierre, ruthlessly executed anyone considered a threat to their regime. Also called **REIGN OF TERROR**.
2 (also **holy terror**) informal a person, especially a child, that causes trouble or annoyance.
– PHRASES **have** (or **hold**) **no terrors for someone** not frighten or worry someone.
– ORIGIN late Middle English: from Old French *terrour*, from Latin *terror*, from *terrere* 'frighten'.

terrorism ▶ **noun** [mass noun] the use of violence and intimidation in the pursuit of political aims.

terrorist ▶ **noun** a person who uses terrorism in the pursuit of political aims.
– DERIVATIVES **terroristic** adjective, **terroristically** adverb.
– ORIGIN late 18th cent.: from French *terroriste*, from Latin *terror* (see **TERROR**). The word was originally applied to supporters of the Jacobins in the French Revolution, who advocated repression and violence in pursuit of the principles of democracy and equality.

terrorize (also **-ise**) ▶ **verb** [with obj.] create and maintain a state of extreme fear and distress in (someone); fill with terror: *he used his private army to terrorize the population* | *the union said staff would not be* ***terrorized into*** *ending their strike.*
– DERIVATIVES **terrorization** noun, **terrorizer** noun.

terror-stricken (also **terror-struck**) ▶ **adjective** feeling or expressing extreme fear.

Terry, Dame (Alice) Ellen (1847–1928), English actress. She played in many of Henry Irving's Shakespearean productions and George Bernard Shaw created a number of roles for her.

terry ▶ **noun** (pl. **-ies**) [mass noun] a fabric with raised uncut loops of thread covering both surfaces, used especially for towels.
– ORIGIN late 18th cent.: of unknown origin.

terse ▶ **adjective** (**terser**, **tersest**) sparing in the use of words; abrupt: *a terse statement.*
– DERIVATIVES **tersely** adverb, **terseness** noun.
– ORIGIN early 17th cent.: from Latin *tersus* 'wiped, polished', from the verb *tergere*. The original sense was 'polished, trim, spruce', (relating to language) 'polished, polite', hence 'concise and to the point' (late 18th cent.).

tertian /ˈtəːʃ(ə)n/ ▶ **adjective** [attrib.] Medicine denoting a form of malaria causing a fever that recurs every second day: *tertian fever.*
• The common benign tertian malaria (or tertian ague) is caused by infection with *Plasmodium vivax* or *P. ovale*, and malignant tertian malaria is caused by *P. falciparum*. Compare with **QUARTAN**.
– ORIGIN late Middle English (*fever*) *terciane*, from Latin (*febris*) *tertiana*, from *tertius* 'third' (the fever recurring every third day by inclusive reckoning).

tertiary /ˈtəːʃ(ə)ri/ ▶ **adjective 1** third in order or level: *most of the enterprises were of tertiary importance* | *the tertiary stage of the disease.*
■ chiefly Brit. relating to or denoting education at a level beyond that provided by schools, especially that provided by a college or university. ■ relating to or denoting the medical treatment provided at a specialist institution.
2 (**Tertiary**) Geology of, relating to, or denoting the first period of the Cenozoic era, between the Cretaceous and Quaternary periods, and comprising the Palaeogene and Neogene sub-periods.
3 Chemistry (of an organic compound) having its functional group located on a carbon atom which is itself bonded to three other carbon atoms.
■ Chemistry (chiefly of amines) derived from ammonia by replacement of three hydrogen atoms by organic groups.
▶ **noun 1** (**the Tertiary**) Geology the Tertiary period or the system of rocks deposited during it.

> The Tertiary lasted from about 65 to 1.6 million years ago. The mammals diversified following the demise of the dinosaurs and became dominant, as did the flowering plants.

2 a lay associate of certain Christian monastic organizations: *a Franciscan tertiary.*
– ORIGIN mid 16th cent. (in sense 2 of the noun): from Latin *tertiarius* 'of the third part or rank', from *tertius* 'third'.

tertiary industry ▶ **noun** [mass noun] Economics the part of a country's economy concerned with the provision of services.

tertiary sector ▶ **noun** the sector of an economy concerned with or relating to tertiary industry.

tertiary structure ▶ **noun** Biochemistry the overall three-dimensional structure resulting from folding and covalent cross-linking of a protein or polynucleotide molecule.

tertium quid /ˌtəːʃɪəm ˈkwɪd, ˌtəːtɪəm/ ▶ **noun** a third thing that is indefinite and undefined but is related to two definite or known things.
– ORIGIN early 18th cent.: from late Latin, translation of Greek *triton ti* 'some third thing'.

Tertullian /təːˈtʌlɪən/ (*c.*160–*c.*240), early Christian theologian; Latin name *Quintus Septimius Florens Tertullianus*. His writings include Christian apologetics and attacks on pagan idolatry and Gnosticism.

tervalent /təːˈveɪl(ə)nt/ ▶ **adjective** Chemistry another term for **TRIVALENT**.

terylene ▶ **noun** [mass noun] Brit. trademark an artificial textile fibre made from a polyester, used to make light, crease-resistant clothing, bed linen, and sails.
– ORIGIN 1940s: formed by inversion of (*polyeth*)*ylene ter*(*ephthalate*).

terza rima /ˌtɛːtsə ˈriːmə/ ▶ **noun** Prosody an arrangement of triplets, especially in iambic pentameter, that rhyme *aba bcb cdc* etc. as in Dante's *Divine Comedy*.
– ORIGIN Italian, literally 'third rhyme'.

terzetto /tɛːtˈsɛtəʊ, təːt-/ ▶ **noun** (pl. **terzettos** or **terzetti** /-ti/) Music a vocal or instrumental trio.
– ORIGIN Italian (see **TERCET**).

TESL ▶ **abbreviation for** teaching of English as a second language.

Tesla /ˈtɛslə/, Nikola (1856–1943), American electrical engineer and inventor, born in what is now Croatia of Serbian descent. He developed the first alternating-current induction motor, as well as several forms of oscillators, the tesla coil, and a wireless guidance system for ships.

tesla /ˈtɛslə, ˈtɛzlə/ (abbrev.: **T**) ▶ **noun** Physics the SI unit of magnetic flux density.
– ORIGIN 1960s: named after N. **TESLA**.

Tesla coil ▶ **noun** a form of induction coil for producing high-frequency alternating currents.

TESOL /ˈtɛsɒl/ ▶ **abbreviation for** teaching of English to speakers of other languages.

TESSA (also **Tessa**) ▶ **noun** (in the UK) a tax-exempt special savings account allowing savers to invest a certain amount in a bank or building society with no tax to pay on the interest, provided that the capital remains in the account for five years (replaced in 1999 by the ISA).
– ORIGIN acronym.

tessellate /ˈtɛsəleɪt/ ▶ **verb** [with obj.] decorate (a floor) with mosaics.
■ Mathematics cover (a plane surface) by repeated use of a single shape, without gaps or overlapping.
– ORIGIN late 18th cent.: from late Latin *tessellat-*, from the verb *tessellare*, from *tessella*, diminutive of *tessera* (see **TESSERA**).

tessellated ▶ **adjective** (of a floor or pavement) decorated with mosaic.
– ORIGIN late 17th cent.: from Italian *tessellato* or Latin *tessellatus* (from *tessellare*, from *tessella*, diminutive of *tessera*: see **TESSERA**) + **-ED**[2].

tessellation /ˌtɛsəˈleɪʃ(ə)n/ ▶ **noun** [mass noun] the process, art, or state of covering a surface or being covered with an arrangement of small pieces that fit closely together but do not overlap, especially in the construction of a mosaic.
■ [count noun] an arrangement of polygons without gaps or overlapping, especially in a repeated pattern.

tessera /ˈtɛs(ə)rə/ ▶ **noun** (pl. **tesserae** /-riː/) a small block of stone, tile, glass, or other material used in the construction of a mosaic.
■ (in ancient Greece and Rome) a small tablet of wood or bone used as a token.
– DERIVATIVES **tesseral** adjective.
– ORIGIN mid 17th cent.: via Latin from Greek, neuter of *tesseres*, variant of *tessares* 'four'.

Tessin /French tɛsɛ̃, German tɛˈsiːn/ French and German name for **TICINO**.

tessitura /ˌtɛsɪˈtjʊərə/ ▶ **noun** Music the range within which most notes of a vocal part fall.
– ORIGIN Italian, literally 'texture', from Latin *textura* (see **TEXTURE**).

test[1] ▶ **noun 1** a procedure intended to establish the quality, performance, or reliability of something, especially before it is taken into widespread use: *no sparking was visible during the tests* | [mass noun] *four fax modems are on test.*
■ a short written or spoken examination of a person's proficiency or knowledge: *a spelling test.* ■ an event or situation that reveals the strength or quality of someone or something by putting them under strain: *this is the first serious test of the peace agreement.* ■ an examination of part of the body or a body fluid for medical purposes, especially by means of a chemical or mechanical procedure rather than simple inspection: *a test for HIV* | *eye tests.* ■ Chemistry a procedure employed to identify a substance or to reveal the presence or absence of a constituent within a substance. ■ the result of a medical examination or analytical procedure: *a positive test for protein.* ■ a means of establishing whether an action, item, or situation is an instance of a specified quality, especially one held to be undesirable: *a statutory test of obscenity.*
2 short for **TEST MATCH**.
3 Metallurgy a movable hearth in a reverberating furnace, used for separating gold or silver from lead.
▶ **verb** [with obj.] take measures to check the quality, performance, or reliability of (something), especially before putting it into widespread use or practice: *this range has not been tested on animals* | [as noun **testing**] *the testing and developing of prototypes* | figurative *a useful way to **test** out ideas before implementation.*
■ reveal the strengths or capabilities of (someone or something) by putting them under strain: *such behaviour would severely test any marriage* | [as adj. **testing**] *a testing time ahead.* ■ give (someone) a short written or oral examination of their proficiency or knowledge: *all children are tested at eleven.* ■ judge or measure (someone's proficiency or knowledge) by means of such an examination. ■ carry out a medical test on (a person, a part of the body, or a body fluid). ■ [no obj., with complement] produce a specified result in a medical test, especially a drugs test or Aids test: *he tested positive for steroids during the race.* ■ Chemistry examine (a substance) by means of a reagent. ■ touch or taste (something) to check that it is acceptable before proceeding further: *she tested the water with the tip of her elbow.*
– PHRASES **put someone/thing to the test** find out how useful, strong, or effective someone or something is. **stand the test of time** last or remain popular for a long time. **test the water** judge people's feelings or opinions before taking further action.
– DERIVATIVES **testability** noun, **testable** adjective, **testee** noun.
– ORIGIN late Middle English (denoting a cupel used to treat gold or silver alloys or ore): via Old French from Latin *testu, testum* 'earthen pot', variant of *testa* 'jug, shell'. Compare with **TEST**[2]. The verb dates from the early 17th cent.

test[2] ▶ **noun** Zoology the shell or integument of some invertebrates and protozoans, especially the chalky shell of a foraminiferan or the tough outer layer of a tunicate.
– ORIGIN mid 19th cent.: from Latin *testa* 'tile, jug, shell'. Compare with **TEST**[1].

testa ▶ **noun** (pl. **testae** /-tiː/) Botany the protective outer covering of a seed; the seed coat.
– ORIGIN late 18th cent.: from Latin, literally 'tile, shell'.

testaceous /tɛˈsteɪʃəs/ ▶ **adjective** chiefly Entomology of a dull brick-red colour.
– ORIGIN mid 17th cent.: from Latin *testaceus* (from *testa* 'tile') + -OUS.

Test Act ▶ **noun 1** (in the UK) an act in force between 1673 and 1828 that made an oath of allegiance to the Church of England and the supremacy of the monarch as its head and repudiation of the doctrine of transubstantiation a condition of eligibility for public office.
2 (in the UK) an act of 1871 relaxing restrictions on university entrance for candidates who were not members of the Church of England.

testament ▶ **noun 1** a person's will, especially the part relating to personal property.
2 something that serves as a sign or evidence of a specified fact, event, or quality: *growing attendance figures are a **testament** to the event's popularity.*
3 (in biblical use) a covenant or dispensation.
■ (**Testament**) a division of the Bible. See also **OLD**

TESTAMENT, NEW TESTAMENT. ■ (**Testament**) a copy of the New Testament.
– ORIGIN Middle English: from Latin *testamentum* 'a will' (from *testari* 'testify'), in Christian Latin also translating Greek *diathēkē* 'covenant'.

testamentary ▶ **adjective** of, relating to, or bequeathed or appointed through a will.
– ORIGIN late Middle English: from Latin *testamentarius*, from *testamentum* 'a will', from *testari* 'testify'.

testate /ˈtɛsteɪt/ ▶ **adjective** [predic.] having made a valid will before one dies.
▶ **noun** a person who has died leaving such a will.
– ORIGIN late Middle English (as a noun): from Latin *testatus* 'testified, witnessed', past participle of *testari*, from *testis* 'a witness'.

testation ▶ **noun** [mass noun] Law the disposal of property by will.

testator /tɛˈsteɪtə/ ▶ **noun** Law a person who has made a will or given a legacy.
– ORIGIN Middle English: from Anglo-Norman French *testatour*, from Latin *testator*, from the verb *testari* 'testify'.

testatrix /tɛˈsteɪtrɪks/ ▶ **noun** (pl. **testatrices** /-trɪsiːz/ or **testatrixes**) Law a woman who has made a will or given a legacy.
– ORIGIN late 16th cent.: from late Latin, feminine of *testator* (see **TESTATOR**).

Test-Ban Treaty an international agreement not to test nuclear weapons in the atmosphere, in space, or under water, signed in 1963 by the US, the UK, and the USSR, and later by more than 100 governments.

test bed ▶ **noun** a piece of equipment used for testing new machinery, especially aircraft engines.

test card ▶ **noun** Brit. a still television picture transmitted outside normal programme hours and designed for use in judging the quality and position of the image.

test case ▶ **noun** Law a case that sets a precedent for other cases involving the same question of law.

test drive ▶ **noun** an act of driving a motor vehicle that one is considering buying, in order to determine its quality.
■ figurative a test of a product prior to purchase or release.
▶ **verb** (**test-drive**) [with obj.] drive (a vehicle) to determine its qualities with a view to buying it.
■ figurative test (a product) prior to purchase or release.

tester[1] ▶ **noun** a person who tests something, especially a new product.
■ a person who tests another's proficiency. ■ a device that tests the functioning of something: *a mains tester.* ■ a sample of a product provided so that customers can try it before buying it.

tester[2] ▶ **noun** a canopy over a four-poster bed.
– ORIGIN late Middle English: from medieval Latin *testerium, testrum*, from a Romance word meaning 'head', based on Latin *testa* 'tile'.

testes plural form of **TESTIS**.

test flight ▶ **noun** a flight during which the performance of an aircraft or its equipment is tested.
– DERIVATIVES **test-fly** verb.

testicle ▶ **noun** either of the two oval organs that produce sperm in men and other male mammals, enclosed in the scrotum behind the penis. Also called **TESTIS**.
– DERIVATIVES **testicular** adjective.
– ORIGIN late Middle English: from Latin *testiculus*, diminutive of *testis* 'a witness' (i.e. to virility).

testicular feminization ▶ **noun** [mass noun] a condition produced in genetically male people by the failure of tissue to respond to male sex hormones, resulting in normal female anatomy but with testes in place of ovaries.

testiculate /tɛˈstɪkjʊlət/ ▶ **adjective** Botany (especially of the twin tubers of some orchids) shaped like a pair of testicles.
– ORIGIN mid 18th cent.: from late Latin *testiculatus*, from *testiculus* (see **TESTICLE**).

testify ▶ **verb** (-ies, -ied) [no obj.] give evidence as a witness in a law court: *he testified against his own commander* | [with clause] *he testified that he had supplied Barry with crack.*
■ serve as evidence or proof of something's existing or being the case: *the bleak lines testify to inner torment.*
– DERIVATIVES **testifier** noun.

– ORIGIN late Middle English: from Latin *testificari*, from *testis* 'a witness'.

testimonial /ˌtɛstɪˈməʊnɪəl/ ▶ **noun** a formal statement testifying to someone's character and qualifications.
■ a public tribute to someone and to their achievements. ■ [often as modifier] (in sport) a game or event held in honour of a player, who typically receives part of the income generated: *he has been granted a testimonial match.*
– ORIGIN late Middle English: from Old French *testimonial* 'testifying, serving as evidence', from late Latin *testimonialis*, from Latin *testimonium* (see **TESTIMONY**).

testimony ▶ **noun** (pl. **-ies**) a formal written or spoken statement, especially one given in a court of law.
■ [mass noun] evidence or proof provided by the existence or appearance of something: *his blackened finger was testimony to the fact that he had played in pain.* ■ archaic a solemn protest or declaration.
– ORIGIN Middle English: from Latin *testimonium*, from *testis* 'a witness'.

testing ground ▶ **noun** an area or field of activity used for the testing of a product or an idea, especially a military site used for the testing of weapons.

testis /ˈtɛstɪs/ ▶ **noun** (pl. **testes** /-tiːz/) Anatomy & Zoology an organ which produces spermatozoa (male reproductive cells). Compare with **TESTICLE**.
– ORIGIN early 18th cent.: from Latin, literally 'a witness' (i.e. to virility). Compare with **TESTICLE**.

test match ▶ **noun** an international cricket or rugby match, typically one of a series, played between teams representing two different countries.

test meal ▶ **noun** Medicine a portion of food of specified quantity and composition, eaten to stimulate digestive secretions which can then be analysed.

testosterone /tɛˈstɒstərəʊn/ ▶ **noun** [mass noun] a steroid hormone that stimulates development of male secondary sexual characteristics, produced mainly in the testes, but also in the ovaries and adrenal cortex.
– ORIGIN 1930s: from **TESTIS** + *sterone* (blend of **STEROL** and **KETONE**).

test paper ▶ **noun 1** a paper set to test the knowledge of a student, especially in preparation for an examination.
2 Chemistry a paper impregnated with an indicator which changes colour under known conditions, used especially to test for acidity.

test piece ▶ **noun 1** a piece of music set to be performed by contestants in a competition.
2 a sample of material on which tests are carried out.

test pilot ▶ **noun** a pilot who flies an aircraft to test its performance.

test pit ▶ **noun** a small preliminary excavation made to gain an idea of the contents or stratigraphy of an archaeological site.

test rig ▶ **noun** an apparatus used for assessing the performance of a piece of mechanical or electrical equipment.

test strip ▶ **noun** a strip of material used in testing, especially (in photography) a strip of sensitized material, sections of which are exposed for varying lengths of time to assess its response.

test tube ▶ **noun** a thin glass tube closed at one end, used to hold small amounts of material for laboratory testing or experiments.
■ [as modifier] denoting things produced or processes performed in a laboratory: *new forms of test-tube life.*

test-tube baby ▶ **noun** informal a baby conceived by in vitro fertilization.

Testudines /tɛˈstjuːdɪniːz/ Zoology an order of reptiles which comprises the turtles, terrapins, and tortoises. They are distinguished by having a shell of bony plates covered with horny scales, and many kinds are aquatic. Also called **CHELONIA**.
– ORIGIN modern Latin (plural), based on Latin *testa* 'shell'.

testudo /tɛˈstjuːdəʊ, -ˈstuː-/ ▶ **noun** (pl. **testudos** or **testudines** /-dɪniːz/) (in ancient Rome) a screen on wheels and with an arched roof, used to protect besieging troops.
■ a protective screen formed by a body of troops

holding their shields above their heads in such a way that the shields overlap.
– ORIGIN late Middle English: from Latin, literally 'tortoise', from *testa* 'tile, shell'.

testy ▶ adjective easily irritated; impatient and somewhat bad-tempered.
– DERIVATIVES **testily** adverb, **testiness** noun.
– ORIGIN late Middle English (in the sense 'headstrong, impetuous'): from Anglo-Norman French *testif*, from Old French *teste* 'head', from Latin *testa* 'shell'.

tetanic /tɪˈtanɪk/ ▶ adjective relating to or characteristic of tetanus, especially in connection with tonic muscle spasm.
– DERIVATIVES **tetanically** adverb.
– ORIGIN early 18th cent.: via Latin from Greek *tetanikos*, from *tetanos* (see TETANUS).

tetanus ▶ noun [mass noun] **1** a bacterial disease marked by rigidity and spasms of the voluntary muscles. See also TRISMUS.
● This disease is caused by the bacterium *Clostridium tetani*; Gram-positive anaerobic rods.
2 Physiology the prolonged contraction of a muscle caused by rapidly repeated stimuli.
– DERIVATIVES **tetanize** (also **-ise**) verb, **tetanoid** adjective.
– ORIGIN late Middle English: from Latin, from Greek *tetanos* 'muscular spasm', from *teinein* 'to stretch'.

tetany /ˈtɛt(ə)ni/ ▶ noun [mass noun] a condition marked by intermittent muscular spasms, caused by malfunction of the parathyroid glands and a consequent deficiency of calcium.
– ORIGIN late 19th cent.: from French *tétanie*, from Latin *tetanus* (see TETANUS).

tetchy (also **techy**) ▶ adjective bad-tempered and irritable.
– DERIVATIVES **tetchily** adverb, **tetchiness** noun.
– ORIGIN late 16th cent.: probably from a variant of Scots *tache* 'blotch, fault', from Old French *teche*.

tête-à-tête /ˌteɪtɑːˈtɛt, ˌteɪtaːˈteɪt/ ▶ noun **1** a private conversation between two people.
2 an S-shaped sofa on which two people can sit face to face.
▶ adjective & adverb involving or happening between two people in private: [as adj.] *a tête-à-tête meal* | [as adv.] *his business was conducted tête-à-tête*.
– ORIGIN late 17th cent.: French, literally 'head-to-head'.

tête-bêche /ˌtɛtˈbɛʃ, French tɛtbɛʃ/ ▶ adjective (of a postage stamp) printed upside down or sideways relative to another.
– ORIGIN French, from *tête* 'head' and *bêche*, contraction of obsolete *béchevet* 'double bedhead'.

tête de cuvée /ˌtɛt də kjuːˈveɪ, ˌteɪt, French tɛt də kyve/ ▶ noun (pl. **têtes de cuvées** pronunc. same) a wine produced from the first pressing of the grapes, generally considered superior in quality.
■ a vineyard producing the best wine in the locality of a village.
– ORIGIN French, literally 'head of the vatful'.

tether ▶ noun a rope or chain with which an animal is tied to restrict its movement.
▶ verb [with obj.] tie (an animal) with a rope or chain so as to restrict its movement: *the horse had been tethered to a post*.
– PHRASES **the end of one's tether** see END.
– ORIGIN late Middle English: from Old Norse *tjóthr*, from a Germanic base meaning 'fasten'.

Tethys /ˈtɛθɪs/ **1** Greek Mythology a goddess of the sea, daughter of Uranus (Heaven) and Gaia (Earth).
2 Astronomy a satellite of Saturn, the ninth closest to the planet and probably composed mainly of ice, discovered by Cassini in 1684 (diameter 1,050 km).
3 Geology an ocean formerly separating the supercontinents of Gondwana and Laurasia, the forerunner of the present-day Mediterranean.

Tet Offensive (in the Vietnam War) an offensive launched in January–February 1968 by the Vietcong and the North Vietnamese army. Timed to coincide with the first day of the Tet (Vietnamese New Year), it was a surprise attack on South Vietnamese cities, notably Saigon. Although repulsed after initial successes, the attack shook US confidence and hastened the withdrawal of its forces.

Teton /ˈtiːtɒn, -t(ə)n/ (also **Teton Sioux**) ▶ noun another term for LAKOTA.

– ORIGIN the name in Dakota, literally 'dwellers on the prairie'.

Tétouan /teɪˈtwɑːn/ a city in northern Morocco; pop. 272,000 (1993).

tetra /ˈtɛtrə/ ▶ noun a small tropical freshwater fish that is typically brightly coloured. Native to Africa and America, many tetras are popular in aquaria.
● Numerous genera and species in the family Characidae, including the **neon tetra**.
– ORIGIN mid 20th cent.: abbreviation of modern Latin *Tetragonopterus* (former genus name), literally 'tetragonal finned'.

tetra- (also **tetr-** before a vowel) ▶ combining form **1** four; having four: *tetramerous* | *tetragram* | *tetrode*.
2 Chemistry (in names of compounds) containing four atoms or groups of a specified kind: *tetracycline*.
– ORIGIN from Greek, from *tettares* 'four'.

tetrachloroethylene /ˌtɛtrəˌklɔːrəʊˈɛθɪliːn, -ˌklɒrəʊ-/ ▶ noun another term for PERCHLOROETHYLENE.

tetrachord ▶ noun Music a scale of four notes, the interval between the first and last being a perfect fourth.
■ historical a musical instrument with four strings.

tetracycline /ˌtɛtrəˈsʌɪkliːn/ ▶ noun Medicine any of a large group of antibiotics with a molecular structure containing four rings.
● These antibiotics are often obtained from bacteria of the genus **Streptomyces**.
– ORIGIN 1950s: from TETRA- + CYCLIC + -INE[4].

tetrad /ˈtɛtrad/ ▶ noun technical a group or set of four.
– ORIGIN mid 17th cent.: from Greek *tetras, tetrad-* 'four, a group of four'.

tetradactyl /ˌtɛtrəˈdaktɪl/ ▶ adjective Zoology (of a vertebrate limb) having four toes or fingers.

tetraethyl lead /ˌtɛtrəˈiːθʌɪl/ ▶ noun [mass noun] Chemistry a toxic colourless oily liquid made synthetically and used as an anti-knock agent in leaded petrol.
● Chem. formula: $Pb(C_2H_5)_4$.

tetrafluoroethylene /ˌtɛtrəˌfluːərəʊˈɛθɪliːn, -ˌflɔː-/ ▶ noun [mass noun] Chemistry a dense colourless gas which is polymerized to make plastics such as polytetrafluoroethylene.
● Chem formula: $F_2C=CF_2$.

tetragonal /tɪˈtrag(ə)n(ə)l/ ▶ adjective of or denoting a crystal system or three-dimensional geometrical arrangement having three axes at right angles, two of them equal.
– DERIVATIVES **tetragonally** adverb.
– ORIGIN late 16th cent.: via late Latin from Greek *tetragōnon* (neuter of *tetragōnos* 'four-angled') + -AL.

tetragram ▶ noun a word consisting of four letters or characters.

Tetragrammaton /ˌtɛtrəˈgramətɒn/ ▶ noun the Hebrew name of God transliterated in four letters as YHWH or JHVH and articulated as Yahweh or Jehovah.
– ORIGIN Greek, neuter of *tetragrammatos* 'having four letters', from *tetra-* 'four' + *gramma, grammat-* 'letter'.

tetrahedrite /ˌtɛtrəˈhiːdrʌɪt, -ˈhɛdrʌɪt/ ▶ noun [mass noun] a grey mineral consisting of a sulphide of antimony, iron, and copper, typically occurring as tetrahedral crystals.

tetrahedron /ˌtɛtrəˈhiːdrən, -ˈhɛd-/ ▶ noun (pl. **tetrahedra** /-drə/ or **tetrahedrons**) a solid having four plane triangular faces; a triangular pyramid.
– DERIVATIVES **tetrahedral** adjective.
– ORIGIN late 16th cent.: from late Greek *tetraedron*, neuter (used as a noun) of *tetraedros* 'four-sided'.

tetrahydrocannabinol /ˌtɛtrəˌhʌɪdrə(ʊ)ˈkanəbɪnɒl, -kəˈnab-/ ▶ noun [mass noun] Chemistry a crystalline compound that is the main active ingredient of cannabis.
● Chem. formula: $C_{21}H_{30}O_2$.

tetrahydrofuran /ˌtɛtrəˌhʌɪdrəʊˈfjʊəran/ ▶ noun [mass noun] Chemistry a colourless liquid used chiefly as a solvent for plastics and as an intermediate in organic syntheses.
● A heterocyclic compound; chem. formula: C_4H_8O.

tetralogy /tɪˈtralədʒi/ ▶ noun (pl. **-ies**) **1** a group of four related literary or operatic works.
■ a series of four ancient Greek dramas, three tragic and one satyric, originally presented together. [ORIGIN: from Greek *tetralogia*.]
2 Medicine a set of four related symptoms or abnormalities frequently occurring together.

tetralogy of Fallot /ˈfaləʊ/ ▶ noun Medicine a congenital heart condition involving four abnormalities occurring together, including a defective septum between the ventricles and narrowing of the pulmonary artery, and accompanied by cyanosis.
– ORIGIN 1920s: named after Etienne L. A. *Fallot* (1850–1911), French physician.

tetramer /ˈtɛtrəmə/ ▶ noun Chemistry a polymer comprising four monomer units.
– DERIVATIVES **tetrameric** adjective.

tetramerous /tɪˈtram(ə)rəs/ ▶ adjective Botany & Zoology having parts arranged in groups of four.
■ consisting of four joints or parts.

tetrameter /tɪˈtramɪtə/ ▶ noun Prosody a verse of four measures.
– ORIGIN early 17th cent.: from late Latin *tetrametrus*, from Greek *tetrametros*, from *tetra-* 'four' + *metron* 'measure'.

Tetra Pak (also **tetrapack**) ▶ noun trademark a type of plasticized cardboard carton for packing milk and other drinks, folded from a single sheet into a box shape.

tetraplegia /ˌtɛtrəˈpliːdʒə/ ▶ noun another term for QUADRIPLEGIA.
– DERIVATIVES **tetraplegic** adjective & noun.
– ORIGIN early 20th cent.: from TETRA- 'four' + PARAPLEGIA.

tetraploid /ˈtɛtrəplɔɪd/ Biology ▶ adjective (of a cell or nucleus) containing four homologous sets of chromosomes.
■ (of an organism or species) composed of such cells.
▶ noun an organism, variety, or species of this type.
– DERIVATIVES **tetraploidy** noun.

tetrapod ▶ noun Zoology a four-footed animal, especially a member of a group which includes all vertebrates higher than fishes.
● Superclass Tetrapoda: the amphibians, reptiles, birds, and mammals.
■ an object or structure with four feet, legs, or supports.
– ORIGIN early 19th cent.: from modern Latin *tetrapodus*, from Greek *tetrapous, tetrapod-* 'four-footed', from *tetra-* 'four' + *pous* 'foot'.

tetrapterous /tɪˈtrapt(ə)rəs/ ▶ adjective Entomology (of an insect) having two pairs of wings.
– ORIGIN early 19th cent.: from modern Latin *tetrapterus* (from Greek *tetrapteros*, from *tetra-* 'four' + *pteron* 'wing') + -OUS.

tetrarch /ˈtɛtrɑːk/ ▶ noun (in the Roman Empire) the governor of one of four divisions of a country or province.
■ one of four joint rulers. ■ archaic a subordinate ruler.
– DERIVATIVES **tetrarchy** noun (pl. **-ies**).
– ORIGIN Old English, from late Latin *tetrarcha*, from Latin *tetrarches*, from Greek *tetrarkhēs*, from *tetra-* 'four' + *arkhein* 'to rule'.

tetraspore ▶ noun Botany a spore occurring in groups of four, in particular (in a red alga) each of four spores produced together, two of which produce male plants and two female.

tetrastich /ˈtɛtrəstɪk/ ▶ noun Prosody a group of four lines of verse.
– ORIGIN late 16th cent.: via Latin from Greek *tetrastikhon* 'having four rows', from *tetra-* 'four' + *stikhon* 'row, line of verse'.

tetrastyle Architecture ▶ noun a building or part of a building, especially a portico, that has four pillars.
▶ adjective (of a building or part of a building) having four pillars.
– ORIGIN early 18th cent.: via Latin from Greek *tetrastulos*, from *tetra-* 'four' + *stulos* 'column'.

tetrasyllable ▶ noun a word consisting of four syllables.
– DERIVATIVES **tetrasyllabic** adjective.

tetrathlon /tɛˈtraθlɒn, -lən/ ▶ noun a sporting contest in which each participant competes in four events, typically riding, shooting, swimming, and running.
– ORIGIN 1950s: from TETRA- 'four' + Greek *athlon* 'contest', on the pattern of *pentathlon*.

tetratomic ▶ adjective Chemistry consisting of four atoms.

tetravalent /ˌtɛtrəˈveɪl(ə)nt/ ▶ adjective Chemistry having a valency of four.

tetrazole /ˈtɛtrəzəʊl/ ▶ noun [mass noun] Chemistry an acidic crystalline compound whose molecule is a

five-membered ring of one carbon and four nitrogen atoms.
• Chem. formula: CH_2N_4.
– ORIGIN late 19th cent.: from **TETRA-** 'four' + **AZO-** + **-OLE**.

tetrazolium /ˌtɛtrəˈzəʊlɪəm/ ▶ **noun** [as modifier] Chemistry a cation derived from tetrazole or one of its derivatives, especially the triphenyl derivative.
■(also **nitroblue tetrazolium**) [mass noun] a yellow dye used as a test for viability in biological material.

tetrode /ˈtɛtrəʊd/ ▶ **noun** a thermionic valve having four electrodes.
– ORIGIN early 20th cent.: from **TETRA-** 'four' + Greek *hodos* 'way'.

tetrodotoxin /ˌtɛtrədə(ʊ)ˈtɒksɪn/ ▶ **noun** [mass noun] a poisonous compound present in the ovaries of certain pufferfishes. It is a powerful neurotoxin.
– ORIGIN early 20th cent.: from modern Latin *Tetrodon* (former genus name, from Greek *tetra-* 'fourfold' + *odous, odont-* 'tooth') + **TOXIN**.

tetrose /ˈtɛtrəʊz, -s/ ▶ **noun** Chemistry any of a group of monosaccharide sugars whose molecules contain four carbon atoms.

tetroxide /tɛˈtrɒksʌɪd/ ▶ **noun** Chemistry an oxide containing four atoms of oxygen in its molecule or empirical formula.

tetter ▶ **noun** chiefly archaic a skin disease in humans or animals causing itchy or pustular patches, such as eczema or ringworm.
– ORIGIN Old English *teter*, of Germanic origin; from an Indo-European root shared by Sanskrit *dadru* 'skin disease'.

Teuton /ˈtjuːt(ə)n/ ▶ **noun** a member of a people who lived in Jutland in the 4th century BC and fought the Romans in France in the 2nd century BC.
■often derogatory a German.
– ORIGIN from Latin *Teutones, Teutoni* (plural), from an Indo-European root meaning 'people' or 'country'.

Teutonic /tjuːˈtɒnɪk/ ▶ **adjective 1** of or relating to the Teutons.
■informal, often derogatory displaying the characteristics popularly attributed to Germans: *making preparations with Teutonic thoroughness.*
2 archaic denoting the Germanic branch of the Indo-European language family.
▶ **noun** [mass noun] archaic the language of the Teutons.
– DERIVATIVES **Teutonicism** noun.

Teutonic Knights a military and religious order of German knights, priests, and lay brothers, originally enrolled *c.*1191 as the Teutonic Knights of St Mary of Jerusalem.

> They became a great sovereign power through conquests made in campaigns against Germany's non-Christian neighbours, such as Prussia and Livonia from 1225. Abolished by Napoleon in 1809, the order was re-established in Vienna as an honorary ecclesiastical institution in 1834 and maintains a titular existence.

Tevere /ˈtevere/ Italian name for **TIBER**.

Tevet /ˈtɛvɛt/ ▶ **noun** variant spelling of **TEBET**.

Tewa /ˈteɪwə/ ▶ **noun** (pl. same or **Tewas**) **1** a member of a Pueblo Indian people of the Rio Grande area in the south-western US.
2 [mass noun] the Tanoan language of this people, with fewer than 3,000 speakers. (Not the same as Tiwa.)
▶ **adjective** of or relating to this people or their language.
– ORIGIN from Tewa *téwa* 'moccasins'.

Tex. ▶ **abbreviation for** Texas.

Texas a state in the southern US, on the border with Mexico, with a coastline on the Gulf of Mexico; pop. 16,986,510; capital, Austin. The area formed part of Mexico until 1836, when it declared independence and became a republic. It became the 28th state of the US in 1845.
– DERIVATIVES **Texan** adjective & noun.

Texas leaguer ▶ **noun** Baseball, dated a fly ball that falls to the ground between the infield and the outfield and results in a base hit.

Texas Ranger ▶ **noun** a member of the Texas State police force (formerly, of certain locally mustered regiments in the federal service during the Mexican War).

Texel /ˈtɛks(ə)l/ ▶ **noun** a sheep of a hardy, hornless breed with a heavy fleece, originally developed on the West Frisian island of Texel.

Tex-Mex ▶ **adjective** (especially of cooking and music) having a blend of Mexican and southern American features originally characteristic of the border regions of Texas and Mexico.
▶ **noun** [mass noun] **1** music or cookery of such a type.
2 a variety of Mexican Spanish spoken in Texas.
– ORIGIN 1940s: blend of *Texan* and *Mexican*.

text ▶ **noun 1** a book or other written or printed work, regarded in terms of its content rather than its physical form: *a text which explores pain and grief.*
■a piece of written or printed material regarded as conveying the authentic or primary form of a particular work: *in some passages it is difficult to establish the original text.* ■ [mass noun] written or printed words, typically forming a connected piece of work: *stylistic features of journalistic text.* ■ [mass noun] Computing data in written form, especially when stored, processed, or displayed in a word processor. ■ [in sing.] the main body of a book or other piece of writing, as distinct from other material such as notes, appendices, and illustrations: *the pictures are clear and relate well to the text.* ■ a script or libretto. ■ a written work chosen or set as a subject of study: *too much concentration on* **set texts** *can turn pupils against reading.* ■ a textbook. ■ a passage from the Bible or other religious work, especially when used as the subject of a sermon. ■ a subject or theme for a discussion or exposition: *he took as his text the fact that Australia is paradise.*
2 (also **text-hand**) [mass noun] fine, large handwriting, used especially for manuscripts.
▶ **verb** send (someone) a text message.
– DERIVATIVES **textless** adjective.
– ORIGIN late Middle English: from Old Northern French *texte*, from Latin *textus* 'tissue, literary style' (in medieval Latin, 'Gospel'), from *text-* 'woven', from the verb *texere*.

textbook ▶ **noun** a book used as a standard work for the study of a particular subject.
▶ **adjective** [attrib.] conforming to or corresponding to a standard or type that is prescribed or widely held by theorists: *he had the presence of mind to carry out a textbook emergency descent.*
– DERIVATIVES **textbookish** adjective.

text editor ▶ **noun** Computing a system or program that allows a user to edit text.

textile ▶ **noun 1** (usu. **textiles**) a type of cloth or woven fabric: *a fascinating range of pottery, jewellery, and textiles.*
■(**textiles**) the branch of industry involved in the manufacture of cloth.
2 informal used by nudists to describe someone wearing clothes, especially on a beach.
▶ **adjective 1** [attrib.] of or relating to fabric or weaving: *the textile industry.*
2 informal used by nudists to describe something relating to or restricted to people wearing clothes.
– ORIGIN early 17th cent.: from Latin *textilis*, from *text-* 'woven', from the verb *texere*.

text message ▶ **noun** an electronic communication sent and received by mobile phone.

text processing ▶ **noun** [mass noun] Computing the manipulation of text, especially the transformation of text from one format to another.

textual ▶ **adjective** of or relating to a text or texts: *textual analysis.*
– DERIVATIVES **textually** adverb.
– ORIGIN late Middle English: from medieval Latin *textualis*, from Latin *textus* (see **TEXT**).

textual criticism ▶ **noun** [mass noun] the process of attempting to ascertain the original wording of a text.

textualist ▶ **noun** a person who adheres strictly to a text, especially that of the scriptures.
– DERIVATIVES **textualism** noun.

textuality ▶ **noun 1** the quality or use of language characteristic of written works as opposed to spoken usage.
2 strict adherence to a text; textualism.

texture ▶ **noun** [mass noun] the feel, appearance, or consistency of a surface or a substance: *skin texture and tone* | *the cheese is firm in texture* | [count noun] *the different colours and textures of bark.*
■the character or appearance of a textile fabric as determined by the arrangement and thickness of its threads: *a dark shirt of rough texture.* ■ Art the tactile quality of the surface of a work of art. ■ the quality created by the combination of the different elements in a work of music or literature: *a closely knit symphonic texture.*
▶ **verb** [with obj.] [usu. as adj. **textured**] give (a surface) a rough or raised texture: *wallcoverings which create a textured finish.*
– DERIVATIVES **textural** adjective, **texturally** adverb, **textureless** adjective.
– ORIGIN late Middle English (denoting a woven fabric or something resembling this): from Latin *textura* 'weaving', from *text-* 'woven', from the verb *texere*.

textured vegetable protein ▶ **noun** [mass noun] a type of protein obtained from soya beans and made to resemble minced meat.

texture mapping ▶ **noun** [mass noun] Computing the application of patterns or images to three-dimensional graphics to enhance the realism of their surfaces.

texturing ▶ **noun** [mass noun] the representation or use of texture, especially in music, fine art, and interior design.

texturize (also **-ise**) ▶ **verb** [with obj.] impart a particular texture to (a product, especially a fabric or foodstuff) in order to make it more attractive.
■cut (hair) in such a way as to remove its weight and create extra fullness.

text wrap ▶ **noun** [mass noun] (in word processing) a facility allowing text to surround embedded features such as pictures.

T-formation ▶ **noun** American Football a T-shaped offensive formation of players.

TFT Electronics ▶ **abbreviation for** thin-film transistor, denoting a technology used to make flat colour display screens, usually for high-end portable computers.

TG ▶ **abbreviation for** ■ Togo (international vehicle registration). ■ transformational grammar or transformational-generative grammar.

T-group ▶ **noun** Psychology a group of people undergoing therapy or training in which they observe and seek to improve their own interpersonal relationships or communication skills.
– ORIGIN 1950s: *T* for *training*.

TGV ▶ **noun** a French high-speed electric passenger train.
– ORIGIN abbreviation of French *train à grande vitesse*.

TGWU ▶ **abbreviation for** (in the UK) Transport and General Workers' Union.

Th ▶ **symbol for** the chemical element thorium.

Th. ▶ **abbreviation for** Thursday.

-th[1] (also **-eth**) ▶ **suffix** forming ordinal and fractional numbers from *four* onwards: *fifth* | *sixty-sixth.*
– ORIGIN Old English *-(o)tha, -(o)the*.

-th[2] ▶ **suffix** forming nouns: **1** (from verbs) denoting an action or process: *birth* | *growth.*
2 (from adjectives) denoting a state: *filth* | *health* | *width.*
– ORIGIN Old English *-thu, -tho, -th*.

-th[3] ▶ **suffix** variant spelling of **-ETH**[2] (as in *doth*).

Thackeray /ˈθakəri/, William Makepeace (1811–63), British novelist. He established his reputation with *Vanity Fair* (1847–8), a satire of the upper middle class of early 19th-century society.

Thaddaeus /ˈθadɪəs/ an apostle named in St Matthew's Gospel, traditionally identified with St Jude.

Thai /tʌɪ/ ▶ **adjective** of or relating to Thailand, its people, or their language.
▶ **noun** (pl. same or **Thais**) **1** a native or national of Thailand, or a person of Thai descent.
■a member of the largest ethnic group in Thailand.
2 [mass noun] the official language of Thailand, spoken by over 20 million people, mainly in central Thailand. It belongs to the Tai language group.
– ORIGIN Thai, literally 'free'.

Thailand a kingdom in SE Asia; pop. 56,303,270 (1990); official language, Thai; capital, Bangkok. Former name (until 1939) **SIAM**.

> A powerful Thai kingdom emerged in the 14th century. In the 19th century it lost territory in the east to France and in the south to Britain. Thailand was occupied by the Japanese in the Second World War; it supported the US in the Vietnam War, later experiencing a large influx of refugees from Cambodia, Laos, and Vietnam. Absolute monarchy was abolished in 1932, the king remaining head of state.

Thailand, Gulf of an inlet of the South China Sea between the Malay Peninsula to the west and Thailand and Cambodia to the east. It was formerly known as the Gulf of Siam.

Thai stick ▶**noun** strong cannabis in leaf form, twisted into a small, tightly packed cylinder ready for smoking.

thakur /'tɑːkʊr, 'tɑːkʊə/ ▶**noun** Indian a respectful title for a nobleman and landowner.
– ORIGIN from Hindi *ṭhākur* 'lord', from Sanskrit *ṭhakkura* 'chief, lord'.

thalamus /'θaləməs/ ▶**noun** (pl. **thalami** /-mʌɪ, -miː/) Anatomy either of two masses of grey matter lying between the cerebral hemispheres on either side of the third ventricle, relaying sensory information and acting as a centre for pain perception.
– DERIVATIVES **thalamic** /θə'lamɪk, 'θaləmɪk/ adjective.
– ORIGIN late 17th cent. (denoting the part of the brain at which a nerve originates): via Latin from Greek *thalamos*.

thalassaemia /ˌθalə'siːmɪə/ (US **thalassemia**) ▶**noun** [mass noun] Medicine any of a group of hereditary haemolytic diseases caused by faulty haemoglobin synthesis, widespread in Mediterranean, African, and Asian countries.
– ORIGIN 1930s: from Greek *thalassa* 'sea' (because the diseases were first known around the Mediterranean) + **-AEMIA**.

thalassic /θə'lasɪk/ ▶**adjective** poetic/literary or technical of or relating to the sea.
– ORIGIN mid 19th cent.: from French *thalassique*, from Greek *thalassa* 'sea'.

thalassotherapy /θəˌlasəʊ'θɛrəpi/ ▶**noun** [mass noun] the use of seawater in cosmetic and health treatment.
– ORIGIN late 19th cent.: from Greek *thalassa* 'sea' + **THERAPY**.

thale cress /θeɪl/ ▶**noun** a small white-flowered plant of north temperate regions, widely used in genetics experiments due to its small number of chromosomes and short life cycle.
• *Arabidopsis thaliana*, family Cruciferae.
– ORIGIN late 18th cent.: named after Johann *Thal* (1542–83), German physician.

thaler /'tɑːlə/ ▶**noun** historical a German silver coin.
– ORIGIN German, earlier form of *Taler* (see **DOLLAR**).

Thales /'θeɪliːz/ (*c.*624–*c.*545 BC), Greek philosopher, mathematician, and astronomer, living at Miletus. Judged by Aristotle to be the founder of physical science, he is also credited with founding geometry. He proposed that water was the primary substance from which all things were derived.

thali /'tɑːli/ ▶**noun** (pl. **thalis**) a set meal at an Indian restaurant, typically consisting of a variety of curry dishes served with rice or chapattis.
■ a metal plate on which Indian food is served.
– ORIGIN from Hindi *thālī*, from Sanskrit *sthālī*.

Thalia /'θeɪlɪə, θə'lʌɪə, 'tɑːlɪə/ **1** Greek & Roman Mythology the Muse of comedy.
2 Greek Mythology one of the Graces.
– ORIGIN Greek, literally 'rich, plentiful'.

thalidomide /θə'lɪdəmʌɪd/ ▶**noun** [mass noun] a drug formerly used as a sedative, but withdrawn in the UK in the early 1960s after it was found to cause congenital malformation or absence of limbs in children whose mothers took the drug during early pregnancy.
– ORIGIN 1950s: from *(ph)thal(ic acid)* + *(im)ido* + *(i)mide*.

thalli plural form of **THALLUS**.

thallium /'θalɪəm/ ▶**noun** [mass noun] the chemical element of atomic number 81, a soft silvery-white metal which occurs naturally in small amounts in iron pyrites, sphalerite, and other ores. Its compounds are very poisonous. (Symbol: **Tl**)
– ORIGIN mid 19th cent.: modern Latin, from Greek *thallos* 'green shoot', because of the green line in its spectrum.

thallophyte /'θalə(ʊ)fʌɪt/ ▶**noun** Botany a plant that consists of a thallus.
– ORIGIN mid 19th cent.: from modern Latin *Thallophyta* (former taxon), from Greek *thallos* (see **THALLUS**) + **-PHYTE**.

thallus /'θaləs/ ▶**noun** (pl. **thalli** /-lʌɪ, -liː/) Botany a plant body that is not differentiated into stem and leaves and lacks true roots and a vascular system. Thalli are typical of algae, fungi, lichens, and some liverworts.
– DERIVATIVES **thalloid** adjective.
– ORIGIN early 19th cent.: from Greek *thallos* 'green shoot', from *thallein* 'to bloom'.

thalweg /'tɑːlvɛg, 'θɑːlwɛg/ ▶**noun** Geology a line connecting the lowest points of successive cross-sections along the course of a valley or river.
– ORIGIN mid 19th cent.: from German, from obsolete *Thal* 'valley, dale' + *Weg* 'way'.

Thames /tɛmz/ a river of southern England, flowing 338 km (210 miles) eastwards from the Cotswolds in Gloucestershire through London to the North Sea.
■ a shipping forecast area covering the southernmost part of the North Sea, roughly as far north as the latitude of northern Norfolk.

thamin /θə'mɪn/ ▶**noun** a reddish-brown deer which lives in low-lying marshy areas of SE Asia.
• *Cervus eldi*, family Cervidae.
– ORIGIN late 19th cent.: from Burmese.

Thammuz /'tamʊz/ (also **Tammuz**) ▶**noun** (in the Jewish calendar) the tenth month of the civil and fourth of the religious year, usually coinciding with parts of June and July.
– ORIGIN from Hebrew *tammūz*.

than ▶**conjunction** & **preposition** **1** introducing the second element in a comparison: [as prep.] *he was much smaller than his son* | [as conjunction] *Jack doesn't know any more than I do.*
2 used in expressions introducing an exception or contrast: [as prep.] *he claims not to own anything* ***other than*** *his home* | [as conjunction] *they observe* ***rather than*** *act.*
3 [conjunction] used in expressions indicating one thing happening immediately after another: ***scarcely*** *was the work completed* ***than*** *it was abandoned.*
– ORIGIN Old English *than(ne)*, *thon(ne)*, *thænne*, originally the same word as **THEN**.

USAGE Traditional grammar holds that personal pronouns following **than** should be in the subjective rather than the objective case: *he is smaller* ***than she*** rather than *he is smaller* ***than her***. This is based on an analysis of **than** by which **than** is a conjunction and the personal pronoun ('she') is standing in for a full clause: *he is smaller* ***than she is***. However, it is arguable that **than** in this context is not a conjunction but a preposition, similar grammatically to words like **with**, **between**, or **for**. In this case the personal pronoun is objective: *he is smaller* ***than her*** is standard in just the same way as, for example, *I work* ***with her*** is standard (not *I work* ***with she***). Whatever the grammatical analysis, the evidence confirms that sentences like *he is smaller* ***than she*** are uncommon in modern English and only ever found in formal contexts. Uses involving the objective personal pronoun, on the other hand, are almost universally accepted. For more explanation, see **usage** at **PERSONAL PRONOUN** and **BETWEEN**.

thana /'θɑːnɑː/ ▶**noun** Indian a police station.
– ORIGIN from Hindi *thānā*, from Sanskrit *sthāna* 'place, station'.

thanage /'θeɪnɪdʒ/ ▶**noun** [mass noun] historical the tenure, land, and rank granted to a thane.
– ORIGIN late Middle English: from Anglo-Norman French (see **THANE**, **-AGE**).

thanatology /ˌθanə'tɒlədʒi/ ▶**noun** [mass noun] the scientific study of death and the practices associated with it, including the study of the needs of the terminally ill and their families.
– DERIVATIVES **thanatological** adjective, **thanatologist** noun.
– ORIGIN mid 19th cent.: from Greek *thanatos* 'death' + **-LOGY**.

Thanatos /'θanətɒs/ (in Freudian theory) the death instinct. Often contrasted with **EROS**.
– ORIGIN from Greek *thanatos* 'death'.

thane /θeɪn/ ▶**noun** historical (in Anglo-Saxon England) a man who held land granted by the king or by a military nobleman, ranking between an ordinary freeman and a hereditary noble.
■ (in Scotland) a man, often the chief of a clan, who held land from a Scottish king and ranked with an earl's son.
– DERIVATIVES **thanedom** noun.
– ORIGIN Old English *theg(e)n* 'servant, soldier', of Germanic origin; related to German *Degen* 'warrior', from an Indo-European root shared by Greek *teknon* 'child', *tokeus* 'parent'.

thang ▶**noun** informal, chiefly US non-standard spelling of **THING** representing Southern US pronunciation, and typically used to denote a feeling or tendency: *yet another dimension of this Canadian groove thang.*

thank ▶**verb** [with obj.] express gratitude to (someone), especially by saying 'Thank you': *Mac* ***thanked*** *her* ***for*** *the meal and left.*
■ used ironically to assign blame or responsibility for something: *you have only yourself to thank for the plight you are in.*
– PHRASES **I will thank you to do something** used to make a request or command and implying a reproach or annoyance: *I'll thank you not to interrupt me again.* **thank goodness** (or **God** or **heavens**) an expression of relief: *thank goodness no one was badly injured.* **thank one's lucky stars** feel grateful for one's good fortune.
– ORIGIN Old English *thancian*, of Germanic origin; related to Dutch and German *danken*; compare with **THANKS**.

thankful ▶**adjective** pleased and relieved: [with clause] *they were thankful that the war was finally over* | [with infinitive] *I was very thankful to be alive.*
■ expressing gratitude and relief: *an earnest and thankful prayer.*
– DERIVATIVES **thankfulness** noun.
– ORIGIN Old English *thancful* (see **THANK**, **-FUL**).

thankfully ▶**adverb** in a thankful manner: *she thankfully accepted the armchair she was offered.*
■ [sentence adverb] used to express pleasure or relief at the situation or outcome that one is reporting; fortunately: *thankfully, everything went smoothly.*
– ORIGIN Old English *thancfullīce* (see **THANKFUL**, **-LY**[2]).

USAGE **Thankfully** has been used for centuries to mean 'in a thankful manner', as in *she accepted the offer* ***thankfully***. Since the 1960s it has also been used as a sentence adverb to mean 'fortunately', as in ***thankfully****, we didn't have to wait.* Although this use has not attracted the same amount of attention as **hopefully**, it has been criticized for the same reasons. It is, however, far commoner now than the traditional use, accounting for more than 80 per cent of citations for **thankfully** in the British National Corpus. For further explanation, see **usage** at **HOPEFULLY**.

thankless ▶**adjective** (of a job or task) difficult or unpleasant and not likely to bring one pleasure or the appreciation of others.
■ (of a person) not expressing or feeling gratitude.
– DERIVATIVES **thanklessly** adverb, **thanklessness** noun.

thank-offering ▶**noun** an offering made as an act of thanksgiving.

thanks ▶**plural noun** an expression of gratitude: *festivals were held to* ***give thanks for*** *the harvest* | *a letter of thanks.*
■ a feeling of gratitude: *they expressed their thanks and wished her well.* ■ another way of saying **THANK YOU**: ***thanks for*** *being so helpful* | *many thanks.*
– PHRASES **no thanks to** used to imply that someone has failed to contribute to, or has hindered, a successful outcome: *we've won, but no thanks to you.* **thanks a million** informal thank you very much. **thanks to** as a result of; due to: *it's thanks to you that he's in this mess.*
– ORIGIN Old English *thancas*, plural of *thanc* '(kindly) thought, gratitude', of Germanic origin; related to Dutch *dank* and German *Dank*, also to **THINK**.

thanksgiving ▶**noun** [mass noun] **1** the expression of gratitude, especially to God: *he offered prayers* ***in thanksgiving for*** *his safe arrival* | [count noun] *he described the service as a thanksgiving.*
2 (**Thanksgiving** or **Thanksgiving Day**) (in North America) an annual national holiday marked by religious observances and a traditional meal including turkey. The holiday commemorates a harvest festival celebrated by the Pilgrim Fathers in 1621, and is held in the US on the fourth Thursday in November. A similar holiday is held in Canada, usually on the second Monday in October.

thank you ▶**exclamation** a polite expression used when acknowledging a gift, service, or compliment, or accepting or refusing an offer: ***thank you for*** *your letter* | *no thank you, I'll give it a miss.*
▶**noun** an instance or means of expressing thanks: *Lucy planned a party as a thank you to hospital staff* | [as modifier] *thank-you letters.*

thar /tɑː/ ▶**noun** variant form of **TAHR**.

Thar Desert /tɑː/ a desert region to the east of the River Indus, lying in the Rajasthan and Gujarat states of NW India and the Punjab and Sind regions of SE Pakistan. Also called **GREAT INDIAN DESERT**.

that ▶**pronoun** (pl. **those**) **1** used to identify a specific person or thing observed or heard by the speaker: *that's his wife over there* | *hello, is that Ben?*

■referring to the more distant of two things near to the speaker (the other, if specified, being identified by 'this'): *this is stronger than that.*

2 referring to a specific thing previously mentioned, known, or understood: *that's a good idea | what are we going to do about that?*

3 [often with clause] used in singling out someone or something and ascribing a distinctive feature to them: *it is part of human nature to be attracted to* **that** *which is aesthetically pleasing | his appearance was* **that** *of an undergrown man | they care about the rights of those less privileged than themselves.*

4 informal, chiefly Brit. expressing strong agreement with a description just given: *'He's a fussy man.' 'He is that.'*

5 (pl. **that**) [relative pronoun] used to introduce a defining clause, especially one essential to identification:

■instead of 'which', 'who', or 'whom': *the woman that owns the place.* ■ instead of 'when' after an expression of time: *the year that Anna was born.*

▶**determiner** (pl. **those**) **1** used to identify a specific person or thing observed or heard by the speaker: *look at that chap there | how much are those brushes?*

■referring to the more distant of two things near to the speaker (the other, if specified, being identified by 'this').

2 referring to a specific thing previously mentioned, known, or understood: *he lived in Mysore at that time | seven people died in that incident.*

3 [usu. with clause] used in singling out someone or something and ascribing a distinctive feature to them: *I have always envied those people who make their own bread.*

4 referring to a specific person or thing assumed as understood or familiar to the person being addressed: *where is that son of yours? | I let him spend all that money on me | Dad got that hunted look.*

▶**adverb** [as submodifier] to such a degree; so: *I would not go that far.*

■used with a gesture to indicate size: *it was that big, perhaps even bigger.* ■ [with negative] informal very: *he wasn't that far away.*

▶**conjunction 1** introducing a subordinate clause expressing a statement or hypothesis: *she said that she was satisfied | it is possible that we have misunderstood.*

■expressing a reason or cause: *he seemed pleased that I wanted to continue.* ■ expressing a result: *she was so tired* **that** *she couldn't think.* ■ [usu. with modal] expressing a purpose, hope, or intention: *we pray that the coming year may be a year of peace | I eat that I may live.*

2 [usu. with modal] poetic/literary expressing a wish or regret: *oh that he could be restored to health.*

– PHRASES **and all that** (or **and that**) informal and that sort of thing; and so on: *other people depend on them for food and clothing and all that.* **at that** see **AT**[1]. **like that 1** of that nature or in that manner: *we need more people like that | don't talk like that.* **2** informal with no preparation or introduction; instantly or effortlessly: *he can't just leave like that.* **not all that** —— not very —: *it was not all that long ago.* **that is** (or **that is to say**) a formula introducing or following an explanation or further clarification of a preceding word or words: *androcentric—that is to say, male-dominated—concepts | He was a long-haired kid with freckles. Last time I saw him, that is.* **that said** even so (introducing a concessive statement): *It's just a gimmick. That said, I'd love to do it.* **that's it** see **IT**[1]. **that's that** there is nothing more to do or say about the matter. —— **that was** as the specified person or thing was formerly known: *General Dunstaple had married Miss Hughes that was.* **that will do** no more is needed or desirable.

– ORIGIN Old English *thæt*, nominative and accusative singular neuter of *se* 'the', of Germanic origin; related to Dutch *dat* and German *das*.

USAGE 1 The word **that** can be omitted in standard English where it introduces a subordinate clause, as in *she said* (***that***) *she was satisfied*. It can also be dropped in a relative clause where the subject of the subordinate clause is not the same as the subject of the main clause, as in *the book* (**that**) *I've just written* ('the book' and 'I' are two different subjects). Where the subject of the subordinate clause and the main clause are the same, use of the word **that** is obligatory, as in *the woman* ***that*** *owns the place* ('the woman' is the subject of both clauses).

2 It is sometimes argued that, in relative clauses, **that** should be used for non-human references, while **who** should be used for human references: *a house* ***that*** *overlooks the park* but *the woman* ***who*** *lives next door*. In practice, while it is true to say that **who** is restricted to human references, the function of **that** is flexible. It has been used for human and non-human references since at least the 11th century. In standard English it is interchangeable with **who** in this context.

3 Is there any difference between the use of **that** and **which** in sentences such as *any book* ***that*** *gets children reading is worth having*, and *any book* ***which*** *gets children reading is worth having*? The general rule is that, in **restrictive relative clauses**, where the relative clause serves to define or restrict the reference to the particular one described, **which** could replace **that**. However, in non-restrictive relative clauses, where the relative clause serves only to give additional information, **that** cannot be used: *this book,* ***which*** *is set in the last century, is very popular with teenagers* but not *this book,* ***that*** *is set in the last century, is very popular with teenagers*.

thataway ▶**adverb** informal, chiefly US **1** in that direction.

2 in that way; like that.

thatch ▶**noun** [mass noun] a roof covering of straw, reeds, palm leaves, or a similar material.

■straw or a similar material used for such a covering. ■ informal the hair on a person's head, especially if thick or unruly. ■ a matted layer of dead stalks, moss, and other material in a lawn.

▶**verb** [with obj.] cover (a roof or a building) with straw or a similar material: [as adj. **thatched**] *thatched cottages.*

– DERIVATIVES **thatcher** noun.

– ORIGIN Old English *theccan* 'cover', of Germanic origin; related to Dutch *dekken* and German *decken*.

Thatcher, Margaret (Hilda), Baroness Thatcher of Kesteven (b.1925), British Conservative stateswoman, Prime Minister 1979–90. She was the country's first woman Prime Minister, and became the longest-serving British Prime Minister of the 20th century. Her period in office was marked by an emphasis on monetarist policies, privatization of nationalized industries, and trade union legislation. She became known for her determination and her emphasis on individual responsibility and enterprise.

– DERIVATIVES **Thatcherism** noun, **Thatcherite** noun & adjective.

thaumatin /ˈθɔːmətɪn/ ▶**noun** [mass noun] a sweet-tasting protein isolated from a West African fruit, used as a sweetener in food.

– ORIGIN 1970s: *thaumat-* from modern Latin *Thaumatococcus daniellii* (name of the plant from which the fruit is obtained), from Greek *thauma*, *thaumat-* 'marvel') + **-IN**[1].

thaumatrope /ˈθɔːmətrəʊp/ ▶**noun** a scientific toy that was devised in the 19th century, consisting of a disc having a different picture on each of its two sides, these appearing to combine into one image when the disc is rapidly rotated.

■another term for **ZOETROPE**.

– ORIGIN early 19th cent.: from Greek *thauma* 'marvel' + *-tropos* '-turning'.

thaumaturge /ˈθɔːmətəːdʒ/ ▶**noun** a worker of wonders and performer of miracles; a magician.

– DERIVATIVES **thaumaturgic** adjective, **thaumaturgical** adjective, **thaumaturgist** noun, **thaumaturgy** noun.

– ORIGIN early 18th cent. (as *thaumaturg*): via medieval Latin from Greek *thaumatourgos*, from *thauma* 'marvel' + *-ergos* '-working'.

thaw ▶**verb** [no obj.] (of ice, snow, or another frozen substance, such as food) become liquid or soft as a result of warming up: *the river thawed and barges of food began to reach the capital* | [as noun **thawing**] *catastrophic summer floods caused by thawing.*

■(**it thaws**, **it is thawing**, etc.) the weather becomes warmer and melts snow and ice. ■ [with obj.] make (something) warm enough to become liquid or soft: *European exporters simply thawed their beef before unloading.* ■ (of a part of the body) become warm enough to stop feeling numb: *Riven began to feel his ears and toes* **thaw out**. ■ become friendlier or more cordial: *she* **thawed out** *sufficiently to allow a smile to appear.* ■ [with obj.] make friendlier or more cordial: *the cast thawed the audience into real pleasure.*

▶**noun** a period of warmer weather that thaws ice and snow: *the thaw came yesterday afternoon.*

■an increase in friendliness or cordiality: *a thaw in relations between the USA and the USSR.*

– ORIGIN Old English *thawian* (verb), of West Germanic origin; related to Dutch *dooien*. The noun (first recorded in Middle English) developed its figurative use in the mid 19th cent.

THC ▶**abbreviation for** tetrahydrocannabinol.

the [called the definite article] ▶**determiner 1** denoting one or more people or things already mentioned or assumed to be common knowledge: *what's the matter? | call the doctor | the phone rang.* Compare with **A**[1].

■used to refer to a person, place, or thing that is unique: *the Queen | the Mona Lisa | the Nile.* ■ informal or archaic denoting a disease or affliction: *I've got the flu.* ■ (with a unit of time) the present; the current: *dish of the day | man of the moment.* ■ informal used instead of a possessive to refer to someone with whom the speaker or person addressed is associated: *I'm meeting the boss | how's the family?* ■ used with a surname to refer to a family or married couple: *the Johnsons were not wealthy.* ■ used before the surname of the chief of a Scottish or Irish clan: *the O'Donoghue.*

2 used to point forward to a following qualifying or defining clause or phrase: *the fuss that he made of her | the top of a bus | I have done the best I could.*

■(chiefly with rulers and family members with the same name) used after a name to qualify it: *George the Sixth | Edward the Confessor | Jack the Ripper.*

3 used to make a generalized reference to something rather than identifying a particular instance: *he taught himself to play the violin | I worry about the future.*

■used with a singular noun to indicate that it represents a whole species or class: *they placed the African elephant on their endangered list.* ■ used with an adjective to refer to those people who are of the type described: *the unemployed.* ■ used with an adjective to refer to something of the class or quality described: *they are trying to accomplish the impossible.* ■ used with the name of a unit to state a rate: *they can do 120 miles to* **the** *gallon | 35p* **in the** *pound.*

4 enough of (a particular thing): *he hoped to publish monthly, if only he could find the money.*

5 (pronounced stressing 'the') used to indicate that someone or something is the best known or most important of that name or type: *he was* **the** *hot young piano prospect in jazz.*

6 used adverbially with comparatives to indicate how one amount or degree of something varies in relation to another: ***the more*** *she thought about it,* ***the more*** *devastating it became.*

■(usu. **all the** ——) used to emphasize the amount or degree to which something is affected: *commodities made all the more desirable by their rarity.*

– ORIGIN Old English *se*, *sēo*, *thæt*, ultimately superseded by forms from Northumbrian and North Mercian *thē*, of Germanic origin; related to Dutch *de*, *dat*, and German *der*, *die*, *das*.

theanthropic /ˌθiːanˈθrɒpɪk/ ▶**adjective** embodying deity in a human form; both divine and human.

– ORIGIN mid 17th cent.: from ecclesiastical Greek *theanthrōpos* 'god-man' (from *theos* 'god' + *anthrōpos* 'human being') + **-IC**.

thearchy /ˈθiːɑːki/ ▶**noun** (pl. **-ies**) [mass noun] archaic rule by a god or gods.

– ORIGIN mid 17th cent.: from ecclesiastical Greek *thearkhia* 'godhead', from *theos* 'god' + *arkhein* 'to rule'.

theatre (US **theater**) ▶**noun** a building or outdoor area in which plays and other dramatic performances are given.

■[mass noun] (often **the theatre**) the activity or profession of acting in, producing, directing, or writing plays: *what made you want to go into the theatre?* ■ [mass noun] a play or other activity or presentation considered in terms of its dramatic quality: *this is intense, moving, and inspiring theatre.* ■ chiefly N. Amer. & W. Indian a cinema. ■ (also **lecture theatre**) a room or hall for lectures with seats in tiers. ■ Brit. an operating theatre. ■ the area in which something happens: *a new* ***theatre of war*** *has been opened up.* ■ [as modifier] denoting weapons for use in a particular region between tactical and strategic: *he was working on theatre defence missiles.*

– ORIGIN late Middle English: from Old French, or from Latin *theatrum*, from Greek *theatron*, from *theasthai* 'behold'.

theatreland ▶**noun** [mass noun] informal the district of a city in which most theatres are situated.

■people professionally involved in theatre, viewed collectively: *theatreland is having a bumper season.*

Theatre of the Absurd ▶**noun** (**the Theatre of the Absurd**) drama using the abandonment of conventional dramatic form to portray the futility of human struggle in a senseless world. Major exponents include Samuel Beckett, Eugène Ionesco, and Harold Pinter.

theatric /θɪˈatrɪk/ ▶ **adjective** another term for **THEATRICAL**.

theatrical ▶ **adjective** of, for, or relating to acting, actors, or the theatre: *theatrical productions*.
▪exaggerated and excessively dramatic: *Henry looked over his shoulder with theatrical caution*.
▶**noun** (usu. **theatricals**) a professional actor or actress: *a boarding house that catered for theatricals*.
– DERIVATIVES **theatricalism** noun, **theatricality** noun, **theatricalization** noun, **theatricalize** (also **-ise**) verb, **theatrically** adverb.
– ORIGIN mid 16th cent.: via late Latin from Greek *theatrikos* (from *theatron* 'theatre') + **-AL**.

theatricals ▶ **plural noun** dramatic performances: *I was persuaded to act in some amateur theatricals*.
▪excessively emotional and dramatic behaviour: *their love affair ended without theatricals*.

theatrics ▶ **plural noun** another term for **THEATRICALS**.

thebe /ˈθeɪbeɪ/ ▶ **noun** (pl. same) a monetary unit of Botswana, equal to one hundredth of a pula.
– ORIGIN Setswana, literally 'shield'.

Thebes /θiːbz/ **1** the Greek name for an ancient city of Upper Egypt, whose ruins are situated on the Nile about 675 km (420 miles) south of Cairo. It was the capital of ancient Egypt under the 18th dynasty (*c*.1550–1290 BC) and is the site of the major temples of Luxor and Karnak.
2 a city in Greece, in Boeotia, north-west of Athens. Thebes became a major military power in Greece following the defeat of the Spartans at the battle of Leuctra in 371 BC. It was destroyed by Alexander the Great in 336 BC. Greek name **Thívai**.
– DERIVATIVES **Theban** adjective & noun.

theca /ˈθiːkə/ ▶ **noun** (pl. **thecae** /-siː/) a receptacle, sheath, or cell enclosing an organ, part, or structure, in particular:
▪Anatomy the loose sheath enclosing the spinal cord. ▪ Zoology a cup-like or tubular structure containing a coral polyp. ▪ Botany either of the lobes of an anther, each containing two pollen sacs. ▪ (also **theca folliculi** /fəˈlɪkjʊlʌɪ/) Anatomy the outer layer of cells of a Graafian follicle.
– DERIVATIVES **thecate** adjective.
– ORIGIN early 17th cent.: via Latin from Greek *thēkē* 'case'.

thecodont /ˈθiːkə(ʊ)dɒnt/ ▶ **noun** a fossil quadrupedal or partly bipedal reptile of the Triassic period, having teeth fixed in sockets in the jaw. Thecodonts are ancestral to the dinosaurs and other archosaurs.
• Order Thecodontia, subdivision Archosauria.
– ORIGIN mid 19th cent.: from modern Latin *Thecodontia*, from Greek *thēkē* 'case' + *odous, odont-* 'tooth'.

thé dansant /ˌteɪ dɒ̃ˈsɒ̃, French te dɑ̃sɑ̃/ ▶ **noun** (pl. **thés dansants** pronunc. same) French term for **TEA DANCE**.

thee ▶ **pronoun** [second person singular] archaic or dialect form of **YOU**, as the singular object of a verb or preposition: *we beseech thee O lord*. Compare with **THOU**[1].
– ORIGIN Old English *thē*, accusative and dative case of *thū* 'thou'.

> **USAGE** The word **thee** is still used in some traditional dialects (e.g. in northern England) and among certain religious groups, but in standard English it is restricted to archaic contexts. For more details on **thee** and **thou**, see **usage** at **THOU**[1].

theft ▶ **noun** [mass noun] the action or crime of stealing: *he was convicted of theft* | [count noun] *the latest theft happened at a garage*.
– ORIGIN Old English *thīefth, thēofth*, of Germanic origin; related to **THIEF**.

thegn /θeɪn/ ▶ **noun** historical an English thane.
– ORIGIN mid 19th cent.: modern representation of Old English *theg(e)n*, adopted to distinguish the Old English use of **THANE** from the Scots use made familiar by Shakespeare.

theine /ˈθiːiːn, ˈθiːɪn/ ▶ **noun** [mass noun] caffeine, especially when it occurs in tea.
– ORIGIN mid 19th cent.: from modern Latin *Thea* (former genus name of the tea plant, from Dutch *thee*) + **-INE**[4].

their ▶ **possessive determiner 1** belonging to or associated with the people or things previously mentioned or easily identified: *parents keen to help their children*.
▪belonging to or associated with a person of unspecified sex: *she heard someone blow their nose loudly*.
2 (**Their**) used in titles: *a double portrait of Their Majesties*.
– ORIGIN Middle English: from Old Norse *their(r)a* 'of them', genitive plural of the demonstrative *sá*; related to **THEM** and **THEY**.

> **USAGE** On the use of **their** in the singular to mean 'his or her', see **usage** at **THEY**.

theirs ▶ **possessive pronoun** used to refer to a thing or things belonging to or associated with two or more people or things previously mentioned: *they think everything is theirs* | *a favourite game of theirs*.
– ORIGIN Middle English: from **THEIR** + **-'s**[1].

theirselves ▶ **pronoun** [third person plural] dialect form of **THEMSELVES**.

theism /ˈθiːɪz(ə)m/ ▶ **noun** [mass noun] belief in the existence of a god or gods, especially belief in one god as creator of the universe, intervening in it and sustaining a personal relation to his creatures. Compare with **DEISM**.
– DERIVATIVES **theist** noun, **theistic** /-ˈɪstɪk/ adjective.
– ORIGIN late 17th cent.: from Greek *theos* 'god' + **-ISM**.

them ▶ **pronoun** [third person plural] **1** used as the object of a verb or preposition to refer to two or more people or things previously mentioned or easily identified: *I bathed the kids and read them stories* | *rows of doors, most of them locked*. Compare with **THEY**.
▪used after the verb 'to be' and after 'than' or 'as': *you reckon that's them?* | *we're better than them*. ▪ [singular] referring to a person of unspecified sex: *how well do you have to know someone before you call them a friend?*
2 archaic themselves: *they bethought them of a new expedient*.
▶**determiner** informal or dialect those: *look at them eyes*.
– ORIGIN Middle English: from Old Norse *theim* 'to those, to them', dative plural of *sá*; related to **THEIR** and **THEM**.

> **USAGE** On the use of **them** in the singular to mean 'him or her', see **usage** at **THEY**.

thematic ▶ **adjective 1** having or relating to subjects or a particular subject: *the orientation of this anthology is essentially thematic*.
▪relating to the collecting of postage stamps with designs connected with the same subject. ▪ Linguistics belonging to, relating to, or denoting the theme of a sentence. ▪ Music of, relating to, or containing melodic subjects: *the concerto relies on the frequent repetition of thematic fragments*.
2 Linguistics of or relating to the theme of an inflected word.
▪(of a vowel) connecting the theme of a word to its inflections. ▪ (of a word) having a vowel connecting its theme to its inflections.
▶**noun 1** (**thematics**) [treated as sing. or pl.] a body of topics for study or discussion.
2 a postage stamp forming part of a set or collection with designs connected with the same subject.
– DERIVATIVES **thematically** adverb.
– ORIGIN late 17th cent.: from Greek *thematikos*, from *thema* (see **THEME**).

thematic apperception test ▶ **noun** Psychology a projective test designed to reveal a person's social drives or needs by their interpretation of a series of pictures of emotionally ambiguous situations.

thematic catalogue ▶ **noun** Music a catalogue giving the opening themes of works as well as their names and other details.

thematic role ▶ **noun** (in Chomskyan linguistics) any of a set of semantic roles that a noun phrase may have in relation to a verb, for example agent, patient, location, source, or goal. Also called **THETA ROLE**.

thematize (also **-ise**) ▶ **verb** [with obj.] present or select (a subject) as a theme.
▪Linguistics place (a word or phrase) at the start of a sentence in order to focus attention on it.
– DERIVATIVES **thematization** noun.

theme ▶ **noun 1** the subject of a talk, a piece of writing, a person's thoughts, or an exhibition; a topic: *the theme of the sermon was reverence* | *a show on the theme of waste and recycling*.
▪Linguistics the first major constituent of a clause, indicating the subject-matter, typically being the subject but optionally other constituents, as in '*smitten* he is not'. Contrasted with **RHEME**. ▪ an idea that recurs in or pervades a work of art or literature. ▪ Music a prominent or frequently recurring melody or group of notes in a composition. ▪ [as modifier] (of music) frequently recurring in or accompanying the beginning and end of a film, play, or musical: *a theme song*. ▪ a setting or ambience given to a leisure venue or activity: *a family fun park with a western theme*. ▪ [as modifier] denoting a restaurant or pub in which the decor and the food and drink served are intended to suggest a particular foreign country, historical period, or other ambience: *American theme restaurants*. ▪ US an essay written by a school pupil on a set subject.
2 Linguistics the stem of a noun or verb; the part to which inflections are added, especially one composed of the root and an added vowel.
3 historical any of the twenty-nine provinces in the Byzantine empire.
▶**verb** [with obj.] give a particular setting or ambience to (a leisure venue or activity): [as adj. **themed**] *Independence Day was celebrated with special themed menus*.
– ORIGIN Middle English: via Old French from Latin *thema*, from Greek, literally 'proposition'; related to *tithenai* 'to set or place'.

theme park ▶ **noun** an amusement park with a unifying setting or idea.

Themis /ˈθɛmɪs/ Greek Mythology a goddess, daughter of Uranus (Heaven) and Gaia (Earth). In Homer she was the personification of order and justice, who convened the assembly of the gods.

Themistocles /θɪˈmɪstəˌkliːz/ (*c*.528–462 BC), Athenian statesman. He helped build up the Athenian fleet, and defeated the Persian fleet at Salamis in 480.

themself ▶ **pronoun** [third person singular] used instead of 'himself' or 'herself' to refer to a person of unspecified sex: *the casual observer might easily think themself back in 1945*.

> **USAGE** The standard reflexive form corresponding to **they** and **them** is **themselves**, as in *they can do it themselves*. The singular form **themself**, first recorded in the 14th century, has re-emerged in recent years corresponding to the singular gender-neutral use of **they**, as in *this is the first step in helping someone to help themself*. The form is not widely accepted in standard English, however. For more details, see **usage** at **THEY**.

themselves ▶ **pronoun** [third person plural] **1** [reflexive] used as the object of a verb or preposition to refer to a group of people or things previously mentioned as the subject of the clause: *countries unable to look after themselves*.
2 [emphatic] used to emphasize a particular group of people or things mentioned: *excellent at organizing others, they may well be disorganized themselves*.
3 [singular] used instead of 'himself' or 'herself' to refer to a person of unspecified sex: *anyone who fancies themselves as a racing driver*.
– PHRASES (**not**) **be themselves** see ***be oneself, not be oneself*** at **BE**. **by themselves** see ***by oneself*** at **BY**.

> **USAGE** On the use of **themselves** in the singular to mean 'himself or herself', see **usage** at **THEY**.

then ▶ **adverb 1** at that time; at the time in question: *I was living in Cairo then* | [after prep.] *Phoebe by then was exhausted* | [as adj.] *he accepted a peerage from the then Prime Minister, Edward Heath*.
2 after that; next; afterwards: *she won the first and then the second game*.
▪also; in addition: *I'm paid a generous salary, and then there's the money I've made at the races*.
3 in that case; therefore: *if you do what I tell you, then there's nothing to worry about* | *well, that's okay then*.
▪used at the end of a sentence to emphasize an inference being drawn: *so you're still here then*. ▪ used to finish off a conversation: *see you in an hour then*.
– PHRASES **but then** (**again**) after all; on the other hand (introducing a contrasting comment): *it couldn't help, but then again, it probably couldn't hurt*. **then and there** immediately.
– ORIGIN Old English *thænne, thanne, thonne*, of Germanic origin; related to Dutch *dan* and German *dann*, also to **THAT** and **THE**.

thenar /ˈθiːnə/ Anatomy ▶ **adjective** of or relating to the rounded fleshy part of the hand at the base of the thumb (the ball of the thumb).
– ORIGIN mid 17th cent.: from Greek, literally 'palm of the hand, sole of the foot'.

t

thenardite /θɛˈnɑːdʌɪt/ ▶ **noun** [mass noun] a white to brownish translucent crystalline mineral occurring in evaporated salt lakes, consisting of anhydrous sodium sulphate.
– ORIGIN mid 19th cent.: from the name of Baron Louis-Jacques *Thénard* (1777–1857), French chemist, + **-ITE**[1].

thence (also **from thence**) ▶ **adverb** formal from a place or source previously mentioned: *they intended to cycle on into France and thence home via Belgium.*
■ as a consequence: *studying maps to assess past latitudes and thence an indication of climate.*
– ORIGIN Middle English *thennes*, from earlier *thenne* (from Old English *thanon*, of West Germanic origin) + **-S**[3] (later respelled *-ce* to denote the unvoiced sound).

USAGE The use of **thence** is similar to **whence** in that **thence** and **from thence** are both used to mean 'from a place or source previously mentioned'. See also **usage** at **WHENCE**.

thenceforth (also **from thenceforth**) ▶ **adverb** archaic or poetic/literary from that time, place, or point onward: *thenceforth he made his life in England.*

thenceforward ▶ **adverb** another term for **THENCEFORTH**.

theo- ▶ **combining form** relating to God or deities: *theocentric | theocracy.*
– ORIGIN from Greek *theos* 'god'.

theobromine /ˌθɪə(ʊ)ˈbrəʊmɪn, -miːn/ ▶ **noun** [mass noun] Chemistry a bitter, volatile compound obtained from cacao seeds. It is an alkaloid resembling caffeine in its physiological effects.
• Chem. formula: $C_7H_8N_4O_2$.
– ORIGIN mid 19th cent.: from modern Latin *Theobroma* (genus name, from Greek *theos* 'god' and *brōma* 'food') + **-INE**[4].

theocentric /ˌθɪə(ʊ)ˈsɛntrɪk/ ▶ **adjective** having God as a central focus: *a theocentric civilization.*

theocracy /θɪˈɒkrəsi/ ▶ **noun** (pl. **-ies**) a system of government in which priests rule in the name of God or a god.
■ (**the Theocracy**) the commonwealth of Israel from the time of Moses until the election of Saul as King.
– DERIVATIVES **theocrat** noun, **theocratic** adjective, **theocratically** adverb.
– ORIGIN early 17th cent.: from Greek *theokratia* (see **THEO-**, **-CRACY**).

Theocritus /θɪˈɒkrɪtəs/ (c.310–c.250 BC), Greek poet, born in Sicily. He is chiefly known for his *Idylls*, hexameter poems presenting the lives of imaginary shepherds which were the model for Virgil's *Eclogues*.

theodicy /θɪˈɒdɪsi/ ▶ **noun** (pl. **-ies**) [mass noun] the vindication of divine providence in view of the existence of evil.
– DERIVATIVES **theodicean** /-ˈsiːən/ adjective.
– ORIGIN late 18th cent.: from French *Théodicée*, the title of a work by Leibniz, from Greek *theos* 'god' + *dikē* 'justice'.

theodolite /θɪˈɒdəlʌɪt/ ▶ **noun** a surveying instrument with a rotating telescope for measuring horizontal and vertical angles.
– DERIVATIVES **theodolitic** adjective.
– ORIGIN late 16th cent. (originally denoting an instrument for measuring horizontal angles): from modern Latin *theodelitus*, of unknown origin.

Theodora /θɪəˈdɔːrə/ (c.500–48), Byzantine empress, wife of Justinian. As Justinian's closest adviser, she exercised a considerable influence on political affairs and the theological questions of the time.

Theodorakis /ˌθɪədəˈrɑːkɪs/, Mikis (b.1925), Greek composer and politician. He was imprisoned by the military government for his left-wing political activities (1967–70). His compositions include the ballet *Antigone* (1958), and the score for the film *Zorba the Greek* (1965).

Theodoric /θɪˈɒdərɪk/ (c.454–526), king of the Ostrogoths 471–526; known as **Theodoric the Great**. At its greatest extent his empire included Italy, Sicily, Dalmatia, and parts of Germany.

Theodosius I /θɪəˈdəʊsɪəs/ (c.346–95), Roman emperor 379–95; full name *Flavius Theodosius*; known as **Theodosius the Great**. Proclaimed co-emperor by the Emperor Gratian in 379, he took control of the Eastern Empire and ended the war with the Visigoths. A pious Christian, in 391 he banned all forms of pagan worship.

theogony /θɪˈɒɡəni/ ▶ **noun** (pl. **-ies**) the genealogy of a group or system of gods.
– ORIGIN early 17th cent.: from Greek *theogonia*, from *theos* 'god' + Greek *-gonia* '-begetting'.

theologian /θɪəˈləʊdʒɪən, -dʒ(ə)n/ ▶ **noun** a person who engages or is an expert in theology.
– ORIGIN late 15th cent.: from French *théologien*, from *théologie* or Latin *theologia* (see **THEOLOGY**).

theological /θɪəˈlɒdʒɪk(ə)l/ ▶ **adjective** of or relating to the study of the nature of God and religious belief.
– DERIVATIVES **theologically** adverb.
– ORIGIN late Middle English (in the sense 'relating to the word of God or the Bible'): from medieval Latin *theologicalis*, from late Latin *theologicus*, from Greek *theologikos*, from *theologia* (see **THEOLOGY**).

theological virtue ▶ **noun** each of the three virtues of faith, hope, and charity. Often contrasted with **NATURAL VIRTUES**.

theologize (also **-ise**) ▶ **verb 1** [no obj.] engage is theological reasoning or speculation.
2 [with obj.] treat (a person or subject) in theological terms.

theology ▶ **noun** (pl. **-ies**) [mass noun] the study of the nature of God and religious belief.
■ religious beliefs and theory when systematically developed: *in Christian theology, God comes to be conceived as Father and Son* | [count noun] *a willingness to tolerate new theologies.*
– DERIVATIVES **theologist** noun.
– ORIGIN late Middle English (originally applying only to Christianity): from French *théologie*, from Latin *theologia*, from Greek, from *theos* 'god' + *-logia* (see **-LOGY**).

theomachy /θɪˈɒmәki/ ▶ **noun** (pl. **-ies**) a war or struggle against God or among or against the gods.
– ORIGIN late 16th cent. (denoting fighting against God): from Greek *theomakhia*, from *theos* 'god' + *-makhia* 'fighting'.

theophany /θɪˈɒf(ə)ni/ ▶ **noun** (pl. **-ies**) a visible manifestation to humankind of God or a god.
– ORIGIN Old English, via ecclesiastical Latin from Greek *theophaneia*, from *theos* 'god' + *phainein* 'to show'.

theophoric /θɪəˈfɒrɪk/ (also **theophorous**) ▶ **adjective** bearing the name of a god.

Theophrastus /θɪəˈfrastəs/ (c.370–c.287 BC), Greek philosopher and scientist, the pupil and successor of Aristotle. The most influential of his works was *Characters*, a collection of sketches of psychological types.

theophylline /θɪəˈfɪliːn, -lɪn/ ▶ **noun** [mass noun] Chemistry a bitter crystalline compound present in small quantities in tea leaves, isomeric with theobromine.
– ORIGIN late 19th cent.: from modern Latin *Thea* (former genus name of the tea plant, from Dutch *thee*) + Greek *phullon* 'leaf' + **-INE**[4].

theorbo /θɪˈɔːbəʊ/ ▶ **noun** (pl. **-os**) a large lute with the neck extended to carry several long bass strings, used for accompaniment in 17th and early 18th century music.
– ORIGIN early 17th cent.: from Italian *tiorba*, of unknown origin.

theorem /ˈθɪərəm/ ▶ **noun** Physics & Mathematics a general proposition not self-evident but proved by a chain of reasoning; a truth established by means of accepted truths.
■ a rule in algebra or other branches of mathematics expressed by symbols or formulae.
– DERIVATIVES **theorematic** /-ˈmatɪk/ adjective.
– ORIGIN mid 16th cent.: from French *théorème*, or via late Latin from Greek *theōrēma* 'speculation, proposition', from *theōrein* 'look at', from *theōros* 'spectator'.

theoretic /θɪəˈrɛtɪk/ ▶ **adjective** another term for **THEORETICAL**.
– ORIGIN early 17th cent. (in the sense 'conjectural'): via late Latin from Greek *theōrētikos*, from *theōrētos* 'that may be seen', from *theōrein* (see **THEOREM**).

theoretical ▶ **adjective** concerned with or involving the theory of a subject or area of study rather than its practical application: *a theoretical physicist* | *the training is task-related rather than theoretical.*
■ based on or calculated through theory rather than experience or practice: *the theoretical value of their work.*
– DERIVATIVES **theoretically** adverb [sentence adverb] *theoretically we might expect this to be true.*

theoretician /ˌθɪərɪˈtɪʃ(ə)n/ ▶ **noun** a person who forms, develops, or studies the theoretical framework of a subject.

theorist ▶ **noun** a person concerned with the theoretical aspects of a subject; a theoretician.

theorize (also **-ise**) ▶ **verb** [no obj.] form a theory or set of theories about something: [as noun **theorizing**] *they are more interested in obtaining results than in political theorizing.*
■ [with obj.] create a theoretical premise or framework for (something): *women should be doing feminism rather than theorizing it.*
– DERIVATIVES **theorization** noun, **theorizer** noun.

theory ▶ **noun** (pl. **-ies**) a supposition or a system of ideas intended to explain something, especially one based on general principles independent of the thing to be explained: *Darwin's theory of evolution.*
■ a set of principles on which the practice of an activity is based: *a theory of education* | [mass noun] *music theory.* ■ an idea used to account for a situation or justify a course of action: *my theory would be that the place has been seriously mismanaged.* ■ Mathematics a collection of propositions to illustrate the principles of a subject.
– PHRASES **in theory** used in describing what is supposed to happen or be possible, usually with the implication that it does not in fact happen: *in theory, things can only get better; in practice, they may well become a lot worse.*
– ORIGIN late 16th cent. (denoting a mental scheme of something to be done): via late Latin from Greek *theōria* 'contemplation, speculation', from *theōros* 'spectator'.

theory-laden ▶ **adjective** denoting a term, concept, or statement which has meaning only as part of some theory, so that its use implies the acceptance of that theory.

theory of games ▶ **noun** another term for **GAME THEORY**.

theosophy /θɪˈɒsəfi/ ▶ **noun** [mass noun] any of a number of philosophies maintaining that a knowledge of God may be achieved through spiritual ecstasy, direct intuition, or special individual relations, especially the movement founded in 1875 as the Theosophical Society by Helena Blavatsky and Henry Steel Olcott (1832–1907).
– DERIVATIVES **theosopher** noun, **theosophic** adjective, **theosophical** adjective, **theosophically** adverb, **theosophist** noun.
– ORIGIN mid 17th cent.: from medieval Latin *theosophia*, from late Greek, from *theosophos* 'wise concerning God', from *theos* 'god' + *sophos* 'wise'.

Theotokos /θɪˈɒtəkɒs/ ▶ **noun** (**the Theotokos**) Mother of God (used in the Eastern Orthodox Church as a title of the Virgin Mary).
– ORIGIN from ecclesiastical Greek, from *theos* 'god' + *-tokos* 'bringing forth'.

Thera /ˈθɪərə/ a Greek island in the southern Cyclades. The island suffered a violent volcanic eruption in about 1500 BC; remains of an ancient Minoan civilization have been preserved beneath the pumice and volcanic debris. Also called **SANTORINI**. Greek name **THÍRA**.

therapeutic /ˌθɛrəˈpjuːtɪk/ ▶ **adjective** of or relating to the healing of disease: *diagnostic and therapeutic facilities.*
■ administered or applied for reasons of health: *a therapeutic shampoo.* ■ having a good effect on the body or mind; contributing to a sense of well-being: *a therapeutic silence.*
– DERIVATIVES **therapeutical** adjective, **therapeutically** adverb, **therapeutist** noun (archaic).
– ORIGIN mid 17th cent.: via modern Latin from Greek *therapeutikos*, from *therapeuein* 'minister to, treat medically'.

therapeutics ▶ **plural noun** [treated as sing.] the branch of medicine concerned with the treatment of disease and the action of remedial agents.
– ORIGIN late 17th cent.: plural of earlier *therapeutic* (noun), from French *thérapeutique*, or via late Latin from Greek *therapeutika*, neuter plural (used as a noun) of *therapeutikos* (see **THERAPEUTIC**).

therapsid /θɛˈrapsɪd/ ▶ **noun** a fossil reptile of a Permian and Triassic order, the members of which are related to the ancestors of mammals.
• Order Therapsida, subclass Synapsida: many families and numerous genera, including the cynodonts.

– ORIGIN early 20th cent.: from modern Latin *Therapsida*, from Greek *thēr* 'beast' + *hapsis, hapsid-* 'arch' (referring to the structure of the skull).

therapy ▶ **noun** (pl. **-ies**) [mass noun] treatment intended to relieve or heal a disorder: *a course of antibiotic therapy* | [count noun] *cancer therapies.*
■ the treatment of mental or psychological disorders by psychological means: *he is currently* **in therapy** | [as modifier] *therapy sessions.*
– DERIVATIVES **therapist** noun.
– ORIGIN mid 19th cent.: from modern Latin *therapia*, from Greek *therapeia* 'healing', from *therapeuein* 'minister to, treat medically'.

Theravada /ˌθɛrəˈvɑːdə/ (also **Theravada Buddhism**) ▶ **noun** [mass noun] the more conservative of the two major traditions of Buddhism (the other being Mahayana), which developed from Hinayana Buddhism. It is practised mainly in Sri Lanka, Burma (Myanmar), Thailand, Cambodia, and Laos.
– ORIGIN from Pali *theravāda*, literally 'doctrine of the elders', from *thera* 'elder, old' + *vāda* 'speech, doctrine'.

there ▶ **adverb 1** in, at, or to that place or position: *we went on to Paris and stayed there eleven days* | [after prep.] *I'm not going in there—it's freezing* | figurative *the opportunity is right there in front of you.*
■ used when pointing or gesturing to indicate the place in mind: *there on the right* | *if anyone wants out,* **there's** *the door!* ■ at that point (in speech, performance, writing, etc.): *'I'm quite—' There she stopped.* ■ in that respect; on that issue: *I don't agree with you there.* ■ [with infinitive] used to indicate one's role in a particular situation: *at the end of the day we are there to make money.*
2 used in attracting someone's attention or calling attention to someone or something: *hello there!* | *there goes the phone.*
3 (usu. **there is/are**) used to indicate the fact or existence of something: *there's a restaurant round the corner* | *there comes a point where you give up.*
▶ **exclamation 1** used to focus attention on something and express satisfaction or annoyance at it: *there, I told you she wouldn't mind!*
2 used to comfort someone: **there, there,** *you must take all of this philosophically.*
– PHRASES **been there, done that** informal used to express past experience of or familiarity with something, especially something now regarded as boring or unwelcome. **be there for someone** be available to provide support or comfort for someone, especially at a time of adversity. **have been there before** informal know all about a situation from experience. **here and there** see HERE. **so there** informal used to express one's defiance or awareness that someone will not like what one has decided or is saying: *you can't share, so there!* **there and then** immediately. **there goes ——** used to express the destruction or failure of something: *there goes my career.* **there it is** that is the situation: *pretty ridiculous, I know, but there it is.* **there or thereabouts** in or very near a particular place or position. ■ approximately: *forty years, there or thereabouts, had elapsed.* **there you are** (or **go**) informal **1** this is what you wanted: *there you are—that'll be £3.80 please.* **2** expressing confirmation, triumph, or resignation: *there you are! I told you the problem was a political one* | *sometimes it is embarrassing, but there you go.* **there you go again** used to criticize someone for behaving in a way that is typical of them. **there you have it** used to emphasize or draw attention to a particular fact: *so there you have it—fish and chips were a West country invention.* ■ used to draw attention to the simplicity of a process or action: *simply turn the handle three times and there you have it.*
– ORIGIN Old English *thǣr, thēr* of Germanic origin; related to Dutch *daar* and German *da*, also to THAT and THE.

thereabouts (also **thereabout**) ▶ **adverb** near that place: *the land is dry in places thereabouts.*
■ used to indicate that a date or figure is approximate: *the notes were written in 1860 or thereabouts.*

thereafter ▶ **adverb** formal after that time: *thereafter their fortunes suffered a steep decline.*

thereanent /ˌðɛːrəˈnɛnt/ ▶ **adverb** Scottish concerning that matter: *optimistic views thereanent.*

thereat ▶ **adverb** archaic or formal **1** at that place.
2 on account of or after that.

thereby ▶ **adverb** by that means; as a result of that: *students perform in hospitals, thereby gaining a deeper awareness of the therapeutic power of music.*
– PHRASES **thereby hangs a tale** used to indicate that there is more to say about something.

therefor ▶ **adverb** archaic for that object or purpose.

therefore ▶ **adverb** for that reason; consequently: *he was injured and therefore unable to play.*

therefrom ▶ **adverb** archaic or formal from that or that place.

therein ▶ **adverb** archaic or formal in that place, document, or respect.

thereinafter ▶ **adverb** archaic or formal in a later part of that document.

thereinbefore ▶ **adverb** archaic or formal in an earlier part of that document.

thereinto ▶ **adverb** archaic or formal into that place.

theremin /ˈθɛrəmɪn/ ▶ **noun** an electronic musical instrument in which the tone is generated by two high-frequency oscillators and the pitch controlled by the movement of the performer's hand towards and away from the circuit.
– ORIGIN early 20th cent.: named after Lev *Theremin* (1896–1993), its Russian inventor.

thereof ▶ **adverb** formal of the thing just mentioned; of that: *the member state or a part thereof.*

thereon ▶ **adverb** formal on or following from the thing just mentioned: *the order of the court and the taxation consequent thereon.*

thereout ▶ **adverb** archaic out of that; from that source.

there's ▶ **contraction of** there is: *there's nothing there.*
■ informal, chiefly Brit. used to make a request or express approval of an action in a patronizing manner: *make a cup of tea, there's a good girl.*

Theresa, Mother see TERESA, MOTHER.

Thérèse of Lisieux, St /tɛˈrɛz, French tɛʀɛz/ variant spelling of TERESA OF LISIEUX, ST.

therethrough ▶ **adverb** archaic through or by reason of that; thereby.

thereto ▶ **adverb** archaic or formal to that or that place: *the third party assents thereto.*

theretofore ▶ **adverb** archaic or formal before that time.

thereunder ▶ **adverb** archaic or formal in accordance with the thing mentioned: *the act and the regulations made thereunder.*

thereunto ▶ **adverb** archaic or formal to that: *his agent thereunto lawfully authorized in writing or by will.*

thereupon ▶ **adverb** formal immediately or shortly after that: *he thereupon returned to Moscow.*

therewith ▶ **adverb** archaic or formal **1** with or in the thing mentioned: *documents lodged therewith.*
2 soon or immediately after that; forthwith: *therewith he rose.*

therewithal ▶ **adverb** archaic together with that; besides: *he was to make a voyage and his fortune therewithal.*

Theria /ˈθɪərɪə/ Zoology a major group of mammals that comprises the marsupials and placentals. Compare with PROTOTHERIA.
• Subclass Theria, class Mammalia.
– DERIVATIVES **therian** noun & adjective.
– ORIGIN modern Latin (plural), from Greek *thēria* 'wild animals'.

theriac /ˈθɪərɪak/ ▶ **noun** [mass noun] archaic an ointment or other medicinal compound used as an antidote to snake venom or other poison.
– ORIGIN late Middle English: from Latin *theriaca* (see TREACLE).

therianthropic /ˌθɪərɪanˈθrɒpɪk/ ▶ **adjective** (especially of a deity) combining the form of an animal with that of a man.
– ORIGIN late 19th cent.: from Greek *thērion* 'wild animal' + *anthrōpos* 'human being' + -IC.

theriomorphic /ˌθɪərɪə(ʊ)ˈmɔːfɪk/ ▶ **adjective** (especially of a deity) having an animal form.
– ORIGIN late 19th cent.: from Greek *thērion* 'wild beast' + -MORPH + -IC.

therm ▶ **noun** a unit of heat, especially as the former statutory unit of gas supplied in the UK equivalent to 100,000 British thermal units or 1.055 × 10^8 joules.
– ORIGIN 1920s: from Greek *thermē* 'heat'.

thermae /ˈθəːmiː/ ▶ **plural noun** (in ancient Greece and Rome) hot baths used for public bathing.
– ORIGIN Latin, from Greek *thermai* 'hot baths', from *thermē* 'heat'.

thermal ▶ **adjective** of or relating to heat.
■ another term for GEOTHERMAL. ■ (of a garment) made of a fabric that provides exceptional insulation to keep the body warm: *thermal underwear.*
▶ **noun 1** an upward current of warm air, used by gliders, balloons, and birds to gain height.
2 (usu. **thermals**) a thermal garment, especially underwear.
– DERIVATIVES **thermally** adverb.
– ORIGIN mid 18th cent. (in the sense 'relating to hot springs'): from French, from Greek *thermē* 'heat'.

thermal capacity ▶ **noun** the number of heat units needed to raise the temperature of a body by one degree.

thermal diffusivity ▶ **noun** the thermal conductivity of a substance divided by the product of its density and its specific heat capacity.

thermal efficiency ▶ **noun** the efficiency of a heat engine measured by the ratio of the work done by it to the heat supplied to it.

thermal imaging ▶ **noun** [mass noun] the technique of using the heat given off by an object to produce an image of it or locate it.

thermal inversion ▶ **noun** see INVERSION (sense 2).

thermalize (also **-ise**) ▶ **verb** attain or cause to attain thermal equilibrium with the environment.
– DERIVATIVES **thermalization** noun.

thermal neutron ▶ **noun** a neutron in thermal equilibrium with its surroundings.

thermal noise ▶ **noun** [mass noun] Electronics electrical fluctuations arising from the random thermal motion of electrons.

thermal paper ▶ **noun** [mass noun] heat-sensitive paper used in thermal printers.

thermal printer ▶ **noun** a printer in which fine heated pins form characters on heat-sensitive paper.

thermal reactor ▶ **noun** a nuclear reactor using thermal neutrons.

thermal shock ▶ **noun** [mass noun] a sudden temperature fluctuation causing stress in an object or substance.

thermal spring ▶ **noun** a spring of naturally hot water.

thermal unit ▶ **noun** a unit for measuring heat.

thermic ▶ **adjective** of or relating to heat.
– ORIGIN mid 19th cent.: from Greek *thermē* 'heat' + -IC.

thermic lance ▶ **noun** a steel pipe packed with steel wool through which a jet of oxygen or other gas may be passed to generate a very hot cutting flame by the burning of the pipe.

Thermidor /ˈθəːmɪdɔː, French tɛʀmidɔʀ/ ▶ **noun** the eleventh month of the French Republican calendar (1793–1805), originally running from 19 July to 17 August.
– DERIVATIVES **Thermidorian** adjective.
– ORIGIN French, from Greek *thermē* 'heat' + *dōron* 'gift'.

thermion /ˈθəːmɪɒn/ ▶ **noun** an ion or electron emitted by a substance at high temperature.
– ORIGIN early 20th cent.: from THERMO- 'of heat' + ION.

thermionic ▶ **adjective** of or relating to electrons emitted from a substance at very high temperature.

thermionic emission ▶ **noun** the emission of electrons from a heated source.

thermionics ▶ **plural noun** [treated as sing.] the branch of science and technology concerned with thermionic emission.

thermionic valve (US **thermionic tube**) ▶ **noun** Electronics a device giving a flow of thermionic electrons in one direction, used especially in the rectification of a current and in radio reception.

thermistor /θəːˈmɪstə/ ▶ **noun** an electrical resistor whose resistance is greatly reduced by heating, used for measurement and control.
– ORIGIN 1940s: contraction of *thermal resistor.*

thermite /ˈθəːmʌɪt/ (also **thermit** /-mɪt/) ▶ **noun** [mass noun] a mixture of finely powdered aluminium and iron oxide that produces a very high temperature on combustion, used in welding and for incendiary bombs.

a cat | ɑː arm | ɛ bed | ɛː hair | ə ago | əː her | ɪ sit | i cosy | iː see | ɒ hot | ɔː saw | ʌ run | ʊ put | uː too | ʌɪ my | aʊ how | eɪ day | əʊ no | ɪə near | ɔɪ boy | ʊə poor | ʌɪə fire | aʊə sour

– ORIGIN early 20th cent.: coined in German from **THERMO-** 'of heat' + **-ITE**[1].

thermo- ▶ combining form relating to heat: *thermodynamics | thermoelectric*.
– ORIGIN from Greek *thermos* 'hot', *thermē* 'heat'.

thermochemistry ▶ noun [mass noun] the branch of chemistry concerned with the quantities of heat evolved or absorbed during chemical reactions.
– DERIVATIVES **thermochemical** adjective.

thermochromic /ˌθəːmə(ʊ)ˈkrəʊmɪk/ ▶ adjective (of a substance) undergoing a reversible change of colour when heated or cooled.

thermocline /ˈθəːmə(ʊ)klʌɪn/ ▶ noun an abrupt temperature gradient in a body of water such as a lake, marked by a layer above and below which the water is at different temperatures.

thermocouple ▶ noun a thermoelectric device for measuring temperature, consisting of two wires of different metals connected at two points, a voltage being developed between the two junctions in proportion to the temperature difference.

thermodynamics ▶ plural noun [treated as sing.] the branch of physical science that deals with the relations between heat and other forms of energy (such as mechanical, electrical, or chemical energy), and, by extension, of the relationships and interconvertibility of all forms of energy.

> The **first law of thermodynamics** states the equivalence of heat and work and reaffirms the principle of conservation of energy. The **second law** states that heat does not of itself pass from a cooler to a hotter body. Another, equivalent, formulation of the second law is that the entropy of a closed system can only increase. The **third law** (also called Nernst's heat theorem) states that it is impossible to reduce the temperature of a system to absolute zero in a finite number of operations.

– DERIVATIVES **thermodynamic** adjective, **thermodynamical** adjective, **thermodynamically** adverb, **thermodynamicist** noun.

thermo-elastic ▶ adjective of or relating to elasticity in connection with heat.

thermoelectric ▶ adjective producing electricity by a difference of temperatures.
– DERIVATIVES **thermoelectrically** adverb, **thermoelectricity** noun.

thermoforming ▶ noun the process of heating a thermoplastic material and shaping it in a mould.

thermogenesis /ˌθəːmə(ʊ)ˈdʒɛnɪsɪs/ ▶ noun [mass noun] the production of heat, especially in a human or animal body.
– DERIVATIVES **thermogenic** adjective.

thermogram ▶ noun a record made by a thermograph.

thermograph ▶ noun an instrument that produces a trace or image representing a record of the varying temperature or infrared radiation over an area or during a period of time.

thermography ▶ noun [mass noun] **1** the use of thermograms to study heat distribution in structures or regions, for example in detecting tumours.
2 a printing technique in which a wet ink image is fused by heat or infrared radiation with a resinous powder to produce a raised impression.
– DERIVATIVES **thermographic** adjective.

thermohaline circulation /ˌθəːmə(ʊ)ˈheɪlʌɪn, -ˈheɪliːn/ ▶ noun [mass noun] Oceanography the movement of seawater in a pattern of flow dependent on variations in temperature, which give rise to changes in salt content and hence in density.

thermokarst /ˈθəːmə(ʊ)kɑːst/ ▶ noun [mass noun] Geology a form of periglacial topography resembling karst, with hollows produced by the selective melting of permafrost.

thermolabile /ˌθəːmə(ʊ)ˈleɪbʌɪl, -bɪl/ ▶ adjective chiefly Biochemistry (of a substance) readily destroyed or deactivated by heat.

thermoluminescence ▶ noun [mass noun] the property of some materials which have accumulated energy over a long period of becoming luminescent when pretreated and subjected to high temperatures, used as a means of dating ancient ceramics and other artefacts.
– DERIVATIVES **thermoluminescent** adjective.

thermolysis /θəːˈmɒlɪsɪs/ ▶ noun [mass noun] Chemistry the breakdown of molecules by the action of heat.
– DERIVATIVES **thermolytic** adjective.

thermometer ▶ noun an instrument for measuring and indicating temperature, typically one consisting of a narrow, hermetically sealed glass tube marked with graduations and having at one end a bulb containing mercury or alcohol which extends along the tube as it expands.
– DERIVATIVES **thermometric** adjective, **thermometrical** adjective, **thermometry** noun.
– ORIGIN mid 17th cent.: from French *thermomètre* or modern Latin *thermometrum*, from **THERMO-** 'of heat' + *-metrum* 'measure'.

thermonuclear ▶ adjective relating to or using nuclear reactions that occur only at very high temperatures.
■ of, relating to, or involving weapons in which explosive force is produced by thermonuclear reactions.

thermophile /ˈθəːmə(ʊ)fʌɪl/ ▶ noun Microbiology a bacterium or other micro-organism that grows best at higher than normal temperatures.
– DERIVATIVES **thermophilic** adjective.

thermopile /ˈθəːmə(ʊ)pʌɪl/ ▶ noun a set of thermocouples arranged for measuring small quantities of radiant heat.

thermoplastic Chemistry ▶ adjective denoting substances (especially synthetic resins) that become plastic on heating and harden on cooling, and are able to repeat these processes. Often contrasted with **THERMOSETTING**.
▶ noun (usu. **thermoplastics**) a substance of this kind.

Thermopylae /θəːˈmɒpɪliː/ a pass between the mountains and the sea in Greece, about 200 km (120 miles) north-west of Athens, originally narrow but now much widened by the recession of the sea. In 480 BC it was the scene of the defence against the Persian army of Xerxes I by 6,000 Greeks; among them were 300 Spartans, all of whom, including their king Leonidas, were killed.

thermoregulate ▶ verb [no obj.] regulate temperature, especially one's own body temperature.
– DERIVATIVES **thermoregulation** noun, **thermoregulatory** adjective.

Thermos (also **Thermos flask**, US also **Thermos bottle**) ▶ noun trademark a vacuum flask.
– ORIGIN early 20th cent.: from Greek, literally 'hot'.

thermosetting ▶ adjective Chemistry denoting substances (especially synthetic resins) which set permanently when heated. Often contrasted with **THERMOPLASTIC**.
– DERIVATIVES **thermoset** adjective & noun.

thermosphere ▶ noun the region of the atmosphere above the mesosphere and below the height at which the atmosphere ceases to have the properties of a continuous medium. The thermosphere is characterized throughout by an increase in temperature with height.

thermostable ▶ adjective chiefly Biochemistry (of a substance) not readily destroyed or deactivated by heat.

thermostat /ˈθəːməstat/ ▶ noun a device that automatically regulates temperature, or that activates a device when the temperature reaches a certain point.
– DERIVATIVES **thermostatic** adjective, **thermostatically** adverb.

thermotropism /ˌθəːmə(ʊ)ˈtrəʊpɪz(ə)m/ ▶ noun [mass noun] Biology the turning or bending of a plant or other organism in response to a directional source of heat.
– DERIVATIVES **thermotropic** adjective.

theropod /ˈθɪərə(ʊ)pɒd/ ▶ noun a carnivorous dinosaur of a group whose members are typically bipedal and range from small and delicately built to very large.
● Suborder Theropoda, order Saurischia; includes the carnosaurs, ornithomimosaurs, coelurosaurs, and dromaeosaurids.
– ORIGIN 1930s: from Greek *thēr* 'beast' + *pous, pod-* 'foot'.

thesaurus /θɪˈsɔːrəs/ ▶ noun (pl. **thesauri** /-rʌɪ/ or **thesauruses**) a book that lists words in groups of synonyms and related concepts.
■ archaic a dictionary or encyclopedia.
– ORIGIN late 16th cent.: via Latin from Greek *thēsauros* 'storehouse, treasure'. The original sense 'dictionary or encyclopedia' was narrowed to the current meaning by the publication of Roget's *Thesaurus of English Words and Phrases* (1852).

these plural form of **THIS**.

Theseus /ˈθiːsɪəs/ Greek Mythology The legendary hero of Athens, son of Poseidon (or, in another account, of Aegeus, king of Athens) and husband of Phaedra. He slew the Cretan Minotaur with the help of Ariadne.

Thesiger /ˈθɛsɪdʒə/, Wilfred (Patrick) (b.1910), English explorer. He explored many countries, notably Saudi Arabia and Oman. Notable works: *Arabian Sands* (1959) and *The Marsh Arabs* (1964).

thesis /ˈθiːsɪs/ ▶ noun (pl. **theses** /-siːz/) **1** a statement or theory that is put forward as a premise to be maintained or proved: *his central thesis is that psychological life is not part of the material world*.
■ (in Hegelian philosophy) a proposition forming the first stage in the process of dialectical reasoning. Compare with **ANTITHESIS**, **SYNTHESIS**.
2 a long essay or dissertation involving personal research, written by a candidate for a university degree: *a doctoral thesis*.
3 /ˈθiːsɪs, ˈθɛsɪs/ Prosody an unstressed syllable or part of a metrical foot in Greek or Latin verse. Often contrasted with **ARSIS**.
– ORIGIN late Middle English (in sense 3): via late Latin from Greek, literally 'placing, a proposition', from the root of *tithenai* 'to place'.

thesp informal ▶ abbreviation for thespian.

thespian /ˈθɛspɪən/ formal or humorous ▶ adjective of or relating to drama and the theatre: *thespian talents*.
▶ noun an actor or actress.
– ORIGIN late 17th cent.: from the name **THESPIS** + **-IAN**.

Thespis /ˈθɛspɪs/ (6th century BC), Greek dramatic poet, regarded as the founder of Greek tragedy.

Thess. ▶ abbreviation for Epistle to the Thessalonians (in biblical references).

Thessalonians, Epistle to the /ˌθɛsəˈləʊnɪənz/ either of two books of the New Testament, letters of St Paul, to the new Church at Thessalonica.

Thessaloníki /ˌθɛsələˈniːki/ a seaport in NE Greece, the second largest city in Greece and capital of the Greek region of Macedonia; pop. 378,000 (1991). Also called **SALONICA**; Latin name **THESSALONICA** /ˌθɛsəˈlɒnɪkə, -ləˈnʌɪkə/.

Thessaly /ˈθɛsəli/ a region of NE Greece. Greek name **THESSALÍA** /ˌθɛsaˈliːa/.
– DERIVATIVES **Thessalian** /θɛˈseɪlɪən/ adjective & noun.

theta /ˈθiːtə/ ▶ noun the eighth letter of the Greek alphabet (Θ, θ), transliterated as 'th'.
■ (**Theta**) [followed by Latin genitive] Astronomy the eighth star in a constellation: *Theta Draconis*. ■ [as modifier] Chemistry denoting a temperature at which a polymer solution behaves ideally as regards its osmotic pressure. ■ [as modifier] denoting electrical activity observed in the brain under certain conditions, consisting of oscillations having a frequency of 4 to 7 hertz: *theta rhythm*.
▶ symbol for ■ (θ) temperature (especially in degrees Celsius). ■ (θ) a plane angle. ■ (θ) a polar coordinate. Often coupled with φ.
– ORIGIN Greek.

theta role ▶ noun another term for **THEMATIC ROLE**.

Thetis /ˈθɛtɪs/ Greek Mythology a sea nymph, mother of Achilles.

theurgy /ˈθiːəːdʒi/ ▶ noun [mass noun] the operation or effect of a supernatural or divine agency in human affairs.
■ a system of white magic practised by the early Neoplatonists.
– DERIVATIVES **theurgic** adjective, **theurgical** adjective, **theurgist** noun.
– ORIGIN mid 16th cent.: via late Latin from Greek *theourgia* 'sorcery', from *theos* 'god' + *-ergos* 'working'.

thew /θjuː/ ▶ noun [mass noun] poetic/literary muscular strength.
■ (**thews**) muscles and tendons perceived as generating such strength.
– DERIVATIVES **thewy** adjective.
– ORIGIN Old English *thēaw* 'usage, custom', (plural) '(personal) manner of behaving', of unknown origin. The sense 'good bodily proportions, muscular development' arose in Middle English.

they ▶ pronoun [third person plural] **1** used to refer to two or more people or things previously mentioned or easily identified: *the two men could get life sentences if they are convicted*.
■ people in general: *the rest, as they say, is history*.

■ informal a group of people in authority regarded collectively: *they cut my water off.*
2 [singular] used to refer to a person of unspecified sex: *ask a friend if they could help.*
– ORIGIN Middle English: from Old Norse *their*, nominative plural masculine of *sá*; related to **THEM** and **THEIR**, also to **THAT** and **THE**.

USAGE The word **they** (with its counterparts **them**, **their**, and **themselves**) as a singular pronoun to refer to a person of unspecified sex has been used since at least the 16th century. In the late 20th century, as the traditional use of **he** to refer to a person of either sex came under scrutiny on the grounds of sexism, this use of **they** has become more common. It is now generally accepted in contexts where it follows an indefinite pronoun such as **anyone**, **no one**, **someone**, or **a person**, as in ***anyone** can join if **they** are a resident* and ***each** to **their** own*. In other contexts, coming after singular nouns, the use of **they** is now common, though less widely accepted, especially in formal contexts. Sentences such as *ask **a friend** if **they** could help* are still criticized for being ungrammatical. Nevertheless, in view of the growing acceptance of **they** and its obvious practical advantages, **they** is used in this dictionary in many cases where **he** would have been used formerly. See also **usage** at **HE** and **SHE**.

they'd ▶ **contraction of** ■ they had. ■ they would.
they'll ▶ **contraction of** they shall; they will.
they're ▶ **contraction of** they are.
they've ▶ **contraction of** they have.
THI ▶ **abbreviation for** temperature–humidity index.
thiabendazole /ˌθʌɪəˈbɛndəzəʊl/ ▶ **noun** [mass noun] Medicine a synthetic compound with anthelmintic properties, derived from thiazole and used chiefly to treat infestation with intestinal nematodes.
– ORIGIN 1960s: from elements from **THIAZOLE** + **BENZENE** + **IMIDAZOLE**.
thiamine /ˈθʌɪəmiːn, -mɪn/ (also **thiamin**) ▶ **noun** [mass noun] Biochemistry a vitamin of the B complex, found in unrefined cereals, beans, and liver, a deficiency of which causes beriberi. It is a sulphur-containing derivative of thiazole and pyrimidine. Also called ***vitamin*** B_1.
thiazide /ˈθʌɪəzʌɪd/ ▶ **noun** Medicine any of a class of sulphur-containing drugs that increase the excretion of sodium and chloride and are used as diuretics and to assist in lowering the blood pressure.
– ORIGIN 1950s: from elements of **THIO-** + **AZINE** + **OXIDE**.
thiazole /θʌɪˈeɪzəʊl/ ▶ **noun** [mass noun] Chemistry a synthetic foul-smelling liquid whose molecule is a ring of one nitrogen, one sulphur, and three carbon atoms.
• Chem. formula: C_3H_3NS.
thick ▶ **adjective 1** with opposite sides or surfaces that are a great or relatively great distance apart: *thick slices of bread | the walls are 5 feet thick.*
■ (of a garment or other knitted or woven item) made of heavy material for warmth or comfort: *a thick sweater.* ■ of large diameter: *thick metal cables.* ■ (of script or type) consisting of broad lines: *a headline in thick black type.*
2 made up of a large number of things or people close together: *his hair was long and thick | the road winds through thick forest.*
■ [predic.] (**thick with**) densely filled or covered with: *the room was thick with smoke |* figurative *the air was thick with rumours.* ■ (of air, the atmosphere, or an odour carried by them) heavy or dense: *a thick odour of dust and perfume.* ■ (of darkness or a substance in the air) so black or dense as to be impossible or difficult to see through: *a motorway pile-up in thick fog.*
3 (of a liquid or a semi-liquid substance) relatively firm in consistency; not flowing freely: *thick mud.*
4 informal of low intelligence; stupid: *he's a bit thick | I've got to shout to get it into your thick head.*
5 (of a voice) not clear or distinct; hoarse or husky.
■ (of an accent) very marked and difficult to understand. ■ (of one's head) having a dull pain or cloudy feeling, especially from illness or excessive drinking.
6 [predic.] informal having a very close, friendly relationship: *he's very **thick with** the new master.*
▶ **noun** (**the thick**) the busiest or most crowded part of something; the middle of something: *the thick of battle.*
▶ **adverb** in or with deep, dense, or heavy mass: *bread spread thick with butter.*
– PHRASES **be thick on the ground** see **GROUND**[1]. **a bit thick** Brit. informal unfair or unreasonable. **give someone** (or **get**) **a thick ear** Brit. informal punish someone (or be punished) with a blow, especially on the ear. **have a thick skin** see **SKIN**. **in** (or **into**) **the thick of something** in (or into) the busiest or most crowded part of something: *we were in the thick of the traffic.* ■ deeply involved in something: *Collins was soon back in the thick of the action.* **thick and fast** rapidly and in great numbers. **(as) thick as a brick** another way of saying ***as thick as two planks*** below. **(as) thick as thieves** informal (of two or more people) very close or friendly; sharing secrets. **(as) thick as two (short) planks** (or **as a plank**) Brit. informal very stupid. **the thick end of something** Brit. the greater part of something: *he was borrowing the thick end of £750 every week.* **through thick and thin** under all circumstances, no matter how difficult: *they stuck together through thick and thin.*
– DERIVATIVES **thickish** adjective, **thickly** adverb [as submodifier] *thickly carpeted corridors.*
– ORIGIN Old English *thicce*, of Germanic origin; related to Dutch *dik* and German *dick*.
thicken ▶ **verb** make or become thick or thicker: [with obj.] *thicken the sauce with flour |* [no obj.] *the fog had thickened.*
– PHRASES **the plot thickens** used when a situation is becoming more and more complicated and puzzling.
thickener ▶ **noun** a substance added to a liquid to make it firmer, especially in cooking.
■ Chemistry an apparatus for the sedimentation of solids from suspension in a liquid.
thickening ▶ **noun** [mass noun] **1** the process or result of becoming broader, deeper, or denser.
■ [count noun] a broader, deeper, or denser area of animal or plant tissue.
2 another term for **THICKENER**.
▶ **adjective** becoming broader, deeper, or denser: *a hazardous journey through thickening fog.*
thicket ▶ **noun** a dense group of bushes or trees.
– ORIGIN Old English *thiccet* (see **THICK**, **-ET**[1]).
thick-film ▶ **adjective** (of a process or device) using or involving a relatively thick solid or liquid film.
■ Electronics denoting a miniature circuit or device based on a metal film.
thickhead ▶ **noun 1** informal a stupid person.
2 another term for **WHISTLER** (in sense 2).
– DERIVATIVES **thickheaded** adjective, **thickheadedness** noun.
thick-knee ▶ **noun** another term for **STONE CURLEW**.
thickness ▶ **noun 1** [mass noun] the distance between opposite sides of something: *the gateway is several feet in thickness |* [count noun] *paving slabs can be obtained in varying thicknesses.*
■ the quality of being broad or deep: *the immense thickness of the walls.* ■ [count noun] a layer of a specified material: *the framework has to support two thicknesses of plasterboard.* ■ [in sing.] a broad or deep part of a specified thing: *the beams were set into the thickness of the wall.*
2 [mass noun] the quality of being dense: *he gave his eyes time to adjust to the thickness of the fog.*
■ the state or quality of being made up of many closely packed parts: *the thickness of his hair.*
▶ **verb** [with obj.] plane or cut (wood) to a desired breadth or depth.
– DERIVATIVES **thicknesser** noun.
– ORIGIN Old English *thicness* (see **THICK**, **-NESS**).
thicko ▶ **noun** (pl. **-os**) informal an unintelligent person.
thickset ▶ **adjective** (of a person or animal) heavily or solidly built; stocky.
thick-skulled (also **thick-witted**) ▶ **adjective** dull and stupid.
thief ▶ **noun** (pl. **thieves**) a person who steals another person's property, especially by stealth and without using force or violence.
– ORIGIN Old English *thīof*, *thēof*, of Germanic origin; related to Dutch *dief* and German *Dieb*, also to **THEFT**.
thieve ▶ **verb** [no obj.] be a thief; steal something: *they began thieving again |* [as adj. **thieving**] *get lost, you thieving swine |* [with obj.] *the students have been thieving my favourite art books.*
– ORIGIN Old English *thēofian*, from *thēof* 'thief'. Transitive uses began in the late 17th cent.
thievery ▶ **noun** [mass noun] the action of stealing another person's property.
thieves plural form of **THIEF**.
thievish ▶ **adjective** of, relating to, or given to stealing.
– DERIVATIVES **thievishly** adverb, **thievishness** noun.
thigh ▶ **noun** the part of the human leg between the hip and the knee.
■ the corresponding part in other animals.
– DERIVATIVES **thighed** adjective [in combination] *a big-thighed man.*
– ORIGIN Old English *thēh*, *thēoh*, *thīoh*, of Germanic origin; related to Dutch *dij*.
thigh bone ▶ **noun** the femur.
thigh-high ▶ **adjective** (of an item of clothing) reaching as far as a person's thigh.
■ at or reaching to the level of a person's thigh: *he waded into the thigh-high river.*
▶ **noun** an item of clothing, especially a garterless stocking, that reaches to a person's thigh.
thigh-slapper ▶ **noun** informal a joke or anecdote considered to be exceptionally funny.
– DERIVATIVES **thigh-slapping** adjective.
thigmotaxis /ˌθɪgməˈtaksɪs/ ▶ **noun** [mass noun] Biology the motion or orientation of an organism in response to a touch stimulus.
– DERIVATIVES **thigmotactic** adjective.
– ORIGIN early 20th cent.: from Greek *thigma* 'touch' + **TAXIS**.
thigmotropism /ˌθɪgmə(ʊ)ˈtrəʊpɪz(ə)m/ ▶ **noun** [mass noun] Biology the turning or bending of a plant or other organism in response to a touch stimulus.
– DERIVATIVES **thigmotropic** adjective.
– ORIGIN early 20th cent.: from Greek *thigma* 'touch' + **TROPISM**.
thill ▶ **noun** historical a shaft, especially one of a pair, used to attach a cart or carriage to the animal drawing it.
– ORIGIN Middle English: of unknown origin.
thiller ▶ **noun** historical a horse pulling a cart or carriage between shafts.
thimble ▶ **noun** a metal or plastic cap with a closed end, worn to protect the finger and push the needle in sewing.
■ a short metal tube or ferrule. ■ Nautical a metal ring, concave on the outside, around which a loop of rope is spliced.
– ORIGIN Old English *thȳmel* 'finger-stall' (see **THUMB**, **-LE**[1]).
thimbleberry ▶ **noun** (pl. **-ies**) a North American blackberry or raspberry with thimble-shaped fruit.
• Genus *Rubus*, family Rosaceae: several species, including *R. odoratus*, which has large fragrant flowers and unpalatable fruit.
thimbleful ▶ **noun** (pl. **-fuls**) a small quantity of liquid, especially alcohol: *a **thimbleful of** brandy.*
thimblerig ▶ **noun** [mass noun] a game involving sleight of hand, in which three inverted thimbles or cups are moved about, contestants having to spot which is the one with a pea or other object underneath.
– DERIVATIVES **thimblerigger** noun.
– ORIGIN early 19th cent.: from **THIMBLE** + **RIG**[2] in the sense 'trick, dodge'.
Thimphu /ˈtɪmpuː, ˈθɪm-/ (also **Thimbu** /ˈtɪmbuː, ˈθɪm-/) the capital of Bhutan, in the Himalayas at an altitude of 2,450 m (8,000 ft); pop. 30,300 (est. 1993).
thin ▶ **adjective** (**thinner**, **thinnest**) **1** having opposite surfaces or sides close together; of little thickness or depth: *thin slices of bread.*
■ (of a person) having little, or too little, flesh or fat on their body: *she was painfully thin.* ■ (of a garment or other knitted or woven item) made of light material for coolness or elegance. ■ (of a garment) having had a considerable amount of fabric worn away. ■ (of script or type) consisting of narrow lines: *tall, thin lettering.*
2 having few parts or members relative to the area covered or filled; sparse: *a depressingly thin crowd | his hair was going thin.*
■ not dense: *the thin cold air of the mountains.* ■ containing much liquid and not much solid substance: *thin soup.* ■ Climbing denoting a route on which the holds are small or scarce.
3 (of a sound) faint and high-pitched: *a thin, reedy little voice.*
■ (of a smile) weak and forced. ■ too weak to justify a result or effect; inadequate: *the evidence is rather thin.*
▶ **adverb** [often in combination] with little thickness or depth: *thin-sliced ham | cut it as thin as possible.*
▶ **verb** (**thinned**, **thinning**) **1** make or become less dense, crowded, or numerous: [with obj.] *the*

t

remorseless fire of archers thinned their ranks | [no obj.] *the trees began to* **thin out** | [as adj. **thinning**] *thinning hair.* ■[with obj.] remove some plants from (a row or area) to allow the others more room to grow: *thin out over-wintered rows of peas.* ■ make or become weaker or more watery: [with obj.] *if the soup is too thick, add a little water to* **thin** *it* **down** | [no obj.] *the blood thins.* **2** make or become smaller in width or thickness: [with obj.] *their effect in thinning the ozone layer is probably slowing the global warming trend* | [no obj.] *the linen had thinned and shrunk with frequent laundering.* **3** [with obj.] Golf hit (a ball) above its centre.

– PHRASES **have a thin time** Brit. informal have a wretched or uncomfortable time. **on thin ice** see **ICE**. **thin air** used to refer to the state of being invisible or non-existent: *she just vanished* **into thin air** | *they seemed to pluck numbers* **out of thin air**. **the thin blue line** informal used to refer to the police, typically in the context of situations of civil unrest. **thin end of the wedge** see **WEDGE**[1]. **thin on the ground** see **GROUND**[1]. **thin on top** informal balding.

– DERIVATIVES **thinly** adverb, **thinness** noun, **thinnish** adjective.

– ORIGIN Old English *thynne*, of Germanic origin; related to Dutch *dun* and German *dünn*, from an Indo-European root shared by Latin *tenuis*.

-thin ▶ **combining form** denoting a specified degree of thinness: *gossamer-thin* | *wafer-thin.*

thine ▶ **possessive pronoun** archaic form of **YOURS**; the thing or things belonging to or associated with thee: *his spirit will take courage from thine.*
▶ **possessive determiner** form of **THY** used before a vowel: *inquire into thine own heart.*

– ORIGIN Old English *thīn*, of Germanic origin; related to German *dein*, also to **THOU**[1].

USAGE The use of **thine** is still found in some traditional dialects but elsewhere it is restricted to archaic contexts. See also **usage** at **THOU**[1].

thin-film ▶ **adjective** (of a process or device) using or involving a very thin solid or liquid film. ■Electronics denoting a miniature circuit or device consisting of a thin layer of metal or semiconductor on a ceramic or glass substrate.

thing ▶ **noun 1** an object that one need not, cannot, or does not wish to give a specific name to: *look at that metal rail thing over there* | *there are lots of things I'd like to buy* | *she was wearing this pink thing.* ■(**things**) personal belongings or clothing: *she began to unpack her things.* ■ [with adj. or noun modifier] (**things**) objects, equipment, or utensils used for a particular purpose: *they cleared away the last few lunch things.* ■ [with negative] (**a thing**) anything (used for emphasis): *she couldn't find a thing to wear.* ■ used to express one's disapproval or contempt for something: *you won't find me smoking those filthy things.* ■ [with postpositive adj.] (**things**) all that can be described in the specified way: *his love for all things English.* ■ used euphemistically to refer to a man's penis. **2** an inanimate material object as distinct from a living sentient being: *I'm not a thing, not a work of art to be cherished.* ■[with adj.] a living creature or plant: *the sea is the primal source of all living things on earth.* ■ [with adj.] used to express and give a reason for one's pity, affection, approval, or contempt for a person or animal: *have a nice weekend in the country, you lucky thing!* | *the lamb was a puny little thing.* **3** an action, activity, event, thought, or utterance: *she said the first thing that came into her head* | *the only thing I could do well was cook.* ■(**things**) circumstances, conditions, or matters that are unspecified: *things haven't gone entirely to plan* | *how are things with you?* ■ an abstract entity or concept: *mourning and depression are not the same thing.* ■ a quality or attribute: *they had one thing in common—they were men of action.* ■ a specimen or type of something: *the game is the latest thing in family fun.* ■ (**one's thing**) informal one's special interest or concern: *reading isn't my thing.* ■ [with adj. or noun modifier] (**a thing**) informal a situation or activity of a specified type or quality: *your being here is just a friendship thing, OK?* **4** (**the thing**) informal what is needed or required: *you need a tonic—and here's just the thing.* ■what is socially acceptable or fashionable: *it wouldn't be quite the thing to go to a royal garden party in wellies.* ■ used to introduce or draw attention to an important fact or consideration: *the thing is, I am going to sell this house.*

– PHRASES **be all things to all men** (or **people**) please everyone, typically by regularly altering one's behaviour or opinions in order to conform to those of others. ■ be able to be interpreted or used differently by different people to their own satisfaction. **be on to a good thing** informal have found a job, situation, or lifestyle that is pleasant, profitable, or easy. **be hearing** (or **seeing**) **things** imagine that one can hear (or see) something that is not in fact there. **a close** (or **near**) **thing** a narrow avoidance of something unpleasant. **do one's own thing** informal follow one's own interests or inclinations regardless of others. **do the —— thing** informal, chiefly N. Amer. engage in the kind of behaviour typically associated with someone or something: *a film in which he does the bad-guy thing.* **do things to** informal have a powerful emotional effect on: *it just does things to me when we kiss.* **for one thing** used to introduce one of two or more possible reasons for something, the remainder of which may or may not be stated: *Why hadn't he arranged to see her at the house? For one thing, it would have been warmer.* **have a thing about** informal have an obsessive interest in or dislike of: *she had a thing about men who wore glasses.* **—— is one thing, —— is another** used to indicate that the second item mentioned is much more serious or important than the first, and cannot be compared to it: *physical attraction was one thing, love was quite another.* **make a** (**big**) **thing of** (or **about**) informal make (something) seem more important than it actually is. **of all things** out of all conceivable possibilities (used to express surprise): *What had he been thinking about? A kitten, of all things.* (**just**) **one of those things** informal used to indicate that one wishes to pass over an unfortunate event or experience by regarding it as unavoidable or to be accepted. **one thing leads to another** used to suggest that the exact sequence of events is too obvious to need recounting, the listener or reader being able to guess easily what happened. **there is only one thing for it** there is only one possible course of action. (**now**) **there's a thing** informal used as an expression of surprise at a particular event or fact. **a thing of the past** a thing that no longer happens or exists. **a thing or two** informal used to refer to useful information that can be imparted or learned: *Teddy taught me a thing or two about wine.* **things that go bump in the night** informal, humorous unexplained and frightening noises at night, regarded as being caused by ghosts.

– ORIGIN Old English, of Germanic origin; related to German *Ding*. Early senses included 'meeting' and 'matter, concern' as well as 'inanimate object'.

thingamabob /ˈθɪŋəməbɒb/ (also **thingumabob**, **thingamajig**, or **thingumajig** /ˈθɪŋəmədʒɪɡ/) ▶ **noun** another term for **THINGUMMY**.

thingummy /ˈθɪŋəmi/ (also **thingamy**) ▶ **noun** (pl. **-ies**) informal used to refer to or address a person or thing whose name one has forgotten, does not know, or does not wish to mention: *one of those thingummies for keeping all the fire tools together.*

– ORIGIN late 18th cent.: from **THING** + a meaningless suffix.

thingy ▶ **noun** (pl. **-ies**) another term for **THINGUMMY**.

think ▶ **verb** (past and past participle **thought**) **1** [with clause] have a particular opinion, belief, or idea about someone or something: *she thought that nothing would be the same again* | [no obj.] *what would John think of her?* | (**be thought**) *it's thought he may have collapsed from shock* | [with infinitive] *up to 300 people were thought to have died.* ■used in questions to express anger or surprise: *What do you think you're doing?* ■ (**I think**) used in speech to reduce the force of a statement or opinion, or to politely suggest or refuse something: *I thought we could go out for a meal.* **2** [no obj.] direct one's mind towards someone or something; use one's mind actively to form connected ideas: *he was thinking about Colin* | *Jack thought for a moment* | [with obj.] *any writer who so rarely produces a book is not thinking deep thoughts.* ■(**think of/about**) take into account or consideration when deciding on a possible action: *you can live how you like, but there's the children to think about.* ■ (**think of/about**) consider the possibility or advantages of (a course of action): *he was thinking of becoming a zoologist.* ■ have a particular mental attitude or approach: *he thought like a general* | [with complement] *one should always think positive.* ■ (**think of**) have a particular opinion of: *I think of him as a friend* | *she did not think highly of modern art.* ■ call something to mind; remember: *lemon thyme is a natural pair with any chicken dish you* **can think of** | [with infinitive] *I hadn't thought to warn Rachel about him.* ■ imagine (an actual or possible situation): *think of being paid a salary to hunt big game!* ■ [usu. with clause] expect: *I never thought we'd raise so much money* | [with infinitive] *she said something he'd never thought to have heard said again.* ■ (**think oneself into**) concentrate on imagining what it would be like to be in (a position or role): *she tried to think herself into the part of Peter's fiancée.*
▶ **noun** [in sing.] informal an act of thinking: *I went for a walk to have a think.*

– PHRASES **have** (**got**) **another think coming** informal used to express the speaker's disagreement with or unwillingness to do something suggested by someone else: *if they think I'm going to do physical jerks, they've got another think coming.* **think again** reconsider something, typically so as to alter one's intentions or ideas. **think aloud** express one's thoughts as soon as they occur. **think better of** decide not to do (something) after reconsideration. **think big** see **BIG**. **think fit** see **FIT**[1]. **think for oneself** have an independent mind or attitude. **think nothing** (or **little**) **of** consider (an activity others regard as odd, wrong, or difficult) as straightforward or normal. **think nothing of it** see **NOTHING**. **think on one's feet** see **FOOT**. **think scorn of** see **SCORN**. **think twice** consider a course of action carefully before embarking on it. **think the world of** see **WORLD**.

– DERIVATIVES **thinkable** adjective.

– ORIGIN Old English *thencan*, of Germanic origin; related to Dutch and German *denken*.

▶ **think back** recall a past event or time: *I keep* **thinking back to** *school.*
think on dialect & N. Amer. think of or about.
think something out consider something in all its aspects before taking action: *the plan had not been properly thought out.*
think something over consider something carefully.
think something through consider all the possible effects or implications of something: *they had failed to think the policy through.*
think something up informal use one's ingenuity to invent or devise something.

thinker ▶ **noun** a person who thinks deeply and seriously. ■a person with highly developed intellectual powers, especially one whose profession involves intellectual activity: *a leading scientific thinker.*

thinking ▶ **adjective** [attrib.] using thought or rational judgement; intelligent: *he seemed a thinking man.*
▶ **noun** [mass noun] the process of using one's mind to consider or reason about something: *the selectors have some thinking to do before the match.* ■a person's ideas or opinions: *his thinking is reflected in his later autobiography.* ■ (**thinkings**) archaic thoughts; meditations.

– PHRASES **good** (or **nice**) **thinking** used as an expression of approval for an ingenious plan, explanation, or observation. **put on one's thinking cap** informal meditate on a problem.

think piece ▶ **noun** an article in a newspaper, magazine, or journal presenting personal opinions, analysis, or discussion, rather than bare facts.

think tank ▶ **noun** a body of experts providing advice and ideas on specific political or economic problems.

– DERIVATIVES **think-tanker** noun.

thin-layer chromatography ▶ **noun** [mass noun] Chemistry chromatography in which compounds are separated on a thin layer of adsorbent material, typically a coating of silica gel on a glass plate or plastic sheet.

thinner ▶ **noun** [mass noun] (also **thinners**) a volatile solvent used to make paint or other solutions less viscous.

thinnings ▶ **plural noun** seedlings, trees, or fruit which have been removed to improve the growth of those remaining.

thin section ▶ **noun** a thin, flat piece of material prepared for examination with a microscope, in particular a piece of rock about 0.03 mm thick, or, for electron microscopy, a piece of tissue about 30 nm thick.
▶ **verb** (**thin-section**) [with obj.] prepare (something) for examination in this way.

thio- ▶ **combining form** Chemistry denoting replacement of oxygen by sulphur in a compound: *thiosulphate.*

– ORIGIN from Greek *theion* 'sulphur'.

b **b**ut | d **d**og | f **f**ew | g **g**et | h **h**e | j **y**es | k **c**at | l **l**eg | m **m**an | n **n**o | p **p**en | r **r**ed | s **s**it | t **t**op | v **v**oice | w **w**e | z **z**oo | ʃ **sh**e | ʒ deci**s**ion | θ **th**in | ð **th**is | ŋ ri**ng** | x lo**ch** | tʃ **ch**ip | dʒ **j**ar

thiocyanate /ˌθʌɪə(ʊ)ˈsʌɪəneɪt/ ▶ **noun** Chemistry a salt containing the anion SCN^-.

thiol /ˈθʌɪɒl/ ▶ **noun** Chemistry an organic compound containing the group —SH, i.e. a sulphur-containing analogue of an alcohol.

thiomersal /ˌθʌɪə(ʊ)ˈməːs(ə)l/ ▶ **noun** [mass noun] an organomercury compound able to inhibit the growth of bacteria and other micro-organisms, used as a medical disinfectant and preservative for biological products.
• Chem. formula: $C_9H_9O_2SHgNa$.
– ORIGIN 1950s; from **THIO-** + *mer(cury)* + *sal(icylate)*.

thionyl /ˈθʌɪənɪl/ ▶ **noun** [as modifier] Chemistry of or denoting the divalent radical =SO.
– ORIGIN 1857: so named by H. Schiff (see **SCHIFF BASE**).

thiopental ▶ **noun** North American term for **THIOPENTONE**.

thiopentone /ˌθʌɪə(ʊ)ˈpɛntəʊn/ ▶ **noun** [mass noun] Medicine a sulphur-containing barbiturate drug used as a general anaesthetic and hypnotic, and (reputedly) as a truth drug.
– ORIGIN 1940s: from **THIO-** + a contraction of **PENTOBARBITONE**.

thioridazine /ˌθʌɪə(ʊ)rɪˈdeɪziːn/ ▶ **noun** [mass noun] Medicine a synthetic compound derived from phenothiazine, used as a tranquillizer, chiefly in the treatment of mental illness.
– ORIGIN 1950s: from **THIO-** + *(pipe)rid(ine)* + **AZINE**.

thiosulphate (US **thiosulfate**) ▶ **noun** Chemistry a salt containing the anion $S_2O_3^{2-}$, i.e. a sulphate with one oxygen atom replaced by sulphur.

thiourea /ˌθʌɪə(ʊ)jʊˈriːə/ ▶ **noun** [mass noun] Chemistry a synthetic crystalline compound used in photography and the manufacture of synthetic resins.
• The sulphur analogue of urea; chem. formula: $SC(NH_2)_2$.

Thíra /ˈθiːra/ Greek name for **THERA**.

thiram /ˈθʌɪram/ ▶ **noun** [mass noun] Chemistry a synthetic sulphur-containing compound used as a fungicide and seed protectant.
• Chem. formula: $(CH_3)_2NCSS_2SCN(CH_3)_2$.
– ORIGIN 1950s: from **THIO-**, *(u)r(ea)*, and *am(ine)*, elements of the systematic name.

third ▶ **ordinal number** constituting number three in a sequence; 3rd: *the third century* | *the third of October* | *Edward the Third.*
■ (**a third/one third**) each of three equal parts into which something is or may be divided: *a third of a mile.* ■ the third finisher or position in a race or competition: *Hill finished third.* ■ the third in a sequence of a vehicle's gears: *he took the corner in third.* ■ Baseball third base. ■ chiefly Brit. the third form of a school or college. ■ thirdly (used to introduce a third point or reason): *second, they are lightly regulated; and third, they do business with non-resident clients.* ■ Music an interval spanning three consecutive notes in a diatonic scale, e.g. C to E (**major third**, equal to two tones) or A to C (**minor third**, equal to a tone and a semitone). ■ Music the note which is higher by this interval than the tonic of a diatonic scale or root of a chord. ■ Brit. a place in the third grade in an examination, especially that for a degree.
– PHRASES **third time lucky** (or US **third time is the charm**) used to express the hope that, after twice failing to accomplish something, one may succeed in the third attempt.
– ORIGIN Old English *thridda*, of Germanic origin; related to Dutch *derde* and German *dritte*, also to **THREE**. The spelling *thrid* was dominant until the 16th cent. (but *thirdda* is recorded in Northumbrian dialect as early as the 10th cent.).

third age ▶ **noun** (**the third age**) Brit. the period in life between middle age and old age, about 55 to 70.
– DERIVATIVES **third ager** noun.

third best ▶ **adjective** good enough to be next after the second-best thing of the same type.
▶ **noun** a level that is less adequate or desirable than best and second best.

third class ▶ **noun** [in sing.] a group of people or things considered together as third best.
■ Brit. a university degree or examination result in the third-highest classification. ■ [mass noun] US a cheap class of mail for the handling of advertising and other printed material that weighs less than 16 ounces and is unsealed. ■ [mass noun] chiefly historical the cheapest and least comfortable accommodation in a train or ship.
▶ **adjective & adverb** of the third-best quality or of lower status: [as adj.] *many indigenous groups are still viewed as third-class citizens.*
■ [as adj.] Brit. of or relating to the third-highest division in a university examination: *he left university with a third-class degree.* ■ US of or relating to a cheap class of mail including advertising and other printed material weighing less than 16 ounces: [as adj.] *third-class mail.* ■ chiefly historical of or relating to the cheapest and least comfortable accommodation in a train or ship: [as adj.] *a suffocating third-class compartment* | [as adv.] *I travelled third class across Europe.*

third country ▶ **noun** a Third World country.

third cousin ▶ **noun** see **COUSIN**.

third-degree ▶ **adjective** [attrib.] **1** denoting burns of the most severe kind, affecting tissue below the skin.
2 Law, chiefly N. Amer. denoting the least serious category of a crime, especially murder.
▶ **noun** (**the third degree**) long and harsh questioning, especially by police, to obtain information or a confession.

third estate ▶ **noun** [treated as sing. or pl.] the common people as part of a country's political system. [ORIGIN: the first two estates were formerly represented by the clergy, and the barons and knights; later the Lords spiritual and the Lords temporal.]
■ (**the Third Estate**) the French bourgeoisie and working class before the Revolution. [ORIGIN: translating French *le tiers état.*]

third eye ▶ **noun 1** Hinduism & Buddhism the 'eye of insight' in the forehead of an image of a deity, especially the god Shiva.
■ the faculty of intuitive insight or prescience.
2 informal term for **PINEAL EYE**.

third eyelid ▶ **noun** informal term for **NICTITATING MEMBRANE**.

third force ▶ **noun** [in sing.] a political group or party acting as a check on conflict between two extreme or opposing groups.
■ (in South Africa) a supposed group thought by some to have carried out acts of violence to incriminate members of left-wing groups representing blacks, and so sow discord among these groups.

third-hand ▶ **adjective 1** (of goods) having had two previous owners: *a third-hand dinner suit.*
2 (of information) acquired from or via several intermediate sources and consequently not authoritative or reliable: *the accounts are third-hand, told years after the event.*
▶ **adverb** from or via several intermediate sources: *I heard about the case third-hand.*

Third International see **INTERNATIONAL** (sense 2).

thirdly ▶ **adverb** in the third place (used to introduce a third point or reason).

third man ▶ **noun** Cricket a fielding position near the boundary behind the slips.
■ a fielder at this position.

third market ▶ **noun** Finance used to refer to trading in listed stock outside the stock exchange.

third party ▶ **noun** a person or group besides the two primarily involved in a situation, especially a dispute.
▶ **adjective** [attrib.] of or relating to a person or group besides the two primarily involved in a situation: *third-party suppliers.*
■ Brit. (of insurance) covering damage or injury suffered by a person other than the insured.

third person ▶ **noun 1** a third party.
2 see **PERSON** (sense 2).

third position ▶ **noun 1** Ballet a posture in which the turned-out feet are placed one in front of the other, so that the heel of the front foot fits into the hollow of the instep of the back foot.
■ a position of the arms in which one is held curved in front of the body and the other curved to the side, both at waist level.
2 Music a position of the left hand on the fingerboard of a stringed instrument nearer to the bridge than the second position, enabling a higher set of notes to be played.

Third Programme one of the three national radio networks of the BBC from 1946 until 1967, when it was replaced by Radio 3.

third rail ▶ **noun** an additional rail supplying electric current, used in some electric railway systems.

third-rate ▶ **adjective** of inferior or very poor quality.
– DERIVATIVES **third-rater** noun.

third reading ▶ **noun** a third presentation of a bill to a legislative assembly, in the UK to debate committee reports and in the US to consider it for the last time.

Third Reich the Nazi regime, 1933–45.

Third Republic the republican regime in France between the fall of Napoleon III (1870) and the German occupation of 1940.

third ventricle ▶ **noun** Anatomy the central cavity of the brain, lying between the thalamus and hypothalamus of the two cerebral hemispheres.

Third World ▶ **noun** (usu. **the Third World**) the developing countries of Asia, Africa, and Latin America.
– ORIGIN first applied in the 1950s by French commentators who used *tiers monde* to distinguish the developing countries from the capitalist and Communist blocs.

thirst ▶ **noun** [mass noun] a feeling of needing or wanting to drink something: *they quenched their thirst with spring water.*
■ lack of the liquid needed to sustain life: *tens of thousands died of thirst and starvation.* ■ (usu. **thirst for**) poetic/literary a strong desire for something: *his thirst for knowledge was mainly academic.*
▶ **verb** [no obj.] archaic (of a person or animal) feel a need to drink something.
■ (usu. **thirst for/after**) poetic/literary have a strong desire for something: *an opponent thirsting for revenge.*
– ORIGIN Old English *thurst* (noun), *thyrstan* (verb), of Germanic origin; related to Dutch *dorst, dorsten* and German *Durst, dürsten.*

thirstland ▶ **noun** S. African a large arid area.

thirsty ▶ **adjective** (**thirstier, thirstiest**) feeling a need to drink something: *the Guides were hot and thirsty.*
■ (of land, plants, or skin) in need of water; dry or parched. ■ (of an engine, plant, or crop) consuming a lot of fuel or water. ■ having or showing a strong desire for something: *Joe was as thirsty for scandal as anyone else.* ■ [attrib.] informal (of activity, weather, or a time) causing the feeling of a need to drink something: *modelling is thirsty work.*
– DERIVATIVES **thirstily** adverb, **thirstiness** noun.

thirteen ▶ **cardinal number** equivalent to the sum of six and seven; one more than twelve, or seven less than twenty; 13: *thirteen miles away* | *a rise of 13 per cent* | *thirteen of the bishops voted against the motion.* (Roman numeral: **xiii** or **XIII**.)
■ a size of garment or other merchandise denoted by thirteen. ■ thirteen years old: *two boys aged eleven and thirteen.*
– DERIVATIVES **thirteenth** ordinal number.
– ORIGIN Old English *thrēotīene* (see **THREE, -TEEN**). The spelling with initial *thi-* is recorded in late Middle English.

Thirteen Colonies the British colonies that ratified the Declaration of Independence in 1776 and thereby became founding states of the US. The colonies were Virginia, Massachusetts, Maryland, Connecticut, Rhode Island, North Carolina, South Carolina, New York, New Jersey, Delaware, New Hampshire, Pennsylvania, and Georgia.

thirty ▶ **cardinal number** (pl. **-ies**) the number equivalent to the product of three and ten; ten less than forty; 30: *thirty or forty years ago* | *thirty were hurt* | *thirty of her school friends.* (Roman numeral: **xxx** or **XXX**)
■ (**thirties**) the numbers from thirty to thirty-nine, especially the years of a century or of a person's life: *a woman in her thirties* | *she was a famous actress in the thirties.* ■ thirty years old: *I've got a long way to go before I'm thirty.* ■ thirty miles an hour: *doing about thirty.* ■ a size of garment or other merchandise denoted by thirty.
– DERIVATIVES **thirtieth** ordinal number, **thirtyfold** adjective & adverb.
– ORIGIN Old English *thrītig* (see **THREE, -TY**[2]). The spelling with initial *thi-* is recorded in literature in the 15th cent., and has been the prevalent form since the 16th cent.

thirty-eight ▶ **noun** a revolver of .38 calibre.

Thirty-nine Articles ▶ **plural noun** a series of points of doctrine historically accepted as representing the teaching of the Church of England.

thirty-second note ▸ **noun** Music, chiefly N. Amer. a demisemiquaver.

thirty-two-mo ▸ **noun** (pl. **-os**) a size of book page that results from folding each printed sheet into thirty-two leaves (sixty-four pages).
■ a book of this size.

thirty-year rule ▸ **noun** a rule that public records may be open to inspection after a lapse of thirty years.

Thirty Years War a European war of 1618–48 which broke out between the Catholic Holy Roman emperor and some of his German Protestant states and developed into a struggle for continental hegemony with France, Sweden, Spain, and the Holy Roman Empire as the major protagonists. It was ended by the Treaty of Westphalia.

this ▸ **pronoun** (pl. **these**) **1** used to identify a specific person or thing close at hand or being indicated or experienced: *is this your bag?* | *he soon knew that this was not the place for him.*
■ used to introduce someone or something: *this is the captain speaking* | *listen to this.* ■ referring to the nearer of two things close to the speaker (the other, if specified, being identified by 'that'): *this is different from that.*
2 referring to a specific thing or situation just mentioned: *the company was transformed and Ward had played a vital role in bringing this about.*
▸ **determiner** (pl. **these**) **1** used to identify a specific person or thing close at hand or being indicated or experienced: *don't listen to this guy* | *these croissants are delicious.*
■ referring to the nearer of two things close to the speaker (the other, if specified, being identified by 'that'): *this one or that one?*
2 referring to a specific thing or situation just mentioned: *there was a court case resulting from this incident.*
3 used with periods of time related to the present: *I thought you were busy all this week* | *how are you this morning?*
■ referring to a period of time that has just passed: *I haven't left my bed these three days.*
4 informal used (chiefly in narrative) to refer to a person or thing previously unspecified: *I turned round and there was this big mummy standing next to us!* | *I've got this problem and I need help.*
▸ **adverb** [as submodifier] to the degree or extent indicated: *they can't handle a job this big* | *he's not used to this much attention.*
– PHRASES **this and that** (or **this, that, and the other**) informal various unspecified things: *they stayed up chatting about this and that.* **this here** informal used to draw attention emphatically to someone or something: *I've slept in this here bed for forty years.*
– ORIGIN Old English, neuter of *thes*, of West Germanic origin; related to **THAT** and **THE**.

Thisbe /ˈθɪzbi/ Roman Mythology a Babylonian girl, lover of Pyramus.

thistle ▸ **noun 1** a widely distributed herbaceous plant of the daisy family, which typically has a prickly stem and leaves and rounded heads of purple flowers.
● *Carlina, Carduus,* and other genera, family Compositae.
2 a plant of this type as the Scottish national emblem.
● This is usually identified as the **cotton thistle** (*Onopordum acanthium*).
– DERIVATIVES **thistly** adjective.
– ORIGIN Old English *thistel*, of Germanic origin; related to Dutch *distel* and German *Distel*.

Thistle, Order of the ▸ **noun** see **ORDER OF THE THISTLE**.

thistledown ▸ **noun** [mass noun] light fluffy down which is attached to thistle seeds, enabling them to be blown about in the wind.

thither /ˈðɪðə/ ▸ **adverb** archaic or poetic/literary to or towards that place: *no trickery had been necessary to attract him thither.*
– ORIGIN Old English *thider*, alteration (by association with **HITHER**) of *thæder*, of Germanic origin; related to **THAT** and **THE**.

Thívai /ˈθiːvɛ/ Greek name for **THEBES** 2.

thixotropy /θɪkˈsɒtrəpi/ ▸ **noun** [mass noun] Chemistry the property of becoming less viscous when subjected to an applied stress, shown for example by some gels which become temporarily fluid when shaken or stirred.
– DERIVATIVES **thixotropic** adjective.

– ORIGIN 1920s: from Greek *thixis* 'touching' + *tropē* 'turning'.

tho' (also **tho**) ▸ **conjunction** & **adverb** informal spelling of **THOUGH**.

thole[1] /θəʊl/ (also **thole pin**) ▸ **noun** a pin, typically one of a pair, fitted to the gunwale of a rowing boat to act as the fulcrum for an oar.
– ORIGIN Old English, of Germanic origin; related to Dutch *dol*.

thole[2] /θəʊl/ ▸ **verb** [with obj.] Scottish or archaic endure (something) without complaint or resistance; tolerate.
– ORIGIN Old English *tholian*, of Germanic origin.

tholeiite /ˈθəʊlɪaɪt/ ▸ **noun** [mass noun] Geology a basaltic rock containing augite and a calcium-poor pyroxene (pigeonite or hypersthene), and with a higher silica content than an alkali basalt.
– DERIVATIVES **tholeiitic** /ˌθəʊlɪˈɪtɪk/ adjective.
– ORIGIN mid 19th cent.: from *Tholei*, the name of a village (now *Tholey*) in the Saarland, Germany, + -ITE[1].

tholos /ˈθɒlɒs/ ▸ **noun** (pl. **tholoi** /-lɔɪ/) Archaeology a dome-shaped tomb of ancient Greek origin, especially one dating from the Mycenaean period.
– ORIGIN Greek.

Thomas[1], Dylan (Marlais) (1914–53), Welsh poet. In 1953 he narrated on radio *Under Milk Wood*, a portrait of a small Welsh town, interspersing poetic alliterative prose with songs and ballads. Other notable works: *Portrait of the Artist as a Young Dog* (prose, 1940).

Thomas[2], (Philip) Edward (1878–1917), English poet. His work offers a sympathetic but unidealized depiction of rural English life, adapting colloquial speech rhythms to poetic metre.

Thomas, St an Apostle; known as **Doubting Thomas**. He earned his nickname by saying that he would not believe that Christ had risen again until he had seen and touched his wounds (John 20:24–9). Feast day, 21 December.

Thomas à Kempis /ə ˈkɛmpɪs/ (c.1380–1471), German theologian; born *Thomas Hemerken*. He is the probable author of *On the Imitation of Christ* (c.1415–24), a manual of spiritual devotion.

Thomas Aquinas, St, see **AQUINAS, ST THOMAS**.

Thomas More, St see **MORE**[1].

Thomism /ˈtəʊmɪz(ə)m/ ▸ **noun** [mass noun] the theology of Thomas Aquinas or of his followers.
– DERIVATIVES **Thomist** noun & adjective, **Thomistic** adjective.

Thompson[1], Daley (b.1958), English athlete, winner of a number of decathlon titles that included gold medals in the Olympic Games of 1980 and 1984.

Thompson[2], Emma (b.1959), English actress and screenwriter. Her films include *Howard's End* (1992), for which she won an Oscar for best actress, and *Sense and Sensibility* (1995), for which she also wrote the Oscar-winning screenplay.

Thompson[3], Flora (Jane) (1876–1947), English writer. She is remembered for her semi-autobiographical trilogy *Lark Rise to Candleford* (1945).

Thompson[4], Francis (1859–1907), English poet. His best-known work, such as 'The Hound of Heaven' (1893), uses powerful imagery to convey intense religious experience.

Thomson[1], James (1700–48), Scottish poet. The words of the song 'Rule, Britannia' (1740) have been attributed to him.

Thomson[2], James (1834–82), Scottish poet, chiefly remembered for the poem 'The City of Dreadful Night' (1874).

Thomson[3], Sir Joseph John (1856–1940), English atomic physicist. He discovered the electron, deducing its existence as a particle smaller than the atom from his experiments. Thomson received the 1906 Nobel Prize for Physics for his researches into the electrical conductivity of gases. His son Sir George Paget Thomson (1892–1975) shared the 1937 Nobel Prize for Physics for his discovery of electron diffraction by crystals.

Thomson[4], Roy Herbert, 1st Baron Thomson of Fleet (1894–1976), Canadian-born British newspaper proprietor and media entrepreneur. He settled in Edinburgh in 1952, buying the *Scotsman*,

and later the *Sunday Times* (1959) and *The Times* (1966).

Thomson[5], Sir William, see **KELVIN**.

Thomson's gazelle ▸ **noun** a light brown gazelle with a dark band along the flanks, living in large herds on the open plains of East Africa.
● *Gazella thomsonii,* family Bovidae.
– ORIGIN late 19th cent.: named after Joseph *Thomson* (1858–94), Scottish explorer.

thong ▸ **noun 1** a narrow strip of leather or other material, used especially as a fastening or as the lash of a whip.
2 an item of clothing fastened by or including such a narrow strip, in particular:
■ a skimpy bathing garment or pair of knickers like a G-string. ■ chiefly N. Amer. another term for **FLIP-FLOP** (in sense 1).
▸ **verb** [with obj.] archaic flog or lash (someone) with a whip.
– DERIVATIVES **thonged** adjective, **thongy** adjective.
– ORIGIN Old English *thwang, thwong,* of Germanic origin; related to German *Zwang* 'compulsion'. Compare with **WHANG**.

Thor /θɔː/ Scandinavian Mythology the god of thunder, the weather, agriculture, and the home, the son of Odin and Freya (Frigga). Thursday is named after him.

thoracic /θɔːˈrasɪk/ ▸ **adjective** Anatomy & Zoology of or relating to the thorax.

thoracic duct ▸ **noun** Anatomy the main vessel of the lymphatic system, passing upwards in front of the spine and draining into the left innominate vein near the base of the neck.

thoracic vertebra ▸ **noun** Anatomy each of the twelve bones of the backbone to which the ribs are attached.

thoracolumbar /ˌθɔːrəkəʊˈlʌmbə/ ▸ **adjective** Anatomy of or relating to the thoracic and lumbar regions of the spine.
■ denoting the sympathetic nervous system.

thoracotomy /ˌθɔːrəˈkɒtəmi/ ▸ **noun** [mass noun] surgical incision into the chest wall.
– ORIGIN late 19th cent.: from Greek *thōrax, thōrāc-* 'chest' + -TOMY.

thorax /ˈθɔːraks/ ▸ **noun** (pl. **thoraces** /ˈθɔːrəsiːz/ or **thoraxes**) Anatomy & Zoology the part of the body of a mammal between the neck and the abdomen, including the cavity enclosed by the ribs, breastbone, and dorsal vertebrae, and containing the chief organs of circulation and respiration; the chest.
■ Zoology the corresponding part of a bird, reptile, amphibian, or fish. ■ Entomology the middle section of the body of an insect, between the head and the abdomen, bearing the legs and wings.
– ORIGIN late Middle English: via Latin from Greek *thōrax*.

Thorazine /ˈθɔːrəziːn/ ▸ **noun** trademark for **CHLORPROMAZINE**.
– ORIGIN 1950s: formed from elements of the systematic name.

Thoreau /ˈθɔːrəʊ/, Henry David (1817–62), American essayist and poet, and a key figure in Transcendentalism. He is best known for his book *Walden, or Life in the Woods* (1854), an account of a two-year experiment in self-sufficiency.

thoria /ˈθɔːrɪə/ ▸ **noun** [mass noun] Chemistry thorium dioxide, a white refractory solid used in making gas mantles and other materials for high-temperature applications.
● Chem. formula: ThO_2.
– ORIGIN mid 19th cent.: from **THORIUM**, on the pattern of words such as *alumina* and *magnesia*.

thorium /ˈθɔːrɪəm/ ▸ **noun** [mass noun] the chemical element of atomic number 90, a white radioactive metal of the actinide series. (Symbol: **Th**)
– ORIGIN mid 19th cent.: named after the god **THOR**.

Thorn /tɔːʊn/ German name for **TORUŃ**.

thorn ▸ **noun 1** a stiff, sharp-pointed, straight or curved woody projection on the stem or other part of a plant.
■ figurative a source of discomfort, annoyance, or difficulty; an irritation or an obstacle: *the issue has become a thorn in renewing the peace talks.* See also *a thorn in someone's side* below.
2 (also **thorn bush** or **thorn tree**) a thorny bush, shrub, or tree, especially a hawthorn.
3 an Old English and Icelandic runic letter, þ or Þ, representing the dental fricatives /ð/ and /θ/. It was

eventually superseded by the digraph *th*. Compare with **ETH**. [ORIGIN: so named from the word of which it was the first letter.]

4 a yellowish-brown woodland moth which rests with the wings raised over the back, with twig-like caterpillars.
• *Ennomos* and other genera, family Geometridae.

– PHRASES **on thorns** continuously uneasy, especially in fear of being detected. **there is no rose without a thorn** proverb every apparently desirable situation has its share of trouble or difficulty. **a thorn in someone's side** (or **flesh**) a source of continual annoyance or trouble: *the pastor has long been a thorn in the side of the regime.*
– DERIVATIVES **thornless** adjective (only in sense 1), **thornproof** adjective (only in sense 1).
– ORIGIN Old English, of Germanic origin; related to Dutch *doorn* and German *Dorn*.

thorn apple ▶ **noun** a poisonous datura with large trumpet-shaped white flowers and toothed leaves, which has become a weed of waste ground in many countries. Also called **JIMSON WEED** in North America.
• *Datura stramonium*, family Solanaceae.
▪ the prickly fruit of this plant, which resembles that of a horse chestnut.

thornback (also **thornback ray**) ▶ **noun** a ray of shallow inshore waters which has spines on the back and tail, in particular:
• a prickly skinned European ray which is often eaten as 'skate' (*Raja clavata*, family Rajidae). • a ray which lives in the warm waters of the Pacific (*Platyrhinoidis triseriata*, family Platyrhinidae).

thornbill ▶ **noun 1** a small Australian warbler with drab plumage and a pointed bill.
• Genus *Acanthiza*, family Acanthizidae: several species.
2 a tropical American hummingbird with a short, sharply pointed bill.
• Family Trochilidae: three genera, in particular *Chalcostigma*, and several species.

Thorndike, Dame (Agnes) Sybil (1882–1976), English actress. She played the title part in the first London production of George Bernard Shaw's *St Joan* (1924).

thorntail ▶ **noun** a tropical American hummingbird with bright green plumage and projecting outer tail feathers.
• Genus *Popelairia*, family Trochilidae: four species.

thornveld /ˈθɔːnvɛlt/ ▶ **noun** [mass noun] S. African land on which the vegetation consists mainly of thorny trees and bushes.
– ORIGIN from **THORN** + Afrikaans *veld* in the sense 'natural uncultivated vegetation'.

thorny ▶ **adjective** (**thornier**, **thorniest**) having many thorns or thorn bushes.
▪ figurative causing distress, difficulty, or trouble: *a thorny problem for our team to solve.*
– DERIVATIVES **thornily** adverb, **thorniness** noun.

thorny devil ▶ **noun** another term for **MOLOCH**.

thorny-headed worm ▶ **noun** a parasitic worm with a thorn-like proboscis for attachment to the gut of vertebrates. Also called **SPINY-HEADED WORM**.
• Phylum Acanthocephala.

thorny oyster ▶ **noun** a bivalve mollusc of warm seas, the pinkish-brown shell of which is heavily ribbed and bears blunt or flattened spines.
• Family Spondylidae: *Spondylus* and other genera.

thorough ▶ **adjective** complete with regard to every detail; not superficial or partial: *planners need a thorough understanding of the subject.*
▪ performed or written with great care and completeness: *officers have made a thorough examination of the wreckage.* ▪ taking pains to do something carefully and completely: *the British authorities are very thorough.* ▪ [attrib.] absolute (used to emphasize the degree of something, typically something unwelcome or unpleasant): *the child is being a thorough nuisance.*
– DERIVATIVES **thoroughly** adverb, **thoroughness** noun.
– ORIGIN Old English *thuruh*, alteration of *thurh* 'through'. Original use was as an adverb and preposition, in senses of *through*. The adjective dates from the late 15th cent., when it also had the sense 'that goes or extends through something', surviving in *thoroughfare*.

thorough bass ▶ **noun** Music basso continuo (see **CONTINUO**).

thoroughbred ▶ **adjective** (of a horse) of pure breed, especially of a breed originating from English mares and Arab stallions and widely used as racehorses.
▪ informal of outstanding quality: *this thoroughbred car affords the luxury of three spoilers.*
▶ **noun** a horse of a thoroughbred breed.
▪ informal an outstanding or first-class person or thing: *this is a real thoroughbred of a record.*

thoroughfare ▶ **noun** a road or path forming a route between two places.
▪ a main road in a town.

thoroughgoing ▶ **adjective** involving or attending to every detail or aspect of something: *a thoroughgoing reform of the whole economy.*
▪ [attrib.] exemplifying a specified characteristic fully; absolute: *a thoroughgoing chocoholic.*

thorough-paced ▶ **adjective** archaic highly skilled or trained.
▪ absolute (used to emphasize the degree to which someone or something exemplifies a characteristic).

thoroughpin ▶ **noun** a swelling of the tendon sheath above the hock of a horse, which may be pressed from inside to outside and vice versa.

thorow-wax /ˈθʌrəwaks/ ▶ **noun** a European plant of the parsley family with yellowish-green flowers, formerly a widespread weed of cornfields.
• Genus *Bupleurum*, family Umbelliferae: two species, including *B. rotundifolium*, which is extinct in the wild in Britain.
– ORIGIN mid 16th cent.: from **THOROUGH** 'through' + **WAX**[2] (because the stem appears to grow through the leaves).

thorp (also **thorpe**) ▶ **noun** [in place names] a village or hamlet: *Scunthorpe.*
– ORIGIN Old English *thorp*, *throp*, of Germanic origin; related to Dutch *dorp* and German *Dorf*.

Thorshavn variant spelling of **TÓRSHAVN**.

Thorvaldsen /ˈtɔːvals(ə)n/ (also **Thorwaldsen**), Bertel (*c.*1770–1844), Danish neoclassical sculptor. Major works include a statue of Jason in Rome (1803) and the tomb of Pius VII (1824–31).

Thos ▶ **abbreviation for** Thomas.

those plural form of **THAT**.

Thoth /θəʊθ, təʊt/ Egyptian Mythology a moon god, the god of wisdom, justice, and writing, patron of the sciences, and messenger of Ra.

thou[1] ▶ **pronoun** [second person singular] archaic or dialect form of **YOU**, as the singular subject of a verb: *thou art fair, o my beloved.* Compare with **THEE**.
– ORIGIN Old English *thu*, of Germanic origin; related to German *du*, from an Indo-European root shared by Latin *tu*.

USAGE In modern English, the personal pronoun **you** (together with the possessives **your** and **yours**) covers a number of uses: it is both singular and plural, both objective and subjective, and both formal and familiar. This has not always been the case. In Old English and Middle English some of these different functions of **you** were supplied by different words. Thus, **thou** was at one time the singular subjective case (*thou art a beast*), while **thee** was the singular objective case (*he cares not for thee*). In addition, the form **thy** (modern equivalent **your**) was the singular possessive determiner and **thine** (modern equivalent **yours**) the singular possessive pronoun, both corresponding to **thee**. The forms **you** and **ye**, on the other hand, were at one time reserved for plural uses. By the 19th century these forms were universal in standard English for both singular and plural, polite and familiar. In present day use, **thou**, **thee**, **thy**, and **thine** survive in some traditional dialects but otherwise are found only in archaic contexts.

thou[2] ▶ **noun** (pl. same or **thous**) informal a thousand.
▪ one thousandth of an inch.
– ORIGIN mid 19th cent.: abbreviation.

though ▶ **conjunction** despite the fact that; although: *though they were speaking in undertones, Percival could hear them.*
▪ [with modal] even if (introducing a possibility): *you will be informed of its progress, slow though that may be.* ▪ however; but (introducing something opposed to or qualifying what has just been said): *her first name was Rose, though no one called her that.*
▶ **adverb** however (indicating that a factor qualifies or imposes restrictions on what was said previously): *I was hunting for work. Jobs were scarce though.*
– PHRASES **as though** see **AS**[1]. **even though** see **EVEN**[1].
– ORIGIN Old English *thēah*, of Germanic origin; related to Dutch and German *doch*; superseded in Middle English by forms from Old Norse *thó*, *thau*.

USAGE On the differences in use between **though** and **although**, see **usage** at **ALTHOUGH**.

thought[1] ▶ **noun 1** an idea or opinion produced by thinking or occurring suddenly in the mind: *Maggie had a sudden thought | I asked him if he had any thoughts on how it had happened | Mrs Oliver's first thought was to get help.*
▪ an idea or mental picture, imagined and contemplated: *the mere thought of Piers with Nicole made her see red.* ▪ (**one's thoughts**) one's mind or attention: *he's very much* ***in our thoughts*** *and prayers.* ▪ an act of considering or remembering someone or something: *she hadn't* ***given a thought to*** *Max for some time.* ▪ (usu. **thought of**) an intention, hope, or idea of doing or receiving something: *he had given up all thoughts of making London his home.*
2 [mass noun] the action or process of thinking: *Sophie sat deep* ***in thought***.
▪ the formation of opinions, especially as a philosophy or system of ideas, or the opinions so formed: *the freedom of thought and action | the traditions of Western thought.* ▪ careful consideration or attention: *I haven't* ***given*** *it much* ***thought***. ▪ concern for another's well-being or convenience: *he is carrying on the life of a single man, with* ***no thought for*** *me.*
– PHRASES **don't give it another thought** informal used to tell someone not to worry when they have apologized for something. **it's the thought that counts** informal used to indicate that it is the kindness behind an act that matters, however imperfect or insignificant the act may be. **a second thought** [with negative] more than the slightest consideration: *not one of them* ***gave a second thought to*** *the risks involved.* **a thought** dated to a small extent; somewhat: *those of us who work at home may find our hands a thought freer.* **take thought** dated reflect or consider. **that's a thought!** informal used to express approval of a comment or suggestion.
– ORIGIN Old English *thōht*, of Germanic origin; related to Dutch *gedachte*, also to **THINK**.

thought[2] past and past participle of **THINK**.

thought control ▶ **noun** [mass noun] the attempt to restrict ideas and impose opinions through censorship and the control of curricula.

thoughtcrime ▶ **noun** an instance of unorthodox or controversial thinking, considered as a criminal offence or as socially unacceptable.
– ORIGIN 1949: from George Orwell's *Nineteen Eighty-Four*.

thought disorder ▶ **noun** [mass noun] Psychiatry a disorder of cognitive organization, characteristic of psychotic mental illness, in which thoughts and conversation appear illogical and lacking in sequence and may be delusional or bizarre in content.

thought experiment ▶ **noun** a mental assessment of the implications of a hypothesis.

thought form ▶ **noun** (often **thought forms**) (especially in Christian theology) a combination of presuppositions, imagery, and vocabulary current at a particular time or place and forming the context for thinking on a subject.

thoughtful ▶ **adjective** absorbed in or involving thought: *brows drawn together in thoughtful consideration.*
▪ showing consideration for the needs of other people: *he was attentive and thoughtful | how very* ***thoughtful of*** *you!* ▪ showing careful consideration or attention: *her work is thoughtful and provocative.*
– DERIVATIVES **thoughtfully** adverb, **thoughtfulness** noun.

thoughtless ▶ **adjective** (of a person or their behaviour) not showing consideration for the needs of other people: *it was* ***thoughtless of*** *her to have rushed out and not said where she would be going.*
▪ without consideration of the possible consequences: *to think a few minutes of thoughtless pleasure could end in this.*
– DERIVATIVES **thoughtlessly** adverb, **thoughtlessness** noun.

thought pattern ▶ **noun** a habit of thinking in a particular way, using particular assumptions.
▪ a quality characterizing someone's thought processes as expressed in language: *thought patterns such as overgeneralization and illogicality.* ▪ another term for **THOUGHT FORM**.

thought police ▶ **noun** [treated as pl.] a group of people who aim or are seen as aiming to suppress ideas that deviate from the way of thinking that they believe to be correct.

t

thought-provoking ▶ adjective stimulating careful consideration or attention: *thought-provoking questions.*

thought-reader ▶ noun a person who can supposedly discern what someone else is thinking.
– DERIVATIVES **thought-reading** noun.

thought reform ▶ noun [mass noun] the systematic alteration of a person's mode of thinking, especially (in Communist China) a process of individual political indoctrination.

thought transference ▶ noun another term for **TELEPATHY**.

thought wave ▶ noun a supposed pattern of energy by which it is claimed that thoughts are transferred from one person to another.

thousand ▶ cardinal number (pl. **thousands** or (with numeral or quantifying word) same) (**a/one thousand**) the number equivalent to the product of a hundred and ten; 1,000: *a thousand metres | two thousand acres | thousands have been killed.* (Roman numeral: **m, M.**)
■(**thousands**) the numbers from one thousand to 9,999: *the cost of repairs could be in the thousands.* ■(usu. **thousands**) informal an unspecified large number: *you'll meet thousands of girls before you find the one you like | I have imagined it a thousand times.*
– DERIVATIVES **thousandfold** adjective & adverb, **thousandth** ordinal number.
– ORIGIN Old English *thūsend*, of Germanic origin; related to Dutch *duizend* and German *Tausend*.

Thousand and One Nights another name for **ARABIAN NIGHTS**.

Thousand Island dressing ▶ noun [mass noun] a dressing for salad or seafood consisting of mayonnaise with ketchup and chopped gherkins.

Thousand Islands **1** a group of about 1,500 islands in a widening of the St Lawrence River, just below Kingston. Some of the islands belong to Canada and some to the US.
2 a group of about 100 small islands off the north coast of Java, forming part of Indonesia. Indonesian name **PULAU SERIBU**.

Thrace /θreɪs/ an ancient country lying west of the Black Sea and north of the Aegean. It is now divided between Turkey, Bulgaria, and Greece.
– DERIVATIVES **Thracian** /ˈθreɪʃ(ə)n/ adjective & noun.

Thrale /θreɪl/, Mrs Hester Lynch (1741–1821), English writer; latterly *Hester Lynch Piozzi*. She was a close friend of Dr Johnson, who lived with her and her husband for several years.

thrall /θrɔːl/ ▶ noun [mass noun] poetic/literary the state of being in someone's power or having great power over someone: *she was **in thrall to** her abusive husband.*
■[count noun] historical a slave, servant, or captive.
– DERIVATIVES **thraldom** (also **thralldom**) noun.
– ORIGIN Old English *thrǣl* 'slave', from Old Norse *thræll*.

thrash ▶ verb [with obj.] beat (a person or animal) repeatedly and violently with a stick or whip: *she thrashed him across the head and shoulders* | [as noun **thrashing**] *what he needs is a good thrashing.*
■hit (something) hard and repeatedly: *the wind screeched and the mast thrashed the deck.* ■[no obj.] make a repeated crashing by or as if by hitting something: *the surf thrashed and thundered.* ■[no obj.] move in a violent and convulsive way: *he lay on the ground **thrashing around** in pain* | [with obj.] *she thrashed her arms, attempting to swim.* ■[no obj.] (**thrash around**) struggle in a wild or desperate way to do something: *two months of thrashing around on my own have produced nothing.* ■informal defeat (someone) heavily in a contest or match: *I thrashed Pete at cards* | [with obj. and complement] *Newcastle were thrashed 8–1 by the Czech team.* ■[no obj., with adverbial of direction] move with brute determination or violent movements: *I wrench the steering wheel back and thrash on up the hill.* ■rare term for **THRESH** (in sense 1).
▶ noun **1** [usu. in sing.] a violent or noisy movement, typically involving hitting something repeatedly: *the thrash of the waves.*
■Brit. informal a party, especially a loud or lavish one. ■informal a fast and exciting motor race or other sporting event.
2 (also **thrash metal**) [mass noun] a style of fast, loud, harsh-sounding rock music, combining elements of punk and heavy metal.
■[count noun] a short, fast, loud piece or passage of rock music.
– ORIGIN Old English, variant of **THRESH** (an early sense). Current senses of the noun date from the mid 19th cent.
▶ **thrash something out** discuss something thoroughly and honestly. ■produce a conclusion by such discussion.

thrasher[1] ▶ noun **1** a person or thing that thrashes.
2 archaic spelling of **THRESHER** (in sense 1).

thrasher[2] ▶ noun a thrush-like American songbird of the mockingbird family, with mainly brown or grey plumage, a long tail, and a downcurved bill.
• Family Mimidae: five genera, in particular *Toxostoma*, and several species.
– ORIGIN early 19th cent.: perhaps from English dialect *thrusher, thresher* 'thrush'.

thrawn /θrɔːn/ ▶ adjective Scottish perverse; ill-tempered: *mother's looking a bit thrawn this morning.*
■twisted; crooked: *a slightly thrawn neck.*
– ORIGIN late Middle English: Scots form of *thrown* (see **THROW**), in the obsolete sense 'twisted, wrung'.

thread ▶ noun **1** a long, thin strand of cotton, nylon, or other fibres used in sewing or weaving.
■[mass noun] cotton, nylon, or other fibres spun into long, thin strands and used for sewing. ■(**threads**) informal, chiefly N. Amer. clothes.
2 a thing resembling a thread in length or thinness, in particular:
■chiefly poetic/literary a long, thin line or piece of something: *the Thames was a thread of silver below them.* ■[in sing.] something abstract or intangible, regarded as weak or fragile: *keeping the tenuous thread of life attached to a dying body.* ■a theme or characteristic, typically forming one of several, running throughout a situation or piece of writing: *a **common thread** running through the scandals was the failure to conduct audits.* ■Computing a group of linked messages posted on the Internet that share a common subject or theme. ■Computing a programming structure or process formed by linking a number of separate elements or subroutines, especially each of the tasks executed concurrently in multithreading.
3 (also **screw thread**) a helical ridge on the outside of a screw, bolt, etc. or on the inside of a cylindrical hole, to allow two parts to be screwed together.
▶ verb [with obj.] **1** pass a thread through the eye of (a needle) or through the needle and guides of (a sewing machine).
■[with obj. and adverbial of direction] pass (a long, thin object or piece of material) through something and into the required position for use: *he threaded the rope through a pulley.* ■[no obj., with adverbial of direction] move carefully or skilfully in and out of obstacles: *she **threaded her way** through the tables.* ■interweave or intersperse as if with threads: *his hair had become ill-kempt and **threaded with** grey.* ■put (beads, chunks of food, or other small objects) together or singly on a thread, chain, or skewer, which runs through the centre of each one: *Constance sat threading beads.*
2 [usu. as adj. **threaded**] cut a screw thread in or on (a hole, screw, or other object).
– PHRASES **hang by a thread** be in a highly precarious state. **lose the** (or **one's**) **thread** be unable to follow what someone is saying or remember what one is going to say next.
– DERIVATIVES **thread-like** adjective.
– ORIGIN Old English *thrǣd* (noun), of Germanic origin; related to Dutch *draad* and German *Draht*, also to the verb **THROW**. The verb dates from late Middle English.

threadbare ▶ adjective (of cloth, clothing, or soft furnishings) becoming thin and tattered with age: *tatty rooms with threadbare carpets* | figurative *the song was a tissue of threadbare clichés.*
■(of a person, building, or room) poor or shabby in appearance.

threader ▶ noun **1** a device for passing a thread through the needle and guides of a sewing machine.
■a factory worker who attaches spools of yarn to a loom.
2 a device for cutting a spiral ridge on the outside of a screw or the inside of a hole.

threadfin ▶ noun a tropical marine fish that has long streamers or rays arising from its pectoral fins, locally important as a food fish.
• Family Polynemidae: several genera and species.

thread mark ▶ noun a mark in the form of a thin line made in banknote paper with highly coloured silk fibres to prevent photographic counterfeiting.

Threadneedle Street a street in the City of London containing the premises of the Bank of England.
– ORIGIN *Threadneedle* from *three-needle*, possibly from a tavern with the arms of the city of London Guild of Needlemakers.

thread vein ▶ noun a very slender vein, especially one on the face that is visible through the skin.

threadworm ▶ noun a very slender parasitic nematode worm, especially a pinworm.

thready ▶ adjective (**threadier**, **threadiest**) **1** of, relating to, or resembling a thread.
2 (of a sound, especially the voice) scarcely audible: *he managed a thready whisper.*
■Medicine (of a person's pulse) scarcely perceptible.

threat ▶ noun **1** a statement of an intention to inflict pain, injury, damage, or other hostile action on someone in retribution for something done or not done: *members of her family have received **death threats**.*
■Law a menace of bodily harm, such as may restrain a person's freedom of action.
2 a person or thing likely to cause damage or danger: *hurricane damage poses a major **threat to** many coastal communities.*
■[in sing.] the possibility of trouble, danger, or ruin: *the company faces the threat of liquidation proceedings* | [mass noun] *thousands of rail freight jobs came **under threat**.*
– ORIGIN Old English *thrēat* 'oppression', of Germanic origin; related to Dutch *verdrieten* 'grieve', German *verdriessen* 'irritate'.

threaten ▶ verb [reporting verb] state one's intention to take hostile action against someone in retribution for something done or not done: [with obj.] *the trade unions threatened a general strike* | [with infinitive] *she forced a scene and Toby threatened to leave* | [with direct speech] *'I might sue for damages,' he threatened.*
■[with obj.] express one's intention to harm or kill (someone): *the men **threatened** staff **with** a handgun.* ■[with obj.] cause (someone or something) to be vulnerable or at risk; endanger: *a broken finger threatened his career | one of four London hospitals **threatened with** closure.* ■[with infinitive] (of a situation or weather conditions) seem likely to produce an unpleasant or unwelcome result: *the dispute threatened to spread to other cities* | [with obj.] *the air was raw and threatened rain.* ■[no obj.] (of something undesirable) seem likely to occur: *unless war threatened, national politics remained the focus of attention.*
– DERIVATIVES **threatener** noun.
– ORIGIN Old English *thrēatnian* 'urge or induce, especially by using threats', from *thrēat* (see **THREAT**).

threatening ▶ adjective having a hostile or deliberately frightening quality or manner: *her mother had received a threatening letter.*
■Law (of behaviour) showing an intention to cause bodily harm. ■(of a person or situation) causing someone to feel vulnerable or at risk: *she was a type he found threatening.* ■(of weather conditions) indicating that bad weather is likely: *black threatening clouds.*
– DERIVATIVES **threateningly** adverb.

three ▶ cardinal number equivalent to the sum of one and two; one more than two; 3: *her three children | a crew of three | a three-bedroom house | all three of them are buried there.* (Roman numeral: **iii** or **III**)
■a group or unit of three people or things: *students clustered in twos or threes.* ■three years old: *she is only three.* ■three o'clock: *I'll come at three.* ■a size of garment or other merchandise denoted by three. ■a playing card or domino with three pips.
– PHRASES **three parts** three out of four equal parts; three quarters.
– ORIGIN Old English *thrīe* (masculine), *thrīo, thrēo* (feminine), of Germanic origin; related to Dutch *drie* and German *drei*, from an Indo-European root shared by Latin *tres* and Greek *treis*.

three-card monte ▶ noun see **MONTE**.

three-card trick ▶ noun [mass noun] a game, traditionally associated with confidence tricksters, in which bets are made on which is the queen among three cards lying face downwards.

three cheers ▶ plural noun see **CHEER**.

three-colour process ▶ noun Photography a means of reproducing natural colours by combining photographic images in the three primary colours.

three-cornered ▶ adjective triangular.
■(especially of a contest) between three people or groups.

three-decker ▶ noun a thing with three levels or layers: [as modifier] *three-decker sandwiches.*

■ informal a novel in three volumes.

three-dimensional ▶ adjective having or appearing to have length, breadth, and depth: *a three-dimensional object.*

■ figurative (of a literary or dramatic work) sufficiently full in characterization and representation of events to be believable.

– DERIVATIVES **three-dimensionality** noun, **three-dimensionally** adverb.

threefold ▶ adjective three times as great or as numerous: *a threefold increase in the number of stolen cars.*

■ having three parts or elements: *the differences are threefold.*

▶ adverb by three times; to three times the number or amount: *the aftershocks intensify threefold each time.*

Three Graces see GRACE.

three-handed ▶ adjective having, using, or requiring three people: *it's a three-handed job.*

three-legged race ▶ noun a race run by pairs of people, one member of each pair having their left leg tied to the right leg of the other.

three-line whip ▶ noun (in the UK) a written notice, underlined three times to denote urgency, to members of a political party to attend a parliamentary vote.

Three Mile Island an island in the Susquehanna River near Harrisburg, Pennsylvania, site of a nuclear power station. In 1979 an accident caused damage to the reactor core, provoking strong reactions against the nuclear industry in the US.

three-peat N. Amer. ▶ verb [no obj.] win a particular sporting championship three times, especially consecutively.

▶ noun [in sing.] a third win of a particular sporting championship, especially the third of three consecutive wins.

– ORIGIN 1980s: from THREE + a shortened form of REPEAT.

threepence /ˈθrɛp(ə)ns, ˈθrʊ-, ˈθrʌ-/ ▶ noun Brit. the sum of three pence, especially before decimalization (1971).

threepenny /ˈθrɛp(ə)ni, ˈθrʊ-, ˈθrʌ-/ ▶ adjective [attrib.] Brit. costing or worth three pence, especially before decimalization (1971).

threepenny bit ▶ noun Brit. historical a coin worth three old pence (1¼ p).

three-phase ▶ adjective (of an electric generator, motor, or other device) designed to supply or use simultaneously three separate alternating currents of the same voltage, but with phases differing by a third of a period.

three-piece ▶ adjective [attrib.] consisting of three separate and complementary items, in particular: ■ (of a set of furniture) consisting of a sofa and two armchairs. ■ (of a set of clothes) consisting of trousers or a skirt with a waistcoat and jacket.

▶ noun a set of three separate and complementary items.

■ a group consisting of three musicians.

three-ply ▶ adjective (of material) having three layers or strands.

▶ noun [mass noun] **1** knitting wool made of three strands.

2 plywood made by gluing together three layers with the grain in different directions.

three-point landing ▶ noun a landing of an aircraft on the two main wheels and the tailwheel or skid simultaneously.

three-point turn ▶ noun a method of turning a vehicle round in a narrow space by moving forwards, backwards, and forwards again in a sequence of arcs.

three-pronged ▶ adjective having three projecting, pointed parts: *a three-pronged hook.*

■ (especially of an attack or operation) having three separate parts.

three-quarter ▶ adjective [attrib.] consisting of three quarters of something (used especially with reference to size, length, or the hour): *a three-quarter length cashmere coat.*

■ (of a view or depiction of a person's face) at an angle between full face and profile.

▶ noun **1** Rugby each of four players in a team positioned across the field behind the halfbacks.

2 (**the three-quarter**) a point in time forty-five

minutes after any full hour of the clock: *the cathedral clock was chiming the three-quarter.*

▶ adverb [as submodifier] to a size or extent of three quarters: *three-quarter grown rabbits.*

three quarters ▶ plural noun three of the four equal parts into which something may be divided: *three quarters of an hour.*

▶ adverb to the extent of three quarters: *Vermont is more than three quarters woodland.*

three-ring circus ▶ noun chiefly US a circus with three rings for simultaneous performances.

■ a public spectacle, especially one with little substance: *his attempt at a dignified resignation turned into a three-ring circus.*

threescore ▶ cardinal number poetic/literary sixty.

threesome ▶ noun a group of three people engaged in the same activity.

■ a game or activity for three people.

three-star ▶ adjective (especially of accommodation or service) given three stars in a grading system in which this denotes a high class or quality, being one grade below four-star.

■ having or denoting the third-highest military rank, distinguished in the US armed forces by three stars on the shoulder piece of the uniform.

three strikes ▶ noun [mass noun] [usu. as modifier] US legislation which provides that an offender's third felony is punishable by life imprisonment or other severe sentence.

– ORIGIN 1990s: from the phrase *three strikes and you're out* (with allusion to baseball).

three-way ▶ adjective involving three directions, processes, or participants: *a three-way race for the presidency* | *a three-way switch.*

three-wheeler ▶ noun a vehicle with three wheels.

Three Wise Men another name for MAGI.

threnody /ˈθrɛnədi/ ▶ noun (pl. **-ies**) a lament.

– DERIVATIVES **threnodial** adjective, **threnodic** adjective, **threnodist** noun.

– ORIGIN mid 17th cent.: from Greek *thrēnōidia*, from *thrēnos* 'wailing' + *ōidē* 'song'.

threonine /ˈθriːəniːn/ ▶ noun [mass noun] Biochemistry a hydrophilic amino acid which is a constituent of most proteins. It is an essential nutrient in the diet of vertebrates.

● Chem. formula: $CH_3CH(OH)CH(NH_2)COOH$.

– ORIGIN 1930s: from *threose* (the name of a tetrose sugar) + -INE[4].

thresh /θrɛʃ/ ▶ verb [with obj.] **1** separate grain from (corn or other crops), typically with a flail or by the action of a revolving mechanism: *machinery that can reap and thresh corn in the same process* | [as noun **threshing**] *farm workers started the afternoon's threshing.*

■ (**thresh something over**) analyse a problem in search of a solution.

2 /θraʃ/ variant spelling of THRASH (in the sense of violent movement).

– ORIGIN Old English *therscan*, later *threscan*, of Germanic origin; related to Dutch *dorsen* and German *dreschen*. Compare with THRASH.

thresher /ˈθrɛʃə/ ▶ noun **1** a person or machine that separates grain from corn or other crops by beating.

2 (also **thresher shark**) a surface-living shark with a long upper lobe to the tail. Threshers often hunt in pairs, lashing the water with their tails to herd fish into a tightly packed shoal.

● *Alopias vulpinus*, family Alopidae.

threshing floor ▶ noun a hard, level surface on which corn or other grain is threshed with a flail.

threshing machine ▶ noun a power-driven machine for separating the grain from corn or other crops.

threshold /ˈθrɛʃəʊld, ˈθrɛʃ.həʊld/ ▶ noun **1** a strip of wood or stone forming the bottom of a doorway and crossed in entering a house or room.

■ [in sing.] a point of entry or beginning: *she was on the threshold of a dazzling career.* ■ the beginning of an airport runway on which an aircraft is attempting to land.

2 the magnitude or intensity that must be exceeded for a certain reaction, phenomenon, result, or condition to occur or be manifested.

■ the maximum level of radiation or a concentration of a substance considered to be acceptable or safe. ■ Physiology & Psychology a limit below which a stimulus causes no reaction: *everyone has a different pain*

threshold. ■ chiefly Brit. a level, rate, or amount at which something such as a tax comes into effect: *the VAT threshold.*

– ORIGIN Old English *therscold, threscold*; related to German dialect *Drischaufel*; the first element is related to THRESH (in a Germanic sense 'tread'), but the origin of the second element is unknown.

threw past of THROW.

thrice /θrʌɪs/ ▶ adverb chiefly formal or poetic/literary three times: *a dose of 25 mg thrice daily.*

■ [as submodifier] extremely; very: *I was thrice blessed.*

– ORIGIN Middle English *thries*, from earlier *thrie* (from Old English *thriga*, related to THREE) + -S[3] (later respelled -ce to denote the unvoiced sound); compare with ONCE.

thrift ▶ noun [mass noun] **1** the quality of using money and other resources carefully and not wastefully: *the values of thrift and self-reliance.*

■ [count noun] US another term for SAVINGS AND LOAN.

2 a European plant which forms low-growing tufts of slender leaves with rounded pink flower heads, growing chiefly on sea cliffs and mountains. Also called SEA PINK.

● *Armeria maritima*, family Plumbaginaceae.

– ORIGIN Middle English (in the sense 'prosperity, acquired wealth, success'): from Old Norse, from *thrifa* 'grasp, get hold of'. Compare with THRIVE.

thriftless ▶ adjective (of a person or their behaviour) spending money in an extravagant and wasteful way.

– DERIVATIVES **thriftlessly** adverb, **thriftlessness** noun.

thrift shop (also **thrift store**) ▶ noun N. Amer. a shop selling second-hand clothes and other household goods, typically to raise funds for a church or charitable institution.

thrifty ▶ adjective (**thriftier**, **thriftiest**) **1** (of a person or their behaviour) using money and other resources carefully and not wastefully.

2 chiefly archaic or dialect (of livestock or plants) strong and healthy.

■ archaic prosperous.

– DERIVATIVES **thriftily** adverb, **thriftiness** noun.

thrill ▶ noun a sudden feeling of excitement and pleasure: *the thrill of jumping out of an aeroplane.*

■ an experience that produces such a feeling. ■ a wave or nervous tremor of emotion or sensation: *a thrill of excitement ran through her.* ■ archaic a throb or pulsation. ■ Medicine a vibratory movement or resonance heard through a stethoscope.

▶ verb **1** [with obj.] cause (someone) to have a sudden feeling of excitement and pleasure: *his kiss thrilled and excited her* | *I'm thrilled to bits* | [as adj. **thrilling**] *a thrilling adventure.*

■ [no obj.] experience such feeling: *thrill to the magic of the world's greatest guitarist.*

2 [no obj., with adverbial] (of an emotion or sensation) pass with a nervous tremor: *the shock of alarm thrilled through her.*

■ [no obj.] poetic/literary quiver or throb.

– PHRASES **the thrill of the chase** pleasure and excitement derived from seeking something desired, especially a sexual relationship with someone. **thrills and spills** the excitement of dangerous sports or entertainments, as experienced by spectators.

– DERIVATIVES **thrillingly** adverb.

– ORIGIN Middle English (as a verb in the sense 'pierce or penetrate'): alteration of dialect *thirl* 'pierce, bore'.

thriller ▶ noun a novel, play, or film with an exciting plot, typically involving crime or espionage.

thrips /θrɪps/ (also **thrip**) ▶ noun (pl. same) a minute black winged insect which sucks plant sap and can be a serious pest of ornamental and food plants when present in large numbers. Thrips swarm on warm still summer days and cause irritation by crawling on the skin. Also called THUNDERBUG, THUNDERFLY.

● Order Thysanoptera: many species, including the **pea thrips** (*Kakothrips robustus*), which can cause considerable losses to pea crops.

– ORIGIN late 18th cent.: via Latin from Greek, literally 'woodworm'.

thrive ▶ verb (past **throve** or **thrived**; past participle **thriven** or **thrived**) [no obj.] (of a child, animal, or plant) grow or develop well or vigorously: *the new baby thrived.*

■ prosper; flourish: *education groups thrive on organization* | [as adj. **thriving**] *a thriving economy.*

– ORIGIN Middle English (originally in the sense 'grow, increase'): from Old Norse *thrífask*, reflexive of *thrífa* 'grasp, get hold of'. Compare with **THRIFT**.

thro' ▶ **preposition**, **adverb**, & **adjective** poetic/literary or informal spelling of **THROUGH**.

throat ▶ **noun** the passage which leads from the back of the mouth of a person or animal.
■ the front part of a person's or animal's neck, behind which the gullet, windpipe, and blood vessels serving the head are situated: *a gold pendant gleamed at her throat.* ■ poetic/literary a voice of a person or a songbird: *from a hundred throats came the cry 'Vive l'Empereur!'* ■ a thing compared to a throat, especially a narrow passage, entrance, or exit. ■ Sailing the forward upper corner of a quadrilateral fore-and-aft sail.
– PHRASES **be at each other's throats** (of people or organizations) quarrel or fight persistently. **force** (or **ram** or **shove**) **something down someone's throat** force ideas or material on a person's attention by repeatedly putting them forward. **grab** (or **take**) **someone by the throat** put one's hands around someone's throat, typically in an attempt to throttle them. ■ (**grab something by the throat**) seize control of something: *Scotland took the game by the throat.* ■ attract someone's undivided attention: *the film grabs you by the throat and refuses to let go.*
– DERIVATIVES **throated** adjective [in combination] *a full-throated baritone.*
– ORIGIN Old English *throte*, *throtu*, of Germanic origin; related to German *Drossel*. Compare with **THROTTLE**.

throatlatch (also **throatlash**) ▶ **noun** a strap passing under a horse's throat to help keep the bridle in position.

throat microphone ▶ **noun** a microphone attached to a speaker's throat and actuated by the larynx.

throatwort ▶ **noun** a tall Eurasian bellflower that is reputed to cure sore throats.
• Genus *Campanula*, family Campanulaceae: several species, in particular *C. trachelium* and *C. latifolia*.

throaty ▶ **adjective** (**throatier**, **throatiest**) **1** (of a sound such as a person's voice or the noise of an engine) deep and rasping: *rich, throaty laughter.*
2 (of an animal, especially a dog) having loose, pendulous skin around the throat.
– DERIVATIVES **throatily** adverb, **throatiness** noun.

throb ▶ **verb** (**throbbed**, **throbbing**) [no obj.] beat or sound with a strong, regular rhythm; pulsate steadily: *the war drums throbbed* | figurative *the crowded streets throbbed with life.*
■ feel pain in a series of regular beats: *her foot throbbed with pain* | [as adj. **throbbing**] *a throbbing headache.*
▶ **noun** [usu. in sing.] a strong, regular beat or sound; a steady pulsation: *the throb of the ship's engines.*
■ a feeling of pain in a series of regular beats.
– ORIGIN late Middle English: probably imitative.

throes /θrəʊz/ ▶ **plural noun** intense or violent pain and struggle, especially accompanying birth, death, or great change: *he convulsed in his death throes.*
– PHRASES **in the throes of** in the middle of doing or dealing with something very difficult or painful: *a friend was in the throes of a divorce.*
– ORIGIN Middle English *throwe* (singular); perhaps related to Old English *thrēa*, *thrawu* 'calamity', influenced by *thrōwian* 'suffer'.

thrombectomy /θrɒmˈbɛktəmi/ ▶ **noun** [mass noun] surgical removal of a thrombus from a blood vessel.

thrombi plural form of **THROMBUS**.

thrombin /ˈθrɒmbɪn/ ▶ **noun** [mass noun] Biochemistry an enzyme in blood plasma which causes the clotting of blood by converting fibrinogen to fibrin.
– ORIGIN late 19th cent.: from Greek *thrombos* 'blood clot' + **-IN**[1].

thrombo- ▶ **combining form** relating to the clotting of blood: *thromboembolism.*
– ORIGIN from Greek *thrombos* 'blood clot'.

thrombocyte /ˈθrɒmbə(ʊ)sʌɪt/ ▶ **noun** another term for **PLATELET**.

thrombocythaemia /ˌθrɒmbə(ʊ)sʌɪˈθiːmɪə/ ▶ **noun** [mass noun] Medicine abnormal proliferation of the cells that produce blood platelets, leading to an excess of platelets in the blood and increasing risk either of thrombosis or of bleeding.

thrombocytopenia /ˌθrɒmbə(ʊ)ˌsʌɪtə(ʊ)ˈpiːnɪə/ ▶ **noun** [mass noun] Medicine deficiency of platelets in the blood. This causes bleeding into the tissues, bruising, and slow blood clotting after injury.
– ORIGIN 1920s: from **THROMBOCYTE** + Greek *penia* 'poverty'.

thromboembolism /ˌθrɒmbəʊˈɛmbəlɪz(ə)m/ ▶ **noun** Medicine obstruction of a blood vessel by a blood clot that has become dislodged from another site in the circulation.
– DERIVATIVES **thromboembolic** adjective.

thrombogenic /ˌθrɒmbə(ʊ)ˈdʒɛnɪk/ ▶ **adjective** Medicine (of a substance or condition) producing coagulation of the blood, especially as predisposing to thrombosis.
– DERIVATIVES **thrombogenicity** noun.

thrombolysis /θrɒmˈbɒlɪsɪs/ ▶ **noun** [mass noun] Medicine the dissolution of a blood clot, especially as induced artificially by infusion of an enzyme into the blood.
– DERIVATIVES **thrombolytic** adjective.

thrombophlebitis /ˌθrɒmbəʊflɪˈbʌɪtɪs/ ▶ **noun** [mass noun] Medicine inflammation of the wall of a vein with associated thrombosis, often occurring in the legs during pregnancy.

thromboplastin /ˌθrɒmbə(ʊ)ˈplastɪn/ ▶ **noun** [mass noun] Biochemistry an enzyme released from damaged cells, especially platelets, which converts prothrombin to thrombin during the early stages of blood coagulation.

thrombose /θrɒmˈbəʊz, -s/ ▶ **verb** affect with or be affected by thrombosis: [with obj.] *the superior mesenteric artery was thrombosed* | [no obj.] *the adjacent capillaries may thrombose* | [as adj. **thrombosed**] *the appearance of the thrombosed vein.*
– ORIGIN late 19th cent.: back-formation from **THROMBOSIS**.

thrombosis /θrɒmˈbəʊsɪs/ ▶ **noun** (pl. **thromboses** /-siːz/) [mass noun] local coagulation or clotting of the blood in a part of the circulatory system: *increased risk of thrombosis* | [count noun] *he died of a coronary thrombosis.*
– DERIVATIVES **thrombotic** adjective.
– ORIGIN early 18th cent.: modern Latin, from Greek *thrombōsis* 'curdling', from *thrombos* 'blood clot'.

thromboxane /θrɒmˈbɒkseɪn/ ▶ **noun** [mass noun] Biochemistry a hormone of the prostacyclin type released from blood platelets, which induces platelet aggregation and arterial constriction.

thrombus /ˈθrɒmbəs/ ▶ **noun** (pl. **thrombi** /-bʌɪ/) a blood clot formed in situ within the vascular system of the body and impeding blood flow.
– ORIGIN mid 19th cent.: modern Latin, from Greek *thrombos* 'lump, blood clot'.

throne ▶ **noun** a ceremonial chair for a sovereign, bishop, or similar figure.
■ (**the throne**) used to signify sovereign power: *the heir to the throne.* ■ humorous a toilet. ■ (**thrones**) (in traditional Christian angelology) the third-highest order of the ninefold celestial hierarchy.
▶ **verb** [with obj.] (usu. **be throned**) poetic/literary place (someone) on a throne: *the king was throned on a rock.*
– ORIGIN Middle English: from Old French *trone*, via Latin from Greek *thronos* 'elevated seat'.

throng ▶ **noun** a large, densely packed crowd of people or animals: *he pushed his way through the throng* | *a throng of birds.*
▶ **verb** [with obj.] (of a crowd) fill or be present in (a place or area): *a crowd thronged the station* | *the pavements are thronged with people.*
■ [no obj., with adverbial of direction] flock or be present in great numbers: *tourists thronged to the picturesque village.*
– ORIGIN Old English (*ge*)*thrang* 'crowd, tumult', of Germanic origin. The early sense of the verb (Middle English) was 'press violently, force one's way'.

throstle /ˈθrɒs(ə)l/ ▶ **noun 1** Brit. old-fashioned term for **SONG THRUSH**.
2 (also **throstle frame**) historical a machine for continuously spinning wool or cotton.
– ORIGIN Old English, of Germanic origin, from an Indo-European root shared by Latin *turdus* 'thrush'. Sense 2 dates from the early 19th cent. and was apparently named from the humming sound of the machine.

throttle ▶ **noun 1** a device controlling the flow of fuel or power to an engine: *the engines were at full throttle.*
2 archaic a person's throat, gullet, or windpipe.
▶ **verb** [with obj.] **1** attack or kill (someone) by choking or strangling them: *she was sorely tempted to throttle him* | figurative *the revolution has throttled the free exchange of information and opinion.*
2 control (an engine or vehicle) with a throttle.
■ (**throttle back** or **down**) reduce the power of an engine or vehicle by use of the throttle.
– DERIVATIVES **throttler** noun.
– ORIGIN late Middle English (as a verb): perhaps a frequentative, from **THROAT**; the noun (dating from the mid 16th cent. in sense 2) is perhaps a diminutive of **THROAT**, but the history of the word is not clear.

through ▶ **preposition** & **adverb 1** moving in one side and out of the other side of (an opening, channel, or location): [as prep.] *stepping boldly through the doorway* | [as adv.] *as soon as we opened the gate they came streaming through.*
■ so as to make a hole or opening in (a physical object): [as prep.] *the lorry smashed through a brick wall* | [as adv.] *a cucumber, slit, but not right through.* ■ moving around or from one side to the other within (a crowd or group): [as prep.] *making my way through the guests.* ■ so as to be perceived from the other side of (an intervening obstacle): [as prep.] *the sun was streaming in through the window* | [as adv.] *the glass in the front door where the moonlight streamed through.* ■ [prep.] expressing the position or location of something beyond or at the far end of (an opening or an obstacle): *the approach to the church is through a gate.* ■ expressing the extent of turning from one orientation to another: [as prep.] *each joint can move through an angle within fixed limits.*
2 continuing in time towards completion of (a process or period): [as prep.] *the goal came midway through the second half* | [as adv.] *to struggle through until pay day.*
■ so as to complete (a particular stage or trial) successfully: [as prep.] *she had come through her sternest test* | [as adv.] *I will struggle through alone rather than ask for help.* ■ from beginning to end of (an experience or activity, typically a tedious or stressful one): [as prep.] *we sat through some very boring speeches* | *she's been through a bad time* | [as adv.] *Karl will see you through, Ingrid.*
3 so as to inspect all or part of (a collection, inventory, or publication): [as prep.] *flipping through the pages of a notebook* | [as adv.] *she read the letter through carefully.*
4 [prep.] N. Amer. up to and including (a particular point in an ordered sequence): *they will be in London from March 24 through May 7.*
5 [prep.] by means of (a process or intermediate stage): *dioxins get into mothers' milk through contaminated food.*
■ by means of (an intermediary or agent): *seeking justice through the proper channels.*
6 [adverb] so as to be connected by telephone: *he put a call through to the Naturalists' Trust Office.*
▶ **adjective 1** [attrib.] (of a means of public transport or a ticket) continuing or valid to the final destination: *a through train from London.*
2 [attrib.] denoting traffic that passes from one side of a place to another in the course of a longer journey: *urban precincts from which through traffic would be excluded.*
■ denoting a road that is open at both ends, allowing traffic free passage from one end to the other: *the village lies on a busy through road.*
3 [attrib.] (of a room) running the whole length of a building.
4 [predic.] (of a team or competitor) having successfully passed to the next stage of a competition: *Swindon Town are through to the third round.*
5 [predic.] informal, chiefly N. Amer. having no prospect of any future relationship, dealings, or success: *she told him she was through with him* | *you and I are through.*
– PHRASES **through and through** in every aspect; thoroughly or completely: *Harriet was a political animal through and through.*
– ORIGIN Old English *thurh* (preposition and adverb), of Germanic origin; related to Dutch *door* and German *durch*. The spelling change to *thr-* appears *c.*1300, becoming standard from Caxton onwards.

through ball ▶ **noun** Soccer a forward pass which goes through the opposing team's defence.

through-composed ▶ **adjective** another term for **DURCHKOMPONIERT**.

throughfall ▶ **noun** [mass noun] the part of rainfall or other precipitation which falls to the forest floor from the canopy.

throughflow ▶ noun [mass noun] the flowing of liquid or air through something.

through-hole ▶ adjective (of an electronic component) having leads which are designed to go through holes to the other side of a circuit board for soldering. Often contrasted with **SURFACE-MOUNT**.

throughother Scottish & Irish ▶ adverb mingled through one another: *their life together had been woven throughother.*
▶ adjective (of a person) disordered; confused.

throughout ▶ preposition & adverb all the way through, in particular:
■ in every part of (a place or object): [as prep.] *it had repercussions throughout Europe* | [as adv.] *the house is in good order throughout.* ■ from beginning to end of (an event or period of time): [as prep.] *the Church of which she was a faithful member throughout her life* | [as adv.] *both MPs retained a smiling dignity throughout.*

through pass ▶ noun another term for **THROUGH BALL**.

throughput ▶ noun the amount of material or items passing through a system or process.

through-ticketing ▶ noun [mass noun] a system whereby a traveller passing through a number of different railway networks can purchase one ticket for the complete journey.

throughway (also **thruway**) ▶ noun N. Amer. a major road or motorway.

throve past of **THRIVE**.

throw ▶ verb (past **threw**; past participle **thrown**) 1 [with obj. and usu. with adverbial] propel (something) with force through the air by a movement of the arm and hand: *I threw a brick through the window.*
■ [with obj. and adverbial or complement] push or force (someone or something) violently and suddenly into a particular physical position or state: *the pilot and one passenger were thrown clear and survived* | *the door was thrown open and a uniformed guard entered the room.* ■ put in place or erect quickly: *the stewards had thrown a cordon across the fairway.* ■ move (a part of the body) quickly or suddenly in a particular direction: *she threw her head back and laughed.* ■ project or cast (light or shadow) in a particular direction: *a chandelier threw its bright light over the walls.* ■ deliver (a punch). ■ direct a particular kind of look or facial expression: *she threw a withering glance at him.* ■ project (one's voice) so that it appears to come from someone or something else, as in ventriloquism. ■ (**throw something off/on**) put on or take off (a garment) hastily: *I tumbled out of bed, threw on my tracksuit, and joined the others.* ■ move (a switch or lever) so as to operate a device. ■ roll (dice). ■ obtain (a specified number) by rolling dice. ■ [with obj.] informal lose (a race or contest) intentionally, especially in return for a bribe. ■ Cricket bowl (the ball) with an illegitimate bent arm action.
2 [with obj. and adverbial] cause to enter suddenly a particular state or condition: *he threw all her emotions into turmoil* | *the bond market was thrown into confusion.*
■ put (someone) in a particular place or state in a rough, abrupt, or summary fashion: *these guys should be thrown in jail.* ■ [with obj.] disconcert; confuse: *she frowned, thrown by this apparent change of tack.*
3 [with obj.] send (one's opponent) to the ground in wrestling, judo, or similar activity.
■ (of a horse) unseat (its rider). ■ (of a horse) lose (a shoe). ■ (of an animal) give birth to (young, especially of a specified kind): *sometimes a completely black calf is thrown.*
4 [with obj.] form (ceramic ware) on a potter's wheel: *further on a potter was throwing pots.*
■ turn (wood or other material) on a lathe. ■ twist (silk or other fabrics) into thread or yarn.
5 [with obj.] have (a fit or tantrum).
6 [with obj.] give or hold (a party).
▶ noun 1 an act of throwing something: *Holding's throw hit the stumps.*
■ an act of throwing one's opponent in wrestling, judo, or similar sport: *a shoulder throw.* ■ Cricket an illegitimate delivery considered to have been thrown rather than properly bowled.
2 a light cover for furniture.
■ short for **THROW RUG**.
3 short for *throw of the dice* below.
4 Geology the extent of vertical displacement in a fault.
5 a machine or device by or on which an object is turned while being shaped.
6 [usu. in sing.] the action or motion of a slide valve or of a crank, eccentric wheel, or cam.
■ the extent of such motion. ■ the distance moved by the pointer of an instrument.
7 (**a throw**) informal used to indicate how much a single item, turn, or attempt costs: *he was offering to draw on-the-spot portraits at £25 a throw.*
– PHRASES **be thrown back on** be forced to rely on (something) because there is no alternative: *we are once again thrown back on the resources of our imagination.* **throw away the key** used to suggest that someone who has been put in prison should or will never be released: *the judge should lock up these robbers and throw away the key.* **throw the baby out with the bathwater** see **BABY**. **throw something back in someone's face** see **FACE**. **throw the bones** see **BONE**. **throw the book at** see **BOOK**. **throw cold water on** see **COLD**. **throw down the gauntlet** see **GAUNTLET**[1]. **throw dust in someone's eyes** seek to mislead or deceive someone by misrepresentation or distraction. **throw good money after bad** incur further loss in a hopeless attempt to recoup a previous loss. **throw one's hand in** withdraw from a card game, especially poker, because one has a poor hand. ■ withdraw from a contest or activity; give up. **throw in one's lot with** see **LOT**. **throw in the towel** (or **sponge**) (of boxers or their seconds) throw a towel (or sponge) into the ring as a token of defeat. ■ abandon a struggle; admit defeat. **throw light on** see **LIGHT**[1]. **throw money at something** see **MONEY**. **throw of the dice** a risky attempt to do or achieve something: *a struggling actor giving it a last throw of the dice as he stages a self-financed production of Hamlet.* **throw oneself on** (or **upon**) **someone's mercy** abjectly ask someone for help, forgiveness, or leniency. **throw up one's hands** raise both hands in the air as an indication of one's exasperation. **throw one's weight about** (or **around**) see **WEIGHT**. **throw one's weight behind** see **WEIGHT**.
– DERIVATIVES **throwable** adjective, **thrower** noun.
– ORIGIN Old English *thrāwan* 'to twist, turn', of West Germanic origin; related to Dutch *draaien* and German *drehen*, from an Indo-European root shared by Latin *terere* 'to rub', Greek *teirein* 'wear out'. Sense 1, expressing propulsion and sudden action, dates from Middle English.

▶ **throw something about** (or **around**) spend money freely and ostentatiously: *I can't abide that, people being well off and throwing their money about.*
throw oneself at appear too eager to become the sexual partner of.
throw something away 1 discard something as useless or unwanted. ■ waste or fail to make use of an opportunity or advantage: *I've thrown away my chances in life.* ■ discard a playing card in a game. **2** (of an actor) deliver a line with deliberate underemphasis for increased dramatic effect.
throw something down dated demolish a building or other structure.
throw something in 1 include something, typically at no extra cost, with something that is being sold or offered: *they cut the price by £100 and threw in the add-on TV adaptor.* **2** make a remark casually as an interjection in a conversation: *he threw in a sensible remark about funding.* **3** Soccer & Rugby return the ball to play by means of a throw-in.
throw oneself into start to do (something) with enthusiasm and vigour: *Evelyn threw herself into her work.*
throw off (of hounds or a hunt) begin hunting.
throw something off 1 rid oneself of something: *he was struggling to throw off a viral-hepatitis problem.* **2** write or utter in an offhand manner: *Thomas threw off the question lightly.*
throw oneself on (or **upon**) attack someone vigorously: *they threw themselves on the enemy.*
throw something open make something accessible: *the market was thrown open to any supplier to compete for contracts.* ■ invite general discussion of or participation in a subject or a debate or other event: *the debate will be thrown open to the audience.*
throw someone out 1 expel someone unceremoniously from a place, organization, or activity. **2** confuse or distract someone from the matter in hand: *do keep quiet or you'll throw me out in my calculations.* **3** Cricket & Baseball put out an opponent by throwing the ball to the wicket or a base.
throw something out 1 discard something as unwanted. **2** (of a court, legislature, or other body) dismiss or reject something brought before it: *the charges were thrown out by the magistrate.* **3** put forward a suggestion tentatively: *a suggestion that Dunne threw out caught many a reader's fancy.* **4** cause numbers or calculations to become inaccurate: *an undisclosed stock option throws out all your figures.* **5** emit or radiate something: *a big range fire that threw out heat like a furnace.* **6** (of a plant) rapidly develop a side shoot, bud, etc.
throw someone over abandon or reject someone as a lover.
throw people together bring people into contact, especially by chance.
throw something together make or produce something hastily, without careful planning or arrangement: *the meal was quickly thrown together at news of Rose's arrival.*
throw up vomit.
throw something up 1 abandon or give up something, especially one's job: *why has he thrown up a promising career in politics?* **2** informal vomit something one has eaten or drunk. **3** produce something and bring it to notice: *he saw the prayers of the Church as a living and fruitful tradition which threw up new ideas.*

throwaway ▶ adjective 1 denoting or relating to products that are intended to be discarded after being used once or a few times: *a throwaway camera* | *we live in a throwaway society.*
2 (of a remark) expressed in a casual or understated way: *some people overreacted to a few throwaway lines.*
▶ noun a thing intended or destined to be discarded after brief use or appeal.
■ a casual or understated remark or idea.

throwback ▶ noun a reversion to an earlier ancestral characteristic: *the eyes could be an ancestral throwback.*
■ a person or thing having the characteristics of a former time: *a lot of his work is a throwback to the fifties.*

throw-in ▶ noun Soccer & Rugby the act of throwing the ball from the sideline to restart play after the ball has gone into touch.

throw-off ▶ noun the release of the hounds at the start of a hunt.

throw-over ▶ adjective denoting a bedspread or other large piece of cloth used as a loose-fitting decorative cover for a piece of furniture.

throw rug ▶ noun another term for **SCATTER RUG**.

throwster ▶ noun a person who twists silk fibres into thread.

thru ▶ preposition, adverb, & adjective chiefly US informal spelling of **THROUGH**.

thrum[1] ▶ verb (**thrummed**, **thrumming**) [no obj.] make a continuous rhythmic humming sound: *the boat's huge engines thrummed in his ears.*
■ [with obj.] strum (the strings of a musical instrument) in a rhythmic way.
▶ noun [usu. in sing.] a continuous rhythmic humming sound: *the steady thrum of rain on the windows.*
– ORIGIN late 16th cent. (as a verb): imitative.

thrum[2] ▶ noun (in weaving) an unwoven end of a warp thread, or a fringe of such ends, left in the loom when the finished cloth is cut away.
■ any short loose thread.
▶ verb (**thrummed**, **thrumming**) [with obj.] cover or adorn (cloth or clothing) with ends of thread.
– DERIVATIVES **thrummer** noun, **thrummy** adjective.
– ORIGIN Old English *thrum* (only in *tungethrum* 'ligament of the tongue'): of Germanic origin; related to Dutch *dreum* 'thrum' and German *Trumm* 'end piece'. The current sense dates from Middle English.

thrush[1] ▶ noun a small or medium-sized songbird, typically having a brown back, spotted breast, and loud song.
● Family Turdidae (the **thrush family**): many genera, in particular *Turdus*, and numerous species. The thrush family also includes the chats, robins, blackbirds, nightingales, redstarts, and wheatears.
– ORIGIN Old English *thrysce*, of Germanic origin; related to **THROSTLE**.

thrush[2] ▶ noun [mass noun] 1 infection of the mouth and throat by a yeast-like fungus, causing whitish patches. Also called **CANDIDIASIS**.
● The fungus belongs to the genus *Candida*, subdivision Deuteromycotina, in particular *C. albicans*.
■ infection of the female genitals with the same fungus.

2 a chronic condition affecting the frog of a horse's foot, causing the accumulation of a dark, foul-smelling substance. Also called **CANKER**.
– ORIGIN mid 17th cent.: origin uncertain; sense 1 possibly related to Swedish *torsk* and Danish *troske*; sense 2 perhaps from dialect *frush* in the same sense, perhaps from Old French *fourchette* 'frog of a horse's hoof'.

thrush nightingale ▶ **noun** a songbird that is closely related to the nightingale and which replaces it in eastern Europe, the Baltic, and western Asia. Also called **SPROSSER**.
• *Luscinia luscinia*, family Turdidae.

thrust ▶ **verb** (past and past participle **thrust**) [with obj. and adverbial of direction] push (something or someone) suddenly or violently in the specified direction: *she thrust her hands into her pockets* | figurative *Howard was thrust into the limelight* | [no obj.] *he* **thrust at** *his opponent with his sword.*
■ [no obj., with adverbial of direction] (of a person) move or advance forcibly: *she thrust through the bramble canes* | *he tried to* **thrust his way** *past her.* ■ [no obj., with adverbial of direction] (of a thing) extend so as to project conspicuously: *beside the boathouse a jetty thrust out into the water.* ■ (**thrust something on/upon**) force (someone) to accept or deal with something: *he felt that fame had been thrust upon him.* ■ [no obj.] (of a man) penetrate the vagina or anus of a sexual partner with forceful movements of the penis.
▶ **noun 1** a sudden or violent lunge with a pointed weapon or a bodily part: *he drove the blade upwards with one powerful thrust.*
■ a forceful attack or effort: *executives led a new thrust in business development.* ■ [in sing.] the principal purpose or theme of a course of action or line of reasoning: *anti-Americanism became* **the main thrust** *of their policy.*
2 [mass noun] the propulsive force of a jet or rocket engine.
■ the lateral pressure exerted by an arch or other support in a building.
3 (also **thrust fault**) Geology a reverse fault of low angle, with older strata displaced horizontally over newer.
– ORIGIN Middle English (as a verb): from Old Norse *thrýsta*; perhaps related to Latin *trudere* 'to thrust'. The noun is first recorded (early 16th cent.) in the sense 'act of pressing'.

thrust bearing ▶ **noun** a bearing designed to take a load in the direction of the axis of a shaft, especially one transmitting the thrust of a propeller shaft to the hull of a ship.

thrust block ▶ **noun** a casting or frame carrying or containing the bearings on which the collars of a propeller shaft press.

thruster ▶ **noun** a person or thing that thrusts, in particular:
■ a small rocket engine on a spacecraft, used to make alterations in its flight path or altitude. ■ a secondary jet or propeller on a ship or offshore rig, used for accurate manoeuvring and maintenance of position. ■ informal a person who is aggressively ambitious. ■ a surfboard or sailboard capable of increased speed and manoeuvrability owing to a more streamlined shape and the provision of one or more additional fins.

thrusting ▶ **noun** [mass noun] the motion of pushing or lungeing suddenly or violently.
■ Geology the pushing upwards of the earth's crust.
▶ **adjective 1** aggressively ambitious: *thrusting entrepreneurs.*
2 (of an object or part of the body) projecting in a conspicuous way: *a thrusting jaw.*

thrust reverser ▶ **noun** Aeronautics a device for reversing the flow of gas from a jet engine so as to produce a retarding backward force.

thrust slice ▶ **noun** Geology a relatively thin, broad mass of rock situated between two approximately parallel thrust faults.

thrust stage ▶ **noun** a stage that extends into the auditorium so that the audience is seated around three sides.

thrutch ▶ **noun** N. English a narrow gorge or ravine.
▶ **verb** [no obj., with adverbial of direction] chiefly Climbing push, press, or squeeze into a space.
– ORIGIN Old English (as a verb), of West Germanic origin.

thruway ▶ **noun** chiefly US informal spelling of **THROUGHWAY**.

Thucydides /θjuːˈsɪdɪdiːz/ (*c.*455–*c.*400 BC), Greek historian. He is remembered for his *History of the Peloponnesian War*, which analyses the origins and course of the war; he fought in the conflict on the Athenian side.

thud ▶ **noun** a dull, heavy sound, such as that made by an object falling to the ground: *Jean heard the thud of the closing door.*
▶ **verb** (**thudded**, **thudding**) [no obj.] move, fall, or strike something with a dull, heavy sound: *the bullets thudded into the dusty ground.*
– PHRASES **with a thud** used to describe a sudden and disillusioning reminder of reality in contrast to someone's dreams or aspirations: *school-leavers have now come back down to earth with a thud.*
– ORIGIN late Middle English (originally Scots): probably from Old English *thyddan* 'to thrust, push'; related to *thoden* 'violent wind'. The noun is recorded first denoting a sudden blast or gust of wind, later the sound of a thunderclap, whence a dull, heavy sound. The verb dates from the early 16th cent.

thudding ▶ **noun** [mass noun] the action of moving, falling, or striking something with a dull, heavy sound: *he heard the hollow thudding of hooves.*
▶ **adjective** [attrib.] used to emphasize the clumsiness or awkwardness of something, especially a remark: *great thudding conversation-stoppers.*
– DERIVATIVES **thuddingly** adverb.

thug ▶ **noun 1** a violent person, especially a criminal. [ORIGIN: mid 19th cent.: extension of sense 2.]
2 (**Thug**) historical a member of a religious organization of robbers and assassins in India. Devotees of the goddess Kali, the Thugs waylaid and strangled their victims, usually travellers, in a ritually prescribed manner. They were suppressed by the British in the 1830s.
– DERIVATIVES **thuggery** noun, **thuggish** adjective, **thuggishly** adverb, **thuggishness** noun.
– ORIGIN early 19th cent. (in sense 2): from Hindi *ṭhag* 'swindler, thief', based on Sanskrit *sthagati* 'he covers or conceals'.

thuggee /θʌˈɡiː/ ▶ **noun** [mass noun] historical the robbery and murder practised by the Thugs in accordance with their ritual.
– DERIVATIVES **thuggism** noun.
– ORIGIN from Hindi *ṭhagī*, from *ṭhag* (see **THUG**).

thuja /ˈθ(j)uːjə/ (also **thuya**) ▶ **noun** an evergreen coniferous tree of a genus that includes the western red cedar. Also called **ARBOR VITAE**.
• Genus *Thuja*, family Cupressaceae.
– ORIGIN modern Latin (genus name), from Greek *thuia*, denoting an African tree formerly included in the genus.

Thule 1 /ˈθjuːli/ a country described by the ancient Greek explorer Pytheas (*c.*310 BC) as being six days' sail north of Britain, most plausibly identified with Norway. It was regarded by the ancients as the northernmost part of the world.
2 /θuːl, θjuːl/ an Eskimo culture widely distributed from Alaska to Greenland *c.*500–1400 AD.
3 /ˈtuːli/ a settlement on the NW coast of Greenland, founded in 1910 by the Danish explorer Knud Rasmussen (1879–1933).

thulium /ˈθ(j)uːlɪəm/ ▶ **noun** [mass noun] the chemical element of atomic number 69, a soft silvery-white metal of the lanthanide series. (Symbol: **Tm**)
– ORIGIN late 19th cent.: modern Latin, from Latin *Thule* (see sense 1 of **THULE**), from Greek *Thoulē*, of unknown origin.

thumb ▶ **noun 1** the short, thick first digit of the human hand, set lower and apart from the other four and opposable to them.
■ the corresponding digit of primates or other mammals. ■ the part of a glove intended to cover the thumb.
▶ **verb** [with obj.] press, move, or touch (something) with one's thumb: *as soon as she thumbed the button, the door slid open.*
■ turn over (pages) with or as if with one's thumb: *I've thumbed my address book and found quite a range of smaller hotels* | [no obj.] *he was* **thumbing through** USA Today *for the umpteenth time.* ■ (usu. **be thumbed**) wear or soil (a book's pages) by repeated handling: *his dictionaries were thumbed and ink-stained.* ■ [no obj.] use one's thumb to indicate something: *he thumbed towards the men behind him.* ■ request or obtain (a free ride in a passing vehicle) by signalling with one's thumb: *three cars passed me and I tried to* **thumb a lift** | [no obj.] *he was* **thumbing his way** *across France*
– PHRASES **be all thumbs** another way of saying **be all fingers and thumbs** (see **FINGER**). **thumb one's nose at** informal show disdain or contempt for. **thumbs up** (or **down**) informal an indication of satisfaction or approval (or of rejection or failure): *plans to build a house on the site have been given the thumbs down by the Department of the Environment.* [ORIGIN: with reference to the signal of approval or disapproval, used by spectators at a Roman amphitheatre; the sense has been reversed, as the Romans used 'thumbs down' to signify that a beaten gladiator had performed well and should be spared, and 'thumbs up' to call for his death.] **under someone's thumb** completely under someone's influence or control.
– DERIVATIVES **thumbed** adjective, **thumbless** adjective.
– ORIGIN Old English *thūma*, of West Germanic origin; related to Dutch *duim* and German *Daumen*, from an Indo-European root shared by Latin *tumere* 'to swell'. The verb dates from the late 16th cent., first in the sense 'play (a musical instrument) with the thumbs'.

thumb index ▶ **noun** a set of lettered grooves cut down the side of a book, especially a diary or dictionary, for easy reference.
– DERIVATIVES **thumb-indexed** adjective.

thumbnail ▶ **noun 1** the nail of the thumb.
2 [usu. as modifier] a very small or concise description, representation, or summary: *a thumbnail sketch.*
■ Computing a small picture of an image or page layout.

thumb nut ▶ **noun** another term for **WING NUT**.

thumb piano ▶ **noun** any of various musical instruments, mainly of African origin, made from strips of metal fastened to a resonator and played by plucking with the fingers and thumbs. Also called **KALIMBA**, **MBIRA**, or **SANSA**.

thumbprint ▶ **noun** an impression or mark made on a surface by the inner part of the top joint of the thumb, especially as used for identifying individuals from the unique pattern of whorls and lines.
■ figurative a distinctive identifying characteristic: *it has an individuality and thumbprint of its own.*

thumbscrew ▶ **noun 1** (usu. **thumbscrews**) an instrument of torture for crushing the thumbs.
2 a screw with a protruding winged or flattened head for turning with the thumb and forefinger.

thumb stick ▶ **noun 1** a tall walking stick with a forked thumb rest at the top.
2 a basic control lever for audio and televisual equipment.

thumbsucker ▶ **noun** US informal, often derogatory a serious piece of journalism which concentrates on the background and interpretation of events rather than on the news or action.

thumbtack ▶ **noun** North American term for **DRAWING PIN**.

thumbwheel ▶ **noun** a control device for electrical or mechanical equipment in the form of a wheel operated with the thumb.

Thummim /ˈθʌmɪm/ ▶ **noun** see **URIM AND THUMMIM**.

thump ▶ **verb** [with obj.] hit (someone or something) heavily, especially with the fist or a blunt implement: *Holman thumped the desk with his hand* | [no obj.] *she thumped on the cottage door.*
■ [with obj. and adverbial of direction] move (something) forcefully, noisily, or decisively: *she picked up the kettle then thumped it down again.* ■ [no obj., with adverbial of direction] move or do something with a heavy deadened sound: *Philip thumped down on the settee.* ■ [no obj.] (of a person's heart or pulse) beat or pulsate strongly, typically because of fear or excitement. ■ (**thump something out**) play a tune enthusiastically but heavy-handedly. ■ informal defeat heavily: [with obj. and complement] *Bristol thumped Rugby 35–13.*
▶ **noun** a heavy dull blow with a person's fist or a blunt implement: *I felt a thump on my back.*
■ a loud deadened sound: *his wife put down her iron with a thump.* ■ a strong heartbeat, especially one caused by fear or excitement.
– DERIVATIVES **thumper** noun.
– ORIGIN mid 16th cent.: imitative.

thumping ▶ **adjective** [attrib.] **1** pounding; throbbing: *the thumping beat of her heart.*
2 informal of an impressive size, extent, or amount: *a thumping 64 per cent majority* | [as submodifier] *a thumping great lie.*

thumri /ˈtʊmriː/ ▶ **noun** (pl. **thumris**) (in Hindustani classical music) a romantic song.

– ORIGIN from Hindi *ṭhumrī*.

thunder ▶ **noun** [mass noun] a loud rumbling or crashing noise heard after a lightning flash due to the expansion of rapidly heated air.
■ a resounding loud deep noise: *you can hear the thunder of the falls in the distance.* ■ used in similes and comparisons to refer to an angry facial expression or tone of voice: *'I am Brother Joachim,' he announced in a voice like thunder.* ■ [as exclamation] dated used to express anger, annoyance, or incredulity: *none of this did the remotest good, but, by thunder, it kept the union activists feeling good.*
▶ **verb** [no obj.] (**it thunders**, **it is thundering**, etc.) thunder sounds: *it began to thunder.*
■ make a loud, deep resounding noise: *the motorcycle thundered into life | the train thundered through the night.* ■ [with obj. and adverbial of direction] strike powerfully: *Briggs thundered home a 30-yard free kick.* ■ speak loudly and forcefully or angrily, especially to denounce or criticize: *he **thundered against** the evils of the age* | [with direct speech] *'Sit down!' thundered Morse with immense authority.*
– DERIVATIVES **thunderer** noun, **thundery** adjective.
– ORIGIN Old English *thunor* (noun), *thunrian* (verb), of Germanic origin; related to Dutch *donder* and German *Donner* (noun), from an Indo-European root shared by Latin *tonare* 'to thunder'.

Thunder Bay a city on an inlet of Lake Superior in SW Ontario; pop. 109,330 (1991). It is one of Canada's major ports.

thunderbird ▶ **noun** **1** a mythical bird thought by some North American Indians to bring thunder.
2 Austral. either of two thickheads (birds) which become noisy before and during thunderstorms.
• The golden whistler (*Pachycephala pectoralis*) and the rufous whistler (*P. rufiventris*), family Pachycephalidae.

thunderbolt ▶ **noun** poetic/literary a flash of lightning with a simultaneous crash of thunder.
■ a supposed bolt or shaft believed to be the destructive agent in a lightning flash, especially as an attribute of a god such as Jupiter or Thor. ■ used in similes and comparisons to refer to a very sudden or unexpected event or item of news, especially of an unpleasant nature: *the full force of what she had been told hit her like a thunderbolt.* ■ informal a very fast and powerful shot, throw, or stroke.

thunderbox ▶ **noun** Brit. informal a primitive or makeshift toilet.

thunderbug ▶ **noun** another term for **THRIPS**.

thunderclap ▶ **noun** a crash of thunder (often used to refer to something startling or unexpected): *the door opened like a thunderclap.*

thundercloud ▶ **noun** a cumulus cloud with a towering or spreading top, charged with electricity and producing thunder and lightning.

thunderflash ▶ **noun** a noisy but harmless pyrotechnic device used especially in military exercises.

thunderfly ▶ **noun** (pl. **-flies**) another term for **THRIPS**.

thunderhead ▶ **noun** a rounded, projecting head of a cumulus cloud, which portends a thunderstorm.

thundering ▶ **adjective** [attrib.] making a resounding, loud, deep noise: *thundering waterfalls.*
■ informal extremely great, severe, or impressive: *a thundering bore* | [as submodifier] *a thundering good read.*
– DERIVATIVES **thunderingly** adverb [as submodifier] *it was so thunderingly dull.*

thunderous ▶ **adjective** of, relating to, or giving warning of thunder: *a thunderous grey cloud.*
■ very loud: *thunderous applause.* ■ (of a person's expression or behaviour) very angry or menacing: *Robin's thunderous mood hadn't lightened.* ■ very powerful or intense: *no goalkeeper cares to face his thunderous shots.*
– DERIVATIVES **thunderously** adverb, **thunderousness** noun.

thunderstorm ▶ **noun** a storm with thunder and lightning and typically also heavy rain or hail.

thunderstruck ▶ **adjective** extremely surprised or shocked: *they were thunderstruck by this revelation.*

thunk[1] ▶ **noun** & **verb** informal term for **THUD**.

thunk[2] informal or humorous past and past participle of **THINK**.

Thur. ▶ **abbreviation for** Thursday.

Thurber /ˈθəːbə/, James (Grover) (1894–1961), American humorist and cartoonist. His collections of essays, stories, and sketches include *My World—And Welcome to It* (1942), which contains the story 'The Secret Life of Walter Mitty'.

thurible /ˈθjʊərɪb(ə)l/ ▶ **noun** a censer.
– ORIGIN late Middle English: from Old French, or from Latin *thuribulum*, from *thus*, *thur-* 'incense' (see **THURIFER**).

thurifer /ˈθjʊərɪfə/ ▶ **noun** an acolyte carrying a censer.
– ORIGIN mid 19th cent.: from late Latin, from Latin *thus*, *thur-* 'incense' (from Greek *thuos* 'sacrifice') + *-fer* '-bearing'.

Thuringia /ˌθjʊəˈrɪndʒɪə/ a densely forested state of central Germany; capital, Erfurt. German name **THÜRINGEN** /ˈtyːrɪŋən/.

Thurs. ▶ **abbreviation for** Thursday.

Thursday ▶ **noun** the day of the week before Friday and following Wednesday: *the committee met **on Thursday** | the music programme for Thursdays in April* | [as modifier] *Thursday morning.*
▶ **adverb** chiefly N. Amer. on Thursday: *he called her up Thursday.*
■ (**Thursdays**) on Thursdays; each Thursday.
– ORIGIN Old English *Thu(n)resdæg* 'day of thunder', translation of late Latin *Jovis dies* 'day of Jupiter' (god associated with thunder): compare with Dutch *donderdag* and German *Donnerstag*.

Thurso /ˈθəːsəʊ/ a fishing port on the northern coast of Scotland, in Highland region, the northernmost town on the mainland of Britain; pop. 8,900 (1981).

thus ▶ **adverb** poetic/literary or formal **1** as a result or consequence of this; therefore: *Burke knocked out Byrne, thus becoming champion.*
2 in the manner now being indicated or exemplified; in this way: *she rang up Susan, and while she was thus engaged Chignell summoned the doctor.*
3 [as submodifier] to this point; so: *the Ryder Cup is the highlight of Torrance's career **thus far**.*
– ORIGIN Old English, of unknown origin.

thusly ▶ **adverb** informal another term for **THUS** (in sense 2): *the review was conducted thusly.*

thuya ▶ **noun** variant spelling of **THUJA**.

thwack ▶ **verb** [with obj.] strike forcefully with a sharp blow: *she thwacked the back of their knees with a cane.*
▶ **noun** a sharp blow: *he hit it with a hefty thwack.*
– ORIGIN late Middle English: imitative.

thwaite /θweɪt/ ▶ **noun** [in place names] a piece of wild land cleared or reclaimed for cultivation: *Bassenthwaite.*
– ORIGIN Middle English: from Old Norse *thveit*, *thveiti* 'paddock', literally 'cut piece'.

thwart /θwɔːt/ ▶ **verb** [with obj.] prevent (someone) from accomplishing something: *he never did anything to thwart his father | he was **thwarted in** his desire to punish Uncle Fred.*
■ oppose (a plan, attempt, or ambition) successfully: *the government had been able to thwart all attempts by opposition leaders to form new parties.*
▶ **noun** a structural crosspiece forming a seat for a rower in a boat.
▶ **preposition** & **adverb** archaic or poetic/literary from one side to another side of; across: [as prep.] *a pink-tinged cloud spread thwart the shore.*
– ORIGIN Middle English *thwerte*, from the adjective *thwert* 'perverse, obstinate, adverse', from Old Norse *thvert*, neuter of *thverr* 'transverse', from an Indo-European root shared by Latin *torquere* 'to twist'.

thy (also **thine** before a vowel) ▶ **possessive determiner** archaic or dialect form of **YOUR**: *honour thy father and thy mother.*
– ORIGIN Middle English *thi* (originally before words beginning with any consonant except *h*), reduced from *thin*, from Old English *thīn* (see **THINE**).

USAGE The use of **thy** is still found in some traditional dialects but elsewhere it is restricted to archaic contexts. See also **usage** at **THOU**[1].

Thyestes /θʌɪˈɛstiːz/ Greek Mythology the brother of Atreus and father of Aegisthus.
– DERIVATIVES **Thyestean** /-ˈɛstɪən/ adjective.

thylacine /ˈθʌɪləsiːn, -sʌɪn, -sɪn/ ▶ **noun** a doglike carnivorous marsupial with stripes across the rump, found only in Tasmania. There have been no confirmed sightings since one was captured in 1933, and it may now be extinct. Also called **TASMANIAN WOLF**.
• *Thylacinus cynocephalus*, family Thylacinidae.
– ORIGIN mid 19th cent.: from modern Latin *Thylacinus* (genus name), from Greek *thulakos* 'pouch'.

thylakoid /ˈθʌɪləkɔɪd/ ▶ **noun** Botany each of a number of flattened sacs inside a chloroplast, bounded by pigmented membranes on which the light reactions of photosynthesis take place, and arranged in stacks or grana.
– ORIGIN 1960s: from German *Thylakoid*, from Greek *thulakoeidēs* 'pouch-like', from *thulakos* 'pouch'.

thyme /tʌɪm/ ▶ **noun** [mass noun] a low-growing aromatic plant of the mint family. The small leaves are used as a culinary herb and the plant yields a medicinal oil.
• Genus *Thymus*, family Labiatae: many species, in particular **common** (or **garden**) **thyme** (*T. vulgaris*).
– DERIVATIVES **thymy** adjective.
– ORIGIN Middle English: from Old French *thym*, via Latin from Greek *thumon*, from *thuein* 'burn, sacrifice'.

thymectomy /θʌɪˈmɛktəmi/ ▶ **noun** (pl. **-ies**) surgical removal of the thymus gland.

thymi plural form of **THYMUS**.

thymic /ˈθʌɪmɪk/ ▶ **adjective** Physiology of or relating to the thymus gland or its functions.

thymidine /ˈθʌɪmɪdiːn/ ▶ **noun** [mass noun] Biochemistry a crystalline nucleoside present in DNA, consisting of thymine linked to deoxyribose.
– ORIGIN early 20th cent.: from **THYMINE** + **-IDE** + **-INE**[4].

thymine /ˈθʌɪmiːn/ ▶ **noun** [mass noun] Biochemistry a compound which is one of the four constituent bases of nucleic acids. A pyrimidine derivative, it is paired with adenine in double-stranded DNA.
• Alternative name; **5-methyluracil**; chem. formula: $C_5H_6N_2O_2$.
– ORIGIN late 19th cent.: from **THYMUS** + **-INE**[4].

thymocyte /ˈθʌɪmə(ʊ)sʌɪt/ ▶ **noun** Physiology a lymphocyte within the thymus gland.
– ORIGIN 1920s: from **THYMUS** + **-CYTE**.

thymol /ˈθʌɪmɒl/ ▶ **noun** [mass noun] Chemistry a white crystalline compound present in oil of thyme and used as a flavouring and preservative.
• Alternative name: **2-isopropyl-5-methylphenol**; chem. formula: $C_{10}H_{13}OH$.
– ORIGIN mid 19th cent.: from Greek *thumon* 'thyme' + **-OL**.

thymoma /ˈθʌɪməʊmə/ ▶ **noun** (pl. **thymomas** or **thymomata** /-mətə/) Medicine a rare, usually benign tumour arising from thymus tissue and sometimes associated with myasthenia gravis.
– ORIGIN early 20th cent.: from **THYMUS** + **-OMA**.

thymus /ˈθʌɪməs/ (also **thymus gland**) ▶ **noun** (pl. **thymi** /-mʌɪ/) a lymphoid organ situated in the neck of vertebrates which produces T-lymphocytes for the immune system. The human thymus becomes much smaller at the approach of puberty.
– ORIGIN late 16th cent. (denoting a growth or tumour resembling a bud): from Greek *thumos* 'excrescence like a thyme bud, thymus gland'.

thyristor /θʌɪˈrɪstə/ ▶ **noun** Electronics a four-layered semiconductor rectifier in which the flow of current between two electrodes is triggered by a signal at a third electrode.
– ORIGIN 1950s: blend of *thyratron*, denoting a kind of thermionic valve (from Greek *thura* 'gate') and **TRANSISTOR**.

thyro- ▶ **combining form** representing **THYROID**.

thyroglobulin /ˌθʌɪrə(ʊ)ˈglɒbjʊlɪn/ ▶ **noun** [mass noun] Biochemistry a protein present in the thyroid gland, from which thyroid hormones are synthesized.

thyroid /ˈθʌɪrɔɪd/ ▶ **noun** **1** (also **thyroid gland**) a large ductless gland in the neck which secretes hormones regulating growth and development through the rate of metabolism.
■ [mass noun] an extract prepared from the thyroid gland of animals and used in treating deficiency of thyroid hormones.
2 (also **thyroid cartilage**) a large cartilage of the larynx, a projection of which forms the Adam's apple in humans.
– ORIGIN early 18th cent. (as an adjective): from Greek (*khondros*) *thureoeidēs* 'shield-shaped (cartilage)', from *thureos* 'oblong shield'.

thyroid-stimulating hormone ▶ **noun** another term for **THYROTROPIN**.

thyrotoxicosis /ˌθʌɪrəʊˌtɒksɪˈkəʊsɪs/ ▶ **noun** another term for **HYPERTHYROIDISM**.

thyrotropin /ˌθʌɪrə(ʊ)ˈtrəʊpɪn/ (also **thyrotrophin**

/-ˈtrəʊfɪn/) ▶ **noun** [mass noun] Biochemistry a hormone secreted by the pituitary gland which regulates the production of thyroid hormones.

thyrotropin-releasing hormone (also **thyrotropin-releasing factor**) ▶ **noun** [mass noun] Biochemistry a hormone secreted by the hypothalamus which stimulates release of thyrotropin.

thyroxine /θʌɪˈrɒksiːn, -sɪn/ ▶ **noun** [mass noun] Biochemistry the main hormone produced by the thyroid gland, acting to increase metabolic rate and so regulating growth and development.
• An iodine-containing amino acid; chem. formula: $C_{15}H_{11}NO_4I_4$.
– ORIGIN early 20th cent.: from **THYROID** + **OX-** 'oxygen' + *in* from **INDOLE** (because of an early misunderstanding of its chemical structure), altered by substitution of **-INE**[4].

thyrsus /ˈθəːsəs/ ▶ **noun** (pl. **thyrsi** /-sʌɪ, -siː/) (in ancient Greece and Rome) a staff or spear tipped with an ornament like a pine cone, carried by Bacchus and his followers.
– ORIGIN Latin, from Greek *thursos* 'plant stalk, Bacchic staff'.

Thysanoptera /ˌθʌɪsəˈnɒpt(ə)rə/ Entomology an order of insects that comprises the thrips.
■ [as plural noun **thysanoptera**] insects of this order; thrips.
– DERIVATIVES **thysanopteran** noun & adjective.
– ORIGIN modern Latin (plural), from Greek *thusanos* 'tassel' + *pteron* 'wing'.

Thysanura /ˌθʌɪsəˈn(j)ʊərə/ Entomology an order of insects that comprises the true, or three-pronged, bristletails.
■ [as plural noun **thysanura**] insects of this order; bristletails.
– DERIVATIVES **thysanuran** noun & adjective.
– ORIGIN modern Latin (plural), from Greek *thusanos* 'tassel' + *oura* 'tail'.

thyself ▶ **pronoun** [second person singular] archaic or dialect form of **YOURSELF**, corresponding to the subject **THOU**[1]: *thou shalt love thy neighbour as thyself.*

Ti ▶ **symbol for** the chemical element titanium.

ti ▶ **noun** North American form of **TE**.

TIA Medicine ▶ **abbreviation for** transient ischaemic attack, particularly affecting the brain of a person susceptible to strokes.

Tia Maria /ˌtiːə məˈriːə/ ▶ **noun** [mass noun] trademark a coffee-flavoured liqueur based on rum, made originally in the Caribbean.
– ORIGIN from Spanish *Tía María*, literally 'Aunt Mary'.

Tiamat /ˈtɪamat, tɪˈɑːmat/ Babylonian Mythology a monstrous she-dragon who was the mother of the first Babylonian gods. She was slain by Marduk.

tian /tjɑ̃/ ▶ **noun** (pl. pronounced same) [mass noun] a dish of finely chopped vegetables cooked in olive oil and then baked au gratin.
■ [count noun] a large oval earthenware cooking pot traditionally used in Provence.
– ORIGIN Provençal, based on Greek *tēganon* 'frying pan'.

Tiananmen Square /ˈtjɛnənmən/ a square in the centre of Beijing adjacent to the Forbidden City, the largest public open space in the world. In spring 1989 government troops opened fire there on unarmed pro-democracy protesters, killing over 2,000.
– ORIGIN Chinese, literally 'square of heavenly peace'.

Tianjin /tjɛnˈdʒɪn/ (also **Tientsin**) a port in NE China, in Hubei province; pop. 5,700,000 (1990).

Tian Shan variant spelling of **TIEN SHAN**.

tiara ▶ **noun 1** a jewelled ornamental band worn on the front of a woman's hair.
2 a high diadem encircled with three crowns and worn by a pope.
■ historical a turban worn by ancient Persian kings.
– ORIGIN mid 16th cent. (denoting the Persian royal headdress): via Latin from Greek, partly via Italian. Sense 1 dates from the early 18th cent.

tiare /tiːˈɑːreɪ/ ▶ **noun** (pl. same) (in Tahiti) a gardenia of a variety bearing fragrant white flowers.
– ORIGIN late 19th cent.: special use of French *tiare* 'tiara'.

tiarella /tɪəˈrɛlə/ ▶ **noun** a small chiefly North American plant of the saxifrage family.
• Genus *Tiarella*, family Saxifragaceae, especially *T. cordifolia*.
– ORIGIN modern Latin, from Latin *tiara* 'turban, tiara' + the diminutive suffix *-ella*.

Tiber /ˈtʌɪbə/ a river of central Italy, upon which Rome stands. It rises in the Tuscan Apennines and flows 405 km (252 miles) generally south-westwards, entering the Tyrrhenian Sea at Ostia. Italian name **TEVERE**.

Tiberias, Lake /tʌɪˈbɪərɪəs/ another name for Sea of Galilee (see **GALILEE, SEA OF**).

Tiberius /tʌɪˈbɪərɪəs/ (42 BC–AD 37), Roman emperor AD 14–37; full name *Tiberius Julius Caesar Augustus*. The adopted successor of his stepfather and father-in-law Augustus, he became increasingly tyrannical and his reign was marked by a growing number of treason trials and executions.

Tibesti Mountains /tɪˈbɛsti/ a mountain range in north central Africa, in the Sahara in northern Chad and southern Libya. It rises to 3,415 m (11,201 ft) at Emi Koussi, the highest point in the Sahara.

Tibet /tɪˈbɛt/ a mountainous country in Asia on the northern side of the Himalayas, since 1965 forming an autonomous region in the west of China; pop. 2,196,000 (1990); official languages, Tibetan and Chinese; capital, Lhasa. Chinese name **XIZANG**.

> Most of Tibet forms a high plateau with an average elevation of over 4,000 m (12,500 ft). Ruled by Buddhist lamas since the 7th century, it was conquered by the Mongols in the 13th century and the Manchus in the 18th. China extended its authority over Tibet in 1951 but gained full control only after crushing a revolt in 1959, during which the country's spiritual leader, the Dalai Lama, escaped to India; he remains in exile and sporadic unrest has continued.

Tibetan ▶ **noun 1** a native of Tibet or a person of Tibetan descent.
2 [mass noun] the Sino-Tibetan language of Tibet, spoken by about 4 million people in Tibet and in neighbouring areas of China, India, and Nepal.
▶ **adjective** of or relating to Tibet, its people, or its language.

Tibetan antelope ▶ **noun** another term for **CHIRU**.

Tibetan Buddhism ▶ **noun** [mass noun] the religion of Tibet, a form of Mahayana Buddhism. It was formed in the 8th century AD from a combination of Buddhism and the indigenous Tibetan religion. The head of the religion is the Dalai Lama.

Tibetan mastiff ▶ **noun** an animal of a breed of large black-and-tan dog with a thick coat and drop ears.

Tibetan spaniel ▶ **noun** an animal of a breed of small white, brown, or black dog with a silky coat of medium length.

Tibetan terrier ▶ **noun** an animal of a breed of grey, black, cream, or particoloured terrier with a thick shaggy coat.

Tibeto-Burman ▶ **adjective** of, relating to, or denoting a division of the Sino-Tibetan language family that includes Tibetan, Burmese, and a number of other languages spoken in mountainous regions of central southern Asia.

tibia /ˈtɪbɪə/ ▶ **noun** (pl. **tibiae** /-bɪiː/) Anatomy the inner and typically larger of the two bones between the knee and the ankle (or the equivalent joints in other terrestrial vertebrates), parallel with the fibula.
■ Zoology the tibiotarsus of a bird. ■ Entomology the fourth segment of the leg of an insect, between the femur and the tarsus.
– DERIVATIVES **tibial** adjective.
– ORIGIN late Middle English: from Latin, 'shin bone'.

tibialis /ˌtɪbɪˈeɪlɪs/ ▶ **noun** Anatomy any of several muscles and tendons in the calf of the leg concerned with movements of the foot.
– ORIGIN late 19th cent.: from Latin, 'relating to the shin bone'.

tibiotarsus /ˌtɪbɪə(ʊ)ˈtɑːsəs/ ▶ **noun** (pl. **tibiotarsi** /-sʌɪ, -siː/) Zoology the bone in a bird's leg corresponding to the tibia, fused at the lower end with some bones of the tarsus.
– ORIGIN late 19th cent.: blend of **TIBIA** and **TARSUS**.

Tibullus /tɪˈbʌləs/, Albius (*c.*50–19 BC), Roman poet. He is known for his elegiac love poetry and for his celebration of peaceful rural life.

tic ▶ **noun** a habitual spasmodic contraction of the muscles, most often in the face.
– ORIGIN early 19th cent.: from French, from Italian *ticchio*.

tic douloureux /tɪk ˌduːləˈruː, -ˈrəː/ ▶ **noun** another term for **TRIGEMINAL NEURALGIA**.
– ORIGIN early 19th cent.: French, literally 'painful tic'.

tich /tɪtʃ/ ▶ **noun** variant spelling of **TITCH**.

Tichborne claimant /ˈtɪtʃbɔːn/ see **ORTON**[1].

Ticino /tɪˈtʃiːnəʊ, Italian tiˈtsino/ a predominantly Italian-speaking canton in southern Switzerland, on the Italian border; capital, Bellinzona. It joined the Swiss Confederation in 1803. French name **TESSIN** /tɛsɛ̃/, German name **TESSIN** /tɛˈsiːn/.

tick[1] ▶ **noun 1** a mark (✓) used to indicate that a textual item is correct or has been chosen or checked.
2 a regular short, sharp sound, especially that made every second by a clock or watch.
■ Brit. informal a moment (used especially to reassure someone that one will return or be ready very soon): *I shan't be a tick | I'll be with you in a tick.*
3 Stock Exchange the smallest recognized amount by which a price of a security or future may fluctuate.
▶ **verb 1** [with obj.] mark (an item) with a tick, typically to show that it has been chosen, checked, or approved: *just tick the appropriate box below.*
■ (**tick something off**) list items one by one in one's mind or during a speech: *he ticked the points off on his fingers.*
2 [no obj.] (of a clock or other mechanical device) make regular short sharp sounds, typically for every second of time passing: *I could hear the clock ticking.*
■ (**tick away/by/past**) (of time) pass (used especially when someone is pressed for time or keenly awaiting an event): *the minutes were ticking away till the actor's appearance.* ■ [with obj.] (**tick something away**) (of a clock or watch) mark the passing of time with regular short sharp sounds: *the little clock ticked the precious minutes away.* ■ proceed or progress: *her book was ticking along nicely.*
– PHRASES **what makes someone tick** informal what motivates someone: *people are curious to know what makes British men tick.*
– ORIGIN Middle English (as a verb in the sense 'pat, touch'): probably of Germanic origin and related to Dutch *tik* (noun), *tikken* (verb) 'pat, touch'. The noun was recorded in late Middle English as 'a light tap'; current senses date from the late 17th cent.
▶ **tick someone off 1** Brit. informal reprimand or rebuke someone: *he was ticked off by Angela* | [as noun **ticking off**] *he got a ticking off from the magistrate.* **2** N. Amer. informal make someone annoyed or angry.
tick over (of an engine) run slowly in neutral. ■ work or function at a basic or minimum level: *they are keeping things ticking over until their father returns.*

tick[2] ▶ **noun 1** a parasitic arachnid which attaches itself to the skin of a terrestrial vertebrate from which it sucks blood, leaving the host when sated. Some species transmit diseases, including tularaemia and Lyme disease.
• Suborder Ixodida, order Acari (or order and subclass).
■ informal a parasitic louse fly, especially the sheep ked.
2 Brit. informal a worthless or contemptible person.
– PHRASES **full** (or **tight**) **as a tick** informal replete after eating (or very drunk).
– ORIGIN Old English *ticia*, of Germanic origin; related to Dutch *teek* and German *Zecke*.

tick[3] ▶ **noun** (in phrase **on tick**) on credit.
– ORIGIN mid 17th cent.: apparently short for **TICKET** in the phrase *on the ticket*, referring to an IOU or promise to pay.

tick[4] ▶ **noun** a fabric case stuffed with feathers or other material to form a mattress or pillow.
■ short for **TICKING**.
– ORIGIN late Middle English: probably Middle Low German, Middle Dutch *tēke*, or Middle Dutch *tīke*, via West Germanic from Latin *theca* 'case', from Greek *thēkē*.

tick bean ▶ **noun** a field bean of a variety with small rounded seeds, used for feeding to pigeons.
– ORIGIN mid 18th cent.: so named from the resemblance of the seeds to dog ticks.

tick-bird ▶ **noun 1** another term for **OXPECKER**.
2 South African term for **CATTLE EGRET**.

ticker ▶ **noun 1** informal a watch.
■ a person's heart.
2 N. Amer. a telegraphic or electronic machine that prints out data on a strip of paper, especially stock market information or news reports.

ticker tape ▶ **noun** a paper strip on which messages are recorded in a telegraphic tape machine.

■[as modifier] denoting a parade or other event in which this or similar material is thrown from windows.

ticket ▶ noun **1** a piece of paper or card that gives the holder a certain right, especially to enter a place, travel by public transport, or participate in an event: *admission is by ticket only.*
■a receipt for goods that have been received. ■ (**ticket to/out of**) a method of getting into or out of (a specified state or situation): *drugs are seen as the only ticket out of poverty | companies that appeared to have a **one-way ticket** to profitability.*
2 a certificate or warrant, in particular:
■an official notice of a traffic offence. ■ a certificate of qualification as a ship's master, pilot, or other crew member. ■ Brit. a certificate of discharge from the army.
3 a label attached to a retail product, giving its price, size, and other details.
4 [in sing.] chiefly N. Amer. a list of candidates put forward by a party in an election: *his presence on the Republican ticket.*
■a set of principles or policies supported by a party in an election: *he stood for office on a strong right-wing, no-nonsense ticket.*
5 (**the ticket**) informal the desirable or correct thing: *a wet spring would be **just the ticket** for the garden.*
6 [with adj.] Scottish & US informal a person of a specified kind: *I think you're all a bunch of sick tickets.*
▶ verb (**ticketed, ticketing**) [with obj.] **1** issue (someone) with an official notice of a traffic or other offence: *park illegally and you are likely to be ticketed.*
2 (**be ticketed**) (of a passenger) be issued with a travel ticket: *passengers can now get electronically ticketed.*
■US be destined or heading for a specified state or position: *they were sure that Downing was ticketed for greatness.*
3 (**be ticketed**) (of a retail product) be marked with a label giving its price, size, and other details.
– PHRASES **be tickets** S. African informal be the end: *if that man talks to the police, it's tickets for him.* **have tickets on oneself** Austral./NZ informal be excessively proud of oneself. **punch one's ticket** US informal deliberately undertake particular assignments that are likely to lead to promotion at work. **write one's (own) ticket** informal, chiefly N. Amer. dictate one's own terms.
– DERIVATIVES **ticketless** adjective.
– ORIGIN early 16th cent. (in the general senses 'short written note' and 'a licence or permit'): shortening of obsolete French *étiquet*, from Old French *estiquet(te)*, from *estiquier* 'to fix', from Middle Dutch *steken*. Compare with **ETIQUETTE**.

ticketed ▶ adjective [attrib.] **1** marked on a ticket: *the ticketed price.*
2 having been issued with a ticket: *ticketed passengers.*

ticket office ▶ noun an office or kiosk where tickets are sold.

ticket of leave ▶ noun Brit. historical a document granting certain concessions, especially leave, to a prisoner or convict who had served part of their time.

ticket tout ▶ noun see **TOUT**[1] (sense 1).

tickety-boo ▶ adjective [predic.] Brit. informal, dated in good order; fine: *everything is tickety-boo.*
– ORIGIN 1930s: perhaps from Hindi *ṭhīk hai* 'all right'.

tickey /ˈtɪkiː/ ▶ noun (pl. **-eys**) S. African a small silver threepenny piece, withdrawn from circulation in 1961.
■informal used as a nickname for a small person.
– PHRASES **on a tickey** in a very small area: *he could turn his car on a tickey.*
– ORIGIN of unknown origin.

tickey-box ▶ noun S. African informal a public telephone.

tickey-draai /ˈtɪkiːˌdrʌɪ/ ▶ noun (pl. **tickey-draais**) S. African a dance involving a fast movement in which couples link hands and spin round on the spot.
■[mass noun] the fast, rhythmical music played to accompany this dance.
– ORIGIN partly translating Afrikaans *tiekiedraai*, from *tiekie* 'threepenny piece' + *draai* 'a turn' (because of the spinning movement).

tick fever ▶ noun [mass noun] any bacterial or rickettsial fever transmitted by the bite of a tick.

ticking ▶ noun [mass noun] a strong, durable material, typically striped, used to cover mattresses.
– ORIGIN mid 17th cent.: from **TICK**[4] + **-ING**[1].

tickle ▶ verb [with obj.] **1** lightly touch or prod (a person or a part of the body) in a way that causes mild discomfort or itching and often laughter: *I tickled him under the ears.*
■[no obj.] (of a part of the body) give a sensation similar to that caused by being touched in this way: *his throat had stopped tickling.* ■ touch with light finger movements: [with obj. and complement] *tickling the safe open took nearly ninety minutes.* ■ catch (a trout) by lightly rubbing it so that it moves backwards into the hand.
2 appeal to (someone's taste, sense of humour, curiosity, etc.): *here are a couple of anecdotes that might **tickle your fancy**.*
■(usu. **be tickled**) cause (someone) amusement or pleasure: *he is tickled by the idea.*
▶ noun [in sing.] an act of tickling someone: *Dad gave my chin a little tickle.*
■a sensation like that of being lightly touched or prodded: *I had a tickle between my shoulder blades.*
– PHRASES **be tickled pink** (or **to death**) informal be extremely amused or pleased. **tickle the ivories** informal play the piano.
– ORIGIN Middle English (in the sense 'be delighted or thrilled'): perhaps a frequentative of **TICK**[1], or an alteration of Scots and dialect *kittle* 'to tickle' (compare with **KITTLE**).

tickler ▶ noun a thing that tickles.
■N. Amer. a memorandum.

ticklish ▶ adjective **1** (of a person) sensitive to being tickled: *I'm ticklish on the feet.*
■(of a cough) characterized by persistent irritation in the throat.
2 (of a situation or problem) difficult to deal with; requiring careful handling: *her skill in evading ticklish questions.*
■(of a person) easily upset.
– DERIVATIVES **ticklishly** adverb, **ticklishness** noun.

tickly ▶ adjective another term for **TICKLISH**.

tickover ▶ noun [mass noun] the lowest number of revolutions per minute that an engine will run at without stalling.

tickseed ▶ noun chiefly N. Amer. another term for **COREOPSIS**.
– ORIGIN mid 16th cent.: so named because of the resemblance of the seed to a parasitic tick.

tick-tack-toe ▶ noun variant spelling of **TIC-TAC-TOE**.

tick-tock ▶ noun [in sing.] the sound of a large clock ticking.
▶ verb [no obj.] make a ticking sound: *the clock on the wall was tick-tocking.*
– ORIGIN mid 19th cent.: imitative; compare with **TICK**[1].

tick trefoil ▶ noun a leguminous North American plant, the pods of which break up into one-seeded joints which adhere to clothing, animals' fur, etc.
● Genus *Desmodium*, family Leguminosae: several species.

ticky-tacky informal, chiefly N. Amer. ▶ noun [mass noun] inferior or cheap material, especially as used in suburban building.
▶ adjective (especially of a building or housing development) made of inferior material; cheap or in poor taste: *ticky-tacky little houses.*
– ORIGIN 1960s: probably a reduplication of **TACKY**[2].

tic-tac (also **tick-tack**) ▶ noun [mass noun] (in the UK) a kind of manual semaphore used by racecourse bookmakers to exchange information.
– ORIGIN mid 16th cent. (denoting a repeated ticking sound): imitative; compare with **TICK-TOCK**. The current usage (originally slang) dates from the late 19th cent.

tic-tac-toe (also **tick-tack-toe**) ▶ noun North American term for **NOUGHTS AND CROSSES**.
– ORIGIN 1960s: imitative; from *tick-tack*, used earlier to denote games in which the pieces made clicking sounds.

tidal ▶ adjective of, relating to, or affected by tides: *the river here is not tidal | strong tidal currents.*
– DERIVATIVES **tidally** adverb.

tidal basin ▶ noun a basin for boats which is accessible or navigable only at high tide.

tidal bore ▶ noun a large wave or bore caused by the constriction of the spring tide as it enters a long, narrow, shallow inlet.

tidal wave ▶ noun an exceptionally large ocean wave, especially one caused by an underwater earthquake or volcanic eruption.
■figurative a widespread or overwhelming manifestation of an emotion or phenomenon: *a **tidal wave of** crime.*

tidbit ▶ noun US spelling of **TITBIT**.

tiddledywink ▶ noun US spelling of **TIDDLYWINK**.

tiddler ▶ noun Brit. informal a small fish, especially a stickleback or minnow.
■a young or unusually small person or thing.
– ORIGIN late 19th cent.: perhaps related to **TIDDLY**[2] or *tittlebat*, a childish form of *stickleback*.

tiddly[1] ▶ adjective (**tiddlier, tiddliest**) informal, chiefly Brit. slightly drunk: *we were all a little bit tiddly.*
– ORIGIN mid 19th cent. (as a noun denoting an alcoholic drink, particularly of spirits): perhaps from slang *tiddlywink*, denoting an unlicensed public house. The current sense dates from the early 20th cent.

tiddly[2] ▶ adjective (**tiddlier, tiddliest**) Brit. informal little; tiny: *a tiddly little pool.*
– ORIGIN mid 19th cent.: variant of colloquial *tiddy*, of unknown origin.

tiddlywink (US **tiddledywink**) ▶ noun **1** (**tiddlywinks**) a game in which small plastic counters are flicked into a central receptacle by being pressed on the edge with a larger counter.
2 a counter used in such a game.
– ORIGIN mid 19th cent.: of unknown origin; perhaps related to **TIDDLY**[1]. The word originally denoted an unlicensed public house, also a game of dominoes. Current senses date from the late 19th cent.

tiddy oggy /ˈtɪdi ˌɒgi/ ▶ noun Brit. dialect or Nautical slang a Cornish pasty.
– ORIGIN probably from West Country dialect *tiddy* 'potato' and Cornish *hogen* 'pastry'.

tide ▶ noun the alternate rising and falling of the sea, usually twice in each lunar day at a particular place, due to the attraction of the moon and sun: *the changing patterns of the tides* | [mass noun] *they were driven on by wind and tide.*
■the water as affected by this: *the rising tide covered the wharf.* ■ figurative a powerful surge of feeling or trend of events: *he drifted into sleep on a tide of euphoria | we must reverse the growing tide of racism sweeping Europe.*
▶ verb [no obj., with adverbial of direction] archaic drift with or as if with the tide.
■(of a ship) work in or out of harbour with the help of the tide.
– DERIVATIVES **tideless** adjective.
– ORIGIN Old English *tīd* 'time, period, era', of Germanic origin; related to Dutch *tijd* and German *Zeit*, also to **TIME**. The sense relating to the sea dates from late Middle English.
▶ **tide someone over** help someone through a difficult period, especially with financial assistance: *she needed a small loan to tide her over.*

-tide ▶ combining form poetic/literary denoting a specified time or season: *springtide.* ■ denoting a festival of the Christian Church: *Shrovetide.*

tideland ▶ noun [mass noun] (also **tidelands**) N. Amer. land that is submerged at high tide.

tideline ▶ noun a line left or reached by the sea on a shore at the highest point of a tide.

tidemark ▶ noun a mark left or reached by the sea on a shore at the highest point of a tide.
■Brit. a mark left on a surface, especially around the inside of a bath or washbasin, at the level reached by water.

tide mill ▶ noun a mill with a waterwheel driven by the tide.

tide rip ▶ noun an area of rough water typically caused by opposing tides or by a rapid current passing over an uneven bottom.

tide table ▶ noun a table indicating the times of high and low tides at a particular place.

tidewaiter ▶ noun historical a customs officer who boarded ships on their arrival to enforce the customs regulations.

tidewater ▶ noun [mass noun] water brought or affected by tides.
■US an area that is affected by tides, especially eastern Virginia: [as modifier] *a large area of tidewater country.*

tideway ▶ noun a channel in which a tide runs, especially the tidal part of a river.

tidings ▶ plural noun poetic/literary news; information: *the bearer of glad tidings.*
– ORIGIN late Old English *tīdung* 'announcement, piece of news', probably from Old Norse *títhindi* 'news of events', from *títhr* 'occurring'.

t

tidy ▶ adjective (**tidier, tidiest**) **1** arranged neatly and in order: *his scrupulously tidy apartment* | figurative *the lives they lead don't fit into tidy patterns.*
■(of a person) inclined to keep things or one's appearance neat and in order: *she was a tidy little girl.* ■ not messy; neat and controlled: *he wrote down her replies in a small, tidy hand.*
2 [attrib.] informal (of an amount, especially of money) considerable: *the book will bring in a tidy sum.*
■used as a general term of approval: *City have the backbone of a tidy side.*
▶ **noun** (pl. **-ies**) **1** (also **tidy-up**) [in sing.] an act or spell of tidying something.
2 [usu. with modifier] a receptacle for holding small objects or waste scraps: *a desk tidy.*
3 chiefly US a detachable ornamental cover for a chair back.
▶ **verb** (**-ies, -ied**) [with obj.] (often **tidy someone/thing up**) bring order to; arrange neatly: *I'd better try to tidy my desk up a bit* | figurative *the Bill is intended to tidy up the law on this matter* | [no obj.] *I'll just go and tidy up.*
■(**tidy something away**) put something away for the sake of neatness: *I was tidying away papers in my office.*
– DERIVATIVES **tidily** adverb, **tidiness** noun.
– ORIGIN Middle English: from the noun **TIDE** + **-Y**[1]. The original meaning was 'timely, opportune'; it later had various senses expressing approval, usually of a person, including 'attractive', 'healthy', and 'skilful'; the sense 'orderly, neat' dates from the early 18th cent.

tie ▶ **verb** (**tying**) **1** [with obj. and usu. with adverbial] attach or fasten (someone or something) with string or similar cord: *they tied Max to a chair* | *her long hair was tied back in a bow.*
■fasten (something) to or around someone or something by means of its strings or by forming the ends into a knot or bow: *Lewis tied on his apron.* ■ form (a string, ribbon, or lace) into a knot or bow: *Renwick bent to tie his shoelace.* ■ form (a knot or bow) in this way: *tie a knot in one end of the cotton.* ■ [no obj.] be fastened with a knot or bow: *a sarong which ties at the waist.* ■ (often **be tied**) restrict or limit (someone) to a particular situation, occupation, or place: *she didn't want to be like her mother, tied to a feckless man.*
2 [with obj.] (often **be tied**) connect; link: *self-respect is closely* ***tied up with*** *the esteem in which one is held by one's fellows.*
■hold together by a crosspiece or tie: *ceiling joists are used to tie the rafter feet.* ■ Music unite (written notes) by a tie. ■ Music perform (two notes) as one unbroken note.
3 [no obj.] achieve the same score or ranking as another competitor or team: *he* ***tied for*** *second in the league* | [with obj.] *Muir tied the score at 5–5.*
▶ **noun** (pl. **-ies**) **1** a piece of string, cord, or similar used for fastening or tying something: *he tightened the tie of his robe.*
■(usu. **ties**) figurative a thing that unites or links people: *it is important that we keep family ties strong.* ■ (usu. **ties**) figurative a thing that restricts someone's freedom of action: *some cities and merchants were freed from feudal ties.* ■a rod or beam holding parts of a structure together. ■ N. Amer. short for **CROSS TIE**. ■ Music a curved line above or below two notes of the same pitch indicating that they are to be played for the combined duration of their time values. ■ US a shoe tied with a lace.
2 a strip of material worn round the collar and tied in a knot at the front with the ends hanging down, typically forming part of a man's smart or formal outfit.
3 a result in a game or other competitive situation in which two or more competitors or teams have the same score or ranking; a draw: *there was a tie for first place.*
■Cricket a game in which the scores are level and both sides have completed their innings, as distinct from a draw (a game left incomplete through lack of time).
4 Brit. a sports match between two or more players or teams in which the winners proceed to the next round of the competition.
– PHRASES **fit to be tied** see **FIT**[1]. **tie someone hand and foot** see **HAND**. **tie someone (up) in knots** see **KNOT**[1]. **tie the knot** see **KNOT**[1]. **tie one on** N. Amer. informal get drunk.
– DERIVATIVES **tieless** adjective.
– ORIGIN Old English *tīgan* (verb), *tēah* (noun), of Germanic origin.
▶ **tie someone down** restrict someone to a particular situation or place: *she didn't want to be tied down by a full-time job.*
tie something in (or **tie in**) cause something to fit or harmonize with something else (or fit or harmonize with something): *her husband is able to* ***tie in*** *his shifts* ***with*** *hers at the hospital* | *she may have developed ideas which don't necessarily* ***tie in with*** *mine.*
tie into N. Amer. informal attack or get to work on vigorously: *tie into breakfast now and let's get a move on.*
tie someone up bind someone's legs and arms together or bind someone to something so that they cannot move or escape: *robbers tied her up and ransacked her home.* ■ (usu. **be tied up**) informal occupy someone to the exclusion of any other activity: *she would be tied up at the meeting all day.*
tie something up 1 bind or fasten something securely with rope, cord, or similar. ■ moor a boat. ■ (often **be tied up**) invest or reserve capital so that it is not immediately available for use: *money tied up in accounts must be left to grow.* **2** bring something to a satisfactory conclusion; settle: *he said he had a business deal to tie up.*

tie-back ▶ **noun** a decorative strip of fabric or cord, typically used for holding an open curtain back from the window.

tie beam ▶ **noun** a horizontal beam connecting two rafters in a roof or roof truss.

tiebreak (also **tiebreaker**) ▶ **noun** a means of deciding a winner from competitors who have tied, in particular (in tennis) a special game to decide the winner of a set when the score is six games all.

tie clip ▶ **noun** an ornamental clip for holding a tie in place.

tied ▶ **adjective 1** fastened or attached with string or similar cord: *a neatly tied package.*
■Music (of two or more notes) united by a tie and performed as one unbroken note.
2 (of a game or contest) with both or more competitors or teams achieving the same score or level of success: *the first tied match in the league* | *a tied vote.*
3 Brit. restricted or limited in some way, in particular:
■(of a house) occupied subject to the tenant's working for its owner: *agricultural workers living in tied accommodation.* ■ (of a public house) owned by a brewery and bound to supply the products produced or specified by that brewery. ■ (of a person or organization) limited to selling the products of only one company. ■ (of aid or an international loan) given subject to the condition that it should be spent on goods or services from the donor or lender.

tie-down ▶ **noun** a device to which something may be attached or secured with rope, cord, or similar.

tie-dye ▶ **noun** [often as modifier] a method of producing textile patterns by tying parts of the fabric to shield it from the dye: *tie-dye T-shirts.*
▶ **verb** [with obj.] dye (a garment or piece of cloth) by such a process.

tief /tiːf/ W. Indian ▶ **verb** [with obj.] steal (something).
▶ **noun** a thief.
– ORIGIN representing a pronunciation of **THIEF**.

tie-in ▶ **noun** a connection or association: *there's a tie-in to another case I'm working on.*
■a book, film, or other product produced to take advantage of a related work in another medium. ■ [as modifier] chiefly N. Amer. denoting sales made conditional on the purchase of an additional item or items from the same supplier.

tie line ▶ **noun** a transmission line connecting parts of a system, especially a telephone line connecting two private branch exchanges.

tienda /tɪˈɛndə/ ▶ **noun** (in the south-western US) a shop, especially a general store.
– ORIGIN mid 19th cent.: Spanish, literally 'tent'.

Tien Shan /tjɛn ˈʃan/ (also **Tian Shan**) a range of mountains lying to the north of the Tarim Basin in the Xinjiang autonomous region and eastern Kyrgyzstan. Extending for about 2,500 km (1,500 miles), it rises to 7,439 m (24,406 ft) at Pik Pobedy.

tiento /ˈtjɛntəʊ/ ▶ **noun** (pl. **-os**) (in 16th- and 17th-century Spanish music) a contrapuntal piece resembling a ricercar, originally for strings and later for organ.
– ORIGIN Spanish, literally 'touch, feel'.

Tientsin /tjɛnˈtʃɪn/ variant of **TIANJIN**.

tiepin ▶ **noun** an ornamental pin for holding a tie in place.

Tiepolo /tɪˈɛpələʊ/, Giovanni Battista (1696–1770), Italian painter. He painted numerous rococo frescoes and altarpieces including the *Antony and Cleopatra* frescoes in the Palazzo Labia, Venice (c.1750), and the decoration of the residence of the Prince-Bishop at Würzburg (1751–3).

tier ▶ **noun** a row or level of a structure, typically one of a series of rows placed one above the other and successively receding or diminishing in size: *a tier of seats* | [in combination] *the room was full of three-tier metal bunks.*
■one of a number of successively overlapping ruffles or flounces on a garment. ■ a level or grade within the hierarchy of an organization or system: *companies have taken out a tier of management to save money.*
– DERIVATIVES **tiered** adjective.
– ORIGIN late 15th cent.: from French *tire* 'sequence, order', from *tirer* 'elongate, draw'.

tierce /tɪəs/ ▶ **noun 1** another term for **TERCE**.
2 Music an organ stop sounding two octaves and a major third above the pitch of the diapason.
3 (in piquet) a sequence of three cards of the same suit.
4 Fencing the third of eight parrying positions.
5 a former measure of wine equal to one third of a pipe, usually equivalent to 35 gallons (about 156 litres).
■archaic a cask containing a certain quantity of provisions, the amount varying with the goods.
– PHRASES **tierce de Picardie** Music a major third in the final chord of a piece in a minor key.
– ORIGIN late Middle English: variant of **TERCE**.

tierced /tɪəst/ (also **tiercé** /ˈtjəːseɪ/) ▶ **adjective** Heraldry divided into three equal parts of different tinctures.
– ORIGIN early 18th cent.: originally as *tiercé* 'divided into three parts', French past participle of *tiercer.*

tiercel /ˈtɪəs(ə)l/ ▶ **noun** variant spelling of **TERCEL**.

tie rod ▶ **noun** a rod acting as a tie in a building or other structure.
■a rod in the steering gear of a motor vehicle.

Tierra del Fuego /tɪˌɛːrə dɛl ˈfweɪgəʊ/ an island at the southern extremity of South America, separated from the mainland by the Strait of Magellan. Discovered by Ferdinand Magellan in 1520, it is now divided between Argentina and Chile.
– ORIGIN Spanish, literally 'land of fire'.

tie-up ▶ **noun 1** a link or connection, especially one between commercial companies: *marketing tie-ups.*
■US a telecommunications link or network.
2 US a building where cattle are tied up for the night.
■a place for mooring a boat.
3 US a traffic hold-up.

TIFF Computing ▶ **abbreviation for** tagged image file format, widely used in desktop publishing.

tiff ▶ **noun** informal a petty quarrel, especially one between friends or lovers: *Joanna had a tiff with her boyfriend.*
– ORIGIN early 18th cent. (denoting a slight outburst of temper): probably of dialect origin.

Tiffany /ˈtɪf(ə)ni/, Louis Comfort (1848–1933), American glass-maker and interior decorator. A leading exponent of American art nouveau, he established an interior decorating firm in New York which produced stained glass, vases, lamps, and mosaic.

tiffany /ˈtɪf(ə)ni/ ▶ **noun** [mass noun] thin gauze muslin.
– ORIGIN early 17th cent.: from Old French *tifanie*, via ecclesiastical Latin from Greek *theophaneia* 'epiphany'. The word is usually taken to be short for *Epiphany silk* or *muslin*, i.e., that worn on Twelfth Night, but may be a humorous allusion to *epiphany* in the sense 'manifestation', tiffany being semi-transparent.

tiffin ▶ **noun** [mass noun] dated or Indian a light meal, especially lunch.
– ORIGIN early 19th cent.: apparently from dialect *tiffing* 'sipping', of unknown origin.

tiffin carrier ▶ **noun** chiefly Indian a set of shallow metal food containers which sit on top of each other inside a hinged metal frame fastened by a clasp.

Tiflis /tɪfˈliːs/ official Russian name (1845–1936) for **TBILISI**.

tig ▶ **noun** & **verb** chiefly Brit. another term for **TAG**[2].
– ORIGIN early 18th cent.: perhaps a variant of the verb **TICK**[1].

tiger ▶ noun **1** a very large solitary cat with a yellow-brown coat striped with black, native to the forests of Asia but becoming increasingly rare.
• *Panthera tigris*, family Felidae.
■used to refer to someone fierce, determined, or ambitious: *despite his wound, he still fought like a tiger | one of the sport's young tigers.* ■ (also **tiger economy**) a dynamic economy of one of the smaller East Asian countries, especially that of Singapore, Taiwan, or South Korea. ■ informal, chiefly Austral./NZ a person with an insatiable appetite for something: *I'm a* ***tiger for*** *a bargain.*
2 used in names of tiger moths and striped butterflies, e.g. **scarlet tiger**, **plain tiger**.
3 (**Tigers**) another term for **TAMIL TIGERS**.
– PHRASES **have a tiger by the tail** (also **be riding a tiger**) have embarked on a course of action which proves unexpectedly difficult but which cannot easily or safely be abandoned.
– ORIGIN Middle English: from Old French *tigre*, from Latin *tigris*, from Greek.

Tiger balm ▶ noun [mass noun] trademark a mentholated ointment widely used in Eastern medicine for a variety of conditions.

tiger beetle ▶ noun a fast-running predatory beetle which has spotted or striped wing cases and flies in sunshine. The larvae live in tunnels from which they snatch passing insect prey.
• Family Cicindelidae: *Cicindela* and other genera.

tiger cat ▶ noun a small forest cat that has a light brown coat with dark stripes and blotches, native to Central and South America.
• *Felis tigrina*, family Felidae.
■any moderate-sized striped cat, such as the ocelot, serval, or margay. ■ Australian term for **QUOLL**.

tiger economy ▶ noun see **TIGER** (sense 1).

tiger fish ▶ noun any of a number of aggressive predatory fish, in particular:
• a large African characin, popular with anglers (*Hydrocynus vittatus*, family Characidae). • an edible fish of the Indo-Pacific (*Therapon jarbua*, family Theraponidae).

tigerish ▶ adjective resembling or likened to a tiger, especially in being fierce and determined: *she was in tigerish mood.*
– DERIVATIVES **tigerishly** adverb.

tiger lily ▶ noun a tall Asian lily which has orange flowers spotted with black or purple.
• *Lilium lancifolium* (or *tigrinum*), family Liliaceae.

tiger maple ▶ noun [mass noun] N. Amer. the timber of an American maple which contains contrasting light and dark lines.

tiger moth ▶ noun a stout moth which has boldly spotted and streaked wings and a hairy caterpillar (woolly bear).
• *Arctia* and other genera, family Arctiidae: many species. See **GARDEN TIGER**.

tiger nut ▶ noun the small dried tuber of a kind of sedge, used locally as food.
• The sedge is *Cyperus esculentus*, family Cyperaceae.

tiger prawn ▶ noun a large edible prawn marked with dark bands, found in the Indian and Pacific oceans.
• Genus *Penaeus*, class Malacostraca: several species, in particular the widely farmed *P. monodon*.

tiger salamander ▶ noun a large North American salamander which is blackish with yellow patches or stripes.
• *Ambystoma tigrinum*, family Ambystomatidae.

tiger's eye (also **tiger eye**) ▶ noun [mass noun] a yellowish-brown semi-precious variety of quartz with a silky or chatoyant lustre, formed by replacement of crocidolite.

tiger shark ▶ noun an aggressive shark of warm seas, with dark vertical stripes on the body.
• *Galeocerdo cuvieri*, family Carcharhinidae.

tiger shrimp ▶ noun another term for **TIGER PRAWN**.

tiger snake ▶ noun **1** a deadly Australian snake, typically marked with brown and yellow bands and active in daylight.
• Genus *Notechis*, family Elapidae: two species, in particular *N. scutatus*.
2 a very slender harmless nocturnal snake found in Africa.
• Genus *Telescopus*, family Colubridae: several species.

tigerwood ▶ noun [mass noun] striped or streaked wood used for cabinetmaking.

tiger worm ▶ noun another term for **BRANDLING**.

tight ▶ adjective **1** fixed, fastened, or closed firmly; hard to move, undo, or open: *she twisted her handkerchief into a tight knot.*
■(of clothes or shoes) close-fitting, especially uncomfortably so: *the dress was too tight for her.* ■ (of a grip) very firm so as not to let go: *she released her tight hold on the dog* | figurative *presidential advisers* ***keep a tight grip on*** *domestic policy.* ■ (of a ship, building, or object) well sealed against something such as water or air: [in combination] *a light-tight container.* ■ (of a formation or a group of people or things) closely or densely packed together: *he levered the bishop out from a tight knot of clerical wives.* ■ (of a community or other group of people) having close relations; secretive: *the folk were far too tight to let anyone know.*
2 (of a rope, fabric, or surface) stretched so as to leave no slack; not loose: *the drawcord pulls tight.*
■(of a part of the body or a bodily sensation) feeling painful and constricted, as a result of anxiety or illness: *there was a tight feeling in his gut.* ■ (of appearance or manner) tense, irritated, or angry: *she gave him a tight smile.* ■ (of a rule, policy, or form of control) strictly imposed: *security was tight at yesterday's ceremony.* ■ (of a game or contest) with evenly matched competitors; very close: *he won in a tight finish.* ■ (of a written work or form) concise, condensed, or well structured: *a tight argument.* ■ (of an organization or group of people) disciplined or professional; well coordinated: *the vocalists are strong and the band is tight.*
3 (of an area or space) having or allowing little room for manoeuvre: *a tight parking spot | it was a tight squeeze in the tiny vestibule.*
■(of a bend, turn, or angle) changing direction sharply; having a short radius. ■ (of money or time) limited or restricted: *David was out of work and money was tight | an ability to work to tight deadlines.* ■ informal (of a person) not willing to spend or give much money; mean.
4 [predic.] informal drunk: *later, at the club, he will get tight on brandy.*
▶ adverb very firmly, closely, or tensely: *he went downstairs, holding tight to the bannisters.*
– PHRASES **run a tight ship** be very strict in managing an organization or operation. **a tight corner** (or **spot** or **place**) a difficult situation: *her talent for talking her way* ***out of tight corners.***
– DERIVATIVES **tightly** adverb, **tightness** noun.
– ORIGIN Middle English (in the sense 'healthy, vigorous', later 'firm, solid'): probably an alteration of *thight* 'firm, solid', later 'close-packed, dense', of Germanic origin; related to German *dicht* 'dense, close'.

tight-ass ▶ noun informal, chiefly N. Amer. an inhibited, repressed, or excessively conventional person.
– DERIVATIVES **tight-assed** adjective.

tighten ▶ verb make or become tight or tighter: [with obj.] *central government has tightened control over local authority spending* | [no obj.] *the revenue laws were tightening up.*
– PHRASES **tighten one's belt** see **BELT**. **tighten the screw** see **SCREW**.

tight end ▶ noun American Football an offensive end who lines up close to the tackle.

tight-fisted ▶ adjective informal not willing to spend or give much money; miserly.

tight-fitting ▶ adjective (of a garment) fitting close to and showing the contours of the body.
■(of a lid or cover) forming a tight seal when placed on a container.

tight head ▶ noun Rugby the prop forward supporting the hooker on the opposite side of the scrum from the loose head.

tight junction ▶ noun Biology a specialized connection of two adjacent animal cell membranes such that the space usually lying between them is absent.

tight-knit (also **tightly knit**) ▶ adjective (of a group of people) united or bound together by strong relationships and common interests: *tight-knit mining communities.*

tight-lipped ▶ adjective with the lips firmly closed, especially as a sign of suppressed emotion or determined reticence: *she stayed tight-lipped and shook her head.*

tight money ▶ noun [mass noun] Finance money or finance that is available only at high rates of interest.

tightrope ▶ noun a rope or wire stretched tightly high above the ground, on which acrobats perform feats of balancing: [as modifier] *a tightrope walker* | figurative *he continues to* ***walk a tightrope*** *between success and failure.*
▶ verb [no obj.] walk or perform on such a rope.

tights ▶ plural noun chiefly Brit. a woman's thin, close-fitting garment, typically made of nylon, cotton, or wool, covering the legs, hips, and bottom.
■a similar garment worn by a dancer or acrobat.

tightwad ▶ noun informal, chiefly US a mean or miserly person.

Tiglath-pileser /ˌtɪglaθpʌɪˈliːzə/ the name of three kings of Assyria, notably:
■Tiglath-pileser I, reigned *c.*1115–*c.*1077 BC. He extended Assyrian territory, taking Cappadocia, reaching Syria, and defeating the king of Babylonia.
■Tiglath-pileser III, reigned *c.*745–727 BC. He brought the Assyrian empire to the height of its power, subduing large parts of Syria and Palestine, and conquered Babylonia.

tignon /ˈtiːjɒn/ ▶ noun a piece of cloth worn as a turban headdress by Creole women from Louisiana.
– ORIGIN Louisana French, from French *tigne*, dialect variant of *teigne* 'moth'.

tigon /ˈtʌɪg(ə)n/ (also **tiglon** /ˈtʌɪglɒn, ˈtɪg-/) ▶ noun the hybrid offspring of a male tiger and a lioness.
– ORIGIN 1920s: portmanteau word from **TIGER** and **LION**.

Tigray /ˈtiːgreɪ/ (also **Tigre**) a province of Ethiopia, in the north of the country, bordering Eritrea; capital, Mekele. An ancient kingdom, Tigray was annexed as a province of Ethiopia in 1855. It engaged in a bitter guerrilla war against the government of Ethiopia 1975–91, during which time the region suffered badly from drought and famine.
– DERIVATIVES **Tigrayan** (also **Tigrean**) adjective & noun.

Tigre[1] variant spelling of **TIGRAY**.

Tigre[2] /ˈtiːgreɪ/ ▶ noun [mass noun] a Semitic language spoken in Eritrea and adjoining parts of Sudan. It is not the language of Tigray, which is Tigrinya.
– ORIGIN the name in Tigre.

tigress ▶ noun a female tiger.
■figurative a fierce or passionate woman.

Tigrinya /tɪˈgriːnjə/ ▶ noun [mass noun] a Semitic language spoken in Tigray, with about 4 million speakers. Compare with **TIGRE**[2].
– ORIGIN the name in Tigrinya.

Tigris /ˈtʌɪgrɪs/ a river in SW Asia, the more easterly of the two rivers of ancient Mesopotamia. It rises in the mountains of eastern Turkey and flows 1,850 km (1,150 miles) south-eastwards through Iraq, passing through Baghdad, to join the Euphrates, forming the Shatt al-Arab, which flows into the Persian Gulf.

Tigua ▶ noun & adjective variant spelling of **TIWA**.

Tihwa /tiːˈhwɑː/ former name (until 1954) for **URUMQI**.

Tijuana /tɪˈ(h)wɑːnə/ a town in NW Mexico, situated just south of the US frontier; pop. 742,690 (1990).

tika /ˈtiːkɑː/ ▶ noun another term for **TILAK**.
– ORIGIN from Hindi *ṭīkā*, from Punjabi *ṭikkā*.

Tikal /tɪˈkɑːl/ an ancient Mayan city in the tropical Petén region of northern Guatemala, with great plazas, pyramids, and palaces. It flourished AD 300–800.

tike ▶ noun variant spelling of **TYKE**.

tiki /ˈtɪki/ ▶ noun (pl. **tikis**) NZ a large wooden or small greenstone image of a human figure.
– ORIGIN Maori, literally 'image'.

tikia /ˈtɪkɪɑː/ ▶ noun an Indian dish consisting of a flat fried cake of spiced meat or mashed potato.
– ORIGIN from Hindi *ṭikiā*.

tikka /ˈtɪkə, ˈtiːkə/ ▶ noun [mass noun] [usu. with modifier] an Indian dish of small pieces of meat or vegetables marinated in a spice mixture.
– ORIGIN from Punjabi *ṭikkā*.

tilak /ˈtɪlʌk/ ▶ noun a mark worn by a Hindu on the forehead to indicate caste, status, or sect, or as an ornament.
– ORIGIN from Sanskrit *tilaka*.

tilapia /tɪˈleɪpɪə, -ˈlap-/ ▶ noun an African freshwater cichlid fish that has been widely introduced to many areas for food, such as St Peter's fish.
• *Tilapia* and related genera, family Cichlidae: several species.
– ORIGIN modern Latin, of unknown origin.

Tilburg /ˈtɪlbəːg/ an industrial city in the southern

Netherlands, in the province of North Brabant; pop. 158,850 (1991).

Tilbury /ˈtɪlb(ə)ri/ the principal container port of London and south-east England, on the north bank of the River Thames.

tilbury /ˈtɪlb(ə)ri/ ▶ **noun** (pl. **-ies**) historical a light, open two-wheeled carriage.
– ORIGIN early 19th cent.: named after its inventor.

tilde /ˈtɪldə/ ▶ **noun** an accent (˜) placed over Spanish *n* when pronounced *ny* (as in *señor*) or Portuguese *a* or *o* when nasalized (as in *São Paulo*), or over a vowel in phonetic transcription, indicating nasalization.
■ a similar symbol used in mathematics and logic to indicate negation, inversion, etc.
– ORIGIN mid 19th cent.: from Spanish, based on Latin *titulus* (see **TITLE**).

tile /tʌɪl/ ▶ **noun** a thin rectangular slab of baked clay, concrete, or other material, used in overlapping rows for covering roofs.
■ a thin square slab of glazed pottery, cork, linoleum, or other material for covering floors, walls, or other surfaces. ■ a thin, flat piece used in Scrabble, mah-jong, and certain other games. ■ Mathematics a plane shape used in tiling.
▶ **verb** [with obj.] (usu. **be tiled**) cover (something) with tiles: *the lobby was tiled in blue.*
■ Computing arrange (two or more windows) on a computer screen so that they do not overlap.
– PHRASES **on the tiles** informal, chiefly Brit. having a lively night out: *it won't be the first time he's spent a night on the tiles.*
– ORIGIN Old English *tigele*, from Latin *tegula*, from an Indo-European root meaning 'cover'.

tilefish ▶ **noun** (pl. same or **-fishes**) a long, slender bottom-dwelling fish of warm seas.
• Several species in the family Malacanthidae (or Branchiostegidae), in particular the large and edible *Lopholatilus chamaeleonticeps* of the Atlantic coast of North America.

tiler ▶ **noun 1** a person who lays tiles: *a roof tiler.*
2 the doorkeeper of a Freemasons' lodge, who prevents outsiders from entering.

tiling ▶ **noun** [mass noun] the action of laying tiles.
■ a surface covered by tiles: *an area of plain tiling.* ■ a technique for displaying several non-overlapping windows on a computer screen. ■ Mathematics a way of arranging identical plane shapes so that they completely cover an area without overlapping.

till[1] ▶ **preposition** & **conjunction** less formal way of saying **UNTIL**.
– ORIGIN Old English *til*, of Germanic origin; related to Old Norse *til* 'to', also ultimately to **TILL**[3].

USAGE In most contexts, **till** and **until** have the same meaning and are interchangeable. The main difference is that **till** is generally considered to be more informal than **until**. **Until** occurs more frequently than **till** in writing—around ten times as often in the British National Corpus. In addition, **until** tends to be the natural choice at the beginning of a sentence: *until very recently, there was still a chance of rescuing the situation.* Interestingly, while it is commonly assumed that **till** is an abbreviated form of **until** (the spellings **'till** and **'til** reflect this), **till** is in fact the earlier form. **Until** appears to have been formed by the addition of Old Norse *und* 'as far as' several hundred years after the date of the first records for **till**.

till[2] ▶ **noun** a cash register or drawer for money in a shop, bank, or restaurant.
– PHRASES **have** (or **with**) **one's fingers** (or **hand**) **in the till** used in reference to theft from one's place of work: *he was caught with his hand in the till and sacked.*
– ORIGIN late Middle English (in the general sense 'drawer or compartment for valuables'): of unknown origin.

till[3] ▶ **verb** [with obj.] prepare and cultivate (land) for crops: *no land was being tilled or crops sown.*
– DERIVATIVES **tillable** adjective.
– ORIGIN Old English *tilian* 'strive for, obtain by effort', of Germanic origin; related to Dutch *telen* 'produce, cultivate' and German *zielen* 'aim, strive', also ultimately to **TILL**[1]. The current sense dates from Middle English.

till[4] ▶ **noun** [mass noun] Geology boulder clay or other unstratified sediment deposited by melting glaciers or ice sheets.
– ORIGIN late 17th cent. (originally Scots, denoting shale): of unknown origin.

tillage /ˈtɪlɪdʒ/ ▶ **noun** [mass noun] the preparation of land for growing crops.
■ land under cultivation: *forty acres of tillage.*

tiller[1] ▶ **noun** a horizontal bar fitted to the head of a boat's rudder post and used for steering.
– ORIGIN late Middle English: from Anglo-Norman French *telier* 'weaver's beam, stock of a crossbow', from medieval Latin *telarium*, from Latin *tela* 'web'.

tiller[2] ▶ **noun** a lateral shoot from the base of the stem, especially in a grass or cereal.
▶ **verb** [no obj.] [usu. as noun **tillering**] develop tillers.
– ORIGIN mid 17th cent. (denoting a sapling arising from the stool of a felled tree): apparently based on Old English *telga* 'bough', of Germanic origin.

tiller[3] ▶ **noun** an implement or machine for breaking up soil; a plough or cultivator.

tilleul /tɪˈjəːl/ ▶ **noun** a lime or linden tree.
■ [mass noun] a tea made from an infusion of the flowers of this tree, originally used as a remedy for headache.
– ORIGIN mid 16th cent.: from French, from a diminutive form of Latin *tilia* 'linden'.

tilley lamp /ˈtɪli/ (also **tilly lamp**) ▶ **noun** trademark a portable oil or paraffin lamp in which air pressure is used to supply the burner with fuel.
– ORIGIN 1930s: from the name of the manufacturers.

Tillich /ˈtɪlɪk/, Paul (Johannes) (1886–1965), German-born American theologian and philosopher. He proposed a form of Christian existentialism. Notable works: *Systematic Theology* (1951–63).

tillite /ˈtɪlʌɪt/ ▶ **noun** [mass noun] Geology sedimentary rock composed of compacted glacial till.

Tilsit /ˈtɪlsɪt/ (also **Tilsit cheese**) ▶ **noun** [mass noun] a semi-hard mildly flavoured cheese.
– ORIGIN named after the town in East Prussia (now Sovetsk, Russia) where it was first produced.

tilt ▶ **verb 1** move or cause to move into a sloping position: [no obj.] *the floor tilted slightly* | figurative *the balance of industrial power tilted towards the workers* | [with obj.] *he tilted his head to one side.*
■ figurative incline or cause to incline towards a particular opinion: [no obj., with adverbial] *he is tilting towards a new economic course.* ■ [with obj.] move (a camera) in a vertical plane.
2 [no obj.] (**tilt at**) historical (in jousting) thrust at with a lance or other weapon: *he tilts at his prey* | figurative *the lonely hero tilting at the system.*
■ (**tilt with**) archaic engage in a contest with: *I resolved never to tilt with a French lady in compliment.*
▶ **noun 1** a sloping position or movement: *the tilt of her head* | *mum's cup was on a tilt.*
■ an upwards or downwards pivoting movement of a camera: *pans and tilts.* ■ an inclination or bias: *the paper's tilt towards the United States.* ■ short for **TILT CAB** or **TILT HAMMER**. ■ Canadian a small hut in a forest. ■ [in place names] a slope or incline: *Glen Tilt.*
2 historical a combat for exercise or sport between two men on horseback with lances; a joust.
■ (**tilt at**) an attempt at winning (something) or defeating (someone), especially in sporting contexts: *a tilt at the European Cup.*
– PHRASES **(at) full tilt** with maximum energy or force; at top speed. **tilt at windmills** attack imaginary enemies or evils. [ORIGIN: with allusion to the story of Don Quixote tilting at windmills, believing they were giants.]
– DERIVATIVES **tilter** noun.
– ORIGIN late Middle English (in the sense 'fall or cause to fall, topple'): perhaps related to Old English *tealt* 'unsteady', or perhaps of Scandinavian origin and related to Norwegian *tylten* 'unsteady' and Swedish *tulta* 'totter'.

tilt cab ▶ **noun** a cab of a lorry or other vehicle which can tilt forwards.

tilth ▶ **noun** [mass noun] cultivation of land; tillage.
■ [in sing.] the condition of tilled soil, especially in respect to suitability for sowing seeds: *he could determine whether the soil was of the right tilth.* ■ prepared surface soil.
– ORIGIN Old English *tilth*, *tilthe*, from *tilian* (see **TILL**[3]).

tilt hammer ▶ **noun** a heavy pivoted hammer used in forging, raised mechanically and allowed to drop on the metal being worked.

tilt yard ▶ **noun** historical a place where jousts took place.

Tim. ▶ **abbreviation for** Timothy (especially in biblical references).

Timaru /ˈtɪməruː/ a port and resort on the east coast of South Island, New Zealand; pop. 27,640 (1991).

timbal /ˈtɪmb(ə)l/ ▶ **noun** archaic a kettledrum.
– ORIGIN late 17th cent.: from French *timbale*, alteration (influenced by *cymbale* 'cymbal') of obsolete *tamballe*, from Spanish *atabal*, from Arabic *aṭ-ṭabl* 'the drum'.

timbale /tamˈbɑːl/ ▶ **noun 1** a dish of finely minced meat or fish cooked with other ingredients in a pastry shell or in a mould.
2 (**timbales**) paired cylindrical drums played with sticks in Latin American dance music.
– ORIGIN French, 'drum' (in sense 1 with reference to the shape of the prepared dish; in sense 2 short for *timbales cubains* or *timbales creoles* 'Cuban' or 'creole drums').

timber ▶ **noun** [mass noun] wood prepared for use in building and carpentry: *the exploitation of forests for timber* | [as modifier] *a small timber building.*
■ trees grown for such wood: *contracts to cut timber.* ■ (usu. **timbers**) a wooden beam or board used in building a house or ship. ■ [as exclamation] used to warn that a tree is about to fall after being cut: *we cried 'Timber!' as our tree fell.* ■ [usu. with adj.] chiefly US personal qualities or character, especially as seen as suitable for a particular role: *she is frequently hailed as presidential timber.*
– ORIGIN Old English in the sense 'a building', also 'building material', of Germanic origin; related to German *Zimmer* 'room', from an Indo-European root meaning 'build'.

timbered ▶ **adjective 1** (of a building) made wholly or partly of timber: *black-and-white timbered buildings.*
■ (of the walls or other surface of a room) covered with wooden panels: *the timbered banqueting hall.*
2 having many trees; wooded.

timber-frame ▶ **adjective** denoting a house or other structure having a wooden frame, traditionally of oak or elm.
▶ **noun** [mass noun] pre-prepared sections of wood used for building a house.
– DERIVATIVES **timber-framed** adjective, **timber-framer** noun, **timber-framing** noun.

timber-getter ▶ **noun** Austral. a lumberjack.

timber hitch ▶ **noun** a knot used in attaching a rope to a log or spar.

timbering ▶ **noun** [mass noun] the action of building with wood.
■ wood as a building material, or finished work built from wood.

timberland ▶ **noun** [mass noun] (also **timberlands**) N. Amer. land covered with forest suitable or managed for timber.

timberline ▶ **noun** chiefly N. Amer. another term for **TREELINE**.

timberman ▶ **noun** (pl. **-men**) **1** a person who works with timber.
2 a greyish-brown longhorn beetle with extremely long antennae, occurring in the old pine forests of northern Europe. The wood-boring larvae live chiefly in fallen or felled trees.
• *Acanthocinus aedilis*, family Cerambycidae.

timber wolf ▶ **noun** a wolf of a large variety found mainly in northern North America, with grey brindled fur. Also called **GREY WOLF**.

timbre /ˈtambə/ ▶ **noun** the character or quality of a musical sound or voice as distinct from its pitch and intensity: *trumpet mutes with different timbres* | [mass noun] *a voice high in pitch but rich in timbre.*
– ORIGIN mid 19th cent.: from French, from medieval Greek *timbanon*, from Greek *tumpanon* 'drum'.

timbrel /ˈtɪmbr(ə)l/ ▶ **noun** archaic a tambourine or similar instrument.
– ORIGIN early 16th cent.: perhaps a diminutive of obsolete *timbre*, in the same sense, from Old French (see **TIMBRE**).

Timbuktu /ˌtɪmbʌkˈtuː/ (also **Timbuctoo**) a town in northern Mali; pop. 20,500 (1976). It was formerly a major trading centre for gold and salt on the trans-Saharan trade routes, reaching the height of its prosperity in the 16th century but falling into decline after its capture by the Moroccans in 1591. French name **TOMBOUCTOU**.
■ used in reference to a remote or extremely distant place: *from here to Timbuktu.*

time ▶ **noun 1** [mass noun] the indefinite continued progress of existence and events in the past, present, and future regarded as a whole: *travel through space and time | one of the greatest wits of all time.*

■the progress of this as affecting people and things: *things were getting better as time passed.* ■ time or an amount of time as reckoned by a conventional standard: *it's eight o'clock New York Time.* ■ (**Time** or **Father Time**) the personification of time, typically as an old man with a scythe and hourglass.

2 a point of time as measured in hours and minutes past midnight or noon: *the time is 9.30.*

■a moment or definite portion of time allotted, used, or suitable for a purpose: *the scheduled departure time | shall we fix a time for the meeting?* ■ (often **time for/to do something**) the favourable or appropriate time to do something; the right moment: *it was time to go | it's time for bed.* ■ (**a time**) an indefinite period: *travelling always distorts one's feelings for a time.* ■ (also **times**) a more or less definite portion of time in history or characterized by particular events or circumstances: *Victorian times | at the time of Galileo | the park is beautiful at this time of year.* ■ (also **times**) the conditions of life during a particular period: *times have changed.* ■ (**the Times**) used in names of newspapers: *the Oxford Times.* ■ (**one's time**) one's lifetime: *I've known a lot of women in my time.* ■ (**one's time**) the successful, fortunate, or influential part of a person's life or career: *in my time that was unheard of.* ■ (**one's time**) the appropriate or expected time for something, in particular childbirth or death: *he seemed old before his time.* ■ an apprenticeship: *engineering officers traditionally* ***served their time*** *as fitters in the yards.* ■ dated a period of menstruation or pregnancy. ■ [mass noun] the normal rate of pay for time spent working: *if called out at the weekend they are paid* ***time and a half.*** ■ the length of time taken to run a race or complete an event or journey: *his time for the mile was 3:49.31.* ■ Brit. the moment at which the opening hours of a public house end: *the landlord* ***called time.*** ■ short for FULL TIME: *he scored the third five minutes from time.* ■ Baseball & American Football a moment at which play stops temporarily within a game: *the umpire* ***called time.***

3 [mass noun] time as allotted, available, or used: *we need more time | it would be a waste of time.*

■informal a prison sentence: *he was* ***doing time*** *for fraud.*

4 an instance of something happening or being done; an occasion: *this is the first time I have got into debt | the nurse came in four times a day.*

■an event, occasion, or period experienced in a particular way: *she was* ***having a rough time of it.***

5 (**times**) (following a number) expressing multiplication: *eleven times four is forty-four.*

6 the rhythmic pattern of a piece of music, as expressed by a time signature: *tunes* ***in waltz time.***

■the tempo at which a piece of music is played or marked to be played.

▶**verb 1** [with obj. and adverbial or infinitive] plan, schedule, or arrange when (something) should happen or be done: *the first track race is timed for 11.15 | the bomb had been timed to go off an hour later.*

■perform (an action) at a particular moment: *Williams timed his pass perfectly from about thirty yards.*

2 [with obj.] measure the time taken by (a process or activity, or a person doing it): *we were timed and given certificates according to our speed |* [with clause] *I timed how long it took to empty that tanker.*

3 [with obj.] (**time something out**) Computing (of a computer or a program) cancel an operation automatically because a predefined interval of time has passed without a certain event happening.

– PHRASES **about time** used to convey that something now happening or about to happen should have happened earlier: *it's about time I came clean and admitted it.* **against time** with utmost speed, so as to finish by a specified time: *he was working against time.* **ahead of time** earlier than expected or required. **ahead of one's time** having ideas too enlightened or advanced to be accepted by one's contemporaries. **all the time** at all times. ■ very frequently or regularly: *we were in and out of each other's flats all the time.* **at one time** in or during a known but unspecified past period: *she was a nurse at one time.* **at the same time 1** simultaneously; at once. **2** nevertheless (used to introduce a fact that should be taken into account): *I can't really explain it, but at the same time I'm not convinced.* **at a time** separately in the specified groups or numbers: *he took the stairs two at a time.* **at times** sometimes; on occasions. **before time** before the due or expected time. **behind time** late. **behind the times** not aware of or using the latest ideas or techniques; out of date. **for the time being** for the present; until some other arrangement is made. **give someone the time of day** [usu. with negative] be pleasantly polite or friendly to someone: *I wouldn't give him the time of day if I could help it.* **half the time** as often as not. **have no time for** be unable or unwilling to spend time on: *he had no time for anything except essays and projects.* ■ dislike or disapprove of: *he's got no time for airheads.* **have the time 1** be able to spend the time needed to do something: *she didn't have the time to look very closely.* **2** know from having a watch what time it is. **in** (**less than**) **no time** very quickly or very soon: *the video has sold 30,000 copies in no time.* **in one's own time 1** (also **in one's own good time**) at a time and a rate decided by oneself. **2** (US **on one's own time**) outside working hours; without being paid. **in time 1** not late; punctual: *I came back* ***in time for*** *Molly's party.* **2** eventually: *there is the danger that he might, in time, not be able to withstand temptation.* **3** in accordance with the appropriate musical rhythm or tempo. **keep good** (or **bad**) **time 1** (of a clock or watch) record time accurately (or inaccurately). **2** (of a person) be habitually punctual (or not punctual). **keep time** play or rhythmically accompany music in time. **lose no time** do a specified thing immediately or as soon as possible: *the administration* ***lost no time in*** *trying to regain the initiative.* **not before time** used to convey that something now happening or about to happen should have happened earlier. **no time** a very short interval or period: *the renovations were done* ***in no time.*** **on time** punctual; punctually: *the train was on time | we paid our bills on time.* **out of time** at the wrong time or period: *I felt that I was born out of time.* **pass the time of day** exchange greetings or casual remarks. **time after time** (also **time and again** or **time and time again**) on very many occasions; repeatedly. **time and tide wait for no man** proverb if you don't make use of a favourable opportunity, you may never get the same chance again. **time immemorial** used to refer to a point of time in the past that was so long ago that people have no knowledge or memory of it: *markets had been held there* ***from time immemorial.*** **time is money** proverb time is a valuable resource, therefore it's better to do things as quickly as possible. **the time of one's life** a period or occasion of exceptional enjoyment. **time out of mind** another way of saying ***time immemorial.*** **time was** there was a time when: *time was, each street had its own specialized trade.* (**only**) **time will tell** the truth or correctness of something will (only) be established at some time in the future.

– ORIGIN Old English *tīma*, of Germanic origin; related to TIDE, which it superseded in temporal senses. The earliest of the current verb senses (dating from late Middle English) is 'do (something) at a particular moment'.

time-and-motion study ▶**noun** a procedure in which the efficiency of an industrial or other operation is evaluated.

time ball ▶**noun** a timepiece consisting of a sphere which at a certain moment each day is allowed to fall down a vertical rod.

time base ▶**noun** Electronics a signal for uniformly and repeatedly deflecting the electron beam of a cathode ray tube.

■a line on the display produced in this way and serving as a time axis.

time bomb ▶**noun** a bomb designed to explode at a preset time.

■figurative a process or procedure causing a problematic situation which will eventually become dangerous if not addressed: *the demographic time bomb.*

time capsule ▶**noun** a container storing a selection of objects chosen as being typical of the present time, buried for discovery in the future.

time clock ▶**noun 1** a clock with a device for recording employees' times of arrival and departure.

2 a switch mechanism activated at preset times by a built-in clock.

time code ▶**noun** Electronics a coded signal on videotape or film giving information about such things as frame number, time of recording, or exposure.

time constant ▶**noun** Physics a time which represents the speed with which a particular system can respond to change, typically equal to the time taken for a specified parameter to vary by a factor of $1-1/e$ (approximately 0.6321).

time-consuming ▶**adjective** taking a lot of or too much time: *an extremely time-consuming process.*

time deposit ▶**noun** a deposit in a bank account that cannot be withdrawn before a set date or for which notice of withdrawal is required.

time division multiplex ▶**noun** [mass noun] Telecommunications a technique for transmitting two or more signals over the same telephone line, radio channel, or other medium. Each signal is sent as a series of pulses or packets, which are interleaved with those of the other signal or signals and transmitted as a continuous stream. Compare with FREQUENCY DIVISION MULTIPLEX.

time domain ▶**noun** Physics time considered as an independent variable in the analysis or measurement of time-dependent phenomena.

time domain reflectometer ▶**noun** see REFLECTOMETER.

time exposure ▶**noun** the exposure of photographic film for longer than the maximum normal shutter setting.

time frame ▶**noun** a period of time, especially a specified period in which something occurs or is planned to take place: *the work had to be done in a time frame of fourteen working days.*

time fuse ▶**noun** a fuse calculated to burn for or explode a bomb, shell, or explosive charge at a specified time.

time-honoured ▶**adjective** [attrib.] (of a custom or tradition) respected or valued because it has existed for a long time.

timekeeper ▶**noun 1** a person who measures or records the amount of time taken, especially in a sports competition.

2 [usu. with adj.] a person regarded as being punctual or not punctual: *we were good timekeepers.*

■a watch or clock regarded as recording time accurately or inaccurately: *these watches are accurate timekeepers.* ■ archaic a clock.

– DERIVATIVES **timekeeping** noun.

time lag ▶**noun** see LAG[1] (sense 1).

time-lapse ▶**adjective** denoting the photographic technique of taking a sequence of frames at set intervals to record changes that take place slowly over time. When the frames are shown at normal speed the action seems much faster.

timeless ▶**adjective** not affected by the passage of time or changes in fashion: *antiques add to the timeless atmosphere of the dining room.*

– DERIVATIVES **timelessly** adverb, **timelessness** noun.

time limit ▶**noun** a limit of time within which something must be done.

– DERIVATIVES **time-limited** adjective.

time line ▶**noun** a pictorial representation of the passage of time as a line.

time lock ▶**noun** a lock fitted with a device that prevents it from being unlocked until a set time.

■a device built into a computer program to stop it operating after a certain time.

▶**verb** (**time-lock**) [with obj.] secure (a door or other locking mechanism) with a time lock.

■link (something) inextricably to a certain period of time: *an overdone theme tends to time-lock a setting and stifle imagination.*

timely ▶**adjective** done or occurring at a favourable or useful time; opportune: *a timely warning.*

– DERIVATIVES **timeliness** noun.

time machine ▶**noun** (in science fiction) a machine capable of transporting a person backwards or forwards in time.

time off ▶**noun** [mass noun] time for rest or recreation away from one's usual work or studies: *we're too busy to* ***take time off.***

time-of-flight ▶**adjective** Physics relating to or denoting techniques and apparatus that depend on the time taken by subatomic particles to traverse a set distance.

timeous /ˈtʌɪməs/ ▶**adjective** chiefly Scottish in good time; sufficiently early: *ensure timeous completion and posting of applications.*

– DERIVATIVES **timeously** adverb.

time out ▶**noun 1** [mass noun] chiefly N. Amer. time for rest or recreation away from one's usual work or studies: *she is* ***taking time out*** *from her hectic tour.*

■[count noun] (**timeout**) a brief break in play in a game of sport: *he called for a timeout from the game.*

2 (**timeout**) Computing a cancellation or cessation that automatically occurs when a predefined interval of time has passed without a certain event occurring.

timepiece ▶ **noun** an instrument, such as a clock or watch, for measuring time.

timer ▶ **noun** **1** an automatic mechanism for activating a device at a preset time: *a video timer.*
■ a person or device that measures or records the amount of time taken by a process or activity.
2 [in combination] used to indicate how many times someone has done something: *for most first-timers the success rate is 45 per cent.*

time-release ▶ **adjective** denoting something, especially a drug preparation, that releases an active substance gradually.

time-resolved ▶ **adjective** Physics & Chemistry relating to or denoting a spectroscopic technique in which a spectrum is obtained at a series of time intervals after excitation of the sample.

time reversal ▶ **noun** Physics a transformation in which the passage of time, and so all velocities, are represented as reversed.

times ▶ **verb** (**timesed**, **timesing**) [with obj.] informal multiply (a number): *you times the six by four to get twenty-four.*
– ORIGIN late 20th cent.: use as a verb of *times* expressing multiplication (dating from late Middle English): see **TIME** sense 5 of the noun.

timescale ▶ **noun** the time allowed for or taken by a process or sequence of events: *climatic changes on a timescale of tens of thousands of years.*

time series ▶ **noun** Statistics a series of values of a quantity obtained at successive times, often with equal intervals between them.

time-served ▶ **adjective** [attrib.] Brit. having completed a period of apprenticeship or training: *all the carpet-fitters are time-served experts.*

time-server ▶ **noun** **1** a person who changes their views to suit the prevailing circumstances or fashion.
2 a person who makes very little effort at work because they are waiting to leave or retire.
– DERIVATIVES **time-serving** adjective.

timeshare ▶ **noun** [mass noun] the arrangement whereby several joint owners have the right to use a property as a holiday home under a time-sharing scheme: *a growing interest in timeshare.*
■ [count noun] a property owned in such a way.

time-sharing ▶ **noun** [mass noun] **1** the operation of a computer system by several users for different operations at the same time.
2 the use of a property as a holiday home at specified times by several joint owners.

time sheet ▶ **noun** a piece of paper for recording the number of hours worked.

time-shift ▶ **verb** **1** [no obj.] move from one period in time to another.
2 [with obj.] record (a television programme) for later viewing.
▶ **noun** (**time shift**) a movement from one period in time to another, especially in a play or film.

time signal ▶ **noun** an audible signal indicating the exact time of day, especially one broadcast by radio at certain times.

time signature ▶ **noun** Music an indication of rhythm following a clef, generally expressed as a fraction with the denominator defining the beat as a division of a semibreve and the numerator giving the number of beats in each bar.

time slice ▶ **noun** Computing a short interval of time during which a computer or its central processor deals uninterruptedly with one user or program, before switching to another.

time span ▶ **noun** a period of time between fixed points or marked by the continuation of a particular process: *the time span of one human life.*

times table ▶ **noun** informal term for **MULTIPLICATION TABLE**.

time switch ▶ **noun** a switch automatically activated at a preset time.

timetable ▶ **noun** a chart showing the departure and arrival times of trains, buses, or planes.
■ a plan of times at which events are scheduled to take place, especially towards a particular end: *the acceleration of the timetable for monetary union.* ■ Brit. a chart showing how the weekly time of a school or college is allotted to classes.
▶ **verb** [with obj.] schedule (something) to take place at a particular time: *German lessons were timetabled on Wednesday and Friday.*

time travel ▶ **noun** [mass noun] (in science fiction) travel through time into the past or the future.
– DERIVATIVES **time traveller** noun.

time trial ▶ **noun** (in various sports) a test of a competitor's individual speed over a set distance, especially a cycling race in which competitors are separately timed.

time warp ▶ **noun** (especially in science fiction) an imaginary distortion of space in relation to time whereby people or objects of one period can be moved to another.

time-wasting ▶ **noun** [mass noun] the action of wasting time.
■ the tactic of slowing down play towards the end of a match to prevent the opposition scoring.
– DERIVATIVES **time-waster** noun.

time-worn ▶ **adjective** damaged or impaired, or made less striking or attractive, as a result of age or much use: *the time-worn faces of the veterans | a time-worn aphorism.*

time zone ▶ **noun** see **ZONE** (sense 1).

timid ▶ **adjective** (**timider**, **timidest**) showing a lack of courage or confidence; easily frightened: *I was too timid to ask for what I wanted.*
– DERIVATIVES **timidity** noun, **timidly** adverb, **timidness** noun.
– ORIGIN mid 16th cent.: from Latin *timidus*, from *timere* 'to fear'.

timing ▶ **noun** [mass noun] the choice, judgement, or control of when something should be done: *one of the secrets of cricket is good timing.*
■ [count noun] a particular point or period of time when something happens. ■ (in an internal-combustion engine) the times when the valves open and close, and the time of the ignition spark, in relation to the movement of the piston in the cylinder.

Timişoara /ˌtɪmɪˈʃwɑːrə/ an industrial city in western Romania; pop. 325,300 (1993). Formerly part of Hungary, the city has substantial Hungarian and German-speaking populations. Hungarian name **TEMESVÁR**.

timocracy /tɪˈmɒkrəsi/ ▶ **noun** (pl. **-ies**) chiefly Philosophy **1** a form of government in which possession of property is required in order to hold office.
2 a form of government in which rulers are motivated by ambition or love of honour.
– DERIVATIVES **timocratic** adjective.
– ORIGIN late 15th cent.: from Old French *timocracie*, via medieval Latin from Greek *timokratia*, from *timē* 'honour, worth' + *-kratia* 'power'. Sense 1 reflects Aristotle's usage, sense 2 Plato's.

timolol /ˈtɪməlɒl/ ▶ **noun** [mass noun] Medicine a synthetic compound which acts as a beta blocker and is used to treat hypertension, migraine, and glaucoma.
• Chem. formula: $C_{13}H_{24}N_4O_3$.
– ORIGIN 1970s: from *tim-* (of unknown origin) + *(propran)olol*.

Timor /ˈtiːmɔː/ the largest of the Lesser Sunda Islands, in the southern Malay Archipelago; pop. East Timor 714,000, West Timor 3,383,500 (est. 1990).

> The island was formerly divided into Dutch West Timor and Portuguese East Timor. In 1950 West Timor was absorbed into the newly formed Republic of Indonesia. In 1975 East Timor declared itself independent but was invaded and occupied by Indonesia (see **EAST TIMOR**).

– DERIVATIVES **Timorese** /ˌtiːmɔːˈriːz/ adjective & noun.

Timor deer ▶ **noun** another term for **RUSA**.

timorous ▶ **adjective** showing or suffering from nervousness or a lack of confidence: *a timorous voice.*
– DERIVATIVES **timorously** adverb, **timorousness** noun.
– ORIGIN late Middle English (in the sense 'feeling fear'): from Old French *temoreus*, from medieval Latin *timorosus*, from Latin *timor* 'fear', from *timere* 'to fear'.

Timor pony ▶ **noun** a small stocky pony of a breed originally from Timor, widely used on ranches in Australia.

Timor Sea an arm of the Indian Ocean between Timor and NW Australia.

timothy (also **timothy grass**) ▶ **noun** [mass noun] a Eurasian grass which is widely grown for grazing and hay. It is naturalized in North America, where many cultivars have been developed.
• *Phleum pratense*, family Gramineae.
– ORIGIN mid 18th cent.: named after *Timothy* Hanson, the American farmer who introduced it to Carolina from New York (*c.*1720).

Timothy, Epistle to either of two books of the New Testament, epistles of St Paul addressed to St Timothy.

Timothy, St (1st century AD), convert and disciple of St Paul. Traditionally he was the first bishop of Ephesus and was martyred in the reign of the Roman emperor Nerva. Feast day, January 22 or 26.

timpani /ˈtɪmpəni/ (also **tympani**) ▶ **plural noun** kettledrums, especially when played by one musician in an orchestra.
– DERIVATIVES **timpanist** noun.
– ORIGIN late 19th cent.: from Italian, plural of *timpano* 'kettledrum', from Latin *tympanum* 'drum' (see **TYMPANUM**).

Timur /tiːˈmʊə/ Tartar name of **TAMERLANE**.

tin ▶ **noun** **1** [mass noun] a silvery-white metal, the chemical element of atomic number 50. (Symbol: **Sn**)
■ short for **TINPLATE**. ■ Brit. informal, dated money.

> Tin is quite a rare element, occurring chiefly in the mineral cassiterite. Pure crystalline tin exists in two allotropic modifications, the metallic form (**white tin**), and a semimetallic form (**grey tin**). It is used in various alloys, notably bronze, and for electroplating iron or steel sheets to make tinplate.

2 a metal container, in particular:
■ chiefly Brit. an airtight sealed container for preserving food, made of tinplate or aluminium; a can: *she had opened **a tin of** beans.* ■ a lidded airtight container made of tinplate or aluminium: *Albert got out the biscuit tin.* ■ the contents of such a container: *how many **tins of** paint would it take?* ■ an open metal container for baking food: *grease a 450 g loaf tin.* ■ Brit. a rectangular loaf of bread baked in such a tin.
▶ **verb** (**tinned**, **tinning**) [with obj.] cover with a thin layer of tin: *the copper pans are correctly tinned inside.*
– PHRASES **have a tin ear** be tone-deaf. **put the tin lid on** another way of saying ***put the lid on*** (see **LID**).
– ORIGIN Old English, of Germanic origin; related to Dutch *tin* and German *Zinn*.

tinamou /ˈtɪnəmuː/ ▶ **noun** a ground-dwelling tropical American bird that looks somewhat like a grouse but is related to the ratites.
• Family Tinamidae: several genera and many species.
– ORIGIN late 18th cent.: via French from Galibi *tinamu*.

Tinbergen[1] /ˈtɪnbəːɡ(ə)n/, Jan (1903–94), Dutch economist. He shared the first Nobel Prize for Economics (1969) with Ragnar Frisch for his pioneering work on econometrics. He was the brother of the zoologist Nikolaas Tinbergen.

Tinbergen[2] /ˈtɪnbəːɡ(ə)n/, Nikolaas (1907–88), Dutch zoologist. From his studies he found that much animal behaviour was innate and stereotyped, and he introduced the concept of displacement activity. Tinbergen shared a Nobel Prize in 1973 with Karl von Frisch and Konrad Lorenz. He was the brother of the economist Jan Tinbergen.

tin can ▶ **noun** a tinplate or aluminium container for preserving food, especially an empty one.

tinctorial /tɪŋ(k)ˈtɔːrɪəl/ ▶ **adjective** technical of or relating to dyeing, colouring, or staining properties.
– ORIGIN mid 17th cent.: from Latin *tinctorius* (from *tinctor* 'dyer', from *tingere* 'to dye or colour') + **-AL**.

tincture /ˈtɪŋ(k)tʃə/ ▶ **noun** **1** a medicine made by dissolving a drug in alcohol: *the remedies can be administered in form of tinctures* | [mass noun] *a bottle containing **tincture of** iodine.*
■ Brit. informal an alcoholic drink.
2 a slight trace of something: *she could not keep **a tincture of** bitterness out of her voice.*
3 Heraldry any of the conventional colours (including the metals and stains, and often the furs) used in coats of arms.
▶ **verb** (**be tinctured**) be tinged, flavoured, or imbued with a slight amount of: *Arthur's affability was tinctured with faint sarcasm.*
– ORIGIN late Middle English (denoting a dye or pigment): from Latin *tinctura* 'dyeing', from *tingere* 'to dye or colour'. Sense 2 (early 17th cent.) comes

from the obsolete sense 'imparted quality', likened to a tint imparted by a dye.

tinder ▶ **noun** [mass noun] dry, flammable material, such as wood or paper, used for lighting a fire.
– DERIVATIVES **tindery** adjective.
– ORIGIN Old English *tynder, tyndre*, of Germanic origin; related to Dutch *tonder* and German *Zunder*.

tinderbox ▶ **noun** historical a box containing tinder, flint, a steel, and other items for kindling fires.

tinder-dry ▶ **adjective** (of vegetation) extremely dry and flammable.

tinder fungus ▶ **noun** a bracket fungus with a hard hoof-like upper surface, growing chiefly on birch and beech. Also called **HOOF FUNGUS**.
● *Fomes fomentarius*, family Polyporaceae, class Hymenomycetes.

tine /tʌɪn/ ▶ **noun** a prong or sharp point, such as that on a fork or antler.
– DERIVATIVES **tined** adjective [in combination] *a three-tined fork*.
– ORIGIN Old English *tind*, of Germanic origin; related to German *Zinne* 'pinnacle'.

tinea /ˈtɪnɪə/ ▶ **noun** technical term for **RINGWORM**.
– ORIGIN late Middle English: from Latin, 'worm'.

tinfoil ▶ **noun** [mass noun] foil made of aluminium or a similar grey metal, used especially for covering or wrapping food.

ting ▶ **noun** a sharp, clear ringing sound, such as when a glass is struck by a metal object.
▶ **verb** [no obj.] emit such a sound.
– ORIGIN late Middle English (as a verb): imitative. The noun dates from the early 17th cent.

tinge ▶ **verb** (**tinging** or **tingeing**) [with obj.] (often **be tinged**) colour slightly: *a mass of white blossom* ***tinged with*** *pink* | [with obj. and complement] *towards the sun the sky was tinged crimson.*
■ figurative have a slight influence on: *this visit will be tinged with sadness.*
▶ **noun** a tendency towards or trace of some colour: *there was a faint pink tinge to the sky.*
■ figurative a slight trace of a feeling or quality.
– ORIGIN late 15th cent.: from Latin *tingere* 'to dip or colour'. The noun dates from the mid 18th cent.

tin glaze ▶ **noun** a glaze made white and opaque by the addition of tin oxide.
– DERIVATIVES **tin-glazed** adjective.

tingle[1] ▶ **verb** [no obj.] (of a person or a part of their body) experience a slight prickling or stinging sensation: *she was tingling with excitement.*
■ [with obj.] cause to experience such a sensation: *a standing ovation that tingled your spine.* ■ [no obj., with adverbial] (of such a sensation) be experienced in a part of one's body: *shivers tingled down the length of her spine.*
▶ **noun** a slight prickling or stinging sensation: *she felt a tingle in the back of her neck* | *a tingle of anticipation.*
– ORIGIN late Middle English: perhaps a variant of **TINKLE**. The original notion was perhaps 'ring in response to a loud noise', but the term was very early applied to the result of hearing something shocking.

tingle[2] ▶ **noun** an S-shaped metal clip used to support heavy panes of glass or slates on a roof.
– ORIGIN Middle English (denoting a small tack): related to Middle High German *zingel* 'small tack or hook', probably from a Germanic base meaning 'fasten'. The current sense dates from the late 19th cent.

tingly ▶ **adjective** (**tinglier**, **tingliest**) causing or experiencing a slight prickling or stinging sensation: *a tingly sense of excitement.*

tin god ▶ **noun** a person, especially a minor official, who is pompous and self-important.
■ an object of unjustified veneration or respect.

tin hat ▶ **noun** informal, chiefly Brit. a soldier's steel helmet.
– PHRASES **put the tin hat on** another way of saying ***put the lid on*** (see **LID**).

tinhorn ▶ **noun** US informal a contemptible person, especially one pretending to have money, influence, or ability.

tinker ▶ **noun 1** (especially in former times) a person who travels from place to place mending pans, kettles, and other metal utensils as a way of making a living.
■ Brit., chiefly derogatory a gypsy or other person living in an itinerant community. ■ Brit. informal a mischievous or persistently naughty child.
2 an act of attempting to repair something.
▶ **verb** [no obj.] attempt to repair or improve something in a casual or desultory way, often to no useful effect: *he spent hours* ***tinkering with*** *the car.*
■ [with obj.] archaic attempt to mend (something) in such a way.
– PHRASES **not give a tinker's curse** (or **cuss** or **damn**) informal not care at all.
– DERIVATIVES **tinkerer** noun.
– ORIGIN Middle English (first recorded in Anglo-Latin as a surname): of unknown origin.

tinkerbird ▶ **noun** a small African barbet with a monotonous metallic call like a hammer striking an anvil, repeated for long periods.
● Genus *Pogonulus*, family Capitonidae: several species. Alternative name: **tinker barbet**.

tinkle ▶ **verb 1** make or cause to make a light, clear ringing sound: [no obj.] *cool water tinkled in the stone fountains* | [with obj.] *the maid tinkled a bell.*
2 [no obj.] informal urinate.
▶ **noun 1** a light, clear ringing sound: *the distant tinkle of a cow bell.*
■ Brit. informal a telephone call: *I'll* ***give them a tinkle****.*
2 informal an act of urinating.
– DERIVATIVES **tinkly** adjective.
– ORIGIN late Middle English (also in the sense 'tingle'): frequentative of obsolete *tink* 'to chink or clink', of imitative origin.

tinktinkie /tɪŋkˈtɪŋki/ ▶ **noun** (pl. **-ies**) South African term for **CISTICOLA**.
– ORIGIN Afrikaans, imitative of its call.

tin Lizzie ▶ **noun** N. Amer. informal, dated a motor car, especially a very early Ford.
– ORIGIN early 20th cent.: *Lizzie*, a pet form of the given name *Elizabeth*.

tinned ▶ **adjective 1** chiefly Brit. (of food) preserved in a sealed airtight container made of tinplate or aluminium: *tinned fruit.*
2 [attrib.] covered or coated in tin or a tin alloy.

tinner ▶ **noun** a tin miner or tinsmith.

tinning ▶ **noun** [mass noun] **1** the action of covering or coating something with tin.
2 tin mining.

tinnitus /tɪˈnʌɪtəs, ˈtɪnɪtəs/ ▶ **noun** [mass noun] Medicine ringing or buzzing in the ears.
– ORIGIN mid 19th cent.: from Latin, from *tinnire* 'to ring, tinkle', of imitative origin.

tinny ▶ **adjective 1** having a displeasingly thin, metallic sound: *tinny music played in the background.*
■ (of an object) made of thin or poor-quality metal: *a tinny little car.* ■ having an unpleasantly metallic taste: *canned artichokes taste somewhat tinny.*
2 Austral./NZ informal lucky. [ORIGIN: early 20th cent.: from *tin* 'luck' (literally 'money, cash') + **-Y**[1].]
▶ **noun** (also **tinnie**) (pl. **-ies**) Austral./NZ informal a can of beer.
– DERIVATIVES **tinnily** adverb, **tinniness** noun.

tin-opener ▶ **noun** chiefly Brit. a tool for opening tins of food.

Tin Pan Alley the name given to a district in New York (28th Street, between 5th Avenue and Broadway) where many songwriters, arrangers, and music publishers were formerly based.
■ [as noun] [usu. as modifier] the world of composers and publishers of popular music.

tinplate ▶ **noun** [mass noun] sheet steel or iron coated with tin.
▶ **verb** [with obj.] [often as adj. **tinplated**] coat (an object) with tin.

tinpot ▶ **adjective** [attrib.] informal (especially of a country or its leader) having or showing poor leadership or organization: *a tinpot dictator.*

tinsel ▶ **noun** [mass noun] a form of decoration consisting of thin strips of shiny metal foil attached to a long piece of thread.
■ showy or superficial attractiveness or glamour: *his taste for the tinsel of the art world.*
– DERIVATIVES **tinselly** adjective.
– ORIGIN late Middle English (denoting fabric either interwoven with metallic thread or spangled): from Old French *estincele* 'spark', or *estinceler* 'to sparkle', based on Latin *scintilla* 'a spark'.

tinselled (US **tinseled**) ▶ **adjective** decorated or adorned with tinsel.
■ showily or superficially attractive or glamorous: *his tinselled sentiments.*

Tinseltown ▶ **noun** [mass noun] derogatory Hollywood, or the superficially glamorous world it represents.

tinsmith ▶ **noun** a person who makes or repairs articles of tin or tinplate.

tinsnips ▶ **plural noun** a pair of clippers for cutting sheet metal.

tin soldier ▶ **noun** a toy soldier made of metal.

tinstone ▶ **noun** another term for **CASSITERITE**.

tint ▶ **noun 1** a shade or variety of colour: *the sky was taking on an apricot tint.*
■ Printing an area of faint even colour printed as a half-tone, used for highlighting overprinted text. ■ a set of parallel engraved lines to give uniform shading. ■ a trace of something: ***a tint of*** *glamour.*
2 an artificial dye for colouring the hair.
■ an application of such a substance: *peering into the mirror to see if any white hair showed after her last tint.*
▶ **verb** [with obj.] (usu. **be tinted**) colour (something) slightly; tinge: *her skin was tinted with delicate colour* | [as adj. **tinted**] *a black car with tinted windows.*
■ dye (someone's hair) with a tint.
– DERIVATIVES **tinter** noun.
– ORIGIN early 18th cent.: alteration (perhaps influenced by Italian *tinta*) of obsolete *tinct* 'to colour, tint', from Latin *tinctus* 'dyeing', from *tingere* 'to dye or colour'.

Tintagel /tɪnˈtadʒəl/ a village on the coast of northern Cornwall. Nearby are the ruins of Tintagel Castle, the legendary birthplace of King Arthur.

tintinnabulation /ˌtɪntɪnabjʊˈleɪʃ(ə)n/ ▶ **noun** a ringing or tinkling sound.
– ORIGIN mid 19th cent.: from Latin *tintinnabulum* 'tinkling bell' (from *tintinnare*, reduplication of *tinnire* 'to ring, tinkle') + **-ATION**.

tinto /ˈtɪntəʊ/ ▶ **noun** (pl. **-os**) [mass noun] Spanish or Portuguese red wine.
– ORIGIN Spanish, literally 'tinted, dark-coloured'.

Tintoretto /ˌtɪntəˈrɛtəʊ/ (1518–94), Italian painter; born *Jacopo Robusti*. His work was typified by a mannerist style, including unusual viewpoints and chiaroscuro effects.

tintype ▶ **noun** historical a photograph taken as a positive on a thin tin plate.

tinware ▶ **noun** [mass noun] kitchen utensils or other articles made of tin or tinplate.

tin whistle ▶ **noun** a small flute-like instrument made from a thin metal tube, with six finger holes of varying size on top and no thumb holes.

tiny ▶ **adjective** (**tinier**, **tiniest**) very small: *a tiny hummingbird.*
▶ **noun** (pl. **-ies**) informal a very young child.
– DERIVATIVES **tinily** adverb, **tininess** noun.
– ORIGIN late 16th cent.: extension of obsolete *tine*, 'small, diminutive', of unknown origin.

-tion ▶ **suffix** forming nouns of action, condition, etc. such as *completion, relation.*
– ORIGIN from Latin participial stems ending in *-t* + **-ION**.

tip[1] ▶ **noun** the pointed or rounded end or extremity of something slender or tapering: *George pressed the tips of his fingers together* | *the northern tip of Scotland.*
■ a small piece or part fitted to the end of an object: *the rubber tip of the walking stick.*
▶ **verb** (**tipped**, **tipping**) [with obj.] **1** [usu. as adj. **tipped**] attach to or cover the end or extremity of: *mountains tipped with snow* | [in combination] *steel-tipped spears.*
■ colour (something) at its end or edge: *velvety red petals tipped with white.*
2 (**tip a page in**) (in bookbinding) paste a single page, typically an illustration, to the neighbouring page of a book by a thin line of paste down its inner margin.
– PHRASES **on the tip of one's tongue** used to indicate that one is almost but not quite able to bring a particular word or name to mind: *his name's on the tip of my tongue!* ■ used to indicate that someone is about to utter a comment or question but thinks better of it: *it was on the tip of his tongue to ask what was the matter.* **the tip of the iceberg** see **ICEBERG**.
– ORIGIN late Middle English: from Old Norse *typpi* (noun), *typpa* (verb), *typptr* 'tipped'; related to **TOP**[1].

tip[2] ▶ **verb** (**tipped**, **tipping**) **1** overbalance or cause to overbalance so as to fall or turn over: [no obj.] *the hay caught fire when the candle* ***tipped over*** | [with obj.] *a youth sprinted past,* ***tipping over*** *her glass.*
■ be or cause to be in a sloping position with one end or side higher than the other: [with obj. and adverbial] *I tipped my seat back, preparing myself for sleep* | [no obj.,

with adverbial] *the car had tipped to one side.* ■ [with obj. and adverbial of direction] cause (the contents of a container) to be emptied out by holding it at an angle: *Sarah tipped the washing-up water down the sink.* ■ [no obj.] (**it tips down**, **it is tipping down**, etc.) Brit. rain heavily.
2 [with obj.] strike or touch lightly: *I tipped his hoof with the handle of a knife.*
■ [with obj. and adverbial of direction] cause (an object) to move somewhere by striking or touching it in this way: *his twenty-yard shot was tipped over the bar by Nixon.*
3 [no obj.] (**tip off**) Basketball put the ball in play by throwing it up between two opponents.
▶ **noun 1** Brit. a place where rubbish is left.
■ informal a dirty or untidy place: *your room's an absolute tip!*
2 Baseball a pitched ball that is slightly deflected by the batter.
– PHRASES **tip one's hand** US informal reveal one's intentions inadvertently. **tip one's hat** (or **cap**) raise or touch one's hat or cap as a way of greeting or acknowledging someone. **tip** (or **turn**) **the scales** (or **balance**) (of a circumstance or event) be the deciding factor; make the critical difference: *her proven current form* ***tips the scales in her favour.*** **tip** (or **turn**) **the scales at** have a weight of (a specified amount): *this phone tips the scales at only 150 g.*
– ORIGIN late Middle English: perhaps of Scandinavian origin, influenced later by **TIP**[1] in the sense 'touch with a tip or point'. Current senses of the noun date from the mid 19th cent.

tip[3] ▶ **noun 1** a sum of money given to someone as a way of rewarding them for their services.
2 a small but useful piece of practical advice.
■ a prediction or piece of expert information about the likely winner of a race or contest: *Barry had a* ***hot tip.***
▶ **verb** (**tipped**, **tipping**) [with obj.] **1** give (someone) a sum of money as a way of rewarding them for their services: [with two objs] *I tipped her five dollars* | [no obj.] *that sort never tip.*
2 (usu. **be tipped**) Brit. predict as likely to win or achieve something: *Christine was widely* ***tipped to*** *get the job.*
– PHRASES **tip someone off** informal give someone information about something, typically in discreet or confidential way: *they were arrested after police were tipped off by local residents.* **tip someone the wink** Brit. informal give someone private information.
– ORIGIN early 17th cent. (in the sense 'give, hand, pass'): probably from **TIP**[1].

tip-and-run ▶ **noun** [mass noun] an informal way of playing cricket in which the batsman must run after every hit.
■ [as modifier] (of a military raid) executed swiftly and followed by immediate withdrawal.

tipcat ▶ **noun** [mass noun] chiefly historical a game in which a piece of wood tapered at both ends is struck at one end with a stick so as to spring up and is then knocked away by the same player.
■ [count noun] a tapered piece of wood of this kind.

tipi ▶ **noun** variant spelling of **TEPEE**.

tip-in ▶ **noun** Basketball a score made by tipping a rebound into the basket.

tip-off ▶ **noun** informal a piece of information, typically one given in a discreet or confidential way.

tipper ▶ **noun 1** (also **tipper truck** or **lorry**) a truck having a rear platform which can be raised at its front end, thus enabling a load to be discharged.
2 [usu. with adj.] a person who leaves a specified sort of tip as a reward for services they have received: *he's a big tipper.*
3 a person who dumps waste, especially illegally.

Tipperary /ˌtɪpəˈrɛːri/ a county in the centre of the Republic of Ireland, in the province of Munster; county town, Clonmel.

tippet ▶ **noun** a woman's long cape or scarf, typically of fur or similar material.
■ a similar ceremonial garment worn especially by the clergy. ■ historical a long, narrow strip of cloth forming part of or attached to a hood or sleeve.
– ORIGIN Middle English: probably from an Anglo-Norman derivative of the noun **TIP**[1].

Tippett /ˈtɪpɪt/, Sir Michael (Kemp) (1905–98), English composer. He established his reputation with the oratorio *A Child of Our Time* (1941), which drew on jazz, madrigals, and spirituals besides classical sources. Other works include five operas, four symphonies, and several song cycles.

Tipp-Ex Brit. trademark ▶ **noun** [mass noun] a type of correction fluid.
▶ **verb** [with obj.] delete with correction fluid.
– ORIGIN 1960s: from German, from *tippen* 'to type' and Latin *ex* 'out'.

tipple ▶ **verb** [no obj.] **1** drink alcohol, especially habitually: *those who liked to tipple and gamble.*
2 (**it tipples down**, **it is tippling down**, etc.) Brit. informal rain heavily: *it was tippling down with rain.*
▶ **noun** informal an alcoholic drink.
– ORIGIN late 15th cent. (in the sense 'sell (alcoholic drink) by retail'): back-formation from **TIPPLER**[1].

tippler[1] ▶ **noun** a habitual drinker of alcohol.
– ORIGIN late Middle English (denoting a retailer of alcoholic liquor): of unknown origin.

tippler[2] ▶ **noun** a revolving frame or cage in which a truck is inverted to discharge its load.
– ORIGIN early 19th cent.: from dialect *tipple* 'tumble over' + **-ER**[1].

tippy ▶ **adjective** N. Amer. inclined to tilt or overturn; unsteady: *they crossed the water in tippy canoes.*

tippy-toe ▶ **verb** [no obj., with adverbial of direction] informal, chiefly US walk on the tips of one's toes; tiptoe: *he tippy-toed around the house.*
– PHRASES **on tippy-toe** (or **tippy-toes**) on the tips of one's toes; on tiptoe: *Kurt was mincing around on tippy-toes.*
– ORIGIN late 19th cent.: alteration of **TIPTOE**.

tipstaff ▶ **noun** a sheriff's officer; a bailiff.
– ORIGIN mid 16th cent. (first denoting a metal-tipped staff): contraction of *tipped staff* (carried by a bailiff).

tipster ▶ **noun** a person who gives tips, especially about the likely winner of a race or contest.

tipsy ▶ **adjective** (**tipsier**, **tipsiest**) slightly drunk.
– DERIVATIVES **tipsily** adverb, **tipsiness** noun.
– ORIGIN late 16th cent.: from the verb **TIP**[2] + **-SY**.

tipsy cake ▶ **noun** Brit. a sponge cake saturated with wine or spirits, typically served with custard.

tip-tilted ▶ **adjective** (especially of a person's nose) turned up at the tip.

tiptoe ▶ **verb** (**tiptoes**, **tiptoed**, **tiptoeing**) [no obj., with adverbial of direction] walk quietly and carefully with one's heels raised and one's weight on the balls of the feet: *Liz tiptoed out of the room.*
– PHRASES **on tiptoe** (or **tiptoes**) (N. Amer. also **on one's tiptoes**) with one's heels raised and one's weight on the balls of the feet, especially in order to move quietly or make oneself taller: *Jane stood on tiptoe to kiss him.*

tip-top ▶ **adjective** of the very best class or quality; excellent: *an athlete in tip-top condition.*
▶ **noun 1** the highest part or point of excellence.
2 N. Amer. a line guide on a fishing rod.

Tiptronic ▶ **noun** trademark a type of electronic gearbox.

tip-up ▶ **adjective** denoting a seat in a theatre or other public place that is designed to tilt up vertically when unoccupied so as to let people pass easily.
■ denoting a rear platform of a truck or lorry that may be raised up, enabling a load to be discharged.
▶ **noun** N. Amer. a device used in ice-fishing in which a wire attached to the rod is tripped, raising a signal flag, when a fish takes the bait.

tirade /tʌɪˈreɪd, tɪ-/ ▶ **noun** a long, angry speech of criticism or accusation: *a tirade of abuse.*
– ORIGIN early 19th cent.: from French, literally 'long speech', from Italian *tirata* 'volley', from *tirare* 'to pull'.

tirailleur /ˌtɪrʌɪˈjəː/ ▶ **noun** chiefly historical a sharpshooter.
– ORIGIN late 18th cent. (originally denoting a skirmisher employed in the wars of the French Revolution): French, from *tirailler* 'shoot independently', from *tirer* 'shoot, draw'.

tiramisu /ˌtɪrəmɪˈsuː/ ▶ **noun** [mass noun] an Italian dessert consisting of layers of sponge cake soaked in coffee and brandy or liqueur with powdered chocolate and mascarpone cheese.
– ORIGIN Italian, from the phrase *tira mi sù* 'pick me up'.

Tirana /tɪˈrɑːnə/ (also **Tiranë**) the capital of Albania, on the Ishm River in central Albania; pop. 210,000 (1990). Founded by the Turks in the 17th century, it became capital of Albania in 1920.

tire[1] ▶ **verb** [no obj.] become in need of rest or sleep; grow weary: *soon the ascent grew steeper and he began to tire.*
■ [with obj.] cause to feel in need of rest or sleep; weary: *the journey had tired her* | *the training* ***tired*** *us* ***out.*** ■ (**tire of**) lose interest in; become bored with: *she will stay with him until he tires of her.* ■ [with obj.] exhaust the patience or interest of; bore: *it tired her that Eddie felt important because he was involved behind the scenes.*
– ORIGIN Old English *tēorian* 'fail, come to an end', also 'become physically exhausted', of unknown origin.

tire[2] ▶ **noun** US spelling of **TYRE**.

tired ▶ **adjective** in need of sleep or rest; weary: *Fisher rubbed his tired eyes* | *she was* ***tired out*** *now that the strain was over.*
■ [predic.] (**tired of**) bored with: *I have to look after these animals when you get tired of them.* ■ (of a thing) no longer fresh or in good condition: *a few boxes of tired vegetables.* ■ (especially of a statement or idea) boring or uninteresting because overfamiliar: *tired clichés like the 'information revolution'.*
– PHRASES **tired and emotional** humorous used euphemistically to indicate that someone is drunk.
– DERIVATIVES **tiredly** adverb, **tiredness** noun.

Tiree /tʌɪˈriː/ an island in the Inner Hebrides, to the west of the isles of Mull and Coll.

tire iron ▶ **noun** US a steel lever for removing tyres from wheel rims.

tireless ▶ **adjective** having or showing great effort or energy: *a tireless campaigner.*
– DERIVATIVES **tirelessly** adverb, **tirelessness** noun.

Tiresias /tʌɪˈriːsɪəs/ Greek Mythology a blind Theban prophet, so wise that even his ghost had its wits and was not a mere phantom. Legends account variously for his wisdom and blindness; some stories hold also that he spent seven years as a woman.

tiresome ▶ **adjective** causing one to feel bored or annoyed: *weeding is a tiresome but essential job.*
– DERIVATIVES **tiresomely** adverb [as submodifier] *a tiresomely predictable attitude*, **tiresomeness** noun.

Tîrgu Mureş /ˌtɪəguː ˈmʊərɛʃ/ a city in central Romania, on the River Mureş; pop. 165,500 (1993).

Tirich Mir /ˌtɪrɪtʃ ˈmɪə/ the highest peak in the Hindu Kush, in NW Pakistan, rising to 7,690 m (25,230 ft).

Tir-nan-Og /ˌtɪənanˈəʊg, Irish ˌtʲiːr nə ˈnoːg/ Irish Mythology a land of perpetual youth, the Irish equivalent of Elysium.
– ORIGIN Irish, literally 'land of the young'.

tiro ▶ **noun** variant spelling of **TYRO**.

Tirol /tiˈroːl/ German name for **TYROL**.

Tiruchirapalli /ˌtɪrʊtʃɪˈrɑːpəli/ a city in Tamil Nadu, southern India; pop. 387,000 (1991). Also called **TRICHINOPOLY**.

'tis chiefly poetic/literary ▶ **contraction of** it is.

Tisa /ˈtiːsa/ Serbian name for **TISZA**.

tisane /tɪˈzan/ ▶ **noun** [mass noun] a herb tea.
– ORIGIN 1930s: from French

Tishri /ˈtɪʃriː/ (also **Tisri** /ˈtɪzriː/) ▶ **noun** (in the Jewish calendar) the first month of the civil and seventh of the religious year, usually coinciding with parts of September and October.
– ORIGIN from Hebrew *tišrī*.

Tisiphone /tɪˈsɪfəni/ Greek Mythology one of the Furies.
– ORIGIN Greek, literally 'the avenger of blood'.

tissue /ˈtɪʃuː, ˈtɪsjuː/ ▶ **noun** [mass noun] **1** any of the distinct types of material of which animals or plants are made, consisting of specialized cells and their products: *inflammation is a reaction of living tissue to infection or injury* | (**tissues**) *the organs and tissues of the body.*
2 tissue paper.
■ [count noun] a disposable piece of absorbent paper, used especially as a handkerchief or for cleaning the skin. ■ rich or fine material of a delicate or gauzy texture: [as modifier] *the blue and silver tissue sari.*
3 [in sing.] an intricate structure or network made from a number of connected items: *such scandalous stories are* ***a tissue of lies.***
– DERIVATIVES **tissuey** adjective (only in sense 2).
– ORIGIN late Middle English: from Old French *tissu* 'woven', past participle of *tistre*, from Latin *texere* 'to weave'. The word originally denoted a rich material, often interwoven with gold or silver threads, later (mid 16th cent.) any woven fabric, hence the notion of 'intricacy'.

tissue culture ▶ **noun** [mass noun] Biology & Medicine the growth in an artificial medium of cells derived from living tissue.
■ [count noun] a cell culture of this kind.

tissue fluid ▶ **noun** [mass noun] Physiology extracellular fluid which bathes the cells of most tissues, arriving via blood capillaries and being removed via the lymphatic vessels.

tissue paper ▶ **noun** [mass noun] thin, soft paper, typically used for wrapping or protecting fragile or delicate articles.

tissue type ▶ **noun** a class of tissues which are immunologically compatible with one another.
▶ **verb** (**tissue-type**) [with obj.] determine the tissue type of.
■[as noun **tissue-typing**] the assessment of the immunological compatibility of tissue from separate sources, particularly prior to organ transplantation.

Tisza /ˈtiːsə/ a river in SE Europe, the longest tributary of the Danube, which rises in the Carpathian Mountains of western Ukraine and flows 960 km (600 miles) westwards into Hungary, then southwards, joining the Danube in Serbia north-west of Belgrade. Serbian name **TISA**.

Tit. ▶ **abbreviation for** Titus (in biblical references).

tit[1] ▶ **noun** a small songbird that searches acrobatically for insects among foliage and branches. Also called **TITMOUSE** or (in North America) **CHICKADEE**.
● Family Paridae: three genera, especially *Parus*, and numerous species. See **BLUE TIT**, **GREAT TIT**.
■used in names of similar or related birds, e.g. **penduline tit**, **New Zealand tit**.
– ORIGIN mid 16th cent.: probably of Scandinavian origin and related to Icelandic *titlingur* 'sparrow'; compare with **TITLING**[2] and **TITMOUSE**. Earlier senses were 'small horse' and 'girl'; the current sense dates from the early 18th cent.

tit[2] ▶ **noun** **1** vulgar slang a woman's breast.
■Brit. a foolish or ineffectual person.
2 military slang a push-button, especially one used to fire a gun or release a bomb.
– PHRASES **get on someone's tits** Brit. vulgar slang irritate someone intensely. **tits and ass** vulgar slang, chiefly N. Amer. (or chiefly Brit. **tits and bums**) used in reference to the use of crudely sexual images of women.
– ORIGIN Old English *tit* 'teat, nipple', of Germanic origin; related to Dutch *tit* and German *Zitze*. The vulgar slang use was originally US and dates from the early 20th cent.

tit[3] ▶ **noun** (in phrase **tit for tat**) the infliction of an injury or insult in return for one that one has suffered: [as modifier] *the conflict staggered on with tit-for-tat assassinations.*
– ORIGIN mid 16th cent.: variant of obsolete *tip for tap*.

Titan /ˈtʌɪt(ə)n/ **1** Greek Mythology any of the older gods who preceded the Olympians and were the children of Uranus (Heaven) and Gaia (Earth). Led by Cronus, they overthrew Uranus; Cronus' son, Zeus, then rebelled against his father and eventually defeated the Titans.
■[as noun **a titan**] a person or thing of very great strength, intellect, or importance: *a titan of American industry.*
2 Astronomy the largest satellite of Saturn, the fifteenth closest to the planet, discovered by C. Huygens in 1655 (diameter 5,150 km). It is unique in having a hazy atmosphere of nitrogen, methane, and oily hydrocarbons.

titanate /ˈtʌɪtəneɪt/ ▶ **noun** Chemistry a salt in which the anion contains both titanium and oxygen, in particular one of the anion TiO_3^{2-}.
– ORIGIN mid 19th cent.: from **TITANIUM** + **-ATE**[1].

titaness /ˈtʌɪtənɪs, -ˈnɛs/ ▶ **noun** a female Titan.

Titania /tɪˈtɑːnɪə, -ˈteɪnɪə/ Astronomy the largest satellite of Uranus, the fourteenth closest to the planet and having an icy surface, discovered by W. Herschel in 1787 (diameter 1,600 km).
– ORIGIN the name of the queen of the fairies in Shakespeare's *A Midsummer Night's Dream*.

Titanic a British passenger liner, the largest ship in the world when she was built and supposedly unsinkable, that struck an iceberg in the North Atlantic on her maiden voyage in April 1912 and sank with the loss of 1,490 lives.

titanic[1] ▶ **adjective** of exceptional strength, size, or power: *a series of titanic explosions.*
– DERIVATIVES **titanically** adverb.
– ORIGIN mid 17th cent. (in the sense 'relating to the sun'): from Greek *titanikos*, from *Titan* (see **TITAN**).

titanic[2] ▶ **adjective** Chemistry of titanium with a valency of four; of titanium(IV). Compare with **TITANOUS**.
– ORIGIN early 19th cent.: from **TITANIUM** + **-IC**.

titaniferous /ˌtʌɪtəˈnɪf(ə)rəs/ ▶ **adjective** (of rocks and minerals) containing or yielding titanium.

titanite /ˈtʌɪtənʌɪt/ ▶ **noun** another term for **SPHENE**.
– ORIGIN late 18th cent.: from **TITANIUM** + **-ITE**[1].

titanium /tʌɪˈteɪnɪəm, tɪ-/ ▶ **noun** [mass noun] the chemical element of atomic number 22, a hard silver-grey metal of the transition series, used in strong, light, corrosion-resistant alloys. (Symbol: **Ti**)
– ORIGIN late 18th cent.: from **TITAN**, on the pattern of *uranium*.

titanium dioxide (also **titanium oxide**) ▶ **noun** [mass noun] a white unreactive solid which occurs naturally as the mineral rutile and is used extensively as a white pigment.
● Chem. formula: TiO_2.

titanium white ▶ **noun** [mass noun] a white pigment consisting chiefly or wholly of titanium dioxide.

titanous /tʌɪˈtanəs/ ▶ **adjective** Chemistry of titanium with a lower valency, usually three. Compare with **TITANIC**[2].
– ORIGIN mid 19th cent.: from **TITANIUM**, on the pattern of words such as *ferrous*.

titbit (N. Amer. **tidbit**) ▶ **noun** a small piece of tasty food.
■a small and particularly interesting item of gossip or information.
– ORIGIN mid 17th cent. (as *tyd bit*, *tid-bit*): from dialect *tid* 'tender' (of unknown origin) + **BIT**[1].

titch (also **tich**) ▶ **noun** Brit. informal a small person.
– ORIGIN 1930s: from *Little Tich*, stage name of Harry Relph (1868–1928), an English music-hall comedian of small stature. He was given the nickname because he resembled Arthur Orton, the *Tich*borne claimant (see **ORTON**[1]).

titchy ▶ **adjective** (**titchier**, **titchiest**) Brit. informal very small: *a titchy theatre.*

titer ▶ **noun** US spelling of **TITRE**.

titfer ▶ **noun** Brit. informal a hat.
– ORIGIN 1930s: abbreviation of rhyming slang *tit for tat*.

tithe /tʌɪð/ ▶ **noun** one tenth of annual produce or earnings, formerly taken as a tax for the support of the church and clergy.
■(in certain religious denominations) a tenth of an individual's income pledged to the church. ■ [in sing.] archaic a tenth of a specified thing: *he hadn't said **a tithe** of the prayers he knew.*
▶ **verb** [with obj.] pay or give as a tithe: *he tithes 10 per cent of his income to the church.*
■historical subject to a tax of one tenth of income or produce.
– DERIVATIVES **tithable** adjective.
– ORIGIN Old English *tēotha* (adjective in the ordinal sense 'tenth', used in a specialized sense as a noun), *tēothian* (verb).

tithe barn ▶ **noun** a barn built to hold tithes paid in kind.

tithing /ˈtʌɪðɪŋ/ ▶ **noun** **1** [mass noun] the practice of taking or paying a tithe.
2 historical (in England) a group of ten householders who lived close together and were collectively responsible for each other's behaviour.
■a rural division, originally regarded as a tenth of a hundred.
– ORIGIN Old English *tēothung* (see **TITHE**, **-ING**[1]).

Tithonus /tɪˈθəʊnəs/ Greek Mythology a Trojan prince with whom the goddess Aurora fell in love. She asked Zeus to make him immortal but omitted to ask for eternal youth, and he became very old and decrepit although he talked perpetually. Tithonus prayed her to remove him from this world and she changed him into a grasshopper, which chirps ceaselessly.

titi[1] /ˈtiːtiː/ (also **titi monkey**) ▶ **noun** (pl. **titis**) a small forest-dwelling monkey of South America.
● Genus *Callicebus*, family Cebidae: several species.
– ORIGIN mid 18th cent.: from Aymara.

titi[2] /ˈtʌɪtʌɪ, ˈtiːtiː/ ▶ **noun** (pl. **titis**) another term for **LEATHERWOOD** (in sense 1).
– ORIGIN early 19th cent.: perhaps of American Indian origin.

Titian[1] /ˈtɪʃ(ə)n/ (*c.*1488–1576), Italian painter; Italian name *Tiziano Vecellio*. The most important painter of the Venetian school, he experimented with vivid colours and often broke conventions of composition. He painted many sensual mythological works, including *Bacchus and Ariadne* (*c.*1518–23).

Titian[2] /ˈtɪʃ(ə)n/ ▶ **adjective** (of hair) bright golden auburn: *a mass of Titian curls.*
– ORIGIN early 19th cent.: from **TITIAN**[1], by association with the bright auburn hair portrayed in many of his works.

Titicaca, Lake /ˌtɪtɪˈkɑːkɑː/ a lake in the Andes, on the border between Peru and Bolivia. At an altitude of 3,809 m (12,497 ft), it is the highest large lake in the world.

titihoya /ˌtɪtɪˈhɔɪə/ ▶ **noun** S. African an African plover related to the lapwing, with a distinctive plaintive cry.
● *Vanellus melanopterus*, family Charadridae. Alternative name: **black-winged plover**.
– ORIGIN 1940s: from Zulu, of imitative origin.

titillate /ˈtɪtɪleɪt/ ▶ **verb** [with obj.] stimulate or excite (someone), especially in a sexual way: *the press are paid to titillate the public* | [as adj. **titillating**] *she let slip titillating details about her clients.*
■archaic lightly touch; tickle.
– DERIVATIVES **titillatingly** adverb, **titillation** noun.
– ORIGIN early 17th cent.: from Latin *titillat-* 'tickled', from the verb *titillare*.

titivate /ˈtɪtɪveɪt/ ▶ **verb** [with obj.] informal make small enhancing alterations to (something): *she slapped on her warpaint and titivated her hair.*
■(**titivate oneself**) make oneself look smart.
– DERIVATIVES **titivation** noun.
– ORIGIN early 19th cent. (in early use, also as *tidivate*): perhaps from **TIDY**, on the pattern of *cultivate*.

USAGE The verbs **titillate** and **titivate** sound alike but do not have the same meaning. **Titillate** is the commoner word (occurring around eight times more frequently in the Oxford Reading Programme), and means 'stimulate or excite', as in *the press are paid to **titillate** the public.* **Titivate**, on the other hand, means 'adorn or smarten up', as in *she **titivated** her hair.*

titlark ▶ **noun** dialect a pipit, especially the meadow pipit.

title ▶ **noun** **1** the name of a book, composition, or other artistic work: *the author and title of the book.*
■a caption or credit in a film or broadcast. ■ a book, magazine, or newspaper considered as a publication: *the company publishes 400 titles a year.*
2 a name that describes someone's position or job: *Leese assumed the title of director-general.*
■a word such as *Lord* or *Dame* that is used before someone's name, or a form that is used instead of someone's name, to indicate high social or official rank: *he will inherit the title of Duke of Marlborough.* ■ a word such as *Mrs* or *Dr* that is used before someone's name to indicate their profession or marital status. ■ a descriptive or distinctive name that is earned or chosen: *the restaurant deserved the title of Best Restaurant of the Year.*
3 the position of being the champion of a major sports competition: *Davis won the world title for the first time in 1981.*
4 [mass noun] Law a right or claim to the ownership of property or to a rank or throne: *a grocery family had **title to** the property* | [count noun] *the buyer acquires a good title to the goods.*
5 (in church use) a fixed sphere of work and source of income as a condition for ordination.
■a parish church in Rome under a cardinal.
▶ **verb** [with obj. and complement] (usu. **be titled**) give a name to (a book, composition, or other work): *a report titled* The Lost Land.
– ORIGIN Old English *titul*, reinforced by Old French *title*, both from Latin *titulus* 'inscription, title'. The word originally denoted a placard or inscription placed on an object, giving information about it, hence a descriptive heading in a book or other composition.

title bar ▶ **noun** Computing a horizontal bar at the top of a window, bearing the name of the program and typically the name of the currently active document.

titled ▶ **adjective** (of a person) having a title indicating high social or official rank.

title deed ▶ **noun** a legal deed or document constituting evidence of a right, especially to ownership of property.

title music ▶ **noun** [mass noun] music played during

the credits at the beginning or end of a television programme or film.

title page ▶ **noun** a page at the beginning of a book giving its title and the names of the author and publisher.

title role ▶ **noun** the part in a play or film from which the work's title is taken.

titling[1] /ˈtʌɪtlɪŋ/ ▶ **noun** [mass noun] the action of providing something with a caption, title, or subtitles.
▪ titles, captions, or subtitles added to something such as a book cover or video. ▪ Printing type consisting only of capital letters and figures which are the full height of the type size.

titling[2] /ˈtɪtlɪŋ/ ▶ **noun** Scottish & N. English the meadow pipit.
– ORIGIN mid 16th cent.: from **TIT**[1] + **-LING**.

titmouse ▶ **noun** (pl. **titmice**) another term for **TIT**[1].
– ORIGIN Middle English: from **TIT**[1] + obsolete *mose* 'titmouse'. The change in the ending in the 16th cent. was due to association with **MOUSE**, probably because of the bird's size and quick movements.

Tito /ˈtiːtəʊ/ (1892–1980), Yugoslav Marshal and statesman, Prime Minister 1945–53 and President 1953–80; born *Josip Broz*. He organized a Communist resistance movement against the German invasion of Yugoslavia (1941). He became head of the new government at the end of the war, establishing Yugoslavia as a non-aligned Communist state with a federal constitution.
– DERIVATIVES **Titoism** noun, **Titoist** noun & adjective.

Titograd /ˈtiːtəʊgrad/ former name (1946–93) for **PODGORICA**.

titrate /tʌɪˈtreɪt, tɪ-/ ▶ **verb** [with obj.] Chemistry ascertain the amount of a constituent in (a solution) by measuring the volume of a known concentration of reagent required to complete a reaction with it, typically using an indicator.
▪ Medicine continuously measure and adjust the balance of (a physiological function or drug dosage).
– DERIVATIVES **titratable** adjective, **titration** noun.
– ORIGIN late 19th cent.: from French *titrer* (from *titre* in the sense 'fineness of alloyed gold or silver)') + **-ATE**[3].

titre /ˈtʌɪtə, ˈtiːtə/ (US **titer**) ▶ **noun** Chemistry the concentration of a solution as determined by titration.
▪ Medicine the concentration of an antibody, as determined by finding the highest dilution at which it is still able to cause agglutination of the antigen.
– ORIGIN mid 19th cent.: from French, from *titrer* (see **TITRATE**).

ti tree ▶ **noun** variant spelling of **TEA TREE** (in sense 1).

titter ▶ **verb** [no obj.] give a short, half-suppressed laugh; giggle: *her stutter caused the children to titter.*
▶ **noun** a short, half-suppressed laugh.
– DERIVATIVES **titterer** noun, **titteringly** adverb.
– ORIGIN early 17th cent.: imitative.

tittivate ▶ **verb** archaic spelling of **TITIVATE**.

tittle ▶ **noun** [in sing.] a tiny amount or part of something: *the rules have* **not** *been altered* **one jot or tittle** *since.*
– ORIGIN late Middle English: from Latin *titulus* (see **TITLE**), in medieval Latin 'small stroke, accent'; the phrase *jot or tittle* is from Matt. 5:18.

tittle-tattle ▶ **noun** [mass noun] idle talk; gossip.
▶ **verb** [no obj.] engage in such talk.
– ORIGIN early 16th cent.: reduplication of **TATTLE**.

tittup /ˈtɪtəp/ ▶ **verb** (**tittuped**, **tittuping** or **tittupped**, **tittupping**) [no obj., with adverbial of direction] chiefly Brit. move with jerky or exaggerated movements: *Nicky came tittupping along in a rakish mood.*
– ORIGIN late 17th cent. (as a noun): perhaps imitative of hoof-beats.

titty (also **tittie**) ▶ **noun** (pl. **-ies**) another term for **TIT**[2].

titubation /ˌtɪtjʊˈbeɪʃ(ə)n/ ▶ **noun** [mass noun] Medicine nodding movement of the head or body, especially as caused by a nervous disorder.
– ORIGIN mid 17th cent.: from Latin *titubatio(n-)*, from *titubare* 'to totter'.

titular /ˈtɪtjʊlə/ ▶ **adjective 1** holding or constituting a purely formal position or title without any real authority: *the queen is titular head of the Church of England | a titular post.*
▪ [attrib.] (of a cleric) nominally appointed to serve a diocese, abbey, or other foundation no longer in existence, and typically in fact having authority in another capacity.
2 denoting a person or thing from whom or which the name of an artistic work or similar is taken: *the work's titular song.*
▪ [attrib.] denoting any of the parish churches in Rome to which cardinals are formally appointed: *the priests of the titular churches.*
– ORIGIN late 16th cent. (in the sense 'existing only in name'): from French *titulaire* or modern Latin *titularis*, from *titulus* (see **TITLE**).

titularly ▶ **adverb** in name or in name only: *he was titularly a chief petty officer.*

Titus /ˈtʌɪtəs/ (AD 39–81), Roman emperor 79–81, son of Vespasian; full name *Titus Vespasianus Augustus*; born *Titus Flavius Vespasianus*. In 70 he ended a revolt in Judaea with the conquest of Jerusalem.

Titus, Epistle to a book of the New Testament, an epistle of St Paul addressed to St Titus.

Titus, St (1st century AD), Greek churchman. A convert and helper of St Paul, he was traditionally the first bishop of Crete. Feast day (in the Eastern Church) 23 August; (in the Western Church) 6 February.

Tiv /tɪv/ ▶ **noun** (pl. same or **Tivs**) **1** a member of a people of SE Nigeria.
2 [mass noun] the Benue-Congo language of this people, with about 1.5 million speakers.
▶ **adjective** of or relating to this people or their language.
– ORIGIN the name in Tiv.

Tiwa /ˈtiːwə/ (also **Tigua**) ▶ **noun** (pl. same or **Tiwas**)
1 a member of a Pueblo Indian people living mainly in the region of Taos, New Mexico.
2 [mass noun] the Tanoan language of this people, with fewer than 5,000 speakers. (Not the same as Tewa.)
▶ **adjective** of or relating to this people or their language.
– ORIGIN the name in Tiwa.

tiyin /tiːˈjɪn/ ▶ **noun** (pl. same or **tiyins**) a monetary unit of Kyrgyzstan, equal to one hundredth of a som.

tizzy (also **tizz**) ▶ **noun** (pl. **-ies**) [in sing.] informal a state of nervous excitement or agitation: *he* **got into a tizzy** *and was talking absolute tosh.*
– ORIGIN 1930s (originally US): of unknown origin.

T-junction ▶ **noun** a junction in the shape of a 'T', in particular a road junction at which one road joins another at right angles without crossing it.

TKO Boxing ▶ **abbreviation for** technical knockout.

Tl ▶ **symbol for** the chemical element thallium.

Tlaxcala /tlɑːsˈkɑːlə/ a state of east central Mexico.
▪ its capital city; pop. 25,000 (est. 1990).

TLC informal ▶ **abbreviation for** tender loving care.

Tlemcen /tlɛmˈsɛn/ a city in NW Algeria; pop. 146,000 (1989). In the 13th–15th centuries it was the capital of a Berber dynasty.

Tlingit /ˈklɪŋkɪt, ˈklɪŋgɪt, ˈtlɪŋ-/ ▶ **noun** (pl. same or **Tlingits**) **1** a member of an American Indian people of the coasts and islands of SE Alaska.
2 [mass noun] the language of this people, which has about 2,000 surviving speakers.
▶ **adjective** of or relating to this people or their language.
– ORIGIN the name in Tlingit.

T-lymphocyte ▶ **noun** Physiology a lymphocyte of a type produced or processed by the thymus gland and actively participating in the immune response. Also called **T-CELL**. Compare with **B-LYMPHOCYTE**.
– ORIGIN 1970s: from *T* for *thymus*.

TM (trademark in the US) ▶ **abbreviation for** Transcendental Meditation.

Tm ▶ **symbol for** the chemical element thulium.

tmesis /ˈtmiːsɪs/ ▶ **noun** (pl. **tmeses** /-siːz/) [mass noun] the separation of parts of a compound word by an intervening word or words, used mainly in informal speech for emphasis (e.g. *can't find it any-blooming-where*).
– ORIGIN mid 16th cent.: from Greek *tmēsis* 'cutting', from *temnein* 'to cut'.

TMV ▶ **abbreviation for** tobacco mosaic virus.

TN ▶ **abbreviation for** ▪ Tennessee (in official postal use). ▪ Tunisia (international vehicle registration).

tn ▶ **abbreviation for** ▪ US ton(s). ▪ town.

TNT ▶ **noun** [mass noun] a high explosive formed from toluene by substitution of three hydrogen atoms with nitro groups. It is relatively insensitive to shock and can be conveniently melted.
• Alternative name: **trinitrotoluene**; chem. formula: $C_7H_5(NO_2)_3$.

to ▶ **preposition 1** expressing motion in the direction of (a particular location): *walking down to the shops | my first visit to Africa.*
▪ expressing location, typically in relation to a specified point of reference: *forty miles to the south of the site | place the cursor to the left of the first word.* ▪ expressing a point reached at the end of a range or after a period of time: *a drop in profits from £105 m to around £75 m | from 1938 to 1945.* ▪ chiefly Brit. (in telling the time) before (the hour specified): *it's five to ten.* ▪ approaching or reaching (a particular condition): *Christopher's expression changed from amazement to joy | she was close to tears.* ▪ expressing the result of a process or action: *smashed to smithereens.*
2 identifying the person or thing affected: *you were terribly unkind to her.*
▪ identifying the recipient or intended recipient of something: *they donated £400 to the hospice | I am deeply grateful to my parents.*
3 identifying a particular relationship between one person and another: *he is married to his cousin Emma | economic adviser to the president.*
▪ in various phrases indicating how something is related to something else (often followed by a noun without a determiner): *made to order | a prelude to disaster.* ▪ indicating a rate of return on something, for example the distance travelled in exchange for fuel used, or an exchange rate that can be obtained in one currency for another: *it only does ten miles to the gallon.* ▪ (**to the**) Mathematics indicating the power (exponent) to which a number is raised: *ten to the minus thirty-three.*
4 indicating that two things are attached: *he had left his dog tied to a drainpipe |* figurative *they are inextricably linked to this island.*
5 concerning or likely to concern (something, especially something abstract): *a threat to world peace | a reference to Psalm 22:18.*
6 governing a phrase expressing someone's reaction to something: *to her astonishment, he smiled.*
7 used to introduce the second element in a comparison: *it's nothing to what it once was.*
8 placed before a debit entry in accounting.
▶ **infinitive marker 1** used with the base form of a verb to indicate that the verb is in the infinitive, in particular:
▪ expressing purpose or intention: *I set out to buy food | we tried to help | I am* **going to** *tell you a story.* ▪ expressing an outcome, result, or consequence: *he was left to die | he managed to escape.* ▪ expressing a cause: *I'm sorry to hear that.* ▪ indicating a desired or advisable action: *I'd love to go to France this summer | we asked her to explain | the leaflet explains how to start a course.* ▪ indicating a proposition that is known, believed, or reported about a specified person or thing: *a house that people believed to be haunted.* ▪ (**about to**) forming a future tense with reference to the immediate future: *he was about to sing.* ▪ after a noun, indicating its function or purpose: *a chair to sit on | something to eat.* ▪ after a phrase containing an ordinal number: *the first person to arrive.*
2 used without a verb following when the missing verb is clearly understood: *he asked her to come but she said she didn't want to.*
▶ **adverb** so as to be closed or nearly closed: *he pulled the door to behind him.*
– ORIGIN Old English *tō* (adverb and preposition), of West Germanic origin; related to Dutch *toe* and German *zu*.

toad ▶ **noun 1** a tailless amphibian with a short stout body and short legs, typically having dry warty skin that can exude poison.
• Several families in the order Anura, in particular Bufonidae, which includes the **European common toad** (*Bufo bufo*).
2 a contemptible or detestable person (used as a general term of abuse): *you're an arrogant little toad.*
– DERIVATIVES **toadish** adjective.
– ORIGIN Old English *tādde, tāda*, abbreviation of *tādige*, of unknown origin.

toad-eater ▶ **noun** archaic a toady.

toadfish ▶ **noun** (pl. same or **-fishes**) any of a number of fishes with a wide flattened head:
• a chiefly bottom-dwelling large-mouthed fish of warm seas that can produce loud grunts (family Batrachoididae: several genera). • Australian term for **PUFFERFISH**.

toadflax ▶ **noun** a Eurasian plant of the figwort family, typically having yellow or purplish snapdragon-like flowers and slender leaves.

• *Linaria* and related genera, family Scrophulariaceae: several species, in particular the common **yellow toadflax** (*L. vulgaris*) and **ivy-leaved toadflax** (*Cymbalaria muralis*).

toad-in-the-hole ▶ **noun** [mass noun] Brit. a dish consisting of sausages baked in batter.

toadlet ▶ **noun 1** a small kind of toad.
• Several genera, including *Pseudophryne* of Australia (family Myobatrachidae), and *Pelophryne* of SE Asia (family Bufonidae).
2 a tiny toad that has recently developed from a tadpole.

toadstone ▶ **noun** a gem, fossil tooth, or other stone formerly supposed to have been formed in the body of a toad, and credited with therapeutic or protective properties.

toadstool ▶ **noun** the spore-bearing fruiting body of a fungus, typically in the form of a rounded cap on a stalk, especially one that is believed to be inedible or poisonous. See also **MUSHROOM**.
– ORIGIN late Middle English: a fanciful name.

toady ▶ **noun** (pl. **-ies**) **1** a person who behaves obsequiously to someone important.
2 Australian term for **PUFFERFISH**.
▶ **verb** (**-ies, -ied**) [no obj.] act in an obsequious way: *she imagined him **toadying to** his rich clients.*
– DERIVATIVES **toadyish** adjective, **toadyism** noun.
– ORIGIN early 19th cent.: said to be a contraction of *toad-eater*, a charlatan's assistant who ate toads; toads were regarded as poisonous, and the assistant's survival was thought to be due to the efficacy of the charlatan's remedy.

to and fro ▶ **adverb** in a constant movement backwards and forwards or from side to side: *she cradled him, rocking him to and fro.*
▶ **verb** [no obj.] (**be toing and froing**) move constantly backwards and forwards: *the ducks were toing and froing* | [as noun **toing and froing**] *it does cost a lot, all this toing and froing up to London.*
■ repeatedly discuss or think about something without making any progress.
▶ **noun** [in sing.] constant movement backwards and forwards: *Wilkie watched the to and fro of their dancing.*
■ constant change in action, attitude, or focus.

toast[1] ▶ **noun 1** [mass noun] sliced bread browned on both sides by exposure to radiant heat, such as a grill or fire.
2 a call to a gathering of people to raise their glasses and drink together in honour of a person or thing, or an instance of drinking in this way: *he raised his glass in a toast to his son.*
■ [in sing.] a person or thing that is very popular or held in high regard by a particular group of people: *he found himself **the toast of** the baseball world.*
▶ **verb** [with obj.] **1** cook or brown (food, especially bread or cheese) by exposure to a grill, fire, or other source of radiant heat: *he sat by the fire and toasted a piece of bread* | [as adj. **toasted**] *a toasted cheese sandwich.*
■ [no obj.] (of food) cook or become brown in this way: *place under a hot grill until the nuts have toasted.* ■ warm (oneself or part of one's body) in front of a fire or other source or heat.
2 drink to the health or in honour of (someone or something) by raising one's glass together with others: *happy families toasting each other's health* | figurative *he is toasted by the trade as the outstanding dealer in children's books.*
– PHRASES **be toast** informal, chiefly N. Amer. be or be likely to become finished, defunct, or dead: *one mistake and you're toast.* **have someone on toast** Brit. informal be in a position to deal with someone as one wishes.
– ORIGIN late Middle English (as a verb in the sense 'burn as the sun does, parch'): from Old French *toster* 'roast', from Latin *torrere* 'parch'. The practice of drinking a toast (sense 2) goes back to the late 17th cent., and originated in naming a lady whose health the company was requested to drink, the idea being that the lady's name flavoured the drink like the pieces of spiced toast that were formerly placed in drinks such as wine.

toast[2] ▶ **verb** [no obj.] [usu. as noun **toasting**] (of a DJ) accompany a reggae backing track or music with improvised rhythmic speech.
– ORIGIN late 20th cent.: perhaps the same word as **TOAST**[1].

toaster ▶ **noun 1** an electrical device for making toast.
2 a DJ who accompanies reggae with improvised rhythmic speech.

toastie ▶ **noun** Brit. informal a toasted sandwich or snack.

toasting fork ▶ **noun** a long-handled fork for making toast in front of a fire.

toastmaster ▶ **noun** an official responsible for proposing toasts, introducing speakers, and making other formal announcements at a large social event.

toastmistress ▶ **noun** a female toastmaster.

toast rack ▶ **noun** a rack for holding slices of toast at table.
■ informal a tram or bus with full-width seats and open sides.

toasty ▶ **adjective** of or resembling toast.
■ chiefly N. Amer. comfortably warm: *a roaring fire may make a home seem toasty.*

Tob. ▶ **abbreviation for** (in biblical references) Tobit (Apocrypha).

tobacco ▶ **noun** (pl. **-os**) **1** [mass noun] a preparation of the nicotine-rich leaves of an American plant, which are cured by a process of drying and fermentation for smoking or chewing.
2 (also **tobacco plant**) the plant of the nightshade family which yields these leaves, native to tropical America. It is widely cultivated in warm regions, especially in the US and China.
• *Nicotiana tabacum*, family Solanaceae. See also **NICOTIANA**.
– ORIGIN mid 16th cent.: from Spanish *tabaco*; said to be from a Carib word denoting a tobacco pipe or from a Taino word for a primitive cigar, but perhaps from Arabic.

tobacco beetle ▶ **noun** another term for **CIGARETTE BEETLE**.

tobacco mosaic virus ▶ **noun** a virus that causes mosaic disease in tobacco, much used in biochemical research.

tobacconist ▶ **noun** chiefly Brit. a shopkeeper who sells cigarettes, tobacco, and other items used by smokers.

tobacco pipe ▶ **noun** another term for **PIPE** (in sense 2).

tobacco plant ▶ **noun** the plant which yields tobacco. See **TOBACCO** (sense 2).
■ an ornamental plant related to this. See **NICOTIANA**.

tobacco-stopper ▶ **noun** an instrument for pressing down the tobacco in a pipe.

Tobago see **TRINIDAD AND TOBAGO**.

Tobit /ˈtəʊbɪt/ a pious Israelite living during the Babylonian Captivity, described in the Apocrypha.
■ a book of the Apocrypha telling the story of Tobit.

toboggan ▶ **noun** a long, light, narrow vehicle, typically on runners, used for sliding downhill over snow or ice.
▶ **verb** [no obj.] [usu. as noun **tobogganing**] ride on a toboggan: *he thought he would enjoy the tobogganing.*
– DERIVATIVES **tobogganer** noun, **tobogganist** noun.
– ORIGIN early 19th cent.: from Canadian French *tabaganne*, from Micmac *topağan* 'sled'.

tobramycin /ˌtɒbrəˈmʌɪsɪn/ ▶ **noun** [mass noun] Medicine a bacterial antibiotic used chiefly to treat pseudomonas infections.
• The drug is obtained from the bacterium *Streptomyces tenebrarius*.
– ORIGIN 1970s: from *to-* (of unknown origin) + Latin *(tene)bra(rius)* 'belonging to darkness' (part of the name of the bacterium) + **-MYCIN**.

Tobruk /təˈbrʊk/ a port on the Mediterranean coast of NE Libya; pop. 94,000 (1984). It was the scene of fierce fighting during the North African campaign in the Second World War. Arabic name **TUBRUQ**.

toby ▶ **noun** (pl. **-ies**) **1** another term for **MOORISH IDOL**.
2 South African term for **PUFFERFISH**.

toby jug ▶ **noun** chiefly Brit. a beer jug or mug in the form of a stout old man wearing a three-cornered hat.
– ORIGIN mid 19th cent.: pet form of the given name *Tobias*, and said to come from an 18th-cent. poem about *Toby Philpot* (with a pun on *fill pot*), a soldier who liked to drink.

TOC ▶ **abbreviation for** (in the UK) train operating company.

Tocantins /ˌtəʊkənˈtiːns/ **1** a river of South America, which rises in central Brazil and flows 2,640 km (1,640 miles) northwards, joining the Pará to enter the Atlantic through a large estuary at Belém.
2 a state of central Brazil; capital, Palmas.

toccata /təˈkɑːtə/ ▶ **noun** a musical composition for a keyboard instrument designed to exhibit the performer's touch and technique.
– ORIGIN early 18th cent.: from Italian, feminine past participle of *toccare* 'to touch'.

Toc H /tɒk ˈeɪtʃ/ (in the UK) a society, originally of ex-service personnel, founded after the First World War for promoting Christian fellowship and social service.
– ORIGIN from *toc* (former telegraphy code for *T*) and *H*, from the initials of *Talbot House*, a soldier's club established in Belgium in 1915.

Tocharian /təˈkɛːrɪən, -ˈkɑːrɪən/ ▶ **noun 1** a member of a central Asian people who inhabited the Tarim Basin in the 1st millennium AD.
2 [mass noun] either of two extinct languages (**Tocharian A** and **Tocharian B**) spoken by this people, the most easterly of known ancient Indo-European languages, surviving in a few documents and inscriptions and showing curious affinities to Celtic and Italic languages.
▶ **adjective** of or relating to this people or their language.
– ORIGIN from French *tocharien*, via Latin from Greek *Tokharoi*, the name of a Scythian tribe (almost certainly unrelated to the Tocharians).

toco /ˈtəʊkəʊ/ (also **toco toucan**) ▶ **noun** (pl. **-os**) the largest and most familiar South American toucan, with mainly black plumage, a white throat and breast, and a massive black-tipped orange bill.
• *Ramphastos toco*, family Ramphastidae.
– ORIGIN late 18th cent.: via Portuguese from Tupi; compare with **TOUCAN**.

tocopherol /tɒˈkɒfərɒl/ ▶ **noun** Biochemistry any of several closely related compounds, found in wheatgerm oil, egg yolk, and leafy vegetables, which collectively constitute vitamin E. They are fat-soluble alcohols with antioxidant properties, important in the stabilization of cell membranes.
– ORIGIN 1930s: from Greek *tokos* 'offspring' + *pherein* 'to bear' + **-OL**.

tocsin /ˈtɒksɪn/ ▶ **noun** archaic an alarm bell or signal.
– ORIGIN late 16th cent.: from Old French *toquassen*, from Provençal *tocasenh*, from *tocar* 'to touch' + *senh* 'signal bell'.

tod ▶ **noun** (in phrase **on one's tod**) Brit. informal on one's own: *I'm going to do something, not just sit here on my tod.*
– ORIGIN 1930s: from rhyming slang *Tod Sloan*, the name of an American jockey (1873–1933).

today ▶ **adverb** on or in the course of this present day: *she's thirty today* | *he will appear in court today.*
■ at the present period of time; nowadays: *millions of people in Britain today cannot afford adequate housing.*
▶ **noun** this present day: *today is a rest day* | *today's match against United.*
■ the present period of time: *the powerful computers of today* | *today's society.*
– PHRASES **today week** Brit. a week from today.
– ORIGIN Old English *tō dæg* 'on (this) day'. Compare with **TOMORROW** and **TONIGHT**.

Todd, Sweeney, a barber who murdered his customers, the central character of a play by George Dibdin Pitt (1799–1855) and of later plays.

toddle ▶ **verb** [no obj. and with adverbial of direction] (of a young child) move with short unsteady steps while learning to walk: *William toddled curiously towards the TV crew.*
■ informal walk or go somewhere in a casual or leisurely way: *they would go for a drink and then toddle off home.*
▶ **noun** [in sing.] a young child's unsteady walk.
– ORIGIN late 16th cent.: of unknown origin.

toddler ▶ **noun** a young child who is just beginning to walk.
– DERIVATIVES **toddlerhood** noun.

toddy ▶ **noun** (pl. **-ies**) [mass noun] **1** a drink made of spirits with hot water, sugar, and sometimes spices.
2 the sap of some kinds of palm, fermented to produce arrack.
– ORIGIN early 17th cent. (in sense 2): from Marathi *tāḍī*, Hindi *tāṛī*, from Sanskrit *tāḍī* 'palmyra'.

toddy cat ▶ **noun** the common palm civet of Asia, which is noted for its habit of stealing toddy from the bamboo tubes placed to collect it from palm trunks.

todger (also **tadger**) ▶ **noun** Brit. informal a man's penis.
– ORIGIN 1950s: of unknown origin.

to-do ▶ **noun** [in sing.] informal a commotion or fuss: *he made a great to-do about fetching a cup.*
– ORIGIN late 16th cent.: from *to do* as in *much to do*, originally meaning 'much needing to be done' but later interpreted as the adjective *much* and a noun; compare with **ADO**.

tody /'təʊdi/ ▶ **noun** (pl. **-ies**) a small insectivorous Caribbean bird related to the motmots, with a large head, long bill, bright green upper parts, and a red throat.
• Family Todidae and genus *Todus*: five species.
– ORIGIN late 18th cent.: from French *todier*, from Latin *todus*, the name of a small bird.

toe ▶ **noun 1** any of the five digits at the end of the human foot: *he cut his big toe on a sharp stone.*
■ any of the digits of the foot of a quadruped or bird. ■ the part of an item of footwear that covers a person's toes.
2 the lower end, tip, or point of something, in particular:
■ the tip of the head of a golf club, furthest from the shaft. ■ the foot or base of a cliff, slope, or embankment. ■ a flattish portion at the foot of an otherwise steep curve on a graph. ■ a section of a rhizome or similar fleshy root from which a new plant may be propagated.
▶ **verb** (**toes**, **toed**, **toeing**) **1** [with obj. and usu. with adverbial] push, touch, or kick (something) with one's toe: *he* ***toed off*** *his shoes and flexed his feet.*
■ Golf strike (the ball) with the toe of the club.
2 [no obj.] (**toe in/out**) walk with the toes pointed in (or out): *he toes out when he walks.*
■ (of a pair of wheels) converge (or diverge) slightly at the front: *on a turn, the inner wheel toes out more.*
– PHRASES **make someone's toes curl** informal bring about an extreme reaction in someone, either of pleasure or of disgust. **on one's toes** ready for any eventuality; alert: *he carries out random spot checks to keep everyone on their toes.* **toe the line** accept the authority, principles, or policies of a particular group, especially under pressure. [ORIGIN: from the literal sense 'stand with the tips of the toes exactly touching a line'.] **toe to toe** (of two people) standing directly in front of one another, especially in order to fight or argue. **turn up one's toes** informal die.
– DERIVATIVES **toed** adjective [in combination] *three-toed feet*, **toeless** adjective.
– ORIGIN Old English *tā*, of Germanic origin; related to Dutch *tee* and German *Zeh*, *Zehe*. Current senses of the verb date from the mid 19th cent.

toea /'təʊeɪə/ ▶ **noun** (pl. same) a monetary unit of Papua New Guinea, equal to one hundredth of a kina.
– ORIGIN Motu, literally 'cone-shaped shell'.

toe box ▶ **noun** a piece of stiffened material between the lining and the toecap of a shoe.

toecap ▶ **noun** a piece of steel or leather constituting or fitted over the front part of a boot or shoe as protection or reinforcement.

toe clip ▶ **noun** a clip on a bicycle pedal to prevent the foot from slipping.

toe-curling ▶ **adjective** informal extremely distasteful, typically because embarrassing or excessively sentimental: *a toe-curling ballad.*
– DERIVATIVES **toe-curlingly** adverb.

toehold ▶ **noun** a small place where a person's foot can be lodged to support them, especially while climbing.
■ a relatively insignificant position from which further progress may be made: *the initiative is helping companies to gain a toehold in the Gulf.*

toe-in /'təʊɪn/ ▶ **noun** [mass noun] a slight forward convergence of a pair of wheels so that they are closer together in front than behind.

toe loop ▶ **noun** Skating a jump, initiated with the help of the supporting foot, in which the skater makes a full turn in the air, taking off from and landing on the outside edge of the same foot.

toenail ▶ **noun 1** the nail at the tip of each toe.
2 a nail driven obliquely through a piece of wood to secure it.
▶ **verb** [with obj.] fasten (a piece of wood) in this way.

toe-out /'təʊɪn/ ▶ **noun** [mass noun] a slight forward divergence of a pair of wheels so that they are closer together behind than in front.

toerag ▶ **noun** Brit. informal a contemptible or worthless person.
– ORIGIN mid 19th cent.: originally denoting a rag wrapped round the foot as a sock or, by extension, the wearer (such as a vagrant).

toe-tapping ▶ **adjective** informal (of music) making one want to tap one's feet; lively.

toey ▶ **adjective** [predic.] Austral./NZ informal (of a person or animal) nervous or restive.

toff Brit. informal ▶ **noun** derogatory a rich or upper-class person.
▶ **verb** (**be toffed up**) dated be smartly dressed: *he was all toffed up in officer's broadcloth.*
– ORIGIN mid 19th cent.: perhaps an alteration of **TUFT**, used to denote a gold tassel worn on the cap by titled undergraduates at Oxford and Cambridge.

toffee ▶ **noun** (pl. **toffees**) [mass noun] **1** a kind of firm or hard sweet which softens when sucked or chewed, made by boiling together sugar and butter, often with other ingredients or flavourings added.
■ [count noun] a small shaped piece of such a sweet.
2 Brit. informal, dated nonsense; rubbish: *his wife swallowed this load of old toffee.*
– PHRASES **not be able to do something for toffee** Brit. informal be totally incompetent at doing something: *Jill said I couldn't sing for toffee.*
– ORIGIN early 19th cent.: alteration of **TAFFY**.

toffee apple ▶ **noun** Brit. an apple coated with a thin layer of toffee and fixed on a stick.

toffee-nosed ▶ **adjective** informal, chiefly Brit. pretentiously superior; snobbish.
– DERIVATIVES **toffee nose** noun.

Tofranil /'tɒfrənɪl/ ▶ **noun** trademark for **IMIPRAMINE**.
– ORIGIN 1950s: of unknown origin.

toft ▶ **noun** Brit. rare a homestead.
– ORIGIN Old English, from Old Norse *topt*.

tofu /'təʊfu:/ ▶ **noun** [mass noun] curd made from mashed soya beans, used chiefly in Asian and vegetarian cookery.
– ORIGIN from Japanese *tōfu*, from Chinese *dòufu*, from *dòu* 'beans' + *fǔ* 'rot, turn sour'.

tog[1] informal ▶ **noun** (**togs**) clothes: *running togs.*
▶ **verb** (**togged**, **togging**) (**be/get togged up/out**) be or get dressed for a particular occasion or activity: *we got togged up in our glad rags.*
– ORIGIN early 18th cent. (as a slang term for a coat or outer garment): apparently an abbreviation of obsolete criminals' slang *togeman(s)* 'a light cloak', from French *toge* or Latin *toga* (see **TOGA**).

tog[2] ▶ **noun** Brit. a unit of thermal resistance used to express the insulating properties of clothes and quilts.
– ORIGIN 1940s: from **TOG**[1], on the pattern of an earlier unit called the *clo* (first element of *clothes*).

toga /'təʊgə/ ▶ **noun** a loose flowing outer garment worn by the citizens of ancient Rome, made of a single piece of cloth and covering the whole body apart from the right arm.
– ORIGIN Latin; related to *tegere* 'to cover'.

together ▶ **adverb 1** with or in proximity to another person or people: *together they climbed the dark stairs* | *they stood together in the kitchen.*
■ so as to touch or combine: *she held her hands together as if she was praying* | *bits of wood nailed together.* ■ in combination; collectively: *taken together, these measures would significantly improve people's chances of surviving a coach crash.* ■ into companionship or close association: *the experience has brought us together.* ■ (of two people) married or in a sexual relationship with each other: *they split up after ten years together.* ■ so as to be united or in agreement: *he won the confidence of the government and the rebels, but could not bring the two sides together.*
2 at the same time: *they both spoke together.*
3 without interruption; continuously: *she sits for hours together in the lotus position.*
▶ **adjective** informal self-confident, level-headed, or well organized: *she looks a very together young woman.*
– PHRASES **together with** as well as; along with: *their meal arrived, together with a carafe of red wine.*
– ORIGIN Old English *tōgædere*, based on the preposition **TO** + a West Germanic word related to **GATHER**. The adjective dates from the 1960s.

togetherness ▶ **noun** [mass noun] the state of being close to another person or other people: *the sense of family togetherness was strong and excluded neighbours.*

Toggenburg /'tɒgənbə:g/ ▶ **noun** a goat of a hornless light brown breed developed in the region of Toggenburg, a valley in the region of St Callen, Switzerland.

toggery ▶ **noun** [mass noun] informal, humorous clothes.

toggle ▶ **noun 1** a short rod of wood or plastic sewn to one side of a coat or other garment, pushed through a hole or loop on the other side and twisted so as to act as a fastener.
■ a pin or other crosspiece put through the eye of a rope or a link of a chain to keep it in place. ■ (also **toggle bolt**) a kind of wall fastener for use on open-backed plasterboard, having a part that springs open or turns through 90° after it is inserted so as to prevent withdrawal. ■ a movable pivoted crosspiece acting as a barb on a harpoon.
2 (also **toggle switch** or **toggle key**) Computing a key or command that is operated the same way but with opposite effect on successive occasions.
▶ **verb 1** [no obj., with adverbial] Computing switch from one effect, feature, or state to another by using a toggle.
2 [with obj.] provide or fasten with a toggle or toggles.
– ORIGIN mid 18th cent. (originally in nautical use): of unknown origin.

toggle switch ▶ **noun 1** an electric switch operated by means of a projecting lever that is moved up and down.
2 Computing another term for **TOGGLE**.

Togliatti /tɒ'ljati/ an industrial city and river port in SW Russia, on the River Volga; pop. 642,000 (1990). It was founded in 1738 but relocated in the mid 1950s to make way for the Kuibyshev reservoir. Former name (until 1964) **STAVROPOL**. Russian name **TOLYATTI**.
– ORIGIN renamed in 1964 after Palmiro *Togliatti* (1893–1964), leader of the Italian Communist Party.

Togo /'təʊgəʊ/ a country in West Africa with a short coastline on the Gulf of Guinea; pop. 3,761,000 (est. 1991); languages, French (official), West African languages; capital, Lomé. Official name **TOGOLESE REPUBLIC**.

The region formerly known as Togoland lay between the military powers of Ashanti and Dahomey and became a centre of the slave trade. It was annexed by Germany in 1884 and divided between France and Britain after the First World War. The western, British section joined Ghana on the latter's independence (1957). The remainder, administered by France under a United Nations mandate after the Second World War, became an independent republic with the name Togo in 1960.

– DERIVATIVES **Togolese** /,təʊgə'li:z/ adjective & noun.

togt /tɒxt/ ▶ **adjective** [attrib.] S. African (of a labourer or their work) hired or paid for by the day; casual.
– ORIGIN Afrikaans, from Dutch *tocht* 'expedition, journey'.

Tohoku /təʊ'həʊku:/ a region of Japan, on the island of Honshu; capital, Sendai.

tohubohu /,təʊhu:'bəʊhu:/ ▶ **noun** informal, chiefly N. Amer. a state of chaos; utter confusion: *a fearful tohubohu.*
– ORIGIN from Hebrew *tōhū wa-ḇōhū* 'emptiness and desolation', translated in Gen. 1:2 (Bible of 1611) as 'without form and void'.

toil ▶ **verb** [no obj.] work extremely hard or incessantly: *we toiled away* | [with infinitive] *Richard toiled to build his editorial team.*
■ [with adverbial of direction] move slowly and with difficulty: *she began to toil up the cliff path.*
▶ **noun** [mass noun] exhausting physical labour: *a life of toil.*
– DERIVATIVES **toiler** noun.
– ORIGIN Middle English (in the senses 'contend verbally' and 'strife'): from Anglo-Norman French *toiler* 'strive, dispute', *toil* 'confusion', from Latin *tudiculare* 'stir about', from *tudicula* 'machine for crushing olives', related to *tundere* 'crush'.

toile /twɑ:l/ ▶ **noun 1** an early version of a finished garment made up in cheap material so that the design can be tested and perfected.
2 [mass noun] a translucent linen or cotton fabric, used for making clothes.
■ short for **TOILE DE JOUY**.
– ORIGIN late Middle English (denoting cloth or canvas for painting on): from French *toile* 'cloth, web', from Latin *tela* 'web'.

toile de Jouy /də ʒwi:/ ▶ **noun** [mass noun] a type of printed calico with a characteristic floral, figure, or landscape design on a light background.
– ORIGIN originally made at *Jouy*-en-Josas, near Paris.

toilet ▶ **noun 1** a large bowl for urinating or defecating into, typically plumbed into a sewage system and with a flushing mechanism; a lavatory: *Liz heard the toilet flush* | figurative *my tenure was* ***down the toilet.***

■a room, building, or cubicle containing one or more of these.

2 [in sing.] the process of washing oneself, dressing, and attending to one's appearance: *her toilet completed, she finally went back downstairs.*

■[as modifier] denoting articles used in this process: *a bathroom cabinet stocked with toilet articles.* ■the cleansing of part of a person's body as a medical procedure.

▶**verb** (**toileted**, **toileting**) [with obj.] [usu. as noun **toileting**] assist or supervise (someone, especially an infant or invalid) in using a toilet.

– ORIGIN mid 16th cent.: from French *toilette* 'cloth, wrapper', diminutive of *toile* (see **TOILE**). The word originally denoted a cloth used as a wrapper for clothes; then (in the 17th cent.) a cloth cover for a dressing table, the articles used in dressing, and the process of dressing, later also of washing oneself (sense 2). In the 19th cent. the word came to denote a dressing room, and, in the US, one with washing facilities; hence, a lavatory (early 20th cent.).

toilet bag ▶**noun** Brit. a waterproof bag for holding toothpaste, soap, and other bathroom items when travelling.

toilet paper ▶**noun** [mass noun] paper in sheets or on a roll for wiping oneself clean after urination or defecation.

toiletries ▶**plural noun** articles used in washing and taking care of one's body, such as soap, shampoo, and toothpaste.

toilet roll ▶**noun** a roll of toilet paper.

toilet set ▶**noun** a set of items used in arranging the hair, typically including a hairbrush, comb, and mirror.

■a set of items formerly used in washing and cleaning oneself, typically including a wash bowl, jug, and chamber pot kept in a bedroom.

toilet soap ▶**noun** soap for washing oneself.

toilet table ▶**noun** old-fashioned term for **DRESSING TABLE**.

toilette /twɑːˈlɛt/ ▶**noun** [in sing.] dated the process of washing oneself, dressing, and attending to one's appearance: *Emily got up to begin her morning toilette.*

– ORIGIN late 17th cent.: French (see **TOILET**).

toilet tissue ▶**noun** another term for **TOILET PAPER**.

toilet-train ▶**verb** [with obj.] teach (a young child) to use the toilet: *she was toilet-trained by the age of one.*

toilet water ▶**noun** a dilute form of perfume. Also called **EAU DE TOILETTE**.

toils ▶**plural noun** poetic/literary used in reference to a situation regarded as a trap: *Henry had become caught in the toils of his own deviousness.*

– ORIGIN early 16th cent. (denoting a net into which a hunted quarry is driven): plural of *toil*, from Old French *toile* 'net, trap' (see **TOILE**).

toilsome ▶**adjective** archaic or poetic/literary involving hard or tedious work.

– DERIVATIVES **toilsomely** adverb, **toilsomeness** noun.

toilworn ▶**adjective** poetic/literary exhausted by punishing physical labour.

Tojo /ˈtəʊdʒəʊ/, Hideki (1884–1948), Japanese military leader and statesman, Prime Minister 1941–4. He initiated the Japanese attack on Pearl Harbor and by 1944 he had assumed virtual control of all political and military decision-making. After Japan's surrender he was tried and hanged as a war criminal.

tokamak /ˈtəʊkəmak/ ▶**noun** Physics a toroidal apparatus for producing controlled fusion reactions in hot plasma.

– ORIGIN 1960s: Russian, from *toroidal'naya kamera s magnitnym polem* 'toroidal chamber with magnetic field'.

Tokay /təʊˈkeɪ/ ▶**noun** [mass noun] a sweet aromatic wine, originally made near Tokaj in Hungary.

tokay /təʊˈkeɪ/ (also **tokay gecko**) ▶**noun** a large grey SE Asian gecko with orange and blue spots, having a loud call that resembles its name.

● *Gekko gecko*, family Gekkonidae.

– ORIGIN mid 18th cent.: from Malay dialect *toke'*, from Javanese *tekèk*, imitative of its call.

toke informal ▶**noun** a pull on a cigarette or pipe, typically one containing cannabis.

▶**verb** [no obj.] smoke cannabis or tobacco: *he muses while toking on a cigarette* | [with obj.] *we toke some grass.*

– DERIVATIVES **toker** noun.

– ORIGIN 1950s: of unknown origin.

Tokelau /ˌtəʊkəˈlaʊː/ a group of three islands in the western Pacific, between Kiribati and Samoa, forming an overseas territory of New Zealand; pop. 1,700 (1994).

token ▶**noun 1** a thing serving as a visible or tangible representation of something abstract: *mistletoe was cut from an oak tree as a token of good fortune.*

■a thing given to or done for someone as an expression of one's feelings: *I wanted to offer you a small token of my appreciation.* ■archaic a characteristic or distinctive sign or mark, especially a badge or favour worn to indicate allegiance to a particular person or party. ■archaic a word or object conferring authority on or serving to authenticate the speaker or holder. ■a staff or other object given to a train driver on a single-track railway as authority to proceed over a given section of line. ■Computing a sequence of bits used in a certain network architecture in which the ability to transmit information is conferred on a particular node by the arrival there of this sequence, which is passed continuously between nodes in a fixed order. ■a person chosen by way of tokenism as a nominal representative of a minority or under-represented group.

2 a voucher that can be exchanged for goods or services, typically one given as a gift or offered as part of a promotional offer: *a record token.*

■a metal or plastic disc used to operate a machine or in exchange for particular goods or services.

3 an individual occurrence of a symbol or string, in particular:

■Linguistics an individual occurrence of a linguistic unit in speech or writing, as contrasted with the type or class of linguistic unit of which it is an instance. Contrasted with **TYPE**. ■Computing the smallest meaningful unit of information in a sequence of data for a compiler.

▶**adjective** done for the sake of appearances or as a symbolic gesture: *cases like these often bring just token fines from magistrates.*

■[attrib.] (of a person) chosen by way of tokenism as a representative of a particular minority or under-represented group: *she took offence at being called the token woman on the force.*

– PHRASES **by the same** (or **that** or **this**) **token** in the same way or for the same reason: *there was little evidence to substantiate the gossip and, by the same token, there was little to disprove it.* **in token of** as a sign or symbol of: *adults exchanging drinks around a pub bar in token of temporary trust and friendship.*

– ORIGIN Old English *tāc(e)n*, of Germanic origin; related to Dutch *teken* and German *Zeichen*, also to **TEACH**.

tokenism ▶**noun** [mass noun] the practice of making only a perfunctory or symbolic effort to do a particular thing, especially by recruiting a small number of people from under-represented groups in order to give the appearance of sexual or racial equality within a workforce.

– DERIVATIVES **tokenistic** adjective.

token money ▶**noun** [mass noun] money where the face value of notes or coins is unrelated to the value of the material of which they are composed.

token ring ▶**noun** Computing a local area network in which a node can only transmit when in possession of a sequence of bits (called the token), which is passed to each node in turn.

tokkin /tɒˈkɪn/ (also **tokkin fund**) ▶**noun** (pl. same or **tokkins**) (in Japan) a type of short-term corporate investment fund managed by a trust bank, providing a reduction of tax liability and other financial advantages.

– ORIGIN Japanese acronym.

tokoloshe /ˈtɒkɒlɒʃ/ ▶**noun** S. African (in African folklore) a mischievous and lascivious hairy water sprite.

– ORIGIN Sesotho, Xhosa, and Zulu.

tokonoma /ˌtɒkəʊˈnəʊmə/ ▶**noun** (in a Japanese house) a recess or alcove, typically a few inches above floor level, for displaying flowers, pictures, and ornaments.

– ORIGIN Japanese.

Tok Pisin /tɒk ˈpɪsɪn/ ▶**noun** [mass noun] an English-based creole used as a commercial and administrative language by over 2 million people in Papua New Guinea. Also called **NEO-MELANESIAN**.

– ORIGIN the name in Tok Pisin, literally 'pidgin talk'.

tok-tokkie /tɒkˈtɒki/ ▶**noun** (pl. **-ies**) S. African **1** [mass noun] a children's game that involves tricking a victim, especially by knocking on a door and running away before it is answered.

2 a dark rounded African beetle which taps its abdomen on the ground, making a rapid tapping sound to attract a mate.

● *Dichtha* and other genera, family Tenebrionidae.

– ORIGIN early 20th cent. (in sense 2): Afrikaans, from Dutch *tokken* 'to tap', of imitative origin.

Tokugawa /ˌtɒkʊˈgɑːwə/ the last shogunate in Japan (1603–1867), founded by Tokugawa Ieyasu (1543–1616). The shogunate was followed by the restoration of imperial power under Meiji Tenno.

Tokyo /ˈtəʊkɪəʊ/ the capital of Japan and capital of Kanto region; pop. 8,163,000 (1990). Formerly called Edo, it was the centre of the military government under the shoguns (1603–1867). It was renamed Tokyo in 1868, when it replaced Kyoto as the imperial capital.

tolar /ˈtɒlɑː/ ▶**noun** the basic monetary unit of Slovenia, equal to 100 stotins.

– ORIGIN Slovene; compare with **THALER**.

tolbooth ▶**noun** variant spelling of **TOLLBOOTH**.

Tolbukhin /tɒlˈbuːkɪn/ former name (1949–91) for **DOBRICH**.

tolbutamide /tɒlˈbjuːtəmʌɪd/ ▶**noun** [mass noun] Medicine a synthetic compound used to lower blood sugar levels in the treatment of diabetes.

● Alternative name: **1-butyl-3-tosylurea**; chem. formula: $C_{12}H_{18}N_2O_3S$.

– ORIGIN 1950s: from *tol(uene)* + *but(yl)* + **AMIDE**.

told past and past participle of **TELL**[1].

tole /təʊl/ (also **tôle** /tɔːl/) ▶**noun** [mass noun] painted, enamelled, or lacquered tin plate used to make decorative domestic objects.

– DERIVATIVES **toleware** noun.

– ORIGIN 1940s: French *tôle*, 'sheet iron', from dialect *taule* 'table', from Latin *tabula* 'flat board'.

Toledo 1 /təˈleɪdəʊ/ a city in central Spain on the River Tagus, capital of Castilla-La Mancha region; pop. 63,560 (1991). It was a pre-eminent city and cultural centre of Castile. Toledan steel and sword blades have been famous since the first century BC.

2 /təˈliːdəʊ/ an industrial city and port on Lake Erie, in NW Ohio; pop. 332,940 (1990).

– DERIVATIVES **Toledan** adjective & noun.

tolerable ▶**adjective** able to be endured: *a stimulant to make life more tolerable.*

■fairly good; mediocre: *he was fond of music and had a tolerable voice.*

– DERIVATIVES **tolerability** noun, **tolerably** adverb [as submodifier] *the welfare state works tolerably well.*

– ORIGIN late Middle English: via Old French from Latin *tolerabilis*, from *tolerare* (see **TOLERATE**).

tolerance ▶**noun 1** [mass noun] the ability or willingness to tolerate something, in particular the existence of opinions or behaviour that one does not necessarily agree with: *the tolerance of corruption* | *an advocate of religious tolerance.*

■the capacity to endure continued subjection to something, especially a drug, transplant, antigen, or environmental conditions, without adverse reaction: *the desert camel shows the greatest tolerance to dehydration* | *species were grouped according to pollution tolerance* | [count noun] *various species of diatoms display different tolerances to acid.* ■diminution in the body's response to a drug after continued use.

2 an allowable amount of variation of a specified quantity, especially in the dimensions of a machine or part: *250 parts in his cars were made to tolerances of one thousandth of an inch.*

– ORIGIN late Middle English (denoting the action of bearing hardship, or the ability to bear pain and hardship): via Old French from Latin *tolerantia*, from *tolerare* (see **TOLERATE**).

tolerance dose ▶**noun** a dose of something toxic, in particular of nuclear radiation, believed to be the maximum that can be taken without harm.

tolerant ▶**adjective 1** showing willingness to allow the existence of opinions or behaviour that one does not necessarily agree with: *we must be* ***tolerant of*** *others* | *a more tolerant attitude towards other religions.*

2 (of a plant, animal, or machine) able to endure specified conditions or treatment: *rye is reasonably*

t

tolerant of drought | [in combination] *fault-tolerant computer systems.*
– DERIVATIVES **tolerantly** adverb (only in sense 1).
– ORIGIN late 18th cent.: from French *tolérant*, present participle of *tolérer*, from Latin *tolerare* (see **TOLERATE**). Compare with earlier **INTOLERANT**.

tolerate ▶ verb [with obj.] allow the existence, occurrence, or practice of (something that one does not necessarily like or agree with) without interference: *a regime unwilling to tolerate dissent.*
■ accept or endure (someone or something unpleasant or disliked) with forbearance: *how was it that she could tolerate such noise?* ■ be capable of continued subjection to (a drug, toxin, or environmental condition) without adverse reaction: *lichens grow in conditions that no other plants tolerate.*
– DERIVATIVES **tolerator** noun.
– ORIGIN early 16th cent. (in the sense 'endure (pain)': from Latin *tolerat-* 'endured', from the verb *tolerare.*

toleration ▶ noun [mass noun] the practice of tolerating something, in particular differences of opinion or behaviour: *the king demanded greater religious toleration.*
– ORIGIN late 15th cent. (denoting the granting of permission by authority): from French *tolération*, from Latin *toleratio(n-)*, from *tolerare* (see **TOLERATE**).

Toleration Act an act of 1689 granting freedom of worship to dissenters (excluding Roman Catholics and Unitarians) on certain conditions. Its real purpose was to unite all Protestants under William III against the deposed Roman Catholic James II.

Tolkien /ˈtɒlkiːn/, J. R. R. (1892–1973), British novelist and literary scholar, born in South Africa; full name *John Ronald Reuel Tolkien*. He is famous for the fantasy adventures *The Hobbit* (1937) and *The Lord of the Rings* (1954–5), set in Middle Earth.

toll[1] /təʊl/ ▶ noun **1** a charge payable for permission to use a particular bridge or road: *motorway tolls* | [as modifier] *a toll bridge.*
■ N. Amer. a charge for a long-distance telephone call.
2 [in sing.] the number of deaths, casualties, or injuries arising from particular circumstances, such as a natural disaster, conflict, or accident: *the toll of dead and injured mounted.*
■ the cost or damage resulting from something: *the environmental toll of the policy has been high.*
▶ verb [with obj.] [usu. as noun **tolling**] charge a toll for the use of (a bridge or road): *the report advocates motorway tolling.*
– PHRASES **take its toll** (or **take a heavy toll**) have an adverse effect, especially so as to cause damage, suffering, or death: *years of pumping iron have taken their toll on his body.*
– ORIGIN Old English (denoting a charge, tax, or duty), from medieval Latin *toloneum*, alteration of late Latin *teloneum*, from Latin *telos* 'tax'. Sense 2 (late 19th cent.) arose from the notion of paying a toll or tribute in human lives (to an adversary or to death).

toll[2] /təʊl/ ▶ verb [no obj.] (of a bell) sound with a slow, uniform succession of strokes, as a signal or announcement: *the bells of the cathedral began to toll for evening service.*
■ [with obj.] cause (a bell) to make such a sound. ■ (of a bell) announce or mark (the time, a service, or a person's death): *the bell of St Mary Le Bow began to toll the curfew.*
▶ noun [in sing.] a single ring of a bell.
– ORIGIN late Middle English: probably a special use of dialect *toll* 'drag, pull'.

tollbooth (also **tolbooth**) ▶ noun **1** a roadside kiosk where drivers or pedestrians must pay to use a bridge or road.
2 Scottish archaic a town hall.
■ a town jail.

toll gate ▶ noun a barrier across a road where drivers or pedestrians must pay to go further.

toll house ▶ noun a small house by a toll gate or toll bridge where money is collected from road users.

tollhouse cookie ▶ noun US a sweet biscuit made with flour, brown sugar, chocolate chips, and sometimes chopped nuts.
– ORIGIN named after the *Toll House* in Whitman, Massachusetts, source of the original recipe.

toll plaza ▶ noun US a row of tollbooths on a toll road.

Tollund Man /ˈtɒlənd/ the well-preserved corpse of

an Iron Age man (*c.*500 BC–AD 400) found in 1950 in a peat bog in central Jutland, Denmark. Around the neck was a plaited leather noose, indicating that Tollund Man had met his death by hanging.
– ORIGIN named after *Tollund* Fen, where it was found.

tollway ▶ noun US a highway for the use of which a charge is made.

Tolpuddle martyrs /ˈtɒlpʌd(ə)l/ six farm labourers from the village of Tolpuddle in Dorset who attempted to form a trade union and were sentenced in 1834 to seven years' transportation on a charge of administering unlawful oaths. Their harsh sentences caused widespread protests, and two years later they were pardoned and repatriated from Australia.

Tolstoy /ˈtɒlstɔɪ/, Count Leo (1828–1910), Russian writer; Russian name *Lev Nikolaevich Tolstoi*. He is best known for the novels *War and Peace* (1863–9), an epic tale of the Napoleonic invasion, and *Anna Karenina* (1873–7).

Toltec /ˈtɒltɛk/ ▶ noun a member of an American Indian people that flourished in Mexico before the Aztecs.
▶ adjective of or relating to this people.
– DERIVATIVES **Toltecan** adjective.
– ORIGIN via Spanish from Nahuatl *toltecatl*, literally 'a person from *Tula*' (see **TULA**).

tolu /təˈluː, ˈtəʊluː/ (also **tolu balsam**) ▶ noun [mass noun] a fragrant brown balsam obtained from a South American tree, used in perfumery and medicine.
● This balsam is obtained mainly from *Myroxylon balsamum*, family Leguminosae.
– ORIGIN late 17th cent.: named after *Santiago de Tolú* in Colombia, from where it was exported.

Toluca /təˈluːkə/ a city in central Mexico, capital of the state of Mexico; pop. 488,000 (1990). It lies at the foot of the extinct volcano Nevado de Toluca, at an altitude of 2,680 m (8,793 ft). Full name **TOLUCA DE LERDO** /deɪ ˈlɛːdəʊ/.

toluene /ˈtɒljʊiːn/ ▶ noun [mass noun] Chemistry a colourless liquid hydrocarbon present in coal tar and petroleum and used as a solvent and in organic synthesis.
● Alternative name: **methylbenzene**; chem. formula: $C_6H_5CH_3$.
– ORIGIN late 19th cent.: from **TOLU** + **-ENE**.

toluidine blue /ˈtɒljʊɪdiːn, tɒˈljuː-/ ▶ noun [mass noun] a synthetic blue dye used chiefly as a stain in biology.
● A thiazine dye; chem. formula: $C_{15}H_{16}ClN_3S$.
– ORIGIN late 19th cent.: *toluidine* from **TOLUENE** + **-IDE** + **-INE**[1].

Tolyatti /tɑˈljɑtʲi/ Russian name for **TOGLIATTI**.

tom[1] ▶ noun **1** the male of various animals, especially a domestic cat.
2 Brit. a female prostitute. [ORIGIN: early 20th cent.: from criminals' slang.]
3 (**Tom**) US informal short for **UNCLE TOM**.
▶ verb (**tommed**, **tomming**) [no obj.] informal **1** (**be tomming**) Brit. work as a prostitute.
2 US (of a black person) behave in an excessively obedient or servile way.
– ORIGIN late Middle English (denoting an ordinary man, surviving in *tomfool*, *tomboy*, and the phrase *Tom, Dick, and Harry*): abbreviation of the given name *Thomas*. Sense 1 dates from the mid 18th cent.

tom[2] ▶ noun (usu. **toms**) informal short for **TOM-TOM**.

tom[3] ▶ noun (usu. **toms**) informal short for **TOMATO**.

tomahawk /ˈtɒməhɔːk/ ▶ noun a light axe used as a tool or weapon by American Indians.
■ Austral./NZ a hatchet.
▶ verb [with obj.] strike or cut with or as if with a tomahawk.
– ORIGIN early 17th cent.: from a Virginia Algonquian language.

tomalley /ˈtɒmali/ ▶ noun N. Amer. the digestive gland of a lobster, which turns green when cooked, and is considered a delicacy.
– ORIGIN mid 17th cent.: from French *taumalin*, from Carib *taumali*.

Tom and Jerry ▶ noun (pl. **-ies**) US a kind of hot spiced rum cocktail, made with eggs.

tomatillo /ˌtɒməˈtiːjəʊ, -ˈtiːjəʊ, -ˈtiːljəʊ/ ▶ noun (pl. **-os**) **1** an edible purple or yellow fruit which is chiefly used for sauces and preserves.

2 the Mexican plant, related to the Cape gooseberry, which bears this fruit.
● *Physalis philadelphica*, family Solanaceae.
– ORIGIN early 20th cent.: from Spanish, diminutive of *tomate* 'tomato'.

tomatine /ˈtɒmətiːn/ (also **tomatin** /ˈtɒmətɪn/) ▶ noun [mass noun] Chemistry a compound of the steroid glycoside class, present in the stems and leaves of the tomato and related plants.
– ORIGIN 1940s: from **TOMATO** + **-INE**[4].

tomato ▶ noun (pl. **-oes**) **1** a glossy red, or occasionally yellow, pulpy edible fruit which is typically eaten as a vegetable or in salad.
■ [mass noun] the bright red colour of a ripe tomato.
2 the South American plant of the nightshade family which produces this fruit. It is widely grown as a cash crop and many varieties have been developed.
● *Lycopersicon esculentum*, family Solanaceae.
– DERIVATIVES **tomatoey** adjective.
– ORIGIN early 17th cent.: from French, Spanish, or Portuguese *tomate*, from Nahuatl *tomatl*.

tomb ▶ noun a large vault, typically an underground one, for burying the dead.
■ an enclosure for a corpse cut in the earth or in rock. ■ a monument to the memory of a dead person, erected over their burial place. ■ used in similes and metaphors to refer to a place or situation that is extremely cold, quiet, or dark, or that forms a confining enclosure: *the house was as quiet as a tomb.* ■ [mass noun] (**the tomb**) poetic/literary death: *none escape the tomb.*
– ORIGIN Middle English: from Old French *tombe*, from late Latin *tumba*, from Greek *tumbos*.

Tombaugh /ˈtɒmbɔː/, Clyde William (1906–97), American astronomer. His chief discovery was that of the planet Pluto on 13 March 1930, which he made from the Lowell Observatory in Arizona. Tombaugh subsequently discovered numerous asteroids.

tombola /tɒmˈbəʊlə/ ▶ noun Brit. a game in which people pick tickets out of a revolving drum and certain tickets win immediate prizes, typically played at a fête or fair.
– ORIGIN late 19th cent.: from French or Italian, from Italian *tombolare* 'turn a somersault'.

tombolo /ˈtɒmbələʊ/ ▶ noun (pl. **-os**) a bar of sand or shingle joining an island to the mainland.
– ORIGIN late 19th cent.: from Italian, literally 'sand dune'.

Tombouctou /tɔ̃buktu/ French name for **TIMBUKTU**.

tomboy ▶ noun a girl who enjoys rough, noisy activities traditionally associated with boys.
– DERIVATIVES **tomboyish** adjective, **tomboyishness** noun.

tombstone ▶ noun **1** a large, flat inscribed stone standing or laid over a grave.
2 (also **tombstone advertisement**) an advertisement listing the underwriters or firms associated with a new issue of shares, bonds, warrants, etc.

tomcat ▶ noun a male domestic cat.

tomcod ▶ noun (pl. same or **tomcods**) a small edible greenish-brown North American fish of the cod family, popular with anglers.
● Genus *Microgadus*, family Gadidae: *M. proximus* of the Pacific coasts, and *M. tomcod* of the Atlantic coasts and fresh water.

Tom Collins ▶ noun a cocktail made from gin mixed with soda, sugar, and lemon or lime juice.
– ORIGIN sometimes said to have been named after a 19th-cent. London bartender.

Tom, Dick, and Harry (also **Tom, Dick, or Harry**) ▶ noun used to refer to ordinary people in general: *he didn't want every Tom, Dick, and Harry knowing their business.*

tome ▶ noun chiefly humorous a book, especially a large, heavy, scholarly one: *a weighty tome.*
– ORIGIN late 16th cent. (denoting one volume of a larger work): from French, via Latin from Greek *tomos* 'section, roll of papyrus, volume'; related to *temnein* 'to cut'.

-tome ▶ combining form **1** denoting an instrument for cutting: *microtome.*
2 denoting a section or segment: *myotome.*
– ORIGIN sense 1 from Greek *-tomon* (neuter) 'that cuts'; sense 2 from Greek *tomē* 'a cutting', both from *temnein* 'to cut'.

tomentum /təˈmɛntəm/ ▶ noun (pl. **tomenta** /-tə/) Botany a layer of matted woolly down on the surface of a plant.
– DERIVATIVES **tomentose** /təˈmɛntəʊs, ˈtəʊ-/ adjective, **tomentous** adjective.
– ORIGIN late 17th cent.: from Latin, literally 'cushion stuffing'.

tomfool ▶ noun dated a foolish person: [as modifier] she was destined to take part in some tomfool caper.

tomfoolery ▶ noun [mass noun] foolish or silly behaviour: the tomfoolery of MPs at question time.

Tomis /ˈtəʊmɪs/ ancient name for CONSTANŢA.

tomme /tɒm/ ▶ noun (pl. pronunc. same) a cheese made in Savoy.
– ORIGIN French.

Tommy ▶ noun (pl. **-ies**) informal **1** a British private soldier. [ORIGIN: pet form of the given name *Thomas*; from a use of the name *Thomas Atkins* in specimens of completed official forms in the British army during the 19th cent.]
2 a Thomson's gazelle.

tommy bar ▶ noun a short bar used to turn a box spanner.

tommy gun ▶ noun informal a type of sub-machine gun.
– ORIGIN 1920s: contraction of *Thompson gun*, named by its designer after John T. *Thompson* (1860–1940), the American army officer who conceived the idea for it.

tommyrot ▶ noun [mass noun] informal, dated nonsense; rubbish: did you ever hear such awful tommyrot?

tommy ruff (also **tommy rough**) ▶ noun see RUFF² (sense 1).

tomogram /ˈtəʊmə(ʊ)gram, ˈtɒm-/ ▶ noun a record obtained by tomography.

tomography /təˈmɒgrəfi/ ▶ noun [mass noun] a technique for displaying a representation of a cross section through a human body or other solid object using X-rays or ultrasound.
– DERIVATIVES **tomographic** adjective.
– ORIGIN 1930s: from Greek *tomos* 'slice, section' + -GRAPHY.

tomorrow ▶ adverb on the day after today: the show opens tomorrow.
■ in the future, especially the near future: East Germany will not disappear tomorrow.
▶ noun the day after today: tomorrow is going to be a special day.
■ the future, especially the near future: today's engineers are tomorrow's buyers.
– PHRASES **as if there was** (or **as though there were**) **no tomorrow** with no regard for the future consequences: I ate as if there was no tomorrow. **tomorrow morning** (or **afternoon** etc.) in the morning (or afternoon etc.) of tomorrow. **tomorrow is another day** used after a bad experience to express one's belief that the future will be better. **tomorrow week** Brit. a week from tomorrow.
– ORIGIN Middle English (as two words): from the preposition TO + MORROW. Compare with TODAY and TONIGHT.

Tompion /ˈtɒmpɪən/, Thomas (c.1639–1713), English clock and watchmaker. He made one of the first balance-spring watches and made two large pendulum clocks for the Royal Greenwich Observatory.

tompion /ˈtɒmpɪən/ ▶ noun variant spelling of TAMPION.

Tomsk /tɒmsk/ an industrial city in southern Siberian Russia, a port on the River Tom; pop. 506,000 (1990).

tom thumb ▶ noun **1** [usu. as modifier] a dwarf variety of a cultivated flower or vegetable: Tom Thumb lettuce.
2 a small wild flower, especially bird's-foot trefoil.
– ORIGIN late 19th cent.: from the name of the hero of a children's story, a ploughman's son who was only as tall as his father's thumb.

tomtit ▶ noun a popular name for any of a number of small active songbirds:
● Brit. the blue tit. ● NZ the black-and-white New Zealand tit (*Petroica macrocephala*, family Eopsaltridae). ● Austral. the yellow-tailed thornbill (*Acanthiza chrysorrhoa*, family Acanthizidae).

tom-tom ▶ noun a medium-sized cylindrical drum, of which one to three may be used in a drum kit.

■ informal a drum played by non-European tribal peoples.
– ORIGIN late 17th cent.: from Hindi *ṭam ṭam*, Telugu *tamaṭama*, of imitative origin.

-tomy ▶ combining form cutting, especially as part of a surgical process: episiotomy.
– ORIGIN from Greek *-tomia* 'cutting', from *temnein* 'to cut'.

ton¹ /tʌn/ (abbrev.: **t** also US **tn**) ▶ noun **1** (also **long ton**) a unit of weight equal to 2,240 lb avoirdupois (1016.05 kg).
■ (also **short ton**) chiefly N. Amer. a unit of weight equal to 2,000 lb avoirdupois (907.19 kg). ■ short for METRIC TON. ■ (also **displacement ton**) a unit of measurement of a ship's weight representing the weight of water it displaces with the load line just immersed, equal to 2,240 lb or 35 cu. ft (0.99 cubic metres). ■ (also **freight ton**) a unit of weight or volume of sea cargo, equal to a metric ton (1,000 kg) or 40 cu. ft. ■ (also **gross ton**) a unit of gross internal capacity, equal to 100 cu. ft (2.83 cubic metres). ■ (also **net** or **register ton**) an equivalent unit of net internal capacity. ■ a unit of refrigerating power able to freeze 2,000 lb of water at 0°C in 24 hours. ■ a measure of capacity for various materials, especially 40 cu. ft of timber.
2 (usu. **a ton of/tons of**) informal a large number or amount: all of a sudden I had tons of friends | that bag of yours weighs a ton.
3 informal, chiefly Brit. a hundred, in particular a speed of 100 mph, a score of 100 or more, or a sum of £100: he scored 102 not out, his third ton of the tour.
– PHRASES **like a ton of bricks** see BRICK.
– ORIGIN Middle English: variant of TUN, both spellings being used for the container and the weight. The senses were differentiated in the late 17th cent.

ton² /tɒ̃/ ▶ noun [mass noun] fashionable style or distinction.
■ (**the ton**) [treated as sing. or pl.] fashionable society.
– ORIGIN French, from Latin *tonus* (see TONE).

tonal /ˈtəʊn(ə)l/ ▶ adjective of or relating to the tone of music, colour, or writing: his ear for tonal colour | the poem's tonal lapses.
■ of or relating to music written using conventional keys and harmony. ■ Phonetics (of a language) expressing semantic differences by varying the intonation given to words or syllables of a similar sound.
– DERIVATIVES **tonally** adverb.
– ORIGIN late 18th cent. (designating church music in plainsong mode): from medieval Latin *tonalis*, from Latin *tonus* (see TONE).

tonalite /ˈtɒn(ə)lʌɪt/ ▶ noun [mass noun] Geology a coarse-grained plutonic rock consisting chiefly of sodic plagioclase, quartz, and hornblende or other mafic minerals.
– DERIVATIVES **tonalitic** adjective.
– ORIGIN late 19th cent.: from *Tonale* Pass, northern Italy, + -ITE¹.

tonality ▶ noun (pl. **-ies**) [mass noun] **1** the character of a piece of music as determined by the key in which it is played or the relations between the notes of a scale or key.
■ [count noun] the harmonic effect of being in a particular key: the first bar would seem set to create a tonality of C major. ■ the use of conventional keys and harmony as the basis of musical composition.
2 the colour scheme or range of tones used in a picture.

tondo /ˈtɒndəʊ/ ▶ noun (pl. **tondi** /-di/) a circular painting or relief.
– ORIGIN late 19th cent.: from Italian, literally 'round object', from *rotondo* 'round', from Latin *rotundus*.

Tone /təʊn/, (Theobald) Wolfe (1763–98), Irish nationalist. In 1794 he induced a French invasion of Ireland to overthrow English rule, which failed. Tone was captured by the British during the Irish insurrection in 1798 and committed suicide in prison.

tone ▶ noun **1** the overall quality of a musical or vocal sound: the piano tone appears monochrome or lacking in warmth.
■ a modulation of the voice expressing a particular feeling or mood: a firm tone of voice. ■ a manner of expression in writing: there was a general tone of ill-concealed glee in the reporting.
2 the general character of a group of people or a place or event: a bell would lower the tone of the place.

■ [mass noun] informal an atmosphere of respectability or class: they don't feel he gives the place tone.
3 a musical sound, especially one of a definite pitch and character.
■ a musical note, warble, or other sound used as a particular signal on a telephone or answering machine. ■ Phonetics (in some languages, such as Chinese) a particular pitch pattern on a syllable used to make semantic distinctions. ■ Phonetics (in some languages, such as English) intonation on a word or phrase used to add functional meaning.
4 (also **whole tone**) a basic interval in classical Western music, equal to two semitones and separating, for example, the first and second notes of an ordinary scale (such as C and D, or E and F sharp); a major second or whole step.
5 [mass noun] the particular quality of brightness, deepness, or hue of a tint or shade of a colour: an attractive colour which is even in tone and texture | [count noun] stained glass in vivid tones of red and blue.
■ the general effect of colour or of light and shade in a picture. ■ [count noun] a slight degree of difference in the intensity of a colour.
6 (also **muscle tone**) [mass noun] the normal level of firmness or slight contraction in a resting muscle.
■ Physiology the normal level of activity in a nerve fibre.
▶ verb [with obj.] **1** give greater strength or firmness to (the body or a part of it): exercise tones up the muscles.
■ [no obj.] (**tone up**) (of a muscle or bodily part) became stronger or firmer.
2 [no obj.] (**tone with**) harmonize with (something) in terms of colour: the rich orange colour of the wood tones beautifully with the yellow roses.
3 Photography give (a monochrome picture) an altered colour in finishing by means of a chemical solution.
– DERIVATIVES **toned** adjective [in combination] the fresh-toned singing.
– ORIGIN Middle English: from Old French *ton*, from Latin *tonus*, from Greek *tonos* 'tension, tone', from *teinein* 'to stretch'.

▶ **tone something down** make something less harsh in sound or colour. ■ make something less extreme or intense: she saw the need to tone down her protests.

tone arm ▶ noun the movable arm supporting the pickup of a record player.

toneburst ▶ noun an audio signal used in testing the transient response of audio components.

tone cluster ▶ noun another term for NOTE CLUSTER.

tone colour ▶ noun Music another term for TIMBRE.

tone-deaf ▶ adjective (of a person) unable to perceive differences of musical pitch accurately.
– DERIVATIVES **tone-deafness** noun.

tone dialling ▶ noun [mass noun] a method of telephone dialling in which each digit is represented by a particular combination of tones.

tone group ▶ noun Phonetics a group of words forming a distinctive unit in an utterance, containing a nucleus and optionally one or more other syllables before and after the nucleus.

tone language ▶ noun Linguistics a language in which variations in pitch distinguish different words.

toneless ▶ adjective (of a voice or musical sound) lacking expression or interest.
– DERIVATIVES **tonelessly** adverb.

toneme /ˈtəʊniːm/ ▶ noun Phonetics a phoneme distinguished from another only by its tone.
– DERIVATIVES **tonemic** adjective.
– ORIGIN 1920s: from TONE, on the pattern of *phoneme*.

tone-on-tone ▶ adjective (of a fabric or design) dyed with or using different shades of the same colour.

tonepad ▶ noun a device generating specific tones to control a device at the other end of a telephone line, where the caller's phone does not generate such tones itself.

tone poem ▶ noun a piece of orchestral music, typically in one movement, on a descriptive or rhapsodic theme.

toner ▶ noun **1** an astringent liquid applied to the skin to reduce oiliness and improve its condition.
■ [with modifier] a device or exercise for making a specified part of the body firmer and stronger: a tummy toner.
2 [mass noun] a black or coloured powder used in xerographic copying processes.
■ [count noun] [usu. with adj. or noun modifier] a chemical bath

for changing the colour or shade of a photographic print, especially as specified: *sepia or blue toners*.

tone row ▶ noun a particular sequence of the twelve notes of the chromatic scale used as a basis for twelve-note (serial) music.

tone unit ▶ noun another term for **TONE GROUP**.

tong¹ ▶ noun a Chinese association or secret society in the US, frequently associated with underworld criminal activity.
– ORIGIN late 19th cent.: from Chinese (Cantonese dialect) *t'ŏng*, literally 'meeting place'.

tong² ▶ verb [with obj.] **1** curl (hair) using tongs.
2 collect (oysters) using oyster tongs.

Tonga¹ /ˈtɒŋə, ˈtɒŋgə/ a country in the South Pacific consisting of an island group south-east of Fiji; pop. 98,000 (est. 1994); official languages, Tongan and English; capital, Nuku'alofa. Also called the **FRIENDLY ISLANDS**.

> The kingdom of Tonga consists of about 170 volcanic and coral islands, of which thirty-six are inhabited. Visited by the Dutch in the early 17th century, Tonga became a British protectorate in 1900 and an independent Commonwealth state in 1970. It has been a constitutional monarchy since 1875.

Tonga² /ˈtɒŋgə/ ▶ noun (pl. same or **Tongas**) **1** a member of any of three peoples of southern Africa, living mainly in Zambia, Malawi, and Mozambique respectively.
2 [mass noun] any of the three different Bantu languages spoken by these peoples.
▶ adjective of or relating to these peoples or their languages.

tonga /ˈtɒŋgə/ ▶ noun a light horse-drawn two-wheeled vehicle used in India.
– ORIGIN from Hindi *tãgā*.

Tongan /ˈtɒŋən, ˈtɒŋg(ə)n/ ▶ adjective of or relating to Tonga or its people or language.
▶ noun **1** a native or national of Tonga.
2 [mass noun] the Polynesian language spoken in Tonga.

Tongariro, Mount /ˌtɒŋgəˈrɪərəʊ/ a mountain in North Island, New Zealand. It rises to a height of 1,968 m (6,457 ft) and is held sacred by the Maoris.

tongs ▶ plural noun (also **a pair of tongs**) **1** an instrument with two movable arms that are joined at one end, used for picking up and holding things: *sugar tongs*.
2 a heated cylindrical device used for curling hair: *curling tongs*.
– ORIGIN Old English *tang(e)* (singular), of Germanic origin; related to Dutch *tang* and German *Zange*.

Tongshan /tɒŋˈʃan/ former name (1912–45) for **XUZHOU**.

tongue ▶ noun **1** the fleshy muscular organ in the mouth of a mammal, used for tasting, licking, swallowing, and (in humans) articulating speech.
■the equivalent organ in other vertebrates, sometimes used (in snakes) as a scent organ or (in chameleons) for catching food. ■ an analogous organ in insects, formed from some of the mouthparts and used in feeding. ■ [mass noun] the tongue of a hoofed mammal, in particular an ox or lamb, as food. ■ used in reference to a person's style or manner of speaking: *he was a redoubtable debater with a caustic tongue*. ■ a particular language: *the prioress chatted to the pedlar in a strange tongue*.
2 a thing resembling or likened to a tongue, in particular:
■a long, low promontory of land. ■ a strip of leather or fabric under the laces in a shoe, attached only at the front end. ■ the free-swinging metal piece inside a bell which is made to strike the tongue to produce the sound. ■ the pin of a buckle. ■ a projecting strip on a wooden board fitting into a groove on another. ■ the vibrating reed of a musical instrument or organ pipe. ■ a jet of flame: *a tongue of flame flashes four feet from the gun*.
▶ verb (**tongues, tongued, tonguing**) [with obj.] **1** Music sound (a note) distinctly on a wind instrument by interrupting the air flow with the tongue.
2 lick or caress with the tongue: *the other horse tongued every part of the colt's mane*.
– PHRASES **find** (or **lose**) **one's tongue** be able (or unable) to express oneself after a shock. **get one's tongue round** pronounce (words): *she found it very difficult to get her tongue round the unfamiliar words*. **the gift of tongues** the power of speaking in unknown languages, regarded as one of the gifts of the Holy Spirit (Acts 2). **give tongue** (of hounds) bark, especially on finding a scent. ■ express one's feelings or opinions freely, sometimes

objectionably so. **keep a civil tongue in one's head** speak politely. (**with**) **tongue in cheek** without really meaning what one is saying or writing. **someone's tongue is hanging out** someone is very eager for something, especially a drink: *the tabloids have their tongues hanging out for this stuff*.
– DERIVATIVES **tongueless** adjective.
– ORIGIN Old English *tunge*, of Germanic origin; related to Dutch *tong*, German *Zunge* and Latin *lingua*.

tongue and groove ▶ noun [mass noun] wooden planking in which adjacent boards are joined by means of interlocking ridges and hollows down their sides.
– DERIVATIVES **tongued-and-grooved** adjective.

tongued ▶ adjective **1** [in combination] having a specified kind of tongue: *the blue-tongued lizard*.
■(in carpentry) constructed using a tongue.
2 (of a note) played by tonguing.

tonguefish ▶ noun (pl. same or **-fishes**) a small teardrop-shaped flatfish of warm seas, which is an important food fish in some areas.
● Family Cynoglossidae: *Symphurus* and other genera; numerous species.

tongue-in-cheek ▶ adjective & adverb with ironic or flippant intent: [as adj.] *her delightful tongue-in-cheek humour* | [as adv.] *'I swear there's a female conspiracy against men!' he complained, tongue-in-cheek*.

tongue-lashing ▶ noun [in sing.] a loud or severe scolding: *the incensed boss gave him a tongue-lashing*.

tongue tie ▶ noun a malformation which restricts the movement of the tongue and causes a speech impediment.

tongue-tied ▶ adjective **1** too shy or embarrassed to speak.
2 having a malformation restricting the movement of the tongue.

tongue-twister ▶ noun a sequence of words or sounds, typically of an alliterative kind, that are difficult to pronounce quickly and correctly, as for example *Peter Piper picked a peck of pickled pepper*.
– DERIVATIVES **tongue-twisting** adjective.

tongue worm ▶ noun a flattened worm-like parasite which infests vertebrates, especially reptiles, having a sucking mouth with hooks for attachment to the lining of the respiratory tract.
● Subphylum Pentastomida, phylum Arthropoda; sometimes regarded as a class of crustacean.

tonic ▶ noun **1** a medicinal substance taken to give a feeling of vigour or well-being.
■something with an invigorating effect: *being needed is a tonic for someone at my age*.
2 short for **TONIC WATER**.
3 Music the first note in a scale which, in conventional harmony, provides the keynote of a piece of music.
▶ adjective **1** giving a feeling of vigour or well-being; invigorating.
2 Music relating to or denoting the first degree of a scale.
3 Phonetics denoting or relating to the syllable within a tone group that has greatest prominence, because it carries the main change of pitch.
4 relating to or restoring normal tone to muscles or other organs.
■Physiology relating to, denoting, or producing continuous muscular contraction.
– DERIVATIVES **tonically** adverb.
– ORIGIN mid 17th cent.: from French *tonique*, from Greek *tonikos* 'of or for stretching', from *tonos* (see **TONE**).

tonic–clonic /ˌtɒnɪ(k)ˈklɒnɪk/ ▶ adjective Medicine of or characterized by successive phases of tonic and clonic spasm (as in *grand mal* epilepsy).

tonicity /təˈnɪsɪti/ ▶ noun [mass noun] **1** muscle tone.
2 Linguistics the pattern of tones or stress in speech.
3 Biology the state of a solution in respect of osmotic pressure: *the tonicity of the fluid*.

tonic sol-fa ▶ noun [mass noun] a system of naming the notes of the scale (usually **doh, ray, me, fah, soh, lah, te**) used especially to teach singing, with doh as the keynote of all major keys and lah as the keynote of all minor keys. See **SOLMIZATION**.

tonic water ▶ noun [mass noun] a carbonated soft drink with a bitter flavour, used as a mixer with gin or other spirits (originally as a stimulant of appetite and digestion).

tonify /ˈtəʊnɪfʌɪ/ ▶ verb (**-ies, -ied**) [with obj.] impart tone to (the body or a part of it).
■(of acupuncture or herbal medicine) increase the available energy of (an organ, part, or system of the body).
– DERIVATIVES **tonification** noun.

tonight ▶ adverb on the present or approaching evening or night: *are you doing anything tonight?*
▶ noun the evening or night of the present day: *tonight is a night to remember*.
– ORIGIN Old English *tō niht*, from the preposition **TO** + **NIGHT**. Compare with **TODAY** and **TOMORROW**.

tonka bean /ˈtɒŋkə/ ▶ noun the black seed of a South American tree, which has a vanilla-like fragrance. The dried beans are cured in rum or other alcohol and then used in perfumery and for scenting and flavouring tobacco, ice cream, and other products.
● The tree is *Dipteryx odorata*, family Leguminosae.
– ORIGIN late 18th cent.: from *tonka*, a local word in Guyana.

Tonkin /tɒnˈkɪn/ a mountainous region of northern Vietnam, centred on the delta of the Red River.

Tonkin, Gulf of an arm of the South China Sea, bounded by the coasts of southern China and northern Vietnam. Its chief port is Haiphong. An incident there in 1964 led to increased US military involvement in the area prior to the Vietnam War.

Tonlé Sap /ˌtɒnleɪ ˈsap/ a lake in central Cambodia, linked to the Mekong River by the Tonlé Sap river.

ton-mile ▶ noun one ton of goods carried one mile, as a unit of traffic.

tonnage ▶ noun [mass noun] weight in tons, especially of cargo or freight: *road convoys carry more tonnage*.
■the size or carrying capacity of a ship measured in tons. ■ shipping considered in terms of total carrying capacity: *the European Community's total tonnage*.
– ORIGIN early 17th cent. (denoting a charge per ton on cargo): from **TON**¹ + **-AGE**.

tonne /tʌn/ ▶ noun another term for **METRIC TON**.
– ORIGIN late 19th cent.: from French; compare with **TON**¹.

tonneau /ˈtɒnəʊ/ ▶ noun **1** the part of a motor car, typically an open car, occupied by the back seats.
■short for **TONNEAU COVER**.
2 a unit of capacity for French wine, especially Bordeaux, usually equally to 900 litres or 198 gallons.
– ORIGIN late 18th cent. (in sense 2): French, literally 'cask, tun'.

tonneau cover ▶ noun a protective cover for the seats in an open car or cabin cruiser when they are not in use.

tonometer /tə(ʊ)ˈnɒmɪtə/ ▶ noun **1** a tuning fork or other instrument for measuring the pitch of musical tones.
2 an instrument for measuring the pressure in a part of the body, such as the eyeball (to test for glaucoma) or a blood vessel.
– ORIGIN early 18th cent.: from Greek *tonos* (see **TONE**) + **-METER**.

tonoplast /ˈtəʊnə(ʊ)plast, -plɑːst/ ▶ noun Botany a membrane which bounds the chief vacuole of a plant cell.
– ORIGIN late 19th cent.: from Greek *tonos* 'tension, tone' + *plastos* 'formed'.

tonsil ▶ noun either of two small masses of lymphoid tissue in the throat, one on each side of the root of the tongue.
– DERIVATIVES **tonsillar** adjective.
– ORIGIN late 16th cent.: from French *tonsilles* or Latin *tonsillae* (plural).

tonsillectomy /ˌtɒnsɪˈlɛktəmi/ ▶ noun (pl. **-ies**) a surgical operation to remove the tonsils.

tonsillitis ▶ noun [mass noun] inflammation of the tonsils.

tonsorial /tɒnˈsɔːrɪəl/ ▶ adjective formal or humorous of or relating to hairdressing.
– ORIGIN early 19th cent.: from Latin *tonsorius* (from *tonsor* 'barber', from *tondere* 'shear, clip') + **-AL**.

tonsure /ˈtɒnsjə, ˈtɒnʃə/ ▶ noun a part of a monk's or priest's head left bare on top by shaving off the hair.
■[in sing.] an act of shaving the top of a monk's or priest's head as a preparation for entering a religious order.

▶**verb** [with obj.] [often as adj. **tonsured**] shave the hair on the crown of.
– ORIGIN late Middle English: from Old French, or from Latin *tonsura*, from *tondere* 'shear, clip'.

tontine /tɒnˈtiːn, ˈtɒn-/ ▶ **noun** an annuity shared by subscribers to a loan or common fund, the shares increasing as subscribers die until the last survivor enjoys the whole income.
– ORIGIN mid 18th cent.: from French, named after Lorenzo *Tonti* (1630–95), a Neapolitan banker who started such a scheme to raise government loans in France (c.1653).

Tonton Macoute /ˌtɒntɒn məˈkuːt/ ▶ **noun** (pl. **Tontons Macoutes** pronunc. same) a member of a notoriously brutal militia formed by President François Duvalier of Haiti, active from 1961–86.
– ORIGIN Haitian French, apparently with reference to an ogre of folk tales.

ton-up ▶ **noun** Brit. informal **1** a speed of 100 mph.
2 a score of 100 or more.

tonus /ˈtəʊnəs/ ▶ **noun** [mass noun] the constant low-level activity of a body tissue, especially muscle tone.
– ORIGIN late 19th cent.: from Latin, from Greek *tonos* 'tension'.

Tony ▶ **noun** (pl. **Tonys**) (in the US) any of a number of awards given annually for outstanding achievement in the theatre in various categories.
– ORIGIN from the nickname of Antoinette Perry (1888–1946), American actress and director.

tony ▶ **adjective** (**tonier**, **toniest**) US informal fashionable among wealthy or stylish people: *a tony restaurant*.
– ORIGIN late 19th cent.: from the noun TONE + -Y¹.

too ▶ **adverb 1** [as submodifier] to a higher degree than is desirable, permissible, or possible; excessively: *he was driving too fast* | *he wore suits that seemed a size too small for him*.
■informal very: *you're too kind.*
2 in addition; also: *is he coming too?*
■moreover (used when adding a further point): *she is a grown woman, and a strong one too.*
– PHRASES **all too** ⸺ used to emphasize that something is the case to an extreme or unwelcome extent: *failures are all too common.* **none too** ⸺ far from; not very: *her sight's none too good.* **only too** see ONLY. **too bad** see BAD. **too besides** W. Indian moreover; also: *'You not listening, and too besides you don't have to shout at the damn bird so!'* **too far** see FAR. **too much** see MUCH. **too right** see RIGHT.
– ORIGIN Old English, stressed form of TO, spelled *too* from the 16th cent.

toodle-oo ▶ **exclamation** informal, dated goodbye: *we'll see you later, toodle-oo!*
– ORIGIN early 20th cent.: perhaps an alteration of French *à tout à l'heure* 'see you soon'.

took past of TAKE.

tool ▶ **noun 1** a device or implement, especially one held in the hand, used to carry out a particular function: *gardening tools.*
■a thing used in an occupation or pursuit: *computers are an essential tool* | *the ability to write clearly is a tool of the trade.* ■a person used or exploited by another: *the beautiful Estella is Miss Havisham's tool.* ■Computing a piece of software that carries out a particular function, typically creating or modifying another program.
2 a distinct design in the tooling of a book.
■a small stamp or roller used to make such a design.
3 vulgar slang a man's penis.
▶**verb 1** [with obj.] (usu. **be tooled**) impress a design on (leather, especially a leather book cover): *volumes bound in green leather and tooled in gold.*
■dress (stone) with a chisel.
2 equip or be equipped with tools for industrial production: [with obj.] *the factory must be tooled to produce the models* | [no obj.] *they were tooling up for British production.*
■(**tool up** or **be tooled up**) Brit. informal be or become armed, especially for criminal activity.
3 [no obj., with adverbial of direction] informal drive or ride in a casual or leisurely manner: *tooling around town in a pink Rolls-Royce.*
– DERIVATIVES **tooler** noun.
– ORIGIN Old English *tōl*, from a Germanic base meaning 'prepare'; compare with TAW¹. The verb dates from the early 19th cent.

toolbar ▶ **noun** Computing (in a program with a graphical user interface) a strip of icons used to perform certain functions.

toolbox ▶ **noun** a box or container for keeping tools in.
■Computing a set of software tools. ■Computing the set of programs or functions accessible from a single menu.

tooling ▶ **noun** [mass noun] **1** assorted tools, especially ones required for a mechanized process.
■the process of making or working something with tools.
2 the ornamentation of a leather book cover with designs impressed by heated tools.

tool kit ▶ **noun** a set of tools, especially one kept in a bag or box and used for a particular purpose.
■Computing a set of software tools.

toolmaker ▶ **noun** a maker of tools, especially a person who makes and maintains tools for use in a manufacturing process.
– DERIVATIVES **toolmaking** noun.

tool post ▶ **noun** the post of a machine tool which holds a cutting tool steady.

tool pusher ▶ **noun** a person who directs the drilling on an oil rig.

tool steel ▶ **noun** [mass noun] hard steel of a quality used for making cutting tools.

toon¹ ▶ **noun** informal a cartoon film.
■a character in such a film.
– ORIGIN 1930s: shortening of CARTOON.

toon² ▶ **noun** non-standard spelling of TOWN, representing Scottish and Northern English pronunciation.

toot ▶ **noun 1** a short, sharp sound made by a horn, trumpet, or similar instrument.
2 informal, chiefly US a snort of a drug, especially cocaine.
■[mass noun] cocaine.
3 N. Amer. informal a spell of drinking and lively enjoyment; a spree: *a sales manager on a toot.*
▶**verb** [with obj.] **1** sound (a horn or similar) with a short, sharp sound: *behind us an impatient motorist tooted a horn.*
■[no obj.] make such a sound: *a car tooted at us.*
2 informal, chiefly US snort (cocaine).
– DERIVATIVES **tooter** noun.
– ORIGIN early 16th cent.: probably from Middle Low German *tūten*, but possibly an independent imitative formation.

tooth ▶ **noun** (pl. **teeth**) **1** each of a set of hard, bony enamel-coated structures in the jaws of most vertebrates, used for biting and chewing.
■a similar hard, pointed structure in invertebrate animals, typically functioning in the mechanical breakdown of food. ■an appetite or liking for a particular thing: *what a tooth for fruit a monkey has!* ■ [mass noun] roughness given to a surface to allow colour or glue to adhere. ■ (**teeth**) figurative genuine force or effectiveness of a body or in a law or agreement: *the Charter would be fine if it had teeth and could be enforced.* ■ (**teeth**) used in curses or exclamations: *Hell's teeth!*
2 a projecting part on a tool or other instrument, especially one of a series that function or engage together, such as a cog on a gearwheel or a point on a saw or comb.
■a projecting part on an animal or plant, especially one of a jagged or dentate row on the margin of a leaf or shell.
– PHRASES **armed to the teeth** formidably armed. **fight tooth and nail** fight very fiercely. **get** (or **sink**) **one's teeth into** work energetically and productively on (a task): *the course gives students something to get their teeth into.* **in the teeth of** directly against (the wind). ■ in spite of or contrary to (opposition or difficulty): *we defended it in the teeth of persecution.* **set someone's teeth on edge** see EDGE.
– DERIVATIVES **toothed** adjective, **tooth-like** adjective.
– ORIGIN Old English *tōth* (plural *tēth*), of Germanic origin; related to Dutch *tand* and German *Zahn*, from an Indo-European root shared by Latin *dent-*, Greek *odont-*.

toothache ▶ **noun** [mass noun] pain in a tooth or teeth: *I've got toothache* | [in sing.] *he has a toothache.*

toothbrush ▶ **noun** a small brush with a long handle, used for cleaning the teeth.

toothbrush moustache ▶ **noun** a short bristly moustache trimmed to a rectangular shape.

toothcarp ▶ **noun** (pl. same) a small fish that resembles the carp but possesses small teeth,

occurring mainly in fresh water in America. Many toothcarp are popular in aquaria.
●Order Cyprinodontiformes: several families, in particular Cyprinodontidae (or Fundulidae) (the egg-laying killifishes and topminnows), and Poeciliidae (the livebearers).

toothcomb ▶ **noun** Brit. used with reference to a very thorough search or analysis of something: *Cropper will have been through the manuscript with a toothcomb* | *the boys have been over the area with a fine toothcomb.*

USAGE The forms **toothcomb** and **fine toothcomb** arose from a misreading of the compound noun **fine-tooth comb**. In modern use all the forms are accepted in standard English.

toothed whale ▶ **noun** a predatory whale having teeth rather than baleen plates. Toothed whales include sperm whales, killer whales, beaked whales, narwhals, dolphins, and porpoises.
●Suborder Odontoceti, order Cetacea: six families and numerous species.

tooth fairy ▶ **noun** a fairy said to take children's milk teeth after they fall out and leave a coin under their pillow.

toothglass ▶ **noun** a glass for holding toothbrushes or dentures, or one used as a tumbler for mouthwash.

toothing ▶ **noun** [mass noun] the teeth on a saw.
■projecting bricks or stones left at the end of a wall to allow its continuation.

toothless ▶ **adjective** having no teeth, typically through old age: *a toothless old man.*
■figurative lacking genuine force or effectiveness: *laws that are well intentioned but toothless.*
– DERIVATIVES **toothlessly** adverb, **toothlessness** noun.

toothpaste ▶ **noun** [mass noun] a thick, soft, moist substance used on a brush for cleaning a person's teeth.

toothpick ▶ **noun** a short pointed piece of wood or plastic used for removing bits of food lodged between the teeth.

tooth powder ▶ **noun** [mass noun] powder used for cleaning the teeth.

tooth shell ▶ **noun** another term for TUSK SHELL.

toothsome ▶ **adjective** (of food) temptingly tasty: *a toothsome morsel.*
■informal (of a person) good-looking; attractive.
– DERIVATIVES **toothsomely** adverb, **toothsomeness** noun.

toothwort ▶ **noun** a Eurasian plant which is parasitic on the roots of hazel and beech, with a thick rhizome bearing rows of tooth-like scales.
●*Lathraea squamaria*, family Scrophulariaceae (or Orobanchaceae).

toothy ▶ **adjective** (**toothier**, **toothiest**) having or showing large, numerous, or prominent teeth: *a toothy smile.*
– DERIVATIVES **toothily** adverb.

tootin' ▶ **adjective** N. Amer. informal used for emphasis: *he said he was damned tootin' he was right.*

tootle ▶ **verb 1** [no obj.] casually make a series of sounds on a horn, trumpet, or similar instrument: *he tootled on the horn.*
■[with obj.] play (an instrument) or make (a sound or tune) in such a way: *the video games tootled their tunes.*
2 [no obj., with adverbial of direction] informal go or travel in a leisurely way: *they were tootling along the coast road.*
▶**noun** [usu. in sing.] **1** an act or sound of casual playing on an instrument such as a horn or trumpet.
2 informal a leisurely journey.
– ORIGIN early 19th cent.: frequentative of TOOT.

too-too ▶ **adverb** & **adjective** informal, dated used affectedly to convey that one finds something excessively annoying or fatiguing: [as adv.] *it had become too-too tiring* | [as adj.] *it is all just too-too.*
– ORIGIN late 19th cent.: reduplication of TOO.

tootsie (also **tootsy**) ▶ **noun** (pl. **-ies**) informal **1** a person's foot.
2 a young woman, especially one perceived as being sexually available.
– ORIGIN mid 19th cent.: humorous diminutive of FOOT.

toot sweet ▶ **adverb** informal immediately: *hop down here toot sweet and let's have a look at it.*
– ORIGIN early 20th cent.: Anglicized form of French *tout de suite.*

Toowoomba /təˈwʊmbə/ a town in Queensland,

Australia, to the west of Brisbane; pop. 75,960 (1991). It was formerly known as The Swamps.

top[1] ▶ **noun 1** [usu. in sing.] the highest or uppermost point, part, or surface of something: *Doreen stood at the top of the stairs | fill the cup almost to the top.* ■ chiefly Brit. the end of something that is furthest from the speaker or a point of reference: *the bus shelter at the top of the road.* ■ (usu. **tops**) the leaves, stems, and shoots of a plant, especially those of a vegetable grown for its root. ■ chiefly Brit. the uppermost creamy layer of milk.
2 a thing or part placed on, fitted to, or covering the upper part of something, in particular: ■ a garment covering the upper part of the body and worn with a skirt, trousers, or shorts. ■ a lid, cover, or cap for something: *beer-bottle tops.* ■ a platform at the head of a ship's mast; especially (in a sailing ship), a platform around the head of each of the lower masts, serving to extend the topmast rigging.
3 (**the top**) the highest or most important rank, level, or position: *her talent will take her right to the top | the people* **at the top** *must be competent.* ■ a person or thing occupying such a position: *I came top in my class.* ■ (**tops**) informal a person or thing regarded as particularly good or pleasant: *cranberry sauce is tops with turkey.* ■ the utmost degree or the highest level: *she shouted at the top of her voice.* ■ Brit. the highest gear of a motor vehicle. ■ [mass noun] the high-frequency component of reproduced sound.
4 short for **TOPSPIN**.
5 (usu. **tops**) a bundle of long wool fibres prepared for spinning.
6 [mass noun] Physics one of six flavours of quark.
▶ **adjective** [attrib.] highest in position, rank, or degree: *the top button of his shirt | a top executive.* ■ chiefly Brit. furthest away from the speaker or a point of reference: *the top end of Fulham Road.*
▶ **verb** (**topped**, **topping**) [with obj.] **1** exceed (an amount, level, or number); be more than: *losses are expected to top £100 m this year.* ■ be at the highest place or rank in (a list, poll, chart, or league): *her debut album topped the charts for five weeks.* ■ be taller than: *he topped her by several inches.* ■ surpass (a person or previous achievement or action); outdo: *he was baffled as to how he could top his past work.* ■ appear as the chief performer or attraction at: *Hopper topped a great night of boxing.* ■ reach the top of (a hill or other stretch of rising ground): *they topped a rise and began a slow descent.*
2 (usu. **be topped**) provide with a top or topping: *toast topped with baked beans.* ■ complete (an outfit) with an upper garment, hat, or item of jewellery: *a white dress topped by a dark cardigan.* ■ remove the top of (a vegetable or fruit) in preparation for cooking. ■ informal kill: *I wasn't sorry when that fellow topped himself.*
3 Golf mishit (the ball or a stroke) by hitting above the centre of the ball.
▶ **adverb** (**tops**) informal at the most: *some civil servant knocking down twenty-eight thousand a year, tops.*
– PHRASES **from top to bottom** completely; thoroughly: *we searched the place from top to bottom.* **from top to toe** completely; all over: *she seemed to glow from top to toe.* **from the top** informal from the beginning: *they rehearsed Act One from the top.* **get on top of** cause (someone) to feel overwhelmed and depressed by their inability to cope: *things had got on top of me.* **off the top of one's head** see **HEAD**. **on top 1** on the highest point or uppermost surface: *a woollen hat with a bobble on top.* ■ on the upper part of the head: *Graeme's going a bit thin on top.* ■ so as to cover; over: *she put on a grey raincoat on top.* **2** in a leading or the dominant position: *United were on top for most of the first half.* **3** in addition: *the price was £75, with VAT on top.* **on top of 1** on the highest point or uppermost surface of: *a town perched on top of a hill.* ■ so as to cover; over: *his habit of wearing one v-neck jumper on top of another.* ■ in close proximity to: *we all lived on top of each other.* **2** in command or control of: *he couldn't* **get on top of** *his work.* **3** in addition to: *on top of everything else he's a brilliant linguist.* **on top of the world** informal happy and elated. **over the top 1** informal, chiefly Brit. to an excessive or exaggerated degree, in particular so as to go beyond reasonable or acceptable limits: *her reactions had been a bit over the top.* **2** chiefly historical over the parapet of a trench and into battle. **top and tail** Brit. **1** remove the top and bottom of (a fruit or vegetable) while preparing it as food. **2** wash the face and bottom of (a baby or small child). **top dollar** N. Amer. informal a very high price: *I pay top dollar for my materials.* **the top of the tree** the highest level of a profession or career. **top ten** (or **twenty** etc.) the first ten (or twenty etc.) records in the pop music charts. **to top it all** as a culminating, typically unpleasant, event or action in a series. **up top** see **UP**.
– DERIVATIVES **topmost** adjective, **topped** adjective [in combination] *a glass-topped table.*
– ORIGIN late Old English *topp* (noun), of Germanic origin; related to Dutch *top* 'summit, crest'.
▶ **top something off 1** (often **be topped off**) finish something in a memorable or notable way: *the festive celebration was topped off with the awarding of prizes.* **2** US informal fill up a partly full tank with fuel.
top out reach an upper limit: *collectors whose budgets tend to top out at about $50,000.*
top something out put the highest structural feature on a building, typically as a ceremony to mark the building's completion.
top someone up informal refill a partly full glass or cup for someone.
top something up add to a number or amount to bring it up to a certain level: *a 0.5 per cent bonus is offered to top up savings rates.* ■ fill up a glass or other partly full container.

top[2] ▶ **noun 1** (also **spinning top**) a conical, spherical, or pear-shaped toy that with a quick or vigorous twist may be set to spin.
2 used in names of top shells, e.g. **strawberry top**.
– ORIGIN late Old English, of unknown origin.

topaz ▶ **noun 1** a precious stone, typically colourless, yellow, or pale blue, consisting of a fluorine-containing aluminium silicate. ■ [mass noun] a dark yellow colour.
2 a large tropical American hummingbird with a yellowish throat and a long tail.
• Genus *Topaza*, family Trochilidae: two species.
– ORIGIN Middle English (denoting a yellow sapphire): from Old French *topace*, via Latin from Greek *topazos*.

topazolite /tə(ʊ)ˈpazəlʌɪt/ ▶ **noun** [mass noun] a yellowish-green variety of andradite (garnet).
– ORIGIN early 19th cent.: from **TOPAZ** + **-LITE**.

top boot ▶ **noun** chiefly historical a high boot with a broad band of a different material or colour at the top.

top brass ▶ **noun** see **BRASS**.

topcoat ▶ **noun 1** an overcoat.
2 an outer coat of paint.

top copy ▶ **noun** the original typed or handwritten copy of a letter or document of which carbon copies have been made.

top dead centre ▶ **noun** the furthest point of a piston's travel, at which it changes from an upward to a downward stroke.

top dog ▶ **noun** informal a person who is successful or dominant in their field: *he was a top dog in the City.*

top-down ▶ **adjective 1** denoting a system of government or management in which actions and policies are initiated at the highest level; hierarchical.
2 proceeding from the general to the particular: *a top-down approach to research.* ■ Computing working from the top or root of a tree-like system towards the branches.

top drawer ▶ **noun** the uppermost drawer in a chest or desk. ■ (**the top drawer**) informal high social position or class: *George and Madge were not* **out of the top drawer**.
▶ **adjective** (**top-drawer**) informal of the highest quality or social class: *a top-drawer performance.*

top dressing ▶ **noun** an application of manure or fertilizer to the surface layer of soil or a lawn.
– DERIVATIVES **top-dress** verb.

tope[1] ▶ **verb** [no obj.] archaic or poetic/literary drink alcohol to excess, especially on a regular basis.
– DERIVATIVES **toper** noun.
– ORIGIN mid 17th cent.: perhaps an alteration of obsolete *top* 'overbalance'; perhaps from Dutch *toppen* 'slant or tilt a ship's yard'.

tope[2] ▶ **noun** (in the Indian subcontinent) a grove or plantation of trees, especially mango trees.
– ORIGIN from Telugu *tōpu* or Tamil *tōppu*.

tope[3] ▶ **noun** another term for **STUPA**.
– ORIGIN from Punjabi *thūp*, *thop* 'barrow, mound', apparently related to Sanskrit *stūpa*.

tope[4] ▶ **noun** a small greyish slender-bodied shark, occurring chiefly in inshore waters.
• Genus *Galeorhinus*, family Carcharhinidae: the East Atlantic *G. galeus*, favoured by British sea anglers, and the commercially important *G. australis* of Australia.
– ORIGIN late 17th cent.: perhaps of Cornish origin.

top edge Cricket ▶ **noun** a shot hit into the air off the upper edge of a bat held sideways.
▶ **verb** (**top-edge**) [with obj.] hit (the ball) in this way; hit a ball delivered by (a bowler) in this way.

topee ▶ **noun** variant spelling of **TOPI**[1].

Topeka /təˈpiːkə/ the state capital of Kansas; pop. 119,880 (1990).

top fermentation ▶ **noun** [mass noun] the process by which ale-type beers are fermented, proceeding for a relatively short period at high temperature with the yeast rising to the top.

top flight ▶ **noun** (**the top flight**) the highest rank or level.
▶ **adjective** [attrib.] of the highest rank or level: *a top-flight batsman.*

top fruit ▶ **noun** [mass noun] Brit. fruit grown on trees rather than bushes.

topgallant /tɒpˈgal(ə)nt, təˈgal-/ ▶ **noun** (also **topgallant mast**) the section of a square-rigged sailing ship's mast immediately above the topmast. ■ (also **topgallant sail**) a sail set on such a mast.

top hamper ▶ **noun** [mass noun] Sailing sails, rigging, or other things above decks creating top-heavy weight or wind-resistant surfaces.

top hat ▶ **noun** a man's formal hat with a high cylindrical crown.

top-heavy ▶ **adjective** disproportionately heavy at the top so as to be in danger of toppling. ■ (of an organization) having a disproportionately large number of people in senior administrative positions. ■ informal (of a woman) having a disproportionately large bust.
– DERIVATIVES **top-heavily** adverb, **top-heaviness** noun.

Tophet /ˈtəʊfɪt/ ▶ **noun** a term for hell.
– ORIGIN late Middle English: from Hebrew *tōpeṯ*, the name of a place in the Valley of Hinnom near Jerusalem used for idolatrous worship, including the sacrifice of children (see Jer. 19:6), and later for burning refuse.

top-hole ▶ **adjective** Brit. informal, dated excellent; first-rate.

tophus /ˈtəʊfəs/ ▶ **noun** (pl. **tophi** /-fʌɪ/) Medicine a deposit of crystalline uric acid and other substances at the surface of joints or in skin or cartilage, typically as a feature of gout.
– ORIGIN early 17th cent.: from Latin, denoting loose porous stones of various kinds.

topi[1] /ˈtəʊpi/ (also **topee**) ▶ **noun** (pl. **topis** or **topees**) chiefly Indian a hat, especially a sola topi.
– ORIGIN from Hindi *topī* 'hat'.

topi[2] /ˈtəʊpi/ ▶ **noun** (pl. same or **topis**) a large African antelope related to the hartebeests, with a pattern of bold black patches on a reddish coat, and thick ridged horns.
• *Damaliscus lunatus*, family Bovidae, in particular the race *D. l. topi* of East Africa. Compare with **TSESSEBI**.
– ORIGIN late 19th cent.: from Mende.

topiary /ˈtəʊpɪəri/ ▶ **noun** (pl. **-ies**) [mass noun] the art or practice of clipping shrubs or trees into ornamental shapes. ■ shrubs or trees clipped into ornamental shapes in such a way: *a cottage surrounded by topiary and flowers.*
– DERIVATIVES **topiarian** /-pɪˈɛːrɪən/ adjective, **topiarist** noun.
– ORIGIN late 16th cent.: from French *topiaire*, from Latin *topiarius* 'ornamental gardener', from *topia opera* 'fancy gardening', from a diminutive of Greek *topos* 'place'.

topic ▶ **noun** a matter dealt with in a text, discourse, or conversation; a subject: *her favourite topic of conversation is her partner.* ■ Linguistics that part of a sentence about which something is said, typically the first major constituent.
– ORIGIN late 15th cent. (originally denoting a set or book of general rules or ideas): from Latin *topica*, from Greek *ta topika*, literally 'matters concerning commonplaces' (the title of a treatise by Aristotle), from *topos* 'a place'.

topical ▶ **adjective 1** (of a subject) of immediate relevance, interest, or importance owing to its relation to current events: *a popular topical affairs programme.* ■ relating to a particular subject; classified according to subject: *foreign or topical stamps.*

2 chiefly Medicine relating or applied directly to a part of the body.
– DERIVATIVES **topicality** noun, **topically** adverb.
– ORIGIN late 16th cent.: from Greek *topikos* + **-AL**. Early use was as a term in logic and rhetoric describing a rule or argument as 'applicable in most but not all cases'.

topicalize (also **-ise**) ▶ verb [with obj.] Linguistics cause (a subject, word, or phrase) to be the topic of a sentence or discourse, typically by placing it first.
– DERIVATIVES **topicalization** noun.

topic sentence ▶ noun a sentence that expresses the main idea of the paragraph in which it occurs.

Topkapi Palace /tɒpˈkɑːpi/ the former seraglio or residence in Istanbul of the sultans of the Ottoman Empire, last occupied by Mahmut II (1808–39) and now a museum.

topknot ▶ noun a knot of hair arranged on the top of the head.
■ a decorative knot or bow of ribbon worn on the top of the head, popular in the 18th century. ■ (in an animal or bird) a tuft or crest of hair or feathers.

topless ▶ adjective (of a woman or a woman's item of clothing) having or leaving the breasts uncovered: *a topless dancer.*
– DERIVATIVES **toplessness** noun.

top-level ▶ adjective of the highest level of importance or prestige: *top-level talks.*

top light ▶ noun **1** a small pane above a main window, which typically opens outwards and upwards.
2 a skylight.

top-line ▶ adjective [attrib.] of the highest quality or ranking: *a top-line act.*

toplofty ▶ adjective US informal haughty and arrogant.

topman ▶ noun (pl. **-men**) chiefly historical **1** a sawyer working the upper handle of a pit saw; a top-sawyer.
2 a sailor on duty in a sailing ship's tops.

topmast /ˈtɒpmɑːst, -məst/ ▶ noun the second section of a square-rigged sailing ship's mast, immediately above the lower mast.

topminnow ▶ noun an American killifish, often seen at the water surface.
● *Fundulus* and other genera in the families Cyprinodontidae (or Fundulidae) (many species), and Poeciliidae (one or two species).

top-notch ▶ adjective informal of the highest quality; excellent: *a top-notch hotel.*
– DERIVATIVES **top-notcher** noun.

top note ▶ noun the highest or a very high note in a piece of music or a singer's vocal range.
■ a dominant scent in a perfume.

topo /ˈtɒpəʊ/ ▶ noun (pl. **-os**) informal, chiefly N. Amer. a topographic map.
■ Climbing a diagram of a mountain with details of routes to the top marked on it.
– ORIGIN 1970s: abbreviation of *topographic* (see **TOPOGRAPHICAL**).

topographical /ˌtɒpəˈɡrafɪkəl/ ▶ adjective of or relating to the arrangement or accurate representation of the physical features of an area: *the topographical features of the river valley.*
■ (of a work of art or an artist) dealing with or depicting places (especially towns), buildings, and natural prospects, in a realistic and detailed manner. ■ Anatomy & Biology relating to or representing the physical distribution of parts or features on the surface of or within an organ or organism.
– DERIVATIVES **topographic** adjective, **topographically** adverb.

topography /təˈpɒɡrəfi/ ▶ noun [mass noun] the arrangement of the natural and artificial physical features of an area: *the topography of the island.*
■ [count noun] a detailed description or representation on a map of such features. ■ Anatomy & Biology the distribution of parts or features on the surface of or within an organ or organism.
– DERIVATIVES **topographer** noun.
– ORIGIN late Middle English: via late Latin from Greek *topographia*, from *topos* 'place' + *-graphia* (see **-GRAPHY**).

topoi plural form of **TOPOS**.

topoisomer /ˌtɒpəʊˈʌɪsəmə/ ▶ noun Biochemistry a topologically distinct isomer, especially of DNA.

topoisomerase /ˌtɒpəʊˈʌɪsəmereɪz/ ▶ noun Biochemistry an enzyme which alters the supercoiled form of a DNA molecule.

– ORIGIN 1970s: from Greek *topos* 'place' + **ISOMER** + **-ASE**.

topological space ▶ noun Mathematics a space which has an associated family of subsets that constitute a topology. The relationships between members of the space are mathematically analogous to those between points in ordinary two- and three-dimensional space.

topology /təˈpɒlədʒi/ ▶ noun **1** [mass noun] Mathematics the study of geometrical properties and spatial relations unaffected by the continuous change of shape or size of figures.
■ [count noun] a family of open subsets of an abstract space such that the union and the intersection of any two of them are members of the family, and which includes the space itself and the empty set.
2 the way in which constituent parts are interrelated or arranged: *the topology of a computer network.*
– DERIVATIVES **topological** adjective, **topologically** adverb, **topologist** noun.
– ORIGIN late 19th cent.: via German from Greek *topos* 'place' + **-LOGY**.

toponym /ˈtɒpənɪm/ ▶ noun a place name, especially one derived from a topographical feature.
– ORIGIN 1930s: from Greek *topos* 'place' + *onuma* 'a name'.

toponymy /təˈpɒnɪmi/ ▶ noun [mass noun] the study of place names.
– DERIVATIVES **toponymic** adjective.
– ORIGIN late 19th cent.: from Greek *topos* 'place' + *onuma* 'name'.

topos /ˈtɒpɒs/ ▶ noun (pl. **topoi** /ˈtɒpɔɪ/) a traditional theme or formula in literature.
– ORIGIN 1940s: from Greek, literally 'place'.

topper ▶ noun **1** a machine that cuts the tops off weeds.
2 US a hard protective lightweight cover or shell mounted on the back or bed of a pickup truck.
■ US a type of camper van mounted on a truck bed.
3 informal a top hat.
4 Brit. informal, dated an exceptionally good person or thing.

toppie /ˈtɒpi/ ▶ noun (pl. **-ies**) S. African **1** informal a middle-aged or elderly man. [ORIGIN: perhaps from Zulu *thopi* 'growing sparsely' (describing thinning hair), or from Hindi *topī* 'hat'.]
2 an African bulbul with a black or dark brown head and crest. [ORIGIN: late 19th cent.: from **TOPKNOT**.]
● Genus *Pycnonotus*, family Pycnonotidae: several species.

topping ▶ adjective Brit. informal, dated excellent: *that really is a topping dress.*
▶ noun a layer of food poured or spread over a base of a different type of food to add flavour.

topping lift ▶ noun a rope or cable on a sailing boat that supports the weight of a boom or yard and can be used to lift it.

topple ▶ verb [no obj., with adverbial of direction] overbalance or become unsteady and fall slowly: *she toppled over when I touched her.*
■ [with obj.] cause to fall in such a way: *the push almost toppled him to the ground* | figurative *disagreement had threatened to topple the government.*
– ORIGIN mid 16th cent. (in the sense 'tumble about'): frequentative of **TOP**[1].

top rope Climbing ▶ noun a rope lowered from above to the lead climber in a group, typically to give assistance at a difficult part of a climb.
▶ verb (**top-rope**) [with obj.] climb (a route or part of one) using a top rope.

topsail /ˈtɒpseɪl, -s(ə)l/ ▶ noun a sail set on a ship's topmast.
■ a fore-and-aft sail set above the gaff.

top-sawyer ▶ noun chiefly historical a sawyer holding the upper handle of a pit saw and standing in the upper position above the saw pit.
■ archaic a distinguished person.

top secret ▶ adjective of the highest secrecy; highly confidential: *the experiments were top secret.*

top shell ▶ noun a marine mollusc which has a low conical shell with a pearly interior, widespread in tropical and temperate seas.
● Family Trochidae, class Gastropoda.

topside ▶ noun **1** [mass noun] Brit. the outer side of a round of beef: *roast topside.*
2 (often **topsides**) the upper part of a ship's side, above the waterline.

▶ adverb on or towards the upper decks of a ship: *we stayed topside.*

Topsider ▶ noun US trademark a casual shoe, typically made of leather or canvas with a rubber sole, designed to be worn on boats.

top-slicing ▶ noun [mass noun] a method of assessing tax chargeable on a lump sum by averaging the sum out over the years it has accrued and charging accordingly.

topsoil ▶ noun [mass noun] the top layer of soil.

topspin ▶ noun [mass noun] a fast forward spinning motion imparted to a ball when throwing or hitting it, often resulting in a curved path or a strong forward motion on rebounding.
– DERIVATIVES **topspinner** noun.

topstitch ▶ verb [no obj.] make a row of continuous stitches on the top or right side of a garment or other article as a decorative feature.

topsy-turvy ▶ adjective & adverb upside down: [as adv.] *the fairground ride turned riders topsy-turvy.*
■ in a state of confusion: [as adj.] *the topsy-turvy months of the invasion.*
▶ noun [in sing.] a state of utter confusion.
– DERIVATIVES **topsy-turvily** adverb, **topsy-turviness** noun.
– ORIGIN early 16th cent.: a jingle apparently based on **TOP**[1] and obsolete *terve* 'overturn'.

top table ▶ noun the table at which the chief guests are placed at a formal dinner.

top-up ▶ noun Brit. an additional or extra amount or portion that restores something to a former level: *you go in once a week for a top-up of the chemotherapy.*

topwater ▶ adjective Fishing, N. Amer. (of a bait) floating on or near the top of the water.

top weight ▶ noun the heaviest weight carried by a horse in a race.
■ a horse carrying this weight.

toque /təʊk/ ▶ noun a woman's small hat, typically having a narrow, closely turned-up brim.
■ historical a small cap or bonnet of such a type worn by a man or woman. ■ a tall white hat with a full pouched crown, worn by chefs.
– ORIGIN early 16th cent.: from French, of unknown origin.

tor /tɔː/ ▶ noun a hill or rocky peak: [in place names] *Glastonbury Tor.*
– ORIGIN Old English *torr*, perhaps of Celtic origin and related to Welsh *tor* 'belly' and Scottish Gaelic *tòrr* 'bulging hill'.

Torah /ˈtɔːrɑː, tɔːˈrɑː/ ▶ noun (usu. **the Torah**) (in Judaism) the law of God as revealed to Moses and recorded in the first five books of the Hebrew scriptures (the Pentateuch).
– ORIGIN from Hebrew *tōrāh* 'instruction, doctrine, law', from *yārāh* 'show, direct, instruct'.

Torbay a borough in Devon, SW England; pop. 121,000 (est. 1991). It was formed in 1968 from the amalgamation of the seaside resorts Torquay, Paignton, and Brixham.

torc /tɔːk/ (also **torque**) ▶ noun historical a neck ornament consisting of a band of twisted metal, worn especially by the ancient Gauls and Britons.
– ORIGIN mid 19th cent.: from French *torque*, from Latin *torques* (see **TORCH**).

torch ▶ noun **1** Brit. a portable battery-powered electric lamp.
■ chiefly historical a portable means of illumination such as a piece of wood or cloth soaked in tallow or an oil lamp on a pole, sometimes carried ceremonially. ■ (usu. **the torch**) figurative used to refer to a valuable quality, principle, or cause, which needs to be protected and maintained: *mountain warlords carried the torch of Greek independence.* ■ chiefly N. Amer. a blowlamp. ■ US informal an arsonist.
▶ verb [with obj.] informal set fire to: *the shops had been looted and torched.*
– PHRASES **carry a torch for** suffer from unrequited love for. **put to the torch** (or **put a torch to**) destroy by burning.
– ORIGIN Middle English: from Old French *torche*, from Latin *torqua*, variant of *torques* 'necklace, wreath', from *torquere* 'to twist'. The current verb sense was originally US slang and dates from the 1930s.

torch-bearer ▶ noun a person who carries a ceremonial torch.
■ figurative a person who leads or inspires others in working towards a valued goal.

torchère /tɔːˈʃɛː/ ▶ noun a tall ornamental flat-topped stand, traditionally used as a stand for a candlestick.
– ORIGIN early 20th cent.: French, from *torche* (see TORCH).

torchlight ▶ noun [mass noun] the light of a torch or torches.
– DERIVATIVES **torchlit** adjective.

torchon /ˈtɔːʃ(ə)n/ (also **torchon lace**) ▶ noun [mass noun] coarse bobbin lace with geometrical designs.
– ORIGIN mid 19th cent.: from French, literally 'duster, dishcloth', from *torcher* 'to wipe'.

torch race ▶ noun a ritual competition held at certain festivals in ancient Greece, in which runners carried lighted torches.

torch song ▶ noun a sad or sentimental song of unrequited love.
– DERIVATIVES **torch singer** noun.

tore¹ past of TEAR¹.

tore² /tɔː/ ▶ noun archaic term for TORUS.
– ORIGIN mid 17th cent.: from French.

toreador /ˈtɒrɪədɔː, ˌtɒrɪəˈdɔː/ ▶ noun a bullfighter, especially one on horseback.
– ORIGIN Spanish, from *torear* 'fight bulls', from *toro* 'bull'.

toreador pants ▶ plural noun chiefly US women's tight-fitting calf-length trousers.

torero /tɒˈrɛːrəʊ/ ▶ noun (pl. **-os**) a bullfighter, especially one on foot.
– ORIGIN Spanish, from *toro* 'bull' (see TOREADOR).

toreutics /təˈruːtɪks/ ▶ plural noun [treated as sing.] the art of making designs in relief or intaglio, especially by chasing, carving, and embossing in metal.
– DERIVATIVES **toreutic** adjective.
– ORIGIN mid 19th cent.: from Greek *toreutikos*, from *toreuein* 'to work in relief'.

torgoch /ˈtɔːɡɒx/ ▶ noun (in Wales) an Arctic charr.
– ORIGIN early 17th cent.: Welsh, from *tor* 'belly' + *coch* 'red'.

tori plural form of TORUS.

toric /ˈtɒrɪk, ˈtɔːrɪk/ ▶ adjective Geometry having the form of a torus or part of a torus.

torii /ˈtɔːriː/ ▶ noun (pl. same) the gateway of a Shinto shrine, with two uprights and two crosspieces.
– ORIGIN Japanese, from *tori* 'bird' + *i* 'sit, perch'.

Torino /tɒˈrinɒ/ Italian name for TURIN.

torment ▶ noun [mass noun] severe physical or mental suffering: *their deaths have left both families in torment.*
■ [count noun] a cause of such suffering: *the journey must have been a torment for them.*
▶ verb [with obj.] cause to experience severe mental or physical suffering: *he was tormented by jealousy.*
■ annoy or provoke in a deliberately unkind way: *every day I have kids tormenting me because they know I live alone.*
– DERIVATIVES **tormentedly** adverb, **tormentingly** adverb, **tormentor** noun.
– ORIGIN Middle English (as both noun and verb referring to the infliction or suffering of torture): from Old French *torment* (noun), *tormenter* (verb), from Latin *tormentum* 'instrument of torture', from *torquere* 'to twist'.

tormentil /ˈtɔːm(ə)ntɪl/ ▶ noun a low-growing Eurasian plant with bright yellow flowers. The root is used in herbal medicine to treat diarrhoea.
● *Potentilla erecta*, family Rosaceae.
– ORIGIN late Middle English: from French *tormentille*, from medieval Latin *tormentilla*, of unknown origin.

torn past participle of TEAR¹.

tornado /tɔːˈneɪdəʊ/ ▶ noun (pl. **-oes** or **-os**) a mobile, destructive vortex of violently rotating winds having the appearance of a funnel-shaped cloud and advancing beneath a large storm system.
■ figurative a person or thing characterized by violent or devastating action or emotion: *a tornado of sexual confusion.*
– DERIVATIVES **tornadic** /-ˈnadɪk/ adjective.
– ORIGIN mid 16th cent. (denoting a violent thunderstorm of the tropical Atlantic Ocean): perhaps an alteration of Spanish *tronada* 'thunderstorm' (from *tronar* 'to thunder') by association with Spanish *tornar* 'to turn'.

Tornio /ˈtɔːnɪəʊ/ a river which rises in NE Sweden and flows 566 km (356 miles) generally southwards, forming the border between Sweden and Finland before emptying into the Gulf of Bothnia. Swedish name **TORNE ÄLV** /ˌtɔːnə ˈɛlv/.

toroid /ˈtɔːrɔɪd, ˈtɔː-/ ▶ noun Geometry a figure of toroidal shape.

toroidal /tɒˈrɔɪd(ə)l, tɔː-/ ▶ adjective Geometry of or resembling a torus.
– DERIVATIVES **toroidally** adverb.

Toronto the capital of Ontario and the largest city in Canada, situated on the north shore of Lake Ontario; pop. 612,300 (1991); metropolitan area pop. 3,550,000 (1991).
– ORIGIN originally named York but renamed *Toronto* in 1834, from a Huron word meaning 'meeting place'.

torpedo ▶ noun (pl. **-oes**) **1** a cigar-shaped self-propelled underwater missile designed to be fired from a ship or submarine or dropped into the water from an aircraft and to explode on reaching a target.
■ US a railway fog signal. ■ US a firework exploding on impact with a hard surface.
2 (also **torpedo ray**) an electric ray.
▶ verb (**-oes, -oed**) [with obj.] attack or sink (a ship) with a torpedo or torpedoes.
■ figurative destroy or ruin (a plan or project): *fighting between the militias torpedoed peace talks.*
– DERIVATIVES **torpedo-like** adjective.
– ORIGIN early 16th cent. (in sense 2): from Latin, literally 'stiffness, numbness', by extension 'electric ray' (which gives a shock causing numbness), from *torpere* 'be numb or sluggish'. Sense 1 dates from the late 18th cent. and first described a timed explosive device for detonation under water.

torpedo boat ▶ noun a small, fast, light warship armed with torpedoes.

torpedo net ▶ noun historical a net made of steel wire, hung in the water round an anchored ship to intercept torpedoes.

torpedo tube ▶ noun a tube in a submarine or other ship from which torpedoes are fired by the use of compressed air or an explosive charge.

torpefy /ˈtɔːpɪfʌɪ/ ▶ verb (**-ies, -ied**) [with obj.] formal make (someone or something) numb, paralysed, or lifeless.
– ORIGIN early 19th cent.: from Latin *torpefacere*, from *torpere* 'be numb or sluggish'.

torpid ▶ adjective mentally or physically inactive; lethargic: *we sat around in a torpid state.*
■ (of an animal) dormant, especially during hibernation.
– DERIVATIVES **torpidity** noun, **torpidly** adverb.
– ORIGIN late Middle English: from Latin *torpidus*, from *torpere* 'be numb or sluggish'.

torpor /ˈtɔːpə/ ▶ noun [mass noun] a state of physical or mental inactivity; lethargy: *they veered between apathetic torpor and hysterical fanaticism.*
– ORIGIN late Middle English: from Latin, from *torpere* 'be numb or sluggish'.

Torquay a resort town in SW England, in Devon, administratively part of Torbay since 1968; pop. 57,500 (1981).

torque /tɔːk/ ▶ noun **1** [mass noun] Mechanics a force that tends to cause rotation.
2 variant spelling of TORC.
▶ verb [with obj.] apply torque or a twisting force to (an object): *he gently torqued the hip joint.*
– DERIVATIVES **torquey** adjective.
– ORIGIN late 19th cent.: from Latin *torquere* 'to twist'.

torque converter ▶ noun a device that transmits or multiplies torque generated by an engine.

Torquemada /ˌtɔːkɪˈmɑːdə, Spanish torkeˈmaða/, Tomás de (*c*.1420–98), Spanish cleric and Grand Inquisitor. A Dominican monk, he became confessor to Ferdinand and Isabella, whom he persuaded to institute the Inquisition in 1478. He was also the prime mover behind the expulsion of the Jews from Spain in and after 1492.

torque wrench ▶ noun a tool for setting and adjusting the tightness of nuts and bolts to a desired value.

torr /tɔː/ ▶ noun (pl. same) a unit of pressure used in measuring partial vacuums, equal to 133.32 pascals.
– ORIGIN 1940s: named after E. TORRICELLI.

Torrens system /ˈtɒr(ə)nz/ ▶ noun Law a system of land title registration, adopted originally in Australia and later in some states of the US and Malaysia.
– ORIGIN mid 19th cent.: named after Sir Robert Torrens (1814–84), first Premier of South Australia.

torrent ▶ noun a strong and fast-moving stream of water or other liquid: *rain poured down in torrents | after the winter rains, the stream becomes a raging torrent.*
■ (**a torrent of/torrents of**) a sudden, violent, and copious outpouring of (something, typically words or feelings): *she was subjected to a torrent of abuse.*
– ORIGIN late 16th cent.: from French, from Italian *torrente*, from Latin *torrent-* 'boiling, roaring', from *torrere* 'parch, scorch'.

torrential ▶ adjective (of rain) falling rapidly and in copious quantities: *a torrential downpour.*
■ (of water) flowing rapidly and with force.
– DERIVATIVES **torrentially** adverb.

Torres Strait /ˈtɒrɪs/ a channel separating the northern tip of Queensland, Australia, from the island of New Guinea and linking the Arafura Sea and the Coral Sea.
– ORIGIN named after the Spanish explorer Luis V. de Torres, the first European to sail along the south coast of New Guinea (1606).

Torricelli /ˌtɒrɪˈtʃɛli/, Evangelista (1608–47), Italian mathematician and physicist. He invented the mercury barometer, with which he demonstrated that the atmosphere exerts a pressure sufficient to support a column of mercury in an inverted closed tube.

Torricellian vacuum /ˌtɒrɪˈtʃɛliən, -ˈsɛliən/ ▶ noun a vacuum formed above the column of mercury in a mercury barometer.

torrid ▶ adjective very hot and dry: *the torrid heat of the afternoon.*
■ full of passionate or highly charged emotions arising from sexual love: *a torrid love affair.* ■ full of difficulty or tribulation: *Wall Street is in for a torrid time in the next few weeks.*
– DERIVATIVES **torridity** noun, **torridly** adverb.
– ORIGIN late 16th cent.: from French *torride* or Latin *torridus*, from *torrere* 'parch, scorch'.

Torridonian /ˌtɒrɪˈdəʊnɪən/ ▶ adjective Geology of, relating to, or denoting the later stage of the Proterozoic aeon in NW Scotland, from about 1100 to 600 million years ago.
■ [as noun **the Torridonian**] this period, or the system of rocks deposited during it.
– ORIGIN late 19th cent.: from the name of Loch Torridon, in north-west Scotland, + -IAN.

torrid zone ▶ noun the hot central belt of the earth bounded by the tropics of Cancer and Capricorn.

torsade /tɔːˈseɪd/ ▶ noun a decorative twisted braid, ribbon, or other strand used as trimming.
■ an artificial plait of hair.
– ORIGIN late 19th cent.: from French, from Latin *tors-* 'twisted', from *torquere* 'to twist'.

torsade de pointes /tɔːˌsɑːd də ˈpwãt/ ▶ noun [mass noun] Medicine a form of tachycardia in which the electrical pulse in the heart undergoes a cyclical variation in strength, giving a characteristic electrocardiogram resembling a twisted fringe of spikes.
– ORIGIN 1960s: French, literally 'twist of spikes'.

torse /tɔːs/ ▶ noun Heraldry a wreath.
– ORIGIN late 16th cent.: from obsolete French, from Latin *torta*, feminine past participle of *torquere* 'twist'.

torsel /ˈtɔːs(ə)l/ ▶ noun another term for TASSEL².

Tórshavn /ˈtɔːshaʊn/ (also **Thorshavn**) the capital of the Faroe Islands, a port on the island of Strømø; pop. 13,680 (1994).

torsion /ˈtɔːʃ(ə)n/ ▶ noun [mass noun] the action of twisting or the state of being twisted, especially of one end of an object relative to the other.
■ the twisting of the cut end of an artery after surgery to impede bleeding. ■ Mathematics the extent to which a curve departs from being planar. ■ Zoology (in a gastropod mollusc) the spontaneous twisting of the visceral hump through 180° during larval development.
– DERIVATIVES **torsional** adjective, **torsionally** adverb, **torsionless** adjective.
– ORIGIN late Middle English (as a medical term denoting colic or in the sense 'twisting' (especially of a loop of the intestine): via Old French from late Latin *torsio(n-)*, variant of *tortio(n-)* 'twisting, torture', from Latin *torquere* 'to twist'.

torsion balance ▶**noun** an instrument for measuring very weak forces by their effect upon a system of fine twisted wire.

torsion bar (also **torsion beam**) ▶**noun** a bar forming part of a vehicle suspension, twisting in response to the motion of the wheels and absorbing their vertical movement.

torsion pendulum ▶**noun** a pendulum that rotates rather than swings.

torsk /tɔːsk/ ▶**noun** a North Atlantic fish of the cod family, occurring in deep water and of some commercial importance. Also called **CUSK**.
• *Brosme brosme*, family Gadidae.
– ORIGIN early 18th cent.: from Norwegian *torsk*, from Old Norse *thorskr*; probably related to *thurr* 'dry'.

torso ▶**noun** (pl. **torsos** or US also **torsi**) the trunk of the human body.
■the trunk of a statue without, or considered independently of, the head and limbs. ■ figurative an unfinished or mutilated thing, especially a work of art or literature: *the Requiem torso was preceded by the cantata*.
– ORIGIN late 18th cent.: from Italian, literally 'stalk, stump', from Latin *thyrsus* (see **THYRSUS**).

tort ▶**noun** Law a wrongful act or an infringement of a right (other than under contract) leading to legal liability.
– ORIGIN Middle English (in the general sense 'wrong, injury'): from Old French, from medieval Latin *tortum* 'wrong, injustice', neuter past participle of Latin *torquere* 'to twist'.

torte /ˈtɔːtə/ ▶**noun** (pl. **torten** /ˈtɔːt(ə)n/ or **tortes**) a sweet cake or tart.
– ORIGIN from German *Torte*, via Italian from late Latin *torta* 'round loaf, cake'. Compare with **TORTILLA**.

Tortelier /tɔːˈtɛlɪeɪ, French tɔʀtəlje/, Paul (1914–90), French cellist. He was noted for his interpretations of Bach and Elgar, and was appointed professor at the Paris Conservatoire in 1957.

tortelli /tɔːˈtɛli/ ▶**plural noun** small pasta parcels stuffed with a cheese or vegetable mixture.
– ORIGIN Italian, plural of *tortello* 'small cake, fritter'.

tortellini /ˌtɔːtəˈliːni/ ▶**noun** tortelli which have been rolled and formed into small rings.
– ORIGIN Italian, plural of *tortellino*, diminutive of *tortello* 'small cake, fritter'.

tortfeasor /ˈtɔːtfiːzə/ ▶**noun** Law a person who commits a tort.
– ORIGIN mid 17th cent.: from Old French *tort-fesor*, from *tort* 'wrong' and *fesor* 'doer'.

torticollis /ˌtɔːtɪˈkɒlɪs/ ▶**noun** [mass noun] Medicine a condition in which the head becomes persistently turned to one side, often associated with painful muscle spasms. Also called **WRYNECK**.
– ORIGIN early 19th cent.: modern Latin, from Latin *tortus* 'crooked, twisted' + *collum* 'neck'.

tortilla /tɔːˈtiːjə/ ▶**noun** (in Mexican cookery) a thin, flat maize pancake, eaten hot or cold, typically with a savoury filling.
■(in Spanish cookery) a thick omelette containing potato and other vegetables, typically served cut into wedges.
– ORIGIN Spanish, diminutive of *torta* 'cake'.

tortious /ˈtɔːʃəs/ ▶**adjective** Law constituting a tort; wrongful.
– DERIVATIVES **tortiously** adverb.
– ORIGIN late Middle English: from Anglo-Norman French *torcious*, from the stem of *torcion* 'extortion, violence', from late Latin *tortio(n-)* (see **TORSION**). The original sense was 'injurious'.

tortoise /ˈtɔːtəs, -tɔɪz/ ▶**noun** **1** a slow-moving typically herbivorous land reptile of warm climates, enclosed in a scaly or leathery domed shell into which it can retract its head and thick legs. Called **TURTLE** in North America.
• Family Testudinidae: numerous genera and species, including the **European tortoise** (*Testudo graeca*).
■Austral. a freshwater turtle.
2 another term for **TESTUDO**.
– DERIVATIVES **tortoise-like** adjective & adverb.
– ORIGIN late Middle English *tortu, tortuce*: from Old French *tortue* and Spanish *tortuga*, both from medieval Latin *tortuca*, of uncertain origin. The current spelling dates from the mid 16th cent.

tortoise beetle ▶**noun** a small flattened leaf beetle with an enlarged thorax and wing cases which cover the entire insect and provide camouflage and protection. The larva carries a construction of faeces and moulted skins for camouflage.
• *Cassida* and other genera, family Chrysomelidae.

tortoiseshell ▶**noun** **1** [mass noun] the semi-transparent mottled yellow and brown shell of certain turtles, typically used to make jewellery or ornaments.
■a synthetic substance made in imitation of this.
2 short for **TORTOISESHELL CAT**.
3 short for **TORTOISESHELL BUTTERFLY**.

tortoiseshell butterfly ▶**noun** a butterfly with mottled orange, yellow, and black markings, and wavy wing margins.
• Genera *Aglais* and *Nymphalis*, subfamily Nymphalinae, family Nymphalidae: several species, including the common Eurasian **small tortoiseshell** (*A. urticae*).

tortoiseshell cat ▶**noun** a domestic cat with markings resembling tortoiseshell.

Tortola /tɔːˈtəʊlə/ the principal island of the British Virgin Islands in the Caribbean. Its chief town, Road Town, is the capital of the British Virgin Islands.
– ORIGIN Spanish, literally 'turtle dove'.

tortrix /ˈtɔːtrɪks/ (also **tortrix moth**) ▶**noun** (pl. **tortrices** /-trɪsiːz/) a small moth with typically green caterpillars that live inside rolled leaves and can be a serious pest of fruit and other trees.
• Family Tortricidae: many species, including *Pammene rhediella*, whose larvae damage apple and plum trees.
– DERIVATIVES **tortricid** noun & adjective.
– ORIGIN late 18th cent.: modern Latin, feminine of Latin *tortor* 'twister', from *torquere* 'to twist'.

tortuous /ˈtɔːtʃʊəs, -tjʊəs/ ▶**adjective** full of twists and turns: *the route is remote and tortuous*.
■excessively lengthy and complex: *a tortuous argument*.
– DERIVATIVES **tortuosity** noun (pl. **-ies**), **tortuously** adverb, **tortuousness** noun.
– ORIGIN late Middle English: via Old French from Latin *tortuosus*, from *tortus* 'twisting, a twist', from Latin *torquere* 'to twist'.

USAGE The two words **tortuous** and **torturous** have different core meanings. **Tortuous** means 'full of twists and turns', as in *a **tortuous** route*. **Torturous** means 'involving or causing torture', as in *a **torturous** five days of fitness training*. In extended senses, however, **tortuous** is used to mean 'excessively lengthy and complex' and hence may become indistinguishable from **torturous**: something which is **tortuous** is often also **torturous**, as in *a **tortuous** piece of bureaucratese; their way had been **tortuous** and very difficult*. Something which is **torturous** need not necessarily also be **tortuous**, however, but the overlap in sense has led to **tortuous** being sometimes used interchangeably with **torturous**, as in *he would at last draw in a **tortuous** gasp of air*.

torture ▶**noun** [mass noun] the action or practice of inflicting severe pain on someone as a punishment or in order to force them to do or say something.
■great physical or mental suffering or anxiety: *the torture I've gone through because of loving you so*. ■ a cause of such suffering or anxiety: *dances were absolute torture because I was so small*.
▶**verb** [with obj.] inflict severe pain on: *most of the victims had been brutally tortured*.
■cause great mental suffering or anxiety to: *he was tortured by grief*.
– DERIVATIVES **torturer** noun.
– ORIGIN late Middle English (in the sense 'distortion, twisting', or a physical disorder characterized by this): via French from late Latin *tortura* 'twisting, torment', from Latin *torquere* 'to twist'.

torturous ▶**adjective** characterized by, involving, or causing pain or suffering: *a torturous five days of fitness training*.
– DERIVATIVES **torturously** adverb.
– ORIGIN late 15th cent.: from Anglo-Norman French, from *torture* 'torture'.

USAGE On the difference between **torturous** and **tortuous**, see usage at **TORTUOUS**.

torula /ˈtɒrʊlə, -(j)ʊlə/ ▶**noun** (pl. **torulae** /-liː/) **1** (also **torula yeast**) a yeast which is cultured for use in medicine and as a food additive, especially as a source of vitamins and protein.
• *Candida utilis*, subdivision Deuteromycotina.
2 a yeast-like fungus composed of chains of rounded cells, several kinds growing on dead vegetation and some causing infections.
• Genus *Torula* (or formerly this genus), subdivision Deuteromycotina: several species, in particular *T. herbarum*, which grows on dead grasses.
– ORIGIN modern Latin (genus name), diminutive of Latin *torus* 'swelling, bolster'.

torulosis /ˌtɒruːˈləʊsɪs, ˌtɒr(j)ʊ-/ ▶**noun** another term for **CRYPTOCOCCOSIS**.

Toruń /ˈtɒrʊn/ an industrial city in northern Poland, on the River Vistula; pop. 200,820 (1990). German name **THORN**.

torus /ˈtɔːrəs/ ▶**noun** (pl. **tori** /-rʌɪ/ or **toruses**) **1** Geometry a surface or solid formed by rotating a closed curve, especially a circle, about a line which lies in the same plane but does not intersect it (e.g. like a ring doughnut).
■a thing of this shape, especially a large ring-shaped chamber used in physical research.
2 Architecture a large convex moulding, typically semicircular in cross section, especially as the lowest part of the base of a column.
3 Anatomy a ridge of bone or muscle: *the maxillary torus*.
4 Botany the receptacle of a flower.
– ORIGIN mid 16th cent. (in sense 2): from Latin, literally 'swelling, bolster, round moulding'. The other senses date from the 19th cent.

Torvill and Dean /ˈtɔːvɪl/ two English ice skaters, **Jayne Torvill** (b.1957) and **Christopher (Colin) Dean** (b.1958). In partnership they won the world ice dancing championships (1981–3), the gold medal in the 1984 Winter Olympics, and the bronze medal in the 1994 Winter Olympics.

Tory ▶**noun** (pl. **-ies**) **1** (in the UK) a member or supporter of the Conservative Party.
■a member of the English political party opposing the exclusion of James II from the succession. It remained the name for members of the English, later British, parliamentary party supporting the established religious and political order until the emergence of the Conservative Party in the 1830s. Compare with **WHIG** (sense 1).
2 US a colonist who supported the British side during the American Revolution.
▶**adjective** of or relating to the British Conservative Party or its supporters: *the Tory party | Tory voters*.
– DERIVATIVES **Toryism** noun.
– ORIGIN mid 17th cent.: probably from Irish *toraidhe* 'outlaw, highwayman', from *tóir* 'pursue'. The word was used of Irish peasants dispossessed by English settlers and living as robbers, and extended to other marauders especially in the Scottish Highlands. It was then adopted *c.*1679 as an abusive nickname for supporters of the Catholic James II.

tosa /ˈtəʊsə/ ▶**noun** a dog of a breed of mastiff originally kept for dogfighting.
– ORIGIN 1940s: from *Tosa*, the name of a former province in Japan.

Toscana /Italian toˈskana/ Italian name for **TUSCANY**.

Toscanini /ˌtɒskəˈniːni/, Arturo (1867–1957), Italian conductor. He was musical director at La Scala in Milan (1898–1903; 1906–8) before becoming a conductor at the Metropolitan Opera, New York (1908–21).

tosh[1] ▶**noun** [mass noun] Brit. informal rubbish; nonsense: *it's sentimental tosh*.
– ORIGIN late 19th cent.: of unknown origin.

tosh[2] ▶**noun** Brit. informal used as a casual form of address, especially to an unknown person.
– ORIGIN 1950s: of unknown origin.

Tosk /tɒsk/ ▶**noun** (pl. same or **Tosks**) **1** a member of one of the main ethnic groups of Albania, living mainly in the south of the country.
2 [mass noun] the dialect of Albanian spoken by this people, with about 4 million speakers, forming the basis for standard Albanian. Compare with **GHEG**.
▶**adjective** of or relating to the Tosks or their dialect.
– ORIGIN from Albanian *Toskë*.

toss ▶**verb** **1** [with obj. and adverbial of direction] throw (something) somewhere lightly, easily, or casually: *Suzy tossed her bag on to the sofa* | [with two objs] *she tossed me a box of matches*.
■[with obj.] (of a horse) throw (a rider) off its back. ■ [with obj.] throw (a coin) into the air in order to make a decision between two alternatives, based on which side of the coin faces uppermost when it lands: *we could just toss a coin* | [no obj.] *he **tossed up** between courgettes and tomatoes and courgettes won*. ■ [with obj.] settle a matter with (someone) by doing this: *I'll **toss you for it***. ■ move or cause to move from side to side

t

or back and forth: [no obj.] *the tops of the olive trees swayed and tossed* | [with obj.] *the yachts were tossed around like toys in the harbour* | [as adj., in combination **-tossed**] *a storm-tossed sea.* ■ [with obj.] jerk (one's head or hair) sharply backwards. ■ [with obj.] shake or turn (food) in a liquid, so as to coat it lightly: *toss the pasta in the sauce.*

2 [with obj.] N. Amer. informal search (a place).

▶**noun 1** an action or instance of tossing something: *a defiant toss of her head* | *the toss of a coin.*

■(**the toss**) the action of tossing a coin as a method of deciding which team has the right to make a particular decision at the beginning of a game: *Somerset won the toss and chose to bat.*

– PHRASES **give** (or **care**) **a toss** [usu. with negative] Brit. informal care at all: *I don't give a toss what you think.* **take a toss** fall off a horse. **toss one's cookies** N. Amer. informal vomit. **tossing the caber** see **CABER**. **toss a pancake** turn a pancake by flipping it into the air so that it lands in the pan on its opposite side.

– ORIGIN early 16th cent.: of unknown origin.

▶**toss oneself/someone off** (or **toss off**) Brit. vulgar slang masturbate.

toss something off 1 drink something rapidly or all at once. **2** produce something rapidly or without thought or effort: *some of the best letters are tossed off in a burst of inspiration.*

tosser ▶**noun 1** [usu. in combination] a person or thing that tosses something: *a contest to find the best pancake-tosser.*

2 Brit. vulgar slang a person who masturbates (used as a term of abuse).

tosspot ▶**noun** informal a habitual drinker (also used as a general term of abuse).

toss-up ▶**noun** informal the tossing of a coin to make a decision between two alternatives.

■a situation in which any of two or more outcomes or options is equally possible or equally attractive: *the choice of restaurant was a toss-up between Indian or Chinese.*

tostada /tɒˈstɑːdə/ (also **tostado** /tɒˈstɑːdəʊ/) ▶**noun** (pl. **tostadas** or **tostados**) a Mexican deep-fried maize flour pancake topped with a seasoned mixture of beans, mincemeat, and vegetables.

– ORIGIN Spanish, literally 'toasted', past participle of *tostar*.

tostone /tɒˈstəʊneɪ/ ▶**noun** a Mexican dish of fried plantain, typically served with a dip.

– ORIGIN Spanish.

tosyl /ˈtəʊsʌɪl, -sɪl/ ▶**noun** [as modifier] Chemistry of or denoting the toluene-4-sulphonyl radical —$SO_2C_6H_4CH_3$, used in organic synthesis.

– ORIGIN 1930s: from German, from *to(luol)* and *s(ulphon)yl*.

tosylate /ˈtəʊsʌɪleɪt, -sɪleɪt/ ▶**noun** Chemistry an ester containing a tosyl group.

tot[1] ▶**noun 1** a very young child.

2 chiefly Brit. a small amount of a strong alcoholic drink such as whisky or brandy: *a tot of brandy.*

– ORIGIN early 18th cent. (originally dialect): of unknown origin.

tot[2] ▶**verb** (**totted**, **totting**) chiefly Brit. [with obj.] (**tot something up**) add up numbers or amounts.

■accumulate something over a period of time: *he totted up 180 League appearances.*

– ORIGIN mid 18th cent.: from archaic *tot* 'set of figures to be added up', abbreviation of **TOTAL** or of Latin *totum* 'the whole'.

tot[3] ▶**verb** (**totted**, **totting**) [no obj.] [usu. as noun **totting**] Brit. informal salvage saleable items from dustbins or rubbish heaps.

– DERIVATIVES **totter** noun.

– ORIGIN late 19th cent.: from slang *tot* 'bone', of unknown origin.

total ▶**adjective 1** [attrib.] comprising the whole number or amount: *a total cost of £4,000.*

2 complete; absolute: *it is a matter of total indifference to me* | *a total stranger.*

▶**noun** the whole number or amount of something: *he scored a total of thirty-three points* | **in total**, *200 people were interviewed.*

▶**verb** (**totalled**, **totalling**; US **totaled**, **totaling**) **1** [with obj.] amount in number to: *they were left with debts totalling £6,260.*

■add up the full number or amount of: *the scores were totalled.*

2 [with obj.] informal, chiefly US damage (something, typically a vehicle) beyond repair; wreck.

■kill or severely injure (someone).

– ORIGIN late Middle English: via Old French from medieval Latin *totalis*, from *totum* 'the whole', neuter of Latin *totus* 'whole, entire'. The verb, at first in the sense 'add up', dates from the late 16th cent.

total allergy syndrome ▶**noun** [mass noun] a condition involving a wide range of symptoms thought to be caused by sensitivity to the chemical substances encountered in the modern environment. Its medical characterization is controversial.

total depravity ▶**noun** [mass noun] Christian Theology the Calvinist doctrine that human nature is thoroughly corrupt and sinful as a result of the Fall.

total eclipse ▶**noun** an eclipse in which the whole of the disc of the sun or moon is obscured.

total harmonic distortion ▶**noun** [mass noun] the distortion produced by an amplifier, as measured in terms of the harmonics of the sinusoidal components of the signal that it introduces.

total heat ▶**noun** another term for **ENTHALPY**.

total internal reflection ▶**noun** [mass noun] Physics the complete reflection of a light ray reaching an interface with a less dense medium when the angle of incidence exceeds the critical angle.

totalitarian /ˌtəʊtalɪˈtɛːrɪən, tə(ʊ)ˌtalɪ-/ ▶**adjective** of or relating to a system of government that is centralized and dictatorial and requires complete subservience to the state: *a totalitarian regime.*

▶**noun** a person advocating such a system of government.

– DERIVATIVES **totalitarianism** noun.

totality ▶**noun** the whole of something: *the totality of their current policies.*

■Astronomy the moment or duration of total obscuration of the sun or moon during an eclipse.

– PHRASES **in its totality** as a whole: *a deeper exploration of life in its totality.*

totalizator (also **totalisator**) ▶**noun** a device showing the number and amount of bets staked on a race, to facilitate the division of the total among those backing the winner.

■another term for **TOTE**[1].

totalize (also **-ise**) ▶**verb** [with obj.] [usu. as adj. **totalizing**] combine into a total.

– DERIVATIVES **totalization** noun.

totalizer ▶**noun** another term for **TOTALIZATOR**.

totally ▶**adverb** completely; absolutely: *the building was totally destroyed by the fire* | [as submodifier] *they came from totally different backgrounds.*

Total Quality Management ▶**noun** [mass noun] a system of management based on the principle that every member of staff must be committed to maintaining high standards of work in every aspect of a company's operations.

total recall ▶**noun** [mass noun] the ability to remember with clarity every detail of the events of one's life or of a particular event, object, or experience.

total war ▶**noun** a war which is unrestricted in terms of the weapons used, the territory or combatants involved, or the objectives pursued, especially one in which the laws of war are disregarded.

totara /ˈtəʊt(ə)rə/ ▶**noun** a large New Zealand coniferous tree which yields useful timber.

• *Podocarpus totara*, family Podocarpaceae.

– ORIGIN mid 19th cent.: from Maori *tōtara*.

tote[1] ▶**noun** (**the tote**) informal a system of betting based on the use of the totalizator, in which dividends are calculated according to the amount staked rather than odds offered.

– ORIGIN late 19th cent.: abbreviation.

tote[2] ▶**verb** [with obj.] informal, chiefly N. Amer. carry, wield, or convey (something heavy or substantial): *here are books well worth toting home* | [as adj., in combination **-toting**] *a gun-toting loner.*

– DERIVATIVES **toter** noun [in combination] *a gun-toter.*

– ORIGIN late 17th cent.: probably of dialect origin.

tote bag ▶**noun** a large bag used for carrying a number of items.

totem /ˈtəʊtəm/ ▶**noun** a natural object or animal that is believed by a particular society to have spiritual significance and that is adopted by it as an emblem.

– DERIVATIVES **totemic** /-ˈtɛmɪk/ adjective, **totemism** noun, **totemist** noun, **totemistic** adjective.

– ORIGIN mid 18th cent.: from Ojibwa *nindoodem* 'my totem'.

totem pole ▶**noun** a pole on which totems are hung or on which the images of totems are carved.

■figurative, chiefly US a hierarchy: *the social totem pole.*

t'other /ˈtʌðə/ (also **tother**) ▶**adjective** & **pronoun** dialect or humorous the other: [as adj.] *we was talking about it t'other day* | [as pronoun] *we were talking of this, that, and t'other.*

– PHRASES **tell t'other from which** Brit. humorous tell one from the other.

– ORIGIN Middle English *the tother*, wrong division of *thet other* 'the other' (*thet*, from Old English *thaet*, the obsolete neuter form of *the*).

totipotent /təʊˈtɪpət(ə)nt/ ▶**adjective** Biology (of an immature or stem cell) capable of giving rise to any cell type or (of a blastomere) a complete embryo.

– ORIGIN early 20th cent.: from Latin *totus* 'whole' + **POTENT**[1].

tot system (also **dop system**) ▶**noun** S. African historical a system according to which labourers, especially those in vineyards, were paid part of their wages in wine.

totter ▶**verb** [no obj., with adverbial] move in a feeble or unsteady way: *a hunched figure tottering down the path.*

■[usu. as adj. **tottering**] (of a building) shake or rock as if about to collapse: *tottering, gutted houses.* ■ figurative be insecure or about to collapse: *the pharmaceutical industry has tottered from crisis to crisis.*

▶**noun** [in sing.] a feeble or unsteady gait.

– DERIVATIVES **totterer** noun, **tottery** adjective.

– ORIGIN Middle English: from Middle Dutch *touteren* 'to swing' (the original sense in English).

totting-up ▶**noun** [mass noun] the adding up of numbers or amounts.

■Brit. the accumulation of penalty points on someone's driving licence, a certain number in a fixed period leading to disqualification.

totty ▶**noun** [mass noun] Brit. informal girls or women collectively regarded as sexually desirable: *loads of Italian totty in tight white shorts.*

■[count noun] a girl or woman, especially one regarded as sexually desirable.

– ORIGIN late 19th cent.: slang word from **TOT**[1].

toucan /ˈtuːk(ə)n/ ▶**noun** a tropical American fruit-eating bird with a massive bill and typically brightly coloured plumage.

• Genera *Ramphastos* and *Andigena*, family Ramphastidae: several species.

– ORIGIN mid 16th cent.: via French and Portuguese from Tupi *tucan*, imitative of its call.

toucanet /ˌtuːk(ə)ˈnɛt/ ▶**noun** a small tropical American toucan with mainly green plumage.

• Family Ramphastidae: three genera, in particular *Aulacorhynchus* and *Selenidera*, and several species.

– ORIGIN early 19th cent.: diminutive of **TOUCAN**.

touch ▶**verb** [with obj.] **1** come so close to (an object) as to be or come into contact with it: *the dog had one paw outstretched, not quite touching the ground.*

■bring one's hand or another part of one's body into contact with: *he touched a strand of her hair* | *she lowered her head to touch his fingers with her lips.* ■ (**touch something to**) move a part of one's body to bring it into contact with: *he gently touched his lips to her cheek.* ■ lightly press or strike (a button or key on a device or instrument) to operate or play it: *he touched a button on the control pad.* ■ [no obj.] (of two people or two or more things, typically ones of the same kind) come into contact with each other: *for a moment their fingers touched.* ■ cause (two or more things, typically ones of the same kind) to come into contact: *we touched wheels and nearly came off the road.* ■ [with obj. and adverbial of direction] strike (the ball) lightly so as to make it move in a specified direction: *he touched back a cross-field ball.* ■ Geometry be tangent to (a curve or surface) at a certain point. ■ informal reach (a specified level or amount): *sales touched twenty grand last year.* ■ [usu. with negative] informal be comparable to in quality or excellence: *there's no one who can touch him at lightweight judo.*

2 handle in order to manipulate, alter, or otherwise affect, especially in an adverse way: *I didn't play her records or touch any of her stuff.*

■cause harm to (someone): *I've got friends who'll pull strings—nobody will dare touch me.* ■ take some of (a store, especially of money) for use: *in three years I haven't touched a cent of the money.* ■ [usu. with negative] consume a small amount of (food or drink): *the pint by his right hand was hardly touched.* ■ [with negative] used to indicate that something is avoided or rejected: *he was good only for the jobs that nobody else would touch.* ■ (**touch someone for**) informal ask someone for (money or some other commodity) as a loan or gift: *he touched me for his fare.*

3 have an effect on; make a difference to: *a tenth of state companies have been touched by privatization.* ■ be relevant to: *some British interests touched other European powers.* ■ (usu. **be touched**) (of a quality or feature) be visible or apparent in the appearance or character of (something): *the trees were beginning to be touched by the colours of autumn.* ■ reach and affect the appearance of: *a wry smile touched his lips.* ■ (**touch something in**) chiefly Art lightly mark in features or other details with a brush or pencil. ■ (often **be touched**) produce feelings of affection, gratitude, or sympathy in: *she was touched by her friend's loyalty.* ■ [as adj. **touched**] informal slightly mad.

▶**noun 1** an act of bringing a part of one's body, typically one's hand, into contact with someone or something: *her touch on his shoulder was hesitant* | [mass noun] *expressions of love through words and touch.* ■ [in sing.] an act of lightly pressing or striking something in order to move or operate it: *you can manipulate images on the screen **at the touch of** a key.* ■ [mass noun] the faculty of perception through physical contact, especially with the fingers: *reading by touch.* ■ [mass noun] a musician's manner of playing keys or strings. ■ [mass noun] the manner in which a musical instrument's keys or strings respond to being played: *Viennese instruments with their too delicate touch.* ■ a light stroke with a pen, pencil, etc. ■ [in sing.] informal, dated an act of asking for and getting money or some other commodity from someone as a loan or gift: *I only tolerated him because he was good for a touch now and then.* ■ [in sing.] archaic a thing or an action that tries out the worth or character of something; a test: *you must **put** your fate **to the touch**.*

2 a small amount; a trace: *add **a touch of** vinegar* | *he retired to bed with **a touch of** flu.* ■ a detail or feature, typically one that gives something a distinctive character: *the film's most inventive touch.* ■ [in sing.] a distinctive manner or method of dealing with something: *later he showed a surer political touch.* ■ [in sing.] an ability to deal with something successfully: *getting caught looks so incompetent, as though we're losing our touch.*

3 [in sing.] Rugby & Soccer the area beyond the sidelines, out of play: *his clearance went directly **into touch*** | figurative *the idea was kicked firmly into touch by the authorities.*

4 Bell-ringing a series of changes shorter than a peal.

– PHRASES **a touch** to a slight degree; a little: *the water was a touch chilly for us.* **in touch 1** in or into communication: *she said that you **kept in touch**, that you wrote* | *ask someone to **put** you **in touch** with other carers.* **2** possessing up-to-date knowledge: *we need to keep in touch with the latest developments.* ■ having an intuitive or empathetic awareness: *you need to be in touch with your feelings.* **lose touch 1** cease to correspond or be in communication: *I **lost touch with** him when he joined the Air Force.* **2** cease to be aware or informed: *we cannot **lose touch with** political reality.* **out of touch** lacking knowledge or information concerning current events and developments: *he seems surprisingly out of touch with recent economic thinking.* ■ lacking in awareness or sympathy: *we have been betrayed by a government out of touch with our values.* **to the touch** used to describe the qualities of something perceived by touching it or the sensations felt by someone who is touched: *the silk was slightly rough to the touch* | *the ankle was swollen and painful to the touch.* **touch base** (**with**) see **BASE**[1]. **touch bottom** reach the ground below a stretch of water with one's feet or a pole. ■ be at the lowest or worst point: *the housing market has touched bottom.* **touch a chord** see **CHORD**[2]. **touch of nature** a display of human feeling with which others sympathize (based on a misinterpretation of Shakespeare's *Troilus and Cressida* III iii. 169). **touch of the sun 1** a slight attack of sunstroke. **2** some time spent in the sunlight: *when you fancy a touch of the sun and some sea air, you can head for the beach.* **touch wood** see **WOOD**. **would not touch something with a bargepole** see **BARGEPOLE**.

– DERIVATIVES **touchable** adjective.

– ORIGIN Middle English: the verb from Old French *tochier*, probably from a Romance word of imitative origin; the noun originally from Old French *touche*, later (in certain senses) directly from the verb.

▶**touch at** (of a ship or someone in it) call briefly at (a port).

touch down 1 Rugby touch the ground with the ball behind the opponents' goal line, scoring a try. ■ American Football score six points by being in possession of the ball behind the opponents' goal line. **2** (of an aircraft or spacecraft) make contact with the ground in landing.

touch something off 1 cause something to ignite or explode by touching it with a match. ■ cause something to happen, especially suddenly: *there was concern that the move could touch off a trade war.* **2** (of a racehorse) defeat another horse in a race by a short margin: *Royal Ballerina was touched off by Intrepidity in the English Oaks.*

touch on (or **upon**) **1** deal brieflywith (a subject) in written or spoken discussion: *he touches upon several themes from the last chapter.* **2** come near to being: *a self-confident manner touching on the arrogant.*

touch someone up Brit. informal caress someone without their consent for sexual pleasure.

touch something up make small improvements to something: *these paints are handy for touching up small areas on walls or ceilings.*

touch-and-go ▶**adjective** (of an outcome, especially one that is desired) possible but very uncertain: *it was touch-and-go whether she could reach the pram before it overturned.*
▶**noun** (pl. **touch-and-goes**) a manoeuvre in which an aircraft touches the ground as in landing and immediately takes off again.

touchback ▶**noun** American Football a ball downed behind one's own goal.

touchdown ▶**noun 1** the moment at which an aircraft's wheels or part of a spacecraft make contact with the ground during landing: *two hours until touchdown.*
2 Rugby an act of touching the ground with the ball behind the opponents' goal line, scoring a try. ■ American Football a six-point score made by carrying or passing the ball into the end zone of the opposing side.

touché /tuːˈʃeɪ/ ▶**exclamation** (in fencing) used as an acknowledgement of a hit by one's opponent. ■ used as an acknowledgement during a discussion of a good or clever point made at one's expense by another person.
– ORIGIN French, literally 'touched', past participle of *toucher.*

toucher ▶**noun** a person or thing that touches. ■ (in bowls) a wood that touches the jack.

touch football ▶**noun** [mass noun] a form of American football in which a ball-carrier is downed by touching instead of tackling.

touch hole ▶**noun** a small hole in early firearms through which the charge is ignited.

touching ▶**adjective** arousing strong feelings of sympathy or of appreciation or gratitude: *your loyalty is very touching* | *a touching reconciliation scene.* [ORIGIN: early 16th cent.: from **TOUCH** + **-ING**[2].]
▶**preposition** concerning; about: *discoveries touching the neglected traditions of the London Boroughs.* [ORIGIN: late Middle English: from French *touchant*, present participle of *toucher* 'to touch'.]
– DERIVATIVES **touchingly** adverb, **touchingness** noun.

touch-in-goal ▶**noun** Rugby the area at the corner of the field bounded by continuations of the touchline and the goal line.

touch judge ▶**noun** Rugby a linesman.

touchline ▶**noun** Rugby & Soccer the boundary line on each side of the field.

touch mark ▶**noun** an official mark made by the manufacturer on items made from pewter.

touch-me-not ▶**noun** a plant of the balsam family, whose ripe seed capsules open explosively when touched, scattering seeds over some distance.
• Genus *Impatiens*, family Balsaminaceae: several species, in particular the yellow balsam (*I. noli-tangere*).

touch needles ▶**plural noun** a set of needles of gold or silver alloy of known compositions, used in testing other alloys on a touchstone.

touch pad ▶**noun** a computer input device in the form of a small panel containing different touch-sensitive areas.

touchpaper ▶**noun** a strip of paper impregnated with nitre, for setting light to fireworks or gunpowder.

touch screen ▶**noun** a display device which allows the user to interact with a computer by touching areas on the screen.

touchstone ▶**noun** a piece of fine-grained dark schist or jasper formerly used for testing alloys of gold by observing the colour of the mark which they made on it. ■ a standard or criterion by which something is judged or recognized: *they tend to regard grammar as the touchstone of all language performance.*

touch-tone (also **Touch-Tone**) ▶**adjective** (of a telephone) having push-buttons and generating tones to dial rather than pulses. ■ (of a service) accessed or controlled by the tones generated by these telephones.
▶**noun** trademark a telephone of this type. ■ one of the set of tones generated by these telephones.

touch-type ▶**verb** [no obj.] [often as noun **touch-typing**] type using all one's fingers and without looking at the keys.
– DERIVATIVES **touch-typist** noun.

touch-up ▶**noun** a quick restoration or improvement made to the appearance or state of something: *the hotels had undergone more than the customary touch-ups and refurbishing.*

touchwood ▶**noun** [mass noun] archaic readily flammable wood used as tinder, especially when made soft by fungi.

touchy ▶**adjective** (**touchier**, **touchiest**) (of a person) oversensitive and irritable. ■ (of an issue or situation) requiring careful handling; delicate: *the monarchy has become a touchy topic.*
– DERIVATIVES **touchily** adverb, **touchiness** noun.
– ORIGIN early 17th cent.: perhaps an alteration of **TETCHY**, influenced by **TOUCH**.

touchy-feely ▶**adjective** informal, often derogatory openly expressing affection or other emotions, especially through physical contact: *touchy-feely guys calling home to talk baby talk to their kids.* ■ characteristic of or relating to such behaviour: *such touchy-feely topics as employees' personal values.*

tough ▶**adjective 1** (of a substance or object) strong enough to withstand adverse conditions or rough or careless handling: *tough rucksacks for climbers.* ■ (of a person or animal) able to endure hardship or pain; physically robust: *she took a tonic, and said that was why she was as tough as old boots.* ■ able to protect one's own interests or maintain one's own opinions without being intimidated by opposition; confident and determined: *she's both sensitive and tough.* ■ demonstrating a strict and uncompromising attitude or approach: *police have been getting tough with drivers* | *tough new laws on tobacco advertising.* ■ (of a person) strong and prone to violence: *tough young teenagers.* ■ (of an area) notorious for violence and crime. ■ (of food, especially meat) difficult to cut or chew.
2 involving considerable difficulty or hardship; requiring great determination or effort: *the training has been quite tough* | *he had a tough time getting into a good college.* ■ used to express sympathy with someone in an unpleasant or difficult situation: *Poor kid. It's **tough on** her.* ■ [often as exclamation] used to express a lack of sympathy with someone: *I feel the way I feel, and if you don't like it, tough.*
– PHRASES **tough it out** informal endure a period of hardship or difficulty. **tough shit** (or **titty**) vulgar slang used to express a lack of sympathy with someone.
– DERIVATIVES **toughish** adjective, **toughly** adverb, **toughness** noun.
– ORIGIN Old English *tōh*, of Germanic origin; related to Dutch *taai* and German *zäh*.

toughen ▶**verb** make or become stronger or more resilient: [with obj.] *he tried to **toughen** his son **up** by sending him to public school* | [no obj.] *a falcon has scaly skin on its legs that toughens up very quickly.* ■ [with obj.] make (rules or a policy) stricter and more harsh: *proposals to toughen up sentencing policy.*
– DERIVATIVES **toughener** noun.

toughie ▶**noun** informal **1** a person who is tough, determined, and not easily daunted.
2 a difficult problem or question: *Who do you admire most? That's a toughie.*

tough love ▶**noun** [mass noun] promotion of a person's welfare, especially that of an addict, child, or criminal, by enforcing certain constraints on them, or requiring them to take responsibility for their actions. ■ N. Amer. a political policy designed to encourage self-help by restricting state benefits.

t

tough-minded ▶ adjective strong, determined, and able to face up to reality.
– DERIVATIVES **tough-mindedness** noun.

Toulon /ˈtuːlɔ̃, French tulɔ̃/ a port and naval base on the Mediterranean coast of southern France; pop. 170,170 (1990).

Toulouse /tuːˈluːz, French tuluz/ a city in SW France on the Garonne River, principal city of the Midi-Pyrénées region; pop. 365,930 (1990).

Toulouse-Lautrec /tuːˌluːz ləʊˈtrɛk, French tuluzlotʀɛk/, Henri (Marie Raymond) de (1864–1901), French painter and lithographer. His reputation is based on his colour lithographs from the 1890s, depicting actors, music-hall singers, prostitutes, and waitresses in Montmartre: particularly well known is the *Moulin Rouge* series (1894).

toupee /ˈtuːpeɪ/ (also **toupet** /ˈtuːpeɪ, ˈtuːpɪt/) ▶ noun a small wig or artificial hairpiece worn to cover a bald spot.
– ORIGIN early 18th cent. (denoting a curl or lock of artificial hair): *toupee*, alteration of French *toupet* 'hair-tuft', diminutive of Old French *toup* 'tuft', ultimately of Germanic origin and related to **TOP**[1].

tour ▶ noun **1** a journey for pleasure in which several different places are visited: *a motoring tour of Scotland.*
■ a short trip to or through a place in order to view or inspect something: *a tour of the White House.*
2 a journey made by performers or a sports team, in which they perform or play in several different places: *Ireland's eight-match tour of New Zealand | she joined the Royal Shakespeare Company* ***on tour.***
■ (**the tour**) (in golf, tennis, and other sports) the annual round of events in which top professionals compete.
3 (also **tour of duty**) a spell of duty on military or diplomatic service: *a tour of duty in Northern Ireland.*
▶ verb [with obj.] make a tour of (an area): *he decided to tour France | [no obj.] he toured in America and Europe.*
■ take (a performer, production, etc.) on tour.
– ORIGIN Middle English (in sense 3; also denoting a circular movement): from Old French, 'turn', via Latin from Greek *tornos* 'lathe'. Sense 1 dates from the mid 17th cent.

touraco ▶ noun variant spelling of **TURACO**.

Tourane /tʊəˈrɑːneɪ/ former name for **DA NANG**.

tour de force /ˌtʊə də ˈfɔːs/ ▶ noun (pl. **tours de force** pronunc. same) a performance or achievement that has been accomplished or managed with great skill: *his novel is a tour de force.*
– ORIGIN French, literally 'feat of strength'.

Tour de France /ˌtʊə də ˈfrɑːns, French tuʀ də fʀɑ̃s/ a French race for professional cyclists held annually since 1903, covering approximately 4,800 km (3,000 miles) of roads in about three weeks, renowned for its mountain stages.

tour d'horizon /ˌtʊə dɒrɪˈzɒ̃, French tuʀ dɔʀizɔ̃/ ▶ noun (pl. **tours d'horizon** pronunc. same) a broad general survey or summary of an argument or event.
– ORIGIN French, literally 'tour of the horizon'.

tour en l'air /ɒ̃ lɛː/ ▶ noun (pl. **tours en l'air** pronunc. same) Ballet a movement in which a dancer jumps straight upwards and completes at least one full revolution in the air before landing.
– ORIGIN French, literally 'turn in the air'.

tourer ▶ noun a car, caravan, or bicycle designed for touring.
■ a person touring with such a vehicle.

Tourette's syndrome /tʊˈrɛts/ ▶ noun [mass noun] Medicine a neurological disorder characterized by involuntary tics and vocalizations and often the compulsive utterance of obscenities.
– ORIGIN late 19th cent.: named after Gilles de la *Tourette* (1857–1904), French neurologist.

touring car ▶ noun a car designed with room for passengers and luggage.
■ a car of this type used in motor racing, as distinct from a racing car.

tourism ▶ noun [mass noun] the commercial organization and operation of holidays and visits to places of interest.

tourist ▶ noun **1** a person who is travelling or visiting a place for pleasure: *the pyramids have drawn tourists to Egypt.*
2 a member of a touring sports team.
▶ verb [no obj.] rare travel as a tourist: *American families touristing abroad.*
– DERIVATIVES **touristic** adjective, **touristically** adverb.

tourist class ▶ noun [mass noun] the cheapest accommodation or seating for passengers in a ship, aircraft, or hotel.
▶ adjective & adverb of, relating to, or by such accommodation or seating: [as adj.] *a tourist-class hotel |* [as adv.] *they had come tourist class from Cairo.*

Tourist Trophy (abbrev.: **TT**) a motorcycle-racing competition held annually on roads in the Isle of Man since 1907.

touristy ▶ adjective informal relating to, appealing to, or visited by tourists (often used to suggest tawdriness or lack of authenticity): *a touristy shopping street.*

tourmaline /ˈtʊəməlɪn, -iːn/ ▶ noun [mass noun] a brittle grey or black mineral which occurs as prismatic crystals in granitic and other rocks. It consists of a boron aluminosilicate and has pyroelectric and polarizing properties.
– ORIGIN mid 18th cent.: from French, based on Sinhalese *tōramalli* 'carnelian'.

Tournai /tʊəˈneɪ, French tuʀnɛ/ a town in Belgium, on the River Scheldt near the French frontier; pop. 67,730 (1991). From the 9th century it was controlled by the counts of Flanders until taken by France in 1188, returning to the Netherlands in 1814. Flemish name **DOORNIK**.

tournament ▶ noun **1** (in a sport or game) a series of contests between a number of competitors, competing for an overall prize.
2 (in the Middle Ages) a sporting event in which two knights (or two groups of knights) jousted on horseback with blunted weapons, each trying to knock the other off, the winner receiving a prize.
■ a modern event involving display of military techniques and exercises: *the Royal Tournament.*
– ORIGIN Middle English (in sense 2): from Anglo-Norman French variants of Old French *torneiement*, from *torneier* 'take part in a tourney' (see **TOURNEY**).

tournedos /ˈtʊənədəʊ/ ▶ noun (pl. same /-dəʊz/) a small round thick cut from a fillet of beef.
– ORIGIN French, from *tourner* 'to turn' + *dos* 'back'.

tournedos Rossini ▶ noun (pl. same) a tournedos served with a crouton and pâté and a Madeira sauce.

tourney /ˈtʊəni, ˈtəːni/ ▶ noun (pl. **-eys**) a tournament, especially a medieval joust.
▶ verb (**-eys**, **-eyed**) [no obj.] take part in such a tournament.
– ORIGIN Middle English: from Old French *tornei* (noun), *torneier* (verb), based on Latin *tornus* 'a turn'.

tourniquet /ˈtʊənɪkeɪ, ˈtɔː-/ ▶ noun a device for stopping the flow of blood through an artery, typically by compressing a limb with a cord or tight bandage.
– ORIGIN late 17th cent.: from French, probably from Old French *tournicle* 'coat of mail', influenced by *tourner* 'to turn'.

tournois /ˈtʊənwɑː, French tuʀnwa/ ▶ adjective [postpositive] historical relating to or denoting a coin struck at Tours, which was one-fifth less in value than that coined at Paris.
– ORIGIN French.

tour operator ▶ noun a travel agent specializing in package holidays.

Tours /tʊə, French tuʀ/ an industrial city in west central France, on the Loire; pop. 133,400 (1990).

tourtière /ˌtʊətɪˈɛː/ (also **tourtiere**) ▶ noun (pl. pronounced same) a kind of meat pie traditionally eaten at Christmas in Canada.
■ a tin or round baking sheet for tarts and pies.
– ORIGIN French.

tousle /ˈtaʊz(ə)l/ ▶ verb [with obj.] [usu. as adj. **tousled**] make (something, especially a person's hair) untidy: *Nathan's tousled head appeared in the hatchway.*
– ORIGIN late Middle English (in the sense 'handle roughly or rudely'): frequentative of dialect *touse* 'handle roughly', of Germanic origin and related to German *zausen*. Compare with **TUSSLE**.

tousle-haired ▶ adjective having untidy hair.

Toussaint L'Ouverture /ˌtuːsã ˌluːvəˈtjʊə, French tusɛ̃ luvɛʀtyʀ/, Pierre Dominique (c.1743–1803), Haitian revolutionary leader. One of the leaders of a rebellion (1791) that emancipated the island's slaves, he was appointed Governor General by the revolutionary government of France in 1797. In 1802 Napoleon (wishing to restore slavery) took over the island and Toussaint died in prison in France.

tout[1] /taʊt/ ▶ verb **1** [with obj.] attempt to sell (something), typically by pestering people in an aggressive or bold manner: *Sanjay was touting his wares |* [no obj.] *shop managers would stand in the street* ***touting for*** *business.*
■ (often **be touted**) attempt to persuade people of the merits of (someone or something): *she was* ***touted as*** *a potential Prime Minister.* ■ Brit. sell (a ticket) for a popular event at a price higher than the official one.
2 [no obj.] US offer racing tips for a share of any resulting winnings.
■ [with obj.] chiefly Brit. spy out the movements and condition of (a racehorse in training) in order to gain information to be used when betting.
▶ noun **1** (also **ticket tout**) Brit. a person who buys up tickets for an event to resell them at a profit.
■ a person soliciting custom or business, typically in an aggressive or bold manner.
2 US a person who offers racing tips for a share of any resulting winnings.
3 N. Irish & Scottish informal an informer.
– DERIVATIVES **touter** noun.
– ORIGIN Middle English *tute* 'look out', of Germanic origin; related to Dutch *tuit* 'spout, nozzle'. Later senses were 'watch, spy on' (late 17th cent.) and 'solicit custom' (mid 18th cent.). The noun was first recorded (early 18th cent.) in the slang use 'thieves' lookout'.

tout[2] /tuː, French tu/ ▶ determiner (often **le tout**) used before the name of a city to refer to its high society or people of importance: *le tout Washington adored him.*
– ORIGIN French, suggested by *le tout Paris* 'all (of) Paris', used to refer to Parisian high society.

tout court /tuː ˈkʊə, French tu kuʀ/ ▶ adverb with no addition or qualification; simply: *he saw it as an illusion, tout court.*
– ORIGIN French, literally 'very short'.

tout de suite /ˌtuː də ˈswiːt, French tu d(ə) sɥit/ ▶ adverb immediately; at once: *she left tout de suite.*
– ORIGIN French, literally 'quite in sequence'.

tout le monde /ˌtuː lə mɒ̃d, French tu lə mɔ̃d/ ▶ noun [treated as sing. or pl.] everyone: *he shouted 'Bon appetit, tout le monde!'*
– ORIGIN French.

tovarish /tɒˈvɑːrɪʃ/ (also **tovarich**) ▶ noun (in the former USSR) a comrade (often used as a form of address).
– ORIGIN from Russian *tovarishch*, from Turkic.

TOW ▶ abbreviation for tube-launched, optically guided, wire-guided (missile).

tow[1] ▶ verb [with obj.] (of a motor vehicle or boat) pull (another vehicle or boat) along with a rope, chain, or tow bar.
■ (of a person) pull (someone or something) along behind one: *she saw Florian towing Nicky along by the hand.*
▶ noun [in sing.] an act of towing a vehicle or boat.
■ a rope or line used to tow a vehicle or boat.
– PHRASES **in tow 1** (also **on tow**) being towed by another vehicle or boat: *his boat was taken in tow by a trawler.* **2** accompanying or following someone: *trying to shop with three children in tow is no joke.*
– DERIVATIVES **towable** adjective.
– ORIGIN Old English *togian* 'draw, drag', of Germanic origin; related to **TUG**. The noun dates from the early 17th cent.

tow[2] ▶ noun [mass noun] the coarse and broken part of flax or hemp prepared for spinning.
■ [count noun] a bundle of untwisted natural or man-made fibres.
– DERIVATIVES **towy** adjective.
– ORIGIN Old English (recorded in *towcræft* 'spinning'), of Germanic origin.

towage ▶ noun [mass noun] **1** [usu. as modifier] the action or process of towing.
2 a charge for towing a boat.

towai /ˈtəʊwʌɪ/ ▶ noun a large New Zealand timber tree related to the kamahi.
• *Weinmannia silvicola*, family Cunoniaceae.
– ORIGIN mid 19th cent.: from Maori.

toward ▶ preposition /təˈwɔːd, twɔːd, tɔːd/ variant of **TOWARDS**.
▶ adjective /ˈtəʊəd/ [predic.] archaic going on; in progress: *is something new toward?*
– ORIGIN Old English *tōweard* (see **TO**, **-WARD**).

towards /təˈwɔːdz, twɔːdz, ˈtɔːdz/ (chiefly N. Amer. also

toward) ▶ preposition **1** in the direction of: *they drove towards the German frontier.*
■ getting closer to achieving (a goal): *moves towards EC political and monetary union.* ■ close or closer to (a particular time): *towards the end of April.*
2 expressing the relation between behaviour or an attitude and the person, thing, or subject at which it is directed or with which it is concerned: *he was warm and tender towards her | our attitude towards death.*
■ paying homage to, especially in a superficial or insincere way: *he gave a nod towards the good work done by the Press Fund.*
3 contributing to the cost of (something): *the council provided a grant towards the cost of new buses.*
– ORIGIN Old English *tōweardes* (see **TO**, **-WARD**).

tow bar ▶ noun a bar fitted to the back of a vehicle, used in towing a trailer or caravan.

tow-coloured ▶ adjective (of hair) very light blonde.

towel ▶ noun **1** a piece of thick absorbent cloth or paper used for drying oneself or wiping things dry. **2** Brit. dated a sanitary towel.
▶ verb (**towelled**, **towelling**; US **toweled**, **toweling**) [with obj.] **1** wipe or dry (a person or thing) with a towel: [with obj. and complement] *she towelled her hair dry.* **2** informal, chiefly Austral./NZ thrash or beat (someone).
– ORIGIN Middle English: from Old French *toaille*, of Germanic origin. Sense 2 of the verb dates from the early 18th cent.; sense 1 from the mid 19th cent.

towel horse ▶ noun a free-standing frame on which to hang towels.

towelling (US **toweling**) ▶ noun [mass noun] thick absorbent cloth, typically cotton with uncut loops, used for towels and robes.

tower ▶ noun a tall narrow building, either free-standing or forming part of a building such as a church or castle.
■ [with modifier] a tall structure that houses machinery, operators, etc. ■ [with modifier] a tall structure used as a receptacle or for storage: *a CD tower.* ■ a tall pile or mass of something: *a titanic tower of garbage.* ■ (**the Tower**) see **TOWER OF LONDON**.
▶ verb [no obj.] **1** rise to or reach a great height: *he seemed to tower over everyone else.*
2 (of a bird) soar up to a great height, especially (of a falcon) so as to be able to swoop down on the quarry.
– PHRASES **tower of strength** see **STRENGTH**.
– DERIVATIVES **towered** adjective (chiefly poetic/literary), **towery** adjective (poetic/literary).
– ORIGIN Old English *torr*, reinforced in Middle English by Old French *tour*, from Latin *turris*, from Greek.

tower block ▶ noun Brit. a tall modern building containing numerous floors of offices or flats.

Tower Bridge a bridge across the Thames in London, famous for its twin towers and for the two bascules of which the roadway consists, able to be lifted to allow the passage of large ships. It was completed in 1894.

towering ▶ adjective [attrib.] extremely tall, especially in comparison with the surroundings: *Hari looked up at the towering buildings.*
■ of exceptional importance or influence: *a majestic, towering album.* ■ of great intensity: *his towering anger.*

Tower of Babel /ˈbeɪb(ə)l/ (in the Bible) a tower built in an attempt to reach heaven, which God frustrated by confusing the languages of its builders so that they could not understand one another (Genesis 11:1–9).
– ORIGIN *Babel* from Hebrew *Bābel* 'Babylon', from Akkadian *bāb ili* 'gate of god'.

Tower of London (also **the Tower**) a fortress by the Thames just east of the City of London. The oldest part, the White Tower, was begun in 1078. It was later used as a state prison, and is now open to the public as a repository of ancient armour and weapons, and of the Crown jewels.

tower of silence ▶ noun a tall open-topped structure on which Parsees traditionally place and leave exposed the body of someone who has died.

tow-headed ▶ adjective having tow-coloured or untidy hair.
– DERIVATIVES **tow-head** noun.

towhee /ˈtəʊ(h)iː, ˈtaʊ-/ ▶ noun a North American songbird of the bunting family, typically with brownish plumage but sometimes black and rufous.

● Genus *Pipilo* (and *Chlorurus*), family Emberizidae (subfamily Emberizinae): several species.
– ORIGIN mid 18th cent.: imitative of the call of *Pipilo erythrophthalmus.*

towing path ▶ noun another term for **TOWPATH**.

towing rope ▶ noun another term for **TOW ROPE**.

towline ▶ noun another term for **TOW ROPE**.

town ▶ noun an urban area with a name, defined boundaries, and local government, that is larger than a village and generally smaller than a city.
■ the particular town under consideration, especially one's own town: *Churchill was in town.* ■ the central part of a neighbourhood, with its business or shopping area: *Rachel left to drive back into town.* ■ Brit. dated the chief city or town of a region: *he has moved to town.* ■ [mass noun] a densely populated area, especially as contrasted with the country or suburbs: *the cultural differences between town and country.* ■ [mass noun] the permanent residents of a university town as distinct from the members of the university: *a rift between the city's town and gown which resulted in a petition to the college.* Often contrasted with **GOWN**. ■ N. Amer. another term for **TOWNSHIP** (in sense 3).
– PHRASES **go to town** informal do something thoroughly, enthusiastically, or extravagantly: *I thought I'd go to town on the redecoration.* **on the town** informal enjoying the entertainments, especially the nightlife, of a city or town: *a lot of guys out for a night on the town.*
– DERIVATIVES **townish** adjective, **townlet** noun, **townward** adjective & adverb, **townwards** adverb.
– ORIGIN Old English *tūn* 'enclosed piece of land, homestead, village', of Germanic origin; related to Dutch *tuin* 'garden' and German *Zaun* 'fence'.

town car ▶ noun US a limousine.

town clerk ▶ noun **1** US a public official in charge of the records of a town.
2 (in the UK, until 1974) the secretary and legal adviser of a town corporation.

town council ▶ noun (especially in the UK) the elected governing body in a municipality.
– DERIVATIVES **town councillor** noun.

town crier ▶ noun historical a person employed to make public announcements in the streets or marketplace of a town.

townee ▶ noun variant spelling of **TOWNIE**.

Townes /taʊnz/, Charles Hard (b.1915), American physicist. His development of microwave oscillators and amplifiers led to his invention of the maser in 1954. Townes later showed that an optical maser (a laser) was possible, though the first working laser was constructed by others. Nobel Prize for Physics (1964).

tow net ▶ noun Biology a dragnet that is towed behind a boat to collect specimens.

town gas ▶ noun Brit., chiefly historical another term for **COAL GAS**.

town hall ▶ noun a building used for the administration of local government.

town house ▶ noun **1** a tall, narrow traditional terrace house, generally having three or more floors.
■ a modern two- or three-storey house built as one of a group of similar houses.
2 a house in a town or city belonging to someone who has another property in the country.
3 archaic a town hall.

townie (also **townee**) ▶ noun informal a person who lives in a town (used especially with reference to their supposed lack of familiarity with rural affairs).

townland ▶ noun (especially in Ireland) a territorial division of land; a township.

town major ▶ noun historical the chief executive officer in a garrison town or fortress.

town mayor ▶ noun Brit. the chairperson of a town council.

town meeting ▶ noun US a meeting of the voters of a town for the transaction of public business.

town planning ▶ noun [mass noun] the planning and control of the construction, growth, and development of a town or other urban area.
– DERIVATIVES **town planner** noun.

townscape ▶ noun the visual appearance of a town or urban area; an urban landscape: *the building's contribution to the townscape | an industrial townscape.*
■ a picture of a town.

township ▶ noun **1** (in South Africa) a suburb or city of predominantly black occupation, formerly officially designated for black occupation by apartheid legislation.
2 S. African a new area being developed for residential or industrial use by speculators.
3 N. Amer. a division of a county with some corporate powers.
■ a district six miles square.
4 Brit. historical a manor or parish as a territorial division.
■ a small town or village forming part of a large parish.
5 Austral./NZ a small town.
– ORIGIN Old English *tūnscipe* 'the inhabitants of a village' (see **TOWN**, **-SHIP**).

townsite ▶ noun N. Amer. a tract of land set apart by legal authority to be occupied by a town and usually surveyed and laid out with streets.

townsman ▶ noun (pl. **-men**) a man living in a particular town or city (often used to contrast with a visitor or a person living in the country).

townspeople (also **townsfolk**) ▶ plural noun people living in a particular town or city.

Townsville an industrial port and resort on the coast of Queensland, NE Australia; pop. 101,400 (1991).

townswoman ▶ noun (pl. **-women**) a woman living in a particular town or city.

Townswomen's Guild (in the UK) a branch of a network of women's organizations, first set up in 1929, that functions as an urban counterpart of the Women's Institute.

towpath (also **towing path**) ▶ noun a path beside a river or canal, originally used as a pathway for horses towing barges.

towplane ▶ noun an aircraft that tows gliders.

tow rope (also **towing rope**) ▶ noun a rope, cable, or other line used in towing.

toxaemia /tɒkˈsiːmɪə/ (US **toxemia**) ▶ noun [mass noun] blood poisoning by toxins from a local bacterial infection.
■ (also **toxaemia of pregnancy**) another term for **PRE-ECLAMPSIA**.
– DERIVATIVES **toxaemic** adjective.
– ORIGIN mid 19th cent.: from **TOXI-** + **-AEMIA**.

toxaphene /ˈtɒksəfiːn/ ▶ noun [mass noun] a synthetic amber waxy solid with an odour of chlorine and camphor, used as an insecticide. It is a chlorinated terpene.
– ORIGIN 1940s: from **TOXIN** + (*cam*)*phene*, a related terpene.

toxi- ▶ combining form representing **TOXIC** or **TOXIN**.

toxic /ˈtɒksɪk/ ▶ adjective poisonous: *the dumping of toxic waste | alcohol is toxic to the ovaries.*
■ of or relating to poison: *toxic hazards.* ■ caused by poison: *toxic liver injury.*
▶ noun (**toxics**) poisonous substances.
– DERIVATIVES **toxically** adverb, **toxicity** noun.
– ORIGIN mid 17th cent.: from medieval Latin *toxicus* 'poisoned', from Latin *toxicum* 'poison', from Greek *toxikon* (*pharmakon*) '(poison for) arrows', from *toxon* 'bow'.

toxicant /ˈtɒksɪk(ə)nt/ ▶ noun a toxic substance introduced into the environment, e.g. a pesticide.
– ORIGIN late 19th cent.: variant of **INTOXICANT**, differentiated in sense.

toxico- ▶ combining form equivalent to **TOXI-**.
– ORIGIN from Greek *toxicon* 'poison'.

toxicology /ˌtɒksɪˈkɒlədʒi/ ▶ noun [mass noun] the branch of science concerned with the nature, effects, and detection of poisons.
– DERIVATIVES **toxicological** adjective, **toxicologically** adverb, **toxicologist** noun.

toxic shock syndrome (abbrev.: **TSS**) ▶ noun [mass noun] acute septicaemia in women, typically caused by bacterial infection from a retained tampon or IUD.

toxigenic /ˌtɒksɪˈdʒɛnɪk/ ▶ adjective (especially of a bacterium) producing a toxin or toxic effect.
– DERIVATIVES **toxigenicity** noun.

toxin /ˈtɒksɪn/ ▶ noun an antigenic poison or venom of plant or animal origin, especially one produced by or derived from micro-organisms and causing disease when present at low concentration in the body.
– ORIGIN late 19th cent.: from **TOXIC** + **-IN**[1].

toxo- ▶ combining form equivalent to **TOXI-**.

toxocara /ˌtɒksəˈkɑːrə/ ▶ noun a parasitic nematode worm, especially a common worm of dogs or cats which is transmissible to humans.
• Genus *Toxocara*, class Phasmida, in particular *T. canis* (in dogs) and *T. cati* (in cats).
– ORIGIN modern Latin, from **TOXO-** (see **TOXI-**) + Greek *kara* 'head'.

toxocariasis /ˌtɒksəʊkəˈrʌɪəsɪs/ ▶ noun [mass noun] infection of a human with the larvae of toxocara worms, causing illness and a risk of blindness from cyst formation in the eye.

toxoid ▶ noun Medicine a chemically modified toxin from a pathogenic micro-organism, which is no longer toxic but is still antigenic and can be used as a vaccine.

toxophilite /tɒkˈsɒfɪlʌɪt/ rare ▶ noun a student or lover of archery.
▶ adjective of or relating to archers and archery.
– DERIVATIVES **toxophily** noun.
– ORIGIN late 18th cent.: from *Toxophilus* (a name invented by Ascham, used as the title of his treatise on archery (1545), from Greek *toxon* 'bow' + *-philos* 'loving') + **-ITE**[1].

toxoplasma /ˌtɒksə(ʊ)ˈplazmə/ ▶ noun a parasitic spore-forming protozoan that can sometimes cause disease in humans.
• Genus *Toxoplasma*, phylum Sporozoa, in particular *T. gondii*.

toxoplasmosis /ˌtɒksəʊplazˈməʊsɪs/ ▶ noun [mass noun] a disease caused by toxoplasmas, transmitted chiefly through undercooked meat, soil, or in cat faeces. Symptoms of infection generally pass unremarked in adults, but can be dangerous to unborn children.

toy ▶ noun **1** an object for a child to play with, typically a model or miniature replica of something: [as modifier] *a toy car.*
■ an object, especially a gadget or machine, regarded as providing amusement for an adult: *in 1914 the car was still a rich man's toy.* ■ a person treated by another as a source of pleasure or amusement rather than with due seriousness: *a man needed a friend, an ally, not an idol or a toy.*
2 [as modifier] denoting a diminutive breed or variety of dog: *a toy poodle.*
– DERIVATIVES **toylike** adjective.
– ORIGIN late Middle English: of unknown origin. The word originally denoted a funny story or remark, later an antic or trick, or a frivolous entertainment. The verb dates from the early 16th cent.
▶ **toy with 1** consider (an idea, movement, or proposal) casually or indecisively. ■ treat (someone) without due seriousness, especially in a superficially amorous way. **2** move or handle (an object) absent-mindedly or nervously. ■ eat or drink in an unenthusiastic or restrained way.

toy boy ▶ noun Brit. informal a male lover who is much younger than his partner.

toyi-toyi /ˈtɔɪtɔɪ/ S. African ▶ noun (pl. **toyi-toyis**) a dance step characterized by high-stepping movements, typically performed at protest gatherings or marches.
▶ verb (**toyi-toyis**, **toyi-toyied**, **toyi-toying** or **toyi-toyiing**) [no obj.] perform such a dance.
– ORIGIN Ndebele and Shona; probably introduced into South Africa by ANC exiles returning from military training in Zimbabwe.

Toynbee[1] /ˈtɔɪnbiː/, Arnold (1852–83), English economist and social reformer. He taught both undergraduates and workers' adult education classes in Oxford and worked with the poor in London's East End. He is best known for his pioneering work *The Industrial Revolution* (1884).

Toynbee[2] /ˈtɔɪnbiː/, Arnold (Joseph) (1889–1975), English historian. He is best known for his twelve-volume *Study of History* (1934–61), in which he traced the pattern of growth, maturity, and decay of different civilizations.

toyon /ˈtɔɪɒn/ ▶ noun an evergreen Californian shrub of the rose family, the fruiting branches of which are used for Christmas decorations.
• *Heteromeles arbutifolia*, family Rosaceae.
– ORIGIN mid 19th cent.: from Mexican Spanish *tollón*.

toytown ▶ adjective [attrib.] resembling a quaint or miniature replica of something: *below you, far away, was a single toytown rooftop.*
■ having no real value, substance, or merit: *toytown tunes, daft haircuts and even dafter trousers.*

Tpr ▶ abbreviation for Trooper.

TQM ▶ abbreviation for Total Quality Management.

TR ▶ abbreviation for Turkey (international vehicle registration).

trabeation /ˌtreɪbɪˈeɪʃ(ə)n/ ▶ noun [mass noun] the use of beams in architectural construction, rather than arches or vaulting.
– DERIVATIVES **trabeated** /ˈtreɪbɪeɪtɪd/ adjective.
– ORIGIN mid 16th cent. (denoting a horizontal beam): formed irregularly from Latin *trabs*, *trab-* 'beam, timber' + **-ATION**.

trabecula /trəˈbɛkjʊlə/ ▶ noun (usu. in pl. **trabeculae** /-liː/) **1** Anatomy each of a series or group of partitions formed by bands or columns of connective tissue, especially a plate of the calcareous tissue forming cancellous bone.
2 Botany any of a number of rod-like structures in plants, e.g. a strand of sterile tissue dividing the cavity in a sporangium.
– DERIVATIVES **trabecular** adjective, **trabeculate** /-lət/ adjective.
– ORIGIN mid 19th cent.: from Latin, diminutive of *trabs* 'beam, timber'.

Trâblous /trɑːˈbluːs/ Arabic name for **TRIPOLI** (sense 2).

Trabzon /ˈtrabz(ə)n/ a port on the Black Sea in northern Turkey; pop. 143,940 (1990). In 1204, after the sack of Constantinople by the Crusaders, an offshoot of the Byzantine Empire was founded with Trabzon as its capital, which was annexed to the Ottoman Empire in 1461. Also called **TREBIZOND**.

tracasserie /trəˈkas(ə)ri/ ▶ noun (usu. **tracasseries**) archaic a fuss; a petty quarrel.
– ORIGIN French, from *tracasser* 'to bustle or fuss'.

trace[1] ▶ verb [with obj.] **1** find or discover by investigation: *police are trying to trace a white van seen in the area.*
■ find or describe the origin or development of: *Bob's book traces his flying career with the RAF.* ■ follow or mark the course or position of (something) with one's eye, mind, or finger: *through the binoculars, I traced the path I had taken the night before.* ■ take (a particular path or route): *a tear traced a lonely path down her cheek.*
2 copy (a drawing, map, or design) by drawing over its lines on a superimposed piece of transparent paper.
■ draw (a pattern or line), especially with one's finger or toe. ■ give an outline of: *the article* **traces out** *some of the connections between education, qualifications, and the labour market.*
▶ noun **1** a mark, object, or other indication of the existence or passing of something: *remove all traces of the old adhesive* | [mass noun] *the aircraft disappeared without trace.*
■ W. Indian & US a beaten path or small road; a track. ■ a physical change in the brain presumed to be caused by a process of learning or memory. ■ Linguistics (in transformational grammar) a slot from which an element has been moved by a transformation. ■ a procedure to investigate the source of something, such as the place from which a telephone call was made, or the origin of a fault in a computer program.
2 a very small quantity, especially one too small to be accurately measured: *his body contained traces of amphetamines* | [as modifier] *trace quantities of PCBs.*
■ a slight indication or barely discernible hint of something: *just a trace of a smile.*
3 a line or pattern displayed by an instrument using a moving pen or a luminous spot on a screen to show the existence or nature of something which is being investigated.
■ a line which represents the projection of a curve or surface on a plane or the intersection of a curve or surface with a plane.
4 Mathematics the sum of the elements in the principle diagonal of a square matrix.
– DERIVATIVES **traceability** noun, **traceable** adjective, **traceless** adjective.
– ORIGIN Middle English (first recorded as a noun in the sense 'path that someone or something takes'): from Old French *trace* (noun), *tracier* (verb), based on Latin *tractus* (see **TRACT**[1]).

trace[2] ▶ noun each of the two side straps, chains, or ropes by which a horse is attached to a vehicle that it is pulling.
– PHRASES **kick over the traces** become insubordinate or reckless.
– ORIGIN Middle English (denoting a pair of traces): from Old French *trais*, plural of *trait* (see **TRAIT**).

trace element ▶ noun a chemical element present only in minute amounts in a particular sample or environment.
■ a chemical element required only in minute amounts by living organisms for normal growth.

trace fossil ▶ noun Geology a fossil of a footprint, trail, burrow, or other trace of an animal rather than of the animal itself.

trace-horse ▶ noun historical a horse put in traces to pull a vehicle.

tracer ▶ noun a person or thing that traces something or by which something may be traced, in particular:
■ a bullet or shell whose course is made visible in flight by a trail of flames or smoke, used to assist in aiming. ■ a substance introduced into a biological organism or other system so that its subsequent distribution may be readily followed from its colour, fluorescence, radioactivity, or other distinctive property. ■ a device which transmits a signal and so can be located when attached to a moving vehicle or other object.

tracery ▶ noun (pl. **-ies**) [mass noun] Architecture ornamental stone openwork, typically in the upper part of a Gothic window.
■ [count noun] a delicate branching pattern: *a tracery of red veins.*
– DERIVATIVES **traceried** adjective.

trachea /trəˈkiːə, ˈtreɪkɪə/ ▶ noun (pl. **tracheae** /-ˈkiːiː/ or **tracheas**) Anatomy a large membranous tube reinforced by rings of cartilage, extending from the larynx to the bronchial tubes and conveying air to and from the lungs; the windpipe.
■ Entomology each of a number of fine chitinous tubes in the body of an insect, conveying air direct to the tissues. ■ Botany any duct or vessel in a plant, providing support and conveying water and salts.
– DERIVATIVES **tracheal** /ˈtreɪkɪəl/ adjective, **tracheate** /ˈtreɪkɪeɪt/ adjective.
– ORIGIN late Middle English: from medieval Latin, from late Latin *trachia*, from Greek *trakheia* (*artēria*) 'rough (artery)', from *trakhus* 'rough'.

tracheid /ˈtreɪkɪɪd/ ▶ noun Botany a type of water-conducting cell in the xylem which lacks perforations in the cell wall.
– ORIGIN late 19th cent.: from German *Tracheïde*, from medieval Latin *trachea* (see **TRACHEA**).

tracheitis /ˌtreɪkɪˈʌɪtɪs/ ▶ noun [mass noun] Medicine inflammation of the trachea, usually secondary to a nose or throat infection.

tracheo- /trəˈkiːəʊ, ˈtrakɪəʊ, ˈtreɪkɪəʊ/ ▶ combining form relating to the trachea: *tracheotomy.*

tracheotomy /ˌtrakɪˈɒtəmi/ (also **tracheostomy** /-ˈɒstəmi/) ▶ noun (pl. **-ies**) Medicine an incision in the windpipe made to relieve an obstruction to breathing.

tracheotomy tube ▶ noun a breathing tube inserted into a tracheotomy.

trachoma /trəˈkəʊmə/ ▶ noun [mass noun] a contagious bacterial infection of the eye in which there is inflamed granulation on the inner surface of the lids.
• The disease is caused by the chlamydial organism *Chlamydia trichomatis*.
– DERIVATIVES **trachomatous** /-ˈkəʊmətəs, -ˈkɒmətəs/ adjective.
– ORIGIN late 17th cent.: from Greek *trakhōma* 'roughness', from *trakhus* 'rough'.

trachyte /ˈtreɪkʌɪt, ˈtrakʌɪt/ ▶ noun [mass noun] Geology a grey fine-grained volcanic rock consisting largely of alkali feldspar.
– ORIGIN early 19th cent. (denoting a volcanic rock with a rough or gritty surface): from Greek *trakhus* 'rough' or *trakhutēs* 'roughness'.

trachytic /trəˈkɪtɪk/ ▶ adjective Geology relating to or denoting a rock texture (characteristic of trachyte) in which crystals show parallel alignment due to liquid flow.

tracing ▶ noun a copy of a drawing, map, or design made by tracing it.
■ a faint or delicate mark or pattern: *tracings of apple blossoms against the deep greens of pines.* ■ another term for **TRACE**[1] (in sense 3). ■ [mass noun] Skating the marking out of a figure on the ice when skating.

tracing paper ▶ noun [mass noun] transparent paper used for tracing maps, drawings, or designs.

track[1] ▶ noun **1** a rough path or minor road,

typically one beaten by use rather than constructed: *follow the track to the farm | a forest track.*
■a prepared course or circuit for athletes, horses, motor vehicles, bicycles, or dogs to race on: *a Formula One Grand Prix track.* ■ [mass noun] the sport of running on such a track. ■ (usu. **tracks**) a mark or line of marks left by a person, animal, or vehicle in passing: *he followed the tracks made by the police cars in the snow.* ■the course or route followed by someone or something (used especially in talking about their pursuit by others): *I didn't want the Russians **on my track.*** ■ figurative a course of action; a way of proceeding: *defence budgeting and procurement do not move along different tracks from defence policy as a whole.*
2 a continuous line of rails on a railway.
■a metal or plastic strip or rail from which a curtain or spotlight may be hung or fitted. ■ a continuous articulated metal band around the wheels of a heavy vehicle such as a tank or bulldozer, intended to facilitate movement over rough or soft ground. ■ Electronics a continuous line of copper or other conductive material on a printed circuit board, used to connect parts of a circuit. ■ Sailing a strip on the mast, boom, or floor of a yacht along which a slide attached to a sail can be moved, used to adjust the position of the sail.
3 a section of a record, compact disc, or cassette tape containing one song or piece of music: *the CD contains early Elvis Presley tracks.* [ORIGIN: originally denoting a groove on a gramophone record.]
■a lengthwise strip of magnetic tape containing one sequence of signals. ■ the soundtrack of a film or video.
4 the transverse distance between a vehicle's wheels.
5 US term for **STREAM** (in sense 3).
▶ **verb** [with obj.] **1** follow the course or trail of (someone or something), typically in order to find them or note their location at various points: *secondary radars that track the aircraft in flight | he tracked Anna to her room.*
■figurative follow and note the course or progress of: *City have been tracking the striker since the summer.* ■ [no obj., with adverbial of direction] follow a particular course: *the storm was tracking across the ground at 30 mph.* ■ (of a stylus) follow (a groove in a record). ■ [no obj., with adverbial of direction] (of a film or television camera) move in relation to the subject being filmed: *the camera eventually tracked away.* [ORIGIN: with reference to early filming when a camera was mobile by means of a track.] ■ (**track something up**) N. Amer. leave a trail of dirty footprints on a surface. ■ (**track something in**) N. Amer. leave a trail of dirt, debris, or snow from one's feet: *the road salt I'd tracked in from the street.*
2 [no obj.] (of wheels) run so that the back ones are exactly in the track of the front ones.
3 [no obj.] Electronics (of a tunable circuit or component) vary in frequency in the same way as another circuit or component, so that the frequency difference between them remains constant.
– PHRASES **in one's tracks** informal where one or something is at that moment; suddenly: *Turner immediately **stopped dead in his tracks.*** **keep** (or **lose**) **track of** keep (or fail to keep) fully aware of or informed about: *she had lost all track of time and had fallen asleep.* **make tracks** (**for**) informal leave (for a place). **off the beaten track** see **BEATEN**. **off the track** departing from the right course of thinking or behaviour. **on the right** (or **wrong**) **track** acting or thinking in a way that is likely to result in success (or failure): *we are on the right track for continued growth.* **on track** acting or thinking in a way that is likely to achieve what is required: *formulas for keeping the economy on track.* **the wrong side of the tracks** informal a poor or less prestigious part of town. [ORIGIN: with reference to the railway tracks of American towns, once serving as a line of demarcation between rich and poor quarters.]
– ORIGIN late 15th cent. (in the sense 'trail, marks left behind'): the noun from Old French *trac*, perhaps from Low German or Dutch *trek* 'draught, drawing'; the verb (current senses dating from the mid 16th cent.) from French *traquer* or directly from the noun.
▶ **track someone/thing down** find someone or something after a thorough or difficult search.
track up (of a horse at the trot) create sufficient impulsion in its hindquarters to cause the hind feet to step on to or slightly ahead of the former position of the forefeet.
track (**square**) **with** Austral. informal carry on a romantic or sexual relationship with.

track[2] ▶ **verb** [with obj. and adverbial of direction] tow (a canoe) along a waterway from the bank.
– ORIGIN early 18th cent.: apparently from Dutch *trekken* 'to draw, pull, or travel'. The change in the vowel was due to association with **TRACK**[1].

trackage ▶ **noun** [mass noun] N. Amer. the tracks or lines of a railway system collectively.

trackball (also **tracker ball**) ▶ **noun** a small ball that is set in a holder and can be rotated by hand to move a cursor on a computer screen.

trackbed ▶ **noun** the foundation structure on which railway tracks are laid.

track circuit ▶ **noun** an electric circuit made in a section of railway track as an aid to signalling, and able to be short-circuited by the presence of a train.

tracker ▶ **noun 1** a person who tracks someone or something by following their trail.
2 a connecting rod in the mechanism of an organ.

track events ▶ **plural noun** athletic events that take place on a running track, as opposed to those involving throwing or other activities. Compare with **FIELD EVENTS**.

tracking ▶ **noun** [mass noun] **1** the action of tracking someone or something.
■Electronics the maintenance of a constant difference in frequency between two or more connected circuits or components. ■ the alignment of the wheels of a vehicle. ■ the formation of a conducting path for an electric current over the surface of an insulating material.
2 US the streaming of school pupils.

tracking station ▶ **noun** a place from which the movements of missiles, aircraft, or satellites are tracked by radar or radio.

tracklayer ▶ **noun 1** a tractor or other vehicle equipped with continuous tracks.
2 N. Amer. another term for **TRACKMAN**.

tracklement ▶ **noun** Brit. a savoury jelly, served with meat.
– ORIGIN 1950s: of unknown origin.

trackless ▶ **adjective 1** (of land) having no paths or tracks on it: *leading travellers into trackless wastelands.*
■poetic/literary not leaving a track or trace.
2 (of a vehicle or component) not running on a track or tracks.

trackman ▶ **noun** (pl. **-men**) a person employed in laying and maintaining railway track.

track record ▶ **noun** the best recorded performance in a particular athletics event at a particular track.
■the past achievements or performance of a person, organization, or product: *he has an excellent track record as an author.*

track rod ▶ **noun** a rod that connects the two front wheels of a motor vehicle and transmits the steering action from the steering column to the wheels.

track shoe ▶ **noun** a running shoe.

trackside ▶ **adjective** adjacent to a railway track.

tracksuit ▶ **noun** a loose, warm set of clothes consisting of a sweatshirt and trousers with an elasticated or drawstring waist, worn when exercising or as casual wear.

trackway ▶ **noun** a path formed by the repeated treading of people or animals.
■an ancient roadway.

trackwork ▶ **noun** [mass noun] railway track and associated equipment.
■work involved in constructing or maintaining railway track.

tract[1] ▶ **noun 1** an area of indefinite extent, typically a large one: *large tracts of natural forest.*
■poetic/literary an indefinitely large extent of something: *the vast tracts of time required to account for the deposition of the strata.*
2 a major passage in the body, large bundle of nerve fibres, or other continuous elongated anatomical structure or region: *the digestive tract.*
– ORIGIN late Middle English (in the sense 'duration or course (of time)'): from Latin *tractus* 'drawing, draught', from *trahere* 'draw, pull'.

tract[2] ▶ **noun** a short treatise in pamphlet form, typically on a religious subject.
– ORIGIN late Middle English (denoting a written work treating a particular topic), apparently an abbreviation of Latin *tractatus* (see **TRACTATE**). The current sense dates from the early 19th cent.

tract[3] ▶ **noun** (in the Roman Catholic Church) an anthem of Scriptural verses formerly replacing the alleluia in certain penitential and requiem Masses.
– ORIGIN late Middle English: from medieval Latin *tractus* (*cantus*) 'drawn-out (song)', past participle of Latin *trahere* 'draw'.

tractable ▶ **adjective** (of a person) easy to control or influence: *underfed children were more tractable.*
■(of a situation or problem) easy to deal with: *trying to make the mathematics tractable.*
– DERIVATIVES **tractability** noun, **tractably** adverb.
– ORIGIN early 16th cent.: from Latin *tractabilis*, from *tractare* 'to handle' (see **TRACTATE**).

Tractarianism /trak'tɛːrɪənɪz(ə)m/ ▶ **noun** [mass noun] another name for **OXFORD MOVEMENT**.
– DERIVATIVES **Tractarian** adjective & noun.
– ORIGIN mid 19th cent.: from *Tracts for the Times*, the title of a series of pamphlets on theological topics started by J. H. Newman and published in Oxford 1833–41, which set out the doctrines on which the movement was based.

tractate /'trakteɪt/ ▶ **noun** formal a treatise.
– ORIGIN late 15th cent.: from Latin *tractatus*, from *tractare* 'to handle', frequentative of *trahere* 'draw'.

traction ▶ **noun** [mass noun] **1** the action of drawing or pulling a thing over a surface, especially a road or track: *a primitive vehicle used in animal traction.*
■motive power provided for such movement, especially on a railway: *the changeover to diesel and electric traction.* ■ locomotives collectively.
2 Medicine the application of a sustained pull on a limb or muscle, especially in order to maintain the position of a fractured bone or to correct a deformity: *his leg is **in traction.***
3 the grip of a tyre on a road or a wheel on a rail: *his car hit a patch of ice and lost traction.*
– ORIGIN late Middle English (denoting contraction, such as that of a muscle): from French, or from medieval Latin *tractio(n-)*, from Latin *trahere* 'draw, pull'. Current senses date from the early 19th cent.

traction engine ▶ **noun** a steam or diesel-powered road vehicle used (especially formerly) for pulling very heavy loads.

tractive /'traktɪv/ ▶ **adjective** [attrib.] relating to or denoting the power exerted in pulling, especially by a vehicle or other machine.

tractor ▶ **noun** a powerful motor vehicle with large rear wheels, used chiefly on farms for hauling equipment and trailers.
– ORIGIN late 18th cent. (in the general sense 'someone or something that pulls'): from Latin, from *tract-* 'pulled', from the verb *trahere*.

tractor beam ▶ **noun** (in science fiction) a hypothetical beam of energy that can be used to move objects such as space ships or hold them stationary.

tractotomy /trak'tɒtəmi/ ▶ **noun** [mass noun] the surgical severing of nerve tracts especially in the medulla of the brain, typically to relieve intractable pain or mental illness, or in research.

tractrix /'traktrɪks/ ▶ **noun** (pl. **tractrices** /-trɪsiːz/) Geometry a curve whose tangents all intercept the *x*-axis at the same distance from the point of contact, being the involute of a catenary.
■one of a class of curves similarly traced by one end of a rigid rod, whose other end moves along a fixed line or curve.
– ORIGIN early 18th cent.: modern Latin, feminine of late Latin *tractor* 'that which pulls' (see **TRACTOR**).

Tracy, Spencer (1900–67), American actor, particularly known for his screen partnership with Katharine Hepburn, with whom he co-starred in films such as *Guess Who's Coming to Dinner?* (1967).

trad informal ▶ **adjective** (especially of music) traditional: *trad jazz.*
▶ **noun** [mass noun] traditional jazz or folk music.
– ORIGIN 1950s: abbreviation.

trade ▶ **noun 1** [mass noun] the action of buying and selling goods and services: *a move to ban all **trade in** ivory | a significant increase in foreign trade | the meat trade.*
■dated, chiefly derogatory the practice of making one's living in business, as opposed to in a profession or from unearned income: *the aristocratic classes were contemptuous of those **in trade.*** ■ [count noun] N. Amer. (in sport) a transfer; an exchange: *players can demand a trade after five years of service.*

2 a skilled job, typically one requiring manual skills and special training: *the fundamentals of the construction trade* | [mass noun] *a carpenter by trade.*
■ (**the trade**) [treated as sing. or pl.] the people engaged in a particular area of business: *in the trade this sort of computer is called 'a client-based system'.* ■ (**the trade**) [treated as sing. or pl.] Brit. people licensed to sell alcoholic drink.
3 (usu. **trades**) a trade wind: *the north-east trades.*
▶**verb** [no obj.] buy and sell goods and services: *middlemen **trading in** luxury goods.*
■ [with obj.] buy or sell (a particular item or product): *she has traded millions of dollars' worth of metals.* ■ (especially of shares or currency) be bought and sold at a specified price: *the dollar was trading where it was in January.* ■ [with obj.] exchange (something) for something else, typically as a commercial transaction: *they trade mud-shark livers for fish oil* | *the hostages were **traded for** arms.* ■ [with obj.] figurative give and receive (typically insults or blows): *they traded a few punches.* ■ [with obj.] N. Amer. transfer (a player) to another club or team.
– PHRASES **trade places** US change places.
– DERIVATIVES **tradable** (or **tradeable**) adjective.
– ORIGIN late Middle English (as a noun): from Middle Low German, literally 'track', of West Germanic origin; related to **TREAD**. Early senses included 'course, way of life', which gave rise in the 16th cent. to 'habitual practice of an occupation', 'skilled handicraft'. The current verb senses date from the late 16th cent.
▶**trade down** (or **up**) sell something in order to buy something similar but less (or more) expensive.
trade something in exchange a used article in part payment for another: *she **traded in** her Ford **for** a Land Rover.*
trade something off exchange something of value, especially as part of a compromise: *the government **traded off** economic advantages **for** political gains.*
trade on take advantage of (something), especially in an unfair way: *the government is trading on fears of inflation.*

Trade Board ▶**noun** Brit. historical a statutory body with members from workers and management, set up to settle disputes and regulate conditions of employment in certain industries.

trade book ▶**noun** a book published by a commercial publisher and intended for general readership.

trade cycle ▶**noun** a regular alternation of periods of increased and decreased economic activity.

trade deficit ▶**noun** the amount by which the cost of a country's imports exceeds the value of its exports.

trade discount ▶**noun** a discount on the retail price of something allowed or agreed between traders or to a retailer by a wholesaler.

trade dispute ▶**noun** a dispute among workers or between employers and workers that is connected with the terms or conditions of employment.

traded option ▶**noun** an option on a stock exchange or futures exchange which can itself be bought and sold.

trade edition ▶**noun** an edition of a book intended for general sale rather than for book clubs or specialist suppliers.

trade gap ▶**noun** another term for **TRADE DEFICIT**.

trade-in ▶**noun** [usu. as modifier] a used article accepted by a retailer in part payment for another.

trade journal ▶**noun** a periodical containing news and items of interest concerning a particular trade.

trade-last ▶**noun** US dated a compliment from a third person that is relayed to the person complimented in exchange for a similarly relayed compliment.

trademark ▶**noun** a symbol, word, or words, legally registered or established by use as representing a company or product.
■ figurative a distinctive characteristic or object: *it had all the trademarks of a Mafia hit.*
▶**verb** [with obj.] [usu. as adj. **trademarked**] provide with a trademark: *they are counterfeiting trademarked goods.*
■ figurative identify (a habit, quality, or way of life) as typical of someone: *his trademarked grandiose style.*

trade name ▶**noun 1** a name that has the status of a trademark.
2 a name by which something is known in a particular trade or profession.

trade-off ▶**noun** a balance achieved between two desirable but incompatible features; a compromise: *a trade-off between objectivity and relevance.*

trade paper ▶**noun** another term for **TRADE JOURNAL**.

trade plates ▶**plural noun** Brit. temporary number plates used by car dealers or manufacturers on unlicensed cars.

trade price ▶**noun** the price paid for goods by a retailer to a manufacturer or wholesaler.

trader ▶**noun** a person who buys and sells goods, currency, or shares.
■ a merchant ship.

Tradescant /ˈtradɪskant/, John (1570–1638), English botanist and horticulturalist. He was the earliest known collector of plants and other natural history specimens, and took part in collecting trips to western Europe, Russia, and North Africa. His son **John** (1608–62) added many plants to his father's collection, which was eventually bequeathed to Elias Ashmole.

tradescantia /ˌtradɪˈskantɪə/ ▶**noun** an American plant with triangular three-petalled flowers, especially a tender kind widely grown as a house plant for its trailing, typically variegated, foliage. Compare with **SPIDERWORT**.
● Genus *Tradescantia*, family Commelinaceae.
– ORIGIN modern Latin, named in honour of J. **TRADESCANT**.

trade secret ▶**noun** a secret device or technique used by a company in manufacturing its products.

tradesman ▶**noun** (pl. **-men**) a person engaged in trading or a trade, typically on a relatively small scale.

tradespeople ▶**plural noun** people engaged in trade.

Trades Union Congress (abbrev: **TUC**) (in the UK) the official representative body of British trade unions, founded in 1868 and meeting annually.

trade surplus ▶**noun** the amount by which the value of a country's exports exceeds the cost of its imports.

trade union (Brit. also **trades union**) ▶**noun** an organized association of workers in a trade, group of trades, or profession, formed to protect and further their rights and interests.

trade unionist (Brit. also **trades unionist**) ▶**noun** a member of a trade union or an advocate of trade unionism.
– DERIVATIVES **trade unionism** noun.

trade-up ▶**noun** a sale of an article in order to buy something similar but more expensive and of higher quality.

trade war ▶**noun** a situation in which countries try to damage each other's trade, typically by the imposition of tariffs or quota restrictions.

trade-weighted ▶**adjective** (especially of exchange rates) weighted according to the importance of the trade with the various countries involved.

trade wind ▶**noun** a wind blowing steadily towards the equator from the north-east in the northern hemisphere or the south-east in the southern hemisphere, especially at sea. Two belts of trade winds encircle the earth, blowing from the tropical high-pressure belts to the low-pressure zone at the equator.
– ORIGIN mid 17th cent.: from the phrase *blow trade* 'blow steadily in the same direction'. Because of the importance of these winds to navigation, 18th-cent. etymologists were led erroneously to connect the word *trade* with 'commerce'

trading ▶**noun** [mass noun] the action of engaging in trade.

trading estate ▶**noun** Brit. a specially designed industrial and commercial area.

trading floor ▶**noun** an area within an exchange or a bank or securities house where dealers trade in shares or other securities.

trading post ▶**noun** a store or small settlement established for trading, typically in a remote place.

trading stamp ▶**noun** a stamp given by some stores to a customer according to the amount spent, and exchangeable in the appropriate number for various articles.

tradition ▶**noun 1** [mass noun] the transmission of customs or beliefs from generation to generation, or the fact of being passed on in this way: *members of different castes have **by tradition** been associated with specific occupations.*
■ [count noun] a long-established custom or belief that has been passed on in this way: *Japan's unique cultural traditions.* ■ [in sing.] an artistic or literary method or style established by an artist, writer, or movement, and subsequently followed by others: *visionary works **in the tradition of** William Blake.*
2 Theology a doctrine believed to have divine authority though not in the scriptures, in particular:
■ [mass noun] (in Christianity) doctrine not explicit in the Bible but held to derive from the oral teaching of Christ and the Apostles. ■ (in Judaism) an ordinance of the oral law not in the Torah but held to have been given by God to Moses. ■ (in Islam) a saying or act ascribed to the Prophet but not recorded in the Koran. See **HADITH**.
– DERIVATIVES **traditionary** adjective, **traditionist** noun, **traditionless** adjective.
– ORIGIN late Middle English: from Old French *tradicion*, or from Latin *traditio(n-)*, from *tradere* 'deliver, betray', from *trans-* 'across' + *dare* 'give'.

traditional ▶**adjective** existing in or as part of a tradition; long-established: *the traditional festivities of the church year.*
■ produced, done, or used in accordance with tradition: *a traditional fish soup.* ■ habitually done, used, or found: *the traditional drinks in the clubhouse.* ■ (of a person or group) adhering to tradition, or to a particular tradition: *traditional Elgarians.* ■ (of jazz) in the style of the early 20th century.
– DERIVATIVES **traditionally** adverb.

traditionalism ▶**noun** [mass noun] the upholding or maintenance of tradition, especially so as to resist change.
■ chiefly historical the theory that all moral and religious truth comes from divine revelation passed on by tradition, human reason being incapable of attaining it.
– DERIVATIVES **traditionalist** noun & adjective, **traditionalistic** adjective.

traduce /trəˈdjuːs/ ▶**verb** [with obj.] speak badly of or tell lies about (someone) so as to damage their reputation.
– DERIVATIVES **traducement** noun, **traducer** noun.
– ORIGIN mid 16th cent. (in the sense 'transport, transmit'): from Latin *traducere* 'lead in front of others, expose to ridicule', from *trans-* 'over, across' + *ducere* 'to lead'.

Trafalgar, Battle of /trəˈfalgə/ a decisive naval battle fought on 21 October 1805 off the cape of Trafalgar on the south coast of Spain during the Napoleonic Wars. The British fleet under Horatio Nelson defeated the combined fleets of France and Spain, which were attempting to clear the way for Napoleon's projected invasion of Britain.

Trafalgar Square a square in central London, planned by John Nash and built between the 1820s and 1840s. It is dominated by Nelson's Column, a memorial to Lord Nelson.

traffic ▶**noun** [mass noun] **1** vehicles moving on a public highway: *a stream of heavy traffic.*
■ a large number of such vehicles: *we were caught in traffic on the motorway.* ■ the movement of other forms of transport or of pedestrians: *Europe's air traffic.* ■ the transportation of goods or passengers: *the increased use of railways for goods traffic.* ■ the messages or signals transmitted through a communications system: *data traffic between remote workstations.*
2 the action of dealing or trading in something illegal: *the **traffic in** stolen cattle.*
3 archaic dealings or communication between people.
▶**verb** (**trafficked**, **trafficking**) [no obj.] deal or trade in something illegal: *the government will vigorously pursue individuals who **traffic in** drugs.*
– DERIVATIVES **trafficker** noun, **trafficless** adjective.
– ORIGIN early 16th cent. (denoting commercial transportation of merchandise or passengers): from French *traffique*, Spanish *tráfico*, or Italian *traffico*, of unknown origin. Sense 1 dates from the early 19th cent.

trafficator /ˈtrafɪkeɪtə/ ▶**noun** Brit. an obsolete kind of signalling device on the side of a motor vehicle, having the form of a small illuminated pointer which could be extended to indicate a change of direction.
– ORIGIN 1930s: blend of **TRAFFIC** and **INDICATOR**.

traffic calming ▶ **noun** [mass noun] the deliberate slowing of traffic in residential areas, by building road humps or other obstructions.
– ORIGIN 1980s: translation of German *Verkehrsberuhigung*.

traffic circle ▶ **noun** North American term for **ROUNDABOUT** (in sense 1).

traffic island ▶ **noun** a small raised area in the middle of a road which provides a safe place for pedestrians to stand and marks a division between two opposing streams of traffic.

traffic jam ▶ **noun** a line or lines of traffic at or virtually at a standstill because of roadworks, an accident, or heavy congestion.

traffic lights (also **traffic light** or **traffic signal**) ▶ **plural noun** a set of automatically operated coloured lights, typically red, amber, and green, for controlling traffic at road junctions, pedestrian crossings, and roundabouts.

traffic pattern ▶ **noun** chiefly N. Amer. a pattern in the air above an airport of permitted lanes for aircraft to follow after take-off or prior to landing.

traffic sign ▶ **noun** a sign conveying information, an instruction, or a warning to drivers.

traffic warden ▶ **noun** Brit. a uniformed official employed to locate and report on infringements of parking regulations.

tragacanth /ˈtraɡəkanθ/ (also **gum tragacanth**) ▶ **noun** [mass noun] a white or reddish plant gum, used in the food, textile, and pharmaceutical industries.
• This gum is obtained from plants of the genus *Astragalus*, family Leguminosae, in particular the Eurasian *A. gummifer*.
– ORIGIN late 16th cent.: from French *tragacante*, via Latin from Greek *tragakantha* 'goat's thorn', from *tragos* 'goat' (because it is browsed by goats) + *akantha* 'thorn' (referring to the shrub's spines).

tragedian /trəˈdʒiːdɪən/ ▶ **noun** an actor who specializes in tragic roles.
■ a writer of tragedies.
– ORIGIN late Middle English (denoting a writer of tragedies): from Old French *tragediane*, from *tragedie* (see **TRAGEDY**).

tragedienne /trəˌdʒiːdɪˈɛn/ ▶ **noun** an actress who specializes in tragic roles.
– ORIGIN mid 19th cent.: from French *tragédienne*, feminine of *tragédien*.

tragedy ▶ **noun** (pl. **-ies**) **1** an event causing great suffering, destruction, and distress, such as a serious accident, crime, or natural catastrophe: *a tragedy that killed 95 people* | [mass noun] *his life had been plagued by tragedy*.
2 a play dealing with tragic events and having an unhappy ending, especially one concerning the downfall of the main character.
■ [mass noun] the dramatic genre represented by such plays: *Greek tragedy*. Compare with **COMEDY**.
– ORIGIN late Middle English: from Old French *tragedie*, via Latin from Greek *tragōidia*, apparently from *tragos* 'goat' (the reason remains unexplained) + *ōidē* 'song, ode'. Compare with **TRAGIC**.

traghetto /traˈɡɛtəʊ/ ▶ **noun** (pl. **traghetti** /traˈɡɛti/) (in Venice) a landing place or jetty for gondolas.
■ a gondola ferry.
– ORIGIN Italian.

tragic ▶ **adjective** causing or characterized by extreme distress or sorrow: *the shooting was a tragic accident*.
■ suffering extreme distress or sorrow: *the tragic parents reached the end of their tether*. ■ of or relating to tragedy in a literary work.
– DERIVATIVES **tragical** adjective, **tragically** adverb.
– ORIGIN mid 16th cent.: from French *tragique*, via Latin from Greek *tragikos*, from *tragos* 'goat', but associated with *tragōidia* (see **TRAGEDY**).

tragic flaw ▶ **noun** less technical term for **HAMARTIA**.

tragic irony ▶ **noun** see **IRONY**[1].

tragicomedy /ˌtradʒɪˈkɒmɪdi/ ▶ **noun** (pl. **-ies**) a play or novel containing elements of both comedy and tragedy.
■ [mass noun] such works as a genre.
– DERIVATIVES **tragicomic** adjective, **tragicomically** adverb.
– ORIGIN late 16th cent.: from French *tragicomédie* or Italian *tragicomedia*, based on Latin *tragicocomoedia*, from *tragicus* (see **TRAGIC**) + *comoedia* (see **COMEDY**).

tragopan /ˈtraɡəpan/ ▶ **noun** an Asian pheasant of highland forests, the male of which has brightly coloured plumage used in courtship.
• Genus *Tragopan*, family Phasianidae: five species.
– ORIGIN modern Latin, from Greek, the name of a horned bird, from *tragos* 'goat' + the name *Pan* (see **PAN**).

tragus /ˈtreɪɡəs/ ▶ **noun** (pl. **tragi** /ˈtreɪɡʌɪ, ˈtreɪdʒʌɪ/) Anatomy & Zoology a prominence on the inner side of the external ear, in front of and partly closing the passage to the organs of hearing.
– ORIGIN late 17th cent.: from late Latin, via Latin from Greek *tragos* 'goat' (with reference to the characteristic tuft of hair that is often present, likened to a goat's beard).

Traherne /trəˈhəːn/, Thomas (1637–74), English religious writer and metaphysical poet. His major prose work *Centuries* (1699) was rediscovered in 1896 and republished as *Centuries of Meditation* (1908). It consists of brief meditations showing his joy in creation and in divine love and is noted for its description of his childhood.

trahison des clercs /ˌtraːɪzɔ̃ deɪ ˈklɛː, French traizɔ̃ de klɛʀ/ ▶ **noun** poetic/literary a betrayal of intellectual, artistic, or moral standards by writers, academics, or artists.
– ORIGIN French, literally 'treason of the scholars', the title of a book by Julien Benda (1927).

trail ▶ **noun 1** a mark or a series of signs or objects left behind by the passage of someone or something: *a trail of blood on the grass*.
■ a track or scent used in following someone or hunting an animal: *police followed his trail to Dorset*. ■ a part, typically long and thin, stretching behind or hanging down from something: *smoke trails* | *trails of ivy*. ■ a line of people or things following behind each other: *we drove down in a trail of tourist cars*.
2 a beaten path through rough country such as a wood or moor.
■ a route planned or followed for a particular purpose: *the tourist trail*. ■ (also **ski trail**) N. Amer. a downhill ski run or cross-country ski route.
3 short for **TRAILER** (in sense 2).
4 the rear end of a gun carriage, resting or sliding on the ground when the gun is unlimbered.
▶ **verb 1** [with adverbial] draw or be drawn along the ground or other surface behind someone or something: [with obj.] *Alex trailed a hand through the clear water* | [no obj.] *her robe trailed along the ground*.
■ [no obj.] (typically of a plant) grow or hang over the edge of something or along the ground: *the roses grew wild, their stems trailing over the banks*. ■ [with obj.] follow (a person or animal), typically by using marks, signs, or scent left behind. ■ [no obj.] be losing to an opponent in a game or contest: [with complement] *the defending champions were trailing 10–5 at half-time*.
2 [no obj., with adverbial of direction] walk or move slowly or wearily: *she trailed behind, whimpering at intervals*.
■ (of the voice or a speaker) fade gradually before stopping: *her voice trailed away*.
3 [with obj.] advertise (something, especially a film or programme) in advance by broadcasting extracts or details.
4 [with obj.] apply (slip) through a nozzle or spout to decorate ceramic ware.
– PHRASES **at the trail** Military with a rifle hanging balanced in one hand and (in Britain) parallel to the ground. **trail arms** Military let a rifle hang in such a way. **trail one's coat** deliberately provoke a quarrel or fight.
– ORIGIN Middle English (as a verb): from Old French *traillier* 'to tow', or Middle Low German *treilen* 'haul (a boat)', based on Latin *tragula* 'dragnet', from *trahere* 'to pull'. Compare with **TRAWL**. The noun originally denoted the train of a robe, later generalized to denote something trailing.

trail bike ▶ **noun** a light motorcycle for use in rough terrain.

trailblazer ▶ **noun** a person who makes a new track through wild country.
■ a pioneer; an innovator: *he was a trailblazer for many ideas that are now standard fare*.
– DERIVATIVES **trailblazing** noun & adjective.

trail boss ▶ **noun** US a foreman in charge of a cattle drive.

trailer ▶ **noun 1** an unpowered vehicle towed by another, in particular:
■ the rear section of an articulated lorry. ■ an open cart. ■ a platform for transporting a boat. ■ US a caravan.
2 an extract or series of extracts from a film or programme used to advertise it in advance.
3 a thing that trails, especially a trailing plant.
▶ **verb** [with obj.] **1** advertise (a film or programme) in advance by broadcasting extracts or details.
2 transport (something) by trailer.

trailer park ▶ **noun** N. Amer. a caravan site.
■ [as modifier] US lacking refinement, taste, or quality; coarse: *her trailer-park bleached perm*.

trailer truck ▶ **noun** US an articulated lorry.

trailing arbutus ▶ **noun** a creeping North American plant of the heather family, with leathery evergreen leaves and clusters of pink or white flowers. Also called **MAYFLOWER**.
• *Epigaea repens*, family Ericaceae.

trailing edge ▶ **noun** the rear edge of a moving body, especially an aircraft wing or propeller blade.
■ Electronics the part of a pulse in which the amplitude diminishes.

trailing wheel ▶ **noun** a wheel on a railway locomotive or other vehicle that is not given direct motive power.

trail mix ▶ **noun** [mass noun] a mixture of dried fruit and nuts eaten as a snack food, originally by walkers and campers.

train ▶ **verb 1** [with obj.] teach (a person or animal) a particular skill or type of behaviour through practice and instruction over a period of time: *the scheme trains people for promotion* | [with obj. and infinitive] *the dogs are trained to sniff out illegal stowaways*.
■ [no obj.] be taught in such a way: *he trained as a plumber*. ■ [usu. as adj. **trained**] cause (a mental or physical faculty) to be sharp, discerning, or developed as a result of instruction or practice: *an alert mind and trained eye give astute evaluations*. ■ cause (a plant) to grow in a particular direction or into a required shape: *they trained crimson ramblers over their houses*. ■ [no obj.] undertake a course of exercise and diet in order to reach or maintain a high level of physical fitness, typically in preparation for participating in a specific sport or event: *she trains three times a week*. ■ cause to undertake such a course of exercise: *the horse was trained in Paris*. ■ [no obj.] (**train down**) reduce one's weight through diet and exercise in order to be fit for a particular event: *he trained down to heavyweight*.
2 [with obj.] (**train something on**) point or aim something, typically a gun or camera, at: *the detective trained his gun on the side door*.
3 [no obj., with adverbial of direction] dated go by train: *Charles trained to London with Emma*.
4 [with obj.] archaic entice (someone) by offering pleasure or a reward.
▶ **noun 1** a series of railway carriages or wagons moved as a unit by a locomotive or by integral motors: *a freight train* | *the journey took two hours **by train***.
2 a succession of vehicles or pack animals travelling in the same direction: *a camel train*.
■ a retinue of attendants accompanying an important person. ■ a series of connected events: *you may be setting in motion a train of events which will cause harm*. ■ [usu. with modifier] a series of gears or other connected parts in machinery: *a **train of gears***.
3 a long piece of material attached to the back of a formal dress or robe that trails along the ground.
4 a trail of gunpowder for firing an explosive charge.
– PHRASES **in train** (of arrangements) well organized or in progress: *an investigation is in train*. **in someone/thing's train** (or **in the train of**) following behind someone or something. ■ figurative as a sequel or consequence: *unemployment brings great difficulties in its train*. **train of thought** the way in which someone reaches a conclusion; a line of reasoning: *I failed to follow his train of thought*.
– DERIVATIVES **trainability** noun, **trainable** adjective.
– ORIGIN Middle English (as a noun in the sense 'delay'): from Old French *train* (masculine), *traine* (feminine), from *trahiner* (verb), from Latin *trahere* 'pull, draw'. Early noun senses were 'trailing part of a robe' and 'retinue'; the latter gave rise to 'line of travelling people or vehicles', later 'a connected series of things'. The early verb sense 'cause (a plant) to grow in a desired shape' was the basis of the sense 'educate, instruct, teach'.

trainband ▶ **noun** historical a division of civilian soldiers in London and other areas, in particular in the Stuart period.

train-bearer ▶ **noun** a person whose job is to hold up the train of a dress or robe.

t

trainee ▶ **noun** a person undergoing training for a particular job or profession.
– DERIVATIVES **traineeship** noun.

trainer ▶ **noun 1** a person who trains people or animals.
■ informal an aircraft or simulator used to train pilots.
2 Brit. a soft shoe, suitable for sports or casual wear.

train ferry ▶ **noun** a ferry that conveys railway carriages across water.

training ▶ **noun** [mass noun] the action of teaching a person or animal a particular skill or type of behaviour: *in-service training for staff.*
■ the action of undertaking a course of exercise and diet in preparation for a sporting event: *you'll have to go into strict training.*
– PHRASES **in** (or **out of**) **training** undergoing (or no longer undergoing) physical training for a sporting event. ■ physically fit (or unfit) as a result of the amount of training one has undertaken.

training college ▶ **noun** (in the UK) a college or school where people, typically prospective teachers, are trained.

training ship ▶ **noun** a ship on which people are taught how to sail and related skills.

training shoe ▶ **noun** another term for **TRAINER** (in sense 2).

training wheels ▶ **plural noun** N. Amer. a pair of small supporting wheels fitted on either side of the rear wheel of a child's bicycle.

trainload ▶ **noun** a number of people or a quantity of a commodity transported by train.

train-mile ▶ **noun** one mile travelled by one train, as a unit of traffic.

train-oil ▶ **noun** [mass noun] chiefly historical oil obtained from the blubber of a whale (and formerly of other sea creatures), especially the right whale.
– ORIGIN mid 16th cent.: from obsolete *train* 'train-oil', from Middle Low German *trän*, Middle Dutch *traen*, literally 'tear' (because it was extracted in droplets).

train set ▶ **noun 1** a set of railway wagons or carriages, often with a locomotive, coupled together for a particular service.
2 Brit. a set of trains, tracks, and other things making up a child's model railway.

train shed ▶ **noun** a large structure providing a shelter over the tracks and platforms of a railway station.

trainsick ▶ **adjective** affected with nausea by the motion of a train.

trainspotter ▶ **noun** Brit. a person who collects train or locomotive numbers as a hobby.
■ often derogatory a person who obsessively studies the minutiae of any minority interest or specialized hobby.
– DERIVATIVES **trainspotting** noun.

traipse /treɪps/ ▶ **verb** [no obj., with adverbial of direction] walk or move wearily or reluctantly: *students had to traipse all over London to attend lectures.*
■ walk about casually or needlessly: *there's people traipsing in and out all the time.*
▶ **noun 1** [in sing.] a tedious or tiring journey on foot.
2 archaic a slovenly woman.
– ORIGIN late 16th cent. (as a verb): of unknown origin. The noun is first recorded in sense 2 in the late 17th cent.

trait /treɪ, treɪt/ ▶ **noun** a distinguishing quality or characteristic, typically one belonging to a person: *the traditionally British trait of self-denigration.*
■ a genetically determined characteristic.
– ORIGIN mid 16th cent.: from French, from Latin *tractus* 'drawing, draught' (see **TRACT**[1]). An early sense was 'stroke of the pen or pencil in a picture', giving rise to the sense 'a particular feature of mind or character' (mid 18th cent.).

traitor ▶ **noun** a person who betrays someone or something, such as a friend, cause, or principle.
– DERIVATIVES **traitorous** adjective, **traitorously** adverb.
– ORIGIN Middle English: from Old French *traitour*, from Latin *traditor*, from *tradere* 'hand over'.
▶ **turn traitor** betray a group or person: *to think of a man like you turning traitor to his class.*

Trajan /ˈtreɪdʒ(ə)n/ (*c.*53–117 AD), Roman emperor 98–117; Latin name *Marcus Ulpius Traianus*. His reign is noted for the many public works undertaken and for the Dacian wars (101–6), which ended in the annexation of Dacia as a province.

trajectory /trəˈdʒɛkt(ə)ri, ˈtradʒɪkt(ə)ri/ ▶ **noun** (pl. **-ies**) **1** the path described by a projectile flying or an object moving under the action of given forces.
2 Geometry a curve or surface cutting a family of curves or surfaces at a constant angle.
– ORIGIN late 17th cent.: from modern Latin *trajectoria* (feminine), from Latin *traject-* 'thrown across', from the verb *traicere*, from *trans-* 'across' + *jacere* 'to throw'.

Trakehner /traˈkeɪnə/ ▶ **noun 1** a saddle horse of a light breed first developed at the Trakehnen stud near Kaliningrad in Russia.
2 a type of fence used in horse trials, which consists of a ditch spanned by centre rails.
– ORIGIN early 20th cent.: from German.

tra la ▶ **exclamation** chiefly ironic expressing joy or gaiety: *off to his life, kids, and wife, tra la.*
– ORIGIN early 19th cent.: imitative of a fanfare or of the refrain of a song.

Tralee /trəˈliː/ the county town of Kerry, a port on the SW coast of the Republic of Ireland; pop. 17,200 (1991).

tram (also **tramcar**) ▶ **noun 1** Brit. a passenger vehicle powered by electricity conveyed by overhead cables, and running on rails laid in a public road.
2 historical a low four-wheeled cart or barrow used in coal mines.
– ORIGIN early 16th cent. (denoting a shaft of a barrow; also in sense 2): from Middle Low German and Middle Dutch *trame* 'beam, barrow shaft'. In the early 19th cent. the word denoted the parallel wheel tracks used in a mine, on which the public tramway was modelled; hence sense 1 (late 19th cent.).

Traminer /trəˈmiːnə/ ▶ **noun** [mass noun] a variety of white wine grape grown chiefly in Germany and Alsace.
■ a white wine with a perfumed bouquet made from this grape.
– ORIGIN named after the Italian village *Termeno*.

tramlines /ˈtramlʌɪn/ ▶ **noun** Brit. rails for a tramcar.
■ informal a pair of parallel lines, in particular the long lines at the sides of a tennis court (enclosing the extra width used in doubles play) or at the side or back of a badminton court. ■ figurative an inflexible principle or course of action.

trammel /ˈtram(ə)l/ ▶ **noun 1** (usu. **trammels**) poetic/literary a restriction or impediment to someone's freedom of action: *we will forge our own future, free from the trammels of materialism.*
2 (also **trammel net**) a dragnet consisting of three layers of netting, designed so that a fish entering through one of the large-meshed outer sections will push part of the finer-meshed central section through the large meshes on the further side, forming a pocket in which the fish is trapped.
3 an instrument consisting of a board with two grooves intersecting at right angles, in which the two ends of a beam compass can slide to draw an ellipse. [ORIGIN: early 18th cent.: so named because the motion of the beam is 'restricted' by the grooves.]
■ a beam compass.
4 US a hook in a fireplace for a kettle.
▶ **verb** (**trammelled**, **trammelling**; US **trammeled**, **trammeling**) [with obj.] deprive of freedom of action: *those less trammelled by convention than himself.*
– ORIGIN late Middle English (in sense 2): from Old French *tramail*, from a medieval Latin variant of *trimaculum*, perhaps from Latin *tri-* 'three' + *macula* 'mesh'.

tramontana /ˌtramɒnˈtɑːnə/ ▶ **noun** a cold north wind blowing in Italy or the adjoining regions of the Adriatic and Mediterranean.
– ORIGIN Italian, 'north wind, Pole Star' (see **TRAMONTANE**).

tramontane /trəˈmɒnteɪn/ ▶ **adjective** rare travelling to, or situated or living on, the other side of mountains.
■ archaic (especially from the Italian point of view) foreign; barbarous.
▶ **noun 1** another term for **TRAMONTANA**.
2 archaic a person who lives on the other side of mountains (used in particular by Italians to refer to people beyond the Alps).
– ORIGIN Middle English (as a noun denoting the Pole Star): from Italian *tramontana* 'Pole Star, north wind', *tramontani* 'people living beyond the Alps', from Latin *transmontanus* 'beyond the mountains', from *trans-* 'across' + *mons, mont-* 'mountain'.

tramp ▶ **verb** [no obj., with adverbial of direction] walk heavily or noisily: *he tramped about the room.*
■ walk through or over a place wearily or reluctantly and for long distances: *we have tramped miles over mountain and moorland.* ■ [with obj.] tread or stamp on: *one of the few wines still tramped by foot.*
▶ **noun 1** a person who travels from place to place on foot in search of work or as a vagrant or beggar.
2 [in sing.] the sound of heavy steps, typically of several people: *the tramp of marching feet.*
3 [in sing.] a long walk, typically a tiring one: *she was freshly returned from a tramp round Norwich.*
4 [usu. as modifier] a cargo vessel that carries goods between many different ports rather than sailing a fixed route: *a tramp steamer.*
5 informal, chiefly US a promiscuous woman.
6 a metal plate protecting the sole of a boot used for digging.
■ the top of the blade of a spade.
– DERIVATIVES **tramper** noun, **trampish** adjective.
– ORIGIN late Middle English (as a verb): probably of Low German origin. The noun dates from the mid 17th cent.

trample ▶ **verb** [with obj.] tread on and crush: *the fence had been trampled down* | [no obj.] *her dog* ***trampled on*** *his tulips.*
■ [no obj.] (**trample on/upon/over**) figurative treat with contempt: *a lay statesman ought not to trample upon the opinions of his Church advisers.*
▶ **noun** poetic/literary an act or the sound of trampling.
– DERIVATIVES **trampler** noun.
– ORIGIN late Middle English (in the sense 'tread heavily'): frequentative of **TRAMP**.

trampoline /ˈtrampəliːn/ ▶ **noun** a strong fabric sheet connected by springs to a frame, used as a springboard and landing area in doing acrobatic or gymnastic exercises. See also **REBOUNDER** (sense 1).
▶ **verb** [no obj.] [usu. as noun **trampolining**] do acrobatic or gymnastic exercises on a trampoline as a recreation or sport: *his hobby is trampolining.*
■ [no obj., with adverbial of direction] leap or rebound from something with a springy base: *she trampolined across the bed.*
– DERIVATIVES **trampolinist** noun.
– ORIGIN late 18th cent.: from Italian *trampolino*, from *trampoli* 'stilts'.

tram road ▶ **noun** historical a road with wooden, stone, or metal tracks for wheels, used by wagons in mining districts.

tramway ▶ **noun 1** Brit. a set of rails which forms the route for a tram.
■ a tram system.
2 historical another term for **TRAM ROAD**.

trance /trɑːns/ ▶ **noun** a half-conscious state characterized by an absence of response to external stimuli, typically as induced by hypnosis or entered by a medium: *she put him into a light trance.*
■ a state of abstraction: *the kind of trance he went into whenever illness was discussed.* ■ (also **trance music**) [mass noun] a type of electronic dance music characterized by hypnotic rhythms and sounds.
▶ **verb** [with obj.] (often **be tranced**) poetic/literary put into a trance: *she's been tranced and may need waking.*
– DERIVATIVES **trancedly** adverb, **trance-like** adjective.
– ORIGIN Middle English (originally as a verb in the sense 'be in a trance'): from Old French *transir* 'depart, fall into trance', from Latin *transire* 'go across'.

tranche /trɑːnʃ/ ▶ **noun** a portion of something, especially money: *they released the first* ***tranche of*** *the loan.*
– ORIGIN late 15th cent.: from Old French, literally 'slice'.

tranexamic acid /ˌtranɛkˈsamɪk/ ▶ **noun** [mass noun] Medicine a synthetic compound derived from cyclohexane which inhibits the breakdown of fibrin in blood clots and is used to treat haemorrhage.
● Chem. formula: $NH_2CH_2C_6H_{10}COOH$.
– ORIGIN 1960s: from elements of the systematic name, *trans-4-aminomethylcyclohexanecarboxylic acid.*

trank ▶ **noun** informal term for **TRANQUILLIZER**.
– DERIVATIVES **tranked** adjective.

tranny (also **trannie**) ▶ **noun** (pl. **-ies**) informal **1** chiefly Brit. a transistor radio.
2 a photographic transparency.
3 N. Amer. the transmission in a motor vehicle.
4 (usu. **trannie**) a transvestite.
– ORIGIN 1960s: abbreviation.

tranquil ▶ **adjective** free from disturbance; calm: *her tranquil gaze | the sea was tranquil.*
– DERIVATIVES **tranquillity** (also **tranquility**) noun, **tranquilly** adverb.
– ORIGIN late Middle English: from French *tranquille* or Latin *tranquillus*.

tranquillize (also **-ise**; US **tranquilize**) ▶ **verb** [with obj.] [usu. as adj. **tranquillizing**] (of a drug) have a calming or sedative effect on.
■ administer such a drug to (a person or animal). ■ poetic/literary make tranquil: *joys that tranquillize the mind.*

tranquillizer (also **-iser**; US also **tranquilizer**) ▶ **noun** a medicinal drug taken to reduce tension or anxiety.

trans ▶ **adjective** Chemistry denoting or relating to a molecular structure in which two particular atoms or groups lie on opposite sides of a given plane in the molecule, in particular denoting an isomer in which substituents at opposite ends of a carbon–carbon double bond are also on opposite sides of the bond: *the trans isomer of stilbene.* Compare with **CIS**.
– ORIGIN independent usage of **TRANS-**.

trans- /trans, trɑːns, -nz/ ▶ **prefix 1** across; beyond: *transcontinental | transgress.*
■ on or to the other side of: *transatlantic | transalpine.* Often contrasted with **CIS-**.
2 through: *transonic.*
■ into another state or place: *transform | translate.* ■ surpassing; transcending: *transfinite.*
3 Chemistry (usu. ***trans-***) denoting molecules with trans arrangements of substituents: trans-*1,2-dichloroethene.*
■ Genetics denoting alleles on different chromosomes.
– ORIGIN from Latin *trans* 'across'.

transact ▶ **verb** [with obj.] conduct or carry out (business).
– DERIVATIVES **transactor** noun.
– ORIGIN late 16th cent.: from Latin *transact-* 'driven through', from the verb *transigere*, from *trans-* 'through' + *agere* 'do, lead'.

transaction ▶ **noun** an instance of buying or selling something; a business deal: *in an ordinary commercial transaction a delivery date is essential.*
■ [mass noun] the action of conducting business. ■ an exchange or interaction between people: *intellectual transactions in the classroom.* ■ (**transactions**) published reports of proceedings at the meetings of a learned society. ■ an input message to a computer system that must be dealt with as a single unit of work.
– DERIVATIVES **transactional** adjective, **transactionally** adverb.
– ORIGIN late Middle English (as a term in Roman Law): from late Latin *transactio(n-)*, from *transigere* 'drive through' (see **TRANSACT**).

transactional analysis ▶ **noun** [mass noun] a system of popular psychology based on the idea that one's behaviour and social relationships reflect an interchange between parental (critical and nurturing), adult (rational), and childlike (intuitive and dependent) aspects of personality established early in life.

transactivation ▶ **noun** [mass noun] Biochemistry activation of a gene at one locus by the presence of a particular gene at another locus, typically following infection by a virus.

transalpine ▶ **adjective** of, related to, or situated in the area beyond the Alps, in particular as viewed from Italy. See also **GAUL**[1].
■ crossing the Alps: *transalpine road freight.*
– ORIGIN late 16th cent.: from Latin *transalpinus*, from *trans-* 'across' + *alpinus* (see **ALPINE**).

transaminase /tranˈzamɪneɪz, trɑːn-, -ˈsa-/ ▶ **noun** Biochemistry an enzyme which catalyses a particular transamination reaction.

transamination /ˌtransamɪˈneɪʃ(ə)n, ˌtrɑːns-, -nz-/ ▶ **noun** [mass noun] Biochemistry the transfer of an amino group from one molecule to another, especially from an amino acid to a keto acid.
– DERIVATIVES **transaminate** verb.

transatlantic ▶ **adjective** crossing the Atlantic: *a transatlantic flight.*
■ concerning countries on both sides of the Atlantic, typically Britain and the US: *the transatlantic relationship.* ■ of, relating to, or situated on the other side of the Atlantic; American (from a British point of view); British or European (from an American point of view).

transaxle ▶ **noun** an integral driving axle and differential gear in a motor vehicle.

Transcaucasia /ˌtranzkɔːˈkeɪʒə, ˌtrɑːnz-, -ˈkeɪzɪə/ a region lying to the south of the Caucasus mountains, between the Black Sea and the Caspian, and comprising the present-day republics of Georgia, Armenia, and Azerbaijan. It was created a republic of the Soviet Union in 1922 as the Transcaucasian Soviet Federated Socialist Republic, but was broken up into its constituent republics in 1936.
– DERIVATIVES **Transcaucasian** adjective.

transceiver ▶ **noun** a device that can both transmit and receive communications, in particular a combined radio transmitter and receiver.
– ORIGIN 1930s: blend of **TRANSMITTER** and **RECEIVER**.

transcend ▶ **verb** [with obj.] be or go beyond the range or limits of (something abstract, typically a conceptual field or division): *this was an issue transcending party politics.*
■ surpass (a person or an achievement).
– ORIGIN Middle English: from Old French *transcendre* or Latin *transcendere*, from *trans-* 'across' + *scandere* 'climb'.

transcendent ▶ **adjective 1** beyond or above the range of normal or merely physical human experience: *the search for a transcendent level of knowledge.*
■ surpassing the ordinary; exceptional: *the conductor was described as a 'transcendent genius'.* ■ (of God) existing apart from and not subject to the limitations of the material universe. Often contrasted with **IMMANENT**. ■ (in scholastic philosophy) higher than or not included in any of Aristotle's ten categories. ■ (in Kantian philosophy) not realizable in experience.
– DERIVATIVES **transcendence** noun, **transcendency** noun, **transcendently** adverb.
– ORIGIN late Middle English: from Latin *transcendent-* 'climbing over', from the verb *transcendere* (see **TRANSCEND**).

transcendental ▶ **adjective 1** of or relating to a spiritual or non-physical realm: *the transcendental importance of each person's soul.*
■ (in Kantian philosophy) presupposed in and necessary to experience; a priori. ■ relating to or denoting Transcendentalism.
2 Mathematics (of a number, e.g. e or π) real but not a root of an algebraic equation with rational coefficients.
■ (of a function) not capable of being produced by the algebraical operations of addition, multiplication, and involution, or the inverse operations.
– DERIVATIVES **transcendentalize** (also **-ise**) verb, **transcendentally** adverb.
– ORIGIN early 17th cent.: from medieval Latin *transcendentalis* (see **TRANSCENDENT**).

transcendentalism ▶ **noun** [mass noun] **1** (**Transcendentalism**) an idealistic philosophical and social movement which developed in New England around 1836 in reaction to rationalism. Influenced by romanticism, Platonism, and Kantian philosophy, it taught that divinity pervades all nature and humanity, and its members held progressive views on feminism and communal living. Ralph Waldo Emerson and Henry David Thoreau were central figures.
2 a system developed by Immanuel Kant, based on the idea that, in order to understand the nature of reality, one must first examine and analyse the reasoning process which governs the nature of experience.
– DERIVATIVES **transcendentalist** (also **Transcendentalist**) noun & adjective.

Transcendental Meditation (abbrev.: **TM**) ▶ **noun** [mass noun] (trademark in the US) a technique for detaching oneself from anxiety and promoting harmony and self-realization by meditation, repetition of a mantra, and other yogic practices, promulgated by an international organization founded by the Indian guru Maharishi Mahesh Yogi (born *c.*1911).

transcode ▶ **verb** [with obj.] convert (language or information) from one form of coded representation to another.

transconductance ▶ **noun** Electronics the ratio of the change in current at the output terminal to the change in the voltage at the input terminal of an active device.

transconjugant /ˌtransˈkɒndʒʊɡənt, ˌtrɑːns, -nz/ ▶ **noun** Biology a plasmid or a bacterial cell which has received genetic material by conjugation with another bacterium.

transcontinental ▶ **adjective** (especially of a railway line) crossing a continent.
■ extending across or relating to two or more continents: *a transcontinental radio audience.*
▶ **noun** Canadian a transcontinental railway or train.
– DERIVATIVES **transcontinentally** adverb.

transcortical /ˌtransˈkɔːtɪk(ə)l, ˌtrɑːns, -nz/ ▶ **adjective** Physiology of or relating to nerve pathways which cross the cerebral cortex of the brain.

transcribe ▶ **verb** [with obj.] put (thoughts, speech, or data) into written or printed form: *each interview was taped and transcribed.*
■ transliterate (foreign characters) or write or type out (shorthand, notes, or other abbreviated forms) into ordinary characters or full sentences. ■ arrange (a piece of music) for a different instrument, voice, or group of these: *his largest early work was **transcribed for** organ.* ■ Biochemistry synthesize (a nucleic acid, typically RNA) using an existing nucleic acid, typically DNA, as a template, so that the genetic information in the latter is copied.
– DERIVATIVES **transcriber** noun.
– ORIGIN mid 16th cent. (in the sense 'make a copy in writing'): from Latin *transcribere*, from *trans-* 'across' + *scribere* 'write'.

transcript ▶ **noun** a written or printed version of material originally presented in another medium.
■ Biochemistry a length of RNA or DNA that has been transcribed respectively from a DNA or RNA template. ■ N. Amer. an official record of a student's work, showing courses taken and grades achieved.
– DERIVATIVES **transcriptive** adjective.
– ORIGIN Middle English: from Old French *transcrit*, from Latin *transcriptum*, neuter past participle of *transcribere* (see **TRANSCRIBE**). The spelling change in the 15th cent. was due to association with the Latin.

transcriptase /tranˈskrɪpteɪz, trɑːn-/ ▶ **noun** [mass noun] Biochemistry an enzyme which catalyses the formation of RNA from a DNA template during transcription, or (**reverse transcriptase**), the formation of DNA from an RNA template in reverse transcription.

transcription ▶ **noun** a written or printed representation of something.
■ [mass noun] the action or process of transcribing something: *the funding covers transcription of nearly illegible photocopies.* ■ an arrangement of a piece of music for a different instrument, voice, or number of these: *a transcription for voice and lute.* ■ a form in which a speech sound or a foreign character is represented. ■ [mass noun] Biochemistry the process by which genetic information represented by a sequence of DNA nucleotides is copied into newly synthesized molecules of RNA, with the DNA serving as a template.
– DERIVATIVES **transcriptional** adjective, **transcriptionally** adverb, **transcriptionist** noun (N. Amer.).
– ORIGIN late 16th cent.: from French, or from Latin *transcriptio(n-)*, from the verb *transcribere* (see **TRANSCRIBE**).

transcutaneous /ˌtranzkjʊˈteɪnɪəs, ˌtrɑːnz-, -ns-/ ▶ **adjective** existing, applied, or measured across the depth of the skin.

transdermal /ˌtranzˈdəːməl, trɑːnz, -ns-/ ▶ **adjective** relating to or denoting the application of a medicine or drug through the skin, typically by using an adhesive patch, so that it is absorbed slowly into the body.

transducer /tranzˈdjuːsə, trɑːnz-, -ns-/ ▶ **noun** a device that converts variations in a physical quantity, such as pressure or brightness, into an electrical signal, or vice versa.
– DERIVATIVES **transduce** verb, **transduction** noun.
– ORIGIN 1920s: from Latin *transducere* 'lead across' (from *trans-* 'across' + *ducere* 'lead') + **-ER**[1].

transect technical ▶ **verb** [with obj.] cut across or make a transverse section in.
▶ **noun** a straight line or narrow section through an object or natural feature or across the earth's surface, along which observations are made or measurements taken.
– DERIVATIVES **transection** noun.
– ORIGIN mid 17th cent. (as a verb): from **TRANS-** 'through' + Latin *sect-* 'divided by cutting' (from the verb *secare*).

transept /ˈtransɛpt, ˈtrɑːn-/ ▶ **noun** (in a cross-shaped church) either of the two parts forming the arms of the cross shape, projecting at right angles from the nave: *the north transept.*
– DERIVATIVES **transeptal** adjective.
– ORIGIN mid 16th cent.: from modern Latin *transeptum* (see **TRANS-**, **SEPTUM**).

transexual ▶ **adjective** & **noun** variant spelling of **TRANSSEXUAL**.

trans-fat ▶ **noun** another term for **TRANS-FATTY ACID**.

trans-fatty acid ▶ **noun** an unsaturated fatty acid with a trans arrangement of the carbon atoms adjacent to its double bonds. Such acids occur especially in margarines and cooking oils as a result of the hydrogenation process.

transfect /tranzˈfɛkt, trɑːnz-, -ns-/ ▶ **verb** [with obj.] Microbiology infect (a cell) with free nucleic acid.
■ introduce (genetic material) in this way.
– DERIVATIVES **transfectant** noun, **transfection** noun.
– ORIGIN 1960s: from **TRANS-** 'across' + **INFECT**, or a blend of **TRANSFER** and **INFECT**.

transfer ▶ **verb** (**transferred**, **transferring**) [with obj.] move (someone or something) from one place to another: *he intends to* **transfer** *the fund's assets* **to** *the Treasury.*
■ move or cause to move to another group, occupation or service: [no obj.] *she transferred to the Physics Department* | [with obj.] *employees have been transferred to the installation team.* ■ (in football and other sports) move or cause to move to another club, typically for a transfer fee. ■ [no obj.] change to another place, route, or means of transport during a journey: *John advised him to transfer from Rome airport to the railway station.* ■ make over the possession of (property, a right, or a responsibility) to someone else. ■ convey (a drawing or design) from one surface to another. ■ [usu. as adj. **transferred**] change (the sense of a word or phrase) by extension or metaphor: *a transferred use of the Old English noun.* ■ redirect (a telephone call) to a new line or extension.
▶ **noun** an act of moving something or someone to another place: *a transfer of wealth to the EC's poorer nations* | [mass noun] *a patient had died after transfer from the County Hospital to St. Peter's.*
■ a change of employment, typically within an organization or field: *she was going to ask her boss for a transfer to the city.* ■ an act of selling or moving a sports player to another club: *his transfer from Rangers cost £800,000.* ■ a conveyance of property, especially stocks and shares, from one person to another. ■ Brit. a small coloured picture or design on paper, which can be transferred to another surface by being pressed or heated: *T-shirts with iron-on transfers.* ■ N. Amer. a ticket allowing a passenger to change from one public transport vehicle to another as part of a single journey.
– DERIVATIVES **transferee** noun, **transferor** noun (chiefly Law), **transferrer** noun.
– ORIGIN late Middle English (as a verb): from French *transférer* or Latin *transferre*, from *trans-* 'across' + *ferre* 'to bear'. The earliest use of the noun (late 17th cent.) was as a legal term in the sense 'conveyance of property'.

transferable /transˈfəːrəb(ə)l, ˈtransf(ə)r-, trɑː-, -nz-/ ▶ **adjective** (typically of financial assets, liabilities or legal rights) able to be transferred or made over to the possession of another person.
– DERIVATIVES **transferability** noun.

transferase /ˈtransf(ə)reɪz, ˈtrɑːns-, -nz-/ ▶ **noun** Biochemistry an enzyme which catalyses the transfer of a particular group from one molecule to another.

transference /ˈtransf(ə)r(ə)ns, ˈtrɑːns-, -nz-/ ▶ **noun** [mass noun] the action of transferring something or the process of being transferred: *education involves the transference of knowledge.*
■ Psychoanalysis the redirection to a substitute, usually a therapist, of emotions that were originally felt in childhood (in a phase of analysis called **transference neurosis**).

transfer factor ▶ **noun** Biology a substance released by antigen-sensitized lymphocytes and capable of transferring the response of delayed hypersensitivity to a non-sensitized cell or individual into which it is introduced.

transfer fee ▶ **noun** Brit. a fee paid by one soccer or rugby club to another for the transfer of a player.

transfer function ▶ **noun** Electronics a mathematical function relating the output or response of a system such as a filter circuit to the input or stimulus.

transfer list Brit. ▶ **noun** a soccer or rugby club's list of players available for transfer.
▶ **verb** (**transfer-list**) [with obj.] (usu. **be transfer-listed**) make (a player) available for transfer.

transfer orbit ▶ **noun** a trajectory by which a spacecraft can pass from one orbit to another at a higher altitude, especially a geostationary orbit.

transfer payment ▶ **noun** Economics a payment made or income received in which no goods or services are being paid for, such as a benefit payment or subsidy.

transferral ▶ **noun** an act of transferring someone or something.

transferrin /transˈfɛrɪn, trɑːns-, -nz-/ ▶ **noun** [mass noun] Biochemistry a protein of the beta globulin group which binds and transports iron in blood serum.
– ORIGIN 1940s: from **TRANS-** 'across' + Latin *ferrum* 'iron' + **-IN**[1].

transfer RNA ▶ **noun** [mass noun] Biochemistry RNA consisting of folded molecules which transport amino acids from the cytoplasm of a cell to a ribosome.

transferware ▶ **noun** [mass noun] pottery decorated with transfers.

transfiguration ▶ **noun** a complete change of form or appearance into a more beautiful or spiritual state: *in this light the junk undergoes a transfiguration; it shines.*
■ (**the Transfiguration**) Christ's appearance in radiant glory to three of his disciples (Matthew 17:2 and Mark 9:2–3). ■ the church festival commemorating this, held on 6 August.
– ORIGIN late Middle English (with biblical reference): from Old French, or from Latin *transfiguratio(n-)*, from the verb *transfigurare* (see **TRANSFIGURE**).

transfigure ▶ **verb** [with obj.] (usu. **be transfigured**) transform into something more beautiful or elevated: *the world is made luminous and is transfigured.*
– ORIGIN Middle English: from Old French *transfigurer* or Latin *transfigurare*, from *trans-* 'across' + *figura* 'figure'.

transfinite ▶ **adjective** Mathematics relating to or denoting a number corresponding to an infinite set in the way that a natural number denotes or counts members of a finite set.

transfix ▶ **verb** [with obj.] **1** (usu. **be transfixed**) cause (someone) to become motionless with horror, wonder, or astonishment: *he was transfixed by the pain in her face* | *she stared at him, transfixed.*
2 pierce with a sharp implement or weapon: *a field mouse is transfixed by the curved talons of an owl.*
– DERIVATIVES **transfixion** noun.
– ORIGIN late 16th cent. (in sense 2): from Latin *transfix-* 'pierced through', from the verb *transfigere*, from *trans-* 'across' + *figere* 'fix, fasten'.

transform ▶ **verb** [with obj.] make a thorough or dramatic change in the form, appearance, or character of: *lasers have transformed cardiac surgery* | *he wanted to* **transform** *himself* **into** *a successful businessman.*
■ [no obj.] undergo such a change. ■ change the voltage of (an electric current). ■ Mathematics change (a mathematical entity) by transformation.
▶ **noun** Mathematics & Linguistics the product of a transformation.
■ a rule for making a transformation.
– DERIVATIVES **transformable** adjective, **transformative** adjective.
– ORIGIN Middle English (as a verb): from Old French *transformer* or Latin *transformare* (see **TRANS-**, **FORM**).

transformation ▶ **noun** a thorough or dramatic change in form or appearance: *British society underwent a radical transformation.*
■ (also **transformation scene**) a sudden dramatic change of scenery on stage. ■ a metamorphosis during the life cycle of an animal. ■ Physics the induced or spontaneous change of one element into another by a nuclear process. ■ Mathematics & Logic a process by which one figure, expression, or function is converted into another which is equivalent in some important respect but is differently expressed or represented. ■ Linguistics a process by which an element in the underlying logical deep structure of a sentence is converted to an element in the surface structure. ■ [mass noun] Biology the genetic alteration of a cell by introduction of extraneous DNA, especially by a plasmid. ■ [mass noun] Biology the heritable modification of a cell from its normal state to a malignant state.
– ORIGIN late Middle English: from Old French, or from late Latin *transformatio(n-)*, from the verb *transformare* (see **TRANSFORM**).

transformational ▶ **adjective** relating to or involving transformation or transformations.
■ of or relating to transformational grammar.
– DERIVATIVES **transformationally** adverb.

transformational grammar ▶ **noun** [mass noun] Linguistics a type of grammar which describes a language in terms of transformations applied to an underlying logical deep structure in order to generate the surface structure of sentences which can actually occur. See also **GENERATIVE GRAMMAR**.

transformer ▶ **noun 1** an apparatus for reducing or increasing the voltage of an alternating current.
2 a person or thing that transforms something.

transform fault ▶ **noun** Geology a strike-slip fault occurring at the boundary between two plates of the earth's crust.

transfuse ▶ **verb** [with obj.] **1** Medicine transfer (blood or its components) from one person or animal to another.
■ inject (liquid) into a blood vessel to replace lost fluid.
2 cause (something or someone) to be permeated or infused by something: *we became transfused by a radiance of joy.*
– ORIGIN late Middle English (in the sense 'cause to pass from one person to another'): from Latin *transfus-* 'poured from one container to another', from the verb *transfundere*, from *trans-* 'across' + *fundere* 'pour'.

transfusion /transˈfjuːʒ(ə)n, trɑːns-, -nz-/ ▶ **noun** an act of transfusing donated blood, blood products, or other fluid into the circulatory system of a person or animal.

transgenic /tranzˈdʒɛnɪk, trɑːnz-, -ns-/ ▶ **adjective** Biology of, relating to, or denoting an organism that contains genetic material into which DNA from an unrelated organism has been artificially introduced.
– ORIGIN 1980s: from **TRANS-** 'across' + **GENE** + **-IC**.

transgenics ▶ **plural noun** [usu. treated as sing.] the branch of biology concerned with transgenic organisms.

transglobal ▶ **adjective** (of an expedition, enterprise, search, or network) moving or extending across or round the world.

transgress ▶ **verb** [with obj.] infringe or go beyond the bounds of (a moral principle or other established standard of behaviour): *she had transgressed an unwritten social law.*
■ Geology (of the sea) spread over (an area of land).
– DERIVATIVES **transgression** noun, **transgressor** noun.
– ORIGIN late 15th cent.: from Old French *transgresser* or Latin *transgress-* 'stepped across', from the verb *transgredi*, from *trans-* 'across' + *gradi* 'go'.

transgressive ▶ **adjective** involving a violation of accepted or imposed boundaries, especially those of social acceptability: *her experiences of transgressive love with both sexes.*
■ of or relating to fiction, cinema, or art in which orthodox cultural, moral, and artistic boundaries are challenged by the representation of unconventional behaviour and the use of experimental forms. ■ Geology (of a stratum) overlapping others unconformably, especially as a result of marine transgression.

tranship ▶ **verb** variant spelling of **TRANS-SHIP**.

transhistorical ▶ **adjective** transcending historical boundaries; eternal: *femininity may not be a transhistorical absolute.*

transhumance /tranzˈhjuːməns, trɑːnz-, -ns-/ ▶ **noun** [mass noun] the action or practice of moving livestock from one grazing ground to another in a seasonal cycle, typically to lowlands in winter and highlands in summer.
– DERIVATIVES **transhumant** adjective.
– ORIGIN early 20th cent.: from French, from the verb *transhumer*, based on Latin *trans-* 'across' + *humus* 'ground'.

transient /ˈtransɪənt, ˈtrɑːns-, -nz-/ ▶ **adjective** lasting only for a short time; impermanent: *a transient cold spell.*

t

■staying or working in a place for a short time only: *the transient nature of the labour force in catering.*
▶**noun 1** a person who is staying or working in a place for a short time only.
2 a momentary variation in current, voltage, or frequency.
– DERIVATIVES **transience** noun, **transiency** noun, **transiently** adverb.
– ORIGIN late 16th cent.: from Latin *transient-* 'going across', from the verb *transire*, from *trans-* 'across' + *ire* 'go'.

transilluminate ▶**verb** [with obj.] pass strong light through (an organ or part of the body) in order to detect disease or abnormality.
– DERIVATIVES **transillumination** noun.

transire /tranˈzʌɪə, trɑː-, -s-, -ʌɪri/ ▶**noun** (in the UK) a customs document on which the cargo loaded on to a ship is listed, issued to prove that the goods listed on it have come from a home port rather than an overseas one.
– ORIGIN late 16th cent.: from Latin *transire* 'go across'.

transistor ▶**noun** a semiconductor device with three connections, capable of amplification in addition to rectification.
■(also **transistor radio**) a portable radio using circuits containing transistors rather than valves.
– ORIGIN 1940s: from **TRANSCONDUCTANCE**, on the pattern of words such as *varistor.*

transistorize (also **-ise**) ▶**verb** [with obj.] [usu. as adj. **transistorized**] design or make with transistors rather than valves: *a transistorized tape recorder.*
– DERIVATIVES **transistorization** noun.

transit ▶**noun** [mass noun] the carrying of people, goods, or materials from one place to another: *a painting was damaged* ***in transit.***
■[count noun] an act of passing through or across a place: *the first west-to-east transit of the Northwest Passage* | [as modifier] *a transit airline passenger.* ■N. Amer. the conveyance of passengers on public transport. ■Astronomy the passage of an inferior planet across the face of the sun, or of a moon or its shadow across the face of a planet. ■Astronomy the apparent passage of a celestial body across the meridian of a place. ■Astrology the passage of a celestial body through a specified sign, house, or area of a chart.
▶**verb** (**transited**, **transiting**) [with obj.] pass across or through (an area): *the new large ships will be too big to transit the Panama Canal.*
■Astronomy (of a planet or other celestial body) pass across (the face of another body, or a meridian). ■Astrology (of a celestial body) pass across (a specified sign, house, or area of a chart).
– ORIGIN late Middle English (denoting passage from one place to another): from Latin *transitus*, from *transire* 'go across'.

transit camp ▶**noun** a camp for the temporary accommodation of groups of people, e.g. refugees or soldiers, who are travelling through a country or region.

transit circle (also **transit instrument**) ▶**noun** another term for **MERIDIAN CIRCLE**.

transition ▶**noun** [mass noun] the process or a period of changing from one state or condition to another: *students* ***in transition*** *from one programme to another* | [count noun] *a transition to multiparty democracy.*
■[count noun] Music a momentary modulation from one key to another. ■[count noun] Physics a change of an atom, nucleus, electron, etc. from one quantum state to another, with emission or absorption of radiation.
– DERIVATIVES **transitionary** adjective.
– ORIGIN mid 16th cent.: from French, or from Latin *transitio(n-)*, from *transire* 'go across'.

transitional ▶**adjective** relating to or characteristic of a process or period of transition.
■(**Transitional**) Architecture of or denoting the last stage of Romanesque style, in which Gothic elements begin to appear.
– DERIVATIVES **transitionally** adverb.

transition curve ▶**noun** a curve of constantly changing radius, used to connect a circular arc to a straight line or to an arc of different curvature.

transition metal (also **transition element**) ▶**noun** Chemistry any of the set of metallic elements occupying a central block (Groups IVB–VIII, IB, and IIB, or 4–12) in the periodic table, e.g. iron, manganese, chromium, and copper. Chemically they show variable valency and a strong tendency to form coordination compounds, and many of their compounds are coloured.

transition point ▶**noun** Chemistry the set of conditions of temperature and pressure at which different phases of the same substance can be in equilibrium.

transition temperature ▶**noun** Physics the temperature at which a substance acquires or loses some distinctive property, in particular superconductivity.

transitive /ˈtransɪtɪv, ˈtrɑːns-, -nz-/ ▶**adjective** **1** Grammar (of a verb or a sense or use of a verb) able to take a direct object (expressed or implied), e.g. *saw* in *he saw the donkey.* The opposite of **INTRANSITIVE**.
2 Logic & Mathematics (of a relation) such that, if it applies between successive members of a sequence, it must also apply between any two members taken in order. For instance, if A is larger than B, and B is larger than C, then A is larger than C.
– DERIVATIVES **transitively** adverb, **transitiveness** noun, **transitivity** noun.
– ORIGIN mid 16th cent. (in the sense 'transitory'): from late Latin *transitivus*, from *transit-* 'gone across' (see **TRANSIT**).

transit lounge ▶**noun** a lounge at an airport for passengers waiting between flights.

transitory /ˈtransɪt(ə)ri, ˈtrɑːns-, -nz-/ ▶**adjective** not permanent: *transitory periods of medieval greatness.*
– DERIVATIVES **transitorily** adverb, **transitoriness** noun.
– ORIGIN late Middle English: from Old French *transitoire*, from Christian Latin *transitorius*, from *transit-* 'gone across' (see **TRANSIT**).

transit visa ▶**noun** a visa allowing its holder to pass through a country only, not to stay there.

Transjordan former name (until 1949) of the region east of the River Jordan now forming the main part of the kingdom of Jordan.
– DERIVATIVES **Transjordanian** adjective.

Transkei /tranˈskʌɪ/ a former homeland established in South Africa for the Xhosa people, now part of the province of Eastern Cape.

transketolase /tranzˈkiːtəleɪz, trɑːnz, -ns-/ ▶**noun** [mass noun] Biochemistry an enzyme which catalyses the transfer of an alcohol group between sugar molecules.

translate /transˈleɪt, trɑːns-, -nz-/ ▶**verb** [with obj.] **1** express the sense of (words or text) in another language: *the German original has been* ***translated into*** *English.*
■[no obj.] be expressed or be capable of being expressed in another language: *shiatsu literally translates as 'finger pressure'.* ■(**translate something into/translate into**) convert or be converted into (another form or medium): [with obj.] *few of Shakespeare's other works have been translated into ballets* | [no obj.] *twenty years of critical success which rarely translated into public acclaim.*
2 move from one place or condition to another: *she had been translated from familiar surroundings to a foreign court.*
■formal move (a bishop or, in Scotland, a minister) to another see or pastoral charge. ■formal remove (a saint's relics) to another place. ■poetic/literary convey (someone, typically still alive) to heaven. ■Biology convert (a sequence of nucleotides in messenger RNA) to an amino-acid sequence in a protein or polypeptide during synthesis.
3 Physics cause (a body) to move so that all its parts travel in the same direction, without rotation or change of shape.
■Mathematics transform (a geometrical figure) in an analogous way.
– DERIVATIVES **translatability** noun, **translatable** adjective.
– ORIGIN Middle English: from Latin *translatus* 'carried across', past participle of *transferre* (see **TRANSFER**).

translation ▶**noun** [mass noun] **1** the process of translating words or text from one language into another: *Cromwell promoted the translation of the Bible into English.*
■[count noun] a written or spoken rendering of the meaning of a word, speech, book, or other text, in another language: *a Spanish translation of Calvin's great work.* ■the conversion of something from one form or medium into another: *the translation of research findings into clinical practice.* ■Biology the process by which a sequence of nucleotide triplets in a messenger RNA molecule gives rise to a specific sequence of amino acids during synthesis of a polypeptide or protein.
2 formal or technical the process of moving something from one place to another: *the translation of the relics of St Thomas of Canterbury.*
■Mathematics movement of a body from one point of space to another such that every point of the body moves in the same direction and over the same distance, without any rotation, reflection, or change in size.
– DERIVATIVES **translational** adjective, **translationally** adverb.
– ORIGIN Middle English: from Old French, or from Latin *translatio(n-)*, from *translat-* 'carried across' (see **TRANSLATE**).

translation table ▶**noun** Computing a table of stored information used in translating one code into another.

translator ▶**noun 1** a person who translates from one language into another, especially as a profession.
■a program that translates from one programming language into another.
2 a television relay transmitter.

transliterate ▶**verb** [with obj.] (usu. **be transliterated**) write or print (a letter or word) using the closest corresponding letters of a different alphabet or language: *names from one language are often* ***transliterated into*** *another.*
– DERIVATIVES **transliteration** noun, **transliterator** noun.
– ORIGIN mid 19th cent.: from **TRANS-** 'across' + Latin *littera* 'letter' + **-ATE**[3].

translocate ▶**verb** [with obj.] chiefly technical move from one place to another: *translocating rhinos to other reserves* | [no obj.] *the cell bodies translocate into the other side of the brain.*
■[with obj.] Physiology & Biochemistry transport (a dissolved substance) within an organism, especially in the phloem of a plant, or actively across a cell membrane. ■[with obj.] Genetics move (a portion of a chromosome) to a new position on the same or another chromosome.
– DERIVATIVES **translocation** noun.

translucent /transˈluːs(ə)nt, trɑːns-, -nz-/ ▶**adjective** (of a substance) allowing light, but not detailed shapes, to pass through; semi-transparent: *her beautiful translucent skin.*
– DERIVATIVES **translucence** noun, **translucency** noun, **translucently** adverb.
– ORIGIN late 16th cent. (in the Latin sense): from Latin *translucent-* 'shining through', from the verb *translucere*, from *trans-* 'through' + *lucere* 'to shine'.

translunar /tranzˈluːnə, trɑːnz-, -ns-/ ▶**adjective** of, relating to, or denoting the trajectory of a spacecraft travelling between the earth and the moon.

transmarine /ˌtranzməˈriːn, ˌtrɑːnz-, -ns-/ ▶**adjective** dated situated or originating on the other side of the sea: *an alien, or a transmarine stranger.*
■of or involving crossing the sea: *some birds make long transmarine migrations.*
– ORIGIN late 16th cent.: from Latin *transmarinus*, from *trans-* 'across' + *marinus* 'marine, of the sea'.

transmembrane /ˌtranzˈmɛmbreɪn, trɑːnz-, -ns-/ ▶**adjective** Biology existing or occurring across a cell membrane: *transmembrane conductance.*

transmigrant ▶**noun** rare a person passing through a country or region in the course of emigrating to another region.
– ORIGIN early 17th cent.: from Latin *transmigrant-* 'migrating across', from the verb *transmigrare* (see **TRANSMIGRATE**).

transmigrate ▶**verb** [no obj.] **1** (of the soul) pass into a different body after death.
2 rare migrate.
– DERIVATIVES **transmigration** noun, **transmigrator** noun, **transmigratory** adjective.
– ORIGIN late Middle English (as an adjective in the sense 'transferred'): from Latin *transmigrat-* 'removed from one place to another', from the verb *transmigrare* (see **TRANS-**, **MIGRATE**).

transmission ▶**noun 1** [mass noun] the action or process of transmitting something or the state of being transmitted: *the transmission of the HIV virus.*
■[count noun] a programme or signal that is broadcast or sent out: *television transmissions.*
2 the mechanism by which power is transmitted from an engine to the axle in a motor vehicle.
– ORIGIN early 17th cent.: from Latin *transmissio* (see **TRANS-**, **MISSION**).

transmission electron microscope ▶**noun**

a form of electron microscope in which an image is derived from electrons which have passed through the specimen, in particular one in which the whole image is formed at once rather than by scanning.

transmission line ▶ **noun** a conductor or conductors designed to carry electricity or an electrical signal over large distances with minimum losses and distortion.

transmissivity /ˌtranzmɪˈsɪvɪti, ˌtrɑːnz-, -ns-/ ▶ **noun** (pl. **-ies**) the degree to which a medium allows something, in particular electromagnetic radiation, to pass through it.

transmit ▶ **verb** (**transmitted**, **transmitting**) [with obj.] cause (something) to pass on from one place or person to another: *knowledge is transmitted from teacher to pupil.*
■ broadcast or send out (an electrical signal or a radio or television programme): *the programme was transmitted on 7 October.* ■ pass on (a disease or trait) to another: [as adj. **transmitted**] *sexually transmitted diseases.* ■ allow (heat, light, sound, electricity, or other energy) to pass through a medium: *the three bones transmit sound waves to the inner ear.* ■ communicate or be a medium for (an idea or emotion): *the theatrical gift of being able to transmit emotion.*
– DERIVATIVES **transmissibility** noun (chiefly Medicine), **transmissible** adjective (chiefly Medicine), **transmissive** adjective, **transmittable** adjective, **transmittal** noun.
– ORIGIN late Middle English: from Latin *transmittere*, from *trans-* 'across' + *mittere* 'send'.

transmittance ▶ **noun** Physics the ratio of the light energy falling on a body to that transmitted through it.

transmitter ▶ **noun** a set of equipment used to generate and transmit electromagnetic waves carrying messages or signals, especially those of radio or television.
■ a person or thing that transmits something: *reggae has established itself as the principal transmitter of the Jamaican language.* ■ short for **NEUROTRANSMITTER**.

transmogrify /tranzˈmɒɡrɪfʌɪ, trɑːnz-, -ns-/ ▶ **verb** (**-ies**, **-ied**) [with obj.] (often **be transmogrified**) usu. humorous transform in a surprising or magical manner: *his home was **transmogrified into** a hippy crash pad.*
– DERIVATIVES **transmogrification** noun.
– ORIGIN mid 17th cent.: of unknown origin.

transmontane /tranzˈmɒnteɪn, trɑːnz-, -mɒnˈteɪn, -ns-/ ▶ **adjective** another term for **TRAMONTANE**.

transmural /tranzˈmjʊːr(ə)l, trɑːnz-, -ns-/ ▶ **adjective** Medicine existing or occurring across the entire wall of an organ or blood vessel.

transmutation /tranzmjuːˈteɪʃ(ə)n, trɑːnz-, -ns-/ ▶ **noun** [mass noun] the action of changing or the state of being changed into another form: *the transmutation of the political economy of the post-war years was complete* | [count noun] *grotesque transmutations.*
■ Physics the changing of one element into another by radioactive decay, nuclear bombardment, or similar processes. ■ Biology, chiefly historical the conversion or transformation of one species into another. ■ the supposed alchemical process of changing base metals into gold.
– DERIVATIVES **transmutational** adjective, **transmutationist** noun.

transmute /tranzˈmjuːt, trɑːnz-, -ns-/ ▶ **verb** change in form, nature, or substance: [with obj.] *the raw material of his experience was **transmuted into** stories* | [no obj.] *the discovery that elements can transmute by radioactivity.*
■ [with obj.] subject (base metals) to alchemical transmutation: *the quest to **transmute** lead **into** gold.*
– DERIVATIVES **transmutability** noun, **transmutable** adjective, **transmutative** adjective, **transmuter** noun.
– ORIGIN late Middle English: from Latin *transmutare*, from *trans-* 'across' + *mutare* 'to change'.

transnational ▶ **adjective** extending or operating across national boundaries: *transnational advertising agencies.*
▶ **noun** a large company operating internationally; a multinational.
– DERIVATIVES **transnationalism** noun, **transnationally** adverb.

transoceanic ▶ **adjective** crossing an ocean: *the transoceanic cable system.*
■ coming from or situated beyond an ocean: *there is a higher rate for letters intended for transoceanic countries.*

transom /ˈtrans(ə)m/ ▶ **noun** the flat surface forming the stern of a boat.
■ a horizontal beam reinforcing the stern of a boat. ■ a strengthening crossbar, in particular one set above a window or door. Compare with **MULLION**. ■ US term for **TRANSOM WINDOW**.
– PHRASES **over the transom** US informal offered or sent without prior agreement; unsolicited: *the editors receive about ten manuscripts a week over the transom.*
– DERIVATIVES **transomed** adjective.
– ORIGIN late Middle English (earlier as *traversayn*): from Old French *traversin*, from the verb *traverser* 'to cross' (see **TRAVERSE**).

transom window ▶ **noun** a window set above the transom of a door or larger window; a fanlight.

transonic /tranˈsɒnɪk, trɑːn-/ (also **trans-sonic**) ▶ **adjective** denoting or relating to speeds close to that of sound.
– ORIGIN 1940s: from **TRANS-** 'through, across' + **SONIC**, on the pattern of words such as *supersonic*.

trans-Pacific ▶ **adjective** crossing the Pacific: *trans-Pacific routes to India.*
■ of or relating to an area beyond the Pacific: *a journal influenced by trans-Pacific pomposity.*

transparence ▶ **noun** rare term for **TRANSPARENCY** (in sense 1).

transparency ▶ **noun** (pl. **-ies**) **1** [mass noun] the condition of being transparent: *the transparency of ice.*
2 a positive transparent photograph printed on transparent plastic or glass, able to be viewed using a slide projector.
– ORIGIN late 16th cent. (as a general term denoting a transparent object): from medieval Latin *transparentia*, from *transparent-* 'shining through' (see **TRANSPARENT**).

transparent /tranˈspar(ə)nt, trɑːn-, -ˈspɛː-/ ▶ **adjective 1** (of a material or article) allowing light to pass through so that objects behind can be distinctly seen: *transparent blue water* | *fine transparent fabrics.*
■ easy to perceive or detect: *the residents will see through any transparent attempt to buy their votes* | *the meaning of the poem is by no means transparent.* ■ having thoughts, feelings, or motives that are easily perceived: *you'd be no good at poker—you're too transparent.* ■ Physics transmitting heat or other electromagnetic rays without distortion. ■ Computing (of a process or interface) functioning without the user being aware of its presence.
– DERIVATIVES **transparently** adverb [as submodifier] *a transparently feeble argument.*
– ORIGIN late Middle English: from Old French, from medieval Latin *transparent-* 'shining through', from Latin *transparere*, from *trans-* 'through' + *parere* 'appear'.

transpersonal ▶ **adjective** of, denoting, or dealing with states or areas of consciousness beyond the limits of personal identity: *the book covers shamanism and transpersonal psychology.*

transpicuous /tranˈspɪkjʊəs, trɑːn-/ ▶ **adjective** rare transparent.
■ easily understood, lucid.
– ORIGIN mid 17th cent.: from modern Latin *transpicuus* (from Latin *transpicere* 'look through') + **-OUS**.

transpierce ▶ **verb** [with obj.] poetic/literary pierce through (someone or something).

transpiration stream ▶ **noun** Botany the flow of water through a plant, from the roots to the leaves, via the xylem vessels.

transpire ▶ **verb** [no obj.] **1** [with clause] (usu. **it transpires**) (of a secret or something unknown) come to be known; be revealed: ***it transpired that** Mark had been baptized a Catholic.*
■ prove to be the case: *as it transpired, he was right.* ■ occur; happen: *I'm going to find out exactly what transpired.*
2 Botany (of a plant or leaf) give off water vapour through the stomata.
– DERIVATIVES **transpiration** noun (only in sense 2).
– ORIGIN late Middle English (in the sense 'emit as vapour through the surface'): from French *transpirer* or medieval Latin *transpirare*, from Latin *trans-* 'through' + *spirare* 'breathe'. Sense 1 (mid 18th cent.) is a figurative use comparable with 'leak out'.

USAGE The standard general sense of **transpire** is 'come to be known' (as in *it **transpired** that Mark had been baptized a Catholic*). From this, a looser sense has developed, meaning 'happen or occur' (*I'm going to find out exactly what **transpired***). This looser sense, first recorded in US English towards the end of the 18th century and listed in US dictionaries from the 19th century, is criticized for being jargon, an unnecessarily long word used where **occur** and **happen** would do just as well. In practice the two senses are indistinguishable in many contexts. The newer sense is common, though, and accounts for around 25 per cent of citations for **transpire** on the Oxford Reading Programme.

transplant ▶ **verb** /transˈplɑːnt, trɑːns-, -nz-/ [with obj.] move or transfer (something) to another place or situation, typically with some effort or upheaval: *it was proposed to transplant the club to the vacant site.*
■ replant (a plant) in another place. ■ transfer (living tissue or an organ) and implant it in another part of the body or in another body.
▶ **noun** /ˈtransplɑːnt, ˈtrɑːns-, -nz-/ an operation in which an organ or tissue is transplanted: *a heart transplant* | [mass noun] *kidneys available for transplant.*
■ an organ or tissue which is transplanted. ■ a plant which has been or is to be transplanted. ■ a person or thing that has been moved to a new place or situation.
– DERIVATIVES **transplantable** /-ˈplɑːntəb(ə)l/ adjective, **transplantation** /-ˈteɪʃ(ə)n/ noun, **transplanter** /-ˈplɑːntə/ noun.
– ORIGIN late Middle English (as a verb describing the repositioning of a plant): from late Latin *transplantare*, from Latin *trans-* 'across' + *plantare* 'to plant'. The noun, first in the sense 'something or someone moved to a new place', dates from the mid 18th cent.

transponder /tranˈspɒndə, trɑːn-/ ▶ **noun** a device for receiving a radio signal and automatically transmitting a different signal.
– ORIGIN 1940s: blend of **TRANSMIT** and **RESPOND**, + **-ER**[1].

transpontine /transˈpɒntʌɪn, trɑːns-, -nz-/ ▶ **adjective** dated on or from the other side of an ocean, in particular the Atlantic as viewed from Britain; American: *she approached the task with typical transpontine enthusiasm.*
– ORIGIN late 19th cent.: from **TRANS-** 'across' + Latin *pontus* 'sea' + **-INE**[1].

transport ▶ **verb** [with obj.] take or carry (people or goods) from one place to another by means of a vehicle, aircraft, or ship: *the bulk of freight traffic was transported by lorry.*
■ historical send (a convict) to a penal colony. ■ figurative cause (someone) to feel that they are in another place or time: *for a moment she was transported to a warm summer garden on the night of a Ball.* ■ (usu. **be transported**) overwhelm (someone) with a strong emotion, especially joy: *she was **transported with** pleasure.*
▶ **noun 1** [mass noun] a system or means of conveying people or goods from place to place by means of a vehicle, aircraft, or ship: *many possess their own forms of transport* | *air transport.*
■ the action of transporting something or the state of being transported: *the transport of crude oil.* ■ [count noun] a large vehicle, ship, or aircraft used to carry troops or stores. ■ [count noun] historical a convict who was transported to a penal colony.
2 (usu. **transports**) an overwhelmingly strong emotion: *art can send people into **transports of** delight.*
– ORIGIN late Middle English: from Old French *transporter* or Latin *transportare*, from *trans-* 'across' + *portare* 'carry'.

transportable ▶ **adjective 1** able to be carried or moved: *the first transportable phones.*
2 historical (of an offender or an offence) punishable by transportation.
▶ **noun** a large portable computer or telephone.
– DERIVATIVES **transportability** noun.

transportation ▶ **noun** [mass noun] **1** the action of transporting someone or something or the process of being transported: *the era of global mass transportation.*
■ a system or means of transporting people or goods: *transportation on the site includes a monorail.*
2 historical the action or practice of transporting convicts to a penal colony.

transport cafe ▶ **noun** Brit. a roadside cafe for drivers of haulage vehicles.

t

transporter ▶ **noun** a person or thing that transports something, in particular:
■ a large vehicle used to carry heavy objects, e.g. cars. ■ (in science fiction) a device that conveys people or things instantaneously from one place to another.

transpose ▶ **verb** [with obj.] **1** cause (two or more things) to change places with each other: *the situation might have been the same if the parties in opposition and government had been transposed.*
2 transfer to a different place or context: *an evacuation order transposed the school from Kent to Shropshire | the themes are transposed from the sphere of love to that of work.*
■ write or play (music) in a different key from the original: *the basses are* **transposed down** *an octave.* ■ Mathematics transfer (a term), with its sign changed, to the other side of an equation. ■ translate into another language: *a sequence of French tales transposed into English.* ■ change into a new form: *he* **transposed** *a gaffe by the mayor* **into** *a public-relations advantage.*
▶ **noun** Mathematics a matrix obtained from a given matrix by interchanging each row and the corresponding column.
– DERIVATIVES **transposable** adjective, **transposal** noun, **transposer** noun.
– ORIGIN late Middle English (also in the sense 'transform, convert'): from Old French *transposer*, from *trans-* 'across' + *poser* 'to place'.

transposing instrument ▶ **noun** an orchestral instrument for which parts are written in a different key from that in which they sound, e.g. the clarinet and many brass instruments.

transposition ▶ **noun** [mass noun] the action of transposing something: *transposition of word order |* [count noun] *a transposition of an old story into a contemporary context.*
■ [count noun] a thing that has been produced by transposing something: *in China, the dragon is a transposition of the serpent.*
– DERIVATIVES **transpositional** adjective.
– ORIGIN mid 16th cent.: from late Latin *transpositio(n-)* (see **TRANS-**, **POSITION**).

transposon /trans'pəʊzɒn, trɑːns-, -nz-/ ▶ **noun** Genetics a chromosomal segment that can undergo transposition, especially a segment of bacterial DNA that can be translocated as a whole between chromosomal, phage, and plasmid DNA in the absence of a complementary sequence in the host DNA. Also called **JUMPING GENE**.
– ORIGIN 1970s: from **TRANSPOSITION** + **-ON**.

transputer /trans'pjuːtə, trɑːns-, -nz-/ ▶ **noun** a microprocessor with integral memory designed for parallel processing.
– ORIGIN 1970s: blend of **TRANSISTOR** and **COMPUTER**.

transracial ▶ **adjective** across or crossing racial boundaries.

transsexual (also **transexual**) ▶ **noun** a person born with the physical characteristics of one sex who emotionally and psychologically feels that they belong to the opposite sex.
▶ **adjective** of or relating to such a person.
– DERIVATIVES **transsexualism** noun, **transsexuality** noun.

trans-ship (also **tranship**) ▶ **verb** (**-shipped**, **-shipping**) [with obj.] transfer (cargo) from one ship or other form of transport to another.
– DERIVATIVES **trans-shipment** noun.

Trans-Siberian Railway a railway running from Moscow east around Lake Baikal to Vladivostok on the Sea of Japan, a distance of 9,311 km (5,786 miles). Begun in 1891 and virtually completed by 1904, it opened up Siberia and advanced Russian interest in eastern Asia.

trans-sonic ▶ **adjective** variant spelling of **TRANSONIC**.

trans-synaptic ▶ **adjective** Physiology occurring or existing across a nerve synapse.

transubstantiate /ˌtransəb'stanʃɪeɪt, ˌtrɑːn-, -sɪ-/ ▶ **verb** [with obj.] (usu. **be transubstantiated**) Christian Theology convert (the substance of the Eucharistic elements) into the body and blood of Christ.
■ formal change the form or substance of (something) into something different.
– ORIGIN late Middle English: from medieval Latin *transubstantiat-* 'changed in substance', from the verb *transubstantiare*, from Latin *trans-* 'across' + *substantia* 'substance'.

transubstantiation ▶ **noun** [mass noun] Christian Theology the conversion of the substance of the Eucharistic elements into the body and blood of Christ at consecration, only the appearances of bread and wine still remaining.

transude /tran'sjuːd, trɑːn-/ ▶ **verb** [with obj.] archaic discharge (a fluid) gradually through pores in a membrane, especially within the body.
■ [no obj.] (of a fluid) be discharged in such a way.
– DERIVATIVES **transudate** noun, **transudation** noun.
– ORIGIN mid 17th cent.: from French *transsuder* (in Old French *tressuer*), from Latin *trans-* 'across' + Latin *sudare* 'to sweat'.

transuranic /ˌtransjʊ'ranɪk, ˌtrɑːns-, -nz-/ ▶ **adjective** Chemistry (of an element) having a higher atomic number than uranium (92).

transurethral /ˌtranzjʊ'riːθrəl, ˌtrɑːnz-/ ▶ **adjective** (of a medical procedure) performed via the urethra.

Transvaal /tranz'vɑːl, trɑːnz-, -ns-/ (also **the Transvaal**) a former province in north-eastern South Africa, lying north of the River Vaal.

> It was first settled by Boers *c.*1840 after the Great Trek, becoming the core of the Boer republic in 1857. Resistance to Britain's annexation of Transvaal in 1877 led to the Boer Wars, after which the Transvaal became a Crown Colony. It became a founding province of the Union of South Africa in 1910. In 1994 it was divided into the provinces of Northern Transvaal, Eastern Transvaal, Pretoria-Witwatersrand-Vereeniging, and the eastern part of North-West Province.

Transvaal daisy ▶ **noun** a South African gerbera, grown for its large brightly coloured daisy-like flowers.
● *Gerbera jamesonii*, family Compositae.

transvalue ▶ **verb** (**transvalues**, **transvalued**, **transvaluing**) [with obj.] (often **be transvalued**) represent (something, typically an idea, custom, or quality) in a different way, altering people's judgement of or reaction to it: *survival strategies are aesthetically* **transvalued into** *weapons of attack.*
– DERIVATIVES **transvaluation** noun.

transversal /tranz'vəːs(ə)l, trɑːnz-, -ns-/ Geometry ▶ **adjective** (of a line) cutting a system of lines.
▶ **noun** a transversal line.
– DERIVATIVES **transversality** noun, **transversally** adverb.
– ORIGIN late Middle English (as a synonym of **TRANSVERSE**): from medieval Latin *transversalis*, from Latin *transversus* 'lying across'.

transverse /tranz'vəːs, trɑːnz-, -ns-/ ▶ **adjective** situated or extending across something: *a transverse beam supports the dashboard.*
– DERIVATIVES **transversely** adverb.
– ORIGIN late Middle English: from Latin *transversus* 'turned across', past participle of *transvertere*, from *trans-* 'across' + *vertere* 'to turn'.

transverse colon ▶ **noun** Anatomy the middle part of the large intestine, passing across the abdomen from right to left below the stomach.

transverse flute ▶ **noun** a flute which is held horizontally when played.

transverse magnet ▶ **noun** a magnet with poles at the sides and not the ends.

transverse wave ▶ **noun** Physics a wave in which the medium vibrates at right angles to the direction of its propagation.

transvestite ▶ **noun** a person, typically a man, who derives pleasure from dressing in clothes appropriate to the opposite sex.
– DERIVATIVES **transvestism** noun, **transvestist** noun (dated), **transvestitism** noun.
– ORIGIN 1920s: from German *Transvestit*, from Latin *trans-* 'across' + *vestire* 'clothe'.

Transylvania /ˌtransɪl'veɪnɪə/ a large tableland region of NW Romania, separated from the rest of the country by the Carpathian Mountains and the Transylvanian Alps. Part of Hungary until it became a principality of the Ottoman Empire in the 16th century, it was returned to Hungary at the end of the 17th century and was incorporated into Romania in 1918.
– DERIVATIVES **Transylvanian** adjective.
– ORIGIN based on Latin *trans* 'across, beyond' + *silva* 'forest'.

trap[1] ▶ **noun** **1** a device or enclosure designed to catch and retain animals, typically by allowing entry but not exit or by catching hold of a part of the body.
■ a curve in the waste pipe from a bath, basin, or toilet that is always full of liquid and prevents gases from coming up the pipe into the building. ■ [with modifier] a container or device used to collect a specified thing: *one fuel filter and water trap are sufficient on the fuel system.* ■ a bunker or other hollow on a golf course. ■ the compartment from which a greyhound is released at the start of a race. ■ figurative a trick by which someone is misled into giving themselves away or otherwise acting contrary to their interests or intentions: *by keeping quiet I was* **walking into a trap**. ■ figurative an unpleasant situation from which it is hard to escape: *they* **fell into the trap** *of relying too little on equity finance.*
2 a device for hurling an object such as a clay pigeon into the air to be shot at.
■ (in the game of trapball) the shoe-shaped device that is hit with a bat to send the ball into the air.
3 chiefly historical a light, two-wheeled carriage pulled by a horse or pony.
4 short for **TRAPDOOR**.
5 informal a person's mouth (used in expressions to do with speaking): *keep your trap shut!*
6 (usu. **traps**) informal a percussion instrument, typically in a jazz band.
▶ **verb** (**trapped**, **trapping**) [with obj.] catch (an animal) in a trap.
■ (often **be trapped**) prevent (someone) from escaping from a place: *twenty workers were trapped by flames.* ■ have (something, typically a part of the body) held tightly by something so that it cannot move or be freed: *he had trapped his finger in a spring-loaded hinge.* ■ induce (someone) to do something they would not otherwise want to do by means of trickery or deception: *I hoped to* **trap** *him* **into** *an admission.* ■ Soccer bring (the ball) under control with the feet or other part of the body on receiving it.
– DERIVATIVES **trap-like** adjective.
– ORIGIN Old English *træppe* (in *coltetræppe* 'Christ's thorn'); related to Middle Dutch *trappe* and medieval Latin *trappa*, of uncertain origin. The verb dates from late Middle English.

trap[2] ▶ **verb** (**trapped**, **trapping**) [with obj.] [usu. as adj. **trapped**] archaic put trappings on (a horse).
– ORIGIN late Middle English: from the obsolete noun *trap* 'trappings', from Old French *drap* 'drape'.

trap[3] (also **traprock**) ▶ **noun** [mass noun] N. Amer. basalt or a similar dark, fine-grained igneous rock.
– ORIGIN late 18th cent.: from Swedish *trapp*, from *trappa* 'stair' (because of the often stair-like appearance of its outcroppings).

trapball ▶ **noun** [mass noun] historical a game in which the player uses a bat to hit a trap (see **TRAP**[1] sense 2) to send a ball into the air and then hits the ball itself.

trap crop ▶ **noun** a crop planted to attract insect pests from another crop, especially one in which the pests fail to survive or reproduce.

trapdoor ▶ **noun** a hinged or removable panel in a floor, ceiling, or roof.
■ a feature or defect of a computer system which allows surreptitious unauthorized access to data belonging to other users.

trapdoor spider ▶ **noun** a spider which lives in a burrow with a hinged cover like a trapdoor.
● Family Ctenizidae, suborder Mygalomorphae.
■ Austral. a funnel-web spider.

trapes ▶ **verb** & **noun** archaic spelling of **TRAIPSE**.

trapeze ▶ **noun** **1** (also **flying trapeze**) a horizontal bar hanging by two ropes and free to swing, used by acrobats in a circus.
2 Sailing a harness attached by a cable to a dinghy's mast, enabling a sailor to balance the boat by leaning backwards far out over the windward side.
– ORIGIN mid 19th cent.: from French *trapèze*, from late Latin *trapezium* (see **TRAPEZIUM**).

Trapezium /trə'piːzɪəm/ (**the Trapezium**) Astronomy the multiple star Theta Orionis, which lies within the Great Nebula of Orion and illuminates it. Four stars are visible in a small telescope and two more with a larger telescope.

trapezium /trə'piːzɪəm/ ▶ **noun** (pl. **trapezia** /-zɪə/ or **trapeziums**) **1** Geometry a type of quadrilateral:
■ Brit. a quadrilateral with one pair of sides parallel. ■ N. Amer. a quadrilateral with no sides parallel. Compare with **TRAPEZOID**.
2 (also **os trapezium**) Anatomy a carpal bone below the base of the thumb.
– ORIGIN late 16th cent.: via late Latin from Greek *trapezion*, from *trapeza* 'table'. The term has been used in anatomy since the mid 19th cent.

trapezium rule ▶ **noun** Mathematics a method of estimating the area under a curve by dividing it into a series of strips, each of which is approximately a trapezium.

trapezius /trəˈpiːzɪəs/ (also **trapezius muscle**) ▶ **noun** (pl. **trapezii** /-zɪʌɪ/) Anatomy either of a pair of large triangular muscles extending over the back of the neck and shoulders and moving the head and shoulder blade.
– ORIGIN early 18th cent.: from modern Latin, from Greek *trapezion* 'trapezium' (because of the shape formed by the muscles).

trapezohedron /ˌtrapɪzə(ʊ)ˈhiːdrən, -ˈhɛd-/ ▶ **noun** (pl. **trapezohedra** /-drə/ or **trapezohedrons**) a solid figure whose faces are trapeziums or trapezoids.
– DERIVATIVES **trapezohedral** adjective.
– ORIGIN early 19th cent.: from **TRAPEZIUM** + **-HEDRON**, on the pattern of words such as *polyhedron*.

trapezoid /ˈtrapɪzɔɪd, trəˈpiːzɔɪd/ ▶ **noun 1** Geometry a type of quadrilateral:
■ Brit. a quadrilateral with no sides parallel. ■ N. Amer. a quadrilateral with one pair of sides parallel. Compare with **TRAPEZIUM**.
2 (also **trapezoid bone**) Anatomy a small carpal bone in the base of the hand, articulating with the metacarpal of the index finger.
– DERIVATIVES **trapezoidal** adjective.
– ORIGIN early 18th cent.: from modern Latin *trapezoides*, from late Greek *trapezoeidēs*, from *trapeza* 'table' (see **TRAPEZIUM**).

trapline ▶ **noun** N. Amer. a series of game traps.

trapper ▶ **noun** a person who traps wild animals, especially for their fur.

trappings ▶ **plural noun** the outward signs, features, or objects associated with a particular situation, role, or thing: *I had the trappings of success.*
■ a horse's ornamental harness.
– ORIGIN late Middle English: derivative of **TRAP**[2].

Trappist ▶ **adjective** of, relating to, or denoting a branch of the Cistercian order of monks founded in 1664 and noted for an austere rule including a vow of silence.
▶ **noun** a member of this order.
– ORIGIN early 19th cent.: from French *trappiste*, from *La Trappe* in Normandy.

traprock ▶ **noun** see **TRAP**[3].

traps ▶ **plural noun** informal personal belongings; baggage: *I was ready to pack my traps and leave.*
– ORIGIN early 19th cent.: perhaps a contraction of **TRAPPINGS**.

trap shooting ▶ **noun** [mass noun] N. Amer. the sport of shooting at clay pigeons released from a spring trap.
– DERIVATIVES **trap shooter** noun.

trash ▶ **noun** [mass noun] **1** chiefly N. Amer. discarded matter; refuse.
■ writing, art, or other cultural items of poor quality: *if they read at all, they read trash.* ■ a person or people regarded as being of very low social standing: *she would have been considered trash.*
2 (also **cane trash**) W. Indian the leaves, tops, and crushed stems of sugar cane, used as fuel.
▶ **verb** [with obj.] **1** informal, chiefly N. Amer. damage or wreck: *my apartment's been totally trashed.*
■ discard: *they trashed the tapes and sent her back into the studio.* ■ Computing kill (a file or process) or wipe (a disk). ■ criticize severely: *trade associations trashed the legislation as deficient.* ■ [as adj. **trashed**] intoxicated with alcohol or drugs: *there was pot, there was booze, but nobody really got trashed.*
2 strip (sugar canes) of their outer leaves to ripen them faster.
– ORIGIN late Middle English: of unknown origin. The verb is first recorded (mid 18th cent.) in sense 2; the other senses have arisen in the 20th cent.

trash can ▶ **noun** North American term for **DUSTBIN**.

trash talk US informal ▶ **noun** [mass noun] insulting or boastful speech intended to demoralize, intimidate, or humiliate someone, especially a sporting opponent.
▶ **verb** [no obj.] (**trash-talk**) use insulting or boastful speech for such a purpose.
– DERIVATIVES **trash talker** noun.

trashy ▶ **adjective** (**trashier**, **trashiest**) (especially of items of popular culture) of poor quality: *trashy novels and formulaic movies.*
– DERIVATIVES **trashily** adverb, **trashiness** noun.

Trás-os-Montes /ˌtraʒuːʃˈmɒntɛʃ/ a mountainous region of NE Portugal, north of the Douro River.
– ORIGIN Portuguese, literally 'beyond the mountains'.

trass (also **tarras**) ▶ **noun** [mass noun] a light-coloured variety of volcanic ash resembling pozzolana, used in making water-resistant cement.
– ORIGIN late 18th cent.: from Dutch *tras*, German *Trass*, based on Latin *terra* 'earth'.

trattoria /ˌtratəˈriːə/ ▶ **noun** an Italian restaurant.
– ORIGIN Italian.

trauma /ˈtrɔːmə, ˈtraʊmə/ ▶ **noun** (pl. **traumas** or **traumata** /-mətə/) a deeply distressing or disturbing experience: *they were reluctant to talk about the traumas of the revolution.*
■ [mass noun] emotional shock following a stressful event or a physical injury, which may be associated with physical shock, and sometimes leads to long-term neurosis. ■ [mass noun] Medicine physical injury.
– ORIGIN late 17th cent.: from Greek, literally 'wound'.

traumatic ▶ **adjective** emotionally disturbing or distressing: *she was going through a traumatic divorce.*
■ relating to or causing psychological trauma. ■ Medicine relating to or denoting physical injury.
– DERIVATIVES **traumatically** adverb.
– ORIGIN mid 19th cent.: via late Latin from Greek *traumatikos*, from *trauma* (see **TRAUMA**).

traumatism ▶ **noun** chiefly technical a traumatic effect or condition.

traumatize (also **-ise**) ▶ **verb** [with obj.] subject to lasting shock as a result of an emotionally disturbing experience or physical injury.
■ Medicine cause physical injury to.
– DERIVATIVES **traumatization** noun.

travail /ˈtraveɪl/ poetic/literary ▶ **noun** [mass noun] (also **travails**) painful or laborious effort: *advice for those who wish to save great sorrow and travail.*
■ labour pains: *a woman in travail.*
▶ **verb** [no obj.] engage in painful or laborious effort.
■ (of a woman) be in labour.
– ORIGIN Middle English: via Old French from medieval Latin *trepalium* 'instrument of torture', from Latin *tres* 'three' + *palus* 'stake'.

travel ▶ **verb** (**travelled**, **travelling**; US also **traveled**, **traveling**) [no obj., with adverbial] make a journey, typically of some length or abroad: *the vessel had been travelling from Libya to Ireland | we travelled thousands of miles.*
■ [with obj.] journey along (a road) or through (a region): *he travelled the world with the army.* ■ [usu. as adj. **travelling**] go or be moved from place to place: *a travelling exhibition.* ■ informal resist motion sickness, damage, or some other impairment on a journey: *he usually* **travels well**, *but he did get a bit upset on a very rough crossing.* ■ be enjoyed or successful away from the place of origin: *accordion music travels well.* ■ (of an object or radiation) move, typically in a constant or predictable way: *light travels faster than sound.* ■ informal (especially of a vehicle) move quickly.
▶ **noun** [mass noun] the action of travelling, typically abroad: *I have a job which involves quite a lot of travel.*
■ [count noun] (**travels**) journeys, especially long or exotic ones: *perhaps you'll write a book about your travels.* ■ [as modifier] (of a device) designed so as to be sufficiently compact for use on a journey: *a travel iron.* ■ the range, rate, or mode of motion of a part of a machine: *two proximity switches detect when the valve has reached the end of its travel.*
– ORIGIN Middle English: variant of **TRAVAIL** and originally in the same sense.

travel agency (also **travel bureau**) ▶ **noun** an agency that makes the necessary arrangements for travellers.
– DERIVATIVES **travel agent** noun.

travelator /ˈtravəleɪtə/ (also **travolator**) ▶ **noun** a moving walkway, typically at an airport.
– ORIGIN 1950s: from **TRAVEL**, suggested by **ESCALATOR**.

travel card ▶ **noun** a prepaid card allowing unlimited travel on buses or trains for a specified period of time: *a one-day travel card.*

travelled /ˈtrav(ə)ld/ ▶ **adjective** [with submodifier or in combination] **1** having travelled to many places: *he was widely travelled.*
2 used by people travelling: *a less well-travelled route.*

traveller (US also **traveler**) ▶ **noun** a person who is travelling or who often travels.
■ a gypsy. ■ (also **New Age traveller**) a person who holds New Age values and leads an itinerant and unconventional lifestyle. ■ Austral. an itinerant worker.

traveller's cheque ▶ **noun** a cheque for a fixed amount that may be cashed or used in payment abroad after endorsement by the holder's signature.

traveller's joy ▶ **noun** a tall scrambling clematis with small fragrant flowers and tufts of grey hairs around the seeds. Native to Eurasia and North Africa, it grows chiefly on calcareous soils. Also called **OLD MAN'S BEARD**.
• *Clematis vitalba*, family Ranunculaceae.

traveller's tale ▶ **noun** a story about the unusual characteristics or customs of a foreign country, regarded as probably exaggerated or untrue.

travelling ▶ **adjective** [attrib.] (of a device) designed so as to be sufficiently compact for use on a journey: *a travelling clock.*

travelling crane ▶ **noun** a crane able to move on rails, especially along an overhead support.

travelling people ▶ **plural noun** people whose lifestyle is nomadic, for example gypsies (a term typically used by such people of themselves).

travelling salesman ▶ **noun** a representative of a firm who visits shops and other businesses to show samples and gain orders.

travelling salesman problem ▶ **noun** a mathematical problem in which one has to find which is the shortest route which passes through each of a set of points once and only once.

travelling scholarship ▶ **noun** a scholarship given to enable the holder to travel for the purpose of study or research.

travelling wave ▶ **noun** Physics a wave in which the medium moves in the direction of propagation.

travelogue ▶ **noun** a film, book, or illustrated lecture about the places visited by or experiences of a traveller.
– ORIGIN early 20th cent.: from **TRAVEL**, on the pattern of *monologue*.

travel-sick ▶ **adjective** (of a person) suffering from nausea caused by the motion of a moving vehicle, boat, or aircraft.
– DERIVATIVES **travel-sickness** noun.

travers /ˈtravəs/ (also **traverse**) ▶ **noun** a movement performed in dressage, in which the horse moves parallel to the side of the arena, with its shoulders carried closer to the wall than its hindquarters and its body curved towards the centre.
– ORIGIN French, from *pied de travers* 'foot askew'.

traverse /ˈtravəs, trəˈvəːs/ ▶ **verb** [with obj.] **1** travel across or through: *he traversed the forest.*
■ extend across or through: *a moving catwalk that traversed a vast cavernous space.* ■ [no obj., with adverbial of direction] cross a hill or mountain by means of a series of sideways movements. ■ ski diagonally across (a slope), losing only a little height. ■ figurative consider or discuss the whole extent of (a subject).
2 [with obj. and adverbial of direction] move (something) back and forth or sideways: *a probe is traversed along the tunnel.*
■ turn (a large gun or other device on a pivot) to face a different direction. ■ [no obj.] (of such a gun or device) be turned in this way.
3 Law deny (an allegation) in pleading.
■ archaic oppose or thwart (a plan).
▶ **noun 1** an act of traversing something.
■ a sideways movement, or a series of such movements, across a rock face from one practicable line of ascent or descent to another. ■ a place where a movement of this type is necessary: *a narrow traverse made lethal by snow and ice.* ■ a movement following a diagonal course made by a skier descending a slope. ■ a zigzag line taken by a ship because winds or currents prevent it from sailing directly towards its destination.
2 a part of a structure that extends or is fixed across something.
■ a gallery extending from side to side of a church or other building.
3 a mechanism enabling a large gun to be turned to face a different direction.
■ [mass noun] the sideways movement of a part in a machine.
4 a single line of survey, usually plotted from compass bearings and chained or paced distances between angular points.
■ a tract surveyed in this way.
5 Military a pair of right-angled bends incorporated in a trench to avoid enfilading fire.
6 variant spelling of **TRAVERS**.
– DERIVATIVES **traversable** adjective, **traversal** noun.

– ORIGIN Middle English (in sense 3 of the verb): from Old French *traverser*, from late Latin *traversare*; the noun is from Old French *travers* (masculine), *traverse* (feminine), partly based on *traverser*.

traverser /trəˈvəːsə/ ▶ **noun** a sideways-moving platform for transferring a railway vehicle from one set of rails to another parallel set.

travertine /ˈtravətɪn/ ▶ **noun** [mass noun] white or light-coloured calcareous rock deposited from mineral springs, used in building.
– ORIGIN late 18th cent.: from Italian *travertino*, *tivertino*, from Latin *tiburtinus* 'of Tibur' (now Tivoli, a district near Rome).

travesty /ˈtravɪsti/ ▶ **noun** (pl. **-ies**) a false, absurd, or distorted representation of something: *the absurdly lenient sentence is **a travesty of** justice.*
▶ **verb** (**-ies**, **-ied**) [with obj.] represent in such a way: *Michael has betrayed the family by travestying them in his plays.*
– ORIGIN mid 17th cent. (as an adjective in the sense 'dressed to appear ridiculous'): from French *travesti* 'disguised', past participle of *travestir*, from Italian *travestire*, from *trans-* 'across' + *vestire* 'clothe'.

travois /trəˈvɔɪ/ ▶ **noun** (pl. same /-ˈvɔɪz/) a type of sledge formerly used by North American Indians to carry goods, consisting of two joined poles pulled by a horse.
– ORIGIN mid 19th cent.: alteration of synonymous *travail*, from French.

travolator ▶ **noun** variant spelling of **TRAVELATOR**.

trawl ▶ **verb** [no obj.] fish with a trawl net or seine: *the boats **trawled for** flounder* | [as noun **trawling**] *restrictions on excessive trawling were urgently needed.*
■ [with obj.] catch with a trawl or seine. ■ search thoroughly: *the Home Office **trawled through** twenty-five-year-old confidential files* | [with obj.] *he trawled his memory and remembered locking the door.* ■ [with obj.] drag or trail (something) through water or other liquid: *she trawled a toe to test the temperature.*
▶ **noun 1** an act of fishing with a trawl net or seine: *they had caught two trout on the lazy trawl up-lake.*
■ a thorough search: *a constant **trawl for** information.*
2 (also **trawl net**) a large wide-mouthed fishing net dragged by a boat along the bottom of the sea or a lake.
3 (also **trawl line**) N. Amer. a long sea-fishing line along which are tied buoys supporting baited hooks on short lines.
– ORIGIN mid 16th cent. (as a verb): probably from Middle Dutch *traghelen* 'to drag' (related to *traghel* 'dragnet'), perhaps from Latin *tragula* 'dragnet'.

trawler ▶ **noun** a fishing boat used for trawling.

tray ▶ **noun** a flat, shallow container with a raised rim, typically used for carrying food and drink, or for holding small items or loose material.
– DERIVATIVES **trayful** noun (pl. **-fuls**).
– ORIGIN late Old English *trīg*, from the Germanic base of **TREE**; the primary sense may have been 'wooden container'.

trayf /treɪf/ ▶ **adjective** another term for **TREFA**.

treacherous ▶ **adjective** guilty of or involving betrayal or deception: *a treacherous Gestapo agent* | *memory is particularly treacherous.*
■ (of ground, water, conditions, etc.) hazardous because of presenting hidden or unpredictable dangers: *a holidaymaker was swept away by treacherous currents.*
– DERIVATIVES **treacherously** adverb, **treacherousness** noun.
– ORIGIN Middle English (in the sense 'involving betrayal'): from Old French *trecherous*, from *trecheor* 'a cheat', from *trechier* 'to cheat'.

treachery ▶ **noun** (pl. **-ies**) [mass noun] betrayal of trust; deceptive action or nature: *his resignation was perceived as an act of treachery* | *the treachery of language* | [count noun] *his distaste for plots and treacheries.*
– ORIGIN Middle English: from Old French *trecherie*, from *trechier* 'to cheat'.

treacle ▶ **noun** [mass noun] chiefly Brit. a thick, sticky dark syrup made from partly refined sugar; molasses.
■ a paler sweeter version of such a syrup; golden syrup.
– DERIVATIVES **treacly** adjective.
– ORIGIN Middle English (originally denoting an antidote against venom): from Old French *triacle*, via Latin from Greek *thēriakē* 'antidote against venom', feminine of *thēriakos* (adjective), from *thērion* 'wild beast'. Current senses date from the late 17th cent.

tread ▶ **verb** (past **trod**; past participle **trodden** or **trod**) [no obj., with adverbial] walk in a specified way: *he trod lightly, trying to make as little contact with the mud as possible* | figurative *the government had to **tread carefully** so as not to offend the judiciary.*
■ (**tread on**) set one's foot down on top of. ■ [with obj.] walk on or along: *shoppers will soon be treading the floors of the new shopping mall.* ■ [with obj. and adverbial] press down into the ground or another surface with the feet: *food and cigarette butts had been **trodden into** the carpet.* ■ [with obj.] crush or flatten something with the feet: *the snow had been **trodden down** by the horses* | [as adj. **trodden**] figurative *the conscientious are **trodden down** into conformity.*
▶ **noun 1** [in sing.] a manner or the sound of someone walking: *I heard the heavy tread of Dad's boots.*
2 (also **tread board**) the top surface of a step or stair.
3 the thick moulded part of a vehicle tyre that grips the road.
■ the part of a wheel that touches the ground or rail. ■ the upper surface of a railway track, in contact with the wheels. ■ the part of the sole of a shoe that rests on the ground.
– PHRASES **tread the boards** (or **stage**) see **BOARD**. **tread on air** see **AIR**. **tread** (or **step**) **on someone's toes** offend someone by encroaching on their area of responsibility. **tread water** maintain an upright position in deep water by moving the feet with a walking movement and the hands with a downward circular motion. ■ figurative fail to advance or make progress: *men who are treading water in their careers.*
– DERIVATIVES **treader** noun.
– ORIGIN Old English *tredan* (as a verb), of West Germanic origin; related to Dutch *treden* and German *treten*.

treadle /ˈtrɛd(ə)l/ ▶ **noun** a lever worked by the foot and imparting motion to a machine.
▶ **verb** [with obj.] operate (a machine) using a treadle.
– ORIGIN Old English *tredel* 'stair, step' (see **TREAD**).

treadmill ▶ **noun** a device formerly used for driving machinery, consisting of a large wheel with steps fitted into its inner surface. It was turned by the weight of people or animals treading the steps.
■ a similar device used today for exercise. ■ figurative a job or situation that is tiring, boring, or unpleasant and from which it is hard to escape: *the soulless treadmill of urban existence.*

treadwheel ▶ **noun** another term for **TREADMILL**.

treason ▶ **noun** (also **high treason**) [mass noun] the crime of betraying one's country, especially by attempting to kill or overthrow the sovereign or government: *they were convicted of treason.*
■ the action of betraying someone or something: *doubt is the ultimate treason against faith.* ■ (**petty treason**) historical the crime of murdering someone to whom the murderer owed allegiance, such as a master or husband.
– DERIVATIVES **treasonous** adjective.
– ORIGIN Middle English: from Anglo-Norman French *treisoun*, from Latin *traditio(n-)* 'handing over', from the verb *tradere*.

USAGE Formerly, there were two types of crime to which the term **treason** was applied: **petty treason**, the crime of murdering one's master, and **high treason**, the crime of betraying one's country. The crime of **petty treason** was abolished in 1828 and in modern use the term **high treason** is now often simply called **treason**.

treasonable ▶ **adjective** (of an offence or offender) punishable as treason or as committing treason: *there was no evidence of treasonable activity.*
– DERIVATIVES **treasonably** adverb.

treasure ▶ **noun 1** [mass noun] a quantity of precious metals, gems, or other valuable objects.
■ [count noun] a very valuable object: *she set out to look at the art treasures.* ■ [count noun] informal a person whom the speaker loves or who is valued for the assistance they can give: *the housekeeper is a real treasure—I don't know what he would do without her.*
▶ **verb** [with obj.] keep carefully (a valuable or valued item).
■ value highly: *the island is treasured by walkers and conservationists* | [as adj. **treasured**] *his library was his most treasured possession.*
– ORIGIN Middle English: from Old French *tresor*, based on Greek *thēsauros* (see **THESAURUS**).

treasure hunt ▶ **noun** a search for treasure.
■ a game in which players search for hidden objects by following a trail of clues.

treasurer ▶ **noun** a person appointed to administer or manage the financial assets and liabilities of a society, company, local authority, or other body.
■ Austral. the minister of finance. ■ (also **Lord Treasurer** or **Lord High Treasurer**) Brit. historical the head of the Exchequer.
– DERIVATIVES **treasurership** noun.
– ORIGIN Middle English: from Old French *tresorier*, from *tresor* (see **TREASURE**), influenced by late Latin *thesaurarius*.

Treasure State informal name for **MONTANA**[1].

treasure trove ▶ **noun** [mass noun] English Law (abolished in 1996) valuables of unknown ownership that are found hidden and declared the property of the Crown.
■ [count noun] a hidden store of valuable or delightful things: *your book is a treasure trove of unspeakable delights.*
– ORIGIN late Middle English: from Anglo-Norman French *tresor trové*, literally 'found treasure'.

treasury ▶ **noun** (pl. **-ies**) **1** the funds or revenue of a state, institution, or society: *the landowners' estates and assets were seized for the imperial treasury.*
■ (**Treasury**) (in some countries) the government department responsible for budgeting for and controlling public expenditure, management of the national debt, and the overall management of the economy.
2 a place or building where treasure is stored.
■ a store or collection of valuable or delightful things: *the old town is a treasury of ancient monuments.*
– ORIGIN Middle English: from Old French *tresorie* (see **TREASURE**).

Treasury bench ▶ **noun** (**the Treasury bench**) (in the UK) the front bench in the House of Commons occupied by the Prime Minister, the Chancellor of the Exchequer, and other members of the government.

Treasury bill ▶ **noun** a short-dated UK or US government security, yielding no interest but issued at a discount on its redemption price.

Treasury bond ▶ **noun** a government bond issued by the Treasury.

Treasury note ▶ **noun** US & historical a note issued by the Treasury for use as currency.

treat ▶ **verb** [with obj.] **1** behave towards or deal with in a certain way: *she had been brutally treated* | *he treated her with grave courtesy.*
■ (**treat something as**) regard something as being of a specified nature with implications for one's actions concerning it: *the names are being treated as classified information.* ■ give medical care or attention to; try to heal or cure: *the two were **treated for** cuts and bruises.* ■ apply a process or a substance to (something) to protect or preserve it or to give it particular properties: *linen creases badly unless it is **treated with** the appropriate finish.* ■ present or discuss (a subject): *the lectures show a striking variation in the level at which subjects are treated.*
2 (**treat someone to**) provide someone with (food, drink, or entertainment) at one's own expense: *he treated her to a slap-up lunch.*
■ give someone (something) as a favour: *he treated her to one of his smiles.* ■ (**treat oneself**) do or have something that gives one great pleasure: *treat yourself—you can diet tomorrow.*
3 [no obj.] negotiate terms with someone, especially an opponent: *propagandists claimed that he was **treating with** the enemy.*
▶ **noun** an event or item that is out of the ordinary and gives great pleasure: *he wanted to take her to the pictures as a treat.*
■ used with a possessive determiner to indicate that the person specified is paying for food, entertainment, etc., for someone else: *'My treat,' he insisted, reaching for the bill.*
– PHRASES —— **a treat** Brit. informal used to indicate that someone or something does something specified very well or satisfactorily: *their tactics worked a treat.* ■ used to indicate that someone is looking attractive: *I don't know whether she can act, but she **looks a treat**.*
– DERIVATIVES **treatable** adjective, **treater** noun.
– ORIGIN Middle English (in the senses 'negotiate' and 'discuss (a subject)'): from Old French *traitier*, from Latin *tractare* 'handle', frequentative of *trahere* 'draw, pull'. The current noun sense dates from the mid 17th cent.

treatise /ˈtriːtɪs, -ɪz/ ▶ **noun** a written work dealing

t

formally and systematically with a subject: *his treatise on Scottish political theory.*
– ORIGIN late Middle English: from Anglo-Norman French *tretis,* from Old French *traitier* (see **TREAT**).

treatment ▶ noun [mass noun] the manner in which someone behaves towards or deals with someone or something: *the directive required equal treatment for men and women in social security schemes.*
 ■ medical care given to a patient for an illness or injury: *I'm receiving treatment for an injured shoulder.* ■ [count noun] a session of medical care or the administration of a dose of medicine: *the patient was given repeated treatments as required.* ■ the use of a chemical, physical, or biological agent to preserve or give particular properties to something: *the treatment of hazardous waste is particularly expensive.* ■ the presentation or discussion of a subject: *comparison with earlier artists is useful in analysis of the treatment of women in her painting.* ■ **(the full treatment)** informal used to indicate that something is done enthusiastically, vigorously, or to an extreme degree: *a bit of soft shoe shuffle got the full treatment.*

treaty ▶ noun (pl. **-ies**) a formally concluded and ratified agreement between states.
– ORIGIN late Middle English: from Old French *traite,* from Latin *tractatus* 'treatise' (see **TRACTATE**).

treaty Indian ▶ noun chiefly Canadian a North American Indian whose people have signed a treaty with the government.

Treaty of Rome, Treaty of Versailles, etc. see **ROME, TREATY OF; VERSAILLES, TREATY OF,** etc.

treaty port ▶ noun historical a port bound by treaty to be open to foreign trade, especially in 19th and early 20th-century China and Japan.

Trebbiano /ˌtrɛbɪˈɑːnəʊ/ ▶ noun [mass noun] a variety of wine grape widely cultivated in Italy and elsewhere.
 ■ a wine made from this grape.
– ORIGIN Italian, from the name of the River *Trebbia,* in northern central Italy.

Trebizond /ˈtrɛbɪzɒnd/ another name for **TRABZON**.

treble[1] ▶ adjective [attrib.] consisting of three parts; threefold: *the fish were caught with large treble hooks dragged through the water.*
 ■ multiplied or occurring three times: *she turned back to make a double and treble check.* ■ used to indicate that a number occurs three times in succession: *call Kate on 0500 403 treble zero.*
▶ predeterminer three times as much or as many: *the tip was at least treble what she would normally have given.*
▶ noun **1** Brit. three sporting victories or championships in the same season, event, etc.: *the victory completed a treble for the horse's trainer.*
 2 Darts a hit on the narrow ring enclosed by the two middle circles of a dartboard, scoring treble.
 3 Brit. a system of betting in which the winnings and stake from the first bet are transferred to a second and then (if successful) to a third.
 4 a threefold quantity or thing, in particular:
 ■ (in showjumping) a fence consisting of three elements. ■ a crochet stitch made with three loops of wool on the hook at a time. ■ a drink of spirits of three times the standard measure.
▶ pronoun a number or amount which is three times as large as a contrasting or usual number or amount: *by virtue of having paid treble, he had a double room to himself.*
▶ verb make or become three times as large or numerous: [with obj.] *rents were doubled and probably trebled* | [no obj.] *his salary has trebled in a couple of years.*
– ORIGIN Middle English: via Old French from Latin *triplus* (see **TRIPLE**).

treble[2] ▶ noun a high-pitched voice, especially a boy's singing voice.
 ■ a boy (or girl) with such a singing voice. ■ a part written for a high voice or an instrument of a high pitch. ■ [as modifier] denoting a relatively high-pitched member of a family of similar instruments: *a treble viol.* ■ (also **treble bell**) the smallest and highest-pitched bell of a ring or set. ■ [mass noun] the high-frequency output of a radio, or audio system, corresponding to the treble in music.
– ORIGIN late Middle English: from **TREBLE**[1], because it was the highest part in a three-part contrapuntal composition.

treble chance ▶ noun [mass noun] Brit. a form of football pool in which different numbers of points are awarded for a draw, an away win, and a home win.

treble clef ▶ noun a clef placing G above middle C on the second-lowest line of the stave.

Treblinka /trɛˈblɪŋkə/ a Nazi concentration camp in Poland in the Second World War, where a great many of the Jews of the Warsaw ghetto were murdered.

trebly ▶ adjective (of sound, especially recorded music) having too much treble; tinny.
▶ adverb [as submodifier] three times as much: *to Katherine, the house was trebly impressive.*

trebuchet /ˈtrɛbjʊʃɛt, -bəʃɛt/ ▶ noun a machine used in medieval siege warfare for hurling large stones or other missiles.
– ORIGIN Middle English: from Old French, from *trebucher* 'overthrow'.

trecento /treɪˈtʃɛntəʊ/ ▶ noun (**the trecento**) the 14th century as a period of Italian art, architecture, or literature.
– ORIGIN Italian, literally '300', shortened from *milletrecento* '1300', used with reference to the years 1300–99.

tree ➤ noun **1** a woody perennial plant, typically having a single stem or trunk growing to a considerable height and bearing lateral branches at some distance from the ground. Compare with **SHRUB**[1].
 ■ (in general use) any bush, shrub, or herbaceous plant with a tall erect stem, e.g. a banana plant.
 2 a wooden structure or part of a structure.
 ■ archaic or poetic/literary the cross on which Christ was crucified. ■ archaic a gibbet.
 3 a thing that has a branching structure resembling that of a tree.
 ■ (also **tree diagram**) a diagram with a structure of branching connecting lines, representing different processes and relationships.
▶ verb (**trees, treed, treeing**) [with obj.] N. Amer. force (a hunted animal) to take refuge in a tree.
 ■ informal, chiefly US force (someone) into a difficult situation.
– PHRASES **out of one's tree** informal, chiefly N. Amer. completely stupid; mad. **up a tree** informal, chiefly N. Amer. in a difficult situation without escape; cornered.
– DERIVATIVES **treeless** adjective, **treelessness** noun, **tree-like** adjective.
– ORIGIN Old English *trēow, trēo*: from a Germanic variant of an Indo-European root shared by Greek *doru* 'wood, spear', *drus* 'oak'.

tree calf ▶ noun [mass noun] calfskin stained with a tree-like design and used in bookbinding.

treecreeper ▶ noun a small songbird with drab plumage and a downcurved bill, which creeps about on the trunks of trees to search for insects. Compare with **CREEPER** (in sense 2).
 ■ a Eurasian and North American bird (*Certhia,* family Certhiidae, in particular the common *C. familiaris*). ■ an Australasian bird (family Climacteridae and genus *Climacteris*).

tree diagram ▶ noun see **TREE** (sense 3).

tree duck ▶ noun another term for **WHISTLING DUCK**.

tree fern ▶ noun a large palm-like fern with a trunk-like stem bearing a crown of large fronds, sometimes reaching a height of 24 m and occurring chiefly in the tropics, particularly the southern hemisphere.
 ● Cyatheaceae and related families, class Filicopsida: seven genera, in particular *Cyathea* and *Dicksonia.*

tree frog ▶ noun an arboreal frog that has long toes with adhesive disks and is typically small and brightly coloured.
 ● Families Hylidae (of Eurasia, America, and Australia) and Rhacophoridae (of Africa and Asia): numerous species, including the common **green tree frog** (*Hyla arborea*) of southern Europe.

tree heath ▶ noun a white-flowered shrub or tree of the heather family, with woody nodules that are used to make briar pipes. It is native to southern Europe and parts of Africa. Also called **BRIAR**[2].
 ● *Erica arborea,* family Ericaceae.

treehopper ▶ noun a tree-dwelling jumping bug that lives chiefly in the tropics. A tall backward-curving projection of the thorax gives the bug a thorn-like appearance for camouflage.
 ● Family Membracidae, suborder Homoptera: many species, including the bright green **buffalo treehopper** (*Stictocephalus bisonia*) of North America.

tree house ▶ noun a structure built in the branches of a tree for children to play in.

tree-hugger ▶ noun informal, chiefly derogatory an environmental campaigner (used in reference to

the practice of embracing a tree in an attempt to prevent it from being felled).
– DERIVATIVES **tree-hugging** noun.

tree kangaroo ▶ noun an agile tree-climbing kangaroo with a long furred tail, and fore- and hindlimbs that are of almost equal length, found in the rainforests of Queensland and New Guinea.
 ● Genus *Dendrolagus,* family Macropodidae: six species.

treeline ▶ noun (on a mountain) the line or altitude above which no trees grow.
 ■ (in high northern (or southern) latitudes) the line north (or south) of which no trees grow.

tree lupin ▶ noun a shrubby yellow-flowered Californian lupin, widely planted to reclaim sandy land.
 ● *Lupinus arboreus,* family Leguminosae.

tree mallow ▶ noun a tall woody-stemmed European mallow of coastal regions.
 ● *Lavatera arborea,* family Malvaceae.

treen ▶ noun [treated as pl.] small domestic wooden objects, especially antiques.
▶ adjective chiefly archaic wooden: *a fine treen sycamore dairy bowl.*
– ORIGIN Old English *trēowen* 'wooden' (see **TREE, -EN**[2]).

treenail (also **trenail** or US **trunnel**) ▶ noun a hard wooden pin used for fastening timbers together.

tree of heaven ▶ noun a fast-growing Chinese ailanthus which is widely cultivated as an ornamental.
 ● *Ailanthus altissima,* family Simaroubaceae.

tree of knowledge (also **tree of knowledge of good and evil**) ▶ noun (in the Bible) the tree in the Garden of Eden bearing the forbidden fruit which Adam and Eve disobediently ate (Gen. 2:9, 3).

tree of life ▶ noun **1** (Tree of Life) (in the Bible) a tree in the Garden of Eden whose fruit imparts eternal life (Gen. 3:22–24).
 ■ an imaginary branching, tree-like structure representing the evolutionary divergence of all living creatures. ■ (in the Kabbalah) a diagram in the form of a tree bearing spheres which represent the sephiroth.
 2 the thuja or arbor vitae.

tree pie ▶ noun a long-tailed tree-dwelling Asian crow, with blackish or brown and grey plumage.
 ● Family Corvidae: three genera, in particular *Dendrocitta,* and several species.
– ORIGIN late 19th cent.: *pie* from **PIE**[2].

tree pipit ▶ noun a widespread Old World pipit which inhabits open country with scattered trees.
 ● *Anthus trivialis,* family Motacillidae.

tree ring ▶ noun each of a number of concentric rings in the cross section of a tree trunk, representing a single year's growth.

tree shrew ▶ noun a small squirrel-like insectivorous mammal with a pointed snout, native to SE Asia, especially Borneo.
 ● Family Tupaiidae and order Scandentia: several genera, in particular *Tupaia;* tree shrews were formerly placed with either the insectivores or the primates.

tree snake ▶ noun a harmless arboreal snake, typically very slender and able to mimic a twig.
 ● Several genera in the family Colubridae, e.g. *Dendrelaphis* and *Ahaetulla* (of Asia), and *Leptophis* and *Oxybelis* (of America).

tree sparrow ▶ noun **1** a Eurasian sparrow with a chocolate brown cap in both sexes, inhabiting agricultural land.
 ● *Passer montanus,* family Passeridae (or Ploceidae).
 2 N. Amer. a migratory sparrow-like songbird of the bunting family, breeding on the edge of the North American tundra.
 ● *Spizella arborea,* family Emberizidae (subfamily Emberizinae).

tree squirrel ▶ noun an arboreal squirrel that is typically active in daylight and does not hibernate.
 ● *Sciurus* and other genera, family Sciuridae: numerous species.

tree structure ▶ noun Computing a structure in which there are successive branchings or subdivisions.

tree surgeon ▶ noun a person who prunes and treats old or damaged trees in order to preserve them.
– DERIVATIVES **tree surgery** noun.

tree toad ▶ noun another term for **TREE FROG**.

tree tomato ▶ noun another term for **TAMARILLO**.

treetop ▶ noun (usu. **treetops**) the uppermost part of a tree.

tree trunk ▶ noun the main woody stem of a tree, from which its branches grow.

trefa /ˈtreɪfə/ (also **trifa** or **trayf**) ▶ adjective (of food) not satisfying the requirements of Jewish law.
– ORIGIN mid 19th cent.: from Hebrew *ṭᵉrēp̄āh* 'the flesh of an animal torn or mauled', from *ṭārap* 'rend'.

trefid /ˈtrɛfɪd/ ▶ adjective variant spelling of **TRIFID** (in sense 2).

trefoil /ˈtrɛfɔɪl, ˈtriːfɔɪl/ ▶ noun a small European plant of the pea family, with yellow flowers and three-lobed cloverlike leaves.
• Genera *Trifolium* and *Lotus*, family Leguminosae: several species, in particular the **bird's-foot trefoil**.
■ a similar or related plant with three-lobed leaves. ■ an ornamental design of three rounded lobes like a clover leaf, used typically in architectural tracery. ■ a thing having three parts; a set of three: *a trefoil of parachutes lowers the shuttle's used rockets to Earth.* ■ [as modifier] denoting something shaped in the form of a trefoil leaf: *trefoil windows.*
– DERIVATIVES **trefoiled** adjective.
– ORIGIN Middle English: from Anglo-Norman French *trifoil*, from Latin *trifolium*, from *tri-* 'three' + *folium* 'leaf'.

trehalose /ˈtriːhələʊs, trɪˈhɑːləʊs, -z/ ▶ noun [mass noun] Chemistry a sugar of the disaccharide class produced by some fungi, yeasts, and similar organisms.
– ORIGIN mid 19th cent.: from *trehala* (from Turkish, denoting a sweet substance derived from insect cocoons) + **-OSE**[2].

trek ▶ noun **1** a long arduous journey, especially one made on foot: *a trek to the South Pole.*
■ (**the Trek**) S. African see **GREAT TREK**. ■ S. African a leg or stage of a journey.
2 [mass noun] S. African informal a person's possessions: *I was at the new flat waiting for my trek to arrive.*
3 S. African a haul of fish caught using a trek net.
▶ verb (**trekked**, **trekking**) **1** [no obj., with adverbial of direction] go on a long arduous journey, typically on foot: *we trekked through the jungle.*
■ historical, chiefly S. African migrate or journey with one's belongings by ox-wagon. ■ [no obj., usu. in imperative] S. African (of an ox) draw a vehicle or pull a load. ■ S. African travel constantly from place to place; lead a nomadic life: *my plan is to trek about seeing the world.*
2 [no obj.] S. African fish using a trek net.
– DERIVATIVES **trekker** noun.
– ORIGIN mid 19th cent.: from South African Dutch *trek* (noun), *trekken* (verb) 'pull, travel'.

Trekkie ▶ noun (pl. **-ies**) informal a fan of the US science-fiction television programme *Star Trek*.

trek net ▶ noun S. African a large fishing net, weighted at one end and fitted with floats on the other so that it hangs vertically in the water, usually dropped from a boat and hauled in from the shore.

trellis ▶ noun (also **trelliswork**) [mass noun] a framework of light wooden or metal bars, chiefly used as a support for fruit trees or creepers, typically fastened against a wall.
▶ verb (**trellised**, **trellising**) [with obj.] [usu. as adj. **trellised**] provide with or enclose in a trellis: *a trellised archway.*
■ support (a climbing plant) with a trellis.
– ORIGIN late Middle English (denoting any latticed screen): from Old French *trelis*, from Latin *trilix* 'three-ply', from *tri-* 'three' + *licium* 'warp thread'. Current senses date from the early 16th cent.

trem (also **trem arm**) ▶ noun informal a tremolo arm.

Trematoda /ˌtrɛməˈtəʊdə/ Zoology a class of flatworms that comprises those flukes that are internal parasites. The monogenean flukes are sometimes also placed in this class. See **FLUKE**[2] (sense 1) and **DIGENEAN**.
– DERIVATIVES **trematode** /ˈtrɛmətəʊd/ noun.
– ORIGIN modern Latin (plural), from Greek *trēmatōdēs* 'perforated', from *trēma* 'hole'.

tremble ▶ verb [no obj.] shake involuntarily, typically as a result of anxiety, excitement, or frailty: *Isobel was trembling with excitement.*
■ be in a state of extreme apprehension: [with infinitive] *I tremble to think that we could ever return to conditions like these.* ■ [usu. as adj. **trembling**] (of a person's voice) sound unsteady or hesitant. ■ shake or quiver slightly: *the earth trembled beneath their feet.*
▶ noun **1** a trembling feeling, movement, or sound: *there was a slight tremble in his voice.*
2 (**the trembles**) informal a physical or emotional condition marked by trembling.
■ another term for **MILK-SICKNESS**.
– PHRASES **all of a tremble** informal extremely agitated or excited.
– DERIVATIVES **tremblingly** adverb.
– ORIGIN Middle English (as a verb): from Old French *trembler*, from medieval Latin *tremulare*, from Latin *tremulus* (see **TREMULOUS**).

trembler ▶ noun **1** Brit. an automatic vibrator for making and breaking an electric circuit, typically used as a fuse for an explosive device sensitive to physical disturbance.
2 a songbird related to the thrashers, found in the Lesser Antilles and named from its habit of violent shaking.
• Genera *Cinclocerthia* and *Ramphocinclus*, family Mimidae: three species.
3 informal an earthquake.

trembling poplar ▶ noun the European aspen.

tremblor /ˈtrɛmblɔː/ ▶ noun US an earth tremor.
– ORIGIN early 20th cent.: alteration of Spanish *temblor* 'shudder', influenced by **TREMBLER**.

trembly ▶ adjective (**tremblier**, **trembliest**) informal shaking or quivering involuntarily: *her eyes were tearful, her hands trembly | she gave a queer trembly laugh.*

tremendous ▶ adjective very great in amount, scale, or intensity: *Penny put in a tremendous amount of time | there was a tremendous explosion.*
■ informal extremely good or impressive; excellent: *the crew did a tremendous job.*
– DERIVATIVES **tremendously** adverb, **tremendousness** noun.
– ORIGIN mid 17th cent.: from Latin *tremendus* (gerundive of *tremere* 'tremble') + **-OUS**.

tremolando /ˌtrɛməˈlandəʊ/ Music ▶ noun (pl. **tremolandi**) another term for **TREMOLO**.
▶ adverb & adjective (especially as a direction) with tremolo.
– ORIGIN Italian, literally 'trembling'.

tremolite /ˈtrɛm(ə)lʌɪt/ ▶ noun [mass noun] a white to grey amphibole mineral which occurs widely in igneous rocks and is characteristic of metamorphosed dolomitic limestones.
– ORIGIN late 18th cent.: from *Tremola* Valley, Switzerland, + **-ITE**[1].

tremolo ▶ noun (pl. **-os**) Music a wavering effect in a musical tone, produced either by rapid reiteration of a note, by rapid repeated slight variation in the pitch of a note, or by sounding two notes of slightly different pitches to produce prominent overtones. Compare with **VIBRATO**.
■ a mechanism in an organ producing such an effect. ■ (also **tremolo arm**) a lever on an electric guitar, used to produce such an effect.
– ORIGIN mid 18th cent.: from Italian.

tremor ▶ noun an involuntary quivering movement: *a disorder that causes tremors and muscle rigidity.*
■ (also **earth tremor**) a slight earthquake. ■ a sudden feeling of fear or excitement: *a tremor of unease.* ■ a tremble or quaver in a person's voice.
▶ verb [no obj.] undergo a tremor or tremors: *a muscle in my jaw tremored uncontrollably.*
– ORIGIN early 17th cent.: from Latin *tremor*, from *tremere* 'to tremble'.

tremulous /ˈtrɛmjʊləs/ ▶ adjective shaking or quivering slightly: *Barbara's voice was tremulous.*
■ timid; nervous: *he gave a tremulous smile.*
– DERIVATIVES **tremulously** adverb, **tremulousness** noun.
– ORIGIN early 17th cent.: from Latin *tremulus* (from *tremere* 'tremble') + **-OUS**.

trenail ▶ noun variant spelling of **TREENAIL**.

trench ▶ noun a long, narrow ditch.
■ such a ditch dug by troops to provide a place of shelter from enemy fire. ■ (**trenches**) a connected system of such ditches forming an army's line. ■ (**the trenches**) the battlefields of northern France and Belgium in the First World War: *the slaughter in the trenches created a new cynicism.* ■ (also **ocean trench**) a long, narrow, deep depression in the ocean bed, typically one running parallel to a plate boundary and marking a subduction zone. ■ a trench coat.
▶ verb **1** [with obj.] dig a trench or trenches in (the ground): *she trenched the terrace to a depth of 6 feet.*
■ turn over the earth of (a field or garden) by digging a succession of adjoining ditches.
2 [no obj.] (**trench on/upon**) archaic border closely on; encroach upon: *this would surely trench very far on the dignity and liberty of citizens.*
– ORIGIN late Middle English (in the senses 'track cut through a wood' and 'sever by cutting'): from Old French *trenche* (noun), *trenchier* (verb), based on Latin *truncare* (see **TRUNCATE**).

trenchant /ˈtrɛn(t)ʃ(ə)nt/ ▶ adjective **1** vigorous or incisive in expression or style: *the White Paper makes trenchant criticisms of health authorities.*
2 archaic or poetic/literary (of a weapon or tool) having a sharp edge: *a trenchant blade.*
– DERIVATIVES **trenchancy** noun (only in sense 1), **trenchantly** adverb (only in sense 1).
– ORIGIN Middle English (in sense 2): from Old French, literally 'cutting', present participle of *trenchier* (see **TRENCH**).

Trenchard /ˈtrɛnʃɑːd/, Hugh Montague, 1st Viscount of Wolfeton (1873–1956), British Marshal of the RAF. As chief of staff (1918) then First Marshal (1927) of the RAF he developed the force as a major element in the British armed services.

trench coat ▶ noun a loose belted, double-breasted raincoat in a military style.
■ a lined or padded waterproof coat worn by soldiers.

trench digging ▶ noun another term for **DOUBLE DIGGING**.

trencher[1] ▶ noun **1** historical a wooden plate or platter for food.
■ a thick slice of bread used as a plate or platter.
2 old-fashioned term for **MORTAR BOARD** (in sense 1).
– ORIGIN Middle English: from Anglo-Norman French *trenchour*, from Old French *trenchier* 'to cut' (see **TRENCH**).

trencher[2] ▶ noun a machine or attachment used in digging trenches.

trencherman ▶ noun (pl. **-men**) [usu. with adj.] humorous a person who eats in a specified manner, typically heartily: *a doughty trencherman who gives the Simpson's beef trolley a good run for its money.*

trench fever ▶ noun [mass noun] a highly contagious rickettsial disease transmitted by lice, that infested soldiers in the trenches in the First World War.

trench foot ▶ noun [mass noun] a painful condition of the feet caused by long immersion in cold water or mud and marked by blackening and death of surface tissue.

trench mortar ▶ noun a light simple mortar designed to propel a bomb into enemy trenches.

trench mouth ▶ noun [mass noun] ulcerative gingivitis.

trench warfare ▶ noun [mass noun] a type of combat in which opposing troops fight from trenches facing each other.

trend ▶ noun a general direction in which something is developing or changing: *an upward trend in sales and profit margins.*
■ a fashion: *the latest trends in modern dance.*
▶ verb [no obj., with adverbial of direction] (especially of geographical features) bend or turn away in a specified direction: *the Richelieu River trending southward to Lake Champlain.*
■ chiefly N. Amer. change or develop in a general direction: *unemployment has been trending upwards.*
– ORIGIN Old English *trendan* 'revolve, rotate', of Germanic origin; compare with **TRUNDLE**. The verb sense 'turn in a specified direction' dates from the late 16th cent., and gave rise to the figurative use 'assume a general tendency' in the mid 19th cent., a development paralleled in the noun.

Trendelenburg position /trɛnˈdɛlənbəːg/ ▶ noun a position, used for pelvic surgery and to treat shock, in which a patient lies face upwards on a tilted table or bed with the pelvis higher than the head.
– ORIGIN late 19th cent.: named after Friedrich *Trendelenburg* (1844–1924), German surgeon.

trendify ▶ verb [with obj.] informal, chiefly derogatory make (something or someone) very fashionable or up to date in style or influence: *the cafe has been trendified to look like a wine bar.*

trend line ▶ noun a line indicating the general course or tendency of something, e.g. a geographical feature or a set of points on a graph.

trendoid informal ▶ noun a person who follows fashion blindly or excessively.
▶ adjective following fashion blindly or extravagantly.

trendsetter ▶ **noun** a person who leads the way in fashion or ideas.
– DERIVATIVES **trendsetting** adjective.

trendy informal ▶ **adjective** (**trendier**, **trendiest**) very fashionable or up to date in style or influence: *I enjoyed being able to go out and buy trendy clothes.*
▶ **noun** (pl. **-ies**) a person who is very fashionable or up to date.
– DERIVATIVES **trendily** adverb, **trendiness** noun.

Trengganu /trɛŋ'gɑːnuː/ (also **Terengganu**) a state of Malaysia, on the east coast of the Malay Peninsula; capital, Kuala Trengganu.

Trent the chief river of central England, which rises in Staffordshire and flows 275 km (170 miles) generally north-eastwards, uniting with the River Ouse 25 km (15 miles) west of Hull to form the Humber estuary.

Trent, Council of an ecumenical council of the Roman Catholic Church, held in three sessions between 1545 and 1563 in Trento. Prompted by the opposition of the Reformation, the council clarified and redefined the Church's doctrine, abolished many ecclesiastical abuses, and strengthened the authority of the papacy. These measures provided the Church with a solid foundation for the Counter-Reformation.

trente et quarante /ˌtrɒteɪkaˈrɒt, French trɑ̃tekarɑ̃t/ ▶ **noun** [mass noun] a gambling game in which cards are turned up on a table marked with red and black diamonds.
– ORIGIN French, literally 'thirty and forty', these being winning and losing numbers respectively in the game.

Trentino-Alto Adige /trɛnˌtiːnəʊ ˌaltəʊ ˈadɪdʒeɪ/ a region of NE Italy; capital, Bolzano. Situated on the border with Austria, it includes the Dolomites.

Trento /ˈtrɛntəʊ/ a city on the Adige River in northern Italy; pop. 102,120 (1990).

Trenton /ˈtrɛnt(ə)n/ the state capital of New Jersey; pop. 88,675 (1990).

trepan /trɪˈpan/ ▶ **noun** **1** chiefly historical a trephine (crown saw) used by surgeons for perforating the skull.
2 a borer for sinking shafts.
▶ **verb** (**trepanned**, **trepanning**) [with obj.] perforate (a person's skull) with a trepan.
– DERIVATIVES **trepanation** /ˌtrɛpəˈneɪʃ(ə)n/ noun.
– ORIGIN late Middle English: the noun via medieval Latin from Greek *trupanon*, from *trupan* 'to bore', from *trupē* 'hole'; the verb from Old French *trepaner*.

trepang /trɪˈpaŋ/ ▶ **noun** another term for **BÊCHE-DE-MER** (in sense 1).
– ORIGIN late 18th cent.: from Malay *teripang*.

trephine /trɪˈfʌɪn, -ˈfiːn/ ▶ **noun** a crown saw used in surgery to remove a circle of tissue or bone.
▶ **verb** [with obj.] operate on with a trephine.
– DERIVATIVES **trephination** /ˌtrɛfɪˈneɪʃ(ə)n/ noun.
– ORIGIN early 17th cent.: from Latin *tres fines* 'three ends', apparently influenced by **TREPAN**.

trepidation ▶ **noun** [mass noun] **1** a feeling of fear or agitation about something that may happen: *the men set off in fear and trepidation.*
2 archaic trembling motion.
– ORIGIN late 15th cent.: from Latin *trepidatio(n-)*, from *trepidare* 'be agitated, tremble', from *trepidus* 'alarmed'.

treponeme /ˈtrɛpəniːm/ (also **treponema** /-ə/) ▶ **noun** a spirochaete bacterium that is parasitic or pathogenic in humans and warm-blooded animals, including the causal agents of syphilis and yaws.
• Genus *Treponema*, order Spirochaetales; Gram-negative.
– DERIVATIVES **treponemal** adjective.
– ORIGIN early 20th cent.: from modern Latin *Treponema*, from Greek *trepein* 'to turn' + *nēma* 'thread'.

trespass ▶ **verb** [no obj.] **1** enter someone's land or property without their permission: *there is no excuse for* **trespassing on** *railway property.*
■ (**trespass on**) make unfair claims on or take advantage of (something): *she really must not trespass on his hospitality.*
2 (**trespass against**) archaic or poetic/literary commit an offence against (a person or a set of rules): *a man who had trespassed against Judaic law.*
▶ **noun** **1** [mass noun] Law entry to a person's land or property without their permission: *the defendants were guilty of trespass* | [count noun] *a mass trespass on the moor.*
2 archaic or poetic/literary a sin; an offence: *the worst trespass against the goddess Venus is to see her naked and asleep.*
– DERIVATIVES **trespasser** noun.
– ORIGIN Middle English (in sense 2): from Old French *trespasser* 'pass over, trespass', *trespas* 'passing across', from medieval Latin *transpassare* (see **TRANS-**, **PASS**[1]).

tress ▶ **noun** (usu. **tresses**) a long lock of a woman's hair: *she was tugging a comb through her long tresses.*
▶ **verb** [with obj.] archaic arrange (a person's hair) into long locks.
– DERIVATIVES **tressed** adjective [often in combination] *a blonde-tressed sex symbol*, **tressy** adjective.
– ORIGIN Middle English: from Old French *tresse*, perhaps based on Greek *trikha* 'threefold'.

tressure /ˈtrɛʃə, ˈtrɛs(j)ʊə/ ▶ **noun** Heraldry a thin border inset from the edge of a shield, narrower than an orle and usually borne double.
■ an ornamental enclosure containing a figure or distinctive device, formerly found on various gold and silver coins.
– ORIGIN Middle English (denoting a ribbon or band for the hair): from Old French *tressour* (see **TRESS**).

trestle ▶ **noun** a framework consisting of a horizontal beam supported by two pairs of sloping legs, used in pairs to support a flat surface such as a table top.
■ short for **TRESTLE TABLE**. ■ (also **trestlework**) an open braced framework used to support an elevated structure such as a bridge. ■ (also **trestletree**) each of a pair of horizontal pieces on a sailing ship's lower mast supporting the topmast.
– ORIGIN Middle English: from Old French *trestel*, based on Latin *transtrum* 'beam'.

trestle table ▶ **noun** a table consisting of a board or boards laid on trestles.

tret /trɛt/ ▶ **noun** [mass noun] historical an allowance of extra weight made to purchasers of certain goods to compensate for waste during transportation.
– ORIGIN late 15th cent: from an Old French variant of *trait* 'draught' (see **TRAIT**).

Tretyakov Gallery /ˈtrɛtjəkɒf/ an art gallery in Moscow, one of the largest in the world. It houses exhibits ranging from early Russian art to contemporary work, and has a huge collection of icons.
– ORIGIN named after P. M. *Tretyakov* (1832–98), who founded it in 1856.

trevally /trɪˈvali/ ▶ **noun** (pl. **-ies**) a marine sporting fish of the Indo-Pacific, which is sometimes caught in large quantities for food.
• *Caranx* and other genera, family Carangidae: several species.
– ORIGIN late 19th cent.: probably an alteration of *cavally* 'horse mackerel', from Spanish *caballo* 'horse'.

Trèves /trɛv/ French name for **TRIER**.

Trevino /trəˈviːnəʊ/, Lee (Buck) (b.1939), American golfer; known as **Supermex**. In 1971 he became the first man to win all three Open championships (Canadian, US, and British) in the same year.

Trevira /trəˈvɪərə/ ▶ **noun** [mass noun] trademark a polyester fibre, used chiefly to make clothes and soft furnishings.
– ORIGIN 1950s: of unknown origin.

Trevithick /trəˈvɪθɪk/, Richard (1771–1833), English engineer. His chief contribution was in the use of high-pressure steam to drive a double-acting engine. Trevithick built the world's first railway locomotive (1804) and many stationary engines.

trews /truːz/ ▶ **plural noun** chiefly Brit. trousers.
■ close-fitting tartan trousers worn by certain Scottish regiments.
– ORIGIN mid 16th cent.: from Irish *triús*, Scottish Gaelic *triubhas* (singular); compare with **TROUSERS**.

trey /treɪ/ ▶ **noun** (pl. **-eys**) a thing having three of something, in particular:
■ a playing card or dice with three spots. ■ US (in basketball) a shot scoring three points.
– ORIGIN late Middle English: from Old French *trei* 'three', from Latin *tres*.

TRH ▶ **abbreviation for** ■ Their Royal Highnesses. ■ Biochemistry thyrotropin-releasing hormone.

tri- /trʌɪ/ ▶ **combining form** three; having three: *triathlon.*
■ Chemistry (in names of compounds) containing three atoms or groups of a specified kind: *trichloroethane.*
– ORIGIN from Latin and Greek, from Latin *tres*, Greek *treis* 'three'.

triable /ˈtrʌɪəb(ə)l/ ▶ **adjective** Law (of an offence) liable to a judicial trial.
■ (of a case or issue) able to be investigated and decided judicially.
– ORIGIN late Middle English: from Anglo-Norman French, from Old French *trier* 'sift' (see **TRY**).

triac /ˈtrʌɪak/ ▶ **noun** Electronics a three-electrode semiconductor device that will conduct in either direction when triggered by a positive or negative signal at the gate electrode.
– ORIGIN 1960s: from **TRIODE** + **AC** (short for *alternating current*).

triacetate /trʌɪˈasɪteɪt/ (also **cellulose triacetate**) ▶ **noun** [mass noun] a form of cellulose acetate containing three acetate groups per glucose monomer, used as a basis for man-made fibres.

triad /ˈtrʌɪad/ ▶ **noun** **1** a group or set of three connected people or things: *the triad of medication, diet, and exercise are necessary in diabetes care.*
■ a chord of three musical notes, consisting of a given note with the third and fifth above it. ■ a Welsh form of literary composition with an arrangement of subjects or statements in groups of three.
2 (also **Triad**) a secret society originating in China, typically involved in organized crime.
■ a member of such a society.
– DERIVATIVES **triadic** adjective (only in sense 1).
– ORIGIN mid 16th cent.: from French *triade*, or via late Latin from Greek *trias*, *triad-*, from *treis* 'three'.

triage /ˈtrʌɪɪdʒ/ ▶ **noun** [mass noun] **1** the action of sorting according to quality.
2 (in medical use) the assignment of degrees of urgency to wounds or illnesses to decide the order of treatment of a large number of patients or casualties.
– ORIGIN early 18th cent.: from French, from *trier* 'separate out'. The medical sense dates from the 1930s, from the military system of assessing the wounded on the battlefield.

trial ▶ **noun** **1** a formal examination of evidence by a judge, typically before a jury, in order to decide guilt in a case of criminal or civil proceedings: *the newspaper accounts of the trial* | [mass noun] *the editor was summoned to* **stand trial** *for libel.*
2 a test of the performance, qualities, or suitability of someone or something: *clinical trials must establish whether the new hip replacements are working.*
■ a sports match to test the ability of players eligible for selection to a team. ■ a test of individual ability on a motorcycle over rough ground or on a road. ■ (**trials**) an event in which horses, dogs, or other animals compete or perform: *horse trials.*
3 a person, thing, or situation that tests a person's endurance or forbearance: *the trials and tribulations of married life.*
▶ **verb** (**trialled**, **trialling**; US **trialed**, **trialing**) **1** [with obj.] test (something, especially a new product) to assess its suitability or performance: *teachers all over the UK are trialling the materials.*
2 [no obj.] (of a horse, dog, or other animal) compete in trials: *the pup trialled on Saturday.*
– PHRASES **on trial** **1** being tried in a court of law. **2** undergoing tests or scrutiny: *water metering has been on trial in England and Wales.* **trial and error** the process of experimenting with various methods of doing something until one finds the most successful.
– ORIGIN late Middle English (as a noun): from Anglo-Norman French, or from medieval Latin *triallum*. The verb dates from the 1980s.

trial balance ▶ **noun** a statement of all debits and credits in a double-entry account book, with any disagreement indicating an error.

trial balloon ▶ **noun** a tentative measure taken or statement made to see how a new policy will be received.
– ORIGIN 1930s: from translation of French *ballon d'essai*.

trial court ▶ **noun** chiefly N. Amer. a court of law where cases are tried in the first place, as opposed to an appeal court.

trialist (Brit. also **triallist**) ▶ **noun** a person who participates in a trial, in particular:
■ a person who takes part in a sports trial or motorcycle trial. ■ a person who takes part in a clinical or market test of a new product.

trial lawyer ▶ **noun** N. Amer. a lawyer who practises in a trial court.

trialogue ▶ **noun** a dialogue between three people.
– ORIGIN mid 16th cent.: formed irregularly from

TRI- 'three' + **DIALOGUE** (the prefix *di-* misinterpreted as 'two').

trial run ▶ **noun** a preliminary test of how a new system or product works.

triangle ▶ **noun 1** a plane figure with three straight sides and three angles: *an equilateral triangle.*
■ a thing shaped like such a figure: *a small triangle of grass.* ■ a situation involving three people or things, especially an emotional relationship involving a couple and a third person with whom one of them is involved. ■ a musical instrument consisting of a steel rod bent into a triangle and sounded by being struck with a small steel rod. ■ a frame used to position the pool balls in snooker and pool. ■ N. Amer. a drawing instrument in the form of a right-angled triangle. ■ (**triangles**) historical a frame of three halberds joined at the top to which a soldier was bound for flogging.
2 a small brownish Eurasian moth of oak and beech woods.
• *Heterogenea asella*, family Limacodidae.
– ORIGIN late Middle English: from Old French *triangle* or Latin *triangulum*, neuter of *triangulus* 'three-cornered' (see **TRI-**, **ANGLE**[1]).

triangle of forces ▶ **noun** Physics a triangle whose sides represent in magnitude and direction three forces in equilibrium.

triangular ▶ **adjective** shaped like a triangle; having three sides and three corners: *dainty triangular sandwiches.*
■ involving three people or parties: *a triangular cricket competition.* ■ (of a pyramid) having a three-sided base.
– DERIVATIVES **triangularity** noun, **triangularly** adverb.
– ORIGIN mid 16th cent.: from late Latin *triangularis*, from Latin *triangulum* (see **TRIANGLE**).

triangular number ▶ **noun** any of the series of numbers (1, 3, 6, 10, 15, etc.) obtained by continued summation of the natural numbers 1, 2, 3, 4, 5, etc.

triangular trade ▶ **noun** [mass noun] a multilateral system of trading in which a country pays for its imports from one country by its exports to another.
■ used to refer to the trade in the eighteenth and nineteenth centuries which involved shipping goods from Britain to West Africa to be exchanged for slaves, these slaves being shipped to the West Indies and exchanged for sugar and other commodities which were in turn shipped back to Britain.

triangulate ▶ **verb** /trʌɪˈaŋgjʊleɪt/ **1** [with obj.] divide (an area) into triangles for surveying purposes.
■ measure and map (an area) by the use of triangles with a known base length and base angles. ■ determine (a height, distance, or location) in this way.
2 [with obj.] form into a triangle or triangles: *the brackets triangulate the frame.*
– ORIGIN mid 19th cent.: from Latin *triangulum* 'triangle' (see **TRIANGLE**) + **-ATE**[3].

triangulation ▶ **noun** [mass noun] **1** (in surveying) the tracing and measurement of a series or network of triangles in order to determine the distances and relative positions of points spread over a territory or region, especially by measuring the length of one side of each triangle and deducing its angles and the length of the other two sides by observation from this baseline.
2 formation of or division into triangles.

triangulation point ▶ **noun** another term for **TRIG POINT**.

Triangulum /trʌɪˈaŋgjʊləm/ Astronomy a small northern constellation (the Triangle), between Andromeda and Aries.
■ [as genitive **Trianguli** /trʌɪˈangjʊliː/] used with preceding letter or numeral to designate a star in this constellation: *the star Beta Trianguli.*
– ORIGIN Latin.

Triangulum Australe /ɒˈstrɑːliː/ Astronomy a small southern constellation (the Southern Triangle), lying in the Milky Way near the south celestial pole.
■ [as genitive **Trianguli Australis** /ɒˈstreɪlɪs/] used with preceding letter or numeral to designate a star in this constellation: *the star Alpha Trianguli Australis.*
– ORIGIN Latin.

Trianon /ˈtriːənɒn, French triɑ̃nɔ̃/ either of two small palaces in the great park at Versailles in France. The larger was built by Louis XIV in 1687; the smaller, built by Louis XV 1762–8, was used first by his mistress Madame du Barry (1743–93) and afterwards by Marie Antoinette.

Triassic /trʌɪˈasɪk/ ▶ **adjective** Geology of, relating to, or denoting the earliest period of the Mesozoic era, between the Permian and Jurassic periods. See also **PERMO-TRIASSIC**.
■ [as noun **the Triassic** or **the Trias**] the Triassic period or the system of rocks deposited during it.

> The Triassic lasted from about 245 to 208 million years ago. Many new organisms appeared following the mass extinctions of the end of the Palaeozoic era, including the earliest dinosaurs and ammonites and the first primitive mammals.

– ORIGIN mid 19th cent.: from late Latin *trias* (see **TRIAD**), because the strata are divisible into three groups, + **-IC**.

triathlon /trʌɪˈaθlɒn, -lən/ ▶ **noun** an athletic contest consisting of three different events, typically swimming, cycling, and long-distance running.
– DERIVATIVES **triathlete** noun.
– ORIGIN 1970s: from **TRI-** 'three', on the pattern of *decathlon.*

triatomic /ˌtrʌɪəˈtɒmɪk/ ▶ **adjective** Chemistry consisting of three atoms.

triaxial /trʌɪˈaksɪəl/ ▶ **adjective** having or relating to three axes, especially in mechanical or astronomical contexts.

tri-axle ▶ **noun** a trailer or articulated lorry with three axles.

triazine /ˈtrʌɪəziːn, trʌɪˈaziːn, -zɪn/ ▶ **noun** Chemistry any of a group of compounds whose molecules contain an unsaturated ring of three carbon and three nitrogen atoms.

triazole /ˈtrʌɪəzəʊl, trʌɪˈazəʊl/ ▶ **noun** any compound whose molecule contains a ring of three nitrogen and two carbon atoms, in particular each of five isomeric compounds containing such a ring with two double bonds.
• Chem. formula: $C_2H_3N_3$

tribade /ˈtrɪbəd/ ▶ **noun** a lesbian, especially one who lies on top of her partner and simulates the movements of the male in heterosexual intercourse.
– DERIVATIVES **tribadism** noun.
– ORIGIN early 17th cent.: from French *tribade*, or via Latin from Greek *tribas*, from *tribein* 'to rub'.

tribal ▶ **adjective** of or characteristic of a tribe or tribes: *tribal people in Malaysia.*
■ chiefly derogatory characterized by a tendency to form groups or by strong group loyalty: *British industrial operatives remained locked in primitive tribal attitudes.*
▶ **noun** (**tribals**) members of tribal communities, especially in the Indian subcontinent.
– DERIVATIVES **tribally** adverb.

tribalism ▶ **noun** [mass noun] the state or fact of being organized in a tribe or tribes: *black tribalism became the excuse for creating ethnic homelands.*
■ chiefly derogatory the behaviour and attitudes that stem from strong loyalty to one's own tribe or social group: *the tribalism which haunts police defensiveness.*

tribalist ▶ **noun** chiefly derogatory an advocate or practitioner of strong loyalty to one's own tribe or social group.
– DERIVATIVES **tribalistic** adjective.

tribasic /trʌɪˈbeɪsɪk/ ▶ **adjective** Chemistry (of an acid) having three replaceable hydrogen atoms.

tribe ▶ **noun 1** a social division in a traditional society consisting of families or communities linked by social, economic, religious, or blood ties, with a common culture and dialect, typically having a recognized leader: *indigenous Indian tribes.*
■ (in ancient Rome) each of several political divisions, originally three, later thirty, ultimately thirty-five. ■ derogatory a distinctive close-knit social or political group: *she made a stand against the social codes of her English middle-class tribe.* ■ derogatory a group or class of people or things: *an outburst against the whole tribe of theoreticians.* ■ (**tribes**) informal large numbers of people: *tribes of children playing under the watchful eyes of nurses.*
2 Biology a taxonomic category that ranks above genus and below family or subfamily, usually ending in *-ini* (in zoology) or *-eae* (in botany).
– ORIGIN Middle English: from Old French *tribu* or Latin *tribus* (singular and plural); perhaps related to *tri-* 'three' and referring to the three divisions of the early people of Rome.

> **USAGE** In historical contexts, the word **tribe** is broadly accepted (*the area was inhabited by Slavic tribes*). However, in contemporary contexts, used to refer to a community living within a traditional society today, the word is problematic. It is strongly associated with past attitudes of white colonialists towards so-called primitive or uncivilized peoples living in remote undeveloped places. For this reason, it is generally preferable to use alternative terms such as **community** or **people**.

tribesman ▶ **noun** (pl. **-men**) a man belonging to a tribe in a traditional society or group.

Tribes of Israel the twelve divisions of ancient Israel, each traditionally descended from one of the twelve sons of Jacob. Ten of the tribes (Asher, Dan, Gad, Issachar, Levi, Manasseh, Naphtali, Reuben, Simeon, and Zebulun, known as the **Lost Tribes**) were deported to captivity in Assyria *c.*720 BC, leaving only the tribes of Judah and Benjamin. Also called **TWELVE TRIBES OF ISRAEL**.

tribespeople ▶ **plural noun** people belonging to a tribe in a traditional society or group.

tribeswoman ▶ **noun** (pl. **-women**) a woman belonging to a tribe in a traditional society or group.

triblet /ˈtrɪblɪt/ ▶ **noun** a cylindrical rod used for forging nuts, rings, tubes, and other rounded metallic objects.
– ORIGIN early 17th cent.: from French *triboulet*, of unknown origin.

tribo- /ˈtrʌɪbəʊ, ˈtrɪbəʊ/ ▶ **combining form** relating to friction: *triboelectricity.*
– ORIGIN from Greek *tribos* 'rubbing'.

triboelectricity ▶ **noun** [mass noun] electric charge generated by friction.

tribology /trʌɪˈbɒlədʒi/ ▶ **noun** [mass noun] the study of friction, wear, lubrication, and the design of bearings; the science of interacting surfaces in relative motion.
– DERIVATIVES **tribological** adjective, **tribologist** noun.

triboluminescence ▶ **noun** [mass noun] the emission of light from a substance caused by rubbing, scratching, or similar frictional contact.
– DERIVATIVES **triboluminescent** adjective.

tribometer /trʌɪˈbɒmɪtə/ ▶ **noun** an instrument for measuring friction in sliding.

tribrach /ˈtrʌɪbrak, ˈtrɪ-/ ▶ **noun** Prosody a metrical foot of three short or unstressed syllables.
– DERIVATIVES **tribrachic** /-ˈbrakɪk/ adjective.
– ORIGIN late 16th cent.: via Latin from Greek *tribrakhus*, from *tri-* 'three' + *brakhus* 'short'.

tribulation /ˌtrɪbjʊˈleɪʃ(ə)n/ ▶ **noun** (usu. **tribulations**) a cause of great trouble or suffering: *the tribulations of being a megastar.*
■ [mass noun] a state of great trouble or suffering: *his time of tribulation was just beginning.*
– ORIGIN Middle English: via Old French from ecclesiastical Latin *tribulatio(n-)*, from Latin *tribulare* 'press, oppress', from *tribulum* 'threshing board (constructed of sharp points)', based on *terere* 'rub'.

tribunal /trʌɪˈbjuːn(ə)l, trɪ-/ ▶ **noun 1** Brit. a body established to settle certain types of dispute: *an industrial tribunal ruled that he was unfairly dismissed.*
2 a court of justice: *an international war crimes tribunal.*
■ a seat or bench for a judge or judges.
– ORIGIN late Middle English (denoting a seat for judges): from Old French, or from Latin *tribunal* 'raised platform provided for magistrate's seats', from *tribunus* (see **TRIBUNE**[1]). Sense 1 dates from the early 20th cent.

tribune[1] ▶ **noun** (also **tribune of the people**) an official in ancient Rome chosen by the plebeians to protect their interests.
■ (also **military tribune**) a Roman legionary officer. ■ figurative a popular leader; a champion of the people.
– DERIVATIVES **tribunate** noun, **tribuneship** noun.
– ORIGIN late Middle English: from Latin *tribunus*, literally 'head of a tribe', from *tribus* 'tribe'.

tribune[2] ▶ **noun 1** an apse in a basilica.
2 a dais or rostrum, especially in a church.
■ a raised area or gallery with seats, especially in a church.
– ORIGIN mid 17th cent. (denoting the principal room in an Italian mansion): via French from Italian, from medieval Latin *tribuna*, alteration of Latin *tribunal* (see **TRIBUNAL**).

Tribune Group a left-wing group within the British Labour Party consisting of supporters of the views put forward in the weekly journal *Tribune*.

tributary /ˈtrɪbjʊt(ə)ri/ ▶ **noun** (pl. **-ies**) **1** a river or stream flowing into a larger river or lake: *the Illinois River, a tributary of the Mississippi.*
2 historical a person or state that pays tribute to another state or ruler: *tributaries of the Chinese empire.*
– ORIGIN late Middle English (in sense 2): from Latin *tributarius*, from *tributum* (see **TRIBUTE**). Sense 1 dates from the early 19th cent.

tribute ▶ **noun 1** an act, statement, or gift that is intended to show gratitude, respect, or admiration: *the video is a tribute to the musicals of the '40s* | [mass noun] *a symposium organized to* ***pay tribute to*** *Darwin.*
■ [in sing.] something resulting from something else and indicating its worth: *his victory in the championship was* ***a tribute to*** *his persistence.*
2 [mass noun] historical payment made periodically by one state or ruler to another, especially as a sign of dependence: *the king had at his disposal plunder and tribute amassed through warfare.*
3 historical a proportion of ore or its equivalent, paid to a miner for his work, or to the owner or lessor of a mine.
– ORIGIN late Middle English (in sense 2): from Latin *tributum*, neuter past participle (used as a noun) of *tribuere* 'assign' (originally 'divide between tribes'), from *tribus* 'tribe'.

tricameral /trʌɪˈkam(ə)r(ə)l/ ▶ **adjective** of or relating to the parliamentary system operating in South Africa between 1983 and 1994, in which the legislature consisted of three ethnically based houses.

tricar /ˈtrʌɪkɑː/ ▶ **noun** Brit. dated a three-wheeled motor car.

tricarboxylic acid cycle /trʌɪˌkɑːbɒkˈsɪlɪk/ ▶ **noun** another term for **KREBS CYCLE**.

tricast /ˈtrʌɪkɑːst/ ▶ **noun** Brit. a bet in which the person betting forecasts the first three horses in a race in the correct order.
– ORIGIN 1970s: from **TRI-** 'three' + the noun **FORECAST**.

trice /trʌɪs/ ▶ **noun** (in phrase **in a trice**) in a moment; very quickly.
– ORIGIN late Middle English *trice* 'a tug', figuratively 'an instant', from Middle Dutch *trīsen* 'pull sharply', related to *trīse* 'pulley'.

Tricel /ˈtrʌɪsɛl/ ▶ **noun** [mass noun] trademark a textile fibre made from cellulose triacetate.
– ORIGIN 1950s: blend of **TRIACETATE** + **CELLULOSE**.

tricentenary ▶ **noun** (pl. **-ies**) another term for **TERCENTENARY**.

tricentennial ▶ **adjective** & **noun** another term for **TERCENTENARY**.

triceps /ˈtrʌɪsɛps/ ▶ **noun** (pl. same) Anatomy any of several muscles having three points of attachment at one end, particularly (also **triceps brachii** /ˈbreɪkɪʌɪ/) the large muscle at the back of the upper arm.
– ORIGIN late 16th cent.: from Latin, literally 'three-headed', from *tri-* 'three' + *-ceps* (from *caput* 'head').

triceratops /trʌɪˈsɛrətɒps/ ▶ **noun** a large quadrupedal herbivorous dinosaur living at the end of the Cretaceous period, having a massive head with two large horns, a smaller horn on the beaked snout, and a bony frill above the neck.
• Genus *Triceratops*, infraorder Ceratopsia, order Ornithischia.
– ORIGIN modern Latin, from Greek *trikeratos* 'three-horned' + *ōps* 'face'.

trichiasis /ˌtrɪkɪˈeɪsɪs, trɪˈkʌɪəsɪs/ ▶ **noun** [mass noun] Medicine ingrowth or introversion of the eyelashes.
– ORIGIN mid 17th cent.: via late Latin from Greek *trikhiasis*, from *trikhian* 'be hairy'.

trichina /ˈtrɪkɪnə, trɪˈkʌɪnə/ ▶ **noun** (pl. **trichinae** /-niː/) a parasitic nematode worm of humans and other mammals, the adults of which live in the small intestine. The larvae form hard cysts in the muscles, where they remain until eaten by the next host.
• Genus *Trichinella*, class Aphasmida (or Adenophorea).
– ORIGIN mid 19th cent.: from modern Latin (former genus name), from Greek *trikhinos* 'of hair'.

Trichinopoly /ˌtrɪtʃɪˈnɒpəli/ another name for **TIRUCHIRAPALLI**.

trichinosis /ˌtrɪkɪˈnəʊsɪs/ ▶ **noun** [mass noun] a disease caused by trichinae, typically from infected meat, characterized by digestive disturbance, fever, and muscular rigidity.
• This disease is typically caused by *Trichinella spiralis*.

trichloroacetic acid /trʌɪˌklɔːrəʊəˈsiːtɪk, -ˌklɒrəʊ-/ (also **trichloracetic acid** /-ˌklɔːrəˈsiːtɪk, -ˌklɒr-/) ▶ **noun** [mass noun] Chemistry a toxic deliquescent crystalline solid used as a solvent, analgesic, and anaesthetic.
• Chem. formula: CCl_3COOH.
– DERIVATIVES **trichloroacetate** noun.

trichloroethane /ˌtrʌɪklɔːrəʊˈiːθeɪn, -klɒr-/ ▶ **noun** [mass noun] Chemistry a colourless non-flammable volatile liquid, used as a solvent and cleaner.
• Alternative name: **1,1,1-trichloroethane**; chem. formula: CCl_3CH_3.

trichloroethylene /ˌtrʌɪklɔːrəʊˈɛθɪliːn, -klɒr-/ ▶ **noun** [mass noun] Chemistry a colourless volatile liquid used as a solvent and formerly as an anaesthetic.
• Chem. formula: $CCl_2{=}CHCl$.

trichlorophenol /ˌtrʌɪklɔːrə(ʊ)ˈfiːnɒl, -klɒr-/ ▶ **noun** [mass noun] Chemistry a synthetic crystalline compound used as an insecticide and preservative and in the synthesis of pesticides.
• Chem. formula: $C_6H_2Cl_3(OH)$; six isomers.

tricho- /ˈtrɪkəʊ, ˈtrʌɪkəʊ/ ▶ **combining form** of or relating to hair: *trichology.*
– ORIGIN from Greek *thrix, trikhos* 'hair'.

trichocyst /ˈtrɪkə(ʊ)sɪst, ˈtrʌɪ-/ ▶ **noun** Biology any of numerous minute rod-like structures, each containing a protrusible filament, found near the surface of ciliates and dinoflagellates.

trichology /trɪˈkɒlədʒi/ ▶ **noun** [mass noun] the branch of medical and cosmetic study and practice concerned with the hair and scalp.
– DERIVATIVES **trichological** adjective, **trichologist** noun.

trichome /ˈtrʌɪkəʊm, ˈtrɪ-/ ▶ **noun** Botany a small hair or other outgrowth from the epidermis of a plant, typically unicellular and glandular.
– ORIGIN late 19th cent.: from Greek *trikhōma*, from *trikhoun* 'cover with hair'.

trichomonad /ˌtrɪkə(ʊ)ˈmɒnad/ ▶ **noun** Zoology & Medicine a parasitic protozoan with four to six flagella and an undulating membrane, infesting the urogenital or digestive system.
• Order Trichomonadida, phylum Parabasilia, kingdom Protista.
– DERIVATIVES **trichomonal** adjective.
– ORIGIN mid 19th cent.: from modern Latin *Trichomonadida* (plural), from Greek *thrix, trikh-* 'hair' + *monas, monad-* 'unit'.

trichomoniasis /ˌtrɪkə(ʊ)məˈnʌɪəsɪs/ ▶ **noun** [mass noun] Medicine an infection caused by parasitic trichomonads, chiefly affecting the urinary tract, vagina, or digestive system.
• Genus *Trichomonas*, in particular *T. vaginalis* (in the reproductive tract) and *T. hominis* (in the large intestine).

Trichoptera /trʌɪˈkɒpt(ə)rə/ Entomology an order of insects that comprises the caddis flies.
■ [as plural noun **trichoptera**] insects of this order.
– DERIVATIVES **trichopteran** noun & adjective.
– ORIGIN modern Latin (plural), from **TRICHO-** 'hair' + *pteron* 'wing'.

trichotomy /trʌɪˈkɒtəmi, trɪ-/ ▶ **noun** (pl. **-ies**) a division into three categories: *the pragmatics–semantics–syntax trichotomy.*
– DERIVATIVES **trichotomous** adjective.
– ORIGIN 17th cent.: from Greek *trikha* 'threefold' from *treis* 'three', on the pattern of *dichotomy*.

trichroic /trʌɪˈkrəʊɪk/ ▶ **adjective** Crystallography (of a crystal) appearing with different colours when viewed along the three crystallographic directions.
– DERIVATIVES **trichroism** /ˈtrʌɪkrəʊɪz(ə)m/ noun.
– ORIGIN late 19th cent.: from Greek *trikhroos* (from *tri-* 'three' + *khrōs* 'colour') + **-IC**.

trichromatic /ˌtrʌɪkrəˈmatɪk/ ▶ **adjective** having or using three colours.
■ having normal colour vision, which is sensitive to all three primary colours.
– DERIVATIVES **trichromatism** noun.

trichrome /ˈtrʌɪkrəʊm/ ▶ **adjective** Biology denoting a stain or method of histological staining in which different tissues are stained, each in one of three different colours.
– ORIGIN early 20th cent.: from **TRI-** 'three' + Greek *khrōma* 'colour'.

trick ▶ **noun 1** a cunning or skilful act or scheme intended to deceive or outwit someone: *he's a double-dealer capable of any mean trick.*
■ a mischievous practical joke: *she thought Elaine was* ***playing*** *some* ***trick on*** *her.* ■ a skilful act performed for entertainment or amusement: *he did conjuring tricks for his daughters.* ■ an illusion: *I thought I saw a flicker of emotion, but it was probably* ***a trick of the light.*** ■ a clever or particular way of doing something: *the trick is to put one ski forward and kneel.*
2 a peculiar or characteristic habit or mannerism: *she had a trick of clipping off certain words and phrases.*
3 (in bridge, whist, and similar card games) a sequence of cards forming a single round of play. One card is laid down by each player, the highest card being the winner.
4 informal a prostitute's client.
5 a sailor's turn at the helm, usually lasting for two or four hours.
▶ **verb** [with obj.] **1** (often **be tricked**) deceive or outwit (someone) by being cunning or skilful: *many people have been tricked by villains with false identity cards.*
■ (**trick someone into**) use deception to make someone do (something): *he tricked her into parting with the money.* ■ (**trick someone out of**) use deception to deprive someone of (something): *two men tricked a pensioner out of several hundred pounds.*
2 Heraldry sketch (a coat of arms) in outline, with the colours indicated by letters or signs.
▶ **adjective** [attrib.] **1** intended or used to deceive or mystify, or to create an illusion: *a trick question.*
2 N. Amer. liable to fail; defective: *a trick knee.*
– PHRASES **do the trick** informal achieve the required result. **every trick in the book** informal every available method of achieving what one wants. **how's tricks?** informal used as a friendly greeting: *'How's tricks in your neck of the woods?'* **not miss a trick** see **MISS**[1]. **the oldest trick in the book** a ruse so hackneyed that it should no longer deceive anyone. **trick or treat** chiefly N. Amer. a children's custom of calling at houses at Halloween with the threat of pranks if they are not given a small gift (often used as a greeting by children doing this). **tricks of the trade** special ingenious techniques used in a profession or craft, especially those that are little known by outsiders. **turn a trick** informal (of a prostitute) have a session with a client. **up to one's (old) tricks** informal misbehaving in a characteristic way.
– DERIVATIVES **tricker** noun, **trickish** adjective (dated).
– ORIGIN late Middle English (as a noun): from an Old French dialect variant of *triche*, from *trichier* 'deceive', of unknown origin. Current senses of the verb date from the mid 16th cent.
▶ **trick someone/thing out** (or **up**) (usu. **be tricked out**) dress or decorate someone or something in an elaborate or showy way: *a Marine* ***tricked out in*** *World War II kit and weaponry.* [ORIGIN: late 15th cent.: perhaps associated with obsolete French *s'estriquer*.]

trick cyclist ▶ **noun** Brit. informal used as a humorous euphemism for a psychiatrist.

trickery ▶ **noun** (pl. **-ies**) [mass noun] the practice of deception: *the dealer resorted to trickery.*

trickle ▶ **verb** [no obj., with adverbial of direction] (of a liquid) flow in a small stream: *a solitary tear trickled down her cheek* | [as adj. **trickling**] *a trickling brook.*
■ [with obj. and adverbial of direction] cause (a liquid) to flow in a small stream: *Philip trickled a line of sauce on his fish fingers.* ■ come or go slowly or gradually: *the details began to trickle out.*
▶ **noun** a small flow of liquid: *a trickle of blood.*
■ a small group or number of people or things moving slowly: *the traffic had dwindled to a trickle.*
▶ **trickle down** (of wealth) gradually benefit the poorest as a result of the increasing wealth of the richest.
– ORIGIN Middle English (as a verb): imitative.

trickle charger ▶ **noun** an electrical charger for batteries that works at a steady slow rate from the mains.

trickle-down ▶ **adjective** (of an economic system) in which the poorest gradually benefit as a result of the increasing wealth of the richest.

trickle irrigation ▶ **noun** [mass noun] the supply of a controlled restricted flow of water to a number of points in a cultivated area.

trickster ▶ **noun** a person who cheats or deceives people.

tricksy ▶ **adjective** (**tricksier, tricksiest**) clever in an ingenious or deceptive way: *tricksy little repro low-level cupboards.*
■ (of a person) playful or mischievous.
– DERIVATIVES **tricksily** adverb, **tricksiness** noun.

tricky ▶ **adjective** (**trickier, trickiest**) (of a task, problem, or situation) requiring care and skill

because difficult or awkward: *applying eyeliner can be a tricky business* | *some things are very tricky to explain.*
▪(of a person or act) deceitful, crafty, or skilful.
– DERIVATIVES **trickily** adverb, **trickiness** noun.

triclad /ˈtrʌɪklad/ ▶ **noun** Zoology a free-living flatworm of an order characterized by having a gut with three branches, including the planarians.
• Order Tricladida, class Turbellaria.
– ORIGIN late 19th cent.: from modern Latin *Tricladida*, from **TRI-** 'three' + Greek *klados* 'branch'.

triclinic /trʌɪˈklɪnɪk/ ▶ **adjective** of or denoting a crystal system or three-dimensional geometrical arrangement having three unequal oblique axes.
– ORIGIN mid 19th cent.: from Greek **TRI-** 'three' + *-clinic*, on the pattern of *monoclinic*.

triclinium /trʌɪˈklɪnɪəm, trɪ-, -ˈklʌɪn-/ ▶ **noun** (pl. **triclinia** /-nɪə/) a dining table with couches along three sides used in ancient Rome.
▪a room containing such a table.
– ORIGIN Latin, from Greek *triklinion*, from *tri-* 'three' + *klinē* 'couch'.

tricolour /ˈtrɪkələ, ˈtrʌɪkʌlə/ (US **tricolor**) ▶ **noun** a flag with three bands or blocks of different colours, especially the French national flag with equal upright bands of blue, white, and red.
▶ **adjective** (also **tricoloured**) having three colours.
– ORIGIN late 18th cent.: from French *tricolore*, from late Latin *tricolor* (see **TRI-**, **COLOUR**).

tricorne /ˈtrʌɪkɔːn/ (also **tricorn**) ▶ **adjective** [attrib.] (of a hat) having a brim turned up on three sides.
▶ **noun** a hat of this kind.
– ORIGIN mid 19th cent.: from French *tricorne* or Latin *tricornis*, from *tri-* 'three' + *cornu* 'horn'.

tricot /ˈtrɪkəʊ, ˈtriː-/ ▶ **noun** [mass noun] a fine knitted fabric made of a natural or man-made fibre.
– ORIGIN late 18th cent.: from French, literally 'knitting', from *tricoter* 'to knit', of unknown origin.

tricoteuse /ˌtrɪkəˈtəːz, French trikɔtøz/ ▶ **noun** (pl. pronounced same) a woman who sits and knits (used in particular in reference to a number of women who did this, during the French Revolution, while attending public executions).
– ORIGIN French, from *tricoter* 'to knit'.

tric-trac ▶ **noun** [mass noun] historical a form of backgammon.
– ORIGIN late 17th cent.: from French, from the clicking sound made by the game pieces.

tricuspid /trʌɪˈkʌspɪd/ ▶ **adjective** **1** having three cusps or points, in particular:
▪denoting a tooth with three cusps or points. ▪denoting a valve formed of three triangular segments, particularly that between the right atrium and ventricle of the heart.
2 [attrib.] of or relating to the tricuspid valve: *tricuspid atresia.*
– ORIGIN late 17th cent.: from **TRI-** 'three' + Latin *cuspis, cuspid-* 'cusp'.

tricycle ▶ **noun** a vehicle similar to a bicycle, but having three wheels, two at the back and one at the front.
▪a three-wheeled motor vehicle for a disabled driver.
▶ **verb** [no obj.] [often as noun **tricycling**] ride on a tricycle.
– DERIVATIVES **tricyclist** noun.

tricyclic /trʌɪˈsʌɪklɪk/ ▶ **adjective** Chemistry (of a compound) having three rings of atoms in its molecule.
▶ **noun** (usu. **tricyclics**) Medicine any of a class of antidepressant drugs having molecules with three fused rings.
– ORIGIN late 19th cent.: from **TRI-** 'three' + Greek *kuklos* 'circle' + **-IC**.

tridactyl /trʌɪˈdaktɪl/ ▶ **adjective** Zoology (of a vertebrate limb) having three toes or fingers.
– ORIGIN early 19th cent.: from **TRI-** 'three' + Greek *daktulos* 'finger'.

trident ▶ **noun** a three-pronged spear, especially as an attribute of Poseidon (Neptune) or Britannia.
▪(**Trident**) a US design of submarine-launched long-range ballistic missile.
– ORIGIN late Middle English: from Latin *trident-*, from *tri-* 'three' + *dens, dent-* 'tooth'.

Tridentine /trɪˈdɛntʌɪn, trʌɪ-/ ▶ **adjective** of or relating to the Council of Trent, especially as the basis of Roman Catholic doctrine.
– ORIGIN from medieval Latin *Tridentinus*, from *Tridentum* 'Trent'.

Tridentine mass ▶ **noun** the Latin Eucharistic liturgy used by the Roman Catholic Church from 1570 to 1964.

triduum /ˈtrɪdjʊəm, ˈtrʌɪ-/ ▶ **noun** [in sing.] (especially in the Roman Catholic Church) a period of three days' observance, specifically Maundy Thursday, Good Friday, and Holy Saturday.
– ORIGIN Latin, from *tri-* 'three' + *dies* 'day'.

tridymite /ˈtrɪdɪmʌɪt/ ▶ **noun** [mass noun] a high-temperature form of quartz found as thin hexagonal crystals in some igneous rocks and stony meteorites.
– ORIGIN mid 19th cent.: from German *Tridymit*, from Greek *tridumos* 'threefold', from *tri-* 'three' + *-dumos* (as in *didumos* 'twin'), because of its occurrence in groups of three crystals.

tried past and past participle of **TRY**. ▶ **adjective** [attrib.] used in various phrases to describe something that has proved effective or reliable before: *novel applications of* ***tried-and-tested*** *methods.*
– PHRASES **the tried and true** something that has proved effective or reliable before: *supermarkets generally stick to the tried and true.*

triene /ˈtrʌɪiːn/ ▶ **noun** Chemistry an unsaturated hydrocarbon containing three double bonds between carbon atoms.

triennial /trʌɪˈɛnɪəl/ ▶ **adjective** recurring every three years: *the triennial meeting of the Association.*
▪lasting for or relating to a period of three years.
▶ **noun** a visitation of an Anglican diocese by its bishop every three years.
– DERIVATIVES **triennially** adverb.
– ORIGIN mid 16th cent.: from late Latin *triennis* (from Latin *tri-* 'three' + *annus* 'year') + **-AL**.

triennium /trʌɪˈɛnɪəm/ ▶ **noun** (pl. **triennia** /-nɪə/ or **trienniums**) a specified period of three years.
– ORIGIN mid 19th cent.: from Latin, from *tri-* 'three' + *annum* 'year'.

Trier /trɪə/ a city on the River Mosel in Rhineland-Palatinate, western Germany; pop. 98,750 (1991). French name **TRÈVES**. Established by a Germanic tribe, the Treveri, *c.*400 BC, Trier is one of the oldest cities in Europe. It was a powerful archbishopric from 815 until the 18th century, but fell into decline after the French occupation in 1797.

trier ▶ **noun** **1** a person who always makes an effort, however unsuccessful they may be: *Kelly was described by her teachers as a real trier.*
2 a person or body responsible for investigating and deciding a case judicially: *the jury is the* ***trier of fact.***

Trieste /trɪˈɛst/ a city in NE Italy, the largest port on the Adriatic and capital of Friuli-Venezia Giulia region; pop. 231,000 (1990). Formerly held by Austria (1382–1918), Trieste was annexed by Italy after the First World War. The Free Territory of Trieste was created after the Second World War but returned to Italy in 1954.

trifa /ˈtrʌɪfə/ ▶ **adjective** another term for **TREFA**.

trifacial nerve /trʌɪˈfeɪʃ(ə)l/ ▶ **noun** another term for **TRIGEMINAL NERVE**.

trifecta /trʌɪˈfɛktə/ ▶ **noun** N. Amer. & Austral./NZ a bet in which the person betting forecasts the first three finishers in a race in the correct order. See also **TRICAST**.
▪[in sing.] a run of three wins or grand events: *today is a trifecta of birthdays.*
– ORIGIN 1970s: from **TRI-** 'three' + **PERFECTA**.

triffid ▶ **noun** (in science fiction) one of a race of predatory plants which are capable of growing to a gigantic size and are possessed of locomotor ability and a poisonous sting.
– ORIGIN coined by John Wyndham in *Day of the Triffids* (1951).

trifid /ˈtrʌɪfɪd/ ▶ **adjective** **1** chiefly Biology partly or wholly split into three divisions or lobes.
2 (also **trefid**) (of an antique spoon) with three notches splitting the end of the handle.
– ORIGIN mid 18th cent.: from Latin *trifidus*, from *tri-* 'three' + *fid-* 'split, divided' (from the verb *findere*).

trifle ▶ **noun** **1** a thing of little value or importance: *we needn't trouble the headmaster over such trifles.*
▪[in sing.] a small amount of something: *the thousand yen he'd paid seemed the merest trifle.*
2 Brit. a cold dessert of sponge cake and fruit covered with layers of custard, jelly, and cream.
▶ **verb** [no obj.] **1** (**trifle with**) treat (someone or something) without seriousness or respect: *he is not a man* ***to be trifled with*** | *men who trifle with women's affections.*
2 archaic talk or act frivolously: *we will not trifle—life is too short.*
▪[with obj.] (**trifle something away**) waste (something, especially time) frivolously.
– PHRASES **a trifle** a little; somewhat: *his methods are a trifle eccentric.*
– DERIVATIVES **trifler** noun.
– ORIGIN Middle English (also denoting an idle story told to deceive or amuse): from Old French *trufle*, by-form of *trufe* 'deceit', of unknown origin. The verb derives from Old French *truffler* 'mock, deceive'.

trifling ▶ **adjective** unimportant or trivial: *a trifling sum.*
– DERIVATIVES **triflingly** adverb.

trifluoperazine /ˌtrʌɪfluːə(ʊ)ˈpɛrəziːn/ ▶ **noun** [mass noun] Medicine an antipsychotic and sedative drug related to phenothiazine.
– ORIGIN mid 20th cent.: from **TRI-** + *fluo(rine)* + *(pi)perazine*.

trifocal ▶ **adjective** (of a pair of glasses) having lenses with three parts with different focal lengths.
▶ **noun** (**trifocals**) a pair of glasses with such lenses.

trifoliate /trʌɪˈfəʊlɪət/ ▶ **adjective** (of a compound leaf) having three leaflets: *dark green trifoliate leaves.*
▪(of a plant) having such leaves. ▪(of an object or design) having the form of such a leaf: *a bronze trifoliate key handle.*

triforium /trʌɪˈfɔːrɪəm/ ▶ **noun** (pl. **triforia** /-rɪə/) a gallery or arcade above the arches of the nave, choir, and transepts of a church.
– ORIGIN early 18th cent.: from Anglo-Latin, of unknown origin.

triform ▶ **adjective** technical composed of three parts: *strawberries nestling among their triform leaves.*

trifurcate ▶ **verb** /ˈtrʌɪfəkeɪt/ [no obj.] divide into three branches or forks.
▶ **adjective** /-ˈfəːkət/ divided into three branches or forks.
– DERIVATIVES **trifurcation** noun.
– ORIGIN mid 19th cent.: from Latin *trifurcus* 'three-forked' (from *tri-* 'three' + *furca* 'fork') + **-ATE**[2].

trig[1] ▶ **noun** [mass noun] informal trigonometry.
– ORIGIN late 19th cent.: abbreviation.

trig[2] US or archaic ▶ **adjective** neat and smart in appearance: *two trig little boys, each in a gray flannel suit.*
▶ **verb** (**trigged**, **trigging**) [with obj.] make neat and smart in appearance: *he has rigged her and trigged her with paint and spar.*
– ORIGIN Middle English (in the sense 'faithful, trusty'): from Old Norse *tryggr*; related to **TRUE**. The current verb sense dates from the late 17th cent.

trigamous /ˈtrɪgəməs/ ▶ **adjective** having three wives or husbands at the same time.
– DERIVATIVES **trigamist** noun, **trigamy** noun.
– ORIGIN mid 19th cent.: from Greek *trigamos* (from *tri-* 'three' + *gamos* 'marriage') + **-OUS**. The nouns *trigamist* and *trigamy* date from the mid 17th cent.

trigeminal nerve /trʌɪˈdʒɛmɪn(ə)l/ ▶ **noun** Anatomy each of the fifth and largest pair of cranial nerves, supplying the front part of the head and dividing into the ophthalmic, maxillary, and mandibular nerves.

trigeminal neuralgia ▶ **noun** [mass noun] Medicine neuralgia involving one or more of the branches of the trigeminal nerves, and often causing severe pain.

trigeminus /trʌɪˈdʒɛmɪnəs/ ▶ **noun** (pl. **trigemini** /-nʌɪ/) Anatomy the trigeminal nerve.
– ORIGIN late 19th cent.: from Latin, literally 'three born at the same birth', extended to mean 'threefold'.

trigger ▶ **noun** a small device that releases a spring or catch and so sets off a mechanism, especially in order to fire a gun: *he pulled the trigger of the shotgun.*
▪an event or thing that causes something to happen: *the trigger for the strike was the closure of a mine.*
▶ **verb** [with obj.] **1** (often **be triggered**) cause (an event or situation) to happen or exist: *an allergy can be triggered by stress or overwork.*
▪cause (a device) to function.
– PHRASES **quick on the trigger** quick to respond.
– DERIVATIVES **triggered** adjective.
– ORIGIN early 17th cent.: from dialect *tricker*, from Dutch *trekker*, from *trekken* 'to pull'.

trigger finger ▶ **noun** **1** the forefinger of the right hand, as that with which the trigger of a gun is typically pulled.
2 [mass noun] Medicine a defect in a tendon causing a

finger to jerk or snap straight when the hand is extended.

triggerfish ▶ noun (pl. same or **-fishes**) a marine fish occurring chiefly in tropical inshore waters. It has a large stout dorsal spine which can be erected and locked into place, allowing the fish to wedge itself into crevices.
• Family Balistidae: numerous genera and species.

trigger hair ▶ noun a hair-like structure which triggers a rapid movement when touched, in particular:
■ Zoology (in a coelenterate) a filament at the mouth of a nematocyst, triggering the emission of the stinging hair. ■ Botany a bristle on the leaf of a Venus flytrap, triggering the closure of the leaf around an insect.

trigger-happy ▶ adjective ready to react violently, especially by shooting, on the slightest provocation: *territory controlled by trigger-happy bandits.*

trigger point ▶ noun a particular circumstance or situation which causes an event to occur: *the army's refusal to withdraw from the territory was the trigger point for military action.*
■ Physiology & Medicine a sensitive area of the body, stimulation or irritation of which causes a specific effect in another part, especially a tender area in a muscle which causes generalized musculoskeletal pain when overstimulated.

Triglav /ˈtriːglaf/ a mountain in the Julian Alps, NW Slovenia, near the Italian border. Rising to 2,863 m (9,392 ft), it is the highest peak in the mountains east of the Adriatic.

triglyceride /trʌɪˈglɪsərʌɪd/ ▶ noun Chemistry an ester formed from glycerol and three fatty acid groups. Triglycerides are the main constituents of natural fats and oils.

triglyph /ˈtrʌɪglɪf/ ▶ noun Architecture a tablet in a Doric frieze with three vertical grooves alternating with metopes.
– DERIVATIVES **triglyphic** adjective.
– ORIGIN mid 16th cent.: via Latin from Greek *trigluphos*, from *tri-* 'three' + *gluphē* 'carving'.

trigon /ˈtrʌɪgɒn/ ▶ noun archaic term for **TRIANGLE**.
■ an ancient triangular lyre or harp. ■ a triangular cutting region formed by three cusps on an upper molar tooth.
– ORIGIN early 17th cent. (in the sense 'triangle'): via Latin from Greek *trigōnon*, neuter of *trigōnos* 'three-cornered'.

trigonal /ˈtrɪg(ə)n(ə)l/ ▶ adjective triangular: *square or trigonal double-sided inserts.*
■ chiefly Biology triangular in cross section: *large trigonal shells.* ■ of or denoting a crystal system or three-dimensional geometrical arrangement having three equal axes separated by equal angles that are not right angles.
– DERIVATIVES **trigonally** adverb.
– ORIGIN late 16th cent.: from medieval Latin *trigonalis*, from Latin *trigonum* (see **TRIGON**).

trigone /trɪˈgəʊn, ˈtrʌɪ-/ ▶ noun Anatomy a triangular region or tissue, particularly the area at the base of the urinary bladder, between the openings of the ureters and urethra.
– ORIGIN mid 19th cent.: from French, from Latin *trigonum* 'triangle'.

trigonometry /ˌtrɪgəˈnɒmɪtri/ ▶ noun [mass noun] the branch of mathematics dealing with the relations of the sides and angles of triangles and with the relevant functions of any angles.
– DERIVATIVES **trigonometric** /-nəˈmɛtrɪk/ adjective, **trigonometrical** adjective.
– ORIGIN early 17th cent.: from modern Latin *trigonometria* (see **TRIGON**, **-METRY**).

trig point ▶ noun Brit. a reference point on high ground used in surveying, typically marked by a small pillar.
– ORIGIN mid 19th cent.: abbreviation of *trigonometrical point.*

trigram /ˈtrʌɪgram/ ▶ noun **1** another term for **TRIGRAPH**.
2 each of the eight figures formed of three parallel lines, each either whole or broken, combined to form the sixty-four hexagrams of the *I Ching.*

trigraph /ˈtrʌɪgrɑːf/ ▶ noun a group of three letters representing one sound, for example German *sch-.*

trihedral /trʌɪˈhiːdr(ə)l, -ˈhɛdr(ə)l/ ▶ adjective (of a solid figure or body) having three sides or faces (in addition to the base or ends); triangular in cross section.
▶ noun a trihedral figure.
– ORIGIN late 18th cent.: from Greek *tri-* 'three' + *hedra* 'base' + **-AL**.

trihedron /trʌɪˈhiːdrən, -ˈhɛdrən/ ▶ noun (pl. **trihedra** /-drə/ or **trihedrons**) a solid figure having three sides or faces (in addition to the base or ends).
– ORIGIN early 19th cent.: from **TRI-** 'three' + **-HEDRON**, on the pattern of words such as *polyhedron.*

trihydric /trʌɪˈhʌɪdrɪk/ ▶ adjective Chemistry (of an alcohol) containing three hydroxyl groups.
– ORIGIN mid 19th cent.: from **TRI-** 'three' + **HYDROGEN** + **-IC**.

triiodomethane /trʌɪˌʌɪədə(ʊ)ˈmiːθeɪn/ ▶ noun another term for **IODOFORM**.

triiodothyronine /trʌɪˌʌɪədə(ʊ)ˈθʌɪrəniːn/ ▶ noun [mass noun] Biochemistry a thyroid hormone similar to thyroxine but having greater potency.

trike informal ▶ noun **1** a tricycle.
2 a kind of ultralight aircraft.
▶ verb [no obj.] ride on a tricycle.
– ORIGIN late 19th cent.: abbreviation.

trilateral ▶ adjective shared by or involving three parties: *trilateral negotiations.*
■ Geometry of, on, or with three sides.
▶ noun a triangle.

trilby ▶ noun (pl. **-ies**) chiefly Brit. a soft felt hat with a narrow brim and indented crown.
– DERIVATIVES **trilbied** adjective.
– ORIGIN late 19th cent.: from the name of the heroine in G. du Maurier's novel *Trilby* (1894), in the stage version of which such a hat was worn.

trilinear ▶ adjective Mathematics of or having three lines.

trilingual ▶ adjective (of a person) speaking three languages fluently.
■ (of a text or an activity) written or conducted in three languages: *CNN have begun offering a trilingual entertainment service.*
– DERIVATIVES **trilingualism** noun.
– ORIGIN mid 19th cent.: from **TRI-** 'three' + Latin *lingua* 'tongue' + **-AL**.

trilithon /trʌɪˈlɪθ(ə)n/ (also **trilith** /ˈtrʌɪlɪθ/) ▶ noun Archaeology a megalithic structure consisting of two upright stones and a third across the top as a lintel.
– ORIGIN mid 18th cent.: from Greek, from *tri-* 'three' + *lithos* 'stone'.

trill ▶ noun a quavering or vibratory sound, especially a rapid alternation of sung or played notes: *they heard the muffled trill of the telephone | the caged bird launched into a piercing trill.*
■ the pronunciation of a consonant, especially *r*, with rapid vibration of the tongue against the hard or soft palate or the uvula.
▶ verb [no obj.] produce a quavering or warbling sound: *a skylark was trilling overhead* | [with direct speech] *'Coming sir,' they both trilled.*
■ [with obj.] sing (a note or song) with a warbling or quavering sound: *trilling a love ballad, she led him to her chair.* ■ [with obj.] pronounce (a consonant) by rapid vibration of the tongue against the hard or soft palate or the uvula.
– ORIGIN mid 17th cent.: from Italian *trillo* (noun), *trillare* (verb).

triller ▶ noun an Australasian and SE Asian songbird of the cuckoo-shrike family, with mainly black and white plumage.
• Family Campephagidae: two genera, in particular *Lalage*, and several species.

trillion ▶ cardinal number (pl. **trillions** or (with numeral) same) a million million (1,000,000,000,000 or 10^{12}).
■ (**trillions**) informal a very large number or amount: *the yammering of trillions of voices.* ■ dated, chiefly Brit. a million million million (1,000,000,000,000,000,000 or 10^{18}).
– DERIVATIVES **trillionth** ordinal number.
– ORIGIN late 17th cent.: from French, from *million*, by substitution of the prefix *tri-* 'three' for the initial letters.

trillium /ˈtrɪlɪəm/ ▶ noun a plant with a solitary three-petalled flower above a whorl of three leaves, native to North America and Asia.
• Genus *Trillium*, family Liliaceae (or Trilliaceae).
– ORIGIN modern Latin, apparently an alteration of Swedish *trilling* 'triplet'.

trilobite /ˈtrʌɪlə(ʊ)bʌɪt, ˈtrɪ-/ ▶ noun a fossil marine arthropod that occurred abundantly during the Palaeozoic era, with a carapace over the forepart, and a segmented hindpart divided longitudinally into three lobes.
• Subphylum Trilobita, phylum Arthropoda: numerous classes and orders.
– ORIGIN mid 19th cent.: from modern Latin *Trilobites*, from Greek *tri-* 'three' + *lobos* 'lobe'.

trilogy ▶ noun (pl. **-ies**) a group of three related novels, plays, films, operas, or albums.
■ (in ancient Greece) a series of three tragedies performed one after the other. [ORIGIN: from Greek *trilogia*.] ■ figurative a group or series of three related things: *a trilogy of cases reflected this development.*

Trim a town in Meath, in the Republic of Ireland, situated to the north-west of Dublin; pop. 18,120 (1991).

trim ▶ verb (**trimmed**, **trimming**) [with obj.] **1** make (something) neat or of the required size or form by cutting away irregular or unwanted parts: *trim the grass using a sharp mower.*
■ [with obj. and adverbial] cut off (irregular or unwanted parts): *he was* **trimming** *the fat* **off** *some pork chops.* ■ figurative reduce the size, amount, or number of (something, typically expenditure or costs): *Congress had to decide which current defence programmes should be trimmed.* ■ [no obj.] (**trim down**) (of a person) lose weight; become slimmer: *he trimmed down from twenty-two stone to a mere eighteen.* ■ firm up or lose weight from (a part of one's body).
2 (usu. **be trimmed**) decorate (something), typically with contrasting items or pieces of material: *a pair of black leather gloves* **trimmed with** *fake fur.*
3 adjust (a sail) to take advantage of the wind.
■ adjust the balance of (a ship or aircraft) by rearranging its cargo. ■ keep or adjust the degree to which (an aircraft) can be maintained at a constant altitude without any control forces being present. ■ [no obj.] adapt one's views to the prevailing political trends for personal advancement.
4 informal, dated get the better of (someone), typically by cheating them out of money.
5 informal, dated rebuke (someone) angrily.
▶ noun [mass noun] **1** additional decoration, typically along the edges of something and in contrasting colour or material: *suede sandals with gold trim* | [count noun] *we painted the buildings off-white with a blue trim.*
■ decorative additions to a vehicle, typically the upholstery or interior lining of a car.
2 [in sing.] an act of cutting off part of something in order to neaten it: *his hair needs a trim.*
■ [count noun] a short piece of film cut out during the final editing stage.
3 the state of being in good order or condition: *no one had been there for months—everything was out of trim.*
4 the degree to which an aircraft can be maintained at a constant altitude without any control forces being present: *the pilot's only problem was the need to constantly readjust the trim.*
5 the way in which a ship floats in the water, especially in relation to the fore-and-aft line.
▶ adjective (**trimmer**, **trimmest**) neat and smart in appearance; in good order: *she kept her husband's clothes neat and trim | a trim little villa.*
■ (of a person or their body) slim and fit: *she has a trim, athletic figure.*
– PHRASES **in trim** slim and fit. ■ Nautical in good order. **trim one's sails** (**to the wind**) make changes to suit one's new circumstances.
– DERIVATIVES **trimly** adverb, **trimness** noun.
– ORIGIN Old English *trymman, trymian* 'make firm, arrange', of which the adjective appears to be a derivative. The word's history is obscure; current verb senses date from the early 16th cent. when usage became frequent and served many purposes: this is possibly explained by spoken or dialect use in the Middle English period not recorded in extant literature.

trimaran /ˈtrʌɪməran/ ▶ noun a yacht with three hulls in parallel.
– ORIGIN 1940s: from **TRI-** + **CATAMARAN**.

trimer /ˈtrʌɪmə/ ▶ noun Chemistry a polymer comprising three monomer units.
– DERIVATIVES **trimeric** adjective.

trimerous /ˈtrɪm(ə)rəs, ˈtrʌɪ-/ ▶ adjective Botany & Zoology having parts arranged in groups of three.
■ consisting of three joints or parts.

trimester /trʌɪˈmɛstə/ ▶ noun a period of three months, especially as a division of the duration of pregnancy.
■ US each of the three terms in an academic year.

t

– DERIVATIVES **trimestral** adjective, **trimestrial** adjective.
– ORIGIN early 19th cent.: from French *trimestre*, from Latin *trimestris*, from *tri-* 'three' + *mensis* 'month'.

trimeter /ˈtrɪmɪtə, ˈtrʌɪ-/ ▶ **noun** Prosody a line of verse consisting of three metrical feet.
– DERIVATIVES **trimetric** adjective, **trimetrical** adjective.
– ORIGIN mid 16th cent.: via Latin from Greek *trimetros*, from *tri-* 'three' + *metron* 'measure'.

trimethoprim /trʌɪˈmɛθə(ʊ)prɪm/ ▶ **noun** [mass noun] Medicine a synthetic antibiotic used to treat malaria and respiratory and urinary infections (usually in conjunction with a sulphonamide).
– ORIGIN 1960s: from *trimeth(yl)* + *o(xy-)* + *p(y)rim(idine)*.

trimix /ˈtrʌɪmɪks/ ▶ **noun** [mass noun] a breathing mixture for deep-sea divers, composed of nitrogen, helium, and oxygen.

trimmer ▶ **noun 1** an implement used for trimming off the unwanted or untidy parts of something: *a hedge trimmer.*
2 a person who adapts their views to the prevailing political trends for personal advancement.
3 a person who decorates something: *window trimmers.*
4 (also **trimmer joist**) Architecture a crosspiece fixed between full-length joists (and often across the end of truncated joists) to form part of the frame of an opening in a floor or roof.
5 a person responsible for trimming the sails of a yacht.
■ a person employed to arrange cargo or fuel in a ship's hold.
6 a small capacitor or other component used to tune a circuit such as a radio set.
7 Austral./NZ informal an excellent or outstanding person or thing.

trimming ▶ **noun 1** [mass noun] the action of cutting off the unwanted or untidy parts of something: *he keeps his hair short by continual trimming.*
■ (**trimmings**) small pieces cut off in such a way: *hedge trimmings.*
2 (usu. **trimmings**) decoration, especially for clothing: *a white romper suit with pink trimmings* | [mass noun] *a party dress with lace trimming.*
■ (**the trimmings**) informal the traditional accompaniments to something, especially a meal or special occasion: *roast turkey* ***with all the trimmings.***

Trimontium /trʌɪˈmɒntɪəm/ Roman name for **PLOVDIV**.

trimpot ▶ **noun** a small potentiometer used to make small adjustments to the value of resistance or voltage in an electronic circuit.

trim tab (also **trimming tab**) ▶ **noun** Aeronautics an adjustable tab or aerofoil attached to a control surface, used to trim an aircraft in flight.

Trimurti /trɪˈmɔːti, trɪˈmʊəti/ Hinduism the trinity of Brahma, Vishnu, and Shiva.
– ORIGIN from Sanskrit *tri* 'three' + *mūrti* 'form'.

Trincomalee /ˌtrɪŋkəməˈliː/ the principal port of Sri Lanka, on the east coast; pop. 44,300 (1981). It was the chief British naval base in SE Asia during the Second World War after the fall of Singapore.

trine /trʌɪn/ Astrology ▶ **noun** an aspect of 120° (one third of a circle): *Venus* ***in trine to*** *Mars* | [as modifier] *a trine aspect.* See also **GRAND TRINE**.
▶ **verb** [with obj.] (of a planet) be in a trine aspect with (another planet or position): *Jupiter trines Pluto all month.*
– ORIGIN late Middle English (in the sense 'made up of three parts'): from Old French *trin(e)*, from Latin *trinus* 'threefold', from *tres* 'three'.

Trini /ˈtrɪni/ ▶ **noun** W. Indian a Trinidadian.
– ORIGIN abbreviation.

Trinidad and Tobago /ˈtrɪnɪdad, təˈbeɪgəʊ/ a country in the Caribbean consisting of two islands off the NE coast of Venezuela; pop. 1,213,700 (1990); languages, English (official), Creoles; capital, Port-of-Spain (on Trinidad).

Much the larger of the two islands is Trinidad, with Tobago to the north-east. Trinidad, inhabited by Arawaks, was visited by Columbus in 1498 and settled by the Spanish; Tobago, occupied by Caribs, was colonized by the French and later the British in the 18th century. Trinidad became British during the Napoleonic Wars and was formally amalgamated with Tobago as a Crown Colony in 1888. Trinidad and Tobago became an independent member state of the Commonwealth in 1962 and finally a republic in 1976.

– DERIVATIVES **Trinidadian** /ˌtrɪnɪˈdeɪdɪən, -ˈdadɪən/ adjective & noun, **Tobagan** adjective & noun, **Tobagonian** /ˌtəʊbəˈgəʊnɪən/ adjective & noun.

Trinitarian /ˌtrɪnɪˈtɛːrɪən/ ▶ **adjective** of or relating to belief in the doctrine of the Trinity.
▶ **noun** a person who believes in the doctrine of the Trinity.
– DERIVATIVES **Trinitarianism** noun.

trinitrotoluene /trʌɪˌnʌɪtrəʊˈtɒljʊiːn/ ▶ **noun** see **TNT**.

trinity ▶ **noun** (pl. **-ies**) (also **the Trinity** or **the Holy Trinity**) the three persons of the Christian Godhead; Father, Son, and Holy Spirit.
■ a group of three people or things: *the wine was the first of a trinity of three excellent vintages.* ■ [mass noun] the state of being three: *God is said to be trinity in unity.*
– ORIGIN Middle English: from Old French *trinite*, from Latin *trinitas* 'triad', from *trinus* 'threefold' (see **TRINE**).

Trinity Brethren ▶ **plural noun** the members of Trinity House.

Trinity House an association founded in 1514 responsible for the licensing of ships' pilots and the construction and maintenance of buoys and lighthouses around the coasts of England and Wales.

Trinity Sunday ▶ **noun** the next Sunday after Pentecost, observed in the Western Christian Church as a feast in honour of the Holy Trinity.

Trinity term ▶ **noun** Brit. (in some universities) the term beginning after Easter.
■ a session of the High Court beginning after Easter.

trinket ▶ **noun** a small ornament or item of jewellery that is of little value.
– DERIVATIVES **trinketry** noun.
– ORIGIN mid 16th cent.: of unknown origin.

trinomial /trʌɪˈnəʊmɪəl/ ▶ **adjective 1** (of an algebraic expression) consisting of three terms.
2 Biology (of a taxonomic name) consisting of three terms where the first is the name of the genus, the second that of the species, and the third that of the subspecies or variety.
▶ **noun 1** an algebraic expression of three terms.
2 Biology a trinomial taxonomic name.
– ORIGIN late 17th cent.: from **TRI-** 'three', on the pattern of *binomial*.

trio ▶ **noun** (pl. **-os**) **1** a set or group of three people or things: *the hotel was run by a trio of brothers.*
■ a group of three musicians: *a jazz trio.* ■ a composition written for three musicians: *Chopin's G minor Trio.* ■ the central, typicallycontrastive, section of a minuet, scherzo, or march. ■ (in piquet) a set of three aces, kings, queens, jacks, or tens held in one hand.
– ORIGIN early 18th cent.: from Italian, from Latin *tres* 'three', on the pattern of *duo*.

triode /ˈtrʌɪəʊd/ ▶ **noun** a thermionic valve having three electrodes.
■ a semiconductor rectifier having three connections.
– ORIGIN early 20th cent.: from **TRI-** 'three' + **ELECTRODE**.

triolet /ˈtriːə(ʊ)lɛt, ˈtrʌɪəlɛt/ ▶ **noun** a poem of eight lines, typically of eight syllables each, rhyming *abaaabab* and so structured that the first line recurs as the fourth and seventh and the second as the eighth.
– ORIGIN mid 17th cent.: from French.

triose /ˈtrʌɪəʊz, -s/ ▶ **noun** Chemistry any of a group of monosaccharide sugars whose molecules contain three carbon atoms.

trio sonata ▶ **noun** a baroque composition written in three parts, two upper parts and one bass, and usually performed with a keyboard continuo.

trioxide ▶ **noun** Chemistry an oxide containing three atoms of oxygen in its molecule or empirical formula.

trip ▶ **verb** (**tripped**, **tripping**) **1** [no obj.] catch one's foot on something and stumble or fall: *he* ***tripped over*** *his cat* | *she* ***tripped up*** *during the penultimate lap.*
■ [with obj.] cause (someone) to do this: *she shot out her foot to* ***trip him up.*** ■ (**trip up**) make a mistake: *taxpayers often trip up by not declaring taxable income.* ■ [with obj.] (**trip someone up**) detect or expose someone in an error, blunder, or inconsistency: *the man was determined to trip him up on his economics.*
2 [no obj., with adverbial] walk, run, or dance with quick light steps: *they tripped up the terrace steps.*
■ (of words) flow lightly and easily: *a name which* ***trips off the tongue*** | *the guest list tripped from her lips.*
3 [with obj.] activate (a mechanism), especially by contact with a switch, catch, or other electrical device: *an intruder trips the alarm.*
■ [no obj.] (of part of an electric circuit) disconnect automatically as a safety measure: *the plugs will trip as soon as any change in current is detected.*
4 [with obj.] Nautical release and raise (an anchor) from the seabed by means of a cable.
■ turn (a yard or other object) from a horizontal to a vertical position for lowering.
5 [no obj.] informal experience hallucinations induced by taking a psychedelic drug, especially LSD: *a couple of boys were tripping.*
6 [no obj., with adverbial of direction] go on a short journey: *when tripping through the Yukon take some time to explore our museums.*
▶ **noun 1** a journey or excursion, especially for pleasure: *Sammy's gone on a school trip* | *a trip to America.*
■ the distance from start to finish of a race: *the dog clocked a tremendous 27.47 secs for the 450 metres trip.*
2 a stumble or fall due to catching one's foot on something.
■ archaic a mistake: *an occasional trip in the performance.*
3 informal a hallucinatory experience caused by taking a psychedelic drug, especially LSD: *acid trips.*
■ an exciting or stimulating experience: *it was quite a trip talking to you.* ■ a self-indulgent attitude or activity: *politics was a sixties trip.*
4 a device that activates or disconnects a mechanism, circuit, etc.
■ an instance of a device deactivating or the power supply disconnecting as a safety measure.
5 archaic a light, lively movement of a person's feet: *yonder comes Dalinda; I know her by her trip.*
– PHRASES **trip the light fantastic** humorous dance, in particular engage in ballroom dancing. [ORIGIN: from 'Trip it as you go On the light fantastic toe' (Milton's *L'Allegro*).]
– ORIGIN Middle English: from Old French *triper*, from Middle Dutch *trippen* 'to skip, hop'.

tripartite /trʌɪˈpɑːtʌɪt/ ▶ **adjective** consisting of three parts: *a tripartite classification.*
■ shared by or involving three parties: *a tripartite coalition government.*
– DERIVATIVES **tripartitely** adverb, **tripartition** noun.
– ORIGIN late Middle English: from Latin *tripartitus*, from *tri-* 'three' + *partitus* 'divided' (past participle of *partiri*).

trip computer ▶ **noun** an electronic odometer, typically with extra capabilities such as the ability to calculate fuel consumption.

tripe ▶ **noun** [mass noun] **1** the first or second stomach of a cow or other ruminant used as food.
2 informal nonsense; rubbish: *you do talk tripe sometimes.*
– ORIGIN Middle English: from Old French, of unknown origin.

trip hammer ▶ **noun** a large, heavy pivoted hammer used in forging, raised by a cam or lever and allowed to drop on the metal being worked.

trip hop ▶ **noun** [mass noun] a style of dance music, usually slow in tempo, that combines elements of hip hop and dub reggae with softer, more ambient sounds.

triphthong /ˈtrɪfθɒŋ/ ▶ **noun** a union of three vowels (letters or sounds) pronounced in one syllable (as in *fire*). Contrasted with **DIPHTHONG**, **MONOPHTHONG**.
■ three written vowel characters representing the sound of a single vowel (as in *beau*).
– DERIVATIVES **triphthongal** adjective.
– ORIGIN mid 16th cent.: from French *triphtongue*, from *tri-* 'three', on the pattern of *diphthong*.

Tripitaka /trɪˈpɪtəkə/ ▶ **noun** (**the Tripitaka**) the sacred canon of Theravada Buddhism, written in the Pali language.
– ORIGIN from Sanskrit *tripiṭaka*, literally 'the three baskets or collections'.

triplane ▶ **noun** an early type of aeroplane with three pairs of wings, one above the other.

triple ▶ **adjective** [attrib.] consisting of or involving three parts, things, or people: *a triple murder* | *triple somersaults.*
■ having three times the usual size, quality, or strength: *a triple dark rum.* ■ (of a person or animal) having done or won something three times: *a triple champion.*
▶ **predeterminer** three times as much or as many: *the copper energy cells had triple the efficiency of silicon cells.*
▶ **noun 1** a set of three things or parts.

t

■an amount that is three times as large as another: *Rowe scored two single centuries and a triple.*
2 (**triples**) a sporting contest in which each side has three players.
3 (**triples**) Bell-ringing a system of change-ringing using seven bells, with three pairs changing places each time.
4 Baseball a hit which enables the batter to reach third base.
▶**verb** [no obj.] become three times as much or as many: *grain prices were expected to triple.*
■[with obj.] multiply (something) by three: *the party more than tripled its share of the vote.*
– DERIVATIVES **triply** adverb.
– ORIGIN Middle English (as an adjective and adverb): from Old French, or from Latin *triplus*, from Greek *triplous*.

triple A ▶**noun 1** [usu. as modifier] Finance the highest grading available from credit rating agencies.
2 the highest competitive level of achievement in baseball.

triple acrostic ▶**noun** an acrostic in which the first, middle, and last letters of each line form hidden words.

Triple Alliance ▶**noun** a union or association between three powers or states, in particular that made in 1668 between England, the Netherlands, and Sweden against France, and that in 1882 between Germany, Austria-Hungary, and Italy against France and Russia.

triple bond ▶**noun** Chemistry a chemical bond in which three pairs of electrons are shared between two atoms.

triple crown ▶**noun 1** (**Triple Crown**) an award or honour for winning a group of three important events in a sport, in particular (in rugby union) victory by one of the four British home countries over all the other three in the same season.
2 the papal tiara.

Triple Entente an early 20th-century alliance between Great Britain, France, and Russia. Originally a series of loose agreements, the Triple Entente began to assume the nature of a more formal alliance as the prospect of war with the Central Powers became more likely, and formed the basis of the Allied powers in the First World War.

triple harp ▶**noun** a large harp without pedals, and with three rows of strings, the middle row providing sharps and flats. Also called **WELSH HARP**.

triple jump ▶**noun 1** (**the triple jump**) an athletic event in which competitors attempt to jump as far as possible by performing a hop, a step, and a jump from a running start.
2 Skating a jump in which the skater makes three full turns while in the air.
▶**verb** (**triple-jump**) [no obj.] (of an athlete) perform a triple jump.
– DERIVATIVES **triple jumper** noun.

triple play ▶**noun** Baseball a defensive play in which three runners are put out.

triple point ▶**noun** Chemistry the temperature and pressure at which the solid, liquid, and vapour phases of a pure substance can coexist in equilibrium.

triple rhyme ▶**noun** a rhyme involving three syllables.

triplet ▶**noun 1** (usu. **triplets**) one of three children or animals born at the same birth.
2 a set or succession of three similar things.
■Music a group of three equal notes to be performed in the time of two or four. ■a set of three rhyming lines of verse.
3 Physics & Chemistry an atomic or molecular state characterized by two unpaired electrons with parallel spins.
■a group of three associated lines close together in a spectrum or electrophoretic gel.
– ORIGIN mid 17th cent.: from **TRIPLE**, on the pattern of *doublet*.

triplet code ▶**noun** Biology the standard version of the genetic code, in which a sequence of three nucleotides on a DNA or RNA molecule codes for a specific amino acid in protein synthesis.

triple time ▶**noun** [mass noun] musical time with three beats to the bar.

triple tonguing ▶**noun** [mass noun] Music a technique in which alternate movements of the tongue are made (typically as in sounding *ttk*) to facilitate rapid playing of a wind instrument.

triplex /ˈtrɪplɛks/ ▶**noun 1** (**Triplex**) [mass noun] Brit. trademark toughened or laminated safety glass, used especially for car windows.
2 [count noun] N. Amer. a building divided into three self-contained residences.
3 Biochemistry a triple-stranded polynucleotide molecule.
▶**adjective** having three parts, in particular:
■N. Amer. (of a residence) on three floors: *his vast triplex apartment.* ■Biochemistry consisting of three polynucleotide strands linked side by side.
▶**verb** (**be triplexed**) (of electrical equipment or systems) be provided or fitted in triplicate so as to ensure reliability.
– ORIGIN early 17th cent. (as an adjective in the sense 'threefold'): from Latin, 'threefold', from *tri-* 'three' + *plicare* 'to fold'. Current specific senses date from the 1920s.

triplicate ▶**adjective** /ˈtrɪplɪkət/ [attrib.] existing in three copies or examples: *triplicate measurements.*
▶**noun** /ˈtrɪplɪkət/ archaic a thing which is part of a set of three copies or corresponding parts: *the triplicate of a letter to the Governor.*
▶**verb** /ˈtrɪplɪkeɪt/ [with obj.] make three copies of (something); multiply by three.
– PHRASES **in triplicate** three times in exactly the same way: *the procedure was repeated in triplicate.* ■existing as a set of three exact copies: *this form is in triplicate and must be handed to all employees.*
– DERIVATIVES **triplication** /-ˈkeɪʃ(ə)n/ noun.
– ORIGIN late Middle English: from Latin *triplicat-* 'made three', from the verb *triplicare*, from *triplex*, *triplic-* 'threefold' (see **TRIPLEX**). The verb dates from the early 17th cent.

triplicity /trɪˈplɪsɪti/ ▶**noun** (pl. **-ies**) rare a group of three people or things.
■[mass noun] archaic the state of being triple.
– ORIGIN late Middle English (as a term in astrology): from late Latin *triplicitas*, from Latin *triplex*, *triplic-* 'threefold' (see **TRIPLEX**).

triploblastic /ˌtrɪplə(ʊ)ˈblastɪk/ ▶**adjective** Zoology having a body derived from three embryonic cell layers (ectoderm, mesoderm, and endoderm), as in all multicellular animals except sponges and coelenterates.
– ORIGIN late 19th cent.: from Greek *triploos* 'threefold' + **-BLAST** + **-IC**.

triploid /ˈtrɪplɔɪd/ Genetics ▶**adjective** (of a cell or nucleus) containing three homologous sets of chromosomes.
■(of an organism or species) composed of triploid cells.
▶**noun** a triploid organism, variety, or species.
– DERIVATIVES **triploidy** noun.

tripmeter ▶**noun** a vehicle instrument that can be set to record the distance of individual journeys.

tripod /ˈtrʌɪpɒd/ ▶**noun 1** a three-legged stand for supporting a camera or other apparatus.
2 archaic a stool, table, or cauldron resting on three legs.
■historical the bronze altar at Delphi on which a priestess sat to utter oracles.
– DERIVATIVES **tripodal** /ˈtrɪpəd(ə)l/ adjective.
– ORIGIN early 17th cent.: via Latin from Greek *tripous*, *tripod-*, from *tri-* 'three' + *pous*, *pod-* 'foot'.

Tripoli /ˈtrɪpəli/ **1** the capital and chief port of Libya, on the Mediterranean coast in the north-west of the country; pop. 990,700 (1984). Founded by Phoenicians in the 7th century BC, its ancient name was Oea. Arabic name **TARABULUS AL-GHARB**, 'western Tripoli'.
2 a port in NW Lebanon; pop. 160,000 (1988). It was founded *c.*700 BC and was the capital of the Phoenician triple federation formed by the city states Sidon, Tyre, and Arvad. Today it is a major port and commercial centre of Lebanon. Arabic name **TARABULUS ASH-SHAM**, 'eastern Tripoli', **TRÂBLOUS**.

tripoli /ˈtrɪpəli/ ▶**noun** another term for **ROTTENSTONE**.
– ORIGIN early 17th cent.: from French, from **TRIPOLI**.

Tripolitania /ˌtrɪpəlɪˈteɪnɪə, trɪˌpɒlɪ-/ a coastal region surrounding Tripoli in North Africa, in what is now NE Libya.
– DERIVATIVES **Tripolitanian** adjective & noun.
– ORIGIN based on Latin *tripolis* 'three cities', referring to the Phoenician cities, Oea (now Tripoli), Leptis Magna, and Sabratha, established there in the 7th cent. BC.

tripos /ˈtrʌɪpɒs/ ▶**noun** [in sing.] the final honours examination for a BA degree at Cambridge University.
– ORIGIN late 16th cent.: alteration of Latin *tripus* 'tripod', with reference to the stool on which a designated graduate (known as the 'Tripos') sat to deliver a satirical speech at the degree ceremony. A sheet of humorous verses (at one time composed by the Tripos) was published on this occasion until the late 19th cent., on the back of which the list of successful candidates for the honours degree in mathematics was originally printed; hence the current sense.

trippant /ˈtrɪp(ə)nt/ ▶**adjective** [usu. postpositive] Heraldry (of a stag or deer) represented as walking. Compare with **PASSANT**.
– ORIGIN mid 17th cent.: from Old French, literally 'walking or springing lightly', present participle of *tripper*.

tripper ▶**noun** Brit. informal a person who goes on a pleasure trip or excursion.

tripple S. African ▶**noun** [in sing.] a horse's gait in which both left and then both right legs move together.
▶**verb** [no obj.] (of a horse or a horse and its rider) move at the pace of a tripple.
– ORIGIN late 19th cent.: from Dutch *trippelen*, from *trippen* 'to skip, trip'.

trippy ▶**adjective** (**trippier**, **trippiest**) informal resembling or inducing the hallucinatory effect produced by taking a psychedelic drug: *trippy house music.*

triptych /ˈtrɪptɪk/ ▶**noun** a picture or relief carving on three panels, typically hinged together vertically and used as an altarpiece.
■a set of three associated artistic, literary, or musical works intended to be appreciated together.
– ORIGIN mid 18th cent. (denoting a set of three writing tablets hinged or tied together): from **TRI-** 'three', on the pattern of *diptych*.

triptyque /trɪpˈtiːk/ ▶**noun** dated a customs permit serving as a passport for a motor vehicle.
– ORIGIN early 20th cent.: from French, literally 'triptych' (because originally the document had three sections).

Tripura /ˈtrɪpʊərə/ a small state in the far north-east of India, on the eastern border of Bangladesh; capital, Agartala. An ancient Hindu kingdom, Tripura acceded to India after independence in 1947, and achieved full status as a state in 1972.

tripwire ▶**noun** a wire stretched close to the ground, working a trap, explosion, or alarm when disturbed and serving to detect or prevent people or animals entering an area.
■a comparatively weak military force employed as a first line of defence, engagement with which will trigger the intervention of strong forces.

triquetra /trʌɪˈkwɛtrə, -ˈkwiːtrə/ ▶**noun** (pl. **triquetrae** /-triː/) a symmetrical triangular ornament of three interlaced arcs used on metalwork and stone crosses.
– ORIGIN late 16th cent. (originally denoting a triangle): from Latin, feminine of *triquetrus* 'three-cornered'.

triquetral (also **triquetral bone**) ▶**noun** Anatomy a carpal bone on the outside of the wrist, articulating with the lunate, hamate, and pisiform bones.
– ORIGIN mid 17th cent.: from Latin *triquetrus* 'three-cornered' + **-AL**.

trireme /ˈtrʌɪriːm/ ▶**noun** an ancient Greek or Roman war galley with three banks of oars. The rowers are believed to have sat in threes on angled benches, rather than in three superimposed banks.
– ORIGIN from Latin *triremis*, from *tri-* 'three' + *remus* 'oar'.

tris[1] /trɪs/ (also **tris buffer**) ▶**noun** [mass noun] a flammable compound which forms a corrosive solution in water and is used as a buffer and emulsifying agent.
• Alternative name: **trishydroxymethylaminomethane**; chem. formula: $(HOCH_2)_3CNH_2$.
– ORIGIN 1950s: from *tris-*, the prefix of the systematic name.

tris[2] /trɪs/ ▶**noun** [mass noun] an organophosphorus compound, used as a flame retardant.
• Alternative name: **tris-2,3-dibromopropylphosphate**; chem. formula: $(Br_2C_3H_5)_3PO_4$.
– ORIGIN 1970s: from *tris-*, the prefix of the systematic name.

trisaccharide /trʌɪˈsakərʌɪd/ ▶ **noun** Chemistry any of the class of sugars whose molecules contain three monosaccharide molecules.

Trisagion /trɪˈsagɪən, -ˈseɪgɪən/ ▶ **noun** a hymn, especially in the Orthodox Church, with a triple invocation of God as holy.
– ORIGIN late Middle English: from Greek, neuter of *trisagios*, from *tris* 'three times' + *hagios* 'holy'.

trisect /trʌɪˈsɛkt/ ▶ **verb** [with obj.] divide (something) into three parts, typically three equal parts.
– DERIVATIVES **trisection** noun, **trisector** noun.
– ORIGIN late 17th cent.: from **TRI-** 'three' + Latin *sect-* 'divided, cut' (from the verb *secare*).

trishaw /ˈtrʌɪʃɔː/ ▶ **noun** a light three-wheeled vehicle with pedals used in the Far East.
– ORIGIN 1940s: from **TRI-** 'three' + **RICKSHAW**.

triskaidekaphobia /ˌtrɪskʌɪdɛkəˈfəʊbɪə/ ▶ **noun** [mass noun] extreme superstition regarding the number thirteen.
– ORIGIN early 20th cent.: from Greek *treiskaideka* 'thirteen' + **-PHOBIA**.

triskelion /trɪˈskɛlɪən/ ▶ **noun** a Celtic symbol consisting of three legs or lines radiating from a centre.
– ORIGIN mid 19th cent.: from **TRI-** 'three' + Greek *skelos* 'leg'.

trismus /ˈtrɪzməs/ ▶ **noun** [mass noun] Medicine spasm of the jaw muscles, causing the mouth to remain tightly closed, typically as a symptom of tetanus. Also called **LOCKJAW**.
– ORIGIN late 17th cent.: from modern Latin, from Greek *trismos* 'a scream, grinding'.

trisomy /ˈtrɪsəmi/ ▶ **noun** Medicine a condition in which an extra copy of a chromosome is present in the cell nuclei, causing developmental abnormalities.
– ORIGIN 1930s: from **TRI-** 'three' + **-SOME**[3].

trisomy-21 ▶ **noun** [mass noun] Medicine the most common form of Down's syndrome, caused by an extra copy of chromosome number 21.

Tristan /ˈtrɪstən/ variant spelling of **TRISTRAM**.

Tristan da Cunha /ˌtrɪstən də ˈkuːnə/ the largest of a small group of volcanic islands in the South Atlantic, 2,112 km (1,320 miles) south-west of the British colony of St Helena, of which it is a dependency; pop. 292 (1996). It was discovered in 1506 by the Portuguese admiral Tristão da Cunha and annexed to Britain in 1816.

tristesse /trɪˈstɛs/ ▶ **noun** [mass noun] poetic/literary a state of melancholy sadness.
– ORIGIN French.

Tristram /ˈtrɪstrəm/ (also **Tristan**) (in medieval legend) a knight who was the lover of Iseult.

trisyllable /trʌɪˈsɪləb(ə)l/ ▶ **noun** a word or metrical foot of three syllables.
– DERIVATIVES **trisyllabic** adjective.

tritagonist /trʌɪˈtag(ə)nɪst, trɪ-/ ▶ **noun** the person who is third in importance, after the protagonist and deuteragonist, in an ancient Greek drama.
– ORIGIN late 19th cent.: from Greek *tritagōnistēs*, from *tritos* 'third' + *agōnistēs* 'actor'.

tritanope /ˈtrɪtənəʊp/ ▶ **noun** a person suffering from tritanopia.

tritanopia /ˌtrɪtəˈnəʊpɪə/ ▶ **noun** [mass noun] a rare form of colour blindness resulting from insensitivity to blue light, causing confusion of greens and blues. Compare with **PROTANOPIA**.
– ORIGIN early 20th cent.: from **TRITO-** 'third' (referring to blue as the third colour in the spectrum) + **AN-**[1] 'without' + **-OPIA**.

trite ▶ **adjective** (of a remark, opinion, or idea) overused and consequently of little import; lacking originality or freshness: *this point may now seem obvious and trite.*
– DERIVATIVES **tritely** adverb, **triteness** noun.
– ORIGIN mid 16th cent.: from Latin *tritus*, past participle of *terere* 'to rub'.

triterpene /trʌɪˈtəːpiːn/ ▶ **noun** Chemistry any of a group of terpenes found in plant gums and resins, having unsaturated molecules based on a unit with the formula $C_{30}H_{48}$.
– DERIVATIVES **triterpenoid** adjective & noun.

tritheism /ˈtrʌɪˌθiːɪz(ə)m/ ▶ **noun** [mass noun] (in Christian theology) the doctrine of or belief in the three persons of the Trinity as three distinct gods.
– DERIVATIVES **tritheist** noun.

tritiated /ˈtrɪtɪeɪtɪd/ ▶ **adjective** Chemistry (of a compound) in which the ordinary isotope of hydrogen has been replaced with tritium.
– DERIVATIVES **tritiation** noun.

triticale /ˌtrɪtɪˈkeɪli/ ▶ **noun** [mass noun] a hybrid cereal produced by crossing wheat and rye, grown as a fodder crop.
– ORIGIN 1950s: modern Latin, from a blend of the genus names *Triticum* 'wheat' and *Secale* 'rye'.

tritium /ˈtrɪtɪəm/ ▶ **noun** [mass noun] Chemistry a radioactive isotope of hydrogen with a mass approximately three times that of the usual isotope. (Symbol: **T**)

> Discovered in 1934, tritium has two neutrons as well as a proton in the nucleus. It occurs in minute traces in nature and can be made artificially from lithium or deuterium in nuclear reactors; it is used as a fuel in thermonuclear bombs.

– ORIGIN 1930s: from modern Latin, from Greek *tritos* 'third'.

trito- /ˈtrɪtəʊ, ˈtrʌɪtəʊ/ ▶ **combining form** third: *tritocerebrum.*
– ORIGIN from Greek *tritos* 'third'.

tritocerebrum /ˌtrɪtə(ʊ)ˈsɛrɪbrəm/ ▶ **noun** (pl. **tritocerebra** /-brə/) Entomology the third and hindmost segment of an insect's brain.

Triton /ˈtrʌɪt(ə)n/ **1** Greek Mythology a minor sea god usually represented as a man with a fish's tail and carrying a trident and shell-trumpet.
2 Astronomy the largest satellite of Neptune, the seventh closest to the planet and having a retrograde orbit and a thin nitrogen atmosphere, discovered in 1846 (diameter 2,700 km).

triton[1] ▶ **noun** a large mollusc which has a tall spiral shell with a large aperture, living in tropical and subtropical seas.
• Genus *Charonia*, family Cymatiidae, class Gastropoda, in particular *C. tritonis*, which is used as a trumpet shell.
– ORIGIN late 18th cent.: from **TRITON**.

triton[2] ▶ **noun** a nucleus of a tritium atom, consisting of a proton and two neutrons.
– ORIGIN 1940s: from **TRITIUM** + **-ON**.

tritone ▶ **noun** Music an interval of three whole tones (an augmented fourth), as between C and F sharp.

triturate /ˈtrɪtjʊreɪt/ ▶ **verb** [with obj.] technical grind to a fine powder.
■ chew or grind (food) thoroughly.
– DERIVATIVES **trituration** noun, **triturator** noun.
– ORIGIN mid 18th cent.: from Latin *triturat-* '(of corn) threshed', from *tritura* 'rubbing' (from the verb *terere*).

triumph ▶ **noun 1** a great victory or achievement: *a garden built to celebrate Napoleon's many triumphs.*
■ [mass noun] the state of being victorious or successful: *the king returned home* ***in triumph***. ■ [mass noun] joy or satisfaction resulting from a success or victory: *'Here it is!' Helen's voice rose* ***in triumph***. ■ a highly successful example of something: *the marriage had been a* ***triumph of*** *togetherness.*
2 the processional entry of a victorious general into ancient Rome.
▶ **verb** [no obj.] **1** achieve a victory; be successful: *they had no chance of* ***triumphing over*** *the Nationalists.*
■ rejoice or exult at a victory or success: *she stopped* ***triumphing over*** *Mrs Ward's failure.*
2 (of a Roman general) ride into ancient Rome after a victory.
– ORIGIN late Middle English: from Old French *triumphe* (noun), from Latin *triump(h)us*, probably from Greek *thriambos* 'hymn to Bacchus'. Current senses of the verb date from the early 16th cent.

triumphal ▶ **adjective** made, carried out, or used in celebration of a great victory or achievement: *a vast triumphal arch | a triumphal procession.*
– ORIGIN late Middle English: from Old French *triumphal* or Latin *triumphalis*, from *triump(h)us* (see **TRIUMPH**).

triumphalism ▶ **noun** [mass noun] excessive exultation over one's success or achievements (used especially in a political context): *an air of triumphalism reigns in his administration.*
– DERIVATIVES **triumphalist** adjective & noun.

triumphant ▶ **adjective** having won a battle or contest; victorious: *two of their triumphant Cup team |* [postpositive] *a comic fairy tale about innocence triumphant.*
■ feeling or expressing jubilation after having won a victory or mastered a difficulty: *he couldn't suppress a triumphant smile.*
– DERIVATIVES **triumphantly** adverb.
– ORIGIN late Middle English (in the sense 'victorious'): from Old French, or from Latin *triumphant-* 'celebrating a triumph', from the verb *triumphare* (see **TRIUMPH**).

triumvir /trʌɪˈʌmvə, ˈtrʌɪəmvə/ ▶ **noun** (pl. **triumvirs** or **triumviri** /-rʌɪ/) (in ancient Rome) each of three public officers jointly responsible for overseeing any of the administrative departments.
– DERIVATIVES **triumviral** adjective.
– ORIGIN Latin, originally as *triumviri* (plural), back-formation from *trium virorum* 'of three men', genitive of *tres viri*.

triumvirate /trʌɪˈʌmvɪrət/ ▶ **noun 1** (in ancient Rome) a group of three men holding power, in particular (**the First Triumvirate**) the unofficial coalition of Julius Caesar, Pompey, and Crassus in 60 BC and (**the Second Triumvirate**) a coalition formed by Antony, Lepidus, and Octavian in 43 BC.
■ a group of three powerful or notable people or things existing in relation to each other: *a triumvirate of three former executive vice-presidents.*
2 the office of triumvir in ancient Rome.
– ORIGIN late 16th cent.: from Latin *triumviratus*, from *triumvir* (see **TRIUMVIR**).

triune /ˈtrʌɪjuːn/ ▶ **adjective** consisting of three in one (used especially with reference to the Trinity): *the triune Godhead.*
– DERIVATIVES **triunity** noun (pl. **-ies**).
– ORIGIN early 17th cent.: from **TRI-** 'three' + Latin *unus* 'one'.

trivalent /trʌɪˈveɪl(ə)nt/ ▶ **adjective** Chemistry having a valency of three.

Trivandrum /trɪˈvandrəm/ the capital of the state of Kerala, a port on the SW coast of India; pop. 524,000 (1991).

trivet ▶ **noun** an iron tripod placed over a fire for a cooking pot or kettle to stand on.
■ an iron bracket designed to hook on to bars of a grate for a similar purpose. ■ a stand or support with three or more legs.
– PHRASES **(as) right as a trivet** Brit. informal perfectly all right; in good health.
– ORIGIN late Middle English: apparently from Latin *tripes, triped-* 'three-legged', from *tri-* 'three' + *pes, ped-* 'foot'.

trivia ▶ **plural noun** details, considerations, or pieces of information of little importance or value: *we fill our days with meaningless trivia.*
– ORIGIN early 20th cent.: from modern Latin, plural of *trivium* 'place where three roads meet', influenced in sense by **TRIVIAL**.

trivial ▶ **adjective** of little value or importance: *huge fines were imposed for trivial offences | trivial details.*
■ (of a person) concerned only with trifling or unimportant things. ■ Mathematics denoting a subgroup that either contains only the identity element or is identical with the given group.
– DERIVATIVES **triviality** noun (pl. **-ies**), **trivially** adverb.
– ORIGIN late Middle English (in the sense 'belonging to the trivium'): from medieval Latin *trivialis*, from Latin *trivium* (see **TRIVIUM**).

trivialize (also **-ise**) ▶ **verb** [with obj.] make (something) seem less important, significant, or complex than it really is: *the problem was either trivialized or ignored by teachers.*
– DERIVATIVES **trivialization** noun.

trivial name ▶ **noun** chiefly Chemistry a name that is in general use although not part of systematic nomenclature: *its common trivial name is citric acid.*
■ chiefly Zoology another term for **SPECIFIC EPITHET**.

trivium /ˈtrɪvɪəm/ ▶ **noun** historical an introductory course at a medieval university involving the study of grammar, rhetoric, and logic. Compare with **QUADRIVIUM**.
– ORIGIN early 19th cent.: from Latin, literally 'place where three roads meet', from *tri-* 'three' + *via* 'road'.

-trix ▶ **suffix** (pl. **-trices** /trɪˈsiːz, ˈtrʌɪsiːz/ or **-trixes**) (chiefly in legal terms) forming feminine agent nouns corresponding to masculine nouns ending in *-tor* (such as *executrix* corresponding to *executor*).
– ORIGIN from Latin.

> **USAGE** The suffix **-trix** has been used since the 15th century to form feminine agent nouns corresponding to masculine forms ending in **-tor**. Although a wide variety of forms has been coined, very few of them have ever had wide currency. In modern use the suffix is found chiefly in legal terms such as **executrix**, **administratrix**, and **testatrix**.

t

tRNA Biology ▶ abbreviation for transfer RNA.

Troad /'trəʊad/ an ancient region of NW Asia Minor, of which ancient Troy was the chief city.

Trobriand Islands /'trəʊbrɪənd/ a small group of islands in the SW Pacific, in Papua New Guinea, situated off the south-eastern tip of the island of New Guinea.

trocar /'trəʊkɑː/ ▶ noun a surgical instrument with a three-sided cutting point enclosed in a tube, used for withdrawing fluid from a body cavity.
– ORIGIN early 18th cent.: from French *trocart, trois-quarts*, from *trois* 'three' + *carre* 'side, face of an instrument'.

trochaic /trə(ʊ)'keɪk/ Prosody ▶ adjective consisting of or featuring trochees.
▶ noun (usu. **trochaics**) a type of verse that consists of or features trochees.
– ORIGIN late 16th cent.: via Latin from Greek *trokhaikos*, from *trokhaios* (see **TROCHEE**).

trochal disc ▶ noun Zoology each of two projections below the neck of the femur (thigh bone) to which muscles are attached.
– ORIGIN mid 19th cent.: *trochal* from Greek *trokhos* 'wheel' + **-AL**.

trochanter /trə'kantə/ ▶ noun 1 Anatomy any of a number of bony protuberances by which muscles are attached to the upper part of the thigh bone.
2 Entomology the small second segment of the leg of an insect, between the coxa and the femur.
– ORIGIN early 17th cent.: from French, from Greek *trokhantēr*, from *trekhein* 'to run'.

trochee /'trəʊkiː/ ▶ noun Prosody a foot consisting of one long or stressed syllable followed by one short or unstressed syllable.
– ORIGIN late 16th cent.: via Latin from Greek *trokhaios* (*pous*) 'running (foot)', from *trekhein* 'to run'.

trochlea /'trɒklɪə/ ▶ noun (pl. **trochleae** /-lɪiː/) Anatomy a structure resembling or acting like a pulley, such as the groove at the lower end of the humerus forming part of the elbow joint.
– ORIGIN late 17th cent.: Latin, 'pulley'; compare with Greek *trokhilia* 'sheave of a pulley'.

trochlear /'trɒklɪə/ ▶ adjective Anatomy of or relating to a part of the body resembling a pulley.

trochlear nerve ▶ noun Anatomy each of the fourth pair of cranial nerves, supplying the superior oblique muscle of the eyeball.

trochoid /'trəʊkɔɪd/ ▶ adjective 1 Anatomy denoting a joint in which one element rotates on its own axis (e.g. the atlas vertebra).
2 Geometry denoting a curve traced by a point on a radius of a circle rotating along a straight line or another circle (a cycloid, epicycloid, or hypocycloid).
3 Zoology having or denoting a form of mollusc shell which is conical with a flat base, like a top shell.
▶ noun 1 a trochoid curve.
2 a trochoid joint.
– DERIVATIVES **trochoidal** adjective.
– ORIGIN early 18th cent.: from Greek *trokhoeidēs* 'wheel-like', from *trokhos* 'wheel'.

trochophore /'trəʊkə(ʊ)fɔː, 'trɒk-/ ▶ noun Zoology the planktonic larva of certain invertebrates, including some molluscs and polychaete worms, having a roughly spherical body, a band of cilia, and a spinning motion.
– ORIGIN late 19th cent.: from Greek *trokhos* 'wheel' + **-PHORE**.

Trockenbeerenauslese /'trɒk(ə)n,bɛːr(ə)n-,aʊslɛɪzə, German 'trɔknbeːrən,aʊsleːzə/ ▶ noun [mass noun] a sweet German white wine made from selected individual grapes picked later than the general harvest and affected by noble rot.
– ORIGIN German, from *trocken* 'dry' + **BEERENAUSLESE**.

troctolite /'trɒktə(ʊ)lʌɪt/ ▶ noun [mass noun] Geology gabbro made up mainly of olivine and calcic plagioclase, often having a spotted appearance likened to a trout's back.
– ORIGIN late 19th cent.: from German *Troklotit*, from Greek *trōktēs*, a marine fish (taken to be 'trout').

trod past and past participle of **TREAD**.

trodden past participle of **TREAD**.

trog¹ ▶ noun Brit. a person regarded as contemptible or socially inferior.
– ORIGIN 1950s: abbreviation of **TROGLODYTE**.

trog² ▶ verb (**trogged**, **trogging**) [no obj., with adverbial of direction] Brit. informal walk heavily or laboriously; trudge: *I left him trogging off to the tube station.*
– ORIGIN 1980s: perhaps a blend of **TRUDGE**, **SLOG**, **TROLL**², and **JOG**.

troglodyte /'trɒglədʌɪt/ ▶ noun (especially in prehistoric times) a person who lived in a cave.
■ a hermit. ■ a person who is regarded as being deliberately ignorant or old-fashioned.
– DERIVATIVES **troglodytic** /-'dɪtɪk/ adjective, **troglodytism** noun.
– ORIGIN late 15th cent.: via Latin from Greek *trōglodutēs*, alteration of the name of an Ethiopian people, influenced by *trōglē* 'hole'.

trogon /'trəʊgɒn/ ▶ noun a bird of tropical American forests, with a long tail and brilliantly coloured plumage.
● Family Trogonidae: several genera, in particular *Trogon*, and many species; the quetzals also belong to this family.
– ORIGIN late 18th cent.: from modern Latin, from Greek *trōgōn*, from *trōgein* 'gnaw'.

troika /'trɔɪkə/ ▶ noun 1 a Russian vehicle pulled by a team of three horses abreast.
■ a team of three horses for such a vehicle.
2 a group of three people working together, especially in an administrative or managerial capacity.
– ORIGIN Russian, from *troe* 'set of three'.

troilism /'trɔɪlɪz(ə)m/ ▶ noun [mass noun] sexual activity involving three participants.
– ORIGIN 1950s: perhaps based on French *trois* 'three'.

Troilus /'trɔɪləs/ Greek Mythology a Trojan prince, the son of Priam and Hecuba, killed by Achilles. In medieval legends of the Trojan war he is portrayed as the forsaken lover of Cressida.

Trojan ▶ adjective of or relating to ancient Troy in Asia Minor: *Trojan legends.*
▶ noun a native or inhabitant of ancient Troy.
– PHRASES **work like a Trojan** (or **Trojans**) work extremely hard.
– ORIGIN Middle English: from Latin *Troianus*, from *Troia* 'Troy'.

Trojan asteroid ▶ noun an asteroid belonging to one of two groups which orbit the sun at the same distance as Jupiter, at the Lagrangian points roughly 60 degrees ahead of it and behind it.
– ORIGIN early 20th cent.: so named because the first asteroids discovered were named after heroes of the Trojan War.

Trojan Horse ▶ noun (in Greek mythology) a hollow wooden statue of a horse in which the Greeks are said to have concealed themselves in order to enter Troy.
■ figurative a person or thing intended secretly to undermine or bring about the downfall of an enemy or opponent: *the rebels may use this peace accord as a Trojan horse to try and take over.* ■ Computing a program designed to breach the security of a computer system while ostensibly performing some innocuous function.

Trojan War the legendary ten-year siege of Troy by a coalition of Greeks, described in Homer's *Iliad*.

The Greeks were attempting to recover Helen, wife of Menelaus, who had been abducted by the Trojan prince Paris. The war ended with the capture of the city by a trick: the Greeks ostensibly ended the siege but left behind a group of men concealed in a hollow wooden horse so large that the city walls had to be breached for it to be drawn inside.

troll¹ /trəʊl, trɒl/ ▶ noun a mythical, cave-dwelling being depicted in folklore as either a giant or a dwarf, typically having a very ugly appearance.
– ORIGIN from Old Norse and Swedish *troll*, Danish *trold*; adopted into English from Scandinavian in the mid 19th cent.

troll² /trəʊl, trɒl/ ▶ verb [no obj.] 1 fish by trailing a baited line along behind a boat: *we trolled for mackerel.*
■ search for something: *a group of companies trolling for partnership opportunities.*
2 [with adverbial of direction] chiefly Brit. walk; stroll: *we all trolled into town.*
3 [with obj.] sing (something) in a happy and carefree way: *he trolled a note or two.*
4 Computing, informal send (an e-mail message or posting on the Internet) intended to provoke a response from the reader by containing errors.
▶ noun 1 [mass noun] the action of trolling for fish.
■ [count noun] a line or bait used in such fishing.
2 Computing, informal an e-mail message or posting on the Internet intended to provoke a response in the reader by containing errors.
– DERIVATIVES **troller** noun.
– ORIGIN late Middle English (in the sense 'stroll, roll'): origin uncertain; compare with Old French *troller* 'wander here and there (in search of game)' and Middle High German *trollen* 'stroll'.

trolley ▶ noun (pl. **-eys**) 1 Brit. a large metal basket or frame on wheels, used for transporting heavy or unwieldy items, such as purchases in a supermarket or luggage at an airport or railway station.
■ a small table on wheels or castors, typically used to convey food and drink. ■ a hospital bed on wheels for transporting patients who are incapable of moving unaided.
2 (also **trolley wheel**) a wheel attached to a pole, used for collecting current from an overhead electric wire to drive a tram.
3 short for **TROLLEYBUS** or **TROLLEY CAR**.
– PHRASES **off one's trolley** Brit. informal mad; insane.
– ORIGIN early 19th cent.: of dialect origin, perhaps from **TROLL**².

trolleybus ▶ noun a bus powered by electricity obtained from overhead wires by means of a pole.

trolley car ▶ noun US a tram powered by electricity obtained from an overhead cable by means of a trolley wheel.

trollius /'trɒlɪəs/ ▶ noun (pl. same) a plant of a genus that comprises the globeflowers.
● Genus *Trollius*, family Ranunculaceae.
– ORIGIN modern Latin, apparently representing German *Trollblume* 'globeflower', from the stem of *trollen* 'to roll' (because of the globular flowers).

trollop ▶ noun dated or humorous a woman perceived as sexually disreputable or promiscuous.
– ORIGIN early 17th cent.: perhaps related to **TRULL**.

Trollope /'trɒləp/, Anthony (1815–82), English novelist. He worked for the General Post Office from 1834 to 1867 and introduced the pillar box to Britain. He is best-known for the six 'Barsetshire' novels, including *The Warden* (1855) and *Barchester Towers* (1857), and for the six political 'Palliser' novels.

trombone ▶ noun a large brass wind instrument with straight tubing in three sections, ending in a bell over the player's left shoulder, different fundamental notes being made using a forward-pointing extendable slide.
■ an organ stop with the quality of such an instrument.
– DERIVATIVES **trombonist** noun.
– ORIGIN early 18th cent.: from French or Italian, from Italian *tromba* 'trumpet'.

trommel /'trɒm(ə)l/ ▶ noun Mining a rotating cylindrical sieve or screen used for washing and sorting pieces of ore or coal.
– ORIGIN late 19th cent.: from German, literally 'drum'.

trompe l'œil /trɒmp 'lɔɪ, French trɔ̃p lœj/ ▶ noun (pl. **trompe l'œils** pronunc. same) [mass noun] visual illusion in art, especially as used to trick the eye into perceiving a painted detail as a three-dimensional object.
■ [count noun] a painting or design intended to create such an illusion.
– ORIGIN French, literally 'deceives the eye'.

Tromsø /'trɒmsəː/ the principal city of Arctic Norway, situated on an island just west of the mainland; pop. 51,330 (1991).

-tron ▶ suffix Physics 1 denoting a subatomic particle: *positron.*
2 denoting a particle accelerator: *cyclotron.*
3 denoting a thermionic valve: *ignitron.*
– ORIGIN from (*elec*)*tron*.

trona /'trəʊnə/ ▶ noun [mass noun] a grey mineral which occurs as an evaporite in salt deposits and consists of a hydrated carbonate and bicarbonate of sodium.
– ORIGIN late 18th cent.: from Swedish, from Arabic *naṭrūn* (see **NATRON**).

tronc /trɒŋk/ ▶ noun (in a hotel or restaurant) a common fund into which tips and service charges are paid for distribution to the staff.
– ORIGIN 1920s: from French, literally 'collecting box'.

Trondheim /'trɒndhʌɪm/ a fishing port in west central Norway; pop. 138,060 (1991). It was the capital of Norway during the Viking period.

Troon /truːn/ a town on the west coast of Scotland, in South Ayrshire; pop. 14,230 (1981). It is noted for its championship golf course.

troop ▶ noun **1** (**troops**) soldiers or armed forces: *UN peacekeeping troops* | [as modifier] (**troop**) *troop withdrawals.*
■ a cavalry unit commanded by a captain. ■ a unit of artillery and armoured formation. ■ a group of three or more Scout patrols.
2 a group of people or animals of a particular kind: *a troop of musicians.*
▶ verb [no obj., with adverbial of direction] (of a group of people) come or go together or in large numbers: *the girls trooped in for dinner.*
■ (of a lone person) walk at a slow or steady pace: *Caroline trooped wearily home from work.*
– PHRASES **troop the colour** Brit. perform the ceremony of parading a regiment's flag along ranks of soldiers.
– ORIGIN mid 16th cent.: from French *troupe*, back-formation from *troupeau*, diminutive of medieval Latin *troppus* 'flock', probably of Germanic origin.

troop carrier ▶ noun a large aircraft or armoured vehicle designed for transporting troops.

trooper ▶ noun **1** a private soldier in a cavalry or armoured unit.
■ a cavalry horse. ■ chiefly Brit. a ship used for transporting troops.
2 Austral. & US a mounted police officer.
■ US a state police officer.
– PHRASES **swear like a trooper** swear a great deal.

troopie ▶ noun (pl. **-ies**) S. African informal a private soldier, especially a national serviceman.

troopship ▶ noun a ship designed or used for transporting troops.

tropaeolum /trə(ʊ)ˈpiːələm/ ▶ noun a Central and South American trailing or climbing plant of a genus that includes the nasturtium and the canary creeper.
● Genus *Tropaeolum*, family Tropaeolaceae.
– ORIGIN modern Latin, from Latin *tropaeum* 'trophy', because of the resemblance of the flower and leaf to a helmet and shield.

trope /trəʊp/ ▶ noun a figurative or metaphorical use of a word or expression.
– ORIGIN mid 16th cent.: via Latin from Greek *tropos* 'turn, way, trope', from *trepein* 'to turn'.

trophallaxis /ˌtrɒfəˈlaksɪs/ ▶ noun [mass noun] Entomology the mutual exchange of regurgitated liquids between adult social insects or between them and their larvae.
– ORIGIN early 20th cent.: from TROPHO- 'nourishment' + Greek *allaxis* 'exchange'.

trophectoderm /trəˈfɛktə(ʊ)dəːm, trəʊ-/ ▶ noun another term for TROPHOBLAST.

trophic /ˈtrəʊfɪk, ˈtrɒfɪk/ ▶ adjective Ecology of or relating to feeding and nutrition.
■ Physiology (of a hormone or its effect) stimulating the activity of another endocrine gland.
– ORIGIN late 19th cent.: from Greek *trophikos*, from *trophē* 'nourishment', from *trephein* 'nourish'.

-trophic ▶ combining form **1** relating to nutrition: *oligotrophic.*
2 relating to maintenance or regulation of a bodily organ or function, especially by a hormone: *gonadotrophic.*
– DERIVATIVES **-trophism** combining form in corresponding nouns, **-trophy** combining form in corresponding nouns.
– ORIGIN from Greek *trophikos*, from *trophē* 'nourishment'.

trophic level ▶ noun Ecology each of several hierarchical levels in an ecosystem, consisting of organisms sharing the same function in the food chain and the same nutritional relationship to the primary sources of energy.

tropho- ▶ combining form relating to nourishment: *trophoblast.*
– ORIGIN from Greek *trophē* 'nourishment'.

trophoblast /ˈtrɒfə(ʊ)blast, ˈtrəʊf-/ ▶ noun Embryology a layer of tissue on the outside of a mammalian blastula, supplying the embryo with nourishment and later forming the major part of the placenta.
– DERIVATIVES **trophoblastic** adjective.

trophozoite /ˌtrɒfəˈzəʊʌɪt, ˌtrəʊfə(ʊ)-/ ▶ noun Zoology & Medicine a growing stage in the life cycle of some sporozoan parasites, when they are absorbing nutrients from the host.

trophy ▶ noun (pl. **-ies**) **1** a cup or other decorative object awarded as a prize for a victory or success.
■ a souvenir of an achievement, especially a part of an animal taken when hunting.
2 (in ancient Greece or Rome) the weapons of a defeated army set up as a memorial of victory.
■ a representation of such a memorial; an ornamental group of symbolic objects arranged for display.
– ORIGIN late 15th cent. (in sense 2, denoting a display of weapons): from French *trophée*, via Latin from Greek *tropaion*, from *tropē* 'a rout', from *trepein* 'to turn'.

trophy wife ▶ noun informal, derogatory a young, attractive wife regarded as a status symbol for an older man.

tropic¹ /ˈtrɒpɪk/ ▶ noun the parallel of latitude 23°26′ north (**tropic of Cancer**) or south (**tropic of Capricorn**) of the equator.
■ Astronomy each of two corresponding circles on the celestial sphere where the sun appears to turn after reaching its greatest declination, marking the northern and southern limits of the ecliptic. ■ (**the tropics**) the region between the tropics of Cancer and Capricorn.
▶ adjective another term for TROPICAL (in sense 1).
– ORIGIN late Middle English (denoting the point on the ecliptic reached by the sun at the solstice): via Latin from Greek *tropikos*, from *tropē* 'turning', from *trepein* 'to turn'.

tropic² /ˈtrəʊpɪk/ ▶ adjective **1** Biology relating to, consisting of, or exhibiting tropism.
2 Physiology variant spelling of TROPHIC.

-tropic ▶ combining form **1** turning towards: *heliotropic.*
2 affecting: *psychotropic.*
3 (especially in names of hormones) equivalent to -TROPHIC.
– ORIGIN from Greek *tropē* 'turn, turning'.

tropical ▶ adjective **1** of, typical of, or peculiar to the tropics: *tropical countries* | *a tropical rainforest.*
■ resembling the tropics, especially in being very hot and humid: *some plants thrived in last year's tropical summer heat.*
2 archaic of or involving a trope; figurative.
– DERIVATIVES **tropically** adverb.

tropical sprue ▶ noun see SPRUE².

tropical storm (also **tropical cyclone**) ▶ noun a localized, very intense low-pressure wind system, forming over tropical oceans and with winds of hurricane force.

tropical year ▶ noun see YEAR (sense 1).

tropicbird ▶ noun a tropical seabird with mainly white plumage and very long central tail feathers.
● Family Phaethontidae and genus *Phaethon*: three species.

tropic of Cancer ▶ noun see TROPIC¹.

tropic of Capricorn ▶ noun see TROPIC¹.

tropism /ˈtrəʊpɪz(ə)m, ˈtrɒp-/ ▶ noun [mass noun] Biology the turning of all or part of an organism in a particular direction in response to an external stimulus.
– ORIGIN late 19th cent.: from Greek *tropos* 'turning' (from *trepein* 'to turn') + -ISM.

tropology /trəˈpɒlədʒi/ ▶ noun [mass noun] the figurative use of language.
■ Christian Theology the figurative interpretation of the scriptures as a source of moral guidance.
– DERIVATIVES **tropological** adjective.
– ORIGIN late Middle English: via late Latin from Greek *tropologia*, from *tropos* (see TROPE).

tropolone /ˈtrɒpələʊn/ ▶ noun [mass noun] Chemistry an organic compound present in various plants, with a molecule based on a seven-membered carbon ring.
● An enolic ketone; chem. formula: $C_7H_6O_2$.
– ORIGIN 1940s: from *tropilidine* (a liquid hydrocarbon) + -OL + -ONE.

tropomyosin /ˌtrəʊpə(ʊ)ˈmʌɪəsɪn/ ▶ noun [mass noun] Biochemistry a protein involved in muscle contraction. It is related to myosin and occurs together with troponin in the thin filaments of muscle tissue.
– ORIGIN 1940s: from Greek *tropos* 'turning' + MYOSIN.

troponin /ˈtrəʊpə(ʊ)nɪn/ ▶ noun [mass noun] Biochemistry a globular protein complex involved in muscle contraction. It occurs with tropomyosin in the thin filaments of muscle tissue.
– ORIGIN 1960s: from TROPOMYOSIN + -*n*- + -IN¹.

tropopause /ˈtrɒpə(ʊ)pɔːz, ˈtrəʊp-/ ▶ noun the interface between the troposphere and the stratosphere.
– ORIGIN early 20th cent.: from Greek *tropos* 'turning' + PAUSE.

troposphere /ˈtrɒpə(ʊ)sfɪə, ˈtrəʊp-/ ▶ noun the lowest region of the atmosphere, extending from the earth's surface to a height of about 6–10 km (the lower boundary of the stratosphere).
– DERIVATIVES **tropospheric** adjective.
– ORIGIN early 20th cent.: from Greek *tropos* 'turning' + SPHERE.

troppo¹ /ˈtrɒpəʊ/ ▶ adverb [usu. with negative] Music (in directions) too much; excessively: *allegro ma non troppo.*
– ORIGIN Italian.

troppo² /ˈtrɒpəʊ/ ▶ adjective Austral./NZ informal mentally disturbed, supposedly as a result of spending too much time in a tropical climate: *have you gone troppo?*
– ORIGIN 1940s: from TROPIC¹ + -O.

Trossachs /ˈtrɒsəks/ (**the Trossachs**) a picturesque wooded valley in central Scotland, between Loch Achray and the lower end of Loch Katrine.

Trot ▶ noun informal, usu. derogatory, chiefly Brit. a Trotskyist or supporter of extreme left-wing views.
– ORIGIN 1960s: abbreviation.

trot ▶ verb (**trotted**, **trotting**) (of a horse or other quadruped) proceed at a pace faster than a walk, lifting each diagonal pair of legs alternately.
■ [with obj.] cause (a horse) to move at such a pace: *he trotted his horse forward.* ■ [no obj., with adverbial of direction] (of a person) run at a moderate pace, typically with short steps. ■ [no obj., with adverbial of direction] informal go or walk briskly: *I may trot round to Portobello market for vegetables.*
▶ noun **1** a trotting pace: *our horses slowed to a trot.*
■ an act or period of trotting: *you might like an early morning trot round the crew deck.* ■ [usu. with adj.] chiefly Austral./NZ a period of luck, especially of a specified kind: *you expect the odd bad trot.* ■ (**the trots**) Austral./NZ informal trotting races: *she was taking me to the trots.*
2 (**the trots**) informal diarrhoea: *a bad case of the trots.*
– PHRASES **on the trot** informal **1** Brit. in succession: *they lost seven matches on the trot.* **2** continually busy: *I've been on the trot all day.*
– ORIGIN Middle English: from Old French *trot* (noun), *troter* (verb), from medieval Latin *trottare*, of Germanic origin.
▶ **trot something out 1** informal produce the same information, story, or explanation that has been produced many times before: *everyone trots out the old excuse.* **2** cause a horse to trot to show its paces.

troth /trəʊθ, trɒθ/ ▶ noun [mass noun] **1** archaic or formal faith or loyalty when pledged in a solemn agreement or undertaking: *a token of troth.*
2 archaic truth.
– PHRASES **pledge** (or **plight**) **one's troth** make a solemn pledge of commitment or loyalty, especially in marriage.
– ORIGIN Middle English: variant of TRUTH.

tro-tro /ˈtrəʊtrəʊ/ ▶ noun (pl. **-os**) (in Ghana) a converted lorry or van used as a public conveyance.
– ORIGIN probably from Akan *tro* 'threepence', with reference to the fare.

Trotsky /ˈtrɒtski/, Leon (1879–1940), Russian revolutionary; born *Lev Davidovich Bronshtein*. He helped to organize the October Revolution with Lenin, and built up the Red Army. He was expelled from the party by Stalin in 1927 and exiled in 1929. He settled in Mexico in 1937, where he was later murdered by a Stalinist assassin.

Trotskyism ▶ noun [mass noun] the political or economic principles of Leon Trotsky, especially the theory that socialism should be established throughout the world by continuing revolution. Trotskyism has generally included elements of anarchism and syndicalism, but the term has come to be used indiscriminately to describe a great many forms of radical socialism.
– DERIVATIVES **Trotskyist** noun & adjective, **Trotskyite** noun & adjective (derogatory).

trotter ▶ noun **1** a horse bred or trained for the sport of trotting.
2 a pig's foot used as food.
■ humorous a human foot.

trotting ▶ noun [mass noun] racing for trotting horses

pulling a two-wheeled vehicle (a sulky) and driver. Also called **HARNESS RACING**.

troubadour /ˈtruːbədɔː/ ▶ **noun** a French medieval lyric poet composing and singing in Provençal in the 11th to 13th centuries, especially on the theme of courtly love.
■ a poet who writes verse to music.
– ORIGIN French, from Provençal *trobador*, from *trobar* 'find, invent, compose in verse'.

trouble ▶ **noun** [mass noun] **1** difficulty or problems: *I had trouble finding somewhere to park | the government's policies* ***ran into trouble*** *|* [count noun] *our troubles are just beginning.*
■ the malfunction of something such as a machine or a part of the body: *their helicopter developed engine trouble.* ■ effort or exertion made to do something, especially when inconvenient: *I wouldn't want to put you to any trouble | most schools found multimedia kits more trouble than they were worth | he's* ***gone to*** *a lot of* ***trouble*** *to help you.* ■ a cause of worry or inconvenience: *the kid had been* ***no trouble*** *up to now.* ■ a particular aspect or quality of something regarded as unsatisfactory or as a source of difficulty: *that's* ***the trouble with*** *capitalism.* ■ a situation in which one is liable to incur punishment or blame: *he's been* ***in trouble with*** *the police.* ■ informal, dated used to refer to the condition of a pregnant unmarried woman: *she's not the first girl who's* ***got*** *herself* ***into trouble.***
2 public unrest or disorder: *there was crowd trouble before and during the match.*
■ **(the Troubles)** any of various periods of civil war or unrest in Ireland, especially in 1919–23 and (in Northern Ireland) since 1968.
▶ **verb** [with obj.] (often **be troubled**) cause distress or anxiety to: *he was not troubled by doubts.*
■ [no obj.] **(trouble about/over/with)** be distressed or anxious about: *there is nothing you need trouble about.* ■ cause (someone) pain: *my legs started to trouble me.* ■ cause (someone) inconvenience (typically used as a polite way of asking someone to do or provide something): *sorry to trouble you | could I* ***trouble*** *you for a receipt?* ■ [no obj., with infinitive] make the effort required to do something: *oh, don't trouble to answer.*
– PHRASES **ask for trouble** informal act in a way that is likely to incur problems or difficulties: *hitching a lift is asking for trouble.* **look for trouble** informal behave in a way that is likely to provoke an argument or fight: *youths take a cocktail of drink and drugs before going out to look for trouble.* **trouble and strife** Brit. rhyming slang wife. **a trouble shared is a trouble halved** proverb talking to someone else about one's problems helps to alleviate them.
– DERIVATIVES **troubler** noun.
– ORIGIN Middle English: from Old French *truble* (noun), *trubler* (verb), based on Latin *turbidus* (see **TURBID**).

troubled ▶ **adjective** beset by problems or conflict: *his troubled private life.*
■ showing distress or anxiety: *his troubled face.*
– PHRASES **troubled waters** a difficult situation or time.

troublemaker ▶ **noun** a person who habitually causes difficulty or problems, especially by inciting others to defy those in authority.
– DERIVATIVES **troublemaking** noun & adjective.

troubleshoot ▶ **verb** [no obj.] [usu. as noun **troubleshooting**] solve serious problems for a company or other organization.
■ trace and correct faults in a mechanical or electronic system.
– DERIVATIVES **troubleshooter** noun.

troublesome ▶ **adjective** causing difficulty or annoyance: *schools are removing troublesome pupils.*
– DERIVATIVES **troublesomely** adverb, **troublesomeness** noun.

trouble spot ▶ **noun** a place where difficulties regularly occur, especially a country or area where there is a continuous cycle of violence.

troublous ▶ **adjective** archaic or poetic/literary full of difficulty or agitation: *those were troublous times.*
– ORIGIN late Middle English: from Old French *troubleus*, from *truble* (see **TROUBLE**).

trough ▶ **noun** a long, narrow open container for animals to eat or drink out of: *a water trough.*
■ a container of a similar shape used for a purpose such as growing plants or mixing chemicals. ■ a channel used to convey a liquid. ■ a long hollow in the earth's surface: *a vast glacial trough.* ■ an elongated region of low barometric pressure. ■ a hollow between two wave crests in the sea. ■ a low level of economic activity. ■ Mathematics a region around the minimum on a curve of variation of a quantity. ■ a point of low achievement or satisfaction: *learning a language is a series of* ***peaks and troughs.***
– ORIGIN Old English *trog*, of Germanic origin; related to Dutch *trog* and German *Trog*, also to **TREE**.

trough shell ▶ **noun** a burrowing marine bivalve mollusc with a thin smooth shell.
• Family Mactridae: *Spisula* and other genera.

trounce ▶ **verb** [with obj.] defeat heavily in a contest: *Essex trounced Cambridgeshire 5–1 in the final.*
■ rebuke or punish severely: *insider dealing has been roundly trounced.*
– DERIVATIVES **trouncer** noun.
– ORIGIN mid 16th cent. (also in the sense 'afflict'): of unknown origin.

troupe ▶ **noun** a group of dancers, actors, or other entertainers who tour to different venues.
– ORIGIN early 19th cent.: from French, literally 'troop'.

trouper ▶ **noun** an actor or other entertainer, typically one with long experience.
■ a reliable and uncomplaining person: *a* ***real trouper,*** *Ma concealed her troubles.*

troupial /ˈtruːpɪəl/ ▶ **noun** a gregarious songbird of the American oriole family, typically having orange and black plumage and yellow eyes.
• Genus *Icterus*, family Icteridae: several species, in particular the tropical American *Icterus icterus*.
– ORIGIN early 19th cent.: from French *troupiale*, alteration of American Spanish *turpial*, of unknown origin.

trouser ▶ **noun** [as modifier] relating to trousers: *his trouser pocket | a trouser press.*
■ a trouser leg: *his trouser was torn.*
▶ **verb** [with obj.] Brit. informal receive or take (something, especially money) for oneself; pocket: *they claimed that he had trousered a £2 million advance.*

trouser clip ▶ **noun** another term for **BICYCLE CLIP**.

trousers (also **a pair of trousers**) ▶ **plural noun** an outer garment covering the body from the waist to the ankles, with a separate part for each leg.
– PHRASES **catch someone with their trousers down** see ***catch someone with their pants down*** at **PANTS**. **wear the trousers** informal be the dominant partner in a relationship.
– DERIVATIVES **trousered** adjective.
– ORIGIN early 17th cent.: from archaic *trouse* (singular) from Irish *triús* and Scottish Gaelic *triubhas* (see **TREWS**), on the pattern of *drawers*.

trouser suit ▶ **noun** Brit. a pair of trousers and a matching jacket worn by women.

trousseau /ˈtruːsəʊ/ ▶ **noun** (pl. **trousseaux** or **trousseaus** /-səʊz/) the clothes, linen, and other belongings collected by a bride for her marriage.
– ORIGIN mid 19th cent.: from French, diminutive of *trousse* 'bundle' (a sense also found in Middle English).

trout ▶ **noun** (pl. same or **trouts**) a chiefly freshwater fish of the salmon family, found in both Eurasia and North America and highly valued for food and game.
• Genera *Salmo* (several species of true trouts, including the European **brown trout** and the **rainbow trout**), and *Salvelinus* (several North American species), family Salmonidae. See also **LAKE TROUT**, **SEA TROUT**.
– PHRASES **old trout** informal an annoying or bad-tempered old person, especially a woman.
– ORIGIN late Old English *truht*, from late Latin *tructa*, based on Greek *trōgein* 'gnaw'.

trouting ▶ **noun** [mass noun] the activity of catching or trying to catch trout, either for food or as a sport.

trout lily ▶ **noun** a North American dog's-tooth violet with yellow flowers, so called from its mottled leaves.
• *Erythronium americanum*, family Liliaceae.

trouvaille /ˈtruːvʌɪ/ ▶ **noun** a lucky find: *one of numerous trouvailles to be gleaned from his book.*
– ORIGIN French, from *trouver* 'find'.

trouvère /truːˈvɛː/ ▶ **noun** a medieval epic poet in northern France in the 11th–14th centuries.
– ORIGIN from Old French *trovere*, from *trover* 'to find'; compare with **TROUBADOUR**.

trove ▶ **noun** a store of valuable or delightful things: *the museum's trove of antique treasure.*
– ORIGIN late 19th cent.: from **TREASURE TROVE**.

trover ▶ **noun** [mass noun] Law common-law action to recover the value of personal property that has been wrongfully disposed of by another person.
– ORIGIN late 16th cent.: from an Anglo-Norman French noun use of Old French *trover* 'to find'.

trow /trəʊ/ ▶ **verb** [with obj.] archaic think or believe: *why, this is strange, I trow!*
– ORIGIN Old English *trūwian*, *trēowian* 'to trust'; related to **TRUCE**.

Trowbridge /ˈtrəʊbrɪdʒ/ a town in SW England, the county town of Wiltshire; pop. 22,980 (1981).

trowel ▶ **noun 1** a small hand-held tool with a flat, pointed blade, used to apply and spread mortar or plaster.
2 a small hand-held tool with a curved scoop for lifting plants or earth.
▶ **verb** (**trowelled**, **trowelling**; US **troweled**, **troweling**) [with obj.] apply or spread with or as if with a trowel.
– ORIGIN Middle English (as a noun): from Old French *truele*, from medieval Latin *truella*, alteration of Latin *trulla* 'scoop', diminutive of *trua* 'skimmer'.

Troy (in Homeric legend) the city of King Priam, besieged for ten years by the Greeks during the Trojan War. It was regarded as having been a purely legendary city until Heinrich Schliemann identified the mound of Hissarlik on the NE Aegean coast of Turkey as the site of Troy. The city was apparently sacked and destroyed by fire in the mid 13th century BC, a period coinciding with the Mycenaean civilization of Greece. Also called **ILIUM**.

troy (in full **troy weight**) ▶ **noun** a system of weights used mainly for precious metals and gems, with a pound of 12 ounces or 5,760 grains. Compare with **AVOIRDUPOIS**.
– ORIGIN late Middle English: from a weight used at the fair of *Troyes* (see **TROYES**[1]).

Troyes[1] /trwʌ, French trwa/ a town in northern France, on the River Seine; pop. 60,755 (1990). It was capital of the former province of Champagne.

Troyes[2], Chrétien de, see **CHRÉTIEN DE TROYES**.

truant ▶ **noun** a pupil who stays away from school without leave or explanation.
▶ **adjective** (of a pupil) being a truant: *truant children.*
■ wandering; straying: *her truant husband.*
▶ **verb** [no obj.] another way of saying ***play truant*** below.
– PHRASES **play truant** (of a pupil) stay away from school without leave or explanation.
– DERIVATIVES **truancy** noun.
– ORIGIN Middle English (denoting a person begging through choice rather than necessity): from Old French, probably ultimately of Celtic origin; compare with Welsh *truan*, Scottish Gaelic *truaghan* 'wretched'.

truce ▶ **noun** an agreement between enemies or opponents to stop fighting or arguing for a certain time: *the guerrillas called a three-day truce.*
– ORIGIN Middle English *trewes*, *trues* (plural), from Old English *trēowa*, plural of *trēow* 'belief, trust', of Germanic origin; related to Dutch *trouw* and German *Treue*, also to **TRUE**.

Trucial States /ˈtruːʃ(ə)l/ former name (until 1971) for **UNITED ARAB EMIRATES**.

truck[1] ▶ **noun 1** a wheeled vehicle, in particular:
■ a large road vehicle, used for carrying goods, materials, or troops; a lorry. ■ Brit. a railway vehicle for carrying freight, especially a small open one. ■ a low flat-topped trolley used for moving heavy items.
2 a railway bogie.
■ each of two axle units on a skateboard, to which the wheels are attached.
3 a wooden disc at the top of a ship's mast or flagstaff, with holes for halyards to slide through.
▶ **verb** [with obj. and adverbial of direction] chiefly N. Amer. convey by truck: *the food was trucked to St Petersburg |* [as noun **trucking**] *industries such as trucking.*
■ [no obj.] drive a truck. ■ [no obj., with adverbial of direction] informal go or proceed, especially in a casual or leisurely way: *my mate walked confidently behind them and trucked on through!*
– DERIVATIVES **truckage** noun.
– ORIGIN Middle English (denoting a solid wooden wheel): perhaps short for **TRUCKLE**[1] in the sense 'wheel, pulley'. The sense 'wheeled vehicle' dates from the late 18th cent.

truck[2] ▶ **noun** [mass noun] **1** archaic barter.
■ chiefly historical the payment of workers in kind or with vouchers rather than money.
2 chiefly archaic small wares.
■ informal odds and ends.

3 N. Amer. market-garden produce, especially vegetables: [as modifier] *a truck garden.*
▶**verb** [with obj.] archaic barter or exchange.
– PHRASES **have** (or **want**) **no truck with** avoid or wish to avoid dealings or being associated with: *we have no truck with that style of gutter journalism.*
– ORIGIN Middle English (as a verb): probably from Old French, of unknown origin; compare with medieval Latin *trocare.*

Truck Acts (in the UK) a series of Acts directed, from 1830 onwards, against the system whereby workers received their wages in the form of vouchers for goods redeemable only at a special shop (often run by the employer). The Acts required wages to be paid in cash.

trucker ▶**noun** a long-distance lorry driver.

truckie ▶**noun** Austral. informal term for **TRUCKER**.

truckle[1] ▶**noun** a small barrel-shaped cheese, especially cheddar.
– ORIGIN late Middle English (denoting a wheel or pulley): from Anglo-Norman French *trocle*, from Latin *trochlea* 'sheaf of a pulley'. The current sense dates from the early 19th cent. and was originally dialect.

truckle[2] ▶**verb** [no obj.] submit or behave obsequiously: *she despised her husband, who truckled to her.*
– DERIVATIVES **truckler** noun.
– ORIGIN mid 17th cent.: figuratively, from **TRUCKLE BED**; an earlier use of the verb was in the sense *sleep in a truckle bed.*

truckle bed ▶**noun** chiefly Brit. a low bed on wheels that can be stored under a larger bed.
– ORIGIN late Middle English: from **TRUCKLE**[1] in the sense 'wheel' + **BED**.

truckload ▶**noun** a quantity of goods that can be transported in a truck: *a truckload of chemicals caught fire.*
■(**a truckload/truckloads of**) informal a large quantity or number of something: *the government had ploughed truckloads of money into this land.*
– PHRASES **by the truckload** informal in large quantities or numbers: *he had charm by the truckload.*

truck stop ▶**noun** North American term for **TRANSPORT CAFE**.

truculent /ˈtrʌkjʊl(ə)nt/ ▶**adjective** eager or quick to argue or fight; aggressively defiant: *the truculent attitude of farmers to cheaper imports.*
– DERIVATIVES **truculence** noun, **truculently** adverb.
– ORIGIN mid 16th cent.: from Latin *truculentus*, from *trux, truc-* 'fierce'.

Trudeau /ˈtruːdəʊ, truːˈdəʊ/, Pierre (Elliott) (b.1919), Canadian Liberal statesman, Prime Minister of Canada 1968–79 and 1980–4. Noted for his commitment to federalism, Trudeau held a provincial referendum in Quebec in 1980, which rejected independence, and saw the transfer of residual constitutional powers from Britain to Canada in 1982.

trudge ▶**verb** [no obj., with adverbial of direction] walk slowly and with heavy steps, typically because of exhaustion or harsh conditions: *I trudged up the stairs | she trudged through blinding snow.*
▶**noun** a difficult or laborious walk: *he began the long trudge back to Stokenchurch Street.*
– DERIVATIVES **trudger** noun.
– ORIGIN mid 16th cent. (as a verb): of unknown origin.

trudgen /ˈtrʌdʒ(ə)n/ ▶**noun** [in sing.] a swimming stroke like the crawl with a scissors movement of the legs.
– ORIGIN late 19th cent.: named after John *Trudgen* (1852–1902), English swimmer.

true ▶**adjective** (**truer, truest**) **1** in accordance with fact or reality: *a true story | of course it's true | that is not true of the people I am talking about.*
■[attrib.] rightly or strictly so called; genuine: *people are still willing to pay for true craftsmanship | we believe in true love.* ■[attrib.] real or actual: *he has guessed my true intentions.* ■said when conceding a point in argument or discussion: *true, it faced north, but you got used to that.*
2 accurate or exact: *it was a true depiction.*
■(of a note) exactly in tune. ■(of a compass bearing) measured relative to true north: *steer 085 degrees true.* ■correctly positioned, balanced, or aligned; upright or level.
3 loyal or faithful: *he was a true friend.*
■[predic.] (**true to**) accurately conforming to (a standard or expectation); faithful to: *this entirely new production remains true to the essence of Lorca's play.*
4 chiefly archaic honest: *we appeal to all good men and true to rally to us.*
▶**adverb 1** chiefly poetic/literary truly: *Hobson spoke truer than he knew.*
2 accurately or without variation.
▶**verb** (**trues, trued, truing** or **trueing**) [with obj.] bring (an object, wheel, or other construction) into the exact shape or position required.
– PHRASES **come true** actually happen or become the case: *dreams can come true.* **out of true** (or **the true**) not in the correct or exact shape or alignment: *take care not to pull the frame out of true.* **many a true word is spoken in jest** proverb a humorous remark not intended to be taken seriously may turn out to be accurate after all. **true as Bob** (or **God**) S. African informal absolutely true: *true as Bob, I nearly went right through the windscreen.* [ORIGIN: *Bob* represents a euphemistic substitution of *God*, the idiom translating obsolete Afrikaans *so waar as God.*] **true to form** (or **type**) being or behaving as expected: *true to type, they took it well.* **true to life** accurately representing real events or objects.
– DERIVATIVES **trueness** noun.
– ORIGIN Old English *trēowe, trȳwe* 'steadfast, loyal'; related to Dutch *getrouw*, German *treu*, also to **TRUCE**.

true bill ▶**noun** US Law a bill of indictment found by a grand jury to be supported by sufficient evidence to justify the hearing of a case.

true-blue ▶**adjective** Brit. staunchly loyal to the Conservative Party.
■US extremely loyal or orthodox: *I'm a dyed-in-the-wool, true-blue patriot.*
▶**noun** (**true blue**) Brit. a staunchly loyal supporter of the Conservative Party.

true-born ▶**adjective** [attrib.] of a specified kind by birth; genuine: *a true-born criminal.*

true bug ▶**noun** see **BUG** (sense 2).

true-hearted ▶**adjective** poetic/literary loyal or faithful: *a true-hearted paladin.*

true horizon ▶**noun** Astronomy see **HORIZON** (sense 1).

true leaf ▶**noun** Botany a foliage leaf of a plant, as opposed to a seed leaf or cotyledon.

true-love knot (also **true-lover's knot**) ▶**noun** a kind of knot with interlacing bows on each side, symbolizing the bonds of love.

Trueman, Fred (b.1931), English cricketer; full name *Frederick Sewards Trueman.* A fast bowler for Yorkshire and England, he became the first bowler to take 300 test wickets (1964).

true north ▶**noun** north according to the earth's axis, not magnetic north.

true rib ▶**noun** a rib which is attached directly to the breastbone. Compare with **FLOATING RIB**.

Truffaut /ˈtruːfəʊ, French tʀyfo/, François (1932–84), French film director. His first feature film, *Les Quatre cents coups* (1959), established him as a leading director of the *nouvelle vague.* Other films include *Jules et Jim* (1961) and *The Last Metro* (1980).

truffle ▶**noun 1** a strong-smelling underground fungus that resembles an irregular, rough-skinned potato, growing chiefly in broad-leaved woodland on calcareous soils. It is considered a culinary delicacy and found, especially in France, with the aid of trained dogs or pigs.
• Family Tuberaceae, subdivision Ascomycotina: *Tuber* and other genera.
2 a soft sweet made of a chocolate mixture, typically flavoured with rum and covered with cocoa.
– ORIGIN late 16th cent.: probably via Dutch from obsolete French *truffle*, perhaps based on Latin *tubera*, plural of *tuber* 'hump, swelling'. Sense 2 dates from the 1920s.

truffled ▶**adjective** (of food) cooked, garnished, or stuffed with truffles: *a truffled turkey.*

truffling ▶**noun** [mass noun] the activity of hunting or rooting for truffles.

trug (also **trug basket**) ▶**noun** Brit. a shallow oblong basket made of strips of wood, traditionally used for carrying garden flowers and produce.
– ORIGIN late Middle English (denoting a basin): perhaps a dialect variant of **TROUGH**.

truism ▶**noun** a statement that is obviously true and says nothing new or interesting: *the truism that you get what you pay for.*
■Logic a proposition that states nothing beyond what is implied by any of its terms.
– DERIVATIVES **truistic** /-ˈɪstɪk/ adjective.

truite au bleu /ˌtrwiːt əʊ ˈbləː/ ▶**noun** [mass noun] a dish consisting of trout cooked with vinegar, which turns the fish blue.
– ORIGIN French, literally 'trout in the blue'.

Trujillo[1] /truːˈhiːjəʊ, -ˈhiːljəʊ/ a city on the coast of NW Peru; pop. 509,310 (1993).

Trujillo[2] /truːˈhiːjəʊ, -ˈhiːljəʊ/, Rafael (1891–1961), Dominican statesman, President of the Dominican Republic 1930–8 and 1942–52; born *Rafael Leónidas Trujillo Molina*; known as **Generalissimo.** Although he was formally President for only two periods, he wielded dictatorial powers from 1930 until his death.

Truk Islands /trʌk/ a group of fourteen volcanic islands and numerous atolls in the western Pacific, in the Caroline Islands group, forming part of the Federated States of Micronesia; pop. 53,700 (est. 1990). There was a Japanese naval base there during the Second World War.

trull /trʌl/ ▶**noun** archaic a prostitute.
– ORIGIN early 16th cent.: from German *Trulle.*

truly ▶**adverb 1** in a truthful way: *he speaks truly.*
■used to emphasize emotional sincerity or seriousness: *time to reflect on what we truly want | it is truly a privilege to be here |* [as submodifier] *I'm truly sorry, but I can't join you today |* [sentence adverb] *truly, I don't understand you sometimes.*
2 to the fullest degree; genuinely or properly: *management does not truly understand or care about the residents |* [as submodifier] *a truly free press.*
■[as submodifier] absolutely or completely (used to emphasize a description): *a truly dreadful song.*
3 in actual fact or without doubt; really: *this is truly a miracle.*
4 archaic loyally or faithfully: *why cannot all masters be served truly?*
– PHRASES **yours truly** used as a formula for ending a letter. ■humorous used to refer to oneself: *the demos will be organized by yours truly.*
– ORIGIN Old English *trēowlīce* 'faithfully' (see **TRUE**, **-LY**[2]).

Truman, Harry S. (1884–1972), American Democratic statesman, 33rd President of the US 1945–53. He authorized the use of the atom bomb against Hiroshima and Nagasaki, introduced the Marshall Plan of emergency aid in 1948 to war-shattered European countries, and involved the US in the Korean War.

Truman Doctrine the principle that the US should give support to countries or peoples threatened by Soviet forces or Communist insurrection. First expressed in 1947 by US President Truman in a speech to Congress seeking aid for Greece and Turkey, the doctrine was seen by the Communists as an open declaration of the cold war.

trumeau /truːˈməʊ/ ▶**noun** (pl. **trumeaux** /-ˈməʊz/) a section of wall or a pillar between two openings, especially a pillar dividing a large doorway in a church.
– ORIGIN late 19th cent.: from French, literally 'calf of the leg'.

trump[1] ▶**noun** (in bridge, whist, and similar card games) a playing card of the suit chosen to rank above the others, which can win a trick where a card of a different suit has been led.
■(**trumps**) the suit having this rank in a particular hand: *the ace of trumps.* ■(in a tarot pack) any of a special suit of 22 cards depicting symbolic and typical figures and scenes. ■(also **trump card**) figurative a valuable resource that may be used, especially as a surprise, in order to gain an advantage: *in this month General Haig decided to play his trump card: the tank.* ■informal, dated a helpful or admirable person. ■Austral./NZ informal a person in authority.
▶**verb** [with obj.] (in bridge, whist, and similar card games) play a trump on (a card of another suit), having no cards of the suit led.
■figurative beat (someone or something) by saying or doing something better: *if the fetus is human life, that trumps any argument about the freedom of the mother.*
– PHRASES **come** (or **turn**) **up trumps** informal, chiefly Brit. (of a person or situation) have a better performance or outcome than expected: *Conrad*

t

came up trumps again, finishing fourth in the 800 metres. ■ be especially generous or helpful: *Mother had been absent throughout, but Aunt Edie had come up trumps.*
– ORIGIN early 16th cent.: alteration of **TRIUMPH**, once used in card games in the same sense.
▶ **trump something up** invent a false accusation or excuse: *they've trumped up charges against her.*

trump² ▶ noun archaic a trumpet or a trumpet blast.
– ORIGIN Middle English: from Old French *trompe*, of Germanic origin; probably imitative.

trumpery archaic ▶ noun (pl. **-ies**) [mass noun] attractive articles of little value or use.
■ practices or beliefs that are superficially or visually appealing but have little real value or worth.
▶ adjective showy but worthless: *trumpery jewellery.*
■ delusive or shallow: *that trumpery hope which lets us dupe ourselves.*
– ORIGIN late Middle English (denoting trickery): from Old French *tromperie*, from *tromper* 'deceive'.

trumpet ▶ noun **1** a brass musical instrument with a flared bell and a bright, penetrating tone. The modern instrument has the tubing looped to form a straight-sided coil, with three valves.
■ an organ reed stop with a quality resembling that of a trumpet. ■ something shaped like a trumpet, especially the tubular corona of a daffodil flower. ■ a sound resembling that of a trumpet, especially the loud cry of an elephant.
2 (**trumpets**) a North American pitcher plant.
• Genus *Sarracenia*, family Sarraceniaceae: several species, in particular **yellow trumpets** (*S. flava*).
▶ verb (**trumpeted**, **trumpeting**) **1** [no obj.] play a trumpet: [as adj. **trumpeting**] *figures of two trumpeting angels.*
■ make a loud, penetrating sound resembling that of a trumpet: *wild elephants trumpeting in the bush.*
2 [with obj.] proclaim widely or loudly: *the press trumpeted another defeat for the government.*
– PHRASES **blow one's trumpet** talk openly and boastfully about one's achievements: *he refused to* ***blow his own trumpet*** *and blushingly declined to speak.*
– ORIGIN Middle English: from Old French *trompette*, diminutive of *trompe* (see **TRUMP²**). The verb dates from the mid 16th cent.

trumpet creeper ▶ noun another term for **TRUMPET VINE**.

trumpeter ▶ noun **1** a person who plays a trumpet.
■ a cavalry or artillery soldier who gives signals with a trumpet.
2 a large gregarious ground-dwelling bird of tropical South American forests, with mainly black plumage and loud trumpeting and booming calls.
• Family Psophiidae and genus *Psophia*: three species.
3 a pigeon of a domestic breed that makes a trumpet-like sound.
4 an edible marine fish with a spiny dorsal fin, found chiefly in cool Australasian waters and said to make a grunting or trumpeting sound when taken out of the water.
• Family Latridae: several genera and species, including the **Tasmanian trumpeter** (*Latris lineata*), prized as food.

trumpeter swan ▶ noun a large migratory swan with a black and yellow bill and a honking call, breeding in northern North America.
• *Cygnus buccinator*, family Anatidae.

trumpetfish ▶ noun (pl. same or **-fishes**) an elongated marine fish with a long narrow snout, resembling a pipefish. It lives around reefs and rocks in tropical waters and typically hangs in a semi-vertical position.
• Family Aulostomidae and genus *Aulostomus*: several species.

trumpet major ▶ noun the chief trumpeter of a cavalry regiment, typically a principal musician in a regimental band.

trumpet shell ▶ noun the shell of a large marine mollusc which can be blown to produce a loud note.
• Several species in the class Gastropoda, in particular the triton (*Charonia tritonis*, family Cymatiidae).

trumpet tree ▶ noun any of a number of tropical American trees, in particular:
• a tree grown in the Caribbean for its numerous trumpet-shaped flowers, which bloom when the tree is leafless (genus *Tabebuia*, family Bignoniaceae). • a cecropia whose hollow branches are used to make wind instruments (*Cecropia peltata*, family Cecropiaceae).

trumpet vine (also **trumpet creeper**) ▶ noun a climbing shrub with orange or red trumpet-shaped flowers, cultivated as an ornamental.
• Genus *Campsis*, family Bignoniaceae: the North American *C. radicans* and the Chinese *C. grandiflora*.

truncal ▶ adjective Medicine of or affecting the trunk of the body, or of a nerve.

truncate ▶ verb /trʌŋˈkeɪt, ˈtrʌŋ-/ [with obj.] [often as adj. **truncated**] shorten (something) by cutting off the top or the end: *a truncated cone shape* | *discussion was truncated by the arrival of tea.*
■ Crystallography replace (an edge or an angle) by a plane, typically so as to make equal angles with the adjacent faces.
▶ adjective /ˈtrʌŋkeɪt/ Botany & Zoology (of a leaf, feather, or other part) ending abruptly as if cut off across the base or tip.
– DERIVATIVES **truncation** noun.
– ORIGIN late 15th cent. (as a verb): from Latin *truncat-* 'maimed', from the verb *truncare*.

truncheon /ˈtrʌn(t)ʃ(ə)n/ ▶ noun chiefly Brit. a short, thick stick carried as a weapon by a police officer.
■ a staff or baton acting as a symbol of authority, especially that used by the Earl Marshal.
– ORIGIN Middle English (denoting a piece broken off (especially from a spear), also a cudgel): from Old French *tronchon* 'stump', based on Latin *truncus* 'trunk'.

trundle ▶ verb [no obj., with adverbial of direction] (of a wheeled vehicle or its occupants) move slowly and heavily, typically in a noisy or uneven way: *ten vintage cars trundled past.*
■ (of a person) move in a similar way: *she could hear him coughing as he trundled out.* ■ [with obj. and adverbial of direction] cause (something, typically a wheeled vehicle) to roll or move in such a way: *we trundled a wheelbarrow down to the river and collected driftwood.*
▶ noun [in sing.] an act of moving in such a way.
– ORIGIN mid 16th cent. (denoting a small wheel or roller): a parallel formation to obsolete or dialect *trendle, trindle* '(cause to) revolve'; related to **TREND**.

trundle bed ▶ noun chiefly N. Amer. a truckle bed.

trunk ▶ noun **1** the main woody stem of a tree as distinct from its branches and roots.
■ the main part of an artery, nerve, or other anatomical structure from which smaller branches arise. ■ an enclosed shaft or conduit for cables or ventilation.
2 a person's or animal's body apart from the limbs and head.
3 the elongated, prehensile nose of an elephant.
4 a large box with a hinged lid for storing or transporting clothes and other articles.
■ US the boot of a motor car.
– DERIVATIVES **trunkful** noun (pl. **-fuls**), **trunkless** adjective.
– ORIGIN late Middle English: from Old French *tronc*, from Latin *truncus*.

trunk call ▶ noun dated, chiefly Brit. a long-distance telephone call made within the same country.

trunkfish ▶ noun (pl. same or **-fishes**) another term for **BOXFISH**.

trunking ▶ noun [mass noun] **1** a system of shafts or conduits for cables or ventilation.
2 the use or arrangement of trunk lines.

trunk line ▶ noun a main line of a railway, telephone system, or other network.

trunk road ▶ noun chiefly Brit. an important main road used for long-distance travel.

trunks ▶ plural noun men's shorts, worn especially for swimming or boxing.
– ORIGIN late 19th cent. (originally US): from an earlier theatrical use denoting short breeches of thin material worn over tights.

trunnel /ˈtrʌn(ə)l/ ▶ noun US variant spelling of **TREENAIL**.

trunnion /ˈtrʌnjən/ ▶ noun a pin or pivot forming one of a pair on which something is supported.
■ a supporting cylindrical projection on each side of a cannon or mortar.
– ORIGIN early 17th cent.: from French *trognon* 'core, tree trunk', of unknown origin.

Truro /ˈtrʊərəʊ/ the county town of Cornwall; pop. 18,560 (1981).

truss ▶ noun **1** a framework, typically consisting of rafters, posts, and struts, supporting a roof, bridge, or other structure: *roof trusses.*
■ a surgical appliance worn to support a hernia, typically a padded belt. ■ a large projection of stone or timber, typically one supporting a cornice.
2 Brit., chiefly historical a bundle of old hay (56 lb), new hay (60 lb), or straw (36 lb).
3 a compact cluster of flowers or fruit growing on one stalk.
4 Sailing a heavy metal ring securing the lower yards to a mast.
▶ verb [with obj.] **1** tie up the wings and legs of (a chicken or other bird) before cooking.
■ tie up (someone) with their arms at their sides: *I found him* ***trussed up*** *in his cupboard.*
2 [usu. as adj. **trussed**] support (a roof, bridge, or other structure) with a truss or trusses.
– DERIVATIVES **trusser** noun.
– ORIGIN Middle English (in the sense 'bundle'): from Old French *trusse* (noun), *trusser* 'pack up, bind in', based on late Latin *tors-* 'twisted', from the verb *torquere*. Sense 1 dates from the mid 17th cent.

trust ▶ noun [mass noun] **1** firm belief in the reliability, truth, ability, or strength of someone or something: *relations have to be built on trust* | *they have been able to win the trust of the others.*
■ acceptance of the truth of a statement without evidence or investigation: *I used only primary sources,* ***taking*** *nothing* ***on trust.*** ■ the state of being responsible for someone or something: *a man in a position of trust.* ■ [count noun] poetic/literary a person or duty for which one has responsibility: *rulership is a trust from God.* ■ [count noun] poetic/literary a hope or expectation: *all the great trusts of womanhood.*
2 Law confidence placed in a person by making that person the nominal owner of property to be held or used for the benefit of one or more others.
■ [count noun] an arrangement whereby property is held in such a way: *a trust was set up* | [mass noun] *the flat will be auctioned and the proceeds* ***put into trust.***
3 [count noun] a body of trustees.
■ an organization or company managed by trustees: *a charitable trust* | [in names] *the Yorkshire Wildlife Trust.* ■ US, dated a large company that has or attempts to gain monopolistic control of a market.
4 W. Indian or archaic commercial credit: *my master lived on trust at an alehouse.*
▶ verb [with obj.] **1** believe in the reliability, truth, ability, or strength of: *I should never have trusted her* | [with obj. and infinitive] *he can be trusted to carry out an impartial investigation* | [as adj. **trusted**] *a trusted adviser.*
■ (**trust someone with**) allow someone to have, use, or look after (someone or something of importance or value) with confidence: *I'd trust you with my life.* ■ (**trust someone/thing to**) commit (someone or something) to the safe keeping of: *they don't like to* ***trust*** *their money* ***to*** *anyone outside the family.* ■ [with clause] have confidence; hope (used as a polite formula in conversation): *I trust that you have enjoyed this book.* ■ [no obj.] have faith or confidence: *she* ***trusted in*** *the powers of justice.* ■ [no obj.] (**trust to**) place reliance on (luck, fate, or something else over which one has little control): *I hurtled down the path, trusting to luck that I wouldn't put a foot wrong.*
2 archaic allow credit to (a customer).
– PHRASES **not trust someone as far as one can throw them** informal not trust or hardly trust a particular person at all. **trust someone to ——** it is characteristic or predictable for someone to act in the specified way: *trust Sam to have all the inside information.*
– DERIVATIVES **trustable** adjective, **truster** noun.
– ORIGIN Middle English: from Old Norse *traust*, from *traustr* 'strong'; the verb from Old Norse *treysta*, assimilated to the noun.

trustbuster ▶ noun informal, chiefly US a person or agency employed to enforce antitrust legislation.

trust company ▶ noun a company formed to act as a trustee or to deal with trusts.

trust corporation ▶ noun English Law a corporation empowered to act as a trustee, provided that it is a registered company which satisfies certain conditions.

trust deed ▶ noun Law a deed of conveyance creating and setting out the conditions of a trust.

trustee ▶ noun Law an individual person or member of a board given control or powers of administration of property in trust with a legal obligation to administer it solely for the purposes specified.
■ a state made responsible for the government of an area by the United Nations.
– DERIVATIVES **trusteeship** noun.

trustee in bankruptcy ▶ noun Law a person taking administrative responsibility for the financial affairs of a bankrupt and the distribution of assets to creditors.

trustful ▶ adjective having or marked by a total

belief in the reliability, truth, ability, or strength of someone.

– DERIVATIVES **trustfully** adverb, **trustfulness** noun.

trust fund ▶ noun a fund consisting of assets belonging to a trust, held by the trustees for the beneficiaries.

trusting ▶ adjective showing or tending to have a belief in a person's honesty or sincerity; not suspicious: *it is foolish to be too **trusting of** other people | a shy and trusting child.*

– DERIVATIVES **trustingly** adverb, **trustingness** noun.

trust territory ▶ noun a territory under the trusteeship of the United Nations or of a state designated by them.

trustworthy ▶ adjective able to be relied on as honest or truthful: *leave a spare key with a trustworthy neighbour.*

– DERIVATIVES **trustworthily** adverb, **trustworthiness** noun.

trusty ▶ adjective (**trustier**, **trustiest**) [attrib.] archaic or humorous having served for a long time and regarded as reliable or faithful: *my trusty old Morris Minor | their trusty steeds.*

▶ noun (pl. **-ies**) a prisoner who is given special privileges or responsibilities in return for good behaviour.

– DERIVATIVES **trustily** adverb, **trustiness** noun.

Truth, Sojourner (*c.*1797–1883), American evangelist and reformer; previously *Isabella Van Wagener.* Born into slavery, she was sold to an Isaac Van Wagener, who released her in 1827. She became a zealous evangelist, preaching in favour of black rights and women's suffrage.

truth ▶ noun (pl. **truths** /truːðz, truːθs/) [mass noun] the quality or state of being true: *he had to accept the truth of her accusation.*
■(also **the truth**) that which is true or in accordance with fact or reality: *tell me the truth | she found out the truth about him.* ■ [count noun] a fact or belief that is accepted as true: *the emergence of scientific truths | the fundamental truths about mankind.*

– PHRASES **in truth** really; in fact: *in truth, she was more than a little unhappy.* **to tell the truth** (or **truth to tell** or **if truth be told**) to be frank (used especially when making an admission or when expressing an unwelcome or controversial opinion): *I think, if truth be told, we were all a little afraid of him.* **the truth, the whole truth, and nothing but the truth** used to emphasize the absolute veracity of a statement. [ORIGIN: part of a statement sworn by witnesses in court.]

– ORIGIN Old English *trīewth, trēowth* 'faithfulness, constancy' (see **TRUE**, **-TH**[2]).

truth condition ▶ noun Logic the condition under which a given proposition is true.
■a statement of this condition, sometimes taken to be the meaning of the proposition.

truth drug ▶ noun a drug supposedly able to induce a state in which a person answers questions truthfully.

truthful ▶ adjective (of a person or statement) telling or expressing the truth; honest: *I think you're confusing being rude with being truthful | I want a truthful answer.*
■(of artistic or literary representation) characterized by accuracy or realism; true to life: *astonishingly truthful acting.*

– DERIVATIVES **truthfully** adverb, **truthfulness** noun.

truth function ▶ noun Logic a function whose truth value is dependent on the truth value of its arguments.

truth table ▶ noun Logic a diagram in rows and columns showing how the truth or falsity of a proposition varies with that of its components.
■Electronics a similar diagram of the outputs from all possible combinations of input.

truth value ▶ noun Logic the attribute assigned to a proposition in respect of its truth or falsehood, which in classical logic has only two possible values (true or false).

try ▶ verb (**-ies**, **-ied**) **1** [no obj.] make an attempt or effort to do something: [with infinitive] *he **tried to** regain his breath | I started to **try and** untangle the mystery | I decided to try writing fiction | none of them tried very hard |* [with obj.] *three times he tried the manoeuvre and three times he failed.*
■(**try for**) attempt to achieve or attain: *they decided to try for another baby.* ■ [with obj.] use, test, or do (something new or different) in order to see if it is suitable, effective, or pleasant: *everyone wanted to know if I'd tried jellied eel | these methods are **tried and tested**.* ■ (**try out for**) N. Amer. compete or audition in order to join (a team) or be given (a post): *she tried out for the team.* ■ [with obj.] go to (a place) or attempt to contact (someone), typically in order to obtain something: *I've tried the apartment, but the number is engaged.* ■ [with obj.] push or pull (a door or window) to determine whether it is locked: *I tried the doors, but they were locked.* ■ [with obj.] make severe demands on (a person or a quality, typically patience): *Mary tried everyone's patience to the limit.*
2 [with obj.] (usu. **be tried**) subject (someone) to trial: *he was arrested and tried for the murder.*
■investigate and decide (a case or issue) in a formal trial: *the case is to be tried by a jury in the Crown Court.*
3 [with obj.] smooth (roughly planed wood) with a plane to give an accurately flat surface.
4 [with obj.] extract (oil or fat) by heating: *some of the fat may be **tried out** and used.*

▶ noun (pl. **-ies**) **1** an effort to accomplish something; an attempt: *he got his membership card on his third try.*
■an act of doing, using, or testing something new or different to see if it is suitable, effective, or pleasant: *she agreed that they should give the idea a try.*
2 Rugby an act of touching the ball down behind the opposing goal line, scoring points and entitling the scoring side to a kick at goal.
■American Football an attempt to score an extra point after a touchdown.

– PHRASES **I** (or **he** etc.) **will try anything once** used to indicate willingness to do or experience something new. **try conclusions with** see **CONCLUSION**. **try something** (**on**) **for size** assess whether something is suitable: *he was trying the role for size.* **try for white** (or **black**) S. African historical (under the apartheid system) attempt to pass oneself off as a white (or black) person by assimilating oneself into a white (or black) community. **try one's hand at** attempt to do (something) for the first time, typically in order to find out if one is good at it: *a chance to try your hand at the ancient art of drystone walling.* **try it on** Brit. informal attempt to deceive or seduce someone: *he was **trying it on with** my wife.* ■ deliberately test someone's patience to see how much one can get away with. **try one's luck** see **LUCK**. **try me** used to suggest that one may be willing to do something unexpected or unlikely: *'You won't use a gun up here.' 'Try me.'*

– ORIGIN Middle English: from Old French *trier* 'sift', of unknown origin. Sense 1 of the noun dates from the early 17th cent.

USAGE Is there any difference between **try to** plus infinitive and **try and** plus infinitive in sentences such as *we should **try to** (or **try and**) help them?* In practice there is little discernible difference in meaning, although there is a difference in formality, with **try to** being regarded as more formal than **try and**. The construction **try and** is grammatically odd, however, in that it cannot be inflected for tense (e.g. sentences like *she **tried and** fix it* or *they are **trying and** renew their visa* are not acceptable, while their equivalents *she **tried to** fix it* or *they are **trying to** renew their visa* undoubtedly are). For this reason **try and** is best regarded as a fixed idiom used only in its infinitive and imperative form. See also **usage** at **AND**.

▶ **try something on** put on an item of clothing to see if it fits or suits one.
try someone/thing out test someone or something new or different to assess their suitability or effectiveness: *I try out new recipes on my daughter.*

trying ▶ adjective difficult or annoying; hard to endure: *it had been a very trying day.*

– DERIVATIVES **tryingly** adverb.

trying plane ▶ noun a long, heavy plane used in smoothing the edges of roughly planed wood.

try-on ▶ noun [in sing.] Brit. informal an attempt to fool or deceive someone.

try-out ▶ noun a test of the potential of someone or something, especially in the context of entertainment or sport.

trypan blue ▶ noun [mass noun] a diazo dye used as a biological stain due to its absorption by macrophages of the reticuloendothelial system.

– ORIGIN early 20th cent.: *trypan* from **TRYPANOSOME**.

trypanosome /ˈtrɪp(ə)nəsəʊm, trɪˈpanə-/ ▶ noun Medicine & Zoology a single-celled parasitic protozoan with a trailing flagellum, infesting the blood.
● Genus *Trypanosoma*, phylum Kinetoplastida, kingdom Protista.

– ORIGIN early 20th cent.: from Greek *trupanon* 'borer' + **-SOME**[3].

trypanosomiasis /ˌtrɪp(ə)nə(ʊ)sə(ʊ)ˈmʌɪəsɪs, trɪˌpanə(ʊ)-/ ▶ noun [mass noun] Medicine any tropical disease caused by trypanosomes and typically transmitted by biting insects, especially sleeping sickness and Chagas' disease.

trypsin /ˈtrɪpsɪn/ ▶ noun [mass noun] a digestive enzyme which breaks down proteins in the small intestine. It is secreted by the pancreas in an inactive form, trypsinogen.

– DERIVATIVES **tryptic** adjective.

– ORIGIN late 19th cent.: from Greek *tripsis* 'friction', from *tribein* 'to rub' (because it was first obtained by rubbing down the pancreas with glycerine), + **-IN**[1].

trypsinogen /trɪpˈsɪnədʒ(ə)n/ ▶ noun [mass noun] Biochemistry an inactive substance secreted by the pancreas, from which the digestive enzyme trypsin is formed in the duodenum.

tryptamine /ˈtrɪptəmiːn/ ▶ noun [mass noun] Biochemistry a compound, of which serotonin is a derivative, produced from tryptophan by decarboxylation.
● A heterocyclic amine; chem. formula: $C_8H_6NCH_2CH_2NH$.

tryptophan /ˈtrɪptəfan/ ▶ noun [mass noun] Biochemistry an amino acid which is a constituent of most proteins. It is an essential nutrient in the diet of vertebrates.
● An indole derivative; chem. formula: $C_8H_6NCH_2CH(NH_2)COOH$.

– ORIGIN late 19th cent.: from *tryptic* 'relating to trypsin' + Greek *phainein* 'appear'.

trysail /ˈtrʌɪs(ə)l/ ▶ noun a small strong fore-and-aft sail set on the mainmast or other mast of a sailing vessel in heavy weather.

try square ▶ noun an implement used to check and mark right angles in constructional work.

tryst /trɪst/ poetic/literary ▶ noun a private, romantic rendezvous between lovers: *a moonlight tryst.*

▶ verb [no obj.] keep a rendezvous of this kind: [as noun **trysting**] *a trysting place.*

– DERIVATIVES **tryster** noun.

– ORIGIN late Middle English (originally Scots): variant of obsolete *trist* 'an appointed place in hunting', from French *triste* or medieval Latin *trista*.

tsamma /ˈtsamə/ (also **tsamma melon**) ▶ noun S. African a watermelon, especially one growing wild in the desert.

– ORIGIN from Nama *tsamas* 'watermelon'.

tsantsa /ˈtsantsə/ ▶ noun a human head shrunk as a trophy by the Jivaros of Ecuador.

– ORIGIN Jivaro.

Tsao-chuang /tʃaʊˈtʃwaŋ/ variant of **ZAOZHUANG**.

tsar /zɑː, tsɑː/ (also **czar** or **tzar**) ▶ noun an emperor of Russia before 1917: [as title] *Tsar Nicholas II.*
■a South Slav ruler in former times, especially one reigning over Serbia in the 14th century. ■ [usu. with adj. or noun modifier] a person with great authority or power in a particular area: *America's new drug tsar.*

– DERIVATIVES **tsardom** noun, **tsarism** noun, **tsarist** noun & adjective.

– ORIGIN from Russian *tsar'*, representing Latin *Caesar*.

tsarevich /ˈzɑːrɪvɪtʃ, ˈtsɑː-, -ˈrjeɪ-/ (also **czarevich**) ▶ noun historical the eldest son of an emperor of Russia.

– ORIGIN Russian, literally 'son of a tsar'.

tsarina /zɑːˈriːnə, tsɑː-/ (also **czarina** or **tzarina**) ▶ noun historical an empress of Russia before 1917.

– ORIGIN via Italian and Spanish from German *Czarin, Zarin*, feminine of *Czar, Zar*.

Tsaritsyn /tsɑːˈriːtsɪn/ former name (until 1925) for **VOLGOGRAD**.

tsatske /ˈtsɒtskə/ ▶ noun variant spelling of **TCHOTCHKE**.

Tsavo National Park /ˈtsɑːvəʊ/ an extensive national park in SE Kenya, established in 1948.

Tselinograd /(t)sɛˈlɪnə(ʊ)ˌgrad/ former name for **AKMOLA**.

tsessebi /tsɛˈseɪbi/ (also **tsessebe** or **sassaby**) ▶ noun a topi (antelope) of a race found mainly in southern Africa.
● *Damaliscus lunatus lunatus*, family Bovidae. Alternative name: **bastard hartebeest**.

– ORIGIN mid 19th cent.: from Setswana.

tsetse /ˈtsɛtsi, ˈtɛtsi/ (also **tsetse fly**) ▶ noun an African bloodsucking fly which bites humans and

other mammals, transmitting sleeping sickness and nagana.
● Genus *Glossina*, family Tabanidae.
– ORIGIN mid 19th cent.: from Setswana.

TSgt ▶ abbreviation for Technical Sergeant.

TSH ▶ abbreviation for thyroid-stimulating hormone.

T-shirt (also **tee shirt**) ▶ noun a short-sleeved casual top, generally made of cotton, having the shape of a T when spread out flat.

tsimmes /'tsɪməs/ (also **tzimmes** or **tzimmis**) ▶ noun (pl. same) a Jewish stew of sweetened vegetables or vegetables and fruit, sometimes with meat.
■figurative a fuss or muddle.
– ORIGIN Yiddish.

Tsimshian /'tʃɪmʃɪən/ ▶ noun (pl. same) **1** a member of an American Indian people of the northern Pacific coast.
2 [mass noun] the Penutian language of this people, now with few speakers.
▶ adjective of or relating to this people or their language.
– ORIGIN from Tsimshian *čamsián*, literally 'inside the Skeena River'.

Tsinan /tsi:'nan/ variant of **JINAN**.

Tsinghai variant of **QINGHAI**.

Tsiolkovsky /ˌtsiːɒlˈkɒfski/, Konstantin (Eduardovich) (1857–1935), Russian aeronautical engineer. Tsiolkovsky carried out pioneering theoretical work on multistage rockets, jet engines, and space flight, and his proposal for the use of liquid fuel pre-dated the work of R. H. Goddard by nearly forty years.

Tskhinvali /tskɪn'vɑːli/ the capital of South Ossetia.

tsk tsk /t(ə)sk t(ə)sk/ ▶ exclamation expressing disapproval or annoyance: *you of all people, Goldie— tsk, tsk.*
▶ verb (**tsk-tsk**) [no obj.] make such an exclamation.
– ORIGIN 1940s: imitative.

Tsonga /'tsɒŋgə/ ▶ noun (pl. same or **Tsongas**) **1** a member of a people living in Transvaal, southern Mozambique, and southern Zimbabwe. Also called **SHANGAAN**.
2 [mass noun] the Bantu language of this people, which has about 3 million speakers.
▶ adjective of or relating to the Tsonga or their language.
– ORIGIN a local name, from either Tsonga or Zulu.

tsotsi /'tsɒtsi/ ▶ noun (pl. **tsotsis**) S. African a young black urban criminal.
■used as an affectionate or contemptuous term for a young man. ■ historical a young black gangster belonging to a group most prominent in the 1940s and 1950s, affecting a special language and flashy dress.
– ORIGIN said to be a Sotho corruption of **ZOOT SUIT**.

tsp ▶ abbreviation for (pl. same or **tsps**) teaspoonful.

T-square ▶ noun a T-shaped instrument for drawing or testing right angles.

TSR Computing ▶ abbreviation for terminate and stay resident, denoting a type of program that remains in the memory of a microcomputer after it has finished running and which can be quickly reactivated.

TSS ▶ abbreviation for toxic shock syndrome.

tsuba /'tsuː.ba/ ▶ noun (pl. same or **tsubas**) a Japanese sword guard, typically elaborately decorated and made of iron or leather.
– ORIGIN Japanese.

tsubo /'tsuː.bəʊ/ ▶ noun (pl. same or **-os**) **1** a Japanese unit of area equal to approximately 3.31 sq. metres (3.95 sq. yards).
2 (in complementary medicine) a point on the face or body to which pressure or other stimulation is applied during treatment.
– ORIGIN Japanese.

tsukemono /ˌtsuːkɪˈməʊnəʊ/ ▶ noun (pl. **-os**) a Japanese side dish of pickled vegetables, usually served with rice.
– ORIGIN Japanese, from *tsukeru* 'pickle' + *mono* 'thing'.

tsunami /tsuː'nɑːmi/ ▶ noun (pl. same or **tsunamis**) a long high sea wave caused by an earthquake or other disturbance.
– ORIGIN late 19th cent.: from Japanese, from *tsu* 'harbour' + *nami* 'wave'.

Tsushima /tsuː.'ʃiːmə/ a Japanese island in the

Korea Strait, between South Korea and Japan. In 1905 it was the scene of a defeat for the Russian navy during the Russo-Japanese War.

tsutsugamushi disease /ˌtsuːtsuːgəˈmʊʃi/ ▶ noun another term for **SCRUB TYPHUS**.
– ORIGIN early 20th cent.: *tsutsugamushi*, from the Japanese name of the mite which transmits the disease.

Tswana /'tswɑːnə/ ▶ noun (pl. same, **Tswanas**, or **Batswana**) **1** a member of a southern African people living in Botswana, South Africa, and neighbouring areas.
2 [mass noun] the language of this people, also called Setswana.
▶ adjective of or relating to the Tswana or their language.
– ORIGIN stem of Setswana *moTswana*, plural *baTswana*.

TT ▶ abbreviation for ■ teetotal. ■ teetotaller. ■ Tourist Trophy. ■ tuberculin-tested.

TTL ▶ noun [mass noun] Electronics a widely used technology for making integrated circuits.
[ORIGIN: abbreviation of *transistor transistor logic*.]
▶ adjective Photography (of a camera focusing system) through-the-lens.

TU ▶ abbreviation for Trade Union.

Tu. ▶ abbreviation for Tuesday.

Tuamotu Archipelago /tuːəˈmɔːtuː/ a group of about eighty coral islands forming part of French Polynesia, in the South Pacific; pop. 12,370 (1988). It is the largest group of coral atolls in the world.

tuan /'tjuː.ən/ ▶ noun another term for **PHASCOGALE**.
– ORIGIN mid 19th cent.: an Aboriginal word.

Tuareg /'twɑː.rɛg/ ▶ noun (pl. same or **Tuaregs**) a member of a Berber people of the western and central Sahara, living mainly in Algeria, Mali, Niger, and western Libya, traditionally as nomadic pastoralists.
▶ adjective of or relating to this people.
– ORIGIN the name in Berber.

tuatara /ˌtuː.əˈtɑːrə, ˌtjuː-/ ▶ noun a nocturnal burrowing lizard-like reptile with a crest of soft spines along its back, now confined to some small islands off New Zealand.
● Order Rhynchocephalia and genus *Sphenodon*: two species, in particular *S. punctatum*. All other members of the order became extinct during the Mesozoic era.
– ORIGIN late 19th cent.: from Maori, from *tua* 'on the back' + *tara* 'spine'.

Tuatha Dé Danann /ˌtuːəhə deɪ 'danən/ ▶ plural noun Irish Mythology the members of an ancient race said to have inhabited Ireland before the historical Irish. Formerly believed to have been a real people, they are credited with the possession of magical powers and great wisdom.
– ORIGIN Irish, literally 'people of the goddess Danann'.

tub ▶ noun **1** a wide, open, deep, typically round container with a flat bottom used for holding liquids, growing plants, etc.: *hydrangeas in a patio tub.*
■a similar small plastic or cardboard container in which food is bought or stored: *a margarine tub.* ■ the contents of such a container or the amount it can contain: *she ate a tub of yogurt.* ■ a washtub. ■ informal, chiefly N. Amer. a bath: *a soak in the tub.* ■ Mining a container for conveying ore, coal, etc.
2 informal, derogatory a short, broad boat that handles awkwardly.
▶ verb (**tubbed**, **tubbing**) [with obj.] **1** [usu. as adj. **tubbed**] plant in a tub: *tubbed fruit trees.*
2 dated wash or bathe (someone or something) in or as in a tub or bath.
■[no obj.] Brit. informal have a bath.
– DERIVATIVES **tubbable** adjective (informal) (in sense 2 of the verb), **tubful** noun (pl. **-fuls**).
– ORIGIN Middle English: probably of Low German or Dutch origin; compare with Middle Low German, Middle Dutch *tubbe*.

tuba ▶ noun a large brass wind instrument of bass pitch, with three to six valves and a broad bell typically facing upwards.
■a powerful reed stop on an organ with the quality of a tuba.
– ORIGIN mid 19th cent.: via Italian from Latin, 'trumpet'.

tubal ▶ adjective of, relating to, or occurring in a tube, especially the Fallopian tubes.

tubal ligation ▶ noun a surgical procedure for

female sterilization which involves severing and tying the Fallopian tubes.

tubal pregnancy ▶ noun Medicine an ectopic pregnancy in which the fetus develops in a Fallopian tube.

tubby ▶ adjective (**tubbier**, **tubbiest**) **1** informal (of a person) short and rather fat. [ORIGIN: referring to the shape of a tub.]
2 (of a sound) lacking resonance; dull. [ORIGIN: referring to the sound of a tub when struck.]
– DERIVATIVES **tubbiness** noun.

tub chair ▶ noun a chair with solid arms continuous with a semicircular back.

tube ▶ noun **1** a long, hollow cylinder of metal, plastic, glass, etc. for holding or transporting something, chiefly liquids or gases: *a plastic tube is connected to the tap and the beer is ready to be pulled.*
■the inner tube of a bicycle tyre. ■ [mass noun] tubing in such a cylindrical form; tubing: *the firm manufactures steel tube for a wide variety of applications.*
2 a thing in the form of or resembling such a cylinder, in particular:
■a flexible metal or plastic container sealed at one end and having a screw cap at the other, for holding a semi-liquid substance ready for use: *a tube of toothpaste.* ■ a rigid cylindrical container: *a tube of Smarties.* ■ Austral. informal a can of beer: *a tube of lager.* ■ [usu. with adj. or noun modifier] Anatomy, Zoology, & Botany a hollow cylindrical organ or structure in an animal body or in a plant (e.g. a Eustachian tube, a sieve tube). ■ (**tubes**) informal a woman's Fallopian tubes: *women with blocked tubes.* ■ a woman's close-fitting garment, typically without darts or other tailoring and made from a single piece of knitted or elasticated fabric: [as modifier] *stretchy tube skirts.* ■ (in surfing) the hollow curve under the crest of a breaking wave. ■ informal a cigarette.
3 Brit. informal (**the tube**) the underground railway system in London: *it wasn't far from where he lived, just a stop further on the tube.*
■a train running on this system: *I caught the tube home.*
4 a sealed container, typically of glass and either evacuated or filled with gas, containing two electrodes between which an electric current can be made to flow.
■a cathode ray tube, especially in a television set. ■ (**the tube**) N. Amer. informal television: *watching the tube in a country bar.* ■ US a thermionic valve.
▶ verb [with obj.] **1** [usu. as adj. **tubed**] provide with a tube or tubes: [in combination] *a giant eight-tubed hookah.*
■informal fit (a racehorse) with a tube to assist breathing, chiefly after a laryngotomy.
2 [with adverbial] convey in a tube.
– PHRASES **go down the tube** (or **tubes**) informal be completely lost or wasted; fail utterly: *the country is going slowly and surely down the tubes.*
– DERIVATIVES **tubeless** adjective, **tube-like** adjective.
– ORIGIN mid 17th cent.: from French *tube* or Latin *tubus*.

tubectomy ▶ noun (pl. **-ies**) another term for **SALPINGECTOMY**.

tube foot ▶ noun (usu. **tube feet**) Zoology (in an echinoderm) each of a large number of small flexible hollow appendages protruding through the ambulacra, used either for locomotion or for collecting food and operated by hydraulic pressure within the water-vascular system.

tube-nosed bat ▶ noun an Old World bat with tubular nostrils.
● a fruit bat found chiefly in New Guinea and Sulawesi (genus *Nyctimene*, family Pteropodidae). ● an insectivorous Asian bat (genus *Murina*, family Vespertilionidae).

tuber ▶ noun **1** a much thickened underground part of a stem or rhizome, e.g. in the potato, serving as a food reserve and bearing buds from which new plants arise.
■a tuberous root, e.g. of the dahlia.
2 Anatomy a rounded swelling or protuberant part.
– ORIGIN mid 17th cent.: from Latin, literally 'hump, swelling'.

tuber cinereum /ˌtjuːbə sɪˈnɪərɪəm/ ▶ noun Anatomy the part of the hypothalamus to which the pituitary gland is attached.
– ORIGIN Latin *cinereum*, neuter of *cinereus* 'ash-coloured'.

tubercle /'tjuːbək(ə)l/ ▶ noun **1** Anatomy, Zoology, & Botany a small rounded projection or protuberance, especially on a bone or on the surface of an animal or plant.
2 Medicine a small nodular lesion in the lungs or other tissues, characteristic of tuberculosis.

– DERIVATIVES **tuberculate** /-ˈbəːkjʊlət/ adjective (only in sense 1).
– ORIGIN late 16th cent.: from Latin *tuberculum*, diminutive of *tuber* (see TUBER).

tubercle bacillus ▶ noun a bacterium that causes tuberculosis.

tubercular /tjʊˈbəːkjʊlə/ ▶ adjective Medicine of, relating to, or affected with tuberculosis: *a tubercular kidney*.
  ■ Biology & Medicine having or covered with tubercles.
▶ noun a person with tuberculosis.

tuberculation /tjʊˌbəːkjʊˈleɪʃ(ə)n/ ▶ noun [mass noun] chiefly Biology the formation or presence of tubercles, especially of a specified type.
– ORIGIN mid 19th cent.: from Latin *tuberculum* (see TUBERCLE) + -ATION.

tuberculin /tjʊˈbəːkjʊlɪn/ ▶ noun [mass noun] a sterile protein extract from cultures of tubercle bacillus, used in a test by hypodermic injection for infection with or immunity to tuberculosis, and also formerly in the treatment of the disease.
– ORIGIN late 19th cent.: from Latin *tuberculum* (see TUBERCLE) + -IN[1].

tuberculin-tested ▶ adjective (of cows or their milk) giving, or from cows giving, a negative response to a tuberculin test.

tuberculoid /tjʊˈbəːkjʊlɔɪd/ ▶ adjective Medicine resembling tuberculosis or its symptoms.
  ■ relating to or denoting the milder of the two principal forms of leprosy, marked by few, well-defined lesions similar to those of tuberculosis, often with loss of feeling in the affected areas. Compare with LEPROMATOUS.

tuberculosis /tjʊˌbəːkjʊˈləʊsɪs/ (abbrev.: **TB**) ▶ noun [mass noun] an infectious bacterial disease characterized by the growth of nodules (tubercles) in the tissues, especially the lungs.
  ● The disease is caused by the bacterium *Mycobacterium tuberculosis* or (especially in animals) a related species; Gram-positive acid-fast rods.

The most common form, **pulmonary tuberculosis** (formerly known as 'consumption'), is caused by inhalation of the bacteria. It was widespread in 19th-century Europe, and still causes 3 million deaths each year in developing countries. The disease can affect other parts of the body, notably the bones and joints and the central nervous system. Its spread is countered by vaccination and by the pasteurization of milk to prevent transmission from cattle. It was once considered incurable, but early X-ray diagnosis permits its arrest by drugs and surgery.

– ORIGIN mid 19th cent.: modern Latin, from Latin *tuberculum* (see TUBERCLE) + -OSIS.

tuberculous /tjʊˈbəːkjʊləs/ ▶ adjective another term for TUBERCULAR.

tuberose /ˈtjuːbərəʊz/ ▶ noun a Mexican plant with heavily scented white waxy flowers and a bulb-like base. Unknown in the wild, it was formerly cultivated as a flavouring for chocolate; the flower oil is used in perfumery.
  ● *Polianthes tuberosa*, family Agavaceae.
▶ adjective variant spelling of TUBEROUS.
– ORIGIN mid 17th cent.: noun from Latin *tuberosa*, feminine of *tuberosus* 'with protuberances'; adjective from Latin *tuberosus*.

tuberous /ˈtjuːb(ə)rəs/ (also **tuberose** /ˈtjuːb(ə)rəʊs/) ▶ adjective **1** Botany of the nature of a tuber. See TUBEROUS ROOT.
  ■ (of a plant) having tubers or a tuberous root.
  2 Medicine characterized by or affected by rounded swellings: *tuberous sclerosis*.
– DERIVATIVES **tuberosity** /-ˈrɒsɪti/ noun.
– ORIGIN mid 17th cent.: from French *tubéreux* or Latin *tuberosus*, from *tuber* (see TUBER).

tuberous root ▶ noun a thick and fleshy root like a tuber but without buds, as in the dahlia.

tubesnout ▶ noun a small inshore fish with a very elongated snout, head, and body, living along the Pacific coast of North America.
  ● *Aulorhynchus flavidus*, the only member of the family Aulorhynchidae.

tube top ▶ noun North American term for BOOB TUBE.

tube well ▶ noun a well consisting of an iron pipe with a solid steel point and lateral perforations near the end, which is driven into the earth until a water-bearing stratum is reached, when a suction pump is applied to the upper end.

tube worm ▶ noun a marine bristle worm, especially a fan worm, which lives in a tube made

from sand particles or in a calcareous tube that it secretes.
  ● Families Serpulidae and Sabellidae, phylum Polychaeta.
  ■ a pogonophoran or vestimentiferan worm.

tubicolous /tjuːˈbɪkələs/ ▶ adjective Zoology (of a marine worm) living in a tube.

tubifex /ˈtjuːbɪfɛks/ ▶ noun a small red annelid worm that lives in fresh water, partly buried in the mud. Also called BLOODWORM.
  ● Genus *Tubifex*, family Tubificidae, class Oligochaeta.
– ORIGIN modern Latin, from Latin *tubus* 'tube' + -fex from *facere* 'make'.

tubing ▶ noun [mass noun] **1** a length or lengths of metal, plastic, glass, etc., in tubular form: *use the plastic tubing to siphon the beer into the bottles*.
  2 N. Amer. the leisure activity of riding on water or snow on a large inflated inner tube.

tubocurarine /ˌtjuːbə(ʊ)ˈkjʊərəriːn/ ▶ noun [mass noun] Medicine a compound of the alkaloid class obtained from curare and used to produce relaxation of voluntary muscles before surgery and in tetanus, encephalitis, and poliomyelitis.
– ORIGIN late 19th cent.: from Latin *tubus* 'tube' + CURARE + -INE[4].

Tubruq /tʊˈbruːk/ Arabic name for TOBRUK.

tub-thumping informal, derogatory ▶ adjective [attrib.] expressing opinions in a loud and violent or dramatic manner: *a tub-thumping speech*.
▶ noun [mass noun] the expression of opinions in such a way.
– DERIVATIVES **tub-thumper** noun.

Tubuai Islands /tuːbuˈwɑːi/ a group of volcanic islands in the South Pacific, forming part of French Polynesia; chief town, Mataura (on the island of Tubuai); pop. 6,500 (1988). Also called the AUSTRAL ISLANDS.

tubular ▶ adjective **1** long, round, and hollow like a tube: *tubular flowers of deep crimson*.
  ■ made from a tube or tubes: *tubular steel chairs*.
  ■ Surfing, chiefly US (of a wave) hollow and well curved.
  2 Medicine of or involving tubules or other tube-shaped structures.
▶ noun **1** short for TUBULAR TYRE.
  2 (**tubulars**) oil-drilling equipment made from tubes.
– ORIGIN late 17th cent.: from Latin *tubulus* 'small tube' + -AR[1].

tubular bells ▶ plural noun an orchestral instrument consisting of a row of vertically suspended metal tubes struck with a mallet.

tubular tyre ▶ noun a completely enclosed tyre cemented on to the wheel rim, used on racing bicycles.

tubule /ˈtjuːbjuːl/ ▶ noun a minute tube, especially as an anatomical structure: *kidney tubules*.
– ORIGIN late 17th cent.: from Latin *tubulus*, diminutive of *tubus* 'tube'.

Tubulidentata /ˌtjuːbjʊlɪdɛnˈtɑːtə, -ˈteɪtə/ Zoology an order of mammals which comprises only the aardvark.
– ORIGIN modern Latin (plural), from TUBULE + Greek *odous, odont-* 'tooth'.

tubulin /ˈtjuːbjʊlɪn/ ▶ noun [mass noun] Biochemistry a protein that is the main constituent of the microtubules of living cells.
– ORIGIN 1960s: from TUBULE + -IN[1].

TUC ▶ abbreviation for (in the UK) Trades Union Congress.

Tucana /tʊˈkɑːnə/ Astronomy a southern constellation (the Toucan), south of Grus and Phoenix. It contains the Small Magellanic Cloud.
  ■ [as genitive **Tucanae** /tʊˈkɑːniː/] used with preceding letter or numeral to designate a star in this constellation: *the star Delta Tucanae*.
– ORIGIN modern Latin.

tuck ▶ verb **1** [with obj. and usu. with adverbial of place] push, fold, or turn (the edges or ends of something, especially a garment or bedclothes) so as to hide them or hold them in place: *he tucked his shirt into his trousers*.
  ■ (**tuck someone in/up**) make someone, especially a child, comfortable in bed by pulling the edges of the bedclothes firmly under the mattress: *Emily was only too willing to be tucked up in bed by nine*. ■ draw (something, especially part of one's body) together into a small space: *she tucked her legs under her*. ■ (often **be tucked**) put (something) away in a specified place or way so as to be hidden, safe,

comfortable, or tidy: *the Colonel was coming towards her, his gun tucked under his arm*.
  2 [with obj.] make a flattened, stitched fold in (a garment or material), typically so as to shorten or tighten it, or for decoration.
▶ noun **1** a flattened, stitched fold in a garment or material, typically one of several parallel folds put in a garment for shortening, tightening, or decoration: *a dress with tucks along the bodice*.
  ■ [usu. with modifier] informal a surgical operation to reduce surplus flesh or fat: *a tummy tuck*.
  2 [mass noun] Brit. informal food, typically cakes and sweets, eaten by children at school as a snack: [as modifier] *a tuck shop*.
  3 (also **tuck position**) (in diving, gymnastics, downhill skiing, etc.) a position with the knees bent and held close to the chest, often with the hands clasped round the shins.
– ORIGIN Old English *tūcian* 'to punish, ill-treat': of West Germanic origin; related to TUG. Influenced in Middle English by Middle Dutch *tucken* 'pull sharply'.
▶ **tuck something away 1** store something in a secure place: *savers are turning to unit trusts as the best place to tuck away their money*. ■ (usu. **be tucked away**) put or keep someone or something in an inconspicuous or concealed place: *the police station was tucked away in a square behind the main street*. **2** informal (in sport) hit the ball to the desired place: *Stewart neatly tucked away the first goal*. **3** informal eat a lot of food.
  tuck in (or **into**) informal eat food heartily: *I tucked into the bacon and scrambled eggs*.

tuckahoe /ˈtʌkəhəʊ/ ▶ noun [mass noun] a root or other underground plant part formerly eaten by North American Indians, in particular:
  ● the starchy rhizome of an arum that grows chiefly in marshland (*Peltandra virginica*, family Araceae). ● the underground sclerotium of a bracket fungus (*Poria cocos*, class Hymenomycetes).
– ORIGIN early 17th cent.: from Virginia Algonquian *tockawhoughe*.

tucker ▶ noun **1** [mass noun] Austral./NZ informal food. [ORIGIN: early 19th cent.: derivative of British English slang *tuck* 'consume (food or drink)'.]
  2 historical a piece of lace or linen worn in or around the top of a bodice or as an insert at the front of a low-cut dress. See also **one's best bib and tucker** at BIB[1].
▶ verb [with obj.] (usu. **be tuckered out**) N. Amer. informal exhaust; wear out.

tucket ▶ noun archaic a flourish on a trumpet.
– ORIGIN late 16th cent.: from obsolete *tuck* 'beat (a drum)', from Old Northern French *toquer*, from the base of TOUCH.

tuck-in ▶ noun Brit. informal, dated a large meal.

tucking ▶ noun [mass noun] a series of stitched tucks in a garment.

tuck-point ▶ verb [with obj.] point (brickwork) with coloured mortar so as to have a narrow groove which is filled with fine white lime putty allowed to project slightly.

tuck position ▶ noun see TUCK (sense 3).

tuco-tuco /ˈtuːkəʊˌtuːkəʊ/ ▶ noun (pl. **-os**) a burrowing rat-like rodent native to South America.
  ● Family Ctenomyidae and genus *Ctenomys*: numerous species.
– ORIGIN mid 19th cent.: imitative of the call of some species.

Tucson /ˈtuːsɒn/ a city in SE Arizona; pop. 405,390 (1990).

tucuxi /tʊˈkuːhi/ ▶ noun (pl. same) a small stout-bodied dolphin with a grey back and pinkish underparts, living along the coasts and rivers from Panama to Brazil and in the Amazon.
  ● *Sotalia fluviatilis*, family Delphinidae.

'tude ▶ noun N. Amer. informal short for ATTITUDE: *the song bristles with lotsa 'tude*.

-tude ▶ suffix forming abstract nouns such as *beatitude, solitude*.
– ORIGIN from French *-tude*, from Latin *-tudo*.

Tudeh /ˈtuːdeɪ/ (also **Tudeh Party**) the Communist Party of Iran.
– ORIGIN Persian, literally 'mass'.

Tudor[1] ▶ adjective of or relating to the English royal dynasty which held the throne from the accession of Henry VII in 1485 until the death of Elizabeth I in 1603.
  ■ of, denoting, or relating to the prevalent

architectural style of the Tudor period, characterized especially by half-timbering.
▶ **noun** a member of this dynasty.

Tudor², Henry, Henry VII of England (see **HENRY**¹).

Tudor³, Mary, Mary I of England (see **MARY**²).

Tudorbethan /ˌtjuːdəˈbiːθ(ə)n/ ▶ **adjective** (of a contemporary house or architectural design) imitative of Tudor and Elizabethan styles.
– ORIGIN 1930s: blend of **TUDOR**¹ and **ELIZABETHAN**.

Tudor rose ▶ **noun** a conventionalized, typically five-lobed figure of a rose used in architectural and other decoration in the Tudor period, in particular a combination of the red and white roses of Lancaster or York adopted as a badge by Henry VII.

Tues. (also **Tue.**) ▶ **abbreviation for** Tuesday.

Tuesday ▶ **noun** the day of the week before Wednesday and following Monday: *come to dinner on Tuesday* | *the following Tuesday* | [as modifier] *Tuesday afternoons.*
▶ **adverb** chiefly N. Amer. on Tuesday: *they're all leaving Tuesday.*
■ (**Tuesdays**) on Tuesdays; each Tuesday: *she works late Tuesdays.*
– ORIGIN Old English *Tiwesdæg*, named after the Germanic god *Tiw* (associated with Mars); translation of Latin *dies Marti* 'day of Mars'; compare with Swedish *tisdag*.

tufa /ˈtjuːfə/ ▶ **noun** [mass noun] a porous rock composed of calcium carbonate and formed by precipitation from water, e.g. around mineral springs.
■ another term for **TUFF**.
– DERIVATIVES **tufaceous** /-ˈfeɪʃəs/ adjective.
– ORIGIN late 18th cent.: from Italian, variant of *tufo* (see **TUFF**).

tuff /tʌf/ ▶ **noun** [mass noun] a light, porous rock formed by consolidation of volcanic ash.
– DERIVATIVES **tuffaceous** /-ˈfeɪʃəs/ adjective.
– ORIGIN mid 16th cent.: via French from Italian *tufo*, from late Latin *tofus*, Latin *tophus* (see **TOPHUS**).

tuffet ▶ **noun** 1 a tuft or clump of something: *grass tuffets.*
2 a footstool or low seat.
– ORIGIN mid 16th cent.: alteration of **TUFT**.

tuft ▶ **noun** a bunch or collection of something, typically threads, grass, or hair, held or growing together at the base: *scrubby tufts of grass.*
■ Anatomy & Zoology a bunch of small blood vessels, respiratory tentacles, or other small anatomical structures.
▶ **verb** [with obj.] 1 (usu. **be tufted**) provide (something) with a tuft or tufts.
2 Needlework make depressions at regular intervals in (a mattress or cushion) by passing a thread through it.
– DERIVATIVES **tufty** adjective.
– ORIGIN late Middle English: probably from Old French *tofe*, of unknown origin. The final -t is typical of phonetic confusion between -f and -ft at the end of words; compare with **GRAFT**¹.

tufted ▶ **adjective** having or growing in a tuft or tufts: *tufted grass.*

tufted duck ▶ **noun** a Eurasian freshwater diving duck with a drooping crest, the male having mainly black and white plumage.
● *Aythya fuligula*, family Anatidae.

Tu Fu /tuː ˈfuː/ (also **Du Fu**) (AD 712–70), Chinese poet. He is noted for his bitter satiric poems attacking social injustice and corruption at court.

tug ▶ **verb** (**tugged**, **tugging**) [with obj.] pull (something) hard or suddenly: *she tugged off her boots* | [no obj.] *he tugged at Tom's coat sleeve.*
■ tow (a ship) by means of a tug or tugs.
▶ **noun** 1 a hard or sudden pull: *another tug and it came loose* | figurative *an overwhelming tug of attraction.*
2 (also **tugboat**) a small, powerful boat used for towing larger boats and ships, especially in harbour.
■ an aircraft towing a glider.
3 a loop from a horse's saddle which supports a shaft or trace.
– PHRASES **tug of love** Brit. informal a dispute over the custody of a child.
– DERIVATIVES **tugger** noun.
– ORIGIN Middle English: from the base of **TOW**¹. The noun is first recorded (late Middle English) in sense 3.

tug of war ▶ **noun** a contest in which two teams pull at opposite ends of a rope until one drags the other over a central line.
■ figurative a situation in which two evenly matched people or factions are striving to keep or obtain the same thing: *a tug of war between builders and environmentalists.*

tugrik /ˈtuːɡriːk/ ▶ **noun** (pl. same or **tugriks**) the basic monetary unit of Mongolia, equal to 100 mongos.
– ORIGIN Mongolian.

tui /ˈtuːi/ ▶ **noun** a large New Zealand honeyeater with glossy blackish plumage and two white tufts at the throat. Also called **PARSON-BIRD**.
● *Prosthemadura novaeseelandiae*, family Meliphagidae.
– ORIGIN mid 19th cent.: from Maori.

tuile /twiːl/ ▶ **noun** (pl. pronounced same) a thin curved biscuit, typically made with almonds.
– ORIGIN French, literally 'tile'.

Tuileries /ˈtwiːləri, French tɥilʁi/ (also **Tuileries Gardens**) formal gardens next to the Louvre in Paris. The gardens are all that remain of the Tuileries Palace, a royal residence begun in 1564 and burnt down in 1871 during the Commune of Paris.
– ORIGIN French, literally 'Tile-works', so named because the palace was built on the site of an ancient tile-works.

Tuinal /ˈt(j)uːnal, -nəl/ ▶ **noun** [mass noun] Medicine, trademark a sedative and hypnotic drug consisting of a combination of two barbiturates.

tuition ▶ **noun** [mass noun] teaching or instruction, especially of individual pupils or small groups.
■ N. Amer. a sum of money charged for this by a college or university: *I'm not paying next year's tuition.*
– DERIVATIVES **tuitional** adjective.
– ORIGIN late Middle English (in the sense 'custody, care'): via Old French from Latin *tuitio(n-)*, from *tueri* 'to watch, guard'. Current senses date from the late 16th cent.

tuk-tuk /ˈtʊktʊk/ ▶ **noun** (in Thailand) a three-wheeled motorized vehicle used as a taxi.
– ORIGIN imitative.

Tula /ˈtuːlə/ 1 an industrial city in European Russia, to the south of Moscow; pop. 543,000 (1990).
2 the ancient capital city of the Toltecs, generally identified with a site near the town of Tula in Hidalgo State, central Mexico.

tularaemia /ˌt(j)uːləˈriːmɪə/ (US **tularemia**) ▶ **noun** [mass noun] a severe infectious bacterial disease of animals transmissible to humans, characterized by ulcers at the site of infection, fever, and loss of weight. Compare with **RABBIT FEVER**.
● This disease is caused by the bacterium *Pasteurella tularense*; Gram-negative rods or cocci.
– DERIVATIVES **tularaemic** adjective.
– ORIGIN 1920s: modern Latin, from *Tulare*, the county in California where it was first observed.

tule /ˈtuːli/ ▶ **noun** US a clubrush that is abundant in marshy areas of California.
● *Scirpus acutus* and *S. validus*, family Cyperaceae.
– ORIGIN mid 19th cent.: via Spanish from Nahuatl *tullin*.

tulip ▶ **noun** a bulbous spring-flowering plant of the lily family, with boldly coloured cup-shaped flowers.
● Genus *Tulipa*, family Liliaceae: numerous complex hybrids.
– ORIGIN late 16th cent.: from French *tulipe*, via Turkish from Persian *dulband* 'turban', from the shape of the expanded flower.

tulip shell ▶ **noun** a predatory marine mollusc with a sculptured spiral shell resembling that of a whelk.
● Family Fasciolariidae, class Gastropoda, in particular *Fasciolaria tulipa*, which is common in the Caribbean.

tulip tree ▶ **noun** a deciduous North American tree which has large distinctively lobed leaves and insignificant tulip-like flowers. Also called **YELLOW POPLAR** or **WHITEWOOD** in North America.
● *Liriodendron tulipifera*, family Magnoliaceae.

tulipwood ▶ **noun** 1 an Australian tree of rainforest and scrub, with heavy black and yellow timber that is used mainly for cabinetmaking.
● *Harpullia pendula*, family Sapindaceae.
2 [mass noun] the pale timber of the tulip tree.

Tull /tʌl/, Jethro (1674–1741), English agriculturalist. In 1701 he invented the seed drill, a machine which could sow seeds in accurately spaced rows at a controlled rate, reducing the need for farm labourers.

Tullamore /ˌtʊləˈmɔː/ the county town of Offaly, in the Republic of Ireland; pop. 8,620 (1991).

tulle /t(j)uːl/ ▶ **noun** [mass noun] a soft, fine silk, cotton, or nylon material like net, used for making veils and dresses.
– ORIGIN early 19th cent.: from *Tulle*, a town in SW France, where it was first made.

tullibee /ˈtʌlɪbiː/ ▶ **noun** (pl. same or **tullibees**) a lake cisco (fish) of a deep-bodied race living in the Great Lakes of Canada.
● *Coregonus artedii tullibee*, family Salmonidae.
– ORIGIN late 18th cent.: from Canadian French *toulibi*, ultimately from Ojibwa.

tulp /tʊlp/ ▶ **noun** S. African an African plant of the iris family, which is grown for its showy flowers but is toxic to livestock.
● Genera *Homeria* and *Moraea*, family Iridaceae: several species, including the **blue tulp** (*M. polystachya*).
– ORIGIN mid 19th cent.: from Afrikaans, from Dutch.

Tulsa /ˈtʌlsə/ a port on the Arkansas River in NE Oklahoma; pop. 367,300 (1990).

tulsi /ˈtʊlsiː/ ▶ **noun** a kind of basil which is cultivated by Hindus as a sacred plant.
● *Ocimum sanctum*, family Labiatae.
– ORIGIN from Hindi *tūlsī*.

Tulsidas /ˈtʊlsɪdɑːs/ (c.1543–1623), Indian poet. A leading Hindu devotional poet, he is chiefly remembered for the *Ramcaritmanas* (c.1574–7), a work consisting of seven cantos based on the Sanskrit epic the Ramayana.

tum ▶ **noun** informal a person's stomach or abdomen.
– ORIGIN mid 19th cent.: abbreviation of **TUMMY**.

tumbaga /tɒmˈbɑːɡə/ ▶ **noun** [mass noun] an alloy of gold and copper commonly used in pre-Columbian South and Central America.
– ORIGIN 1930s: from Spanish, from Malay *tembaga* 'copper, brass'.

tumble ▶ **verb** 1 [no obj., with adverbial] (typically of a person) fall suddenly, clumsily, or headlong: *she pitched forward, tumbling down the remaining stairs.*
■ move or rush in a headlong or uncontrolled way: *police and dogs tumbled from the vehicle.* ■ (of something abstract) fall rapidly in amount or value: *property prices tumbled.* ■ [with obj.] dry (washing) in a tumble-dryer. ■ [with obj.] rumple; disarrange: [as adj. **tumbled**] *his tumbled bedclothes.* ■ [with obj.] informal have sexual intercourse with (someone).
2 [no obj.] (**tumble to**) informal understand the meaning or hidden implication of (a situation): *she'll ring again as soon as she tumbles to what she's done.*
3 [no obj.] perform acrobatic feats, typically handsprings and somersaults in the air.
■ (of a breed of pigeon) repeatedly turn over backwards in flight.
4 [with obj.] clean (castings, gemstones, etc.) in a tumbling barrel.
▶ **noun** 1 a sudden or headlong fall: *I took a tumble in the nettles.*
■ a rapid fall in amount or value: *a tumble in share prices.* ■ an untidy or confused arrangement or state: *her hair was a tumble of untamed curls.* ■ informal an act of sexual intercourse. ■ a handspring, somersault in the air, or other acrobatic feat.
2 US informal a friendly sign of recognition, acknowledgement, or interest: *not a soul gave him a tumble.*
– ORIGIN Middle English (as a verb, also in the sense 'dance with contortions'): from Middle Low German *tummelen*; compare with Old English *tumbian* 'to dance'. The sense was probably influenced by Old French *tomber* 'to fall'. The noun, first in the sense 'tangled mass', dates from the mid 17th cent.

tumblebug ▶ **noun** N. Amer. a dung beetle that rolls balls of dung along the ground.

tumbledown ▶ **adjective** (of a building or structure) falling or fallen into ruin; dilapidated.

tumble-dryer ▶ **noun** a machine that dries washed clothes by spinning them in hot air inside a rotating drum.
– DERIVATIVES **tumble-dry** verb (**-dries**, **-dried**).

tumblehome ▶ **noun** [mass noun] the inward slope of the upper part of a boat's sides.

tumbler ▶ **noun** 1 a drinking glass with straight sides and no handle or stem. [ORIGIN: formerly having a rounded bottom so as not to stand upright.]

2 an acrobat, especially one who performs somersaults.
■a pigeon of a breed that repeatedly turns over backwards in flight.
3 (also **tumbler-dryer**) another term for **TUMBLE-DRYER**.
4 a pivoted piece in a lock that holds the bolt until lifted by a key.
■a notched pivoted plate in a gunlock.
5 an electrical switch worked by pushing a small sprung lever.
6 another term for **TUMBLING BARREL**.
– DERIVATIVES **tumblerful** noun (pl. **-fuls**).

tumbleweed ▶ noun [mass noun] N. Amer. & Austral. a plant of arid regions which breaks off near the ground in late summer, forming light globular masses which are tumbled about by the wind.
● Genera *Salsola* (family Chenopodiaceae) and *Amaranthus* (family Amaranthaceae).

tumbling barrel ▶ noun a revolving device containing an abrasive substance, in which castings, gemstones, or other hard objects can be cleaned by friction.

tumbling bay ▶ noun chiefly historical an outfall from a river, reservoir, or canal, or the pool into which this flows.

tumbril /'tʌmbr(ə)l, -bril/ (also **tumbrel**) ▶ noun historical an open cart that tilted backwards to empty out its load, in particular one used to convey condemned prisoners to the guillotine during the French Revolution.
■a two-wheeled covered cart which carried tools or ammunition for an army.
– ORIGIN Middle English (originally denoting a type of cucking-stool): from Old French *tomberel*, from *tomber* 'to fall'.

tumefy /'tjuːmɪfʌɪ/ ▶ verb (**-ies, -ied**) [no obj.] become swollen.
– DERIVATIVES **tumefaction** noun.
– ORIGIN late 16th cent. (in the sense 'cause to swell'): from French *tuméfier*, from Latin *tumefacere*, from *tumere* 'to swell'.

tumescent /tjʊ'mɛs(ə)nt/ ▶ adjective swollen or becoming swollen, especially as a response to sexual arousal.
– DERIVATIVES **tumescence** noun, **tumescently** adverb.
– ORIGIN mid 19th cent.: from Latin *tumescent-* 'beginning to swell', from the verb *tumescere*, from *tumere* 'to swell'.

tumid /'tjuːmɪd/ ▶ adjective (especially of a part of the body) swollen: *a tumid belly.*
■figurative (especially of language or literary style) pompous or bombastic: *tumid oratory.*
– DERIVATIVES **tumidity** noun, **tumidly** adverb.
– ORIGIN mid 16th cent.: from Latin *tumidus*, from *tumere* 'to swell'.

tummler /'tʊmlə/ ▶ noun US a person who makes things happen, in particular a professional entertainer whose function is to encourage an audience, guests at a resort, etc. to participate in the entertainments or activities.
■a professional comedian.
– ORIGIN 1960s: Yiddish, from German *tummeln* 'to stir'.

tummy ▶ noun (pl. **-ies**) informal a person's stomach or abdomen: [as modifier] *a tummy upset.*
– ORIGIN mid 19th cent.: child's pronunciation of **STOMACH**.

tummy button ▶ noun informal a person's navel.

tumorigenesis /ˌtjuːmərɪ'dʒɛnɪsɪs/ ▶ noun [mass noun] the production or formation of a tumour or tumours.

tumorigenic /ˌtjuːmərɪ'dʒɛnɪk/ ▶ adjective capable of forming or tending to form tumours.
– DERIVATIVES **tumorigenicity** noun.

tumour (US **tumor**) ▶ noun a swelling of a part of the body, generally without inflammation, caused by an abnormal growth of tissue, whether benign or malignant.
■archaic a swelling of any kind.
– DERIVATIVES **tumorous** adjective.
– ORIGIN late Middle English: from Latin *tumor*, from *tumere* 'to swell'.

tump /tʌmp/ ▶ noun chiefly dialect [often in place names] **1** a small rounded hill or mound; a tumulus.
2 a clump of trees, shrubs, or grass.
– ORIGIN late 16th cent.: of unknown origin.

tumpline /'tʌmplʌɪn/ ▶ noun N. Amer. a sling for carrying a load on the back, with a strap which passes round the forehead.
■a strap of this kind.
– ORIGIN late 18th cent.: based on Algonquian (*mat*)*tump* + the noun **LINE**[1].

tumult ▶ noun [usu. in sing.] a loud, confused noise, especially one caused by a large mass of people: *a tumult of shouting and screaming broke out.*
■[mass noun] confusion or disorder: *the whole neighbourhood was in a state of fear and tumult* | figurative *his personal tumult ended when he began writing songs.*
– ORIGIN late Middle English: from Old French *tumulte* or Latin *tumultus.*

tumultuous /tjʊ'mʌltjʊəs/ ▶ adjective making a loud, confused noise; uproarious: *tumultuous applause.*
■excited, confused, or disorderly: *a tumultuous crowd* | figurative *a tumultuous personal life.*
– DERIVATIVES **tumultuously** adverb, **tumultuousness** noun.
– ORIGIN mid 16th cent.: from Old French *tumultuous* or Latin *tumultuosus*, from *tumultus* (see **TUMULT**).

tumulus /'tjuːmjʊləs/ ▶ noun (pl. **tumuli** /-lʌɪ, -liː/) an ancient burial mound; a barrow.
– ORIGIN late Middle English: from Latin; related to *tumere* 'swell'.

tun ▶ noun **1** a large beer or wine cask.
■a brewer's fermenting-vat.
2 an imperial measure of capacity, equal to 4 hogsheads.
3 (also **tun shell**) a large marine mollusc which has a rounded barrel-like shell with broad spirals.
● Family Tonnidae, class Gastropoda.
▶ verb (**tunned, tunning**) [with obj.] archaic store (wine or other alcoholic drinks) in a tun.
– ORIGIN Old English *tunne*, from medieval Latin *tunna*, probably of Gaulish origin.

tuna[1] ▶ noun (pl. same or **tunas**) a large and active predatory schooling fish of warm seas, extensively fished commercially and popular as a game fish. See also **TUNNY**.
● *Thunnus* and other genera, family Scombridae: several species, including the albacore, bigeye, bluefin, skipjack, and yellowfin.
– ORIGIN late 19th cent.: from American Spanish, from Spanish *atún* 'tunny'.

tuna[2] ▶ noun N. Amer. **1** the edible fruit of a prickly pear cactus.
2 a cactus that produces such fruit, widely cultivated in Mexico.
● Genus *Opuntia*, family Cactaceae: many species, in particular *O. tuna* of Central America and the Caribbean.
– ORIGIN mid 16th cent.: via Spanish from Taino.

Tunbridge Wells a spa town in Kent, SE England; pop. 58,140 (1981). Founded in the 1630s after the discovery of iron-rich springs, the town was patronized by royalty throughout the 17th and 18th centuries. Official name **ROYAL TUNBRIDGE WELLS**.

tundish /'tʌndɪʃ/ ▶ noun Brit. a broad open container or large funnel with one or more holes at the bottom, used especially in plumbing or metal-founding.

tundra /'tʌndrə/ ▶ noun a vast, flat, treeless Arctic region of Europe, Asia, and North America in which the subsoil is permanently frozen.
– ORIGIN late 16th cent.: from Lappish.

tundra swan ▶ noun an Arctic-breeding migratory swan with a yellow and black bill, often known by the names of its constituent races (Bewick's swan and whistling swan).
● *Cygnus columbianus*, family Anatidae.

tune ▶ noun a melody, especially one which characterizes a certain piece of music: *she left the theatre humming a cheerful tune.*
▶ verb [with obj.] **1** adjust (a musical instrument) to the correct or uniform pitch: *he tuned the harp for me.*
■adjust (a receiver circuit such as a radio or television) to the frequency of the required signal: *the radio was tuned to the BBC* | [no obj.] *they tuned in to watch the cricket.* ■ adjust (an engine) or balance (mechanical parts) so that a vehicle runs smoothly and efficiently. ■ (usu. **be tuned**) figurative adjust or adapt (something) to a particular purpose or situation: *the animals are finely tuned to life in the desert.* ■ [no obj.] (**tune into**) figurative become sensitive to: *you must tune into the needs of loved ones.*
2 [with two objs] S. African informal tell (someone) (something): *he starts tuning you stories about his youth.* [ORIGIN: transferred use of *tune* 'adjust, put right'.]
– PHRASES **be tuned in** informal be aware of, sensitive to, or able to understand something: *it's important to be tuned in to your child's needs.* **call the tune** see **CALL**. **change one's tune** see **CHANGE**. **in** (or **out of**) **tune** with correct (or incorrect) pitch or intonation. ■ (of a motor engine or other machine) properly (or poorly) adjusted. ■ figurative in (or not in) agreement or harmony: *he was out of tune with conventional belief.* **there's many a good tune played on an old fiddle** proverb someone's abilities do not depend on their being young. **to the tune of** informal amounting to or involving (a specified considerable sum): *he was in debt to the tune of forty thousand pounds.*
– DERIVATIVES **tunable** (also **tuneable**) adjective.
– ORIGIN late Middle English: unexplained alteration of **TONE**. The verb is first recorded (late 15th cent.) in the sense 'celebrate in music, sing'.
▶ **tune out** informal stop listening or paying attention.
tune something out exclude a sound or transmission of a particular frequency.
tune up (of a musician) adjust one's instrument to the correct or uniform pitch.
tune something up adjust something so that it performs at its most efficient.

tuneful ▶ adjective having a pleasing tune; melodious.
– DERIVATIVES **tunefully** adverb, **tunefulness** noun.

tuneless ▶ adjective not pleasing to listen to; unmelodious.
– DERIVATIVES **tunelessly** adverb, **tunelessness** noun.

tuner ▶ noun a person who tunes musical instruments, especially pianos.
■an electronic device for tuning a guitar or other instrument. ■ an electronic device for varying the frequency to which a radio or television is tuned. ■ a separate unit for detecting and preamplifying a programme signal and supplying it to an audio amplifier. ■ a person who tunes car engines or other machines.

tunesmith ▶ noun informal a composer of popular music or songs.

tune-up ▶ noun an act of tuning something up: *take your car in for a tune-up if it's an older model.*
■chiefly US a sporting event that serves as a practice for a subsequent event: *a tune-up for the college's fall league.*

tung oil ▶ noun [mass noun] an oil used as a drying agent in inks, paints, and varnishes.
● This oil is obtained from the seeds of trees of the genus *Aleurites*, family Euphorbiaceae.
– ORIGIN late 19th cent.: *tung*, from Chinese.

tungstate /'tʌŋsteɪt/ ▶ noun Chemistry a salt in which the anion contains both tungsten and oxygen, especially one of the anion WO_4^{2-}.
– ORIGIN early 19th cent.: from **TUNGSTEN** + **-ATE**[1].

tungsten /'tʌŋst(ə)n/ ▶ noun [mass noun] the chemical element of atomic number 74, a hard steel-grey metal of the transition series. It has a very high melting point (3410°C) and is used to make electric light filaments. (Symbol: **W**).
– ORIGIN late 18th cent.: from Swedish, from *tung* 'heavy' + *sten* 'stone'.

tungsten carbide ▶ noun [mass noun] a very hard grey compound made by reaction of tungsten and carbon at high temperatures, used in making engineering dies, cutting and drilling tools, etc.
● Chem. formula: WC; some forms also contain W_2C.

tungstite /'tʌŋstʌɪt/ ▶ noun [mass noun] a yellow mineral consisting of hydrated tungsten oxide, typically occurring as a powdery coating on tungsten ores.
– ORIGIN mid 19th cent.: from **TUNGSTEN** + **-ITE**[1].

Tungus /'tʊŋɡs, tʊŋ'ɡuːs/ ▶ noun (pl. same) a member of the northern Evenki people of Siberia.
■older term for **EVENKI** (the language).
– ORIGIN the name in Yakut.

Tungusic /tʊŋ'ɡuːsɪk/ ▶ adjective of, relating to, or denoting a small family of Altaic languages of Siberia and northern China.
▶ noun this family of languages collectively.

Tunguska /tʊŋ'ɡuːskə/ two rivers in Siberian Russia, the **Lower Tunguska** and **Stony Tunguska**, flowing westwards into the Yenisei River through the forested, sparsely populated Tunguska Basin. The area was the scene in 1908 of a devastating explosion believed to have been due to the disintegration in the atmosphere of a meteorite or small comet.

tunic ▶ noun **1** a loose garment, typically sleeveless and reaching to the wearer's knees, as worn in ancient Greece and Rome.
■ a loose, thigh-length garment, worn typically by women over a skirt or trousers. ■ a gymslip.
2 a close-fitting short coat as part of a uniform, especially a police or military uniform.
3 Biology & Anatomy an integument or membrane enclosing or lining an organ or part.
■ Botany any of the concentric layers of a plant bulb, e.g. an onion. ■ Zoology the rubbery outer coat of a sea squirt.
– ORIGIN Old English, from Old French *tunique* or Latin *tunica*.

tunica /ˈtjuːnɪkə/ ▶ noun (pl. **tunicae** /-kiː/) **1** Anatomy a membranous sheath enveloping or lining an organ.
2 Botany the outer layer or layers of cells in an apical meristem, which contribute to surface growth.
– ORIGIN late 17th cent.: from Latin, literally 'tunic'.

tunicate /ˈtjuːnɪkət, -keɪt/ ▶ noun Zoology a marine invertebrate of a group which includes the sea squirts and salps. They have a rubbery or hard outer coat and two siphons to draw water into and out of the body.
● Subphylum Urochordata: three classes.
▶ adjective (usu. **tunicated**) Botany (of a plant bulb, e.g. an onion) having concentric layers.
– ORIGIN mid 18th cent.: from Latin *tunicatus*, past participle of *tunicare* 'clothe with a tunic', from *tunica* (see TUNICA).

tunicle /ˈtjuːnɪk(ə)l/ ▶ noun a short liturgical vestment which is traditionally worn over the alb by a subdeacon at celebrations of the Mass.
– ORIGIN late Middle English: from Old French *tunicle* or Latin *tunicula*, diminutive of *tunica* (see TUNICA).

tuning ▶ noun [mass noun] the action or process of tuning something: *an electronic instrument requires no tuning.*
■ the extent to which a musical instrument, performance, or ensemble is in tune: *at times the tuning is uncertain, and the solos often lack conviction.* ■ a particular key or set of pitches to which an instrument, especially one with strings, is tuned: *E-flat tuning.* ■ the facility on a radio allowing for the reception of different stations, frequencies, or wavelengths. ■ Electronics the variation of the resonant frequency of an oscillatory circuit.

tuning fork ▶ noun a two-pronged steel device used by musicians, which vibrates when struck to give a note of specific pitch.

tuning peg ▶ noun any of the pegs in the neck of a stringed musical instrument around which the strings are wound, and which are turned to adjust their tension and so tune the instrument.

Tunis /ˈtjuːnɪs/ the capital of Tunisia, a port on the Mediterranean coast of North Africa; pop. 596,650 (1984).

Tunisia /tjuːˈnɪzɪə/ a country in North Africa; pop. 8,223,000 (est. 1991); official language, Arabic; capital, Tunis.

Tunisia has a Mediterranean coastline and extends south into the Sahara Desert. Phoenician coastal settlements developed into the commercial empire of Carthage (near modern Tunis). The area was conquered by the Arabs in the 7th century and became part of the Ottoman Empire in the 16th century; a French protectorate was established in 1886. The rise of nationalism led to independence and the establishment of a republic in 1956–7.

– DERIVATIVES **Tunisian** adjective & noun.

tunnel ▶ noun **1** an artificial underground passage, especially one built through a hill or under a building, road, or river.
■ an underground passage dug by a burrowing animal. ■ [in sing.] a passage in a sports stadium by which players enter or leave the field.
2 short for WIND TUNNEL (in sense 1).
3 a long, half-cylindrical enclosure used to protect plants, typically made of clear plastic stretched over hoops.
▶ verb (**tunnelled**, **tunnelling**; US **tunneled**, **tunneling**) **1** [no obj., with adverbial of direction] dig or force a passage underground or through something: *he tunnelled under the fence* | (**tunnel one's way**) *the insect tunnels its way out of the plant.*
2 [no obj.] Physics (of a particle) pass through a potential barrier.
– PHRASES **light at the end of the tunnel** see LIGHT[1].

– DERIVATIVES **tunneller** noun.
– ORIGIN late Middle English (in the senses 'tunnel-net' and 'flue of a chimney'): from Old French *tonel*, diminutive of *tonne* 'cask'. Sense 1 of the noun dates from the mid 18th cent.

tunnel diode ▶ noun Electronics a two-terminal semiconductor diode using tunnelling electrons to perform high-speed switching operations.

tunnel kiln ▶ noun an industrial kiln in which ceramic items being fired are carried on trucks along a continuously heated passage.

tunnel of love ▶ noun a fairground amusement for couples involving a train- or boat-ride through a darkened tunnel.

tunnel vision ▶ noun [mass noun] defective sight in which objects cannot be properly seen if not close to the centre of the field of view.
■ informal the tendency to focus exclusively on a single or limited objective or view.

tunny (also **tunny fish**) ▶ noun (pl. same or **-ies**) a tuna, especially the bluefin.
– ORIGIN mid 16th cent.: from French *thon*, via Latin from Greek *thunnos*.

tun shell ▶ noun see TUN (sense 3).

tup /tʌp/ ▶ noun chiefly Brit. a ram.
▶ verb (**tupped**, **tupping**) [with obj.] **1** [often as noun **tupping**] chiefly Brit. (of a ram) copulate with (a ewe).
■ vulgar slang (of a man) have sexual intercourse with (a woman).
2 N. English informal head-butt (someone) in a fight.
– ORIGIN Middle English: of unknown origin.

Tupamaro /ˌtuːpəˈmɑːrəʊ/ ▶ noun (pl. **-os**) a member of a Marxist urban guerrilla organization in Uruguay that was active mainly in the late 1960s and early 1970s.
– ORIGIN 1960s: from *Tupac Amarú*, the name of an 18th-cent. Inca leader.

Tupelo /ˈt(j)uːpələʊ/ a city in NE Mississippi; pop. 30,685 (1990).

tupelo /ˈt(j)uːpɪləʊ/ ▶ noun (pl. **-os**) a North American or Asian tree of damp and swampy habitats, which yields useful timber.
● Genus *Nyssa*, family Nyssaceae: several species, in particular *N. sylvatica* (also called PEPPERIDGE).
– ORIGIN mid 18th cent.: from Creek, from *ito* 'tree' + *opílwa* 'swamp'.

Tupi /ˈtuːpi/ ▶ noun (pl. same or **Tupis**) **1** a member of a group of American Indian peoples living in scattered areas throughout the Amazon valley.
2 [mass noun] any of the languages of these peoples, which constitute a branch of the Tupi-Guarani language family.
▶ adjective of or relating to these peoples or their languages.
– DERIVATIVES **Tupian** adjective.
– ORIGIN a local name.

Tupi-Guarani ▶ noun [mass noun] a South American Indian language family whose principal members are Guarani and the Tupian languages.
▶ adjective of, relating to, or denoting these languages.

tupik /ˈtuːpɪk/ ▶ noun a hut or tent made of animal skins used by Inuits in the Canadian Arctic as a summer dwelling.
– ORIGIN from Inuit *tupiq*.

tuppence ▶ noun Brit. variant spelling of TWOPENCE.

tuppenny ▶ adjective Brit. variant spelling of TWOPENNY.

Tupperware /ˈtʌpəwɛː/ ▶ noun [mass noun] trademark a range of plastic containers used chiefly for storing food.
– ORIGIN 1950s: from *Tupper*, the name of the American manufacturer, + WARE[1].

tuque /tuːk/ ▶ noun Canadian a close-fitting knitted stocking cap.
– ORIGIN Canadian French form of TOQUE.

tur /tʊə/ ▶ noun a wild goat native to the Caucasian mountains.
● Genus *Capra*, family Bovidae: two species.
– ORIGIN late 19th cent.: from Russian.

turaco /ˈtʊərəkəʊ/ (also **touraco**) ▶ noun (pl. **-os**) a fruit-eating African bird with brightly coloured plumage, a prominent crest, and a long tail. Also called LOERIE or LOURIE in South Africa.
● Family Musophagidae (the **turaco family**): three genera, especially *Musophaga* and *Tauraco*, and several species. The

turaco family also includes the go-away birds and plantain-eaters.
– ORIGIN mid 18th cent.: from French *touraco*, from a West African word.

Turanian /tjʊˈreɪnɪən/ ▶ adjective dated of, relating to, or denoting the languages of central Asia, particularly those of the Uralic and Altaic families, or the peoples that speak them.
– ORIGIN late 18th cent.: from Persian *Tūrān*, the region beyond the Oxus, + -IAN.

turban ▶ noun **1** a man's headdress, consisting of a long length of cotton or silk wound round a cap or the head, worn especially by Muslims and Sikhs.
2 (also **turban shell**) a marine mollusc with a sculptured spiral shell and a distinctive operculum which is smooth on the inside and sculptured and typically patterned on the outside.
● Family Turbinidae, class Gastropoda: *Turbo* and other genera.
– DERIVATIVES **turbaned** (also **turbanned**) adjective.
– ORIGIN mid 16th cent.: via French from Turkish *tülbent*, from Persian *dulband*. Compare with TULIP.

turbary /ˈtəːb(ə)ri/ ▶ noun (in full **common of turbary**) (pl. **-ies**) [mass noun] Brit. the legal right to cut turf or peat for fuel on common ground or on another person's ground.
■ [count noun] a place where turf or peat is dug or cut under such a right.
– ORIGIN late Middle English: from Anglo-Norman French *turberie*, from Old French *tourbe* 'turf'.

Turbellaria /ˌtəːbɪˈlɛːrɪə/ Zoology a class of typically free-living flatworms which have a ciliated surface and a simple branched gut with a single opening.
– DERIVATIVES **turbellarian** adjective & noun.
– ORIGIN modern Latin (plural), from Latin *turbella* 'bustle, stir', diminutive of *turba* 'crowd'.

turbid /ˈtəːbɪd/ ▶ adjective (of a liquid) cloudy, opaque, or thick with suspended matter: *the turbid estuary* | figurative *a turbid piece of cinéma vérité.*
– DERIVATIVES **turbidity** noun, **turbidly** adverb, **turbidness** noun.
– ORIGIN late Middle English (in the figurative sense): from Latin *turbidus*, from *turba* 'a crowd, a disturbance'.

turbidimeter /ˌtəːbɪˈdɪmɪtə/ ▶ noun an instrument for measuring the turbidity of a liquid suspension, usually as a means of determining the surface area of the suspended particles.
– DERIVATIVES **turbidimetric** adjective, **turbidimetry** noun.

turbidite /ˈtəːbɪdʌɪt/ ▶ noun Geology a sediment or rock deposited by a turbidity current.
– DERIVATIVES **turbiditic** adjective.
– ORIGIN 1950s: from *turbidity* (see TURBID) + -ITE[1].

turbidity current ▶ noun an underwater current flowing swiftly downslope owing to the weight of sediment it carries.

turbinal /ˈtəːbɪn(ə)l/ ▶ noun (usu. **turbinals**) Anatomy & Zoology each of three thin curved shelves of bone in the sides of the nasal cavity in humans and other warm-blooded vertebrates, covered in mucous membrane.
– ORIGIN late 16th cent. (as an adjective in the sense 'top-shaped'): from Latin *turbo*, *turbin-* 'spinning top' + -AL.

turbinate /ˈtəːbɪnət/ ▶ adjective chiefly Zoology (especially of a shell) shaped like a spinning top or inverted cone.
■ Anatomy relating to or denoting the turbinals.
▶ noun (also **turbinate bone**) Anatomy another term for TURBINAL.
– ORIGIN mid 17th cent.: from Latin *turbinatus*, from *turbo*, *turbin-* (see TURBINE).

turbine /ˈtəːbʌɪn, -ɪn/ ▶ noun a machine for producing continuous power in which a wheel or rotor, typically fitted with vanes, is made to revolve by a fast-moving flow of water, steam, gas, air, or other fluid.
– ORIGIN mid 19th cent.: from French, from Latin *turbo*, *turbin-* 'spinning top, whirl'.

turbit /ˈtəːbɪt/ ▶ noun a stoutly built pigeon of a domestic breed with a neck frill and short beak.
– ORIGIN late 17th cent.: apparently from Latin *turbo* 'spinning top', from its shape.

turbo /ˈtəːbəʊ/ ▶ noun (pl. **-os**) short for TURBOCHARGER.
■ a motor vehicle equipped with a turbocharger.

turbo- ▶ combining form having or driven by a turbine: *turboshaft.*
– ORIGIN from TURBINE.

turboboost ▶ **noun** [mass noun] the increase in speed or power produced by turbocharging a car's engine or, specifically, when the turbocharger becomes activated.

turbocharge ▶ **verb** [with obj.] [often as adj. **turbocharged**] equip (an engine or vehicle) with a turbocharger.

turbocharger ▶ **noun** a supercharger driven by a turbine powered by the engine's exhaust gases.

turbo diesel ▶ **noun** a turbocharged diesel engine.
▪a vehicle equipped with such an engine.

turbofan ▶ **noun** a jet engine in which a turbine-driven fan provides additional thrust.
▪an aircraft powered by such an engine.

turbogenerator ▶ **noun** a large electricity generator driven by a steam turbine.

turbojet ▶ **noun** a jet engine in which the jet gases also operate a turbine-driven compressor for compressing the air drawn into the engine.
▪an aircraft powered by such an engine.

turboprop ▶ **noun** a jet engine in which a turbine is used to drive a propeller.
▪an aircraft powered by such an engine.

turboshaft ▶ **noun** a gas turbine engine in which the turbine drives a shaft other than a propeller shaft.

turbosupercharger ▶ **noun** another term for **TURBOCHARGER**.

turbot ▶ **noun** (pl. same or **turbots**) a European flatfish of inshore waters, which has large bony tubercles on the body and is prized as food.
• *Scophthalmus maximus*, family Scophthalmidae (or Bothidae).
▪used in names of similar flatfishes, e.g. **black turbot**.
– ORIGIN Middle English: from Old French, of Scandinavian origin.

turbulence ▶ **noun** [mass noun] violent or unsteady movement of air or water, or of some other fluid: *the plane shuddered as it entered some turbulence*.
▪figurative conflict; confusion: *a time of political turbulence*.
– ORIGIN late Middle English: from Old French, or from late Latin *turbulentia*, from *turbulentus* 'full of commotion' (see **TURBULENT**).

turbulent /ˈtəːbjʊl(ə)nt/ ▶ **adjective** characterized by conflict, disorder, or confusion; not controlled or calm: *the country's turbulent 20-year history | her turbulent emotions*.
▪(of air or water) moving unsteadily or violently: *the turbulent sea*. ▪technical of, relating to, or denoting flow of a fluid in which the velocity at any point fluctuates irregularly and there is continual mixing rather than a steady or laminar flow pattern.
– DERIVATIVES **turbulently** adverb.
– ORIGIN late Middle English: from Latin *turbulentus* 'full of commotion', from *turba* 'crowd'.

Turco /ˈtəːkəʊ/ ▶ **noun** (pl. **-os**) historical an Algerian soldier in the French army.
– ORIGIN mid 19th cent.: from Spanish, Portuguese, and Italian, literally 'Turk'.

Turco- (also **Turko-**) ▶ **combining form** Turkish; Turkish and ...: *Turco-Tartar*.
▪relating to Turkey.

Turcoman ▶ **noun** variant spelling of **TURKOMAN**.

turd ▶ **noun** vulgar slang a lump of excrement.
▪a person regarded as obnoxious or contemptible.
– ORIGIN Old English *tord*, of Germanic origin.

tureen /tjʊˈriːn, tə-/ ▶ **noun** a deep covered dish from which soup is served.
– ORIGIN mid 18th cent.: alteration of earlier *terrine*, from French *terrine* (see **TERRINE**), feminine of Old French *terrin* 'earthen', based on Latin *terra* 'earth'.

turf ▶ **noun** (pl. **turfs** or **turves**) [mass noun] **1** grass and the surface layer of earth held together by its roots: *they walked across the springy turf*.
▪[count noun] a piece of such grass and earth cut from the ground. ▪peat used for fuel.
2 (**the turf**) horse racing or racecourses generally: *he spent his money gambling on the turf*.
3 informal an area regarded as someone's personal territory; one's home ground: *the team will play Canada on their home turf this summer*.
▪a person's sphere of influence or activity: *we're in similar businesses but we cover different turf*.
▶**verb 1** [with obj. and adverbial] informal, chiefly Brit. force (someone) to leave somewhere: *they were turfed off the bus*.
2 [with obj.] [often as adj. **turfed**] cover (a patch of ground) with turf: *a turfed lawn*.
– ORIGIN Old English, of Germanic origin; related to Dutch *turf* and German *Torf*, from an Indo-European root shared by Sanskrit *darbha* 'tuft of grass'.

turf accountant ▶ **noun** Brit. formal a bookmaker.

Turfan Depression /ˈtʊəfan, tʊəˈfan/ (also **Turpan**) a low-lying area in Xinjiang, western China, descending to 154 m (505 ft) below sea level, with an area of 50,000 sq. km (20,000 sq. miles). It is China's lowest point below sea level.

turfman ▶ **noun** (pl. **-men**) chiefly US a devotee of horse racing, especially one who owns or trains horses.

turf war (also **turf battle**) ▶ **noun** informal, chiefly N. Amer. an acrimonious dispute between rival groups over territory or a particular sphere of influence.
– ORIGIN 1970s: from the notion of a *war* over *turf* in the informal sense 'area regarded as personal territory' (originally the area controlled by, for example, a street gang or criminal).

turfy ▶ **adjective** (**turfier**, **turfiest**) covered with or consisting of turf; grassy: *a turfy plain*.
▪of or like peat; peaty: *I inhaled the turfy air*.

Turgenev /təːˈgeɪnjɛf, tʊəˈgɛnjɛf/, Ivan (Sergeevich) (1818–83), Russian novelist, dramatist, and short-story writer. His novels, such as *Fathers and Sons* (1862), examine individual lives to illuminate the social, political, and philosophical issues of the day.

turgescent /təːˈdʒɛs(ə)nt/ ▶ **adjective** chiefly technical becoming or seeming swollen or distended.
– DERIVATIVES **turgescence** noun.
– ORIGIN early 18th cent.: from Latin *turgescent-* 'beginning to swell', from the verb *turgescere*, from *turgere* 'to swell'.

turgid /ˈtəːdʒɪd/ ▶ **adjective** swollen and distended or congested: *a turgid and fast-moving river*.
▪(of language or style) tediously pompous or bombastic: *some turgid verses on the death of Prince Albert*.
– DERIVATIVES **turgidity** noun, **turgidly** adverb.
– ORIGIN early 17th cent.: from Latin *turgidus*, from *turgere* 'to swell'.

turgor /ˈtəːgə/ ▶ **noun** [mass noun] chiefly Botany the state of turgidity and resulting rigidity of cells (or tissues), typically due to the absorption of fluid.
– ORIGIN late 19th cent.: from late Latin, from *turgere* 'to swell'.

Turin /tjʊˈrɪn/ a city in NW Italy on the River Po, capital of Piedmont region; pop. 991,870 (1990). Turin was the capital of the kingdom of Sardinia from 1720 and became the first capital of a unified Italy (1861–4). Italian name **TORINO**.

Turing /ˈtjʊərɪŋ/, Alan Mathison (1912–54), English mathematician. He developed the concept of a theoretical computing machine, a key step in the development of the first computer, and carried out important code-breaking work in the Second World War. He also investigated artificial intelligence.

Turing machine ▶ **noun** a mathematical model of a hypothetical computing machine which can use a predefined set of rules to determine a result from a set of input variables.

Turing test ▶ **noun** a test for intelligence in a computer, requiring that a human being should be unable to distinguish the machine from another human being by using the replies to questions put to both.

Turin Shroud a relic, preserved at Turin since 1578, venerated as the winding-sheet in which Christ's body was wrapped for burial. It bears the imprint of the front and back of a human body as well as markings that correspond to the traditional stigmata. Scientific tests carried out in 1988 dated the shroud to the 13th–14th centuries.

turion /ˈt(j)ʊərɪən/ ▶ **noun** Botany (in some aquatic plants) a wintering bud which becomes detached and remains dormant at the bottom of the water.
– ORIGIN early 18th cent.: from French, from Latin *turio(n-)* 'a shoot'.

turista /t(j)ʊˈrɪstə/ ▶ **noun** [mass noun] informal, chiefly US diarrhoea as suffered by holidaymakers when visiting certain foreign countries.
– ORIGIN Spanish, literally 'tourist'.

Turk ▶ **noun 1** a native or national of Turkey, or a person of Turkish descent.
2 historical a member of any of the ancient central Asian peoples who spoke Turkic languages, including the Seljuks and Ottomans.
3 archaic a member of the ruling Muslim population of the Ottoman Empire.
– ORIGIN late Middle English: via Old French from Turkish *türk*.

Turkana /təːˈkɑːnə/ ▶ **noun** (pl. same) **1** a member of an East African people living between Lake Turkana and the Nile.
2 [mass noun] the Nilotic language of the Turkana, spoken by about 250,000 people.
▶**adjective** of or relating to the Turkana or their language.
– ORIGIN a local name.

Turkana, Lake a salt lake in NW Kenya, with no outlet. It was visited in 1888 by the Hungarian explorer Count Teleki (1845–1916), who named it Lake Rudolf after the Crown Prince of Austria. It was given its present name in 1979.

Turkestan /ˌtəːkɪˈstɑːn, -ˈstan/ (also **Turkistan**) a region of central Asia between the Caspian Sea and the Gobi Desert, inhabited mainly by Turkic peoples. It is divided by the Pamir and Tien Shan mountains into eastern Turkestan, now the Xinjiang autonomous region of China, and western Turkestan, which comprises present-day Turkmenistan, Kazakhstan, Uzbekistan, Tajikistan, and Kyrgyzstan.

Turkey a country comprising the whole of the Anatolian peninsula in western Asia, with a small enclave in SE Europe to the west of Istanbul; pop. 56,473,000 (1990); official language, Turkish; capital, Ankara.

Turkey was the centre of the Ottoman Empire, established in the late Middle Ages and largely maintained until its collapse at the end of the First World War, in which Turkey supported the Central Powers. The nationalist leader Kemal Atatürk expelled the minority Greek population and established the modern republic of Turkey in the 1920s. Turkey was neutral in the Second World War but is a member of NATO.

turkey ▶ **noun** (pl. **-eys**) **1** a large mainly domesticated game bird native to North America, having a bald head and (in the male) red wattles. It is prized as food, especially on festive occasions such as Christmas and (in the US) Thanksgiving.
• *Meleagris gallopavo*, family Meleagridae (or Phasianidae).
▪[mass noun] the flesh of the turkey as food.
2 informal, chiefly US something that is extremely or completely unsuccessful, especially a play or film.
▪a stupid or inept person.
– PHRASES **like turkeys voting for Christmas** informal used to suggest that a particular action or decision is hopelessly self-defeating. **talk turkey** N. Amer. informal discuss something frankly and straightforwardly.
– ORIGIN mid 16th cent.: short for **TURKEYCOCK** or *turkeyhen*, originally applied to the guineafowl (which was imported through Turkey), and then erroneously to the American bird.

turkey buzzard ▶ **noun** North American term for **TURKEY VULTURE**.

turkey call ▶ **noun** chiefly US an instrument used by hunters to decoy the wild turkey by imitating its characteristic gobbling sound.

turkeycock ▶ **noun** a male turkey.
▪a pompous or self-important person.

turkey oak ▶ **noun** a southern European oak with a domed spreading crown and acorn cups with long outward-pointing scales.
• *Quercus cerris*, family Fagaceae.

Turkey red ▶ **noun** [mass noun] a scarlet textile dye obtained from madder or alizarin.
▪the colour of this dye. ▪cotton cloth dyed with this, popular in the 19th century.

turkey shoot ▶ **noun** informal, chiefly US a situation, typically in a war, in which the aggressor has an overwhelming advantage.

turkey trot ▶ **noun** a kind of ballroom dance to ragtime music which originated in the US and was popular in the early 20th century.

turkey vulture ▶ **noun** a common American vulture with black plumage and a bare red head.
• *Cathartes aura*, family Cathartidae.

Turkic /ˈtəːkɪk/ ▶ **adjective** of, relating to, or denoting a large group of closely related Altaic languages of western and central Asia, including Turkish, Azerbaijani, Kazakh, Kyrgyz, Uighur, Uzbek, and Tatar.
▶**noun** [mass noun] the Turkic languages collectively.
– ORIGIN mid 19th cent.: from **TURK** + **-IC**.

t

Turkish ▶ **adjective** of or relating to Turkey or to the Turks or their language.
■ historical relating to or associated with the Ottoman Empire.
▶ **noun** [mass noun] the official language of Turkey, a Turkic language spoken by about 50 million people. It was written in the Arabic script until 1928, when the Roman alphabet was adopted.

Turkish bath ▶ **noun** a cleansing or relaxing treatment that involves a period of time spent sitting in a room filled with very hot air or steam, generally followed by washing and massage.
■ a building or room where such a treatment is available.

Turkish carpet (also **Turkish rug**) ▶ **noun** a rug woven in Turkey in a traditional fashion, typically with a bold coloured design and thick wool pile, or made elsewhere in this style.

Turkish coffee ▶ **noun** [mass noun] very strong black coffee served with the fine grounds in it.

Turkish delight ▶ **noun** [mass noun] a sweet consisting of flavoured gelatin coated in icing sugar.

Turkish slipper ▶ **noun** a soft heelless slipper with a turned-up toe.

Turkish towel ▶ **noun** a towel made of cotton terry towelling.

Turkish Van (in full **Turkish Van cat**) ▶ **noun** a cat of a long-haired breed, with a white body, auburn markings on the head and tail, and light orange eyes.
– ORIGIN 1960s: named after the town of *Van*, Turkey.

Turkistan variant spelling of **TURKESTAN**.

Turkmen /'tə:kmən/ ▶ **noun** (pl. same or **Turkmens**) **1** a member of a group of Turkic peoples inhabiting the region east of the Caspian Sea and south of the Aral Sea, now comprising Turkmenistan and parts of Iran and Afghanistan.
2 [mass noun] the Turkic language of these peoples, having about 3 million speakers.
▶ **adjective** of or relating to the Turkmens, their language, or the region which they inhabit.
– ORIGIN from Persian *turkmān*, from Turkish *türkmen*; also influenced by Russian *turkmen*.

Turkmenistan /tə:k,menɪ'stɑ:n, -'stan/ a republic in central Asia, lying between the Caspian Sea and Afghanistan; pop. 3,861,000 (est. 1992); languages, Turkoman (official), Russian; capital, Ashgabat. Also called **TURKMENIA** /-'mi:nɪə/.

Turkmenistan is dominated by the Karakum Desert, which occupies about 90 per cent of the country. Previously part of Turkestan, from 1924 it formed a separate constituent republic of the USSR; Turkmenistan became an independent republic within the Commonwealth of Independent States in 1991.

Turko- ▶ **combining form** variant spelling of **TURCO-**.

Turkoman /'tə:kə(ʊ)mən/ (also **Turcoman**) ▶ **noun** (pl. **Turkomans**) **1** another term for **TURKMEN**.
2 (also **Turkoman carpet** or **rug**) a kind of large, soft, richly coloured rug made by the Turkmens.
– ORIGIN early 17th cent.: from medieval Latin *Turcomannus*, French *turcoman*, from Persian *turkmān* (see **TURKMEN**).

Turks and Caicos Islands /'keɪkɒs/ a British dependency in the Caribbean, comprising two island groups between Haiti and the Bahamas; pop. 12,350 (1990); capital, Cockburn Town (on the island of Grand Turk).

Turk's cap ▶ **noun** any of a number of plants which have parts that are said to resemble a turban or similar headdress, in particular:
• (also **Turk's cap lily**) the martagon lily. • (also **Turk's cap cactus**) a barrel-shaped Caribbean cactus (*Melocactus communis*, family Cactaceae).

Turk's head ▶ **noun** an ornamental knot resembling a turban in shape, made in the end of a rope to form a stopper.

Turku /'tʊəku:/ an industrial port in SW Finland; pop. 159,180 (1990). It was the capital of Finland until 1812. Swedish name **ÅBO**.

turlough /'tʊələʊx/ ▶ **noun** (in Ireland) a low-lying area on limestone which becomes flooded in wet weather through the welling up of groundwater from the rock.
– ORIGIN late 17th cent.: from Irish *turloch*, from *tur* 'dry' + *loch* 'lake'.

turmeric /'tə:mərɪk/ ▶ **noun** [mass noun] **1** a bright yellow aromatic powder obtained from the rhizome of a plant of the ginger family, used for flavouring and colouring in Asian cookery and formerly as a fabric dye.
2 the Asian plant from which this rhizome is obtained.
• *Curcuma longa*, family Zingiberaceae.
– ORIGIN late Middle English (earlier as *tarmaret*): perhaps from French *terre mérite* and modern Latin *terra merita*, literally 'deserving earth', perhaps an alteration of an oriental word.

turmoil ▶ **noun** [mass noun] a state of great disturbance, confusion, or uncertainty: *the country was in turmoil* | *he endured years of inner turmoil.*
– ORIGIN early 16th cent.: of unknown origin.

turn ▶ **verb 1** move or cause to move in a circular direction wholly or partly around an axis or point: [no obj.] *the big wheel was turning* | [with obj.] *I turned the key in the door and crept in.*
■ [with obj. and adverbial] move (something) so that it is in a different position in relation to its surroundings or its previous position: *we waited in suspense for him to turn the cards over.* ■ [with obj.] move (a page) over so that it is flat against the previous or next page: *she turned a page noisily* | [no obj.] *turn to page five for the answer.* ■ change or cause to change direction: [no obj., with adverbial of direction] *we turned round and headed back to the house.* ■ [with obj. and adverbial] aim, point, or direct (something): *she turned her head towards me* | *the government has now turned its attention to primary schools.* ■ [no obj.] change the position of one's body so that one is facing in a different direction: *Charlie turned and looked at his friend.* ■ [no obj.] (of the tide) change from flood to ebb or vice versa. ■ [with obj.] pass round (the flank or defensive lines of an army) so as to attack it from the side or rear. ■ [with obj.] perform (a somersault or cartwheel). ■ [with obj.] twist or sprain (an ankle). ■ [with obj. and adverbial] fold or unfold (fabric or a piece of a garment) in the specified way: *he turned up the collar of his coat.* ■ [with obj.] remake (a garment or a sheet), putting the worn outer side on the inside. ■ [with obj.] [usu. as adj. **turned**] Printing set or print (a type or letter) upside down. ■ [with obj.] archaic bend back (the edge of a blade) so as to make it blunt.
2 [no obj., with complement or adverbial] change in nature, state, form, or colour; become: *Emmeline turned pale* | *the slight drizzle turned into a downpour.*
■ [with obj. and complement or adverbial] cause to change in such a way; cause to become: *potatoes are covered with sacking to keep the light from turning them green.* ■ [no obj.] (of leaves) change colour in the autumn. ■ [with obj.] pass the age or time of: *I've just turned forty.* ■ (with reference to milk) make or become sour: [with obj.] *the thunder had turned the milk.* ■ (with reference to the stomach) make or become nauseated: [with obj.] *the smell was bad enough to turn the strongest stomach.* ■ [with obj. and complement or adverbial] send or put into a specified place or condition: *the dogs were turned loose on the crowd.*
3 [no obj.] (**turn to**) start doing or becoming involved with: *in 1939 he turned to films in earnest.*
■ go on to consider next: *we can now turn to another aspect of the problem.* ■ go to for help, advice, or information: *who can she turn to?* ■ have recourse to (something, especially something dangerous or unhealthy): *he turned to drink and drugs for solace.*
4 [with obj.] shape (something) on a lathe: *the faceplate is turned rather than cast.*
■ give a graceful or elegant form to: [as adj., with submodifier] (**turned**) *a production full of so many finely turned words.* ■ make (a profit).
▶ **noun 1** an act of moving something in a circular direction around an axis or point: *a safety lock requiring four turns of the key.*
■ a change of direction when moving: *they made a left turn and picked up speed.* ■ a development or change in circumstances or a course of events: *life has* ***taken a turn for the better.*** ■ a time when one specified period of time ends and another begins: *the turn of the century.* ■ a bend or curve in a road, path, river, etc.: *the twists and turns in the passageways.* ■ a place where a road meets or branches off another; a turning. ■ [mass noun] Cricket deviation in the direction of the ball when bouncing off the pitch. ■ (**the turn**) the beginning of the second nine holes of a round of golf: *he made the turn in one under par.* ■ a change of the tide from ebb to flow or vice versa. ■ one round in a coil of rope or other material.
2 an opportunity or obligation to do something that comes successively to each of a number of people: *it was his turn to speak.*
■ a short performance, especially one of a number given by different performers in succession: *a comic turn.* ■ a performer giving such a performance.
3 a short walk or ride: *why don't you* ***take a turn*** *around the garden?*
4 informal a shock: *you gave us quite a turn!*
■ a brief feeling or experience of illness: *tell me how you feel when you have these funny turns.*
5 the difference between the buying and selling price of stocks or other financial products.
■ a profit made from such a difference.
6 Music a melodic ornament consisting of the principal note with those above and below it.
– PHRASES **at every turn** on every occasion; continually: *her name seemed to come up at every turn.* **by turns** one after the other; alternately: *he was by turns amused and mildly annoyed by her.* **do someone a good** (or **bad**) **turn** do something that is helpful (or unhelpful) for someone. **in turn** in succession; one after the other: *everyone* ***took it in turn*** *to attack my work.* ■ (also **in one's/its turn**) used to convey that an action, process, or situation is the result or product of a previous one: *he would shout until she, in her turn, lost her temper.* **not know which way** (or **where**) **to turn** not know what to do; be completely at a loss. **not turn a hair** see **HAIR**. **one good turn deserves another** proverb if someone does you a favour, you should take the chance to repay it. **on the turn** at a turning point; in a state of change: *my luck is on the turn.* ■ (of certain foods or liquids) going off: *the smell of meat on the turn.* **out of turn** at a time when it is not one's turn. **speak** (or **talk**) **out of turn** speak in a tactless or foolish way. **take turns** (or **take it in turns**) (of two or more people) do something alternately or in succession. **to a turn** to exactly the right degree (used especially in relation to cooking): *beefburgers done to a turn.* **turn and turn about** chiefly Brit. one after another; in succession: *the two men were working in rotation, turn and turn about.* **turn one's back on** see **BACK**. **turn the** (or **a**) **corner 1** pass round a corner into another street. **2** pass the critical point and start to improve. **turn a deaf ear** see **DEAF**. **turn one's hand to something** see **HAND**. **turn one's head** see **HEAD**. **turn heads** see **HEAD**. **turn an honest penny** see **HONEST**. **turn in one's grave** see **GRAVE**[1]. **turn of mind** a particular way of thinking: *people with a practical turn of mind.* **turn of speed** the ability to go fast when necessary. **turn on one's heel** see **HEEL**[1]. **turn the other cheek** see **CHEEK**. **turn over a new leaf** start to act or behave in a better or more responsible way. **turn something over in one's mind** think about or consider something thoroughly. **turn round and do** (or **say**) **something** informal used to convey that someone's actions or words are perceived as unexpected, unwelcome, or confrontational: *then she just turned round and said she wasn't coming after all.* **turn the scales** see **SCALE**[2]. **turn the tables** see **TABLE**. **turn tail** informal turn round and run away. **turn the tide** reverse the trend of events. **turn something to (good) account** see **ACCOUNT**. **turn a trick** see **TRICK**. **turn turtle** see **TURTLE**. **turn up one's nose at** see **NOSE**.
– ORIGIN Old English *tyrnan*, *turnian* (verb), from Latin *tornare*, from *tornus* 'lathe', from Greek *tornos* 'lathe, circular movement'; probably reinforced in Middle English by Old French *turner*. The noun (Middle English) is partly from Anglo-Norman French *tourn*, partly from the verb.
▶ **turn about** move so as to face in the opposite direction: *Alice turned about and walked down the corridor.*
turn against (or **turn someone against**) become (or cause someone to become) hostile towards: *public opinion turned against him.*
turn something around chiefly N. Amer. see ***turn something round.***
turn someone away refuse to allow someone to enter or pass through a place.
turn back (or **turn someone/thing back**) go (or cause to go) back in the direction in which one has come: *they turned back before reaching the church.*
turn someone down reject an offer or application made by someone: *the RAF turned him down on medical grounds.*
turn something down 1 reject something offered or proposed: *his novel was turned down by publisher after publisher.* **2** adjust a control on an electrical device to reduce the volume, heat, etc.
turn in informal go to bed in the evening.
turn someone in hand someone over to the authorities.
turn something in give something to someone in authority: *I've turned in my resignation.* ■ produce or

achieve a particular score or a performance of a specified quality.

turn off leave one road in order to join another.

turn someone off informal cause someone to feel bored, disgusted, or sexually repelled.

turn something off stop the operation or flow of something by means of a tap, switch, or button: *remember to turn off the gas.* ▪ operate a tap or switch in order to do this.

turn on 1 suddenly attack (someone) physically or verbally: *he turned on her with cold savagery.* **2** have as the main topic or point of interest: *for most businessmen, the central questions will turn on taxation.*

turn someone on informal excite or stimulate the interest of someone, especially sexually.

turn something on start the flow or operation of something by means of a tap, switch, or button: *she turned on the TV.* ▪ operate a tap or switch in order to do this.

turn someone on to informal cause someone to become interested or involved in (something, especially drugs): *he turned her on to heroin.*

turn out 1 prove to be the case: *the job turned out to be beyond his rather limited abilities.* **2** go somewhere in order to do something, especially to attend a meeting, to play in a match, or to vote: *over 75 per cent of the electorate turned out to vote.*

turn someone out 1 eject or expel someone from a place. **2** Military call a guard from the guardroom. **3** (**be turned out**) be dressed in the manner specified: *she was smartly turned out and as well groomed as always.*

turn something out 1 extinguish a light. **2** produce something: *the plant takes 53 hours to turn out each car.* **3** empty something, especially one's pockets. ▪ Brit. clean out a drawer, room, etc. by taking out and reorganizing its contents. **4** tip prepared food from a mould or other container.

turn over (of an engine) start or continue to run properly.

turn someone over to deliver someone to the care or custody of (another person or body, especially one in authority): *they turned him over to the police.*

turn something over 1 cause an engine to run. **2** transfer control or management of something to someone else: *a plan to* **turn** *the pub* **over to** *a new manager.* **3** change the function or use of something: *the works was* **turned over to** *the production of aircraft parts.* **4** informal rob a place. **5** (of a business) have a turnover of a specified amount: *last year the company turned over £12 million.*

turn something round (or **around**) **1** prepare a ship or aircraft for its return journey. **2** reverse the previously poor performance of something, especially a company, and make it successful.

turn up 1 be found, especially by chance, after being lost: *all the missing documents had turned up.* **2** put in an appearance; arrive: *half the guests failed to turn up.*

turn something up 1 increase the volume or strength of sound, heat, etc. by turning a knob or switch on a device. **2** reveal or discover something: *New Yorkers confidently expect the inquiry to turn up nothing.* **3** shorten a garment by raising the hem.

turnabout ▶ **noun** a sudden and complete change or reversal of policy, opinion, or of a situation: *the move was a significant turnabout for the company.*

turnaround (also **turnround**) ▶ **noun 1** an abrupt or unexpected change, especially one that results in a more favourable situation: *it was a remarkable* **turnaround** *in his fortunes.*

2 the process of completing or the time needed to complete a task, especially one involving receiving something, processing it, and sending it out again: *a seven-day turnaround.*

▪the process of or time taken for unloading and reloading a ship, aircraft, or vehicle.

3 N. Amer. a space for vehicles to turn round in, especially one at the end of a driveway.

turnback ▶ **noun** a part of a garment that is folded back: [as modifier] *the jacket has turnback cuffs.*

turnbuckle ▶ **noun** a coupling with internal screw threads used to connect two rods, lengths of boat's rigging, etc. lengthwise or to regulate their length or tension.

turncoat ▶ **noun** a person who deserts one party or cause in order to join an opposing one.

turncock ▶ **noun** historical a waterworks official responsible for turning on water at the mains.

turndown ▶ **noun 1** a rejection or refusal.

2 a decline in something; a downturn.

▶ **adjective** (of a collar) turned down.

Turner, J. M. W. (1775–1851), English painter; full name *Joseph Mallord William Turner.* He made his name with landscapes and stormy seascapes, becoming increasingly concerned with depicting the power of light by the use of primary colours, often arranged in a swirling vortex. Notable works: *Rain, Steam, Speed* (1844); *The Fighting Téméraire* (1838).

turner ▶ **noun 1** a person who is skilled in turning wood on a lathe.

2 an implement that can be used to turn or flip something over: *a pancake turner.*

– ORIGIN Middle English: from Old French *torneor,* from late Latin *tornator,* from the verb *tornare* (see **TURN**).

Turner's syndrome ▶ **noun** [mass noun] Medicine a genetic defect in which affected women have only one X chromosome, causing developmental abnormalities and infertility.

– ORIGIN named after Henry Hubert *Turner* (1892–1970), the American physician who described it.

turnery ▶ **noun** [mass noun] the action or skill of making objects on a lathe.

▪objects made on a lathe.

turning ▶ **noun 1** a place where a road branches off another: *take the first turning on the right.*

2 [mass noun] the action or skill of using a lathe.

▪(**turnings**) shavings of wood resulting from turning wood on a lathe.

turning circle ▶ **noun** the smallest circle in which a vehicle or vessel can turn without reversing.

turning point ▶ **noun** a time at which a decisive change in a situation occurs, especially one with beneficial results: *this could be the turning point in Nigel's career.*

turnip ▶ **noun 1** a round root with white or cream flesh which is eaten as a vegetable and also has edible leaves.

▪a similar or related root, especially a swede.

2 the European plant of the cabbage family which produces this root.

• *Brassica rapa,* family Cruciferae: 'rapifera' group.

3 informal a large, thick, old-fashioned watch.

– DERIVATIVES **turnipy** adjective.

– ORIGIN mid 16th cent.: first element of unknown origin + **NEEP**.

turnip moth ▶ **noun** a moth with drab forewings and pearly hindwings, the caterpillar of which is the most harmful of cutworms in Britain.

• *Agrotis segetum,* family Noctuidae.

turnip tops (US **turnip greens**) ▶ **plural noun** the leaves of a turnip eaten as a vegetable.

turnkey ▶ **noun** (pl. **-eys**) archaic a jailer.

▶ **adjective** of or involving the provision of a complete product or service that is ready for immediate use: *turnkey systems for telecommunications customers.*

turn-off ▶ **noun 1** a junction at which a road branches off from a main road: *Adam missed the turn-off to the village.*

2 [usu. in sing.] informal a person or thing that causes someone to feel bored, disgusted, or sexually repelled: *he smelled of carbolic soap, a dreadful turn-off.*

3 an instance of turning or switching something off.

turn-on ▶ **noun 1** [usu. in sing.] informal a person or thing that causes someone to feel excited or sexually aroused: *tight jeans are a real turn-on.*

2 an instance of turning or switching something on.

turnout ▶ **noun 1** [usu. in sing.] the number of people attending or taking part in an event, especially the number of people voting in an election.

2 N. Amer. a road turning.

▪a point at which a railway track diverges; a set of points. ▪ N. Amer. a widened place in a road for cars to pass each other or park temporarily.

3 a carriage or other horse-drawn vehicle with its horse or horses.

4 [in sing.] the way in which a person or thing is equipped or dressed: *his turnout was exceedingly elegant.*

5 [mass noun] Ballet the ability to rotate the legs outward in the hip socket.

turnover ▶ **noun 1** the amount of money taken by a business in a particular period: *a turnover approaching £4 million.*

2 the rate at which employees leave a workforce and are replaced.

▪the rate at which goods are sold and replaced in a shop.

3 a small pie made by folding a piece of pastry over on itself to enclose a sweet filling: *an apple turnover.*

4 US (in a game) a loss of possession of the ball to the opposing team.

turnpike ▶ **noun 1** historical a toll gate.

▪(also **turnpike road**) a road on which a toll was collected at such a gate. ▪ US a motorway, especially one on which a toll is charged.

2 historical a spiked barrier fixed in or across a road or passage as a defence against sudden attack.

turnround ▶ **noun** another term for **TURNAROUND**.

turnsick ▶ **noun** dialect term for **STURDY**.

turn signal ▶ **noun** N. Amer. an indicator on a vehicle.

turnsole ▶ **noun** a Mediterranean plant of the spurge family, whose flowers are said to turn with the sun.

• *Chrozophora tinctoria* (family Euphorbiaceae), from which a blue or purple dye was formerly obtained.

– ORIGIN late Middle English: from Old French *tournesole,* based on Latin *tornare* (see **TURN**) + *sol* 'sun'.

turnspit ▶ **noun** historical a servant whose job was to turn a spit on which meat was roasting.

▪a dog kept to perform this task by running on a treadmill connected to the spit.

turns ratio ▶ **noun** the ratio of the number of turns on the primary coil of an electrical transformer to the number on the secondary, or vice versa.

turnstile ▶ **noun** a mechanical gate consisting of revolving horizontal arms fixed to a vertical post, allowing only one person at a time to pass through.

turnstone ▶ **noun** a small short-billed wading bird of the sandpiper family that turns over stones to feed on small animals beneath them.

• Genus *Arenaria,* family Scolopacidae: two species, in particular the (**ruddy**) **turnstone** (*A. interpres*), breeding in northern Eurasia and northern Canada.

turntable ▶ **noun** a circular revolving platform for turning a railway locomotive or other vehicle.

▪a circular revolving plate supporting a gramophone record as it is played.

turntable ladder ▶ **noun** Brit. a power-operated extending and revolving ladder mounted on a fire engine.

turn-up ▶ **noun** Brit. **1** (usu. **turn-ups**) the end of a trouser leg folded upwards on the outside.

2 [in sing.] informal an unusual or unexpected event or occurrence; a surprise: *fancy you being in New York too—what* **a turn-up for the books.**

Turpan Depression variant of **TURFAN DEPRESSION**.

turpentine /ˈtəːp(ə)ntʌɪn/ ▶ **noun 1** (also **oil of turpentine**) [mass noun] a volatile pungent oil distilled from gum turpentine or pine wood, used in mixing paints and varnishes and in liniment.

▪(also **crude turpentine** or **gum turpentine**) an oleoresin secreted by certain trees, especially pines, and distilled to make rosin and oil of turpentine.

2 (also **turpentine tree**) any of a number of trees which yield turpentine or a similar resin, in particular:

• a coniferous tree of the pine family (*Larix, Pinus,* and other genera, family Pinaceae). • the terebinth.

▶ **verb** [with obj.] apply turpentine to.

– ORIGIN Middle English: from Old French *ter(e)bentine,* from Latin *ter(e)binthina (resina)* '(resin) of the turpentine tree', from *terebinthus* (see **TEREBINTH**).

Turpin, Dick (1706–39), English highwayman. He was a cattle and deer thief in Essex before entering into partnership with Tom King, a notorious highwayman. Turpin was hanged at York for horse-stealing.

turpitude /ˈtəːpɪtjuːd/ ▶ **noun** [mass noun] formal depravity; wickedness: *acts of* **moral turpitude.**

– ORIGIN late 15th cent.: from French, or from Latin *turpitudo,* from *turpis* 'disgraceful, base'.

turps ▶ **noun** [mass noun] informal turpentine.

– ORIGIN early 19th cent.: abbreviation.

turquoise /ˈtəːkwɔɪz, -kwɑːz/ ▶ **noun** [mass noun] **1** a semi-precious stone, typically opaque and of a

greenish-blue or sky-blue colour, consisting of a hydrated phosphate of copper and aluminium. **2** a greenish-blue colour like that of this stone: [as modifier] *the turquoise waters of the bay.*
– ORIGIN late Middle English: from Old French *turqueise* 'Turkish (stone)'.

turret ▶ noun **1** a small tower on top of a larger tower or at the corner of a building or wall, typically of a castle. ■a low, flat armoured tower, typically one that revolves, for a gun and gunners in a ship, aircraft, fort, or tank. ■ a rotating holder for tools, especially on a lathe. **2** (also **turret shell**) a mollusc with a long, slender, pointed spiral shell, typically brightly coloured and living in tropical seas.
● Family Turitellidae, class Gastropoda: *Turitella* and other genera.
– DERIVATIVES **turreted** adjective.
– ORIGIN Middle English: from Old French *tourete*, diminutive of *tour* 'tower'.

turret lathe ▶ noun another term for **CAPSTAN LATHE**.

turron /tʊˈrɒn/ ▶ noun [mass noun] a kind of Spanish confectionery resembling nougat, made from almonds and honey.
– ORIGIN from Spanish *turrón*.

turtle ▶ noun **1** (also **sea turtle**) a large marine reptile with a bony or leathery shell and flippers, coming ashore annually on sandy beaches to lay eggs.
● Families Cheloniidae (seven species) and Dermochelyidae (the leatherback).
■[mass noun] the flesh of a sea turtle, especially the green turtle, used chiefly for soup. **2** a freshwater reptile related to the sea turtles and tortoises, typically having a flattened shell. Called **TERRAPIN** in South Africa and India and **TORTOISE** in Australia.
● Order Chelonia: several families, in particular Emydidae and Kinosternidae.
■N. Amer. any reptile of this order, including the terrapins and tortoises. **3** Computing a directional cursor in a computer graphics system which can be instructed to move around a screen.
– PHRASES **turn turtle** (chiefly of a boat) turn upside down.
– ORIGIN mid 16th cent.: apparently an alteration of French *tortue* (see **TORTOISE**).

turtle bug ▶ noun a bug or beetle with a turtle-like carapace, especially a olive-brown European shield bug which frequents grassy places.
● The shield bug is *Podops inuncta*, family Pentatomidae.

turtle dove ▶ noun a small Old World dove with a soft purring call, noted for the apparent affection shown for its mate.
● Genus *Streptopelia*, family Columbidae: several species, in particular the migratory European and North African *S. turtur*, with a reddish-brown back and pinkish breast.
– ORIGIN Middle English: *turtle* from Old English *turtla*, *turtle* 'turtle dove' (from Latin *turtur*, of imitative origin).

turtle-grass ▶ noun [mass noun] a submerged marine flowering plant found in the Caribbean, with long grass-like leaves.
● *Thalassia testudinum*, family Hydrocharitaceae.

turtlehead ▶ noun a North American plant which produces spikes of pink or white flowers which are said to resemble the head of a turtle.
● Genus *Chelone*, family Scrophulariaceae.

turtleneck ▶ noun **1** Brit. a high, round, close-fitting neck on a knitted garment. ■a sweater with a neck of this type. ■ North American term for **POLO NECK**.

turtleshell ▶ noun another term for **TORTOISESHELL**.

turves plural form of **TURF**.

Tuscan /ˈtʌskən/ ▶ adjective **1** of or relating to Tuscany, its inhabitants, or the form of Italian spoken there, which is a standard variety widely taught to foreign learners. **2** relating to or denoting a classical order of architecture resembling the Doric but lacking all ornamentation.
▶ noun **1** a native or inhabitant of Tuscany. **2** [mass noun] the form of Italian spoken in Tuscany. **3** [mass noun] the Tuscan order of architecture.
– ORIGIN late Middle English (as a noun denoting an

Etruscan): via French from Latin *Tuscanus*, from *Tuscus* 'an Etruscan'.

Tuscany /ˈtʌskəni/ a region of west central Italy, on the Ligurian Sea; capital, Florence. Italian name **TOSCANA**.

Tuscarora /ˌtʌskəˈrɔːrə/ ▶ noun (pl. same or **Tuscaroras**) **1** an American Indian people forming part of the Iroquois confederacy, originally inhabiting the Carolinas and later New York State. **2** [mass noun] the extinct Iroquoian language of this people.
▶ adjective of or relating to the Tuscarora or their language.
– ORIGIN the name in Iroquois.

tush[1] /tʌʃ/ ▶ exclamation archaic or humorous expressing disapproval, impatience, or dismissal: *tush, these are trifles and mere old wives' tales.*
– ORIGIN natural utterance: first recorded in late Middle English.

tush[2] /tʌʃ/ ▶ noun a long pointed tooth, in particular a canine tooth of a male horse. ■a stunted tusk of some Indian elephants.
– ORIGIN Old English *tusc* (see **TUSK**).

tush[3] /tʊʃ/ ▶ noun informal, chiefly N. Amer. a person's buttocks.
– ORIGIN 1960s (as *tushie*): from Yiddish *tokhes*, from Hebrew *taḥat* 'beneath'.

tushy /ˈtʊʃi/ ▶ noun (pl. **-ies**) another term for **TUSH**[3].

tusk ▶ noun a long, pointed tooth, especially one specially developed so as to protrude from the closed mouth, as in the elephant, walrus, or wild boar. ■a long, tapering object or projection resembling such a tooth.
– DERIVATIVES **tusked** adjective, **tusky** adjective (poetic/literary).
– ORIGIN Old English *tux*, variant of *tusc* (see **TUSH**[2]).

tusker ▶ noun an elephant or wild boar with well-developed tusks.

tusk shell ▶ noun a burrowing mollusc with a slender tusk-shaped shell, which is open at both ends and typically white, and a three-lobed foot.
● Class Scaphopoda, in particular the genus *Dentalium*.

tussah /ˈtʌsə/ ▶ noun variant form of **TUSSORE**.

Tussaud /təˈsɔːd, French tyso/, Madame (1761–1850), French founder of Madame Tussaud's waxworks, resident in Britain from 1802; née *Marie Grosholtz*. She took death masks in wax of prominent victims of the French Revolution and later toured Britain with her wax models. In 1835 she founded a permanent waxworks exhibition in Baker Street, London.

tussie-mussie /ˈtʌsɪmʌsi/ ▶ noun (pl. **-ies**) a small bunch of flowers or aromatic herbs.
– ORIGIN late Middle English: of unknown origin.

tussive /ˈtʌsɪv/ ▶ adjective Medicine relating to coughing.
– ORIGIN mid 19th cent.: from Latin *tussis* 'a cough' + -IVE.

tussle ▶ noun a vigorous struggle or scuffle, typically in order to obtain or achieve something: *there was a tussle for the ball.*
▶ verb [no obj.] engage in such a struggle or scuffle: *the demonstrators tussled with police.*
– ORIGIN late Middle English (as a verb, originally Scots and northern English): perhaps a diminutive of dialect *touse* 'handle roughly' (see **TOUSLE**).

tussock /ˈtʌsək/ ▶ noun **1** a small area of grass that is thicker or longer than the grass growing around it. **2** (also **tussock moth**) a woodland moth whose adults and brightly coloured caterpillars both bear tufts of irritant hairs. The caterpillars can be a pest of trees, damaging fruit and stripping leaves.
● Family Lymantriidae: many genera.
– DERIVATIVES **tussocky** adjective.
– ORIGIN mid 16th cent.: perhaps an alteration of dialect *tusk* 'tuft', of unknown origin.

tussock grass ▶ noun a grass which grows in tussocks.
● Genera *Poa*, *Nassella*, or *Deschampsia*, family Gramineae: several species, in particular *D. cespitosa*, a coarse fodder grass of the northern hemisphere.

tussore /ˈtʌsɔː, ˈtʌsə/ (also **tussah**) ▶ noun (also **tussore silk**) [mass noun] coarse silk from the larvae of the tussore moth and related species.
– ORIGIN late 16th cent. (denoting the silk): from Hindi *tasar*, from Sanskrit *tasara* 'shuttle'.

tussore moth ▶ noun a silk moth that is sometimes kept in India and China, with caterpillars (**tussore silkworms**) that yield a strong but coarse brown silk.
● *Antheraea mylitta*, family Saturniidae.

tut ▶ exclamation, noun, & verb short for **TUT-TUT**.

Tutankhamen /ˌtuːtənˈkɑːmən/ (also **Tutankhamun** /-kɑːˈmuːn/) (died *c*.1352 BC), Egyptian pharaoh of the 18th dynasty, reigned *c*.1361–*c*.1352 BC. His tomb, containing a wealth of rich and varied contents, was discovered virtually intact by the English archaeologist Howard Carter in 1922.

tutee /tjuːˈtiː/ ▶ noun a student or pupil of a tutor.

tutelage /ˈtjuːtɪlɪdʒ/ ▶ noun [mass noun] protection of or authority over someone or something; guardianship: *the organizations remained under firm government tutelage.* ■instruction; tuition: *he felt privileged to be under the tutelage of an experienced actor.*
– ORIGIN early 17th cent.: from Latin *tutela* 'keeping', (from *tut*- 'watched', from the verb *tueri*) + -AGE.

tutelary /ˈtjuːtɪləri/ (also **tutelar** /-tɪlə/) ▶ adjective serving as a protector, guardian, or patron: *the tutelary spirits of these regions.* ■of or relating to protection or a guardian: *the state maintained a tutelary relation with the security police.*
– ORIGIN early 17th cent.: from Latin *tutelarius*, from *tutela* 'keeping' (see **TUTELAGE**).

Tuthmosis III /tʌθˈməʊsɪs/ (died *c*.1450 BC), son of Tuthmosis II, Egyptian pharaoh of the 18th dynasty *c*.1504–*c*.1450. His reign was marked by extensive building; the monuments he erected included Cleopatra's Needles (*c*.1475).

tutor ▶ noun a private teacher, typically one who teaches a single pupil or a very small group. ■chiefly Brit. a university or college teacher responsible for the teaching and supervision of assigned students. ■ US an assistant lecturer in a college or university. ■ Brit. a book of instruction in a particular subject.
▶ verb [with obj.] act as a tutor to (a single pupil or a very small group): *his children were privately tutored.* ■[no obj.] work as a tutor.
– DERIVATIVES **tutorage** noun, **tutorship** noun.
– ORIGIN late Middle English: from Old French *tutour* or Latin *tutor*, from *tueri* 'to watch, guard'.

tutorial ▶ adjective of or relating to a tutor or a tutor's tuition: *tutorial sessions | a tutorial college.*
▶ noun a period of tuition given by a university or college tutor to an individual or very small group. ■an account or explanation of a subject, printed or on a computer screen, intended for private study.
– ORIGIN early 18th cent.: from Latin *tutorius* (see **TUTOR**) + -AL.

tutsan /ˈtʌts(ə)n/ ▶ noun a Eurasian St John's wort with large aromatic leaves and a berry-like fruit, formerly used medicinally.
● *H. androsaemum*, family Guttiferae.
– ORIGIN late Middle English: from Anglo-Norman French *tutsaine* 'all wholesome'.

Tutsi /ˈtʊtsi/ ▶ noun (pl. same or **Tutsis**) a member of a people forming a minority of the population of Rwanda and Burundi but who formerly dominated the Hutu majority. Historical antagonism between the peoples led in 1994 to large-scale ethnic violence, especially in Rwanda.
▶ adjective of or relating to this people.
– ORIGIN a local name. See also **WATUSI**.

tutti /ˈtoti/ Music ▶ adverb & adjective (especially as a direction) with all voices or instruments together.
▶ noun (pl. **tuttis**) a passage to be performed in this way.
– ORIGIN Italian, plural of *tutto* 'all', from Latin *totus*.

tutti-frutti /ˌtuːtɪˈfruːti/ ▶ noun (pl. **tutti-fruttis**) [mass noun] a type of ice cream containing or flavoured with mixed fruits and sometimes nuts.
– ORIGIN Italian, literally 'all fruits'.

tut-tut (also **tut**) ▶ exclamation expressing disapproval or annoyance: *tut-tut, Robin, you disappoint me.*
▶ noun such an exclamation: *tut-tuts of disapproval.*
▶ verb (**tut-tutted**, **tut-tutting**) [no obj.] make such an exclamation: *Aunt Mary tut-tutted at all the goings-on.*
– ORIGIN natural utterance (representing a reduplicated clicking sound made by the tongue against the teeth): first recorded in English in the early 16th cent.

Tutu /ˈtuːtuː/, Desmond (Mpilo) (b.1931), South

African clergyman. As General Secretary of the South African Council of Churches (1979–84) he became a leading voice in the struggle against apartheid. He was archbishop of Cape Town 1986–96. Nobel Peace Prize (1984).

tutu[1] /ˈtuːtuː/ ▶ **noun** a female ballet dancer's costume consisting of a bodice and an attached skirt incorporating numerous layers of fabric, this being either short and stiff and projecting horizontally from the waist (the **classical tutu**) or long, soft, and bell-shaped (the **romantic tutu**).
– ORIGIN early 20th cent.: from French, child's alteration of *cucu*, informal diminutive of *cul* 'buttocks'.

tutu[2] /ˈtuːtuː/ ▶ **noun** a New Zealand shrub which bears poisonous purplish-black berries.
• *Coriaria arborea*, family Coriariaceae.
– ORIGIN mid 19th cent.: from Maori.

Tuva /ˈtuːvə/ an autonomous republic in south central Russia, on the border with Mongolia; pop. 314,000 (1990); capital, Kyzyl. Former name **TANNU-TUVA**.

Tuvalu /tuːˈvɑːluː/ a country in the SW Pacific consisting of a group of nine main islands, formerly called the Ellice Islands; pop. 8,500 (est. 1988); official languages, English and Tuvaluan (local Austronesian language); capital, Funafuti. The islands formed part of the British colony of the Gilbert and Ellice Islands but separated from the Gilberts after a referendum in 1975. Tuvalu became independent within the Commonwealth in 1978.
– DERIVATIVES **Tuvaluan** /ˌtuːvəˈluːən, tuːˈvɑːluən/ adjective & noun.

tu-whit tu-whoo ▶ **noun** a stylized representation of the cry of the tawny owl.
– ORIGIN late 16th cent.: imitative.

tux ▶ **noun** informal, chiefly US a tuxedo.

tuxedo /tʌkˈsiːdəʊ/ ▶ **noun** (pl. **-os** or **-oes**) chiefly US a man's dinner jacket.
■ a suit of formal evening clothes including such a jacket.
– DERIVATIVES **tuxedoed** adjective.
– ORIGIN late 19th cent.: from *Tuxedo* Park, the site of a country club in New York, where it was first worn.

Tuxtla Gutiérrez /ˌtʊstlə ˌɡuːtɪˈɛːrɛz/ a city in SE Mexico, capital of the state of Chiapas; pop. 295,615 (1990).

tuyère /twiːˈjɛː, tuː-/ ▶ **noun** a nozzle through which air is forced into a smelter, furnace, or forge.
– ORIGIN late 18th cent.: French, from *tuyau* 'pipe'.

Tuzla /ˈtʊzlə/ a town in NE Bosnia; pop. 132,000 (1991). The town, a Muslim enclave, suffered damage and heavy casualties when besieged by Bosnian Serb forces between 1992 and 1994.

TV ▶ **abbreviation for** ■ television (the system or a set): *anything good on TV tonight?* ■ transvestite.

TVA ▶ **abbreviation for** (in the US) Tennessee Valley Authority.

TV dinner ▶ **noun** a prepared pre-packed meal that only requires heating before it is ready to eat.

TVEI ▶ **abbreviation for** (in the UK) Technical and Vocational Educational Initiative, a national scheme encouraging students to gain practical experience of technology and industry, often through work placement.

Tver /tvɛː/ an industrial port in European Russia, on the River Volga north-west of Moscow; pop. 454,000 (1990). It was known as Kalinin, in honour of President Kalinin, from 1931 until 1991.

TVP trademark ▶ **abbreviation for** textured vegetable protein.

Twa /twɑː/ ▶ **noun** (pl. same or **Twas**) a member of a pygmy people inhabiting parts of Burundi, Rwanda, and Zaire (Democratic Republic of Congo).
▶ **adjective** of or relating to the Twa.
– ORIGIN a local word meaning 'foreigner, outsider'.

twaddle informal ▶ **noun** [mass noun] trivial or foolish speech or writing; nonsense: *he dismissed the novel as self-indulgent twaddle.*
▶ **verb** [no obj.] archaic talk or write in a trivial or foolish way: *what is that old fellow twaddling about?*
– DERIVATIVES **twaddler** noun.
– ORIGIN late 18th cent.: alteration of earlier *twattle*, of unknown origin.

Twain, Mark (1835–1910), American novelist and humorist; pseudonym of *Samuel Langhorne Clemens*. His best-known novels, *The Adventures of Tom Sawyer* (1876) and *The Adventures of Huckleberry Finn* (1885), give a vivid evocation of Mississippi frontier life.

twain ▶ **cardinal number** archaic term for **TWO**: *he split it in twain.*
– PHRASES **never the twain shall meet** used to suggest that two things are too different to exist alongside each other: *families were either 'church' or 'chapel' and never the twain shall meet.* [ORIGIN: from Rudyard Kipling's 'Oh, East is East, and West is West, and never the twain shall meet'. (*Barrack-room Ballads* (1892)).]
– ORIGIN Old English *twegen*, masculine of *twā* (see **TWO**).

twaite shad /tweɪt/ ▶ **noun** a European shad (fish) with a deep blue back, silvery sides, and some spotting.
• *Alosa fallax*, family Clupeidae.
– ORIGIN early 17th cent. (as *twaite*): of unknown origin.

twang ▶ **noun** a strong ringing sound such as that made by the plucked string of a musical instrument or a released bowstring.
■ a nasal or other distinctive manner of pronunciation or intonation characteristic of the speech of an individual, area, or country: *an American twang.*
▶ **verb** make or cause to make such a sound: [no obj.] *a spring twanged beneath him.*
■ [with obj.] play (an instrument) in such a way as to produce such sounds: *some old men were twanging banjos.* ■ [with obj.] utter (something) with a nasal twang: *the announcer was twanging out all the details.*
– DERIVATIVES **twangy** adjective.
– ORIGIN mid 16th cent.: imitative.

'twas archaic or poetic/literary ▶ **contraction of** it was.

twat /twɒt, twat/ ▶ **noun** vulgar slang a woman's genitals.
■ a person regarded as stupid or obnoxious.
▶ **verb** [with obj.] Brit. informal hit or punch (someone).
– ORIGIN mid 17th cent.: of unknown origin.

twayblade ▶ **noun** an orchid with a slender spike of greenish or brownish flowers and a single pair of broad leaves near the base.
• Genus *Listera*, family Orchidaceae: several species, including the Eurasian **common twayblade** (*L. ovata*).
– ORIGIN late 16th cent.: from *tway* (variant of **TWAIN**) + **BLADE**, translating Latin *bifolium*.

tweak ▶ **verb** [with obj.] **1** twist or pull (something) sharply: *he tweaked the boy's ear.*
2 informal improve (a mechanism or system) by making fine adjustments to it: *engineers tweak the car's operating systems during the race.*
▶ **noun 1** a sharp twist or pull.
2 informal a fine adjustment to a mechanism or system.
– ORIGIN early 17th cent.: probably an alteration of dialect *twick* 'pull sharply'; related to **TWITCH**.

twee ▶ **adjective** (**tweer**, **tweest**) Brit., chiefly derogatory excessively or affectedly quaint, pretty, or sentimental: *although the film's a bit twee, it's watchable.*
– DERIVATIVES **tweely** adverb, **tweeness** noun.
– ORIGIN early 20th cent.: representing a child's pronunciation of **SWEET**.

Tweed a river which rises in the Southern Uplands of Scotland and flows generally eastwards, crossing into NE England and entering the North Sea at Berwick-upon-Tweed. For part of its lower course it forms the border between Scotland and England.

tweed ▶ **noun** [mass noun] a rough-surfaced woollen cloth, typicallyof mixed flecked colours, originally produced in Scotland: [as modifier] *a tweed sports jacket.*
■ (**tweeds**) clothes made of this material: *boisterous Englishwomen in tweeds.*
– ORIGIN mid 19th cent.: originally a misreading of *tweel*, Scots form of **TWILL**, influenced by association with the river *Tweed*.

Tweedledum and Tweedledee ▶ **noun** a pair of people or things that are virtually indistinguishable.
– ORIGIN originally names applied to the composers Bononcini (1670–1747) and Handel, in a 1725 satire by John Byrom (1692–1763); they were later used for two identical characters in Lewis Carroll's *Through the Looking Glass*.

tweedy ▶ **adjective** (**tweedier**, **tweediest**) (of a garment) made of tweed cloth: *a tweedy suit.*
■ informal (of a person) habitually wearing tweed clothes: *a stout, tweedy woman.* ■ informal of a robust traditional or rural character (by association with the country gentry who traditionally wear tweeds): *a tweedy gathering of the Cheshire young farmers.*
– DERIVATIVES **tweedily** adverb, **tweediness** noun.

Tween ▶ **noun** trademark any of a class of compounds used especially as emulsifiers and surfactants. They are derivatives of fatty acid esters of sorbitan.
– ORIGIN 1940s: of unknown origin.

'tween archaic or poetic/literary ▶ **contraction of** between.

'tween decks ▶ **plural noun** Nautical the space between the decks of a ship, especially that between the continuous inside decks below the main or upper deck.

tweeny ▶ **noun** (pl. **-ies**) archaic, informal a maid who assisted two other members of a domestic staff.
– ORIGIN late 19th cent.: from *between-maid*, a servant assisting two others.

tweet (also **tweet tweet**) ▶ **noun** the chirp of a small or young bird.
▶ **verb** [no obj.] make a chirping noise: *the birds were tweeting in the branches.*
– ORIGIN mid 19th cent.: imitative.

tweeter ▶ **noun** a loudspeaker designed to reproduce high frequencies.

tweeze ▶ **verb** [with obj.] pluck, grasp, or pull with or as if with tweezers: *the brows were tweezed to an almost invisible line.*
– ORIGIN 1930s: back-formation from *tweezer* (see **TWEEZERS**).

tweezers ▶ **plural noun** (also **a pair of tweezers**) a small instrument like a pair of pincers for plucking out hairs and picking up small objects.
– ORIGIN mid 17th cent.: extended form of obsolete *tweeze* 'case of surgical instruments', shortening of *etweese*, plural of **ETUI**.

twelfth /twɛlfθ/ ▶ **ordinal number** constituting number twelve in a sequence; 12th: *the twelfth of November | his twelfth birthday | the twelfth in a series of essays.*
■ (**a twelfth/one twelfth**) each of twelve equal parts into which something is or may be divided. ■ Music an interval or chord spanning an octave and a fifth in the diatonic scale, or a note separated from another by this interval. ■ (**the Twelfth** or **the Glorious Twelfth**) (in the UK) 12 August, the day on which the grouse-shooting season begins. ■ (**the Twelfth**) 12 July, celebrated by upholders of Protestant supremacy in Ireland as the anniversary of William III's victory over James II at the Battle of the Boyne.
– DERIVATIVES **twelfthly** adverb, **twelvefold** adjective & adverb.

Twelfth Day ▶ **noun** archaic term for **TWELFTH NIGHT**.

twelfth man ▶ **noun** Cricket a player nominated to act as a reserve in a game, typically carrying out duties such as fielding as a substitute, taking out drinks, etc.

Twelfth Night ▶ **noun** 6 January, the feast of the Epiphany.
■ strictly, the evening of 5 January, the eve of the Epiphany and formerly the twelfth and last day of Christmas festivities.

twelve ▶ **cardinal number** equivalent to the product of three and four; two more than ten; 12: *he walked twelve miles | there are just twelve of us in all | a twelve-string guitar.* (Roman numeral: **xii** or **XII**.)
■ a group or unit of twelve people or things. ■ twelve years old: *a small blonde girl of about twelve.* ■ twelve o'clock: *it's half past twelve.* ■ a size of garment or other merchandise denoted by twelve. ■ (**the Twelve**) the twelve Apostles. ■ (**12**) Brit. (of a film) classified as suitable for people of 12 years and over.
– ORIGIN Old English *twelf(e)*, from the base of **TWO** + a second element (probably expressing the sense 'left over'); of Germanic origin and related to Dutch *twaalf* and German *zwölf*. Compare with **ELEVEN**.

twelve-bar ▶ **adjective** denoting or relating to a musical structure based around a sequence lasting twelve bars and typically consisting of three chords, the basic unit of much blues and rock and roll music.
▶ **noun** a song or piece of music having such a structure.

twelve-bore ▶ **noun** a shotgun with a bore corresponding to the diameter of a round bullet of which twelve constitute a pound in weight.

twelve-gauge ▶ **noun** North American term for **TWELVE-BORE**.

twelvemo ▶ **noun** another term for **DUODECIMO**.

t

twelvemonth ▶ noun archaic a year.

twelve-note (also **twelve-tone**) ▶ adjective denoting a system of musical composition using the twelve chromatic notes of the octave on an equal basis without dependence on a key system. Developed by Arnold Schoenberg, the technique is central to serialism and involves the transposition and inversion of a fixed sequence of pitches.

Twelve Tables a set of laws drawn up in ancient Rome in 451 and 450 BC, embodying the most important rules of Roman law.

Twelve Tribes of Israel see **TRIBES OF ISRAEL**.

Twentieth Century Fox a US film production company formed in 1935 by the merger of the Fox Company with Twentieth Century. Under production head Darryl F. Zanuck (1902–79) the company pioneered widescreen film techniques.

twenty ▶ cardinal number (pl. **-ies**) the number equivalent to the product of two and ten; ten less than thirty; 20: *twenty or thirty years ago | twenty of us stood and waited | a twenty-foot aerial.* (Roman numeral: **xx** or **XX**.)
■ (**twenties**) the numbers from twenty to twenty-nine, especially the years of a century or of a person's life: *he's in his late twenties.* ■ twenty years old: *he's about twenty.* ■ twenty miles an hour. ■ a size of garment or other merchandise denoted by twenty.
– DERIVATIVES **twentieth** ordinal number, **twentyfold** adjective & adverb.
– ORIGIN Old English *twentig*, from the base of **TWO** + **-TY**².

twenty-eight ▶ noun Austral. a ringneck parrot of a race having a call that resembles the word 'twenty-eight'.
• *Barnardius zonarius semitorquatus*, family Psittacidae; a subspecies of the Port Lincoln parrot.

twenty-four-hour clock (also **24-hour clock**) ▶ noun a method of measuring the time based on the full twenty-four hours of the day, rather than dividing it into two units of twelve hours.

twenty-four hours ▶ noun W. Indian a long-legged arboreal lizard of tropical America, related to the anoles.
• *Polychrus marmoratus*, family Iguanidae.
– ORIGIN so named from the superstition that a person touched by one will die within twenty-four hours.

twenty-one ▶ noun [mass noun] the card game blackjack or pontoon.

twenty-twenty (also **20/20**) ▶ adjective denoting vision of normal acuity.
– ORIGIN the Snellen fraction for normal visual acuity (see **SNELLEN TEST**).

'twere archaic or poetic/literary ▶ contraction of it were.

twerp (also **twirp**) ▶ noun informal a silly or annoying person.
– ORIGIN late 19th cent.: of unknown origin.

Twi /twiː, tʃwiː/ ▶ noun (pl. same or **Twis**) **1** a member of an Akan-speaking people of Ghana.
2 another term for **AKAN** (the language).
▶ adjective of or relating to this people or their language.
– ORIGIN the name in Akan.

twibill /ˈtwʌɪbɪl/ ▶ noun archaic a double-bladed battleaxe.
– ORIGIN Old English *twibile* 'axe with two cutting edges', from *twi-* 'double' + **BILL**³.

twice ▶ adverb two times; on two occasions: *the earl married twice | the tablets should be taken twice a day.*
■ double in degree or quantity: *I'm twice your age | an engine twice as big as the original.*
– PHRASES **once bitten, twice shy** see **BITE**. **think twice** see **THINK**.
– ORIGIN late Old English *twiges*, from the base of **TWO** + **-S**³ (later respelled *-ce* to denote the unvoiced sound); compare with **ONCE**.

twice-born ▶ adjective having undergone a renewal of faith or life, in particular:
■ (of a Hindu) belonging to one of the three highest castes, especially as an initiated Brahmin. ■ (of a Christian) born-again.

twiddle ▶ verb [with obj.] twist, move, or fiddle with (something), typically in a purposeless or nervous way: *she twiddled the dials on the radio* | [no obj.] *he began twiddling with the curtain cord.*
■ [no obj.] archaic turn or move in a twirling way.
▶ noun an act of twisting or fiddling with something: *one twiddle of a button.*
■ a twisted or curled mark or design: *twiddles and twirls.*
■ a rapid or intricate series of musical notes: *gay little twiddles from the clarinet.*
– PHRASES **twiddle one's thumbs** rotate one's thumbs round each other with the fingers linked together. ■ be bored or idle because one has nothing to do.
– DERIVATIVES **twiddler** noun, **twiddly** adjective.
– ORIGIN mid 16th cent. (in the sense 'trifle'): apparently imitative, combining the notion *twirl* or *twist* with that of trifling action expressed by *fiddle*.

twig¹ ▶ noun a slender woody shoot growing from a branch or stem of a tree or shrub.
■ Anatomy a small branch of a blood vessel or nerve.
– DERIVATIVES **twigged** adjective, **twiggy** adjective.
– ORIGIN Old English *twigge*, of Germanic origin; related to Dutch *twijg* and German *Zweig*, also to **TWAIN** and **TWO**.

twig² ▶ verb (**twigged**, **twigging**) [no obj.] Brit. informal understand or realize something: *it was amazing that Graham hadn't twigged before.*
■ [with obj.] archaic perceive; observe: *nine days now since my eyes have twigged any terra firma.*
– ORIGIN mid 18th cent.: of unknown origin.

twig furniture ▶ noun [mass noun] N. Amer. a rustic style of furniture in which the natural state of the wood is retained as an aesthetic feature.

twilight /ˈtwʌɪlʌɪt/ ▶ noun [mass noun] the soft glowing light from the sky when the sun is below the horizon, caused by the reflection of the sun's rays from the atmosphere.
■ the period of the evening during which this takes place, between daylight and darkness: *a pleasant walk in the woods at twilight.* ■ [in sing.] figurative a period or state of obscurity, ambiguity, or gradual decline: *he was in the twilight of his career.*
– ORIGIN late Middle English: from Old English *twi-* 'two' (used in an obscure sense in this compound) + **LIGHT**¹.

twilight home ▶ noun a residential home for the elderly.

twilight of the gods Scandinavian & Germanic Mythology the destruction of the gods and the world in a final conflict with the powers of evil. Also called **GÖTTERDÄMMERUNG**, **RAGNARÖK**.
– ORIGIN translating Icelandic *ragna rökr* (see **RAGNARÖK**).

twilight sleep ▶ noun [mass noun] Medicine a state of partial narcosis or stupor without total loss of consciousness, in particular a state induced by an injection of morphine and scopolamine, formerly popular for use during childbirth.

twilight zone ▶ noun **1** an urban area that is becoming dilapidated, with decrepit housing and accompanying social and economic degeneration.
2 a conceptual area which is undefined or intermediate: *the twilight zone between the middle and working classes.*
■ a sphere of experience which appears sinister or dangerous because of its uncertainty, unpredictability, or ambiguity: *schizophrenia isolates the individual in a twilight zone of terror.*
3 the lowest level of the ocean to which light can penetrate.

twilit (also **twilighted**) ▶ adjective dimly illuminated by or as if by twilight: *the deserted twilit street.*
■ relating to or denoting the period of twilight: *twilit hours.*
– ORIGIN mid 19th cent.: past participle of the literary verb *twilight*.

twill ▶ noun [mass noun] a fabric so woven as to have a surface of diagonal parallel ridges.
▶ verb [with obj.] [usu. as adj. **twilled**] weave (fabric) in this way: *twilled cotton.*
– ORIGIN Middle English: from a Scots and northern English variant of obsolete *twilly*, from Old English *twi-* 'two', suggested by Latin *bilix* 'two-threaded'.

'twill archaic or poetic/literary ▶ contraction of it will.

twin ▶ noun **1** one of two children or animals born at the same birth.
■ a person or thing that is exactly like another: *there was a bruise on his cheek, **a twin to** the one on mine.* ■ (**the Twins**) the zodiacal sign or constellation Gemini.
2 something containing or consisting of two matching or corresponding parts, in particular:
■ a twin-bedded room. ■ a twin-engined aircraft. ■ a twinned crystal.
▶ adjective [attrib.] forming, or being one of, a pair born at one birth: *she gave birth to twin boys | her twin sister.*
■ forming a matching, complementary, or closely connected pair: *the twin problems of economic failure and social disintegration.* ■ Botany growing in pairs: *twin seed leaves.* ■ (of a bedroom) containing two single beds. ■ (of a crystal) twinned.
▶ verb (**twinned**, **twinning**) [with obj.] (usu. **be twinned**) Brit. link (a town or district) with another in a different country or cause (two towns or districts) to be linked, for the purposes of friendship and cultural exchange: *the Russian city of Kostroma is **twinned with** Durham.*
■ link; combine: *the company twinned its core business of brewing with that of distilling.*
– ORIGIN late Old English *twinn* 'double', from *twi-* 'two'; related to Old Norse *tvinnr*. Current verb senses date from late Middle English.

twin bed ▶ noun one of a pair of matching single beds, particularly in a hotel or guest room intended for two people.
– DERIVATIVES **twin-bedded** adjective.

twin-cam ▶ adjective denoting an engine having two camshafts.

twin city ▶ noun either of two neighbouring cities lying close together.
■ (**the Twin Cities**) N. Amer. Minneapolis and St Paul in Minnesota. ■ a city which has been twinned with another.

twine ▶ noun [mass noun] strong thread or string consisting of two or more strands of hemp or cotton twisted together.
▶ verb [with obj.] cause to wind or spiral round something: *she **twined** her arms **round** his neck.*
■ [no obj.] (of a plant) grow so as to spiral round a support: *runner beans twined round canes.* ■ interlace: *a spray of jasmine was twined in her hair.*
– DERIVATIVES **twiner** noun.
– ORIGIN Old English *twīn* 'thread, linen', from the Germanic base of *twi-* 'two'; related to Dutch *twijn*.

twin-engined ▶ adjective (chiefly of an aircraft) having two engines.

twinflower ▶ noun a slender evergreen trailing plant with pairs of very small trumpet-shaped pink flowers in the leaf axils, native to coniferous woodland in northern latitudes.
• *Linnaea borealis*, family Caprifoliaceae.

twinge ▶ noun a sudden, sharp localized pain: *he felt a twinge in his knee.*
■ a brief experience of an emotion, typically an unpleasant one: *Kate felt **a twinge of** guilt.*
▶ verb (**twingeing** or **twinging**) [no obj.] (of a part of the body) suffer a sudden, sharp localized pain: *stop the exercises if the tummy twinges.*
– ORIGIN Old English *twengan* 'pinch, wring', of Germanic origin. The noun dates from the mid 16th cent.

twinkie ▶ noun (pl. **-ies**) US **1** trademark a small finger-shaped sponge cake with a white synthetic cream filling.
2 informal, offensive a gay or effeminate man.
– ORIGIN late 20th cent.: probably related to **TWINKLE**.

twinkle ▶ verb [no obj.] (of a star or light, or a shiny object) shine with a gleam that changes constantly from bright to faint: *the lights twinkled in the distance.*
■ (of a person's eyes) sparkle, especially with amusement. ■ smile so that one's eyes sparkle: *'Aha!' he said, **twinkling at** her.* ■ [no obj., with adverbial] (of a person's feet) move lightly and rapidly: *his sandalled feet twinkled over the ground.*
▶ noun a sparkle or gleam in a person's eyes.
■ a light which appears continually to grow brighter and fainter: *the distant twinkle of the lights.*
– PHRASES **in a twinkling** (or **the twinkling of an eye**) in an instant; very quickly.
– DERIVATIVES **twinkler** noun, **twinkly** adjective.
– ORIGIN Old English *twinclian* (verb), of Germanic origin.

twinkle-toed ▶ adjective informal nimble and quick on one's feet: *a twinkle-toed midfielder.*

twinkletoes ▶ noun informal a person who is nimble and quick on their feet.

twin-lens ▶ adjective (of a camera) having two identical sets of lenses, either for taking stereoscopic pictures, or with one forming an image for viewing and the other an image to be photographed (**twin-lens reflex**).

twinned ▶ adjective (of a crystal) that is a composite consisting of two (or sometimes more) parts which are reversed in orientation with respect to each other (typically by reflection in a particular plane).

twinning ▶ noun [mass noun] the bearing of twins: *the study showed an increased level of twinning in cattle.* ■ the occurrence or formation of twinned crystals.

twin paradox ▶ noun Physics the apparent paradox arising from relativity theory that if one of a pair of twins makes a long journey at near the speed of light and then returns, he or she will have aged less than the twin who remains behind.

twin-screw ▶ adjective (of a ship) having two propellers on separate shafts with opposite twists.

twinset ▶ noun chiefly Brit. a woman's matching cardigan and jumper.

twinspot ▶ noun an African waxbill with white-spotted black underparts, the male typically having a reddish face and breast.
• *Hypargos* and related genera, family Estrildidae: several species.

twin town ▶ noun Brit. a town which has established official or social links with another, typically in a different country.

twin-tub ▶ adjective (of a washing machine) having two separate top-loading drums, one for washing and the other for spin-drying.
▶ noun a washing machine of this kind.

twirl ▶ verb [no obj.] spin quickly and lightly round, especially repeatedly: *she twirled in delight to show off her new dress.*
■ [with obj.] cause to rotate: *she twirled her fork in the pasta.*
▶ noun an act of spinning: *Kate did a twirl in front of the mirror.*
■ a spiralling or swirling shape, especially a flourish made with a pen.
– DERIVATIVES **twirler** noun, **twirly** adjective.
– ORIGIN late 16th cent.: probably an alteration (by association with **WHIRL**) of *tirl*, a variant of archaic *trill* 'twiddle, spin'.

twirp ▶ noun variant spelling of **TWERP**.

twist ▶ verb [with obj.] **1** form into a bent, curling, or distorted shape: *a strip of metal is twisted to form a hollow tube* | *her pretty features twisted into a fearsome expression.*
■ [with obj. and adverbial] form (something) into a particular shape by taking hold of one or both ends and turning them: *she twisted her handkerchief into a knot.* ■ [with obj. and adverbial] turn or bend into a specified position or in a specified direction: *he grabbed the man and twisted his arm behind his back.* ■ (**twist something off**) remove something by pulling and rotating it: *beetroot can be stored once the leaves have been twisted off.* ■ [no obj.] move one's body so that the shoulders and hips are facing in different directions: *she twisted in her seat to look at the buildings.* ■ [no obj., with adverbial] move in a wriggling or writhing fashion: *he* ***twisted himself*** *free.* ■ injure (a joint) by wrenching it: *he twisted his ankle trying to avoid his opponent's lunge.* ■ distort or misrepresent the meaning of (words): *he twisted my words to make it seem that I'd claimed she was a drug addict.* ■ [as adj. **twisted**] (of a personality or a way of thinking) unpleasantly or unhealthily abnormal: *a man with a twisted mind.*
2 cause to rotate around something that remains stationary; turn: *she twisted her ring round and round on her finger.*
■ [with obj. and adverbial] wind around or through something: *she twisted a lock of hair around her finger.* ■ move or cause to move around each other; interlace: [with obj.] *she twisted her hands together nervously* | *the machine twists together strands to make a double yarn.* ■ make (something) by interlacing or winding strands together. ■ [no obj.] take or have a winding course: *the railway lines twist and turn round the hills.*
3 [no obj.] dance the twist.
4 Brit. informal cheat; defraud.
5 [no obj.] (in pontoon) request, deal, or be dealt a card face upwards.
▶ noun **1** an act of turning something so that it moves in relation to something that remains stationary: *the taps needed a single twist to turn them on.*
■ an act of turning one's body or part of one's body: *with a sudden twist, she got away from him.* ■ (**the twist**) a dance with a twisting movement of the body, popular in the 1960s. ■ [mass noun] the extent of twisting of a rod or other object. ■ [mass noun] force producing twisting; torque. ■ [mass noun] forward motion combined with rotation about an axis. ■ the rifling in the bore of a gun: *barrels with a 1:24 inch twist.*
2 a thing with a spiral shape: *a barley sugar twist.*
■ Brit. a paper packet with twisted ends. ■ a small quantity of tobacco, sugar, salt, or a similar substance, wrapped in such a packet. ■ a curled piece of lemon peel used to flavour a drink.
3 a distorted shape: *he had a cruel twist to his mouth.*
■ an unusual feature of a person's personality, typically an unhealthy one. ■ Brit. informal a swindle.
4 a point at which something turns or bends: *the car negotiated the twists and turns of the mountain road.*
■ an unexpected development of events: *it was soon time for the next* ***twist of fate*** *in his extraordinary career.* ■ a new treatment or outlook; a variation: *she takes conventional subjects and gives them a twist.*
5 [mass noun] a fine strong thread consisting of twisted strands of cotton or silk.
6 Brit. a drink consisting of two ingredients mixed together.
7 a carpet with a tightly curled pile.
– PHRASES **round the twist** Brit. informal out of one's mind; crazy: *the games she plays* ***drive me round the twist.*** **twist someone's arm** informal persuade someone to do something that they are or might be reluctant to do. **twist in the wind** be left in a state of suspense or uncertainty. **twist someone around one's little finger** see **LITTLE FINGER**. **twists and turns** intricate or convoluted dealings or circumstances: *the twists and turns of her political career.*
– DERIVATIVES **twisty** adjective.
– ORIGIN Old English (as a noun), of Germanic origin; probably from the base of **TWIN** and **TWINE**. Current verb senses date from late Middle English.

twist drill ▶ noun a drill with a twisted body like that of an auger.

twisted pair ▶ noun Electronics a cable consisting of two wires twisted round each other, used especially for telephone or computer applications.

twisted-stalk ▶ noun a plant of the lily family with bell-shaped flowers carried on bent or twisted stalks, native to the temperate regions of Russia and North America.
• Genus *Streptopus*, family Liliaceae.

twister ▶ noun **1** Brit. informal a swindler; a dishonest person.
2 N. Amer. a tornado.

twist-grip ▶ noun a control operated manually by twisting, especially one serving as a handgrip for operating the throttle on a motorcycle or for changing gear on a bicycle.

twist-lock ▶ noun a locking device for securing freight containers to the trailers on which they are transported.

twistor /ˈtwɪstə/ ▶ noun Physics a complex variable used in some descriptions of space–time.

twist tie ▶ noun a small piece of plastic-covered wire, to be twisted around the neck of a plastic bag as a closure.

twit[1] ▶ noun informal, chiefly Brit. a silly or foolish person.
– DERIVATIVES **twittish** adjective.
– ORIGIN 1930s (earlier dialect, in the sense 'tale-bearer'): perhaps from **TWIT**[2].

twit[2] informal ▶ verb (**twitted**, **twitting**) [with obj.] dated tease or taunt (someone), especially in a good-humoured way.
▶ noun [in sing.] N. Amer. a state of nervous excitement: *we're in a twit about your visit.*
– ORIGIN Old English *ætwītan* 'reproach with', from *æt* 'at' + *wītan* 'to blame'.

twitch ▶ verb **1** give or cause to give a short, sudden jerking or convulsive movement: [no obj.] *he saw her lips twitch and her eyelids flutter* | [with obj.] *the dog twitched his ears.*
■ [with obj. and adverbial] cause to move in a specified direction by giving a sharp pull: *he twitched a cigarette out of a packet.*
2 [with obj.] use a twitch to subdue (a horse).
▶ noun **1** a short, sudden jerking or convulsive movement: *his mouth gave a slight twitch.*
■ a sudden pull or jerk: *he gave a twitch at his moustache.* ■ a sudden sharp sensation; a pang: *he felt* ***a twitch of*** *annoyance.*
2 a stick with a small noose attached to one end. The noose may be twisted around the upper lip or the ear of a horse to subdue it, especially during veterinary procedures.
– ORIGIN Middle English: of Germanic origin; related to Old English *twiccian* 'to pluck, pull sharply'.

twitcher ▶ noun a person or thing that twitches.
■ Brit. informal a birdwatcher whose main aim is to collect sightings of rare birds.

twitch grass ▶ noun [mass noun] couch grass.
– ORIGIN late 16th cent.: *twitch*, alteration of **QUITCH**.

twitchy ▶ adjective (**twitchier**, **twitchiest**) informal nervous; anxious: *she felt twitchy about the man hovering in the background.*
■ given to twitching: *a mouse with a twitchy nose.*

twite /twʌɪt/ ▶ noun a Eurasian moorland finch related to the linnet, having streaky brown plumage with a pink rump.
• *Acanthis flavirostris*, family Fringillidae.
– ORIGIN mid 16th cent.: imitative of its call.

twitten /ˈtwɪt(ə)n/ ▶ noun Brit. dialect a narrow path or passage between two walls or hedges.
– ORIGIN early 19th cent.: perhaps related to Low German *twiete* 'alley, lane'.

twitter ▶ verb [no obj.] (of a bird) give a call consisting of repeated light tremulous sounds.
■ talk in a light, high-pitched voice: *old ladies in the congregation twittered.* ■ talk rapidly and at length in an idle or trivial way: *he* ***twittered on*** *about buying a new workshop.*
▶ noun a series of short, high-pitched calls or sounds: *his words were cut off by a faint electronic twitter.*
■ [mass noun] idle or ignorant talk: *drawing-room twitter.*
– PHRASES **in** (or **of**) **a twitter** informal in a state of agitation or excitement.
– DERIVATIVES **twitterer** noun, **twittery** adjective.
– ORIGIN late Middle English (as a verb): imitative.

'twixt ▶ contraction of betwixt.

twizzle informal or dialect ▶ verb spin or cause to spin around.
▶ noun a twisting or spinning movement.
– ORIGIN late 18th cent.: probably imitative, influenced by **TWIST**.

two ▶ cardinal number equivalent to the sum of one and one; one less than three; 2: *two years ago* | *a romantic weekend for two in Paris* | *two of Amy's friends.* (Roman numeral: **ii** or **II**.)
■ a group or unit of two people or things: *they would straggle home in ones and twos.* ■ two years old: *he is only two.* ■ two o'clock: *the pub closed at two.* ■ a size of garment or other merchandise denoted by two. ■ a playing card or domino with two pips.
– PHRASES **a —— or two** (or **two or three ——**) used to denote a small but unspecified number: *a minute or two had passed.* **be two a penny** see **PENNY**. **in two** in or into two halves or pieces: *he tore the piece of paper in two.* **in two shakes** (**of a lamb's tail**) see **SHAKE**. **it takes two to tango** see **TANGO**[1]. **put two and two together** draw an obvious conclusion from what is known or evident. ■ (**put two and two together and make five**) draw a plausible but incorrect conclusion from what is known or evident. **that makes two of us** one is in the same position or holds the same opinion as the previous speaker: *'I haven't a clue!' 'That makes two of us.'* **two by two** (or **two and two**) side by side in pairs. **two can play at that game** used to assert that another person's bad behaviour can be copied to that person's disadvantage. **two's company, three's a crowd** used to indicate that two people, especially lovers, should be left alone together. **two heads are better than one** proverb it's helpful to have the advice or opinion of a second person.
– ORIGIN Old English *twā* (feminine and neuter) of Germanic origin; related to Dutch *twee* and German *zwei*, from an Indo-European root shared by Latin and Greek *duo*. Compare with **TWAIN**.

two-bit ▶ adjective [attrib.] N. Amer. informal insignificant, cheap, or worthless: *some two-bit town.*

two-by-four ▶ noun a length of wood with a rectangular cross section nominally two inches by four inches.
■ [usu. as modifier] W. Indian & US a small or insignificant thing, typically a building: *they lived in a two-by-four shack of one bedroom.*

twoc /twɒk/ ▶ verb (**twocced**, **twoccing**) [with obj.] Brit. informal steal (a car): *people are fed up with having their cars twocced.*
– DERIVATIVES **twoccer** noun.
– ORIGIN 1990s: acronym from *taken without owner's consent.*

two-cycle ▶ adjective another term for **TWO-STROKE**.

two-dimensional ▶ adjective having or appearing to have length and breadth but no depth.
■ lacking depth or substance; superficial: *a nether world of two-dimensional heroes and villains.*
– DERIVATIVES **two-dimensionality** noun, **two-dimensionally** adverb.

t

two-edged ▶ adjective double-edged.

two-faced ▶ adjective insincere and deceitful.

two fingers ▶ plural noun [often treated as sing.] another term for **V-SIGN** (chiefly in sense 1).

two-fisted ▶ adjective US strong, virile, and straightforward.

twofold ▶ adjective twice as great or as numerous: *a twofold increase in the risk.*
■ having two parts or elements: *the twofold demands of the business and motherhood.*
▶ adverb so as to double; to twice the number or amount: *use increased more than twofold from 1979 to 1989.*

two-handed ▶ adjective & adverb having, using, or requiring the use of two hands.
– DERIVATIVES **two-handedly** adverb.

two-hander ▶ noun a play for two actors.

two-horse ▶ adjective (of a race or other contest) in which only two of the competitors or participants are likely winners.

twoness ▶ noun [mass noun] the fact or state of being two; duality.

twopence /ˈtʌp(ə)ns/ ▶ noun Brit. the sum of two pence, especially before decimalization (1971).
■ [with negative] informal a trivial sum; anything at all: *he didn't care twopence for her.*

twopenn'orth /tuːˈpɛnəθ/ ▶ noun an amount of something that is worth or costs twopence.
■ a paltry or insignificant amount.
– PHRASES **add** (or **put in**) **one's twopenn'orth** informal contribute one's opinion.

twopenny /ˈtʌp(ə)ni/ ▶ adjective [attrib.] Brit. costing or worth two pence, especially before decimalization (1971).

twopenny-halfpenny ▶ adjective Brit. informal not worthy of consideration or respect; worthless and unimportant: *a twopenny-halfpenny dictator.*

two-phase ▶ adjective (of an electric generator, motor, or other device) designed to supply or use simultaneously two separate alternating currents of the same voltage, but with phases differing by half a period.

two-piece ▶ adjective denoting something consisting of two matching items: *a two-piece suit.*
▶ noun a thing consisting of two matching parts, especially a suit.

two-ply ▶ adjective (of a material or yarn) consisting of two layers or strands.
▶ noun [mass noun] **1** a yarn consisting of two strands.
2 plywood made by gluing together two layers with the grain in different directions.

two-seater ▶ noun a vehicle or piece of furniture with seating for two people.

two shot ▶ noun a cinema or television shot of two people together.

two-sided ▶ adjective having two sides: *a colourful two-sided leaflet.*
■ having two aspects: *the two-sided nature of the debate.*

twosome ▶ noun a pair of people considered together.
■ a game or dance for or involving two people.

two-star ▶ adjective given two stars in a grading system in which this denotes a low middle standard, being the next above one-star: *a two-star award in the Michelin guide.*
■ having or denoting the fourth-highest military rank, distinguished in the US armed forces by two stars on the shoulder piece of the uniform.
▶ noun [mass noun] petrol with two-star grading.

two-state ▶ adjective capable of existing in either of two states or conditions.

two-step ▶ noun a round dance with a sliding step in march or polka time.

two-stroke ▶ adjective denoting an internal-combustion engine having its power cycle completed in one up-and-down movement of the piston.
■ denoting a vehicle having such an engine.
▶ noun a two-stroke engine or vehicle.

two-tailed ▶ adjective Statistics (of a test) testing for deviation from the null hypothesis in both directions.

two-tailed pasha ▶ noun see **PASHA**.

two-time ▶ verb [with obj.] informal deceive or be unfaithful to (a lover or spouse).
▶ adjective [attrib.] denoting someone who has done or experienced something twice: *a two-time winner of the event.*
– DERIVATIVES **two-timer** noun.

two-tone ▶ adjective having two different shades or colours: *a two-tone jacket.*
■ emitting or consisting of two different sounds, typically alternately and at intervals: *a two-tone pulse signal.*

two-toned ▶ adjective another term for **TWO-TONE**.

'twould archaic ▶ contraction of it would.

two-up ▶ noun (in Australia and New Zealand) a gambling game in which two coins are tossed in the air and bets are laid as to whether both will fall heads or tails uppermost.

two-up two-down ▶ noun Brit. informal a house with two reception rooms downstairs and two bedrooms upstairs.

two-way ▶ adjective allowing or involving movement or communication in opposite directions: *a two-way radio* | *make the interview a two-way process.*
■ (of a switch) permitting a current to be switched on or off from either of two points.
– PHRASES **two-way street** a situation or relationship involving mutual or reciprocal action or obligation: *trust is a two-way street.*

two-way mirror ▶ noun a panel of glass that can be seen through from one side and is a mirror on the other.

two-wheeler ▶ noun a bicycle or motorcycle.

TX ▶ abbreviation for Texas (in official postal use).

-ty[1] ▶ suffix forming nouns denoting quality or condition such as *beauty, royalty.*
– ORIGIN via Old French from Latin *-tas, -tat-.*

-ty[2] ▶ suffix denoting specified groups of ten: *forty* | *ninety.*
– ORIGIN Old English *-tig.*

Tyburn /ˈtaɪbəːn/ a place in London, near Marble Arch, where public hangings were held *c.*1300–1783.
– ORIGIN named after a tributary of the Thames, which flows in an underground culvert nearby.

tychism /ˈtaɪkɪz(ə)m/ ▶ noun [mass noun] Philosophy the doctrine that account must be taken of the element of chance in reasoning or explanation of the universe.
– ORIGIN late 19th cent.: from Greek *tukhē* 'chance' + **-ISM**.

Tycho Brahe see **BRAHE**.

tycoon /taɪˈkuːn/ ▶ noun **1** a wealthy, powerful person in business or industry: *a newspaper tycoon.*
2 a title applied by foreigners to the shogun of Japan in power between 1857 and 1868.
– ORIGIN mid 19th cent.: from Japanese *taikun* 'great lord'.

Tyddewi /tɪˈðewi/ Welsh name for **ST DAVID'S**.

tying present participle of **TIE**.

tying-up ▶ noun another term for **AZOTURIA** in horses.

tyke (also **tike**) ▶ noun **1** [usu. with adj.] informal a small child, especially one regarded as cheeky or badly behaved: *is the little tyke up to his tricks again?*
■ [usu. as modifier] Canadian an initiation level of sports competition for young children: *tyke hockey.*
2 dated, chiefly Brit. an unpleasant or coarse man.
3 a dog, especially a mongrel.
4 (also **Yorkshire tyke**) Brit. informal a person from Yorkshire.
5 Austral./NZ informal, derogatory a Roman Catholic. [ORIGIN: early 20th cent.: alteration of **TAIG**.]
– ORIGIN late Middle English (in senses 2 and 3): from Old Norse *tík* 'bitch'.

Tylenol /ˈtaɪlənɒl/ ▶ noun chiefly US trademark for **PARACETAMOL**.

Tyler[1], John (1790–1862), American Whig statesman, 10th President of the US 1841–5.

Tyler[2], Wat (d.1381), English leader of the Peasants' Revolt of 1381. He captured Canterbury and went on to take London and secure Richard II's concession to the rebels' demands, which included the lifting of the newly imposed poll tax. He was killed by royal supporters.

tylopod /ˈtaɪlə(ʊ)pɒd/ ▶ noun Zoology an even-toed ungulate mammal of a group that comprises the camels, llamas, and their extinct relatives. They are distinguished by bearing their weight on the sole pads of the feet rather than on the hoofs, and they do not chew the cud.
● Suborder Tylopoda, order Artiodactyla: family Camelidae.
– ORIGIN late 19th cent.: from modern Latin *Tylopoda,* from Greek *tulos* 'knob' or *tulē* 'callus, cushion' + *pous, pod-* 'foot'.

tympan /ˈtɪmpən/ ▶ noun **1** (in letterpress printing) a layer of packing, typically of paper, placed between the platen and the paper to be printed to equalize the pressure over the whole forme.
2 Architecture another term for **TYMPANUM**.
– ORIGIN late 16th cent. (in sense 1): from French *tympan* or Latin *tympanum* (see **TYMPANUM**). Sense 2 dates from the early 18th cent.

tympana plural form of **TYMPANUM**.

tympani ▶ plural noun variant spelling of **TIMPANI**.

tympanic /tɪmˈpanɪk/ ▶ adjective **1** Anatomy of, relating to, or having a tympanum.
2 resembling or acting like a drumhead.

tympanic bone ▶ noun Zoology a small bone supporting the tympanic membrane in some vertebrates.

tympanic membrane ▶ noun a membrane forming part of the organ of hearing, which vibrates in response to sound waves. In humans and other higher vertebrates it forms the eardrum, between the outer and middle ear.

tympanites /ˌtɪmpəˈnaɪtiːz/ ▶ noun [mass noun] Medicine swelling of the abdomen with air or gas.
– DERIVATIVES **tympanitic** adjective.
– ORIGIN late Middle English: via late Latin from Greek *tumpanitēs,* from *tumpanon* (see **TYMPANUM**).

tympanum /ˈtɪmpənəm/ ▶ noun (pl. **tympanums** or **tympana** /-nə/) **1** Anatomy & Zoology the tympanic membrane or eardrum.
■ Entomology a membrane covering the hearing organ on the leg or body of some insects, sometimes adapted (as in cicadas) for producing sound. ■ archaic a drum.
2 Architecture a vertical recessed triangular space forming the centre of a pediment, typically decorated.
■ a similar space over a door between the lintel and the arch.
– ORIGIN early 17th cent.: via Latin from Greek *tumpanon* 'drum', based on *tuptein* 'to strike'.

tympany /ˈtɪmpəni/ ▶ noun another term for **TYMPANITES** (used especially in veterinary medicine).
– ORIGIN early 16th cent.: from Greek *tumpanias,* from *tumpanon* (see **TYMPANUM**).

Tyndale /ˈtɪnd(ə)l/, William (*c.*1494–1536), English translator and Protestant martyr. Faced with ecclesiastical opposition to his project for translating the Bible into English, Tyndale left England in 1524. His translations of the Bible later formed the basis of the Authorized Version. He was burnt at the stake as a heretic in Antwerp.

Tyndall /ˈtɪnd(ə)l/, John (1820–93), Irish physicist. He is best known for his work on heat but he also worked on diamagnetism, the transmission of sound, and the scattering of light by suspended particles (becoming the first person to explain the blue colour of the sky).

Tyne a river in NE England, formed by the confluence of two headstreams, the North Tyne, which rises in the Cheviot Hills, and the South Tyne, which rises in the northern Pennines. It flows generally eastwards, entering the North Sea at Tynemouth.
■ a shipping forecast area covering English coastal waters roughly from Flamborough Head in the south to Berwick in the north.

Tyne and Wear /wɪə/ a metropolitan county of NE England.

Tyneside an industrial conurbation on the banks of the River Tyne, in NE England, stretching from Newcastle-upon-Tyne to the coast.
– DERIVATIVES **Tynesider** noun.

Tynwald /ˈtɪnw(ə)ld/ the parliament of the Isle of Man. It meets annually and consists of the governor (representing the sovereign) and council acting as the upper house, and an elected assembly called the House of Keys.
– ORIGIN from Old Norse *thing-vǫllr* 'place of assembly', from *thing* 'assembly' + *vǫllr* 'field'.

type ▶ noun **1** a category of people or things having common characteristics: *this type of heather grows better in a drier habitat* | *blood types.*

■a person, thing, or event considered as a representative of such a category: *it's not the type of car I'd want my daughter to drive* | *I'm an adventurous type.* ■[with adj. or noun modifier] informal a person of a specified character or nature: *two sporty types in tracksuits.* ■(**one's type**) informal the sort of person one likes or finds attractive: *she's not really my type.* ■Linguistics an abstract category or class of linguistic item or unit, as distinct from actual occurrences in speech or writing. Contrasted with **TOKEN**.

2 a person or thing symbolizing or exemplifying the ideal or defining characteristics of something: *she characterized his witty sayings as the type of modern wisdom.*

■an object, conception, or work of art serving as a model for subsequent artists. ■Botany & Zoology an organism or taxon chosen as having the essential characteristics of its group. ■short for **TYPE SPECIMEN**.

3 [mass noun] printed characters or letters: *bold or italic type.*

■[count noun] a piece of metal with a raised letter or character on its upper surface, for use in letterpress printing. ■such pieces collectively.

4 a design on either side of a medal or coin.

5 Theology a foreshadowing in the Old Testament of a person or event of the Christian dispensation.

▶**verb** [with obj.] **1** write (something) on a typewriter or computer by pressing the keys: *he* **typed out** *the second draft* | [no obj.] *I am learning how to type.*

2 Medicine determine the type to which (a person or their blood or tissue) belongs: *the kidney was typed.*

3 short for **TYPECAST**.

– PHRASES **in type** Printing composed and ready for printing.

– DERIVATIVES **typal** adjective (rare).

– ORIGIN late 15th cent. (in the sense 'symbol, emblem'): from French, or from Latin *typus*, from Greek *tupos* 'impression, figure, type', from *tuptein* 'to strike'. The use in printing dates from the early 18th cent.; the general sense 'category with common characteristics' arose in the mid 19th cent.

-type ▶**suffix** (forming adjectives) resembling or having the characteristics of a specified thing: *the dish-type radio telescope* | *a champagne-type fizzy wine.*

Type A ▶**noun** a personality type characterized by ambition, impatience, and competitiveness, and thought to be susceptible to stress and heart disease.

type approval ▶**noun** [mass noun] official confirmation from a government or other body that a manufactured item meets required specifications.

Type B ▶**noun** a personality type characterized as easy-going and thought to have low susceptibility to stress.

typecast ▶**verb** (past and past participle **-cast**) [with obj.] (usu. **be typecast**) assign (an actor or actress) repeatedly to the same type of role, as a result of the appropriateness of their appearance or previous success in such roles: *he tends to be typecast as the caring, intelligent male.*

■represent or regard (a person or their role) as a stereotype: *people are not as likely to be typecast by their accents as they once were.*

typeface ▶**noun** Printing a particular design of type.

type founder ▶**noun** Printing a designer and maker of metal type.

– DERIVATIVES **type foundry** noun.

type locality ▶**noun 1** Botany & Zoology the place in which a type specimen was found.

2 Geology a place where deposits regarded as defining the characteristics of a particular geological formation or period occur.

type metal ▶**noun** [mass noun] Printing an alloy of lead, tin, and antimony, used for casting type.

typescript ▶**noun** a typed copy of a text.

typeset ▶**verb** (**-setting**; past and past participle **-set**) [with obj.] arrange or generate the type for (a piece of text to be printed).

– DERIVATIVES **typesetting** noun.

typesetter ▶**noun** Printing a person who typesets text.

■a typesetting machine.

type site ▶**noun 1** Archaeology a site where objects or materials regarded as defining the characteristics of a particular period were found.

2 another term for **TYPE LOCALITY** (in sense 1).

type species ▶**noun** Botany & Zoology the species on which a genus is based and with which the genus name remains associated during any taxonomic revision.

type specimen ▶**noun** Botany & Zoology the specimen, or each of a set of specimens, on which the description and name of a new species is based. See also **HOLOTYPE**, **SYNTYPE**.

typewriter ▶**noun** an electric, electronic, or manual machine with keys for producing print-like characters one at a time on paper inserted round a roller.

– DERIVATIVES **typewriting** noun, **typewritten** adjective.

typhlitis /tɪˈflʌɪtɪs/ ▶**noun** [mass noun] Medicine inflammation of the caecum.

– DERIVATIVES **typhlitic** adjective.

– ORIGIN mid 19th cent.: modern Latin, from Greek *tuphlon* 'caecum or blind gut' (from *tuphlos* 'blind') + **-ITIS**.

typhoid (also **typhoid fever**) ▶**noun** [mass noun] an infectious bacterial fever with an eruption of red spots on the chest and abdomen and severe intestinal irritation.

●Typhoid is caused by the bacterium *Salmonella typhi*: Gram-negative rods.

– DERIVATIVES **typhoidal** adjective.

– ORIGIN early 19th cent.: from **TYPHUS** + **-OID**.

Typhoid Mary ▶**noun** (pl. **Typhoid Marys**) informal a transmitter of undesirable opinions, sentiments, or attitudes.

– ORIGIN the nickname of *Mary* Mallon (died 1938), an Irish-born cook who transmitted typhoid fever in the US.

typhoon /tʌɪˈfuːn/ ▶**noun** a tropical storm in the region of the Indian or western Pacific oceans.

– DERIVATIVES **typhonic** adjective.

– ORIGIN late 16th cent.: partly via Portuguese from Arabic *ṭūfān* (perhaps from Greek *tuphōn* 'whirlwind'); reinforced by Chinese dialect *tai fung* 'big wind'.

typhus /ˈtʌɪfəs/ ▶**noun** [mass noun] an infectious disease caused by rickettsiae, characterized by a purple rash, headaches, fever, and usually delirium, and historically a cause of high mortality during wars and famines. There are several forms, transmitted by vectors such as lice, ticks, mites, and rat fleas. Also called **SPOTTED FEVER**.

– DERIVATIVES **typhous** adjective.

– ORIGIN mid 17th cent.: modern Latin, from Greek *tuphos* 'smoke, stupor', from *tuphein* 'to smoke'.

typical ▶**adjective** having the distinctive qualities of a particular type of person or thing: *a typical day* | *a typical example of 1930s art deco* | *typical symptoms.*

■characteristic of a particular person or thing: *he brushed the incident aside with typical good humour.* ■informal showing the characteristics expected of or popularly associated with a particular person, situation, or thing: *'Typical woman!' John said disapprovingly.* ■representative as a symbol; symbolic: *the pit is typical of hell.*

– DERIVATIVES **typicality** /-ˈkalɪti/ noun, **typically** adverb [sentence adverb] *typically, she showed no alarm* | [as submodifier] *a typically British stiff upper lip.*

– ORIGIN early 17th cent.: from medieval Latin *typicalis*, via Latin from Greek *tupikos*, from *tupos* (see **TYPE**).

typify ▶**verb** (**-ies**, **-ied**) [with obj.] be characteristic or a representative example of: *tough, low-lying vegetation typifies this arctic area.*

■represent; symbolize: *the sun typified the Greeks, and the moon the Persians.*

– DERIVATIVES **typification** noun, **typifier** noun.

– ORIGIN mid 17th cent.: from Latin *typus* (see **TYPE**) + **-FY**.

typing ▶**noun** [mass noun] the action or skill of writing something by means of a typewriter or computer: *they learned shorthand and typing* | [as modifier] *typing errors.*

■writing produced in such a way: *five pages of typing.*

typist ▶**noun** a person who is skilled in using a typewriter or computer keyboard, especially one who is employed for this purpose.

typo /ˈtʌɪpəʊ/ ▶**noun** (pl. **-os**) informal a typographical error.

– ORIGIN early 19th cent.: abbreviation.

typography /tʌɪˈpɒɡrəfi/ ▶**noun** [mass noun] the art or process of setting and arranging types and printing from them.

■the style and appearance of printed matter.

– DERIVATIVES **typographer** noun, **typographic** adjective, **typographical** adjective, **typographically** adverb.

– ORIGIN early 17th cent.: from French *typographie* or modern Latin *typographia* (see **TYPE**, **-GRAPHY**).

typology ▶**noun** (pl. **-ies**) **1** a classification according to general type, especially in archaeology, psychology, or the social sciences: *a typology of Saxon cremation vessels.*

■[mass noun] study or analysis using such classification.

2 [mass noun] the study and interpretation of types and symbols, originally especially in the Bible.

– DERIVATIVES **typological** /-əˈlɒdʒɪk(ə)l/ adjective, **typologist** noun.

– ORIGIN mid 19th cent. (in sense 2): from Greek *tupos* 'type' + **-LOGY**.

Tyr /tɪə/ Scandinavian Mythology the god of battle, identified with Mars, after whom Tuesday is named.

tyramine /ˈtʌɪrəmiːn/ ▶**noun** [mass noun] Biochemistry a compound which occurs naturally in cheese and other foods and can cause dangerously high blood pressure in people taking a monoamine oxidase inhibitor.

●An amine related to tyrosine; chem. formula: $C_6H_4(OH)CH_2CH_2NH_2$.

– ORIGIN early 20th cent.: from *tyr(osine)* + **AMINE**.

tyrannical /tɪˈranɪk(ə)l, tʌɪ-/ ▶**adjective** exercising power in a cruel or arbitrary way: *her father was portrayed as tyrannical and unloving.*

■characteristic of tyranny; oppressive and controlling: *a momentary quieting of her tyrannical appetite.*

– DERIVATIVES **tyrannically** adverb.

– ORIGIN mid 16th cent.: from Old French *tyrannique*, via Latin from Greek *turannikos*, from *turannos* (see **TYRANT**).

tyrannicide /tɪˈranɪsʌɪd, tʌɪ-/ ▶**noun** [mass noun] the killing of a tyrant.

■[count noun] the killer of a tyrant.

– DERIVATIVES **tyrannicidal** adjective.

– ORIGIN mid 17th cent.: from French, from Latin *tyrannicida* 'killer of a tyrant', *tyrannicidium* 'killing of a tyrant' (see **TYRANT**, **-CIDE**).

tyrannize /ˈtɪrənʌɪz/ (also **-ise**) ▶**verb** [with obj.] rule or treat (someone) despotically or cruelly: *she tyrannized her family* | [no obj.] *he* **tyrannizes over** *the servants.*

– ORIGIN late 15th cent.: from French *tyranniser*, from *tyran* 'tyrant'.

tyrannosaur /tɪˈranəsɔː, tʌɪ-/ (also **tyrannosaurus** /tɪˌranəˈsɔːrəs/) ▶**noun** a very large bipedal carnivorous dinosaur of the late Cretaceous period, with powerful jaws and small claw-like front legs.

●Family Tyrannosauridae, infraorder Carnosauria, suborder Theopoda: several species, in particular *Tyrannosaurus rex*.

– ORIGIN modern Latin, from Greek *turannos* 'tyrant' + *sauros* 'lizard', on the pattern of *dinosaur*.

tyrannulet /tʌɪˈranjʊlɪt/ ▶**noun** a small tropical American bird of the tyrant flycatcher family, typically with drab greyish or greenish plumage.

●Family Tyrannidae: several genera and many species.

– ORIGIN diminutive based on modern Latin *Tyrannus* (genus name), from Greek *turannos* 'tyrant'.

tyranny ▶**noun** (pl. **-ies**) [mass noun] cruel and oppressive government or rule: *refugees who managed to escape Nazi tyranny* | [count noun] *the removal of the regime may be the end of a tyranny.*

■[count noun] a state under such cruel and oppressive government. ■cruel, unreasonable, or arbitrary use of power or control: *she resented his rages and his tyranny* | figurative *the tyranny of the nine-to-five day* | [count noun] *his father's tyrannies.* ■(especially in ancient Greece) rule by one who has absolute power without legal right.

– DERIVATIVES **tyrannous** adjective, **tyrannously** adverb.

– ORIGIN late Middle English: from Old French *tyrannie*, from late Latin *tyrannia*, from Latin *turannus* (see **TYRANT**).

tyrant /ˈtʌɪr(ə)nt/ ▶**noun 1** a cruel and oppressive ruler: *the tyrant was deposed by popular demonstrations.*

■a person exercising power or control in a cruel, unreasonable, or arbitrary way: *her father was a tyrant and a bully.* ■(especially in ancient Greece) a ruler who seized absolute power without legal right.

2 a tyrant flycatcher.

– ORIGIN Middle English: from Old French, via Latin from Greek *turannos*.

tyrant flycatcher ▶**noun** a New World perching

bird that resembles the Old World flycatchers in behaviour, typically with brightly coloured plumage.
● Family Tyrannidae: many genera and numerous species.
– ORIGIN mid 18th cent.: so named because of its aggressive behaviour towards other birds approaching its nest.

Tyre /'tʌɪə/ a port on the Mediterranean in southern Lebanon; pop. 14,000 (1988). Founded in the 2nd millennium BC as a colony of Sidon, it was for centuries a Phoenician port and trading centre.
– DERIVATIVES **Tyrian** adjective & noun.

tyre (US **tire**) ▶ noun a rubber covering, typically inflated or surrounding an inflated inner tube, placed round a wheel to form a soft contact with the road.
■ a strengthening band of metal fitted around the rim of a wheel, especially of a railway vehicle.
– ORIGIN late 15th cent. (denoting the curved pieces of iron plate with which carriage wheels were formerly shod): perhaps a variant of archaic *tire*, shortening of **ATTIRE** (because the tyre was the 'clothing' of the wheel).

tyre gauge ▶ noun a portable pressure gauge for measuring the air pressure in a tyre.

Tyrian purple ▶ noun see **PURPLE**.

tyro /'tʌɪrəʊ/ (also **tiro**) ▶ noun (pl. **-os**) a beginner or novice.
– ORIGIN late Middle English: from Latin *tiro*, medieval Latin *tyro* 'recruit'.

Tyrode's solution /'tʌɪrəʊdz/ (also **Tyrode's**) ▶ noun [mass noun] Biology & Medicine a type of physiological saline solution.
– ORIGIN 1920s: named after Maurice V. *Tyrode* (1878–1930), American pharmacologist.

Tyrol /tɪ'rəʊl/ an Alpine state of western Austria; capital, Innsbruck. The southern part was ceded to Italy after the First World War. German name **TIROL**.
– DERIVATIVES **Tyrolean** /ˌtɪrə'liːən/ adjective & noun, **Tyrolese** adjective & noun.

Tyrolean finish ▶ noun a rough-textured plaster finish for an exterior wall.

Tyrone /tɪ'rəʊn/ one of the Six Counties of Northern Ireland, formerly an administrative area; pop. 143,900 (1981); chief town, Omagh.

tyrosinase /'tʌɪrəsɪneɪz, tʌɪ'rɒs-/ ▶ noun [mass noun] Biochemistry a copper-containing enzyme which catalyses the formation of quinones from phenols and polyphenols (e.g. melanin from tyrosine).
– ORIGIN late 19th cent.: from **TYROSINE** + **-ASE**.

tyrosine /'tʌɪrəsiːn/ ▶ noun [mass noun] Biochemistry a hydrophilic amino acid which is a constituent of most proteins and is important in the synthesis of some hormones.
● Chem. formula: $C_6H_4(OH)CH_2CH(NH_2)COOH$.
– ORIGIN mid 19th cent.: formed irregularly from Greek *turos* 'cheese' + **-INE**[4].

Tyrrhene /'tɪriːn/ ▶ adjective & noun archaic term for **ETRUSCAN**.
– ORIGIN late Middle English: from Latin *Tyrrhenus* 'Etruscan'.

Tyrrhenian /tɪ'riːnɪən/ ▶ adjective of, relating to, or denoting the Tyrrhenian Sea or the surrounding region.
■ archaic Etruscan.
▶ noun archaic an Etruscan.

Tyrrhenian Sea a part of the Mediterranean Sea between mainland Italy and the islands of Sicily and Sardinia.

Tyson /'tʌɪs(ə)n/, Mike (b.1966), American boxer; full name *Michael Gerald Tyson*. He became undisputed world heavyweight champion in 1987, winning the WBA, WBC, and IBF titles. He was imprisoned in 1992 for rape; after his release in 1995 he reclaimed the WBC and WBA titles in the following year.

tystie /'tʌɪsti, 'tiːsti/ ▶ noun (pl. **-ies**) chiefly Scottish another term for **BLACK GUILLEMOT**.
– ORIGIN late 18th cent.: of Norse origin.

Tyumen /tju'mɛn/ a city in west Siberian Russia, in the eastern foothills of the Ural Mountains; pop. 487,000 (1990). Founded in 1586, it is regarded as the oldest city in Siberia.

tyuyamunite /ˌtjuːjə'muːnʌɪt/ ▶ noun [mass noun] a yellowish earthy mineral which is an ore of uranium. It consists of a hydrated vanadate of calcium and uranium.
– ORIGIN early 20th cent.: from *Tyuya Muyun*, the name of a Kyrgyz village, + **-ITE**[1].

tzar ▶ noun variant spelling of **TSAR**.

Tzara /'zɑːrə/, Tristan (1896–1963), Romanian-born French poet; born *Samuel Rosenstock*. He was one of the founders of the Dada movement and wrote its manifestos. His poetry, with its continuous flow of unconnected images, helped form the basis for surrealism.

tzarina ▶ noun variant spelling of **TSARINA**.

tzatziki /tsat'siːki/ ▶ noun [mass noun] a Greek side dish of yogurt with cucumber, garlic, and often mint.
– ORIGIN modern Greek.

tzedakah /tsɛ'dɒkə/ ▶ noun [mass noun] (among Jewish people) charitable giving, typically seen as a moral obligation.
– ORIGIN from Hebrew *sĕḏāqāh* 'righteousness'.

Tzeltal /tsɛl'tɑːl, 'tsɛltɑːl; s-/ ▶ noun (pl. same or **Tzeltals**) **1** a member of an American Indian people inhabiting parts of southern Mexico. **2** [mass noun] the Mayan language of this people.
▶ adjective of or relating to this people or their language.
– ORIGIN Spanish name of one of the three regions of the Mexican state of *Chiapas*, of uncertain origin.

tzigane /tsɪ'gɑːn/ ▶ noun (pl. same or **tziganes**) a Hungarian gypsy.
– ORIGIN mid 18th cent.: from French, from Hungarian *c(z)igány*.

tzimmes (also **tzimmis**) ▶ noun variant spelling of **TSIMMES**.

T-zone ▶ noun the central part of a person's face, including the forehead, nose, and chin, especially as having oilier skin than the rest of the face.
– ORIGIN *T* designating the shape of the area defined.

Tzotzil /'tsəʊtsɪl, tsəʊt'sɪl, s-/ ▶ noun (pl. same or **Tzotzils**) **1** a member of an American Indian people inhabiting parts of southern Mexico. **2** [mass noun] the Mayan language of this people.
▶ adjective of or relating to this people or their language.
– ORIGIN the name in Tzotzil.

Tzu-po /tsuː'pəʊ/ variant of **ZIBO**.

Uu

U¹ /juː/ (also **u**) ▶ noun (pl. **Us** or **U's**) **1** the twenty-first letter of the alphabet.
■denoting the next after T in a set of items, categories, etc.
2 (**U**) a shape like that of a capital U, especially a cross section: [in combination] *U-shaped glaciated valleys.*

U² /juː/ ▶ abbreviation for ■ (in names of sports clubs) United: *Newcastle U.* ■ Brit. universal (denoting films classified as suitable without restriction). ■ Uruguay (international vehicle registration).
▶ symbol for the chemical element uranium.

U³ /juː/ ▶ adjective informal, chiefly Brit. (of language or social behaviour) characteristic of or appropriate to the upper social classes: *U manners.*
– ORIGIN abbreviation of **UPPER CLASS**; coined in 1954 by Alan S. C. Ross, professor of linguistics, the term was popularized by its use in Nancy Mitford's *Noblesse Oblige* (1956).

U⁴ /uː/ ▶ noun a Burmese title of respect before a man's name, equivalent to Mr: *U Thien San.*

u ▶ abbreviation Physics denoting quantum states or wave functions which change sign on inversion through the origin. The opposite of **G**. [ORIGIN: from German *ungerade* 'odd'.]
▶ symbol for [in combination] (in units of measurement) micro- (10^{-6}). [ORIGIN: substituted for **MU**.]

UAE ▶ abbreviation for United Arab Emirates.

uakari /wəˈkɑːri/ ▶ noun (pl. **uakaris**) a short-tailed monkey with a long, coarse coat and a bare red, white, or black face, found in the Amazon rainforest.
● Genus *Cacajao*, family Cebidae: two or three species.
– ORIGIN mid 19th cent.: from Tupi.

UB40 ▶ noun (in the UK) a card issued to a person registered as unemployed.

ubac /ˈjuːbak/ ▶ noun Geography a mountain slope which receives little sunshine, especially one facing north. Compare with **ADRET**.
– ORIGIN 1930s: from French, apparently from Latin *opacus* 'shady'.

Ubaid /uːˈbeɪd/ ▶ adjective Archaeology of, relating to, or denoting a pre-urban culture in Mesopotamia, dated to the 5th millennium BC.
■ [as noun **the Ubaid**] the Ubaid culture or period.
– ORIGIN from the name of the tell Al '*Ubaid* near Ur in the Euphrates valley.

Ubanghi Shari /juːˌbaŋɡi ˈʃɑːri/ former name (until 1958) for **CENTRAL AFRICAN REPUBLIC**.

U-bend ▶ noun a section of a pipe, in particular of a waste pipe, shaped like a U.

Übermensch /ˈuːbəˌmɛnʃ/ ▶ noun the ideal superior man of the future who could rise above conventional Christian morality to create and impose his own values, originally described by Nietzsche in *Thus Spake Zarathustra* (1883–5). Also called **SUPERMAN** and **OVERMAN**.
– ORIGIN German, literally 'superhuman person'.

ubiety /juːˈbʌɪti/ ▶ noun [mass noun] poetic/literary the condition of being in a definite place.
– ORIGIN late 17th cent.: from medieval Latin *ubietas*, from Latin *ubi* 'where'.

-ubility ▶ suffix forming nouns from or corresponding to adjectives ending in *-uble* (such as *solubility* from *soluble*).

ubiquinone /juːˈbɪkwɪnəʊn/ ▶ noun Biochemistry any of a class of compounds which occur in all living cells and which act as electron-transfer agents in cell respiration. They are substituted quinones.
– ORIGIN 1950s: blend of **UBIQUITOUS** and **QUINONE**.

ubiquitarian /juːˌbɪkwɪˈtɛːrɪən/ Christian Theology ▶ noun a person, typically a Lutheran, who believes that Christ is present everywhere at all times.
▶ adjective relating to or believing in such a doctrine.
– DERIVATIVES **ubiquitarianism** noun.
– ORIGIN mid 17th cent.: from modern Latin *ubiquitarius* (from Latin *ubique* 'everywhere') + **-AN**.

ubiquitin /juːˈbɪkwɪtɪn/ ▶ noun [mass noun] Biochemistry a compound found in living cells which plays a role in the degradation of defective and superfluous proteins. It is a single-chain polypeptide.
– ORIGIN 1970s: from **UBIQUITOUS** + **-IN**¹.

ubiquitous /juːˈbɪkwɪtəs/ ▶ adjective present, appearing, or found everywhere: *his ubiquitous influence was felt by all the family | cowboy hats are ubiquitous among the male singers.*
– DERIVATIVES **ubiquitously** adverb, **ubiquitousness** noun, **ubiquity** noun.
– ORIGIN mid 19th cent.: from modern Latin *ubiquitas* (from Latin *ubique* 'everywhere', from *ubi* 'where') + **-OUS**.

-uble ▶ suffix (forming adjectives) able to: *voluble.*
■ able to be: *soluble.* Compare with **-ABLE**.
– ORIGIN from French, from Latin *-ubilis.*

-ubly ▶ suffix forming adverbs corresponding to adjectives ending in *-uble* (such as *volubly* corresponding to *voluble*).

U-boat ▶ noun a German submarine used in the First or Second World War.
– ORIGIN from German *U-boot*, abbreviation of *Unterseeboot* 'undersea boat'.

UBR ▶ abbreviation for uniform business rate (a tax on business property in England and Wales).

ubuntu /ʊˈbʊntʊ/ ▶ noun [mass noun] S. African a quality that includes the essential human virtues; compassion and humanity.
– ORIGIN Xhosa and Zulu.

UC ▶ abbreviation for University College.

u.c. ▶ abbreviation for upper case.

UCAS /ˈjuːkas/ ▶ abbreviation for (in the UK) Universities and Colleges Admissions Service (created by the amalgamation of UCCA and PCAS in the 1993–4 academic year).

UCCA /ˈʌkə/ ▶ abbreviation for (in the UK) Universities Central Council on Admissions (incorporated into UCAS in the 1993–4 academic year).

Uccello /uːˈtʃɛləʊ, uˈtsɛllo/, Paolo (c.1397–1475), Italian painter; born *Paolo di Dono*. His paintings are associated with the early use of perspective and include *The Rout of San Romano* (c.1454–7) and *A Hunt in a Forest* (after 1460), one of the earliest known paintings on canvas.

UDA ▶ abbreviation for Ulster Defence Association (a Loyalist paramilitary organization).

udal /ˈjuːd(ə)l/ ▶ noun [mass noun] Law a kind of freehold tenure based on uninterrupted possession, formerly practised in northern Europe and still in use in Orkney and Shetland.
– ORIGIN late 15th cent.: from Old Norse *othal* 'property held by inheritance', of Germanic origin.

UDC ▶ abbreviation for ■ (in the UK) Urban Development Corporation. ■ historical (in the UK) Urban District Council.

udder ▶ noun the mammary gland of female cattle, sheep, goats, horses, and related ungulates, hanging near the hind legs as a bag-like organ with two or more teats.
– DERIVATIVES **uddered** adjective [in combination].
– ORIGIN Old English *ūder*, of West Germanic origin; related to Dutch *uier* and German *Euter*.

UDI ▶ abbreviation for unilateral declaration of independence.

Udmurt /ˈʊdmʊət/ ▶ noun **1** a member of a people of central Russia, living mainly in Udmurtia.
2 [mass noun] the Finno-Ugric language of this people, with about 500,000 speakers. Formerly called **VOTYAK**.
▶ adjective of, relating to, or denoting this people or their language.

Udmurtia /ʊdˈmʊətɪə/ an autonomous republic in central Russia; pop. 1,619,000 (1990); capital, Izhevsk. Also called **UDMURT REPUBLIC** /ˈʊdmʊət/.

udon /ˈuːdɒn/ ▶ noun [mass noun] (in Japanese cookery) wheat pasta made in thick strips.
– ORIGIN Japanese.

UDR ▶ abbreviation for Ulster Defence Regiment (a former reserve unit of the British army based in Northern Ireland).

UEFA /juːˈiːfə, -ˈeɪfə/ ▶ abbreviation for Union of European Football Associations, the governing body of soccer in Europe.

UF ▶ abbreviation for urea-formaldehyde.

Ufa /uːˈfɑː/ the capital of Bashkiria, in the Ural Mountains; pop. 1,094,000 (1990).

Uffizi /ʊˈfiːtsi/ an art gallery and museum in Florence, housing one of Europe's finest art collections.

UFO ▶ noun (pl. **UFOs**) a mysterious object seen in the sky for which it is claimed no orthodox scientific explanation can be found.
– ORIGIN 1950s: acronym from *unidentified flying object.*

ufology /juːˈfɒlədʒi/ ▶ noun [mass noun] the study of UFOs.
– DERIVATIVES **ufological** adjective, **ufologist** noun.

ugali /uːˈɡɑːli/ ▶ noun [mass noun] a type of maize porridge eaten in east and central Africa.
– ORIGIN Kiswahili.

Uganda /juːˈɡandə/ a landlocked country in East Africa; pop. 16,876,000 (est. 1991); languages, English (official), Swahili, and other languages; capital, Kampala.

Ethnically and culturally diverse, Uganda became a British protectorate in 1894 and an independent Commonwealth state in 1962. The country was ruled 1971–9 by the brutal dictator Idi Amin, who came to power after an army coup. His overthrow, with Tanzanian military support, was followed by several years of conflict, partly resolved in 1986 by the formation of a government under President Yoweri Museveni.

– DERIVATIVES **Ugandan** adjective & noun.

Ugarit /ʊˈɡɑːrɪt, ˈjuːɡərɪt/ an ancient port and

Bronze Age trading city in northern Syria, founded in Neolithic times and destroyed by the Sea Peoples in about the 12th century BC. Its people spoke a Semitic language written in a distinctive cuneiform alphabet.
- DERIVATIVES **Ugaritic** /ˌjuːgəˈrɪtɪk/ adjective & noun.

ugh ▶ exclamation informal used to express disgust or horror: *Ugh—what's this disgusting object?*
- ORIGIN mid 18th cent.: imitative.

Ugli fruit /ˈʌɡli/ ▶ noun (pl. same) trademark a mottled green and yellow citrus fruit which is a hybrid of a grapefruit and tangerine.
- This fruit is obtained from the tree *Citrus × tangelo*, family Rutaceae.
- ORIGIN 1930s: *ugli*, alteration of UGLY.

ugly ▶ adjective (**uglier, ugliest**) unpleasant or repulsive, especially in appearance: *she thought she was ugly and fat* | *the ugly sound of a fire alarm* | [as noun **the ugly**] *he instinctively shrinks from the ugly.*
- ■ (of a situation or mood) involving or likely to involve violence or other unpleasantness: *the mood in the room turned ugly.* ■ unpleasantly suggestive; causing disquiet: *ugly rumours persisted that there had been a cover-up.* ■ morally repugnant: *racism and its most ugly manifestations, racial attacks and harassment.*
- DERIVATIVES **uglification** noun, **uglify** verb, **uglily** adverb, **ugliness** noun.
- ORIGIN Middle English: from Old Norse *uggligr* 'to be dreaded', from *ugga* 'to dread'.

ugly American ▶ noun informal an American who behaves offensively when abroad.

ugly duckling ▶ noun a person who turns out to be beautiful or talented against all expectations.
- ORIGIN from the title of one of Hans Christian Andersen's fairy tales, in which the 'ugly duckling' becomes a swan.

Ugrian /ˈuːɡrɪən, ˈjuː-/ ▶ adjective another term for UGRIC.

Ugric /ˈuːɡrɪk, ˈjuː-/ ▶ adjective of, relating to, or denoting a branch of the Finno-Ugric language family including only Hungarian and the Ob-Ugric languages.
- ORIGIN from Russian *ugry* (the name of a people dwelling east of the Urals) + -IC.

uh[1] ▶ exclamation **1** used to express hesitation: *I was just, uh, passing by.*
2 used in questions to invite agreement or further comment or to express a lack of understanding: *You want to get there pretty bad, uh?*
- ORIGIN 1960s: imitative.

uh[2] ▶ determiner non-standard spelling of the indefinite article A[1], used to represent black English: *crabs in uh basket.*
▶ preposition non-standard spelling of OF, used to represent black English: *a house full uh young 'uns.*

UHF ▶ abbreviation for ultra-high frequency.

uh-huh ▶ exclamation used to express assent or as a non-committal response to a question or remark: *'Do you understand?' 'Uh-huh.'*
- ORIGIN 1920s: imitative.

uhlan /ˈuːlɑːn, ˈjuː-, ʊˈlɑːn/ ▶ noun historical a cavalryman armed with a lance as a member of various European armies.
- ORIGIN mid 18th cent.: via French and German from Polish (h)*ulan*, from Turkish *oğlan* 'youth, servant'.

uh-oh ▶ exclamation an expression of alarm, dismay, or realization of a difficulty: *'Uh-oh! Take cover!'*

UHT ▶ abbreviation for ultra heat treated (a process typically used to extend the shelf life of milk).

uh-uh ▶ exclamation used to express a negative response to a question or remark.
- ORIGIN 1920s: imitative.

Uighur /ˈwiːɡə/ (also **Uigur, Uygur**) ▶ noun **1** a member of a Turkic people of NW China, particularly the Xinjiang region, and adjoining areas.
2 [mass noun] the Turkic language of this people, which has about 7 million speakers.
▶ adjective of or relating to this people or their language.
- ORIGIN the name in Uighur.

uillean pipes /ˈɪlɪn, ˈɪlən/ ▶ plural noun Irish bagpipes played resting on the knee using bellows worked by the elbow, and having three extra pipes on which chords can be played.
- ORIGIN early 20th cent.: from Irish *píob uilleann*, literally 'pipe of the elbow'.

uintathere /juːˈɪntəθɪə/ ▶ noun an early fossil hoofed mammal of the Eocene epoch, with a heavy rhinoceros-like body and a grotesque head with several bony horn-like swellings and long canine teeth.
- Family Uintatheriidae, order Dinocerata, including *Uintatherium.*
- ORIGIN late 19th cent.: from modern Latin *Uintatherium*, from *Uinta*(h), the name of a mountain range in Utah, US (where remains were found), + Greek *thērion* 'wild beast'.

Uist /ˈjuːɪst/ two islands in the Outer Hebrides, **North Uist** and **South Uist**, lying to the south of Lewis and Harris and separated from each other by the island of Benbecula.

ujamaa /ˌʊdʒɑːˈmɑː/ ▶ noun [mass noun] (in Tanzania) a socialist system of village cooperatives based on equality of opportunity and self-help, established in the 1960s.
- ORIGIN Kiswahili, literally 'brotherhood', from *jamaa* 'family', from Arabic *jamāʿa* 'community'.

Ujiyamada /ˌuːjɪjɑːˈmɑːdə/ former name (until 1956) for ISE.

Ujjain /ˈuːdʒʌɪn/ a city in west central India, in Madhya Pradesh; pop. 376,000 (1991).

Ujung Pandang /uːˌdʒʊŋ panˈdaŋ/ the chief seaport of the island of Sulawesi in Indonesia; pop. 944,300 (1990). Former name (until 1973) MAKASSAR.

UK ▶ abbreviation for United Kingdom.

UKAEA ▶ abbreviation for United Kingdom Atomic Energy Authority.

ukase /juːˈkeɪz/ ▶ noun (in tsarist Russia) a decree with the force of law.
- ■ an arbitrary or peremptory command.
- ORIGIN from Russian *ukaz* 'ordinance, edict', from *ukazat* 'show, decree'.

uke ▶ noun informal short for UKULELE.

ukiyo-e /uːˌkiːjəʊˈeɪ/ ▶ noun [mass noun] a school of Japanese art depicting subjects from everyday life, dominant in the 17th–19th centuries.
- ORIGIN Japanese, from *ukiyo* 'fleeting world' + *e* 'picture'.

Ukraine /juːˈkreɪn/ (also **the Ukraine**) a country in eastern Europe, to the north of the Black Sea; pop. 51,999,000 (est. 1991); languages, Ukrainian and Russian; capital, Kiev.

Ukraine was united with Russia, with the capital at Kiev, in the 9th century. After a period of division between Poland, Russia, and the Ottoman Empire it was reunited with Russia in 1785. Briefly independent following the 1917 revolution, it became one of the original constituent republics (and the third largest) of the USSR. In 1991, on the break-up of the Soviet Union, Ukraine became an independent republic within the Commonwealth of Independent States.

- ORIGIN from obsolete Russian *ukraina* 'frontier regions', from *u* 'at' + *krai* 'edge'.

Ukrainian ▶ noun **1** a native or national of Ukraine, or a person of Ukrainian descent.
2 [mass noun] the Eastern Slavic language of Ukraine, which has about 60 million speakers worldwide.
▶ adjective of or relating to Ukraine, its people, or their language.

ukulele /ˌjuːkəˈleɪli/ ▶ noun a small four-stringed guitar of Hawaiian origin.
- ORIGIN late 19th cent.: from Hawaiian, literally 'jumping flea'.

Ulala /ˌuːlɑːˈlɑː/ former name (until 1932) for GORNO-ALTAISK.

ulama ▶ noun variant spelling of ULEMA.

Ulan Bator /ˌuːlɑːn ˈbɑːtə/ (also **Ulaanbaatar**) the capital of Mongolia; pop. 575,000 (1990). Former name (until 1924) URGA.

Ulanova /uːˈlɑːnəvə/, Galina (Sergeevna) (1910–98), Russian ballet dancer. She gave notable interpretations of *Swan Lake* and *Giselle*, and also danced the leading roles, composed especially for her, in all three of Prokofiev's ballets.

Ulan-Ude /uːˌlɑːnuːˈdeɪ/ an industrial city in southern Siberian Russia, capital of the republic of Buryatia; pop. 359,000 (1990). Former name (until 1934) VERKHNEUDINSK.

-ular ▶ suffix forming adjectives, sometimes corresponding to nouns ending in *-ule* (such as *pustular* corresponding to *pustule*), but often without diminutive force (as in *angular, granular*).
- DERIVATIVES **-ularity** suffix forming corresponding nouns.

- ORIGIN from Latin *-ularis*.

ulcer ▶ noun an open sore on an external or internal surface of the body, caused by a break in the skin or mucous membrane which fails to heal. Ulcers range from small, painful sores in the mouth to bedsores and serious lesions of the stomach or intestine.
- ■ figurative a moral blemish or corrupting influence: *he's a con man with an incurable ulcer called gambling.*
- DERIVATIVES **ulcered** adjective, **ulcerous** adjective.
- ORIGIN late Middle English: from Latin *ulcus, ulcer-*.

ulcerate ▶ verb [no obj.] develop into or become affected by an ulcer.
- DERIVATIVES **ulceration** noun, **ulcerative** adjective.
- ORIGIN late Middle English: from Latin *ulcerat-* 'made ulcerous', from the verb *ulcerare.*

-ule ▶ suffix forming diminutive nouns such as *capsule, pustule.*
- ORIGIN from Latin *-ulus, -ula, -ulum.*

Uleåborg /ˌuːlɛəʊˈbɔːrj/ Swedish name for OULU.

ulema /ˈʊləmə, ˈuːlɪmə, uːlɪˈmɑː/ (also **ulama**) ▶ noun [treated as sing. or pl.] a body of Muslim scholars who are recognized as having specialist knowledge of Islamic sacred law and theology.
- ■ a member of such a body.
- ORIGIN from Arabic *ʿulamā*, plural of *ʿalim* 'learned', from *ʿalima* 'know'.

-ulent ▶ suffix (forming adjectives) abounding in; full of: *fraudulent* | *purulent*. Compare with -LENT.
- DERIVATIVES **-ulence** suffix forming corresponding nouns.
- ORIGIN from Latin *-ulentus.*

ulexite /ˈjuːlɛksʌɪt/ ▶ noun [mass noun] a mineral occurring on alkali flats as rounded masses of small white crystals. It is a hydrated borate of sodium and calcium.
- ORIGIN mid 19th cent.: from George L. *Ulex* (died 1883), German chemist, + -ITE[1].

Ulfilas /ˈʊlfɪlas/ (also **Wulfila**) (c.311–c.381), bishop and translator. Believed to be of Cappadocian descent, he became bishop of the Visigoths in 341. His translation of the Bible from Greek into Gothic (of which fragments survive) is the earliest known translation of the Bible into a Germanic language. Ulfilas is traditionally held to have invented the Gothic alphabet, based on Latin and Greek characters.

Ulhasnagar /ˌuːlhəsˈnʌɡə/ a city in western India, in the state of Maharashtra; pop. 369,000 (1991).

ullage /ˈʌlɪdʒ/ ▶ noun [mass noun] the amount by which a container falls short of being full.
- ■ loss of liquid, by evaporation or leakage.
- ORIGIN late Middle English: from Anglo-Norman French *ulliage*, from Old French *euillier* 'fill up', based on Latin *oculus* 'eye' (with reference to a container's bunghole).

ullage rocket ▶ noun an auxiliary rocket engine used in weightless conditions to provide sufficient acceleration to maintain the flow of liquid propellant from the tank.

Ulm /ʊlm/ an industrial city on the Danube in Baden-Württemberg, southern Germany; pop. 112,170 (1991).

ulmo /ˈʌlməʊ/ ▶ noun a Chilean eucryphia tree which is sometimes cultivated as an ornamental.
- *Eucryphia cordifolia*, family Eucryphiaceae.
- ORIGIN Spanish.

ulna /ˈʌlnə/ ▶ noun (pl. **ulnae** /-niː/ or **ulnas**) the thinner and longer of the two bones in the human forearm, on the side opposite to the thumb. Compare with RADIUS (in sense 2).
- ■ the corresponding bone in a quadruped's foreleg or a bird's wing.
- DERIVATIVES **ulnar** adjective.
- ORIGIN late Middle English (denoting the humerus): from Latin; related to ELL[1].

U-lock ▶ noun another term for D-LOCK.

-ulous ▶ suffix forming adjectives such as *incredulous, garrulous.*
- ORIGIN from Latin *-ulosus, -ulus.*

Ulpian /ˈʌlpɪən/ (died c.228), Roman jurist, born in Phoenicia; Latin name *Domitius Ulpianus*. His numerous legal writings provided one of the chief sources for Justinian's *Digest* of 533.

Ulsan /uːlˈsɑːn/ an industrial port on the south coast of South Korea; pop. 682,980 (1990).

Ulster a former province of Ireland, in the north of the island. The nine counties of Ulster are now

divided between Northern Ireland (Antrim, Down, Armagh, Londonderry, Tyrone, and Fermanagh) and the Republic of Ireland (Cavan, Donegal, and Monaghan).
■(in general use) Northern Ireland.
– DERIVATIVES **Ulsterman** noun (pl. **-men**), **Ulsterwoman** noun (pl. **-women**).

ulster ▶ **noun** a man's long, loose overcoat of rough cloth, typically with a belt at the back.
– ORIGIN late 19th cent.: from **ULSTER**, where it was originally sold.

Ulster Democratic Unionist Party an extreme Loyalist political party in Northern Ireland, co-founded by Ian Paisley in 1972.

Ulster Unionist Council (abbrev.: **UUC**) a political party in Northern Ireland seeking to maintain the union with Britain. Founded in 1905, the UUC is regarded as being more moderate than the Ulster Democratic Unionist Party.

ult. ▶ **abbreviation for** ■ ultimate. ■ ultimo.

ulterior ▶ **adjective** existing beyond what is obvious or admitted; intentionally hidden: *could there be an ulterior motive behind his request?*
■beyond what is immediate or present; coming in the future: *ulterior pay promised to the mariners.*
– ORIGIN mid 17th cent.: from Latin, literally 'further, more distant'.

ultimata plural form of **ULTIMATUM**.

ultimate ▶ **adjective** being or happening at the end of a process; final: *their ultimate aim was to force his resignation.*
■being the best or most extreme example of its kind: *the ultimate accolade.* ■ basic or fundamental: *the ultimate constituents of anything that exists are atoms.* ■ Physics denoting the maximum possible strength or resistance beyond which an object breaks.
▶ **noun 1** (**the ultimate**) the best achievable or imaginable of its kind: ***the ultimate in** decorative luxury.*
2 a final or fundamental fact or principle.
– DERIVATIVES **ultimacy** noun (pl. **-ies**), **ultimately** adverb.
– ORIGIN mid 17th cent.: from late Latin *ultimatus*, past participle of *ultimare* 'come to an end'.

ultima Thule ▶ **noun** a distant unknown region; the extreme limit of travel and discovery.
– ORIGIN Latin, literally 'furthest Thule' (see **THULE**).

ultimatum ▶ **noun** (pl. **ultimatums** or **ultimata** /-tə/) a final demand or statement of terms, the rejection of which will result in retaliation or a breakdown in relations: *the British government **issued an ultimatum to** Hitler to cease invasion of Poland.*
– ORIGIN mid 18th cent.: from Latin, neuter past participle of *ultimare* 'come to an end'.

ultimo /ˈʌltɪməʊ/ (abbrev.: **ult.** or **ulto**) ▶ **adjective** [postpositive] dated of last month: *the 3rd ultimo.*
– ORIGIN from Latin *ultimo mense* 'in the last month'.

ultimobranchial /ˌʌltɪmə(ʊ)ˈbraŋkɪəl/ ▶ **adjective** Zoology relating to or denoting a gland in the neck which in many lower vertebrates regulates the calcium level in the body.

ultisol /ˈʌltɪsɒl/ ▶ **noun** Soil Science a highly weathered leached red or reddish-yellow acid soil with a clay-rich B horizon, occurring in warm, humid climates.
– ORIGIN 1960s: from **ULTIMATE** + Latin *solum* 'soil'.

ultra informal ▶ **noun** an extremist.
▶ **adverb** [as submodifier] very: *ultra modern furniture.*
– ORIGIN early 19th cent.: an independent usage of **ULTRA-**, originally as an abbreviation of French *ultra-royaliste*.

ultra- ▶ **prefix 1** beyond; on the other side of: *ultramontane.* Often contrasted with **CIS-**.
2 extreme; to an extreme degree: *ultramicroscopic.*
– ORIGIN from Latin *ultra* 'beyond'.

ultrabasic ▶ **adjective** Geology relating to or denoting igneous rocks having a silica content less than 45 per cent by weight.

ultracentrifuge ▶ **noun** a very fast centrifuge used to precipitate large biological molecules from solution or separate them by their different rates of sedimentation.
▶ **verb** [with obj.] subject to the action of an ultracentrifuge.
– DERIVATIVES **ultracentrifugation** noun.

ultracold ▶ **adjective** Physics (of a neutron) having an energy of the order of 10^{-7} eV or less.

ultradian /ʌlˈtreɪdɪən/ ▶ **adjective** Physiology (of a rhythm or cycle) having a period of recurrence shorter than a day but longer than an hour. Compare with **INFRADIAN**.
– ORIGIN 1960s: from **ULTRA-** 'beyond' (being of greater frequency than circadian) + **-IAN**.

ultrafiltration ▶ **noun** [mass noun] filtration using a medium fine enough to retain colloidal particles, viruses, or large molecules.

ultra-high frequency (abbrev.: **UHF**) ▶ **noun** a radio frequency in the range 300 to 3,000 MHz.

ultraist ▶ **noun** a holder of extreme opinions.
– DERIVATIVES **ultraism** noun.

ultralight ▶ **adjective** extremely lightweight.
▶ **noun** chiefly N. Amer. another term for **MICROLIGHT**.

ultramafic /ˌʌltrəˈmafɪk/ ▶ **adjective** Geology relating to or denoting igneous rocks composed chiefly of mafic minerals.

ultramarine ▶ **noun** [mass noun] a brilliant deep blue pigment originally obtained from lapis lazuli.
■an imitation of such a pigment, made from powdered fired clay, sodium carbonate, sulphur, and resin. ■ a brilliant deep blue colour.
– ORIGIN late 16th cent.: from medieval Latin *ultramarinus* 'beyond the sea'; the name of the pigment is from obsolete Italian (*azzurro*) *oltramarino*, literally '(azure) from overseas'.

ultramicroscope ▶ **noun** an optical microscope used to detect particles smaller than the wavelength of light by illuminating them at an angle and observing the light scattered by the Tyndall effect against a dark background.

ultramicroscopic ▶ **adjective** too small to be seen by an ordinary optical microscope.
■of or relating to an ultramicroscope.

ultramontane /ˌʌltrəˈmɒnteɪn/ ▶ **adjective 1** advocating supreme papal authority in matters of faith and discipline. Compare with **GALLICAN**.
2 situated on the other side of the Alps from the point of view of the speaker.
▶ **noun** a person advocating supreme papal authority.
– DERIVATIVES **ultramontanism** noun.
– ORIGIN late 16th cent. (denoting a representative of the Roman Catholic Church north of the Alps): from medieval Latin *ultramontanus*, from Latin *ultra* 'beyond' + *mons, mont-* 'mountain'.

ultramundane /ˌʌltrəˈmʌndeɪn/ ▶ **adjective** poetic/literary existing outside the known world, the solar system, or the universe.
– ORIGIN mid 17th cent.: from late Latin *ultramundanus*, from *ultra* 'beyond' + *mundanus* (from *mundus* 'world').

ultrasaurus /ˈʌltrəsɔːrəs/ ▶ **noun** a late Jurassic dinosaur related to brachiosaurus, known from only a few bones but probably the tallest ever animal, and possibly the heaviest at up to 130 tons.
● Genus *Ultrasaurus*, infraorder Sauropoda, order Saurischia.
– ORIGIN modern Latin, from Latin *ultra* 'beyond' + Greek *sauros* 'lizard'.

ultrashort ▶ **adjective** (of radio waves) having a wavelength significantly shorter than that of the usual short waves, in particular shorter than 10 metres (i.e. of a VHF frequency above 30 MHz).

ultrasonic ▶ **adjective** of or involving sound waves with a frequency above the upper limit of human hearing.
– DERIVATIVES **ultrasonically** adverb.

ultrasonics ▶ **plural noun** [treated as sing.] the science and application of ultrasonic waves.
■[treated as sing. or pl.] ultrasonic waves; ultrasound.

ultrasonography /ˌʌltrəsəˈnɒɡrəfi/ ▶ **noun** [mass noun] Medicine a technique using echoes of ultrasound pulses to delineate objects or areas of different density in the body.
– DERIVATIVES **ultrasonographic** adjective.

ultrasound ▶ **noun** [mass noun] sound or other vibrations having an ultrasonic frequency, particularly as used in medical imaging.
■[count noun] an ultrasound scan, especially one of a pregnant woman to examine the fetus.

ultrastructure ▶ **noun** Biology fine structure, especially within a cell, that can be seen only with the high magnification obtainable with an electron microscope.

ultraviolet Physics ▶ **adjective** (of electromagnetic radiation) having a wavelength shorter than that of the violet end of the visible spectrum but longer than that of X-rays.
■(of equipment or techniques) using or concerned with this radiation: *an ultraviolet telescope.*
▶ **noun** [mass noun] the ultraviolet part of the spectrum; ultraviolet radiation.

> Ultraviolet radiation spans wavelengths from about 10 nm to 400 nm, and is an important component of sunlight, although the ozone layer prevents much of it from reaching the earth's surface. While ultraviolet is necessary for the production of vitamin D_2 in the skin, it is now known that excessive exposure can be harmful, causing skin cancer and genetic mutation.

ultra vires /ˌʌltrə ˈvʌɪriːz, ˌʊltrɑː ˈviːreɪz/ ▶ **adjective & adverb** Law beyond one's legal power or authority: [as adj.] *jurisdictional errors render the decision ultra vires.*
– ORIGIN Latin, literally 'beyond the powers'.

ulu /ˈuːluː/ ▶ **noun** (pl. **ulus**) an Eskimo woman's short-handled knife with a broad crescent-shaped blade.
– ORIGIN Inuit.

ululate /ˈjuːljʊleɪt, ˈʌl-/ ▶ **verb** [no obj.] howl or wail as an expression of strong emotion, typically grief: *women were ululating as the body was laid out.*
– DERIVATIVES **ululant** adjective, **ululation** noun.
– ORIGIN early 17th cent.: from Latin *ululat-* 'howled, shrieked', from the verb *ululare*, of imitative origin.

Ulundi /ʊˈlʊndi/ a town in KwaZulu/Natal, South Africa, formerly capital of Zululand and KwaZulu.

Uluru /ʊˈlʊəruː/ Aboriginal name for **AYERS ROCK**.

Ulyanov /uːlˈjɑːnɒf/, Vladimir Ilich, see **LENIN**.

Ulyanovsk /uːlˈjɑːnəfsk/ former name (1924–92) for **SIMBIRSK**.

Ulysses /ˈjuːlɪsiːz/ **1** Roman Mythology Roman name for **ODYSSEUS**.
2 a space probe of the European Space Agency, launched in 1990 to investigate the polar regions of the sun.

um ▶ **exclamation** expressing hesitation or a pause in speech: *anyway, um, where was I?*
– ORIGIN natural utterance: first recorded in English in the early 17th cent.

-um ▶ **suffix** variant spelling of **-IUM** (in sense 1).

U-matic ▶ **noun** [mass noun] trademark a system for recording and playing audio-visual material and videos, mainly restricted to professional use.
– ORIGIN 1970s: *U* from the shape of the path followed by the tape around the drum and heads of the machine + *-matic* from **AUTOMATIC**.

Umayyad /ʊˈmʌɪjad/ (also **Omayyad**) ▶ **noun** a member of a Muslim dynasty that ruled the Islamic world from AD 660 (or 661) to 750 and Moorish Spain 756–1031. The dynasty claimed descent from Umayya, a distant relative of Muhammad.
▶ **adjective** of or relating to this dynasty.

Umayyad Mosque a mosque in Damascus, Syria, built AD 705–15 on the site of a church dedicated to St John the Baptist.

Umbanda /ʊmˈbandə/ ▶ **noun** [mass noun] a Brazilian folk religion combining elements of macumba, Roman Catholicism, and South American Indian practices.
– ORIGIN Portuguese.

umbel /ˈʌmb(ə)l/ ▶ **noun** Botany a flower cluster in which stalks of nearly equal length spring from a common centre and form a flat or curved surface, characteristic of the parsley family.
– DERIVATIVES **umbellate** adjective.
– ORIGIN late 16th cent.: from obsolete French *umbelle* or Latin *umbella* 'sunshade', diminutive of *umbra* (see **UMBRA**).

umbellifer /ʌmˈbɛlɪfə/ ▶ **noun** Botany a plant of the parsley family.
● Family Umbelliferae: numerous genera and species.
– DERIVATIVES **umbelliferous** adjective.
– ORIGIN early 18th cent.: from obsolete French *umbellifère*, from Latin *umbella* 'parasol' + *-fer* 'bearing'.

umber /ˈʌmbə/ ▶ **noun 1** [mass noun] a natural pigment resembling but darker than ochre, normally dark yellowish-brown in colour (**raw umber**) or dark brown when roasted (**burnt umber**).
■the colour of this pigment.
2 a brownish moth with colouring that resembles tree bark.
● Several species in the family Geometridae, including the **mottled umber** (*Erannis defoliaria*), whose female is wingless and the caterpillar a pest of trees and fruit bushes.
– ORIGIN mid 16th cent.: from French (*terre d'*)*ombre* or Italian (*terra di*) *ombra*, literally '(earth of) shadow', from Latin *umbra* 'shadow' or *Umbra* (feminine) 'Umbrian'.

umbilical /ʌmˈbɪlɪk(ə)l, ˌʌmbɪˈlʌɪk(ə)l/ ▶ adjective relating to or affecting the navel or umbilical cord: *the umbilical artery.*
■ figurative extremely close; inseparable: *the umbilical link between commerce and international rugby.* ■ (of a pipe or cable) connecting someone or something to a source of essential supplies.
▶ noun short for UMBILICAL CORD.
− DERIVATIVES **umbilically** adverb.
− ORIGIN mid 16th cent.: from French *ombilical*, or based on Latin *umbilicus* (see UMBILICUS).

umbilical cord ▶ noun a flexible cord-like structure containing blood vessels and attaching a human or other mammalian fetus to the placenta during gestation.
■ a flexible cable, pipe, or other line carrying essential services or supplies.

umbilicate /ʌmˈbɪlɪkət/ ▶ adjective Botany & Zoology (especially of the cap of a fungus) having a central depression.
■ (of a shell) having an umbilicus.

umbilicus /ʌmˈbɪlɪkəs, ˌʌmbɪˈlʌɪkəs/ ▶ noun (pl. **umbilici** /-sʌɪ/ or **umbilicuses**) Anatomy the navel.
■ Zoology a depression or hole at the centre of the shell whorls of some gastropod molluscs and many ammonites. ■ Zoology a hole at each end of the hollow shaft of a feather.
− ORIGIN late 17th cent.: from Latin: related to Greek *omphalos*, also to NAVEL.

umbles ▶ plural noun variant spelling of NUMBLES.

umbo /ˈʌmbəʊ/ ▶ noun (pl. **umbones** /-ˈbəʊniːz/ or **umbos**) **1** historical the central boss of a shield.
2 Biology a rounded knob or protuberance.
■ Zoology the highest point of each valve of a bivalve shell. ■ Botany a central swelling on the cap of a mushroom or toadstool.
− DERIVATIVES **umbonal** adjective (chiefly Zoology), **umbonate** adjective (chiefly Botany).
− ORIGIN early 18th cent.: from Latin, 'shield boss'.

umbra /ˈʌmbrə/ ▶ noun (pl. **umbras** or **umbrae** /-briː/) the fully shaded inner region of a shadow cast by an opaque object, especially the area on the earth or moon experiencing the total phase of an eclipse. Compare with PENUMBRA.
■ Astronomy the dark central part of a sunspot. ■ [mass noun] chiefly poetic/literary shadow or darkness.
− DERIVATIVES **umbral** adjective.
− ORIGIN late 16th cent. (denoting a phantom or ghost): from Latin, literally 'shade'.

umbrage /ˈʌmbrɪdʒ/ ▶ noun [mass noun] **1** offence or annoyance: *she took umbrage at his remarks.*
2 archaic shade or shadow, especially as cast by trees.
− DERIVATIVES **umbrageous** adjective.
− ORIGIN late Middle English (in sense 2): from Old French, from Latin *umbra* 'shadow'. An early sense was 'shadowy outline', giving rise to 'ground for suspicion', whence the current notion of 'offence'.

umbrella ▶ noun **1** a device consisting of a circular canopy of cloth on a folding metal frame supported by a central rod, used as protection against rain.
■ figurative a protecting force or influence: *the American nuclear umbrella over the west.* ■ a screen of fighter aircraft or anti-aircraft artillery. ■ [usu. as modifier] a thing that includes or contains many different elements or parts: *an umbrella organization.*
2 Zoology the gelatinous disc of a jellyfish, which it contracts and expands to move through the water.
− DERIVATIVES **umbrellaed** adjective, **umbrella-like** adjective.
− ORIGIN early 17th cent.: from Italian *ombrella*, diminutive of *ombra* 'shade', from Latin *umbra* (see UMBRA).

umbrellabird ▶ noun a large tropical American cotinga with black plumage, a radiating crest, and typically long wattles.
● Genus *Cephalopterus*, family Cotingidae: three species.

umbrella fund ▶ noun an offshore investment fund which invests only in other investment funds.

umbrella pine ▶ noun **1** another term for STONE PINE.
2 a tall Japanese evergreen conifer related to the redwoods, with leaves growing in umbrella-like whorls.
● *Sciadopitys verticillata*, family Taxodiaceae.

umbrella plant ▶ noun a tropical Old World sedge which has stiff green stems, each terminating in a whorl of arching green leaf-like bracts. It is commonly grown as a house plant.
● *Cyperus involucratus*, family Cyperaceae.

umbrella tree ▶ noun either of two small trees or shrubs with leaves or leaflets arranged in umbrella-like whorls:
● an Australian plant which is widely grown elsewhere as a house plant (*Schefflera actinophylla*, family Araliaceae). ● a North American magnolia (*Magnolia tripetala*, family Magnoliaceae).

Umbria /ˈʌmbrɪə/ a region of central Italy, in the valley of the Tiber; capital, Perugia.

Umbrian ▶ adjective of or relating to Umbria, its people, or their languages.
▶ noun **1** a native or inhabitant of Umbria, especially in pre-Roman times.
2 [mass noun] an extinct Italic language of central Italy, related to Oscan and surviving in inscriptions mainly of the 2nd and 1st centuries BC.

Umbrian School a Renaissance school of Italian painting, to which Raphael and Perugino belonged.

Umbriel /ˈʌmbrɪəl/ Astronomy a satellite of Uranus, the thirteenth closest to the planet, discovered in 1851 (diameter 1,190 km).
− ORIGIN named after a sprite in *The Rape of the Lock* by Alexander Pope.

umbriferous /ʌmˈbrɪf(ə)rəs/ ▶ adjective poetic/literary providing shade.
− ORIGIN early 17th cent.: from Latin *umbrifer* (from *umbra* 'shade' + *-fer* 'bearing') + -OUS.

Umbundu see MBUNDU.

Umeå /ˈuːmɛɔː/ a city in NE Sweden, on an inlet of the Gulf of Bothnia; pop. 91,260 (1990).

umfaan /ʊmˈfɑːn, ʌm-/ ▶ noun (pl. **umfaans**, **abafana**, or **bafana**) S. African (among Zulu-speaking people) a young man who has gone through initiation but is not yet married.
■ offensive a black male domestic servant.
− ORIGIN from Zulu *umfana* 'boy'.

umiak /ˈuːmɪak/ ▶ noun an Eskimo open boat made of wood and skin, traditionally rowed by women.
− ORIGIN from Inuit *umiaq*.

umlaut /ˈʊmlaʊt/ Linguistics ▶ noun a mark (¨) used over a vowel, especially in German, to indicate a different vowel quality.
■ [mass noun] the process in Germanic languages by which the quality of a vowel was altered in certain phonetic contexts, resulting for example in the differences between modern German *Mann* and *Männer*.
▶ verb [with obj.] modify (a form or a sound) by using an umlaut.
− ORIGIN mid 19th cent.: from German *Umlaut*, from *um* 'about' + *Laut* 'sound'.

umma /ˈʊmə/ (also **ummah**) ▶ noun the whole community of Muslims bound together by ties of religion.
− ORIGIN Arabic, literally 'people, community'.

Umm al Qaiwain /ˌʊm al kʌɪˈwʌɪn/ one of the seven member states of the United Arab Emirates; pop. 35,100 (1995).

ump ▶ noun informal, chiefly N. Amer. an umpire.
− ORIGIN early 20th cent.: abbreviation.

umph ▶ noun variant spelling of OOMPH.

umpire ▶ noun (in some sports) an official who watches a game or match closely to enforce the rules and arbitrate on matters arising from the play.
■ a person chosen to arbitrate between contending parties.
▶ verb [no obj.] act as an umpire.
■ [with obj.] act as umpire in (a game or match).
− DERIVATIVES **umpirage** noun, **umpireship** noun.
− ORIGIN late Middle English (originally as *noumpere*) (denoting an arbitrator): from Old French *nonper* 'not equal'. The *n* was lost by wrong division of *a noumpere*; compare with ADDER[1].

umpteen informal ▶ cardinal number indefinitely many; a lot of: *you need umpteen pieces of identification to cash a cheque* | *umpteen of them arrived at once.*
− DERIVATIVES **umpteenth** ordinal number.
− ORIGIN early 20th cent.: humorous formation based on -TEEN.

Umtali /ʊmˈtɑːli/ former name (until 1982) for MUTARE.

umu /ˈʊmʊ/ ▶ noun a Maori oven consisting of a hollow in the earth in which food is cooked on heated stones.
− ORIGIN Maori.

Umwelt /ˈʊmvɛlt/ ▶ noun (pl. **Umwelten** /-t(ə)n/) (in ethology) the world as it is experienced by a particular organism.

− ORIGIN German, literally 'environment'.

UN ▶ abbreviation for United Nations.

un-[1] ▶ prefix **1** (added to adjectives, participles, and their derivatives) denoting the absence of a quality or state; not: *unabashed* | *unacademic* | *unrepeatable.*
■ the reverse of (usually with an implication of approval or disapproval, or with another special connotation): *unselfish* | *unprepossessing* | *unworldly.*
2 (added to nouns) a lack of: *unrest* | *untruth.*
− ORIGIN Old English, of Germanic origin; from an Indo-European root shared by Latin *in-* and Greek *a-*.

USAGE The prefixes **un-** and **non-** both mean 'not', but there is often a distinction in terms of emphasis. **un-** tends to be stronger and less neutral than **non-**: consider the differences between **unacademic** and **non-academic**, for example (*his language was refreshingly unacademic; a non-academic life suits him*).

un-[2] ▶ prefix added to verbs: **1** denoting the reversal or cancellation of an action or state: *untie* | *unsettle.*
2 denoting deprivation, separation, or reduction to a lesser state: *unmask* | *unman.*
■ denoting release: *unburden* | *unhand.*
− ORIGIN Old English *un-*, *on-*, of Germanic origin; related to Dutch *ont-* and German *ent-*.

'un informal ▶ contraction of one: *a good 'un* | *a wild 'un.*

UNA ▶ abbreviation for United Nations Association.

unabashed ▶ adjective not embarrassed, disconcerted, or ashamed: *he was unabashed by the furore his words provoked.*
− DERIVATIVES **unabashedly** adverb.

unabated ▶ adjective without any reduction in intensity or strength: *the storm was raging unabated.*
− DERIVATIVES **unabatedly** adverb.

unable ▶ adjective [with infinitive] lacking the skill, means, or opportunity to do something: *she was unable to conceal her surprise.*

unabridged ▶ adjective (of a text) not cut or shortened; complete: *an unabridged edition.*

unabsorbed ▶ adjective not taken in or soaked up; not absorbed: *unabsorbed nutrients.*

unacademic ▶ adjective not adopting or characteristic of a scholarly approach or language: *his language was refreshingly unacademic.*
■ (of a person) not suited or drawn to academic study.

unaccented ▶ adjective having no accent, stress, or emphasis: *his English is fluent and unaccented.*

unacceptable ▶ adjective not satisfactory or allowable: *unacceptable behaviour.*
− DERIVATIVES **unacceptability** noun, **unacceptably** adverb.

unaccommodating ▶ adjective not fitting in with the wishes or demands of others; unhelpful.

unaccompanied ▶ adjective having no companion or escort: *no unaccompanied children allowed.*
■ (of a piece of music) sung or played without instrumental accompaniment: *they sang unaccompanied.* ■ (of a state, condition, or event) taking place without something specified taking place at the same time: *the political change was unaccompanied by social change.*

unaccomplished ▶ adjective **1** showing little skill.
2 not accomplished or carried out.

unaccountable ▶ adjective **1** unable to be explained: *a strange and unaccountable fact.*
■ (of a person or their behaviour) unpredictable and strange.
2 (of a person, organization, or institution) not required or expected to justify actions or decisions; not responsible for results or consequences.
− DERIVATIVES **unaccountability** noun, **unaccountably** adverb.

unaccounted ▶ adjective (**unaccounted for**) not included in (an account or calculation) through being lost or disregarded: *a substantial amount of money is unaccounted for.*

unaccustomed ▶ adjective not familiar or usual; out of the ordinary: *they finished their supper with unaccustomed speed.*
■ [predic.] (**unaccustomed to**) not familiar with or used to: *the visitors were unaccustomed to country roads.*
− DERIVATIVES **unaccustomedly** adverb.

unacknowledged ▶ adjective (of a state, action, or event) existing or having taken place but not

accepted, recognized, or admitted to: *her unacknowledged feelings.*
■ (of a person or their work) deserving but not receiving praise or recognition.

una corda /ˌuːnə ˈkɔːdə/ Music ▶ adverb & adjective (especially as a direction) using the soft pedal on a piano.
▶ noun a device in a piano that shifts the mechanism slightly to one side when the soft pedal is depressed, so that the hammers do not strike all of the strings when sounding each note and the tone is therefore quieter.
– ORIGIN Italian, literally 'one string'.

unacquainted ▶ adjective [predic.] (**unacquainted with**) having no experience of or familiarity with: *I regret that I am unacquainted with the place.*
■ (of two or more people) not having met before; not knowing each other.

unaddressed ▶ adjective **1** not considered or dealt with: *wider questions remain unaddressed.*
2 (of a letter or other item sent in the post) having no address written or printed on it.

unadjusted ▶ adjective (especially of figures or statistics) not adjusted or refined: *the unadjusted jobless total increased last month.*

unadopted ▶ adjective Brit. (of a road) taken over for maintenance by a local authority.

unadorned ▶ adjective not adorned; plain.

unadulterated ▶ adjective not mixed or diluted with any different or extra elements; complete and absolute: *pure, unadulterated jealousy.*
■ (of food or drink) having no inferior added substances; pure: *unadulterated whole-milk yogurt.*

unadventurous ▶ adjective not offering, involving, or eager for new or stimulating things: *he was the unadventurous type | an unadventurous menu.*
– DERIVATIVES **unadventurously** adverb.

unadvertised ▶ adjective existing or taking place without being made public.

unadvisable ▶ adjective another term for **INADVISABLE**.

unadvisedly ▶ adverb in an unwise or rash manner: *they enter into nothing lightly or unadvisedly.*

unaesthetic ▶ adjective not visually pleasing; unattractive.
■ not motivated by aesthetic principles.

unaffected ▶ adjective **1** feeling or showing no effects or changes: *the walks are suitable only for people who are unaffected by vertigo.*
2 (of a person) without artificiality or insincerity.
– DERIVATIVES **unaffectedly** adverb, **unaffectedness** noun.

unaffectionate ▶ adjective feeling, showing, or having no fondness or tenderness.

unaffiliated ▶ adjective not officially attached to or connected with an organization or group.

unaffordable ▶ adjective too expensive to be afforded by the average person: *medical care has become unaffordable.*

unafraid ▶ adjective [predic.] feeling no fear or anxiety: *she was calm and unafraid.*

unaggressive ▶ adjective tending not to attack without provocation; not hostile or violent.

unaided ▶ adjective needing or having no assistance; without help: *she can no longer walk unaided.*

unalienable ▶ adjective another term for **INALIENABLE**.

unaligned ▶ adjective not placed or arranged in a straight line, in parallel, or in correct relative positions.
■ not allied with or giving support to a particular organization or cause.

unalike ▶ adjective [predic.] (of two or more subjects) differing from each other; not similar: *they are unalike in personality.*

unalleviated ▶ adjective not alleviated; relentless: *a time of unalleviated misery.*

unalloyed ▶ adjective (of metal) not alloyed; pure: *unalloyed copper.*
■ (chiefly of emotions) complete and unreserved: *unalloyed delight.*

unalterable ▶ adjective not able to be changed.
– DERIVATIVES **unalterableness** noun, **unalterably** adverb.

unaltered ▶ adjective remaining the same; unchanged: *many buildings survive unaltered.*

unambiguous ▶ adjective not open to more than one interpretation: *instructions should be unambiguous.*
– DERIVATIVES **unambiguity** noun, **unambiguously** adverb.

unambitious ▶ adjective not motivated or driven by a strong desire or determination to succeed.
■ (of a plan or piece of work) not involving anything new, exciting, or demanding.
– DERIVATIVES **unambitiously** adverb, **unambitiousness** noun.

unambivalent ▶ adjective having or showing no mixed feelings or contradictory ideas.
– DERIVATIVES **unambivalently** adverb.

un-American ▶ adjective not in accordance with American characteristics: *such un-American concepts as subsidized medicine and free education.*
■ US, chiefly historical contrary to the interests of the US and therefore treasonable.
– DERIVATIVES **un-Americanism** noun.

Unami /uːˈnɒmi/ ▶ noun see **DELAWARE**[2] (in sense 2).
– ORIGIN the name in Unami.

unamiable ▶ adjective not having a friendly manner; not pleasant.

unamplified ▶ adjective not amplified.

unamused ▶ adjective not responding in a positive way to something intended to be amusing; feeling somewhat annoyed or disapproving: *she was unamused by some of the things written about her.*

unanalysable (US **unanalyzable**) ▶ adjective not able to be explained or interpreted through methodical examination: *unanalysable recorded data.*

unanalysed (US **unanalyzed**) ▶ adjective not revealed, explained, or interpreted through methodical examination.

unanchored ▶ adjective not anchored or securely fixed.

unaneled /ˌʌnəˈniːld/ ▶ adjective archaic having died without receiving extreme unction; unanointed.

Unani /juːˈnɑːni/ ▶ noun [mass noun] [usu. as modifier] a system of medicine practised in parts of India, thought to be derived via medieval Muslim physicians from Byzantine Greece. It is sometimes contrasted with the Ayurvedic system.
– ORIGIN from Arabic *Yūnānī* 'Greek'.

unanimous /juːˈnanɪməs/ ▶ adjective (of two or more people) fully in agreement: *the doctors were unanimous in their diagnoses.*
■ (of an opinion, decision, or vote) held or carried by everyone involved.
– DERIVATIVES **unanimity** /ˌjuːnəˈnɪmɪti/ noun, **unanimously** adverb.
– ORIGIN early 17th cent.: from Latin *unanimus* (from *unus* 'one' + *animus* 'mind') + **-ous**.

unannounced ▶ adjective not made known; not publicized.
■ without previous notice or arrangement and therefore unexpected: *he arrived unannounced.*

unanswerable ▶ adjective unable to be answered: *unanswerable questions concerning our own mortality.*
■ unable to be disclaimed or proved wrong: *the case for abolishing the fee is unanswerable.*
– DERIVATIVES **unanswerably** adverb.

unanswered ▶ adjective not answered or responded to: *unanswered letters.*

unanticipated ▶ adjective not expected or predicted.

unapologetic ▶ adjective not acknowledging or expressing regret: *he remained unapologetic about his decision.*
– DERIVATIVES **unapologetically** adverb.

unapparent ▶ adjective not visible or in evidence.

unappealable ▶ adjective Law (of a case or ruling) not able to be referred to a higher court for review.

unappealing ▶ adjective not inviting or attractive: *the company faces some unappealing choices.*
– DERIVATIVES **unappealingly** adverb.

unappeasable ▶ adjective not able to be pacified, placated, or satisfied.

unappeased ▶ adjective not pacified, placated, or satisfied.

unappetizing (also **-ising**) ▶ adjective not inviting or attractive; unwholesome.
– DERIVATIVES **unappetizingly** adverb.

unappreciated ▶ adjective not fully understood, recognized, or valued: *she had been brought up in a family where she felt unappreciated and undervalued.*

unappreciative ▶ adjective not fully understanding, recognizing, or valuing something: *they were unappreciative of country problems.*

unapprehended ▶ adjective **1** not perceived or understood.
2 not seized in the name of the law; not arrested.

unapproachable ▶ adjective (of a person or institution) not welcoming or friendly.
■ archaic (of a place) remote and inaccessible.
– DERIVATIVES **unapproachability** noun, **unapproachably** adverb.

unapproved ▶ adjective not officially accepted or sanctioned: *they deposit waste on unapproved sites.*

unapt ▶ adjective not appropriate or suitable in the circumstances: *it is not an unapt word.*
– DERIVATIVES **unaptly** adverb, **unaptness** noun.

unarguable ▶ adjective not open to disagreement; indisputable: *unarguable proof of conspiracy.*
■ not able to be discussed or asserted.
– DERIVATIVES **unarguably** adverb.

unarmed ▶ adjective not equipped with or carrying weapons: *he was shooting unarmed civilians.*

unarmed combat ▶ noun [mass noun] a mode of combat in which weapons are not used.

unarticulated ▶ adjective not mentioned or coherently expressed: *repressed hurt and previously unarticulated anger are explored.*

unary /ˈjuːnəri/ ▶ adjective (especially of a mathematical operation) consisting of or involving a single component or element.

unashamed ▶ adjective expressed or acting openly and without guilt or embarrassment: *an unashamed emotionalism.*
– DERIVATIVES **unashamedly** adverb, **unashamedness** noun.

unasked ▶ adjective (of a question) not asked.
■ (of an action) not invited or requested: *the memories he had poured unasked into her head.* ■ (**unasked for**) not sought or requested: *unasked-for advice.*

unassailable ▶ adjective unable to be attacked, questioned, or defeated: *an unassailable lead.*
– DERIVATIVES **unassailability** noun, **unassailably** adverb.

unassertive ▶ adjective (of a person) not having or showing a confident and forceful personality.
– DERIVATIVES **unassertively** adverb, **unassertiveness** noun.

unassigned ▶ adjective not allocated or set aside for a specific purpose.

unassimilated ▶ adjective (especially of a people, an idea, or a culture) not absorbed or integrated into a wider society or culture.
– DERIVATIVES **unassimilable** adjective.

unassisted ▶ adjective not helped by anyone or anything: *medically unassisted births | I could never find the place unassisted.*

unassociated ▶ adjective not connected or associated: *the issue is being raised by thousands of unassociated individuals.*

unassuaged ▶ adjective not soothed or relieved: *her unassuaged grief.*
– DERIVATIVES **unassuageable** adjective.

unassuming ▶ adjective not pretentious or arrogant; modest: *he was an unassuming and kindly man.*
– DERIVATIVES **unassumingly** adverb, **unassumingness** noun.

unattached ▶ adjective not working for or belonging to a particular body or organization.
■ not married or having an established partner; single.

unattainable ▶ adjective not able to be reached or achieved: *an unattainable goal.*
– DERIVATIVES **unattainableness** noun, **unattainably** adverb.

unattempted ▶ adjective not previously attempted or embarked upon; untried.

unattended ▶ adjective not noticed or dealt with: *her behaviour went unnoticed and unattended to.*
■ not supervised or looked after: *it is not acceptable for parents to leave children unattended at that age.*

unattractive ▶ adjective not pleasing or appealing to look at.

■having no inviting or beneficial features: *if the revised bid is unattractive, it may not be accepted.*
– DERIVATIVES **unattractively** adverb, **unattractiveness** noun.

unattributed ▶ adjective (of a quotation, story, or work of art) not ascribed to any source; of unknown or unpublished provenance.
– DERIVATIVES **unattributable** adjective, **unattributably** adverb.

unaudited ▶ adjective (of financial accounts) not having been officially examined.

unauthentic ▶ adjective not made or done in a way that reflects tradition or faithfully resembles an original.
– DERIVATIVES **unauthentically** adverb.

unauthenticated ▶ adjective not proven or validated: *an unauthenticated report.*

unauthorized (also **-ised**) ▶ adjective not having official permission or approval: *an unauthorized meeting.*

unavailable ▶ adjective not able to be used or obtained; not at someone's disposal: *material which is unavailable to the researcher.*
■(of a person) not free to do something; otherwise occupied: *the men were unavailable for work.*
– DERIVATIVES **unavailability** noun.

unavailing ▶ adjective achieving little or nothing; ineffective: *their efforts were unavailing.*
– DERIVATIVES **unavailingly** adverb.

unavoidable ▶ adjective not able to be avoided, prevented, or ignored; inevitable: *the natural and unavoidable consequences of growing old.*
– DERIVATIVES **unavoidability** noun, **unavoidably** adverb.

unavowed ▶ adjective not openly or publicly declared; unstated: *an underlying, unavowed hostility.*

unawakened ▶ adjective not aware of or roused to particular sensations or feelings.

unaware ▶ adjective [predic.] having no knowledge of a situation or fact: *they were unaware of his absence.*
▶ adverb variant of **UNAWARES**.
– DERIVATIVES **unawareness** noun.

unawares (also **unaware**) ▶ adverb without being aware of a situation: *the photographer had caught her unawares.*
– ORIGIN mid 16th cent.: from **UNAWARE** + **-S**³.

unawed ▶ adjective not filled with awe.

unbacked ▶ adjective **1** having no financial, material, or moral support.
2 (of a horse) having no backers in a race.
3 having no backing layer: *unbacked hessian.*

unbalance ▶ verb [with obj.] make (someone or something) unsteady so that they tip or fall.
■upset or disturb the equilibrium of (a state of affairs or someone's state of mind): *this sharing can often unbalance even the closest of relationships.*
▶ noun a lack of symmetry, balance, or stability.

unbalanced ▶ adjective not keeping or showing an even balance; not evenly distributed.
■(of a person) emotionally or mentally disturbed. ■(of an account) not giving accurate, fair, or equal coverage to all aspects; partial: *this may give an unbalanced impression of the competition.*

unban ▶ verb (**unbanned**, **unbanning**) [with obj.] remove a ban on (a person, group, or activity).

unbar ▶ verb (**unbarred**, **unbarring**) [with obj.] remove the bars from (a gate or door); unlock.

unbearable ▶ adjective not able to be endured or tolerated: *the heat was getting unbearable.*
– DERIVATIVES **unbearableness** noun, **unbearably** adverb [as submodifier] *it was unbearably hot.*

unbeatable ▶ adjective not able to be defeated or exceeded in a contest or commercial market: *the shop sells bikes at unbeatable prices.*
■extremely good; outstanding: *views from the patio are unbeatable.*

unbeaten ▶ adjective not defeated or surpassed: *they were the only side to remain unbeaten.*
■Cricket (of a batsman) not out in his or her side's innings.

unbeautiful ▶ adjective without beauty.
– DERIVATIVES **unbeautifully** adverb.

unbecoming ▶ adjective (especially of clothing or a colour) not flattering: *a stout lady in an unbecoming striped sundress.*
■(of a person's attitude or behaviour) not fitting or appropriate; unseemly: *it was unbecoming for a university to do anything so crass as advertising its wares.*
– DERIVATIVES **unbecomingly** adverb, **unbecomingness** noun.

unbefitting ▶ adjective not appropriate; unsuitable: *unbefitting conduct.*
– DERIVATIVES **unbefittingly** adverb, **unbefittingness** noun.

unbeholden ▶ adjective formal owing no one any duty or thanks; free of any obligation.

unbeknown (also **unbeknownst**) ▶ adjective [predic.] (**unbeknown to**) without the knowledge of (someone): *unbeknown to me, she made some enquiries.*
– ORIGIN mid 17th cent.: from **UN**-¹ 'not' + archaic *beknown* 'known'.

unbelief ▶ noun [mass noun] lack of religious belief; an absence of faith.
– DERIVATIVES **unbeliever** noun, **unbelieving** adjective, **unbelievingly** adverb.

unbelievable ▶ adjective not able to be believed; unlikely to be true: *unbelievable or not, it happened.*
■so great or extreme as to be difficult to believe; extraordinary: *your audacity is unbelievable.*
– DERIVATIVES **unbelievability** noun, **unbelievably** adverb [as submodifier] *he worked unbelievably long hours.*

unbeloved ▶ adjective not loved: *he is unbeloved of the society in which his creations are set.*

unbelt ▶ verb [with obj.] remove or undo the belt of (a garment): *he unbelted his kimono.*

unbelted ▶ adjective (of a garment) without a belt.
■(of a person) not wearing a belt, in particular a vehicle seat belt.

unbend ▶ verb (past and past participle **unbent**) **1** make or become straight from a bent or twisted form or position: [with obj.] *I had trouble unbending my cramped knees* | [no obj.] *he unbent from the cockpit as she passed.*
■[no obj.] become less reserved, formal, or strict: *you could be fun too, you know, if you'd only unbend a little.*
2 [with obj.] Sailing unfasten (sails) from yards and stays.
■cast (a cable) loose. ■ untie (a rope).

unbending ▶ adjective reserved, formal, or strict in one's behaviour or attitudes; austere and inflexible.
– DERIVATIVES **unbendingly** adverb, **unbendingness** noun.

unbiased (also **unbiassed**) ▶ adjective showing no prejudice for or against something; impartial.

unbiblical ▶ adjective not found in, authorized by, or based on the Bible.

unbiddable ▶ adjective not easily controlled; unruly or disobedient.

unbidden ▶ adjective without having been commanded or invited: *unbidden guests.*
■(especially of a thought or feeling) arising without conscious effort: *unbidden tears came to his eyes.*

unbind ▶ verb (past and past participle **unbound**) [with obj.] release from bonds or restraints.

unbirthday ▶ noun humorous any day except one's birthday: [as modifier] *an unbirthday present.*
– ORIGIN 1871: coined by Lewis Carroll in *Through the Looking Glass.*

unbleached ▶ adjective (especially of paper or cloth) not made whiter or lighter by a chemical process: *unbleached cotton.*

unblemished ▶ adjective not damaged or marked in any way.

unblended ▶ adjective not mixed with other types of the same substance: *unblended whisky.*

unblessed (also **unblest**) ▶ adjective not blessed: *to us, unblessed by our own children, he was almost a son.*

unblind ▶ verb [with obj.] conduct (a test or experiment) in such a way that it is not blind.

unblinking ▶ adjective (of a person or their gaze or eyes) not blinking.
– DERIVATIVES **unblinkingly** adverb.

unblock ▶ verb [with obj.] remove an obstruction from (something, especially a pipe or drain).
■Bridge play in such a way that (a long suit) becomes established.

unblown ▶ adjective informal (of a vehicle or its engine) not provided with a turbocharger.

unblushing ▶ adjective not feeling or showing embarrassment or shame.
– DERIVATIVES **unblushingly** adverb.

unbolt ▶ verb [with obj.] open (a door or window) by drawing back a bolt.

unbookish ▶ adjective not particularly interested in reading and studying.

unborn ▶ adjective (of a baby) not yet born.

unbosom ▶ verb [with obj.] archaic disclose (one's thoughts or secrets): *she unbosomed herself to a trusty female friend.*

unbothered ▶ adjective showing or feeling a lack of concern about or interest in something: *she was unbothered by the mess in the sink.*

unbound¹ ▶ adjective not bound or tied up: *her hair was unbound* | figurative *they were unbound by convention.*
■(of printed sheets) not bound together. ■ (of a bound book) not provided with a proper or permanent cover. ■ Chemistry & Physics not held by a chemical bond, gravity, or other physical force: *unbound electrons.*

unbound² past and past participle of **UNBIND**.

unbounded ▶ adjective having or appearing to have no limits: *the possibilities are unbounded.*
– DERIVATIVES **unboundedly** adverb, **unboundedness** noun.

unbowed ▶ adjective not having submitted to pressure or demands: *they are unbowed by centuries of colonial rule.*

unbrace ▶ verb [with obj.] remove a support from.

unbranded ▶ adjective **1** (of a product) not bearing a brand name: *unbranded computer systems.*
2 (of livestock) not branded with the owner's mark.

unbreachable ▶ adjective not able to be breached or overcome: *a virtually unbreachable position.*

unbreakable ▶ adjective not liable to break or able to be broken easily: *the flask is guaranteed unbreakable* | *an unbreakable code.*

unbreathable ▶ adjective (of air) not fit or pleasant to breathe.

unbribable ▶ adjective (of a person) not susceptible to bribery.

unbridgeable ▶ adjective (of a gap or difference) not able to be bridged or made less significant: *a seemingly unbridgeable cultural abyss.*

unbridled ▶ adjective uncontrolled; unconstrained: *a moment of unbridled ambition* | *unbridled lust.*

unbroken ▶ adjective not broken, fractured, or damaged: *an unbroken glass.*
■not interrupted or disturbed; continuous: *a night of sleep unbroken by nightmares.* ■(of a record) not surpassed: *a 13-year unbroken record of increasing profits.* ■(of a horse) not tamed or accustomed to being ridden. ■(of land) not cultivated.
– DERIVATIVES **unbrokenly** adverb, **unbrokenness** noun.

unbruised ▶ adjective not bruised.

unbuckle ▶ verb [with obj.] unfasten the buckle of (something, especially a belt or shoe).

unbuild ▶ verb (past and past participle **unbuilt**) [with obj.] demolish or destroy (something, especially a building or system).
■[as adj. **unbuilt**] (of buildings or land) not yet built or built on: *a slope of unbuilt land.*

unbundle ▶ verb [with obj.] **1** market or charge for (items or services) separately rather than as part of a package.
2 split (a company or conglomerate) into its constituent businesses, especially prior to selling them off.
– DERIVATIVES **unbundler** noun (only in sense 2).

unburden ▶ verb [with obj.] relieve (someone) of something that is causing anxiety or distress: *the need to unburden yourself to someone who will listen.*
■(usu. **be unburdened**) not cause (someone) hardship or distress: *they are unburdened by expectations of success.*

unburied ▶ adjective (especially of a dead body) not buried.

unburnt (also **unburned**) ▶ adjective not damaged or destroyed by fire.
■(especially of bricks) not exposed to heat in a kiln.

unbury ▶ verb (**-ies**, **-ied**) [with obj.] remove (something) from under the ground.

unbusinesslike ▶ adjective not businesslike.

unbutton ▶ verb [with obj.] unfasten the buttons of (a garment).
■[no obj.] informal relax and become less inhibited: *unbutton a little, Molly.*

uncaged ▶ adjective released from or not confined in a cage.

uncalled ▶ adjective not summoned or invited.

■**(uncalled for)** (especially of a person's behaviour) undesirable and unnecessary: *uncalled-for remarks.*

uncanny ▶ adjective (**uncannier, uncanniest**) strange or mysterious, especially in an unsettling way: *an uncanny feeling that she was being watched.*
– DERIVATIVES **uncannily** adverb, **uncanniness** noun.
– ORIGIN late 16th cent. (originally Scots in the sense 'relating to the occult, malicious'): from **UN-**[1] 'not' + **CANNY.**

uncanonical ▶ adjective not conforming to or ordered by canon law.
■not belonging to a literary or other canon.
– DERIVATIVES **uncanonically** adverb.

uncap ▶ verb (**uncapped, uncapping**) [with obj.] remove the lid or cover from.
■remove a limit or restriction on (a price, rate, or amount).

uncapped ▶ adjective chiefly Brit. (of a player) never having been chosen as a member of a particular sports team, especially a national one.

uncared ▶ adjective (**uncared for**) not looked after properly: *it was sad to see the old place uncared for and neglected.*

uncaring ▶ adjective not displaying sympathy or concern for others: *an uncaring father.*
■not feeling interest in or attaching importance to something: *she had always been uncaring of her appearance.*
– DERIVATIVES **uncaringly** adverb.

uncarpeted ▶ adjective (of a floor) not covered with a carpet or carpeting.

uncase ▶ verb [with obj.] remove from a cover or case.

uncashed ▶ adjective (of a cheque or money order) not yet cashed.

uncatchable ▶ adjective not able to be caught, in particular (of an athlete or sports team) not able or likely to be equalled or bettered.

unceasing ▶ adjective not coming to an end; continuous: *the unceasing efforts of the staff.*
– DERIVATIVES **unceasingly** adverb.

uncelebrated ▶ adjective not publicly acclaimed: *an uncelebrated but indispensable role.*

uncensored ▶ adjective not censored.

unceremonious ▶ adjective having or showing a lack of courtesy or dignity; rough or abrupt: *he was known for his strong views and unceremonious manners.*
– DERIVATIVES **unceremoniously** adverb, **unceremoniousness** noun.

uncertain ▶ adjective not able to be relied on; not known or definite: *an uncertain future.*
■(of a person) not completely confident or sure of something: *I was uncertain how to proceed.*
– PHRASES **in no uncertain terms** clearly and forcefully: *she has already refused me, in no uncertain terms.*
– DERIVATIVES **uncertainly** adverb.

uncertainty ▶ noun (pl. **-ies**) [mass noun] the state of being uncertain: *times of uncertainty and danger.*
■[count noun] (usu. **uncertainties**) something that is uncertain or that causes one to feel uncertain: *financial uncertainties.*

uncertainty principle ▶ noun Physics the principle that the momentum and position of a particle cannot both be precisely determined at the same time.

uncertified ▶ adjective not officially recognized as having a certain status or meeting certain standards: *uncertified accountants.*
■not attested or confirmed in a formal statement.

unchain ▶ verb [with obj.] remove the chains fastening or securing (someone or something).

unchallengeable ▶ adjective not able to be disputed, opposed, or defeated: *the unchallengeable truth of these basic facts.*
– DERIVATIVES **unchallengeably** adverb.

unchallenged ▶ adjective not disputed or questioned: *the report's findings did not go unchallenged.*
■(especially of a person in power) not opposed or defeated: *a position of unchallenged supremacy.* ■not called on to prove one's identity or allegiance: *they walked unchallenged into a hospital and stole a baby.*

unchallenging ▶ adjective (of a task or situation) not testing one's abilities: *my job was unchallenging.*
■not threatening someone's position: *his voice was gentle and unchallenging.*

---

unchancy ▶ adjective (**unchancier, unchanciest**) chiefly Scottish unlucky, inauspicious, or dangerous.

unchangeable ▶ adjective not liable to variation or able to be altered: *personality characteristics are virtually unchangeable.*
– DERIVATIVES **unchangeability** noun, **unchangeableness** noun, **unchangeably** adverb.

unchanged ▶ adjective not changed; unaltered: *an unchanged side for tonight's home game.*

unchanging ▶ adjective not changing; remaining the same: *the party stood for unchanging principles.*
– DERIVATIVES **unchangingly** adverb.

unchaperoned ▶ adjective unaccompanied; unsupervised.

uncharacteristic ▶ adjective not typical of a particular person or thing: *an uncharacteristic display of temper.*
– DERIVATIVES **uncharacteristically** adverb.

uncharged ▶ adjective not charged, in particular:
■not accused of an offence under the law: *she was released uncharged.* ■ not carrying an electric charge. ■ not charged to a particular account: *an uncharged fixed cost.*

uncharismatic ▶ adjective lacking the charm and attractiveness that can inspire enthusiasm in others.

uncharitable ▶ adjective (of a person's behaviour or attitude towards others) unkind; unsympathetic: *this uncharitable remark possibly arose out of jealousy.*
– DERIVATIVES **uncharitableness** noun, **uncharitably** adverb.

uncharted ▶ adjective (of an area of land or sea) not mapped or surveyed.

unchartered ▶ adjective not having a charter or written constitution.

unchaste ▶ adjective relating to or engaging in sexual activity, especially of an illicit or extramarital nature: *unchaste subjects in art.*
– DERIVATIVES **unchastely** adverb, **unchastity** noun.

unchastened ▶ adjective (of a person) not restrained or subdued: *he was unchastened and ready for fresh mischief.*

unchecked ▶ adjective (especially of something undesirable) not controlled or restrained: *prices rose unchecked, hitting the poor worst of all.*
■not examined, especially in order to determine the accuracy, quality, or condition of something.

unchivalrous ▶ adjective (of a man or his behaviour) discourteous, especially towards women.
– DERIVATIVES **unchivalrously** adverb.

unchosen ▶ adjective not chosen.

unchristian ▶ adjective not professing Christianity or its teachings.
■informal (of a person or their behaviour) unkind, unfair, or morally wrong.
– DERIVATIVES **unchristianly** adverb.

unchurch ▶ verb [with obj.] officially exclude (someone) from participation in the Christian sacraments; excommunicate.
■deprive (a building) of its status as a church.

unchurched ▶ adjective [attrib.] not belonging to or connected with a church.

uncial /ˈʌnsɪəl, -ʃ(ə)l/ ▶ adjective **1** of or written in a majuscule script with rounded unjoined letters which is found in European manuscripts of the 4th–8th centuries and from which modern capital letters are derived.
2 rare of or relating to an inch or an ounce.
▶ noun an uncial letter or script.
■a manuscript in uncial script.
– ORIGIN mid 17th cent.: from Latin *uncialis,* from *uncia* 'inch'. Sense 1 is in the late Latin sense of *unciales litterae* 'uncial letters', the original application of which is unclear.

unciform /ˈʌnsɪfɔːm/ ▶ adjective another term for **UNCINATE.**
■dated denoting the hamate bone of the wrist.

uncinariasis /ˌʌnsɪnəˈrʌɪəsɪs/ ▶ noun another term for **ANCYLOSTOMIASIS.**
– ORIGIN early 20th cent.: from modern Latin *Uncinaria* (the name of a genus of hookworms) + **-IASIS.**

uncinate /ˈʌnsɪnət, -eɪt/ ▶ adjective chiefly Anatomy having a hooked shape.
– ORIGIN mid 18th cent.: from Latin *uncinatus,* from *uncinus* 'hook'.

---

uncirculated ▶ adjective (especially of a note or coin) that has not been in circulation.

uncircumcised ▶ adjective (of a boy or man) not circumcised.
■archaic irreligious or heathen.
– DERIVATIVES **uncircumcision** noun.

uncivil ▶ adjective discourteous; impolite.
– DERIVATIVES **uncivilly** adverb.

uncivilized (also **-ised**) ▶ adjective (of a place or people) not considered to be socially, culturally, or morally advanced.
■impolite; bad-mannered.

unclad ▶ adjective **1** unclothed; naked.
2 not provided with cladding: *unclad girders.*

unclaimed ▶ adjective not demanded or requested as being something one has a right to: *unclaimed benefits.*

unclasp ▶ verb [with obj.] unfasten (a clasp or similar device): *they unclasped their seat belts.*
■release the grip of: *I unclasped her fingers from my hair.*

unclassifiable ▶ adjective not able to be assigned to a particular class or category.

unclassified ▶ adjective not arranged in or assigned to classes or categories: *many texts remain unclassified or uncatalogued.*
■(of information or documents) not designated as secret. ■ Brit. (of a road) not classified according to the overall system of road numbering. ■ Brit. denoting a university degree without honours. ■ Brit. (of a grade in an examination) denoting a fail.

uncle ▶ noun the brother of one's father or mother or the husband of one's aunt.
■informal an unrelated older male friend, especially of a child. ■ archaic, informal a pawnbroker.
– PHRASES **cry** (or **say** or **yell**) **uncle** N. Amer. informal surrender or admit defeat. **Uncle Tom Cobley** (or **Cobleigh**) **and all** Brit. informal used to denote a long list of people. [ORIGIN: with allusion to the ballad *Widdicombe Fair* in G. Bantock's *One Hundred Songs of England.*]
– ORIGIN Middle English: from Old French *oncle,* from late Latin *auunculus,* alteration of Latin *avunculus* 'maternal uncle' (see **AVUNCULAR**).

-uncle ▶ suffix forming chiefly diminutive nouns: *carbuncle* | *peduncle.*
– ORIGIN from Old French *-oncle, -uncle,* or from Latin *-unculus,* a special form of *-ulus.*

unclean ▶ adjective dirty: *the firm was fined for operating in unclean premises.*
■morally wrong: *unclean thoughts.* ■(of food) regarded in a particular religion as impure and unfit to be eaten: *pork is an unclean meat for Muslims.* ■(in biblical use) ritually impure; (of a spirit) evil.
– DERIVATIVES **uncleanness** noun.
– ORIGIN Old English *unclæne* (see **UN-**[1], **CLEAN**).

uncleanliness ▶ noun [mass noun] the state of being dirty: *head lice and general uncleanliness in schools.*

uncleanly ▶ adjective archaic term for **UNCLEAN.**

unclear ▶ adjective not easy to see, hear, or understand: *the motive for this killing is unclear.*
■not obvious or definite; ambiguous: *their future remains unclear.* ■having or feeling doubt or confusion: *users are still unclear about what middleware does.*
– DERIVATIVES **unclearly** adverb, **unclearness** noun.

uncleared ▶ adjective not having been cleared or cleared up, in particular:
■(of a cheque) not having passed through a clearing house and been paid to the payee's account. ■(of land) not cleared of vegetation before cultivation.

unclench ▶ verb [with obj.] release (a clenched part of the body): *slowly she unclenched her fist.*
■[no obj.] relax from a clenched state.

Uncle Sam a personification of the federal government or citizens of the US.
– ORIGIN early 19th cent.: said (from the time of the first recorded instances) to have arisen as a facetious expansion of the letters US.

Uncle Tom ▶ noun derogatory, chiefly N. Amer. a black man considered to be excessively obedient or servile.
– ORIGIN 1920s: from the name of the hero of H. B. Stowe's *Uncle Tom's Cabin* (1852).

unclimbed ▶ adjective (of a mountain or rock face) not previously climbed: *the unclimbed south ridge.*
– DERIVATIVES **unclimbable** adjective.

uncloak ▶ verb [with obj.] poetic/literary uncover; reveal.

unclog ▶ verb (**unclogged, unclogging**) [with obj.]

remove accumulated glutinous matter from.

unclose ▶ verb rare open.

unclosed ▶ adjective not closed.

unclothe ▶ verb [with obj.] remove the clothes from (oneself or someone).

unclouded ▶ adjective (of the sky) not dark or overcast: *you wake up to sunshine and unclouded skies.* ■ not troubled or spoiled by anything: *six months of unclouded happiness.*

uncluttered ▶ adjective not having or impeded by too many objects, details, or elements: *the rooms were plain and uncluttered.*

unco /ˈʌŋkə/ Scottish ▶ adjective unusual or remarkable.
▶ adverb [as submodifier] remarkably; very: *it's got an unco fine taste.*
▶ noun (pl. **-os**) a stranger.
■ (**uncos**) news.
– PHRASES **the unco guid** /gɪd/ chiefly derogatory strictly religious people.
– ORIGIN late Middle English (in the sense 'unknown, strange'): alteration of UNCOUTH.

uncoated ▶ adjective not covered with a coating of a particular substance.

uncoil ▶ verb straighten or cause to straighten from a coiled or curled position: [no obj.] *the rope uncoiled like a snake* | [with obj.] *she uncoiled her feather boa.*

uncollected ▶ adjective (especially of money) not collected or claimed: *the reward remained uncollected.* ■ left awaiting collection: *bursting sacks of uncollected refuse.* ■ (of literary works) not previously published.

uncoloured (US **uncolored**) ▶ adjective having no colour; neutral in colour.
■ not influenced, especially in a negative way: *explanations which are uncoloured by the observer's feelings.*

uncombed ▶ adjective (of a person's hair) not combed: *his hair was matted and uncombed.*

uncomely ▶ adjective archaic or humorous (especially of a woman) not attractive: *she was nineteen and not uncomely.*
■ archaic not agreeable or suitable.

uncomfortable ▶ adjective causing or feeling slight pain or physical discomfort: *athlete's foot is a painful and uncomfortable condition.*
■ causing or feeling unease or awkwardness: *he began to feel uncomfortable at the man's hard stare* | *an uncomfortable silence.*
– DERIVATIVES **uncomfortableness** noun, **uncomfortably** adverb [as submodifier] *the house was dark and uncomfortably cold.*

uncomfy ▶ adjective informal not comfortable.

uncomment ▶ verb [with obj.] Computing change (a piece of text within a program) from being a comment to be part of the program that is run by the computer.

uncommercial ▶ adjective not making, intended to make, or allowing a profit.

uncommitted ▶ adjective not committed to a particular course or policy: *uncommitted voters.*
■ (of resources) not pledged or set aside for future use: *there is very little uncommitted money to fund new policies.* ■ (of a person) not pledged to remain in a long-term emotional relationship with someone.

uncommon ▶ adjective out of the ordinary; unusual: *prostate cancer is not uncommon in men over 60* | *an uncommon name.*
■ [attrib.] remarkably great (used for emphasis): *an uncommon amount of noise.*
▶ adverb [as submodifier] archaic remarkably: *he was uncommon afraid.*
– DERIVATIVES **uncommonly** adverb [as submodifier] *an uncommonly large crowd,* **uncommonness** noun.

uncommunicative ▶ adjective (of a person) unwilling to talk or impart information.
– DERIVATIVES **uncommunicatively** adverb, **uncommunicativeness** noun.

uncompanionable /ʌnkəmˈpanjənəb(ə)l/ ▶ adjective not friendly and sociable.

uncompensated ▶ adjective (of a person or expense) not compensated or reimbursed.
■ (of an action) not compensated for: *uncompensated exploitation of the Third World.*

uncompetitive ▶ adjective (with reference to business or commerce) not competitive: *that would destroy jobs and make industry uncompetitive.*
■ characterized by a desire to avoid fair competition: *uncompetitive practices.*

– DERIVATIVES **uncompetitively** adverb, **uncompetitiveness** noun.

uncomplaining ▶ adjective not complaining; resigned: *she was uncomplaining, accepting of her lot.*
– DERIVATIVES **uncomplainingly** adverb.

uncompleted ▶ adjective not completed.

uncomplicated ▶ adjective simple or straightforward: *he was an extraordinarily uncomplicated man.*
– DERIVATIVES **uncomplicatedly** adverb **uncomplicatedness** noun.

uncomplimentary ▶ adjective not complimentary; negative or insulting: *uncomplimentary remarks.*

uncompounded ▶ adjective not mixed.
■ (of a word) not made up of two or more existing words.

uncomprehending ▶ adjective showing or having an inability to comprehend something: *an uncomprehending silence.*
– DERIVATIVES **uncomprehendingly** adverb.

uncompromising ▶ adjective showing an unwillingness to make concessions to others, especially by changing one's ways or opinions.
■ harsh or relentless: *the uncompromising ugliness of her home.*
– DERIVATIVES **uncompromisingly** adverb, **uncompromisingness** noun.

unconcealed ▶ adjective (especially of an emotion) not concealed; obvious: *Sophia looked around her with unconcealed curiosity.*

unconcern ▶ noun [mass noun] a lack of worry or interest, especially when surprising or callous.

unconcerned ▶ adjective showing a lack of worry or interest, especially when this is surprising or callous: *Scott seemed unconcerned by his companion's problem.*
– DERIVATIVES **unconcernedly** adverb.

unconcluded ▶ adjective not yet brought to a conclusion: *unconcluded agreements.*

unconditional ▶ adjective not subject to any conditions: *unconditional surrender.*
– DERIVATIVES **unconditionality** noun, **unconditionally** adverb.

unconditioned ▶ adjective 1 not subject to conditions or to an antecedent condition; unconditional.
2 relating to or denoting instinctive reflexes or other behaviour not formed or influenced by conditioning or learning: *an unconditioned response.*
3 not subjected to a conditioning process: *waste in its raw, unconditioned form.*

unconfessed ▶ adjective not acknowledged: *the hope that remains unconfessed.*
■ (of a sin) not confessed to a priest.

unconfident ▶ adjective not confident; hesitant.
– DERIVATIVES **unconfidently** adverb.

unconfined ▶ adjective not confined to a limited space: *sows should be unconfined at farrowing.*
■ (of joy or excitement) very great: *joy was unconfined.*

unconfirmed ▶ adjective not confirmed as to truth or validity: *an unconfirmed report of shots being fired.*

unconformable ▶ adjective Geology (of rock strata in contact) marking a discontinuity in the geological record, and typically not having the same direction of stratification.
– DERIVATIVES **unconformably** adverb.

unconformity ▶ noun Geology a surface of contact between two groups of unconformable strata.
■ [mass noun] the condition of being unconformable.

uncongenial ▶ adjective (of a person) not friendly or pleasant to be with: *uncongenial dining companions.*
■ unsuitable and therefore unlikely to promote success or well-being: *the religious climate proved **uncongenial** to such ideas.*

unconnected ▶ adjective not joined together or to something else: *the earth wire was left unconnected.*
■ not associated or linked in a sequence: *two unconnected events* | *the question was **unconnected** to anything they had been discussing.* ■ not having relatives in important or influential positions.
– DERIVATIVES **unconnectedly** adverb, **unconnectedness** noun.

unconquerable ▶ adjective (especially of a place, people, or emotion) not conquerable: *an unconquerable pride.*
– DERIVATIVES **unconquerably** adverb.

unconquered ▶ adjective not conquered.

unconscionable /ʌnˈkɒnʃ(ə)nəb(ə)l/ ▶ adjective not right or reasonable: *the unconscionable conduct of his son.*
■ unreasonably excessive: *shareholders have had to wait an unconscionable time for the facts to be established.*
– DERIVATIVES **unconscionably** adverb.
– ORIGIN mid 16th cent.: from UN-1 'not' + obsolete *conscionable,* from **CONSCIENCE** (interpreted as a plural) + -ABLE.

unconscious ▶ adjective not awake and aware of and responding to one's environment: *the boy was beaten unconscious.*
■ done or existing without one realizing: *he would wipe back his hair in an unconscious gesture of annoyance.* ■ [predic.] (**unconscious of**) unaware of: *'What is it?' he said again, unconscious of the repetition.*
▶ noun (**the unconscious**) the part of the mind which is inaccessible to the conscious mind but which affects behaviour and emotions.
– DERIVATIVES **unconsciously** adverb, **unconsciousness** noun.

unconsecrated ▶ adjective not consecrated.

unconsenting ▶ adjective not consenting.

unconsidered ▶ adjective disregarded and unappreciated: *a snapper-up of unconsidered trifles.*
■ (of a statement or action) not thought about in advance, and therefore rash or harsh.

unconsolable ▶ adjective inconsolable.
– DERIVATIVES **unconsolably** adverb.

unconstitutional ▶ adjective not in accordance with the political constitution or with procedural rules.
– DERIVATIVES **unconstitutionality** noun, **unconstitutionally** adverb.

unconstrained ▶ adjective not restricted or limited: *unconstrained growth.*
– DERIVATIVES **unconstrainedly** adverb.

unconstricted ▶ adjective not constricted.

unconstructed ▶ adjective chiefly N. Amer. (of a garment) unstructured.

unconsulted ▶ adjective not consulted for information or an opinion.

unconsumed ▶ adjective (especially of food or fuel) not consumed.

unconsummated ▶ adjective (of a marriage or other relationship) not having been consummated.

uncontainable ▶ adjective (especially of an emotion) very strong: *his uncontainable enthusiasm.*

uncontaminated ▶ adjective not contaminated: *uncontaminated air and food.*

uncontentious ▶ adjective not causing or likely to cause an argument: *an uncontentious view.*

uncontested ▶ adjective not contested: *these claims have not gone uncontested.*
– DERIVATIVES **uncontestedly** adverb.

uncontradicted ▶ adjective (of a statement) not contradicted.

uncontrived ▶ adjective not artificially created.
■ not appearing artificial: *the whole effect was uncontrived.*

uncontrollable ▶ adjective not controllable: *her brother had an uncontrollable temper.*
– DERIVATIVES **uncontrollableness** noun, **uncontrollably** adverb.

uncontrolled ▶ adjective not controlled.
– DERIVATIVES **uncontrolledly** adverb.

uncontroversial ▶ adjective not controversial.
– DERIVATIVES **uncontroversially** adverb.

uncontroverted ▶ adjective of which the truth or validity is not disputed.

unconventional ▶ adjective not based on or conforming to what is generally done or believed: *his unconventional approach to life.*
– DERIVATIVES **unconventionality** noun, **unconventionally** adverb.

unconverted ▶ adjective not converted, in particular:
■ (of a building) not adapted to a different use. ■ not having adopted a different religion, belief, or practice: *unconverted pagans.* ■ Rugby (of a try) not followed by a successful kick at goal.

unconvinced ▶ adjective not certain that something is true or can be relied on or trusted: *Parisians remain **unconvinced that** the project will be approved.*

unconvincing ▶ adjective failing to make someone believe that something is true or valid: *she felt the lie was unconvincing.*
  ■ failing to impress: *a slightly bizarre and unconvincing fusion of musical forces.*
– DERIVATIVES **unconvincingly** adverb.

uncooked ▶ adjective not cooked; raw.

uncool ▶ adjective informal not fashionable or impressive: *an uncool haircut.*

uncooperative ▶ adjective unwilling to help others or do what they ask.
– DERIVATIVES **uncooperatively** adverb.

uncoordinated ▶ adjective **1** badly organized: *expensive mistakes resulting from uncoordinated manufacturing strategies.*
  2 (of a person or their movements) clumsy.

uncork ▶ verb [with obj.] pull the cork out of (a bottle or other container).
  ■ N. Amer. informal (in a game or sport) deliver (a kick, throw, or punch): *Stulce uncorked the best throw of his career.*

uncorrected ▶ adjective not corrected.

uncorroborated ▶ adjective not confirmed or supported by other evidence or information: *the unreliability of uncorroborated confessions.*

uncorrupted ▶ adjective not corrupted: *Lucinda is uncorrupted by nefarious influences.*

uncountable ▶ adjective too many to be counted (usually in hyperbolic use): *she'd spent uncountable nights in this very bed.*
– DERIVATIVES **uncountability** noun, **uncountably** adverb.

uncountable noun (also **uncount noun**) ▶ noun another term for **MASS NOUN** (in sense 1).

uncounted ▶ adjective not counted.
  ■ very numerous: *uncounted millions of dollars.*

uncouple ▶ verb [with obj.] disconnect (something, especially a railway vehicle that has been coupled to another).
  ■ [no obj.] become disconnected. ■ release (hunting dogs) from being fastened together in couples.

uncourtly ▶ adjective not courteous or refined.

uncouth ▶ adjective (of a person or their appearance or behaviour) lacking good manners, refinement, or grace: *he is unwashed, uncouth, and drunk most of the time.*
  ■ (especially of art or language) lacking sophistication or delicacy: *uncouth sketches of peasants.* ■ archaic (of a place) uncomfortable, especially because of remoteness or poor conditions.
– DERIVATIVES **uncouthly** adverb, **uncouthness** noun.
– ORIGIN Old English *uncūth* 'unknown', from **UN-**¹ 'not' + *cūth* (past participle of *cunnan* 'know, be able').

uncovenanted ▶ adjective not bound by or in accordance with a covenant or agreement.
  ■ not promised by or based on a covenant, especially a covenant with God.

uncover ▶ verb [with obj.] remove a cover or covering from: *he uncovered the face of the dead man.*
  ■ discover (something previously secret or unknown): *further evidence has been uncovered.* ■ [no obj.] archaic remove one's hat, especially as a mark of respect.

uncreate ▶ verb [with obj.] poetic/literary destroy.

uncreated ▶ adjective (especially of a divine being) existing without having been created.
  ■ not yet created.

uncreative ▶ adjective not having or involving imagination or original ideas.

uncredited ▶ adjective (of a person or their work) not publicly acknowledged as being part of something, especially a publication or broadcast.

uncritical ▶ adjective not expressing criticism or using one's critical faculties: *an uncritical acceptance of the results.*
  ■ not in accordance with the principles of critical analysis: *uncritical reasoning.*
– DERIVATIVES **uncritically** adverb.

uncropped ▶ adjective not cropped.

uncross ▶ verb [with obj.] move (something) back from a crossed position: *the reporter uncrossed his legs.*

uncrossed ▶ adjective not crossed, in particular:
  ■ (of a person's legs or arms) not folded across each other. ■ Brit. (of a cheque) not crossed.

uncrowded ▶ adjective not filled with a large number of people: *miles of uncrowded beaches.*

uncrown ▶ verb [with obj.] deprive (a monarch) of their ruling position.

uncrowned ▶ adjective not formally crowned as a monarch.

uncrushable ▶ adjective (of a fabric) resistant to creasing.

uncrushed ▶ adjective not crushed.

UNCSTD ▶ abbreviation for United Nations Conference on Science and Technology for Development.

UNCTAD /ˈʌŋ(k)tad/ ▶ abbreviation for United Nations Conference on Trade and Development.

unction /ˈʌŋ(k)ʃ(ə)n/ ▶ noun [mass noun] **1** formal the action of anointing someone with oil or ointment as a religious rite or as a symbol of investiture as a monarch.
  ■ [count noun] the oil or ointment so used. ■ short for **EXTREME UNCTION**.
  2 archaic treatment with a medicinal oil or ointment.
  ■ [count noun] an ointment: *mercury in the form of unctions.*
  3 a manner of expression arising or apparently arising from deep emotion, especially as intended to flatter: *the headlines gloated with the kind of effusive unction only the English press can muster.*
– ORIGIN late Middle English: from Latin *unctio(n-)*, from *unguere* 'anoint'. Sense 3 arises from the link between religious fervour and 'anointing' with the Holy Spirit.

unctuous /ˈʌŋ(k)tjʊəs/ ▶ adjective **1** (of a person) excessively or ingratiatingly flattering; oily: *he seemed anxious to please but not in an unctuous way.*
  2 (chiefly of minerals) having a greasy or soapy feel.
– DERIVATIVES **unctuously** adverb, **unctuousness** noun.
– ORIGIN late Middle English (in the sense 'greasy'): from medieval Latin *unctuosus*, from Latin *unctus* 'anointing', from *unguere* 'anoint'.

uncultivated ▶ adjective (of land) not used for growing crops.
  ■ (of a person) not highly educated.

uncultured ▶ adjective not characterized by good taste, manners, or education: *to my uncultured palate most of the wines were good.*

uncurbed ▶ adjective not restrained or kept in check: *their activities continue to be largely uncurbed.*

uncured ▶ adjective **1** (of a person) not restored to health.
  2 (of meat, fish, tobacco, or animal skins) not preserved by salting, drying, or smoking.

uncurl ▶ verb straighten or cause to straighten from a curled position: [no obj.] *in spring the new leaves uncurl* | [with obj.] *the doctor uncurled his fingers.*

uncurtained ▶ adjective (of a window) not provided with a curtain or curtains.

uncut ▶ adjective not cut: *her hair was left uncut.*
  ■ (of a text, film, or performance) complete; unabridged. ■ (of a stone, especially a diamond) not shaped by cutting. ■ (of alcohol or a drug) not diluted or adulterated: *large amounts of uncut heroin.* ■ chiefly historical (of a book) with the edges of its pages not slit open or trimmed off. ■ (of fabric) having its pile loops intact.

undamaged ▶ adjective not harmed or damaged: *buildings undamaged during the war.*

undated ▶ adjective not provided or marked with a date: *most of his letters are undated.*

undaunted ▶ adjective not intimidated or discouraged by difficulty, danger, or disappointment: *they were undaunted by the huge amount of work needed.*
– DERIVATIVES **undauntedly** adverb, **undauntedness** noun.

undead ▶ adjective (of a fictional being, especially a vampire) technically dead but still animate.

undecagon /ʌnˈdɛkəg(ə)n/ ▶ noun another term for **HENDECAGON**.
– ORIGIN early 18th cent.: formed irregularly from Latin *undecim* 'eleven', on the pattern of *decagon*.

undeceive ▶ verb [with obj.] tell (someone) that an idea or belief is mistaken: *they took her for a nun and Mary said nothing to undeceive them.*

undecidable ▶ adjective not able to be firmly established or refuted.
  ■ Logic (of a proposition or theorem) not able to be proved or disproved.

– DERIVATIVES **undecidability** noun.

undecided ▶ adjective (of a person) not having made a decision: *the jury remained undecided.*
  ■ not settled or resolved: *the match was still undecided.* ▶ noun a person who has not decided how they are going to vote in an election.
– DERIVATIVES **undecidedly** adverb.

undecipherable ▶ adjective (of speech or writing) not able to be read or understood.

undeclared ▶ adjective not publicly announced, admitted, or acknowledged: *undeclared war.*
  ■ (especially of taxable income or dutiable goods) not declared.

undecorated ▶ adjective **1** not adorned or decorated: *the walls were completely undecorated.*
  2 (of a member of the armed forces) not honoured with an award.

undee /ˈʌndeɪ/ ▶ adjective variant spelling of **UNDY**.

undefeated ▶ adjective not defeated, especially in a battle or other contest: *the undefeated champion.*

undefended ▶ adjective not defended: *undefended frontiers* | *legal aid for undefended divorces.*

undefiled ▶ adjective not defiled; pure.

undefined ▶ adjective not clear or defined: *undefined areas of jurisdiction* | *he felt an undefined longing.*
– DERIVATIVES **undefinable** adjective, **undefinably** adverb.

undelete ▶ verb [with obj.] Computing cancel the deletion of (text or a file).

undelivered ▶ adjective not delivered: *undelivered letters.*

undemanding ▶ adjective (especially of a task or person) not demanding: *undemanding clerical jobs.*

undemocratic ▶ adjective not relating or according to democratic principles: *an undemocratic regime.*
– DERIVATIVES **undemocratically** adverb.

undemonstrated ▶ adjective not shown to exist or be true.

undemonstrative ▶ adjective (of a person) not tending to express feelings, especially of affection, openly: *the English are an undemonstrative lot.*
– DERIVATIVES **undemonstratively** adverb, **undemonstrativeness** noun.

undeniable ▶ adjective unable to be denied or disputed: *it is an undeniable fact that some dogs are easier to train than others.*
– DERIVATIVES **undeniably** adverb [sentence adverb] *the topic is undeniably an important one.*

undenominational ▶ adjective not attached to any specific religious denomination.

undented ▶ adjective (of a surface) not marked with a dent.

undependable ▶ adjective not trustworthy and reliable: *evidence is scarce and often undependable.*

under ▶ preposition **1** extending or directly below: *vast stores of gas under the North Sea* | *the streams that ran under the melting glaciers.*
  ■ below (something covering or protecting): *under several feet of water* | *a hot plate under an insulated lid.*
  2 at a lower level or layer than: *the room under his study.*
  ■ behind (a physical surface): *it was written on the new canvas under a gluey coating.* ■ behind or hidden behind (an appearance): *he had a deep sense of fun under his quiet exterior.* ■ lower in grade or rank than: *under him in the hierarchy.*
  3 used to express dominance or control: *I was under his spell.*
  ■ during (a specified time period): *the coinage standard was reformed under Elizabeth I.* ■ as a reaction to or undergoing the pressure of (something): *the sofa creaked under his weight* | *certain institutions may be under threat.* ■ as provided for by the rules of; in accordance with: *flowers supplied under contract by a local florist.* ■ used to express grouping or classification: *file it under 'lost'* | *published under his own name.* ■ Computing within the environment of (a particular operating system): *the program runs under DOS.*
  4 lower than (a specified amount, rate, or norm): *they averaged just under 2.8 per cent.*
  5 undergoing (a process): *under construction.*
  ■ in an existent state of: *children living under difficult circumstances.* ■ planted with: *fields under wheat.*
  ▶ adverb **1** extending or directly below something: *weaving the body through the crossbars, over and under, over and under.*

2 under water: *he was floating for some time but suddenly went under.* ■ affected by an anaesthetic; unconscious: *the operation was quick; she was only under for 15 minutes.* – PHRASES **under way** having started and making progress. ■ (of a boat) moving through the water: *no time was lost in getting under way.* [ORIGIN: mid 18th cent. (as a nautical term): from Dutch *onderweg*.] – DERIVATIVES **undermost** adjective. – ORIGIN Old English, of Germanic origin; related to Dutch *onder* and German *unter*.

under- ▶ prefix **1** below; beneath: *underclothes* | *undercover.* ■ lower in status; subordinate: *undersecretary.* **2** insufficiently; incompletely: *undernourished.*

underachieve ▶ verb [no obj.] do less well than is expected, especially in school work. – DERIVATIVES **underachievement** noun, **underachiever** noun.

underact ▶ verb [no obj.] act a part in a play or film in an overly restrained or unemotional way.

under age ▶ adjective (of a person) too young to engage legally in a particular activity, especially drinking alcohol or having sex. ■ [attrib.] (of an activity) engaged in by people who are under age: *under-age drinking.*

underarm ▶ adjective & adverb (of a throw or stroke in sport) made with the arm or hand below shoulder level: [as adj.] *a good length underarm serve* | [as adv.] *bowling underarm.* ▶ noun a person's armpit: [as modifier] *use an underarm deodorant.*

underbelly ▶ noun (pl. **-ies**) the soft underside or abdomen of an animal. ■ figurative an area vulnerable to attack: *these multinationals have a soft underbelly.* ■ figurative a hidden unpleasant or criminal part of society.

underbid ▶ verb (**-bidding**; past and past participle **-bid**) [with obj.] (in an auction or competitive tendering) make a lower bid than (someone). ■ Bridge make a lower bid on (one's hand) than its strength warrants. ▶ noun a bid that is lower than another or than is justified. – DERIVATIVES **underbidder** noun.

underbite ▶ noun (in non-technical use) the projection of the lower teeth beyond the upper.

underbody ▶ noun (pl. **-ies**) the underside of a road vehicle, ship, or animal's body.

underbred ▶ adjective dated ill-mannered; rude.

underbridge ▶ noun a bridge spanning an opening under a railway or road.

underbrush ▶ noun [mass noun] N. Amer. shrubs and small trees forming the undergrowth in a forest.

undercapitalize (also **-ise**) ▶ verb [with obj.] provide (a company) with insufficient capital to achieve desired results. – DERIVATIVES **undercapitalization** noun.

undercard ▶ noun the list of less important bouts on the same bill as a main boxing match.

undercarriage ▶ noun a wheeled structure beneath an aircraft, typically retracted when not in use, which receives the impact on landing and supports the aircraft on the ground. ■ the supporting frame under the body of a vehicle.

undercast ▶ verb (past and past participle **-cast**) [with obj.] (usu. **be undercast**) allocate the parts in (a play or film) to insufficiently skilled actors.

undercharge ▶ verb [with obj.] **1** charge (someone) a price or amount that is too low. **2** give less than the proper charge to (an electric battery). ▶ noun a charge that is insufficient.

underclass ▶ noun the lowest social stratum in a country or community, consisting of the poor and unemployed.

undercliff ▶ noun a terrace or lower cliff formed by a landslip.

undercling Climbing ▶ noun a handhold which faces down the rock face. ▶ verb [no obj.] climb using such handholds.

underclothes ▶ plural noun clothes worn under others, typically next to the skin. – DERIVATIVES **underclothing** noun.

undercoat ▶ noun **1** a layer of paint applied after the primer and before the topcoat.

2 an animal's underfur or down. ▶ verb [with obj.] apply a coat of undercoat to (something).

underconsumption ▶ noun [mass noun] Economics purchase of goods and services at a level lower than that of their supply.

undercook ▶ verb [with obj.] [usu. as adj. **undercooked**] cook (something) insufficiently: *undercooked meats.*

undercool ▶ verb another term for **SUPERCOOL**.

undercount ▶ verb [with obj.] enumerate (something, especially a sector of a population in a census) at a lower figure than the actual figure. ▶ noun a count or figure that is inaccurately low. ■ the amount by which such a count or figure falls short of the actual figure.

undercover ▶ adjective **1** (of a person or their activities) involved in or involving secret work within a community or organization, especially for the purposes of police investigation or espionage: *an undercover police operation.* **2** provided with shelter: *undercover seating.* ▶ adverb as an undercover agent: *he worked undercover in Northern Ireland.*

undercroft ▶ noun the crypt of a church. – ORIGIN late Middle English: from **UNDER-** + the rare term *croft* 'crypt', from Middle Dutch *crofte* 'cave', from Latin *crypta*.

undercurrent ▶ noun a current of water below the surface and moving in a different direction from any surface current. ■ figurative an underlying feeling or influence, especially one that is contrary to the prevailing atmosphere and is not expressed openly: *racial undercurrents.*

undercut ▶ verb (**-cutting**; past and past participle **-cut**) [with obj.] **1** offer goods or services at a lower price than (a competitor): *these industries have been undercut by more efficient foreign producers.* **2** cut or wear away the part below or under (something, especially a cliff). ■ figurative weaken; undermine: *the chairman denied his authority was being undercut.* ■ cut away material to leave (a carved design) in relief. **3** Tennis strike (a ball) with backspin so that it rises high in the air. ▶ noun **1** a space formed by the removal or absence of material from the lower part of something, such as a cliff, a coal seam, or part of a carving in relief. ■ N. Amer. a notch cut in a tree trunk to guide its fall when felled. **2** Brit. the underside of a sirloin of beef.

underdamp ▶ verb [with obj.] Physics damp (a system) incompletely, so as to allow a few oscillations after a single disturbance.

underdetermine ▶ verb [with obj.] (usu. **be underdetermined**) account for (a theory or phenomenon) with less than the amount of evidence needed for proof or certainty. – DERIVATIVES **underdetermination** noun.

underdeveloped ▶ adjective not fully developed: *underdeveloped kidneys* | *the community services are underfunded and underdeveloped.* ■ (of a country or region) not advanced economically. ■ (of a photographic film) not developed sufficiently to give a normal image. – DERIVATIVES **underdevelopment** noun.

underdog ▶ noun a competitor thought to have little chance of winning a fight or contest. ■ a person who has little status in society.

underdone ▶ adjective (of food) insufficiently cooked.

underdrawing ▶ noun [mass noun] sketched lines made by a painter as a preliminary guide, and subsequently covered with layers of paint. ■ [count noun] such a preliminary sketch.

underdress ▶ verb [no obj.] (also **be underdressed**) dress too plainly or too informally: *without a pinstripe you'd be underdressed.*

undereducated ▶ adjective poorly educated.

underemphasize (also **-ise**) ▶ verb [with obj.] (usu. **be underemphasized**) place insufficient emphasis on: *history is underemphasized in the curriculum.* – DERIVATIVES **underemphasis** noun.

underemployed ▶ adjective (of a person) not having enough paid work or not doing work that makes full use of their skills and abilities. – DERIVATIVES **underemployment** noun.

underestimate ▶ verb [with obj.] estimate (something) to be smaller or less important than it

really is: *the government has grossly underestimated the extent of the problem.* ■ regard (someone) as less capable than they really are: *he had underestimated the new President.* ▶ noun [usu. in sing.] an estimate that is too low. – DERIVATIVES **underestimation** noun.

underexpose ▶ verb [with obj.] Photography expose (film or an image) for too short a time. – DERIVATIVES **underexposure** noun.

underfed ▶ adjective insufficiently fed or nourished.

underfelt ▶ noun [mass noun] Brit. felt laid under a carpet for extra support.

under-fives ▶ plural noun chiefly Brit. children who are less than five years old, especially those who are not in full-time education.

underfloor ▶ adjective (especially of a heating system) situated or operating beneath the floor.

underflow ▶ noun **1** an undercurrent. ■ a horizontal flow of water through the ground, especially one underneath a river bed. **2** [mass noun] Computing the generation of a number that is too small to be represented in the device meant to store it.

underfoot ▶ adverb under one's feet; on the ground: *it was very muddy underfoot* | figurative *genuine rights were being trodden underfoot.* ■ constantly present and in one's way: *the last thing my mother wanted was a child underfoot.* ▶ adjective [attrib.] of or relating to the state of the ground, especially in a horse race.

underframe ▶ noun the substructure of a motor vehicle or railway carriage. ■ the supporting frame of a chair seat or table top.

underfund ▶ verb [with obj.] (usu. **be underfunded**) provide with insufficient funding. – DERIVATIVES **underfunding** noun.

underfur ▶ noun [mass noun] an inner layer of short, fine fur or down underlying an animal's outer fur, providing warmth and waterproofing.

undergarment ▶ noun an article of underclothing.

undergird ▶ verb [with obj.] secure or fasten from the underside, especially by a rope or chain passed underneath. ■ formal provide support or a firm basis for.

underglaze ▶ adjective (of decoration on pottery) done before the glaze is applied. ■ (of colours) used in such decoration. ▶ noun a colour or design applied in this way.

undergo ▶ verb (**-goes**; past **-went**; past participle **-gone**) [with obj.] experience or be subjected to (something, typically something unpleasant, painful, or arduous): *the baby underwent a life-saving brain operation.* – ORIGIN Old English *undergān* 'undermine' (see **UNDER-**, **GO**[1]).

undergrad ▶ noun informal an undergraduate.

undergraduate ▶ noun a student at a university who has not yet taken a first degree.

underground ▶ adverb beneath the surface of the ground: *miners working underground.* ■ in or into secrecy or hiding, especially as a result of carrying out subversive political activities: *many were forced to go underground by the government.* ▶ adjective situated beneath the surface of the ground: *an underground car park.* ■ of or relating to the secret activities of people working to subvert an established order: *Czech underground literature.* ■ of or denoting a group or movement seeking to explore alternative forms of lifestyle or artistic expression: *radical and experimental: the New York underground art scene.* ▶ noun **1** (often **the Underground**) Brit. an underground railway, especially the one in London: *travel chaos on the Underground* | *he'd gone home by underground.* **2** a group or movement organized secretly to work against an existing regime. ■ a group or movement seeking to explore alternative forms of lifestyle or artistic expression: *the late sixties underground.* ▶ verb [with obj.] lay (cables) below ground level.

underground economy ▶ noun North American term for **BLACK ECONOMY**.

underground mutton ▶ noun [mass noun] Austral. informal rabbit meat.

Underground Railroad (in the US) a secret network for helping slaves escape from the South to the North and Canada in the years before the American Civil War.

undergrowth ▶ noun [mass noun] a dense growth of shrubs and other plants, especially under trees in woodland.

underhand ▶ adjective **1** acting or done in a secret or dishonest way: *underhand dealings.*
2 another term for UNDERARM: *underhand bowling* | [as adv.] *I served underhand.*
■ with the palm of the hand upward or outward: *an underhand grip.*
– ORIGIN Old English in the sense 'in or into subjection, under control' (see UNDER-, HAND).

underhanded ▶ adjective another term for UNDERHAND: *underhanded practices.*
– DERIVATIVES **underhandedly** adverb.

underhung ▶ adjective another term for UNDERSHOT (in sense 2).

underinsured ▶ adjective (of a person) having inadequate insurance cover.
– DERIVATIVES **underinsurance** noun.

underinvest ▶ verb [no obj.] fail to invest sufficient money or resources in a project or enterprise: *we persistently underinvest in historic buildings.*
– DERIVATIVES **underinvestment** noun.

underlay¹ ▶ verb (past and past participle **-laid**) [with obj.] (usu. **be underlaid**) place something under (something else), especially to support or raise it: *the green fields are underlaid with limestone.*
▶ noun [mass noun] something placed under or behind something else, especially material laid under a carpet for protection or support.
■ Music the manner in which the words are fitted to the notes of a piece of vocal music.
– ORIGIN Old English *underlecgan* (see UNDER-, LAY¹).

underlay² past tense of UNDERLIE.

underlease ▶ noun & verb another term for SUBLEASE.

underlet ▶ verb (**-letting**; past and past participle **-let**) another term for SUBLEASE.

underlever ▶ noun a lever behind the trigger guard on a rifle.

underlie ▶ verb (**-lying**; past **-lay**; past participle **-lain**) [with obj.] (especially of a layer of rock or soil) lie or be situated under (something).
■ be the cause or basis of (something): *the fundamental issue which underlies the conflict* | [as adj. **underlying**] *the underlying causes of poverty and drug addiction.*
– ORIGIN Old English *underlicgan* 'be subject or subordinate to' (see UNDER-, LIE¹).

underlife ▶ noun (pl. **underlives**) a way of living with which the general public do not normally come into contact.

underline ▶ verb [with obj.] draw a line under (a word or phrase) to give emphasis or indicate special type.
■ emphasize (something): *the improvement in retail sales was underlined by these figures.*
▶ noun **1** a line drawn under a word or phrase, especially for emphasis.
2 the line of the lower part of an animal's body.

underlinen ▶ noun [mass noun] archaic underclothes, especially those made of linen.

underling ▶ noun (usu. **underlings**) chiefly derogatory a person lower in status or rank.

underlip ▶ noun the lower lip of a person or animal.

underlying present participle of UNDERLIE.

underman ▶ verb (**-manned**, **-manning**) [with obj.] (usu. **be undermanned**) fail to provide with enough workers or crew: *the public prosecutor's offices are hopelessly undermanned.*

undermanager ▶ noun a manager who is subordinate to another manager.

undermentioned ▶ adjective Brit. mentioned at a later place in a book or document.

undermine ▶ verb [with obj.] erode the base or foundation of (a rock formation).
■ dig or excavate beneath (a building or fortification) so as to make it collapse. ■ figurative damage or weaken (someone or something), especially gradually or insidiously: *this could undermine years of hard work.*
– DERIVATIVES **underminer** noun.
– ORIGIN Middle English: from UNDER- + the verb MINE², probably suggested by Middle Dutch *ondermineren.*

underneath ▶ preposition & adverb **1** situated directly below (something else): [as prep.] *our bedroom's right underneath theirs* | [as adv.] *his eyes were*

red-rimmed with black bags underneath | [as adj.] *on longer hair, the underneath layers can be permed to give extra body.*
■ situated on a page directly below (a picture or another piece of writing): [as prep.] *four names written neatly underneath each other* | [as adv.] *there was writing underneath.*
2 so as to be concealed by (something else): [as prep.] *money changed hands underneath the table* | figurative *underneath his aloof air, Nicky was a warm and open young man* | [as adv.] *paint peeling off in flakes to reveal greyish plaster underneath.*
■ partly or wholly concealed by (a garment): [as prep.] *she could easily see the broadness of his shoulders underneath a tailored white sports shirt* | [as adv.] *undoing her jacket to reveal nothing but a clingy bra underneath.*
▶ noun [in sing.] the part or side of something facing towards the ground; the underside.
– ORIGIN Old English *underneothan*; compare with BENEATH.

undernourished ▶ adjective having insufficient food or other substances for good health and condition: *undernourished children.*
– DERIVATIVES **undernourishment** noun.

underoccupancy ▶ noun [mass noun] Brit. (with reference to holiday or hospital accommodation) the state of not being occupied to the expected or advertised capacity.

underpaid past and past participle of UNDERPAY.

underpainting ▶ noun [mass noun] paint subsequently overlaid with another layer or with a finishing coat.

underpants ▶ plural noun an undergarment, especially for men or boys, covering the lower part of the body and having two holes for the legs.

underpart ▶ noun a lower part or portion of something.
■ (underparts) the underside of an animal's body, especially when of a specified colour or pattern.

underpass ▶ noun a road or pedestrian tunnel passing under another road or a railway.

underpay ▶ verb (past and past participle **-paid**) pay too little to (someone).
■ pay less than is due for (something): [as adj. **underpaid**] *late or underpaid tax.*
– DERIVATIVES **underpayment** noun.

underperform ▶ verb [no obj.] perform less well than expected.
■ [with obj.] increase in value less than: *the shares have underperformed the market.*
– DERIVATIVES **underperformance** noun.

underpin ▶ verb (**-pinned**, **-pinning**) [with obj.] support (a building or other structure) from below by laying a solid foundation below ground level or by substituting stronger for weaker materials.
■ support, justify, or form the basis for: *the theme of honour underpinning the two books.*

underpinning ▶ noun a solid foundation laid below ground level to support or strengthen a building.
■ a set of ideas, motives, or devices which justify or form the basis for something: *the theoretical underpinning for free-market economics.*

underplant ▶ verb [with obj.] plant or cultivate the ground around (a tall plant) with smaller plants: *the roses are underplanted with pink and white bulbs.*

underplay ▶ verb [with obj.] perform (something) in a restrained way: *the violins underplayed the romantic element in the music.*
■ represent (something) as being less important than it really is: *I do not wish to underplay the tragedies that have occurred.*

underplot ▶ noun a subordinate plot in a play, novel, or similar work.

underpopulated ▶ adjective having an insufficient or very small population.
– DERIVATIVES **underpopulation** noun.

underpowered ▶ adjective lacking sufficient mechanical, electrical, or other power.

underprepared ▶ adjective not having prepared sufficiently to carry out a task.

underprice ▶ verb [with obj.] sell or offer at too low a price: *water shares were underpriced.*

underprivileged ▶ adjective (of a person) not enjoying the same standard of living or rights as the majority of people in a society.

underproduce ▶ verb [with obj.] **1** produce less of (a commodity) than is wanted or needed.

2 (often as adj. **underproduced**) record or produce (a song or film) in such a basic way that it appears rough or unfinished.
– DERIVATIVES **underproduction** noun.

underproof ▶ adjective containing less alcohol than proof spirit does.

underprop ▶ verb (**-propped**, **-propping**) [with obj.] archaic support, especially with a prop.

underrate ▶ verb [with obj.] [often as adj. **underrated**] underestimate the extent, value, or importance of (someone or something): *a very underrated film.*

under-read ▶ verb (past and past participle **-read**) [no obj.] (of a gauge or dial) show a reading lower than the true one.

under-record ▶ verb [with obj.] record (a number or amount) as being lower than it really is.
■ record (data or information) insufficiently or inadequately: *such conditions had been markedly under-recorded in medical inspection.*

under-rehearsed ▶ adjective (of a performance or performer) insufficiently rehearsed.

under-report ▶ verb [with obj.] fail to report (something, especially news or data) fully.

under-represent ▶ verb [with obj.] provide with insufficient or inadequate representation: *women are under-represented at high levels.*
– DERIVATIVES **under-representation** noun.

under-resourced ▶ adjective provided with insufficient resources: *an overstretched and under-resourced service.*
– DERIVATIVES **under-resourcing** noun.

undersaturated ▶ adjective technical falling short of being saturated with a particular constituent.
– DERIVATIVES **undersaturation** noun.

underscore ▶ verb another term for UNDERLINE.
▶ noun another term for UNDERLINE (in sense 1).

undersea ▶ adjective of, relating to, or situated below the sea or the surface of the sea.

underseal chiefly Brit. ▶ verb [with obj.] coat (the underpart of a motor vehicle) with waterproof material as protection against rust.
▶ noun [mass noun] waterproof coating used in this way.

undersecretary ▶ noun (pl. **-ies**) a subordinate official, in particular (in the UK) a junior minister or senior civil servant, or (in the US) the principal assistant to a member of the cabinet.

undersell ▶ verb (past and past participle **-sold**) [with obj.] sell something at a lower price than (a competitor).
■ promote or rate (something) insufficiently; undervalue.

underset ▶ verb (**-setting**; past and past participle **-set**) [with obj.] rare place (something) under something else, especially for support.
▶ noun another term for UNDERCURRENT.

undersexed ▶ adjective having unusually weak sexual desires.

undersheriff ▶ noun a deputy sheriff.

undershirt ▶ noun chiefly N. Amer. an undergarment worn under a shirt; a vest.

undershoot ▶ verb (past and past participle **-shot**) [with obj.] fall short of (a point or target): *the figure undershot the government's original estimate.*
■ (of an aircraft) land short of (the runway).
▶ noun an act of undershooting.

undershorts ▶ plural noun chiefly N. Amer. underpants.

undershot past and past participle of UNDERSHOOT. ▶ adjective **1** (of a waterwheel) turned by water flowing under it.
2 denoting or having a lower jaw which projects beyond the upper jaw.

underside ▶ noun the bottom or lower side or surface of something: *the butterfly's wings have a mottled brown pattern on the underside.*
■ figurative the less favourable aspect of something: *the sordid underside of the glamorous 1980s.*

undersigned ▶ adjective [usu. as plural noun **the undersigned**] formal whose signature is appended: *we, the undersigned, wish to protest at the current activities of the company.*

undersized (also **undersize**) ▶ adjective of less than the usual size.

underskirt ▶ noun a skirt worn under another; a petticoat.

underslung ▶ adjective suspended from the underside of something: *helicopters hover to lift underslung loads.*

■(of a vehicle chassis) hanging lower than the axles.

undersoil ▶ **noun** [mass noun] subsoil.

undersold past and past participle of **UNDERSELL**.

undersow ▶ **verb** (past participle **-sown**) [with obj.] sow (a later-growing crop) on land already seeded with another crop.

underspend ▶ **verb** (past and past participle **-spent**) [no obj.] spend too little.
■[with obj.] spend less than (a specified or allocated amount): *schools have underspent their training budgets.*
▶ **noun** [in sing.] an act of underspending: *areas in the year's budget where there has been an underspend.*

understaff ▶ **verb** [with obj.] provide (an organization) with too few members of staff to operate effectively: [as adj. **understaffed**] *the department is understaffed and overworked.*
– DERIVATIVES **understaffing** noun.

understairs ▶ **adjective** in the space below the staircase: *an understairs storage cupboard.*

understand ▶ **verb** (past and past participle **-stood**) **1** [with obj.] perceive the intended meaning of (words, a language, or speaker): *he didn't understand a word I said* | *he could usually **make himself understood*** | [with clause] *she understood what he was saying.*
■perceive the significance, explanation, or cause of (something): *she didn't really understand the situation* | [with clause] *he couldn't understand why we burst out laughing* | [no obj.] *you don't understand—she has left me.* ■ be sympathetically or knowledgeably aware of the character or nature of: *Picasso understood colour* | [with clause] *I understand how you feel.* ■interpret or view (something) in a particular way: *as the term is usually understood, legislation refers to regulations and directives.*
2 [with clause] infer something from information received (often used as a polite formula in conversation): *I understand you're at art school* | [with obj.] *as I understood it she was flying back to the States tomorrow.*
■[with obj.] (often **be understood**) regard (a missing word, phrase, or idea) as present; supply mentally: *'present company excepted' is always understood when sweeping generalizations are being made.* ■ [with obj.] (often **be understood**) assume to be the case; take for granted: *he liked to play the field, that was understood.*
– DERIVATIVES **understander** noun.
– ORIGIN Old English *understandan* (see **UNDER-**, **STAND**).

understandable ▶ **adjective** able to be understood: *though his accent was strange, the words were perfectly understandable.*
■to be expected; natural, reasonable, or forgivable: *such fears are understandable* | ***it is understandable that** mistakes occur sometimes.*
– DERIVATIVES **understandability** noun, **understandably** adverb [sentence adverb] *understandably, Richard did not believe me.*

understanding ▶ **noun** [mass noun] the ability to understand something; comprehension: *foreign visitors with little understanding of English.*
■the power of abstract thought; intellect: *a child of sufficient intelligence and understanding.* ■ an individual's perception or judgement of a situation: *my understanding was that he would try to find a new supplier.* ■ sympathetic awareness or tolerance: *a problem which needs to be handled with understanding.* ■ [count noun] an informal or unspoken agreement or arrangement: *he and I have an understanding* | *he had only been allowed to come **on the understanding that** he would be on his best behaviour.*
▶ **adjective 1** sympathetically aware of other people's feelings; tolerant and forgiving: *people expect their doctor to be understanding.*
2 archaic having insight or good judgement.
– DERIVATIVES **understandingly** adverb.

understate ▶ **verb** [with obj.] describe or represent (something) as being smaller or less good or important than it really is: *the press have understated the extent of the problem.*
– DERIVATIVES **understater** noun.

understated ▶ **adjective** presented or expressed in a subtle and effective way: *understated elegance.*
– DERIVATIVES **understatedly** adverb.

understatement ▶ **noun** [mass noun] the presentation of something as being smaller or less good or important than it really is: *a master of English understatement* | [count noun] *to say I am delighted is an understatement.*

understeer ▶ **verb** [no obj.] (of a motor vehicle) have a tendency to turn less sharply than is intended: *the turbo understeers on very fast bends.*
▶ **noun** [mass noun] the tendency of a vehicle to turn in such a way.

understood past and past participle of **UNDERSTAND**.

understorey ▶ **noun** (pl. **-eys**) Ecology a layer of vegetation beneath the main canopy of a forest.

understrapper ▶ **noun** informal, dated an assistant or junior official.

understudy ▶ **noun** (pl. **-ies**) (in the theatre) a person who learns another's role in order to be able to act at short notice in their absence.
▶ **verb** (**-ies**, **-ied**) [with obj.] study (a role or actor) as an understudy: *he had to understudy Prospero.*

undersubscribed ▶ **adjective** (of a course or event) having more places available than applications.
■(of a share issue) having fewer applications for shares than there are shares available.

undersurface ▶ **noun** the lower or under surface of something.

underswell ▶ **noun** an undercurrent.

undertake ▶ **verb** (past **-took**; past participle **-taken**) [with obj.] commit oneself to and begin (an enterprise or responsibility); take on: *a firm of builders undertook the construction work.*
■[usu. with infinitive] promise to do a particular thing: *the firm undertook to keep price increases to a minimum.* ■ [with clause] guarantee or affirm something; give as a formal pledge: *a lorry driver implicitly **undertakes that** he is reasonably skilled as a driver.*

undertaker ▶ **noun** a person whose business is preparing dead bodies for burial or cremation and making arrangements for funerals.

undertaking ▶ **noun 1** a formal pledge or promise to do something: *I give **an undertaking that** we shall proceed with the legislation.*
■a task that is taken on; an enterprise: *a mammoth undertaking that involved digging into the side of a cliff face.* ■ a company or business: *industrial undertakings ranging from textiles to rubber.* ■ [mass noun] the action of undertaking to do something: *the knowing undertaking of an obligation.*
2 [mass noun] the management of funerals as a profession.

undertenant ▶ **noun** a subtenant.
– DERIVATIVES **undertenancy** noun (pl. **-ies**).

underthings ▶ **plural noun** underclothes.

underthrust Geology ▶ **verb** (past and past participle **-thrust**) [with obj.] force (a crustal plate or other body of rock) beneath another formation.
■be forced underneath (another formation).
▶ **noun** an instance of such forced movement.

undertint ▶ **noun** a subdued or delicate tint.

undertone ▶ **noun** a subdued or muted tone of sound or colour: *they were talking in undertones.*
■an underlying quality or feeling: *the sexual undertones of most advertising.*

undertook past participle of **UNDERTAKE**.

undertow ▶ **noun** another term for **UNDERCURRENT**.

undertrial ▶ **noun** Indian informal a person who is on trial in a court of law.

undertrick ▶ **noun** Bridge a trick by which the declarer falls short of his or her contract.

underuse /ʌndəˈjuːz/ ▶ **verb** [with obj.] [usu. as adj. **underused**] use (something) below the optimum level: *massive acreages of underused land.*
▶ **noun** /ʌndəˈjuːs/ [mass noun] insufficient use: *underuse of existing services.*

underutilize (also **-ise**) ▶ **verb** [with obj.] underuse (something).
– DERIVATIVES **underutilization** noun.

undervalue ▶ **verb** (**-values**, **-valued**, **-valuing**) [with obj.] [often as adj. **undervalued**] rate (something) insufficiently highly; fail to appreciate: *the skills of the housewife remain undervalued in society.*
■underestimate the financial value of (something): *the company's assets were undervalued in its balance sheet.*
▶ **noun** a price below the real value.
– DERIVATIVES **undervaluation** noun.

undervest ▶ **noun** a vest worn as an undergarment.

underwater ▶ **adjective** & **adverb** situated, occurring, or done beneath the surface of the water: [as adj.] *there are underwater volcanoes in the region* | [as adv.] *the seal spent a lot of time underwater.*

underwear ▶ **noun** [mass noun] clothing worn under other clothes, typically next to the skin.

underweight ▶ **adjective** below a weight considered normal or desirable: *he was thirty pounds underweight.*
■Finance having less investment in a particular area than is considered desirable or appropriate: *the company is still underweight in Japan.*
▶ **verb** [with obj.] apply too little weight to (something): *we feared the hot-air balloon had been underweighted.*
▶ **noun** [mass noun] insufficient weight.

underwent past of **UNDERGO**.

underwhelm ▶ **verb** [with obj.] (usu. **be underwhelmed**) humorous fail to impress or make a positive impact on (someone); disappoint: *American voters seem underwhelmed by the choices for president.*
– ORIGIN 1950s: suggested by **OVERWHELM**.

underwing ▶ **noun 1** the hindwing of an insect, especially when it is normally hidden by a forewing.
2 the underside of a bird's wing.
3 (also **underwing moth**) [usu. with modifier] a moth with drab forewings and brightly coloured hindwings, typically yellow with a black terminal band.
• Several genera in the family Noctuidae.

underwire ▶ **noun** a semicircular wire support stitched under each cup of a bra.
– DERIVATIVES **underwired** adjective.

underwood ▶ **noun** [mass noun] small trees and shrubs growing beneath taller timber trees.

underwork ▶ **verb** [with obj.] (usu. **be underworked**) impose too little work on (someone).

underworld ▶ **noun 1** the world of criminals or of organized crime.
2 the mythical abode of the dead, imagined as being under the earth.

underwrite ▶ **verb** (past **-wrote**; past participle **-written**) [with obj.] **1** sign and accept liability under (an insurance policy), thus guaranteeing payment in case loss or damage occurs.
■accept (a liability or risk) in this way.
2 (of a bank or other financial institution) engage to buy all the unsold shares in (an issue of new shares).
■undertake to finance or otherwise support or guarantee (something): *they were willing to underwrite, in part, the construction of a ship.*
3 archaic write (something) below something else, especially other written matter.
– DERIVATIVES **underwriter** noun.

undescended ▶ **adjective** Medicine (of a testicle) remaining in the abdomen instead of descending normally into the scrotum.

undeserved ▶ **adjective** not warranted, merited, or earned: *an undeserved term of imprisonment.*
– DERIVATIVES **undeservedly** adverb.

undeserving ▶ **adjective** not deserving or worthy of something positive, especially help or praise.
– DERIVATIVES **undeservingly** adverb.

undesigned ▶ **adjective** unintended.
– DERIVATIVES **undesignedly** adverb.

undesirable ▶ **adjective** not wanted or desirable because harmful, objectionable, or unpleasant: *the drug's undesirable side effects.*
▶ **noun** a person considered to be objectionable in some way.
– DERIVATIVES **undesirability** noun, **undesirableness** noun, **undesirably** adverb.

undesired ▶ **adjective** (especially of an act or consequence) not wanted or desired.

undesirous ▶ **adjective** [predic.] formal not wanting or wishing something: *the prince was **undesirous of** seeing the Lady Anne.*

undetectable ▶ **adjective** not able to be detected.
– DERIVATIVES **undetectability** noun, **undetectably** adverb.

undetected ▶ **adjective** not detected or discovered: *the thieves escaped undetected.*

undetermined ▶ **adjective** not authoritatively decided or settled: *the acquisition will result in an as yet undetermined number of lay-offs.*
■not known: *the bus was travelling with an undetermined number of passengers when it crashed.*

undeterred ▶ **adjective** [predic.] persevering with something despite setbacks: *he was undeterred by these disasters.*

undeveloped ▶ **adjective** not having been developed: *undeveloped coal reserves.*
■not having developed: *undeveloped buds and shoots.*

b **but** | d **dog** | f **few** | g **get** | h **he** | j **yes** | k **cat** | l **leg** | m **man** | n **no** | p **pen** | r **red** | s **sit** | t **top** | v **voice** | w **we** | z **zoo** | ʃ **she** | ʒ **decision** | θ **thin** | ð **this** | ŋ **ring** | x **loch** | tʃ **chip** | dʒ **jar**

undeviating ▶ adjective showing no deviation; constant and steady: *the undeviating loyalty of his wife.*
– DERIVATIVES **undeviatingly** adverb.

undiagnosed ▶ adjective not diagnosed or having been subject to diagnosis.

undid past of **UNDO**.

undies ▶ plural noun informal articles of underwear, especially those of a woman or girl.
– ORIGIN early 20th cent.: abbreviation.

undifferenced ▶ adjective Heraldry (of arms) not made distinct by a mark of difference.

undifferentiated ▶ adjective not different or differentiated.

undigested ▶ adjective (of food) not digested.
■ (of information, facts, or ideas) not having been properly assessed, considered, or understood.

undignified ▶ adjective appearing foolish and unseemly; lacking in dignity: *an undignified exit.*

undiluted ▶ adjective (of a liquid) not diluted.
■ not moderated or weakened in any way: *a sudden surge of pure, undiluted happiness.*

undiminished ▶ adjective not diminished, reduced, or lessened: *his enthusiasm for the game remains undiminished.*

undine /'ʌndiːn/ ▶ noun a female spirit or nymph imagined as inhabiting water.
– ORIGIN early 19th cent.: from modern Latin *undina* (a word invented by Paracelsus), from Latin *unda* 'a wave'.

undiplomatic ▶ adjective being or appearing insensitive and tactless.
– DERIVATIVES **undiplomatically** adverb.

undirected ▶ adjective lacking direction; without a particular aim, purpose, or target: *she was full of ineffectual undirected anger.*

undiscerning ▶ adjective lacking judgement, insight, or taste: *an undiscerning audience.*

undischarged ▶ adjective not discharged: *an undischarged bankrupt | an undischarged gun.*

undisciplined ▶ adjective lacking in discipline; uncontrolled in behaviour or manner.

undisclosed ▶ adjective not revealed or made known publicly: *the precise terms of the agreement remained undisclosed.*

undiscovered ▶ adjective not discovered: *the novel had lain undiscovered for years among his papers.*

undiscriminating ▶ adjective not having or showing good judgement or taste.

undiscussed ▶ adjective not discussed.

undisguised ▶ adjective (of a feeling) not disguised or concealed; open: *she looked at him with undisguised contempt.*
– DERIVATIVES **undisguisedly** adverb.

undismayed ▶ adjective not dismayed or discouraged by a setback.

undisputed ▶ adjective not disputed or called in question; accepted.

undistinguishable ▶ adjective indistinguishable.

undistinguished ▶ adjective lacking distinction; unexceptional: *an undistinguished career.*

undistorted ▶ adjective not distorted: *it may be difficult to provide undistorted information.*

undistributed ▶ adjective not distributed.

undistributed middle ▶ noun Logic a fallacy arising from the failure of the middle term of a syllogism to refer to all the members of a class in at least one premise.

undisturbed ▶ adjective not disturbed: *a quiet weekend of undisturbed tranquillity | the tombs had lain undisturbed for 2,500 years.*

undivided ▶ adjective not divided, separated, or broken into parts.
■ concentrated on or devoted completely to one object: *I can now give you my undivided attention.*

undo ▶ verb (**undoes**; past **undid**; past participle **undone**) [with obj.] **1** unfasten, untie, or loosen (something): *the knot was difficult to undo.*
2 cancel or reverse the effects or results of (a previous action or measure): *there wasn't any way Evelyn could undo the damage.*
■ cancel (the last command executed by a computer).
3 formal cause the downfall or ruin of: *Iago's hatred of women undoes him.*
▶ noun Computing a feature of a computer program that

allows a user to cancel or reverse the last command executed.
– ORIGIN Old English *undōn* (see **UN-²**, **DO¹**).

undock ▶ verb [with obj.] **1** separate (a spacecraft) from another in space.
2 take (a ship) out of a dock.

undocumented ▶ adjective **1** not recorded in or proved by documents.
2 N. Amer. not having the appropriate legal document or licence: *undocumented immigrants.*

undoing ▶ noun [in sing.] a person's ruin or downfall: *he knew of his ex-partner's role in his undoing.*
■ the cause of such ruin or downfall: *that complacency was to be their undoing.*

undomesticated ▶ adjective not domesticated: *I never cook for him and I am totally undomesticated.*

undone ▶ adjective **1** not tied or fastened: *the top few buttons of his shirt were undone.*
2 not done or finished: *he had left his homework undone.*
3 formal or humorous (of a person) ruined by a disastrous or devastating setback or reverse: *I am undone!*

undoubtable ▶ adjective rare not able to be doubted; indubitable.
– DERIVATIVES **undoubtably** adverb.

undoubted ▶ adjective not questioned or doubted by anyone: *her undoubted ability.*
– DERIVATIVES **undoubtedly** adverb.

UNDP ▶ abbreviation for United Nations Development Programme.

undrained ▶ adjective not emptied of water; not drained: *undrained marshes.*

undramatic ▶ adjective lacking the qualities expected in drama: *an undramatic libretto.*
■ unexciting: *research tends to be undramatic and unglamorous.*

undraped ▶ adjective not covered with cloth or drapery.
■ (especially of a model or subject in art) naked.

undrawn ▶ adjective **1** (of curtains) not drawn across the window; open.
2 (of money) not drawn from a bank account.

undreamed /ʌnˈdriːmd, -ˈdrɛmt/ (Brit. also **undreamt** /ʌnˈdrɛmt/) ▶ adjective (**undreamed of**) not thought to be possible (used to express pleasant surprise at the amount, extent, or level of something): *she is now enjoying undreamed-of success.*

undress ▶ verb [no obj.] take off one's clothes: *she undressed and climbed into bed | I went into the bathroom to get undressed.*
■ [with obj.] take the clothes off (someone else).
▶ noun [mass noun] **1** the state of being naked or only partially clothed: *women in various states of undress.*
2 Military ordinary clothing or uniform, as opposed to that worn on ceremonial occasions. Compare with **FULL DRESS**.

undressed ▶ adjective **1** wearing no clothes; naked: *he was undressed and ready for bed.*
2 not treated, processed, or prepared for use: *undressed deerskin | a rough, undressed stone slab.*
3 (of food) not having a dressing: *an undressed salad.*

undrinkable ▶ adjective not fit to be drunk because of impurity or poor quality.

UNDRO ▶ abbreviation for United Nations Disaster Relief Office.

undue ▶ adjective unwarranted or inappropriate because excessive or disproportionate: *this figure did not give rise to undue concern.*
– DERIVATIVES **unduly** adverb.

undue influence ▶ noun [mass noun] Law influence by which a person is induced to act otherwise than by their own free will or without adequate attention to the consequences.

undulant /'ʌndjʊl(ə)nt/ ▶ adjective having a rising and falling motion or appearance like that of waves; undulating.
– ORIGIN mid 19th cent.: from Latin *undulant-* 'moving like a wave', from the verb *undulare.*

undulant fever ▶ noun [mass noun] brucellosis in humans.
– ORIGIN late 19th cent.: so named because of the intermittent fever associated with the disease.

undulate ▶ verb /'ʌndjʊleɪt/ [no obj.] move with a smooth wave-like motion: *her body undulated to the thumping rhythm of the music.*

■ [usu. as adj. **undulating**] have a wavy form or outline: *delightful views over undulating countryside.*
▶ adjective /'ʌndjʊlət/ Botany & Zoology (especially of a leaf) having a wavy surface or edge.
– DERIVATIVES **undulately** adverb, **undulation** noun, **undulatory** adjective.
– ORIGIN mid 17th cent.: from late Latin *undulatus*, from Latin *unda* 'a wave'.

undutiful ▶ adjective not respectful or obedient.
– DERIVATIVES **undutifully** adverb, **undutifulness** noun.

undy /'ʌndi/ (also **undee**) ▶ adjective [usu. postpositive] Heraldry another term for **WAVY**.

undyed ▶ adjective (of fabric) not dyed; of its natural colour.

undying ▶ adjective (especially of an emotion) lasting forever: *promises of undying love.*
– DERIVATIVES **undyingly** adverb.

unearned ▶ adjective not earned or deserved: *unearned privileges.*
■ Baseball (of a run) resulting from an error by the fielding side.

unearned income ▶ noun [mass noun] income from investments rather than from work.

unearned increment ▶ noun an increase in the value of land or property without labour or expenditure on the part of the owner.

unearth ▶ verb [with obj.] **1** find (something) in the ground by digging.
■ discover (something hidden, lost, or kept secret) by investigation or searching: *they have done all they can to unearth the truth.*
2 drive (an animal, especially a fox) out of a hole or burrow.

unearthly ▶ adjective **1** unnatural or mysterious, especially in a disturbing way: *unearthly quiet.*
2 informal unreasonably early or inconvenient: *a job which involves getting up at an unearthly hour.*
– DERIVATIVES **unearthliness** noun.

unease ▶ noun [mass noun] anxiety or discontent: *public unease about defence policy.*

uneasy ▶ adjective (**uneasier, uneasiest**) causing or feeling anxiety; troubled or uncomfortable: *she felt guilty now and a little uneasy | an uneasy silence.*
– DERIVATIVES **uneasily** adverb, **uneasiness** noun.

uneatable ▶ adjective not fit to be eaten.

uneaten ▶ adjective not eaten: *salad lying uneaten on the plate.*

uneconomic ▶ adjective unprofitable: *the closure of uneconomic pits.*
■ constituting an inefficient use of money or other resources: *it may be uneconomic to repair some goods.*

uneconomical ▶ adjective wasteful of money or other resources; not economical: *the old buses eventually become uneconomical to run.*
– DERIVATIVES **uneconomically** adverb.

unedifying ▶ adjective (especially of an event taking place in public) distasteful; unpleasant: *the unedifying sight of the two leaders screeching conflicting proposals.*
– DERIVATIVES **unedifyingly** adverb.

unedited ▶ adjective (of material for publication or broadcasting) not edited.

uneducated ▶ adjective having or showing a poor level of education.
– DERIVATIVES **uneducable** adjective.

unelectable ▶ adjective (of a candidate or party) very likely to be defeated at an election.

unelected ▶ adjective (of an official) not elected: *unelected bureaucrats.*

unembarrassed ▶ adjective not feeling or showing embarrassment.

unembellished ▶ adjective not embellished or decorated: *the unembellished truth.*

unemotional ▶ adjective not having or showing strong feelings: *a flat, unemotional voice.*
– DERIVATIVES **unemotionally** adverb.

unemphatic ▶ adjective (especially of tone or a gesture) not emphatic: *an unemphatic 'yes'.*
– DERIVATIVES **unemphatically** adverb.

unemployable ▶ adjective (of a person) not able or likely to get paid employment because of a lack of skills or qualifications.
▶ noun an unemployable person.
– DERIVATIVES **unemployability** noun.

unemployed ▶ adjective (of a person) without a

paid job but available to work: *I was unemployed for three months* | [as plural noun **the unemployed**] *a training programme for the long-term unemployed.*
■(of a thing) not in use.

unemployment ▶ noun [mass noun] the state of being unemployed.
■the number or proportion of unemployed people: *a time of high unemployment.*

unemployment benefit ▶ noun [mass noun] payment made by the state or a trade union to an unemployed person.

unenclosed ▶ adjective (especially of land) not enclosed: *the unenclosed uplands of Wales.*

unencumbered ▶ adjective not having any burden or impediment: *he needed to travel light and unencumbered.*
■free of debt or other financial liability.

unending ▶ adjective having or seeming to have no end: *the charity rescues children from unending poverty.*
■countless or continual: *unending demands.*
– DERIVATIVES **unendingly** adverb, **unendingness** noun.

unendowed ▶ adjective not endowed, especially by donated funds.

unendurable ▶ adjective not able to be tolerated or endured: *cries of unendurable suffering.*
– DERIVATIVES **unendurably** adverb.

unenforceable ▶ adjective (especially of an obligation or law) impossible to enforce.

unengaged ▶ adjective not occupied or engaged.

un-English ▶ adjective not considered characteristic of English people or the English language.

unenjoyable ▶ adjective (of an activity or occasion) not giving pleasure.

unenlightened ▶ adjective not having or showing an enlightened outlook: *unenlightened rules.*
– DERIVATIVES **unenlightening** adjective, **unenlightenment** noun.

unentangle ▶ verb another term for DISENTANGLE.

unenterprising ▶ adjective not having or showing initiative or entrepreneurial ability.

unenthusiastic ▶ adjective not having or showing enthusiasm: *an unenthusiastic response.*
– DERIVATIVES **unenthusiastically** adverb.

unenviable ▶ adjective difficult, undesirable, or unpleasant: *an unenviable reputation for drunkenness.*
– DERIVATIVES **unenviably** adverb.

unenvied ▶ adjective not regarded with envy.

UNEP ▶ abbreviation for United Nations Environment Programme.

unequal ▶ adjective **1** not equal in quantity, size, or value: *two rooms of unequal size* | *unequal odds.*
■not fair, evenly balanced, or having equal advantage: *the ownership of capital is unequal in this country.*
2 [predic.] not having the ability or resources to meet a challenge: *she felt unequal to the task before her.*
▶ noun a person or thing considered to be different from another in status or level.
– DERIVATIVES **unequally** adverb.

unequalled (US **unequaled**) ▶ adjective superior to all others in performance or extent: *a range of facilities unequalled in London* | *trout of unequalled quality.*

unequipped ▶ adjective [predic.] not equipped with the necessary items or skills: *kids unequipped to deal with the situation.*

unequivocal ▶ adjective leaving no doubt; unambiguous: *an unequivocal answer* | *he was unequivocal in condemning the violence.*
– DERIVATIVES **unequivocally** adverb, **unequivocalness** noun.

unerring ▶ adjective always right or accurate: *an unerring sense of direction.*
– DERIVATIVES **unerringly** adverb, **unerringness** noun.

unescapable ▶ adjective unable to be avoided or denied.

UNESCO /juːˈnɛskəʊ/ (also **Unesco**) an agency of the United Nations set up in 1945 to promote the exchange of information, ideas, and culture.
– ORIGIN acronym from *United Nations Educational, Scientific, and Cultural Organization.*

unescorted ▶ adjective not escorted, especially for protection, security, or as a mark of rank.

unessential ▶ adjective & noun another term for INESSENTIAL.

unestablished ▶ adjective not established.
■not forming part of the permanent staff: *an unestablished professor of anatomy.*

unethical ▶ adjective not morally correct: *it is unethical to torment any creature for entertainment.*
– DERIVATIVES **unethically** adverb.

unevangelical ▶ adjective not evangelical.

uneven ▶ adjective not level or smooth: *the floors are cracked and uneven.*
■not regular, consistent, or equal: *the uneven distribution of resources.* ■(of a contest) not equally balanced: *Fran struggled briefly but soon gave up the uneven match.*
– DERIVATIVES **unevenly** adverb, **unevenness** noun.
– ORIGIN Old English *unefen* 'not corresponding exactly' (see UN-[1], EVEN[1]).

uneven bars ▶ plural noun North American term for ASYMMETRIC BARS.

uneventful ▶ adjective not marked by interesting or exciting events.
– DERIVATIVES **uneventfully** adverb, **uneventfulness** noun.

unexamined ▶ adjective not investigated or examined: *widely held but largely unexamined preconceptions.*

unexampled ▶ adjective formal having no precedent or parallel: *a regime which brought such unexampled disaster on its people.*

unexceptionable ▶ adjective not open to objection, but not particularly new or exciting: *the unexceptionable belief that society should be governed by law.*
– DERIVATIVES **unexceptionableness** noun, **unexceptionably** adverb.

> **USAGE** There is a clear distinction in meaning between **exceptionable** ('open to objection') and **exceptional** ('out of the ordinary; very good'). However, this distinction has become blurred in the negative forms **unexceptionable** and **unexceptional**. Strictly speaking, **unexceptionable** means 'not open to objection', as in *this view is unexceptionable in itself*, while **unexceptional** means 'not out of the ordinary; usual', as in *the hotel was adequate but unexceptional*. But, although the distinction may be clear in these two examples, the meaning of **unexceptionable** is often indeterminate between 'not open to objection' and 'ordinary', as in *the food was bland and unexceptionable* or *the candidates were pretty unexceptionable*.

unexceptional ▶ adjective not out of the ordinary; usual: *an unexceptional movie.*
– DERIVATIVES **unexceptionally** adverb.

unexcitable ▶ adjective (of a person) not easily excited.
– DERIVATIVES **unexcitability** noun.

unexciting ▶ adjective not exciting; dull.

unexecuted ▶ adjective not executed, carried out, or put into effect: *unexecuted schemes for redeveloping the main buildings.*

unexercised ▶ adjective not made use of or put into practice: *the enemy left no manner of cruelty unexercised that day.*
■(of a person) not taking exercise; unfit.

unexhausted ▶ adjective (especially of resources or reserves) not exhausted.

unexpected ▶ adjective not expected or regarded as likely to happen: *his death was totally unexpected* | [as noun **the unexpected**] *he seemed to have a knack for saying the unexpected.*
– DERIVATIVES **unexpectedly** adverb [as submodifier] *an unexpectedly high price,* **unexpectedness** noun.

unexpired ▶ adjective (of an agreement or period of time) not yet having come to an end: *the unexpired portion of the lease.*

unexplainable ▶ adjective unable to be explained or accounted for: *unexplainable rages.*
– DERIVATIVES **unexplainably** adverb.

unexplained ▶ adjective not described or made clear; unknown: *the reason for her summons was as yet unexplained.*
■not accounted for or attributable to an identified cause: *cot death is still an unexplained phenomenon.*

unexploded ▶ adjective (of a bomb or other explosive device) not having exploded.

unexploited ▶ adjective (of resources) not used to maximum benefit: *unexploited reserves of natural gas.*

unexplored ▶ adjective (of a country or area) not investigated or mapped.
■not evaluated or discussed in detail: *the research focuses on an unexplored theme in European history.*

unexposed ▶ adjective covered or protected; not vulnerable.
■[predic.] not introduced to or acquainted with something: *a person unexposed to spiritualist traditions.* ■[predic.] not made public; concealed: *no secrets were left unexposed.* ■(of photographic film) not subjected to light.

unexpressed ▶ adjective (of a thought or feeling) not communicated or made known: *he thought it best to leave his doubts unexpressed.*
■Genetics (of a gene) not appearing in a phenotype.

unexpurgated ▶ adjective (of a text) complete and containing all the original material; uncensored.

unfaceable ▶ adjective (of a situation or circumstance) not able to be confronted or dealt with.

unfading ▶ adjective not losing brightness, vitality, or strength.
– DERIVATIVES **unfadingly** adverb.

unfailing ▶ adjective without error or fault: *his unfailing memory for names.*
■reliable or constant: *his mother had always been an unfailing source of reassurance.*
– DERIVATIVES **unfailingly** adverb, **unfailingness** noun.

unfair ▶ adjective not based on or behaving according to the principles of equality and justice: *at times like these the legal system appears inhuman and unfair.*
■unkind, inconsiderate, or unreasonable: *you're unfair to criticize like that, she's never done you any harm.* ■not following the rules of a game or sport: *he was sent off for unfair play.*
– DERIVATIVES **unfairly** adverb, **unfairness** noun.
– ORIGIN Old English *unfæger* 'not beautiful' (see UN-[1], FAIR[1]).

unfaithful ▶ adjective not faithful, in particular:
■engaging in sexual relations with a person other than one's regular partner in contravention of a previous promise or understanding: *you haven't been unfaithful to him, have you?* | *her unfaithful husband.* ■disloyal, treacherous, or insincere: *she felt that to sell the house would be unfaithful to her parent's memory.*
– DERIVATIVES **unfaithfully** adverb, **unfaithfulness** noun.

unfaltering ▶ adjective not faltering; steady; resolute: *her unfaltering energy and determination.*
– DERIVATIVES **unfalteringly** adverb.

unfamiliar ▶ adjective not known or recognized: *his voice was unfamiliar to her.*
■unusual or uncharacteristic: *the yellow taxicab was an unfamiliar sight on these roads.* ■[predic.] (**unfamiliar with**) not having knowledge or experience of: *the organization was set up to advise people who might be unfamiliar with legal procedures.*
– DERIVATIVES **unfamiliarity** noun.

unfancied ▶ adjective (of a sports team or racehorse) not considered likely to win.

unfashionable ▶ adjective not fashionable or popular at a particular time: *they lived in an unfashionable part of London.*
– DERIVATIVES **unfashionableness** noun, **unfashionably** adverb.

unfashioned ▶ adjective chiefly poetic/literary not made into a specific shape; formless.

unfasten ▶ verb [with obj.] open the fastening of; undo (something): *Allie stands before the mirror unfastening her earrings* | [as adj. **unfastened**] *he had left the door unfastened.*
■[no obj.] become loose or undone.

unfathered ▶ adjective dated having no known or acknowledged father; illegitimate.
■chiefly poetic/literary of unknown or obscure origin: *unfathered rumours.*

unfatherly ▶ adjective not having or showing the affectionate or protective characteristics associated with a father.
– DERIVATIVES **unfatherliness** noun.

unfathomable ▶ adjective incapable of being fully explored or understood: *her grey eyes were dark with some unfathomable emotion.*
■(of water or a natural feature) impossible to measure the extent of.
– DERIVATIVES **unfathomableness** noun, **unfathomably** adverb.

unfathomed ▶ adjective not fully explored or understood.
■ (of water) of unascertained depth.

unfavourable (US **unfavorable**) ▶ adjective
1 expressing or showing a lack of approval or support: *single mothers are often the target of unfavourable press attention.*
2 adverse; inauspicious: *it would be unwise to sell the company while the economic circumstances are so unfavourable.*
– DERIVATIVES **unfavourableness** noun, **unfavourably** adverb.

unfavourite (US **unfavorite**) ▶ adjective [attrib.] informal least favourite; most disliked.

unfazed ▶ adjective [predic.] informal not disconcerted or perturbed: *the protestors were unfazed by the prospect of arrest.*

unfeasible ▶ adjective inconvenient or impractical: *childcare is expensive, making the return to work unfeasible for many women.*
– DERIVATIVES **unfeasibility** noun, **unfeasibly** adverb.

unfed ▶ adjective not having been fed.

unfeeling ▶ adjective unsympathetic, harsh, or callous.
■ lacking physical sensation or sensitivity.
– DERIVATIVES **unfeelingly** adverb, **unfeelingness** noun.
– ORIGIN late Old English *unfēlende* 'insensible' (see `UN-`[1], **FEELING**).

unfeigned ▶ adjective genuine; sincere: *a broad smile of unfeigned delight.*
– DERIVATIVES **unfeignedly** adverb.

unfelt ▶ adjective not felt or experienced.

unfeminine ▶ adjective not having or showing qualities traditionally associated with women.
– DERIVATIVES **unfemininity** noun.

unfenced ▶ adjective not provided with fences.

unfermented ▶ adjective not fermented.

unfertile ▶ adjective not fertile; infertile.

unfertilized (also **-ised**) ▶ adjective not fertilized: *an unfertilized egg | unfertilized land.*

unfetter ▶ verb [with obj.] [usu. as adj. **unfettered**] release from restraint or inhibition: *his imagination is unfettered by the laws of logic.*

unfilial ▶ adjective not having or showing the qualities associated with a son or daughter.
– DERIVATIVES **unfilially** adverb.

unfilled ▶ adjective not filled: *there are a number of unfilled posts in this area of nursing.*

unfiltered ▶ adjective **1** not filtered: *unfiltered tap water.*
2 (of a cigarette) not provided with a filter.

unfinished ▶ adjective not finished or concluded; incomplete: *her last novel is unfinished.*
■ (of an object) not having been given an attractive surface appearance as the final stage of manufacture.

unfit ▶ adjective **1** [predic.] (of a thing) not of the necessary quality or standard to meet a particular purpose: *the land is unfit for food crops.*
■ (of a person) not having the requisite qualities or skills to undertake something competently: *she is unfit to have care and control of her children.*
2 (of a person) not in good physical condition, typically as a result of failure to take regular exercise.
▶ verb (**unfitted**, **unfitting**) [with obj.] archaic make (something or someone) unsuitable; disqualify.
– DERIVATIVES **unfitly** adverb, **unfitness** noun.

unfitted ▶ adjective **1** [predic.] (of a person) not fitted or suited for a particular task or vocation: *she was unfitted for marriage.*
2 (of furniture) not fitted.

unfitting ▶ adjective not fitting or suitable; unbecoming: *certain occupations were held unfitting for baptized believers.*
– DERIVATIVES **unfittingly** adverb.

unfixed ▶ adjective not fixed, in particular:
■ not fixed in a definite place or position; unfastened; loose: *the green cloth cover had become unfixed in a dozen places.* ■ uncertain or variable: *a being of unfixed gender.*
– DERIVATIVES **unfix** verb.

unflagging ▶ adjective tireless; persistent: *his apparently unflagging enthusiasm impressed her.*
– DERIVATIVES **unflaggingly** adverb.

unflappable ▶ adjective informal having or showing calmness in a crisis.
– DERIVATIVES **unflappability** noun, **unflappably** adverb.

unflattering ▶ adjective not flattering: *the reviews of the book were very unflattering | an unflattering portrait.*
– DERIVATIVES **unflatteringly** adverb.

unflavoured (US **unflavored**) ▶ adjective (of food or drink) not containing additional flavourings.

unfledged ▶ adjective (of a bird) not yet fledged.
■ figurative (of a person) inexperienced; youthful.

unfleshed ▶ adjective chiefly poetic/literary not covered with flesh.

unflinching ▶ adjective not showing fear or hesitation in the face of danger or difficulty: *he has shown unflinching determination throughout the campaign.*
– DERIVATIVES **unflinchingly** adverb.

unfocused (also **unfocussed**) ▶ adjective (of a person or their eyes) not seeing clearly; appearing glazed or expressionless.
■ (of an optical device) not adjusted to focus. ■ (of a lens) not making incident light rays meet at a single point. ■ (of an object of vision) not in focus; indistinct. ■ (of feelings or plans) without a specific aim or direction: *my aspirations to write history were real but unfocused.*

unfold ▶ verb open or spread out from a folded position: [with obj.] *he unfolded the map and laid it out on the table |* [no obj.] *a Chinese paper flower that unfolds in water.*
■ [with obj.] reveal or disclose (thoughts or information): *Miss Eva unfolded her secret exploits to Mattie.* ■ [no obj.] (of information or a sequence of events) be revealed or disclosed: *there was a fascinating scene unfolding before me.*
– DERIVATIVES **unfoldment** noun US.
– ORIGIN Old English *unfealdan* (see **UN-**[2], **FOLD**[1]).

unforced ▶ adjective not produced by effort; natural: *an unforced cheerfulness.*
■ not compelled or constrained: *his retirement was an unforced departure.*
– DERIVATIVES **unforcedly** adverb.

unforeseeable ▶ adjective not able to be anticipated or predicted: *too many unforeseeable political consequences could arise from such a decision.*

unforeseen ▶ adjective not anticipated or predicted.

unforetold ▶ adjective poetic/literary not foretold; unpredicted.

unforgettable ▶ adjective impossible to forget; very memorable: *that unforgettable first kiss.*
– DERIVATIVES **unforgettably** adverb.

unforgivable ▶ adjective so bad as to be unable to be forgiven or excused: *losing your temper with him was unforgivable.*
– DERIVATIVES **unforgivably** adverb.

unforgiven ▶ adjective not forgiven: *the catalogue of unforgiven wrongs simply grows and grows.*

unforgiving ▶ adjective not willing to forgive or excuse people's faults or wrongdoings: *he was always a proud and unforgiving man.*
■ (of conditions) harsh; hostile: *the moor can be a wild and unforgiving place in bad weather.*
– DERIVATIVES **unforgivingly** adverb, **unforgivingness** noun.

unforgotten ▶ adjective not forgotten.

unformed ▶ adjective without a definite form or shape: *she packed the unformed butter into the mould.*
■ not having developed or been developed fully: *he had an ambitious, albeit unformed, idea for a novel | unformed youths.*

unformulated ▶ adjective not formulated: *the unformulated rules of society.*

unforthcoming ▶ adjective [predic.] **1** (of a person) not willing to divulge information: *the sergeant seemed unforthcoming, so he enquired at the gate.*
2 (of something required) not ready or made available when wanted or needed: *with money unforthcoming from the company, the project has had to be delayed.*

unfortified ▶ adjective not fortified: *there seems to have been an unfortified village on the site | unfortified wines.*

unfortunate ▶ adjective having or marked by bad fortune; unlucky: *the unfortunate Cunningham was sacked.*
■ (of a circumstance) unfavourable or inauspicious: *the delay at the airport was an unfortunate start to our holiday.* ■ regrettable or inappropriate: *his unfortunate remark silenced the gathering.*
▶ noun (often **unfortunates**) a person who suffers bad fortune.
■ archaic a person who is considered immoral or lacking in religious faith or instruction, especially a prostitute.

unfortunately ▶ adverb [sentence adverb] it is unfortunate that: *unfortunately, we do not have the time to interview every applicant.*

unfounded ▶ adjective having no foundation or basis in fact: *her persistent fear that she had cancer was unfounded.*
– DERIVATIVES **unfoundedly** adverb, **unfoundedness** noun.

UNFPA ▶ abbreviation for United Nations Fund for Population Activities.

unframed ▶ adjective (especially of a picture) not having a frame.

unfree ▶ adjective deprived or devoid of liberty.
– DERIVATIVES **unfreedom** noun.

unfreeze ▶ verb (past **unfroze**; past participle **unfrozen**) [with obj.] cause (something) to thaw.
■ [no obj.] become thawed. ■ remove restrictions on the use or transfer of (an asset).

unfrequented ▶ adjective (of a place) visited only rarely: *a region with only a few unfrequented tracks.*

unfriended ▶ adjective poetic/literary without friends: *murder left innocent people bereft and unfriended.*

unfriendly ▶ adjective (**unfriendlier**, **unfriendliest**) not friendly: *she shot him an unfriendly glance.*
– DERIVATIVES **unfriendliness** noun.

unfrock ▶ verb another term for **DEFROCK**.

unfroze past of **UNFREEZE**.

unfrozen[1] past participle of **UNFREEZE**.

unfrozen[2] ▶ adjective not or no longer frozen: *larvae remain unfrozen under the ice.*

unfruitful ▶ adjective **1** not producing good or helpful results; unproductive: *the meeting was unfruitful.*
2 not producing fruit or crops; unfertile.
– DERIVATIVES **unfruitfully** adverb, **unfruitfulness** noun.

unfulfilled ▶ adjective not carried out or brought to completion: *it was his unfulfilled ambition to write.*
■ not having fully utilized or exploited one's abilities or character.
– DERIVATIVES **unfulfillable** adjective, **unfulfilling** adjective.

unfunded ▶ adjective not funded, in particular:
■ not receiving public funds: *a new education bill remained unfunded.* ■ (of a debt) repayable on demand rather than having been converted into a more or less permanent debt at fixed interest. ■ denoting or relating to a pension scheme without a pension fund, the current beneficiaries being paid by a former employer from revenue or contributions by present employees.

unfunny ▶ adjective (**unfunnier**, **unfunniest**) (especially of something intended to be funny) not amusing: *a hideously unfunny spoof film.*
– DERIVATIVES **unfunnily** adverb, **unfunniness** noun.

unfurl ▶ verb make or become spread out from a rolled or folded state, especially in order to be open to the wind: [with obj.] *a man was unfurling a sail |* [no obj.] *the flags unfurl.*

unfurnished ▶ adjective **1** (of a house or flat) without furniture, especially available to be rented without furniture: *an unfurnished apartment.*
2 archaic not supplied: *he is unfurnished with the ideas of justice.*

unfussy ▶ adjective not fussy: *a simple unfussy design.*
– DERIVATIVES **unfussily** adverb.

ungainly ▶ adjective (of a person or movement) awkward; clumsy: *an ungainly walk.*
– DERIVATIVES **ungainliness** noun.
– ORIGIN mid 17th cent.: from **UN-**[1] 'not' + obsolete *gainly* 'graceful', based on Old Norse *gegn* 'straight'.

ungainsayable /ˌʌŋɡeɪnˈseɪəb(ə)l/ ▶ adjective formal undeniable; irrefutable.

ungallant ▶ adjective not gallant.
– DERIVATIVES **ungallantly** adverb.

ungeared ▶ adjective **1** (of a vehicle) not having gears or gearing.

2 (of a company or its balance sheet) having or showing no debt.

ungenerous ▸ adjective not generous; mean.
– DERIVATIVES **ungenerously** adverb, **ungenerousness** noun.

ungenial ▸ adjective not genial.

ungentle ▸ adjective not gentle: *an ungentle grip.*
– DERIVATIVES **ungentleness** noun, **ungently** adverb.

ungentlemanly ▸ adjective not appropriate to or behaving like a gentleman: *an ungentlemanly lack of sportsmanship.*
– DERIVATIVES **ungentlemanliness** noun.

unget-at-able ▸ adjective informal inaccessible.

ungifted ▸ adjective not having any exceptional talents.

ungird ▸ verb [with obj.] archaic release or take off by undoing a belt or girth.

ungiving ▸ adjective (of a person) cold or stubborn in relationships with other people.
▪(of a material) not bending or pliable; stiff.

unglamorous ▸ adjective lacking glamour and excitement: *an unglamorous family car.*

unglazed ▸ adjective not glazed: *unglazed porcelain.*

ungloved ▸ adjective not wearing a glove or gloves.

unglued ▸ adjective not or no longer stuck: *grease particles come unglued from the plate.*
▪informal (of a person or state of mind) confused and emotionally strained: *it had been a long day, and tempers were becoming unglued.*

ungodly ▸ adjective irreligious or immoral: *ungodly lives of self-obsession, lust, and pleasure.*
▪informal unreasonably early or inconvenient: *I've been troubled by telephone calls at ungodly hours.*
– DERIVATIVES **ungodliness** noun.

ungovernable ▸ adjective impossible to control or govern.
– DERIVATIVES **ungovernability** noun, **ungovernably** adverb.

ungraceful ▸ adjective lacking grace; clumsy.
– DERIVATIVES **ungracefully** adverb, **ungracefulness** noun.

ungracious ▸ adjective **1** not polite or friendly: *after Anna's kindness I wouldn't want to seem ungracious.*
2 not graceful or elegant.
– DERIVATIVES **ungraciously** adverb, **ungraciousness** noun.

ungrammatical ▸ adjective not conforming to grammatical rules; not well formed: *ungrammatical sentences.*
– DERIVATIVES **ungrammaticality** noun (pl. **-ies**), **ungrammatically** adverb, **ungrammaticalness** noun.

ungraspable ▸ adjective impossible to comprehend or understand.

ungrateful ▸ adjective not feeling or showing gratitude: *she's so ungrateful for everything we do.*
– DERIVATIVES **ungratefully** adverb, **ungratefulness** noun.

ungreen ▸ adjective (of a product or practice) harmful to the environment; not ecologically acceptable: *an ungreen commercial development.*
▪(of a person or organization) not supporting protection of the environment.
– DERIVATIVES **ungreenly** adverb.

ungrounded ▸ adjective **1** having no basis or justification; unfounded: *ungrounded fears.*
2 not electrically earthed.
3 [predic.] (**ungrounded in**) not properly instructed or proficient in (a subject or activity).

ungroup ▸ verb [with obj.] Computing separate (items) from a group formed within a word-processing or graphics package.

ungrudging ▸ adjective not grudging: *he showed her ungrudging courtesy and kindness.*
– DERIVATIVES **ungrudgingly** adverb.

ungual /ˈʌŋɡw(ə)l/ ▸ adjective Zoology & Medicine of, relating to, or affecting a nail, hoof, or claw.
– ORIGIN mid 19th cent.: from Latin *unguis* 'nail' + **-AL**.

unguard ▸ verb [with obj.] (in bridge and whist) expose (a high card) to a risk of defeat by discarding low cards in the same suit.

unguarded ▸ adjective without protection or a guard: *the museum was unguarded at night.*
▪not well considered; careless: *an unguarded remark.*

– DERIVATIVES **unguardedly** adverb, **unguardedness** noun.

unguent /ˈʌŋɡwənt/ ▸ noun a soft greasy or viscous substance used as ointment or for lubrication.
– ORIGIN late Middle English: from Latin *unguentum*, from *unguere* 'anoint'.

unguessable ▸ adjective impossible to guess or imagine: *a manor of an unguessable antiquity.*

unguiculate /ʌŋˈɡwɪkjʊlət/ ▸ adjective Zoology having one or more nails or claws.
▪Botany (of a petal) having a narrow stalk-like base.
– ORIGIN early 19th cent.: from modern Latin *unguiculatus*, from Latin *unguiculus* 'fingernail, toenail', diminutive of *unguis* 'nail'.

unguided ▸ adjective not guided in a particular path or direction; left to take its own course.
▪(of a missile) not directed by remote control or internal equipment.

unguis /ˈʌŋɡwɪs/ ▸ noun (pl. **ungues** /-wiːz/) Zoology a nail, claw, or fang.
– ORIGIN early 18th cent.: from Latin.

ungulate /ˈʌŋɡjʊlət, -leɪt/ ▸ noun Zoology a hoofed mammal.
●Former order Ungulata, now divided into two unrelated orders (see **ARTIODACTYLA** and **PERISSODACTYLA**).
– ORIGIN early 19th cent.: from late Latin *ungulatus*, from Latin *ungula* 'hoof'.

unguled /ˈʌŋɡjuːld/ ▸ adjective Heraldry (of an animal) having hoofs of a specified different tincture.

unhallowed ▸ adjective not formally consecrated: *unhallowed ground.*
▪unholy; wicked: *unhallowed retribution.*

unhampered ▸ adjective not impeded or encumbered: *a press unhampered by government censorship.*

unhand ▸ verb [with obj.] [usu. in imperative] archaic or humorous release (someone) from one's grasp: *'Unhand me, sir!' she cried.*

unhandled ▸ adjective not handled, in particular (of an animal) not tamed.

unhandsome ▸ adjective [often with negative] not handsome: *Bobby was not unhandsome in his uniform.*

unhandy ▸ adjective **1** not easy to handle or manage; awkward.
2 not skilful in using the hands.
– DERIVATIVES **unhandily** adverb, **unhandiness** noun.

unhang ▸ verb (past and past participle **unhung**) rare [with obj.] take down from a hanging position.

unhappen ▸ verb [no obj.] (of an occurrence) become as though never having happened; be reversed: *things had happened that could never unhappen.*

unhappily ▸ adverb in an unhappy manner.
▪[sentence adverb] unfortunately: *unhappily, such days do not come too often.*

unhappy ▸ adjective (**unhappier**, **unhappiest**) not happy: *an unhappy marriage.*
▪[predic.] (**unhappy at/about/with**) not satisfied or pleased with (a situation): *many were unhappy about the scale of the cuts.* ▪unfortunate: *an unhappy coincidence.*
– DERIVATIVES **unhappiness** noun.

unharmed ▸ adjective [often as complement] not harmed; uninjured: *all the hostages were released unharmed.*

unharmful ▸ adjective not harmful.

unharmonious ▸ adjective not harmonious.

unharness ▸ verb [with obj.] remove a harness from (a horse or other animal).

unhasp ▸ verb [with obj.] archaic unfasten.

unhatched ▸ adjective (of an egg or young bird) not yet hatched.

UNHCR an agency of the United Nations set up in 1951 to aid, protect, and monitor refugees.
– ORIGIN abbreviation of *United Nations High Commission for Refugees.*

unhealed ▸ adjective not yet healed.

unhealthful ▸ adjective harmful to health.
– DERIVATIVES **unhealthfulness** noun.

unhealthy ▸ adjective (**unhealthier**, **unhealthiest**) harmful to health: *an unhealthy diet.*
▪not having or showing good health: *his skin looked pale and unhealthy.* ▪(of a person's attitude or behaviour) not sensible or well balanced; abnormal and harmful: *an unhealthy obsession with fast cars.*
– DERIVATIVES **unhealthily** adverb, **unhealthiness** noun.

unheard ▸ adjective not heard or listened to: *my protests went unheard.*
■(**unheard of**) not previously known of or done: *sales tax was unheard of in Kansas up until 1937* | *wines from unheard-of villages.*

unheated ▸ adjective not heated.

unhedged ▸ adjective **1** not bounded by a hedge.
2 (of an investment or investor) not protected against loss by balancing or compensating contracts or transactions.

unheeded ▸ adjective heard or noticed but disregarded: *my protest went unheeded.*

unheedful ▸ adjective [predic.] not noticing or paying attention: *I charged down the stairs, unheedful of the missing bannister.*

unheeding ▸ adjective not paying attention: *Mary, unheeding, watched the television.*
– DERIVATIVES **unheedingly** adverb.

unheimlich /ʊnˈhaɪmlɪx/ ▸ adjective uncanny; weird.
– ORIGIN German.

unhelpful ▸ adjective not helpful: *several complained that the staff were unhelpful.*
– DERIVATIVES **unhelpfully** adverb, **unhelpfulness** noun.

unheralded ▸ adjective not previously announced, expected, or recognized.

unheroic ▸ adjective not heroic: *an unheroic death.*
– DERIVATIVES **unheroically** adverb.

unhesitating ▸ adjective without doubt or hesitation; immediate: *war merits unequivocal and unhesitating condemnation.*
– DERIVATIVES **unhesitatingly** adverb.

unhindered ▸ adjective not hindered or obstructed.

unhinge ▸ verb [with obj.] **1** [usu. as adj. **unhinged**] make (someone) mentally unbalanced: *I thought she must be unhinged by grief.*
▪deprive of stability or fixity; throw into disorder.
2 take (a door) off its hinges.

unhistoric ▸ adjective not historic or historical.

unhistorical ▸ adjective not in accordance with history or with historical analysis.
– DERIVATIVES **unhistorically** adverb.

unhitch ▸ verb [with obj.] unhook or unfasten (something tethered to or caught on something else).

unholy ▸ adjective (**unholier**, **unholiest**) sinful; wicked.
▪denoting an alliance with potentially harmful implications between two or more parties that are not natural allies. ▪informal awful; dreadful (used for emphasis): *she was making an unholy racket.*
– DERIVATIVES **unholiness** noun.
– ORIGIN Old English *unhālig* (see **UN-¹**, **HOLY**).

unhonoured ▸ adjective not given public praise or respect.

unhood ▸ verb [with obj.] remove the hood from (a falcon, horse, or someone held captive).

unhook ▸ verb [with obj.] unfasten or detach (something that is held or caught by a hook).

unhoped ▸ adjective (**unhoped for**) exceeding hope or expectation: *an unhoped-for piece of good luck.*

unhorse ▸ verb [with obj.] drag or cause to fall from a horse.

unhoused ▸ adjective having no accommodation or shelter: *the poor remain unhoused.*

unhouseled /ʌnˈhaʊz(ə)ld/ ▸ adjective archaic (of a person) not having received the Eucharist.
– ORIGIN mid 16th cent.: from **UN-¹** 'not' + the past participle of obsolete *housel* 'offer the Eucharist to', from *housel* 'Eucharist'.

unhuman ▸ adjective not resembling or having the qualities of a human being.

unhung¹ ▸ adjective (especially of a picture) not hanging or hung.

unhung² past and past participle of **UNHANG**.

unhurried ▸ adjective moving, acting, or taking place without haste or urgency.
– DERIVATIVES **unhurriedly** adverb.

unhurt ▸ adjective [predic.] not hurt or harmed.

unhusk ▸ verb [with obj.] remove a husk or shell from (a seed or fruit): [as adj. **unhusked**] *unhusked rice.*

unhygienic ▸ adjective not clean or sanitary: *damp, unhygienic accommodation.*

u

– DERIVATIVES **unhygienically** adverb.

unhyphenated ▶ adjective (of a word or phrase) not written with a hyphen.

uni ▶ noun (pl. **unis**) informal university.
– ORIGIN late 19th cent.: abbreviation.

uni- ▶ combining form one; having or consisting of one: *unicellular* | *unicycle*.
– ORIGIN from Latin *unus* 'one'.

Uniate /ˈjuːnɪeɪt/ (also **Uniat**) ▶ adjective denoting or relating to any community of Christians in eastern Europe or the Near East that acknowledges papal supremacy but retains its own liturgy.
▶ noun a member of such a community.
– ORIGIN mid 19th cent.: from Russian *uniat*, from *uniya*, from Latin *unio* (see **UNION**).

uniaxial /juːnɪˈaksɪəl/ ▶ adjective having or relating to a single axis.
■ (of crystals) having one optic axis, as in the hexagonal, trigonal, and tetragonal systems.

unibody ▶ noun (pl. **-ies**) a single moulded unit forming both the bodywork and chassis of a vehicle.

unicameral /juːnɪˈkam(ə)r(ə)l/ ▶ adjective (of a legislative body) having a single legislative chamber.
– ORIGIN mid 19th cent.: from **UNI-** 'one' + Latin *camera* 'chamber' + **-AL**.

UNICEF /ˈjuːnɪsɛf/ an agency of the United Nations established in 1946 to help governments (especially in developing countries) improve the health and education of children and their mothers.
– ORIGIN acronym from *United Nations Children's* (originally *International Children's Emergency*) *Fund*.

unicellular ▶ adjective Biology (of protozoans, certain algae, spores, etc.) consisting of a single cell.
■ (of an evolutionary or developmental stage) characterized by the formation or presence of a single cell or cells.

unicity /juːˈnɪsɪti/ ▶ noun [mass noun] rare the fact of being or consisting of one, or of being united as a whole.
■ the fact or quality of being unique.

unicolour (also **unicoloured**) (US **-color** or **-colored**) ▶ adjective of one colour.

unicom ▶ noun a radio communications system of a type used at small airports.

unicorn ▶ noun 1 a mythical animal typically represented as a horse with a single straight horn projecting from its forehead.
■ a heraldic representation of such an animal, with a twisted horn, a deer's feet, a goat's beard, and a lion's tail.
2 historical a carriage drawn by three horses, two abreast and one leader.
■ a team of three horses arranged in such a way.
– ORIGIN Middle English: via Old French from Latin *unicornis*, from *uni-* 'single' + *cornu* 'horn', translating Greek *monokerōs*.

unicorn fish ▶ noun any of a number of fishes with a horn-like projection on the head:
● an Indo-Pacific surgeonfish (genus *Naso*, family Acanthuridae). ● a crestfish with a dorsal fin that extends forward from the head (*Lophotes fiskii*, family Lophotidae).

unicorn root ▶ noun [mass noun] US any of a number of plants in the lily family, especially those with roots having medicinal uses, in particular:
● the blazing star (*Chamaelirium luteum*). ● colic root.

unicum /ˈjuːnɪkəm/ ▶ noun (pl. **unica**) rare a unique example or specimen.
– ORIGIN late 19th cent.: from Latin, neuter of *unicus* 'unique'.

unicursal /juːnɪˈkɜːs(ə)l/ ▶ adjective Mathematics relating to or denoting a curve or surface which is closed and can be drawn or swept out in a single movement.
– ORIGIN mid 19th cent.: from **UNI-** 'one' + Latin *cursus* 'course' + **-AL**.

unicuspid ▶ adjective having one cusp or point.
▶ noun a tooth with a single cusp, especially a canine tooth.

unicycle ▶ noun a cycle with a single wheel, typically used by acrobats.
– DERIVATIVES **unicyclist** noun.

unidea'd ▶ adjective archaic having no ideas.

unideal ▶ adjective not satisfying one's perception of what is perfect: *we have all had unideal parents.*

unidentifiable ▶ adjective unable to be identified: *an unidentifiable accent.*

unidentified ▶ adjective not recognized or identified: *a picture of an unidentified motorcyclist.*

unidimensional ▶ adjective having one dimension: *a unidimensional model.*

unidiomatic ▶ adjective not using or containing expressions natural to a native speaker of a language.

unidirectional ▶ adjective moving or operating in a single direction.
– DERIVATIVES **unidirectionality** noun, **unidirectionally** adverb.

UNIDO /juːˈniːdəʊ/ ▶ abbreviation for United Nations Industrial Development Organization.

uniface ▶ adjective (of a coin or medallion) having one side blank or unfinished.

unification ▶ noun [mass noun] the process of being united or made into a whole.
– DERIVATIVES **unificatory** adjective.

Unification Church an evangelistic religious and political organization founded in 1954 in Korea by Sun Myung Moon. Also called **HOLY SPIRIT ASSOCIATION FOR THE UNIFICATION OF WORLD CHRISTIANITY**.

unified field theory ▶ noun Physics a theory that describes two or more of the four interactions (electromagnetic, gravitational, weak, and strong) previously described by separate theories.

uniflow ▶ adjective [attrib.] involving flow in one direction (used especially with reference to the flow of steam or gases through the cylinder in a steam or internal-combustion engine): *a uniflow engine.*

uniform ▶ adjective 1 not changing in form or character; remaining the same in all cases and at all times: *blocks of stone of uniform size.*
■ of a similar form or character to another or others: *a uniform package of amenities at a choice of hotels.*
2 denoting a garment forming part of a person's uniform: *black uniform jackets.*
▶ noun 1 the distinctive clothing worn by members of the same organization or body or by children attending certain schools: *airline pilots in dark blue uniforms* | [mass noun] *an officer in uniform.*
■ informal, chiefly N. Amer. a police officer wearing a uniform: *uniforms were already on the scene.*
2 a code word representing the letter U, used in radio communication.
▶ verb [with obj.] make uniform.
– DERIVATIVES **uniformly** adverb.
– ORIGIN mid 16th cent. (as an adjective): from French *uniforme* or Latin *uniformis* (see **UNI-**, **FORM**). Sense 1 of the noun dates from the mid 18th cent.

uniformed ▶ adjective (of a person) wearing a uniform: *uniformed police officers.*

uniformitarianism ▶ noun [mass noun] Geology the theory that changes in the earth's crust during geological history have resulted from the action of continuous and uniform processes. Often contrasted with **CATASTROPHISM**.
– DERIVATIVES **uniformitarian** adjective & noun.

uniformity ▶ noun (pl. **-ies**) [mass noun] the quality or state of being uniform: *an attempt to impose administrative and cultural uniformity.*
– ORIGIN late Middle English: from Old French *uniformite* or late Latin *uniformitas*, from Latin *uniformis* (see **UNIFORM**).

Uniformity, Act of (in British history) any of four acts (especially that of 1662) establishing the foundations of the English Protestant Church and securing uniformity in public worship and use of a particular Book of Common Prayer.

unify /ˈjuːnɪfʌɪ/ ▶ verb (**-ies**, **-ied**) make or become united, uniform, or whole: [with obj.] *the government hoped to centralize and unify the nation* | [no obj.] *opposition groups struggling to unify around the goal of replacing the regime* | [as adj. **unified**] *a unified system of national education.*
– DERIVATIVES **unifier** noun.
– ORIGIN early 16th cent.: from French *unifier* or late Latin *unificare* 'make into a whole'.

unijunction ▶ noun Electronics a negative resistance device consisting of a rectifying p–n junction in the middle of a length of semiconducting material that has an ohmic contact at each end, used as a switching element.

unilateral ▶ adjective 1 (of an action or decision) performed by or affecting only one person, group, or country involved in a particular situation, without the agreement of another or the others: *unilateral nuclear disarmament.*
2 relating to, occurring on, or affecting only one side of an organ or structure, or of the body.
– DERIVATIVES **unilaterally** adverb.

Unilateral Declaration of Independence (abbrev.: **UDI**) the declaration of independence from the United Kingdom made by Rhodesia under Ian Smith in 1965. See **ZIMBABWE**.

unilateralism ▶ noun [mass noun] the process of acting, reaching a decision, or espousing a principle unilaterally.
– DERIVATIVES **unilateralist** noun & adjective.

unilingual ▶ adjective conducted in, concerned with, or speaking only one language.
– DERIVATIVES **unilingually** adverb.

unilluminated ▶ adjective not illuminated.

unillustrated ▶ adjective having no illustrations.

unilocular /juːnɪˈlɒkjʊlə/ ▶ adjective Botany & Zoology having, consisting of, or characterized by only one loculus or cavity; single-chambered.

unimaginable ▶ adjective difficult or impossible to imagine or comprehend: *lives of almost unimaginable deprivation.*
– DERIVATIVES **unimaginably** adverb.

unimaginative ▶ adjective not readily using or demonstrating the use of the imagination; stolid and somewhat dull.
– DERIVATIVES **unimaginatively** adverb, **unimaginativeness** noun.

unimodal ▶ adjective having or involving one mode.
■ (of a statistical distribution) having one maximum.

unimodular ▶ adjective Mathematics having a determinant of ±1.

unimolecular ▶ adjective Chemistry consisting of or involving a single molecule.

unimpaired ▶ adjective not weakened or damaged: *unimpaired mobility.*

unimpassioned ▶ adjective having or showing no emotion or intensity: *a flat, unimpassioned voice.*

unimpeachable ▶ adjective not able to be doubted, questioned, or criticized; entirely trustworthy: *an unimpeachable witness.*
– DERIVATIVES **unimpeachably** adverb.

unimpeded ▶ adjective not obstructed or hindered: *an unimpeded view across the headland.*
– DERIVATIVES **unimpededly** adverb.

unimportance ▶ noun [mass noun] the state or fact of lacking in importance or significance: *the relative unimportance of wider kin ties in British culture.*

unimportant ▶ adjective lacking in importance or significance: *trivial and unimportant details.*

unimposing ▶ adjective not imposing or grandly impressive.
– DERIVATIVES **unimposingly** adverb.

unimpressed ▶ adjective feeling no admiration, interest, or respect.

unimpressionable ▶ adjective (of a person) not easily moved or influenced.

unimpressive ▶ adjective evoking no admiration or respect; not striking.
– DERIVATIVES **unimpressively** adverb, **unimpressiveness** noun.

unimproved ▶ adjective not made better.
■ (of land) not cleared or cultivated.

unincorporated ▶ adjective 1 (of a company or other organization) not formed into a legal corporation: *an unincorporated business.*
2 not included as part of a whole.
■ N. Amer. (of territory) not designated as belonging to a particular country, town, or area.

uninfected ▶ adjective not harbouring a disease-causing organism.
■ Computing not affected with a virus.

uninflamed ▶ adjective (of a part of the body) not affected by inflammation: *an uninflamed appendix.*

uninflected ▶ adjective 1 Grammar (of a word or a language) not undergoing changes to express particular grammatical functions or attributes: *English is largely uninflected.*
2 not varying in intonation or pitch: *her voice was flat and uninflected.*

uninfluenced ▶ adjective [predic.] not influenced or affected: *styles of dress relatively uninfluenced by popular fashion.*

u

uninfluential ▶ adjective having little or no influence.

uninformative ▶ adjective not providing particularly useful or interesting information.

uninformed ▶ adjective not having or showing awareness or understanding of the facts: *uninformed criticism of conservation projects.*

uninhabitable ▶ adjective (of a place) unsuitable for living in.

uninhabited ▶ adjective (of a place) without inhabitants: *small uninhabited islands.*

uninhibited ▶ adjective expressing one's feelings or thoughts unselfconsciously and without restraint: *fits of uninhibited laughter.*
– DERIVATIVES **uninhibitedly** adverb, **uninhibitedness** noun.

uninitiated ▶ adjective without special knowledge or experience: [as plural noun **the uninitiated**] *the discussion wasn't easy to follow for the uninitiated.*

uninjured ▶ adjective (of a person or part of the body) not harmed or damaged.

uninspired ▶ adjective **1** lacking in imagination or originality: *he writes repetitive and uninspired poetry.*
2 (of a person) not filled with excitement: *they were uninspired by the Nationalist Party.*

uninspiring ▶ adjective not producing excitement or interest: *an uninspiring game that United scarcely deserved to win.*
– DERIVATIVES **uninspiringly** adverb.

uninstructed ▶ adjective (of a person) not taught or having learned a subject or skill.
■ (of behaviour) not acquired by teaching; natural or spontaneous: *her own instinctive, uninstructed response.*

uninsulated ▶ adjective not insulated.

uninsurable ▶ adjective not eligible for insurance cover: *some risky activities are uninsurable at any price.*

uninsured ▶ adjective not covered by insurance: *an uninsured driver.*

unintelligent ▶ adjective having or showing a low level of intelligence: *a good-natured but unintelligent boy.*
– DERIVATIVES **unintelligence** noun, **unintelligently** adverb.

unintelligible ▶ adjective impossible to understand: *dolphin sounds are **unintelligible to** humans.*
– DERIVATIVES **unintelligibility** noun, **unintelligibly** adverb.

unintended ▶ adjective not planned or meant: *the unintended consequences of people's actions.*

unintentional ▶ adjective not done on purpose: *the translation added a layer of unintentional comedy.*
– DERIVATIVES **unintentionally** adverb.

uninterested ▶ adjective not interested in or concerned about something or someone: *I was totally **uninterested in** boys | an uninterested voice.*
– DERIVATIVES **uninterestedly** adverb, **uninterestedness** noun.

> **USAGE** On the meaning and use of **uninterested** and **disinterested**, see usage at **DISINTERESTED**.

uninteresting ▶ adjective not arousing curiosity or interest: *the scenery is dull and uninteresting.*
– DERIVATIVES **uninterestingly** adverb, **uninterestingness** noun.

uninterpretable ▶ adjective impossible to explain or understand in terms of meaning or significance.

uninterrupted ▶ adjective without a break in continuity: *an uninterrupted flow of traffic.*
■ (of a view) unobstructed.
– DERIVATIVES **uninterruptedly** adverb.

uninterruptible ▶ adjective not able to be broken in continuity: *an uninterruptible power supply.*

uninventive ▶ adjective not showing creativity or original thought: *the oils were sensitively painted but uninventive in design.*
– DERIVATIVES **uninventively** adverb, **uninventiveness** noun.

uninvestigated ▶ adjective not systematically investigated: *uninvestigated deaths in custody.*

uninvited ▶ adjective (of a person) attending somewhere or doing something without having been asked: *their privacy was disrupted by a series of uninvited guests.*
■ (of a thought or act) involuntary, unwelcome, or unwarranted: *strange uninvited thoughts crossed her mind.*
– DERIVATIVES **uninvitedly** adverb.

uninviting ▶ adjective (especially of a place or prospect) not attractive: *the house was dark and uninviting.*
– DERIVATIVES **uninvitingly** adverb.

uninvoked ▶ adjective (of a god, spirit, or power) not invoked or called on in prayer.

uninvolved ▶ adjective not connected or concerned with someone or something, especially on an emotional level.

union ▶ noun **1** [mass noun] the action or fact of joining together or being joined together, especially in a political context: *he was opposed to closer political or economic union with Europe* | [count noun] *a currency union between the two countries.*
■ a state of harmony or agreement: *they live in perfect union.* ■ [count noun] a marriage: *their union had not been blessed with children.* ■ (**the Union**) historical the uniting of the English and Scottish crowns in 1603, of the English and Scottish parliaments in 1707, or of the parliaments of Great Britain and Ireland in 1801.
2 an organized association of workers formed to protect and further their rights and interests; a trade union: *the National Farmers' Union.*
■ a club, society, or association formed by people with a common interest or purpose: *members of the Students' Union.* ■ short for **RUGBY UNION**. ■ Brit. historical a number of parishes consolidated for the purposes of administering the Poor Laws. ■ (also **union workhouse** or **house**) a workhouse set up by such a group of parishes. ■ Brit. an association of independent Churches, especially Congregational or Baptist, for purposes of cooperation. ■ (in the Indian subcontinent) a local administrative unit comprising several rural villages.
3 (also **Union**) a political unit consisting of a number of states or provinces with the same central government, in particular:
■ the United States, especially from its founding by the original thirteen states in 1787–90 to the secession of the Confederate states in 1860–1. ■ the United Kingdom. ■ South Africa. ■ (also **the Federal Union**) the northern states of the United States which opposed the seceding Confederate states in the American Civil War.
4 Mathematics the set that comprises all the elements (and no others) contained in any of two or more given sets.
■ [mass noun] the operation of forming such a set.
5 a joint or coupling for pipes.
6 a part of a flag with an emblem symbolizing national union, typically occupying the upper corner next to the staff.
7 [mass noun] a fabric made of two or more different yarns, typically cotton and linen or silk.
– ORIGIN late Middle English: from Old French, or from ecclesiastical Latin *unio(n-)* 'unity', from Latin *unus* 'one'.

Union, Act of (in British history) either of the parliamentary acts by which the countries of the United Kingdom were brought together as a political whole. By the first Act of Union (1707) Scotland was joined with England to form Great Britain. The second Act of Union (1801) established the United Kingdom of Great Britain and Ireland. Wales had been incorporated with England in 1536.

union-bashing ▶ noun [mass noun] informal active or vocal opposition to trade unions and their rights.

union catalogue ▶ noun a list of the combined holdings of several libraries.

Union flag ▶ noun another term for **UNION JACK** (in sense 1).

union house ▶ noun see **UNION** (sense 2).

unionist ▶ noun **1** a member of a trade union.
■ an advocate or supporter of trade unions.
2 (**Unionist**) a person in Northern Ireland, especially a member of a political party, supporting or advocating union with Great Britain.
■ historical a member of a British political party formed in 1886 which supported maintenance of the parliamentary union between Great Britain and Ireland. ■ a person who opposed secession during the American Civil War of 1861–5.
– DERIVATIVES **unionism** noun, **unionistic** adjective.

unionize (also **-ise**) ▶ verb become or cause to become members of a trade union.
– DERIVATIVES **unionization** noun.

unionized (also **-ised**) ▶ adjective (of workers or their workplace) belonging to, or having workers belonging to, a trade union: *unionized factories.*

Union Jack ▶ noun **1** the national flag of the United Kingdom, consisting of red and white crosses on a blue background and formed by combining the flags of St George, St Andrew, and St Patrick. Also called **UNION FLAG**. [ORIGIN: originally a small British union flag flown as the jack of a ship.]
2 (**union jack**) (in the US) a small flag consisting of the union from the national flag, flown at the bows of vessels in harbour.

Union of Myanmar official name for **BURMA**.

Union of Soviet Socialist Republics (abbrev.: **USSR**) full name of **SOVIET UNION**.

union shop ▶ noun a place of work where all employees must belong to a trade union or join one within an agreed time. Compare with **CLOSED SHOP**.

union suit ▶ noun N. Amer. dated a single undergarment covering the body and legs, worn by men and boys.

Union Territory any of several territories of India which are administered by the central government.

union workhouse ▶ noun see **UNION** (sense 2).

uniparous /juːˈnɪp(ə)rəs/ ▶ adjective chiefly Zoology producing a single young at a birth.
– ORIGIN mid 17th cent.: from modern Latin *uniparus* (from Latin *uni-* 'one' + *-parus* 'bearing') + **-OUS**.

uniped /ˈjuːnɪpɛd/ ▶ noun rare a person or animal having only one foot or leg.
– ORIGIN early 19th cent.: from **UNI-** 'one' + *pes, ped-* 'foot'.

unipersonal ▶ adjective rare comprising, or existing as, one person only.

uniplanar ▶ adjective lying in one plane.

unipod /ˈjuːnɪpɒd/ ▶ noun a one-legged support for a camera.
– ORIGIN 1930s: from **UNI-** 'one', suggested by **TRIPOD**.

unipolar ▶ adjective having or relating to a single pole or kind of polarity: *a unipolar magnetic charge.*
■ (of psychiatric illness) characterized by either depressive or (more rarely) manic episodes but not both. ■ (of a nerve cell) having only one axon or process. ■ Electronics (of a transistor or other device) using charge carriers of a single polarity.
– DERIVATIVES **unipolarity** /-ˈlarɪti/ noun.

unipotent /ˌjuːnɪˈpəʊt(ə)nt/ ▶ adjective **1** Mathematics (of a subgroup) having only one idempotent element.
2 Biology (of an immature or stem cell) capable of giving rise to only one cell type.

unique ▶ adjective being the only one of its kind; unlike anything else: *the situation was unique in modern British politics | original and unique designs.*
■ particularly remarkable, special, or unusual: *a unique opportunity to see the spectacular Bolshoi Ballet.* ■ [predic.] (**unique to**) belonging or connected to (one particular person, group, or place): *a style of architecture that is unique to Portugal.*
▶ noun archaic a unique person or thing.
– DERIVATIVES **uniquely** adverb, **uniqueness** noun.
– ORIGIN early 17th cent.: from French, from Latin *unicus*, from *unus* 'one'.

> **USAGE** There is a set of adjectives—including **unique**, **complete**, **equal**, **infinite**, and **perfect**—whose core meaning embraces a mathematically absolute concept and which therefore, according to a traditional argument, cannot be modified by adverbs such as **really**, **quite**, or **very**. For example, since the core meaning of **unique** (from Latin 'one') is 'being only one of its kind', it is logically impossible, the argument goes, to submodify it: it either is 'unique' or it is not, and there are no in-between stages. In practice the situation in the language is more complex than this. Words like **unique** have a core sense but they often also have a secondary, less precise sense: in this case, the meaning 'very remarkable or unusual', as in a ***really unique** opportunity*. In its secondary sense, **unique** does not relate to an absolute concept, and so the use of submodifying adverbs is grammatically acceptable.

unironed ▶ adjective (of clothes or other fabric articles) not smoothed with an iron.

uniserial ▶ adjective Botany & Zoology arranged in or consisting of one series or row.

unisex ▶ adjective (especially of clothing or hairstyles) designed to be suitable for both sexes.

▶**noun** [mass noun] a style in which men and women look and dress in a similar way.

unisexual ▶**adjective** (of an organism) either male or female; not hermaphrodite.
■Botany (of a flower) having either stamens or pistils but not both.
– DERIVATIVES **unisexuality** noun, **unisexually** adverb.

UNISON /ˈjuːnɪs(ə)n/ ▶**noun** (in the UK) a trade union formed in 1993 and representing employees in the health service and public sector.

unison /ˈjuːnɪs(ə)n/ ▶**noun** [mass noun] **1** simultaneous performance or utterance of action or speech: *'Yes, sir,' said the girls* ***in unison****.*
2 Music coincidence in pitch of sounds or notes: *the flutes play* ***in unison with*** *the violas.*
■[count noun] a combination of notes, voices, or instruments at the same pitch or (especially when singing) in octaves: *good unisons are formed by flutes, oboes, and clarinets.*
▶**adjective** [attrib.] performed in unison.
– DERIVATIVES **unisonous** adjective.
– ORIGIN late Middle English (in sense 2): from Old French, or from late Latin *unisonus*, from Latin *uni-* 'one' + *sonus* 'sound'.

unison string ▶**noun** a string in a piano or other instrument tuned to the same pitch (or to a pitch an octave higher) as another string and meant to be sounded with it.

unissued ▶**adjective** (especially of shares) not yet issued.

unit ▶**noun 1** an individual thing or person regarded as single and complete, especially for purposes of calculation; each of the individuals or collocations into which a complex whole may be analysed: *large areas of land made up of smaller units | the sentence as a unit of grammar | the family unit.*
■a device that has a specified function, especially one forming part of a complex mechanism: *the gearbox and transmission unit.* ■a piece of furniture or equipment for fitting with others like it or made of complementary parts: *a sink unit.* ■a self-contained section of accommodation in a larger building or group of buildings: *one- and two-bedroom units.* ■a part of an institution such as a hospital having a special function: *the intensive-care unit.* ■a subdivision of a larger military grouping: *he returned to Germany with his unit.* ■a self-contained part of a course: *students take three compulsory core units.* ■an item manufactured: [as modifier] *unit cost.* ■US a police car: *he eased into his unit and flicked the siren on.* ■Brit. the smallest measure of investment in a unit trust.
2 a quantity chosen as a standard in terms of which other quantities may be expressed: *a unit of measurement | fifty units of electricity.*
3 the number one.
■(**units**) the digit before the decimal point in decimal notation, representing an integer less than ten.
– ORIGIN late 16th cent. (as a mathematical term): from Latin *unus*, probably suggested by **DIGIT**.

UNITA /juːˈniːtə/ an Angolan nationalist movement founded in 1966 by Jonas Savimbi (b.1934) to fight Portuguese rule. After independence was achieved in 1975 UNITA continued to fight against the ruling Marxist MPLA, with help from South Africa.
– ORIGIN acronym from Portuguese *União Nacional para a Independencia Total de Angola.*

UNITAR /juːˈniːtɑː/ ▶**abbreviation for** United Nations Institute for Training and Research.

unitard /ˈjuːnɪtɑːd/ ▶**noun** a tight-fitting one-piece garment of stretchable fabric which covers the body from the neck to the knees or feet.
– ORIGIN 1960s: from **UNI-** 'single' + **LEOTARD**.

Unitarian /ˌjuːnɪˈtɛːrɪən/ ▶**noun** Theology a person, especially a Christian, who asserts the unity of God and rejects the doctrine of the Trinity.
■a member of a Church or religious body maintaining this belief and typically rejecting formal dogma in favour of a rationalist and inclusivist approach to belief.
▶**adjective** of or relating to the Unitarians.
– DERIVATIVES **Unitarianism** noun.
– ORIGIN late 17th cent.: from modern Latin *unitarius* (from Latin *unitas* 'unity') + **-AN**.

unitarist /ˈjuːnɪt(ə)rɪst/ ▶**noun** an advocate of a unitary system of government.

unitary /ˈjuːnɪt(ə)ri/ ▶**adjective 1** single; uniform: *a sort of unitary wholeness.*
■of or relating to a system of government or organization in which the powers of the separate constituent parts are vested in a central body: *a unitary rather than a federal state.*
2 of or relating to a unit or units.
– DERIVATIVES **unitarily** adverb, **unitarity** /-ˈtarɪti/ noun.

unitary authority (also **unitary council**) ▶**noun** (chiefly in the UK) an administrative division of local government established in place of, or as an alternative to, a two-tier system of local councils.

unit cell ▶**noun** Crystallography the smallest group of atoms which has the overall symmetry of a crystal, and from which the entire lattice can be built up by repetition in three dimensions.

unite ▶**verb** come or bring together for a common purpose or action: [no obj.] *he called on the party to unite* | [with obj.] *they are united by their love of cars.*
■come or bring together to form a unit or whole, especially in a political context: [no obj.] *the two Germanys officially united* | [with obj.] *he aimed to unite Italy and Sicily under his imperial crown | his work unites theory and practice.* ■[with obj.] archaic join in marriage: *Lady Midlothian united herself to a man of bad character.*
– DERIVATIVES **unitive** adjective.
– ORIGIN late Middle English: from Latin *unit-* 'joined together', from the verb *unire*, from *unus* 'one'.

united ▶**adjective** joined together politically, for a common purpose, or by common feelings: *women acting together in a united way.*
■Brit. used in names of soccer and other sports teams formed by amalgamation: *Oxford United.*
– DERIVATIVES **unitedly** adverb.

United Arab Emirates (abbrev.: **UAE**) an independent state on the south coast of the Persian Gulf, west of the Gulf of Oman; population 2,377,400 (1995); official language, Arabic; capital, Abu Dhabi. The United Arab Emirates was formed in 1971 by the federation of the independent sheikhdoms formerly called the Trucial States: Abu Dhabi, Ajman, Dubai, Fujairah, Ras al Khaimah (joined early 1972), Sharjah, and Umm al Qaiwain.

United Arab Republic (abbrev.: **UAR**) a former political union established by Egypt and Syria in 1958. It was seen as the first step towards the creation of a pan-Arab union in the Middle East, but only Yemen entered into loose association with it (1958–66) and Syria withdrew in 1961. Egypt retained the name United Arab Republic until 1971.

United Artists a US film production company founded in 1919 by Charlie Chaplin, Douglas Fairbanks, Mary Pickford, and D. W. Griffith, formed to make films without the artistic strictures of the larger companies.

United Free Church a Presbyterian Church in Scotland formed in 1900 by the union of the Free Church of Scotland with the United Presbyterian Church. In 1929 the majority of its congregation joined the established Church of Scotland.

United Kingdom (abbrev.: **UK**) a country of western Europe consisting of England, Wales, Scotland, and Northern Ireland; pop. 55,700,000 (1991); official language, English; capital, London. Full name **UNITED KINGDOM OF GREAT BRITAIN AND NORTHERN IRELAND.**

England (which had incorporated Wales in the 16th century) and Scotland have had the same monarch since 1603, when James VI of Scotland succeeded to the English crown as James I; the kingdoms were formally united by the Act of Union in 1707. An Act of Parliament joined Great Britain and Ireland in 1801, but the Irish Free State (later the Republic of Ireland) broke away in 1921. The UK became a member of the EC in 1973.

United Nations (abbrev.: **UN**) an international organization of countries set up in 1945, in succession to the League of Nations, to promote international peace, security, and cooperation.

Its members, originally the countries that fought against the Axis Powers in the Second World War, now number more than 150 and include most sovereign states of the world, the chief exceptions being Switzerland and North and South Korea. Administration is by a secretariat headed by the Secretary General. The chief deliberative body is the General Assembly, in which each member state has one vote; recommendations are passed but are not binding on members, and in general have had little effect on world politics. The Security Council bears the primary responsibility for the maintenance of peace and security, and may call on members to take action, chiefly peacekeeping action, to enforce its decisions. The UN's headquarters are in New York.

United Presbyterian Church a Presbyterian Church in Scotland formed in 1847. In 1900 it joined with the Free Church of Scotland to form the United Free Church.

United Provinces historical **1** the seven provinces united in 1579 and forming the basis of the republic of the Netherlands.
2 an Indian administrative division formed by the union of Agra and Oudh and called Uttar Pradesh since 1950.

United Provinces of Central America a former federal republic in Central America, formed in 1823 to unite the states of Guatemala, El Salvador, Honduras, Nicaragua, and Costa Rica, all newly independent from Spain. The federation collapsed in 1838.

United Reformed Church a Church formed in 1972 by the union of the Congregational Church in England and Wales with the Presbyterian Church in England. Most of the Churches of Christ in the UK joined the union in 1981.

USAGE The correct term is **United Reformed Church**, although it is sometimes called **United Reform Church** in general use.

United States (abbrev.: **US**) a country occupying most of the southern half of North America and including also Alaska and the Hawaiian Islands; pop. 248,709,870 (1990); official language, English; capital, Washington DC. Full name **UNITED STATES OF AMERICA.**

The US is a federal republic comprising fifty states and the Federal District of Columbia. It originated in the American War of Independence, the successful rebellion of the British colonies on the east coast in 1775–83. The original thirteen states which formed the Union drew up a federal constitution in 1787, and George Washington was elected the first President in 1789. In the 19th century the territory of the US was extended across the continent through the westward spread of pioneers and settlers (at the expense of the American Indian peoples), and acquisitions such as that of Texas and California from Mexico in the 1840s. After a long period of isolation in foreign affairs the US participated on the Allied side in both world wars, and came out of the cold war as the world's leading military and economic power.

unitholder ▶**noun** chiefly Brit. a person with an investment in a unit trust.

unitize (also **-ise**) ▶**verb** [with obj.] form into a unit; unite into a whole.
■[usu. as adj. **unitized**] package (cargo) into unit loads: *a unitized load.* ■convert (an investment trust) into a unit trust.

unit-linked ▶**adjective** Brit. denoting or relating to a life assurance policy or other investment in which the premiums or payments are invested in a unit trust.

unit matrix ▶**noun** another term for **IDENTITY MATRIX.**

unit membrane ▶**noun** Biology a lipoprotein membrane which encloses many cells and cell organelles and is composed of two electron-dense layers enclosing a less dense layer.

unit train ▶**noun** N. Amer. a train transporting a single commodity.

unit trust ▶**noun** Brit. a trust formed to manage a portfolio of stock exchange securities, in which small investors can buy units.

unit vector ▶**noun** Mathematics a vector which has a magnitude of one.

unity ▶**noun** (pl. **-ies**) [mass noun] **1** the state of being united or joined as a whole, especially in a political context: *European unity | economic unity.*
■harmony or agreement between people or groups: *their leaders called for unity between opposing factions.* ■the state of forming a complete and pleasing whole, especially in an artistic context: *the repeated phrase gives the piece unity and cohesion.* ■[count noun] a thing forming a complex whole: *they speak of the three parts as a unity.* ■[count noun] each of the three dramatic principles requiring limitation of the supposed time of a drama to that occupied in acting it or to a single day (**unity of time**), use of one scene throughout (**unity of place**), and concentration on the development of a single plot (**unity of action**).
2 Mathematics the number one.
– ORIGIN Middle English: from Old French *unite*, from Latin *unitas*, from *unus* 'one'.

Univ. ▶**abbreviation for** University.

univalent ▶**adjective 1** /juːˈnɪvəl(ə)nt/ Biology (of a chromosome) remaining unpaired during meiosis.
2 /ˌjuːnɪˈveɪl(ə)nt/ Chemistry another term for **MONOVALENT.**
▶**noun** /juːˈnɪvəl(ə)nt/ Biology a univalent chromosome.

u

a **cat** | ɑː **arm** | ɛ **bed** | ɛː **hair** | ə **ago** | əː **her** | ɪ **sit** | i **cosy** | iː **see** | ɒ **hot** | ɔː **saw** | ʌ **run** | ʊ **put** | uː **too** | ʌɪ **my** | aʊ **how** | eɪ **day** | əʊ **no** | ɪə **near** | ɔɪ **boy** | ʊə **poor** | ʌɪə **fire** | aʊə **sour**

univalve Zoology ▶**adjective** having one valve or shell.
▶**noun** another term for *gastropod* (see **GASTROPODA**).

Universal a US film production company formed in 1912.

universal ▶**adjective** of, affecting, or done by all people or things in the world or in a particular group; applicable to all cases: *universal adult suffrage | the incidents caused universal concern.*
■Logic denoting a proposition in which something is asserted of all of a class. Contrasted with **PARTICULAR**. ■ Linguistics denoting or relating to a grammatical rule, set of rules, or other linguistic feature that is found in all languages. ■(of a tool or machine) adjustable to or appropriate for all requirements; not restricted to a single purpose or position.
▶**noun** a person or thing having universal effect, currency, or application, in particular:
■Logic a universal proposition. ■ Philosophy a term or concept of general application. ■ Philosophy a nature or essence signified by a general term. ■ Linguistics a universal grammatical rule or linguistic feature.
– DERIVATIVES **universality** noun.
– ORIGIN late Middle English: from Old French, or from Latin *universalis*, from *universus* (see **UNIVERSE**).

universal compass ▶**noun** a pair of compasses with legs that may be extended for large circles.

universal donor ▶**noun** a person of blood group O, who can in theory donate blood to recipients of any ABO blood group.

universal indicator ▶**noun** [mass noun] Chemistry a mixture of dyes that changes colour gradually over a range of pH and is used (especially as indicator paper) in testing for acids and alkalis.

universalist ▶**noun 1** Christian Theology a person who believes that all humankind will eventually be saved.
2 a person advocating loyalty to and concern for others without regard to national or other allegiances.
▶**adjective 1** Christian Theology of or relating to universalists.
2 universal in scope or character.
– DERIVATIVES **universalism** noun, **universalistic** adjective.

universalize (also **-ise**) ▶**verb** [with obj.] give a universal character or application to (something, especially something abstract): *theories that universalize experience.*
■bring into universal use; make available for all: *attempts to universalize basic education.*
– DERIVATIVES **universalizability** noun, **universalization** noun.

universal joint (also **universal coupling**) ▶**noun** a coupling or joint which can transmit rotary power by a shaft at any selected angle.

universally ▶**adverb** by everyone; in every case: *progress is not always universally welcomed.*

Universal Postal Union (abbrev.: **UPU**) an agency of the United Nations that regulates international postal affairs.

universal product code ▶**noun** more formal term for **BAR CODE**.

universal quantifier ▶**noun** Logic a formal expression used in asserting that a stated general proposition is true of all the members of the delineated universe or class.

universal recipient ▶**noun** a person of blood group AB, who can in theory receive donated blood of any ABO blood group.

universal set ▶**noun** Mathematics & Logic the set containing all objects or elements and of which all other sets are subsets.

universal suffrage ▶**noun** [mass noun] the right of almost all adults to vote in political elections.

Universal Time (also **Universal Time Coordinated**) another term for **GREENWICH MEAN TIME**.

universe ▶**noun** (**the universe**) all existing matter and space considered as a whole; the cosmos. The universe is believed to be at least 10 billion light years in diameter and contains a vast number of galaxies; it has been expanding since its creation in the big bang about 13 billion years ago.
■a particular sphere of activity, interest, or experience: *the front parlour was the hub of her universe.* ■ (Logic also **universe of discourse**) another term for **UNIVERSAL SET**.
– ORIGIN late Middle English: from Old French *univers* or Latin *universum*, neuter of *universus* 'combined into one, whole', from *uni-* 'one' + *versus* 'turned' (past participle of *vertere*).

university ▶**noun** (pl. **-ies**) a high-level educational institution in which students study for degrees and academic research is done: *I went to* ***university*** *at the Sorbonne | his daughter is* ***at university.***
– PHRASES **the university of life** the experience of life regarded as a means of instruction.
– ORIGIN Middle English: from Old French *universite*, from Latin *universitas* 'the whole', in late Latin 'society, guild', from *universus* (see **UNIVERSE**).

University of the Third Age ▶**noun** an organization providing courses of education for retired or elderly people.

univocal /ˌjuːnɪˈvəʊk(ə)l, juːˈnɪvək(ə)l/ ▶**adjective** Philosophy & Linguistics (of a word or term) having only one possible meaning; unambiguous: *a univocal set of instructions.*
– DERIVATIVES **univocality** noun, **univocally** adverb.

Unix /ˈjuːnɪks/ ▶**noun** [mass noun] Computing, trademark a widely used multi-user operating system.
– ORIGIN 1970s: from **UNI-** 'one' + a respelling of **-ICS**, on the pattern of an earlier less compact system called *Multics*.

unjoin ▶**verb** [with obj.] archaic detach; separate.

unjoined ▶**adjective** not joined together.

unjoint ▶**verb** [with obj.] rare separate or dislocate the joints of.

unjointed ▶**adjective** lacking a joint or joints; consisting of a single piece: *a flat, unjointed surface.*

unjust ▶**adjective** not based on or behaving according to what is morally right and fair: *resistance to unjust laws.*
– DERIVATIVES **unjustly** adverb, **unjustness** noun.

unjustifiable ▶**adjective** not able to be shown to be right or reasonable: *an unjustifiable restriction on their freedom.*
– DERIVATIVES **unjustifiably** adverb [sentence adverb] *they seemed, unjustifiably, to be taking things out on the students.*

unjustified ▶**adjective 1** not shown to be right or reasonable: *unjustified price increases.*
2 Printing (of printed text) not justified.

unkempt /ʌnˈkɛm(p)t/ ▶**adjective** (especially of a person) having an untidy or dishevelled appearance: *they were unwashed and unkempt.*
– DERIVATIVES **unkemptly** adverb, **unkemptness** noun.
– ORIGIN late Middle English: from **UN-**[1] 'not' + *kempt* 'combed' (past participle of archaic *kemb*, related to **COMB**).

unkept ▶**adjective 1** (of a commitment or undertaking) not honoured or fulfilled: *unkept appointments and broken promises.*
2 not tidy or cared for.

unkillable ▶**adjective** not able to be killed.

unkind ▶**adjective** inconsiderate and harsh to others: *you were terribly* ***unkind to*** *her | he was the butt of some unkind jokes | it was* ***unkind of*** *her to criticize.*
– DERIVATIVES **unkindly** adverb, **unkindness** noun.

unking ▶**verb** [with obj.] archaic remove (a monarch) from power.

unkink ▶**verb** straighten or become straight.

unknit ▶**verb** (**unknitted**, **unknitting**) [with obj.] separate (things that are joined, knotted, or interlocked).

unknot ▶**verb** (**unknotted**, **unknotting**) **1** [with obj.] release or untie the knot or knots in: *he swiftly unknotted his tie.*
2 [no obj.] (of a muscle) relax after being tense and hard: *his shoulders unknotted.*

unknowable ▶**adjective** not able to be known: *the total cost is unknowable.*
– DERIVATIVES **unknowability** noun.

unknowing ▶**adjective** not knowing or aware: *the lions moved stealthily towards their unknowing victims.*
▶**noun** [mass noun] lack of awareness or knowledge.
– DERIVATIVES **unknowingly** adverb, **unknowingness** noun.

unknown ▶**adjective** not known or familiar: *exploration into unknown territory | his whereabouts are* ***unknown to*** *his family.*
■(of a performer or artist) not well known or famous.
▶**noun** an unknown person or thing: *she is a relative unknown.*
■Mathematics an unknown quantity or variable: *find the unknown in the following equations.* ■ (**the unknown**) that which is unknown: *our fear of the unknown.*
– PHRASES **unknown to** without the knowledge of.
– DERIVATIVES **unknownness** noun.

unknown quantity ▶**noun** a person or thing whose nature, value, or significance cannot be determined or is not yet known.

Unknown Soldier (also **Unknown Warrior**) ▶**noun** an unidentified representative member of a country's armed forces killed in war, given burial with special honours in a national memorial.

unlabelled (US **unlabeled**) ▶**adjective** without a label; not labelled: *bottles of unlabelled white wine.*

unlaboured (US **unlabored**) ▶**adjective** done with ease or fluency: *flexibility and unlaboured movement.*

unlace ▶**verb** [with obj.] undo the laces of (a shoe or garment).

unlade /ʌnˈleɪd/ ▶**verb** [with obj.] archaic unload (a ship or cargo).

unladen ▶**adjective** not carrying a load: *unladen, the boat heeled to starboard.*

unladen weight ▶**noun** the weight of a vehicle when not loaded with goods.

unladylike ▶**adjective** not behaving or dressing in a way considered appropriate for a well-bred woman or girl: *Sharon gave an unladylike snort.*
■(of an activity or occupation) not considered suitable for a woman or girl.

unlaid[1] ▶**adjective** not laid: *the table was still unlaid.*

unlaid[2] past and past participle of **UNLAY**.

unlamented ▶**adjective** (of a person who has died or something that has gone or finished) not mourned or regretted.

unlash ▶**verb** [with obj.] unfasten (something securely tied with a cord or rope): *he unlashed the dinghy.*

unlatch ▶**verb** [with obj.] unfasten the latch of (a door or gate).

unlawful ▶**adjective** not conforming to, permitted by, or recognized by law or rules: *the use of unlawful violence | they claimed the ban was unlawful.*
– DERIVATIVES **unlawfully** adverb, **unlawfulness** noun.

unlawful assembly ▶**noun** English Law, historical a meeting of three or more people likely to cause a breach of the peace or to endanger the public.

unlay ▶**verb** (past and past participle **unlaid**) [with obj.] Nautical untwist (a rope) into separate strands.
– ORIGIN early 18th cent.: from **UN-**[2] (expressing reversal) + **LAY**[1].

unleaded ▶**adjective 1** (especially of petrol) without added lead.
2 not covered, weighted, or framed with lead.
3 Printing (of type) with no space or leads added between lines.
▶**noun** [mass noun] petrol without added lead.

unlearn ▶**verb** (past and past participle **unlearned** or **unlearnt**) [with obj.] discard (something learned, especially a bad habit or false or outdated information) from one's memory: *teachers are being asked to unlearn rigid rules for labelling and placing children.*

unlearned[1] /ʌnˈləːnd, -ˈləːnɪd/ ▶**adjective** (of a person) not well educated.
– DERIVATIVES **unlearnedly** adverb.

unlearned[2] /ʌnˈləːnd/ (also **unlearnt** /-ˈləːnt/) ▶**adjective** not having been learned: *she found herself on the stage, lines unlearned.*
■not needing to be learned because innate: *the unlearned responses of our inner world.*

unleash ▶**verb** [with obj.] release from a leash or restraint: *they dig up badger setts and unleash terriers into them |* figurative *the failure of the talks could unleash more fighting.*

unleavened ▶**adjective** (of bread) made without yeast or other raising agent.

unless ▶**conjunction** except if (used to introduce the case in which a statement being made is not true or valid): *unless you have a photographic memory, repetition is vital | manuscripts cannot be returned unless accompanied by a self-addressed envelope.*
– ORIGIN late Middle English: from **ON** or **IN** (assimilated through lack of stress to **UN-**[1]) + **LESS**.

unlettered ▶**adjective** (of a person) poorly educated or illiterate.

unliberated ▶**adjective** (of a person or their

behaviour) not liberated: *she never minded housework—Jenny said she was appallingly unliberated.*

unlicensed (also **unlicenced**) ▶ adjective not having an official licence: *unlicensed weapons.* ■ chiefly Brit. (of premises) not having a licence for the sale of alcoholic liquor: *unlicensed restaurants.*

unlighted ▶ adjective unlit.

unlike ▶ preposition different from; not similar to: *a large house not unlike Mr Shah's | they were unlike anything ever seen before.* ■ in contrast to; differently from: *unlike Elena he was not superstitious.* ■ uncharacteristic of (someone): *he sounded irritable, which was unlike him.* ▶ adjective [predic.] dissimilar or different from each other: *they seemed utterly unlike, despite being twins.* ■ (**unlike to/from**) archaic not like; different from: *he was very unlike to any other man.*
– DERIVATIVES **unlikeness** noun.
– ORIGIN Middle English: perhaps originally an alteration of Old Norse *úlíkr*; compare with Old English *ungelíc* 'not of the same kind, not comparable'.

USAGE The use of **unlike** as a conjunction, as in *she was behaving unlike she'd ever behaved before*, is not considered standard English. It can be avoided by using **as** with a negative instead: *she was behaving as she'd never behaved before.*

unlikeable (also **unlikable**) ▶ adjective (especially of a person) not likeable: *a thoroughly unlikeable bully.*

unlikely ▶ adjective (**unlikelier**, **unlikeliest**) not likely to happen, be done, or be true; improbable: *an unlikely explanation | it is unlikely that they will ever be used | [with infinitive] the change is unlikely to affect many people.*
– DERIVATIVES **unlikelihood** noun, **unlikeliness** noun.

unlimber ▶ verb [with obj.] detach (a gun) from its limber so that it can be used. ■ chiefly US unpack or unfasten (something) ready for use: *we had to unlimber some of the gear.*

unlimited ▶ adjective not limited or restricted in terms of number, quantity, or extent: *offshore reserves of gas and oil are not unlimited.* ■ (of a company) not limited. ■ Mathematics (of a problem) having an infinite number of solutions.
– DERIVATIVES **unlimitedly** adverb, **unlimitedness** noun.

unlined[1] ▶ adjective not marked or covered with lines: *her face was still unlined | unlined paper.*

unlined[2] ▶ adjective (of a container or garment) without a lining: *unlined curtains.*

unlink ▶ verb [with obj.] make no longer connected: [as adj. **unlinked**] *three previously unlinked murders.*

unliquidated ▶ adjective (of a debt) not cleared or paid off.

unlisted ▶ adjective not included on a list. ■ denoting or relating to a company whose shares are not listed on a stock exchange. ■ chiefly N. Amer. another term for **EX-DIRECTORY**. ■ Brit. (of a building) not having listed status.

unlistenable ▶ adjective (especially of music) impossible or unbearable to listen to.

unlit ▶ adjective **1** not provided with lighting: *an unlit staircase.* **2** not having been set light to: *his unlit pipe.*

unlivable ▶ adjective not able to be lived in; uninhabitable: *humanity had made the world unlivable.*

unlived ▶ adjective (**unlived-in**) not appearing to be used or inhabited; not homely or comfortable.

unload ▶ verb [with obj.] **1** remove goods from (a vehicle, ship, container, etc.): *she hadn't finished unloading the car.* ■ remove (goods) from a vehicle, ship, container, etc. ■ [no obj.] (of a vehicle, ship, container, etc.) have goods removed: *the street was jammed with vans unloading.* ■ informal get rid of (something unwanted): *he had unloaded his depreciating stock on his unsuspecting wife.* ■ chiefly US give expression to (oppressive thoughts or feelings): *the meeting had been a chance for her to unload some of her feelings about her son.* **2** remove (ammunition) from a gun or (film) from a camera.
– DERIVATIVES **unloader** noun.

unlock ▶ verb [with obj.] undo the lock of (something) using a key: *he unlocked the door to his room.* ■ make (something previously inaccessible or unexploited) available for use: *the campaign has helped us unlock rich reserves of talent among our employees.*

unlocked ▶ adjective not locked: *unlocked doors.*

unlooked ▶ adjective (**unlooked-for**) unexpected; unforeseen: *in his family he found unlooked-for happiness.*

unloose ▶ verb [with obj.] undo; let free: *his first action must be to unloose that knotted necktie | figurative she unloosed a salvo of condescension.*

unloosen ▶ verb another term for **UNLOOSE**.

unlovable (also **unloveable**) ▶ adjective not lovable: *a very unlovable child.*
– DERIVATIVES **unlovability** noun.

unloved ▶ adjective not loved.

unlovely ▶ adjective not attractive; ugly.
– DERIVATIVES **unloveliness** noun.

unloving ▶ adjective not loving: *an unloving father.*
– DERIVATIVES **unlovingly** adverb, **unlovingness** noun.

unlucky ▶ adjective (**unluckier**, **unluckiest**) having, bringing, or resulting from bad luck: *an unlucky defeat | [with infinitive] the visitors were unlucky to have a goal disallowed.*
– DERIVATIVES **unluckily** adverb, **unluckiness** noun.

unmade ▶ adjective **1** (of a bed) not having the bedclothes arranged tidily ready for sleeping in. **2** Brit. (of a road) without a hard, smooth surface.

unmaidenly ▶ adjective not befitting or characteristic of a young, sexually inexperienced woman.
– DERIVATIVES **unmaidenliness** noun.

unmake ▶ verb (past and past participle **unmade**) [with obj.] reverse or undo the making of; annul: *Parliament can make and unmake any law whatever.*

unman ▶ verb (**unmanned**, **unmanning**) [with obj.] poetic/literary deprive of qualities traditionally associated with men, such as self-control or courage: *sitting in the dock awaiting a sentence will unman the stoutest heart.*

unmanageable ▶ adjective difficult or impossible to manage, manipulate, or control: *his behaviour was becoming unmanageable at home.*
– DERIVATIVES **unmanageableness** noun, **unmanageably** adverb.

unmanaged ▶ adjective **1** not controlled or regulated: *a critique of unmanaged capitalism.* **2** (of land) left wild; in a natural state.

unmanly ▶ adjective not manly: *unmanly behaviour.*
– DERIVATIVES **unmanliness** noun.

unmanned ▶ adjective not having or needing a crew or staff: *an unmanned level crossing.*

unmannered ▶ adjective not affected or artificial in style.

unmannerly ▶ adjective not having or showing good manners: *uncouth, unmannerly fellows.*
– DERIVATIVES **unmannerliness** noun.

unmapped ▶ adjective (of an area or feature) not represented on a geographical map. ■ unexplored: *unmapped corners of Africa.* ■ Biology (of a gene or chromosome) not yet mapped.

unmarked ▶ adjective **1** not marked: *an unmarked police car | his skin was unmarked.* ■ Linguistics (of a word or other linguistic unit) having a more general meaning or use than a corresponding marked term: *'duck' is unmarked, whereas 'drake' is marked.* **2** not noticed: *it's a pleasure to reward them for work which might otherwise go unmarked.*

unmarketable ▶ adjective not marketable.

unmarried ▶ adjective not married; single.

unmask ▶ verb [with obj.] expose the true character of or hidden truth about: *the trial unmasked him as a complete charlatan.* ■ [often as adj. **unmasked**] remove the mask from: *an unmasked gunman.*
– DERIVATIVES **unmasker** noun.

unmatchable ▶ adjective incapable of being matched, equalled, or rivalled.
– DERIVATIVES **unmatchably** adverb.

unmatched ▶ adjective not matched or equalled: *he has a talent unmatched by any other politician.*

unmatured ▶ adjective not yet matured: *unmatured cheese.*

unmeaning ▶ adjective having no meaning or significance; meaningless: *a sweet, unmeaning smile.*
– DERIVATIVES **unmeaningly** adverb.

unmeant ▶ adjective not meant or intended: *an unmeant threat.*

unmeasurable ▶ adjective not able to be measured objectively: *the unmeasurable qualities of a scientist.*
– DERIVATIVES **unmeasurably** adverb.

unmeasured ▶ adjective **1** not having been measured: *unmeasured risk factors.* **2** chiefly poetic/literary immense; limitless: *he is regarded by his congregation with unmeasured adoration.*

unmediated ▶ adjective without anyone or anything intervening or acting as an intermediate; direct.

unmelodious ▶ adjective not melodious; discordant: *an unmelodious chorus of horns.*
– DERIVATIVES **unmelodiously** adverb.

unmelted ▶ adjective not melted: *unmelted snow.*

unmemorable ▶ adjective not memorable.
– DERIVATIVES **unmemorably** adverb.

unmentionable ▶ adjective too embarrassing, offensive, or shocking to be spoken about: *the unmentionable subject of incontinence.* ▶ noun (usu. **unmentionables**) chiefly humorous a person or thing that is too shocking or embarrassing to be mentioned by name: *wearing nothing but fig leaves over their unmentionables.*
– DERIVATIVES **unmentionability** noun, **unmentionableness** noun, **unmentionably** adverb.

unmentioned ▶ adjective not mentioned: *a monument unmentioned in all the architectural guides.*

unmerchantable ▶ adjective not suitable for purchase or sale.

unmerciful ▶ adjective cruel or harsh; showing no mercy.
– DERIVATIVES **unmercifully** adverb, **unmercifulness** noun.

unmerited ▶ adjective not deserved or merited: *an unmerited insult.*

unmet ▶ adjective (of a requirement) not achieved or fulfilled: *an unmet need.*

unmetalled ▶ adjective Brit. (of a road) not having a hard surface of road metal.

unmethodical ▶ adjective not orderly and systematic.
– DERIVATIVES **unmethodically** adverb.

unmetrical ▶ adjective not composed in or using metre: *an unmetrical poet.*

unmilitary ▶ adjective not typical of, suitable for, or connected with the military.

unmindful ▶ adjective [predic.] not conscious or aware: *Danielle seemed unmindful of her parents' plight.*
– DERIVATIVES **unmindfully** adverb, **unmindfulness** noun.

unmissable ▶ adjective **1** so good that it should not be missed: *the special effects make this an unmissable treat.* **2** so clear or obvious that it cannot be missed.

unmistakable (also **unmistakeable**) ▶ adjective not able to be mistaken for anything else; very distinctive: *the unmistakable sound of his laughter.*
– DERIVATIVES **unmistakability** noun, **unmistakably** adverb.

unmitigated ▶ adjective [attrib.] absolute; unqualified: *the tour had been an unmitigated disaster.*
– DERIVATIVES **unmitigatedly** adverb.

unmixed ▶ adjective not mixed: *bold unmixed colours.*

unmixed blessing ▶ noun [usu. with negative] a situation or thing having advantages and no disadvantages: *motherhood is not an unmixed blessing.*

unmodernized (also **-ised**) ▶ adjective (especially of a building) not modernized; retaining the original features.

unmodified ▶ adjective not modified.

unmodulated ▶ adjective not modulated.

unmolested ▶ adjective not pestered or molested; left in peace: *they allowed him to pass unmolested.*

unmoor ▶ verb [with obj.] release the moorings of (a vessel).

unmoral ▶ adjective not influenced by or concerned with morality. Compare with **IMMORAL**.
– DERIVATIVES **unmorality** noun.

unmothered ▶ adjective deprived of or without a mother or maternal care.

unmotherly ▶ adjective not having or showing the affectionate feelings associated with a mother.

unmotivated ▶ adjective **1** not having interest in or enthusiasm for something, especially work or study.
2 without a reason or motive: *an unmotivated attack.*

unmounted ▶ adjective not mounted.

unmourned ▶ adjective not mourned: *he would die alone and unmourned.*

unmoved ▶ adjective [predic.] not affected by emotion or excitement: *he was clearly unmoved by her outburst.*
■ not changed in one's purpose or intention: *her opponents were unmoved and plan to return to court.* ■ not changed in position: *their shares were unmoved at 25p.*
– DERIVATIVES **unmovable** (also **unmoveable**) adjective.

unmoving ▶ adjective **1** not moving; still: *Claudia sat unmoving behind her desk.*
2 not stirring any emotion.

unmown ▶ adjective not mown: *unmown grass.*

unmuffle ▶ verb [with obj.] free from something that muffles or conceals.

unmurmuring ▶ adjective poetic/literary not complaining.
– DERIVATIVES **unmurmuringly** adverb.

unmusical ▶ adjective not pleasing to the ear.
■ unskilled in or indifferent to music.
– DERIVATIVES **unmusicality** noun, **unmusically** adverb, **unmusicalness** noun.

unmutilated ▶ adjective not mutilated.

unmuzzle ▶ verb [with obj.] remove a muzzle from (an animal).
■ figurative allow (a person or the press) to express their views freely and without censorship.

unmuzzled ▶ adjective (of an animal) not wearing a muzzle.

unnameable (also **unnamable**) ▶ adjective not able to be named, especially because too bad or horrific: *his mind was blank with an unnameable fear.*

unnamed ▶ adjective not named.

unnatural ▶ adjective contrary to the ordinary course of nature; abnormal: *death by unnatural causes.*
■ not existing in nature; artificial: *the artificial turf looks an unnatural green.* ■ affected or stilted: *the formal tone of the programmes caused them to sound stilted and unnatural.* ■ lacking feelings of kindness and sympathy that are considered to be natural: *they condemned her as an unnatural woman.*
– DERIVATIVES **unnaturally** adverb, **unnaturalness** noun.

unnavigable ▶ adjective (of a waterway or sea) not able to be sailed on by ships or boats.
– DERIVATIVES **unnavigability** noun.

unnecessary ▶ adjective not needed: *the police had used unnecessary violence.*
■ more than is needed; excessive: *good construction is essential to avoid unnecessary waste.* ■ (of a remark) not appropriate and likely to be offensive or impertinent.
▶ plural noun (**unnecessaries**) unnecessary things.
– DERIVATIVES **unnecessarily** adverb, **unnecessariness** noun.

unneeded ▶ adjective not needed: *the disposal of unneeded assets.*

unneighbourly ▶ adjective not neighbourly.
– DERIVATIVES **unneighbourliness** noun.

unnerve ▶ verb [with obj.] make (someone) lose courage or confidence: [as adj. **unnerving**] *an unnerving experience.*
– DERIVATIVES **unnervingly** adverb.

unnoticeable ▶ adjective not easily observed or noticed: *the reverberation will be so slight as to be unnoticeable.*
– DERIVATIVES **unnoticeably** adverb.

unnoticed ▶ adjective [usu. as complement] not noticed: *a deliberate kick that went unnoticed by the referee.*

unnumbered ▶ adjective **1** not marked with or assigned a number.
2 not counted, typically because very great.

UNO ▶ abbreviation for United Nations Organization.

unobjectionable ▶ adjective not objectionable; acceptable: *much of the above would be unobjectionable to most Marxists.*
– DERIVATIVES **unobjectionably** adverb.

unobliging ▶ adjective not helpful or cooperative.

unobscured ▶ adjective not obscured.

unobservable ▶ adjective not able to be observed.

unobservant ▶ adjective not observant.
– DERIVATIVES **unobservantly** adverb.

unobserved ▶ adjective not observed: *their courtship has not gone unobserved by Giles.*

unobstructed ▶ adjective not obstructed: *an unobstructed view of the traffic lights.*

unobtainable ▶ adjective not able to be obtained.

unobtrusive ▶ adjective not conspicuous or attracting attention: *corrections should be neat and unobtrusive.*
– DERIVATIVES **unobtrusively** adverb, **unobtrusiveness** noun.

unoccupied ▶ adjective not occupied: *the house has been unoccupied for some time.*

unoffended ▶ adjective not having taken offence.

unoffending ▶ adjective not causing offence; harmless.

unofficial ▶ adjective not officially authorized or confirmed: *unofficial reports said that dozens of people were injured.*
– DERIVATIVES **unofficially** adverb.

unoiled ▶ adjective not oiled: *unoiled hinges.*

unopened ▶ adjective not opened: *unopened mail.*

unopposed ▶ adjective not opposed; unchallenged: *she was elected unopposed as leader.*

unordained ▶ adjective not having been ordained as a priest or minister.

unordered ▶ adjective not put in order; unarranged or disorderly.
■ not ordered or asked for.

unordinary ▶ adjective not ordinary; unusual.

unorganized (also **-ised**) ▶ adjective not organized: *a sea of unorganized data.*

unoriginal ▶ adjective lacking originality; derivative: *an uninteresting and unoriginal essay.*
– DERIVATIVES **unoriginality** noun, **unoriginally** adverb.

unornamental ▶ adjective not ornamental; plain.

unornamented ▶ adjective not having any decoration.

unorthodox ▶ adjective contrary to what is usual, traditional, or accepted; not orthodox: *he frequently upset other scholars with his unorthodox views.*
– DERIVATIVES **unorthodoxly** adverb, **unorthodoxy** noun.

unostentatious ▶ adjective not ostentatious: *he was generous in a quiet, unostentatious way.*
– DERIVATIVES **unostentatiously** adverb, **unostentatiousness** noun.

unowned ▶ adjective **1** not having an owner.
2 not admitted to; unacknowledged: *the unowned anger of all the smiling females of unenlightened times.*

unpack ▶ verb [with obj.] open and remove the contents of (a suitcase, bag, or package): *she unpacked her suitcase* | [no obj.] *he unpacked and put everything away.*
■ remove (something) from a suitcase, bag, or package: *we unpacked the sandwiches.* ■ figurative analyse (something) into its component elements: *let us unpack this question.* ■ Computing convert (data) from a compressed form to a usable form.
– DERIVATIVES **unpacker** noun.

unpaid ▶ adjective **1** (of a debt) not yet discharged by payment: *unpaid bills.*
2 (of work or a period of leave) undertaken without payment: *unpaid labour in the home.*
■ (of a person) not receiving payment for work done.

unpainted ▶ adjective not painted.

unpaired ▶ adjective **1** not arranged in pairs.
2 not forming one of a pair.

unpalatable ▶ adjective not pleasant to taste.
■ difficult to put up with or accept: *the unpalatable fact that many of the world's people are starving.*
– DERIVATIVES **unpalatability** noun, **unpalatably** adverb.

unparalleled ▶ adjective having no parallel or equal; exceptional: *the sudden rise in unemployment is unparalleled in the post-war period.*

unpardonable ▶ adjective (of a fault or offence) too severe to be pardoned; unforgivable: *an unpardonable sin.*
– DERIVATIVES **unpardonableness** noun, **unpardonably** adverb.

unparliamentary ▶ adjective (especially of language) contrary to the rules or procedures of parliament: *an unparliamentary expression.*

unpasteurized (also **-ised**) ▶ adjective not pasteurized: *unpasteurized milk.*

unpatented ▶ adjective not patented: *an unpatented invention.*

unpatriotic ▶ adjective not patriotic.
– DERIVATIVES **unpatriotically** adverb.

unpatronizing (also **-ising**) ▶ adjective not showing condescension.
– DERIVATIVES **unpatronizingly** adverb.

unpaved ▶ adjective not paved: *unpaved streets.*

unpeeled ▶ adjective not peeled: *an unpeeled orange.*

unpeg ▶ verb (**unpegged**, **unpegging**) [with obj.] unfasten by the removal of pegs: *she hastily unpegged her washing.*
■ cease to maintain a fixed relationship between (a currency) and another currency.

unpeople ▶ verb [with obj.] [usu. as adj. **unpeopled**] empty of people; depopulate.

unperceived ▶ adjective [usu. as complement] not perceived; unobserved: *the full significance of this went unperceived.*

unperceptive ▶ adjective not perceptive.
– DERIVATIVES **unperceptively** adverb, **unperceptiveness** noun.

unperfected ▶ adjective not perfected: *an unperfected sketch.*

unperforated ▶ adjective not perforated.

unperformed ▶ adjective not having been performed: *an unperformed play.*

unperfumed ▶ adjective not perfumed.

unperson ▶ noun (pl. **-persons**) a person whose name or existence is denied or ignored, especially because of a political misdemeanour.

unpersuadable ▶ adjective not able to be persuaded; obstinate.

unpersuaded ▶ adjective not persuaded; unconvinced.

unpersuasive ▶ adjective not persuasive.
– DERIVATIVES **unpersuasively** adverb.

unperturbed ▶ adjective not perturbed or concerned: *Kenneth seems unperturbed by the news.*
– DERIVATIVES **unperturbedly** adverb.

unphilosophical ▶ adjective not following philosophical principles or method.
– DERIVATIVES **unphilosophic** adjective (archaic), **unphilosophically** adverb.

unphysical ▶ adjective not in accordance with the laws or principles of physics; not corresponding to a physically possible situation.

unphysiological ▶ adjective not in accordance with normal physiological conditions.
– DERIVATIVES **unphysiologic** adjective, **unphysiologically** adverb.

unpick ▶ verb [with obj.] undo the sewing of (stitches or a garment): *I unpicked the seams of his trousers.*
■ figurative carefully analyse the different elements of, especially in order to find faults.

unpicked ▶ adjective **1** (of a flower, fruit, or vegetable) not picked: *unpicked tomatoes.*
2 not selected.

unpicturesque ▶ adjective not picturesque.

unpin ▶ verb (**unpinned**, **unpinning**) [with obj.] unfasten or detach by removing a pin or pins.
■ Chess release (a pinned piece or pawn), e.g. by moving away the piece it is shielding.

unpitied ▶ adjective not pitied.

unpitying ▶ adjective not feeling or showing pity.
– DERIVATIVES **unpityingly** adverb.

unplaceable ▶ adjective not able to be placed or classified: *an unplaceable accent.*

unplaced ▶ adjective not having or assigned to a specific place.
■ chiefly Horse Racing not one of the first three to finish in a race or competition.

unplanned ▶ adjective not planned: *an unplanned pregnancy.*

unplanted ▶ adjective (of land) uncultivated.

unplayable ▶ adjective not able to be played or played on: *unplayable deliveries* | *an unplayable winter pitch.*
■ (of music) too difficult or bad to perform.
– DERIVATIVES **unplayably** adverb.

unpleasant ▶ adjective causing discomfort, unhappiness, or revulsion; disagreeable: *an unpleasant smell* | *the symptoms are extremely unpleasant.*
■ (of a person or their manner) unfriendly and inconsiderate; rude: *when drunk, he could become very unpleasant.*
– DERIVATIVES **unpleasantly** adverb.

unpleasantness ▶ noun [mass noun] the state or quality of being unpleasant.
■ bad feeling or quarrelling between people.

unpleasantry ▶ noun (pl. **-ies**) **1** (**unpleasantries**) disagreeable matters or comments: *the day-to-day unpleasantries of dealing with an alien administration.*
2 [mass noun] dated quarrelling or other disagreeable behaviour: *a little unpleasantry with the authorities.*

unpleasing ▶ adjective not giving satisfaction, especially of an aesthetic kind: *the sound was not unpleasing.*
– DERIVATIVES **unpleasingly** adverb.

unpleasure ▶ noun [mass noun] Psychoanalysis the sense of inner pain, discomfort, or anxiety which results from the blocking of an instinctual impulse by the ego.

unploughed (US **unplowed**) ▶ adjective **1** (of an area of land) not having been ploughed.
2 N. Amer. (of a road) not cleared of snow by a snowplough.

unplucked ▶ adjective not plucked: *unplucked eyebrows.*

unplug ▶ verb (**unplugged**, **unplugging**) [with obj.] **1** disconnect (an electrical device) by removing its plug from a socket: *she unplugged the fridge.*
2 remove an obstacle or blockage from: *a procedure to unplug blocked arteries.*

unplugged ▶ adjective trademark (of pop or rock music) performed or recorded with acoustic rather than electrically amplified instruments.

unplumbed ▶ adjective **1** not fully explored or understood: *one-dimensional performances that leave the play's psychological depths unplumbed.*
2 (of a building or room) not having water and drainage pipes installed and connected.
– DERIVATIVES **unplumbable** adjective.

unpoetic ▶ adjective not having a style of expression characteristic of poetry.
– DERIVATIVES **unpoetical** adjective.

unpointed ▶ adjective **1** not having a sharpened or tapered tip.
2 (of a Semitic language) written without dots or small strokes to indicate vowels or distinguish consonants.
3 (of brickwork, a brick structure, or tiling) having joints that are not filled in or repaired.

unpolished ▶ adjective not having a polished surface: *his shoes were unpolished.*
■ unrefined in style or behaviour: *his work is unpolished and sometimes incoherent.*

unpolitic ▶ adjective rare term for IMPOLITIC.

unpolitical ▶ adjective not concerned with politics: *large numbers of otherwise unpolitical people responded to the war.*

unpolled ▶ adjective **1** (of a voter) not having voted, or registered to vote, at an election.
■ (of a vote) not cast at or registered for an election.
2 (of a person) not included in an opinion poll.

unpolluted ▶ adjective not contaminated with noxious or poisonous substances.

unpopular ▶ adjective not liked or popular: *unpopular measures* | *Luke was unpopular with most of the teachers.*
– DERIVATIVES **unpopularity** noun.

unpopulated ▶ adjective (of a place) having no inhabitants: *three missiles landed in unpopulated areas.*
■ (of a printed circuit board) having no components fitted.

unposed ▶ adjective (of a photograph) not having an artificially posed subject.

unpossessed ▶ adjective not owned.
■ [predic.] (**unpossessed of**) not having (an ability, quality, or characteristic): *the money men are unpossessed of the social graces.*

unpowered ▶ adjective having no fuel-burning source of power for propulsion.

unpractical ▶ adjective another term for IMPRACTICAL (in sense 1).
– DERIVATIVES **unpracticality** noun.

unpractised (US **unpracticed**) ▶ adjective (of a person or faculty) not trained or experienced: *to the unpractised eye, the result might appear a hotchpotch.*
■ (of an action or performance) not often done before.

unprecedented /ʌnˈprɛsɪdɛntɪd/ ▶ adjective never done or known before: *the government took the unprecedented step of releasing confidential correspondence.*
– DERIVATIVES **unprecedentedly** adverb.

unpredictable ▶ adjective not able to be predicted: *the unpredictable weather of the Scottish islands.*
■ (of a person) behaving in a way that is not easily predicted: *he is emotional and unpredictable.*
– DERIVATIVES **unpredictability** noun, **unpredictably** adverb.

unpredicted ▶ adjective (of an event or result) unforeseen: *the unpredicted change of weather.*

unprejudiced ▶ adjective not having or showing a dislike or distrust based on fixed or preconceived ideas.

unpremeditated ▶ adjective (of an act, remark, or state) not thought out or planned beforehand: *it was a totally unpremeditated attack.*
– DERIVATIVES **unpremeditatedly** adverb.

unprepared ▶ adjective [predic.] not ready or able to deal with something: *she was totally **unprepared for** what happened next* | *the transformation **caught** them unprepared.*
■ [with infinitive] not willing to do something: *they were unprepared to accept what was proposed.* ■ (of a thing) not made ready for use: *paintings on unprepared canvas.*
– DERIVATIVES **unpreparedness** noun.

unprepossessing ▶ adjective not attractive or appealing to the eye.

unpresentable ▶ adjective not clean, smart, or decent enough to be seen in public.

unpressed ▶ adjective (of food or drink) not shaped, squeezed, or obtained by pressure.
■ (of clothing) unironed.

unpressurized (also **-ised**) ▶ adjective (of a gas or its container) not having raised pressure that is produced or maintained artificially.
■ (of an aircraft cabin) not having normal atmospheric pressure maintained at a high altitude.

unpretending ▶ adjective archaic not pretentious or false: *unpretending sympathy.*

unpretentious ▶ adjective not attempting to impress others with an appearance of greater importance, talent, or culture than is actually possessed.
■ (of a place) pleasantly simple and functional; modest.
– DERIVATIVES **unpretentiously** adverb, **unpretentiousness** noun.

unpriced ▶ adjective having no marked or stated price.

unprimed ▶ adjective not made ready for use or action, in particular:
■ (of wood, canvas, or metal) not covered with primer or undercoat. ■ Biology & Medicine (of a cell) not having an induced susceptibility or proclivity.

unprincipled ▶ adjective (of a person or their behaviour) not acting in accordance with moral principles: *the public's dislike of unprincipled press behaviour.*

unprintable ▶ adjective (of words, comments, or thoughts) too offensive or shocking to be published: *Peter's first reply was unprintable.*
– DERIVATIVES **unprintably** adverb.

unprinted ▶ adjective (of a book or piece of writing) not published: *unprinted law reports.*

unprivileged ▶ adjective not having special rights, advantages, or immunities.

unproblematic ▶ adjective not constituting or presenting a problem or difficulty: *none of these approaches is unproblematic.*
– DERIVATIVES **unproblematical** adjective, **unproblematically** adverb.

unprocessed ▶ adjective not processed: *fresh, unprocessed food.*

unproclaimed ▶ adjective not announced officially or publicly.

unproductive ▶ adjective not producing or able to produce large amounts of goods, crops, or other commodities: *unproductive land must be reforested.*

■ (of an activity or period) not achieving much; not very useful: *unproductive meetings.*
– DERIVATIVES **unproductively** adverb, **unproductiveness** noun.

unprofessional ▶ adjective below or contrary to the standards expected in a particular profession: *a report on unprofessional conduct.*
– DERIVATIVES **unprofessionalism** noun, **unprofessionally** adverb.

unprofitable ▶ adjective (of a business or activity) not yielding profit or financial gain: *the mines became increasingly unprofitable.*
■ (of an activity) not beneficial or useful: *there has been much unprofitable speculation.*
– DERIVATIVES **unprofitability** noun, **unprofitably** adverb.

unprogressive ▶ adjective not favouring or implementing social reform or new, typically liberal, ideas.

unpromising ▶ adjective not giving hope of future success or good results: *the boy's natural intellect had survived in unpromising circumstances.*
– DERIVATIVES **unpromisingly** adverb.

unprompted ▶ adjective said, done, or acting without being encouraged or assisted: *unprompted remarks.*

unpronounceable ▶ adjective (of a word or name) too difficult to say.
– DERIVATIVES **unpronounceably** adverb.

unpropitious ▶ adjective (of a circumstance) not giving or indicating a good chance of success; unfavourable.
– DERIVATIVES **unpropitiously** adverb.

unprosperous ▶ adjective rare not enjoying or bringing financial success.

unprotected ▶ adjective not protected or kept safe from harm or injury: *a high, unprotected plateau* | *health-care workers remained **unprotected against** hepatitis B infection.*
■ (of a dangerous machine or mechanism) not fitted with safety guards. ■ (of sexual intercourse) performed without a condom. ■ Computing (of data or a memory location) able to be accessed or used without restriction.

unprotesting ▶ adjective not objecting to what someone has said or done.
– DERIVATIVES **unprotestingly** adverb.

unproud ▶ adjective not having a high opinion of one's worth or accomplishments.

unprovable ▶ adjective unable to be demonstrated by evidence or argument as true or existing: *the hypothesis is not merely unprovable, but false.*
– DERIVATIVES **unprovability** noun.

unproven /ʌnˈpruːv(ə)n, -ˈprəʊ-/ (also **unproved** /-ˈpruːvd/) ▶ adjective not demonstrated by evidence or argument as true or existing: *long-standing but unproven allegations* | *the risks are unproven.*
■ (of a new or alternative product, system, or treatment) not tried and tested.

unprovided ▶ adjective not provided.
■ (**unprovided with**) not equipped with (something useful or necessary). ■ (**unprovided for**) (of a dependant) not supplied with sufficient money to cover the cost of living: *he left a widow and children totally unprovided for.*

unprovoked ▶ adjective (of an attack, or a display of aggression or emotion) not caused by anything done or said: *acts of unprovoked aggression.*
■ (of a person) not provoked to do something.

unpublicized (also **-ised**) ▶ adjective not made widely known.

unpublished ▶ adjective (of a piece of writing or music) not issued in print for public sale or consumption.
■ (of an author) having no writings issued in print.
– DERIVATIVES **unpublishable** adjective.

unpunctual ▶ adjective not happening or doing something at the agreed or proper time.
– DERIVATIVES **unpunctuality** noun.

unpunctuated ▶ adjective (of a continuing event) not interrupted or marked by something occurring at intervals: *we wished for sleep unpunctuated by the cry of gulls.*
■ (of text) not containing punctuation marks.

unpunished ▶ adjective [as complement] (of an offence or offender) not receiving a penalty or sanction as retribution for transgression: *I can't allow such a mistake to go unpunished.*

unpurified ▶ adjective not made pure: *unpurified water.*

unputdownable ▶ adjective informal (of a book) so engrossing that one cannot stop reading it.

unqualified ▶ adjective 1 (of a person) not officially recognized as a practitioner of a particular profession or activity through having satisfied the relevant conditions or requirements.
■[usu. with infinitive] not competent or sufficiently knowledgeable to do something: *I am singularly unqualified to write about football.*
2 without reservation or limitation; total: *the experiment was not an unqualified success.*
– DERIVATIVES **unqualifiedly** adverb.

unquantifiable ▶ adjective impossible to express or measure in terms of quantity.

unquantified ▶ adjective not expressed or measured in terms of quantity: *we now have abundant, if unquantified, evidence.*

unquenchable ▶ adjective not able to be quenched: *his enthusiasm was unquenchable.*
– DERIVATIVES **unquenchably** adverb.

unquenched ▶ adjective not quenched.

unquestionable ▶ adjective not able to be disputed or doubted: *his musicianship is unquestionable.*
– DERIVATIVES **unquestionability** noun, **unquestionably** adverb [sentence adverb] *unquestionably, the loss of his father was a grievous blow.*

unquestioned ▶ adjective not disputed or doubted; certain: *his loyalty to John is unquestioned.*
■not examined or enquired into: *an unquestioned assumption.* ■ not subjected to questioning.

unquestioning ▶ adjective accepting something without dissent or doubt: *an unquestioning acceptance of the traditional curriculum.*
– DERIVATIVES **unquestioningly** adverb.

unquiet ▶ adjective not inclined to be quiet or inactive; restless: *she prowled at night like an unquiet spirit.*
■uneasy; anxious: *her unquiet desperation.*
– DERIVATIVES **unquietly** adverb, **unquietness** noun.

unquotable ▶ adjective not able to be quoted.

unquote ▶ verb see *quote —— unquote* at QUOTE.

unquoted ▶ adjective not quoted or listed on a stock exchange.

unrated ▶ adjective not having received a rating or assessment.
■US (of a film) not allocated an official classification, typically because regarded as unsuitable for general release. ■ informal not highly regarded.

unravel ▶ verb (**unravelled**, **unravelling**; US **unraveled**, **unraveling**) [with obj.] 1 undo (twisted, knitted, or woven threads).
■[no obj.] (of twisted, knitted, or woven threads) become undone: *part of the crew neck had unravelled.* ■ unwind (something wrapped around another object): *he unravelled the cellophane from a small cigar.*
2 investigate and solve or explain (something complicated or puzzling): *they were attempting to unravel the cause of death.*
■[no obj.] begin to fail or collapse: *his painstaking diplomacy of the last eight months could quickly unravel.*

unreachable ▶ adjective unable to be reached or contacted.
– DERIVATIVES **unreachableness** noun, **unreachably** adverb.

unreached ▶ adjective not yet reached, especially by those seeking to convert people to Christianity.

unread ▶ adjective (of a book or document) not read.
■archaic (of a person) not well read.

unreadable ▶ adjective not clear enough to read; illegible.
■too dull or difficult to be worth reading: *a heavy, unreadable novel.*
– DERIVATIVES **unreadability** noun, **unreadably** adverb.

unready ▶ adjective [predic.] not prepared for a situation or activity: *she was young and unready for motherhood.*
■archaic slow to act; hesitant.
– DERIVATIVES **unreadiness** noun.

unreal ▶ adjective so strange as to appear imaginary; not seeming real: *in the half-light the tiny cottages seemed unreal.*
■unrealistic: *unreal expectations.* ■ informal, chiefly N. Amer. incredible; amazing.
– DERIVATIVES **unreality** noun, **unreally** adverb.

unrealism ▶ noun [mass noun] lack of realism.

unrealistic ▶ adjective not realistic: *it was unrealistic to expect changes to be made overnight.*
– DERIVATIVES **unrealistically** adverb.

unrealizable (also **-isable**) ▶ adjective not able to be achieved or made to happen: *the summit might generate unrealizable public expectations.*

unrealized (also **-ised**) ▶ adjective not achieved or created: *an unrealized plan for a full-length novel.*
■not converted into money: *unrealized property assets.*

unreason ▶ noun [mass noun] inability to act or think reasonably.
– ORIGIN Middle English (in the senses 'unreasonable intention' and 'impropriety'): from UN-[1] 'lack of' + REASON.

unreasonable ▶ adjective not guided by or based on good sense: *your attitude is completely unreasonable.*
■beyond the limits of acceptability or fairness: *an unreasonable request.*
– DERIVATIVES **unreasonableness** noun, **unreasonably** adverb.

unreasoned ▶ adjective not based on good sense or logic: *an unreasoned reaction to the idea.*

unreasoning ▶ adjective not guided by or based on good sense; illogical: *unreasoning panic.*
– DERIVATIVES **unreasoningly** adverb.

unreceptive ▶ adjective not receptive, especially to new suggestions or ideas.

unreciprocated ▶ adjective not reciprocated: *his feelings for her were unreciprocated.*

unreckoned ▶ adjective not calculated or taken into account.

unreclaimed ▶ adjective (especially of land) not reclaimed.

unrecognizable (also **-isable**) ▶ adjective not able to be recognized or identified from previous encounters.
– DERIVATIVES **unrecognizably** adverb.

unrecognized (also **-ised**) ▶ adjective not identified from previous encounters or knowledge.
■not acknowledged as valuable or valid.

unrecompensed ▶ adjective not rewarded or made amends for.

unreconciled ▶ adjective not reconciled: *unreconciled conflict.*

unreconstructed ▶ adjective 1 not reconciled or converted to the current political theory or movement: *unreconstructed Communists.*
2 not rebuilt.

unrecorded ▶ adjective not recorded.
– DERIVATIVES **unrecordable** adjective.

unrecoverable ▶ adjective not able to be recovered or corrected.

unrectified ▶ adjective not corrected or amended.

unredeemable ▶ adjective not able to be redeemed: *an unredeemable defect.*

unredeemed ▶ adjective not redeemed.

unredressed ▶ adjective not corrected or compensated for: *unredressed grievances and protests.*

unreel ▶ verb [with obj. and adverbial] unwind (something wrapped around another object): *she unreeled the plug from her headset.*
■[no obj., with adverbial] (of a film) wind from one reel to another during projection.

unreeve ▶ verb (past **unrove**) [with obj.] Nautical withdraw (a rope) from a securing ring or block.

unrefined ▶ adjective not processed to remove impurities or unwanted elements: *unrefined sugar.*
■(of a person or their behaviour) not elegant or cultured.

unreflecting ▶ adjective 1 not engaging in reflection or thought: *an unreflecting hedonist.*
2 not reflecting light.
– DERIVATIVES **unreflectingly** adverb, **unreflectingness** noun, **unreflective** adjective.

unreformed ▶ adjective not changed or improved.

unregarded ▶ adjective not respected or considered; ignored: *her sarcasm went unregarded.*

unregenerate /ˌʌnrɪˈdʒɛn(ə)rət/ ▶ adjective not reforming or showing repentance; obstinately wrong or bad.
– DERIVATIVES **unregeneracy** noun, **unregenerately** adverb.

unregistered ▶ adjective not officially recognized and recorded: *unregistered births.*

unregulated ▶ adjective not controlled or supervised by regulations or laws.

unrehearsed ▶ adjective not practised before a performance: *spontaneous and unrehearsed music.*

unrelated ▶ adjective not related: *unrelated facts | households containing two or more unrelated people.*
– DERIVATIVES **unrelatedness** noun.

unrelaxed ▶ adjective tense.

unreleased ▶ adjective (especially of a film or recording) not released.

unrelenting ▶ adjective not yielding in strength, severity, or determination: *the heat was unrelenting.*
■(of a person or their behaviour) not giving way to kindness or compassion: *unrelenting opponents.*
– DERIVATIVES **unrelentingly** adverb, **unrelentingness** noun.

unreliable ▶ adjective not able to be relied upon: *he's lazy and unreliable | unreliable information.*
– DERIVATIVES **unreliability** noun, **unreliably** adverb.

unrelieved ▶ adjective lacking variation or change; monotonous: *flowing gowns of unrelieved black.*
■not provided with relief; not aided or assisted.
– DERIVATIVES **unrelievedly** adverb.

unreligious ▶ adjective indifferent or hostile to religion.
■not connected with religion.

unremarkable ▶ adjective not particularly interesting or surprising: *his early childhood was unremarkable | an unremarkable house.*
– DERIVATIVES **unremarkably** adverb.

unremarked ▶ adjective not mentioned or remarked upon; unnoticed: *she let his bitterness go unremarked.*

unremembered ▶ adjective not remembered; forgotten.

unremitting ▶ adjective never relaxing or slackening; incessant: *unremitting drizzle.*
– DERIVATIVES **unremittingly** adverb, **unremittingness** noun.

unremorseful ▶ adjective lacking feelings of regret or guilt.
– DERIVATIVES **unremorsefully** adverb.

unremovable ▶ adjective not able to be removed.

unremunerative ▶ adjective bringing little or no profit or income: *unremunerative research work.*
– DERIVATIVES **unremuneratively** adverb.

unrenewable ▶ adjective not able to be renewed: *unrenewable fossil fuels.*
– DERIVATIVES **unrenewed** adjective.

unrepealed ▶ adjective not repealed.

unrepeatable ▶ adjective not able to be done or made again.
■too offensive or shocking to be said again.
– DERIVATIVES **unrepeatability** noun.

unrepentant ▶ adjective showing no regret for one's wrongdoings.
– DERIVATIVES **unrepentantly** adverb.

unreported ▶ adjective not reported: *many human rights abuses went unreported.*

unrepresentative ▶ adjective not typical of a class, group, or body of opinion: *an unrepresentative minority.*
– DERIVATIVES **unrepresentativeness** noun.

unrepresented ▶ adjective not represented.

unrequested ▶ adjective not asked for.

unrequited ▶ adjective (of a feeling, especially love) not returned or rewarded.
– DERIVATIVES **unrequitedly** adverb, **unrequitedness** noun.

unreserve ▶ noun [mass noun] archaic lack of reserve; frankness.

unreserved ▶ adjective 1 without reservations; complete: *he has had their unreserved support.*
■frank and open: *a tall, unreserved young man.*
2 not set apart for a particular purpose or booked in advance: *unreserved grandstand seats.*
– DERIVATIVES **unreservedly** adverb, **unreservedness** noun.

unresisted ▶ adjective not resisted.

unresisting ▶ adjective not showing, producing, or putting up any resistance.
– DERIVATIVES **unresistingly** adverb.

unresolvable ▶ adjective not able to be resolved.

unresolved ▶ adjective (of a problem, question, or

dispute) not resolved: *a number of issues remain unresolved.*
■archaic (of a person) uncertain of what to think or do.
– DERIVATIVES **unresolvedly** /-vɪdli/ adverb, **unresolvedness** noun.

unresponsive ▶ adjective not responsive: *these symptoms may be* **unresponsive to** *conventional treatment.*
– DERIVATIVES **unresponsively** adverb, **unresponsiveness** noun.

unrest ▶ noun [mass noun] a state of dissatisfaction, disturbance, and agitation in a group of people, typically involving public demonstrations or disorder: *the very worst years of industrial unrest.*
■a feeling of disturbance and dissatisfaction in a person: *the frenzy and unrest of her own life.*

unrested ▶ adjective (of a person) not refreshed by rest: *she woke feeling unrested.*

unresting ▶ adjective ceaselessly active.
– DERIVATIVES **unrestingly** adverb.

unrestored ▶ adjective not repaired or renovated: *an unrestored farmhouse.*

unrestrained ▶ adjective not restrained or restricted: *a display of unrestrained delight.*
– DERIVATIVES **unrestrainedly** adverb, **unrestrainedness** noun.

unrestricted ▶ adjective not limited or restricted: *unrestricted access to both military bases.*
– DERIVATIVES **unrestrictedly** adverb.

unreturned ▶ adjective not reciprocated or responded to: *the pain of unreturned love.*

unrevised ▶ adjective not revised; in an original form: *the manuscript was unrevised when he died.*

unrevoked ▶ adjective not revoked or annulled; still in force.

unrewarded ▶ adjective not rewarded: *he gave untiring and unrewarded service.*

unrewarding ▶ adjective not rewarding or satisfying: *it was dull, unrewarding work.*

unrhymed ▶ adjective without rhymes; not rhymed.

unridden ▶ adjective not ridden or never having been ridden.

unriddle ▶ verb [with obj.] rare solve; explain.

unrideable (also **unridable**) ▶ adjective not able to be ridden.

unrig ▶ verb (**unrigged**, **unrigging**) [with obj.] remove the rigging from (a ship).
■archaic or dialect undress (someone).

unrighteous ▶ adjective formal not righteous; wicked.
– DERIVATIVES **unrighteously** adverb, **unrighteousness** noun.
– ORIGIN Old English *unrihtwīs* (see UN-[1], RIGHTEOUS).

unrip ▶ verb (**unripped**, **unripping**) [with obj.] rare open by ripping: *he carefully unripped one of the seams.*

unripe ▶ adjective not ripe: *unripe fruit.*
– DERIVATIVES **unripeness** noun.

unrisen ▶ adjective not having risen: *the unrisen sun.*

unrivalled (US **unrivaled**) ▶ adjective better than everyone or everything of the same type: *the paper's coverage of foreign news is unrivalled.*

unrivet ▶ verb (**unriveted**, **unriveting**) [with obj.] rare undo, unfasten, or detach by the removal of rivets.

unroadworthy ▶ adjective (of a vehicle) not roadworthy.

unrobe ▶ verb less common term for DISROBE.

unroll ▶ verb open or cause to open out from a rolled-up state: [no obj.] *the blanket unrolled as he tugged it* | [with obj.] *two carpets had been unrolled.*

unromantic ▶ adjective not romantic.
– DERIVATIVES **unromantically** adverb.

unroofed ▶ adjective not provided with a roof.

unroot ▶ verb uproot (something).

unrope ▶ verb [no obj.] Climbing detach oneself from a rope.

unrounded ▶ adjective not rounded.
■Phonetics (of a vowel) pronounced with the lips not rounded.

unrove past of UNREEVE.

unruffled ▶ adjective not disordered or disarranged: *the unruffled waters of the lake.*
■(of a person) not agitated or disturbed; calm.

unruled ▶ adjective 1 poetic/literary not ruled,

governed, or under control: *men with passions unruled.*
2 (of paper) not having ruled lines.

unruly ▶ adjective (**unrulier**, **unruliest**) disorderly and disruptive and not amenable to discipline or control: *complaints about unruly behaviour.*
■(of hair) difficult to keep neat and tidy.
– DERIVATIVES **unruliness** noun.
– ORIGIN late Middle English: from UN-[1] 'not' + archaic *ruly* 'amenable to discipline or order' (from RULE).

UNRWA ▶ abbreviation for United Nations Relief and Works Agency.

unsaddle ▶ verb [with obj.] remove the saddle from (a horse or other ridden animal).
■dislodge from a saddle.

unsafe ▶ adjective 1 not safe; dangerous: *drinking water in some areas may be unsafe.*
2 Law (of a verdict or conviction) not based on reliable evidence and likely to constitute a miscarriage of justice.
– DERIVATIVES **unsafely** adverb, **unsafeness** noun.

unsafe sex ▶ noun [mass noun] sexual activity in which precautions are not taken to reduce the risk of spreading sexually transmitted diseases, especially Aids.

unsaid[1] past and past participle of UNSAY.

unsaid[2] ▶ adjective not said or uttered: *the rest of the remark he left unsaid.*

unsalaried ▶ adjective not being paid or involving the payment of a salary: *an unsalaried post.*

unsaleable (also **unsalable**) ▶ adjective not able to be sold: *the house proved unsaleable.*
– DERIVATIVES **unsaleability** noun.

unsalted ▶ adjective not salted: *unsalted butter.*

unsanctified ▶ adjective not sanctified.

unsanctioned ▶ adjective not sanctioned.

unsanitary ▶ adjective not sanitary: *the unsanitary conditions in the orphanage.*

unsatisfactory ▶ adjective unacceptable because poor or not good enough: *an unsatisfactory situation.*
■Law another term for UNSAFE.
– DERIVATIVES **unsatisfactorily** adverb, **unsatisfactoriness** noun.

unsatisfied ▶ adjective not satisfied: *the compromise left all sides unsatisfied.*

unsatisfying ▶ adjective not satisfying: *an unsatisfying relationship.*
– DERIVATIVES **unsatisfyingly** adverb.

unsaturated ▶ adjective Chemistry (of organic molecules) having carbon–carbon double or triple bonds and therefore not containing the greatest possible number of hydrogen atoms.
– DERIVATIVES **unsaturation** noun.

unsaved ▶ adjective not saved, in particular (in Christian use) not having had one's soul saved from damnation.

unsavoury (US **unsavory**) ▶ adjective disagreeable to taste, smell, or look at.
■disagreeable and unpleasant because morally disreputable: *an unsavoury reputation.*
– DERIVATIVES **unsavourily** adverb, **unsavouriness** noun.

unsay ▶ verb (past and past participle **unsaid**) [with obj.] withdraw or retract (a statement).

unsayable ▶ adjective not able to be said, especially because considered too controversial or offensive to mention.

unscalable ▶ adjective not able to be scaled or climbed: *a prison with unscalable walls.*

unscaled ▶ adjective (of a mountain) not yet climbed: *they had climbed a hitherto unscaled peak.*

unscarred ▶ adjective not scarred or damaged: *he did not escape unscarred.*

unscathed ▶ adjective [predic.] without suffering any injury, damage, or harm: *I came through all those perils unscathed.*

unscented ▶ adjective not scented: *unscented soap.*

unscheduled ▶ adjective not scheduled: *his plane made an unscheduled stop.*

unscholarly ▶ adjective not showing the learning and attention to detail characteristic of a scholar.
– DERIVATIVES **unscholarliness** noun (rare).

unschooled ▶ adjective not educated at or made to attend school: *unschooled children.*

■lacking knowledge or training in a particular field: *she was* **unschooled in** *the niceties of royal behaviour.*
■ not affected or artificial; natural and spontaneous.
■ uncontrolled; undisciplined: *he reacts with intense, unschooled emotion.*

unscientific ▶ adjective 1 not in accordance with scientific principles or methodology: *our whole approach is hopelessly unscientific.*
2 lacking knowledge of or interest in science.
– DERIVATIVES **unscientifically** adverb.

unscramble ▶ verb [with obj.] restore (something that has been scrambled) to an intelligible, readable, or viewable state.
– DERIVATIVES **unscrambler** noun.

unscreened ▶ adjective 1 not subjected to testing or investigation by screening: *transfusion with unscreened blood.*
■not filtered or sorted using a screen.
2 (of a film or programme) not shown or broadcast: *copies of the unscreened episodes.*
3 not provided with or hidden by a screen.

unscrew ▶ verb (with reference to a lid or other object held in place by a spiral thread) unfasten or be unfastened by twisting: [with obj.] *Will unscrewed the cap from a metal flask* | [no obj.] *the spout usually unscrews or lifts off easily.*
■[with obj.] detach, open, or slacken (something) by removing or loosening the screws holding it in place.

unscripted ▶ adjective said or delivered without a prepared script; impromptu.

unscriptural ▶ adjective not in accordance with the Bible: *sacraments deemed unscriptural by Luther.*

unscrupulous ▶ adjective having or showing no moral principles; not honest or fair.
– DERIVATIVES **unscrupulously** adverb, **unscrupulousness** noun.

unseal ▶ verb [with obj.] remove or break the seal of: *she slowly unsealed the envelope.*

unsealed ▶ adjective not sealed: *unsealed envelopes.*
■chiefly Austral./NZ (of a road) not surfaced with bitumen or a similar substance.

unsearchable ▶ adjective poetic/literary unable to be clearly understood; inscrutable.
– DERIVATIVES **unsearchableness** noun, **unsearchably** adverb.

unseasonable ▶ adjective (of weather) unusual for the time of year: *an unseasonable warm spell.*
■untimely; inopportune.
– DERIVATIVES **unseasonableness** noun, **unseasonably** adverb.

unseasonal ▶ adjective (especially of weather) unusual or inappropriate for the time of year: *temperatures rose to an unseasonal 12°C.*

unseasoned ▶ adjective 1 (of food) not flavoured with salt, pepper, or other spices.
2 (of timber) not treated or matured.
■(of a person) inexperienced.

unseat ▶ verb [with obj.] cause (someone) to fall from a horse or bicycle.
■remove from a position of power or authority.

unseaworthy ▶ adjective (of a boat or ship) not in a good enough condition to sail on the sea.

unsecured ▶ adjective 1 (of a loan) made without an asset given as security.
■(of a creditor) having made such a loan.
2 not made secure or safe.

unseeable ▶ adjective not able to be seen; invisible.

unseeded ▶ adjective 1 (chiefly of a competitor in a sports tournament) not seeded.
2 (of a grape) not having seeds.

unseeing ▶ adjective with one's eyes open but without noticing or seeing anything.
– DERIVATIVES **unseeingly** adverb.

unseemly ▶ adjective (of behaviour or actions) not proper or appropriate: *an unseemly squabble.*
– DERIVATIVES **unseemliness** noun.

unseen ▶ adjective not seen or noticed: *it seemed she might escape unseen.*
■not foreseen or predicted: *unseen problems.* ■ chiefly Brit. (of a passage for translation in a test or examination) not previously read or prepared.
▶ noun Brit. an unseen passage for translation.

unsegregated ▶ adjective not segregated or set apart from the rest or from others.

unselective ▶ adjective not selective.

unselfconscious ▶ adjective not suffering from

u

or exhibiting self-consciousness; not shy or embarrassed.
– DERIVATIVES **unselfconsciously** adverb, **unself-consciousness** noun.

unselfish ▶ adjective willing to put the needs or wishes of others before one's own: *unselfish devotion.*
– DERIVATIVES **unselfishly** adverb, **unselfishness** noun.

unsensational ▶ adjective not sensational or seeking to provoke interest or excitement at the expense of accuracy.
– DERIVATIVES **unsensationally** adverb.

unsentimental ▶ adjective not displaying or influenced by sentimental feelings.
– DERIVATIVES **unsentimentally** adverb.

unserious ▶ adjective not serious; light-hearted.

unserved ▶ adjective (of a person or section of society) not attended to or catered for.
■ Law (of a writ or summons) not officially delivered to a person. ■ (of a female animal) not mated with a male.

unserviceable ▶ adjective not in working order or fulfilling its function adequately; unfit for use.
– DERIVATIVES **unserviceability** noun.

unsettle ▶ verb [with obj.] cause to feel anxious or uneasy; disturb: *the crisis has unsettled financial markets* | [as adj.] **unsettling** *an unsettling conversation.*
– DERIVATIVES **unsettlement** noun, **unsettlingly** adverb.

unsettled ▶ adjective **1** lacking stability: *an unsettled childhood.*
■ worried and uneasy: *she felt edgy and unsettled.* ■ liable to change; unpredictable: *a spell of unsettled weather.* ■ not yet resolved: *one important question remains unsettled.* ■ (of a bill) not yet paid.
2 (of an area) having no settlers or inhabitants.
– DERIVATIVES **unsettledness** noun.

unsewn binding ▶ noun Brit. another term for **PERFECT BINDING**.

unsex ▶ verb [with obj.] deprive of gender, sexuality, or the characteristic attributes or qualities of one or other sex.

unsexy ▶ adjective (**unsexier**, **unsexiest**) not sexually attractive or exciting.

unshackle ▶ verb [with obj.] (usu. **be unshackled**) release from shackles, chains, or other physical restraints: *his feet were unshackled.*
■ figurative liberate; set free.

unshaded ▶ adjective **1** (of a light bulb or lamp) not having a shade or cover.
■ not screened from direct light.
2 (of an area of a diagram) not shaded with pencil lines or a block of colour.

unshadowed ▶ adjective not covered or darkened by a shadow or shadows.

unshakeable (also **unshakable**) ▶ adjective (of a belief, feeling, or opinion) strongly felt and unable to be changed: *an unshakeable faith in God.*
■ unable to be disputed or questioned: *an unshakeable alibi.*
– DERIVATIVES **unshakeability** noun, **unshakeably** adverb.

unshaken ▶ adjective not disturbed from a firm position or state; steadfast and unwavering: *their trust in him remained unshaken.*
– DERIVATIVES **unshakenly** adverb.

unshaped ▶ adjective having a vague, ill-formed, or unfinished shape.

unshared ▶ adjective not shared with or by another or others.

unsharp ▶ adjective Photography (of a picture or image) not well defined.
– DERIVATIVES **unsharpness** noun.

unshaved ▶ adjective unshaven.

unshaven ▶ adjective not having recently shaved or been shaved.

unsheathe ▶ verb [with obj.] draw or pull out (a knife, sword, or similar weapon) from its sheath or covering.

unshed ▶ adjective (of tears) welling in a person's eyes but not falling on their cheeks.

unshelled ▶ adjective not extracted from its shell: *unshelled peanuts.*

unshielded ▶ adjective not protected or shielded.

unship ▶ verb (**unshipped**, **unshipping**) [with obj.] chiefly Nautical remove (an oar, mast, or other object)

from its fixed or regular position: *they unshipped the oars.*
■ unload (a cargo) from a ship or boat.

unshockable ▶ adjective impossible to shock, horrify, or disgust: *most doctors are fairly unshockable.*
– DERIVATIVES **unshockability** noun.

unshod ▶ adjective not wearing shoes.

unshorn ▶ adjective (of a person's hair) not cut.

unshrinking ▶ adjective unhesitating; fearless.
– DERIVATIVES **unshrinkingly** adverb.

unsighted ▶ adjective lacking the power of sight: *blind or unsighted people.*
■ (especially in sport) prevented from having a clear view of something. ■ not seen: *a distant unsighted object.*

unsightly ▶ adjective unpleasant to look at; ugly: *an unsightly rubbish tip.*
– DERIVATIVES **unsightliness** noun.

unsigned ▶ adjective **1** not identified or authorized by a person's signature: *an unsigned cheque.*
■ (of a musician or sports player) not having signed a contract of employment.
2 Mathematics & Computing not having a plus or minus sign, or a bit representing this.

unsinkable ▶ adjective (of a ship or boat) unable to be sunk: *the supposedly unsinkable ship hit an iceberg.*
– DERIVATIVES **unsinkability** noun.

unsisterly ▶ adjective not showing the support and affection which is thought to be characteristic of a sister.

unsized ▶ adjective (of fabric, paper, or a wall) not treated with size.

unskilful (also chiefly US **unskillful**) ▶ adjective not having or showing skill.
– DERIVATIVES **unskilfully** adverb, **unskilfulness** noun.

unskilled ▶ adjective not having or requiring special skill or training: *unskilled manual workers.*

unslakeable (also **unslakable**) ▶ adjective not able to be quenched or satisfied: *her unslakeable desire.*

unsleeping ▶ adjective not or never sleeping: *much of that night she lay unsleeping.*
– DERIVATIVES **unsleepingly** adverb.

unsliced ▶ adjective (especially of a commercially produced loaf of bread) not having been cut into slices.

unsling ▶ verb (past and past participle **unslung**) [with obj.] remove (something) from the place where it has been slung or suspended.

unsmiling ▶ adjective (of a person or their manner or expression) serious or unfriendly; not smiling.
– DERIVATIVES **unsmilingly** adverb, **unsmilingness** noun.

unsmoked ▶ adjective **1** (of meat or fish) not cured by exposure to smoke: *smoked and unsmoked bacon.*
2 (of tobacco or a cigarette) not having been smoked.

unsnap ▶ verb (**unsnapped**, **unsnapping**) [with obj.] unfasten or open with a brisk movement and a sharp sound: *he put the case on the table and unsnapped the clasps.*

unsnarl ▶ verb [with obj.] disentangle; sort out.

unsociable ▶ adjective not enjoying or making an effort to behave sociably in the company of others: *Terry was grumpy and unsociable.*
■ not conducive to friendly social relations: *watching TV is a fairly unsociable activity.*
– DERIVATIVES **unsociability** noun, **unsociableness** noun, **unsociably** adverb.

USAGE There is some overlap in the use of the adjectives **unsociable**, **unsocial**, and **antisocial**, but they also have distinct core meanings. Generally speaking, **unsociable** means 'not enjoying the company of others', as in *Terry was grumpy and unsociable*. **Antisocial** means 'contrary to the laws and customs of a society', as in *aggressive and antisocial behaviour*. **Unsocial** is usually restricted to the sense '(of hours) falling outside the normal working day', as in *employees were expected to work unsocial hours*.

unsocial ▶ adjective (of the hours of work of a job) falling outside the normal working day and thus socially inconvenient.
■ causing annoyance and disapproval in others; antisocial: *the unsocial behaviour of young teenagers.* ■ not seeking the company of others.
– DERIVATIVES **unsocially** adverb.

unsoiled ▶ adjective not stained or dirty.

unsold ▶ adjective (of an item) not sold.

unsolicited ▶ adjective not asked for; given or done voluntarily: *unsolicited junk mail.*
– DERIVATIVES **unsolicitedly** adverb.

unsolvable ▶ adjective not able to be solved.
– DERIVATIVES **unsolvability** noun.

unsolved ▶ adjective not solved: *an unsolved mystery.*

unsophisticated ▶ adjective lacking refined worldly knowledge or tastes.
■ not complicated or highly developed; basic: *unsophisticated computer software.*
– DERIVATIVES **unsophisticatedly** adverb, **unsophisticatedness** noun, **unsophistication** noun.

unsorted ▶ adjective not sorted or arranged: *a mass of unsorted papers.*

unsought ▶ adjective not searched for, requested, or desired.

unsound ▶ adjective not safe or robust; in poor condition: *the tower is structurally unsound.*
■ not based on sound evidence or reasoning and therefore unreliable or unacceptable: *activities deemed to be environmentally unsound.* ■ (of a person) not competent, reliable, or holding acceptable views. ■ injured, ill, or diseased, especially (of a horse) lame.
– DERIVATIVES **unsoundly** adverb, **unsoundness** noun.

unsounded[1] ▶ adjective not uttered, pronounced, or made to sound.

unsounded[2] ▶ adjective unfathomed.

unsoured ▶ adjective not soured: *unsoured milk.*

unsown ▶ adjective not having been sown.

unsparing ▶ adjective **1** merciless; severe: *he is unsparing in his criticism of the arms trade.*
2 given freely and generously: *she had won her mother's unsparing approval.*
– DERIVATIVES **unsparingly** adverb, **unsparingness** noun.

unspeakable ▶ adjective not able to be expressed in words: *I felt an unspeakable tenderness towards her.*
■ too bad or horrific to express in words.
– DERIVATIVES **unspeakableness** noun, **unspeakably** adverb.

unspeaking ▶ adjective not speaking; silent.

unspecialized (also **-ised**) ▶ adjective not specialized.

unspecific ▶ adjective not specific; vague: *he was unspecific about his relationship with Marian.*

unspecified ▶ adjective not stated clearly or exactly: *an unspecified number of people.*

unspectacular ▶ adjective not spectacular; unremarkable: *she had been an unspectacular student.*
– DERIVATIVES **unspectacularly** adverb.

unspent ▶ adjective not spent.
■ not exhausted or used up: *he shook with unspent rage.*

unspilled (also **unspilt**) ▶ adjective not spilt.

unspiritual ▶ adjective not spiritual; worldly: *the clergymen were deplorably unspiritual.*
– DERIVATIVES **unspirituality** noun, **unspiritually** adverb.

unspoilt (also **unspoiled**) ▶ adjective not spoilt, in particular (of a place) not marred by development: *unspoilt countryside.*

unspoken ▶ adjective not expressed in speech; tacit: *an unspoken assumption.*

unsponsored ▶ adjective not supported or promoted by a sponsor.

unspool ▶ verb [no obj.] unwind from or as if from a spool.
■ (of a film) be screened. ■ [with obj.] show (a film).

unsporting ▶ adjective not fair, generous, or sportsmanlike: *the unsporting behaviour of some of the crowd.*
– DERIVATIVES **unsportingly** adverb.

unsportsmanlike ▶ adjective unsporting.

unspotted ▶ adjective not marked with spots.

unsprayed ▶ adjective not having been sprayed, especially with pesticides or other chemicals.

unsprung ▶ adjective not provided with springs.

unstable ▶ adjective (**unstabler**, **unstablest**) prone to change, fail, or give way; not stable: *the unstable cliff tops* | *an unstable government.*

■prone to psychiatric problems or sudden changes of mood: *he was mentally unstable.*
– DERIVATIVES **unstableness** noun, **unstably** adverb.

unstable equilibrium ▶ noun Physics a state of equilibrium in which a small disturbance will produce a large change.

unstageable ▶ adjective (of a play) impossible or very difficult to present to an audience.

unstained ▶ adjective not stained.

unstamped ▶ adjective **1** not marked by stamping. **2** not having a postage stamp affixed.

unstarched ▶ adjective (especially of fabric or clothing) not starched.

unstated ▶ adjective not stated or declared: *a series of unstated assumptions.*

unstatesmanlike ▶ adjective not suitable for or befitting a statesman.

unsteady ▶ adjective (**unsteadier**, **unsteadiest**) **1** liable to fall or shake; not firm: *he was very unsteady on his feet.* **2** not uniform or regular.
– DERIVATIVES **unsteadily** adverb, **unsteadiness** noun.

unstep ▶ verb (**unstepped**, **unstepping**) [with obj.] detach (a mast) from its step.

unstick ▶ verb (past and past participle **unstuck**) **1** [with obj.] cause to become no longer stuck together. **2** [no obj.] Brit. informal (of an aircraft) take off. ■[with obj.] cause (an aircraft) to take off. ▶ noun [in sing.] Brit. informal the moment at which an aircraft takes off.
– PHRASES **come** (or **get**) **unstuck** become separated or unfastened. ■informal fail completely: *all their clever ideas came unstuck.*

unstinted ▶ adjective given without restraint; liberal: *they received unstinted praise.*
– DERIVATIVES **unstintedly** adverb.

unstinting ▶ adjective given or giving without restraint; unsparing: *he was unstinting in his praise.*
– DERIVATIVES **unstintingly** adverb.

unstirred ▶ adjective not moved, agitated, or stirred.

unstitch ▶ verb [with obj.] undo the stitches of.

unstop ▶ verb (**unstopped**, **unstopping**) [with obj.] free (something) from obstruction: *he must unstop the sink.* ■remove the stopper from (a bottle or other container).

unstoppable ▶ adjective impossible to stop or prevent: *an unstoppable left-foot volley.*
– DERIVATIVES **unstoppability** noun, **unstoppably** adverb.

unstopper ▶ verb [with obj.] remove the stopper from (a bottle or other container): *he unstoppered the jar.*

unstrained ▶ adjective **1** not forced or produced by effort: *a lovely warm unstrained smile.* **2** not subjected to straining or stretching.

unstrap ▶ verb (**unstrapped**, **unstrapping**) [with obj.] undo the strap or straps of. ■release (someone or something) by undoing straps: *they unstrapped themselves.*

unstreamed ▶ adjective Brit. (of schoolchildren, a class, or a school) not arranged in streams.

unstressed ▶ adjective **1** Phonetics (of a syllable) not pronounced with stress: *an unstressed syllable.* **2** not subjected to stress: *a well-balanced, unstressed person.*

unstring ▶ verb (past and past participle **unstrung**) [with obj.] **1** [usu. as adj. **unstrung**] unnerve: *a mind unstrung by loneliness.* **2** remove or relax the string or strings of (a bow or musical instrument). **3** remove from a string: *unstringing the beads from the rosary.*

unstructured ▶ adjective without formal organization or structure: *an unstructured interview.* ■(of a garment) made with little or no interfacing or other material which would give definition to its shape.

unstuck past and past participle of UNSTICK.

unstudied ▶ adjective not laboured or artificial; natural: *she had an unstudied grace in every step.*
– DERIVATIVES **unstudiedly** adverb.

unstuffed ▶ adjective not containing stuffing.

unstuffy ▶ adjective **1** friendly, informal, and approachable: *colourful and unstuffy periodicals.*
2 having fresh air or ventilation.

unstylish ▶ adjective not elegant, fashionable, or stylish.

unsubdued ▶ adjective not restrained or subdued.

unsubjugated ▶ adjective not subjugated.

unsubstantial ▶ adjective having little or no solidity, reality, or factual basis.
– DERIVATIVES **unsubstantiality** noun, **unsubstantially** adverb.

unsubstantiated ▶ adjective not supported or proven by evidence: *unsubstantiated claims.*

unsubtle ▶ adjective not subtle; obvious; clumsy: *a grindingly unsubtle joke.*
– DERIVATIVES **unsubtly** adverb.

unsuccess ▶ noun [mass noun] lack of success: *I had done two shows with spectacular unsuccess.*

unsuccessful ▶ adjective not successful: *an unsuccessful attempt to enter Parliament.*
– DERIVATIVES **unsuccessfully** adverb, **unsuccessfulness** noun.

unsugared ▶ adjective not sweetened with sugar.

unsuitable ▶ adjective not fitting or appropriate: *the display is unsuitable for young children.*
– DERIVATIVES **unsuitability** noun, **unsuitableness** noun, **unsuitably** adverb.

unsuited ▶ adjective [predic.] not right or appropriate: *he was totally unsuited for the job.*

unsullied ▶ adjective not spoiled or made impure: *an unsullied reputation.*

unsummoned ▶ adjective not summoned: *these visions appeared, unsummoned.*

unsung ▶ adjective not celebrated or praised: *Harvey is one of the unsung heroes of the industrial revolution.*

unsupervised ▶ adjective not done or acting under supervision: *unsupervised visits | a safe garden where children may play unsupervised.*

unsupportable ▶ adjective another term for INSUPPORTABLE.
– DERIVATIVES **unsupportably** adverb.

unsupported ▶ adjective (of a structure, object, or person) not supported physically: *a toddler who can stand unsupported.* ■not borne out by evidence or facts: *the assumption was unsupported by evidence.* ■(of a person or activity) not given financial or other assistance. ■ Computing (of a program, language, or device) not having assistance for the user available from a manufacturer or system manager.

unsupportive ▶ adjective not providing encouragement or emotional help.

unsure ▶ adjective not feeling, showing, or done with confidence and certainty: *she was feeling nervous, unsure of herself* | [with clause] *she was unsure how to reply.* ■(of a fact) not fixed or certain: *the date is unsure.*
– DERIVATIVES **unsurely** adverb, **unsureness** noun.

unsurfaced ▶ adjective (of a road or path) not provided with a durable upper layer.

unsurmountable ▶ adjective not able to be overcome; insurmountable.

unsurpassable ▶ adjective not able to be exceeded in quality or degree.
– DERIVATIVES **unsurpassably** adverb.

unsurpassed ▶ adjective better or greater than any other: *the quality of workmanship is unsurpassed.*

unsurprised ▶ adjective not feeling or showing surprise at something unexpected: *he replied in a flat and unsurprised voice.*

unsurprising ▶ adjective not unexpected and so not causing surprise: *the outcome of this sombre film is unsurprising.*
– DERIVATIVES **unsurprisingly** adverb [sentence adverb] *unsurprisingly, recession is the theme of most reports.*

unsusceptible ▶ adjective **1** not likely or liable to be influenced or harmed by a particular thing: *infants are relatively unsusceptible to infections.* **2** [predic.] (**unsusceptible of**) not capable or admitting of: *their meaning is unsusceptible of analysis.*
– DERIVATIVES **unsusceptibility** noun.

unsuspected ▶ adjective not known or thought to exist or be present; not imagined possible: *the actor displays an unsuspected talent for comedy.* ■(of a person) not regarded with suspicion.
– DERIVATIVES **unsuspectedly** adverb.

unsuspecting ▶ adjective (of a person or animal) not aware of the presence of danger; feeling no
suspicion: *anti-personnel mines lie in wait for their unsuspecting victims.*
– DERIVATIVES **unsuspectingly** adverb, **unsuspectingness** noun.

unsuspicious ▶ adjective not having or showing suspicion.
– DERIVATIVES **unsuspiciously** adverb.

unsustainable ▶ adjective not able to be maintained at the current rate or level: *macroeconomic instability led to an unsustainable boom.* ■Ecology upsetting the ecological balance by depleting natural resources: *unsustainable fishing practices.* ■ not able to be upheld or defended: *both remarks are unsustainable.*
– DERIVATIVES **unsustainably** adverb.

unsustained ▶ adjective not prolonged for an extended period or without interruption.

unswayed ▶ adjective [predic.] (of a person) not influenced or affected: *investors are unswayed by suggestions that the numbers are overblown.*

unsweetened ▶ adjective (of food or drink) without sugar or a similar substance having been added: *unsweetened grapefruit juice.*

unswept ▶ adjective (of an area) not cleaned by having the dirt or litter on it swept up.

unswerving ▶ adjective not changing or becoming weaker; steady or constant: *unswerving loyalty.*
– DERIVATIVES **unswervingly** adverb.

unsworn ▶ adjective Law (of testimony or evidence) not given under oath.

unsymmetrical ▶ adjective another term for ASYMMETRICAL.
– DERIVATIVES **unsymmetrically** adverb.

unsympathetic ▶ adjective not feeling, showing, or expressing sympathy: *I'm not being unsympathetic, but I can't see why you put up with him.* ■[predic.] not showing approval or favour towards an idea or action: *they were initially unsympathetic towards the cause of Irish freedom.* ■ (of a person) not friendly or cooperative; unlikeable: *a totally unsympathetic character.*
– DERIVATIVES **unsympathetically** adverb.

unsystematic ▶ adjective not done or acting according to a fixed plan or system; unmethodical.
– DERIVATIVES **unsystematically** adverb.

untack[1] ▶ verb [with obj.] detach (something) by the removal of tacks.

untack[2] ▶ verb [with obj.] remove the saddle and bridle from (a horse).

untainted ▶ adjective not contaminated, polluted, or tainted: *the paper was untainted by age.*

untaken ▶ adjective **1** (of a region or person) not taken by force; uncaptured. **2** (of an action) not put into effect: *hard decisions have been left untaken.*

untalented ▶ adjective (of a person) not having a natural aptitude or skill.

untameable (also **untamable**) ▶ adjective (of an animal) not capable of being domesticated. ■not capable of being controlled: *her untameable mop of thick black hair.*

untamed ▶ adjective not domesticated or otherwise controlled.

untangle ▶ verb [with obj.] free from a tangled or twisted state: *fishermen untangle their nets.* ■make (something complicated or confusing) easier to understand or deal with.

untanned ▶ adjective **1** (of a person or their skin) not tanned by exposure to the sun. **2** (of animal skin) not converted into leather by tanning: *untanned hides.*

untapped ▶ adjective (of a resource) not yet exploited or used: *the vast untapped potential of individual women and men.*

untarnished ▶ adjective (of metal or metalware) not having lost its lustre, especially as a result of exposure to air or moisture. ■figurative not made less valuable or respected: *his ministers enjoyed an untarnished reputation.*

untasted ▶ adjective (of food or drink) not sampled or tested for flavour.

untaught ▶ adjective (of a person) not trained by teaching: *she is totally untaught and will not listen.* ■not acquired by teaching; natural or spontaneous: *by untaught instinct they know that scent means food.*

untaxed ▶ adjective not subject to taxation.

■(of an item, income, etc.) not having had the required tax paid on it.

unteachable ▶ adjective (of a pupil or skill) unable to be taught.

untechnical ▶ adjective not having or requiring technical knowledge.

untempered ▶ adjective not moderated or lessened by anything: *the products of a technological mastery untempered by political imagination.*
■(of a material) not brought to the proper hardness or consistency.

untenable ▶ adjective (especially of a position or view) not able to be maintained or defended against attack or objection: *this argument is clearly untenable.*
– DERIVATIVES **untenability** noun, **untenably** adverb.

untended ▶ adjective not cared for or looked after; neglected: *untended gravestones.*

untenured ▶ adjective (of a teacher, lecturer, or other professional) not having a permanent post.
■(of an academic or other post) not permanent.

Untermensch /ˈʊntəmɛn(t)ʃ, German ˈʊntɐmɛnʃ/ ▶ noun (pl. **Untermenschen** /-mɛn(t)ʃ(ə)n, German -mɛnʃn/) a person considered racially or socially inferior.
– ORIGIN German, literally 'underperson'.

untested ▶ adjective (of an idea, product, or person) not subjected to examination, experiment, or experience; unproven: *analyses based on dubious and untested assumptions.*
– DERIVATIVES **untestable** adjective.

untether ▶ verb [with obj.] release or free from a tether: *I reached the horses and untethered them.*

unthanked ▶ adjective without receiving thanks: *the women's kind gesture did not go unthanked.*

unthankful ▶ adjective not feeling or showing pleasure, relief, or gratitude.
– DERIVATIVES **unthankfully** adverb, **unthankfulness** noun.

unthaw ▶ verb N. Amer. melt or thaw: [with obj.] *the warm weather helped unthaw the rail lines.*

untheorized (also **-ised**) ▶ adjective not given a theoretical premise or framework.

unthinkable ▶ adjective (of a situation or event) too unlikely or undesirable to be considered a possibility: *it was unthinkable that John could be dead* | [as noun **the unthinkable**] *the unthinkable happened—I spoke up.*
– DERIVATIVES **unthinkability** noun, **unthinkably** adverb [as submodifier] *a land of unthinkably vast spaces.*

unthinking ▶ adjective expressed, done, or acting without proper consideration of the consequences: *she was at pains to correct unthinking prejudices.*
– DERIVATIVES **unthinkingly** adverb, **unthinkingness** noun.

unthought ▶ adjective not formed by the process of thinking.
■(**unthought of**) not imagined or dreamed of: *the old develop interests unthought of in earlier years.*

unthread ▶ verb [with obj.] take (a thread) out of a needle.
■remove (an object) from a thread.

unthreatening ▶ adjective not having a hostile or frightening quality or manner: *the nymphet image renders women safe, unthreatening, and biddable.*
– DERIVATIVES **unthreatened** adjective.

unthrifty ▶ adjective 1 not using money and other resources carefully; wasteful.
2 chiefly archaic or dialect (of livestock or plants) not strong and healthy.
– DERIVATIVES **unthriftily** adverb, **unthriftiness** noun.

unthrone ▶ verb archaic term for **DETHRONE**.

untidy ▶ adjective (**untidier**, **untidiest**) not arranged neatly and in order: *the place was dreadfully untidy.*
■(of a person) not inclined to keep one's possessions or appearance neat and in order.
– DERIVATIVES **untidily** adverb, **untidiness** noun.

untie ▶ verb (**untying**) [with obj.] undo or unfasten (a cord or knot): *she knelt to untie her laces.*
■undo a cord or similar fastening that binds (someone or something): *Morton undid the parcel.*
– ORIGIN Old English *untigan* (see **UN-²**, **TIE**).

untied ▶ adjective 1 not fastened or knotted.
2 (of an international loan or aid) not given subject to the condition that it should be used for purchases from the donor country.

until ▶ preposition & conjunction up to (the point in

time or the event mentioned): [as prep.] *the kidnappers have given us until October 11th to deliver the documents* | *he held the office until his death* | [as conjunction] *you don't know what you can achieve until you try.*
– ORIGIN Middle English: from Old Norse *und* 'as far as' + **TILL**¹ (the sense thus duplicated).

> **USAGE** On the differences between until and till, see usage at **TILL**¹.

untilled ▶ adjective (of land) not prepared and cultivated for crops.

untimely ▶ adjective (of an event or act) happening or done at an unsuitable time: *Dave's untimely return.*
■(of a death or end) happening too soon or sooner than normal: *his untimely death in military action.*
▶ adverb archaic at a time that is unsuitable or premature: *the moment was very untimely chosen.*
– DERIVATIVES **untimeliness** noun.

untinged ▶ adjective [predic.] (**untinged by/with**) not in the slightest affected by: *a cold-blooded killing untinged by any remorse on your part.*

untiring ▶ adjective (of a person or their actions) continuing at the same rate without loss of vigour: *his untiring efforts in commissioning ecological reports.*
– DERIVATIVES **untiringly** adverb.

untitled ▶ adjective 1 (of a book, composition, or other artistic work) having no name.
2 (of a person) not having a title indicating high social or official rank: *lesser untitled officials.*
■(of a sports player) not a champion.

unto ▶ preposition 1 archaic term for **TO**: *do unto others as you would be done by* | *I say unto you, be gone.*
2 archaic term for **UNTIL**: *marriage was forever—unto death.*
– ORIGIN Middle English: from **UNTIL**, with **TO** replacing **TILL**¹ (in its northern dialect meaning 'to').

untold ▶ adjective 1 [attrib.] too much or too many to be counted or measured: *thieves caused untold damage.*
2 (of a story or event) not narrated or recounted: *no event, however boring, is left untold.*
– ORIGIN Old English *unteald* 'not counted' (see **UN-¹**, **TOLD**).

untoned ▶ adjective 1 (of a person's body) lacking in tone or muscular definition.
2 (especially of music) lacking in variation of tone or subtlety.

untouchable ▶ adjective 1 not able or allowing to be touched or affected: *a receptionist looking gorgeous and untouchable.*
■unable to be matched or rivalled: *when the band retreat to ambience and minimalism, they are untouchable.*
2 of or belonging to the lowest-caste Hindu group or the people outside the caste system.
▶ noun a member of the lowest-caste Hindu group or a person outside the caste system. Contact with untouchables is traditionally held to defile members of higher castes.
– DERIVATIVES **untouchability** noun.

> **USAGE** In senses relating to the traditional Hindu caste system, the term **untouchable** and the social restrictions accompanying it were declared illegal in the constitution of India in 1949 and of Pakistan in 1953. The official term today is **scheduled caste**.

untouched ▶ adjective 1 not handled, used, or tasted: *Annabel pushed aside her untouched plate.*
■(of a subject) not treated in writing or speech; not discussed: *no detail is left untouched.*
2 not affected, changed, or damaged in any way: *Prague was relatively untouched by the war.*

untoward ▶ adjective unexpected and inappropriate or inconvenient: *both tried to behave as if nothing untoward had happened* | *untoward jokes and racial remarks.*
– DERIVATIVES **untowardly** adverb, **untowardness** noun.

untraceable ▶ adjective unable to be found, discovered, or traced: *many use false addresses and are untraceable.*
– DERIVATIVES **untraceably** adverb.

untraced ▶ adjective not found or discovered by investigation: *patients with untraced records.*

untracked ▶ adjective (of land) not previously explored or traversed; without a path or tracks: *the Saxons usually hid in the untracked marshlands.*

– PHRASES **get untracked** US get into one's stride or find good form, especially in sporting contexts.

untraditional ▶ adjective not existing in or as part of a tradition; not customary or long-established.

untrained ▶ adjective not having been trained in a particular skill: *self-styled doctors untrained in diagnosis* | *to the untrained eye, the two products look remarkably similar.*
– DERIVATIVES **untrainable** adjective.

untrammelled (US also **untrammeled**) ▶ adjective not deprived of freedom of action or expression; not restricted or hampered: *a mind untrammelled by convention.*

untransferable ▶ adjective not able to be transferred to another place, occupation, or person.

untransformed ▶ adjective not having been transformed in form, appearance, or character.

untranslatable /ˌʌntransˈleɪtəb(ə)l, ˌʌntrɑːns-, -z-/ ▶ adjective (of a word, phrase, or text) not able to have its sense expressed in another language: *an untranslatable German pun.*
– DERIVATIVES **untranslatability** noun.

untravelled (US also **untraveled**) ▶ adjective (of a person) not having travelled much.
■(of a road or region) not journeyed along or through: *an unknown and untravelled wilderness.*

untreatable ▶ adjective (of a patient, disease, or other condition) for whom or which no medical care is available or possible.

untreated ▶ adjective 1 (of a patient, disease, or other condition) not given medical care: *untreated cholera can kill up to half of those infected.*
2 not preserved, improved, or altered by the use of a chemical, physical, or biological agent: *untreated sewage is pumped directly into the sea.*

untrendy ▶ adjective informal not very fashionable or up to date: *his untrendy long hair.*

untried ▶ adjective 1 not yet tested to discover quality or reliability; inexperienced: *he chose two untried actors for leading roles.*
2 Law (of an accused person) not yet subjected to a trial in court.

untrimmed ▶ adjective not having been trimmed.

untrodden ▶ adjective (of a surface) not having been walked on: *untrodden snow.*

untroubled ▶ adjective not feeling, showing, or affected by anxiety or problems: *a man untroubled by a guilty conscience* | *an untroubled gaze.*

untrue ▶ adjective 1 not in accordance with fact or reality; false or incorrect: *these suggestions are totally untrue* | *a malicious and untrue story.*
2 [predic.] not faithful or loyal.
3 incorrectly positioned or balanced; not upright or level.
– DERIVATIVES **untruly** adverb.
– ORIGIN Old English *untrēowe* 'unfaithful' (see **UN-¹**, **TRUE**).

untrussed ▶ adjective (of a chicken or other bird prepared for eating) having had its wings and legs unfastened before cooking: *an untrussed chicken.*

untrusting ▶ adjective not tending to believe in other people's honesty or sincerity; suspicious.

untrustworthy ▶ adjective not able to be relied on as honest or truthful.
– DERIVATIVES **untrustworthiness** noun.

untruth ▶ noun (pl. **untruths**) a lie or false statement (often used euphemistically): *they go off and tell untruths about organizations for which they worked.*
■[mass noun] the quality of being false.
– ORIGIN Old English *untrēowth* 'unfaithfulness' (see **UN-¹**, **TRUTH**).

untruthful ▶ adjective saying or consisting of something that is false or incorrect: *companies issuing untruthful recruitment brochures.*
– DERIVATIVES **untruthfully** adverb, **untruthfulness** noun.

untuck ▶ verb [with obj.] free the edges or ends of (something) from being hidden or held in place.

untucked ▶ adjective with the edges or ends hanging loose; not tucked in: *an untucked shirt.*

untuned ▶ adjective not tuned or properly adjusted.

untuneful ▶ adjective not having a pleasing melody; unmusical: *an untuneful hymn.*
– DERIVATIVES **untunefully** adverb.

unturned ▶ adjective not turned: *unturned soil.*

untutored ▶ adjective not formally taught or

trained: *the species are all much the same to the untutored eye.*

untwine ▶ verb make or become unwound or untwisted: [with obj.] *Robyn untwined her fingers.*

untwist ▶ verb open or cause to open from a twisted position: [with obj.] *he untwisted the wire and straightened it out.*

untying present participle of **UNTIE**.

untypical ▶ adjective not having the distinctive qualities of a particular type of person or thing; unusual or uncharacteristic: *the harsh dissonances give a sound which is quite untypical of that period.*
– DERIVATIVES **untypically** adverb [as submodifier] *I'll keep this review untypically short* | [sentence adverb] *not untypically, one large painting took her five months.*

unusable ▶ adjective not fit to be used: *the steps were overgrown and unusable.*

unused ▶ adjective 1 not being, or never having been, used: *any unused equipment will be welcomed back.*
2 [predic.] (**unused to**) not familiar with or accustomed to something: *unused to spicy food, she took a long mouthful of water.*

unusual ▶ adjective not habitually or commonly occurring or done: *the government has taken the unusual step of calling home its ambassador* | *it was unusual for Dennis to be late.*
▪ remarkable or interesting because different from or better than others: *a man of unusual talent.*
– DERIVATIVES **unusually** adverb [sentence adverb] *unusually for a city hotel, it is set around a lovely garden* | [as submodifier] *he made an unusually large number of mistakes,* **unusualness** noun.

unutterable ▶ adjective too great, intense, or awful to describe: *there was an unutterable sadness around Medina del Campo* | *I felt an unutterable fool.*
– DERIVATIVES **unutterably** adverb [as submodifier] *Juliet climbed the stairs, feeling unutterably weary.*

unuttered ▶ adjective (of words or thoughts) not spoken or expressed.

unvalued ▶ adjective 1 not considered to be important or beneficial: *he felt unvalued.*
2 archaic not valued or appraised with regard to monetary worth.

unvanquished ▶ adjective (of an opponent or obstacle) not conquered or overcome.

unvaried ▶ adjective not involving change: *a plain, unvaried diet.*

unvarnished ▶ adjective not covered with varnish.
▪ (of a statement or manner) plain and straightforward: *please tell me the unvarnished truth.*

unvarying ▶ adjective not changing; constant or uniform: *the unvarying routine of parsonage life.*
– DERIVATIVES **unvaryingly** adverb [as submodifier] *they found her to be unvaryingly polite,* **unvaryingness** noun.

unveil ▶ verb [with obj.] remove a veil or covering from, in particular uncover (a new monument or work of art) as part of a public ceremony: *the Princess unveiled a plaque* | [as noun **unveiling**] *the unveiling of the memorial.*
▪ show or announce publicly for the first time: *the Home Secretary has unveiled plans to crack down on crime.*

unventilated ▶ adjective (of a room or space) not provided with fresh air.

unverifiable ▶ adjective not able to be verified: *an unverifiable hypothesis.*

unverified ▶ adjective not having been verified.

unversed ▶ adjective [predic.] (**unversed in**) not experienced or skilled in; not knowledgeable about: *he was unversed in Washington ways.*

unviable ▶ adjective not capable of working successfully; not feasible: *the commission found the plan to be financially unviable.*
– DERIVATIVES **unviability** noun.

unviolated ▶ adjective not violated or desecrated.

unvisited ▶ adjective (of a place) having had no people visit it: *Antarctica remained unvisited until the late 18th century.*

unvitiated /ʌnˈvɪʃɪeɪtɪd/ ▶ adjective archaic pure and uncorrupted.

unvoiced ▶ adjective 1 not expressed in words; unuttered: *a person's unvoiced thoughts.*
2 Phonetics (of a speech sound) uttered without vibration of the vocal cords.

unwaged ▶ adjective chiefly Brit. (of a person) out of

work or doing unpaid work: *unwaged adults claiming income support.*
▪ (of work) unpaid: *recognition of unwaged work.*

unwalled ▶ adjective (of a place) without enclosing or defensive walls.

unwanted ▶ adjective not or no longer desired: *affairs can lead to unwanted pregnancies* | *she felt unwanted.*

unwarlike ▶ adjective not disposed towards war or hostilities.

unwarned ▶ adjective (of a person) not warned in advance about something.

unwarrantable ▶ adjective not able to be authorized or sanctioned; unjustifiable: *an unwarrantable intrusion into personal matters.*
– DERIVATIVES **unwarrantably** adverb.

unwarranted ▶ adjective not justified or authorized: *I am sure your fears are unwarranted.*

unwary ▶ adjective not cautious of possible dangers or problems: *accidents can happen to the unwary traveller* | [as plural noun **the unwary**] *hidden traps for the unwary.*
– DERIVATIVES **unwarily** adverb, **unwariness** noun.

unwashed ▶ adjective not having been washed.
– PHRASES **the (great) unwashed** derogatory the mass or multitude of ordinary people.

unwatchable ▶ adjective (of a film or television programme) too poor, tedious, or disturbing to be viewed.

unwatched ▶ adjective not looked at or observed.

unwatered ▶ adjective not supplied or sprinkled with water.

unwavering ▶ adjective not wavering; steady or resolute: *she fixed him with an unwavering stare.*
– DERIVATIVES **unwaveringly** adverb.

unweaned ▶ adjective (of an infant or other young mammal) not accustomed to food other than its mother's milk.

unwearable ▶ adjective (of a garment) not fit to be worn.

unwearied ▶ adjective not tired or becoming tired.
– DERIVATIVES **unweariedly** adverb.

unwearying ▶ adjective never tiring or slackening.
– DERIVATIVES **unwearyingly** adverb.

unwed (also **unwedded**) ▶ adjective not married: *an unwed teenage mother.*
– DERIVATIVES **unweddedness** noun.

unweight ▶ verb [with obj.] momentarily stop pressing heavily on (a ski or skateboard) in order to make a turn more easily.
– ORIGIN 1930s: back-formation from **UNWEIGHTED**.

unweighted ▶ adjective 1 without a weight attached.
2 Statistics (of a figure or sample) not adjusted or biased to reflect importance or value.

unwelcome ▶ adjective (of a guest or new arrival) not gladly received: *guards kept out unwelcome visitors.*
▪ not much needed or desired: *unwelcome attentions from men.*
– DERIVATIVES **unwelcomely** adverb, **unwelcomeness** noun.

unwelcoming ▶ adjective having an inhospitable or uninviting atmosphere or appearance: *Jean crept into her cold and unwelcoming bed.*
▪ (of a person or their manner) not friendly towards someone arriving or approaching.

unwell ▶ adjective [predic.] ill: *he was admitted to hospital for tests after feeling unwell.*

unwept ▶ adjective chiefly poetic/literary (of a person) not mourned or lamented.

unwhipped ▶ adjective Brit. (of an MP or vote) not subject to a party whip.

unwholesome ▶ adjective not characterized by or conducive to health or moral well-being: *the use of the living room as sleeping quarters led to unwholesome crowding.*
– DERIVATIVES **unwholesomely** adverb, **unwholesomeness** noun.

unwieldy ▶ adjective (**unwieldier, unwieldiest**) difficult to carry or move because of its size, shape, or weight: *the first mechanical clocks were large and unwieldy.*
▪ (of a system or bureaucracy) too big or badly organized to function efficiently.

– DERIVATIVES **unwieldily** adverb, **unwieldiness** noun.
– ORIGIN late Middle English (in the sense 'lacking strength, infirm'): from UN-[1] 'not' + WIELDY (in the obsolete sense 'active').

unwilling ▶ adjective [often with infinitive] not ready, eager, or prepared to do something: *he was unwilling to take on that responsibility* | *unwilling conscripts.*
– DERIVATIVES **unwillingly** adverb, **unwillingness** noun.
– ORIGIN Old English *unwillende* (see UN-[1], WILLING).

unwind ▶ verb (past and past participle **unwound**) undo or be undone after winding or being wound: [with obj.] *Ella unwound the long woollen scarf from her neck* | [no obj.] *the net unwinds from the reel.*
▪ [no obj.] relax after a period of work or tension: *the Grand Hotel is a superb place to unwind.*

unwinking ▶ adjective (of a stare or a shining light) steady; unwavering: *the lights shone unwinking in the still air* | *unwinking blue eyes.*
– DERIVATIVES **unwinkingly** adverb.

unwinnable ▶ adjective not able to be won: *an immoral and unwinnable war.*

unwisdom ▶ noun [mass noun] folly; lack of wisdom: *it stresses the unwisdom of fathers leaving their children.*
– ORIGIN Old English *unwīsdōm* (see UN-[1], WISDOM).

unwise ▶ adjective (of a person or action) not wise or sensible; foolish: *it is unwise to rely on hearsay evidence* | *unwise policy decisions.*
– DERIVATIVES **unwisely** adverb [sentence adverb] *unwisely, she repeated the remark to her mother.*
– ORIGIN Old English *unwīs* (see UN-[1], WISE[1]).

unwished ▶ adjective not wanted or desired.

unwithered ▶ adjective not withered.

unwitnessed ▶ adjective (especially of an event) not witnessed.

unwitting ▶ adjective (of a person) not aware of the full facts: *an unwitting accomplice.*
▪ not done on purpose; unintentional: *we are anxious to rectify the unwitting mistakes made in the past.*
– DERIVATIVES **unwittingly** adverb [sentence adverb] *quite unwittingly you played right into my hands that night,* **unwittingness** noun.
– ORIGIN Old English *unwitende* 'not knowing or realizing' (see UN-[1], WIT[2]).

unwomanly ▶ adjective not having or showing qualities traditionally associated with women: *initiative of any overt sort was considered unwomanly.*
– DERIVATIVES **unwomanliness** noun.

unwonted /ʌnˈwəʊntɪd/ ▶ adjective [attrib.] unaccustomed or unusual: *there was an unwonted gaiety in her manner.*
– DERIVATIVES **unwontedly** adverb [as submodifier] *she was unwontedly shy and subdued,* **unwontedness** noun.

unwooded ▶ adjective 1 not having many trees.
2 (of a wine) not stored in a wooden cask.

unworkable ▶ adjective not able to function or be carried out successfully; impractical: *an unworkable scheme.*
▪ (of a material) not able to be worked: *the alloy becomes brittle and almost unworkable.*
– DERIVATIVES **unworkability** noun, **unworkably** adverb.

unworked ▶ adjective not cultivated, mined, or carved: *unworked fields* | *unworked flint nodules.*

unworkmanlike ▶ adjective badly done or made.

unworldly ▶ adjective (of a person) not having much awareness of the realities of life, in particular not motivated by material or practical considerations: *she was so shrewd in some ways, but hopelessly unworldly in others.*
▪ not seeming to belong to this planet; strange: *the unworldly monolith loomed four stories high.*
– DERIVATIVES **unworldliness** noun.

unworn ▶ adjective not damaged or shabby-looking as a result of much use: *the tyres appear unworn, even after many fast miles* | *unworn carpeting.*
▪ (of a garment) never worn.

unworried ▶ adjective [predic.] not anxious or uneasy: *foreign investors are largely unworried by the government's fall.*

unworthy ▶ adjective (**unworthier, unworthiest**) not deserving effort, attention, or respect: *he was unworthy of trust and unfit to hold office.*
▪ (of a person's action or behaviour) not acceptable, especially from someone with a good reputation or social position: *such a suggestion is unworthy of the*

Honourable Gentleman. ■ having little value or merit: *many pieces are unworthy and ungrammatical.*
– DERIVATIVES **unworthily** adverb, **unworthiness** noun.

unwound[1] ▶ **adjective** (of a clock or watch) not wound or wound up.

unwound[2] past and past participle of **UNWIND**.

unwounded ▶ **adjective** not hurt or injured.

unwrap ▶ **verb** (**unwrapped**, **unwrapping**) [with obj.] remove the wrapping from a package: *children excitedly unwrapping and playing with their new presents.*

unwrinkled ▶ **adjective** (especially of fabric or the skin) free from wrinkles.

unwritable ▶ **adjective** not able to be written.

unwritten ▶ **adjective** not recorded in writing: *documenting unwritten languages.*
■ (especially of a law) resting originally on custom or judicial decision rather than on statute: *an unwritten constitution.* ■ (of a convention) understood and accepted by everyone, although not formally established: *the unwritten rules of social life.*

unyielding ▶ **adjective** (of a mass or structure) not giving way to pressure; hard or solid: *the Atlantic hurled its waves at the unyielding rocks.*
■ (of a person or their behaviour) unlikely to be swayed; resolute: *his unyielding faith.*
– DERIVATIVES **unyieldingly** adverb, **unyieldingness** noun.

unyoke ▶ **verb** [with obj.] release (a pair of animals) from a yoke.
■ [no obj.] archaic cease work.

unzip ▶ **verb** (**unzipped**, **unzipping**) [with obj.] unfasten the zip fastener of.
■ Computing decompress (a file) that has previously been compressed.

up ▶ **adverb 1** towards the sky or a higher position: *he jumped up | two of the men hoisted her up | the curtain went up.*
■ upstairs: *she made her way up to bed.* ■ out of bed: *Miranda hardly ever got up for breakfast | he had been up for hours.* ■ (of the sun) visible in the sky after daybreak: *the sun was already up when they set off.* ■ expressing movement towards or position in the north: *driving up to Inverness to see the old man.* ■ to or at a place perceived as higher: *going for a walk up to the shops.* ■ towards or in the capital or a major city: *give me a ring when you're up in London.* ■ Brit. at or to a university, especially Oxford or Cambridge: *they were up at Cambridge about the same time.* ■ (of food that has been eaten) regurgitated from the stomach: *I was ill and vomited up everything.* ■ [as exclamation] used as a command to a soldier or an animal to stand up and be ready to move or attack: *up, boys, and at 'em.*
2 to the place where someone is: *Dot didn't hear Mrs Parvis come creeping up behind her.*
3 at or to a higher level of intensity, volume, or activity: *she turned the volume up | liven up the graphics | US environmental groups had been stepping up their attack on GATT.*
■ at or to a higher price, value, or rank: *sales are up 22.8 per cent at $50.2 m | unemployment is up and rising.* ■ winning or at an advantage by a specified margin: *United were 3–1 up at half time | we came away £300 up on the evening.*
4 into the desired or a proper condition: *the government agreed to set up a committee of inquiry.*
■ so as to be finished or closed: *I've got a bit of paperwork to finish up | he zipped up the holdall.*
5 into a happy mood: *I don't think anything's going to cheer me up.*
6 displayed on a noticeboard or other publicly visible site: *sticking up posters to advertise concerts.*
■ (of points in a game) scored or registered on a scoreboard.
7 (of sailing) against the current or the wind.
■ (of a ship's helm) moved round to windward so that the rudder is to leeward.
8 Baseball at bat: *every time up, he had a different stance.*
▶ **preposition** from a lower to a higher point on (something); upwards along: *she climbed up a flight of steps.*
■ from one end to another of (a street or other area), not necessarily with any noticeable change in altitude: *cycling up St Giles towards North Oxford | walking up the street.* ■ to a higher part of (a river or stream), away from the sea: *a cruise up the Rhine.* ■ informal at or to (a place, typically one considered interesting or sophisticated): *going up the Palais.*
▶ **adjective 1** [attrib.] directed or moving towards a higher place or position: *the up escalator.*
■ relating to or denoting trains travelling towards the major point on a route: *the first up train.* ■ Physics denoting a flavour of quark having a charge of $+\frac{2}{3}$. Protons and neutrons are thought to be composed of combinations of up and down quarks.
2 [predic.] (of the road) being repaired.
3 (of a jockey) in the saddle.
4 [predic.] in a cheerful mood; ebullient: *the mood here is resolutely up.*
■ Brit. dated (of a drink) effervescent; frothy.
5 [predic.] (of a computer system) functioning properly: *the system is now up.*
6 [predic.] at an end: *his contract was up in three weeks | time's up.*
▶ **noun** informal a period of good fortune: *you can't have ups all the time in football.*
▶ **verb** (**upped**, **upping**) **1** [no obj.] (**up and do something**) informal do something abruptly or boldly: *she upped and left him.*
2 [with obj.] cause (a level or amount) to be increased: *capacity will be upped by 70 per cent next year.*
3 [with obj.] lift (something) up: *everybody was cheering and upping their glasses.*
■ [no obj.] (**up with**) informal, chiefly W. Indian & US raise or pick up (something): *this woman ups with a stone.*
– PHRASES **it is all up with** informal it is the end or there is no hope for (someone or something). **on the up and up** informal **1** Brit. steadily improving or becoming more successful. **2** chiefly N. Amer. honest or sincere. **something is up** informal something unusual or undesirable is happening or afoot. **up against** close to or in contact with: *crowds pressed up against the police barricades.* ■ informal confronted with or opposed by: *I began to think of what teachers are up against today.* ■ (**up against it**) informal facing some serious but unspecified difficulty: *they play better when they're up against it.* **up and about** no longer in bed (after sleep or an illness). **up and doing** active; busy: *a normal young chap wants to be up and doing.* **up and down 1** moving upwards and downwards: *bouncing up and down.* **2** to and fro: *pacing up and down in front of her desk.* ■ [as prep.] to and fro along: *strolling up and down the corridor.* **3** in various places throughout: *in clubs up and down the country.* **4** informal in varying states or moods; changeable: *my relationship with her was up and down.* **up and running** (especially of a computer system) in operation; functioning: *the new computer is up and running.* **up the ante** see **ANTE**. **up before** appearing for a hearing in the presence of: *we'll have to come up before a magistrate.* **up for 1** available for: *the house next door is up for sale.* **2** being considered for: *he had been up for promotion.* **3** due for: *his contract is up for renewal in June.* **up for it** informal ready to take part in a particular activity: *Nigel was really up for it, as always.* **up hill and down dale** all over the place: *he led me up hill and down dale till my feet were dropping off.* **up on** well informed about: *he was up on the latest methods.* **up sticks** see **STICK**[1]. **up to 1** as far as: *I could reach just up to his waist.* ■ (also **up until**) until: *up to now I hadn't had a relationship.* **2** indicating a maximum amount: *the process is expected to take up to two years.* **3** [with negative or in questions] as good as; good enough for: *I was not up to her standards.* ■ capable of or fit for: *he is simply not up to the job.* **4** the duty, responsibility, or choice of (someone): *it was up to them to gauge the problem.* **5** informal occupied or busy with: *what's he been up to?* **up top** Brit. informal in the brain (with reference to intelligence): *a man with nothing much up top.* **up with ——** an exclamation expressing support for a stated person or thing. **up yours** vulgar slang an exclamation expressing contemptuous defiance or rejection of someone. **what's up?** informal **1** what is going on? **2** what is the matter?: *what's up with you?*
– ORIGIN Old English *up(p)*, *uppe*, of Germanic origin; related to Dutch *op* and German *auf*.

up- ▶ **prefix 1** (added to verbs and their derivatives) upwards: *upturned | upthrow.*
■ to a more recent time: *update.*
2 (added to nouns) denoting motion up: *upriver | uphill.*
3 (added to nouns) higher: *upland | upstroke*
■ increased: *up-tempo.*

up-anchor ▶ **verb** [no obj.] (of a ship) weigh anchor.

up-and-coming ▶ **adjective** (of a person beginning a particular activity or occupation) making good progress and likely to become successful: *up-and-coming young players.*
– DERIVATIVES **up-and-comer** noun.

up-and-over ▶ **adjective** (of a door, typically one to a garage) opened by being raised and pushed back into a horizontal position.

up-and-under ▶ **noun** Rugby a high kick that allows time for fellow team members to reach the point where the ball will come down.

Upanishad /uːˈpanɪʃad/ ▶ **noun** each of a series of Hindu sacred treatises written in Sanskrit *c.*800–200 BC, expounding the Vedas in predominantly mystical and monistic terms.
– ORIGIN from Sanskrit, literally 'sitting near (i.e. at the feet of a master)', from *upa* 'near' + *ni-ṣad* 'sit down'.

upas /ˈjuːpəs/ (also **upas tree**) ▶ **noun** a tropical Asian tree, the milky sap of which has been used as arrow poison and for ritual purposes.
● *Antiaris toxicaria*, family Moraceae.
■ (in folklore) a Javanese tree alleged to poison its surroundings and said to be fatal to approach.
– ORIGIN late 18th cent.: from Malay (*pohun*) *upas* 'poison'.

upbeat ▶ **noun** (in music) an unaccented beat preceding an accented beat.
▶ **adjective** informal cheerful; optimistic.

upbraid ▶ **verb** [with obj.] find fault with (someone); scold: *he was upbraided for his slovenly appearance.*
– ORIGIN late Old English *upbrēdan* 'allege (something) as a basis for censure', based on **BRAID** in the obsolete sense 'brandish'. The current sense dates from Middle English.

upbringing ▶ **noun** the treatment and instruction received by a child from its parents throughout its childhood: *she had had a Christian upbringing | he was a countryman by upbringing.*
– ORIGIN late 15th cent.: from obsolete *upbring* 'to rear' (see **UP-**, **BRING**).

upbuild ▶ **verb** (past and past participle **-built**) [with obj.] chiefly poetic/literary construct or develop (something).

up card ▶ **noun** chiefly US a playing card turned face up on the table, especially the top card of the waste heap in rummy.

upcast ▶ **noun** (also **upcast shaft**) a shaft through which air leaves a mine.
▶ **verb** (past and past participle **-cast**) [with obj.] cast (something) upward: [as adj. **upcast**] *upcast light.*

upchuck N. Amer. informal ▶ **verb** vomit: [no obj.] *don't let her upchuck on him* | [with obj.] *I almost upchucked my toasted marshmallows.*
▶ **noun** [mass noun] matter vomited from the stomach.

upcoast ▶ **adverb** & **adjective** further up the coast.

upcoming ▶ **adjective** forthcoming; about to happen: *the upcoming election.*

upcountry ▶ **adverb** & **adjective** in or towards the interior of a country; inland: [as adv.] *she comes from somewhere up-country* | [as adj.] *a little up-country town.*

update ▶ **verb** /ʌpˈdeɪt/ [with obj.] make (something) more modern or up to date: *security measures are continually updated and improved* | [as adj. **updated**] *an updated list of subscribers.*
■ give (someone) the latest information about something: *the reporter promised to keep the viewers updated.*
▶ **noun** /ˈʌpdeɪt/ an act of bringing something or someone up to date, or an updated version of something: *an update on recently published crime figures.*
– DERIVATIVES **updatable** adjective (Computing).

Updike /ˈʌpdʌɪk/, John (Hoyer) (b.1932), American novelist, poet, and short-story writer. He is noted for his quartet of novels *Rabbit, Run* (1960), *Rabbit Redux* (1971), *Rabbit is Rich* (Pulitzer Prize, 1981), and *Rabbit at Rest* (Pulitzer Prize, 1990).

updoming /ˈʌpdəʊmɪŋ/ ▶ **noun** [mass noun] Geology the upward deformation of a rock mass into a dome shape.

updraught (US **updraft**) ▶ **noun** an upward current or draught of air.

upend ▶ **verb** [with obj.] set or turn (something) on its end or upside down: *she upended a can of soup over the portions* | [as adj. **upended**] *an upended box.*
■ [no obj.] (of a swimming duck or other waterbird) submerge the head and foreparts in order to feed, so that the tail is raised in the air.

upfield ▶ **adverb 1** (in sport) in or to a position nearer to the opponents' end of a field.
2 Physics in a direction corresponding to increasing field strength.

upflung ▶ **adjective** chiefly poetic/literary (especially of

u

b **but** | d **dog** | f **few** | g **get** | h **he** | j **yes** | k **cat** | l **leg** | m **man** | n **no** | p **pen** | r **red** | s **sit** | t **top** | v **voice** | w **we** | z **zoo** | ʃ **she** | ʒ **decision** | θ **thin** | ð **this** | ŋ **ring** | x **loch** | tʃ **chip** | dʒ **jar**

limbs) flung upwards, especially in a gesture of helplessness or alarm.

upfront informal ▶ **adverb** (usu. **up front**) **1** at the front; in front: *he can play up front or in defence.* **2** (of a payment) in advance.
▶ **adjective 1** bold, honest, and frank: *he'd been upfront about his intentions.*
2 [attrib.] (of a payment) made in advance.
3 chiefly US at the front or the most prominent position: *a literary weekly with an upfront section modelled on the New Yorker.*

upgrade ▶ **verb** [with obj.] raise (something) to a higher standard, in particular improve (equipment or machinery) by adding or replacing components: [as adj. **upgraded**] *upgraded computers.*
■ raise (an employee) to a higher grade or rank.
▶ **noun** an act of upgrading something.
■ an improved or more modern version of something, especially a piece of computing equipment.
– PHRASES **on the upgrade** improving; progressing.
– DERIVATIVES **upgradeability** (also **upgradability**) noun, **upgradeable** (also **upgradable**) adjective.

upgrowth ▶ **noun** [mass noun] the process or result of growing upwards.
■ [count noun] an upward growth.

uphaul ▶ **noun** a rope used for hauling up a boat's sail or centreboard.

upheaval ▶ **noun** a violent or sudden change or disruption to something: *major upheavals in the financial markets* | [mass noun] *times of political upheaval.*
■ an upward displacement of part of the earth's crust.

upheave ▶ **verb** [with obj.] poetic/literary heave or lift up (something, especially part of the earth's surface): *the area was first upheaved from the primeval ocean.*

Up-Helly-Aa /ˌʌphɛlɪˈɑː/ (also **Up-Helly-A'**) ▶ **noun** an annual festival held at Lerwick in the Shetland Islands, celebrated as the revival of a traditional midwinter fire festival.
– ORIGIN variant of Scots *Uphaliday,* denoting Epiphany as the end of the Christmas holiday.

uphill ▶ **adverb** in an ascending direction up a hill or slope: *follow the track uphill.*
▶ **adjective** sloping upwards; ascending: *the journey is slightly uphill.*
■ figurative requiring great effort; difficult: *an uphill struggle to gain worldwide recognition.*
▶ **noun** an upward slope.

uphold ▶ **verb** (past and past participle **-held**) [with obj.] confirm or support (something which has been questioned): *the court upheld his claim for damages.*
■ maintain (a custom or practice): *they uphold a tradition of not causing distress to living creatures.*
– DERIVATIVES **upholder** noun.

upholster /ʌpˈhəʊlstə, -ˈhɒl-/ ▶ **verb** [with obj.] provide (furniture) with a soft, padded covering: *the chairs were upholstered in red velvet* | [as adj. **upholstered**] *an upholstered stool.*
■ cover the walls or furniture in (a room) with textiles.
– ORIGIN mid 19th cent.: back-formation from **UPHOLSTERER**.

upholsterer ▶ **noun** a person who upholsters furniture, especially professionally.
– ORIGIN early 17th cent.: from the obsolete noun *upholster* (from **UPHOLD** in the obsolete sense 'keep in repair') + **-STER**.

upholstery ▶ **noun** [mass noun] soft, padded textile covering that is fixed to furniture such as armchairs and sofas.
■ the art or practice of fitting such a covering.

upkeep ▶ **noun** [mass noun] the process of keeping something in good condition: *we will be responsible for the upkeep of the access road.*
■ financial or material support of a person or animal: *payments for the children's upkeep.*

upland ▶ **noun** [mass noun] (also **uplands**) an area of high or hilly land: *conservation of areas of upland.*

upland cotton ▶ **noun** [mass noun] cotton of a type grown in the US, which typically yields medium- and short-stapled forms of cotton.
● *Gossypium hirsutum* var. *latifolium,* family Malvaceae.

uplift ▶ **verb** [with obj.] **1** [usu. as adj. **uplifted**] lift (something) up; raise: *her uplifted face.*
■ (**be uplifted**) (of an island, mountain, etc.) be created by an upward movement of the earth's surface.
2 elevate or stimulate (someone) morally or spiritually: [as adj. **uplifting**] *an uplifting tune.*
▶ **noun 1** an act of raising something.

■ Geology the upward movement of part of the earth's surface.
■ [mass noun] (often as modifier) support, especially for a woman's bust, from a garment: *an uplift bra.*
2 a morally or spiritually elevating influence: *their love will prove an enormous uplift.*
– DERIVATIVES **uplifter** noun.

uplighter (also **uplight**) ▶ **noun** a light placed or designed to throw illumination upwards.
– DERIVATIVES **uplighting** noun.

uplink ▶ **noun** a communications link to a satellite.
▶ **verb** [with obj.] provide (someone) with or send (something) by such a link: *I can uplink fax transmissions to a satellite.*

upload Computing ▶ **verb** [with obj.] transfer (data) to a larger computer system.
▶ **noun** [mass noun] the action or process of transferring data in such a way.

upmarket ▶ **adjective & adverb** chiefly Brit. towards or relating to the more expensive or affluent sector of the market: [as adj.] *an upmarket housing estate* | [as adv.] *they used their newly acquired cash to move a little upmarket.*

upmost ▶ **adjective** another term for **UPPERMOST**.

upon ▶ **preposition** more formal term for **ON**, especially in abstract senses: *it was based upon two principles* | *a school's dependence upon parental support.*
– ORIGIN Middle English: from **UP** + **ON**, suggested by Old Norse *upp á.*

USAGE The preposition **upon** has the same core meaning as the preposition **on**. However, in modern English **upon** tends to be restricted to more formal contexts or to established phrases and idioms, as in *once upon a time* and *row upon row of seats.*

upper[1] ▶ **adjective 1** situated above another part: *his upper arm* | *the upper atmosphere.*
■ higher in position or status: *the upper end of the social scale.*
2 situated on higher ground.
■ situated to the north: [in place names] *Upper California.*
3 Geology & Archaeology denoting a younger (and hence usually shallower) part of a stratigraphic division or archaeological deposit or the period in which it was formed or deposited: *the Upper Palaeolithic age.*
▶ **noun** the part of a boot or shoe above the sole.
– PHRASES **have** (or **gain**) **the upper hand** have or gain advantage or control over someone or something. **on one's uppers** informal extremely short of money. **the upper crust** informal the upper classes.
– ORIGIN Middle English: from the adjective **UP** + **-ER**[2].

upper[2] ▶ **noun** (usu. **uppers**) informal a stimulating drug, especially amphetamine.
– ORIGIN 1960s: from the verb **UP** + **-ER**[1].

Upper Austria a state of NW Austria; capital, Linz. German name **OBERÖSTERREICH**.

Upper Canada the mainly English-speaking region of Canada north of the Great Lakes and west of the Ottawa River, in what is now southern Ontario.

upper case ▶ **noun** [mass noun] capital letters as opposed to small letters (lower case): *the keywords must be in upper case* | [as modifier] *upper-case letters.*
– ORIGIN referring originally to two type cases positioned on an angled stand, the case containing the capital letters being higher and further away from the compositor.

upper chamber ▶ **noun** another term for **UPPER HOUSE**.

upper circle ▶ **noun** the tier of seats in a theatre above the dress circle.

upper class ▶ **noun** [treated as sing. or pl.] the social group that has the highest status in society, especially the aristocracy.
▶ **adjective** of, relating to, or characteristic of such a group: *upper-class accents.*

upperclassman ▶ **noun** (pl. **-men**) US a junior or senior in high school or college.

uppercut ▶ **noun** a punch delivered with an upwards motion and the arm bent.
■ Baseball an upward batting stroke, typically resulting in a fly ball.

upper house ▶ **noun** the higher house in a bicameral parliament or similar legislature.
■ (**the Upper House**) (in the UK) the House of Lords.

uppermost ▶ **adjective** (also **upmost**) highest in place, rank, or importance: *the uppermost windows* | *her father was uppermost in her mind.*

▶ **adverb** at or to the highest or most important position: *investors put environmental concerns uppermost on their list.*

upper regions ▶ **plural noun** archaic or poetic/literary the sky or heaven.

upper school ▶ **noun** a secondary school for children aged from about fourteen upwards, generally following on from a middle school.
■ the section of a school which comprises or caters for the older pupils.

Upper Volta former name (until 1984) for **BURKINA**.

upper works ▶ **plural noun** the parts of a ship that are above the water when it is fully laden.

uppish ▶ **adjective** informal arrogantly self-assertive.
– DERIVATIVES **uppishly** adverb, **uppishness** noun.

uppity ▶ **adjective** informal self-important; arrogant: *an uppity MP and his lady wife.*
– ORIGIN late 19th cent.: a fanciful formation from **UP**.

Uppsala /ˈʊpsɑːlə/ a city in eastern Sweden; pop. 167,500 (1990). Its university, founded in 1477, is the oldest in northern Europe.

upraise ▶ **verb** [with obj.] raise (something) to a higher level: [as adj. **upraised**] *an upraised arm.*

uprate ▶ **verb** [with obj.] **1** increase the value of (a payment or benefit): *income support will be uprated by an unspecified amount.*
2 improve the performance of; upgrade: *the gas plants are to be expanded and uprated.*

upright ▶ **adjective 1** vertical; erect: *the posts must be in an upright position.*
■ (of a piano) having vertical strings. ■ greater in height than breadth: *an upright freezer.* ■ denoting a device designed to be used in a vertical position: *an upright vacuum cleaner.* ■ denoting a chair with a straight back and typically no arms.
2 (of a person or their behaviour) strictly honourable or honest: *an upright member of the community.*
▶ **adverb** in or into a vertical position: *she was sitting upright in bed.*
▶ **noun 1** a post or rod fixed vertically, especially as a structural support: *the stone uprights of the parapet.*
2 an upright piano.
– DERIVATIVES **uprightly** adverb, **uprightness** noun.
– ORIGIN Old English *upriht,* of Germanic origin; related to Dutch *oprecht* and German *aufrecht* (see **UP**, **RIGHT**).

uprise ▶ **verb** (past **-rose**; past participle **-risen**) [no obj.] archaic or poetic/literary rise to a standing or elevated position: *bright and red uprose the morning sun.*

uprising ▶ **noun** an act of resistance or rebellion; a revolt: *an armed uprising.*

upriver ▶ **adverb & adjective** towards or situated at a point nearer the source of a river: [as adv.] *the salmon heads upriver to spawn* | [as adj.] *they headed for the upriver side.*

uproar ▶ **noun** a loud and impassioned noise or disturbance: *the room was in an uproar* | [mass noun] *the assembly dissolved in uproar.*
■ a public expression of protest or outrage: *it caused an uproar in the press.*
– ORIGIN early 16th cent.: from Middle Dutch *uproer,* from *op* 'up' + *roer* 'confusion', associated with **ROAR**.

uproarious ▶ **adjective** characterized by or provoking loud noise or uproar: *an uproarious party.*
■ provoking loud laughter; very funny.
– DERIVATIVES **uproariously** adverb, **uproariousness** noun.

uproot ▶ **verb** [with obj.] pull (something, especially a tree or plant) out of the ground: *the elephant's trunk is powerful enough to uproot trees.*
■ move (someone) from their home or a familiar location: *my father travelled constantly and uprooted his family several times.* ■ figurative eradicate; destroy: *a revolution is necessary to uproot the social order.*
– DERIVATIVES **uprooter** noun.

uprose past of **UPRISE**.

uprush ▶ **noun** a sudden upward surge or flow, especially of a feeling: *an uprush of joy.*

UPS ▶ **abbreviation for** uninterruptible power supply.

ups-a-daisy ▶ **exclamation** variant spelling of **UPSY-DAISY**.

ups and downs ▶ **plural noun** a succession of both good and bad experiences: *I have my ups and downs.*

■rises and falls, especially in the value or success of something: *the ups and downs of the market.*

upscale ▶ adjective & adverb N. Amer. upmarket.

upset ▶ verb /ʌpˈsɛt/ (**-setting**; past and past participle **-set**) [with obj.] **1** make (someone) unhappy, disappointed, or worried: *the accusation upset her* | [as adj. **upsetting**] *a painful and upsetting divorce.*
2 knock (something) over: *he upset a tureen of soup.* ■cause disorder in (something); disrupt: *the dam will upset the ecological balance.* ■ disturb the digestion of (a person's stomach); cause (someone) to feel nauseous or unwell.
3 [often as noun **upsetting**] shorten and thicken the end or edge of (a metal bar, wheel rim, or other object), especially by hammering or pressure when heated.
▶ noun /ˈʌpsɛt/ **1** a state of being unhappy, disappointed, or worried: *domestic upsets* | [mass noun] *a legal dispute will cause worry and upset.*
2 an unexpected result or situation, especially in a sports competition: *they caused one of last season's league upsets by winning 27–15.*
3 a disturbance of a person's digestive system: *a stomach upset.*
▶ adjective **1** /ʌpˈsɛt/ [predic.] unhappy, disappointed, or worried: *she looked pale and upset.*
2 /ˈʌpsɛt/ (of a person's stomach) having disturbed digestion, especially because of something eaten.
– DERIVATIVES **upsetter** noun, **upsettingly** adverb.

upset price ▶ noun the lowest acceptable selling price for a property in an auction; a reserve price.

upshift ▶ verb [no obj.] change to a higher gear in a motor vehicle. ■[with obj.] increase: *stricter driving laws that upshifted the penalties for drunk-driving.*
▶ noun a change to a higher gear. ■an increase in something.

upshot ▶ noun [in sing.] the final or eventual outcome or conclusion of a discussion, action, or series of events: *the upshot of the meeting was that he was on the next plane to New York.*

upside ▶ noun [in sing.] **1** the positive aspect of something.
2 an upward movement of share prices.

upside down ▶ adverb & adjective with the upper part where the lower part should be; in an inverted position: [as adv.] *the bar staff put the chairs upside down on the tables* | [as adj.] *an upside-down canoe.* ■in or into total disorder or confusion: [as adv.] *burglars have turned our house upside down.*
– ORIGIN Middle English: originally *up so down*, perhaps in the sense 'up as if down'.

upside-down cake ▶ noun a sponge cake that is baked over a layer of fruit in syrup and inverted for serving.

upside-down catfish ▶ noun a small freshwater catfish that habitually swims upside down, enabling it to browse on algae on the undersides of floating leaves. Native to central Congo, it is popular in aquaria.
● *Synodontis nigriventris,* family Mochokidae.

upsides ▶ adverb (especially in horse racing) alongside; on a level: *the horse came upsides.* ■(**upsides with**) archaic even or equal with.
– ORIGIN early 18th cent.: from **UPSIDE** in the sense 'upper part' + the adverbial suffix *-s.*

upsilon /ʌpˈsʌɪlən, juːp-, ˈʊpsɪlɒn, ˈjuːp-/ ▶ noun the twentieth letter of the Greek alphabet (Υ, υ), transliterated as 'u' or (chiefly in English words derived through Latin) as 'y'.
■(**Upsilon**) [followed by Latin genitive] Astronomy the twentieth star in a constellation: *Upsilon Scorpii.* ■ (also **upsilon particle**) Physics a meson thought to contain a *b* quark bound to its antiparticle, produced in particle accelerators.
– ORIGIN Greek, literally 'slender U', from *psilos* 'slender', referring to the need to distinguish upsilon from the diphthong *oi*: in late Greek the two had the same pronunciation.

upslope ▶ noun an upward slope.
▶ adverb & adjective at or towards a higher point on a slope.

upstage ▶ adverb & adjective at or towards the back of a theatre stage: [as adv.] *Hamlet turns to face upstage* | [as adj.] *an upstage exit.* ■[as adj.] informal, dated superior; aloof.
▶ verb [with obj.] divert attention from (someone) towards oneself; outshine: *they were totally upstaged by their co-star in the film.*

■(of an actor) move towards the back of a stage to make (another actor) face away from the audience.

upstairs ▶ adverb on or to an upper floor of a building: *I tiptoed upstairs.*
▶ adjective (also **upstair**) [attrib.] situated on an upper floor: *an upstairs bedroom.*
▶ noun an upper floor: *she was cleaning the upstairs.*

upstand ▶ noun an upright structure or object. ■a turned-up edge of a flat surface or sheeting, especially in a roof space where it meets the wall.

upstanding ▶ adjective **1** honest; respectable: *an upstanding member of the community.*
2 standing up; erect: *upstanding feathered plumes.* ■(of an animal) strong and healthy.

upstart ▶ noun **1** derogatory a person who has risen suddenly to wealth or high position, especially one who behaves arrogantly: *the upstarts who dare to challenge the legitimacy of his rule* | [as modifier] *an upstart leader.*
2 Gymnastics a series of movements on the parallel or asymmetric bars, by which a gymnast swings to a position in which their body is supported by their arms above the bar, especially at the start of a routine.

upstate US ▶ adjective & adverb of, in, or to a part of a state remote from its large cities, especially the northern part: [as adj.] *upstate New York.*
▶ noun such an area: *visiting farmers from upstate.*
– DERIVATIVES **upstater** noun.

upstream ▶ adverb & adjective moving or situated in the opposite direction from that in which a stream or river flows; nearer to the source: [as adv.] *a lone motor cruiser rumbled upstream* | [as adj.] *the upstream stretch of the Nene.*
■Biology situated in or towards the part of a sequence of genetic material where transcription takes place earlier than at a given point. ■at a stage in the process of gas or oil extraction and production before the raw material is ready for refining.

upstroke ▶ noun a stroke made upwards: *the upstroke of the whale's tail.*

upsurge ▶ noun an upward surge in the strength or quantity of something; an increase: *an upsurge in separatist activity.*

upswell ▶ noun rare an increase or upsurge.

upswept ▶ adjective curved, sloping, or directed upwards: *an upswept moustache.* ■(of the hair) brushed or held upwards and off the face: *an elegant upswept style.*

upswing ▶ noun an increase in strength or quantity; an upward trend: *an upswing in economic activity.*

upsy-daisy (also **ups-a-daisy, oops-a-daisy**) ▶ exclamation expressing encouragement to a child who has fallen or is being lifted.
– ORIGIN mid 19th cent.: alteration of earlier *up-a-daisy*; compare with **LACKADAISICAL**.

uptake ▶ noun [mass noun] the action of taking up or making use of something that is available: *the uptake of free school meals.* ■the taking in or absorption of a substance by a living organism or bodily organ: *the uptake of glucose into the muscles.*
– PHRASES **be quick (or slow) on the uptake** informal be quick (or slow) to understand something.

uptempo ▶ adjective & adverb Music played with a fast or increased tempo: [as adj.] *uptempo guitar work.*

upthrow Geology ▶ verb [with obj.] [usu. as adj. **upthrown**] displace (a rock formation) upwards.
▶ noun an upward displacement of rock strata.

upthrust ▶ noun Physics the upward force that a liquid or gas exerts on a body floating in it. ■Geology another term for **UPLIFT**.
▶ verb [with obj.] [usu. as adj. **upthrust**] thrust (something) upwards: *Turco's upthrust beard.*

uptick ▶ noun US a small increase.

uptight ▶ adjective informal anxious or angry in a tense and overly controlled way: *he is so uptight about everything.*

uptime ▶ noun [mass noun] time during which a machine, especially a computer, is in operation.

up to date ▶ adjective incorporating the latest developments and trends: *a modern, up-to-date hospital.* ■incorporating or aware of the latest information.

up to the minute ▶ adjective incorporating the very latest information or developments: *it is fitted with up-to-the-minute security devices.*

uptown chiefly N. Amer. ▶ adjective of, in, or characteristic of the residential area of a town or city. ■of or characteristic of an affluent area or people: *I don't pay uptown prices.*
▶ adverb in or into such an area.
▶ noun a residential area in a town or city.
– DERIVATIVES **uptowner** noun.

uptrend ▶ noun an upward tendency.

upturn ▶ noun an improvement or upward trend, especially in economic conditions or someone's fortunes: *an upturn in the economy.*
▶ verb [with obj.] [usu. as adj. **upturned**] turn (something) upwards or upside down: *a sea of upturned faces.*

UPU ▶ abbreviation for Universal Postal Union.

uPVC ▶ abbreviation for unplasticized polyvinyl chloride, a rigid, chemically resistant form of PVC used for pipework, window frames, and other structures.

upward ▶ adverb (also **upwards**) towards a higher place, point, or level: *she peered upward at the sky.*
▶ adjective moving, pointing, or leading to a higher place, point, or level: *an upward trend in sales.*
– PHRASES **upwards** (or **upward**) **of** more than.
– ORIGIN Old English *upweard(es)* (see **UP, -WARD**).

upwardly ▶ adverb in an upward direction.
– PHRASES **upwardly mobile** see **MOBILE**.

upwarp Geology ▶ noun a broad elevated area of the earth's surface.
▶ verb (**be upwarped**) (of part of the earth's surface) be elevated to form an upwarp.

upwelling ▶ noun a rising up of seawater, magma, or other liquid.
▶ adjective (especially of emotion) building up or gathering strength: *upwelling grief.*

upwind /ʌpˈwɪnd/ ▶ adverb & adjective against the direction of the wind: [as adv.] *you learn how to sail upwind* | [as adj.] *the upwind wing tip.*

Ur /əː, ʊə/ an ancient Sumerian city formerly on the Euphrates, in southern Iraq. It was one of the oldest cities of Mesopotamia, dating from the 4th millennium BC, and reached its zenith in the late 3rd millennium BC.

ur- /ʊə/ ▶ combining form primitive; original; earliest: *urtext.*
– ORIGIN from German.

uracil /ˈjʊərəsɪl/ ▶ noun [mass noun] Biochemistry a compound found in living tissue as a constituent base of RNA. In DNA it is replaced by thymine.
● A pyrimidine derivative; chem. formula: $C_4H_4N_2O_2$.
– ORIGIN late 19th cent.: from *ur(ea)* + *ac(etic)* + **-IL**.

uraemia /jʊˈriːmɪə/ (US **uremia**) ▶ noun [mass noun] Medicine a raised level in the blood of urea and other nitrogenous waste compounds that are normally eliminated by the kidneys.
– DERIVATIVES **uraemic** adjective.
– ORIGIN mid 19th cent.: modern Latin, from Greek *ouron* 'urine' + *haima* 'blood'.

uraeus /jʊˈriːəs/ ▶ noun (pl. **uraei** /jʊˈriːʌɪ/) a representation of a sacred serpent as an emblem of supreme power, worn on the headdresses of ancient Egyptian deities and sovereigns.
– ORIGIN mid 19th cent.: modern Latin, from Greek *ouraios,* representing the Egyptian word for 'cobra'.

Ural-Altaic ▶ adjective of, relating to, or denoting a hypothetical language group formerly proposed to include both the Uralic and the Altaic languages.

Uralic /jʊˈralɪk/ ▶ adjective **1** of, relating to, or denoting a family of languages spoken from northern Scandinavia to western Siberia, comprising the Finno-Ugric and Samoyedic groups.
2 of or relating to the Ural Mountains or the surrounding areas.
▶ noun [mass noun] the Uralic languages collectively.

Ural Mountains /ˈjʊərəl/ (also **the Urals**) a mountain range in northern Russia, extending 1,600 km (1,000 miles) southwards from the Arctic Ocean to the Aral Sea, in Kazakhstan, rising to 1,894 m (6,214 ft) at Mount Narodnaya. It forms part of the conventional boundary between Europe and Asia.

Urania /jʊˈreɪnɪə/ Greek & Roman Mythology the Muse of astronomy.
– ORIGIN Greek, literally 'heavenly (female)'.

uraninite /jʊˈranɪnʌɪt/ ▶ noun [mass noun] a black, grey, or brown mineral which consists mainly of uranium dioxide and is the chief ore of uranium.
– ORIGIN late 19th cent.: from **URANO-**[2] + **-ITE**[1].

uranium /jʊˈreɪnɪəm/ ▶ **noun** [mass noun] the chemical element of atomic number 92, a grey dense radioactive metal used as a fuel in nuclear reactors. (Symbol: **U**)

Uranium is a chemically reactive metal belonging to the actinide series. Becquerel discovered radioactivity in uranium in 1896, and its capacity to undergo fission led to its use as a source of energy, though the fissile isotope, uranium-235, has to be separated from the more common uranium-238 before it can be used in nuclear weapons. The atom bomb exploded over Hiroshima in 1945 contained uranium-235.

– ORIGIN late 18th cent.: modern Latin, from **URANUS**: compare with **TELLURIUM**.

urano-[1] /ˈjʊər(ə)nəʊ/ ▶ **combining form** relating to the heavens: *uranography*.
– ORIGIN from Greek *ouranos* 'heavens, sky'.

urano-[2] /ˈjʊər(ə)nəʊ/ ▶ **combining form** representing **URANIUM**.

uranography /ˌjʊərəˈnɒɡrəfi/ ▶ **noun** [mass noun] archaic the branch of astronomy concerned with describing and mapping the stars.
– DERIVATIVES **uranographer** noun, **uranographic** adjective.

Uranus /ˈjʊərənəs, jʊˈreɪnəs/ **1** Greek Mythology a personification of heaven or the sky, the most ancient of the Greek gods and first ruler of the universe. He was overthrown and castrated by his son Cronus.
2 Astronomy a distant planet of the solar system, seventh in order from the sun, discovered by William Herschel in 1781.

Uranus orbits between Jupiter and Neptune at an average distance of 2,870 million km from the sun. It has an equatorial diameter of 50,800 km, and is one of the gas giants. The planet is bluish-green in colour, having an upper atmosphere consisting almost entirely of hydrogen and helium. There are at least seventeen satellites, the largest of which are Oberon and Titania, and a faint ring system.

uranyl /ˈjʊər(ə)nʌɪl, ˈjʊər(ə)nɪl/ ▶ **noun** [as modifier] Chemistry the cation UO_2^{2+}, present in some compounds of uranium: *uranyl acetate*.
– ORIGIN mid 19th cent.: from **URANIUM** + **-YL**.

Urartian /ʊˈrɑːtɪən/ ▶ **adjective** of or relating to the ancient kingdom of Urartu in eastern Anatolia (*c.*1500–585 BC).
▶ **noun 1** a native or inhabitant of ancient Urartu.
2 [mass noun] the language of Urartu, related to Hurrian.

urban ▶ **adjective** in, relating to, or characteristic of a town or city: *the urban population*.
– DERIVATIVES **urbanism** noun, **urbanist** noun.
– ORIGIN early 17th cent.: from Latin *urbanus*, from *urbs, urb-* 'city'.

urban district ▶ **noun** Brit. historical a group of urban communities governed by an elected council.

urbane /əːˈbeɪn/ ▶ **adjective** (of a person, especially a man) suave, courteous, and refined in manner.
– DERIVATIVES **urbanely** adverb.
– ORIGIN mid 16th cent. (in the sense 'urban'): from French *urbain* or Latin *urbanus* (see **URBAN**).

urbanite ▶ **noun** informal a person who lives in a town or city.

urbanity ▶ **noun** [mass noun] **1** suavity, courteousness, and refinement of manner.
2 urban life.
– ORIGIN mid 16th cent.: from French *urbanité* or Latin *urbanitas*, from *urbanus* 'belonging to the city' (see **URBAN**).

urbanize (also **-ise**) ▶ **verb** make or become urban in character: [with obj.] *once an agrarian society, the island has recently been urbanized* | [as adj. **urbanized**] *urbanized areas*.
– DERIVATIVES **urbanization** noun.

urban myth (also chiefly US **urban legend**) ▶ **noun** an entertaining story or piece of information circulated as though true, especially one purporting to involve someone vaguely related or known to the teller.

urban renewal ▶ **noun** [mass noun] the redevelopment of areas within a large city, typically involving the clearance of slums.

urbs /əːbz/ ▶ **noun** chiefly poetic/literary the city, especially as a symbol of harsh or busy modern life.
– ORIGIN Latin.

URC ▶ **abbreviation for** United Reformed Church.

urchin /ˈəːtʃɪn/ ▶ **noun 1** a mischievous young child, especially one who is poorly or raggedly dressed.
■archaic a goblin.
2 chiefly dialect a hedgehog.
■short for **SEA URCHIN**.
– ORIGIN Middle English *hirchon, urchon* 'hedgehog', from Old Northern French *herichon*, based on Latin *hericius* 'hedgehog'.

Urdu /ˈʊəduː, ˈəːduː/ ▶ **noun** [mass noun] an Indic language closely related to Hindi but written in the Persian script and having many loanwords from Persian and Arabic. It is the official language of Pakistan, and is also widely used in India and elsewhere, with about 50 million speakers worldwide.
– ORIGIN from Persian (*zabān-i-)urdū* '(language of the) camp' (because it developed as a lingua franca after the Muslim invasions between the occupying armies and the local people of the region around Delhi), *urdū* being from Turkic *ordu* (see **HORDE**).

-ure ▶ **suffix** forming nouns: **1** denoting an action, process, or result: *censure* | *closure* | *scripture*.
2 denoting an office or function: *judicature*.
3 denoting a collective: *legislature*.
– ORIGIN from Old French *-ure*, from Latin *-ura*.

urea /jʊˈriːə, ˈjʊərɪə/ ▶ **noun** [mass noun] Biochemistry a colourless crystalline compound which is the main nitrogenous breakdown product of protein metabolism in mammals and is excreted in urine.
● Chem. formula: $CO(NH_2)_2$.
– ORIGIN early 19th cent.: modern Latin, from French *urée*, from Greek *ouron* 'urine'.

ureaplasma /ˌjʊərɪəˈplazmə/ ▶ **noun** a small bacterium related to the mycoplasmas, characterized by the ability to metabolize urea.
● Genus *Ureaplasma*, order Mycoplasmatales.

ureide /ˈjʊərɪʌɪd/ ▶ **noun** Chemistry any of a group of compounds which are acyl derivatives of urea.

uremia ▶ **noun** US spelling of **URAEMIA**.

ureter /jʊˈriːtə, ˈjʊərɪtə/ ▶ **noun** Anatomy & Zoology the duct by which urine passes from the kidney to the bladder or cloaca.
– DERIVATIVES **ureteral** adjective, **ureteric** /jʊərɪˈtɛrɪk/ adjective.
– ORIGIN late 16th cent.: from French *uretère* or modern Latin *ureter*, from Greek *ourētēr*, from *ourein* 'urinate'.

urethane /ˈjʊərɪθeɪn, jʊˈrɛθeɪn/ ▶ **noun** [mass noun] Chemistry a synthetic crystalline compound used in making pesticides and fungicides, and formerly as an anaesthetic.
● Alternative name: **ethyl carbamate**; chem. formula: $CO(NH_2)OC_2H_5$.
■short for **POLYURETHANE**.
– ORIGIN mid 19th cent.: from French *uréthane* (see **UREA, ETHANE**).

urethra /jʊˈriːθrə/ ▶ **noun** Anatomy & Zoology the duct by which urine is conveyed out of the body from the bladder, and which in male vertebrates also conveys semen.
– DERIVATIVES **urethral** adjective.
– ORIGIN mid 17th cent.: from late Latin, from Greek *ourēthra*, from *ourein* 'urinate'.

urethritis /ˌjʊriːˈθrʌɪtɪs/ ▶ **noun** [mass noun] Medicine inflammation of the urethra.

Urey /ˈjʊəri/, Harold Clayton (1893–1981), American chemist. He discovered deuterium in 1932, pioneered the use of isotope labelling, and became director of the Manhattan project at Columbia University. Nobel Prize for Chemistry (1934).

Urga /ˈʊəɡə/ former name (until 1924) for **ULAN BATOR**.

urge ▶ **verb** [with obj. and usu. infinitive] try earnestly or persistently to persuade (someone) to do something: *he urged her to come and stay with us* | [with direct speech] *'Do try to relax,' she urged*.
■recommend or advocate (something) strongly: *I urge caution in interpreting these results* | [with clause] *they are urging that more treatment facilities be provided*. ■[with obj. and adverbial] encourage (a person or animal) to move more quickly or in a particular direction: *drawing up outside the house, he urged her inside*. ■(**urge someone on**) encourage someone to continue or succeed in something: *he could hear her voice urging him on*.
▶ **noun** a strong desire or impulse: *the urge for revenge*.
– ORIGIN mid 16th cent.: from Latin *urgere* 'press, drive'.

urgent ▶ **adjective** (of a state or situation) requiring immediate action or attention: *the situation is far more urgent than politicians are admitting*.
■(of an action or event) done or arranged in response to such a situation: *she needs urgent treatment*. ■(of a person or their manner) earnest and persistent in response to such a situation: *an urgent whisper*.
– DERIVATIVES **urgency** noun, **urgently** adverb.
– ORIGIN late 15th cent.: from Old French, from Latin *urgent-* 'pressing, driving', from the verb *urgere* (see **URGE**).

urger /ˈəːdʒə/ ▶ **noun** Austral. informal a person who gives tips at a race meeting.
■a person who takes advantage of others; a racketeer.

-uria ▶ **combining form** in nouns denoting that a substance is present in the urine, especially in excess: *glycosuria*.
– ORIGIN modern Latin, from Greek *-ouria*, from *ouron* 'urine'.

Uriah /jʊˈrʌɪə/ (in the Bible) a Hittite officer in David's army, whom David, desiring his wife Bathsheba, caused to be killed in battle (2 Sam. 11).

urial /ˈʊərɪəl/ ▶ **noun** (pl. same) a wild sheep with long legs and relatively small horns, native to central Asia.
● *Ovis vignei*, family Bovidae.
– ORIGIN mid 19th cent.: from Punjabi *ūrial*.

uric acid ▶ **noun** [mass noun] Biochemistry an almost insoluble compound which is a breakdown product of nitrogenous metabolism. It is the main excretory product in birds, reptiles, and insects.
● A bicyclic acid derived from purine; chem. formula: $C_5H_4N_4O_3$.
– DERIVATIVES **urate** noun.
– ORIGIN early 19th cent.: *uric* from French *urique*, from *urine* (see **URINE**).

uridine /ˈjʊərɪdiːn/ ▶ **noun** [mass noun] Biochemistry a compound formed by partial hydrolysis of RNA. It is a nucleoside containing uracil linked to ribose.
– ORIGIN early 20th cent.: from *ur(acil)* + **-IDE** + **-INE**[4].

Urim and Thummim ▶ **plural noun** historical two objects of a now unknown nature, possibly used for divination, worn on the breastplate of a Jewish high priest.
– ORIGIN from Hebrew.

urinal /jʊˈrʌɪn(ə)l, ˈjʊərɪn(ə)l/ ▶ **noun** a bowl or other receptacle, typically attached to a wall in a public toilet, into which men may urinate.
– ORIGIN Middle English (denoting a glass container for the medical inspection of urine): via Old French from Latin *urinal*, from *urina* (see **URINE**).

urinalysis /ˌjʊərɪˈnalɪsɪs/ ▶ **noun** (pl. **urinalyses** /-siːz/) [mass noun] Medicine analysis of urine by physical, chemical, and microscopical means to test for the presence of disease, drugs, etc.

urinary ▶ **adjective** of or relating to urine.
■of, relating to, or denoting the system of organs, structures, and ducts by which urine is produced and discharged, in mammals comprising the kidneys, ureters, bladder, and urethra.

urinate ▶ **verb** [no obj.] discharge urine; pass water.
– DERIVATIVES **urination** noun.
– ORIGIN late 16th cent.: from medieval Latin *urinat-* 'urinated', from the verb *urinare*.

urine /ˈjʊərɪn, -rʌɪn/ ▶ **noun** [mass noun] a watery, typically yellowish fluid stored in the bladder and discharged through the urethra. It is one of the body's chief means of eliminating excess water and salt, and also contains nitrogen compounds such as urea and other waste substances removed from the blood by the kidneys.
– ORIGIN Middle English: via Old French from Latin *urina*.

uriniferous tubule /ˌjʊərɪˈnɪf(ə)rəs/ ▶ **noun** another term for **KIDNEY TUBULE**.

URL Computing ▶ **abbreviation for** uniform (or universal) resource locator, the address of a World Wide Web page.

urn ▶ **noun 1** a tall, rounded vase with a stem and base, especially one used for storing the ashes of a cremated person.
2 a large metal container with a tap, in which tea or coffee is made and kept hot, or water for making such drinks is boiled: *a tea urn*.
▶ **verb** [with obj.] archaic place (something) in an urn.
– ORIGIN late Middle English: from Latin *urna*; related to *urceus* 'pitcher'.

urnfield Archaeology ▶ **noun** a prehistoric cemetery of the European late Bronze Age and early Iron Age, in which cremated remains were placed in pottery vessels (cinerary urns) and buried.
▶ **adjective** (often **Urnfield**) of, relating to, or denoting a people or culture characterized by burial in this form of cemetery. The **Urnfield complex** is equated

with the Hallstatt culture and is dated to *c.*1200–800 BC.

uro-¹ ▶ **combining form** of or relating to urine or the urinary organs: *urogenital.*
– ORIGIN from Greek *ouron* 'urine'.

uro-² ▶ **combining form** Zoology relating to a tail or the caudal region: *urodele.*
– ORIGIN from Greek *oura* 'tail'.

uroboros /jʊərə(ʊ)ˈbɒrəs/ (also **ouroboros**) ▶ **noun** a circular symbol depicting a snake, or less commonly a dragon, swallowing its tail, as an emblem of wholeness or infinity.
– DERIVATIVES **uroboric** adjective.
– ORIGIN 1940s: from Greek (*drakōn*) *ouroboros* '(snake) devouring its tail'.

Urochordata /jʊərə(ʊ)kɔːˈdeɪtə/ Zoology a group of chordate animals that comprises the tunicates.
• Subphylum Urochordata, phylum Chordata.
– DERIVATIVES **urochordate** noun & adjective.
– ORIGIN modern Latin (plural), from **URO-**² 'tail' + **CHORDATA**.

Urodela /jʊərə(ʊ)ˈdiːlə/ Zoology an order of amphibians that comprises the newts and salamanders, which retain the tail as adults. Also called **CAUDATA**.
– DERIVATIVES **urodele** /ˈjʊərə(ʊ)diːl/ noun & adjective.
– ORIGIN modern Latin (plural), from **URO-**² 'tail' + Greek *dēlos* 'evident'.

urodynamics ▶ **plural noun** [treated as sing.] Medicine the diagnostic study of pressure in the bladder, in treating incontinence.
– DERIVATIVES **urodynamic** adjective.

urogenital ▶ **adjective** of, relating to, or denoting both the urinary and genital organs.

urography /jʊˈrɒgrəfi/ ▶ **noun** another term for **PYELOGRAPHY**.
– DERIVATIVES **urogram** noun.

urokinase /jʊərə(ʊ)ˈkʌɪneɪz/ ▶ **noun** [mass noun] Biochemistry an enzyme produced in the kidneys which promotes the conversion of plasminogen to plasmin and can be used to dissolve blood clots.

urolagnia /jʊərə(ʊ)ˈlagnɪə/ ▶ **noun** [mass noun] a tendency to derive sexual pleasure from the sight or thought of urination. Also called **UROPHILIA**.
– ORIGIN early 20th cent.: from **URO-**¹ 'of urine' + Greek *lagneia* 'lust'.

urolithiasis /jʊərə(ʊ)lɪˈθʌɪəsɪs/ ▶ **noun** [mass noun] Medicine the formation of stony concretions in the bladder or urinary tract.

urology /jʊˈrɒlədʒi/ ▶ **noun** [mass noun] the branch of medicine and physiology concerned with the function and disorders of the urinary system.
– DERIVATIVES **urologic** adjective, **urological** adjective, **urologist** noun.

uronic acid /jʊˈrɒnɪk/ ▶ **noun** Biochemistry any of a class of compounds which are derived from sugars by oxidizing a $—CH_2OH$ group to an acid group ($—COOH$).
– ORIGIN 1920s: *uronic* from **URO-**¹ 'urine' + **-IC**, with the insertion of *-n-*.

urophilia /jʊərə(ʊ)ˈfɪlɪə/ ▶ **noun** another term for **UROLAGNIA**.

uropod /ˈjʊərə(ʊ)pɒd/ ▶ **noun** Zoology the sixth and last pair of abdominal appendages of lobsters and related crustaceans, forming part of the tail fan.
– ORIGIN late 19th cent.: from **URO-**² 'tail' + Greek *pous, pod-* 'pod'.

uropygium /jʊərə(ʊ)ˈpɪdʒɪəm/ ▶ **noun** Zoology the rump of a bird, supporting the tail feathers.
– DERIVATIVES **uropygial** adjective.
– ORIGIN late 18th cent.: via medieval Latin from Greek *ouropugion.*

uroscopy /jʊˈrɒskəpi/ ▶ **noun** [mass noun] Medicine, historical the diagnostic examination of urine by simple inspection.

urostyle /ˈjʊərə(ʊ)stʌɪl/ ▶ **noun** Zoology a long bone formed from fused vertebrae at the base of the vertebral column in some lower vertebrates, especially frogs and toads.

Ursa Major /ˌəːsə ˈmeɪdʒə/ Astronomy one of the largest and most prominent northern constellations (the Great Bear). The seven brightest stars form a familiar formation variously called the Plough, Big Dipper, or Charles's Wain, and include the Pointers.
■ [as genitive **Ursae Majoris** /ˌəːsiː məˈdʒɔːrɪs/] used with preceding letter or numeral to designate a star in this constellation: *the star Delta Ursae Majoris.*
– ORIGIN Latin, from the story in Greek mythology that the nymph Callisto was turned into a bear and placed as a constellation in the heavens by Zeus.

Ursa Minor /ˈmʌɪnə/ Astronomy a northern constellation (the Little Bear), which contains the north celestial pole and the pole star Polaris. The brightest stars form a shape that is also known as the Little Dipper.
■ [as genitive **Ursae Minoris** /mɪˈnɔːrɪs/] used with preceding letter or numeral to designate a star in this constellation: *the star Alpha Ursae Minoris.*
– ORIGIN Latin.

ursine /ˈəːsʌɪn, -ɪn/ ▶ **adjective** of, relating to, or resembling bears.
– ORIGIN mid 16th cent.: from Latin *ursinus*, from *ursus* 'bear'.

Ursula, St /ˈəːsjʊlə/ a legendary British saint and martyr, said to have been put to death with 11,000 virgins after being captured by Huns near Cologne while on a pilgrimage.

Ursuline /ˈəːsjʊlʌɪn, -lɪn/ ▶ **noun** a nun of an order founded by St Angela Merici (1470–1540) at Brescia in 1535 for nursing the sick and teaching girls.
▶ **adjective** of or relating to this order.
– ORIGIN from St *Ursula*, the founder's patron saint (see **URSULA, ST**), + **-INE**¹.

urtext /ˈuːətɛkst/ ▶ **noun** (pl. **urtexte** /-tə/) an original or the earliest version of a text, to which later versions can be compared.

urticaria /ˌəːtɪˈkɛːrɪə/ ▶ **noun** [mass noun] Medicine a rash of round, red weals on the skin which itch intensely, sometimes with dangerous swelling, caused by an allergic reaction, typically to specific foods. Also called **NETTLERASH** or **HIVES**.
– ORIGIN late 18th cent.: modern Latin, from Latin *urtica* 'nettle', from *urere* 'to burn'.

urticate /ˈəːtɪkeɪt/ ▶ **verb** [no obj.] cause a stinging or prickling sensation like that given by a nettle: [as adj. **urticating**] *the urticating hairs.*
– DERIVATIVES **urtication** noun.
– ORIGIN mid 19th cent.: from medieval Latin *urticat-* 'stung', from the verb *urticare*, from Latin *urtica* (see **URTICARIA**).

Uruguay /ˈjʊərəgwʌɪ, Spanish uruˈɣwaj/ a country on the Atlantic coast of South America south of Brazil; pop. 3,110,000 (est. 1991); official language, Spanish; capital, Montevideo.

> Uruguay was liberated from Spanish colonial rule in 1825, and in the early 20th century was moulded into South America's first welfare state. Civil unrest beginning in the 1960s, and particularly fighting against the Marxist Tupamaro guerrillas, led to a period of military rule, but civilian government was restored in 1985.

– DERIVATIVES **Uruguayan** adjective & noun.

Uruk /ˈʊrʊk/ an ancient city in southern Mesopotamia, to the north-west of Ur. One of the greatest cities of Sumer, it was built in the 5th millennium BC and is associated with the legendary hero Gilgamesh. Arabic name **WARKA**; biblical name **ERECH**.

Urumqi /ʊˈrʊmtʃi/ (also **Urumchi**) the capital of Xinjiang autonomous region in NW China; pop. 1,110,000 (1990). Former name (until 1954) **TIHWA**.

urus /ˈjʊərəs/ ▶ **noun** another term for **AUROCHS**.
– ORIGIN early 17th cent.: from Latin, from Greek *ouros.*

urushiol /ʊˈruːʃɪɒl/ ▶ **noun** [mass noun] Biochemistry an oily liquid which is the main constituent of Japanese lacquer and is responsible for the irritant properties of poison ivy and other plants. It consists of a mixture of catechol derivatives.
– ORIGIN early 20th cent.: from Japanese *urushi* 'Japanese lacquer' + **-OL**.

US ▶ **abbreviation for** ■ Brit. undersecretary. ■ United States. ■ Brit. informal unserviceable; useless.

us ▶ **pronoun** [first person plural] **1** used by a speaker to refer to himself or herself and one or more other people as the object of a verb or preposition: *let us know* | *we asked him to come with us* | *both of us.* Compare with **WE**.
■ used after the verb 'to be' and after 'than' or 'as': *it's us or them* | *they are richer than us.* ■ N. Amer. informal to or for ourselves: *we got us some good hunting.*
2 informal me: *give us a kiss.*
– PHRASES **one of us** a person recognized as an accepted member of a particular group, typically one that is exclusive in some way. **us and them** (or **them and us**) expressing a sense of division within a group of people: *negotiations were hampered by an 'us and them' attitude between management and unions.*
– ORIGIN Old English *ūs*, accusative and dative of **WE**, of Germanic origin; related to Dutch *ons* and German *uns.*

> **USAGE** Is it correct to say *they are richer than* **us**, or is it better to say *they are richer than* **we** (*are*)? See usage at **PERSONAL PRONOUN** and **THAN**.

USA ▶ **abbreviation for** ■ United States of America. ■ United States Army.

usable (also **useable**) ▶ **adjective** able or fit to be used: *usable information.*
– DERIVATIVES **usability** noun.

USAF ▶ **abbreviation for** United States Air Force.

usage ▶ **noun** [mass noun] the action of using something or the fact of being used: *a survey of water usage* | *the usage of equipment.*
■ the way in which a word or phrase is normally and correctly used. ■ habitual or customary practice, especially as creating a right, obligation, or standard.
– ORIGIN Middle English (in the sense 'customary practice'): from Old French, from *us* 'a use' (see **USE**).

usance /ˈjuːz(ə)ns/ ▶ **noun** [mass noun] archaic **1** another term for **USAGE**.
2 the time allowed for the payment of foreign bills of exchange, according to law or commercial practice.
– ORIGIN late Middle English: from Old French, from the base of the verb *user* 'to use'.

USD ▶ **abbreviation for** United States dollar.

USDA ▶ **abbreviation for** United States Department of Agriculture.

use ▶ **verb 1** /juːz/ [with obj.] take, hold, or deploy (something) as a means of accomplishing a purpose or achieving a result; employ: *she used her key to open the front door* | *the poem uses simple language.*
■ take or consume (an amount) from a limited supply of something: *we have used all the available funds.* ■ exploit (a person or situation) for one's own advantage: *I couldn't help feeling that she was using me.* ■ [with obj. and adverbial] treat (someone) in a particular way: *use your troops well and they will not let you down.* ■ apply (a name or title) to oneself: *she still used her maiden name professionally.* ■ (**one could use**) informal one would like or benefit from: *I could use another cup of coffee.* ■ informal take (an illegal drug).
2 /juːst/ [in past, with infinitive] (**used to**) describing an action or state of affairs that was done repeatedly or existed for a period in the past: *this road used to be a dirt track* | *I used to give him lifts home.*
3 /juːst/ (**be/get used to**) be or become familiar with someone or something through experience: *she was used to getting what she wanted* | *he's weird, but you just have to get used to him.*
▶ **noun** /juːs/ [mass noun] the action of using something or the state of being used for some purpose: *a member of staff is present when the pool is* **in use** | *theatre owners were charging too much for* **the use of** *their venues.*
■ the ability or power to exercise or manipulate something, especially one's mind or body: *the horse lost* **the use of** *his hind legs.* ■ [count noun] a purpose for or way in which something can be used: *the herb has various culinary uses.* ■ the value or advantage of something: *it was no use trying to persuade her* | *what's the use of crying?* ■ Law, historical the benefit or profit of lands, especially lands that are in the possession of another who holds them solely for the beneficiary. ■ the characteristic ritual and liturgy of a church or diocese. ■ the action of taking or habitual consumption of a drug.
– PHRASES **have its** (or **one's**) **uses** informal be useful on certain occasions or in certain respects. **have no use for** be unable to find a purpose for; have no need for: *he had no use for a single glove.* ■ informal dislike or be impatient with. **make use of** use for a purpose. ■ benefit from: *they were educated enough to make use of further training.* **use and wont** formal established custom. **use someone's name** quote someone as an authority or reference.
– ORIGIN Middle English: the noun from Old French *us*, from Latin *usus*, from *uti* 'to use'; the verb from Old French *user*, based on Latin *uti.*

USAGE 1 The construction **used to** is standard, but difficulties arise with the formation of negatives and questions. Traditionally, **used to** behaves as a modal verb, so that questions and negatives are formed without the auxiliary verb **do**, as in *it* ***used not to*** *be like that* and **used** *she* **to** *come here?* In modern English this question form is now regarded as very formal or old-fashioned and the use with **do** is broadly accepted as standard, as in ***did*** *they* ***use to*** *come here?* Negative constructions with **do**, on the other hand (as in *it* ***didn't use to*** *be like that*), though common, are informal and are not generally accepted.
2 There is sometimes confusion over whether to use the form **used to** or **use to**, which has arisen largely because the pronunciation is the same in both cases. Except in negatives and questions, the correct form is **used to**: *we* ***used to*** *go to the cinema all the time*, not *we* ***use to*** *go to the cinema all the time*. However, in negatives and questions using the auxiliary verb **do**, the correct form is **use to**, because the form of the verb required is the infinitive: ***I didn't use to*** *like mushrooms*, not ***I didn't used to*** *like mushrooms*.

▶**use something up** consume or expend the whole of something: *the money was soon used up.* ■ find a purpose for something that is left over: *I might use up all my odd scraps of wool to make a scarf.* ■ (**be used up**) informal (of a person) be worn out, especially with overwork: *she was tired and used up.*

useable ▶ **adjective** variant spelling of **USABLE**.

use-by date ▶ **noun** chiefly Brit. a date marked on a perishable product, especially a foodstuff, indicating the recommended date by which it should be used or consumed.

used /juːzd/ ▶ **adjective 1** having already been used: *scrawling on the back of a used envelope.*
2 second-hand: *a used car.*

useful ▶ **adjective** able to be used for a practical purpose or in several ways: *aspirin are useful for headaches.*
■ informal very able or competent in a particular area: *a useful pace bowler.*
– PHRASES **make oneself useful** do something that is of some value or benefit to someone: *make yourself useful—get Jenny a drink.*
– DERIVATIVES **usefully** adverb, **usefulness** noun.

useful load ▶ **noun** the load carried by an aircraft in addition to its own weight.

useless ▶ **adjective** not fulfilling or not expected to achieve the intended purpose or desired outcome: *a piece of useless knowledge | we tried to pacify him but it was useless.*
■ informal having no ability or skill in a specified activity or area: *he was useless at football.*
– DERIVATIVES **uselessly** adverb, **uselessness** noun.

Usenet Computing an Internet service consisting of thousands of newsgroups.

user ▶ **noun 1** a person who uses or operates something, especially a computer or other machine.
■ a person who takes illegal drugs; an addict. ■ a person who manipulates others for their own gain: *he was a gifted user of other people.*
2 [mass noun] Law the continued use or enjoyment of a right.

user-definable ▶ **adjective** Computing having a function or meaning that can be specified and varied by a user.

user-friendly ▶ **adjective** (of a machine or system) easy to use or understand: *the search software is user-friendly.*
– DERIVATIVES **user-friendliness** noun.

user-hostile ▶ **adjective** (of a machine or system) difficult to use or understand.

user interface ▶ **noun** Computing the means by which the user and a computer system interact, in particular the use of input devices and software.

username ▶ **noun** Computing an identification used by a person with access to a computer network.

user-oriented ▶ **adjective** (of a machine or system) designed with the user's convenience given priority.

ushabti /ʊˈʃabti/ ▶ **noun** (pl. **ushabtis**) variant form of **SHABTI**.

usher ▶ **noun 1** a person who shows people to their seats, especially in a theatre or cinema or at a wedding.
■ an official in a law court whose duties include swearing in jurors and witnesses and keeping order. ■ Brit. a person employed to walk before a person of high rank on special occasions.
2 archaic an assistant teacher.
▶ **verb** [with obj. and adverbial of direction] show or guide (someone) somewhere: *a waiter ushered me to a table.*
■ figurative cause or mark the start of (something new): *the railways* ***ushered in*** *an era of cheap mass travel.*
– ORIGIN late Middle English (denoting a doorkeeper): from Anglo-Norman French *usser*, from medieval Latin *ustiarius*, from Latin *ostiarius*, from *ostium* 'door'.

usherette ▶ **noun** a woman who shows people to their seats in a cinema or theatre.

Ushuaia /uːˈswʌɪə/ a port in Argentina, in Tierra del Fuego; pop. 11,000 (1980). It is the southernmost town in the world.

Üsküdar /ˌuːskʊˈdɑːr/ a suburb of Istanbul, on the eastern side of the Bosporus where it joins the Sea of Marmara; pop. 395,620 (1990). Former name **SCUTARI**.

US Marines a US armed service (part of the US navy), founded in 1775 and trained to operate on land and at sea.

USN ▶ **abbreviation for** United States Navy.

usnic acid /ˈʌznɪk/ ▶ **noun** [mass noun] Biochemistry a yellow crystalline compound which is present in many lichens and is used as an antibiotic.
• A tricyclic phenol; chem. formula: $C_{18}H_{16}O_7$.
– ORIGIN mid 19th cent.: *usnic* from medieval Latin *usnea* (from Arabic *ushnah* 'moss') + **-IC**.

Usonian /juːˈsəʊnɪən/ ▶ **adjective** of or relating to the United States: *the Usonian city.*
■ relating to or denoting the style of buildings designed in the 1930s by Frank Lloyd Wright, characterized by inexpensive construction and flat roofs.
▶ **noun** a native or inhabitant of the United States.
■ a house built in the 1930s by Frank Lloyd Wright.

Uspallata Pass /ˌuːspəˈjɑːtə/ a pass over the Andes near Santiago, in southern South America.

usquebaugh /ˈʌskwɪbɔː/ ▶ **noun** [mass noun] chiefly Irish & Scottish whisky.
– ORIGIN late 16th cent.: from Irish and Scottish Gaelic *uisge beatha* 'water of life'; compare with **WHISKY**.

USS ▶ **abbreviation for** United States Ship, used in the names of ships in the US navy: *USS Saratoga.*

USSR historical ▶ **abbreviation for** Union of Soviet Socialist Republics.

Ust-Abakanskoe /ˌuːstabəˈkɑːnskəʊjɛ/ former name (until 1931) for **ABAKAN**.

ustad /ʊsˈtɑːd/ ▶ **noun** Indian an expert or highly skilled person, especially a musician.
– ORIGIN from Urdu *ustād*.

Ustashe /uːˈstɑːʃi/ (also **Ustashas** or **Ustashi**) ▶ **plural noun** [treated as sing. or pl.] the members of a Croatian extreme nationalist movement that engaged in terrorist activity before the Second World War and ruled Croatia with Nazi support after Yugoslavia was invaded and divided by the Germans in 1941.
– ORIGIN from Serbo-Croat *Ustaše* 'rebels'.

Ustinov[1] /uːˈstiːnɒf/ former name (1984–7) for **IZHEVSK**.

Ustinov[2] /ˈjuːstɪnɒf/, Sir Peter (Alexander) (b.1921), British actor, director, and dramatist, of Russian descent. He has written and acted in a number of plays, including *Romanoff and Juliet* (1956). Notable films: *Spartacus* (1960) and *Death on the Nile* (1978).

usual ▶ **adjective** habitually or typically occurring or done; customary: *he carried out his usual evening routine | their room was a shambles* ***as usual.***
▶ **noun** (**the/one's usual**) informal the drink someone habitually orders or prefers.
■ the thing which is typically done or present: *the band was a bit sick of playing all the usuals.*
– DERIVATIVES **usually** adverb *March usually has the heaviest rainfall*, **usualness** noun.
– ORIGIN late Middle English: from Old French, or from late Latin *usualis*, from Latin *usus* 'a use' (see **USE**).

usucaption /ˌjuːzjʊˈkapʃ(ə)n/ (also **usucapion** /ˌjuːzjʊˈkeɪpɪən/) ▶ **noun** [mass noun] Roman Law, chiefly historical the acquisition of a title or right to property by uninterrupted and undisputed possession for a prescribed term.
– ORIGIN mid 17th cent.: from medieval Latin *usucaptio(n-)*, from *usucapere* 'acquire by prescription', from *usu* 'by use' + *capere* 'take'.

usufruct /ˈjuːzjʊfrʌkt/ ▶ **noun** [mass noun] Roman Law the right to enjoy the use and advantages of another's property short of the destruction or waste of its substance.
– DERIVATIVES **usufructuary** adjective & noun.
– ORIGIN early 17th cent.: from medieval Latin *usufructus*, from Latin *usus (et) fructus* 'use (and) enjoyment', from *usus* 'a use' + *fructus* 'fruit'.

Usumbura /ˌuːzəmˈbʊərə/ former name (until 1962) for **BUJUMBURA**.

usurer /ˈjuːʒ(ə)rə/ ▶ **noun** a person who lends money at unreasonably high rates of interest.
– ORIGIN Middle English: from Anglo-Norman French, from Old French *usure*, from Latin *usura* (see **USURY**).

usurious /juːˈʒʊərɪəs, juːˈzj-/ ▶ **adjective** of or relating to the practice of usury: *they lend money at usurious rates.*
– DERIVATIVES **usuriously** adverb.

usurp /juːˈzəːp, jʊˈsəːp/ ▶ **verb** [with obj.] take (a position of power or importance) illegally or by force: *Richard usurped the throne.*
■ take the place of (someone in a position of power) illegally; supplant: *the Hanoverian dynasty had usurped the Stuarts.* ■ [no obj.] (**usurp on/upon**) archaic encroach or infringe upon (someone's rights): *the Church had usurped upon the domain of the state.*
– DERIVATIVES **usurpation** /ˌjuːzəˈpeɪʃ(ə)n, ˌjuːs-/ noun, **usurper** noun.
– ORIGIN Middle English (in the sense 'appropriate (a right) wrongfully)': from Old French *usurper*, from Latin *usurpare* 'seize for use'.

usury /ˈjuːʒ(ə)ri/ ▶ **noun** [mass noun] the action or practice of lending money at unreasonably high rates of interest.
■ archaic interest at such rates.
– ORIGIN Middle English: from Anglo-Norman French *usurie*, or from medieval Latin *usuria*, from Latin *usura*, from *usus* 'a use' (see **USE**).

UT ▶ **abbreviation for** ■ Universal Time. ■ Utah (in official postal use).

Utah /ˈjuːtɔː, -tɑː/ a state in the western US; pop. 1,722,850 (1990); capital, Salt Lake City. The region became part of Mexico in 1821 and was ceded to the US in 1848, becoming the 45th state of the US in 1896.
– DERIVATIVES **Utahan** /juːˈtɔːən, -ˈtɑːən/ adjective & noun.

utahraptor /ˈjuːtɔːˌraptə/ ▶ **noun** a large dromaeosaurid dinosaur, the remains of which were discovered in Utah in 1992. It was twice the size of deinonychus.
• Genus *Utahraptor*, family Dromaeosauridae, suborder Theropoda.
– ORIGIN modern Latin, from **UTAH** + **RAPTOR**.

Utamaro /ˌuːtəˈmɑːrəʊ/, Kitagawa (1753–1806), Japanese painter and printmaker; born *Kitagawa Nebsuyoshi*. A leading exponent of the ukiyo-e school, he was noted for his sensual depictions of women.

UTC ▶ **abbreviation for** Universal Time Coordinated. Also expanded as **COORDINATED UNIVERSAL TIME**.

Utd ▶ **abbreviation for** United (in names of soccer teams): *Scunthorpe Utd.*

Ute /juːt/ ▶ **noun** (pl. same or **Utes**) **1** a member of an American Indian people living chiefly in Colorado, Utah, and New Mexico.
2 [mass noun] the Uto-Aztecan language of this people, now with few speakers.
▶ **adjective** of or relating to this people or their language.
– ORIGIN from Spanish *Yuta*; compare with **PAIUTE**.

ute /juːt/ ▶ **noun** Austral./NZ informal a utility vehicle; a pickup.
– ORIGIN 1940s: abbreviation.

utensil ▶ **noun** a tool, container, or other article, especially for household use.
– ORIGIN late Middle English (denoting domestic implements or vessels collectively): from Old French *utensile*, from medieval Latin, neuter of Latin *utensilis* 'usable', from *uti* 'to use' (see **USE**).

uteri plural form of **UTERUS**.

uterine /ˈjuːtərɪn, -rʌɪn/ ▶ **adjective** of or relating to the uterus or womb: *uterine contractions.*
■ [attrib.] born of the same mother but not having the same father: *a uterine sister.*

– ORIGIN late Middle English: from **UTERUS** + **-INE**[1], or, in the sense 'born of the same mother', from late Latin *uterinus*.

uterus ▶ noun (pl. **uteri** /-rʌɪ/) the womb (as a bodily organ, especially in medical and technical contexts).
– ORIGIN Latin.

Uther Pendragon /ˈjuːθə pɛnˈdrag(ə)n/ (in Arthurian legend) king of the Britons and father of Arthur.

utile[1] /ˈjuːtʌɪl/ ▶ adjective rare advantageous.
– ORIGIN late 15th cent.: via Old French from Latin *utilis*, from *uti* 'to use'.

utile[2] /ˈjuːtiːli/ ▶ noun a large tropical African hardwood tree with timber that is widely used as a substitute for mahogany.
● *Entandrophragma utile*, family Meliaceae.
– ORIGIN 1950s: modern Latin, specific epithet (see above).

utilitarian /jʊˌtɪlɪˈtɛːrɪən/ ▶ adjective **1** designed to be useful or practical rather than attractive.
2 Philosophy of, relating to, or adhering to the doctrine of utilitarianism: *a utilitarian theorist*.
▶ noun Philosophy an adherent of utilitarianism.

utilitarianism ▶ noun [mass noun] the doctrine that actions are right if they are useful or for the benefit of a majority.
■ the doctrine that an action is right in so far as it promotes happiness, and that the greatest happiness of the greatest number should be the guiding principle of conduct.

> The most famous exponents of utilitarianism were Jeremy Bentham and J. S. Mill. It has been criticized for focusing on the consequences rather than the motive or intrinsic nature of an action, for the difficulty of adequately comparing the happiness of different individuals, and for failing to account for the value placed on concepts such as justice and equality.

utility ▶ noun (pl. **-ies**) **1** [mass noun] the state of being useful, profitable, or beneficial.
■ (in game theory or economics) a measure of that which is sought to be maximized in any situation involving a choice.
2 a public utility.
3 Computing a utility program.
4 Austral./NZ a utility vehicle.
▶ adjective [attrib.] **1** useful, especially through being able to perform several functions: *a utility truck*.
■ denoting a player capable of playing in several different positions in a sport.
2 functional rather than attractive: *utility clothing*.
– ORIGIN late Middle English: from Old French *utilite*, from Latin *utilitas*, from *utilis* 'useful'.

utility function ▶ noun Economics a mathematical function which ranks alternatives according to their utility to an individual.

utility knife ▶ noun a knife with a small sharp blade, often retractable, designed to cut wood, cardboard, and other materials.

utility pole ▶ noun North American term for **TELEGRAPH POLE**.

utility program ▶ noun Computing a program for carrying out a routine function.

utility room ▶ noun a room equipped with appliances for washing and other domestic work.

utility vehicle (also **utility truck**) ▶ noun a truck with low sides designed for carrying small loads.

utilize (also **-ise**) ▶ verb [with obj.] make practical and effective use of: *vitamin C helps your body utilize the iron present in your diet*.
– DERIVATIVES **utilizable** adjective, **utilization** noun, **utilizer** noun.
– ORIGIN early 19th cent.: from French *utiliser*, from Italian *utilizzare*, from *utile* (see **UTILE**[1]).

-ution ▶ suffix (forming nouns) equivalent to **-ATION** (as in *solution*).
– ORIGIN via French from Latin *-utio(n-)*.

utmost ▶ adjective [attrib.] most extreme; greatest: *a matter of the utmost importance*.
▶ noun (**the utmost**) the greatest or most extreme extent or amount: *a plot that stretches credulity to the utmost*.
– PHRASES **do one's utmost** do the most that one is able: *Dan was doing his utmost to be helpful*.
– ORIGIN Old English *ūt(e)mest* 'outermost' (see **OUT**, **-MOST**).

Uto-Aztecan /ˌjuːtəʊˈaztɛk(ə)n/ ▶ noun [mass noun] a language family of Central America and western North America including Nahuatl (the language of the Aztecs), Shoshone, and Paiute.
▶ adjective of, relating to, or denoting this language family.

Utopia /juːˈtəʊpɪə/ ▶ noun an imagined place or state of things in which everything is perfect. The word was first used in the book *Utopia* (1516) by Sir Thomas More. The opposite of **DYSTOPIA**.
– ORIGIN based on Greek *ou* 'not' + *topos* 'place'.

Utopian ▶ adjective modelled on or aiming for a state in which everything is perfect; idealistic.
▶ noun an idealistic reformer.
– DERIVATIVES **Utopianism** noun.

utopian socialism ▶ noun [mass noun] socialism achieved by the moral persuasion of capitalists to surrender the means of production peacefully to the people. It was advocated by Johann Fichte and Robert Owen among others.

Utrecht /juːˈtrɛxt/ a city in the central Netherlands, capital of a province of the same name; pop. 231,230 (1991).

Utrecht, Peace of a series of treaties (1713–14) ending the War of the Spanish Succession. The disputed throne of Spain was given to the French Philip V, but the union of the French and Spanish thrones was forbidden. The House of Hanover succeeded to the British throne and the former Spanish territories in Italy were ceded to the Habsburgs.

Utrecht velvet ▶ noun [mass noun] a strong, thick plush velvet, used in upholstery.

utricle /ˈjuːtrɪk(ə)l/ ▶ noun a small cell, sac, or bladder-like protuberance in an animal or plant.
■ (also **utriculus** /juːˈtrɪkjʊləs/) the larger of the two fluid-filled cavities forming part of the labyrinth of the inner ear (the other being the sacculus). It contains hair cells and otoliths which send signals to the brain concerning the orientation of the head.
– DERIVATIVES **utricular** /juːˈtrɪkjʊlə/ adjective.
– ORIGIN mid 18th cent.: from French *utricule* or Latin *utriculus*, diminutive of *uter* 'leather bag'.

Utrillo /juːˈtrɪləʊ, French ytrijo/, Maurice (1883–1955), French painter, chiefly known for his depictions of Paris street scenes.

Utsire /ʊtˈsɪərə/ a small island off the coast of southern Norway to the north-west of Stavanger. The shipping forecast area **North Utsire** covers Norwegian coastal waters immediately to the north of the island, while **South Utsire** covers the area to the south, as far as the mouth of the Skagerrak.

Uttar Pradesh /ˌʊtə prəˈdɛʃ/ a large state in northern India, bordering on Tibet and Nepal; capital, Lucknow. It was formed in 1950 from the United Provinces of Agra and Oudh.

utter[1] ▶ adjective [attrib.] complete; absolute: *Charlotte stared at her in utter amazement*.
– DERIVATIVES **utterly** adverb [as submodifier] *he looked utterly ridiculous*.
– ORIGIN Old English *ūtera*, *ūttra* 'outer', comparative of *ūt* 'out'; compare with **OUTER**.

utter[2] ▶ verb [with obj.] **1** make (a sound) with one's voice: *he uttered an exasperated snort*.
■ say (something) aloud: *they are busily scribbling down every word she utters*.
2 Law put (forged money) into circulation.
– DERIVATIVES **utterable** adjective, **utterer** noun.
– ORIGIN late Middle English: from Middle Dutch *ūteren* 'speak, make known, give currency to (coins)'.

utterance ▶ noun a spoken word, statement, or vocal sound.
■ [mass noun] the action of saying or expressing something aloud: *the simple utterance of a few platitudes*. ■ Linguistics an uninterrupted chain of spoken or written language.

uttermost ▶ adjective & noun another term for **UTMOST**.

Uttley /ˈʌtli/, Alison (1884–1976), English author. She is remembered for her children's books, particularly the 'Little Grey Rabbit' series (1929 onwards) and the 'Sam Pig' stories (1940 onwards).

U-turn ▶ noun the turning of a vehicle in a U-shaped course so as to face in the opposite direction.
■ a change of plan, especially a reversal of political policy: *another U-turn by the government*.

UUC ▶ abbreviation for Ulster Unionist Council.

UV ▶ abbreviation for ultraviolet.

UVA ▶ abbreviation for ultraviolet radiation of relatively long wavelengths.

uvarovite /uːˈvarə(ʊ)vʌɪt/ ▶ noun [mass noun] an emerald green variety of garnet, containing chromium.
– ORIGIN mid 19th cent.: from the name of Count Sergei S. *Uvarov* (1785–1855), Russian statesman, + **-ITE**[1].

UVB ▶ abbreviation for ultraviolet radiation of relatively short wavelengths.

UVC ▶ abbreviation for ultraviolet radiation of very short wavelengths, which does not penetrate the earth's ozone layer.

uvea /ˈjuːvɪə/ ▶ noun the pigmented layer of the eye, lying beneath the sclera and cornea, and comprising the iris, choroid, and ciliary body.
– DERIVATIVES **uveal** adjective.
– ORIGIN late Middle English (denoting the choroid layer of the eye): from medieval Latin, from Latin *uva* 'grape'.

uveitis /ˌjuːvɪˈʌɪtɪs/ ▶ noun [mass noun] Medicine inflammation of the uvea.

uvula /ˈjuːvjʊlə/ ▶ noun (pl. **uvulae** /-liː/) Anatomy (also **palatine uvula**) a fleshy extension at the back of the soft palate which hangs above the throat.
■ a similar fleshy, hanging structure in any organ of the body, particularly one at the opening of the bladder.
– ORIGIN late Middle English: from late Latin, diminutive of Latin *uva* 'grape'.

uvular /ˈjuːvjʊlə/ ▶ adjective **1** Phonetics (of a sound) articulated with the back of the tongue and the uvula, as *r* in French and *q* in Arabic.
2 Anatomy of or relating to the uvula.
▶ noun Phonetics a uvular consonant.

uxorial /ʌkˈsɔːrɪəl/ ▶ adjective of or relating to a wife.
– ORIGIN early 19th cent.: from Latin *uxor* 'wife' + **-IAL**.

uxoricide /ʌkˈsɔːrɪsʌɪd/ ▶ noun [mass noun] the killing of one's wife.
■ [count noun] a man who kills his wife.
– DERIVATIVES **uxoricidal** adjective.
– ORIGIN mid 19th cent.: from Latin *uxor* 'wife' + **-CIDE**.

uxorilocal /ˌʌksɒrɪˈləʊk(ə)l/ ▶ adjective another term for **MATRILOCAL**.
– ORIGIN 1930s: from Latin *uxorius* 'of a wife' (from *uxor* 'wife') + **LOCAL**.

uxorious /ʌkˈsɔːrɪəs/ ▶ adjective having or showing a great or excessive fondness for one's wife.
– DERIVATIVES **uxoriously** adverb, **uxoriousness** noun.
– ORIGIN late 16th cent.: from Latin *uxoriosus*, from *uxor* 'wife'.

Uygur ▶ noun & adjective variant spelling of **UIGHUR**.

Uzbek /ˈʊzbɛk, ˈʌz-/ ▶ noun **1** a member of a Turkic people living mainly in the republic of Uzbekistan and also in Turkmenistan, Tajikistan, Kazakhstan, and Afghanistan.
■ a native or national of Uzbekistan.
2 [mass noun] the Turkic language of Uzbekistan, having some 16 million speakers.
▶ adjective of or relating to Uzbekistan, the Uzbeks, or their language.
– ORIGIN the name in Uzbek.

Uzbekistan /ʊzˌbɛkɪˈstɑːn, ʌz-, -ˈstan/ an independent republic in central Asia, lying south and south-east of the Aral Sea; pop. 20,955,000 (est. 1991); official language, Uzbek; capital, Tashkent.

> Uzbekistan was formerly a constituent republic of the USSR (established in 1924). It became independent within the Commonwealth of Independent States on the break-up of the Soviet Union in 1991.

Uzi /ˈuːzi/ ▶ noun a type of sub-machine gun of Israeli design.
– ORIGIN 1950s: from *Uziel* Gal, the Israeli army officer who designed it.

Vv

V[1] (also **v**) ▶ **noun** (pl. **Vs** or **V's**) **1** the twenty-second letter of the alphabet.
■ denoting the next after U in a set of items, categories, etc.
2 (also **vee**) a shape like that of a letter V: [in combination] *deep, V-shaped valleys.*
■ [as modifier] denoting an internal-combustion engine with a number of cylinders arranged in two rows at an angle to each other in a V-shape: *a V-engine | a 32-valve V8 power plant.*
3 the Roman numeral for five.

V[2] ▶ **abbreviation for** ■ Vatican City (international vehicle registration). ■ volt(s).
▶ **symbol for** ■ the chemical element vanadium. ■ voltage or potential difference: *V = IR.* ■ (in mathematical formulae) volume: *pV = nRT.*

v ▶ **abbreviation for** ■ Grammar verb. ■ (in textual references) verse. ■ verso. ■ versus. ■ very. ■ (in textual references) *vide.*
▶ **symbol for** velocity.

V-1 ▶ **noun** a small flying bomb powered by a simple jet engine, used by the Germans in the Second World War. Also called **DOODLEBUG.**
– ORIGIN abbreviation of German *Vergeltungswaffe* 'reprisal weapon'.

V-2 ▶ **noun** a rocket-powered flying bomb, which was the first ballistic missile, used by the Germans in the Second World War.
– ORIGIN see **V-1.**

VA ▶ **abbreviation for** ■ (in the UK) Order of Victoria and Albert. ■ (in the US) Veterans' Administration. ■ Vicar Apostolic. ■ Vice Admiral. ■ Virginia (in official postal use).

Va ▶ **abbreviation for** Virginia.

Vaal /vɑːl/ a river of South Africa, the chief tributary of the Orange River, rising in the Drakensberg Mountains and flowing 1,200 km (750 miles) south-westwards to the Orange River near Douglas, in Northern Cape. For much of its length it forms the border between North-West Province and Free State.

Vaasa /'vɑːsə/ a port in western Finland, on the Gulf of Bothnia; pop. 53,430 (1990). Swedish name **VASA.**

vac ▶ **noun** Brit. **1** informal term for **VACATION.**
2 informal term for **VACUUM CLEANER.**

vacancy ▶ **noun** (pl. **-ies**) **1** an unoccupied position or job: *a vacancy for a shorthand typist.*
■ an available room in a hotel or other establishment providing accommodation.
2 [mass noun] empty space: *Cathy stared into vacancy, seeing nothing.*
■ emptiness of mind; lack of intelligence or understanding: *vacancy, vanity, and inane deception.*

vacant ▶ **adjective** (of a place) not occupied; empty: *40 per cent of the offices are still vacant.*
■ (of a position or employment) not filled: *the President resigned and the post was left vacant.* ■ (of a person or their expression) having or showing no intelligence or interest: *a vacant stare.*
– DERIVATIVES **vacantly** adverb.
– ORIGIN Middle English: from Old French, or from Latin *vacant-* 'remaining empty', from the verb *vacare.*

vacant possession ▶ **noun** [mass noun] Brit. the right of a purchaser to exclusive use of a property on completion of the sale, any previous occupant having moved out.

vacate /veɪˈkeɪt, vəˈkeɪt/ ▶ **verb** [with obj.] **1** leave (a place that one previously occupied): *rooms must be vacated by noon on the last day of your holiday.*
■ give up (a position or employment): *he vacated his office as Director.*
2 Law cancel or annul (a judgement, contract, or charge).
– ORIGIN mid 17th cent. (as a legal term, also in the sense 'make ineffective'): from Latin *vacat-* 'left empty', from the verb *vacare.*

vacation ▶ **noun 1** a fixed holiday period between terms in universities and law courts.
■ chiefly N. Amer. a holiday: *he took a vacation in the south of France | people come here on vacation.*
2 [mass noun] the action of leaving something one previously occupied: *his marriage was the reason for the vacation of his fellowship.*
▶ **verb** [no obj.] chiefly US take a holiday: *I was vacationing in Europe with my family.*
– DERIVATIVES **vacationer** noun, **vacationist** noun.
– ORIGIN late Middle English: from Old French, or from Latin *vacatio(n-)*, from *vacare* 'be unoccupied' (see **VACATE**).

vacationland ▶ **noun** US an area providing attractions for holidaymakers.

vaccinate /'vaksɪneɪt/ ▶ **verb** [with obj.] treat with a vaccine to produce immunity against a disease; inoculate: *all the children were vaccinated against tuberculosis.*
– DERIVATIVES **vaccination** noun, **vaccinator** noun.

vaccine /'vaksiːn, -ɪn/ ▶ **noun** Medicine a substance used to stimulate the production of antibodies and provide immunity against one or several diseases, prepared from the causative agent of a disease, its products, or a synthetic substitute, treated to act as an antigen without inducing the disease: *there is no vaccine against HIV infection.*
■ Computing a program designed to detect computer viruses, and prevent them from operating.
– ORIGIN late 18th cent.: from Latin *vaccinus*, from *vacca* 'cow' (because of the early use of the cowpox virus against smallpox).

vaccinia /vakˈsɪnɪə/ ▶ **noun** [mass noun] Medicine cowpox, or the virus which causes it.
– ORIGIN early 19th cent.: modern Latin, from Latin *vaccinus* (see **VACCINE**).

Vacherin /'vaʃ(ə)rã/ ▶ **noun** [mass noun] a type of soft French or Swiss cheese made from cow's milk.
– ORIGIN French, from earlier *vachelin*, from *vache* 'cow'.

vacillate /'vasɪleɪt/ ▶ **verb** [no obj.] alternate or waver between different opinions or actions; be indecisive: *I had for a time vacillated between teaching and journalism.*
– DERIVATIVES **vacillation** noun, **vacillator** noun.
– ORIGIN late 16th cent. (in the sense 'sway unsteadily'): from Latin *vacillat-* 'swayed', from the verb *vacillare.*

vacua plural form of **VACUUM.**

vacuole /'vakjʊəʊl/ ▶ **noun** Biology a space or vesicle within the cytoplasm of a cell, enclosed by a membrane and typically containing fluid.
■ a small cavity or space in tissue, especially in nervous tissue as the result of disease.
– DERIVATIVES **vacuolar** /'vakjʊələ/ adjective, **vacuolation** noun.
– ORIGIN mid 19th cent.: from French, diminutive of Latin *vacuus* 'empty'.

vacuous /'vakjʊəs/ ▶ **adjective** having or showing a lack of thought or intelligence; mindless: *a vacuous smile | vacuous slogans.*
■ archaic empty.
– DERIVATIVES **vacuity** /vəˈkjuːɪti/ noun, **vacuously** adverb, **vacuousness** noun.
– ORIGIN mid 17th cent. (in the sense 'empty of matter'): from Latin *vacuus* 'empty' + **-OUS.**

vacuum /'vakjʊəm/ ▶ **noun** (pl. **vacuums** or **vacua** /-jʊə/) **1** a space entirely devoid of matter.
■ a space or container from which the air has been completely or partly removed. ■ [usu. in sing.] a gap left by the loss, death, or departure of someone or something formerly playing a significant part in a situation or activity: *the political vacuum left by the death of the Emperor.*
2 (pl. **vacuums**) informal a vacuum cleaner.
▶ **verb** [with obj.] informal clean with a vacuum cleaner: *the room needs to be vacuumed.*
– PHRASES **in a vacuum** (of an activity or a problem to be considered) isolated from the context normal to it and in which it can best be understood or assessed.
– ORIGIN mid 16th cent.: modern Latin, neuter of Latin *vacuus* 'empty'.

vacuum brake ▶ **noun** a railway vehicle brake operated by changes in pressure in a continuous pipe which is generally kept exhausted of air by a pump and controls similar brakes throughout the train.

vacuum cleaner ▶ **noun** an electrical apparatus that by means of suction collects dust and small particles from floors and other surfaces.
– DERIVATIVES **vacuum-clean** verb.

vacuum distillation ▶ **noun** [mass noun] Chemistry distillation of a liquid under reduced pressure, enabling it to boil at a lower temperature than normal.

vacuum extraction ▶ **noun** [mass noun] the application of reduced pressure to extract something, particularly to assist childbirth or as a method of abortion, or as a technique for removing components of a chemical mixture.

vacuum extractor ▶ **noun** a cup-shaped appliance for performing vacuum extraction in childbirth. Also called **VENTOUSE.**

vacuum flask ▶ **noun** chiefly Brit. a container that keeps a drink or other fluid hot by means of a double wall enclosing a vacuum.

vacuum gauge ▶ **noun** a gauge for testing pressure after the production of a vacuum.

vacuum-pack ▶ **verb** [with obj.] seal (a product) in a pack or wrapping after any air has been removed so that the pack or wrapping is tight and firm: [as adj.] **vacuum-packed**] *vacuum-packed cheese.*

vacuum pump ▶ **noun** a pump used for creating a vacuum.

vacuum tube ▶ **noun** a sealed glass tube

containing a near-vacuum which allows the free passage of electric current.

VAD historical ▶ abbreviation for Voluntary Aid Detachment, a British organization of first-aid workers and nurses.

vada /'vɑːdə/ (also **wada**) ▶ noun an Indian dish consisting of a ball made from ground lentils and deep-fried.
– ORIGIN from Hindi *vaḍā*.

vade mecum /ˌvɑːdi 'meɪkəm, ˌveɪdi, 'miːkəm/ ▶ noun a handbook or guide that is kept constantly at hand for consultation.
– ORIGIN early 17th cent.: modern Latin, literally 'go with me'.

Vadodara /və'dəʊdərə/ a city in the state of Gujarat, western India; pop. 1,021,000 (1991). The capital of the former state of Baroda, the city was known as Baroda until 1976.

vadose /'veɪdəʊs/ ▶ adjective relating to or denoting underground water above the water table. Compare with **PHREATIC**.
– ORIGIN late 19th cent.: from Latin *vadosus*, from *vadum* 'shallow expanse of water'.

Vaduz /va'dʊts/ the capital of Liechtenstein; pop. 4,870 (est. 1990).

vagabond ▶ noun a person who wanders from place to place without a home or job.
■ informal, dated a rascal; a rogue.
▶ adjective [attrib.] having no settled home.
▶ verb [no obj.] archaic wander about as or like a vagabond.
– DERIVATIVES **vagabondage** noun.
– ORIGIN Middle English (originally denoting a criminal): from Old French, or from Latin *vagabundus*, from *vagari* 'wander'.

vagal ▶ adjective of or relating to the vagus nerve.

vagarious /və'gɛːrɪəs/ ▶ adjective rare erratic and unpredictable in behaviour or direction.
– ORIGIN late 18th cent. (in the sense 'changing, inconstant'): from **VAGARY** + **-OUS**.

vagary /'veɪg(ə)ri/ ▶ noun (pl. **-ies**) (usu. **vagaries**) an unexpected and inexplicable change in a situation or in someone's behaviour: *the vagaries of the weather.*
– ORIGIN late 16th cent. (also as a verb in the sense 'roam'): from Latin *vagari* 'wander'.

vagi plural form of **VAGUS**.

vagina /və'dʒʌɪnə/ ▶ noun (pl. **vaginas** or **vaginae** /-niː/) the muscular tube leading from the external genitals to the cervix of the uterus in women and most female mammals.
■ Botany & Zoology any sheath-like structure, especially a sheath formed round a stem by the base of a leaf.
– DERIVATIVES **vaginal** adjective.
– ORIGIN late 17th cent.: from Latin, literally 'sheath, scabbard'.

vagina dentata /dɛn'tɑːtə/ ▶ noun the motif of a vagina with teeth, occurring in folklore and fantasy and said to symbolize male fears of the dangers of sexual intercourse.
– ORIGIN early 20th cent.: *dentata*, feminine of Latin *dentatus* 'having teeth'.

vaginal plug ▶ noun Zoology a secretion which blocks the vagina of some rodents and insectivores after mating.

vaginismus /ˌvadʒɪ'nɪzməs/ ▶ noun [mass noun] painful spasmodic contraction of the vagina in response to physical contact or pressure (especially in sexual intercourse).
– ORIGIN mid 19th cent.: modern Latin, from Latin *vagina* (see **VAGINA**).

vaginitis /ˌvadʒɪ'nʌɪtɪs/ ▶ noun [mass noun] inflammation of the vagina.

vaginosis /ˌvadʒɪ'nəʊsɪs/ ▶ noun [mass noun] a bacterial infection of the vagina causing a smelly white discharge.

vagotomy /veɪ'gɒtəmi/ ▶ noun (pl. **-ies**) [mass noun] a surgical operation in which one or more branches of the vagus nerve are cut, typically to reduce the rate of gastric secretion (e.g. in treating peptic ulcers).
– DERIVATIVES **vagotomized** adjective.

vagrant /'veɪgr(ə)nt/ ▶ noun a person without a settled home or regular work who wanders from place to place and lives by begging.
■ archaic a wanderer. ■ Ornithology a bird that has strayed or been blown from its usual range or migratory route. Also called **ACCIDENTAL**.

▶ adjective [attrib.] characteristic of, relating to, or living the life of a vagrant: *vagrant beggars.*
■ moving from place to place; wandering: *vagrant whales.* ■ poetic/literary moving or occurring unpredictably; inconstant: *the vagrant heart of my mother.*
– DERIVATIVES **vagrancy** noun, **vagrantly** adverb.
– ORIGIN late Middle English: from Anglo-Norman French *vagarant* 'wandering about', from the verb *vagrer.*

vague ▶ adjective of uncertain, indefinite, or unclear character or meaning: *many patients suffer vague symptoms.*
■ thinking or communicating in an unfocused or imprecise way: *he had been very vague about his activities.*
– DERIVATIVES **vaguely** adverb, **vagueness** noun, **vaguish** adjective.
– ORIGIN mid 16th cent.: from French, or from Latin *vagus* 'wandering, uncertain'.

vagus /'veɪgəs/ ▶ noun (pl. **vagi** /-dʒʌɪ, -gʌɪ/) (also **vagus nerve**) Anatomy each of the tenth pair of cranial nerves, supplying the heart, lungs, upper digestive tract, and other organs of the chest and abdomen.
– ORIGIN mid 19th cent.: from Latin (see **VAGUE**).

vail /veɪl/ ▶ verb [with obj.] archaic take off or lower (one's hat or crown) as a token of respect or submission.
■ [no obj.] take off one's hat or otherwise show respect or submission to someone.
– ORIGIN Middle English (originally in the sense 'lower (one's eyes, weapon, banner, etc.) as a sign of submission'): shortening of obsolete *avale*, from Old French *avaler* 'to lower', from *a val* 'down' (literally 'in the valley').

vain ▶ adjective 1 having or showing an excessively high opinion of one's appearance, abilities, or worth: *their flattery made him vain.*
2 [attrib.] producing no result; useless: *a vain attempt to tidy up the room* | *the vain hope of finding work.*
■ having no meaning or likelihood of fulfilment: *a vain boast.*
– PHRASES **in vain** without success or a result: *they waited in vain for a response.* **take someone's name in vain** use someone's name in a way that shows a lack of respect.
– DERIVATIVES **vainly** adverb.
– ORIGIN Middle English (in the sense 'devoid of real worth'): via Old French from Latin *vanus* 'empty, without substance'.

vainglory ▶ noun [mass noun] poetic/literary inordinate pride in oneself or one's achievements; excessive vanity.
– DERIVATIVES **vainglorious** adjective, **vaingloriously** adverb, **vaingloriousness** noun.
– ORIGIN Middle English: suggested by Old French *vaine gloire*, Latin *vana gloria*.

vair /vɛː/ ▶ noun [mass noun] **1** fur obtained from a variety of red squirrel, used in the 13th and 14th centuries as a trimming or lining for garments.
2 Heraldry fur represented by interlocking rows of shield-shaped or bell-shaped figures which are typically alternately blue and white, as a tincture.
– ORIGIN Middle English: via Old French from Latin *varius* (see **VARIOUS**).

vairy /'vɛːri/ ▶ adjective Heraldry of a pattern resembling vair but usually in other colours.

Vaishnava /'vʌɪʃnəvə/ ▶ noun a member of one of the main branches of modern Hinduism, devoted to the worship of the god Vishnu as the supreme being. Compare with **SAIVA**.
– ORIGIN from Sanskrit *vaiṣnava.*

Vaisya /'vʌɪsjə, -ʃjə/ (also **Vaishya**) ▶ noun a member of the third of the four Hindu castes, comprising the merchants and farmers.
– ORIGIN from Sanskrit *vaiśya* 'peasant, labourer'.

vajra /'vʌdʒrə/ ▶ noun (in Buddhism and Hinduism) a thunderbolt or mythical weapon, especially one wielded by the god Indra.
– ORIGIN Sanskrit.

valance /'val(ə)ns/ (also **valence**) ▶ noun a length of decorative drapery attached to the canopy or frame of a bed in order to screen the structure or the space beneath it.
■ a sheet with a deep pleated or gathered border that is designed to hang down over the mattress and sides of a bed. ■ a length of decorative drapery hung above a window to screen the curtain fittings. ■ a protective panel screening the wheels of a vehicle.
– DERIVATIVES **valanced** adjective.

– ORIGIN late Middle English: perhaps Anglo-Norman French, from a shortened form of Old French *avaler* 'descend' (see **VAIL**).

vale[1] /veɪl/ ▶ noun a valley (used in place names or as a poetic term): *the Vale of Glamorgan.*
– PHRASES **vale of tears** poetic/literary the world regarded as a scene of trouble or sorrow.
– ORIGIN Middle English: from Old French *val*, from Latin *vallis, valles.*

vale[2] /'vɑːleɪ/ archaic ▶ exclamation farewell.
▶ noun a written or spoken farewell.
– ORIGIN Latin, literally 'be well!, be strong!', imperative of *valere.*

valediction /ˌvalɪ'dɪkʃ(ə)n/ ▶ noun [mass noun] the action of saying farewell: *he spread his palm in valediction.*
■ [count noun] a statement or address made at or as a farewell: *his official memorial valediction.*
– ORIGIN mid 17th cent.: based on Latin *vale* 'goodbye' + *dicere* 'to say', on the pattern of *benediction.*

valedictorian /ˌvalɪdɪk'tɔːrɪən/ ▶ noun (in North America) a student who delivers the valedictory at a graduation ceremony.

valedictory /ˌvalɪ'dɪkt(ə)ri/ ▶ adjective serving as a farewell: *a valedictory wave.*
▶ noun (pl. **-ies**) a farewell address.

valence[1] /'veɪl(ə)ns/ ▶ noun Chemistry & Linguistics another term for **VALENCY**.
■ [as modifier] relating to or denoting electrons involved in or available for chemical bond formation: *molecules with unpaired valence electrons.*

valence[2] ▶ noun variant spelling of **VALANCE**.

Valencia /və'lɛnsɪə, Spanish ba'lenθja, -sja/ **1** an autonomous region of eastern Spain, on the Mediterranean coast. It was formerly a Moorish kingdom (1021–1238).
■ its capital, a port on the Mediterranean coast; pop. 777,430 (1991).
2 a city in northern Venezuela; pop. 903,080 (1991).

Valenciennes /ˌvalɒ̃'sjɛn/ ▶ noun [mass noun] a type of bobbin lace.
– ORIGIN named after a town in NE France, where it was made in the 17th and 18th cents.

valency /'veɪl(ə)nsi/ ▶ noun (pl. **-ies**) Chemistry, chiefly Brit. the combining power of an element, especially as measured by the number of hydrogen atoms it can displace or combine with: *carbon always has a valency of 4.* Compare with **VALENCE**[1].
■ Linguistics the number of grammatical elements with which a particular word, especially a verb, combines in a sentence.
– ORIGIN early 17th cent.: from late Latin *valentia* 'power, competence', from *valere* 'be well or strong'.

valentine ▶ noun a card sent, often anonymously, on St Valentine's Day, 14 February, to a person one loves or is attracted to.
■ a person to whom one sends such a card or whom one asks to be one's sweetheart.
– ORIGIN late Middle English (denoting a person chosen (sometimes by lot) as a sweetheart or special friend): from Old French *Valentin*, from Latin *Valentinus.*

Valentine, St either of two early Italian saints (who may have been the same person) traditionally commemorated on 14 February—a Roman priest martyred c.269 and a bishop of Terni martyred at Rome. St Valentine was regarded as the patron of lovers.

Valentino /ˌvalən'tiːnəʊ/, Rudolph (1895–1926), Italian-born American actor; born *Rodolfo Guglielmi di Valentina d'Antonguolla*. He played the romantic hero in silent films such as *The Sheikh* (1921).

Valera, Eamon de, see **DE VALERA**.

Valerian /və'lɪərɪən/ (d.260), Roman emperor 253–60; Latin name *Publius Licinius Valerianus.* He renewed the persecution of the Christians initiated by Decius.

valerian /və'lɪərɪən/ ▶ noun a Eurasian plant which typically bears clusters of small pink or white flowers.
● Family Valerianaceae: several species, in particular **common valerian** (*Valeriana officinalis*), a valued medicinal herb, and the Mediterranean **red valerian** (*Centranthus ruber*), grown for its spurred flowers which attract butterflies.
■ [mass noun] a drug obtained from the root of common valerian, used as a stimulant and antispasmodic.
– ORIGIN late Middle English: from Old French *valeriane*, from medieval Latin *valeriana* (*herba*),

apparently the feminine of *Valerianus* 'of Valerius' (a personal name).

valeric acid /və'lɛrɪk, -'lɪərɪk/ ▶ **noun** Chemistry another term for **PENTANOIC ACID**.
– DERIVATIVES **valerate** noun.
– ORIGIN mid 19th cent.: *valeric* from **VALERIAN** + **-IC**.

Valéry /ˌvale'riː, French valeʀi/, (Ambroise) Paul (Toussaint Jules) (1871–1945), French poet, essayist, and critic. His poetry includes *La Jeune parque* (1917) and 'Le Cimetière marin' (1922).

valet /'valɪt, 'valeɪ/ ▶ **noun 1** a man's personal male attendant, responsible for his clothes and appearance.
■a hotel employee performing such duties for guests.
2 a person employed to clean or park cars.
▶ **verb** (**valeted**, **valeting**) [with obj.] **1** act as a valet to (a particular man).
■[no obj.] work as a valet.
2 clean (a car), especially on the inside.
– ORIGIN late 15th cent. (denoting a footman acting as an attendant to a horseman): from French; related to **VASSAL**.

valeta ▶ **noun** variant spelling of **VELETA**.

valetudinarian /ˌvalɪtjuːdɪ'nɛːrɪən/ ▶ **noun** a person who is unduly anxious about their health.
■a person suffering from poor health.
▶ **adjective** showing undue concern about one's health.
■suffering from poor health.
– DERIVATIVES **valetudinarianism** noun.
– ORIGIN early 18th cent.: from Latin *valetudinarius* 'in ill health' (from *valetudo* 'health', from *valere* 'be well') + **-AN**.

valetudinary /ˌvalɪ'tjuːdɪn(ə)ri/ ▶ **adjective** & **noun** (pl. **-ies**) another term for **VALETUDINARIAN**.

valgus /'valgəs/ ▶ **noun** [mass noun] Medicine a deformity involving oblique displacement of part of a limb away from the midline. The opposite of **VARUS**.
– ORIGIN early 19th cent.: from Latin, literally 'knock-kneed'.

Valhalla /val'halə/ Scandinavian Mythology a palace in which heroes killed in battle were believed to feast with Odin for eternity.
– ORIGIN modern Latin, from Old Norse *Valhǫll*, from *valr* 'the slain' + *hǫll* 'hall'.

valiant ▶ **adjective** possessing or showing courage or determination: *she made a valiant effort to hold her anger in check* | *a valiant warrior*.
– DERIVATIVES **valiantly** adverb.
– ORIGIN Middle English (also in the sense 'robust, well-built'): from Old French *vailant*, based on Latin *valere* 'be strong'.

valid ▶ **adjective** actually supporting the intended point or claim; acceptable as cogent: *a valid criticism*.
■legally binding due to having been executed in compliance with the law: *a valid contract*. ■ legally acceptable: *the visas are valid for thirty days*.
– DERIVATIVES **validity** noun, **validly** adverb.
– ORIGIN late 16th cent.: from French *valide* or Latin *validus* 'strong', from *valere* 'be strong'.

validate ▶ **verb** [with obj.] check or prove the validity or accuracy of (something): *all analytical methods should be validated in respect of accuracy*.
■demonstrate or support the truth or value of: *acclaim was seen as a means of validating one's existence*. ■ make or declare legally valid.
– DERIVATIVES **validation** noun.
– ORIGIN mid 17th cent. (in the sense 'make legally valid'): from medieval Latin *validat-* 'made legally valid', from the verb *validare*, from Latin *validus* (see **VALID**).

valine /'veɪliːn/ ▶ **noun** [mass noun] Biochemistry an amino acid which is a constituent of most proteins. It is an essential nutrient in the diet of vertebrates.
• Chem. formula: $(CH_3)_2CHCH(NH_2)COOH$.
– ORIGIN early 20th cent.: from *val(eric acid)* + **-INE**[4].

valise /və'liːz/ ▶ **noun** a small travelling bag or suitcase.
– ORIGIN early 17th cent.: from French, from Italian *valigia*; compare with medieval Latin *valesia*, of unknown origin.

Valium /'valɪəm/ ▶ **noun** trademark for **DIAZEPAM**.
– ORIGIN 1960s: of unknown origin.

Valkyrie /val'kɪəri, 'valkɪri/ ▶ **noun** Scandinavian Mythology each of Odin's twelve handmaids who conducted the slain warriors of their choice from the battlefield to Valhalla.
– ORIGIN from Old Norse *Valkyrja*, literally 'chooser of the slain', from *valr* 'the slain' + *kyrja* 'chooser'.

Valladolid /ˌvaləd̪ə'liːd, Spanish bajaðo'lið/ **1** a city in northern Spain, capital of Castilla-León region; pop. 345,260 (1991). It was the principal residence of the kings of Castile in the 15th century.
2 former name (until 1828) for **MORELIA**.

vallecula /va'lɛkjʊlə/ ▶ **noun** (pl. **valleculae** /-liː/) Anatomy & Botany a groove or furrow.
– DERIVATIVES **vallecular** adjective.
– ORIGIN mid 19th cent.: from a late Latin variant of Latin *vallicula*, diminutive of Latin *vallis* 'valley'.

Valle d'Aosta /ˌvaleɪ dɑː'ɒstə/ an Alpine region in the north-western corner of Italy; capital, Aosta.

Valletta /və'lɛtə/ the capital and chief port of Malta; pop. 9,240 (1987); urban harbour area pop. 102,000 (1992).
– ORIGIN named after Jean de *Valette*, Grand Master of the Knights of St John, who built the town after the victory over the Turks in 1565.

valley ▶ **noun** (pl. **-eys**) **1** a low area of land between hills or mountains, typically with a river or stream flowing through it.
2 Architecture an internal angle formed by the intersecting planes of a roof, or by the slope of a roof and a wall.
– ORIGIN Middle English: from Old French *valee*, based on Latin *vallis*, *valles*; compare with **VALE**[1].

valley fever (also **San Joaquin valley fever**) ▶ **noun** [mass noun] N. Amer. informal term for **COCCIDIOIDOMYCOSIS**.

Valley Forge the site on the Schuylkill River in Pennsylvania, about 32 km (20 miles) to the north-west of Philadelphia, where George Washington's Continental Army spent the winter of 1777–8 in conditions of extreme hardship.

Valley Girl ▶ **noun** US informal a fashionable and affluent teenage girl from the San Fernando valley in southern California.

Valley of the Kings a valley near ancient Thebes in Egypt where the pharaohs of the New Kingdom (*c*.1550–1070 BC) were buried.

vallum /'valəm/ ▶ **noun** (in ancient Rome) a defensive wall, rampart, or stockade.
– ORIGIN Latin, collective from *vallus* 'stake, palisade'.

Valois[1] /'valwɑː/ **1** a medieval duchy of northern France, home of the Valois dynasty.
2 the French royal house from the accession of Philip VI in 1328 to the death of Henry III (1589).

Valois[2], Dame Ninette de, see **DE VALOIS**.

Valona /va'lona/ Italian name for **VLORË**.

valonia /va'ləʊnɪə/ ▶ **noun** (also **valonia oak**) an evergreen oak tree native to southern Europe and western Asia. See also **ALEPPO GALL**.
• *Quercus macrolepis*, family Fagaceae.
■the acorn cups of this tree, which yield a black dye and are used in tanning.
– ORIGIN early 18th cent.: from Italian *vallonia*, based on Greek *balanos* 'acorn'.

valor ▶ **noun** US spelling of **VALOUR**.

valorize /'valərʌɪz/ (also **-ise**) ▶ **verb** [with obj.] give or ascribe value or validity to (something): *the culture valorizes the individual*.
■raise or fix the price or value of (a commodity or currency) by artificial means, especially by government action.
– DERIVATIVES **valorization** noun.
– ORIGIN 1920s: back-formation from *valorization* (from French *valorisation*, from *valeur* 'value').

valour (US **valor**) ▶ **noun** [mass noun] great courage in the face of danger, especially in battle: *the medals are awarded for acts of valour*.
– DERIVATIVES **valorous** adjective.
– ORIGIN Middle English (denoting worth derived from personal qualities or rank): via Old French from late Latin *valor*, from *valere* 'be strong'.

Valparaíso /ˌvalpə'rʌɪzəʊ, Spanish balpara'iso/ the principal port of Chile, in the centre of the country, near the capital Santiago; pop. 276,740 (1992).

Valpolicella /ˌvalpɒlɪ'tʃɛlə/ ▶ **noun** [mass noun] red Italian wine made in the Val Policella district.

valproic acid /val'prəʊɪk/ ▶ **noun** [mass noun] Chemistry a synthetic crystalline compound with anticonvulsant properties, used (generally as salts) in the treatment of epilepsy.
• Alternative name: **2-propylpentanoic acid**; chem. formula: $C_7H_{15}COOH$.
– DERIVATIVES **valproate** noun.
– ORIGIN 1970s: *valproic* from *valeric* (see **VALERIC ACID**) + *pro(pyl)* + **-IC**.

Valsalva manoeuvre /val'salvə/ ▶ **noun** Medicine the action of attempting to exhale with the nostrils and mouth, or the glottis, closed. This increases pressure in the middle ear and the chest, as when bracing to lift heavy objects, and is used as a means of equalizing pressure in the ears.
– ORIGIN late 19th cent.: named after Antonio M. *Valsalva* (1666–1723), Italian anatomist.

valse /vals, vɔːls/ ▶ **noun** (pl. pronounced same) French term for **WALTZ** (especially as used in the titles of pieces of music).
– ORIGIN late 18th cent.: via French from German *Walzer*.

valuable ▶ **adjective** worth a great deal of money: *a valuable antique*.
■extremely useful or important: *my time is valuable*.
▶ **noun** (usu. **valuables**) a thing that is of great worth, especially a small item of personal property: *put all your valuables in the hotel safe*.
– DERIVATIVES **valuably** adverb.

valuable consideration ▶ **noun** [mass noun] Law legal consideration having some economic value, which is necessary for a contract to be enforceable.

valuation ▶ **noun** an estimation of something's worth, especially one carried out by a professional valuer: *it is wise to obtain an independent valuation*.
■the monetary worth of something, especially as estimated by a valuer.
– DERIVATIVES **valuate** verb chiefly US.

valuator ▶ **noun** archaic a person who makes valuations; a valuer.

value ▶ **noun 1** [mass noun] the regard that something is held to deserve; the importance or preciousness of something: *your support is of great value*.
■the material or monetary worth of something: *prints seldom rise in value* | [count noun] *equipment is included up to a total value of £500*. ■ the worth of something compared to the price paid or asked for it: *at £12.50 the book is* **good value**. ■ the usefulness of something considered in respect of a particular purpose: *some new drugs are of great value in treating cancers*.
2 (**values**) a person's principles or standards of behaviour; one's judgement of what is important in life: *they internalize their parents' rules and values*.
3 the numerical amount denoted by an algebraic term; a magnitude, quantity, or number: *the mean value of x* | *an accurate value for the mass of Venus*.
4 Music the relative duration of the sound signified by a note.
5 Linguistics the meaning of a word or other linguistic unit.
■the quality or tone of a spoken sound; the sound represented by a letter.
6 Art the relative degree of lightness or darkness of a particular colour: *the artist has used adjacent colour values as the landscape recedes*.
▶ **verb** (**values**, **valued**, **valuing**) [with obj.] **1** (often **be valued**) estimate the monetary worth of (something): *his estate was* **valued at** *£45,000*.
2 consider (someone or something) to be important or beneficial; have a high opinion of: *she had come to value her privacy and independence* | [as adj. **valued**] *a valued friend*.
– PHRASES **value for money** Brit. used in reference to something that is well worth the money spent on it: *this camera is really good value for money*.
– ORIGIN Middle English: from Old French, feminine past participle of *valoir* 'be worth', from Latin *valere*.

value added ▶ **noun** [mass noun] Economics the amount by which the value of an article is increased at each stage of its production, exclusive of initial costs.
▶ **adjective** [attrib.] (of goods) having features added to a basic line or model for which the buyer is prepared to pay extra.
■(of a company) offering specialized or extended services in a commercial area.

value added tax (abbrev.: **VAT**) ▶ **noun** [mass noun] a tax on the amount by which the value of an article has been increased at each stage of its production or distribution.

value analysis ▶ **noun** [mass noun] the systematic and critical assessment by an organization of every feature of a product to ensure that its cost is no greater than is necessary to carry out its functions.

V

value engineering ▶ **noun** [mass noun] the modification of designs and systems according to value analysis.

value-free ▶ **adjective** free from criteria imposed by subjective values or standards; purely objective: *real science could and should be value-free.*

value judgement ▶ **noun** an assessment of something as good or bad in terms of one's standards or priorities.

value-laden ▶ **adjective** presupposing the acceptance of a particular set of values: *governments' judgements are value-laden.*

valueless ▶ **adjective** having no value; worthless: *cherished but valueless heirlooms.*
– DERIVATIVES **valuelessness** noun.

value-neutral ▶ **adjective** not presupposing the acceptance of any particular values.

valuer ▶ **noun** chiefly Brit. a person whose job is to estimate or assess the value of something that is to be purchased.

value received ▶ **noun** [mass noun] Finance used on a bill of exchange to indicate that the bill is a means of paying for goods or services to the value of the bill.

valuta /vəˈljuːtə, -ˈluː-/ ▶ **noun** [mass noun] the value of one currency with respect to its exchange rate with another.
■ foreign currency: *these internal flights supply valuta to the cash-starved confederation.*
– ORIGIN late 19th cent.: from Italian, literally 'value'.

valvate /ˈvalveɪt/ ▶ **adjective** Botany (of sepals or other parts) having adjacent edges abutting rather than overlapping. Compare with **IMBRICATE**.
– ORIGIN early 19th cent.: from Latin *valvatus* 'having folding doors', from *valva* 'valve'.

valve ▶ **noun** a device for controlling the passage of fluid through a pipe or duct, especially an automatic device allowing movement in one direction only.
■ Brit. short for **THERMIONIC VALVE**. ■ Music a cylindrical mechanism in a brass instrument which, when depressed or turned, admits air into different sections of tubing and so extends the range of available notes. ■ Anatomy & Zoology a membranous fold in a hollow organ or tubular structure, such as a blood vessel or the digestive tract, which maintains the flow of the contents in one direction by closing in response to any pressure from reverse flow. ■ Zoology each of the halves of the hinged shell of a bivalve mollusc or brachiopod, or of the parts of the compound shell of a barnacle. ■ Botany each of the halves or sections into which a dry fruit (especially a pod or capsule) dehisces.
– DERIVATIVES **valved** adjective [in combination] *a branchiopod has a two-valved outer covering*, **valveless** adjective.
– ORIGIN late Middle English (denoting a leaf of a folding or double door): from Latin *valva*.

valve gear ▶ **noun** the mechanism that controls the opening and closing of the cylinder valves in a steam engine or internal-combustion engine.

valve head ▶ **noun** the part of a vertically opening valve that is lifted off the valve aperture to open the valve.

valvular ▶ **adjective** relating to, having, or acting as a valve or valves: *valvular heart disease | three pairs of valvular apertures.*
– ORIGIN late 18th cent.: from modern Latin *valvula* (diminutive of Latin *valva* 'leaf of a door') + **-AR**[1].

valvulitis /ˌvalvjʊˈlʌɪtɪs/ ▶ **noun** [mass noun] Medicine inflammation of the valves of the heart.

vambrace /ˈvambreɪs/ ▶ **noun** historical a piece of armour for the arm, especially the forearm.
– ORIGIN Middle English: from an Anglo-Norman French shortening of Old French *avantbras*, from *avant* 'before' + *bras* 'arm'. Compare with **VAMPLATE**.

vamoose /vəˈmuːs/ ▶ **verb** [no obj.] informal depart hurriedly: *we'd better vamoose before we're caught.*
– ORIGIN mid 19th cent.: from Spanish *vamos* 'let us go'.

vamp[1] ▶ **noun 1** the upper front part of a boot or shoe.
2 (in jazz and popular music) a short, simple introductory passage, usually repeated several times until otherwise instructed.
▶ **verb 1** [no obj.] repeat a short, simple passage of music: *the band was vamping gently behind his busy lead guitar.*
2 [with obj.] attach a new upper to (a boot or shoe).
■ (**vamp something up**) informal repair or improve something: *the production values have been vamped up.*
– ORIGIN Middle English (denoting the foot of a stocking): shortening of Old French *avantpie*, from *avant* 'before' + *pie* 'foot'. The musical sense of the verb developed from the general sense 'improvise'.

vamp[2] informal ▶ **noun** a woman who uses sexual attraction to exploit men.
▶ **verb** [with obj.] blatantly set out to attract: *she had not vamped him like some wicked Jezebel.*
– DERIVATIVES **vampish** adjective, **vampishly** adverb, **vampy** adjective.
– ORIGIN early 20th cent.: abbreviation of **VAMPIRE**.

vampire /ˈvampʌɪə/ ▶ **noun 1** a corpse supposed, in European folklore, to leave its grave at night to drink the blood of the living by biting their necks with long pointed canine teeth.
■ figurative a person who preys ruthlessly on others: *the protectionist vampires in the Congress.*
2 (also **vampire bat**) a small bat that feeds on the blood of mammals or birds using its two sharp incisor teeth and anticoagulant saliva, found mainly in tropical America. See also **FALSE VAMPIRE**.
● Family Desmodontidae (or Phyllostomidae): three species, in particular the **common vampire** (*Desmodus rotundus*).
3 (also **vampire trap**) Theatre a small spring trapdoor used for sudden disappearances from a stage.
– DERIVATIVES **vampiric** /-ˈpɪrɪk/ adjective.
– ORIGIN mid 18th cent.: from French, from Hungarian *vampir*, perhaps from Turkish *uber* 'witch'.

vampirism /ˈvampʌɪrɪz(ə)m/ ▶ **noun** [mass noun] the action or practices of a vampire.

vamplate /ˈvampleɪt/ ▶ **noun** historical a circular plate on a spear or lance designed to protect the hand.
– ORIGIN Middle English: from Anglo-Norman French *vauntplate*, from *avant* 'before' + *plate* 'thin plate'. Compare with **VAMBRACE**.

van[1] ▶ **noun** a covered motor vehicle, typically without side windows, used for transporting goods or people.
■ Brit. an enclosed railway vehicle for conveying something other than passengers. ■ Brit. a caravan.
– ORIGIN early 19th cent.: shortening of **CARAVAN**.

van[2] ▶ **noun** (**the van**) the foremost part of a company of people moving or preparing to move forwards, especially the foremost division of an advancing military force: *in the van were the foremost chiefs and some of the warriors astride horses.*
■ figurative the forefront: *he was in the van of the movement to encourage the cultivation of wild flowers.*
– ORIGIN early 17th cent.: abbreviation of **VANGUARD**.

van[3] ▶ **noun 1** archaic a winnowing fan.
2 archaic or poetic/literary a bird's wing.
– ORIGIN late Middle English: dialect variant of **FAN**[1], probably reinforced by Old French *van* or Latin *vannus*.

van[4] ▶ **noun** Tennis, Brit. informal term for **ADVANTAGE**.
– ORIGIN 1920s: abbreviation.

Van, Lake /van/ a large salt lake in the mountains of eastern Turkey.

vanadate /ˈvanədeɪt/ ▶ **noun** Chemistry a salt in which the anion contains both vanadium and oxygen, especially one of the anion VO_4^{3-}.
– ORIGIN mid 19th cent.: from **VANADIUM** + **-ATE**[1].

vanadinite /vəˈnadɪnʌɪt/ ▶ **noun** [mass noun] a rare reddish-brown mineral consisting of a vanadate and chloride of lead, typically occurring as an oxidation product of lead ores.
– ORIGIN mid 19th cent.: from **VANADIUM** + **-ITE**[1].

vanadium /vəˈneɪdɪəm/ ▶ **noun** [mass noun] the chemical element of atomic number 23, a hard grey metal of the transition series, used to make alloy steels. (Symbol: **V**)
– ORIGIN mid 19th cent.: modern Latin, from Old Norse *Vanadis* (a name of the Scandinavian goddess Freyja).

Van Allen /van ˈalən/, James Alfred (b.1914), American physicist. He used balloons and rockets to study cosmic radiation in the upper atmosphere, showing that specific zones of high radiation were the result of charged particles from the solar wind being trapped in two belts around the earth.

Van Allen belt ▶ **noun** each of two regions of intense radiation partly surrounding the earth at heights of several thousand kilometres.

vanaspati /vəˈnʌspəˌtiː/ ▶ **noun** [mass noun] a type of thick vegetable oil used in India.
– ORIGIN from Sanskrit *vanas-pati*, literally 'lord of the wood, lord of plants'.

Vanbrugh /ˈvanbrə/, Sir John (1664–1726), English architect and dramatist. His comedies include *The Relapse* (1696) and *The Provok'd Wife* (1697); among his architectural works are Castle Howard in Yorkshire (1702) and Blenheim Palace in Oxfordshire (1705), both produced in collaboration with Nicholas Hawksmoor.

Van Buren /van ˈbjʊərən/, Martin (1782–1862), American Democratic statesman, 8th President of the US 1837–41.

vancomycin /ˌvaŋkəˈmʌɪsɪn/ ▶ **noun** [mass noun] Medicine a bacterial antibiotic used against resistant strains of streptococcus and staphylococcus.
● This antibiotic is obtained from the bacterium *Streptomyces orientalis*.
– ORIGIN 1950s: from *vanco-* (of unknown origin) + **-MYCIN**.

Vancouver[1] /vanˈkuːvə/ a city and port in British Columbia, SW Canada, situated on the mainland opposite Vancouver Island; pop. 471,840 (1991); metropolitan area pop. 1,602,500. It is the largest city in western Canada and its chief Pacific port.

Vancouver[2] /vanˈkuːvə/, George (1757–98), English navigator. He led an exploration of the coasts of Australia, New Zealand, and Hawaii (1791–2), and later charted much of the west coast of North America between southern Alaska and California.

Vancouver Island a large island off the Pacific coast of Canada, in SW British Columbia. Its capital, Victoria, is the capital of British Columbia. It became a British Crown Colony in 1849, later uniting with British Columbia to join the Dominion of Canada.

V. & A. ▶ **abbreviation for** Victoria and Albert Museum.

Vanda /ˈvanda/ Swedish name for **VANTAA**.

vandal ▶ **noun 1** a person who deliberately destroys or damages public or private property: *the rear window of the car was smashed by vandals.*
2 (**Vandal**) a member of a Germanic people that ravaged Gaul, Spain, Rome (455), and North Africa in the 4th–5th centuries.
– ORIGIN from Latin *Vandalus*, of Germanic origin. Sense 1 dates from the mid 17th cent.

vandalism ▶ **noun** [mass noun] action involving deliberate destruction of or damage to public or private property.
– DERIVATIVES **vandalistic** adjective, **vandalistically** adverb.

vandalize (also **-ise**) ▶ **verb** [with obj.] deliberately destroy or damage (public or private property): *stations have been wrecked and vandalized beyond recognition.*

van de Graaff generator /ˌvan də ˈɡrɑːf/ ▶ **noun** Physics a machine devised to generate electrostatic charge by means of a vertical endless belt collecting charge from a voltage source and transferring it to a large insulated metal dome, where a high voltage is produced.
– ORIGIN mid 20th cent.: named after Robert Jemison *Van de Graaf* (1901–67), American physicist.

Vanderbijlpark /ˈvandəbʌɪlˌpɑːk/ a steel-manufacturing city in South Africa, in the province of Gauteng, south of Johannesburg; pop. 540,140 (1985) (with Vereeniging).

Vanderbilt /ˈvandəbɪlt/, Cornelius (1794–1877), American businessman and philanthropist. He amassed a fortune from shipping and railroads, and made an endowment to found Vanderbilt University in Nashville, Tennessee (1873).

Van der Hum /ˌvan də ˈhʌm/ ▶ **noun** [mass noun] a South African brandy-based liqueur made with naartjies.
– ORIGIN perhaps from a personal name.

Van der Post /ˌvan də ˈpɒst/, Sir Laurens (Jan) (1906–96), South African explorer and writer. His books, including *Venture to the Interior* (1952) and *The Lost World of the Kalahari* (1958), combine travel writing and descriptions of fauna with philosophical speculation.

van der Waals forces /ˌvan də ˈwɑːlz, ˈvɑːlz/ ▶ **plural noun** Chemistry weak, short-range electrostatic attractive forces between uncharged molecules,

arising from the interaction of permanent or transient electric dipole moments.
– ORIGIN late 19th cent.: named after Johannes *van der Waals* (1837–1923), Dutch physicist.

van de Velde[1] /ˌvan də ˈvɛldə/ the name of a family of Dutch painters:
■ **Willem** (1611–93); known as **Willem van de Velde the Elder**. He painted marine subjects and was official artist to the Dutch fleet. He also worked for Charles II.
■ **Willem** (1633–1707), son of Willem the Elder; known as **Willem van de Velde the Younger**. He was also a notable marine artist who painted for Charles II.
■ **Adriaen** (1636–72); son of Willem the Elder. He painted landscapes, portraits, and biblical and genre scenes.

van de Velde[2] /ˌvan də ˈvɛldə/, Henri (Clemens) (1863–1957), Belgian architect, designer, and teacher, who pioneered the development of art nouveau design and architecture in Europe. His buildings include the Werkbund Theatre in Cologne (1914).

Van Diemen's Land /van ˈdiːmənz/ former name (until 1855) for TASMANIA.

Van Dyck /van ˈdʌɪk/ (also **Vandyke**), Sir Anthony (1599–1641), Flemish painter. He is famous for his portraits of members of the English court, which determined the course of portraiture in England for more than 200 years.

Vandyke /vanˈdʌɪk/ (also **vandyke**) ▶ noun **1** a broad lace or linen collar with an edge deeply cut into large points (in imitation of a style frequently depicted in portraits by Sir Anthony Van Dyck), fashionable in the 18th century.
■ each of a number of large deep-cut points on the border or fringe of a garment or piece of material.
2 (also **Vandyke beard**) a neat, pointed beard.
▶ adjective [attrib.] denoting a style of garment or decorative design associated with the portraits of Van Dyck: *a Vandyke handkerchief.*

Vandyke brown ▶ noun [mass noun] a deep rich brown.

vane ▶ noun a broad blade attached to a rotating axis or wheel which pushes or is pushed by wind or water and forms part of a machine or device such as a windmill, propeller, or turbine.
■ short for WEATHERVANE. ■ the flat part on either side of the shaft of a feather. ■ a broad, flat projecting surface designed to guide the motion of a projectile, such as a feather on an arrow or a fin on a torpedo.
– DERIVATIVES **vaned** adjective [usu. in combination] *a three-vaned windmill.*
– ORIGIN late Middle English: dialect variant of obsolete *fane* 'banner', of Germanic origin.

Vänern /ˈvɛːnən/ a lake in SW Sweden, the largest lake in Sweden and the third largest in Europe.

vanessid /vəˈnɛsɪd/ ▶ noun Entomology a butterfly of a group that includes many of the better known kinds found in temperate regions. Compare with NYMPHALID.
● Subfamily Nymphalinae, family Nymphalidae (formerly the family Vanessidae).
– ORIGIN early 20th cent.: from modern Latin *Vanessidae*, from *Vanessa* (female given name adopted as a genus name).

Van Eyck /van ˈʌɪk/, Jan (c.1370–1441), Flemish painter. He made innovative use of oils, bringing greater flexibility, richer and denser colour, and a wider range from light to dark. Notable works: *The Adoration of the Lamb* (known as the Ghent Altarpiece, 1432) in the church of St Bavon in Ghent and *The Arnolfini Marriage* (1434).

vang /vaŋ/ ▶ noun Sailing each of two guy ropes running from the end of a gaff to the deck.
■ (also **boom vang**) a fitting used to pull a boat's boom down and help control the shape of the sail.
– ORIGIN mid 18th cent.: variant of obsolete *fang*, denoting a gripping device, from Old Norse *fang* 'grasp', of Germanic origin.

vanga /ˈvaŋɡə/ (also **vanga shrike**) ▶ noun a shrike-like songbird found in Madagascar.
● Family Vangidae: several genera and species.
– ORIGIN mid 19th cent.: modern Latin (genus name), from Latin, literally 'mattock' (because of the shape of the bill).

Van Gogh /van ˈɡɒx, ˈɡɒf/, Vincent (Willem) (1853–90), Dutch painter. He is best known for his post-Impressionist work, influenced by contact with Impressionist painting and Japanese woodcuts after he moved to Paris in 1886. His most famous

pictures include several studies of sunflowers and *A Starry Night* (1889). Suffering from severe depression, he cut off part of his own ear and eventually committed suicide.

vanguard ▶ noun a group of people leading the way in new developments or ideas: *the experimental spirit of the modernist vanguard.*
■ a position at the forefront of new developments or ideas: *the prototype was in the vanguard of technical development.* ■ the foremost part of an advancing army or naval force.
– ORIGIN late Middle English (denoting the foremost part of an army): shortening of Old French *avan(t)garde*, from *avant* 'before' + *garde* 'guard'.

vanilla ▶ noun **1** [mass noun] a substance obtained from vanilla pods or produced artificially and used to flavour sweet foods or to impart a fragrant scent to cosmetic preparations: [as modifier] *vanilla ice cream.*
■ ice cream flavoured with vanilla: *four scoops of vanilla with hot fudge sauce.* ■ [as modifier] of the colour of vanilla ice cream: *a vanilla dress.*
2 a tropical climbing orchid which has fragrant flowers and long pod-like fruit.
● Genus *Vanilla*, family Orchidaceae: many species, in particular *V. planifolia*, the chief commercial source of vanilla pods.
■ (also **vanilla pod**) the fruit of this plant which is cured and then either used in cookery or processed to extract an essence which is used for flavour and fragrance.
▶ adjective (also **plain vanilla**) having no special or extra features; ordinary: *it will be able to do tricks that plain vanilla CD-ROMs can't.*
– ORIGIN mid 17th cent.: from Spanish *vainilla* 'pod', diminutive of *vaina* 'sheath, pod', from Latin *vagina* 'sheath'. The spelling change was due to association with French *vanille*.

vanillin ▶ noun [mass noun] Chemistry a fragrant compound which is the essential constituent of vanilla.
● Alternative name: **3-methoxy-4-hydroxybenzaldehyde**; chem. formula: $CH_3OC_6H_3(OH)CHO$.
– ORIGIN mid 19th cent.; from VANILLA + -IN[1].

vanish ▶ verb [no obj.] **1** disappear suddenly and completely: *Moira vanished without trace.*
■ gradually cease to exist: *the environment is under threat—hedgerows and woodlands are vanishing.*
2 Mathematics become zero.
– ORIGIN Middle English: shortening of Old French *e(s)vaniss-*, lengthened stem of *e(s)vanir*, from Latin *evanescere* 'die away'.

vanishing cream ▶ noun [mass noun] dated a cream or ointment that leaves no visible trace when rubbed into the skin.

vanishingly ▶ adverb [as submodifier] in such a manner or to such a degree as almost to become invisible, non-existent, or negligible: *an event of vanishingly small probability.*

vanishing point ▶ noun **1** the point at which receding parallel lines viewed in perspective appear to converge.
2 [in sing.] the point at which something that has been growing smaller or increasingly faint disappears altogether: *rates of interest dwindled to vanishing point.*

vanitas /ˈvanɪtɑːs/ ▶ noun a still-life painting of a 17th-century Dutch genre containing symbols of death or change as a reminder of their inevitability.
– ORIGIN Latin, literally 'vanity'.

Vanitory unit /ˈvanɪt(ə)ri/ ▶ noun trademark a vanity unit.
– ORIGIN 1950s: *Vanitory* from VANITY, on the pattern of *lavatory*.

vanity ▶ noun (pl. **-ies**) **1** [mass noun] excessive pride in or admiration of one's own appearance or achievements: *it flattered his vanity to think I was in love with him* | [count noun] *the personal vanities and ambitions of politicians.*
■ [as modifier] denoting a person or company publishing works at the author's expense: *a vanity press.*
2 [mass noun] the quality of being worthless or futile: *the vanity of human wishes.*
3 N. Amer. a dressing table.
– ORIGIN Middle English: from Old French *vanite*, from Latin *vanitas*, from *vanus* 'empty' (see VAIN).

vanity case ▶ noun a small case fitted with a mirror and compartments for make-up.

Vanity Fair the world regarded as a place of

frivolity and idle amusement (originally with reference to Bunyan's *Pilgrim's Progress*).

vanity mirror ▶ noun a small mirror used for applying make-up, especially one fitted in a motor vehicle.

vanity plate ▶ noun N. Amer. a vehicle licence plate bearing a distinctive or personalized combination of letters, numbers, or both.

vanity table ▶ noun a dressing table.

vanity unit ▶ noun a unit consisting of a washbasin set into a flat top with cupboards beneath.

van Leyden, Lucas, see LUCAS VAN LEYDEN.

vanquish /ˈvaŋkwɪʃ/ ▶ verb [with obj.] defeat thoroughly: *he successfully vanquished his rival.*
– DERIVATIVES **vanquishable** adjective, **vanquisher** noun.
– ORIGIN Middle English: from Old French *vencus*, *venquis* (past participle and past tense of *veintre*), *vainquiss-* (lengthened stem of *vainquir*), from Latin *vincere* 'conquer'.

Vantaa /ˈvantɑː/ a city in southern Finland; pop. 154,930 (1990). Swedish name VANDA.

vantage /ˈvɑːntɪdʒ/ (usu. **vantage point**) ▶ noun a place or position affording a good view of something: *from my vantage point I could see into the front garden* | figurative *the past is continuously reinterpreted from the vantage point of the present.*
– ORIGIN Middle English: from Anglo-Norman French, shortening of Old French *avantage* 'advantage'.

Vanuatu /ˌvanuːˈɑːtuː/ a country consisting of a group of islands in the SW Pacific; pop. 156,000 (est. 1991); official languages, Bislama, English, and French; capital, Vila. The islands were administered jointly by Britain and France as the condominium of the New Hebrides. Vanuatu became an independent republic within the Commonwealth in 1980.
– DERIVATIVES **Vanuatuan** adjective & noun.

vapid /ˈvapɪd/ ▶ adjective offering nothing that is stimulating or challenging: *tuneful but vapid musical comedies.*
– DERIVATIVES **vapidity** noun, **vapidly** adverb.
– ORIGIN mid 17th cent. (used originally in description of drinks as 'lacking in flavour'): from Latin *vapidus*.

vapor ▶ noun US spelling of VAPOUR.

vaporetto /ˌvapəˈrɛtəʊ/ ▶ noun (pl. **vaporetti** /-ti/ or **vaporettos**) (in Venice) a canal boat (originally a steamboat, now a motor boat) used for public transport.
– ORIGIN Italian, diminutive of *vapore* 'steam', from Latin *vapor*.

vaporize (also **-ise**) ▶ verb convert or be converted into vapour: [with obj.] *there is a large current which is sufficient to vaporize carbon* | [no obj.] *cold gasoline does not vaporize readily.*
– DERIVATIVES **vaporable** adjective, **vaporizable** adjective, **vaporization** noun.

vaporizer ▶ noun a device that generates a particular substance in the form of vapour, especially for medicinal inhalation.

vapour (US **vapor**) ▶ noun [mass noun] a substance diffused or suspended in the air, especially one normally liquid or solid: *dense clouds of smoke and toxic vapour* | [count noun] *petrol vapours.*
■ [count noun] Physics a gaseous substance that is below its critical temperature, and can therefore be liquefied by pressure alone. Compare with GAS. ■ (**the vapours**) dated a sudden feeling of faintness or nervousness or a state of depression.
▶ verb [no obj.] talk in a vacuous, boasting, or pompous way: *he was vapouring on about the days of his youth.*
– DERIVATIVES **vaporous** adjective, **vaporousness** noun, **vapourish** adjective (archaic), **vapoury** adjective.
– ORIGIN late Middle English: from Old French, or from Latin *vapor* 'steam, heat'. The current verb sense dates from the early 17th cent.

vapour barrier ▶ noun a thin layer of impermeable material, typically polythene sheeting, included in building construction to prevent moisture from damaging the fabric of the building.

vapour density ▶ noun Chemistry the density of a particular gas or vapour relative to that of hydrogen at the same pressure and temperature.

vapourer (also **vapourer moth**) ▶ noun a day-flying

tussock moth, the female of which is wingless and lays eggs on the cocoon from which she emerged.
• Genus *Orgyia*, family Lymantriidae: several species, in particular *O. antiqua*, which is often seen in towns.

vapour lock ▶ **noun** an interruption in the flow of a liquid through a fuel line or other pipe as a result of vaporization of the liquid.

vapour pressure ▶ **noun** Chemistry the pressure of a vapour in contact with its liquid or solid form.

vapour trail ▶ **noun** a trail of condensed water from an aircraft or rocket at high altitude, seen as a white streak against the sky.

vapourware (US **vaporware**) ▶ **noun** [mass noun] Computing, informal software or hardware that has been advertised but is not yet available to buy, either because it is only a concept or because it is still being written or designed.

vaquero /və'kɛːrəʊ/ ▶ **noun** (pl. **-os**) (in Spanish-speaking parts of the USA) a cowboy; a cattle driver.
– ORIGIN Spanish, from *vaca* 'cow'.

VAR ▶ **abbreviation for** value-added reseller, a company that adds extra features to products it has bought before selling them on. ■ value at risk, a method of quantifying the risk of holding a financial asset.

var. ▶ **abbreviation for** variety.

varactor /və'raktə/ ▶ **noun** a semiconductor diode with a capacitance dependent on the applied voltage.
– ORIGIN 1950s: from elements of *variable reactor*.

Varah /'vɑːrə/, (Edward) Chad (b.1911), English clergyman, founder of the Samaritans.

Varanasi /və'rɑːnəsi/ a city on the Ganges, in Uttar Pradesh, northern India; pop. 926,000 (1991). It is a holy city and a place of pilgrimage for Hindus, who undergo ritual purification in the Ganges. Former name **BENARES**.

Varangian /və'randʒɪən/ ▶ **noun** any of the Scandinavian voyagers who travelled by land and up rivers into Russia in the 9th and 10th centuries AD, establishing the Rurik dynasty and gaining great influence in the Byzantine Empire.
– ORIGIN from medieval Latin *Varangus* (a name ultimately from Old Norse, probably based on *vár* 'pledge') + **-IAN**.

Varangian guard the bodyguard of the later Byzantine emperors, comprising Varangians and later also Anglo-Saxons.

vardo /'vɑːdəʊ/ (also **varda** /'vɑːdə/) ▶ **noun** (pl. **vardos** or **vardas**) a gypsy caravan.
– ORIGIN early 19th cent.: from Romany.

varec /'varɛk/ ▶ **noun** [mass noun] seaweed, especially kelp.
– ORIGIN late 17th cent.: from French *varec(h)*, from Old Norse; related to **WRECK**.

Varese /və'reɪzeɪ, -zi/ a town in Lombardy, northern Italy; pop. 87,970 (1990).

Varèse /va'rɛz/, Edgar(d) (1883–1965), French-born American composer. His music explored dissonance, unusual orchestration, and (from the 1950s) tape-recording and electronic instruments.

Vargas /'vɑːgəs/, Getúlio Dornelles (1883–1954), Brazilian statesman, President 1930–45 and 1951–4. After seizing power he ruled as a virtual dictator until overthrown by a coup. Returned to power after elections in 1951, he later committed suicide after widespread calls for his resignation.

Vargas Llosa /ˌvɑːgəs 'ljəʊsə, 'jəʊsə/, (Jorge) Mario (Pedro) (b.1936), Peruvian novelist, dramatist, and essayist. Novels include *Aunt Julia and the Scriptwriter* (1977) and *The War of the End of the World* (1982).

variable ▶ **adjective** **1** not consistent or having a fixed pattern; liable to change: *the quality of hospital food is highly variable | awards can be for highly variable amounts.*
■ (of a wind) tending to change direction. ■ Mathematics (of a quantity) able to assume different numerical values. ■ Botany & Zoology (of a species) liable to deviate from the typical colour or form, or to occur in different colours or forms.
2 able to be changed or adapted: *the drill has variable speed.*
■ (of a gear) designed to give varying ratios or speeds.
▶ **noun** an element, feature, or factor that is liable to vary or change: *there are too many variables involved to make any meaningful predictions.*
■ Mathematics a quantity which during a calculation is assumed to vary or be capable of varying in value. ■ Computing a data item that may take on more than one value during or between programs. ■ Astronomy short for **VARIABLE STAR**. ■ (**variables**) the region of light, variable winds to the north of the NE trade winds or (in the southern hemisphere) between the SE trade winds and the westerlies.
– DERIVATIVES **variability** noun, **variableness** noun, **variably** adverb.
– ORIGIN late Middle English: via Old French from Latin *variabilis*, from *variare* (see **VARY**).

variable cost ▶ **noun** a cost that varies with the level of output.

variable-geometry ▶ **adjective** denoting a swing-wing aircraft.

variable star ▶ **noun** Astronomy a star whose brightness changes, either irregularly or regularly.

variance ▶ **noun** [mass noun] the fact or quality of being different, divergent, or inconsistent: *her light tone was* ***at variance with*** *her sudden trembling.*
■ the state or fact of disagreeing or quarrelling: *they were* ***at variance with*** *all their previous allies.* ■ chiefly Law a discrepancy between two statements or documents. ■ US Law an official dispensation from a rule or regulation, typically a building regulation. ■ Statistics a quantity equal to the square of the standard deviation.
– ORIGIN Middle English: via Old French from Latin *variantia* 'difference', from the verb *variare* (see **VARY**).

variant ▶ **noun** a form or version of something that differs in some respect from other forms of the same thing or from a standard: *clinically distinct variants of malaria |* [as modifier] *a variant spelling.*
– ORIGIN late Middle English (as an adjective in the sense 'tending to vary'): from Old French, literally 'varying', present participle of *varier* (see **VARY**). The noun dates from the mid 19th cent.

variate /'vɛːrɪət/ ▶ **noun** Statistics a quantity having a numerical value for each member of a group, especially one whose values occur according to a frequency distribution.
– ORIGIN late 19th cent.: from Latin *variatus* 'diversified', past participle of *variare* (see **VARY**).

variation ▶ **noun** **1** a change or slight difference in condition, amount, or level, typically with certain limits: *regional variations in house prices |* [mass noun] *the figures showed marked variation from year to year.*
■ Astronomy a deviation of a celestial body from its mean orbit or motion. ■ Mathematics a change in the value of a function due to small changes in the values of its argument or arguments. ■ (also **magnetic variation**) the angular difference between true north and magnetic north at a particular place. ■ [mass noun] Biology the occurrence of an organism in more than one distinct colour or form.
2 a different or distinct form or version of something: *hurling is an Irish variation of hockey.*
■ Music a version of a theme, modified in melody, rhythm, harmony, or ornamentation, so as to present it in a new but still recognizable form: *Elgar's Enigma Variations |* figurative ***variations on*** *the perennial theme of marital discord.* ■ Ballet a solo dance as part of a performance.
– DERIVATIVES **variational** adjective.
– ORIGIN late Middle English (denoting variance or conflict): from Old French, or from Latin *variatio(n-)*, from the verb *variare* (see **VARY**).

variationist ▶ **noun** a person who studies variations in usage among different speakers of the same language.

variceal /ˌvarɪ'siːəl/ ▶ **adjective** Zoology & Medicine of, relating to, or involving a varix.
– ORIGIN 1960s: from Latin *varix*, *varic-*, on the pattern of words such as *corneal* and *laryngeal*.

varicella /ˌvarɪ'sɛlə/ ▶ **noun** [mass noun] Medicine technical term for **CHICKENPOX**.
■ (also **varicella-zoster**) a herpesvirus that causes chickenpox and shingles; herpes zoster.
– ORIGIN late 18th cent.: modern Latin, irregular diminutive of **VARIOLA**.

varices plural form of **VARIX**.

varicocele /'varɪkə(ʊ)ˌsiːl/ ▶ **noun** Medicine a mass of varicose veins in the spermatic cord.
– ORIGIN mid 18th cent.: from Latin *varix*, *varic-* 'dilated vein' + **-CELE**.

varicoloured /'vɛːrɪˌkʌləd/ (US **varicolored**) ▶ **adjective** consisting of several different colours.
– ORIGIN mid 17th cent.: from Latin *varius* 'diverse' + **COLOURED**.

varicose /'varɪkəʊs, -kəs, -z/ ▶ **adjective** [attrib.] affected by a condition causing the swelling and tortuous lengthening of veins, most often in the legs: *varicose veins.*
– DERIVATIVES **varicosed** adjective, **varicosity** noun.
– ORIGIN late Middle English: from Latin *varicosus*, from *varix* (see **VARIX**).

varied ▶ **adjective** incorporating a number of different types or elements; showing variation or variety: *the phenomena were very varied | a long and varied career.*
– DERIVATIVES **variedly** adverb.

variegated /'vɛːrɪgeɪtɪd, 'vɛːrɪə-/ ▶ **adjective** exhibiting different colours, especially as irregular patches or streaks: *variegated yellow bricks.*
■ Botany (of a plant or foliage) having or consisting of leaves that are edged or patterned in a second colour, especially white as well as green. ■ marked by variety: *his variegated and amusing observations.*
– DERIVATIVES **variegation** /-'geɪʃ(ə)n/ noun.
– ORIGIN mid 17th cent.: from Latin *variegat-* 'made varied' (from the verb *variegare*, from *varius* 'diverse') + **-ED**[2].

varietal /və'rʌɪət(ə)l/ ▶ **adjective** **1** (of a wine or grape) made from or belonging to a single specified variety of grape.
2 chiefly Botany & Zoology of, relating to, characteristic of, or forming a variety: *varietal names.*
▶ **noun** a varietal wine.
– DERIVATIVES **varietally** adverb.

varietist /və'rʌɪətɪst/ ▶ **noun** dated a person who enjoys sexual variety.

variety ▶ **noun** (pl. **-ies**) **1** [mass noun] the quality or state of being different or diverse; the absence of uniformity, sameness, or monotony: *it's the variety that makes my job so enjoyable.*
■ (**a variety of**) a number or range of things of the same general class that are different or distinct in character or quality: *the centre offers a variety of leisure activities.* ■ [count noun] a thing which differs in some way from others of the same general class or sort; a type: *fifty varieties of fresh and frozen pasta.* ■ a form of television or theatre entertainment consisting of a series of different types of act, such as singing, dancing, and comedy: [as modifier] *a variety show.*
2 Biology a taxonomic category that ranks below subspecies (where present) or species, its members differing from others of the same subspecies or species in minor but permanent or heritable characteristics. Varieties are more often recognized in botany, in which they are designated in the style *Apium graveolens* var. *dulce*. Compare with **FORM** (in sense 3) and **SUBSPECIES**.
■ a cultivated form of a plant. See **CULTIVAR**. ■ a plant or animal which varies in some trivial respect from its immediate parent or type.
– PHRASES **variety is the spice of life** proverb new and exciting experiences make life more interesting.
– ORIGIN late 15th cent.: from French *variété* or Latin *varietas*, from *varius* (see **VARIOUS**).

variety meats ▶ **plural noun** N. Amer. offal.

variety store ▶ **noun** N. Amer. a small shop selling a wide range of inexpensive items.

varifocal /ˌvɛːrɪ'fəʊk(ə)l/ ▶ **adjective** denoting a lens that allows an infinite number of focusing distances for near, intermediate, and far vision.
▶ **noun** (**varifocals**) varifocal glasses.

variform /'vɛːrɪfɔːm/ ▶ **adjective** (of a group of things) differing from one another in form: *variform languages.*
■ (of a single thing or a mass) consisting of a variety of forms or things: *a variform education.*
– ORIGIN mid 17th cent.: from Latin *varius* 'diverse' + **-FORM**.

varimax /'vɛːrɪmaks/ ▶ **noun** [mass noun] Statistics a method of factor analysis in which uncorrelated factors are sought by a rotation that maximizes the variance of the factor loadings.
– ORIGIN 1950s: blend of **VARIANCE** and **MAXIMUM**.

variola /və'rʌɪələ/ ▶ **noun** Medicine technical term for **SMALLPOX**.
– DERIVATIVES **variolar** adjective, **variolous** adjective (archaic).
– ORIGIN late 18th cent.: from medieval Latin, literally 'pustule, pock', from Latin *varius* 'diverse'.

varioloid /'vɛːrɪəlɔɪd/ Medicine ▶ **adjective** resembling smallpox.
▶ **noun** [mass noun] a mild form of smallpox affecting people who have already had the disease or have been vaccinated against it.

b **b**ut | d **d**og | f **f**ew | g **g**et | h **h**e | j **y**es | k **c**at | l **l**eg | m **m**an | n **n**o | p **p**en | r **r**ed | s **s**it | t **t**op | v **v**oice | w **w**e | z **z**oo | ʃ **sh**e | ʒ deci**s**ion | θ **th**in | ð **th**is | ŋ ri**ng** | x lo**ch** | tʃ **ch**ip | dʒ **j**ar

variometer /ˌvɛːrɪˈɒmɪtə/ ▶ **noun 1** a device for indicating an aircraft's rate of climb or descent.
2 an inductor whose total inductance can be varied by altering the relative position of two coaxial coils connected in series, or by permeability tuning, and so usable to tune an electric circuit.
3 an instrument for measuring variations in the intensity of the earth's magnetic field.

variorum /ˌvɛːrɪˈɔːrəm/ ▶ **adjective** (of an edition of an author's works) having notes by various editors or commentators.
▪including variant readings from manuscripts or earlier editions.
▶ **noun** a variorum edition.
– ORIGIN early 18th cent.: genitive plural of *varius* 'diverse', from Latin *editio cum notis variorum* 'edition with notes by various (commentators)'.

various ▶ **adjective** different from one another; of different kinds or sorts: *dresses of various colours* | *his grievances were many and various.*
▪having or showing different properties or qualities: *their environments are locally various.*
▶ **determiner & pronoun** more than one; individual and separate: [as determiner] *various people arrived late* | [as pronoun] ***various of*** *her friends had called.*
– DERIVATIVES **variousness** noun.
– ORIGIN late Middle English: from Latin *varius* 'changing, diverse' + **-OUS**.

USAGE In standard English the word **various** is normally used as an adjective and determiner. It is sometimes also used as a pronoun followed by **of**, as in ***various of*** *her friends had called.* Although this pronoun use is similar to that of words such as **several** and **many** (e.g. ***several of*** *her friends had called*), it is sometimes regarded as incorrect.

variously ▶ **adverb** in several or different ways: *his early successes can be variously accounted for.*

Variscan /vəˈrɪsk(ə)n/ ▶ **adjective** Geology another term for **HERCYNIAN**.
– ORIGIN early 20th cent.: from Latin *Varisci* (the name of a Germanic tribe) + **-AN**.

varistor /vɛːˈrɪstə, və-/ ▶ **noun** a semiconductor diode with resistance dependent on the applied voltage.
– ORIGIN 1930s: contraction of *varying resistor.*

varix /ˈvɛːrɪks/ ▶ **noun** (pl. **varices** /ˈvarɪsiːz/) **1** Medicine a varicose vein.
2 Zoology each of the ridges on the shell of a gastropod mollusc, marking a former position of the aperture.
– ORIGIN late Middle English: from Latin.

varlet /ˈvɑːlɪt/ ▶ **noun** historical a man or boy acting as an attendant or servant.
▪archaic an unprincipled rogue or rascal.
– DERIVATIVES **varletry** noun.
– ORIGIN late Middle English: from Old French, variant of *valet* 'attendant' (see **VALET**). The sense 'rogue' dates from the mid 16th cent.

varmint /ˈvɑːmɪnt/ ▶ **noun** N. Amer. or dialect, informal a troublesome wild animal, especially a fox.
▪a troublesome and mischievous person, especially a child.
– ORIGIN mid 16th cent.: alteration of **VERMIN**.

Varna /ˈvɑːnə/ a port and resort in eastern Bulgaria, on the western shores of the Black Sea; pop. 320,640 (1990).

varna /ˈvɑːnə/ ▶ **noun** each of the four Hindu castes, Brahman, Kshatriya, Vaisya, and Sudra.
– ORIGIN Sanskrit, literally 'colour, class'.

varnish ▶ **noun** [mass noun] resin dissolved in a liquid for applying on wood, metal, or other materials to form a hard, clear, shiny surface when dry.
▪short for **NAIL VARNISH**. ▪[in sing.] archaic an external or superficially attractive appearance of a specific quality: *an outward varnish of civilization.*
▶ **verb** [with obj.] apply varnish to: *we stripped the floor and varnished it* | [with obj. and complement] *her toenails were varnished red.*
– DERIVATIVES **varnisher** noun.
– ORIGIN Middle English: from Old French *vernis*, from medieval Latin *veronix* 'fragrant resin, sandarac' or medieval Greek *berenikē*, probably from *Berenice*, a town in Cyrenaica.

Varro /ˈvarəʊ/, Marcus Terentius (116–27 BC), Roman scholar and satirist. His works covered many subjects, including philosophy, agriculture, the Latin language, and education.

varroa /ˈvarəʊə/ (also **varroa mite**) ▶ **noun** a microscopic mite which is a debilitating parasite of the honeybee, causing loss of honey production.
• *Varroa jacobsoni*, order (or subclass) Acari.
– ORIGIN 1970s: modern Latin, from **VARRO** (with reference to his work on bee-keeping) + **-A**[1].

varsity ▶ **noun** (pl. **-ies**) Brit. dated or S. African university: *he had his hair cut as soon as he got back from varsity.*
▪[as modifier] Brit. (especially of a sporting event or team) of or relating to a university, especially Oxford or Cambridge: *a varsity match.* ▪chiefly N. Amer. a sports team representing a university or college.
– ORIGIN mid 17th cent.: shortening of **UNIVERSITY**, reflecting an archaic pronunciation.

Varuna /ˈvʌrʊnə/ Hinduism one of the gods in the Rig Veda. Originally the sovereign lord of the universe and guardian of cosmic law, he is known in later Hinduism as god of the waters.

varus /ˈvɛːrəs/ ▶ **noun** [mass noun] Medicine a deformity involving oblique displacement of part of a limb towards the midline. The opposite of **VALGUS**.
– ORIGIN early 19th cent.: from Latin, literally 'bent, crooked'.

varve /vɑːv/ ▶ **noun** Geology a pair of thin layers of clay and silt of contrasting colour and texture which represent the deposit of a single year (summer and winter) in a lake. Such layers can be measured to determine the chronology of glacial sediments.
– DERIVATIVES **varved** adjective.
– ORIGIN early 20th cent.: from Swedish *varv* 'layer'.

vary ▶ **verb (-ies, -ied)** [no obj.] differ in size, amount, degree, or nature from something else of the same general class: *the properties* ***vary in*** *price* | [as adj. **varying**] *varying degrees of success.*
▪change from one condition, form, or state to another: *your skin's moisture content varies according to climatic conditions.* ▪[with obj.] introduce modifications or changes into (something) so as to make it different or less uniform: *he tried to vary his diet.*
– DERIVATIVES **varyingly** adverb.
– ORIGIN Middle English: from Old French *varier* or Latin *variare*, from *varius* 'diverse' .

vas /vas/ ▶ **noun** (pl. **vasa** /ˈveɪsə/) Anatomy a vessel or duct.
– DERIVATIVES **vasal** /ˈveɪs(ə)l/ adjective.
– ORIGIN late 16th cent.: from Latin, literally 'vessel'.

Vasa /ˈvɑːsə/ Swedish name for **VAASA**.

Vasarely /ˌvasəˈrɛli/, Viktor (1908–97), Hungarian-born French painter. A pioneer of op art, he was best known for a style of geometric abstraction that used repeated geometric forms and interacting colours to create visual disorientation.

Vasari /vəˈsɑːri/, Giorgio (1511–74), Italian painter, architect, and biographer. His *Lives of the Most Excellent Painters, Sculptors, and Architects* (1550, enlarged 1568) laid the basis for later study of art history in the West.

vasbyt /ˈfasbeɪt/ ▶ **verb** [no obj.] S. African be stoical: *I am expected to vasbyt and bite back my tears.*
– ORIGIN Afrikaans, literally 'bite hard'.

Vasco da Gama /ˈvaskəʊ/ see **DA GAMA**.

vascular /ˈvaskjʊlə/ ▶ **adjective** Anatomy, Zoology, & Medicine of, relating to, affecting, or consisting of a vessel or vessels, especially those which carry blood: *vascular disease* | *the vascular system.*
▪Botany relating to or denoting the plant tissues (xylem and phloem) which conduct water, sap, and nutrients in flowering plants, ferns, and their relatives.
– DERIVATIVES **vascularity** /-ˈlarɪti/ noun.
– ORIGIN late 17th cent.: from modern Latin *vascularis*, from Latin *vasculum* (see **VASCULUM**).

vascular bundle ▶ **noun** Botany a strand of conducting vessels in the stem or leaves of a plant, typically with phloem on the outside and xylem on the inside.

vascular cryptogam ▶ **noun** Botany a plant of the division Pteridophyta, i.e. a fern, horsetail, or clubmoss.

vascular cylinder ▶ **noun** another term for **STELE** (in sense 1).

vascularize (also **-ise**) ▶ **verb** [with obj.] Biology & Anatomy provide (a tissue or structure) with vessels, especially blood vessels; make vascular: [as adj. **vascularized**] *the endocrine glands are highly vascularized tissues.*
– DERIVATIVES **vascularization** noun.

vascular plant ▶ **noun** Botany a plant that is characterized by the presence of conducting tissue.
• Subkingdom Tracheophyta: divisions Pteridophyta (ferns, horsetails, and clubmosses) and Spermatophyta (cycads, conifers, and flowering plants).

vasculature /ˈvaskjʊlətʃə/ ▶ **noun** Anatomy the vascular system of a part of the body and its arrangement: *diseases affecting the pulmonary vasculature.*

vasculitis /ˌvaskjʊˈlʌɪtɪs/ ▶ **noun** (pl. **vasculitides** /-ˈlʌɪtɪdiːz/) [mass noun] Medicine inflammation of a blood vessel or blood vessels.
– DERIVATIVES **vasculitic** /-ˈlɪtɪk/ adjective.

vasculum /ˈvaskjʊləm/ ▶ **noun** (pl. **vascula** /-lə/) Botany a collecting box for plants, typically in the form of a flattened cylindrical metal case with a lengthwise opening, carried by a shoulder strap.
– ORIGIN late 18th cent.: from Latin, diminutive of *vas* 'vessel'.

vas deferens /ˈdɛfərɛnz/ ▶ **noun** (pl. **vasa deferentia** /ˌdɛfəˈrɛnʃɪə/) Anatomy the duct which conveys sperm from the testicle to the urethra.
– ORIGIN late 16th cent.: from **VAS** + Latin *deferens* 'carrying away', present participle of *deferre.*

vase ▶ **noun** a decorative container without handles, typically made of glass or china and used as an ornament or for displaying cut flowers.
– DERIVATIVES **vaseful** noun (pl. **-fuls**).
– ORIGIN late Middle English: from French, from Latin *vas* 'vessel'.

vasectomy /vəˈsɛktəmi/ ▶ **noun** (pl. **-ies**) the surgical cutting and sealing of part of each vas deferens, typically as a means of sterilization.
– DERIVATIVES **vasectomize** (also **-ise**) verb.

vaseline /ˈvasɪliːn/ ▶ **noun** [mass noun] trademark a type of petroleum jelly used as an ointment and lubricant.
▶ **verb** [with obj.] cover or smear with this.
– ORIGIN late 19th cent.: formed irregularly from German *Wasser* + Greek *elaion* 'oil' + **-INE**[4].

vase shell ▶ **noun** a predatory mollusc of warm seas, with a heavy ribbed shell that has blunt spines and is typically pale with chestnut markings.
• Genus *Vasum*, family Vasidae, class Gastropoda.

vaso- /ˈveɪzəʊ/ ▶ **combining form** of or relating to a vessel or vessels, especially blood vessels: *vasoconstriction.*
– ORIGIN from Latin *vas* 'vessel'.

vasoactive ▶ **adjective** Physiology affecting the diameter of blood vessels (and hence blood pressure).

vasoconstriction ▶ **noun** [mass noun] the constriction of blood vessels, which increases blood pressure.
– DERIVATIVES **vasoconstrictive** adjective, **vasoconstrictor** noun.

vasodilation (also **vasodilatation** /-ˌdʌɪləˈteɪʃ(ə)n/) ▶ **noun** the dilatation of blood vessels, which decreases blood pressure.
– DERIVATIVES **vasodilator** noun, **vasodilatory** adjective.

vasomotor ▶ **adjective** [attrib.] causing or relating to the constriction or dilatation of blood vessels.
▪denoting a region in the medulla of the brain (the **vasomotor centre**) which regulates blood pressure by controlling reflex alterations in the heart rate and the diameter of the blood vessels, in response to stimuli from receptors in the circulatory system or from other parts of the brain.

vasopressin /ˌveɪzəʊˈprɛsɪn/ ▶ **noun** [mass noun] Biochemistry a pituitary hormone which acts to promote the retention of water by the kidneys and increase blood pressure.
– ORIGIN 1920s: from *vasopressor* 'causing constriction in blood vessels' + **-IN**[1].

vasovagal /ˌveɪzəʊveɪg(ə)l/ ▶ **adjective** [attrib.] Medicine relating to or denoting a temporary fall in blood pressure, with pallor, fainting, sweating, and nausea, caused by overactivity of the vagus nerve, especially as a result of stress.

vassal /ˈvas(ə)l/ ▶ **noun** historical a holder of land by feudal tenure on conditions of homage and allegiance.
▪a person or country in a subordinate position to another: [as modifier] *a vassal state of the Chinese empire.*
– DERIVATIVES **vassalage** noun.
– ORIGIN late Middle English: via Old French from medieval Latin *vassallus* 'retainer', of Celtic origin; compare with **VAVASOUR**.

V

vast ▶ adjective of very great extent or quantity; immense: *a vast plain full of orchards.*
▶ noun archaic an immense space.
– DERIVATIVES **vastly** adverb, **vastness** noun.
– ORIGIN late Middle English: from Latin *vastus* 'void, immense'.

vastation /vaˈsteɪʃ(ə)n/ ▶ noun [mass noun] poetic/literary the action or process of emptying or purifying someone or something, typically violently or drastically.
– ORIGIN mid 16th cent.: from Latin *vastatio(n-)*, from *vastare* 'lay waste'.

Västerås /ˌvɛstəˈrɒs/ a port on Lake Mälaren in eastern Sweden; pop. 119,760 (1990).

VAT ▶ abbreviation for value added tax.

vat ▶ noun **1** a large tank or tub used to hold liquid, especially in industry: *a vat of hot tar.*
2 (also **vat dye**) a water-insoluble dye, such as indigo, that is applied to a fabric in a reducing bath which converts it to a soluble form, the colour being obtained on subsequent oxidation in the fabric fibres.
▶ verb (**vatted**, **vatting**) [with obj.] (often **be vatted**) place or treat in a vat.
– ORIGIN Middle English: southern and western dialect variant of obsolete *fat* 'container', of Germanic origin; related to Dutch *vat* and German *Fass.*

vatic /ˈvatɪk/ ▶ adjective poetic/literary describing or predicting what will happen in the future.
– ORIGIN early 17th cent.: from Latin *vates* 'prophet' + -IC.

Vatican ▶ noun (usu. **the Vatican**) the palace and official residence of the Pope in Rome.
■ [treated as sing. or pl.] the administrative centre of the Roman Catholic Church.
– ORIGIN mid 16th cent.: from French, or from Latin *Vaticanus*, the name of a hill in Rome.

Vatican City an independent papal state in the city of Rome, the seat of government of the Roman Catholic Church; pop. 1,000 (est. 1991). It covers an area of 44 hectares (109 acres) around St Peter's Basilica and the palace of the Vatican. Having been suspended after the incorporation of the former Papal States into Italy in 1870, the temporal power of the Pope was restored by the Lateran Treaty of 1929.

Vatican Council ▶ noun each of two general councils of the Roman Catholic Church, held in 1869–70 and 1962–5. The first (**Vatican I**) proclaimed the infallibility of the Pope when speaking *ex cathedra*; the second (**Vatican II**) made numerous reforms, abandoning the universal Latin liturgy and acknowledging ecumenism.

vaticinate /vaˈtɪsɪneɪt/ ▶ verb [no obj.] rare foretell the future.
– DERIVATIVES **vaticinal** adjective, **vaticination** noun, **vaticinator** noun, **vaticinatory** adjective.
– ORIGIN early 17th cent.: from Latin *vaticinat-* 'prophesied', from the verb *vaticinari*, from *vates* 'prophet'.

VATman ▶ noun (pl. **-men**) Brit. informal a customs and excise officer who deals with VAT.

Vättern /ˈvɛt(ə)n/ a large lake in southern Sweden.

vatu /ˈvatuː/ ▶ noun (pl. same) the basic monetary unit of Vanuatu, equal to 100 centimes.
– ORIGIN Bislama.

Vaud /vəʊ/ a canton on the shores of Lake Geneva in western Switzerland; capital, Lausanne. German name **WAADT**.

vaudeville /ˈvɔːdəvɪl, ˈvəʊd-/ ▶ noun [mass noun] a type of entertainment popular chiefly in the US in the early 20th century, featuring a mixture of speciality acts such as burlesque comedy and song and dance.
■ [count noun] a stage play on a trivial theme with interspersed songs. ■ [count noun] archaic a satirical or topical song with a refrain.
– DERIVATIVES **vaudevillian** adjective & noun.
– ORIGIN mid 18th cent.: from French, earlier *vau de ville* (or *vire*), said to be a name given originally to songs composed by Olivier Basselin, a 15th-cent. fuller born in *Vau de Vire* in Normandy.

Vaudois¹ /ˈvəʊdwɑː/ ▶ adjective of or relating to Vaud, its people, or their dialect of French.
▶ noun (pl. same) **1** a native of Vaud.
2 [mass noun] the French dialect spoken in this region.

– ORIGIN French.

Vaudois² /ˈvəʊdwɑː/ ▶ noun (pl. same) historical a member of the Waldenses religious sect.
▶ adjective of or relating to the Waldenses.
– ORIGIN mid 16th cent.: French, representing medieval Latin *Valdensis* (see **WALDENSES**).

Vaughan¹ /vɔːn/, Henry (1621–95), Welsh religious writer and metaphysical poet.

Vaughan² /vɔːn/, Sarah (Lois) (1924–90), American jazz singer and pianist. She was notable for her vocal range, her use of vibrato, and her improvisational skills.

Vaughan Williams, Ralph (1872–1958), English composer. His strongly melodic music frequently reflects his interest in Tudor composers and English folk songs. Notable works: *Fantasia on a Theme by Thomas Tallis* (1910), *A London Symphony* (1914), and the Mass in G minor (1922).

vault¹ /vɔːlt/ ▶ noun **1** a roof in the form of an arch or a series of arches, typical of churches and other large, formal buildings.
■ poetic/literary a thing resembling an arched roof, especially the sky: *the vault of heaven.* ■ Anatomy the arched roof of a cavity, especially that of the skull: *the cranial vault.*
2 a large room or chamber used for storage, especially an underground one.
■ a secure room in a bank in which valuables are stored. ■ a chamber beneath a church or in a graveyard used for burials.
▶ verb [with obj.] [usu. as adj. **vaulted**] provide (a building or room) with an arched roof or roofs: *a vaulted arcade.*
■ make (a roof) in the form of a vault: *there was a high ceiling, vaulted with cut slate.*
– ORIGIN Middle English: from Old French *voute*, based on Latin *volvere* 'to roll'.

vault² /vɔːlt/ ▶ verb [no obj., with adverbial of direction] leap or spring while supporting or propelling oneself with one or both hands or with the help of a pole: *he vaulted over the gate.*
■ [with obj.] jump over (an obstacle) in such a way: *Ryker vaulted the barrier.*
▶ noun an act of vaulting.
– DERIVATIVES **vaulter** noun.
– ORIGIN mid 16th cent.: from Old French *volter* 'to turn (a horse), gambol', based on Latin *volvere* 'to roll'.

vaulting ▶ noun [mass noun] **1** ornamental work in a vaulted roof or ceiling.
2 the action of vaulting over obstacles as a gymnastic or athletic exercise.

vaulting horse ▶ noun a padded wooden block used for vaulting over by gymnasts and athletes.

vaunt /vɔːnt/ ▶ verb [with obj.] [usu. as adj. **vaunted**] boast about or praise (something), especially excessively: *the much vaunted information superhighway.*
▶ noun archaic a boast.
– DERIVATIVES **vaunter** noun, **vauntingly** adverb.
– ORIGIN late Middle English: the noun a shortening of obsolete *avaunt* 'boasting, a boast'; the verb (originally in the sense 'use boastful language') from Old French *vanter*, from late Latin *vantare*, based on Latin *vanus* 'vain, empty'.

vavasory /ˈvavəs(ə)ri/ ▶ noun (pl. **-ies**) historical the estate of a vavasour.
– ORIGIN early 17th cent.: from Old French *vavasorie* or medieval Latin *vavasoria* (see **VAVASOUR**).

vavasour /ˈvavəsʊə/ ▶ noun historical a vassal owing allegiance to a great lord and having other vassals under him.
– ORIGIN Middle English: from Old French *vavas(s)our*, from medieval Latin *vavassor*, perhaps from *vassus vassorum* 'vassal of vassals'.

Vavilov /ˈvavɪlɒf/, Nikolai (Ivanovich) (1887–c.1943), Soviet plant geneticist. He amassed a considerable collection of new plants, utilizing their genetic resources for crop improvement.

VC ▶ abbreviation for ■ Vice-Chairman. ■ Vice-Chancellor. ■ Vice-Consul. ■ Victoria Cross.

V-chip ▶ noun a computer chip installed in a television receiver that can be programmed by the user to block or scramble material containing a special code in its signal indicating that it is deemed violent or sexually explicit.

VCR ▶ abbreviation for video cassette recorder.

VD ▶ abbreviation for venereal disease.

VDU ▶ abbreviation for visual display unit.

've informal ▶ abbreviation for have (usually after the pronouns I, you, we, and they): *we've tried our best.*

veal ▶ noun [mass noun] the flesh of a calf, used as food.
– ORIGIN Middle English: from Anglo-Norman French *ve(e)l*, from Latin *vitellus*, diminutive of *vitulus* 'calf'.

veal crate ▶ noun a partitioned area with restricted light and space in which a calf is reared for slaughter so as to ensure the whiteness of the meat.

Veblen /ˈvɛblən/, Thorstein (Bunde) (1857–1929), American economist and social scientist. His works include the critique of capitalism *The Theory of the Leisure Class* (1899) and *The Theory of Business Enterprise* (1904).

vector /ˈvɛktə/ ▶ noun **1** Mathematics & Physics a quantity having direction as well as magnitude, especially as determining the position of one point in space relative to another.
■ a matrix with one row or one column. ■ a course to be taken by an aircraft. ■ [as modifier] Computing denoting a type of graphical representation using lines to construct the outlines of objects.
2 an organism, typically a biting insect or tick, that transmits a disease or parasite from one animal or plant to another.
■ Genetics a bacteriophage or plasmid which transfers genetic material into a cell, or from one bacterium to another.
▶ verb [with obj. and adverbial of direction] (often **be vectored**) direct (an aircraft in flight) to a desired point.
– DERIVATIVES **vectorial** /-ˈtɔːrɪəl/ adjective, **vectorially** adverb, **vectorization** noun (only in sense 1 of the noun), **vectorize** (also **-ise**) verb (only in sense 1 of the noun).
– ORIGIN mid 19th cent.: from Latin, literally 'carrier', from *vehere* 'convey'.

vector field ▶ noun Mathematics a function of a space whose value at each point is a vector quantity.

vector processor ▶ noun Computing a processor that is able to process sequences of data with a single instruction.

vector product ▶ noun Mathematics the product of two real vectors in three dimensions which is itself a vector at right angles to both the original vectors. Its magnitude is the product of the magnitudes of the original vectors and the sine of the angle between their directions. Also called **CROSS PRODUCT**.
■ Written as a × b.

vector space ▶ noun Mathematics a space consisting of vectors, together with the associative and commutative operation of addition of vectors, and the associative and distributive operation of multiplication of vectors by scalars.

VED ▶ abbreviation for vehicle excise duty.

Veda /ˈveɪdə, ˈviːdə/ ▶ noun [treated as sing. or pl.] the most ancient Hindu scriptures, written in early Sanskrit and containing hymns, philosophy, and guidance on ritual for the priests of Vedic religion. Believed to have been directly revealed to seers among the early Aryans in India, and preserved by oral tradition, the four chief collections are the Rig Veda, Sama Veda, Yajur Veda, and Atharva Veda.
– ORIGIN Sanskrit, literally '(sacred) knowledge'.

vedalia beetle /vɪˈdeɪlɪə/ ▶ noun an Australian ladybird which has been introduced into California and elsewhere to control scale insects.
● *Rodolia cardinalis*, family Coccinellidae.
– ORIGIN late 19th cent.: modern Latin *Vedalia* (former genus name), of unknown origin.

Vedanta /vɪˈdɑːntə, -ˈda-, vɛ-/ ▶ noun [mass noun] a Hindu philosophy based on the doctrine of the Upanishads, especially in its monistic form.
– DERIVATIVES **Vedantic** adjective, **Vedantist** noun.
– ORIGIN from Sanskrit *vedānta*, from *veda* (see **VEDA**) + *anta* 'end'.

VE day ▶ noun the day (8 May) marking the Allied victory in Europe in 1945.
– ORIGIN VE, abbreviation of *Victory in Europe*.

Vedda /ˈvɛdə/ ▶ noun a member of an aboriginal people inhabiting the forests of Sri Lanka.
– ORIGIN from Sinhalese *vaddā* 'hunter'.

vedette /vɪˈdɛt/ ▶ noun **1** historical a mounted sentry positioned beyond an army's outposts to observe the movements of the enemy.
2 chiefly N. Amer. a leading star of stage, screen, or television.
– ORIGIN late 17th cent.: from French, literally

'scout', from an alteration of southern Italian *veletta*, perhaps based on Spanish *velar* 'keep watch'.

Vedic /ˈveɪdɪk, ˈviː-/ ▶ **adjective** of or relating to the Veda or Vedas.
▶ **noun** [mass noun] the language of the Vedas, an early form of Sanskrit.
– ORIGIN from French *védique* or German *vedisch* (see **VEDA**).

Vedic religion ▶ **noun** [mass noun] the ancient religion of the Aryan peoples who entered NW India from Persia *c.*2000–1200 BC. It was the precursor of Hinduism, and its beliefs and practices are contained in the Vedas.

Its characteristics included ritual sacrifice to many gods, especially Indra, Varuna, and Agni; social classes (varnas) that formed the basis of the caste system; and the emergence of the priesthood which dominated orthodox Brahmanism from *c.*900 BC. Transition to classical Hinduism began in about the 5th century BC.

vee ▶ **noun** the letter V.
■ a thing shaped like a V: *a vee of geese goes over.*

veejay ▶ **noun** informal, chiefly N. Amer. a person who introduces and plays popular music videos.
– ORIGIN 1980s: representing a pronunciation of *VJ*, short for *video jockey*, on the pattern of *deejay*.

veena /ˈviːnə/ (also **vina**) ▶ **noun** an Indian stringed instrument, with four main and three auxiliary strings. The southern type has a lute-like body; the older northern type has a tubular body and a gourd fitted to each end as a resonator.
– ORIGIN from Sanskrit *vīṇā*.

veep ▶ **noun** US informal a vice-president.
– ORIGIN 1940s: from the initials *VP*.

veer[1] ▶ **verb** [no obj., with adverbial of direction] change direction suddenly: *an oil tanker that had veered off course.*
■ figurative suddenly change an opinion, subject, type of behaviour, etc.: *the conversation eventually veered away from theatrical things.* ■ (of the wind) change direction clockwise around the points of the compass: *the wind veered a point.* The opposite of **BACK**.
▶ **noun 1** a sudden change of direction.
2 American Football an offensive play using a modified T-formation with a split backfield, which allows the quarterback the option of passing to the fullback, pitching to a running back, or running with the ball.
– ORIGIN late 16th cent.: from French *virer*, perhaps from an alteration of Latin *gyrare* (see **GYRATE**).

veer[2] ▶ **verb** [with obj.] Nautical, dated slacken or let out (a rope or cable) in a controlled way.
– ORIGIN late Middle English: from Middle Dutch *vieren*.

veery /ˈvɪəri/ ▶ **noun** a North American woodland thrush with a brown back and speckled breast.
● *Catharus fuscescens*, family Turdidae.
– ORIGIN mid 19th cent.: perhaps imitative.

veg[1] /vɛdʒ/ ▶ **noun** (pl. same) Brit. informal a vegetable or vegetables: *meat and two veg.*
– ORIGIN late 19th cent.: abbreviation.

veg[2] /vɛdʒ/ ▶ **verb** (**vegges, vegging, vegged**) [no obj.] informal relax to the point of complete inertia: *they were **vegging out** in front of the TV.*
– ORIGIN 1920s: abbreviation of **VEGETATE**.

Vega[1] /ˈveɪɡə, Spanish ˈbeɣa/, Lope de (1562–1635), Spanish dramatist and poet; full name *Lope Felix de Vega Carpio*. He is regarded as the founder of Spanish drama.

Vega[2] /ˈviːɡə/ Astronomy the fifth brightest star in the sky, and the brightest in the constellation Lyra, overhead in summer to observers in the northern hemisphere.
– ORIGIN via Spanish or medieval Latin from Arabic, literally 'the falling vulture'.

vega /ˈveɪɡə/ ▶ **noun** (in Spain and Spanish America) a large plain or valley, typically a fertile and grassy one.
– ORIGIN Spanish and Catalan.

vegan ▶ **noun** a person who does not eat or use animal products: [as modifier] *a vegan diet.*
– ORIGIN 1940s: from **VEGETARIAN** + **-AN**.

Vegeburger ▶ **noun** trademark for **VEGGIE BURGER**.

Vegemite /ˈvɛdʒɪmʌɪt/ ▶ **noun** [mass noun] Austral./NZ trademark a type of savoury spread made from concentrated yeast extract.
– ORIGIN 1920s: from **VEGETABLE**, on the pattern of *marmite*.

vegetable /ˈvɛdʒtəb(ə)l, ˈvɛdʒɪtə-/ ▶ **noun 1** a plant or part of a plant used as food, typically as accompaniment to meat or fish, such as a cabbage, potato, turnip, or bean.
2 informal, offensive a person who is incapable of normal mental or physical activity, especially through brain damage.
■ informal a person with a dull or inactive life: *I thought I'd sort of flop back and be a vegetable for a bit.*
▶ **adjective** [attrib.] of or relating to vegetables as food: *a vegetable garden | vegetable soup.*
■ of or relating to plants or plant life, especially as distinct from animal life or mineral substances: *vegetable matter.*
– ORIGIN late Middle English (in the sense 'growing as a plant'): from Old French, or from late Latin *vegetabilis* 'animating', from Latin *vegetare* (see **VEGETATE**). The noun dates from the late 16th cent.

vegetable butter ▶ **noun** [mass noun] a vegetable fat with the consistency of butter.

vegetable ivory ▶ **noun** [mass noun] a hard white material obtained from the endosperm of the ivory nut.

vegetable marrow ▶ **noun** see **MARROW** (sense 1).

vegetable oil ▶ **noun** [mass noun] an oil derived from plants, e.g. rapeseed oil, olive oil, sunflower oil.

vegetable oyster ▶ **noun** [mass noun] the edible root of salsify, the taste of which is said to resemble that of oysters.

vegetable sheep ▶ **noun** a New Zealand plant of the daisy family, which has greyish hairy leaves and forms hummocks which look like sheep from a distance.
● *Raoulia eximia*, family Compositae.

vegetable spaghetti ▶ **noun** [mass noun] Brit. an edible squash of a variety with slightly stringy flesh which when cooked has a texture and appearance like that of spaghetti.

vegetable sponge ▶ **noun** another term for **LOOFAH**.

vegetable tallow ▶ **noun** [mass noun] vegetable fat used as tallow.

vegetal /ˈvɛdʒɪt(ə)l/ ▶ **adjective 1** formal of or relating to plants: *a vegetal aroma.*
2 [attrib.] Embryology of or relating to that pole of the ovum or embryo that contains the less active cytoplasm, and frequently most of the yolk, in the early stages of development: *vegetal cells | the vegetal region.*
– ORIGIN late Middle English: from medieval Latin *vegetalis*, from Latin *vegetare* 'animate'. Sense 2 dates from the early 20th cent.

vegetarian ▶ **noun** a person who does not eat meat, and sometimes other animal products, especiallyfor moral, religious, or health reasons.
▶ **adjective** of or relating to the exclusion of meat or other animal products from the diet: *a vegetarian restaurant.*
– DERIVATIVES **vegetarianism** noun.
– ORIGIN mid 19th cent.: formed irregularly from **VEGETABLE** + **-ARIAN**.

vegetate ▶ **verb** [no obj.] **1** live or spend a period of time in a dull, inactive, unchallenging way: *if she left him there alone, he'd sit in front of the television set and vegetate.*
2 dated (of a plant or seed) grow; sprout.
■ [with obj.] cause plants to grow in or cover (a place).
– ORIGIN early 17th cent.: from Latin *vegetat-* 'enlivened', from the verb *vegetare*, from *vegetus* 'active', from *vegere* 'be active'.

vegetated ▶ **adjective** covered with vegetation or plant life: *densely vegetated wetlands.*

vegetation ▶ **noun** [mass noun] **1** plants considered collectively, especially those found in a particular area or habitat: *the chalk cliffs are mainly sheer with little vegetation.*
2 the action or process of vegetating.
– DERIVATIVES **vegetational** adjective.
– ORIGIN mid 16th cent. (in sense 2): from medieval Latin *vegetatio(n-)* 'power of growth', from the verb *vegetare* (see **VEGETATE**).

vegetative /ˈvɛdʒɪtətɪv, -teɪtɪv/ ▶ **adjective 1** Biology of, relating to, or denoting reproduction or propagation achieved by asexual means, either naturally (budding, rhizomes, runners, bulbs, etc.) or artificially (grafting, layering, or taking cuttings): *vegetative spores | a vegetative replicating phase.*
■ of, relating to, or concerned with growth rather than sexual reproduction: *environmental factors trigger the switch from vegetative to floral development.*
2 of or relating to vegetation or plant life: *diverse vegetative types.*
3 Medicine (of a person) alive but comatose and without apparent brain activity or responsiveness. See **PERSISTENT VEGETATIVE STATE**.
– DERIVATIVES **vegetatively** adverb, **vegetativeness** noun.
– ORIGIN late Middle English (in sense 2): from Old French *vegetatif, -ive* or medieval Latin *vegetativus* (see **VEGETATE**).

vegetative cell ▶ **noun** Botany & Microbiology a cell of a bacterium or unicellular alga that is actively growing rather than forming spores.

veggie (also **vegie**) ▶ **noun** & **adjective** informal
1 another term for **VEGETARIAN**.
2 chiefly N. Amer. another term for **VEGETABLE**.
– ORIGIN 1970s: abbreviation.

veggie burger (also trademark **Vegeburger**) ▶ **noun** a savoury cake resembling a hamburger but made with vegetable protein, soya, etc., instead of meat.

vehement /ˈviːɪm(ə)nt/ ▶ **adjective** showing strong feeling; forceful, passionate, or intense: *her voice was low but vehement | vehement criticism.*
– DERIVATIVES **vehemence** noun, **vehemently** adverb.
– ORIGIN late Middle English (describing pain or temperature, in the sense 'intense, high in degree'): from French *véhément* or Latin *vehement-* 'impetuous, violent', perhaps from an unrecorded adjective meaning 'deprived of mind', influenced by *vehere* 'carry'.

vehicle ▶ **noun 1** a thing used for transporting people or goods, especially on land, such as a car, lorry, or cart.
2 a thing used to express, embody, or fulfil something: *I use paint as a **vehicle for** my ideas.*
■ a substance that facilitates the use of a drug, pigment, or other material mixed with it. ■ a privately controlled company through which an individual or organization conducts a particular kind of business, especially investment. ■ a film, television programme, song, etc. that is intended to display the leading performer to the best advantage.
– DERIVATIVES **vehicular** /vɪˈhɪkjʊlə/ adjective (only in sense 1).
– ORIGIN early 17th cent.: from French *véhicule* or Latin *vehiculum*, from *vehere* 'carry'.

veil ▶ **noun** a piece of fine material worn by women to protect or conceal the face: *a white bridal veil.*
■ a piece of linen or other fabric forming part of a nun's headdress, resting on the head and shoulders. ■ a thing that conceals, disguises, or obscures something: *shrouded in an eerie veil of mist.* ■ Botany a membrane which is attached to the immature fruiting body of some toadstools and ruptures in the course of development, either (**universal veil**) enclosing the whole fruiting body or (**partial veil**) joining the edges of the cap to the stalk. ■ (in Jewish antiquity) the piece of precious cloth separating the sanctuary from the body of the Temple or the Tabernacle.
▶ **verb** [with obj.] cover with or as though with a veil: *she veiled her face.*
■ [usu. as adj. **veiled**] partially conceal, disguise, or obscure: *a thinly veiled threat.*
– PHRASES **beyond the veil** in a mysterious or hidden place or state, especially the unknown state of life after death. **draw a veil over** avoid discussing or calling attention to (something), especially because it is embarrassing or unpleasant. **take the veil** become a nun.
– DERIVATIVES **veilless** adjective.
– ORIGIN Middle English: from Anglo-Norman French *veil(e)*, from Latin *vela*, plural of *velum* (see **VELUM**).

veiling ▶ **noun** [mass noun] **1** the action of wearing or covering someone or something with a veil: *the fundamentalist campaign for the veiling of women.*
2 a light gauzy fabric used for veils.

vein ▶ **noun 1** any of the tubes forming part of the blood circulation system of the body, carrying mainly oxygen-depleted blood towards the heart. Compare with **ARTERY**.
■ (in general and figurative use) a blood vessel: *he felt the adrenalin course through his veins.* ■ (in plants) a slender rib running through a leaf or bract, typically dividing or branching, and containing a vascular bundle. ■ (in insects) a hardened branching rib that forms part of the supporting framework of a wing,

V

consisting of an extension of the tracheal system; a nervure. ∎ a streak or stripe of a different colour in wood, marble, cheese, etc. ∎ a fracture in rock containing a deposit of minerals or ore and typically having an extensive course underground. ∎ figurative a source of a specified quality or other abstract resource: *he managed to tap into the thick vein of discontent to his own advantage.*

2 [in sing.] a distinctive quality, style, or tendency: *he closes his article in a somewhat humorous vein.*

– DERIVATIVES **veinless** adjective, **veinlet** noun, **vein-like** adjective & adverb, **veiny** adjective (**veinier**, **veiniest**).

– ORIGIN Middle English: from Old French *veine*, from Latin *vena*. The earliest senses were 'blood vessel' and 'small natural underground channel of water'.

veined ▸ adjective marked with or as if with veins: [in combination] *a blue-veined cheese.*

veining ▸ noun [mass noun] a pattern of lines, streaks, or veins: *the marble's characteristic surface veining.*

veinous ▸ adjective having prominent or noticeable veins. Compare with **VENOUS**.

veinstone ▸ noun another term for **GANGUE**.

veitchberry /ˈviːtʃb(ə)ri, -bɛri/ ▸ noun (pl. **-ies**) a bushy plant which is a hybrid of a raspberry and a blackberry, first produced in 1925.
● *Rubus inermis* × *idaeus*, family Rosaceae.
∎ the edible fruit of this plant, which resembles a mulberry.
– ORIGIN 1920s: from *Veitch*, the surname of a family of nurserymen, + **BERRY**.

Vela /ˈviːlə/ Astronomy a southern constellation (the Sails), lying partly in the Milky Way between Carina and Pyxis and originally part of Argo.
∎ [as genitive **Velorum** /vɪˈlɔːrəm/] used with preceding letter or numeral to designate a star in this constellation: *the star Gamma Velorum.*
– ORIGIN Latin, plural of *velum* 'sail'.

vela plural form of **VELUM**.

velamen /vɪˈleɪmən/ ▸ noun (pl. **velamina** /-mɪnə/) Botany an outer layer of empty cells in the aerial roots of epiphytic orchids and aroids.
– ORIGIN late 19th cent.: from Latin, from *velare* 'to cover'.

velar /ˈviːlə/ ▸ adjective **1** of or relating to a veil or velum.
2 Phonetics (of a speech sound) pronounced with the back of the tongue near the soft palate, as in *k* and *g* in English.
▸ noun a velar sound.
– ORIGIN early 18th cent.: from Latin *velaris*, from *velum* (see **VELUM**).

velaric airstream /vɪˈlarɪk/ ▸ noun Phonetics the creation of an ingressive airstream in the mouth by use of tongue contact with the velum, used to make clicks. Contrasted with **PULMONIC AIRSTREAM**.

velarium /vɪˈlɛːrɪəm/ ▸ noun (pl. **velaria** /-rɪə/) a large awning of a type used in ancient Rome to cover a theatre or amphitheatre as a protection against the weather, now more commonly used as an inner ceiling to improve acoustics.
– ORIGIN Latin.

velarization /ˌviːlərʌɪˈzeɪʃ(ə)n/ ▸ noun [mass noun] Phonetics a secondary articulation involving movement of the back of the tongue towards the velum.
– DERIVATIVES **velarize** verb.

Velázquez /vɪˈlaskwɪz, Spanish beˈlaskeθ, -kes/, Diego Rodríguez de Silva y (1599–1660), Spanish painter, court painter to Philip IV. His portraits humanized the formal Spanish tradition of idealized figures. Notable works: *Pope Innocent X* (1650), *The Toilet of Venus* (known as The Rokeby Venus, c.1651), and *Las Meninas* (c.1656).

Velázquez de Cuéllar /deɪ ˈkwejɑː, ˈkweɪljɑː, Spanish de ˈkwejar/, Diego (c.1465–1524), Spanish conquistador. After sailing with Columbus to the New World in 1493, he began the conquest of Cuba in 1511; he later initiated expeditions to conquer Mexico.

Velcro /ˈvɛlkrəʊ/ ▸ noun [mass noun] trademark a fastener for clothes or other items, consisting of two strips of thin plastic sheet, one covered with tiny loops and the other with tiny flexible hooks, which adhere when pressed together and can be separated when pulled apart deliberately.

▸ verb [with obj. and adverbial] fasten, join, or fix with such a fastener.
– DERIVATIVES **Velcroed** adjective.
– ORIGIN 1960s: from French *velours croché* 'hooked velvet'.

veld /vɛlt/ (also **veldt**) ▸ noun [mass noun] open, uncultivated country or grassland in southern Africa. It is conventionally divided by altitude into highveld, middleveld, and lowveld.
– ORIGIN Afrikaans, from Dutch, literally 'field'.

Velde, van de[1], Henri, see **VAN DE VELDE**[2].

Velde, van de[2], Willem and sons, see **VAN DE VELDE**[1].

veldskoen /ˈfɛltskʊn, ˈfɛls-/ ▸ noun a strong suede or leather shoe or boot.
∎ S. African used as a symbol of conservative or reactionary attitudes: [as modifier] *he is a veldskoen bitter-ender.*
– ORIGIN Afrikaans, literally 'field shoe'.

veleta /vəˈliːtə/ (also **valeta**) ▸ noun a ballroom dance in triple time, faster than a waltz and with partners side by side.
– ORIGIN early 20th cent.: from Spanish, literally 'weathervane'.

veliger /ˈviːlɪdʒə/ ▸ noun Zoology the final larval stage of certain molluscs, having two ciliated flaps for swimming and feeding.
– ORIGIN late 19th cent.: from **VELUM** + Latin *-ger* 'bearing'.

velleity /vɛˈliːɪti/ ▸ noun (pl. **-ies**) formal a wish or inclination not strong enough to lead to action: *the notion intrigued me, but remained a velleity.*
– ORIGIN early 17th cent.: from medieval Latin *velleitas*, from Latin *velle* 'to wish'.

Velleius Paterculus /vɛˌleɪəs pəˈtəːkjʊləs/ (c.19 BC–c.30 AD), Roman historian and soldier. His *Roman History*, covering the period from the early history of Rome to AD 30, is notable for its eulogistic depiction of Tiberius.

vellum /ˈvɛləm/ ▸ noun [mass noun] fine parchment made originally from the skin of a calf.
– ORIGIN late Middle English: from Old French *velin*, from *veel* (see **VEAL**).

velocimeter /ˌvɛlə(ʊ)ˈsɪmɪtə/ ▸ noun an instrument for measuring velocity.
– DERIVATIVES **velocimetry** noun.
– ORIGIN mid 19th cent.: from Latin *velox, veloc-* 'swift' + **-METER**.

velocipede /vɪˈlɒsɪpiːd/ ▸ noun historical an early form of bicycle propelled by working pedals on cranks fitted to the front axle.
∎ US a child's tricycle.
– DERIVATIVES **velocipedist** noun.
– ORIGIN early 19th cent.: from French *vélocipède*, from Latin *velox, veloc-* 'swift' + *pes, ped-* 'foot'.

velociraptor /vɪˌlɒsɪˈraptə/ ▸ noun a small dromaeosaurid dinosaur of the late Cretaceous period.
● Genus *Velociraptor*, family Dromaeosauridae, suborder Theropoda.
– ORIGIN modern Latin, from Latin *velox, veloc-* 'swift' + **RAPTOR**.

velocity /vɪˈlɒsɪti/ ▸ noun (pl. **-ies**) the speed of something in a given direction: *the velocities of the emitted particles.*
∎ (in general use) speed: *the tank shot backwards at an incredible velocity.* ∎ (also **velocity of circulation**) Economics the rate at which money changes hands within an economy.
– ORIGIN late Middle English: from French *vélocité* or Latin *velocitas*, from *velox, veloc-* 'swift'.

velocity profile ▸ noun Physics the variation in velocity along a line at right angles to the general direction of flow.

velodrome /ˈvɛlədrəʊm/ ▸ noun a cycle-racing track, typically with steeply banked curves.
∎ a stadium containing such a track.
– ORIGIN late 19th cent.: from French *vélodrome*, from *vélo* 'bicycle' + *-drome* (see **-DROME**).

velour /vəˈlʊə/ (also **velours**) ▸ noun [mass noun] a plush woven fabric resembling velvet, chiefly used for soft furnishings and hats.
∎ [count noun] dated a hat made of such fabric.
– ORIGIN early 18th cent.: from French *velours* 'velvet', from Old French *velour, velous*, from Latin *villosus* 'hairy', from *villus* (see **VELVET**).

velouté /vəˈluːteɪ/ ▸ noun [mass noun] a sauce made

from a roux of butter and flour with chicken, veal, or pork stock.
– ORIGIN French, literally 'velvety'.

velum /ˈviːləm/ ▸ noun (pl. **vela** /-lə/) chiefly Anatomy, Zoology, & Botany a membrane or membranous structure, typically covering another structure or partly obscuring an opening, in particular:
∎ Anatomy the soft palate. ∎ Zoology a membrane, typically bordering a cavity, especially in certain molluscs, medusae, and other invertebrates. ∎ Botany the veil of a toadstool.
– ORIGIN mid 18th cent.: from Latin, literally 'sail, curtain, covering, veil'.

velvet ▸ noun [mass noun] a closely woven fabric of silk, cotton, or nylon, that has a thick short pile on one side.
∎ soft downy skin that covers a deer's antler while it is growing.
– PHRASES **on velvet** informal, dated in an advantageous or prosperous position.
– DERIVATIVES **velveted** adjective, **velvety** adjective.
– ORIGIN Middle English: from Old French *veluotte*, from *velu* 'velvety', from medieval Latin *villutus*, from Latin *villus* 'tuft, down'.

velvet ant ▸ noun an ant-like velvety-bodied insect that is related to the wasps. The female is wingless and the larvae parasitize the young of bees and wasps in the nest.
● Family Mutillidae, superfamily Scolioidea: numerous species, including the European *Mutilla europaea*.

velveteen ▸ noun [mass noun] a cotton fabric with a pile resembling velvet.
∎ (**velveteens**) dated trousers made of this fabric.

velvetleaf ▸ noun [mass noun] a Eurasian plant of the mallow family, with large heart-shaped velvety leaves and yellow flowers. It is naturalized in North America, where it has become a serious weed of farmland.
● *Abutilon theophrasti*, family Malvaceae.

velvet revolution ▸ noun a non-violent political revolution, especially the relatively smooth change from Communism to a Western-style democracy in Czechoslovakia at the end of 1989.
– ORIGIN translating Czech *sametová revoluce*.

velvet worm ▸ noun an onychophoran.

Ven. ▸ abbreviation for Venerable (as the title of an archdeacon): *the Ven. William Davies.*

vena cava /ˌviːnə ˈkeɪvə/ ▸ noun (pl. **venae cavae** /-ni· ·viː/) a large vein carrying deoxygenated blood into the heart. There are two in humans, the **inferior vena cava** (carrying blood from the lower body) and the **superior vena cava** (carrying blood from the head, arms, and upper body).
– ORIGIN late 16th cent.: from Latin, literally 'hollow vein'.

venal /ˈviːn(ə)l/ ▸ adjective showing or motivated by susceptibility to bribery: *why should these venal politicians care how they are rated?* | *their generosity had been at least partly venal.*
– DERIVATIVES **venality** noun, **venally** adverb.
– ORIGIN mid 17th cent. (in the sense 'available for purchase', referring to merchandise or a favour): from Latin *venalis*, from *venum* 'thing for sale'.

venation /vɪˈneɪʃ(ə)n/ ▸ noun [mass noun] Biology the arrangement of veins in a leaf or in an insect's wing.
∎ the system of venous blood vessels in an animal.
– DERIVATIVES **venational** adjective.
– ORIGIN mid 17th cent.: from Latin *vena* 'vein' + **-ATION**.

vend ▸ verb [with obj.] offer (small items, especially food) for sale, either from a stall or from a slot machine: *there was a man vending sticky cakes and ices.*
∎ Law or formal sell (something).
– DERIVATIVES **vendible** adjective.
– ORIGIN early 17th cent. (in the sense 'be sold'): from French *vendre* or Latin *vendere* 'sell', from *venum* 'something for sale' + a variant of *dare* 'give'.

Venda[1] /ˈvɛndə/ a former homeland established in South Africa for the Venda people, now part of Northern Province.

Venda[2] /ˈvɛndə/ ▸ noun (pl. same or **Vendas**) **1** a member of a people living in Northern Transvaal and southern Zimbabwe.
2 [mass noun] the Bantu language of this people, which has about 600,000 speakers.
▸ adjective of or relating to this people or their language.

- ORIGIN the stem of Venda *Muvenda* (in sense 1), *Tshivenda* (in sense 2).

vendace /ˈvɛndɪs/ ▶ noun an edible whitefish found in lakes in northern Europe. In Britain it is now confined to two lakes in the English Lake District.
● *Coregonus albula*, family Salmonidae.
- ORIGIN mid 18th cent.: from obsolete French *vendese*, from a base related to Welsh *gwyn* 'white'.

vendange /vɒ̃ˈdɒ̃ʒ, French vɑ̃dɑ̃ʒ/ ▶ noun (pl. pronounced same) (in France) the grape harvest.
- ORIGIN French.

Vendemiaire /vɛnˌdɛmɪˈɛː/ (also **Vendémiaire** /French vɑ̃demjɛːʁ/) ▶ noun the first month of the French Republican calendar (1793–1805), originally running from 22 September to 21 October.
- ORIGIN French, from Latin *vindemia* 'vintage'.

vender ▶ noun US variant spelling of VENDOR.

vendetta /vɛnˈdɛtə/ ▶ noun a blood feud in which the family of a murdered person seeks vengeance on the murderer or the murderer's family.
■ a prolonged bitter quarrel with or campaign against someone: *he has accused the British media of pursuing a vendetta against him.*
- ORIGIN mid 19th cent.: from Italian, from Latin *vindicta* 'vengeance'.

vendeuse /vɒ̃ˈdəːz, French vɑ̃døz/ ▶ noun a saleswoman, especially one in a fashionable dress shop.
- ORIGIN French.

vending machine ▶ noun a machine that dispenses small articles such as food, drinks, or cigarettes when a coin or token is inserted.

vendor (US also **vender**) ▶ noun a person or company offering something for sale, especially a trader in the street: *an Italian ice-cream vendor.*
■ /also ˈvɛndɔː/ Law the seller in a sale, especially of property.
- ORIGIN late 16th cent.: from Anglo-Norman French *vendour* (see VEND).

vendor placing ▶ noun [mass noun] Finance a type of placing used as a method of financing a takeover in which the purchasing company issues its own shares as payment to the company being bought, with the pre-arranged agreement that these shares are then placed with investors in exchange for cash.

vendue /vɛnˈdjuː/ ▶ noun US & W. Indian a public auction.
- ORIGIN late 17th cent.: via Dutch from French dialect *vendue* 'sale', from *vendre* 'to sell'.

veneer /vɪˈnɪə/ ▶ noun a thin decorative covering of fine wood applied to a coarser wood or other material.
■ a layer of wood used to make plywood. ■ [in sing.] an attractive appearance that covers or disguises someone or something's true nature or feelings: *her veneer of composure cracked a little.*
▶ verb [with obj.] [usu. as adj. **veneered**] cover (something) with a decorative layer of fine wood.
■ cover or disguise (someone or something's true nature) with an attractive appearance.
- ORIGIN early 18th cent. (earlier as *fineer*): from German *furni(e)ren*, from Old French *fournir* 'furnish'.

veneering ▶ noun [mass noun] **1** material used as veneer.
2 the action of covering something with a veneer.

venepuncture /ˈvɛnɪˌpʌŋ(k)tʃə, ˈviːnɪ-/ (chiefly N. Amer. also **venipuncture**) ▶ noun [mass noun] the puncture of a vein as part of a medical procedure, typically to withdraw a blood sample or for an intravenous injection.
- ORIGIN 1920s: from Latin *vena* 'vein' + PUNCTURE.

venerable ▶ adjective accorded a great deal of respect, especially because of age, wisdom, or character: *a venerable statesman.*
■ (in the Anglican Church) a title given to an archdeacon. ■ (in the Roman Catholic Church) a title given to a deceased person who has attained a certain degree of sanctity but has not been fully beatified or canonized.
- DERIVATIVES **venerability** noun, **venerableness** noun, **venerably** adverb.
- ORIGIN late Middle English: from Old French, or from Latin *venerabilis*, from the verb *venerari* (see VENERATE).

venerate /ˈvɛnəreɪt/ ▶ verb [with obj.] (often be **venerated**) regard with great respect; revere: *Philip of Beverley was venerated as a saint.*

- DERIVATIVES **veneration** noun, **venerator** noun.
- ORIGIN early 17th cent.: from Latin *venerat-* 'adored, revered', from the verb *venerari.*

venereal /vɪˈnɪərɪəl/ ▶ adjective of or relating to sexual desire or sexual intercourse.
■ of or relating to venereal disease.
- DERIVATIVES **venereally** adverb.
- ORIGIN late Middle English: from Latin *venereus* (from *venus, vener-* 'sexual love') + -AL.

venereal disease ▶ noun a disease typically contracted by sexual intercourse with a person already infected; a sexually transmitted disease.

venereology /vɪˌnɪərɪˈɒlədʒi/ ▶ noun [mass noun] the branch of medicine concerned with venereal diseases.
- DERIVATIVES **venereological** adjective, **venereologist** noun.

venery[1] /ˈvɛn(ə)ri/ ▶ noun [mass noun] archaic sexual indulgence.
- ORIGIN late Middle English: from medieval Latin *veneria*, from *venus, vener-* 'sexual love'.

venery[2] /ˈvɛn(ə)ri/ ▶ noun [mass noun] archaic hunting.
- ORIGIN late Middle English: from Old French *venerie*, from *vener* 'to hunt', from Latin *venari.*

venesection /ˌvɛnɪˈsɛkʃ(ə)n, ˌviːnɪ-/ ▶ noun another term for PHLEBOTOMY.
- ORIGIN mid 17th cent.: from medieval Latin *venae sectio(n-)* 'cutting of a vein'.

Venetia /vɪˈniːʃə/ a region of NE Italy; capital, Venice. Italian name **VENETO** /ˈvɛneto/.
- ORIGIN named after the *Veneti*, the pre-Roman inhabitants of the region.

Venetian ▶ adjective of or relating to Venice or its people.
▶ noun **1** a native or citizen of Venice.
■ [mass noun] the dialect of Italian spoken in Venice.
2 (**venetians**) venetian blinds.
- ORIGIN late Middle English: from Old French *Venicien*, assimilated to medieval Latin *Venetianus*, from Latin *Venetia* 'Venice'.

venetian blind ▶ noun a window blind consisting of horizontal slats which can be pivoted to control the amount of light that passes through it.

Venetian glass ▶ noun another term for MURANO GLASS.

Venetian red ▶ noun [mass noun] a reddish-brown pigment consisting of ferric oxide.
■ a strong reddish-brown colour.

Venetian window ▶ noun a window with three separate openings, the central one being arched and taller than the others.

Venezia /veˈnɛttsja/ Italian name for VENICE.

Venezuela /ˌvɛnɪˈzweɪlə, Spanish beneˈswela, -θwela/ a republic on the north coast of South America, with a coastline on the Caribbean Sea; pop. 20,191,000 (est. 1991); official language, Spanish; capital, Caracas.

Colonized by the Spanish in the 16th century, Venezuela won its independence in 1821 after a ten-year struggle, but did not finally emerge as a separate nation until its secession from federation with Colombia (1830). It is a major oil-exporting country, with the industry based on the area around Lake Maracaibo in the north-west.

- DERIVATIVES **Venezuelan** adjective & noun.
- ORIGIN Spanish, literally 'little Venice', named by early explorers when they saw native houses built on stilts over water.

vengeance /ˈvɛn(d)ʒ(ə)ns/ ▶ noun [mass noun] punishment inflicted or retribution exacted for an injury or wrong.
- PHRASES **with a vengeance** used to emphasize the degree to which something occurs or is true: *her headache was back with a vengeance.*
- ORIGIN Middle English: from Old French, from *venger* 'avenge'.

vengeful ▶ adjective seeking to harm someone in return for a perceived injury: *a vengeful ex-con.*
- DERIVATIVES **vengefully** adverb, **vengefulness** noun.
- ORIGIN late 16th cent.: from obsolete *venge* 'avenge' (see VENGEANCE), on the pattern of *revengeful.*

venial /ˈviːnɪəl/ ▶ adjective Christian Theology denoting a sin that is not regarded as depriving the soul of divine grace. Often contrasted with MORTAL.
■ (of a fault or offence) slight and pardonable.
- DERIVATIVES **veniality** /-ˈalɪti/ noun, **venially** adverb.
- ORIGIN Middle English: via Old French from late Latin *venialis*, from *venia* 'forgiveness'.

Venice /ˈvɛnɪs/ a city in NE Italy, capital of Venetia region; pop. 317,840 (1990). Italian name **VENEZIA**.

Situated on a lagoon of the Adriatic, it is built on numerous islands that are separated by canals and linked by bridges. It was a powerful republic in the Middle Ages and from the 13th to the 16th centuries a leading sea power, controlling trade to the Levant and ruling parts of the eastern Mediterranean. After the Napoleonic Wars Venice was placed under Austrian rule and was incorporated into a unified Italy in 1866.

venipuncture ▶ noun chiefly N. Amer. variant spelling of VENEPUNCTURE.

venison /ˈvɛnɪs(ə)n, ˈvɛnɪz(ə)n/ ▶ noun [mass noun] meat from a deer.
- ORIGIN Middle English: from Old French *veneso(u)n*, from Latin *venatio(n-)* 'hunting', from *venari* 'to hunt'.

Venite /vɪˈnʌɪti, vɪˈniːti, -teɪ/ ▶ noun Psalm 95 used as a canticle in Christian liturgy, chiefly at matins.
- ORIGIN Latin, literally 'come ye', the first word of the psalm.

Venn diagram ▶ noun a diagram representing mathematical or logical sets pictorially as circles or closed curves within an enclosing rectangle (the universal set), common elements of the sets being represented by intersections of the circles.
- ORIGIN early 20th cent.: named after John *Venn* (1834–1923), English logician.

vennel /ˈvɛn(ə)l/ ▶ noun chiefly Scottish a narrow lane or passage between buildings; an alley.
- ORIGIN late Middle English: from Old French *venele*, from medieval Latin *venella*, diminutive of Latin *vena* 'vein'.

venogram /ˈviːnə(ʊ)gram/ ▶ noun Medicine an image produced by venography.

venography /vɪˈnɒɡrəfi/ ▶ noun [mass noun] Medicine radiography of a vein after injection of a radiopaque fluid.
- DERIVATIVES **venographic** /ˌviːnə(ʊ)ˈɡrafɪk/ adjective, **venographically** adverb.
- ORIGIN 1930s: from Latin *vena* 'vein' + -GRAPHY.

venom ▶ noun [mass noun] poisonous fluid secreted by animals such as snakes and scorpions and typically injected into prey or aggressors by biting or stinging.
■ figurative extreme malice and bitterness shown in someone's attitudes, speech, or actions: *his voice was full of venom.*
- DERIVATIVES **venomed** adjective.
- ORIGIN Middle English: from Old French *venim*, variant of *venin*, from an alteration of Latin *venenum* 'poison'.

venomous /ˈvɛnəməs/ ▶ adjective (of animals, especially snakes, or their parts) secreting venom; capable of injecting venom by means of a bite or sting.
■ figurative (of a person or their behaviour) full of malice or spite: *she replied with a venomous glance.*
- DERIVATIVES **venomously** adverb, **venomousness** noun.
- ORIGIN Middle English: from Old French *venimeux*, from *venim* (see VENOM).

venous /ˈviːnəs/ ▶ adjective of or relating to a vein or the veins.
- DERIVATIVES **venosity** /vɪˈnɒsɪti/ noun, **venously** adverb.
- ORIGIN early 17th cent.: from Latin *venosus* 'venose', from *vena* 'vein'.

vent[1] ▶ noun an opening that allows air, gas, or liquid to pass out of or into a confined space.
■ [mass noun] figurative release or expression of a strong emotion, energy, etc.: *children give vent to their anger in various ways.* ■ the opening of a volcano, through which lava and other materials are emitted. ■ chiefly Scottish a flue of a chimney. ■ historical the touch hole of a gun. ■ the anus, especially one in a lower animal such as a fish that serves for both excretion and reproduction.
▶ verb [with obj.] **1** give free expression to (a strong emotion): *we vent our spleen on drug barons.*
2 provide with an outlet for air, gas, or liquid: *tumble-dryers must be vented to the outside.*
■ discharge or expel (air, gas, or liquid) through an outlet: *the plant was isolated and the gas vented.* ■ permit air to enter (a beer cask).
- DERIVATIVES **ventless** adjective.
- ORIGIN late Middle English: partly from French *vent* 'wind', from Latin *ventus*, reinforced by French *évent*, from *éventer* 'expose to air', based on Latin *ventus* 'wind'.

vent[2] ▶ noun a slit in a garment, especially in the

lower edge of the back of a coat through the seam.
– ORIGIN late Middle English: alteration of dialect *fent*, from Old French *fente* 'slit', based on Latin *findere* 'cleave'.

venter ▶ **noun** Zoology the underside or abdomen of an animal.
– ORIGIN early 18th cent.: from Latin, literally 'belly'.

ventiduct /ˈvɛntɪdʌkt/ ▶ **noun** Architecture an air passage, especially for ventilation.
– ORIGIN early 17th cent.: from Latin *ventus* 'wind' + *ductus* 'duct'.

ventifact /ˈvɛntɪfakt/ ▶ **noun** Geology a stone shaped by the erosive action of wind-blown sand.
– ORIGIN early 20th cent.: from Latin *ventus* 'wind' + *factum*, neuter past participle of *facere* 'make'.

ventil /ˈvɛntɪl/ ▶ **noun** Music **1** a valve in a wind instrument.
2 a shutter for regulating the airflow in an organ.
– ORIGIN late 19th cent.: from German, from Italian *ventile*, from medieval Latin *ventile* 'sluice', from Latin *ventus* 'wind'.

ventilate ▶ **verb** [with obj.] **1** cause air to enter and circulate freely in (a room, building, etc.): [as adj., in combination **-ventilated**] *gas heaters should only ever be used in well-ventilated rooms.*
■(of air) purify or freshen (something) by blowing on or through it: *a colossus ventilated by the dawn breeze.* ■Medicine subject to artificial respiration. ■archaic oxygenate (the blood). ■informal kill (someone) by shooting: *I pull out a gun and ventilate her dinner companion.*
2 discuss or examine (an opinion, issue, complaint, etc.) in public: *he used the club to ventilate an ongoing complaint.*
– ORIGIN late Middle English (in the sense 'winnow, scatter'): from Latin *ventilat-* 'blown, winnowed', from the verb *ventilare*, from *ventus* 'wind'. The sense 'cause air to circulate in' dates from the mid 18th cent.

ventilation ▶ **noun** [mass noun] **1** the provision of fresh air to a room, building, etc.
■Medicine the supply of air to the lungs, especially by artificial means.
2 public discussion or examination of an opinion, issue, complaint, etc.
– ORIGIN late Middle English (in the sense 'current of air'): from Old French, or from Latin *ventilatio(n-)*, from the verb *ventilare* (see **VENTILATE**). Sense 1 dates from the mid 17th cent.

ventilator ▶ **noun 1** an appliance or aperture for ventilating a room or other space.
2 Medicine appliance for artificial respiration; a respirator.

ventilatory /ˈvɛntɪlə,t(ə)ri/ ▶ **adjective** Physiology of, relating to, or serving for the provision of air to the lungs or respiratory system.

Ventolin /ˈvɛntəlɪn/ ▶ **noun** trademark for **SALBUTAMOL**.
– ORIGIN 1960s: perhaps from **VENTILATE** + **-OL** + **-IN**[1].

Ventose /vɒ̃ˈtəʊz/ (also **Ventôse** /French vɑ̃toz/) ▶ **noun** the sixth month of the French Republican calendar (1793–1805), originally running from 19 February to 20 March.
– ORIGIN French *Ventôse*, from Latin *ventosus* 'windy', from *ventus* 'wind'.

ventouse /ˈvɛntuːs/ ▶ **noun** Medicine a vacuum extractor for use in assisting childbirth.
– ORIGIN 1960s: from French, literally 'cupping-glass', based on Latin *ventus* 'wind'.

ventral ▶ **adjective** Anatomy, Zoology, & Botany of, on, or relating to the underside of an animal or plant; abdominal: *a ventral nerve cord | the ventral part of the head.* Compare with **DORSAL**.
– DERIVATIVES **ventrally** adverb.
– ORIGIN late Middle English: from Latin *venter, ventr-* 'belly' + **-AL**.

ventral fin ▶ **noun** Zoology another term for **PELVIC FIN**.
■an unpaired fin on the underside of certain fishes. ■a single vertical fin under the fuselage or tail of an aircraft.

ventre à terre /,vɒ̃tr(ə) ɑː ˈtɛː, French vɑ̃tʀ a tɛʀ/ ▶ **adverb** at full speed (used especially of a horse's movement or its representation in painting).
– ORIGIN French, literally '(with) belly to the ground'.

ventricle /ˈvɛntrɪk(ə)l/ ▶ **noun** Anatomy a hollow part or cavity in an organ, in particular:
■each of the two main chambers of the heart, left and right. ■each of the four connected fluid-filled cavities in the centre of the brain.
– DERIVATIVES **ventricular** /-ˈtrɪkjʊlə/ adjective.
– ORIGIN late Middle English: from Latin *ventriculus*, diminutive of *venter* 'belly'.

ventriculography /vɛn,trɪkjʊˈlɒgrəfi/ ▶ **noun** [mass noun] Medicine radiography of the ventricles of the brain with the cerebral fluid replaced by air (pneumoencephalography) or radiopaque material or labelled with a radionuclide.

ventriloquist /vɛnˈtrɪləkwɪst/ ▶ **noun** a person who can speak or utter sounds so that they seem to come from somewhere else, especially an entertainer who makes their voice appear to come from a dummy of a person or animal.
– DERIVATIVES **ventriloquial** /,vɛntrɪˈləʊkwɪəl/ adjective, **ventriloquism** noun, **ventriloquize** (also **-ise**) verb, **ventriloquy** noun.
– ORIGIN mid 17th cent.: from modern Latin *ventriloquium* (from Latin *venter* 'belly' + *loqui* 'speak') + **-IST**.

ventrolateral /,vɛntrə(ʊ)ˈlatər(ə)l/ ▶ **adjective** Biology situated towards the junction of the ventral and lateral sides.
– DERIVATIVES **ventrolaterally** adverb.

ventromedial /,vɛntrə(ʊ)ˈmiːdɪəl/ ▶ **adjective** Biology situated towards the middle of the ventral side.
– DERIVATIVES **ventromedially** adverb.

venture ▶ **noun** a risky or daring journey or undertaking: *pioneering ventures into little-known waters.*
■a business enterprise involving considerable risk.
▶ **verb** [no obj., with infinitive or adverbial] dare to do something or go somewhere that may be dangerous or unpleasant: *she **ventured out** into the blizzard.*
■dare to do or say something that may be considered audacious (often used as a polite expression of hesitation or apology): *may I venture to add a few comments? | I ventured to write to her |* [with obj.] *he ventured the opinion that Putt was now dangerously insane.* ■[with obj.] expose (something) to the risk of loss: *his fortune is ventured in an expedition over which he has no control.*
– PHRASES **at a venture** archaic trusting to chance rather than to previous consideration or preparation: *a man drew a bow at a venture.* **nothing ventured, nothing gained** proverb you can't expect to achieve anything if you never take any risks.
– ORIGIN late Middle English (in the sense 'adventure', also 'risk the loss of'): shortening of **ADVENTURE**.

venture capital ▶ **noun** [mass noun] capital invested in a project in which there is a substantial element of risk, typically a new or expanding business.
– DERIVATIVES **venture capitalist** noun.

venturer ▶ **noun** archaic a person who undertakes or shares in a trading venture.

Venture Scout ▶ **noun** a member of the Scout Association aged between 16 and 20.

venturesome ▶ **adjective** willing to take risks or embark on difficult or unusual courses of action.
– DERIVATIVES **venturesomely** adverb, **venturesomeness** noun.

Venturi /vɛnˈtjʊəri/, Robert (Charles) (b.1925), American architect, pioneer of postmodernist architecture. Among his buildings are the Humanities Classroom Building of the State University of New York (1973) and the Sainsbury Wing of the National Gallery in London (1991).

venturi /vɛnˈtjʊəri/ ▶ **noun** (pl. **venturis**) a short piece of narrow tube between wider sections for measuring flow rate or exerting suction.
– ORIGIN late 19th cent.: named after Giovanni B. *Venturi* (1746–1822), Italian physicist.

venue /ˈvɛnjuː/ ▶ **noun** the place where something happens, especially an organized event such as a concert, conference, or sports event: *the river could soon be the venue for a powerboat world championship event.*
■English Law the county or district within which a criminal or civil case must be heard.
– ORIGIN late 16th cent. (denoting a thrust or bout in fencing; also in the Law sense): from Old French, literally 'a coming', feminine past participle of *venir* 'come' from Latin *venire*.

venule /ˈvɛnjuːl/ ▶ **noun** Anatomy a very small vein, especially one collecting blood from the capillaries.
– ORIGIN mid 19th cent.: from Latin *venula*, diminutive of *vena* 'vein'.

Venus 1 Roman Mythology a goddess, worshipped as the goddess of love in classical Rome though apparently a spirit of kitchen gardens in earlier times. Greek equivalent **APHRODITE**. [ORIGIN: Latin.]
■[as noun **a Venus**] chiefly poetic/literary a beautiful woman.
2 Astronomy the second planet from the sun in the solar system, the brightest celestial object after the sun and moon and frequently appearing in the twilight sky as the evening or morning star.

Venus orbits between Mercury and the earth at an average distance of 108 million km from the sun. It is almost equal in size to the earth, with a diameter of 12,104 km, and shows phases similar to the moon. The planet is completely covered by clouds consisting chiefly of sulphuric acid droplets, and no surface detail can be seen by telescope. There is a dense atmosphere of carbon dioxide, which traps the heat of the sun by the greenhouse effect to produce a surface temperature of 460°C. The planet has no natural satellite.

3 (also **venus**, **Venus shell**, or (chiefly US) **Venus clam**) a burrowing marine bivalve mollusc with clearly defined growth lines on the shell.
● *Venus*, *Venerupis*, and other genera, family Veneridae.
– DERIVATIVES **Venusian** /vɪˈnjuːzɪən/ adjective & noun.

Venusberg /ˈviːnəsbəːg/ ▶ **noun** (in German legend) the court of Venus.

Venus de Milo /də ˈmʌɪləʊ, ˈmiːləʊ/ a classical sculpture of Aphrodite dated to *c.*100 BC. It was discovered on the Greek island of Melos in 1820 and is now in the Louvre in Paris.
– ORIGIN French, 'Venus of Melos'.

Venus flytrap (also **Venus's flytrap**) ▶ **noun** a small carnivorous bog plant with hinged leaves that spring shut on and digest insects which land on them. Native to the south-eastern US, it is also kept as an indoor plant.
● *Dionaea muscipula*, family Droseraceae.

Venus's comb ▶ **noun** another term for **SHEPHERD'S NEEDLE**.

Venus's flower basket ▶ **noun** a slender upright glass sponge with a filmy lattice-like skeleton.
● Genus *Euplectella*, class Hexactinellida.

Venus's girdle ▶ **noun** a large, almost transparent comb jelly with a flattened ribbon-like body, living chiefly in warmer seas.
● Genus *Cestum*, phylum Ctenophora.

Venus's looking glass ▶ **noun** a blue-flowered plant of the bellflower family, whose shiny brown seeds inside their open capsule supposedly resemble ladies' looking glasses.
● Two species in the family Campanulaceae: *Legousia hybrida* of Europe, and *Triodanis perfoliata* of North America.

vera causa /,vɛːrə ˈkaʊzə/ ▶ **noun** (pl. **verae causae** /,vɛːriː ˈkaʊziː/) chiefly historical (in Newtonian philosophy) the true cause of a natural phenomenon, by an agency whose existence is independently evidenced.
– ORIGIN Latin, literally 'real cause'.

veracious /vəˈreɪʃəs/ ▶ **adjective** formal speaking or representing the truth.
– DERIVATIVES **veraciously** adverb, **veraciousness** noun.
– ORIGIN late 17th cent.: from Latin *verax, verac-* (from *verus* 'true') + **-IOUS**.

veracity /vəˈrasɪti/ ▶ **noun** [mass noun] conformity to facts; accuracy: *officials expressed doubts concerning the veracity of the story.*
■habitual truthfulness: *voters should be concerned about his veracity and character.*
– ORIGIN early 17th cent.: from French *véracité* or medieval Latin *veracitas*, from *verax* 'speaking truly' (see **VERACIOUS**).

Veracruz /,vɪərəˈkruːz, Spanish beraˈkruθ, -krus/ **1** a state of east central Mexico, with a long coastline on the Gulf of Mexico; capital, Jalapa Enriquez.
2 a city and port of Mexico, in Veracruz state, on the Gulf of Mexico; pop. 327,520 (1990).

veranda (also **verandah**) ▶ **noun** a roofed platform along the outside of a house, level with the ground floor.
■Austral./NZ a roof over the pavement in front of a shop.
– DERIVATIVES **verandaed** adjective.
– ORIGIN early 18th cent.: from Hindi *varaṇḍā*, from Portuguese *varanda* 'railing, balustrade'.

verapamil /vəˈrapəmɪl/ ▶ **noun** [mass noun] Medicine a synthetic compound which acts as a calcium

antagonist and is used to treat angina pectoris and cardiac arrhythmias.
– ORIGIN 1960s: from *v(al)er(onitr)il(e)* (from **VALERIC ACID** + **NITRILE**), with the insertion of -*apam*- (of unknown origin).

veratrine /ˈvɛrətriːn, -ɪn/ ▶ noun [mass noun] Chemistry a poisonous substance consisting of a mixture of alkaloids which occurs in the seeds of sabadilla and related plants.
– ORIGIN early 19th cent.: from French *vératrine*, from Latin *veratrum* 'hellebore'.

veratrum /vəˈreɪtrəm/ ▶ noun (pl. **veratrums**) a plant of a genus that includes the false helleborines.
● Genus *Veratrum*, family Liliaceae.
– ORIGIN modern Latin, from Latin, literally 'hellebore'.

verb ▶ noun Grammar a word used to describe an action, state, or occurrence, and forming the main part of the predicate of a sentence, such as *hear*, *become*, *happen*.
– DERIVATIVES **verbless** adjective.
– ORIGIN late Middle English: from Old French *verbe* or Latin *verbum* 'word, verb'.

verbal ▶ adjective 1 relating to or in the form of words: *the root of the problem is visual rather than verbal* | *verbal abuse*.
■spoken rather than written; oral: *a verbal agreement*. ■ tending to talk a lot: *he's very verbal*.
2 Grammar of, relating to, or derived from a verb: *a verbal adjective*.
▶ noun 1 Grammar a word or words functioning as a verb.
■a verbal noun.
2 [mass noun] Brit. informal abuse; insults: *I'd go out on the pitch and get verbal from the crowd*.
■lengthy meaningless talk; verbiage: *the actors give it some verbal about how it's an honour just to be nominated*.
3 (**verbals**) informal the lyrics of a song or the dialogue of a film.
4 (usu. **verbals**) Brit. informal a verbal statement containing a damaging admission alleged to have been made to the police, and offered as evidence by the prosecution.
▶ verb (**verballed**, **verballing**) [with obj.] Brit. informal attribute a damaging statement to (a suspect), especially dishonestly.
– DERIVATIVES **verbally** adverb.
– ORIGIN late 15th cent. (describing a person who deals with words rather than things): from French, or from late Latin *verbalis*, from *verbum* 'word' (see **VERB**).

USAGE It is sometimes said that the true sense of the adjective **verbal** is 'of or concerned with words', whether spoken or written (as in **verbal** *abuse*), and that it should not be used to mean 'spoken rather than written' (as in *a verbal agreement*). For this sense, it is said that the adjective **oral** should be used instead. In practice, however, **verbal** is well established in this sense and, in certain idiomatic phrases (such as *a verbal agreement*), cannot be simply replaced by **oral**.

verbalism ▶ noun [mass noun] concentration on forms of expression rather than content.
■ [count noun] a verbal expression. ■ excessive or empty use of language.
– DERIVATIVES **verbalist** noun, **verbalistic** adjective.

verbalize (also **-ise**) ▶ verb 1 [with obj.] express (ideas or feelings) in words, especially by speaking out loud: *they are unable to verbalize their real feelings*.
2 [no obj.] speak, especially at excessive length and with little real content: *the dangers of verbalizing about art*.
3 [with obj.] make (a word, especially a noun) into a verb.
– DERIVATIVES **verbalizable** adjective, **verbalization** noun, **verbalizer** noun.

verbal noun ▶ noun Grammar a noun formed as an inflection of a verb and partly sharing its constructions, such as *smoking* in *smoking is forbidden*. See **-ING**[1].

verbascum /vəˈbaskəm/ ▶ noun a plant of a genus that comprises the mulleins.
● Genus *Verbascum*, family Scrophulariaceae.
– ORIGIN modern Latin, from Latin, literally 'mullein'.

verbatim /vəˈbeɪtɪm/ ▶ adverb & adjective in exactly the same words as were used originally: [as adv.] *subjects were instructed to recall the passage verbatim* | [as adj.] *your quotations must be verbatim*.

– ORIGIN late 15th cent.: from medieval Latin, from Latin *verbum* 'word'. Compare with **LITERATIM**.

verbena /vəˈbiːnə/ ▶ noun a chiefly American herbaceous plant which bears heads of bright showy flowers, widely cultivated as a garden ornamental.
● Genus *Verbena*, family Verbenaceae: many species, in particular a group of complex cultivars (*V.* × *hybrida*).
– ORIGIN modern Latin, from Latin, literally 'sacred bough', in medieval Latin 'vervain'.

verbiage /ˈvəːbɪɪdʒ/ ▶ noun [mass noun] speech or writing that uses too many words or excessively technical expressions.
– ORIGIN early 18th cent.: from French, from obsolete *verbeier* 'to chatter', from *verbe* 'word' (see **VERB**).

verbose /vəˈbəʊs/ ▶ adjective using or expressed in more words than are needed: *much academic language is obscure and verbose*.
– DERIVATIVES **verbosely** adverb, **verbosity** noun.
– ORIGIN late 17th cent.: from Latin *verbosus*, from *verbum* 'word'.

verboten /vəˈbəʊt(ə)n, German fɛɐˈboːtn̩/ ▶ adjective forbidden, especially by an authority.
– ORIGIN German.

verb phrase ▶ noun Grammar the part of a sentence containing the verb and any direct or indirect object, but not the subject.

verdant /ˈvəːd(ə)nt/ ▶ adjective (of countryside) green with grass or other rich vegetation.
■of the bright green colour of lush grass: *a deep, verdant green*.
– DERIVATIVES **verdancy** noun, **verdantly** adverb.
– ORIGIN late 16th cent.: perhaps from Old French *verdeant*, present participle of *verdoier* 'be green', based on Latin *viridis* 'green'.

verd-antique /ˌvəːdanˈtiːk/ ▶ noun [mass noun] a green ornamental marble consisting of serpentine with calcite and dolomite.
■verdigris on ancient bronze or copper. ■ a green form of porphyry.
– ORIGIN mid 18th cent.: from obsolete French, literally 'antique green'.

Verdelho /vəːˈdɛljuː, -ljəʊ/ ▶ noun (pl. **-os**) a white grape originally grown in Madeira, now also in Portugal, Sicily, Australia, and South Africa.
■[mass noun] a medium Madeira made from this grape.
– ORIGIN Portuguese.

verderer /ˈvəːd(ə)rə/ ▶ noun Brit. a judicial officer of a royal forest.
– ORIGIN mid 16th cent.: from Anglo-Norman French, based on Latin *viridis* 'green'.

Verdi /ˈvɛːdi, Italian ˈverdi/, Giuseppe (Fortunino Francesco) (1813–1901), Italian composer. His many operas, such as *La Traviata* (1853), *Aida* (1871), and *Otello* (1887), emphasize the dramatic element, treating personal stories on a heroic scale and often against backgrounds that reflect his political interests. He is also famous for his *Requiem* (1874).

Verdicchio /vɛːˈdiːkɪəʊ/ ▶ noun [mass noun] a variety of white wine grape grown in the Marche region of Italy.
■a dry white wine made from this grape.
– ORIGIN Italian.

verdict ▶ noun a decision on an issue of fact in a civil or criminal case or an inquest: *the jury returned a verdict of not guilty*.
■an opinion or judgement: *this seems a fair verdict on the tabloids*.
– ORIGIN Middle English: from Anglo-Norman French *verdit*, from Old French *veir* 'true' (from Latin *verus*) + *dit* (from Latin *dictum* 'saying').

verdigris /ˈvəːdɪgriː, -griːs/ ▶ noun [mass noun] a bright bluish-green encrustation or patina formed on copper or brass by atmospheric oxidation, consisting of basic copper carbonate.
– ORIGIN Middle English: from Old French *verte-gres*, earlier *vert de Grece* 'green of Greece'.

verdigris agaric ▶ noun a toadstool with a slimy blue-green cap and dark brown gills, found in both Eurasia and North America.
● *Stropharia aeruginosa*, family Strophariaceae, class Hymenomycetes.

verdin /ˈvəːdɪn/ ▶ noun a small songbird with a grey body and yellowish head, found in the semi-deserts of south-western North America.
● *Auriparus flaviceps*, family Remizidae.
– ORIGIN late 19th cent.: from French, literally 'yellowhammer'.

verditer /ˈvəːdɪtə/ ▶ noun [mass noun] a light blue or bluish-green pigment, typically prepared by adding chalk or whiting to a solution of copper nitrate, used in making crayons and as a watercolour.
▶ adjective of this colour.
– ORIGIN early 16th cent.: from Old French *verd de terre*, literally 'earth green'.

Verdun, Battle of /vɛːˈdʌn, French vɛʁdœ̃/ a long and severe battle in 1916, during the First World War, at the fortified town of Verdun in NE France.

verdure /ˈvəːdjə, -jʊə/ ▶ noun [mass noun] lush green vegetation.
■the fresh green colour of such vegetation. ■ poetic/literary a condition of freshness.
– DERIVATIVES **verdured** adjective, **verdurous** adjective.
– ORIGIN late Middle English: via French from Old French *verd* 'green', from Latin *viridis*.

Vereeniging /fəˈriːnɪkɪŋ, fəˈreɪnɪxɪŋ/ a city in South Africa, in the province of Gauteng; pop. 773,590 (1991) (with Vanderbijlpark).

verge[1] ▶ noun an edge or border: *they came down to the verge of the lake*.
■an extreme limit beyond which something specified will happen: *I was on the verge of tears*. ■ Brit. a grass edging such as that by the side of a road or path. ■ Architecture an edge of tiles projecting over a gable.
▶ verb [no obj.] (**verge on**) approach (something) closely; be close or similar to (something): *despair verging on the suicidal*.
– ORIGIN late Middle English: via Old French from Latin *virga* 'rod'. The current verb sense dates from the late 18th cent.

verge[2] ▶ noun a wand or rod carried before a bishop or dean as an emblem of office.
– ORIGIN late Middle English: from Latin *virga* 'rod'.

verge[3] ▶ verb [no obj., with adverbial of direction] incline in a certain direction or towards a particular state: *his style verged into the art nouveau school*.
– ORIGIN early 17th cent. (in the sense 'descend (to the horizon)'): from Latin *vergere* 'to bend, incline'.

vergence ▶ noun [mass noun] 1 Physiology the simultaneous movement of the pupils of the eyes towards or away from one another during focusing.
2 Geology the direction in which a fold is inclined or overturned: *a zone of opposing fold vergence*.
– ORIGIN 1980s: common element of **CONVERGENCE** and **DIVERGENCE**.

verger ▶ noun 1 an official in a church who carries a rod before a bishop or dean as a symbol of office.
2 an officer who carries a rod before a bishop or dean as a symbol of office.
– DERIVATIVES **vergership** noun.
– ORIGIN Middle English (in sense 2): from Anglo-Norman French (see **VERGE**[2]).

Vergil variant spelling of **VIRGIL**.

verglas /ˈvɛːglɑː/ ▶ noun [mass noun] a thin coating of ice or frozen rain on an exposed surface.
– ORIGIN late 19th cent.: French, from *verre* 'glass' + *glas* (now *glace*) 'ice'.

veridical /vɪˈrɪdɪk(ə)l/ ▶ adjective formal truthful.
■coinciding with reality: *such memories are not necessarily veridical*.
– DERIVATIVES **veridicality** noun, **veridically** adverb.
– ORIGIN mid 17th cent.: from Latin *veridicus* (from *verus* 'true' + *dicere* 'say') + **-AL**.

veriest ▶ adjective [attrib.] (**the veriest**) chiefly archaic used to emphasize the degree to which a description applies to someone or something: *everyone but the veriest greenhorn knows by now*.
– ORIGIN early 16th cent.: superlative of **VERY**.

verification ▶ noun [mass noun] the process of establishing the truth, accuracy, or validity of something: *the verification of official documents*.
■[often as modifier] Philosophy the establishment by empirical means of the validity of a proposition. ■ the process of ensuring that procedures laid down in weapons limitation agreements are followed.
– ORIGIN early 16th cent.: from Old French or from medieval Latin *verificatio(n-)*, from the verb *verificare* (see **VERIFY**).

verification principle ▶ noun Philosophy the characteristic doctrine of logical positivism, that a statement which cannot be verified is strictly meaningless.

verify /ˈvɛrɪfʌɪ/ ▶ verb (**-ies**, **-ied**) [with obj.] (often **be verified**) make sure or demonstrate that (something) is true, accurate, or justified: *his*

conclusions have been verified by later experiments | [with clause] 'Can you verify that the guns are licensed?'
■Law swear to or support (a statement) by affidavit.
– DERIVATIVES **verifiable** adjective, **verifiably** adverb, **verifier** noun.
– ORIGIN Middle English (as a legal term): from Old French *verifier*, from medieval Latin *verificare*, from *verus* 'true'.

verily ▶ adverb archaic truly; certainly: [sentence adverb] *verily these men are mad.*
– ORIGIN Middle English: from **VERY** + **-LY**[2], suggested by Old French *verrai(e)ment*.

verisimilitude /ˌvɛrɪsɪˈmɪlɪtjuːd/ ▶ noun [mass noun] the appearance of being true or real: *the detail gives the novel some verisimilitude.*
– DERIVATIVES **verisimilar** adjective.
– ORIGIN early 17th cent.: from Latin *verisimilitudo*, from *verisimilis* 'probable', from *veri* (genitive of *verus* 'true') + *similis* 'like'.

verismo /vɛˈrɪzməʊ/ ▶ noun [mass noun] realism in the arts, especially late 19th-century Italian opera.
■this genre of opera, as composed principally by Puccini, Mascagni, and Leoncavallo.
– ORIGIN Italian.

veristic /vɪəˈrɪstɪk/ ▶ adjective (of art or literature) extremely or strictly naturalistic.
– DERIVATIVES **verism** noun, **verist** noun & adjective.
– ORIGIN late 19th cent.: from Latin *verum* (neuter) 'true' or Italian *vero* 'true' + **-IST** + **-IC**.

veritable ▶ adjective [attrib.] used as an intensifier, often to qualify a metaphor: *the early 1970s witnessed a veritable price explosion.*
– DERIVATIVES **veritably** adverb.
– ORIGIN late Middle English: from Old French, from *verite* 'truth' (see **VERITY**). Early senses included 'true' and 'speaking the truth', later 'genuine, actual'.

vérité /ˈvɛrɪteɪ, French veˈrite/ ▶ noun [mass noun] a genre of film, television, and radio programmes emphasizing realism and naturalism.
– ORIGIN French, literally 'truth'.

verity /ˈvɛrɪti/ ▶ noun (pl. **-ies**) a true principle or belief, especially one of fundamental importance: *the eternal verities.*
■[mass noun] truth: *irrefutable, objective verity.*
– ORIGIN late Middle English: from Old French *verite*, from Latin *veritas*, from *verus* 'true'.

verjuice /ˈvɜːdʒuːs/ ▶ noun [mass noun] a sour juice obtained from crab apples, unripe grapes, or other fruit, used in cooking and formerly in medicine.
– ORIGIN Middle English: from Old French *vertjus*, from *vert* 'green' + *jus* 'juice'.

Verkhneudinsk /ˌvɛːxnjɛˈuːdɪnsk/ former name (until 1934) for **ULAN-UDE**.

verkrampte /fɛːˈkramptə/ (also **verkramp** /fɛːˈkramp/) S. African ▶ adjective politically or socially conservative or reactionary, especially as regards apartheid.
▶ noun a person holding bigoted and reactionary views.
– DERIVATIVES **verkramptheid** noun.
– ORIGIN Afrikaans, literally 'narrow, cramped'.

Verlaine /vɛːˈlɛn, French vɛʁlɛn/, Paul (1844–96), French symbolist poet. Notable collections of poetry include *Poèmes saturniens* (1867), *Fêtes galantes* (1869), and *Romances sans paroles* (1874).

verligte /fɛːˈlɪxtə/ (also **verlig**) S. African ▶ adjective progressive or enlightened, especially as regards apartheid.
▶ noun a person holding progressive and enlightened views.
– DERIVATIVES **verligtheid** noun.
– ORIGIN Afrikaans, literally 'enlightened'.

Vermeer /vɜːˈmɪə/, Jan (1632–75), Dutch painter. He generally painted domestic genre scenes, for example *The Kitchen-Maid* (c.1658). His work is distinguished by its clear design and simple form.

vermeil /ˈvɜːmeɪl, -mɪl/ ▶ noun [mass noun] [often as modifier] **1** gilded silver or bronze.
2 poetic/literary vermilion.
– ORIGIN late Middle English (in sense 2): from Old French (see **VERMILION**).

vermi- ▶ combining form of or relating to a worm or worms, especially parasitic ones: *vermiform.*
– ORIGIN from Latin *vermis* 'worm'.

vermian /ˈvɜːmɪən/ ▶ adjective **1** poetic/literary relating to or resembling a worm; worm-like.
2 Anatomy of or relating to the vermis of the brain.

– ORIGIN late 19th cent.: from Latin *vermis* 'worm' + **-IAN**.

vermicelli /ˌvɜːmɪˈtʃɛli, ˌvɜːmɪˈ-, -ˈsɛli/ ▶ plural noun
1 pasta made in long slender threads.
2 Brit. shreds of chocolate used to decorate cakes or other sweet foods.
– ORIGIN Italian, plural of *vermicello*, diminutive of *verme* 'worm', from Latin *vermis*.

vermicide /ˈvɜːmɪsʌɪd/ ▶ noun a substance that is poisonous to worms.

vermicular /vəˈmɪkjʊlə/ ▶ adjective **1** like a worm in form or movement; vermiform.
2 of, denoting, or caused by intestinal worms.
– ORIGIN late 17th cent.: from medieval Latin *vermicularis*, from Latin *vermiculus*, diminutive of *vermis* 'worm'.

vermiculate /vəˈmɪkjʊlət/ ▶ adjective **1** another term for **VERMICULAR**.
2 another term for **VERMICULATED**.
– ORIGIN early 17th cent.: from Latin *vermiculatus*, past participle of *vermiculari* 'be full of worms' (see **VERMICULAR**).

vermiculated ▶ adjective **1** (especially of the plumage of a bird) marked with sinuous or wavy lines.
2 archaic worm-eaten.

vermiculite /vəˈmɪkjʊlʌɪt/ ▶ noun [mass noun] a yellow or brown mineral found as an alteration product of mica and other minerals, used for insulation or as a moisture-retentive medium for growing plants.
– ORIGIN early 19th cent.: from Latin *vermiculari* 'be full of worms' (because on expansion due to heat, it shoots out forms resembling small worms) + **-ITE**[1].

vermiform ▶ adjective chiefly Zoology or Anatomy resembling or having the form of a worm.

vermiform appendix ▶ noun technical term for **APPENDIX** (in sense 1).

vermifuge /ˈvɜːmɪfjuːdʒ/ ▶ noun Medicine an anthelmintic medicine.

vermilion /vəˈmɪljən/ (also **vermillion**) ▶ noun [mass noun] a brilliant red pigment made from mercury sulphide (cinnabar).
■a brilliant red colour: *a lateral stripe of vermilion* | [as modifier] *vermilion streaks of sunset.*
– ORIGIN Middle English: from Old French *vermeillon*, from *vermeil*, from Latin *vermiculus*, diminutive of *vermis* 'worm'.

vermin ▶ noun [treated as pl.] wild mammals and birds which are believed to be harmful to crops, farm animals, or game, or which carry disease, e.g. foxes, rodents, and insect pests.
■parasitic worms or insects. ■ figurative people perceived as despicable and as causing problems for the rest of society: *the vermin who ransacked her house.*
– DERIVATIVES **verminous** adjective.
– ORIGIN Middle English (originally denoting animals such as reptiles and snakes): from Old French, based on Latin *vermis* 'worm'.

verminate ▶ verb [no obj.] [usu. as adj. **verminating**] archaic breed or become infested with vermin.
– DERIVATIVES **vermination** noun.
– ORIGIN late 17th cent.: from Latin *verminat-* 'full of worms', from the verb *verminare*, from *vermis* 'worm'.

vermis /ˈvɜːmɪs/ ▶ noun Anatomy the rounded and elongated central part of the cerebellum, between the two hemispheres.
– ORIGIN late 19th cent.: from Latin, literally 'worm'.

Vermont /vəˈmɒnt/ a state in the north-eastern US, on the border with Canada; pop. 562,760 (1990); capital, Montpelier. Explored and settled by the French during the 17th and 18th centuries, it became an independent republic in 1777 and the 14th state of the US in 1791.
– DERIVATIVES **Vermonter** noun.

vermouth /ˈvɜːməθ, vəˈmuːθ/ ▶ noun [mass noun] a red or white wine flavoured with aromatic herbs, chiefly made in France and Italy and drunk mixed with gin.
– ORIGIN from French *vermout*, from German *Wermut* 'wormwood'.

vernaccia /vəˈnatʃə/ ▶ noun [mass noun] a variety of wine grape grown in the San Gimignano area of Italy and in Sardinia.
■a strong dry white wine made from this grape.
– ORIGIN Italian.

vernacular /vəˈnakjʊlə/ ▶ noun **1** (usu. **the**

vernacular) the language or dialect spoken by the ordinary people in a particular country or region: *he wrote in the vernacular to reach a larger audience.*
■[with adj. or noun modifier] informal the terminology used by people belonging to a specified group or engaging in a specialized activity: [mass noun] *gardening vernacular.*
2 [mass noun] architecture concerned with domestic and functional rather than monumental buildings: *buildings in which Gothic merged into farmhouse vernacular.*
▶ adjective **1** (of language) spoken as one's mother tongue; not learned or imposed as a second language.
■(of speech or written works) using such a language: *vernacular literature.*
2 (of architecture) concerned with domestic and functional rather than monumental buildings.
– DERIVATIVES **vernacularism** noun, **vernacularity** noun, **vernacularize** (also **-ise**) verb, **vernacularly** adverb.
– ORIGIN early 17th cent.: from Latin *vernaculus* 'domestic, native' (from *verna* 'home-born slave') + **-AR**[1].

vernal /ˈvɜːn(ə)l/ ▶ adjective of, in, or appropriate to spring: *the vernal freshness of the land.*
– DERIVATIVES **vernally** adverb.
– ORIGIN mid 16th cent.: from Latin *vernalis*, from *vernus* 'of the spring', from *ver* 'spring'.

vernal equinox ▶ noun another term for **SPRING EQUINOX**.
■Astronomy another term for *First Point of Aries* (see **ARIES**).

vernal grass (also **sweet vernal grass**) ▶ noun [mass noun] a sweet-scented Eurasian grass which is sometimes grown as a meadow or hay grass.
● *Anthoxanthum odoratum*, family Gramineae.

vernalization (also **-isation**) ▶ noun [mass noun] the cooling of seed during germination in order to accelerate flowering when it is planted.
– DERIVATIVES **vernalize** (also **-ise**) verb.
– ORIGIN 1930s: translation of Russian *yarovizatsiya*.

vernation /vəˈneɪʃ(ə)n/ ▶ noun [mass noun] Botany the arrangement of bud scales or young leaves in a leaf bud before it opens. Compare with **AESTIVATION**.
– ORIGIN late 18th cent.: from modern Latin *vernatio(n-)*, from Latin *vernare* 'to grow (as in the spring)', from *vernus* (see **VERNAL**).

Verne /vɜːn/, Jules (1828–1905), French novelist. One of the first writers of science fiction, he often anticipated later scientific and technological developments, as in *Twenty Thousand Leagues under the Sea* (1870). Other novels include *Around the World in Eighty Days* (1873).

Verner's Law /ˈvɜːnəz, ˈvəːnəz/ Linguistics the observation that voiceless fricatives in Germanic predicted by Grimm's Law became voiced if the preceding syllable in the corresponding Indo-European word was unstressed.
– ORIGIN late 19th cent.: named after Karl A. *Verner* (1846–96), Danish philologist.

verneuk /fəˈ(r)njuːk/ ▶ verb [with obj.] S. African informal swindle: *it was just a ruse to verneuk them.*
– DERIVATIVES **verneuker** noun.
– ORIGIN Afrikaans, from Dutch *verneuken*.

vernicle /ˈvɜːnɪk(ə)l/ ▶ noun another term for **VERONICA** (in sense 2).
– ORIGIN Middle English: from Old French, alteration of *vernique*, from medieval Latin *veronica*.

vernier /ˈvɜːnɪə/ ▶ noun a small movable graduated scale for obtaining fractional parts of subdivisions on a fixed main scale of a barometer, sextant, or other measuring instrument.
– ORIGIN mid 18th cent.: named after Pierre *Vernier* (1580–1637), French mathematician.

vernier engine ▶ noun another term for **THRUSTER** (on a spacecraft).
– ORIGIN mid 20th cent.: named after P. *Vernier* (see **VERNIER**).

vernissage /ˌvɛːnɪˈsɑːʒ/ ▶ noun (pl. pronounced same) a private view of paintings before public exhibition.
– ORIGIN French, literally 'varnishing', originally referring to the day prior to an exhibition when artists were allowed to retouch and varnish hung work.

vernix /ˈvɜːnɪks/ ▶ noun (in full **vernix caseosa** /ˌkeɪsɪˈəʊsə/) [mass noun] a greasy deposit covering the skin of a baby at birth.

– ORIGIN late 16th cent.: from medieval Latin, variant of *veronix* 'fragrant resin' (see **VARNISH**).

Verny /ˈvɛːni/ former name (until 1921) for **ALMATY**.

Vero board /ˈvɛrəʊ, ˈvɪərəʊ/ ▶ **noun** Brit. trademark a type of board used to make electronic circuits, where some of the electrical connections are formed by strips of copper on the underside of the board.

Verona /vəˈrəʊnə/ a city on the River Adige, in NE Italy; pop. 258,950 (1990).

veronal /ˈvɛrən(ə)l/ ▶ **noun** another term for **BARBITONE**.

– ORIGIN early 20th cent.: from German, from **VERONA** + **-AL**.

Veronese /ˌvɛrəˈneɪzeɪ, -zi/, Paolo (c.1528–88), Italian painter; born *Paolo Caliari*. He gained many commissions in Venice, including the painting of frescoes in the Doges' Palace. He is particularly known for his richly coloured feast scenes (for example *The Marriage at Cana*, 1562).

veronica ▶ **noun 1** a herbaceous plant of north temperate regions, typically with upright stems bearing narrow pointed leaves and spikes of blue or purple flowers.
• Genus *Veronica*, family Scrophulariaceae: many species, including the speedwells.
2 a cloth supposedly impressed with an image of Christ's face. [ORIGIN: see **VERONICA, ST**.]
■ a picture of Christ's face similar to this.
3 the movement of a matador's cape away from a charging bull. [ORIGIN: said to be by association of the attitude of the matador with the depiction of St *Veronica* holding out a cloth to Christ (see **VERONICA, ST**).]

– ORIGIN early 16th cent.: from medieval Latin, from the given name *Veronica*.

Veronica, St /vəˈrɒnɪkə/ a woman of Jerusalem who offered her headcloth to Christ on the way to Calvary, to wipe the blood and sweat from his face. The cloth is said to have retained the image of his features.

veronique /ˌvɛrəˈniːk/ ▶ **adjective** [postpositive] denoting a dish, typically of fish or chicken, prepared or garnished with grapes.

– ORIGIN from the French given name *Véronique*.

Verrazano-Narrows Bridge /ˌvɛrəˈzɑːnəʊ/ a suspension bridge across New York harbour between Brooklyn and Staten Island, the longest in the world when it was completed in 1964.

– ORIGIN named after Giovanni da *Verrazano* (1485–1528), Italian explorer.

verre églomisé /vɛː ˌeɪɡlɒmiːˈzeɪ, French vɛʀ eɡlɔmize/ ▶ **noun** [mass noun] glass decorated on the back with engraved gold or silver leaf or paint.

– ORIGIN early 20th cent.: French, from *verre* 'glass' + *églomisé*, from *Glomy*, the name of an 18th-cent. Parisian picture-framer.

verruca /vəˈruːkə/ ▶ **noun** (pl. **verrucae** /-kiː, -siː/ or **verrucas**) a contagious and usually painful wart on the sole of the foot; a plantar wart.
■ (in medical use) a wart of any kind.

– DERIVATIVES **verrucose** /ˈvɛrʊkəʊz, vəˈruː-/ adjective, **verrucous** /ˈvɛrʊkəs, vəˈruː-/ adjective.

– ORIGIN late Middle English: from Latin.

Versace /vɛːˈsɑːtʃeɪ, -tʃi, Italian verˈsatʃe/, Gianni (1946–97), Italian fashion designer. He was shot dead outside his home in Miami.

Versailles /vɛːˈsʌɪ/ a palace built for Louis XIV near the town of Versailles, south-west of Paris. It was built around a château belonging to Louis XIII, which was transformed by additions in the grand French classical style.

Versailles, Treaty of 1 a treaty which terminated the War of American Independence in 1783.
2 a treaty signed in 1919 which brought a formal end to the First World War.

> The treaty redivided the territory of the defeated Central Powers, restricted Germany's armed forces, and established the League of Nations. It left Germany smarting under what it considered a vindictive settlement while not sufficiently restricting its ability eventually to rearm and seek forcible redress.

versal /ˈvəːs(ə)l/ ▶ **adjective** of or relating to a style of ornate capital letter used to start a verse, paragraph, etc., in a manuscript, typically built up by inking between pen strokes and with long, rather flat serifs.
▶ **noun** a versal letter.

– ORIGIN late 19th cent.: from Latin *vers-* 'turned' + **-AL**, influenced by **VERSE**.

versant /ˈvəːs(ə)nt/ ▶ **noun** a region of land sloping in one general direction.

– ORIGIN mid 19th cent.: from French, present participle (used as a noun) of *verser* 'tilt over', from Latin *versare*.

versatile ▶ **adjective 1** able to adapt or be adapted to many different functions or activities: *a versatile sewing machine* | *he was versatile enough to play on either wing*.
2 archaic changeable; inconstant.

– DERIVATIVES **versatilely** adverb, **versatility** noun.

– ORIGIN early 17th cent. (in the sense 'inconstant, fluctuating'): from French, or from Latin *versatilis*, from *versat-* 'turned about, revolved', from the verb *versare*, frequentative of *vertere* 'to turn'.

vers de société /ˌvɛ də səʊsɪeɪˈteɪ, sɒ-, French vɛʀ də sɔsjete/ ▶ **noun** [mass noun] verse dealing with topics provided by polite society in a light, witty style.

– ORIGIN French, literally 'verse of society'.

verse ▶ **noun** [mass noun] writing arranged with a metrical rhythm, typically having a rhyme: *a lament in verse* | [as modifier] *verse drama*.
■ [count noun] a group of lines that form a unit in a poem or song; a stanza: *the second verse*. ■ [count noun] each of the short numbered divisions of a chapter in the Bible or other scripture. ■ [count noun] a versicle. ■ [count noun] archaic a line of poetry. ■ [count noun] a passage in an anthem for a soloist or a small group of voices.
▶ **verb** [no obj.] archaic speak in or compose verse; versify.

– DERIVATIVES **verselet** noun.

– ORIGIN Old English *fers*, from Latin *versus* 'a turn of the plough, a furrow, a line of writing', from *vertere* 'to turn'; reinforced in Middle English by Old French *vers*, from Latin *versus*.

versed ▶ **adjective** (**versed in**) experienced or skilled in; knowledgeable about: *a solicitor* **well versed** *in employment law*.

– ORIGIN early 17th cent.: from French *versé* or Latin *versatus*, past participle of *versari* 'be engaged in'.

versed sine ▶ **noun** Mathematics unity minus cosine.
■ Architecture the rise of an arch of a bridge.

verset /ˈvəːsɪt/ ▶ **noun** Music a short prelude or interlude for organ.

– ORIGIN Middle English (denoting a versicle): from Old French, diminutive of *vers* 'verse'.

versicle /ˈvəːsɪk(ə)l/ ▶ **noun** (usu. **versicles**) a short sentence said or sung by the minister in a church service, to which the congregation gives a response.

– ORIGIN Middle English: from Old French *versicule* or Latin *versiculus*, diminutive of *versus* (see **VERSE**).

versicoloured /ˈvəːsɪˌkʌləd/ (US **versicolored**) ▶ **adjective** archaic **1** changing from one colour to another in different lights.
2 variegated.

– ORIGIN early 18th cent.: from Latin *versicolor* (from *versus* 'turned' + *color* 'colour') + **-ED**[2].

versify ▶ **verb** (**-ies**, **-ied**) [with obj.] turn into or express in verse: *it was never suggested that Wordsworth should simply versify Coleridge's ideas* | [as noun **versifying**] *a talent for versifying*.

– DERIVATIVES **versification** noun, **versifier** noun.

– ORIGIN late Middle English: from Old French *versifier*, from Latin *versificare*, from *versus* (see **VERSE**).

versin /ˈvəːsɪn, -sʌɪn/ (also **versine**) ▶ **noun** Mathematics another term for **VERSED SINE**.

– ORIGIN early 19th cent.: abbreviation.

version ▶ **noun 1** a particular form of something differing in certain respects from an earlier form or other forms of the same type of thing: *a revised version of the paper was produced for a later meeting* | *they produce yachts in both standard and master versions*.
■ a particular edition or translation of a book or other work: *the English version will be published next year*. ■ [usu. with modifier] an adaptation of a novel, piece of music, etc. into another medium or style: *a film version of a wonderfully funny cult novel*. ■ a particular updated edition of a piece of computer software. ■ an account of a matter from a particular person's point of view: *he told her his version of events*.
2 [mass noun] Medicine the manual turning of a fetus in the womb to make delivery easier.

– DERIVATIVES **versional** adjective.

– ORIGIN late Middle English (in the sense 'translation'): from French, or from medieval Latin *versio(n-)*, from Latin *vertere* 'to turn'.

vers libre /vɛː ˈliːbr(ə), French vɛʀ libʀ/ ▶ **noun** another term for **FREE VERSE**.

– ORIGIN French, literally 'free verse'.

verso /ˈvəːsəʊ/ ▶ **noun** (pl. **-os**) **1** a left-hand page of an open book, or the back of a loose document. Contrasted with **RECTO**.
2 the reverse of something such as a coin or painting.

– ORIGIN mid 19th cent.: from Latin *verso* (*folio*) 'on the turned (leaf)'.

verst /vəːst/ ▶ **noun** a Russian measure of length, about 1.1 km (0.66 mile).

– ORIGIN from Russian *versta*.

Verstehen /fɛːˈʃteɪən, German fɛɐ̯ˈʃteːən/ ▶ **noun** [mass noun] Sociology empathic understanding of human behaviour.

– ORIGIN German, literally 'understanding'.

versus (abbrev.: **v**, **v.**, or **vs**) ▶ **preposition** against (especially in sporting and legal use): *England versus Australia*.
■ as opposed to; in contrast to: *weighing up the pros and cons of organic versus inorganic produce*.

– ORIGIN late Middle English: from a medieval Latin use of Latin *versus* 'towards'.

vert /vəːt/ ▶ **noun** [mass noun] green, as a heraldic tincture: [postpositive] *three piles vert*.

– ORIGIN late Middle English (as an adjective): via Old French from Latin *viridis* 'green'.

vertebra /ˈvəːtɪbrə/ ▶ **noun** (pl. **vertebrae** /-breɪ, -briː/) each of the series of small bones forming the backbone, having several projections for articulation and muscle attachment, and a hole through which the spinal cord passes.

> In the human spine (or vertebral column) there are seven cervical vertebrae (in the neck), twelve thoracic vertebrae (to which the ribs are attached), and five lumbar vertebrae (in the lower back). In addition, five fused vertebrae form the sacrum, and four the coccyx.

– DERIVATIVES **vertebral** adjective.

– ORIGIN early 17th cent.: from Latin, from *vertere* 'to turn'.

vertebral column ▶ **noun** another term for **SPINAL COLUMN**.

vertebrate /ˈvəːtɪbrət/ ▶ **noun** an animal of a large group distinguished by the possession of a backbone or spinal column, including mammals, birds, reptiles, amphibians, and fishes. Compare with **INVERTEBRATE**.
• Subphylum Vertebrata, phylum Chordata: seven classes.
▶ **adjective** of or relating to the vertebrates.

– ORIGIN early 19th cent.: from Latin *vertebratus* 'jointed', from *vertebra* (see **VERTEBRA**).

vertex /ˈvəːtɛks/ ▶ **noun** (pl. **vertices** /-tɪsiːz/ or **vertexes**) **1** the highest point; the top or apex.
■ Anatomy the crown of the head.
2 Geometry each angular point of a polygon, polyhedron, or other figure.
■ a meeting point of two lines that form an angle. ■ the point at which an axis meets a curve or surface.

– ORIGIN late Middle English: from Latin, 'whirlpool, crown of a head, vertex', from *vertere* 'to turn'.

vertical ▶ **adjective 1** at right angles to a horizontal plane; in a direction, or having an alignment, such that the top is directly above the bottom: *the vertical axis* | *keep your back vertical*.
2 archaic denoting a point at the zenith or the highest point of something.
3 Anatomy of or relating to the crown of the head.
4 involving different levels of a hierarchy or progression, in particular:
■ involving all the stages from the production to the sale of a class of goods. ■ (especially of the transmission of disease or genetic traits) passed from one generation to the next.
▶ **noun 1** (usu. **the vertical**) a vertical line or plane: *the columns incline several degrees away from the vertical*.
2 an upright structure: *we remodelled the opening with a simple lintel and unadorned verticals*.
3 short for **VERTICAL TASTING**.
4 the distance between the highest and lowest points of a ski area: *the resort claims a vertical of 2100 metres*.

– DERIVATIVES **verticality** noun, **verticalize** (also **-ise**) verb, **vertically** adverb.

– ORIGIN mid 16th cent. (in the sense 'directly overhead'): from French, or from late Latin *verticalis*, from *vertex* (see **VERTEX**).

vertical angles ▶ **plural noun** Mathematics each of

V

the pairs of opposite angles made by two intersecting lines.

vertical fin ▶ **noun** Zoology any of the unpaired fins in the midline of a fish's body, i.e. a dorsal, anal, or caudal fin.

vertical integration ▶ **noun** [mass noun] the combination in one firm of two or more stages of production normally operated by separate firms.

vertical market ▶ **noun** a market comprising all the potential purchasers in a particular occupation or industry.

vertical stabilizer ▶ **noun** Aeronautics US term for **FIN**.

vertical tasting ▶ **noun** a tasting in order of year of several different vintages of a particular wine.

vertical thinking ▶ **noun** [mass noun] chiefly Brit. the solving of problems using conventional logical processes. Contrasted with **LATERAL THINKING**.

verticillium /ˌvəːtɪˈsɪlɪəm/ ▶ **noun** a fungus of a genus which includes a number that cause wilt in plants.
● Genus *Verticillium*, subdivision Deuteromycotina, in particular *V. albo-atrum* and *V. dahliae*.
■ [mass noun] wilt caused by such fungi.
– ORIGIN modern Latin, from Latin *verticillus* 'whorl of a spindle'.

vertiginous /vəːˈtɪdʒɪnəs/ ▶ **adjective** causing vertigo, especially by being extremely high or steep: *vertiginous drops to the valleys below.*
■ relating to or affected by vertigo.
– DERIVATIVES **vertiginously** adverb.
– ORIGIN early 17th cent.: from Latin *vertiginosus*, from *vertigo* 'whirling about' (see **VERTIGO**).

vertigo /ˈvəːtɪɡəʊ/ ▶ **noun** [mass noun] a sensation of whirling and loss of balance, associated particularly with looking down from a great height, or caused by disease affecting the inner ear or the vestibular nerve; giddiness.
– ORIGIN late Middle English: from Latin, 'whirling', from *vertere* 'to turn'.

vertisol /ˈvəːtɪsɒl/ ▶ **noun** Soil Science a clayey soil with little organic matter which occurs in regions having distinct wet and dry seasons.
– ORIGIN 1960s: from **VERTICAL** + Latin *solum* 'soil'.

vertu ▶ **noun** variant spelling of **VIRTU**.

Verulamium /ˌvɛrʊˈleɪmɪəm/ Roman name for **ST ALBANS**.

vervain /ˈvəːveɪn/ ▶ **noun** [mass noun] a widely distributed herbaceous plant with small blue, white, or purple flowers and a long history of use as a magical and medicinal herb.
● *Verbena officinalis*, family Verbenaceae.
– ORIGIN late Middle English: from Old French *verveine*, from Latin *verbena* (see **VERBENA**).

verve ▶ **noun** [mass noun] vigour and spirit or enthusiasm: *Kollo sings with supreme verve and flexibility.*
– ORIGIN late 17th cent. (denoting special talent in writing): from French, 'vigour', earlier 'form of expression', from Latin *verba* 'words'.

vervet /ˈvəːvɪt/ (also **vervet monkey**) ▶ **noun** a common African guenon with greenish-brown upper parts and a black face. Compare with **GREEN MONKEY**, **GRIVET**.
● *Cercopithecus aethiops*, family Cercopithecidae, in particular the race *C. a. pygerythrus* of southern and eastern Africa.
– ORIGIN late 19th cent.: from French, of unknown origin.

Verviers /ˈvɛːvɪeɪ, French vɛrvje/ a manufacturing town in eastern Belgium; pop 53,480. (1991).

Verwoerd /fəˈvʊət/, Hendrik (Frensch) (1901–66), South African statesman, Prime Minister 1958–66. As Minister of Bantu Affairs (1950–8) he developed the segregation policy of apartheid. As Premier he banned the ANC and the Pan-Africanist Congress in 1960, following the Sharpeville massacre. He withdrew South Africa from the Commonwealth and declared it a republic in 1961.

Verwoerdian /fəˈvʊədɪən/ ▶ **adjective** S. African of or relating to grand apartheid, especially as it involved geographically based racial segregation.

very ▶ **adverb** used for emphasis:
■ in a high degree: *very large | very quickly | very much so.* ■ [with superlative or **own**] used to emphasize that the following description applies without qualification: *the very best quality | his very own car.*
▶ **adjective** actual; precise (used to emphasize the exact identity of a particular person or thing): *those were his very words | he might be phoning her at this very moment | transformed **before our very eyes**.*
■ emphasizing an extreme point in time or space: *from the very beginning of the book | at the very back of the skull.* ■ with no addition of or contribution from anything else; mere: *the very thought of drink made him feel sick.* ■ archaic real, genuine: *the very God of Heaven.*
– PHRASES **not very 1** in a low degree: *'Bad news?' 'Not very.'* **2** far from being: *I'm not very impressed.* **the very idea!** see **IDEA**. **the very same** see **SAME**. **very good** (or **well**) an expression of consent.
– ORIGIN Middle English (as an adjective in the sense 'real, genuine'): from Old French *verai*, based on Latin *verus* 'true'.

Very light /ˈvɛri, ˈvɪəri/ ▶ **noun** a flare fired into the air from a pistol for signalling or for temporary illumination.
– ORIGIN early 20th cent.: named after Edward W. *Very* (1847–1910), American naval officer.

Very pistol /ˈvɛri, ˈvɪəri/ ▶ **noun** a hand-held gun used for firing a Very light.

Very Reverend ▶ **noun** a title given to a dean in the Anglican Church: *the Very Reverend James Wilkins.*

VESA ▶ **abbreviation for** Video Electronics Standards Association, a US-based organization that defines formats for displays and buses used in computers.

Vesak /ˈvɛsak/ (also **Wesak** or **Visākha**) ▶ **noun** [mass noun] the most important Buddhist festival, taking place at the full moon when the sun is in the zodiacal sign of Taurus, and commemorating the birth, enlightenment, and death of the Buddha.
■ the month in which this festival occurs.
– ORIGIN Sinhalese *vesak*, via Pali from Sanskrit *vaiśākha*, denoting the month April–May.

Vesalius /vɪˈseɪlɪəs/, Andreas (1514–64), Flemish anatomist, the founder of modern anatomy. His major work, *De Humani Corporis Fabrica* (1543), contained accurate descriptions of human anatomy, but owed much of its great historical impact to the woodcuts of his dissections.

vesical /ˈvɛsɪk(ə)l, ˈviː-/ ▶ **adjective** Anatomy & Medicine of, relating to, or affecting the urinary bladder: *vesical function | the vesical artery.*
– ORIGIN late 18th cent.: from Latin *vesica* 'bladder' + **-AL**.

vesicant /ˈvɛsɪkənt, ˈviː-/ ▶ **adjective** tending to cause blistering.
▶ **noun** an agent that causes blistering.
– ORIGIN late Middle English: from late Latin *vesicant-* 'forming pustules', from the verb *vesicare*, from *vesica* 'bladder'.

vesica piscis /ˌvɛsɪkə ˈpɪskɪs, ˈviː-/ ▶ **noun** (pl. **vesicae** /ˈvɛsɪkiː, ˈviː-/) a pointed oval figure used as an architectural feature and as an aureole enclosing figures such as Christ or the Virgin Mary in medieval art. Also called **MANDORLA**.
– ORIGIN Latin, literally 'fish's bladder'.

vesicate /ˈvɛsɪkeɪt, ˈviː-/ ▶ **verb** [with obj.] chiefly Medicine raise blisters on.
■ [no obj.] form blisters.
– DERIVATIVES **vesication** noun, **vesicatory** adjective & noun.
– ORIGIN mid 17th cent.: from late Latin *vesicat-* 'having pustules', from *vesica* 'bladder'.

vesicle /ˈvɛsɪk(ə)l, ˈviː-/ ▶ **noun** a fluid- or air-filled cavity or sac, in particular:
■ Anatomy & Zoology a small fluid-filled bladder, sac, cyst, or vacuole within the body. ■ Botany an air-filled swelling in a plant, especially a seaweed. ■ Geology a small cavity in volcanic rock, produced by gas bubbles. ■ Medicine a small blister full of clear fluid.
– DERIVATIVES **vesicular** adjective, **vesiculated** adjective, **vesiculation** noun.
– ORIGIN late 16th cent.: from French *vésicule* or Latin *vesicula*, diminutive of *vesica* 'bladder'.

vesicoureteric reflux /ˌvɛsɪkəʊjʊərɪˈtɛrɪk, ˈviː-/ ▶ **noun** [mass noun] Medicine flow of urine from the bladder back into the ureters, arising from defective valves and causing a high risk of kidney infection.
– ORIGIN mid 20th cent.: *vesicoureteric* from Latin *vesica* 'bladder' + *ureteric* (see **URETER**).

Vespasian /vɛˈspeɪʒ(ə)n/ (AD 9–79), Roman emperor 69–79 and founder of the Flavian dynasty; Latin name *Titus Flavius Vespasianus*. He was acclaimed emperor by the legions in Egypt during the civil wars following the death of Nero and gained control of Italy after the defeat of Vitellius. His reign saw the restoration of financial and military order and the initiation of a public building programme.

vesper ▶ **noun** evening prayer: [as modifier] *vesper service.* See also **VESPERS**.
■ archaic evening. ■ (**Vesper**) poetic/literary Venus as the evening star.
– ORIGIN late Middle English: from Latin *vesper* 'evening (star)'.

vesper rat ▶ **noun** an arboreal and nocturnal South American rat which builds nests in trees.
● Genera *Nyctomys* and *Otonyctomys*, family Muridae.

vespers ▶ **noun** a service of evening prayer in the Divine Office of the Western Christian Church (sometimes said earlier in the day).
■ a service of evening prayer in other churches.
– ORIGIN late 15th cent.: from Old French *vespres* 'evensong', from Latin *vesperas* (accusative plural), on the pattern of *matutinas* 'matins'.

vesper sparrow ▶ **noun** a small North American songbird related to the buntings, having streaked brown plumage and known for its evening song.
● *Pooecetes gramineus*, family Emberizidae (subfamily Emberizidae).

vespertilionid /ˌvɛspətɪlɪˈɒnɪd/ ▶ **noun** Zoology a bat of a large family (Vespertilionidae) that includes most of the typical insectivorous bats of northern temperate regions.
– ORIGIN late 19th cent.: from modern Latin *Vespertilionidae* (plural), from Latin *vespertilio* 'bat'.

vespertine /ˈvɛspətʌɪn, -tɪn/ ▶ **adjective** technical or poetic/literary of, relating to, occurring, or active in the evening.
– ORIGIN late Middle English: from Latin *vespertinus*, from *vesper* 'evening'.

Vespucci /vɛˈspuːtʃi/, Amerigo (1451–1512), Italian merchant and explorer. He travelled to the New World, reaching the coast of Venezuela on his first voyage (1499–1500) and exploring the Brazilian coastline in 1501–2. The Latin form of his first name is believed to have given rise to the name of America.

vessel ▶ **noun 1** a ship or large boat.
2 a hollow container, especially one used to hold liquid, such as a bowl or cask.
■ (chiefly in or alluding to biblical use) a person, especially regarded as holding or embodying a particular quality: *giving honour unto the wife, as unto the weaker vessel.*
3 Anatomy & Zoology a duct or canal holding or conveying blood or other fluid. See also **BLOOD VESSEL**.
■ Botany any of the tubular structures in the vascular system of a plant, serving to conduct water and mineral nutrients from the root.
– ORIGIN Middle English: from Anglo-Norman French *vessel(e)*, from late Latin *vascellum*, diminutive of *vas* 'vessel'.

vest ▶ **noun 1** Brit. an undergarment worn on the upper part of the body, typically having no sleeves.
2 a similar garment worn on the upper part of the body for a particular purpose or activity: *a running vest | a bulletproof vest.*
■ US & Austral. a waistcoat or sleeveless jacket. ■ a piece of material showing at the neck of a woman's dress.
▶ **verb 1** [with obj.] (usu. **be vested in**) confer or bestow (power, authority, property, etc.) on someone: *executive power is vested in the President.*
■ (usu. **be vested with**) give (someone) the legal right to power, property, etc.: *the socialists came to be vested with the power of legislation.* ■ [no obj.] (**vest in**) (of power, property, etc.) come into the possession of: *the bankrupt's property vests in his trustee.*
2 [no obj.] (of a chorister or member of the clergy) put on vestments.
■ [with obj.] poetic/literary dress (someone): *the Speaker vested him with a rich purple robe.*
– PHRASES **play** (or **keep**) **one's cards close to one's vest** see **CHEST**.
– ORIGIN late Middle English (as a verb): from Old French *vestu* 'clothed', past participle of *vestir*, from Latin *vestire*; the noun (early 17th cent., denoting a loose outer garment) from French *veste*, via Italian from Latin *vestis* 'garment'.

Vesta 1 Roman Mythology the goddess of the hearth and household. Her temple in Rome contained no image but a fire which was kept constantly burning and was tended by the Vestal Virgins.
2 Astronomy asteroid 4, discovered in 1807. It is the brightest asteroid and the third largest (diameter 501 km), and appears to consist of basaltic rock.

vesta ▶ noun chiefly historical a short wooden or wax match.
– ORIGIN mid 19th cent.: from the name of the goddess VESTA.

vestal ▶ adjective of or relating to the Roman goddess Vesta: *a vestal temple.*
■ poetic/literary chaste; pure.
▶ noun a vestal virgin.
■ poetic/literary a chaste woman, especially a nun.

Vestal Virgin (also **vestal virgin**) ▶ noun (in ancient Rome) a virgin consecrated to Vesta and vowed to chastity, sharing the charge of maintaining the sacred fire burning on the goddess's altar.

vested interest ▶ noun [usu. in sing.] a personal stake or involvement in an undertaking or state of affairs, especially one with an expectation of financial gain: *banks have a vested interest in the growth of their customers.*
■ a person or group having such a personal stake or involvement: *the problem is that the authorities are a vested interest.* ■ Law an interest (usually in land or money held in trust) recognized as belonging to a particular person.

vestee ▶ noun North American term for WAISTCOAT.

Vesterålen /ˈvɛstəˌrɔːlən/ a group of islands of Norway, north of the Arctic Circle.

vestiary /ˈvɛstɪəri/ ▶ adjective poetic/literary of or relating to clothes or dress.
▶ noun (pl. **-ies**) a room or building in a monastery or other large establishment in which clothes are kept.
– ORIGIN Middle English (denoting a vestry): from Old French *vestiarie*, from Latin *vestiarium* (see VESTRY).

vestibular /vɛˈstɪbjʊlə/ ▶ adjective chiefly Anatomy of or relating to a vestibule, particularly that of the inner ear, or more generally to the sense of balance.

vestibule /ˈvɛstɪbjuːl/ ▶ noun **1** an antechamber, hall, or lobby next to the outer door of a building.
■ an enclosed entrance compartment in a railway carriage.
2 Anatomy a chamber or channel communicating with or opening into another, in particular:
■ the central cavity of the labyrinth of the inner ear. ■ the part of the mouth outside the teeth. ■ the space in the vulva into which both the urethra and vagina open.
– DERIVATIVES **vestibuled** adjective.
– ORIGIN early 17th cent. (denoting the space in front of the main entrance of a Roman or Greek building): from French, or from Latin *vestibulum* 'entrance court'.

vestibulocochlear nerve /vɛˌstɪbjʊləʊˈkɒklɪə/ ▶ noun Anatomy each of the eighth pair of cranial nerves, conveying sensory impulses from the organs of hearing and balance in the inner ear to the brain. The vestibulocochlear nerve on each side branches into the **vestibular nerve** and the **cochlear nerve**.

vestibulo-ocular reflex /vɛˌstɪbjʊləʊˈɒkjʊlə/ ▶ noun the reflex by which balance is maintained when the visual field is in motion.

vestige /ˈvɛstɪdʒ/ ▶ noun a trace of something that is disappearing or no longer exists: *the last vestiges of colonialism.*
■ [usu. with negative] the smallest amount (used to emphasize the absence of something): *he waited patiently, but without a vestige of sympathy.* ■ Biology a part or organ of an organism which has become reduced or functionless in the course of evolution.
– ORIGIN late Middle English: from French, from Latin *vestigium* 'footprint'.

vestigial /vɛˈstɪdʒɪəl, -dʒ(ə)l/ ▶ adjective forming a very small remnant of something that was once much larger and more noticeable: *he felt a vestigial flicker of anger from last night.*
■ Biology (of an organ or part of the body) degenerate, rudimentary, or atrophied, having become functionless in the course of evolution: *the vestigial wings of kiwis are entirely hidden.*
– DERIVATIVES **vestigially** adverb.

vestimentary /ˌvɛstɪˈmɛnt(ə)ri/ ▶ adjective formal of or relating to clothing or dress: *lack of vestimentary rigour.*
– ORIGIN early 19th cent.: from Latin *vestimentum* 'clothing' + -ARY[1].

vestimentiferan /ˌvɛstɪmɛnˈtɪfərən/ ▶ noun Zoology a very large marine worm which lives in upright tubes near hydrothermal vents, subsisting on the products of chemoautotrophic bacteria.
● Order Vestimentifera, phylum Pogonophora; sometimes regarded as a separate phylum.
– ORIGIN late 20th cent.: from modern Latin *Vestimentifera* (from Latin *vestimentum* 'clothing' + -fer 'bearing') + -AN.

vestiture /ˈvɛstɪtʃə, -tʃə/ ▶ noun [mass noun] archaic clothing.
– ORIGIN mid 19th cent.: based on Latin *vestire* 'clothe'.

Vestmannaeyjar /ˌvɛstmanəˈeɪjɑːr/ Icelandic name for WESTMANN ISLANDS.

vestment ▶ noun (usu. **vestments**) a chasuble or other robe worn by the clergy or choristers during services.
■ archaic a garment, especially a ceremonial or official robe.
– ORIGIN Middle English: from Old French *vestiment*, from Latin *vestimentum*, from *vestire* 'clothe' (see VEST).

vest-pocket ▶ adjective [attrib.] N. Amer. (especially of a reference book) small enough to fit into a pocket: *a series of popular vest-pocket dictionaries.*
■ very small in size or scale: *a vest-pocket park.*

vestry ▶ noun (pl. **-ies**) a room or building attached to a church, used as an office and for changing into ceremonial vestments.
■ a meeting of parishioners, originally in a vestry, for the conduct of parochial business.
– ORIGIN late Middle English: probably from an Anglo-Norman French alteration of Old French *vestiarie*, from Latin *vestiarium*.

vestryman ▶ noun (pl. **-men**) a member of a parochial vestry.

vesture ▶ noun [mass noun] poetic/literary clothing; dress: *a man garbed in ancient vesture.*
– ORIGIN Middle English: from Old French, based on Latin *vestire* 'clothe'.

vesuvianite /vɪˈsuːvɪənʌɪt/ ▶ noun another term for IDOCRASE.
– ORIGIN late 19th cent.: from VESUVIUS + -AN + -ITE[1].

Vesuvius /vɪˈsuːvɪəs/ an active volcano near Naples, in southern Italy, 1,277 m (4,190 ft) high. A violent eruption in AD 79 buried the towns of Pompeii and Herculaneum.

vet[1] ▶ noun a veterinary surgeon.
▶ verb (**vetted**, **vetting**) [with obj.] make a careful and critical examination of (something): *proposals for vetting large takeover bids.*
■ (often **be vetted**) Brit. investigate (someone) thoroughly, especially in order to ensure that they are suitable for a job requiring secrecy, loyalty, or trustworthiness: *each applicant will be vetted by police* | [as noun **vetting**] *the vetting of people who work with children.*
– ORIGIN mid 19th cent: abbreviation of VETERINARY or VETERINARIAN.

vet[2] ▶ noun N. Amer. informal a veteran.
– ORIGIN mid 19th cent.: abbreviation.

vetch ▶ noun a widely distributed scrambling herbaceous plant of the pea family, which is cultivated as a silage or fodder crop. See also TARE[1].
● Genus *Vicia*, family Leguminosae: several species, in particular the European **common vetch** (*V. sativa*).
– ORIGIN Middle English: from Anglo-Norman French *veche*, from Latin *vicia*.

vetchling ▶ noun a widely distributed scrambling plant related to the vetches, typically having fewer leaflets.
● Genus *Lathyrus*, family Leguminosae.

veteran ▶ noun a person who has had long experience in a particular field, especially military service: *a veteran of two world wars.*
■ an ex-serviceman or -servicewoman.
– ORIGIN early 16th cent.: from French *vétéran* or Latin *veteranus*, from *vetus* 'old'.

veteran car ▶ noun Brit. an old style or model of car, specifically one made before 1916, or (strictly) before 1905. Compare with VINTAGE CAR.

Veterans Day ▶ noun (in the US) a public holiday held on the anniversary of the end of the First World War (11 November) to honour US veterans and victims of all wars. It replaced Armistice Day in 1954.

veterinarian /ˌvɛt(ə)rɪˈnɛːrɪən/ ▶ noun North American term for VETERINARY SURGEON.

veterinary /ˈvɛt(ə)rɪnri, ˈvɛt(ə)nri/ ▶ adjective of or relating to the diseases, injuries, and treatment of farm and domestic animals: *a veterinary nurse.*
▶ noun (pl. **-ies**) dated a veterinary surgeon.
– ORIGIN late 18th cent.: from Latin *veterinarius*, from *veterinae* 'cattle'.

veterinary surgeon ▶ noun Brit. a person qualified to treat diseased or injured animals.

vetiver /ˈvɛtɪvə/ (also **vetivert**) ▶ noun [mass noun] a fragrant extract or essential oil obtained from the root of an Indian grass, used in perfumery and aromatherapy.
● The grass is *Vetiveria zizanioides*, family Gramineae.
– ORIGIN mid 19th cent.: from French *vétiver*, from Tamil *veṭṭivēr*, from *vēr* 'root'.

vetkoek /ˈfɛtkʊk/ ▶ noun (pl. same, **vetkoeks**, or **vetkoeke**) S. African a small, unsweetened cake of deep-fried dough.
■ [mass noun] deep-fried dough.
– ORIGIN Afrikaans, from *vet* 'fat' + *koek* 'cake'.

veto /ˈviːtəʊ/ ▶ noun (pl. **-oes**) a constitutional right to reject a decision or proposal made by a law-making body: *the legislature would have a veto over appointments to key posts.*
■ such a rejection. ■ a prohibition: *his veto on our drinking after the meal was annoying.*
▶ verb (**-oes**, **-oed**) [with obj.] exercise a veto against (a decision or proposal made by a law-making body): *the president vetoed the bill.*
■ refuse to accept or allow: *the film star often has a right to veto the pictures used for publicity.*
– DERIVATIVES **vetoer** noun.
– ORIGIN early 17th cent.: from Latin, literally 'I forbid', used by Roman tribunes of the people when opposing measures of the Senate.

vex ▶ verb [with obj.] make (someone) feel annoyed, frustrated, or worried, especially with trivial matters: *the memory of the conversation still vexed him* | [as adj. **vexing**] *the most vexing questions for policy-makers.*
■ [no obj.] W. Indian be annoyed, irritated, or unhappy. ■ archaic cause distress to: *thou shalt not vex a stranger.*
▶ adjective chiefly W. Indian angry; annoyed: *I ain't vex with you.*
– DERIVATIVES **vexer** noun, **vexingly** adverb.
– ORIGIN late Middle English: from Old French *vexer*, from Latin *vexare* 'shake, disturb'.

vexation ▶ noun [mass noun] the state of being annoyed, frustrated, or worried: *Jenna bit her lip in vexation.*
■ [count noun] something that causes annoyance, frustration, or worry: *the new VAT rules have brought vexations in their wake.*
– ORIGIN late Middle English: from Old French, or from Latin *vexatio(n-)*, from *vexare* (see VEX).

vexatious ▶ adjective causing or tending to cause annoyance, frustration, or worry: *the vexatious questions posed by software copyrights.*
■ Law denoting an action or the bringer of an action that is brought without sufficient grounds for winning, purely to cause annoyance to the defendant.
– DERIVATIVES **vexatiously** adverb, **vexatiousness** noun.

vexed ▶ adjective **1** [attrib.] (of a problem or issue) difficult and much debated; problematic: *the vexed question of exactly how much money the government is going to spend.*
2 annoyed, frustrated, or worried: *I'm very vexed with you!*
– DERIVATIVES **vexedly** adverb.

vexillology /ˌvɛksɪˈlɒlədʒi/ ▶ noun [mass noun] the study of flags.
– DERIVATIVES **vexillological** adjective, **vexillologist** noun.
– ORIGIN 1950s: from Latin *vexillum* 'flag' + -LOGY.

vexillum /vɛkˈsɪləm/ ▶ noun (pl. **vexilla** /-lə/) **1** a Roman military standard or banner, especially one of a maniple. [ORIGIN: Latin, from *vehere* 'carry'.]
■ a body of troops under such a standard. ■ a flag attached to a bishop's staff. ■ a processional banner or cross.
2 Botany the standard of a papilionaceous flower.
3 Ornithology the vane of a feather.

VFR ▶ abbreviation for visual flight rules, used to regulate the flying and navigating of an aircraft under conditions of good visibility.

VG ▶ abbreviation for ■ very good. ■ Vicar General.

VGA ▶ **abbreviation for** videographics array, a standard for defining colour display screens for computers.

vgc ▶ **abbreviation for** very good condition (used in advertisements).

VHF ▶ **abbreviation for** very high frequency (denoting radio waves of a frequency of *c.*30–300 MHz and a wavelength of *c.*1–10 metres).

VHS trademark ▶ **abbreviation for** video home system, denoting the video system and tape used by domestic video recorders and some camcorders.

VHS-C trademark ▶ **abbreviation for** VHS compact, denoting a video system used by some camcorders, which records signals in VHS format on smaller video cassettes.

VI ▶ **abbreviation for** Virgin Islands.

via ▶ **preposition** travelling through (a place) en route to a destination: *came to Europe via Turkey.*
■by way of; through: *most people buy a home with a mortgage via a building society.* ■ by means of: *a file sent via electronic mail.*
– ORIGIN late 18th cent.: from Latin, ablative of *via* 'way, road'.

Via Appia /ˌviːə ˈapɪə, ˌvʌɪə/ Latin name for **APPIAN WAY**.

viable /ˈvʌɪəb(ə)l/ ▶ **adjective** capable of working successfully; feasible: *the proposed investment was economically viable.*
■Botany (of a seed or spore) able to germinate. ■ Biology (of a plant, animal, or cell) capable of surviving or living successfully, especially under particular environmental conditions. ■ Medicine (of a fetus or unborn child) able to live after birth.
– DERIVATIVES **viability** noun, **viably** adverb.
– ORIGIN early 19th cent.: from French, from *vie* 'life', from Latin *vita*.

Via Crucis /ˈkruːtʃɪs/ ▶ **noun** another term for ***the way of the Cross*** (see **WAY**). [ORIGIN: Latin.]
■figurative a lengthy and distressing or painful procedure: *we embarked on a Via Crucis of tired comic formulae.*

via dolorosa /ˌdɒləˈrəʊzə/ ▶ **noun** (**the Via Dolorosa**) the route believed to have been taken by Christ through Jerusalem to Calvary.
■figurative a distressing or painful journey or process: *he commenced a via dolorosa to the coast.*
– ORIGIN Latin, literally 'painful path'.

viaduct ▶ **noun** a long bridge-like structure, typically a series of arches, carrying a road or railway across a valley or other low ground.
– ORIGIN early 19th cent.: from Latin *via* 'way', on the pattern of *aqueduct*.

vial /ˈvʌɪəl/ ▶ **noun** a small container, typically cylindrical and made of glass, used especially for holding liquid medicines.
– ORIGIN Middle English: alteration of **PHIAL**.

via media /ˈmiːdɪə, ˈmedɪə/ ▶ **noun** formal a middle way or compromise between extremes: *the settlement is a via media between Catholicism and Protestantism.*
– ORIGIN Latin.

viand /ˈvʌɪənd/ ▶ **noun** poetic/literary (usu. **viands**) an item of food: *an unlimited assortment of viands.*
– ORIGIN late Middle English: from Old French *viande* 'food', from an alteration of Latin *vivenda*, neuter plural gerundive of *vivere* 'to live'.

via negativa /ˌnɛgəˈtiːvə/ ▶ **noun** Theology a way of describing something by saying what it is not, especially denying that any finite concept of attribute can be identified with or used of God or ultimate reality.
– ORIGIN Latin, literally 'negative path'.

viatical settlement /vʌɪˈatɪk(ə)l/ ▶ **noun** an arrangement whereby a person with a terminal illness sells their life insurance policy to a third party for less than its mature value, in order to benefit from the proceeds while alive. See also **DEATH FUTURES**.
– ORIGIN 1990s: *viatical* from Latin *viaticus* 'relating to a journey or departing' + **-AL**.

viaticum /vʌɪˈatɪkəm/ ▶ **noun** (pl. **viatica** /-kə/) **1** the Eucharist as given to a person near or in danger of death.
2 archaic a supply of provisions or an official allowance of money for a journey.
– ORIGIN mid 16th cent.: from Latin, neuter of *viaticus*, from *via* 'road'.

vibe ▶ **noun** informal **1** (usu. **vibes**) a person's emotional state or the atmosphere of a place as communicated to and felt by others: *we've been picking up some bad vibes on that guy.* [ORIGIN: abbreviation of *vibrations*.]
2 (**vibes**) another term for **VIBRAPHONE**.

vibist /ˈvʌɪbɪst/ ▶ **noun** a musician who plays the vibraphone.

vibraculum /vʌɪˈbrakjʊləm, vɪ-/ ▶ **noun** (pl. **vibracula** /-lə/) Zoology (in some bryozoans) any of a number of modified zooids that bear a long whip-like seta, serving to prevent other organisms from settling on the colony. Compare with **AVICULARIUM**.
– DERIVATIVES **vibracular** adjective.
– ORIGIN mid 19th cent.: modern Latin, from Latin *vibrare* (see **VIBRATE**).

vibrant ▶ **adjective** full of energy and enthusiasm: *a vibrant cosmopolitan city.*
■quivering; pulsating: *Rose was* ***vibrant with*** *anger.* ■ (of colour) bright and striking. ■ (of sound) strong or resonating: *his vibrant voice.*
– DERIVATIVES **vibrancy** noun, **vibrantly** adverb.
– ORIGIN early 17th cent. (in the sense 'moving rapidly, vibrating'): from Latin *vibrant-* 'shaking to and fro', from the verb *vibrare* (see **VIBRATE**).

vibraphone /ˈvʌɪbrəfəʊn/ ▶ **noun** a musical percussion instrument with a double row of tuned metal bars, each above a tubular resonator containing a motor-driven rotating vane, giving a vibrato effect.
– DERIVATIVES **vibraphonist** noun.
– ORIGIN 1920s: from **VIBRATO** + **-PHONE**.

vibrate ▶ **verb** move or cause to move continuously and rapidly to and fro: [no obj.] *the cabin started to vibrate* | [with obj.] *the bumblebee vibrated its wings for a few seconds.*
■[no obj.] (**vibrate with**) quiver with (a quality or emotion): *his voice vibrated with terror.* ■ [no obj.] (of a sound) resonate; continue to be heard: *a low rumbling sound that began to vibrate through the car.* ■ [no obj.] (of a pendulum) swing to and fro.
– ORIGIN late Middle English (in the sense 'give out (light or sound) as if by vibration'): from Latin *vibrat-* 'moved to and fro', from the verb *vibrare*.

vibratile /ˈvʌɪbrətʌɪl/ ▶ **adjective** Biology (of cilia, flagella, or other small appendages) capable of or characterized by oscillatory motion.
– ORIGIN early 19th cent.: alteration of **VIBRATORY**, on the pattern of words such as *pulsatile*.

vibration ▶ **noun** an instance of vibrating: *powerful vibrations from an earthquake* | [mass noun] *the big-capacity engine generated less vibration.*
■Physics an oscillation of the parts of a fluid or an elastic solid whose equilibrium has been disturbed or of an electromagnetic wave. ■ (**vibrations**) informal a person's emotional state, the atmosphere of a place, or the associations of an object, as communicated to and felt by others.
– DERIVATIVES **vibrational** adjective.
– ORIGIN mid 17th cent.: from Latin *vibratio(n-)*, from the verb *vibrare* (see **VIBRATE**).

vibrato /vɪˈbrɑːtəʊ/ ▶ **noun** [mass noun] Music a rapid, slight variation in pitch in singing or playing some musical instruments, producing a stronger or richer tone. Compare with **TREMOLO**.
– ORIGIN mid 19th cent.: Italian, past participle of *vibrare* 'vibrate'.

vibrator ▶ **noun** a device that vibrates or causes vibration, in particular:
■a device used for massage or sexual stimulation. ■ a device for compacting concrete before it has set. ■ Music a reed in a reed organ.

vibratory /ˈvʌɪbrət(ə)ri, vʌɪˈbreɪt(ə)ri/ ▶ **adjective** of, relating to, or causing vibration.

vibrio /ˈvɪbrɪəʊ, ˈvʌɪ-/ ▶ **noun** (pl. **-os**) Medicine a water-borne bacterium of a group that includes some pathogenic kinds that cause cholera, gastro-enteritis, and septicaemia.
● *Vibrio* and related genera; motile Gram-negative bacteria occurring as curved flagellated rods.
– ORIGIN modern Latin, from Latin *vibrare* 'vibrate'.

vibrissae /vʌɪˈbrɪsiː/ ▶ **plural noun** Zoology long stiff hairs growing around the mouth or elsewhere on the face of many mammals, used as organs of touch; whiskers.
■Ornithology coarse bristle-like feathers growing around the gape of certain insectivorous birds that catch insects in flight.
– ORIGIN late 17th cent.: from Latin, literally 'nostril hairs'.

vibrotactile /ˌvʌɪbrə(ʊ)ˈtaktʌɪl/ ▶ **adjective** relating to or involving the perception of vibration through touch.

viburnum /vɪˈbəːnəm, vʌɪ-/ ▶ **noun** a shrub or small tree of temperate and warm regions, typically bearing flat or rounded clusters of small white flowers.
● Genus *Viburnum*, family Caprifoliaceae: many species and ornamental hybrids, including the guelder rose and wayfaring tree.
– ORIGIN modern Latin, from Latin, 'wayfaring tree'.

Vic. ▶ **abbreviation for** Victoria.

vicar ▶ **noun** (in the Church of England) an incumbent of a parish where tithes formerly passed to a chapter or religious house or layman.
■(in other Anglican Churches) a member of the clergy deputizing for another. ■ (in the Roman Catholic Church) a representative or deputy of a bishop. ■ (in the US Episcopal Church) a clergyman in charge of a chapel. ■ a cleric or choir member appointed to sing certain parts of a cathedral service.
– DERIVATIVES **vicarship** noun.
– ORIGIN Middle English: via Anglo-Norman French from Old French *vicaire*, from Latin *vicarius* 'substitute', from *vic-* 'change, turn, place' (compare with **VICE**³).

vicarage ▶ **noun** the residence of a vicar.
■historical the benefice or living of a vicar.

vicar apostolic ▶ **noun** a Roman Catholic missionary.
■a titular bishop.

vicar general ▶ **noun** (pl. **vicars general**) an Anglican official serving as a deputy or assistant to a bishop or archbishop.
■(in the Roman Catholic Church) a bishop's representative in matters of jurisdiction or administration.

vicarial /vɪˈkɛːrɪəl, vʌɪ-/ ▶ **adjective** archaic of, relating to, or serving as a vicar.

vicariance /vɪˈkɛːrɪəns, vʌɪ-/ ▶ **noun** [mass noun] Biology the geographical separation of a population, typically by a physical barrier such as a mountain range or river, resulting in a pair of closely related species.
– ORIGIN 1950s: from Latin *vicarius* 'substitute' + **-ANCE**.

vicariate /vɪˈkɛːrɪət, vʌɪ-/ ▶ **noun** the office or authority of a vicar.
■a church or parish ministered to by a vicar.

vicarious /vɪˈkɛːrɪəs, vʌɪ-/ ▶ **adjective** experienced in the imagination through the feelings or actions of another person: *this catalogue brings vicarious pleasure in luxury living.*
■acting or done for another: *a vicarious atonement.*
– DERIVATIVES **vicariously** adverb, **vicariousness** noun.
– ORIGIN mid 17th cent.: from Latin *vicarius* 'substitute' (see **VICAR**) + **-OUS**.

Vicar of Christ ▶ **noun** (in the Roman Catholic Church) a title of the Pope.

vice¹ /vʌɪs/ ▶ **noun** [mass noun] immoral or wicked behaviour.
■criminal activities involving prostitution, pornography, or drugs. ■ [count noun] an immoral or wicked personal characteristic. ■ [count noun] a weakness of character or behaviour; a bad habit: *cigars happen to be my father's vice.* ■ (also **stable vice**) [count noun] a bad or neurotic habit of stabled horses, typically arising as a result of boredom.
– DERIVATIVES **viceless** adjective.
– ORIGIN Middle English: via Old French from Latin *vitium*.

vice² /vʌɪs/ (US **vise**) ▶ **noun** a metal tool with movable jaws which are used to hold an object firmly in place while work is done on it, typically attached to a workbench.
– DERIVATIVES **vice-like** adjective.
– ORIGIN Middle English (denoting a screw or winch): from Old French *vis*, from Latin *vitis* 'vine'.

vice³ /ˈvʌɪsi/ ▶ **preposition** as a substitute for: *the letter was drafted by David Hunt, vice Bevin who was ill.*
– ORIGIN Latin, ablative of *vic-* 'change'.

vice⁴ /vʌɪs/ ▶ **noun** informal short for **VICE-PRESIDENT**, **VICE ADMIRAL**, etc.

vice- ▶ **combining form** next in rank to, and typically denoting capacity to deputize for: *vice admiral* | *vice-president.*
– ORIGIN from Latin *vice* 'in place of' (compare with **VICE**³).

V

vice admiral ▶ **noun** a high rank of naval officer, above rear admiral and below admiral.

vice anglais /vis ɑ̃glɛ/ ▶ **noun** [in sing.] chiefly humorous a vice considered characteristic of the English, especially the use of corporal punishment for sexual stimulation.
– ORIGIN French, literally 'English vice'.

vice chamberlain ▶ **noun** a deputy chamberlain, especially (in the UK) the deputy of the Lord Chamberlain.

vice chancellor ▶ **noun** a deputy chancellor, especially one of a British university who discharges most of its administrative duties.

vicegerent /vʌɪsˈdʒɪər(ə)nt, -ˈdʒɛ-/ ▶ **noun** formal a person exercising delegated power on behalf of a sovereign or ruler.
▪a person regarded as an earthly representative of God or a god, especially the Pope.
– DERIVATIVES **vicegerency** noun (pl. **-ies**).
– ORIGIN mid 16th cent.: from medieval Latin *vicegerent-* '(person) holding office', from Latin *vic-* 'office, place, turn' + *gerere* 'carry on, hold'.

Vicente /vɪˈsɛnti/, Gil (*c.*1465–*c.*1536), Portuguese dramatist and poet. He is regarded as Portugal's most important dramatist; many of his works were written to commemorate national or court events and include religious dramas, farces, pastoral plays, and satirical comedies.

Vicenza /vɪˈtʃɛntsə/ a city in NE Italy; pop. 109,330 (1990).

vice-president ▶ **noun** an official or executive ranking below and deputizing for a president.
– DERIVATIVES **vice-presidency** noun (pl. **-ies**), **vice-presidential** adjective.

viceregal ▶ **adjective** of or relating to a viceroy.

vicereine /ˈvʌɪsreɪn/ ▶ **noun** the wife of a viceroy.
▪a female viceroy.
– ORIGIN early 19th cent.: from French, from *vice-* 'in place of' + *reine* 'queen'.

vice ring ▶ **noun** a group of criminals involved in organizing illegal prostitution.

viceroy /ˈvʌɪsrɔɪ/ ▶ **noun** a ruler exercising authority in a colony on behalf of a sovereign.
– DERIVATIVES **viceroyal** adjective, **viceroyship** noun.
– ORIGIN early 16th cent.: from archaic French, from *vice-* 'in place of' + *roi* 'king'.

viceroyalty (also **Viceroyalty**) ▶ **noun** (pl. **-ies**) the office, position, or authority of a viceroy.
▪a territory governed by a viceroy.

vice squad ▶ **noun** a department or division of a police force that enforces laws against prostitution, drug abuse, illegal gambling, etc.

vice versa /ˌvʌɪs ˈvəːsə, vʌɪsə/ ▶ **adverb** with the main items in the preceding statement the other way round: *cruise from Cairo to Aswan or vice versa.*
– ORIGIN early 17th cent.: from Latin, literally 'in-turned position'.

Vichy /ˈviːʃi/ a town in south central France; pop. 28,050 (1990). A noted spa town, it is the source of an effervescent mineral water.

During the Second World War the town was the headquarters of the regime that was set up after the German occupation of northern France, to administer unoccupied France and the colonies. Never recognized by the Allies, the regime functioned as a puppet government for the Nazis.

vichyssoise /ˌviːʃiːˈswɑːz/ ▶ **noun** [mass noun] a soup made with potatoes, leeks, and cream and typically served chilled.
– ORIGIN French (feminine) 'of *Vichy*' (see **VICHY**).

vicinage /ˈvɪsɪnɪdʒ/ ▶ **noun** chiefly US another term for **VICINITY**.
– ORIGIN Middle English: from Old French *vis(e)nage*, from an alteration of Latin *vicinus* 'neighbour'.

vicinal /ˈvɪsɪn(ə)l, vɪˈsʌɪn(ə)l/ ▶ **adjective** rare neighbouring; adjacent.
▪(especially of a railway or road) serving a neighbourhood; local. ▪Chemistry relating to or denoting substituents attached to adjacent atoms in a ring or chain.
– ORIGIN early 17th cent.: from French, or from Latin *vicinalis*, from *vicinus* 'neighbour'.

vicinity ▶ **noun** (pl. **-ies**) the area near or surrounding a particular place: *the number of people living in the immediate vicinity was small.*
▪[mass noun] archaic proximity in space or relationship: *the abundance and vicinity of country seats.*
– ORIGIN mid 16th cent. (in the sense 'proximity'): from Latin *vicinitas*, from *vicinus* 'neighbour'.

vicious ▶ **adjective 1** deliberately cruel or violent: *a vicious assault.*
▪(of an animal) wild and dangerous to people. ▪figurative serious or dangerous: *a vicious flu bug.* ▪poetic/literary immoral: *every soul on earth, virtuous or vicious, shall perish.*
2 archaic (of language or a line of reasoning) imperfect; defective.
– DERIVATIVES **viciously** adverb, **viciousness** noun.
– ORIGIN Middle English (in the sense 'characterized by immorality'): from Old French *vicious* or Latin *vitiosus*, from *vitium* 'vice'.

vicious circle (also **vicious cycle**) ▶ **noun** a sequence of reciprocal cause and effect in which two or more elements intensify and aggravate each other, leading inexorably to a worsening of the situation.

vicious spiral ▶ **noun** Brit. see **SPIRAL** (sense 2).

vicissitude /vɪˈsɪsɪtjuːd, vʌɪ-/ ▶ **noun** (usu. **vicissitudes**) a change of circumstances or fortune, typically one that is unwelcome or unpleasant: *her husband's sharp vicissitudes of fortune.*
▪[mass noun] poetic/literary alternation between opposite or contrasting things: *the vicissitude of the seasons.*
– DERIVATIVES **vicissitudinous** /-ˈtjuːdɪnəs/ adjective.
– ORIGIN early 17th cent. (in the sense 'alternation'): from French, or from Latin *vicissitudo*, from *vicissim* 'by turns', from *vic-* 'turn, change'.

Vicksburg /ˈvɪksbəːg/ a city on the Mississippi River, in western Mississippi; pop. 20,910 (1990). In 1863, during the American Civil War, it was successfully besieged by Union forces. It was the last Confederate-held outpost on the river and its loss effectively split the secessionist states in half.

Vico /ˈviːkəʊ/, Giambattista (1668–1744), Italian philosopher. In *Scienza Nuova* (1725) he asserted that civilizations are subject to recurring cycles of barbarism, heroism, and reason, accompanied by corresponding cultural, linguistic, and political modes. His historicist approach influenced later philosophers such as Marx.

vicomte /ˈviːkɔ̃t, ˈviːkɒmt, French vikɔ̃t/ ▶ **noun** (pl. pronounced same) a French nobleman corresponding in rank to a British or Irish viscount.
– ORIGIN French.

vicomtesse /ˌvikɔ̃ˈtɛs, ˌviːkɒnˈtɛs, French vikɒmtɛs/ ▶ **noun** (pl. pronounced same) a French noblewoman corresponding in rank to a British or Irish viscountess.
– ORIGIN French.

victim ▶ **noun** a person harmed, injured, or killed as a result of a crime, accident, or other event or action.
▪a person who is tricked or duped: *the victim of a hoax.* ▪a living creature killed as a religious sacrifice.
– PHRASES **fall victim to** be hurt, killed, damaged, or destroyed by: *many streams have fallen victim to the recent drought.*
– ORIGIN late 15th cent. (denoting a creature killed as a religious sacrifice): from Latin *victima*.

victimize (also **-ise**) ▶ **verb** [with obj.] single (someone) out for cruel or unjust treatment: *they are victimized by racism or discriminatory barriers.*
– DERIVATIVES **victimization** noun, **victimizer** noun.

victimless ▶ **adjective** used to describe a crime in which there is no injured party.

victimology ▶ **noun** (pl. **-ies**) [mass noun] the study of the victims of crime and the psychological effects on them of their experience.
▪the possession of an outlook, arising from real or imagined victimization, which seems to glorify and indulge the state of being a victim.

victim support ▶ **noun** [mass noun] the provision of advice and counselling to victims of crime.

victor ▶ **noun 1** a person who defeats an enemy or opponent in a battle, game, or other competition.
2 a code word representing the letter V, used in radio communication.
– ORIGIN Middle English: from Anglo-Norman French *victo(u)r* or Latin *victor*, from *vincere* 'conquer'.

Victor Emmanuel II (1820–78), ruler of the kingdom of Sardinia 1849–61 and first king of united Italy 1861–78. He hastened the drive towards Italian unification by appointing Cavour as Premier of Piedmont in 1852. After being crowned king of Italy he added Venetia to the kingdom in 1866 and Rome in 1870.

Victor Emmanuel III (1869–1947), last king of Italy 1900–46. He invited Mussolini to form a government in 1922 and lost all political power. After the loss of Sicily to the Allies (1943), he acted to dismiss Mussolini and conclude an armistice.

Victoria[1] /vɪkˈtɔːrɪə/ **1** a state of SE Australia; pop. 4,394,000 (est. 1990); capital, Melbourne. Originally a district of New South Wales, it became a separate colony in 1851 and was federated with the other states of Australia in 1901.
2 a port at the southern tip of Vancouver Island, capital of British Columbia; pop. 262,220 (1991).
3 the capital of the Seychelles, a port on the island of Mahé; pop. 24,000 (est. 1987).
4 the capital of Hong Kong; pop. 590,771 (1981).

Victoria[2] /vɪkˈtɔːrɪə/ (1819–1901), queen of Great Britain and Ireland 1837–1901 and empress of India 1876–1901. She took an active interest in the policies of her ministers, but largely retired from public life after Prince Albert's death in 1861. Her reign was the longest in British history.

Victoria[3] /vɪkˈtɔːrɪə, Spanish bikˈtorja/, Tomás Luis de (1548–1611), Spanish composer. His music, all of it religious, resembles that of Palestrina in its contrapuntal nature; it includes motets, masses, and hymns.

Victoria[4] /vɪkˈtɔːrɪə/ (also **victoria**) ▶ **noun** historical a light four-wheeled horse-drawn carriage with a collapsible hood, seats for two passengers, and an elevated driver's seat in front.
– ORIGIN late 19th cent.: named after Queen *Victoria* (see **VICTORIA**[2]).

Victoria, Lake the largest lake in Africa, with shores in Uganda, Tanzania, and Kenya, and drained by the Nile. Also called **VICTORIA NYANZA**.

Victoria and Albert Museum (abbrev.: **V & A**) a national museum of fine and applied art in South Kensington, London, created in 1852 and having collections principally of pictures, textiles, ceramics, and furniture.

Victoria Cross (abbrev.: **VC**) ▶ **noun** a decoration awarded for conspicuous bravery in the Commonwealth armed services, instituted by Queen Victoria in 1856.

Victoria Day ▶ **noun** (in Canada) the Monday preceding May 24, observed as a national holiday to commemorate the birthday of Queen Victoria.

Victoria de Durango full name for **DURANGO**.

Victoria Falls a spectacular waterfall 109 m (355 ft) high, on the River Zambezi, on the Zimbabwe–Zambia border. Its native name is Mosi-oa-tunya, 'the smoke that thunders'.

Victoria Island an island in the Canadian Arctic, in the Northwest Territories.

Victoria lily ▶ **noun** a tropical South American water lily which has gigantic floating leaves with raised sides.
• Genus *Victoria*, family Nymphaeaceae: two species.

Victorian ▶ **adjective** of or relating to the reign of Queen Victoria: *a Victorian house.*
▪of or relating to the attitudes and values of this period, regarded as characterized especially by a stifling and prudish moral earnestness.
▶**noun** a person who lived during the Victorian period.
– DERIVATIVES **Victorianism** noun.

Victoriana ▶ **plural noun** articles, especially collectors' items, from the Victorian period.
▪matters or attitudes relating to or characteristic of this period.

Victoria Nile the upper part of the White Nile, between Lake Victoria and Lake Albert.

Victoria Nyanza /nɪˈanzə/ another name for Lake Victoria (see **VICTORIA, LAKE**).

Victoria Peak a mountain on Hong Kong Island, rising to 554 m (1,818 ft).

Victoria plum ▶ **noun** Brit. a plum of a large red dessert variety.

Victoria sandwich (also **Victoria sponge**) ▶ **noun** Brit. a cake consisting of two layers of sponge with a jam filling.

victorious ▶ **adjective** having won a victory; triumphant: *a victorious army | the team defied the odds and emerged victorious.*
▪of or characterized by victory: *he'd participated in the victorious campaigns of the Franco-Prussian War.*
– DERIVATIVES **victoriously** adverb, **victoriousness** noun.
– ORIGIN late Middle English: from Anglo-Norman

V

French *victorious*, from Latin *victoriosus*, from *victoria* (see **VICTORY**).

victor ludorum /luːˈdɔːrəm/ ▶ noun Brit. a boy or man who is the overall champion in a sports competition, especially at a school or college.
– ORIGIN Latin, literally 'victor of the games'.

Victory the flagship of Lord Nelson at the Battle of Trafalgar, launched in 1765. It has been restored, and is now on display in dry dock at Portsmouth.

victory ▶ noun (pl. **-ies**) an act of defeating an enemy or opponent in a battle, game, or other competition: *an election victory* | [mass noun] *they won their heat and went on to victory in the final*.
– ORIGIN Middle English: from Anglo-Norman French *victorie*, from Latin *victoria*.

victory bond ▶ noun a bond issued by a government during or immediately after a major war.

victory roll ▶ noun a roll performed by an aircraft as a sign of triumph, typically after a successful mission.

victory sign ▶ noun a signal of triumph or celebration made by holding up the hand with the palm outwards and the first two fingers spread apart to represent the letter V.

victrix /ˈvɪktrɪks/ ▶ noun (pl. **victrices** /-trɪsiːz/) rare a female victor or champion.
– ORIGIN Latin, feminine of *victor* (see **VICTOR**).

victrix ludorum ▶ noun Brit. a girl or woman who is the overall champion in sports competition, especially at a school or college.
– ORIGIN Latin, feminine of **VICTOR LUDORUM**.

victual /ˈvɪt(ə)l/ dated ▶ noun (**victuals**) food or provisions, typically as prepared for consumption.
▶ verb (**victualled**, **victualling**; US **victualed**, **victualing**) [with obj.] provide with food or other stores: *the ship wasn't even properly victualled*.
■ [no obj.] archaic obtain or lay in food or other stores: *a voyage of such length, that no ship could victual for*. ■ [no obj.] eat: *victual with me next Saturday*.
– ORIGIN Middle English: from Old French *vitaille*, from late Latin *victualia*, neuter plural of Latin *victualis*, from *victus* 'food'; related to *vivere* 'to live'. The pronunciation still represents the early spelling *vittel*; later spelling has been influenced by the Latin form.

victualler /ˈvɪt(ə)lə/ (US **victualer**) ▶ noun **1** (also **licensed victualler**) Brit. a person who is licensed to sell alcoholic liquor.
2 dated a person providing or selling food or other provisions.
■ a ship providing supplies for troops or other ships.
– ORIGIN late Middle English: from Old French *vitaill(i)er*, from *vitaille* (see **VICTUAL**).

vicuña /vɪˈkjuːnjə, -kuː-, vɪˈkuːnə/ ▶ noun a wild relative of the llama, inhabiting mountainous regions of South America and valued for its fine silky wool.
● *Vicugna vicugna*, family Camelidae.
■ [mass noun] cloth made from this wool or an imitation of it.
– ORIGIN early 17th cent.: from Spanish, from Quechua.

vicus /ˈvʌɪkəs, ˈviːkəs/ ▶ noun (pl. **vici** /ˈvʌɪkiː, ˈviːkiː/) the smallest unit of ancient Roman municipal administration, consisting of a village or part of a town.
■ a medieval European township.
– ORIGIN Latin, literally 'group of dwellings'.

Vic-Wells Ballet a ballet company set up by Ninette de Valois, based first at the Old Vic and from 1931 established at Sadler's Wells Theatre. The company later became the Sadler's Wells Ballet which in turn became part of the newly formed Royal Ballet.

vid ▶ noun informal short for **VIDEO**.

Vidal /vɪˈdɑːl/, Gore (b.1925), American novelist, dramatist, and essayist; born *Eugene Luther Vidal*. His novels, many of them satirical comedies, include *Williwaw* (1946) and *Myra Breckenridge* (1968).

vide /ˈvɪdeɪ, ˈviː-, ˈvʌɪdi/ ▶ verb [with obj., in imperative] see; consult (used as an instruction in a text to refer the reader to a specified passage, book, author, etc., for fuller or further information): *vide the comments cited in Schlosser*.
– ORIGIN Latin, 'see!', imperative of *videre*.

videlicet /vɪˈdɛlɪsɛt, vʌɪ-, -kɛt/ ▶ adverb more formal term for **VIZ.**

– ORIGIN Latin, from *videre* 'to see' + *licet* 'it is permissible'.

video ▶ noun (pl. **-os**) [mass noun] the system of recording, reproducing, or broadcasting moving visual images on or from videotape.
■ [count noun] a film or other piece of material recorded on videotape. ■ [count noun] a video cassette: *a blank video* | [mass noun] *the film will soon be released on video*. ■ [count noun] a short film made by a pop or rock group to accompany a song when broadcast on television. ■ [count noun] Brit. a video recorder.
▶ verb (**-oes**, **-oed**) [with obj.] make a video recording of (something broadcast on television).
■ film (someone or something) with a video camera.
– ORIGIN 1930s: from Latin *videre* 'to see', on the pattern of *audio*.

video amplifier ▶ noun a device designed to amplify the wide range of frequencies present in video signals and deliver the signal to the picture tube of a television set.

video camera ▶ noun a camera for recording images on videotape or for transmitting them to a monitor screen.

video card ▶ noun Computing a printed circuit board controlling output to a display screen.

video cassette recorder ▶ noun another term for **VIDEO RECORDER**.

videoconference ▶ noun an arrangement in which television sets linked to telephone lines are used to enable a group of people in several different locations to communicate with each other in sound and vision.
– DERIVATIVES **videoconferencing** noun.

video diary ▶ noun a record on videotape of a notable period of someone's life, or of a particular event, made using a camcorder.

videodisc ▶ noun a CD-ROM or other disc used to store visual images.

videofit ▶ noun a picture of someone sought by the police, built up on a computer screen by selecting and combining facial features according to witnesses' descriptions.

video frequency ▶ noun a frequency in the range used for video signals in television.

video game ▶ noun a game played by electronically manipulating images produced by a computer program on a television screen or display.

videogram ▶ noun a pre-recorded video of a commercial film or television programme.

videographics ▶ plural noun visual images produced using computer technology.
■ [treated as sing.] the manipulation of video images using a computer.

videography ▶ noun [mass noun] the process or art of making video films.
– DERIVATIVES **videographer** noun.

video jockey ▶ noun a person who introduces and plays music videos on television.

video nasty ▶ noun Brit. informal a film on video that contains scenes that are considered to be gratuitously and offensively violent or pornographic.

video-on-demand ▶ noun [mass noun] a system in which viewers choose their own filmed entertainment, by means of a PC or interactive TV system, from a wide available selection.

videophile ▶ noun an enthusiast for or devotee of video recordings or video technology.

videophone ▶ noun a telephone device transmitting and receiving a visual image as well as sound.

video piracy ▶ noun [mass noun] the unauthorized and illegal production and sale of copies of commercial video films.
– DERIVATIVES **video pirate** noun.

VideoPlus ▶ noun [mass noun] trademark a system for identifying broadcast television programmes by a numerical code which can be input into a video recorder in order to preset recording.

video recorder ▶ noun a device which, when linked to a television set, can be used for recording on and playing videotapes.
– DERIVATIVES **video recording** noun.

videotape ▶ noun [mass noun] magnetic tape for recording and reproducing visual images and sound.

■ [count noun] a video cassette. ■ a film or other piece of material recorded on videotape.
▶ verb another term for **VIDEO**: *his arrest was videotaped*.

videotelephony ▶ noun [mass noun] the transmission of video signals along telephone wires.

videotex (also **videotext**) ▶ noun [mass noun] an electronic information system such as teletext or viewdata.
– ORIGIN 1970s: from **VIDEO** + **TEXT**.

vidicon ▶ noun Electronics a small television camera tube in which the image is formed on a transparent electrode coated with photoconductive material, the current from which varies as it is scanned by a beam of low-speed electrons.
– ORIGIN 1950s: from the initial elements of **VIDEO** and *iconoscope* (an early television camera tube).

vidiot /ˈvɪdɪət/ ▶ noun N. Amer. informal a habitual, undiscriminating watcher of television or videotapes.
– ORIGIN 1960s: blend of **VIDEO** and **IDIOT**.

vie /vʌɪ/ ▶ verb (**vying**) [no obj.] compete eagerly with someone in order to do or achieve something: *the athletes were vying for a place in the British team*.
– ORIGIN mid 16th cent.: probably a shortening of obsolete *envy*, via Old French from Latin *invitare* 'challenge'.

vie de Bohème /ˌviː də bəʊˈɛm/ ▶ noun [mass noun] (usu. **la vie de Bohème**) an unconventional or informal way of life, especially as practised by an artist or writer.
– ORIGIN French, literally 'bohemian's life'.

vielle /vɪˈɛl/ ▶ noun a hurdy-gurdy.
– ORIGIN mid 18th cent.: from French, from Old French *viele* (see **VIOL**).

Vienna /vɪˈɛnə/ the capital of Austria, situated in the north-east of the country on the River Danube; pop. 1,533,180 (1991). From 1278 to 1918 it was the seat of the Habsburgs. It has long been a centre of the arts, especially music; Mozart, Beethoven, and the Strauss family were among the great composers who lived and worked there. German name **WIEN**.
– DERIVATIVES **Viennese** /vɪəˈniːz/ adjective & noun.

Vienna, Congress of an international conference held 1814–15 to agree the settlement of Europe after the Napoleonic Wars. The guiding principle of the settlement was the restoration and strengthening of hereditary and sometimes despotic rulers; the result was a political stability that lasted for three or four decades.

Vienna Circle a group of empiricist philosophers, scientists, and mathematicians active in Vienna from the 1920s until 1938, including Rudolf Carnap and Kurt Gödel. Their work laid the foundations of logical positivism.

Vienna sausage ▶ noun a small frankfurter made of pork, beef, or veal.

Vienna Secession ▶ noun see **SECESSION**.

Viennese coffee ▶ noun [mass noun] a blend of coffee flavoured with fig extract.

Viennese waltz ▶ noun a waltz characterized by a slight anticipation of the second beat of the bar and having a romantic quality.
■ a piece of music written in this style.

Vientiane /ˌvjɛnˈtjɑːn/ the capital and chief port of Laos, on the Mekong River; pop. 377,400 (1985).

Vierwaldstättersee /ˌfiːɐˈvalt ˌʃtɛtɐˌzeː/ German name for Lake Lucerne (see **LUCERNE, LAKE**).

Vietcong /vjɛtˈkɒŋ/ ▶ noun (pl. same) a member of the Communist guerrilla movement in Vietnam which fought the South Vietnamese government forces 1954–75 with the support of the North Vietnamese army and opposed the South Vietnam and US forces in the Vietnam War.
– ORIGIN Vietnamese, literally 'Vietnamese Communist'.

Vietminh /vjɛtˈmɪn/ ▶ noun (pl. same) a member of a Communist-dominated nationalist movement, formed in 1941, that fought for Vietnamese independence from French rule. Members of the Vietminh later joined with the Vietcong.
– ORIGIN from Vietnamese *Viet-Nam Dôc-Lâp Dông-Minh* 'Vietnamese Independence League'.

Vietnam /vjɛtˈnam/ a country in SE Asia, with a coastline on the South China Sea; pop. 67,843,000 (est. 1991); official language, Vietnamese; capital, Hanoi.

> Traditionally dominated by China, Vietnam came under French influence between 1862 and 1954. After the Second World War the Vietminh defeated the French, who then withdrew. Vietnam was partitioned along the 17th parallel between Communist North Vietnam (capital, Hanoi) and non-Communist South Vietnam (capital, Saigon). The Vietnam War between the North and the US-backed South ended in the victory of the North in 1975 and the reunification of the country under a Communist regime in the following year.

– ORIGIN from Vietnamese *Viet*, the name of the inhabitants, + *nam* 'south'.

Vietnamese ▶ **adjective** of or relating to Vietnam, its people, or their language.
▶ **noun** (pl. same) **1** a native or national of Vietnam, or a person of Vietnamese descent.
2 [mass noun] the language of Vietnam, spoken by about 60 million people. It probably belongs to the Mon-Khmer group, although much of its vocabulary is derived from Chinese.

Vietnamese pot-bellied pig ▶ **noun** a pig of a small, dark breed with short legs and a large stomach, sometimes kept as a pet.

Vietnamization (also **-isation**) ▶ **noun** [mass noun] (in the Vietnam War) the US policy of withdrawing its troops and transferring the responsibility and direction of the war effort to the government of South Vietnam.

Vietnam War a war between Communist North Vietnam and US-backed South Vietnam.

> Since the partition of Vietnam in 1954 the Communist North had attempted to unite the country as a Communist state, fuelling US concern over the possible spread of Communism in SE Asia. After two US destroyers were reportedly fired on in the Gulf of Tonkin in 1964, a US army was sent to Vietnam, supported by contingents from South Korea, Australia, New Zealand, and Thailand, while American aircraft bombed North Vietnamese forces and areas of Cambodia. The Tet Offensive of 1968 damaged US confidence and US forces began to be withdrawn, finally leaving in 1973. The North Vietnamese captured the southern capital Saigon to end the war in 1975.

vieux jeu /vjəː 'ʒəː, French vjø ʒø/ ▶ **adjective** old-fashioned; hackneyed: *a joke that was vieux jeu even in my day.*
– ORIGIN French, literally 'old game'.

view ▶ **noun 1** [mass noun] the ability to see something or to be seen from a particular place: *the end of the tunnel came into view* | [count noun] *they stood on the bar to get a better view.*
■ [count noun] a sight or prospect, typically of attractive natural scenery, that can be taken in by the eye from a particular place: *a fine view of the castle.* ■ [count noun] a work of art depicting such a sight. ■ [count noun] the visual appearance or an image of something when looked at in a particular way: *an aerial view of the military earthworks.* ■ [count noun] an inspection of things for sale by prospective purchasers, especially of works of art at an exhibition.
2 a particular way of considering or regarding something; an attitude or opinion: *strong political views.*
▶ **verb 1** [with obj.] look at or inspect (something): *the public can view the famous hall with its unique staircase.*
■ inspect (a house or other property) with the intention of possibly buying or renting it. ■ watch (something) on television. ■ Hunting see (a fox) break cover.
2 [with obj. and adverbial] regard in a particular light or with a particular attitude: *farmers are viewing the rise in rabbit numbers with concern.*
– PHRASES **in full view** clearly visible. **in view** visible to someone: *the youth was keeping him in view.* ■ as one's aim or objective: *the operation they* ***had in view.*** ■ in one's mind when forming a judgement: *it is important to* ***have in view*** *the position reached at the beginning of the 1970s.* **in view of** because or as a result of. **on view** (especially of a work of art) being shown or exhibited to the public. ■ easily visible: *it is advisable not to leave handbags on view.* **with a view to** with the hope, aim, or intention of.
– DERIVATIVES **viewable** adjective.
– ORIGIN Middle English: from Anglo-Norman French *vieue*, feminine past participle of *veoir* 'see', from Latin *videre*. The verb dates from the early 16th cent.

viewdata ▶ **noun** [mass noun] a news and information service in which computer data is sent by a telephone link and displayed on a television screen.

viewer ▶ **noun 1** a person who looks at or inspects something.
■ a person watching television or a film.
2 a device for looking at film transparencies or similar photographic images.

viewership ▶ **noun** [treated as sing. or pl.] the audience for a particular television programme or channel.

viewfinder ▶ **noun** a device on a camera showing the field of view of the lens, used in framing and focusing the picture.

viewgraph ▶ **noun** a graph or other data produced as a transparency for projection on to a screen or for transmission during a teleconference.

view halloo ▶ **noun** a shout given by a hunter on seeing a fox break cover.

viewing ▶ **noun** [mass noun] the action of inspecting or looking at something: *the owner may allow viewing by appointment.*
■ the action of watching something on television: *it is quite unsuitable for family viewing.* ■ [count noun] an opportunity to see something, especially a work of art.

viewless ▶ **adjective** not having or affording a pleasant sight or prospect.

viewpoint ▶ **noun** another term for **POINT OF VIEW**.

viewport ▶ **noun** a window in a spacecraft or in the conning tower of an oil rig.
■ Computing a framed area on a display screen for viewing information.

viff (also **VIFF**) Aeronautics, informal ▶ **noun** [mass noun] a technique used by a vertical take-off aircraft to change direction abruptly by altering the direction of thrust of the aircraft's jet engines.
▶ **verb** [no obj.] (of a vertical take-off aircraft) change direction in such a way.
– ORIGIN 1970s: acronym from *vectoring in forward flight.*

vig ▶ **noun** short for **VIGORISH**.

viga /'viːɡə/ ▶ **noun** US a rough-hewn roof timber or rafter, especially in an adobe building.
– ORIGIN Spanish.

Vigée-Lebrun /ˌviːʒeɪlə'brəːn, French viʒeləbʀœ̃/, (Marie Louise) Élisabeth (1755–1842), French painter. She is known for her portraits of women and children, especially Marie Antoinette and Lady Hamilton.

vigesimal /vɪ'dʒɛsɪm(ə)l, vʌɪ-/ ▶ **adjective** rare relating to or based on the number twenty.
– ORIGIN mid 17th cent.: from Latin *vigesimus* (from *viginti* 'twenty') + **-AL**.

vigil /'vɪdʒɪl/ ▶ **noun 1** a period of keeping awake during the time usually spent asleep, especially to keep watch or pray: *my birdwatching vigils lasted for hours* | *as he lay in a coma the family* ***kept vigil.***
■ a stationary, peaceful demonstration in support of a particular cause, typically without speeches.
2 (in the Christian Church) the eve of a festival or holy day as an occasion of religious observance.
■ (**vigils**) nocturnal devotions.
– ORIGIN Middle English (in sense 2): via Old French from Latin *vigilia*, from *vigil* 'awake'.

vigilance ▶ **noun** [mass noun] the action or state of keeping careful watch for possible danger or difficulties.
– ORIGIN late 16th cent.: from French, or from Latin *vigilantia*, from *vigilare* 'keep awake', from *vigil* (see **VIGIL**).

vigilance committee ▶ **noun** US a body of vigilantes.

vigilant ▶ **adjective** keeping careful watch for possible danger or difficulties: *the burglar was spotted by vigilant neighbours.*
– DERIVATIVES **vigilantly** adverb.
– ORIGIN late 15th cent.: from Latin *vigilant-* 'keeping awake', from the verb *vigilare*, from *vigil* (see **VIGIL**).

vigilante /ˌvɪdʒɪ'lanti/ ▶ **noun** a member of a self-appointed group of citizens who undertake law enforcement in their community without legal authority, typically because the legal agencies are thought to be inadequate.
– DERIVATIVES **vigilantism** noun.
– ORIGIN mid 19th cent.: from Spanish, literally 'vigilant'.

vigneron /'viːnjərɒ̃, French viɲ(ə)ʀɔ̃/ ▶ **noun** a person who cultivates grapes for winemaking.
– ORIGIN French, from *vigne* 'vine'.

vignette /viː'njɛt, vɪ-/ ▶ **noun 1** a brief evocative description, account, or episode.
2 a small illustration or portrait photograph which fades into its background without a definite border.
■ a small ornamental design filling a space in a book or carving, typically based on foliage.
▶ **verb** [with obj.] portray (someone) in the style of a vignette.
■ produce (a photograph) in the style of a vignette by softening or shading away the edges of the subject.
– DERIVATIVES **vignettist** noun.
– ORIGIN late Middle English (in sense 2; also as an architectural term denoting a carved representation of a vine): from French, diminutive of *vigne* 'vine'.

Vignola /vɪ'njəʊlə/, Giacomo Barozzi da (1507–73), Italian architect. His designs were mannerist in style and include the Palazzo Farnese near Viterbo (1559–73) and the church of Il Gesù in Rome (begun 1568).

Vigny /'viːnji/, Alfred Victor, Comte de (1797–1863), French poet, novelist, and dramatist. His poetry reveals his faith in 'man's unconquerable mind'. Other works include the play *Chatterton* (1835).

Vigo[1] /'viːɡəʊ/ a port on the Atlantic in Galicia, NW Spain; pop. 276,570 (1991).

Vigo[2] /'viːɡəʊ/, Jean (1905–34), French film director. His experimental films, which combine lyrical, surrealist, and realist elements, include *Zéro de conduite* (1933) and *L'Atalante* (1934).

vigor ▶ **noun** US spelling of **VIGOUR**.

vigorish ▶ **noun** US informal **1** [in sing.] an excessive rate of interest on a loan, typically one from an illegal moneylender.
2 [mass noun] the percentage deducted from a gambler's winnings by the organizers of a game.
– ORIGIN early 20th cent.: probably from Yiddish, from Russian *vyigrysh* 'gain, winnings'.

vigoro /'vɪɡ(ə)rəʊ/ ▶ **noun** [mass noun] an Australian team ball game combining elements of cricket and baseball, traditionally played by women.
– ORIGIN 1930s: apparently from **VIGOROUS**.

vigorous ▶ **adjective** (of a person) strong, healthy, and full of energy.
■ characterized by or involving physical strength, effort, or energy: *vigorous aerobic exercise.* ■ (of language) forceful: *a vigorous denial.* ■ (of a plant) growing strongly.
– DERIVATIVES **vigorously** adverb, **vigorousness** noun.
– ORIGIN Middle English: via Old French from medieval Latin *vigorosus*, from Latin *vigor* (see **VIGOUR**).

vigour (US **vigor**) ▶ **noun** [mass noun] physical strength and good health.
■ effort, energy, and enthusiasm: *they set about the new task with vigour.* ■ strong, healthy growth of a plant.
– DERIVATIVES **vigourless** adjective.
– ORIGIN Middle English: from Old French, from Latin *vigor*, from *vigere* 'be lively'.

vihara /vɪ'hɑːrə/ ▶ **noun** a Buddhist temple or monastery.
– ORIGIN Sanskrit.

vihuela /vɪ'(h)weɪlə/ ▶ **noun** a type of early Spanish stringed musical instrument, in particular:
■ (**vihuela de mano** /deɪ 'manəʊ/) a type of guitar.
■ (**vihuela de arco** /deɪ 'ɑːkəʊ/) a type of viol.
– ORIGIN mid 19th cent.: Spanish.

Vijayawada /ˌvɪdʒʌɪə'wɑːdə/ a city on the Krishna River in Andhra Pradesh, SE India; pop. 701,000 (1991).

Viking[1] /'vʌɪkɪŋ/ ▶ **noun** any of the Scandinavian seafaring pirates and traders who raided and settled in many parts of NW Europe in the 8th–11th centuries.
▶ **adjective** of or relating to the Vikings or the period in which they lived.
– ORIGIN from Old Norse *víkingr*, from *vík* 'creek' or Old English *wīc* 'camp, dwelling place'.

Viking[2] /'vʌɪkɪŋ/ a shipping forecast area covering the open sea between southern Norway and the Shetland Islands.

Viking[3] /'vʌɪkɪŋ/ either of two American space probes sent to Mars in 1975, each of which consisted of a lander that conducted experiments on the surface and an orbiter.

Vila /'viːlə/ (also **Port Vila**) the capital of Vanuatu, on the SW coast of the island of Efate; pop. 20,000 (1992).

vilayet /vɪ'lɑːjɛt/ ▶ **noun** (in Turkey, and formerly in the Ottoman Empire) a major administrative district or province with its own governor.
– ORIGIN Turkish, from Arabic *wilāya(t)* 'government, administrative district'.

V

vile ▶ adjective extremely unpleasant: *he has a vile temper | vile smells.*
▪morally bad; wicked: *as vile a rogue as ever lived.* ▪ archaic of little worth or value.
– DERIVATIVES **vilely** adverb, **vileness** noun.
– ORIGIN Middle English: via Old French from Latin *vilis* 'cheap, base'.

vilify /ˈvɪlɪfʌɪ/ ▶ verb (**-ies**, **-ied**) [with obj.] speak or write about in an abusively disparaging manner: *he has been vilified in the press.*
– DERIVATIVES **vilification** /-fɪˈkeɪʃ(ə)n/ noun, **vilifier** noun.
– ORIGIN late Middle English (in the sense 'lower in value'): from late Latin *vilificare*, from Latin *vilis* 'of low value' (see **VILE**).

vill ▶ noun (in medieval England) the smallest administrative unit under the feudal system, consisting of a number of houses and their adjacent lands, roughly corresponding to the modern parish.
– ORIGIN early 17th cent.: from Anglo-Norman French, from Latin *villa* 'country house'.

Villa /ˈviːjə, ˈviːljə/, Pancho (1878–1923), Mexican revolutionary; born *Doroteo Arango*. After playing a prominent role in the revolution of 1910–11 he overthrew the dictatorial regime of General Victoriano Huerta in 1914 together with Venustiano Carranza, but then rebelled against Carranza's regime with Emiliano Zapata.

villa ▶ noun (especially in continental Europe) a large and luxurious country residence in its own grounds.
▪a large country house of Roman times, having an estate and consisting of farm and residential buildings arranged around a courtyard. ▪ Brit. a detached or semi-detached house in a residential district, typically one that is Victorian or Edwardian in style. ▪ a rented holiday home abroad.
– ORIGIN early 17th cent.: from Italian, from Latin.

Villafranchian /ˌvɪləˈfraŋkɪən/ ▶ adjective of, relating to, or denoting an age (or stage) in Europe crossing the boundary of the Upper Pliocene and Lower Pleistocene, lasting from about 3 to 1 million years ago.
▪[as noun **the Villafranchian**] the Villafranchian age or stage, or the system of deposits laid down during it.
– ORIGIN late 19th cent.: from French *villafranchien*, from *Villafranca* d'Asti, the village in northern Italy near which exposures of this period occur.

village ▶ noun a group of houses and associated buildings, larger than a hamlet and smaller than a town, situated in a rural area.
▪a self-contained district or community within a town or city, regarded as having features characteristic of village life: *the Olympic village.* ▪ US a small municipality with limited corporate powers. ▪ Austral./NZ a select suburban shopping centre.
– DERIVATIVES **villager** noun, **villagey** adjective.
– ORIGIN late Middle English: from Old French, from Latin *villa* 'country house'.

village idiot ▶ noun chiefly archaic a person of very low intelligence resident and well-known in a village.

villagization /ˌvɪlɪdʒʌɪˈzeɪʃ(ə)n/ (also **-isation**) ▶ noun [mass noun] (in Africa and Asia) the concentration of the population in villages as opposed to scattered settlements, typically to ensure more efficient control and distribution of services such as health care and education.
▪the transfer of land to the communal control of villagers.

Villahermosa /ˌviːjəɛːˈməʊsə, Spanish bijaerˈmosa/ a city in SE Mexico, capital of the state of Tabasco; pop. 390,160 (1990). Full name **VILLAHERMOSA DE SAN JUAN BAUTISTA** /deɪ san ˌhwɑːn baʊˈtiːstə, Spanish ðe saŋ xwan bauˈtista/.

villain /ˈvɪlən/ ▶ noun **1** a person guilty or capable of a crime or wickedness.
▪the person or thing responsible for specified trouble, harm, or damage: *the industrialized nations are the real environmental villains.* ▪ (in a play or novel) a character whose evil actions or motives are important to the plot: *a pantomime villain.*
2 archaic variant spelling of **VILLEIN**.
– ORIGIN Middle English (in the sense 'a rustic, boor'): from Old French *vilein*, based on Latin *villa* (see **VILLA**).

villainous ▶ adjective relating to, constituting, or guilty of wicked or criminal behaviour: *the villainous crimes of the terrorists.*
▪informal extremely bad or unpleasant: *a villainous smell.*
– DERIVATIVES **villainously** adverb, **villainousness** noun.

villainy ▶ noun (pl. **-ies**) [mass noun] wicked or criminal behaviour: *the villainy of professional racketeers* | [count noun] *minor villainies.*
– ORIGIN Middle English: from Old French *vilenie*, from *vilein* (see **VILLAIN**).

Villa-Lobos /ˌvɪləˈləʊbɒs/, Heitor (1887–1959), Brazilian composer. He used folk music in many of his instrumental compositions, notably the nine *Bachianas brasileiras* (1930–45).

villancico /ˌviːjanˈsiːkəʊ/ ▶ noun (pl. **-os** /-əʊz/) a form of Spanish and Portuguese song with short stanzas and a refrain, originally a folk song, later used in sacred music, and now especially as a Christmas carol.
– ORIGIN Spanish, diminutive of *villano* 'peasant'.

villanella /ˌvɪləˈnɛlə/ ▶ noun (pl. **villanelle** /ˌvɪləˈnɛleɪ/ or **villanellas**) a form of Italian part-song originating in Naples in the 16th century, in rustic style with a vigorous rhythm.
– ORIGIN Italian, feminine of *villanello* 'rural', diminutive of *villano* 'peasant'.

villanelle /ˌvɪləˈnɛl/ ▶ noun a pastoral or lyrical poem of nineteen lines, with only two rhymes throughout, and some lines repeated.
– ORIGIN late 19th cent.: from French, from Italian *villanella* (see **VILLANELLA**).

-ville ▶ combining form informal used in fictitious place names with reference to a particular quality: *dullsville.*
– ORIGIN from French *ville* 'town', used in many US town names.

villein /ˈvɪlən, -eɪn/ ▶ noun (in medieval England) a feudal tenant entirely subject to a lord or manor to whom he paid dues and services in return for land.
– ORIGIN Middle English: variant of **VILLAIN**.

villeinage /ˈvɪlənɪdʒ, -leɪn-/ ▶ noun [mass noun] historical the tenure or status of a villein.

villi plural form of **VILLUS**.

Villon /ˈviːjɒ̃, French vijɔ̃/, François (*fl.c.*1460), French poet; born *François de Montcorbier* or *François des Loges*. He is best known for *Le Lais* or *Le Petit testament* (1456) and the longer, more serious *Le Grand testament* (1461).

villous /ˈvɪləs/ ▶ adjective Anatomy (of a structure, especially the epithelium) covered with villi.
▪Medicine (of a condition) affecting the villi: *villous atrophy.* ▪ Botany shaggy.

villus /ˈvɪləs/ ▶ noun (pl. **villi** /-lʌɪ, -liː/) Anatomy any of numerous minute elongated projections set closely together on a surface, typically increasing its surface area for the absorption of substances, in particular:
▪a finger-like projection of the lining of the small intestine. ▪ a fold of the chorion.
– ORIGIN early 18th cent.: from Latin, literally 'shaggy hair'.

Vilnius /ˈvɪlnɪəs/ the capital of Lithuania; pop. 593,000 (1991).

vim ▶ noun [mass noun] informal energy; enthusiasm: *in his youth he was full of vim and vigour.*
– ORIGIN mid 19th cent. (originally US): perhaps from Latin, accusative of *vis* 'energy'.

Vimy Ridge, Battle of /ˈviːmi/ an Allied attack on the German position of Vimy Ridge, near Arras, during the First World War. One of the key points on the Western Front, it had long resisted assaults, but on 9 April 1917 it was taken by Canadian troops in fifteen minutes, at the cost of heavy casualties.

VIN ▶ abbreviation for vehicle identification number.

vin /vã, French vɛ̃/ ▶ noun [mass noun] [usu. with modifier] French wine: *vin blanc.*
– ORIGIN French, literally 'wine'.

vina ▶ noun variant spelling of **VEENA**.

vinaceous /vʌɪˈneɪʃəs/ ▶ adjective of the colour of red wine.
– ORIGIN late 17th cent.: from Latin *vinaceus* (from *vinum* 'wine') + **-OUS**.

vinaigrette /ˌvɪnɪˈgrɛt, ˌvɪneɪ-/ ▶ noun **1** (also **vinaigrette dressing**) [mass noun] salad dressing of oil, wine vinegar, and seasoning.
2 historical a small ornamental bottle for holding smelling salts.
– ORIGIN French, diminutive of *vinaigre* 'vinegar'.

vinblastine /vɪnˈblastiːn/ ▶ noun [mass noun] Medicine a cytotoxic compound of the alkaloid class obtained from the Madagascar periwinkle and used to treat Hodgkin's disease and other cancers of the lymphatic system.
– ORIGIN 1960s: from modern Latin *Vinca* (see **VINCA**) + (*leuco*)*blast* (a cell from which a leucocyte develops) + **-INE**[4].

vinca /ˈvɪŋkə/ ▶ noun another term for **PERIWINKLE**[1].
– ORIGIN 1930s: from modern Latin *Vinca* (genus name), from late Latin *pervinca* (see **PERIWINKLE**[1]).

Vincent de Paul, St (1581–1660), French priest. He devoted his life to work among the poor and the sick and established institutions to continue his work, including the Daughters of Charity (Sisters of Charity of St Vincent de Paul) (1633). Feast day, 19 July.

Vincentian /vɪnˈsɛnʃ(ə)n/ ▶ noun another name for **LAZARIST**.

Vinci, Leonardo da, see **LEONARDO DA VINCI**.

vincible /ˈvɪnsɪb(ə)l/ ▶ adjective poetic/literary (of an opponent or obstacle) able to be overcome or conquered.
– DERIVATIVES **vincibility** noun.
– ORIGIN mid 16th cent.: from Latin *vincibilis*, from *vincere* 'to overcome'.

vincristine /vɪnˈkrɪstiːn/ ▶ noun [mass noun] Medicine a cytotoxic compound of the alkaloid class obtained from the Madagascar periwinkle and used to treat acute leukaemia and other cancers.
– ORIGIN 1960s: from modern Latin *Vinca* (see **VINCA**) + a second element perhaps based on **CRISTA** + **-INE**[4].

vinculum /ˈvɪŋkjʊləm/ ▶ noun (pl. **vincula** /-lə/)
1 Anatomy a connecting band of tissue, such as that attaching a flexor tendon to the bone of a finger or toe.
2 Mathematics a horizontal line drawn over a group of terms in a mathematical expression to indicate that they are to be operated on as a single entity by the preceding or following operator.
– DERIVATIVES **vincular** adjective.
– ORIGIN mid 17th cent. (in the sense 'bond, tie'): from Latin, literally 'bond', from *vincire* 'bind'. The term has been used in anatomy since the mid 19th cent.

vindaloo /ˌvɪndəˈluː/ ▶ noun [mass noun] a highly spiced hot Indian curry made with meat or fish.
– ORIGIN probably from Portuguese *vin d'alho* 'wine and garlic (sauce)', from *vinho* 'wine' + *alho* 'garlic'.

vin de garde /ˌvã də ˈgɑːd/ ▶ noun (pl. **vins de garde**) [mass noun] wine which will significantly improve in quality if left to mature.
– ORIGIN French, literally 'wine for keeping'.

vin de paille /ˈpɑːj/ ▶ noun (pl. **vins de paille**) [mass noun] a rich dessert wine made chiefly in the Jura region from grapes dried or partly dried in the sun on straw mats or wire frames.
– ORIGIN French, literally 'straw wine'.

vin de table /ˈtɑːbl(ə)/ ▶ noun (pl. **vins de table**) [mass noun] French table wine of reasonable quality, suitable for accompanying a meal.
– ORIGIN French, literally 'table wine'.

vin d'honneur /vã dɒˈnəː, French vɛ̃ dɔnœʀ/ ▶ noun (pl. **vins d'honneur**) [mass noun] wine formally offered in honour of a special guest.
▪[count noun] a reception at which wine is offered for such a purpose.
– ORIGIN French, literally 'wine of honour'.

vindicate /ˈvɪndɪkeɪt/ ▶ verb [with obj.] clear (someone) of blame or suspicion: *hospital staff were vindicated by the inquest verdict.*
▪show or prove to be right, reasonable, or justified: *more sober views were vindicated by events.*
– DERIVATIVES **vindicable** adjective, **vindication** noun, **vindicator** noun, **vindicatory** adjective.
– ORIGIN mid 16th cent. (in the sense 'deliver, rescue'): from Latin *vindicat-* 'claimed, avenged', from the verb *vindicare*, from *vindex*, *vindic-* 'claimant, avenger'.

vindicative /ˈvɪndɪˌkətɪv/ ▶ adjective archaic
1 another term for **VINDICTIVE**.
2 serving to vindicate someone or something.

vindictive /vɪnˈdɪktɪv/ ▶ adjective having or showing a strong or unreasoning desire for revenge: *the criticism was both vindictive and personalized.*
– DERIVATIVES **vindictively** adverb, **vindictiveness** noun.

V

– ORIGIN early 17th cent.: from Latin *vindicta* 'vengeance' + -IVE.

vin du pays /vã ˌd(j)uː peɪˈiː, French vɛ̃ dy pei/ (also **vin de pays**) ▶ noun (pl. **vins du pays**) [mass noun] the third-highest French classification of wine, indicating that the wine meets certain standards including area of production, strength, and quality.
■ French wine produced locally.
– ORIGIN French, literally 'wine of the region'.

Vine, Frederick John (b.1939), English geologist. Vine and his colleague **Drummond H. Matthews** (1931–97) contributed to the theory of plate tectonics, showing that magnetic data from the earth's crust under the Atlantic Ocean provided evidence for sea-floor spreading.

vine ▶ noun a climbing or trailing woody-stemmed plant related to the grapevine.
● *Vitis* and other genera, family Vitaceae.
■ used in names of climbing or trailing plants of other families, e.g. **Russian vine**. ■ the slender stem of a trailing or climbing plant.
– DERIVATIVES **viny** adjective.
– ORIGIN Middle English: from Old French, from Latin *vinea* 'vineyard, vine', from *vinum* 'wine'.

vine dresser ▶ noun a person who prunes, trains, and cultivates vines.

vinegar ▶ noun [mass noun] a sour-tasting liquid containing acetic acid, obtained by fermenting dilute alcoholic liquids, typically wine, cider, or beer, and used as a condiment or for pickling.
■ figurative sourness or peevishness of behaviour, character, or speech: *her aggrieved tone held a touch of vinegar.*
– DERIVATIVES **vinegarish** adjective, **vinegary** adjective.
– ORIGIN Middle English: from Old French *vyn egre*, based on Latin *vinum* 'wine' + *acer* 'sour'.

vinery ▶ noun (pl. **-ies**) a greenhouse for grapevines.
■ a vineyard.

vineyard ▶ noun a plantation of grapevines, typically producing grapes used in winemaking.
■ figurative a sphere of action or labour (in allusion to Matt. 20:1): *women professors labouring in feminist vineyards.*

vingt-et-un /ˌvãteɪˈɜːn, French vɛ̃teœ̃/ ▶ noun [mass noun] the card game pontoon or blackjack.
– ORIGIN French, literally 'twenty-one'.

vinho verde /ˌviːnəʊ ˈvɛːdi/ ▶ noun [mass noun] a young Portuguese wine, not allowed to mature.
– ORIGIN Portuguese, literally 'green wine'.

vini- ▶ combining form of or relating to wine: *viniculture.*
– ORIGIN from Latin *vinum* 'wine'.

viniculture /ˈvɪnɪˌkʌltʃə/ ▶ noun [mass noun] the cultivation of grapevines for winemaking.
– DERIVATIVES **vinicultural** adjective, **viniculturist** noun.
– ORIGIN late 19th cent.: from Latin *vinum* 'wine' + CULTURE, on the pattern of words such as *agriculture.*

vinification /ˌvɪnɪfɪˈkeɪʃ(ə)n/ ▶ noun [mass noun] the conversion of grape juice or other vegetable extract into wine by fermentation.
– DERIVATIVES **vinify** verb (**-ies, -ied**).

vining /ˈvaɪnɪŋ/ ▶ noun [mass noun] the separation of leguminous crops from their vines and pods.
▶ adjective [attrib.] (of a plant) growing as a vine with climbing or trailing woody stems.

vin jaune /vã ˈʒɒn, French vɛ̃ ʒɔn/ ▶ noun (pl. **vins jaunes**) [mass noun] a strong yellowish white wine made in the Jura region of eastern France from the Sauvignon grape.
– ORIGIN French, literally 'yellow wine'.

Vinland the region of the NE coast of North America which was visited in the 11th century by Norsemen led by Leif Ericsson. It was so named from the report that grapevines were found growing there. The exact location is uncertain.

Vinnytsya /ˈviːnɪtsjə/ a city in central Ukraine; pop. 379,000 (1990). Russian name **VINNITSA** /ˈviːnɪtsə/.

vino /ˈviːnəʊ/ ▶ noun (pl. **-os**) [mass noun] Spanish or Italian wine.
■ informal, chiefly Brit. wine, typically that which is cheap or of inferior quality.
– ORIGIN Spanish and Italian, 'wine'.

vino da tavola /da ˈtɑːvɒlə/ ▶ noun [mass noun] Italian wine of reasonable quality, suitable for drinking with a meal.

– ORIGIN Italian, literally 'table wine'.

vin ordinaire /vã ˌɔːdɪˈnɛː, French vɛ̃ ɔrdinɛr/ ▶ noun (pl. **vins ordinaires**) [mass noun] cheap table wine for everyday use.
– ORIGIN French, literally 'ordinary wine'.

vinous /ˈvaɪnəs/ ▶ adjective of, resembling, or associated with wine: *a vinous smell.*
■ fond of or influenced by drinking wine: *his vinous companion.* ■ of the reddish colour of wine.
– DERIVATIVES **vinosity** noun, **vinously** adverb.
– ORIGIN late Middle English: from Latin *vinum* 'wine' + -OUS.

Vinson Massif /ˌvɪns(ə)n maˈsiːf/ the highest mountain range in Antarctica, in Ellsworth Land, rising to 5,140 m (16,863 ft).

vint /vɪnt/ ▶ verb [with obj.] (usu. **be vinted**) produce (wine or another alcoholic drink).
– ORIGIN mid 19th cent.: back-formation from VINTAGE.

vintage ▶ noun the year or place in which wine, especially wine of high quality, was produced.
■ a wine of high quality made from the crop of a single identified district in a good year. ■ [mass noun] poetic/literary wine. ■ the harvesting of grapes for winemaking. ■ the grapes or wine produced in a particular season. ■ the time that something of quality was produced: *rifles of various sizes and vintages.*
▶ adjective of, relating to, or denoting wine of high quality: *vintage claret.*
■ denoting something of high quality, especially something from the past or characteristic of the best period of a person's work: *a vintage Sherlock Holmes adventure.*
– ORIGIN late Middle English: alteration (influenced by VINTNER) of earlier *vendage*, from Old French *vendange*, from Latin *vindemia* (from *vinum* 'wine' + *demere* 'remove').

vintage car ▶ noun Brit. an old style or model of car, specifically one made between 1917 and 1930.

vintage port ▶ noun [mass noun] port of special quality, all of one year, bottled early and aged in the bottle.

vintager ▶ noun a person who harvests grapes.

vintner /ˈvɪntnə/ ▶ noun a wine merchant.
– ORIGIN late Middle English: via Anglo-Latin from Old French *vinetier*, from medieval Latin *vinetarius*, from Latin *vinetum* 'vineyard', from *vinum* 'wine'.

vinyl /ˈvaɪn(ə)l/ ▶ noun 1 [mass noun] synthetic resin or plastic consisting of polyvinyl chloride or a related polymer, used especially for wallpapers and other covering materials and formerly as the standard material for gramophone records before the introduction of compact discs: *fans had to wait almost a year before the song eventually appeared on vinyl* | [count noun] *light-reflecting vinyls can be hung in the usual way.*
2 /also ˈvaɪnʌɪl, -nɪl/ [as modifier] Chemistry of or denoting the unsaturated hydrocarbon radical —CH=CH$_2$, derived from ethylene by removal of a hydrogen atom: *a vinyl group.*
– ORIGIN mid 19th cent.: from Latin *vinum* 'wine' + -YL.

vinyl acetate ▶ noun [mass noun] Chemistry a colourless liquid ester used in the production of polyvinyl acetate and other commercially important polymers.
● Chem. formula: $CH_2CHOCOCH_3$.

vinyl chloride ▶ noun [mass noun] Chemistry a colourless toxic gas used in the production of polyvinyl chloride and other commercially important polymers.
● Chem. formula: CH_2CHCl.

viol /ˈvaɪəl/ ▶ noun a musical instrument of the Renaissance and baroque periods, typically six-stringed, held vertically and played with a bow.
– ORIGIN late 15th cent. (originally denoting a violin-like instrument): from Old French *viele*, from Provençal *viola*; probably related to FIDDLE.

viola[1] /vɪˈəʊlə/ ▶ noun an instrument of the violin family, larger than the violin and tuned a fifth lower.
– ORIGIN early 18th cent.: from Italian and Spanish; compare with VIOL.

viola[2] /ˈvaɪələ/ ▶ noun a plant of a genus that includes the pansies and violets.
● Genus *Viola*, family Violaceae: many species.
– ORIGIN modern Latin, from Latin, literally 'violet'.

violaceous /ˌvaɪəˈleɪʃəs/ ▶ adjective **1** of a violet colour.
2 Botany of, relating to, or denoting plants of the violet family (Violaceae).
– ORIGIN mid 17th cent.: from Latin *violaceus* (from *viola* 'violet') + -OUS.

viola da braccio /vɪˌəʊlə da ˈbraːtʃɪəʊ/ ▶ noun an early musical instrument of the violin family (as distinct from a viol), specifically one corresponding to the modern viola.
– ORIGIN Italian, literally 'viol for the arm'.

viola da gamba /ˈɡambə/ (also **viol da gamba**) ▶ noun a viol, specifically a bass viol (corresponding to the modern cello).
– ORIGIN Italian, literally 'viol for the leg'.

viola d'amore /daˈmɔːreɪ/ ▶ noun a sweet-toned 18th-century musical instrument similar to a viola, but with six or seven strings, and additional sympathetic strings below the fingerboard.
– ORIGIN Italian, literally 'viol of love'.

violate ▶ verb [with obj.] break or fail to comply with (a rule or formal agreement): *they violated the terms of a ceasefire.*
■ fail to respect (someone's peace, privacy, or rights): *they denied that human rights were being violated.* ■ treat (something sacred) with irreverence or disrespect: *he was accused of violating a tomb.* ■ rape or sexually assault (someone).
– DERIVATIVES **violator** noun, **violable** adjective (rare).
– ORIGIN late Middle English: from Latin *violat-* 'treated violently', from the verb *violare.*

violation ▶ noun [mass noun] the action of violating someone or something: *the aircraft were in violation of UN resolutions.*

violence ▶ noun [mass noun] behaviour involving physical force intended to hurt, damage, or kill someone or something.
■ strength of emotion or an unpleasant or destructive natural force: *the violence of her own feelings.* ■ Law the unlawful exercise of physical force or intimidation by the exhibition of such force.
– PHRASES **do violence to** damage or adversely affect.
– ORIGIN Middle English: via Old French from Latin *violentia*, from *violent-* 'vehement, violent' (see VIOLENT).

violent ▶ adjective using or involving physical force intended to hurt, damage, or kill someone or something: *a violent confrontation with riot police.*
■ (especially of an emotion or unpleasant or destructive natural force) very strong or powerful: *violent dislike* | *the violent eruption killed 1,700 people.* ■ (of a colour) vivid. ■ Law involving an unlawful exercise or exhibition of force.
– DERIVATIVES **violently** adverb.
– ORIGIN Middle English (in the sense 'having a marked or powerful effect'): via Old French from Latin *violent-* 'vehement, violent'.

violent storm ▶ noun a wind of force 11 on the Beaufort scale (56–63 knots or 103–117 kph).

violet ▶ noun **1** a herbaceous plant of temperate regions, typically having purple, blue, or white five-petalled flowers, one petal of which forms a landing pad for pollinating insects.
● Genus *Viola*, family Violaceae (the **violet family**): many species, including the **dog violet** and **sweet violet**. See also VIOLA[2].
■ used in names of similar-flowered plants of other families, e.g. **African violet**.
2 [mass noun] a bluish-purple colour seen at the end of the spectrum opposite red.
▶ adjective of a bluish-purple colour.
– ORIGIN Middle English: from Old French *violette*, diminutive of *viole*, from Latin *viola* 'violet'.

violet-ear ▶ noun a tropical American hummingbird with green or brown plumage and a glittering purple patch behind each eye.
● Genus *Colibri*, family Trochilidae: four species.

violet snail (also **violet sea snail**) ▶ noun a small marine snail which drifts on the surface of the sea attached to a raft of bubbles. The shell is typically purple-violet and the animal emits a violet fluid when attacked.
● Family Janthinidae, class Gastropoda.

violin ▶ noun a stringed musical instrument of treble pitch, played with a horsehair bow. The classical European violin was developed in the 16th century. It has four strings and a body of characteristic rounded shape, narrowed at the middle and with two f-shaped soundholes.

– DERIVATIVES **violinist** noun.
– ORIGIN late 16th cent.: from Italian *violino*, diminutive of *viola* (see VIOLA[1]).

violist ▶ noun **1** /vɪˈəʊlɪst/ a viola player.
2 /ˈvaɪəlɪst/ a viol player.

viologen /vaɪˈɒlədʒ(ə)n/ ▶ noun Chemistry any of a series of synthetic compounds related to the weedkiller paraquat, used as redox indicators. They contain heteroaromatic cations of the general formula $(C_5H_4NR)_2^{2+}$.
– ORIGIN 1930s: from VIOLET (because of the purple colour when electrochemically reduced) + -GEN.

violoncello /ˌvaɪələnˈtʃɛləʊ, ˌviːə-/ ▶ noun formal term for CELLO.
– DERIVATIVES **violoncellist** noun.
– ORIGIN early 18th cent.: Italian, diminutive of *violone* (see VIOLONE).

violone /vɪəˈləʊneɪ, -niː/ ▶ noun an early form of double bass, especially a large bass viol.
– ORIGIN Italian, augmentative of *viola* (see VIOLA[1]).

VIP ▶ abbreviation for ■ Biochemistry vasoactive intestinal polypeptide (or peptide), a substance which acts as a neurotransmitter, especially in the brain and gastrointestinal tract. ■ very important person.

vipassana /vɪˈpasənə/ (also **Vipassana**) ▶ noun [mass noun] (in Theravada Buddhism) meditation involving concentration on the body or its sensations, or the insight which this provides.
– ORIGIN Pali, literally 'inward vision'.

viper /ˈvaɪpə/ ▶ noun a venomous snake with large hinged fangs, typically having a broad head and stout body, with dark patterns on a lighter background.
● Family Viperidae: numerous genera and species. See also PIT VIPER, ADDER[1].
■ a spiteful or treacherous person.
– PHRASES **viper in one's bosom** a person who betrays those who have helped them.
– DERIVATIVES **viperine** /-raɪn/ adjective, **viperish** adjective, **viperous** adjective.
– ORIGIN early 16th cent.: from French *vipère* or Latin *vipera*, from *vivus* 'alive' + *parere* 'bring forth'.

viperfish ▶ noun (pl. same or **-fishes**) a small, elongated deep-sea fish that has large jaws with long protruding fangs.
● Family Chauliodontidae: several genera and species.

viper's bugloss ▶ noun a bristly Eurasian plant of the borage family, with pink buds which open to blue flowers. It was formerly used in the treatment of snake bites.
● *Echium vulgare*, family Boraginaceae.

viper's grass ▶ noun [mass noun] scorzonera, the juice of which was formerly believed to be a remedy for snake bites.

viraemia /vaɪˈriːmɪə/ (also **viremia**) ▶ noun [mass noun] Medicine the presence of viruses in the blood.
– DERIVATIVES **viraemic** adjective.
– ORIGIN 1940s: from VIRUS + -AEMIA.

virago /vɪˈrɑːgəʊ, -ˈreɪgəʊ/ ▶ noun (pl. **-os** or **-oes**) a domineering, violent, or bad-tempered woman.
■ archaic a woman of masculine strength or spirit; a female warrior.
– ORIGIN Old English (used only as the name given by Adam to Eve, following the Vulgate), from Latin 'heroic woman, female warrior', from *vir* 'man'. The current sense dates from late Middle English.

viral /ˈvaɪr(ə)l/ ▶ adjective of the nature of, caused by, or relating to a virus or viruses.
– DERIVATIVES **virally** adverb.

Virchow /ˈvɜːkaʊ, German ˈfɪrço/, Rudolf Karl (1821–1902), German physician and pathologist, founder of cellular pathology. He argued that the cell was the basis of life and that diseases were reflected in specific cellular abnormalities. Virchow also stressed the importance of environmental factors in disease.

virelay /ˈvɪrəleɪ/ ▶ noun a short lyric poem of a type originating in France in the 14th century, consisting of short lines arranged in stanzas with only two rhymes, the end rhyme of one stanza being the chief one of the next.
– ORIGIN late Middle English: from Old French *virelai*.

virement /ˈvaɪəm(ə)nt, ˈvɪəmɒ̃/ ▶ noun [mass noun] Finance, Brit. the process of transferring items from one financial account to another.

– ORIGIN early 20th cent.: from French, from *virer* 'to turn'.

viremia ▶ noun variant spelling of VIRAEMIA.

vireo /ˈvɪrɪəʊ/ ▶ noun (pl. **-os**) a small American songbird, typically having a green or grey back and yellow or white underparts.
● Family Vireonidae (the **vireo family**): two genera, especially *Vireo*, and several species. The vireo family also includes the greenlets and pepper-shrikes.
– ORIGIN mid 19th cent.: from Latin, perhaps denoting a greenfinch.

virescent /vɪˈrɛs(ə)nt/ ▶ adjective poetic/literary greenish.
– DERIVATIVES **virescence** noun, **virescently** adverb.
– ORIGIN early 19th cent.: from Latin *virescent-* 'turning green', inceptive of *virere* 'be green'.

virga /ˈvɜːgə/ ▶ noun (pl. **virgae** /ˈvɜːgiː/) Meteorology a mass of streaks of rain appearing to hang under a cloud and evaporating before reaching the ground.
– ORIGIN 1940s: from Latin, literally 'rod, stripe'.

virgate /ˈvɜːgət/ ▶ noun Brit. historical a varying measure of land, typically 30 acres.
– ORIGIN mid 17th cent.: from Latin *virgatus*, from *virga* 'rod'.

virger ▶ noun chiefly archaic variant spelling of VERGER.

Virgil /ˈvɜːdʒɪl/ (also **Vergil**) (70–19 BC), Roman poet; Latin name *Publius Vergilius Maro*. He wrote three major works: the *Eclogues*, ten pastoral poems, blending traditional themes of Greek bucolic poetry with contemporary political and literary themes; the *Georgics*, a didactic poem on farming; and the *Aeneid* (see AENEID).
– DERIVATIVES **Virgilian** adjective.

virgin ▶ noun a person, typically a woman, who has never had sexual intercourse.
■ a naive, innocent, or inexperienced person, especially in a particular context: *a political virgin*. ■ **(the Virgin)** the mother of Jesus; the Virgin Mary. ■ a woman who has taken a vow to remain a virgin. ■ **(the Virgin)** the zodiacal sign or constellation Virgo. ■ Entomology a female insect that produces eggs without being fertilized.
▶ adjective **1** [attrib.] being, relating to, or appropriate for a virgin: *his virgin bride*.
2 not yet used or exploited: *acres of virgin forests*.
■ (of clay) not yet fired. ■ (of wool) not yet, or only once, spun or woven. ■ (of olive oil) obtained from the first pressing of olives. ■ (of metal) made from ore by smelting.
– ORIGIN Middle English: from Old French *virgine*, from Latin *virgo*, *virgin-*.

virginal ▶ adjective being, relating to, or appropriate for a virgin: *virginal shyness*.
▶ noun (usu. **virginals**) an early spinet with the strings parallel to the keyboard, typically rectangular, and popular in 16th and 17th century houses. [ORIGIN: perhaps because usually played by young women (see origin below).]
– DERIVATIVES **virginalist** noun, **virginally** adverb.
– ORIGIN late Middle English: from Old French, or from Latin *virginalis*, from *virgo* 'young woman'.

virgin birth ▶ noun **1** **(the Virgin Birth)** the doctrine of Christ's birth from a mother, Mary, who was a virgin.
2 [mass noun] Zoology parthenogenesis.

virgin comb ▶ noun a honeycomb that has been used only once for honey and never for storing eggs.

virgin honey ▶ noun [mass noun] honey taken from a virgin comb, or drained from the comb without heat or pressure.

Virginia[1] a state of the eastern US, on the Atlantic coast; pop. 6,187,360 (1990); capital, Richmond. It was the site of the first permanent European settlement in North America in 1607, and was named in honour of Elizabeth I, the 'Virgin Queen'. It was one of the original thirteen states of the Union (1788).
– DERIVATIVES **Virginian** noun & adjective.

Virginia[2] ▶ noun [mass noun] a type of tobacco grown and manufactured in Virginia.
■ [count noun] a cigarette made of such tobacco.
– DERIVATIVES **Virginian** noun & adjective.

Virginia Beach a city and resort on the Atlantic coast of SE Virginia; pop. 393,000 (1990).

Virginia bluebell ▶ noun a North American woodland plant of the borage family, bearing nodding blue trumpet-shaped flowers.
● *Mertensia virginica*, family Boraginaceae.

Virginia creeper ▶ noun a North American vine which is chiefly cultivated for its red autumn foliage.
● Genus *Parthenocissus*, family Vitaceae: several species, in particular *P. quinquefolia*.

Virginian snakeroot ▶ noun see SNAKEROOT.

Virginia opossum ▶ noun a cat-sized opossum with a greyish body and a white face, widespread throughout North and Central America.
● *Didelphis virginiana*, family Didelphidae.

Virginia reel ▶ noun a lively North American country dance performed by a number of couples facing each other in parallel lines.

Virginia stock (also **Virginian stock**) ▶ noun a low-growing sweetly scented Mediterranean plant with white, pink, or lilac flowers.
● *Malcolmia maritima*, family Cruciferae.

Virgin Islands a group of Caribbean islands at the eastern extremity of the Greater Antilles, divided between British and US administration.

The islands were settled, mainly in the 17th century, by British and Danish sugar planters, who introduced African slaves. The British Virgin Islands consists of about forty islands in the north-east of the group; pop. 16,750 (est. 1991); capital, Road Town (on Tortola). The remaining islands (about fifty) make up the US unincorporated territory of the Virgin Islands; pop. 101,800 (1990); capital, Charlotte Amalie (on St Thomas).

virginity ▶ noun [mass noun] the state of never having had sexual intercourse: *I lost my virginity*.
■ the state of being naive, innocent, or inexperienced in a particular context: *he could claim no political virginity*.
– ORIGIN Middle English: from Old French *virginite*, from Latin *virginitas*, from *virgo* (see VIRGIN).

Virgin Mary mother of Jesus (see MARY[1]).

virgin queen ▶ noun **1** an unfertilized queen bee.
2 **(the Virgin Queen)** Queen Elizabeth I of England, who died unmarried.

virgin's bower ▶ noun a North American clematis.
● *Clematis virginiana*, family Ranunculaceae.

Virgo /ˈvɜːgəʊ/ **1** Astronomy a large constellation (the Virgin), said to represent a maiden or goddess associated with the harvest. It contains several bright stars, the brightest of which is Spica, and a dense cluster of galaxies.
■ [as genitive **Virginis** /ˈvɜːdʒɪnɪs/] used with preceding letter or numeral to designate a star in this constellation: *the star Gamma Virginis*.
2 Astrology the sixth sign of the zodiac, which the sun enters about 23 August.
■ **(a Virgo)** (pl. **-os**) a person born when the sun is in this sign.
– DERIVATIVES **Virgoan** noun & adjective (only in sense 2).
– ORIGIN Latin.

virgo intacta /ˌvɜːgəʊ ɪnˈtaktə/ ▶ noun chiefly Law a girl or woman who has never had sexual intercourse, originally a virgin whose hymen is intact.
– ORIGIN Latin, literally 'untouched virgin'.

virgule /ˈvɜːgjuːl/ ▶ noun another term for SLASH (in sense 2).
– ORIGIN mid 19th cent.: from French, literally 'comma', from Latin *virgula*, diminutive of *virga* 'rod'.

viridescent /ˌvɪrɪˈdɛs(ə)nt/ ▶ adjective greenish or becoming green.
– DERIVATIVES **viridescence** noun.
– ORIGIN mid 19th cent.: from late Latin *viridescent-* 'becoming green', from the verb *viridescere*, from Latin *viridis* 'green'.

viridian /vɪˈrɪdɪən/ ▶ noun [mass noun] a bluish-green pigment consisting of hydrated chromium hydroxide.
■ the bluish-green colour of this.
– ORIGIN late 19th cent.: from Latin *viridis* 'green' (from *virere* 'be green') + -IAN.

virile ▶ adjective (of a man) having strength, energy, and a strong sex drive.
■ having or characterized by strength and energy: *a strong, virile performance of the Mass*.
– DERIVATIVES **virility** noun.
– ORIGIN late 15th cent. (in the sense 'characteristic of a man'): from French *viril* or Latin *virilis*, from *vir* 'man'.

virilism /ˈvɪrɪlɪz(ə)m/ ▶ noun [mass noun] Medicine the condition which results from virilization.

virilization /ˌvɪrɪlaɪˈzeɪʃ(ə)n/ (also **-isation**) ▶ noun [mass noun] Medicine the development of male physical characteristics (such as muscle bulk, body hair, and deep voice) in a female or precociously in a boy, typically as a result of excess androgen production.

virilocal /ˌvɪrɪˈləʊk(ə)l/ ▶ **adjective** another term for **PATRILOCAL**.
– ORIGIN 1940s: from Latin *virilis* 'of a man' + **LOCAL**.

virino /vɪˈriːnəʊ/ ▶ **noun** (pl. **-os**) Microbiology a hypothetical infectious particle postulated as the cause of scrapie, BSE, and CJD, consisting of non-coding nucleic acid in a protective coat made from host cell proteins. Compare with **PRION**[2].
– ORIGIN 1970s: from **VIRUS** + the diminutive suffix *-ino*.

virion /ˈvʌɪrɪɒn/ ▶ **noun** Microbiology the complete, infective form of a virus outside a host cell, with a core of RNA and a capsid.
– ORIGIN 1950s: from **VIRUS** + **-ON**.

viroid /ˈvʌɪrɔɪd/ ▶ **noun** Microbiology an infectious entity affecting plants, smaller than a virus and consisting only of nucleic acid without a protein coat.

virology /vʌɪˈrɒlədʒi/ ▶ **noun** [mass noun] the branch of science that deals with the study of viruses.
– DERIVATIVES **virological** adjective, **virologically** adverb, **virologist** noun.

viropexis /ˌvʌɪrə(ʊ)ˈpɛksɪs/ ▶ **noun** [mass noun] Microbiology the process by which a virus particle becomes attached to a cell wall and incorporated into the cell by phagocytosis.
– ORIGIN 1940s: from **VIRUS** + Greek *pēxis* 'fixing'.

virtu /vəːˈt(j)uː/ (also **vertu**) ▶ **noun** [mass noun] **1** knowledge of or expertise in the fine arts.
■ curios or objets d'art collectively.
2 poetic/literary the good qualities inherent in a person or thing.
– PHRASES **article** (or **object**) **of virtu** an article that is interesting because of its antiquity, beauty, quality of workmanship, etc.
– ORIGIN early 18th cent.: from Italian *virtù* 'virtue'; the variant *vertu* is an alteration, as if from French.

virtual /ˈvəːtjʊəl/ ▶ **adjective** almost or nearly as described, but not completely or according to strict definition: *the virtual absence of border controls*.
■ Computing not physically existing as such but made by software to appear to do so: *a virtual computer*. See also **VIRTUAL REALITY**. ■ Optics relating to the points at which rays would meet if produced backwards. ■ Mechanics relating to or denoting infinitesimal displacements of a point in a system. ■ Physics denoting particles or interactions with extremely short lifetimes and (owing to the uncertainty principle) indefinitely great energies, postulated as intermediates in some processes.
– DERIVATIVES **virtuality** /-jʊˈalɪti/ noun.
– ORIGIN late Middle English (also in the sense 'possessing certain virtues'): from medieval Latin *virtualis*, from Latin *virtus* 'virtue', suggested by late Latin *virtuosus*.

virtual image ▶ **noun** Optics an optical image formed from the apparent divergence of light rays from a point, as opposed to an image formed from their actual divergence.

virtually ▶ **adverb** nearly; almost: *virtually all those arrested were accused* | *the college became virtually bankrupt*.
■ Computing by means of virtual reality techniques.

virtual memory (also **virtual storage**) ▶ **noun** [mass noun] Computing memory that appears to exist as main storage although most of it is supported by data held in secondary storage, transfer between the two being made automatically as required.

virtual reality ▶ **noun** [mass noun] Computing the computer-generated simulation of a three-dimensional image or environment that can be interacted with in a seemingly real or physical way by a person using special electronic equipment, such as a helmet with a screen inside or gloves fitted with sensors.

virtue /ˈvəːtjuː, -tʃuː/ ▶ **noun** **1** [mass noun] behaviour showing high moral standards: *paragons of virtue*.
■ [count noun] a quality considered morally good or desirable in a person: *patience is a virtue*. ■ [count noun] a good or useful quality of a thing: *Mike was extolling the virtues of the car* | [mass noun] *there's no virtue in suffering in silence*. ■ [mass noun] archaic virginity or chastity, especially of a woman.
2 (**virtues**) (in traditional Christian angelology) the seventh highest order of the ninefold celestial hierarchy.
– PHRASES **by** (or **in**) **virtue of** because or as a result of. **make a virtue of** derive benefit or advantage from submitting to (an unwelcome obligation or unavoidable circumstance).
– DERIVATIVES **virtueless** adjective.
– ORIGIN Middle English: from Old French *vertu*, from Latin *virtus* 'valour, merit, moral perfection', from *vir* 'man'.

virtuoso /ˌvəːtjʊˈəʊzəʊ, -səʊ/ ▶ **noun** (pl. **virtuosi** /-si/ or **virtuosos**) a person highly skilled in music or another artistic pursuit: *a celebrated clarinet virtuoso* | [as modifier] *virtuoso guitar playing*.
■ a person with a special knowledge of or interest in works of art or curios.
– DERIVATIVES **virtuosic** adjective, **virtuosity** noun.
– ORIGIN early 17th cent.: from Italian, literally 'learned, skilful', from late Latin *virtuosus* (see **VIRTUOUS**).

virtuous ▶ **adjective** having or showing high moral standards: *she considered herself very virtuous because she neither drank nor smoked*.
■ archaic (especially of a woman) chaste.
– DERIVATIVES **virtuously** adverb, **virtuousness** noun.
– ORIGIN Middle English: from Old French *vertuous*, from late Latin *virtuosus*, from *virtus* 'virtue'.

virtuous circle ▶ **noun** a recurring cycle of events, the result of each one being to increase the beneficial effect of the next.

virulent /ˈvɪrʊl(ə)nt, ˈvɪrjʊ-/ ▶ **adjective** **1** (of a disease or poison) extremely severe or harmful in its effects.
■ (of a pathogen, especially a virus) highly infective.
2 bitterly hostile: *a virulent attack on liberalism*.
– DERIVATIVES **virulence** noun, **virulently** adverb.
– ORIGIN late Middle English (originally describing a poisoned wound): from Latin *virulentus*, from *virus* 'poison' (see **VIRUS**).

virus /ˈvʌɪrəs/ ▶ **noun** an infective agent that typically consists of a nucleic acid molecule in a protein coat, is too small to be seen by light microscopy, and is able to multiply only within the living cells of a host: [as modifier] *a virus infection*.
■ informal an infection or disease caused by such an agent. ■ figurative a harmful or corrupting influence: *the virus of cruelty that is latent in all human beings*. ■ (also **computer virus**) a piece of code which is capable of copying itself and typicallyhas a detrimental effect, such as corrupting the system or destroying data.
– ORIGIN late Middle English (denoting the venom of a snake): from Latin, literally 'slimy liquid, poison'. The earlier medical sense, superseded by the current use as a result of improved scientific understanding, was 'a substance produced in the body as the result of disease, especially one that is capable of infecting others with the same disease'.

Vis. ▶ **abbreviation for** Viscount.

visa /ˈviːzə/ ▶ **noun** an endorsement on a passport indicating that the holder is allowed to enter, leave, or stay for a specified period of time in a country.
– ORIGIN mid 19th cent.: via French from Latin *visa*, past participle (neuter plural) of *videre* 'to see'.

visage /ˈvɪzɪdʒ/ ▶ **noun** [usu. in sing.] poetic/literary a person's face, with reference to the form or proportions of the features: *an elegant, angular visage*.
■ a person's facial expression: *there was something hidden behind his visage of cheerfulness*. ■ figurative the surface of an object presented to view: *the moonlit visage of the port's whitewashed buildings*.
– DERIVATIVES **visaged** adjective [in combination] *a stern-visaged old man*.
– ORIGIN Middle English: via Old French from Latin *visus* 'sight', from *videre* 'to see'.

visagiste /ˌviːzɑːˈʒiːst/ ▶ **noun** a make-up artist.
– ORIGIN French.

Visākha /vɪˈsɑːkə/ ▶ **noun** variant spelling of **VESAK**.

Visakhapatnam /vɪˌsɑːkəˈpʌtnəm/ a port on the coast of Andhra Pradesh, in SE India; pop. 750,000 (1991).

vis-à-vis /ˌviːzɑːˈviː, French vizavi/ ▶ **preposition** in relation to; with regard to: *many agencies now have a unit to deal with women's needs vis-à-vis employment*.
■ as compared with; as opposed to: *the advantage for US exports is the value of the dollar vis-à-vis other currencies*.
▶ **adverb** archaic in a position facing a specified or implied subject: *he was there* **vis-à-vis** *with Miss Arundel*.
▶ **noun** (pl. same) **1** a person or group occupying a corresponding position to that of another person or group in a different area or domain; a counterpart: *his admiration for the US armed services extends to their vis-à-vis, the Russian military*.
2 a face-to-face meeting: *the dreaded vis-à-vis with his boss*.
– ORIGIN mid 18th cent.: French, literally 'face to face', from Old French *vis* 'face'.

Visby /ˈvɪzbi, Swedish ˈviːsbyː/ a port on the west coast of the Swedish island of Gotland, of which it is the capital; pop. 57,110 (1990).

Visc. ▶ **abbreviation for** Viscount.

viscacha /vɪˈskatʃə/ ▶ **noun** a large South American burrowing rodent of the chinchilla family, sometimes hunted for its fur and flesh.
● Genera *Lagidium* and *Lagostomus*, family Chinchillidae: four species.
– ORIGIN early 17th cent.: via Spanish from Quechua *(h)uiscacha*.

viscera /ˈvɪs(ə)rə/ ▶ **plural noun** (sing. **viscus**) the internal organs in the main cavities of the body, especially those in the abdomen, e.g. the intestines.
– ORIGIN mid 17th cent.: from Latin, plural of *viscus* (see **VISCUS**).

visceral ▶ **adjective** of or relating to the viscera: *the visceral nervous system*.
■ relating to deep inward feelings rather than to the intellect: *the voters' visceral fear of change*.
– DERIVATIVES **viscerally** adverb.

viscerotropic /ˌvɪs(ə)rə(ʊ)ˈtrəʊpɪk, -ˈtrɒpɪk/ ▶ **adjective** (of a micro-organism) tending to attack or affect the viscera.

viscid /ˈvɪsɪd/ ▶ **adjective** glutinous; sticky: *the viscid mucus lining of the intestine*.
– DERIVATIVES **viscidity** noun.
– ORIGIN mid 17th cent.: from late Latin *viscidus*, from Latin *viscum* 'birdlime'.

viscoelasticity /ˌvɪskəʊɛlaˈstɪsɪti, -iːla-, -ɪla-/ ▶ **noun** [mass noun] Physics the property of a substance of exhibiting both elastic and viscous behaviour, the application of stress causing temporary deformation if the stress is quickly removed but permanent deformation if it is maintained.
– DERIVATIVES **viscoelastic** adjective.

viscometer /vɪsˈkɒmɪtə/ ▶ **noun** an instrument for measuring the viscosity of liquids.
– DERIVATIVES **viscometric** adjective, **viscometrically** adverb, **viscometry** noun.
– ORIGIN late 19th cent.: from late Latin *viscosus* 'viscous' + **-METER**.

Visconti /vɪsˈkɒnti/, Luchino (1906–76), Italian film and theatre director; full name *Don Luchino Visconti, Conte di Modrone*. His films include *The Leopard* (1963) and *Death in Venice* (1971). His first film, *Obsession* (1942), was regarded as the forerunner of neo-realism.

viscose /ˈvɪskəʊz, -kəʊs/ ▶ **noun** [mass noun] a viscous orange-brown solution obtained by treating cellulose with sodium hydroxide and carbon disulphide, used as the basis of manufacturing rayon fibre and transparent cellulose film.
■ rayon fabric or fibre made from this.
– ORIGIN late 19th cent.: from late Latin *viscosus*, from Latin *viscus* 'birdlime'.

viscosimeter /vɪskəˈsɪmɪtə/ ▶ **noun** another term for **VISCOMETER**.

viscosity /vɪˈskɒsɪti/ ▶ **noun** (pl. **-ies**) [mass noun] the state of being thick, sticky, and semi-fluid in consistency, due to internal friction.
■ [count noun] a quantity expressing the magnitude of such friction, as measured by the force per unit area resisting a flow in which parallel layers unit distance apart have unit speed relative to one another.
– ORIGIN late Middle English: from Old French *viscosite* or medieval Latin *viscositas*, from late Latin *viscosus* (see **VISCOUS**).

viscount /ˈvʌɪkaʊnt/ ▶ **noun** a British nobleman ranking above a baron and below an earl.
– DERIVATIVES **viscountcy** noun.
– ORIGIN late Middle English: from Old French *visconte*, from medieval Latin *vicecomes*, *vicecomit-* (see **VICE-**, **COUNT**[2]).

viscountess /ˈvʌɪkaʊntɪs/ ▶ **noun** the wife or widow of a viscount.
■ a woman holding the rank of viscount in her own right.

viscounty ▶ **noun** the land under the authority of a particular viscount.

viscous /ˈvɪskəs/ ▶ **adjective** having a thick, sticky

V

consistency between solid and liquid; having a high viscosity: *viscous lava.*
– DERIVATIVES **viscously** adverb, **viscousness** noun.
– ORIGIN late Middle English: from Anglo-Norman French *viscous* or late Latin *viscosus*, from Latin *viscum* 'birdlime'.

viscus /ˈvɪskəs/ singular form of **VISCERA**.
– ORIGIN Latin.

vise ▶ **noun** US spelling of **VICE**[2].

Vishnu /ˈvɪʃnuː/ Hinduism a god, originally a minor Vedic god, now regarded by his worshippers as the supreme deity and saviour, by others as the preserver of the cosmos in a triad with Brahma and Shiva. Vishnu is considered by Hindus to have had nine earthly incarnations or avatars, including Rama, Krishna, and the historical Buddha; the tenth avatar will herald the end of the world.
– DERIVATIVES **Vishnuism** noun, **Vishnuite** noun & adjective.
– ORIGIN from Sanskrit *Viṣṇu*.

visibility ▶ **noun** [mass noun] the state of being able to see or be seen: *a reduction in police presence and visibility on the streets.*
■ the distance one can see as determined by light and weather conditions: *visibility was down to 15 yards.* ■ the degree to which something has attracted general attention; prominence: *the issue began to lose its visibility.*
– ORIGIN late Middle English: from French *visibilite* or late Latin *visibilitas*, from Latin *visibilis* (see **VISIBLE**).

visible ▶ **adjective** **1** able to be seen: *the church spire is visible from miles away.*
■ Physics (of light) within the range of wavelengths to which the eye is sensitive. ■ able to be perceived or noticed easily: *a visible improvement.* ■ in a position of public prominence: *a highly visible member of the royal entourage.*
2 of or relating to imports or exports of tangible commodities: *the visible trade gap.*
▶ **noun** (**visibles**) visible imports or exports.
– DERIVATIVES **visibleness** noun, **visibly** adverb *he was visibly uncomfortable.*
– ORIGIN Middle English: from Old French, or from Latin *visibilis*, from *videre* 'to see'.

Visigoth /ˈvɪzɪɡɒθ/ ▶ **noun** a member of the branch of the Goths who invaded the Roman Empire between the 3rd and 5th centuries AD and ruled much of Spain until overthrown by the Moors in 711.
– DERIVATIVES **Visigothic** adjective.
– ORIGIN from late Latin *Visigothus*, the first element possibly meaning 'west' (compare with **OSTROGOTH**).

vision ▶ **noun** **1** [mass noun] the faculty or state of being able to see: *she had defective vision.*
■ the ability to think about or plan the future with imagination or wisdom: *the organization had lost its vision and direction.* ■ [count noun] a mental image of what the future will or could be like: *a socialist vision of society.* ■ the images seen on a television screen.
2 an experience of seeing someone or something in a dream or trance, or as a supernatural apparition: *the idea came to him in a vision.*
■ (often **visions**) a vivid mental image, especially a fanciful one of the future: *he **had visions of** becoming the Elton John of his time.* ■ a person or sight of unusual beauty.
▶ **verb** [with obj.] rare imagine.
– DERIVATIVES **visional** adjective, **visionless** adjective.
– ORIGIN Middle English (denoting a supernatural apparition): via Old French from Latin *visio(n-)*, from *videre* 'to see'.

visionary ▶ **adjective** **1** (especially of a person) thinking about or planning the future with imagination or wisdom: *a visionary leader.*
■ archaic (of a scheme or idea) not practical.
2 of, relating to, or able to see visions in a dream or trance, or as a supernatural apparition: *a visionary experience.*
■ archaic existing only in a vision or in the imagination.
▶ **noun** (pl. **-ies**) a person with original ideas about what the future will or could be like.
– DERIVATIVES **visionariness** noun.

vision mixer ▶ **noun** Brit. a person whose job is to select and manipulate images in television broadcasting or recording.
■ a piece of equipment used for this purpose.
– DERIVATIVES **vision mixing** noun.

vision quest ▶ **noun** an attempt to achieve a vision of a future guardian spirit, traditionally undertaken at puberty by boys of the Plains Indian peoples, typically through fasting or self-torture.

visit ▶ **verb** (**visited**, **visiting**) [with obj.] **1** go to see and spend time with (someone) socially: *I came to visit my grandmother.*
■ go to see and spend time in (a place) as a tourist. ■ stay temporarily with (someone) or at (a place) as a guest: *we hope you enjoy your stay and will visit us again* | [no obj.] *I don't live here—I'm only visiting.* ■ go to see (someone or something) for a specific purpose, such as to make an inspection or to receive or give professional advice or help: *inspectors visit all the hotels.* ■ [no obj.] (**visit with**) N. Amer. go to see (someone) socially: *he went out to visit with his pals.* ■ [no obj.] US informal chat: *there was nothing to do but visit with one another.* ■ (chiefly in biblical use) (of God) come to (a person or place) in order to bring comfort or salvation.
2 (often **be visited**) inflict (something harmful or unpleasant) on someone: *the mockery **visited upon** him by his schoolmates.*
■ (of something harmful or unpleasant) afflict (someone): *they were **visited with** epidemics of a strange disease.* ■ archaic punish (a person or a wrongful act): *offences were visited with the loss of eyes or ears.*
▶ **noun** an act of going or coming to see a person or place socially, as a tourist, or for some other purpose: *a visit to the doctor.*
■ a temporary stay with a person or at a place. ■ US an informal conversation.
– DERIVATIVES **visitable** adjective.
– ORIGIN Middle English: from Old French *visiter* or Latin *visitare* 'go to see', frequentative of *visare* 'to view', from *videre* 'to see'.

visitant ▶ **noun** chiefly poetic/literary a supernatural being or agency; an apparition.
■ archaic a visitor or guest. ■ Ornithology a visitor.
▶ **adjective** archaic or poetic/literary paying a visit: *the housekeeper was abrupt with the poor visitant niece.*
– ORIGIN late 16th cent.: from French, or from Latin *visitant-* 'going to see', from the verb *visitare* (see **VISIT**).

visitation ▶ **noun** **1** an official or formal visit, in particular:
■ (in church use) an official visit of inspection, especially one by a bishop to a church in his diocese. ■ a pastoral or charitable visit, especially to the sick or poor. ■ the appearance of a divine or supernatural being. ■ informal an unwelcome or unduly protracted social visit. ■ US a gathering with the family of a deceased person before the funeral. ■ [mass noun] US Law a divorced person's right to spend time with their children in the custody of a former spouse.
2 a disaster or difficulty regarded as a divine punishment: *a visitation of the plague.*
3 (**the Visitation**) the visit of the Virgin Mary to Elizabeth related in Luke 1:39–56.
■ the festival commemorating this on 31 May (formerly 2 July).
– ORIGIN Middle English: from Old French, or from late Latin *visitatio(n-)*, from the verb *visitare* (see **VISIT**).

visitatorial /ˌvɪzɪtəˈtɔːrɪəl/ ▶ **adjective** another term for **VISITORIAL**.

visiting ▶ **adjective** [attrib.] (of a person) on a visit to a person or place: *a visiting speaker.*
■ (of an academic) working for a fixed period of time at another institution: *a visiting professor.*

visiting card ▶ **noun** Brit. a card bearing a person's name and address, sent or left in lieu of a formal social or business visit.

visiting fireman ▶ **noun** US informal an important visitor to a city or organization who is given an official welcome and especially cordial treatment.
■ a visitor or tourist who is accorded special attention because they are expected to spend extravagantly.

visitor ▶ **noun** a person visiting a person or place, especially socially or as a tourist.
■ (usu. **visitors**) a member of a sports team on tour or playing away from home. ■ Brit. a person with the right or duty of occasionally inspecting and reporting on a college or other academic institution. ■ Ornithology a migratory bird present in a locality for only part of the year.
– ORIGIN late Middle English: from Anglo-Norman French *visitour*, from Old French *visiter* (see **VISIT**).

visitorial ▶ **adjective** of or relating to an official visitor or visitation: *visitorial jurisdiction.*

visitors' book ▶ **noun** chiefly Brit. a book in which visitors to a public building write their names and addresses, and sometimes remarks.

Visking /ˈvɪskɪŋ/ (also **Visking tubing**) ▶ **noun** [mass noun] trademark a type of seamless cellulose tubing used as a membrane in dialysis and as an edible casing for sausages.
– ORIGIN 1930s: named after the *Visking* Corporation of Chicago, US.

vis medicatrix naturae /vɪs mɛdɪˌkeɪtrɪks ˈnatʃərʌɪ/ ▶ **noun** [mass noun] the body's natural ability to heal itself.
– ORIGIN Latin, 'the healing power of nature'.

visna /ˈvɪznə/ ▶ **noun** [mass noun] Veterinary Medicine a fatal disease of sheep in which there is progressive demyelination of neurons in the brain and spinal cord, caused by the maedi virus.
– ORIGIN 1950s: from Old Norse, 'to wither'.

visor /ˈvʌɪzə/ (also **vizor**) ▶ **noun** a movable part of a helmet that can be pulled down to cover the face.
■ a screen for protecting the eyes from unwanted light, especially one at the top of a vehicle windscreen. ■ N. Amer. a stiff peak at the front of a cap. ■ historical a mask.
– DERIVATIVES **visored** adjective.
– ORIGIN Middle English: from Anglo-Norman French *viser*, from Old French *vis* 'face', from Latin *visus* (see **VISAGE**).

Visqueen /ˈvɪskwiːn/ ▶ **noun** [mass noun] trademark a durable polyethylene sheeting, used in various building applications and in the manufacture of waterproof household articles.
– ORIGIN 1940s: from **VISKING**, with humorous alteration of *-king* to *-queen*.

vista ▶ **noun** a pleasing view, especially one seen through a long, narrow opening: *a vista of church spires.*
■ a mental view of a succession of remembered or anticipated events: *vistas of freedom seemed to open ahead of him.*
– ORIGIN mid 17th cent.: from Italian, literally 'view', from *visto* 'seen', past participle of *vedere* 'see', from Latin *videre*.

vista dome ▶ **noun** N. Amer. an observation compartment in the roof of a railway carriage.

Vistavision ▶ **noun** [mass noun] US trademark a form of widescreen cinematography employing standard 35 mm film in such a way as to give a larger projected image using ordinary methods of projection.

Vistula /ˈvɪstjʊlə/ a river in Poland which rises in the Carpathian Mountains and flows 940 km (592 miles) generally northwards, through Cracow and Warsaw, to the Baltic near Gdańsk. Polish name **WISŁA**.

visual /ˈvɪʒʊəl, -zj-/ ▶ **adjective** of or relating to seeing or sight: *visual perception.*
▶ **noun** (usu. **visuals**) a picture, piece of film, or display used to illustrate or accompany something.
– DERIVATIVES **visuality** noun, **visually** adverb.
– ORIGIN late Middle English (originally describing a beam imagined to proceed from the eye and make vision possible): from late Latin *visualis*, from Latin *visus* 'sight', from *videre* 'to see'. The current noun sense dates from the 1950s.

visual agnosia ▶ **noun** [mass noun] Medicine a condition in which a person can see but cannot recognize or interpret visual information, due to a disorder in the parietal lobes.

visual aid ▶ **noun** **1** (usu. **visual aids**) an item of illustrative matter, such as a film, slide, or model, designed to supplement written or spoken information so that it can be understood more easily.
2 a device used to improve vision, such as a magnifying glass or glasses.

visual angle ▶ **noun** Optics the angle formed at the eye by rays from the extremities of an object viewed.

visual binary ▶ **noun** Astronomy a binary star of which the components are sufficiently far apart to be resolved by an optical telescope.

visual cortex ▶ **noun** Anatomy the part of the cerebral cortex that receives and processes sensory nerve impulses from the eyes.

visual display unit (abbrev.: **VDU**) ▶ **noun** Computing, chiefly Brit. a device for displaying input signals as characters on a screen, typically incorporating a keyboard.

visual field ▶ **noun** another term for **FIELD OF VISION**.

visualize (also **-ise**) ▶ **verb** [with obj.] **1** form a mental

image of; imagine: *it is not easy to visualize the future.* **2** make (something) visible to the eye: *the DNA was visualized by staining with ethidium bromide.*
– DERIVATIVES **visualizable** adjective, **visualization** noun.

visual purple ▶ noun [mass noun] a purplish-red light-sensitive pigment present in the retinas of humans and many other animal groups.

visual ray ▶ noun Optics an imaginary line representing the path of light from an object to the eye.

visuomotor /ˈvɪʒʊə(ʊ),məʊtə, -zj-/ ▶ adjective [attrib.] relating to or denoting the coordination of movement and visual perception by the brain.

visuospatial /ˌvɪʒjʊəʊˈspeɪʃ(ə)l, -zj-/ ▶ adjective [attrib.] Psychology relating to or denoting the visual perception of the spatial relationships of objects.

vital ▶ adjective **1** absolutely necessary; essential: *secrecy is of vital importance | it is vital that the system is regularly maintained.*
■indispensable to the continuance of life: *the vital organs.*
2 full of energy; lively: *a beautiful, vital girl.*
3 archaic fatal: *the wound is vital.*
▶ noun (**vitals**) the body's important internal organs.
– DERIVATIVES **vitally** adverb [as submodifier] *eating sensibly is vitally important for health.*
– ORIGIN late Middle English (describing the animating principle of living beings, also in sense 2): via Old French from Latin *vitalis*, from *vita* 'life'. The sense 'essential' dates from the early 17th cent.

vital capacity ▶ noun the greatest volume of air that can be expelled from the lungs after taking the deepest possible breath.

vital force ▶ noun [mass noun] the energy or spirit which animates living creatures; the soul.
■Philosophy (in some theories, particularly that of Bergson) a hypothetical force, independent of physical and chemical forces, regarded as being the causative factor in the evolution and development of living organisms. [ORIGIN: translating French *élan vital*.] ■[count noun] a person or thing that gives something vitality and strength: *he was a vital force in British music.*

vitalism ▶ noun [mass noun] the theory that the origin and phenomena of life are dependent on a force or principle distinct from purely chemical or physical forces.
– DERIVATIVES **vitalist** noun & adjective, **vitalistic** adjective.
– ORIGIN early 19th cent.: from French *vitalisme*, or from **VITAL** + **-ISM**.

vitality ▶ noun [mass noun] the state of being strong and active; energy: *changes that will give renewed vitality to our democracy.*
■the power giving continuance of life, present in all living things: *the vitality of seeds.*
– ORIGIN late 16th cent.: from Latin *vitalitas*, from *vitalis* (see **VITAL**).

vitalize /ˈvʌɪt(ə)lʌɪz/ (also **-ise**) ▶ verb [with obj.] give strength and energy to: *yoga calms and vitalizes body and mind.*
– DERIVATIVES **vitalization** noun.

vital signs ▶ plural noun clinical measurements, specifically pulse rate, temperature, respiration rate, and blood pressure, that indicate the state of a patient's essential body functions.

vital statistics ▶ plural noun **1** quantitative data concerning the population, such as the number of births, marriages, and deaths.
2 informal the measurements of a woman's bust, waist, and hips.

vitamin /ˈvɪtəmɪn, ˈvʌɪt-/ ▶ noun any of a group of organic compounds which are essential for normal growth and nutrition and are required in small quantities in the diet because they cannot be synthesized by the body.
– ORIGIN early 20th cent.: from Latin *vita* 'life' + **AMINE**, because vitamins were originally thought to contain an amino acid.

vitamin A ▶ noun another term for **RETINOL**.

vitamin B ▶ noun [mass noun] any of a group of substances (the **vitamin B complex**) which are essential for the working of certain enzymes in the body and, although not chemically related, are generally found together in the same foods. They include thiamine (**vitamin B_1**), riboflavin (**vitamin B_2**), pyridoxine (**vitamin B_6**), and cyanocobalamin (**vitamin B_{12}**).

vitamin C ▶ noun another term for **ASCORBIC ACID**.

vitamin D ▶ noun [mass noun] any of a group of vitamins found in liver and fish oils, essential for the absorption of calcium and the prevention of rickets in children and osteomalacia in adults. They include calciferol (**vitamin D_2**) and cholecalciferol (**vitamin D_3**).

vitamin E ▶ noun another term for **TOCOPHEROL**.

vitamin H ▶ noun chiefly US another term for **BIOTIN**.

vitaminize (also **-ise**) ▶ verb [with obj.] add vitamins to (food): [as adj. **vitaminized**] *vitaminized biscuits.*

vitamin K ▶ noun [mass noun] any of a group of vitamins found mainly in green leaves and essential for the blood-clotting process. They include phylloquinone (**vitamin K_1**) and menaquinone (**vitamin K_2**).

vitamin M ▶ noun chiefly US another term for **FOLIC ACID**.

vitamin P ▶ noun [mass noun] chiefly US the bioflavonoids, regarded collectively as a vitamin.

Vitebsk /ˈvʲitʲipsk/ Russian name for **VITSEBSK**.

vitelli plural form of **VITELLUS**.

vitellin /vɪˈtɛlɪn, vʌɪ-/ ▶ noun [mass noun] Biochemistry the chief protein constituent of egg yolk.
– ORIGIN mid 19th cent.: from **VITELLUS** + **-IN**[1].

vitelline /vɪˈtɛlʌɪn, vʌɪ-, -lɪn/ ▶ adjective Zoology & Embryology of or relating to the yolk (or yolk sac) of an egg or embryo, or to yolk-producing organs.
– ORIGIN late Middle English (in the sense 'coloured like egg yolk'): from medieval Latin *vitellinus*, from *vitellus* (see **VITELLUS**).

vitelline membrane ▶ noun Embryology a transparent membrane surrounding and secreted by the fertilized ovum, preventing the entry of further spermatozoa.

Vitellius /vɪˈtɛlɪəs/, Aulus (15–69), Roman emperor. He was acclaimed emperor in January 69 by the legions in Germany during the civil wars that followed the death of Nero. He defeated Otho but was killed by the supporters of Vespasian.

vitellogenin /vɪˌtɛlə(ʊ)ˈdʒɛnɪn, ˌvɪt(ə)ləʊˈdʒɛnɪn/ ▶ noun Biochemistry a protein present in the blood, from which the substance of egg yolk is derived.
– ORIGIN 1960s: from **VITELLUS** + **-GEN** + **-IN**[1].

vitello tonnato /vɪˈtɛləʊ tɒˈnɑːtəʊ/ ▶ noun [mass noun] an Italian dish consisting of roast or poached veal served cold in a tuna and anchovy mayonnaise.
– ORIGIN Italian, from *vitello* 'veal' + *tonno* 'tuna'.

vitellus /vɪˈtɛləs, vʌɪ-/ ▶ noun [mass noun] Embryology the yolk of an egg or ovum.
– ORIGIN early 18th cent.: from Latin, literally 'yolk'.

vitiate /ˈvɪʃɪeɪt/ ▶ verb [with obj.] formal spoil or impair the quality or efficiency of: *development programmes have been vitiated by the rise in population.*
■destroy or impair the legal validity of.
– DERIVATIVES **vitiation** noun, **vitiator** noun.
– ORIGIN mid 16th cent.: from Latin *vitiat-* 'impaired', from the verb *vitiare*, from *vitium* (see **VICE**[1]).

viticulture /ˈvɪtɪˌkʌltʃə/ ▶ noun [mass noun] the cultivation of grapevines.
■the study of grape cultivation.
– DERIVATIVES **viticultural** adjective, **viticulturist** noun.
– ORIGIN late 19th cent.: from Latin *vitis* 'vine' + **CULTURE**, on the pattern of words such as *agriculture*.

Viti Levu /ˌviːtiː ˈlɛvuː/ the largest of the Fiji islands. Its chief settlement is Suva.

vitiligo /ˌvɪtɪˈlʌɪɡəʊ/ ▶ noun [mass noun] Medicine a condition in which the pigment is lost from areas of the skin, causing whitish patches, often with no clear cause. Also called **LEUCODERMA**.
– ORIGIN late 16th cent.: from Latin, literally 'tetter'.

Vitoria /vɪˈtɔːrɪə, Spanish biˈtorja/ a city in NE Spain, capital of the Basque Provinces; pop. 208,570 (1991). In 1813 Wellington defeated a French force there, and thus freed Spain from French domination.

Vitória /vɪˈtɔːrɪə/ a port in eastern Brazil, capital of the state of Espírito Santo; pop. 276,170 (1990).

vitrectomy /vɪˈtrɛktəmi/ ▶ noun [mass noun] the surgical operation of removing the vitreous humour from the eyeball.

vitreous /ˈvɪtrɪəs/ ▶ adjective like glass in appearance or physical properties.
■(of a substance) derived from or containing glass: *toilet and bidet are made of vitreous china.*
– DERIVATIVES **vitreousness** noun.
– ORIGIN late Middle English: from Latin *vitreus* (from *vitrum* 'glass') + **-OUS**.

vitreous humour ▶ noun [mass noun] the transparent jelly-like tissue filling the eyeball behind the lens. Compare with **AQUEOUS HUMOUR**.

vitrescent /vɪˈtrɛs(ə)nt/ ▶ adjective rare capable of or susceptible to being turned into glass.
– DERIVATIVES **vitrescence** noun.
– ORIGIN mid 18th cent.: from Latin *vitrum* 'glass' + **-ESCENT**.

vitriform /ˈvɪtrɪfɔːm/ ▶ adjective having the form or appearance of glass.

vitrify /ˈvɪtrɪfʌɪ/ ▶ verb (**-ies**, **-ied**) [with obj.] (often **be vitrified**) convert (something) into glass or a glass-like substance, typically by exposure to heat.
– DERIVATIVES **vitrifaction** /-ˈfakʃ(ə)n/ noun, **vitrifiable** adjective, **vitrification** /-fɪˈkeɪʃ(ə)n/ noun.
– ORIGIN late Middle English: from French *vitrifier* or based on Latin *vitrum* 'glass'.

vitrine /ˈvɪtriːn/ ▶ noun a glass display case.
– ORIGIN French, from *vitre* 'glass pane'.

vitriol /ˈvɪtrɪəl/ ▶ noun [mass noun] archaic or poetic/literary sulphuric acid.
■figurative cruel and bitter criticism: *her mother's sudden gush of fury and vitriol.*
– DERIVATIVES **vitriolic** adjective.
– ORIGIN late Middle English (denoting the sulphate of various metals): from Old French, or from medieval Latin *vitriolum*, from Latin *vitrum* 'glass'.

Vitruvius /vɪˈtruːvɪəs/ (*fl.* 1st century BC), Roman architect and military engineer; full name *Marcus Vitruvius Pollio*. He wrote a comprehensive ten-volume treatise on architecture which includes matters such as acoustics and water supply as well as the more obvious aspects of architectural design, decoration, and building.

Vitsebsk /ˈviːtsjɛbsk/ a city in NE Belarus; pop. 356,000 (1990). Russian name **VITEBSK**.

vitta /ˈvɪtə/ ▶ noun (pl. **vittae** /ˈvɪtiː/) Zoology a band or stripe of colour.
– ORIGIN early 19th cent.: from Latin, literally 'band, chaplet'.

vittle ▶ noun archaic variant spelling of **VICTUAL**.

vituperate /vɪˈtjuːpəreɪt, vʌɪ-/ ▶ verb [with obj.] archaic blame or insult (someone) in strong or violent language.
– DERIVATIVES **vituperator** noun.
– ORIGIN mid 16th cent.: from Latin *vituperat-* 'censured, disparaged', from the verb *vituperare*, from *vitium* 'fault' + *parare* 'prepare'.

vituperation ▶ noun [mass noun] bitter and abusive language: *no one else attracted such vituperation from him.*

vituperative /vɪˈtjuːp(ə)rətɪv, vʌɪ-/ ▶ adjective bitter and abusive: *the criticism soon turned into a vituperative attack.*

Vitus, St /ˈvʌɪtəs/ (died *c.*300), Christian martyr. He was the patron of those who suffered from epilepsy and certain nervous disorders, including St Vitus's dance (Sydenham's chorea). Feast day, 15 June.

viva[1] /ˈvʌɪvə/ Brit. ▶ noun short for **VIVA VOCE**.
▶ verb (**vivas**, **vivaed** /-vəd/ or **viva'd**, **vivaing**) [with obj.] (often **be vivaed**) subject (someone) to an oral examination.

viva[2] /ˈviːvə/ ▶ exclamation long live! (used to express acclaim or support for a specified person or thing): *'Viva Mexico!'*
▶ noun a cry of this as a salute or cheer.
– ORIGIN Italian.

vivace /vɪˈvɑːtʃeɪ/ Music ▶ adverb & adjective (especially as a direction) in a lively and brisk manner.
▶ noun a passage or movement marked to be performed in this manner.
– ORIGIN Italian, 'brisk, lively', from Latin *vivax, vivac-*.

vivacious /vɪˈveɪʃəs, vʌɪ-/ ▶ adjective (especially of a woman) attractively lively and animated.
– DERIVATIVES **vivaciously** adverb, **vivaciousness** noun, **vivacity** noun.
– ORIGIN mid 17th cent.: from Latin *vivax, vivac-* 'lively, vigorous' (from *vivere* 'to live') + **-IOUS**.

Vivaldi /vɪˈvaldi/, Antonio (Lucio) (1678–1741), Italian composer and violinist, one of the most important baroque composers. His feeling for texture and melody is evident in his numerous

V

compositions such as *The Four Seasons* (concerto, 1725).

vivarium /vʌɪˈvɛːrɪəm, vɪ-/ ▶ noun (pl. **vivaria** /-rɪə/) an enclosure, container, or structure adapted or prepared for keeping animals under semi-natural conditions for observation or study or as pets; an aquarium or terrarium.
− ORIGIN early 17th cent.: from Latin, literally 'warren, fish pond', from *vivus* 'living', from *vivere* 'to live'.

vivat /ˈviːvat, ˈviː-/ ▶ exclamation & noun Latin term for **VIVA**[2].

viva voce /ˌvʌɪvə ˈvəʊtʃeɪ, ˈvəʊtʃi/ ▶ adjective (especially of an examination) oral rather than written.
▶ adverb orally rather than in writing.
▶ noun (also **viva**) Brit. an oral examination, typically for an academic qualification.
− ORIGIN mid 16th cent.: from medieval Latin, literally 'with the living voice'.

Vivekananda /ˌvɪveɪkɑːˈnɑːndə/, Swami (1863–1902), Indian spiritual leader and reformer; born *Narendranath Datta*. He spread the teachings of the Indian mystic Ramakrishna and introduced Vedantic philosophy to the US and Europe.

vive la difference /ˌviːv lɑː ˌdɪfəˈrɒns/ ▶ exclamation chiefly humorous an expression of approval of difference, especially that between the sexes.
− ORIGIN from French *vive la différence*, literally 'long live the difference'.

viverrid /vɪˈvɛrɪd, vʌɪ-/ ▶ noun Zoology a mammal of the civet family (Viverridae).
− ORIGIN early 20th cent.: from modern Latin *Viverridae*, from Latin *viverra* 'ferret'.

vivers /ˈvʌɪvəz/ ▶ plural noun Scottish food; provisions.
− ORIGIN mid 16th cent.: from French *vivres*, from *vivre* 'to live', from Latin *vivere*.

vivianite /ˈvɪvɪənʌɪt/ ▶ noun [mass noun] a mineral consisting of a phosphate of iron which occurs as a secondary mineral in ore deposits. It is colourless when fresh but becomes blue or green with oxidization.
− ORIGIN early 19th cent.: named after John H. *Vivian* (1785–1855), British mineralogist, + **-ITE**[1].

vivid ▶ adjective 1 producing powerful feelings or strong, clear images in the mind: *memories of that evening were still vivid | a vivid description.*
■(of a colour) intensely deep or bright.
2 archaic (of a person or animal) lively and vigorous.
− DERIVATIVES **vividly** adverb, **vividness** noun.
− ORIGIN mid 17th cent.: from Latin *vividus*, from *vivere* 'to live'.

vivify /ˈvɪvɪfʌɪ/ ▶ verb (**-ies, -ied**) [with obj.] enliven or animate: *outings vivify learning for children.*
− DERIVATIVES **vivification** /-fɪˈkeɪʃ(ə)n/ noun.
− ORIGIN late Middle English: from French *vivifier*, from late Latin *vivificare*, from Latin *vivus* 'living', from *vivere* 'to live'.

viviparous /vɪˈvɪp(ə)rəs, vʌɪ-/ ▶ adjective Zoology (of an animal) bringing forth live young which have developed inside the body of the parent. Compare with **OVIPAROUS** and **OVOVIVIPAROUS**.
■Botany (of a plant) reproducing from buds which form plantlets while still attached to the parent plant, or from seeds which germinate within the fruit.
− DERIVATIVES **viviparity** /ˌvɪvɪˈparɪti/ noun, **viviparously** adverb.
− ORIGIN mid 17th cent.: from Latin *viviparus* (from *vivus* 'alive' + *-parus* 'bearing') + **-OUS**.

viviparous lizard ▶ noun a small brownish-grey Eurasian lizard which gives birth to live young which have hatched from eggs inside the female.
● *Lacerta vivipara*, family Lacertidae. Alternative name: **common lizard**.

vivisect /ˈvɪvɪsɛkt, ˌvɪvɪˈsɛkt/ ▶ verb [with obj.] perform vivisection on (an animal) (used only by people who are opposed to the practice).
− DERIVATIVES **vivisector** noun.
− ORIGIN mid 19th cent.: back-formation from **VIVISECTION**.

vivisection ▶ noun [mass noun] the practice of performing operations on live animals for the purpose of experimentation or scientific research (used only by people who are opposed to such work).
■figurative ruthlessly sharp and detailed criticism or analysis: *the vivisection of America's seamy underbelly.*
− DERIVATIVES **vivisectionist** noun & adjective.

− ORIGIN early 18th cent.: from Latin *vivus* 'living', on the pattern of *dissection*.

vixen ▶ noun a female fox.
■a spiteful or quarrelsome woman.
− DERIVATIVES **vixenish** adjective
− ORIGIN late Middle English *fixen*, perhaps from the Old English adjective *fyxen* 'of a fox'. The *v-* is from the form of the word in southern English dialect.

Viyella /vʌɪˈɛlə/ ▶ noun [mass noun] trademark a fabric made from a twilled mixture of cotton and wool.
− ORIGIN late 19th cent.: from *Via Gellia*, a valley in Derbyshire where it was first made.

viz. ▶ adverb namely; in other words (used especially to introduce a gloss or explanation): *the first music reproducing media, viz., the music box and the player piano.*
− ORIGIN abbreviation of **VIDELICET**, *z* being a medieval Latin symbol for *-et*.

vizard /ˈvɪzəd/ ▶ noun archaic a mask or disguise.
− ORIGIN mid 16th cent.: alteration of **VISOR**.

vizier /vɪˈzɪə, ˈvɪzɪə/ ▶ noun historical a high official in some Muslim countries, especially in Turkey under Ottoman rule.
− DERIVATIVES **vizierate** /-rət/ noun, **vizierial** /vɪˈzɪərɪəl/ adjective, **viziership** noun.
− ORIGIN mid 16th cent.: via Turkish from Arabic *wazīr* 'caliph's chief counsellor'.

vizor ▶ noun variant spelling of **VISOR**.

vizsla /ˈvɪʒlə/ ▶ noun a dog of a breed of golden-brown pointer with large drooping ears.
− ORIGIN 1940s: from the name of a town in Hungary.

VJ ▶ abbreviation for video jockey.

VJ day ▶ noun the day (15 August) in 1945 on which Japan ceased fighting in the Second World War, or the day (2 September) when Japan formally surrendered.
− ORIGIN VJ, abbreviation of *Victory over Japan*.

Vlach /vlak/ ▶ noun a member of the indigenous population of Romania and Moldova, claiming descent from the inhabitants of the Roman province of Dacia.
▶ adjective of or relating to this people.
− ORIGIN from a Slavic word meaning 'foreigner', from a Germanic word related to Old English *Wælisc* (see **WELSH**). Compare with **WALLACHIA**.

Vladikavkaz /ˌvladɪkafˈkɑːs/ a city in SW Russia, capital of the autonomous republic of North Ossetia; pop. 306,000 (1990). Former names **ORDZHONIKIDZE** (1931–44 and 1954–93) and **DZAUDZHIKAU** (1944–54).

Vladimir /ˈvladɪˌmɪə, vləˈdiːmɪə/ a city in European Russia, east of Moscow; pop. 353,000 (1990).

Vladimir I (956–1015), grand prince of Kiev 980–1015; known as **Vladimir the Great**; canonized as **St Vladimir**. His marriage to a sister of the Byzantine emperor Basil II resulted in his conversion to Christianity and in Christianity in Russia developing in close association with the Orthodox Church. Feast day, 15 July.

Vladivostok /ˌvladɪˈvɒstɒk/ a city in the extreme south-east of Russia, on the coast of the Sea of Japan, capital of Primorsky; pop. 643,000 (1990). It is the chief port of Russia's Pacific coast.

Vlaminck /vlaˈmaŋk, French vlamɛ̃k/, Maurice de (1876–1958), French painter and writer. With Derain and Matisse he became a leading exponent of fauvism, though later his colour became more subdued.

vlast /vlast/ ▶ noun (pl. **vlasti** /-ti/) [mass noun] (in countries of the former USSR) political power or authority.
■(**the vlasti**) members of the government; people holding political power.
− ORIGIN Russian.

vlei /fleɪ, vlʌɪ/ ▶ noun S. African a shallow natural pool of water.
■[mass noun] low-lying, marshy ground, covered with water during the rainy season.
− ORIGIN Afrikaans, from Dutch *vallei* 'valley'.

vlei rat ▶ noun see **SWAMP RAT**.

VLF ▶ abbreviation for very low frequency (denoting radio waves of frequency 3–30 kHz and wavelength 10–100 km).

Vlissingen /ˈvlɪsɪŋə(n)/ Dutch name for **FLUSHING**.

Vlorë /ˈvlɔːrə/ a port in SW Albania, on the Adriatic

coast; pop. 55,800 (1990). Also called **VLONA** /ˈvləʊnə/, Italian name **VALONA**.

VLSI Electronics ▶ abbreviation for very large-scale integration, the process of integrating hundreds of thousands of components on a single silicon chip.

Vltava /ˈvəltəvə/ a river of the Czech Republic, which rises in the Bohemian Forest on the German–Czech border and flows 435 km (270 miles) generally northwards, passing through Prague before joining the Elbe north of the city. German name **MOLDAU**.

VN ▶ abbreviation for Vietnam (international vehicle registration).

V-neck ▶ noun a neckline of a garment, having straight sides meeting at a point to form a V-shape.
■a garment with a neckline of this type.
− DERIVATIVES **V-necked** adjective.

VO ▶ abbreviation for (in the UK) Royal Victorian Order.

vobla /ˈvɒblə/ ▶ noun [mass noun] dried and smoked roach eaten in Russia as a delicacy.
− ORIGIN Russian.

vocable /ˈvəʊkəb(ə)l/ ▶ noun a word, especially with reference to form rather than meaning.
− ORIGIN late Middle English (denoting a name): from French, or from Latin *vocabulum*, from *vocare* 'call'.

vocabulary ▶ noun (pl. **-ies**) the body of words used in a particular language.
■a part of such a body of words used on a particular occasion or in a particular sphere: *the vocabulary of law |* [mass noun] *the term became part of business vocabulary.* ■ the body of words known to an individual person: *he had a wide vocabulary.* ■ a list of difficult or unfamiliar words with an explanation of their meanings, accompanying a piece of specialist or foreign-language text. ■ a range of artistic or stylistic forms, techniques, or movements: *dance companies have their own vocabularies of movement.*
− ORIGIN mid 16th cent. (denoting a list of words with definitions or translations): from medieval Latin *vocabularius*, from Latin *vocabulum* (see **VOCABLE**).

vocal ▶ adjective 1 of or relating to the human voice: *non-linguistic vocal effects like laughs and sobs.*
■Anatomy used in the production of speech sounds: *the vocal apparatus.*
2 expressing opinions or feelings freely or loudly: *he was vocal in condemning the action.*
3 (of music) consisting of or incorporating singing.
▶ noun (often **vocals**) a part of a piece of music that is sung.
■a musical performance involving singing.
− DERIVATIVES **vocality** noun, **vocally** adverb.
− ORIGIN late Middle English: from Latin *vocalis*, from *vox, voc-* (see **VOICE**). Current senses of the noun date from the 1920s.

vocal cords (also **vocal folds**) ▶ plural noun folds of membranous tissue which project inwards from the sides of the larynx to form a slit across the glottis in the throat, and whose edges vibrate in the airstream to produce the voice.

vocalese /ˌvəʊkəˈliːz/ ▶ noun [mass noun] a style of singing in which singers put words to jazz tunes, especially to previously improvised instrumental solos.

vocalic /və(ʊ)ˈkalɪk/ ▶ adjective Phonetics of, relating to, or consisting of a vowel or vowels.

vocalise /ˌvəʊkəˈliːz, ˈvəʊkəliːz/ ▶ noun Music a singing exercise using individual syllables or vowel sounds to develop flexibility and control of pitch and tone.
■a vocal passage consisting of a melody without words: *the second movement is in the spirit of a vocalise.*

vocalism ▶ noun 1 [mass noun] the use of the voice or vocal organs in speech.
■the skill or art of exercising the voice in singing.
2 Phonetics a vowel sound or articulation.
■a system of vowels used in a given language.

vocalist ▶ noun a singer, typically one who regularly performs with a jazz or pop group.

vocalize /ˈvəʊk(ə)lʌɪz/ (also **-ise**) ▶ verb [with obj.]
1 utter (a sound or word): *the child vocalizes a number of distinct sounds |* [no obj.] *a warbler vocalized from a reed bed.*
■express (something) with words: *Gillie could scarcely vocalize her responses.* ■ [no obj.] Music sing with several notes to one vowel.

2 Phonetics change (a consonant) to a semivowel or vowel.
3 write (a language such as Hebrew) with vowel points.
– DERIVATIVES **vocalization** noun, **vocalizer** noun.

vocal sac ▶**noun** Zoology (in many male frogs) a loose fold of skin on each side of the mouth, which can be inflated to produce sound.

vocal score ▶**noun** a musical score showing the voice parts in full, but with the accompaniment reduced or omitted.

vocation /və(ʊ)ˈkeɪʃ(ə)n/ ▶**noun** a strong feeling of suitability for a particular career or occupation: *not all of us have a vocation to be nurses or doctors.*
■ a person's employment or main occupation, especially regarded as particularly worthy and requiring great dedication: *her vocation as a poet.* ■ a trade or profession.
– ORIGIN late Middle English: from Old French, or from Latin *vocatio(n-)*, from *vocare* 'to call'.

vocational ▶**adjective** of or relating to an occupation or employment: *they supervised prisoners in vocational activities.*
■ (of education or training) directed at a particular occupation and its skills.
– DERIVATIVES **vocationalism** noun, **vocationalize** (also **-ise**) verb, **vocationally** adverb.

vocative /ˈvɒkətɪv/ Grammar ▶**adjective** relating to or denoting a case of nouns, pronouns, and adjectives in Latin and other languages, used in addressing or invoking a person or thing.
▶**noun** a word in the vocative case.
■ (**the vocative**) the vocative case.
– ORIGIN late Middle English: from Old French *vocatif, -ive* or Latin *vocativus*, from *vocare* 'to call'.

vociferate /və(ʊ)ˈsɪfəreɪt/ ▶**verb** [no obj.] shout, complain, or argue loudly or vehemently: *he then began to vociferate pretty loudly* | [with obj.] *he entered, vociferating curses.*
– DERIVATIVES **vociferant** adjective, **vociferation** noun.
– ORIGIN late 16th cent.: from Latin *vociferat-* 'exclaimed', from the verb *vociferari*, from *vox* 'voice' + *ferre* 'carry'.

vociferous ▶**adjective** (especially of a person or speech) vehement or clamorous: *he was a vociferous opponent of the takeover.*
– DERIVATIVES **vociferously** adverb, **vociferousness** noun.

vocoder /vəʊˈkəʊdə/ ▶**noun** a synthesizer that produces sounds from an analysis of speech input.
– ORIGIN 1930s: from **VOICE** + **CODE** + **-ER**[1].

VOD ▶**abbreviation for** video-on-demand.

vodka /ˈvɒdkə/ ▶**noun** [mass noun] an alcoholic spirit of Russian origin made by distillation of rye, wheat, or potatoes.
– ORIGIN Russian, diminutive of *voda* 'water'.

vodun /ˈvəʊduːn/ ▶**noun** another term for **VOODOO**.
– ORIGIN Fon, 'fetish'.

voe /vəʊ/ ▶**noun** a small bay or creek in Orkney or Shetland.
– ORIGIN late 17th cent.: from Norwegian *våg*, from Old Norse *vágr*.

voetsak /ˈfʊtsak/ ▶**verb** [no obj., usu. in imperative] S. African informal go away: *voetsak out of here!* | [as exclamation] *150,000 rand for a Mercedes? Voetsak!*
– ORIGIN South African Dutch, contraction of Dutch *voort seg ik!* 'away, say I!'.

voetstoots /ˈfʊtˌstʊəts/ ▶**adverb** & **adjective** S. African Law (of a sale or purchase) without guarantee or warranty; at the buyer's risk: [as adv.] *the property is sold voetstoots* | [as adj.] *auctions are voetstoots deals.*
■ without reservation or qualification: [as adv.] *I'm not entirely in favour of school uniforms voetstoots.*
– ORIGIN Afrikaans, from the Dutch phrase *met de voet te stoten* 'to push with the foot'.

vogue ▶**noun** [usu. in sing.] the prevailing fashion or style at a particular time: *the vogue is to make realistic films.*
■ [mass noun] general acceptance or favour; popularity: *crochet garments are* **in vogue** *this season.*
▶**adjective** [attrib.] popular; fashionable: *'citizenship' was to be the government's vogue word.*
– DERIVATIVES **voguish** adjective.
– ORIGIN late 16th cent. (in *the vogue*, denoting the foremost place in popular estimation): from French, from Italian *voga* 'rowing, fashion', from *vogare* 'row, go well'.

voice ▶**noun 1** the sound produced in a person's larynx and uttered through the mouth, as speech or song: *Meg raised her voice* | [mass noun] *a worried tone of voice.*
■ an agency by which a particular point of view is expressed or represented: *once the proud voice of middle-class conservatism, the paper had fallen on hard times.* ■ [in sing.] the right to express an opinion: *the new electoral system gives minority parties a voice.* ■ a particular opinion or attitude expressed: *a dissenting voice.* ■ the ability to speak or sing: *she'd* **lost her voice**. ■ (usu. **voices**) the supposed utterance of a guiding spirit, typically giving instructions or advice. ■ the distinctive tone or style of a literary work or author: *she had strained and falsified her literary voice.*
2 Music the range of pitch or type of tone with which a person sings, such as soprano or tenor.
■ a vocal part in a composition. ■ a constituent part in a fugue. ■ each of the notes or sounds able to be produced simultaneously by a musical instrument (especially an electronic one) or a computer. ■ (in an electronic musical instrument) each of a number of preset or programmable tones.
3 [mass noun] Phonetics sound uttered with resonance of the vocal cords (used in the pronunciation of vowels and certain consonants).
4 Grammar a form or set of forms of a verb showing the relation of the subject to the action: *the passive voice.*
▶**verb** [with obj.] **1** express (something) in words: *get teachers to voice their opinions on important subjects.*
2 [usu. as adj. **voiced**] Phonetics utter (a speech sound) with resonance of the vocal cords (e.g. *b, d, g, v, z*).
3 Music regulate the tone quality of (organ pipes).
– PHRASES **give voice to** allow (a particular emotion, opinion, or point of view) to be expressed. ■ allow (a person or group) to express their emotions, opinion, or point of view. **in voice** in proper vocal condition for singing or speaking: *the soprano is in marvellous voice.* **with one voice** in complete agreement; unanimously.
– DERIVATIVES **voiced** adjective [in combination] *deep-voiced*, **voicer** noun (only in sense 3 of the verb).
– ORIGIN Middle English: from Old French *vois*, from Latin *vox, voc-*.

voice box ▶**noun** the larynx.

voice channel ▶**noun** Telecommunications a channel with a bandwidth sufficiently great to accommodate speech.

voice coil ▶**noun** Telecommunications a coil that drives the cone of a loudspeaker according to the signal current flowing in it.
■ a similar coil with the converse function in a moving-coil microphone.

voiceful ▶**adjective** poetic/literary possessing a voice: *the swelling of the voiceful sea.*

voiceless ▶**adjective** mute; speechless: *how could he have remained voiceless in the face of her cruelty?*
■ not expressed: *the air was charged with voiceless currents of thought.* ■ (of a person or group) lacking the power or right to express an opinion or exert control over affairs. ■ Phonetics (of a speech sound) uttered without resonance of the vocal cords (e.g. *f, k, p, s, t*).
– DERIVATIVES **voicelessly** adverb, **voicelessness** noun.

voicemail ▶**noun** [mass noun] a centralized electronic system which can store messages from telephone callers.

Voice of America an official US radio station founded in 1942, operated by the Board for International Broadcasting, that broadcasts around the world in English and other languages.

voice-over ▶**noun** a piece of narration in a film or broadcast, not accompanied by an image of the speaker.
▶**verb** [with obj.] narrate (spoken material) for a film or broadcast in this way.

voiceprint ▶**noun** a visual record of speech, analysed with respect to frequency, duration, and amplitude.
– ORIGIN 1960s: from the noun **VOICE**, on the pattern of *fingerprint*.

voice vote ▶**noun** a vote taken by noting the relative strength and volume of calls of *aye* and *no*.

void /vɔɪd/ ▶**adjective 1** not valid or legally binding: *the contract was void.*
■ (of speech or action) ineffectual; useless: *all the stratagems you've worked out are rendered void.*
2 completely empty: *void spaces surround the tanks.*
■ [predic.] (**void of**) free from; lacking: *what were once the masterpieces of literature are now void of meaning.* ■ formal (of an office or position) vacant.
3 [predic.] (in bridge and whist) having been dealt no cards in a particular suit.
▶**noun 1** a completely empty space: *the black void of space.*
■ an emptiness caused by the loss of something: *the void left by the collapse of Communism.* ■ an unfilled space in a wall, building, or structure.
2 (in bridge and whist) a suit in which a player is dealt no cards.
▶**verb** [with obj.] **1** chiefly US declare that (something) is not valid or legally binding: *the Supreme court voided the statute.*
2 discharge or drain away (water, gases, etc.).
■ chiefly Medicine excrete (waste matter). ■ [usu. as adj. **voided**] empty or evacuate (a container or space).
– DERIVATIVES **voidable** adjective, **voidness** noun.
– ORIGIN Middle English (in the sense 'unoccupied'): from a dialect variant of Old French *vuide*; related to Latin *vacare* 'vacate'; the verb partly a shortening of **AVOID**, reinforced by Old French *voider*.

voidance ▶**noun** [mass noun] the action of voiding something or the state of being voided: *the voidance of exhaust gases.*
■ [count noun] chiefly Law an annulment of a contract. ■ [count noun] Christian Church a vacancy in a benefice.
– ORIGIN late Middle English: from Old French, from the verb *voider* (see **VOID**).

voided ▶**adjective** Heraldry (of a bearing) having the central area cut away so as to show the field.

voila /vwʌˈlɑː/ ▶**exclamation** there it is; there you are: *'Voila!' she said, producing a pair of strappy white sandals.*
– ORIGIN French *voilà*.

voile /vɔɪl, vwɑːl/ ▶**noun** [mass noun] a thin, semi-transparent fabric of cotton, wool, or silk.
– ORIGIN late 19th cent.: French, literally 'veil'.

voir dire /ˌvwɑː ˈdɪə/ (also **voire dire**) ▶**noun** Law a preliminary examination of a witness by a judge or counsel.
– ORIGIN Law French, from Old French *voir* 'true' + *dire* 'say'.

voix celeste /ˌvwʌ səˈlɛst/ ▶**noun** French term for **VOX ANGELICA**.
– ORIGIN late 19th cent.: French, literally 'heavenly voice'.

Vojvodina /vɔɪˈvɒdɪnə/ a mainly Hungarian-speaking province of northern Serbia, on the Hungarian border; capital, Novi Sad.

vol. ▶**abbreviation for** volume.

Volans /ˈvəʊlənz/ Astronomy an inconspicuous southern constellation (the Flying Fish), between Carina and the south celestial pole.
■ [as genitive **Volantis** /və(ʊ)ˈlantɪs/] used with preceding letter or numeral to designate a star in this constellation: *the star Beta Volantis.*
– ORIGIN Latin, from the former name *Piscis Volans*.

volant /ˈvəʊlənt/ ▶**adjective** Zoology (of an animal) able to fly or glide: *newly volant young.*
■ of, relating to, or characterized by flight: *volant ways of life.* ■ [usu. postpositive] Heraldry represented as flying: *a falcon volant.* ■ poetic/literary moving rapidly or lightly: *her sails caught a volant wind.*
– ORIGIN mid 16th cent. (as a military term in the sense 'capable of rapid movement'): from French, literally 'flying', present participle of *voler*, from Latin *volare* 'to fly'.

Volapük /ˈvɒləˌp(j)uːk/ ▶**noun** [mass noun] an artificial language devised in 1879 for universal use by a German cleric, Johann M. Schleyer, and based on extremely modified forms of words from English and Romance languages, with complex inflections.
– ORIGIN from *vol* representing English *world* + *-a-* (as a connective) + *pük* representing English *speak* or *speech*.

volar /ˈvəʊlə/ ▶**adjective** Anatomy relating to the palm of the hand or the sole of the foot.
– ORIGIN early 19th cent.: from Latin *vola* 'hollow of hand or foot' + **-AR**[1].

volatile /ˈvɒlətʌɪl/ ▶**adjective 1** (of a substance) easily evaporated at normal temperatures.
2 liable to change rapidly and unpredictably, especially for the worse: *the political situation was becoming more volatile.*
■ (of a person) liable to display rapid changes of emotion. ■ (of a computer's memory) retaining data only as long as there is a power supply connected.
▶**noun** (usu. **volatiles**) a volatile substance.

– DERIVATIVES **volatility** noun.
– ORIGIN Middle English (in the sense 'creature that flies', also, as a collective, 'birds'): from Old French *volatil* or Latin *volatilis*, from *volare* 'to fly'.

volatile oil ▶ noun another term for **ESSENTIAL OIL**.

volatilize /və'latɪlʌɪz, 'vɒlətɪlʌɪz/ (also **-ise**) ▶ verb [with obj.] cause (a substance) to evaporate or disperse in vapour.
■ [no obj.] become volatile; evaporate.
– DERIVATIVES **volatilizable** adjective, **volatilization** noun.

vol-au-vent /'vɒlə(ʊ)vɒ̃/ ▶ noun a small round case of puff pastry filled with a savoury mixture, typically of meat or fish in a richly flavoured sauce.
– ORIGIN French, literally 'flight in the wind'.

volcanic ▶ adjective of, relating to, or produced by a volcano or volcanoes.
■ figurative (especially of a feeling or emotion) bursting out or liable to burst out violently: *the kind of volcanic passion she'd felt last night.*
– DERIVATIVES **volcanically** adverb.
– ORIGIN late 18th cent.: from French *volcanique*, from *volcan* (see **VOLCANO**).

volcanic bomb ▶ noun see **BOMB** (sense 2).

volcanic glass ▶ noun another term for **OBSIDIAN**.

volcanicity ▶ noun another term for **VOLCANISM**.

volcaniclastic /vɒlˌkanɪ'klastɪk/ ▶ adjective Geology relating to or denoting a clastic rock which contains volcanic material.

volcanic neck ▶ noun see **NECK** (sense 2).

volcanism /'vɒlkənɪz(ə)m/ (also **vulcanism**) ▶ noun [mass noun] Geology volcanic activity or phenomena.

volcano ▶ noun (pl. **-oes** or **-os**) a mountain or hill, typically conical, having a crater or vent through which lava, rock fragments, hot vapour, and gas are or have been erupted from the earth's crust.
■ figurative an intense suppressed emotion; a situation liable to burst out suddenly: *what volcano of emotion must have been boiling inside that youngster.*
– ORIGIN early 17th cent.: from Italian, from Latin *Volcanus* 'Vulcan'.

volcanology /ˌvɒlkə'nɒlədʒi/ (also **vulcanology**) ▶ noun [mass noun] the scientific study of volcanoes.
– DERIVATIVES **volcanological** adjective, **volcanologist** noun.

vole ▶ noun a small, typically burrowing, mouse-like rodent with a rounded muzzle, found in both Eurasia and North America.
• Subfamily Microtinae (or Arvicolinae), family Muridae: several genera, in particular *Microtus*, and numerous species.
– ORIGIN early 19th cent. (originally *vole-mouse*): from Norwegian *voll(mus)* 'field (mouse)'.

volet /'vɒleɪ/ ▶ noun a panel or wing of a triptych.
– ORIGIN mid 19th cent.: from French, literally 'shutter', from *voler* 'to fly'.

Volga /'vɒlgə/ the longest river in Europe, which rises in NW Russia and flows 3,688 km (2,292 miles) generally eastwards to Kazan, where it turns south-eastwards to the Caspian Sea. It has been dammed at several points to provide hydroelectric power, and is navigable for most of its length.

Volgograd /'vɒlgəgrad/ an industrial city in SW Russia, situated at the junction of the Don and Volga Rivers; pop. 1,005,000 (1990). Former names **TSARITSYN** (until 1925) and **STALINGRAD** (1925–61).

volition /və'lɪʃ(ə)n/ ▶ noun [mass noun] the faculty or power of using one's will: *without conscious volition she backed into her office.*
– PHRASES **of** (or **by** or **on**) **one's own volition** voluntarily: *they choose to leave early of their own volition.*
– DERIVATIVES **volitional** adjective, **volitionally** adverb, **volitive** adjective (formal or technical).
– ORIGIN early 17th cent. (denoting a decision or choice made after deliberation): from French, or from medieval Latin *volitio(n-)*, from *volo* 'I wish'.

volk /fɒlk/ ▶ noun (pl. **volke**) S. African a nation; a people.
■ [treated as pl.] people belonging to a particular group or country: *English-speaking volk.* ■ [treated as pl.] (among Afrikaans-speakers) coloured or black farm workers.
■ [treated as pl.] (**die/the volk**) the members of the Afrikaner nation.
– ORIGIN Dutch and Afrikaans.

Völkerwanderung /'fəːlkəˌvaːndərʊŋ, German 'fœlkɐˌvandərʊŋ/ ▶ noun a migration of peoples, especially that of Germanic and Slavic peoples into Europe from the 2nd to the 11th centuries.
– ORIGIN German, from *Völker* 'nations' + *Wanderung* 'migration'.

völkisch /'fəːlkɪs, German 'fœlkɪʃ/ (also **volkisch** /'fɒlkɪs/) ▶ adjective (of a person or ideology) populist or nationalist, and typically racist: *völkisch ideas and traditions.*
– ORIGIN German.

volley ▶ noun (pl. **-eys**) **1** a number of bullets, arrows, or other projectiles discharged at one time: *the infantry let off a couple of volleys.*
■ a series of utterances directed at someone in quick succession: *he unleashed a volley of angry questions.*
2 (in sport, especially tennis or soccer) a strike or kick of the ball made before it touches the ground.
▶ verb (**-eys**, **-eyed**) [with obj.] (in sport, especially tennis or soccer) strike or kick (the ball) before it touches the ground: *he volleyed home the cross.*
■ score (a goal) with such a shot. ■ utter or discharge in quick succession: *the dog was volleying joyful barks.*
– DERIVATIVES **volleyer** noun.
– ORIGIN late 16th cent.: from French *volée*, based on Latin *volare* 'to fly'.

volleyball ▶ noun [mass noun] a game for two teams, usually of six players, in which a large ball is hit by hand over a high net, the aim being to score points by making the ball reach the ground on the opponent's side of the court.

Vologda /'vɒləgdə/ a city in northern Russia; pop. 286,000 (1990).

Volos /'vɒlɒs/ a port on an inlet of the Aegean Sea, in Thessaly, eastern Greece; pop. 77,190 (1991). Greek name **VÓLOS** /'vɔlɔs/.

volplane /'vɒlpleɪn/ Aeronautics ▶ noun a controlled dive or downward flight at a steep angle, especially by an aeroplane with the engine shut off.
▶ verb [no obj., with adverbial of direction] (of an aeroplane) make such a dive or downward flight.
– ORIGIN early 20th cent.: from French *vol plané*, literally 'glided flight'.

vols ▶ abbreviation for volumes (in sense 1).

Volscian /'vɒlʃ(ə)n/ ▶ noun a member of an ancient Italic people who fought the Romans in Latium in the 5th and 4th centuries BC until absorbed into Rome after their final defeat in 304 BC.
▶ adjective of or relating to the Volscians.
– ORIGIN from Latin *Volsci* (the name of the people) + **-AN**.

Volstead Act /'vɒlstɛd/ a law which enforced alcohol prohibition in the US from 1920–33.
– ORIGIN named after Andrew J. *Volstead* (1860–1947), American legislator.

volt[1] /vəʊlt, vɒlt/ (abbrev.: **V**) ▶ noun the SI unit of electromotive force, the difference of potential that would carry one ampere of current against one ohm resistance.
– ORIGIN late 19th cent.: named after A. *Volta* (see **VOLTA**[2]).

volt[2] /vɒlt, vəʊlt/ ▶ noun variant spelling of **VOLTE**.
▶ verb [no obj.] Fencing make a quick movement to avoid a thrust.
– ORIGIN late 17th cent.: from French *volter* (see **VOLTE**).

Volta[1] /'vɒltə/ a river of West Africa, which is formed in central Ghana by the junction of its headwaters, the Black Volta, the White Volta, and the Red Volta, which rise in Burkina. At Akosombo in SE Ghana the river has been dammed, creating Lake Volta, one of the world's largest man-made lakes.

Volta[2] /'vɒltə/, Alessandro Giuseppe Antonio Anastasio, Count (1745–1827), Italian physicist. Volta is best known for the voltaic pile or electrochemical battery (1800), the first device to produce a continuous electric current.

voltage ▶ noun Physics an electromotive force or potential difference expressed in volts.

voltage clamp Physiology ▶ noun a constant electrical potential applied to a cell membrane, typically in order to measure ionic currents.
▶ verb (**voltage-clamp**) [with obj.] apply a voltage clamp to (a membrane, cell, etc.).

voltage divider ▶ noun a series of resistors or capacitors which can be tapped at any intermediate point to produce a specific fraction of the voltage applied between its ends.

Voltaic ▶ adjective & noun another term for **GUR**.

voltaic /vɒl'teɪɪk/ ▶ adjective of or relating to electricity produced by chemical action in a primary battery; galvanic.
– ORIGIN early 19th cent.: from the name of A. *Volta* (see **VOLTA**[2]) + **-IC**.

Voltaire /vɒl'tɛː, French vɔltɛʀ/ (1694–1778), French writer, dramatist, and poet; pseudonym of *François-Marie Arouet*. He was a leading figure of the Enlightenment, and frequently came into conflict with the Establishment as a result of his radical views and satirical writings. Notable works: *Lettres philosophiques* (1734) and the satire *Candide* (1759).

volte /vɒlt, vəʊlt/ (also **volt**) ▶ noun **1** Fencing a sudden quick jump or other movement to escape a thrust, especially a swinging round of the rear leg to turn the body sideways.
2 a movement performed in dressage and classical riding, in which a horse describes a circle of 6 yards diameter.
– ORIGIN late 17th cent. (as a fencing term): from French, from Italian *volta* 'a turn', from *volgere* 'to turn'. Sense 2 dates from the early 18th cent.

volte-face /vɒlt'fas, -'fɑːs/ ▶ noun an act of turning round so as to face in the opposite direction.
■ an abrupt and complete reversal of attitude, opinion, or position: *a remarkable volte-face on taxes.*
– ORIGIN early 19th cent.: from French, from Italian *voltafaccia*, based on Latin *volvere* 'to roll' + *facies* 'appearance, face'.

voltmeter ▶ noun an instrument for measuring electric potential in volts.

voluble /'vɒljʊb(ə)l/ ▶ adjective speaking or spoken incessantly and fluently: *she was as voluble as her husband was silent.*
– DERIVATIVES **volubility** noun, **volubleness** noun, **volubly** adverb.
– ORIGIN late 16th cent.: from French, or from Latin *volubilis*, from *volvere* 'to roll'. Earlier use in late Middle English included the senses 'rotating about an axis' and 'having a tendency to change', also meanings of the Latin word.

volume ▶ noun **1** a book forming part of a work or series.
■ a single book or a bound collection of printed sheets. ■ a consecutive sequence of issues of a periodical. ■ historical a scroll of parchment or papyrus containing written matter.
2 [mass noun] the amount of space that a substance or object occupies, or that is enclosed within a container, especially when great: *the sewer could not cope with the volume of rainwater* | [count noun] *a volume of air.*
■ the amount or quantity of something, especially when great: *changes in the volume of consumer spending.* ■ (**a volume of/volumes of**) a certain, typically large amount of something: *the volumes of data handled are vast.* ■ fullness or expansive thickness of something, especially of a person's hair.
3 [mass noun] quantity or power of sound; degree of loudness: *he turned the volume up on the radio.*
– ORIGIN late Middle English (originally denoting a roll of parchment containing written matter): from Old French *volum(e)*, from Latin *volumen* 'a roll', from *volvere* 'to roll'. An obsolete meaning 'size or extent (of a book)' gave rise to sense 2.

volumetric /ˌvɒljʊ'mɛtrɪk/ ▶ adjective of or relating to the measurement of volume.
■ (of chemical analysis) based on measuring the volumes of reagents, especially by titration.
– DERIVATIVES **volumetrically** adverb.
– ORIGIN mid 19th cent.: from **VOLUME** + **METRIC**[1].

volumetric efficiency ▶ noun the ratio of the volume of fluid actually displaced by a piston or plunger to its swept volume.

voluminous /və'ljuːmɪnəs/ ▶ adjective occupying or containing much space; large in volume, in particular:
■ (of clothing or drapery) loose and ample. ■ (of writing) very lengthy and full. ■ (of a writer) producing many books.
– DERIVATIVES **voluminously** adverb, **voluminousness** noun.
– ORIGIN early 17th cent.: partly from late Latin *voluminosus* 'having many coils', partly from Latin *volumen, volumin-* (see **VOLUME**).

volumize (also **-ise**) ▶ verb [with obj.] (of a product or styling technique) give body to (hair).
– DERIVATIVES **volumizer** noun.

voluntarism ▶ noun [mass noun] **1** the principle of relying on voluntary action (used especially with

V

reference to the involvement of voluntary organizations in social welfare).
■historical (especially in the 19th century) the principle that the Church or schools should be independent of the state and supported by voluntary contributions.
2 Philosophy the doctrine that the will is a fundamental or dominant factor in the individual or the universe.
– DERIVATIVES **voluntarist** noun & adjective.
– ORIGIN mid 19th cent.: formed irregularly from **VOLUNTARY**.

voluntary ▶ **adjective** done, given, or acting of one's own free will: *we are funded by voluntary contributions.*
■working, done, or maintained without payment: *a voluntary helper.* ■ Physiology under the conscious control of the brain. ■ Law (of a conveyance or disposition) made without return in money or other consideration.
▶ **noun** (pl. **-ies**) **1** an organ solo played before, during, or after a church service.
■historical a piece of music performed extempore, especially as a prelude to other music, or composed in a free style.
2 (in a competition) a special performance left to the performer's choice.
– DERIVATIVES **voluntarily** adverb, **voluntariness** noun.
– ORIGIN late Middle English: from Old French *volontaire* or Latin *voluntarius*, from *voluntas* 'will'.

voluntary-aided ▶ **adjective** (in the UK) denoting a voluntary school, funded mainly by the local authority.

voluntary-controlled ▶ **adjective** (in the UK) denoting a voluntary school fully funded by the local authority.

voluntaryism /ˈvɒlənt(ə)rɪˌɪz(ə)m/ ▶ **noun** less common term for **VOLUNTARISM** (in sense 1).
– DERIVATIVES **voluntaryist** noun.

voluntary school ▶ **noun** (in the UK) a school which, though not established by the local education authority, is funded mainly or entirely by it, and which typically encourages a particular set of religious beliefs.

Voluntary Service Overseas (abbrev.: **VSO**) a British charitable organization founded in 1958 to promote voluntary work in developing countries.

voluntary simplicity ▶ **noun** [mass noun] a philosophy or way of life that rejects materialism in favour of human and spiritual values, and is characterized by minimal consumption, environmental responsibility, and community cooperation.

volunteer ▶ **noun 1** a person who freely offers to take part in an enterprise or undertake a task.
■a person who works for an organization without being paid. ■ a person who freely enrols for military service rather than being conscripted, especially a member of a force formed by voluntary enrolment and distinct from the regular army. ■ a plant that has not been deliberately planted. ■ Law a person to whom a voluntary conveyance or deposition is made.
▶ **verb** [no obj.] freely offer to do something: *140 men and women volunteered for redundancy* | [with infinitive] *I rashly volunteered to be a contestant.*
■[with obj.] offer (help) in such a way: *he volunteered his services as a driver for the convoy.* ■ [reporting verb] say or suggest something without being asked: [with obj.] *it never paid to volunteer information* | [with direct speech] *'Her name's Louise,' Christina volunteered.* ■work for an organization without being paid. ■ [with obj.] commit (someone) to a particular undertaking, typically without consulting them: *he was volunteered for parachute training by friends.*
– ORIGIN late 16th cent. (as a noun, with military reference): from French *volontaire* 'voluntary'. The change in the ending was due to association with **-EER**.

volunteerism ▶ **noun** [mass noun] chiefly N. Amer. the use or involvement of volunteer labour, especially in community services.

Volunteer State informal name for **TENNESSEE**.

volupté /ˌvɒlʊpˈteɪ, French vɔlypte/ ▶ **noun** [mass noun] poetic/literary the quality of being voluptuous or sensual.
– ORIGIN French.

voluptuary /vəˈlʌptjʊəri/ ▶ **noun** (pl. **-ies**) a person devoted to luxury and sensual pleasure.
▶ **adjective** concerned with luxury and sensual pleasure: *a voluptuary decade when high living was in style.*
– ORIGIN early 17th cent.: from Latin *volupt(u)arius*, from *voluptas* 'pleasure'.

voluptuous /vəˈlʌptjʊəs/ ▶ **adjective** of, relating to, or characterized by luxury or sensual pleasure: *long curtains in voluptuous crimson velvet.*
■(of a woman) curvaceous and sexually attractive.
– DERIVATIVES **voluptuously** adverb, **voluptuousness** noun.
– ORIGIN late Middle English: from Old French *voluptueux* or Latin *voluptuosus*, from *voluptas* 'pleasure'.

volute /vəˈl(j)uːt/ ▶ **noun 1** Architecture a spiral scroll characteristic of Ionic capitals and also used in Corinthian and composite capitals.
2 a deep-water marine mollusc with a thick spiral shell which is colourful and prized by collectors.
• Family Volutidae, class Gastropoda: *Voluta* and other genera.
▶ **adjective** forming a spiral curve or curves: *spoked wheels with outside volute springs.*
– DERIVATIVES **voluted** adjective.
– ORIGIN mid 16th cent.: from French, or from Latin *voluta*, feminine past participle of *volvere* 'to roll'.

volution ▶ **noun 1** poetic/literary a rolling or revolving motion.
2 a single turn of a spiral or coil.
– ORIGIN late 15th cent.; from late Latin *volutio(n-)*, from Latin *volut-* 'rolled', from the verb *volvere*.

volva /ˈvɒlvə/ ▶ **noun** Botany (in certain fungi) a veil which encloses the fruiting body, often persisting after rupture as a sheath at the base of the stalk.
– ORIGIN mid 18th cent.: modern Latin, from Latin *volvere* 'to roll, wrap round'.

volvox /ˈvɒlvɒks/ ▶ **noun** Biology a green single-celled aquatic organism which forms minute free-swimming spherical colonies.
• Genus *Volvox*, division Chlorophyta (or phylum Chlorophyta, kingdom Protista).
– ORIGIN modern Latin, from Latin *volvere* 'to roll'.

volvulus /ˈvɒlvjʊləs/ ▶ **noun** (pl. **volvuli** /ˈvɒlvjʊlʌɪ, -liː/ or **volvuluses**) Medicine an obstruction caused by twisting of the stomach or intestine.
– ORIGIN late 17th cent.: modern or medieval Latin, from Latin *volvere* 'to roll'.

Volzhsky /ˈvɒlʒski/ an industrial city in SW Russia, on the Volga; pop. 275,000 (1990).

vomer /ˈvəʊmə/ ▶ **noun** Anatomy the small thin bone separating the left and right nasal cavities in humans and most vertebrates.
– ORIGIN early 18th cent.: from Latin, literally 'ploughshare' (because of the shape).

vomit ▶ **verb** (**vomited**, **vomiting**) [no obj.] eject matter from the stomach through the mouth: *the sickly stench made him want to vomit* | [with obj.] *she used to* **vomit up** *her food.*
■[with obj.] emit (something) in an uncontrolled stream or flow: *the machine vomited fold after fold of paper.*
▶ **noun 1** [mass noun] matter vomited from the stomach.
2 archaic an emetic.
– DERIVATIVES **vomiter** noun.
– ORIGIN late Middle English: from Old French *vomite* (noun) or Latin *vomitus*, from *vomere* 'to vomit'.

vomitorium /ˌvɒmɪˈtɔːrɪəm/ ▶ **noun** (pl. **vomitoria** /-rɪə/) **1** each of a series of entrance or exit passages in an ancient Roman amphitheatre or theatre.
2 a place in which, according to popular misconception, the ancient Romans are supposed to have vomited during feasts to make room for more food.
– ORIGIN Latin.

vomitory /ˈvɒmɪt(ə)ri/ ▶ **adjective 1** denoting the entrance or exit passages in a theatre or amphitheatre.
2 rare relating to or inducing vomiting.
▶ **noun** (pl. **-ies**) another term for **VOMITORIUM** (in sense 1).
– ORIGIN early 17th cent.: from Latin *vomitorius*, based on *vomere* 'to vomit', partly as an Anglicization of Latin *vomitorium* (see **VOMITORIUM**).

vomitous ▶ **adjective** chiefly N. Amer. nauseating.

vomitus /ˈvɒmɪtəs/ ▶ **noun** [mass noun] chiefly Medicine matter that has been vomited.
– ORIGIN early 20th cent.: from Latin.

von Braun see **BRAUN**[3].

Vonnegut /ˈvɒnɪgət/, Kurt (b.1922), American novelist and short-story writer. His works blend elements of realism, science fiction, fantasy, and satire, and include *Slaughterhouse-Five* (1969).

von Neumann see **NEUMANN**.

von Recklinghausen's disease /ˈrɛklɪŋˌhaʊz(ə)nz/ ▶ **noun** [mass noun] **1** a hereditary disease in which numerous benign tumours develop in various parts of the body, especially the skin and the fibrous sheaths of the nerves. It is a form of neurofibromatosis.
2 a disease in which the bones are weakened as a result of excessive secretion of the parathyroid hormone, leading to bowing and fracture of long bones and sometimes deformities of the chest and spine. Also called ***osteitis fibrosa cystica***.
– ORIGIN early 20th cent.: named after Friedrich *von Recklinghausen* (1833–1910), German pathologist.

von Sternberg /ˈstəːnbəːg/, Josef (1894–1969), Austrian-born American film director. His best-known film *Der Blaue Engel* (1930; *The Blue Angel*) made Marlene Dietrich an international star.

von Willebrand's disease /ˈwɪləbrand/ ▶ **noun** [mass noun] Medicine an inherited disorder characterized by a tendency to bleed, caused by deficiency or abnormality of a plasma coagulation factor (**von Willebrand factor**).
– ORIGIN 1940s: named after Erik A. *von Willebrand* (1870–1949), Finnish physician.

voodoo ▶ **noun** [mass noun] a black religious cult practised in the Caribbean and the southern US, combining elements of Roman Catholic ritual with traditional African magical and religious rites, and characterized by sorcery and spirit possession.
■[count noun] a person skilled in such practice.
▶ **verb** (**voodoos**, **voodooed**) [with obj.] affect (someone) by the practice of such witchcraft.
– DERIVATIVES **voodooism** noun, **voodooist** noun.
– ORIGIN early 19th cent.: from Louisiana French, from Kwa *vodũ*.

Voortrekker /ˈfʊə(r)ˌtrɛkə(r)/ ▶ **noun** S. African historical a member of one of the groups of Dutch-speaking people who migrated by wagon from the Cape Colony into the interior from 1836 onwards, in order to live beyond the borders of British rule.
■a member of an Afrikaner youth movement similar to the Boy Scouts and Girl Guides. ■ a person who explores or initiates new areas of thought and action; a pioneer.
– ORIGIN Afrikaans, from Dutch *voor* 'fore' + *trekken* 'to travel'.

VOR ▶ **abbreviation for** VHF omnirange, denoting a type of navigation system using a series of radio beacons.

voracious /vəˈreɪʃəs/ ▶ **adjective** wanting or devouring great quantities of food: *he had a voracious appetite.*
■having a very eager approach to an activity: *his voracious reading of literature.*
– DERIVATIVES **voraciously** adverb, **voraciousness** noun, **voracity** noun.
– ORIGIN mid 17th cent.: from Latin *vorax*, *vorac-* (from *vorare* 'devour') + **-IOUS**.

Vorarlberg /ˈfɔːˌrɑːlbəːg, German ˈfoːɐˌarlbɛrk/ an Alpine state of western Austria; capital, Bregenz.

Voronezh /vəˈrɒnɛʒ/ a city in Russia, south of Moscow; pop. 895,000 (1990).

Voroshilovgrad /ˌvɒrəˈʃiːləfgrad/ former name (1935–58 and 1970–91) for **LUHANSK**.
– ORIGIN named in honour of Marshal Kliment *Voroshilov* (1881–1969), Soviet military and political leader.

-vorous /v(ə)rəs/ ▶ **combining form** feeding on a specified food: *carnivorous* | *herbivorous*.
– DERIVATIVES **-vora** /v(ə)rə/ combining form in corresponding names of groups, **-vore** /vɔː/ combining form in corresponding names of individuals within such groups.
– ORIGIN from Latin *-vorus* (from *vorare* 'devour') + **-OUS**.

Vorstellung /ˈfɔːˌʃtɛlʊŋ, German ˈfoːɐˌʃtɛlʊŋ/ ▶ **noun** (pl. **Vorstellungen** /-ˌʃtɛlʊŋ(ə)n/) Philosophy a mental image or idea produced by prior perception of an object, as in memory or imagination, rather than by actual perception.
– ORIGIN German.

vortex /ˈvɔːtɛks/ ▶ **noun** (pl. **vortexes** or **vortices** /-tɪsiːz/) a mass of whirling fluid, especially a whirlpool or whirlwind.
■figurative something regarded as a whirling mass: *a swirling vortex of emotions.*
– DERIVATIVES **vortical** adjective, **vortically** adverb, **vorticity** /vɔːˈtɪsɪti/ noun, **vorticose** adjective, **vorticular** /vɔːˈtɪkjʊlə/ adjective.

V

– ORIGIN mid 17th cent.: from Latin *vortex, vortic-,* literally 'eddy', variant of **VERTEX**.

vorticella /ˌvɔːtɪˈsɛlə/ ▶ noun Zoology a sedentary, single-celled aquatic animal with a contractile stalk and a bell-shaped body bearing a ring of cilia.
● Genus *Vorticella,* phylum Ciliophora, kingdom Protista.
– ORIGIN late 18th cent.: modern Latin, diminutive of Latin *vortex, vortic-* 'eddy'.

Vorticist /ˈvɔːtɪsɪst/ ▶ noun historical a member of a British artistic movement of 1914–15 influenced by cubism and futurism and favouring machine-like forms.
– DERIVATIVES **Vorticism** noun.
– ORIGIN from Latin *vortex, vortic-* 'eddy' + **-IST**.

Vosges /vəʊʒ/ a mountain system of eastern France, in Alsace near the border with Germany.

Vostok /ˈvɒstɒk/ a series of six manned Soviet orbiting spacecraft, the first of which, launched in April 1961, carried the first man in space (Yuri Gagarin).

votary /ˈvəʊt(ə)ri/ ▶ noun (pl. **-ies**) a person, such as a monk or nun, who has made vows of dedication to religious service.
■ a devoted follower, adherent, or advocate of someone or something: *he was a votary of John Keats.*
– DERIVATIVES **votarist** noun.
– ORIGIN mid 16th cent.: from Latin *vot-* 'vowed' (from the verb *vovere*) + **-ARY**[1].

vote ▶ noun a formal indication of a choice between two or more candidates or courses of action, expressed typically through a ballot or a show of hands.
■ an act of expressing such an indication of choice: *they are ready to put it to a vote.* ■ (**the vote**) the choice expressed collectively by a body of electors or by a specified group: *the nationalist vote in Northern Ireland.* ■ (**the vote**) the right to indicate a choice in an election.
▶ verb [no obj.] give or register a vote: *they voted against the resolution* | [with complement] *I voted Labour.*
■ [with obj. and adverbial or complement] cause (someone) to gain or lose a particular post or honour by means of a vote: *incompetent judges are voted out of office.* ■ [with clause] informal used to express a wish to follow a particular course of action: *I vote we have one more game.* ■ [with obj.] (of a legislature) grant or confer by vote. ■ [with obj.] (**vote something down**) reject (something) by means of a vote.
– PHRASES **vote of confidence** a vote showing that a majority continues to support the policy of a leader or governing body. **vote of no confidence** (or **vote of censure**) a vote showing that a majority does not support the policy of a leader or governing body. **vote with one's feet** informal indicate an opinion by being present or absent or by some other course of action.
– DERIVATIVES **voteless** adjective.
– ORIGIN late Middle English: from Latin *votum* 'a vow, wish', from *vovere* 'to vow'. The verb dates from the mid 16th cent.

vote bank ▶ noun (in the Indian subcontinent) a group of people who can be relied upon to vote together in support of the same party.

voter ▶ noun a person who votes or has the right to vote at an election.

voting booth ▶ noun US term for **POLLING BOOTH**.

voting machine ▶ noun (especially in the US) a machine for the automatic registering of votes.

votive ▶ adjective offered or consecrated in fulfilment of a vow: *votive offerings.*
▶ noun an object offered in this way, such as a candle used as a vigil light.
– ORIGIN late 16th cent.: from Latin *votivus,* from *votum* (see **VOTE**). The original sense was 'expressing a desire', preserved in **VOTIVE MASS**.

votive Mass ▶ noun (in the Roman Catholic Church) a Mass celebrated for a special purpose or occasion.

Votyak /ˈvɒtjak/ ▶ noun former term for **UDMURT** (the language).

vouch ▶ verb [no obj.] (**vouch for**) assert or confirm as a result of one's own experience the truth or accuracy of (something): *the explosive used is of my own formulation, and I can vouch for its efficiency.*
■ confirm the identity or good character of (someone): *he was refused entrance until someone could vouch for him.*
– ORIGIN Middle English (as a legal term in the sense 'summon (a person) to court to prove title to

property'): from Old French *voucher* 'summon', based on Latin *vocare* 'to call'.

voucher /ˈvaʊtʃə/ ▶ noun a small printed piece of paper that entitles the holder to a discount, or that may be exchanged for goods or services.
■ a receipt.
– ORIGIN early 17th cent.: from **VOUCH**.

vouchsafe ▶ verb [with two objs] (often **be vouchsafed**) give or grant (something) to (someone) in a gracious or condescending manner: *it is a blessing vouchsafed him by heaven.*
■ [with obj.] reveal or disclose (information): *you'd never vouchsafed that interesting titbit before.*
– ORIGIN Middle English: originally as the phrase *vouch something safe* on someone, i.e. 'warrant the secure conferment of (something on someone)'.

voulu /vuˈluː, French vuly/ ▶ adjective poetic/literary lacking in spontaneity; contrived.
– ORIGIN French, literally 'wanted, wished', past participle of *vouloir.*

voussoir /ˈvuːswɑː/ ▶ noun Architecture a wedge-shaped or tapered stone used to construct an arch.
– ORIGIN early 18th cent: via French from popular Latin *volsorium,* based on Latin *volvere* 'to roll'. The word, borrowed from Old French, was also used for a time in late Middle English.

Vouvray /ˈvuːvreɪ, French vuvrɛ/ ▶ noun [mass noun] dry white wine, either still or sparkling, produced in the Vouvray district of the Loire Valley.
– ORIGIN French.

vow ▶ noun a solemn promise.
■ (**vows**) a set of such promises committing one to a prescribed role, calling, or course of action, typically to marriage or a monastic career.
▶ verb **1** [reporting verb] solemnly promise to do a specified thing: [with clause] *he vowed that his government would not tolerate a repeat of the disorder* | [with direct speech] *one fan vowed, 'I'll picket every home game'.*
2 [with obj.] archaic dedicate to someone or something, especially a deity: *I vowed myself to this enterprise.*
– ORIGIN Middle English: from Old French *vou,* from Latin *votum* (see **VOTE**); the verb from Old French *vouer.*

vowel ▶ noun a speech sound which is produced by comparatively open configuration of the vocal tract, with vibration of the vocal cords but without audible friction, and which is a unit of the sound system of a language than forms the nucleus of a syllable. Contrasted with **CONSONANT**.
■ a letter representing such a sound, such as *a, e, i, o, u.*
– DERIVATIVES **vowelled** (US **voweled**) adjective [usu. in combination], **vowelless** adjective, **vowelly** adjective.
– ORIGIN Middle English: from Old French *vouel,* from Latin *vocalis* (*littera*) 'vocal (letter)'.

vowel gradation ▶ noun another term for **ABLAUT**.

vowel harmony ▶ noun [mass noun] the phenomenon in some languages, e.g. Turkish, for all the vowels in a word to be members of the same sub-class, for example all front vowels or all back vowels.

vowel height ▶ noun [mass noun] Phonetics the degree to which the tongue is raised or lowered in the articulation of a particular vowel.

vowelize (also **-ise**) ▶ verb [with obj.] supply (something such as a Hebrew or shorthand text) with vowel points or signs representing vowels.

vowel point ▶ noun each of a set of marks indicating vowels in writing phonetically explicit text in Semitic languages such as Hebrew and Arabic.

vowel shift ▶ noun Phonetics a phonetic change in a vowel or vowels.
■ (**the Great Vowel Shift**) a series of changes between medieval and modern English affecting the long vowels of the standard language.

vox angelica /ˌvɒks anˈdʒɛlɪkə/ ▶ noun a soft stop on an organ or harmonium which is tuned slightly sharp to produce a tremolo effect.
– ORIGIN mid 19th cent.: from late Latin, literally 'angelic voice'.

voxel /ˈvɒksɛl/ ▶ noun (in computer-based modelling or graphic simulation) each of an array of elements of volume that constitute a notional three-dimensional space, especially each of an array of discrete elements into which a representation of a three-dimensional object is divided.

– ORIGIN 1970s: from the initial letters of **VOLUME** and **ELEMENT**, with the insertion of -x- for ease of pronunciation.

vox humana /hjuːˈmɑːnə/ ▶ noun an organ stop with a tone supposedly resembling the human voice.
– ORIGIN early 18th cent.: from Latin, literally 'human voice'.

vox pop ▶ noun [mass noun] Brit. informal popular opinion as represented by informal comments from members of the public, especially when broadcast or published: *paragraphs of vox pop.*
– ORIGIN 1960s: abbreviation of **VOX POPULI**.

vox populi /ˈpɒpjʊliː, -lʌɪ/ ▶ noun [in sing.] the opinions or beliefs of the majority.
– ORIGIN mid 16th cent.: from Latin, literally 'the people's voice'.

voyage ▶ noun a long journey involving travel by sea or in space: *a six-year voyage to Jupiter* | figurative *writing a biography is a voyage of discovery.*
▶ verb [no obj., with adverbial of direction] go on a long journey, typically by sea or in space: *he has voyaged through places like Venezuela and Peru.*
■ [with obj.] archaic sail over or along (a sea or river).
– DERIVATIVES **voyageable** adjective (archaic), **voyager** noun.
– ORIGIN Middle English (as a noun denoting a journey): from Old French *voiage,* from Latin *viaticum* 'provisions for a journey' (in late Latin 'journey').

Voyager either of two American space probes launched in 1977 to investigate the outer planets. Voyager 1 encountered Jupiter and Saturn, while Voyager 2 reached Jupiter, Saturn, Uranus, and finally Neptune (1989).

voyageur /ˌvwajaˈʒəː, ˌvɔɪə-/ ▶ noun historical (in Canada) a boatman employed by the fur companies in transporting goods and passengers to and from the trading posts on the lakes and rivers.
– ORIGIN French, literally 'voyager', from *voyager* 'to travel'.

voyeur /vwʌˈjəː, vɔɪ-/ ▶ noun a person who gains sexual pleasure from watching others when they are naked or engaged in sexual activity.
■ a person who enjoys seeing the pain or distress of others.
– DERIVATIVES **voyeurism** noun, **voyeuristic** adjective, **voyeuristically** adverb.
– ORIGIN early 20th cent.: from French, from *voir* 'see'.

VP ▶ abbreviation for Vice-President.

VPL informal ▶ abbreviation for visible panty line.

VR ▶ abbreviation for ■ Queen Victoria. [ORIGIN: abbreviation of Latin *Victoria Regina.*] ■ variant reading. ■ virtual reality.

VRAM ▶ noun Electronics a type of RAM used in computer display cards.
– ORIGIN 1990s: abbreviation of *video RAM.*

VRML Computing ▶ abbreviation for virtual reality modelling language.

vroom informal ▶ verb [no obj.] (of an engine in a vehicle) make a roaring sound by being run at very high speed.
■ [with obj.] cause (an engine in a vehicle) to make such a sound in this way. ■ [no obj., with adverbial of direction] (of a vehicle or its driver) travel at great speed: *she still had the car and she would vroom up at midnight.*
▶ noun the roaring sound of an engine or motor vehicle.
▶ exclamation used to express or imitate such a sound to suggest speed or acceleration: *press the ignition button and vroom!*
– ORIGIN 1960s: imitative.

vrouw /vraʊ/ (also **vrow**) ▶ noun [usu. as title] chiefly S. African a woman or wife, especially of Dutch origin.
– ORIGIN Dutch.

VS ▶ abbreviation for Veterinary Surgeon.

vs ▶ abbreviation for versus.

V-sign ▶ noun **1** Brit. a sign resembling the letter V made with the first two fingers pointing up and the back of the hand facing outwards, used as a gesture of abuse or contempt.
2 a similar sign made with the palm of the hand facing outwards, used as a symbol or gesture of victory.

VSO ▶ abbreviation for Voluntary Service Overseas.

VSOP ▶ abbreviation for Very Special Old Pale, a kind of brandy.

VT ▶ abbreviation for Vermont (in official postal use).

Vt ▶ abbreviation for Vermont.

VTO ▶ abbreviation for vertical take-off.

VTOL ▶ abbreviation for vertical take-off and landing.

VTR ▶ abbreviation for videotape recorder.

vug /vʌg/ ▶ noun Geology a cavity in rock, lined with mineral crystals.
– DERIVATIVES **vuggy** adjective, **vugular** adjective.
– ORIGIN early 19th cent.: from Cornish *vooga*.

Vuillard /ˈvwiːɑː, French vwijaʀ/, (Jean) Édouard (1868–1940), French painter and graphic artist. A member of the Nabi Group, he produced decorative panels, murals, paintings, and lithographs, particularly of domestic interiors and portraits.

Vulcan Roman Mythology the god of fire. Greek equivalent **HEPHAESTUS**.

Vulcanian /vʌlˈkeɪnɪən/ ▶ adjective Geology relating to or denoting a type of volcanic eruption marked by periodic explosive events.
– ORIGIN early 20th cent.: from *Vulcano*, the name of a volcano in the Lipari Islands, Italy, + -**IAN**.

vulcanism /ˈvʌlkənɪz(ə)m/ ▶ noun variant spelling of **VOLCANISM**.

vulcanite /ˈvʌlkənʌɪt/ ▶ noun [mass noun] hard, black vulcanized rubber.
– ORIGIN mid 19th cent.: from **VULCAN** + -**ITE**[1].

vulcanize /ˈvʌlkənʌɪz/ (also -**ise**) ▶ verb [with obj.] harden (rubber or rubber-like material) by treating it with sulphur at a high temperature.
– DERIVATIVES **vulcanizable** adjective, **vulcanization** noun, **vulcanizer** noun.
– ORIGIN early 19th cent. (in the sense 'throw into a fire'): from **VULCAN** + -**IZE**.

vulcanology ▶ noun variant spelling of **VOLCANOLOGY**.

vulgar ▶ adjective lacking sophistication or good taste; unrefined: *a vulgar check suit.*
■ making explicit and offensive reference to sex or bodily functions; coarse and rude: *a vulgar joke.*
■ dated characteristic of or belonging to the masses.
– DERIVATIVES **vulgarity** noun (pl. -**ies**), **vulgarly** adverb.
– ORIGIN late Middle English: from Latin *vulgaris*, from *vulgus* 'common people'. The original senses were 'used in ordinary calculations' (surviving in **VULGAR FRACTION**) and 'in ordinary use, used by the people' (surviving in **VULGAR TONGUE**).

vulgar fraction ▶ noun Brit. a fraction expressed by numerator and denominator, not decimally.

vulgarian /vʌlˈgɛːrɪən/ ▶ noun an unrefined person, especially one with newly acquired power or wealth.

vulgarism ▶ noun a word or expression that is considered inelegant, especially one that makes explicit and offensive reference to sex or bodily functions.
■ archaic an instance of rude or offensive behaviour.

vulgarize (also -**ise**) ▶ verb [with obj.] make less refined: *her voice, vulgarized by its accent, was full of caressing tones.*
■ make commonplace or less subtle or complex: [as adj. **vulgarized**] *a vulgarized version of the argument.*
– DERIVATIVES **vulgarization** noun.

vulgar Latin ▶ noun [mass noun] informal Latin of classical times.

vulgar tongue ▶ noun (**the vulgar tongue**) dated the national or vernacular language of a people (used typically to contrast such a language with Latin).

Vulgate /ˈvʌlgeɪt, -gət/ ▶ noun **1** the principal Latin version of the Bible, prepared mainly by St Jerome in the late 4th century, and (as revised in 1592) adopted as the official text for the Roman Catholic Church.
2 (**vulgate**) [in sing.] formal common or colloquial speech: *I required a new, formal language in which to address him, not the vulgate.*
– ORIGIN from Latin *vulgata* (*editio*(*n-*)) '(edition) prepared for the public', feminine past participle of *vulgare*, from *vulgus* 'common people'.

vuln /vʌln/ ▶ verb [with obj.] Heraldry wound.
– ORIGIN late 16th cent.: formed irregularly from Latin *vulnerare* 'to wound'.

vulnerable ▶ adjective exposed to the possibility of being attacked or harmed, either physically or emotionally: *we were in a vulnerable position | small fish are vulnerable to predators.*
■ Bridge (of a partnership) liable to higher penalties, either by convention or through having won one game towards a rubber.
– DERIVATIVES **vulnerability** noun (pl. -**ies**), **vulnerableness** noun, **vulnerably** adverb.
– ORIGIN early 17th cent.: from late Latin *vulnerabilis*, from Latin *vulnerare* 'to wound', from *vulnus* 'wound'.

vulnerary /ˈvʌln(ə)rəri/ archaic ▶ adjective (of a drug, plant, etc.) of use in the healing of wounds.
▶ noun (pl. -**ies**) a medicine of this kind.
– ORIGIN late 16th cent.: from Latin *vulnerarius*, from *vulnus* 'wound'.

Vulpecula /vʌlˈpɛkjʊlə/ Astronomy an inconspicuous northern constellation (the Fox), lying in the Milky Way between Cygnus and Aquila.
■ [as genitive **Vulpeculae** /-liː/] used with preceding letter or numeral to designate a star in this constellation: *the star Alpha Vulpeculae.*
– ORIGIN Latin, diminutive of *vulpes* 'fox'.

vulpine /ˈvʌlpʌɪn/ ▶ adjective of or relating to a fox or foxes.
■ crafty; cunning: *Karl gave a vulpine smile.*
– ORIGIN early 17th cent.: from Latin *vulpinus*, from *vulpes* 'fox'.

vulture /ˈvʌltʃə/ ▶ noun **1** a large bird of prey with the head and neck more or less bare of feathers, feeding chiefly on carrion and reputed to gather with others in anticipation of the death of a sick or injured animal or person.
● Order Accipitriformes: the **Old World vultures** (family Accipitridae, especially *Gyps* and *Aegypius*) and the **New World vultures** (with the condors in the family Cathartidae).
2 a contemptible person who preys on or exploits others.
– DERIVATIVES **vulturine** /-rʌɪn/ adjective, **vulturish** adjective, **vulturous** adjective.
– ORIGIN late Middle English: from Anglo-Norman French *vultur*, from Latin *vulturius*.

vulva /ˈvʌlvə/ ▶ noun Anatomy the female external genitals.
■ Zoology the external opening of the vagina or reproductive tract in a female mammal or nematode.
– DERIVATIVES **vulval** adjective, **vulvar** adjective.
– ORIGIN late Middle English: from Latin, literally 'womb'.

vulvitis /vʌlˈvʌɪtɪs/ ▶ noun [mass noun] Medicine inflammation of the vulva.

VV. ▶ abbreviation for ■ verses. ■ volumes.

Vyatka /ˈvjɑːtkə/ an industrial town in north central European Russia, on the Vyatka River; pop. 487,000 (1990). Former name (1934–92) **KIROV**.

vygie /ˈfeɪxi/ ▶ noun (pl. -**ies**) S. African another term for **MESEMBRYANTHEMUM**.
– ORIGIN 1920s: from Afrikaans, from Dutch *vyg* 'fig' + the diminutive suffix -*ie*.

vying present participle of **VIE**.

Ww

W¹ (also **w**) ▶ **noun** (pl. **Ws** or **W's**) **1** the twenty-third letter of the alphabet.
  ■denoting the next after V in a set of items, categories, etc.
  2 a shape like that of a letter W: [in combination] *the W-shaped northern constellation of Cassiopeia.*

W² ▶ **abbreviation for** ■ (in tables of sports results) games won. ■ watt(s). ■ West or Western: *104° W | W Europe.* ■ Cricket (on scorecards) wicket(s). ■ women's (clothes size).
  ▶ **symbol for** ■ the chemical element tungsten. [ORIGIN: from modern Latin *wolframium.*]

w ▶ **abbreviation for** ■ weight. ■ Cricket (on scorecards) wide(s). ■ with.

WA ▶ **abbreviation for** ■ Washington (State) (in official postal use). ■ Western Australia.

Wa /wɑː/ ▶ **noun** (pl. same or **Was**) **1** a member of a hill people living on the borders of China and Burma (Myanmar).
  2 [mass noun] the language of this people, belonging to the Mon-Khmer family.
  ▶ **adjective** of, relating to, or denoting this people or their language.

Waadt /vɑːt/ German name for **VAUD**.

Waaf /waf/ ▶ **noun** (in the UK) a member of the Women's Auxiliary Air Force (1939–48, subsequently reorganized as part of the Women's Royal Air Force).
  – ORIGIN acronym.

Waal /vɑːl/ a river of the south central Netherlands. The most southerly of two major distributaries of the Rhine, it flows for 84 km (52 miles) from the point where the Rhine forks, just west of the border with Germany, to the estuary of the Meuse (Maas) on the North Sea.

wabbit /ˈwabɪt/ ▶ **adjective** [predic.] Scottish exhausted; slightly unwell: *I'm feeling a bit wabbit.*
  – ORIGIN late 19th cent.: of unknown origin.

wabi /ˈwabi/ ▶ **noun** [mass noun] (in Japanese art) a quality of austere and serene beauty expressing a mood of spiritual solitude recognized in Zen Buddhist philosophy.
  – ORIGIN Japanese, literally 'solitude'.

waboom /ˈvɑːbʊəm/ ▶ **noun** S. African a protea with large pale yellow flowers and reddish timber.
  ● *Protea nitida*, family Proteaceae.
  – ORIGIN from South African Dutch *wagenboom,* literally 'wagon tree', so named by colonists who found the wood suitable for making felloes.

WAC ▶ **abbreviation for** (in the US) Women's Army Corps.

wack¹ ▶ **noun** Brit. informal used as a familiar term of address, chiefly in Liverpool.
  – ORIGIN 1960s: of unknown origin.

wack² informal, chiefly US ▶ **noun 1** a crazy or eccentric person.
  2 [mass noun] worthless or stupid work, or talk; rubbish: *this track is a load of wack.*
  ▶ **adjective** bad; inferior: *a wack radio station.*
  – ORIGIN 1930s: probably a back-formation from **WACKY**.

wacke /ˈwakə/ ▶ **noun** [mass noun] Geology a sandstone of which the mud matrix in which the grains are embedded amounts to between 15 and 75 per cent of the mass.
  – ORIGIN early 19th cent.: from German, from Middle High German *wacke* 'large stone', Old High German *wacko* 'pebble'.

wacked ▶ **adjective** variant spelling of **WHACKED**.

wacko (also **whacko**) informal, chiefly N. Amer. ▶ **adjective** mad; insane: *wacko fundamentalists.*
  ▶ **noun** (pl. **-os** or **-oes**) a crazy person.
  – ORIGIN 1970s: from **WACKY** + **-O**.

wacky (also **whacky**) ▶ **adjective** (**wackier**, **wackiest**) informal funny or amusing in a slightly odd or peculiar way: *a wacky chase movie.*
  – DERIVATIVES **wackily** adverb, **wackiness** noun.
  – ORIGIN mid 19th cent. (originally dialect): from the noun **WHACK** + **-Y¹**.

wacky baccy ▶ **noun** [mass noun] Brit. informal cannabis.

wad /wɒd/ ▶ **noun 1** a lump or bundle of a soft material, used for padding, stuffing, or wiping: *a wad of lint-free rag.*
  ■chiefly historical a disc of felt or another material used to keep powder or shot in place in a gun barrel. ■ a portion of tobacco or another narcotic when used for chewing. ■ Brit., chiefly military slang a bun, cake, sandwich, or other piece of food.
  2 a bundle of paper, banknotes, or documents: *a wad of A5 paper.*
  ■informal a large amount of something, especially money: *she was working on TV and had wads of money.* ■ [mass noun] informal money.
  ▶ **verb** (**wadded**, **wadding**) [with obj.] [usu. as adj. **wadded**] **1** compress (a soft material) into a lump or bundle: *a knob of wadded lint.*
  2 line or stuff (a garment or piece of furniture) with wadding: *a pair of wadded socks.*
  ■stop up (an aperture or a gun barrel) with a bundle or lump of soft material: *he had something wadded behind his teeth.*
  – ORIGIN mid 16th cent. (denoting wadding): perhaps related to Dutch *watten,* French *ouate* 'padding, cotton wool'.

wada ▶ **noun** variant spelling of **VADA**.

wadcutter ▶ **noun** chiefly US a bullet designed to cut a neat hole in a paper range target.

wadding ▶ **noun** [mass noun] soft, thick material used to line garments or pack fragile items, especially cotton wool formed into a fleecy layer.
  ■a material from which wads for guns are made.

waddle ▶ **verb** [no obj., with adverbial of direction] walk with short steps and a clumsy swaying motion: *three geese waddled across the road.*
  ▶ **noun** [in sing.] a waddling gait: *I walk with a waddle.*
  – DERIVATIVES **waddler** noun.
  – ORIGIN late 16th cent.: perhaps a frequentative of **WADE**.

waddy /ˈwɒdi/ ▶ **noun** (pl. **-ies**) an Australian Aboriginal's war club.
  ■Austral./NZ a club or stick, especially a walking stick.
  – ORIGIN from Dharuk *wadi* 'tree, stick, club'.

Wade¹, George (1673–1748), English soldier. He was responsible for the construction of a network of roads and bridges in the Scottish Highlands to facilitate government control of the Jacobite clans after the 1715 uprising.

Wade², (Sarah) Virginia (b.1945), English tennis player. She won many singles titles, including the US Open (1968), the Italian championship (1971), the Australian Open (1972), and Wimbledon (1977).

wade ▶ **verb** [no obj., with adverbial] walk through water or another liquid or soft substance: *in the absence of any jetty we waded ashore.*
  ■[with obj.] walk through (something filled with water): *I had waded ditches instead of attempting to find easier crossing places.* ■ (**wade through**) read laboriously through (a long piece of writing). ■ (**wade into**) informal get involved in (something) vigorously or forcefully: *Seb waded into the melee and started to beat off the boys.* ■ (**wade into**) informal attack (someone) physically or in argument: *Vincent waded into his father with such anger.* ■ (**wade in**) informal make a vigorous attack or intervention: *Nicola waded in and grabbed the baby.*
  ▶ **noun** [in sing.] an act of wading.
  – DERIVATIVES **wadable** (also **wadeable**) adjective.
  – ORIGIN Old English *wadan* 'move onward', also 'penetrate', from a Germanic word meaning 'go (through)', from an Indo-European root shared by Latin *vadere* 'go'.

Wade–Giles ▶ **noun** a system of romanized spelling for transliterating Chinese, devised by the British diplomat Sir Thomas Francis Wade (1818–95), professor of Chinese at Cambridge, and modified by his successor Herbert Allen Giles (1845–1935). It has been largely superseded by Pinyin.

wader ▶ **noun 1** a person or animal, especially a bird, that wades, in particular:
  ■chiefly Brit. a wading bird of the order Charadriiformes, which comprises the sandpipers, plovers, and their allies. Also called **SHOREBIRD**, especially in North America. ■ chiefly N. Amer. a wading bird of the order Ciconiiformes, which comprises the herons, storks, and their allies.
  2 (**waders**) high waterproof boots, or a waterproof garment for the legs and body, used especially by anglers when fishing.

wadi /ˈwɑːdi, ˈwɒdi/ (also **wady**) ▶ **noun** (pl. **wadis** or **wadies**) (in certain Arabic-speaking countries) a valley, ravine, or channel that is dry except in the rainy season.
  – ORIGIN early 17th cent.: from Arabic *wādī.*

Wadi Halfa /ˌwɒdi ˈhalfə, ˌwɑːdi/ a town in northern Sudan, on the border with Egypt. It is situated on the Nile at the southern end of Lake Nasser and is the terminus of the railway from Khartoum.

wading pool ▶ **noun** North American term for **PADDLING POOL**.

WAF ▶ **abbreviation for** (in the US) Women in the Air Force.
  ▶ **noun** a member of the WAF.

wafer ▶ **noun** a very thin light crisp sweet biscuit, especially one of a kind eaten with ice cream.
  ■a thin disc of unleavened bread used in the Eucharist. ■ (also **wafer seal**) a disc of red paper stuck on a legal document as a seal. ■ Electronics a very thin slice of a semiconductor crystal used as the substrate for solid-state circuitry. ■ historical a small disc of dried paste formerly used for fastening letters or holding papers together. ■ a round, thin piece of something: *a wafer of turf.*

▶ **verb** [with obj.] rare fasten or seal (a letter, document, etc.) with a wafer.
– DERIVATIVES **wafery** adjective.
– ORIGIN late Middle English: from an Anglo-Norman French variant of Old French *gaufre* (see **GOFFER**), from Middle Low German *wāfel* 'waffle'; compare with **WAFFLE**[2].

wafer-thin ▶ **adjective** & **adverb** very thin or thinly: [as adj.] *plates of wafer-thin metal* | [as adv.] *slicing meats wafer-thin*.

Waffen SS /ˈvaf(ə)n/ ▶ **noun** (**the Waffen SS**) the combat units of the SS in Nazi Germany during the Second World War.
– ORIGIN German *Waffen* 'armed'.

waffle[1] informal ▶ **verb** [no obj.] **1** chiefly Brit. speak or write, especially at great length, without saying anything important or useful: *he waffled on about everything that didn't matter.*
2 US fail to make up one's mind: *Joseph had been waffling over where to go.*
▶ **noun 1** [mass noun] chiefly Brit. lengthy but trivial or useless talk or writing.
2 US a failure to make up one's mind: *his waffle on abortion.*
– DERIVATIVES **waffler** noun, **waffly** adjective.
– ORIGIN late 17th cent. (originally in the sense 'yap, yelp'): frequentative of dialect *waff* 'yelp', of imitative origin.

waffle[2] ▶ **noun** a small crisp batter cake, baked in a waffle iron and eaten hot with butter or syrup.
▶ **adjective** denoting a style of fine honeycomb weaving or a fabric woven to give a honeycomb effect.
– ORIGIN mid 18th cent.: from Dutch *wafel*; compare with **WAFER** and **GOFFER**.

waffle iron ▶ **noun** a utensil, typically consisting of two shallow metal pans hinged together, used for baking waffles.

waft /wɒft, wɑːft/ ▶ **verb** pass or cause to pass easily or gently through or as if through the air: [no obj., with adverbial of direction] *the smell of stale fat wafted out from the cafe* | [with obj., and adverbial of direction] *each breeze would waft pollen round the house.*
▶ **noun 1** a gentle movement of air.
■ a scent or odour carried on such a movement of air.
2 (also **weft**) Nautical, historical a knotted ensign, garment, etc. displayed by a ship as a signal. [ORIGIN: Perhaps related to Scots and northern *waff* 'a signal, waving of something in the hand', a variant of **WAVE**.]
– ORIGIN early 16th cent. (in the sense 'escort (a ship)'): back-formation from obsolete *wafter* 'armed convoy vessel', from Low German, Dutch *wachter*, from *wachten* 'to guard'. A sense 'convey by water' gave rise to the current use of the verb.

WAG ▶ **abbreviation for** Gambia (international vehicle registration).
– ORIGIN from *West Africa Gambia.*

wag[1] ▶ **verb** (**wagged**, **wagging**) (with reference to an animal's tail) move or cause to move rapidly to and fro: [no obj.] *his tail began to wag* | [with obj.] *the dog went out, wagging its tail.*
■ [with obj.] move (an upwards-pointing finger) from side to side to signify a warning or reprimand: *she wagged a finger at Elinor.* ■ [no obj.] (used of a tongue, jaw, or chin, as representing a person) talk, especially in order to gossip or spread rumours: *this is a small island and tongues are beginning to wag.*
▶ **noun** a single rapid movement from side to side: *a chirpy wag of the head.*
– PHRASES **how the world wags** dated how affairs are going or being conducted. **the tail wags the dog** see **TAIL**[1].
– ORIGIN Middle English (as a verb): from the Germanic base of Old English *wagian* 'to sway'.

wag[2] ▶ **noun 1** dated a person who makes facetious jokes.
2 Austral./NZ informal a truant: *Boogie plays the wag from school.*
– ORIGIN mid 16th cent. (denoting a young man or mischievous boy, also used as a term of endearment to an infant): probably from obsolete *waghalter* 'person likely to be hanged' (see **WAG**[1], **HALTER**).

wage ▶ **noun** (usu. **wages**) a fixed regular payment, typically paid on a daily or weekly basis, made by an employer to an employee, especially to a manual or unskilled worker: *we were struggling to get better wages.* Compare with **SALARY**.
■ (**wages**) Economics the part of total production that is

the return to labour as earned income as distinct from the remuneration received by capital as unearned income. ■ figurative the result or effect of doing something considered wrong or unwise: *disasters are the wages of sin.*
▶ **verb** [with obj.] carry on (a war or campaign): *it is necessary to destroy their capacity to wage war.*
– ORIGIN Middle English: from Anglo-Norman French and Old Northern French, of Germanic origin; related to **GAGE**[1] and **WED**.

waged ▶ **adjective** having or relating to regular paid employment: *a larger class of waged workers.*

wage drift ▶ **noun** [mass noun] the tendency for the average level of wages actually paid to rise above wage rates through increases in overtime and other factors.

wager ▶ **noun** & **verb** more formal term for **BET**.
– ORIGIN Middle English (also in the sense 'solemn pledge'): from Anglo-Norman French *wageure*, from *wager* 'to wage'.

wager of battle ▶ **noun** historical a form of trial by which someone's guilt or innocence was decided by personal combat between the parties or their champions.

wager of law ▶ **noun** historical a form of trial in which the defendant was required to produce witnesses who would swear to his or her innocence.

wages council ▶ **noun** (in the UK) one of a number of statutory bodies, now abolished, consisting of workers' and employers' representatives responsible for determining wages in particular industries.

wage slave ▶ **noun** informal a person who is wholly dependent on income from employment, typically employment of an arduous or menial nature.
– DERIVATIVES **wage slavery** noun.

Wagga Wagga /ˌwɒgə ˈwɒgə/ a town on the Murrumbidgee River, in New South Wales, SE Australia; pop. 40,875 (1991).

waggery ▶ **noun** (pl. **-ies**) [mass noun] dated waggish behaviour or remarks; jocularity.
■ [count noun] archaic a waggish action or remark.

waggish ▶ **adjective** dated humorous in a playful, mischievous, or facetious manner: *a waggish riposte.*
– DERIVATIVES **waggishly** adverb, **waggishness** noun.

waggle ▶ **verb** informal move or cause to move with short quick movements from side to side or up and down: [no obj.] *his arm waggled* | [with obj.] *Mary waggled a glass at them.*
■ [with obj.] swing (a golf club) loosely to and fro over the ball before playing a shot.
▶ **noun** an act of waggling.
– ORIGIN late 16th cent.: frequentative of **WAG**[1].

waggle dance ▶ **noun** a waggling movement performed by a honeybee at the hive or nest, to indicate to other bees the direction and distance of a source of food.

waggler ▶ **noun** Fishing a type of long float designed to be especially sensitive to movement of the bait, chiefly used in semi-still water.

waggly ▶ **adjective** moving with quick short movements from side to side or up and down: *a waggly tail.*

wag-'n-bietjie /ˈvaxəˌbiki/ ▶ **noun** S. African any of a number of shrubs bearing strong curved thorns, in particular:
● a plant related to asparagus (genus *Asparagus*, family Liliaceae, in particular *A. capensis*). ● a wait-a-bit.
– ORIGIN late 18th cent.: from Afrikaans, literally 'wait a bit'.

Wagner /ˈvɑːgnə/, (Wilhelm) Richard (1813–83), German composer. He developed an operatic genre which he called music drama, synthesizing music, drama, verse, legend, and spectacle. Notable works: *The Flying Dutchman* (opera, 1841), *Der Ring des Nibelungen* (a cycle of four operas, 1847–74), *Tristan and Isolde* (music drama, 1859), and the *Siegfried Idyll* (1870).
– DERIVATIVES **Wagnerian** adjective & noun.

Wagner tuba ▶ **noun** a brass instrument of baritone pitch with an oval shape and upward-pointing bell, combining features of the tuba and the French horn and first used in Wagner's *Der Ring des Nibelungen.*

wagon (Brit. also **waggon**) ▶ **noun 1** a vehicle used for transporting goods or another specified purpose: *a timber wagon* | *a breakdown wagon.*

■ a four-wheeled trailer for agricultural use. ■ Brit. a railway freight vehicle; a truck. ■ a light horse-drawn vehicle, especially a covered one used by early settlers in North America and elsewhere. ■ chiefly N. Amer. a wheeled cart or hut used as a food stall. ■ a vehicle like a caravan used by gypsies or circus performers. ■ informal short for **STATION WAGON**.
– PHRASES **hitch one's wagon to a star** see **HITCH**. **on the wagon** informal teetotal: *Agnes was thinking of going on the wagon again.*
– ORIGIN late 15th cent.: from Dutch *wagen*; related to **WAIN**.

wagoner (Brit. also **waggoner**) ▶ **noun** the driver of a horse-drawn wagon.
– ORIGIN mid 16th cent.: from Dutch *wagenaar*, from *wagen* (see **WAGON**).

wagonette (Brit. also **waggonette**) ▶ **noun** a four-wheeled horse-drawn pleasure vehicle, typically open, with facing side seats and one or two seats arranged crosswise in front.

wagon-lit /ˌvagɔ̃ˈliː/, French *vagɔli/ ▶ **noun** (pl. **wagons-lits** pronunc. same) a sleeping car on a Continental railway.
– ORIGIN French.

wagonload ▶ **noun** an amount of something that can be carried in one wagon: *a wagonload of food.*

wagon-roof (also **wagon-vault**) ▶ **noun** another term for **BARREL VAULT**.

wagon train ▶ **noun** historical a convoy or train of covered horse-drawn wagons, as used by pioneers or settlers in North America.

wagtail ▶ **noun** a slender Eurasian and African songbird with a long tail that is frequently wagged up and down, typically living by water. See also **WILLY WAGTAIL**.
● Family Motacillidae: two genera, in particular *Motacilla*, and several species.

wah ▶ **exclamation** Indian used to express admiration or anger.
– ORIGIN from Hindi *vāh*.

wahey /wəˈheɪ/ ▶ **exclamation** used to express delight, pleasure, or exhilaration.
– ORIGIN 1970s: imitative.

Wahhabi /wəˈhɑːbi/ (also **Wahabi**) ▶ **noun** (pl. **Wahabis**) a member of a strictly orthodox Sunni Muslim sect founded by Muhammad ibn Abd al-Wahhab (1703–92). It advocates a return to the early Islam of the Koran and Sunna, rejecting later innovations; the sect is still the predominant religious force in Saudi Arabia.
– DERIVATIVES **Wahhabism** noun.

wahine /wɑːˈhiːni/ ▶ **noun** NZ a Maori woman or wife.
– ORIGIN Maori.

wahoo[1] /wɑːˈhuː/ ▶ **noun 1** (also **wahoo elm**) a North American elm which yields useful timber. [ORIGIN: perhaps from Creek *ahá-hwa* 'walnut'.]
● *Ulmus alata*, family Ulmaceae.
2 a North American spindle tree. [ORIGIN: from Dakota.]
● Genus *Euonymus*, family Celastraceae: two species.
3 a large predatory tropical marine fish of the mackerel family, prized as a game fish. [ORIGIN: early 20th cent.: of unknown origin.]
● *Acanthocybium solanderi*, family Scombridae.

wahoo[2] /wɑːˈhuː/ ▶ **exclamation** N. Amer. another word for **YAHOO**[2].
– ORIGIN 1940s: probably a natural exclamation.

wah-wah (also **wa-wa**) ▶ **noun** [mass noun] a musical effect achieved on brass instruments by alternately applying and removing a mute and on an electric guitar by controlling the output from the amplifier with a pedal.
■ [count noun] a pedal for producing such an effect on an electric guitar.
– ORIGIN 1920s: imitative.

waiata /ˈwaɪətə/ ▶ **noun** a Maori song.
– ORIGIN Maori.

waif ▶ **noun** a homeless and helpless person, especially a neglected or abandoned child: *she is foster-mother to various waifs and strays.*
■ an abandoned pet animal.
– DERIVATIVES **waifish** adjective.
– ORIGIN late Middle English: from an Anglo-Norman French variant of Old Northern French *gaif*, probably of Scandinavian origin. Early use was often in *waif and stray*, as a legal term denoting a piece of property found and, if unclaimed, falling to the lord of the manor.

Waikato /waɪˈkɑːtəʊ/ the longest river of New

Zealand, which flows 434 km (270 miles) generally north-westwards from Lake Taupo, at the centre of North Island, to the Tasman Sea.

Waikiki /ˈwʌɪkɪˌkiː/ a Hawaiian beach resort, a suburb of Honolulu, on the island of Oahu, in Hawaii.

wail ▶ **noun** a prolonged high-pitched cry of pain, grief, or anger: *Christopher let out a wail.*
■ a sound resembling this: *the wail of an air-raid siren.*
▶ **verb** [no obj.] give such a cry of pain, grief, or anger: *Tina ran off wailing* | [with direct speech] *'But why?' she wailed.*
■ make a sound resembling such a cry: *the wind wailed and buffeted the timber structure.* ■ [with obj.] poetic/literary manifest or feel deep sorrow for; lament: *she wailed her wretched life.*
– DERIVATIVES **wailer** noun, **wailful** adjective (poetic/literary), **wailingly** adverb.
– ORIGIN Middle English: from Old Norse; related to **WOE**.

Wailing Wall a high wall in Jerusalem said to stand on the site of Herod's temple, where Jews traditionally pray and lament on Fridays.

Wain, John (Barrington) (1925–94), English writer and critic. One of the Angry Young Men of the early 1950s, he was later professor of poetry at Oxford (1973–8).

wain ▶ **noun** archaic a wagon or cart.
■ (**the Wain**) short for **CHARLES'S WAIN**.
– ORIGIN Old English *wæg(e)n*, of Germanic origin; related to Dutch *wagen* and German *Wagen*, also to **WAY** and **WEIGH**[1].

wainscot /ˈweɪnskɒt/ ▶ **noun 1** [in sing.] an area of wooden panelling on the lower part of the walls of a room.
■ [mass noun] Brit. historical imported oak of fine quality, used mainly to make panelling.
2 a drab yellowish to brown-coloured European moth.
● *Mythimna* and other genera, family Noctuidae: several species.
▶ **verb** (**wainscoted**, **wainscoting** or **wainscotted**, **wainscotting**) [with obj.] line (a room or wall) with wooden panelling.
– ORIGIN Middle English: from Middle Low German *wagenschot*, apparently from *wagen* 'wagon' + *schot*, probably meaning 'partition'. Sense 2 dates from the early 19th cent.

wainscoting (also **wainscotting**) ▶ **noun** [mass noun] wooden panelling that lines the lower part of the walls of a room.
■ material for such panelling.

wainwright ▶ **noun** historical a wagon-builder.

WAIS Computing ▶ **abbreviation for** wide area information service, designed to provide access to information across a computer network.

waist ▶ **noun** the part of the human body below the ribs and above the hips.
■ the circumference of this: *her waist has reduced from 35 to 28 inches.* ■ a narrowing of the trunk of the body at this point: *the last time you had a waist was around 1978.* ■ the part of a garment encircling or covering the waist. ■ the point at which a garment is shaped so as to narrow between the ribcage and the hips: *a jacket with a high waist.* ■ US a blouse or bodice. ■ a narrow part in the middle of anything, such as a violin, an hourglass, the body of a wasp, etc. ■ the middle part of a ship, between the forecastle and the quarterdeck.
– DERIVATIVES **waisted** adjective [in combination] *high-waisted*, **waistless** adjective.
– ORIGIN late Middle English: apparently representing an Old English word from the Germanic root of **WAX**[2].

waistband ▶ **noun** a strip of cloth forming the waist of a garment such as a skirt or a pair of trousers.

waist cloth ▶ **noun** a loincloth.

waistcoat /ˈweɪs(t)kəʊt, ˈwɛskɪt/ ▶ **noun** Brit. a close-fitting waist-length garment, typically having no sleeves or collar and buttoning down the front, worn especially by men over a shirt and under a jacket.

waist-deep (also **waist-high**) ▶ **adjective** & **adverb** of or at a depth to reach the waist: [as adj.] *the waist-deep water* | [as adv.] *Ellwood stood waist-high in the water.*
■ of or at a height to reach the waist: [as adj.] *a ruin surrounded by waist-high grass and nettles.*

waistline ▶ **noun** an imaginary line around a person's body at the waist, especially with respect to its size: *eliminating inches from the waistline.*
■ the shaping and position of the waist of a garment. ■ an imaginary line around a car or other vehicle at the level of the bottom of the windows.

wait ▶ **verb** [no obj.] **1** stay where one is or delay action until a particular time or until something else happens: *he did not wait for a reply* | *Vera did not* ***wait on*** *a Home Office ruling* | [with infinitive] *Ben stood on the street corner waiting to cross* | [with obj.] *I had to wait my turn to play.*
■ remain in readiness for some purpose: *he found the funicular car waiting on the platform.* ■ be left until a later time before being dealt with: *we shall need a statement later, but that will have to wait.* ■ [with obj.] informal defer (a meal) until a person's arrival: *he will wait supper for me.* ■ [usu. as noun **waiting**] (of a vehicle) remain parked for a short time at the side of a road: *Holmes admitted parking a car in a no-waiting zone.* ■ (**wait on/upon**) await the convenience of: *to see the full series, we will have to wait on the BBC.*
2 (**cannot wait**) used to indicate that one is eagerly impatient to do something or for something to happen: *I can't wait for tomorrow* | [with infinitive] *I can't wait to get started again.*
3 act as a waiter or waitress, serving food and drink: *a local man was employed to* ***wait on*** *them at table* | [with obj.] *we had to wait tables in the mess hall.*
▶ **noun 1** [in sing.] a period of waiting: *we had a long wait.*
2 (**waits**) Brit. archaic street singers of Christmas carols.
■ historical official bands of musicians maintained by a city or town.
– PHRASES **in wait** watching for an enemy or potential victim and preparing to attack them: *he decided to* ***lie in wait for*** *the thief.* **wait and see** wait to find out what will happen before doing or deciding something. **wait for it** Brit. informal do not act before the proper moment: *patrol—wait for it—halt!* **you wait** used to convey a threat, warning, or promise: *you wait until your Dad gets in!*
▶ **wait on** (or **upon**) **1** act as an attendant to (someone): *a maid was appointed to wait on her.* ■ archaic pay a respectful visit to. **2** Austral./NZ & N. English informal not do a particular thing until something else happens: *wait on, I've an important message for you.* ■ be patient.
wait up 1 not go to bed until someone arrives or something happens. **2** N. Amer. go more slowly or stop until someone catches up.
– ORIGIN Middle English: from Old Northern French *waitier*, of Germanic origin; related to **WAKE**[1]. Early senses included 'lie in wait (for)', 'observe carefully', and 'be watchful'.

wait-a-bit (also **wait-a-bit thorn**) ▶ **noun** chiefly S. African an African bush with hooked thorns that catch the clothing, in particular an acacia.
– ORIGIN translating Afrikaans **WAG-'N-BIETJIE**.

Waitangi, Treaty of /wʌɪˈtaŋi/ a treaty signed in 1840 at the settlement of Waitangi in New Zealand, which formed the basis of the British annexation of New Zealand. Subsequent contraventions of the treaty by the British led to the Maori Wars.

Waitangi Day ▶ **noun** the anniversary of the signing of the Treaty of Waitangi, celebrated as a public holiday in New Zealand on 6 February since 1960.

waiter ▶ **noun 1** a man whose job is to serve customers at their tables in a restaurant.
2 a person who waits for a time, event, or opportunity.
3 a small tray; a salver.

waiting ▶ **noun** [mass noun] **1** the action of staying where one is or delaying action until a particular time or until something else happens.
2 the action or occupation of working as a waiter or waitress.
3 official attendance at court. See also **LADY-IN-WAITING**.

waiting game ▶ **noun** a tactic in which one refrains from action for a time in order to act more effectively at a later date or stage: *policemen were last night playing a waiting game outside a country cottage.*

waiting list ▶ **noun** a list of people waiting for something, especially housing or admission to a hospital or school.

waiting room ▶ **noun** a room provided for the use of people who are waiting to be seen by a doctor or dentist or who are waiting in a station for a bus or train.

wait list ▶ **noun** North American term for **WAITING LIST**.
▶ **verb** (**wait-list**) [with obj.] put (someone) on a waiting list.

waitperson ▶ **noun** chiefly US a waiter or waitress (used as a neutral alternative).

waitress ▶ **noun** a woman whose job is to serve customers at their tables in a restaurant.

waitressing ▶ **noun** [mass noun] the action or occupation of working as a waitress.

waitron ▶ **noun** US a waiter or waitress (used as a neutral alternative).

waitstaff ▶ **noun** [treated as sing. or pl.] US waiters and waitresses collectively.

wait state ▶ **noun** the condition of computer software or hardware being unable to process further instructions while waiting for some event such as the completion of a data transfer.

waive ▶ **verb** [with obj.] refrain from insisting on or using (a right or claim): *he will waive all rights to the money.*
■ refrain from applying or enforcing (a rule, restriction, or fee): *her tuition fees would be waived.*
– ORIGIN Middle English (originally as a legal term relating to removal of the protection of the law): from an Anglo-Norman French variant of Old French *gaiver* 'allow to become a waif, abandon'.

waiver ▶ **noun** an act or instance of waiving a right or claim.
■ a document recording such waiving of a right or claim.

Wajda /ˈvʌɪdə/, Andrzej (b.1929), Polish film director. Notable films: *Ashes and Diamonds* (1958), *Man of Iron* (1981), and *Danton* (1983).

waka /ˈwaka/ ▶ **noun** NZ a traditional Maori canoe.
– ORIGIN Maori.

Wakamba /waˈkambə/ plural form of **KAMBA**.

wakame /ˈwakameɪ/ ▶ **noun** [mass noun] an edible brown seaweed used, typically in dried form, in Chinese and Japanese cookery.
● *Undaria pinnitafida*, class Phaeophyceae.
– ORIGIN Japanese.

Wakashan /waˈkaʃ(ə)n/ ▶ **adjective** of, relating to, or denoting a small family of almost extinct American Indian languages of the northern Pacific coast, including Kwakiutl and Nootka.
▶ **noun** [mass noun] this family of languages.
– ORIGIN from Nootka *waukash* 'good' (said to have been applied to the people by Captain Cook) + **-AN**.

wake[1] ▶ **verb** (past **woke** or US, dialect, or archaic **waked**; past participle **woken** or US, dialect, or archaic **waked**) **1** emerge or cause to emerge from a state of sleep; stop sleeping: [no obj.] *she* ***woke up*** *feeling better* | [with obj.] *I wake him gently.*
■ [no obj.] (**wake up to**) become alert to or aware of: *he needs to wake up to reality.* ■ [with obj.] figurative cause (something) to stir or come to life: *it wakes desire in others.*
2 [with obj.] dialect, chiefly Irish or US hold a vigil beside (someone who has died): *we waked Jim last night.*
▶ **noun 1** a watch or vigil held beside the body of someone who has died, sometimes accompanied by ritual observances including eating and drinking.
2 (**wakes**) [treated as sing.] chiefly historical (in some parts of the UK) a festival and holiday held annually in a rural parish, originally on the feast day of the patron saint of the church. [ORIGIN: probably from Old Norse *vaka*.]
– PHRASES **wake up and smell the coffee** [usu. in imperative] informal, chiefly N. Amer. become aware of the realities of a situation, however unpleasant.
– DERIVATIVES **waker** noun.
– ORIGIN Old English (recorded only in the past tense *wōc*), also partly from the weak verb *wacian* 'remain awake, hold a vigil', of Germanic origin; related to Dutch *waken* and German *wachen*; compare with **WATCH**.

wake[2] ▶ **noun** a trail of disturbed water or air left by the passage of a ship or aircraft.
■ figurative used to refer to the aftermath or consequences of something: *the committee was set up* ***in the wake of*** *the inquiry.*
– ORIGIN late 15th cent. (denoting a track made by a person or thing): probably via Middle Low German from Old Norse *vǫk*, *vaka* 'hole or opening in ice'.

wakeboarding ▶ **noun** [mass noun] the sport of

W

riding on a short, wide board resembling a surfboard and performing acrobatic manoeuvres while being towed behind a motor boat.
– DERIVATIVES **wakeboard** noun.
– ORIGIN 1990s: from **WAKE**[2], on the pattern of *surfboarding*.

Wakefield a town in northern England, a unitary council formerly in Yorkshire; pop. 75,840 (1981).

wakeful ▶ **adjective** (of a person) unable or not needing to sleep: *he had been wakeful all night*.
■ alert and vigilant. ■ (of a period of time) passed with little or no sleep: *wakeful nights*.
– DERIVATIVES **wakefully** adverb, **wakefulness** noun.

waken ▶ **verb** poetic/literary term for **WAKE**[1] (in sense 1).
– ORIGIN Old English *wæcnan* 'be aroused', of Germanic origin; related to **WAKE**[1].

wake-robin ▶ **noun** **1** Brit. another term for **CUCKOO PINT**.
2 N. Amer. another term for **TRILLIUM**.

wake-up ▶ **noun** [in sing.] an instance of a person waking up or being woken up.
– PHRASES **be a wake-up** Austral./NZ informal be fully alert or aware: *I'm a wake-up to you*.

wake-up call ▶ **noun** chiefly N. Amer. a telephone call notifying the person called that a previously agreed time to wake up has arrived.
■ figurative a person or thing that causes people to become fully alert to an unsatisfactory situation and to take action to remedy it: *today's statistics will be a wake-up call for the administration*.

wakey-wakey ▶ **exclamation** informal used to rouse or wake someone.
– ORIGIN 1940s: reduplicated extension of the verb **WAKE**[1].

Wakhan Salient /wəˈkɑːn/ a narrow corridor of land, 300 km in length, in the north-eastern corner of Afghanistan.

waking ▶ **noun** [mass noun] the state of being awake: *he hangs between sleeping and waking*.

wakizashi /ˌwakɪˈzaʃi/ ▶ **noun** (pl. same) a Japanese sword shorter than a katana.
– ORIGIN Japanese, from *waki* 'side' + *sasu* 'wear at one's side'.

Waksman /ˈwaksmən/, Selman Abraham (1888–1973), Russian-born American microbiologist. He discovered the antibiotic streptomycin, used especially against tuberculosis. Nobel Prize for Physiology or Medicine (1952).

WAL ▶ **abbreviation for** Sierra Leone (international vehicle registration).
– ORIGIN from *West Africa Leone*.

Walachia variant spelling of **WALLACHIA**.

Waldenses /wɒlˈdɛnsiːz/ ▶ **plural noun** a puritan religious sect based originally in southern France, now chiefly in Italy and America, founded *c.*1170 by Peter Valdes (d.1205), a merchant of Lyons.
– DERIVATIVES **Waldensian** adjective & noun.

Waldheim /ˈvaldhʌɪm, German ˈvalthaɪm/, Kurt (b.1918), Austrian diplomat and statesman, President 1986–92. He was Secretary General of the United Nations 1972–81. During the presidential election campaign of 1986 he denied allegations that as an army intelligence officer he had had direct knowledge of Nazi atrocities during the Second World War.

waldo /ˈwɔːldəʊ/ ▶ **noun** (pl. **-oes**) a remote-controlled device for handling objects.
– ORIGIN 1940s: named after *Waldo* F. Jones, a fictional inventor described by Robert Heinlein in a science-fiction story.

Waldorf salad /ˈwɔːldɔːf/ ▶ **noun** a salad made from apples, walnuts, celery, and mayonnaise.
– ORIGIN named after the *Waldorf*-Astoria Hotel in New York, where it was first served.

waldrapp /ˈwɔːldrap/ ▶ **noun** an ibis with a bare red head and mainly dark metallic green plumage, now breeding only in Morocco.
• *Geronticus eremita*, family Threskiornithidae. Alternative names: **hermit ibis**, **bald ibis**.
– ORIGIN 1920s: from German, from *Wald* 'forest' + *Rapp*, variant of *Rabe* 'raven'.

Waldsterben /ˈvaltˌʃtɛːb(ə)n, German ˈvaltˌʃtɛrbn/ ▶ **noun** [mass noun] disease and death in forest trees in central Europe as a result of atmospheric pollution.
– ORIGIN 1980s: from German, from *Wald* 'forest' + *Sterben* 'death'.

wale ▶ **noun** **1** a ridge on a textured woven fabric such as corduroy.
2 Nautical a horizontal wooden strip fitted as strengthening to a boat's side.
3 a horizontal band around a woven basket.
– ORIGIN late Old English *walu* 'stripe, weal'.

wale knot (also **wall knot**) ▶ **noun** a knot made at the end of a rope by intertwining strands to prevent unravelling or act as a stopper.

Waler /ˈweɪlə/ ▶ **noun** **1** a horse of a light breed from Australia, especially from New South Wales.
2 informal a native or inhabitant of Australia, especially New South Wales.

Wales a principality of Great Britain and the United Kingdom, to the west of central England; pop. 2,798,200 (1991); capital, Cardiff. Welsh name **CYMRU**.

> The Celtic inhabitants of Wales successfully maintained independence against the Anglo-Saxons who settled in England following the withdrawal of the Romans. Norman colonization from England began in the 12th century, and their control over the country was assured by Edward I's conquest (1277–84). Edward began the custom of making the English sovereign's eldest son Prince of Wales. Wales was formally brought into the English legal and parliamentary system by Henry VIII (1536), but has retained a distinct cultural identity. In 1997 a referendum narrowly approved proposals for a Welsh assembly, which was inaugurated in 1999.

Wales, Prince of see **PRINCE OF WALES**; **CHARLES, PRINCE**.

Wałęsa /vaˈwɛnsə/, Lech (b.1943), Polish trade unionist and statesman, President 1990–5. The founder of Solidarity (1980), he was imprisoned 1981–2 after the movement was banned. After Solidarity's landslide victory in the 1989 elections he became President. Nobel Peace Prize (1983).

wali /ˈwɑːliː/ ▶ **noun** the governor of a province in an Arab country.
– ORIGIN from Arabic (*al-*)*wālī*.

walk ▶ **verb** **1** [no obj., usu. with adverbial] move at a regular and fairly slow pace by lifting and setting down each foot in turn, never having both feet off the ground at once: *I walked across the lawn* | *she turned and walked a few paces*.
■ use similar movements but of a different part of one's body or a support: *he could walk on his hands carrying a plate on one foot*. ■ go on foot for recreation and exercise: *you can walk in 21,000 acres of mountain and moorland*. ■ [with obj.] travel along or over (a route or area) on foot: *the police department has encouraged officers to walk the beat*. ■ (of a quadruped) proceed with the slowest gait, always having at least two feet on the ground at once. ■ [with obj.] ride (a horse) at this pace: *he walked his horse towards her*. ■ informal (of a thing) go missing (typically used to suggest that it has been stolen): *anything walks if it is not properly secured and locked*. ■ N. Amer. informal abandon or suddenly withdraw from a job, commitment, or situation. ■ N. Amer. informal be released from suspicion or from a charge: *had any of the others come clean during the trial, he might have walked*. ■ used to suggest that someone has achieved a state or position easily or undeservedly: *no one has the right to walk straight into a well-paid job for life*. ■ (of a ghost) be present and visible: *the ghosts of Bannockburn walked abroad*. ■ archaic used to describe the way in which someone lives or behaves: *walk humbly with your God*. ■ Cricket (of a batsman) leave the field without waiting to be given out by the umpire. ■ Baseball reach first base automatically after not hitting at four balls pitched outside the strike zone. ■ [with obj.] Baseball allow or enable (a batter) to do this.
2 [with obj. and adverbial of direction] cause or enable (someone or something) to walk or move as though walking: *she walked her fingers over the dresses*.
■ guide, accompany, or escort (someone) on foot: *he walked her home to her door* | figurative *a meeting to walk parents through the complaint process*. ■ [with obj.] take (a domestic animal, typically a dog) out for exercise: *she spotted a man walking his retriever*. ■ [with obj.] train and look after (a hound puppy).
▶ **noun** **1** an act of travelling or an excursion on foot: *he was too restless to sleep, so he went out for a walk*.
■ [in sing.] used to indicate the time that it will take someone to reach a place on foot or the distance that they must travel: *the library is within five minutes' walk*. ■ a route recommended or marked out for recreational walking. ■ a path. ■ chiefly Brit. the round followed by a postman. ■ a part of a forest under one keeper. ■ the place where a gamecock is kept. ■ chiefly Brit. a farm where a hound puppy is sent for training and to accustom it to various surroundings.
2 [in sing.] an unhurried rate of movement on foot: *they crossed the field at a leisurely walk*.
■ the slowest gait of an animal. ■ a person's manner of walking: *the spring was back in his walk*.
3 Baseball an instance of reaching first base automatically after not hitting at four balls pitched outside the strike zone.
– PHRASES **walk all over** informal treat in a thoughtless, disrespectful, and exploitative manner: *you don't want to let the cops walk all over you*. ■ defeat easily. **walk before one can run** grasp the basic skills before attempting something more difficult. **walking encyclopedia** (also **walking dictionary**) informal a person who has an impressive knowledge of facts or words. **walk the boards** see **BOARD**. **walk it** **1** make a journey on foot rather than riding or in a vehicle. **2** informal achieve a victory easily. **walk Matilda** see **MATILDA**[2]. **walk someone off their feet** walk with someone until they are exhausted. **walk of life** the position within society that someone holds or the part of society to which they belong as a result of their job or social status: *the courses attracted people from all walks of life*. **walk on air** see **AIR**. **walk on eggshells** be extremely cautious about one's words or actions. **walk one's talk** chiefly N. Amer. suit one's actions to one's words. **walk the plank** see **PLANK**. **walk the streets** **1** walk freely in a town or city. **2** work as a prostitute. **walk the wards** dated gain experience as a clinical medical student. **win in a walk** US win without effort or competition.
– DERIVATIVES **walkable** adjective.
– ORIGIN Old English *wealcan* 'roll, toss', also 'wander', of Germanic origin. The sense 'move about', and specifically 'go about on foot', arose in Middle English.
▶ **walk away** easily, casually, or irresponsibly abandon a situation in which one is involved or for which one is responsible.
walk away with informal another way of saying ***walk off with***.
walk in on enter suddenly or unexpectedly. ■ intrude on: *he was clearly not expecting her to walk in on him just then*.
walk into informal encounter or become involved in through ignorance or carelessness: *I had walked into a situation from which there was no escape*.
walk off with informal **1** steal. **2** win: *the group walked off with a silver medal*.
walk something off take exercise on foot in order to undo the effects of a heavy meal.
walk out **1** depart suddenly or angrily. ■ leave one's job suddenly. ■ go on strike. ■ abandon someone or something towards which one has responsibilities: *he walked out on his wife*. **2** Brit. informal, dated go for walks in courtship: *you were walking out with Tom*.
walk over **1** informal another way of saying ***walk all over***. **2** traverse (a racecourse) without needing to hurry, because one has no opponents or only inferior ones.
walk up! Brit. used by a showman as an invitation to a circus or other show: *walk up and have a look*.

walkabout ▶ **noun** chiefly Brit. an informal stroll among a crowd conducted by an important visitor.
■ Austral. a journey on foot undertaken by an Australian Aboriginal in order to live in the traditional manner.
– PHRASES **go walkabout** wander around from place to place in a protracted or leisurely way. ■ (of an Australian Aboriginal) wander into the bush away from white society in order to live in the traditional manner.

walkathon ▶ **noun** informal a long-distance walk organized as a fund-raising event.
– ORIGIN 1930s: from **WALK**, on the pattern of *marathon*.

Walker[1], Alice (Malsenior) (b.1944), American writer and critic. Notable novels: *The Color Purple* (Pulitzer Prize, 1982) and *Possessing the Secret of Joy* (1992).

Walker[2], John (b.1952), New Zealand athlete. He was the first athlete to run a mile in less than 3 minutes 50 seconds (1975).

walker ▶ **noun** a person who walks, especially for exercise or enjoyment.
■ a device for helping a baby learn to walk, consisting of a harness set into a frame on wheels. ■ short for **WALKING FRAME**.

Walker Cup a golf tournament held every two years and played between teams of male amateurs from the US and from Great Britain and Ireland, first held in 1922. The tournament was instituted by George Herbert Walker, a former President of the US Golf Association.

walkies informal ▶ **exclamation** a command to a dog to prepare for a walk.
▶ **noun** a spell of walking with a dog.
– PHRASES **go** (or **take a dog**) **walkies** take a dog for a walk. ■ (**go walkies**) go missing, especially as a result of theft: *the fund went walkies.*

walkie-talkie ▶ **noun** a portable two-way radio.

walk-in ▶ **adjective** 1 (especially of a storage area) large enough to walk into: *a walk-in cupboard.*
2 (of a service) available for customers or clients without the need for an appointment: *a walk-in clinic.*

walking bass ▶ **noun** Music a bass part in 4/4 time in which a note is played on each beat of the bar and which typically moves up and down the scale in small steps.

walking fern ▶ **noun** a North American fern with long slender tapering fronds that form new plantlets where the tips touch the ground, typically growing on limestone.
● *Asplenium* (or *Camptosorus*) *rhizophyllus*, family Aspleniaceae.

walking frame ▶ **noun** Brit. a frame used by disabled or infirm people for support while walking, typically made of metal tubing with rubber feet.

walking leaf ▶ **noun** another term for **WALKING FERN**.

walking leg ▶ **noun** Zoology (in certain arthropods, especially crustaceans) a limb used for walking.

walking papers ▶ **plural noun** informal, chiefly US notice of dismissal from a job: *the reporter has been given his walking papers.*

walking shoe ▶ **noun** a sturdy, practical shoe with good treads, suitable for regular or extensive walking.

walking stick ▶ **noun** 1 a stick with a curved handle used for support when walking.
2 (also **walking-stick insect**) North American term for **STICK INSECT**.

walking tour ▶ **noun** a sightseeing tour made on foot.

walking wounded ▶ **plural noun** (usu. **the walking wounded**) people who have been injured in a battle or major accident but who are still able to walk.

Walkman ▶ **noun** (pl. **Walkmans** or **Walkmen**) trademark a type of personal stereo.

walk-on ▶ **adjective** [attrib.] denoting a small non-speaking part in a play or film.
▶ **noun** a person who plays such a part.
■ US a sports player with no regular status in a team.

walkout ▶ **noun** a sudden angry departure, especially as a protest or strike.

walkover ▶ **noun** an easy victory: *they won in a 12–2 walkover.*

walk-through ▶ **noun** 1 an undemanding task.
■ an unchallenging role in a play or other performance. ■ a perfunctory or lacklustre performance.
2 a rough rehearsal of a play, film, or other performance, without an audience or cameras.
■ Computing a product review of software carried out before release.
3 Computing a software model of a building or other object in which the user can simulate walking around or through.
▶ **adjective** [attrib.] (of a building or other structure) permitting access from either end: *a walk-through gallery.*

walk-up N. Amer. ▶ **adjective** (of a building) allowing access to the upper floors by stairs only; having no lift: *a walk-up hotel.*
■ (of a room or flat) accessed in this way.
▶ **noun** a building of this kind.

walkway ▶ **noun** a passage or path for walking along, especially a raised passageway connecting different sections of a building or a wide path in a park or garden.

wall ▶ **noun** 1 a continuous vertical brick or stone structure that encloses or divides an area of land: *a garden wall* | *farmland traversed by drystone walls.*
■ a side of a building or room, typically forming part of

the building's structure. ■ any high vertical surface or facade, especially one that is imposing in scale: *the eastern wall of the valley* | figurative *a wall of sound.* ■ a thing perceived as a protective or restrictive barrier: *a wall of silence.* ■ Soccer a line of defenders forming a barrier against a free kick taken near the penalty area. ■ short for **CLIMBING WALL**. ■ Mining the rock enclosing a lode or seam. ■ Anatomy & Zoology the membranous outer layer or lining of an organ or cavity: *the wall of the stomach.* ■ Biology see **CELL WALL**. ■ (**the Wall**) short for **BERLIN WALL**.
2 another term for **WALL BROWN**.
▶ **verb** [with obj.] enclose (an area) within walls, especially to protect it or lend it some privacy: *housing areas that are walled off from the indigenous population.*
■ (**wall something up**) block or seal a place by building a wall around or across it: *one doorway has been walled up.* ■ (**wall someone/thing in/up**) confine or imprison someone or something in a restricted or sealed place: *the grey tenements walled in the space completely.*
– PHRASES **between you and me and the wall** see **BEDPOST**. **drive someone up the wall** informal make someone very irritated or angry. **go to the wall** informal 1 (of a business) fail; go out of business. 2 support someone or something, no matter what the cost to oneself: *the tendency for poets to go to the wall for their beliefs.* **hit the wall** (of an athlete) experience a sudden loss of energy in a long race. **off the wall** N. Amer. informal 1 eccentric or unconventional. 2 (of a person) angry: *the president was off the wall about the article.* 3 (of an accusation) without basis or foundation. **walls have ears** proverb be careful what you say as people may be eavesdropping. **wall-to-wall** (of a carpet or other floor covering) fitted to cover an entire floor. ■ informal denoting great extent or number: *wall-to-wall customers.*
– DERIVATIVES **wall-less** adjective.
– ORIGIN Old English, from Latin *vallum* 'rampart', from *vallus* 'stake'.

wallaby ▶ **noun** (pl. **-ies**) an Australasian marsupial that is similar to, but smaller than, a kangaroo.
● Family Macropodidae: several genera and numerous species.
■ (**the Wallabies**) informal the Australian international rugby union team.
– PHRASES **on the wallaby** (**track**) Austral. informal (of a person) unemployed and having no fixed address.
– ORIGIN early 19th cent.: from Dharuk *walabi* or *waliba.*

Wallace[1], Alfred Russel (1823–1913), English naturalist and a founder of zoogeography. He independently formulated a theory of the origin of species that was very similar to that of Charles Darwin.

Wallace[2], (Richard Horatio) Edgar (1875–1932), English novelist, screenwriter, and dramatist, noted for his crime novels.

Wallace[3], Sir William (c.1270–1305), Scottish national hero. He was a leader of Scottish resistance to Edward I, defeating the English army at Stirling in 1297. After Edward's second invasion of Scotland in 1298 Wallace was defeated and subsequently executed.

Wallacea /wɒˈleɪsɪə/ Zoology a zoogeographical area constituting a transition zone between the Oriental and Australian regions, east of Wallace's line. It is generally held to comprise Sulawesi and other islands between the two continental shelves.
– DERIVATIVES **Wallacean** adjective.
– ORIGIN 1920s: from the name of A. R. *Wallace* (see **WALLACE**[1]).

Wallace's line Zoology a hypothetical line, proposed by Alfred Russel Wallace, marking the boundary between the Oriental and Australian zoogeographical regions. Wallace's line is now placed along the continental shelf of SE Asia. To the west of the line Asian mammals predominate, while to the east of it the fauna is dominated by marsupials.

Wallachia /wɒˈleɪkɪə/ (also **Walachia**) a former principality of SE Europe, between the Danube and the Transylvanian Alps. In 1861 it was united with Moldavia to form Romania.
– DERIVATIVES **Wallachian** adjective & noun.
– ORIGIN based on a variant of **VLACH**.

wallah /ˈwɒlə/ ▶ **noun** [in combination or with modifier] Indian or informal a person concerned or involved with a specified thing or business: *a paan-wallah.*

■ a native or inhabitant of a specified place: *Bombay wallahs.*
– ORIGIN from the Hindi suffix *-vālā* 'doer' (commonly interpreted in the sense 'fellow'), from Sanskrit *pālaka* 'keeper'.

wallaroo /ˌwɒləˈruː/ ▶ **noun** a large Australian kangaroo, the female of which is paler than the male.
● Genus *Macropus*, family Macropodidae: two species, in particular the **common wallaroo** (*M. robustus*).
– ORIGIN early 19th cent.: from Dharuk *waларu.*

Wallasey /ˈwɒləsi/ a town in NW England on the Wirral Peninsula; pop. 62,530 (1981).

wall bar ▶ **noun** (usu. **wall bars**) Brit. one of a set of parallel horizontal bars attached to the wall of a gymnasium, on which exercises are performed.

wallboard ▶ **noun** [mass noun] chiefly N. Amer. a type of board made from wood pulp, plaster, or other material, used for covering walls and ceilings.
■ [count noun] a piece of such board.

wall brown ▶ **noun** a brown Eurasian butterfly with orange markings on the wings, which breeds on grasses.
● *Lasiommata megera*, subfamily Satyrinae, family Nymphalidae.

wallchart ▶ **noun** a chart or poster designed for display on a wall as a teaching aid or source of information.

wallcovering ▶ **noun** [mass noun] material such as wallpaper or textured fabric used as a decorative covering for interior walls.

wallcreeper ▶ **noun** a Eurasian songbird related to the nuthatches, having mainly grey plumage with broad bright red wings, and living among rocks in mountainous country.
● *Tichodroma muraria*, family Sittidae (or Tichodromadidae).

wall cress ▶ **noun** another term for **ARABIS**.

Wallenberg /ˈvɑːlənbɜːɡ/, Raoul (1912–?), Swedish diplomat. In 1944 in Budapest he helped many thousands of Jews to escape death by issuing them with Swedish passports. In 1945 he was arrested by Soviet forces and imprisoned in Moscow. Although the Soviet authorities stated that Wallenberg had died in prison in 1947, his fate remains uncertain.

Waller /ˈwɒlə/, Fats (1904–43), American jazz pianist, songwriter, bandleader, and singer; born *Thomas Wright Waller*. He was the foremost exponent of the New York 'stride school' of piano playing.

wallet ▶ **noun** a pocket-sized, flat, folding holder for money and plastic cards.
■ archaic a bag for holding provisions, especially when travelling, typically used by pedlars and pilgrims.
– ORIGIN late Middle English (denoting a bag for provisions): probably via Anglo-Norman French from a Germanic word related to **WELL**[2]. The current sense (originally US) dates from the mid 19th cent.

wall eye ▶ **noun** 1 an eye with a streaked or opaque white iris.
■ an eye squinting outwards.
2 (**walleye**) a North American pikeperch with large, opaque silvery eyes. It is a commercially valuable food fish and a popular sporting fish.
● *Stizostedion vitreum*, family Percidae.
– DERIVATIVES **wall-eyed** adjective.
– ORIGIN early 16th cent.: back-formation from earlier *wall-eyed*, from Old Norse *vagleygr*; related to Icelandic *vagl* 'film over the eye'.

wallflower ▶ **noun** 1 a southern European plant with fragrant yellow, orange-red, dark red, or brown flowers, cultivated for its early spring blooming.
● *Cheiranthus cheiri*, family Cruciferae.
2 informal a person who has no one to dance with or who feels shy, awkward, or excluded at a party.

wall game (also **Eton wall game**) ▶ **noun** (in the UK) an early form of football played traditionally at Eton College, in which, in a series of scrimmages, players attempt to take the ball past the opposing team while keeping the ball against a wall.

wall hanging ▶ **noun** a large decorative piece of fabric or other material to be hung on the wall of a room.

wall-hung ▶ **adjective** another term for **WALL-MOUNTED**.

walling ▶ **noun** [mass noun] 1 a length of wall: *it has high perimeter walling.*

2 the action of building a wall.

Wallis, Sir Barnes Neville (1887–1979), English inventor. His designs include the bouncing bomb used against the Ruhr dams in Germany in the Second World War.

Wallis and Futuna Islands /fəˈtjuːnə/ an overseas territory of France comprising two groups of islands to the west of Samoa in the central Pacific; pop. 15,400 (est. 1988); capital, Mata-Utu.

wall knot ▶ noun another term for **WALE KNOT**.

wall lizard ▶ noun a small brownish-grey Eurasian lizard which typically has black and white bars on the tail, frequently seen on walls and rocks.
● Genus *Podarcis*, family Lacertidae: several species, in particular *P. muralis*.

wall-mounted ▶ adjective fixed to a wall.

Wall of Death ▶ noun a fairground sideshow in which a motorcyclist uses gravitational force to ride around the inside walls of a vertical cylinder.

Walloon /wɒˈluːn/ ▶ noun **1** a member of a people who speak a French dialect and live in southern and eastern Belgium and neighbouring parts of France. Compare with **FLEMING**[1].
2 [mass noun] the French dialect spoken by this people.
▶ adjective of or concerning the Walloons or their language.
– ORIGIN from French *Wallon*, from medieval Latin *Wallo(n-)*, from the same Germanic origin as **WELSH**.

wallop informal ▶ verb (**walloped**, **walloping**) [with obj.] strike or hit (someone or something) very hard: *they walloped the back of his head with a stick* | figurative *they were tired of getting walloped with income taxes.*
■ heavily defeat (an opponent).
▶ noun **1** a heavy blow or punch.
■ [in sing.] figurative, chiefly US a potent effect: *the script packs a wallop.*
2 [mass noun] Brit. alcoholic drink, especially beer.
– ORIGIN Middle English (as a noun denoting a horse's gallop): from Old Northern French *walop* (noun), *waloper* (verb), perhaps from a Germanic phrase meaning 'run well', from the bases of **WELL**[1] and **LEAP**. Compare with **GALLOP**. From 'gallop' the senses 'bubbling noise of a boiling liquid' and then 'sound of a clumsy movement' arose, leading to the current senses.

walloper ▶ noun informal **1** a person or thing that wallops someone or something.
2 N. English a person or thing that is strikingly big.
■ a blatant lie.
3 Austral. a policeman.

walloping informal ▶ noun [in sing.] a beating: *she gave him a good walloping.*
▶ adjective [attrib.] large and powerful: *a walloping shock.*

wallow ▶ verb [no obj.] **1** (chiefly of large mammals) roll about or lie relaxed in mud or water, especially to keep cool, avoid biting insects, or spread scent: *there were watering places where buffalo liked to wallow.*
■ (of a boat or aircraft) roll from side to side: *the small jet wallowed in the sky.*
2 (**wallow in**) (of a person) indulge in an unrestrained way in (something that creates a pleasurable sensation): *I was wallowing in the luxury of the hotel* | *he had been wallowing in self-pity.*
▶ noun **1** an act of wallowing: *a wallow in nostalgia.*
2 an area of mud or shallow water where mammals go to wallow, typically developing into a depression in the ground over long use.
– DERIVATIVES **wallower** noun.
– ORIGIN Old English *walwian* 'to roll about', of Germanic origin, from an Indo-European root shared by Latin *volvere* 'to roll'.

wall painting ▶ noun a painting made directly on a wall, such as a fresco or mural.

wallpaper ▶ noun [mass noun] paper that is pasted in vertical strips over the walls of a room to provide a decorative or textured surface.
■ figurative a thing, especially music, that provides a bland or unvaried background: *soothing sonic wallpaper.* ■ Computing an optional background pattern or picture on a computer screen.
▶ verb [with obj.] apply wallpaper to (a wall or room).

wall pass ▶ noun Soccer a short pass to a teammate who immediately returns it; a one-two.

wall pepper ▶ noun the yellow stonecrop.

wall plate ▶ noun a timber laid horizontally in or on a wall as a support for a girder, rafter, or joist.

wall plug ▶ noun **1** a fibre or plastic dowel inserted into a drilled hole to provide a gripping base for a screw.
2 an electric socket in a wall.

wall pocket ▶ noun a receptacle for small household items, designed to hang on a wall.
■ a vase having one flat side, designed to be hung on a wall.

wall rock ▶ noun Geology the rock adjacent to or enclosing a vein, hydrothermal ore deposit, fault, or other geological feature.

wall rocket ▶ noun a yellow-flowered European plant which resembles mustard and emits a foul smell when crushed.
● *Diplotaxis muralis*, family Cruciferae.

wall rue ▶ noun a small delicate spleenwort (fern) which resembles rue, growing on walls and rocks in both Europe and North America and sensitive to atmospheric pollution.
● *Asplenium ruta-muraria*, family Aspleniaceae.

Wall Street a street at the south end of Manhattan, where the New York Stock Exchange and other leading American financial institutions are located.
■ used allusively to refer to the American money market or financial interests.
– ORIGIN named after a wooden stockade which was built in 1653 around the original Dutch settlement of New Amsterdam.

Wall Street Crash the collapse of prices on the New York Stock Exchange in October 1929, a major factor in the early stages of the Depression.

wall tent ▶ noun N. Amer. a tent with nearly perpendicular sides; a frame tent.

wall unit ▶ noun a piece of furniture having various sections, typically shelves and cupboards, designed to stand against a wall.

wallwasher ▶ noun a lighting fixture designed to illuminate a wall evenly without lighting the floor.

wally ▶ noun (pl. **-ies**) Brit. informal a silly or inept person.
– ORIGIN 1960s: perhaps a shortened form of the given name *Walter*. There are many theories of the origin: one story tells of a *Wally* who became separated from companions at a 1960s pop festival; the name, announced many times over a loudspeaker, was taken up as a chant by the crowd.

walnut ▶ noun **1** the large wrinkled edible seed of a deciduous tree, consisting of two halves contained within a hard shell which is enclosed in a green fruit.
2 (also **walnut tree**) the tall tree which produces this nut, with compound leaves and valuable ornamental timber that is used chiefly in cabinetmaking and gun stocks.
● Genus *Juglans*, family Juglandaceae: several species, including the **common** (or **English**) **walnut** (*J. regia*).
– ORIGIN late Old English *walh-hnutu*, from a Germanic compound meaning 'foreign nut'.

Walpole[1] /ˈwɔːlpəʊl/, Horace, 4th Earl of Orford (1717–97), English writer and Whig politician, son of Sir Robert Walpole. He wrote *The Castle of Otranto* (1764), one of the first Gothic novels.

Walpole[2] /ˈwɔːlpəʊl/, Sir Hugh (Seymour) (1884–1941), British novelist, born in New Zealand. He is best known for *The Herries Chronicle* (1930–3), a historical sequence set in the Lake District.

Walpole[3] /ˈwɔːlpəʊl/, Sir Robert, 1st Earl of Orford (1676–1745), British Whig statesman, First Lord of the Treasury and Chancellor of the Exchequer 1715–17 and 1721–42, father of Horace Walpole. Walpole is generally regarded as the first British Prime Minister, having presided over the cabinet for George I and George II.

Walpurgisnacht /valˈpʊrɡɪsnaxt/ ▶ noun German for **WALPURGIS NIGHT**.

Walpurgis night /valˈpʊəɡɪs/ ▶ noun (in German folklore) the night of April 30 (May Day's eve), when witches meet on the Brocken mountain and hold revels with the Devil.
– ORIGIN named after St *Walburga*, an English nun who in the 8th cent. helped to convert the Germans to Christianity; her feast day coincided with an ancient pagan festival whose rites were intended to give protection from witchcraft.

Walras' law /ˈvalrɑːs/ Economics a law stating that the total value of goods and money supplied equals that of goods and money demanded.

– ORIGIN 1940s: named after M. E. Léon *Walras* (1834–1910), French economist.

walrus ▶ noun a large gregarious marine mammal related to the eared seals, having two large downward-pointing tusks and found in the Arctic Ocean.
● *Odobenus rosmarus*, the only member of the family Odobenidae.
– ORIGIN early 18th cent.: probably from Dutch *walrus*, perhaps by an inversion of elements (influenced by *walvis* 'whale-fish') of Old Norse *hrosshvalr* 'horse-whale'.

walrus moustache ▶ noun a long, thick, drooping moustache.

Walsall /ˈwɔːlsɔːl, ˈwɒl-/ an industrial town in the Midlands of England; pop. 255,600 (1991).

Walsingham /ˈwɔːlsɪŋəm, ˈwɒl-/, Sir Francis (c.1530–90), English politician. As Secretary of State to Queen Elizabeth I he developed a spy network that gathered information about Catholic plots against Elizabeth I.

Walter Mitty the hero of a story (by James Thurber) who indulged in extravagant daydreams of his own triumphs.
■ [as noun] [often as modifier] used to refer to a person who fantasizes about a life much more exciting and glamorous than their own life: *my client is very much a Walter Mitty character.*

Walton[1] /ˈwɔːlt(ə)n, ˈwɒl-/, Ernest Thomas Sinton (1903–95), Irish physicist. In 1932 he succeeded, with Sir John Cockcroft, in splitting the atom. Nobel Prize for Physics (1951, shared with Cockcroft).

Walton[2] /ˈwɔːlt(ə)n, ˈwɒl-/, Izaak (1593–1683), English writer. He is chiefly known for *The Compleat Angler* (1653; largely rewritten, 1655) which combines practical information on fishing with folklore, interspersed with pastoral songs and ballads.

Walton[3] /ˈwɔːlt(ə)n, ˈwɒl-/, Sir William (Turner) (1902–83), English composer. Notable works: *Façade* (1921–3, a setting of poems by Edith Sitwell for recitation), the oratorio *Belshazzar's Feast* (1930–1), and film scores for three Shakespeare plays and the film *The Battle of Britain* (1969).

waltz /wɔːl(t)s, wɒl-/ ▶ noun a dance in triple time performed by a couple who as a pair turn rhythmically round and round as they progress around the dance floor.
■ a piece of music written for or in the style of this dance.
▶ verb [no obj.] dance a waltz: *I waltzed across the floor with the lieutenant.*
■ [with obj. and adverbial of direction] guide (someone) in or as if in a waltz: *he waltzed her round the table.* ■ [no obj., with adverbial of direction] move or act lightly, casually, or inconsiderately: *you can't just waltz in and expect to make a mark* | *it is the third time that he has waltzed off with the coveted award.*
– PHRASES **waltz Matilda** see **MATILDA**[2].
– ORIGIN late 18th cent.: from German *Walzer*, from *walzen* 'revolve'.

waltzer ▶ noun a person who dances the waltz.
■ a fairground ride in which cars spin round as they are carried round an undulating track.

Walvis Bay /ˈwɔːlvɪs/ a port in Namibia; pop. 25,000 (1980). It was administratively an exclave of the former Cape Province, South Africa until it was transferred to Namibia in 1994.

wambenger /ˈwɒmbɛŋɡə/ ▶ noun another term for **PHASCOGALE**.
– ORIGIN perhaps from Nyungar.

Wampanoag /ˌwɑːmˈpɑːnəʊəɡ/ ▶ noun (pl. same or **Wampanoags**) a member of a confederacy of American Indian peoples of SE Massachusetts.
▶ adjective of, relating to, or denoting these people.
– ORIGIN Narragansett, literally 'easterners'.

wampum /ˈwɒmpəm/ ▶ noun [mass noun] historical a quantity of small cylindrical beads made by North American Indians from shells, strung together and worn as a decorative belt or other decoration or used as money.
– ORIGIN from Algonquian *wampumpeag*, from *wap* 'white' + *umpe* 'string' + the plural suffix *-ag*.

WAN ▶ abbreviation for ■ Computing wide area network.
■ Nigeria (international vehicle registration).
[ORIGIN: from *West Africa Nigeria*.]

wan /wɒn/ ▶ adjective (of a person's complexion or appearance) pale and giving the impression of

illness or exhaustion: *she was looking wan and bleary-eyed.*
■(of light) pale; weak: *the wan dawn light.* ■ (of a smile) weak; strained. ■ poetic/literary (of the sea) without lustre; dark and gloomy.
– DERIVATIVES **wanly** adverb, **wanness** /ˈwɒnnɪs/ noun.
– ORIGIN Old English *wann* 'dark, black', of unknown origin.

wand ▶ **noun** a long, thin stick or rod, in particular:
■a stick or rod thought to have magic properties, held by a magician, fairy, or conjuror and used in casting spells or performing tricks: *the fairy godmother waves her magic wand and grants the heroine's wishes.* ■ a staff or rod held as a symbol of office. ■ informal a conductor's baton. ■ a hand-held electronic device which can be passed over a bar code to read the encoded data. ■ a device emitting a laser beam, used especially to create a pointer on a projected image or text. ■ a small stick with a brush at one end used for the application of mascara: *a mascara wand.* ■ (**wands**) one of the suits in some tarot packs, corresponding to batons in others.
– ORIGIN Middle English: from Old Norse *vǫndr*, probably of Germanic origin and related to **WEND** and **WIND**².

wander ▶ **verb** [no obj., with adverbial of direction] walk or move in a leisurely, casual, or aimless way: *he wandered aimlessly through the narrow streets.*
■[no obj.] move slowly away from a fixed point or place: *please don't **wander off** again* | figurative *his attention had wandered.* ■ (of a road or river) wind with gentle twists and turns in a particular direction; meander. ■ [with obj.] move or travel slowly through or over (a place or area): *she found her wandering the streets.* ■ [no obj.] be unfaithful to one's regular sexual partner.
▶ **noun** an act or instance of wandering: *she'd go on wanders like that in her nightgown.*
– DERIVATIVES **wanderer** noun.
– ORIGIN Old English *wandrian*, of West Germanic origin; related to **WEND** and **WIND**².

wandering albatross ▶ **noun** a very large albatross of southern oceans, having white plumage with black wings and a wingspan of up to 3.3 m.
● *Diomedea exulans*, family Diomedeidae.

wandering Jew ▶ **noun 1** a legendary person said to have been condemned by Christ to wander the earth until the second advent.
■a person who never settles down.
2 a tender trailing tradescantia, typically having striped leaves which are suffused with purple.
● Genus *Tradescantia*, family Commelinaceae: *T. albiflora* and *T. pendula* (formerly *Zebrina pendula*).

wandering sailor ▶ **noun** either of two creeping plants:
● creeping jenny. ● ivy-leaved toadflax. See **TOADFLAX**.

Wanderjahr /ˈvandəjɑː/ ▶ **noun** (pl. **Wanderjahre**) /-rə/ chiefly N. Amer. a year spent travelling abroad, typically immediately before or after a university or college course.
– ORIGIN late 19th cent.: German, literally 'wander year'.

wanderlust ▶ **noun** [mass noun] a strong desire to travel: *a man consumed by wanderlust.*
– ORIGIN early 20th cent.: from German *Wanderlust*.

wanderoo /ˌwɒndəˈruː/ ▶ **noun** (in Sri Lanka) a leaf monkey or langur.
● Genus *Presbytis*, family Cercopithecidae: the purple-faced leaf monkey (*P. vetulus*), or the hanuman (*P. entellus*).
– ORIGIN late 17th cent.: from Sinhalese *wanderu* 'monkey'.

Wandervogel /ˈvandəˌfəʊgəl, German ˈvandɐˌfoːgl/ ▶ **noun** (pl. **Wandervögel** /-fəːgəl, German -føːgl/) a member of a German youth organization founded at the end of the 19th century for the promotion of outdoor activities and folk culture.
■a wanderer, especially someone who travels the world on foot.
– ORIGIN German, literally 'bird of passage'.

W

wane¹ ▶ **verb** [no obj.] (of the moon) have a progressively smaller part of its visible surface illuminated, so that it appears to decrease in size.
■(especially of a condition or feeling) decrease in vigour, power, or extent; become weaker: *confidence in the dollar waned.*
– PHRASES **on the wane** becoming weaker, less vigorous, or less extensive: *the epidemic was on the wane.*
– ORIGIN Old English *wanian* 'lessen', of Germanic origin; related to Latin *vanus* 'vain'.

wane² ▶ **noun** the amount by which a plank or log is bevelled or falls short of a squared shape.
– DERIVATIVES **waney** adjective.
– ORIGIN mid 17th cent.: from **WANE**¹.

Wanganui /ˌwɒŋgəˈnuːi/ a port in New Zealand, on the west coast of North Island; pop. 41,210 (1991).

wangle informal ▶ **verb** [with obj.] obtain (something that is desired) by persuading others to comply or by manipulating events: *I wangled an invitation to her flat* | *I think we should be able to **wangle it** so that you can start tomorrow.*
▶ **noun** an act or an instance of obtaining something in such a way: *they regarded the coalition as a wangle.*
– DERIVATIVES **wangler** noun.
– ORIGIN late 19th cent. (first recorded as printers' slang): of unknown origin; perhaps based on the verb **WAGGLE**.

wank Brit. vulgar slang ▶ **verb** [no obj.] (typically of a man) masturbate.
▶ **noun** an act of masturbating.
– ORIGIN 1940s: of unknown origin.
▶ **wank oneself/someone off** (or **wank off**) masturbate.

Wankel engine /ˈwaŋk(ə)l, ˈvaŋ-/ ▶ **noun** a rotary internal-combustion engine in which a curvilinear, triangular, eccentrically pivoted piston rotates in an elliptical chamber, forming three combustion spaces that vary in volume as it turns.
– ORIGIN 1960s: named after Felix Wankel (1902–88), German engineer.

wanker ▶ **noun** Brit. vulgar slang a person who masturbates (used as a term of abuse).

Wankie /ˈwɑːŋki/ former name (until 1982) for **HWANGE**.

wanna informal ▶ **contraction of** want to; want a.

wannabe /ˈwɒnəbi/ ▶ **noun** informal, derogatory a person who tries to be like someone else or to fit in with a particular group of people: *a star-struck wannabe.*
– ORIGIN 1980s: representing a pronunciation of *want to be*.

want ▶ **verb 1** [with obj.] have a desire to possess or do (something); wish for: *I want an apple* | [with infinitive] *we want to go to the beach* | [with obj. and infinitive] *she wanted me to go to her room* | [no obj.] *I'll give you a lift into town if you want.*
■wish to consult or speak to (someone): *Tony wants me in the studio.* ■ (usu. **be wanted**) (of the police) desire to question or apprehend (a suspected criminal): *he is wanted by the police in connection with an arms theft.* ■ desire (someone) sexually: *I've wanted you since the first moment I saw you.* ■ [with present participle] informal, chiefly Brit. (of a thing) require to be attended to in a specified way: *the wheel wants greasing.* ■ [with infinitive] informal ought, should, or need to do something: *you don't want to believe everything you hear.* ■ [no obj.] (**want in/into/out/away**) informal, chiefly US desire to be in or out of a particular place or situation: *if anyone wants out, there's the door.*
2 [no obj.] chiefly archaic lack or be short of something desirable or essential: *you shall **want for nothing** while you are with me.*
■[with obj.] (chiefly used in expressions of time) be short of or lack (a specified amount or thing): *it **wanted** twenty minutes **to** midnight* | *it **wants** a few minutes **of** five o'clock.*
▶ **noun 1** [mass noun] chiefly archaic a lack or deficiency of something: *Victorian houses which are **in want of** repair* | *it won't be through want of trying.*
■the state of being poor and in need of essentials; poverty: *freedom from want.*
2 a desire for something: *the expression of our wants and desires.*
– PHRASES **for want of** because of a lack of (something): *for want of a better location we ate our picnic lunch in the cemetery.*
– ORIGIN Middle English: the noun from Old Norse *vant*, neuter of *vanr* 'lacking'; the verb from Old Norse *vanta* 'be lacking'. The original notion of 'lack' was early extended to 'need' and from this developed the sense 'desire'.

want ad ▶ **noun** US informal a classified advertisement in a newspaper or magazine; a small ad.

wanting ▶ **adjective** [predic.] lacking in a certain required or necessary quality: *they weren't **wanting in** confidence* | *the English batting technique has been **found** sadly **wanting**.*
■not existing or supplied; absent: *mandibles are wanting in many of these insects.* ■ informal deficient in intelligence.

want list (also **wants list**) ▶ **noun** a list of stamps, books, recordings, or similar items required by a collector.

wanton ▶ **adjective 1** (of a cruel or violent action) deliberate and unprovoked: *sheer wanton vandalism.*
2 (especially of a woman) sexually immodest or promiscuous.
■poetic/literary growing profusely; luxuriant: *where wanton ivy twines.* ■ poetic/literary lively; playful: *a wanton fawn.*
▶ **noun** archaic a sexually immodest or promiscuous woman.
▶ **verb** [no obj.] archaic or poetic/literary **1** play; frolic.
2 behave in a sexually immodest or promiscuous way.
– DERIVATIVES **wantonly** adverb, **wantonness** noun.
– ORIGIN Middle English *wantowen* 'rebellious, lacking discipline', from *wan-* 'badly' + Old English *togen* 'trained' (related to **TEAM** and **TOW**¹).

wapentake /ˈwɒp(ə)nteɪk, ˈwap-/ ▶ **noun** historical (in the UK) a subdivision of certain northern and midland English counties, corresponding to a hundred in other counties.
– ORIGIN late Old English *wǣpen(ge)tæc*, from Old Norse *vápnatak*, from *vápn* 'weapon' + *taka* 'take', perhaps with reference to voting in an assembly by a show of weapons.

wapiti /ˈwɒpɪti/ ▶ **noun** (pl. **wapitis**) a red deer of a large race native to North America. Also called **ELK** in North America.
● *Cervus elaphus canadensis*, family Cervidae; it is sometimes treated as a separate species (*C. canadensis*).
– ORIGIN early 19th cent.: from Shawnee, literally 'white rump'.

waqf /vʌkf/ ▶ **noun** (pl. same) an endowment made by a Muslim to a religious, educational, or charitable cause.
– ORIGIN from Arabic, literally 'stoppage, immobilization (of ownership of property)', from *waqafa* 'come to a standstill'.

War. ▶ **abbreviation for** Warwickshire.

war ▶ **noun** [mass noun] a state of armed conflict between different nations or states or different groups within a nation or state: *Japan **declared war on** Germany* | *Iran and Iraq had been **at war** for six years.*
■[count noun] a particular armed conflict: *after the war, they emigrated to America.* ■ a state of competition, conflict, or hostility between different people or groups: *she was **at war with** her parents* | [count noun] *a price war among tour operators.* ■ a sustained effort to deal with or end a particular unpleasant or undesirable situation or condition: *the authorities are **waging war against** all forms of smuggling* | [count noun] *a **war on** drugs.*
▶ **verb** (**warred**, **warring**) [no obj.] engage in a war: *small states warred against each another* | figurative *conflicting emotions warred within her.*
– PHRASES **go to war** declare, begin, or see active service in a war. **go to the wars** archaic serve as a soldier. **have been in the wars** informal have been hurt or injured. **war clouds** a threatening situation of instability in international relations: *the war clouds were looming.* **war of attrition** a prolonged war or period of conflict during which each side seeks to gradually wear out the other by a series of small-scale actions. **war of nerves** see **NERVE**. **war of words** a prolonged debate conducted by means of the spoken or printed word. **war to end all wars** a war, especially the First World War, regarded as making subsequent wars unnecessary.
– ORIGIN late Old English *werre*, from an Anglo-Norman French variant of Old French *guerre*, from a Germanic base shared by **WORSE**.

waragi /ˈwarəgi/ ▶ **noun** [mass noun] (in Uganda) a strong alcoholic drink made from bananas or cassava.
– ORIGIN from Kiswahili *wargi*.

war artist ▶ **noun** an artist employed to draw or paint events and situations arising during a war.

waratah /ˈwɔːrətɑː, ˌwɒrəˈtɑː/ ▶ **noun** an Australian shrub which bears slender leathery leaves and clusters of crimson flowers.
● Genus *Telopea*, family Proteaceae: several species, in particular *T. speciosissima*, which is the emblem of New South Wales.
– ORIGIN late 18th cent.: from Dharuk *warata*.

war baby ▶ **noun** a child born in wartime, especially one fathered illegitimately by a serviceman.

Warbeck /ˈwɔːbɛk/, Perkin (1474–99), Flemish

claimant to the English throne. In an attempt to overthrow Henry VII, he claimed to be one of the Princes in the Tower. After attempting to begin a revolt he was captured and imprisoned in the Tower of London in 1497 and later executed.

warbird ▶ **noun** a vintage military aircraft.

warble[1] ▶ **verb** [no obj.] (of a bird) sing softly and with a succession of constantly changing notes: *larks were warbling in the trees.*
■(of a person) sing in a trilling or quavering voice: *he warbled in an implausible soprano.*
▶ **noun** a warbling sound or utterance.
– ORIGIN late Middle English (as a noun in the sense 'melody'): from Old Northern French *werble* (noun), *werbler* (verb), of Germanic origin; related to **WHIRL**.

warble[2] ▶ **noun** a swelling or abscess beneath the skin on the back of cattle, horses, and other mammals, caused by the presence of the larva of a warble fly.
■the larva causing this.
– ORIGIN late Middle English: of uncertain origin.

warble fly ▶ **noun** a large fly which lays its eggs on the legs of mammals such as cattle and horses. The larvae migrate internally to the host's back, where they form a small lump with a breathing hole, dropping to the ground later when fully grown.
• Genus *Hypoderma*, family Oestridae: several species, including the widespread *H. bovis*.

warbler ▶ **noun** **1** any of a number of small insectivorous songbirds that typically have a warbling song:
• an Old World bird of the family Sylviidae, which includes the blackcap, whitethroat, and chiffchaff. • (also **wood warbler**) N. Amer. a New World bird of the family Parulidae. • Austral. an Australasian bird of the family Acanthizidae.
2 informal a person who sings in a trilling or quavering voice.

warbonnet ▶ **noun** an elongated slender fish of the North Pacific that has branched tentacles above the eye, over the back of the head, and at the front of the long dorsal fin.
• Genus *Chirolophis*, family Stichaeidae: several species.

war bonnet ▶ **noun** see **BONNET** (sense 1).

war bride ▶ **noun** a woman who marries a man whom she met while he was on active service.

Warburg[1] /ˈwɔːbəːɡ, German ˈvaːɐbʊrk/, Aby (Moritz) (1866–1929), German art historian. From 1905 he built up a library in Hamburg, dedicated to preserving the classical heritage of Western culture. In 1933 it was transferred to England and housed in the Warburg Institute (part of the University of London).

Warburg[2] /ˈwɔːbəːɡ, German ˈvaːɐbʊrk/, Otto Heinrich (1883–1970), German biochemist. He pioneered the use of the techniques of chemistry for biochemical investigations, especially for his work on intracellular respiration. Nobel Prize for Physiology or Medicine (1931); he was prevented by the Nazi regime from accepting a second one in 1944 because of his Jewish ancestry.

war chest ▶ **noun** a reserve of funds used for fighting a war.
■a sum of money used for conducting a campaign or business.

war crime ▶ **noun** an action carried out during the conduct of a war that violates accepted international rules of war.
– DERIVATIVES **war criminal** noun.

war cry ▶ **noun** a call made to rally soldiers for battle or to gather together participants in a campaign.

Ward, Mrs Humphry (1851–1920), English writer and anti-suffrage campaigner, niece of Matthew Arnold; née *Mary Augusta Arnold*. She is best known for several novels dealing with social and religious themes, especially *Robert Elsmere* (1888). An active opponent of the women's suffrage movement, she became the first president of the Anti-Suffrage League in 1908.

ward ▶ **noun** **1** a separate room in a hospital, typically one allocated to a particular type of patient: *a children's ward* | [as modifier] *a ward sister.*
2 an administrative division of a city or borough that typically elects and is represented by a councillor or councillors.
3 a child or young person under the care and control of a guardian appointed by their parents or a court.
■[mass noun] archaic guardianship or the state of being subject to a guardian: *the ward and care of the Crown.*
4 (usu. **wards**) any of the internal ridges or bars in a lock which prevent the turning of any key which does not have grooves of corresponding form or size.
■the corresponding grooves in the bit of a key.
5 [mass noun] archaic the action of keeping a lookout for danger: *I saw them keeping ward at one of those huge gates.*
6 historical an area of ground enclosed by the encircling walls of a fortress or castle.
▶ **verb** [with obj.] **1** archaic guard; protect: *it was his duty to ward the king.*
2 admit (a patient) to a hospital ward.
– PHRASES **ward of court** a child or young person for whom a guardian has been appointed by the Court of Chancery or who has become directly subject to the authority of that court.
– DERIVATIVES **wardship** noun.
– ORIGIN Old English *weard* (in sense 5, also 'body of guards'), *weardian* 'keep safe, guard', of Germanic origin; reinforced in Middle English by Old Northern French *warde* (noun), *warder* (verb) 'guard'.
▶ **ward someone/thing off** prevent from harming or affecting one: *she put up a hand as if to ward him off.*

-ward (also **-wards**) ▶ **suffix** added to nouns of place or destination and to adverbs of direction :
1 (usu. **-wards**) (forming adverbs) towards the specified place or direction: *eastwards* | *homewards.*
2 (usu. **-ward**) (forming adjectives) turned or tending towards: *onward* | *upward.*
– ORIGIN Old English *-weard*, from a Germanic base meaning 'turn'.

war dance ▶ **noun** a ceremonial dance performed before a battle or to celebrate victory.

warden ▶ **noun** a person responsible for the supervision of a particular place or thing or for ensuring that regulations associated with it are obeyed: *the warden of a local nature reserve* | *an air-raid warden.*
■Brit. the head of certain schools, colleges, or other institutions. ■ a prison officer. ■ chiefly US a prison governor.
– DERIVATIVES **wardenship** noun.
– ORIGIN Middle English (originally denoting a guardian or protector): from Anglo-Norman French and Old Northern French *wardein*, variant of Old French *guarden* 'guardian'.

warder ▶ **noun** chiefly Brit. a prison guard.
– ORIGIN late Middle English (denoting a watchman or sentinel): from Anglo-Norman French *wardere*, from Old Northern French *warder* 'to guard'. The current sense dates from the mid 19th cent.

ward heeler ▶ **noun** US informal, chiefly derogatory a person who assists in a political campaign by canvassing votes for a party and performing menial tasks for its leaders.

Wardian case /ˈwɔːdɪən/ ▶ **noun** chiefly historical a glass-sided airtight case used for growing ferns or other plants indoors or for transporting living plants over long distances.
– ORIGIN mid 19th cent.: named after Nathaniel B. Ward (1791–1868), the English botanist who invented it.

Wardour Street /ˈwɔːdə/ ▶ **noun** **1** used allusively to refer to the British film industry.
2 [as modifier] denoting the pseudo-archaic diction affected by some modern writers of historical novels.
– ORIGIN the name of a street in central London, formerly mainly occupied by dealers in antique furniture, now the site of the central offices of the British film industry.

wardress ▶ **noun** chiefly Brit. a female prison guard.

wardrobe ▶ **noun** a large, tall cupboard in which clothes may be hung or stored.
■a person's entire collection of clothes: *her wardrobe is extensive.* ■ the costume department or costumes of a theatre or film company: [as modifier] *a wardrobe assistant.* ■ a department of a royal or noble household in charge of clothing.
– ORIGIN Middle English (in the sense 'private chamber'): from Old Northern French *warderobe*, variant of Old French *garderobe* (see **GARDEROBE**).

wardrobe mistress ▶ **noun** a woman in charge of the construction and organization of the costumes in a theatrical company.

wardrobe trunk ▶ **noun** chiefly US a trunk fitted with rails and shelves for use as a travelling wardrobe.

wardroom ▶ **noun** a commissioned officers' mess on board a warship.

ward round ▶ **noun** visits paid by a doctor in a hospital to each of the patients in their care or in a particular ward or wards.

war drum ▶ **noun** a drum beaten as a summons or an accompaniment to battle.

-wards ▶ **suffix** variant spelling of **-WARD**.

ware[1] /wɛː/ ▶ **noun** [mass noun] [usu. with adj. or noun modifier] pottery, typically that of a specified type: *blue-and-white majolica ware* | (**wares**) *Minoan potters produced an astonishing variety of wares.*
■manufactured articles of a specified type: *crystal ware* | *aluminium ware.* ■ (**wares**) articles offered for sale: *traders in the street markets displayed their wares.*
– ORIGIN Old English *waru* 'commodities', of Germanic origin, perhaps the same word as Scots *ware* 'cautiousness', and having the primary sense 'object of care'; related to **WARE**[3].

ware[2] /wɛː/ (also **'ware**) ▶ **verb** [in imperative] beware (used as a warning cry, typically in a hunting context).
– ORIGIN Old English *warian* 'be on one's guard', from a Germanic base meaning 'observe, take care'.

ware[3] /wɛː/ ▶ **adjective** [predic.] archaic aware: *thou speak'st wiser than thou art ware of.*
– ORIGIN Old English *wær*, from the Germanic base of **WARE**[2].

ware[4] /ˈvɑːrə/ ▶ **adjective** S. African loyal; genuine.
– ORIGIN Afrikaans, 'true'.

warehou /ˈwɑːrəˌhaʊ/ ▶ **noun** (pl. same) NZ a marine fish of coastal Australasian waters. See **SEA BREAM**.
– ORIGIN mid 19th cent.: from Maori.

warehouse /ˈwɛːhaʊs/ ▶ **noun** a large building where raw materials or manufactured goods may be stored prior to their export or distribution for sale.
■a large wholesale or retail store: *a discount warehouse.*
▶ **verb** /also -haʊz/ [with obj.] store (goods) in a warehouse.
■place (imported goods) in a bonded warehouse pending the payment of import duty. ■ US informal place (someone, typically a prisoner or a psychiatric patient) in a large, impersonal institution in which their problems are not satisfactorily addressed.

warehouse club ▶ **noun** an organization which operates from a large out-of-town store and sells goods in bulk at discounted prices to business and private customers who must first become club members.

warehouseman ▶ **noun** (pl. **-men**) a person who is employed in, manages, or owns a warehouse.

warehouse party ▶ **noun** a large public party with dancing held in a warehouse or similar building, typically organized without official permission.

warehousing ▶ **noun** [mass noun] **1** the practice or process of storing goods in a warehouse.
■warehouses considered collectively. ■ US informal the practice of placing people, typically prisoners or psychiatric patients, in large, impersonal institutions.
2 Stock Exchange the building up of a holding of shares in a company by buying numerous small lots of shares in the names of nominees, in order to make a takeover bid while remaining anonymous.

war establishment ▶ **noun** the level of equipment and manning laid down for a military unit in wartime.

warfare ▶ **noun** [mass noun] engagement in or the activities involved in war or conflict: *guerrilla warfare.*

warfarin /ˈwɔːfərɪn/ ▶ **noun** [mass noun] a water-soluble compound with anticoagulant properties, used as a rat poison and in the treatment of thrombosis.
• A coumarin derivative; chem. formula: $C_{19}H_{16}O_4$.
– ORIGIN 1950s: from the initial letters of *Wisconsin Alumni Research Foundation* + *-arin* on the pattern of *coumarin*.

war game ▶ **noun** a military exercise carried out to test or improve tactical expertise.
■a simulated military conflict carried out as a game, leisure activity, or exercise in personal development.
▶ **verb** [with obj.] (**war-game**) US engage in (a campaign or course of action) using the strategies of such a military exercise: *there seemed to be no point war-gaming an election 15 months away.*

W

a cat | ɑː arm | ɛ bed | ɛː hair | ə ago | əː her | ɪ sit | i cosy | iː see | ɒ hot | ɔː saw | ʌ run | ʊ put | uː too | ʌɪ my | aʊ how | eɪ day | əʊ no | ɪə near | ɔɪ boy | ʊə poor | ʌɪə fire | aʊə sour

– DERIVATIVES **war-gamer** noun.

war gaming ▶ **noun** [mass noun] the action of playing a war game as a leisure activity or exercise in personal development.
■ US the action of engaging in a campaign or course of action using the strategies of a military exercise.

war grave ▶ **noun** a grave of a serviceman who has died on active service, especially one among a number of graves in a site serving as a monument.

warhead ▶ **noun** the explosive head of a missile, torpedo, or similar weapon.

Warhol /ˈwɔːhəʊl/, Andy (*c.*1928–87), American painter, graphic artist, and film-maker; born *Andrew Warhola*. A major exponent of pop art, he achieved fame for a series of silk-screen prints and acrylic paintings of familiar objects (such as Campbell's soup tins) and famous people (such as Marilyn Monroe), treated with objectivity and precision.
– DERIVATIVES **Warholian** adjective.

warhorse ▶ **noun** (in historical contexts) a powerful horse ridden in a battle.
■ informal an elderly person such as a soldier, politician, or sports player who has fought many campaigns or contests.

Warka /wəˈkɑː/ Arabic name for **URUK**.

warlike ▶ **adjective** disposed towards or threatening war; hostile: *a warlike clan.*
■ (of plans, preparations, or munitions) directed towards or prepared for war.

war loan ▶ **noun** [mass noun] stock issued by the British government to raise funds at a time of war.

warlock ▶ **noun** a man who practises witchcraft; a sorcerer.
– ORIGIN Old English *wǣrloga* 'traitor, scoundrel, monster', also 'the Devil', from *wǣr* 'covenant' + an element related to *lēogan* 'belie, deny'. From its application to the Devil, the word was transferred in Middle English to a person in league with the devil, and hence a sorcerer. It was chiefly Scots until given wider currency by Sir Walter Scott.

warlord ▶ **noun** a military commander, especially an aggressive regional commander with individual autonomy.

Warlpiri /ˈwɔːlpəri/ ▶ **noun** [mass noun] an Australian Aboriginal language of Northern Territory, with about 2,800 speakers.

warm ▶ **adjective 1** of or at a fairly or comfortably high temperature: *a warm September evening* | [as complement] *I walked quickly to keep warm.*
■ (of clothes or coverings) made of a material that helps the body to retain heat; suitable for cold weather: *a warm winter coat.* ■ (of a colour) containing red, yellow, or orange tones: *her fair colouring suited soft, warm shades.* ■ Hunting (of a scent or trail) fresh; strong. ■ (of a soil) quick to absorb heat or retaining heat.
2 having, showing, or expressive of enthusiasm, affection, or kindness: *they exchanged warm, friendly smiles* | *a warm welcome.*
■ archaic characterized by lively or heated disagreement: *a warm debate arose.* ■ archaic sexually explicit or titillating.
3 [predic.] informal (especially in children's games) close to discovering something or guessing the correct answer: *we're getting warmer, sir.*
▶ **verb** make or become warm: [with obj.] *I stamped my feet to **warm** them **up*** | figurative *the film warmed our hearts* | [no obj.] *it's a bit chilly in here, but it'll soon **warm up**.*
■ [with obj.] informal spank (someone's buttocks): *I'll warm your bum if you don't come here this instant.*
▶ **noun 1** (**the warm**) a warm place or area: *stay in the warm, I've made up the fire for you.*
■ [in sing.] an act of warming something or oneself: *he had a cup of tea and a warm by the kitchen range.*
2 short for **BRITISH WARM**.
– PHRASES **keep something warm for someone** hold or occupy a place or post until another person is ready to do so. **(as) warm as toast** pleasantly warm. **wrap up warm** (or **be wrapped up warm**) put on (or have on) plenty of clothes to protect oneself against cold weather.
– DERIVATIVES **warmer** noun [usu. in combination] *a towel-warmer*, **warmish** adjective, **warmly** adverb, **warmness** noun.
– ORIGIN Old English *wearm* (adjective), *werman*, *wearmian* (verb), of Germanic origin; related to Dutch and German *warm*, from an Indo-European root shared by Latin *formus* 'warm' and Greek *thermos* 'hot'.
▶ **warm down** recover from strenuous physical exertion by doing gentle stretches and exercises.
warm to/towards (or US **warm up to/towards**) begin to like (someone). ■ become more interested in or enthusiastic about (something): *she was warming to her theme.*
warm up prepare for physical exertion or a performance by exercising or practising gently beforehand: *the band were warming up.* ■ (of an engine or electrical appliance) reach a temperature high enough to allow it to operate efficiently. ■ become livelier or more animated: *after several more rounds, things began to warm up in the bar.*
warm something up (or US **over**) reheat previously cooked food. ■ amuse or entertain an audience or crowd so as to make them more receptive to the main act.

war machine ▶ **noun 1** the military resources of a country organized for waging war.
2 an instrument or weapon of war.

warmblood ▶ **noun** a horse of a breed that is a cross between an Arab or similar breed and another breed of the draught or pony type.

warm-blooded ▶ **adjective 1** relating to or denoting animals (chiefly mammals and birds) which maintain a constant body temperature, typicallyabove that of the surroundings, by metabolic means; homeothermic.
2 ardent; passionate.
– DERIVATIVES **warm-bloodedness** noun.

warm-down ▶ **noun** a series of gentle exercises designed to relax the body after strenuous physical exertion.

warmed-up (N. Amer. **warmed-over**) ▶ **adjective 1** (of food or drink) reheated: *a warmed-up airline meal.*
2 (of a person) ready for physical exertion or a performance having exercised or practised gently; limbered-up.
3 (of an engine, electrical appliance, or musical instrument) operating efficiently having reached a high enough temperature or been prepared in some other way.
4 (of an idea or product) second-hand; stale.

war memorial ▶ **noun** a monument commemorating those killed in a war.

warm front ▶ **noun** Meteorology the boundary of an advancing mass of warm air, in particular the leading edge of the warm sector of a low-pressure system.

warm-hearted ▶ **adjective** (of a person or their actions) sympathetic and kind.
– DERIVATIVES **warm-heartedly** adverb, **warm-heartedness** noun.

warming pan ▶ **noun** historical a wide, flat brass pan on a long handle, filled with hot coals and used for warming a bed.

warmonger /ˈwɔːmʌŋgə/ ▶ **noun** a sovereign or political leader or activist who encourages or advocates aggression or warfare towards other nations or groups.
– DERIVATIVES **warmongering** noun & adjective.

warmth ▶ **noun** [mass noun] the quality, state, or sensation of being warm; moderate and comfortable heat: *the warmth of the sun on her skin.*
■ enthusiasm, affection, or kindness: *she smiled with real warmth.* ■ vehemence or intensity of emotion: *'Of course not,' he snapped, with a warmth that he regretted.*

warm-up ▶ **noun** a period or act of preparation for a match, performance, or exercise session, involving gentle exercise or practice.
■ (**warm-ups**) N. Amer. a garment worn during light exercise or training; a tracksuit. ■ a period before a stage performance in which the audience is amused or entertained in order to make it more receptive to the main act.

warm work ▶ **noun** [mass noun] **1** physical action that makes one warm through exertion.
2 archaic dangerous conflict.

warn ▶ **verb** [reporting verb] inform someone in advance of an impending or possible danger, problem, or other unpleasant situation: [with obj.] *his father had **warned** him **of** what might happen* | [with direct speech] *'He's going to humiliate you,' John warned* | [with clause] *the union warned that its members were close to going on strike.*
■ give someone forceful or cautionary advice about their actions or conduct: [with obj.] *he **warned** the chancellor **against** raising taxes* | [with obj. and infinitive] *they warned people not to keep large amounts of cash in their homes* | [no obj.] *they **warned against** false optimism.*
– PHRASES **warn someone off the course** Horse Racing prohibit someone who has broken the laws of the Jockey Club from riding or running horses at meetings under the Jockey Club's jurisdiction.
– DERIVATIVES **warner** noun.
– ORIGIN Old English *war(e)nian*, *wearnian*, from a West Germanic base meaning 'be cautious'; compare with **WARE**[3].
▶ **warn someone off** tell someone forcefully or threateningly to go or keep away from somewhere. ■ advise someone forcefully against (a particular thing or course of action): *he has been warned off booze.*

Warner Brothers a US film production company founded in 1923 by the brothers Harry, Jack, Sam, and Albert Warner.

warning ▶ **noun** a statement or event that indicates a possible or impending danger, problem, or other unpleasant situation: *police issued a warning about fake £20 notes* | [mass noun] *suddenly and without any warning, the army opened fire* | [as modifier] *a red warning light.*
■ [mass noun] cautionary advice: *a word of warning—don't park illegally.* ■ [mass noun] advance notice of something: *she had only had four days' warning before leaving Berlin.* ■ an experience or sight that serves as a cautionary example to others: *his sad death should be a warning to everyone.*
– DERIVATIVES **warningly** adverb.
– ORIGIN Old English *war(e)nung* (see **WARN**, **-ING**[1]).

warning coloration ▶ **noun** [mass noun] Zoology conspicuous colouring that warns a predator that an animal is unpalatable or poisonous.

warning track ▶ **noun** Baseball a strip around the outside of the outfield which warns approaching fielders of the proximity of a wall.

warning triangle ▶ **noun** a triangular red frame, made of reflective material, carried by motorists to be set up on the road as a danger signal in case of a breakdown or other hazard.

War of 1812 a conflict between the US and the UK (1812–14), prompted by restrictions on US trade resulting from the British blockade of French and allied ports during the Napoleonic Wars, and by British and Canadian support for American Indians trying to resist westward expansion. It was ended by a treaty which restored all conquered territories to their owners before outbreak of war.

War of American Independence see **AMERICAN INDEPENDENCE, WAR OF**.

War Office a former department of the British government that was in charge of the army (incorporated into the Ministry of Defence in 1964).

War of Jenkins's Ear see **JENKINS'S EAR, WAR OF**.

warp ▶ **verb 1** become or cause to become bent or twisted out of shape, typically as a result of the effects of heat or dampness: [no obj.] *wood has a tendency to warp* | [with obj.] *moisture had warped the box.*
■ [with obj.] cause to become abnormal or strange; have a distorting effect on: *your judgement has been warped by your obvious dislike of him* | [as adj. **warped**] *a warped sense of humour.*
2 [with obj. and adverbial of direction] move or tow (a ship) along by hauling on a rope attached to a stationary object ashore.
■ [no obj., with adverbial of direction] (of a ship) move or be towed in such a way.
3 [with obj.] (in weaving) arrange (yarn) so as to form the warp of a piece of cloth.
4 [with obj.] cover (land) with a deposit of alluvial soil by natural or artificial flooding.
▶ **noun 1** a twist or distortion in the shape or form of something: *the head of the racket had a curious warp.*
■ figurative an abnormality or perversion in a person's character. ■ [as modifier] relating to or denoting (fictional or hypothetical) space travel by means of distorting space–time: *the craft possessed warp drive* | *warp speed.*
2 [in sing.] (in weaving) the threads on a loom over and under which other threads (the weft) are passed to make cloth: *the warp and weft are the basic constituents of all textiles* | figurative *rugby is woven into the warp and weft of South African society.*
3 a rope attached at one end to a fixed point and used for moving or mooring a ship.
4 [mass noun] archaic alluvial sediment; silt.

W

– DERIVATIVES **warpage** noun (usu. in sense 1 of the verb), **warper** noun.
– ORIGIN Old English *weorpan* (verb), *wearp* (noun), of Germanic origin; related to Dutch *werpen* and German *werfen* 'to throw'. Early verb senses included 'throw', 'fling open', and 'hit (with a missile)'; the sense 'bend' dates from late Middle English. The noun was originally a term in weaving (see sense 2).

warpaint ▶ noun [mass noun] a pigment or paint traditionally used in some societies, especially those of North American Indians, to decorate the face and body before battle.
■ informal elaborate or excessively applied make-up.

warpath ▶ noun (in phrase **on the warpath**) in an angry and aggressive state about a conflict or dispute: *he intends to go on the warpath with a national campaign to reverse the decision.*
– ORIGIN with reference to American Indians heading towards a battle with an enemy.

war pension ▶ noun a pension paid to someone who is disabled or bereaved by war.

warplane ▶ noun an aeroplane designed and equipped to engage in air combat or to drop bombs.

war poet ▶ noun a poet writing at the time of and on the subject of war, especially one on military service during the First World War.

warragal ▶ noun & adjective variant spelling of **WARRIGAL**.

warrant ▶ noun **1** a document issued by a legal or government official authorizing the police or some other body to make an arrest, search premises, or carry out some other action relating to the administration of justice: *magistrates issued a warrant for his arrest | an extradition warrant.*
■ a document that entitles the holder to receive goods, money, or services: *we'll issue you with a travel warrant.* ■ Finance a negotiable security allowing the holder to buy shares at a specified price at or before some future date. ■ [mass noun] [usu. with negative] justification or authority for an action, belief, or feeling: *there is **no warrant for** this assumption.*
2 an official certificate of appointment issued to an officer of lower rank than a commissioned officer.
▶ verb [with obj.] justify or necessitate (a certain course of action): *there is not enough new evidence to warrant a reference to the Court of Appeal.*
■ officially affirm or guarantee: *the vendor warrants the accuracy of the report.*
– PHRASES **I** (or **I'll**) **warrant** (**you**) dated used to express the speaker's certainty about a fact or situation: *I'll warrant you'll thank me for it in years to come.*
– DERIVATIVES **warranter** noun.
– ORIGIN Middle English (in the senses 'protector' and 'safeguard', also, as a verb, 'keep safe from danger'): from variants of Old French *guarant* (noun), *guarantir* (verb), of Germanic origin; compare with **GUARANTEE**.

warrantable ▶ adjective (of an action or statement) able to be authorized or sanctioned; justifiable: *a warrantable assertion.*
– DERIVATIVES **warrantableness** noun, **warrantably** adverb.

warrant card ▶ noun a document of authorization and identification carried by a police officer.

warrantee ▶ noun Law a person to whom a warranty is given.

warrant officer ▶ noun a rank of officer in the army, RAF, or US navy, below the commissioned officers and above the NCOs.

warrantor /ˈwɒrəntə/ ▶ noun a person or company that provides a warranty.

warranty ▶ noun (pl. **-ies**) a written guarantee, issued to the purchaser of an article by its manufacturer, promising to repair or replace it if necessary within a specified period of time: *the car comes with a three-year warranty* | [mass noun] *as your machine is under warranty, I suggest getting it checked.*
■ (in an insurance contract) an engagement by the insured party that certain statements are true or that certain conditions shall be fulfilled, the breach of it invalidating the policy. ■ [mass noun] [usu. with negative] archaic justification or grounds for an action or belief: *you have no warranty for such an audacious doctrine.*
– ORIGIN Middle English: from Anglo-Norman French *warantie*, variant of *garantie* (see **GUARANTY**). Early use was as a legal term denoting a covenant annexed to a conveyance of property, in which the vendor affirmed the security of the title.

Warren[1], Earl (1891–1974), American judge. As Chief Justice of the Supreme Court (1953–69) he did much to improve civil liberties and is also remembered for heading the Warren Commission (1964) into the assassination of President Kennedy.

Warren[2], Robert Penn (1905–89), American poet, novelist, and critic. An advocate of New Criticism, he was the first person to win Pulitzer Prizes in both fiction and poetry categories and in 1986 he was made the first American Poet Laureate.

warren ▶ noun (also **rabbit warren**) a network of interconnecting rabbit burrows.
■ a densely populated or labyrinthine building or district: *a warren of narrow gas-lit streets.* ■ Brit. historical an enclosed piece of land set aside for breeding game, especially rabbits.
– ORIGIN late Middle English: from an Anglo-Norman French and Old Northern French variant of Old French *garenne* 'game park', of Gaulish origin.

warrener ▶ noun historical a gamekeeper.
■ a person in charge of a rabbit warren, either as owner or on behalf of its owner.
– ORIGIN late Middle English: from Anglo-Norman French *warener*, from *warenne* 'game park'.

warrigal /ˈwɒrɪg(ə)l/ (also **warragal**) Austral. ▶ noun
1 a dingo dog.
2 a wild or untamed horse.
3 another term for **MYALL** (in sense 2).
▶ adjective (of a plant) not cultivated: *warrigal melons.*
■ untamed; undisciplined: *half a dozen warrigal knockabout men, proper tearaway types.*
– ORIGIN from Dharuk *warrigal* 'wild dingo'.

warring /ˈwɔːrɪŋ/ ▶ adjective [attrib.] (of two or more people or groups) in conflict with each other: *warring factions | a warring couple.*

Warrington /ˈwɒrɪŋtən/ an industrial town on the River Mersey in NW England; pop. 82,520 (1981).

warrior ▶ noun (especially in former times) a brave or experienced soldier or fighter.
– ORIGIN Middle English: from Old Northern French *werreior*, variant of Old French *guerreior*, from *guerreier* 'make war', from *guerre* 'war'.

Warsaw /ˈwɔːsɔː/ the capital of Poland, on the River Vistula; pop. 1,655,660 (1990). The city suffered severe damage and the loss of 700,000 lives during the Second World War and was almost completely rebuilt. Polish name **WARSZAWA** /varˈʃava/.

Warsaw Pact a treaty of mutual defence and military aid signed at Warsaw on 14 May 1955 by Communist states of Europe under Soviet influence, in response to the admission of West Germany to NATO. The Pact was dissolved in 1991.

warship ▶ noun a ship equipped with weapons and designed to take part in warfare at sea.

Wars of Religion another term for **FRENCH WARS OF RELIGION**.

Wars of the Roses the 15th-century English civil wars between the Houses of York and Lancaster, represented by white and red roses respectively, during the reigns of Henry VI, Edward IV, and Richard III. The struggle was largely ended in 1485 by the defeat and death of the Yorkist king Richard III at the Battle of Bosworth and the accession of the Lancastrian Henry Tudor (Henry VII), who united the two houses by marrying Elizabeth, daughter of Edward IV.

wart ▶ noun a small, hard, benign growth on the skin, caused by a virus.
■ any rounded excrescence on the skin of an animal or the surface of a plant. ■ informal an obnoxious or objectionable person. ■ an undesirable or disfiguring feature: *few products are without their warts.*
– PHRASES **warts and all** informal including features or qualities that are not appealing or attractive: *Philip must learn to accept me, warts and all.*
– DERIVATIVES **warty** adjective.
– ORIGIN Old English *wearte*, of Germanic origin; related to Dutch *wrat* and German *Warze*.

wart-biter ▶ noun a large mottled green or brown bush cricket that inhabits coarse grassland in Europe.
● *Decticus verrucivorus*, family Tettigoniidae.
– ORIGIN mid 19th cent.: so named from the reputed former use in Sweden of such crickets to bite off warts.

wart disease ▶ noun [mass noun] a fungal disease of potatoes which produces warty outgrowths on the tubers.
● The fungus is *Synchytrium endobioticum*, subdivision Mastigomycotina.

warthog ▶ noun an African wild pig with a large head, warty lumps on the face, and curved tusks.
● *Phacochoerus aethiopicus*, family Suidae.

wartime ▶ noun [mass noun] a period during which a war is taking place.

war-torn ▶ adjective (of a place) racked or devastated by war: *a war-torn republic.*

wart snake ▶ noun a large aquatic fish-eating snake with coarse-textured scales which give it a file-like appearance, native to SE Asia and Australia. Also called **FILE SNAKE**.
● Family Achrochordidae and genus *Achrochordus*: three species, e.g. the **Asian wart snake** (*A. arafurae*).

warty newt ▶ noun another term for **CRESTED NEWT**.

Warwick[1] /ˈwɒrɪk/ the county town of Warwickshire, in central England, on the River Avon; pop. 21,990 (1981).

Warwick[2] /ˈwɒrɪk/, Richard Neville, Earl of (1428–71), English statesman; known as **Warwick the Kingmaker**. During the Wars of the Roses he fought first on the Yorkist side, helping Edward IV to gain the throne (1461), and then on the Lancastrian side, briefly restoring Henry VI to the throne (1470). Warwick was killed at the battle of Barnet.

Warwickshire a county of central England; county town, Warwick.

wary ▶ adjective (**warier**, **wariest**) feeling or showing caution about possible dangers or problems: *dogs which have been mistreated often remain very **wary of** strangers | a wary look.*
– DERIVATIVES **warily** adverb, **wariness** noun.
– ORIGIN late 15th cent.: from **WARE**[3] + **-Y**[1].

was first and third person singular past of **BE**.

wasabi /wəˈsɑːbi/ ▶ noun [mass noun] a Japanese plant with a thick green root which tastes like strong horseradish and is used in cookery, especially in powder or paste form as an accompaniment to raw fish.
● *Eutrema wasabi*, family Cruciferae.
– ORIGIN early 20th cent.: from Japanese.

Wash. ▶ abbreviation for Washington.

wash ▶ verb **1** [with obj.] clean with water and, typically, soap or detergent: *Auntie Lou had washed all their clothes | he **washed down** the woodwork in the kitchen.*
■ [no obj.] clean oneself, especially one's hands and face with soap and water. ■ [with obj. and adverbial] remove (a stain or dirt) from something by cleaning with water and detergent: *they have to keep washing the mould off the walls* | figurative *all that hate can't wash away the guilt.* ■ [no obj., with adverbial] (of dirt or a stain) be removed in such a way: *the dirt on his clothes would easily wash out.* ■ [no obj., with adverbial] (of fabric, a garment, or dye) withstand cleaning to a specified degree without shrinking or fading: *a linen-mix yarn which washes well.* ■ [no obj.] do one's laundry: *I need someone to cook and wash for me.* ■ (usu. **be washed**) poetic/literary wet or moisten (something) thoroughly: *you are beautiful with your face washed with rain.*
2 [with obj. and adverbial of direction] (of flowing water) carry (someone or something) in a particular direction: *floods washed away the bridges.*
■ [no obj., with adverbial of direction] be carried by flowing water: *an oil slick washed up on the beaches.* ■ [no obj., with adverbial of direction] (especially of waves) sweep, move, or splash in a particular direction: *the sea began to wash along the decks.* ■ [with obj.] (usu. **be washed**) (of a river, sea, or lake) flow through or lap against (a country, coast, etc.): *offshore islands washed by warm blue seas.* ■ [no obj.] (**wash over**) (of a feeling) affect (someone) suddenly: *a deep feeling of sadness washed over her.* ■ [no obj.] (**wash over**) occur all around without greatly affecting (someone): *she allowed the babble of conversation to wash over her.* ■ [with obj.] sift metallic particles from (earth or gravel) by running water through it.
3 [with obj.] (usu. **be washed**) brush with a thin coat of dilute paint or ink: *the walls were washed with shades of umber.*
■ (**wash something with**) coat inferior metal with (a film of gold or silver from a solution).
4 [no obj., with negative] informal seem convincing or genuine: *charm won't wash with this crew.*

W

▶**noun 1** [usu. in sing.] an act of washing something or an instance of being washed: *her hair needs a wash.*
■a quantity of clothes needing to be or just having been washed: *she hung out her Tuesday wash.* ■ [mass noun] a medicinal or cleansing solution, especially one applied to the skin: *antiseptic skin wash.*
2 [in sing.] the disturbed water or air behind a moving boat or aircraft or the sound made by this: *the wash of a smart motor boat.*
■the surging of water or breaking of waves or the sound made by this: *the wash of waves on the pebbled beach.*
3 (**the Wash**) an inlet of the North Sea on the east coast of England between Norfolk and Lincolnshire.
4 a layer of paint or metal spread thinly on a surface: *the walls were covered with a pale lemon wash.*
5 [mass noun] silt or gravel carried by a stream or river and deposited as sediment.
■[count noun] a sandbank exposed only at low tide.
6 [mass noun] kitchen slops and other food waste fed to pigs.
7 [mass noun] malt fermenting in preparation for distillation.
8 [in sing.] US informal a situation or result that is of no benefit to either of two opposing sides.
– PHRASES **come out in the wash** informal be resolved eventually with no lasting harm: *he's not happy but he assures me it'll all come out in the wash.* **in the wash** (of clothes, bedlinen, or similar) put aside for washing or in the process of being washed. **wash one's dirty linen** (or **laundry**) **in public** informal discuss or argue about one's personal affairs in public. **wash one's hands** go to the toilet (used euphemistically). **wash one's hands of** disclaim responsibility for: *the social services washed their hands of his daughter.* [ORIGIN: originally with biblical allusion to Matt. 27:24.]
– ORIGIN Old English *wæscan* (verb), of Germanic origin; related to Dutch *wassen*, German *waschen*, also to **WATER**.

▶**wash something down** accompany or follow food with a drink: *bacon and eggs washed down with a cup of tea.*
wash out (or **wash someone out**) N. Amer. be excluded (or exclude someone) from a course or position after a failure to meet the required standards: *a lot of them had washed out of pilot training.*
wash something out 1 clean the inside of something with water. **2** wash something, especially a garment, quickly or briefly: *I don't have time to wash a blouse out every night.* **3** (usu. **be washed out**) cause an event to be postponed or cancelled because of rain: *their match against Australia was washed out.* **4** (of a flood or downpour) make a breach in a road.
wash up 1 (also **wash something up**) chiefly Brit. clean crockery and cutlery after use. **2** US clean one's hands and face.

washable ▶**adjective** (especially of fabric or clothes) able to be washed without shrinkage or other damage: *washable curtains.*
– DERIVATIVES **washability** noun.

wash-and-wear ▶**adjective** (of a garment or fabric) easily washed, drying quickly, and not needing to be ironed.

washbag ▶**noun** Brit. a toilet bag.

washbasin ▶**noun** a basin, typically fixed to a wall or on a pedestal, used for washing one's hands and face.

washboard ▶**noun 1** a board made of ridged wood or a sheet of corrugated zinc, used when washing clothes as a surface against which to scrub them.
■a similar board played as a percussion instrument by scraping. ■ [mass noun] chiefly N. Amer. the surface of a worn, uneven road. ■ [as modifier] denoting a man's stomach that is lean and has well-defined muscles.
2 a board fixed along the side of a boat to prevent water from spilling in over the edge.
▶**verb** [with obj.] [usu. as adj. **washboarded**] chiefly N. Amer. cause ridges to develop in (a road or road surface): *a road left washboarded by winter frost.*

wash bottle ▶**noun** Chemistry a bottle, typically plastic, with a nozzle for directing a stream of liquid on to something.
■a bottle containing liquid through which gases are passed for purification.

washcloth ▶**noun** N. Amer. a facecloth.

washday ▶**noun** a day on which a household's

clothes, bedlinen, etc. are washed, especially when the same day each week.

washdown ▶**noun** an act of washing someone or something thoroughly, in particular an act of washing oneself completely at a washbasin.
■[as modifier] denoting a toilet having a flushing system in which the pan is automatically washed down.

wash drawing ▶**noun** a picture or sketch made by laying on washes of watercolour, typically in monochrome, over a pen or pencil drawing.

washed out ▶**adjective** faded by or as if by sunlight or repeated washing: *washed-out jeans.*
■(of a person) pale and tired.

washed-up ▶**adjective** deposited by the tide on a shore: *washed-up jellyfish.*
■informal no longer effective or successful: *a washed-up actress.*

washer ▶**noun 1** [usu. with modifier] a person or device that washes something: *a glass washer.*
■a washing machine. ■ a windscreen washer. ■ Austral. a facecloth.
2 a small flat ring made of metal, rubber, or plastic fixed under a nut or the head of a bolt to spread the pressure when tightened or between two joining surfaces as a spacer or seal.

washer-dryer ▶**noun** a washing machine with an inbuilt tumble-dryer.

washer-up ▶**noun** (pl. **washers-up**) Brit. a person whose job or task it is to wash the crockery, cutlery, and other utensils in a kitchen.

washerwoman ▶**noun** (pl. **-women**) a woman whose occupation is washing clothes.

washery ▶**noun** (pl. **-ies**) (in the mining industry) a place where coal is washed.

washeteria ▶**noun** another term for **LAUNDERETTE**.
– ORIGIN 1950s: from **WASH**, on the pattern of *cafeteria.*

wash-hand basin ▶**noun** another term for **WASHBASIN**.

wash-hand stand ▶**noun** another term for **WASHSTAND**.

wash house ▶**noun** an outhouse or room in which clothes are washed.

washing ▶**noun** [mass noun] the action of washing oneself or laundering clothes, bedlinen, etc.
■a quantity of clothes, bedlinen, etc. that is to be washed or has just been washed: *she took her washing around to the launderette.*

washing line ▶**noun** a clothes line.

washing machine ▶**noun** a machine for washing clothes, bedlinen, etc.

washing powder ▶**noun** [mass noun] chiefly Brit. detergent in the form of a powder for washing clothes, bedlinen, etc.

washing soda ▶**noun** [mass noun] sodium carbonate, used dissolved in water for washing and cleaning.

Washington[1] **1** a state of the north-western US, on the Pacific coast; pop. 4,866,690 (1990); capital, Olympia. It became the 42nd state in 1889.
2 the capital of the US; pop. 606,900 (1990). It is coextensive with the District of Columbia, a federal district on the Potomac River with boundaries on the states of Virginia and Maryland. Founded in 1790, during the presidency of George Washington, it was planned and built as a capital city. Full name **WASHINGTON DC**.
3 an industrial town in NE England, designated as a new town in 1964; pop. 48,830 (1981).
– DERIVATIVES **Washingtonian** noun & adjective.

Washington[2], Booker T. (1856–1915), American educationist; full name *Booker Taliaferro Washington.* A leading commentator for black Americans, Washington established the Tuskegee Institute in Alabama (1881). His support for segregation and his emphasis on black people's vocational skills attracted criticism from other black leaders.

Washington[3], George (1732–99), American general and statesman, 1st President of the US 1789–97. Washington helped win the War of Independence by keeping his army together through the winter at Valley Forge and winning a decisive battle at Yorktown (1781). He chaired the convention at Philadelphia (1787) that drew up the American Constitution and subsequently served two terms as

President, following a policy of neutrality in international affairs.

washing-up ▶**noun** [mass noun] Brit. the process of washing used crockery, cutlery, and other kitchen utensils: *they've finished the washing-up.*
■crockery, cutlery, and other kitchen utensils that are to be washed: *the sink is full of washing-up.*

washland ▶**noun** [mass noun] land that is periodically flooded by a river or stream.

wash leather ▶**noun** [mass noun] dated chamois or a similar leather.

washout ▶**noun 1** [usu. in sing.] informal an event that is spoiled by constant or heavy rain.
■a disappointing failure: *the film was branded a colossal washout.*
2 a breach in a road or railway track caused by flooding.
■Geology a channel cut into a sedimentary deposit by rushing water and filled with younger material.
3 Medicine the removal of material or a substance from the body or a part of it, either by washing with a fluid, or by allowing it to be eliminated over a period.

washrag ▶**noun** US term for **FACECLOTH**.

washroom ▶**noun** N. Amer. a room with washing and toilet facilities.

washstand ▶**noun** chiefly historical a piece of furniture designed to hold a jug, bowl, or basin for the purpose of washing one's hands and face.

washtub ▶**noun** a large metal tub used for washing clothes and linen.

wash-up ▶**noun 1** an act of washing, especially washing oneself or crockery.
■Brit. informal a person employed to wash dishes in the kitchen of a restaurant or hotel.
2 informal a debrief or follow-up discussion.

wash-wipe ▶**noun** a vehicle's built-in window-cleaning system, comprising windscreen wipers and water bottle.

washy ▶**adjective** (**washier, washiest**) **1** archaic (of food or drink) too watery: *washy potatoes.*
■lacking in strength or vigour; insipid: *a weak and washy production.*
2 (of a colour) having a faded appearance.
– DERIVATIVES **washiness** noun.

wasn't ▶**contraction of** was not.

Wasp ▶**noun** N. Amer. an upper- or middle-class American white Protestant, considered to be a member of the most powerful group in society.
– DERIVATIVES **Waspish** adjective, **Waspy** adjective.
– ORIGIN 1960s: acronym from *white Anglo-Saxon Protestant.*

wasp ▶**noun 1** a social winged insect which has a narrow waist and a sting and is typically yellow with black stripes. It constructs a paper nest from wood pulp and raises the larvae on a diet of insects.
●Family Vespidae, superfamily Vespoidea, order Hymenoptera: several genera, in particular *Vespula* and *Polistes.*
2 a solitary winged insect with a narrow waist, mostly distantly related to the social wasps and including many parasitic kinds.
●Several superfamilies in the sections Aculeata (digger, mason, and potter wasps) and Parasitica (parasitic wasps and gall wasps), order Hymenoptera.
– DERIVATIVES **wasp-like** adjective.
– ORIGIN Old English *wæfs, wæps, wæsp*, of West Germanic origin, from an Indo-European root shared by Latin *vespa*; perhaps related to **WEAVE**[1] (from the web-like form of its nest).

wasp beetle ▶**noun** a black and yellow longhorn beetle that mimics the appearance and behaviour of a wasp.
●*Clytus arietis*, family Cerambycidae.

waspie ▶**noun** (pl. **-ies**) dated a woman's corset or belt designed to accentuate a slender waist.
– ORIGIN 1950s: diminutive of *wasp* from **WASP WAIST**.

waspish ▶**adjective** readily expressing anger or irritation: *he had a waspish tongue.*
– DERIVATIVES **waspishly** adverb, **waspishness** noun.

wasp waist ▶**noun** a very narrow or tightly corseted waist.
– DERIVATIVES **wasp-waisted** adjective.

wassail /ˈwɒseɪl, ˈwɒsl, ˈwɑ-/ archaic ▶**noun** [mass noun] spiced ale or mulled wine drunk during celebrations for Twelfth Night and Christmas Eve.
■lively and noisy festivities involving the drinking of plentiful amounts of alcohol; revelry.

▶**verb 1** [no obj.] drink plentiful amounts of alcohol and enjoy oneself with others in a noisy, lively way.
■[with obj.] historical (in SW England) drink to (fruit trees, typically apple trees) in a custom intended to ensure a fruitful crop.
2 go from house to house at Christmas singing carols: *here we go a-wassailing.*
– DERIVATIVES **wassailer** noun.
– ORIGIN Middle English *wæs hæil* 'be in (good) health!': from Old Norse *ves heill* (compare with **HAIL**[2]). The drinking formula *wassail* (and the reply *drinkhail* 'drink good health') were probably introduced by Danish-speaking inhabitants of England, and then spread, so that by the 12th cent. the usage was considered by the Normans to be characteristic of Englishmen.

wassail bowl (also **wassail cup**) ▶**noun** a large bowl in which wassail was made and from which it was dispensed for the drinking of toasts.

Wassermann test /'vɑːsəmən/ ▶**noun** Medicine a diagnostic test for syphilis using a specific antibody reaction (the **Wassermann reaction**) of the patient's blood serum.
– ORIGIN early 20th cent.: named after August P. Wassermann (1866–1925), German pathologist.

wast /wɒst, wəst/ archaic or dialect second person singular past of **BE**.

wastage ▶**noun** [mass noun] **1** the action or process of losing or destroying something by using it carelessly or extravagantly: *the wastage of natural resources.*
■the amount of something lost or destroyed in such a way: *wastage was cut by 50 per cent.*
2 (also **natural wastage**) the reduction in the size of a workforce as a result of voluntary resignation or retirement rather than enforced redundancy.
■the number of people leaving a job or further educational establishment before they have completed their training or education.
3 the weakening or deterioration of a part of the body, typically as a result of illness or lack of use: *the wastage of muscle tissue.*

waste ▶**verb 1** [with obj.] use or expend carelessly, extravagantly, or to no purpose: *we can't afford to waste electricity* | *I don't use the car, so why should I* ***waste*** *precious money* ***on*** *it?*
■(usu. **be wasted on**) bestow or expend on an unappreciative recipient: *her small talk was wasted on this guest.* ■ (usu. **be wasted**) fail to make full or good use of: *we're wasted in this job.* ■ deliberately dispose of (surplus stock).
2 [no obj.] (of a person or a part of the body) become progressively weaker and more emaciated: *she was dying of Aids, visibly* ***wasting away*** | [as adj. **wasting**] *a wasting disease.*
■[with obj.] archaic cause to do this: *these symptoms wasted the patients very much.*
3 [with obj.] poetic/literary devastate or ruin (a place): *he seized their cattle and wasted their country.*
■N. Amer. informal kill or severely injure (someone).
4 [no obj.] poetic/literary (of time) pass away; be spent: *the years were wasting.*
▶**adjective** [attrib.] **1** (of a material, substance, or by-product) eliminated or discarded as no longer useful or required after the completion of a process: *ensure that waste materials are disposed of responsibly* | *plants produce oxygen as a waste product.*
2 (of an area of land, typically in a city or town) not used, cultivated, or built on: *a patch of waste ground.*
▶**noun 1** an act or instance of using or expending something carelessly, extravagantly, or to no purpose: *it's a waste of time trying to argue with him* | [mass noun] *they had learned to avoid waste.*
■[mass noun] archaic the gradual loss or diminution of something: *he was pale and weak from waste of blood.*
2 [mass noun] material that is not wanted; the unusable remains or by-products of something: *nuclear waste* | (**wastes**) *hazardous industrial wastes.*
3 (usu. **wastes**) a large area of barren, typically uninhabited land: *the icy wastes of the Antarctic.*
4 [mass noun] Law damage to an estate caused by an act or by neglect, especially by a life-tenant.
5 short for **WASTE PIPE**.
– PHRASES **go to waste** be unused or expended to no purpose. **lay waste to** (or **lay something** (**to**) **waste**) completely destroy: *a land laid waste by war.* **waste one's breath** see **BREATH**. **waste of space** informal a person perceived as useless or incompetent. **waste not, want not** proverb if you use a commodity or resource carefully and without extravagance you will never be in need. **waste words** see **WORD**.
– ORIGIN Middle English: from Old Northern French *wast(e)* (noun), *waster* (verb), based on Latin *vastus* 'unoccupied, uncultivated'.

wastebasket ▶**noun** a waste-paper basket.

waste bin ▶**noun** an all-purpose rubbish bin of varying sizes for use either indoors or outdoors.

wasted ▶**adjective 1** used or expended carelessly, extravagantly, or to no purpose: *wasted fuel* | *a wasted opportunity.*
■(of an action) not producing the desired result: *I'm sorry you've had a wasted journey.*
2 (of a person or a part of the body) weak and emaciated: *her wasted arm.*
■informal under the influence of alcohol or illegal drugs: *he looked kind of wasted.*

waste-disposal unit (also **waste disposer**) ▶**noun** an electrically operated device fitted to the waste pipe of a kitchen sink for grinding up food waste.

wasteful ▶**adjective** (of a person, action, or process) using or expending something of value carelessly, extravagantly, or to no purpose: *wasteful energy consumption.*
– DERIVATIVES **wastefully** adverb, **wastefulness** noun.

wastegate ▶**noun** a device in a turbocharger which regulates the pressure at which exhaust gases pass to the turbine by opening or closing a vent to the exterior.

wasteland ▶**noun** [mass noun] an unused area of land that has become barren or overgrown.
■a bleak, unattractive, and unused or neglected urban or industrial area: *the restoration of industrial wasteland* | [count noun] figurative *the mid 70s are now seen as something of a cultural wasteland.*

waste-paper basket ▶**noun** chiefly Brit. a receptacle for small quantities of rubbish.

waste pipe ▶**noun** a pipe carrying waste water, such as that from a sink, bath, or shower, to a drain.

waster ▶**noun** a wasteful person or thing: *you are a great waster of time.*
■informal a person who does little or nothing of value.
■ a discarded piece of defective pottery.

wastrel /'weɪstr(ə)l/ ▶**noun 1** poetic/literary a wasteful or good-for-nothing person.
2 archaic a waif; a neglected child.
– ORIGIN late 16th cent. (denoting a strip of waste land): from the verb **WASTE** + **-REL**.

watch ▶**verb 1** [with obj.] look at or observe attentively, typically over a period of time: *Lucy watched him go* | [no obj.] *as she watched, two women came into the garden* | [with clause] *everyone stopped to watch what was going on.*
■keep under careful or protective observation: *a large set of steel doors,* ***watched over*** *by a single guard.* ■ secretly follow or spy on: *he told me my telephones were tapped and that I was being watched.* ■ follow closely or maintain an interest in: *the girls watched the development of this relationship with incredulity.* ■ exercise care, caution, or restraint about: *most women watch their diet during pregnancy* | [with clause] *you should watch what you say!* ■ [no obj.] (**watch for**) look out or be on the alert for: *in spring and summer, watch for kingfishers* | ***watch out for*** *broken glass.* ■ [no obj.] [usu. in imperative] (**watch out**) be careful: *credit-card fraud is on the increase, so watch out.* ■ (**watch it/yourself**) [usu. in imperative] informal be careful (used as a warning or threat): *if anyone finds out, you're dead meat, so watch it.*
2 [no obj.] archaic remain awake for the purpose of religious observance: *she watched whole nights in the church.*
▶**noun 1** a small timepiece worn typically on a strap on one's wrist.
2 [usu. in sing.] an act or instance of carefully observing someone or something over a period of time: *the security forces have been* ***keeping a close watch on*** *our activities.*
■a period of vigil during which a person is stationed to look out for danger or trouble, typically during the night: *Murray took the last watch before dawn.* ■ a fixed period of duty on a ship, usually lasting four hours. ■ (also **starboard** or **port watch**) the officers and crew on duty during one such period. ■ a spell of duty worked by firefighters or police officers; a shift. ■ figurative the period someone spends in a particular role or job. ■ (usu. **the watch**) historical a watchman or group of watchmen who patrolled and guarded the streets of a town before the introduction of the police force.
3 [in sing.] [with adj.] informal a film or programme considered in terms of its appeal to the public: *this movie's an engrossing watch.*
– PHRASES **be on the watch** be carefully looking out for something, especially a possible danger. **keep watch** stay on the lookout for danger or trouble. **watch one's** (or **someone's**) **back** protect oneself (or someone else) against danger from an unexpected quarter. **watch one's mouth** see **MOUTH**. **the watches of the night** poetic/literary the hours of night, portrayed as a time when one cannot sleep. **watch the pennies** see **PENNY**. **watch one's step** see **STEP**. **watch this space** see **SPACE**. **watch the time** ensure that one is aware of the time in order to avoid being late. **watch the world go by** spend time observing other people going about their business.
– DERIVATIVES **watcher** noun [often in combination] *a badger-watcher.*
– ORIGIN Old English *wæcce* 'watchfulness', *wæccende* 'remaining awake'; related to **WAKE**[1]. The sense 'small timepiece' probably developed by way of a sense 'alarm device attached to a clock'.

watcha ▶**exclamation** variant spelling of **WOTCHA**[2].

watchable ▶**adjective** (of a film or television programme) moderately enjoyable to watch.
– DERIVATIVES **watchability** noun.

watch cap ▶**noun** a close-fitting knitted cap of a kind worn by members of the US Navy in cold weather.

watch case ▶**noun** a metal case enclosing the works of a watch.

watch chain ▶**noun** a metal chain securing a pocket watch.

Watch Committee ▶**noun** historical (in the UK) the committee of a county borough council dealing with policing and public lighting.

watchdog ▶**noun** a dog kept to guard private property.
■a person or group whose occupation or function is to monitor the practices of companies providing a particular service or utility: *the consumer watchdog for transport in London.*
▶**verb** (**-dogged**, **-dogging**) [with obj.] maintain surveillance over (a person, activity, or situation): *how can we watchdog our investments?*

watchfire ▶**noun** a fire maintained during the night as a signal or for the use of someone who is on watch.

watchful ▶**adjective** watching or observing someone or something closely; alert and vigilant: *they attended dances under the* ***watchful eye*** *of their father.*
■archaic wakeful; sleepless.
– DERIVATIVES **watchfully** adverb, **watchfulness** noun.

watch glass ▶**noun** Brit. a glass disc covering the dial of a watch.
■a concave glass disc used in a laboratory to hold material for use in experiments.

watching brief ▶**noun** Law, Brit. a brief held by a barrister to follow a case on behalf of a client who is not directly involved.
■an interest in a proceeding in which one is not directly or immediately concerned.

watchkeeper ▶**noun** a person who keeps watch or acts as a lookout, especially on board a ship.

watch list ▶**noun** a list of individuals, groups, or items that require close surveillance, typically for legal or political reasons.

watchmaker ▶**noun** a person who makes and repairs watches and clocks.
– DERIVATIVES **watchmaking** noun.

watchman ▶**noun** (pl. **-men**) a man employed to look after an empty building, especially at night.
■historical a member of a body of people employed to keep watch in a town at night.

watchnight ▶**noun** a religious service held on New Year's Eve or Christmas Eve.
■historical a religious service extending over midnight, held on a monthly basis by Wesleyan Methodists.

watch spring ▶**noun** a mainspring in a watch.

watchtower ▶**noun** a tower built to create an elevated observation point.

watchword ▶**noun** a word or phrase expressing a

W

person's or group's core aim or belief: *environmental quality will be a watchword for the nineties.*
■ archaic a military password.

water ▶ **noun** [mass noun] **1** a colourless, transparent, odourless, tasteless liquid which forms the seas, lakes, rivers, and rain and is the basis of the fluids of living organisms.
■ this as supplied to houses or commercial establishments through pipes and taps: *each bedroom has a washbasin with hot and cold water* | [as modifier] *water pipes.* ■ one of the four elements in ancient and medieval philosophy and in astrology (considered essential to the nature of the signs Cancer, Scorpio, and Pisces): [as modifier] *a water sign.* ■ (usu. **the waters**) the water of a mineral spring, typically as used medicinally for bathing in or drinking: *you can take the waters at the Pump Room.* ■ [with modifier] a solution of a specified substance in water: *ammonia water.* ■ urine: *drinking alcohol will make you need to* ***pass water*** *more often.* ■ (**waters**) the amniotic fluid surrounding a fetus in the womb, especially as discharged in a flow shortly before birth: *I think my waters have broken.*

Water is a compound of oxygen and hydrogen (chem. formula: H_2O) with highly distinctive physical and chemical properties: it is able to dissolve many other substances; its solid form (ice) is *less* dense than the liquid form; its boiling point, viscosity, and surface tension are unusually high for its molecular weight, and it is partially dissociated into hydrogen and hydroxyl ions.

2 (**the water**) a stretch or area of water, such as a river, sea, or lake: *the lawns ran down to the water's edge.*
■ the surface of such an area of water: *she ducked under the water.* ■ [as modifier] found in, on, or near such areas of water: *a water plant.* ■ (**waters**) the water of a particular sea, river, or lake: *the waters of Hudson Bay* | figurative *the government are taking us into unknown waters with these changes in the legislation.* ■ (**waters**) an area of sea regarded as under the jurisdiction of a particular country: *Japanese coastal waters.*
3 the quality of transparency and brilliance shown by a diamond or other gem.
4 Finance capital stock which represents a book value greater than the true assets of a company.
▶ **verb 1** [with obj.] pour or sprinkle water over (a plant or an area of ground), typically in order to encourage plant growth: *I went out to water the geraniums.*
■ give a drink of water to (an animal): *they stopped to water the horses and to refresh themselves.* ■ [no obj.] (of an animal) drink water. ■ (usu. **be watered**) (of a river) flow through (an area of land): *the valley is watered by the River Dee.* ■ take a fresh supply of water on board (a ship or steam train): *the ship was watered and fresh livestock taken aboard.* ■ Finance increase (a company's debt, or nominal capital) by the issue of new shares without a corresponding addition to assets.
2 [no obj.] (of the eyes) become full of moisture or tears: *Rory blinked, his eyes watering.*
■ (of the mouth) produce saliva, typically in response to the sight or smell of appetizing food: *the smell of frying bacon made Hilary's mouth water.*
3 [with obj.] dilute or adulterate (a drink, typically an alcoholic one) with water: *staff at the club had been* ***watering down*** *the drinks.*
■ (**water something down**) make a statement or proposal less forceful or controversial by changing or leaving out certain details: *the army's report of its investigation was considerably watered down.*
– PHRASES **by water** using a ship or boat for travel or transport: *at the end of the lake was a small kiosk, accessible only by water.* **cast one's bread upon the waters** see **BREAD**. **like water** in great quantities: *George was spending money like water.* **make water** (of a ship or boat) take in water through a leak. **of the first water** (of a diamond or pearl) of the greatest brilliance and transparency. ■ (typically of someone or something perceived as undesirable or annoying) extreme or unsurpassed of their kind: *she was a bore of the first water.* **under water** submerged; flooded. **the water of life** whisky. **water off a duck's back** see **DUCK**[1]. **water on the brain** informal hydrocephalus. **water under the bridge** (or N. Amer. **water over the dam**) used to refer to events or situations that are in the past and consequently no longer to be regarded as important or as a source of concern.
– DERIVATIVES **waterer** noun, **waterless** adjective.
– ORIGIN Old English *wæter* (noun), *wæterian* (verb), of Germanic origin; related to Dutch *water*, German *Wasser*, from an Indo-European root shared by Russian *voda* (compare with **VODKA**), also by Latin *unda* 'wave' and Greek *hudōr* 'water'.

W

water bag ▶ **noun** a bag made of leather, canvas, or other material, used for carrying water.

water bailiff ▶ **noun** Brit. **1** an official who enforces fishing laws.
2 historical a customs officer at a port.

water-based ▶ **adjective 1** (of a substance or solution) using or having water as a medium or main ingredient: *a water-based paint.*
2 (of a sporting activity) carried out on water.

water bath ▶ **noun** Chemistry a container of water heated to a given temperature, used for heating substances placed in smaller containers.

water bear ▶ **noun** a minute animal with a short plump body and four pairs of stubby legs, living in water or in the film of water on plants such as mosses.
● Phylum Tardigrada.

Water Bearer (**the Water Bearer**) the zodiacal sign or constellation Aquarius.

waterbed ▶ **noun** a bed with a water-filled rubber or plastic mattress.

water beetle ▶ **noun** any of a large number of beetles that live in fresh water.
● Several families, in particular Dytiscidae (the predatory diving beetles) and Hydrophilidae (scavenging beetles).

waterbird ▶ **noun** a bird that frequents water, especially one that habitually wades or swims in fresh water.

water birth ▶ **noun** a birth in which the mother spends the final stages of labour in a birthing pool, with delivery taking place either in or out of the water.

water biscuit ▶ **noun** a thin, crisp unsweetened biscuit made from flour and water.

water blinks ▶ **noun** see **BLINKS**.

waterblommetjie /ˈvɑːtə(r)ˌblɒməki/ ▶ **noun** (pl. **-ies**) South African term for **WATER HAWTHORN**.
– ORIGIN 1950s: Afrikaans, literally 'little water flower'.

water bloom ▶ **noun** another term for **ALGAL BLOOM**.

water boatman ▶ **noun 1** (also **lesser water boatman**) an aquatic bug which spends much of its time on the bottom, using its front legs to sieve food from the water and its hair-fringed rear legs for swimming.
● Family Corixidae, suborder Heteroptera: *Corixa*, *Sigara*, and other genera.
2 another term for **BACKSWIMMER**.

waterbody ▶ **noun** (pl. **-ies**) a body of water forming a physiographical feature, for example a sea or a reservoir.

water bomber ▶ **noun** Canadian an aircraft used for extinguishing forest fires by dropping water.

water-borne ▶ **adjective** (of a vehicle or goods) conveyed by, travelling on, or involving travel or transport on water.
■ (of a disease) communicated or propagated by contaminated water.

waterbrash ▶ **noun** [mass noun] a sudden flow of saliva associated with indigestion.
– ORIGIN early 19th cent.: from **WATER** + dialect *brash* 'eruption of fluid from the stomach'.

waterbuck ▶ **noun** a large African antelope occurring near rivers and lakes in the savannah.
● *Kobus ellipsiprymnus*, family Bovidae.

water buffalo ▶ **noun** a large black domesticated buffalo with heavy swept-back horns, used as a beast of burden throughout the tropics.
● Genus *Bubalus*, family Bovidae: the domesticated *B. bubalis*, descended from the wild *B. arnee*, which is confined to remote parts of India and SE Asia.

water butt ▶ **noun** a large barrel used for catching and storing rainwater.

water calla ▶ **noun** another term for **BOG ARUM**.

water cannon ▶ **noun** a device that ejects a powerful jet of water, typically used to disperse a crowd.

Water Carrier (**the Water Carrier**) the zodiacal sign or constellation Aquarius.

water chestnut ▶ **noun 1** (also **Chinese water chestnut**) the tuber of a tropical sedge which is widely used in oriental cookery, its white flesh remaining crisp after cooking.
2 the sedge which yields this tuber, which is cultivated in flooded fields in SE Asia.
● *Eleocharis tuberosa*, family Cyperaceae.
3 (also **water caltrop**) an aquatic plant with small white flowers, producing an edible rounded seed with two large projecting horns.
● *Trapa natans*, family Trapaceae.

water clock ▶ **noun** historical a clock that used the flow of water to measure time.

water closet ▶ **noun** dated a flush toilet.
■ a room containing such a toilet.

watercock ▶ **noun** a brown and grey aquatic Asian rail, the male of which develops black plumage and a red frontal shield in the breeding season.
● *Gallicrex cinerea*, family Rallidae.

watercolour (US **watercolor**) ▶ **noun** [mass noun] (also **watercolours**) artists' paint made with a water-soluble binder such as gum arabic, and thinned with water rather than oil, giving a transparent colour.
■ [count noun] a picture painted with watercolours. ■ the art of painting with watercolours, especially using a technique of producing paler colours by diluting rather than by adding white.
– DERIVATIVES **watercolourist** noun.

water cooler ▶ **noun** a dispenser of cooled drinking water, typically used in places of work.
■ [as modifier] US informal denoting the type of informal conversation or socializing among office workers that takes place in the communal area in which such a dispenser is located: *a water-cooler conversation.*

watercourse ▶ **noun** a brook, stream, or artificially constructed water channel.
■ the bed along which this flows.

watercraft ▶ **noun** (pl. same) **1** a boat or other vessel that travels on water.
2 [mass noun] skill in sailing and other activities which take place on water.

watercress ▶ **noun** [mass noun] a Eurasian cress which grows in running water and whose pungent leaves are used in salad.
● *Nasturtium officinale*, family Cruciferae.

water cricket ▶ **noun** a predatory water bug that runs on the surface film of water, related to the pond skater but with shorter legs. Called **WATER STRIDER** in North America.
● Family Veliidae, suborder Heteroptera: several genera, in particular *Velia*.

water crowfoot ▶ **noun** see **CROWFOOT**.

water cure ▶ **noun** chiefly historical a session of treatment by hydropathy.

water cycle ▶ **noun** the cycle of processes by which water circulates between the earth's oceans, atmosphere, and land, involving precipitation as rain and snow, drainage in streams and rivers, and return to the atmosphere by evaporation and transpiration.

water deer (also **Chinese water deer**) ▶ **noun** a small deer without antlers, the male having a pair of tusk-like canine teeth, native to China and Korea.
● *Hydropotes inermis*, family Cervidae.

water diviner ▶ **noun** Brit. a person who searches for underground water by using a dowsing rod.

waterdog ▶ **noun** an aquatic North American salamander which is a smaller relative of the mud puppy, typically living in flowing water.
● Genus *Necturus*, family Proteidae: several species.

water dropwort ▶ **noun** a widely distributed poisonous plant of the parsley family, which grows in wet habitats.
● Genus *Oenanthe*, family Umbelliferae: several species, in particular *O. crocata* of Europe.

water drum ▶ **noun 1** a West African instrument played by striking a bowl or gourd floating upside down in a pail of water.
2 an American Indian drum partly filled with water to adjust the pitch and timbre.

watered silk ▶ **noun** [mass noun] silk that has been treated in such a way as to give it a wavy, lustrous finish.

waterfall ▶ **noun** a cascade of water falling from a height, formed when a river or stream flows over a precipice or steep incline.

water fern ▶ **noun 1** a small aquatic or semiaquatic fern which is either free-floating or anchored by the roots, found chiefly in tropical and warm countries.
● Families Azollaceae, Marsileaceae and Salviniaceae: many species, in particular the minute floating *Azolla filiculoides* of tropical America, which has been naturalized elsewhere.

2 an Australian fern with large coarse fronds, typically growing in marshy areas and rainforests.
● Genus *Blechnum*, family Blechnaceae: several species.

water flea ▶ noun another term for **DAPHNIA**.

Waterford a county in the south-east of the Republic of Ireland, in the province of Munster; main administrative centre, Dungarvan.
■ its county town, a port on an inlet of St George's Channel; pop. 40,345 (1991).

Waterford glass ▶ noun [mass noun] fine clear, colourless flint glassware first manufactured in Waterford in the 18th and 19th centuries.

waterfowl ▶ plural noun ducks, geese, or other large aquatic birds, especially when regarded as game.

waterfront ▶ noun a part of a town that borders the sea or a lake or river.

water garden ▶ noun a garden with pools or a stream, for growing aquatic plants.

water gas ▶ noun [mass noun] a fuel gas consisting mainly of carbon monoxide and hydrogen, made by passing steam over incandescent coke.

Watergate a US political scandal in which an attempt to bug the national headquarters of the Democratic Party (in the Watergate building in Washington DC) led to the resignation of President Nixon (1974).

watergate ▶ noun a gate of a town or castle opening on to a lake, river, or sea.
■ archaic a sluice; a floodgate.

water glass ▶ noun **1** [mass noun] a solution of sodium or potassium silicate. It solidifies on exposure to air and is used to make silica gel and for preserving eggs and hardening artificial stone.
2 an instrument for making observations beneath the surface of water, consisting of a bucket with a glass bottom.

water gun ▶ noun N. Amer. a water pistol.

water hammer ▶ noun [mass noun] a knocking noise in a water pipe that occurs when a tap is turned off briskly.

water hawthorn ▶ noun [mass noun] an ornamental water plant with long oval floating leaves and erect aromatic flower spikes, native to the Cape of Good Hope where the flower spikes are used in cooking.
● *Aponogeton distachyus*, family Aponogetonaceae.

water hemlock ▶ noun a highly poisonous European plant of the parsley family, which grows in ditches and marshy ground. Also called **COWBANE**.
● *Cicuta virosa*, family Umbelliferae.

waterhen ▶ noun an aquatic rail, especially a moorhen or related bird.
● Genera *Gallinula* and *Amaurornis*, family Rallidae.

waterhole ▶ noun a depression in which water collects, especially one that is regularly drunk from by animals.

Waterhouse, Alfred (1830–1905), English architect. His designs include the Manchester Assize courts (1859) and Town Hall (1869–77), and the Natural History Museum in London (1873–81).

water hyacinth ▶ noun [mass noun] a free-floating tropical American water plant which has been introduced elsewhere as an ornamental and in some warmer regions has become a serious weed of waterways.
● *Eichhornia crassipes*, family Pontederiaceae.

water ice ▶ noun a dessert consisting of frozen fruit juice or flavoured water and sugar.

watering can ▶ noun a portable water container with a long spout and a detachable perforated cap, used for watering plants.

watering hole ▶ noun a waterhole from which animals regularly drink.
■ informal a pub or bar.

watering place ▶ noun a watering hole.
■ a spa or seaside resort.

water injection ▶ noun [mass noun] (in the oil industry) the forcing of water into a reservoir formation, in particular as a technique of secondary recovery.

water jacket ▶ noun a casing containing water placed around something to protect it from extremes of temperature.
– DERIVATIVES **water-jacketed** adjective.

water jump ▶ noun an obstacle in a jumping competition or steeplechase, where a horse must jump over or into water.

water knot ▶ noun a kind of knot used to join two fishing lines.

waterleaf ▶ noun a North American woodland plant with bell-shaped flowers and leaves that appear to be stained with water.
● Genus *Hydrophyllum*, family Hydrophyllaceae.

water lettuce ▶ noun [mass noun] a tropical aquatic plant of the arum family which forms a floating rosette of leaves.
● *Pistia stratiotes*, family Araceae.

water level ▶ noun **1** the height reached by the water in a reservoir, river, storage tank, or similar.
■ another term for **WATER TABLE**.
2 an implement which uses water to indicate the horizontal.

water lily ▶ noun an ornamental aquatic plant with large round floating leaves and large, typically cup-shaped, floating flowers.
● Family Nymphaeaceae: several genera and many species, including the Eurasian **white water lily** (*Nymphaea alba*, with numerous cultivars), and the widely distributed **yellow water lily** or brandy-bottle (*Nuphar luteum*).

waterline ▶ noun **1** the level normally reached by the water on the side of a ship.
■ the level reached by the sea or a river visible as a line on a rock face, beach, or riverbank. ■ any of various structural lines of a ship, parallel with the surface of the water, representing the contour of the hull at various heights above the keel.
2 a linear watermark in paper.

waterlogged ▶ adjective saturated with or full of water: *the race was called off after parts of the course were found to be waterlogged.*
– ORIGIN mid 18th cent.: past participle of the verb *waterlog* 'make (a ship) unmanageable by flooding', from **WATER** + the verb **LOG**[1].

Waterloo, Battle of /ˌwɔːtəˈluː/ a battle fought on 18 June 1815 near the village of Waterloo (in what is now Belgium), in which Napoleon's army was defeated by the British (under the Duke of Wellington) and Prussians. The allied pursuit caused Napoleon's army to disintegrate entirely, ending his bid to return to power.
■ [as noun **a Waterloo**] a decisive defeat or failure: *the coach rued the absence of his top player as his team met their Waterloo.*

water main ▶ noun the main pipe in a water supply system.

waterman ▶ noun (pl. **-men**) a boatman.
■ an oarsman who has attained a particular level of knowledge or skill.

watermark ▶ noun a faint design made in some paper during manufacture that is visible when held against the light and typically identifies the maker.
▶ verb [with obj.] mark with such a design.

water mass ▶ noun a large body of seawater that is distinguishable by its characteristic temperature and salinity range.

water meadow ▶ noun a meadow that is periodically flooded by a stream or river.

water measurer ▶ noun a long, thin aquatic bug which walks slowly on the surface film of water and spears small prey with its beak.
● Genus *Hydrometra*, family Hydrometridae, suborder Heteroptera: several species.

watermelon ▶ noun **1** the large melon-like fruit of a plant of the gourd family, with smooth green skin, red pulp, and watery juice.
2 the African plant which yields this fruit.
● *Citrullus lanatus*, family Cucurbitaceae.

water milfoil ▶ noun see **MILFOIL** (sense 2).

watermill ▶ noun a mill worked by a waterwheel.

water moccasin ▶ noun another term for **COTTONMOUTH**.

water nymph ▶ noun (in folklore and classical mythology) a nymph inhabiting or presiding over water, especially a naiad or nereid.

water of crystallization ▶ noun [mass noun] Chemistry water molecules forming an essential part of the crystal structure of some compounds.

water opossum ▶ noun another term for **YAPOK**.

water ouzel ▶ noun dialect term for **DIPPER** (in sense 1).

water parsnip ▶ noun a tall plant of the parsley family which lives in or near water.

● *Sium latifolium* and *Berula erecta*, family Umbelliferae.

water pepper ▶ noun a widely distributed plant of the dock family which grows in wet ground, with peppery-tasting leaves and sap which is a skin irritant.
● Genus *Polygonum*, family Polygonaceae: several species, in particular *P. hydropiper*.

water pipe ▶ noun **1** a pipe for conveying water.
2 a pipe for smoking tobacco, cannabis, etc., that draws the smoke through water to cool it.

water pipit ▶ noun a dark-coloured European pipit that frequents waterside habitats.
● *Anthus spinoletta*, family Motacillidae; formerly thought to be conspecific with the rock pipit.

water pistol ▶ noun a toy pistol that shoots a jet of water.

waterplane ▶ noun the horizontal plane which passes through a floating ship on a level with the waterline.

water plantain ▶ noun an aquatic or marshland plant of north temperate regions, with leaves that resemble those of plantains and a tall stem bearing numerous pink flowers.
● Genus *Alisma*, family Alismataceae.

water polo ▶ noun [mass noun] a seven-a-side game played by swimmers in a pool, with a ball like a football that is thrown into the opponents' net. The game developed in Britain from about 1870.

water power ▶ noun [mass noun] power that is derived from the weight or motion of water, used as a force to drive machinery.
– DERIVATIVES **water-powered** adjective.

waterproof ▶ adjective impervious to water: *a waterproof hat.*
■ not liable to be washed away by water: *waterproof ink.*
▶ noun Brit. a garment, especially a coat, that keeps out water.
▶ verb [with obj.] make impervious to water.
– DERIVATIVES **waterproofer** noun, **waterproofness** noun.

water purslane ▶ noun a creeping Eurasian plant of damp places and bare ground.
● *Lythrum portula*, family Lythraceae.

water rail ▶ noun a secretive Eurasian marshbird with dark grey and brown plumage, making loud grunts and squeals in the breeding season.
● *Rallus aquaticus*, family Rallidae.

water rat ▶ noun a large semiaquatic rat-like rodent.
● Several genera in the family Muridae, in particular *Hydromys* of Australasia.
■ Brit. another term for **WATER VOLE**.

water rate ▶ noun (usu. **water rates**) a charge made for the use of a public water supply.

water-repellent ▶ adjective not easily penetrated by water, especially as a result of being treated for such a purpose with a surface coating.

water-resistant ▶ adjective able to resist the penetration of water to some degree but not entirely.
– DERIVATIVES **water-resistance** noun.

Waters, Muddy (1915–83), American blues singer and guitarist; born *McKinley Morganfield*. Waters impressed new rhythm-and-blues bands such as the Rolling Stones, who took their name from his 1950 song.

waterscape ▶ noun a landscape in which an expanse of water is a dominant feature.

water scorpion ▶ noun a mainly tropical predatory water bug with grasping forelegs, breathing from the surface via a bristle-like 'tail'.
● Family Nepidae, suborder Heteroptera: several genera and species, including the European *Nepa cinerea*.

watershed ▶ noun an area or ridge of land that separates waters flowing to different rivers, basins, or seas.
■ an event or period marking a turning point in a course of action or state of affairs: *these works mark a watershed in the history of music.* ■ Brit. the time after which programmes that are regarded as unsuitable for children are broadcast on television.
– ORIGIN early 19th cent.: from **WATER** + *shed* in the sense 'ridge of high ground' (related to **SHED**[2]), suggested by German *Wasserscheide*.

water shoot ▶ noun a vigorous but unproductive shoot from the trunk, main branch, or root of a tree.

water shrew ▶ **noun** a large semiaquatic shrew that preys on aquatic invertebrates.
• Four genera, family Soricidae: several species, in particular the **Eurasian water shrew** (*Neomys fodiens*) and the **American water shrew** (*Sorex palustris*).

waterside ▶ **noun** the edge of or area adjoining a sea, lake, or river.

waterski ▶ **noun** (pl. **-skis**) each of a pair of skis enabling the wearer to skim the surface of the water when towed by a motor boat.
▶ **verb** [no obj.] skim the surface of water on waterskis.
– DERIVATIVES **waterskier** noun.

water slide ▶ **noun** a slide into a swimming pool, typically flowing with water and incorporating a number of twists and turns.

water snake ▶ **noun** a harmless snake which is a powerful swimmer and spends part of its time in fresh water hunting for prey. Water snakes are found in Africa, Asia, and America.
• *Natrix* and other genera, family Colubridae: several species.

water softener ▶ **noun** a device or substance that softens hard water by removing certain minerals.

water soldier ▶ **noun** an aquatic European plant with slender spiny-toothed leaves in submerged rosettes that rise to the surface at flowering time.
• *Stratiotes aloides*, family Hydrocharitaceae.

water spider ▶ **noun** a semiaquatic spider.
• Several species, including the European *Argyroneta aquatica* (family Argyronetidae), which lives in an underwater dome of silk filled with air. See also **RAFT SPIDER**.

water splash ▶ **noun** Brit. a water-filled dip in a road.

water sports ▶ **plural noun** sports that are carried out on water, such as waterskiing and windsurfing.
■ informal sexual activity involving urination.

waterspout ▶ **noun** a rotating column of water and spray formed by a whirlwind occurring over the sea or other body of water.

water starwort ▶ **noun** a widely distributed slender-leaved plant which grows in water or on mud and is sometimes used in aquaria.
• Genus *Callitriche*, family Callitrichaceae.

water stick insect ▶ **noun** a very long, slender European water bug related to the water scorpion, which waits motionless in the vegetation for prey to pass.
• *Ranatra linearis*, family Nepidae, suborder Heteroptera.

water stone ▶ **noun** a whetstone used with water rather than oil.

water strider ▶ **noun** North American term for **POND SKATER** and **WATER CRICKET**.

water table ▶ **noun** the level below which the ground is saturated with water.

waterthrush ▶ **noun** a thrush-like North American warbler related to the ovenbird, found near woodland streams and swamps.
• Genus *Seiurus*, family Parulidae: two species.

watertight ▶ **adjective** closely sealed, fastened, or fitted so that no water enters or passes through: *a watertight seal.*
■ (of an argument or account) unable to be disputed or questioned: *their alibis are watertight.*

water torture ▶ **noun** [mass noun] a form of torture in which the victim is exposed to the incessant dripping of water on the head or to the sound of dripping.

water tower ▶ **noun** a tower supporting an elevated water tank, whose height creates the pressure required to distribute the water through a piped system.

water-tube boiler ▶ **noun** a form of boiler in which steam is generated by circulating water through tubes exposed to the source of heat (as opposed to the more usual arrangement in which tubes carry hot gases through the water).

water-vascular system ▶ **noun** Zoology (in an echinoderm) a network of water vessels in the body, the tube feet being operated by hydraulic pressure within the vessels.

water violet ▶ **noun** an aquatic plant of the primrose family, with lilac flowers and finely divided submerged leaves.
• *Hottonia palustris*, family Primulaceae.

water vole ▶ **noun** a large semiaquatic vole which excavates burrows in the banks of rivers.
• Genera *Arvicola* and *Microtus*, family Muridae: three species, in particular the **European water vole** (*A. terrestris*) and the **American water vole** (*M. richardsoni*).

waterway ▶ **noun** **1** a river, canal, or other route for travel by water.
2 a thick plank at the outer edge of a deck of a boat along which a channel is hollowed for water to run off by.

waterweed ▶ **noun** [mass noun] **1** any aquatic plant with inconspicuous flowers.
2 a submerged aquatic American plant which is grown in ornamental ponds.
• Genus *Elodea*, family Hydrocharitaceae: several species, in particular Canadian pondweed.

waterwheel ▶ **noun** a large wheel driven by flowing water, used to work machinery or to raise water to a higher level.

water wings ▶ **plural noun** inflated floats that may be fixed to the arms of someone learning to swim to give increased buoyancy.

water witch (also **water-witcher**) ▶ **noun** US a water diviner.
– DERIVATIVES **water witching** noun.

waterworks ▶ **plural noun** **1** [treated as sing.] an establishment for managing a water supply.
2 informal used to refer to the shedding of tears: *'Don't turn on the waterworks,' he advised.*
■ Brit. used as a humorous euphemism for the urinary system.

watery ▶ **adjective** consisting of, containing, or resembling water: *a watery fluid.*
■ thin or tasteless as a result of containing too much water: *watery coffee.* ■ weak; pale: *watery sunshine.* ■ (of a person's eyes) full of or running with tears. ■ (of the sky) threatening rain.
– DERIVATIVES **wateriness** noun.
– ORIGIN Old English *wæterig* (see **WATER**, **-Y**[1]).

Watford a town in Hertfordshire, SE England; pop. 74,460 (1981).

Watling Street a Roman road (now largely underlying modern roads) running north-westwards across England, from Richborough in Kent through London and St Albans to Wroxeter in Shropshire.

Watson[1], James Dewey (b.1928), American biologist. Together with Francis Crick he proposed a model for the structure of the DNA molecule. He shared the Nobel Prize for Physiology or Medicine with Crick and Maurice Wilkins in 1962.

Watson[2], John Broadus (1878–1958), American psychologist, founder of the school of behaviourism. He held that the role of the psychologist was to discern, through observation and experimentation, the innate behaviour and acquired behaviour in an individual.

Watson-Watt, Sir Robert Alexander (1892–1973), Scottish physicist. He led a team that developed radar into a practical system for locating aircraft; this played a vital role in the Second World War.

Watt, James (1736–1819), Scottish engineer. Among his many innovations he greatly improved the efficiency of the Newcomen steam engine, which was then adopted for a variety of purposes. He also introduced the term *horsepower*.

watt (abbrev.: **W**) ▶ **noun** the SI unit of power, equivalent to one joule per second, corresponding to the rate of energy in an electric circuit where the potential difference is one volt and the current one ampere.
– ORIGIN late 19th cent.: named after J. **WATT**.

wattage ▶ **noun** an amount of electrical power expressed in watts.
■ the operating power of a lamp or other electrical appliance expressed in watts.

Watteau /ˈwɒtəʊ/, Jean Antoine (1684–1721), French painter, of Flemish descent. An initiator of the rococo style, he is also known for his invention of the *fête galante*.

watt-hour ▶ **noun** a measure of electrical energy equivalent to a power consumption of one watt for one hour.

wattle[1] /ˈwɒt(ə)l/ ▶ **noun** **1** [mass noun] a material for making fences, walls, etc., consisting of rods or stakes interlaced with twigs or branches.
■ [count noun] dialect a wicker hurdle.
2 chiefly Austral. an acacia.
• Genus *Acacia*, family Leguminosae: many species, including the **golden wattle**.
▶ **verb** [with obj.] make, enclose, or fill up with wattle.
– ORIGIN Old English *watul*, of unknown origin.

wattle[2] /ˈwɒt(ə)l/ ▶ **noun** a coloured fleshy lobe hanging from the head or neck of the turkey and some other birds.
– DERIVATIVES **wattled** adjective.
– ORIGIN early 16th cent.: of unknown origin.

wattle and daub ▶ **noun** [mass noun] a material formerly or traditionally used in building walls, consisting of a network of interwoven sticks and twigs covered with mud or clay.

wattlebird ▶ **noun** **1** the largest of the honeyeaters found in Australia, with a wattle hanging from each cheek.
• Genus *Anthochaera* (and *Melidectes*), family Meliphagidae: four species.
2 a songbird of a New Zealand family distinguished by wattles hanging from the base of the bill.
• Family Callaeidae: the saddleback and the kokako, together with the extinct huia.

wattle-eye ▶ **noun** a small African flycatcher with a coloured patch of bare skin around or above the eye, typically having black and white plumage.
• Genus *Platysteira*, family Platysteiridae (or Monarchidae): several species.

wattmeter ▶ **noun** a meter for measuring electric power in watts.

Watts[1], George Frederick (1817–1904), English painter and sculptor. He is best known for his portraits of public figures, including Gladstone, Tennyson, and J. S. Mill. He was married to the actress Ellen Terry from 1864 to 1877.

Watts[2], Isaac (1674–1748), English hymn writer and poet, remembered for hymns such as 'O God, Our Help in Ages Past' (1719).

Watusi /wəˈtuːsi/ (also **Watutsi** /wəˈtʊtsi/) ▶ **noun** **1** [treated as pl.] the Tutsi people collectively (now dated in English use).
2 an energetic dance popular in the 1960s.
▶ **verb** [no obj.] dance the Watusi.
– ORIGIN a local name, from the plural prefix *wa-* + **TUTSI**.

Waugh /wɔː/, Evelyn (Arthur St John) (1903–66), English novelist. His work was profoundly influenced by his conversion to Roman Catholicism in 1930. Notable works: *Decline and Fall* (1928); *Brideshead Revisited* (1945).

waul /wɔːl/ ▶ **verb** [no obj.] give a loud plaintive cry like that of a cat.
– ORIGIN early 16th cent.: imitative.

wave ▶ **verb** **1** [no obj.] move one's hand to and fro in greeting or as a signal: *he waved to me from the train.*
■ [with obj.] move (one's hand or arm, or something held in one's hand) to and fro: *he waved a sheaf of papers in the air.* ■ move to and fro with a swaying or undulating motion while remaining fixed to one point: *the flag waved in the wind.* ■ [with obj.] convey (a greeting or other message) by moving one's hand or something held in it to and fro: *we waved our farewells* | [with two objs] *she waved him goodbye.* ■ [with obj. and adverbial of direction] instruct (someone) to move in a particular direction by moving one's hand: *he waved her back.*
2 [with obj.] style (hair) so that it curls slightly: *her hair had been carefully waved for the evening.*
■ [no obj.] (of hair) grow with a slight curl: [as adj. **waving**] *thick, waving grey hair sprouted back from his forehead.*
▶ **noun** **1** a long body of water curling into an arched form and breaking on the shore: *he was swept out to sea by a freak wave.*
■ a ridge of water between two depressions in open water: *gulls and cormorants bobbed on the waves.* ■ a shape seen as comparable to a breaking wave: *a wave of treetops stretched to the horizon.* ■ (**the waves**) poetic/literary the sea. ■ an intense burst of a particular feeling or emotion: *horror came over me in waves* | *a new wave of apprehension assailed her.* ■ a sudden occurrence of or increase in a specified phenomenon: *a wave of strikes had effectively paralysed the government.*
2 a gesture or signal made by moving one's hand to and fro: *he gave a little wave and walked off.*
3 a slightly curling lock of hair: *his hair was drying in unruly waves.*
■ a tendency to curl in a person's hair: *her hair has a slight natural wave.*
4 Physics a periodic disturbance of the particles of a substance which may be propagated without net movement of the particles, such as in the passage of undulating motion, heat, or sound. See also **STANDING WAVE** and **TRAVELLING WAVE**.
■ a single curve in the course of this motion. ■ a similar variation of an electromagnetic field in the propagation of light or other radiation through a medium or vacuum.

W

b **b**ut | d **d**og | f **f**ew | g **g**et | h **h**e | j **y**es | k **c**at | l **l**eg | m **m**an | n **n**o | p **p**en | r **r**ed | s **s**it | t **t**op | v **v**oice | w **w**e | z **z**oo | ʃ **sh**e | ʒ deci**s**ion | θ **th**in | ð **th**is | ŋ ri**ng** | x lo**ch** | tʃ **ch**ip | dʒ **j**ar

– PHRASES **make waves** informal create a significant impression: *he has already made waves as a sculptor.* ■ cause trouble: *I don't want to risk her welfare by making waves.*
– DERIVATIVES **waveless** adjective, **wave-like** adjective & adverb.
– ORIGIN Old English *wafian* (verb), from the Germanic base of **WAVER**; the noun by alteration (influenced by the verb) of Middle English *wawe* '(sea) wave'.

▶**wave something aside** dismiss something as unnecessary or irrelevant: *he waved the objection aside and carried on.*
wave someone/thing down use one's hand to give a signal to stop to a driver or vehicle.

waveband ▶ noun a range of wavelengths falling between two given limits, used in radio transmission.

wave equation ▶ noun Mathematics a differential equation expressing the properties of motion in waves.

waveform ▶ noun Physics a curve showing the shape of a wave at a given time.

wavefront ▶ noun Physics a surface containing points affected in the same way by a wave at a given time.

wave function ▶ noun Physics a function that satisfies a wave equation and describes the properties of a wave.

waveguide ▶ noun a metal tube or other device confining and conveying microwaves.

wavelength /ˈweɪvlɛŋθ, -lɛŋkθ/ ▶ noun Physics the distance between successive crests of a wave, especially points in a sound wave or electromagnetic wave. (Symbol: λ)
■ this distance as a distinctive feature of radio waves from a transmitter. ■ figurative a person's ideas and way of thinking, especially as it affects their ability to communicate with others: *when we met we hit it off immediately—we're* **on the same wavelength**.

wavelet ▶ noun a small wave of water; a ripple.

wave machine ▶ noun a machine that creates waves in the water in a swimming pool.

wave mechanics ▶ plural noun [treated as sing.] Physics a method of analysis of the behaviour of atomic phenomena with particles represented by wave equations.

wave number ▶ noun Physics the number of waves in a unit distance.

wave packet ▶ noun Physics a group of superposed waves which together form a travelling localized disturbance, especially one described by Schrödinger's equation and regarded as representing a particle.

waver ▶ verb [no obj.] shake with a quivering motion: *the flame wavered in the draught.*
■ become unsteady or unreliable: *his love for her had never wavered.* ■ be undecided between two opinions or courses of action; be irresolute: *she never* **wavered from** *her intention.*
– DERIVATIVES **waverer** noun, **waveringly** adverb, **wavery** adjective.
– ORIGIN Middle English: from Old Norse *vafra* 'flicker', of Germanic origin. Compare with **WAVE**.

WAVES ▶ plural noun the women's section of the US Naval Reserve, established in 1942, or, since 1948, of the US Navy.
– ORIGIN acronym from *Women Appointed* (later *Accepted*) *for Volunteer Emergency Service.*

wavetable ▶ noun Computing a file or memory device containing data that represents a sound such as a piece of music.

wave theory ▶ noun Physics, historical the theory that light is propagated through the ether by a wave motion imparted to the ether by the molecular vibrations of the radiant body.

wave train ▶ noun a group of waves of equal or similar wavelengths travelling in the same direction.

wavicle /ˈweɪvɪk(ə)l/ ▶ noun Physics an entity having characteristic properties of both waves and particles.
– ORIGIN 1920s: blend of **WAVE** and **PARTICLE**.

wavy ▶ adjective (**wavier**, **waviest**) (of a line or surface) having or consisting of a series of undulating and wave-like curves: *she had long, wavy hair.*
■ [usu. postpositive] Heraldry divided or edged with a line formed of alternating shallow curves.
– DERIVATIVES **wavily** adverb, **waviness** noun.

wa-wa ▶ noun variant spelling of **WAH-WAH**.

wax¹ ▶ noun [mass noun] a sticky yellowish mouldable substance secreted by honeybees as the material of honeycomb; beeswax.
■ a white translucent material obtained by bleaching and purifying this substance and used for such purposes as making candles, modelling, and as a basis of polishes. ■ [count noun] a figure made of this substance. ■ a similar viscous substance, typically a lipid or hydrocarbon. ■ informal used in reference to gramophone records: *he didn't get* **on wax** *until 1959.*
▶ verb [with obj.] **1** cover or treat (something) with wax or a similar substance, typically to polish or protect it: *I washed and waxed the floor.*
■ remove unwanted hair from (a part of the body) by applying wax and then peeling off the wax and hairs together.
2 informal make a recording of: *he waxed a series of tracks that emphasized his lead guitar work.*
– DERIVATIVES **waxer** noun.
– ORIGIN Old English *wæx*, *weax*, of Germanic origin; related to Dutch *was* and German *Wachs*. The verb dates from late Middle English.

wax² ▶ verb [no obj.] (of the moon between new and full) have a progressively larger part of its visible surface illuminated, increasing its apparent size.
■ poetic/literary become larger or stronger: *his anger waxed.* ■ [with complement] begin to speak or write about something in the specified manner: *they* **waxed lyrical** *about the old days.*
– PHRASES **wax and wane** undergo alternate increases and decreases: *green sentiment has waxed and waned.*
– ORIGIN Old English *weaxan*, of Germanic origin; related to Dutch *wassen* and German *wachsen*, from an Indo-European root shared by Greek *auxanein* and Latin *augere* 'to increase'.

wax³ ▶ noun [usu. in sing.] Brit. informal, dated a fit of anger: *she is* **in a wax** *about the delay to the wedding.*
– ORIGIN mid 19th cent.: origin uncertain; perhaps from phrases such as *wax angry.*

waxberry ▶ noun a shrub with berries that have a waxy coating, in particular a bayberry.

waxbill ▶ noun a small finch-like Old World songbird, typically brightly coloured and with a red bill that resembles sealing wax in colour.
● Family Estrildidae (the **waxbill family**): about three genera, especially *Estrilda*, and several species. The waxbill family also includes the avadavats, mannikins, cordon-bleu, Java sparrow, zebra finch, etc., many popular as cage birds.

waxcloth (also **waxed cloth**) ▶ noun [mass noun] cloth that has been impregnated with wax to make it waterproof.
■ cloth that is impregnated with oil for covering floors and tables; oilcloth.

waxed jacket ▶ noun an outdoor jacket made of a fabric that has been impregnated with wax to make it waterproof.

waxed paper ▶ noun [mass noun] paper that has been impregnated with wax to make it waterproof or greaseproof, used especially in cooking and the wrapping of foodstuffs.

waxen ▶ adjective having a smooth, pale, translucent surface or appearance like that of wax: *a canopy of waxen, creamy blooms.*
■ archaic or poetic/literary made of wax: *a waxen effigy.*

wax flower ▶ noun a plant bearing flowers with a waxy appearance:
● an Australian shrub with white or pink flowers (genus *Eriostemon*, family *Rutaceae*). ● a hoya.

wax light ▶ noun historical a taper or candle made from wax.

wax moth ▶ noun a brownish moth which lays its eggs in beehives. The caterpillars cover the combs with silken tunnels and feed on beeswax.
● Genera *Galleria* and *Achroea*, family Pyralidae: several species, in particular *G. mellonella*.

wax myrtle ▶ noun another term for **BAYBERRY**.

wax painting ▶ noun another term for **ENCAUSTIC**.

wax palm ▶ noun either of two South American palm trees from which wax is obtained:
● an Andean palm with a stem coated in a mixture of resin and wax (*Ceroxylon alpinum*, family Palmae). ● a carnauba.

waxpod ▶ noun a dwarf French bean of a variety with yellow, stringless pods.

wax resist ▶ noun [mass noun] a process similar to batik used in pottery and printing.

wax tree (also **Japanese wax tree**) ▶ noun an East Asian tree with white berries that produce a wax which is used as a substitute for beeswax.
● *Rhus succedanea*, family Anacardiaceae.

waxwing ▶ noun a crested Eurasian and American songbird with mainly pinkish-brown plumage, having small tips like red sealing wax to some wing feathers.
● Genus *Bombycilla*, family Bombycillidae: three species, in particular the (**Bohemian**)**waxwing** (*B. garrulus*).

waxwork ▶ noun a lifelike dummy modelled in wax.
■ (**waxworks**) [treated as sing.] an exhibition of wax dummies.

waxy¹ ▶ adjective (**waxier**, **waxiest**) resembling wax in consistency or appearance: *waxy potatoes.*
– DERIVATIVES **waxily** adverb, **waxiness** noun.

waxy² ▶ adjective (**waxier**, **waxiest**) Brit. informal, dated angry; bad-tempered.

way /weɪ/ ▶ noun **1** a method, style, or manner of doing something: *I hated their way of cooking potatoes with their jackets on | there are two ways of approaching this problem.*
■ a person's characteristic or habitual manner of behaviour or expression: *it was not his way to wait passively for things to happen.* ■ (**ways**) the customary modes of behaviour or practices of a group: *my years of acclimatization to British ways.* ■ [in sing.] the typical manner in which something happens or in which someone or something behaves: *he was showing off, as is the way with adolescent boys.* ■ [in sing.] formal or Scottish a person's occupation or line of business.
2 a road, track, path, or street for travelling along: [in place names] *No. 3, Church Way.*
■ [usu. in sing.] a course of travel or route taken in order to reach a place: *can you tell me the way to Leicester Square?* ■ a means of entry or exit from somewhere, such as a door or gate: *I nipped out the back way.* ■ [in sing.] (also N. Amer. informal **ways**) a distance travelled or to be travelled; the distance from one place to another: *they still had a long way ahead of them* | figurative *the area's wine industry still has some way to go to full maturity.* ■ [in sing.] a period between one point in time and another: *September was a long way off.* ■ [in sing.] travel or motion along a particular route; the route along which someone or something would travel if unobstructed: *Christine tried to follow but Martin blocked her way.* ■ [in sing.] a specified direction: *we just missed another car coming the other way.* ■ (**ways**) parts into which something divides or is divided: *the national vote split three ways.* ■ (**one's way**) used with a verb and adverbial phrase to intensify the force of an action or to denote movement or progress: *I shouldered my way to the bar.* ■ [mass noun] forward motion or momentum of a ship or boat through water: *the dinghy lost way and drifted towards the shore.*
3 [in sing.] [with modifier or possessive] informal a particular area or locality: *the family's main estate over Maidenhead way.*
4 a particular aspect of something; a respect: *I have changed in every way.*
5 [in sing.] [with adj.] a specified condition or state: *the family was in a poor way.*
6 (**ways**) a sloping structure down which a new ship is launched.
▶ adverb informal at or to a considerable distance or extent; far (used before an adverb or preposition for emphasis): *his understanding of what constitutes good writing is way off target | my grandchildren are way ahead of others their age.*
■ [as submodifier] chiefly N. Amer. much: *I was cycling way too fast.* ■ [usu. as submodifier] extremely; really (used for emphasis): *the guys behind the bar were way cool.* [ORIGIN: shortening of **AWAY**.]
– PHRASES **across** (Brit. also **over**) **the way** nearby, especially on the opposite side of the street. **all the way** see **ALL**. **be on one's way** have started one's journey. ■ [in imperative] ((**be**) **on your way**) informal go away: *on your way, and stop wasting my time!* **by a long way** by a great amount; by far. **by the way 1** incidentally (used to introduce a minor topic not connected with what was being spoken about previously): *oh, by the way, while you were away I had a message.* **2** during the course of a journey: *you will have a fine view of Moray Firth by the way.* **by way of 1** so as to pass through or across; via: *he travelled by way of Canterbury.* **2** constituting; as a form of: *'I can't help it,' shouted Tom by way of apology.* **3** by means of: *non-compliance with the regulations is punishable by way of a fine.* **come one's way** happen

W

or become available to one: *he did whatever jobs came his way.* **find a way** discover a means of obtaining one's object. **get** (or **have**) **one's** (**own**) **way** get or do what one wants in spite of opposition. **give way 1** yield to someone or something: *he was not a man to give way to this kind of pressure.* ■ (of a support or structure) be unable to carry a load or withstand a force; collapse or break. ■ (**give way to**) allow oneself to be overcome by or to succumb to (an emotion or impulse): *she gave way to a burst of weeping.* **2** allow someone or something to be or go first: *give way to traffic coming from the right.* ■ (**give way to**) be replaced or superseded by: *Alan's discomfort gave way to anger.* **3** (of rowers) row hard. **go all** (or **the whole**) **way** continue a course of action to its conclusion. ■ informal have full sexual intercourse with someone. **go out of one's way** [usu. with infinitive] make a special effort to do something: *Mrs Mott went out of her way to be courteous to Sara.* **go one's own way** act independently or as one wishes, especially against contrary advice. **go one's way 1** (of events, circumstances, etc.) be favourable to one: *I was just hoping things went my way.* **2** leave: *one by one the staff went their way.* **go someone's way** travel in the same direction as someone: *wait for Owen, he's going your way.* **have it your** (**own**) **way** [in imperative] informal used to indicate angrily that although one disagrees with something someone has said or proposed, one is not going to argue further: *have it your way–we'll go to Princetown.* **have it both ways** see **BOTH**. **have a way with** have a particular talent for dealing with or ability in: *she's got a way with animals.* **have a way with one** have a charming and persuasive manner. **have one's way with** humorous have sexual intercourse with (someone) (typically implying that it is against their wishes or better judgement). **in more ways than one** used to indicate that a statement has more than one meaning: *Shelley let her hair down in more ways than one.* **in a way** (or **in some ways** or **in one way**) to a certain extent, but not altogether or completely (used to reduce the effect of a statement): *in some ways television is more challenging than theatre.* **in the family way** see **FAMILY**. **in the** (or **one's**) **way** forming an obstacle or hindrance to movement or action: *his head was in the way of my view.* **in the way of** another way of saying ***by way of*** (sense 2) above. **in someone/thing's** (**own**) **way** if regarded from a particular standpoint appropriate to that person or thing: *it's a good enough book in its way.* **in no way** not at all. **keep** (or **stay**) **out of someone's way** avoid someone. **know one's way around** (or **about**) be familiar with (an area, procedure, or subject). **lead the way** go first along a route to show someone the way. ■ be a pioneer in a particular activity. **look the other way** deliberately avoid seeing or noticing someone or something. **no two ways about it** see **NO**. **one way and another 1** taking most aspects or considerations into account: *it's been quite a day one way and another.* **2** another way of saying ***one way or the other*** below. **one way or the other** (or **one way and another**) used to indicate that something is the case for any of various unspecified reasons: *one way or another she brought it on herself.* ■ by some means: *he wants to get rid of me one way or another.* ■ whichever of two given alternatives is the case: *the question is not yet decided, one way or the other.* **on the** (or **one's**) **way** in the course of a journey: *I'll tell you on the way home.* **on the** (or **its**) **way** about to arrive or happen: *there's more snow on the way.* ■ informal (of a child) conceived but not yet born. **on the** (or **one's**) **way out** in the process of leaving. ■ informal going out of fashion or favour. ■ informal dying. **the other way round** (or **around**; Brit. also **about**) in the opposite position or direction. ■ the opposite of what is expected or supposed: *it was you who sought me out, not the other way round.* **out of the way 1** (of a place) remote. **2** dealt with or finished: *economic recovery will begin once the election is out of the way.* ■ (of a person) no longer an obstacle or hindrance to someone's plans: *why did Josie want her out of the way?* **3** [usu. with negative] unusual, exceptional, or remarkable: *he'd seen nothing out of the way.* **out of one's way** not on one's intended route. **put someone in the way of** dated give someone the opportunity of. **that way** used euphemistically to indicate that someone is homosexual: *he was a bit that way.* **to someone's** (or **one's**) **way of thinking** in someone's (or one's) opinion. **way back** (US also **way back when**) informal long ago. **the way of the Cross 1** the journey of Jesus to the place of his crucifixion. **2** a set of images representing the Stations of the Cross. **3** figurative the suffering and self-sacrifice of a Christian. **way of life** the typical pattern of behaviour of a person or group: *the rural way of life.* **the way of the world** the manner in which people typically behave or things typically happen (used to express one's resignation to it): *all those millions of pounds are not going to create many jobs, but that's the way of the world.* **ways and means** the methods and resources at someone's disposal for achieving something: *the company is seeking ways and means of safeguarding jobs.* **way to go** N. Amer. informal used to express pleasure, approval, or excitement.

– ORIGIN Old English *weg*, of Germanic origin; related to Dutch *weg* and German *Weg*, from a base meaning 'move, carry'.

-way ▶ **suffix** equivalent to **-WAYS**.

wayang /ˈwɑːjaŋ/ ▶ **noun** [mass noun] (in Indonesia and Malaysia) a theatrical performance employing puppets or human dancers.

■ (also **wayang kulit**) a Javanese and Balinese shadow puppet play.

– ORIGIN Javanese.

waybill ▶ **noun** a list of passengers or goods being carried on a vehicle.

waybread ▶ **noun** [mass noun] Brit. archaic the Eurasian common plantain, with broad rounded leaves.

• *Plantago major*, family Plantaginaceae.

– ORIGIN Old English *wegbrǣde* (see **WAY**, **BROAD**).

wayfarer ▶ **noun** poetic/literary a person who travels on foot.

– DERIVATIVES **wayfaring** noun.

wayfaring tree ▶ **noun** a white-flowered Eurasian shrub which has berries at different stages of ripening (green, red, and black) occurring together, growing chiefly on calcareous soils.

• *Viburnum lantana*, family Caprifoliaceae.

Wayland the Smith /ˈweɪlənd/ (also **Weland**) Scandinavian & Anglo-Saxon Mythology a smith with supernatural powers, in English legend supposed to have his forge in a Neolithic chambered tomb (**Wayland's Smithy**) on the downs in SW Oxfordshire.

waylay ▶ **verb** (past and past participle **waylaid**) [with obj.] stop or interrupt (someone) and detain them in conversation or trouble them in some other way: *he waylaid me on the stairs.*

– DERIVATIVES **waylayer** noun.

way leave ▶ **noun** a right of way granted by a landowner, generally in exchange for payment and typically for purposes such as the erection of telegraph wires or laying of pipes.

waymark ▶ **noun** (also **waymarker**) a sign forming one of a series used to mark out a route, especially a footpath or bridle path.

▶ **verb** [with obj.] identify (a route) with such a sign.

Wayne, John (1907–79), American actor; born *Marion Michael Morrison*. Associated with the film director John Ford from 1930, Wayne became a Hollywood star with *Stagecoach* (1939) and appeared in classic westerns such as *The Searchers* (1956) and *True Grit* (1969), for which he won an Oscar.

way-out ▶ **adjective** informal regarded as extremely unconventional, unusual, or avant-garde.

waypoint ▶ **noun** a stopping place on a journey.

■ the computer-checked coordinates of each stage of a flight or sea journey.

-ways ▶ **suffix** forming adjectives and adverbs of direction or manner: *edgeways* | *lengthways*. Compare with **-WISE**.

wayside ▶ **noun** the edge of a road.

– PHRASES **fall by the wayside** fail to persist in an endeavour or undertaking: *many readers will fall by the wayside as the terminology becomes more complicated.* [ORIGIN: with biblical allusion to Luke 8:5.]

wayside pulpit ▶ **noun** a board placed outside a place of worship, displaying a religious text or maxim.

way station ▶ **noun** N. Amer. a stopping point on a journey.

■ a minor station on a railway.

wayward ▶ **adjective** difficult to control or predict because of unusual or perverse behaviour: *her wayward, difficult sister* | figurative *his wayward emotions.*

– DERIVATIVES **waywardly** adverb, **waywardness** noun.

– ORIGIN late Middle English: shortening of obsolete *awayward* 'turned away'; compare with **FROWARD**.

way-worn ▶ **adjective** archaic weary with travelling.

wayzgoose /ˈweɪzguːs/ ▶ **noun** (pl. **wayzgooses**) Brit. historical an annual summer dinner or outing held by a printing house for its employees.

– ORIGIN mid 18th cent. (earlier *waygoose*): of unknown origin.

wazir /wəˈzɪə/ ▶ **noun** another term for **VIZIER**.

wazzock /ˈwazək/ ▶ **noun** Brit. informal a stupid or annoying person.

– ORIGIN 1980s: of unknown origin.

Wb ▶ **abbreviation for** weber(s).

WBA ▶ **abbreviation for** World Boxing Association.

WBC ▶ **abbreviation for** World Boxing Council.

W boson ▶ **noun** another term for **W PARTICLE**.

WC ▶ **abbreviation for** ■ Brit. water closet. ■ (of a region) west central.

WCC ▶ **abbreviation for** World Council of Churches.

we ▶ **pronoun** [first person plural] **1** used by a speaker to refer to himself or herself and one or more other people considered together: *shall we have a drink?*

■ used to refer to the speaker together with other people regarded in the same category: *nobody knows kids better than we teachers do.* ■ people in general: *we should eat as varied and well-balanced a diet as possible.*

2 used in formal contexts for or by a royal person, or by a writer or editor, to refer to himself or herself: *in this section we discuss the reasons.*

3 used condescendingly to refer to the person being addressed: *how are we today?*

– ORIGIN Old English, of Germanic origin; related to Dutch *wij* and German *wir*.

WEA ▶ **abbreviation for** (in the UK) Workers' Educational Association.

weak ▶ **adjective 1** lacking the power to perform physically demanding tasks; lacking physical strength and energy: *she was recovering from flu, and was very weak.*

■ lacking political or social power or influence: *the central government had grown too weak to impose order* | [as plural noun **the weak**] *the new king used his powers to protect the weak.* ■ (of a crew, team, or army) containing too few members or members of insufficient quality. ■ (of a faculty or part of the body) not able to fulfil its functions properly: *he had a weak stomach.* ■ of a low standard; performing or performed badly: *the choruses on this recording are weak.* ■ not convincing or logically forceful: *the argument is an extremely weak one* | *a weak plot.* ■ exerting only a small force: *a weak magnetic field.*

2 liable to break or give way under pressure; easily damaged: *the salamander's tail may be broken off at a weak spot near the base.*

■ lacking the force of character to hold to one's own decisions, beliefs, or principles; irresolute. ■ (of a belief, emotion, or attitude) not held or felt with such conviction or intensity as to prevent its being abandoned or dispelled: *their commitment to the project is weak.* ■ not in a secure financial position: *people have no faith in weak banks.* ■ (of prices or a market) having a downward tendency.

3 lacking intensity or brightness: *a weak light from a single street lamp.*

■ (of a liquid or solution) lacking flavour or effectiveness through being heavily diluted: *a cup of weak coffee.* ■ displaying or characterized by a lack of enthusiasm or energy: *she managed a weak, nervous smile.* ■ (of features) not striking or strongly marked: *his beard covered a weak chin.* ■ (of a syllable) unstressed.

4 Grammar denoting a class of verbs in Germanic languages that form the past tense and past participle by addition of a suffix (in English, typically *-ed*).

5 Physics of, relating to, or denoting the weakest of the known kinds of force between particles, which acts only at distances less than about 10^{-15} cm, is very much weaker than the electromagnetic and the strong interactions, and conserves neither strangeness, parity, nor isospin.

– PHRASES **the weaker sex** [treated as sing. or pl.] dated, derogatory women regarded collectively. **weak at the knees** helpless with emotion. **the weak link** the point at which a system, sequence, or organization is most vulnerable; the least dependable element or member.

– DERIVATIVES **weakish** adjective.

– ORIGIN Old English *wāc* 'pliant', 'of little worth', 'not steadfast', reinforced in Middle English by Old Norse *veikr*, from a Germanic base meaning 'yield, give way'.

weaken ▶ **verb** make or become weaker in power, resolve, or physical strength: [with obj.] *fault lines had weakened and shattered the rocks* | [no obj.] *his resistance had weakened.*
– DERIVATIVES **weakener** noun.

weak ending ▶ **noun** Prosody an unstressed syllable in a place at the end of a line of verse that normally receives a stress.

weakfish ▶ **noun** (pl. same or **-fishes**) a large slender-bodied marine fish living along the east coast of North America, popular as a food fish and for sport. Also called **SEA TROUT**.
● *Cynoscion regalis*, family Sciaenidae.
– ORIGIN late 18th cent.: from obsolete Dutch *weekvisch*, from *week* 'soft' + *visch* 'fish'.

weak interaction ▶ **noun** Physics interaction at short distances between subatomic particles mediated by the weak force.

weak-kneed ▶ **adjective** weak and shaky as a result of fear or excitement.
■ lacking in resolve or courage; cowardly.

weakling ▶ **noun** a person or animal that is physically weak and frail.
■ an ineffectual or cowardly person.

weakly ▶ **adverb** in a way that lacks strength or force: *she leaned weakly against the wall.*
▶ **adjective** (**weaklier**, **weakliest**) sickly; not robust.
– DERIVATIVES **weakliness** noun.

weak-minded ▶ **adjective** lacking determination, emotional strength, or intellectual capacity.
– DERIVATIVES **weak-mindedness** noun.

weakness ▶ **noun** [mass noun] the state or condition of lacking strength: *the country's weakness in international dealings.*
■ [count noun] a quality or feature regarded as a disadvantage or fault: *you must recognize your product's strengths and weaknesses.* ■ [count noun] a person or thing that one is unable to resist or likes excessively: *you're his one weakness—he should never have met you.* ■ [in sing.] (**weakness for**) a self-indulgent liking for: *his weakness for prawn cocktails.*

weak sister ▶ **noun** US informal a weak, ineffectual, or unreliable member of a group.

weal¹ /wiːl/ (also chiefly Medicine **wheal**) ▶ **noun** a red, swollen mark left on flesh by a blow or pressure.
■ Medicine an area of the skin which is temporarily raised, typically reddened, and usually accompanied by itching.
▶ **verb** [with obj.] mark with a weal.
– ORIGIN early 19th cent.: variant of **WALE**, influenced by obsolete *wheal* 'suppurate'.

weal² /wiːl/ ▶ **noun** [mass noun] formal that which is best for someone or something: *I am holding this trial behind closed doors in the public weal.*
– ORIGIN Old English *wela* 'wealth, well-being', of West Germanic origin; related to **WELL**¹.

Weald /wiːld/ a formerly wooded district including parts of Kent, Surrey, and East Sussex.
– ORIGIN Old English, variant of *wald* (see **WOLD**).

Weald clay ▶ **noun** [mass noun] Geology a series of beds of clay, sandstone, limestone, and ironstone, forming the top of the Wealden strata in southern England and containing abundant fossil remains.

Wealden /ˈwiːld(ə)n/ ▶ **adjective** Brit. of or relating to the Weald.
■ denoting a style of timber house built in the Weald in the late medieval and Tudor periods. ■ Geology relating to or denoting a series of Lower Cretaceous estuarine and freshwater deposits best exemplified in the Weald.

wealth ▶ **noun** [mass noun] an abundance of valuable possessions or money: *he used his considerable wealth to bribe officials.*
■ the state of being rich; material prosperity: *some people buy boats and cars to display their wealth.* ■ plentiful supplies of a particular resource: *the country's mineral wealth.* ■ [in sing.] a plentiful supply of a particular desirable thing: *the tables and maps contain a wealth of information.* ■ archaic well-being; prosperity.
– ORIGIN Middle English *welthe*, from **WELL**¹ or **WEAL**², on the pattern of *health*.

wealth tax ▶ **noun** a tax levied on personal capital.

wealthy ▶ **adjective** (**wealthier**, **wealthiest**) having a great deal of money, resources, or assets; rich: *the wealthy nations of the world* | [as plural noun **the wealthy**] *the burden of taxation on the wealthy.*
– DERIVATIVES **wealthily** adverb.

wean¹ ▶ **verb** [with obj.] accustom (an infant or other young mammal) to food other than its mother's milk.
■ accustom (someone) to managing without something on which they have become dependent or of which they have become excessively fond: *the doctor tried to **wean** her **off** the sleeping pills.* ■ (**be weaned on**) be strongly influenced by (something), especially from an early age: *I was weaned on a regular diet of Hollywood fantasy.*
– ORIGIN Old English *wenian*, of Germanic origin; related to Dutch *wennen* and German *entwöhnen*.

wean² ▶ **noun** Scottish & N. English a young child.
– ORIGIN late 17th cent.: contraction of *wee ane* 'little one'.

weaner ▶ **noun** a calf, lamb, or pig weaned during the current year.

weanling ▶ **noun** a newly weaned animal.

weapon ▶ **noun** a thing designed or used for inflicting bodily harm or physical damage: *nuclear weapons.*
■ figurative a means of gaining an advantage or defending oneself in a conflict or contest: *resignation threats had long been a weapon in his armoury.*
– DERIVATIVES **weaponed** adjective, **weaponless** adjective.
– ORIGIN Old English *wǣp(e)n*, of Germanic origin; related to Dutch *wapen* and German *Waffe*.

weaponry ▶ **noun** [treated as sing. or pl.] weapons regarded collectively.

wear¹ ▶ **verb** (past **wore**; past participle **worn** /wɔːn/)
1 [with obj.] have on one's body or a part of one's body as clothing, decoration, protection, or for some other purpose: *he was wearing a dark suit* | *firemen wearing breathing apparatus.*
■ habitually have on one's body or be dressed in: *although she was a widow, she didn't wear black.* ■ exhibit or present (a particular facial expression or appearance): *they wear a frozen smile on their faces.* ■ [with obj. and complement or adverbial] have (one's hair or beard) at a specified length or arranged in a specified style: *the students wore their hair long.* ■ (of a ship) fly (a flag).
2 [with obj. and adverbial or complement] damage, erode, or destroy by friction or use: *the track has been worn down in part to bare rock.*
■ [no obj., with adverbial or complement] undergo such damage, erosion, or destruction: *mountains are wearing down with each passing second.* ■ [with obj.] form (a hole, path, etc.) by constant friction or use: *the water was forced up through holes it had worn.*
3 [no obj., with adverbial] withstand continued use or life in a specified way: *a carpet-type finish seems to **wear well**.*
■ [with obj.] [usu. with negative] Brit. informal tolerate; accept: *the environmental health people wouldn't wear it.*
4 [no obj.] (**wear on**) (of a period of time) pass, especially slowly or tediously: *as the afternoon wore on he began to look unhappy.*
■ [with obj.] poetic/literary pass (a period of time) in some activity: *spinning long stories, wearing half the day.*
▶ **noun** [mass noun] **1** the wearing of something or the state of being worn as clothing: *some new tops for wear in the evening.*
2 [with modifier] clothing suitable for a particular purpose or of a particular type: *evening wear.*
3 damage or deterioration sustained from continuous use: *you need to make a deduction for **wear and tear** on all your belongings.*
■ the capacity for withstanding continuous use without such damage: *old things were relegated to the bedrooms because there was plenty of wear left in them.*
– PHRASES **in wear** being regularly worn. **wear one's heart on one's sleeve** see **HEART**. **wear oneself to a shadow** see **SHADOW**. **wear thin** be gradually used up or become less convincing or acceptable: *his patience was wearing thin* | *the joke had started to wear thin.* **wear the trousers** see **TROUSERS**.
– DERIVATIVES **wearability** noun, **wearable** adjective, **wearer** noun.
– ORIGIN Old English *werian*, of Germanic origin, from an Indo-European root shared by Latin *vestis* 'clothing'.
▶ **wear someone/thing down** overcome someone or something by persistence.
wear off lose effectiveness or intensity.
wear something out (or **wear out**) **1** use or be used until no longer in good condition or working order: *wearing out the stair carpet* | *the type was used again and again until it wore out.* **2** (**wear someone/thing out**) exhaust or tire someone or something: *an hour of this wandering wore out Lampard's patience.*

wear² ▶ **verb** (past and past participle **wore**) [with obj.] Sailing bring (a ship) about by turning its head away from the wind: *Shannon gives the order to **wear ship**.* Compare with **TACK**¹ (in sense 2), **GYBE**.
– ORIGIN early 17th cent.: of unknown origin.

wearing ▶ **adjective** mentally or physically tiring.
– DERIVATIVES **wearingly** adverb.

wearing course ▶ **noun** the top layer of a road surface which is worn down by traffic.

wearisome ▶ **adjective** causing one to feel tired or bored.
– DERIVATIVES **wearisomely** adverb, **wearisomeness** noun.

weary ▶ **adjective** (**wearier**, **weariest**) feeling or showing tiredness, especially as a result of excessive exertion or lack of sleep: *he gave a long, weary sigh.*
■ reluctant to see or experience any more of; tired of: *she was **weary of** their constant arguments* | [in combination] *war-weary Americans.* ■ calling for a great amount of energy or endurance; tiring and tedious: *the weary journey began again.*
▶ **verb** (**-ies, -ied**) **1** [with obj.] cause to become tired: *she was wearied by her persistent cough.*
■ [no obj.] (**weary of**) grow tired of or bored with: *she wearied of the sameness of her life.*
2 [no obj.] chiefly Scottish be distressed; fret: *don't think I'm wearying about not being able to paint any more.*
– DERIVATIVES **weariless** adjective, **wearily** adverb, **weariness** noun, **wearyingly** adverb.
– ORIGIN Old English *wērig*, *wǣrig*, of West Germanic origin.

weasel ▶ **noun** a small slender carnivorous mammal related to, but smaller than, the stoat.
● Genus *Mustela*, family Mustelidae (the **weasel family**): several species, in particular *M. nivalis* of northern Eurasia and northern North America. The family also includes the polecats, minks, martens, skunks, wolverine, otters, and badgers.
■ Irish term for **STOAT**. ■ figurative, informal a deceitful or treacherous person.
▶ **verb** (**weaselled**, **weaselling**; US **weaseled**, **weaseling**) [no obj.] achieve something by use of cunning or deceit: *she suspects me of trying to **weasel** my way into his affections.*
■ chiefly US behave or talk evasively.
– DERIVATIVES **weaselly** adjective.
– ORIGIN Old English *wesle*, *wesule*, of West Germanic origin; related to Dutch *wezel* and German *Wiesel*.

weasel-faced ▶ **adjective** (of a person) having a face with unattractively thin, sharp, or pointed features.

weasel's snout ▶ **noun** a small wild Eurasian snapdragon with reddish-purple flowers, naturalized in Britain and North America.
● *Misopates* (formerly *Antirrhinum*) *orontium*, family Scrophulariaceae.

weasel words ▶ **plural noun** words or statements that are intentionally ambiguous or misleading.

weather ▶ **noun** [mass noun] the state of the atmosphere at a place and time as regards heat, cloudiness, dryness, sunshine, wind, rain, etc.: *if the weather's good we can go for a walk.*
■ cold, wet, and unpleasant or unpredictable atmospheric conditions; the elements: *stone walls provide shelter from wind and weather.* ■ [as modifier] denoting the side from which the wind is blowing, especially on board a ship; windward: *the weather side of the yacht.* Contrasted with **LEE**.
▶ **verb** [with obj.] **1** wear away or change the appearance or texture of (something) by long exposure to the atmosphere: [with obj. and complement] *his skin was weathered almost black by his long outdoor life* | [as adj. **weathered**] *chemically weathered rock.*
■ [no obj.] (of rock or other material) be worn away or altered by such processes: *the ice sheet preserves specimens that would **weather away** more quickly in other regions.* ■ [usu. as noun **weathering**] Falconry allow (a hawk) to spend a period perched in the open air.
2 come safely through (a storm).
■ withstand (a difficulty or danger): *this year has tested industry's ability to weather recession.* ■ Sailing (of a ship) get to the windward of (a cape).
3 make (boards or tiles) overlap downwards to keep out rain.
■ (in building) slope or bevel (a surface) to throw off rain.

– PHRASES **in all weathers** in every kind of weather, both good and bad. **keep a weather eye on** observe very carefully, especially for changes or developments. **make heavy weather of** informal have unnecessary difficulty in dealing with (a task or problem). [ORIGIN: from the nautical phrase *make good* or *bad weather of it*, referring to a ship in a storm.] **under the weather** informal slightly unwell or in low spirits.
– ORIGIN Old English *weder*, of Germanic origin; related to Dutch *weer* and German *Wetter*, probably also to the noun WIND[1].

weather balloon ▶ noun a balloon equipped with meteorological apparatus which is sent into the atmosphere to provide information about the weather.

weather-beaten ▶ adjective damaged or worn by exposure to the weather: *a tiny weather-beaten church.*
■(of a person or a person's face) having skin that is lined and tanned or reddened through prolonged time spent outdoors.

weatherboard chiefly Brit. ▶ noun a sloping board attached to the bottom of an outside door to keep out the rain.
■each of a series of horizontal boards nailed to outside walls with edges overlapping to keep out the rain.
▶ verb [with obj.] fit or supply with weatherboards.

weatherboarding ▶ noun [mass noun] weatherboards collectively.

weatherbound ▶ adjective prevented by bad weather from travelling or proceeding with a course of action.

weather chart ▶ noun a map showing the state of the weather over a large area.

weathercock ▶ noun a weathervane in the form of a cockerel.
▶ verb [no obj.] (of a boat or aircraft) tend to turn to head into the wind.

weatherfish ▶ noun (pl. same or **-fishes**) a yellowish-brown freshwater loach which is reputed to become restless at the approach of stormy weather.
●Genus *Misgurnus*, family Cobitidae: the European *M. fossilis*, and the Asian *M. anguillicaudatus*, which has also been introduced to North America.

weather gage ▶ noun see GAUGE (sense 3).

weathergirl ▶ noun informal a woman who broadcasts a description and forecast of weather conditions.

weather glass ▶ noun dated a barometer.

weather helm ▶ noun [mass noun] Nautical a tendency in a sailing ship to head into the wind if the tiller is released.

weather house ▶ noun a toy hygroscope in the form of a small house with figures of a man and woman standing in two porches, the man coming out of his porch in wet weather and the woman out of hers in dry.

weatherly ▶ adjective Sailing (of a boat) able to sail close to the wind without drifting to leeward.
– DERIVATIVES **weatherliness** noun.

weatherman ▶ noun (pl. **-men**) a man who broadcasts a description and forecast of weather conditions.

weather map ▶ noun another term for WEATHER CHART.

weatherproof ▶ adjective resistant to the effects of bad weather, especially rain: *the building is structurally sound and weatherproof.*
▶ verb [with obj.] make (something) resistant to the effects of bad weather, especially rain.

weather station ▶ noun an observation post where weather conditions and meteorological data are observed and recorded.

weatherstrip ▶ noun a strip of rubber, metal, or other material used to seal the edges of a door or window against rain and wind.
▶ verb (**-stripped, -stripping**) [with obj.] apply such a strip to (a door or window).
– DERIVATIVES **weatherstripping** noun.

weatherstruck joint ▶ noun another term for STRUCK JOINT.

weathertight ▶ adjective (of a building) sealed against rain and wind.

weather tile ▶ noun each of a series of overlapping tiles used to cover a wall.

weathervane ▶ noun a revolving pointer to show the direction of the wind, typically mounted on top of a building.

weather-worn ▶ adjective eroded or altered by being exposed to the weather: *a weather-worn gravestone.*

weave[1] ▶ verb (past **wove**; past participle **woven** or **wove**) [with obj.] form (fabric or a fabric item) by interlacing long threads passing in one direction with others at a right angle to them: *linen was woven in the district.*
■form (thread) into fabric in this way: *some thick mohairs can be difficult to weave.* ■ [no obj.] [usu. as noun **weaving**] make fabric in this way, typically by working at a loom: *cotton spinning and weaving was done in mills.* ■(**weave something into**) include something as an integral part or element of (a woven fabric): *a gold pattern was woven into the material.* ■ make (basketwork or a wreath) by interlacing rods or flowers. ■ make (a complex story or pattern) from a number of interconnected elements: *he weaves colourful, cinematic plots.* ■ (**weave something into**) include an element in (such a story or pattern): *interpretative comments are woven into the narrative.*
▶ noun [usu. with adj.] a particular style or manner in which something is woven: *scarlet cloth of a very fine weave.*
– ORIGIN Old English *wefan*, of Germanic origin, from an Indo-European root shared by Greek *huphē* 'web' and Sanskrit *ūrṇavābhi* 'spider', literally 'wool-weaver'. The current noun sense dates from the late 19th cent.

weave[2] ▶ verb [no obj.] twist and turn from side to side while moving somewhere in order to avoid obstructions: *he had to weave his way through the crowds.*
■take evasive action in an aircraft, typically by moving it from side to side. ■(of a horse) repeatedly swing the head and forepart of the body from side to side (considered to be a vice).
– PHRASES **get weaving** Brit. informal set briskly to work; begin action.
– ORIGIN late 16th cent.: probably from Old Norse *veifa* 'to wave, brandish'.

weaver ▶ noun **1** a person who weaves fabric.
2 (also **weaver bird**) a finch-like songbird of tropical Africa and Asia, related to the sparrows and building elaborately woven nests.
●Family Ploceidae: several genera, in particular *Ploceus*, and numerous species.

weaver ant ▶ noun a tropical ant which builds its nest between leaves that are fastened together using silk secreted by the larvae.
●Genera *Oecophylla* and *Camponotus*, family Formicidae.

weaver's knot ▶ noun a sheet bend used for joining threads in weaving.

web ▶ noun **1** a network of fine threads constructed by a spider from fluid secreted by its spinnerets, used to catch its prey.
■a similar filmy network spun by some insect larvae, especially communal caterpillars. ■ figurative a complex system of interconnected elements, especially one perceived as a trap or danger: *he found himself caught up in a web of bureaucracy.* ■ (**the Web**) short for WORLD WIDE WEB.
2 a membrane between the toes of a swimming bird or other aquatic animal.
■a thin flat part connecting thicker or more solid parts in machinery.
3 a roll of paper used in a continuous printing process.
■the endless wire mesh in a papermaking machine on which such paper is made.
4 a piece of woven fabric.
▶ verb (**webbed, webbing**) [no obj., with adverbial] move or hang so as to form a web-like shape: *an intricate transportation network webs from coast to coast.*
■[with obj.] (usu. **be webbed**) cover with or as though with a web: *she noticed his tanned skin, webbed with fine creases.*
– DERIVATIVES **web-like** adjective.
– ORIGIN Old English *web(b)* 'woven fabric', of Germanic origin; related to Dutch *web*, also to WEAVE. Early use of the verb was in the sense 'weave (fabric) on a loom'.

Webb[1], (Gladys) Mary (1881–1927), English novelist. Her novels, such as *Gone to Earth* (1917) and *Precious Bane* (1924), are representative of much regional English fiction popular at the beginning of the century.

Webb[2], (Martha) Beatrice (1858–1943) and Sidney

(James), Baron Passfield (1859–1947), English socialists, economists, and historians. They were prominent members of the Fabian Society and helped to establish the London School of Economics (1895).

webbed ▶ adjective **1** (of the feet of a swimming bird or other aquatic animal) having the toes connected by a membrane.
■Medicine (of fingers or toes) abnormally united for all or part of their length by a fold of skin.
2 (of a band or strip of tough material) made from webbing or similar fabric: *a webbed girth.*

webbing ▶ noun [mass noun] **1** strong, closely woven fabric used for making items such as straps and belts, and for supporting the seats of upholstered chairs.
■the system of belts, pouches, and straps worn by a soldier as part of his combat uniform.
2 the part of a baseball glove between the thumb and forefinger.

Weber[1] /ˈveɪbə, German ˈveːbɐ/, Carl Maria (Friedrich Ernst) von (1786–1826), German composer. He is regarded as the founder of the German romantic school of opera. Notable operas: *Der Freischütz* (1817–21), *Euryanthe* (1822–3).

Weber[2] /ˈveɪbə, German ˈveːbɐ/, Max (1864–1920), German economist and sociologist, regarded as one of the founders of modern sociology. Notable works: *The Protestant Ethic and the Spirit of Capitalism* (1904) and *Economy and Society* (1922).

Weber[3] /ˈveɪbə, German ˈveːbɐ/, Wilhelm Eduard (1804–91), German physicist. He proposed a unified system for electrical units and determined the ratio between the units of electrostatic and electromagnetic charge.

weber /ˈveɪbə/ (abbrev.: **Wb**) ▶ noun the SI unit of magnetic flux, causing the electromotive force of one volt in a circuit of one turn when generated or removed in one second.
– ORIGIN late 19th cent.: named after W. E. *Weber* (see WEBER[3]).

Webern /ˈveɪb(ə)n, German ˈveːbɐn/, Anton (Friedrich Ernst) von (1883–1945), Austrian composer, a leading exponent of serialism. His music is marked by its brevity: the atonal *Five Pieces for Orchestra* (1911–13) lasts under a minute.

web-footed ▶ adjective (of a swimming bird or other aquatic animal) having webbed feet.

webmaster ▶ noun Computing a person who is responsible for a particular server on the World Wide Web.

web offset ▶ noun [mass noun] offset printing on continuous paper fed from a reel.

web page ▶ noun Computing a document connected to the World Wide Web and viewable by anyone with an Internet connection and a browser.

web site ▶ noun Computing a location connected to the Internet that maintains one or more pages on the World Wide Web.

web-spinner ▶ noun a slender mainly tropical insect with a soft brownish body, living under stones or logs in a tunnel of silk produced by glands on the front legs.
●Order Embioptera: several families.

Webster[1], John (*c.*1580–*c.*1625), English dramatist. Notable works: *The White Devil* (1612) and *The Duchess of Malfi* (1623), both revenge tragedies.

Webster[2], Noah (1758–1843), American lexicographer. His *American Dictionary of the English Language* (1828) was the first dictionary to give comprehensive coverage of American usage.

web wheel ▶ noun a wheel with a plate instead of spokes, or one with rim, spokes, and centre made in one piece, as in the balance wheel of a clock or watch.

webwork ▶ noun a mesh or network of links or connecting pieces: *a webwork of beams and girders.*

webworm ▶ noun N. Amer. a caterpillar which spins a web in which to rest or feed. When present in large numbers it can become a serious pest.
●*Loxostega* and other genera, family Pyralidae.

Wed. ▶ abbreviation for Wednesday.

wed ▶ verb (**wedding**; past and past participle **wedded** or **wed**) [with obj.] chiefly formal or archaic get married to: *he was to wed the king's daughter.*
■[no obj.] get married: *they wed a week after meeting* | (**be wed**) *after a three-month engagement, they were wed in*

London. ■ give or join in marriage: *will you wed your daughter to him?* ■ [as adj. **wedded**] of or concerning marriage: *a celebration of 25 years' wedded bliss.* ■ combine (two factors or qualities, especially desirable ones): *in this album he weds an excellent programme with a distinctive vocal style.* ■ (**be wedded to**) be obstinately attached or devoted to (an activity, belief, or system): *the government was wedded to budgetary orthodoxy.*
– ORIGIN Old English *weddian*, from the Germanic base of Scots *wed* 'a pledge'; related to Latin *vas* 'surety', also to **GAGE**[1].

we'd ▶ contraction of we had: *we'd already been on board.*
■ we should or we would: *we'd like to make you an offer.*

Weddell Sea /ˈwɛd(ə)l/ an arm of the Atlantic Ocean, off the coast of Antarctica.
– ORIGIN named after the British explorer James *Weddell* (1787–1834), who visited it in 1823.

Weddell seal ▶ noun a large mottled grey seal with a small head, ranging farther south than any other seal and breeding on the fast ice of Antarctica.
• *Leptonychotes weddelli*, family Phocidae.
– ORIGIN early 20th cent.: named after James *Weddell* (see **WEDDELL SEA**).

wedding ▶ noun a marriage ceremony, especially considered as including the associated celebrations.
– ORIGIN Old English *weddung* (see **WED**, **-ING**[1]).

wedding band ▶ noun chiefly N. Amer. a wedding ring.

wedding bells ▶ plural noun bells rung to celebrate a wedding (used to allude to the likelihood of marriage between two people): *the two were seen going everywhere together, and all her friends could hear wedding bells.*

wedding breakfast ▶ noun Brit. a celebratory meal eaten just after a wedding (at any time of day) by the couple and their guests.

wedding cake ▶ noun a rich iced cake, typically in two or more tiers, served at a wedding reception.
■ [as modifier] denoting a building or architectural style that is very decorative or ornate: *a wedding-cake mansion.*

wedding day ▶ noun the day or anniversary of a wedding.

wedding march ▶ noun a piece of march music played at the entrance of the bride or the exit of the couple at a wedding.

wedding night ▶ noun the night after a wedding (especially with reference to its consummation).

wedding ring ▶ noun a ring worn by a married person, given to them by their spouse at their wedding.

wedding tackle ▶ noun another term for **TACKLE** (in sense 1).

Wedekind /ˈveɪdəkɪnd, German ˈveːdəkɪnt/, Frank (1864–1918), German dramatist. A key figure of expressionist drama, he scandalized contemporary German society with the explicit and sardonic portrayal of sexual awakening in *The Awakening of Spring* (1891).

wedge[1] ▶ noun a piece of wood, metal, or some other material having one thick end and tapering to a thin edge, that is driven between two objects or parts of an object to secure or separate them.
■ an object or piece of something having such a shape: *a wedge of cheese.* ■ a formation of people or animals with such a shape. ■ a golf club with a low, angled face for maximum loft. ■ a shot made with such a club. ■ a shoe, typically having a fairly high heel, of which the heel and sole form a solid block, with no gap under the instep. ■ a heel of this kind.
▶ verb **1** [with obj.] fix in position using a wedge: [with obj. and complement] *the door was wedged open.*
2 [with obj. and adverbial] force into a narrow space: *she wedged her holdall between two bags.*
– PHRASES **drive a wedge between** separate: *the general aimed to drive a wedge between the city and its northern defences.* ■ cause disagreement or hostility between: *I'm not trying to drive a wedge between you and your father.* **thin end of the wedge** informal an action or procedure of little importance in itself, but likely to lead to more serious developments.
– DERIVATIVES **wedge-like** adjective.
– ORIGIN Old English *wecg* (noun), of Germanic origin; related to Dutch *wig*.

wedge[2] ▶ verb [with obj.] prepare (pottery clay) for use by cutting, kneading, and throwing down to homogenize it and remove air pockets.
– ORIGIN late 17th cent.: of unknown origin.

wedgebill ▶ noun an Australian songbird of the logrunner family, with a wedge-shaped bill, long tail, and upright crest.
• *Sphenostoma cristatum*, family Orthonychidae.

wedge-shaped ▶ adjective **1** (of a solid object) tapering to a thin edge at one end.
2 (of a plane shape) tapering to a point; V-shaped.

wedge shell ▶ noun a marine bivalve mollusc which has a somewhat triangular shell.
• Family Donacidae: *Donax* and other genera.

wedgie ▶ noun informal a shoe with a wedged heel.

Wedgwood /ˈwɛdʒwʊd/ ▶ noun [mass noun] trademark ceramic ware made by the English potter Josiah Wedgwood (1730–95) and his successors. Wedgwood is most associated with the powder-blue stoneware pieces with white embossed cameos that first appeared in 1775.
■ a powder-blue colour characteristic of this stoneware.

wedlock ▶ noun [mass noun] the state of being married.
– PHRASES **born in** (or **out of**) **wedlock** born of married (or unmarried) parents.
– ORIGIN late Old English *wedlāc* 'marriage vow', from *wed* 'pledge' (related to **WED**) + the suffix *-lāc* (denoting action).

Wednesday ▶ noun the day of the week before Thursday and following Tuesday: *a report goes before the councillors* **on Wednesday** | *they finish early on Wednesdays* | [as modifier] *on a Wednesday morning.*
▶ adverb chiefly N. Amer. on Wednesday: *see you Wednesday.*
■ (**Wednesdays**) on Wednesdays; each Wednesday: *Wednesdays, the jazz DJ hosts a jam session.*
– ORIGIN Old English *Wōdnesdæg*, named after the Germanic god **ODIN**; translation of late Latin *Mercurii dies*; compare with Dutch *woensdag*.

Weds. ▶ abbreviation for Wednesday.

wee[1] ▶ adjective (**weer**, **weest**) chiefly Scottish little: *when I was just a wee bairn.*
– ORIGIN Middle English (originally a noun use in Scots, usually as *a little wee* 'a little bit'): from Old English *wēg(e)* (see **WEY**).

wee[2] informal, chiefly Brit. ▶ noun [in sing.] an act of urinating.
■ [mass noun] urine.
▶ verb (**wees**, **weed**) [no obj.] urinate.
– ORIGIN 1930s: imitative.

weebill ▶ noun a very small Australian warbler with an olive back, yellow underparts, and a short stubby bill.
• *Smicrornis brevirostris*, family Acanthizidae.

weed ▶ noun **1** a wild plant growing where it is not wanted and in competition with cultivated plants.
■ [mass noun] any wild plant growing in salt or fresh water. ■ [mass noun] informal cannabis. ■ (**the weed**) informal tobacco. ■ informal a person regarded as contemptibly feeble. ■ informal a leggy, loosely built horse.
▶ verb [with obj.] remove unwanted plants from (an area of ground or the plants cultivated in it): *I was weeding a flower bed.*
■ (**weed something out**) remove something, especially inferior or unwanted items or members from a group or collection: *we must raise the level of research and weed out the poorest work.*
– DERIVATIVES **weeder** noun, **weedless** adjective.
– ORIGIN Old English *wēod* (noun), *wēodian* (verb), of unknown origin; related to Dutch *wieden* (verb).

weedgrown ▶ adjective overgrown with weeds.

weedicide ▶ noun a chemical weedkiller.

weedkiller ▶ noun a substance used to destroy weeds.

weeds ▶ plural noun short for **WIDOW'S WEEDS**.

weed whacker ▶ noun chiefly US a strimmer.

weedy ▶ adjective (**weedier**, **weediest**) **1** containing or covered with many weeds: *a weedy path led to the gate.*
■ of the nature of or resembling a weed: *a weedy species of plant.*
2 informal (of a person) thin and physically weak in appearance.
– DERIVATIVES **weediness** noun.

Wee Free ▶ noun a member of the minority group nicknamed the **Wee Free Kirk** which stood apart from the Free Church of Scotland when the majority amalgamated with the United Presbyterian Church to form the United Free Church in 1900. The group continued to call itself the Free Church of Scotland after this date.

weejuns /ˈwiːdʒənz/ ▶ plural noun trademark, chiefly US moccasin-style shoes for casual wear.
– ORIGIN 1950s: a fanciful formation.

week ▶ noun a period of seven days: *the course lasts sixteen weeks* | *he'd cut the grass a week ago.*
■ the period of seven days generally reckoned from and to midnight on Saturday night: *she has an art class twice a week.* ■ workdays as opposed to the weekend; the five days from Monday to Friday: *I work during the week, so I can only get to this shop on Saturdays.* ■ the time spent working in this period: *she works a 48-hour week.* ■ informal, chiefly Brit. used after the name of a day to indicate that something will happen seven days after that day: *the programme will be broadcast on Sunday week.*
– PHRASES **a week on ——** used to state that something is due to happen seven days after the specified day or date: *we'll be back a week on Friday.* **week in, week out** every week without exception.
– ORIGIN Old English *wice*, of Germanic origin; related to Dutch *week* and German *Woche*, from a base probably meaning 'sequence, series'.

weekday ▶ noun a day of the week other than Sunday or Saturday.

weekend ▶ noun Saturday and Sunday, especially regarded as a time for leisure: *she spent the weekend camping* | [as modifier] *a weekend break.*
▶ verb [no obj., with adverbial] informal spend a weekend somewhere: *he was weekending in the country.*

weekender ▶ noun a person who spends time in a particular place only at weekends.
■ Austral. informal a holiday cottage. ■ a small pleasure boat.

week-long ▶ adjective [attrib.] lasting for a week: *a week-long visit to New Zealand.*

weekly ▶ adjective [attrib.] done, produced, or occurring once a week: *there was a weekly dance on Wednesdays.*
■ relating to or calculated in terms of a week: *the difference in weekly income is £29.10.*
▶ adverb once a week: *interviews were given weekly.*
▶ noun (pl. **-ies**) a newspaper or periodical issued every week.

weel ▶ adverb, adjective, & exclamation Scottish form of **WELL**[1].

ween ▶ verb [no obj.] archaic be of the opinion; think or suppose: *he, I ween, is no sacred personage.*
– ORIGIN Old English *wēnan*, of Germanic origin; related to Dutch *wanen* 'imagine', German *wähnen* 'suppose wrongly', also to **WISH**.

weenie ▶ noun another term for **WIENER**.

weeny ▶ adjective (**weenier**, **weeniest**) informal tiny.
– ORIGIN late 18th cent.: from **WEE**[1], on the pattern of *tiny*; compare with **TEENY**.

weep ▶ verb (past and past participle **wept**) [no obj.] **1** shed tears: *a grieving mother wept over the body of her daughter* | [with obj.] *he wept bitter tears at her cruelty.*
■ utter or express with tears: [with direct speech] *'No!' she wept.* ■ [with obj.] archaic mourn for; shed tears over: *a young widow weeping her lost lord.*
2 exude liquid: *she rubbed one of the sores, making it weep.*
▶ noun [in sing.] a fit or spell of shedding tears.
– ORIGIN Old English *wēpan* (verb), of Germanic origin, probably imitative.

weeper ▶ noun **1** a person who weeps.
■ historical a hired mourner at a funeral. ■ a small image of a mourner on a monument. ■ US another term for **WEEPIE**.
2 (**weepers**) historical funeral garments, in particular:
■ a man's crape hatband worn at funerals. ■ a widow's black crape veil and white cuffs.

weepie (also **weepy**) ▶ noun (pl. **-ies**) informal a sentimental or emotional film, novel, or song.

weeping ▶ adjective [attrib.] **1** shedding tears.
■ exuding liquid.
2 used in names of tree and shrub varieties with drooping branches, e.g. **weeping cherry**.
– DERIVATIVES **weepingly** adverb.

Weeping Cross ▶ noun historical a wayside cross for penitents to pray at.

weeping widow ▶ noun a mushroom which has a buff cap with purplish-black gills that appear to

W

secrete drops of fluid when damp, found commonly in both Eurasia and North America.
• *Lacrymaria velutina*, family Coprinaceae, class Hymenomycetes.

weeping willow ▶ **noun** a Eurasian willow with trailing branches and foliage reaching down to the ground, widely grown as an ornamental in waterside settings.
• Genus *Salix*, family Salicaceae: several species and hybrids, in particular *S.* × *chrysocoma*.

weepy ▶ **adjective** (**weepier**, **weepiest**) informal tearful; inclined to weep: *a weepy clingy child.*
■ sentimental: *a weepy made-for-TV movie.*
▶ **noun** variant spelling of **WEEPIE**.
– DERIVATIVES **weepily** adverb, **weepiness** noun.

weever (also **weever fish**) ▶ **noun** a small, long-bodied fish with eyes at the top of the head and venomous dorsal spines. It occurs along East Atlantic coasts, typically buried in the sand with just the eyes and spines protruding.
• Family Trachinidae: several genera and species.
– ORIGIN early 17th cent.: perhaps a transferred use of Old French *wivre* 'serpent, dragon', from Latin *vipera* 'viper'.

weevil /ˈwiːv(ə)l, ˈwiːvɪl/ ▶ **noun** a small beetle with an elongated snout, the larvae of which typically develop inside seeds, stems, or other plant parts. Many are pests of crops or stored foodstuffs.
• Curculionidae and other families in the superfamily Curculionoidea: numerous genera.
■ informal any small insect that damages stored grain.
– DERIVATIVES **weevily** adjective.
– ORIGIN Old English *wifel* 'beetle', from a Germanic base meaning 'move briskly'.

wee-wee informal, chiefly Brit. ▶ **noun** a child's word for urine.
▶ **verb** [no obj.] urinate.
– ORIGIN 1930s: imitative.

w.e.f. Brit. ▶ **abbreviation for** with effect from: *a budget to allocate w.e.f. 1st April.*

weft[1] ▶ **noun** [in sing.] (in weaving) the crosswise threads on a loom over and under which other threads (the warp) are passed to make cloth.
– ORIGIN Old English *weft(a)*, of Germanic origin; related to **WEAVE**[1].

weft[2] ▶ **noun** variant spelling of **WAFT** (in sense 2).

Wegener /ˈveɪɡənə, German ˈveːɡənɐ/, Alfred Lothar (1880–1930), German meteorologist and geologist. He was the first serious proponent of the theory of continental drift.

Wehrmacht /ˈvɛːrmɑːxt, German ˈveːɐmaxt/ the German armed forces, especially the army, from 1921 to 1945.
– ORIGIN German, literally 'defensive force'.

Wei /weɪ/ the name of several dynasties which ruled in China, especially that of AD 386–535.

wei ch'i /weɪ ˈtʃiː/ ▶ **noun** [mass noun] a traditional Chinese board game of territorial possession and capture.
– ORIGIN Chinese, from *wei* 'surround' + *ch'i* 'chess'.

Weichsel /ˈvʌɪks(ə)l/ ▶ **noun** [usu. as modifier] Geology the final Pleistocene glaciation in northern Europe, corresponding to the Devensian of Britain (and possibly the Würm of the Alps).
■ the system of deposits laid down at this time.
– DERIVATIVES **Weichselian** /vʌɪkˈsiːlɪən/ adjective & noun.
– ORIGIN 1930s: from the German name of the River Vistula in Poland.

Weifang /weɪˈfaŋ/ a city in Shandong province, eastern China; pop. 3,037,500 (1990). Former name **WEIHSIEN**.

weigela /wʌɪˈdʒiːlə/ ▶ **noun** an Asian flowering shrub of the honeysuckle family, which has pink, red, or yellow flowers and is a popular ornamental.
• Genus *Weigela*, family Caprifoliaceae: several species, in particular *W. florida*.
– ORIGIN modern Latin, named after Christian E. Weigel (1748–1831), German physician.

weigh[1] ▶ **verb 1** [with obj.] find out how heavy (someone or something) is, typically using scales: *weigh yourself on the day you begin the diet | the vendor weighed the vegetables.*
■ have a specified weight: *when the twins were born they weighed ten pounds.* ■ balance in the hands to guess or as if to guess the weight of: *she picked up the brick and weighed it in her right hand.* ■ (**weigh something out**) measure and take from a larger quantity of a substance a portion of a particular weight: *she weighed out two ounces of loose tobacco.* ■ [no obj.] (**weigh on**) be depressing or burdensome to: *his unhappiness would weigh on my mind so much.*
2 assess the nature or importance of, especially with a view to a decision or action: *the consequences of the move would need to be very carefully weighed.*
■ (**weigh something against**) compare the importance of one factor with that of (another): *they need to weigh benefit against risk.* ■ [no obj.] influence a decision or action; be considered important: *the evidence weighed heavily against him.*
– PHRASES **weigh anchor** see **ANCHOR**. **weigh one's words** carefully choose the way one expresses something.
– DERIVATIVES **weighable** adjective, **weigher** noun.
– ORIGIN Old English *wegan*, of Germanic origin; related to Dutch *wegen* 'weigh', German *bewegen* 'move', from an Indo-European root shared by Latin *vehere* 'convey'. Early senses included 'transport from one place to another' and 'raise up'.
▶ **weigh someone down** be heavy and cumbersome to someone: *my waders and fishing gear weighed me down.* ■ be oppressive or burdensome to someone: *she was weighed down by the responsibility of looking after her sisters.*
weigh in (chiefly of a boxer or jockey) be officially weighed before or after a contest: *Mason* ***weighed in at*** *17st 10 lb.*
weigh in at informal be of (a specified weight). ■ informal cost (a specified amount).
weigh in with informal make a forceful contribution to a competition or argument by means of: *I like to weigh in with a few goals.*
weigh into informal join in forcefully or enthusiastically: *they weighed into the election campaign.* ■ attack physically or verbally: *he weighed into the companies for their high costs.*
weigh out (of a jockey) be weighed before a race.
weigh someone/thing up carefully assess someone or something: *the coach weighed up his team's opponents.*

weigh[2] ▶ **noun** (in phrase **under weigh**) Nautical another way of saying ***under way*** (see **UNDER**).
– ORIGIN late 18th cent.: from an erroneous association with *weigh anchor* (see **WEIGH**[1]).

weighbridge ▶ **noun** a machine for weighing vehicles, set into the ground to be driven on to.

weigh-in ▶ **noun** an official or regular weighing of something or someone, for example of boxers before a fight.

weight ▶ **noun 1** [mass noun] a body's relative mass or the quantity of matter contained by it, giving rise to a downward force; the heaviness of a person or thing: *he was at least fifteen stone in weight.*
■ Physics the force exerted on the mass of a body by a gravitational field. Compare with **MASS**. ■ the quality of being heavy: *as he came upstairs the boards creaked under his weight.* ■ [count noun] a unit or system of units used for expressing how much an object or quantity of matter weighs. ■ [count noun] a piece of metal known to weigh a definite amount and used on scales to determine how heavy an object or quantity of a substance is. ■ the amount that a jockey is expected or required to weigh, or the amount that a horse can easily carry. ■ the surface density of cloth, used as a measure of its quality.
2 a heavy object, especially one being lifted or carried.
■ a heavy object used to give an impulse or act as a counterpoise in a mechanism. ■ a heavy object thrown by a shot-putter. ■ (**weights**) blocks or discs of metal or other heavy material used in weightlifting or weight training.
3 [mass noun] the ability of someone or something to influence decisions or actions: *a recommendation by the committee will carry great weight.*
■ the importance attached to something: *individuals differ in the weight they attach to various aspects of a job.* ■ Statistics a factor associated with one of a set of numerical quantities, used to represent its importance relative to the other members of the set.
▶ **verb** [with obj.] **1** hold (something) down by placing a heavy object on top of it: *a mug half filled with coffee* ***weighted down*** *a stack of papers.*
■ make (something) heavier by attaching a heavy object to it, especiallyso as to make it stay in place: *the jugs were covered with muslin veils weighted with coloured beads.*
2 attach importance or value to: *speaking, reading, and writing should be weighted equally in the assessment.*
■ (**be weighted**) be planned or arranged so as to put a specified person, group, or factor in a position of advantage or disadvantage: *the balance of power is weighted in favour of the government.* ■ Statistics multiply the components of (an average) by factors to take account of their importance.
3 assign a handicap weight to (a horse).
4 treat (a fabric) with a mineral to make it seem thicker and heavier.
– PHRASES **put on** (or **lose**) **weight** become fatter (or thinner). **throw one's weight about** (or **around**) informal be unpleasantly self-assertive. **throw one's weight behind** informal use one's influence to help support. **the weight of the world** used in reference to a very heavy burden of worry or responsibility: *he continues to carry the weight of the world on his shoulders.* **be a weight off one's mind** come as a great relief after one has been worried. **worth one's weight in gold** (of a person) exceedingly useful or helpful.
– ORIGIN Old English *(ge)wiht*, of Germanic origin; related to Dutch *wicht* and German *Gewicht*. The form of the word has been influenced by **WEIGH**[1].

weight belt ▶ **noun** a belt to which weights are attached, designed to help divers stay submerged.

weighted average ▶ **noun** Statistics an average resulting from the multiplication of each component by a factor reflecting its importance.

weighting ▶ **noun** [mass noun] allowance or adjustment made in order to take account of special circumstances or compensate for a distorting factor.
■ Brit. an extra amount of wages or salary paid especially to allow for a higher cost of living in a particular area: *London weighting of £1,750 is payable.* ■ emphasis or priority: *they will give due weighting to quality as well as price.*

weightless ▶ **adjective** (of a body, especially in an orbiting spacecraft) not apparently acted on by gravity.
– DERIVATIVES **weightlessly** adverb, **weightlessness** noun.

weightlifting ▶ **noun** [mass noun] the sport or activity of lifting barbells or other heavy weights. There are two standard lifts in modern weightlifting: the single-movement lift from floor to extended position (the **snatch**), and the two-movement lift from floor to shoulder position, and from shoulders to extended position (the **clean and jerk**).
– DERIVATIVES **weightlifter** noun.

weight training ▶ **noun** [mass noun] physical training that involves lifting weights.

weight-watcher ▶ **noun** a person who is concerned about their weight, especially one who diets.
– DERIVATIVES **weight-watching** noun & adjective.
– ORIGIN from the proprietary name *Weight Watchers*, an organization promoting dietary control as a means of slimming.

weighty ▶ **adjective** (**weightier**, **weightiest**) weighing a great deal; heavy: *a weighty candelabra.*
■ of great seriousness and importance: *he threw off all weighty considerations of state.* ■ having a great deal of influence on events or decisions.
– DERIVATIVES **weightily** adverb, **weightiness** noun.

Weihsien /weɪˈʃjɛn/ former name for **WEIFANG**.

Weil /vʌɪl, French vɛj/, Simone (1909–43), French essayist, philosopher, and mystic. During the Second World War she joined the resistance movement in England and died of tuberculosis while weakened by voluntary starvation in identification with her French compatriots.

Weill /vʌɪl/, Kurt (1900–50), German composer, resident in the US from 1935. He is best known for the operas he wrote with Bertolt Brecht, political satires including *The Threepenny Opera* (1928).

Weil's disease /vʌɪlz/ ▶ **noun** [mass noun] a severe, sometimes fatal, form of leptospirosis transmitted by rats via contaminated water.
– ORIGIN late 19th cent.: named after H. Adolf *Weil* (1848–1916), German physician.

Weimar /ˈvʌɪmɑː, German ˈvaɪmar/ a city in Thuringia, central Germany; pop. 59,100 (1991). It was famous in the late 18th and early 19th century for its intellectual and cultural life.

Weimaraner /ˈvʌɪməˌrɑːnə, ˈwʌɪ-/ ▶ **noun** a dog of a thin-coated, typically grey breed of pointer used as a gun dog.
– ORIGIN 1940s: from German, from **WEIMAR** in Germany, where the breed was developed.

Weimar Republic the German republic of 1919–

W

33, so called because its constitution was drawn up at Weimar. The republic was faced with huge reparation costs deriving from the Treaty of Versailles as well as soaring inflation and high unemployment. The 1920s saw a growth in support for right-wing groups and the Republic was eventually overthrown by the Nazi Party of Adolf Hitler.

Weinberg /ˈwʌɪnbəːg/, Steven (b.1933), American theoretical physicist. He devised a theory to unify electromagnetic interactions and the weak forces within the nucleus of an atom, for which he shared the Nobel Prize for Physics in 1979.

Weinstube /ˈvʌɪnˌʃtuːbə, -stuːbə, German ˈvaɪnˌʃtuːbə/ ▶ **noun** (pl. **Weinstuben** /-ˌʃtuːb(ə)n, -stuːb(ə)n, German -ˌʃtuːbn/) a small German wine bar or tavern.
– ORIGIN German, literally 'wine room'.

weir ▶ **noun** a low dam built across a river to raise the level of water upstream or regulate its flow.
■ an enclosure of stakes set in a stream as a trap for fish.
– ORIGIN Old English *wer*, from *werian* 'dam up'.

weird ▶ **adjective** suggesting something supernatural; uncanny: *the weird crying of a seal.*
■ informal very strange; bizarre: *a weird coincidence | all sorts of* **weird and wonderful** *characters.* ■ archaic connected with fate.
▶ **noun** archaic, chiefly Scottish a person's destiny.
▶ **verb** [with obj.] (**weird someone out**) N. Amer. informal induce a sense of disbelief or alienation in someone.
– DERIVATIVES **weirdly** adverb, **weirdness** noun.
– ORIGIN Old English *wyrd* 'destiny', of Germanic origin. The adjective (late Middle English) originally meant 'having the power to control destiny', and was used especially in *the Weird Sisters*, originally referring to the Fates, later the witches in Shakespeare's *Macbeth*; the latter use gave rise to the sense 'unearthly' (early 19th cent.).

weirdie (also **weirdy**) ▶ **noun** (pl. **-ies**) another term for **WEIRDO**.

weirdo ▶ **noun** (pl. **-os**) informal a person whose dress or behaviour seems strange or eccentric.

weird sisters ▶ **plural noun** (usu. **the weird sisters**) the Fates.
■ witches, especially those in Shakespeare's *Macbeth*.

Weismann /ˈvʌɪsmən, German ˈvaɪsman/, August Friedrich Leopold (1834–1914), German biologist, one of the founders of modern genetics. He expounded the theory of germ plasm, which ruled out the transmission of acquired characteristics, and suggested that variability in individuals came from the recombination of chromosomes during reproduction.
– DERIVATIVES **Weismannism** noun, **Weismannist** noun & adjective.

Weissmuller /ˈwʌɪsˌmʊlə/, Johnny (1904–84), American swimmer and actor; full name *John Peter Weissmuller*. He won three Olympic gold medals in 1924 and two in 1928. In the 1930s and 1940s he was the star of the Tarzan films.

Weisswurst /ˈvʌɪsvəːst/ (also **weisswurst**) ▶ **noun** [mass noun] whitish German sausage made chiefly of veal.
– ORIGIN German, literally 'white sausage'.

Weizmann /ˈvʌɪtsmən, ˈwʌɪzmən/, Chaim (Azriel) (1874–1952), Russian-born Israeli statesman, President 1949–52. He played an important role in persuading the US government to recognize the new state of Israel (1948) and became its first President.

weka /ˈwɛkə/ ▶ **noun** a large flightless New Zealand rail with heavily built legs and feet.
● *Gallirallus australis*, family Rallidae.
– ORIGIN mid 19th cent.: from Maori, imitative of its cry.

Welamo /ˈwɛləməʊ/ ▶ **noun** (pl. same or **Welamos**) **1** a member of a people living mainly in SW Ethiopia.
2 [mass noun] the Omotic language of this people.
▶ **adjective** of or relating to this people or their language.

Weland /ˈwɛlənd/ variant of **WAYLAND THE SMITH**.

welch /wɛltʃ/ ▶ **verb** variant spelling of **WELSH**.

welcome ▶ **noun** an instance or manner of greeting someone: *you will receive a warm welcome |* [mass noun] *he went to meet them with his hand stretched out in welcome.*
■ a pleased or approving reaction: *the announcement received an immediate welcome from childcare agencies.*
▶ **exclamation** used to greet someone in a glad or friendly way: **welcome to** *the Wildlife Park.*
▶ **verb** [with obj.] greet (someone arriving) in a glad, polite, or friendly way: *hotels should welcome guests in their own language |* [as adj. **welcoming**] *a welcoming smile.*
■ be glad to entertain (someone) or receive (something): *we welcome any comments.* ■ react with pleasure or approval to (an event or development): *the bank's decision to cut its rates was widely welcomed.*
▶ **adjective** (of a guest or new arrival) gladly received: *I'm pleased to see you, lad—you're welcome.*
■ very pleasing because much needed or desired: *after your walk, the tea room serves a welcome cuppa | the news will be most* **welcome to** *those whose jobs will now be safeguarded.* ■ [predic., with infinitive] allowed or invited to do a specified thing: *we arrange a framework of activities which you are welcome to join.* ■ [predic.] (**welcome to**) used to indicate that one is relieved to be relinquishing the control or possession of something to another: *the job is all yours and you're welcome to it!*
– PHRASES **make someone welcome** receive and treat someone hospitably. **outstay** (or **overstay**) **one's welcome** stay as a visitor longer than one is wanted. **you are welcome** used as a polite response to thanks.
– DERIVATIVES **welcomely** adverb, **welcomeness** noun, **welcomer** noun, **welcomingly** adverb.
– ORIGIN Old English *wilcuma* 'a person whose coming is pleasing', *wilcumian* (verb), from *wil-* 'desire, pleasure' + *cuman* 'come'. The first element was later changed to *wel-* 'well', influenced by Old French *bien venu* or Old Norse *velkominn*.

Welcome Wagon ▶ **noun** N. Amer. trademark a vehicle bringing gifts and samples from local merchants to newcomers in a community.

weld[1] ▶ **verb** [with obj.] join together (metal pieces or parts) by heating the surfaces to the point of melting with a blowpipe, electric arc, or other means, and uniting them by pressing, hammering, etc.: *the truck had spikes welded to the back.*
■ forge (an article) by such means. ■ unite (pieces of plastic or other material) by melting or softening of surfaces in contact. ■ figurative cause to combine and form a harmonious or effective whole: *cross-curricular themes would* **weld** *the curriculum* **together**.
▶ **noun** a welded joint.
– DERIVATIVES **weldability** noun, **weldable** adjective, **welder** noun.
– ORIGIN late 16th cent. (in the sense 'become united'): alteration (probably influenced by the past participle) of **WELL**[2] in the obsolete sense 'melt or weld (heated metal)'.

weld[2] ▶ **noun** a widely distributed plant related to mignonette, yielding a yellow dye.
● *Reseda luteola*, family Resedaceae.
■ [mass noun] the yellow dye made from this plant, which has been used since Neolithic times and was a popular colour for Roman wedding garments.
– ORIGIN late Middle English: related to Dutch *wouw*, perhaps also to **WOLD**.

weldmesh ▶ **noun** [mass noun] trademark wire mesh formed by welding together two series of parallel wires crossing at right angles.

welfare ▶ **noun** [mass noun] the health, happiness, and fortunes of a person or group: *they don't give a damn about the welfare of their families.*
■ statutory procedure or social effort designed to promote the basic physical and material well-being of people in need: *the protection of rights to education, housing, and welfare.* ■ chiefly N. Amer. financial support given for this purpose.
– ORIGIN Middle English: from the adverb **WELL**[1] + the verb **FARE**.

welfare state ▶ **noun** a system whereby the state undertakes to protect the health and well-being of its citizens, especially those in financial or social need, by means of grants, pensions, and other benefits. The foundations for the modern welfare state in the UK were laid by the Beveridge Report of 1942; proposals such as the establishment of a National Health Service and the National Insurance Scheme were implemented by the Labour administration in 1948.
■ a country practising such a system.

welfare to work ▶ **noun** [mass noun] (in the UK) the government policy of encouraging unemployed people and others receiving state benefits to find a job, for example by paying a fee to their new employers.

welfare work ▶ **noun** [mass noun] organized effort to promote the basic physical and material well-being of people in need.
– DERIVATIVES **welfare worker** noun.

welfarism ▶ **noun** [mass noun] the principles or policies associated with a welfare state.
– DERIVATIVES **welfarist** noun & adjective.

welkin /ˈwɛlkɪn/ ▶ **noun** poetic/literary the sky.
■ heaven.
– PHRASES **make the welkin ring** make a very loud sound: *the crew made the welkin ring with its hurrahs.*
– ORIGIN Old English *wolcen* 'cloud, sky', of West Germanic origin; related to Dutch *wolk* and German *Wolke*.

Welkom /ˈwɛlkəm, ˈvɛl-/ a town in central South Africa, in Free State; pop. 185,500 (1985).

well[1] ▶ **adverb** (**better**, **best**) **1** in a good or satisfactory way: *the whole team played well.*
■ in a way that is appropriate to the facts or circumstances: *you did well to come and tell me |* [as submodifier, in combination] *a well-timed exit.* ■ so as to have a fortunate outcome: *his campaign was not going well.* ■ in a kind way: *the animals will remain loyal to humans if treated well.* ■ with praise or approval: *people spoke well of him | the film was quite well reviewed at the time.* ■ with equanimity: *she took it very well, all things considered.* ■ profitably; advantageously: *she would marry well or not at all.* ■ in a condition of prosperity or comfort: *they lived well and were generous with their money.* ■ archaic luckily; opportunely: *hail fellow, well met.*
2 in a thorough manner: *add the mustard and lemon juice and mix well.*
■ to a great extent or degree (often used for emphasis): *the visit had been planned well in advance |* [as submodifier, in combination] *a well-loved mother.* ■ intimately; closely: *he knew my father very well.* ■ [as submodifier] Brit. informal very; extremely: *he was well out of order.* ■ [with submodifier] used as an intensifier: *I should bloody well hope so.*
3 [with modal] very probably; in all likelihood: *being short of breath may well be the first sign of asthma.*
■ without difficulty: *she could well afford to pay for the reception herself.* ■ with good reason: *'What are we doing here?' 'You may well ask.'*
▶ **adjective** (**better**, **best**) [predic.] **1** in good health; free or recovered from illness: *I don't feel very well | it would be some time before Sarah was completely well |* [attrib.] informal *I am not a well man.*
■ in a satisfactory state or position: *all is not well in post-Soviet Russia.*
2 sensible; advisable: *it would be well to know just what this suggestion entails.*
▶ **exclamation** used to express a range of emotions including surprise, anger, resignation, or relief: *Well, really! The manners of some people!*
■ used when pausing to consider one's next words: *well, I suppose I could fit you in at 3.45.* ■ used to mark the end of a conversation or activity: *well, cheers, Tom—I must fly.* ■ used to indicate that one is waiting for an answer or explanation from someone: *Well? You promised to tell me all about it.*
– PHRASES **all's well that ends well** see **ALL**. **all very well** see **ALL**. **as well 1** in addition; too: *the museum provides hours of fun and a few surprises as well | a shop that sold books* **as well as** *newspapers.* **2** (**as well** or **just as well**) with equal reason or an equally good result: *I* **may as well** *have a look.* ■ sensible, appropriate, or desirable: *it would be as well to let him go.* **as well he** (or **she** etc.) **might** (or **may**) used to convey the speaker's opinion that a reaction is appropriate or unsurprising: *she sounded rather chipper, as well she might, given her bright prospects.* **be well away** Brit. informal having made considerable or easy progress: *If we got Terry to do that, we'd be well away.* ■ be fast asleep or very drunk. **be well out of** Brit. informal be fortunate to be no longer involved in (a situation). **be well up on** (or **in**) know a great deal about (a particular thing). **do well for oneself** be successful, typically in material or financial terms. **leave** (or **let**) **well** (US **enough**) **alone** refrain from interfering with or trying improve something that is satisfactory or adequate as it is. **very well** used to express agreement or understanding: *oh very well then, come in.* (**all**) **well and good** used to express acceptance of a first statement before introducing a contradictory or confirming second statement: *that's all well and good, but why didn't he phone her to say so?* **well and truly** completely: *Leith was well and*

W

truly rattled. **well enough** to a reasonable degree: *he liked Isobel well enough, but wouldn't want to make a close friend of her.*

– DERIVATIVES **wellness** noun.

– ORIGIN Old English *wel(l)*, of Germanic origin; related to Dutch *wel* and German *wohl*; probably also to the verb WILL¹. Vowel lengthening in Middle English gave rise to the current Scots form WEEL.

> USAGE The adverb **well** is often used in combination with past participles to form adjectival compounds: **well adjusted**, **well intentioned**, **well known**, and so on. As far as hyphenation is concerned, the general stylistic principle is that if the adjectival compound is placed attributively (i.e. it comes before the noun), it should be hyphenated (*a well-intentioned remark*) but that if it is placed predicatively (i.e. standing alone after the verb), it should not be hyphenated (*her remarks were well intentioned*). In this dictionary, the unhyphenated form is generally the only one given, although the hyphenated form may be seen in illustrative examples.

well² ▶ noun **1** a shaft sunk into the ground to obtain water, oil, or gas.
■ a plentiful source or supply: *she could feel a deep well of sympathy and compassion.* ■ archaic a water spring or fountain. ■ (**Wells**) [in place names] a place where there are mineral springs: *Tunbridge Wells.* ■ short for INKWELL. ■ a depression made to hold liquid: *put the flour on a flat surface and make a well to hold the eggs.*
2 an enclosed space in the middle of a building, giving room for stairs or a lift, or to allow light or ventilation.
■ Brit. the place in a law court where the clerks and ushers sit.
3 Physics a region of minimum potential: *a gravity well.*
▶ verb [no obj., with adverbial] (of a liquid) rise up to the surface and spill or be about to spill: *tears were beginning to well in her eyes.*
■ (of an emotion) arise and become more intense: *all the old bitterness began to well up inside her again.*

– ORIGIN Old English *wella*, of Germanic origin; related to Dutch *wel* and German *Welle* 'a wave'.

we'll ▶ contraction of we shall; we will.

well adjusted ▶ adjective successfully altered or moved so as to achieve a desired fit, appearance, or result: *her eyes were well adjusted to the darkness.*
■ (of a person) mentally and emotionally stable.

well advised ▶ adjective [with infinitive] sensible; wise: *you would be well advised to obtain legal advice.*

Welland Canal /ˈwɛlənd/ (also **Welland Ship Canal**) a canal in southern Canada, 42 km (26 miles) long, linking Lake Erie with Lake Ontario, bypassing Niagara Falls and forming part of the St Lawrence Seaway.

well appointed ▶ adjective (of a building or room) having a high standard of equipment or furnishing.

well behaved ▶ adjective conducting oneself in an appropriate manner: *the crowd was very well behaved.*
■ (of a computer program) communicating with hardware via standard operating system calls rather than directly and therefore able to be used on different machines.

well-being ▶ noun [mass noun] the state of being comfortable, healthy, or happy: *an improvement in the patient's well-being.*

well born ▶ adjective from a noble or wealthy family.

well bred ▶ adjective having or showing good breeding or manners.

well built ▶ adjective (of a person) large and strong.
■ of strong, solid construction: *the well-built and massively thick walls.*

well conducted ▶ adjective properly organized or carried out: *responsible, well-conducted businesses.*
■ archaic well behaved.

well connected ▶ adjective acquainted with or related to people with prestige or influence.

well covered ▶ adjective Brit. informal slightly plump.

well deck ▶ noun an open space on the main deck of a ship, lying at a lower level between the forecastle and poop.

well disposed ▶ adjective having a positive, sympathetic, or friendly attitude towards someone or something: *the company is well disposed to the idea of partnership.*

well done ▶ adjective **1** (of a task or undertaking) carried out successfully: *the*

decoration is very well done | [postpositive] *the satisfaction of a job well done.*
2 (of meat) thoroughly cooked.
▶ exclamation used to express congratulation or approval: *Well done—you've worked very hard!*

well dressed ▶ adjective wearing smart or fashionable clothes.

well dressing ▶ noun [mass noun] the decoration of wells with flowers at Whitsuntide, especially in Derbyshire, as an ancient custom originally associated with the belief in water deities.

well earned ▶ adjective fully merited or deserved: *a well-earned rest.*

well endowed ▶ adjective having plentiful supplies of a resource: *the country is well endowed with mineral resources.*
■ well provided with money; wealthy. ■ informal, humorous (of a man) having large genitals. ■ informal, humorous (of a woman) large-breasted.

Welles /wɛlz/, (George) Orson (1915–85), American film director and actor. His realistic radio dramatization in 1938 of H. G. Wells's *The War of the Worlds* persuaded many listeners that a Martian invasion was really happening. Notable films: *Citizen Kane* (1941) and *The Third Man* (1949).

well favoured (US **well favored**) ▶ adjective having special advantages, especially good looks.

well fed ▶ adjective having good meals regularly.

well formed ▶ adjective correctly or attractively proportioned or shaped.
■ (especially of a sentence or phrase) constructed according to grammatical rules. ■ conforming to the formation rules of a logical system.

well found ▶ adjective (chiefly of a boat) well equipped and maintained.

well founded ▶ adjective (especially of a suspicion or belief) based on good evidence or reasons: *their apprehensions were well founded.*

well groomed ▶ adjective (especially of a person) clean, tidy, and smart.

well grounded ▶ adjective based on good evidence or reasons.
■ having a good training in or knowledge of a subject: *boys who are well grounded in traditional academic subjects.*

well head ▶ noun **1** the place where a spring comes out of the ground.
2 the structure over a well, typically an oil or gas well.

well heeled ▶ adjective informal wealthy.

well house ▶ noun a small building or room enclosing a well and its apparatus.

well hung ▶ adjective **1** informal (of a man) having large genitals.
2 (of meat or game) hung until sufficiently dry, tender, or high before cooking.

wellie ▶ noun variant spelling of WELLY.

well informed ▶ adjective having or showing much knowledge about a wide range of subjects, or about one particular subject.

Wellington¹ the capital of New Zealand, situated at the southern tip of North Island; pop. 150,300 (1991). It became the capital in 1865, when the seat of government was moved from Auckland.

Wellington², Arthur Wellesley, 1st Duke of (1769–1852), British soldier and Tory statesman, Prime Minister 1828–30 and 1834; known as the **Iron Duke**. He served as commander of the British forces in the Peninsular War (1808–14) and in 1815 defeated Napoleon at the Battle of Waterloo, so ending the Napoleonic Wars.

wellington (also **wellington boot**) ▶ noun chiefly Brit. a knee-length waterproof rubber or plastic boot.

– ORIGIN early 19th cent.: named after the 1st Duke of Wellington (see WELLINGTON²).

wellingtonia /ˌwɛlɪŋˈtəʊnɪə/ ▶ noun the giant redwood.

– ORIGIN mid 19th cent.: modern Latin, from the former binomial *Wellingtonia gigantea* (from WELLINGTON²).

well intentioned ▶ adjective having or showing good intentions despite a lack of success or fortunate results: *well-intentioned advice.*

well judged ▶ adjective showing careful consideration or much skill.

well kept ▶ adjective (especially of property) kept clean, tidy, and in good condition.

■ (of a secret) not told to anyone or made widely known.

well knit ▶ adjective (of a person) strongly and compactly built.

well known ▶ adjective known widely or thoroughly: *a well-known television personality.*

well made ▶ adjective strongly or skilfully constructed: *a well-made film.*
■ (of a person) having a good, strong build.

well matched ▶ adjective (of two or more people or items) appropriate for or very similar to each other: *a fiercely contested quarter-final between two well-matched sides.*

well meaning (also **well meant**) ▶ adjective well intentioned: *well-meaning friends.*

well-nigh ▶ adverb chiefly poetic/literary almost: *a task that is well-nigh impossible.*

well off ▶ adjective wealthy: *her family are quite well off.*
■ in a favourable situation or circumstances: *they were well off without her.*

well oiled ▶ adjective **1** [predic.] informal drunk.
2 (especially of an organization) operating smoothly: *the ruling party's well-oiled political machine.*

well pleased ▶ adjective highly gratified or satisfied: *Moore paused, well pleased with the effect.*

well preserved ▶ adjective (of something old) having remained in good condition.
■ (of an old person) showing little sign of ageing.

well rounded ▶ adjective having a pleasing curved shape: *the guitar has a well-rounded neck.*
■ (of a person) plump. ■ (of a person) having a personality that is fully developed in all aspects. ■ (of a phrase or sentence) carefully composed and balanced.

Wells, H. G. (1866–1946), English novelist; full name Herbert George Wells. He wrote some of the earliest science-fiction novels, such as *The War of the Worlds* (1898), which combined political satire with warnings about the powers of science.

well set ▶ adjective (of a construction) firmly established; solidly fixed or arranged.
■ (also **well-set-up**) (of a person) strongly built.

Wells, Fargo, & Co. /ˈfɑːɡəʊ/ a US transportation company founded in 1852 by the businessmen Henry Wells (1805–78) and William Fargo (1818–81) and others. It carried mail to and from the newly developed West, founded a San Francisco bank, and later ran a stagecoach service.

well spent ▶ adjective (of money or time) usefully or profitably expended: *time spent in taking stock is time well spent.*

well spoken ▶ adjective (of a person) speaking in an educated and refined manner.

wellspring ▶ noun poetic/literary term for WELL HEAD (in sense 1).

well tempered ▶ adjective (of a person or animal) having a cheerful or emotionally stable disposition.
■ (of a process or activity) properly regulated, controlled, or moderated.

well thumbed ▶ adjective (of a book, magazine, etc.) having been read often and bearing marks of frequent handling.

well-to-do ▶ adjective wealthy; prosperous: *a well-to-do family.*

well travelled (US **well traveled**) ▶ adjective **1** (of a person) having travelled widely.
2 (of a route) much frequented by travellers.

well tried ▶ adjective having been used often and therefore known to be reliable: *well-tried tactics.*

well trodden ▶ adjective much frequented by travellers: *a well-trodden path.*

well turned ▶ adjective **1** (of a compliment, phrase, or verse) elegantly expressed.
2 (especially of an ankle or leg) having an elegant and attractive shape.

well upholstered ▶ adjective (of a chair or sofa) having plenty of padding.
■ humorous (of a person) fat.

well used ▶ adjective much used: *a well-used route.*
■ worn or shabby through much use, handling, or wear: *a well-used wax jacket.*

well-wisher ▶ noun a person who desires happiness or success for another, or who expresses such a desire.

well woman ▶ noun [as modifier] Brit. denoting a clinic

or other establishment providing health advice and check-ups for problems specific to women. (Equivalent 'well man' clinics for men are relatively unusual.)

well worn ▶ **adjective** showing the signs of extensive use or wear: *a well-worn leather armchair.*
■ (of a phrase, idea, or joke) used or repeated so often that it no longer has interest or significance.

well wrought ▶ **adjective** skilfully constructed or put together: *a well-wrought argument.*

welly (also **wellie**) ▶ **noun** (pl. **-ies**) Brit. informal **1** short for **WELLINGTON**.
2 [mass noun] power or vigour: *I like big, fat voices with plenty of welly.*

wels /wɛls, vɛls/ ▶ **noun** a large freshwater catfish that occurs from central Europe to central Asia. It has been known to reach a length of 5 m and a weight of over 300 kg. Also called **SHEATFISH**.
● *Silurus glanis*, family Siluridae.
– ORIGIN late 19th cent.: from German *Wels*.

Welsbach /'wɛlzbak, German 'vɛlsbax/, Carl Auer von, see **AUER**.

Welsh ▶ **adjective** of or relating to Wales, its people, or their Celtic language.
▶ **noun 1** [mass noun] the Celtic language of Wales, spoken by about 500,000 people (mainly bilingual in English). Descended from the Brythonic language spoken in most of Roman Britain, it has been strongly revived after a long decline.
2 [as plural noun **the Welsh**] the people of Wales collectively.
– DERIVATIVES **Welshness** noun.
– ORIGIN Old English *Welisc*, *Wælisc*, from a Germanic word meaning 'foreigner', from Latin *Volcae*, the name of a Celtic people.

welsh (also **welch**) ▶ **verb** [no obj.] (**welsh on**) fail to honour (a debt or obligation incurred through a promise or agreement): *banks began welshing on their agreement not to convert dollar reserves into gold.*
– DERIVATIVES **welsher** noun.
– ORIGIN mid 19th cent.: of unknown origin.

Welsh Black ▶ **noun** an animal of a black-coated breed of cattle developed in North Wales, now generally kept for both meat and milk production.

Welsh corgi ▶ **noun** see **CORGI**.

Welsh dragon ▶ **noun** a red heraldic dragon as the emblem of Wales.

Welsh dresser ▶ **noun** a piece of wooden furniture with cupboards and drawers in the lower part and open shelves in the upper part.

Welsh harp ▶ **noun** another term for **TRIPLE HARP**. Compare with **CELTIC HARP**.

Welshman ▶ **noun** (pl. **-men**) a male native or national of Wales, or a man of Welsh descent.

Welsh mountain pony ▶ **noun** a small, strong, slender pony of a hardy breed, used as a riding pony or in harness.

Welsh mountain sheep ▶ **noun** a sheep of a small hardy breed developed in the uplands of Wales.

Welsh onion ▶ **noun** an Asian onion that forms clusters of slender bulbs which resemble salad (spring) onions. It is the onion most commonly used in SE Asia.
● *Allium fistulosum*, family Liliaceae (or Alliaceae).
– ORIGIN early 18th cent. (as *Welch onion*): *Welsh* from German *welsch* 'foreign'.

Welsh poppy ▶ **noun** a yellow- or orange-flowered European poppy of shady rocky places.
● *Meconopsis cambrica*, family Papaveraceae.

Welsh rarebit (also **Welsh rabbit**) ▶ **noun** another term for **RAREBIT**.

Welsh springer ▶ **noun** see **SPRINGER** (sense 1).

Welsh terrier ▶ **noun** a stocky, rough-coated, typically black-and-tan terrier of a breed with a square muzzle and drop ears.

Welshwoman ▶ **noun** (pl. **-women**) a female native or national of Wales, or a woman of Welsh descent.

welt ▶ **noun 1** a leather rim sewn round the edge of a shoe upper to which the sole is attached.
■ a ribbed, reinforced, or decorative border of a garment or pocket.
2 another term for **WEAL**[1].
■ a heavy blow.
▶ **verb** [with obj.] **1** provide with a welt.
2 strike (someone or something) hard and heavily: *I could have welted her.*

■ [no obj.] develop a raised scar: *his lip was beginning to thicken and welt from the blow.*
– ORIGIN late Middle English: of unknown origin.

Weltanschauung /'vɛlt,anʃaʊʊŋ, German 'vɛlt,anʃaʊʊŋ/ ▶ **noun** (pl. **Weltanschauungen** /-(ə)n/) a particular philosophy or view of life; the world view of an individual or group.
– ORIGIN German, from *Welt* 'world' + *Anschauung* 'perception'.

welter[1] ▶ **verb** [no obj.] poetic/literary move in a turbulent fashion: *the streams foam and welter.*
■ lie steeped in blood with no help or care.
▶ **noun** a large number of items in no order; a confused mass: *there's such a welter of conflicting rules.*
■ a state of general disorder: *the attack petered out in a welter of bloody, confused fighting.*
– ORIGIN Middle English (in the sense 'writhe, wallow'): from Middle Dutch, Middle Low German *welteren*.

welter[2] ▶ **noun** short for **WELTERWEIGHT**.

welterweight ▶ **noun** [mass noun] a weight in boxing and other sports intermediate between lightweight and middleweight. In the amateur boxing scale it ranges from 63.5–67 kg.
■ [count noun] a boxer or other competitor of this weight.
– ORIGIN early 19th cent.: *welter* of unknown origin.

Weltschmerz /'vɛlt,ʃmɛːts, German 'vɛlt,ʃmɛrts/ ▶ **noun** [mass noun] a feeling of melancholy and world-weariness.
– ORIGIN German, from *Welt* 'world' + *Schmerz* 'pain'.

Welty /'wɛlti/, Eudora (b.1909), American novelist, short-story writer, and critic. Welty's novels chiefly focus on life in the South and contain Gothic elements; they include *The Optimist's Daughter* (1972), which won the Pulitzer Prize.

Wembley Stadium a sports stadium in Wembley, NW London. The FA Cup Final and the England football team's home matches are played there.

wen[1] ▶ **noun** a boil or other swelling or growth on the skin, especially a sebaceous cyst.
■ archaic an outstandingly large or overcrowded city: *the great wen of London.*
– ORIGIN Old English *wen(n)*, of unknown origin; compare with Low German *wehne* 'tumour, wart'.

wen[2] (also **wyn**) ▶ **noun** a runic letter, used in Old and Middle English, later replaced by *w*.
– ORIGIN Old English, literally 'joy'; so named because it is the first letter of the word. Compare with sense 3 of **THORN** and sense 2 of **ASH**[2].

Wenceslas /'wɛnsɪslas, 'wɛnsəslas/ (also **Wenceslaus** /-laʊs/) (1361–1419), king of Bohemia (as Wenceslas IV) 1378–1419. He became king of Germany, Holy Roman emperor, and King of Bohemia in the same year, but was deposed by the German Electors in 1400.

Wenceslas, St (also **Wenceslaus**) (*c*.907–29), Duke of Bohemia and patron saint of the Czech Republic; also known as **Good King Wenceslas**. He worked to Christianize the people of Bohemia but was murdered by his brother; he later became venerated as a martyr. Feast day, 28 September.

wench /wɛn(t)ʃ/ ▶ **noun** archaic or humorous a girl or young woman.
■ archaic a prostitute.
▶ **verb** [no obj.] archaic (of a man) consort with prostitutes.
– DERIVATIVES **wencher** noun.
– ORIGIN Middle English: abbreviation of obsolete *wenchel* 'child, servant, prostitute'; perhaps related to Old English *wancol* 'unsteady, inconstant'.

Wen-Chou /wɛn'tʃaʊ/ variant of **WENZHOU**.

Wend /wɛnd/ ▶ **noun** another term for **SORB**.
– ORIGIN from German *Wende*, of unknown origin.

wend ▶ **verb** [no obj., with adverbial] (**wend one's way**) go in a specified direction, typically slowly or by an indirect route: *they wended their way across the city.*
– ORIGIN Old English *wendan* 'to turn, depart', of Germanic origin; related to Dutch and German *wenden*, also to **WIND**[2].

wendigo /'wɛndɪɡəʊ/ ▶ **noun** variant spelling of **WINDIGO**.

Wendish /'wɛndɪʃ/ ▶ **adjective & noun** another term for **SORBIAN**.

Wendy house ▶ **noun** Brit. a toy house large enough for children to play in.
– ORIGIN named after the house built around *Wendy* in Barrie's play *Peter Pan*.

Wensleydale /'wɛnzlɪdeɪl/ ▶ **noun 1** [mass noun] a type of white cheese with a crumbly texture.
2 a sheep of a breed with long wool.
– ORIGIN named after *Wensleydale* in Yorkshire.

went past of **GO**[1].

wentletrap /'wɛnt(ə)ltrap/ ▶ **noun** a marine mollusc which has a tall spiral shell with many whorls that are ringed with oblique ridges. Also called **STAIRCASE SHELL**.
● Family Epitoniidae, class Gastropoda: numerous species, including the European **common wentletrap** (*Clathrus clathrus*).
– ORIGIN mid 18th cent.: from Dutch *wenteltrap*, literally 'winding stair'.

Wenzhou /wɛn'dʒəʊ/ (also **Wen-Chou**) an industrial city in Zhejiang province, eastern China; pop. 1,650,400 (1990).

wept past and past participle of **WEEP**.

were second person singular past, plural past, and past subjunctive of **BE**.

we're ▶ **contraction of** we are.

weren't ▶ **contraction of** were not.

werewolf /'wɛːwʊlf, 'wɪə-, 'wəː-/ ▶ **noun** (pl. **werewolves**) (in myth or fiction) a person who changes for periods of time into a wolf, typically when there is a full moon.
– ORIGIN late Old English *werewulf*; the first element has usually been identified with Old English *wer* 'man'. In modern use the word has been revived through folklore studies.

werf /vɛrf/ ▶ **noun** (pl. **werfs** or **werven**) S. African a farm homestead and farmyard.
■ (in traditional African society) a group of dwellings under the control of one headman. ■ the temporary settlement of a nomadic group.
– ORIGIN from archaic and dialect Dutch, literally 'raised ground on which a house is built'.

Werner[1] /'vɛːnə, German 'vɛrnə/, Abraham Gottlob (1749–1817), German geologist. He was the chief exponent of the theory of Neptunism, eventually shown to be incorrect, and attempted to establish a universal stratigraphic sequence.

Werner[2] /'vɛːnə, French vɛrnɛr/, Alfred (1866–1919), French-born Swiss chemist. He showed that stereochemistry was general to the whole of chemistry and was a pioneer in the study of coordination compounds. Nobel Prize for Chemistry (1913).

Werner's syndrome /'wəːnəz, 'vɛː-/ ▶ **noun** [mass noun] Medicine a rare hereditary syndrome causing rapid premature ageing, susceptibility to cancer, and other disorders.
– ORIGIN 1930s: named after Carl O. *Werner* (1879–1936), German physician.

Wernicke's area /'wəːnɪkəz, 'vɛː-/ ▶ **noun** Anatomy a region of the brain concerned with the comprehension of language, located in the cortex of the dominant temporal lobe. Damage in this area causes **Wernicke's aphasia**, characterized by superficially fluent, grammatical speech but an inability to use or understand more than the most basic nouns and verbs.
– ORIGIN late 19th cent.: named after Karl *Wernicke* (1848–1905), German neuropsychiatrist.

Wernicke's encephalopathy (also **Wernicke's syndrome**) ▶ **noun** [mass noun] Medicine a neurological disorder caused by thiamine deficiency, typically from chronic alcoholism or persistent vomiting, and marked by mental confusion, abnormal eye movements, and unsteady gait.
– ORIGIN late 19th cent.: named after K. *Wernicke* (see **WERNICKE'S AREA**).

wert /wəːt/ archaic second person singular past of **BE**.

Wesak /'vɛsak/ ▶ **noun** variant spelling of **VESAK**.

Weser /'veɪzə, German 'veːzɐ/ a river of NW Germany, which is formed at the junction of the Werra and Fulda Rivers in Lower Saxony and flows 292 km (182 miles) northwards to the North Sea near Bremerhaven.

Wesker /'wɛskə/, Arnold (b.1932), English dramatist. His writing is associated with the British kitchen-sink drama of the 1950s. Notable plays: *Roots* (1959) and *Chips with Everything* (1962).

Wesley /'wɛzli/, John (1703–91), English preacher and co-founder of Methodism. Wesley was a committed Christian evangelist who won many working-class converts, often through open-air preaching. The opposition they encountered from the Church establishment led to the Methodists forming a separate denomination in 1791. His brother **Charles** (1707–88) was also a founding Methodist, and both wrote many hymns.

Wesleyan ▶ adjective of, relating to, or denoting the teachings of John Wesley or the main branch of the Methodist Church which he founded.
▶ noun a follower of Wesley or adherent of the main Methodist tradition.
– DERIVATIVES **Wesleyanism** noun.

Wessex the kingdom of the West Saxons, established in Hampshire in the early 6th century and gradually extended by conquest to include much of southern England. The name was revived in the 19th century by Thomas Hardy to designate the south-western counties of England (especially Dorset) in which his novels are set.

West[1], Benjamin (1738–1820), American painter, resident in Britain from 1763. He became historical painter to George III in 1769 and the second president of the Royal Academy in 1792. Notable works: *The Death of General Wolfe* (1771).

West[2], Mae (1892–1980), American actress and dramatist. She made her name on Broadway in her own comedies *Sex* (1926) and *Diamond Lil* (1928), memorable for their spirited approach to sexual matters, before embarking on her successful Hollywood career in the 1930s.

West[3], Dame Rebecca (1892–1983), Irish-born British writer and feminist; born *Cicily Isabel Fairfield*. She is best remembered for her study of the Nuremberg trials *The Meaning of Treason* (1949). Other notable works: *The Fountain Overflows* (novel, 1957).

west ▶ noun (usu. **the west**) **1** the direction towards the point of the horizon where the sun sets at the equinoxes, on the left-hand side of a person facing north, or the part of the horizon lying in this direction: *the evening sun glowed from the west | a patrol aimed to create a diversion to the west of the city.*
■ the compass point corresponding to this.
2 the western part of the world or of a specified country, region, or town: *it will become windy in the west.*
■ (usu. **the West**) Europe and North America seen in contrast to other civilizations. ■ (usu. **the West**) historical the non-Communist states of Europe and North America, contrasted with the former Communist states of eastern Europe. ■ (usu. **the West**) the western part of the United States, especially the states west of the Mississippi.
3 [as name] (**West**) Bridge the player sitting to the right of North and partnering East.
▶ adjective **1** [attrib.] lying towards, near, or facing the west: *the west coast.*
■ (of a wind) blowing from the west.
2 of or denoting the western part of a specified area, city, or country or its inhabitants: *West Africa.*
▶ adverb to or towards the west: *he faced west and watched the sunset | the accident happened a mile west of Bowes.*
– PHRASES **go west** Brit. informal be killed or lost; meet with disaster.
– ORIGIN Old English, of Germanic origin; related to Dutch and German *west*, from an Indo-European root shared by Greek *hesperos*, Latin *vesper* 'evening'.

West Africa the western part of the African continent, especially the countries bounded by and including Mauritania, Mali, and Niger in the north and Gabon in the south.

West Bank a region west of the River Jordan and north-west of the Dead Sea. It contains Jericho, Hebron, Nablus, Bethlehem, and other settlements. It became part of Jordan in 1948 and was occupied by Israel following the Six Day War of 1967. In 1993 an agreement was signed which granted limited autonomy to the Palestinians, who comprise 97 per cent of its inhabitants; withdrawal of Israeli troops began in 1994.

West Bengal a state in eastern India; capital, Calcutta. It was formed in 1947 from the predominantly Hindu area of former Bengal.

westbound ▶ adjective leading or travelling towards the west: *I need a westbound train.*

West Bromwich /ˈbrɒmɪtʃ/ an industrial town in the Midlands of England; pop. 154,530 (1981).

West Country the south-western counties of England.

West End the entertainment and shopping area of London to the west of the City.

westering ▶ adjective poetic/literary (especially of the sun) nearing the west.
– ORIGIN mid 17th cent.: from the literary verb *wester*, from WEST.

westerly ▶ adjective & adverb in a westward position or direction: [as adj.] *the westerly end of Sunset Boulevard* | [as adv.] *our plan was to keep westerly.*
■ (of a wind) blowing from the west: [as adj.] *a stiff westerly breeze.*
▶ noun (often **westerlies**) a wind blowing from the west.
■ (**westerlies**) the belt of prevailing westerly winds in medium latitudes in the southern hemisphere.
– ORIGIN late 15th cent.: from obsolete *wester* 'western' + -LY[1].

western ▶ adjective **1** [attrib.] situated in the west, or directed towards or facing the west: *there will be showers in some western areas.*
■ (of a wind) blowing from the west.
2 (usu. **Western**) living in or originating from the west, in particular Europe or the United States: *Western society.*
■ of, relating to, or characteristic of the west or its inhabitants: *the history of western art.* ■ historical of or originating from the non-Communist states of Europe and North America in contrast to the Eastern bloc.
▶ noun a film, television drama, or novel about cowboys in western North America, especially in the late 19th and early 20th centuries.
– DERIVATIVES **westernmost** adjective.
– ORIGIN Old English *westerne* (see WEST, -ERN).

Western Australia a state comprising the western part of Australia; pop. 1,642,700 (1990); capital, Perth. It was colonized by the British in 1826, and was federated with the other states of Australia in 1901.

Western blot ▶ noun Biochemistry an adaptation of the Southern blot procedure, used to identify specific amino-acid sequences in proteins.
– ORIGIN suggested by SOUTHERN BLOT.

Western Cape a province of south-western South Africa, formerly part of Cape Province; capital, Cape Town.

Western Church the part of the Christian Church historically originating in the Latin Church of the Western Roman Empire, including the Roman Catholic Church and the Anglican, Lutheran, and Reformed Churches, especially as distinct from the Eastern Orthodox Church.

Western Empire the western part of the Roman Empire, after its division in AD 395.

westerner ▶ noun a native or inhabitant of the west, especially of western Europe or North America.

Western European Union (abbrev.: **WEU**) an association formed in 1955 from the former Western Union, with the addition of Italy and West Germany, chiefly in order to coordinate defence and promote economic cooperation.

Western Front the zone of fighting in western Europe in the First World War, in which the German army engaged the armies to its west, i.e. France, the UK (and its dominions), and, from 1917, the US. For most of the war the front line stretched from the Vosges mountains in eastern France through Amiens to Ostend in Belgium.

Western Ghats see GHATS.

Western hemisphere the half of the earth containing the Americas.

western hemlock ▶ noun a large coniferous North American tree with flattened needles of two different sizes, grown for pulp and as an ornamental.
● *Tsuga heterophylla*, family Pinaceae.

Western Isles another name for HEBRIDES.
■ an administrative region of Scotland, consisting of the Outer Hebrides; administrative centre, Stornoway.

westernize (also **-ise**) ▶ verb [with obj.] (usu. **be westernized**) cause (a country, person, or system) to adopt or be influenced by the cultural, economic, or political systems of Europe and North America: *the agreement provided for the legal system to be westernized* | [as adj. **westernized**] *the more westernized parts of the city.*
■ [no obj.] be in the process of adopting or being influenced by the systems of the West: [as adj. **westernizing**] *a westernizing tribe.*
– DERIVATIVES **westernization** noun, **westernizer** noun.

Western Ocean former term for ATLANTIC OCEAN.

Western Roman Empire see ROMAN EMPIRE.

Western saddle ▶ noun a saddle with a deep seat, high pommel and cantle, and broad stirrups.

Western Sahara a region of NW Africa, on the Atlantic coast between Morocco and Mauritania; pop. 186,500 (est. 1989); capital, La'youn.

> The region was formerly an overseas Spanish province, called Spanish Sahara. After the Spanish withdrew in 1976 it was renamed and annexed by Morocco and Mauritania. Mauritania withdrew in 1979 and Morocco extended its control over the entire region. A liberation movement, the Polisario Front, which had launched a guerrilla war against the Spanish in 1973, continued its struggle against Morocco in an attempt to establish an independent Saharawi Arab Democratic Republic; a ceasefire came into effect in 1991.

Western Samoa see SAMOA.

western sandwich ▶ noun N. Amer. a sandwich having an omelette filling containing onion, green pepper, and ham.

western swing ▶ noun [mass noun] a style of country music influenced by jazz, popular in the 1930s.

Western Union an association of West European nations (Belgium, France, Luxembourg, the Netherlands, and the UK) formed in 1948 with similar aims to, and later superseded by, the Western European Union.

Western Wall another name for WAILING WALL.

Western Zhou see ZHOU.

Westfalen /ˈvɛstˈfaːlən/ German name for WESTPHALIA.

West Flanders a province of NW Belgium; capital, Bruges.

West Frisian Islands see FRISIAN ISLANDS.

West Germanic ▶ noun [mass noun] the western group of Germanic languages, comprising High and Low German, Dutch, Frisian, and English.
▶ adjective of or relating to West Germanic.

West Germany see GERMANY.

West Glamorgan a former county of South Wales, formed in 1974 and dissolved in 1996.

West Highland terrier /wɛst ˈhʌɪlənd ˈtɛrɪə/ ▶ noun a dog of a small, short-legged breed of terrier with a white coat and erect ears and tail, developed in the West Highlands.

Westie ▶ noun (pl. **-ies**) informal a West Highland terrier.

West Indian ▶ noun a native or national of any of the islands of the West Indies.
■ a person of West Indian descent.
▶ adjective of or relating to the West Indies or its people.

West Indian satinwood ▶ noun see SATINWOOD.

West Indies a chain of islands extending from the Florida peninsula to the coast of Venezuela, lying between the Caribbean and the Atlantic.

> They consist of three main island groups, the Greater and Lesser Antilles and the Bahamas lying further to the north. Originally inhabited by Arawak and Carib Indians, the islands were visited by Columbus in 1492 and named by him in the belief that he had reached the coast of India.

westing ▶ noun [mass noun] distance travelled or measured westward, especially at sea.
■ [count noun] a figure or line representing westward distance on a map.

Westinghouse, George (1846–1914), American engineer. His achievements covered several fields but he is best known for developing vacuum-operated safety brakes and electrically controlled signals for railways. He built up a huge company to manufacture his products.

West Irian another name for IRIAN JAYA.

Westmann Islands /ˈvɛstmən, ˈwɛst-/ a group of fifteen volcanic islands off the south coast of Iceland. Icelandic name VESTMANNAEYJAR.

Westmeath /wɛstˈmiːθ/ a county of the Republic of Ireland, in the province of Leinster; county town, Mullingar.

West Midlands a metropolitan county of central England.

Westminster an inner London borough which contains the Houses of Parliament and many government offices. Full name **CITY OF WESTMINSTER**.

■used in reference to the British Parliament: *Westminster enforced successive cuts in pay.*

Westminster, Palace of the building in Westminster in which the British Parliament meets; the Houses of Parliament. The present building, designed by Sir Charles Barry, was formally opened in 1852. The original palace, a royal residence until it was damaged by fire in 1512, was destroyed by a fire in 1834.

Westminster, Statute of a statute of 1931 recognizing the equality of status of the dominions as autonomous communities within the British Empire, and giving their legislatures independence from British control.

Westminster Abbey the collegiate church of St Peter in Westminster, originally the abbey church of a Benedictine monastery. Nearly all the kings and queens of England have been crowned in Westminster Abbey; it is also the burial place of many of England's monarchs and of some of the nation's leading figures.

Westminster Confession a Calvinist doctrinal statement which was issued by the synod appointed to reform the English and Scottish Churches in 1643, and became widely accepted among Presbyterian Churches.

Westmorland /ˈwestmələnd/ a former county of NW England. In 1974 it was united with Cumberland and northern parts of Lancashire to form the county of Cumbria.

west-north-west ▶ noun the direction or compass point midway between west and north-west.

Weston-super-Mare /ˌwestənˌsuːpəˈmɛː, -ˌsjuːpə-/ a resort in SW England, on the Bristol Channel; pop. 62,260 (1981).

Westphalia /westˈfeɪlɪə/ a former province of NW Germany. Previously a duchy of the archbishop of Cologne, it became a province of Prussia in 1815. In 1946 the major part was incorporated in the state of North Rhine–Westphalia, the northern portion becoming part of Lower Saxony. German name **WESTFALEN**.

– DERIVATIVES **Westphalian** adjective & noun.

Westphalia, Treaty of the peace accord (1648) which ended the Thirty Years War, signed simultaneously in Osnabrück and Münster.

West Point (in full **West Point Academy**) the US Military Academy, founded in 1802, located on the site of a former strategic fort on the west bank of the Hudson River in New York State.

West Saxon ▶ noun **1** a native or inhabitant of the Anglo-Saxon kingdom of Wessex.
2 [mass noun] the dialect of Old English used by the West Saxons.
▶ adjective of or relating to the West Saxons or their dialect.

West Side the western part of any of several North American cities or boroughs, especially the island borough of Manhattan, New York.

west-south-west ▶ noun the direction or compass point midway between west and south-west.

West Sussex a county of SE England; county town, Chichester. It was formed in 1974 from part of the former county of Sussex.

West Virginia a state of the eastern US; pop. 1,793,480 (1990); capital, Charleston. It separated from Virginia during the American Civil War (1861) and became the 35th state of the US in 1863.

– DERIVATIVES **West Virginian** noun & adjective.

westward ▶ adjective towards the west: *the journey covers eight time zones in a westward direction.*
▶ adverb (also **westwards**) in a westerly direction: *a track leads westwards through the glen.*
▶ noun (**the westward**) a direction or region towards the west: *he sees a light to the westward.*

– DERIVATIVES **westwardly** adverb.

West Yorkshire a metropolitan county of northern England.

wet ▶ adjective (**wetter**, **wettest**) **1** covered or

saturated with water or another liquid: *she followed, slipping on the wet rock.*

■(of the weather) rainy: *a wet, windy evening.* ■(of paint, ink, plaster, or a similar substance) not yet having dried or hardened. ■(of a baby or young child) having urinated in its nappy or underwear. ■ involving the use of water or liquid: *wet methods of photography.* ■ Nautical (of a ship) liable to take in water over her bows or sides.
2 Brit. informal showing a lack of forcefulness or strength of character; feeble: *they thought the cadets were a bit wet.*
■Conservative with liberal tendencies, especially as regarded by right-wing Conservatives.
3 informal (of a country or region or of its legislation) allowing the free sale of alcoholic drink.
■(of a person) addicted to alcohol.
▶ verb (**wetting**; past and past participle **wet** or **wetted**) [with obj.] cover or touch with liquid; moisten: *he wetted a finger and flicked through the pages* | [as noun **wetting**] *it was a velvet cap, and a wetting would ruin it.*
■(especially of a baby or young child) urinate in or on: *while dreaming the child wet the bed.* ■(**wet oneself**) urinate involuntarily. ■ dialect infuse (tea) by pouring on boiling water.
▶ noun **1** [mass noun] liquid that makes something damp: *I could feel the wet of his tears.*
■(**the wet**) rainy weather: *the race was held in the wet.* ■ [count noun] Brit. informal a drink: *I took a wet from my bottle.*
2 Brit. informal a person lacking forcefulness or strength of character.
■a Conservative with liberal tendencies.

– PHRASES **all wet** N. Amer. completely wrong. **wet the baby's head** Brit. informal celebrate a baby's birth with a drink, typically an alcoholic one. **wet behind the ears** informal lacking experience; immature. **wet through** (or **to the skin**) with one's clothes soaked; completely drenched. **wet one's whistle** informal have a drink.

– DERIVATIVES **wetly** adverb, **wetness** noun, **wettable** adjective, **wettish** adjective.

– ORIGIN Old English *wǣt* (adjective and noun), *wǣtan* (verb); related to **WATER**.

weta /ˈwetə/ ▶ noun a large brown wingless insect related to the grasshoppers, with long spiny legs and wood-boring larvae, found only in New Zealand.
● Family Stenopelmatidae: several genera, including *Deinacrida* (the **giant wetas**).

– ORIGIN mid 19th cent.: from Maori.

wetback ▶ noun US informal, derogatory a Mexican living in the US, especially one who is an illegal immigrant.

– ORIGIN 1920s: so named from the practice of swimming the Rio Grande to reach the US.

wet bar ▶ noun N. Amer. a bar or counter in the home for serving alcoholic drinks.

wet blanket ▶ noun informal a person who spoils other people's fun by failing to join in with or by disapproving of their activities.

wet bulb ▶ noun one of the two thermometers of a psychrometer, the bulb of which is enclosed in wetted material so that water is constantly evaporating from it and cooling the bulb.

wet cell ▶ noun a primary electric cell in which the electrolyte is a liquid.

wet dock ▶ noun a dock in which water is maintained at a level at which a ship is able to float.

wet dream ▶ noun an erotic dream that causes involuntary ejaculation of semen.

wet fish ▶ noun [mass noun] fresh fish, as opposed to fish which has been frozen, cooked, or dried.

wet fly ▶ noun an artificial fishing fly designed to sink below the surface of the water.

wether /ˈwɛðə/ ▶ noun a castrated ram.

– ORIGIN Old English, of Germanic origin; related to Dutch *weer* and German *Widder*.

wetland ▶ noun [mass noun] (also **wetlands**) land consisting of marshes or swamps; saturated land.

wet lease ▶ noun an arrangement covering the hire of an aircraft including the provision of a flight crew and sometimes fuel.
▶ verb (**wet-lease**) [with obj.] hire (an aircraft) using such an arrangement.

wet look ▶ noun [in sing.] an artificially wet or shiny appearance, in particular one possessed by a

clothing fabric or achieved by applying a type of gel to the hair.
▶ adjective (**wet-look**) having or giving a shiny or wet appearance: *her hair was spiky with wet-look gel.*

wet nurse ▶ noun chiefly historical a woman employed to suckle another woman's child.
▶ verb (**wet-nurse**) [with obj.] act as a wet nurse to.
■informal look after (someone) as though they were a helpless infant.

wet pack ▶ noun **1** a session of hydrotherapy in which the body is wrapped in wet cloth.
2 a washbag.

wet plate ▶ noun Photography a sensitized collodion plate exposed in the camera while the collodion is moist.

wet rot ▶ noun [mass noun] **1** a brown fungal rot affecting timber with a high moisture content.
2 (also **wet rot fungus**) the fungus that causes this.
● *Coniophora puteana*, family Coniophoraceae, class Hymenomycetes, and other species.

wetsuit ▶ noun a close-fitting rubber garment typically covering the entire body, worn for warmth in water sports or diving.

wetting agent ▶ noun a chemical that can be added to a liquid to reduce its surface tension and make it more effective in spreading over and penetrating surfaces.

wetware ▶ noun [mass noun] human brain cells or thought processes regarded as analogous to, or in contrast with, computer systems.
■(chiefly in science fiction) computer technology in which the brain is linked to artificial systems, or used as a model for artificial systems based on biochemical processes.

WEU ▶ abbreviation for Western European Union.

we've ▶ contraction of we have.

Wexford /ˈweksfəd/ a county of the Republic of Ireland, in the south-east in the province of Leinster.
■its county town, a port on the Irish Sea; pop. 9,540 (1991).

wey /weɪ/ ▶ noun a former unit of weight or volume varying with different kinds of goods, e.g. 3 cwt. of cheese.

– ORIGIN Old English *wǣg(e)*, *wēg(e)* 'balance, weight', of Germanic origin; related to **WEIGH**[1].

Weyden /ˈveɪd(ə)n/, Rogier van der (*c*.1400–64), Flemish painter; French name *Rogier de la Pasture*. He was particularly influential in the development of Dutch portrait painting. Notable works: *The Last Judgement* and *The Deposition in the Tomb* (both *c*.1450).

Weymouth[1] /ˈweɪməθ/ a resort and port on the coast of Dorset, southern England; pop. 38,400 (1981).

Weymouth[2] /ˈweɪməθ/ ▶ noun (also **Weymouth bit**) a simple curb bit, used especially in a double bridle.
■(also **Weymouth bridle**) a double bridle in which the curb bit is a Weymouth bit.

– ORIGIN late 18th cent.: of unknown origin.

w.f. Printing ▶ abbreviation for wrong fount (used as a proof-reading mark).

WFTU ▶ abbreviation for World Federation of Trade Unions.

Wg Cdr ▶ abbreviation for Wing Commander.

whack informal ▶ verb [with obj.] strike forcefully with a sharp blow: *his attacker whacked him on the head* | [no obj.] *she found a stick to whack at the branches.*
■defeat in a contest: [with obj. and complement] *the team were whacked six-nil.* ■ [with obj. and adverbial] put or push (something) roughly or carelessly in a specified place or direction: *he whacks a tape into the cassette recorder.* ■ US murder: *he was whacked while sitting in his car.*
▶ noun **1** a sharp or resounding blow.
2 a try or attempt: *we decided to take a whack at spotting the decade's trends.*
3 Brit. a specified share of or contribution to something: *motorists pay a fair whack for the use of the roads through taxes.*

– PHRASES **out of whack** chiefly N. Amer. & Austral. out of order; not working: *all their calculations were out of whack.* **top** (or **full**) **whack** chiefly Brit. the maximum price or rate: *the car has a top whack of 107 mph.*

– DERIVATIVES **whacker** noun.

– ORIGIN early 18th cent.: imitative, or perhaps an alteration of **THWACK**.

▶ **whack off** vulgar slang masturbate.

whacked (also **whacked out**) ▶ **adjective** informal, chiefly Brit. completely exhausted: *I'm not staying long—I'm whacked.*
■chiefly US under the influence of drugs: *a sixteen-year-old whacked out on acid.*

whacking Brit. informal ▶ **adjective** [attrib.] very large: *she poured us two whacking drinks* | [as submodifier] *he dug a whacking great hole.*

whacko[1] ▶ **exclamation** Brit. informal, dated used to express delight and enthusiasm: *Home Friday. Whacko!*
– ORIGIN 1940s: from the noun **WHACK** + **-O**.

whacko[2] ▶ **adjective** & **noun** (pl. **-os**) variant spelling of **WACKO**.

whacky ▶ **adjective** variant spelling of **WACKY**.

whale[1] ▶ **noun** (pl. same or **whales**) a very large marine mammal with a streamlined hairless body, a horizontal tail fin, and a blowhole on top of the head for breathing.
● Order Cetacea. See **BALEEN WHALE** and **TOOTHED WHALE**.
– PHRASES **a whale of a ——** informal an exceedingly good example of a particular thing: *you've been doing a whale of a job.* **have a whale of a time** enjoy oneself very much.
– ORIGIN Old English *hwæl*, of Germanic origin.

whale[2] ▶ **verb** [with obj.] informal, chiefly US beat; hit: *Dad came upstairs and whaled me* | [no obj.] *they whaled at the water with their paddles.*
– ORIGIN late 18th cent.: variant of **WALE**.

whaleback ▶ **noun** a thing that is shaped like a whale's back, especially an arched structure over the bow or stern part of the deck of a steamer, or a large elongated hill: [as modifier] *a whaleback ridge.*

whalebird ▶ **noun** a prion (so called because often found in the vicinity of whales or whaling vessels).

whaleboat ▶ **noun** a long rowing boat with a bow at either end for easy manoeuvrability, formerly used in whaling.

whalebone ▶ **noun** [mass noun] an elastic horny substance which grows in a series of thin parallel plates in the upper jaw of some whales and is used by them to strain plankton from the seawater. Also called **BALEEN**.
■strips of this substance, much used formerly as stays in corsets and dresses: [as modifier] *a whalebone bodice.*
■ bone or ivory from a whale or walrus.

whalebone whale ▶ **noun** another term for **BALEEN WHALE**.

whale-headed stork ▶ **noun** an African stork with grey plumage and a very large bill shaped like a clog. Also called **SHOEBILL**.
● *Balaeniceps rex*, the only member of the family Balaenicipitidae.

whale oil ▶ **noun** [mass noun] oil obtained from the blubber of a whale, formerly used in oil lamps or for making soap.

whaler ▶ **noun 1** a whaling ship.
■a seaman engaged in whaling.
2 any of a number of large slender-bodied sharks:
● a shark that typically occurs inshore and is sometimes found in rivers (genus *Carcharhinus*, family Carcharhinidae), including the Australian *C. brachyurus*. ● another term for **BLUE SHARK**.
3 Austral. informal a tramp, especially one who follows the course of a river.

whale shark ▶ **noun** a very large tropical shark which typically swims close to the surface, where it feeds chiefly on plankton. It is the largest known fish.
● *Rhincodon typus*, the sole member of the family Rhincodontidae.

whaling ▶ **noun** [mass noun] the practice or industry of hunting and killing whales for their oil, meat, or whalebone.

wham informal ▶ **exclamation** used to express the sound of a forcible impact: *the bombs landed—wham!—right on target.*
■used to express the idea of a sudden, dramatic, and decisive occurrence: *he asked me out for a drink, and—wham!—that was it.*
▶ **verb** (**whammed**, **whamming**) [no obj., with adverbial] strike something forcefully: *trucks whammed into each other.*
■make a loud sound as of a forceful impact: *my heart was whamming away like a drum.*
– ORIGIN 1920s: imitative.

wham-bam informal ▶ **adjective** characterized by quick or violent action: *Hollywood wanted a wham-bam end to the plot.*
▶ **exclamation** used to express the idea of a sudden or dramatic occurrence or change of events: *Wham-bam!—we were sitting in a wreck at the foot of the cliff.*
– PHRASES **wham-bam-thank-you-ma'am** used in reference to sexual activity conducted roughly and quickly, without tenderness.
– ORIGIN 1950s (as *wham-bang*): from **WHAM** + **BAM** or the verb **BANG**[1].

whammo ▶ **exclamation** another word for **WHAM**.

whammy ▶ **noun** (pl. **-ies**) informal an event with a powerful and unpleasant effect; a blow: *the third whammy was the degradation of the financial system.* See also **DOUBLE WHAMMY**.
■chiefly US an evil or unlucky influence: *I've come to put the whammy on them.*
– ORIGIN 1940s: from the noun **WHAM** + **-Y**[1]; associated from the 1950s with the cartoon strip *Li'l Abner*, in which the hillbilly Evil-Eye Fleegle could 'shoot a whammy' (to put a curse on somebody) by pointing a finger with one eye open, and a 'double whammy' with both eyes open.

whanau /ˈwɑːnaʊ/ ▶ **noun** (pl. same) NZ an extended family or community of related families who live together in the same area.
– ORIGIN Maori.

whang informal ▶ **verb** [no obj., with adverbial] make or produce a resonant noise: *the cheerleader whanged on a tambourine.*
■[no obj.] drive at speed: *we whanged round the bend.* ■ [with obj.] strike or throw heavily and loudly: *he whanged down the receiver.*
▶ **noun** a noisy blow: *he gave a whang with his hammer.*
– ORIGIN late 17th cent. (in the sense 'strike as if with a thong'): variant of **THONG**; senses describing noise are imitative.

Whangarei /ˌwaŋgəˈreɪ/ a port on the NE coast of North Island, New Zealand; pop. 44,180 (1991).

whap ▶ **verb** (**whapped**, **whapping**) & **noun** chiefly US variant spelling of **WHOP**.

whare /ˈwɒri/ ▶ **noun** a Maori hut or house.
– ORIGIN Maori.

wharf /wɔːf/ ▶ **noun** (pl. **wharves** or **wharfs**) a level quayside area to which a ship may be moored to load and unload.
– ORIGIN late Old English *hwearf*, of Germanic origin.

wharfage ▶ **noun** [mass noun] accommodation provided at a wharf for the loading, unloading, or storage of goods.
■payment made for such accommodation.

wharfie ▶ **noun** Austral./NZ informal a person who works at a wharf; a waterside worker or labourer.

wharfinger /ˈwɔːfɪn(d)ʒə/ ▶ **noun** an owner or keeper of a wharf.
– ORIGIN Middle English: from **WHARFAGE** + **-ER**[1].

Wharton /ˈwɔːt(ə)n/, Edith (Newbold) (1862–1937), American novelist and short-story writer, resident in France from 1907. Her novels are concerned with the conflict between social and individual fulfilment. They include *The Age of Innocence* (1920), which won a Pulitzer Prize.

wharves plural form of **WHARF**.

what ▶ **pronoun 1** [interrogative pronoun] asking for information specifying something: *what is your name?* | *I'm not sure what you mean.*
■asking for repetition of something not heard or confirmation of something not understood: *what? I can't hear you* | *you did what?*
2 [relative pronoun] the thing or things that (used in specifying something): *what we need is a commitment.*
■(referring to the whole of an amount) whatever: *I want to do what I can to make a difference.*
3 (in exclamations) emphasizing something surprising or remarkable: *what some people do for a crust!*
▶ **determiner 1** [interrogative determiner] asking for information specifying something: *what time is it?* | *do you know what excuse he gave me?*
2 [relative determiner] (referring to the whole of an amount) whatever: *he had been robbed of what little money he had.*
3 (in exclamations) how great or remarkable: [as determiner] *what luck!* | [as predeterminer] *what a fool she was.*
▶ **interrogative adverb 1** to what extent?: *what does it matter?*
2 used to indicate an estimate or approximation: *see you, what, about four?*
3 informal, dated used for emphasis or to invite agreement: *pretty poor show, what?*
– PHRASES **and** (or **or**) **what have you** informal and/or anything else similar: *for a binder try soup, gravy, cream, or what have you.* **and what not** informal and other similar things. **give someone what for** see **GIVE**. **what about ——? 1** used when asking for information or an opinion on something: *what about the practical angle?* **2** used to make a suggestion: *what about a walk?* **what-d'you-call-it** (or **what's-its name**) informal used as a substitute for a name not recalled. **what for?** informal for what reason? **what if ——? 1** what would result if ——?: *what if nobody shows up?* **2** what does it matter if ——?: *what if our house is a mess? I'm clean.* **what is more** and as an additional point; moreover. **what next** see **NEXT**. **what of ——?** what is the news concerning ——? **what of it?** why should that be considered significant? **what's-his** (or **-its**) **-name** another term for *what-d'you-call-it*. **what say ——?** used to make a suggestion: *what say we call a tea break?* **what's what** informal what is useful or important: *I'll teach her what's what.* **what with** because of (used typically to introduce several causes of something): *what with the drought and the neglect, the garden is in a sad condition.*
– ORIGIN Old English *hwæt*, of Germanic origin; related to Dutch *wat* and German *was*, from an Indo-European root shared by Latin *quod*.

whatchamacallit /ˈwɒtʃəməˌkɔːlɪt/ ▶ **noun** another word for **WHATSIT**.

whate'er /wɒtˈɛː/ poetic/literary ▶ **contraction** of whatever.

whatever ▶ **relative pronoun** & **determiner** used to emphasize a lack of restriction in referring to any thing or amount, no matter what: [as pronoun] *do whatever you like* | [as determiner] *take whatever action is needed.*
■regardless of what: [as pronoun] *you have our support, whatever you decide* | [as determiner] *whatever decision he made I would support it.*
▶ **interrogative pronoun** used for emphasis instead of 'what' in questions, typically expressing surprise or confusion: *whatever is the matter?*
▶ **adverb 1** [with negative] at all; of any kind (used for emphasis): *they received no help whatever.*
2 informal no matter what happens: *we told him we'd back him whatever.*
– PHRASES **or whatever** informal or anything similar: *use chopped herbs, nuts, garlic, or whatever.* **whatever next** see **NEXT**.

> **USAGE** In the emphatic use (***whatever** was she thinking of?*) **whatever** is also written as two words. See **usage** at **HOWEVER**.

whatnot ▶ **noun 1** informal used to refer to an item or items that are not identified but are felt to have something in common with items already named: *little flashing digital displays, electric zooms and whatnots* | [mass noun] *pictures and books and manuscripts and whatnot.*
2 a stand with shelves for small objects.

whatsit ▶ **noun** informal a person or thing whose name one cannot recall, does not know, or does not wish to specify: *'Let's say two o'clock on the whatsit of May?'* | *he's a right old interfering whatsit.*

whatso ▶ **pronoun** & **determiner** archaic whatever: [as pronoun] *whatso goes into their brain comes out as prose.*
– ORIGIN Middle English: reduced form of Old English *swā hwæt swā* 'so what so'.

whatsoe'er /ˌwɒtsəʊˈɛː/ poetic/literary ▶ **contraction** of whatsoever.

whatsoever ▶ **adverb** [with negative] at all (used for emphasis): *I have no doubt whatsoever.*
▶ **determiner** & **pronoun** archaic whatever.

what-you-see-is-what-you-get ▶ **adjective** see **WYSIWYG**.

whaup /(h)wɔːp/ ▶ **noun** chiefly Scottish another term for **CURLEW**.
– ORIGIN mid 16th cent.: imitative of its cry.

wheal ▶ **noun** variant spelling of **WEAL**[1].

wheat ▶ **noun** [mass noun] a cereal which is the most important kind grown in temperate countries, the grain of which is ground to make flour for bread, pasta, pastry, etc.
● Genus *Triticum*, family Gramineae: several species, including **bread wheat** (*T. aestivum*) and **durum wheat**, and many distinctive cultivars.
■the grain of this plant.
– PHRASES **separate the wheat from the chaff** see **CHAFF**[1].
– ORIGIN Old English *hwǣte* of Germanic origin;

W

related to Dutch *weit*, German *Weizen*, also to **WHITE**.

wheat belt ▶ **noun** (**the wheat belt**) a region where wheat is the chief agricultural product.

wheat bunt ▶ **noun** see **BUNT**[2].

wheatear ▶ **noun** a mainly Eurasian and African songbird related to the chats, with black and buff or black and white plumage and a white rump.
● Genus *Oenanthe*, family Turdidae: several species, in particular the grey-backed (**northern**) **wheatear** (*O. oenanthe*) of Eurasia and NE Canada.
– ORIGIN late 16th cent.: apparently from **WHITE** (assimilated to **WHEAT**) + **ARSE** (assimilated to **EAR**[2]).

wheaten ▶ **adjective** (especially of bread) made of wheat.
■ of a colour resembling that of wheat; a pale yellow-beige.

wheaten terrier ▶ **noun** a terrier of a breed with a pale golden soft wavy coat.

wheatgerm ▶ **noun** [mass noun] a nutritious foodstuff of a dry floury consistency consisting of the extracted embryos of grains of wheat.

wheatgrass ▶ **noun** another term for **COUCH**[2].

wheatmeal ▶ **noun** [mass noun] flour made from wheat from which some of the bran and germ has been removed.

Wheatstone /ˈwiːtstən/, Sir Charles (1802–75), English physicist and inventor. He is best known for his electrical inventions which included an electric clock, the Wheatstone bridge, the rheostat, and with Sir W. F. Cooke, the electric telegraph.

Wheatstone bridge ▶ **noun** a simple circuit for measuring an unknown resistance by connecting it so as to form a quadrilateral with three known resistances and applying a voltage between a pair of opposite corners.

whee ▶ **exclamation** used to express delight, excitement, or exhilaration: *as the car began to bump down the track he felt a lightening of his spirits—whee!*
– ORIGIN natural exclamation: first recorded in English in the 1920s.

wheech /hwiːx, hwiːk/ ▶ **verb** [with obj.] Scottish snatch or remove (something) quickly: *I wheeched the duvet off Gavin's bed.*
■ [no obj., with adverbial of direction] rush; dash.
– ORIGIN early 19th cent.: symbolic.

wheedle ▶ **verb** [no obj.] employ endearments or flattery to persuade someone to do something or give one something: *you can contrive to wheedle your way on to a playing field* | [with direct speech] *'Please, for my sake,' he wheedled.*
■ [with obj.] (**wheedle someone into doing something**) coax or persuade someone to do something. ■ [with obj.] (**wheedle something out of**) coax or persuade (someone) to say or give something.
– DERIVATIVES **wheedler** noun, **wheedlingly** adverb.
– ORIGIN mid 17th cent.: perhaps from German *wedeln* 'cringe, fawn', from *Wedel* 'tail, fan'.

wheel ▶ **noun** **1** a circular object that revolves on an axle and is fixed below a vehicle or other object to enable it to move over the ground.
■ a circular object that revolves on an axle and forms part of a machine. ■ (**the wheel**) used in reference to the cycle of a specified condition or set of events: *the final release from the wheel of life.* ■ (**the wheel**) historical a large wheel used as an instrument of punishment or torture, especially by binding someone to it and breaking their limbs: *a man sentenced to be broken on the wheel.*
2 a machine or structure having a wheel as its essential part.
■ (**the wheel**) a steering wheel (used in reference to driving or steering a vehicle or vessel): *his crew know when he wants to take the wheel.* ■ a device with a revolving disc or drum used in various games of chance. ■ a system, or a part of a system, regarded as a relentlessly moving machine: *the wheels of justice.*
3 (**wheels**) informal a car: *she's got wheels now.*
4 a thing resembling a wheel in form or function, in particular a cheese made in the form of a shallow disc.
5 an instance of wheeling; a turn or rotation.
6 US informal short for **BIG WHEEL** (in sense 2).
7 a set of short lines, typically five in number and rhyming, concluding the stanza of a poem.
▶ **verb** **1** [with obj.] push or pull (a vehicle with wheels): *the tea trolley was wheeled out.*
■ [with obj. and adverbial of direction] carry (someone or something) in or on a vehicle with wheels: *a young woman is wheeled into the operating theatre.* ■ (**wheel something in/on/out**) informal produce something that is unimpressive because it has been frequently seen or heard before: *the old journalistic arguments have been wheeled out.*
2 [no obj.] (of a bird or aircraft) fly in a wide circle or curve: *the birds wheeled and dived.*
■ turn round quickly so as to face another way: *Robert wheeled round to see the face of Mr Mafouz.* ■ turn or seem to turn on an axis or pivot: *the stars wheeled through the sky.*
– PHRASES **on someone's wheel** close behind someone when they are driving or cycling. **on wheels 1** by, or travelling by, car or bicycle: *a journey on wheels.* ■ (of a service) brought to one's home or district; mobile. ■ Brit. informal smoothly: *the business ran on wheels.* **2** Brit. informal used to emphasize one's distaste or dislike of the person or thing mentioned: *she was a bitch on wheels.* **silly as a wheel** Austral. very silly. **wheel and deal** engage in commercial or political scheming, especially unscrupulously: [as noun **wheeling and dealing**] *the wheeling and dealing of the Wall Street boom years.* **the wheel of Fortune** the wheel which the deity Fortune is fabled to turn as a symbol of random luck or change. **wheels within wheels** used to indicate that a situation is complicated and affected by secret or indirect influences.
– DERIVATIVES **wheeled** adjective [in combination] *a four-wheeled cart*, **wheelless** adjective.
– ORIGIN Old English *hwēol* (noun), of Germanic origin, from an Indo-European root shared by Sanskrit *cakra* 'wheel, circle' and Greek *kuklos* 'circle'.

wheel and axle ▶ **noun** a simple lifting machine consisting of a rope which unwinds from a wheel on to a cylindrical drum or shaft joined to the wheel to provide mechanical advantage.

wheel arch ▶ **noun** an arch-shaped cavity in the body of a vehicle, which houses a wheel.

wheelback ▶ **adjective** (of a chair) with a back incorporating the design of a wheel.

wheelbarrow ▶ **noun** a small cart with a single wheel at the front and two supporting legs and two handles at the rear, used typically for carrying loads in building work or gardening.

wheelbase ▶ **noun** the distance between the front and rear axles of a vehicle: [in combination] *a short-wheelbase model.*

wheel brace ▶ **noun** **1** a tool for screwing and unscrewing nuts on the wheel of a vehicle.
2 a hand drill worked by turning a wheel.

wheelchair ▶ **noun** a chair built on wheels for an invalid or disabled person, either pushed by another person or propelled by the occupant.

wheel clamp ▶ **noun** a device for immobilizing an illegally parked car.
▶ **verb** (**wheel-clamp**) [with obj.] clamp (an illegally parked car) with such a device.

wheel dog ▶ **noun** the dog harnessed nearest to the sleigh in a dog team.

Wheeler, John Archibald (b.1911), American theoretical physicist. Wheeler worked with Niels Bohr on nuclear fission, and collaborated with Richard Feynman on problems concerning the retarded effects of action at a distance.

wheeler ▶ **noun** **1** [in combination] a vehicle having a specified number of wheels: *a huge sixteen-wheeler truck.*
2 a wheelwright.
3 a horse harnessed next to the wheels of a cart and behind a leading horse.

wheeler-dealer (also **wheeler and dealer**) ▶ **noun** a person who engages in commercial or political scheming.
– DERIVATIVES **wheeler-dealing** noun.

wheel horse ▶ **noun** a horse harnessed nearest the wheels of a vehicle.
■ figurative, chiefly US a responsible and hard-working person, especially an experienced and conscientious member of a political party.

wheelhouse ▶ **noun** **1** a part of a boat or ship serving as a shelter for the person at the wheel.
2 Archaeology a stone-built circular house with inner partition walls radiating like the spokes of a wheel, found in western and northern Scotland and dating chiefly from about 100 BC to AD 100.

wheelie ▶ **noun** informal a trick or manoeuvre whereby a bicycle or motorcycle is ridden for a short distance with the front wheel raised off the ground.

wheelie bin (also **wheely bin**) ▶ **noun** Brit. informal a large refuse bin set on wheels.

wheel lock ▶ **noun** historical a kind of gunlock having a steel wheel that rubbed against a flint.
■ a gun having such a gunlock.

wheelman ▶ **noun** (pl. **-men**) chiefly N. Amer. a person who drives a car or takes the wheel of a boat.
■ a cyclist.

wheel set ▶ **noun** a pair of wheels attached to an axle.

wheelsman ▶ **noun** (pl. **-men**) N. Amer. a person who steers a ship or boat.

wheelspin ▶ **noun** [mass noun] rotation of a vehicle's wheels without traction.

wheel well ▶ **noun** a recess in a vehicle in which a wheel is located.

wheelwright ▶ **noun** chiefly historical a person who makes or repairs wooden wheels.

wheely bin ▶ **noun** variant spelling of **WHEELIE BIN**.

wheen /wiːn/ ▶ **noun** [in sing.] chiefly Scottish a considerable amount or number: *a wheen of pennies.*
– ORIGIN late Middle English: from Old English *hwēne* 'in some degree'.

wheesht /wiːʃt/ ▶ **exclamation** variant of **WHISHT**.

wheeze ▶ **verb** [no obj.] (of a person) breathe with a whistling or rattling sound in the chest, as a result of obstruction in the air passages: *the illness often leaves her wheezing.*
■ [with obj.] utter with such a sound: *he could barely wheeze out his pleas for a handout* | [with direct speech] *'Don't worry son,' he wheezed.* ■ [no obj., with adverbial of direction] walk or move slowly with such a sound: *she wheezed up the hill towards them.* ■ (of a device) make an irregular rattling or spluttering sound: *the engine coughed, wheezed, and shrieked into life.*
▶ **noun** [usu. in sing.] **1** a sound of or as of a person wheezing: *I talk with a wheeze.*
2 Brit. informal a clever or amusing scheme, idea, or trick: *a new wheeze to help farmers.*
– DERIVATIVES **wheezer** noun, **wheezingly** adverb.
– ORIGIN late Middle English: probably from Old Norse *hvæsa* 'to hiss'.

wheezy ▶ **adjective** making the sound of a person wheezing: *a wheezy laugh.*
– DERIVATIVES **wheezily** adverb, **wheeziness** noun.

whelk[1] ▶ **noun** a predatory marine mollusc with a heavy pointed spiral shell, some kinds of which are edible.
● Family Buccinidae, class Gastropoda: *Buccinum* and other genera.
– ORIGIN Old English *wioloc*, *weoloc*, of unknown origin; the spelling with *wh-* was perhaps influenced by **WHELK**[2].

whelk[2] ▶ **noun** archaic a pimple.
– ORIGIN Old English *hwylca*, related to *hwelian* 'suppurate'.

whelm /wɛlm/ archaic or poetic/literary ▶ **verb** [with obj.] engulf, submerge, or bury (someone or something): *a swimmer whelmed in a raging storm.*
■ [no obj., with adverbial of direction] flow or heap up abundantly: *the brook whelmed up from its source.*
▶ **noun** an act or instance of flowing or heaping up abundantly; a surge: *the whelm of the tide.*
– ORIGIN Middle English: representing an Old English form parallel to *hwelfan* 'overturn (a vessel)'.

whelp ▶ **noun** chiefly archaic a puppy.
■ a cub. ■ a boy or young man (often as a disparaging form of address). ■ (**whelps**) a set of projections on the barrel of a capstan or windlass.
▶ **verb** [with obj.] (of a female dog) give birth to (a puppy): *Copper whelped seven puppies* | [no obj.] *a bitch due to whelp.*
– PHRASES **in whelp** (of a female dog) pregnant.
– ORIGIN Old English *hwelp* (noun), of Germanic origin; related to Dutch *welp* and German *Welf*.

when ▶ **interrogative adverb** at what time: *when did you last see him?* | [with prep.] *since when have you been interested?*
■ how soon: *when can I see you?* ■ in what circumstances: *when would such a rule be justifiable?*
▶ **relative adverb** at or on which (referring to a time or circumstance): *Saturday is the day when I get my hair done.*
▶ **conjunction** **1** at or during the time that: *I loved maths when I was at school.*

W

▪after: *call me when you've finished.* ▪ at any time that; whenever: *can you spare five minutes when it's convenient?*
2 after which; and just then (implying suddenness): *he had just drifted off to sleep when the phone rang.*
3 in view of the fact that; considering that: *why bother to paint it when you can photograph it with the same effect?*
4 although; whereas: *I'm saying it now when I should have told you long ago.*
– ORIGIN Old English *hwanne, hwenne*; of Germanic origin; related to German *wenn* 'if', *wann* 'when'.

whence (also **from whence**) formal or archaic ▶ **interrogative adverb** from what place or source: *whence does Parliament derive this power?*
▶ **relative adverb** from which; from where: *the Ural mountains, whence the ore is procured.*
▪to the place from which: *he will be sent back whence he came.* ▪ as a consequence of which: *whence it followed that the strategies were obsolete.*
– ORIGIN Middle English *whennes*, from earlier *whenne* (from Old English *hwanon*, of Germanic origin) + **-s**[3] (later respelled *-ce* to denote the unvoiced sound).

USAGE Strictly speaking, **whence** means 'from what place', as in ***whence** did you come?* Thus, the preposition **from** in ***from whence** did you come?* is redundant and its use is considered incorrect by some. The use with **from** is very common, though (occurring in more than 20 per cent of citations for **whence** in the British National Corpus), and has been used by reputable writers since the 14th century. It is now broadly accepted in standard English.

whencesoever ▶ **relative adverb** formal or archaic from whatever place or source.

whene'er /wɛnˈɛː/ poetic/literary ▶ **contraction** of whenever.

whenever ▶ **conjunction** at whatever time; on whatever occasion (emphasizing a lack of restriction): *you can ask for help whenever you need it.*
▪every time that: *the springs in the armchair creak whenever I change position.*
▶ **interrogative adverb** used for emphasis instead of 'when' in questions, typically expressing surprise or confusion: *whenever shall we get there?*
– PHRASES **or whenever** informal or at any time: *if you lay eyes on him, either tonight or tomorrow or whenever, call me straight away.*

when-issued ▶ **adjective** Finance, chiefly US of or relating to trading in securities which have not yet been issued.

whensoe'er /ˌwɛnsəʊˈɛː/ poetic/literary ▶ **contraction** of whensoever.

whensoever ▶ **conjunction** & **adverb** formal word for **WHENEVER**.

whenua /ˈfɛnuːə/ ▶ **noun** [mass noun] NZ land.
– ORIGIN Maori.

where ▶ **interrogative adverb** in or to what place or position: *where do you live?* | [with prep.] *I wonder where they will take us to.*
▪in what direction or respect: *where does the argument lead?* ▪ in or from what source: *where did you read that?* ▪ in or to what situation or condition: *just where is all this leading us?*
▶ **relative adverb 1** at, in, or to which (used after reference to a place or situation): *I first saw him in Paris, where I lived in the early sixties.*
2 the place or situation in which: *this is where I live.*
▪in or to a place or situation in which: *sit where I can see you* | *where people were concerned, his threshold of boredom was low.* ▪ in or to any place in which; wherever: *he was free to go where he liked.*
– ORIGIN Old English *hwǣr*, of Germanic origin; related to Dutch *waar* and German *wo*.

whereabouts ▶ **interrogative adverb** where or approximately where: *whereabouts do you come from?*
▶ **noun** [treated as sing. or pl.] the place where someone or something is: *his whereabouts remain secret.*

whereafter ▶ **relative adverb** formal after which: *dinner was taken at a long wooden table, whereafter we sipped liqueurs in front of a roaring fire.*

whereas ▶ **conjunction** in contrast or comparison with the fact that: *you treat the matter lightly, whereas I myself was never more serious.*
▪(especially in legal preambles) taking into consideration the fact that.

whereat ▶ **relative adverb** & **conjunction** archaic or formal at which: *they demanded an equal share in the high command, whereat negotiations broke down.*

whereby ▶ **relative adverb** by which: *a system whereby people could vote by telephone.*

where'er /wɛːrˈɛː/ poetic/literary ▶ **contraction** of wherever.

wherefore archaic ▶ **interrogative adverb** for what reason: *she took an ill turn, but wherefore I cannot say.*
▶ **relative adverb** & **conjunction** as a result of which: [as conjunction] *truly he cared for me, wherefore I title him with all respect.*
– PHRASES **whys and wherefores** see **WHY**.

wherefrom ▶ **relative adverb** archaic from which or from where: *one day you may lose this pride of place wherefrom you now dominate.*

wherein formal ▶ **adverb 1** [relative adverb] in which: *the situation wherein the information will eventually be used.*
2 [interrogative adverb] in what place or respect?: *so wherein lies the difference?*

whereof /wɛːrˈɒv/ ▶ **relative adverb** formal of what or which: *I know whereof I speak.*

whereon ▶ **relative adverb** archaic on which: *the cliff side whereon I walked.*

wheresoe'er /ˌwɛːsəʊˈɛː/ poetic/literary ▶ **contraction** of wheresoever.

wheresoever ▶ **adverb** & **conjunction** formal word for **WHEREVER**.

whereto /wɛːˈtuː/ ▶ **relative adverb** archaic or formal to which: *young ambition's ladder, whereto the climber-upward turns his face.*

whereupon ▶ **conjunction** immediately after which: *he qualified in February, whereupon he was promoted to Sergeant.*

wherever ▶ **relative adverb** in or to whatever place (emphasizing a lack of restriction): *meet me wherever you like.*
▪in all places; regardless of where: *it should be available wherever you go to shop.*
▶ **interrogative adverb** used for emphasis instead of 'where' in questions, typically expressing surprise or confusion: *wherever can he have gone to?*
▶ **conjunction** in every case when: *use wholegrain breakfast cereals wherever possible.*
– PHRASES **or wherever** informal or any similar place: *it is bound to have originated in Taiwan or wherever.*

USAGE In the emphatic use (***wherever** can he have got to?*) the one-word form **wherever** may also be written as two words. See **usage** at **HOWEVER**.

wherewith ▶ **relative adverb** formal or archaic with or by which: *the instrumental means wherewith the action is performed.*

wherewithal ▶ **noun** [usu. with infinitive] (**the wherewithal**) the money or other means needed for a particular purpose: *they lacked the wherewithal to pay.*

wherry /ˈwɛri/ ▶ **noun** (pl. **-ies**) a light rowing boat used chiefly for carrying passengers.
▪Brit. a large light barge.
– DERIVATIVES **wherryman** noun (pl. **-men**).
– ORIGIN late Middle English: of unknown origin.

whet /wɛt/ ▶ **verb** (**whetted**, **whetting**) [with obj.] sharpen the blade of (a tool or weapon): *her husband is whetting his knife.*
▪excite or stimulate (someone's desire, interest, or appetite): *here's an extract to whet your appetite.*
▶ **noun** archaic a thing that stimulates appetite or desire: *he swallowed his two dozen oysters as a whet.*
– DERIVATIVES **whetter** noun (rare).
– ORIGIN Old English *hwettan*, of Germanic origin; related to German *wetzen*, based on an adjective meaning 'sharp'.

whether ▶ **conjunction** expressing a doubt or choice between alternatives: *he seemed undecided* ***whether*** *to* ***go or stay*** | *it is still not clear* ***whether or not*** *he realizes.*
▪expressing an enquiry or investigation (often used in indirect questions): *I'll see whether she's at home.* ▪ indicating that a statement applies whichever of the alternatives mentioned is the case: *I'm going* ***whether*** *you like it* ***or not****.*
– PHRASES **whether or no 1** whether or not: *the only issue arising would be whether or no the publication was defamatory.* **2** archaic in any case: *God help us, whether or no!*
– ORIGIN Old English *hwæther, hwether*, of Germanic origin; related to German *weder* 'neither'.

USAGE On the difference between **whether** and **if**, see **usage** at **IF**.

whetstone ▶ **noun** a fine-grained stone used for sharpening cutting tools.

whew /hwjuː, fjuː/ ▶ **exclamation** used to express surprise, relief, or a feeling of being very hot or tired: *Whew—and I thought it was serious!*
– ORIGIN late Middle English: imitative; compare with **PHEW**.

whey /weɪ/ ▶ **noun** [mass noun] the watery part of milk that remains after the formation of curds.
– ORIGIN Old English *hwæg, hweg*, of Germanic origin; related to Dutch *wei*.

whey-faced ▶ **adjective** (of a person) pale, especially as a result of ill health, shock, or fear.

which ▶ **interrogative pronoun** & **determiner** asking for information specifying one or more people or things from a definite set: [as pronoun] *which are the best varieties of grapes for long keeping?* | ***which of*** *the suspects murdered him?* | [as determiner] *which way is the wind blowing?*
▶ **relative pronoun** & **determiner** used referring to something previously mentioned when introducing a clause giving further information: [as pronoun] *a conference in Vienna which ended on Friday* | [after prep.] *it was a crisis for which he was totally unprepared* | [as determiner, after prep.] *your claim ought to succeed,* ***in which case*** *the damages will be substantial.*
– PHRASES **which is which** used when two or more people or things are difficult to distinguish from each other: *there is no confusion as to which is which.*
– ORIGIN Old English *hwilc*, from the Germanic bases of **WHO** and **ALIKE**.

USAGE On the differences between **which** and **that** in relative clauses, see **usage** at **THAT**.

whichaway US informal or dialect ▶ **interrogative adverb**
1 in which direction?
2 how? in which way?
▶ **relative adverb** however; in whatever way.
– PHRASES **every whichaway** in a disorderly fashion: *books are skewed and lounge against one another every whichaway.*

whichever ▶ **relative determiner** & **pronoun** used to emphasize a lack of restriction in selecting one of a definite set of alternatives: [as determiner] *choose whichever brand you prefer* | [as pronoun] *their pension should be increased annually in line with earnings or prices, whichever is the higher.*
▪regardless of which: [as determiner] *they were in a position to intercept him whichever way he ran* | [as pronoun] *whichever they choose, we must accept it.*

whichsoever ▶ **determiner** & **pronoun** archaic whichever: [as pronoun] *on any occasion whichsoever it be.*

whicker ▶ **verb** [no obj.] (of a horse) give a soft breathy whinny.
▶ **noun** a sound of this type.
– ORIGIN mid 17th cent. (in the sense 'to snigger, titter'): imitative.

whidah ▶ **noun** archaic spelling of **WHYDAH**.

whiff[1] ▶ **noun 1** a smell that is only smelt briefly or faintly: *I* ***caught a whiff*** *of peachy perfume.*
▪[in sing.] Brit. informal an unpleasant smell. ▪ [in sing.] an act of sniffing or inhaling, typically so as to determine or savour a scent: *one whiff of clothing and Fido was off.* ▪ [in sing.] a trace or hint of something bad, menacing, or exciting: *here was a man with a whiff of danger about him.*
2 a puff or breath of air or smoke.
3 N. Amer. informal (chiefly in baseball or golf) an unsuccessful attempt to hit the ball.
▶ **verb 1** [with obj.] get a brief or faint smell of: *he could whiff the slightest reek.*
▪[no obj.] Brit. informal give off an unpleasant smell.
2 [no obj.] N. Amer. informal (chiefly in baseball or golf) try unsuccessfully to hit the ball.
– ORIGIN late 16th cent. (originally in the senses 'gust of wind' and 'inhalation of tobacco smoke', also, as a verb, 'blow with a slight gust'): imitative.

whiff[2] ▶ **noun** another term for **MEGRIM**[2].
– ORIGIN early 18th cent.: perhaps from **WHIFF**[1].

whiffle ▶ **verb** [no obj., with adverbial of direction] (of the wind) blow lightly in a specified direction: *as we walked, air began whiffling down off Bald Peak.*
▪move lightly as if blown by a puff of air: *the geese came whiffling down on to the grass.* ▪ [with obj.] blow or move (something) with or as if with a puff of air: *the mouse whiffled its whiskers.*
▶ **noun 1** a slight movement of air or the sound of such a movement.
2 (also **whiffle cut**) US informal a very short haircut worn by US soldiers in the Second World War.

– ORIGIN mid 16th cent.: frequentative (verb), diminutive (noun) of **WHIFF**[1].

whiffletree ▶ noun US a swingletree.
– ORIGIN mid 19th cent.: variant of **WHIPPLETREE**.

whiffy ▶ adjective (**whiffier**, **whiffiest**) Brit. informal having an unpleasant smell: *whiffy socks*.

Whig historical ▶ noun **1** a member of the British reforming and constitutional party that sought the supremacy of Parliament and was eventually succeeded in the 19th century by the Liberal Party. **2** a supporter of the American Revolution.
■a member of an American political party in the 19th century, succeeded by the Republicans.
3 a 17th-century Scottish Presbyterian.
4 [as modifier] denoting a historian who interprets history as the continuing and inevitable victory of progress over reaction.
– DERIVATIVES **Whiggery** noun, **Whiggish** adjective, **Whiggism** noun.
– ORIGIN probably a shortening of Scots *whiggamore*, the nickname of 17th-cent. Scottish rebels, from *whig* 'to drive' + **MARE**[1].

while ▶ noun **1** a period of time: *we chatted for a while* | *she retired a little while ago*.
■(**a while**) for some time: *can I keep it a while?*
2 (**the while**) at the same time; meanwhile: *he starts to draw, talking the while*.
■poetic/literary during the time that: *beseeching him, the while his hand she wrung*.
▶ conjunction **1** during the time that; at the same time as: *nothing much changed while he was away*.
2 whereas (indicating a contrast): *one person wants out, while the other wants the relationship to continue*.
■in spite of the fact that; although: *while I wouldn't recommend a night-time visit, by day the area is full of interest*.
▶ relative adverb during which: *the period while the animal remains alive*.
▶ verb [with obj.] (**while time away**) pass time in a leisurely manner: *a diversion to while away the long afternoons*.
▶ preposition N. English until: *father will be happy while dinner time*.
– PHRASES **worth while** (or **worth one's while**) worth the time or effort spent.
– ORIGIN Old English *hwīl* 'period of time', of Germanic origin; related to Dutch *wijl*, German *Weile*; the conjunction is an abbreviation of Old English *thā hwīle the* 'the while that'.

USAGE **1** On the distinction between **worth while** and **worthwhile**, see usage at **WORTHWHILE**.
2 In dialects of Northern England **while** is used to mean 'until', as in *I waited while six o'clock*. This use is not standard English, however.

whiles ▶ conjunction archaic form of **WHILE**.
– ORIGIN Middle English: originally in adverbs such as *somewhiles* 'formerly', *otherwhiles* 'at times'.

while-you-wait ▶ adjective [attrib.] (of a service) performed immediately: *a while-you-wait swab test*.

whilom /ˈwʌɪləm/ archaic ▶ adverb formerly; in the past: *the wistful eyes which whilom glanced down upon the fields*.
▶ adjective former; erstwhile: *a whilom circus acrobat*.
– ORIGIN Old English *hwīlum* 'at times', dative plural of *hwīl* (see **WHILE**).

whilst ▶ conjunction & relative adverb chiefly Brit. while.
– ORIGIN late Middle English: from **WHILES** + -*t* as in **AGAINST**.

whim ▶ noun **1** a sudden desire or change of mind, especially one that is unusual or unexplained: *she bought it on a whim* | [mass noun] *he appeared and disappeared at whim*.
2 archaic a windlass for raising ore or water from a mine.
– ORIGIN late 17th cent.: of unknown origin. Sense 2 (mid 18th cent.) is a transferred use.

whimbrel /ˈwɪmbr(ə)l/ ▶ noun a small migratory curlew of northern Eurasia and northern Canada, with a striped crown and a trilling call.
● *Numenius phaeopus*, family Scolopacidae.
– ORIGIN mid 16th cent.: from **WHIMPER** or synonymous dialect *whimp* (imitative of the bird's call) + -**REL**.

whimper ▶ verb [no obj.] (of a person or animal) make a series of low, feeble sounds expressive of fear, pain, or discontent: *a child in a bed nearby began to whimper*.
■[with direct speech] say something in a low, feeble voice expressive of such emotions: '*He's not dead, is he?*' *she whimpered*.
▶ noun a low, feeble sound expressive of such emotions: *she gave a little whimper of protest*.
■(**a whimper**) a feeble or anticlimatic tone or ending: *their first appearance in the top flight ended with a whimper rather than a bang*. [ORIGIN: with allusion to T. S. Eliot's 'This is the way the world ends Not with a bang but a whimper' (Hollow Men, 1925).]
– DERIVATIVES **whimperer** noun, **whimperingly** adverb.
– ORIGIN early 16th cent.: from dialect *whimp* 'to whimper', of imitative origin.

whimsical ▶ adjective **1** playfully quaint or fanciful, especially in an appealing and amusing way: *a whimsical sense of humour*.
2 acting or behaving in a capricious manner: *the whimsical arbitrariness of autocracy*.
– DERIVATIVES **whimsicality** noun, **whimsically** adverb.

whimsy (also **whimsey**) ▶ noun (pl. -**ies** or -**eys**) [mass noun] playfully quaint or fanciful behaviour or humour: *the film is an awkward blend of whimsy and moralizing*.
■[count noun] a whim. ■[count noun] a thing that is fanciful or odd: *the stone carvings and whimsies*.
– ORIGIN early 17th cent. (in the sense 'caprice'): probably based on **WHIM-WHAM**.

whim-wham ▶ noun archaic a quaint and decorative object; a trinket.
■a whim: *the follies and whim-whams of the metropolis*.
– ORIGIN early 16th cent.: fanciful reduplication.

whin[1] ▶ noun [mass noun] chiefly N. English furze; gorse.
– ORIGIN late Middle English: probably of Scandinavian origin; compare with Swedish *ven* 'bent grass'.

whin[2] (also **whinstone**) ▶ noun [mass noun] Brit. hard, dark basaltic rock such as that of the Whin Sill in Northern England.
– ORIGIN Middle English: of unknown origin.

whinchat /ˈwɪntʃat/ ▶ noun a small Eurasian and North African songbird related to the stonechat, with a brown back and orange-buff underparts.
● *Saxicola rubetra*, family Turdidae.
– ORIGIN late 17th cent.: from **WHIN**[1] + **CHAT**[2].

whine ▶ noun a long, high-pitched complaining cry: *the dog gave a small whine*.
■a long, high-pitched unpleasant sound: *the whine of the engine*. ■a complaining tone of voice. ■a feeble or petulant complaint: *a constant whine about the quality of public services*.
▶ verb [no obj.] give or make a long, high-pitched complaining cry or sound: *the dog whined and scratched at the back door*.
■[reporting verb] complain in a feeble or petulant way: [no obj.] *the waitress whined about the increased work* | [with direct speech] '*What about him?*' *he whined*.
– DERIVATIVES **whiner** noun, **whiningly** adverb, **whiny** adjective.
– ORIGIN Old English *hwīnan* 'whistle through the air', related to **WHINGE**. The noun dates from the mid 17th cent.

whinge Brit. informal ▶ verb (**whingeing**) [no obj.] complain persistently and in a peevish or irritating way: *stop whingeing and get on with it!*
▶ noun an act of complaining in such a way.
– DERIVATIVES **whingeingly** adverb, **whinger** noun, **whingy** adjective.
– ORIGIN late Old English *hwinsian*, of Germanic origin; related to German *winseln*; compare with **WHINE**.

whinny ▶ noun (pl. -**ies**) a gentle, high-pitched neigh.
▶ verb (-**ies**, -**ied**) [no obj.] (of a horse) make such a sound: *the pony whinnied and tossed his head happily*.
– ORIGIN late Middle English (as a verb): imitative. The noun dates from the early 19th cent.

whinstone ▶ noun another term for **WHIN**[2].

whip ▶ noun **1** a strip of leather or length of cord fastened to a handle, used for flogging or beating a person or for urging on an animal.
■figurative a thing causing mental or physical pain or acting as a stimulus to action: *councils are attempting to find new sites under the whip of a powerful agency*.
2 a thing or person resembling a whip in form or function: *a licorice whip*.
■a slender, unbranched shoot or plant. ■short for **WHIPPER-IN**. ■short for **WHIP AERIAL**. ■[with modifier] N. Amer. a scythe for cutting specified crops: *a grass whip*. ■a rope-and-pulley hoisting apparatus.

3 an official of a political party appointed to maintain parliamentary discipline among its members, especially so as to ensure attendance and voting in debates.
■Brit. a written notice from such an official requesting attendance for voting. See also **THREE-LINE WHIP**. ■(**the whip**) Brit. party membership of a Member of Parliament or other elected body: *he asked for the whip to be withdrawn from them*.
4 [mass noun] a dessert consisting of cream or eggs beaten into a light fluffy mass with fruit, chocolate, or other ingredients.
5 [in sing.] a violent striking or beating movement.
■a fast movement in a specified direction: *cleaning may consist of a quick dust or whip round*.
▶ verb (**whipped**, **whipping**) [with obj.] **1** beat (a person or animal) with a whip or similar instrument, especially as a punishment or to urge them on.
■(of a flexible object or rain or wind) strike or beat violently: *the wind whipped their faces* | [no obj.] *ferns and brambles whipped at him*. ■beat (cream, eggs, or other food) into a froth. ■(**whip someone into**) urge or rouse someone into (a specified state or position): *the radio host whipped his listeners into a frenzy*. ■informal (of a player or team) defeat (a person or team) heavily in a sporting contest.
2 [no obj., with adverbial of direction] move fast or suddenly in a specified direction: *I whipped round the corner*.
■[with obj. and adverbial of direction] take out or move (something) fast or suddenly: *he whipped out his revolver and shot him*.
3 Brit. informal steal (something): *the escaper had whipped his overcoat*.
4 bind (something) with spirally wound twine.
■sew or gather (something) with overcast stitches.
– PHRASES **the whip hand** a position of power or control over someone. **whips of** Austral./NZ large quantities of: *tea with whips of sugar*. [ORIGIN: late 19th cent.: from British English dialect *whips* 'lashings'.] **whip someone's ass** see **ASS**[2].
– DERIVATIVES **whip-like** adjective, **whipper** noun.
– ORIGIN Middle English: probably from Middle Low German and Middle Dutch *wippen* 'swing, leap, dance', from a Germanic base meaning 'move quickly'. The noun is partly from the verb, reinforced by Middle Low German *wippe* 'quick movement'.
▶ whip in act as whipper-in.
whip someone up deliberately excite someone into having a strong feeling or reaction: *Dad had managed to whip himself up into a fantastic rage*.
whip something up 1 cause water, sand, etc., to rise up and be flung about in a violent manner: *the sea was whipped up by a force-nine gale*. ■stimulate a particular feeling in someone: *we tried hard to whip up interest in the products*. **2** make or prepare something, typically something to eat, very quickly.

whip aerial (also **whip antenna**) ▶ noun an aerial in the form of a long flexible wire or rod with a connection at one end.

whip and tongue grafting ▶ noun [mass noun] a method of grafting in which both stock and scion are cut diagonally and their surfaces are provided with matching tongues which interlock when the graft is tied.

whipbird ▶ noun a long-tailed Australian songbird of the logrunner family, with a call like the crack of a whip.
● Genus *Psophodes*, family Orthonychidae: two species.

whipcord ▶ noun [mass noun] **1** thin, tough, tightly twisted cord used for making the flexible end part of whips.
2 a closely woven ribbed worsted fabric, used for making garments such as jodhpurs.

whip graft ▶ noun (in horticulture) a simple graft in which both stock and scion are cut diagonally.

whiplash ▶ noun **1** [usu. in sing.] the lashing action of a whip: figurative *he cringed before the icy whiplash of Curtis's tongue*.
■the flexible part of a whip or something resembling it.
2 [mass noun] injury caused by a severe jerk to the head, typically in a motor accident.
▶ verb [with obj.] jerk or jolt (someone or something) suddenly, typically so as to cause injury: *the force of impact had whiplashed the man's head*.
■[no obj., with adverbial of direction] move suddenly and forcefully, like a whip being cracked: *he rammed the yacht, sending its necklace of lights whiplashing from the bridge*.

whipless ▶ adjective Brit. (of an MP) having formally

w

relinquished, or been deprived of, party membership.

whip pan ▶ noun a camera panning movement fast enough to give a blurred picture.
▶ verb (**whip-pan**) [no obj.] pan quickly to give a blurred picture.

whipped ▶ adjective **1** [attrib.] having been flogged or beaten with a whip: *a whipped dog.*
■ [predic.] N. Amer. informal worn out; exhausted.
2 (of cream, eggs, or other food) beaten into a froth.

whipper-in ▶ noun (pl. **whippers-in**) a huntsman's assistant who brings straying hounds back into the pack.

whippersnapper ▶ noun informal a young and inexperienced person considered to be presumptuous or overconfident.
– ORIGIN late 17th cent.: perhaps representing *whipsnapper*, expressing noise and unimportance.

whippet ▶ noun a dog of a small slender breed originally produced as a cross between the greyhound and the terrier or spaniel, bred for racing.
– ORIGIN early 17th cent.: partly from obsolete *whippet* 'move briskly'.

whipping ▶ noun **1** a thrashing or beating with a whip or similar implement: *she saw scars on his back from the whippings* | [mass noun] *whipping was to be abolished as a punishment*
2 [mass noun] cord or twine used to bind or cover a rope.

whipping boy ▶ noun a person who is blamed or punished for the faults or incompetence of others.
– ORIGIN extended use of the original term (mid 17th cent.) denoting a boy educated with a young prince or other royal person and punished instead of him.

whipping cream ▶ noun [mass noun] fairly thick cream containing enough butterfat to make it suitable for whipping.

whipping post ▶ noun historical a post to which offenders were tied in order to be whipped as a public punishment.

whippletree /'wɪp(ə)ltriː/ ▶ noun archaic term for **SWINGLETREE**.
– ORIGIN mid 18th cent.: apparently from **WHIP** + **TREE**.

whippoorwill /'wɪpəwɪl/ ▶ noun a North and Central American nightjar with a distinctive call.
● *Caprimulgus vociferus*, family Caprimulgidae.
– ORIGIN early 18th cent.: imitative of its call.

whippy ▶ adjective flexible; springy: *new growths of whippy sapling twigs.*
– DERIVATIVES **whippiness** noun.

whip-round ▶ noun [usu. in sing.] Brit. informal a collection of contributions of money from a group of people for a particular purpose.

whipsaw ▶ noun a saw with a narrow blade and a handle at both ends, used typically by two people.
▶ verb (past participle **-sawn** or **-sawed**) [with obj.] US cut with a whipsaw: *he was whipsawing lumber.*
■ informal subject to two difficult situations or opposing pressures at the same time: *the army has been whipsawed by a shrinking budget and a growing pool of recruits.* ■ informal compel to do something. ■ (usu. **be whipsawed**) Stock Exchange, informal subject to a double loss, as when buying a security before the price falls and selling before the price rises.

whip scorpion ▶ noun an arachnid that resembles a scorpion, with stout pincer-like mouthparts and a long slender tail-like appendage, living in leaf litter and under stones in tropical and semi-tropical regions.
● Order Uropygi.

whip snake ▶ noun any of a number of slender fast-moving snakes which often feed on lizards and catch their prey by pursuing it, in particular:
● a harmless snake found in Eurasia, America, and Africa (*Coluber* and other genera, family Colubridae, including the Eurasian *C. viridiflavus*). ● a venomous Australian snake (*Desmansia* and other genera, family Elapidae, including the widespread *D. psammophis*).

whipstitch ▶ noun an overcast stitch.
▶ verb [with obj.] sew (something) with such stitches.

whipstock ▶ noun the handle of a whip.

whiptail (also **whiptail lizard**) ▶ noun a slender long-tailed American lizard with an alert manner and a jerky gait.
● Genus *Cnemidophorus*, family Teiidae: several species.

whiptail wallaby ▶ noun a wallaby with a very long slender tail and a distinctive white facial stripe, native to woodlands of NE Australia. Also called **PRETTY-FACE WALLABY**.
● *Macropus parryi*, family Macropodidae.

whipworm ▶ noun a parasitic nematode worm with a stout posterior and slender anterior part, especially one that infests the intestines of domestic animals.
● Genus *Trichuris*, class Aphasmida (or Adenophorea).

whir ▶ noun & verb variant spelling of **WHIRR**.

whirl ▶ verb move or cause to move rapidly round and round: [no obj.] *leaves whirled in eddies of wind* | [with obj.] *I whirled her round the dance hall.*
■ move or cause to move rapidly: [no obj., with adverbial of direction] *Sybil stood waving as they whirled past* | [with obj. and adverbial of direction] *he was whirled into the bushes.* ■ [no obj.] (of the head, mind, or senses) seem to spin round: *Kate made her way back to the office, her mind whirling.* ■ [no obj., with adverbial of direction] (of thoughts or mental images) follow each other in bewildering succession: *a kaleidoscope of images whirled through her brain.*
▶ noun [in sing.] a rapid movement round and round.
■ frantic activity of a specified kind: *the event was all part of the mad social whirl.* ■ [with adj. or noun modifier] a specified kind of sweet or biscuit with a spiral shape: *a hazelnut whirl.*
– PHRASES **give something a whirl** informal give something a try. **in a whirl** in a state of confusion.
– DERIVATIVES **whirler** noun, **whirlingly** adverb.
– ORIGIN Middle English: the verb probably from Old Norse *hvirfla* 'turn about'; the noun partly from Middle Low German, Middle Dutch *wervel* 'spindle', or from Old Norse *hvirfill* 'circle', from a Germanic base meaning 'rotate'.

whirligig ▶ noun **1** a toy that spins round, for example a top or windmill.
■ another term for **ROUNDABOUT** (in sense 2).
2 [in sing.] a thing regarded as hectic or constantly changing: *the whirligig of time.*
3 (also **whirligig beetle**) a small black predatory beetle which swims rapidly in circles on the surface of still or slow-moving water and dives when alarmed.
● Family Gyrinidae: *Gyrinus* and other genera.
– ORIGIN late Middle English: from **WHIRL** + obsolete *gig* 'whipping-top'.

whirling dervish ▶ noun see **DERVISH**.

whirling disease ▶ noun [mass noun] a disease of trout caused by a parasitic protozoan, affecting the balance of the fish and causing it to swim with a whirling motion.
● The protozoan is *Myxosoma cerebralis*, phylum Sporozoa.

whirlpool ▶ noun a quickly rotating mass of water in a river or sea into which objects may be drawn, typically caused by the meeting of conflicting currents.
■ figurative a turbulent situation from which it is hard to escape: *he was drawing her down into an emotional whirlpool.* ■ (also **whirlpool bath**) a heated pool in which hot aerated water is continuously circulated.

whirlwind ▶ noun a column of air moving rapidly round and round in a cylindrical or funnel shape.
■ used in similes and metaphors to describe a very energetic or tumultuous person or process: *a whirlwind of activity* | [as modifier] *a whirlwind romance.*
– PHRASES **(sow the wind and) reap the whirlwind** suffer serious consequences as a result of one's actions. [ORIGIN: with biblical allusion to Hos. 8:7.]

whirlybird ▶ noun informal, chiefly N. Amer. a helicopter.

whirr (also **whir**) ▶ verb (**whirred**, **whirring**) [no obj.] (especially of a machine or a bird's wings) make a low, continuous, regular sound: *the ceiling fans whirred in the smoky air.*
▶ noun a sound of such a type: *the whirr of the projector.*
– ORIGIN late Middle English (in the sense 'move with a whirring sound'): probably of Scandinavian origin; compare with **WHIRL**.

whisht /(h)wɪʃt/ (also **wheesht**, **whist**) ▶ exclamation chiefly Scottish & Irish hush (used to demand silence): *'Whisht, child. Away and do what you're told.'*
– PHRASES **hold one's whisht** keep silent.
– ORIGIN natural exclamation: first recorded in English in the mid 16th cent.

whisk ▶ verb **1** [with obj. and adverbial of direction] take or move (someone or something) in a particular direction suddenly and quickly: *his jacket was whisked away for dry-cleaning.*
■ move (something) through the air with a light, sweeping movement: *hippopotamuses spread their scents by whisking their tails.*
2 [with obj.] beat or stir (a substance, especially cream or eggs) with a light, rapid movement.
▶ noun **1** a utensil for whipping eggs or cream.
2 (also **fly whisk**) a bunch of grass, twigs, or bristles for removing dust or flies.
3 [in sing.] a brief, rapid action or movement: *a whisk round St Basil's cathedral.*
– ORIGIN late Middle English: of Scandinavian origin.

whisker ▶ noun **1** a long projecting hair or bristle growing from the face or snout of many mammals.
■ (**whiskers**) the hair growing on a man's face, especially on his cheeks. ■ a single crystal of a material in the form of a filament with no dislocations.
2 (a **whisker**) informal a very small amount: *they won the election by a whisker.*
– PHRASES **have** (or **have grown**) **whiskers** informal (especially of a story) be very old. **within a whisker of** informal extremely close or near to doing, achieving, or suffering something.
– DERIVATIVES **whiskered** adjective, **whiskery** adjective.
– ORIGIN late Middle English (originally denoting a bundle of feathers, twigs, etc., used for whisking): from the verb **WHISK** + **-ER**[1].

whiskered bat ▶ noun a small brown myotis bat native to Eurasia.
● Genus *Myotis*, family Vespertilionidae: several species, in particular the common and widespread *M. mystacinus*.

whisky ▶ noun (pl. **-ies**) **1** (Irish **whiskey**) [mass noun] a spirit distilled from malted grain, especially barley or rye.
2 (**whiskey**) a code word representing the letter W, used in radio communication.
– ORIGIN early 18th cent.: abbreviation of obsolete *whiskybae*, variant of **USQUEBAUGH**.

whisky jack ▶ noun N. Amer. informal another term for **GREY JAY**.

whisky mac ▶ noun a drink consisting of whisky and ginger wine mixed in equal amounts.

whisky sour ▶ noun a drink consisting of whisky mixed with lemon or lime juice.

whisper ▶ verb [no obj.] speak very softly using one's breath rather than one's throat, especially for the sake of secrecy: *Alison was whispering in his ear* | [with obj.] *he managed to whisper a faint goodbye* | [with direct speech] *'Are you all right?' he whispered.*
■ poetic/literary (of leaves, wind, or water) rustle or murmur softly. ■ (**be whispered**) be rumoured: *it was whispered that he would soon die.*
▶ noun a soft or confidential tone of voice; a whispered word or phrase: *she spoke in a whisper.*
■ poetic/literary a soft rustling or murmuring sound: *the thunder of the surf became a muted whisper.* ■ a rumour or piece of gossip: *whispers of a blossoming romance.* ■ [usu. in sing.] a slight trace; a hint: *he didn't show even a whisper of interest.*
– DERIVATIVES **whisperer** noun, **whispery** adjective.
– ORIGIN Old English *hwisprian*, of Germanic origin; related to German *wispeln*, from the imitative base of **WHISTLE**.

whispering campaign ▶ noun a systematic circulation of a rumour, typically in order to damage someone's reputation.

whispering gallery ▶ noun a gallery or dome with acoustic properties such that a faint sound may be heard round its entire circumference.

whist[1] /wɪst/ ▶ noun [mass noun] a card game, usually for two pairs of players, in which points are scored according to the number of tricks won.
– ORIGIN mid 17th cent. (earlier as *whisk*): perhaps from **WHISK** (with reference to whisking away the tricks); perhaps associated with **WHIST**[2].

whist[2] /(h)wɪst/ ▶ exclamation variant spelling of **WHISHT**.

whistle ▶ noun **1** a clear, high-pitched sound made by forcing breath through a small hole between partly closed lips, or between one's teeth.
■ a similar sound, especially one made by a bird, machine, or the wind. ■ an instrument used to produce such a sound, especially for giving a signal.
2 Brit. a suit. [ORIGIN: from rhyming slang *whistle and flute*.]
▶ verb **1** [no obj.] emit a clear, high-pitched sound by forcing breath through a small hole between one's lips or teeth: *the audience cheered and whistled.*

W

■ express surprise, admiration, or derision by making such a sound: *Bob whistled. 'You look beautiful!' he said.* ■ [with obj.] produce (a tune) in such a way. ■ (especially of a bird or machine) produce a similar sound: *the kettle began to whistle.* ■ [no obj., with adverbial] produce such a sound by moving rapidly through the air or a narrow opening: *the wind was whistling down the chimney.* ■ blow an instrument that makes such a sound, especially as a signal: *the referee did not whistle for a foul.* ■ [with obj.] (**whistle someone/thing up**) summon something or someone by making such a sound.

2 (**whistle for**) wish for or expect (something) in vain: *you can go home and whistle for your wages.*

– PHRASES **blow the whistle on** informal bring an illicit activity to an end by informing on the person responsible. **(as) clean as a whistle** extremely clean or clear. ■ informal free of incriminating evidence: *the cops raided the warehouse but the place was clean as a whistle.* **whistle something down the wind** let something go; abandon something. ■ archaic turn a trained hawk loose by casting it off with the wind. **whistle in the dark** pretend to be unafraid. **whistle in the wind** try unsuccessfully to influence something that cannot be changed.

– ORIGIN Old English *(h)wistlian* (verb), *(h)wistle* (noun), of Germanic origin; imitative and related to Swedish *vissla* 'to whistle'.

whistle-blower ▶ **noun** a person who informs on someone engaged in an illicit activity.

Whistler /ˈwɪslə/, James (Abbott) McNeill (1834–1903), American painter and etcher. Notable works: *Arrangement in Grey and Black: The Artist's Mother* (portrait, 1872).

whistler ▶ **noun 1** a person who whistles.
■ an atmospheric radio disturbance heard as a whistle that falls in pitch, caused by lightning.
2 a robust Australasian and Indonesian songbird with a strong and typically hooked bill and a loud melodious call. Also called **THICKHEAD**.
• Family Pachycephalidae: four genera, in particular *Pachycephala*, and many species.
3 North American term for **HOARY MARMOT**.

whistle-stop ▶ **adjective** [attrib.] very fast and with only brief pauses: *a whistle-stop tour of Britain.*
▶ **noun** N. Amer. a small unimportant town on a railway.
■ a brief pause in a tour by a politician for an electioneering speech.

whistling duck ▶ **noun** a long-legged duck with an upright stance and a whistling call, often perching on branches. Also called **TREE DUCK**.
• Genus *Dendrocygna*, family Anatidae: several species.

whistling kettle ▶ **noun** a kettle fitted with a spout that whistles as steam is forced through it when the kettle is boiling.

whistling swan ▶ **noun** a bird of the North American race of the tundra swan, breeding in northern Canada and overwintering on the coasts of the US.
• *Cygnus columbianus columbianus*, family Anatidae.

Whit ▶ **noun** short for **WHITSUNTIDE**.
▶ **adjective** of, connected with, or following Whit Sunday: *Whit Monday.*

whit ▶ **noun** [in sing.] a very small part or amount: *the last whit of warmth was drawn off by the setting sun.*
– PHRASES **every whit** wholly: *my mother was fond of her and I shall be every whit as fond.* **not** (or **never**) **a whit** not at all: *Sara had not changed a whit.*
– ORIGIN late Middle English: apparently an alteration of obsolete *wight* 'small amount'.

Whitby a town on the coast of North Yorkshire, NE England; pop. 13,380 (1981).

Whitby, Synod of a conference held in Whitby in 664 that resolved the differences between the Celtic and Roman forms of Christian worship in England, in particular the method of calculating the date of Easter. King Oswy (612–70) of Northumbria decided in favour of Rome, and England as a result effectively severed the connection with the Celtic Church.

White[1], Gilbert (1720–93), English clergyman and naturalist. He wrote many letters to friends on aspects of natural history in his native village of Selborne, Hampshire; these were published in 1789 as *The Natural History and Antiquities of Selborne*, which has remained in print ever since.

White[2], Patrick (Victor Martindale) (1912–90), Australian novelist, born in Britain. White's reputation is chiefly based on his two novels *The Tree of Man* (1955) and *Voss* (1957). Nobel Prize for Literature (1973).

White[3], T. H. (1906–64), British novelist, born in India; full name *Terence Hanbury White*. He is best known for the tetralogy *The Once and Future King*, his reworking of the Arthurian legend that began with *The Sword in the Stone* (1937).

white ▶ **adjective 1** of the colour of milk or fresh snow, due to the reflection of all visible rays of light; the opposite of black: *a sheet of white paper.*
■ approaching such a colour; very pale: *her face was white with fear.* ■ figurative morally or spiritually pure; innocent and untainted: *he is as pure and white as the driven snow.* ■ (of a plant) having white flowers or pale-coloured fruit. ■ (of a tree) having light-coloured bark. ■ (of wine) made from white grapes, or dark grapes with the skins removed, and having a yellowish colour. ■ Brit. (of coffee or tea) served with milk or cream. ■ (of glass) transparent; colourless. ■ (of bread) made from a light-coloured, sifted, or bleached flour.
2 (also **White**) belonging to or denoting a human group having light-coloured skin (chiefly used of peoples of European extraction): *a white farming community.*
■ of or relating to such people: *white Australian culture.* ■ S. African, historical reserved by law for those classified as white. ■ S. African, offensive impudent or cheeky (used of black people): *don't get white with me.*
3 historical counter-revolutionary or reactionary. Contrasted with **RED** (in sense 2).
▶ **noun 1** [mass noun] white colour or pigment: *garnet-red flowers flecked with white* | [count noun] *the woodwork was an immaculate white.*
■ white clothes or material: *he was dressed from head to foot in white.* ■ (**whites**) white clothes, especially as worn for playing cricket or tennis, or as naval uniform, or in the context of washing: *wash whites separately to avoid them being dulled.* ■ white wine. ■ (**White**) the player of the white pieces in chess or draughts. ■ [count noun] a white thing, in particular the white ball (the cue ball) in snooker or billiards. ■ the outer part (white when cooked) which surrounds the yolk of an egg; the albumen.
2 the visible pale part of the eyeball around the iris.
3 (also **White**) a member of a light-skinned people, especially one of European extraction.
4 [with modifier] a white or cream butterfly which has dark veins or spots on the wings. It can be a serious crop pest.
• *Pieris* and other genera, family Pieridae. See also **CABBAGE WHITE**.
▶ **verb** [with obj.] archaic paint or turn (something) white: *your passion hath whited your face.*
– PHRASES **bleed someone/thing white** drain someone or something of wealth or resources. **whited sepulchre** poetic/literary a hypocrite. [ORIGIN: with biblical allusion to Matt 23:27.] **white man's burden** the task which white colonizers believed they had to impose their civilization on the black inhabitants of their colonies. [ORIGIN: from Rudyard Kipling's *The White Man's Burden* (1899).] **whiter than white** extremely white. ■ morally beyond reproach.
– DERIVATIVES **whitely** adverb, **whiteness** noun, **whitish** adjective.
– ORIGIN late Old English *hwīt*, of Germanic origin; related to Dutch *wit* and German *weiss*, also to **WHEAT**.

USAGE The term **white** has been used to refer to the skin colour of Europeans or people of European extraction since the early 17th century. Unlike other labels for skin colour such as **red** or **yellow**, **white** has not been generally used in a derogatory way. In modern contexts there is a growing tendency to prefer to use terms which relate to geographical origin rather than skin colour: hence the current preference in the US for **African American** rather than **black** and **European** rather than **white**.

▶ **white out** (of vision) become impaired by exposure to sudden bright light. ■ (of a person) lose colour vision as a prelude to losing consciousness.
white something out 1 obliterate a mistake with white correction fluid. ■ cover one's face or facial blemishes completely with make-up. **2** impair someone's vision with a sudden bright light.

white admiral ▶ **noun** a butterfly which has dark brown wings bearing a broad white band.
• Subfamily Limenitinae, family Nymphalidae: several genera, in particular *Ladoga* (including the European *L. camilla*) and *Basilarchia* (American species).

white ant ▶ **noun** another term for **TERMITE**.

White Army ▶ **noun** any of the armies which opposed the Bolsheviks during the Russian Civil War of 1918–21.

white arsenic ▶ **noun** [mass noun] an extremely toxic soluble white solid made by burning arsenic.
• Alternative name: **arsenic trioxide**; chem. formula: As_2O_3.

whitebait ▶ **noun** [mass noun] the small silvery-white young of herrings, sprats, and similar marine fish, eaten in numbers as food.

white balance ▶ **noun** the colour balance on a video camera.
■ a control or system for adjusting this.

white bass ▶ **noun** a North American freshwater bass with dark horizontal stripes.
• *Morone chrysops*, family Percichthyidae.

white bat ▶ **noun** a bat with white fur found mainly in Central America.
• Genus *Diclidurus*, family Emballonuridae (four species, in particular *D. virgo*, also called **GHOST BAT**); and *Ectophylla alba* (family Phyllostomidae).

whitebeam ▶ **noun** a European tree related to the rowan, with red berries and hairy oval leaves that are white underneath.
• *Sorbus aria*, family Rosaceae.

white belt ▶ **noun** a white belt worn by a beginner in judo or karate.
■ a person wearing such a belt.

white birch ▶ **noun** chiefly N. Amer. a birch tree with white bark, especially the paper birch or the European silver birch.

white blood cell ▶ **noun** less technical term for **LEUCOCYTE**.

whiteboard ▶ **noun** a wipeable board with a white surface used for teaching or presentations.
■ Computing an area common to several users or applications, where they can exchange information, in particular as handwriting or graphics.

white book ▶ **noun** a book of rules, standards, or records, especially an official government report, bound in white.
■ (**White Book**) Law (in England and Wales) a book setting out the rules of practice and procedure in the Supreme Court.

white-bread ▶ **adjective** N. Amer. informal of, belonging to, or representative of the white middle classes; not progressive, radical, or innovative: *one of the West's more white-bread political institutions.*

white bryony ▶ **noun** see **BRYONY** (sense 1).

white cedar ▶ **noun 1** a North American tree of the cypress family.
• *Thuja* and other genera, family Cupressaceae: several species, in particular *Thuja occidentalis*, which yields timber and medicinal oil.
2 chiefly Austral. the chinaberry.

white cell ▶ **noun** less technical term for **LEUCOCYTE**.

white Christmas ▶ **noun** a Christmas during which there is snow on the ground.

white clover ▶ **noun** a creeping white-flowered European clover which is an important fodder plant. Also called **DUTCH CLOVER**.
• *Trifolium repens*, family Leguminosae.

whitecoat ▶ **noun** Canadian an infant harp seal, which has whitish fur.

white-collar ▶ **adjective** of or relating to the work done or those who work in an office or other professional environment.
■ denoting non-violent crime committed by white-collar workers, especially fraud.

white currant ▶ **noun** a cultivated variety of redcurrant with pale edible berries. The berries are insipid and generally used for jams and jellies, in combination with other fruits.

white dwarf ▶ **noun** Astronomy a small very dense star that is typically the size of a planet. A white dwarf is formed when a low-mass star has exhausted all its central nuclear fuel and lost its outer layers as a planetary nebula.

white elephant ▶ **noun** a possession that is useless or troublesome, especially one that is expensive to maintain or difficult to dispose of.
– ORIGIN from the story that the kings of Siam gave such animals as a gift to courtiers considered obnoxious, in order to ruin the recipient by the great expense incurred in maintaining the animal.

white ensign ▶ **noun** a white flag carrying a St

George's cross with the Union Jack in the top corner next to the flagstaff, flown by the Royal and most Commonwealth navies and the Royal Yacht Squadron.

white-eye ▶ noun a small Old World songbird with a ring of white feathers around the eye.
● Family Zosteropidae: several genera, in particular *Zosterops*, and numerous species.

whiteface ▶ noun 1 [mass noun] white stage make-up.
2 chiefly N. Amer. a Hereford cow or bull.
3 an Australian warbler with a white face.
● Genus *Aphelocephala*, family Acanthizidae: three species.

White Father ▶ noun 1 a white man regarded by people of a non-white race as having authority over them.
2 a member of the Society of Missionaries of Africa, a Roman Catholic order founded in Algiers in 1868.
– ORIGIN translating French *Père Blanc*.

white feather ▶ noun a white feather given to someone as a sign that the giver considers them a coward.
– PHRASES **show the white feather** Brit. dated behave in a cowardly fashion.
– ORIGIN late 18th cent.: with reference to a white feather in the tail of a game bird, being a mark of bad breeding.

white finger ▶ noun informal term for **RAYNAUD'S DISEASE**.

white fir ▶ noun a silver fir.
● Genus *Abies*, family Pinaceae: several species, in particular *Abies concolor*.

whitefish ▶ noun (pl. same or **-fishes**) a mainly freshwater fish of the salmon family, widely used as food.
● *Coregonus* and other genera, family Salmonidae: several species. See **CISCO**, **HOUTING**, **POWAN**, and **VENDACE**.

white fish ▶ noun [mass noun] fish with pale flesh, such as plaice, halibut, cod, and haddock. Compare with **RED FISH**.

white flag ▶ noun a white flag or cloth used as a symbol of surrender, truce, or a desire to parley.

white flour ▶ noun [mass noun] fine wheat flour, typically bleached, from which most of the bran and germ have been removed.

whitefly ▶ noun (pl. same or **-flies**) a minute winged bug covered with powdery white wax, damaging plants by feeding on the sap and coating them with honeydew.
● Family Aleyrodidae, suborder Homoptera: numerous genera and species.

white-footed mouse ▶ noun a common deer mouse with white feet, found in the US and Mexico.
● *Peromyscus leucopus*, family Muridae.

whitefront (also **white-fronted goose**) ▶ noun a migratory goose with mainly grey plumage and a white forehead, breeding in northern Eurasia and North America.
● Genus *Anser*, family Anatidae: two species.

white gold ▶ noun [mass noun] a silver-coloured alloy of gold with nickel, platinum, or another metal.

white goods ▶ plural noun 1 large electrical goods used domestically such as refrigerators and washing machines, typically white in colour. Compare with **BROWN GOODS**.
2 archaic domestic linen.

Whitehall a street in Westminster, London, in which many government offices are located.
■ used as an allusive reference to the British Civil Service. ■ used as an allusive reference to the British government, its offices, or its policy: *a pledge was given by Whitehall to protect British troops in Bosnia.*

Whitehead, Alfred North (1861–1947), English philosopher and mathematician. He is remembered chiefly for *Principia Mathematica* (1910–13), on which he collaborated with his pupil Bertrand Russell. However, he was concerned to explain more generally the connections between mathematics, theoretical science, and ordinary experience.

whitehead ▶ noun 1 informal a pale or white-topped pustule on the skin.
2 a small New Zealand songbird with a white head and underparts, found only on North Island.
● *Mohoua albicilla*, family Pachycephalidae (or Acanthizidae).

white heat ▶ noun [mass noun] the temperature or state of something that is so hot that it emits white light.
■ [in sing.] figurative a state of intense passion or activity.

white hole ▶ noun Astronomy a hypothetical celestial object which expands outwards from a space–time singularity and emits energy, in the manner of a time-reversed black hole.

white hope ▶ noun a person expected to bring much success to a team or organization: *the great white hope of the Tory Left.*

Whitehorse the capital of Yukon Territory in NW Canada; pop. 21,650 (1991). Situated on the Alaska Highway, it is the centre of a copper-mining and fur-trapping region.

white horses ▶ plural noun white-crested waves at sea.

white-hot ▶ adjective at white heat: *a shower of white-hot embers.*

White House (**the White house**) 1 the official residence of the US president in Washington DC.
■ the US president, presidency, or government: *the White House denounced the charge.*
2 the Russian parliament building.

white information ▶ noun [mass noun] positive information about a person's creditworthiness held by a bank or similar institution.

white knight ▶ noun a person or thing that comes to someone's aid.
■ a person or company making an acceptable counter offer for a company facing a hostile takeover bid.

white-knuckle ▶ adjective [attrib.] (especially of a fairground ride) designed to cause excitement or tension.
– ORIGIN 1970s: with reference to the effect caused by gripping tightly to steady oneself.

white-knuckled ▶ adjective informal (of a person) showing signs of extreme tension due to fear or anger.

white-label ▶ adjective denoting a musical recording for which the fully printed commercial label is not yet available, and which has been supplied with a plain white label before general release for promotional purposes.
▶ noun (**white label**) a recording released in such a way.

White Lady ▶ noun a cocktail made with gin, orange liqueur, and lemon juice.

white land ▶ noun [mass noun] open land not designated for development or change of use, or on which development is not allowed.

white lead ▶ noun [mass noun] a white pigment consisting of a mixture of lead carbonate and lead hydroxide.

white lie ▶ noun a harmless or trivial lie, especially one told to avoid hurting someone's feelings.

white light ▶ noun [mass noun] apparently colourless light, for example ordinary daylight. It contains all the wavelengths of the visible spectrum at equal intensity.

white lightning ▶ noun [mass noun] US illicit home-made whiskey, typically colourless and distilled from corn.

white lime ▶ noun [mass noun] lime mixed with water as a coating for walls; whitewash.

white list ▶ noun informal a list of people or products viewed with approval.

white magic ▶ noun [mass noun] magic used only for good purposes.
– DERIVATIVES **white magician** noun.

white matter ▶ noun [mass noun] the paler tissue of the brain and spinal cord, consisting mainly of nerve fibres with their myelin sheaths. Compare with **GREY MATTER**.

white meat ▶ noun [mass noun] pale meat such as poultry, veal, and rabbit. Often contrasted with **RED MEAT**.

white metal ▶ noun [mass noun] a white or silvery alloy, especially a tin-based alloy used for the surfaces of bearings.

white meter ▶ noun a meter for measuring the off-peak consumption of electricity.

white mouse ▶ noun an albino form of the house mouse, widely bred as a pet and laboratory animal.

whiten ▶ verb make or become white: [with obj.] *snow whitened the mountain tops* | [no obj.] *she gripped the handle until her knuckles whitened.*

– DERIVATIVES **whitener** noun.

white night ▶ noun 1 a sleepless night. [ORIGIN: translating French *nuit blanche*.]
2 a night when it is never properly dark, as in high latitudes in summer.

White Nile the name for the main, western branch of the Nile between the Ugandan–Sudanese border and its confluence with the Blue Nile at Khartoum.

white noise ▶ noun [mass noun] Physics noise containing many frequencies with equal intensities.

white oil ▶ noun a colourless petroleum distillate, especially liquid paraffin, used medicinally and in the food and plastic industries.

white-out ▶ noun 1 a dense blizzard, especially in polar regions.
■ a weather condition in which the features and horizon of snow-covered country are indistinguishable due to uniform light diffusion.
2 [mass noun] white correction fluid for covering typing or writing mistakes.
3 a loss of colour vision due to rapid acceleration, often prior to a loss of consciousness.

White Paper ▶ noun (in the UK) a government report giving information or proposals on an issue.

white park cattle ▶ noun see **PARK CATTLE**.

white pepper ▶ noun [mass noun] the husked ripe or unripe berries of the pepper (see **PEPPER** sense 1), typically ground and used as a condiment.

white phosphorus ▶ noun see **PHOSPHORUS**.

white pine ▶ noun any of a number of coniferous trees with whitish timber, in particular:
● a North American tree which yields high-quality timber that is valued for intricate work (*Pinus strobus*, family Pinaceae). ● NZ the kahikatea.

white pointer ▶ noun another term for **GREAT WHITE SHARK**.

white poplar ▶ noun a Eurasian poplar with lobed leaves that are white underneath and grey-green above. Also called **ABELE**.
● *Populus alba*, family Salicaceae.

white pudding ▶ noun [mass noun] a kind of sausage made of oatmeal and suet.

white rhinoceros ▶ noun a very large two-horned African rhinoceros with broad lips.
● *Ceratotherium simum*, family Rhinocerotidae.

white rose ▶ noun the emblem of Yorkshire or the House of York.

White Russia former name for **BELARUS**.

White Russian ▶ noun dated a Belorussian.
■ an opponent of the Bolsheviks during the Russian Civil War.
▶ adjective dated Belorussian.
■ of or relating to the opponents of the Bolsheviks.

white sage ▶ noun see **SAGE**[1] (sense 2).

white sale ▶ noun a shop's sale of household linen.

white sandalwood ▶ noun see **SANDALWOOD**.

White Sands an area of white gypsum salt flats in central New Mexico, designated a national monument in 1933. It is surrounded by a large missile-testing range, which, in 1945, was the site of the detonation of the first nuclear weapon.

white sauce ▶ noun [mass noun] a sauce of flour, melted butter, and milk or cream.

White Sea an inlet of the Barents Sea on the coast of NW Russia.

white sea bass ▶ noun see **SEA BASS**.

white shark ▶ noun see **GREAT WHITE SHARK**.

white sheep ▶ noun another term for **DALL SHEEP**.

white-shoe ▶ adjective US informal denoting a company, especially a law firm, owned and run by members of the WASP elite, generally regarded as cautious and conservative.
– ORIGIN with reference to the white shoes fashionable among Ivy League college students in the 1950s.

white slave ▶ noun a woman tricked or forced into prostitution, typically one taken to a foreign country for this purpose.
– DERIVATIVES **white slaver** noun, **white slavery** noun.

whitesmith ▶ noun a person who makes articles out of metal, especially tin.
■ a polisher or finisher of metal goods.

b **b**ut | d **d**og | f **f**ew | g **g**et | h **h**e | j **y**es | k **c**at | l **l**eg | m **m**an | n **n**o | p **p**en | r **r**ed | s **s**it | t **t**op | v **v**oice | w **w**e | z **z**oo | ʃ **sh**e | ʒ deci**s**ion | θ **th**in | ð **th**is | ŋ ri**ng** | x lo**ch** | tʃ **ch**ip | dʒ **j**ar

– ORIGIN Middle English: from **WHITE** (denoting 'white iron', i.e. tin) + **SMITH**.

white snakeroot ▶ noun see **SNAKEROOT**.

white spirit ▶ noun [mass noun] Brit. a volatile colourless liquid distilled from petroleum, used as a paint thinner and solvent.

white sugar ▶ noun [mass noun] purified sugar.

white-tailed deer (US also **whitetail**) ▶ noun a reddish to greyish American deer with white on the belly and the underside of the tail.
● *Odocoileus virginianus*, family Cervidae.

whitethorn ▶ noun the hawthorn.

whitethroat ▶ noun a migratory Eurasian and North African warbler with a grey head and white throat.
● Genus *Sylvia*, family Sylviidae: three species, in particular the common *S. communis*.

white tie ▶ noun a white bow tie worn by men as part of full evening dress.
■ [mass noun] full evening dress with a white bow tie: *he was wearing immaculate white tie and tails.*
▶ adjective (of an event) requiring full evening dress to be worn, including a white bow tie.

white-toothed shrew ▶ noun an aggressive shrew with white teeth, native to Eurasia and Africa.
● Genus *Crocidura*, family Soricidae: numerous species. The **pygmy white-toothed shrew** (*C. etruscus*) is the smallest known terrestrial mammal.

white trash ▶ noun [mass noun] N. Amer. derogatory poor white people, especially those living in the southern US.

white truffle ▶ noun an underground fungus eaten in Europe as a delicacy. Also called **TARTUFO**.
● *Tuber magnatum*, family Tuberaceae, subdivision Ascomycotina. Alternative name: **Piedmont truffle**.

white vitriol ▶ noun [mass noun] archaic crystalline zinc sulphate.

whitewall ▶ noun 1 (also **whitewall tyre**) a tyre with a white stripe round the outside, or a white side wall.
2 [as modifier] N. Amer. denoting a haircut in which the sides of the head are shaved and the top and back are left longer.

whitewash ▶ noun 1 [mass noun] a solution of lime and water or of whiting, size, and water, used for painting walls white.
■ [in sing.] a deliberate concealment of someone's mistakes or faults in order to clear their name.
2 a victory by the same side in every game of a series.
▶ verb [with obj.] 1 [usu. as adj. **whitewashed**] paint (a wall, building, or room) with whitewash.
■ try to clear (someone or their name) by deliberately concealing their mistakes or faults: *his wife must have wanted to whitewash his reputation.* ■ deliberately conceal (someone's mistakes or faults): *this is not to whitewash the actual political practice of the government.*
2 defeat (an opponent) in every game of a series.
[ORIGIN: originally US, extension of *whitewash* 'to clear of liability for debts' (relating to bankruptcy).]
– DERIVATIVES **whitewasher** noun.

white water ▶ noun [mass noun] [often as modifier] fast shallow stretches of water in a river: *white-water rafting.*

white wedding ▶ noun Brit. a traditional wedding at which the bride wears a formal white dress.

white whale ▶ noun another term for **BELUGA** (in sense 1).

white willow ▶ noun a Eurasian streamside willow which has narrow leaves with silky white hairs on both sides, and the bark of which contains salicin.
● *Salix alba*, family Salicaceae.

white-winged chough ▶ noun see **CHOUGH** (sense 2).

white witch ▶ noun a person, typically a woman, who practises magic for altruistic purposes.

whitewood ▶ noun 1 [mass noun] light-coloured wood, especially when made up into furniture and ready for staining, varnishing, or painting.
2 chiefly N. Amer. any of a number of trees which yield pale timber, in particular:
● a silver fir (*Abies alba*, family Pinaceae). ● a basswood. ● the tulip tree.

whitework ▶ noun [mass noun] embroidery worked in white thread on a white ground.

white worm ▶ noun a burrowing marine bristle

worm which is bluish-white with iridescent pink shading and a grey dorsal line.
● *Nephtys hombergi*, family Nephtyidae.

whitey ▶ noun (pl. **-eys**) informal, derogatory used by black people to refer to a white person.
■ [in sing.] white people collectively: *her ambitions are thwarted by whitey in publishing.*
▶ adjective [usu. in combination] with a whitish tinge: *a whitey-grey colour.*

whither archaic or poetic/literary ▶ interrogative adverb to what place or state: *whither are we bound?* | *they asked people whither they would emigrate.*
■ what is the likely future of: *whither modern architecture?*
▶ relative adverb to which (with reference to a place): *the barbecue had been set up by the lake, whither Matthew and Sara were conducted.*
■ to whatever place; wherever: *we could drive whither we pleased.*
– ORIGIN Old English *hwider*, from the Germanic base of **WHICH**; compare with **HITHER** and **THITHER**.

whithersoever ▶ relative adverb archaic wherever: *she was free to drift whithersoever she chose.*

whiting[1] ▶ noun (pl. same) 1 a slender-bodied marine fish of the cod family, which lives in shallow European waters and is a commercially important food fish.
● *Merlangius merlangus*, family Gadidae.
2 [usu. with modifier] any of a number of similar marine fishes, in particular:
● a fish of the Indo-Pacific (family Sillaginidae), including the commercially important *Sillaginoides punctatus* of Australia.
● the northern kingfish of eastern North America.
– ORIGIN Middle English: from Middle Dutch *wijting*, from *wijt* 'white'.

whiting[2] ▶ noun [mass noun] ground chalk used for purposes such as whitewashing and cleaning metal plate.

Whitlam /ˈwɪtləm/, (Edward) Gough (b.1916), Australian Labor statesman, Prime Minister 1972–5. Whitlam ended compulsory military service and relaxed the immigration laws. In 1975 he refused to call a general election and became the first elected Prime Minister to be dismissed by the British Crown.

whitleather ▶ noun [mass noun] leather that has been prepared by dressing with alum and salt so as to retain its natural colour.
– ORIGIN late Middle English: from **WHITE** + **LEATHER**.

Whitley Council /ˈwɪtli/ ▶ noun a negotiating body for discussing and settling matters of industrial relations, pay and conditions, and related issues.
– ORIGIN early 20th cent.: named after John H. Whitley (1866–1935), chairman of a committee (1916) which recommended such bodies.

whitlow /ˈwɪtloʊ/ ▶ noun an abscess in the soft tissue near a fingernail or toenail.
– ORIGIN late Middle English (also as *whitflaw*, *-flow*), apparently from **WHITE** + **FLAW**[1] in the sense 'crack', but perhaps related to Dutch *fijt* 'whitlow'.

whitlow-grass ▶ noun [mass noun] a dwarf European plant with a rosette of leaves at the base of a low flowering stem, growing widely on rocks and walls. It was formerly believed to cure whitlows.
● Genus *Erophila*, family Cruciferae: several species, in particular *E. verna*.

Whitman, Walt (1819–92), American poet. In 1855 he published the free verse collection *Leaves of Grass*, incorporating 'I Sing the Body Electric' and 'Song of Myself'; eight further editions followed in Whitman's lifetime.

Whitney, Eli (1765–1825), American inventor. He conceived the idea of mass-producing interchangeable parts. This he applied in his fulfilment of a contract (1797) to supply muskets.

Whitney, Mount a mountain in the Sierra Nevada in California. Rising to 4,418 m (14,495 ft), it is the highest peak in the continental US outside Alaska.

Whitsun /ˈwɪts(ə)n/ ▶ noun Whitsuntide.
– ORIGIN Middle English: from **WHIT SUNDAY**, reduced as if from *Whitsun Day*.

Whit Sunday ▶ noun the seventh Sunday after Easter, a Christian festival commemorating the descent of the Holy Spirit at Pentecost (Acts 2). Also called **PENTECOST**.

– ORIGIN late Old English *Hwīta Sunnandæg*, literally 'white Sunday', probably with reference to the white robes of those newly baptized at Pentecost.

Whitsuntide /ˈwɪts(ə)ntaɪd/ ▶ noun the weekend or week including Whit Sunday.

Whittier /ˈwɪtɪə/, John Greenleaf (1807–92), American poet and abolitionist. He is best known for his poems on rural themes, especially 'Snow-Bound' (1866).

Whittington, Dick (d.1423), English merchant and Lord Mayor of London; full name *Sir Richard Whittington*. Whittington was a mercer who became Lord Mayor three times (1397–8; 1406–7; 1419–20). The legend of his early life as a poor orphan was first recorded in 1605.

Whittle, Sir Frank (1907–96), English aeronautical engineer, test pilot, and inventor of the jet aircraft engine. He took out the first patent for a turbojet engine in 1930 and in 1941 the first flight using Whittle's jet engine was made.

whittle ▶ verb [with obj.] carve (wood) into an object by repeatedly cutting small slices from it.
■ carve (an object) from wood in this way. ■ (**whittle something away/down**) reduce something in size, amount, or extent by a gradual series of steps: *the shortlist of fifteen was whittled down to five* | [no obj.] *the censors had whittled away at the racy dialogue.*
– ORIGIN mid 16th cent.: from dialect *whittle* 'knife'.

Whitworth ▶ noun [as modifier] denoting a standard series of screw threads in imperial sizes.
– ORIGIN late 19th cent.: from the name of Sir Joseph Whitworth (1803–1887), English engineer.

whiz-bang (also **whizz-bang**) informal ▶ noun (especially during the First World War) a low-velocity shell.
■ chiefly N. Amer. a resounding success: *Dan was a whiz-bang at mechanical things.*
▶ adjective chiefly N. Amer. lively or sensational; fast-paced: *a whizz-bang publicity campaign.*

whizz (also **whiz**) ▶ verb (**whizzed**, **whizzing**) 1 [no obj., with adverbial of direction] move quickly through the air with a whistling or whooshing sound: *the Iraqi missiles whizzed past* | figurative *the weeks whizzed by.*
■ (**whizz through**) do or deal with quickly: *Audrey would whizz through a few chores in the shop.* ■ [with obj. and adverbial of direction] cause (someone or something) to move or go fast: *Derek had whizzed them round the factory.* ■ [with obj.] cause to rotate in a machine, especially a food processor: *whiz the mixture to a smooth paste.*
2 [no obj.] informal urinate.
▶ noun 1 a whistling or whooshing sound made by something moving fast through the air.
■ [in sing.] informal a fast movement or tour: *a quick whizz around the research-and-development facility.*
2 (also **wiz**) informal a person who is extremely clever at something: *fancy yourself as a whizz at puzzles?* [ORIGIN: early 20th cent.: influenced by **WIZARD**.]
3 N. Amer. informal an act of urinating.
4 [mass noun] Brit. informal amphetamines.
– ORIGIN mid 16th cent.: imitative.

whizz-kid (also **whiz-kid**) ▶ noun informal a young person who is outstandingly skilful or successful at something: *a computer whizz-kid.*

whizzo (also **wizzo**) ▶ adjective [often as exclamation] informal, dated excellent.

whizzy ▶ adjective technologically innovative or advanced: *boggle your eyes at the whizzy visuals.*

WHO ▶ abbreviation for World Health Organization.

who ▶ pronoun 1 [interrogative pronoun] what or which person or people: *who is that woman?* | *I wonder who that letter was from.*
2 [relative pronoun] used to introduce a clause giving further information about a person or people previously mentioned: *Joan Fontaine plays the mouse who married the playboy.*
■ archaic the person that; whoever: *who holds the sea, perforce doth hold the land.*
– PHRASES **as who should say** archaic as if to say: *he meekly bowed to him, as who should say 'Proceed.'* **who am I** (or **are you, is he**, etc.) **to do something** what right or authority do I (or you, he, etc.) have to do something: *who am I to object?* **who goes there?** see **GO**[1].
– ORIGIN Old English *hwā*, of Germanic origin; related to Dutch *wie* and German *wer*.

USAGE 1 A continuing debate in English usage is the question of when to use **who** and when to use **whom**. According to formal grammar, **who** forms the subjective case and so should be used in subject position in a sentence, as in *who decided this?* The form **whom**, on the other hand, forms the objective case and so should be used in object position in a sentence, as in *whom do you think we should support?*; *to whom do you wish to speak?* Although there are some speakers who still use **who** and **whom** according to the rules of formal grammar as stated here, there are many more who rarely use **whom** at all; its use has retreated steadily and is now largely restricted to formal contexts. The normal practice in modern English is to use **who** instead of **whom** (and, where applicable, to put the preposition at the end of the sentence): *who do you wish to speak to?*; *who do you think we should support?* Such uses are today broadly accepted in standard English. In the British National Corpus, for example, **who** is around fifteen times more frequently used for the objective case than **whom**.
2 On the use of **who** and **that** in relative clauses see **usage** at **THAT**.

whoa /wəʊ/ ▶ **exclamation** used as a command to a horse to make it stop or slow down.
■ informal used as a greeting, to express surprise or interest, or to command attention: *whoa, that's huge!*
– ORIGIN late Middle English: variant of **HO**[2].

who'd ▶ **contraction of** ■ who had: *some Americans who'd arrived after lunch.* ■ who would: *he knew many of the people who'd be there.*

whodunnit (US **whodunit**) ▶ **noun** informal a story or play about a murder in which the identity of the murderer is not revealed until the end.
– ORIGIN 1930s: from *who done it?*, non-standard form of *who did it?*

whoe'er /huːˈɛː/ poetic/literary ▶ **contraction of** whoever.

whoever ▶ **relative pronoun** the person or people who; any person who: *whoever wins should be guaranteed an Olympic place.*
■ regardless of who: *come out, whoever you are.*
▶ **interrogative pronoun** used for emphasis instead of 'who' in questions, typically expressing surprise or confusion: *whoever would want to make up something like that?*

USAGE In the emphatic use (*whoever does he think he is?*) **whoever** is also written as two words. See **usage** at **HOWEVER**.

whole ▶ **adjective 1** [attrib.] all of; entire: *he spent the whole day walking | she wasn't telling the whole truth.*
■ used to emphasize a large extent or number: *disputes on a whole range of issues.*
2 in an unbroken or undamaged state; in one piece: *owls usually swallow their prey whole.*
■ [attrib.] (of milk, blood, or other substances) with no part removed. ■ [predic.] healthy: *all people should be whole in body, mind, and spirit.*
▶ **noun 1** a thing that is complete in itself: *the subjects of the curriculum form a coherent whole.*
2 (**the whole**) all of something: *the effects will last for the whole of his life.*
▶ **adverb** [as submodifier] informal used to emphasize the novelty or distinctness of something: *the man who's given a whole new meaning to the term 'cowboy'.*
– PHRASES **as a whole** as a single unit and not as separate parts; in general: *a healthy economy is in the best interests of society as a whole.* **in whole** entirely or fully: *a number of stone churches survive in whole or in part.* **in the whole** (**wide**) **world** anywhere; of all: *he was the nicest person in the whole world.* **on the whole** taking everything into account; in general. **the whole nine yards** informal, chiefly N. Amer. everything possible or available: *send in the troops, aircraft, nuclear submarine experts, the whole nine yards.*
– DERIVATIVES **wholeness** noun.
– ORIGIN Old English *hāl*, of Germanic origin; related to Dutch *heel* and German *heil*, also to **HAIL**[2]. The spelling with *wh-* (reflecting a dialect pronunciation with *w-*) first appeared in the 15th cent.

whole cloth ▶ **noun** [mass noun] cloth of the full size as manufactured, as distinguished from a piece cut off for a garment or other item.
– PHRASES **out of** (**the**) **whole cloth** N. Amer. informal totally false: *she created conspiracy theories out of the whole cloth.*

wholefood ▶ **noun** [mass noun] (also **wholefoods**) Brit. food that has been processed or refined as little as possible and is free from additives or other artificial substances.

wholegrain ▶ **adjective** made with or containing whole unprocessed grains of something: *wholegrain mustard.*

wholehearted ▶ **adjective** showing or characterized by complete sincerity and commitment: *you have my wholehearted support.*
– DERIVATIVES **wholeheartedly** adverb, **wholeheartedness** noun.

whole-life ▶ **adjective** [attrib.] relating to or denoting a life insurance policy that pays a specified amount only on the death of the person insured.

wholemeal Brit. ▶ **adjective** denoting flour or bread made from whole grains of wheat, including the husk or outer layer.
▶ **noun** [mass noun] wholemeal bread or flour.

whole note ▶ **noun** Music, chiefly N. Amer. a semibreve.

whole number ▶ **noun** a number without fractions; an integer.

wholesale ▶ **noun** [mass noun] the selling of goods in large quantities to be retailed by others.
▶ **adverb** being sold in such a way: *bottles from this region sell wholesale at about £72 a case.*
■ on a large scale: *the safety clauses seem to have been taken wholesale from union documents.*
▶ **adjective** done on a large scale; extensive: *the wholesale destruction of Iraqi communications.*
▶ **verb** [with obj.] sell (goods) in large quantities at low prices to be retailed by others.
– DERIVATIVES **wholesaler** noun.
– ORIGIN late Middle English: originally as *by whole sale* 'in large quantities'.

wholescale ▶ **adjective** another term for **WHOLESALE**.

wholesome ▶ **adjective** conducive to or suggestive of good health and physical well-being: *the food is plentiful and very wholesome.*
■ conducive to or promoting moral well-being: *good wholesome fun.*
– DERIVATIVES **wholesomely** adverb, **wholesomeness** noun.
– ORIGIN Middle English: probably already in Old English (see **WHOLE**, **-SOME**[1]).

whole step ▶ **noun** Music an interval of a (whole) tone.

whole-time ▶ **adjective** & **adverb** another term for **FULL-TIME**.
– DERIVATIVES **whole-timer** noun.

whole-tone scale ▶ **noun** Music a scale consisting entirely of intervals of a tone, with no semitones.

wholewheat ▶ **noun** [mass noun] [usu. as modifier] whole grains of wheat including the husk or outer layer: *wholewheat pasta.*

wholism ▶ **noun** variant spelling of **HOLISM**.

wholly /ˈhəʊlli, ˈhəʊli/ ▶ **adverb** entirely; fully: *she found herself given over wholly to sensation | [as submodifier] the distinction is not wholly clear.*
– ORIGIN Middle English: probably already in Old English (see **WHOLE**, **-LY**[2]).

wholly-owned ▶ **adjective** denoting a company all of whose shares are owned by another company.

whom ▶ **pronoun** used instead of 'who' as the object of a verb or preposition: [interrogative pronoun] *whom did he marry?* | [relative pronoun] *her mother, in whom she confided, said it wasn't easy for her.*

USAGE On the use of **who** and **whom**, see **usage** at **WHO**.

whomever ▶ **pronoun** chiefly formal or poetic/literary used instead of 'whoever' as the object of a verb or preposition: *I'll sing whatever I like to whomever I like.*

whomp /wɒmp/ informal ▶ **verb** [with obj.] strike heavily; thump: *whomp the club head on the ground* | [no obj.] *giant comet chunks whomped into Jupiter.*
■ defeat decisively: *that was our last fight and I whomped him good.*
▶ **noun** a dull heavy sound.
▶ **whomp something up** N. Amer. produce something quickly: *I might whomp up a couple of gallons of spaghetti sauce.*
– ORIGIN 1920s: imitative.

whomso ▶ **pronoun** archaic used instead of 'whoso' as the object of a verb or preposition: *whomso thou meetest, say thou this to each.*

whomsoever ▶ **relative pronoun** formal used instead of 'whosoever' as the object of a verb or preposition: *they supported his right to marry whomsoever he chose.*

whoomph /wʊm(p)f/ (also **whoomp** /wʊmp/) ▶ **noun** a sudden loud sound, such as that made by a muffled or distant explosion: *the distant whoomph of anti-aircraft shells bursting.*
– ORIGIN 1950s: imitative.

whoop /huːp, wuːp/ ▶ **noun 1** a loud cry of joy or excitement.
■ a hooting cry or sound: *the whoop of fast-approaching sirens.* ■ a long rasping indrawn breath, typically of someone with whooping cough.
2 (in motorcycling or cycling) a bump or dip on an off-road racetrack or rally course.
▶ **verb** [no obj.] give or make a whoop: *all at once they were **whooping with** laughter.*
– PHRASES **not give** (or **care**) **a whoop** US informal, dated be totally indifferent. **whoop it up** informal enjoy oneself or celebrate in a noisy way. ■ US create or stir up excitement or enthusiasm.
– ORIGIN Middle English: probably imitative.

whoopee informal ▶ **exclamation** /wʊˈpiː/ expressing wild excitement or joy.
▶ **noun** /ˈwʊpi/ [mass noun] wild revelry: *hours of parades and whoopee.*
■ [count noun] dated a wild party.
– PHRASES **make whoopee 1** celebrate wildly. **2** have sexual intercourse.

whoopee cushion ▶ **noun** a rubber cushion that makes a sound like the breaking of wind when someone sits on it.

whooper /ˈhuːpə, ˈw-/ (also **whooper swan**) ▶ **noun** a large migratory swan with a black and yellow bill and a loud trumpeting call, breeding in northern Eurasia and Greenland.
• *Cygnus cygnus*, family Anatidae.

whooping cough /ˈhuːpɪŋ/ ▶ **noun** [mass noun] a contagious bacterial disease chiefly affecting children, characterized by convulsive coughs followed by a whoop. Also called **PERTUSSIS**.
• The organism responsible is *Bordetella pertussis*, a Gram-negative bacterium intermediate between a coccus and a bacillus.

whooping crane /ˈhuːpɪŋ, ˈw-/ ▶ **noun** a large mainly white crane with a trumpeting call, breeding in central Canada and now endangered.
• *Grus americana*, family Gruidae.

whoops (also **whoops-a-daisy**) ▶ **exclamation** informal expressing mild dismay or regret (used when someone has had an accident or made a mistake): *Whoops! I nearly dropped it.*
– ORIGIN 1920s: probably an alteration of **UPSY-DAISY**; compare with **OOPS**.

whoopsie /ˈwʊpsi, ˈwuː-/ ▶ **noun** (pl. **-ies**) Brit. informal used euphemistically to refer to a piece of excrement.

whoosh /wʊʃ, wuːʃ/ (also **woosh**) ▶ **verb** [no obj., with adverbial of direction] move quickly or suddenly with a rushing sound: *a train whooshed by* | [as adj. **whooshing**] *there was a loud whooshing noise.*
■ [with obj. and adverbial or complement] move (something) in such a way: *he whooshed the curtains open.*
▶ **noun** a sudden movement accompanied by a rushing sound: *there was a big whoosh of air.*
▶ **exclamation** used to imitate such a movement and sound.
– ORIGIN mid 19th cent.: imitative.

whop /wɒp/ (chiefly US also **whap**) informal ▶ **verb** (**whopped**, **whopping**) [with obj.] hit hard: *Smith whopped him on the nose.*
▶ **noun** a heavy blow or the sound of such a blow.
■ the regular pulsing sound of a helicopter rotor.
– ORIGIN late Middle English (in the sense 'take or put sharply'): variant of dialect *wap* 'strike', of unknown origin.

whopper ▶ **noun** informal a thing that is extremely or unusually large: *the novel is a 1,079 page whopper.*
■ a gross or blatant lie.

whopping ▶ **adjective** informal very large: *a whopping £74 million loss* | [as submodifier] *a whopping great lie.*

whore ▶ **noun** derogatory a prostitute.
■ a promiscuous woman.
▶ **verb** [no obj.] (of a woman) work as a prostitute: *she spent her life whoring for dangerous men.*
■ [often as noun **whoring**] (of a man) use the services of prostitutes: *he lived by night, indulging in his two hobbies, whoring and eating.* ■ debase oneself by doing something for unworthy motives, typically to make money: *he had never whored after money.*
– PHRASES **the Whore of Babylon** derogatory the

W

Roman Catholic Church. [ORIGIN: with biblical allusion to Rev. 17:1, 5, etc.).]
– ORIGIN late Old English *hōre*, of Germanic origin; related to Dutch *hoer* and German *Hure*, from an Indo-European root shared by Latin *carus* 'dear'.

whoredom ▶ **noun** [mass noun] dated prostitution or other promiscuous sexual activity.

whorehouse ▶ **noun** informal a brothel.

whoremaster ▶ **noun** archaic a whoremonger.

whoremonger ▶ **noun** archaic a person who has dealings with prostitutes, especially a sexually promiscuous man.

whoreson /ˈhɔːs(ə)n/ ▶ **noun** archaic an unpleasant or greatly disliked person.
– ORIGIN Middle English: from **WHORE** + **SON**, suggested by Anglo-Norman French *fiz a putain*.

Whorf /wɔːf/, Benjamin Lee (1897–1941), American linguist and insurance worker, known for his contribution to the Sapir-Whorf hypothesis. A student of linguistics in his spare time, Whorf studied Hopi and other American Indian languages and attended Edward Sapir's courses at Yale.

whorish /ˈhɔːrɪʃ/ ▶ **adjective** belonging to or characteristic of a prostitute.
– DERIVATIVES **whorishly** adverb, **whorishness** noun.

whorl /wɔːl, wəːl/ ▶ **noun** a coil or ring, in particular:
■ Zoology each of the turns or convolutions in the shell of a gastropod or ammonoid mollusc. ■ Botany a set of leaves, flowers, or branches springing from the stem at the same level and encircling it. ■ Botany (in a flower) each of the sets of organs, especially the petals and sepals, arranged concentrically round the receptacle. ■ a complete circle in a fingerprint. ■ chiefly historical a small wheel or pulley in a spinning wheel, spinning machine, or spindle.
▶ **verb** [no obj.] poetic/literary spiral or move in a twisted and convoluted fashion: *the dances are kinetic kaleidoscopes where steps whorl into wildness.*
– DERIVATIVES **whorled** adjective.
– ORIGIN late Middle English (denoting a small flywheel): apparently a variant of **WHIRL**, influenced by Old English *wharve* 'whorl of a spindle'.

whortleberry /ˈwəːt(ə)lˌb(ə)ri, -ˈbɛri/ ▶ **noun** a bilberry.
– ORIGIN late 16th cent.: dialect variant of Middle English *hurtleberry*, of unknown origin.

who's ▶ **contraction of** ■ who is: *who's that?* ■ who has: *who's done the reading?*

USAGE A common written mistake is to confuse **who's** with **whose**. The form **who's** represents a contraction of 'who is' or 'who has', while **whose** is a possessive pronoun or determiner used in questions, as in ***whose** is this?* or ***whose** turn is it?*

whose ▶ **interrogative possessive determiner** & **pronoun** belonging to or associated with which person: [as determiner] *whose round is it?* | [as pronoun] *a Mini was parked at the kerb and Juliet wondered whose it was.*
▶ **relative possessive determiner** of whom or which (used to indicate that the following noun belongs to or is associated with the person or thing mentioned in the previous clause): *he's a man whose opinion I respect.*
– ORIGIN Old English *hwæs*, genitive of *hwā* 'who' and *hwæt* 'what'.

whosesoever ▶ **relative pronoun** & **determiner** formal whoever's: [as determiner] *the story will have been told you by your fathers, whosesoever sons you are.*

whosever ▶ **relative pronoun** & **determiner** rare belonging to or associated with whichever person; whoever's: [as pronoun] *the choice, whosever it was, is interesting* | [as determiner] *she dialled whosever number she could still remember.*

whoso ▶ **pronoun** archaic term for **WHOEVER**: *whoso took such things into account was a fool.*
– ORIGIN Middle English: shortening Old English *swā hwā swā* 'so who so'.

whosoever ▶ **pronoun** formal term for **WHOEVER**: *a belief that whosoever steals will be blinded.*

who's who ▶ **noun** a list or directory of facts about notable people.

wh-question ▶ **noun** a question in English introduced by a wh-word, that requires information in answer, rather than *yes* or *no*.

whump /wʌmp, wʊmp/ ▶ **noun** [usu. in sing.] a dull thudding sound: *the horse fell with a great whump.*
▶ **verb** [no obj., with adverbial] make such a sound: *he pitched a snowball that whumped into the car.*
■ [with obj.] strike (something) heavily with such a sound: *she began whumping him on his lower back.*
– ORIGIN late 19th cent.: imitative.

whup /wʌp/ ▶ **verb** (**whupped**, **whupping**) [with obj.] informal, chiefly N. Amer. beat; thrash: *they would whup him and send him home.*
■ defeat convincingly: *if you lined up our guys against the 49ers, they'd get whupped.*
– ORIGIN late 19th cent.: variant of **WHIP**.

wh-word ▶ **noun** Grammar any of a class of English words used to introduce questions and relative clauses. The main wh-words are *why, who, which, what, where, when,* and *how*.

why ▶ **interrogative adverb** for what reason or purpose: *why did he do it?*
■ [with negative] used to make or agree to a suggestion: *why don't I give you a lift?*
▶ **relative adverb** (with reference to a reason) on account of which; for which: ***the reason why** flu jabs need repeating every year is that the virus changes.*
■ the reason for which: *each has faced similar hardships, and perhaps that is why they are friends.*
▶ **exclamation 1** expressing surprise or indignation: *Why, that's absurd!*
2 used to add emphasis to a response: *'You think so?' 'Why, yes.'*
▶ **noun** (pl. **whys**) a reason or explanation: *the **whys and wherefores** of these procedures need to be explained to students.*
– PHRASES **why so?** for what reason or purpose?
– ORIGIN Old English *hwī, hwȳ* 'by what cause', instrumental case of *hwæt* 'what', of Germanic origin.

Whyalla /wʌɪˈalə/ a steel-manufacturing town on the coast of South Australia, on the Spencer Gulf; pop. 25,525 (1991).

whydah /ˈwɪdə/ (also **whyda**) ▶ **noun** an African weaver bird, the male of which has a black back and a very long black tail used in display flight.
● Genus *Vidua*, family Ploceidae: several species.
■ another term for **WIDOWBIRD**.
– ORIGIN late 18th cent. (originally *widow-bird*): alteration by association with *Whidah* (now Ouidah), a town in Benin.

Whymper /ˈwɪmpə/, Edward (1840–1911), English mountaineer. After seven attempts he finally succeeded in climbing the Matterhorn in 1865, but on the way down four of his fellow climbers fell to their deaths.

WI ▶ **abbreviation for** ■ West Indies. ■ Wisconsin (in official postal use). ■ Brit. Women's Institute.

wibble ▶ **verb** [no obj.] informal **1** another term for **WOBBLE**: *his chin was wibbling over the edge of his violin.*
2 speak or write, especially at great length, without saying anything important or useful: *why was he allowed to wibble on about the game?*
– DERIVATIVES **wibbly** adjective.
– ORIGIN late 19th cent.: independent usage of the first element of the reduplication *wibble-wobble*.

Wicca /ˈwɪkə/ ▶ **noun** [mass noun] the religious cult of modern witchcraft, especially an initiatory tradition founded in England in the mid 20th century and claiming its origins in pre-Christian pagan religions.
– DERIVATIVES **Wiccan** adjective & noun.
– ORIGIN representing Old English *wicca* 'witch'.

Wichita /ˈwɪtʃɪtɔː/ a city in southern Kansas, on the River Arkansas; pop. 304,000 (1990).

wick[1] ▶ **noun** a strip of porous material up which liquid fuel is drawn by capillary action to the flame in a candle, lamp, or lighter.
■ Medicine a gauze strip inserted in a wound to drain it.
▶ **verb** [with obj.] absorb or draw off (liquid) by capillary action: *these excellent socks will **wick away** the sweat* | [no obj.] *synthetics with hollow fibres that wick well.*
– PHRASES **dip one's wick** vulgar slang (of a man) have sexual intercourse. **get on someone's wick** Brit. informal annoy someone.
– ORIGIN Old English *wēoce*, of West Germanic origin; related to Dutch *wiek* and German *Wieche* 'wick yarn'.

wick[2] ▶ **noun 1** [in place names] a town, hamlet, or district: *Hampton Wick* | *Warwick.*
2 dialect a dairy farm.
– ORIGIN Old English *wīc* 'dwelling place', probably based on Latin *vicus* 'street, village'.

wick[3] ▶ **adjective** N. English quick, lively, or active: *Martha's approaching her century and as wick as a flea.*
– ORIGIN mid 18th cent.: variant of **QUICK**.

wicked ▶ **adjective** (**wickeder**, **wickedest**) evil or morally wrong: *a wicked and unscrupulous politician.*
■ intended to or capable of harming someone or something: *he should be punished for his wicked driving.* ■ informal extremely unpleasant: *despite the sun, the wind outside was wicked.* ■ playfully mischievous: *Ben has a wicked sense of humour.* ■ informal excellent; wonderful: *Sophie makes wicked cakes.*
– PHRASES **no rest** (or **peace**) **for the wicked** humorous the speaker's heavy workload or lack of tranquillity is due to their sinful life. [ORIGIN: with biblical allusion to Isa. 48:22, 57:21.]
– DERIVATIVES **wickedly** adverb, **wickedness** noun.
– ORIGIN Middle English: probably from Old English *wicca* 'witch' + **-ED**[1].

wicker ▶ **noun** [mass noun] pliable twigs, typically of willow, plaited or woven to make items such as furniture and baskets: [as modifier] *a wicker chair.*
– ORIGIN Middle English: of Scandinavian origin; compare with Swedish *viker* 'willow'; related to *vika* 'to bend'.

wickerwork ▶ **noun** [mass noun] wicker.
■ furniture or other items made of wicker.

wicket ▶ **noun 1** Cricket each of the sets of three stumps with two bails across the top at either end of the pitch, defended by a batsman.
■ the prepared strip of ground between these two sets of stumps. ■ the dismissal of a batsman; each of ten dismissals regarded as marking a division of a side's innings: *Darlington won by four wickets.*
2 (also **wicket door** or **wicket gate**) a small door or gate, especially one beside or in a larger one.
■ US an opening in a door or wall, often fitted with glass or a grille and used for selling tickets or a similar purpose. ■ US a croquet hoop.
– PHRASES **at the wicket** Cricket **1** batting: *the batsman remained at the wicket.* **2** by the wicketkeeper: *he was **caught at the wicket** chasing a wide one.* **keep wicket** Cricket be a wicketkeeper. **lose a wicket** Cricket (of the batting side) have a batsman dismissed. **a sticky wicket** Cricket a pitch that has been drying after rain and is difficult to bat on. ■ [in sing.] informal a tricky or awkward situation: *I might be **on a sticky wicket** if I used that line.* **over the wicket** Cricket (referring to which side of the wicket a bowler runs when bowling) to the left of the wicket if a right-handed bowler and the right of the wicket if a left-handed bowler. **round the wicket** Cricket (referring to which side of the wicket a bowler runs when bowling) to the right of the wicket if a right-handed bowler and the left of the wicket if a left-handed bowler. **take a wicket** Cricket (of a bowler or a fielding side) dismiss a batsman.
– ORIGIN Middle English (in the sense 'small door or grille'): from Anglo-Norman French and Old Northern French *wiket*; origin uncertain, usually referred to the Germanic root of Old Norse *víkja* 'to turn, move'. Cricket senses date from the late 17th cent.

wicketkeeper ▶ **noun** Cricket a fielder stationed close behind a batsman's wicket and typically equipped with gloves and pads.
– DERIVATIVES **wicketkeeping** noun.

wickiup /ˈwɪkɪʌp/ ▶ **noun** an American Indian hut consisting of an oval frame covered with brushwood or grass.
– ORIGIN Algonquian.

Wicklow /ˈwɪkləʊ/ a county of the Republic of Ireland, in the east, in the province of Leinster.
■ its county town, on the Irish Sea; pop. 5,850 (1991).

widdershins /ˈwɪdəʃɪnz/ (also **withershins**) ▶ **adverb** chiefly Scottish in a direction contrary to the sun's course, considered as unlucky; anticlockwise.
– ORIGIN early 16th cent.: from Middle Low German *weddersins*, from Middle High German *widersinnes*, from *wider* 'against' + *sin* 'direction'; the second element was associated with Scots *sin* 'sun'.

widdle informal ▶ **verb** [no obj.] urinate.
▶ **noun** an act of urinating.
■ [mass noun] urine.
– ORIGIN 1950s: alteration of **PIDDLE**.

wide ▶ **adjective** (**wider**, **widest**) **1** of great or more than average width: *a wide road.*
■ (after a measurement and in questions) from side to side: *it measures 15 cm long by 12 cm wide* | *how wide do you think this house is?* ■ open to the full extent: *wide eyes.* ■ considerable: *tax revenues have undershot Treasury projections by a wide margin.*

2 including a great variety of people or things: *a wide range of opinion.*
■spread among a large number of people or over a large area: *wider share ownership.* ■[in combination] extending over the whole of: *an industry-wide trend.*
3 at a considerable or specified distance from a point or mark: *the ball was* **wide of** *the leg stump.*
■(especially in soccer) at or near the side of the field: *he played in a wide left position.*
▶**adverb 1** to the full extent: *his eyes opened wide.*
2 far from a particular point or mark: *he hit the safety fence after a local rider inside him drifted wide.*
■(especially in football) at or near the side of the field: *he will play wide on the right.*
▶**noun** Cricket a ball that is judged to be too wide of the stumps for the batsman to play, for which an extra is awarded to the batting side.
– PHRASES **give someone/thing a wide berth** see **BERTH**. **wide awake** fully awake. **wide of the mark** a long way away from an intended target. ■ inaccurate: *Dickie's memory is somewhat wide of the mark.* **wide open 1** stretching over an outdoor expanse: *the wide open spaces of Montana.* **2** offering a great variety of opportunities: *suddenly the whole world was* **wide open to** *her.* **3** (of a contest) of which the outcome is not predictable. **4** vulnerable, especially to attack.
– DERIVATIVES **wideness** noun, **widish** adjective.
– ORIGIN Old English *wīd* 'spacious, extensive', *wīde* 'over a large area', of Germanic origin.

wide-angle ▶**adjective** (of a lens) having a short focal length and hence a field covering a wide angle.

wide area network (abbrev.: **WAN**) ▶**noun** a computer network in which the computers connected may be far apart, generally having a radius of more than 1 km.

wideawake ▶**noun** a soft felt hat with a low crown and wide brim.
– ORIGIN mid 19th cent.: punningly so named, because the hat does not have a nap.

wide ball ▶**noun** Cricket another term for **WIDE**.

wide-band ▶**adjective** (of a radio, or other device or activity involving broadcasting) having or using a wide band of frequencies or wavelengths.

widebody (also **wide-bodied**) ▶**adjective** [attrib.] having a wide body, in particular:
■(of a large jet aeroplane) having a wide fuselage. ■ chiefly US (of a tennis racket) having a wide head.
▶**noun** (pl. **-ies**) **1** a large jet aeroplane with a wide fuselage.
2 US a tennis racket with a wide head.
3 US informal a large, heavily built person, especially one who plays a team sport.

wide boy ▶**noun** Brit. informal a man involved in petty criminal activities.

wide-eyed ▶**adjective** having one's eyes wide open in amazement.
■figurative innocent: *people think of Pinocchio as the wide-eyed, sweet-voiced puppet.*
▶**adverb** with one's eyes wide open in amazement: *we looked at each other wide-eyed.*

widely ▶**adverb 1** over a wide area or at a wide interval: *he smiled widely and held out a hand | a tall man with widely spaced eyes.*
■to a large degree in nature or character (used to describe considerable variation or difference): *lending policies vary widely between different banks |* [as submodifier] *people in widely different circumstances.*
2 over a large area or range; extensively: *Deborah has travelled widely |* [as submodifier] *she was widely read.*
■by many people or in many places: *credit cards are widely accepted.*

widen ▶**verb** make or become wider: [with obj.] *the incentive to dredge and widen the river |* [no obj.] *his grin widened | the lane* **widened out** *into a small clearing.*
– DERIVATIVES **widener** noun.

wideout ▶**noun** a wide receiver.

wide-ranging ▶**adjective** covering an extensive range: *a wide-ranging discussion.*

wide receiver ▶**noun** American Football an offensive player positioned away from the line, used primarily as a pass receiver.

widescreen ▶**adjective** [attrib.] designed with or for a screen presenting a wide field of vision in relation to its height: *a widescreen TV.*
▶**noun** a cinema or television screen presenting a wide field of vision in relation to its height.
■[mass noun] a film format presenting a wide field of vision in relation to height.

widespread ▶**adjective** found or distributed over a large area or number of people: *there was widespread support for the war.*

widgeon ▶**noun** variant spelling of **WIGEON**.

widger /ˈwɪdʒə/ ▶**noun** a spatula used in gardening to transplant seedlings.
– ORIGIN 1950s: a word from a nonsense definition used in a series of memory tests.

widget /ˈwɪdʒɪt/ ▶**noun** informal a gadget or mechanical device, in particular:
■Computing a component of a user interface which operates in a particular way. ■ (in some beer cans) a plastic device which introduces nitrogen into the beer, giving it a creamy head in imitation of draught beer.
– ORIGIN 1930s (originally US): perhaps an alteration of **GADGET**.

Widnes /ˈwɪdnɪs/ a town on the River Mersey in Cheshire, NW England; pop. 55,930 (1981).

widow ▶**noun 1** a woman who has lost her husband by death and has not married again.
■[with modifier] humorous a woman whose husband is often away participating in a specified sport or activity: *my wife has been a golf widow for the last 30 years.*
2 Printing a last word or short last line of a paragraph falling at the top of a page or column and considered undesirable.
3 a widowbird.
▶**verb** [with obj.] [usu. as adj. **widowed**] make into a widow or widower: *she had to care for her widowed mother.*
– ORIGIN Old English *widewe*, from an Indo-European root meaning 'be empty'; compare with Sanskrit *vidh* 'be destitute', Latin *viduus* 'bereft, widowed', and Greek *ēitheos* 'unmarried man'.

widowbird ▶**noun** an African weaver bird, the male of which has mainly black plumage and typically a long tail used in leaping displays.
● Genus *Euplectes*, family Ploceidae: several species.
■another term for **WHYDAH**.

widower ▶**noun** a man who has lost his wife by death and has not married again.

widow finch ▶**noun** S. African an indigobird or a widowbird.

widowhood ▶**noun** [mass noun] the state or period of being a widow or widower.

widow-maker ▶**noun** informal a thing with the potential to kill men.
■Canadian a dead branch caught precariously high in a tree which may fall on a person below.

widow's cruse ▶**noun** [in sing.] an apparently small supply that proves inexhaustible.
– ORIGIN with biblical allusion to 1 Kings 17:10–16.

widow's mite ▶**noun** a small monetary contribution from someone who is poor.
– ORIGIN with biblical allusion to Mark 12:43.

widow's peak ▶**noun** a V-shaped growth of hair towards the centre of the forehead, especially one left by a receding hairline in a man.

widow's walk ▶**noun** N. Amer. a railed or balustraded platform built on a roof, originally in early New England houses, typically for providing an unimpeded view of the sea.
– ORIGIN 1930s: with reference to its use as a viewpoint for the hoped-for return of a seafaring husband.

widow's weeds ▶**plural noun** black clothes worn by a widow in mourning.
– ORIGIN early 18th cent. (earlier as *mourning weeds*): *weeds* (obsolete in the general sense 'garments') is from Old English *wǣd(e)*, of Germanic origin.

width /wɪtθ, wɪdθ/ ▶**noun** [mass noun] the measurement or extent of something from side to side; the lesser of two or the least of three dimensions of a body: *the yard was about seven feet* **in width** | [count noun] *the shoe comes in a variety of widths.*
■[count noun] a piece of something at its full extent from side to side: *a single* **width of** *hardboard.* ■ [count noun] the sideways extent of a swimming pool as a measure of the distance swum. ■ the quality of covering or accepting a broad range of things; scope: *the width of experience required for these positions.*
– ORIGIN early 17th cent.: from **WIDE** + **-TH**², on the pattern of *breadth* (replacing *wideness*).

widthways (also **widthwise**) ▶**adverb** in a direction parallel with a thing's width: *fold the pastry in half widthways.*

wield ▶**verb** [with obj.] hold and use (a weapon or tool): *a masked raider wielding a handgun.*
■have and be able to use (power or influence): *faction leaders wielded enormous influence within the party.*
– DERIVATIVES **wielder** noun.
– ORIGIN Old English *wealdan, wieldan* 'govern, subdue, direct', of Germanic origin; related to German *walten.*

wieldy ▶**adjective** (**wieldier, wieldiest**) easily controlled or handled: *the beefy Bentley is far from wieldy.*
– ORIGIN late 16th cent.: back-formation from **UNWIELDY**.

Wien /viːn/ German name for **VIENNA**.

Wiener /ˈwiːnə/, Norbert (1894–1964), American mathematician. He is best known for establishing the science of cybernetics in the late 1940s. Wiener made major contributions to the study of stochastic processes, integral equations, harmonic analysis, and related fields.

wiener /ˈwiːnə/ (also informal **weenie, wienie** /ˈwiːni/) ▶**noun** N. Amer. **1** a frankfurter or similar sausage.
2 vulgar slang a man's penis.
■informal a stupid, boring, or contemptible person.
– ORIGIN early 20th cent.: abbreviation of German *Wienerwurst* 'Vienna sausage'.

Wiener schnitzel ▶**noun** [mass noun] a dish consisting of a thin slice of veal that is breaded, fried, and garnished.
– ORIGIN from German, literally 'Vienna cutlet'.

Wiesbaden /ˈviːzbɑːd(ə)n, German ˈviːsbaːdn/ a city in western Germany, the capital of the state of Hesse, situated on the Rhine opposite Mainz; pop. 264,020 (1991). It has been a popular spa town since Roman times.

Wiesel /ˈwiːz(ə)l/, Elie (b.1928), Romanian-born American human rights campaigner, novelist, and academic; full name *Eliezer Wiesel.* A survivor of Auschwitz and Buchenwald, Wiesel became an authority on the Holocaust, documenting and publicizing Nazi war crimes. Nobel Peace Prize (1986).

Wiesenthal /ˈviːz(ə)ntɑːl/, Simon (b.1908), Austrian Jewish investigator of Nazi war crimes. After spending three years in concentration camps he began a campaign to bring Nazi war criminals to justice, tracing some 1,000 unprosecuted criminals including Adolf Eichmann.

wife ▶**noun** (pl. **wives**) a married woman considered in relation to her husband.
■[with modifier] the wife of a man with a specified occupation: *a clergy wife.* ■ archaic or dialect a woman, especially an old or uneducated one.
– PHRASES **take a woman to wife** archaic marry a woman.
– DERIVATIVES **wifehood** noun, **wifeless** adjective, **wife-like** adjective, **wifeliness** noun, **wifely** adjective.
– ORIGIN Old English *wīf* 'woman', of Germanic origin; related to Dutch *wijf* and German *Weib.*

wife-swapping ▶**noun** [mass noun] informal the practice within a group of married couples of exchanging sexual partners on a casual basis.

wifey ▶**noun** (pl. **-eys**) informal a condescending way of referring to a man's wife.

Wiffle ball ▶**noun** US trademark a light perforated ball used in a type of baseball.
■[mass noun] a game played with such a ball.
– ORIGIN 1950s: *Wiffle*, variant of **WHIFFLE**.

wifie ▶**noun** (pl. **-ies**) Scottish a woman.
– ORIGIN late 18th cent.: diminutive of **WIFE**.

wig¹ ▶**noun** a covering for the head made of real or artificial hair, typically worn by judges and barristers in law courts or by people trying to conceal their baldness.
– DERIVATIVES **wigged** adjective, **wigless** adjective.
– ORIGIN late 17th cent.: shortening of **PERIWIG**.

wig² ▶**verb** (**wigged, wigging**) [with obj.] Brit. informal, dated rebuke (someone) severely: *I had often occasion to wig him for getting drunk.*
– ORIGIN early 19th cent.: apparently from **WIG**¹, perhaps from **BIGWIG** and associated with a rebuke given by a person in authority.
▶**wig out** informal, chiefly US become deliriously excited; go completely wild.

Wigan /ˈwɪɡ(ə)n/ a town in NW England, near Manchester; pop. 88,900 (1981).

wigeon /ˈwɪdʒ(ə)n/ (also **widgeon**) ▶**noun** a dabbling duck with mainly reddish-brown and grey plumage, the male having a whistling call.
● Genus *Anas*, family Anatidae: three species, in particular the

W

European wigeon (*A. penelope*) and the **American wigeon** (*A. americana*).
– ORIGIN early 16th cent.: perhaps of imitative origin and suggested by **PIGEON**[1].

wigging ▶ **noun** Brit. informal, dated a severe rebuke.

wiggle ▶ **verb** move or cause to move up and down or from side to side with small rapid movements: [with obj.] *Vi wiggled her toes* | [no obj.] *my tooth was wiggling about.*
▶ **noun** a movement of such a kind: *a slight wiggle of the hips.*
■ a deviation in a line: *a wiggle on a chart.*
– PHRASES **get a wiggle on** US informal get moving; hurry.
– DERIVATIVES **wiggly** adjective (**wigglier, wiggliest**).
– ORIGIN Middle English: from Middle Low German and Middle Dutch *wiggelen* (frequentative).

wiggler ▶ **noun** a person or thing that wiggles or causes something to wiggle.
■ Physics a magnet designed to make a beam of particles in an accelerator follow a sinusoidal path, in order to increase the amount of radiation they produce.

wiggy ▶ **adjective** (**wiggier, wiggiest**) informal, chiefly N. Amer. emotionally uncontrolled or weird: *Arkansas has its wiggy side.*
– ORIGIN 1960s: from US slang *wig out* (see **WIG**[2]).

Wight a shipping forecast area covering the English Channel roughly between the Strait of Dover and the meridian of Poole.

wight ▶ **noun** [usu. with adj.] archaic or dialect a person of a specified kind, especially one regarded as unfortunate: *he always was an unlucky wight.*
■ poetic/literary a spirit, ghost, or other supernatural being.
– ORIGIN Old English *wiht* 'thing, creature', of Germanic origin; related to Dutch *wicht* 'little child' and German *Wicht* 'creature'.

Wight, Isle of see **ISLE OF WIGHT**.

Wigtownshire /ˈwɪɡtənʃɪə, -ʃə/ a former county of SW Scotland. It became a part of the region of Dumfries and Galloway in 1975.

wig tree ▶ **noun** the smoke tree.
– ORIGIN mid 19th cent.: so named because of its hair-like arrangement of flowers.

wigwag ▶ **verb** (**wigwagged, wigwagging**) [no obj.] US informal move to and fro: *the wipers were wigwagging to keep the windscreen clear.*
■ signal by waving an arm, flag, light, or other object: *Ned furiously wigwagged at her.*
– ORIGIN late 16th cent.: reduplication of **WAG**[1].

wigwam ▶ **noun** a dome-shaped hut or tent made by fastening mats, skins, or bark over a framework of poles, used by some North American Indian peoples.
■ a pyramidal framework of poles used to support runner beans, sweet peas, and other climbing plants.
– ORIGIN early 17th cent.: from Ojibwa *wigwaum*, Algonquian *wikiwam* 'their house'.

Wilberforce /ˈwɪlbəfɔːs/, William (1759–1833), English politician and social reformer. He was a prominent campaigner for the abolition of the slave trade, his efforts resulting in its outlawing in the British West Indies (1807) and in the 1833 Slavery Abolition Act.

wilco ▶ **exclamation** expressing compliance or agreement, especially acceptance of instructions received by radio.
– ORIGIN 1940s (originally in military use): abbreviation of *will comply.*

Wilcox, Ella Wheeler (1850–1919), American poet, novelist, and short-story writer. She wrote many volumes of romantic verse, the most successful one being *Poems of Passion* (1883).

Wilcoxon test /ˈwɪlkɒks(ə)n/ ▶ **noun** another term for **SIGNED-RANK TEST**.
– ORIGIN 1960s: named after Frank *Wilcoxon* (1892–1965), Irish statistician.

wild ▶ **adjective 1** (of an animal or plant) living or growing in the natural environment; not domesticated or cultivated.
■ (of people) not civilized; barbarous: *the wild tribes from the north.* ■ (of scenery or a region) desolate-looking: *the wild coastline of Cape Wrath.*
2 uncontrolled or unrestrained, especially in pursuit of pleasure: *she went through a wild phase of drunken parties and desperate affairs.*
■ haphazard, especially rashly so: *a wild guess.* ■ extravagant or unreasonable; fanciful: *who, even* **in their wildest dreams**, *could have anticipated such a victory?* ■ stormy: *the wild sea.* ■ informal very enthusiastic or excited: *I'm not wild about the music.* ■ informal very angry. ■ (of looks, appearance, etc.) indicating distraction: *her wild eyes were darting back and forth.* ■ (of a playing card) deemed to have any value, suit, colour, or other property in a game at the discretion of the player holding it. See also **WILD CARD**.
▶ **noun** (**the wild**) a natural state or uncultivated or uninhabited region: *kiwis are virtually extinct* **in the wild.**
■ (**the wilds**) a remote uninhabited or sparsely inhabited area: *he spent a year in* **the wilds of** *Canada.*
▶ **verb** [with obj.] W. Indian treat (someone or something) harshly, so that they become untrusting or nervous.
– PHRASES **run wild** (of an animal, plant, or person) grow or develop without restraint or discipline: *these horses have been running wild since they were born* | figurative *her imagination had run wild.* **wild and woolly** uncouth in appearance or behaviour.
– DERIVATIVES **wildish** adjective, **wildly** adverb, **wildness** noun.
– ORIGIN Old English *wilde*, of Germanic origin; related to Dutch and German *wild*.

wild arum ▶ **noun** another term for **CUCKOO PINT**.

wild boar ▶ **noun** see **BOAR** (sense 1).

wild card ▶ **noun** a playing card that can have any value, suit, colour, or other property in a game at the discretion of the player holding it.
■ a person or thing whose influence is unpredictable or whose qualities are uncertain. ■ Computing a character that will match any character or sequence of characters in a search. ■ an opportunity to enter a sports competition without having to take part in qualifying matches or be ranked at a particular level. ■ a player or team given such an opportunity.

wildcat ▶ **noun 1** a small native Eurasian and African cat that is typically grey with black markings and a bushy tail, noted for its ferocity.
• *Felis silvestris*, family Felidae, the African race of which is believed to be the ancestor of the domestic cat.
■ any of the smaller members of the cat family, especially (N. Amer.) the bobcat. ■ a hot-tempered or ferocious person, typically a woman.
2 an exploratory oil well.
▶ **adjective** [attrib.] (of a strike) sudden and unofficial: *legislation to curb wildcat strikes.*
■ commercially unsound or risky.
▶ **verb** [no obj.] US prospect for oil.

wildcatter ▶ **noun** US a prospector who sinks exploratory oil wells.

wild-caught ▶ **adjective** (of an animal) taken from the wild rather than bred from captive stock.

wild cherry ▶ **noun** another term for **GEAN**.

wild dagga ▶ **noun** [mass noun] S. African a preparation of a southern African plant of the mint family, used similarly to cannabis.
• The plant is *Leonotis leonurus*, family Labiatae.

wild dog ▶ **noun** a wild member of the dog family, especially the hunting dog of Africa, the dhole of India, or the dingo of Australia.

wild duck ▶ **noun** another term for **MALLARD**.

Wilde, Oscar (Fingal O'Flahertie Wills) (1854–1900), Irish dramatist, novelist, poet, and wit. His advocacy of 'art for art's sake' is evident in his only novel, *The Picture of Dorian Gray* (1890). As a dramatist he achieved success with the comedies *Lady Windermere's Fan* (1892) and *The Importance of Being Earnest* (1895). Wilde was imprisoned (1895–7) for homosexual offences and died in exile.

wildebeest /ˈwɪldəbiːst, ˈvɪ-/ ▶ **noun** (pl. same or **wildebeests**) another term for **GNU**.
– ORIGIN early 19th cent.: from Afrikaans, literally 'wild beast'.

Wilder[1] /ˈwʌɪldə/, Billy (b.1906), Austrian-born American film director and screenwriter; born *Samuel Wilder.* He earned recognition as a writer-director with the *film noir* classic *Double Indemnity* (1944). Other films include *The Apartment* (1960), which won three Oscars.

Wilder[2] /ˈwʌɪldə/, Thornton (Niven) (1897–1975), American novelist and dramatist. He won several Pulitzer Prizes. Notable works: *The Bridge of San Luis Rey* (novel, 1927) and *Our Town* (play, 1938).

wilder /ˈwɪldə/ ▶ **verb** [with obj.] archaic cause to lose one's way; lead or drive astray: *unknowne Lands, where we have wildered ourselves.*
■ perplex; bewilder: *the sad Queen, wildered of thought.*
– ORIGIN early 17th cent.: origin uncertain; perhaps based on **WILDERNESS**.

wilderness ▶ **noun** [usu. in sing.] an uncultivated, uninhabited, and inhospitable region.
■ a neglected or abandoned area of a garden or town. ■ figurative a position of disfavour, especially in a political context: *the man who led the Labour Party out of the wilderness* | [as modifier] *his wilderness years.*
– PHRASES **a voice in the wilderness** an unheeded advocate of reform (see Matt. 3:3 etc.).
– ORIGIN Old English *wildēornes* 'land inhabited only by wild animals', from *wild dēor* 'wild deer' + **-NESS**.

wild-eyed ▶ **adjective** (of a person or animal) with an expression of panic or desperation in the eyes.
■ figurative emotionally volatile, typically fearful or desperate: *wild-eyed manic depressives.*

wildfire ▶ **noun 1** [mass noun] historical a combustible liquid such as Greek fire that was readily ignited and difficult to extinguish, used especially in warfare.
2 less common term for **WILL-O'-THE-WISP**.
– PHRASES **spread like wildfire** spread with great speed: *the news had spread like wildfire.*

wild flower ▶ **noun** a flower of an uncultivated variety or a flower growing freely without human intervention.

wildfowl ▶ **plural noun** game birds, especially aquatic ones; waterfowl.

wild garlic ▶ **noun** another term for **RAMSONS**.

wild ginger ▶ **noun** [mass noun] a North American plant with an aromatic root which is used as a ginger substitute.
• *Asarum canadense*, family Aristolochiaceae.

wild goose chase ▶ **noun** a foolish and hopeless search for or pursuit of something unattainable.

wild horse ▶ **noun** a domestic horse that has returned to the wild, or that is allowed to live under natural conditions; a feral horse.
■ a horse that has not been broken in. ■ a wild animal of the horse family.
– PHRASES **wild horses wouldn't ——** used to convey that nothing could persuade or force someone to do something: *wild horses wouldn't have kept me away.*

wild hyacinth ▶ **noun** Scottish term for **BLUEBELL** (in sense 1).

wilding[1] /ˈwʌɪldɪŋ/ ▶ **noun** [mass noun] US informal the activity by a gang of youths of going on a protracted and violent rampage in a public place, attacking or mugging people at random.
– ORIGIN 1980s: from the adjective **WILD** + **-ING**[1].

wilding[2] /ˈwʌɪldɪŋ/ (also **wildling** /-lɪŋ/) ▶ **noun** a wild plant, especially an apple tree descended from cultivated varieties, or its fruit.
– ORIGIN early 16th cent.: from the adjective **WILD** + **-ING**[3].

wildlife ▶ **noun** [mass noun] wild animals collectively; the native fauna (and sometimes flora) of a region.

wildlife park ▶ **noun** see **PARK** (sense 1).

wild man ▶ **noun** a man with a fierce or wildly unruly nature.
■ the image of a primitive or uncivilized man as a symbol of the wild side of human nature or of seasonal fertility. ■ a supposed manlike animal such as a yeti.

wild man of the woods ▶ **noun** dated an orang-utan.
– ORIGIN translating the Malay word for the animal.

wild mustard ▶ **noun** [mass noun] charlock.

wild oat ▶ **noun** an Old World grass which is related to the cultivated oat and is commonly found as a weed of other cereals.
• *Avena fatua*, family Gramineae.
– PHRASES **sow one's wild oats** see **OAT**.

wild pitch Baseball ▶ **noun** a pitch which is not hit by the batter and cannot be stopped by the catcher, enabling a base-runner to advance.
▶ **verb** (**wild-pitch**) [with obj.] enable (a base-runner) to advance by making such a pitch.

wild rice ▶ **noun** [mass noun] a tall aquatic American grass related to rice, with edible grains that are traditionally eaten by American Indians.
• *Zizania aquatica*, family Gramineae.

wild service tree ▶ **noun** see **SERVICE TREE**.

wild silk ▶ **noun** [mass noun] coarse silk produced by wild silkworms, especially tussore.

wild type ▶ **noun** [mass noun] Genetics a strain, gene, or characteristic which prevails among individuals in

W

natural conditions, as distinct from an atypical mutant type.

wild water ▶ **noun** another term for **WHITE WATER**.

Wild West the western US in a time of lawlessness in its early history. The Wild West was the last of a succession of frontiers formed as settlers moved gradually further west. The frontier was officially declared closed in 1890.

wildwood ▶ **noun** chiefly poetic/literary an uncultivated wood or forest that has been allowed to grow naturally.

wile ▶ **noun** (**wiles**) devious or cunning stratagems employed in manipulating or persuading someone to do what one wants.
▶ **verb** [with obj.] **1** archaic lure; entice: *she could be neither driven nor wiled into the parish kirk.*
2 (**wile time away**) another way of saying ***while time away***. See **WHILE**.
– ORIGIN Middle English: perhaps from an Old Norse word related to *vél* 'craft'.

wilful (US also **willful**) ▶ **adjective** (of an immoral or illegal act or omission) intentional; deliberate: *wilful acts of damage.*
■ having or showing a stubborn and determined intention to do as one wants, regardless of the consequences or effects: *the pettish, wilful side of him.*
– DERIVATIVES **wilfully** adverb, **wilfulness** noun.
– ORIGIN Middle English: from the noun **WILL**[2] + **-FUL**.

wilga /ˈwɪlgə/ ▶ **noun** a small white-flowering Australian tree which is resistant to drought and a valuable source of fodder.
• *Geijera parviflora*, family Rutaceae.
– ORIGIN late 19th cent.: from Wiradhuri *wilgar*.

Wilhelm I /ˈvɪlhɛlm/ (1797–1888), king of Prussia 1861–88 and emperor of Germany 1871–88. He became the first emperor of Germany after Prussia's victory against France in 1871. The latter part of his reign was marked by the rise of German socialism, to which he responded with harsh, repressive measures.

Wilhelm II /ˈvɪlhɛlm/ (1859–1941), emperor of Germany 1888–1918, grandson of Wilhelm I and also of Queen Victoria; known as **Kaiser Wilhelm**. After forcing Bismarck to resign in 1890 he proved unable to exercise a strong or consistent influence over German policies. He was vilified by Allied propaganda as the author of the First World War. In 1918 he abdicated and went into exile.

Wilhelmina /ˌwɪləˈmiːnə/, (1880–1962), queen of the Netherlands 1890–1948. During the Second World War she maintained a government in exile in London, and through frequent radio broadcasts became a symbol of resistance to the Dutch people. She returned to the Netherlands in 1945.

Wilhelmshaven /ˈvɪlhɛlmzˌhɑːv(ə)n/ a port and resort in NW Germany, on the North Sea; pop. 91,150 (1991). It was a major naval base until 1945.

Wilkes Land /wɪlks/ a region of Antarctica with a coast on the Indian Ocean. It is claimed by Australia.
– ORIGIN named after the American naval officer Charles Wilkes (1798–1877), who sighted and surveyed it between 1838 and 1842.

Wilkie, Sir David (1785–1841), Scottish painter. He made his name with the painting *Village Politicians* (1806). His style contributed to the growing prestige of genre painting.

Wilkins, Maurice Hugh Frederick (b.1916), New Zealand-born British biochemist and molecular biologist. From X-ray diffraction analysis of DNA, he and his colleague Rosalind Franklin confirmed the double helix structure proposed by Francis Crick and James Watson in 1953. Nobel Prize for Physiology or Medicine (1962, shared with Crick and Watson).

will[1] ▶ **modal verb** (3rd sing. present **will**; past **would**) **1** expressing the future tense: *you will regret it when you are older.*
■ expressing a strong intention or assertion about the future: *come what may, I will succeed.*
2 expressing inevitable events: *accidents will happen.*
3 expressing a request: *will you stop here, please.*
■ expressing desire, consent, or willingness: *will you have a cognac?*
4 expressing facts about ability or capacity: *a rock so light that it will float on water | your tank will hold about 26 gallons.*
5 expressing habitual behaviour: *she will dance for hours.*
■ (pronounced stressing 'will') indicating annoyance about the habitual behaviour described: *he will keep intruding.*
6 expressing probability or expectation about something in the present: *they will be miles away by now.*
– PHRASES **will do** informal expressing willingness to carry out a request or suggestion: *'Might be best to check.' 'Righty-ho, will do.'*
– ORIGIN Old English *wyllan*, of Germanic origin; related to Dutch *willen*, German *wollen*, from an Indo-European root shared by Latin *velle* 'will, wish'.

USAGE On the differences in use between **will** and **shall**, see usage at **SHALL**.

will[2] ▶ **noun 1** [usu. in sing.] the faculty by which a person decides on and initiates action: *she has an iron will | a battle of wills between children and their parents |* [mass noun] *an act of will.*
■ (also **will power**) [mass noun] control deliberately exerted to do something or to restrain one's own impulses: *a stupendous effort of will.* ■ a deliberate or fixed desire or intention: *Jane had not wanted them to stay **against their will** |* [with infinitive] *the will to live.* ■ the thing that one desires or ordains: *the disaster was God's will.*
2 a legal document containing instructions as to what should be done with one's money and property after one's death.
▶ **verb** [with obj.] **1** chiefly formal or poetic/literary intend, desire, or wish (something) to happen: *he was doing what the saint willed |* [with clause] *marijuana, dope, grass—call it what you will.*
■ [with obj. and infinitive] make or try to make (someone) do something or (something) happen by the exercise of mental powers: *reluctantly he willed himself to turn and go back | she stared into the fog, willing it to clear.*
2 (**will something to**) bequeath something to (someone) by the terms of one's will.
■ [with clause] leave specified instructions in one's will: *he willed that his body should be given to the hospital.*
– PHRASES **at will** at whatever time or in whatever way one pleases: *it can be moulded and shaped at will | he was shoved around at will.* **have a will of one's own** have a wilful character. **have one's will** archaic obtain what one wants. **if you will** said when politely inviting a listener or reader to do something or when using an unusual or fanciful term: *imagine, if you will, a typical silversmith's shop.* **where there's a will there's a way** proverb determination will overcome any obstacle. **with the best will in the world** however good one's intentions (used to imply that success in a particular undertaking is unlikely although desired). **with a will** energetically and resolutely.
– DERIVATIVES **willed** adjective [in combination] *I'm strong-willed*, **willer** noun.
– ORIGIN Old English *willa* (noun), *willian* (verb), of Germanic origin; related to Dutch *wil*, German *Wille* (nouns), also to **WILL**[1] and the adverb **WELL**[1].

Willard /ˈwɪlɑːd/, Emma (1787–1870), American educational reformer. She founded a boarding school in Vermont (1814) to teach subjects not then available to women, such as mathematics and philosophy.

willemite /ˈwɪləmʌɪt/ ▶ **noun** [mass noun] a mineral, typically greenish-yellow and fluorescent, consisting of a silicate of zinc.
– ORIGIN mid 19th cent.: from the name of *Willem* I (1772–1843), king of the Netherlands, + **-ITE**[1].

Willemstad /ˈwɪləmstɑːt, ˈvɪl-/ the capital of the Netherlands Antilles, situated on the SW coast of the island of Curaçao; pop. 50,000 (est. 1993).

willet /ˈwɪlɪt/ ▶ **noun** (pl. same or **willets**) a large North American sandpiper.
• *Catoptrophorus semipalmatus*, family Scolopacidae.
– ORIGIN mid 19th cent.: imitative of its call, *pill-will-willet*.

willful ▶ **adjective** US variant spelling of **WILFUL**.

William the name of two kings of England and two of Great Britain and Ireland:
■ **William I** (*c*.1027–87), reigned 1066–87, the first Norman king of England; known as **William the Conqueror**. He invaded England and defeated Harold II at the Battle of Hastings (1066). He introduced Norman institutions and customs (including feudalism) and instigated the Domesday Book.
■ **William II** (*c*.1060–1100), son of William I, reigned 1087–1100; known as **William Rufus**. William crushed rebellions in 1088 and 1095 and also campaigned against his brother Robert, Duke of Normandy (1089–96), ultimately acquiring the duchy. He was killed by an arrow while out hunting.
■ **William III** (1650–1702), grandson of Charles I, husband of Mary II, reigned 1689–1702; known as **William of Orange**. In 1688 he deposed James II at the invitation of disaffected politicians and, having accepted the Declaration of Rights, was crowned along with his wife Mary.
■ **William IV** (1765–1837), son of George III, reigned 1830–7; known as **the Sailor King**. Having served in the Royal Navy, he came to the throne after the death of his brother George IV. In 1834 he intervened in political affairs by imposing the Conservative Robert Peel as Prime Minister, despite a Whig majority in Parliament.

William I[1] (1143–1214), grandson of David I, king of Scotland 1165–1214; known as **William the Lion**. He attempted to reassert Scottish independence but was forced to pay homage to Henry II of England after being captured by him in 1174.

William I[2] (1533–84), prince of the House of Orange, first stadtholder (chief magistrate) of the United Provinces of the Netherlands 1572–84; known as **William the Silent**. He led a revolt against Spain from 1568 and was assassinated by a Spanish agent.

William of Occam /ˈɒkəm/ (also **Ockham**) (*c*.1285–1349), English philosopher and Franciscan friar. A defender of nominalism, he is known for the maxim called 'Occam's razor'.

William of Orange, William III of Great Britain and Ireland (see **WILLIAM**).

William Rufus, William II of England (see **WILLIAM**).

Williams[1], Hank (1923–53), American country singer and songwriter; born *Hiram King Williams*. Williams had the first of many country hits, 'Lovesick Blues', in 1949; 'Your Cheatin' Heart' (recorded 1952) was released after his sudden death.

Williams[2], John (Christopher) (b.1941), Australian guitarist and composer. He made his name as a recitalist, noted for an eclectic repertoire that includes both classical and popular music.

Williams[3], J. P. R. (b.1949), Welsh rugby union player; full name *John Peter Rhys Williams*. One of the leading fullbacks of the 1970s, Williams played for his country and for the British Lions.

Williams[4], Tennessee (1911–83), American dramatist; born *Thomas Lanier Williams*. He achieved success with *The Glass Menagerie* (1944) and *A Streetcar Named Desire* (1947), which deal with the tragedy of vulnerable heroines living in fragile fantasy worlds shattered by brutal reality. Other notable works: *Cat on a Hot Tin Roof* (1955) and *The Night of the Iguana* (1962).

Williams[5], William Carlos (1883–1963), American poet, essayist, novelist, and short-story writer. His poetry is characterized by avoidance of emotional content and the use of American vernacular. Collections include *Spring and All* (1923).

Williams[6] ▶ **noun** a dessert pear of an early green variety.
– ORIGIN early 19th cent.: named after its first distributor in England.

Williamsburg /ˈwɪljəmzbəːg/ a city in SE Virginia, between the James and York Rivers; pop. 11,530 (1990). It was the state capital of Virginia from 1699, when it was renamed in honour of William III, until 1799, when Richmond became the capital.

Williamson, Henry (1895–1977), English novelist. His works include *Tarka the Otter* (1927) and the fifteen-volume semi-autobiographical sequence *A Chronicle of Ancient Sunlight* (1951–69).

William the Conqueror, William I of England (see **WILLIAM**).

willie ▶ **noun** variant spelling of **WILLY**.

willies ▶ **plural noun** (**the willies**) informal a strong feeling of nervous discomfort: *that room **gave** him **the willies**.*
– ORIGIN late 19th cent. (originally US): of unknown origin.

willie wagtail (also **willy wagtail**) ▶ **noun** Austral. a common Australian monarch flycatcher with striking black and white plumage.

W

● *Rhipidura leucophrys*, family Monarchidae. Aternative name: **black and white fantail**.

■Brit. informal the pied wagtail.

willing ▶ **adjective** [often with infinitive] ready, eager, or prepared to do something: *he was quite willing to compromise.*

■given or done readily: *willing and prompt obedience.*

– PHRASES **show willing** see **SHOW**.

– DERIVATIVES **willingly** adverb, **willingness** noun.

williwaw /ˈwɪlɪwɔː/ ▶ **noun** a sudden violent squall blowing offshore from a mountainous coast.

– ORIGIN mid 19th cent.: of unknown origin.

will-o'-the-wisp ▶ **noun** a phosphorescent light seen hovering or floating at night on marshy ground, thought to result from the combustion of natural gases.

■figurative a person or thing that is difficult or impossible to find, reach, or catch.

– ORIGIN early 17th cent.: originally as *Will with the wisp*, the sense of *wisp* being 'handful of (lighted) hay'.

willow (also **willow tree**) ▶ **noun** a tree or shrub of temperate climates which typically has narrow leaves, bears catkins, and grows near water. Its pliant branches yield osiers for basketry, and the timber has various uses.

● Genus *Salix*, family Salicaceae: many species.

– ORIGIN Old English *welig*, of Germanic origin; related to Dutch *wilg*.

willow grouse ▶ **noun** a common Eurasian and North American grouse with reddish-brown and white plumage, turning mainly white in winter.

● *Lagopus lagopus*, family Tetraonidae (or Phasianidae). See also **RED GROUSE**.

willowherb ▶ **noun** a plant of temperate regions that typically has willow-like leaves and pink or pale purple flowers.

● *Epilobium* and related genera, family Onagraceae: many species, including the common **great hairy willowherb** (*E. hirsutum*) of Eurasia, and the rosebay.

willow pattern ▶ **noun** a conventional design representing a Chinese scene in blue on white pottery, typically showing three figures on a bridge, with a willow tree and two birds above: [as modifier] *a willow-pattern plate.*

willow ptarmigan ▶ **noun** North American term for **WILLOW GROUSE**.

willow tit ▶ **noun** a Eurasian tit (songbird) with mainly grey-brown plumage, a dull black cap, and white cheeks.

● *Parus montanus*, family Paridae.

willow warbler ▶ **noun** a small migratory Eurasian leaf warbler with mainly drab plumage and a tuneful song.

● Genus *Phylloscopus*, family Sylviidae: several species, in particular the common and widespread *P. trochilus*.

willowware ▶ **noun** chiefly US pottery with a willow-pattern design.

willow wren ▶ **noun** Brit. another term for **WILLOW WARBLER**.

willowy ▶ **adjective 1** bordered, shaded, or covered by willows: *willowy meadow land.*

2 (of a person) tall, slim, and lithe.

will power ▶ **noun** see **WILL**[2] (sense 1).

Wills, William John (1834–61), English explorer. In 1860 he was a member, with two others, of Robert Burke's expedition to cross Australia from south to north, but he died of starvation on the return journey.

willy (also **willie**) ▶ **noun** (pl. **-ies**) Brit. informal a penis.

– ORIGIN early 20th cent.: pet form of the given name *William*.

willy-nilly ▶ **adverb 1** whether one likes it or not: *he would be forced to collaborate willy-nilly.*

2 without direction or planning; haphazardly: *politicians expanded spending programmes willy-nilly.*

– ORIGIN early 17th cent.: later spelling of *will I, nill I* 'I am willing, I am unwilling'.

willy wagtail ▶ **noun** variant spelling of **WILLIE WAGTAIL**.

willy-willy ▶ **noun** (pl. **-ies**) Austral./NZ a whirlwind or dust storm.

– ORIGIN from Yindjibarndi (an Aboriginal language of western Australia).

Wilms' tumour /wɪlmz, vɪlmz/ ▶ **noun** a malignant tumour of the kidney, of a type that occurs in young children.

– ORIGIN early 20th cent.: named after Max *Wilms* (1867–1918), German surgeon.

Wilson[1], Sir Angus (Frank Johnstone) (1913–91), English novelist and short-story writer. His works display his satiric wit, acute social observation, and a love of the macabre and the farcical. Notable novels: *The Old Men at the Zoo* (1961).

Wilson[2], Charles Thomson Rees (1869–1959), Scottish physicist. He is chiefly remembered for inventing the cloud chamber, which became a major tool of particle physicists. Nobel Prize for Physics (1927).

Wilson[3], Edmund (1895–1972), American critic, essayist, and short-story writer. He is remembered chiefly for works of literary and social criticism which include *Patriotic Gore: Studies in the Literature of the American Civil War* (1962).

Wilson[4], Edward Osborne (b.1929), American social biologist. He has worked principally on social insects, extrapolating his findings to the social behaviour of other animals including humans. Notable works: *Sociobiology: the New Synthesis* (1975).

Wilson[5], (James) Harold, Baron Wilson of Rievaulx (1916–95), British Labour statesman, Prime Minister 1964–70 and 1974–6. In both terms of office he faced severe economic problems. His government introduced a number of social reforms, including comprehensive schooling, and renegotiated Britain's terms of entry into the European Economic Community, which was confirmed after a referendum in 1975.

Wilson[6], John Tuzo (1908–93), Canadian geophysicist. Wilson was a pioneer in the study of plate tectonics, introducing the term *plate* in this context and identifying transform faults.

Wilson[7], (Thomas) Woodrow (1856–1924), American Democratic statesman, 28th President of the US 1913–21. He eventually took America into First World War in 1917 and played a leading role in the peace negotiations and the formation of the League of Nations. Nobel Peace Prize (1919).

wilt[1] ▶ **verb** [no obj.] (of a plant, leaf, or flower) become limp through heat, loss of water, or disease; droop.

■(of a person) lose one's energy or vigour. ■ [with obj.] leave (mown grass or a forage crop) in the open to dry partially before being collected for silage.

▶ **noun** [mass noun] [usu. with modifier] any of a number of fungal or bacterial diseases of plants characterized by wilting of the foliage.

– ORIGIN late 17th cent. (originally dialect): perhaps an alteration of dialect *welk* 'lose freshness', of Low German origin.

wilt[2] archaic second person singular of **WILL**[1].

Wilton ▶ **noun** a woven carpet resembling a Brussels carpet but with a velvet pile.

– ORIGIN late 18th cent.: from *Wilton*, the name of a town in southern England, noted for the manufacture of carpets.

Wilts. ▶ **abbreviation for** Wiltshire.

Wiltshire a county of southern England; county town, Trowbridge.

wily /ˈwʌɪli/ ▶ **adjective** (**wilier**, **wiliest**) skilled at gaining an advantage, especially deceitfully: *his wily opponents.*

– DERIVATIVES **wilily** adverb, **wiliness** noun.

Wimbledon /ˈwɪmb(ə)ld(ə)n/ an annual international tennis championship on grass for individual players and pairs, held at the headquarters of the All England Lawn Tennis and Croquet Club in the London suburb of Wimbledon. Now one of the world's major tennis championships, it has been played since 1877.

wimmin ▶ **plural noun** non-standard spelling of 'women' adopted by some feminists to avoid the word ending *-men*.

WIMP[1] ▶ **noun** [often as modifier] Computing a set of software features and hardware devices (such as windows, icons, mice, and pull-down menus) designed to simplify or demystify computing operations for the user.

– ORIGIN 1980s: acronym.

WIMP[2] ▶ **noun** Physics a hypothetical subatomic particle of large mass which interacts only weakly with ordinary matter, postulated as a constituent of the dark matter of the universe.

– ORIGIN 1980s: acronym from *weakly interacting massive particle*.

wimp informal ▶ **noun** a weak and cowardly or unadventurous person.

▶ **verb** [no obj.] (**wimp out**) withdraw from a course of action or a stated position in a way that is seen as feeble or cowardly.

– DERIVATIVES **wimpish** adjective, **wimpishly** adverb, **wimpishness** noun, **wimpy** adjective.

– ORIGIN 1920s: origin uncertain, perhaps from **WHIMPER**.

wimple ▶ **noun** a cloth headdress covering the head, neck, and the sides of the face, formerly worn by women and still worn by some nuns.

– DERIVATIVES **wimpled** adjective.

– ORIGIN late Old English *wimpel*, of Germanic origin; related to German *Wimpel* 'pennon, streamer'.

Wimshurst machine /ˈwɪmzhəːst/ ▶ **noun** a device for generating an electric charge by turning glass discs in opposite directions (now used mainly for demonstration purposes in schools).

– ORIGIN late 19th cent.: named after James *Wimshurst* (1832–1903), English engineer.

win ▶ **verb** (**winning**; past and past participle **won**) [with obj.] **1** be successful or victorious in (a contest or conflict): *the government is winning the battle against inflation* | [no obj.] *a determination to win* | [with complement] *Sunderland won 2–1.*

2 acquire or secure as a result of a contest, conflict, bet, or other endeavour: *there are hundreds of prizes to be won* | [with two objs] *the sort of play that won them the World Cup so brilliantly.*

■gain (a person's attention, support, or love), typically gradually or by effort: *you will find it difficult to win back their attention.* ■ (**win someone over**) gain the support or favour of someone by action or persuasion: *her sense of humour had won him over at once.* ■ [no obj.] (**win out/through**) manage to succeed or achieve something by effort: *a determination to win through against all the odds.* ■ archaic manage to reach (a place) by effort: *many lived to win the great cave.* ■ obtain (ore) from a mine.

3 dry (hay) by exposure to the air.

▶ **noun** a successful result in a contest, conflict, bet, or other endeavour; a victory: *a win against France.*

– PHRASES **one can't win** informal said when someone feels that no course of action open to them will bring success or please people. **win the day** be victorious in battle, sport, or argument. **win or lose** whether one succeeds or fails: *win or lose, the important thing for him is to set a good example to his side.* **win** (or **earn**) **one's spurs** historical gain a knighthood by an act of bravery. ■ informal gain one's first distinction or honours. **you can't win them all** (or **win some, lose some**) informal said to express consolation or resignation after failure in a contest.

– DERIVATIVES **winless** adjective, **winnable** adjective.

– ORIGIN Old English *winnan* 'strive, contend' also 'subdue and take possession of, acquire', of Germanic origin.

wince[1] ▶ **verb** [no obj.] give a slight involuntary grimace or shrinking movement of the body out of pain or distress: *he winced at the disgust in her voice.*

▶ **noun** [in sing.] a slight grimace or shrinking movement caused by pain or distress.

– DERIVATIVES **wincer** noun, **wincingly** adverb.

– ORIGIN Middle English (originally in the sense 'kick restlessly from pain or impatience'): from an Anglo-Norman French variant of Old French *guenchir* 'turn aside'.

wince[2] ▶ **noun** Brit. a roller for moving textile fabric through a dyeing vat.

– ORIGIN late 17th cent. (in the sense 'winch'): variant of **WINCH**.

wincey ▶ **noun** (pl. **-eys**) [mass noun] Brit. a strong, lightweight twilled fabric, typically made of a mixture of wool with cotton or linen.

– ORIGIN early 19th cent.: apparently an alteration of *woolsey* in **LINSEY-WOOLSEY**.

winceyette /ˌwɪnsɪˈɛt/ ▶ **noun** [mass noun] Brit. a lightweight napped flannelette, used especially for nightclothes and undergarments.

winch ▶ **noun 1** a hauling or lifting device consisting of a rope or chain winding around a horizontal rotating drum, turned by a crank or by motor or other power source; a windlass.

■Brit. the reel of a fishing rod. ■ another term for **WINCE**[2].

2 the crank of a wheel or axle.

▶ **verb** [with obj.] hoist or haul with a winch.

– DERIVATIVES **wincher** noun.

– ORIGIN late Old English *wince* 'reel, pulley', of Germanic origin; related to the verb **WINK**. The verb dates from the early 16th cent.

Winchester[1] /ˈwɪntʃɪstə/ a city in southern England, the county town of Hampshire; pop. 35,660 (1981). Known to the Romans as Venta Belgarum, it became capital of the West Saxon kingdom of Wessex in 519. It is the site of Winchester College, the oldest public school in England, founded by the bishop of Winchester William of Wykeham (1324–1404) in 1382.

Winchester[2] /ˈwɪntʃɪstə/ ▶ **noun 1** (also **Winchester rifle**) trademark a breech-loading side-action repeating rifle. [ORIGIN: named after Oliver F. *Winchester* (1810–80), the American manufacturer of the rifle.] **2** (in full **Winchester disk** or **drive**) Computing a disk drive in a sealed unit containing a high-capacity hard disk and the read-write heads. [ORIGIN: so named because its original numerical designation corresponded to the calibre of the rifle (see sense 1).]

winchester ▶ **noun** Brit. a large cylindrical bottle for holding liquids.

– ORIGIN early 18th cent.: originally applied to containers holding a bushel, gallon, or quart, according to an obsolete system of measurement with standards kept at *Winchester* (see **WINCHESTER**[1]).

Winckelmann /ˈvɪŋk(ə)lman/, Johann (Joachim) (1717–68), German archaeologist and art historian, born in Prussia. He took part in the excavations at Pompeii and Herculaneum and his best-known work, *History of the Art of Antiquity* (1764), was particularly influential in popularizing the art and culture of ancient Greece.

wind[1] /wɪnd/ ▶ **noun 1** the perceptible natural movement of the air, especially in the form of a current of air blowing from a particular direction: *the wind howled about the building* | *an easterly wind* | [mass noun] *gusts of wind.*
■ [mass noun] [as modifier] relating to or denoting energy obtained from harnessing the wind with windmills or wind turbines. ■ used to suggest something very fast, unrestrained, or changeable: *run like the wind* | *she could be as free and easy as the wind.* ■ used in reference to an influence or tendency that cannot be resisted: *a wind of change.* ■ used in reference to an impending situation: *he had seen which way the wind was blowing.* ■ the rush of air caused by a fast-moving body. ■ a scent carried by the wind, indicating the presence or proximity of an animal or person.
2 [mass noun] breath as needed in physical exertion or in speech.
■ the power of breathing without difficulty while running or making a similar continuous effort: *he waited while Jez got his wind back.*
3 [mass noun] Brit. air swallowed while eating or gas generated in the stomach and intestines by digestion.
■ empty, pompous, or boastful talk; meaningless rhetoric.
4 [mass noun] air or breath used for sounding an organ or a wind instrument.
■ (also **winds**) [treated as sing. or pl.] wind instruments, or specifically woodwind instruments, forming a band or a section of an orchestra: *these passages are most suitable for wind alone* | [as modifier] *wind players.*
▶ **verb** [with obj.] **1** (often **be winded**) cause (someone) to have difficulty breathing because of exertion or a blow to the stomach: *the fall nearly winded him.*
2 Brit. make (a baby) bring up wind after feeding by patting its back: *Paddy's wife handed him their six-month-old daughter to be winded.*
3 detect the presence of (a person or animal) by scent: *the birds could not have seen us or winded us.*
4 /wʌɪnd/ (past and past participle **winded** or **wound** /waʊnd/) poetic/literary sound (a bugle or call) by blowing: *but scarce again his horn he wound.*

– PHRASES **before the wind** Sailing with the wind blowing from astern. **get wind of** informal begin to suspect that (something) is happening; hear a rumour of: *Mortimer got wind of a plot being hatched.* [ORIGIN: referring originally to the scent of game in hunting.] **it's an ill wind that blows nobody any good** proverb few things are so bad that no one profits from them. **off the wind** Sailing with the wind on the quarter. **on a wind** Sailing against a wind on either bow. **put** (or **have**) **the wind up** Brit. informal alarm or frighten (or be alarmed or frightened): *he was trying to put the wind up him with stories of how hard teaching was.* **sail close to** (or **near**) **the wind 1** Sailing sail as nearly against the wind as is consistent with using its force. **2** informal verge on indecency, dishonesty, or disaster. **take the wind out of someone's sails** frustrate someone by unexpectedly anticipating an action or remark. **to the wind(s)** (or **the four winds**) in all directions: *my little flock scatters to the four winds.* ■ so as to be abandoned or neglected: *I threw my friends' advice to the winds.* [ORIGIN: from 'And fear of death deliver to the winds' (Milton's *Paradise Lost*).]

– DERIVATIVES **windless** adjective.

– ORIGIN Old English, of Germanic origin; related to Dutch *wind* and German *Wind*, from an Indo-European root shared by Latin *ventus*.

wind[2] /wʌɪnd/ ▶ **verb** (past and past participle **wound** /waʊnd/) **1** [no obj., with adverbial of direction] move in or take a twisting or spiral course: *the path wound among olive trees.*
2 [with obj. and adverbial] pass (something) around a thing or person so as to encircle or enfold: *he wound a towel around his midriff.*
■ repeatedly twist or coil (a length of something) around itself or a core: *Anne wound the wool into a ball.* ■ [no obj., with adverbial] be twisted or coiled in such a way: *large vines wound round every tree.* ■ wrap or surround (a core) with a coiled length of something: *devices wound with copper wire.*
3 [with obj.] make (a clock or other device, typically one operated by clockwork) operate by turning a key or handle: *he* **wound up** *the clock every Saturday night* | *she was winding the gramophone.*
■ turn (a key or handle) repeatedly round and round: *I wound the handle as fast as I could.* ■ [with obj. and adverbial of direction] cause (an audio or video tape or a film) to move back or forwards to a desired point: *I forgot how to wind the film on.* ■ [with obj. and adverbial of direction] hoist or draw (something) with a windlass, winch, or similar device.
▶ **noun 1** a twist or turn in a course.
2 a single turn made when winding.

– ORIGIN Old English *windan* 'go rapidly', 'twine', of Germanic origin; related to **WANDER** and **WEND**.

▶ **wind down** (of a mechanism, especially one operated by clockwork) gradually lose power. ■ informal (of a person) relax after stress or excitement. ■ (also **wind something down**) draw or bring gradually to a close: *business began to wind down as people awaited the new regime.*
wind up informal **1** arrive or end up in a specified state, situation, or place: *Kevin winds up in New York.* **2** another way of saying ***wind something up*** (in sense 2): *he wound up by attacking Nonconformists.*
wind someone up 1 Brit. informal tease or irritate someone: *she's only winding me up.* **2** (usu. **be wound up**) make tense or angry: *he was clearly wound up and frantic about his daughter.*
wind something up 1 arrange the affairs of and dissolve a company: *the company has since been wound up.* **2** gradually or finally bring an activity to a conclusion: *the experiments had to be wound up because the funding stopped.* **3** informal increase the tension, intensity, or power of something: *he wound up the engine.*

windage ▶ **noun** [mass noun] the air resistance of a moving object, such as a vessel or a rotating machine part, or the force of the wind on a stationary object.
■ the effect of the wind in deflecting a missile such as a bullet.

Windaus /ˈvɪndaʊs/, Adolf (1876–1959), German organic chemist. He did pioneering work on the chemistry and structure of steroids and their derivatives, notably cholesterol. He also investigated the D vitamins and vitamin B_1, and discovered histamine. Nobel Prize for Chemistry (1928).

windbag ▶ **noun** informal, derogatory a person who talks at length but says little of any value.

– DERIVATIVES **windbaggery** noun.

wind band ▶ **noun** a group of musicians playing mainly woodwind instruments.

windbound ▶ **adjective** (of a sailing ship) unable to sail because of extreme or contrary winds.

windbreak ▶ **noun** a thing, such as a row of trees or a fence, wall, or screen, that provides shelter or protection from the wind.

windbreaker ▶ **noun** US trademark another term for **WINDCHEATER**.

windburn ▶ **noun** [mass noun] reddening and soreness of the skin caused by prolonged exposure to the wind.

– DERIVATIVES **windburned** (also **windburnt**) adjective.

windcheater ▶ **noun** chiefly Brit. a wind-resistant jacket with a close-fitting neck, waistband, and cuffs.

windchest ▶ **noun** a chest or box in an organ which receives wind from the bellows and admits it to the pipes or reeds.

wind chill ▶ **noun** [mass noun] the cooling effect of wind blowing on a surface.

wind chimes ▶ **plural noun** a decorative arrangement of small pieces of glass, metal, or shell suspended from a frame, typically hung near a door or window so as make a tinkling sound in the draught.

wind-down ▶ **noun** [in sing.] a gradual lessening of activity, intensity, or scale as something comes to an end: *the wind-down of space exploration.*

winder /ˈwʌɪndə/ ▶ **noun** a device or mechanism used to wind something, especially something such as a watch or clock or the film in a camera.

Windermere /ˈwɪndəmɪə/ a lake in Cumbria, in the south-eastern part of the Lake District. At about 17 km (10 miles) in length, it is the largest lake in England. The town of Windermere lies on its eastern shores.

windfall ▶ **noun** an apple or other fruit blown down from a tree or bush by the wind.
■ a piece of unexpected good fortune, typically one that involves receiving a large amount of money: [as modifier] *windfall profits.*

windfall tax (also **windfall profits tax**) ▶ **noun** a tax levied on an unforeseen or unexpectedly large profit, especially one regarded to be excessive or unfairly obtained.

wind farm ▶ **noun** an area of land with a group of energy-producing windmills or wind turbines.

windflower ▶ **noun** an anemone.

windgall ▶ **noun** a small painless swelling just above the fetlock of a horse, caused by inflammation of the tendon sheath.

wind gap ▶ **noun** a valley cut through a ridge by erosion by a river which no longer follows a course through the valley.

wind gauge ▶ **noun** an anemometer.

wind harp ▶ **noun** another term for **AEOLIAN HARP**.

Windhoek /ˈwɪnthʊk, ˈvɪnt-/ the capital of Namibia, situated in the centre of the country; pop. 58,600 (1992). It was the capital of the former German protectorate of South West Africa from 1892 until 1919, emerging as capital of independent Namibia in 1990.

windhover ▶ **noun** dialect a kestrel.

Windies ▶ **plural noun** informal West Indians, especially the West Indian cricket team.

windigo /ˈwɪndɪgəʊ/ (also **wendigo**) ▶ **noun** (pl. **-os** or **-oes**) (in the folklore of the northern Algonquian Indians) a cannibalistic giant; a person who has been transformed into a monster by the consumption of human flesh.

– ORIGIN from Ojibwa *wintiko*.

winding /ˈwʌɪndɪŋ/ ▶ **noun** [mass noun] the action of winding something or of moving in a twisting or spiral course.
■ (**windings**) twisting movements: *the windings of the stream.* ■ [count noun] an electrical conductor that is wound round a magnetic material, especially one encircling part of the stator or rotor of an electric motor or generator or forming part of a transformer. ■ (**windings**) things that wind or are wound round something.
▶ **adjective** following a twisting or spiral course: *our bedroom was at the top of a winding staircase.*

winding engine ▶ **noun** a powered winch or similar machine used for hauling or hoisting heavy loads.

winding sheet ▶ **noun** a sheet in which a corpse is wrapped for burial; a shroud.

wind instrument ▶ **noun** a musical instrument in which sound is produced by the vibration of air, typically by the player blowing into the instrument.
■ a woodwind instrument as distinct from a brass instrument.

b **b**ut | d **d**og | f **f**ew | g **g**et | h **h**e | j **y**es | k **c**at | l **l**eg | m **m**an | n **n**o | p **p**en | r **r**ed | s **s**it | t **t**op | v **v**oice | w **w**e | z **z**oo | ʃ **sh**e | ʒ deci**s**ion | θ **th**in | ð **th**is | ŋ ri**ng** | x lo**ch** | tʃ **ch**ip | dʒ **j**ar

windjammer ▶ noun **1** historical a merchant sailing ship.
2 US another term for **WINDCHEATER**.

windlass ▶ noun a winch, especially one on a ship or in a harbour.
▶ verb [with obj.] haul or lift (something) with a windlass.
– ORIGIN late Middle English: probably an alteration of obsolete *windas*, via Anglo-Norman French from Old Norse *vindáss*, literally 'winding pole'.

wind load (also **wind loading**) ▶ noun Engineering the force on a structure arising from the impact of wind on it.

wind machine ▶ noun a machine used in the theatre or in film-making for producing a blast of air or imitating the sound of wind.
■ a wind-driven turbine for producing electricity.

windmill ▶ noun a building with sails or vanes that turn in the wind and generate power to grind corn into flour.
■ a similar structure used to generate electricity or draw water. ■ Brit. a toy consisting of a stick with curved vanes attached that turn in the wind. ■ a propeller, especially one used formerly on an autogiro.
▶ verb [with obj.] move (one's arms) around in a circle in a manner suggestive of the rotating sails or vanes of a windmill.
■ [no obj.] (of one's arms) move in such a way. ■ [no obj.] (of the propeller or rotor of an aircraft, or the aircraft itself) spin unpowered.
– PHRASES **fling** (or **throw**) **one's cap over the windmill(s)** dated act recklessly or unconventionally. **tilt at windmills** see **TILT**.

window ▶ noun **1** an opening in the wall or roof of a building or vehicle that is fitted with glass in a frame to admit light or air and allow people to see out.
■ a pane of glass filling such an opening: *thieves smashed a window and took £600.* ■ an opening in a wall or screen through which customers are served in a bank, ticket office, or similar building. ■ a space behind the window of a shop where goods are displayed for sale: [as modifier] *beautiful window displays.*
2 a thing resembling such an opening in form or function, in particular:
■ a transparent panel on an envelope to show an address. ■ Computing a framed area on a display screen for viewing information. ■ (**window on/into/to**) a means of observing and learning about: *television is a window on the world.* ■ Physics a range of electromagnetic wavelengths for which a medium (especially the atmosphere) is transparent.
3 an interval or opportunity for action: *the parliamentary recess offers a good window for a bid.*
■ an interval during which atmospheric and astronomical circumstances are suitable for the launch of a spacecraft.
4 [mass noun] strips of metal foil dispersed in the air to obstruct radar detection. [ORIGIN: military code word.]
– PHRASES **go out (of) the window** informal (of a plan or pattern of behaviour) no longer exist; disappear. **window of opportunity** a favourable opportunity for doing something that must be seized immediately if it is not to be missed. **window of vulnerability** an opportunity to attack something that is at risk (especially as a cold war claim that America's land-based missiles were easy targets for a Soviet first strike). **windows of the soul** organs of sense, especially the eyes.
– DERIVATIVES **windowless** adjective.
– ORIGIN Middle English: from Old Norse *vindauga*, from *vindr* 'wind' + *auga* 'eye'.

window box ▶ noun a long narrow box in which flowers and other plants are grown, placed on an outside window sill.

window cleaner ▶ noun a person who is employed to clean windows.
■ [mass noun] a substance used for cleaning windows.

window dressing ▶ noun [mass noun] the arrangement of an attractive display in a shop window.
■ an adroit but superficial or actually misleading presentation of something, designed to create a favourable impression: *the government's effort has amounted to little more than window dressing.*

windowed ▶ adjective **1** having a window or windows for admitting light or air: [in combination] *a row of bay-windowed houses.*

2 Computing having or using framed areas on a display screen for viewing information.

window frame ▶ noun a supporting frame for the glass of a window.

windowing ▶ noun [mass noun] Computing the use of windows for the simultaneous display of more than one item on a screen.

window ledge ▶ noun another term for **WINDOW SILL**.

windowpane ▶ noun **1** a pane of glass in a window.
2 a broad flatfish with numerous dark spots, found in the western Atlantic. Also called **SAND DAB**.
● *Scophthalmus aquosus,* family Scophthalmidae (or Bothidae).

Windows ▶ plural noun [treated as sing.] trademark a GUI operating system for personal computers.

window seat ▶ noun a seat below a window, especially one in a bay or alcove.
■ a seat next to a window in an aircraft, train, or other vehicle.

window-shop ▶ verb [no obj.] look at the goods displayed in shop windows, especially without intending to buy anything: [as noun **window-shopping**] *window-shopping is the favourite pastime of all New Yorkers.*
– DERIVATIVES **window-shopper** noun.

window sill ▶ noun a ledge or sill forming the bottom part of a window.

window tax ▶ noun Brit. historical a tax on windows or similar openings that was abolished in 1851.

wind pack ▶ noun [mass noun] snow which has been compacted by the wind.

windpipe ▶ noun the air passage from the throat to the lungs; the trachea.

wind rock ▶ noun [mass noun] damage to the roots of young plants, caused by the movement of the stem in the wind.

wind rose ▶ noun a diagram showing the relative frequency of wind directions at a place.

windrow ▶ noun a long line of raked hay, corn sheaves, or peats laid out to dry in the wind.
■ N. Amer. a long line of material heaped up by the wind.

windsail ▶ noun historical a long wide tube or funnel of sailcloth used to convey air to the lower parts of a ship.

Windscale former name (1947–81) for **SELLAFIELD**.

wind scorpion ▶ noun another term for **SUN SPIDER**.

windscreen ▶ noun Brit. a glass screen at the front of a motor vehicle.

windscreen wiper (N. Amer. **windshield wiper**) ▶ noun a power-operated device for keeping a windscreen clear of rain, typically with a rubber blade on an arm that moves in an arc.

wind shear ▶ noun [mass noun] variation in wind velocity occurring along a direction at right angles to the wind's direction and tending to exert a turning force.

windshield ▶ noun North American term for **WINDSCREEN**.

windslab ▶ noun [mass noun] a thick crust formed on the surface of soft snow by the wind, of a kind liable to slip and create an avalanche.

windsock ▶ noun a light, flexible cylinder or cone mounted on a mast to show the direction and strength of the wind, especially at an airfield.

Windsor[1] **1** a town in southern England, on the River Thames opposite Eton; pop. 31,540 (1981).
2 an industrial city and port in Ontario, southern Canada, on Lake Erie opposite the US city of Detroit; pop. 223,240 (1991).

Windsor[2] the name of the British royal family since 1917. Previously Saxe-Coburg-Gotha, it was changed in response to anti-German feeling in the First World War.

Windsor, Duke of the title conferred on Edward VIII on his abdication in 1936.

Windsor Castle a royal residence at Windsor, founded by William the Conqueror on the site of an earlier fortress and extended by his successors, particularly Edward III. The castle was severely damaged by fire in 1992.

Windsor chair ▶ noun a wooden dining chair with a semicircular back supported by upright rods.

Windsor knot ▶ noun a large, loose triangular knot in a necktie, produced by making extra turns when tying.

Windsor tie ▶ noun dated, chiefly US a wide silk bias-cut necktie, tied in a loose double knot.

wind sprint ▶ noun Athletics a form of exercise involving moving from a walk or slow run to a faster run and repeatedly reversing the process.

windstorm ▶ noun chiefly N. Amer. a storm with very strong wind but little or no rain or snow; a gale.

wind-sucking ▶ noun [mass noun] (in a horse) habitual behaviour involving repeated arching of the neck and sucking in and swallowing air, often accompanied by a grunting sound.

windsurfer ▶ noun a person who takes part in windsurfing.
■ (trademark in the US) a sailboard.

windsurfing ▶ noun [mass noun] the sport or pastime of riding on water on a sailboard.
– DERIVATIVES **windsurf** verb.

windswept ▶ adjective **1** (of a place) exposed to strong winds: *the windswept moors.*
2 (of a person or their appearance) untidy after being exposed to the wind: *his windswept hair.*

wind tunnel ▶ noun a tunnel-like apparatus for producing an airstream of known velocity past models of aircraft, buildings, etc., in order to investigate flow or the effect of wind on the full-size object.
■ an open space through which strong winds are channelled by surrounding tall buildings.

wind turbine ▶ noun a turbine having a large vaned wheel rotated by the wind to generate electricity.

wind-up ▶ noun **1** Brit. informal an attempt to tease or irritate someone.
2 an act of concluding or finishing something: *a company wind-up.*
3 Baseball the motions of a pitcher preparing to pitch the ball.

windward ▶ adjective & adverb facing the wind or on the side facing the wind: [as adj.] *the windward side of the boat.* Contrasted with **LEEWARD**.
▶ noun [mass noun] the side or direction from which the wind is blowing: *he had beaten to windward across St Austell Bay.*
– PHRASES **to windward of** dated in an advantageous position in relation to: *I happen to have got to windward of the young woman.*

Windward Islands a group of islands in the eastern Caribbean. Constituting the southern part of the Lesser Antilles, they include Martinique, Dominica, St Lucia, Barbados, St Vincent and the Grenadines, and Grenada. Their name refers to their position further upwind, in terms of the prevailing south-easterly winds, than the Leeward Islands.

windy[1] /ˈwɪndi/ ▶ adjective (**windier**, **windiest**) **1** (of weather, a period of time, or a place) marked by or exposed to strong winds: *a very windy day.*
■ resembling the wind in sound or force: *Pratt's sigh was windy.*
2 Brit. suffering from, marked by, or causing an accumulation of gas in the alimentary canal.
■ informal using or expressed in many words that sound impressive but mean little: *the way to save time in an exam is by omitting windy phrases.*
3 [predic.] Brit. informal (of a person) nervous or anxious about something.
– DERIVATIVES **windily** adverb, **windiness** noun.
– ORIGIN Old English *windig* (see **WIND**[1], **-Y**[1]).

windy[2] /ˈwaɪndi/ ▶ adjective (of a road or river) following a curving or twisting course.

wine[1] ▶ noun [mass noun] an alcoholic drink made from fermented grape juice.
■ [with modifier] an alcoholic drink made from the fermented juice of specified other fruits or plants: *a glass of elderflower wine.* ■ short for **WINE RED**.
▶ verb [with obj.] (**wine and dine someone**) entertain someone by offering them drinks or a meal: *members of Congress have been lavishly wined and dined by lobbyists for years.*
■ [no obj.] (of a person) take part in such entertainment: *we wined and dined with Edwin's and Bernard's friends.*
– PHRASES **good wine needs no bush** proverb there's no need to advertise or boast about something of good quality as people will always discover its merits. **wine, women, and song** the hedonistic life of drinking, sexual pleasure, and carefree

entertainment proverbially required by men. [ORIGIN: proverbial; compare with the anonymous couplet (found in the Luther room at Wartburg) *Wer nicht liebt Wein, Weib und Gesang Der bleibt ein Narr sein Leben lang* 'Who loves not wine, woman, and song, He is a fool his whole life long'.]

– DERIVATIVES **winey** (also **winy**) adjective.

– ORIGIN Old English *wín*, of Germanic origin; related to Dutch *wijn*, German *Wein*, based on Latin *vinum*.

wine² ▶ verb [no obj.] W. Indian dance with rhythmic gyratory movements of the pelvic region: *the crowd jumped and wined and churned the field into mud.*

– ORIGIN from WIND², influenced by TWINE.

wine bar ▶ noun a bar or small restaurant where wine is the main drink available.

wineberry ▶ noun **1** a bristly deciduous shrub native to China and Japan, producing scarlet berries used in cookery.
● *Rubus phoenicolasius*, family Rosaceae.
■ the fruit of this bush.
2 another term for MAKO².

winebibber ▶ noun archaic or poetic/literary a habitual drinker of alcohol.

– DERIVATIVES **winebibbing** noun & adjective.

wine bottle ▶ noun a glass bottle for wine, the standard size holding 75 cl or 26⅔ fl. oz.

wine box ▶ noun a square carton of wine with a dispensing tap.

wine cellar ▶ noun a cellar in which wine is stored.
■ a stock of wine.

wine glass ▶ noun a glass with a stem and foot, used for drinking wine.

– DERIVATIVES **wineglassful** noun (pl. **-fuls**).

winegrower ▶ noun a cultivator of grapes for wine.

wine gum ▶ noun a small coloured fruit-flavoured sweet made with gelatin.

wine list ▶ noun a list of the wines available in a restaurant.
■ a restaurant's selection or stock or wines.

winemaker ▶ noun a producer of wine; a winegrower.

winemaking ▶ noun [mass noun] the production of wine.

wine of origin ▶ noun (in South Africa) an official designation on wine-bottle labels, indicating that the wine has been certified as originating from a recognized region or estate and also as being of a particular cultivar or vintage.

wine press ▶ noun a press in which grapes are squeezed in making wine.

wine red ▶ noun [mass noun] a dark red colour like that of red wine.

wine route ▶ noun (in South Africa) a touring route taking in several wine farms which are within easy driving distance of one another and are open to the public for wine tasting and the sale of wine.

winery ▶ noun (pl. **-ies**) chiefly US an establishment where wine is made.

Winesap ▶ noun a large red American apple, used for cooking and as a dessert apple.

wineskin ▶ noun an animal skin sewn up and used to hold wine.

wine tasting ▶ noun an event at which people taste and compare a number of wines.
■ [mass noun] the action of judging the quality of wine by tasting it.

– DERIVATIVES **wine taster** noun.

wine vinegar ▶ noun [mass noun] vinegar made from wine rather than malt.

wine waiter ▶ noun Brit. a waiter responsible for serving wine.

wing ▶ noun **1** any of a number of specialized paired appendages that enable some animals to fly, in particular:
■ (in a bird) a modified forelimb that bears large feathers. ■ (in a bat or pterosaur) a modified forelimb with skin stretched between or behind the fingers. ■ (in most insects) each of two or four flat extensions of the thoracic cuticle, either transparent or covered in scales. ■ the meat on the wing bone of a bird used as food. ■ (usu. **wings**) figurative power or means of flight or rapid motion: *time flies by on wings.*

2 a rigid horizontal structure that projects from both sides of an aircraft and supports it in the air.
■ (**wings**) a pilot's certificate of ability to fly a plane, indicated by a badge representing a pair of wings: *Michael earned his wings as a commercial pilot.*
3 a part that projects, in particular:
■ Brit. a raised part of the body of a car or other vehicle above the wheel. ■ [usu. with adj. or noun modifier] a part of a large building, especially one that projects from the main part: *the maternity wing at South Cleveland Hospital.* ■ Anatomy a lateral part or projection of an organ or structure. ■ Botany a thin membranous appendage of a fruit or seed that is dispersed by the wind.
4 a group within a political party or other organization that holds particular views or has a particular function: *Sinn Fein, the political wing of the IRA.*
5 a side area, or a person or activity associated with that area, in particular:
■ (**the wings**) the sides of a theatre stage out of view of the audience. ■ (in soccer, rugby, and hockey) the part of the field close to the sidelines. ■ (also **wing forward**) an attacking player positioned near to one of the sidelines. ■ a flank of a battle array.
6 an air force unit of several squadrons or groups.

▶ verb **1** [no obj., with adverbial of direction] travel on wings or fly: *George satisfied his keen urge to fly by winging homewards with the Royal Air Force.*
■ move, travel, or be sent quickly, as if flying: *the prize will be winging its way to you.* ■ [with obj. and adverbial of direction] send or convey (something) quickly, as if by air: *just jot down the title on a postcard and wing it to us.* ■ [with obj.] archaic enable (someone or something) to fly or move rapidly: *the convent was at some distance, but fear would wing her steps.*
2 [with obj.] shoot (a bird) in the wing, so as to prevent flight without causing death: *one bird was winged for every bird killed.*
■ wound (someone) superficially, especially in the arm or shoulder.
3 (**wing it**) informal speak or act without preparation; improvise: *a little boning up puts you ahead of the job-seekers who try to wing it.* [ORIGIN: from theatrical slang, originally meaning 'to play a role without properly knowing the text' (either by relying on a prompter in the wings or by studying the part in the wings between scenes).]

– PHRASES **in the wings** ready to do something or to be used at the appropriate time: *older councillors were replaced by technocrats waiting in the wings.* **on the wing** (of a bird) in flight. **on a wing and a prayer** with only the slightest chance of success. **on wings** used suggest happiness by reference to the light movement or feeling of flying: *'I'm on wings,' she admitted. 'It's wonderful seeing the palace brightened up.'* **spread** (or **stretch** or **try**) **one's wings** extend one's activities and interests or start new ones. **take wing** (of a bird, insect, or other winged creature) fly away. ■ depart swiftly; flee: *Louise took wing for America.* **under one's wing** in or into one's protective care.

– DERIVATIVES **wingless** adjective, **wing-like** adjective.

– ORIGIN Middle English (originally in the plural): from Old Norse *vængir*, plural of *vængr*.

wing back ▶ noun Soccer a player who plays in a wide position on the field, taking part both in attack and defence.

wingbeat ▶ noun one complete set of motions of a wing in flying.

wing case ▶ noun each of a pair of modified toughened forewings which cover the functional wings in certain insects, especially an elytron of a beetle.

wing chair ▶ noun a high-backed armchair with side pieces projecting from the back, originally in order to protect the sitter from drafts.

wing chun /wɪŋ ˈtʃʊn/ ▶ noun [mass noun] a simplified form of kung fu used principally as a system of self-defence.

– ORIGIN Chinese, apparently from Yim *Wing Chun* (*fl.* mid 18th cent.) by whom the system was developed.

Wingco ▶ noun (pl. **-os**) military slang short for WING COMMANDER.

wing collar ▶ noun a high stiff shirt collar with turned-down corners.

wing commander ▶ noun a rank of officer in the RAF, above squadron leader and below group captain.

wing covert ▶ noun (in a bird's wing) each of the smaller feathers covering the bases of the flight feathers.

wing dam ▶ noun a dam or barrier built into a stream to deflect the current.

wingding ▶ noun informal, chiefly N. Amer. a lively event or party.

– ORIGIN 1920s (in the sense 'spasm, seizure', especially one associated with drug-taking): of unknown origin.

winged ▶ adjective **1** having wings for flight: *the earliest winged insects.*
2 having one or more lateral parts, appendages, or projections: *her winged spectacles.*

winged bean ▶ noun a tropical Asian pea plant which has four-sided pods with longitudinal flanges. The entire pod and the roots are edible.
● *Psophocarpus tetragonolobus*, family Leguminosae.

Winged Victory ▶ noun a winged statue of Nike, the Greek goddess of victory, especially the Nike of Samothrace (*c*.200 BC) preserved in the Louvre in Paris.

winged words ▶ plural noun poetic/literary highly apposite or significant words.

winger ▶ noun **1** an attacking player on the wing in soccer, hockey, and other sports.
2 [in combination] a member of a specified political wing: *a left-winger.*

wing forward ▶ noun see WING (in sense 5 of the noun).

wing half ▶ noun Soccer, dated a halfback positioned towards the right or left side of the field.

winglet ▶ noun **1** a little wing.
■ a vertical projection on the tip of an aircraft wing for reducing drag.

wingman ▶ noun (pl. **-men**) **1** a pilot whose aircraft is positioned behind and outside the leading aircraft in a formation.
2 another term for WINGER (in sense 1).

wing mirror ▶ noun a rear-view mirror projecting from the side of a motor vehicle.

wing nut ▶ noun **1** a nut with a pair of projections for the fingers to turn it on a screw.
2 an Asian tree of the walnut family, with a deeply fissured trunk, compound leaves, and characteristic broad-winged nutlets.
● Genus *Pterocarya*, family Juglandaceae.

wingover ▶ noun a manoeuvre in which an aircraft turns at the top of a steep climb and flies back along its original path.

wing oyster ▶ noun an edible marine bivalve mollusc with a flattened fragile shell, the hinge of which bears wing-like projections.
● Family Pteriidae: *Pteria* and other genera.

wing sail ▶ noun a rigid or semi-rigid structure similar to an aircraft wing fixed vertically on a boat to provide thrust from the action of the wind.

wing shooting ▶ noun [mass noun] the shooting of birds in flight.

wingspan (also **wingspread**) ▶ noun the maximum extent across the wings of an aircraft, bird, or other flying animal, measured from tip to tip.

wingstroke ▶ noun another term for WINGBEAT.

wing tip ▶ noun the tip of the wing of an aircraft, bird, or other animal.
■ (also **wingtip shoe**) N. Amer. a shoe with a toecap having a backward extending point and curving sides, resembling the shape of a wing.

wing walking ▶ noun [mass noun] acrobatic stunts performed on the wings of an airborne aircraft as a public entertainment.

wink ▶ verb [no obj.] close and open one eye quickly, typically to indicate that something is a joke or a secret or as a signal of affection or greeting: *he winked at Nicole as he passed.*
■ (**wink at**) pretend not to notice (something bad or illegal): *the authorities winked at their illegal trade.* ■ (of a bright object or a light) shine or flash intermittently.
▶ noun an act of closing and opening one eye quickly, typically as a signal: *Barney gave him a knowing wink.*

– PHRASES **as easy as winking** informal very easy or easily. **in the wink of an eye** (or **in a wink**) very quickly. **not sleep** (or **get**) **a wink** (or **not get a wink of sleep**) not sleep at all.

– ORIGIN Old English *wincian* 'close the eyes', of Germanic origin; related to German *winken* 'to wave', also to WINCE¹.

winkle ▶ **noun 1** a small herbivorous shore-dwelling mollusc with a spiral shell. Also called **PERIWINKLE**[2].
● Family Littorinidae, class Gastropoda: many genera and species, including the common and edible *Littorina littorea*.
2 informal a child's term for a penis.
▶ **verb** [with obj.] (**winkle something out**) chiefly Brit. extract or obtain something with difficulty: *I swore I wasn't going to tell her, but she **winkled** it all **out of** me.*
– DERIVATIVES **winkler** noun.
– ORIGIN late 16th cent.: shortening of **PERIWINKLE**[2].

winkle-picker ▶ **noun** Brit. informal a shoe with a long pointed toe, popular in the 1950s.

Winnebago /ˌwɪnəˈbeɪɡəʊ/ ▶ **noun** (pl. same or **-os**) **1** a member of an American Indian people formerly living in eastern Wisconsin and now mainly in southern Wisconsin and Nebraska.
2 [mass noun] the Siouan language of this people, now with few speakers.
3 (pl. **-os**) US trademark a motor vehicle with living accommodation used when travelling long distances or camping.
▶ **adjective** of or relating to the Winnebago people or their language.
– ORIGIN Algonquian, literally 'person of the dirty water', referring to the muddy Fox River.

winner /ˈwɪnə/ ▶ **noun** a person or thing that wins something: *a Nobel Prize winner.*
■ a goal or shot that wins a match or point. ■ Bridge a card that can be relied on to win a trick. ■ informal a thing that is a success or is likely to be successful: *the changes failed to make the soap opera a winner.*
– PHRASES **be on** (or **on to**) **a winner** be following a course or plan that is likely to bring rewards.

winning /ˈwɪnɪŋ/ ▶ **adjective 1** [attrib.] gaining, resulting in, or relating to victory in a contest or competition: *a winning streak.*
2 attractive; endearing: *a winning smile.*
▶ **noun** (**winnings**) money won, especially by gambling: *he went to collect his winnings.*
– DERIVATIVES **winningly** adverb (only in sense 2 of the adjective).

winningest ▶ **adjective** US informal having achieved the most success in competition: *the winningest coach in pro-football history.*

winning post ▶ **noun** a post marking the end of a race.

Winnipeg /ˈwɪnɪpɛɡ/ the capital of Manitoba, situated in the south of the province at the confluence of the Assiniboine and Red Rivers, to the south of Lake Winnipeg; pop. 612,770 (1991). First settled as a French trading post in 1738, it became a trading post of the Hudson's Bay Company in 1821. It grew rapidly after the arrival of the railway in 1881.

Winnipeg, Lake a large lake in the province of Manitoba in Canada, to the north of the city of Winnipeg. Fed by the Saskatchewan, Winnipeg, and Red Rivers from the east and south, the lake is drained by the Nelson River, which flows north-eastwards to Hudson Bay.

winnow ▶ **verb 1** [with obj.] blow a current of air through (grain) in order to remove the chaff.
■ remove (chaff) from grain: *women **winnow** the chaff **from** piles of unhusked rice.* ■ reduce the number in a set of (people or things) gradually until only the best ones are left: *the contenders had been winnowed to five.* ■ find or identify (a valuable or useful part of something): *amidst this welter of confusing signals, it's difficult to **winnow out** the truth.* ■ identify and remove (the least valuable or useful people or things): *guidelines that would help **winnow out** those not fit to be soldiers.*
2 [no obj.] poetic/literary (of the wind) blow: *the autumn wind winnowing its way through the grass.*
■ [with obj.] (of a bird) fan (the air) with wings.
– DERIVATIVES **winnower** noun.
– ORIGIN Old English *windwian*, from *wind* (see **WIND**[1]).

wino ▶ **noun** (pl. **-os**) informal a person who drinks excessive amounts of cheap wine or other alcohol, especially one who is homeless.

winsome ▶ **adjective** attractive or appealing in appearance or character: *a winsome smile.*
– DERIVATIVES **winsomely** adverb, **winsomeness** noun.
– ORIGIN Old English *wynsum*, from *wyn* 'joy' + **-SOME**[1].

winter ▶ **noun** the coldest season of the year, in the northern hemisphere from December to February and in the southern hemisphere from June to August: *the tree has a good crop of berries in winter* | [as modifier] *the winter months.*
■ Astronomy the period from the winter solstice to the vernal equinox. ■ (**winters**) poetic/literary years: *he seemed a hundred winters old.*
▶ **adjective** [attrib.] (of fruit) ripening late in the year: *a winter apple.*
■ (of wheat or other crops) sown in autumn for harvesting the following year.
▶ **verb** [no obj., with adverbial of place] (especially of a bird) spend the winter in a particular place: *birds wintering in the Channel.*
■ [with obj.] keep or feed (plants or cattle) during winter.
– DERIVATIVES **winterer** noun, **winterless** adjective, **winterly** adjective.
– ORIGIN Old English, of Germanic origin; related to Dutch *winter* and German *Winter*, probably also to **WET**.

winter aconite ▶ **noun** see **ACONITE** (sense 2).

winterberry ▶ **noun** (pl. **-ies**) a North American holly with toothed, non-prickly leaves and berries which persist through the winter.
● Genus *Ilex*, family Aquifoliaceae: several species, in particular *I. verticillata*.

winterbourne ▶ **noun** Brit. a stream, typically on chalk or limestone, which flows only after wet weather.
– ORIGIN Old English *winterburna* (see **WINTER**, **BURN**[2]).

winter cherry ▶ **noun** a plant of the nightshade family, with cherry-like fruit which ripens in winter.
● Several species in the family Solanaceae, in particular *Solanum capsicastrum*, which is grown as a pot plant, and the Chinese lantern plant.

winter count ▶ **noun** a pictorial record or chronicle of the events of each year, kept by various North American Indian peoples.

winter cress ▶ **noun** a bitter-tasting cress of north temperate regions.
● Genus *Barbarea*, family Cruciferae: several species, in particular *B. vulgaris*.

winter flounder ▶ **noun** a common flatfish of the western Atlantic, having cryptic grey-brown coloration and popular as food in winter in North America.
● *Pseudopleuronectes americanus*, family Pleuronectidae.

winter garden ▶ **noun** a garden of plants, such as evergreens, that flourish in winter.
■ a conservatory in which flowers and other plants are grown in winter.

wintergreen ▶ **noun 1** a North American plant from which a pungent oil is obtained:
● the checkerberry or a related shrub whose leaves produce oil.
● a birch tree whose bark produces oil (*Betula lenta*, family Betulaceae).
■ (also **oil of wintergreen**) [mass noun] a pungent oil containing methyl salicylate, now obtained from this birch tree or made synthetically, used medicinally and as a flavouring.
2 a low-growing plant of acid soils in north temperate regions, with spikes of white bell-shaped flowers.
● *Pyrola* and other genera, family Pyrolaceae.
– ORIGIN mid 16th cent.: the plants so named because of remaining green in winter, suggested by Dutch *wintergroen*, German *Wintergrün*.

Winterhalter /ˈvɪntəˌhaltə, German ˈvɪntɐˌhaltɐ/, Franz Xavier (1806–73), German painter. He painted many portraits of European royalty and aristocracy.

winter heliotrope ▶ **noun** a plant of the daisy family, which produces fragrant lilac flowers in winter.
● *Petasites fragrans*, family Compositae.

winterize (also **-ise**) ▶ **verb** [with obj.] (usu. **be winterized**) chiefly N. Amer. adapt or prepare (something, especially a house) for use in cold weather: *the house was winterized to extend the period of time it could be let.*
– DERIVATIVES **winterization** noun.

winter jasmine ▶ **noun** a yellow-flowered Chinese jasmine which blooms during the winter.
● *Jasminum nudiflorum*, family Oleaceae.

winter moth ▶ **noun** a moth that emerges in the winter, the female of which has only vestigial wings. It was formerly a major pest of fruit trees.
● Several species in the family Geometridae, in particular *Operophtera brumata*.

Winter Olympics an international contest of winter sports held every four years at a two year interval from the summer games. They have been held separately from the main games since 1924.

Winter Palace the former Russian imperial residence in St Petersburg, stormed in the Revolution of 1917 and later used as a museum and art gallery.

winter quarters ▶ **plural noun** accommodation for the winter, especially for soldiers.

winter sleep ▶ **noun** [mass noun] hibernation.

winter solstice ▶ **noun** the solstice at midwinter, at the time of the shortest day, about 22 December in the northern hemisphere and 21 June in the southern hemisphere.
■ Astronomy the solstice in December.

winter sports ▶ **plural noun** sports performed on snow or ice, such as skiing and ice skating.

winter squash ▶ **noun** a squash which has a hard rind and may be stored.
● Cultivars of *Cucurbita moschata* and *C. maxima*, family Cucurbitaceae.

wintersweet ▶ **noun** a deciduous Chinese shrub which produces heavily scented yellow flowers in winter before the leaves appear.
● *Chimonanthus praecox*, family Calycanthaceae.

Winterthur /ˈvɪntəˌtʊə, German ˈvɪntɐˌtuːɐ/ an industrial town in northern Switzerland; pop. 85,680 (1990).

winter-tide ▶ **noun** poetic/literary term for **WINTERTIME**.

wintertime /ˈwɪntətʌɪm/ ▶ **noun** the season or period of winter.

Winter War the war between the USSR and Finland in 1939–40. Heavily outnumbered by invading Soviet troops, the Finns were defeated and forced to cede western Karelia to the Soviet Union. Also called **RUSSO-FINNISH WAR**.

wintry (also **wintery**) ▶ **adjective** (**wintrier**, **wintriest**) characteristic of winter, especially in feeling or looking very cold and bleak: *a wintry landscape.*
– DERIVATIVES **wintrily** adverb, **wintriness** noun.
– ORIGIN Old English *wintrig* (see **WINTER**, **-Y**[1]).

win-win ▶ **adjective** [attrib.] of or denoting a situation in which each party benefits in some way: *we are aiming for a win-win situation.*

WIP ▶ **abbreviation for** work in progress (chiefly in business and financial contexts).

wipe ▶ **verb** [with obj.] clean or dry (something) by rubbing its surface with a cloth, a piece of paper, or one's hand: *Paulie wiped his face with a handkerchief* | *he **wiped down** the kitchen wall.*
■ [with obj. and adverbial] remove (dirt or moisture) from something by rubbing its surface with a cloth, a piece of paper, or one's hand: *she wiped away a tear.* ■ clean (something) by rubbing it against a surface: *the man wiped his hands on his hips.* ■ [with obj. and adverbial] spread (a liquid) over a surface by rubbing: *gently wipe the lotion over the eyelids.* ■ [with obj. and adverbial] figurative remove or eliminate (something) completely: *things have happened to wipe the smile off Kate's face.* ■ erase (data) from a magnetic medium. ■ pass (a swipe card) over the electronic device that reads it. ■ pass (a light pen) over a bar code. ■ Austral./NZ informal reject or dismiss (a person or idea): *you can wipe that idea, if that's what you're thinking.*
▶ **noun 1** an act of wiping.
2 a piece of disposable absorbent cloth, especially one treated with a cleansing agent, for wiping something clean.
3 a cinematographic effect in which an existing picture seems to be wiped out by a new one as the boundary between them moves across the screen.
– PHRASES **wipe someone's eye** Brit. informal, dated get the better of someone. **wipe the floor with** informal inflict a humiliating defeat on: *they wiped the floor with us in a 3–0 win.* **wipe the slate clean** forgive or forget past faults or offences; make a fresh start.
– DERIVATIVES **wipeable** adjective.
– ORIGIN Old English *wīpian*, of Germanic origin; related to **WHIP**.
▶ **wipe something off** subtract an amount from a value or debt: *the crash wiped 24 per cent off stock prices.*
wipe out informal be capsized by a wave while surfing. ■ N. Amer. fall over or off a vehicle.
wipe someone out 1 kill a large number of people: *the plague had wiped out whole villages.* **2** (usu. **be wiped out**) ruin someone financially. **3** informal

W

exhaust or intoxicate someone.

wipe something out eliminate something completely: *their life savings were wiped out.*

wipe-out ▶ noun informal an instance of complete destruction: *a nuclear wipe-out.* ■ a fall from a surfboard. ■ the obliteration of one radio signal by another.

wiper ▶ noun **1** a windscreen wiper. **2** an electrical contact which moves across a surface. **3** a cam or tappet.

WIPO ▶ abbreviation for World Intellectual Property Organization.

Wiradhuri /ˈwɪˈradʒəri/ ▶ noun [mass noun] an Aboriginal language of SE Australia, now extinct.

wire ▶ noun **1** [mass noun] metal drawn out into the form of a thin flexible thread or rod. ■ [count noun] a piece of such metal. ■ a length or quantity of wire used, for example, for fencing or to carry an electric current. ■ an electronic listening device that can be concealed on a person. **2** informal a telegram or cablegram.
▶ verb [with obj.] **1** install electric circuits or wires in: *wiring a plug* | *electricians **wired up** searchlights.* ■ connect (someone or something) to a piece of electronic equipment: *a microphone wired to a loudspeaker.* **2** provide, fasten, or reinforce with wires: *they wired his jaw.* **3** informal, chiefly US send a telegram or cablegram to: *she wired her friend for advice.* ■ [with two objs] send (money) to (someone) by means of a telegram or cablegram: *he was expecting a friend in Australia to wire him $1,500.* **4** snare (an animal) with wire. **5** (usu. **be wired**) Croquet obstruct (a ball, shot, or player) by a hoop.
– PHRASES **by wire** by telegraph. **down to the wire** informal used to denote a situation whose outcome is not decided until the very last minute: *it was probable that the test of nerves would go down to the wire.* **get one's wires crossed** see **CROSS**. **under the wire** N. Amer. informal at the last possible opportunity; just in time.
– DERIVATIVES **wirer** noun.
– ORIGIN Old English *wīr*; of Germanic origin, probably from the base of Latin *viere* 'plait, weave'.

wire brush ▶ noun a brush with tough wire bristles for cleaning hard surfaces. ■ a brush with wire strands, used on cymbals to produce a soft metallic sound.
▶ verb (**wire-brush**) [with obj.] clean (something) with a wire brush.

wire cloth ▶ noun [mass noun] cloth woven from wire.

wire-cutter ▶ noun (usu. **wire-cutters**) a tool for cutting wire.

wired ▶ adjective informal **1** making use of computers and information technology to transfer or receive information, especially by means of the Internet: *the economic arguments for getting your business wired.* **2** [predic.] in a nervous, tense, or edgy state: *not much sleep lately—I'm a little wired.* ■ under the influence of drugs or alcohol.

wire-draw ▶ verb (past **-drew**; past participle **-drawn**) [with obj.] [often as noun **wire-drawing**] draw out (metal) into wire by passing it through a series of holes of diminishing diameter in a steel plate. ■ figurative, archaic refine (an argument or idea) excessively, in such a way that it becomes strained or forced.
– DERIVATIVES **wire-drawer** noun.

wireframe ▶ noun Computing a skeletal three dimensional model in which only lines and vertices are represented.

wire fraud ▶ noun [mass noun] chiefly US financial fraud involving the use of telecommunications or information technology.

wire gauge ▶ noun a gauge for measuring the diameter of wire. ■ the diameter of wire; any of a series of standard sizes in which wire is made.

wire gauze ▶ noun [mass noun] a stiff gauze woven from wire.

wire grass ▶ noun [mass noun] chiefly N. Amer. & Austral. a grass with tough wiry stems.
● Genera *Aristida* and *Poa*, family Gramineae: several species, including the European *P. compressa*, which has become naturalized in North America.

wire-guided ▶ adjective (of a missile) directed by

means of electrical signals transmitted along fine connecting wires which uncoil during the missile's flight.

wire-haired ▶ adjective (especially of a dog breed) having stiff or wiry hair: *a wire-haired terrier.*

wireless ▶ noun dated, chiefly Brit. **1** (also **wireless set**) a radio receiving set. **2** [mass noun] broadcasting or telegraphy using radio signals.
▶ adjective lacking or not requiring wires.

wireline ▶ noun **1** a telegraph or telephone wire. **2** (in the oil industry) a cable for lowering and raising tools and other equipment in a well shaft. ■ an electric cable used to connect measuring devices in an oil well with indicating or recording instruments at the surface.

wireman ▶ noun (pl. **-men**) **1** chiefly US an installer or repairer of electric wiring. **2** a journalist working for a news agency.

wire mattress ▶ noun a mattress supported by wires stretched in a frame.

wirepuller ▶ noun N. Amer. informal a person, especially a politician, who exerts control or influence from behind the scenes.
– DERIVATIVES **wirepulling** noun.

wire rope ▶ noun a length of rope made from wires twisted together as strands.

wire service ▶ noun chiefly N. Amer. a news agency that supplies syndicated news by wire to newspapers, radio, and television stations.

wire stripper ▶ noun a tool for removing the insulation from electric wires.

wiretapping ▶ noun [mass noun] the practice of connecting a listening device to a telephone line to monitor conversations secretly.
– DERIVATIVES **wiretap** noun & verb, **wiretapper** noun.

wire-walker ▶ noun an acrobat who walks along and performs feats on a tightrope.

wire wheel ▶ noun a wheel on a car, especially a sports car, having narrow metal spokes.

wire wool ▶ noun Brit. another term for **STEEL WOOL**.

wireworm ▶ noun the worm-like larva of a click beetle. Many wireworms feed on the underground parts of plants and can cause damage to arable and other crops.

wiring ▶ noun [mass noun] a system of wires providing electric circuits for a device or building. ■ the installation of this. ■ informal the structure of the nervous system or brain perceived as determining a basic or innate pattern of behaviour.

Wirral /ˈwɪrəl/ a peninsula on the coast of NW England, between the estuaries of the Rivers Dee and Mersey. Full name **THE WIRRAL PENINSULA**.

Wirtschaftswunder /ˈvɪətʃafts,vʊndə, German ˈvɪrtʃafts,vʊndə/ ▶ noun an economic miracle, especially the economic recovery of the Federal Republic of West Germany after the Second World War.
– ORIGIN German.

Wirtshaus /ˈvɪətshaʊs, German ˈvɪrtshaʊs/ ▶ noun (pl. **Wirtshäuser** /-hɔɪzə, German -hɔʏzɐ/) a hostel or inn in a German-speaking country.
– ORIGIN German, literally 'house of the innkeeper'.

wiry ▶ adjective (**wirier**, **wiriest**) resembling wire in form and texture: *his wiry black hair.* ■ (of a person) lean, tough, and sinewy: *Bernadette was a small, wiry woman.*
– DERIVATIVES **wirily** adverb, **wiriness** noun.

Wis. ▶ abbreviation for Wisconsin.

wis ▶ verb (**wisses**, **wissed**, **wissing**) [no obj.] archaic know well: *and, you wis, Lord Julian is a hasty man.*
– ORIGIN early 16th cent.: originally in *I wis*, alteration of the obsolete adverb *iwis* 'certainly', erroneously interpreted as 'I know' (associated with *wist*, past tense of **WIT**²).

Wisconsin¹ /wɪsˈkɒnsɪn/ a state in the northern US, bordering on Lakes Superior (in the north-west) and Michigan (in the east); pop. 4,891,770 (1990); capital, Madison. Ceded to Britain by the French in 1763 and acquired by the US in 1783 as part of the former Northwest Territory, it became the 30th state of the US in 1848.
– DERIVATIVES **Wisconsinite** noun.

Wisconsin² /wɪsˈkɒnsɪn/ ▶ noun [usu. as modifier] Geology the last (or last two) of the Pleistocene glaciations

of North America, approximating to the Weichsel of northern Europe.
■ the system of deposits laid down at this time.

Wisd. ▶ abbreviation for (in biblical references) Wisdom of Solomon (Apocrypha).

Wisden /ˈwɪzdən/, John (1826–84), English cricketer. He is remembered as the publisher of *Wisden Cricketers' Almanack*, an annual publication which first appeared in 1864.

wisdom ▶ noun [mass noun] the quality of having experience, knowledge, and good judgement; the quality of being wise.
■ the soundness of an action or decision with regard to the application of such experience, knowledge, and good judgement: *some questioned the wisdom of building the dam so close to an active volcano.* ■ the body of knowledge and principles that develops within a specified society or period: *oriental wisdom.*
– PHRASES **in someone's wisdom** used ironically to suggest that an action is not well judged: *in their wisdom they decided to dispense with him.*
– ORIGIN Old English *wīsdōm* (see **WISE**¹, **-DOM**).

wisdom literature ▶ noun [mass noun] the biblical books of Job, Proverbs, Ecclesiastes, Song of Songs, Wisdom of Solomon, and Ecclesiasticus collectively.
■ similar works, especially from the ancient Near East, containing proverbial sayings and practical maxims.

Wisdom of Solomon a book of the Apocrypha ascribed to Solomon and containing a meditation on wisdom. The book is thought actually to date from about 1st century BC to the 1st century AD.

wisdom tooth ▶ noun each of the four hindmost molars in humans which usually appear at about the age of twenty.

wise¹ ▶ adjective having or showing experience, knowledge, and good judgement: *she seems kind and wise* | *a wise precaution.*
■ responding sensibly or shrewdly to a particular situation: *it would be wise to discuss the matter with the chairman of the committee.* ■ [predic.] having knowledge in a specified subject: *he is wise in the ways of haute couture.* ■ [predic.] (**wise to**) informal alert to or aware of: *at seven she was already wise to the police.*
– PHRASES **be wise after the event** understand and assess an event or situation only after its implications have become obvious. **be none** (or **not any**) **the wiser** know no more than before.
– DERIVATIVES **wisely** adverb.
– ORIGIN Old English *wīs*, of Germanic origin; related to Dutch *wijs* and German *weise*, also to **WIT**².
▶ **wise up** [often in imperative] informal become alert to or aware of something: *wise up to the flavours of North Africa.*

wise² ▶ noun archaic the manner or extent of something: *he did it this wise.*
– PHRASES **in no wise** not at all.
– ORIGIN Old English *wīse*, of Germanic origin; related to **WIT**².

-wise ▶ suffix forming adjectives and adverbs of manner or respect such as *clockwise*, *otherwise*. Compare with **-WAYS**.
■ informal with respect to; concerning: *security-wise, there are few problems.*
– ORIGIN from **WISE**².

USAGE In modern English the suffix **-wise** is attached to nouns to form a sentence adverb meaning 'concerning or with respect to', as in **confidence-wise**, **tax-wise**, **price-wise**, **time-wise**, **news-wise**, and **culture-wise**. The suffix is very productive and widely used in modern English but most of the words so formed are considered inelegant or not good English style.

wiseacre /ˈwʌɪzeɪkə/ ▶ noun a person with an affectation of wisdom or knowledge, regarded with scorn or irritation by others; a know-all.
– ORIGIN late 16th cent.: from Middle Dutch *wijsseggher* 'soothsayer', probably from the Germanic base of **WIT**². The assimilation to **ACRE** remains unexplained.

wisecrack informal ▶ noun a clever and pithy spoken witticism.
▶ verb [no obj.] make a wisecrack: [as noun **wisecracking**] *his warmth, boisterousness, and constant wisecracking.*
– DERIVATIVES **wisecracker** noun.

wise guy informal ▶ noun **1** a person who speaks and behaves as if they know more than others. **2** US a member of the Mafia.

wise man ▶ noun a man versed in magic, witchcraft, or astrology. See also **THREE WISE MEN**.

wisenheimer /ˈwʌɪz(ə)nˌhʌɪmə/ ▶ noun US informal a person who behaves in an irritatingly smug or arrogant fashion, typically by making clever remarks and displaying their knowledge.
– ORIGIN early 20th cent.: from **WISE** + the suffix *-(n)heimer* found in surnames such as *Oppenheimer*.

wisent /ˈwiːz(ə)nt/ ▶ noun the European bison. See **BISON**.
– ORIGIN mid 19th cent.: from German; related to **BISON**.

wise saw ▶ noun a proverbial saying.

wise woman ▶ noun chiefly historical a woman considered to be knowledgeable in matters such as herbal healing, magic charms, or other traditional lore.

wish ▶ verb [no obj.] feel or express a strong desire or hope for something that is not easily attainable; want something that cannot or probably will not happen: *we wished for peace* | [with clause] *he wished that he had practised the routines.*
▪ silently invoke such a hope or desire, especially in a ritualized way: *I closed my eyes and wished.* ▪ [with infinitive] feel or express a desire to do something: *they wish to become involved.* ▪ [with obj. and infinitive] ask (someone) to do something or that (something) be done: *I wish it to be clearly understood.* ▪ [with two objs] express a desire for (the success or good fortune) of (someone): *they wish her every success.* ▪ [with obj.] (**wish something on**) hope that something unpleasant will happen to: *I would not wish it on the vilest soul.*
▶ noun a desire or hope for something to happen: *the union has reiterated its wish for an agreement* | [with infinitive] *it is their wish to continue organizing similar exhibitions.*
▪ (usu. **wishes**) an expression of such a desire, typically in the form of a request or instruction: *she must carry out her late father's wishes.* ▪ an invocation or recitation of a hope or desire: *he makes a wish.* ▪ (usu. **wishes**) an expression of a desire for someone's success or good fortune: *they had received kindness and good wishes from total strangers.* ▪ a thing or event that is or has been desired; an object of desire: *the petitioners eventually got their wish.*
– PHRASES **if wishes were horses, beggars would ride** proverb if you could achieve your aims simply by wishing for them, life would be very easy. **wish someone well** feel or express a desire for someone's well-being. **the wish is father to the thought** proverb we believe a thing because we wish it to be true.
– DERIVATIVES **wisher** noun [in combination] *an ill-wisher.*
– ORIGIN Old English *wȳscan*, of Germanic origin; related to German *wünschen*, also to **WEEN** and **WONT**.

USAGE Is it more correct to say *I wish I were rich* or *I wish I was rich*? On the question of the use of the subjunctive mood, see **usage** at **SUBJUNCTIVE**.

wishbone ▶ noun **1** a forked bone (the furcula) between the neck and breast of a bird. According to a popular custom, this bone from a cooked bird is broken by two people, the holder of the longer portion that results being entitled to make a wish.
2 an object of similar shape, in particular:
▪ a forked element in the suspension of a motor vehicle or aircraft, typically attached to a wheel at one end with the two arms hinged to the chassis. ▪ Sailing a boom in two halves which curve outwards around a sail and meet aft of it.

wish book ▶ noun N. Amer. informal a mail-order catalogue.

wishful ▶ adjective having or expressing a desire or hope for something to happen.
▪ expressing or containing a desire or hope for something impractical or unfeasible: *without resources the proposed measures were merely wishful thinking.*
– DERIVATIVES **wishfully** adverb, **wishfulness** noun.

wish-fulfilment ▶ noun [mass noun] the satisfying of unconscious desires in dreams or fantasies.

wishing well ▶ noun a well into which one drops a coin and makes a wish.

wish list ▶ noun a list of desired things or occurrences.

wish-wash ▶ noun [mass noun] informal a weak or watery drink: *one pot of wish-wash called 'tea'.*
▪ insipid or excessively sentimental talk or writing: *this isn't just emotional wish-wash.*
– ORIGIN late 18th cent.: reduplication of **WASH**.

wishy-washy ▶ adjective (of drink or liquid food such as soup) weak; watery.
▪ feeble or insipid in quality or character; lacking strength or boldness: *wishy-washy liberalism.*
– ORIGIN early 18th cent.: reduplication of **WASHY**.

Wisła /ˈviswa/ Polish name for **VISTULA**.

wisp ▶ noun a small thin or twisted bunch, piece, or amount of something: *wisps of smoke rose into the air.*
▪ a small bunch of hay or straw used for drying or grooming a horse. ▪ a small thin person, typicallya child: *a fourteen-year-old wisp of a girl.*
– DERIVATIVES **wispily** adverb, **wispiness** noun, **wispy** adjective (**wispier, wispiest**).
– ORIGIN Middle English: origin uncertain; perhaps related to **WHISK**.

Wissenschaft /ˈvɪs(ə)nʃaft/ ▶ noun [mass noun] the systematic pursuit of knowledge, learning, and scholarship (especially as contrasted with its application).
– ORIGIN German, literally 'knowledge'.

wist past and past participle of **WIT**².

Wistar rat /ˈwɪstə, ˈwɪstɑː/ ▶ noun Biology & Medicine a rat of a strain developed for laboratory purposes.
– ORIGIN 1930s: named after the *Wistar* Institute of Anatomy and Biology, Philadelphia, US.

wisteria /wɪˈstɪərɪə/ (also **wistaria** /-ˈstɛːrɪə/) ▶ noun a climbing shrub of the pea family, with hanging clusters of pale bluish-lilac flowers. Native to East Asia and North America, ornamental varieties are widely grown on walls and pergolas.
● Genus *Wisteria*, family Leguminosae: several species.
– ORIGIN modern Latin, named after Caspar *Wistar* (or *Wister*) (1761–1818), American anatomist.

wistful ▶ adjective having or showing a feeling of vague or regretful longing: *a wistful smile.*
– DERIVATIVES **wistfully** adverb, **wistfulness** noun.
– ORIGIN early 17th cent.: apparently from obsolete *wistly* 'intently', influenced by **WISHFUL**.

wit¹ ▶ noun [mass noun] **1** mental sharpness and inventiveness; keen intelligence: *he does not lack perception or native wit.*
▪ (**wits**) the intelligence required for normal activity; basic human intelligence: *he needed all his wits to figure out the way back.*
2 a natural aptitude for using words and ideas in a quick and inventive way to create humour: *his caustic wit cuts through the humbug.*
▪ [count noun] a person who has such an aptitude: *she is such a wit.*
– PHRASES **be at one's wits' end** be overwhelmed with difficulties and at a loss as to what to do next. **be frightened** (or **scared**) **out of one's wits** be extremely frightened; be immobilized by fear. **gather** (or **collect**) **one's wits** allow oneself to think calmly and clearly in a demanding situation. **have** (or **keep**) **one's wits about one** be constantly alert and vigilant. **live by one's wits** earn money by clever and sometimes dishonest means, having no regular employment. **pit one's wits against** compete with (someone or something).
– DERIVATIVES **witted** adjective [in combination] *slow-witted.*
– ORIGIN Old English *wit(t), gewit(t)*, denoting the mind as the seat of consciousness, of Germanic origin; related to Dutch *weet* and German *Witz*, also to **WIT**².

wit² ▶ verb (**wot, witting**; past and past participle **wist**) [no obj.] **1** archaic have knowledge: *I addressed a few words to the lady you wot of* | [with obj.] *I wot that but too well.*
2 (**to wit**) that is to say (used to make clearer or more specific something already said or referred to): *the textbooks show an irritating parochialism, to wit an almost total exclusion of papers not in English.*
– ORIGIN Old English *witan*, of Germanic origin; related to Dutch *weten* and German *wissen*, from an Indo-European root shared by Sanskrit *veda* 'knowledge' and Latin *videre* 'see'.

witan /ˈwɪtən/ ▶ noun another term for **WITENAGEMOT**.
– ORIGIN representing the Old English plural of *wita* 'wise man'.

witblits /ˈvətbləts/ ▶ noun S. African a type of raw spirits, especially one that has been illicitly distilled, in particular:
▪ a raw brandy made from peaches and other fruit. ▪ a colourless spirit made from grapes left from winemaking.
– ORIGIN Afrikaans, from *wit* 'white' + *blits* 'lightning'.

witch ▶ noun **1** a woman thought to have evil magic powers. Witches are popularly depicted as wearing a black cloak and pointed hat, and flying on a broomstick.
▪ a follower or practitioner of modern witchcraft; a Wiccan priest or priestess. ▪ informal an ugly or unpleasant old woman; a hag. ▪ a girl or woman capable of enchanting or bewitching a man.
2 an edible North Atlantic flatfish which is of some commercial value.
● *Glyptocephalus cynoglossus*, family Pleuronectidae.
▶ verb [with obj.] (of a witch) cast an evil spell on: *Mrs Mucharski had somehow witched the house.*
▪ (of a girl or woman) enchant (a man): *she witched Jake.*
– PHRASES **as cold as** (or **colder than**) **a witch's tit** informal very cold.
– DERIVATIVES **witchlike** adjective, **witchy** adjective.
– ORIGIN Old English *wicca* (masculine), *wicce* (feminine), *wiccian* (verb); current senses of the verb are probably a shortening of **BEWITCH**.

witch ball ▶ noun a ball of decorated, typically coloured or silvered blown glass, originally used as a charm against witchcraft.

witchcraft ▶ noun [mass noun] the practice of magic, especially black magic; the use of spells and the invocation of spirits. See also **WICCA**.

witch doctor ▶ noun (among tribal peoples) a magician credited with powers of healing, divination, and protection against the magic of others.

witch elm ▶ noun variant spelling of **WYCH ELM**.

witchery ▶ noun [mass noun] the practice of magic: *warding off evil spirits and acts of witchery.*
▪ compelling power exercised by beauty, eloquence, or other attractive or fascinating qualities.

witches' broom ▶ noun [mass noun] dense twiggy growth in a tree caused by infection with fungus (especially rusts), mites, or viruses.

witches' butter ▶ noun [mass noun] a black gelatinous European fungus which forms folded cup-like masses on dead wood.
● *Exidia plana*, family Tremellaceae, class Hymenomycetes.

witches' sabbath ▶ noun see **SABBATH** (sense 2).

witchetty /ˈwɪtʃɪti/ (also **witchetty grub**) ▶ noun (pl. **-ies**) a large whitish wood-eating larva of a beetle or moth, eaten as food by some Aboriginals.
– ORIGIN from Adnyamathanha *wityu* 'hooked stick (for extracting grubs)' + *varti* 'grub'.

witch grass ▶ noun [mass noun] a tough creeping grass that can become an invasive weed:
● couch grass. ● (also **old witch grass**) a North American grass (*Panicum capillare*, family Gramineae).

witch hazel (also **wych hazel**) ▶ noun a shrub with fragrant yellow flowers which is widely grown as an ornamental. American species flower in autumn and Asian species in winter.
● Genus *Hamamelis*, family Hamamelidaceae: several species, especially *H. virginiana*, which is the source of the lotion.
▪ [mass noun] an astringent lotion made from the bark and leaves of this plant.
– ORIGIN mid 16th cent.: *witch*, variant of *wych* (see **WYCH ELM**).

witch-hunt ▶ noun historical a search for and subsequent persecution of a supposed witch.
▪ informal a campaign directed against a person or group holding unorthodox or unpopular views.
– DERIVATIVES **witch-hunting** noun.

witching ▶ noun [mass noun] the practice of witchcraft.
– PHRASES **the witching hour** midnight (with reference to the belief that witches are active and magic takes place at that time). [ORIGIN: with allusion to *the witching time of night* from Shakespeare's *Hamlet* (III. ii. 377).]

witchweed ▶ noun [mass noun] a small parasitic plant which attaches itself to the roots of other plants. Native to the Old World tropics and southern Africa, it can cause serious damage to crops such as maize and sugar.
● Genus *Striga*, family Scrophulariaceae.

witenagemot /ˈwɪt(ə)nəgɪˌməʊt/ ▶ noun historical an Anglo-Saxon national council or parliament. Also called **WITAN**.
– ORIGIN Old English, from *witena*, genitive plural of *wita* 'wise man' + *gemōt* 'meeting' (compare with **MOOT**).

with ▶ preposition **1** accompanied by (another person or thing): *a nice steak with a bottle of red wine.*
▪ in the same direction as: *marine mammals generally*

W

swim with the current. ■ along with (with reference to time): *wisdom comes with age.*
2 possessing (something) as a feature or accompaniment: *a flower-sprigged blouse with a white collar.*
■ marked by or wearing: *a tall dark man with a scar on one cheek | a small man with thick glasses.*
3 indicating the instrument used to perform an action: *cut it with a knife | treatment with acid before analysis.*
■ indicating the material used for some purpose: *fill the bowl with water.*
4 in opposition to: *a row broke out with another man.*
5 indicating the manner or attitude of the person doing something: *with great reluctance.*
6 indicating responsibility: *leave it with me.*
7 in relation to: *my father will be angry with me.*
8 employed by: *she's with the Inland Revenue now.*
■ using the services of: *I bank with the TSB.*
9 affected by (a particular fact or condition): *with no hope | in bed with lumbago.*
■ indicating the cause of an action or condition: *trembling with fear | the paper was yellow with age.*
10 indicating separation or removal from something: *to part with one's dearest possessions | their jobs could be dispensed with.*
– PHRASES **away** (or **off** or **out** etc.) **with** used in exhortations to take or send someone or something away, in, out, etc.: *off with his head.* **be with someone 1** agree with or support someone: *we're all with you on this one.* **2** informal follow someone's meaning: *I'm not with you.* **with it** informal **1** knowledgeable about and following modern ideas and fashions: *a young, with-it film buyer.* **2** [usu. with negative] alert and comprehending: *I'm not really with it this morning.* **3** in addition; besides: *he seems a decent lad, and clever with it.* **with that** at that point; immediately after saying or doing something dramatic: *with that, she flounced out of the room.*
– ORIGIN Old English, probably a shortening of a Germanic preposition related to obsolete English *wither* 'adverse, opposite'.

withal /wɪˈðɔːl/ archaic ▶ **adverb** in addition; as a further factor or consideration: *the whole is light and portable, and ornamental withal.*
■ all the same; nevertheless (used when adding something that contrasts with a previous comment): *she gave him a grateful smile, but rueful withal.*
▶ **preposition** with (used at the end of a clause): *we sat with little to nourish ourselves withal but vile water.*
– ORIGIN Middle English: originally as *with all.*

withdraw ▶ **verb** (past **-drew**; past participle **-drawn**) **1** [with obj.] remove or take away (something) from a particular place or position: *slowly Ruth withdrew her hand from his.*
■ take back or away (something bestowed, proposed, or used): *the party threatened to withdraw its support for the government.* ■ take (money) out of an account: *normally you can withdraw up to £50 in cash.* ■ say that (a statement one has made) is untrue or unjustified: *he failed to withdraw his remarks and apologize.* ■ [no obj.] (of a man) practise coitus interruptus.
2 [no obj.] leave or come back from a place, especially a war zone: *Iraqi forces withdrew from Kuwait.*
■ [with obj.] cause (someone) to leave or come back from a place, especially a war zone: *both countries agreed to withdraw their troops.* ■ no longer participate in an activity or be a member of a team or organization: *his rival withdrew from the race on the second lap.* ■ depart to another room or place, especially in search of quiet or privacy. ■ retreat from contact or communication with other people: *he went silent and withdrew into himself.* ■ [with obj.] remove (a child) from class for remedial teaching.
3 [no obj.] cease to take an addictive drug: *for the cocaine user, it is possible to withdraw without medication.*
– ORIGIN Middle English: from the prefix *with-* 'away' + the verb **DRAW**.

withdrawal ▶ **noun** [mass noun] the action of withdrawing something: *the withdrawal of legal aid.*
■ [count noun] an act of taking money out of an account. ■ the action of ceasing to participate in an activity: *Italy's withdrawal from NATO.* ■ the process of ceasing to take an addictive drug.
– PHRASES **withdrawal symptoms** the unpleasant physical reaction that accompanies the process of ceasing to take an addictive drug.

withdrawing room ▶ **noun** archaic term for **DRAWING ROOM**.

withdrawn past participle of **WITHDRAW**.
▶ **adjective** not wanting to communicate with other people: *a disorder characterized by withdrawn and fearful behaviour.*

withe /wɪθ, wɪð, wʌɪð/ ▶ **noun** variant spelling of **WITHY**.

wither ▶ **verb 1** [no obj.] (of a plant) become dry and shrivelled: *the grass had withered to an unappealing brown | [as adj.* **withered**] *withered leaves.*
■ (of a person, limb, or the skin) become shrunken or wrinkled from age or disease: [as adj. **withered**] *a girl with a withered arm.* ■ cease to flourish; fall into decay or decline: *programmes would* **wither away** *if they did not command local support.* ■ (**wither away**) (of the state in Marxist theory) cease to exist because no longer necessary after the dictatorship of the proletariat has implemented the necessary changes in society.
2 [with obj.] cause harm or damage to: *a business that can wither the hardiest ego.*
■ mortify (someone) with a scornful look or manner: *his clipped tone withered Sylvester.*
– PHRASES **wither on the vine** fail to be implemented or dealt with because of neglect or inaction.
– ORIGIN late Middle English: apparently a variant of **WEATHER**, ultimately differentiated for certain senses.

withering ▶ **adjective 1** intended to make someone feel mortified or humiliated: *a withering look.*
2 (of heat) intense; scorching.
▶ **noun** [mass noun] the action of becoming dry and shrivelled.
■ the action of declining or decaying: *the withering of the PLO's revolutionary threat.*
– DERIVATIVES **witheringly** adverb (usu. in sense 1 of the adjective).

witherite /ˈwɪðərʌɪt/ ▶ **noun** [mass noun] a rare white mineral consisting of barium carbonate, occurring especially in veins of galena.
– ORIGIN late 18th cent.: from the name of William *Withering* (1741–99), the English physician and scientist who first described it, + **-ITE**[1].

withers ▶ **plural noun** the highest part of a horse's back, lying at the base of the neck above the shoulders. The height of a horse is measured to the withers.
– ORIGIN early 16th cent.: apparently a reduced form of *widersome*, from obsolete *wither-* 'against, contrary' (as the part that resists the strain of the collar) + a second element of obscure origin.

withershins /ˈwɪðəʃɪnz/ ▶ **adverb** variant spelling of **WIDDERSHINS**.

withhold ▶ **verb** (past and past participle **-held**) [with obj.] refuse to give (something that is due to or is desired by another): *the name of the dead man is being withheld* | [as noun **withholding**] *the withholding of consent to treatment.*
■ suppress or hold back (an emotion or reaction).
– DERIVATIVES **withholder** noun.
– ORIGIN Middle English: from the prefix *with-* 'away' + the verb **HOLD**[1].

withholding tax ▶ **noun** a tax deducted at source, especially one levied by some countries on interest or dividends paid to a person resident outside that country.

within ▶ **preposition** inside (something): *the spread of fire within the building.*
■ inside the range of (an area or boundary): *property located within the green belt.* ■ inside the range of (a specified action or perception): *within reach.* ■ not further off than (used with distances): *he lives within a few miles of Oxford.* ■ occurring inside (a particular period of time): *sold out within two hours | 33% offended again within two years of being released.* ■ inside the bounds set by (a concept, argument, etc.): *full cooperation within the terms of the treaty.*
▶ **adverb** inside; indoors: *enquire within.*
■ internally or inwardly: *beauty coming from within.*
– PHRASES **within doors** indoors.
– ORIGIN late Old English *withinnan* 'on the inside'

without ▶ **preposition 1** in the absence of: *he went to Sweden without her.*
■ not having the use or benefit of: *the first person to make the ascent without oxygen.* ■ [often with verbal noun] in circumstances in which the action mentioned does not happen: *they sat looking at each other without speaking.*
2 archaic or poetic/literary outside: *the barbarians without the gates.*
▶ **adverb** archaic or poetic/literary outside: *the enemy without.*
▶ **conjunction** archaic or dialect without it being the case that: *he won't be able to go without we know it.*
■ unless: *I'd never have known you without you spoke to me.*
– PHRASES **do without** see **DO**[1]. **go without** see **GO**[1].
– ORIGIN Old English *withūtan* 'on the outside'.

with-profits ▶ **adjective** Brit. (of an insurance policy) allowing the holder to receive a share of the profits made by the company, typically in the form of a bonus.

withstand ▶ **verb** (past and past participle **-stood**) [with obj.] remain undamaged or unaffected by; resist: *the structure had been designed to withstand winds of more than 100 mph.*
■ offer strong resistance or opposition to (someone or something).
– DERIVATIVES **withstander** noun.
– ORIGIN Old English *withstandan*, from the prefix *with-* 'against' + the verb **STAND**.

withy /ˈwɪði/ (also **withe**) ▶ **noun** (pl. **withies** or **withes**) a tough flexible branch of an osier or other willow, used for tying, binding, or basketry.
■ another term for **OSIER**.
– ORIGIN Old English *wīthig*, of Germanic origin; related to German *Weide*.

witless ▶ **adjective** foolish; stupid: *a witless retort.*
■ [as complement] to such an extent that one cannot think clearly or rationally: *I was scared witless.*
– DERIVATIVES **witlessly** adverb, **witlessness** noun.
– ORIGIN Old English *witlēas* 'crazy, dazed' (see **WIT**[1], **-LESS**).

witling ▶ **noun** archaic, usu. derogatory a person who considers themselves to be witty.

witloof /ˈwɪtluːf/ ▶ **noun** [mass noun] chicory of a broad-leaved variety grown for blanching.
– ORIGIN late 19th cent.: from Dutch, literally 'white leaf'.

witness ▶ **noun 1** a person who sees an event, typically a crime or accident, take place: *police are appealing for* **witnesses to** *the accident | I was witness to one of the most amazing comebacks in sprinting history.*
■ a person giving sworn testimony to a court of law or the police. ■ a person who is present at the signing of a document and signs it themselves to confirm this.
2 [mass noun] evidence; proof: *the memorial service was* **witness to** *the wide circle of his interest.*
■ used to refer to confirmation or evidence given by signature, under oath, or otherwise: **in witness thereof**, *the parties sign this document.* ■ open profession of one's religious faith through words or actions: *he told us of faithful Christian witness by many in his country.* ■ (also **witness mark**) [count noun] a line or remnant of an original surface on a workpiece to show how much material has been removed or the shape of the original outline.
▶ **verb 1** [with obj.] see (an event, typically a crime or accident) take place: *staff who witnessed the murder.*
■ have knowledge of (an event or change) from personal observation or experience: *what we are witnessing is the birth of a dangerously liberal orthodoxy.* ■ (of a time, place, or other context) be the setting in which (a particular event) takes place: *the 1980s witnessed an unprecedented increase in the scope of the electronic media.* ■ be present as someone signs (a document) or gives (their signature) to a document and sign it oneself to confirm this: *the clerk witnessed her signature.* ■ [in imperative] look at (used to introduce a fact illustrating a preceding statement): *the nuclear family is a vulnerable institution—witness the rates of marital breakdown.*
2 [no obj.] (**witness to**) give or serve as evidence of; testify to: *his writings witness to an inner toughness.*
■ (of a person) openly profess one's religious faith in: *one of the purposes of his coming was to nerve the disciples to witness to Jesus.*
– PHRASES **as God is my witness** (or **God be my witness**) an invocation of God as confirmation of the truth of a statement: *God be my witness, sir, I didn't!* **call someone or something to witness** archaic appeal or refer to someone or something for confirmation or evidence of something.
– ORIGIN Old English *witnes* (see **WIT**[1], **-NESS**).

witness box (US **witness stand**) ▶ **noun** Law the place in a court where a witness stands to give evidence.

Wittenberg /ˈvɪt(ə)nbəːg, German ˈvɪtnbɛrk/ a town in eastern Germany, on the River Elbe north-east of Leipzig; pop. 87,000 (1991). It was the scene in 1517 of Martin Luther's campaign against the Roman Catholic Church, which was a major factor in the rise of the Reformation.

witter ▶ **verb** [no obj.] Brit. informal speak at length about

trivial matters: *she'd been **wittering on** about Jennifer and her illness.*
– ORIGIN early 19th cent. (originally Scots and dialect): probably imitative.

Wittgenstein /ˈvɪtɡənstʌɪn/, Ludwig (Josef Johann) (1889–1951), British philosopher, born in Austria. His two major works, *Tractatus Logico-Philosophicus* (1921) and *Philosophical Investigations* (1953), examine language and its relationship to the world.

witticism ▶ **noun** a witty remark.
– ORIGIN 1677: coined by Dryden from **WITTY**, on the pattern of *criticism*.

witting ▶ **adjective** done in full awareness or consciousness; deliberate: *the witting and unwitting complicity of the institutions.*
■ (of a person) conscious or aware of the full facts of a situation: *there is no proof that the Chinese were witting accomplices.*
– DERIVATIVES **wittingly** adverb.
– ORIGIN late Middle English: from **WIT**[2] + **-ING**[2].

wittol /ˈwɪt(ə)l/ ▶ **noun** archaic a man who is aware and tolerant of his wife's infidelity; an acquiescent cuckold.
– ORIGIN late Middle English: apparently from **WIT**[2] + the last syllable (with the loss of *-d*) of **CUCKOLD**.

witty ▶ **adjective** (**wittier**, **wittiest**) showing or characterized by quick and inventive verbal humour: *a witty remark* | *Marlowe was charming and witty.*
– DERIVATIVES **wittily** adverb, **wittiness** noun.
– ORIGIN Old English *wit(t)ig* 'having wisdom' (see **WIT**[1], **-Y**[1]).

Witwatersrand /wɪtˈwɔːtəzˌrand/ (**the Witwatersrand**) a region of South Africa, around the city of Johannesburg. Consisting of a series of parallel rocky ridges, it forms a watershed between the Vaal and Olifant Rivers. The region contains rich gold deposits, first discovered in 1886. Also called **THE RAND**.
– ORIGIN Afrikaans, literally 'ridge of white waters'.

wivern ▶ **noun** archaic spelling of **WYVERN**.

wives plural form of **WIFE**.

wiz ▶ **noun** variant spelling of **WHIZZ** (in sense 2).

wizard ▶ **noun 1** a man who has magical powers, especially in legends and fairy tales.
■ a person who is very skilled in a particular field or activity: *a financial wizard.*
2 Computing a help feature of a software package that automates complex tasks by asking the user a series of easy-to-answer questions.
▶ **adjective** informal, dated, chiefly Brit. wonderful; excellent.
– DERIVATIVES **wizardly** adjective (only in sense 1 of the noun).
– ORIGIN late Middle English (in the sense 'philosopher, sage'): from **WISE**[1] + **-ARD**.

wizardry ▶ **noun** [mass noun] the art or practice of magic: *Merlin used his powers of wizardry for good.*
■ great skill in a particular area of activity: *Pless's wizardry with a bat.* ■ the product of such skill: *the car is full of hi-tech wizardry.*

wizen ▶ **adjective** archaic variant of **WIZENED**.

wizened /ˈwɪz(ə)nd/ ▶ **adjective** shrivelled or wrinkled with age: *a wizened, weather-beaten old man.*
– ORIGIN early 16th cent.: past participle of archaic *wizen* 'shrivel', of Germanic origin.

wizzo ▶ **adjective** variant spelling of **WHIZZO**.

wk ▶ **abbreviation for** week: *75 mg per day for 3 wks.*

Władysław II /vwadˈiswaf/ see **LADISLAUS II**.

WLTM ▶ **abbreviation for** would like to meet (used in lonely hearts advertisements).

Wm ▶ **abbreviation for** William.

WMO ▶ **abbreviation for** World Meteorological Organization.

WNW ▶ **abbreviation for** west-north-west.

WO ▶ **abbreviation for** Warrant Officer.

wo ▶ **exclamation** variant spelling of **WHOA**.

woad /wəʊd/ ▶ **noun** [mass noun] a yellow-flowered European plant of the cabbage family. It was formerly widely grown in Britain as a source of blue dye, which was extracted from the leaves after they had been dried, powdered, and fermented.
● *Isatis tinctoria*, family Cruciferae.
■ the dye obtained from this plant, now superseded by synthetic products.
– ORIGIN Old English *wād*, of Germanic origin; related to Dutch *wede* and German *Waid*.

wobbegong /ˈwɒbɪɡɒŋ/ (also **wobbegon**) ▶ **noun** a brown Australian carpet shark with pale markings, living in shallow waters around reefs.
● *Orectolobus maculatus*, family Orectolobidae.
– ORIGIN mid 19th cent.: probably from a New South Wales Aboriginal language.

wobble ▶ **verb** [no obj.] move unsteadily from side to side: *the table wobbles where the leg is too short.*
■ [with obj.] cause to move in such a way. ■ [with adverbial of direction] move in such a way in a particular direction: *they wobble around on their bikes.* ■ (of the voice) tremble; quaver: *her voice wobbled dangerously, but she brought it under control.* ■ figurative hesitate or waver between different courses of action; vacillate: *the President wobbled on Bosnia.*
▶ **noun** an unsteady movement from side to side.
■ a tremble or quaver in the voice. ■ a moment of hesitation or vacillation.
– ORIGIN mid 17th cent. (earlier as *wabble*): of Germanic origin; compare with Old Norse *vafla* 'waver'; related to the verb **WAVE**.

wobble-board ▶ **noun** Austral. a piece of fibreboard used as a musical instrument, which, when held in both hands and flexed, produces a low, rhythmic booming sound.

wobbler ▶ **noun 1** a person or thing that wobbles.
■ (in angling) a lure that wobbles and does not spin.
2 another term for **WOBBLY**: *Mum threw a wobbler.*

Wobblies ▶ **plural noun** popular name for members of **INDUSTRIAL WORKERS OF THE WORLD**.
– ORIGIN early 20th cent.: of unknown origin.

wobbly ▶ **adjective** (**wobblier**, **wobbliest**) tending to move unsteadily from side to side: *the car had a wobbly wheel.*
■ (of a person or their legs) weak and unsteady from illness, tiredness, or anxiety. ■ (of a person, action or state) uncertain, wavering, or insecure: *the evening gets off to a wobbly start.* ■ (of a speaker, singer, or voice) having a tendency to move out of tone or slightly vary in pitch. ■ (of a line or handwriting) not straight or regular; shaky.
▶ **noun** [in sing.] Brit. informal a fit of temper or panic: *my daughter **threw a wobbly** when I wouldn't let her play.*
■ (**the wobblies**) a fit of panic: *the driver was having an attack of the wobblies.*
– DERIVATIVES **wobbliness** noun.

Wodehouse /ˈwʊdhaʊs/, Sir P. G. (1881–1975), English writer; full name *Pelham Grenville Wodehouse*. His best-known works are humorous stories of the upper-class world of Bertie Wooster and his valet Jeeves, the first of which appeared in 1917.

Woden /ˈwəʊd(ə)n/ another name for **ODIN**.

wodge ▶ **noun** Brit. informal a large piece or amount of something: *he slapped **a wodge of** notes down on the counter.*
– ORIGIN mid 19th cent.: alteration of **WEDGE**[1].

woe ▶ **noun** often humorous great sorrow or distress: *the Everton tale of woe continued.*
■ (**woes**) things that cause sorrow or distress; troubles: *to add to his woes, customers have been spending less.*
– PHRASES **woe betide someone** (or **woe to someone**) used humorously to warn someone that they will be in trouble if they do a specified thing: *woe betide anyone wearing the wrong colour!* **woe is me!** an ironical or humorous exclamation of sorrow or distress.
– ORIGIN natural exclamation of lament: recorded as *wā* in Old English and found in several Germanic languages.

woebegone /ˈwəʊbɪɡɒn/ ▶ **adjective** sad or miserable in appearance: *don't look so woebegone, Joanna.*
– ORIGIN Middle English (in the sense 'afflicted with grief'): from **WOE** + *begone* 'surrounded' (past participle of obsolete *bego* 'go around, beset').

woeful ▶ **adjective** characterized by, expressive of, or causing sorrow or misery: *her face was woeful.*
■ very bad; deplorable: *the remark was enough to establish his woeful ignorance about the theatre.*
– DERIVATIVES **woefully** adverb [as submodifier] *the police response was woefully inadequate*, **woefulness** noun.

wog[1] ▶ **noun** Brit. offensive a person who is not white.
– ORIGIN 1920s: of unknown origin.

wog[2] ▶ **noun** Austral. informal an illness or infection, typically a minor one: *a flu wog struck.*
– ORIGIN 1930s: of unknown origin.

woggle ▶ **noun** a loop or ring of leather or cord through which the ends of a Scout's neckerchief are threaded.
– ORIGIN 1930s: of unknown origin.

Wöhler /ˈvəːlə, German ˈvøːlɐ/, Friedrich (1800–82), German chemist. His synthesis of urea from ammonium cyanate in 1828 demonstrated that organic compounds could be made from inorganic compounds. He was also the first to isolate the elements aluminium and beryllium.

wok ▶ **noun** a bowl-shaped frying pan used typically in Chinese cookery.
– ORIGIN Chinese (Cantonese dialect).

woke past of **WAKE**[1].

woken past participle of **WAKE**[1].

Woking /ˈwəʊkɪŋ/ a town in Surrey, SE England; pop. 81,770 (1981).

wold /wəʊld/ ▶ **noun** [often in place names] (usu. **wolds**) (in Britain) a piece of high, open, uncultivated land or moor: *the Lincolnshire Wolds.*
– ORIGIN Old English *wald* 'wooded upland', of Germanic origin; perhaps related to **WILD**. Compare with **WEALD**.

Wolf /vɒlf/, Hugo (Philipp Jakob) (1860–1903), Austrian composer. He is chiefly known as a composer of lieder, some of which are settings of Goethe and Heinrich Heine.

wolf ▶ **noun** (pl. **wolves**) **1** a wild carnivorous mammal which is the largest member of the dog family, living and hunting in packs. It is native to both Eurasia and North America, but is much persecuted and has been widely exterminated.
● *Canis lupus*, family Canidae; it is the chief ancestor of the domestic dog.
■ used in names of similar or related mammals, e.g. **maned wolf**, **Tasmanian wolf**.
2 used in similes and metaphors to refer to a rapacious, ferocious, or voracious person or thing.
■ informal a man who habitually seduces women. ■ N. Amer. informal a homosexual who habitually seduces men or adopts an active role with a partner.
3 a harsh or out-of-tune effect produced when playing particular notes or intervals on a musical instrument, caused either by the instrument's construction or by divergence from equal temperament.
▶ **verb** [with obj.] devour (food) greedily: *he **wolfed down** his breakfast.*
– PHRASES **cry wolf** call for help when it is not needed, with the effect that one is not believed when one really does need help. [ORIGIN: with allusion to the fable of the shepherd boy who deluded people with false cries of 'Wolf!'.] **hold** (or **have**) **a wolf by the ears** be in a precarious position. **keep the wolf from the door** have enough money to avert hunger or starvation (used hyperbolically): *I work part-time to pay the mortgage and keep the wolf from the door.* **throw someone to the wolves** leave someone to be roughly treated or criticized without trying to help or defend them. **a wolf in sheep's clothing** a person or thing that appears friendly or harmless but is really hostile. [ORIGIN: with biblical allusion to Matt. 7:15.]
– DERIVATIVES **wolfish** adjective, **wolfishly** adverb, **wolf-like** adjective.
– ORIGIN Old English *wulf*, of Germanic origin; related to Dutch *wolf* and German *Wolf*, from an Indo-European root shared by Latin *lupus* and Greek *lukos*. The verb dates from the mid 19th cent.

Wolf Cub ▶ **noun** chiefly Brit. former term for **CUB SCOUT**.

Wolfe[1], James (1727–59), British general. One of the leaders of the expedition sent to seize French Canada, he commanded the attack on the French capital, Quebec (1759). He was fatally wounded while leading his troops to victory on the Plains of Abraham, the scene of the battle which led to British control of Canada.

Wolfe[2], Thomas (Clayton) (1900–38), American novelist. His intense, romantic works, including his first, autobiographical novel *Look Homeward Angel* (1929), dwell idealistically on America.

Wolfe[3], Tom (b.1931), American writer; born *Thomas Kennerley Wolfe Jr.* Having been a news reporter for the *Washington Post* and the *Herald Tribune*, he examined contemporary American culture in *The Electric Kool-Aid Acid Test* (1968) and the novel *The Bonfire of the Vanities* (1988).

Wolfenden Report /ˈwʊlf(ə)nd(ə)n/ a study produced in 1957 by the Committee on Homosexual Offences and Prostitution in Britain which recommended the legalization of homosexual relations between consenting adults.

wolf fish ▶ noun a large long-bodied marine fish with a long-based dorsal fin and sharp doglike teeth, which lives in deep waters of the northern hemisphere. Also called **CATFISH**, **SEA WOLF**.
● Family Anarhichadidae: several genera and species, including the edible *Anarhichas lupus*.

wolfhound ▶ noun a dog of a large breed originally used to hunt wolves.

wolf pack ▶ noun a group of people or things that operate as a hunting and attacking pack, in particular a group of attacking submarines or aircraft.

wolfram /ˈwʊlfrəm/ ▶ noun [mass noun] tungsten or its ore, especially as a commercial commodity.
– ORIGIN mid 18th cent.: from German, assumed to be a miners' term, perhaps from *Wolf* 'wolf' + Middle High German *rām* 'soot', probably originally a pejorative term referring to the ore's inferiority to tin, with which it occurred.

wolframite ▶ noun [mass noun] a black or brown mineral which is the chief ore of tungsten. It consists of a tungstate of iron and manganese.

wolfsbane /ˈwʊlfsbeɪn/ ▶ noun a northern European aconite.
● Genus *Aconitum*, family Ranunculaceae: several species, in particular the purple-flowered *A. lycoctonum*.

Wolfsburg /ˈvɒlfsbəːg/ an industrial city on the Mittelland Canal in Lower Saxony, NW Germany; pop. 128,995 (1991).

wolfskin /ˈwʊlfskɪn/ ▶ noun the skin or pelt of a wolf.

wolf snake ▶ noun a harmless Old World snake with long upper teeth:
● a small nocturnal African snake (genus *Lycophidion*, family Colubridae), including the **Cape wolf snake** (*L. capense*).
● a medium-sized Asian snake (genus *Ophites* (formerly *Lycodon*), family Colubridae), including the **common wolf snake** or carpet snake (*O. aulicus*).

Wolfson /ˈwʊlfs(ə)n/, Sir Isaac (1897–1991), Scottish businessman and philanthropist. He established the Wolfson Foundation in 1955 for promoting and funding medical research and education. Colleges in both Oxford and Cambridge now bear his name.

wolf spider ▶ noun a fast-moving ground spider which runs after and springs on its prey.
● Family Lycosidae, order Araneae.

wolf whistle ▶ noun a whistle with a rising and falling pitch, directed towards someone to express sexual attraction or admiration.
▶ verb (**wolf-whistle**) [with obj.] whistle in such a way at: *fans wolf-whistled her as she took off her jacket* | [no obj.] *they wolf-whistled at me.*

Wollaston /ˈwɒləst(ə)n/, William Hyde (1766–1828), English chemist and physicist. He discovered palladium and rhodium, and pioneered techniques in powder metallurgy. Wollaston also demonstrated that static and current electricity were the same, invented a kind of slide rule for use in chemistry, and was the first to observe the dark lines in the solar spectrum.

wollastonite /ˈwɒləstənʌɪt/ ▶ noun [mass noun] a white or greyish mineral typically occurring in tabular masses in metamorphosed limestone. It is a silicate of calcium and is used as a source of rock wool.
– ORIGIN early 19th cent.: from the name of W. H. *Wollaston* (see **WOLLASTON**) + **-ITE**[1].

Wollongong /ˈwʊləŋɡɒŋ/ a city on the coast of New South Wales, SE Australia; pop. 211,420 (1991).

Wollstonecraft /ˈwɒlstənˌkrɑːft/, Mary (1759–97), English writer and feminist, of Irish descent. Her best-known work, *A Vindication of the Rights of Woman* (1792), defied assumptions about male supremacy and championed educational equality for women. In 1797 she married William Godwin and died shortly after giving birth to their daughter Mary Shelley.

Wolof /ˈwəʊlɒf/ ▶ noun (pl. same or **Wolofs**) **1** a member of a people living in Senegal and Gambia. **2** [mass noun] the Niger-Congo language of this people, which has about 2 million speakers.
▶ adjective of or relating to the Wolof or their language.
– ORIGIN the name in Wolof.

Wolsey /ˈwʊlzi/, Thomas (c.1474–1530), English prelate and statesman; known as **Cardinal Wolsey**. Wolsey dominated foreign and domestic policy in the early part of Henry VIII's reign, but incurred royal displeasure through his failure to secure the

papal dispensation necessary for Henry's divorce from Catherine of Aragon. He was arrested on a charge of treason and died on his way to trial.

Wolstonian /wɒlˈstəʊnɪən/ ▶ adjective Geology of, relating to, or denoting the penultimate Pleistocene glaciation in Britain, identified with the Saale of northern Europe (and perhaps the Riss of the Alps).
■ [as noun **the Wolstonian**] the Wolstonian glaciation or the system of deposits laid down during it.
– ORIGIN 1960s: from *Wolston*, the name of a village in Warwickshire, + **-IAN**.

Wolverhampton /ˌwʊlvəˈhæmpt(ə)n/ an industrial city in the Midlands, north-west of Birmingham; pop. 239,800 (1991).

wolverine /ˈwʊlvəriːn/ ▶ noun a heavily built short-legged carnivorous mammal with a long brown coat and a bushy tail, native to the tundra and forests of arctic and subarctic regions.
● *Gulo gulo*, family Mustelidae.
– ORIGIN late 16th cent. (earlier as *wolvering*): formed obscurely from *wolv-*, plural stem of **WOLF**.

Wolverine State informal name for **MICHIGAN**.

wolves plural form of **WOLF**.

woma /ˈwəʊmə/ ▶ noun a brownish-grey Australian python found in sandy desert areas.
● *Aspidites ramsayi*, family Pythonidae.
– ORIGIN 1930s: from Diyari (an Aboriginal language of South Australia).

woman ▶ noun (pl. **women**) an adult human female.
■ a female worker or employee. ■ a wife, girlfriend, or lover: *he wondered whether Billy had his woman with him.* ■ [with modifier] a female person associated with a particular place, activity, or occupation: *a young Clacton woman.* ■ [in sing.] female adults in general: *woman is intuitive.* ■ a female who is paid to clean someone's house and carry out general domestic duties. ■ a peremptory form of address to a woman: *don't be daft, woman.*
– PHRASES **be one's own woman** see **OWN**. **the little woman** a condescending way of referring to a man's wife. **my good woman** Brit. dated a patronizing form of address to a woman: *you're mistaken, my good woman.* **woman of letters** a female scholar or author. **woman of the streets** dated used euphemistically to refer to a prostitute. **woman of the world** see **WORLD**. **woman to woman** in a direct and frank way between two women.
– DERIVATIVES **womanless** adjective, **womanlike** adjective.
– ORIGIN Old English *wifmon*, *-man* (see **WIFE**, **MAN**), a formation peculiar to English, the ancient word being **WIFE**.

-woman ▶ combining form in nouns denoting:
■ a female of a specified nationality: *Englishwoman.* ■ a woman of specified origin or place of abode: *Yorkshirewoman.* ■ a woman belonging to a distinct specified group: *laywoman.* ■ a woman having a specified occupation or professional status: *chairwoman* | *saleswoman.* ■ a woman skilled in or associated with a specified activity, especially a craft or sport: *needlewoman* | *oarswoman.*

womanhood ▶ noun [mass noun] the state or condition of being a woman: *she was on the very brink of womanhood.*
■ the qualities considered to be natural to or characteristic of a woman: *Mary was cultivated as an ideal of womanhood.* ■ women considered collectively: *half of Britain's womanhood is dress size 14 and over.*

womanish ▶ adjective derogatory suitable to or characteristic of a woman: *he confused introspection with womanish indecision.*
■ (of a man) effeminate; unmanly: *Burden thought him a weak womanish fool.*
– DERIVATIVES **womanishly** adverb, **womanishness** noun.

womanism ▶ noun [mass noun] a form of feminism that acknowledges women's natural contribution to society (used by some in distinction to the term *feminism* and its association with white women).
– DERIVATIVES **womanist** noun.

womanize (also **-ise**) ▶ verb [no obj.] (of a man) engage in numerous casual sexual affairs with women (used to express disapproval): [as noun *womanizing*] *there were rumours that his womanizing had now become intolerable.*
– DERIVATIVES **womanizer** noun.

womankind ▶ noun [mass noun] women considered collectively: *she said she acted for womankind in bringing a sexual harassment claim against him.*

womanly ▶ adjective relating to or having the characteristics of a woman or women: *her smooth, womanly skin.*
■ (of a girl's or woman's body) fully developed and curvaceous: *I've got a womanly figure.*
– DERIVATIVES **womanliness** noun.

woman of the bedchamber ▶ noun (in the UK) a female attendant to the queen or queen mother, ranking in the royal household below lady of the bedchamber.

womb ▶ noun the organ in the lower body of a woman or female mammal where offspring are conceived and in which they gestate before birth; the uterus.
– DERIVATIVES **womb-like** adjective.
– ORIGIN Old English *wamb*, *womb*, of Germanic origin.

wombat /ˈwɒmbat/ ▶ noun a burrowing plant-eating Australian marsupial which resembles a small bear with short legs.
● Family Vombatidae: two genera and three species, in particular the **common wombat** (*Vombatus ursinus*).
– ORIGIN late 18th cent.: from Dharuk.

women plural form of **WOMAN**.

womenfolk ▶ plural noun the women of a particular family or community considered collectively.

Women's Institute (abbrev.: **WI**) ▶ noun an organization of women, especially in rural areas, who meet regularly and participate in crafts, cultural activities, and social work. Now worldwide, it was first set up in Ontario, Canada, in 1897, and in Britain in 1915.

women's lib ▶ noun informal short for **WOMEN'S LIBERATION**.
– DERIVATIVES **women's libber** noun.

women's liberation ▶ noun [mass noun] the liberation of women from inequalities and subservient status in relation to men, and from attitudes causing these (now generally replaced by the term *feminism*).

women's movement ▶ noun a broad movement campaigning for women's liberation and rights.

women's page ▶ noun a page of a newspaper or magazine devoted to topics intended to be of special interest to women.

women's rights ▶ plural noun rights that promote a position of legal and social equality of women with men.

women's studies ▶ plural noun [usu. treated as sing.] academic courses in sociology, history, literature, and psychology which focus on the roles, experiences, and achievements of women in society.

women's suffrage ▶ noun [mass noun] the right of women to vote.

womenswear ▶ noun [mass noun] clothing for women.

women's work ▶ noun [mass noun] work traditionally and historically undertaken by women, especially tasks of a domestic nature such as cooking, needlework, and child rearing.

womyn /ˈwɪmɪn/ ▶ plural noun non-standard spelling of 'women' adopted by some feminists in order to avoid the word ending *-men*.

won[1] past and past participle of **WIN**.

won[2] /wɒn/ ▶ noun (pl. same) the basic monetary unit of North and South Korea, equal to 100 jun in North Korea and 100 jeon in South Korea.
– ORIGIN from Korean *wăn*.

Wonder, Stevie (b.1950), American singer, songwriter, and musician; born *Steveland Judkins Morris*. His repertoire has included soul, rock, funk, and romantic ballads, as heard on albums such as *Innervisions* (1973). He has been blind since birth.

wonder ▶ noun [mass noun] a feeling of surprise mingled with admiration, caused by something beautiful, unexpected, unfamiliar, or inexplicable: *he had stood in front of it, observing the intricacy of the ironwork with the wonder of a child.*
■ the quality of a person or thing that causes such a feeling: *Athens was a place of wonder and beauty.* ■ [count noun] a strange or remarkable person, thing, or event: *the electric tramcar was looked upon as the wonder of the age.* ■ [as modifier] having remarkable properties or abilities: *a wonder drug.* ■ [in sing.] a surprising event or situation: *it is a wonder that losses are not much greater.*

▶**verb** [no obj.] **1** desire or be curious to know something: *how many times have I written that, I wonder?* | [with clause] *I can't help wondering how Georgina's feeling.*
■[with clause] used to express a polite question or request: *I wonder whether you have thought more about it?* ■ feel doubt: *even hereditary peers are inclined to **wonder about** the legitimacy of the place.*
2 feel admiration and amazement; marvel: *people stood by and **wondered at** such bravery* | [as adj. **wondering**] *a wondering look on her face.*
■be surprised: *if I feel compassion for her, it is not to be wondered at.*
– PHRASES **I shouldn't wonder** informal I think it likely. **no** (or **little** or **small**) **wonder** it is not surprising: ***it is little wonder that** the fax machine is so popular.* **nine days'** (or **seven-day** or **one-day**) **wonder** something that attracts enthusiastic interest for a short while but is then ignored or forgotten. **wonders will never cease** an exclamation of great surprise at something pleasing. **work** (or **do**) **wonders** have a very beneficial effect on someone or something: *a good night's sleep can work wonders for mind and body.*
– DERIVATIVES **wonderer** noun, **wonderingly** adverb.
– ORIGIN Old English *wundor* (noun), *wundrian* (verb), of Germanic origin; related to Dutch *wonder* and German *Wunder*, of unknown ultimate origin.

wonderful ▶**adjective** inspiring delight, pleasure, or admiration; extremely good; marvellous: *they all think she's wonderful* | *the climate was wonderful all the year round.*
– DERIVATIVES **wonderfully** adverb [as submodifier] *the bed was wonderfully comfortable*, **wonderfulness** noun.
– ORIGIN late Old English *wunderfull* (see **WONDER**, **-FUL**).

wonderland ▶**noun** a land or place full of wonderful things: *London was a wonderland of historical sites, museums, theatres, shops, and entertainment.*

wonderment ▶**noun** [mass noun] a state of awed admiration or respect: *Corbett shook his head in silent wonderment.*

wonder-of-the-world ▶**noun** W. Indian a succulent plant which forms plantlets in notches in the leaf margins under dry conditions. It originated in Madagascar and is used medicinally.
● *Bryophyllum pinnatum*, family Crassulaceae.

wonderstruck ▶**adjective** (of a person) experiencing a sudden feeling of awed delight or wonder.

wonder-worker ▶**noun** a person who performs miracles or wonders.
– DERIVATIVES **wonder-working** adjective.

wondrous ▶**adjective** poetic/literary inspiring a feeling of wonder or delight; marvellous: *this wondrous city.*
▶**adverb** [as submodifier] archaic marvellously; wonderfully: *she is grown wondrous pretty.*
– DERIVATIVES **wondrously** adverb, **wondrousness** noun.
– ORIGIN late 15th cent.: alteration of obsolete *wonders* (adjective and adverb), genitive of **WONDER**, on the pattern of *marvellous.*

wonga /ˈwɒŋɡə, ˈvɒŋɡə/ ▶**noun** [mass noun] Brit. informal money: *you want to earn a lot more wonga.*
– ORIGIN 1980s: perhaps from Romany *wongar* 'coal', also 'money'.

wonk ▶**noun 1** N. Amer. informal, derogatory a studious or hard-working person: *any kid with an interest in science was a wonk.*
■a person who takes an excessive interest in minor details of political policy: *he is a **policy wonk** in tune with a younger generation of voters.*
2 Nautical slang an incompetent or inexperienced sailor, especially a naval cadet.
– ORIGIN 1920s: of unknown origin.

wonky ▶**adjective** (**wonkier**, **wonkiest**) Brit. informal crooked; off-centre; askew: *you have a wonky nose and a crooked mouth.*
■(of a thing) unsteady; shaky: *they sat drinking, perched on the wonky stools.* ■ faulty: *your sense of judgement is a bit wonky at the moment.*
– DERIVATIVES **wonkily** adverb, **wonkiness** noun.
– ORIGIN early 20th cent.: fanciful formation.

wont /wəʊnt/ ▶**adjective** [predic., with infinitive] poetic/literary (of a person) in the habit of doing something; accustomed: *he was wont to arise at 5.30 every morning.*
▶**noun** (**one's wont**) formal or humorous one's customary behaviour in a particular situation: *Constance, as was her wont, had paid her little attention.*
▶**verb** (3rd sing. present **wonts** or **wont**; past and past participle **wont** or **wonted**) archaic make or be or become accustomed: [with obj.] *wont thy heart to thoughts hereof* | [no obj., with infinitive] *sons wont to nurse their Parents in old age.*
– ORIGIN Old English *gewunod*, past participle of *wunian*, 'dwell, be accustomed', of Germanic origin.

won't ▶**contraction of** will not.

wonted /ˈwəʊntɪd/ ▶**adjective** poetic/literary habitual; usual: *the place had sunk back into its wonted quiet.*
– ORIGIN late Middle English: from **WONT**.

wonton /wɒnˈtɒn/ ▶**noun** (in Chinese cookery) a small round dumpling or roll with a savoury filling, usually eaten boiled in soup.
– ORIGIN from Chinese (Cantonese dialect) *wān t'ān.*

woo ▶**verb** (**woos**, **wooed**) [with obj.] try to gain the love of (someone, typically a woman), especially with a view to marriage: *he wooed her with quotes from Shakespeare.*
■seek the favour, support, or custom of: *pop stars are being wooed by film companies eager to sign them up.*
– DERIVATIVES **wooable** adjective, **wooer** noun.
– ORIGIN late Old English *wōgian* (intransitive), *āwōgian* (transitive), of unknown origin.

Wood[1], Mrs Henry (1814–87), English novelist; née *Ellen Price*. Her ingenious and sensational plots about murders, thefts, and forgeries make her one of the forerunners of the modern detective novelist. Notable works: *East Lynne* (1861).

Wood[2], Sir Henry (Joseph) (1869–1944), English conductor. In 1895 he instituted the first of the Promenade Concerts, which he conducted every year until he died. He arranged the *Fantasia on British Sea Songs* (including 'Rule, Britannia') which remains a regular feature of the last night of the promenade concert season.

Wood[3], Natalie (1938–81), American actress. She played the vulnerable adolescent heroine of *Rebel Without A Cause* (1955), and similar roles in *Cry in the Night* (1956), *West Side Story* (1961), and *Inside Daisy Clover* (1966).

wood ▶**noun 1** [mass noun] the hard fibrous material that forms the main substance of the trunk or branches of a tree or shrub.
■such material when cut and used as timber or fuel: *a large table made of dark, polished wood* | [count noun] *best quality woods were used for joinery.* ■ (**the wood**) wooden barrels used for storing alcoholic drinks: *wines **from the wood**.* ■ [count noun] a golf club with a wooden or other head that is relatively broad from face to back (often with a numeral indicating the degree to which the face is angled to loft the ball). ■ [count noun] a shot made with such a club. ■ another term for **BOWL**[2] (in sense 1).
2 (also **woods**) an area of land, smaller than a forest, that is covered with growing trees: *a thick hedge divided the wood from the field* | *a long walk in the woods.*
– PHRASES **cannot see the wood** (or N. Amer. **the forest**) **for the trees** fail to grasp the main issue because of over-attention to details. **out of the wood** (or **woods**) out of danger or difficulty. **touch** (or chiefly N. Amer. **knock on**) **wood** said in order to prevent a confident statement from bringing bad luck: *I haven't been banned yet, touch wood.* [ORIGIN: with reference to the custom of touching something wooden to ward off bad luck.]
– DERIVATIVES **woodless** adjective.
– ORIGIN Old English *wudu*, from a Germanic word related to Welsh *gwŷdd* 'trees'.

wood alcohol ▶**noun** [mass noun] crude methanol made by distillation from wood.

wood-and-iron ▶**adjective** S. African (of a building) consisting of a wooden frame and corrugated iron walls and roof.

wood anemone ▶**noun** a spring-flowering Eurasian anemone with pink-tinged white flowers, growing in woodland and shady places.
● *Anemone nemorosa*, family Ranunculaceae.

wood ant ▶**noun** a large reddish-brown European ant found chiefly in woodland, living in nest mounds which it defends by spraying formic acid at the attacker.
● *Formica rufa*, family Formicidae.

wood avens ▶**noun** a yellow-flowered Eurasian plant which favours damp shady habitats. Also called **HERB BENNET**.
● *Geum urbanum*, family Rosaceae.

woodbine ▶**noun** [mass noun] either of two climbing plants:
● Brit. the common honeysuckle. ● US Virginia creeper.

woodblock ▶**noun** a block of wood, especially one forming part of a floor.
■a block of wood from which woodcut prints are made. ■ a print made in such a way. ■ a hollow wooden block used as a percussion instrument.

woodcarving ▶**noun** [mass noun] the action or skill of carving wood to make functional or ornamental objects.
■[count noun] an object made in this way.
– DERIVATIVES **woodcarver** noun.

woodchat (also **woodchat shrike**) ▶**noun** a shrike of southern Europe, North Africa, and the Middle East, having black and white plumage with a chestnut head.
● *Lanius senator*, family Laniidae.

woodchip ▶**noun** a chip of wood.
■(also **woodchip paper**) [mass noun] chiefly Brit. wallpaper with woodchips embedded in it to give a grainy surface texture.

woodchuck ▶**noun** a North American marmot with a heavy body and short legs.
● *Marmota monax*, family Sciuridae.
– ORIGIN late 17th cent.: alteration (by association with **WOOD**) of an American Indian name; compare with Cree *wuchak, otchock.*

woodcock ▶**noun** (pl. same) a woodland bird of the sandpiper family, with a long bill, brown camouflaged plumage, and a distinctive display flight.
● Genus *Scolopax*, family Scolopacidae: several species, in particular the **Eurasian woodcock** (*S. rusticola*), which is sometimes regarded as a game bird.

woodcraft ▶**noun** [mass noun] chiefly N. Amer. **1** skill in woodwork.
2 knowledge of woodland, especially with reference to camping and other outdoor pursuits.

woodcut ▶**noun** a print of.a type made from a design cut in a block of wood, formerly widely used for illustrations in books. Compare with **WOOD ENGRAVING**.
■[mass noun] the technique of making such prints.

woodcutter ▶**noun 1** a person who cuts down trees or branches, especially for fuel.
2 a person who makes woodcuts.
– DERIVATIVES **woodcutting** noun.

wood duck ▶**noun** a tree-nesting North American duck, the male of which has brightly coloured plumage. Also called **CAROLINA DUCK**.
● *Aix sponsa*, family Anatidae.

wooded ▶**adjective** (of an area of land) covered with woods or many trees: *a wooded valley.*
■another term for **WOODEN**.

wooden ▶**adjective 1** made of wood: *a wooden spoon* | *she closed the heavy wooden door.*
2 like or characteristic of wood: *a kind of dull wooden sound.*
■stiff and awkward in movement or manner: *she is one of the most wooden actresses of all time.*
– DERIVATIVES **woodenly** adverb (only in sense 2), **woodenness** noun (only in sense 2).

wood engraving ▶**noun** a print made from a finely detailed design cut into the end grain of a block of wood. Compare with **WOODCUT**.
■[mass noun] the technique of making such prints.
– DERIVATIVES **wood engraver** noun.

wooden-head ▶**noun** informal a stupid person.
– DERIVATIVES **wooden-headed** adjective, **wooden-headedness** noun.

wooden spoon ▶**noun** a spoon made of wood and used especially in cooking.
■chiefly Brit. a real or imaginary prize given in fun to the person who is last in a race or competition. [ORIGIN: originally a spoon given to the candidate coming last in the Cambridge mathematical tripos.]

woodentop ▶**noun** informal, derogatory **1** a uniformed policeman.
2 a soldier belonging to the Guards.

wood fibre ▶**noun** [mass noun] fibre obtained from wood and used especially in the manufacture of paper.

woodgrain ▶**noun** a pattern of fibres seen in a cut surface of wood.
■[as modifier] denoting a surface or finish imitating such a pattern: *the doors are available in woodgrain finish.*

W

woodgrouse ▶ noun a grouse that frequents woodland, especially a capercaillie, spruce grouse, or willow grouse.

wood hedgehog ▶ noun another term for HEDGEHOG FUNGUS.

wood-hoopoe ▶ noun a long-tailed African bird with a long slender downcurved bill and blackish plumage with a blue or green gloss.
● Genus *Phoeniculus*, family Phoeniculidae: several species.

wood ibis ▶ noun 1 a stork with a slightly downcurved bill and a bare face or head, found in America and Africa. Also called WOOD STORK.
● Genus *Mycteria*, family Ciconiidae: the black-faced *M. americana* of America, and the red-faced *M. ibis* of Africa.
2 (**crested wood ibis**) a mainly brown ibis with a greenish crest, found only in Madagascar.
● *Lophotibis cristata*, family Threskiornithidae.

woodland ▶ noun [mass noun] (also **woodlands**) land covered with trees: *large areas of ancient woodland.*

woodlander ▶ noun an inhabitant of woodland.

woodlark ▶ noun a small European and North African lark with a short tail and melodious song, frequenting open ground with scattered trees.
● *Lullula arborea*, family Alaudidae.

woodlouse ▶ noun (pl. **woodlice**) a small terrestrial crustacean with a greyish segmented body and seven pairs of legs, living in damp habitats.
● *Oniscus* and other genera, order Isopoda.

woodman ▶ noun (pl. **-men**) chiefly historical a person working in woodland, especially a forester or woodcutter.

wood mouse ▶ noun a dark brown Eurasian mouse with a long tail and large eyes. Also called FIELD MOUSE.
● Genus *Apodemus*, family Muridae: several species, in particular the widespread *A. sylvaticus.*

wood mushroom ▶ noun an edible mushroom with a white cap and brown gills, smelling strongly of aniseed and found in woodland in both Eurasia and North America.
● *Agaricus silvicola*, family Agaricaceae, class Hymenomycetes.

woodnote ▶ noun poetic/literary a natural and untrained musical note resembling the song of a bird.

wood nymph ▶ noun 1 (in folklore and classical mythology) a nymph inhabiting woodland, especially a dryad or hamadryad.
2 a brown American butterfly of grassy habitats and light woodland, with large eyespots on the forewings and smaller ones on the hindwings.
● Genus *Cercyonis*, subfamily Satyrinae, family Nymphalidae: several species.

woodpecker ▶ noun a bird with a strong bill and a stiff tail, which climbs tree trunks to find insects and drums on dead wood to mark territory.
● Family Picidae (the **woodpecker family**): many genera and numerous species. The woodpecker family also includes the wrynecks, piculets, flickers, and sapsuckers.

wood pigeon ▶ noun a large Eurasian and African pigeon with mainly grey plumage, using wing claps in display flight.
● Genus *Columba*, family Columbidae: several species, in particular the widespread *C. palumbus* (also called RINGDOVE).

woodpile ▶ noun a stack of wood stored for fuel.

wood pulp ▶ noun [mass noun] wood fibre reduced chemically or mechanically to pulp and used in the manufacture of paper.

woodrat ▶ noun 1 a rat-like rodent that accumulates a mound of sticks and debris in the nest hole, native to North and Central America. Also called PACK RAT.
● *Neotoma* and other genera, family Muridae: many species.
2 (usu. **wood rat**) a forest-dwelling rat found in southern Asia.
● *Rattus*, *Cremnomys*, and other genera, family Muridae.

woodruff (also **sweet woodruff**) ▶ noun a white-flowered Eurasian plant with whorled leaves, smelling of new-mown hay when dried or crushed.
● *Galium odoratum*, family Rubiaceae.
– ORIGIN Old English *wudurofe*, from *wudu* 'wood' + an element of unknown meaning.

Woodruff key ▶ noun a key whose cross section is part circular, to fit into a curved keyway in a shaft, and part rectangular, used chiefly in machinery.
– ORIGIN late 19th cent.: named after the *Woodruff* Manufacturing Company, Hartford, Connecticut, US.

woodrush ▶ noun a grass-like plant that typically has long flat leaves fringed with long hairs.
● Genus *Luzula*, family Juncaceae: many species.

wood sage ▶ noun a yellow-flowered European plant of the mint family, growing in dry shady places.
● *Teucrium scorodonia*, family Labiatae.

woodscrew ▶ noun a tapering metal screw with a sharp point.

woodshed ▶ noun a shed where wood for fuel is stored.
– PHRASES **something nasty in the woodshed** Brit. informal a shocking or distasteful thing that has been kept secret. **take someone to the woodshed** US informal, dated reprove or punish someone, especially discreetly.

woodsia /ˈwʊdzɪə/ ▶ noun a small tufted fern that grows among rocks in mountains in temperate and cool regions.
● Genus *Woodsia*, family Woodsiaceae.
– ORIGIN modern Latin, named after Joseph *Woods* (1776–1864), English architect and botanist.

wood slave ▶ noun W. Indian a Central American gecko with a tail that is swollen at the base, often found living in houses. It is widely regarded, falsely, as deadly.
● *Thecadactylus rapicauda*, family Gekkonidae.

woodsman ▶ noun (pl. **-men**) a person living or working in woodland, especially a forester, hunter, or woodcutter.

woodsmoke ▶ noun [mass noun] the smoke from a wood fire.

wood sorrel ▶ noun a creeping Eurasian woodland plant, with clover-like leaves and pink or white flowers that are typically streaked with purple.
● *Oxalis acetosella*, family Oxalidaceae.

wood spirit ▶ noun another term for WOOD ALCOHOL.

wood stain ▶ noun a commercially produced substance for colouring wood.

woodstar ▶ noun a very small American hummingbird found in tropical forests, with a green back and typically a red or purple throat.
● Family Trochilidae: several genera and species.

Woodstock a small town in New York State, situated in the south-east near Albany. It gave its name in the summer of 1969 to a huge rock festival held some 96 km (60 miles) to the south-west.

wood stork ▶ noun another term for WOOD IBIS (in sense 1).

woodswallow ▶ noun a long-winged Australasian and South Asian bird related to the Australian butcher-birds, feeding on insects in flight.
● Family Artamidae and genus *Artamus*: several species.

woodsy ▶ adjective N. Amer. of, relating to, or characteristic of wood or woodland: *trails through woodsy countryside* | *the woodsy smells of cedar and pine.*
– ORIGIN mid 19th cent.: formed irregularly from WOOD (differentiated from *woody*).

wood thrush ▶ noun a thrush of eastern North America, with a brown back, a dark-spotted white breast, and a loud liquid song.
● *Hylocichla mustelina*, family Turdidae.

wood tick ▶ noun a North American tick which infests wild and domestic animals, often found clinging to plants and responsible for transmitting spotted fever.
● Genus *Dermacentor*, family Ixodidae, in particular *D. andersoni.*

woodturning ▶ noun [mass noun] the action of shaping wood with a lathe.
– DERIVATIVES **woodturner** noun.

wood warbler ▶ noun a migratory European leaf warbler found in woodland, with plaintive calls and a trilling song.
● *Phylloscopus sibilatrix*, family Sylviidae.
■ any New World warbler of the family Parulidae.

Woodward, Robert Burns (1917–79), American organic chemist. He was the first to synthesize quinine, cholesterol, chlorophyll, and vitamin B_{12}, and with the Polish-born American chemist Roald Hoffmann (b.1937) discovered symmetry-based rules governing the course of rearrangement reactions involving cyclic intermediates. Nobel Prize for Chemistry (1965).

woodwasp ▶ noun another term for HORNTAIL.

woodwind ▶ noun [treated as sing. or pl.] wind instruments other than brass instruments forming a section of an orchestra, including flutes, oboes, clarinets, and bassoons: *striking passages for woodwind and brass.*

wood wool ▶ noun [mass noun] Brit. a mass of fine soft wood shavings, typically used as a packing material.

wood woolly foot ▶ noun see WOOLLY FOOT.

woodwork ▶ noun [mass noun] 1 the wooden parts of a room or building, such as window frames or doors: *the woodwork was painted blue.*
■ (**the woodwork**) informal the wooden frame of a goal.
2 Brit. the activity or skill of making things from wood: *he taught woodwork at night school.*
– PHRASES **come out of the woodwork** (of an unpleasant person or thing) emerge from obscurity; be revealed.
– DERIVATIVES **woodworker** noun.

woodworking ▶ noun another term for WOODWORK (in sense 2).

woodworm ▶ noun the wood-boring larva of the furniture beetle.
■ [mass noun] the damaged condition of wood resulting from infestation with this larva.

woody ▶ adjective (**woodier**, **woodiest**) (of an area of land) covered with trees: *a woody dale.*
■ made of, resembling, or suggestive of wood: *cut out the woody central core before boiling.* ■ Botany (of a plant or its stem) of the nature of or consisting of wood; lignified.
– DERIVATIVES **woodiness** noun.

woodyard ▶ noun a yard where wood is chopped or stored.

woody nightshade ▶ noun see NIGHTSHADE.

woof[1] /wʊf/ ▶ noun the barking sound made by a dog.
▶ verb 1 [no obj.] (of a dog) bark: *the dog started to woof.*
■ US black slang say something in an ostentatious or aggressive manner: *mister, you weren't just woofing—you can cook.*
2 another term for WOLF: *Mike and Coleman were woofing down fried eggs and hash browns.*
– ORIGIN early 19th cent.: imitative.

woof[2] /wuːf/ ▶ noun another term for WEFT.
– ORIGIN Old English *ōwef*, a compound from the base of WEAVE[1]; Middle English *oof* later became *woof* by association with WARP in the phrase *warp and woof.*

woofer /ˈwuːfə, ˈwʊfə/ ▶ noun a loudspeaker designed to reproduce low frequencies.
– ORIGIN 1930s: from the verb WOOF[1] + -ER[1].

woofter /ˈwʊftə, ˈwuːftə/ ▶ noun Brit. informal, derogatory an effeminate or homosexual man.
– ORIGIN 1970s: alteration of POOFTER.

wool ▶ noun [mass noun] 1 the fine soft curly or wavy hair forming the coat of a sheep, goat, or similar animal, especially when shorn and prepared for use in making cloth or yarn.
■ yarn or textile fibre made from such hair.
2 a thing resembling such hair in form or texture, in particular:
■ [with modifier] the soft underfur or down of some other mammals: *beaver wool.* ■ [with modifier] a metal or mineral made into a mass of fine fibres: *lead wool.*
– PHRASES **pull the wool over someone's eyes** deceive someone by telling untruths.
– DERIVATIVES **wool-like** adjective.
– ORIGIN Old English *wull*, of Germanic origin; related to Dutch *wol* and German *Wolle*, from an Indo-European root shared by Latin *lana* 'wool', *vellus* 'fleece'.

wool clip ▶ noun [mass noun] the total quantity of wool shorn from a particular flock or in a particular area in the course of a year.

Woolf /wʊlf/, (Adeline) Virginia (1882–1941), English novelist, essayist, and critic; born *Adeline Virginia Stephen.* A member of the Bloomsbury Group, she gained recognition with *Jacob's Room* (1922). Subsequent novels, such as *Mrs Dalloway* (1925) and *To the Lighthouse* (1927), characterized by their poetic Impressionism, established her as an exponent of modernism.

wool-gathering ▶ noun [mass noun] indulgence in aimless thought or dreamy imagining; absent-mindedness: *a vacant daze that leads to formless wool-gathering.*
– DERIVATIVES **wool-gather** verb.

wool grower ▶ noun a breeder of sheep for wool.

woollen (US **woolen**) ▶ **adjective** [attrib.] of or relating to the production of wool: *the woollen industry | a woollen mill.*
■ made wholly or partly of wool: *thick woollen blankets.*
▶ **noun** (usu. **woollens**) an article of clothing made of wool.
– ORIGIN late Old English *wullen* (see **WOOL**, **-EN**²).

Woolley, Sir (Charles) Leonard (1880–1960), English archaeologist. He directed a British–American excavation of the Sumerian city of Ur (1922–34) which uncovered rich royal tombs and thousands of clay tablets.

woolly ▶ **adjective** (**woollier**, **woolliest**) **1** made of wool: *a red woolly hat.*
■ (of an animal, plant, or part) bearing or naturally covered with wool or hair resembling wool. ■ resembling wool in texture or appearance: *woolly wisps of cloud.*
2 vague or confused in expression or character: *woolly thinking.*
■ (of a sound) indistinct or distorted: *an opaque and woolly recording.*
▶ **noun** (pl. **-ies**) informal **1** (usu. **woollies**) chiefly Brit. a garment made of wool, especially a pullover.
2 Austral. a sheep.
– DERIVATIVES **woolliness** noun (only in sense 2 of the adjective).

woolly bear ▶ **noun 1** a large hairy caterpillar, especially that of a tiger moth.
2 the small hairy larva of a carpet beetle or museum beetle, which is destructive to carpets and zoological collections.

woollybutt ▶ **noun** an Australian eucalyptus with thick fibrous bark.
• Several species in the genus *Eucalyptus*, family Myrtaceae.

woolly foot (also **wood woolly foot**) ▶ **noun** a yellowish-brown toadstool with a slender stem, the base of which bears long woolly hairs, found commonly in woodland in both Eurasia and North America.
• *Collybia peronata*, family Tricholomataceae, class Hymenomycetes.

woolly mammoth ▶ **noun** a mammoth that was adapted to the cold periods of the Pleistocene, with a long shaggy coat, small ears, and a thick layer of fat. Individuals are sometimes found frozen in the permafrost of Siberia.
• *Mammuthus primigenius*, family Elephantidae.

woolly rhinoceros ▶ **noun** an extinct two-horned Eurasian rhinoceros that was adapted to the cold periods of the Pleistocene, with a long woolly coat.
• Genus *Coelodonta*, family Rhinocerotidae.

woolly spider monkey ▶ **noun** a large spider monkey with long thin limbs and tail, dense woolly fur, and a large protruding belly, native to the rainforests of SE Brazil.
• *Brachyteles arachnoides*, family Cebidae.

woolman ▶ **noun** (pl. **-men**) chiefly historical a wool merchant or dealer.

Woolmark ▶ **noun** an international quality symbol for wool instituted by the International Wool Secretariat.

woolpack ▶ **noun** historical a bale of wool.

Woolsack ▶ **noun** (in the UK) the Lord Chancellor's wool-stuffed seat in the House of Lords. It is said to have been adopted in Edward III's reign as a reminder to the Lords of the importance to England of the wool trade.
■ (**the woolsack**) the position of Lord Chancellor.

woolshed ▶ **noun** Austral./NZ a large shed for shearing and baling wool.

wool-sorters' disease ▶ **noun** see **ANTHRAX**.

wool-stapler ▶ **noun** archaic a person who buys wool from a producer, grades it, and sells it to a manufacturer.

wool work ▶ **noun** [mass noun] needlework executed in wool on a canvas foundation.

Woolworth, Frank Winfield (1852–1919), American businessman. He opened his first shop selling low-priced goods in 1879 and from this built a large international chain of stores.

Woomera /ˈwuːm(ə)rə/ a town in central South Australia, the site of a vast military testing ground used in the 1950s for nuclear tests and since the 1960s for tracking space satellites.

woomera /ˈwuːm(ə)rə/ ▶ **noun** Austral. an Aboriginal stick used to throw a dart or spear more forcibly.
– ORIGIN from Dharuk *wamara.*

woomph /wuːmf, wʊmf/ ▶ **adverb** & **exclamation** used to imitate a sound like that of a sudden blow or impact accompanied by an expulsion of air.

woonerf /ˈvuːnəːf/ ▶ **noun** (pl. **woonerven** /-əːv(ə)n/ or **woonerfs**) a road in which devices for reducing or slowing the flow of traffic have been installed.
– ORIGIN 1970s: from Dutch, from *wonen* 'reside' + *erf* 'premises, ground'.

woopie /ˈwuːpi, ˈwʊpi/ (also **woopy**) ▶ **noun** (pl. **-ies**) informal, chiefly N. Amer. an affluent retired person able to pursue an active lifestyle.
– ORIGIN 1980s: elaboration of the acronym from *well-off older person.*

Woop Woop /ˈwʊp wʊp/ ▶ **noun** Austral./NZ informal a humorous name for a remote outback town or district.
– ORIGIN 1920s: mock Aboriginal.

woosh ▶ **verb**, **noun**, **exclamation**, & **adverb** variant spelling of **WHOOSH**.

woozy ▶ **adjective** (**woozier**, **wooziest**) informal unsteady, dizzy, or dazed: *I still felt woozy from all the pills.*
– DERIVATIVES **woozily** adverb, **wooziness** noun.
– ORIGIN late 19th cent.: of unknown origin.

wop ▶ **noun** offensive an Italian or other southern European.
– ORIGIN early 20th cent. (originally US): origin uncertain, perhaps from Italian *guappo* 'bold, showy', from Spanish *guapo* 'dandy'.

Worcester¹ /ˈwʊstə/ a cathedral city in western England, on the River Severn, the administrative centre of Worcestershire; pop. 81,000 (1991). It was the scene in 1651, during the English Civil War, of a battle in which Oliver Cromwell defeated a Scottish army under Charles II. It has been a centre of porcelain manufacture since 1751.

Worcester² /ˈwʊstə/ (also **Royal Worcester**) ▶ **noun** [mass noun] trademark porcelain made at Worcester in a factory founded in 1751.

Worcester sauce (also **Worcestershire sauce**) ▶ **noun** [mass noun] a pungent sauce containing soy sauce and vinegar, first made in Worcester.

Worcestershire a county of west central England, part of Hereford and Worcester between 1974 and 1998.

Worcs. ▶ **abbreviation for** Worcestershire.

word ▶ **noun** a single distinct meaningful element of speech or writing, used with others (or sometimes alone) to form a sentence and typically shown with a space on either side when written or printed.
■ a single distinct conceptual unit of language, comprising inflected and variant forms. ■ (usu. **words**) something that someone says or writes; a remark or piece of information: *his grandfather's words had been meant kindly | a word of warning.* ■ [mass noun] speech as distinct from action: *he conforms in word and deed to the values of a society that he rejects.* ■ [with negative] (**a word**) even the smallest amount of something spoken or written: *don't believe a word of it.* ■ (**one's word**) a person's account of the truth, especially when it differs from that of another person: *in court it would have been his word against mine.* ■ (**one's word**) a promise or assurance: *everything will be taken care of—you have my word.* ■ (**words**) the text or spoken part of a play, opera, or other performed piece; a script: *he had to learn his words.* ■ (**words**) angry talk: *her father would have* **had words with** *her about that.* ■ [mass noun] a message; news: *I was afraid to leave Edinburgh in case there was word from the War Office.* ■ a command, password, or motto: *someone* **gave me the word** *to start playing.* ■ a basic unit of data in a computer, typically 16 or 32 bits long.
▶ **verb** [with obj.] choose and use particular words in order to say or write (something): *he words his request in a particularly ironic way* | [as adj., with submodifier] (**worded**) *a strongly worded letter of protest.*
– PHRASES **at a word** as soon as requested: *ready to leave again at a word.* **be as good as one's word** do what one has promised to do. **have a word** speak briefly to someone: *I'll just* **have a word with** *him.* **have a word in someone's ear** speak to someone privately and discreetly, especially to give them a warning. **in other words** expressed in a different way; that is to say. **in so many words** [often with negative] in the way mentioned: *I haven't told him in so many words, but he'd understand.* **in a word** briefly. **keep one's word** do what one has promised. **a man/woman of his/her word** a person who keeps their promises. **(on/upon) my word** an exclamation of surprise or emphasis: *my word, you were here quickly!* **of few words** taciturn: *he's a man of few words.* **put something into words** express something in speech or writing: *he felt a vague disappointment which he couldn't put into words.* **put words into someone's mouth** falsely or inaccurately report what someone has said. ■ prompt or encourage someone to say something that they may not otherwise have said. **take someone at their word** interpret a person's words literally or exactly, especially by believing them or doing as they suggest. **take the words out of someone's mouth** say what someone else was about to say. **take someone's word (for it)** believe what someone says or writes without checking for oneself. **too —— for words** informal extremely ——: *going around by the road was too tedious for words.* **waste words 1** talk in vain. **2** talk at length. **the Word (of God) 1** the Bible, or a part of it. **2** Jesus Christ (see **LOGOS**). **word for word** in exactly the same or, when translated, exactly equivalent words. **word of honour** a solemn promise: *I'll be good to you always, I give you my word of honour.* **word of mouth** spoken language; informal or unofficial discourse. **the word on the street** informal a rumour or piece of information currently being circulated. **words fail me** used to express one's disbelief or dismay. **a word to the wise** a hint or brief explanation given, that being all that is required.
– DERIVATIVES **wordage** noun, **wordless** adjective, **wordlessly** adverb, **wordlessness** noun.
– ORIGIN Old English, of Germanic origin; related to Dutch *woord* and German *Wort*, from an Indo-European root shared by Latin *verbum* 'word'.
▶ **word up** [as imperative] black English listen: *word up, my brother, you got me high as a kite.*

-word ▶ **combining form** denoting a slang word, or one that may be offensive or have a negative connotation, specified by the word's first letter: *the F-word.*

word association ▶ **noun** [mass noun] the spontaneous and unreflective production of other words in response to a given word, as a game, a prompt to creative thought or memory, or a technique in psychiatric evaluation.

word blindness ▶ **noun** less technical term for **ALEXIA**, or (less accurately) for **DYSLEXIA**.

wordbook ▶ **noun** a study book containing lists of words and meanings or other related information.

word break (also **word division**) ▶ **noun** Printing a point at which a word is split between two lines of text by means of a hyphen.

word class ▶ **noun** a category of words of similar form or function; a part of speech.

word deafness ▶ **noun** [mass noun] an inability to identify spoken words, resulting from a brain defect such as Wernicke's aphasia.

word game ▶ **noun** a game involving the making or selection of words.

wording ▶ **noun** [mass noun] the words used to express something; the way in which something is expressed: *the standard form of wording for a consent letter.*

word length ▶ **noun** [mass noun] Computing the number of bits in a word.

word order ▶ **noun** the sequence of words in a sentence, especially as governed by grammatical rules and as affecting meaning.

word-perfect ▶ **adjective** (of an actor or speaker) knowing by heart the words for one's part or speech.

word picture ▶ **noun** a vivid description in writing.

wordplay ▶ **noun** [mass noun] the witty exploitation of the meanings and ambiguities of words, especially in puns.

word problem ▶ **noun** Mathematics the problem of determining whether two different products are equal, or two sequences of operations are equivalent.

word processing ▶ **noun** [mass noun] the production, storage, and manipulation of text on a word processor.
– DERIVATIVES **word-process** verb.

word processor ▶ **noun** a purpose-built computer or program for storing, manipulating, and formatting text entered from a keyboard and providing a printout.

word salad ▶ **noun** [mass noun] a confused or

W

unintelligible mixture of seemingly random words and phrases, specifically (in psychiatry) as a form of speech indicative of advanced schizophrenia.

wordsearch ▶ **noun** a puzzle consisting of letters arranged in a grid, containing several hidden words written in any direction.

wordsmith ▶ **noun** a skilled user of words.

word square ▶ **noun** a puzzle requiring the discovery of a set of words of equal length written one under another to read the same down as across, e.g. *too old ode*.

Wordsworth[1], Dorothy (1771–1855), English diarist, sister of William Wordsworth. Her *Grasmere Journal* (1800–3) documents her intense response to nature.

Wordsworth[2], William (1770–1850), English poet. Much of his work was inspired by the Lake District. His *Lyrical Ballads* (1798), which was composed with Coleridge and included 'Tintern Abbey', was a landmark in romanticism. Other notable poems: 'I Wandered Lonely as a Cloud' (sonnet, 1815) and *The Prelude* (1850). He was appointed Poet Laureate in 1843.

word wrap ▶ **noun** [mass noun] a feature on a word processor that automatically moves a word that is too long to fit on a line to the beginning of the next line.

wordy ▶ **adjective** (**wordier**, **wordiest**) using or expressed in rather too many words: *a wordy and repetitive account.*

■archaic consisting of words: *on the publication of Worcester's dictionary, a wordy war arose.*

– DERIVATIVES **wordily** adverb, **wordiness** noun.

– ORIGIN Old English *wordig* (see **WORD**, **-Y**[1]).

wore[1] past of **WEAR**[1].

wore[2] past and past participle of **WEAR**[2].

work ▶ **noun** [mass noun] **1** activity involving mental or physical effort done in order to achieve a purpose or result: *he was tired after a day's work in the fields.*

■[in combination or with modifier] (**works**) chiefly Brit. operations of building or repair: *extra costs caused by additional building works.* ■ (**works**) [treated as sing.] chiefly Brit. a place or premises for industrial activity, typically manufacturing: [with modifier] *he found a job in the locomotive works.*

2 such activity as a means of earning income; employment: *I'm still looking for work.*

■the place where one engages in such activity: *I was returning home from work on a packed subway.* ■ the period of time spent during the day engaged in such activity: *he was going to the theatre after work.* ■ [count noun] W. Indian a job: *I decided to get a work.*

3 a task or tasks to be undertaken; something a person or thing has to do: *they made sure the work was progressing smoothly.*

■the materials for this: *she frequently took work home with her.* ■ (**works**) Theology good or moral deeds: *the Clapham sect was concerned with works rather than with faith.*

4 something done or made: *her work hangs in all the main American collections.*

■the result of the action of a specified person or thing: *the bombing had been* **the work of** *a German-based cell.* ■ [count noun] a literary or musical composition or other piece of fine art: *a work of fiction.* ■ (**works**) all such pieces by a particular author, composer, or artist, regarded collectively: *the works of Schubert fill several feet of shelf space.* ■ a piece of embroidery, sewing, or knitting, typically made using a specified stitch or method. ■ [count noun] (usu. **works**) Military a defensive structure.

5 (**works**) the operative part of a clock or other machine: *she could almost hear the tick of its works.*

6 Physics the exertion of force overcoming resistance or producing molecular change.

7 (**the works**) informal everything needed, desired, or expected: *the heavens put on a show: sheet lightning, hailstones, the works.*

▶ **verb** (past and past participle **worked** or archaic **wrought**) [no obj.] **1** be engaged in physical or mental activity in order to achieve a purpose or result, especially in one's job; do work: *an engineer who had been* **working on** *a design for a more efficient wing* | *new contracts forcing employees to work longer hours.*

■be employed, typically in a specified occupation or field: *Taylor has* **worked in** *education for 17 years.* ■ [with obj.] W. Indian be engaged in (a particular occupation): *I worked fireman on ships.* ■ (**work in**) (of an artist) produce articles or pictures using (a particular material or medium): *he works in clay over a very strong frame.* ■ [with obj.] produce (an article or design) using a specified material or sewing stitch: *the castle itself is* **worked in** *tent stitch.* ■ [with obj.] set to or keep at work: *Jane is working you too hard.* ■ [with obj.] cultivate (land) or extract materials from (a mine or quarry): *contracts and leases to work the mines.* ■ [with obj.] practise one's occupation or operate in or at (a particular place): *I worked a few clubs and so forth.* ■ make efforts to achieve something; campaign: *an organization* **working for** *a better life for people diagnosed or treated as having mental illness.*

2 (of a machine or system) operate or function, especially properly or effectively: *his cell phone doesn't work unless he goes to a high point.*

■(of a machine or a part of it) run; go through regular motions: *it's designed to go into a special 'rest' state when it's not working.* ■ (especially of a person's features) move violently or convulsively: *hair wild, mouth working furiously.* ■ [with obj.] cause (a device or machine) to operate: *teaching customers how to work a VCR.* ■ (of a plan or method) have the desired result or effect: *the desperate ploy had worked.* ■ [with obj.] bring about; produce as a result: *with a dash of blusher here and there, you can work miracles.* ■ [with obj.] informal arrange or contrive: *the chairman was prepared to work it for Phillip if he was interested.* ■ (**work on/upon**) exert influence or use one's persuasive power on (someone or their feelings): *she worked upon the sympathy of her associates.* ■ [with obj.] use one's persuasive power to stir the emotions of (a person or group of people): *the born politician's art of working a crowd.*

3 [with obj. and adverbial or complement] bring (a material or mixture) to a desired shape or consistency by hammering, kneading, or some other method: *work the mixture into a paste with your hands.*

■bring into a specified state, especially an emotional state: *Harold had worked himself into a minor rage.*

4 move or cause to move gradually or with difficulty into another position, typically by means of constant movement or pressure: [with obj. and adverbial or complement] *comb from tip to root, working out the knots at the end* | [no obj., with adverbial or complement] *its stanchion bases were already working loose.*

■[with adverbial] Sailing make progress to windward, with repeated tacking: *trying to work to windward in light airs.*

– PHRASES **at work** engaged in work. ■ in action: *researchers were convinced that one infectious agent was at work.* **give someone the works** informal **1** tell someone everything. **2** treat someone harshly. ■ kill someone. **have one's work cut out** be faced with a hard or lengthy task. **in the works** chiefly N. Amer. being planned, worked on, or produced. **set to work** (or **set someone to work**) begin or cause to begin work. **a spanner** (or N. Amer. **monkey wrench**) **in the works** a person or thing that prevents the successful implementation of a plan. **the work of ——** a task occupying a specified amount of time: *it was the work of a moment to discover the tiny stab wound.* **work one's ass** (**butt**, etc.) **off** vulgar slang work extremely hard. **work one's fingers to the bone** see **BONE**. **work to rule** chiefly Brit. (typically as a form of industrial action) follow official working rules and hours exactly in order to reduce output and efficiency. ■ a form of industrial action of this type. **work one's passage** pay for one's journey on a ship with work instead of money. **work one's way through university** (or **college**, etc.) obtain the money for educational fees or one's maintenance as a student by working. **work one's will on/upon** accomplish one's purpose on: *she set a coiffeur to work his will on her hair.* **work wonders** see **WONDER**.

– DERIVATIVES **workless** adjective.

– ORIGIN Old English *weorc* (noun), *wyrcan* (verb), of Germanic origin; related to Dutch *werk* and German *Werk*, from an Indo-European root shared by Greek *ergon*.

▶ **work something in** include or incorporate something, typically in something spoken or written.

work something off 1 discharge a debt by working. **2** reduce or get rid of something by work or activity: *one of those gimmicks for working off aggression.*

work out 1 (of an equation) be capable of being solved. ■ (**work out at**) be calculated at: *the losses work out at $2.94 a share.* **2** have a good or specified result: *things don't always work out that way.* **3** engage in vigorous physical exercise or training, typically at a gym.

work someone out understand someone's character.

work something out 1 solve a sum or determine an amount by calculation. ■ solve or find the answer to something: *I couldn't work out whether it was a band playing or a record.* **2** plan or devise something in detail: *work out a seating plan.* **3** poetic/literary accomplish or attain something with difficulty: *malicious fates are bent on working out an ill intent.* **4** (usu. **be worked out**) work a mine until it is exhausted of minerals. **5** another way of saying ***work something off*** above.

work someone over informal treat someone with violence; beat someone severely: *the coppers had worked him over a little just for the fun of it.*

work to follow or operate within the constraints of (a plan or system): *working to tight deadlines.*

work up to proceed gradually towards (something more advanced or intense): *the course starts with landing technique, working up to jumps from an enclosed platform.*

work someone up (often **get worked up**) gradually bring someone, especially oneself, to a state of intense excitement, anger, or anxiety: *he got all worked up and started shouting and swearing.*

work something up 1 bring something gradually to a more complete or satisfactory state: *painters were accustomed to working up compositions from drawings.* **2** develop or produce by activity or effort: *despite the cold, George had already worked up a fair sweat.*

-work ▶ **combining form** denoting things or parts made of a specified material or with specified tools: *silverwork* | *fretwork.*

■denoting a mechanism or structure of a specified kind: *bridgework* | *clockwork.* ■ denoting ornamentation of a specified kind, or articles having such ornamentation: *knotwork.*

workable ▶ **adjective 1** able to be worked, fashioned, or manipulated: *more flour and salt can be added until they make a workable dough.*

2 capable of producing the desired effect or result; practicable; feasible: *a workable peace settlement.*

– DERIVATIVES **workability** noun, **workably** adverb.

workaday ▶ **adjective** of or relating to work or one's job.

■not special, unusual, or interesting in any way; ordinary: *your humble workaday PC.*

workaholic ▶ **noun** informal a person who compulsively works excessively hard and unusually long hours.

– DERIVATIVES **workaholism** noun.

workalike ▶ **noun** Computing a computer which is able to use the software of another specified machine without special modification.

■a piece of software identical in function to another software package.

workaround ▶ **noun** Computing a method for overcoming a problem or limitation in a program or system.

work-basket (also **work-bag**) ▶ **noun** a basket (or bag) used for storing sewing materials.

workbench ▶ **noun** a bench at which carpentry or other mechanical or practical work is done.

workboat ▶ **noun** a boat used for carrying out various kinds of work such as fishing or transporting freight.

workbook ▶ **noun** a student's book containing instruction and exercises relating to a particular subject.

workbox ▶ **noun** a portable box used for storing or holding tools and materials for activities such as sewing.

work camp ▶ **noun** a camp at which community work is done, especially by young volunteers.

■another term for **LABOUR CAMP**.

workday ▶ **noun** a day on which one works: *Saturdays were workdays for him.*

worker ▶ **noun 1** a person or animal that works, in particular:

■[with adj. or noun modifier] a person who does a specified type of work: *a farm worker.* ■ an employee, especially one who does manual or non-executive work. ■ (**workers**) used in Marxist or leftist contexts to refer to the working class. ■ [with adj.] a person who works in a specified way: *she's a good worker.* ■ informal a person who works hard: *I got a reputation for being a worker.* ■ (in social insects such as bees, wasps, ants, and termites) a neuter or undeveloped female which is usually the most numerous caste and does the basic work of the colony.

2 a creator or producer of a specified thing: *he was a bogus worker of miracles.*

worker priest ▶ **noun** a Roman Catholic or Anglican priest who engages part-time in ordinary secular work.

work ethic ▶ **noun** [in sing.] the principle that hard work is intrinsically virtuous or worthy of reward. See also **PROTESTANT ETHIC**.

work experience ▶ **noun** [mass noun] short-term experience of employment, typically arranged for older pupils by schools.

workfare ▶ **noun** [mass noun] a welfare system which requires some work or attendance for training from those receiving benefits.
– ORIGIN 1960s: from **WORK** + a shortened form of **WELFARE**.

workflow ▶ **noun** the sequence of industrial, administrative, or other processes through which a piece of work passes from initiation to completion.

workforce ▶ **noun** [treated as sing. or pl.] the people engaged in or available for work, either in a country or area or in a particular firm or industry.

work function ▶ **noun** Physics the minimum quantity of energy which is required to remove an electron to infinity from the surface of a given solid, usually a metal. (Symbol: φ)

work group ▶ **noun** a group within a workforce who normally work together.
■ Computing a group of this type who share data via a local network. ■ a small group of trainees, formed to practise or develop a skill.

work-harden ▶ **verb** [with obj.] [often as noun **work-hardening**] Metallurgy toughen (a metal) as a result of cold-working.

workhorse ▶ **noun** a horse used for work on a farm.
■ a person or machine that dependably performs hard work over a long period of time: *the aircraft was the standard workhorse of Soviet medium-haul routes.*

workhouse ▶ **noun 1** historical (in the UK) a public institution in which the destitute of a parish received board and lodging in return for work.
2 US a prison in which petty offenders are expected to work.

working ▶ **adjective** [attrib.] **1** having paid employment: *the size of the working population.*
■ engaged in manual labour: *the vote is no longer sufficient protection for the working man.* ■ relating to, suitable for, or for the purpose of work: *improvements in living and working conditions.* ■ (of an animal) used in farming, hunting, or for guard duties; not kept as a pet or for show. ■ (of something possessed) sufficient to work with: *they have a working knowledge of contract law.* ■ (of a theory, definition, or title) used as the basis for work or argument and likely to be developed, adapted, or improved later: *the working hypothesis is tested and refined through discussion.*
2 functioning or able to function: *the mill still has a working waterwheel.*
■ (of parts of a machine) moving and causing a machine to operate: *the working parts of a digital watch.*
▶ **noun 1** [mass noun] the action of doing work.
■ the action of extracting minerals from a mine: *opencast working arouses considerable opposition.* ■ [count noun] (usu. **workings**) a mine or a part of a mine from which minerals are being extracted. ■ [count noun] a scheduled duty or trip performed by a locomotive, train, bus, or other vehicle: *locomotive 37418 is often seen on this working.*
2 (**workings**) the way in which a machine, organization, or system operates: *we will be less secretive about the workings of government.*
■ the record of the successive calculations made in solving a mathematical problem: *show details of workings, where appropriate, in your answer book.*

working capital ▶ **noun** [mass noun] Finance the capital of a business which is used in its day-to-day trading operations, calculated as the current assets minus the current liabilities. Also called **NET CURRENT ASSETS**.

working class ▶ **noun** [treated as sing. or pl.] the social group consisting of people who are employed for wages, especially in manual or industrial work: *the housing needs of the working classes.*
▶ **adjective** of, relating to, or characteristic of people belonging to such a group: *a working-class community.*

working day ▶ **noun** chiefly Brit. a day on which one usually works; a workday.
■ the part of the day devoted or allotted to work: *a long working day.*

working drawing ▶ **noun** a scale drawing which serves as a guide for the construction or manufacture of something such as a building or machine.

working girl ▶ **noun** informal a woman who goes out to work rather than remaining at home.
■ used euphemistically to refer to a prostitute.

working load ▶ **noun** the maximum load that a machine or other structure is designed to bear.

working memory ▶ **noun** Psychology the part of short-term memory which is concerned with immediate conscious perceptual and linguistic processing.
■ Computing an area of high-speed memory used to store programs or data currently in use.

working party (also **working group**) ▶ **noun** Brit. a committee or group appointed to study and report on a particular question and make recommendations based on its findings.

working storage ▶ **noun** [mass noun] Computing a part of a computer's memory that is used by a program for the storage of intermediate results or other temporary items.

Workington a port on the coast of Cumbria, NW England; pop. 26,120 (1981).

workload ▶ **noun** the amount of work to be done by someone or something: *he had been given three deputies to ease his workload.*

workman ▶ **noun** (pl. **-men**) a man employed to do manual labour.
■ [with adj.] a person with specified skill in a job or craft: *you check it through, like all good workmen do.*
– PHRASES **a bad workman always blames his tools** proverb a person who has done something badly will seek to lay the blame on their equipment rather than admit their own lack of skill.

workmanlike ▶ **adjective** showing efficient competence: *a steady, workmanlike approach.*

workmanship ▶ **noun** [mass noun] the degree of skill with which a product is made or a job done: *cracks on the M25 were caused by poor workmanship.*

workmate ▶ **noun** chiefly Brit. a person with whom one works.

work of art ▶ **noun** a creative product with strong imaginative or aesthetic appeal.

workout ▶ **noun** a session of vigorous physical exercise or training.

workpeople ▶ **plural noun** Brit. people in paid employment, especially in manual or industrial labour.

work permit ▶ **noun** an official document giving a foreigner permission to take a job in a country.

workpiece ▶ **noun** an object being worked on with a tool or machine.

workplace ▶ **noun** a place where people work, such as an office or factory.

work rate ▶ **noun** the rate at which work is done.
■ the amount of energy that is expended in sport or physical exercise.

work release ▶ **noun** [mass noun] leave of absence from prison by day enabling a prisoner to continue in normal employment.

workroom ▶ **noun** a room for working in, especially one equipped for a particular kind of work.

works council ▶ **noun** chiefly Brit. a group of employees representing a workforce in discussions with their employers.

worksheet ▶ **noun 1** a paper listing questions or tasks for students.
2 a paper for recording work done or in progress.
■ Computing a data file created and used by a spreadsheet program, which takes the form of a matrix of cells when displayed.

workshop ▶ **noun 1** a room or building in which goods are manufactured or repaired.
2 a meeting at which a group of people engage in intensive discussion and activity on a particular subject or project.
▶ **verb** [with obj.] present a performance of (a dramatic work), using intensive group discussion and improvisation in order to explore aspects of the production prior to formal staging: *the play was workshopped briefly at the Shaw Festival.*

work-shy ▶ **adjective** (of a person) lazy and disinclined to work.

worksite ▶ **noun** an area where an industry is located or where work takes place.

workspace ▶ **noun** [mass noun] space in which to work: *the kitchen is all white, with maximum workspace.*
■ [count noun] an area rented or sold for commercial purposes. ■ [count noun] Computing a memory storage facility for temporary use.

workstation ▶ **noun 1** a general purpose computer with a higher performance level than a personal computer.
2 an area where work of a particular nature is carried out, such as a specific location on a manufacturing assembly line.

work study ▶ **noun** [mass noun] (in business or industry) a system of assessing methods of working so as to achieve the maximum output and efficiency.

work surface ▶ **noun** another term for **WORKTOP**.

worktop ▶ **noun** Brit. a flat surface for working on, especially in a kitchen.

workweek ▶ **noun** N. Amer. the total number of hours or days worked in a week: *we need a shorter workweek and protected benefits for contract workers.*

world ▶ **noun 1** (usu. **the world**) the earth, together with all of its countries, peoples, and natural features: *he was doing his bit to save the world.*
■ (**the world**) all of the people, societies, and institutions on the earth: [as modifier] *world affairs.* ■ [as modifier] denoting one of the most important or influential people or things of its class: *they had been brought up to regard Britain as a world power.* ■ another planet like the earth: *the possibility of life on other worlds.*
2 a part or aspect of human life or of the natural features of the earth, in particular:
■ a region or group of countries: *the English-speaking world.* ■ a period of history: *the ancient world.* ■ a group of living things: *the animal world.* ■ the people, places, and activities to do with a particular thing: *they were a legend in the world of British theatre.* ■ human and social interaction: *he has almost completely withdrawn from the world | how inexperienced she is in the ways of the world.* ■ (**one's world**) a person's life and activities: *he felt his whole world had collapsed.* ■ [in sing.] a stage of human life, either mortal or after death: *in this world and the next.* ■ secular interests and affairs: *parents are not viewed as the primary educators of their own children, either in the world or in the church.*
– PHRASES **be not long for this world** have only a short time to live. **the best of both** (or **all possible**) **worlds** the benefits of widely differing situations, enjoyed at the same time. **bring someone into the world** give birth to or assist at the birth of someone. **come into the world** be born. **come up** (or **go down**) **in the world** rise (or drop) in status, especially by becoming richer (or poorer). **in the world** used for emphasis in questions, especially to express astonishment or disbelief: *why in the world did you not reveal yourself sooner?* **look for all the world like** look precisely like (used for emphasis): *fossil imprints that look for all the world like motorcycle tracks.* **man** (or **woman**) **of the world** a person who is experienced in the ways of sophisticated society. **not do something for the world** not do something whatever the inducement: *I wouldn't miss it for the world.* **out of this world** informal extremely enjoyable or impressive: *a herb and lemon dressing that's out of this world.* **see the world** travel widely and gain wide experience. **think the world of** have a very high regard for (someone): *I thought the world of my father.* **the world and his wife** Brit. a large number of people; everybody: *now all the world and his wife seems to have heard of them.* **the world, the flesh, and the devil** all forms of temptation to sin. **a** (or **the**) **world of** a very great deal of: *there's a world of difference between being alone and being lonely.* (**all**) **the world over** everywhere on the earth. **worlds apart** very different or distant.
– ORIGIN Old English *w(e)oruld*, from a Germanic compound meaning 'age of man'; related to Dutch *wereld* and German *Welt*.

World Bank an international banking organization established to control the distribution of economic aid between member nations, and to make loans to them in times of financial crisis. See also **INTERNATIONAL BANK FOR RECONSTRUCTION AND DEVELOPMENT**.

W

world-beater ▸ noun a person or thing that is better than all others in its field.

world-class ▸ adjective (of a person, thing, or activity) of or among the best in the world.

World Council of Churches (abbrev.: **WCC**) an association established in 1948 to promote unity among the many different Christian Churches. Its member Churches number over 300, and include virtually all Christian traditions except Roman Catholicism and Unitarianism. Its headquarters are in Geneva.

World Cup ▸ noun a competition between teams from several countries in a sport, in particular an international soccer tournament held every four years.
■ a trophy awarded for such a competition.

world English ▸ noun [mass noun] the English language including all of its regional varieties, such as North American, Australian, New Zealand, and South African English.
■ a basic form of English, consisting of features common to all regional varieties.

world fair (also **world's fair**) ▸ noun an international exhibition of the industrial, scientific, technological, and artistic achievements of the participating nations.

world-famous ▸ adjective known throughout the world: *the world-famous tenor José Carreras.*

World Federation of Trade Unions (abbrev.: **WFTU**) an association of trade unions founded in 1945, with headquarters in Prague. In 1949 most of the representatives from non-Communist countries withdrew and founded the International Confederation of Free Trade Unions; the WFTU is now composed largely of groups from developing countries.

World Health Organization (abbrev.: **WHO**) an agency of the United Nations, established in 1948 to promote health and control communicable diseases. It assists in the efforts of member governments, and pursues biomedical research through some 500 collaborating research centres throughout the world. Its headquarters are in Geneva.

World Heritage Site ▸ noun a natural or man-made site, area, or structure recognized as being of outstanding international importance and therefore as deserving special protection. Sites are nominated to and designated by the World Heritage Convention (an organization of UNESCO).

World Intellectual Property Organization (abbrev.: **WIPO**) an organization, established in 1967 and an agency of the United Nations from 1974, for cooperation between governments in matters concerning patents, trademarks, and copyright, and the transfer of technology between countries. Its headquarters are in Geneva.

world language ▸ noun a language known or spoken in many countries.
■ an artificial language for international use.

world line ▸ noun Physics a curve in space–time joining the positions of a particle throughout its existence.

worldling ▸ noun a cosmopolitan and sophisticated person.

worldly ▸ adjective (**worldlier**, **worldliest**) of or concerned with material values or ordinary life rather than a spiritual existence: *his ambitions for worldly success.*
■ (of a person) experienced and sophisticated.
– PHRASES **worldly goods** (or **possessions** or **wealth**) everything that someone owns.
– DERIVATIVES **worldliness** noun.
– ORIGIN Old English *woruldlic* (see **WORLD**, **-LY**[1]).

worldly-wise ▸ adjective prepared by experience for life's difficulties; not easily shocked or deceived: *Lisa was sufficiently worldly-wise to understand the situation.*
– DERIVATIVES **worldly wisdom** noun.

World Meteorological Organization (abbrev.: **WMO**) an agency of the United Nations, established in 1950 with the aim of facilitating worldwide cooperation in meteorological observations, research, and services. Its headquarters are in Geneva.

world music ▸ noun [mass noun] traditional music from the developing world.

■ Western popular music incorporating elements of such music.

world order ▸ noun a system controlling events in the world, especially a set of arrangements established internationally for preserving global political stability.

world power ▸ noun a country that has significant influence in international affairs.

world-ranking ▸ adjective (of a creative artist, sports player, or other person in the public eye) among the best in the world.

World Series the professional championship for major league baseball, played at the end of the season between the champions of the American League and the National League. It was first played in 1903.

World Service a service of the British Broadcasting Corporation that transmits radio programmes in English and over thirty other languages around the world twenty-four hours a day. A worldwide television station was established in 1991 on a similar basis.

world's fair ▸ noun see **WORLD FAIR**.

world-shaking ▸ adjective (in hyperbolic use) of supreme importance or having a momentous effect: *a world-shaking announcement.*

world soul ▸ noun Philosophy the immanent cause or principle of life, order, consciousness, and self-awareness in the physical world.
– ORIGIN mid 19th cent.: translating German *Weltgeist.*

World Trade Center a complex of buildings in New York featuring twin skyscrapers 110 storeys high, designed by Minoru Yamasaki and completed in 1972. The towers were completely destroyed on 11 September 2001 when two airliners hijacked by Islamic fundamentalist terrorists were flown into them.

World Trade Organization (abbrev.: **WTO**) an international body founded in 1995 to promote international trade and economic development by reducing tariffs and other restrictions.

world view ▸ noun a particular philosophy of life or conception of the world: *a Christian world view revolves around the battle of good and evil.*

world war ▸ noun a war involving many large nations in all different parts of the world. The name is commonly given to the wars of 1914–18 and 1939–45, although only the second of these was truly global. See **FIRST WORLD WAR**, **SECOND WORLD WAR**.

World War I another term for **FIRST WORLD WAR**.

World War II another term for **SECOND WORLD WAR**.

world-weary ▸ adjective feeling or indicating feelings of weariness, boredom, or cynicism as a result of long experience of life: *a tired and slightly world-weary voice.*
– DERIVATIVES **world-weariness** noun.

worldwide ▸ adjective extending or reaching throughout the world: *worldwide sales of television rights.*
▸ adverb throughout the world: *she travels worldwide as a consultant.*

World Wide Fund for Nature (abbrev.: **WWF**) an international organization established (as the World Wildlife Fund) in 1961 to raise funds for projects including the conservation of endangered species or of valuable habitats. Its headquarters are in Gland, Switzerland.

World Wide Web Computing a widely used information system on the Internet, which provides facilities for documents to be connected to other documents by hypertext links, enabling the user to search for information by moving from one document to another.

WORM ▸ abbreviation for write-once read-many, denoting a type of computer memory device.

worm ▸ noun **1** any of a number of creeping or burrowing invertebrate animals with long slender soft bodies and no limbs.
● Phyla Annelida (segmented worms), Nematoda (roundworms), and Platyhelminthes (flatworms), and up to twelve minor phyla.
■ short for **EARTHWORM**. ■ (**worms**) intestinal or other internal parasites. ■ used in names of long slender insect larvae, especially those in fruit or wood, e.g. **army worm**, **woodworm**. ■ used in names of other

animals that resemble worms in some way, e.g. **slow-worm**, **shipworm**. ■ a maggot supposed to eat dead bodies buried in the ground: *food for worms.*
■ Computing a self-replicating program able to propagate itself across a network, typically having a detrimental effect.
2 informal a weak or despicable person (used as a general term of contempt).
3 a helical device or component, in particular:
■ the threaded cylinder in a worm gear. ■ the coiled pipe of a still in which the vapour is cooled and condensed.
▸ verb **1** [no obj., with adverbial of direction] move with difficulty by crawling or wriggling: *I wormed my way along the roadside ditch.*
■ (**worm one's way into**) insinuate one's way into: *the educated dealers may later worm their way into stockbroking.* ■ [with obj. and adverbial of direction] move (something) into a confined space by wriggling it: *I wormed my right hand between my body and the earth.*
■ (**worm something out of**) obtain information from (someone) by cunning persistence: *I did manage to worm a few details out of him.*
2 [with obj.] treat (an animal) with a preparation designed to expel parasitic worms.
3 [with obj.] Nautical, archaic make (a rope) smooth by winding thread between the strands.
– PHRASES (**even**) **a worm will turn** proverb (even) a meek person will resist or retaliate if pushed too far.
– DERIVATIVES **worm-like** adjective.
– ORIGIN Old English *wyrm* (noun), of Germanic origin; related to Latin *vermis* 'worm' and Greek *rhomox* 'woodworm'.

worm cast (also **worm casting**) ▸ noun a convoluted mass of soil, mud, or sand thrown up by an earthworm or lugworm on the surface after passing through the worm's body.

worm-charming ▸ noun [mass noun] the sport of enticing worms from their burrows.
– DERIVATIVES **worm-charmer** noun.

worm-eaten ▸ adjective (of organic tissue) eaten into by worms: *a worm-eaten corpse.*
■ (of wood or a wooden object) full of holes made by woodworm.

wormer ▸ noun a substance administered to animals or birds to expel parasitic worms.

wormery ▸ noun (pl. **-ies**) a container, typically with transparent walls, in which worms are kept for study or bred to be used in making compost or as bait for fishing.

wormfish ▸ noun (pl. same or **-fishes**) a small elongated or eel-like marine fish of warm shallow waters.
● *Microdesmus* and other genera, family Microdesmidae.

worm-fishing ▸ noun [mass noun] the activity or practice of angling with worms for bait.

worm gear ▸ noun a mechanical arrangement consisting of a toothed wheel worked by a short revolving cylinder (worm) bearing a screw thread.

worm grass ▸ noun [mass noun] W. Indian American wormseed.

wormhole ▸ noun a hole made by a burrowing insect larva or worm in wood, fruit, books, or other materials.
■ Physics a hypothetical connection between widely separated regions of space–time.

worm lizard ▸ noun **1** a subterranean burrowing reptile which resembles an earthworm, being blind, apparently segmented, and typically without limbs.
● Suborder Amphisbaenia, order Squamata: four families and numerous species.
2 a legless lizard.

Worms /vɔːmz, German vɔrms/ an industrial town in western Germany, on the Rhine north-west of Mannheim; pop. 77,430 (1991). It was the scene in 1521 of the condemnation of Martin Luther's teaching, at the Diet of Worms.

Worms, Diet of see **DIET OF WORMS**.

wormseed ▸ noun [mass noun] a plant whose seeds have anthelmintic properties:
● (also **Levant wormseed**) santonica. ● (also **American wormseed**) an American plant of the goosefoot family (*Chenopodium ambrosioides*, family Chenopodiaceae).

worm's-eye view ▸ noun a view as seen from below or from a humble position: *a worm's-eye view of international diplomacy.*

worm shell ▸ noun **1** a marine mollusc with a

shell that forms loose irregular coils, giving it a worm-like appearance.
• Family Vermetidae, class Gastropoda: *Vermetus* and other genera, including the European **giant worm shell** (*V. gigas*).
2 the twisted calcareous tube of a sedentary marine bristle worm, typically attached to a stone or mollusc shell.
• The worms belong to *Serpula* and other genera, class Polychaeta.

worm snake ▶ **noun 1** a small harmless North American snake which resembles an earthworm.
• *Carphophis amoena*, family Colubridae.
2 another term for **BLIND SNAKE**.

worm tube ▶ **noun** the calcareous or sandy tube of some sedentary marine worms, such as fan worms.

wormwheel ▶ **noun** the wheel of a worm gear.

wormwood ▶ **noun 1** a woody shrub with a bitter aromatic taste, used as an ingredient of vermouth and absinthe and in medicine.
• Genus *Artemisia*, family Compositae: several species, in particular the Eurasian *A. absinthium*.
2 [mass noun] figurative a state or source of bitterness or grief.
– ORIGIN Old English *wermōd*. The change in spelling in late Middle English was due to association with **WORM** and **WOOD**. Compare with **VERMOUTH**.

wormy ▶ **adjective** (**wormier**, **wormiest**) **1** (of organic tissue) infested with or eaten into by worms: *the prisoners received wormy vegetables*.
■ (of wood or a wooden object) full of holes made by woodworm.
2 informal (of a person) weak, abject, or revolting.
– DERIVATIVES **worminess** noun.

worn past participle of **WEAR**[1]. ▶ **adjective** damaged and shabby as a result of much use: *his knees were encased in worn plus fours*.
■ very tired: *his face looked worn and old*.

worn out ▶ **adjective 1** (of a person or animal) extremely tired; exhausted: *you look worn out*.
2 damaged or shabby to the point of being no longer usable: *worn-out shoes*.
■ (of an idea, method, or system) used so often or existing for so long as to be considered valueless: *he portrayed the Tories as the party of worn-out ideas*.

worriment ▶ **noun** US archaic or humorous term for **WORRY**.

worrisome ▶ **adjective** chiefly N. Amer. causing anxiety or concern: *a worrisome problem*.
– DERIVATIVES **worrisomely** adverb.

worrit /ˈwʌrɪt/ ▶ **verb** (**worrited**, **worriting**) & **noun** Brit. archaic another term for **WORRY**.
– ORIGIN late 18th cent.: apparently an alteration of **WORRY**.

worry ▶ **verb** (**-ies**, **-ied**) **1** [no obj.] give way to anxiety or unease; allow one's mind to dwell on difficulty or troubles: *he* ***worried about*** *his soldier sons in the war* | [with clause] *I began to worry whether I had done the right thing*.
■ [with obj.] cause to feel anxiety or concern: *there was no need to worry her* | *I've been* ***worrying myself sick*** *over my mother* | [with obj. and clause] *he is worried that we are not sustaining high employment* | [as adj. **worrying**] *the level of inflation has improved but remains worrying*. ■ [as adj. **worried**] expressing anxiety: *there was a worried frown on his face*. ■ [with obj.] cause annoyance to: *the noise never really stops, but it doesn't worry me*.
2 [with obj.] (of a dog or other carnivorous animal) tear at or pull about with the teeth: *I found my dog contentedly worrying a bone*.
■ (of a dog) chase and attack (livestock, especially sheep). ■ [no obj.] (**worry at**) pull at or fiddle with repeatedly: *he began to worry at the knot in the cord*.
▶ **noun** (pl. **-ies**) [mass noun] a state of anxiety and uncertainty over actual or potential problems: *her son had been a constant source of worry to her*.
■ [count noun] a source of anxiety: *the idea is to secure peace of mind for people whose greatest worry is fear of attack*.
– PHRASES **not to worry** informal used to reassure someone by telling them that a situation is not serious: *not to worry—no harm done*.
– DERIVATIVES **worriedly** adverb, **worrier** noun, **worryingly** adverb [as submodifier] *trade deficits are worryingly large*.
– ORIGIN Old English *wyrgan* 'strangle', of West Germanic origin. In Middle English the original sense of the verb gave rise to the meaning 'seize by the throat and tear', later figuratively 'harass', whence 'cause anxiety to' (early 19th century, the date also of the noun).
▶ **worry something out** discover or devise the solution to a problem or answer to a question by persistent thought: *children should be allowed to pause in their reading to worry out a meaning*.

worry beads ▶ **plural noun** a string of beads that one fingers and moves in order to calm oneself.

worryguts ▶ **noun** informal a person who tends to dwell unduly on difficulty or troubles.

worrywart ▶ **noun** North American term for **WORRYGUTS**.

wors /vɔːs/ ▶ **noun** [mass noun] S. African sausage.
– ORIGIN Afrikaans, from Dutch *worst* 'sausage'.

worse ▶ **adjective 1** of poorer quality or lower standard; less good or desirable: *the accommodation was awful and the food was worse*.
■ more serious or severe: *the movement made the pain worse*. ■ more reprehensible or evil: *it is worse to intend harm than to be indifferent*. ■ [predic. or as complement] in a less satisfactory or pleasant condition; more ill or unhappy: *he felt worse, and groped his way back to bed*.
▶ **adverb** less well or skilfully: *the more famous I became the worse I painted*.
■ more seriously or severely: *the others had been drunk too, worse than herself*. ■ [sentence adverb] used to introduce a statement of circumstances felt by the speaker to be more serious or undesirable than others already mentioned: *The system will find it hard to sort out property disputes. Even worse, the law will discourage foreign investment*.
▶ **noun** [mass noun] a more serious or unpleasant event or circumstance: *the small department was already stretched to the limit, but worse was to follow*.
■ (**the worse**) a less good, favourable, or pleasant condition: *the weather changed for the worse*.
– PHRASES **none the worse for** not adversely affected by: *we were none the worse for our terrible experience*. ■ not to be considered inferior on account of: *she was non-academic and none the worse for that*. **or worse** used to suggest a possibility that is still more serious or unpleasant than one already considered, but that the speaker does not wish or need to specify: *the child might be born blind or worse*. **so much the worse for ——** used to suggest that a problem, failure, or other unfortunate event or situation is the fault of the person specified and that the speaker does not feel any great concern about it: *if they were daft enough to believe it, so much the worse for them*. **the worse for drink** rather drunk: *he was somewhat the worse for drink at his farewell party*. **the worse for wear** informal **1** damaged by use or weather over time; battered and shabby. **2** (of a person) feeling rather unwell, especially as a result of drinking too much alcohol. **worse luck** see **LUCK**. **worse off** in a less advantageous position; less fortunate or prosperous.
– ORIGIN Old English *wyrsa*, *wiersa* (adjective), *wiers* (adverb), of Germanic origin; related to **WAR**.

worsen ▶ **verb** make or become worse: [no obj.] *her condition worsened on the flight* | [with obj.] *arguing actually worsens the problem* | [as adj. **worsening**] *Romania's rapidly worsening economic situation*.

worship ▶ **noun** [mass noun] the feeling or expression of reverence and adoration for a deity: *worship of the Mother Goddess* | *ancestor worship*.
■ the acts or rites that make up a formal expression of reverence for a deity; a religious ceremony or ceremonies: *the church was opened for public worship*. ■ adoration or devotion comparable to religious homage, shown towards a person or principle: *Krushchev threw the worship of Stalin overboard*. ■ archaic honour given to someone in recognition of their merit. ■ [as title] (**His/Your Worship**) chiefly Brit. used in addressing or referring to an important or high-ranking person, especially a magistrate or mayor: *we were soon joined by His Worship the Mayor*.
▶ **verb** (**worshipped**, **worshipping**; US also **worshiped**, **worshiping**) [with obj.] show reverence and adoration for (a deity); honour with religious rites: *the Maya built jungle pyramids to worship their gods*.
■ treat (someone or something) with the reverence and adoration appropriate to a deity: *she adores her sons and they worship her*. ■ [no obj.] take part in a religious ceremony: *he went to the cathedral because he chose to worship in a spiritually inspiring building*.
– DERIVATIVES **worshipper** (US also **worshiper**) noun.
– ORIGIN Old English *weorthscipe* 'worthiness, acknowledgement of worth' (see **WORTH**, **-SHIP**).

worshipful ▶ **adjective** feeling or showing reverence and adoration: *her voice was full of worshipful admiration*.
■ archaic entitled to honour or respect. ■ (**Worshipful**) Brit. used in titles given to justices of the peace and to certain old companies or their officers: *the Worshipful Company of Goldsmiths*.
– DERIVATIVES **worshipfully** adverb, **worshipfulness** noun.

worst ▶ **adjective** of the poorest quality or the lowest standard: *the speech was the worst he had ever made*.
■ least pleasant, desirable, or tolerable: *they were to stay in the worst conditions imaginable*. ■ most severe, serious, or dangerous: *at least 32 people died in Australia's worst bus accident*. ■ least suitable or advantageous: *the worst time to take out a bond is when rates are low but rise suddenly*.
▶ **adverb** most severely or seriously: *manufacturing and mining are the industries worst affected by falling employment*.
■ least well, skilfully, or pleasingly: *he was voted the worst dressed celebrity*. ■ [sentence adverb] used to introduce the fact or circumstance that the speaker considers most serious or unpleasant: *her mother had rejected her, and worst of all, her adoptive father turned out to be a cheat and a deceiver*.
▶ **noun** the most serious or unpleasant thing that could happen: *when I saw the ambulance outside her front door, I began to* ***fear the worst***.
■ the most serious, dangerous, or unpleasant part or stage of something: *there are signs that the recession is past its worst*.
▶ **verb** [with obj.] (usu. **be worsted**) get the better of; defeat: *this was not the time for a deep discussion—she was tired and she would be worsted*.
– PHRASES **at its** (or **someone's**) **worst** in the most unpleasant, unimpressive, or unattractive state of which someone or something is capable: *nothing's working at the moment, so I suppose you've seen us at our worst*. ■ at the most severe or serious point or level: *harsh lines appeared in his face when his rheumatism was at its worst*. **at worst** (or **the worst**) in the most serious case: *at worst the injury could mean months in hospital*. ■ under the most unfavourable interpretation: *the cabinet's reaction to the crisis was at best ineffective and at worst irresponsible*. **be one's own worst enemy** see **ENEMY**. **do one's worst** do as much damage as one can (often used to express defiance in the face of threats): *let them do their worst—he would never surrender*. **get** (or **have**) **the worst of it** be in the least advantageous or successful position; suffer the most. **if the worst comes to the worst** if the most serious or difficult circumstances arise.
– ORIGIN Old English *wierresta*, *wyrresta* (adjective), *wierst*, *wyrst* (adverb), of Germanic origin; related to **WORSE**.

worst-case ▶ **adjective** (of a projected development) characterized by the worst of the possible foreseeable circumstances: *in the* ***worst-case scenario***, *coastal resorts and communities face disaster*.

worsted /ˈwʊstɪd/ ▶ **noun** [mass noun] a fine smooth yarn spun from combed long-staple wool.
■ fabric made from such yarn, having a close-textured surface with no nap: [as modifier] *a worsted suit*.
– ORIGIN Middle English: from *Worstead*, the name of a parish in Norfolk, England.

wort /wəːt/ ▶ **noun 1** [in combination] used in names of plants and herbs, especially those used formerly as food or medicinally, e.g. **butterwort**, **lungwort**, **woundwort**.
■ archaic such a plant or herb.
2 [mass noun] the sweet infusion of ground malt or other grain before fermentation, used to produce beer and distilled malt liquors.
– ORIGIN Old English *wyrt*, of Germanic origin; related to **ROOT**[1].

Worth, Charles Frederick (1825–95), English couturier, resident in France from 1845. Regarded as the founder of Parisian *haute couture*, he is noted for designing gowns with crinolines and for introducing the bustle.

worth ▶ **adjective** [predic.] equivalent in value to the sum or item specified: *jewellery worth £450 was taken*.
■ sufficiently good, important, or interesting to justify a specified action; deserving to be treated or regarded in the way specified: *the museums in the district are well worth a visit*. ■ used to suggest that the specified course of action may be advisable: *the company's service schemes are worth checking out*. ■ having income or property amounting to a specified sum: *she is worth £10 million*.
▶ **noun** [mass noun] the value equivalent to that of someone or something under consideration; the level at which someone or something deserves to

W

be valued or rated: *they had to listen to every piece of gossip and judge its worth.*
▪ an amount of a commodity equivalent to a specified sum of money: *he admitted stealing 10,000 pounds' worth of computer systems.* ▪ the amount that could be achieved or produced in a specified time: *the companies have debts greater than two years' worth of their sales.* ▪ high value or merit: *he is noble, and gains his position by showing his inner worth.*
– PHRASES **for all someone is worth** informal **1** as energetically or enthusiastically as someone can: *he thumps the drums for all he's worth.* **2** so as to obtain everything one can from someone: *the youths milked him for all he was worth and then disappeared.* **for what it is worth** used to present a comment, suggestion, or opinion without making a claim as to its importance or validity: *for what it's worth, she's very highly thought of abroad.* **worth it** informal sufficiently good, enjoyable, or successful to repay any effort, trouble, or expense: *it requires a bit of patience to learn, bit it's well worth it.* **worth one's salt** see **SALT**. **worth one's while** (or **worth while**) see **WHILE**.
– ORIGIN Old English *w(e)orth* (adjective and noun), of Germanic origin; related to Dutch *waard* and German *wert*.

Worthing /ˈwəːðɪŋ/ a town on the south coast of England, in West Sussex; pop. 92,050 (1980).

worthless ▶ **adjective** having no real value or use: *that promise is worthless.*
▪ (of a person) having no good qualities; deserving contempt: *Joan had been deserted by a worthless husband.*
– DERIVATIVES **worthlessly** adverb, **worthlessness** noun.

worthwhile ▶ **adjective** worth the time, money, or effort spent; of value or importance: *extra lighting would make a worthwhile contribution to road safety.*
– DERIVATIVES **worthwhileness** noun.

USAGE When the adjective **worthwhile** is used attributively (i.e. before the noun) it is always written as one word: *a* ***worthwhile*** *cause.* However, when it is used predicatively (i.e. it stands alone and comes after the verb) it may be written as either one or two words: *we didn't think it was* ***worthwhile/ worth while.***

worthy ▶ **adjective** (**worthier**, **worthiest**) deserving effort, attention, or respect: *generous donations to worthy causes.*
▪ showing or characterized by good intent but lacking in humour or imagination: *worthy but tedious advice.* ▪ having or showing the qualities or abilities that merit recognition in a specified way: *issues* ***worthy of*** *further consideration.* ▪ good enough; suitable: *no composer was considered* ***worthy of*** *the name until he had written an opera.*
▶ **noun** (pl. **-ies**) often derogatory or humorous a person notable or important in a particular sphere: *schools governed by local worthies.*
– DERIVATIVES **worthily** adverb, **worthiness** noun.
– ORIGIN Middle English: from **WORTH** + **-Y**[1].

-worthy ▶ **combining form** deserving of a specified thing: *newsworthy.*
▪ suitable or fit for a specified thing: *roadworthy.*
– ORIGIN from **WORTHY**.

wot[1] ▶ **pronoun**, **determiner**, & **interrogative adverb** non-standard spelling of **WHAT**, chiefly representing informal or humorous use.

wot[2] singular present of **WIT**[2].

Wotan /ˈwəʊtɑːn/ another name for **ODIN**.

wotcha[1] (also **wotcher**) ▶ **exclamation** Brit. informal used as a friendly or humorous greeting: *wotcha, Dunc—thanks for turning out.*
– ORIGIN late 19th cent.: corruption of *what cheer?*

wotcha[2] (also **watcha**) ▶ **exclamation** non-standard contraction of:
▪ what are you: *hey, watcha gonna do?* ▪ what have you: *wotcha got this hammer for then?* ▪ what do you: *wotcha want to make a mess like that for?*

would ▶ **modal verb** (3rd sing. present **would**) **1** past of **WILL**[1], in various senses: *he said he would be away for a couple of days | he wanted out, but she wouldn't leave | the windows would not close.*
2 (expressing the conditional mood) indicating the consequence of an imagined event or situation: *he would lose his job if he were identified.*
▪ (**I would**) used to give advice: *I wouldn't drink that if I were you.*
3 expressing a desire or inclination: *I would love to work in America | would you like some water?*
4 expressing a polite request: *would you pour the wine, please?*
▪ expressing willingness or consent: *who would live here?*
5 expressing a conjecture, opinion, or hope: *I would imagine that they'll want to keep it | I guess some people would consider it brutal | I would have to agree.*
6 chiefly derogatory used to make a comment about behaviour that is typical: *they would say that, wouldn't they?*
7 [with clause] poetic/literary expressing a wish or regret: *would that he had lived to finish it.*
– ORIGIN Old English *wolde*, past of *wyllan* (see **WILL**[1]).

USAGE On the differences in use between **would** and **should**, see **usage** at **SHOULD**.

would-be often derogatory ▶ **adjective** [attrib.] desiring or aspiring to be a specified type of person: *a would-be actress who dresses up as Marilyn Monroe.*
▶ **noun** informal a person who desires or aspires to be a particular type: *a seemingly endless queue of journalists and would-bes formed.*

wouldn't ▶ **contraction of** would not.
– PHRASES **I wouldn't know** informal used to indicate that one can't be expected to know the answer to someone's question or to comment on a matter: *'It was a lot better than last year's dance.' 'I wouldn't know about that.'*

wouldst archaic second person singular of **WOULD**.

Woulfe bottle /wʊlf/ ▶ **noun** Chemistry a glass bottle with two or more necks, used for passing gases through liquids.
– ORIGIN early 19th cent.: named after Peter *Woulfe* (*c.*1727–1803), English chemist.

wound[1] /wuːnd/ ▶ **noun** an injury to living tissue caused by a cut, blow, or other impact, typically one in which the skin is cut or broken.
▪ an injury to a person's feelings or reputation: *the new crisis has opened old wounds.*
▶ **verb** [with obj.] (often **be wounded**) inflict an injury on (someone): *the sergeant was seriously wounded* | [as adj. **wounded**] *a wounded soldier.*
▪ injure (a person's feelings): *you really wounded his pride when you turned him down* | [as adj. **wounded**] *her wounded feelings.*
– DERIVATIVES **woundingly** adverb, **woundless** adjective.
– ORIGIN Old English *wund* (noun), *wundian* (verb), of Germanic origin; related to Dutch *wond* and German *Wunde*, of unknown ultimate origin.

wound[2] past and past participle of **WIND**[2].

Wounded Knee, Battle of the last major confrontation (1890) between the US Army and American Indians, at the village of Wounded Knee on a reservation in South Dakota. More than 300 largely unarmed Sioux men, women, and children were massacred. A civil rights protest at the site in 1973 led to clashes with the authorities.

woundwort ▶ **noun** a hairy Eurasian plant resembling a dead-nettle, formerly used in the treatment of wounds.
● Genus *Stachys*, family Labiatae: several species.

wove past of **WEAVE**[1].

woven past participle of **WEAVE**[1]. ▶ **adjective** (of fabric) formed by interlacing long threads passing in one direction with others at a right angle to them: *women in striped, woven shawls.*
▪ (of basketwork or a wreath) made by interlacing items such as cane, stems, flowers, or leaves. ▪ [with submodifier] (of a complex story or pattern) made in a specified way from a number of interconnected elements: *a neatly woven tale of intrigue in academia.*

wove paper ▶ **noun** [mass noun] paper made on a wire-gauze mesh so as to have a uniform unlined surface. Compare with **LAID PAPER**.
– ORIGIN early 19th cent.: *wove*, variant of **WOVEN**.

wow[1] informal ▶ **exclamation** (also **wowee**) expressing astonishment or admiration: *'Wow!' he cried enthusiastically.*
▶ **noun** a sensational success: *your play's a wow.*
▶ **verb** [with obj.] impress and excite (someone) greatly: *they wowed audiences on their recent British tour.*
– ORIGIN natural exclamation: first recorded in Scots in the early 16th cent.

wow[2] ▶ **noun** [mass noun] slow pitch fluctuation in sound reproduction, perceptible in long notes. Compare with **FLUTTER** (sense 1).
– ORIGIN mid 20th cent.: imitative.

wowser /ˈwaʊzə/ ▶ **noun** Austral./NZ informal a person who is publicly critical of others and the pleasures they seek; a killjoy.
▪ a teetotaller.
– ORIGIN late 19th cent.: of obscure origin.

woylie /ˈwɔɪli/ ▶ **noun** (pl. **-ies**) a nocturnal rat-kangaroo that has a tail with a black crest of hair and a bushy tip, which it uses to carry nest material.
● *Bettongia penicillata*, family Potoroidae. Alternative name: **brush-tailed bettong**.
– ORIGIN 1920s: probably from an Aboriginal word of Western Australia.

WP ▶ **abbreviation for** word processing or word processor.

w.p. ▶ **abbreviation for** weather permitting: *I hope to arrive in London that evening (w.p.).*

W particle ▶ **noun** Physics a heavy charged elementary particle considered to transmit the weak interaction between other elementary particles.
– ORIGIN *W*, the initial letter of *weak*.

wpb ▶ **abbreviation for** waste-paper basket.

WPC ▶ **abbreviation for** (in the UK) woman police constable: *WPC Larkin described the incident.*

wpm ▶ **abbreviation for** words per minute (used after a number to indicate typing speed).

WRAC ▶ **abbreviation for** Women's Royal Army Corps (in the UK, until 1993).

wrack[1] ▶ **verb** variant spelling of **RACK**[1].

USAGE On the complicated relationship between **wrack** and **rack**, see **usage** at **RACK**[1].

wrack[2] ▶ **noun** [mass noun] any of a number of coarse brown seaweeds which grow on the shoreline, frequently each kind forming a distinct band in relation to high- and low-water marks. Many have air bladders for buoyancy.
● Genera *Fucus*, *Ascophyllum*, and *Pelvetia*, class Phaeophyceae.
– ORIGIN early 16th cent.: apparently from **WRACK**[4]; compare with **VAREC**.

wrack[3] (also **rack**) ▶ **noun** a mass of high, thick, fast-moving cloud: *there was a thin moon, a wrack of cloud.*
– ORIGIN late Middle English: variant of **RACK**[5].

wrack[4] ▶ **noun** archaic or dialect a wrecked ship; a shipwreck.
▪ [mass noun] wreckage.
– ORIGIN late Middle English: from Middle Dutch *wrak*; related to **WREAK** and **WRECK**.

WRAF ▶ **abbreviation for** Women's Royal Air Force (in the UK, until 1994).

wraith /reɪθ/ ▶ **noun** a ghost or ghostlike image of someone, especially one seen shortly before or after their death.
▪ used in similes and metaphors to describe a pale, thin, or insubstantial person or thing: *heart attacks had reduced his mother to a wraith.* ▪ poetic/literary a wisp or faint trace of something: *a sea breeze was sending a grey* ***wraith of*** *smoke up the slopes.*
– DERIVATIVES **wraithlike** adjective.
– ORIGIN early 16th cent. (originally Scots): of unknown origin.

Wrangel Island /ˈraŋg(ə)l/ an island in the East Siberian Sea, off the coast of NE Russia. It was named after the Russian admiral and explorer Baron Ferdinand Wrangel (1794–1870).

wrangle ▶ **noun** a dispute or argument, typically one that is long and complicated: *an insurance wrangle is holding up compensation payments.*
▶ **verb 1** [no obj.] have such a dispute or argument: [as noun **wrangling**] *weeks of political wrangling.*
2 [with obj.] US round up, herd, or take charge of (livestock): *the horses were wrangled early.*
– ORIGIN late Middle English: compare with Low German *wrangeln*, frequentative of *wrangen* 'to struggle'; related to **WRING**.

wrangler ▶ **noun 1** US a person in charge of horses or other livestock on a ranch.
2 a person engaging in a lengthy and complicated quarrel or dispute.
3 (at Cambridge University) a person placed in the first class of the mathematical tripos.

wrap ▶ **verb** (**wrapped**, **wrapping**) **1** [with obj.] cover or enclose (someone or something) in paper or soft material: *he* ***wrapped up*** *the Christmas presents | Leonora wrapped herself in a large white bath towel.*
▪ clasp; embrace: *she wrapped him in her arms.*
2 [with obj.] (**wrap something round/around**) arrange paper or soft material round (someone or something), typically as a covering or for warmth

or protection: *wrap the bandage around the injured limb.*
■ place an arm, finger, or leg round (someone or something): *he wrapped an arm around her waist.* ■ informal crash a vehicle into (a stationary object): *Richard wrapped his car around a telegraph pole.*
3 [with obj.] Computing cause (a word or unit of text) to be carried over to a new line automatically as the margin is reached, or to fit around embedded features such as pictures.
■ [no obj.] (of a word or unit or text) be carried over in such a way.
4 [no obj.] informal finish filming or recording: *we wrapped on schedule three days later.*
▶ **noun 1** a loose outer garment or piece of material.
■ [as modifier] denoting a garment having one part overlapping another; wrap-around: *a wrap skirt.* ■ [mass noun] paper or soft material used for wrapping: *plastic food wrap.* ■ (usu. **wraps**) figurative a veil of secrecy maintained about something, especially a new project: *details of the police operation are being kept* ***under*** *wraps.* ■ Brit. informal a small packet of a powdered illegal drug.
2 [usu. in sing.] informal the end of a session of filming or recording: *right, it's a wrap.*
– PHRASES **be wrapped up in** be so engrossed or absorbed in (something) that one does not notice other people or things.
– ORIGIN Middle English: of unknown origin.
▶ **wrap up** (or **wrap someone up**) **1** put on (or dress someone in) warm clothes: *wrap up warm | Tim was well wrapped up against the weather.* **2** (also **wrap it up**) [in imperative] Brit. informal be quiet; stop talking or making a noise.
wrap something up complete or conclude a discussion or agreement: *they hope to wrap up negotiations within sixty days.* ■ win a game or competition: *Australia wrapped up the series 4–0.*

wrap-around ▶ **adjective** [attrib.] curving or extending round at the edges or sides: *a wrap-around windscreen.*
■ (also **wrap-over**) (of a garment) having one part overlapping another and fastened loosely: *a wrap-around skirt.*
▶ **noun 1** (also **wrap-over**) a wrap-around garment.
2 (**wraparound**) Computing a facility by which a linear sequence of memory locations or screen positions is treated as a continuous circular series.

wrapped past participle of **WRAP**. ▶ **adjective** Austral. informal overjoyed; delighted: *the new minister declared that he was wrapped.* [ORIGIN: 1960s: blend of *wrapped (up)* 'engrossed' and **RAPT**.]

wrapper ▶ **noun 1** a piece of paper, plastic, or foil covering and protecting something sold.
■ a cover enclosing a newspaper or magazine for posting. ■ the dust jacket of a book. ■ chiefly US a tobacco leaf of superior quality enclosing a cigar.
2 chiefly US a loose robe or gown.

wrapping ▶ **noun** [mass noun] paper or soft material used to cover or enclose someone or something: *she took the cellophane wrapping off the box.*

wrapping paper ▶ **noun** [mass noun] strong or decorative paper for wrapping parcels or presents.

wrap-up N. Amer. ▶ **noun** a summary or résumé, in particular:
■ a review of a sporting event. ■ an overview of the products of one company or in one field.
▶ **adjective** serving to summarize, complete, or conclude something: *200 campaign volunteers celebrated during wrap-up festivities.*

wrasse /ras/ ▶ **noun** (pl. same or **wrasses**) a marine fish with thick lips and strong teeth, typically brightly coloured with marked differences between the male and female.
• Family Labridae: numerous genera and species.
– ORIGIN late 17th cent.: from Cornish *wrah*; related to Welsh *gwrach*, literally 'old woman'.

wrath /rɒθ, rɔːθ/ ▶ **noun** extreme anger (chiefly used for humorous or rhetorical effect): *he hid his pipe for fear of incurring his father's wrath.*
– ORIGIN Old English *wrǣththu*, from *wrāth* (see **WROTH**).

wrathful ▶ **adjective** poetic/literary full of or characterized by intense anger: *natural calamities seemed to be the work of a wrathful deity.*
– DERIVATIVES **wrathfully** adverb, **wrathfulness** noun.

wrathy ▶ **adjective** N. Amer. informal, dated another term for **WRATHFUL**.

wreak ▶ **verb** [with obj.] cause (a large amount of damage or harm): *torrential rainstorms* ***wreaked havoc*** *yesterday | the environmental damage wreaked by ninety years of phosphate mining.*
■ inflict (vengeance): *he was determined to* ***wreak*** *his revenge* ***on*** *the girl who had rejected him.* ■ archaic avenge (someone who has been wronged): *grant me some knight to wreak me for my son.*
– DERIVATIVES **wreaker** noun.
– ORIGIN Old English *wrecan* 'drive (out), avenge', of Germanic origin; related to Dutch *wreken* and German *rächen*; compare with **WRACK**[4], **WRECK**, and **WRETCH**.

USAGE In the phrase **wrought havoc**, as in *they* ***wrought havoc*** *on the countryside*, **wrought** is an archaic past tense of **work** and is not, as is sometimes assumed, a past tense of **wreak**.

wreath ▶ **noun** (pl. **wreaths** /riːðz, riːθs/) **1** an arrangement of flowers, leaves, or stems fastened in a ring and used for decoration or for laying on a grave.
■ a carved representation of such a wreath. ■ a similar ring made of or resembling soft, twisted material: *a gold wreath.* ■ Heraldry a representation of such a ring below a crest (especially where it joins a helmet). ■ a curl or ring of smoke or cloud: *wreaths of mist swirled up into the cold air.*
2 archaic, chiefly Scottish a snowdrift.
– ORIGIN Old English *writha*, related to **WRITHE**.

wreathe /riːð/ ▶ **verb** [with obj.] (usu. **be wreathed**) cover, surround, or encircle (something): *he sits wreathed in smoke | his face was wreathed in smiles.*
■ [with obj. and adverbial of direction] poetic/literary twist or entwine (something flexible) round or over something: *shall I once more wreathe my arms about Antonio's neck?* ■ form (flowers, leaves, or stems) into a wreath. ■ [no obj., with adverbial of direction] (especially of smoke) move with a curling motion: *he watched the smoke wreathe into the night air.*
– ORIGIN mid 16th cent.: partly a back-formation from archaic *wrethen*, past participle of **WRITHE**, reinforced by **WREATH**.

wreck ▶ **noun** the destruction of a ship at sea; a shipwreck: *the survivors of the wreck.*
■ a ship destroyed in such a way: *the salvaging of treasure from wrecks.* ■ [mass noun] Law goods brought ashore by the sea from a wreck: *the profits of wreck.* ■ something, especially a vehicle or building, that has been badly damaged or destroyed: *the plane was reduced to a smouldering wreck |* figurative *the wreck of their marriage.* ■ the disorganized remains of something that has suffered damage or destruction. ■ N. Amer. a road or rail crash: *a train wreck.* ■ a person whose physical or mental health or strength has failed: *the scandal left the family emotional wrecks.*
▶ **verb** [with obj.] (usu. **be wrecked**) cause the destruction of (a ship) by sinking or breaking up: *he was drowned when his ship was wrecked.*
■ involve (someone) in such a wreck: *sailors who had the misfortune to be wrecked on these coasts.* ■ [no obj.] [usu. as noun **wrecking**] chiefly historical cause the destruction of a ship in order to steal the cargo: *the locals reverted to the age-old practice of wrecking.* ■ [no obj.] archaic suffer or undergo shipwreck. ■ destroy or severely damage (a structure, vehicle, or similar): *the blast wrecked 100 houses.* ■ spoil completely: *an eye injury wrecked his chances of a professional career.* ■ [no obj.] [usu. as noun **wrecking**] chiefly N. Amer. engage in breaking up badly damaged vehicles, demolishing old buildings, or similar activities to obtain usable spares or scrap.
– ORIGIN Middle English (as a legal term denoting wreckage washed ashore): from Anglo-Norman French *wrec*, from the base of Old Norse *reka* 'to drive'; related to **WREAK**.

wreckage ▶ **noun** [mass noun] the remains of something that has been badly damaged or destroyed: *firemen had to cut him free from the wreckage of the car.*

wrecked ▶ **adjective 1** having been wrecked: *an old wrecked barge lay upside down | a wrecked marriage.*
2 informal drunk: *they got wrecked on tequila.*

wrecker ▶ **noun** a person or thing that wrecks, damages, or destroys something: [in combination] *she was cast as a home-wrecker.*
■ chiefly N. Amer. a person who breaks up damaged vehicles, demolishes old buildings, salvages wrecked ships, etc. to obtain usable spares or scrap. ■ N. Amer. a recovery vehicle. ■ chiefly historical a person on the shore who tries to bring about a shipwreck in order to plunder or profit from the wreckage.

wreckfish ▶ **noun** (pl. same or **-fishes**) a large heavy-bodied fish of warm Atlantic waters, the young of which are often found associated with driftwood or wreckage.
• *Polyprion americanus*, family Serranidae.

wrecking ball ▶ **noun** a heavy metal ball swung from a crane into a building to demolish it.

Wrecsam /ˈrɛksam/ Welsh name for **WREXHAM**.

Wren[1], Sir Christopher (1632–1723), English architect. Following the Fire of London (1666) Wren was responsible for the design of the new St Paul's Cathedral (1675–1711) and many of the city's churches. Other works include the Greenwich Observatory (1675) and a partial rebuilding of Hampton Court (1689–94).

Wren[2], P. C. (1885–1941), English novelist; full name *Percival Christopher Wren*. He is best known for his romantic adventure stories dealing with life in the French Foreign Legion, the first of which was *Beau Geste* (1924).

Wren[3] ▶ **noun** (in the UK) a member of the former Women's Royal Naval Service.
– ORIGIN early 20th cent.: originally in the plural, from the abbreviation **WRNS**.

wren ▶ **noun 1** a small short-winged songbird found chiefly in the New World.
• Family Troglodytidae: many genera and numerous species, in particular the very small *Troglodytes troglodytes* (North American name: **winter wren**), which has a short cocked tail and is the only wren that occurs in the Old World.
2 [usu. with modifier] any of a number of small songbirds that resemble the true wrens in size or appearance:
• Brit. a small warbler or kinglet, e.g. **willow-wren**, **golden-crested wren**. • Austral. a bird of the family Maluridae or Acanthizidae. See **EMU-WREN**, **FAIRY WREN**. • NZ a bird of the family Xenicidae. • a Central or South American bird of the families Formicariidae, Polioptilidae, etc., e.g. **ant-wren**.
– ORIGIN Old English *wrenna*, of Germanic origin.

wrench ▶ **noun 1** [usu. in sing.] a sudden violent twist or pull: *with a wrench Tony wriggled free.*
■ figurative an act of leaving someone or something that causes sadness or distress: *it will be a real wrench to leave after eight years.*
2 an adjustable tool like a spanner, used for gripping and turning nuts or bolts.
3 Mechanics a combination of a couple with a force along its axis.
▶ **verb** [with obj.] pull or twist (someone or something) suddenly and violently: *Casey grabbed the gun and wrenched it from my hand |* [with obj. and complement] *she wrenched herself free of his grip |* [no obj.] figurative *the betrayal wrenched at her heart.*
■ injure (a part of the body) as a result of a sudden twisting movement: *she slipped and wrenched her ankle.* ■ turn (something, especially a nut or bolt) with a wrench. ■ archaic distort to fit a particular theory or interpretation: *to wrench our Bible to make it fit a misconception of facts.*
– ORIGIN late Old English *wrencan* 'twist', of unknown origin.

wrench fault ▶ **noun** another term for **STRIKE-SLIP FAULT**.

wrentit ▶ **noun** a long-tailed North American songbird that is the only American member of the babbler family, with dark plumage.
• *Chamaea fasciata*, family Timaliidae.

wrest /rɛst/ ▶ **verb** [with obj.] forcibly pull (something) from a person's grasp: *Leila tried to wrest her arm from his hold.*
■ take (something, especially power or control) from someone or something else after considerable effort or difficulty: *they wanted to allow people to wrest control of their lives from impersonal bureaucracies.* ■ archaic distort the meaning or interpretation of (something) to suit one's own interests or views: *you appear convinced of my guilt, and wrest every reply I have made.*
▶ **noun** archaic a key for tuning a harp or piano.
– ORIGIN Old English *wrǣstan* 'twist, tighten', of Germanic origin; related to Danish *vriste*, also to **WRIST**.

wrestle ▶ **verb** [no obj.] take part in a fight, either as sport or in earnest, that involves grappling with one's opponent and trying to throw or force them to the ground: *as the policeman* ***wrestled with*** *the gunman a shot rang out.*
■ [with obj. and adverbial] force (someone) into a particular position or place by fighting in such a way: *the security guards wrestled them to the ground.* ■ figurative struggle with a difficulty or problem: *for over a year David* ***wrestled with*** *a guilty conscience.* ■ [with obj. and adverbial] move or manipulate (something) in a specified way with difficulty and some physical effort: *she wrestled the keys out of the ignition.*

W

▶ **noun** [in sing.] a wrestling bout or contest: *a wrestle to the death.*
■ a hard struggle: *a lifelong wrestle with depression.*
– DERIVATIVES **wrestler** noun.
– ORIGIN Old English, frequentative of *wrǣstan* 'wrest'.

wrestling ▶ **noun** [mass noun] the sport or activity of grappling with an opponent and trying to throw or hold them down on the ground, typically according to a code of rules.

> Popular in ancient Egypt, China, and Greece, wrestling was introduced to the Olympic Games in 704 BC; many of the holds and throws used now are the same as those of antiquity. The two main competition styles are Graeco-Roman (in which holds below the waist are prohibited) and freestyle, which has become a popular televised sport. See also **SUMO**.

wrest pin ▶ **noun** a pin to which the strings of a piano or harpsichord are attached.

wrest plank (also **wrest block**) ▶ **noun** the part of a piano or harpsichord holding the wrest pins.

wretch ▶ **noun** an unfortunate or unhappy person: *can the poor wretch's corpse tell us anything?*
■ informal a despicable or contemptible person: *ungrateful wretches.*
– ORIGIN Old English *wrecca* (also in the sense 'banished person'), of West Germanic origin; related to German *Recke* 'warrior, hero', also to the verb **WREAK**.

wretched ▶ **adjective** (**wretcheder**, **wretchedest**) (of a person) in a very unhappy or unfortunate state: *I felt so wretched because I thought I might never see you again.*
■ of poor quality; very bad: *the wretched conditions of the slums.* ■ used to express anger or annoyance: *she disliked the wretched man intensely.*
– DERIVATIVES **wretchedly** adverb [as submodifier] *a wretchedly poor country*, **wretchedness** noun.
– ORIGIN Middle English: formed irregularly from **WRETCH** + **-ED**[1].

Wrexham /ˈrɛksəm/ a mining and industrial town in NE Wales; pop. 40,930 (1981). Welsh name **WRECSAM**.

wriggle ▶ **verb** [no obj.] twist and turn with quick writhing movements: *she kicked and wriggled but he held her firmly.*
■ [with obj.] cause to move in such a way: *she wriggled her bare, brown toes.* ■ [no obj., with adverbial of direction] move in a particular direction with wriggling movements: *Susie wriggled out of her clothes.* ■ (**wriggle out of**) avoid (something) by devious means: *don't try and wriggle out of your contract.*
▶ **noun** [in sing.] a wriggling movement: *she gave an impatient little wriggle.*
– DERIVATIVES **wriggler** noun, **wriggly** adjective.
– ORIGIN late 15th cent.: from Middle Low German *wriggelen*, frequentative of *wriggen* 'twist, turn'.

Wright[1], Billy (1924–94), English footballer; full name *William Ambrose Wright*. A wing-half and latterly a defender, he was the first player to make more than a hundred appearances for his country (105 altogether, ninety as captain).

Wright[2], Frank Lloyd (1869–1959), American architect. His 'prairie-style' houses revolutionized American domestic architecture. Notable buildings include the Kaufmann House, which incorporated a waterfall, in Pennsylvania (1935–9) and the Guggenheim Museum of Art in New York (1956–9).

Wright[3], Orville (1871–1948) and Wilbur (1867–1912), American aviation pioneers. In 1903 the Wright brothers were the first to make brief powered sustained and controlled flights in an aeroplane, which they had designed and built themselves. They were also the first to make and fly a fully practical powered aeroplane (1905) and passenger-carrying aeroplane (1908).

wright ▶ **noun** archaic a maker or builder.
■ Scottish & N. English a carpenter or joiner.
– ORIGIN Old English *wryhta*, *wyrhta*, of West Germanic origin; related to **WORK**.

wring ▶ **verb** (past and past participle **wrung** /rʌŋ/) [with obj.] squeeze and twist (something) to force liquid from it: *she* **wrung** *the cloth* **out** *in the sink.*
■ [with obj. and adverbial] extract (liquid) by squeezing and twisting something: *I wrung out the excess water.* ■ break (an animal's neck) by twisting it forcibly. ■ squeeze (someone's hand) tightly, especially with sincere emotion. ■ [with obj. and adverbial] obtain (something) with difficulty or effort: *few concessions were wrung from the government.* ■ cause pain or distress to: *the letter must have wrung her heart.*
▶ **noun** [in sing.] an act of squeezing or twisting something.
– PHRASES **wring one's hands** clasp and twist one's hands together as a gesture of great distress, especially when one is powerless to change the situation.
– ORIGIN Old English *wringan* (verb), of West Germanic origin; related to Dutch *wringen*, also to **WRONG**.

wringer ▶ **noun** a device such as a mangle for wringing water from wet clothes, mops, or other objects.
– PHRASES **put someone through the wringer** (or **the mangle**) informal subject someone to a very stressful experience, especially a severe interrogation.

wringing ▶ **adjective** extremely wet; soaked: *the sweat was worse though—he was wringing* | [as submodifier] *my jacket's wringing wet!*
▶ **noun** [mass noun] the action of wringing something.

wrinkle ▶ **noun 1** a slight line or fold in something, especially fabric or the skin of the face.
■ informal a minor difficulty; a snag: *the organizers have the wrinkles pretty well ironed out.*
2 informal a clever innovation, or useful piece of information or advice: *learning the wrinkles from someone more experienced saves time.*
▶ **verb** [with obj.] [often as adj. **wrinkled**] make or cause lines or folds in (something, especially fabric or the skin): *Dotty's wrinkled stockings.*
■ grimace and cause wrinkles on (a part of the face): *he sniffed and wrinkled his nose.* ■ [no obj.] form or become marked with lines or folds: *her brow wrinkled.*
– ORIGIN late Middle English: origin obscure, possibly a back-formation from the Old English past participle *gewrinclod* 'sinuous' (of which no infinitive is recorded).

wrinkly ▶ **adjective** (**wrinklier**, **wrinkliest**) having many lines or folds: *he's old and wrinkly.*
▶ **noun** (also **wrinklie**) (pl. **-ies**) Brit. informal, humorous or derogatory an old person: *none of the wrinklies looked pleased to see their visitors.*

wrist ▶ **noun 1** the joint connecting the hand with the forearm. See also **CARPUS**.
■ the equivalent joint (the carpal joint) in the foreleg of a quadruped or the wing of a bird. ■ the part of a garment covering the wrist; a cuff.
2 (also **wrist pin**) (in a machine) a stud projecting from a crank as an attachment for a connecting rod.
– ORIGIN Old English, of Germanic origin, probably from the base of **WRITHE**.

wristband ▶ **noun** a strip of material worn round the wrist, in particular:
■ a small strap or bracelet, especially one used for identity purposes or as a fashion item. ■ a strip of absorbent material worn during sport or strenuous exercise to soak up sweat. ■ the cuff of a shirt or blouse.

wrist-drop ▶ **noun** [mass noun] paralysis of the muscles which normally raise the hand at the wrist and extend the fingers, typically caused by nerve damage.

wristlet ▶ **noun** a band or bracelet worn on the wrist, typically as an ornament.

wrist pin ▶ **noun** another term for **WRIST** (in sense 2).

wristwatch ▶ **noun** a watch worn on a strap round the wrist.

wristwork ▶ **noun** [mass noun] the action of working the hand without moving the arm, especially in fencing and ball games.

wristy ▶ **adjective** Cricket & Tennis (of a stroke) performed using a pronounced movement of the wrist: *he uses a fast, wristy swing to hit his forehand.*

writ[1] ▶ **noun** a form of written command in the name of a court or other legal authority to act, or abstain from acting, in some way.
■ chiefly Brit. a Crown document summoning a peer to Parliament or ordering the election of a member or members of Parliament. ■ (**one's writ**) one's power to enforce compliance or submission; one's authority: *you have business here which is out of my writ and competence.*
– PHRASES **one's writ runs** one has authority of a specified extent or kind: *Whitewall is the one area where his writ runs.*
– ORIGIN Old English, as a general term denoting written matter, from the Germanic base of **WRITE**.

writ[2] ▶ **verb** archaic past participle of **WRITE**.
– PHRASES **writ large** clear and obvious: *the unspoken question writ large upon Rose's face.* ■ in a stark or exaggerated form: *bribing people by way of tax allowances is the paternalistic state writ large.*

write ▶ **verb** (past **wrote**; past participle **written**) [with obj.] **1** mark (letters, words, or other symbols) on a surface, typically paper, with a pen, pencil, or similar implement: *he wrote his name on the paper* | *Alice* **wrote down** *the address* | [no obj.] *he wrote very neatly in blue ink.*
■ [no obj.] have the ability to mark coherent letters or words in this way: *he couldn't read or write.* ■ fill out or complete (a sheet, cheque, or similar) in this way: *he had to write a cheque for £800.* ■ Canadian & S. African take (an exam or test): *I wrote Prof. Weldon's Middle English exam last week.* ■ [no obj.] write in a cursive hand, as opposed to printing individual letters.
2 compose, write, and send (a letter) to someone: *I wrote a letter* **to** *Alison* | [with two objs] *I wrote him a short letter* | [no obj.] *he wrote almost every day.*
■ chiefly N. Amer. write and send a letter to (someone): *Mother wrote me and told me about poor Simon's death.* ■ [no obj.] (**write in**) write to an organization, especially a broadcasting station, with a question, suggestion, or opinion: *write in with your query.*
3 compose (a text or work) for written or printed reproduction or publication; put into literary form and set down in writing: *I didn't know you wrote poetry* | [no obj.] *he wrote under a pseudonym* | *he had written about the beauty of Andalusia.*
■ compose (a musical work): *he has written a song specifically for her.* ■ (**write someone into/out of**) add or remove a character to or from (a long-running story or series). ■ archaic describe in writing: *if I could write the beauty of your eyes.*
4 [with obj. and adverbial] Computing enter (data) into a specified storage medium or location in store.
5 underwrite (an insurance policy).
– PHRASES **be nothing to write home about** informal be very mediocre or unexceptional. **be** (or **have something**) **written all over one** (or **one's face**) informal used to convey that the presence of a particular quality or feeling is clearly revealed by a person's expression: *guilt was written all over his face.* **be written in stone** see **STONE**. (**and**) **that's all she wrote** N. Amer. informal used to convey that there is or was nothing more to be said about a matter: *we were arguing about who should pay the bill, but he pulled out a couple of hundreds and that's all she wrote.*
– DERIVATIVES **writable** adjective.
– ORIGIN Old English *wrītan* 'score, form (letters) by carving, write', of Germanic origin; related to German *reissen* 'sketch, drag'.
▶ **write something down** reduce the nominal value of stock or goods.
write someone in chiefly US (when voting) add the name of someone not on the original list of candidates and vote for them.
write something off 1 (**write someone/thing off**) dismiss someone or something as insignificant: *they were written off as a bunch of no-hopers.* **2** cancel the record of a bad debt; acknowledge the loss of or failure to recover an asset: *he urged the banks to write off debt owed by poorer countries.* ■ Brit. damage a vehicle so badly that it cannot be repaired or is not worth repairing.
write something up write a full or formal account of something: *I was too tired to write up my notes.* ■ make entries to bring a diary or similar record up to date: *he wrote up a work journal which has never been published.*

write-back ▶ **noun** [mass noun] Finance the process of restoring to profit a provision for bad or doubtful debts previously made against profits and no longer required.

write-down ▶ **noun** Finance a reduction in the estimated or nominal value of an asset.

write-in ▶ **noun 1** US a vote cast for an unlisted candidate by writing their name on a ballot paper: *the results showed 70 blank ballots and 770 write-ins.*
■ a candidate for whom votes are cast in such a way.
2 a demonstration of public opinion in the form of mass letters of protest: *the* Blackpool Evening Gazette *has launched a write-in.*

write-off ▶ **noun 1** a vehicle, aircraft, or other object that is too badly damaged to be repaired.
■ a worthless or ineffectual person or thing: *the* Morning Star *was a write-off, its credibility rating below zero.*

W

2 Finance a cancellation from an account of a bad debt or worthless asset.

write-once ▶ adjective Computing denoting a memory or storage device, typically an optical one, on which data, once written, cannot be modified.

write-protect ▶ verb [with obj.] Computing protect (a disk) from accidental writing or erasure, as by removing the cover from a notch in casing.
▶ adjective denoting a notch or other device which fulfils this function.

writer ▶ noun a person who has written a particular text: *the writer of the letter.*
■ a person who writes books, stories, or articles as a job or regular occupation: *the distinguished travel writer Freya Stark.* ■ [with adj.] a person who writes in a specified way: *Dickens was a prolific writer.* ■ a composer of musical works: *a writer of military music.* ■ Computing a device that writes data to a storage medium. ■ [with adj.] a person who has a specified kind of handwriting: *neat writers.* ■ Brit. historical a scribe. ■ Brit. archaic a clerk, especially in the navy or in government offices.
– PHRASES **writer's block** the condition of being unable to think of what to write or how to proceed with writing. **writer's cramp** pain or stiffness in the hand caused by excessive writing.
– ORIGIN Old English *wrītere* (see **WRITE**).

writer-in-residence ▶ noun (pl. **writers-in-residence**) a writer holding a temporary residential post in an academic establishment, in order to share his or her professional insights.

writerly ▶ adjective of or characteristic of a professional author: *the mixture of writerly craft and stamina which Greene had.*
■ consciously literary: *novels as tricksy and writerly as those of Robbe-Grillet.*

writer to the Signet ▶ noun historical (in Scotland) a senior solicitor conducting cases in the Court of Session.
– ORIGIN originally a clerk in the Secretary of State's office who prepared writs for the royal Signet.

write-up ▶ noun a full written account.
■ a newspaper or magazine article giving the author's opinion of a recent event, performance, or product.

writhe /rʌɪð/ ▶ verb [no obj.] make continual twisting, squirming movements or contortions of the body: *he writhed in agony on the ground.*
■ [with obj.] cause to move in such a way: *a snake writhing its body in a sinuous movement.* ■ (**writhe in/with/at**) respond with great emotional or physical discomfort to (a violent or unpleasant emotion or thought): *she bit her lip, writhing in suppressed fury.*
▶ noun rare a twisting, squirming movement.
– ORIGIN Old English *wrīthan* 'make into coils, plait, fasten with a cord', of Germanic origin; related to **WREATHE**.

writhen /ˈrɪð(ə)n/ (also **wrythen**) ▶ adjective **1** poetic/literary twisted or contorted out of normal shape or form.
2 (of antique glass or silver) having spirally twisted ornamentation.
– ORIGIN Old English in the sense 'plaited, entwined', archaic past participle of **WRITHE**.

writing ▶ noun [mass noun] **1** the activity or skill of marking coherent words on paper and composing text: *parents want schools to concentrate on reading, writing, and arithmetic.*
■ the activity or occupation of composing text for publication: *she made a decent living from writing.*
2 written work, especially with regard to its style or quality: *the writing is straightforward and accessible.*
■ (**writings**) books, stories, articles, or other written works: *he was introduced to the writings of Gertrude Stein.* ■ (**the Writings**) the Hagiographa.
3 a sequence of letters, words, or symbols marked on paper or some other surface: *a leather product with gold writing on it.*
■ handwriting: *his writing looked crabbed.*
– PHRASES **in writing** in written form, especially as proof of an agreement or grievance: *he asked them to put their complaints in writing.* **the writing** (or N. Amer. **handwriting**) **is on the wall** there are clear signs that something unpleasant or unwelcome is going to happen: *the writing was on the wall for the old system.* [ORIGIN: with biblical allusion to Dan. 5:5, 25–8.]

writing case ▶ noun a portable case for holding writing materials and paper.

writing desk ▶ noun a piece of furniture with a surface for writing on and with drawers and other compartments for pens and paper.

writing pad ▶ noun a pad of paper for writing on.

writing paper ▶ noun [mass noun] paper of good quality used for writing, especially letter-writing.

writ of execution ▶ noun Law a judicial order that a judgement be enforced.

writ of summons ▶ noun Law (in England and Wales) a writ by which an action is started in the High Court.

written past participle of **WRITE**.

WRNS historical ▶ abbreviation for (in the UK) Women's Royal Naval Service.

Wrocław /ˈvrɒtswɑːf/ an industrial city on the Oder River in western Poland; pop. 643,220 (1990). Held by the Habsburgs from the 16th century, it was taken by Prussia in 1741. It passed to Poland in 1945. German name **BRESLAU**.

wrong ▶ adjective **1** not correct or true: *that is the wrong answer.*
■ [predic.] mistaken: *I was wrong about him being on the yacht that evening.* ■ unsuitable or undesirable: *they asked all the wrong questions.* ■ [predic.] in a bad or abnormal condition; amiss: *something was wrong with the pump.*
2 unjust, dishonest, or immoral: *they were wrong to take the law into their own hands | it was wrong of me to write you such an angry note.*
▶ adverb in an unsuitable or undesirable manner or direction: *what am I doing wrong?*
■ with an incorrect result: *she guessed wrong.*
▶ noun an unjust, dishonest, or immoral action: *I have done you a great wrong.*
▶ verb [with obj.] act unjustly or dishonestly towards (someone): *please forgive me these things and the people I have wronged.*
■ mistakenly attribute bad motives to; misrepresent: *perhaps I wrong him.*
– PHRASES **get someone wrong** misunderstand someone, especially by falsely imputing malice. **get (hold of) the wrong end of the stick** misunderstand something. **go down the wrong way** (of food) enter the windpipe instead of the gullet. **go wrong** develop in an undesirable way. **in the wrong** responsible for a quarrel, mistake, or offence. **the wrong way round** in the opposite of the normal or desirable orientation, direction, or sequence. **two wrongs don't make a right** proverb the fact that someone has done something unjust or dishonest is no justification for acting in a similar way.
– DERIVATIVES **wronger** noun, **wrongly** adverb, **wrongness** noun.
– ORIGIN late Old English *wrang*, from Old Norse *rangr* 'awry, unjust'; related to **WRING**.

wrongdoing ▶ noun [mass noun] illegal or dishonest behaviour: *the head of the bank has denied any wrongdoing.*
– DERIVATIVES **wrongdoer** noun.

wrong-foot ▶ verb [with obj.] Brit. (in a game) play so as to catch (an opponent) off balance: *Cook wrong-footed the defence with a low free kick.*
■ put (someone) in a difficult or embarrassing situation by saying or doing something that they do not expect: *an announcement regarded as an attempt to wrong-foot the opposition.*

wrongful ▶ adjective (of an act) not fair, just, or legal: *he is suing the police for wrongful arrest.*
– DERIVATIVES **wrongfully** adverb, **wrongfulness** noun.

wrong-headed ▶ adjective having or showing bad judgement; misguided: *this approach is both wrong-headed and naive.*
– DERIVATIVES **wrong-headedly** adverb, **wrong-headedness** noun.

wrong side ▶ noun the reverse side of a fabric.
– PHRASES **born on the wrong side of the blanket** see **BLANKET**. **get out of bed on the wrong side** see **BED**. **on the wrong side of 1** out of favour with: *she knew not to get on the wrong side of him.* **2** somewhat more than (a specified age): *he cheerfully admits he is the wrong side of fifty.* **on the wrong side of the tracks** see **TRACK**[1]. **wrong side out** inside out.

wrong'un ▶ noun Brit. informal **1** a person of bad character.
2 Cricket another term for **GOOGLY**.
– ORIGIN late 19th cent.: contraction of *wrong one*.

wrot /rɒt/ ▶ noun [mass noun] timber with one or more surfaces planed smooth.
– ORIGIN 1930s: alteration of **WROUGHT**.

wrote past tense of **WRITE**.

wroth /rəʊθ, rɒθ/ ▶ adjective archaic angry: *Sir Leicester is majestically wroth.*
– ORIGIN Old English *wrāth*, of Germanic origin; related to Dutch *wreed* 'cruel', also to **WRITHE**.

wrought /rɔːt/ ▶ adjective (of metals) beaten out or shaped by hammering.
– ORIGIN Middle English: archaic past and past participle of **WORK**.

wrought iron ▶ noun [mass noun] a tough malleable form of iron suitable for forging or rolling rather than casting, obtained by puddling pig iron while molten. It is nearly pure but contains some slag in the form of filaments.

wrought up ▶ adjective [predic.] upset and anxious: *she didn't get too wrought up about things.*

wrung past and past participle of **WRING**.

WRVS ▶ abbreviation for (in the UK) Women's Royal Voluntary Service.

wry /rʌɪ/ ▶ adjective (**wryer**, **wryest** or **wrier**, **wriest**) **1** using or expressing dry, especially mocking, humour: *a wry smile | wry comments.*
2 (of a person's face or features) twisted into an expression of disgust, disappointment, or annoyance.
■ archaic (of the neck or features) distorted or turned to one side.
– DERIVATIVES **wryly** adverb, **wryness** noun.
– ORIGIN early 16th cent. (in the sense 'contorted'): from Old English *wrīgian* 'tend, incline', in Middle English 'deviate, swerve, contort'.

wrybill ▶ noun a small New Zealand plover with grey and white plumage and a bill that bends to the right.
• *Anarhynchus frontalis*, family Charadriidae.

wrymouth ▶ noun an elongated marine fish with a long-based spiny dorsal fin and an oblique mouth that is almost vertical. It occurs in the NW Atlantic and the North Pacific.
• Family Cryptacanthodidae: several genera and species.

wryneck ▶ noun **1** an Old World bird of the woodpecker family, with brown camouflaged plumage and a habit of twisting and writhing the neck when disturbed.
• Genus *Jynx*, family Picidae: two species, in particular the **northern wryneck** (*J. torquilla*) of Eurasia.
2 another term for **TORTICOLLIS**.

wrythen ▶ adjective variant spelling of **WRITHEN**.

WSW ▶ abbreviation for west-south-west.

wt ▶ abbreviation for weight.

WTO ▶ abbreviation for World Trade Organization.

Wu /wuː/ ▶ noun [mass noun] a dialect of Chinese spoken in Jiangsu and Zhejiang provinces and the city of Shanghai. It has an estimated 80 million speakers.
– ORIGIN the name in Chinese.

wuff /wʌf/ ▶ noun a dog's low suppressed bark.
▶ verb [no obj.] (of a dog) give such a bark.
– ORIGIN early 19th cent.: imitative.

Wuhan /wuːˈhan/ a port in eastern China, the capital of Hubei province; pop. 3,710,000 (1990). Situated at the confluence of the Han and the Yangtze Rivers, it is a conurbation consisting of three adjacent towns (Hankow, Hanyang, and Wuchang), administered jointly since 1950.

Wu-hsi variant of **WUXI**.

wulfenite /ˈwʊlfənʌɪt/ ▶ noun [mass noun] an orange-yellow mineral consisting of a molybdate of lead, typically occurring as tabular crystals.
– ORIGIN mid 19th cent.: from the name of F. X. von *Wulfen* (1728–1805), Austrian scientist, + **-ITE**[1].

Wulfila /ˈwʊlfɪlə/ variant spelling of **ULFILAS**.

Wunderkammer /ˈvʊndəˌkamə, German ˈvʊndɐˌkamɐ/ ▶ noun (pl. **Wunderkammern** /-ˌkaməːn, German -ˌkamɐn/) a place where a collection of curiosities and rarities is exhibited.
– ORIGIN German, literally 'wonder chamber'.

wunderkind /ˈvʊndəkɪnd/ ▶ noun (pl. **wunderkinds** or **wunderkinder** /-kɪndə/) a person who achieves great success when relatively young.
– ORIGIN late 19th cent.: from German, from *Wunder* 'wonder' + *Kind* 'child'.

Wundt /vʊnt/, Wilhelm (1832–1920), German psychologist. He was the founder of psychology as a separate discipline, establishing a laboratory devoted to its study.

W

wunnerful ▶ adjective non-standard spelling of **WONDERFUL**, representing US or dialect pronunciation.

Wuppertal /ˈvʊpətɑːl, German ˈvʊpɐtaːl/ an industrial city in western Germany, in North Rhine-Westphalia north-east of Düsseldorf; pop. 385,460 (1991).

Wurlitzer /ˈwɜːlɪtsə/ ▶ noun trademark a large pipe organ or electric organ, especially one used in the cinemas of the 1930s.
– ORIGIN named after Rudolf *Wurlitzer* (1831–1914), the German-born American instrument-maker who founded the manufacturing company.

Würm /vʊəm/ ▶ noun [usu. as modifier] Geology the final Pleistocene glaciation in the Alps, possibly corresponding to the Weichsel of northern Europe.
■ the system of deposits laid down at this time.
– ORIGIN early 20th cent.: the former name of the Starnberger See, a lake in Bavaria.

wurst /vɜːst, vʊəst, w-/ ▶ noun [mass noun] German or Austrian sausage.
– ORIGIN from German *Wurst*.

wurtzite /ˈwɜːtsʌɪt, ˈwɔːt-/ ▶ noun [mass noun] a mineral consisting of zinc sulphide, typically occurring as brownish-black pyramidal crystals.
– ORIGIN mid 19th cent.: from the name of Charles A. *Wurtz* (1817–84), French chemist, + **-ITE**[1].

Würzburg /ˈvʊətsbəːɡ, German ˈvʏrtsbʊrk/ an industrial city on the River Main in Bavaria, southern Germany; pop. 128,500 (1991).

wushu /wuːˈʃuː/ ▶ noun [mass noun] the Chinese martial arts.
– ORIGIN from Chinese *wǔshù*, from *wǔ* 'military' + *shù* 'art'.

wuss /wʊs/ ▶ noun informal a weak or ineffectual person (often used as a general term of abuse).
– DERIVATIVES **wussy** noun (pl. **-ies**) & adjective.
– ORIGIN late 20th cent. (originally North American slang): of unknown origin.

Wuxi /wuːˈʃiː/ (also **Wu-hsi**) a city on the Grand Canal in Jiangsu province, eastern China; pop. 930,000 (est. 1990).

wuz /wʌz/ ▶ verb non-standard spelling of **WAS**, representing dialect or informal pronunciation.

WV ▶ abbreviation for West Virginia (in official postal use).

W.Va ▶ abbreviation for West Virginia.

WWF ▶ abbreviation for ■ World Wide Fund for Nature. ■ World Wrestling Federation.

WWI ▶ abbreviation for World War I.

WWII ▶ abbreviation for World War II.

WWW ▶ abbreviation for World Wide Web.

WY ▶ abbreviation for Wyoming (in official postal use).

Wyandot /ˈwʌɪəndɒt/ (also **Wyandotte**) ▶ noun **1** a member of an American Indian community formed by Huron-speaking peoples, originally in Ontario, now living mainly in Oklahoma and Quebec.
2 [mass noun] the extinct Iroquoian language of this people.
3 (usu. **Wyandotte**) a domestic chicken of a medium-sized American breed.
▶ adjective of or relating to the Wyandot people or their language.
– ORIGIN mid 18th cent.: from French *Ouendat*, from Huron *Wendat*.

Wyatt[1] /ˈwʌɪət/, James (1746–1813), English architect. He was both a neoclassicist and a leading figure in the Gothic revival, the latter seen most notably in his design for Fonthill Abbey in Wiltshire (1796–1807).

Wyatt[2] /ˈwʌɪət/, Sir Thomas (1503–42), English poet. He went to Italy (1527) as a diplomat in the service of Henry VIII; this visit probably stimulated his translation of Petrarch. His work also includes sonnets, rondeaux, songs for the lute, and satires.

wych elm /wɪtʃ/ (also **witch elm**) ▶ noun a European elm with large rough leaves, chiefly growing in woodland or near flowing water.
● *Ulmus glabra*, family Ulmaceae.
– ORIGIN early 17th cent.: *wych*, used in names of trees with pliant branches, from Old English *wic(e)*, apparently from a Germanic root meaning 'bend'; related to **WEAK**.

Wycherley /ˈwɪtʃəli/, William (c.1640–1716), English dramatist. His Restoration comedies are characterized by their acute examination of sexual morality and marriage conventions. Notable works: *The Country Wife* (1675).

wych hazel ▶ noun variant spelling of **WITCH HAZEL**.

Wyclif /ˈwɪklɪf/ (also **Wycliffe**), John (c.1330–84), English religious reformer. He criticized the wealth and power of the Church and upheld the Bible as the sole guide for doctrine; his teachings were disseminated by itinerant preachers and are regarded as precursors of the Reformation. Wyclif instituted the first English translation of the complete Bible. His followers were known as Lollards.

Wye a river which rises in the mountains of western Wales and flows 208 km (132 miles) generally south-eastwards, entering the Severn estuary at Chepstow. In its lower reaches it forms part of the border between Wales and England.

wye ▶ noun a support or other structure shaped like a Y, in particular:
■ N. Amer. a triangle of railway track, used for turning locomotives or trains. ■ (in plumbing) a short pipe with a branch joining it at an acute angle.
– ORIGIN mid 19th cent.: the letter Y represented as a word.

Wykehamist /ˈwɪkəmɪst/ ▶ noun a past or present member of Winchester College.
▶ adjective of or relating to Winchester College.
– ORIGIN mid 18th cent.: from modern Latin *Wykehamista*, from the name of William of *Wykeham* (1324–1404), bishop of Winchester and founder of the college.

wyn /wɪn/ ▶ noun variant spelling of **WEN**[2].

wynd /wʌɪnd/ ▶ noun Scottish & N. English a narrow street or alley: [as name] *Friars Wynd*.
– ORIGIN Middle English: apparently from the stem of the verb **WIND**[2].

Wyndham /ˈwɪndəm/, John (1903–69), English writer of science fiction; pseudonym of *John Wyndham Parkes Lucas Beynon Harris*. His fiction often examines the psychological impact of catastrophe. Notable novels: *The Day of the Triffids* (1951), *The Chrysalids* (1955), and *The Midwich Cuckoos* (1957).

Wynette /wɪˈnɛt/, Tammy (1942–98), American country singer; born *Tammy Wynette Pugh*. Her unique lamenting voice brought her success with songs such as 'Apartment No. 9' (1966) and 'Stand by Your Man' (1968).

Wyo. ▶ abbreviation for Wyoming.

Wyoming /wʌɪˈəʊmɪŋ/ a state in the west central US; pop. 453,590 (1990); capital, Cheyenne. Acquired as part of the Louisiana Purchase in 1803, it became the 44th state of the US in 1890.
– DERIVATIVES **Wyomingite** noun.

WYSIWYG /ˈwɪzɪwɪɡ/ (also **wysiwyg**) ▶ adjective Computing denoting the representation of text on-screen in a form exactly corresponding to its appearance on a printout.
– ORIGIN 1980s: acronym from *what you see is what you get*.

wyvern /ˈwʌɪv(ə)n/ ▶ noun Heraldry a winged two-legged dragon with a barbed tail.
– ORIGIN late Middle English (denoting a viper): from Old French *wivre*, from Latin *vipera*.

w

X¹ (also **x**) ▶ noun (pl. **Xs** or **X's**) **1** the twenty-fourth letter of the alphabet.
■denoting the next after W in a set of items, categories, etc. ■denoting an unknown or unspecified person or thing: *there is nothing in the data to tell us whether X causes Y or Y causes X.* ■ (**x**) (used in describing play in bridge) denoting an unspecified card other than an honour. ■ (usu. **x**) the first unknown quantity in an algebraic expression, usually the independent variable. [ORIGIN: the introduction of *x*, *y*, and *z* as symbols of unknown quantities is due to Descartes (*Géométrie*, 1637), who took *z* as the first unknown and then proceeded backwards in the alphabet.] ■ (usu. **x**) denoting the principal or horizontal axis in a system of coordinates: [in combination] *the x-axis.*
2 a cross-shaped written symbol, in particular:
■used to indicate a position on a map or diagram. ■ used to indicate a mistake or incorrect answer. ■ used in a letter or message to symbolize a kiss. ■ used to indicate one's vote on a ballot paper. ■ used in place of the signature of a person who cannot write.
3 a shape like that of a letter X: *two wires in the form of an X* | [in combination] *an X-shaped cross.*
4 the Roman numeral for ten.

X² ▶ symbol for films classified as suitable for adults only (replaced in the UK in 1983 by *18*, and in the US in 1990 by *NC–17*).

-x ▶ suffix forming the plural of many nouns ending in *-u* taken from French: *tableaux.*
– ORIGIN from French.

X-acto knife /ɪɡ'zaktəʊ/ ▶ noun N. Amer. trademark a utility knife with a very sharp replaceable blade.
– ORIGIN 1940s: respelling of the adjective **EXACT** + **-O**.

Xanadu /'zanədu:/ ▶ noun (pl. **Xanadus**) used to convey an impression of a place as almost unattainably luxurious or beautiful: *three architects and a planner combine to create a Xanadu.*
– ORIGIN alteration of *Shang-tu*, the name of an ancient city in SE Mongolia, as portrayed in Coleridge's poem *Kubla Khan* (1816).

Xanax /'zanaks/ ▶ noun trademark for **ALPRAZOLAM**.

Xankändi /,xɑːnkən'diː/ the capital of Nagorno-Karabakh in southern Azerbaijan; pop. 58,000 (1990). Russian name **STEPANAKERT**.

xanthan gum /'zanθan/ ▶ noun [mass noun] Chemistry a substance produced by bacterial fermentation or synthetically and used in foods as a gelling agent and thickener. It is polysaccharide composed of glucose, mannose, and glucuronic acid.
– ORIGIN 1960s: from the modern Latin name of the bacterium *Xanthomonas campestris* + **-AN**.

xanthene /'zanθiːn/ ▶ noun [mass noun] Chemistry a yellowish crystalline compound, whose molecule contains two benzene rings joined by a methylene group and an oxygen atom, and whose derivatives include brilliant, often fluorescent dyes such as fluorescein and rhodamines.
● Chem. formula: $C_{13}H_{10}O$.
– ORIGIN late 19th cent.: from Greek *xanthos* 'yellow' + **-ENE**.

Xanthian Marbles /'zanθɪən/ sculptures found in 1838 at the site of the ancient Lycian town of Xanthus (now in Turkey), which are now in the British Museum. The figures are Assyrian in

character and are believed to have been executed before 500 BC.

xanthic acid /'zanθɪk/ ▶ noun Chemistry an organic acid containing the group —OCS₂H, examples of which are typically reactive solids.
– DERIVATIVES **xanthate** /'zanθeɪt/ noun.
– ORIGIN early 19th cent.: *xanthic* from Greek *xanthos* 'yellow' + **-IC**.

xanthine /'zanθiːn/ ▶ noun [mass noun] Biochemistry a crystalline compound found in blood and urine which is an intermediate in the metabolic breakdown of nucleic acids to uric acid.
● A purine derivative; chem. formula: $C_5H_4N_4O_2$.
■[count noun] any of the derivatives of this, including caffeine and related alkaloids.
– ORIGIN mid 19th cent.: from *xanthic* (from Greek *xanthos* 'yellow' + **-IC**) + **-INE**⁴.

Xanthippe /zan'θɪpi/ (also **Xantippe** /-'tɪpi/) (5th century BC), wife of the philosopher Socrates. Her allegedly bad-tempered behaviour towards her husband has made her proverbial as a shrew.

xanthoma /zan'θəʊmə/ ▶ noun (pl. **xanthomas** or **xanthomata** /-mətə/) Medicine an irregular yellow patch or nodule on the skin, caused by deposition of lipids.
– ORIGIN mid 19th cent.: from Greek *xanthos* 'yellow' + **-OMA**.

xanthophyll /'zanθə(ʊ)fɪl/ ▶ noun [mass noun] Biochemistry a yellow or brown carotenoid plant pigment which causes the autumn colours of leaves.
– ORIGIN mid 19th cent.: from Greek *xanthos* 'yellow' + *phullon* 'leaf'.

Xavier, St Francis /'zavɪə, 'zeɪv-/ (1506–52), Spanish Catholic missionary; known as **the Apostle of the Indies**. One of the original seven Jesuits, from 1540 he travelled to southern India, Sri Lanka, Malacca, the Moluccas, and Japan, making thousands of converts. Feast day, 3 December.

X chromosome ▶ noun Genetics (in humans and other mammals) a sex chromosome, two of which are normally present in female cells (designated XX) and only one in male cells (designated XY). Compare with **Y CHROMOSOME**.

xd ▶ abbreviation for ex dividend.

Xe ▶ symbol for the chemical element xenon.

xebec /'ziːbɛk/ (also **zebec**) ▶ noun historical a small three-masted Mediterranean sailing ship with lateen and square sails.
– ORIGIN mid 18th cent.: alteration (influenced by Spanish *xabeque*) of French *chebec*, via Italian from Arabic *šabbāk*.

Xenakis /zɛ'nɑːkɪs/, Iannis (b.1922), French composer and architect, of Greek descent. He is noted for his use of electronic and aleatory techniques in music.

Xenarthra /zɛ'nɑːθrə/ Zoology an order of mammals that comprises the edentates. Also called **EDENTATA**.
– DERIVATIVES **xenarthran** noun & adjective.
– ORIGIN modern Latin (plural), from **XENO-** 'strange' + Greek *arthron* 'joint' (because of the peculiar accessory articulations in the vertebrae).

xeno- ▶ combining form relating to a foreigner or foreigners: *xenophobia.*

■other; different in origin: *xenograft.*
– ORIGIN from Greek *xenos* 'stranger, foreigner', (adjective) 'strange'.

xenobiotic /,zɛnə(ʊ)bʌɪ'ɒtɪk/ ▶ adjective relating to or denoting a substance, typically a synthetic chemical, that is foreign to the body or to an ecological system.
▶ noun (usu. **xenobiotics**) a substance of this kind.

xenocryst /'zɛnə(ʊ)krɪst/ ▶ noun Geology a crystal in an igneous rock which is not derived from the original magma.
– ORIGIN late 19th cent.: from **XENO-** 'foreign' + **CRYSTAL**.

xenogamy /zɛ'nɒɡəmi/ ▶ noun [mass noun] Botany fertilization of a flower by pollen from a flower on a genetically different plant. Compare with **GEITONOGAMY**.
– DERIVATIVES **xenogamous** adjective.

xenogeneic /,zɛnə(ʊ)dʒɪ'niːɪk, -'neɪɪk/ ▶ adjective Immunology denoting, relating to, or involving tissues or cells belonging to individuals of different species. Compare with **ALLOGENEIC**.

xenograft ▶ noun a tissue graft or organ transplant from a donor of a different species from the recipient.

xenolith /'zɛnə(ʊ)lɪθ/ ▶ noun Geology a piece of rock within an igneous mass which is not derived from the original magma but has been introduced from elsewhere, especially the surrounding country rock.

xenon /'zɛnɒn, 'ziː-/ ▶ noun [mass noun] the chemical element of atomic number 54, a member of the noble gas series. It is obtained by distillation of liquid air, and is used in some specialized electric lamps. (Symbol: **Xe**)
– ORIGIN late 19th cent.: from Greek, neuter of *xenos* 'strange'.

Xenophanes /zɛ'nɒfəniːz/ (c.570–c.480 BC), Greek philosopher. A member of the Eleatic school, he argued for a form of pantheism, criticizing belief in anthropomorphic gods.

xenophobia ▶ noun [mass noun] intense or irrational dislike or fear of people from other countries.
– DERIVATIVES **xenophobe** noun, **xenophobic** adjective.

Xenophon /'zɛnəf(ə)n/ (c.435–c.354 BC), Greek historian, writer, and military leader. From 401 he fought with Cyrus the Younger against Artaxerxes II, and led an army of 10,000 Greek mercenaries in their retreat of about 1,500 km (900 miles) after Cyrus was killed; the campaign and retreat are recorded in the *Anabasis*. Other notable writings include the *Hellenica*, a history of Greece.

Xenopus /'zɛnəpəs/ ▶ noun the African clawed toad, much used in embryological research and formerly in pregnancy testing, as it produces eggs in response to substances in the urine of a pregnant woman.
● *Xenopus laevis*, family Pipidae.
– ORIGIN late 19th cent.: modern Latin, from **XENO-** 'strange' + Greek *pous* 'foot'.

xenotime /'zɛnə(ʊ)tʌɪm/ ▶ noun [mass noun] a yellowish-brown mineral which occurs in some igneous rocks and consists of a phosphate of yttrium and other rare-earth elements.

● Composition: native yttrium phosphate.

– ORIGIN mid 19th cent.: from **XENO-**, apparently erroneously for Greek *kenos* 'vain, empty', + *timē* 'honour' (because it was wrongly supposed to contain a new metal).

xenotransplantation ▶ noun [mass noun] the process of grafting or transplanting organs or tissues between members of different species.

– DERIVATIVES **xenotransplant** noun.

xeric /ˈzɪərɪk, ˈzɛ-/ ▶ adjective Ecology (of an environment or habitat) containing little moisture; very dry. Compare with **HYDRIC** and **MESIC**[1].

– ORIGIN 1920s: from **XERO-** 'dry' + **-IC**.

xeriscape /ˈzɪərɪskeɪp, ˈzɛ-/ chiefly US ▶ noun [mass noun] a style of landscape design requiring little or no irrigation or other maintenance, used in arid regions.

■ [count noun] a garden or landscape created in such a style.

▶ verb [with obj.] landscape (an area) in such a style.

– ORIGIN 1980s: from **XERIC** + **-SCAPE**.

xero- /ˈzɪərəʊ, ˈzɛrəʊ/ ▶ combining form dry: *xeroderma* | *xerophyte*.

– ORIGIN from Greek *xēros* 'dry'.

xeroderma /ˌzɪərə(ʊ)ˈdəːmə, ˌzɛ-/ ▶ noun [mass noun] any of various diseases characterized by extreme dryness of the skin, especially a mild form of ichthyosis.

– ORIGIN mid 19th cent.: modern Latin, from **XERO-** 'dry' + Greek *derma* 'skin'.

xeroderma pigmentosum /ˌpɪɡmɛnˈtəʊsəm/ ▶ noun [mass noun] a rare hereditary defect of the enzyme system that repairs DNA after damage from ultraviolet rays, resulting in extreme sensitivity to sunlight and a tendency to develop skin cancer.

– ORIGIN late 19th cent.: *pigmentosum*, neuter of Latin *pigmentosus* 'pigmented'.

xerography ▶ noun [mass noun] a dry copying process in which black or coloured powder adheres to parts of a surface remaining electrically charged after being exposed to light from an image of the document to be copied.

– DERIVATIVES **xerographic** adjective, **xerographically** adverb.

xerophilous /zɪəˈrɒfɪləs, zɛ-/ ▶ adjective Botany & Zoology (of a plant or animal) adapted to a very dry climate or habitat, or to conditions where moisture is scarce.

– DERIVATIVES **xerophile** noun.

xerophthalmia /ˌzɪərɒfˈθalmɪə, ˌzɛ-/ ▶ noun [mass noun] Medicine abnormal dryness of the conjunctiva and cornea of the eye, with inflammation and ridge formation, typically associated with vitamin A deficiency.

xerophyte /ˈzɪərə(ʊ)fʌɪt, ˈzɛ-/ ▶ noun Botany a plant which needs very little water.

– DERIVATIVES **xerophytic** adjective.

Xerox /ˈzɪərɒks, ˈzɛ-/ ▶ noun [mass noun] trademark a xerographic copying process.

■ [count noun] a copy made using such a process. ■ [count noun] a machine for copying by xerography.

▶ verb (**xerox**) [with obj.] copy (a document) by such a process.

– ORIGIN 1950s: an invented name, based on **XEROGRAPHY**.

Xerxes I /ˈzəːksiːz/ (*c.*519–465 BC), son of Darius I, king of Persia 486–465. His invasion of Greece achieved victories in 480 at Artemisium and Thermopylae, but defeats at Salamis (480) and Plataea (479) forced him to withdraw.

x-height ▶ noun the height of a lower-case x, considered characteristic of a given typeface or script.

Xhosa /ˈkəʊsə, ˈkɔːsə/ ▶ noun (pl. same or **Xhosas**) 1 a member of a South African people traditionally living in the Eastern Cape Province. They form the second largest ethnic group in South Africa after the Zulus.

2 [mass noun] the Bantu language of this people, related to Zulu and spoken by about 6 million people.

▶ adjective of or relating to this people or their language.

– ORIGIN from the stem of Xhosa *umXhosa* (plural *amaXhosa*).

xi /ksAɪ, ɡzAɪ, sAɪ, zAɪ/ ▶ noun the fourteenth letter of the Greek alphabet (Ξ, ξ), transliterated as 'x'.

■ (**Xi**) [followed by Latin genitive] Astronomy the fourteenth star in a specified constellation: *Xi Cygni*.

– ORIGIN Greek.

Xiamen /ʃɑːˈmɛn/ (also **Hsia-men**) a port in Fujian province, SE China; pop. 639,400 (1990). Also called **AMOY**.

Xian /ʃiːˈan/ (also **Hsian** or **Sian**) an industrial city in central China, capital of Shaanxi province; pop. 2,710,000 (1990). The city has been inhabited since the 11th century BC, having previously been the capital of the Han, Sui, and Tang dynasties. Former names **CHANGAN**, **SIKING**.

Xiang /ʃiːˈaŋ/ (also **Hsiang**) ▶ noun [mass noun] a dialect of Chinese spoken by about 36 million people, mainly in Hunan province.

Ximenes de Cisneros variant spelling of **JIMÉNEZ DE CISNEROS**.

Xingtai /ʃɪŋˈtAɪ/ a city in NE China, situated to the south of Shijiazhuang in the province of Hebei; pop. 1,167,000 (1986).

Xingú /ʃɪŋˈɡuː/ a South American river, which rises in the Mato Grosso of western Brazil and flows 1,979 km (1,230 miles) generally northwards to join the Amazon delta.

Xining /ʃiːˈnɪŋ/ (also **Hsining** or **Sining**) a city in north central China, capital of Qinghai province; pop. 697,700 (1990).

Xinjiang /ʃɪnˈdʒjaŋ/ (also **Sinkiang**) an autonomous region of NW China, on the border with Mongolia and Kazakhstan; pop. 15,156,000 (1990); capital, Urumqi.

-xion ▶ suffix forming nouns such as *fluxion*.

– ORIGIN from Latin participial stems (see also **-ION**).

xiphisternum /ˌzɪfɪˈstəːnəm/ ▶ noun Anatomy the lowest part of the sternum; the xiphoid process.

– ORIGIN mid 19th cent.: from Greek *xiphos* 'sword' + **STERNUM**.

xiphoid process /ˈzɪfɔɪd/ (also **xiphoid cartilage**) ▶ noun Anatomy the cartilaginous section at the lower end of the sternum, which is not attached to any ribs, and gradually ossifies during adult life.

– ORIGIN mid 18th cent. (as *xiphoid cartilage*): *xiphoid* from Greek *xiphoeidēs*, from *xiphos* 'sword'.

X-irradiation ▶ noun [mass noun] irradiation with X-rays.

Xizang /ʃiːˈzaŋ/ Chinese name for **TIBET**.

XL ▶ abbreviation for extra large (as a clothes size).

Xmas /ˈkrɪsməs, ˈɛksməs/ ▶ noun informal term for **CHRISTMAS**.

– ORIGIN *X* representing the initial chi of Greek *Khristos* 'Christ'.

XMS ▶ abbreviation for extended memory system, a system for increasing the amount of memory available to a personal computer.

xoanon /ˈzəʊənɒn/ ▶ noun (pl. **xoana** /-nə/) (in ancient Greece) a primitive wooden image of a deity.

– ORIGIN early 18th cent.: from Greek; related to *xein* 'carve'.

XOR ▶ noun another term for **EXCLUSIVE OR**.

X-rated ▶ adjective pornographic or indecent: *there was some X-rated humour.*

■ historical (of a film) given an X classification (see **X**[2]).

X-ray ▶ noun 1 an electromagnetic wave of high energy and very short wavelength (between ultraviolet light and gamma rays), which is able to pass through many materials opaque to light.

■ [as modifier] informal denoting an apparent or supposed faculty for seeing beyond an outward form: *you didn't need X-ray eyes to know what was going on.*

2 a photographic or digital image of the internal composition of something, especially a part of the body, produced by X-rays being passed through it

and being absorbed to different degrees by different materials.

■ an act of photographing someone or something in this way: *he will have an X-ray today* | [mass noun] *would you send her for X-ray?*

3 a code word representing the letter X, used in radio communication.

▶ verb [with obj.] photograph or examine with X-rays: *luggage bound for the hold is X-rayed.*

– ORIGIN translation of German *X-Strahlen* (plural), from *X-* (because, when discovered in 1895, the nature of the rays was unknown) + *Strahl* 'ray'.

X-ray astronomy ▶ noun [mass noun] the branch of astronomy concerned with the detection and measurement of high-energy electromagnetic radiation emitted by celestial objects.

X-ray crystallography ▶ noun [mass noun] the study of crystals and their structure by means of the diffraction of X-rays by the regularly spaced atoms of crystalline materials.

X-ray fish ▶ noun a small almost transparent freshwater fish with an opaque body cavity. Native to South America, it is popular in aquaria.

● *Pristella riddlei*, family Characidae.

X-ray tube ▶ noun Physics a device for generating X-rays by accelerating electrons to high energies and causing them to strike a metal target from which the X-rays are emitted.

xu /suː/ ▶ noun (pl. same) a monetary unit of Vietnam, equal to one hundredth of a dong.

– ORIGIN Vietnamese, from French *sou*.

Xuzhou /ʃuːˈdʒəʊ/ (also **Hsu-chou**, **Suchow**) a city in Jiangsu province, eastern China; pop. 910,000 (est. 1990). Former name (1912–45) **TONGSHAN**.

xylem /ˈzAɪləm/ ▶ noun [mass noun] Botany the vascular tissue in plants which conducts water and dissolved nutrients upwards from the root and also helps to form the woody element in the stem. Compare with **PHLOEM**.

– ORIGIN late 19th cent.: from Greek *xulon* 'wood' + the passive suffix *-ēma*.

xylene /ˈzAɪliːn/ ▶ noun [mass noun] Chemistry a volatile liquid hydrocarbon obtained by distilling wood, coal tar, or petroleum, and used in fuels and solvents, and in chemical synthesis.

● Alternative name: **dimethylbenzene**; chem. formula: $C_6H_4(CH_3)_2$; three isomers.

– ORIGIN mid 19th cent.: from **XYLO-** 'of wood' + **-ENE**.

xylitol /ˈzAɪlɪtɒl/ ▶ noun [mass noun] Chemistry a sweet-tasting crystalline alcohol derived from xylose, present in some plant tissues and used as an artificial sweetener in foods.

● Chem. formula: $CH_2OH(CHOH)_3CH_2OH$.

– ORIGIN late 19th cent.: from **XYLOSE** + **-ITE**[1] + **-OL**.

xylo- /ˈzAɪləʊ/ ▶ combining form of or relating to wood: *xylophagous* | *xylophone*.

– ORIGIN from Greek *xulon* 'wood'.

xylography /zAɪˈlɒɡrəfi/ ▶ noun [mass noun] rare the art of making woodcuts or wood engravings, especially by a relatively primitive technique.

– DERIVATIVES **xylographic** adjective.

xylophagous /zAɪˈlɒfəɡəs/ ▶ adjective Zoology (especially of an insect larva or mollusc) feeding on or boring into wood.

xylophone ▶ noun a musical instrument played by striking a row of wooden bars of graduated length with one or more small wooden or plastic beaters.

– DERIVATIVES **xylophonic** adjective, **xylophonist** noun /zAɪˈlɒfənɪst/.

– ORIGIN mid 19th cent.: from **XYLO-** 'of wood' + **-PHONE**.

xylose /ˈzAɪləʊz, -s/ ▶ noun [mass noun] Chemistry a sugar of the pentose class which occurs widely in plants, especially as a component of hemicelluloses.

xystus /ˈzɪstəs/ ▶ noun (pl. **xysti** /-tAɪ/) 1 (in ancient Greece) a long portico used by athletes for exercise. 2 (in ancient Rome) a garden walk or terrace.

– ORIGIN Latin, from Greek *xustos* 'smooth', from *xuein* 'to scrape'.

Yy

Y¹ (also **y**) ▶ noun (pl. **Ys** or **Y's**) **1** the twenty-fifth letter of the alphabet.
■ denoting the next after X in a set of items, categories, etc. ■ denoting a second unknown or unspecified person or thing: *the claim that chemical X causes birth defect Y.* ■ (usu. **y**) the second unknown quantity in an algebraic expression, usually the dependent variable. [ORIGIN: the introduction of *x*, *y*, and *z* as symbols of unknown quantities is due to Descartes (see **X¹**).] ■ (usu. **y**) denoting the secondary or vertical axis in a system of coordinates: [in combination] *the y-axis.*
2 (**Y**) a shape like that of a capital Y: [in combination] *rows of tiny Y-shaped motifs.*

Y² ▶ abbreviation for ■ yen: *Y140.* ■ N. Amer. informal a YMCA or YWCA hostel: *Scott was living at the Y.*
▶ symbol for the chemical element yttrium.

y ▶ abbreviation for year(s): *orbital period (Pluto): 248.5y.*

-y¹ ▶ suffix forming adjectives: **1** (from nouns and adjectives) full of; having the quality of: *messy* | *milky* | *mousy.*
■ with depreciatory reference: *boozy* | *tinny.*
2 (from verbs) inclined to; apt to: *sticky.*
– ORIGIN Old English *-ig*, of Germanic origin.

-y² (also **-ey** or **-ie**) ▶ suffix forming diminutive nouns, pet names, etc.: *aunty* | *Tommy* | *nightie.*
■ forming verbs: *shinny.*
– ORIGIN Middle English: originally Scots.

-y³ ▶ suffix forming nouns: **1** denoting a state, condition, or quality: *honesty* | *jealousy* | *orthodoxy.*
2 denoting an action or its result: *blasphemy* | *victory.*
– ORIGIN from French *-ie*, from Latin *-ia*, *-ium*, or Greek *-eia*, *-ia.*

ya /jə, jɑ/ ▶ pronoun & possessive determiner non-standard spelling of **YOU** or **YOUR**, used to represent informal or US pronunciation.

yaar /jɑː/ ▶ noun Indian informal a friendly form of address.
– ORIGIN via Hindi from Arabic *yar.*

yabber ▶ verb [no obj.] informal chatter.
– ORIGIN probably from Wuywurung (an Aboriginal language).

yabby (also **yabbie**) ▶ noun (pl. **-ies**) Austral. a small freshwater crayfish.
● Genus *Charax*, infraorder Astacidea, in particular the common *C. destructor.*
■ another term for **NIPPER** (in sense 4).
– ORIGIN late 19th cent.: from Wemba-wemba (an Aboriginal language).

yacht /jɒt/ ▶ noun a medium-sized sailing boat equipped for cruising or racing.
■ [with modifier] a powered boat or small ship equipped for cruising, typically for private or official use: *a steam yacht.*
▶ verb [no obj.] race or cruise in a yacht.
– ORIGIN mid 16th cent.: from early modern Dutch *jaghte*, from *jaghtschip* 'fast pirate ship', from *jag(h)t* 'hunting' + *schip* 'ship'.

yachtie ▶ noun informal a yachtsman or yachtswoman.

yachting ▶ noun [mass noun] the sport or pastime of racing or sailing in yachts.

yachtsman ▶ noun (pl. **-men**) a man who sails yachts.

yachtswoman ▶ noun (pl. **-women**) a woman who sails yachts.

yack ▶ noun & verb variant spelling of **YAK²**.

yacker ▶ noun variant spelling of **YAKKA**.

yackety-yak ▶ noun & verb another term for **YAK²**.
– ORIGIN 1950s: imitative.

yaffle ▶ noun dialect another term for **GREEN WOODPECKER**.
– ORIGIN late 18th cent.: imitative of its call.

Yafo /'jɑːfɔː/ Hebrew name for **JAFFA¹**.

yag ▶ noun a synthetic crystal of yttrium aluminium garnet, used in certain lasers and as an imitation diamond in jewellery.
– ORIGIN 1960s: acronym from *ytrium aluminium garnet.*

yagé /'jɑːʒeɪ/ ▶ noun another term for **AYAHUASCA**.
– ORIGIN 1920s: from American Spanish.

Yagi antenna /'jɑːgi/ (also **Yagi aerial**) ▶ noun a highly directional radio aerial made of several short rods mounted across an insulating support and transmitting or receiving a narrow band of frequencies.
– ORIGIN 1940s: named after Hidetsugu Yagi (1886–1976), Japanese engineer.

yagna /'jʌgnɑː, -nɪə/ ▶ noun variant spelling of **YAJNA**.

yah¹ ▶ exclamation yes (used in representations of upper-class speech): *we can go right now, ok, yah.*

yah² ▶ exclamation expressing derision: *yah, you missed!*
– ORIGIN natural exclamation: first recorded in English in the early 17th cent.

yah³ ▶ pronoun non-standard spelling of **YOU**, used in representing informal or dialectal speech.

yahoo¹ /'jɑːhuː, jə'huː/ ▶ noun informal a rude, noisy, or violent person.
– ORIGIN mid 18th cent.: from the name of an imaginary race of brutish creatures in Swift's *Gulliver's Travels* (1726).

yahoo² /jɑː'huː, ja-/ ▶ exclamation expressing great joy or excitement: *yahoo—my plan worked!*
– ORIGIN natural exclamation: first recorded in English in the 1970s.

yahrzeit /'jɑːtsʌɪt/ ▶ noun (among Jews) the anniversary of someone's death, especially a parent's.
– ORIGIN mid 19th cent.: Yiddish, literally 'anniversary time'.

Yahweh /'jɑːweɪ/ (also **Yahveh** /-veɪ/) ▶ noun a form of the Hebrew name of God used in the Bible. The name came to be regarded by Jews (*c.*300 BC) as too sacred to be spoken, and the vowel sounds are uncertain.
– ORIGIN from Hebrew *YHWH* with added vowels; compare with **JEHOVAH**.

Yahwist /'jɑːwɪst/ (also **Yahvist** /-vɪst/) ▶ noun the postulated author or authors of parts of the first six books of the Bible, in which God is regularly named *Yahweh.* Compare with **ELOHIST**.

yajna /'jʌgnɑː, -nɪə/ (also **yagna**) ▶ noun Hinduism a ritual sacrifice with a specific objective.
– ORIGIN from Sanskrit *yajña* 'worship, sacrifice'.

Yajur Veda /jʌdʒʊə 'veɪdə, -'viːdə/ Hinduism one of the four Vedas, based on a collection of sacrificial formulae in early Sanskrit used in the Vedic religion by the priest in charge of sacrificial ritual.
– ORIGIN from Sanskrit *yajus* 'sacrificial formula' and **VEDA**.

yak¹ ▶ noun a large domesticated wild ox with shaggy hair, humped shoulders, and large horns, used in Tibet as a pack animal and for its milk, meat, and hide.
● Genus *Bos*, family Bovidae; the domesticated *B. grunniens*, descended from the wild *B. mutus*, which is still found rarely at high altitude.
– ORIGIN late 18th cent.: from Tibetan *gyag.*

yak² (also **yack** or **yackety-yak**) informal ▶ noun [in sing.] a trivial or unduly persistent conversation.
▶ verb (**yakked**, **yakking**) [no obj.] talk at length about trivial or boring subjects.
– ORIGIN 1950s: imitative.

yakitori /jakɪ'tɔːri/ ▶ noun [mass noun] a Japanese dish of chicken pieces grilled on a skewer.
– ORIGIN Japanese, from *yaki* 'grilling, toasting' + *tori* 'bird'.

yakka /'jakə/ (also **yacker**) ▶ noun [mass noun] Austral./NZ informal work, especially of a strenuous physical kind.
– ORIGIN from Jagara (an Aboriginal language of Queensland) *yaga* 'to work'.

Yakut /jʌ'kʊt/ ▶ noun (pl. same or **Yakuts**) **1** a member of an indigenous people living in scattered settlements in northern Siberia.
2 [mass noun] the Turkic language of this people, which has some 300,000 speakers spread over 2 million square miles.
▶ adjective of or relating to this people or their language.
– ORIGIN via Russian from Yakut.

Yakutia /jʌ'kʊtɪə/ an autonomous republic in eastern Russia; pop. 1,081,000 (1989); capital, Yakutsk. It is the coldest inhabited region of the world, with 40 per cent of its territory lying to the north of the Arctic Circle. Official name **REPUBLIC OF SAKHA**.

Yakutsk /jʌ'kʊtsk/ a city in eastern Russia, on the Lena River, capital of the republic of Yakutia; pop. 187,000 (1990).

yakuza /jə'kuːzə/ ▶ noun (pl. same) a Japanese gangster or racketeer.
– ORIGIN Japanese, from *ya* 'eight' + *ku* 'nine' + *za* 'three', referring to the worst hand in a gambling game.

Yale ▶ noun [often as modifier] trademark a type of lock with a latch bolt and a flat key with a serrated edge.
– ORIGIN mid 19th cent.: named after Linus *Yale* Jr (1821–68), the American locksmith who invented the mechanism it uses.

Yale University a university at New Haven, Connecticut, one of the most prestigious in the US. It was founded in 1701.

Yalie /'jeɪli/ ▶ noun (pl. **-ies**) US informal a student or graduate of Yale University.

y'all /jɔːl/ ▶ contraction of you-all.

Yalta Conference /'jaltə/ a meeting between the Allied leaders Churchill, Roosevelt, and Stalin in February 1945 at Yalta, a Crimean port on the Black Sea. The leaders planned the final stages of the

Second World War and agreed the subsequent territorial division of Europe.

Yalu /ˈjɑːluː/ a river of eastern Asia, which rises in the mountains of Jilin province in NE China and flows about 800 km (500 miles) generally south-westwards to the Yellow Sea, forming most of the border between China and North Korea.

yam ▶ noun **1** the edible starchy tuber of a climbing plant, widely distributed in tropical and sub-tropical countries.
2 the plant which yields this tuber.
● Genus *Dioscorea*, family Dioscoreaceae: many species.
3 N. Amer. a sweet potato.
– ORIGIN late 16th cent.: from Portuguese *inhame* or obsolete Spanish *iñame*, probably of West African origin.

Yama /ˈjɑːmə/ (in Hindu mythology) the first man to die. He became the guardian, judge, and ruler of the dead, and is represented as carrying a noose and riding a buffalo.
– ORIGIN from Sanskrit *yama* 'restraint' (from *yam* 'restrain').

Yamamoto /ˌjaməˈməʊtəʊ/, Isoroku (1884–1943), Japanese admiral. As Commander-in-Chief of the Combined Fleet (air and naval forces) from 1939, he was responsible for planning the Japanese attack on Pearl Harbor (1941).

Yamasaki /ˌjaməˈsɑːki/, Minoru (1912–86), American architect. He designed the influential barrel-vaulted St Louis Municipal Airport Terminal (1956) and the World Trade Center in New York (1972).

Yamato-e /jaˈmɑːtəʊˌeɪ/ ▶ noun [mass noun] a style of decorative painting in Japan during the 12th and early 13th centuries, characterized by strong colour and flowing lines.
– ORIGIN Japanese, from *Yamato* 'Japan' + *e* 'picture'.

yam bean ▶ noun a Central American climbing plant of the pea family, which has been cultivated for its edible tubers (jicama) since pre-Columbian times.
● *Pachyrhizus erosus*, family Leguminosae.

yammer informal or dialect ▶ noun [mass noun] loud and sustained or repetitive noise: *the yammer of their animated conversation* | *the yammer of enemy fire*.
▶ verb [no obj.] make a loud repetitive noise.
■ talk volubly.
– DERIVATIVES **yammerer** noun.
– ORIGIN late Middle English (as a verb meaning 'lament, cry out'): alteration of earlier *yomer*, from Old English *geōmrian* 'to lament', suggested by Middle Dutch *jammeren*.

Yamoussoukro /jamuːˈsuːkrəʊ/ the capital of the Ivory Coast; pop. 120,000 (est. 1986). It was designated as capital in 1983, replacing Abidjan.

Yamuna /ˈjʌmʊnə/ Hindi name for **JUMNA**.

Yancheng /janˈtʃɛŋ/ (also **Yen-cheng**) a city in Jiangsu province, eastern China; pop. 1,265,000 (1986).

yandy Austral. ▶ verb (**-ies**, **-ied**) [with obj.] separate (grass seed or a mineral) from the surrounding refuse by shaking it in a special shallow dish.
▶ noun (pl. **-ies**) a shallow dish used for such a process.
– ORIGIN from an Aboriginal word.

yang ▶ noun (in Chinese philosophy) the active male principle of the universe, characterized as male and creative and associated with heaven, heat, and light. Contrasted with **YIN**.
– ORIGIN from Chinese *yáng* 'male genitals', 'sun', 'positive'.

Yangon /janˈɡɒn/ Burmese name for **RANGOON**.

Yangshao /janˈʃaʊ/ ▶ noun [usu. as modifier] Archaeology a Neolithic civilization of northern China, dated to *c.*5000–2700 BC and preceding the Longshan period. It is marked by pottery painted with naturalistic designs of fish and human faces and abstract patterns of triangles, spirals, arcs, and dots.
– ORIGIN named after *Yang Shao Cun*, the first settlement of this period to be excavated (1921).

Yangtze /ˈjaŋtsi/ the principal river of China, which rises as the Jinsha in the Tibetan highlands and flows 6,380 km (3,964 miles) southwards then generally eastwards through central China, entering the East China Sea at Shanghai. Also called **CHANG JIANG**.

Yank ▶ noun informal **1** often derogatory a person who lives in, or is from, the US.

2 US another term for **YANKEE** (in sense 2).

yank informal ▶ verb [with obj.] pull with a jerk: *her hair was yanked, and she screamed* | [with obj. and adverbial] *he yanked her to her feet* | [no obj.] *Liz yanked at her arm*.
▶ noun [in sing.] a sudden hard pull: *one of the other girls gave her ponytail a yank*.
– ORIGIN late 18th cent. (as a Scots word in the sense 'sudden sharp blow'): of unknown origin.

Yankee ▶ noun informal **1** often derogatory another term for **YANK** (in sense 1).
2 US an inhabitant of New England or one of the northern states.
■ historical a Federal soldier in the Civil War.
3 a bet on four or more horses to win (or be placed) in different races.
4 (also **Yankee jib**) Sailing a large jib set forward of a staysail in light winds.
5 used in radio communication as a code word representing the letter Y.
– ORIGIN mid 18th cent.: origin uncertain; recorded in the late 17th cent. as a nickname; perhaps from Dutch *Janke*, diminutive of *Jan* 'John'.

Yankee Doodle ▶ noun **1** (also **Yankee Doodle Dandy**) a song popular during the War of American Independence, now regarded as a national song.
2 another term for **YANKEE** (in senses 1 and 2).

Yanomami /ˌjanəˈmɑːmi/ (also **Yanomamö** /-ˌmɑːməʊ/) ▶ noun (pl. same) **1** a member of an American Indian people living mainly in the forests of southern Venezuela and northern Brazil.
2 [mass noun] either of the two related languages of this people.
▶ adjective of or relating to this people or their language.
– ORIGIN the name in Yanomami, literally 'people'.

Yanqui /ˈjaŋki/ ▶ noun variant spelling of **YANKEE**, typically used in Latin American contexts.

Yantai /janˈtʌɪ/ (also **Yen-tai**) a port on the Yellow Sea in Shandong province, eastern China; pop. 3,204,600 (1990). Former name (3rd century BC–15th century) **CHEFOO**.

yantra /ˈjantrə/ ▶ noun a geometrical diagram, or any object, used as an aid to meditation in tantric worship.
– ORIGIN Sanskrit, literally 'device for holding or fastening'.

Yao¹ /jaʊ/ ▶ noun (pl. same) **1** a member of an East African people living to the east and south of Lake Nyasa.
2 [mass noun] the Bantu language of this people, with over a million speakers.
▶ adjective of or relating to this people or their language.
– ORIGIN the local name.

Yao² /jaʊ/ ▶ noun (pl. same) **1** a member of a mountain-dwelling people of the Guangxi, Hunan, Yunnan, Guangdong, and Guizhou provinces of China.
2 [mass noun] the language of this people. Also called **MIEN**.
▶ adjective of or relating to this people or their language.
– ORIGIN from Chinese *Yáo*, literally 'precious jade'.

Yaoundé /jaˈʊndeɪ/ the capital of Cameroon; pop. 800,000 (est. 1992).

yap ▶ verb (**yapped**, **yapping**) [no obj.] give a sharp, shrill bark: *the dachshunds yapped at his heels*.
■ informal talk at length in an irritating manner.
▶ noun a sharp, shrill bark.
– DERIVATIVES **yapper** noun.
– ORIGIN early 17th cent. (denoting a dog that yaps): imitative.

yapok /ˈjapɒk/ ▶ noun a semiaquatic carnivorous opossum with dark-banded grey fur and webbed hind feet, native to tropical America. Also called **WATER OPOSSUM**.
● *Chironectes minimus*, family Didelphidae.
– ORIGIN early 19th cent.: from *Oyapock*, the name of a north Brazilian river.

yapp ▶ noun [mass noun] Brit. a form of bookbinding with a limp leather cover projecting to fold over the edges of the leaves, typically used for bibles.
– ORIGIN late 19th cent.: named after William *Yapp*, a London bookseller, for whom this style of binding was first made (*c.*1860).

yappy ▶ adjective (**yappier**, **yappiest**) informal (of a dog) inclined to bark in a sharp, shrill way.
■ inclined to talk foolishly or at length.

Yaqui /ˈjaki/ ▶ noun (pl. same or **Yaquis**) **1** a member of an American Indian people of NW Mexico and Arizona.
2 [mass noun] the Uto-Aztecan language of this people.
▶ adjective of or relating to this people or their language.
– ORIGIN Spanish, from earlier *Hiaquis*, from Yaqui *Hiaki*.

yarak /ˈjarak/ ▶ noun (in phrase **in yarak**) (of a trained hawk) fit and in a proper condition for hunting.
– ORIGIN mid 19th cent.: perhaps from Persian *yārakī* 'strength, ability' or from Turkish *yaraḡ* 'readiness'.

yarborough /ˈjɑːb(ə)rə/ ▶ noun (in bridge or whist) a hand with no card above a nine.
– ORIGIN early 20th cent.: named after the Earl of *Yarborough* (died 1897), said to have bet 1000 to 1 against its occurrence.

yard¹ ▶ noun **1** (abbrev.: **yd**) a unit of linear measure equal to 3 feet (0.9144 metre).
■ (**yards of**) informal a great length: *yards and yards of fine lace*. ■ a square or cubic yard, especially of sand or other building materials.
2 a cylindrical spar, tapering to each end, slung across a ship's mast for a sail to hang from.
3 US informal one hundred dollars; a one hundred dollar note.
– PHRASES **by the yard** in large numbers or quantities: *golf continues to inspire books by the yard.*
– ORIGIN Old English *gerd* (in sense 2), of West Germanic origin; related to Dutch *gard* 'twig, rod' and German *Gerte*.

yard² ▶ noun **1** chiefly Brit. a piece of uncultivated ground adjoining a building, typically one enclosed by walls or other buildings.
■ an area of land used for a particular purpose or business: *a builder's yard*. ■ N. Amer. the garden of a house. ■ S. African a plot of land, or the grounds of a building, accommodating a number of small rooms which are let out as living space.
2 W. Indian a house and the land attached.
■ a residential compound in an urban area comprising a number of small rented dwellings around a shared open area. ■ (**Yard**) (especially among expatriate Jamaicans) home; Jamaica.
▶ verb [with obj.] **1** N. Amer. store or transport (wood) in or to a timber yard.
2 put (farm animals) into an enclosure: *sheep should be yarded even in the spring*.
■ [no obj.] (of moose) gather as a herd for the winter.
– PHRASES **the Yard** Brit. informal term for **SCOTLAND YARD**.
– ORIGIN Old English *geard* 'building, home, region', from a Germanic base related to Russian *gorod* 'town'. Compare with **GARDEN** and **ORCHARD**.

yardage ▶ noun **1** a distance or length measured in yards: *the caddie was working out yardages from tee to green*.
2 [mass noun] archaic the use of a yard for storage or the keeping of animals, or payment for such use.

yardang /ˈjɑːdaŋ/ ▶ noun a sharp irregular ridge of sand lying in the direction of the prevailing wind in exposed desert regions, formed by the wind erosion of adjacent material which is less resistant.
– ORIGIN early 20th cent.: from Turkish, ablative of *yar* 'steep bank'.

yardarm ▶ noun the outer extremity of a ship's yard.
– PHRASES **the sun is over the yardarm** dated used to refer to the time of day when it is permissible to begin drinking.

yardbird ▶ noun US informal **1** a new military recruit, especially one assigned to menial tasks.
2 a convict.
– ORIGIN 1940s: perhaps suggested by **JAILBIRD**.

Yardie /ˈjɑːdi/ informal ▶ noun (among Jamaicans) a fellow Jamaican.
■ (in the UK) a member of a Jamaican or West Indian gang of criminals.
▶ adjective [attrib.] of or characteristic of Jamaicans.
– ORIGIN 1980s: from Jamaican English, literally 'house, home'.

yardman ▶ noun (pl. **-men**) **1** a person working in a railway or timber yard.
2 US a person who does various outdoor jobs.

yard of ale ▶ noun Brit. the amount of beer (typically two to three pints) held by a narrow glass about a yard high.
■ a glass of this kind.

yard sale ▶**noun** N. Amer. a sale of miscellaneous second-hand items held in the garden of a private house.

yardstick ▶**noun** a measuring rod a yard long, typically divided into inches.
■a standard used for comparison: *league tables are not the only yardstick of schools' performance.*

yare /jɛː/ ▶**adjective** US (of a ship) moving lightly and easily; easily manageable.
– ORIGIN Old English *gearu* 'prepared, ready', of Germanic origin; related to Dutch *gaar* 'done, dressed' and German *gar* 'ready'.

yarmulke /ˈjɑːmʊlkə/ (also **yarmulka**) ▶**noun** a skullcap worn in public by Orthodox Jewish men or during prayer by other Jewish men.
– ORIGIN early 20th cent.: from Yiddish *yarmolke*.

yarn ▶**noun 1** [mass noun] spun thread used for knitting, weaving, or sewing.
2 informal a long or rambling story, especially one that is implausible.
■Austral./NZ a chat.
▶**verb** [no obj.] informal tell a long or implausible story: *they were yarning about local legends and superstitions.*
■Austral./NZ chat; talk: *he sat yarning to his mother.*
– PHRASES **spin a yarn** see **SPIN**.
– ORIGIN Old English *gearn*; of Germanic origin, related to Dutch *garen*.

yarn-dyed ▶**adjective** (of fabric) dyed as yarn, before being woven.

Yaroslavl /ˈjɑːrəsˌlɑːv(ə)l/ a port in European Russia, on the River Volga north-east of Nizhni Novgorod; pop. 636,000 (1990).

yarraman /ˈjarəmən/ ▶**noun** (pl. **yarramans** or **yarramen** /-mɛn/) Austral. a horse.
– ORIGIN probably from an Aboriginal root meaning 'teeth'.

yarran /ˈjarən/ ▶**noun** a small Australian acacia with durable scented timber.
• *Acacia omalophylla*, family Leguminosae.
– ORIGIN late 19th cent.: from Kamilaroi (and related languages) *yarraan*.

yarrow ▶**noun** a Eurasian plant with feathery leaves and heads of small white or pale pink aromatic flowers, which has long been used in herbal medicine. Also called **MILFOIL**.
• *Achillea millefolium*, family Compositae.
– ORIGIN Old English *gearwe*, of West Germanic origin; related to Dutch *gerwe*.

yashmak /ˈjaʃmak/ ▶**noun** a veil concealing all of the face except the eyes, worn by some Muslim women in public.
– ORIGIN mid 19th cent.: via Arabic from Turkish.

yataghan /ˈjatəgan/ ▶**noun** chiefly historical a sword without a guard and typically with a double-curved blade, used in Muslim countries.
– ORIGIN from Turkish *yatağan*.

Yates's correction ▶**noun** Statistics a correction for the discreteness of the data that is made in the chi-square test when the number of cases in any class is small and there is one degree of freedom.
– ORIGIN 1930s: named after Frank *Yates* (1902–94), English statistician.

yatra /ˈjɑːtrɑː/ ▶**noun** Indian a procession or pilgrimage, especially one with a religious purpose.
– ORIGIN from Sanskrit *yātrā* 'journey', from *yā* 'go'.

yatter informal ▶**verb** [no obj.] talk incessantly; chatter.
▶**noun** [mass noun] incessant talk.
– ORIGIN early 19th cent.: imitative, perhaps suggested by **YAMMER** and **CHATTER**.

yaupon /ˈjɔːpɒn/ (also **yaupon holly**) ▶**noun** a North American holly, the leaves of which have emetic properties and were formerly used as a tea by American Indians.
• *Ilex vomitoria*, family Aquifoliaceae.
– ORIGIN early 18th cent.: a North American Indian word.

yautia /jaʊˈtiːə/ ▶**noun** a tropical American plant of the arum family which is cultivated for its edible tubers.
• Genus *Xanthosoma*, family Araceae: several species, in particular the tannia.
– ORIGIN late 19th cent.: American Spanish, from Maya *yaaj* 'wound, poison' + *té* 'mouth' with reference to its caustic properties.

yaw ▶**verb** [no obj.] (of a moving ship or aircraft) twist or oscillate about a vertical axis: [with adverbial of direction] *the jet yawed sharply to the right.*
▶**noun** [mass noun] twisting or oscillation of a moving ship or aircraft about a vertical axis.
– ORIGIN mid 16th cent.: of unknown origin.

yawl ▶**noun** a two-masted fore-and-aft-rigged sailing boat with the mizzenmast stepped far aft so that the mizzen boom overhangs the stern.
■historical a ship's jolly boat with four or six oars.
– ORIGIN late 16th cent.: from Middle Low German *jolle* or Dutch *jol*, of unknown origin; compare with **JOLLY**[2].

yawn ▶**verb** [no obj.] involuntarily open one's mouth wide and inhale deeply due to tiredness or boredom: *he began yawning and looking at his watch.*
■[usu. as adj. **yawning**] be wide open: *a yawning chasm.*
▶**noun** a reflex act of opening one's mouth wide and inhaling deeply due to tiredness or boredom.
■informal a thing that is considered boring or tedious: *a long period of your life is a yawn to everyone.*
– DERIVATIVES **yawningly** adverb.
– ORIGIN Old English *geonian*, of Germanic origin, from an Indo-European root shared by Latin *hiare* and Greek *khainein*. Current noun senses date from the early 18th cent.

yawner ▶**noun** informal a thing that is considered extremely boring: *the game was a real yawner.*

yawp ▶**noun** a harsh or hoarse cry or yelp.
■[mass noun] N. Amer. foolish or noisy talk.
▶**verb** [no obj.] shout or exclaim hoarsely.
■N. Amer. talk foolishly or noisily.
– DERIVATIVES **yawper** noun.
– ORIGIN Middle English (as a verb): imitative. The noun dates from the early 19th cent.

yaws ▶**plural noun** [treated as sing.] a contagious disease of tropical countries, caused by a bacterium that enters skin abrasions and gives rise to small crusted lesions which may develop into deep ulcers. Also called **FRAMBOESIA**.
• The bacterium is the spirochaete *Treponema pallidum* subsp. *pertenue*.
– ORIGIN late 17th cent.: probably from Carib *yaya*, from a South American Indian language.

yay[1] /jeɪ/ ▶**exclamation** informal expressing triumph, approval, or encouragement: *Yay! Great, Julie!*
– ORIGIN 1960s: perhaps an alteration of **YEAH**.

yay[2] /jeɪ/ (also **yea**) ▶**adverb** informal, chiefly N. Amer. (with adjectives of measure) so; to this extent: *I knew him when he was yay big.*
■to a considerable degree; much: *yay later.*
– ORIGIN 1960s: probably a variant of the adverb **YEA**[1].

Yayoi /ˈjɑːjɔɪ/ ▶**noun** [usu. as modifier] Archaeology a Japanese culture following the Jomon period and dated to *c*.300 BC–AD 300. It was marked by the introduction of rice cultivation, and the appearance of large burial mounds has suggested the emergence of an increasingly powerful ruling class.
– ORIGIN early 20th cent.: Japanese, the name of a street in Tokyo where its characteristic pottery (chiefly wheel-made) was first discovered.

Yb ▶**symbol for** the chemical element ytterbium.

Y chromosome ▶**noun** Genetics (in humans and other mammals) a sex chromosome which is normally present only in male cells, which are designated XY. Compare with **X CHROMOSOME**.

yclept /ɪˈklɛpt/ ▶**adjective** [predic.] archaic or humorous by the name of: *a lady yclept Eleanora.*
– ORIGIN Old English *gecleopod*, past participle of *cleopian* 'call', of Germanic origin.

yd ▶**abbreviation for** yard (measure).

ye[1] ▶**pronoun** [second person plural] archaic or dialect plural form of **THOU**[1]: *gather ye rosebuds, while ye may.*
– PHRASES **ye gods!** an exclamation of astonishment.
– ORIGIN Old English *gē*, of Germanic origin; related to Dutch *gij* and German *ihr*.

USAGE The history of the use of **ye** is complex. In the earliest period it was used only as the plural subjective form. In the 13th century it came to be used in the singular, equivalent to **thou**. In the 15th century, when **you** had become the dominant subjective form, **ye** came to be used as an objective singular and plural (equivalent to **thee** and **you**). Various uses survive in modern dialects.

ye[2] ▶**determiner** pseudo-archaic term for **THE**: *Ye Olde Cock Tavern.*
– ORIGIN graphic variant; in late Middle English þ (see **THORN**) came to be written identically with y, so that *the* could be written *ye*. This spelling (usually y[e]) was kept as a convenient abbreviation in handwriting down to the 19th cent., and in printers' types during the 15th and 16th cents., but it was never pronounced as 'ye'.

yea[1] archaic or formal ▶**adverb** yes: *she has the right to say yea or nay.*
■used for emphasis, especially to introduce a stronger or more accurate word than one just used: *he was full, yea, crammed with anxieties.*
▶**noun** an affirmative answer: *the British government would give the final yea or nay.*
■(in the US Congress) an affirmative vote.
– ORIGIN Old English *gēa*, *gē*, of Germanic origin; related to Dutch and German *ja*.

yea[2] ▶**adverb** variant spelling of **YAY**[2].

Yeager /ˈjeɪgə/, Chuck (b.1923), American pilot; full name *Charles Elwood Yeager*. He became the first person to break the sound barrier when he piloted the Bell X-1 rocket research aircraft at high altitude to a level-flight speed of 670 mph in 1947.

yeah (also **yeh**) ▶**exclamation** & **noun** non-standard spelling of **YES**, representing informal pronunciation.

yean /jiːn/ ▶**verb** [with obj.] archaic (of a sheep or goat) give birth to (a lamb or kid).
– ORIGIN late Middle English: perhaps representing an Old English verb related to *ēanian* 'to lamb'.

year /jɪə, jəː/ ▶**noun 1** the time taken by the earth to make one revolution around the sun.

The length of the year depends on the manner of calculation. For ordinary purposes the important period is the **tropical year** (also called **astronomical year**, **equinoctial year**, or **solar year**) which is the time between successive spring or autumn equinoxes, or winter or summer solstices, roughly 365 days, 5 hours, 48 minutes, and 46 seconds in length. This period thus marks the regular cycle of the seasons. See also **SIDEREAL YEAR**, **ANOMALISTIC YEAR**.

2 (also **calendar year** or **civil year**) the period of 365 days (or 366 days in leap years) starting from the first of January, used for reckoning time in ordinary affairs.
■a period of the same length as this starting at any point: *the year starting July 1.* ■[with adj.] such a period regarded in terms of the quality of produce, typically wine: *single-vineyard wine of a good year.* ■a similar period used for reckoning time according to other calendars: *the Muslim year.*
3 (**one's years**) one's age or time of life: *she had a composure well beyond her years.*
4 (**years**) informal a very long time; ages: *it's going to take years to put that right.*
5 a set of students grouped together as being of roughly similar ages, mostly entering a school or college in the same academic year: *most of the girls in my year were leaving school at the end of the term.*
– PHRASES **in the year of grace** (or **Our Lord**) —— in the year —— AD: *he was murdered in the year of grace 1618.* [ORIGIN: *year of grace*, suggested by medieval Latin *anno gratiae*, used by chroniclers.] —— **of the year** a person or thing chosen as outstanding in a specified field or of a specified kind in a particular year: *the sports personality of the year.* **put years on** (or **take years off**) **someone** make someone feel or look older (or younger). **a year and a day** the period specified in some legal matters to ensure the completion of a full year. **the year dot** see **DOT**[1]. **year in, year out** continuously or repeatedly over a period of years: *they rented the same bungalow year in, year out.*
– ORIGIN Old English *gē(a)r*, of Germanic origin; related to Dutch *jaar* and German *Jahr*, from an Indo-European root shared by Greek *hōra* 'season'.

yearbook ▶**noun** an annual publication giving current information and listing events or aspects of the previous year, especially in a particular field: *The Rugby Union Yearbook.*
■N. Amer. a book containing photographs of the senior class in a school or university and details of school activities in the previous year.

year class ▶**noun** Zoology the individual animals of a particular species (especially a fish) that were born in any one year.

year end ▶**noun** the end of the financial year.

yearling ▶**noun** an animal (especially a sheep, calf, or foal) a year old, or in its second year.
■a racehorse in the calendar year after its year of foaling.
▶**adjective** [attrib.] **1** having lived or existed for a year; a year old: *a yearling calf.*

y

■of or relating to an animal that is a year old: *the yearling market.*

2 Finance denoting a bond issued by a local authority and redeemable after one year.]

year-long ▶ adjective [attrib.] lasting for or throughout a year: *his year-long battle with lung cancer.*

yearly ▶ adjective & adverb happening or produced once a year or every year: [as adj.] *yearly visits to Africa* | [as adv.] *rent was paid yearly.*
– ORIGIN Old English *gēarlic* (see YEAR, -LY¹).

yearn /jəːn/ ▶ verb [no obj.] have an intense feeling of loss or lack and longing for something: [with infinitive] *they yearned to go home* | [as noun **yearning**] *he felt a yearning for the mountains.*
■archaic be filled with compassion or warm feeling: *no fellow spirit yearned towards her.*
– DERIVATIVES **yearner** noun, **yearningly** adverb.
– ORIGIN Old English *giernan*, from a Germanic base meaning 'eager'.

year-on-year ▶ adjective (of figures, prices, etc.) as compared with the corresponding ones from a year earlier.

year-round ▶ adjective happening or continuing throughout the year: *an indoor pool for year-round use.*

years of discretion ▶ plural noun another term for AGE OF DISCRETION.

yeast ▶ noun [mass noun] a microscopic fungus consisting of single oval cells that reproduce by budding, and capable of converting sugar into alcohol and carbon dioxide.
● Genus *Saccharomyces*, subdivision Ascomycotina.
■a greyish-yellow preparation of this obtained chiefly from fermented beer, used as a fermenting agent, to raise bread dough, and as a food supplement. ■ [count noun] Biology any unicellular fungus that reproduces vegetatively by budding or fission, including forms such as candida that can cause disease.
– DERIVATIVES **yeast-like** adjective.
– ORIGIN Old English, of Germanic origin; related to Dutch *gist* and German *Gischt* 'froth, yeast', from an Indo-European root shared by Greek *zein* 'to boil'.

yeasty ▶ adjective (**yeastier**, **yeastiest**) of, resembling, or containing yeast: *the yeasty smell of rising dough.*
■figurative characterized by or producing upheaval or agitation; in a state of turbulence, typically a creative or productive one: *the yeasty days of yesterday's revolution.*
– DERIVATIVES **yeastily** adverb, **yeastiness** noun.

Yeats /jeɪts/, W. B. (1865–1939), Irish poet and dramatist; full name *William Butler Yeats*. His play *The Countess Cathleen* (1892) and his collection of stories *The Celtic Twilight* (1893) stimulated Ireland's theatrical, cultural, and literary revival. Notable poetry: *The Tower* (1928), containing 'Sailing to Byzantium' and 'Leda and the Swan', and *The Winding Stair* (1929). Nobel Prize for Literature (1923).

yech /jɛx, jɛk/ (also **yecch**) ▶ exclamation informal expressing aversion or disgust.
– DERIVATIVES **yechy** adjective.
– ORIGIN 1960s: imitative; compare with YUCK.

yeehaw (also **yeehah**) ▶ exclamation N. Amer. an expression of enthusiasm or exuberance, typically associated with cowboys or rural inhabitants of the southern US.
– ORIGIN natural exclamation: first recorded in American English in the 1970s.

yegg ▶ noun US informal a burglar or safe-breaker.
– ORIGIN early 20th cent.: of unknown origin.

yeh ▶ exclamation variant spelling of YEAH.
▶ pronoun non-standard spelling of YOU, used to represent various accents or dialects: *are yeh all right, lads?*

Yekaterinburg /jɛˌkatəˈriːnbəːɡ/ (also **Ekaterinburg**) an industrial city in central Russia, in the eastern foothills of the Urals; pop. 1,372,000 (1990). Former name (1924–91) SVERDLOVSK.
– ORIGIN named in honour of *Ekaterina*, the wife of Peter the Great, who founded the city in 1721.

Yekaterinodar /jəˌkatəˈriːnəˌdɑː/ (also **Ekaterinodar**) former name (until 1922) for KRASNODAR.

Yekaterinoslav /jəˌkatəˈriːnəˌslɑːf/ (also **Ekaterinoslav**) former name (1787–1926) for DNIPROPETROVSK.

Yelizavetpol /jəˌliːzəˈvjɛtpɒl/ (also **Elizavetpol**) former Russian name (1804–1918) for GÄNCÄ.

yell ▶ noun a loud, sharp cry, especially of pain, surprise, or delight; a shout.
■US an organized cheer, especially one used to support a sports team. ■ Brit. informal, dated an extremely amusing person or thing.
▶ verb [no obj.] give a loud, sharp cry: *you heard me losing my temper and yelling at her.*
– ORIGIN Old English *g(i)ellan* (verb), of Germanic origin; related to Dutch *gillen* and German *gellen*.

yellow ▶ adjective **1** of the colour between green and orange in the spectrum, a primary subtractive colour complementary to blue; coloured like ripe lemons or egg yolks: *curly yellow hair.*
■offensive having a naturally yellowish or olive skin (as used to describe Chinese or Japanese people). ■ denoting a warning of danger which is thought to be near but not actually imminent: *he put Camp Visoko on yellow alert.*
2 informal cowardly: *he'd better get back there quick and prove he's not yellow.*
■archaic showing jealousy or suspicion.
3 (of a book or newspaper) unscrupulously sensational: *he based his judgement on headlines and yellow journalism.*
▶ noun **1** [mass noun] yellow colour or pigment: *the craft detonated in a blaze of red and yellow* | [count noun] *painted in vivid blues and yellows.*
■yellow clothes or material: *everyone dresses in yellow.*
2 a yellow ball or piece in a game or sport, especially the yellow ball in snooker.
3 [with modifier] a moth or butterfly that is predominantly yellow in colour, in particular:
● a butterfly related to the brimstones and sulphurs (*Eurema, Colias*, and other genera, family Pieridae). See also CLOUDED YELLOW. ● a small European moth (several species in the family Geometridae).
4 (**yellows**) any of a number of plant diseases in which the leaves turn yellow, typically caused by viruses and transmitted by insects.
▶ verb [no obj.] become a yellow colour, especially with age: *the cream paint was beginning to yellow* | [as adj. **yellowing**] *yellowing lace curtains* | [as adj. **yellowed**] *a yellowed newspaper cutting.*
– PHRASES **the yellow peril** offensive the political or military threat regarded as being posed by the Chinese or by the peoples of SE Asia.
– DERIVATIVES **yellowish** adjective, **yellowly** adverb, **yellowness** noun, **yellowy** adjective.
– ORIGIN Old English *geolu, geolo*, of West Germanic origin; related to Dutch *geel* and German *gelb*, also to GOLD.

yellow archangel ▶ noun see ARCHANGEL (sense 2).

yellow arsenic ▶ noun another term for ORPIMENT.

yellowback ▶ noun historical a cheap novel in a yellow board binding.

yellow-belly ▶ noun informal **1** a coward.
2 any of a number of animals with yellow underparts.
– DERIVATIVES **yellow-bellied** adjective.

yellow bile ▶ noun historical another term for CHOLER.

yellowbill ▶ noun any of a number of birds with yellow bills.
● the African yellow-billed duck (*Anas undulata*, family Anatidae). ● the African yellow-billed cuckoo (*Ceuthmochares aereus*, family Cuculidae). ● N. Amer. the black scoter (*Melanitta nigra*, family Anatidae).

Yellow Book an illustrated literary periodical published quarterly in the UK between 1894 and 1897, associated with the Aesthetic Movement. Often controversial, it contained contributions from writers including Max Beerbohm, Henry James, Edmund Gosse, Arnold Bennett, and H. G. Wells. The art editor was Aubrey Beardsley.
– ORIGIN so named because of its distinctive yellow binding.

yellow bunting ▶ noun another term for YELLOWHAMMER.

yellowcake ▶ noun [mass noun] impure uranium oxide obtained during processing of uranium ore.
– ORIGIN 1950s; so named because it is obtained as a yellow precipitate.

yellow card ▶ noun (in soccer and some other games) a yellow card shown by the referee to a player being cautioned. Compare with RED CARD.

▶ verb (**yellow-card**) [with obj.] (of the referee) caution (a player) by showing them a yellow card.

yellow dog ▶ noun N. Amer. **1** a dog, typically a mongrel, with yellowish fur.
2 informal a contemptible person or thing.

yellow earth ▶ noun [mass noun] a yellowish loess occurring in northern China.

yellow fever ▶ noun [mass noun] a tropical virus disease affecting the liver and kidneys, causing fever and jaundice and often fatal. It is transmitted by mosquitoes.

yellowfin (also **yellowfin tuna**) ▶ noun a widely distributed, commercially important tuna that has yellow anal and dorsal fins.
● *Thunnus albacares*, family Scombridae.

yellow flag ▶ noun **1** a ship's yellow or quarantine flag (denoting the letter Q), indicating a request for customs clearance when flown alone.
■Motor Racing a yellow flag used to signal to drivers that there is a hazard such as oil or a crashed car ahead.
2 a yellow-flowered iris which grows by water and in marshy places, native to Europe.
● *Iris pseudacorus*, family Iridaceae.

yellow ground ▶ noun [mass noun] Geology kimberlite that is exposed at the surface and has become yellow as a result of atmospheric oxidation.

yellowhammer ▶ noun a common Eurasian bunting, the male of which has a yellow head, neck, and breast.
● *Emberiza citrinella*, family Emberizidae (subfamily Emberizinae).
– ORIGIN mid 16th cent.: *-hammer* is perhaps from Old English *amore* (a kind of bird), possibly conflated with *hama* 'feathers'.

Yellowhammer State informal name for ALABAMA.

yellowhead ▶ noun a rare New Zealand songbird with a yellow head and underparts, found only on South Island.
● *Mohoua ochrocephala*, family Pachycephalidae (or Acanthizidae).

yellow jack ▶ noun archaic term for YELLOW FEVER.

yellow jacket ▶ noun N. Amer. informal a wasp or hornet.

yellow jasmine ▶ noun an ornamental climbing shrub with fragrant yellow flowers, native to the south-eastern US. Its rhizome yields the drug gelsemium.
● *Gelsemium sempervirens*, family Loganiaceae.

yellow jersey ▶ noun (in a cycling race involving stages) a yellow jersey worn each day by the rider who is ahead on time over the whole race to that point, and presented to the rider with the shortest overall time at the finish of the race.

Yellowknife /ˈjɛləʊnʌɪf/ the capital of the Northwest Territories in Canada, on the north shore of the Great Slave Lake; pop. 11,860 (1991).

yellowlegs ▶ noun a migratory sandpiper that resembles the greenshank but has yellowish legs, breeding in northern Canada.
● Genus *Tringa*, family Scolopacidae: two species.

yellow line ▶ noun (in the UK) a line painted along the side of the road in yellow to denote parking restrictions.

yellow metal ▶ noun [mass noun] a form of brass containing about 60 parts copper and 40 parts zinc, with a little lead.

Yellow Pages ▶ plural noun (trademark in the UK) a telephone directory, or a section of one, printed on yellow paper and listing businesses and other organizations according to the goods or services they offer.

yellow pepper ▶ noun a yellow variety of the sweet pepper.

yellow poplar ▶ noun North American term for TULIP TREE.

yellow rain ▶ noun [mass noun] a yellow substance reported as falling in SE Asia, alleged to be a chemical warfare agent but now believed to consist of bee droppings.

yellow rattle ▶ noun a partly parasitic yellow-flowered plant whose ripe seeds are shed into a pouch which rattles when shaken, found in both Europe and eastern North America.
● *Rhinanthus minor*, family Scrophulariaceae.

Yellow River the second largest river in China,

which rises in the mountains of west central China and flows over 4,830 km (3,000 miles) in a huge semicircle before entering the gulf of Bo Hai. Chinese name **HUANG HO**.

Yellow Sea an arm of the East China Sea, separating the Korean peninsula from the east coast of China. Chinese name **HUANG HAI**.

yellow spot ▶ **noun** the region of greatest visual acuity around the fovea of the eye; the macula lutea (see **MACULA**).

yellow stainer (also **yellow-staining mushroom**) ▶ **noun** an inedible European mushroom with a whitish cap and purplish-brown gills, the flesh having an unpleasant smell and staining yellow when cut or bruised.
• *Agaricus xanthodermus*, family Agaricaceae, class Hymenomycetes.

Yellowstone National Park a national park in NW Wyoming and Montana. It contains Old Faithful, a geyser which erupts every 45 to 80 minutes to a height of about one hundred feet.

yellow-tail ▶ **noun 1** (also **yellow-tail moth**) a white tussock moth with a tuft of yellow hairs on the tip of the abdomen. The caterpillars have irritant hairs and can be a pest of fruit trees.
• *Euproctis similis*, family Lymantriidae.
2 (usu. **yellowtail**) (pl. same or **yellowtails**) a marine fish which has yellow coloration on the tail, especially a fish of the jack family.
• Several species, especially of the genus *Seriola*, family Carangidae.

yellowthroat ▶ **noun** a small American warbler with a bright yellow throat.
• Genus *Geothlypis*, family Parulidae: several species.

yellow underwing ▶ **noun** an underwing moth which has hindwings that are yellow with a black terminal band.
• *Noctua* and other genera, family Noctuidae: several species, including the **large yellow underwing** (*N. pronuba*), the larva of which is a destructive cutworm.

yellow-wood ▶ **noun** any of a number of trees which have yellowish timber or yield a yellow dye, in particular:
• a North American tree of the pea family (*Cladrastis lutea*, family Leguminosae). • a podocarp tree.

yellow-wort ▶ **noun** a European plant of the gentian family, with yellow flowers and paired leaves that are joined around the stem, growing in calcareous grassland.
• *Blackstonia perfoliata*, family Gentianaceae.

yelp ▶ **noun** a short sharp cry, especially of pain or alarm: *she uttered a yelp as she bumped into a table*.
▶ **verb** [no obj.] utter such a cry: *my dogs were yelping as if badly hurt*.
– DERIVATIVES **yelper** noun.
– ORIGIN Old English *g(i)elpan* (verb) 'to boast', from a Germanic imitative base. From late Middle English 'cry or sing with a loud voice' the current sense arose in the 16th cent.

Yeltsin /ˈjɛltsɪn/, Boris (Nikolaevich) (b.1931), Russian statesman, President of the Russian Federation 1991–9. Impatient with the slow pace of Gorbachev's reforms, Yeltsin resigned from the Communist Party after becoming President of the Russian Soviet Federative Socialist Republic in 1990. As President of the independent Russian Federation he faced opposition to his reforms and in 1993 survived an attempted coup, but was re-elected in 1996.

Yemen /ˈjɛmən/ a country in the south and south-west of the Arabian peninsula; pop. 12,533,000 (est. 1991); official language, Arabic; capital, Sana'a.

An Islamic country since the mid 7th century, Yemen was part of the Ottoman Empire from the 16th century. It came under increasing British influence in the 19th century, and the port of Aden was developed as a British military base. After the Second World War civil war between royalist and republican forces ended with British withdrawal and the partition of the country (1967). South Yemen declared itself independent as the People's Democratic Republic of Yemen, the North becoming the Yemen Arab Republic. In 1990 the countries reunited to form the Republic of Yemen; in 1994 the South briefly seceded but was defeated in a short civil war.

– DERIVATIVES **Yemeni** adjective & noun.

Yemenite ▶ **noun** another term for *Yemeni* (see **YEMEN**).
■ a Jew who was, or whose ancestors were, formerly resident in Yemen.
▶ **adjective** of or relating to Yemeni Arabs or Jews.
– ORIGIN from Arabic *yamanī* 'Yemeni' + **-ITE**[1].

yen[1] ▶ **noun** (pl. same) the basic monetary unit of Japan.
– ORIGIN from Japanese *en* 'round'.

yen[2] informal ▶ **noun** [in sing.] a longing or yearning: [with infinitive] *she always had a yen to be a writer*.
▶ **verb** (**yenned**, **yenning**) [no obj.] feel a longing or yearning: *it's no use yenning for the old simplicities*.
– ORIGIN late 19th cent. (in the sense 'craving (of a drug addict) for a drug'): from Chinese *yǎn*.

Yen-cheng /jɛnˈtʃɛŋ/ variant of **YANCHENG**.

Yenisei /ˌjɛnɪˈseɪ/ a river in Siberia, which rises in the mountains on the Mongolian border and flows 4,106 km (2,566 miles) generally northwards to the Arctic coast, emptying into the Kara Sea.

yenta /ˈyɛntə/ ▶ **noun** N. Amer. **1** a woman who is a gossip or busybody.
2 a vulgar person.
– ORIGIN 1920s: Yiddish, originally a given name.

Yen-tai /jɛnˈtʌɪ/ variant of **YANTAI**.

yeoman /ˈjəʊmən/ ▶ **noun** (pl. **-men**) **1** historical a man holding and cultivating a small landed estate; a freeholder.
■ a person qualified for certain duties and rights, such as to serve on juries and vote for the knight of the shire, by virtue of possessing free land of an annual value of 40 shillings.
2 historical a servant in a royal or noble household, ranking between a sergeant and a groom or a squire and a page.
3 Brit. a member of the yeomanry force.
4 (also **yeoman of signals**) (in the Royal and other Commonwealth navies) a petty officer concerned with signalling.
■ a petty officer in the US navy performing clerical duties on board ship.
– PHRASES **yeoman service** efficient or useful help in need.
– DERIVATIVES **yeomanly** adjective.
– ORIGIN Middle English: probably from **YOUNG** + **MAN**.

Yeoman of the Guard ▶ **noun** a member of the British sovereign's bodyguard, first established by Henry VII, now having only ceremonial duties and wearing Tudor dress as uniform. Also called **BEEFEATER**.
■ used erroneously to refer to a Yeoman Warder.

yeomanry ▶ **noun** [treated as sing. or pl.] historical a group of men who held and cultivated small landed estates.
■ (in Britain) a volunteer cavalry force raised from such a group (1794–1908).

Yeoman Usher ▶ **noun** (in the UK) the deputy of Black Rod.

Yeoman Warder ▶ **noun** a warder at the Tower of London. Also called **BEEFEATER**.

yeow ▶ **exclamation** used to express pain or shock.
– ORIGIN natural exclamation: first recorded in American English in the 1920s.

yep (also **yup**) ▶ **exclamation** & **noun** non-standard spelling of **YES**, representing informal pronunciation.

yer /jə/ ▶ **pronoun** non-standard spelling of **YOU**, used in representing dialectal speech.
▶ **possessive determiner** non-standard spelling of **YOUR**, used in representing dialectal speech.
▶ **contraction of** you are, used in representing dialectal speech.

-yer ▶ **suffix** variant spelling of **-IER** especially after *w* (as in *lawyer*, *sawyer*).

yerba /ˈjəːbə/ (also **yerba maté** /ˈmateɪ/) ▶ **noun** another term for **MATÉ**.
– ORIGIN early 19th cent.: from Spanish, literally 'herb'.

yerba buena /ˈbweɪnə/ ▶ **noun** [mass noun] a trailing aromatic herb with whitish or lilac flowers, related to savory. Native to the western US, it has been used medicinally and as a local tea.
• *Satureja douglasii*, family Labiatae.
– ORIGIN mid 19th cent.: from Spanish, literally 'good herb'.

Yerevan /ˌjɛrɪˈvan/ (also **Erevan**) the capital of Armenia; pop. 1,202,000 (1990).

yes ▶ **exclamation 1** used to give an affirmative response: *'Do you understand?' 'Yes.'*
■ expressing agreement with a positive statement just made: *'That was a grand evening.' 'Yes, it was.'* ■ expressing contradiction of a negative statement: *'You don't want to go.' 'Yes, I do.'*
2 used as a response to someone addressing one or otherwise trying to attract one's attention: *'Oh, Mr Lawrence.' 'Yes?'*
3 used to question a remark or ask for more detail about it: *'It should be easy to check.' 'Oh yes? How?'*
■ asked at the end of a statement to indicate the expectation of agreement: *you think I perhaps killed Westbourne, yes?*
4 encouraging someone to continue speaking: *'When you bought those photographs …' 'Yes?'*
5 expressing delight: *plenty to eat, including hot hamburger sandwiches (yes!)*.
▶ **noun** (pl. **yeses** or **yesses**) an affirmative answer or decision, especially in voting: *answering with assured and ardent yeses*.
– PHRASES **yes and no** partly and partly not: *'Did it come as a surprise to you?' 'Yes and no.'*
– ORIGIN Old English *gēse*, *gīse*, probably from an unrecorded phrase meaning 'may it be so'.

yeshiva /jəˈʃiːvə/ ▶ **noun** an Orthodox Jewish college or seminary.
– ORIGIN from Hebrew *yĕšīḇāh*.

yes-man ▶ **noun** (pl. **-men**) informal a weak person who always agrees with their political leader or their superior at work.

yessir /ˈjɛsə, jɛsˈsəː/ informal ▶ **exclamation** used to express assent, especially to a superior: *'Do you understand me?' 'Yessir!'*
■ N. Amer. used to express emphatic affirmation: *yessir the food was cheap*.
▶ **verb** [with obj.] defer to (someone) as a superior, or indicate agreement to (someone): *you're used to people yessirring you left and right*.
– ORIGIN early 20th cent.: alteration of *yes sir*.

yessum /ˈjɛsəm/ ▶ **exclamation** US dated, chiefly black English used as a polite form of assent addressed to a woman: *'You feel all right?' she asked. 'Yessum.'*
– ORIGIN early 20th cent.: alteration of *yes ma'am*.

yester- ▶ **combining form** poetic/literary or archaic of yesterday: *yestereve*.
– ORIGIN Old English *geostran*, of Germanic origin; related to Dutch *gisteren* and German *gestern* 'yesterday', from an Indo-European root shared by Latin *heri* and Greek *khthes*.

yesterday ▶ **adverb** on the day before today: *he returned to a hero's welcome yesterday*.
■ in the recent past: *everything seems to have been built yesterday*.
▶ **noun** the day before today: *yesterday was Tuesday*.
■ the recent past: *yesterday's best-sellers*.
– PHRASES **yesterday morning** (or **afternoon** etc.) in the morning (or afternoon etc.) of yesterday. **yesterday's man** a man, especially a politician, whose career is finished or past its peak. **yesterday's news** a person or thing that is no longer of interest.
– ORIGIN Old English *giestran dæg* (see **YESTER-**, **DAY**).

yesteryear ▶ **noun** poetic/literary last year or the recent past, especially as nostalgically recalled: *the snows of yesteryear have gone*.

yet ▶ **adverb 1** up until the present or a specified or implied time; by now or then: *I haven't told anyone else yet | aren't you ready to go yet? | I **have yet to** be convinced |* [with superlative] *the congress was widely acclaimed as the best yet*.
■ [with negative] as soon as the present or a specified or implied time: *wait, don't go yet*. ■ from now into the future for a specified length of time: *I hope to continue for some time yet*. ■ referring to something that will or may happen in the future: *further research may yet explain the enigma | I know she's alive and I'll find her yet*.
2 still; even (used to emphasize increase or repetition): *snow, snow, and yet more snow | yet another diet book | the rations were reduced **yet again***.
3 nevertheless; in spite of that: *every week she gets worse, and yet it could go on for years*.
▶ **conjunction** but at the same time; but nevertheless: *the path was dark, yet I slowly found my way*.
– PHRASES **as yet** see **AS**[1]. **nor yet** and also not.
– ORIGIN Old English *gīet(a)*, of unknown origin.

yeti /ˈjɛti/ ▶ **noun** a large hairy creature resembling a human or bear, said to live in the highest part of the Himalayas.
– ORIGIN 1930s: from Tibetan *yeh-teh* 'little manlike animal'.

yeuch /jɪəx, jɪˈʌːx, jiːʌx/ ▶ **exclamation** informal expressing disgust or strong distaste.
– ORIGIN 1970s: imitative.

Yevtushenko /ˌjɛftʊˈʃɛŋkəʊ/, Yevgeni (Aleksandrovich) (b.1933), Russian poet. *Third Snow*

(1955) and *Zima Junction* (1956) were regarded as encapsulating the feelings and aspirations of the post-Stalin generation, and he incurred official hostility because of the outspoken nature of some of his poetry, notably *Babi Yar* (1961).

yew ▶ noun (also **yew tree**) a coniferous tree which has red berry-like fruits, and most parts of which are highly poisonous. Yews are linked with folklore and superstition and can live to a great age; the timber is used in cabinetmaking and (formerly) to make longbows.
● Genus *Taxus*, family Taxaceae: several species, in particular *T. baccata* of Europe.
– ORIGIN Old English *īw*, *ēow*, of Germanic origin.

yez ▶ pronoun non-standard spelling of **YOUSE**, used in representing dialectal speech.

Y-fronts ▶ plural noun Brit. trademark men's or boys' underpants with a branching seam at the front in the shape of an upside-down Y.

Yggdrasil /ˈɪɡdrəsɪl/ Scandinavian Mythology a huge ash tree located at the centre of the earth, with three roots, one extending to Niflheim (the underworld), one to Jotunheim (land of the giants), and one to Asgard (land of the gods).
– ORIGIN from Old Norse *yg(g)drasill*, apparently from *Yggr* 'Odin' + *drasill* 'horse'.

YHA ▶ abbreviation for (in the UK) Youth Hostels Association.

yi ▶ pronoun non-standard spelling of **YOU**, used in representing Scottish speech.

Yichun /jiːˈtʃʊn/ (also **I-chun**) a city in Heilongjiang province, NE China; pop. 882,200 (1990).

Yid ▶ noun informal, offensive a Jew.
– ORIGIN late 19th cent.: back-formation from **YIDDISH**.

Yiddish /ˈjɪdɪʃ/ ▶ noun [mass noun] a language used by Jews in central and eastern Europe before the Holocaust. It was originally a German dialect with words from Hebrew and several modern languages, and still has some 200,000 speakers, mainly in the US, Israel, and Russia.
▶ adjective of or relating to this language.
– ORIGIN late 19th cent.: from Yiddish *yidish (daytsh)* 'Jewish German'.

Yiddisher ▶ noun a person speaking Yiddish.

Yiddishism ▶ noun 1 a Yiddish word or idiom, especially one adopted into another language.
2 [mass noun] advocacy of Yiddish culture.
– DERIVATIVES **Yiddishist** noun (only in sense 2).

Yiddishkeit /ˈjɪdɪʃˌkʌɪt/ ▶ noun [mass noun] the quality of being Jewish; the Jewish way of life or its customs and practices.
– ORIGIN late 19th cent.: from Yiddish *yidishkeyt*.

yield ▶ verb 1 [with obj.] produce or provide (a natural, agricultural, or industrial product): *the land yields grapes and tobacco.*
■ (of an action or process) produce or deliver (a result or gain): *this method yields the same results.* ■ (of a financial or commercial process or transaction) generate (a specified financial return): *such investments yield direct cash returns.*
2 [no obj.] give way to arguments, demands, or pressure: *the Western powers now yielded when they should have resisted* | *he yielded to the demands of his partners.*
■ [with obj.] relinquish possession of (something); give (something) up: *they might yield up their secrets* | *they are forced to yield ground.* ■ [with obj.] cease to argue about: *I yielded the point.* ■ give right of way to other traffic. ■ (of a mass or structure) give way under force or pressure: *he reeled into the house as the door yielded.*
▶ noun the full amount of an agricultural or industrial product: *the milk yield was poor.*
■ a financial return: *an annual dividend yield of 20 per cent.*
– DERIVATIVES **yielder** noun (usu. in sense 1).
– ORIGIN Old English *g(i)eldan* 'pay, repay', of Germanic origin. The senses 'produce, bear' and 'surrender' arose in Middle English.

yield curve ▶ noun Finance a curve on a graph in which the yield of fixed-interest securities is plotted against the length of time they have to run to maturity.

yield gap ▶ noun Finance the difference between the return on government-issued securities and that on ordinary shares.

yielding ▶ adjective 1 (of a substance or object)

giving way under pressure; not hard or rigid: *she dropped on to the yielding cushions.*
■ (of a person) complying with the requests or desires of others: *a gentle, yielding person.*
2 [in combination] giving a product or generating a financial return of a specified amount: *higher-yielding wheat.*
– DERIVATIVES **yieldingly** adverb.

yield point ▶ noun Physics the stress beyond which a material becomes plastic.

yield strength ▶ noun Physics (in materials that do not exhibit a well-defined yield point) the stress at which a specific amount of plastic deformation is produced, usually taken as 0.2 per cent of the unstressed length.

yield stress ▶ noun Physics the value of stress at a yield point or at the yield strength.

yikes ▶ exclamation informal expressing shock and alarm, often for humorous effect: *I had a dip in the 40 degree pool (yikes!).*
– ORIGIN 1970s: of unknown origin; compare with **YOICKS**.

yin ▶ noun (in Chinese philosophy) the passive female principle of the universe, characterized as female and sustaining and associated with earth, dark, and cold. Contrasted with **YANG**.
– ORIGIN from Chinese *yīn* 'feminine', 'moon', 'shade'.

Yinchuan /jɪnˈtʃwan/ the capital of Ningxia, an autonomous region of China, on the Yellow River; pop. 658,000 (est. 1986).

yip /jɪp/ ▶ noun a short, sharp cry or yelp, especially of excitement or delight.
▶ verb (**yipped**, **yipping**) [no obj.] give such a cry or yelp.
– ORIGIN early 20th cent. (originally US): imitative.

yippee ▶ exclamation expressing wild excitement or delight.
– ORIGIN natural exclamation: first recorded in American English in the 1920s.

yippie ▶ noun (pl. **-ies**) a member of a group of politically active hippies, originally in the US.
– ORIGIN 1960s: acronym from *Youth International Party* + the suffix *-ie*, suggested by **HIPPY**[1].

yips ▶ plural noun (**the yips**) informal extreme nervousness causing a golfer to miss easy putts.
– ORIGIN mid 20th cent.: of unknown origin.

Yishuv /jɪˈʃuːv, ˈjɪʃʊv/ the Jewish community or settlement in Palestine during the 19th century and until the formation of the state of Israel in 1948.
– ORIGIN from Hebrew *yiššūb* 'settlement'.

Yizkor /ˈjɪzkə/ ▶ noun (pl. same or **Yizkors**) a memorial service held by Jews on certain holy days for deceased relatives or martyrs.
– ORIGIN from Hebrew *yizkōr*, literally 'may (God) remember'.

-yl ▶ suffix Chemistry forming names of radicals: *hydroxyl* | *phenyl*.
– ORIGIN from Greek *hulē* 'wood, material'.

ylang-ylang /ˌiːlaŋˈiːlaŋ/ (also **ilang-ilang**) ▶ noun
1 [mass noun] a sweet-scented essential oil obtained from the flowers of a tropical tree, used in perfumery and aromatherapy.
2 the yellow-flowered tree, native to Malaya and the Philippines, from which this oil is obtained.
● *Cananga odorata*, family Annonaceae.
– ORIGIN late 19th cent.: from Tagalog *ilang-ilang*.

ylem /ˈiːlɛm/ ▶ noun [mass noun] Astronomy (in the big bang theory) the primordial matter of the universe, originally conceived as composed of neutrons at high temperature and density.
– ORIGIN 1940s: from late Latin *hylem* (accusative) 'matter'.

ylid /ˈɪlɪd/ (also **ylide** /ˈɪlʌɪd/) ▶ noun Chemistry a compound having an uncharged molecule containing a negatively charged carbon atom directly bonded to a positively charged atom of sulphur, phosphorus, nitrogen, or another element.
– ORIGIN 1950s: from **-YL** + **-IDE**.

YMCA ▶ noun a welfare movement with branches all over the world that began in London in 1844.
■ a hostel run by this association.
– ORIGIN abbreviation of *Young Men's Christian Association*.

Ymir /ˈiːmə/ Scandinavian Mythology the primeval giant from whose body the gods created the world.

-yne ▶ suffix Chemistry forming names of unsaturated compounds containing a triple bond: *ethyne*.
– ORIGIN alteration of **-INE**[4].

Ynys Môn /ˌʌnɪs ˈmɔːn/ Welsh name for **ANGLESEY**.

yo[1] ▶ exclamation informal used to greet someone, attract their attention, or express excitement.
– ORIGIN natural exclamation: first recorded in late Middle English.

yo[2] ▶ pronoun non-standard spelling of **YOU**, used to represent black English.
▶ possessive determiner non-standard spelling of **YOUR**, used to represent black English.

yob ▶ noun Brit. informal a rude, noisy, and aggressive young man.
– DERIVATIVES **yobbish** adjective, **yobbishly** adverb, **yobbishness** noun, **yobby** adjective.
– ORIGIN mid 19th cent.: back slang for **BOY**.

yobbery ▶ noun [mass noun] behaviour characteristic of a yob: *yobbery seems to have replaced wit in politics.*

yobbo ▶ noun (pl. **-os** or **-oes**) Brit. informal another term for **YOB**.

yock (also **yok**) ▶ noun US informal a laugh, especially a loud hearty one.
– ORIGIN 1930s (theatrical slang): probably imitative.

yocto- /ˈjɒktəʊ/ ▶ combining form (used in units of measurement) denoting a factor of 10^{-24}: *yoctojoule.*
– ORIGIN adapted from **OCTO-**, on the pattern of combining forms such as *peta-* and *exa-*.

yod /jɒd/ ▶ noun 1 the tenth and smallest letter of the Hebrew alphabet.
2 Phonetics the semivowel or glide /j/.
3 Astrology another term for **FINGER OF GOD**.
– ORIGIN from Hebrew *yōd*; related to *yad* 'hand'.

yodel /ˈjəʊd(ə)l/ ▶ verb (**yodelled**, **yodelling**; US **yodeled**, **yodeling**) [no obj.] practise a form of singing or calling marked by rapid alternation between the normal voice and falsetto.
▶ noun a song, melody, or call delivered in such a way.
– DERIVATIVES **yodeller** noun.
– ORIGIN early 19th cent.: from German *jodeln*.

yoga ▶ noun [mass noun] a Hindu spiritual and ascetic discipline, a part of which, including breath control, simple meditation, and the adoption of specific bodily postures, is widely practised for health and relaxation.

> The yoga widely known in the West is based on **hatha yoga**, which forms one aspect of the ancient Hindu system of religious and ascetic observance and meditation, the highest form of which is **raja yoga** and the ultimate aim of which is spiritual purification and self-understanding leading to *samadhi* or union with the divine.

– DERIVATIVES **yogic** adjective.
– ORIGIN Sanskrit, literally 'union'.

yogh /jɒɡ/ ▶ noun a Middle English letter (ʒ) used mainly where modern English has *gh* and *y*.
– ORIGIN Middle English: of unknown origin.

yogi ▶ noun (pl. **yogis**) a person who is proficient in yoga.
– ORIGIN from Sanskrit *yogī*, from *yoga* (see **YOGA**).

yogic flying ▶ noun [mass noun] a technique used chiefly by Transcendental Meditation practitioners which involves thrusting oneself off the ground while in the lotus position.

yogurt /ˈjɒɡət, ˈjəʊ-/ (also **yoghurt** or **yoghourt**) ▶ noun [mass noun] a semi-solid sourish food prepared from milk fermented by added bacteria.
– ORIGIN early 17th cent.: from Turkish *yoğurt*.

Yogyakarta /ˌjɒɡjəˈkɑːtə/ (also **Jogjakarta**) a city in south central Java, Indonesia; pop. 412,000 (1990). It was formerly the capital of Indonesia (1945–9).

yo-heave-ho ▶ exclamation & noun another term for **HEAVE-HO**.

yohimbe /jəʊˈhɪmbeɪ/ ▶ noun a tropical West African tree from which the drug yohimbine is obtained.
● *Pausinystalia johimbe*, family Rubiaceae.
– ORIGIN late 19th cent.: a local word.

yohimbine /jəʊˈhɪmbiːn/ ▶ noun [mass noun] Chemistry a toxic crystalline compound obtained from the bark of the yohimbe tree, used as an adrenergic blocking agent and also as an aphrodisiac in the treatment of impotence.
● An alkaloid; chem. formula: $C_{21}H_{26}O_3N_2$.
– ORIGIN late 19th cent.: from **YOHIMBE** + **-INE**[4].

yo-ho-ho (also **yo-ho**) ▶ exclamation 1 dated used to attract attention.

2 Nautical, archaic a seaman's chant used while hauling ropes or performing other strenuous work.

yoicks /jɔɪks/ ▶ **exclamation** used by fox-hunters to urge on the hounds.
– ORIGIN mid 18th cent.: of unknown origin.

yok ▶ **noun** variant spelling of **YOCK**.

yoke ▶ **noun 1** a wooden crosspiece that is fastened over the necks of two animals and attached to the plough or cart that they are to pull.
■ (pl. same or **yokes**) a pair of animals coupled together in such a way: *a yoke of oxen.* ■ archaic the amount of land that one pair of oxen could plough in a day. ■ a frame fitting over the neck and shoulders of a person, used for carrying pails or baskets. ■ used of something that is regarded as oppressive or burdensome: *the yoke of imperialism.* ■ used of something that represents a bond between two parties: *the yoke of marriage.*
2 something resembling or likened to such a crosspiece, in particular:
■ a part of a garment that fits over the shoulders and to which the main part of the garment is attached, typically in gathers or pleats. ■ the crossbar of a rudder, to whose ends ropes are fastened. ■ a bar of soft iron between the poles of an electromagnet. ■ (in ancient Rome) an arch of three spears under which a defeated army was made to march. ■ chiefly N. Amer. a control lever in an aircraft.
▶ **verb** [with obj.] put a yoke on (a pair of animals); couple or attach with or to a yoke: *a plough drawn by a camel and donkey yoked together* | figurative *Hong Kong's dollar has been* **yoked to** *America's.*
– ORIGIN Old English *geoc* (noun), *geocian* (verb), of Germanic origin; related to Dutch *juk*, German *Joch*, from an Indo-European root shared by Latin *jugum* and Greek *zugon*, also by Latin *jungere* 'to join'.

yokel ▶ **noun** an uneducated and unsophisticated person from the countryside.
– ORIGIN early 19th cent.: perhaps figuratively from dialect *yokel* 'green woodpecker'.

Yokohama /ˌjəʊkəʊˈhɑːmə/ a seaport on the island of Honshu, Japan; pop. 3,220,000 (1990). It is a major port and the second largest city in Japan.

yokozuna /ˌjəʊkəˈzuːnə/ ▶ **noun** (pl. same) a grand champion sumo wrestler.
– ORIGIN Japanese, from *yoko* 'crosswise' + *tsuna* 'rope' (originally denoting a kind of belt presented to the champion).

yolk /jəʊk/ ▶ **noun** the yellow internal part of a bird's egg, which is surrounded by the white, is rich in protein and fat, and nourishes the developing embryo.
■ [mass noun] Zoology the corresponding part in the ovum or larva of all egg-laying vertebrates and many invertebrates.
– DERIVATIVES **yolked** adjective [also in combination], **yolkless** adjective, **yolky** adjective.
– ORIGIN Old English *geol(o)ca*, from *geolu* 'yellow'.

yolk sac ▶ **noun** Zoology a membranous sac containing yolk attached to the embryos of reptiles and birds and the larvae of some fishes.
■ a sac lacking yolk in the early embryo of a mammal.

Yom Kippur /jɒm ˈkɪpə, kɪˈpʊə/ ▶ **noun** the most solemn religious fast of the Jewish year, the last of the ten days of penitence that begin with Rosh Hashana (the Jewish New Year). Also called **DAY OF ATONEMENT**.
– ORIGIN Hebrew.

Yom Kippur War the Israeli name for the Arab-Israeli conflict in 1973. Arab name **OCTOBER WAR**.

> The war lasted for less than three weeks; it started on the festival of Yom Kippur (in that year, 6 October) when Egypt and Syria simultaneously attacked Israeli forces from the south and north respectively. The Syrians were repulsed and the Egyptians were surrounded. A ceasefire followed and disengagement agreements over the Suez area were signed in 1974 and 1975.

yomp Brit. informal ▶ **verb** [no obj., with adverbial of direction] (of a soldier) march with heavy equipment over difficult terrain: *squaddies yomping over the hills.*
▶ **noun** a march of such a kind: *a 60 km yomp.*
– ORIGIN 1980s: of unknown origin.

yon poetic/literary or dialect ▶ **determiner & adverb** yonder; that: [as determiner] *there's some big ranches yon side of the Sierra.*
▶ **pronoun** yonder person or thing: *what do you make of yon?*
– PHRASES **hither and yon** another term for **HITHER AND THITHER**.
– ORIGIN Old English *geon*, of Germanic origin; related to German *jener* 'that one'.

yonder ▶ **adverb** archaic or dialect at some distance in the direction indicated; over there: *there's a ford south of here, about nine miles yonder.*
▶ **determiner** archaic or dialect that or those (used to refer to something situated at a distance): *what light through yonder window breaks?*
▶ **noun (the yonder)** the far distance: *attempting to fly off into* **the wide blue yonder**.
– ORIGIN Middle English: of Germanic origin; related to Dutch *ginder* 'over there', also to **YON**.

yoni /ˈjəʊni/ ▶ **noun** (pl. **yonis**) Hinduism the vulva, especially as a symbol of divine procreative energy conventionally represented by a circular stone. Compare with **LINGAM**.
– ORIGIN Sanskrit, literally 'source, womb, female genitals'.

yonks ▶ **plural noun** Brit. informal a very long time: *I haven't seen him* **for yonks**.
– ORIGIN 1960s: origin unknown; perhaps related to *donkey's years* (see **DONKEY**).

yoof ▶ **noun** non-standard spelling of **YOUTH**, used humorously or ironically to refer to young people collectively: [as modifier] *yoof culture.*

yoo-hoo ▶ **exclamation** a call used to attract attention to one's arrival or presence: *Yoo-hoo!—Is anyone there?*
▶ **verb** [no obj.] (of a person) make such a call.
– ORIGIN natural exclamation: first recorded in English in the 1920s.

yore ▶ **noun** (in phrase **of yore**) poetic/literary of long ago or former times (used in nostalgic or mock-nostalgic recollection): *a great empire in days of yore.*
– ORIGIN Old English *geāra*, *geāre*, of unknown origin.

York a city in northern England, on the River Ouse, a unitary council formerly in Yorkshire; pop. 100,600 (1991). The Romans occupied the site, known as Eboracum, from AD 71 until about AD 400; in AD 867 it was taken by the Vikings. It is the seat of the Archbishop of York and is noted for its magnificent cathedral, York Minster.
– ORIGIN from Danish *Jorvik*.

york ▶ **verb** [with obj.] Cricket (of a bowler) bowl out (a batsman) with a ball that pitches under the bat.
– ORIGIN late 19th cent.: back-formation from **YORKER**.

York, Archbishop of ▶ **noun** the archbishop of the northern province of the Church of England. The office carries the title of Primate of England.

York, Cape a cape extending into the Torres Strait at the north-east tip of Australia, in Queensland.

York, House of the English royal house which ruled England from 1461 (Edward IV) until the defeat and death of Richard III in 1485, with a short break in 1470–1 (the restoration of Henry VI).

> Descended from Edmund of Langley (1341–1402), 1st Duke of York and 5th son of Edward III, the House of York fought the Wars of the Roses with the House of Lancaster, both houses being branches of the Plantagenet line. Lancaster eventually prevailed, through their descendants, the Tudors, but the houses were united when the victorious Henry VII married Elizabeth, the eldest daughter of Edward IV (1486).

yorker ▶ **noun** Cricket a ball bowled so that it pitches immediately under the bat.
– ORIGIN probably from **YORK**, suggesting its introduction by Yorkshire players.

Yorkie ▶ **noun** (pl. **-ies**) informal Yorkshire terrier.

Yorkist historical ▶ **noun** an adherent or a supporter of the House of York, especially in the Wars of the Roses.
▶ **adjective** of or relating to the House of York: *the town rallied itself to the Yorkist cause.*

Yorks. ▶ **abbreviation for** Yorkshire.

Yorkshire a former county of northern England, traditionally divided into East, West, and North Ridings. Since 1996 the northern part of the area has formed the county of North Yorkshire, while the rest of the Yorkshire area consists of unitary councils.
– DERIVATIVES **Yorkshireman** noun (pl. **-men**), **Yorkshirewoman** noun (pl. **-women**).

Yorkshire fog ▶ **noun** [mass noun] a common pasture grass with soft downy leaves, native to Eurasia.
● *Holcus lanatus*, family Gramineae.
– ORIGIN late 19th cent.: *fog* from **FOG**[2].

Yorkshire pudding ▶ **noun** [mass noun] a baked batter pudding typically eaten with roast beef.

Yorkshire terrier ▶ **noun** a dog of a small long-haired blue-grey and tan breed of terrier.

Yoruba /ˈjɒrʊbə/ ▶ **noun** (pl. same or **Yorubas**) **1** a member of an African people of SW Nigeria and Benin.
2 [mass noun] the language of this people, which belongs to the Kwa group. It is an official language of Nigeria, with over 16 million speakers.
▶ **adjective** of or relating to the Yoruba or their language.
– ORIGIN the name in Yoruba.

Yorvik /ˈjɔːvɪk/ (also **Jorvik**) Viking name for **YORK**.

Yosemite National Park /jə(ʊ)ˈsɛmɪti/ a national park in the Sierra Nevada in central California. It includes Yosemite Valley, with its sheer granite cliffs and Yosemite Falls, the highest waterfall in the US.

Yoshkar-Ola /jaʃˌkɑːrəˈlɑː/ the capital of the republic of Mari El, in Russia; pop. 246,000 (1990).

yotta- /ˈjɒtə/ ▶ **combining form** (used in units of measurement) denoting a factor of 10^{24}: *yottameter.*
– ORIGIN apparently adapted from Italian *otto* 'eight' (see also **YOCTO-**).

you ▶ **pronoun** [second person singular or plural] **1** used to refer to the person or people that the speaker is addressing: *are you listening?* | *I love you.*
■ used to refer to the person being addressed together with other people regarded in the same class: *you Americans.* ■ used in exclamations to address one or more people: *you fools* | *hey, you!*
2 used to refer to any person in general: *after a while, you get used to it.*
– PHRASES **you and yours** you together with your family and close friends. **you-know-who** (or **you-know-what**) used to refer to someone (or something) known to the hearer without specifying their identity: *the minister was later to be sacked by you-know-who.*
– ORIGIN Old English *ēow*, accusative and dative of *gē* (see **YE**[1]), of West Germanic origin; related to Dutch *u* and German *euch*. During the 14th cent. *you* began to replace **YE**[1], **THOU**[1], and **THEE**; by the 17th cent. it had become the ordinary second person pronoun for any number and case.

you-all (also **y'all**) ▶ **pronoun** US informal you (used to refer to more than one person): *how are you-all?*

you'd ▶ **contraction of** ■ you had: *you'd better remember it.* ■ you would: *I was afraid you'd ask me that.*

you'll ▶ **contraction of** you will; you shall: *you'll find many exciting features.*

Young[1], Brigham (1801–77), American Mormon leader. He succeeded Joseph Smith as the leader of the Mormons in 1844, and established their headquarters at Salt Lake City, Utah.

Young[2], Neil (Percival) (b.1945), Canadian singer, songwriter, and guitarist. He performs both solo and with his group Crazy Horse, combining plaintive acoustic material with distinctively distorted electric-guitar playing. Notable albums: *Harvest* (1972).

Young[3], Thomas (1773–1829), English physicist, physician, and Egyptologist. His major work in physics concerned the wave theory of light. He also played a major part in the deciphering of the Rosetta Stone.

young ▶ **adjective** (**younger**, **youngest**) having lived or existed for only a short time: *a young girl* | [as plural noun **the young**] *the young are amazingly resilient.*
■ not as old as the norm or as would be expected: *more people were dying young.* ■ [attrib.] relating to, characteristic of, or consisting of young people: *young love* | *the Young Communist League.* ■ immature or inexperienced: *she's very* **young for her age**. ■ having the qualities popularly associated with young people, such as enthusiasm and optimism: *all those who are* **young at heart**. ■ (**the Younger**) used to denote the younger of two people of the same name: *Pitt the Younger.* ■ (**younger**) [postpositive] Scottish denoting the heir of a landed commoner: *Hugh Magnus Macleod, younger of Macleod.*
▶ **noun** [treated as pl.] offspring, especially of an animal before or soon after birth: *this species carries its young.*
– DERIVATIVES **youngish** adjective.
– ORIGIN Old English *g(e)ong*, of Germanic origin; related to Dutch *jong* and German *jung*, also to **YOUTH**; from an Indo-European root shared by Latin *juvenis*.

y

young adult offender ▶ noun Law (in the UK) a criminal between 18 and 20 years of age.

youngberry ▶ noun (pl. **-ies**) a bramble of a variety which bears large edible reddish-black fruit. First cultivated in the US, it is believed to be a hybrid of a dewberry.
– ORIGIN 1920s: named after B. M. *Young* (*fl.* 1905), the American horticulturalist who first raised it.

younger hand ▶ noun (in card games for two players, e.g. piquet) the player who receives a complete hand after the other, i.e. the dealer.

young fustic ▶ noun the smoke tree.

young gun ▶ noun informal a young man perceived as assertive and aggressively self-confident.

Young Italy a movement founded by Giuseppe Mazzini in 1831 to work towards a united Italian republic. In the 1830s and 1840s the movement plotted against the Italian governments. It failed to gain popular support but was nevertheless a significant stimulus to the Risorgimento.

young lady ▶ noun a woman who is not far advanced in life; a girl.
■ a form of address used by an adult to a girl, often in anger: *I don't know what's got into you, young lady.* ■ dated a girlfriend.

youngling ▶ noun poetic/literary a young person or animal.

young man ▶ noun a man who is not far advanced in life; a boy.
■ a form of address used by an adult to a boy, often in anger: *don't waste my time, young man.* ■ dated a boyfriend.

young offender ▶ noun Law (in the UK) a criminal between 14 and 17 years of age.
■ (in Canada) a criminal between 12 and 17 years of age.

young offender institution ▶ noun Law (in the UK) an institution for the detention of criminals between the ages of 14 and 20, replacing the former detention centres and youth custody centres.

young person ▶ noun Law (in the UK) a person generally between 14 and 17 years of age.

Young Pretender see STUART[1].

Young's modulus ▶ noun Physics a measure of elasticity, equal to the ratio of the stress acting on a substance to the strain produced.
– ORIGIN mid 19th cent.: named after T. *Young* (see YOUNG[3]).

youngster ▶ noun a child, young person, or young animal.

youngstock ▶ noun [usu. treated as pl.] young farm animals.

Young Turk ▶ noun a member of a revolutionary party in the Ottoman Empire who carried out the revolution of 1908 and deposed the sultan Abdul Hamid II.
■ a young person eager for radical change to the established order.

young 'un ▶ noun informal a youngster.

younker /ˈjʌŋkə/ ▶ noun dated a youngster.
– ORIGIN early 16th cent. (denoting a young nobleman): from Middle Dutch *jonckher*, from *jonc* 'young' + *hēre* 'lord'. Compare with JUNKER.

your /jɔː, jʊə/ ▶ possessive determiner 1 belonging to or associated with the person or people that the speaker is addressing: *what is your name?*
2 belonging to or associated with any person in general: *the sight is enough to break your heart.*
■ informal used to denote someone or something that is familiar or typical of its kind: *I'm just your average man in the street* | *she is one of your chatty types.*
3 (**Your**) used when addressing the holder of certain titles: *Your Majesty* | *Your Excellency.*
– ORIGIN Old English *ēower*, genitive of *gē* (see YE[1]), of Germanic origin; related to German *euer*.

Yourcenar /ˈjʊəsənɑː, French juʀsə(ə)naʀ/, Marguerite (1903–87), French writer. Many of her novels are meticulous historical reconstructions, including *Mémoires d'Hadrian* (1951). Her interest in male homosexuality is reflected in the novel *Alexis ou le Traité du vain combat* (1929).

you're /jɔː, jə, jʊə/ ▶ contraction of you are: *you're an angel, Deb!*

yourn /jɔːn, jʊən/ ▶ possessive pronoun regional or archaic form of YOURS.

yours ▶ possessive pronoun 1 used to refer to a thing or things belonging to or associated with the person or people that the speaker is addressing: *the choice is yours* | *it's no business of yours.*
■ (chiefly in commercial use) your letter: *Mr Smythe has sent me yours of the 15th inst. regarding the vacancy.*
2 used in formulas ending a letter: *Yours sincerely, John Watson* | *Yours, Jim Lindsay.*
– PHRASES **up yours** see UP. **you and yours** see YOU. **yours truly** see TRULY.

yourself ▶ pronoun [second person singular] (pl. **yourselves**) **1** [reflexive] used to refer to the person being addressed as the object of a verb or preposition when they are also the subject of the clause: *help yourselves, boys* | *see for yourself.*
2 [emphatic] you personally (used to emphasize the person being addressed): *you're going to have to do it yourself.*
– PHRASES **(not) be yourself** see **be oneself**, **not be oneself** at BE. **by yourself** see **by oneself** at BY. **how's yourself?** informal how are you? (used especially after answering a similar enquiry).

youse /juːz/ (also **yous**) ▶ pronoun dialect you (usually more than one person).

youth ▶ noun (pl. **youths**) **1** [in sing.] the period between childhood and adult age: *he had been a keen sportsman in his youth.*
■ [mass noun] the state or quality of being young, especially as associated with vigour, freshness, or immaturity: *she imagined her youth and beauty fading.* ■ an early stage in the development of something: *this publishing sector is no longer in its youth.*
2 [treated as sing. or pl.] young people considered as a group: *black youth has experienced high levels of racial discrimination* | [as modifier] *youth culture.*
■ [count noun] a young man: *he was attacked by a gang of youths.*
– ORIGIN Old English *geoguth*, of Germanic origin; related to Dutch *jeugd*, German *Jugend*, also to YOUNG.

youth club (also **youth centre**) ▶ noun a place or organization providing leisure activities for young people.

youth court ▶ noun a court of law responsible for the trial of young offenders, (in the UK) replacing the former juvenile courts.

youth custody centre ▶ noun Law (formerly in the UK) a centre for the detention of criminals between the ages of 15 and 20 for periods exceeding four months, replaced by young offender institutions.

youthful ▶ adjective young or seeming young: *people aspiring to remain youthful.*
■ typical or characteristic of young people: *youthful enthusiasm.*
– DERIVATIVES **youthfully** adverb, **youthfulness** noun.

youth hostel ▶ noun a place providing cheap accommodation aimed mainly at young people on walking or cycling tours.
▶ verb (**youth-hostel**) [no obj.] travel around, staying the night in such places: *we went youth-hostelling together.*
– DERIVATIVES **youth-hosteller** noun.

Youth Training Scheme a government-sponsored scheme introduced in Britain in 1983 to offer job experience and training for unemployed school-leavers.

you've ▶ contraction of you have: *you've changed.*

yow /jaʊ/ ▶ pronoun non-standard spelling of YOU, used to represent speech in various dialects.

yowl /jaʊl/ ▶ noun a loud wailing cry, especially one of pain or distress.
▶ verb [no obj.] make such a cry: *he yowled as he touched one of the hot plates.*
– ORIGIN Middle English: imitative.

yo-yo (trademark in the UK) ▶ noun (pl. **-os**) a toy consisting of a pair of joined discs with a deep groove between them in which string is attached and wound, which can be spun alternately downward and upward by its weight and momentum as the string unwinds and rewinds.
■ [often as modifier] a thing that repeatedly falls and rises again: *the yo-yo syndrome of repeatedly losing weight and gaining it again.* ■ informal, chiefly N. Amer. a stupid, insane, or unpredictable person.
▶ verb (**-oes**, **-oed**) [no obj., usu. with adverbial of direction] move up and down; fluctuate: *popularity polls yo-yo up and down with the flow of events.*
■ [with obj.] manipulate or manoeuvre (someone or something): *I don't want the job if it means he gets to yo-yo me around.*

– ORIGIN early 20th cent.: of unknown origin.

Ypres /ˈiːpr(ə), French ipʀ/ a town in NW Belgium, near the border with France, in the province of West Flanders; pop. 35,235 (1990). Ypres was the scene of some of the bitterest fighting of the First World War (see YPRES, BATTLE OF). Flemish name IEPER.

Ypres, Battle of each of three battles on the Western Front near Ypres during the First World War in 1914, 1915, and 1917. See also PASSCHENDAELE, BATTLE OF.

yr ▶ abbreviation for ■ year or years. ■ younger. ■ your.

yrs ▶ abbreviation for ■ years. ■ yours (as a formula ending a letter).

Yr Wyddfa /ʌr ˈwɪðva/ Welsh name for SNOWDON.

YT ▶ abbreviation for Yukon Territory (in official postal use).

YTS ▶ abbreviation for Youth Training Scheme.

ytterbium /ɪˈtəːbɪəm/ ▶ noun [mass noun] the chemical element of atomic number 70, a silvery-white metal of the lanthanide series. (Symbol: **Yb**)
– ORIGIN late 19th cent.: modern Latin, from *Ytterby*, the name of a Swedish quarry where it was first found.

yttrium /ˈɪtrɪəm/ ▶ noun [mass noun] the chemical element of atomic number 39, a greyish-white metal generally included among the rare-earth elements. (Symbol: **Y**)
– ORIGIN early 19th cent.: modern Latin, from *Ytterby* (see YTTERBIUM).

Yuan /jʊˈɑːn/ a dynasty that ruled China AD 1279–1368, established by the Mongols under Kublai Khan. It preceded the Ming dynasty.

yuan /jʊˈɑːn/ ▶ noun (pl. same) the basic monetary unit of China, equal to 10 jiao or 100 fen.
– ORIGIN Chinese, literally 'round'; compare with YEN[1].

Yuan Jiang /jʊˌɑːn ˈdʒjaŋ/ Chinese name for RED RIVER (in sense 1).

yuca /ˈjuːkə/ ▶ noun chiefly US another term for CASSAVA.
– ORIGIN Carib.

Yucatán /jʊkəˈtɑːn/ a state of SE Mexico, at the northern tip of the Yucatán Peninsula; capital, Mérida.
– ORIGIN adapted from a Maya name for the language of the Mayan Indians of Oaxaca, Mexico.

Yucatán Peninsula a peninsula in southern Mexico, lying between the Gulf of Mexico and the Caribbean Sea.

Yucatec /ˈjuːkətɛk/ ▶ noun (pl. same or **Yucatecs**) **1** a member of an American Indian people of the Yucatán peninsula in eastern Mexico.
■ informal a native or inhabitant of the peninsula or the state of Yucatán.
2 [mass noun] the Mayan language of the Yucatec people, with about 500,000 speakers.
▶ adjective of or relating to the Yucatec or their language.
– DERIVATIVES **Yucatecan** adjective.
– ORIGIN from Spanish *yucateco*.

yucca /ˈjʌkə/ ▶ noun a plant of the agave family with sword-like leaves and spikes of white bell-shaped flowers that are dependent upon the yucca moth for fertilization, native to warm regions of North America and Mexico. Also called ADAM'S NEEDLE.
● Genus *Yucca*, family Agavaceae: many species, including the Spanish bayonet.
– ORIGIN mid 16th cent. (denoting cassava): from Carib.

yucca moth ▶ noun a small white American moth which lays its eggs in the ovary of a yucca plant. While doing so it deposits a ball of pollen on the stigma, thereby fertilizing the seeds on which the larvae feed.
● Genus *Tegeticula*, family Incurvariidae: several species, in particular *T. yuccasella*.

yuck (also **yuk**) informal ▶ exclamation used to express strong distaste or disgust: *'Raw herrings! Yuck!'*
▶ noun [mass noun] something messy or disgusting: *I can't bear the sight of blood and yuck.*
– ORIGIN 1960s (originally US): imitative.

yucky (also **yukky**) ▶ adjective (**yuckier**, **yuckiest**) informal messy or disgusting: *yucky green-grey slushy cabbage.*

Yue /jjə)ˈweɪ, jʊˈeɪ/ ▶ noun another term for CANTONESE (the language)

yuga /ˈjʊgə/ ▶ noun Hinduism any of the four ages of the life of the world.
– ORIGIN Sanskrit.

Yugoslav /ˈjuːgə(ʊ)slɑːv, ˌjuːgə(ʊ)ˈslɑːv/ ▶ noun a native or national of Yugoslavia or its former constituent republics, or a person of Yugoslav descent.
▶ adjective of or relating to Yugoslavia, its former constituent republics, or its people.
– ORIGIN from Austrian German *Jugoslav*, from Serbo-Croat *jug* 'south' + **SLAV**.

Yugoslavia /ˌjuːgə(ʊ)ˈslɑːvɪə/ a federation of states in SE Europe, in the Balkans.

The country was formed as the Kingdom of Serbs, Croats, and Slovenes in the peace settlements at the end of the First World War. It comprised Serbia, Montenegro, and the former South Slavic provinces of the Austro-Hungarian empire, and assumed the name of Yugoslavia in 1929; its capital was Belgrade. After the Second World War, during which Yugoslavia was invaded by Germany, the country emerged as a non-aligned Communist federal republic under Marshal Tito. In 1990 Communist rule was formally ended. Four of the six constituent republics (Slovenia, Croatia, Bosnia–Herzegovina, and Macedonia) then seceded amid serious civil and ethnic conflict. The two remaining republics, Serbia and Montenegro, declared a new federal republic of Yugoslavia in 1992.

– DERIVATIVES **Yugoslavian** adjective & noun.

yuh /jə/ ▶ pronoun non-standard spelling of **YOU**, used in representing black English speech.
▶ possessive determiner non-standard spelling of **YOUR**, used in representing black English speech.

Yuit /ˈjuːɪt/ ▶ noun (pl. same or **Yuits**) & adjective another term for **YUPIK**.
– ORIGIN Siberian Yupik, literally 'people'.

yuk ▶ exclamation & noun variant spelling of **YUCK**.

yukata /jʊˈkɑːtə/ ▶ noun (pl. same or **yukatas**) a light cotton kimono.
– ORIGIN Japanese, from *yu* 'hot water' (because originally worn indoors after a bath) + *kata(bira)* 'light kimono'.

yukky ▶ adjective variant spelling of **YUCKY**.

Yukon /ˈjuːkɒn/ a river of NW North America, which rises in Yukon Territory, NW Canada, and flows 3,020 km (1,870 miles) westwards through central Alaska to the Bering Sea.

Yukon stove ▶ noun a lightweight portable stove consisting of a small metal box divided into firebox and oven.

Yukon Territory a territory of NW Canada, on the border with Alaska; pop. 26,900 (1991); capital, Whitehorse. The population increased briefly during the Klondike gold rush (1897–9).

yulan /ˈjuːlən/ ▶ noun a Chinese magnolia with showy white flowers.
● *Magnolia heptapeta*, family Magnoliaceae.
– ORIGIN early 19th cent.: from Chinese *yùlán*, from *yù* 'gem' + *lán* 'plant'.

Yule ▶ noun archaic term for **CHRISTMAS**.
– ORIGIN Old English *gēol(a)* 'Christmas Day'; compare with Old Norse *jól*, originally applied to a heathen festival lasting twelve days, later to Christmas.

yule log ▶ noun a large log traditionally burnt in the hearth on Christmas Eve.
■ a log-shaped chocolate cake eaten at Christmas.

Yuletide ▶ noun archaic term for **CHRISTMAS**.

Yuma /ˈjuːmə/ ▶ noun (pl. same or **Yumas**) a member of an American Indian people living mainly in SW Arizona.
▶ adjective of or relating to this people.
– ORIGIN from Pima *yumĭ*.

Yuman ▶ noun [mass noun] the language of the Yuma people, belonging to the Hokan group and nearly extinct.
▶ adjective of or relating to the Yuma people or their language.
– ORIGIN from **YUMA** + **-AN**.

yummy ▶ adjective (**yummier**, **yummiest**) informal (of food) delicious: *yummy cream cakes*.
■ highly attractive and desirable: *I scooped up this yummy young man.*
– ORIGIN late 19th cent.: from **YUM-YUM** + **-Y**[1].

yum-yum (also **yum**) informal ▶ exclamation used to express pleasure at eating, or at the prospect of eating, a particular food.
▶ adjective (of food) delicious.
– ORIGIN late 19th cent.: imitative.

Yunnan /juːˈnan/ a province of SW China, on the border with Vietnam, Laos, and Burma; capital, Kunming.

yup[1] ▶ exclamation & noun variant spelling of **YEP**.

yup[2] ▶ noun short for **YUPPIE**.

Yupik /ˈjuːpɪk/ ▶ noun (pl. same or **Yupiks**) **1** a member of an Eskimo people of Siberia, the Aleutian Islands, and Alaska.
2 [mass noun] any of the languages of this people, a division of the Eskimo-Aleut family, with around 3,000 speakers.
▶ adjective of or relating to this people or their languages.
– ORIGIN from Alaskan Yupik *Yup'ik* 'real person'.

yuppie (also **yuppy**) ▶ noun (pl. **-ies**) informal, derogatory a well-paid young middle-class professional who works in a city job and has a luxurious lifestyle.
– DERIVATIVES **yuppiedom** noun.
– ORIGIN 1980s: elaboration of the acronym from *young urban professional*.

yuppie flu (also **yuppie disease**) ▶ noun informal derogatory term for **CHRONIC FATIGUE SYNDROME**.

yuppify ▶ verb (**-ies**, **-ied**) [with obj.] informal, derogatory make more affluent and upmarket in keeping with the taste and lifestyle of yuppies: *Kreuzberg is slowly being yuppified with smart little eating places.*
– DERIVATIVES **yuppification** noun.

yurt /jʊət, jəːt/ ▶ noun a circular tent of felt or skins on a collapsible framework, used by nomads in Mongolia, Siberia, and Turkey.
– ORIGIN from Russian *yurta*, via French or German from Turkic *jurt*.

yus /jʌs/ ▶ exclamation & noun non-standard spelling of **YES**, used in representing dialectal speech.

Yuzovka /ˈjuːzəfkə/ former name (1872–1924) for **DONETSK**.
– ORIGIN named in honour of John Hughes (1814–89), a Welshman who established its first ironworks.

YV ▶ abbreviation for Venezuela (international vehicle registration).

YWCA ▶ noun a welfare movement with branches in many countries that began in Britain in 1855.
■ a hostel run by this association.
– ORIGIN abbreviation of *Young Women's Christian Association*.

Zz

Z¹ /zɛd, US ziː/ (also **z**) ▶ **noun** (pl. **Zs** or **Z's**) **1** the twenty-sixth letter of the alphabet.
■denoting the next after Y in a set of items, categories, etc. ■ denoting a third unknown or unspecified person or thing: *X sold a car to Y (a car dealer) who in turn sold it to Z (a finance company)*. ■(usu. **z**) the third unknown quantity in an algebraic expression. [ORIGIN: the introduction of *x*, *y*, and *z* as symbols of unknown quantities is due to Descartes (see **X¹**).] ■ (usu. **z**) denoting the third axis in a three-dimensional system of coordinates: [in combination] *the z-axis.*
2 a shape like that of a capital Z: [in combination] *the same old Z-shaped crack in the paving stone.*
3 used in repeated form to represent the sound of buzzing or snoring.
– PHRASES **catch some** (or **a few**) **Zs** informal, chiefly N. Amer. get some sleep.

Z² ▶ **abbreviation for** Zambia (international vehicle registration).
▶ **symbol for** Chemistry atomic number.

ZA ▶ **abbreviation for** South Africa (international vehicle registration).
– ORIGIN from Afrikaans *Zuid Afrika.*

zabaglione /ˌzabaˈljəʊni/ ▶ **noun** [mass noun] an Italian sweet made of whipped and heated egg yolks, sugar, and Marsala wine, served hot or cold.
– ORIGIN Italian.

Zabrze /ˈzabʒə/ an industrial and mining city in Upper Silesia, southern Poland; pop. 205,000 (1990). From 1915 to 1945 it was a German city bearing the name Hindenburg, after the Field Marshal.

Zacatecas /ˌzakəˈteɪkəs, Spanish sakaˈtekas, θaka-/ a state of north central Mexico.
■its capital, a silver-mining city situated at an altitude of 2,500 m (8,200 ft); pop. 165,000 (1980).

zaffre /ˈzafə/ (also **zaffer**) ▶ **noun** [mass noun] impure cobalt oxide, formerly used to make smalt and blue enamels.
– ORIGIN mid 17th cent.: from Italian *zaffera* or French *safre.*

zaftig /ˈzaftɪg/ (also **zoftig**) ▶ **adjective** N. Amer. informal (of a woman) having a full, rounded figure; plump.
– ORIGIN 1930s: Yiddish, from German *saftig* 'juicy'.

zag ▶ **noun** a sharp change of direction in a zigzag course: *we travelled in a series of zigs and zags.*
▶ **verb** (**zagged**, **zagging**) [no obj.] make a sharp change of direction: *a long path zigged and zagged through the woods.*
– ORIGIN late 18th cent.: shortening of ZIGZAG.

Zagazig /ˈzagəzɪg/ (also **Zaqaziq**) a city in the Nile delta, northern Egypt; pop. 279,000 (1991).

Zagreb /ˈzaːɡrɛb/ the capital of Croatia; pop. 706,700 (1991).

Zagros Mountains /ˈzagrɒs/ a range of mountains in western Iran, rising to 4,548 m (14,921 ft) at Zard Kuh. Most of Iran's oilfields lie along the western foothills.

zaibatsu /zʌɪˈbatsuː/ ▶ **noun** (pl. same) a large Japanese business conglomerate.
– ORIGIN Japanese, from *zai* 'wealth' + *batsu* 'clique'.

Zaire /zʌɪˈɪə/ (also **Zaïre**) a large equatorial country in central Africa with a short coastline on the Atlantic Ocean; pop. 38,473,000 (est. 1991); languages, French (official), Kongo, Lingala, Swahili, and other languages; capital, Kinshasa. Official name (from 1997) DEMOCRATIC REPUBLIC OF CONGO.

Zaire is a former Belgian colony, which was known as the Congo Free State (1885–1908) and the Belgian Congo (1908–60). Independence in 1960 was followed by civil war and UN intervention. General Mobutu seized control in a coup in 1965, changing the name of the country from the Republic of the Congo to Zaire in 1971, and remained in power until he was overthrown in 1997 by Laurent Kabila, who changed the country's name again. The country experienced a huge influx of refugees following the violence in Rwanda in 1994.

– DERIVATIVES **Zairean** /-ˈɪərɪən/ (also **Zairian**) adjective & noun.

zaire /zʌɪˈɪə/ ▶ **noun** (pl. same) the basic monetary unit of Zaire (Democratic Republic of Congo), equal to 100 makuta.
– ORIGIN from *Zaire*, a local name for the Congo River in central Africa.

Zaire River a major river of central Africa, which rises as the Lualaba in northern Zaire and flows 4,630 km (2,880 miles) westwards, then south-westwards to form the border between the Congo and Zaire, before emptying into the Atlantic. Also called the CONGO.

zakat /zəˈkɑːt/ ▶ **noun** [mass noun] obligatory payment made annually under Islamic law on certain kinds of property and used for charitable and religious purposes.
– ORIGIN via Persian and Urdu from Arabic *zakā(t)* 'almsgiving'.

Zakinthos /ˈzakɪnθɒs/ (also **Zakynthos**) a Greek island off the SW coast of mainland Greece, in the Ionian Sea, one of the Ionian Islands; pop. 32,750 (1991). Also called ZANTE.

Zakopane /ˌzakɔˈpɑːneɪ/ a winter-sports resort in the Tatra Mountains of southern Poland; pop. 28,630 (1990).

zakuska /zaˈkuːska/ (also **zakouska**) ▶ **noun** (pl. **zakuski** or **zakuskas**) a substantial Russian hors d'oeuvre item such as caviar sandwiches or vegetables with sour cream dip, all served with vodka.
– ORIGIN Russian.

zalcitabine /zalˈsɪtəbiːn/ ▶ **noun** another term for DIDEOXYCYTIDINE.
– ORIGIN 1990s: from *zal-* (of unknown origin) + -citabine apparently formed by arbitrary alteration of CYTIDINE.

Zambezi /zamˈbiːzi/ a river of East Africa, which rises in NW Zambia and flows for 2,560 km (1,600 miles) southwards through Angola and Zaire (Democratic Republic of Congo) to the Victoria Falls, turning eastwards along the border between Zambia and Zimbabwe, before crossing Mozambique and entering the Indian Ocean.

Zambia /ˈzambɪə/ a landlocked country in central Africa, divided from Zimbabwe by the Zambezi River; pop. 8,373,000 (est. 1991); languages, English (official), various Bantu languages; capital, Lusaka.

Formerly the British protectorate of Northern Rhodesia, Zambia became an independent republic within the Commonwealth in 1964, under Kenneth Kaunda (President 1964–91). Zambia's economy was adversely affected by its involvement in the Zimbabwe independence struggle (1965–79).

– DERIVATIVES **Zambian** adjective & noun.

Zamboanga /ˌzambəʊˈaŋɡə/ a port on the west coast of Mindanao, in the southern Philippines; pop. 442,000 (1990).

zambra /ˈzambrə/ ▶ **noun** a kind of flamenco dance.
– ORIGIN late 17th cent.: Spanish.

zami /ˈzami/ ▶ **noun** W. Indian a lesbian.
– ORIGIN French Creole, from French *les amis* 'friends'.

zamia /ˈzeɪmɪə/ (Austral. also **zamia palm**) ▶ **noun** an American or Australian cycad, some kinds of which produce roots or seeds that are edible after careful preparation.
● Genera *Zamia* (of America) and *Macrozamia* (of Australia), family Zamiaceae.
– ORIGIN early 19th cent.: modern Latin, from *zamiae*, misreading (in Pliny) of *azaniae* 'pine cones'.

zamindar /zəˈmiːndɑː/ ▶ **noun** Indian a landowner, especially one who leases his land to tenant farmers.
– ORIGIN via Urdu from Persian *zamīndār*, from *zamīn* 'land' + -*dār* 'holder'.

zamindari /zəˈmiːndəri, ˌzəmiːnˈdɑːri/ (also **zemindari** or **zamindary**) ▶ **noun** [mass noun] Indian historical the system under which zamindars held land.
■the office or territory of a zamindar.
– ORIGIN Urdu.

Zande /ˈzandi/ (also **Azande** /aˈzandi/) ▶ **noun** (pl. same or **Azande** /aˈzandi/) **1** a member of a central African people of mixed ethnic origin.
2 [mass noun] the Niger-Congo language of this people, with over a million speakers mainly in northern Zaire (Democratic Republic of Congo) and Sudan.
▶ **adjective** of or relating to this people or their language.
– ORIGIN the name in Zande.

zander /ˈzandə/ ▶ **noun** (pl. same) a large predatory freshwater perch native to northern and central Europe, where it is a valuable food fish. It has been introduced into Britain and western Europe. Also called PIKEPERCH.
● *Stizostedion lucioperca*, family Percidae.
– ORIGIN mid 19th cent.: from German *Zander*.

Zantac /ˈzantak/ ▶ **noun** trademark for RANITIDINE.
– ORIGIN late 20th cent.: probably from Z- + ANTACID.

Zante /ˈzanti/ another name for ZAKINTHOS.

ZANU ▶ **abbreviation for** Zimbabwe African National Union.

Zanuck /ˈzanək/, Darryl F. (1902–79), American film producer; full name *Darryl Francis Zanuck*. He was the controlling executive of Twentieth Century Fox, and its president from 1965 until his retirement in 1971.

ZANU–PF ▶ **abbreviation for** Zimbabwe African National Union–Patriotic Front.

zany ▶ **adjective** (**zanier**, **zaniest**) amusingly unconventional and idiosyncratic: *zany humour.*
▶ **noun** an erratic or eccentric person:
■historical a comic performer partnering a clown, whom he imitated in an amusing way.
– DERIVATIVES **zanily** adverb, **zaniness** noun.
– ORIGIN late 16th cent.: from French *zani* or Italian *zan(n)i*, Venetian form of *Gianni*, *Giovanni* 'John',

b **b**ut | d **d**og | f **f**ew | g **g**et | h **h**e | j **y**es | k **c**at | l **l**eg | m **m**an | n **n**o | p **p**en | r **r**ed | s **s**it | t **t**op | v **v**oice | w **w**e | z **z**oo | ʃ **sh**e | ʒ deci**s**ion | θ **th**in | ð **th**is | ŋ ri**ng** | x lo**ch** | tʃ **ch**ip | dʒ **j**ar

stock name of the servants acting as clowns in the *commedia dell'arte*.

Zanzibar /ˌzanzɪˈbɑː/ an island off the coast of East Africa, part of Tanzania; pop. 640,580 (1988). Under Arab rule from the 17th century, Zanzibar was a prosperous trading port. It became a British protectorate in 1890 and an independent Commonwealth state in 1963, but in the following year the sultan was overthrown and the country became a republic, uniting with Tanganyika to form Tanzania.
– DERIVATIVES **Zanzibari** adjective & noun.

Zaozhuang /zaʊˈʒwaŋ/ (also **Tsao-chuang**) a city in Shandong province, eastern China; pop. 3,191,900 (1990).

zap informal ▶ verb (**zapped**, **zapping**) **1** [with obj.] destroy or obliterate: *zap the enemy's artillery before it can damage your core units* | *it's vital to zap stress fast.* **2** [with obj. and adverbial of direction] cause to move suddenly and rapidly in a specified direction: *the boat zapped us up river.*
■ [no obj., with adverbial of direction] move suddenly and rapidly, especially between television channels or sections of videotape by use of a remote control: *video recorders mean the audience will zap through the ads.*
▶ noun a sudden effect or event that makes a dramatic impact, especially a sudden burst of energy or sound: *the eggs get an extra zap of UV light.*
– ORIGIN 1920s (originally US): imitative.

Zapata /zəˈpɑːtə, Spanish saˈpata, θa-/, Emiliano (1879–1919), Mexican revolutionary. Zapata attempted to implement his programme of agrarian reform by means of guerrilla warfare. From 1914 he and Pancho Villa fought against the regimes of General Huerta and Venustiano Carranza.

zapateado /zaˌpatɪˈɑːdəʊ/ ▶ noun (pl. **-os**) a flamenco dance with rhythmic stamping of the feet.
– ORIGIN mid 19th cent.: Spanish, from *zapato* 'shoe'.

Zaporizhzhya /ˌzapɒˈrɪʒjə/ an industrial city of Ukraine, on the Dnieper River; pop. 891,000 (1990). It developed as a major industrial centre after the construction of a hydroelectric dam in 1932. Russian name **ZAPOROZHYE** /zəpɑˈrɔʒjɛ/; former name (until 1921) **ALEKSANDROVSK**.

Zapotec /ˈzapɒtɛk/ ▶ noun (pl. same or **Zapotecs**) **1** a member of an American Indian people living in and around Oaxaca in southern Mexico. **2** [mass noun] the Otomanguean language of this people, with some 300,000 speakers.
▶ adjective of or relating to the Zapotec or their language.
– ORIGIN from Spanish *zapoteco*, from Nahuatl *tzapoteca*, plural of *tzapotecatl*, literally 'person of the place of the sapodilla'.

Zappa /ˈzapə/, Frank (1940–93), American rock singer, musician, and songwriter. In 1965 he formed the Mothers of Invention, who combined psychedelic rock with elements of jazz and satire. In Zappa's later career he often mixed flowing guitar improvisations with scatological humour.

zapper ▶ noun informal **1** a remote control for a television, video, or other piece of electronic equipment. **2** N. Amer. an electronic device used for killing insects: *a bug zapper.*

zappy ▶ adjective (**zappier**, **zappiest**) informal lively; energetic: *Radio 4's zappiest chat show.*

ZAPU /ˈzɑːpuː/ ▶ abbreviation for Zimbabwe African People's Union.

Zaqaziq variant spelling of **ZAGAZIG**.

Zaragoza /ˌθaraˈɡoθa, ˌsaraˈɡosa/ Spanish name for **SARAGOSSA**.

Zarathustra /ˌzaraˈθʊstrə/ the Avestan name for the Persian prophet Zoroaster.
– DERIVATIVES **Zarathustrian** adjective & noun.

zarda /ˈzɑːdɑː/ ▶ noun [mass noun] Indian chewing tobacco flavoured with spices.
– ORIGIN from Persian and Urdu *zardah*, from Persian *zard* 'yellow'.

zari /ˈʒɑːriː/ ▶ noun [mass noun] [usu. as modifier] a type of gold thread used decoratively on Indian clothing.
– ORIGIN from Urdu *zarī*, from Persian *zar* 'gold'.

Zaria /ˈzɑːrɪə/ a city in northern Nigeria; pop. 345,200 (1991).

zariba /zəˈriːbə/ (also **zareba**) ▶ noun (in Sudan and neighbouring countries) a thorn fence fortifying a camp or village.
– ORIGIN from Arabic *zarība* 'cattle pen'.

Zarqa /ˈzɑːkə/ (also **Az Zarqa**) a city in north-western Jordan; pop. 359,000 (1991).

zarzuela /θaːˈθweɪlə, Spanish θarˈθwela, sarˈswela/ ▶ noun **1** a Spanish traditional form of musical comedy. **2** [mass noun] a Spanish dish of various kinds of seafood cooked in a rich sauce.
– ORIGIN Spanish, apparently from a place name.

Zatopek /ˈzatəpɛk/, Emil (1922–2000), Czech long-distance runner. In the 1952 Olympic Games he won gold medals in the 5,000 metres, 10,000 metres, and marathon.

zax ▶ noun variant spelling of **SAX**².

zazen /zɑːˈzɛn/ ▶ noun [mass noun] Zen meditation, usually conducted in the lotus position.
– ORIGIN Japanese, from *za* 'sitting' + *zen* (see **ZEN**).

Z boson ▶ noun another term for **Z PARTICLE**.

Z-DNA ▶ noun [mass noun] Biochemistry DNA in which the double helix has a left-handed rather than the usual right-handed twist and the sugar phosphate backbone follows a zigzag course.

zeal ▶ noun [mass noun] great energy or enthusiasm in pursuit of a cause or an objective: *his zeal for privatization* | *Laura brought a missionary zeal to her work.*
– ORIGIN late Middle English: via ecclesiastical Latin from Greek *zēlos*.

Zealand /ˈziːlənd/ the principal island of Denmark, situated between the Jutland peninsula and the southern tip of Sweden. Its chief city is Copenhagen. Danish name **SJÆLLAND**.

zealot /ˈzɛlət/ ▶ noun a person who is fanatical and uncompromising in pursuit of their religious, political, or other ideals.
■ (**Zealot**) historical a member of an ancient Jewish sect aiming at a world Jewish theocracy and resisting the Romans until AD 70.
– DERIVATIVES **zealotry** noun.
– ORIGIN mid 16th cent. (in the sense 'member of an ancient Jewish sect'): via ecclesiastical Latin from Greek *zēlōtēs*, from *zēloun* 'be jealous', from *zēlos* (see **ZEAL**).

zealous /ˈzɛləs/ ▶ adjective having or showing zeal: *the council was extremely zealous in the application of the regulations.*
– DERIVATIVES **zealously** adverb, **zealousness** noun.
– ORIGIN early 16th cent.: from a medieval Latin derivative of Latin *zelus* 'zeal, jealousy'.

zebec ▶ noun variant spelling of **XEBEC**.

zebra /ˈzɛbrə, ˈziːbrə/ ▶ noun **1** an African wild horse with black-and-white stripes and an erect mane.
● Genus *Equus*, family Equidae: three species, in particular the **common zebra** (*E. burchellii*). See also **QUAGGA**.
2 a large butterfly with pale bold stripes on a dark background, in particular:
● a yellow and black American butterfly (*Heliconius charitonius*, subfamily Heliconiinae, family Nymphalidae). ● (also **Malayan zebra**) a black and white Asian butterfly (*Graphium delesserti*, family Papilionidae).
3 (also **zebra fish**) S. African a silvery-gold sea bream with vertical black stripes.
● *Diplodus cervinus*, family Sparidae.
– ORIGIN early 17th cent.: from Italian, Spanish, or Portuguese, originally in the sense 'wild ass', perhaps ultimately from Latin *equiferus*, from *equus* 'horse' + *ferus* 'wild'.

zebra crossing ▶ noun Brit. an area of road painted with broad white stripes, where vehicles must stop if pedestrians wish to cross.

zebra finch ▶ noun a small Australian waxbill with black and white stripes on the face, popular as a cage bird.
● *Poephila guttata*, family Estrildidae.

zebra mussel ▶ noun a small freshwater bivalve mollusc with zigzag markings on the shell, sometimes becoming a pest due to the blocking of water pipes.
● *Dreissena polymorpha*, family Dreissenidae.

zebra plant ▶ noun a Brazilian calathea with leaves which are horizontally banded in light and dark green and purple.
● *Calathea zebrina*, family Marantaceae.

zebra spider ▶ noun a small European jumping spider with black and white stripes.
● *Salticus scenicus*, family Salticidae.

zebrawood ▶ noun any of a number of tropical trees which produce ornamental striped timber that is used chiefly in cabinetmaking.
● Species in several families, such as *Connarus guianensis* (family Connaraceae) of Guyana, and *Diospyros marmorata* (family Ebenaceae) of the Andaman Islands.

zebu /ˈziːbuː/ ▶ noun another term for **BRAHMIN** (in sense 3).
– ORIGIN late 18th cent.: from French *zébu*, of unknown origin.

Zebulun /ˈzɛbjʊlən/ (also **Zebulon**) (in the Bible) a Hebrew patriarch, son of Jacob and Leah (Gen. 30:20).
■ the tribe of Israel traditionally descended from him.

Zech. ▶ abbreviation for Zechariah (in biblical references).

Zechariah /ˌzɛkəˈrʌɪə/ a Hebrew minor prophet of the 6th century BC.
■ a book of the Bible including his prophecies.

zed ▶ noun Brit. the letter Z.
– ORIGIN late Middle English: from French *zède*, via late Latin from Greek *zēta* (see **ZETA**).

Zedekiah /ˌzɛdɪˈkʌɪə/ (in the Bible) the last king of Judaea, who rebelled against Nebuchadnezzar and was carried off to Babylon into captivity (2 Kings 24–5, 2 Chron. 36).

zedoary /ˈzɛdəʊəri/ ▶ noun an Indian plant related to turmeric, with an aromatic rhizome.
● *Curcuma zedoaria*, family Zingiberaceae.
■ [mass noun] a ginger-like substance made from this rhizome, used in medicine, perfumery, and dyeing.
– ORIGIN late Middle English: from medieval Latin *zedoarium*, from Persian *zadwār*.

zee ▶ noun US the letter Z.
– ORIGIN late 17th cent.: variant of **ZED**.

Zeebrugge /ˈziːbrʊɡə, ˈzeɪ-/ a seaport on the coast of Belgium, linked by canal to Bruges.

Zeeland /ˈziːlənd, ˈzeɪ-/ an agricultural province of the south-western Netherlands, at the estuary of the Maas and Scheldt Rivers; capital, Middelburg.

Zeeman effect /ˈziːmən, ˈzeɪ-/ ▶ noun [mass noun] Physics the splitting of the spectrum line into several components by the application of a magnetic field.
– ORIGIN late 19th cent.: named after Pieter *Zeeman* (1865–1943), Dutch physicist.

zeera /ˈʒɪːrɑː/ ▶ noun variant spelling of **JEERA**.

Zeffirelli /ˌzɛfəˈrɛli, Italian dzeffiˈrɛlli/, Franco (b.1923), Italian film and theatre director; born *Gianfranco Corsi*. His operatic productions are noted for the opulence of their sets and costumes. Notable films: *Romeo and Juliet* (1968), *Brother Sun, Sister Moon* (1973), and the TV film *Jesus of Nazareth* (1977).

zein /ˈziːɪn/ ▶ noun [mass noun] Biochemistry the principal protein of maize.
– ORIGIN early 19th cent.: from modern Latin *Zea* (genus name of maize) + **-IN**¹.

Zeiss /zʌɪs, German tsaɪs/, Carl (1816–88), German optical instrument-maker. He established a workshop in Jena in 1846, which developed into the company which bears his name today.

zeitgeber /ˈzʌɪtɡeɪbə/ ▶ noun Physiology a cue given by the environment to reset the internal body clock.
– ORIGIN mid 20th cent.: from German *Zeitgeber*, from *Zeit* 'time' + *Geber* 'giver'.

zeitgeist /ˈzʌɪtɡʌɪst/ ▶ noun [in sing.] the defining spirit or mood of a particular period of history as shown by the ideas and beliefs of the time: *the story captured the zeitgeist of the late 1960s.*
– ORIGIN mid 19th cent.: from German *Zeitgeist*, from *Zeit* 'time' + *Geist* 'spirit'.

Zen (also **Zen Buddhism**) ▶ noun [mass noun] a Japanese school of Mahayana Buddhism emphasizing the value of meditation and intuition rather than ritual worship or study of scriptures.

Zen Buddhism was introduced to Japan from China in the 12th century, and has had a profound cultural influence. The aim of Zen is to achieve sudden enlightenment (satori) through meditation in a seated posture (zazen), usually under the guidance of a teacher and often using paradoxical statements (koans) to transcend rational thought.

– DERIVATIVES **Zenist** (also **Zennist**) noun (rare).
– ORIGIN Japanese, literally 'meditation', from Chinese *chán* 'quietude', from Sanskrit *dhyāna* 'meditation'.

zenana /zɛˈnɑːnə/ ▶ noun (in India and Iran) the part of a house for the seclusion of women.

– ORIGIN from Persian and Urdu *zanānah*, from *zan* 'woman'.

Zend /zɛnd/ ▶ **noun** an interpretation of the Avesta, each Zend being part of the Zend-Avesta.
– ORIGIN from Persian *zand* 'interpretation'.

Zend-Avesta ▶ **noun** the Zoroastrian sacred writings, comprising the Avesta (the text) and Zend (the commentary).

Zener /'zi:nə/ (in full **Zener diode**) ▶ **noun** Electronics a form of semiconductor diode in which at a critical reverse voltage a large reverse current can flow.
– ORIGIN 1950s: named after Clarence M. *Zener* (1905–93), American physicist.

Zener cards /'zi:nə/ ▶ **noun** a set of 25 cards each with one of five different symbols, used in ESP research.
– ORIGIN 1930s: named after Karl E. *Zener* (1903–61), American psychologist.

zenith /'zɛnɪθ/ ▶ **noun** [in sing.] the highest point reached by a celestial or other object: *the sun was well past the zenith | the missile reached its zenith and fell.*
■ the point in the sky or celestial sphere directly above an observer. The opposite of **NADIR**. ■ the time at which something is most powerful or successful: *in 1977, punk was at its zenith.*
– DERIVATIVES **zenithal** adjective.
– ORIGIN late Middle English: from Old French or medieval Latin *cenit*, based on Arabic *samt* (*ar-ra's*) 'path (over the head)'.

zenithal projection ▶ **noun** a map projection in which a part of the globe is projected on to a plane tangential to the centre of the part, showing the correct directions of all points from the centre.

Zeno[1] /'zi:nəʊ/ (*fl.* 5th century BC), Greek philosopher. A member of the Eleatic school, he defended Parmenides' theories by formulating paradoxes which appeared to demonstrate the impossibility of motion, one of which shows that once Achilles has given a tortoise a start he can never overtake it, since each time he arrives where it was, it has already moved on.

Zeno[2] /'zi:nəʊ/ (*c.*335–*c.*263 BC), Greek philosopher, founder of Stoicism; known as **Zeno of Citium**. He founded the school of Stoic philosophy (*c.*300) (see **STOICISM**), but all that remains of his treatises are fragments of quotations.

Zenobia /zɛ'nəʊbɪə/ (3rd century AD), queen of Palmyra *c.*267–272. She conquered Egypt and much of Asia Minor. When she proclaimed her son emperor, the Roman emperor Aurelian attacked, defeated, and captured her.

zeolite /'zi:əlʌɪt/ ▶ **noun** any of a large group of minerals consisting of hydrated aluminosilicates of sodium, potassium, calcium, and barium. They can be readily dehydrated and rehydrated, and are used as cation exchangers and molecular sieves.
– DERIVATIVES **zeolitic** /-'lɪtɪk/ adjective.
– ORIGIN late 18th cent.: from Swedish and German *zeolit*, from Greek *zein* 'to boil' + **-LITE** (from their characteristic swelling when heated in the laboratory).

Zeph. ▶ **abbreviation for** Zephaniah (in biblical references).

Zephaniah /ˌzɛfə'nʌɪə/ a Hebrew minor prophet of the 7th century BC.
■ a book of the Bible containing his prophecies.

zephyr /'zɛfə/ ▶ **noun** **1** poetic/literary a soft gentle breeze.
2 [mass noun] historical a fine cotton gingham.
■ [count noun] a very light article of clothing.
– ORIGIN late Old English *zefferus*, denoting a personification of the west wind, via Latin from Greek *zephuros* '(god of the) west wind'. Sense 1 dates from the late 17th cent.

Zeppelin[1] /'zɛp(ə)lɪn/, Ferdinand (Adolf August Heinrich), Count von (1838–1917), German aviation pioneer. An army officer until his retirement in 1890, he devoted the rest of his life to the development of the dirigible airship named after him.

Zeppelin[2] /'zɛp(ə)lɪn/ ▶ **noun** historical a large German dirigible airship of the early 20th century, long and cylindrical in shape and with a rigid framework. Zeppelins were used during the First World War for reconnaissance and bombing, and after the war as passenger transports until the 1930s.

zepto- /'zɛptəʊ/ ▶ **combining form** (used in units of measurement) denoting a factor of 10^{-21}: *zeptosecond*.
– ORIGIN adapted from **SEPTI-**, on the pattern of combining forms such as *peta-* and *exa-*.

Zermatt /'zɜ:mat, German tsɛʁ'mat/ an Alpine ski resort and mountaineering centre near the Matterhorn, in southern Switzerland.

zero /'zɪərəʊ/ ▶ **cardinal number** (pl. **-os**) no quantity or number; nought; the figure 0: *figures from zero to nine | you've left off a zero—it should be five hundred million.*
■ a point on a scale or instrument from which a positive or negative quantity is reckoned: *the gauge dropped to zero* | [as modifier] *a zero rate of interest.* ■ the temperature corresponding to 0° on the Celsius scale (32° Fahrenheit), marking the freezing point of water: *the temperature was below zero.* ■ [usu. as modifier] Linguistics the absence of an actual word or morpheme to realize a syntactic or morphological phenomenon: *the zero plural in 'three sheep'.* ■ the lowest possible amount or level; nothing at all: *I rated my chances as zero.* ■ short for **ZERO HOUR**. ■ informal a worthless or contemptibly undistinguished person: *her husband is an absolute zero.*
▶ **verb** (**-oes**, **-oed**) [with obj.] **1** adjust (an instrument) to zero: *zero the counter when the tape has rewound.*
2 set the sights of (a gun) for firing.
– ORIGIN early 17th cent.: from French *zéro* or Italian *zero*, via Old Spanish from Arabic *ṣifr* 'cipher'.
▶ **zero in** take aim with a gun or missile: *jet fighters* **zeroed in on** *the rebels' positions.* ■ focus one's attention: *they* **zeroed in on** *the clues he gave away about.*

zero-based (also **zero-base**) ▶ **adjective** Finance (of a budget or budgeting) having each item costed anew, rather than in relation to its size or status in the previous budget.

zero-coupon bond ▶ **noun** a bond that is issued at a deep discount to its face value but pays no interest.

zero crossing ▶ **noun** Mathematics the point at which a function crosses the horizontal axis as its value passes through zero and changes sign.

zero-emission ▶ **adjective** denoting a road vehicle that emits no pollutants from its exhaust.

zero G ▶ **abbreviation for** zero gravity.

zero gravity ▶ **noun** [mass noun] Physics the state or condition in which there is no apparent force of gravity acting on a body, either because the force is locally weak, or because both the body and its surroundings are freely and equally accelerating under the force.

zero-graze ▶ **verb** [with obj.] [usu. as noun **zero-grazing**] feed (cattle) with cut grass brought to them instead of putting them out to pasture.

zero hour ▶ **noun** the time at which a planned operation, typically a military one, is set to begin.

zero option ▶ **noun** a disarmament proposal for the total removal of certain types of weapons on both sides.

zero-point ▶ **adjective** Physics relating to or denoting properties and phenomena in quantized systems at absolute zero.

zero-rated ▶ **adjective** Finance, Brit. denoting goods or services that are taxable for VAT, but with a tax rate of zero.
– DERIVATIVES **zero rating** noun.

zero-sum ▶ **adjective** [attrib.] (of a game or situation) in which whatever is gained by one side is lost by the other.

zeroth /'zɪərəʊθ/ ▶ **adjective** [attrib.] immediately preceding what is regarded as first in a series.
– ORIGIN late 19th cent.: from **ZERO** + **-TH**[1].

zero tolerance ▶ **noun** [mass noun] non-acceptance of anti-social behaviour, typically by strict and uncompromising application of the law.

zest ▶ **noun** [mass noun] **1** great enthusiasm and energy: *they campaigned with zest and intelligence* | [in sing.] *she had a great* **zest for** *life.*
■ a quality of excitement and piquancy: *I used to try to beat past records to add zest to my monotonous job.*
2 the outer coloured part of the peel of citrus fruit, used as flavouring.
– DERIVATIVES **zestful** adjective, **zestfully** adverb, **zestfulness** noun, **zesty** adjective.
– ORIGIN late 15th cent.: from French *zeste* 'orange or lemon peel', of unknown origin.

zester ▶ **noun** a kitchen utensil for removing fine shreds of zest from citrus fruit.

zeta /'zi:tə/ ▶ **noun** the sixth letter of the Greek alphabet (**Z**, **ζ**), transliterated as 'z'.
■ (**Zeta**) [followed by Latin genitive] Astronomy the sixth star in a constellation: *Zeta Ursae Majoris.*
– ORIGIN Greek.

zeta potential ▶ **noun** Chemistry the potential difference existing between the surface of a solid particle immersed in a conducting liquid (e.g. water) and the bulk of the liquid.

zetetic /zɪ'tɛtɪk/ ▶ **adjective** rare proceeding by inquiry.
– ORIGIN mid 17th cent.: from Greek *zētētikos*, from *zētein* 'seek'.

zetta- /'zɛtə/ ▶ **combining form** (used in units of measurement) denoting a factor of 10^{21}: *zettahertz*.
– ORIGIN apparently adapted from Italian *sette* 'seven' (see also **ZEPTO-**).

zeugma /'zju:gmə/ ▶ **noun** a figure of speech in which a word applies to two others in different senses (e.g. *John and his driving licence expired last week*) or to two others of which it semantically suits only one (e.g. *with weeping eyes and hearts*). Compare with **SYLLEPSIS**.
– DERIVATIVES **zeugmatic** adjective.
– ORIGIN late Middle English: via Latin from Greek, from *zeugnunai* 'to yoke'; related to *zugon* 'yoke'.

Zeus /zju:s/ Greek Mythology the supreme god, the son of Cronus (whom he dethroned) and Rhea, and husband of Hera. Zeus was the protector and ruler of humankind, the dispenser of good and evil, and the god of weather and atmospheric phenomena (such as rain and thunder). Roman equivalent **JUPITER**.
– ORIGIN Greek: related to Sanskrit *dyauḥ* 'sky'.

Zeuxis /'zju:ksɪs/ (*fl.* late 5th century BC), Greek painter, born at Heraclea in southern Italy. His works are known only through the reports of ancient writers, who make reference to monochrome techniques and his use of shading to create an illusion of depth, while his verisimilitude is the subject of many anecdotes.

ZEV ▶ **abbreviation for** zero-emission vehicle.

Zhangjiakou /ˌdʒaŋdʒjɑ:'kəʊ/ (also **Changchiakow**) a city situated on the Great Wall in Hebei province, NE China; pop. 719,600 (1990). Mongolian name **KALGAN**.

Zhanjiang /dʒan'dʒjaŋ/ (also **Chan-chiang**) a port in Guangdong province, southern China; pop. 1,048,700 (1990).

Zhdanov /'ʒdɑ:nɒf/ former name (1948–89) for **MARIUPOL**.
– ORIGIN named after the Soviet Politburo official Andrei *Zhdanov*, the defender of Leningrad during the siege of 1941–4.

Zhejiang /dʒɛ'dʒjaŋ/ (also **Chekiang**) a province of eastern China; capital, Hangzhou.

Zhengzhou /dʒɛŋ'dʒəʊ/ (also **Chengchow**) the capital of Henan province, in NE central China; pop. 1,660,000 (1990).

Zhenjiang /dʒɛn'dʒjaŋ/ (also **Chen-chiang**, **Chinkiang**) a port in Jiangsu province, on the Yangtze River, eastern China; pop. 1,280,000 (1990).

Zhitomir /ʒi'tomʲir/ Russian name for **ZHYTOMYR**.

zho ▶ **noun** variant spelling of **DZO**.

Zhongshan /dʒɒŋ'ʃan/ (also **Chung-shan**) a city in Guangdong province, SE China; pop. 1,073,000 (est. 1986).

Zhou /dʒəʊ/ (also **Chou**) a dynasty which ruled in China from the 11th century BC to 256 BC.

> The dynasty's rule is commonly divided into **Western Zhou** (which ruled from a capital in the west of the region near Xian until 771 BC) and **Eastern Zhou** (which ruled after 771 BC from a capital based in the east). The rule of the Eastern Zhou, although weak and characterized by strife, saw the Chinese classical age of Confucius and Lao-tzu.

Zhou Enlai /ˌdʒəʊ ɛn'lʌɪ/ (also **Chou En-lai**) (1898–1976), Chinese Communist statesman, Prime Minister of China 1949–76. A founder of the Chinese Communist Party, he organized a Communist workers' revolt in 1927 in Shanghai in support of the Kuomintang forces surrounding the city. As Premier, he was a moderating influence during the Cultural Revolution and presided over the moves towards détente with the US in 1972–3.

Zhukov /'ʒu:kɒf/, Georgi (Konstantinovich) (1896–1974), Soviet military leader, born in Russia. In the course of the Second World War he defeated the Germans at Stalingrad (1943), lifted the siege of

Zhytomyr /ʒɪˈtɒmɪə/ an industrial city in central Ukraine; pop. 296,000 (1990). Russian name **ZHITOMIR**.

Zia ul-Haq /ˌzɪə ʊlˈhak/, Muhammad (1924–88), Pakistani general and statesman, President 1978–88. As Chief of Staff he led the coup which deposed President Zulfikar Bhutto in 1977. He banned all political parties and began to introduce strict Islamic laws.

Zibo /ziːˈbəʊ, dzəˈbəʊ/ (also **Tzu-po**) a city in Shandong province, eastern China; pop. 2,484,200 (1990).

zidovudine /zɪˈdɒvjʊdiːn, -ˈdəʊ-/ ▶ noun [mass noun] Medicine an antiviral drug used in the treatment of Aids. It slows the growth of HIV infection in the body, but is not curative.
● A thymidine derivative; chem. formula: $C_{10}H_{13}N_5O_4$.
– ORIGIN 1980s; arbitrary alteration of **AZIDO-THYMIDINE**.

Ziegfeld /ˈziːɡfɛld/, Florenz (1869–1932), American theatre manager. In 1907 he produced the first of a series of revues in New York, based on those of the Folies-Bergère, entitled the *Ziegfeld Follies*. Among the many famous performers he promoted were W. C. Fields and Fred Astaire.

ziff ▶ noun Austral./NZ informal, dated a beard.
– ORIGIN early 20th cent.: of unknown origin.

ZIF socket ▶ noun a type of socket for mounting electronic devices that is designed not to stress or damage them during insertion.
– ORIGIN late 20th cent.: ZIF, acronym from *zero insertion force*.

zig ▶ noun a sharp change of direction in a zigzag course: *he went round and round in zigs and zags.*
▶ verb (**zigged**, **zigging**) [no obj.] make a sharp change of direction: *we zigged to the right.*
– ORIGIN 1960s: by abbreviation of **ZIGZAG**.

ziggurat /ˈzɪɡʊrat/ ▶ noun (in ancient Mesopotamia) a rectangular stepped tower, sometimes surmounted by a temple. Ziggurats are first attested in the late 3rd millennium BC and probably inspired the biblical story of the Tower of Babel (Gen. 11:1–9).
– ORIGIN from Akkadian *ziqqurratu*.

zigzag ▶ noun a line or course having abrupt alternate right and left turns: *she traced a zigzag on the metal with her finger.*
■ a turn on such a course: *the road descends in a series of sharp zigzags.*
▶ adjective having the form of a zigzag; veering to right and left alternately: *when chased by a predator, some animals take a zigzag course.*
▶ adverb so as to move right and left alternately: *she drives zigzag across the city.*
▶ verb (**zigzagged**, **zigzagging**) [no obj.] have or move along in a zigzag course: *the path zigzagged between dry rises in the land.*
– DERIVATIVES **zigzaggedly** adverb.
– ORIGIN early 18th cent.: from French, from German *Zickzack*, symbolic of alternation of direction, first applied to fortifications.

zilch /zɪltʃ/ informal ▶ pronoun nothing: *I did absolutely zilch.*
▶ determiner not any; no: *the character has zilch class.*
– ORIGIN 1960s: of unknown origin.

zilla /ˈzɪlə/ (also **zillah**) ▶ noun an administrative district in India, containing several parganas.
– ORIGIN from Persian and Urdu *zila'* 'division'.

zillion ▶ cardinal number informal an extremely large number of people or things: *we had zillions of customers.*
– DERIVATIVES **zillionth** adjective.
– ORIGIN 1940s: from Z (perhaps as a symbol of an unknown quantity) + **MILLION**.

zillionaire ▶ noun informal an extremely rich person.

Zimbabwe /zɪmˈbɑːbwi, -weɪ/ a landlocked country in SE Africa, divided from Zambia by the Zambezi River; pop. 10,080,000 (est. 1991); languages, English (official), Shona, Ndebele, and other languages; capital, Harare.

Formerly known as Southern Rhodesia, the country was a self-governing British colony from 1923. In 1965 the white minority government of the colony (then called Rhodesia) issued a unilateral declaration of independence (UDI) under its Prime Minister, Ian Smith. Despite UN sanctions, illegal independence lasted until 1979, when the Lancaster House Agreement led to all-party elections (1980) and black majority rule under Robert Mugabe. The country then became an independent republic and a member of the Commonwealth.

– DERIVATIVES **Zimbabwean** /-wɪən, -weɪən/ adjective & noun.
– ORIGIN from Shona *dzimbabwe* 'walled grave', originally referring to *Great Zimbabwe*, a complex of stone ruins in one of the country's fertile valleys, the remains of a city at the centre of a flourishing civilization in the 14th and 15th centuries.

Zimbabwe African National Union (abbrev.: **ZANU** or **ZANU–PF**) a Zimbabwean political party formed in 1963 as a guerrilla organization and led from 1975 by Robert Mugabe.

Having formed an alliance (called the Patriotic Front) with ZAPU in 1976 to coordinate opposition to white rule, ZANU won a large majority in the first post-independence elections (1980). ZANU and ZAPU ruled Zimbabwe as a coalition until a rift developed between them in 1982; in 1987, however, the parties agreed formally to merge, adopting the name ZANU–PF on merger in 1989.

Zimbabwe African People's Union (abbrev.: **ZAPU**) a Zimbabwean political party formed in 1961 as a guerrilla organization and led by Joshua Nkomo. It merged with ZANU in 1989.

Zimmer /ˈzɪmə/ (also **Zimmer frame**) ▶ noun trademark a kind of walking frame.
– ORIGIN 1950s: from *Zimmer* Orthopaedic Limited, the name of the manufacturer.

zinc ▶ noun [mass noun] the chemical element of atomic number 30, a silvery-white metal which is a constituent of brass and is used for coating (galvanizing) iron and steel to protect against corrosion. (Symbol: **Zn**)
■ [usu. as modifier] galvanized iron or steel, especially as the material of domestic utensils or corrugated roofs: *a zinc roof.*
▶ verb [with obj.] [usu. as adj.] (**zinced** /ˈzɪŋ(k)t/) coat (iron) with zinc or a zinc compound to prevent rust.
– ORIGIN mid 17th cent.: from German *Zink*, of unknown origin.

zinc blende ▶ noun another term for **SPHALERITE**.

zinc chromate ▶ noun [mass noun] a toxic yellow insoluble powder, used as a pigment.
● Chem. formula: $ZnCrO_4$.

zinc finger ▶ noun Biochemistry a finger-like loop of peptides enclosing a bound zinc ion at one end, typically part of a larger protein molecule (in particular one regulating transcription).

zincite /ˈzɪŋkʌɪt/ ▶ noun [mass noun] a rare deep red or orange-yellow mineral consisting chiefly of zinc oxide, occurring typically as granular or foliated masses.
– ORIGIN mid 19th cent.: from **ZINC** + **-ITE**[1].

zinco ▶ noun (pl. **-os**) an etched letterpress printing plate made of zinc.

zinc ointment ▶ noun [mass noun] ointment containing zinc oxide, used for various skin conditions.

zinc white ▶ noun [mass noun] a white pigment consisting of zinc oxide.

zindabad /ˈzɪndɑːbɑːd/ ▶ exclamation Indian used to express approbation: *Pakistan zindabad!*
– ORIGIN from Urdu *zindābād* 'may (a person) live!'.

'zine ▶ noun informal a magazine, especially a fanzine.

zineb /ˈzɪnɛb/ ▶ noun [mass noun] a white compound used as a fungicidal powder on vegetables and fruit.
● Alternative name: **zinc ethylene bisdithiocarbamate**; chem. formula: $C_4H_6N_2S_4Zn$.
– ORIGIN 1950s; from *zin(c)* + *e(thylene)* + *b(is-)* from the systematic name.

Zinfandel /ˈzɪnfand(ə)l/ ▶ noun [mass noun] a variety of wine grape grown in California.
■ a red or blush dry wine made from this grape.
– ORIGIN of unknown origin.

zing informal ▶ noun [mass noun] energy, enthusiasm, or liveliness: *he was expected to add some zing to the lacklustre team.*
▶ verb [no obj., with adverbial of direction] move swiftly: *he could send an arrow zinging through the air.*
■ [with obj.] US attack or criticize sharply: *he zinged the budget deal in interviews with journalists.*
– DERIVATIVES **zingy** adjective.

– ORIGIN early 20th cent.: imitative.

zinger ▶ noun informal, chiefly US a striking or amusing remark: *open a speech with a zinger.*
■ an outstanding person or thing: *a zinger of a shot.*

Zinjanthropus /zɪnˈdʒanθrəpəs/ ▶ noun a genus name sometimes applied to Nutcracker man.
– ORIGIN 1950s: modern Latin, from Arabic *Zinj*, the early medieval name for East Africa, + Greek *anthrōpos* 'man'.

Zinnemann /ˈzɪnəmən/, Fred (1907–97), Austrian-born American film director. He joined MGM in 1937 and won Oscars for the short *That Mothers Might Live* (1938) and the feature films *From Here to Eternity* (1953) and *A Man For All Seasons* (1966).

zinnia /ˈzɪnɪə/ ▶ noun an American plant of the daisy family, which is widely cultivated for its bright showy flowers.
● Genus *Zinnia*, family Compositae.
– ORIGIN modern Latin, named after Johann G. *Zinn* (1727–59), German physician and botanist.

Zion /ˈzʌɪən/ (also **Sion**) ▶ noun the hill of Jerusalem on which the city of David was built.
■ the citadel of ancient Jerusalem. ■ Jerusalem. ■ (in Christian thought) the heavenly city or kingdom of heaven. ■ the Jewish people or religion. ■ the Christian Church. ■ a Nonconformist chapel.
– ORIGIN Old English, from ecclesiastical Latin *Sion*, from Hebrew *ṣiyōn*.

Zionism /ˈzʌɪənɪz(ə)m/ ▶ noun [mass noun] **1** a movement for (originally) the re-establishment and (now) the development and protection of a Jewish nation in what is now Israel. It was established as a political organization in 1897 under Theodor Herzl, and was later led by Chaim Weizmann.
2 (in southern Africa) a religious movement represented by a group of independent Churches which practise a form of Christianity incorporating elements of traditional African beliefs.
■ the beliefs and practices of this movement.
– DERIVATIVES **Zionist** noun & adjective.

zip ▶ noun **1** (also **zip fastener**) chiefly Brit. a device consisting of two flexible strips of metal or plastic with interlocking projections closed or opened by pulling a slide along them, used to fasten garments, bags, and other items.
■ [as modifier] denoting something fastened by such a device: *a zip pocket.*
2 [mass noun] informal energy; vigour: *he's full of zip.*
▶ pronoun (also **zippo**) N. Amer. informal nothing at all: *you got zip to do with me and my kind, buddy.*
▶ verb (**zipped**, **zipping**) **1** [with obj.] fasten with a zip: *he zipped up his waterproof.*
■ (**zip someone up**) fasten the zip of a garment that someone is wearing: *he zipped himself up.* ■ Computing compress (a file) so that it takes less space in storage.
2 [no obj., with adverbial of direction] informal move at high speed: *swallows zipped back and forth across the lake.*
■ [with obj. and adverbial] cause to move or be delivered or dealt with rapidly: *he zipped a pass out to his receiver.*
– ORIGIN mid 19th cent.: imitative.

zip code (also **ZIP code**) ▶ noun US a postal code consisting of five or nine digits.
– ORIGIN 1960s: *Zip*, acronym from *zone improvement plan*.

zip gun ▶ noun US informal a cheap home-made or makeshift gun: *I made the zip gun in class out of a toy airplane launcher.*

zipless ▶ adjective informal (of a sexual encounter) brief, uncomplicated, and passionate.
– ORIGIN 1970s: from the phrase *Zipless Fuck*, in Erica Jong's *Fear of Flying.*

ziplock (also trademark **Ziploc**) ▶ adjective denoting a sealable plastic bag with a two-part strip along the opening that can be pressed together and readily reopened.

zipper chiefly US ▶ noun a zip fastener.
▶ verb [with obj.] fasten or provide (something) with a zipper: *he wore a running suit zippered up tight.*

zipperhead ▶ noun US offensive an oriental person.

Zippo ▶ noun (pl. **-os**) trademark a type of cigarette lighter with a hinged lid, using petrol as fuel.
– ORIGIN 1930s: of unknown origin.

zippo ▶ pronoun another term for **ZIP**.

zippy ▶ adjective (**zippier**, **zippiest**) informal bright, fresh, or lively: *a zippy, zingy, almost citrusy tang.*
■ fast or speedy: *the car is zippy around town.*
– DERIVATIVES **zippily** adverb, **zippiness** noun.

zip-up ▶ adjective [attrib.] chiefly Brit. (of a garment, pocket, bag, etc.) able to be fastened with a zip: *a white zip-up jacket.*

zircaloy /ˈzəːkəlɔɪ/ (also **zircalloy**) ▶ **noun** [mass noun] an alloy of zirconium, tin, and other metals, used chiefly as cladding for nuclear reactor fuel.
– ORIGIN 1950s: from **ZIRCONIUM** + **ALLOY**.

zircon /ˈzəːk(ə)n/ ▶ **noun** [mass noun] a mineral occurring as prismatic crystals, typically brown but sometimes in translucent forms of gem quality. It consists of zirconium silicate and is the chief ore of zirconium.
– ORIGIN late 18th cent.: from German *Zirkon*; compare with **JARGON**[2].

zirconia /zəːˈkəʊnɪə/ ▶ **noun** [mass noun] zirconium dioxide, a white solid used in ceramic glazes and refractory coatings, and as a synthetic substitute for diamonds in jewellery.
• Chem. formula: ZrO_2.
– ORIGIN late 18th cent.: from **ZIRCON** + **-IA**[1].

zirconium /zəːˈkəʊnɪəm/ ▶ **noun** [mass noun] the chemical element of atomic number 40, a hard silver-grey metal of the transition series. (Symbol: **Zr**)
– ORIGIN early 19th cent.: modern Latin, from **ZIRCON**.

zit ▶ **noun** informal a spot on the skin.
– ORIGIN 1960s: of unknown origin; apparently originally teenagers' slang in North American English.

zither /ˈzɪðə/ ▶ **noun** a musical instrument consisting of a flat wooden soundbox with numerous strings stretched across it, placed horizontally and played with the fingers and a plectrum. It is used especially in central European folk music.
– DERIVATIVES **zitherist** noun.
– ORIGIN mid 19th cent.: from German, from Latin *cithara* (see **CITTERN**).

ziti /ˈziːti/ ▶ **plural noun** pasta in the form of tubes resembling large macaroni.
– ORIGIN Italian.

zizz informal, chiefly Brit. ▶ **noun** [in sing.] **1** a whizzing or buzzing sound: *there's a nasty zizz from the engine.*
2 a short sleep: *Philip's having a zizz.*
▶ **verb** [no obj.] **1** make a whizzing or buzzing sound: *the banger started zizzing furiously.*
2 doze; sleep: *when everyone inside the building had zizzed off he sneaked inside.*
– ORIGIN early 19th cent.: imitative.

zloty /ˈzlɒti/ ▶ **noun** (pl. same, **zlotys**, or **zloties**) the basic monetary unit of Poland, equal to 100 groszy.
– ORIGIN Polish, literally 'golden'.

Zn ▶ **symbol for** the chemical element zinc.

Zoantharia /ˌzəʊanˈθɛːrɪə/ Zoology a group of coelenterates with polyps that bear more than eight tentacles, including the sea anemones and stony corals.
• Subclass Zoantharia, class Anthozoa.
– DERIVATIVES **zoantharian** noun & adjective.
– ORIGIN modern Latin (plural), from Greek *zōion* 'animal' + *anthos* 'flower'.

zodiac /ˈzəʊdɪak/ ▶ **noun** Astrology a belt of the heavens within about 8° either side of the ecliptic, including all apparent positions of the sun, moon, and most familiar planets. It is divided into twelve equal divisions or signs (Aries, Taurus, Gemini, Cancer, Leo, Virgo, Libra, Scorpio, Sagittarius, Capricorn, Aquarius, Pisces).
■ a representation of the signs of the zodiac or of a similar astrological system.

The supposed significance of the movements of the sun, moon, and planets within the zodiacal band forms the basis of astrology. However, the modern constellations do not represent equal divisions of the zodiac, and the ecliptic now passes through a thirteenth (Ophiuchus). Also, owing to precession, the signs of the zodiac now roughly correspond to the constellations that bear the names of the *preceding* signs.

– DERIVATIVES **zodiacal** /zə(ʊ)ˈdʌɪək(ə)l/ adjective.
– ORIGIN late Middle English: from Old French *zodiaque*, via Latin from Greek *zōidiakos*, from *zōidion* 'sculptured animal figure', diminutive of *zōion* 'animal'.

zodiacal light ▶ **noun** [mass noun] Astronomy a faint elongated cone of light sometimes seen in the night sky, extending from the horizon along the ecliptic. It is thought to be due to the reflection of sunlight from particles of ice and dust within the plane of the solar system.

zodiacal sign ▶ **noun** see **SIGN** (sense 3).

zoetrope /ˈzəʊɪtrəʊp/ ▶ **noun** a 19th-century optical toy consisting of a cylinder with a series of pictures on the inner surface that, when viewed through slits with the cylinder rotating, give an impression of continuous motion. Also called **THAUMATROPE**.
– ORIGIN mid 19th cent.: formed irregularly from Greek *zōē* 'life' + *-tropos* 'turning'.

Zoffany /ˈzɒfəni/, Johann (*c.*1733–1810), German-born painter, resident in England from 1758. Many of his earlier paintings depict scenes from the contemporary theatre and feature the actor David Garrick (e.g. *The Farmer's Return*, 1762).

zoftig /ˈzɒftɪg/ ▶ **adjective** N. Amer. variant spelling of **ZAFTIG**.

Zog I /zɒg/ (1895–1961), Albanian statesman and ruler, Prime Minister 1922–4, President 1925–8, and king 1928–39; full name *Ahmed Bey Zogu*. He initially headed a republican government, proclaiming himself king in 1928. His autocratic rule resulted in relative political stability, but when the country was invaded by Italy in 1939 he went into exile. He abdicated in 1946 after Albania became a Communist state.

Zohar /ˈzəʊhɑː/ ▶ **noun** the chief text of the Jewish Kabbalah, presented as an allegorical or mystical interpretation of the Pentateuch.
– ORIGIN from Hebrew *zōhar*, literally 'light, splendour'.

zoisite /ˈzɔɪsʌɪt/ ▶ **noun** [mass noun] a greyish-white or greyish-green crystalline mineral consisting of a basic silicate of calcium and aluminium.
– ORIGIN early 19th cent.: from the name of Baron S. von Edelstein *Zois* (1747–1819), Austrian scholar, + **-ITE**[1].

zokor /ˈzəʊkɔː/ ▶ **noun** a mole rat of eastern Asia that builds up large food stores in its burrows, found in high-altitude grasslands.
• Genus *Myospalax*, family Muridae: six species.
– ORIGIN a local name in the Altai Mountains.

zol /zɒl/ ▶ **noun** (pl. **zols** or **zolle**) S. African a hand-rolled cigarette, especially of cannabis.
■ [mass noun] cannabis.
– ORIGIN of unknown origin.

Zola /ˈzəʊlə, French zɔla/, Émile (Édouard Charles Antoine) (1840–1902), French novelist and critic. His series of twenty novels collectively entitled *Les Rougon-Macquart* (1871–93), including *Nana* (1880), *Germinal* (1885), and *La Terre* (1887), attempts to show how human behaviour is determined by environment and heredity.

Zollinger–Ellison syndrome /ˌzɒlɪndʒəˈɛlɪs(ə)n/ ▶ **noun** [mass noun] Medicine a condition in which a gastrin-secreting tumour or hyperplasia of the islet cells in the pancreas causes overproduction of gastric acid, resulting in recurrent peptic ulcers.
– ORIGIN 1950s: named after Robert M. *Zollinger* (1903–92) and Edwin H. *Ellison* (1918–70), American physicians.

Zöllner illusion /ˈtsəːlnə/ ▶ **plural noun** an optical illusion in which long parallel lines appear to diverge or converge when crossed by rows of short oblique lines.
– ORIGIN late 19th cent.: named after Johann K. F. *Zöllner* (1834–82), German physicist.

Zollverein /ˈzɒlfəˌrʌɪn, German ˈtsɔlfɛɐˌaɪn/ ▶ **noun** historical the customs union of German states in the 19th century.
– ORIGIN from German *Zoll* 'customs' + *Verein* 'union'.

zombie ▶ **noun** a corpse said to be revived by witchcraft, especially in certain African and Caribbean religions.
■ informal a person who is or appears lifeless, apathetic, or completely unresponsive to their surroundings.
– DERIVATIVES **zombielike** adjective.
– ORIGIN early 19th cent.: of West African origin; compare with Kikongo *zumbi* 'fetish'.

zombify /ˈzɒmbɪfʌɪ/ ▶ **verb** [with obj.] [usu. as adj. **zombified**] informal deprive of energy or vitality: *exhausted, screaming kids and their zombified parents.*

zona pellucida /ˌzəʊnə pɪˈluːsɪdə/ ▶ **noun** (pl. **zonae pellucidae** /ˌzəʊniː pɪˈluːsɪdiː/) Anatomy & Zoology the thick transparent membrane surrounding a mammalian ovum before implantation.
– ORIGIN mid 19th cent.: from Latin, literally 'pellucid girdle'.

zonation /zəʊˈneɪʃ(ə)n/ ▶ **noun** [mass noun] distribution in zones or regions of definite character: *quartz grains can exhibit zonation and rounding.*
■ Ecology the distribution of plants or animals into specific zones according to such parameters as altitude or depth, each characterized by its dominant species.

zone ▶ **noun 1** [usu. with adj. or noun modifier] an area or stretch of land having a particular characteristic, purpose, or use, or subject to particular restrictions: *a pedestrian zone* | figurative *United are still in the relegation zone.*
■ (also **time zone**) a range of longitudes where a common standard time is used. ■ chiefly Botany & Zoology an encircling band or stripe of distinctive colour, texture, or character.
2 archaic a belt or girdle worn round a person's body.
▶ **verb** [with obj.] **1** divide into or assign to zones, in particular:
■ [often as noun **zoning**] divide (a town or stretch of land) into areas subject to particular planning restrictions: *an experimental system of zoning.* ■ designate (a specific area) for use or development in such a manner: *the land is zoned for housing.*
2 archaic encircle as or with a band or stripe.
– DERIVATIVES **zonal** adjective, **zonally** adverb.
– ORIGIN late Middle English: from French, or from Latin *zona* 'girdle', from Greek *zōnē*.
▶ **zone out** US informal fall asleep or lose concentration or consciousness: *I just zoned out for a moment.* [ORIGIN: compare with sense 3 of **ZONED**.]

zoned ▶ **adjective 1** divided into zones, in particular (of land) designated for a particular type of use or development: *zoned housing land.*
2 chiefly Botany & Zoology marked with circles or bands of colour: *strongly zoned leaves.*
3 US informal under the influence of drugs or alcohol: *she's zoned on downers* | *a **zoned-out** hippie.* [ORIGIN: 1970s: blend of **ZONKED** and **STONED**.]

zone plate ▶ **noun** a plate of glass marked out into concentric zones or rings alternately transparent and opaque, used like a lens to bring light to a focus.

zone refining ▶ **noun** [mass noun] a method of purifying a crystalline solid, typically a semiconductor or metal, by causing a narrow molten zone to travel slowly along an otherwise solid rod or bar to one end, at which impurities become concentrated.

zone therapy ▶ **noun** [mass noun] a system of alternative medicine (such as reflexology) in which different parts of the feet or hands are associated with different parts of the body.

zonk informal ▶ **verb 1** [with obj.] hit or strike: *Charley really zonked me.*
2 fall or cause to fall suddenly and heavily asleep or lose consciousness: [no obj.] *I always just **zonk out** and sleep straight through* | [with obj.] *I go rowing because it **zonks** me **out**.*
▶ **exclamation** expressing the sound of a blow or heavy impact: *she let it go and zonk, it was in the water again.*
– ORIGIN 1940s: imitative.

zonked ▶ **adjective** informal under the influence of drugs or alcohol: *the others got zonked on acid* | *a **zonked-out** beach bum.*
■ exhausted; tired out: *we hit the sack, zonked out.*

zonule /ˈzəʊnjuːl/ ▶ **noun** technical, chiefly Anatomy a small zone.

zonure /ˈzəʊnjʊə/ ▶ **noun** another term for **GIRDLED LIZARD**.
– ORIGIN late 19th cent.: from modern Latin *Zonurus* (former genus name), from Greek *zōnē* 'girdle' + *oura* 'tail'.

zoo ▶ **noun** an establishment which maintains a collection of wild animals, typically in a park or gardens, for study, conservation, or display to the public.
■ a situation characterized by confusion and disorder: *it's a zoo in the lobby.*
– ORIGIN mid 19th cent.: abbreviation of **ZOOLOGICAL GARDEN**, originally applied specifically to that of Regent's Park, London.

zoo- ▶ **combining form** of animals; relating to animal life: *zoogeography.*
– ORIGIN from Greek *zōion* 'animal'.

zoogeographical region /ˌzuːə(ʊ)dʒɪə(ʊ)ˈgrafɪk(ə)l, ˌzəʊə(ʊ)-/ ▶ **noun** Zoology each of a number of major areas of the earth having a characteristic fauna (especially mammals). They include the

Palaearctic, Ethiopian, Oriental, Australian, Nearctic, and Neotropical regions. Also called **FAUNAL REGION**.

zoogeography /ˌzuːə(ʊ)dʒɪˈɒɡrəfi, ˌzəʊə(ʊ)-, ˌzuːˈdʒɪ-/ ▶ noun [mass noun] the branch of zoology that deals with the geographical distribution of animals.
– DERIVATIVES **zoogeographer** noun, **zoogeographic** adjective, **zoogeographical** adjective, **zoogeographically** adverb.

zooid /ˈzuːɔɪd, ˈzəʊ-, ˈzuːɪd/ ▶ noun Zoology an animal arising from another by budding or division, especially each of the individuals which make up a colonial organism and typically have different forms and functions.
– DERIVATIVES **zooidal** /zuːˈɔɪd(ə)l, zəʊ-, ˈzuːɪd(ə)l/ adjective.
– ORIGIN mid 19th cent.: from **ZOO-** 'relating to animals' + -**OID**.

zookeeper ▶ noun an animal attendant employed in a zoo.
■ a zoo owner or director.

zoolatry /zuːˈɒlətri, zəʊ-/ ▶ noun [mass noun] rare the worship of animals.

zoological /ˌzuːəˈlɒdʒɪk(ə)l, ˌzəʊə-/ ▶ adjective of or relating to zoology: *zoological classification*.
■ of or relating to animals: *eighty zoological woodcuts*.
– DERIVATIVES **zoologically** adverb.

zoological garden ▶ noun dated a zoo.

zoology /zuːˈɒlədʒi, zəʊ-/ ▶ noun [mass noun] the scientific study of the behaviour, structure, physiology, classification, and distribution of animals.
■ the animal life of a particular area or time: *the zoology of Russia's vast interior*.
– DERIVATIVES **zoologist** noun.
– ORIGIN mid 17th cent.: from modern Latin *zoologia* (see **ZOO-**, **-LOGY**).

zoom ▶ verb [no obj., with adverbial of direction] **1** (especially of a car or aircraft) move or travel very quickly: *we watched the fly zooming about | he jumped into his car and zoomed off.*
■ [no obj.] (of prices) rise sharply: *the share index zoomed by about 136 points.*
2 (of a camera) change smoothly from a long shot to a close-up or vice versa: *the camera zoomed in for a close-up of his face | zoom out for a wide view of the garden again.*
■ [with obj.] cause (a lens or camera) to do this.
▶ noun a camera shot that changes smoothly from a long shot to a close-up or vice versa: [as modifier] *the zoom button.*
■ short for **ZOOM LENS**.
▶ exclamation used to express sudden fast movement: *then suddenly, zoom!, he's off.*
– ORIGIN late 19th cent.: imitative.

zoom lens ▶ noun a lens allowing a camera to change smoothly from a long shot to a close-up or vice versa by varying the focal length.

zoomorphic /ˌzuːə(ʊ)ˈmɔːfɪk, ˌzəʊə(ʊ)-, zuːˈmɔːfɪk/ ▶ adjective having or representing animal forms or gods of animal form: *pottery decorated with anthropomorphic and zoomorphic designs.*
– DERIVATIVES **zoomorphism** noun.
– ORIGIN late 19th cent.: from **ZOO-** 'of animals' + Greek *morphē* 'form' + -**IC**.

zoonosis /ˌzuːəˈnəʊsɪs, ˌzəʊə-/ ▶ noun (pl. **zoonoses** /-siːz/) a disease which can be transmitted to humans from animals.
– DERIVATIVES **zoonotic** adjective.
– ORIGIN late 19th cent.: from **ZOO-** 'of animals' + Greek *nosos* 'disease'.

zoophyte /ˈzuːəfʌɪt, ˈzəʊə-, ˈzuːfʌɪt/ ▶ noun Zoology dated a plant-like animal, especially a coral, sea anemone, sponge, or sea lily.
– ORIGIN early 17th cent.: from Greek *zōiophuton* (see **ZOO-**, **-PHYTE**).

zooplankton /ˈzuːə(ʊ)ˌplaŋ(k)t(ə)n, ˈzəʊə(ʊ)-, ˈzuːˌplaŋ(k)t(ə)n/ ▶ noun [mass noun] Biology plankton consisting of small animals and the immature stages of larger animals.

zoospore /ˈzuːəspɔː, ˈzəʊə-, ˈzuːˌspɔː/ ▶ noun Biology a spore of certain algae, fungi, and protozoans, capable of swimming by means of a flagellum. Also called **SWARMER**.

zoot suit ▶ noun a man's suit of an exaggerated style, characterized by a long loose jacket with padded shoulders and high-waisted tapering trousers, popular in the 1940s.

– ORIGIN 1940s: rhyming formation on **SUIT**.

zooxanthella /ˌzəʊəzanˈθɛlə/ ▶ noun (pl. **zooxanthellae** /-liː/) Biology a yellowish-brown symbiotic dinoflagellate present in large numbers in the cytoplasm of many marine invertebrates.
– DERIVATIVES **zooxanthellate** adjective.
– ORIGIN late 19th cent.: modern Latin, from **ZOO-** 'of animals' + Greek *xanthos* 'yellow' + the diminutive suffix -*ella*.

zori /ˈzɔːri, ˈzɒri/ ▶ noun (pl. **zoris**) a traditional Japanese style of flip-flop, originally made with a straw sole.
– ORIGIN Japanese.

zorilla /zɒˈrɪlə/ ▶ noun a black and white carnivorous mammal that resembles a skunk, inhabiting arid regions of southern Africa. Also called **STRIPED POLECAT**.
● *Ictonyx striatus*, family Mustelidae.
– ORIGIN late 18th cent.: via French from Spanish *zorrilla*, diminutive of *zorro* 'fox'.

Zoroaster /ˌzɒrəʊˈastə/ (*c*.628–*c*.551 BC), Persian prophet and founder of Zoroastrianism; Avestan name *Zarathustra*. Little is known of his life, but traditionally he was born in Persia and began to preach the tenets of what was later called Zoroastrianism after receiving a vision from Ahura Mazda.

Zoroastrianism /ˌzɒrəʊˈastrɪə̯nɪz(ə)m/ ▶ noun [mass noun] a monotheistic pre-Islamic religion of ancient Persia founded by Zoroaster in the 6th century BC.

> According to the teachings of Zoroaster the supreme god, Ahura Mazda, created twin spirits, one of which chose truth and light, the other untruth and darkness. Later writings present a more dualistic cosmology in which the struggle is between Ahura Mazda (Ormazd) and the evil spirit Ahriman. The scriptures of Zoroastrianism are the Zend-Avesta. It survives today in isolated areas of Iran and in India, where followers are known as Parsees.

– DERIVATIVES **Zoroastrian** adjective & noun.

zorro /ˈzɒrəʊ/ ▶ noun (pl. **-os**) a doglike fox found in the forests and savannah of South America.
● Genus *Dusicyon*, family Canidae: two species, in particular the crab-eating fox (*D. thous*).
– ORIGIN mid 19th cent.: from Spanish, 'fox'.

Zouave /zuːˈɑːv, zwɑːv/ ▶ noun **1** a member of a light-infantry corps in the French army, originally formed of Algerians and long retaining their oriental uniform.
2 (**zouaves**) women's trousers with wide tops, tapering to a narrow ankle.
– ORIGIN mid 19th cent.: from French, from Kabyle *Zouaoua*, the name of a tribe.

Zoug /zug/ French name for **ZUG**.

zouk /zuːk/ ▶ noun [mass noun] an exuberant style of popular music combining Caribbean and Western elements and having a fast heavy beat.
– ORIGIN 1970s: Guadeloupian Creole, literally 'to party'.

zounds /zaʊndz/ ▶ exclamation archaic or humorous expressing surprise or indignation.
– ORIGIN late 16th cent.: contraction from (*God*)'s *wounds* (i.e. those of Christ on the Cross).

Zovirax /ˈzəʊvɪraks, zə(ʊ)ˈvʌɪraks/ ▶ noun trademark for **ACYCLOVIR**.

zowie /ˈzaʊi, zaʊˈiː/ ▶ exclamation US informal expressing astonishment or admiration.
– ORIGIN natural exclamation: first recorded in American English in the early 20th cent.

Z particle ▶ noun Physics a heavy uncharged elementary particle considered to transmit the weak interaction between other elementary particles.

ZPG ▶ abbreviation for zero population growth.

Z-plan ▶ noun Architecture the ground plan of a type of Scottish castle having a central block with two towers at diagonally opposite corners.

Z-plasty ▶ noun [mass noun] a technique in orthopaedic and cosmetic surgery in which one or more Z-shaped incisions are made, the diagonals forming one straight line, and the two triangular sections so formed are drawn across the diagonal before being stitched.

Zr ▶ symbol for the chemical element zirconium.

ZRE ▶ abbreviation for Zaire (international vehicle registration).

Zsigmondy /ˈʃɪgmɒndi/, Richard Adolph (1865–1929), Austrian-born German chemist. He investigated the properties of various colloidal

solutions and invented the ultramicroscope for counting colloidal particles. Nobel Prize for Chemistry (1925).

zucchetto /tsuːˈkɛtəʊ/ ▶ noun (pl. **-os**) a Roman Catholic cleric's skullcap: black for a priest, purple for a bishop, red for a cardinal, and white for the Pope.
– ORIGIN mid 19th cent.: from Italian *zucchetta*, diminutive of *zucca* 'gourd, head'.

zucchini /zʊˈkiːni/ ▶ noun (pl. same or **zucchinis**) chiefly N. Amer. a courgette.
– ORIGIN Italian, plural of *zucchino*, diminutive of *zucca* 'gourd'.

Zug /tsuːg/ a mainly German-speaking canton in central Switzerland. The smallest canton, it joined the confederation in 1352.
■ its capital; pop. 21,500 (1990). French name **ZOUG**.

zugzwang /ˈzʌgzwaŋ, ˈzuːg-/ ▶ noun [mass noun] Chess a situation in which the obligation to make a move in one's turn is a serious, often decisive, disadvantage: *black is in zugzwang.*
– ORIGIN early 20th cent.: from German *Zug* 'move' + *Zwang* 'compulsion'.

Zuider Zee /ˌzʌɪdə ˈziː, ˈzeɪ/ a former large shallow inlet of the North Sea, in the Netherlands. In 1932 a dam across its entrance was completed, and large parts have been drained and reclaimed as polders. The remainder forms the IJsselmeer.
– ORIGIN Dutch, literally 'southern sea'.

Zulu /ˈzuːluː/ ▶ noun **1** a member of a South African people living mainly in KwaZulu/Natal province.
■ [mass noun] the Bantu language of this people, related to Xhosa and spoken by over 6 million people.
2 a code word representing the letter Z, used in radio communication.
▶ adjective of or relating to the Zulu people or language.

> The Zulus formed a powerful military empire in southern Africa during the 19th century before being defeated in a series of engagements with white Afrikaner and British settlers. Some Zulus still live under the traditional clan system in the province of KwaZulu/Natal, but many now work in the cities. In recent years the Zulu Inkatha movement has been drawn into violent clashes with other black groups in South Africa, particularly the Xhosa, and also into conflict with the outgoing government and the African National Congress in the period of transfer to majority rule, over future constitutional arrangements and demands for Zulu autonomy.

– ORIGIN from the stem of Zulu *umZulu*, (plural *amaZulu*).

Zululand see **KWAZULU**.

Zuni /ˈzuːni/ (also **Zuñi** /ˈzuːɲi/) ▶ noun (pl. same or **Zunis**) **1** a member of a Pueblo Indian people of western New Mexico.
2 [mass noun] the language of this people, with about 3,000 speakers.
▶ adjective of or relating to this people or their language.

zuppa inglese /ˌ(t)zʊpə ɪŋˈgleɪzei, -zi/ ▶ noun [mass noun] a rich Italian dessert resembling trifle.
– ORIGIN Italian, literally 'English soup'.

Zurbarán /ˌzʊəbəˈrɑːn, Spanish θurbaˈran, surba-/, Francisco de (1598–1664), Spanish painter. Official painter to Seville from 1628, he carried out commissions for many churches and for Philip IV, for whom he painted *The Defence of Cadiz* (1634) and the series *The Labours of Hercules* (1634). Much of his subject matter is religious.

Zurich /ˈzjʊərɪk, German ˈtsyːrɪç/ a city in north central Switzerland, situated on Lake Zurich; pop. 342,860 (1990). The largest city in Switzerland, it is a major international financial centre.

ZW ▶ abbreviation for Zimbabwe (international vehicle registration).

Zwickau /ˈtsvɪkaʊ/ a mining and industrial city in SE Germany, in Saxony; pop. 112,565 (1991).

Zwingli /ˈtsvɪŋli/, Ulrich (1484–1531), Swiss Protestant reformer, the principal figure of the Swiss Reformation. He rejected papal authority and many orthodox doctrines, and although he had strong local support in Zurich, his ideas met with fierce resistance in some regions. Zwingli was killed in the civil war that resulted from his reforms.
– DERIVATIVES **Zwinglian** adjective & noun.

zwitterion /ˈzwɪtərʌɪən, ˈtsvɪ-/ ▶ noun Chemistry a molecule or ion having separate positively and negatively charged groups.
– DERIVATIVES **zwitterionic** adjective.

– ORIGIN early 20th cent.: from German, from *Zwitter* 'a hybrid' + *Ion* 'ion'.

Zwolle /ˈzwɒlə/ a town in the eastern Netherlands, capital of Overijssel province; pop. 95,570 (1991).

Zworykin /ˈzwɔːrɪkɪn, zvəˈriːkɪn/, Vladimir (Kuzmich) (1889–1982), Russian-born American physicist and television pioneer. He invented a precursor of the television camera, the first to scan the image electronically.

zydeco /ˈzʌɪdɪkəʊ/ ▶ noun [mass noun] a kind of black American dance music originally from southern Louisiana, typically featuring accordion and guitar.
– ORIGIN 1960s: Louisiana Creole, possibly from a pronunciation of French *les haricots* in a dance-tune title.

zygo- ▶ combining form relating to joining or pairing: *zygodactyl*.
– ORIGIN from Greek *zugon* 'yoke'.

zygodactyl /ˌzʌɪɡə(ʊ)ˈdaktɪl, zɪɡ-/ ▶ adjective (of a bird's feet) having two toes pointing forward and two backward.
▶ noun a bird with zygodactyl feet.
– DERIVATIVES **zygodactylous** adjective.

zygoma /zʌɪˈɡəʊmə, zɪɡ-/ ▶ noun (pl. **zygomata** /-tə/) Anatomy the bony arch of the cheek formed by connection of the zygomatic and temporal bones.
– DERIVATIVES **zygomatic** adjective.
– ORIGIN late 17th cent.: from Greek *zugōma*, from *zugon* 'yoke'.

zygomatic arch ▶ noun Anatomy the zygoma.

zygomatic bone ▶ noun Anatomy the bone that forms the prominent part of the cheek and the outer side of the eye socket.

zygomatic process ▶ noun Anatomy a projection of the temporal bone that forms part of the zygoma.

zygomorphic /ˌzʌɪɡə(ʊ)ˈmɔːfɪk, ˌzɪɡ-/ ▶ adjective Botany (of a flower) having only one plane of symmetry, as in a pea or snapdragon; bilaterally symmetrical. Compare with **ACTINOMORPHIC**.
– DERIVATIVES **zygomorphy** noun.

Zygoptera /zʌɪˈɡɒptərə/ Entomology a group of insects which comprises the damselflies. Compare with **ANISOPTERA**.
● Suborder Zygoptera, order Odonata.
– DERIVATIVES **zygopteran** noun & adjective.
– ORIGIN modern Latin (plural), from Greek *zugon* 'yoke' + *pteron* 'wing'.

zygospore /ˈzʌɪɡə(ʊ)spɔː/ ▶ noun Biology the thick-walled resting cell of certain fungi and algae, arising from the fusion of two similar gametes. Compare with **OOSPORE**.

zygote /ˈzʌɪɡəʊt/ ▶ noun Biology a diploid cell resulting from the fusion of two haploid gametes; a fertilized ovum.
– DERIVATIVES **zygotic** /-ˈɡɒtɪk/ adjective.
– ORIGIN late 19th cent.: from Greek *zugōtos* 'yoked', from *zugoun* 'to yoke'.

zygotene /ˈzʌɪɡə(ʊ)tiːn/ ▶ noun [mass noun] Biology the second stage of the prophase of meiosis, following leptotene, during which homologous chromosomes begin to pair.

Zyklon B /ˈzʌɪklɒn/ ▶ noun [mass noun] hydrogen cyanide adsorbed on or released from a carrier in the form of small tablets, used as an insecticidal fumigant and by the Nazis as a lethal gas.
– ORIGIN 1930s: from German, of unknown origin.

zymase /ˈzʌɪmeɪz/ ▶ noun [mass noun] Biochemistry a mixture of enzymes obtained from yeast which catalyse the breakdown of sugars in alcoholic fermentation.
– ORIGIN late 19th cent.: from French, from Greek *zumē* 'leaven'.

zymo- /ˈzʌɪməʊ/ (also **zym-** before a vowel) ▶ combining form relating to enzymes or fermentation: *zymogen* | *zymase*.
– ORIGIN from Greek *zumē* 'leaven'.

zymogen /ˈzʌɪmə(ʊ)dʒ(ə)n/ ▶ noun Biochemistry an inactive substance which is converted into an enzyme when activated by another enzyme.

zymotic disease ▶ noun archaic a contagious disease, regarded as developing after infection like the fermenting of yeast.

zymurgy /ˈzʌɪməːdʒi/ ▶ noun [mass noun] the study or practice of fermentation in brewing, winemaking, or distilling.
– ORIGIN mid 19th cent.: from Greek *zumē* 'leaven', on the pattern of *metallurgy*.

Zyrian /ˈzɪrɪən/ ▶ noun former term for **KOMI**[2] (the language).